CROCKFORD'S
CLERICAL DIRECTORY

2010 – 2011

CROCKFORD'S
CLERICAL DIRECTORY
101ST EDITION

2010-2011

A directory of the clergy
of the Church of England
the Church in Wales
the Scottish Episcopal Church
the Church of Ireland

SINCE 1858

CHURCH HOUSE PUBLISHING

Crockford's Clerical Directory published December 2009 for The Archbishops' Council by:

Church House Publishing
Church House
Great Smith Street
London SW1P 3AZ

101st edition (2010–2011) © The Archbishops' Council 2009.

Please send any corrections to the Compiler, Crockford (address as above), Tel (020) 7898 1012
Fax (020) 7898 1769 E-mail crockford@c-of-e.org.uk

ISBN 978 0 7151 1042 3 (hardback)
     978 0 7151 1043 0 (paperback)

QR

203

Jacket and cover design by Aubrey Design

Typeset by
RefineCatch Ltd,
Bungay, Suffolk

Printed in the UK by
CPI William Clowes
Beccles NR34 7TL

CONTENTS

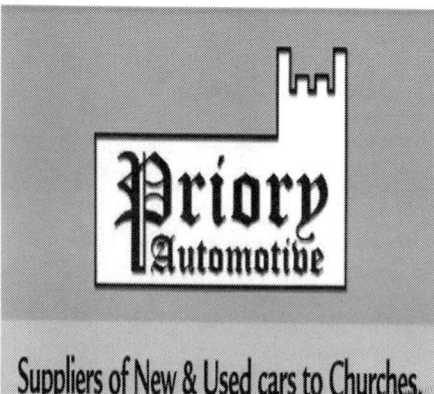
INDEX TO ADVERTISEMENTS

Advertisements can be found on the following pages

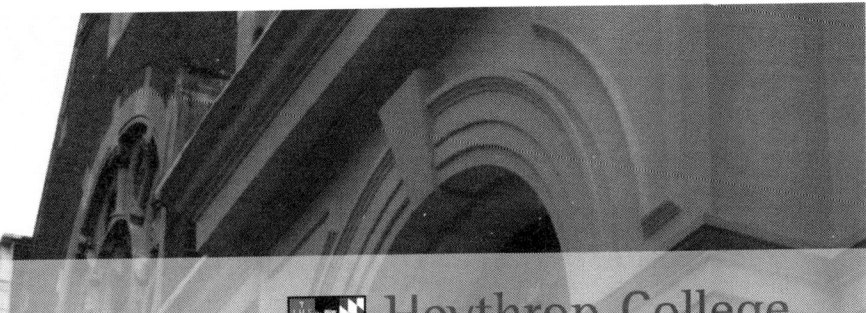

Heythrop College

The Specialist Philosophy and Theology College
of the University of London

With a foundation dating back to 1614,
Heythrop College, University of London offers
a wide range of undergraduate and postgraduate
degree and diploma programmes.

Specialising in Theology and Philosophy,
Heythrop has one of the largest
teaching faculties in its subject areas supported
by one of the oldest and most important libraries
of its kind in the UK

For more information on what Heythrop can offer
please see www.heythrop.ac.uk or contact
enquiries@heythrop.ac.uk.

Heythrop College University of London Kensington Square London W8 5HN   020 7795 6600
www.heythrop.ac.uk

The Anglican Association

(Founded 1969)
Registered charity No: 1002192

SAFEGUARDING THE ANGLICAN MIND
AND
SEEKING TO RESTORE IT

We uphold Canon A5
and proclaim and maintain
the Church of England's theological integrity

http://www.anglicanassociation.co.uk

15

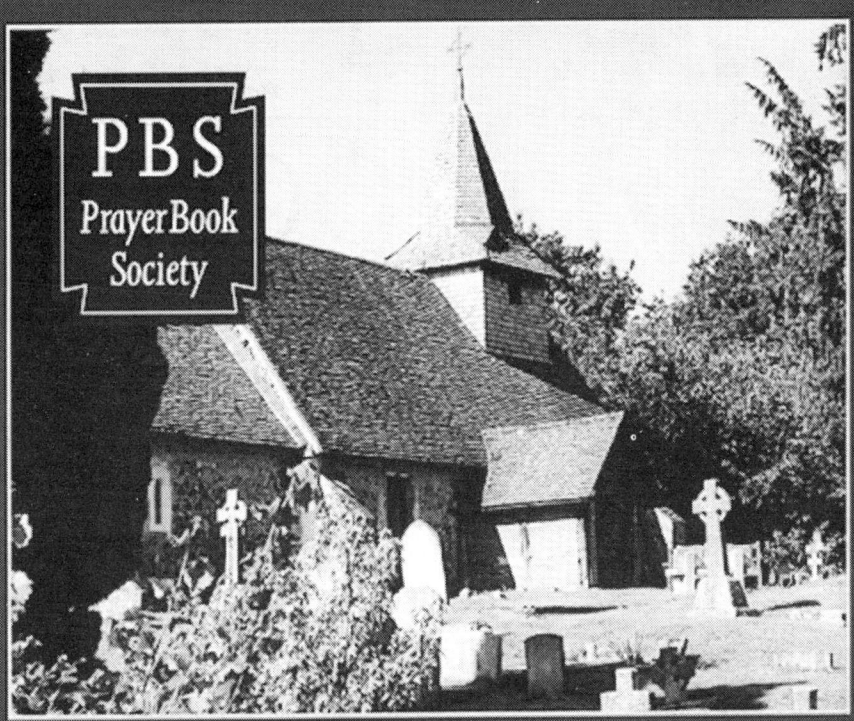

Do you value Anglican Services and music where the Book of Common Prayer is used?

One of the Society's aims is to ensure its continued use for this and future generations. To this end it promotes the prestigious Cranmer Awards for Young People.

It runs ordinands' training projects, produces academic journals sold through the mail order book service and holds a residential conference annually when members are addressed by quality speakers from religion, the arts and broadcasting.

Every member receives five magazines a year.

To find out more and to obtain a membership form please contact Ian Woodhead on 01380 870384 or join online at: www.pbs.org.uk

The Prayer Book Society Registered Charity No. 1099295. Co. Limited by Guarantee No.4786973

Bringing hope and aid to the persecuted Church

Barnabas Fund

PRAYER   AID
          INFORMATION   ADVOCACY

We support:
- Clergy
- Theological students
- Churches
- Christians suffering for their faith

"When I am visiting a country where Christians are under pressure, quite often a minister or a lay person will ask quietly whether I know about Barnabas Fund. When I say, "Yes," their eyes light up and they tell me how Barnabas has encouraged them with a church building, a school or medical assistance. It is this kind of ministry that needs to be supported by prayers and by generosity so that the situation of our brothers and sisters is eased a little by our love."

The Rt Revd Dr Michael Nazir-Ali

MARLBOROUGH COLLEGE

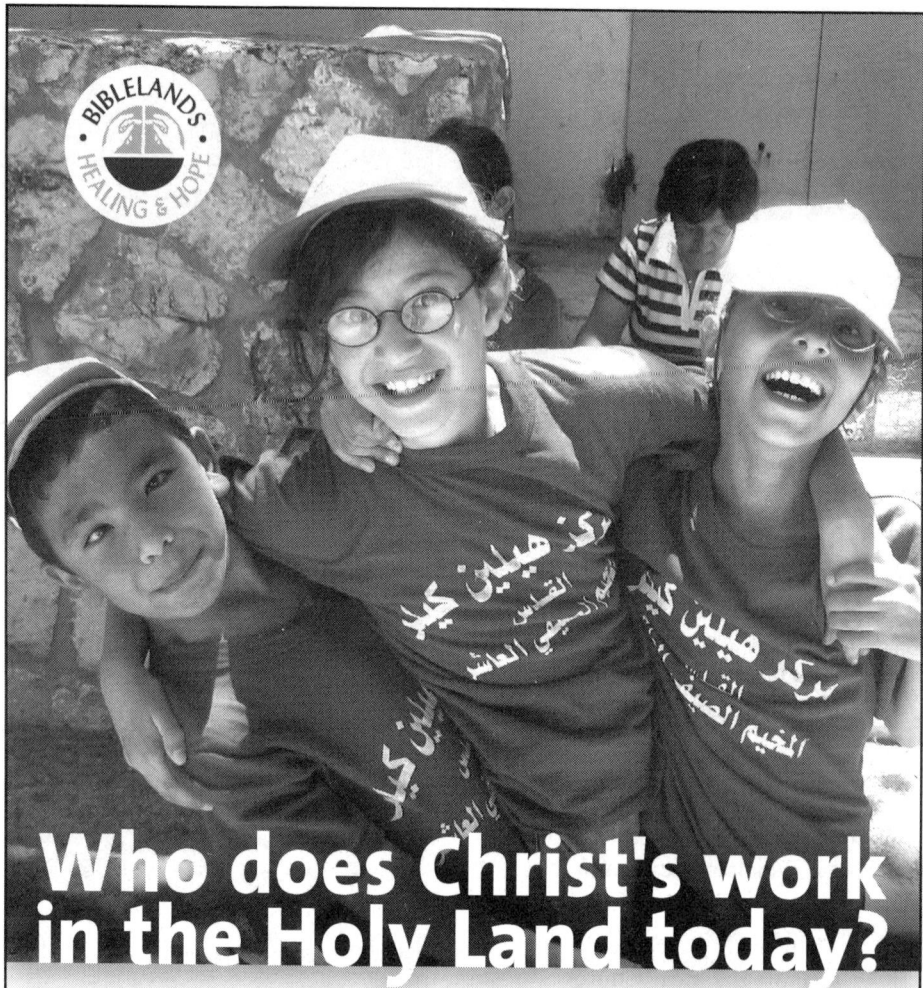

Who does Christ's work in the Holy Land today?

Bible*Lands* is a Christian agency serving the poor, vulnerable and disadvantaged in the lands of the Bible – regardless of their faith or nationality.

Our vision is to enable and resource local Christian partners working in the areas of **education, health** and **community development**.

For further information, resources or to invite a guest speaker, please contact us on:

**01494 897950
www.biblelands.org.uk**

Bible*Lands*, PO Box 50, High Wycombe, Buckinghamshire HP15 7QU
Email: info@biblelands.org.uk   Reg. Charity No. 1076329

The Church and Community Fund

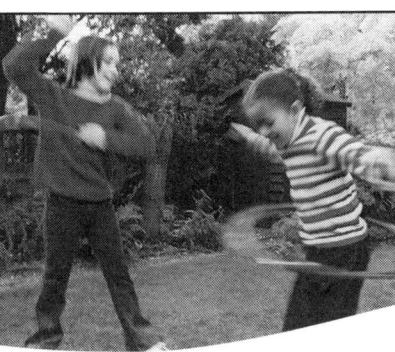

The CCF can offer grants in support of exciting and innovative parish or Diocesan community projects. Projects that show imagination in responding to need and can help to bridge the gap between the Church and the local community are particularly welcome.

- We award £400,000+ every year to exciting church and community projects! We have a strong focus on current initiatives in the Church and regularly support projects in line with the Church's focus on Fresh Expressions, developing the use of Church Buildings, Social Outreach and Youth Evangelism;

- We have helped employ Youth Workers, renovate old Church halls for use as lively community centres, reordered Church buildings to enable them to be used more flexibly and have helped Churches provide hot meals for the homeless;

- We also give an annual grant to the Archbishops' Council in support of the national functions of the Church.

We warmly welcome donations and legacies in support of our work. We support the local Church in responding to the needs of their community throughout the country in both rural and urban areas, bringing about lasting change in some of the neediest parts of England.

Please go to www.churchandcommunityfund.org.uk, call 020 7898 1541/1767 or email us at ccf@c-of-e.org.uk

The Church and Community Fund, Church House, Great Smith Street, London, SW1P 3AZ

The Church and Community Fund is an exempted charity under the trusteeship of The Archbishops' Council of the Church of England (1074857). It exists to support the mission of the Church of England.

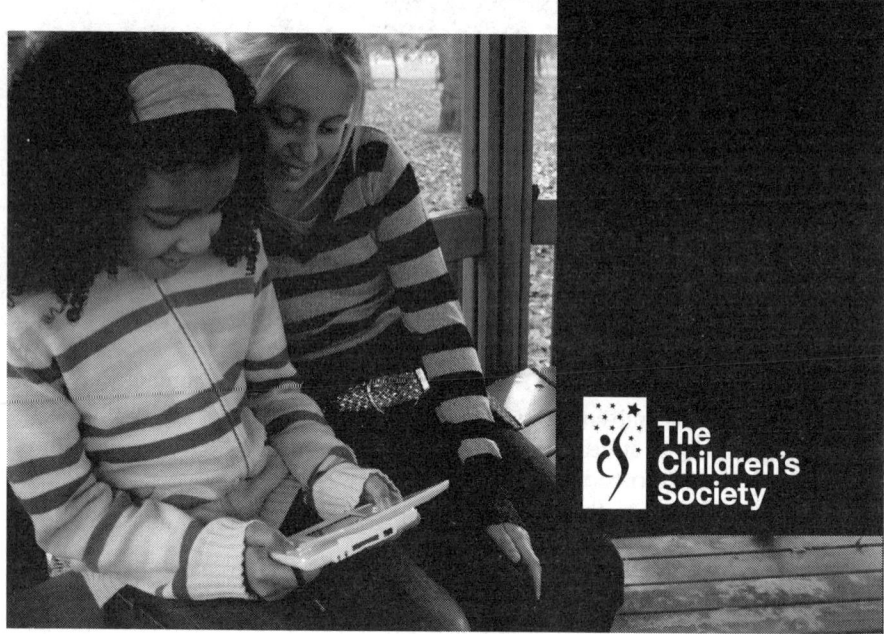

The Kingdom of God belongs to such as these...

The Children's Society is a leading children's charity committed to making childhood better for all children in the UK. Founded in 1881 as The Church of England Central Home for Waifs and Strays by Sunday school teacher, Edward Rudolf, our Christian values have remained the same for over 128 years. We believe in creating a society, which models the values of the Kingdom of God: love, justice and forgiveness.

There are a number of ways to get involved with The Children's Society, such as using our worship resources to reach out to children and young people in your community, fundraising and volunteering or through raising awareness and prayer.

The Children's Society also works together with The Church of England Children's Work Advisers and the Liturgical Commission to produce a number of liturgical resources to support you in your ministry:

- **Christingle** – Advent, Christmas and Ephipany seasons
- **Leaves of Life** – Eastertide
- **Halloween Choice** – Season of All Saints in October

For further information on free support resources and how to get involved visit **www.childrenssociety.org.uk** or call our Supporter Action Line on **0845 300 1148**.

Together we can make childhood better for all children

INTRODUCTION

This, the one hundredth and first edition of *Crockford's Clerical Directory*, provides details as at 3 August 2009 of more than 26,000 clergy and deaconesses in the Church of England (including the Diocese in Europe), the Church in Wales, the Scottish Episcopal Church, and the Church of Ireland. It also includes in the main biographical section those Michaelmas ordinands of whom we were notified in advance.

First published in 1858, the publication of *Crockford* now spans one and a half centuries. The Oxford University Press purchased the copyright for *Crockford* in 1921, publishing thirty-six editions before transferring ownership to the Church Commissioners and the Central Board of Finance, on economic grounds, sixty years later. This is the third edition under the sole ownership of the Archbishops' Council.

The publishing, design, advertising, selling and distribution of the directory are carried out by Church House Publishing in partnership with the *Crockford* Department, who are responsible for the actual compilation of the text. The information that generates the biographical entries is stored on a database, which is updated daily. Much of this information is obtained from the direct link with the Church Commissioners' central clergy pay-roll. Any alterations to this pay-roll (for example, changes of address or appointment) are automatically reflected on the *Crockford* database. However, nearly 8,500 (almost one-third) of the clergy are not on the central pay-roll. These are principally non-stipendiary ministers, those engaged in some form of ministry outside the parochial system (such as hospital, university, prison or service chaplains) and those serving in Wales, Scotland and Ireland. In maintaining the records of these clergy, we continue to rely greatly on the assistance of bishops' secretaries and diocesan offices, and information contained in diocesan directories, year books and the Church Press. We are also grateful for the help provided by the central authorities of the Church in Wales, the Scottish Episcopal Church, the Church of Ireland, the Ministry of Defence, the Hospital Chaplaincies Council, and our various overseas contacts.

A tremendous amount of help has come from the clergy themselves. We are enormously grateful to all those who have provided us with information, and have helped to minimize omissions and errors. For reasons of time, space and consistency, we are unable to include all the information clergy request us to publish, and we apologise that it has not been possible to respond to each letter individually. We are also grateful to Richard Christmas and Angela Florence, who have been responsible for most of the work in compiling the directory.

We are always glad to be informed of amendments to entries, and we particularly appreciate any information about clergy whose addresses are not currently known to us (see list on p. 1249). Information relating to omissions or amendments should be sent to the *Crockford* Department; requests for archival information from earlier editions should be addressed in writing to Lambeth Palace Library; and requests for other information which cannot be found on the Church of England's web site (at www..cofe.anglican.org) should be addressed to the Communications Office.

Crockford Department	*The Librarian*	*The Communications Office*
Church House	*Lambeth Palace Library*	*Church House*
Great Smith Street	*Lambeth Palace*	*Great Smith Street*
London SW1P 3AZ	*London SE1 7JU*	*London SW1P 3AZ*
Tel (020) 7898 1012	Tel (020) 7898 1400	Tel (020) 7898 1463
	Fax (020) 7928 7932	
E-mail crockford@c-of-e.org.uk	E mail lpl.staff@c-of-e.org.uk	E-mail feedback@c-of-e.org.uk

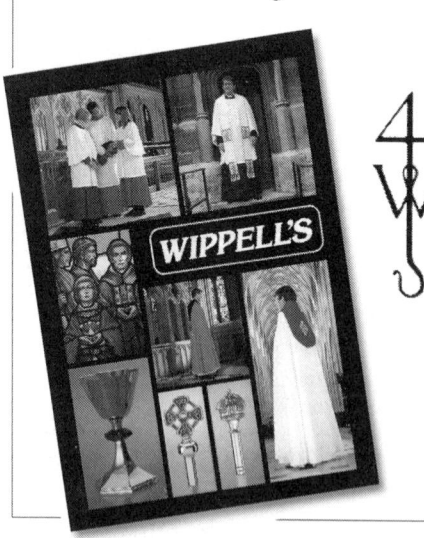

JOHN CROCKFORD

John Crockford was the eldest child of a Somerset schoolmaster and his wife, John and Hannah Crockford; and by 1841 he was working as an attorney's clerk in Taunton, Somerset. John Crockford Sr was described in 1869 as Gentleman, of Rowbarton near Taunton. By his early twenties he was in business as a printer and publisher at 29 Essex Street, Strand; and it was from that address that *Crockford* was first published in 1858. On 6 December of the same year, John Crockford moved to new business premises at 346 Strand and 19 Wellington Street North.

His private address at that time was 16 Oakley Square, Hampstead Road; though by 1865 he had moved to 10 Park Road, Haverstock Hill.

Crockford's business association of more than two decades with Edward William Cox (1809–1879) had begun in 1843, when the *Law Times* first appeared. Both men are claimed as publisher – Crockford by Boase in *Modern English Biography*; Cox by the *Athenaeum* and by *Notes and Queries*. There is similar lack of agreement over other publications, such as the ill-fated *Critic*. "[Crockford] tried to establish a literary paper, the *Critic*. To this he brought all his great ability, but after fifteen years he gave it up in despair" (*Notes and Queries*): whereas the *Dictionary of National Biography* has it that Cox became "proprietor of . . . two other papers called respectively 'The Critic' and 'The Royal Exchange'."

The truth appears to be that the two men, who shared the same business address in Essex Street, were joint founders of a number of projects. Cox – the elder, more established and richer man – was often the financier and named publisher, with Crockford as the manager of the undertaking. Each had his own specialities: Cox, called to the bar in 1843, and successively Recorder of Helston & Falmouth (1857–1868) and of Portsmouth (1868–1879), was no doubt the leader in the establishment of the *Law Times*, to which, in *DNB*'s words, he "thenceforth devoted . . . the larger portion of his time and attention." But the legend which has arisen that Cox, restrained by professional ethics from using his own name, chose, almost at random, the name of one of his clerks to bear the title of his new clerical directory in 1858 – thus, in the words of the first postwar editor (probably Newman) bestowing "a more than tomb-stone meed of remembrance" – cannot be substantiated. As the jubilee account of the *Field* notes, Crockford was an equal partner in the success of the joint enterprises: "It was John Crockford who purchased the paper for Mr Cox. He obtained it from Mr Benjamin Webster for a trifling sum . . . In a short time the net profits amounted to 20,000*l*. a year. The management was placed under Crockford's control. He was a splendid man of business" (*Notes and Queries*).

The first *Clerical Directory* (1858), "A Biographical and Statistical Book of Reference for facts relating to the clergy and the Church", seems to have been assembled in a very haphazard fashion, with names added "as fast as they could be obtained", out of alphabetical order and with an unreliable index. By 1860 the *Directory* had become a very much more useful work of reference; and by 1917, with the absorption of its only serious rival, the *Clergy List*, reigned supreme.

No more than glimpses survive of Crockford's personality, and those mostly from the account of him given by John C. Francis, in the *Field* jubilee article already referred to. "I had occasion to call upon him a short time before his death, when we joined in a hearty laugh over his former furious attacks upon the *Athenaeum*. 'Dilke's Drag' he used to call it, and would accuse it of 'vulgar insolence and coxcombry' and 'the coarsest vulgarity'. As we parted he said, 'You have the *Athenaeum* to be proud of, and we have the *Field*.' "

John Crockford died suddenly at his home on 13 January 1865, at the age of 41. He left a widow, Annie (née Ellam) whom he married on 24 December 1847 at St Pancras Old Church. A daughter, Florence Annie, was born in St Pancras in 1852. (Florence married Arthur Brownlow in 1875 and had a son called Frederick.) His very brief will, proved 6 February 1865 at the Principal Probate Registry, left everything to his widow. His personal effects were valued at less than £1,000, but the family must have lived in some style, since one of the witnesses to the will was the resident coachman. Crockford's widow moved to 4 Upper Eton Place, Tavistock Hill, and died there on 26 July 1868.

BRENDA HOUGH

A request from the *Dictionary of National Biography* for a notice of the life of John Crockford led to the preparation of this article, a shorter version of which appeared in *The Dictionary of National Biography: Missing Persons*, 1993. For the information from the 1841 Census, and the record of Crockford's daughter Florence, we are indebted to Mr Ken Rhoades, of Kent.

A USER'S GUIDE TO *CROCKFORD*

Who is included in Crockford?
Crockford includes details of over 26,000 clergy and deaconesses of the Church of England, the Church in Wales, the Scottish Episcopal Church and the Church of Ireland. Clergy currently serving overseas qualify for inclusion if they have trained or have been licensed in this country (see **Overseas clergy**). Clergy who have died since the last edition are listed on p. 1271. Generally, clergy who have resigned their offices (but not their orders) are included unless they are known to have been received into another Church. A small number of clergy are excluded at their own request.

Readers and lay workers are not included: please consult diocesan directories. The *Who's Who* section of *The Church of England Year Book* (published annually by Church House Publishing and covering most aspects of the life and institutions of the Church of England) lists members of General Synod and principal members of staff of the Church's central organizations.

Addresses and telephone numbers
Where more than one telephone number is given, the first will normally relate to the address shown.

Addressing the clergy
See p. *31*.

Appointment details in the *Biographies* section
These reflect the legal pastoral situation prevailing at 3 August 2009, the date of the compilation of this edition of *Crockford*. Conventional districts, proprietary chapels and local ecumenical projects are also recorded. Benefice names are only recorded once in a biographical entry when they apply to successive appointments.

Crockford does not record group ministries, informal local arrangements, areas of special responsibility, emeritus appointments (except as reflected in the style of address), licence or permission to officiate when held in conjunction with another appointment from the same diocese, commissary appointments, examining chaplaincies, or secular appointments (except for educational or charitable posts).

Appointments held before ordination are not included (apart from service as a deaconess) unless they straddle the date of ordination.

Archbishops overseas
The presiding (arch-)bishop or metropolitan of each of the provinces of the Anglican Communion is listed in the main *Biographies* section, cross-referenced as appropriate, together with the Moderator of each of the united churches.

Archdeaconries
See *Archdeaconries, deaneries and rural deans* on p. 996.

Archdeacons
Look up the place name in *Biographies*: this is cross-referenced to a personal name.

Bishops (diocesan, area, suffragan, and provincial episcopal visitors)
Look up the place name in *Biographies*: this is cross-referenced to a personal name. See also p. 946, which lists the diocesan, area, suffragan and assistant bishops by diocese, as well as provincial episcopal visitors.

Bishops (assistant)
See *Bishops in England, Wales, Scotland and Ireland* on p. 946.

Bishops in the House of Lords
See p. 949.

Bishops overseas
See *Bishops of Anglican dioceses overseas* on p. 1239, and *Bishops of united churches* on p. 1261. Further information about the Anglican Communion can be found in *The Church of England Year Book*.

Bishops and archbishops, former
A list of former archbishops and bishops (diocesan and suffragan) will be found on p. 950.

Boundaries, provincial and diocesan
Maps of England and Wales, Scotland and Ireland, showing provincial and diocesan boundaries and cathedral cities, will be found on p. 1276.

Cathedral clergy
See *Cathedrals* on p. 989 for full-time cathedral clergy. The list does not include honorary appointments.

Chapel Royal
See *Royal Peculiars* on p. 991.

Christian names
The name by which a person prefers to be known, if not the first Christian name, is underlined (for example, SMITH, David <u>John</u> prefers to be called John). Names 'in religion' or names not part of a person's legal name are shown in parentheses.

Church: how to find the names of clergy responsible for a particular church
Look up the place name in the appropriate *Benefices and churches* section, see p. 1004: if the entry is in bold type, the names of all clergy are listed and can be cross-referenced in the *Biographies* section; if the place name is not in bold type, the name of the benefice is given where the names of all clergy will be found.

Church: how to find the names of clergy responsible for a particular church when there is a vacancy
If the benefice is vacant, the telephone number of the clergy house is usually given in the appropriate *Benefices and churches* section to enable contact to be made with a new incumbent or priest-in-charge. The deanery reference (e.g. *Guildf 2*) following the benefice name cross-refers to *Archdeaconries, deaneries and rural deans* on p. 996 by means of which the name of the rural dean responsible for the vacant benefice can be found.

College chaplains
See p. 1233 for chaplains at universities, colleges of further education, colleges of higher education, sixth-form colleges, and schools.

Corrections
Please send notice of any corrections to:
Crockford Compiler, Church House, Great Smith Street, London SW1P 3AZ
Tel (020) 7898 1012 Fax (020) 7898 1769 E-mail crockford@c-of-e.org.uk

Crockford
The full title is *Crockford's Clerical Directory*. *Crockford* (not *Crockford's*) is an accepted abbreviation. See also the biography of John Crockford on p. 23.

Deaconesses
See separate section on p. 945.

Deacons
See *Biographies* section.

Deaneries
See rural or area deans below.

Deans
Look up the place name in *Biographies*: this is cross-referenced to a personal name. See also *Cathedrals* on p. 989, and *Royal Peculiars* on p. 991.

Diocesan offices
Details of the diocesan offices in England, Wales, Scotland and Ireland can be found on p. 992.

E-mail addresses
These are provided where known. See after the telephone and/or fax number.

Europe, chaplains in
See *Chaplains of the Diocese of Gibraltar in Europe* on p. 1216.

Fax numbers
The exchange number is only given if different from that of the preceding telephone number.

Hospital chaplains
Whole-time and part-time hospital chaplains are listed under their NHS trusts on p. 1223. Cross-references have been inserted for individual hospitals.

Lay workers
Lay workers are not included in *Crockford*: please consult diocesan directories.

London churches
See *English benefices and churches* on p. 1004. City and Guild churches are listed under LONDON CITY CHURCHES and LONDON GUILD CHURCHES. In other cases, see under church name (e.g. LANGHAM PLACE (All Souls), WESTMINSTER (St Matthew)).

Married or single?
Crockford does not provide information on marital status. However, we have included the form of address Miss, Mrs or Ms where requested. Where there has been a change of surname, a cross-reference may be found from the previous name.

Non-stipendiary clergy
Non-stipendiary clergy are listed in the main *Biographies* section.

Ordination courses
See *Theological colleges and courses* on p. 1237.

Overseas clergy
Clergy who are on the *Crockford* database and who are currently serving overseas qualify for inclusion. Service overseas has in the past been recorded simply by country, though higher office (e.g. as bishop or archdeacon) has also been noted. Other eligible appointments are now being added on request.

Overseas addresses and telephone numbers are given as required by a user in the UK, and include the international access and country codes, as well as the area code. If dialling from within the country concerned, the user will need to omit the international access and country codes, and dial zero immediately before the area code.

Patronage
The patron of each benefice is listed under the benefice name in *English benefices and churches* on p. 1004.

Prison chaplains
See p. 1221.

Proprietary chapels
See *English benefices and churches* on p. 1004.

Provincial episcopal visitors
Look up the place name in *Biographies*: this is cross-referenced to a personal name. See also p. 946, which lists the diocesan, area, suffragan and assistant bishops and provincial episcopal visitors.

Provosts
Look up the place name in *Biographies*: this is cross-referenced to a personal name. See also *Cathedrals* on p. 989.

Queen's Chaplains
See *Royal Peculiars* on p. 991.

Readers
Readers are not included in *Crockford*: please consult diocesan directories.

Religious orders
For members of religious orders where the Christian name alone is commonly used (e.g. Brother Aidan) a cross-reference is provided to the surname. Names 'in religion' not forming part of a person's legal name will be shown in parentheses. Details of religious communities are provided in *The Church of England Year Book*.

Retired clergy
The description 'rtd' does not imply that ministry has ceased, only that clergy so described are now in receipt of a pension. All eligible appointments are now recorded.

Rural or area deans
See *Archdeaconries, deaneries and rural deans* on p. 996. To find who is the rural dean of a particular church, look up the place or benefice name in the appropriate *Benefices* section: the deanery reference (e.g. *Guildf 2*) following the benefice name cross-refers to *Archdeaconries, deaneries and rural deans* on p. 996 where the name of the rural dean responsible can be found.

School chaplains
See p. 1235 for chaplains in schools.

Service chaplains
See p. 1219.

Sixth-form colleges
See p. 1234.

Theological colleges and courses
See p. 1237.

University chaplains
See p. 1233.

HOW TO ADDRESS THE CLERGY

In offering the advice below, we do not intend to imply that other practices are necessarily to be discouraged (for example, the use of Father as in 'Father Smith'). A good deal depends on circumstances, and, where a personal preference is known, it is usually good practice to follow it.

The following notes show acceptable current usage

(a) on an envelope or formal listing
(b) in starting a social letter or in speech, and
(c) when referring to a member of the clergy

Category (a) is not open to much variation, owing to the formality of the context, but categories (b) and (c) will often vary according to circumstances. It is always acceptable to use the appropriate Christian name in place of initials (for example, the Revd Alice Smith). In the absence of any style or title conferred by a post, all deacons and priests are styled 'The Reverend', and all who have been consecrated bishop are styled 'The Right Reverend'.

For abbreviations, see paragraph 13 below.

1 Deacons and Priests
(a) The Reverend A B Smith
(b) Mr/Mrs/Miss/Ms Smith (unless it is known that some other style is preferred – the title Vicar or Rector is acceptable only if the person so addressed really is the incumbent of the parish where you live or worship)
(c) The Reverend A B Smith at the first mention, and Mr/Mrs/Miss/Ms Smith thereafter

Notes 1 The form 'Reverend Smith' or 'The Reverend Smith' should *never* be used this side of the Atlantic. If the Christian name or initials are not known, the correct forms are
    (a) The Reverend—Smith, *or* The Reverend Mr/Mrs/Miss/Ms Smith
    (b) Mr/Mrs/Miss/Ms Smith
    (c) The Reverend Mr/Mrs/Miss/Ms Smith at the first mention, and Mr/Mrs/Miss/Ms Smith thereafter

  2 There is no universally accepted way of addressing an envelope to a married couple of whom both are in holy orders. We recommend the style 'The Reverend A B and the Reverend C D Smith'.

2 Prebendaries
(a) The Reverend Prebendary A B Smith
(b) Prebendary Smith
(c) Prebendary Smith

3 Canons (both Residentiary and Honorary)
(a) The Reverend Canon A B Smith
(b) Canon Smith
(c) Canon Smith

4 Archdeacons
(a) The Venerable the Archdeacon of X
(b) Archdeacon, *or more formally* Mr/Madam Archdeacon
(c) The Archdeacon of X at the first mention, and the Archdeacon thereafter

Notes 1 In the case of an archdeacon (or dean/provost, bishop, or archbishop) in office, the style above is to be preferred. The personal name should be used only for the purpose of identification.

  2 For an archdeacon emeritus, the correct forms are
    (a) The Venerable A B Smith
    (b) Archdeacon
    (c) Archdeacon Smith

5 Deans and Provosts
(a) The Very Reverend the Dean/Provost of X
(b) Dean/Provost, *or more formally* Mr/Madam Dean/Provost
(c) The Dean/Provost of X at the first mention, and the Dean thereafter (see also note 1 to paragraph 4 above)

6 Bishops, Diocesan and Suffragan
(a) The Right Reverend the Bishop of X, *or* The Right Reverend the Lord Bishop of X
(b) Bishop, *or more formally* My Lord
(c) The Bishop of X at the first mention, and the Bishop thereafter (see also note 1 to paragraph 4 above)

Notes 1 The use of 'Lord' before 'Bishop' is diminishing. It is a matter of individual preference whether it should be used.
     2 The Bishop of London is a Privy Councillor, and has the style 'The Right Reverend and Right Honourable the Lord Bishop of London'.
     3 The Bishop of Meath and Kildare is styled 'The Most Reverend'.

7 Assistant and Retired Bishops
(a) The Right Reverend A B Smith
(b) Bishop
(c) Bishop Smith

8 Archbishops
(a) The Most Reverend the Lord Archbishop of X
(b) Archbishop, *or more formally* Your Grace
(c) The Archbishop of X at the first mention, and the Archbishop thereafter (see also note 1 to paragraph 4 above)

Notes 1 The Archbishops of Canterbury and York, being Privy Councillors, also have 'Right Honourable' included in their style (for example, The Most Reverend and Right Honourable the Lord Archbishop of Canterbury).
     2 The presiding bishop of the Scottish Episcopal Church is the Primus, and the correct forms are
       (a) The Most Reverend the Primus
       (b) Primus
       (c) Primus
     3 A retired archbishop properly reverts to the status of bishop, but may be given as a courtesy the style of an archbishop.

9 Chaplains to the Armed Services
(a) The Reverend A B Smith RN (*or* CF *or* RAF)
(b) Padre, *or* Padre Smith
(c) The Padre, *or* Padre Smith

10 Titled Clerics
Where a member of the clergy also holds a temporal title, this is always preceded in writing by the ecclesiastical one.

Barons (other than retired archbishops)
(a) The Reverend the Lord Smith of Y
(b) Lord Smith
(c) The Reverend the Lord Smith at the first mention, and Lord Smith thereafter

Baronets
(a) The Reverend Sir Alan Smith Bt
(b) Sir Alan Smith or Sir Alan
(c) The Reverend Sir Alan Smith at the first mention, and Sir Alan Smith thereafter

Knights
An ordained priest may be appointed to an order of knighthood, but will not normally receive the accolade or title. The appropriate designation will follow the name or

ecclesiastical title (for example, The Right Reverend the Bishop of X, KCVO). If he was knighted *before* he was ordained, he will retain his title.

11 Ordained Members of Religious Orders

(a) The Reverend Alan/Alice Smith XYZ; The Reverend Brother Alan/Sister Alice XYZ
(b) Father, Father Smith, *or* Father Alan; Brother Alan/Sister Alice
(c) The Reverend Alan/Alice Smith; Father Alan Smith; Father Smith; Brother Alan/Sister Alice

Notes 1 A name 'in religion', shown in parentheses in the biographical entry, should be used in preference to the baptismal name or initials. Sometimes the surname is not used. In this Directory, however, the entry will be found under the surname, whether it is normally used or not, and, if appropriate, a cross-reference is given under the Christian name.
2 Some orders use 'Brother' and 'Sister' for lay and ordained members without distinction, along with Christian names.
3 It is customary to specify the religious order by giving the appropriate letters after the name.

12 Academics

When a member of the clergy holds more than one title, the ecclesiastical one is normally used.

Professor	(a)	The Reverend Canon A B Smith
also Canon	(b)	Canon Smith, *or* Professor Smith, according to context
	(c)	Canon Smith, *or* Professor Smith, according to context
Canon	(a)	The Reverend Canon A B Smith (degree)
also Doctor	(b)	Canon Smith, *or* Dr Smith, according to context
	(c)	Canon Smith, *or* Dr Smith, according to context

13 Abbreviations

The following abbreviations are in common use

Reverend:	Revd *or* Rev
Father:	Fr
Right Reverend:	Rt Revd *or* Rt Rev
Prebendary:	Preb
Venerable:	Ven

Reverend, Right Reverend, Very Reverend, Most Reverend and Venerable, whether abbreviated or not, should always be preceded by the definite article.

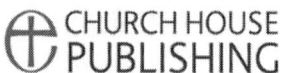

ABBREVIATIONS USED IN CROCKFORD'S CLERICAL DIRECTORY

A

AAAI .... Associate, Institute of Administrative Accountants
AB .... Bachelor of Arts (USA)
ABEng............... Associate Member of the Association of Building Engineers
ABIA................ Associate, Bankers' Institute of Australasia
ABIPP .... Associate, British Institute of Professional Photography
ABIST .... Associate, British Institute of Surgical Technology
ABM .... Advisory Board of Ministry (now Ministry Division)
ABPsS .... Associate, British Psychological Society (now see AFBPsS)
ABSM .... Associate, Birmingham and Midland Institute School of Music
ACA .... Associate, Institute of Chartered Accountants
ACC .... Anglican Consultative Council
ACCA .... Associate, Chartered Association of Certified Accountants (formerly AACCA)
ACCM.............. Advisory Council for the Church's Ministry (now Ministry Division)
ACCS .... Associate, Corporation of Secretaries
ACCTS............. Association for Christian Conferences, Teaching, and Service
ACE.................. Associateship of the College of Education
.... Member, Association of Conference Executives
ACF.................. Army Cadet Force
ACIArb .... Associate, Chartered Institute of Arbitrators
ACIB .... Associate, Chartered Institute of Bankers (formerly AIB)
ACIBS.............. Associate, Chartered Institute of Bankers in Scotland
ACII .... Associate, Chartered Insurance Institute
ACIOB .... Associate, Chartered Institute of Building
ACIPA .... Associate, Chartered Institute of Patent Agents
ACIPD .... Associate, Chartered Institute of Personnel and Development
ACIS................. Associate, Institute of Chartered Secretaries and Administrators
ACIT .... Associate, Chartered Institute of Transport
ACMA .... Associate, Chartered Institute of Management Accountants (formerly ACWA)
ACMI............... Associate, Chartered Management Institute (formerly AIMgt)
ACORA .... Archbishops' Commission on Rural Areas
ACP.................. Associate, College of Preceptors
ACS .... Additional Curates Society
ACSM .... Associate, Camborne School of Mines
ACT.................. Australian Capital Territory
.... Australian College of Theology
ACUPA .... Archbishops' Commission on Urban Priority Areas
ACertCM .... Archbishop of Canterbury's Certificate in Church Music
AD.................... Area Dean
AEdRD .... Associateship in Educational Research and Development

AFAIM .... Associate Fellow, Australian Institute of Management
AFBPsS............ Associate Fellow, British Psychological Society (formerly ABPsS)
AFC .... Air Force Cross
AFIMA .... Associate Fellow, Institute of Mathematics and its Applications
AFOM .... Associate, Faculty of Occupational Medicine
AGSM .... Associate, Guildhall School of Music and Drama
AHSM *or* AHA Associate, Institute of Health Service Management (formerly Administrators)
AIA .... Associate, Institute of Actuaries
AIAS .... Associate, Incorporated Association of Architects and Surveyors
AIAT .... Associate, Institute of Animal Technicians
AIDS................. Acquired Immunity Deficiency Syndrome
AIFST............... Associate, Institute of Food Science and Technology
AIGCM............. Associate, Incorporated Guild of Church Musicians
AIIM .... Associate, Institute of Investment Management
AIL.................... Associate, Institute of Linguists
AIMLS.............. Associate, Institute of Medical Laboratory Sciences
AIMSW............. Associate, Institute of Medical Social Work
AIMgt .... Associate, Institute of Management (now see ACMI)
AIPM .... Associate, Institute of Personnel Management (now see ACIPD)
AITI .... Associate, Institute of Taxation in Ireland
AKC .... Associate, King's College London
ALA .... Associate, Library Association
ALAM .... Associate, London Academy of Music
ALBC................ Associate, London Bible College
ALCD .... Associate, London College of Divinity
ALCM............... Associate, London College of Music
ALSM .... Associate, Lancashire School of Music
AM .... Albert Medal
.... Master of Arts (USA)
AMA .... Associate, Museums Association
AMASI .... Associate Member of the Architects and Surveyors Institute
AMCST............. Associate, Manchester College of Science and Technology
AMCT............... Associate, Manchester College of Technology
AMIBF .... Associate Member, Institute of British Foundrymen
AMIC................ Associate Member, Institute of Counselling
AMICME .... Associate Member, Institute of Cast Metal Engineers
AMIDHE........... Associate Member, Institute of Domestic Heating Engineers
AMIEHO........... Associate Member, Institution of Environmental Health Officers
AMIM............... Associate Member, Institute of Metals
AMIMMM .... Associate Member, Institute of Materials, Minerals and Mining
AMIMinE .... Associate Member, Institute of Mining Engineers

AMITD............. Associate Member, Institute of Training and Development (now see ACIPD)
AMIW............... Associate Member, Institute of Welfare (formerly AMIWO)
AMInstT .... Associate Member, Institute of Transport
AMInstTA .... Associate Member, Institute of Transport Administration
AMRSH............ Associate Member, Royal Society of Health
AMSIA .... Associate Member, Society of Investment Analysts
AMusLCM .... Associate in Music, London College of Music
AMusTCL......... Associate in Music, Trinity College of Music London
ANC.................. African National Congress
AO.................... Officer, Order of Australia
APhS .... Associate, Philosophical Society of England
ARAM .... Associate, Royal Academy of Music
ARCA .... Associate, Royal College of Art
ARCIC .... Anglican-Roman Catholic International Commission
ARCM.............. Associate, Royal College of Music
ARCO .... Associate, Royal College of Organists
ARCO(CHM) ... Associate, Royal College of Organists with Diploma in Choir Training
ARCS .... Associate, Royal College of Science
ARCST............. Associate, Royal College of Science and Technology (Glasgow)
ARCT............... Associate, Royal Conservatory of Music Toronto
ARCUK .... Architects' Registration Council of the United Kingdom
ARHistS........... Associate, Royal Historical Society
ARIAM............ Associate, Royal Irish Academy of Music
ARMCM .... Associate, Royal Manchester College of Music
ARPS .... Associate, Royal Photographic Society
ARSCM .... Associate, Royal School of Church Music
ARSM.............. Associate, Royal School of Mines
AS..................... Associate in Science (USA)
ASCA .... Associate, Society of Company and Commercial Accountants
ASSP .... Society of All Saints Sisters of the Poor
ASVA .... Associate, Incorporated Society of Valuers and Auctioneers
ATC.................. Air Training Corps
ATCL .... Associate, Trinity College of Music London
ATD .... Art Teacher's Diploma
ATI.................... Associate, Textile Institute
ATII.................. Associate Member, Institute of Taxation
ATL................... Association of Teachers and Lecturers
ATV................... Associated Television
ATh(SA)........... Associate in Theology (South Africa)
AVCM .... Associate, Victoria College of Music
Ab..................... (Diocese of) Aberdeen and Orkney
Aber................... Aberdeen
Abp................... Archbishop
Abth .... Aberystwyth
Ad..................... Advanced
AdDipEd........... Advanced Diploma in Education

Admin .... Administration

.... Administrative

.... Administrator

Adn.................. Archdeacon

Adnry .... Archdeaconry

Adv .... Adviser

.... Advisory

Agric................ Agricultural

.... Agriculture

Aid.................. Aidan

.... Aidan's

alt................... alternate

Andr .... Andrew

.... Andrew's

.... Andrews

Angl................ Anglican

.... Anglicans

Ant .... Anthony

.... Anthony's

Appt .... Appointment

Arg .... (Diocese of) Argyll and The Isles

Arm .... (Diocese of) Armagh

Assn................ Association

Assoc .... Associate

Asst................. Assistant

Aug .... Augustine

.... Augustine's

Aus .... Australian

Aux .... Auxiliaries

.... Auxiliary

B

b...................... Born

B & W .... (Diocese of) Bath and Wells

B or Bapt .... Baptist

.... Baptist's

BA .... Bachelor of Arts

BA(Econ) .... Bachelor of Arts in Economics

BA(Ed) .... Bachelor of Arts in Education

BA(QTS) .... Bachelor of Arts (Qualified Teacher Status)

BA(ThM) .... Bachelor of Arts in Theology in Ministry

BA(Theol) .... Bachelor of Arts in Theology

BAI .... Bachelor of Engineering (also see BE and BEng)

BAO .... Bachelor of Obstetrics

BASc .... Bachelor of Applied Science

BAdmin........... Bachelor of Administration

BAgr .... Bachelor of Agriculture

BAgrSc .... Bachelor of Agricultural Science

BAppSc(OT) ..... Bachelor of Applied Science (Occupational Therapy)

BArch .... Bachelor of Architecture

BBA................. Bachelor of Business Administration

BBC................. British Broadcasting Corporation

BBS .... Bachelor of Business Studies

BC .... British Columbia (Canada)

BCA .... Bachelor of Commerce and Administration

BCC................. British Council of Churches (now CTBI)

BCE................. Bachelor of Civil Engineering

BCL................. Bachelor of Civil Law

BCMS .... Bible Churchmen's Missionary Society (now Crosslinks)

BCh or BChir .... Bachelor of Surgery (also see BS and ChB)

BChD .... Bachelor of Dental Surgery

BCom or BComm ... Bachelor of Commerce

BCombStuds ..... Bachelor of Combined Studies

BCommWelf..... Bachelor of Community Welfare

BD .... Bachelor of Divinity

BDA .... Bachelor of Dramatic Art

BDQ .... Bachelor of Divinity Qualifying Examination

BDS .... Bachelor of Dental Surgery

BDSc .... Bachelor of Dental Science

BDiv .... Bachelor of Divinity

BE.................... Bachelor of Engineering (also see BAI and BEng)

BEM................. British Empire Medal

BEc.................. Bachelor of Economics (Australia)

BEcon............... Bachelor of Economics (USA)

BEd .... Bachelor of Education

BEdSt .... Bachelor of Educational Studies

BEng................ Bachelor of Engineering (also see BAI and BE)

BFA .... Bachelor of Fine Arts

BFBS .... British and Foreign Bible Society

BHSc .... Bachelor of Health Sciences

BIE .... Bachelor of Industrial Engineering (USA)

BL.................... Bachelor of Law

BLib .... Bachelor of Librarianship

BLitt .... Bachelor of Letters

BM .... Bachelor of Medicine (also see MB)

BM, BCh .... Conjoint degree of Bachelor of Medicine, Bachelor of Surgery

BMMF............. Bible and Medical Missionary Fellowship (now Interserve)

BMU .... Board for Mission and Unity

BMedSci........... Bachelor of Medical Science

BMet .... Bachelor of Metallurgy

BMin .... Bachelor of Ministry

BMus............... Bachelor of Music (also see MusB and MusBac)

BMusEd .... Bachelor of Music Education

BN .... Bachelor of Nursing

BNC .... Brasenose College

BPR&TM.......... Bachelor of Parks, Recreation and Tourism Management

BPaed .... Bachelor of Paediatrics

BPh or BPhil ..... Bachelor of Philosophy

BPharm .... Bachelor of Pharmacy

BPhil(Ed).......... Bachelor of Philosophy (Education)

BRE................. Bachelor of Religious Education (USA)

BRF................. Bible Reading Fellowship

BS .... Bachelor of Science (also see BSc)

.... Bachelor of Surgery (also see BCh, BChir and ChB)

BSB .... Brotherhood of St Barnabas

BSE .... Bachelor of Science in Engineering (also see BScEng)

BSEd .... Bachelor of Science in Education (USA)

BSP.................. Brotherhood of St Paul

BSS .... Bachelor of Social Studies

BSSc .... Bachelor of Social Science (also see BSocSc)

BSW .... Bachelor of Social Work

BSc .... Bachelor of Science (also see BS)

BSc(Econ) .... Bachelor of Science in Economics

BSc(Soc).......... Bachelor of Science (Sociology)

BScAgr .... Bachelor of Science in Agriculture

BScEcon .... Bachelor of Science in Economics

BScEng............. Bachelor of Science in Engineering (also see BSE)

BScFor.............. Bachelor of Science in Forestry

BScTech............ Bachelor of Technical Science

BSocAdmin .... Bachelor of Social Administration

BSocSc.............. Bachelor of Social Science (also see BSSc)

BT..................... Bachelor of Teaching

BTS .... Bachelor of Theological Studies

BTech .... Bachelor of Technology

BTh or BTheol .. Bachelor of Theology (also see STB)

BVM&S............ Bachelor of Veterinary Medicine and Surgery

BVSc................ Bachelor of Veterinary Science

BVetMed .... Bachelor of Veterinary Medicine (also see VetMB)

Ball .... Balliol

Ban .... (Diocese of) Bangor

Barn.................. Barnabas

.... Barnabas's

Bart................... Bartholomew

.... Bartholomew's

Bd .... Board

Bedf .... Bedford

Belf .... Belfast

BèsL .... Bachelier ès lettres

Bibl................... Biblical

Birm .... (Diocese of) Birmingham

Blackb .... (Diocese of) Blackburn

Bp..................... Bishop

Br...................... British

Bradf .... (Diocese of) Bradford

Bre .... (Diocese of) Brechin

Brig................... Brigadier

Bris .... (Diocese of) Bristol

Bt...................... Baronet

C

C .... Curate

c....................... Consecrated

C & O .... (Diocese of) Cashel and Ossory (united dioceses of Cashel, Waterford, Lismore, Ossory, Ferns and Leighlin)

C of E .... Church of England

C of S............... Church of Scotland

C&G................. City and Guilds

C, C & R .... (Diocese of) Cork, Cloyne and Ross

C-in-c............... Curate-in-charge

c/o .... Care of

CA .... Church Army

.... Member, Institute of Chartered Accountants of Scotland

CA(Z)............... Member, Institute of Chartered Accountants of Zimbabwe

CACTM .... Central Advisory Council for the Ministry (now Ministry Division)

CANDL .... Church and Neighbourhood Development in London

CARA .... Care and Resources for people affected by AIDS/HIV

CARE .... Christian Action Research and Education

CASA .... Anglican Church of the Southern Cone of America

CB .... Companion, Order of the Bath

CBDTI .... Carlisle and Blackburn Diocesan Training Institute

CBE.................. Commander, Order of the British Empire

CBIM .... Companion, British Institute of Management

CBiol .... Chartered Biologist

CCBI .... Council of Churches for Britain and Ireland (now see CTBI)

CCC .... Corpus Christi College

.... Council for the Care of Churches

CCCS .... Commonwealth and Continental Church Society

CCWA .... Churches Community Work Alliance

CChem .... Chartered Chemist

CD.................... Canadian Forces Decoration

.... Conventional District (also see ED)

CDir .... Chartered Director

CECD .... Church of England Council for the Deaf

CECS................ Church of England Children's Society (now known as the Children's Society)

CEMS .... Church of England Men's Society

CETD................ Certificate in the Education of the Deaf

CEng .... Chartered Engineer

CEnv................. Chartered Environmentalist

CF .... Chaplain to the Forces

CGA.................. Community of the Glorious Ascension

CGeol .... Chartered Geologist

CH	Companion of Honour	Cert	Certificat(e)	DBE	Dame Commander, Order of the British Empire
CIO	Church Information Office	CertEd	Certificate of Education	DBF	Diocesan Board of Finance
CIPFA	Chartered Institute of Public Finance and Accountancy	CertFE	Certificate of Further Education	DBP	Diocesan Board of Patronage
CITC	Church of Ireland Theological College	CertHE	Certificate in Higher Education	DC	District of Columbia (USA)
CJGS	Community of the Companions of Jesus the Good Shepherd	Ch	Christ	DCC	Diploma in Crisis Counselling of the Institute of Counselling
			Christ's		
			Church	DCL	Doctor of Civil Law
CMD	Cambridge Mission to Delhi (now see USPG)	Ch Ch	Christ Church	DCYW	Diploma in Community and Youth Work
CME	Continuing Ministerial Education	ChB	Bachelor of Surgery (also see BCh, BChir and BS)	DCnL	Doctor of Canon Law
CMG	Companion, Order of St Michael and St George	Chan	Chancellor	DD	Doctor of Divinity
		Chapl	Chaplain	DDS	Doctor of Dental Surgery
CMJ	Church's Ministry among Jewish People		Chaplaincies	DEHC	Diploma in the Education of Handicapped Children
			Chaplaincy		
CMP	Company of Mission Priests		Chaplains	DEd	Doctor of Education (also see EdD)
CMS	Church Mission Society (formerly Church Missionary Society)	Chas	Charles		
			Charles's	DEng	Doctor of Engineering
		Chelmsf	(Diocese of) Chelmsford	DFC	Distinguished Flying Cross
CMath	Chartered Mathematician	Chelt	Cheltenham	DFM	Distinguished Flying Medal (Canada)
COPEC	Conference on Politics, Economics and Community	Ches	(Diocese of) Chester		
		Chich	(Diocese of) Chichester	DHA	District Health Authority
CORAT	Christian Organizations Research and Advisory Trust	Chmn	Chairman	DHL	Doctor of Humane Letters
			Chairwoman	DHSc	Doctor of Health Science
CORE	City Outreach through Renewal Evangelism	Chpl	Chapel	DHumLit	Doctor of Humane Letters
		Chr	Christian	DL	Deputy Lieutenant
			Christians	DLSc	Doctor of Legal Science
CP	Community Priest	Chris	Christopher	DLitt	Doctor of Letters (also see LittD)
CPA	Chartered Patent Agent (formerly FCIPA)		Christopher's		
		Chrys	Chrysostom	DLitt et Phil	Doctor of Letters and Philosophy
CPAS	Church Pastoral Aid Society		Chrysostom's		
CPEng	Chartered Professional Engineer (of Institution of Engineers of Australia)	Chu	Churchill	DMin	Doctor of Ministry
		Cl-in-c	Cleric-in-charge	DMinTh	Doctor of Ministry and Theology
		Clem	Clement		
CPFA	Member Chartered Institute of Public Finance and Accountancy (formerly IPFA)		Clement's	DOE	Department of the Environment
		Cllr	Councillor/Counsellor		
		Clogh	(Diocese of) Clogher	DPhil	Doctor of Philosophy (also see PhD)
		Co	Company		
CPM	Colonial Police Medal		County	DProf	Doctor in Professional Studies
CPhys	Chartered Physicist of the Institute of Physics		Counties		
		Co-ord	Co-ordinator	DRCOG	Diploma of the Royal College of Obstetricians and Gynaecologists
CPsychol	Chartered Member, British Psychological Society		Co-ordinating		
		Col	Colonel		
CQSW	Certificate of Qualification in Social Work	Coll	College	DSC	Distinguished Service Cross
		Colleg	Collegiate	DSM	Distinguished Service Medal
CR	Community of the Resurrection (Mirfield)	Comdr	Commander	DSO	Companion, Distinguished Service Order
		Comdr OM (Italy)	Commander, Order of Merit of the Italian Republic		
CSA	Community of St Andrew			DST	Doctor of Sacred Theology (also see STD)
CSC	Community of the Sisters of the Church	Commn	Commission		
		Commr	Commissioner	DSc	Doctor of Science (also see ScD)
CSD	Community of St Denys	Comp	Comprehensive		
CSF	Community of St Francis	Conf	Confederation	DSc(Eng)	Doctor of Science in Engineering
CSG	Company of the Servants of God		Conference		
		Conn	(Diocese of) Connor	DSocSc	Doctor of Social Science
CSMV	Community of St Mary the Virgin	Corp	Corporation	DTI	Department of Trade and Industry
		Coun	Council		
CSP	Community of St Peter	Cov	(Diocese of) Coventry	DTech	Doctor of Technology
CSS	Certificate in Social Service	Cttee	Committee	DTh	Doctor of Theology (also see ThD)
CSSM	Children's Special Service Mission	Cust	Custodian		
			Custody	DUP	Docteur de l'Université de Paris
CSWG	Community of the Servants of the Will of God	Cuth	Cuthbert		
			Cuthbert's	DUniv	Doctor of the University
CSci	Chartered Scientist	Cypr	Cyprian	Darw	Darwin
CSocSc	Certificate in Social Science		Cyprian's	Dav	David
CStat	Chartered Statistician				David's
CTABRSM	Certificate of Teaching, Associated Board of the Royal Schools of Music			Dep	Deputy
		D		Dept	Department
CTBI	Churches Together in Britain and Ireland (formerly CCBI)	d	Ordained Deacon	DèsS	Docteur ès sciences
		D & D	(Diocese of) Down and Dromore	DèsL	Docteur ès lettres
CUF	Church Urban Fund			Det	Detention
CVO	Commander, Royal Victorian Order	D & G	(Diocese of) Dublin and Glendalough	Dio	Diocese
				Dioc	Diocesan
CWME	Commission on World Mission and Evangelism	D & R	(Diocese of) Derry and Raphoe	Dip	Diploma
		D&C	Dean and Chapter	DipAE	Diploma in Adult Education
CY	Church and Youth	DACE	Diploma in Adult and Continuing Education	DipAdEd	Diploma in Advanced Education
CYCW	Certificate in Youth and Community Work				
		DAES	Diploma in Advanced Educational Studies	DipCOT	Diploma of the College of Occupational Therapists
CYFA	Church Youth Fellowships Association	DAPC	Diploma in Advanced Psychological Counselling	DipEd	Diploma in Education
Cam	Cambridge			DipHE	Diploma in Higher Education
Can	Canon	DASAE	Diploma of Advanced Study in Adult Education		
Cand	Candidate			DipOT	Diploma in Occupational Therapy
	Candidate's	DASE	Diploma in the Advanced Study of Education		
	Candidates'			DipSW	Diploma in Social Work
Cant	(Diocese of) Canterbury	DASHE	Diploma in Advanced Studies in Higher Education	Dir	Director
Capt	Captain			Distr	District
Carl	(Diocese of) Carlisle	DASS	Diploma in Applied Social Studies	Div	Divinity
Cath	Catharine/Catherine			Div Test	Divinity Testimonium
	Catharine's/Catherine's	DASSc	Diploma in Applied Social Science	Dn	Deacon
Cathl	Cathedral			Dn-in-c	Deacon-in-charge
Cdre	Commodore	DArch	Doctor of Architecture	Dom	Domestic
Cen	Centre	DB	Bachelor of Divinity (USA)	Down	Downing
	Center			Dr	Doctor
	Central			Dr rer nat	Doctor of Natural Science

DrTheol............ Doctor of Theology (Germany)
Dss.................... Deaconess
dss.................. Admitted Deaconess
Dub .... Dublin
Dur................... (Diocese of) Durham

E

E .... East
.... Eastern
EAMTC .... East Anglian Ministerial Training Course
EC .... Emergency Commission
ED................... Ecclesiastical District (also see CD)
.... Efficiency Decoration
EMMTC.......... East Midlands Ministry Training Course
EN(G) .... Enrolled Nurse (General)
EN(M).............. Enrolled Nurse (Mental)
ERD .... Emergency Reserve Decoration
ERMC.............. Eastern Region Ministry Course
ESC .... Ecole Superieure de Commerce
ESMI................ Elderly, Sick and Mentally Infirm
Ecum .... Ecumenical
.... Ecumenics
.... Ecumenism
Ed .... Editor
.... Editorial
EdD .... Doctor of Education (also see DEd)
EdM .... Master of Education (USA) (also see MEd)
Edin................. (Diocese of) Edinburgh
Edm................. Edmund
.... Edmund's
Educn .... Education
.... Educational
Edw .... Edward
.... Edward's
Eliz .... Elizabeth
.... Elizabeth's
Em................... Emanuel
.... Emmanuel
Emb.................. Embassy
EngD................ Doctor of Engineering
EngTech .... Engineering Technician
Episc................ Episcopal
.... Episcopalian
Eur................... (Diocese of) Gibraltar in Europe
.... Europe
.... European
EurIng .... European Engineer
Ev .... Evangelist
.... Evangelist's
.... Evangelists
Evang .... Evangelical
.... Evangelism
Ex .... (Diocese of) Exeter
Exam .... Examining
Exec................. Executive
Exor................. Executor
Ext .... Extension

F

F&HE .... Further and Higher Education
FAA................. Fellow, Institution of Administrative Accountants
FACOG .... Fellow, American College of Obstetricians and Gynaecologists
FADO .... Fellow, Association of Dispensing Opticians
FAEB .... Fellow, Academy of Environmental Biology (India)
FAIM .... Fellow, Australian Institute of Management
FAIWCW......... Fellow, Australian Institute of Welfare and Community Workers
FASI .... Fellow, Architects' and Surveyors' Institute
FBA.................. Fellow, British Academy

FBCO............... Fellow, British College of Ophthalmic Opticians (Optometrists)
FBCS................ Fellow, British Computer Society
FBCartS .... Fellow, British Cartographic Society
FBDO .... Fellow, Association of British Dispensing Opticians
FBEng.............. Fellow, Association of Building Engineers
FBIM .... Fellow, British Institute of Management (formerly MBIM)
FBIS................. Fellow, British Interplanetary Society
FBIST.............. Fellow, British Institute of Surgical Technologists
FBOA............... Fellow, British Optical Association
FBPICS............ Fellow, British Production and Inventory Control Society
FBPsS.............. Fellow, British Psychological Society
FBS .... Fellow, Burgon Society
FCA .... Fellow, Institute of Chartered Accountants
FCCA............... Fellow, Chartered Association of Certified Accountants (formerly FACCA)
FCFI .... Fellow, Clothing and Footwear Institute
FCIArb .... Fellow, Chartered Institute of Arbitrators
FCIB .... Fellow, Chartered Institute of Bankers
.... Fellow, Corporation of Insurance Brokers
FCIE .... Fellow, Association of Charity Independent Examiners
FCIH................ Fellow, Chartered Institute of Housing
FCII .... Fellow, Chartered Insurance Institute
FCILA .... Fellow, Chartered Institute of Loss Adjusters
FCIM .... Fellow, Chartered Institute of Marketing (formerly FInstM)
FCIOB .... Fellow, Chartered Institute of Building
FCIPD .... Fellow, Chartered Institute of Personnel and Development
FCIS................. Fellow, Institute of Chartered Secretaries and Administrators
FCIT .... Fellow, Chartered Institute of Transport
FCMA............... Fellow, Chartered Institute of Management Accountants
FCMI .... Fellow, Chartered Management Institute (formerly FIMgt)
FCO .... Foreign and Commonwealth Office
FCOptom.......... Fellow, College of Optometrists
FCP .... Fellow, College of Preceptors
FCollP.............. Ordinary Fellow, College of Preceptors
FDA .... Foundation Degree in Arts
FDS.................. Fellow in Dental Surgery
FDSRCPSGlas.. Fellow in Dental Surgery, Royal College of Physicians and Surgeons of Glasgow
FDSRCS........... Fellow in Dental Surgery, Royal College of Surgeons of England
FE..................... Further Education
FEPA................ Fellow, Evangelical Preachers' Association
FFA .... Fellow, Institute of Financial Accountants
FFAEM............. Fellow, Faculty of Accident and Emergency Medicine
FFARCS........... Fellow, Faculty of Anaesthetists, Royal College of Surgeons of England
FFChM............. Fellow, Faculty of Church Music

FFDRCSI .... Fellow, Faculty of Dentistry, Royal College of Surgeons in Ireland
FFHom .... Fellow, the Faculty of Homoeopathy
FFOM............... Fellow, Faculty of Occupational Medicine
FFPH .... Fellow, Faculty of Public Health (formerly FFPHM)
FFPHM .... Fellow, Faculty of Public Health Medicine (now see FFPH)
FFPM .... Fellow, Faculty of Pharmaceutical Medicine
FGA .... Fellow, Gemmological Association
FGCM .... Fellow, Guild of Church Musicians
FGMS .... Fellow, Guild of Musicians and Singers
FGS .... Fellow, Geological Society of London
FHA .... Fellow, Institute of Hospital Administrators (now see FHSM)
FHCIMA .... Fellow, Hotel Catering and Institutional Management Association
FHSM .... Fellow, Institute of Health Services Management
FIA.................... Fellow, Institute of Actuaries
FIBMS .... Fellow, Institute of Biomedical Sciences
FIBiol .... Fellow, Institute of Biology
FICE .... Fellow, Institution of Civil Engineers
FICM .... Fellow, Institution of Commercial Managers
FICS................. Fellow, International College of Surgeons
FIChemE .... Fellow, Institution of Chemical Engineers
FIDiagE .... Fellow, Institute of Diagnostic Engineers
FIED................. Fellow, Institution of Engineering Designers
FIEE................. Fellow, Institution of Electrical Engineers (formerly FIERE)
FIEEE .... Fellow, Institute of Electrical and Electronics Engineers (NY)
FIERE............... Fellow, Institution of Electronic and Radio Engineers (now see FIEE)
FIFireE............. Fellow, Institution of Fire Engineers
FIHT................. Fellow of the Institution of Highways and Transportation
FIHospE .... Fellow, Institute of Hospital Engineering
FIIM .... Fellow, Institution of Industrial Managers (formerly FIPlantE)
FIL .... Fellow, Institute of Linguists
FIMA................ Fellow, Institute of Mathematics and its Applications
FIMI .... Fellow, Institute of the Motor Industry
FIMLS .... Fellow, Institute of Medical Laboratory Sciences
FIMM .... Fellow, Institution of Mining and Metallurgy (now see FIMMM)
FIMMM .... Fellow, Institute of Materials, Minerals and Mining
FIMS .... Fellow, Institute of Management Specialists
FIMarEST .... Fellow, Institute of Marine Engineering, Science and Technology
FIMechE........... Fellow, Institution of Mechanical Engineers
FINucE .... Fellow, Institution of Nuclear Engineers
FIOSH .... Fellow, Institute of Occupational Safety and Health
FIPD .... Fellow, Institute of Personnel Development
FIPEM .... Fellow, Institute of Physics and Engineering in Medicine

FIQA .... Fellow, Institute of Quality Assurance
FISM .... Fellow, Institute of Supervisory Management
FIST .... Fellow, Institute of Science and Technology
FIStructE .... Fellow, Institution of Structural Engineers
FInstAM .... Fellow, Institute of Administrative Management
FInstD .... Fellow, Institute of Directors
FInstE .... Fellow, Institute of Energy
FInstLEx .... Fellow, Institute of Legal Executives
FInstMC .... Fellow, Institute of Measurement and Control
FInstP .... Fellow, Institute of Physics
FInstSMM .... Fellow, Institute of Sales and Marketing Management
FInstTT .... Fellow, Institute of Travel and Tourism
FKC .... Fellow, King's College London
FLA .... Fellow, Library Association
FLAME .... Family Life and Marriage Education
FLCM .... Fellow, London College of Music
FLIA .... Fellow, Life Insurance Association
FLS .... Fellow, Linnean Society
FMA .... Fellow, Museums Association
FNI .... Fellow, Nautical Institute
FPS .... Fellow, Pharmaceutical Society of Great Britain
FPhS .... Fellow, Philosophical Society of England
FRACI .... Fellow, Royal Australian Chemical Institute
FRAI .... Fellow, Royal Anthropological Institute
FRAM .... Fellow, Royal Academy of Music
FRAS .... Fellow, Royal Asiatic Society
.... Fellow, Royal Astronomical Society
FRAeS .... Fellow, Royal Aeronautical Society
FRCA .... Fellow, Royal College of Anaesthetists
FRCGP .... Fellow, Royal College of General Practitioners
FRCM .... Fellow, Royal College of Music
FRCO .... Fellow, Royal College of Organists
FRCOG .... Fellow, Royal College of Obstetricians and Gynaecologists
FRCOphth .... Fellow, Royal College of Ophthalmologists
FRCP .... Fellow, Royal College of Physicians
FRCP(C) .... Fellow, Royal College of Physicians of Canada
FRCPCH .... Fellow, Royal College of Paediatrics and Child Health
FRCPEd .... Fellow, Royal College of Physicians Edinburgh
FRCPGlas .... Fellow, Royal College of Physicians and Surgeons, Glasgow (also see FRCSGlas)
FRCPath .... Fellow, Royal College of Pathologists
FRCPsych .... Fellow, Royal College of Psychiatrists
FRCR .... Fellow, Royal College of Radiologists
FRCS .... Fellow, Royal College of Physicians and Surgeons of England
FRCSE or FRCSEd .... Fellow, Royal College of Surgeons of Edinburgh
FRCSGlas .... Fellow, Royal College of Physicians and Surgeons, Glasgow (also see FRCPGlas)
FRCSI .... Fellow, Royal College of Surgeons in Ireland
FRCVS .... Fellow, Royal College of Veterinary Surgeons
FREng .... Fellow, Royal Academy of Engineering

FRGS .... Fellow, Royal Geographical Society
FRHS .... Fellow, Royal Horticultural Society
FRHistS .... Fellow, Royal Historical Society
FRIAS .... Fellow, Royal Incorporation of Architects of Scotland
FRIBA .... Fellow, Royal Institute of British Architects
FRICS .... Fellow, Royal Institution of Chartered Surveyors (formerly FLAS and FSI)
FRIN .... Fellow, Royal Institute of Navigation
FRINA .... Fellow, Royal Institution of Naval Architects
FRIPH .... Fellow, Royal Institute of Public Health
FRMetS .... Fellow, Royal Meteorological Society
FRPharmS .... Fellow, Royal Pharmaceutical Society
FRS .... Fellow, Royal Society
FRSA .... Fellow, Royal Society of Arts
FRSAI .... Fellow, Royal Society of Antiquaries of Ireland
FRSC .... Fellow, Royal Society of Canada
.... Fellow, Royal Society of Chemistry (formerly FRIC)
FRSCM .... Hon Fellow, Royal School of Church Music
FRSE .... Fellow, Royal Society of Edinburgh
FRSH .... Fellow, Royal Society for Public Health
FRSL .... Fellow, Royal Society of Literature
FRSM .... Fellow, Royal Society of Medicine
FRSocMed .... Fellow, Royal Society of Medicine
FRTPI .... Fellow, Royal Town Planning Institute
FSA .... Fellow, Society of Antiquaries
FSAScot .... Fellow, Royal Society of Antiquaries of Scotland
FSCA .... Fellow, Royal Society of Company and Commercial Accountants
FSJ .... Fellowship of St John the Evangelist
FSR .... Fellowship Diploma of the Society of Radiographers
FSS .... Fellow, Royal Statistical Society
FTC .... Flying Training Command
FTCL .... Fellow, Trinity College of Music London
FTII .... Fellow, Institute of Taxation
FVCM .... Fellow, Victoria College of Music
FWeldI .... Fellow, Institute of Welding
Fell .... Fellow
Fitzw .... Fitzwilliam
Foundn .... Foundation
Fran .... Francis
.... Francis's

G

G&C .... Gonville and Caius
GB .... Great Britain
GBSM .... Graduate of the Birmingham School of Music
GCMG .... Knight Grand Cross, Order of St Michael and St George
GCVO .... Knight Grand Cross, Royal Victorian Order
GFS .... Girls' Friendly Society
GGSM .... Graduate Diploma of the Guildhall School of Music and Drama
GIBiol .... Graduate of the Institute of Biology
GIFireE .... Graduate of the Institute of Fire Engineers
GIMechE .... Graduate of the Institution of Mechanical Engineers
GIPE .... Graduate of the Institution of Production Engineers

GInstP .... Graduate of the Institute of Physics
GLCM .... Graduate Diploma of the London College of Music
GM .... George Medal
GMus .... Graduate Diploma in Music
GMusRNCM .... Graduate in Music of the Royal Northern College of Music
GNSM .... Graduate of the Northern School of Music
GRIC .... Graduate Membership, Royal Institute of Chemistry
GRNCM .... Graduate of the Royal Northern College of Music
GRSC .... Graduate of the Royal School of Chemistry
GRSM .... Graduate of the Royal Schools of Music
GSM .... (Member of) Guildhall School of Music and Drama
GTCL .... Graduate Diploma of Trinity College of Music, London
Gabr .... Gabriel
.... Gabriel's
Gd .... Good
Gen .... General
Geo.................... George
.... George's
Gib .... Gibraltar
Glam .... Glamorgan
Glas .... (Diocese of) Glasgow and Galloway
.... Glasgow
Glos .... Gloucestershire
Glouc................. (Diocese of) Gloucester
Gov.................... Governor
Gp .... Group
Gr .... Grammar
GradCIPD .... Graduate of the Chartered Institute of Personnel and Development
GradIPM........... Graduate of the Institute of Personnel Management
Greg.................. Gregory
.... Gregory's
Gt .... Great
Gtr.................... Greater
Guildf .... (Diocese of) Guildford

H

H....................... Holy
H&FE .... Higher and Further Education
HA..................... Health Authority
HDipEd............. Higher Diploma in Education
HE..................... Higher Education
HIV .... Human Immunodeficiency Virus
HM..................... Her (or His) Majesty
HMI .... Her (or His) Majesty's Inspector (or Inspectorate)
HMS.................. Her (or His) Majesty's Ship
HQ..................... Headquarters
HTV................... Harlech Television
HVCert............. Health Visitor's Certificate
Hatf .... Hatfield
Hd .... Head
Heref................. (Diocese of) Hereford
Hertf................. Hertford
Hist................... Historic
.... Historical
.... History
Ho .... House
Hon .... Honorary
.... Honourable
HonDLaws......... Honorary Doctor of Laws
HonFChS.......... Honorary Fellow, Society of Chiropodists
HonRCM .... Honorary Member, Royal College of Music
Hosp.................. Hospital

I

I .... Incumbent
IAAP .... International Association for Analytical Psychology
IBA.................... Independent Broadcasting Authority

ICF .... Industry Churches Forum (formerly Industrial Christian Fellowship)
ICM.................. Irish Church Missions
ICS .... Intercontinental Church Society
IDC .... Inter-Diocesan Certificate
IDWAL .... Inter-Diocesan West Africa Link
IEAB .... Igreja Episcopal Anglicana do Brasil
IEng................. Incorporated Engineer (formerly TEng(CEI))
IFES .... International Fellowship of Evangelical Students
ILEA .... Inner London Education Authority
IME.................. Initial Ministerial Education
IMinE.............. Institution of Mining Engineers
INSEAD .... Institut Européen d'Administration des Affaires
IPFA .... Member, Chartered Institute of Public Finance and Accountancy
ISO .... Imperial Service Order
IT...................... Information Technology
ITV .... Independent Television
IVF .... Inter-Varsity Fellowship of Evangelical Unions (now see UCCF)
IVS .... International Voluntary Service
Imp.................. Imperial
Inc .... Incorporated
Ind .... Industrial
.... Industry
Info.................. Information
Insp.................. Inspector
Inst .... Institut
.... Institute
.... Institution
Intercon........... Intercontinental
Internat............ International
Interpr .... Interpretation
Is....................... Island
.... Islands
.... Isle
.... Isles

J

JCD .... Doctor of Canon Law
JCL................... Licentiate in Canon Law
JD..................... Doctor of Jurisprudence
JEM.................. Jerusalem and the East Mission (now see JMECA)
JMECA .... Jerusalem and Middle East Church Association (formerly JEM)
JP...................... Justice of the Peace
Jas.................... James
.... James's
Jes .... Jesus
Jo .... John
.... John's
Jos.................... Joseph
.... Joseph's
Jt...................... Joint
Jun .... Junior

K

K....................... King
.... King's
K, E & A .... (Diocese of) Kilmore, Elphin and Ardagh
KA.................... Knight of St Andrew, Order of Barbados
KBE .... Knight Commander, Order of the British Empire
KCB.................. Knight Commander, Order of the Bath
KCMG .... Knight Commander, Order of St Michael and St George
KCVO............... Knight Commander, Royal Victorian Order
KPM .... King's Police Medal
Kath .... Katharine/Katherine
.... Katharine's/Katherine's
Kt .... Knight

L

L & K .... (Diocese of) Limerick and Killaloe (united dioceses of Limerick, Ardfert, Aghadoe, Killaloe, Kilfenora, Clonfert, Kilmacduagh and Emly)
LASI................. Licentiate, Ambulance Service Institute
LBIPP.............. Licentiate, British Institute of Professional Photography
LCC.................. London County Council
LCL................... Licentiate in Canon Law
LCP................... Licentiate, College of Preceptors
LCST................. Licentiate, College of Speech Therapists
LCTP................ Lancashire and Cumbria Theological Partnership
LDS.................. Licentiate in Dental Surgery
LDiv................. Licentiate in Divinity
LEA.................. Local Education Authority
LEP .... Local Ecumenical Partnership
LGCM .... Lesbian and Gay Christian Movement
LGSM .... Licentiate, Guildhall School of Music and Drama
LICeram........... Licentiate, Institute of Ceramics
LIMA .... Licentiate, Institute of Mathematics and its Applications
LLA................... Lady Literate in Arts
LLAM............... Licentiate, London Academy of Music and Dramatic Art
LLB .... Bachelor of Laws
LLCM............... Licentiate, London College of Music
LLCM(TD)....... Licentiate, London College of Music (Teachers' Diploma)
LLD .... Doctor of Laws
LLM.................. Master of Laws
LMH................. Lady Margaret Hall
LMPA............... Licentiate Master, Photographers' Association
LNSM .... Local Non-stipendiary Minister (or Ministry)
LOROS............. Leicestershire Organization for the Relief of Suffering
LRAM .... Licentiate, Royal Academy of Music
LRCP................ Licentiate, Royal College of Physicians
LRCPI.............. Licentiate, Royal College of Physicians of Ireland
LRCSEng .... Licentiate of the Royal College of Surgeons in England
LRCSI .... Licentiate, Royal College of Surgeons in Ireland
LRPS................ Licentiate, Royal Photographic Society
LRSC................ Licentiate, Royal Society of Chemistry
LRSM .... Licentiate Diploma of the Royal Schools of Music
LSE .... London School of Economics and Political Science
LSHTM............. London School of Hygiene and Tropical Medicine
LSIAD .... Licentiate, Society of Industrial Artists and Designers
LSocEth .... Licence en Sociologie-Ethnologie
LTCL................ Licentiate, Trinity College of Music London
LTh................... Licentiate in Theology (also see LST)
LVCM............... Licentiate, Victoria College of Music
LVO .... Lieutenant, Royal Victorian Order
LWCMD .... Licentiate, Welsh College of Music and Drama
Lamp................ Lampeter
Lanc.................. Lancaster
Laur.................. Laurence
.... Laurence's
Lawr................. Lawrence
.... Lawrence's
Ld .... Lord

Ldr.................... Leader
Lect................... Lecturer
Leic................... (Diocese of) Leicester
Leon .... Leonard
.... Leonard's
LèsL .... Licencié ès lettres
Lib.................... Librarian
.... Library
Lic .... Licence
.... Licensed
.... Licentiate
LicTh................ Licence in Theology
Lich .... (Diocese of) Lichfield
Linc .... (Diocese of) Lincoln
Lit..................... Literature
LittD .... Doctor of Letters (also see DLitt)
Liturg............... Liturgical
Liv .... (Diocese of) Liverpool
Llan .... (Diocese of) Llandaff
Lon .... (Diocese of) London
Loughb.............. Loughborough
Lt...................... Lieutenant
.... Little
Ltd.................... Limited

M

M & K .... (Diocese of) Meath and Kildare
MA .... Master of Arts
MA(Ed)............ Master of Arts in Education
MA(MM)......... Master of Arts in Mission and Ministry
MA(TS)............ Master of Arts in Theological Studies
MA(Theol)....... Master of Arts in Theology
MAAIS .... Member, Association of Archaeological Illustrators and Surveyors
MAAT............... Member, Association of Accounting Technicians
MACC............... Member, Australian College of Chaplains
MACE............... Member, Australian College of Educators
MACT............... Member, Association of Corporate Treasurers
MAE .... Member, Academy of Experts
MAJA............... Member, Association of Jungian Analysts
MAMIT .... Member, Associate of Meat Inspectors Trust
MAPsS .... Member, Australian Psychological Society
MASI .... Member, Architects and Surveyors Institute
MAT.................. Master of Arts and Teaching (USA)
MATA............... Member, Animal Technicians' Association
MATCA........... Member, Air Traffic Control Association
MATM.............. Master of Arts in Theology and Ministry
MAgrSc............ Master of Agricultural Science
MArAd .... Master of Archive Administration
MArch............... Master of Architecture
MB .... Bachelor of Medicine (also see BM)
MB,BS or MB,ChB .... Conjoint degree of Bachelor of Medicine, Bachelor of Surgery
MBA .... Master of Business Administration
MBACP............. Member, British Association for Counselling and Psychotherapy
MBAOT............ Member, British Association of Occupational Therapists (formerly MAOT)
MBAP................ Member, British Association of Psychotherapists
MBASW .... Member, British Association of Social Workers
MBATOD .... Member, British Association of Teachers of the Deaf
MBC.................. Metropolitan (or Municipal) Borough Council
MBCS .... Member, British Computer Society

MBChA	Member, British Chiropody Association
MBE	Member, Order of the British Empire
MBES	Member, Biological Engineering Society
MBEng	Member, Association of Building Engineers
MBIM	Member, British Institute of Management (later MIMgt)
MBKSTS	Member, British Kinematograph, Sound and Television Society
MBPsS	Member, British Psychological Society
MC	Military Cross
MCA	Member, Institute of Chartered Accountants
MCB	Master in Clinical Biochemistry
MCCDRCS	Member in Clinical Community Dentistry, Royal College of Surgeons
MCD	Master of Civic Design
MCE	Master of Civil Engineering
MCIArb	Member, Chartered Institute of Arbitrators
MCIBS	Member, Chartered Institute of Bankers in Scotland
MCIBSE	Member, Chartered Institute of Building Service Engineers
MCIEH	Member, Chartered Institute of Enviromental Health (formerly MIEH)
MCIH	Member, Chartered Institute of Housing (formerly MIH)
MCIJ	Member, Chartered Institute of Journalists
MCIM	Member, Chartered Institute of Marketing (formerly MInstM)
MCIMA	Member, Chartered Institute of Management Accountants
MCIOB	Member, Chartered Institute of Building
MCIPD	Member, Chartered Institute of Personnel and Development
MCIPS	Member, Chartered Institute of Purchasing and Supply
MCIT	Member, Chartered Institute of Transport
MCIWEM	Member, Chartered Institution of Water and Enviromental Management
MCL	Master of Canon Law
MCLIP	Member, Chartered Institute of Library and Information Professionals
MCMI	Member, Chartered Management Institute (formerly MBIM & MIMgt)
MCS	Master of Christian Spirituality
	Master of Christian Studies
MCSD	Member, Chartered Society of Designers
MCSP	Member, Chartered Society of Physiotherapy
MCST	Member, College of Speech Therapists
MCT	Member, Association of Corporate Treasurers
MChOrth	Master of Orthopaedic Surgery
MChS	Member, Society of Chiropodists
MChemA	Master in Chemical Analysis
MCollP	Member, College of Preceptors
MCom	Master of Commerce
MCommH	Master of Community Health
MD	Doctor of Medicine
MDA	Master of Defence Administration
MDiv	Master of Divinity
ME	Master of Engineering (also see MEng)
MEHS	Member, Ecclesiastical History Society
MEd	Master of Education
MEng	Master of Engineering
MFA	Master of Fine Art
MFHom	Member, Faculty of Homeopathy
MFOM	Member, Faculty of Occupational Medicine
MGDSRCS	Membership in General Dental Surgery, Royal College of Surgeons of England
MHCIMA	Member, Hotel Catering and Institutional Management Association
MHSM	Member, Institute of Health Services Management
MHSc	Master of Health Science
MHort (RHS)	Master of Horticulture, Royal Horticultural Society
MHums	Master of Humanities
MIA	Malawi Institute of Architects
MIAAP	Member, International Association for Analytical Psychology
MIAAS	Member, Incorporated Association of Architects and Surveyors
MIAM	Member, Institute of Administrative Management
MIAP	Member, Institution of Analysts and Programmers
MIAT	Member, Institute of Asphalt Technology
MIBC	Member, Institute of Business Counsellors
MIBCO	Member, Institution of Building Control Officers
MIBF	Member, Institute of British Foundrymen
MIBiol	Member, Institute of Biology
MICA	Member, International Cartographic Association
MICAS	Member, Institute of Chartered Accountants of Scotland
MICE	Member, Institution of Civil Engineers (formerly AMICE)
MICFM	Member, Institute of Charity Fundraising Managers
MICFor	Member, Institute of Chartered Foresters
MICM	Member, Institute of Credit Management
MICS	Member, Institute of Chartered Shipbrokers
MIChemE	Member, Institution of Chemical Engineers
MICorrST	Member, Institution of Corrosion Science and Technology
MIE	Member, Institute of Engineers and Technicians
MIEAust	Member, Institute of Engineers and Technicians Australia
MIED	Member, Institute of Engineering Designers
MIEE	Member, Institution of Electrical Engineers (formerly AMIEE & MIERE)
MIEEE	Member, Institute of Electrical and Electronics Engineers (NY)
MIEEM	Member, Institute of Ecology and Environmental Management
MIET	Member, Institution of Engineering and Technology
MIElecIE	Corporate Member, Institution of Electrical and Electronics Incorporated Engineers
MIEx	Member, Institute of Export
MIGasE	Member, Institution of Gas Engineers
MIHEEM	Member, Institute of Healthcare Engineering and Estate Management
MIHT	Member, Institution of Highways and Transportation
MIIExE	Member, Institute of Incorporated Executive Engineers
MIIM	Member, Institution of Industrial Managers
MIInfSc	Member, Institute of Information Scientists
MIL	Member, Institute of Linguists
MILT	Member, Institute of Logistics and Transport
MIM	Member, Institute of Metals (formerly Institution of Metallurgists)
MIMA	Member, Institute of Management Accountants
	Member, Institute of Mathematics and its Applications
MIMC	Member, Institute of Management Consultants
MIMI	Member, Institute of the Motor Industry
MIMarEST	Member, Institute of Marine Engineering, Science and Technology
MIMechE	Member, Institution of Mechanical Engineers (formerly AMIMechE)
MIMunE	Member, Institution of Municipal Engineers
MINucE	Member, Institution of Nuclear Engineers
MIOSH	Member, Institution of Occupational Safety and Health
MIOT	Member, Institute of Operating Theatre Technicians
MIPI	Member, Institute of Private Investigators
MIPR	Member, Institute of Public Relations
MIProdE	Member, Institution of Production Engineers
MIQA	Member, Institute of Quality Assurance
MIRSE	Member, Institution of Railway Signal Engineers
MISE	Member, Institute of Sales Engineers
MISM	Member, Institute of Supervisory Management
MISW	Member, Institute of Social Welfare
MIStructE	Member, Institution of Structural Engineers
MITMA	Member, Institute of Trade Mark Agents
MITPA	Member, International Tax Planning Association
MIW	Member, Institute of Welfare (formerly MIWO)
MInstC(Glas)	Member, Institute of Counselling (Glasgow)
MInstD	Member, Institute of Directors
MInstE	Member, Institute of Energy
MInstGA	Member, Institute of Group Analysis
MInstP	Member, Institute of Physics
MInstPI	Member, Institute of Patentees and Inventors
MInstPS	Corporate Member, Institute of Purchasing and Supply
MInstPkg	Member, Institute of Packaging
MInstTA	Member, Institute of Transport Administration
ML	Master of Leadership
MLI	Member, Landscape Institute
MLL	Master of Laws
MLS	Master of Library Studies
MLib	Master of Librarianship
MLitt	Master of Letters
MM	Military Medal
MMCET	Martyrs' Memorial and Church of England Trust
MMS	Member, Institute of Management Services
MMath	Master of Mathematics
MMedSc	Master of Medical Science
MMet	Master of Metallurgy
MMin	Master of Ministry
MMinTheol	Master in Ministry and Theology
MMus	Master of Music (also see MusM)
MN	Master of Nursing
MNI	Member, Nautical Institute
MOD	Ministry of Defence

MPA .... Master of Public Administration
MPH .... Master of Public Health
MPS .... Master of Professional Studies
MPhil .... Master of Philosophy
MPhys .... Master of Physics
MPsychSc......... Master of Psychological Science
MRAC .... Member, Royal Agricultural College
MRAeS .... Member, Royal Aeronautical Society
MRCGP .... Member, Royal College of General Practitioners
MRCO............. Member, Royal College of Organists
MRCOG .... Member, Royal College of Obstetricians and Gynaecologists
MRCP .... Member, Royal College of Physicians
MRCPath .... Member, Royal College of Pathologists
MRCPsych .... Member, Royal College of Psychiatrists
MRCS .... Member, Royal College of Surgeons
MRCSE............ Member, Royal College of Surgeons of Edinburgh
MRCVS............ Member, Royal College of Veterinary Surgeons
MRIA............... Member, Royal Irish Academy
MRICS............. Member, Royal Institution of Chartered Surveyors
MRIN .... Member, Royal Institute of Navigation
MRINA .... Member, Royal Institution of Naval Architects
MRIPHH......... Member, Royal Institute of Public Health and Hygiene
MRPharmS....... Member, Royal Pharmaceutical Society (formerly MPS)
MRSC .... Member, Royal Society of Chemistry (formerly MRIC)
MRSH.............. Member, Royal Society for the Promotion of Health
MRSL .... Member, Order of the Republic of Sierra Leone
MRST .... Member, Royal Society of Teachers
MRTPI............. Member, Royal Town Planning Institute
MRTvS............. Member, Royal Television Society
MRelSc............ Master of Religious Science
MS.................... Master of Science (USA)
.... Master of Surgery
MSAICE.......... Member, South African Institution of Civil Engineers
MSE .... Master of Science in Engineering (USA)
.... Minister (or Ministers) in Secular Employment
MSERT .... Member, Society of Electronic and Radio Technicians
MSHAA........... Member, Society of Hearing Aid Audiologists
MSI .... Member, Securities Institute
MSIAD .... Member, Society of Industrial Artists and Designers
MSOSc............ Member, Society of Ordained Scientists
MSOTS .... Member, Society for Old Testament Study
MSR .... Member, Society of Radiographers
MSSCh............ Member, School of Surgical Chiropody
MSSTh............ Member, Society for the Study of Theology
MSSc .... Master of Social Science (also see MSocSc)
MSTSD............ Member, Society of Teachers of Speech and Drama
MSW .... Master of Social Work
MSacMus......... Master of Sacred Music
MSc .... Master of Science
MSc(Econ) .... Master of Science in Economics
MScRel............ Maitrise es Sciences Religieuses

MSci .... Master of Natural Sciences
MSoc................. Maitrise en Sociologie
MSocSc .... Master of Social Sciences (also see MSSc)
MSocWork .... Master of Social Work (USA)
MSt.................. Master of Studies
MTD .... Master of Transport Design
MTS .... Master of Theological Studies
MTech .... Master of Technology
MTh or MTheol Master of Theology (also see STM and ThM)
MU................... Mothers' Union
MVO .... Member, Royal Victorian Order
Magd .... Magdalen/Magdalene
.... Magdalen's/Magdalene's
Man .... (Diocese of) Manchester
Man Dir .... Managing Director
Mansf.............. Mansfield
Marg................. Margaret
.... Margaret's
Matt................. Matthew
.... Matthew's
Mert................. Merton
MesL................ Lettres Modernes
Metrop .... Metropolitan
Mgt.................. Management
Mich .... Michael
.... Michael's
.... Michael and All Angels
Midl................. Midlands
Mil.................. Military
Min.................. Minister
.... Ministries
.... Ministry
.... Minor
Minl................. Ministerial
Miss................. Mission
.... Missions
.... Missionary
Missr................ Missioner
Mon................. (Diocese of) Monmouth
Mor .... (Diocese of) Moray, Ross and Caithness
Mt.................... Mount
MusB or MusBac Bachelor of Music (also see BMus)
MusD or MusDoc Doctor of Music
MusM............... Master of Music (also see MMus)

N

N...................... North
.... Northern
NACRO .... National Association for the Care and Rehabilitation of Offenders
NASA............... National Aeronautics and Space Administration (USA)
NCEC .... National Christian Education Council
NE................... North East
NEITE .... North East Institute for Theological Education
NEOC .... North East Oecumenical Course (formerly North East Ordination Course)
NHS .... National Health Service
NIDA .... National Institute of Dramatic Art
NJ.................... New Jersey
NOC................ Northern Ordination Course
NS .... Nova Scotia (Canada)
NSM................ Non-stipendiary Minister (or Ministry)
NSPCC............ National Society for the Prevention of Cruelty to Children
NSW................ New South Wales (Australia)
NT .... New Testament
NTMTC........... North Thames Ministerial Training Course
NUI .... National University of Ireland
NUU .... New University of Ulster
NW................... North West/Northwestern
NWT .... North West Territories (Canada)
NY................... New York (USA)
NZ................... New Zealand

Nat .... National
Nath .... Nathanael/Nathaniel
.... Nathanael's/Nathaniel's
Newc............... (Diocese of) Newcastle
Nic.................. Nicholas/Nicolas
.... Nicholas's/Nicolas's
Nor.................. (Diocese of) Norwich
Northn............. Northampton
Nottm.............. Nottingham
Nuff................. Nuffield

O

OAM .... Medal of the Order of Australia
OBE................. Officer, Order of the British Empire
OBI................. Order of British India
OCF ,.............. Officiating Chaplain to the Forces
OGS .... Oratory of the Good Shepherd
OH................... Ohio
OHP .... Order of the Holy Paraclete
OLM .... Ordained Local Minister (or Ministry)
OM.................. Order of Merit
OM(Ger).......... Order of Merit of Germany
OMF .... Overseas Missionary Fellowship
ONZ................ Order of New Zealand
OSB .... Order of St Benedict
OSP .... Order of St Paul
OT .... Old Testament
Offg .... Officiating
Offic................ Officiate
Ord .... Ordained
.... Ordinands
.... Ordination
Org .... Organization
.... Organizer
.... Organizing
Ox................... (Diocese of) Oxford

P

P .... Patron(s)
.... Priest
p....................... Ordained Priest
P in O .... Priest in Ordinary
P-in-c .... Priest-in-charge
PBS................. Pengeran Bintang Sarawak (Companion of the Order of the Star, Sarawak)
PC................... Perpetual Curate
.... Privy Counsellor
PCC................. Parochial Church Council
PEV .... Provincial Episcopal Visitor
PGCE.............. Postgraduate Certificate in Education
PGDE.............. Postgraduate Diploma in Education
PM................... Priest Missioner
PO .... Post Office
PQCSW........... Post-Qualifying Certificate in Social Work
PV................... Priest Vicar
Par .... Parish
.... Parishes
Paroch .... Parochial
Past................. Pastoral
Patr................. Patrick
.... Patrick's
.... Patronage
Pemb............... Pembroke
Penn................ Pennsylvania (USA)
Perm................ Permission
Pet................... (Diocese of) Peterborough
.... Peter
.... Peter's
Peterho .... Peterhouse
PhB................. Bachelor of Philosophy
PhC................. Pharmaceutical Chemist
PhD................. Doctor of Philosophy (also see DPhil)
PhD(Educ)....... Doctor of Philosophy in Education
PhL................. Licentiate of Philosophy
Phil .... Philip
.... Philip's
plc................... public limited company
Poly................. Polytechnic

Portsm	(Diocese of) Portsmouth
Preb	Prebendary
Prec	Precentor
Prep	Preparatory
Pres	President
Prin	Principal
Pris	Prison
	Prisons
Prof	Professor
	Professorial
Progr	Program
	Programme
	Programmes
Prop	Proprietary
Prov	Province
	Provincial
Pt	Point

Q

QC	Queen's Counsel
QGM	Queen's Gallantry Medal
QHC	Honorary Chaplain to The Queen
QN	Queen's Nurse
QPM	Queen's Police Medal
QSM	Queen's Service Medal
QSO	Queen's Service Order of New Zealand
QTS	Qualified Teacher Status
QUB	The Queen's University of Belfast
QVRM	Queen's Volunteer Reserve Medal
Qld	Queensland
Qu	Queen
	Queen's
	Queens'

R

R	Rector
	Royal
R and D	Research and Development
R of O	Reserve of Officers
R&SChTrust	Rochester and Southwark Church Trust
RAAF	Royal Australian Air Force
RAChD	Royal Army Chaplains' Department
RAD or RADD	Royal Association in Aid of Deaf People (formerly Deaf and Dumb)
RADA	Royal Academy of Dramatic Art
RADICLE	Residential and Drop-in Centre London Enterprises
RAEC	Royal Army Educational Corps
RAF	Royal Air Force
RAFVR	Royal Air Force Volunteer Reserve
RAM	(Member) Royal Academy of Music
RAN	Royal Australian Navy
RANSR	Royal Australian Naval Strategic Reserve
RAuxAF	Royal Auxiliary Air Force
RC	Roman Catholic
RCA	Royal College of Art
RCAF	Royal Canadian Air Force
RCM	Royal College of Music
RCN	Royal Canadian Navy
	Royal College of Nursing
RCNT	Registered Clinical Nurse Teacher
RCPS	Royal College of Physicians and Surgeons
RCS	Royal College of Surgeons of England
RCSE	Royal College of Surgeons of Edinburgh
RD	Royal Navy Reserve Decoration
	Rural Dean
RE	Religious Education
RFN	Registered Fever Nurse
RGN	Registered General Nurse
RHV	Registered Health Visitor

RIA	Royal Irish Academy
RIBA	(Member) Royal Institute of British Architects (formerly ARIBA)
RLSMD	Royal London School of Medicine and Dentistry
RM	Registered Midwife
RMA or RMC	Royal Military Academy (formerly College), Sandhurst
RMCM	Royal Manchester College of Music
RMCS	Royal Military College of Science, Shrivenham
RMHN	Registered Mental Health Nurse
RMN	Registered Mental Nurse
RN	Registered Nurse (Canada)
	Royal Navy
RN(MH)	Registered Nurse (for the mentally handicapped)
RNIB	Royal National Institute for the Blind
RNLI	Royal National Lifeboat Institution
RNMH	Registered Nurse for the Mentally Handicapped
RNR	Royal Naval Reserve
RNT	Registered Nurse Tutor
RNVR	Royal Naval Volunteer Reserve
RNZN	Royal New Zealand Navy
RS	Religious Studies
RSAMD	Royal Scottish Academy of Music and Drama
RSCM	(Member) Royal School of Church Music
RSCN	Registered Sick Children's Nurse
RTCert	Certified Reality Therapist
RTE	Radio Telefis Eireann
RVC	Royal Veterinary College
RVO	Royal Victorian Order
Reg	Registered
Relig	Religion(s)
	Religious
Relns	Relations
Rem	Remand
Rep	Representative
Res	Residence
	Resident
	Residential
	Residentiary
Resp	Responsibility
Resurr	Resurrection
Revd	Reverend
Rich	Richard
	Richard's
Ripon	Ripon and Leeds
Rob	Robinson
Roch	(Diocese of) Rochester
Rt	Right
Rtd or rtd	Retired

S

S	South
	Southern
S & B	(Diocese of) Swansea and Brecon
S & M	(Diocese of) Sodor and Man
SA	Salvation Army
SAMS	South American Mission Society
SAOMC	St Albans and Oxford Ministry Course
SAP	(Member) Society of Analytical Psychologists
SCM	State Certified Midwife
	Student Christian Movement
SE	South East
SEITE	South East Institute for Theological Education
SEN	State Enrolled Nurse
SHARE	Shelter Housing and Renewal Experiment
SM	Master of Science (USA)
SMF	Society for the Maintenance of the Faith
SNTS	Society for New Testament Studies
SNWTP	Southern North West Training Partnership

SOAS	School of Oriental and African Studies
SOMA	Sharing of Ministries Abroad
SOSc	Society of Ordained Scientists
SPCK	Society for Promoting Christian Knowledge
SPG	Society for the Propagation of the Gospel (now see USPG)
SRCh	State Registered Chiropodist
SRD	State Registered Dietician
SRN	State Registered Nurse
SROT	State Registered Occupational Therapist
SRP	State Registered Physiotherapist
SS	Saints
	Saints'
	Sidney Sussex
SSB	Society of the Sisters of Bethany
SSC	Solicitor before the Supreme Court (Scotland)
SSEES	School of Slavonic and East European Studies
SSF	Society of St Francis
SSJ	Society of St John of Jerusalem
SSJE	Society of St John the Evangelist
SSM	Society of the Sacred Mission
STB	Bachelor of Theology (also see BTh)
STD	Doctor of Sacred Theology (also see DST)
STETS	Southern Theological Education and Training Scheme
STL	Reader (or Professor) of Sacred Theology
STM	Master of Theology (also see MTh or MTheol and ThM)
STV	Scottish Television
STh	Scholar in Theology (also see ThSchol)
	Student in Theology
SW	South West
SWJ	Servants with Jesus
SWMTC	South West Ministry Training Course
Sacr	Sacrist
	Sacristan
Sarum	(Diocese of) Salisbury
Sav	Saviour
	Saviour's
ScD	Doctor of Science (also see DSc)
Sch	School
Sec	Secretary
Selw	Selwyn
Sem	Seminary
Sen	Senior
Sheff	(Diocese of) Sheffield
Shep	Shepherd
So	Souls
	Souls'
Soc	Social
	Society
Southn	Southampton
Sqn Ldr	Squadron Leader
St	Saint
St Alb	(Diocese of) St Albans
	St Alban
	St Alban's
St And	(Diocese of) St Andrews, Dunkeld and Dunblane
St As	(Diocese of) St Asaph
St D	(Diocese of) St Davids
St E	(Diocese of) St Edmundsbury and Ipswich
Ste	Sainte
Steph	Stephen
	Stephen's
Sub	Substitute
Succ	Succentor
Suff	Suffragan
Supt	Superintendent
S'wark	(Diocese of) Southwark
S'well	(Diocese of) Southwell and Nottingham
	Southwell
Syn	Synod

T

T, K & A.........	(Diocese of) Tuam, Killala and Achonry
TA	Territorial Army
TAVR	Territorial and Army Volunteer Reserve
TC	Technician Certificate
TCD	Trinity College, Dublin
TCert	Teacher's Certificate
TD	Team Deacon
....	Territorial Efficiency Decoration
TDip.....	Teacher's Diploma
TEAR.....	The Evangelical Alliance Relief
TEM.....	Territorial Efficiency Medal
TEng.....	Senior Technician Engineer
TISEC	Theological Institute of the Scottish Episcopal Church
TM	Team Minister (or Ministry)
TP.....	Team Priest
TR	Team Rector
TS	Training Ship
TSB	Trustee Savings Bank
TV	Team Vicar
....	Television
TVS	Television South
Tas	Tasmania
Tech	Technical
....	Technological
....	Technology
temp.....	temporarily
Th	Theologian
....	Theological
....	Theology
ThA	Associate of Theology
ThB	Bachelor of Theology (USA)
ThD	Doctorate in Theology (also see DTh)
ThL	Theological Licentiate
ThM	Master of Theology (also see MTh or MTheol and STM)
ThSchol	Scholar in Theology (also see STh)
Thos	Thomas
....	Thomas's
Tim	Timothy
....	Timothy's
Tr	Trainer
....	Training

Treas	Treasurer
....	Treasurer's
Trin	Trinity

U

UAE	United Arab Emirates
UCCF	Universities and Colleges Christian Fellowship of Evangelical Unions (formerly IVF)
UCD.....	University College, Dublin
UEA.....	University of East Anglia
UED.....	University Education Diploma
UK	United Kingdom
UKRC.....	United Kingdom Register of Counsellors
UMCA	Universities' Mission to Central Africa (now see USPG)
UMIST.....	University of Manchester Institute of Science and Technology
UNISA.....	University of South Africa
UPA.....	Urban Priority Area (or Areas)
URC	United Reformed Church
US or USA.....	United States (of America)
USCL.....	United Society for Christian Literature
USPG.....	United Society for the Propagation of the Gospel (formerly SPG, UMCA, and CMD)
UWE	University of the West of England
UWIST.....	University of Wales Institute of Science and Technology
Univ.....	University

V

V	Vicar
....	Virgin
....	Virgin's

VRD.....	Royal Naval Volunteer Reserve Officers' Decoration
VRSM	Volunteer Reserves Service Medal
Ven	Venerable
VetMB.....	Bachelor of Veterinary Medicine (also see BVetMed)
Vic	Victoria (Australia)
Vin.....	Vincent
....	Vincent's
Voc.....	Vocational
....	Vocations

W

W.....	West
....	Western
w.....	with
W/Cdr.....	Wing Commander
WCC.....	World Council of Churches
WEC.....	Worldwide Evangelism Crusade
WEMTC	West of England Ministerial Training Course
WMMTC.....	West Midlands Ministerial Training Course
WRAF	Women's Royal Air Force
Wadh.....	Wadham
Wakef	(Diocese of) Wakefield
Westf.....	Westfield
Westmr	Westminster
Wilts.....	Wiltshire
Win.....	(Diocese of) Winchester
Wm.....	William
Wolfs.....	Wolfson
Wolv.....	Wolverhampton
Worc	(Diocese of) Worcester

Y

YMCA	Young Men's Christian Association
YOI.....	Young Offender Institution
YWAM.....	Youth with a Mission

46

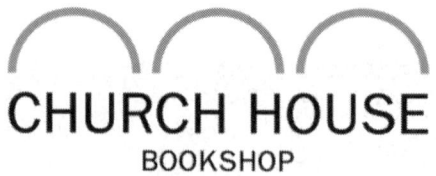

A

AAGAARD, Angus Robert. b 64. Moray Ho Coll of Educn CQSW86. Ripon Coll Cuddesdon BTh93. **d** 93 **p** 94. C Taunton St Andr *B & W* 93-97; TV Southampton (City Cen) *Win* 97-01; TR N Lambeth *S'wark* from 01. *St Anselm's Vicarage, 286 Kennington Road, London SE11 5DU* Tel (020) 7735 3415 Fax 7735 3403 Mobile 07810-646644

ABAYOMI-COLE, Bimbisara Alfred (<u>Bimbi</u>). b 58. CCC Ox BA80 MA85. Trin Coll Bris BA94. **d** 94 **p** 95. C Deptford St Pet *S'wark* 94-98; V Crofton St Paul *Roch* from 98. *St Paul's Vicarage, 2 Oakwood Road, Orpington BR6 8JH* Tel and fax (01689) 852939 *or* 850697
E-mail bimbiabayomi_cole@hotmail.com

ABBEY, Canon Anthony James. b 36. Selw Coll Cam BA59 MA63 ARCO61. Ely Th Coll 59. **d** 61 **p** 62. C Wanstead St Mary *Chelmsf* 61-63; C Laindon w Basildon 63-67; R Sandon 67-76; V Epping St Jo 76-92; Hon Can Chelmsf Cathl 85-01; P-in-c Doddinghurst and Mountnessing 92-01; rtd 01; Perm to Offic *Worc* from 01. *Canons Piece, 2 The Squires, Blackminster, Evesham WR11 7XN* Tel (01386) 834119
E-mail anthony@canonspiece.fsnet.co.uk

ABBOTT, Barry Joseph. b 59. Sunderland Univ BA98 MCIEH. NEOC 89. **d** 92 **p** 93. NSM Bishopwearmouth Ch Ch *Dur* 92-98; NSM Silksworth 98-00; P-in-c Lumley 00-04; AD Chester-le-Street 02-04; P-in-c Whickham 04-08; R from 08. *The Rectory, Church Chare, Whickham, Newcastle upon Tyne NE16 4SH* Tel 0191-488 7197 Mobile 07801-074909

ABBOTT, Christopher Ralph. b 38. Univ of Wales (Lamp) BA59. Wells Th Coll 59. **d** 61 **p** 62. C Camberwell St Giles *S'wark* 61-67; C Portsea St Mary *Portsm* 67-70; V Charlton St Luke 70-87; P-in-c Gt Milton *Ox* 87-88; P-in-c Lt Milton 87-88; R Gt w Lt Milton and Gt Haseley 88-93; R Chailey *Chich* 93-00; Chapl Chailey Heritage Hosp Lewes 95-00; rtd 00; Perm to Offic *Chich* from 01; Chapl SSB from 02; Hon C Purbrook *Portsm* from 03. *6 Winchfield Crescent, Havant PO9 3SP* Tel (023) 9247 7376
E-mail christopherabbott@jonty.fsnet.co.uk

ABBOTT, David John. b 52. CertEd. St Jo Coll Nottm. **d** 87 **p** 88. C Biddulph *Lich* 87-90; C Tunbridge Wells St Jas *Roch* 90-92; TV Tunbridge Wells St Jas w St Phil 92-98; V Sunnyside w Bourne End *St Alb* from 98; RD Berkhamsted from 04. *The Vicarage, Ivy House Lane, Berkhamsted HP4 2PP* Tel (01442) 865100
E-mail ssvicarage@yahoo.co.uk

ABBOTT, David Robert. b 49. Edin Univ BD72. Qu Coll Birm 72. **d** 74 **p** 75. C Kirkby *Liv* 74-78; C Ditton St Mich 78-80; R Ashton in Makerfield H Trin from 80. *The Rectory, North Ashton, Wigan WN4 0QF* Tel (01942) 727241

ABBOTT, Miss Geraldine <u>Mary</u>. b 33. SRN55 SCM58 Open Univ BA77 Lon Univ MTh85. Oak Hill Th Coll BA82. **dss** 86 **d** 87 **p** 94. Tutor Oak Hill Coll 86-96; St Alb St Paul *St Alb* 86-94; Hon Par Dn 87-94; Hon C from 94. *2 Wheatleys, St Albans AL4 9UE* Tel (01727) 860869

ABBOTT, Mrs Kathleen Frances. b 60. STETS 96. **d** 99 **p** 00. NSM St Helens and Sea View *Portsm* 99-02; P-in-c Wootton from 02. *The Rectory, 32 Church Road, Wootton Bridge, Ryde PO33 4PX* Tel and fax (01983) 882213
E-mail kath.abbott@btinternet.com

ABBOTT, Canon Nigel Douglas Blayney. b 37. Open Univ BA87. Bps' Coll Cheshunt 58. **d** 61 **p** 62. C Northampton St Mich *Pet* 61-64; C Wanstead St Mary *Chelmsf* 64-66; Chapl St Jo Sch Tiffield 66-69; V Earls Barton *Pet* 69-73; V Cov H Trin 73-80; Provost St Jo Cathl Oban 80-86; R Oban St Jo 80-86; TR Hemel Hempstead *St Alb* 86-96; RD Hemel Hempstead 94-96; R Much Hadham 96-02; Hon Can St Alb 96-02; rtd 02; Perm to Offic *Ely* from 03. *1 Cambridge Road, Ely CB7 4HJ* Tel (01353) 662256
E-mail ndbabbot@waitrose.com

ABBOTT, Peter John. b 48. CQSW86. St Mich Coll Llan 94. **d** 96 **p** 97. C Neath w Llantwit 96-98; C Merthyr Tydfil Ch Ch 98-00; P-in-c Llangeinor w Nantymoel and Wyndham 00-02; V Cwm Ogwr 02-03; TV Ebbw Vale *Mon* from 03. *New Cwm Vicarage, 19 Crosscombe Terrace, Cwm, Ebbw Vale NP23 7SP* Tel (01495) 371588

ABBOTT, Richard. b 43. **d** 07 **p** 08. OLM Bisley and W End *Guildf* from 07. *241 Arethusa Way, Bisley, Woking GU24 9BU* Tel (01483) 481540 Mobile 07810-800114
E-mail richard_abbott@hotmail.co.uk

ABBOTT, Stephen Anthony. b 43. K Coll Cam BA65 MA69 Edin Univ BD68 Harvard Univ ThM69. Edin Th Coll 66. **d** 69 **p** 70. C Deal St Leon *Cant* 69-72; Chapl K Coll Cam 72-75; C

Cambridge St Matt *Ely* 75-76; Asst Chapl Bris Univ and Hon C Clifton St Paul 77-80; Perm to Offic *Bris* 81-04; P-in-c Mangotsfield from 04. *The Vicarage, St James Place, Mangotsfield, Bristol BS16 9JA* Tel 0117-956 0510
E-mail stephen.abbott@withleigh.freeserve.co.uk

ABBOTT, Stephen John. b 62. Qu Mary Coll Lon LLB83. Linc Th Coll BTh92. **d** 92 **p** 93. C E Dereham and Scarning *Nor* 92-95; TV Penistone and Thurlstone *Wakef* 95-97; R Brandon and Santon Downham w Elveden *St E* 97-00; P-in-c Gt Barton 00-04; Perm to Offic 04-08; R Bansfield from 08. *The Vicarage, Church Road, Wickhambrook, Newmarket CB8 8XH* Tel and fax (01440) 820288 Mobile 07742-396523
E-mail sj.abbott@lineone.net

ABBOTT, Mrs Valerie Ann. b 45. Keele Univ BA68. Trin Coll Bris MLitt00. **d** 00 **p** 01. NSM Knowle St Martin *Bris* 00-01; NSM Brislington St Chris and St Cuth 01-04; NSM Mangotsfield from 04. *The Vicarage, St James Place, Mangotsfield, Bristol BS16 9JA* Tel 0117-956 0510 Mobile 07979-997968 E-mail val.abbott@btinternet.com

ABDY, John Channing. b 38. Nottm Univ BA63. Cuddesdon Coll 63. **d** 65 **p** 66. C Leagrave *St Alb* 65-69; C N Mymms 69-72; V Kings Walden 72-79; V S Woodham Ferrers *Chelmsf* 79-85; V Walthamstow St Pet 85-91; V Burrington and Churchill *B & W* 91-06; rtd 06. *Sunnyside Cottage, Whitford Road, Musbury, Axminster EX13 7AP* Tel (01297) 552847
E-mail jcabdy@icdonline.co.uk

ABECASSIS, Joanna Margaret. b 54. Girton Coll Cam BA75 MA79 PhD81. WEMTC 99. **d** 02 **p** 03. C Tavistock and Gulworthy *Ex* 02-07; TV Totnes w Bridgetown, Berry Pomeroy etc from 07. *The Vicarage, Week, Dartington, Totnes TQ9 6JL* Tel (01803) 868304 E-mail joanna@abecassis.freeserve.co.uk

ABEL, David John. b 31. S'wark Ord Course 71. **d** 74 **p** 75. NSM Crowhurst *S'wark* 74-85; NSM Lingfield and Crowhurst 85-92; Perm to Offic *S'wark* 92-98; *Chich* 98-07; *St E* from 03. *13 Church Street, Boxford, Sudbury CO10 5DU* Tel (01787) 211765

ABELL, Canon Brian. b 37. Nottm Univ BA61 DipEd Leeds Univ MA95. Cuddesdon Coll 61. **d** 63 **p** 64. C Lightcliffe *Wakef* 63-66; C-in-c Mixenden CD 66-68; Lect Linc Coll of Tech 68-69; Chapl Trent Coll Nottm 70-74; V Thorner *Ripon* 74-82; V Far Headingley St Chad 82-86; Deputation Appeals Org CECS 86-89; V Masham and Healey *Ripon* 89-00; Hon Can Ripon Cathl 99-00; rtd 00; Perm to Offic *Ripon* from 00. *Manor Garth, 1 Manor Road, Harrogate HG2 0HP* Tel and fax (01423) 526112
E-mail b.abell@btinternet.com

ABELL, George Derek. b 31. Selw Coll Cam BA54 MA68. Qu Coll Birm 54. **d** 56 **p** 57. C Stoke upon Trent *Lich* 56-60; C Wolverhampton 60-64; R Bridgnorth St Mary *Heref* 64-70; P-in-c Oldbury 64-70; R Atherton N Australia 70-73; R Withington w Westhide and Weston Beggard *Heref* 73-81; R Withington w Westhide 81-83; P-in-c Sutton St Nicholas w Sutton St Michael 76-81; R 81-83; Preb Heref Cathl 82-83; V Basing *Win* 83-88; rtd 88; Perm to Offic *Heref* 88-04. *25 Eastfield Court, Church Street, Faringdon SN7 8SL* Tel (01367) 240731

ABELL, Peter John. b 45. Chich Th Coll 67. **d** 70 **p** 71. C Churchdown St Jo *Glouc* 70-74; Chapl RAF 74-98; R Kilkhampton w Morwenstow *Truro* from 98. *The Rectory, East Road, Kilkhampton, Bude EX23 9QS* Tel and fax (01288) 321314 E-mail rectorkilkstow@aol.com

ABERDEEN AND ORKNEY, Bishop of. See GILLIES, The Rt Revd Robert Arthur

ABERDEEN AND ORKNEY, Dean of. See NIMMO, The Very Revd Alexander Emsley

ABERDEEN, Provost of. See KILGOUR, The Very Revd Richard Eifl

✠**ABERNETHY, The Rt Revd Alan Francis.** b 57. QUB BA78 BD89. CITC. **d** 81 **p** 82 **c** 07. C Dundonald *D & D* 81-84; C Lecale Gp 84-86; I Helen's Bay 86-90; I Ballyholme 90-07; Preb Down Cathl 00-07; Cen Dir of Ords 04-07; Bp Conn from 07. *1 Marlborough Gate, Marlborough Park, Malone, Belfast BT9 6GB* Tel (028) 9066 1942
E-mail bishop@connor.anglican.org

ABINGTON, David John Barringer. b 48. EAMTC 91. **d** 94 **p** 95. C Newport w Longford and Chetwynd *Lich* 94-96; C Newport w Longford, Chetwynd and Forton 96-98; R Adderley, Ash, Calverhall, Ightfield etc 98-02; R Brading w Yaverland *Portsm*

1

from 02. *The Vicarage, The Mall, Brading, Sandown PO36 0DE* Tel (01983) 407262 Mobile 07855-086978

ABLETT, Edwin John. b 37. Clifton Th Coll 64. **d** 67 **p** 68. C Sneinton St Chris w St Phil *S'well* 67-70; R High and Gd Easter w Margaret Roding *Chelmsf* 70-73; SAMS Chile 73-75; C Gt Baddow *Chelmsf* 75-78; V Newchapel *Lich* 78-82; V S Westoe *Dur* 82-86; V Tibshelf *Derby* 86-00; rtd 00; Perm to Offic *St D* from 00. *25 Eden Road, West End, Southampton SO18 3QW* Tel (023) 8047 4784 E-mail john.copihue@btinternet.com

ABLETT, Mrs Jennifer Vera. b 46. **d** 00 **p** 01. OLM Henley, Claydon and Barham *St E* from 00. *10 Phillipps Road, Barham, Ipswich IP6 0AZ* Tel (01473) 830205

ABRAHAM, Brian. b 42. **d** 00 **p** 01. OLM Burscough Bridge *Liv* from 00. *4 Mere Court, Burscough, Ormskirk L40 0TQ* Tel (01704) 892547

ABRAHAM, Canon David Alexander. b 37. AKC61. **d** 62 **p** 63. C Oswestry St Oswald *Lich* 62-63; C Gt Wyrley 63-65; C Sprowston *Nor* 65-67; V Ormesby w Scratby 67-81; R Oxborough w Foulden and Caldecote 81-87; R Cockley Cley w Gooderstone 81-87; V Didlington 81-87; R Gt and Lt Cressingham w Threxton 81-87; R Hilborough w Bodney 81-87; P-in-c Nor St Giles 87-96; Chapl Asst Norfolk and Nor Hosp 87 91; V Thorpe St Matt *Nor* 96-00; Hon Can Nor Cathl 95-00; rtd 00; Perm to Offic *Nor* from 00. *170 Desmond Drive, Old Catton, Norwich NR6 7JW* Tel (01603) 402797

ABRAHAM, Estelle Pamela. b 46. C F Mott Coll of Educn TCert69. **d** 04 **p** 05. OLM Bolton Breightmet St Jas *Man* 04-06; OLM Leverhulme 06-07; NSM Witchford w Wentworth *Ely* from 08; NSM Haddenham from 08; NSM Wilburton from 08. *31A Hardwicke Fields, Haddenham, Ely CB6 3TW* Tel (01353) 740120 E-mail pam.abraham@ntlworld.com

ABRAHAM, Canon John Callis Harford. b 31. Univ of W Aus BA52. Westcott Ho Cam 53. **d** 55 **p** 56. C Wigan St Anne *Liv* 55-57; C Northam Perth Australia 57-60; R Wongan Hills 60-62; Vice-Warden Wollaston Th Coll and R Graylands 63-67; P-in-c City Beach 66-67; Lic to Offic *Birm* 67-68; R Applecross Perth Australia 68-76; Can Perth 71-84; R Leeming 76-79; Chapl Home Miss 79-81; R Wembley 81-89; R Albany 90-94; Can Bunbury 92-94; rtd 94. *10 Royston Park, Pioneer Road, Albany WA 6330, Australia* Tel (0061) (8) 9841 1809

ABRAHAM, Richard James. b 42. Liv Univ BA63. Ridley Hall Cam 64. **d** 66 **p** 67. C Warrington St Ann *Liv* 66-70; C Golborne 70-73; V Bickershaw 73-78; V Ewerby w Evedon *Linc* 78-82; R Kirkby Laythorpe w Asgarby 78-82; R Kirkby Laythorpe 82-03; rtd 03. *23 Londesborough Way, Metheringham, Lincoln LN4 3HW*

ABRAHAMS, Peter William. b 42. Southn Univ BA77. Sarum Th Coll 77. **d** 78 **p** 79. C Bitterne Park *Win* 78-82; C Old Brumby *Linc* 82-84; V Mitcham Ascension *S'wark* 84-91; TV Riverside *Ox* 91-06; rtd 06; Perm to Offic *Ox* from 06. *17 Snowberry Close, Wokingham RG41 4AQ* Tel 0118-989 3072 E-mail frapeter@aol.com

ABRAM, Paul Robert Carrington. b 36. MVO07. Keble Coll Ox BA62 MA65. Chich Th Coll 60. **d** 62 **p** 63. C Redcar *York* 62-65; CF 65-89; V Salcombe *Ex* 89-96; Miss to Seafarers from 89; rtd 96; Chapl to The Queen 96-06; Chapl St Pet-ad-Vincula at HM Tower of Lon 96-06; Dep P in O 96-06. *Paddock End, Kimpton, Andover SP11 8PG* Tel (01264) 772349

ABRAM, Steven James. b 50. Lon Univ BD76. Oak Hill Th Coll 71. **d** 76 **p** 77. C Biddulph *Lich* 76-79; C Heatherlands St Jo *Sarum* 79-83; Libya 83-84; C Stratford-on-Avon w Bishopton *Cov* 84; V Alderholt *Sarum* 84-90; V Daubhill *Man* 90-04; TV Mid Trent *Lich* from 07. *St Peter's House, 2 Vicarage Way, Hixon, Stafford ST18 0FT* Tel (01889) 270418 E-mail sj@abram.org.uk

ABREY, Mark Evans John. b 66. Ripon Coll Cuddesdon BTh93. **d** 93 **p** 94. C W Derby St Mary *Liv* 93-97; P-in-c Anfield St Marg 97-01; Chapl R Liverpool Children's NHS Trust 95-99; V Chase *Ox* from 01; P-in-c Ascott under Wychwood 01-07. *The Vicarage, Church Road, Chadlington, Chipping Norton OX7 3LY* Tel (01608) 676572 E-mail mark@abreys.com

ABREY, Philip James. b 51. NOC 82. **d** 85 **p** 86. NSM Hindley All SS *Liv* 85-90; C Caversham St Pet and Mapledurham etc *Ox* 90-00; Min Caversham Park LEP 90-00; Co Ecum Officer (Berks) 96-00; Perm to Offic *Cov* 01-07; Chapl HM Pris The Mount from 02. *HM Prison, The Mount, Molyneux Avenue, Bovingdon, Hemel Hempstead HP3 0NZ* Tel (01442) 834363 E-mail philip.abrey@hmps.gsi.gov.uk

ABSALOM, Alexander James David Edward. b 69. St Jo Coll Dur BA91. Cranmer Hall Dur 92. **d** 94 **p** 95. C Cranham Park *Chelmsf* 94-98; Perm to Offic *Sheff* 98-05; Miss P Philadelphia St Thos 05-07; USA from 07. *5907 Pecan Grove Place, Edmond OK 73034, USA* Tel (001) (405) 749 8044 E-mail alex@theabsaloms.net

ABSOLON, Michael John. b 33. St Jo Coll Cam BA54 MA59 Lon Hosp BChir57 MB57 FRCS FRCOphth. Wycliffe Hall Ox 95. **d** 96 **p** 97. NSM Micheldever and E Stratton, Woodmancote etc *Win* 96-98; NSM Chipping Campden w Ebrington *Glouc* 99-05; Perm to Offic from 05. *Oakham House, Ebrington, Chipping Campden GL55 6NL* Tel (01386) 593123

ABUJA, Bishop of. *See* AKINOLA, The Most Revd Peter Jasper

ABULEMOI, Joseph Oriho. *See* CHOUFAR, Joseph Oriho Abulemoi

ACARNLEY, Rita Kay. b 57. Girton Coll Cam BA79 MA83 Newc Univ MA94 St Jo Coll Dur BA98. Cranmer Hall Dur 96. **d** 99 **p** 00. NSM Humshaugh w Simonburn and Wark *Newc* 99-00; Tutor TISEC and Prov Local Collaborative Min Officer Scotland 00-03; R Stonehaven and Catterline *Bre* 03-07; P-in-c Muchalls 03-07. *13 Midtown, Poolewe, Achnasheen IV22 2LW* Tel (01445) 781315 E-mail ritaacarnley@dunelm.org.uk

ACCRA, Bishop of. *See* AKROFI, The Most Revd Justice Ofei

ACHESON, Denise Mary. BTh. **d** 05 **p** 06. C Ballyholme *D & D* 05-08; I Dunmurry *Conn* from 08. *The Rectory, 27 Church Avenue, Dunmurry, Belfast BT17 9RS* Tel (028) 9061 0984 E-mail denise.acheson@gmail.com

ACHESON, James Malcolm. b 48. BNC Ox BA70 MA73. Sarum & Wells Th Coll 83. **d** 85 **p** 86. C Highgate St Mich *Lon* 85-88; TV Tisbury *Sarum* and Offg Chapl RAF 88-94; R Storrington *Chich* from 94. *The Rectory, Rectory Road, Storrington, Pulborough RH20 4EF* Tel (01903) 742888

ACHONRY, Dean of. *Vacant*

ACHURCH, Peter William Hammond. b 37. Ridley Coll Melbourne 82. **d** 82 **p** 84. C Port Lincoln Australia 82-84; P-in-c Elliston w Lock and Wuddina 86; R 87-89; Par P Leigh Creek 89-93; TV Madeley *Heref* 00-05; rtd 05. *34 Birchall Road, Goolwa Beach SA 5214, Australia* Tel (0061) (08) 8555 3279

ACKERLEY, Glyn James. b 57. Kent Univ MA04. Cranmer Hall Dur 84. **d** 87 **p** 88. C Tonbridge SS Pet and Paul *Roch* 87-90; R Willingham *Ely* 90-94; R Rampton 90-94; V Chatham St Phil and St Jas *Roch* from 94; Dioc Dir of Ords from 09. *The Vicarage, 139 Sussex Drive, Walderslade, Chatham ME5 0NR* Tel (01634) 861108 *or* 862498 E-mail glyn.ackerley@diocese-rochester.org

ACKERMAN, David Michael. b 71. Westmr Coll Ox BTh95 Brighton Univ PGCE98. Pontificum Institutum Internationale Angelicum Rome STB01 MA02. **d** 01 **p** 02. In RC Ch 01-04; C Fairford and Kempsford w Whelford *Glouc* 05-08; P-in-c Sherborne, Windrush, the Barringtons etc from 08; Dioc Ecum Officer from 08. *The Vicarage, Windrush, Burford OX18 4TS* Tel (01451) 844276 Mobile 07916-348719 E-mail dmackerman@hotmail.com

ACKFORD, Christopher Mark. b 60. Univ Coll Lon BDS83 K Coll Lon MSc89. Ripon Coll Cuddesdon 02. **d** 04 **p** 05. C Bracknell *Ox* 04-07; TV Aylesbury w Bierton and Hulcott from 07. *The Vicarage, St James Way, Bierton, Aylesbury HP22 5ED* Tel (01296) 424466 Mobile 07780-554032 E-mail mark@ackford.wanadoo.co.uk

ACKLAM, Leslie Charles. b 46. Birm Univ BEd71. Ripon Coll Cuddesdon 78. **d** 80 **p** 81. C Chingford St Anne *Chelmsf* 80-83; C Spalding *Linc* 83-85; V Spalding St Paul 85-93; P-in-c Linc St Faith and St Martin w St Pet 93-06; Chapl Linc Univ from 06. *14 Nettleham Close, Lincoln LN2 1SJ* Tel (01522) 879513 *or* 886079 E-mail leslie.acklam@ntlworld.com *or* lacklam@lincoln.ac.uk

ACKLAND, Canon John Robert Warwick. b 47. **d** 82 **p** 83. NSM Shooters Hill Ch Ch *S'wark* 82-88; NSM Mottingham St Andr 82-94; NSM Woolwich St Thos 94-96; NSM Bellingham St Dunstan 96-03; Hon Chapl S'wark Cathl 98-03; P-in-c Perry Hill St Geo w Ch Ch and St Paul 03-04; V from 04; Hon Can S'wark Cathl from 05. *The Vicarage, Vancouver Road, London SE23 2AF* Tel (020) 8699 7676 *or* 8699 7202 Mobile 07831-516662 E-mail johnackland1@aol.com

ACKROYD, David Andrew. b 66. Coll of Ripon & York St Jo BA90 St Jo Coll Dur BA97. Cranmer Hall Dur 94. **d** 97 **p** 98. C Lilleshall and Sheriffhales *Lich* 97-01; Asst Chapl R Wolv Hosps NHS Trust 01-02; C Ogley Hay *Lich* 02-03. *45 Lowland Road, Cannock WS12 4ND* Tel and sandra@btinternet.com

ACKROYD, Dennis. b 36. Cranmer Hall Dur 67. **d** 70 **p** 71. C Newcastle w Butterton *Lich* 70-73; C Horsell *Guildf* 73-77; P-in-c Moreton and Woodsford w Tincleton *Sarum* 77-82; R 82-86; RD Dorchester 79-85; R Ewhurst *Guildf* 86-94; V Cleckheaton St Luke and Whitechapel *Wakef* 94-02; rtd 02; Perm to Offic *Sarum* from 03. *17 Charles Street, Weymouth DT4 7JG* Tel (01305) 778122

ACKROYD, Eric. b 29. Leeds Univ BA51 Liv Univ MA71 Leic Univ MA(Ed)86. St Jo Coll Dur 53. **d** 55 **p** 56. C Newland St Jo *York* 55-58; Succ Birm Cathl 58-60; Chapl Sch Bruton 61-66; Lect Kirkby Fields Coll of Educn Liv 67-72; Sen Lect Nene Coll of HE Northn 72-85; rtd 85. *14 Phippsville Court, St Matthew's Parade, Northampton NN2 7JW* Tel (01604) 713328

ACKROYD, John Michael. b 32. Lon Univ BSc53. Ripon Hall Ox 71. **d** 73 **p** 74. C Keighley *Bradf* 73-76; TV 76-81; V Keighley All SS 81; V Whalley *Blackb* 81-97; Chapl Calderstones Hosp Clitheroe 81-93; Chapl Calderstones NHS Trust 93-97; rtd 97; Perm to Offic *Blackb* from 97. *1 Calder Vale, Whalley, Clitheroe BB7 9SR* Tel (01254) 823943

ACKROYD, Peter Michael. b 60. Jes Coll Cam BA82 MA86 Fontainebleau MBA87 Edin Univ PhD02. Wycliffe Hall Ox BA93 MA00. **d** 94 **p** 95. C Denton Holme *Carl* 94-97; Sec Proclamation Trust 97-00; V Wootton *St Alb* from 02. *The Vicarage, Church Road, Wootton, Bedford MK43 9HF* Tel (01234) 768391 E-mail ackroyds@lineone.net

ACKROYD, Ruth. b 49. **d** 04 **p** 05. NSM Hoole *Ches* from 04. *Strathmore, Ashby Place, Hoole, Chester CH2 3AG* Tel (01244) 344529 E-mail r.ackroyd@chester.ac.uk

ACONLEY, Carole Ann. b 51. Hull Univ BTh01. NEOC 99. **d** 02 **p** 03. NSM Langtoft w Foxholes, Butterwick, Cottam etc *York* from 02. *Hawthorn Farm, Langtoft, Driffield YO25 3BT* Tel (01377) 267219 E-mail revdcarole@ic24.net

ACREMAN, John. b 53. Oak Hill Th Coll 86. **d** 88 **p** 89. C Iver *Ox* 88-92; R Hook Norton w Gt Rollright, Swerford etc from 92. *The Rectory, Hook Norton, Banbury OX15 5QQ* Tel (01608) 737223 E-mail acreman@xalt.co.uk

ACWORTH, The Ven Richard Foote. b 36. SS Coll Cam BA62 MA65. Cuddesdon Coll 61. **d** 63 **p** 64. C Fulham St Etheldreda *Lon* 63-64; C Langley All SS and Martyrs *Man* 64-66; C Bridgwater St Mary w Chilton Trinity *B & W* 66-69; V Yatton 69-81; V Yatton Moor 81; P-in-c Taunton St Jo 81-84; P-in-c Taunton St Mary 81-85; V 85-93; Preb Wells Cathl 87-93; Adn Wells, Can Res and Preb Wells Cathl 93-03; rtd 03; Perm to Offic *B & W* from 04. *Corvedale Cottage, Ganes Terrace, Croscombe, Wells BA5 3QJ* Tel (01749) 342242

ACWORTH, Richard John Philip. b 30. Ch Ch Ox BA52 MA56 Paris Univ DèsL70. **d** 63 **p** 63. In RC Ch 63-67; C Walthamstow St Mary w St Steph *Chelmsf* 68-70; P-in-c Lt Sampford 70-76; P-in-c Gt Sampford 74-76; Lect Bath Coll of HE 76-77; Lect Th Derby Lonsdale Coll 77-83; Derbyshire Coll of HE 83-88; P-in-c Newton Tracey, Alverdiscott, Huntshaw etc *Ex* 88-96; TR Newton Tracey, Horwood, Alverdiscott etc 96-98; RD Torrington 94-97; rtd 98; Perm to Offic *Portsm* from 98. *91 Oaklands Road, Havant PO9 2RL* Tel (023) 9245 0567

ADAIR, Raymond. b 33. Ripon Hall Ox 70. **d** 72 **p** 73. C Knottingley *Wakef* 72-75; C Sandal St Helen 75-77; V Sandal St Cath 77-87; V Brownhill 87-97; rtd 97; Perm to Offic *Wakef* from 99. *15 Chestnut Fold, Upper Lane, Netherton, Wakefield WF4 4HW* Tel (01924) 274640

ADAIR, Canon William Matthew. b 52. Open Univ BA. CITC 77. **d** 77 **p** 78. C Portadown St Mark *Arm* 77-78; Asst Chapl Miss to Seamen 78-80; C Lisburn Ch Ch Cathl 80-84; I Kildress w Altedesert *Arm* 84-92; I Portadown St Columba from 92; Dioc Sec Min of Healing 95-99; Can Arm Cathl from 08. *St Columba's Rectory, 81 Loughgall Road, Portadown, Craigavon BT62 4EG* Tel (028) 3833 2746

ADAM, Canon David. b 36. Kelham Th Coll 54. **d** 59 **p** 60. C Auckland St Helen *Dur* 59-63; C Owton Manor CD 63-67; V Danby *York* 67-90; Can and Preb York Minster 89-90; V Holy Is *Newc* 90-03; rtd 03; Perm to Offic *Newc* from 03. *The Old Granary, Warren Mill, Belford NE70 7EE* Tel (01668) 214770

ADAM, Gordon Angus James. b 62. SEITE 97. **d** 00 **p** 01. NSM Kentish Town St Silas and H Trin w St Barn *Lon* 00-03; NSM Boxmoor St Jo *St Alb* from 03. *167 Long Chaulden, Hemel Hempstead HP1 2JH* Tel and fax (01442) 216539 Mobile 07721-020334 E-mail gaja1962@aol.com

ADAM, Lawrence. b 38. NOC 82. **d** 82 **p** 83. C Thornton-le-Fylde *Blackb* 82-86; Dioc Video Production Co-ord 85-97; P-in-c Scorton 86-91; C W Burnley All SS 91-97; P-in-c Ashton St Jas *Man* 97-99; TV Ashton 00-03; rtd 03; Perm to Offic *Ches* from 03. *23 Dryden Avenue, Cheadle SK8 2AW*

ADAM, Lindsay Anne. See YATES, Lindsay Anne

ADAM, Michael MacIntosh. b 48. Sarum & Wells Th Coll. **d** 84 **p** 85. C Stamford Hill St Thos *Lon* 84-87; rtd 88; Perm to Offic *Lon* 88-07. *16 Barkway Court, 58 Queens Drive, London N4 2YG*

ADAM, Canon Peter James Hedderwick. b 46. Lon Univ BD73 MTh76 Dur Univ PhD81. Ridley Coll Melbourne ThL69. **d** 70 **p** 71. Australia 70-72, 73-74 and from 82; C Ivanhoe St Jas 70-72; C Rosanna 72; Hon C Holborn St Geo w H Trin and St Bart *Lon* 72-73; C Essendon St Thos and Tutor Ridley Coll 73-74; Tutor St Jo Coll Dur 75-82; Hon C Dur St Cuth 75-82; P-in-c Carlton St Jude 82-88; V 88-01; Adn Melbourne 88-91; Chapl Melbourne Univ 95-01; Can Melbourne from 96; Prin Ridley Coll from 01. *160 The Avenue, Parkville Vic 3053, Australia* Tel (0061) (3) 9207 4800 Fax 9387 5099 E-mail principal@ridley.unimelb.edu.au

ADAM, William Jonathan. b 69. Man Univ BA91 Univ of Wales (Cardiff) LLM03. Westcott Ho Cam 92 Bossey Ecum Inst Geneva. **d** 94 **p** 95. C Beaconsfield *Ox* 94-97; C Witney 97-98; TV 98-02; P-in-c Girton *Ely* 02-07; R from 07; Dioc Ecum Officer from 02. *The Rectory, 42 Church Lane, Girton, Cambridge CB3 0JP* Tel and fax (01223) 276235 E-mail wja@luxmundi.co.uk

ADAMS, Mrs Alison Mary. b 51. Girton Coll Cam MA73 Birm Univ BMus76 CertEd77 Sheff Univ MPhil93. EMMTC 94. **d** 91 **p** 98. NSM Burbage w Aston Flamville *Leic* 97-05; Dir Bloxham Project 00-05; Chapl HM YOI Glen Parva from 06. *HM Young Offender Institution, Glen Parva, Tiger's Road, Wigston LE18 4TN* Tel 0116-228 4100

ADAMS, Amanda Elaine. QUB BSc BTh. **d** 06 **p** 07. C Ballymena w Ballyclug *Conn* 06-09; I Ballyrashane w Kildollagh from 09. *9 Sandelwood Avenue, Coleraine BT52 1JW* Tel (028) 7034 3061

ADAMS, Anthony John. b 42. St Jo Coll Nottm 83. **d** 85 **p** 86. C Wellesbourne *Cov* 85-89; R Weddington and Caldecote 89-01; P-in-c Butlers Marston and the Pillertons w Ettington 01-07; P-in-c Alderminster and Halford 01-07; P-in-c Tredington and Darlingscott w Newbold on Stour 04-07; R Stourdene Gp from 07. *The Vicarage, Warwick Road, Ettington, Stratford-upon-Avon CV37 7SH* Tel (01789) 748137 E-mail stour.dene5@btinternet.com

ADAMS, Anthony Paul. b 41. SAOMC 95. **d** 98 **p** 99. NSM Banbury St Hugh *Ox* 98-01; P-in-c Wootton w Glympton and Kiddington 01-04; P-in-c Broughton and Duddon *Carl* from 04. *The Vicarage, Broughton-in-Furness LA20 6HS* Tel (01229) 716305 E-mail adamsfamily2@btinternet.com

ADAMS, Brian Hugh. b 32. Pemb Coll Ox BA54 MA57. Sarum & Wells Th Coll 77. **d** 79 **p** 80. Hon C Crediton *Ex* 79-81; Chapl St Brandon's Sch Clevedon 81-85; C Street w Walton *B & W* 86-85; RD Glastonbury 89-92 and 93-97; V Baltonsborough w Butleigh and W Bradley 88-97; rtd 97; Perm to Offic *B & W* from 99. *Manor Cottage, Weir Lane, Yeovilton, Yeovil BA22 8EU* Tel (01935) 840462 E-mail adamsbj@btinternet.com

ADAMS, Brian Peter. b 47. FInstD FRSA Avery Hill Coll CertEd70. Ox Ord Course 90. **d** 93 **p** 94. NSM Tonbridge SS Pet and Paul *Roch* 93-99; P-in-c Chatham St Mary w St Jo from 99. *The Rectory, 65 Maidstone Road, Chatham ME4 6DP* Tel (01634) 351065 *or* 351069 Mobile 07778-777824 Fax 351069 E-mail brian.adams@diocese-rochester.org

ADAMS, Bridget Ruth. b 52. Sussex Univ BSc74 DPhil78. SAOMC 03. **d** 06 **p** 07. NSM Bushey *St Alb* from 06. *Beech Tree House, The Pathway, Radlett WD7 8JB* Tel (01923) 853967 Mobile 07906-075419 E-mail bridgetbth@aol.com

ADAMS, Mrs Celia. b 39. R Holloway Coll Lon BSc60 Cam Univ CertEd61. Sarum & Wells Th Coll 86. **d** 88 **p** 94. NSM Canley *Cov* 88-91; NSM Cov N Deanery 91-92; C Coventry Caludon 92-97; Asst to Dioc Dir of Educn 92-93; Asst Chapl Geo Eliot Hosp NHS Trust Nuneaton 97-01; rtd 01; Perm to Offic *Ban* and *Cov* from 01. *22 Frankwell Street, Tywyn LL36 9EW* Tel (01654) 711604

ADAMS, The Ven Charles Alexander. b 29. MBE73 CBE82 JP. AKC59. **d** 60 **p** 61. C Bishopwearmouth St Mich w St Hilda *Dur* 60-63; C Ox SS Phil and Jas 63-66; C Tunbridge Wells St Barn *Roch* 66-68; St Vincent from 68; Miss to Seafarers from 68; Can Kingstown Cathl from 73; Adn St Vincent & The Grenadines 76-98; rtd 98. *St Mary's Rectory, Bequia, Northern Grenadines, St Vincent and the Grenadines* Tel (001784) 458 3234 Fax 457 3532 E-mail caadams@caribsurf.com

ADAMS, Christopher John. b 40. **d** 98 **p** 99. C Luton St Fran *St Alb* 98-05; rtd 06; Perm to Offic *St Alb* from 06. *91 Byron Road, Luton LU4 0HX* Tel (01582) 529373 E-mail chrisandsallyadams@ntlworld.com

ADAMS, David. See ADAMS, John David Andrew

ADAMS, David James. b 58. Trin Coll Bris 95. **d** 97 **p** 98. C Wirksworth *Derby* 97-00; P-in-c Seale and Lullington 00-02; R Seale and Lullington w Coton in the Elms 02-05; CF from 05; *rio* MOD Chaplains (Army) Tel (01980) 615804 Fax 615800

ADAMS, David John Anthony. b 46. QUB BSc70. Bris Sch of Min 81. **d** 84 **p** 85. NSM Sea Mills *Bris* 84-97; C Henbury 97-00; V Longwell Green from 00; AD Kingswood and S Glos from 06. *The Vicarage, 85 Bath Road, Longwell Green, Bristol BS30 9DF* Tel 0117-932 3714 Mobile 07803-330727 E-mail djaadams@surfaid.org

ADAMS, Donald John. b 46. St Jo Coll Nottm 86. **d** 88 **p** 89. C Byfleet *Guildf* 88-93; P-in-c E Molesey St Mary 93-03; Perm to Offic *S'wark* 96-03; rtd 03. *4 Boxbush Close, South Cerney, Cirencester GL7 5XS* Tel (01285) 852009 E-mail cada.adams@virgin.net

ADAMS, Douglas George. b 39. St Luke's Coll Ex CertEd69 MEd87 ALBC65. SW Minl Tr Course 86. **d** 89 **p** 90. NSM Bude Haven and Marhamchurch *Truro* 89-93; P-in-c St Mewan 93-04; P-in-c Mevagissey and St Ewe 00-04; Chapl Mt Edgcumbe Hospice 93-96; rtd 04; Perm to Offic *Truro* from 05. *9 Arundel Terrace, Bude EX23 8LS* Tel (01288) 353842 E-mail douglasadams@tiscali.co.uk

ADAMS, Gillian. See WILTON, Mrs Gillian Linda

ADAMS, Godfrey Bernard. b 47. **d** 93 **p** 94. OLM Saddleworth *Man* from 93. *11 Springmeadow Lane, Uppermill, Oldham OL3 6EP* Tel (01457) 875126 E-mail godfreyadams@compuserve.com

ADAMS, Hubert Theodore. b 28. FCA. **d** 98 **p** 99. OLM Blurton *Lich* from 98. *12 Wakefield Road, Stoke-on-Trent ST4 5PT* Tel (01782) 415364

ADAMS, Ian Robert. b 57. R Holloway Coll Lon BA79. Ridley Hall Cam 95. **d** 97 **p** 98. C Thame *Ox* 97-04; Ldr mayBe 04-09; Missional Community Developer CMS from 09. *Old Walls, Fore*

Street, Aveton Gifford, Kingsbridge TQ7 4LL Tel (01548) 550388 Mobile 07889-906983 E-mail ian@thestillpoint.org.uk

ADAMS, Canon James Michael. b 49. Man Univ LLB71 Lon Univ PGCE79. St Jo Coll Nottm 80. **d** 82 **p** 83. C Luton St Mary *St Alb* 82-85; TV Cove St Jo *Guildf* 85-92; V Chislehurst Ch Ch *Roch* from 92; Hon Can Roch Cathl from 09. *Christ Church Vicarage, 62 Lubbock Road, Chislehurst BR7 5JX* Tel (020) 8467 3185 *or* tel and fax 8325 3557 E-mail mmichaelccc@aol.com

ADAMS, Mrs Jayne Maxine. b 57. Westhill Coll Birm CertEd78. WMMTC 94. **d** 97 **p** 98. NSM Cotteridge *Birm* 97-99; NSM Nechells 99-05; NSM Bournville from 05. *40 Middle Park Drive, Northfield, Birmingham B31 2FL* Tel 0121-476 0206 E-mail jane.adams21.freeserve.co.uk

ADAMS, John. b 38. Lon Univ DipEd66 Open Univ BA79. Linc Th Coll 68. **d** 70 **p** 71. C Skipton H Trin *Bradf* 70-72; C Bassingham *Linc* 72-73; Chapl St Piers Hosp Sch Lingfield 73-74; Hon C Keighley *Bradf* 76-79; P-in-c Bredenbury and Wacton w Grendon Bishop *Heref* 79-84; P-in-c Edwyn Ralph and Collington w Thornbury 79-84; P-in-c Pencombe w Marston Stannett and Lt Cowarne 79-84; V Macclesfield St Jo *Ches* 84-87; R Wimblington *Ely* 87-90; V Manea 87-90; R Hallaton w Horninghold, Allexton, Tugby etc *Leic* 90-96; P-in-c Moulton *Linc* 96-97; V 97-03; rtd 03; Perm to Offic *Linc* from 03. *17 Linden Drive, Burgh le Marsh, Skegness PE24 5BP* Tel (01754) 810366

ADAMS, Canon John Christopher Ronald. b 29. St Paul's Coll Grahamstown. **d** 55 **p** 56. C Bulawayo St Marg S Rhodesia 55-61; R Shabani 61-66; C Northolt Park St Barn *Lon* 67-68; C W Brompton St Mary 68-69; C Umtali Zimbabwe 69-71; R Melfort and P-in-c Cranborne 71-75; Lic to Offic 75-98; rtd 98; Perm to Offic *S'wark* from 01. *The College of St Barnabas, Blackberry Lane, Lingfield RH7 6NJ* Tel (01342) 872838

ADAMS, John David Andrew. b 37. TCD BA60 MA64 BD69 Div Test61 Reading Univ MEd74. **d** 62 **p** 63. C Belfast St Steph *Conn* 62-65; Asst Master Lacunza Academy Spain 65-67; Asst Master Tower Ramparts Sch Ipswich 67-70; Asst Master Robert Haining Sch Surrey 70-74; Hd Master St Paul's Secondary Sch Addlestone 74-82; Hd Master Weydon Secondary Sch Farnham 82-98; NSM Bourne *Guildf* 80-99; NSM The Bourne and Tilford 99-07; Chapl to The Queen 94-07; Consultant to Secondary Schs 98-07. *Brookside Farm, Oast House Crescent, Farnham GU9 0NP* Tel (01252) 726888 E-mail j.david_adams@ntworld.com

ADAMS, John Mark Arthur. b 67. Reading Univ BSc89. St Jo Coll Nottm MA98 MPhil07. **d** 99 **p** 00. C Skegby *S'well* 99-02; C Bletchley *Ox* 02-07; P-in-c Mansfield St Jo *S'well* from 07; P-in-c Ladybrook from 09. *The Vicarage, St John Street, Mansfield NG18 1QH* Tel (01623) 660822 *or* 625999

ADAMS, John Peter. b 42. Lon Univ BD69. Oak Hill Th Coll 65. **d** 70 **p** 71. C Whitnash *Cov* 70-73; Hon Asst Chapl Basle *Eur* 73-74; Chapl Davos 74-75; Chapl Düsseldorf 75-76; C Gt Baddow *Chelmsf* 77-80; Miss Eur Chr Miss 80-91; Perm to Offic *Chelmsf* 80-91; Hon Asst Chapl Vienna *Eur* 90-91; Asst Chapl Zürich 91-95; P-in-c Harmondsworth *Lon* 95-99; TV Shebbear, Buckland Filleigh, Sheepwash etc *Ex* 99-02; rtd 02; Perm to Offic *Ex* from 02. *The Leas, Kingscott, Torrington EX38 7JW* Tel (01805) 622161 E-mail john@adams1100.freeserve.co.uk

ADAMS, John Richard. b 38. St D Coll Lamp BA62 Lich Th Coll 62. **d** 64 **p** 65. C Falmouth K Chas *Truro* 64-68; C Bath Twerton-on-Avon *B & W* 68-72; C Milton *Win* 72-79; P-in-c Weymouth St Edm *Sarum* 79-90; V 90-95; Chapl Westhaven Hosp Weymouth 79-94; P-in-c The Winterbournes and Compton Valence 95-03; rtd 03. *1 Manor Barn, Bothenhampton, Bridport DT6 4BJ* Tel (01308) 422808

ADAMS, Jonathan Henry. b 48. St Andr Univ MA73. Cranmer Hall Dur 73. **d** 76 **p** 77. C Upperby St Jo *Carl* 76-78; C Sunderland St Chad *Dur* 78-82; Soc Resp Officer 83-91; TV Willington *Newc* 91-96; Local Min Development Officer 91-96; P-in-c Byker St Silas 96-01; Perm to Offic from 01. *5A Tunstall Vale, Sunderland SR2 7HP* Tel 0191-525 1881 E-mail jonathan@openroad.fsnet.co.uk

ADAMS, Margaret Anne. *See* FREEMAN, Mrs Margaret Anne

ADAMS, Mark. *See* ADAMS, John Mark Arthur

ADAMS, Martin Philip. b 57. Open Univ BA99. Sarum & Wells Th Coll 88. **d** 90 **p** 91. C Sandringham w W Newton *Nor* 90-93; P-in-c Docking w The Birchams and Stanhoe w Barwick 93-95; V Docking, the Birchams, Stanhoe and Sedgeford 95-97; V Orrell *Liv* 97-03; R Aughton St Mich 03-08; Dir Dioc OLM Scheme from 03; Dir Studies SNWTP from 08. *The Vicarage, Intake Lane, Bickerstaffe, Ormskirk L39 0HW* Tel (01695) 727607 Mobile 07939-396934 E-mail martin.adams@liverpool.anglican.org

ADAMS, Michael. *See* ADAMS, Canon James Michael

ADAMS, Canon Michael John. b 48. St Jo Coll Dur BA77. Ripon Coll Cuddesdon 77. **d** 79 **p** 80. C Falmouth K Chas *Truro* 79-81; C St Buryan, St Levan and Sennen 81-83; P-in-c Lanlivery w Luxulyan 83-84; V 84-88; V St Agnes 88-99; V Newquay from 99; RD Powder 90-96; Hon Can Truro Cathl from 03; Perm to

Offic *Ex* from 94. *20 St Michael's Road, Newquay TR7 1RA* Tel and fax (01637) 872096 E-mail vicar@st-michaels-newquay.org.uk

ADAMS, Nicholas Stephen. b 68. K Coll Lon BA04. Westcott Ho Cam 06. **d** 09. C Fishponds St Jo *Bris* from 09; C Fishponds All SS from 09; C Fishponds St Mary from 09; C Bristol St Aid w St Geo from 09; C E Bris St Ambrose and St Leon from 09; C Two Mile Hill St Mich from 09. *15 Bexley Road, Bristol BS16 3SS* Tel 0117-965 9792 Mobile 07952-005137 E-mail nickadams100@hotmail.com

ADAMS, Nigel David. b 40. Sarum & Wells Th Coll 86. **d** 88 **p** 89. C Tile Hill *Cov* 88-91; C Coventry Caludon 91-92; TV 92-97; Asst Chapl HM YOI Onley 92-95; Sub Chapl HM Pris Birm 95-01; P-in-c Nuneaton St Mary *Cov* 97-01; rtd 01; Perm to Offic *Ban and Cov* from 01; AD Ystumaner *Ban* from 05. *22 Frankwell Street, Tywyn LL36 9EW* Tel (01654) 711604

ADAMS, Olugboyega Adeoye. b 55. Illinois Univ BSc81 Univ of Kansas MSc82 Lon Univ PhD93. EMMTC 99. **d** 02 **p** 03. C Glenfield *Leic* 02-05; V Peckham St Mary Magd *S'wark* from 05. *St Mary's Vicarage, 22 St Mary's Road, London SE15 2DW* Tel (020) 7639 4596 E-mail olu.adams@ukgateway.net

ADAMS, Peter. Bris Univ CertEd52 Lon Univ AdDipEd72. Oak Hill Th Coll 91. **d** 91 **p** 92. NSM Towcester w Easton Neston *Pet* 91-95; Perm to Offic *Ex* from 94. *Longmeads, Bovey Tracey, Newton Abbot TQ13 9LZ* Tel (01626) 832518

ADAMS, Canon Peter. b 37. K Coll Lon AKC65 Trin Coll Cam MA70. St Boniface Warminster 65. **d** 66 **p** 67. C Clapham H Trin *S'wark* 66-70; Chapl Trin Coll Cam 70-75; Warden Trin Coll Cen Camberwell 75-83; V Camberwell St Geo *S'wark* 75-83; RD Camberwell 80-83; P-in-c W Dulwich All SS and Em 83-85; V 85-92; V Addington 92-02; Hon Can S'wark Cathl 99-02; rtd 03; Perm to Offic *S'wark* from 04. *26 Mansfield Road, South Croydon CR2 6HN* Tel (020) 8680 3191 E-mail canon.adams@talk21.com

ADAMS, Peter Anthony. b 48. K Coll Lon BD70 AKC70 MTh72. **d** 72 **p** 74. Lic to Offic *Eur* 72-73; C Ashford *Cant* 73-79; P-in-c Ramsgate H Trin 79-86; P-in-c Ramsgate St Geo 84-86; R Ramsgate H Trin and St Geo from 86. *Holy Trinity Rectory, Winterstoke Way, Ramsgate CT11 8AG* Tel and fax (01843) 593593

ADAMS, Peter Harrison. b 41. Tyndale Hall Bris 63. **d** 68 **p** 69. C Kendal St Thos *Carl* 68-71; C W Bromwich Gd Shep w St Jo *Lich* 71-75; R Aldham *Chelmsf* 76-81; R Marks Tey 76-81; R Marks Tey w Aldham and Lt Tey 81-85; Dioc Missr 85-06; rtd 06; Through Faith Miss Ev from 06; Hon C Colchester St Jo *Chelmsf* from 85. *4 St Jude Gardens, Colchester CO4 0QJ* Tel (01206) 854041 E-mail peter@through-faith-missions.org

ADAMS, Canon Raymond William. b 58. Reading Univ BA79. Oak Hill Th Coll BA85. **d** 85 **p** 86. C Blackpool St Thos *Blackb* 85-88; C Padiham 88-90; TV Rodbourne Cheney *Bris* 90-02; RD Cricklade 97-99; V Haydon Wick from 02; Hon Can Bris Cathl from 09. *The Vicarage, 54 Furlong Close, Swindon SN25 1QP* Tel (01793) 634258 E-mail r.adams4@ntlworld.com

ADAMS, Richard. *See* ADAMS, John Richard

ADAMS, Richard John. b 48. Leeds Univ BA70. SAOMC 94. **d** 97 **p** 98. C N Hinksey and Wytham *Ox* 97-01; V Fence-in-Pendle and Higham *Blackb* from 01. *The Vicarage, 12 Wheatcroft Avenue, Fence, Burnley BB12 9QL* Tel (01282) 617316 E-mail richard@gwyneth.net

ADAMS, Roger Charles. b 36. Em Coll Cam BA60 MA64. Tyndale Hall Bris 60. **d** 62 **p** 63. C Longfleet *Sarum* 62-65; C Uphill *B & W* 66-71; R Ramsden Crays w Ramsden Bellhouse *Chelmsf* 71-78; SW Area Sec BFBS 78-84; P-in-c Plymouth St Aug *Ex* 84-85; TV Plymouth Em w Efford 85-90; V Paignton Ch Ch 90-01; rtd 01; Perm to Offic *Ex* from 01. *171 Elburton Road, Plymouth PL9 8HY* Tel (01752) 407287

ADAMS, Ms Ruth Helen. b 73. St Jo Coll Dur BA94 TCD BTh97. CITC 94. **d** 97 **p** 98. C Drumragh w Mountfield *D & R* 97-99; Chapl Trin Coll Cam 00-06; P-in-c Bar Hill *Ely* from 06. *108 Stonefield, Bar Hill, Cambridge CB23 8TE* Tel (01954) 789369

ADAMS, Stephen Paul. b 56. Ex Univ BSc78. Sarum & Wells Th Coll 85. **d** 87 **p** 88. C Swansea St Nic *S & B* 87-88; C Llwynderw 88-91; R Badby w Newham and Charwelton w Fawsley etc *Pet* 91-97; R Abington 97-06; RD Northn 01-06; Dean Min Development St Mich Coll Llan from 06. *St Michael's College, 54 Cardiff Road, Llandaff, Cardiff CF5 2YJ* Tel (029) 2056 3379 Fax 2083 8008

ADAMS (née DABIN), Susan. b 51. NTMTC 96. **d** 00 **p** 01. NSM Hullbridge *Chelmsf* 00-03 and from 07; NSM Rawreth w Rettendon from 07; NSM Ashingdon w S Fambridge 03-07. *49 Crouch Avenue, Hullbridge, Hockley SS5 6BS* Tel (01702) 231825 E-mail susan@secretarybird.fslife.co.uk

ADAMS, Theo. *See* ADAMS, Hubert Theodore

ADAMS, William Thomas. b 47. Ches Coll of HE CertEd69 Open Univ BA74 Leic Univ MA91. EAMTC 97. **d** 00 **p** 01. NSM Helmdon w Stuchbury and Radstone etc *Pet* 00-03; NSM

Astwell Gp 03-05; R from 05. *Brookdale, Mill Road, Whitfield, Brackley NN13 5TQ* Tel (01280) 850683
E-mail rector@astwellbenefice.co.uk

ADAMSON, Anthony Scott. b 49. Newc Univ BA70. Cranmer Hall Dur 75. **d** 78 **p** 79. C High Elswick St Paul *Newc* 78-86; C Benwell 86-92; V Tweedmouth 92-05; P-in-c Scremerston and Spittal 02-05; AD Norham 00-05; I Stranorlar w Meenglas and Kilteevogue *D & R* from 06. *The Rectory, Stranorlar, Co Donegal, Republic of Ireland* Tel (00353) (74) 913 1081
E-mail tkadamson@eircom.net

ADAMSON, Arthur John. b 38. Keble Coll Ox BA61 MA65. Tyndale Hall Bris 61. **d** 63 **p** 64. C Redhill H Trin *S'wark* 63-66; Chapl Trent Park Coll of Educn 66-69; C Enfield Ch Ch Trent Park *Lon* 66-70; Ind Chapl and V Battersea St Geo w St Andr *S'wark* 70-74; R Reedham *Nor* 74-80; Min Beighton and Moulton 75-80; P-in-c Cantley w Limpenhoe and Southwood 77-80; R Oulton St Mich 80-90; Chapl Lothingland Hosp 80-90; R Laceby *Linc* 90-98; R Laceby and Ravendale Gp 98-03; rtd 03; Perm to Offic *Pet* from 03. *24 Mill Lane, Cottesmore, Oakham LE15 7DL* Tel (01572) 812816 E-mail ajaca@compuserve.com *or* ajohnadamson@aol.com

ADAMSON, Paul. b 35. Leeds Univ BA58. Coll of Resurr Mirfield. **d** 60 **p** 61. C Southwick St Columba *Dur* 60-63; Br Guiana 63-66; Guyana 66-75; C Benwell St Jas *Newc* 75-77; V Cowgate 77-83; V Prudhoe 83-93; TV N Tyne and Redesdale 93-98; TR 98-00; RD Bellingham 98-00; rtd 00; Perm to Offic *Newc* from 01. *11 Carham Close, Corbridge NE45 5NA* Tel (01434) 633274

ADAN, Howard Keith. b 62. **d** 01 **p** 02. C Amsterdam w Den Helder and Heiloo *Eur* 01-04; Asst Chapl 04-07; Angl Chapl Amsterdam Airport Schiphol 04-07. *Address temp unknown*
E-mail adans@xs4all.nl

ADDENBROOKE, Keith Paul. b 67. Warwick Univ BSc90 MA05 Lanc Univ MA03. Qu Coll Birm BA07. **d** 07 **p** 08. C Upton (Overchurch) *Ches* from 07. *43 Grafton Drive, Wirral CH49 0TX*

ADDENBROOKE, Peter Homfray. b 38. Trin Coll Cam BA59 MA68 Ex Univ PGCE60. Lich Th Coll 61. **d** 63 **p** 64. C Bakewell *Derby* 63-67; C Horsham *Chich* 67-73; P-in-c Colgate 73-98; Adv for Past Care and Counselling 73-93; rtd 98; Perm to Offic *Chich* from 99. *Oaks, Forest Road, Colgate, Horsham RH12 4SZ* Tel (01293) 851362

ADDINGTON, David John. b 47. FInstLEx72 FCIArb96. St Jo Coll Nottm 98. **d** 01 **p** 03. Asst P Warwick St Mary Bermuda 03-08; Chapl Miss to Seafarers from 05; Hon C March St Jo *Ely* from 08. *79 New Park, March PE15 8RT* Tel and fax (01354) 650139 Mobile 07775-796543

ADDISON, David John Frederick. b 37. K Coll Dur BA60 DipEd62 Birm Univ MA79 Bris Univ MLitt93. Wells Th Coll 64. **d** 66 **p** 71. C Rastrick St Matt *Wakef* 66-67; Perm to Offic *Bradf* 67-71; Hon C Manningham St Luke 71-73; Perm to Offic *Glouc* 77-79; Hon C Bisley w Oakridge 79-81; V Newland and Redbrook w Clearwell 81-02; Chapl R Forest of Dean Coll 89-02; Perm to Offic *Glouc* 02-08 and *Mon* 04-08; TV Langtree *Ox* from 08. *The Vicarage, Crabtree Corner, Ipsden, Wallingford OX10 6BN* Tel (01491) 682832 Mobile 07815-806313

ADDISON, Philip Ives. b 29. K Coll Dur 49. Ely Th Coll 59. **d** 61 **p** 62. C Waltham Cross *St Alb* 61-64; C Bedford St Paul 64-66; Chapl Bedford N Wing Hosp 64-66; Chapl RN 66-70; V Foleshill St Laur *Cov* 70-74; C in-c Halsham *York* 74-78; V Owthorne and Rimswell w Withernsea 74-99; Chapl Withernsea Hosp 74-99; rtd 99; Perm to Offic *York* from 99. *10 Park Avenue, Beverley HU17 7AT* Tel (01482) 872714

ADEKANYE, The Ven Joseph (Kehinde). b 47. Oak Hill Th Coll BA84 Liv Inst of Educn MA98. Immanuel Coll Ibadan. **d** 72 **p** 73. Nigeria 72-80, 84-97 and from 00; Lect Abp Vining Coll of Th Akure from 94; Perm to Offic *Liv* 97-00. *Archbishop Vining College, PO Box 3, Akure, Nigeria* Tel (00234) (34) 233031

ADEKUNLE, Elizabeth. **d** 07 **p** 08. C Homerton St Luke *Lon* from 07. *9 Stanford Mews, London E8 1JA* Tel (020) 7254 5408
E-mail lizadeola@yahoo.co.uk

ADEMOLA, Canon Ade. b 62. Goldsmiths' Coll Lon BA91 N Lon Univ MA94. NTMTC 95. **d** 98 **p** 99. NSM Lt Ilford St Barn *Chelmsf* 98-02; V Leyton Em from 02; Can Ibadan from 03. *Emmanuel Vicarage, 149 Hitcham Road, London E17 8HL* Tel (020) 8539 2200 Mobile 07941-029084
E-mail orison@ademola.eu

ADENEKAN, Latiff Aremu. b 38. **d** 04 **p** 05. OLM Tulse Hill H Trin and St Matthias *S'wark* 04-08; Perm to Offic 08-09. *Address temp unknown* E-mail latiff95@hotmail.com

ADENEY, Harold Walter. b 14. OBE76. Qu Coll Cam BA35 MB BChir38 MA53. Trin Coll Bris. **d** 75 **p** 76. Burundi 75-82; Perm to Offic *St Alb* 83-98 and *Nor* 92-05. *Eckling Grange Residential Home, Norwich Road, Dereham NR20 3BB* Tel (01362) 690239

ADESANYA, The Ven Stephen Adedotun. b 57. Ogun State Univ MEd97 Ado-Ekiti State Univ Ph D03. Evang Th Faculty Osijek Croatia BTh91. **d** 91 **p** 92. Nigeria 91-07; Adn Iwade and V Italupe Em 03-07; Perm to Offic *S'wark* 07-09; P-in-c Romaldkirk w Laithkirk *Ripon* from 09; P-in-c Startforth and

Bowes and Rokeby w Brignall from 09. *35 Low Startforth Road, Startforth, Barnard Castle DL12 9AU* Tel (01833) 631697 Mobile 07950-713797 E-mail dtndsny@yahoo.com

ADETAYO, Mrs Abigail Olufunke. b 47. SRN74 SCM75 Greenwich Univ PGCE07. SEITE 06. **d** 09. *158 Torridon Road, London SE6 1RD* Tel and fax (020) 8695 1713 Mobile 07746-035727 E-mail jadetayo@aol.com

ADEY, John Douglas. b 33. Man Univ BSc54. Coll of Resurr Mirfield 56. **d** 58 **p** 59. C Forton *Portsm* 58-64; C Northolt St Mary *Lon* 64-67; V Snibston *Leic* 67-72; V Outwood *Wakef* 72-78; V Clifton 78; V Upton Priory *Ches* 79-81; V Hyde St Thos 81-82; V Newton in Mottram 82-89; R Roos and Garton w Tunstall, Grimston and Hilston *York* 89-92; C Woodchurch *Ches* 92-95; C Coppenhall 95-98; rtd 98; Perm to Offic *Portsm* from 98. *90A Winter Road, Southsea PO4 9BX* Tel (023) 9273 4116

ADEY HUISH, Helen Louise. b 59. Bris Univ BA81 Qu Coll Cam PhD87. SAOMC 01. **d** 04 **p** 05. NSM Banbury *Ox* 04-07; Chapl Ox Radcliffe Hosps NHS Trust from 07. *Timberhurst, The Green, Shenington, Banbury OX15 6NE* Tel (01295) 670285 *or* (01865) 229104 E-mail adey.huish@onetel.com *or* louise.adeyhuish@orh.nhs.uk

ADFIELD, Richard Ernest. b 31. Oak Hill Th Coll 62. **d** 64 **p** 65. C Bedworth *Cov* 64-67; V Whitehall Park St Andr Hornsey Lane *Lon* 67-77; V Kensington St Helen w H Trin 77-86; V Turnham Green Ch Ch 86-92; rtd 92; Perm to Offic *Chich* from 92; Chapl Brighton and Sussex Univ Hosps NHS Trust 02-03; Chapl Whittington Coll Felbridge from 03. *363 Hangleton Road, Hove BN3 7LQ* Tel (01273) 732538

✠**ADIE, The Rt Revd Michael Edgar.** b 29. CBE94. St Jo Coll Ox BA52 MA56 Surrey Univ DUniv95. Westcott Ho Cam 52. **d** 54 **p** 55 **c** 83. C Pallion *Dur* 54-57; Abp's Dom Chapl *Cant* 57-60; V Sheff St Mark Broomhall 60-69; RD Hallam 66-69; R Louth w Welton-le-Wold *Linc* 69-75; P-in-c N w S Elkington 69-75; TR Louth 75-76; V Morton w Hacconby 76-83; Adn Linc 77-83; Can and Preb Linc Cathl 77-83; Bp Guildf 83-94; rtd 95; Perm to Offic *Portsm* from 95; Hon Asst Bp Portsm from 95; Hon Asst Bp Chich from 96. *Greenslade, Froxfield, Petersfield GU32 1EB* Tel (01730) 827266

ADLAM, David John. b 47. **d** 06 **p** 07. OLM Dickleburgh and The Pulhams *Nor* from 06. *Weggs Farm, Common Road, Dickleburgh, Diss IP21 4PJ* Tel (01379) 741200 Fax 741800 Mobile 07860-417158 E-mail john@adlams.net

ADLAM, Keith Richard. b 44. STETS 00. **d** 03 **p** 04. NSM Binstead and Havenstreet St Pet *Portsm* 03-07; NSM Northwood from 07; NSM Gurnard from 07; NSM Cowes St Faith from 07. *23 Queen's Road, Ryde PO33 3BG* Tel (01983) 616903 Fax 810270 E-mail revkeith@kjr-group.co.uk

ADLEY, Ernest George. b 38. Leeds Univ BA61. Wells Th Coll 62. **d** 64 **p** 65. C Bideford *Ex* 64-67; C Yeovil St Mich *B & W* 67-70; V Taunton Lyngford 70-79; R Skegness and Winthorpe *Linc* 79-91; R Wantage Downs *Ox* 91-03; rtd 03; Perm to Offic *Ox* from 04. *13 Pixton Close, Didcot OX11 0BX* Tel (01235) 210395

ADLINGTON, David John. b 51. AKC73. K Coll Lon 70 St Aug Coll Cant 73. **d** 74 **p** 75. C Clapham St Paul *S'wark* 74-77; C Bethnal Green St Matt *Lon* 77-80; P-in-c Stepney St Pet w St Benet 80-84; PV and Succ O'wall Succ Llan Cathl 84-87; PV and Succ Llan Cathl 88-91; Dioc Dir of Educn 91-00; V St Hilary 91-94; TV Cowbridge 94-95; C Whitchurch 95-00; P-in-c Folkestone St Mary and St Eanswythe *Cant* 00-02; V Cowbridge 94-95; C Whitchurch 95-00; P-in-c Folkestone St Mary and St Eanswythe *Cant* 00-02; V 02-09; P-in-c Elham w Denton and Wootton from 09; Hon Min Can Cant Cathl from 01. *The Vicarage, Vicarage Lane, Elham, Canterbury CT4 6TT* Tel (01303) 840219

ADMAN, Fayaz. b 63. Pakistan Adventist Sem Sheikhupura BA94. St Thos Th Coll Karachi 97. **d** 98 **p** 99. Dn St Jo Cathl Peshawar Pakistan 98-99; P 00-03; Presbyter Peshawar City All SS 99-00; Bp's Chapl 01-03; V Charsada, Shabqadar and Ghalana 00-04; C S Rochdale *Man* 04-07; P-in-c Bolton St Paul w Em from 07; P-in-c Daubhill from 07. *Emmanuel Vicarage, Edward Street, Bolton BL3 5LQ* Tel (01204) 393282
E-mail revfadman_bpchp_dop@hotmail.com

ADNETT, Roy Gumley. b 14. Tyndale Hall Bris 39. **d** 42 **p** 43. C Blackb Ch Ch 42-44; C Denton Holme *Carl* 44-46; V Constable Lee *Man* 46-49; R Peldon w Gt and Lt Wigborough *Chelmsf* 49-55; V Chilcompton *B & W* 55-80; RD Midsomer Norton 78-81; R Chilcompton w Downside and Stratton on the Fosse 80-81; rtd 81; Perm to Offic *Leic* 81-96. *Bosbury, St James Close, Pangbourne, Reading RG8 7AP* Tel 0118-984 3781

ADOYO, Miss Eugeniah Ombwayo. b 54. Lon Bible Coll 84 Westmr Coll Ox BA86 MPhil90. dss 82 **d** 91 **p** 91. Kenya 82-94; Internat Sec Crosslinks 94-97; Hon C Hatcham St Jas *S'wark* 94-97; C S'wark Ch Ch and Chapl S Lon Ind Miss 97-02; TV Plaistow and N Canning Town *Chelmsf* from 02. *St Philip's Vicarage, 19 Abbey Street, London E13 8DT* Tel (020) 7474 4596
E-mail eugeniah@fsmail.net

ADSETTS, Ms Marilyn Ann. b 47. St Jo Coll York CertEd69 Leeds Univ BEd70 Spurgeon's Coll Lon MTh00. EAMTC 98. **d** 00 **p** 01. C Rushmere *St E* 00-03; V Rhymney *Mon* 03-07; rtd

07. *Grace House, 15 Weston Park, Weston under Penyard, Ross-on-Wye HR9 7FR* E-mail mbygrace@aol.com

ADU-BOACHIE, Francis. b 60. Oak Hill Th Coll. **d** 95 **p** 96. C Stonebridge St Mich *Lon* 95-01; V Wembley St Jo from 01. *The Vicarage, 3 Crawford Avenue, Wembley HA0 2HX* Tel (020) 8902 0273 E-mail francis@adu-boachie.freeserve.co.uk

ADYERI, James Joloba. b 58. Redcliffe Coll 96 Chelt & Glouc Coll of HE BA99. United Th Coll Bangalore 91. **d** 84 **p** 85. Uganda 85-88, 89-91, 92-96 and from 99; India 88-89 and 91-92; Perm to Offic *Glouc* 96-99. *PO Box 84, Mityana, Uganda* Tel (00256) (46) 23 36

AFFLECK, John. b 20. Liv Univ LLB48. K Coll Lon 68 St Aug Coll Cant 71. **d** 71 **p** 72. C Hutton *Chelmsf* 71-74; P-in-c Hawkchurch, Fishpond, Bettiscombe, Marshwood etc *Sarum* 74-80; R Marshwood Vale 80-86; rtd 86; Perm to Offic *Sarum* from 86. *23 St Nicholas Hospital, St Nicholas Road, Salisbury SP1 2SW* Tel (01722) 334659

AFFLECK, Stuart John. b 47. AKC69. St Aug Coll Cant. **d** 70 **p** 71. C Prittlewell St Mary *Chelmsf* 70-75; Asst Chapl Charterhouse Sch Godalming 75-78; Chapl 78-80; Warden Pilsdon Community 80-94; Perm to Offic *S'wark* from 03; rtd 07. *3 Chislehurst Road, Richmond TW10 6PW*

AGAR, George. b 40. Edin Univ BSc63 Ox Univ PGCE64. NOC 92. **d** 94 **p** 95. Hd Biddulph High Sch Stoke-on-Trent 94-96; NSM Sandbach *Ches* 94-99; NSM Hartford from 99. *128 Middlewich Road, Sandbach CW11 1FH* Tel (01270) 760191 E-mail georgea@stjohnshartford.org

AGASSIZ, David John Lawrence. b 42. St Pet Hall Ox BA64 MA67 Imp Coll Lon PhD94. Ripon Hall Ox 64. **d** 66 **p** 67. C Southampton St Mary w H Trin *Win* 66-71; V Enfield St Jas *Lon* 71-80; P-in-c Grays Thurrock *Chelmsf* 80-83; P-in-c Grays All SS 81-84; P-in-c Lt Thurrock St Mary 81-84; P-in-c W Thurrock 81-83; P-in-c Grays SS Pet and Paul, S Stifford and W Thurrock 83-84; TR Grays Thurrock 84-90; Hon Can Chelmsf Cathl 90-93; Dioc Development Rep 90-93; Kenya 98-00; Perm to Offic *S'wark* 02-07 and B & W from 08. *The Garden House, Stafford Place, Weston-super-Mare BS23 2QZ* Tel (01934) 620486 Mobile 07813-566957 E-mail dagassiz@tiscali.co.uk

AGBELUSI, Dele Omotayo. b 51. Ahmadu Bello Univ Zaria MSc81 Oak Hill Th Coll BA99. Immanuel Coll Ibadan. **d** 86 **p** 87. Nigeria 86-96; C Edmonton All SS w St Mich *Lon* 97-99; V Hornsey Ch Ch from 99. *Christ Church Vicarage, 32 Crescent Road, London N8 8AX* Tel (020) 8340 1656 *or* 8340 1566 E-mail agbelusi@aol.com

AGER, David George. b 52. Lon Univ BA73 Solicitor 77. SWMTC 01. **d** 04 **p** 05. NSM Deane Vale B & W 04-09; NSM Taunton St Jas from 09; Bp's Officer for Ord NSM (Taunton Adnry) from 09. *14 Morgans Rise, Bishops Hull, Taunton TA1 5HW* Tel (01823) 335424 Mobile 07887-893918 E-mail ager@talk21.com

AGGETT, Miss Vivienne Cecilia. b 33. Sarum & Wells Th Coll 86. **d** 88 **p** 94. C Binley *Cov* 88-91; C Hednesford *Lich* 91-96; rtd 96; Perm to Offic *Cov* from 98 and *Lich* from 04; Asst Chapl Gtr Athens *Eur* 01-08. *Batsi, 845 03 Andros, Greece* Tel (0030) (2282) 041102 Mobile 6936-295647 E-mail aggett@otenet.gr

AGGREY, Solomon Samuel. b 49. BSc76. Immanuel Coll Ibadan MA84. **d** 80 **p** 82. Nigeria 80-88; Miss Partner CMS from 88; C Gorton Em and Gorton St Jas *Man* 93-95. *68 Booth Street, Denton, Manchester M34 3HY*

AGNEW, Kenneth David. b 33. Jes Coll Cam BA58 MA62. Clifton Th Coll 58. **d** 60 **p** 61. C Lozells St Silas *Birm* 60-63; C Skellingthorpe *Linc* 63-68; C Birchwood 68-72; R Willand *Ex* 72-00; RD Cullompton 89-95; rtd 00; Perm to Offic *B & W* from 01. *Eastgate, 14 Limington Road, Ilchester, Yeovil BA22 8LX* Tel (01935) 842010

AGNEW, Kevin Raymond Christopher. b 59. Chich Th Coll. **d** 94 **p** 95. C Eastbourne St Mary *Chich* 94-98; V Roughey from 98. *Roffey Vicarage, 52 Shepherds Way, Horsham RH12 4LX* Tel (01403) 265333

AGNEW, Stephen Mark. b 54. Univ of Wales (Ban) BSc76 Southn Univ BTh81. Sarum & Wells Th Coll 76. **d** 79 **p** 80. C Wilmslow *Ches* 79-84; V Crewe St Jo 84-90; Chapl Bromsgrove Sch 90-99; V Claines St Jo *Worc* from 99. *The Vicarage, Claines Lane, Worcester WR3 7RN* Tel (01905) 754772 Mobile 07762-250749 E-mail revsmagnew@yahoo.com

AHON, Ahon Bol Nyuar. b 62. **d** 01 **p** 03. Uganda 01-03; Lic to Offic *Birm* from 03; Hon Chapl Birm Cathl from 03. *224 Highters Heath Lane, Birmingham B14 4NZ* Tel 07956-165426 (mobile) E-mail de_nyuar@yahoo.com

AHRENS, Irene Karla Elisabeth. b 40. Berlin Univ Bonn Univ PhD69 Lon Bible Coll BA92 K Coll Lon MTh93. SEITE 93. **d** 95 **p** 96. NSM Kew St Phil and All SS w St Luke *S'wark* 95-99; Asst Chapl Berlin *Eur* from 00. *Wildpfad 26, 14193 Berlin, Germany* Tel (0049) (30) 8972 8552 E-mail irene.ahrens@epost.de

AIDLEY, Jessica-Jil Stapleton. b 42. Westf Coll Lon BSc67 UEA PhD73 PGCE84. **d** 99 **p** 00. OLM High Oak, Hingham and Scoulton w Wood Rising *Nor* 99-04; Perm to Offic *Mon* 04-05;

NSM Rockfield and Dingestow Gp from 05. *The Yew Tree, Lydart, Monmouth NP25 4RH* Tel (01600) 713075 E-mail j.aidley@btopenworld.com

AIKEN, Nicholas John. b 58. Sheff Univ BA. Wycliffe Hall Ox 80. **d** 82 **p** 83. C Ashtead *Guildf* 82-86; Dioc Youth Officer 86-93; R Wisley w Pyrford from 93; RD Woking 03-08. *The Rectory, Aviary Road, Woking GU22 8TH* Tel (01932) 352914 E-mail rector@wisleywithpyrford.org

AIKEN, Simon Mark. b 62. St Andr Univ MTheol85. Ripon Coll Cuddesdon 86. **d** 88 **p** 89. C Burnley St Matt w H Trin *Blackb* 88-91; C Heyhouses on Sea 91-94; V Musbury 94-99; V Longridge 99-06; Sub Dean Bloemfontein from 06. *PO Box 1523, Bloemfontein 9300, South Africa* Tel (0027) (51) 448 3010

AINGE, Canon David Stanley. b 47. Brasted Place Coll 68. Oak Hill Th Coll 70. **d** 73 **p** 74. C Bitterne *Win* 73-77; C Castle Church *Lich* 77-79; P-in-c Beccentree St Alb *Chelmsf* 79-89; P-in-c Beccentree St Jo 85-89; TR Beccentree S 89-91; RD Barking and Dagenham 86-91; V Leyton St Mary w St Edw 91-96; P-in-c Leyton St Luke 91-96; V Leyton St Mary w St Edw and St Luke 96-03; RD Waltham Forest 94-00; R Gt Dunmow and Barnston from 03; Hon Can Chelmsf Cathl from 97. *The Vicarage, The Charters, Church End, Dunmow CM6 2SJ* Tel (01371) 872504 E-mail vicar@stmarysgreatdunmow.org.uk *or* davidainge@aol.com

AINSCOUGH, Malcolm Ralph. b 52. Liv Univ BEd76. St Mich Coll Llan 85. **d** 87 **p** 88. C Fleur-de-Lis *Mon* 87-90; C Chepstow 90-91; TV Cwmbran 91-95; V Newport St Steph and H Trin 95-03; R Hasland *Derby* from 03; V Temple Normanton from 03. *The Rectory, 49 Churchside, Hasland, Chesterfield S41 0JX* Tel (01246) 232486 E-mail ainscoughm@fsmail.net

AINSLEY, Canon Anthony Dixon. b 29. Oriel Coll Ox BA52 MA57 UNISA BA74. St Steph Ho Ox 53. **d** 55 **p** 56. C Burnley St Cath *Blackb* 55-60; S Africa 60-80; P-in-c Nqamakwe 62-68; P-in-c Idutywa 73-80; Adn All SS 73-80; Can St Jo Cathl Umtata 73-80; Hon Can from 81; Chapl Bordeaux w Riberac, Cahors, Duras etc *Eur* 81; V Blackpool St Steph *Blackb* 81-94; rtd 94; Perm to Offic *Bradf* 94-99. *PO Box 26239, Hout Bay, 7872 South Africa*

AINSLEY, Peter Dixon. b 32. OBE87. St Steph Ho Ox 58. **d** 60 **p** 61. C Bury St Thos *Man* 60-62; Chapl RN 62-87; Chapl HM Pris Liv 87-88; Chapl HM Pris Garth 88-95; rtd 95; Perm to Offic *Blackb* and *Liv* from 95. *21 Ridge Close, Southport PR9 8JU*

AINSWORTH, Mrs Janina Helen Margaret. b 50. Ripon Coll Cuddesdon. **d** 05 **p** 06. NSM E Farnworth and Kearsley *Man* 05-07; Chief Educn Officer Abps' Coun from 07. *Church House, Great Smith Street, London SW1P 3AZ* Tel (020) 7898 1500 Fax 7898 1520 E-mail janina.ainsworth@c-of-e.org.uk *or* jan@ainsworths.org.uk

AINSWORTH, Mark John. b 64. Lon Univ MTh92. Wycliffe Hall Ox 86. **d** 89 **p** 90. C Chipping Barnet w Arkley *St Alb* 89-93; USA from 93. *270 Bent Road, Wyncote PA 19095-1503, USA* Tel (001) (215) 517 8568 E-mail mjaec@earthlink.net

AINSWORTH, Michael Ronald. b 50. K Coll Lon LLB71 LLM72 Trin Hall Cam BA74 MA79. Westcott Ho Cam 72. **d** 75 **p** 76. C Scotforth *Blackb* 75-78; Chapl St Martin's Coll of Educn 78-82; Chapl NOC 82-89; R Withington St Chris *Man* 89-94; TR Worsley 94-07; Adn Eccles 00-05; Hon Can Man Cathl 04-07; R St Geo-in-the-East w St Paul *Lon* from 07. *St George's Rectory, 16 Cannon Street Road, London E1 0BH* Tel (020) 7680 9634 E-mail michael@ainsworth.org.uk

AINSWORTH, Paul Henry. b 46. JP. Man Poly BA81. NOC 85. **d** 88 **p** 89. NSM Salterhebble All SS *Wakef* 88-92; C Golcar 92-96; TV Moor Allerton *Ripon* from 96. *St Stephen's Vicarage, Tynwald Drive, Leeds LS17 5DR* Tel 0113-268 7338 E-mail batandball1@btopenworld.com

AINSWORTH, Peter. b 34. Lon Univ BD57. Coll of Resurr Mirfield 69. **d** 70 **p** 71. C Leeds St Wilfrid *Ripon* 70-74; TV Tong *Bradf* 74-77; V Fairweather Green 77-94; rtd 94; Perm to Offic *Wakef* 94-02 and *York* from 03. *34 Dulverton Hall, Esplanade, Scarborough YO11 2AR* Tel (01723) 340134

AINSWORTH-SMITH, Canon Ian Martin. b 41. MBE06. Selw Coll Cam BA64 MA68. Westcott Ho Cam 64. **d** 66 **p** 67. C Mill Hill Jo Keble Ch *Lon* 66-69; USA 69-71; C Purley St Mark *S'wark* 71-73; Chapl St Geo Hosp Lon 73-94; Chapl St Geo Healthcare NHS Trust Lon 94-06; Hon Can S'wark Cathl 95-06; rtd 06; Perm to Offic *B & W* from 06; Dioc Adv Hosp Chapl from 07. *Knutsford Cottage, North Street, Milverton, Taunton TA4 1LG* Tel (01823) 400365 E-mail jeanianas@btinternet.com

AIPO RONGO, Bishop of. See AYONG, The Most Revd James Simon

AIRD, Robert Malcolm. b 31. Lon Univ BSc54. Westcott Ho Cam 75. **d** 77 **p** 78. C Burnham *B & W* 77-79; P-in-c Taunton Lyngford 79-84; V 84-87; R Dulverton and Brushford 87-94; rtd 96. *Arran Cottage, East Street, Chulmleigh EX18 7DD* Tel (01769) 581042

AIRD, Wendy Elizabeth. b 41. SEITE. **d** 00 **p** 01. NSM Streatham Immanuel and St Andr *S'wark* 00-05; NSM Chevington *Newc* from 05; P-in-c from 08; NSM Shilbottle 05-08. *98 The Farnes,*

St John's Estate, South Broomhill, Morpeth NE65 9TH Tel (01670) 760890 Mobile 07711-301813
E-mail chevvic@btinternet.com

AIREY, Robert William. b 54. **d** 99 **p** 00. OLM Holcombe *Man* 99-08; OLM Holcombe and Hawkshaw from 09. *4 Pine Street, Haslingden, Rossendale BB4 5ND* Tel (01706) 224743

AIREY, Simon Christopher. b 60. Trin Coll Bris BA87. **d** 87 **p** 88. C Wilton *B & W* 87-90; Chapl Scargill Ho 90-93; TV Kingswood *Bris* 93-96; Asst P Nether Springs Northumbria Community 96-98 and 02-03; C Bath Abbey w St Jas *B & W* 98-02; C Nailsea Ch Ch w Tickenham 03-09; Chapl Grey Coll Dur from 09. *The Chaplain's Office, Grey College, South Road, Durham DH1 3LG* Tel 0191-334 5593 E-mail s.c.airey@durham.ac.uk

AISBITT, Joanne. *See* LISTER, Mrs Joanne

AISBITT, Michael. b 60. St Pet Coll Ox BA81 MA84. Westcott Ho Cam 81. **d** 84 **p** 85. C Norton St Mary *Dur* 84-87; C Kirkleatham *York* 87-90; V S Bank 90-96; R Whitby 96-97; TR Whitby w Aislaby and Ruswarp 97-00; R Attleborough w Besthorpe *Nor* 00-09; RD Thetford and Rockland 03-09. *16 The Acres, Stokesley, Middlesbrough TS9 5QA* E-mail m_aisbitt@hotmail.com

AISBITT, Osmond John. b 35. St Chad's Coll Dur BA57. **d** 61 **p** 62. C Ashington *Newc* 61-64; C Blyth St Mary 64-68; V Cleckheaton St Jo *Wakef* 68-75; V Horbury 75-78; V Horbury w Horbury Bridge 78-97; rtd 97; Perm to Offic *Carl* 97-00 and from 02; P-in-c Nerja and Almuécar *Eur* 00-02. *8 Stonecross Gardens, Ulverston LA12 7HA* Tel (01229) 585622

AITCHISON, Charles Baillie. b 45. New Coll Dur BEd85 Bede Coll Dur TCert67 Newc Univ DAES74 ACP69. LNSM course 85. **d** 93 **p** 98. NSM Peebles *Edin* from 93; NSM Innerleithen from 93. *45 Whitehaugh Park, Peebles EH45 9DB* Tel (01721) 729750 *or* tel and fax 724008

AITKEN, Christopher William Mark. b 53. Dur Univ BA75. Westcott Ho Cam 76. **d** 79 **p** 80. C Finchley St Mary *Lon* 79-82; C Radlett *St Alb* 82-85; V Sprowston *Nor* 85-90; R Beeston St Andr 85-90; R Sprowston w Beeston 90-93; Chapl Sherborne Sch 93-04; Hd Master St Lawr Coll Ramsgate from 04. *Headmaster's House, St Lawrence College, College Road, Ramsgate CT11 7AE* Tel (01843) 572900
E-mail cwmaitken@talk21.com *or* hm@slcuk.com

AITKEN, Leslie St John Robert. b 41. Open Univ BA75. Cranmer Hall Dur 62. **d** 65 **p** 66. C Worc St Barn w Ch Ch 65-69; C Halesowen 69-73; P-in-c Wyche 73-80; R Blackley St Pet *Man* 80-99; Chapl Booth Hall Hosp Man 80-89; R Sutton, Huttoft and Anderby *Linc* 99-06; rtd 06. *17 Old School Mews, Spilsby PE23 5QU*

AITKEN, Valerie Anne. b 46. STETS 01. **d** 04 **p** 05. NSM Perivale *Lon* from 04. *22 Woodfield Road, London W5 1SH* Tel (020) 8997 6819 Mobile 07944-873168
E-mail valerie.aitken2@btinternet.com

AITKEN, William Stuart. b 35. FCFI MSIAD CertEd. Cant Sch of Min 79. **d** 82 **p** 83. NSM Roch 82-86; C Orpington All SS 86-88; R Burham and Wouldham 88-96; Dioc Communications Officer 88-96; rtd 96; Perm to Offic *Roch* from 96. *18 Commissioners Road, Rochester ME2 4EB* Tel (01634) 715892

AITON, Janice Haran. MA79 Jordanhill Coll Glas PGCE80, TISEC 98. **d** 01 **p** 02. C St Andrews St Andr *St And* 01-04; Dunboyne Union *M & K* from 04. *1 The Close, Plunkett Hall, Dunboyne, Co Meath, Republic of Ireland* Tel and fax (00353) (1) 825 3288

AITON, Canon Robert Neilson. b 36. Univ of Wales BA59 DipEd60. Chich Th Coll 74. **d** 76 **p** 77. C E Grinstead St Swithun *Chich* 76-83; R Lavant 83-90; V Durrington *Chich* 90-01; Can and Preb Chich Cathl from 99; rtd 01; Lic to Offic *Chich* from 01. *Fieldings, Joys Croft, Chichester PO19 4NJ* Tel (01243) 781728
E-mail maiton@talk21.com

AJAEFOBI, Joseph Obichukwu. b 63. Anambra State Univ of Tech Nigeria BEng88 Loughb Univ PhD04. Trin Coll Umuahia 90. **d** 92 **p** 93. Chapl Nkpor H Innocents Nigeria 92-00; Perm to Offic *Leic* from 01; Asst Chapl Loughb Univ from 05. *15 Stirling Avenue, Loughborough LE11 4LJ* Tel 07796-672212 (mobile)
E-mail joeajaefobi@yahoo.co.uk

✠**AJETUNMOBI, The Rt Revd Jacob Ademola.** b 48. Middx Univ BA93. Igbaja Sem Nigeria BTh73 Lon Bible Coll BA80. **d** 83 **p** 83 **c** 99. Bp's Chapl and V Ilesa St Marg Nigeria 83-88; Chapl to Nigerian Students in UK (CMS) 88-99; Miss Partner CMS 88-99; Bp Ibadan S from 99. *59 Milton Avenue, London NW10 8PL, or c/o Bishopscourt, PO Box 166, Ibadan, Nigeria* Tel and fax (020) 8969 2379 Fax (00234) (22) 810 1413
E-mail jacajet@aol.com

AJUKA, Sampson. b 72. Qu Coll Birm BA08. **d** 08. C Venice w Trieste *Eur* from 08. *Chaplain's House, Dorsoduro 253, 30123 Venezia, Italy* Tel (0039) (049) 897 7503 Mobile 339-405 2466 E-mail sampress@yahoo.com

✠**AKINOLA, The Most Revd Peter Jasper.** b 44. Virginia Th Sem MTS81 Hon DD93. **d** 78 **p** 79 **c** 89. V Abuja St Jas Nigeria 78-79; V Suleja St Jas 81-84; Prov Missr 84-89; Bp Abuja from

89; Abp Prov III from 97; Primate All Nigeria from 00. *PO Box 212, ADCP, Abuja, Nigeria* Tel (00234) (9) 523 6928 *or* 523 0989 Fax 523 0986 Mobile 90-805853
E-mail abuja@anglican.skannet.com.ng

AKKER, Derek Alexander. b 46. Bradf Univ MA83. NOC 85. **d** 88 **p** 89. C Mossley *Man* 88-90; C Bury St Pet 90-92; V Lever Bridge 92-97; TV Wolstanton *Lich* 97-99; V Hattersley *Ches* 99-09; rtd 09. *54 Purbeck Drive, Bury BL8 1JQ* Tel 0161-797 0105 E-mail d.akker@btclick.com

AKRILL, Dean. b 71. York Univ BA97. Ripon Coll Cuddesdon BTh00. **d** 00 **p** 01. C Swinton *Sheff* 00-01; C Wath-upon-Dearne 01-04; V Mosbrough 04-08; C Sprowston w Beeston *Nor* from 08. *The Newlands, 15 Blue Boar Lane, Norwich NR7 8RX* E-mail dean@sprowston.org.uk

✠**AKROFI, The Most Revd Justice Ofei.** b 42. Cen Connecticut State Univ USA BSc72 MEd73 Hon DHL00. Yale Div Sch MDiv76. **d** 76 **p** 76 **c** 96. Chapl Adisadel Coll Accra Ghana 76-78; Chapl Ridge Ch 78-81; Dean Accra 82-96; Bp Accra from 96; Abp W Africa from 03. *Bishopscourt, PO Box GP 8, Accra, Ghana* Tel (00233) (21) 662292 *or* 663595 Fax 668822
E-mail bishopakrofi@yahoo.com

ALAN MICHAEL, Brother. *See* PATERSON, Alan

ALASAUKKO-OJA, Tuomas. *See* MÄKIPÄÄ, Tuomas

ALBAN-JONES, Timothy Morris. b 64. MBE03. Warwick Univ BA85. Ripon Coll Cuddesdon 85. **d** 88 **p** 89. C Tupsley *Heref* 88-93; TV Ross 93-00; P-in-c Soham *Ely* 00-01; P-in-c Wicken 00-01; V Soham and Wicken from 02. *The Vicarage, Cross Green, Soham, Ely CB7 5DU* Tel (01353) 720423
E-mail vicar@soham.org.uk

ALBERS, Johannes Reynoud (Joop). b 47. Hogeschool Holland BTh92 Amsterdam Univ MTh. EAMTC 99. **d** 00 **p** 01. C Voorschoten *Eur* 00-02; C Amsterdam w Den Helder and Heiloo 02-04; Asst Chapl from 04; Angl Chapl Amsterdam Airport Schiphol from 07. *Dorpsweg 134, 1697 KH Schellinkhout, The Netherlands* Tel (0031) (22) 950 1611 *or* (61) 009 8239
E-mail joopalbers@quicknet.nl

ALBON, Lionel Frederick Shapland. b 31. CEng MIMechE60. St Alb Minl Tr Scheme 80. **d** 83 **p** 84. NSM Bromham w Oakley *St Alb* 83-88; NSM Bromham w Oakley and Stagsden 88-89; Ind Chapl 89-96; rtd 96; Lic to Offic *St Alb* 96-09; Perm to Offic from 09. *38 Glebe Rise, Sharnbrook, Bedford MK44 1JB* Tel (01234) 781560 E-mail lionel@albon.fsnet.co.uk

ALBY, Harold Oriel. b 45. Witwatersrand Univ BA68 MA77. Sarum Th Coll 68. **d** 71 **p** 72. S Africa 71-89; C Germiston St Boniface 71-74; C Johannesburg Cathl 74-75; R Ermelo w Piet Retief 57-78; R Potchefstroom 78-82; R Boksburg 82-89; P-in-c Forton *Portsm* 89-96; V Milton from 96. *St James's Vicarage, 287 Milton Road, Southsea PO4 8PG* Tel (023) 9273 2786

ALCOCK, Edwin James. b 31. AKC57. **d** 58 **p** 59. C Old St Pancras w Bedford New Town St Matt *Lon* 58-62; C Hillingdon St Andr 62-81; V N Acton St Gabr 81-01; rtd 01; Perm to Offic *Lon* from 01. *17 Westfields Road, London W3 0AX* Tel (020) 8896 2748

ALCOCK, Mrs Linda Mary. b 45. St Gabr Coll Lon TCert67. SAOMC 96. **d** 99 **p** 00. OLM Shires' Edge *Ox* from 99. *Copperfields, Swan Lane, Great Bourton, Banbury OX17 1QR* Tel (01295) 750744

ALCOCK, Terry. **d** 08 **p** 09. NSM Narraghmore and Timolin w Castledermot etc *D & G* from 08. *Lacken, Blessington, Co Wicklow, Republic of Ireland* Tel (00353) 87-054 8544 (mobile)

ALDCROFT, Malcolm Charles. b 44. Leeds Univ MA94. NOC 79. **d** 82 **p** 83. NSM Alverthorpe *Wakef* 82-85; NSM Horbury Junction 85-93; Sub Chapl HM Pris and YOI New Hall 94-97; Sub Chapl HM Pris Wakef 96-97; R Cupar and Ladybank *St And* 97-05; Chapl Stratheden Hosp Fife 97-05; Dioc Miss Officer and Min Development Co-ord *Mor* 05-07; Hon C Arpafeelie, Cromarty and Fortrose 05-07; Hon C St Andrews All SS *St And* from 08; TV Edin St Mich and All SS from 08. *14 Cherry Lane, Cupar KY15 5DA* Tel (01334) 650264
E-mail m33aldcroft@tiscali.co.uk

ALDEN, Andrew Michael. b 65. Bris Univ BA88 Ex Univ PGCE89 Lon Univ MA98. Wycliffe Hall Ox 01. **d** 03 **p** 04. C Weston-super-Mare St Paul *B & W* 03-07; V from 07. *Somerset House, 20 Addiscombe Road, Weston-super-Mare BS23 4LT* Tel (01934) 621120 E-mail revandrewalden@btinternet.com

ALDEN, Mrs Pamela Ann (Pat). b 42. St Gabr Coll Lon TCert67. **d** 02 **p** 03. OLM Camberwell St Giles w St Matt *S'wark* 02-07; NSM Camberwell St Phil and St Mark from 07. *189 Upland Road, London SE22 0DG* Tel (020) 8693 5207 Fax 8693 6408 Mobile 07710-283710 E-mail pat@alphaplus.co.uk

ALDER, Mrs Anne-Louise. b 63. STETS 99. **d** 02 **p** 03. C Cowes H Trin and St Mary *Portsm* 02-05; C Cowes St Faith 05-06; C Newport St Thos 06-07; P-in-c Shipdham w E and W Bradenham *Nor* from 07. *The Rectory, Church Close, Shipdham, Thetford IP25 7LX* Tel (01362) 820234 *or* 821593
E-mail louise.alder@lineone.net

ALDER, Eric Reginald Alfred. b 23. St Luke's Coll Ex 47 Lon Univ BA55 Cam Inst of Educn 64. Chich Th Coll 70. **d** 71 **p** 72. C Deal St Leon w Sholden *Cant* 71-80; P-in-c Woodnesborough

80-83; P-in-c Worth 80-83; P-in-c Staple 80-83; V Woodnesborough w Worth and Staple 83-90; rtd 90; Perm to Offic *Cant* from 90. *3 Hackington Terrace, Canterbury CT2 7HE* Tel (01227) 766783

ALDERMAN, Canon John David. b 49. Man Univ BA71 Selw Coll Cam BA79 MA80 Lon Inst of Educn PGCE72. Ridley Hall Cam 77. **d** 80 **p** 81. C Hartley Wintney, Elvetham, Winchfield etc 80-83; V Bursledon 83-92; R Dibden 92-05; Hon Can Win Cathl 01-05; AD Lyndhurst 04-05; Patr Sec CPAS from 05. *CPAS, Athena Drive, Tachbrook Park, Warwick CV34 6NG* Tel (01926) 458457 E-mail jalderman@cpas.org.uk

ALDERSLEY, Ian. b 42. FIBMS68. Wycliffe Hall Ox 89. **d** 91 **p** 92. C Allestree *Derby* 91-94; R Brailsford w Shirley and Osmaston w Edlaston 94-06; P-in-c Yeaveley 05-06; P-in-c Ruishton w Thornfalcon *B & W* from 06; P-in-c Creech St Michael from 08. *The Vicarage, Church Lane, Ruishton, Taunton TA3 5LL* Tel (01823) 442269 E-mail ian@aldersley.fsbusiness.co.uk

ALDERSON, Gary. ERMC. **d** 08 **p** 09. NSM Wellingborough St Mark *Pet* from 08. *75 Chatsworth Drive, Wellingborough NN8 5FD* Tel (01933) 402770 E-mail gary.alderson@btinternet.com

ALDERSON, Mrs Maureen. b 40. WMMTC 90. **d** 93 **p** 94. NSM Yardley St Cypr Hay Mill *Birm* 93-96; P-in-c 96-00; V 00-02; P-in-c Gainford and Winston *Dur* 02-07. *5 St Michaels Court, Northallerton DL7 8YX* Tel (01609) 779265

ALDERSON, Major Robin David Marsh. b 44. **d** 04 **p** 05. OLM Alde River *St E* 04-07; NSM Brandeston w Kettleburgh and Easton from 07. *The Cloisters, Sandy Lane, Snape, Saxmundham IP17 1SD* Tel and fax (01728) 688255 Mobile 07790-242002

ALDERSON, Roger James Ambrose. b 47. Lon Univ BD70 AKC71 Man Univ 76 Liv Inst of Educn PGCE93. St Aug Coll Cant. **d** 71 **p** 72. C Lawton Moor *Man* 71-75; C Barton w Peel Green 75-76; R Heaton Norris St Thos 76-85; V Bedford Leigh 85-92; V Cleadon Park *Dur* 99-07; rtd 07. *73 West Drive, Sunderland SR6 7SL* Tel 0191-536 1236 Mobile 07710-722817

ALDERTON-FORD, Canon Jonathan Laurence. b 57. St Jo Coll Nottm BTh85. **d** 85 **p** 86. C Gaywood, Bawsey and Mintlyn *Nor* 85-87; C Herne Bay Ch Ch *Cant* 87-90; Min Bury St Edmunds St Mary *St E* 90-91; Min Moreton Hall Estate CD 91-94; V Bury St Edmunds Ch Ch from 94; Hon Can St E Cathl from 08. *18 Heldhaw Road, Bury St Edmunds IP32 7ER* Tel (01284) 769956 or tel and fax 725391 E-mail ccmh@iname.com *or* revdjonathanford@minister.com

ALDIS, John Arnold. b 43. Univ of Wales (Cardiff) BA65 Lon Univ BD67. Clifton Th Coll 65. **d** 69 **p** 70. C Tonbridge SS Pet and Paul *Roch* 69-72; C St Marylebone All So w SS Pet and Jo *Lon* 72-77; Overseas Service Adv CMS 77-80; C Welling *Roch* 77-80; V Leic H Trin w St Jo 80-89; Hon Can Leic Cathl 88-89; V W Kowloon St Andr Hong Kong 89-99; Sen Chapl Protestant Ch Oman 00-01; V Watford *St Alb* 02-08; rtd 08. *7 Springfield Court, Stonehouse GL10 2JF* Tel (01453) 822325 E-mail john.aldis@btinternet.com

ALDIS, Miss Rosemary Helen. b 40. Southn Univ BSc62 Ox Univ Inst of Educn DipEd63 Keele Univ MSc67. All Nations Chr Coll MA99. **d** 05 **p** 05. NSM Gabalfa *Llan* from 05. *94 Glendower Court, Velindre Road, Cardiff CF14 2TZ* Tel (029) 2062 6337 E-mail aldisrosemary@omf.net

ALDOUS, Alexander Charles Victor. b 56. Southn Univ BA81 K Alfred's Coll Win PGCE83. S Dios Minl Tr Scheme 91. **d** 94 **p** 95. Chapl Oundle Sch 94-97; Chapl Benenden Sch 98-01; Chapl Oakham Sch from 02. *75 Station Road, Oakham LE15 6QT* Tel (01572) 723941 *or* 758591 E-mail aa@oakham.rutland.sch.uk

ALDOUS, John Herbert. b 37. CQSW83. Bp Otter Coll 94. **d** 96 **p** 00. Hon Gosport Ch Ch *Portsm* 96-00; NSM Rowner 00-02; R Sabie St Pet S Africa 02-05; rtd 05; Perm to Offic Dio Natal from 05. *PO Box 522, Munster, 4278 South Africa* Tel (0027) (39) 312 0415

ALDRIDGE, Mrs Anne Louise. b 59. Nottm Univ BEd80. EAMTC 96. **d** 99 **p** 00. NSM Milton *Ely* 99-04; Deputy Chapl Team Ldr Cam Univ Hosps NHS Foundn Trust from 04. *Addenbrooke's Hospital, Hills Road, Cambridge CB2 0QQ* Tel (01223) 217769 Fax 216520 E-mail r.aldridge@ntlworld.com

ALDRIDGE, Christopher John. b 35. Trin Hall Cam BA57 MA61. Ripon Hall Ox 59. **d** 60 **p** 61. C Coalville *Leic* 60-64; P-in-c Clifton St Fran *S'well* 64-72; V Gospel Lane St Mich *Birm* 72-90; V Selly Oak St Mary 90-00; rtd 00; Perm to Offic *Birm* from 00. *4 Paradise Lane, Birmingham B28 0DS* Tel 0121-777 0446

ALDRIDGE, Canon Harold John. b 42. Oak Hill Th Coll 65. **d** 69 **p** 70. C Rawtenstall St Mary *Man* 69-72; CMJ 72-76; C Woodford Wells *Chelmsf* 76-79; TV Washfield, Stoodleigh, Withleigh etc *Ex* 79-86; V Burton *Ches* 86-90; P-in-c Shotwick 90; V Burton and Shotwick 91-07; Dioc Clergy Widows and Retirement Officer 91-07; RD Wirral S 96-06; Hon Can Ches Cathl 98-07; Chapl Clatterbridge Hosp Wirral 86-91; Chapl Wirral Hosp NHS Trust 91-97; Chapl Wirral and W Cheshire

Community NHS Trust 97-03; Chapl Cheshire and Wirral Partnerships NHS Trust 03-07; rtd 07. *Tedda Junction, 9 Moorhouse Close, Chester CH2 2HU* Tel (01244) 371628

ALDRIDGE, Mark Richard. b 58. Oak Hill Th Coll BA89. **d** 89 **p** 90. C Combe Down w Monkton Combe and S Stoke *B & W* 89-90; C Woodside Park St Barn *Lon* 90-94; P-in-c Cricklewood St Gabr and St Mich 94-99; V 99-04; Min Oak Tree Angl Fellowship from 04. *100 Creffield Road, London W3 9PX* Tel (020) 8993 2060 E-mail marka@oaktree.org.uk

ALEXANDER, Ann Maria. b 58. Surrey Univ BA01. Cuddesdon Coll 07. **d** 09. C Chiswick St Nic w St Mary *Lon* from 09. *64A Grove Park Road, London W4 3SB* Tel 07961-853343 (mobile) E-mail annejmi@ntlworld.com

ALEXANDER, David Graham. b 61. Ridley Hall Cam 87. **d** 89 **p** 90. C New Barnet St Jas *St Alb* 89-93; C Northwood H Trin *Lon* 93-95; V Stopsley *St Alb* from 95. *The Vicarage, 702 Hitchin Road, Luton LU2 7UJ* Tel (01582) 729194 Fax 450375 E-mail stopsley@aol.com

ALEXANDER, Douglas Keith. b 45. Ripon Coll Cuddesdon 87. **d** 89 **p** 90. C Thorpe St Matt *Nor* 89-92; P-in-c Lakenham St Alb 92-97; Chapl Nor City Coll of F&HE 92-97; TV Barnham Broom 97-00; TV Barnham Broom and Upper Yare 00-04; TR from 04; RD Dereham in Mitford from 08. *The Rectory, The Street, Reymerston, Norwich NR9 4AG* Tel and fax (01362) 858377 Mobile 07876-572724 E-mail doug.alexander@btinternet.com

ALEXANDER, Prof Freda. b 41. Girton Coll Cam BA62 Edin Univ PhD67 Lon Univ MSc81. TISEC 06. **d** 08. NSM Edin St Jo from 08. *79 Great King Street, Edinburgh EH3 6RN* Tel 0131-557 4474 E-mail freda.alexander1@btinternet.com

ALEXANDER, James Crighton. b 43. Qu Coll Cam BA65 MA69. Cuddesdon Coll 68. **d** 68 **p** 69. C Much Wenlock w Bourton *Heref* 68-72; V Oakington *Ely* from 72; P-in-c Dry Drayton 85-95. *The Vicarage, 99 Water Lane, Oakington, Cambridge CB24 3AL* Tel (01223) 232396 E-mail liesl@free2live.org.uk

ALEXANDER, Canon James Douglas. b 27. Linc Th Coll 57. **d** 58 **p** 59. C Frodingham *Linc* 58-61; V Alvingham w N and S Cockerington 61-65; V Keddington 61-65; R Gunhouse w Burringham 65-70; R Peterhead *Ab* 70-76; R Aberdeen St Mary 76-95; Miss to Seafarers 78-06; Can St Andr Cathl from 79; Chapl HM Pris Aber 82-06; P-in-c Cove Bay *Ab* 85-90; rtd 95; Dioc Supernumerary *Ab* from 95. *21 Whitehall Road, Aberdeen AB25 2PP* Tel (01224) 643202

ALEXANDER, Jane Louise. *See* MacLAREN, Mrs Jane Louise

ALEXANDER, Mrs Jean Ann. b 44. Southn Univ BTh00 SRN65 SCM67. Ripon Coll Cuddesdon 06. **d** 07 **p** 08. NSM Lytchett Minster *Sarum* from 07. *1 Palmers Orchard, Lytchett Matravers, Poole BH16 6HG* Tel (01202) 631033 E-mail jean.alexander1@virgin.net

ALEXANDER, Julius Erik Louis. b 66. Wycliffe Hall Ox 89. **d** 92 **p** 93. C Hoole *Ches* 92-94; C Offerton 94-98; TV Upper Holloway *Lon* 98-03; Asst Chapl Southn Univ Hosps NHS Trust 03-06; Chapl Oakhaven Hospice Trust from 06. *Oakhaven Hospice Trust, Lower Pennington Lane, Lymington SO41 8ZZ* Tel (01590) 677773 Fax 677582 E-mail jalexander@blueyonder.co.uk

ALEXANDER, Canon Loveday Constance Anne. b 47. Somerville Coll Ox BA69 MA78 DPhil78. NOC 98. **d** 99 **p** 00. NSM Alderley Edge *Ches* from 99; Can Th Ches Cathl from 03; Perm to Offic *Sheff* from 00. *5 Nevill Road, Bramhall, Stockport SK7 3ET* Tel 0161-439 7946 E-mail loveday.alexander@btinternet.com

ALEXANDER, Michael George. b 47. Open Univ BA90 DipEd91. Sarum & Wells Th Coll 74. **d** 77 **p** 78. C Wednesfield *Lich* 77-80; C Tettenhall Wood 80-83; Distr Min 83-85; Dioc Adv in Adult and Youth Educn *Derby* 85-89; V Hazlewood 85-89; V Turnditch 85-89; Par Educn Adv (Laity Development) 89-96; Dioc Laity Development Adv 96-00; Dioc Dir Studies Bp's Centres of Learning 96-00; P-in-c Ticknall, Smisby and Stanton-by-Bridge 00-01; P-in-c Barrow-on-Trent w Twyford and Swarkestone 00-01; V Ticknall, Smisby and Stanton by Bridge etc 01-07; RD Melbourne 02-07; P-in-c Loscoe from 07; C Morley w Smalley and Horsley Woodhouse from 07; RD Heanor from 09. *The Vicarage, 80 Main Road, Smalley, Ilkeston DE7 6EF* Tel (01332) 880380 E-mail mike.alexander@ticvic.fsnet.co.uk

ALEXANDER, Nicholas Edward. b 68. Leic Poly BSc90. Oak Hill Th Coll BA06. **d** 06 **p** 07. C Linc Minster Gp from 06. *23 Montaigne Crescent, Lincoln LN2 4QN* Tel (01522) 529811 E-mail nickalexander110@hotmail.com

ALEXANDER, Peter John. b 36. CQSW73. Oak Hill Th Coll 92. **d** 95 **p** 96. NSM Aspenden, Buntingford and Westmill *St Alb* 95-02; rtd 02; Perm to Offic *Nor* from 02. *Dellgate, 4 The Dell, Bodham, Holt NR25 6NG* Tel (01263) 588126 E-mail peter.brenda@tiscali.co.uk

ALEXANDER, Mrs Rachel Clare. b 57. EAMTC 96. **d** 99 **p** 00. NSM Mattishall w Mattishall Burgh, Welborne etc *Nor* 99-02; Perm to Offic 02-03; NSM Rugby St Matt *Cov* 03-04. *Minstrels,*

50 Dereham Road, Mattishall, Dereham NR20 3NS Tel (01362) 858655 E-mail rachel@ralexander.fsnet.co.uk

ALEXANDER, Robert. b 37. Lon Univ LLB60 St Cath Coll Ox BA62. St Steph Ho Ox 60. **d** 63 **p** 64. C Kensington St Mary Abbots w St Geo *Lon* 63-68; C Notting Hill 71-74; TV 74-79; Australia from 79; rtd 02. *302/27 Neutral Street, North Sydney NSW 2060, Australia* Tel and fax (0061) (2) 9954 0543 E-mail robalexand@bigpond.com

ALEXANDER, Sarah Louise. b 72. Wycliffe Hall Ox 02. **d** 04 **p** 05. C Enfield Ch Ch Trent Park *Lon* 04-08; C Newbury *Ox* from 08. *14 Strawberry Hill, Newbury RG14 1XJ* Tel (01635) 41922 Mobile 07889-146141 E-mail sarah-alex1@yahoo.co.uk

ALEXANDER, Wilfred Robert Donald. b 35. TCD BA58 MA80. **d** 63 **p** 63. C Raheny w Coolock *D & G* 63-67; Min Can St Patr Cathl Dublin 65-67; Hon C Herne Hill St Paul *S'wark* 68-70; Asst Master Gosforth Gr Sch 71-76; Hon C Long Benton St Mary *Newc* 74-76; Chapl St Mary and St Anne's Sch Abbots Bromley 76-80; V Cauldon *Lich* 80-83; V Waterfall 80-83; P-in-c Calton 80-83; P-in-c Grindon 80-83; V Blackb St Luke w St Phil 83-89; V Rainhill *Liv* 89-92; R Croft w Southworth 92-99; C Croft w Southworth and Newchurch 99-01; rtd 01. *16 Hawkshaw Close, Birchwood, Warrington WA3 7NF* Tel (01925) 851472

ALEXANDER-YATES, Tristan Nathaniel. b 66. SEITE 99. **d** 03 **p** 04. NSM Eltham H Trin *S'wark* from 03; Asst Chapl Qu Eliz Hosp NHS Trust from 07. *St Kentigern House, 31 Fairfield Grove, London SE7 8UA* Tel (020) 8853 2257 *or* 8709 9240 Mobile 07970-016009 E-mail tristalex@aol.com

ALFORD, John. b 35. Nottm Univ BSc58 DipEd76. Qu Coll Birm 74. **d** 77 **p** 78. NSM Edgmond *Lich* 77-87; C Cheadle 87-88; C Cheadle w Freehay 88-89; P-in-c Wootton Wawen *Cov* 89-95; P-in-c Grafham *Ely* 95-00; P-in-c Ellington 95-00; P-in-c Easton 95-00; P-in-c Spaldwick w Barham and Woolley 95-00; V 00-01; rtd 01; Perm to Offic *Ely* from 01. *4 Armstrong Close, Perry, Huntingdon PE28 0DF* Tel (01480) 812075 E-mail margaretalford@aol.com

ALFORD, Mrs Rosalie Grace. b 40. Bedf Coll Lon BA61 Lon Univ PGCE62. STETS 95. **d** 98 **p** 99. NSM Wadhurst *Chich* from 98; NSM Stonegate from 98. *Content, 1 Ingoldsby Cottages, Faircrouch Lane, Wadhurst TN5 6PP* Tel (01892) 782974 E-mail rosaliealford@btinternet.com

ALIDINA (née LINGARD), Jennifer Mary. b 59. Ox Min Course 05. **d** 07 **p** 08. C Chipping Norton *Ox* from 07. *Candleford, 4 Langston Villas, Station Road, Kingham, Chipping Norton OX7 6UW* Tel (01608) 659076 E-mail jennyalidina@freeuk.com

ALKER, Adrian. b 49. Wadh Coll Ox BA70 Lanc Univ MA71. Ripon Coll Cuddesdon 77. **d** 79 **p** 80. C W Derby St Mary *Liv* 79-83; Dioc Youth Officer *Carl* 83-88; V Sheff St Mark Broomhill 88-08; Dioc Dir of In-Service Tr 90-08; Hon Can Sheff Cathl 05-08; Dir Miss Resourcing *Ripon* from 08. *Ripon and Leeds Diocesan Office, St Mary's Street, Leeds LS9 7DP* Tel 0113-200 0559

ALKIRE, Sabina Marie. b 69. Illinois Univ BA89 Magd Coll Ox MPhil94 MSc95 DPhil99. **d** 00 **p** 02. NSM Washington St Alb and Washington St Phil USA 00-03; NSM Boston St Steph 05-07; Chapl Assoc Magd Coll Ox from 06; NSM Cowley St Jo *Ox* from 08. *3 Mansfield Road, Oxford OX1 3TB* Tel (01865) 271529 Fax 281801 Mobile 07792-505847 E-mail sabina.alkire@qeh.ox.ac.uk

ALLABY, Miss Mary Dorothea. b 60. Bedf Coll Lon BA82 W Sussex Inst of HE PGCE83. Trin Coll Bris 88. **d** 92 **p** 94. Par Dn Ipsley *Worc* 92-94; C 94-96; TV Bloxwich *Lich* 96-02; V Trent Vale 02-03. *Address withheld by request* E-mail mary@allaby.freeserve.co.uk

ALLABY, Simon Arnold Kenworthy. b 65. St Chad's Coll Dur BA88. Trin Coll Bris 88. **d** 90 **p** 91. C Preston on Tees *Dur* 90-93; C Chester le Street 93-99; R Ardingly *Chich* 99-05. *Sound of Luing, Hurst Road, Hassocks BN6 9NL* Tel 07837-637113 (mobile) E-mail simon@sixnineteen.com

ALLAIN CHAPMAN, Ms Justine Penelope Heathcote. b 67. K Coll Lon BA88 AKC88 PGCE89 Nottm Univ MDiv93. Linc Th Coll 91. **d** 93 **p** 94. C Forest Hill *S'wark* 93-96; TV Clapham Team 96-01; V Clapham St Paul 02-04; Dir Miss & Past Studies SEITE from 04; Vice Prin from 07. *SEITE Ground Floor Offices, Sun Pier House, Medway Street, Chatham ME4 4HF* Tel (01634) 846683 E-mail j.allain-chapman@seite.co.uk

ALLAN, Andrew John. b 47. Westcott Ho Cam 76. **d** 79 **p** 80. C Whitstable All SS w St Pet *Cant* 79-84; C Whitstable 84-86; P-in-c Littlebourne 86-87; P-in-c Ickham w Wickhambreaux and Stodmarsh 86-87; R Littlebourne and Ickham w Wickhambreaux etc from 87. *The Vicarage, Church Road, Littlebourne, Canterbury CT3 1UA* Tel (01227) 721233

ALLAN, Canon Archibald Blackie. b 35. Edin Th Coll 57. **d** 60 **p** 61. C Aberdeen St Jo 60-63; R 82-00; Chapl St Paul's Cathl Dundee 63-68; P-in-c Aberdeen St Clem 68-76; Vice-Provost St Andr Cathl 76-82; Can 88-00; Hon Can from 01; rtd 00. *32 Craigiebuckler Terrace, Aberdeen AB15 8SX* Tel (01224) 316636

ALLAN, Donald James. b 35. Sarum & Wells Th Coll 63. **d** 65 **p** 66. C Royton St Paul *Man* 65-71; V Middleton Junction 71-78; P-in-c Finmere w Mixbury *Ox* 78-83; R Finmere w Mixbury, Cottisford, Hardwick etc 83; Chapl Westcliff Hosp 83-87; V Westcliff St Andr *Chelmsf* 83-87; R Goldhanger w Lt Totham 87-01; rtd 01; P-in-c St Goran w Caerhays *Truro* 01-06. *23 Stirrup Close, Wimborne BH21 2UQ* Tel (01202) 880645 E-mail donald.allan2@btinternet.com

ALLAN, Jeanette Winifred. b 40. ALA63. St And Dioc Tr Course 79. **dss** 81 **d** 86 **p** 94. NSM Hillfoot's TM *St And* 81-86; NSM Bridge of Allan *St And* 86-88; NSM Dunblane 88-98; R Glenrothes 98-06; rtd 06; Lic to Offic *St And* from 07. *Pernettya, Sinclairs Street, Dunblane FK15 0AH* Tel (01786) 821151 E-mail pernettya@googlemail.com

ALLAN, John. *See* ALLAN, Andrew John.

ALLAN, John William. b 58. St Olaf Coll Minnesota BA80 Birm Univ 86. Trin Lutheran Sem Ohio MDiv84 Qu Coll Birm 90. **d** 91 **p** 92. In Lutheran Ch (USA) 84-86; C Newport w Longford and Chetwynd *Lich* 91-94; P-in-c Longdon 94-01; Local Min Adv (Wolverhampton) 94-01; V Alrewas from 01; V Wychnor from 01; RD Lich from 04. *The Vicarage, Church Road, Alrewas, Burton-on-Trent DE13 7BT* Tel (01283) 790486 E-mail john.allan@lichfield.anglican.org

ALLAN, Peter Burnaby. b 52. Clare Coll Cam BA74 MA78 St Jo Coll Dur BA82. Cranmer Hall Dur 80. **d** 83 **p** 84. C Chaddesden St Mary *Derby* 83-86; C Brampton St Thos 86-89; TV Halesworth w Linstead, Chediston, Holton etc *St E* 89-94; TR Trunch *Nor* 94-03; R Ansley and Arley *Cov* from 03; RD Nuneaton from 06. *The Vicarage, 60 Birmingham Road, Ansley, Nuneaton CV10 9PS* Tel (024) 7639 6403 *or* 7639 6036 E-mail peter@allan49.fsworld.co.uk

ALLAN, Peter George. b 50. Wadh Coll Ox BA72 MA76. Coll of Resurr Mirfield 72. **d** 75 **p** 76. C Stevenage St Geo *St Alb* 75-78; Chapl Wadh Coll and C Ox St Mary V w St Cross and St Pet 78-82; CR from 85. *House of the Resurrection, Stocks Bank Road, Mirfield WF14 0BN* Tel (01924) 494318

ALLANDER, William Edward Morgell Kidd. b 15. TCD BA37 MA40. CITC 37. **d** 38 **p** 39. C Knock *D & D* 38-43; Hd of Trin Coll Miss Belf 43-46; Lic to Offic *Lon* 46-51; C Foleshill St Laur *Cov* 53-55; P-in-c Wood End 55-57; V 57-64; V Atherstone 64-73; I Rathcooney Union *C, C & R* 73-88; rtd 88. *12 Richmond Estate, Blackrock, Cork, Republic of Ireland* Tel (00353) (21) 429 3352 Fax 429 3642 E-mail wallander@eircom.net

ALLARD, John Ambrose. b 30. Bps' Coll Cheshunt 63. **d** 65 **p** 66. C Leigh-on-Sea St Marg *Chelmsf* 65-69; P-in-c Rawreth w Rettendon 69-70; R 70-72; V Barkingside St Fran 73-84; V E Ham St Geo 84-86; V St Osyth 86-95; rtd 95; Perm to Offic *Nor* and *St E* 97-02; Hon C Muchalls and Stonehaven *Bre* 03-07. *23 St Nicholas Drive, Banchory AB31 5YG* Tel (01330) 822761

ALLARD, Roderick George. b 44. Lon Univ BA77 Sheff Poly MSc88 Loughb Coll of Educn CertEd96. NOC 97. **d** 99 **p** 00. NSM Charlesworth and Dinting Vale *Derby* from 99. *16 Springmeadow, Charlesworth, Glossop SK13 5HP* Tel (01457) 866278 Mobile 07798-843283

ALLARDICE, Alexander Edwin. b 49. SRN. Chich Th Coll 73. **d** 76 **p** 77. C Rugeley *Lich* 76-79; C Felixstowe St Jo *St E* 79-81; TV Ipswich St Fran 81-87; C Lostwithiel *Truro* 87-90; C Boconnoc w Bradoc 87-90; C St Veep 87-90; C St Winnow 87-90; R Lostwithiel, St Winnow w St Nectan's Chpl etc 90-97; R Mevagissey and St Ewe 97-99; rtd 99; Perm to Offic *Truro* from 99. *4 Pensylva, St Austell PL25 4RW* Tel and fax (01726) 77695 E-mail alex.allardice@classicfm.net

ALLBERRY, Samuel. b 75. Wycliffe Hall Ox BTh03. **d** 05 **p** 06. NSM Ox St Ebbe w H Trin and St Pet 05-08; C Maidenhead St Andr and St Mary from 08. *St Mary's Close, 14 High Street, Maidenhead SL6 1YY* Tel (01628) 638866 E-mail sam_allberry@yahoo.co.uk

ALLBERRY, William Alan John. b 49. Ch Coll Cam BA70 MA71. Ripon Coll Cuddesdon 84. **d** 86 **p** 87. C Brixton St Matt *S'wark* 86-90; V Wandsworth St Paul 90-98; R Esher *Guildf* from 98; RD Emly 01-06. *The Rectory, 4 Esher Place Avenue, Esher KT10 8PY* Tel and fax (01372) 462611 E-mail rector@esher.org *or* william.allberry@btopenworld.com

ALLBUTT, Mavis Miriam. **d** 98 **p** 99. OLM Meir *Lich* 98-08; P-in-c from 08. *The Vicarage, 715 Uttoxeter Road, Stoke-on-Trent ST3 5PY* Tel (01782) 313347 E-mail mavis.allbutt@btinternet.com

ALLCHIN, Canon Arthur Macdonald (Donald). b 30. Ch Ch Ox BA51 MA55 BLitt56 Bucharest Th Inst Hon DD77 Lambeth DD06. Cuddesdon Coll 54. **d** 56 **p** 57. C Kensington St Mary Abbots w St Geo *Lon* 56-60; Lib Pusey Ho 60-69; Warden Community of Sisters of the Love of God Ox 68-73; Can Res and Lib Cant Cathl 73-87; Hon Prov Can Cant Cathl 88-92; Dir St Theosevia Cen for Chr Spirituality 87-94; Hon Prof Univ of N Wales Ban from 93; rtd 94; Lic to Offic *Cant* 94-97; Perm to Offic *Ban* from 97. *1 Trem yr Wyddfa, Bangor LL57 2ER* Tel (01248) 353744

ALLCHIN, Miss Maureen Ann. b 50. Edge Hill Coll of HE CertEd71 Sussex Univ MA93. S Dios Minl Tr Scheme 88. **d** 91

p 94. Hd Past Faculty Steyning Gr Sch 79-92; NSM Southwick St Mich *Chich* 91-92; C Storrington 93-95; TV Bridport *Sarum* 95-05; Lic to Offic 05-06; P-in-c Canalside Benefice 06-08; Lic to Offic from 08. *4 Northfields, Bulkington, Devizes SN10 1SE* Tel (01380) 828931 E-mail maureen@mallchin.co.uk

ALLCOCK, Jeremy Robert. b 63. Trin Coll Bris BA92. **d** 92 **p** 93. C Walthamstow St Luke *Chelmsf* 92-96; V E Ham St Paul 96-05; V Paddington St Steph w St Luke *Lon* from 05. *St Stephen's Vicarage, 25 Talbot Road, London W2 5JF* Tel (020) 7792 2283 E-mail jeme6@aol.com

ALLCOCK, Peter Michael. b 37. Oak Hill Th Coll 65. **d** 68 **p** 69. C Upper Tulse Hill St Matthias *S'wark* 68-71; C Dunkeswell and Dunkeswell Abbey *Ex* 71-72; P-in-c Luppitt and Monkton 72-75; V Okehampton w Inwardleigh 75-80; TV Solihull *Birm* 80-85; V Highbury New Park St Aug *Lon* 85-99; V E and W Horndon w Lt Warley and Childerditch *Chelmsf* 99-02; rtd 02; Perm to Offic *Birm* and *Cov* 03-05; NSM Shepshed and Oaks in Charnwood *Leic* 05-07. *10 Arden Close, Balsall Common, Coventry CV7 7NY* Tel (01676) 532346 E-mail pma946078@aol.com

ALLDRIT, Nicolas Sebastian Fitz-Ansculf. b 41. St Edm Hall Ox BA63 MA69 DPhil69. Cuddesdon Coll 72. **d** 72 **p** 73. C Limpsfield and Titsey *S'wark* 72-81; Tutor Linc Th Coll 81-96; Sub-Warden 88-96; R Witham Gp *Linc* 97-07; rtd 07; Perm to Offic *Pet* from 07. *104 Orchard Hill, Little Billing, Northampton NN3 9AG* Tel (01604) 407115

ALLEN, Andrew Stephen. b 55. Nottm Univ BPharm77 MPS. St Steph Ho Ox 78. **d** 81 **p** 82. C Gt Ilford St Mary *Chelmsf* 81-83; C Luton All SS w St Pet *St Alb* 83-86; TV Chambersbury 86-91; TV Brixham w Churston Ferrers and Kingswear *Ex* 91-01; TR 01-06; P-in-c Upton cum Chalvey *Ox* 06-08; TR from 08. *St Mary's Rectory, 34 Upton Park, Slough SL1 2DE* Tel and fax (01753) 529988 E-mail andrewallen@fastmail.com

ALLEN, Beverley Carole. See PINNELL, Ms Beverley Carole

ALLEN, Brian. See ALLEN, Frank Brian

ALLEN, Brian. b 58. Oak Hill NSM Course 90. **d** 93 **p** 94. NSM W Norwood St Luke *S'wark* 93-02; NSM Gipsy Hill Ch Ch 02-08. *76 Bradley Road, London SE19 3NS* Tel (020) 8771 4282 or 8686 8282

ALLEN, Brian Stanley. b 24. Roch Th Coll 65. **d** 67 **p** 68. C Roch 67-74; P-in-c Drypool St Jo *York* 74-80; TV Drypool 80; V Marlpool *Derby* 80-87; rtd 87; Perm to Offic *York* from 90. *22 Sycamore Terrace, York YO30 7DN* Tel (01904) 653418

ALLEN, Miss Charlotte. b 79. St Jo Coll Dur BA00 Anglia Poly Univ MA03. Westcott Ho Cam 00. **d** 03 **p** 04. C Southwick *Chich* 03-07; V Portchester *Portsm* from 07. *The Vicarage, 164 Castle Street, Portchester, Fareham PO16 9QH* Tel (023) 9238 1414 E-mail charlie.allen@btconnect.com

ALLEN, Christopher Dennis. b 50. Fitzw Coll Cam BA73 MA77. Cuddesdon Coll 74. **d** 76 **p** 77. C Kettering St Andr *Pet* 76-79; C Pet H Spirit Bretton 79-82; R Bardney *Linc* 82-87; V Knighton St Mary Magd *Leic* from 87. *The Vicarage, Church Lane, Leicester LE2 3WG* Tel (0116-270 5730 E-mail vicar@knightonparish.org

ALLEN, Christopher Leslie. b 56. Leeds Univ BA78. St Jo Coll Nottm 79. **d** 80 **p** 81. C Birm St Martin 80-85; Tv and Ed Pathfinders 85-89; Hd 89-92; Midl Youth Dept Co-ord CPAS 85-89; Hon C Selly Park St Steph and St Wulstan *Birm* 86-92; V Hamstead St Bernard 92-95; NSM Kidderminster St Mary and All SS w Trimpley etc *Worc* 03-05; Perm to Offic from 05. *17 Alder Avenue, Kidderminster DY10 2LD* Tel and fax (01562) 820702 Mobile 07956-303037 E-mail chris.allen@ukonline.co.uk

ALLEN, David. b 38. Llan Dioc Tr Scheme. **d** 76 **p** 77. C Fairwater *Llan* 76-84; Chapl Bp of Llan Hosp 83-97; Lic to Offic *Llan* from 84. *1 Kenley Close, Llandaff, Cardiff CF5 2PA* Tel (029) 2056 0252

ALLEN, David Edward. b 70. Van Mildert Coll Dur BSc91. Ripon Coll Cuddesdon BA94. **d** 95 **p** 96. C Grantham *Linc* 95-99; C W Hampstead St Jas *Lon* 99-01; C Kilburn St Mary w All So and W Hampstead St Jas 01-02; V Finsbury St Clem w St Barn and St Matt from 02; Chapl Moorfields Eye Hosp NHS Trust from 04. *St Clement's Vicarage, King Square, London EC1V 8DA* Tel (020) 7251 0706 E-mail davideallen@blueyonder.co.uk

ALLEN, Derek. b 57. MCIOB89. **d** 99 **p** 00. OLM Bacup Ch Ch *Man* 99-04; OLM Bacup and Stacksteads from 04. *180 New Line, Bacup OL13 9RU* Tel (01706) 875960 E-mail allen.newline@cwcom.net

ALLEN, Canon Francis Arthur Patrick. b 26. Em Coll Saskatoon Div Test 52. **d** 51 **p** 52. Miss Nipawin Canada 51-52; Miss Meadow Lake 52-54; Miss Medstead 54-57; C Bishopwearmouth St Nic *Dur* 57-59; Chapl Miss to Seamen Kobe Japan 59-63; Hon Can Kobe from 63; V Kingston upon Hull St Matt *York* 63-67; P-in-c Oberon Australia 67; R 68-73; P-in-c Cobar 73-75; Chapl Torres Strait 76-78; R Waikerie 78-82; R Willunga 82-89; R Bamaga 89-91; rtd 91. *48 Rodriguez Avenue, Blackheath NSW 2785, Australia* Tel (0061) (2) 4787 8143

ALLEN, Frank Brian. b 47. K Coll Lon BD AKC71. **d** 71 **p** 72. C Leam Lane *Dur* 71-74; C Tynemouth Ch Ch *Newc* 74-78; Chapl Preston Hosp N Shields 74-78; Chapl Newc Poly 78-84; V Newc St Hilda 84-88; Chapl Nottm Mental Illness and Psychiatric Unit 88-89; Chapl for Mental Health Newc Mental Health Unit 89-94; Chapl Newc City Health NHS Trust 94-96; Chapl Team Leader from 96; Visiting Fell Newc Univ from 96. *Trust Chaplaincy Centre, St Nicholas Hospital, Gosforth, Newcastle upon Tyne NE3 3XT* Tel 0191-273 6666 ext 28465 Fax 232 2840 E-mail brian_allen63@hotmail.com *or* brian.allen@nmht.nhs.uk

ALLEN, Canon Geoffrey Gordon. b 39. Sarum Th Coll 64. **d** 66 **p** 67. C Langley Marish *Ox* 66-70; Miss to Seamen 70-82; Chapl Rotterdam w Schiedam *Eur* 78-82; Asst Chapl The Hague 84-93; Chapl Voorschoten 84-93; Can Brussels Cathl 89-04; Adn NW Eur 93-04; Chapl E Netherlands 93-04; P-in-c Haarlem 95-02; rtd 04. *Hans Brandts Buyslaan 22, 6952 BK Dieren, The Netherlands* Tel (0031) (313) 412533 E-mail geoffrey@archdeacon.demon.nl

ALLEN, Giles David. b 70. RCM BMus91 Leeds Univ MA05. Coll of Resurr Mirfield 92. **d** 95 **p** 96. C Palmers Green St Jo *Lon* 95-99; V Lund *Blackb* from 99. *Lund Vicarage, Church Lane, Clifton, Preston PR4 0ZE* Tel (01772) 683617 E-mail giles.lund@tiscali.co.uk

ALLEN, Gordon Richard. b 29. St Jo Coll Dur BA54 MA58. **d** 55 **p** 56. C N Meols *Liv* 55-58; Uganda 58-63; V Lathom *Liv* 64-68; USA from 68; rtd 94. *237 Emery's Bridge Road, South Berwick ME 03908-1935, USA*

ALLEN, Hugh Edward. b 47. Bp Otter Coll Chich CertEd. Sarum & Wells Th Coll 79. **d** 81 **p** 82. C Frome St Jo *B & W* 81-85; R Old Cleeve, Leighland and Treborough 85-97; RD Exmoor 92-97; P-in-c The Stanleys *Glouc* 97-99; Perm to Offic *B & W* 99-05; P-in-c Charlton Musgrove, Cucklington and Stoke Trister from 05; RD Bruton from 06; RD Cary from 06. *The Rectory, Rowls Lane, Cucklington, Wincanton BA9 9PY* Tel (01747) 841416 E-mail hallenarkwood@yahoo.co.uk

ALLEN, Mrs Jacqueline Lesley. b 54. EMMTC 99. **d** 02 **p** 03. NSM Huthwaite *S'well* 02-05; P-in-c Shireoaks from 05; Asst Chapl Notts Healthcare NHS Trust from 07. *1 Potter's Nook, Shireoaks, Worksop S81 8NF* Tel (01909) 479350 E-mail jackie@serv77.netscapeonline.com

ALLEN, Jamie. See ALLEN, Timothy James

ALLEN, Mrs Jane Rosemary. b 39. Cartrefle Coll of Educn BA83 PGCE84. St As & Ban Minl Tr Course 99. **d** 00 **p** 01. C Llandudno *Ban* 00-05; TV from 05. *The Wyngarth, 11 Abbey Road, Llandudno LL30 2EE* Tel (01492) 860531 E-mail revmil@hotmail.com

ALLEN, Johan. b 49. Lanc Univ CertEd75 Roehampton Inst BEd88. S'wark Ord Course 05. **d** 08. NSM W Streatham St Jas *S'wark* from 08. *54 Leigham Vale, London SW16 2JQ* Tel (020) 7564 8588 Mobile 07743-156786 E-mail johanallen@btinternet.com

ALLEN, John Catling. b 25. Leeds Univ BA50. Coll of Resurr Mirfield 50. **d** 52 **p** 53. C Knowle H Nativity *Bris* 52-54; C De Beauvoir Town St Pet *Lon* 54-57; C Beckenham St Barn *Roch* 57-60; V Orpington St Andr 60-66; V Linc St Jo 66-84; C Tynemouth Ch Ch w H Trin *Newc* 85-87; C N Shields 87-89; rtd 89; Hon C Gt and Lt Torrington and Frithelstock *Ex* from 89. *7 St Barnabas, The Beauchamp Community, Newland, Malvern WR13 5AX* Tel (01684) 899390

ALLEN, John Clement. b 32. K Coll Lon 54. **d** 58 **p** 59. C Middlesbrough St Martin *York* 58-60; C Northallerton w Kirby Sigston 60-64; V Larkfield *Roch* 64-70; R Ash 70-79; R Ridley 70-79; RD Cobham 76-79; R Chislehurst St Nic 79-97; rtd 97; Perm to Offic *Sarum* from 97. *The Peppergarth, 9 Lane Fox Terrace, Penny Street, Sturminster Newton DT10 1DE* Tel (01258) 473754

ALLEN, The Very Revd John Edward. b 32. Univ Coll Ox BA56 MA63 Fitzw Coll Cam BA68. Westcott Ho Cam 66. **d** 68 **p** 69. C Deal St Leon *Cant* 68-71; P-in-c Clifton St Paul *Bris* 71-78; Chapl Bris Univ 71-78; P-in-c Chippenham St Andr w Tytherton Lucas 78-82; Provost Wakef 82-97; rtd 97; Perm to Offic *York* from 98. *The Glebe Barn, Main Street, Sawdon, Scarborough YO13 9DY* Tel (01723) 859854

ALLEN, John Michael. b 27. Cuddesdon Coll 71. **d** 72 **p** 73. C Shrewsbury St Giles *Lich* 72-75; V Hengoed w Gobowen 75-82; V Burghill *Heref* 82-85; RD Heref Rural 83-85; TV Bracknell *Ox* 85-92; rtd 92; Perm to Offic *Heref* 93-05. *4 Denehyrst Court, York Road, Guildford GU1 4EA* Tel (01483) 569623

ALLEN, Mrs Kathleen. b 46. NOC 88. **d** 91 **p** 94. NSM Colne H Trin *Blackb* 91-94; NSM Colne Ch Ch 94-98; NSM Colne and Villages 98-06; rtd 06. *80 Stoddens Road, Burnham-on-Sea TA8 2DB* Tel (01278) 793627 E-mail kathleen@k-allen.fsnet.co.uk

ALLEN, Malcolm. b 60. Open Th Coll BA00. Trin Coll Bris 94. **d** 96 **p** 97. C Skirbeck H Trin *Linc* 96-00; TV Cheltenham St Mark *Glouc* 00-09; TR Bishop's Cleeve and Woolstone w

Gotherington etc from 09. *The Rectory, 4 Church Approach, Bishops Cleeve, Cheltenham GL52 8NG* Tel (01242) 677851
E-mail malcallen147@btinternet.com

ALLEN, Michael Edward Gerald. b 26. Selw Coll Cam BA50 MA53. Chich Th Coll 50. **d** 52 **p** 53. C Farncombe *Guildf* 52-56; R Bentley 56-60; V Baswich *Lich* 60-75; V Highbrook and W Hoathly *Chich* 75-91; RD Cuckfield 77-88; rtd 91; Perm to Offic *Chich* from 91. *2 Hill Lodge, 13 St John's Road, Eastbourne BN20 7NQ* Tel (01323) 728240

ALLEN, Michael Stephen. b 37. Nottm Univ BA60. Cranmer Hall Dur 60. **d** 62 **p** 63. C Sandal St Helen *Wakef* 62-66; Hon C Tile Cross *Birm* 66-70; V 72-84; Hon C Bletchley *Ox* 70-72; Vice-Prin Aston Tr Scheme 84-91; Hon C Boldmere *Birm* 85-91; P-in-c Easton w Colton and Marlingford *Nor* 91-93; Local Min Officer 91-93; Dioc Adv in Adult Educn *S'well* 93-02; rtd 02; Perm to Offic *S'well* from 02. *3 Grenville Rise, Arnold, Nottingham NG5 8EW* Tel 0115-967 9515
E-mail msa@amd.fsnet.co.uk

ALLEN, Patricia. *See* LEWER ALLEN, Mrs Patricia

ALLEN, Patrick Charles Benedict. b 55. St Steph Ho Ox 83. **d** 86 **p** 87. C Bethnal Green St Matt w St Jas the Gt *Lon* 86-90; C Kenton 90-92; V Plumstead St Nic *S'wark* 92-94; In RC Ch 94-97; Asst to RD Battersea 97-98; P-in-c Lavender Hill Ascension 97-00; P-in-c Battersea St Pet and St Paul 97-98; P-in-c Battersea St Phil w St Bart 98-00; V Lavender Hill Ascension etc 00-08; P-in-c Sutton on Plym *Ex* from 08; P-in-c Plymouth St Simon and St Mary from 08. *St John's Vicarage, 3 Alma Street, Plymouth PL4 0NL* Tel (01752) 664191

ALLEN, Peter Henry. b 34. Nottm Univ BA66. Kelham Th Coll 58. **d** 66 **p** 67. C Salisbury St Martin *Sarum* 66-70; C Melksham 70-73; C Paignton Ch Ch *Ex* 73-76; P-in-c W Holloway St Dav *Lon* 76-77; V Barnsbury St Dav w St Clem 77-84; P-in-c Brentford St Faith 84-87; TV Brentford 87-91; TV Catford (Southend) and Downham *S'wark* 91-01; rtd 01; Perm to Offic *Roch* from 01. *17 Mayfield Road, Belvedere DA17 6DX* Tel (01322) 412903 Mobile 07939-580266
E-mail peterbeth@ntlworld.com

ALLEN, Peter John. b 34. Leic Coll of Educn CertEd74 Leic Univ BEd75 MA79. EAMTC 89. **d** 92 **p** 93. NSM Ketton w Tinwell *Pet* 92-94; NSM Easton on the Hill, Collyweston w Duddington etc 94-96; Chapl St Pet Via del Mar Chile 96-99; NSM Culworth w Sulgrave and Thorpe Mandeville etc *Pet* 00-04; rtd 04; Perm to Offic *Pet* from 04. *18 Scythe Road, Daventry NN11 0WN* Tel (01327) 300596
E-mail peterjallen@tinyworld.co.uk

ALLEN, Canon Peter John Douglas. b 35. Jes Coll Cam BA61 MA64 PGCE67. Westcott Ho Cam 60. **d** 62 **p** 63. C Wyken *Cov* 62-65; C Boston Ch of Advent USA 65-66; Chapl Jes Coll Cam 66-72; Chapl K Sch Cant 72-87; Hon Min Can Cant Cathl 73-87; Second Master and Sen Chapl Sedbergh Sch Cumbria 87-93; P-in-c Edin St Ninian 93-06; Prec and Can St Mary's Cathl 94-06; Tutor Edin Th Coll 94-01; rtd 06; Chapl Edin Academy from 99; Chapl Fettes Coll Edin 02-07. *12A Grosvenor Crescent, Edinburgh EH12 5EL* Tel 0131-337 0027

ALLEN, Peter Richard. b 62. Qu Coll Birm BA04. **d** 04 **p** 05. C Hackenthorpe *Sheff* 04-07; TV Gleadless 07-08; Chapl for Sport from 07. *60 Hollybank Crescent, Sheffield S12 2BP* Tel 07772-926278 (mobile) E-mail prallen3@yahoo.co.uk

ALLEN, Philip Gerald. b 48. Trin Coll Bris 71. **d** 73 **p** 74. C Portsea St Luke *Portsm* 73-75; C-in-c 75-79; C Southsea St Jude 75-79; P-in-c Gatten St Paul 79-85; V from 85. *St Paul's Vicarage, St Paul's Crescent, Shanklin PO37 7AW* Tel (01983) 862027

ALLEN, Richard. **d** 06 **p** 07. NSM Ottery St Mary, Alfington, W Hill, Tipton etc *Ex* from 06. *Timbertops, Salston Ride, Salston, Ottery St Mary EX11 1RH*

ALLEN, Richard James. b 46. Wells Th Coll 69. **d** 71 **p** 72. C Upholland *Liv* 71-75; TV 76-79; TV Padgate 79-85; V Weston-super-Mare St Andr Bournville *B & W* 85-93; V Williton from 93; P-in-c St Decumans from 08; Chapl Somerset Primary Care Trust from 93. *The Vicarage, 16 Bridge Street, Williton, Taunton TA4 4NR* Tel (01984) 632626
E-mail vicar@dickallen.freeserve.co.uk

ALLEN, Richard John. b 55. City Univ BSc76 FCOptom80. ERMC 04. **d** 07 **p** 08. NSM Lexden *Chelmsf* from 07. *22 Fitzwilliam Road, Colchester CO3 3RZ* Tel (01206) 578051 Mobile 07713-625014 E-mail richard.allen@zen.co.uk

ALLEN, Richard John Slaney. b 54. St 00 **p** 01. NSM Tooting All SS *S'wark* 00-04; NSM Streatham Ch Ch w St Marg 05-08; Asst Chapl SW Lon and St George's Mental Health NHS Trust from 03. *9 Roman Rise, London SE19 1JG* Tel (020) 8761 3968

ALLEN, Richard Lee. b 41. Liv Inst of Educn TCert67. NOC 80. **d** 83 **p** 84. NSM Colne Ch Ch *Blackb* 83-90; P-in-c Trawden 91-98; NSM Colne and Villages 98-06; Chapl Burnley Health Care NHS Trust 99-03; Chapl E Lancs Hosps NHS Trust 03-06; rtd 06. *80 Stoddens Road, Burnham-on-Sea TA8 2DB* Tel (01278) 793627

ALLEN, Roger Charles Brews. b 44. Loughb Univ BTech66 Solicitor 77. **d** 92 **p** 93. OLM S Elmham and Ilketshall *St E*

92-95; OLM Bungay H Trin w St Mary from 95. *33A Earsham Street, Bungay NR35 1AF* Tel (01986) 896927
E-mail rallen@zetnet.co.uk

ALLEN, Roy Vernon. b 43. Open Univ BA81 Birm Univ MA84. Sarum Th Coll 67. **d** 70 **p** 71. C Hall Green Ascension *Birm* 70-74; V Temple Balsall 74-78; P-in-c Smethwick St Steph 78-81; V Smethwick St Mich 78-81; V Smethwick SS Steph and Mich 81-86; V Marston Green from 86. *The Vicarage, Elmdon Road, Birmingham B37 7BT* Tel 0121-779 2492
E-mail roy_v_allen@hotmail.com

ALLEN, Canon Steven. b 49. Nottm Univ BA73. St Jo Coll Nottm 73. **d** 75 **p** 76. C Gt Horton *Bradf* 75-80; V 89-02; V Upper Armley *Ripon* 80-89; RD Bowling and Horton *Bradf* 98-02; Hon Can Bradf Cathl from 00; Dioc Tr Officer from 02. *48 Toller Grove, Bradford BD9 5NP* Tel (01274) 482059
E-mail steve.allen@bradford.anglican.org

ALLEN, Stuart Philip. b 73. St Cath Coll Ox BA95. Oak Hill Th Coll BA02. **d** 02 **p** 03. C Burford w Fulbrook, Taynton, Asthall etc *Ox* 02-06; Tutor Proclamation Trust from 06; Hon C Tooting Graveney St Nic *S'wark* from 06. *7 Crowborough Road, London SW17 9QB* Tel (020) 8672 7658 E-mail spa@proctrust.org.uk

ALLEN, Mrs Susan Rosemary. b 47. Warwick Univ BSc68 Trevelyan Coll Dur PGCE69. Sarum Th Coll 93. **d** 96 **p** 97. C Goldsworth Park *Guildf* 96-01; TV Hemel Hempstead *St Alb* from 01. *33 Cragavon Road, Hemel Hempstead HP2 6BA* Tel (01442) 270585 E-mail revsue33@googlemail.com

ALLEN, Thomas Davidson. b 49. QUB BA. CITC 81. **d** 84 **p** 85. C Magheralin w Dollingstown *D & D* 84-86; I Kilwarlin Upper w Kilwarlin Lower 86-91; I Maghera w Killelagh *D & R* 91-03; I Donaghcloney w Waringstown *D & D* from 03. *The Rectory, 54 Banbridge Road, Waringstown, Craigavon BT66 7QD* Tel (028) 3888 1218 E-mail tallen@talk21.com

ALLEN, Thomas Henry. b 42. NOC 87. **d** 90 **p** 91. C Upholland *Liv* 90-93; TV Walton-on-the-Hill 93-07; rtd 07. *13 Crosgrove Road, Liverpool L4 8TE* Tel 0151-476 9705

ALLEN, Timothy James. b 71. Warwick Univ BA93. Ripon Coll Cuddesdon BTh99. **d** 99 **p** 00. C Nuneaton St Mary *Cov* 99-02; V Seend, Bulkington and Poulshot *Sarum* 02-03; Hon C Winslow w Gt Horwood and Addington *Ox* 03-05; V Gt Cornard *St E* 05-09; V New Plymouth St Mary New Zealand from 09. *37 Vivian Street, New Plymouth 4310, New Zealand* Tel (0064) (6) 758 3111 E-mail stmnp@xtra.co.nz

ALLEN, Zachary Edward. b 52. Warwick Univ BA74. Ripon Coll Cuddesdon 78. **d** 81 **p** 82. C Bognor *Chich* 81-84; C Rusper and Roughey 84-86; TV Carl H Trin and St Barn 86-90; Chapl Strathclyde Ho Hosp Carl 86-90; V Findon w Clapham and Patching *Chich* 90-01; V Rustington from 01. *The Vicarage, Claigmar Road, Rustington, Littlehampton BN16 2NL* Tel (01903) 784749

ALLEYNE, Sir John Olpherts Campbell, Bt. b 28. Jes Coll Cam BA50 MA55. **d** 55 **p** 56. C Southampton St Mary w H Trin *Win* 55-58; Chapl Cov Cathl 58-62; Chapl Clare Hall Cam 62-66; Chapl Bris Cathl 66-68; Area Sec (SW England) Toc H 68-71; V Speke All SS *Liv* 71-73; TR Speke St Aid 73-76; R Win St Matt 76-93; rtd 93; Perm to Offic *Guildf* from 93. *2 Ash Grove, Guildford GU2 9UT* Tel (01483) 573021

ALLFORD, Judith Mary. b 55. Sheff Univ BA Lon Univ BD. Trin Coll Bris 77. **dss** 86 **d** 87 **p** 94. Par Dn Deptford St Jo w H Trin *S'wark* 87-91; Asst Chapl Dulwich Hosp 91-93; Asst Chapl K Coll Hosp Lon 91-95; Asst Chapl King's Healthcare NHS Trust 93-95; Chapl N Surrey Primary Care Trust from 95. *St Peter's Hospital, Guildford Road, Chertsey KT16 0PZ* Tel (01932) 872000 ext 3324 E-mail judith.allford@asph.nhs.uk

ALLIES, Lorna Gillian. b 46. UEA BSc93 Sheff Univ EdD01. **d** 05 **p** 06. OLM Thurton *Nor* 05-07; NSM Bunwell, Carleton Rode, Tibenham, Gt Moulton etc 07-09; P-in-c Rackheath and Salhouse from 09; Dioc Rural Adv from 06. *The Rectory, 56 Green Lane West, Rackheath, Norwich NR13 6PG* Tel (01603) 720097 *or* 263801 Mobile 07706-482284
E-mail l.allies@btinternet.com

ALLIN, Philip Ronald. b 43. Reading Univ MA96 Birm Univ CQSW. Lich Th Coll 71. **d** 71 **p** 72. C Sutton in Ashfield St Mary *S'well* 71-74; Chapl to Sutton Cen 74-76; Lic to Offic 74-76; P-in-c Grove 76-77; R Ordsall 76-80; V Mansfield St Mark 81-83; TR Hermitage and Hampstead Norreys, Cold Ash etc *Ox* 83-96; OCF 83-96; Chapl Nine o'clock Service *Sheff* 96-03; rtd 03; Bp's Adv in Past Care and Counselling *Sheff* 03-08; Warden of Spiritual Direction *Dur* from 08. *Hareholme House, New Brancepeth, Durham DH7 7HH* Tel 0191-373 9743

ALLINGTON, Andrew William. b 57. ACA81 Sheff Univ BA78. Cranmer Hall Dur BA95. **d** 95 **p** 96. C Clifton *York* 95-99; P-in-c Stainforth *Sheff* 99-02; V from 02. *The Vicarage, Field Road, Stainforth, Doncaster DN7 5AQ* Tel (01302) 841295
E-mail allingtonandrew@hotmail.com

ALLINSON, Capt Paul Timothy. b 63. CA Tr Coll 82 Edin Th Coll 89. **d** 91 **p** 92. C Peterlee *Dur* 91-94; C Shadforth and Sherburn w Pittington 94-97; P-in-c Byers Green 97-04; P-in-c Seaton Carew from 04; P-in-c Greatham from 09; Dioc

Children's Adv from 94. *6 Front Street, Greatham, Hartlepool TS25 2ER* Tel (01429) 872626 Mobile 07888-726535
E-mail revdpaul@lineone.net

ALLISON, Elliott Desmond. b 36. UNISA BA64 K Coll Lon MTh74. S Africa Federal Th Coll. **d** 69 **p** 70. *Flat 1, 20 Southview Gardens, Worthing BN11 5JA*

ALLISON, James Timothy. b 61. Man Univ BSc83. Oak Hill Th Coll BA89. **d** 89 **p** 90. C Walkden Moor *Man* 89-93; Chapl Huddersfield Univ 93-98; V Erringden from 98; RD Calder Valley from 06. *The Vicarage, Brier Hey Lane, Mytholmroyd, Hebden Bridge HX7 5PJ* Tel (01422) 883130
E-mail erringden@aol.com

ALLISON, Keith. b 34. Dur Univ BA59. Ely Th Coll 59. **d** 61 **p** 62. C Sculcoates *York* 61-64; C Stainton-in-Cleveland 64-65; C Leeds St Pet *Ripon* 65-70; V Micklefield *York* 70-74; V Appleton-le-Street w Amotherby 74-78; P-in-c Barton le Street 77-78; P-in-c Salton 77-80; R Amotherby w Appleton and Barton-le-Street 78-82; Chapl Lister Hosp Stevenage 82-90; P-in-c St Ippolyts *St Alb* 82-85; V 85-90; Chapl Hitchin Hosp 86-90; Chapl Shotley Bridge Gen Hosp 90-94; Chapl NW Dur HA 90-94; Sen Chapl N Dur Acute Hosps NHS Trust 94-98; Sen Chapl N Dur Healthcare NHS Trust 98-00; rtd 00. *2 Middlewood Road, Lanchester, Durham DH7 0HL* Tel (01207) 529046

ALLISON, Michael John. b 33. Leeds Univ BSc97 ATI58. Wilson Carlile Coll 05. **d** 05 **p** 06. NSM Windhill *Bradf* from 05. *33 Busy Lane, Shipley BD18 1DX* Tel (01274) 587194
E-mail m.john.allison@talktalk.net

ALLISON, Susan Ann. b 61. EMMTC 06. **d** 06 **p** 07. C Gt and Lt Coates w Bradley *Linc* from 06. *26 Meadowbank, Grimsby DN37 9PG* Tel (01472) 751213 Mobile 07920-133329
E-mail sue.allison1@ntlworld.com

ALLISTER, The Ven Donald Spargo. b 52. Peterho Cam BA74 MA77. Trin Coll Bris 74. **d** 76 **p** 77. C Hyde St Geo *Ches* 76-79; C Sevenoaks St Nic *Roch* 79-83; V Birkenhead Ch Ch *Ches* 83-89; R Cheadle 89-02; RD Cheadle 99-02; Adn Ches from 02. *The Rectory, Chester Road, Delamere, Northwich CW8 2HS* Tel (01606) 882184 *or* (01244) 620444 Fax (01606) 301911 *or* (01244) 620456 E-mail donald.allister@chester.anglican.org

ALLISTER, John Charles. b 77. Ch Coll Cam MA00 MSci00 St Anne's Coll Ox PGCE01. Wycliffe Hall Ox BA08. **d** 09. C Hurdsfield *Ches* from 09. *138 Brocklehurst Avenue, Macclesfield SK10 2RQ* Tel 07092-119317 (mobile)
E-mail john.allister@cantab.net

ALLMAN, Mrs Susan. b 56. Bris Univ BA77. WEMTC 93. **d** 96 **p** 97. NSM Henleaze *Bris* 96-99; C Southmead 99-02; V Two Mile Hill St Mark from 02; Partnership P E Bris from 08. *5 Lodgeside Gardens, Bristol BS15 1NY* Tel 0117-937 1371 Mobile 07775-977298 E-mail susanrev@hotmail.co.uk

ALLMARK, Leslie. b 48. Open Univ BA90. **d** 01 **p** 02. OLM Halliwell St Luke *Man* 01-08; rtd 08. *75 Crosby Road, Bolton BL1 4EJ* Tel (01204) 845795
E-mail leslie@lallmark.freeserve.co.uk

ALLON-SMITH, Roderick David. b 51. Leic Univ BA PhD Cam Univ MA. Ridley Hall Cam 79. **d** 82 **p** 83. C Kinson *Sarum* 82-86; V Westwood *Cov* 86-96; RD Cov S 92-96; P-in-c Radford Semele 96-04; Dioc Dir Par Development and Evang 01-03; Dioc Missr *Dur* from 04; AD Dur from 08. *5 Beechways, Durham DH1 4LG* Tel 0191-384 4330
E-mail allonsmith@bigfoot.com

ALLPORT, David Jack. b 55. Ox Univ BA MEd. Qu Coll Birm 78. **d** 80 **p** 81. C Abingdon w Shippon *Ox* 80-83; C-in-c Woodgate Valley CD *Birm* 83-91; Perm to Offic *Lich* from 91. *122 Cherry Tree Avenue, Walsall WS5 4JL* Tel (01922) 640059

ALLRED, Frank. b 23. Tyndale Hall Bris 62. **d** 64 **p** 65. C Halliwell St Pet *Man* 64-67; V Ravenhead *Liv* 67-75; R Chadwell *Chelmsf* 75-82; V Theworth H Trin *York* 82-86; rtd 87; Perm to Offic *York* from 87. *12 Viking Road, Bridlington YO16 6TW* Tel (01262) 677321

ALLSO, Michael Neal. b 48. FRICS72 MCIArb73 MAE00. SWMTC 95. **d** 98 **p** 99. NSM Ex St Thos and Em 98-01; NSM Colyton, Southleigh, Offwell, Widworthy etc 01-03; NSM Colyton, Musbury, Southleigh and Branscombe 03-04; C Widecombe-in-the-Moor, Leusdon, Princetown etc 04-07; C Ashburton, Bickington, Buckland in the Moor etc 07-08; NSM Dunster, Carhampton, Withycombe w Rodhuish etc *B & W* from 08. *Tanglewood, Main Road, Carhampton, Minehead TA24 6NQ* E-mail frmichaelallso@aol.com

ALLSOP, Anthony James. b 37. AKC62. **d** 63 **p** 64. C Leytonstone St Marg w St Columba *Chelmsf* 63-68; V Gt Ilford St Alb 68-80; V Gainsborough St Jo *Linc* 80-85; V Hockerill *St Alb* 85-02; Chapl Herts and Essex Hosp Bp's Stortford 85-95; Chapl Essex and Herts Community NHS Trust 95-01; Chapl N Essex Mental Health Partnership NHS Trust 01-02; rtd 02; Perm to Offic *Ches* from 03. *63 Longdown Road, Congleton CW12 4QH* Tel (01260) 280628

ALLSOP, Mrs Beryl Anne. b 45. EMMTC 94. **d** 97 **p** 98. NSM Clipstone *S'well* 97-00; NSM Blidworth w Rainworth from 00. *The Vicarage, 2 Kirks Croft, Blidworth, Mansfield NG21 0QU* Tel (01623) 792306 E-mail beryl@faithfulfish.co.uk

ALLSOP, David George. b 48. Wycliffe Hall Ox. **d** 99 **p** 00. C Chenies and Lt Chalfont, Latimer and Flaunden *Ox* 99-02; P-in-c 02-08; R from 08. *The Rectory, Chenies, Rickmansworth WD3 6ER* Tel (01923) 284433 Mobile 07818-441431
E-mail cheniesrectory@aol.com

ALLSOP, Patrick Leslie Fewtrell. b 52. Fitzw Coll Cam BA74 MA78. Ripon Coll Cuddesdon BA78 MA83. **d** 79 **p** 80. C Barrow St Matt *Carl* 79-82; Chapl Eton Coll 82-88; Chapl K Sch Roch 89-02; Hon PV Roch Cathl 89-97; Chapl St Paul's Sch Barnes from 02. *St Paul's School, Lonsdale Road, London SW13 9JT* Tel (020) 8746 5434

ALLSOP, Peter William. b 33. Kelham Th Coll 58. **d** 58 **p** 59. C Woodford St Barn *Chelmsf* 58-61; C Upholland *Liv* 61-65; V Wigan St Geo 65-71; P-in-c Marham *Ely* 71-72; TV Fincham 72-76; V Trawden *Blackb* 76-90; C Marton 90-92; C S Shore H Trin 92-98; rtd 98; Perm to Offic *Blackb* from 98. *31 Lomond Avenue, Blackpool FY3 9QL* Tel (01253) 696624
E-mail peter.w.allsop@talktalk.net

ALLSOPP, The Ven Christine. b 47. Aston Univ BSc68. S Dios Minl Tr Scheme 86. **d** 89 **p** 94. C Caversham St Pet and Mapledurham etc *Ox* 89-94; C Bracknell 94; TV 94-98; P-in-c Bourne Valley *Sarum* 98-00; TR 00-05; RD Alderbury 99-05; Can and Preb Sarum Cathl 02-05; Adn Northn *Pet* from 05; Can Pet Cathl from 05. *11 The Drive, Northampton NN1 4RZ* Tel (01604) 714015 Fax 792016
E-mail archdeacon@aofn.wanadoo.co.uk

ALLSOPP, Mark Dennis. b 66. Cuddesdon Coll 93. **d** 96 **p** 97. C Hedworth *Dur* 96-98; C Gt Aycliffe 98-00; TV Gt Aycliffe and Chilton 00-04; P-in-c Kirklevington and High and Low Worsall *York* 04-08; Chapl HM YOI Kirklevington Grange 04-08; Chapl RN from 08. *Royal Naval Chaplaincy Service, Mail Point 1-2, Leach Building, Whale Island, Portsmouth PO2 8BY* Tel (023) 9262 5055 Fax 9262 5134 E-mail mark@dallsopp.fsworld.co.uk

ALLSOPP, Mrs Patricia Ann. b 48. St Mary's Coll Chelt CertEd69. Qu Coll Birm. **d** 00 **p** 01. C Upton-on-Severn, Ripple, Earls Croome etc *Worc* 00-04; P-in-c Finstall 04-05; V 05-08; RD Bromsgrove 06-08; rtd 08. *35 Cosby Road, Littlethorpe, Leicester LE19 2HG* E-mail rev.tricia@ukonline.co.uk

ALLSOPP, Stephen Robert. b 50. BSc71 MSc72 PhD75. Mon Dioc Tr Scheme 81. **d** 84 **p** 85. NSM Trevethin *Mon* 84-88; Asst Chapl K Sch Roch 88-07; Chapl K Prep Sch 99-07; rtd 07; Hon PV Roch Cathl from 89. *117 Prince's Street, Rochester ME1 2EA* Tel (01634) 409878
E-mail stephen.allsopp@diocese-rochester.org

ALLSWORTH, Peter Thomas. b 44. St Mich Coll Llan 93. **d** 93 **p** 94. C Prestatyn *St As* 93-96; V Esclusham 96-06; C Rhyl w St Ann from 06. *10 Tirionfa, Rhuddlan, Rhyl LL18 6LT* Tel (01745) 590683

ALLTON, Canon Paul Irving. b 38. Man Univ BA60. **d** 63 **p** 64. C Kibworth Beauchamp *Leic* 63-66; C Reading St Mary V *Ox* 66-70; R Caston and V Griston *Nor* 70-75; P-in-c Sturston w Thompson and Tottington 70-75; V Hunstanton St Mary w Lt Ringstead 75-80; V Holme-next-the-Sea 75-80; V Hunstanton St Mary w Ringstead Parva, Holme etc 80-85; RD Heacham and Rising 81-85; Hon Can Nor Cathl 85-93; TR Lowestoft and Kirkley 85-93; TR Keynsham *B & W* 93-96; TR Gaywood *Nor* 96-01; rtd 01; Perm to Offic *Nor* from 01. *Rustic Lodge, 79 Hall Lane, West Winch, King's Lynn PE33 0PJ* Tel (01553) 840355

ALLUM, Jeremy Warner. b 32. Wycliffe Hall Ox 60. **d** 62 **p** 63. C Hornchurch St Andr *Chelmsf* 62-67; P-in-c W Derby St Luke *Liv* 67-69; V 69-75; P-in-c Boulton *Derby* 75-90; RD Melbourne 86-90; V Hathersage 90-98; rtd 98; Perm to Offic *Derby* from 98. *32 Sandown Avenue, Mickleover, Derby DE3 0QQ* Tel (01332) 231253

ALLWOOD, Linda Angela Fredrika. b 76. Newc Univ BA00. Cranmer Hall Dur 01. **d** 03 **p** 04. C Northampton St Giles *Pet* 03-06; Perm to Offic *St E* from 06. *29 Warren Hill Road, Woodbridge IP12 4DU* Tel (01394) 384575 Mobile 07939-001160 E-mail linda_allwood@hotmail.com

ALLWRIGHT, Mrs Janet Margaret. b 40. Oak Hill Th Coll 87. **d** 90 **p** 94. NSM Galleywood Common *Chelmsf* 90-93; NSM Downham w S Hanningfield 93-99; Chapl HM Pris Bullwood Hall 98-03; TV Canvey Is *Chelmsf* 03-06; rtd 06; Perm to Offic *Chelmsf* from 06. *26 Chaplin Close, Chelmsford CM2 8QW* Tel (01245) 265499 E-mail revdjanet@supanet.com

ALMOND, Kenneth Alfred. b 36. EMMTC 76 Linc Th Coll 78. **d** 79 **p** 80. C Boston *Linc* 79-82; V Surfleet 82-87; RD Elloe W 86-96; V Spalding St Jo w Deeping St Nicholas 87-98; rtd 98; Perm to Offic *Linc* from 99. *1 Buckingham Close, Fishtoft, Boston PE21 9QB* Tel and fax (01205) 352805
E-mail ken.hilary@btopenworld.com

ALP, Mrs Elaine Alison. b 54. Oak Hill Th Coll 87. **d** 00. Dn-in-c Blackb St Mich w St Jo and H Trin 00-02; Par Dn Fleetwood St Nic 02-06; Perm to Offic 06-07; Hon C Ribbleton from 07. *25 Rose Lane, Preston PR1 6HH* Tel (01772) 798483
E-mail deaconalison@hotmail.com

ALSBURY, Colin. b 56. Ch Ch Ox BA77 MA81. Ripon Coll Cuddesdon 77. **d** 80 **p** 81. C Oxton *Ches* 80-84; V Crewe All SS and St Paul 84-92; Ind Chapl 92-95; V Kettering St Andr *Pet* 95-02; V Frome St Jo *B & W* from 02; V Woodlands from 02. *St John's Vicarage, Vicarage Close, Frome BA11 1QL* Tel (01373) 472853 E-mail colin.alsbury@zetnet.co.uk

ALTHAM, Donald. b 40. Liv Univ BA62. NOC 87. **d** 90 **p** 91. NSM Ramsbottom St Jo and St Paul *Man* 90-96; NSM Holcombe 99-04; NSM Walmersley from 04; NSM Bircle from 04; Chapl Asst Burnley Health Care NHS Trust 93-03; Chapl Asst E Lancs Hosps NHS Trust from 03. *387 Whalley Road, Ramsbottom, Bury BL0 0ER* Tel (01706) 822025

✠**ALVAREZ-VELAZQUEZ, The Rt Revd David Andres.** b 41. Inter American Univ Puerto Rico BA62 Caribbean Cen of Advanced Studies MS82. NY Th Sem MDiv65. **d** 65 **p** 65 **c** 87. Puerto Rico from 65; C St Mich 65; Chapl Episc Cathl Sch 65-67; R St Mark 67-70; R St Jo Cathl 70-79; Trujillo Alto St Hilda 79-87; Bp Puerto Rico from 87. *PO Box 902, Saint Just Station, Saint Just, 00978, Puerto Rico* Tel (001) (787) 761 9800 Mobile 376 4125 Fax 761 0320 E-mail iep@spiderlinkpr.net

ALVEY, Martyn Clifford. b 53. EMMTC 96. **d** 99 **p** 00. NSM Burton Joyce w Bulcote and Stoke Bardolph *S'well* 99-02; C Worksop St Jo 02-06; P-in-c Worksop Ch Ch from 06; AD Worksop 04-06. *34 Boscombe Road, Worksop S81 7SB* Tel (01909) 473998 E-mail martynalvey@btinternet.com

AMAT-TORREGROSA, Gabriel José. b 42. R Superior Coll of Music Madrid MA63. Bapt Th Sem Ruschlikon Zürich 64. **d** 71 **p** 72. Spain 71-98; Asst Chapl Zürich *Eur* 98-07; P-in-c Marseille w Aix-en-Provence from 08. *84 boulevard Baille, 13006 Marseille, France* E-mail gjamat@hotmail.com

AMBANI, Stephen Frederick. b 45. Univ of Wales (Lamp) BA90. St Jo Coll Nottm 86 CA Tr Coll Nairobi 70. **d** 83 **p** 83. Kenya 83-93; C Glan Ely *Llan* 93-95; C Whitchurch 95-97; V Nantymoel w Wyndham 97-99; V Tonyrefail w Gilfach Goch and Llandyfodwg 99-03; V Tonyrefail w Gilfach Goch 04; rtd 05. *78 Heol-y-Mynydd, Hendreforgan, Gilfach Goch, Porth CF39 8UR* Tel (01443) 670588

AMBROSE, James Field. b 51. Newc Univ BA73. Cranmer Hall Dur. **d** 80 **p** 81. C Barrow St Geo w St Luke *Carl* 80-83; C Workington St Jo 83-85; R Montford w Shrawardine and Fitz *Lich* 85-88; Ch Radio Officer BBC Radio Shropshire 85-88; Chapl RAF 88-92; Voc and Min Adv CPAS 92-99; TV Syston *Leic* 99-06; C Leic Martyrs 06-07; V Heald Green St Cath *Ches* from 07; Chapl St Ann's Hospice Manchester from 07. *The Vicarage, 217 Outwood Road, Heald Green, Cheadle SK8 3JS* Tel 0161-437 4614 *or* 437 3685 E-mail jfambrose@btinternet.com

AMBROSE, John George. b 30. Lon Univ BD Ox Univ PGCE. **d** 74 **p** 75. C Rayleigh *Chelmsf* 74-79; V Hadleigh St Barn 79-95; rtd 95; Perm to Offic *Chelmsf* from 95. *9 Fairview Gardens, Leigh-on-Sea SS9 3PD* Tel (01702) 474632

AMBROSE, Thomas. b 47. Sheff Univ BSc69 PhD73 Em Coll Cam BA77 MA84. Westcott Ho Cam 75. **d** 78 **p** 79. C Morpeth *Newc* 78-81; C N Gosforth 81-84; R March St Jo *Ely* 84-93; RD March 89-93; P-in-c Witchford w Wentworth 93-99; Dioc Dir of Communications 93-99; Chapl K Sch Ely 94-96; V Trumpington *Ely* 99-08. *229 Arbury Road, Cambridge CB4 2JJ* Tel 07711-263083 (mobile) E-mail tom.ambrose@ely.anglican.org

AMELIA, Alison. b 67. Hull Univ BA03 St Jo Coll Dur BA05 Cranmer Hall Dur 03. **d** 05 **p** 06. C Nunthorpe *York* 05-06; C Hessle 06-09; Chapl United Lincs Hosps NHS Trust from 09. *36 Peterborough Way, Sleaford NG34 8TW* Tel (01529) 414373 E-mail aamelia333@yahoo.com

AMES, Jeremy Peter. b 49. K Coll Lon BD71 AKC71. **d** 72 **p** 73. C Kennington St Jo *S'wark* 72-75; Chapl RN 75-04; Chapl RN Engineering Coll 86-89; USA 91-93; Dir of Ords RN 00-04; QHC 02-04; Master St Nic Hosp Salisbury from 04. *The Master's House, St Nicholas Hospital, Salisbury SP1 2SW* Tel (01722) 336874 E-mail cyberjpa@aol.com

AMES, Reginald John. b 27. Bps' Coll Cheshunt 51. **d** 54 **p** 55. C Edmonton St Alphege *Lon* 54-58; C Mill Hill Jo Keble Ch 58-60; P-in-c Northwood Hills St Edm 61-64; V 64-92; rtd 92; Hon C Moffat *Glas* 92-01; Lic to Offic from 92. *Oakbank, Lochwood, Beattock, Moffat DG10 9PS* Tel (01683) 300381

AMES-LEWIS, Canon Richard. b 45. Em Coll Cam BA66 MA70. Westcott Ho Cam 76. **d** 78 **p** 79. C Bromley St Mark *Roch* 78-81; C Edenbridge 81-84; V 84-91; P-in-c Crockham Hill H Trin 84-91; P-in-c Barnes St Mary *S'wark* 91-97; TR Barnes 97-00; RD Richmond and Barnes 94-00; TR E Dereham and Scarning *Nor* 00-06; P-in-c Swanton Morley w Beetley w E Bilney and Hoe 02-06; TR Dereham and Distr 06-09; RD Dereham in Mitford 03-08; Hon Can Nor Cathl 06-09; rtd 09. *21 Victoria Street, Cambridge CB1 1JP* Tel (01223) 300615 E-mail ameslewis@btinternet.com

AMEY, Graham George. b 44. Lon Univ BD70. Tyndale Hall Bris 67. **d** 72 **p** 72. C Hornsey Rise St Mary *Lon* 71-74; C St Helens St Helen *Liv* 74-79; V Liv All So Springwood 79-91; V Whiston 91-02; V Aigburth from 02. *St Anne's Vicarage, 389 Aigburth Road, Liverpool L17 6BH* Tel 0151-727 1101

AMEY, John Mark. b 59. Ripon Coll Cuddesdon 98. **d** 00 **p** 01. C Winchmore Hill St Paul *Lon* 00-04; V Sutton *Ely* from 04; R Witcham w Mepal from 04; Chapl ATC from 03. *The Vicarage, 7 Church Lane, Sutton, Ely CB6 2RQ* Tel (01353) 778645 Mobile 07905-122090 E-mail mark.amey@ely.anglican.org

AMEY, Phillip Mark. b 73. STETS 03. **d** 06 **p** 07. C Southsea H Spirit *Portsm* from 06. *219 Fawcett Road, Southsea PO4 0DH* Tel (023) 9243 2784 E-mail phillip.amey@ntlworld.com

AMIS, Ronald. b 37. Linc Th Coll 74. **d** 76 **p** 77. C Grantham w Manthorpe *Linc* 76-78; C Grantham 78-79; P-in-c Holbeach Hurn 79-81; V Long Bennington w Foston 81-91; V Corby Glen 91-93; RD Grantham 90-92; rtd 93; Perm to Offic *Pet* 93-03 and from 09; *Ches* 06-08. *9 Cotton End, Bretton, Peterborough PE3 9TF* Tel (01733) 261152

AMOR, Peter David Card. b 28. AKC53. **d** 54 **p** 55. C St Margaret's-on-Thames *Lon* 54; C Leighton Buzzard *St Alb* 54-58; C Toxteth Park St Agnes *Liv* 58-62; C-in-c Aldershot Ascension CD *Guildf* 62-65; V Bingley H Trin *Bradf* 65-72; V The Collingbournes *Sarum* 72-75; R The Collingbournes and Everleigh 75-77; V Thorpe *Guildf* 77-85; P-in-c Monks Risborough *Ox* 85-89; R 89-94; rtd 94; Perm to Offic *Ox* from 97. *1 Culverton Hill, Princes Risborough HP27 0DZ* Tel (01844) 345236

AMOS, Alan John. b 44. OBE79. K Coll Lon BD66 MTh67 AKC67. St Steph Ho Ox 68. **d** 69 **p** 70. C Hoxton H Trin w St Mary *Lon* 69-72; Lebanon 73-82; Lect Liturg Studies Westcott Ho Cam 82-85; Vice-Prin 85-89; Prin Cant Sch of Min 89-94; Co-Prin SEITE 94-96; Chapl Medway NHS Foundn Trust 96-09; Hon PV Roch Cathl 95-04; Hon Can 04-09; P-in-c Newington w Hartlip and Stockbury *Cant* from 09; P-in-c Upchurch w Lower Halstow from 09; P-in-c Iwade from 09. *Penny Cross, Keycol Hill, Newington, Sittingbourne ME9 8NE* Tel (01795) 842913 E-mail alanmedway@btinternet.com

AMOS, Brother. *See* YONGE, James Mohun

AMOS, Colin James. b 62. Univ of Wales (Lamp) BA83 CQSW85. Ridley Hall Cam 93. **d** 93 **p** 94. C Aberdare *Llan* 93-96; V Port Talbot St Theodore from 96; AD Margam from 08. *St Theodore's Vicarage, Talbot Road, Port Talbot SA13 1LB* Tel (01639) 883935 Fax 760104 E-mail fr.amos@ntlworld.com

AMYES, Emma Charlotte. b 65. Redcliffe Coll BA01. Ridley Hall Cam. **d** 04 **p** 05. C Hucclecote *Glouc* from 04. *18 Millfields, Hucclecote, Gloucester GL3 3NH* Tel (01452) 371003 Mobile 07866-808635 E-mail emma.amyes@virgin.net

AMYES, Geoffrey Edmund. b 74. Bris Univ BSc96 Cam Univ BTh04. Ridley Hall Cam 01. **d** 04 **p** 05. C Hucclecote *Glouc* from 04. *18 Millfields, Hucclecote, Gloucester GL3 3NH* Tel (01452) 371003 Mobile 07792-519910 E-mail g.amyes@virgin.net

AMYS, Richard James Rutherford. b 58. Trin Coll Bris BA90. **d** 90 **p** 91. C Whitnash *Cov* 90-93; P-in-c Gravesend H Family w Ifield *Roch* 93-95; R 95-99; R Eastington, Frocester, Haresfield etc *Glouc* from 99. *The Rectory, Mill End Lane, Eastington, Stonehouse GL10 3SG* Tel and fax (01453) 822437 Mobile 07796-956050 E-mail richardjramys@aol.com

ANAN, Gabriel Jaja. b 48. Univ of E Lon MA96 Regents Th Coll BA92 MCIT92. NTMTC 00. **d** 03 **p** 04. NSM Victoria Docks St Luke *Chelmsf* 03 07; NSM Forest Gate St Saw w W Ham St Matt 07-09; NSM N Woolwich w Silvertown from 09. *41 Camel Road, London E16 2DE* Tel (020) 7473 6003 Mobile 07734-707887 E-mail gabriel58@hotmail.com

ANAND, Jessie Nesam Nallammal. b 54. Madurai Univ BSc75 BEd76 Annamalai Univ MA84. Tamilnadu Th Sem BD91 New Coll Edin MTh94 EMMTC 02. **d** 03 **p** 04. NSM Birstall and Wanlip *Leic* 03-05; NSM Emmaus Par Team 05-07; Perm to Offic *S'wark* from 07. *All Saints' Vicarage, 100 Prince of Wales Drive, London SW11 4BD* Tel (020) 7622 3809 Mobile 07811-189358 E-mail jessieanand@yahoo.co.uk

ANAND, The Very Revd Sekar Anand Asir. b 53. Madurai Univ BSc75 Serampore Univ BD79 New Coll Edin MTh93 Annamalai Univ MA99. **d** 80 **p** 81. C Nayaith St Jo India 80-82; R Tuticorin St Paul 82-84; Sec Tirunelveli Children's Miss 84-91; C Edin St Pet 91-92; Hon C Burmantofts St Steph and St Agnes *Ripon* 92-93; C Edin St Mark 93-95; Provost Palayamcottai Cathl India 95-00; C Leic Resurr 00-07; C Battersea Fields *S'wark* from 07. *All Saints' Vicarage, 100 Prince of Wales Drive, London SW11 4BD* Tel (020) 7622 3809 E-mail anandjessie@yahoo.co.uk

ANCRUM, John. b 28. Clifton Th Coll 55. **d** 58 **p** 59. C Branksome St Clem *Sarum* 58-61; C Sparkhill St Jo *Birm* 61-63; V Tibshelf *Derby* 63-70; Canada 70-74; P-in-c Salwarpe *Worc* 74-75; P-in-c Tibberton w Bredicot and Warndon 75-76; P-in-c Hadzor w Oddingley 76-78; Lic to Offic *Chelmsf* 78-81; Chapl HM Pris Stafford 81-82; Chapl HM Pris Dartmoor 82-89; Lic to Offic *Ex* 88-89; rtd 89; Perm to Offic *Ex* from 89. *14 Merrivale View Road, Dousland, Yelverton PL20 6NS*

ANDAYI, Elphas Ombuna. b 57. St Phil Th Coll Maseno 78. **d** 79 **p** 81. Kenya 79-98 and from 99; Provost Butere 92-97; C Sparkhill w Greet and Sparkbrook *Birm* 98-99. *PO Box 199, Bukura, Kenya* Tel (00254) (333) 20038 Fax 20412

ANDERS, Mrs Erika Gertrud. b 45. ACT 88 St Jo Coll Nottm 99. **d** 92 **p** 02. C Proserpine St Paul Australia 92; C Hamburg *Eur* 99-07; Asst Chapl from 07. *Niendorfer Kirchenweg 5C, 22459 Hamburg, Germany* Tel (0049) (40) 582850 Fax 582841 Mobile 162-700 0404 E-mail erika.anders@fco.gov.uk

ANDERS, Jonathan Cyril. b 36. Wycliffe Hall Ox 69. **d** 71 **p** 72. C Prescot *Liv* 71-74; C-in-c 74-76; R Wavertree St Mary 76-81; V Aigburth 81-01; rtd 01; Perm to Offic *Liv* from 03. *3 Silverleigh, Liverpool L17 5BL* Tel 0151-728 9997

ANDERS, Roger John. b 38. Man Univ LLB61. NOC 91. **d** 94 **p** 95. NSM New Mills *Derby* 94-97; NSM Buxton w Burbage and King Sterndale 97-98; NSM Adderley, Ash, Calverhall, Ightfield etc *Lich* 98-03; R from 03. *The Rectory, Moreton Say, Market Drayton TF9 3RS* Tel and fax (01630) 638110 E-mail anders@u.genie.co.uk

ANDERSEN, Paul John. b 49. Univ of Alabama BA. Protestant Th Sem Virginia MDiv77. **d** 77 **p** 83. USA 77-82; Belize 82-84; Chapl Zagreb *Eur* 84-85; Chapl Belgrade 85-86; USA 86-89; India 89-91; Sierra Leone 92-93; Chapl Valletta *Eur* 94-96; Chapl Skopje 96-98; NSM Worcester St Luke USA 98-00; NSM S Barre Ch Ch 00-02; R Milford Trin Ch 02-06, *Christ Church Parish (Episcopal), PO Box 15, Christchurch VA 23031, USA* Tel (001) (804) 758 2006 E-mail paulandersen@earthlink.net

ANDERSON, Albert Geoffrey (Geoff). b 42. Ex Univ BA65 MA67. Qu Coll Birm. **d** 75 **p** 76. C Helsby and Ince *Ches* 75-77; C Helsby and Dunham-on-the-Hill 77-78; TV Gleadless *Sheff* 78-85; V Thorpe Hesley 85-92; R Ribbesford w Bewdley and Dowles *Worc* 92-03; rtd 03. *2 Waterworks Road, Worcester WR1 3EX* Tel (01905) 612634 E-mail ga@priest.com

ANDERSON, Alice Calder. b 50. Moray Ho Coll of Educn DipEd76. Local Minl Tr Course 90. **d** 93 **p** 95. NSM Edin St Barn from 93. *20 Pentland Road, Bonnyrigg EH19 2LG* Tel 0131-654 0506

ANDERSON, Mrs Ann. b 57. Cranmer Hall Dur 01. **d** 03 **p** 04. C Chester le Street *Dur* 03-07; P-in-c Hetton-Lyons w Eppleton 07; R from 07. *The Rectory, Houghton Road, Hetton-le-Hole, Houghton le Spring DH5 9PH* Tel 0191-517 3102

ANDERSON, Preb Brian Arthur. b 42. Sarum Th Coll 75. **d** 78 **p** 79. C Plymouth St Jas Ham *Ex* 78-80; Org Sec CECS *B & W, Ex* and *Truro* 80-89; TV Saltash *Truro* 89-94; RD E Wivelshire 91-94; P-in-c St Breoke and Egloshayle 94-96; R 96-02; RD Trigg Minor and Bodmin 95-02; P-in-c Torpoint from 02; P-in-c Antony w Sheviock from 02; Preb St Endellion from 99. *The Rectory, Sheviock, Torpoint PL11 3EH* Tel (01503) 230622 Mobile 07710-231219 E-mail sheriock@tiscali.co.uk

ANDERSON, Brian Glaister. b 35. K Coll Lon 57. **d** 79 **p** 79. Chapl St Fran Sch Hooke 79; C Croydon St Jo *Cant* 80-83; Dep Chapl HM Youth Cust Cen Glen Parva 83-84; Chapl HM YOI Hewell Grange 84-89; Chapl HM Rem Cen Brockhill 84-89; Chapl HM Pris Parkhurst 89-96; rtd 96. *28 Chase Farm Close, Waltham Chase, Southampton SO32 2UD* Tel (01489) 896880 Mobile 07900-272006 E-mail brianders@btinternet.com

ANDERSON, David. b 19. Selw Coll Cam BA41 MA45. Wycliffe Hall Ox 47. **d** 49 **p** 50. C Bishopwearmouth St Gabr *Dur* 49-52; Tutor St Aid Birkenhead 52-56; Chapl Heswall Nautical Sch 52-53; Warden Melville Hall Ibadan Nigeria 56-58; Prin Immanuel Coll Ibadan 58-62; Can Ibadan 58-62; Prin Wycliffe Hall Ox 62-69; Sen Lect Wall Hall Coll Aldenham 70-74; Prin Lect 74-84; rtd 84; Perm to Offic *Dur* 84-02. *16 Manor Park, Borrowash, Derby DE72 3LP* Tel (01332) 664426

ANDERSON, David Graham. b 33. MICE MIStructE. St Mich Coll Llan 85. **d** 88 **p** 89. C Llanishen and Lisvane *Llan* 88-90; C Fazeley *Lich* 90-94; Perm to Offic *Heref* 96-01 and *Llan* 01-08. *6 Dorchester Way, Belmont, Hereford HR2 7ZP* Tel (01432) 272974

ANDERSON, David Lee. b 75. Westmr Coll Ox BTh96. Ripon Coll Cuddesdon MTh98. **d** 98 **p** 99. C Balderton *S'well* 98-02; V Harworth 02-07; P-in-c Longridge *Blackb* from 07. *The Vicarage, Church Street, Longridge, Preston PR3 3WA* Tel (01772) 783281 E-mail vicaroflongridge@aol.com

ANDERSON, David Richard. b 58. Lanc Univ BEd79. EAMTC 96. **d** 99 **p** 00. C N Walsham w Antingham *Nor* 99-02; R Stalham, E Ruston, Brunstead, Sutton and Ingham 02-06; P-in-c Smallburgh w Dilham w Honing and Crostwight 05-06; TV Wrexham *St As* from 06; Chapl St Jos High Sch Wrexham from 06. *All Saints' Vicarage, 55 Princess Street, Wrexham LL13 7US* Tel (01978) 266145 E-mail revdanderson@bigfoot.com

ANDERSON, Digby Carter. b 44. Reading Univ BA Brunel Univ MPhil73 PhD77. **d** 85 **p** 86. NSM Luton St Sav *St Alb* from 85. *17 Hardwick Place, Woburn Sands, Milton Keynes MK17 8QQ* Tel (01908) 584526

ANDERSON, Donald Whimbey. b 31. Trin Coll Toronto BA54 MA58 LTh57 STB57 ThD71. **d** 56 **p** 57. Canada 57-59, 75-88 and from 96; Japan 59-74; Philippines 74-75; Dir Ecum Affairs ACC 88-96; rtd 96. *The Centre on the Religious Life, PO Box 19, Little Britain ON K0M 2C0, Canada* Tel and fax (001) (705) 786 3330 E-mail dwa@nexicom.net

ANDERSON, Geoff. See ANDERSON, Albert Geoffrey

ANDERSON, Mrs Gillian Ann. b 52. NTMTC 05. **d** 08 **p** 09. NSM Lambourne w Abridge and Stapleford Abbotts *Chelmsf* 08-09; NSM Loughton St Jo from 09. *33 Tower Road, Epping CM16 5EN* Tel (01992) 561002 Mobile 07954-429153 E-mail gillanderson@ntlworld.com

ANDERSON, Gordon Stuart. b 49. St Jo Coll Nottm. **d** 82 **p** 83. C Hattersley *Ches* 82-86; C Dagenham *Chelmsf* 86-91; TV Mildenhall *St E* 91-01; V Southminster *Chelmsf* from 01; P-in-c Steeple from 08; RD Maldon and Dengie from 06. *The Vicarage, Burnham Road, Southminster CM0 7ES* Tel (01621) 772300 Mobile 07759-550990 E-mail gandr42@btinternet.com

ANDERSON, Graeme Edgar. b 59. Poly of Wales BSc82. St Jo Coll Nottm MTh02. **d** 02 **p** 03. C Brislington St Luke *Bris* 02-05; C Galleywood Common *Chelmsf* 05-09; P-in-c Radcliffe-on-Trent and Shelford *S'well* from 09. *The Vicarage, 2 Vicarage Lane, Radcliffe-on-Trent, Nottingham NG12 2FB* Tel 0115-933 2203 Mobile 07840-926736 E-mail graemeandjudy@gmail.com

ANDERSON, Hugh Richard Oswald. b 35. Roch Th Coll 68. **d** 70 **p** 71. C Minehead *B & W* 70-76; C Darley w S Darley *Derby* 76-80; R Hasland 80-94; V Temple Normanton 80-94; rtd 94; Perm to Offic *Derby* from 94. *32 Barry Road, Brimington, Chesterfield S43 1PX* Tel (01246) 551020

ANDERSON, James. b 36. Magd Coll Ox BA59 MA64 Leeds Univ MA00. **d** 02 **p** 03. NSM Holme and Seaton Ross Gp *York* 02-08; P-in-c The Beacon from 08. *The Rectory, Rudston Road, Burton Agnes, Driffield YO25 4NE* Tel (01262) 490217

ANDERSON, James Frederick Wale. b 34. G&C Coll Cam BA58 MA62. Cuddesdon Coll 60. **d** 62 **p** 63. C Leagrave *St Alb* 62-65; C Eastleigh *Win* 65-70; R Sherfield-on-Loddon 70-86; P-in-c Stratfield Saye w Hartley Wespall 75-86; R Sherfield-on-Loddon and Stratfield Saye etc 86-87; R Newton Valence, Selborne and E Tisted w Colemore 87-99; rtd 99; Chapl Surrey Hants Borders NHS Trust 01-04; Hon C Farnham *Guildf* 01-04. *1 Potter's Gate, Farnham GU9 7EJ* Tel (01252) 710728

ANDERSON, Canon James Raffan. b 33. FRSA90 Edin Univ MA54. Edin Th Coll 56. **d** 58 **p** 59. Chapl St Andr Cathl 58-59; Prec St Andr Cathl 59-62; CF (TA) 59-67; Chapl Aber Univ 60-62; Chapl Glas Univ 62-69; Chapl Lucton Sch 69-71; Chapl Barnard Castle Sch 71-74; Asst Dir of Educn *Blackb* 74-78; P-in-c Whitechapel 74-78; Bp's Officer for Miss Cov 78-87; Hon Can Cov Cathl 83-87; Miss Sec Gen Syn Bd for Miss and Unity 87-92; rtd 92; Perm to Offic *Blackb* from 98. *Eccles Moss Farm, Bleasdale Road, Whitechapel, Preston PR3 2ER* Tel and fax (01995) 641280 E-mail jamesanders@onetel.com

ANDERSON (née FLAHERTY), Mrs Jane Venitia. b 68. Oak Hill Th Coll BA92. **d** 93 **p** 94. C Timperley *Ches* 93-97; C Cheshunt *St Alb* 97-99; P-in-c N Springfield *Chelmsf* from 99. *The Vicarage, St Augustine's Way, Beardsley Drive, Springfield, Chelmsford CM1 6GX* Tel (01245) 466160 E-mail revjaney@aol.com

ANDERSON, Jeffrey. b 56. Cranmer Hall Dur. **d** 07 **p** 08. C Chester le Street *Dur* from 07. *The Rectory, Houghton Road, Hetton-le-Hole, Houghton le Spring DH5 9PH* Tel 0191-517 3102

ANDERSON, Jeremy. See ANDERSON, Brian Glaister

ANDERSON, Jeremy Dudgeon. b 41. Edin Univ BSc63. Trin Coll Bris 75. **d** 77 **p** 78. C Bitterne *Win* 77-81; TV Wexcombe *Sarum* 81-91; Evang Enabler (Reading Deanery) *Ox* 91-96; V Epsom Common Ch Ch *Guildf* 96-00; C Kinson *Sarum* 00-06; rtd 06. *The Croft, Church Road, Crowborough TN6 1ED* Tel (01892) 655825

ANDERSON, Mrs Joanna Elisabeth. b 53. St Andr Univ MTheol75. EMMTC 85. **d** 88 **p** 95. Par Dn Crosby *Linc* 88-92; Warden Iona Community *Arg* 92-95; R S Trin Broads *Nor* 95-02; Dir Body, Mind, Spirit Project 02-05; R Stiffkey and Bale *Nor* 05-09; C Hexham *Newc* from 09. *29 Robson Drive, Beaumont Park, Hexham NE46 2HZ* Tel (01434) 604935 E-mail revanderson@aol.com

ANDERSON, John Robert. b 75. QUB BD96 TCD MPhil98. CITC 96. **d** 98 **p** 99. C Magherafelt *Arm* 98-02; C Ballymena w Ballyclug *Conn* 02-05; I Billy w Derrykeighan from 05; Bp's Dom Chapl from 08. *158 Castlecat Road, Derrykeighan, Ballymoney BT53 8AP* Tel (028) 2074 1241

ANDERSON, Canon Keith Bernard. b 36. Qu Coll Cam BA60 MA64. Tyndale Hall Bris 60. **d** 62 **p** 63. C Bootle St Leon *Liv* 62-65; Lect Can Warner Mem Coll Buye Burundi 66-73; Lect Mweya United Th Sem 74; Dir Studies Dio Nakuru Kenya 74-77; Dir RE Dio Mt Kenya E 78-83; Hon Can Mt Kenya E from 82; P-in-c Newnham and Doddington w Wychling *Cant* 83-88; Chapl Cannes w Grasse *Eur* 88-94; Dir and Chapl Mulberry Ho High Ongar 94-95; TV Horley *S'wark* 96-01; rtd 01; Perm to Offic *S'wark* 01-05 and *Chich* from 01. *93 Rusper Road, Horsham RH12 4BJ* Tel (01403) 262185 E-mail kb.anderson@virgin.net

ANDERSON, Canon Keith Edward. b 42. Fitzw Coll Cam BA77 MA83 MRCS83. Ridley Hall Cam 74. **d** 77 **p** 78. C Goodmayes All SS *Chelmsf* 77-80; Chapl Coll of SS Mark and Jo Plymouth *Ex* 80-87; RD Plymouth Moorside 83-86; V Northampton H

Sepulchre w St Andr and St Lawr *Pet* 87-98; RD Northn 92-98; Adv for Min Willesden *Lon* 98-03; Can Res Win Cathl and Adv for Ord Min Development *Win* 03-08; rtd 08. *49 Chaundler Road, Winchester SO23 7HW* Tel (01962) 853429
E-mail keith.anderson20@btinternet.com

ANDERSON, Kenneth. b 38. G&C Coll Cam BA62 MA66. Westcott Ho Cam 63. **d** 65 **p** 66. C Nor St Steph 65-68; Chapl Norfolk and Nor Hosp 65-68; C Wareham w Arne *Sarum* 68-71; Chapl Sherborne Sch 71-83; Zimbabwe 83-94; Chapl Trevelyan and Van Mildert Coll *Dur* 95-04; Dioc Voc Adv 95-04; rtd 04. *39 Hallgarth Street, Durham DH1 3AT* Tel 0191-383 0628 *or* 374 3770

ANDERSON, Martin Edward. b 73. Humberside Univ BA95 St Jo Coll Dur BA02. Cranmer Hall Dur 99. **d** 02 **p** 03. C Gt Aycliffe and Chilton *Dur* 02-05; TV Sunderland 05-07; Chapl Sunderland Minster from 07. *21 Thornhill Terrace, Sunderland SR2 7JL* Tel 0191-567 2231
E-mail martin.anderson@durham.anglican.org

ANDERSON, Michael. b 38. **d** 06 **p** 07. NSM Dungeon Hill and The Caundles w Folke and Holwell *Sarum* 06-07; NSM Vale of White Hart 07-09; Lic to RD Sherborne from 09. *Tiley House, Middlemarsh, Sherborne DT9 5QL* Tel (01300) 345375 Mobile 07966-664319 E-mail michael@tileyhouse.freeserve.co.uk

ANDERSON, Canon Michael Garland. b 42. Clifton Th Coll 62. **d** 66 **p** 67. C Fareham St Jo *Portsm* 66-69; C Worting *Win* 69-74; V Hordle 74-07; RD Lyndhurst 82-00; Hon Can Win Cathl 92-07; rtd 07. *20 Forestlake Avenue, Ringwood BH24 1QU* Tel (01425) 471490 E-mail canon.m.g.anderson@ukgateway.net

ANDERSON, Canon Michael John Austen. b 35. AKC60. **d** 66 **p** 67. C Southall Ch Redeemer *Lon* 66-69; C Hampstead Garden Suburb 69-73; V St Mimms St Giles 73-80; V The Brents and Davington w Oare and Luddenham *Cant* 80-86; V Margate All SS 86-00; Hon Can Cant Cathl 97-00; rtd 00; Perm to Offic *Cant* from 01. *Camwa Ash, Bull Lane, Boughton-under-Blean, Faversham ME13 9AH* Tel (01227) 752352 Mobile 07885-211863

ANDERSON, Nicholas Patrick. b 53. Lanc Univ BA87. Allen Hall 79. **d** 81 **p** 82. In RC Ch 81-89; C Gt Crosby St Faith *Liv* 89-92; C Walton-on-the-Hill 92-95; V Pemberton St Fran Kitt Green 95-04; V Rainhill from 04. *St Ann's Vicarage, View Road, Prescot L35 0LE* Tel 0151-426 4666

ANDERSON, Mrs Pearl Ann. b 46. St Andr Univ MA68 MCIPD74. Cant Sch of Min 90. **d** 93 **p** 00. Par Dn Epping St Jo *Chelmsf* 93-95; Adv to Coun for Soc Resp *Roch* and *Cant* 95-02; Asst Chief Exec Ch in Soc *Roch* and *Cant* 02-06; Hon C Biddenden and Smarden 00-06; rtd 06; Perm to Offic *Roch* from 95 and *Cant* from 06. *1 Gibbs Hill, Headcorn, Ashford TN27 9UD* Tel (01622) 890043 Mobile 07811-209448
E-mail pearlanderson@btinternet.com

ANDERSON, Peter John. b 44. Nottm Univ BA65 BA73 Ex Univ CertEd66. St Jo Coll Nottm. **d** 74 **p** 75. C Otley *Bradf* 74-77; TV Marfleet *York* 77-84; V Greasbrough *Sheff* 84-95; I Clonmel Union *C, C & R* 95-02; I Rathcooney Union 95-02; Chapl Cannes *Eur* 02-09; rtd 09. *100 route de la Colle, 06140 Tourrettes-sur-Loup, France* Tel (0033) (9) 50 41 68 40
E-mail pjhwander@yahoo.com

ANDERSON, Peter Scott. b 49. Nottm Univ BTh72 CertEd. Kelham Th Coll 68. **d** 74 **p** 75. C Shett St Cecilia Parson Cross 74-77; C Leytonstone St Marg w St Columba *Chelmsf* 77-81; P-in-c Forest Gate St Edm 81-89; V 89-90; P-in-c Plaistow 90-94; V Willesden Green St Andr and St Fran *Lon* 94-08, V Lewisham St Mary *S'wark* from 08. *Lewisham Vicarage, 48 Lewisham Park, London SE13 6QZ* Tel (020) 8690 2682 *or* 8690 1585
E-mail peter@scottanderson.freeserve.co.uk

ANDERSON, Philip Gregory. b 80. Keble Coll Ox BA01. Ripon Coll Cuddesdon BA04. **d** 05 **p** 06. C Prescot *Liv* 05-09; Chapl Liv Hope Univ from 09. *Liverpool Hope University, Hope Park, Liverpool L16 9JD* Tel 07773-582920 (mobile)
E-mail philipanderson@merseymail.com

ANDERSON, Canon Roderick Stephen. b 43. Cant Univ (NZ) BSc63 PhD67 New Coll Ox BA72. Wycliffe Hall Ox 70. **d** 73 **p** 74. C Bradf Cathl 73-75; C Allerton 76-78; V Cottingley 78-94; V Heaton St Barn 94-09; C from 09; RD Airedale 88-95; Hon Can Bradf Cathl from 94. *The Vicarage, Parsons Road, Heaton, Bradford BD9 4AY* Tel (01274) 496712 *or* 499354 Mobile 07900-675350 E-mail rod.anderson@bradford.anglican.org *or* rod@kiwityke.org.uk

ANDERSON, Canon Rosemary Ann. b 36. Ex Univ BA59. NOC 83. **dss** 86 **d** 87 **p** 94. Oldham St Paul *Man* 86-87; Hon Par Dn 87-89; Bp's Adv for Women's Min 88-99; Par Dn Roughtown 93-94; P-in-c 94-99; Hon Can Man Cathl 96-99; rtd 99; Perm to Offic *Man* 99-03. *11E Rhodes Hill, Lees, Oldham OL4 5EA* Tel 0161-620 1549

ANDERSON, Scott. *See* ANDERSON, Peter Scott

ANDERSON, Stephen George. b 54. Liv Univ BA75 ACIB. NOC 05. **d** 08 **p** 09. NSM Gt Shelford *Ely* from 08. *3 Dukes Meadow, Stapleford, Cambridge CB22 5BH* Tel (01223) 843859 Mobile 07889-003588 E-mail fr.stephen.anderson@googlemail.com

ANDERSON, Timothy George. b 59. Ealing Coll of HE BA82. Wycliffe Hall Ox 83. **d** 86 **p** 87. C Harold Wood *Chelmsf* 86-90; C Whitfield *Derby* 90-95; P-in-c Wolverhampton St Luke *Lich* 95-98; V 98-01; I Dundonald *D & D* from 01. *St Elizabeth's Rectory, 26 Ballyregan Road, Dundonald, Belfast BT16 1HY* Tel (028) 9048 3153 *or* 9048 2644
E-mail t.j.anderson@btinternet.com

ANDERSON, Timothy James Lane. b 59. Pemb Coll Ox BA80 MA90. St Jo Coll Nottm 89. **d** 93 **p** 94. C Reigate St Mary *S'wark* 93-95; Perm to Offic *S'well* from 95. *3 Dale Lane, Beeston, Nottingham NG9 4EA* Tel 0115-922 4773

ANDERSON-MacKENZIE, Janet Melanie. b 70. Edin Univ BSc93 PhD97 Trin Coll Bris MA07. WEMTC 01. **d** 04 **p** 05. C Woolavington w Cossington and Bawdrip *B & W* 04-05; C Wellington and Distr 05-08; P-in-c Box w Hazlebury and Ditteridge *Bris* from 08. *The Vicarage, Church Lane, Box, Corsham SN13 8NR* Tel and fax (01225) 744458
E-mail janet@anderson-mackenzie.co.uk

ANDERTON, David Edward. b 60. Leeds Poly BSc92. St Jo Coll Nottm 02. **d** 04 **p** 05. C Daybrook *S'well* 04-06; C Hucknall Torkard 06-09; TV Newark from 09. *3 Swinderby Close, Newark NG24 2SY* Tel (01636) 610485 Mobile 07751-269412
E-mail d.anderton1@btinternet.com

ANDERTON, David Ernest. b 36. CEng68 MIMechE68. **d** 00 **p** 01. OLM Eccleston Ch Ch *Liv* 00-06; rtd 06. *16 Croxteth Drive, Rainford, St Helens WA11 8JZ* Tel (01744) 637600 Mobile 07751-038014

ANDERTON, Mrs Elaine Irene. b 73. Sussex Univ BA96. WMMTC 06. **d** 09. C Smestow Vale *Lich* from 09. *39 Wrottesley Road, Tettenhall, Wolverhampton WV6 8SG* Tel (01902) 741663 *or* 758894

ANDERTON, Frederic Michael. b 31. Pemb Coll Cam MA57 IAAP. Westcott Ho Cam 64. **d** 66 **p** 67. C St John's Wood *Lon* 66-69; C All Hallows by the Tower etc 70-77; C St Giles Cripplegate w St Bart Moor Lane etc 77-82; C Zürich *Eur* 82-86; Perm to Offic *Lon* 94-00; rtd 96. *61 Brassey Road, Winchester SO22 6SB* Tel (01962) 856326 Fax 852851
E-mail robin.anderton@lineone.net

ANDERTON, Peter. b 45. Sarum & Wells Th Coll 80. **d** 82 **p** 83. C Adel *Ripon* 82-86; P-in-c Dacre w Hartwith 86-90; P-in-c Thornthwaite w Thruscross and Darley 88-90; V Dacre w Hartwith and Darley w Thornthwaite 90-91; V Owton Manor *Dur* 91-02; V Torrisholme *Blackb* 02-03; P-in-c Hunslet St Mary *Ripon* 03; V Hunslet w Cross Green 03-07; rtd 07. *133 Westbrooke Avenue, Hartlepool TS25 5HZ*
E-mail fr.peter@ntlworld.com

ANDREW, Brian. b 31. Oak Hill Th Coll 75. **d** 77 **p** 78. C Broadwater St Mary *Chich* 77-81; R Nettlebed w Bix and Highmore *Ox* 81-87; V Shenstone *Lich* 87-96; rtd 96; Perm to Offic *Ex* from 97 and *Derby* from 01. *18 Shaldon Drive, Littleover, Derby DE23 6HZ* Tel (01332) 768259

ANDREW, David Neil. b 62. Down Coll Cam BA83 MA87 PhD88. Ridley Hall Cam 93. **d** 93 **p** 94. C Heatherlands St Jo *Sarum* 93-98; P-in-c White Waltham w Shottesbrooke *Ox* from 98; P-in-c Waltham St Lawrence from 07. *The Vicarage, Waltham Road, White Waltham, Maidenhead SL6 3JD* Tel (01628) 822000

ANDREW, David Shore. b 39. Liv Univ BA61 CertEd62. OLM course 97. **d** 99 **p** 00. NSM Birkenshaw w Hunsworth *Wakef* from 99. *448 Oxford Road, Gomersal, Cleckheaton BD19 4LD* Tel (01274) 873339

ANDREW, Donald. b 35. Tyndale Hall Bris 63. **d** 66 **p** 67. C Croydon Ch Ch Broad Green *Cant* 66-69; C Ravenhead *Liv* 69-72; Scripture Union 72-77; V Rushen *S & M* 77-82; TR Heworth H Trin *York* 82-00; rtd 00; Perm to Offic *York* from 05. *60 Viking Road, Bridlington YO16 6TW* Tel (01262) 601273

ANDREW, Frank. b 17. St D Coll Lamp BA49 Ely Th Coll 50. **d** 51 **p** 52. C Howden *York* 51-55; V Mosbrough *Sheff* 55-59; C-in-c Greenhill CD 59-65; V Greenhill 65-69; R March St Jo *Ely* 69-77; R March St Mary 71-77; RD March 73-77; R Catworth Magna 77-83; R Covington 77-83; R Tilbrook 77-83; rtd 83; Perm to Offic *Chich* from 83. *11 Romney Close, Seaford BN25 3TR* Tel (01323) 897352

ANDREW, Jeremy Charles Edward. b 68. St Jo Coll Dur BA01. Cranmer Hall Dur 98. **d** 01. C Newquay *Truro* 01-04; P-in-c Perranzabuloe from 04; P-in-c Crantock 05-06; C Crantock w Cubert 06-07; P-in-c from 07. *The Vicarage, Cocks, Perranporth TR6 0AT* Tel (01872) 573375

ANDREW, John. b 60. St Mich Coll Llan 98. **d** 00 **p** 01. C Oystermouth *S & B* 00-06; V Upper Wye 06-07; P-in-c Swansea St Nic 07-08; rtd 09. *13 Park Street, Mumbles, Swansea SA3 4DA* Tel (01792) 360408

ANDREW, Canon John Gerald Barton. b 31. OBE. Keble Coll Ox BA55 MA58 Cuttington Univ Coll Liberia Hon DD76 Kentucky Sem Hon DD76 Nashotah Ho Wisconsin Hon DD77 Gen Th Sem NY Hon DD96. Cuddesdon Coll 54. **d** 56 **p** 57. C Redcar *York* 56-59; C Rumson St Geo USA 59-60; Abp's Dom Chapl *York* 60-61; Abp's Dom Chapl *Cant* 61-65; Abp's Sen Chapl 65-69; Six Preacher Cant Cathl 67-72; V Preston St Jo

Blackb 69-72; RD Preston 70-72; R New York St Thos USA 72-96; rtd 96; Perm to Offic *B & W* 97-99. *414 East 52nd Street, New York NY 10022-6458, USA* Tel (001) (212) 355 0064

ANDREW, Jonathan William. b 50. Univ Coll Ox MA78 FCA80. Ripon Coll Cuddesdon 02. **d** 04 **p** 05. NSM Hersham *Guildf* from 04. *Orchard, 6 Westacres, Esher KT10 9JE* Tel (01372) 479776 Mobile 07968-765188
E-mail curate.stpeters@btinternet.com

ANDREW, Michael Paul. b 51. Leic Univ CertEd73. Chich Th Coll 80. **d** 83 **p** 84. C Par *Truro* 83-86; Hon Chapl Miss to Seamen 86; P-in-c Salford Ordsall St Clem *Man* 86-91; P-in-c Hammersmith St Jo *Lon* 91-04; Perm to Offic *Ex* from 06. *8 East Park Avenue, Plymouth PL4 6PF* Tel 07515-472547 (mobile)
E-mail paul@dunvykryn.go-plus.net

ANDREW, Paul Roland. b 70. Oak Hill Th Coll BA06. **d** 06 **p** 07. C Plymouth Em, St Paul Efford and St Aug *Ex* from 06. *10 Venn Crescent, Plymouth PL3 5PJ* Tel (01752) 299264
E-mail paulosandrews@blueyonder.co.uk

ANDREW, Philip John. b 62. Nottm Univ BSc84. St Jo Coll Nottm MTh02. **d** 02 **p** 03. C Reading Greyfriars *Ox* 02-06; V Reigate St Mary S'*work* from 06. *St Mary's Vicarage, 76 Church Street, Reigate RH2 0SP* Tel (01737) 242973
E-mail phil.andrew@tiscali.co.uk

ANDREW, Sydney William. b 55. Cranmer Hall Dur 82. **d** 85 **p** 86. C Horncastle w Low Toynton *Linc* 85-88; V Worlaby 88-93; V Bonby 88-93; V Elsham 88-93; rtd 93; Lic to Offic *Linc* 93-95; Hon C Brocklesby Park 95-04; Hon C Croxton 96-04; Hon C Caistor Gp from 04. *10 Bentley Lane, Grasby, Barnetby DN38 6AW* Tel (01652) 628586
E-mail bridget.revdoc@clara.co.uk

ANDREW, Canon William Hugh. b 32. Selw Coll Cam BA56 MA60. Ridley Hall Cam 56. **d** 58 **p** 59. C Woking St Mary *Guildf* 58-61; C Farnborough 61-64; V Gatten St Paul *Portsm* 64-71; R Weymouth St Mary *Sarum* 71-76; V Heatherlands St Jo 76-82; Can and Preb Sarum Cathl 81-86; R Alderbury and W Grimstead 82-86; Perm to Offic *Bris* 86-88; Communications Dir Bible Soc 86-94; Communications Consultant 94-97; Hon C The Lydiards *Bris* 88-94; C W Swindon and the Lydiards 94-96; Hon C 96-98; rtd 96; Perm to Offic *Win* from 98. *31 Charnock Close, Hordle, Lymington SO41 0GU* Tel (01425) 627220

ANDREWES, Nicholas John. b 64. Southn Univ BA87 La Sainte Union Coll PGCE88. Cranmer Hall Dur BTh93. **d** 96 **p** 97. C Dovecot *Liv* 96-00; TV Pendleton *Man* 00-03; P-in-c Lower Crumpsall w Cheetham St Mark from 03. *26 Saltire Gardens, Salford M7 4BG* Tel and fax 0161-792 3123
E-mail nick.andrewes@virgin.net

ANDREWES UTHWATT, Henry. b 25. Jes Coll Cam BA49 MA51. Wells Th Coll 49. **d** 51 **p** 52. C Fareham H Trin *Portsm* 51-55; C Haslemere *Guildf* 55-59; C Wimbledon S'*work* 59-61; V W Wimbledon Ch 61-73; V Yeovil St Jo w Preston Plucknett *B & W* 73-76; TR Yeovil 76-82; V Burrington and Churchill 82-90; RD Locking 87-90; rtd 90; Perm to Offic *B & W* from 90; Chapl Partis Coll Bath 91-08; Chapl Bath and West Community NHS Trust from 91. *1 Glencairn Court, Bath BA2 4HB* Tel (01225) 482220

ANDREWS, Anthony Brian. b 33. Lon Univ BA54 AKC58. Coll of Resurr Mirfield 56. **d** 58 **p** 59. C Haggerston St Columba *Lon* 58-60; C N Hammersmith St Kath 60-63; V Goldthorpe *Sheff* 63-74; V Notting Hill St Mich and Ch Ch *Lon* from 74. *St Michael's Vicarage, 35 St Lawrence Terrace, London W10 5SR* Tel (020) 8969 0776 Fax 8969 0805
E-mail a.b.a@btinternet.com *or* archangel@supanet.com

ANDREWS, Anthony Frederick. b 25. K Coll Lon 54. **d** 55 **p** 56. C Kentish Town St Jo *Lon* 55-58; C Belmont 58-60; R Evershot, Frome St Quinton, Melbury Bubb etc *Sarum* 60-66; CF 66-69; C Bridgwater St Mary w Chilton Trinity *B & W* 69-70; R Cossington 70-73; C Highworth w Sevenhampton and Inglesham etc *Bris* 75-84; P-in-c Bishopstone w Hinton Parva 84-88; rtd 88. *Burford House, Highworth, Swindon SN6 7AD* Tel (01793) 762796

ANDREWS, Anthony John. b 35. S'work Ord Course 75. **d** 80 **p** 81. NSM Cheam S'*work* 80-83; C Epsom St Martin *Guildf* 83-86; V Barton *Portsm* 86-89; Chapl Northwick Park and St Mark's NHS Trust Harrow 90-98; C Regent's Park St Mark *Lon* 98-00; rtd 00; Perm to Offic *Lon* from 00. *112 Albury Drive, Pinner HA5 3RG*

ANDREWS, Benjamin. b 75. St Steph Ho Ox 97. **d** 00 **p** 01. C Whitchurch *Llan* 00-03; C Newton Nottage 03-05; C Cardiff St Mary and St Steph w St Dyfrig etc from 05. *St Paul's Vicarage, Llanmaes Street, Cardiff CF11 7LR* Tel (029) 2022 8707 E-mail frbenandrews@aol.com

ANDREWS, Canon Brian Keith. b 39. Keble Coll Ox BA62 MA69. Coll of Resurr Mirfield 62. **d** 64 **p** 65. C Is of Dogs Ch Ch and St Jo w St Luke *Lon* 64-68; C Hemel Hempstead *St Alb* 68-71; TV 71-79; V Abbots Langley 79-05; RD Watford 88-94; Hon Can St Alb 94-05; rtd 05. *High Pleck, Littleworth, Amberley, Stroud GL5 5AG* Tel (01453) 873068

ANDREWS, Canon Christopher Paul. b 47. Fitzw Coll Cam BA70 MA73. Westcott Ho Cam 69. **d** 72 **p** 73. C Croydon St Jo

Cant 72-75; C Gosforth All SS *Newc* 75-79; TV Newc Epiphany 80-87; RD Newc Cen 82-87; V Alnwick and Chapl Alnwick Infirmary 87-96; R Grantham *Linc* from 96; RD Grantham from 09; Can and Preb Linc Cathl from 04; Chapl United Lincs Hosps NHS Trust 99-01. *The Rectory, 4 Church Street, Grantham NG31 6RR* Tel (01476) 563710 *or* 572932
E-mail chris@stwulframs.com
or chris-p-andrews@hotmail.com

ANDREWS, Clive Frederick. b 43. St Jo Coll Nottm 81. **d** 83 **p** 84. C Leic St Jas 83-86; Ind Chapl 86-90; Hon TV Melton Gt Framland 89-90; TV Clifton S'*well* 90-92; P-in-c Gamston w Eaton and W Drayton 92-94; R 94-08; P-in-c Elkesley w Bothamsall 92-08; Chapl Bramcote Sch Notts 92-08; rtd 08. *13 Church Close, Louth LN11 9LR* Tel (01507) 600293
E-mail cliveand@waitrose.com

ANDREWS, Edward Robert. b 33. Brasted Th Coll 60 St Mich Coll Llan 62. **d** 64 **p** 65. C Kingswinford St Mary *Lich* 64-69; Chapl RAF 69-88; R St Just-in-Roseland w Philleigh *Truro* 88-99; rtd 99; Perm to Offic *Ex* from 00. *2 Langale, Gunsdown Villas, Station Road, South Molton EX36 3EA* Tel (01769) 572386

ANDREWS, Frances. b 24. EMMTC 73. **dss** 78 **d** 87 **p** 94. Porchester S'*well* 78-86; Asst Chapl Nottm City Hosp 86-88; Hon C Gedling S'*well* 88-92; NSM Epperstone 92-95; NSM Gonalston 92-95; NSM Oxton 92-95; rtd 95; Perm to Offic S'*well* 95-05. *Address temp unknown*

ANDREWS, Preb John Colin. b 47. Open Univ BA93. Sarum & Wells Th Coll 78. **d** 80 **p** 81. C Burnham *B & W* 80-84; V Williton 84-92; P-in-c Ashwick w Oakhill and Binegar 92-02; Dioc Communications Officer from 92; TV Yatton Moor from 02; Preb Wells Cathl from 04. *Cherry Tree House, Ham Lane, Kingston Seymour, Clevedon BS21 6XE* Tel (01934) 830208
E-mail john.andrews@bathwells.anglican.org

ANDREWS, Preb John Douglas. b 19. Keble Coll Ox BA39 MA44. Chich Th Coll 40. **d** 42 **p** 43. C S Bermondsey St Aug S'*wark* 42-44; C Lambeth St Jo w All SS 44-46; C Towcester w Easton Neston *Pet* 46-50; C Shrewsbury H Cross *Lich* 50-52; V Ettingshall 52-59; V Walsall St Andr 59-68; V Penkhull 68-80; P-in-c Ellenhall w Ranton 80-86; P-in-c Chebsey 80-86; Preb Lich Cathl 81-86; rtd 86; Perm to Offic *Heref* and *Lich* 86-01; York from 01. *28 Dulverton Hall, Esplanade, Scarborough YO11 2AR* Tel (01723) 340128

ANDREWS, John Elfric. b 35. Ex Coll Ox BA59 MA63. Wycliffe Hall Ox 59. **d** 61 **p** 62. C Pittville All SS *Glouc* 61-66; Cand Sec Lon City Miss 66-92; Lic to Offic S'*wark* 66-92; R Kingham w Churchill, Daylesford and Sarsden *Ox* 92-99; rtd 99; Perm to Offic *St E* from 01. *4 St George's Road, Felixstowe IP11 9PL* Tel (01394) 283557 E-mail john.andrew@care4free.net

ANDREWS, John Francis. b 34. Jes Coll Cam BA58 MA62. S'wark Ord Course 78. **d** 81 **p** 82. NSM Upper Norwood All SS S'*wark* 81-87; NSM Dulwich St Barn 89-92; NSM S Dulwich St Steph 92-95; Perm to Offic S'*wark* 95-01 and 01-07. *1 Kennington Square, Wareham BH20 4JR* Tel (01929) 555311

ANDREWS, John George William. b 42. Qu Coll Birm 65. **d** 68 **p** 69. C Smethwick St Matt w St Chad *Birm* 68-71; CF 71-97; P-in-c Lyme Regis *Sarum* 97-98; TV Golden Cap Team 98-03; rtd 03. *North Gate House, Stapleton Lane, Ashburton, Newton Abbot TQ13 7AE*

ANDREWS, John Robert. b 42. Nottm Coll of Educn CertEd63 FRSA92 FCMI92. **d** 04 **p** 05. OLM Farewell *Lich* from 04. *1 Chaseley Gardens, Burntwood WS7 9DJ* Tel (01543) 674354 Mobile 07711-246656
E-mail johnrobert.andrews@btinternet.com

ANDREWS, Judith Marie. b 47. Avery Hill Coll CertEd68. **d** 00 **p** 01. OLM Wilford Peninsula *St E* 00-08; TV from 08. *Hillside, Tower Hill, Hollesley, Woodbridge IP12 3QX* Tel (01394) 411642
E-mail judith.andrews@btopenworld.com

ANDREWS, Keith. b 47. St Mich Coll Llan 79. **d** 81 **p** 82. C Penarth w Lavernock *Llan* 81-85; V Nantymoel w Wyndham 85-91; RD Bridgend 89-93; R Coychurch w Llangan and St Mary Hill 91-98; V Caerau St Cynfelin from 98. *The Vicarage, Cymmer Road, Caerau, Maesteg CF34 0YR* Tel (01656) 736500

ANDREWS, Morey Alisdair Christopher. b 66. Leic Poly BSc91 MRICS91. St Jo Coll Nottm MA99. **d** 99 **p** 00. C Yate New Town *Bris* 99-02; C Downend 02-06; V Eynsham and Cassington *Ox* from 06. *The Vicarage, 45 Acre End Street, Eynsham, Witney OX29 4PF* Tel (01865) 881323 *or* 881450
E-mail moreyandrews@onetel.com

ANDREWS, Paul Douglas. b 54. Univ of Wales (Abth) BLib76 PhD99. SAOMC. **d** 00 **p** 01. NSM Kempston and Biddenham *St Alb* 00-03; C Leighton Buzzard w Eggington, Hockliffe etc 03-05; TV Billington, Egginton, Hockliffe etc 06-08; P-in-c St Neots *Ely* from 08. *The Vicarage, Church Street, St Neots PE19 2BU* Tel (01480) 472297
E-mail p.d.andrews@btinternet.com

ANDREWS, Ms Penny. b 73. Humberside Univ BA94 Liv Univ MA05. St Jo Coll Nottm 06. **d** 08. C Much Woolton *Liv* from 08. *25 Linkside Road, Liverpool L25 9NX* Tel 0151-428 9458 Mobile 07522-472272 E-mail revpenny@gmail.com

ANDREWS, Peter Alwyne. b 44. Lon Univ BSc67. Westcott Ho Cam 70. **d** 73 **p** 74. C Barnoldswick w Bracewell *Bradf* 73-76; C Maltby *Sheff* 76-78; V Bradf St Oswald Chapel Green 78-85; V Hanwell St Thos *Lon* from 85. *St Thomas's Vicarage, 182 Boston Road, London W7 2AD* Tel (020) 8567 5280 Fax 8567 1061 E-mail thomashanwell@btinternet.com

ANDREWS, Peter Douglas. b 52. SEN72 SRN78. St Steph Ho Ox 86. **d** 88 **p** 89. C Perry Barr *Birm* 88-92; TV Swindon New Town *Bris* 92-98; V Streatham St Pet *S'wark* from 98. *St Peter's Vicarage, 113 Leigham Court Road, London SW16 2NS* Tel (020) 8769 2922 E-mail rpeterandrews@aol.com

ANDREWS, Raymond Cyril. b 50. SEITE 00. **d** 03 **p** 04. C E Dulwich St Jo *S'wark* 03-07; P-in-c S'wark St Geo w St Alphege and St Jude from 07. *St George's Vicarage, Manciple Street, London SE1 4LW* Tel (020) 7407 2796 Mobile 07930-695571 E-mail revrayandrews@aol.com

ANDREWS, Richard John. b 57. Bris Univ BA78 CertEd79. Ripon Coll Cuddesdon 82. **d** 84 **p** 85. C Kidderminster St Mary and All SS, Trimpley etc *Worc* 84-87; Chapl Derbyshire Coll of HE 87-89; Hon C Derby Cathl 87-89; V Chellaston 89-93; V Spondon 93-05; TR Dunstable *St Alb* from 05; RD Dunstable from 09. *The Rectory, 8 Furness Avenue, Dunstable LU6 3BN* Tel (01582) 703271 E-mail rector@dunstableparish.org.uk

ANDREWS, Robert. *See* ANDREWS, Edward Robert

ANDREYEV, Michael. b 62. Hatf Coll Dur BA85. Wycliffe Hall Ox BA93 MA03. **d** 96 **p** 97. C Surbiton Hill Ch Ch *S'wark* 96-01; NSM Stapenhill w Cauldwell *Derby* 02-03; P-in-c 03-06; V from 06. *3 Stapenhill Road, Burton-on-Trent DE15 9AF* Tel (01283) 530320 E-mail staff@st.peters.fsnet.co.uk

ANETTS, Roy. b 55. Qu Coll Birm 06. **d** 09. NSM Acocks Green *Birm* from 09. *99 Vibart Road, Birmingham B26 2AB* Tel 0121-786 1674 Mobile 07967-542237 E-mail snowyanetts@hotmail.com

ANGEL, Andrew Richard. b 67. St Pet Coll Ox BA89 Lon Inst of Educn PGCE90 Surrey Univ MA94 Cant Ch Ch Univ MA06. St Jo Coll Nottm PhD04. **d** 02 **p** 03. C Dartford Ch Ch *Roch* 02-05; Tutor SEITE from 05. *21 Grizedale Close, Rochester ME1 2UX* Tel (01634) 202889 E-mail revandyangel@hotmail.com

ANGEL, Gervais Thomas David. b 36. Ch Ch Ox BA59 MA62 Bris Univ MEd78 Lon Univ PGCE72. Wycliffe Hall Ox 57. **d** 61 **p** 62. C Aberystwyth St Mich *St D* 61-65; Tutor Clifton Th Coll 65-71; Dean of Studies Trin Coll Bris 71-81; Dir of Studies 81-90; Area Sec (W and SW) SAMS 90-92; NSM Stoke Gifford *Bris* 92-02; rtd 02; Perm to Offic *Bris* from 02. *82 Oak Close, Little Stoke, Bristol BS34 6RD* Tel (01454) 618081 Mobile 07967-441426 Fax 0117-904 8588 E-mail gervais.angel@blueyonder.co.uk

ANGEL, Robin Alan. b 41. St Mich Coll Llan. **d** 89 **p** 90. C Whitchurch *Llan* 89-94; V Aberpergwm and Blaengwrach 94-01; V Caerau w Ely 01-03; V Porth w Trealaw 03-06; rtd 06. *54 Mardy Crescent, Caerphilly CF83 1PU*

ANGELL, Miss Elizabeth Patricia. b 54. Univ of Wales (Ban) BA72. Trin Coll Bris BA08. **d** 08 **p** 09. C Syston *Leic* from 08. *St Hilda's Vicarage, 25 Ling Dale, East Goscote, Leicester LE7 3XW* Tel 0116-260 0470 E-mail elizabethangell49@btinternet.com

ANGELL, Geoffrey. b 63. St Jo Coll Nottm. **d** 01 **p** 02. C Daventry, Ashby St Ledgers, Braunston etc *Pet* 01-04; C Oakham, Hambleton, Egleton, Braunston and Brooke 04-07; P-in-c Barrowden and Wakerley w S Luffenham etc from 07. *The Rectory, 11 Church Lane, Barrowden, Oakham LE15 8ED* Tel (01572) 747192 E-mail revgeoff@artangells.com

ANGELO, Brother. *See* DEACON, Donald

ANGIER, Patrick John Mark. b 61. Leic Univ BSc83. Trin Coll Bris. **d** 03 **p** 04. C Stratford-upon-Avon, Luddington etc *Cov* 03-06; V Prestbury *Ches* from 06. *Meadowside, New Road, Prestbury, Macclesfield SK10 4HP* Tel (01625) 820246 Mobile 07971-923668 E-mail patrick.angier@btinternet.com

ANGLE, John Edwin George. b 42. Lon Bible Coll BD65 Liv Univ AdDipEd73 Univ of Wales MEd75. WEMTC 92. **d** 94 **p** 95. NSM Clevedon St Andr and Ch Ch *B & W* 94-97; NSM Worle 97-98; P-in-c Camelot Par 98-01; R 01-06; Warden of Readers Wells Adnry 02-05; rtd 06; Perm to Offic *B & W* from 06. *14 Farthing Combe, Axbridge BS26 2DR* Tel (01934) 733695 E-mail johnangle@btinternet.com

ANGOVE, Ms Helen Teresa. b 71. Bath Univ BEng93. Ripon Coll Cuddesdon BTh97. **d** 97 **p** 98. C Bridgwater St Mary, Chilton Trinity and Durleigh *B & W* 97-01; P-in-c Elstree *St Alb* 01-03; USA from 03. *Address temp unknown* E-mail htangove@yahoo.com

ANGUS, Canon Edward. b 39. Man Univ BA60. Qu Coll Birm. **d** 62 **p** 63. C Chorley St Geo *Blackb* 62-65; C S Shore H Trin 65-68; R Bretherton 68-75; V Altham w Clayton le Moors 76-90; V Preesall 90-04; RD Garstang 96-01; Hon Can Blackb Cathl 98-04; rtd 04; Perm to Offic *Blackb* from 04. *14 Lazenby Avenue, Fleetwood FY7 8QH* Tel (01253) 686817

ANI, Joel Osita. b 72. Qu Coll Birm BA08. **d** 08. C Telford Park *S'wark* 08-09; C Clapham Park All SS from 09. *6 Blenheim Gardens, London SW2 5DB* Tel (020) 8674 1889 Mobile 07903-234444 E-mail joel_ani123@yahoo.com

ANITA, Sister. *See* COOK, Sister Anita Isabel

ANKER, Malcolm. b 39. Univ of Wales BA61. Bps' Coll Cheshunt 61. **d** 63 **p** 64. C Marfleet *York* 63-66; C Cottingham 66-69; V Skirlaugh w Long Riston 69-74; V Elloughton and Brough w Brantingham 74-84; V Tadcaster 84-86; V Tadcaster w Newton Kyme 86-91; V Oatlands *Guildf* 91-05; rtd 05. *10 Pegasus Close, Haslemere GU27 3SZ* Tel (01428) 651630

ANKER-PETERSEN, Robert Brian. b 52. Aber Univ MTh88. Wycliffe Hall Ox BA79 MA88. **d** 93 **p** 94. C Perth St Ninian *St And* 93-96; Bp's Researcher on Ch's Min of Healing from 93; Dir Bield Retreat and Healing Cen from 93; Dioc Dir of Healing from 97. *Blackruthven House, Tibbermore, Perth PH1 1PY* Tel (01738) 583238 Fax 583828 E-mail robin@bieldatblackruthven.org.uk

ANKERS, Charles William (Bill). b 42. FIMI. NEOC 89. **d** 93 **p** 95. NSM York St Luke 93-95; C Kexby w Wilberfoss 95-98; Asst Chapl HM Pris Full Sutton 95-98; V Norton juxta Malton *York* from 98. *The Vicarage, 80 Langton Road, Norton, Malton YO17 9AE* Tel (01653) 692741

ANKETELL, Jeyarajan. b 41. Lon Univ BSc62 PhD67 MInstP. Coll of Resurr Mirfield 69. **d** 73 **p** 74. Asst Chapl Newc Univ 73-75; Asst Chapl Lon Univ 75-77; Teacher 78-05; Lic to Offic *S'wark* 81-83; Chasetown High Sch 85-05; NSM Lich St Mary w St Mich 86-96; NSM Lich St Mich w St Mary and Wall from 96. *7 Wissage Lane, Lichfield WS13 6DQ* Tel (01543) 262211 E-mail jeyan.anketell@ntlworld.com

ANN-MARIA, Sister. *See* STUART, Sister Ann-Marie Lindsay

ANNANCY, Felix. b 62. **d** 87 **p** 88. C Fenton *Lich* 87-88; Ghana 88-98 and from 00; C Stalybridge St Paul *Ches* 98-00. *PO Box 329, Aksombo, Eastern Region, Ghana*

ANNAS, Canon Geoffrey Peter. b 53. Sarum & Wells Th Coll. **d** 83 **p** 84. C S'wark H Trin w St Matt 83-87; TV Walworth 87-94; Warden Pemb Coll Miss Walworth 87-94; V Southampton Thornhill St Chris *Win* from 94; Hon Can Win Cathl from 07. *St Christopher's Vicarage, 402 Hinkler Road, Southampton SO19 6DF* Tel (023) 8044 8537

ANNE, Sister. *See* PROUDLEY, Sister Anne

ANNIS, Herman North. b 28. Lich Th Coll 62. **d** 64 **p** 65. C Kilburn St Aug *Lon* 64-67; C Toxteth Park St Agnes *Liv* 67-70; V 70-82; V Hempton and Pudding Norton 82-84; P-in-c Sculthorpe w Dunton and Doughton 82-84; V Northampton H Trin *Pet* 84-95; rtd 95; Hon C Brighton St Bart *Chich* 95-99. *2 rue de la Liberté, 53500 St Denis-de-Gastines, France* Tel (0033) (2) 43 00 69 66

ANNIS, Jennifer Mary. b 49. Middx Univ BA95. Oak Hill Th Coll 92. **d** 95 **p** 97. NSM Digswell and Panshanger *St Alb* 95-97; NSM Codicote 97-98 and 99-00; Tanzania 98-99; Chapl ATC from 99. *Glanafon, Trecwn, Haverfordwest SA62 5XT* Tel (01348) 840563

ANNIS, Rodney James. b 43. Ex Univ BA75 MA79 PhD86. Ripon Coll Cuddesdon 75. **d** 76 **p** 77. C Brixham *Ex* 76-77; Asst Chapl Ex Univ 77-80; Chapl Ex Sch 77-80; C Boston *Linc* 80-84; Chapl Trin Hall Cam 84-87; Chapl St Edw K and Martyr Cam *Ely* 84-87; V Bush Hill Park St Steph *Lon* from 87. *St Stephen's Vicarage, 43A Village Road, Enfield EN1 2ET*

ANNON, Jacqueline. b 62. **d** 01 **p** 02. OLM Tooting All SS *S'wark* 01-04. *31 Hamilton Road, London SE27 9RZ* Tel (020) 8670 7441

ANNS, Pauline Mary. *See* HIGHAM, Canon Pauline Mary

ANSAH, Canon Kwesi Gyebi Ababio (George). b 54. Oak Hill Th Coll BTh97. Simon of Cyrene Th Inst 90. **d** 93 **p** 94. C Peckham St Mary Magd *S'wark* 93-96; V W Dulwich Em from 96; Hon Can Kumasi from 04. *Emmanuel Vicarage, 94 Clive Road, London SE21 8BU* Tel (020) 8670 2793 Mobile 07771-783693 E-mail gkansa@aol.com

ANSCOMBE, John Thomas. b 51. Ex Univ BA72. Cranmer Hall Dur. **d** 74 **p** 75. C Upper Armley *Ripon* 74-77; C Leeds St Geo 78-81; Exec Producer Scripture Union 81-96; Hon C Beckenham Ch Ch *Roch* from 96. *22 Hawthornedene Road, Bromley BR2 7DY* Tel and fax (020) 8462 4831 Mobile 07736-070160 E-mail john.anscombe@diocese-rochester.org

ANSELL, Antony Michael. b 49. St Jo Coll Nottm 78. **d** 80 **p** 81. C Harrow Weald St Mich *Lon* 80-84; Hon C Ches Square St Mich w St Phil 86-88; Hon C Mayfair Ch Ch 88-02; Perm to Offic *Win* from 02. *Fullerton Mill, Fullerton, Andover SP11 7LA* Tel (01264) 861076 Mobile 07855-943615 E-mail a.ansell@andover.co.uk

ANSELL, John Christopher. b 49. Sarum & Wells Th Coll 79. **d** 81 **p** 82. C Dartford St Alb *Roch* 81-84; C Leybourne and Larkfield 84-88; TV Mortlake w E Sheen *S'wark* 88-98; V Mitcham SS Pet and Paul from 98. *The Vicarage, 11 Vicarage Gardens, Mitcham CR4 3BL* Tel (020) 8646 0666 or 8648 1566 Mobile 07974-432562 E-mail jsansell@hotmail.com *or* mitchamparishchurch@uk2.net

ANSELL

ANSELL, Mrs Mandy. b 47. **d** 04 **p** 05. OLM Rockland St Mary w Hellington, Bramerton etc *Nor* from 04. *44 The Street, Rockland St Mary, Norwich NR14 7AH* Tel (01508) 538654 E-mail mandy.ansell44@gmail.com

ANSELL, Philip Harding. b 67. LMH Ox BA89 Rob Coll Cam BA92. Ridley Hall Cam. **d** 93 **p** 94. C Rainham w Wennington *Chelmsf* 93-97; C Rodbourne Cheney *Bris* 97-01; V Moseley St Agnes *Birm* from 01. *St Agnes' Vicarage, 5 Colmore Crescent, Birmingham B13 9SJ* Tel and fax 0121-449 0368

ANSELL, Stuart Adrian. b 59. Ripon Coll Cuddesdon 95. **d** 97 **p** 98. C Cheadle w Freehay *Lich* 97-00; P-in-c Silverdale 00-03; V from 03; V Keele from 03. *21 Pepper Street, Silverdale, Newcastle ST5 6QJ* Tel (01782) 616804

ANSELM, Brother. *See* SMYTH, Robert Andrew Laine

ANSON (née DRAX), Mrs Elizabeth Margaret. b 57. St Jo Coll Nottm 91. **d** 94 **p** 95. C Kimberworth *Sheff* 94-95; C Doncaster St Mary 95-97; rtd 97. *62 School Green Lane, Sheffield S10 4GR*

ANSON, Harry. b 35. FInstFF79. St Jo Coll Nottm 83. **d** 88 **p** 03. NSM Ayr *Glas* 88-93; Hon Chapl Miss to Seamen 91-93; rtd 94. *Fairvine, Balbinny, Aberlemno, Forfar DD8 3PF* Tel and fax (01307) 830446 Mobile 07790-470660 E-mail h2avro@hotmail.com

ANSTEY, Nigel John. b 55. Cranmer Hall Dur 84. **d** 87 **p** 88. C Plumstead St Jo w St Jas and St Paul *S'wark* 87-91; TV Ipswich St Fran *St E* 91-97; TV Walthamstow *Chelmsf* from 97. *St Luke's Vicarage, 17A Greenleaf Road, London E17 6QQ* Tel (020) 8520 2885 E-mail nigel.anstey@btinternet.com

ANSTICE, John Neville. b 39. Lon Univ BSc63. Cuddesdon Coll 69. **d** 71 **p** 72. C Stonebridge St Mich *Lon* 71-74; Chapl Woodbridge Sch 74-76; TV Droitwich *Worc* 76-80; P-in-c Salwarpe 76-79; Perm to Offic *Chich* from 80; rtd 99. *10 Selham Close, Crawley RH11 0EH* Tel (01293) 535654

ANTELL, Roger Howard. b 47. Lon Univ BD71 Warwick Univ MSc79 Ox Univ MTh99. Ripon Coll Cuddesdon 97. **d** 99 **p** 00. C Ashchurch *Glouc* 99-03; R Stoke Prior, Wychbold and Upton Warren *Worc* from 03. *The Rectory, Fish House Lane, Stoke Prior, Bromsgrove B60 4JT* Tel (01527) 832501 E-mail roger.antell@btinternet.com

ANTHAPURUSHA. b 53. Bangalore Univ BA77 Jnana Deepa Vidyapeeth Poona BPh80 Delhi Univ MA83 MPhil84 Serampore Th Coll BD87. Bp's Coll Calcutta 85. **d** 87 **p** 88. India 87-99; Bethany Chr Trust Edin 01-02; C Bistre *St As* from 02. *11 Bron yr Eglwys, Mynydd Isa, Mold CH7 6YQ* Tel (01352) 753465 E-mail apurusha@bronyreglwys.fsnet.co.uk

ANTHONY, Ian Charles. b 47. NW Ord Course 76. **d** 79 **p** 80. NSM Lt Lever *Man* from 79. *36 Meadow Close, Little Lever, Bolton BL3 1LG* Tel (01204) 791437

ANTHONY, Peter Benedict. b 79. Magd Coll Ox BA02 MA05. St Steph Ho Ox 03 Ven English Coll Rome 05. **d** 06 **p** 07. C Hendon St Mary and Ch Ch *Lon* 06-09; Jun Dean St Steph Ho Ox from 09. *St Stephen's House, 16 Marston Street, Oxford OX4 1JX* Tel (01865) 247874 Mobile 07949-005550 E-mail peterbanthony@hotmail.com

ANTHONY, Miss Sheila Margaret. b 52. Wycliffe Hall Ox BTh04. **d** 04 **p** 05. C Bideford, Northam, Westward Ho!, Appledore etc *Ex* 04-08; P-in-c Bluntisham cum Earith w Colne and Woodhurst *Ely* from 08; P-in-c Holywell w Needingworth from 08. *The Rectory, Rectory Road, Bluntisham, Huntingdon PE28 3LN* Tel (01487) 740456

ANTHONY MARY, Father. *See* HIRST, Anthony Melville

ANTOINE, Emma Louise. b 72. Newc Univ BA96. Westcott Ho Cam 02. **d** 05 **p** 06. C High Wycombe *Ox* 05-06; C Wokingham All SS 06-09. *The Rectory, 6 Edge Lane, Manchester M21 9JF* Tel 0161-881 3063 E-mail revemma@hotmail.co.uk

AOKO, Mrs Olushola Ibiwunmi. b 55. SEITE 03. **d** 06 **p** 07. C Bermondsey St Mary w St Olave, St Jo etc *S'wark* from 06. *22 Reverdy Road, London SE1 5QE* Tel (020) 7064 1250 Mobile 07896-337578 E-mail shol1012@yahoo.co.uk

AOTEAROA, Bishop of. *See* TUREI, The Most Revd William Brown

ap GWILYM, Gwynn. b 50. Univ of Wales (Ban) BA71 MA76. Wycliffe Hall Ox BA84 MA89 MPhil00. **d** 84 **p** 85. C Ynyscynhaearn w Penmorfa and Porthmadog *Ban* 84-86; R Penegoes and Darowen w Llanbryn-Mair 86-97; R Mallwyd w Cemais, Llanymawddwy, Darowen etc 97-02; P-in-c Penyfai *Llan* 02-05; P-in-c Cardiff Dewi Sant 05-07; Language Officer Ch in Wales from 07. *The Rectory, Llandough Hill, Llandough, Penarth CF64 2NA* Tel (029) 2071 0890

ap IORWERTH, Geraint. b 50. Univ of Wales (Cardiff) MPhil90 Open Univ BA78. Burgess Hall Lamp 69 Westmr Past Foundn 73 St Mich Coll Llan 73. **d** 74 **p** 75. C Holyhead w Rhoscolyn *Ban* 74-78; R Pennal w Corris and Esgairgeiliog from 78; Co-Founder and Ldr Order of Sancta Sophia from 87. *The Rectory, Pennal, Machynlleth SY20 9JS* Tel and fax (01654) 791216 E-mail apennal@ouvip.com

APPELBE, Canon Frederick Charles. b 52. CITC 87. **d** 87 **p** 88. C Waterford w Killea, Drumcannon and Dunhill *C & O* 87-90; C Taney *D & G* 90-92; I Rathmichael from 92; Can Ch Ch Cathl

Dublin from 02. *Rathmichael Rectory, Shankill, Co Dublin, Republic of Ireland* Tel (00353) (1) 282 2803 Fax 258 6080 Mobile 87-248 2410 E-mail rathmichael@dublin.anglican.org

APPLEBY, Anthony Robert Nightingale. b 40. K Coll Lon AKC62. St Boniface Warminster 62. **d** 63 **p** 64. C Cov St Mark 63-67; CF 67-95; R Dulverton and Brushford *B & W* 95-02; rtd 02. *9 Ashleigh Park, Bampton, Tiverton EX16 9LF* Tel (01398) 331122

APPLEBY, David. b 60. St Jo Coll Dur BA04. Cranmer Hall Dur 02. **d** 04 **p** 05. C W Acklam *York* 04-08; R Aylestone St Andr w St Jas *Leic* from 08. *9 Springfield Road, Leicester LE2 3BB* Tel 0116-270 8295

APPLEBY, Janet Elizabeth. b 58. Bris Univ BSc80 MSc81 Newc Poly BA90. Cranmer Hall Dur 01. **d** 03 **p** 04. C Newc H Cross 03-06; TV Willington from 06. *The Vicarage, Berwick Drive, Wallsend NE28 9ED* Tel 0191-262 7518 E-mail janet.appleby@dunelm.org.uk

APPLEBY, Miss Janet Mohr. b 32. Lon Univ TCert53 BA79 Sussex Univ MA(Ed)74. Chich Th Coll 90. **d** 91 **p** 95. NSM Rottingdean *Chich* 91-95; NSM Stantonbury and Willen *Ox* 95-02; Perm to Offic 02-07. *Address temp unknown*

APPLEBY, Ms Jennie. b 58. Southlands Coll Lon CertEd81. Cranmer Hall Dur 01. **d** 03 **p** 04. C Marton-in-Cleveland *York* 03-05; C Coatham and Dormanstown 05-08; R Emmaus Par Team *Leic* from 08. *The Rectory, 9 Springfield Road, Leicester LE2 3BB* Tel 0116-270 6097

APPLEBY, Mrs Melanie Jayne. b 65. RGN86. Ripon Coll Cuddesdon 01. **d** 03 **p** 04. C Reddish *Man* 03-06; TV Wythenshawe from 06. *William Temple Vicarage, Robinswood Road, Manchester M22 0BU* Tel 0161-437 3194 Mobile 07876-191572 E-mail melanieappleby@hotmail.com

APPLEFORD, Kenneth Henry. b 30. Portsm Dioc Tr Course 91. **d** 92. NSM Portsea St Mary *Portsm* 92-00; rtd 00. *124 Stride Avenue, Portsmouth PO3 6HN* Tel (023) 9281 4685

APPLEFORD, Canon Patrick Robert Norman. b 25. Trin Coll Cam BA49 MA54. Chich Th Coll 50. **d** 52 **p** 53. C Poplar All SS w St Frideswide *Lon* 52-58; Chapl Bps' Coll Cheshunt 58-61; Educn Sec USPG 61-66; Dean Lusaka 66-72; P-in-c Sutton St Nicholas w Sutton St Michael *Heref* 73-75; Dir of Educn *Chelmsf* 75-90; Can Chelmsf Cathl 78-90; rtd 90; Perm to Offic *Chelmsf* from 90. *35 Sowerberry Close, Chelmsford CM1 4YB* Tel (01245) 443508

APPLEGATE, The Ven John. b 56. Bris Univ BSc78. Trin Coll Bris PhD85. **d** 84 **p** 85. C Collyhurst *Man* 84-87; Asst Chapl Monsall Hosp 84-87; C Broughton St Jas w St Clem and St Matthias 87-94; R Broughton St Jo 94-96; TR Broughton 96-02; AD Salford 97-02; Research Fell and Lect Man Univ from 00; Bp's Adv Hosp Chapl 02-08; Adn Bolton 02-08; Dir SNWTP from 08. *University of Chester, Crab Lane, Warrington WA2 0DB* Tel (01925) 534373 E-mail snwtpprincipal@chester.ac.uk

APPLETON, Mrs Bonita. b 55. Man Univ MA08. St Jo Coll Nottm 91. **d** 93 **p** 94. C Camberley St Paul *Guildf* 93-96; TV Cove St Jo 96-03; Dioc Par Resources Officer from 03; NSM Knaphill w Brookwood from 06. *Diocesan House, Quarry Street, Guildford GU1 3XG* Tel (01483) 790330 E-mail bonnie.appleton@cofeguildford.org.uk

APPLETON, John Bearby. b 42. Linc Th Coll 74. **d** 76 **p** 77. C Selby Abbey *York* 76-79; C Epsom St Barn *Guildf* 79-82; V Linc All SS 82-94; rtd 02. *33 South End, Osmotherley, Northallerton DL6 3BN*

APPLETON, Canon Ronald Percival. b 15. St Pet Hall Ox BA36 MA40. Ridley Hall Cam 36. **d** 38 **p** 39. C Hunsingore w Cowthorpe *Ripon* 38-39; C High Harrogate Ch Ch 39-42; C Bromley SS Pet and Paul *Roch* 42-44; R Knockholt 44-53; V Bromley Common St Luke 53-62; V Winchcombe, Gretton, Sudeley Manor etc *Glouc* 62-86; RD Winchcombe 63-86; Hon Can Glouc Cathl 80-86; rtd 86; Perm to Offic *Glouc* 86-97; Perm to Offic *Worc* from 97. *1 Abbey Croft, Pershore WR10 1JQ* Tel (01386) 553023

APPLIN, David Edward. b 39. Oak Hill Th Coll 63. **d** 65 **p** 66. C Ox St Clem 65-69; C Felixstowe SS Pet and Paul *St E* 69-71; Lic to Offic *Win* 71-91; Travelling Sec Ruanda Miss 71-74; Home Sec 74-77; Gen Sec 77-81; Dir Overseas Personnel Dept TEAR Fund 82-87; Overseas Dir 87-92; Hon C Kempshott *Win* 91-92; R Awbridge w Sherfield English 92-97; Exec Dir Samaritan's Purse Internat from 95. *Flat 4, 25 Christchurch Road, St Cross, Winchester SO23 9SU* Tel (01962) 865678

APPS, Anthony Howard. b 22. Ch Coll Cam BA47 MA51. **d** 49 **p** 50. C Poplar All SS w St Frideswide *Lon* 49-55; V Mile End Old Town H Trin 55-66; V Myddleton Square St Mark 66-82; rtd 82; Perm to Offic *York* from 82. *18 Longworth Way, Guisborough TS14 6DG* Tel (01287) 637939

APPS, Bryan Gerald. b 37. Univ of Wales (Lamp) BA59 St Cath Coll Ox BA61 MA65. Wycliffe Hall Ox 59. **d** 61 **p** 62. C Southampton St Alb *Win* 61-65; C Andover w Foxcott 65-69; P-in-c Freemantle 69-72; R 73-78; V Pokesdown All SS 78-03; rtd 03; Hon C Bournemouth Town Cen *Win* from 03. *14 Bartlett*

18

Drive, Bournemouth BH7 7JT Tel (01202) 418360
E-mail bryanapps@talk21.com

APPS, David Ronald. b 34. Univ of Wales (Lamp) BA57. Sarum Th Coll 57. **d** 59 **p** 60. C Southbourne St Chris *Win* 59-62; C Weeke 62-67; V Alton All SS 67-80; V Charlestown *Truro* 80-97; Miss to Seamen 80-97; rtd 99. *12 Walnut Close, Exminster, Exeter EX6 8SZ* Tel (01392) 823672

APTED, Peter John. b 43. Middx Univ MA01. NTMTC 95. **d** 98 **p** 99. NSM Feltham *Lon* 98-01; TV Horsham *Chich* from 01. *St Leonard's Vicarage, Cambridge Road, Horsham RH13 5ED* Tel (01403) 266903 E-mail peter@revapted.freeserve.co.uk

APTHORP, The Ven Arthur Norman. b 24. Pemb Coll Cam BA47 MA50. Chich Th Coll 48. **d** 50 **p** 51. C Henfield *Chich* 50-52; C Hove All SS 52-56; R Narembeen Australia 57-60; R Boulder 60-66; R Northam 66-72; R Kalgoorlie and Boulder 72-78; Hon Can Perth 73-77 and 79-89; R Dianella 78-82; R Merredin 82-89; Adn of the Country (Perth) 82-87; Adn of the Goldfields 87-89; rtd 89. *67 Brookton Highway, Brookton WA 6306, Australia* Tel (0061) (8) 9642 1046

AQUILINA, Ivan Dominic. b 66. Univ of Malta BA95 BA97 Educn Division Malta PGCE96 Leeds Univ MA02. Coll of Resurr Mirfield 98. **d** 00 **p** 01. C Leam Lane *Dur* 00-01; C Jarrow 01-04; C St Marylebone All SS *Lon* 04-07; V Sevenoaks St Jo *Roch* from 07. *St John's Vicarage, 62 Quakers Hall Lane, Sevenoaks TN13 3TX* Tel (01732) 451710 Mobile 07947-139263 E-mail fatheraquilina@btinternet.com

AQUILON-ELMQVIST, Mrs Gunilla. **p** 91. Sweden 91-05; C Wexford w Ardcolm and Killurin *C & O* from 05. *The Rectory, Killinick, Co Wexford, Republic of Ireland* Tel (00353) (53) 915 8764 Fax 58277 Mobile 87-056 7595
E-mail gunilla.aquilon-elmqvist@svenskakyrkan.se

ARANZULLA, John Paul. b 71. G&C Coll Cam BA94 Oak Hill Th Coll BA01. K Coll Lon 01. **d** 04 **p** 05. C Muswell Hill St Jas w St Matt *Lon* 04-08; Crosslinks Italy from 08. *via Guibotti 14, 40134 Bologna, Italy*

ARBER, Gerald Kenneth Walter. b 37. Open Univ BA87. Oak Hill NSM Course 81. **d** 84 **p** 85. NSM Romford St Edw *Chelmsf* 84-95; NSM Cranham from 95. *5 Hill Grove, Romford RM1 4JP* Tel (01708) 750070

ARCH, Ian Michael. b 75. Univ Coll Dur MSc97 Peterho Cam BA02. Westcott Ho Cam 00. **d** 03 **p** 04. C Bromborough *Ches* 03-05; Chapl Ches Univ from 05. *85 Parkgate Road, Chester CH1 4AQ* Tel (01244) 372003 *or* 375444 Fax 398820
E-mail ian.arch@dunelm.org.uk

ARCHER, Alan Robert. b 38. AKC56. Lich Th Coll 65. **d** 68 **p** 69. C Lower Mitton *Worc* 68-71; C Foley Park 71-74; V Warndon 74-79; P-in-c Clifton upon Teme 79-81; P-in-c Lower Sapey 79-81; P-in-c The Shelsleys 79-81; V Malvern Wells and Wyche 81-83; TV Braunstone *Leic* 83-91; P-in-c Bemerton *Sarum* 91-93; Dioc Link Officer for ACUPA 92-94; rtd 03. *15 Summerfield Road, Stourport-on-Severn DY13 9BE* Tel (01299) 822983

ARCHER, David John. b 69. Ridley Hall Cam. **d** 05 **p** 06. C Abingdon *Ox* 05-09; R Purley from 09. *The Rectory, 1 Westridge Avenue, Purley, Reading RG8 8DE* Tel 0118-941 7727
E-mail revd.archer@btinternet.com

ARCHER, Graham John. b 58. Lanc Univ BSc79. St Jo Coll Nottm 82. **d** 85 **p** 86. C Ipswich St Matt *St E* 85-89; C Walton 89-95; P-in-c 95-99; Chapl Local Health Partnerships NHS Trust 96-99; P-in-c Portswood Ch Ch *Win* 99-05; V from 05; P-in-c Portswood St Denys from 00. *The Vicarage, 36 Brookvale Road, Southampton SO17 1QR* Tel (023) 8055 4277
E-mail vicar@highfield.org.uk

ARCHER, John Thomas. b 28. GIMechE68 CQSW83. EMMTC 79. **d** 80 **p** 81. NSM Derby St Thos 80-86; V Edlington *Sheff* 87-98; rtd 98; Perm to Offic *Lich* from 04. *Little Croft, 20 Adderley, Cheadle, Stoke-on-Trent ST10 2NJ* Tel (01538) 751541

ARCHER, Keith Malcolm. b 40. Man Univ BA61 MA80 Magd Coll Cam BA67 MA72. Ridley Hall Cam 66. **d** 68 **p** 69. C Newland St Jo *York* 68-72; Hon C Kersal Moor *Man* 72-79; Ind Chapl 72-93; V Weaste 93-09; TV Pendleton 08-09; TV Salford All SS from 09. *The Vicarage, 43 Derby Road, Salford M6 5YD* Tel 0161-736 5819 E-mail keitharcher@weaste.in2home.co.uk

ARCHER, Michael James. b 67. St Jo Coll Dur BA90 St Edm Coll Cam PhD95. Ridley Hall Cam 92. **d** 94 **p** 95. C Littleover *Derby* 94-97; C Edgware *Lon* 97-98; TV 98-01; P-in-c Bletchley *Ox* from 01. *101 Whalley Drive, Bletchley, Milton Keynes MK3 6HX* Tel (01908) 630305

ARCHER, Michael John. b 37. Trin Coll Bris 76. **d** 78 **p** 79. C Kinson *Sarum* 78-81; C Harpenden St Nic *St Alb* 81-88; P-in-c Rashcliffe and Lockwood *Wakef* 88-00; rtd 00; Perm to Offic *Truro* from 02. *Seaview Cottage, Porthallow, Helston TR12 6PW* Tel (01326) 280502

ARCHER, Neill John. b 61. UEA BA82. NTMTC 96. **d** 99 **p** 00. C Ripley *Derby* 99-02; C Forster Tuncurry Australia 02-03; Perm to Offic *Lon* 03-04; P-in-c Malmesbury w Westport and Brokenborough *Bris* from 04. *The Vicarage, Holloway, Malmesbury SN16 9BA* Tel (01666) 823126 Mobile 07946-540720 E-mail neilljarcher@tiscali.co.uk

ARCHER, Sarah Elizabeth. *See* HARTLEY, Sarah Elizabeth
ARCHIBALD, Peter Ben. b 83. Robert Gordon Univ Aber BSc04. St Steph Ho Ox BTh08. **d** 08 **p** 09. C Middlesbrough All SS *York* from 08. *14 Chipchase Road, Middlesbrough TS5 6EY* Tel 07793-535628 (mobile) E-mail benarchibald@hotmail.com

ARCUS, Jeffrey. b 40. NW Ord Course 72. **d** 75 **p** 76. C Halliwell St Thos *Man* 75-78; C Walmsley 78-81; P-in-c Bury Ch King 81-82; TV Bury Ch King w H Trin 82-93; V Ramsbottom St Jo and St Paul 93-05; C Edenfield and Stubbins 04-05; TV Ramsbottom and Edenfield 05-08; rtd 08. *12 Carrwood Hey, Ramsbottom, Bury BL0 9QT* Tel (01706) 822312

ARDAGH-WALTER, Christopher Richard. b 35. Univ of Wales (Lamp) BA58. Chich Th Coll 58. **d** 60 **p** 61. C Heavitree *Ex* 60-64; C Redcar *York* 64-67; C King's Worthy *Win* 67-69; C-in-c Four Marks CD 70-73; V Four Marks 73-76; P-in-c Eling, Testwood and Marchwood 76-78; TR Totton 76-84; R The Sherbornes w Pamber 84-88; V Froyle and Holybourne 88-95; C Verwood *Sarum* 95-97; rtd 97; Perm to Offic *Win* from 98 and *Ox* from 01. *2 Bunkers Hill, Newbury RG14 6TF* Tel (01635) 41128 E-mail ctaw@a-walter.freeserve.co.uk

✠**ARDEN, The Rt Revd Donald Seymour.** b 16. CBE81. Leeds Univ BA37. Coll of Resurr Mirfield 37. **d** 39 **p** 40 **c** 61. C Hatcham St Cath *S'wark* 39-40; C Potten End w Nettleden *St Alb* 41-43; S Africa 44-61; Can Zululand 59-61; Bp Nyasaland 61-64; Bp S Malawi 71-81; Abp Cen Africa 71-80; Asst Bp Willesden *Lon* 81-94; Hon Asst Bp Lon from 94; P-in-c Uxbridge St Marg 81-86; rtd 86; Hon C N Harrow St Alb *Lon* from 86. *6 Frobisher Close, Pinner HA5 1NN* Tel (020) 8866 6009 Fax 8868 8013 E-mail ardendj@yahoo.co.uk

ARDFERT AND AGHADOE, Archdeacon of. *Vacant*

ARDILL, Robert William Brian. b 40. QUB BSc63 PhD67 SOSc. Ox NSM Course 80 St Jo Coll Nottm 84. **d** 83 **p** 85. NSM Sunninghill *Ox* 83-84; Hon Chapl R Holloway Coll *Lon* 83-84; C Lenton *S'well* 85-87; Perm to Offic *Leic* 92-95; C Harpenden St Nic *St Alb* 95-00; R N Tawton, Bondleigh, Sampford Courtenay etc *Ex* from 00. *The Rectory, Essington Close, North Tawton EX20 2EX* Tel (01837) 82645
E-mail brian.ardill@googlemail.com

ARDING, Richard. b 52. ACIB84. Oak Hill Th Coll 90. **d** 92 **p** 93. C Bromley Common St Aug *Roch* 92-96; V Wilmington from 96; RD Dartford from 07. *The Vicarage, 1 Curate's Walk, Dartford DA2 7BJ* Tel (01322) 220561 Mobile 07773-104767
E-mail richard.arding@diocese-rochester.org

ARDIS, Canon Edward George. b 54. Dur Univ BA76. CITC 76. **d** 78 **p** 79. C Dublin Drumcondra w N Strand and St Barn *D & G* 78-81; C Dublin St Bart w Leeson Park 81-84; I Ardamine w Kiltennel, Glascarrig etc *C & O* 84-89; Can Tuam Cathl 89-03; Dean Killala 89-03; I Killala w Dunfeeny, Crossmolina etc 89-94; I Killala w Dunfeeny, Crossmolina, Kilmoremoy etc 94-03; Dir of Ords 95-03; I Dublin Irishtown w Donnybrook *D & G* from 03; Can Ch Ch Cathl Dublin from 08. *St Mary's Rectory, 4 Ailesbury Grove, Donnybrook, Dublin 4, Republic of Ireland* Tel (00353) (1) 269 2090 Mobile 87-419 6071 E-mail donnybrook@dublin.anglican.org

ARDIS, John. **d** 06 **p** 07. C Dublin Ch Ch Cathl Gp 06-08; Dean's V Cork Cathl from 08. *23 Firgrove Gardens, Bishopstown, Cork, Republic of Ireland* Tel (00353) (21) 454 6615 *or* 496 3387 Mobile 87-680 7289

ARDLEY, Annett Susan. *See* ROSE, Annette Susan
ARDOUIN, Timothy David Peter. St Mich Coll Llan. **d** 08 **p** 09. C Gorseinon *S & B* from 08. *28 Bryneithin Road, Gorseinon, Swansea SA4 4XA* Tel 07871-420089 (mobile)

ARENS, Johannes. b 69. Heythrop Coll Lon MTh97. **d** 96 **p** 97. Old Catholic Ch Germany 96-04; TV Harrogate St Wilfrid *Ripon* 04-06; V Manston from 06. *Manston Vicarage, Church Lane, Leeds LS15 8JB* Tel 0113-264 2206
E-mail johannes.arens@gmx.net

ARGENTINA, Bishop of. *See* VENABLES, The Most Revd Gregory James

ARGLES, Mrs Christine. b 57. Bris Univ BA00. Trin Coll Bris 00. **d** 02 **p** 03. C Nailsea Ch Ch w Tickenham *B & W* 02-05; Chapl Weston Area Health Trust 05-07; Chapl Cardiff and Vale NHS Trust from 07. *Cardiff and Vale NHS Trust, Cardigan House, Heath Park, Cardiff CF14 4XW* Tel (029) 2074 7747 Mobile 07763-476127 E-mail chrisargles@aol.com

ARGUILE, Canon Roger Henry William. b 43. Dur Univ LLB64 Keble Coll Ox BA70 MA75. St Steph Ho Ox 69 Ripon Hall Ox 70. **d** 71 **p** 72. C Walsall *Lich* 71-76; TV Blakenall Heath 76-83; TV Stafford 83-95; P-in-c St Neots *Ely* 95-97; V 97-07; Hon Can Ely Cathl 01-07; RD St Neots 02-07; rtd 07. *10 Marsh Lane, Wells-next-the-Sea NR23 1EG* Tel (01328) 711788
E-mail arguile@btinternet.com

ARGYLE, Douglas Causer. b 17. St Jo Coll Cam BA39 MA43. Ridley Hall Cam 39. **d** 41 **p** 42. C Somercotes *Derby* 41-44; CF (EC) 44-47; Chapl Repton Sch *Derby* 47-59; Chapl Gresham's Sch Holt 59-74; P-in-c Eastleach w Southrop *Glouc* 74-82; rtd 82; Perm to Offic *Glouc* from 82. *East Lynn, London Road, Fairford GL7 4AR* Tel (01285) 713235

ARGYLE, Edward Charles. b 55. Edith Cowan Univ (Aus) BSocSc99. St Barn Coll Adelaide 77. **d** 80 **p** 80. C Whitford Australia 80-82; C Gt Yarmouth *Nor* 83-85; I Kilcooley w Littleon, Crohane and Fertagh *C & O* 85-94; Can Ossory and Leighlin Cathls 90-94; Min Cranbrook w Mt Barker Australia 95-05; R Albany 02-05; P-in-c Jerramungup 05-07; P-in-c Williams from 07. *14 Adam Street, PO Box 113, Williams WA 6391, Australia* Tel (0061) (8) 9885 1174 Mobile 428-514119 E-mail edwarda@westnet.com.au

ARGYLL AND THE ISLES, Bishop of. *See* SHAW, The Rt Revd Alexander Martin

ARGYLL AND THE ISLES, Dean of. *See* MacCALLUM, The Very Revd Norman Donald

ARKELL, Kevin Paul. b 53. Preston Poly BTh86 Leeds Univ MA95. Sarum & Wells Th Coll 84. **d** 86 **p** 87. C S Petherton w the Seavingtons *B & W* 86-88; P-in-c Gt Harwood St Bart *Blackb* 88-90; V 90-95; TR Darwen St Pet w Hoddlesden 95-03; Acting RD Darwen 97-98; AD Blackb and Darwen 98-03; P-in-c Pokesdown All SS *Win* from 03; P-in-c Bournemouth St Clem from 08. *All Saints' Vicarage, 14 Stourwood Road, Bournemouth BH6 3QP* Tel and fax (01202) 423747 Mobile 07971-800083 E-mail kevin.arkell@ntlworld.com

ARMAGH, Archbishop of. *See* HARPER, The Most Revd Alan Edwin Thomas

ARMAGH, Archdeacon of. *See* HOEY, The Ven Raymond George

ARMAGH, Dean of. *See* ROOKE, The Very Revd Patrick William

ARMAN, Canon Brian Robert. b 54. St Jo Coll Dur BA77. Cranmer Hall Dur 74. **d** 78 **p** 79. C Lawrence Weston *Bris* 78-82; C Bishopston 82-88; R Filton from 88; P-in-c Horfield St Greg 03-05; Hon Can Bris Cathl from 01. *The Rectory, Station Road, Bristol BS34 7BE* Tel 0117-979 1128

ARMES, John Andrew. b 55. SS Coll Cam BA77 MA81 Man Univ PhD96. Sarum & Wells Th Coll 77. **d** 79 **p** 80. C Walney Is *Carl* 79-82; Chapl to Agric 82-86; TV Greystoke, Matterdale and Mungrisdale 82-86; TV Watermillock 82-86; TV Man Whitworth 86-88; TR 88-94; Chapl Man Univ 86-94; P-in-c Goodshaw and Crawshawbooth 94-98; AD Rossendale 94-98; R Edin St Jo from 98. *1 Ainslie Place, Edinburgh EH3 6AR* Tel 0131-225 5004 *or* 229 7565 Fax 229 2561 E-mail johnarmes@btconnect.com

ARMITAGE, Richard Norris. b 51. AKC. St Aug Coll Cant 73. **d** 74 **p** 75. C Chapelthorpe *Wakef* 74-77; C W Bromwich All SS *Lich* 77-82; P-in-c Ketley 82-83; V Oakengates 82-83; V Ketley and Oakengates 83-89; V Evesham *Worc* 89-96; V Evesham w Norton and Lenchwick 96-05; RD Evesham 00-05; Chapl Wilts Constabulary *Bris* from 05. *The Rectory, Churchway, Blunsdon, Swindon SN26 7DG* Tel (01793) 729592 E-mail richard.armitage@wiltshire.pnn.police.uk

ARMITAGE, Susan. b 46. Th Ext Educn Coll 91. **d** 92 **p** 95. Pretoria Corpus Christi S Africa 92-97; C Fawley *Win* 97-00; C Chandler's Ford 00-04; TV Wylye and Till Valley *Sarum* from 04. *The Vicarage, Chapel Lane, Shrewton, Salisbury SP3 4BX* Tel (01980) 620580 E-mail sue.armitage@dial.pipex.com

ARMITSTEAD, Margaretha Catharina Maria. b 65. Free Univ of Amsterdam MA89. SAOMC 00. **d** 03 **p** 04. C Littlemore *Ox* 03-06; P-in-c from 06. *The Vicarage, St Nicholas Road, Oxford OX4 4PP* Tel (01865) 748003 E-mail margreetarmitstead@btinternet.com

ARMITT, Andy John. b 68. Moorlands Bible Coll 88 Trin Coll Bris BA00. **d** 00 **p** 01. C Millhouses H Trin *Sheff* 00-03; R Bisley and W End *Guildf* from 03. *The Rectory, Clews Lane, Bisley, Woking GU24 9DY* Tel and fax (01483) 473377 Mobile 07811-909782 E-mail parishofbisleyandwestend@hotmail.com

ARMSON, Canon John Moss. b 39. Selw Coll Cam BA61 MA64 St Andr Univ PhD65. Coll of Resurr Mirfield 64. **d** 66 **p** 67. C Notting Hill St Jo *Lon* 66-69; Chapl and Fell Down Coll Cam 69-73; Chapl Westcott Ho Cam 73-76; Vice-Prin 76-82; Prin Edin Th Coll 82-89; Can St Mary's Cathl 82-89; Can Res Roch Cathl 89-01; rtd 01; Member Hengrave Ecum Community 01-03; Perm to Offic *Heref* from 03. *Mill Bank, Rowlestone, Hereford HR2 0DS* Tel (01981) 241046 E-mail j.armson@virgin.net

ARMSTEAD, Geoffrey Malcolm. b 32. K Coll Lon BD56 AKC56 Nottm Univ AdDipEd73 Heythrop Coll Lon MA05. St Boniface Warminster 56. **d** 57 **p** 57. C Weymouth H Trin *Sarum* 57-60; C Mortlake w E Sheen *S'wark* 60-63; Chapl Fen Sch Wandsworth 63-74; Dep Hd Master Harriet Costello Sch 74-91; Acting Hd Master 91-92; Perm to Offic *Win* 74-92 and from 01; V Win St Bart 92-01; rtd 01. *Polecat Cottage, Polecat Corner, Tunworth, Basingstoke RG25 2LA* Tel (01256) 471650 E-mail geoffrey@armstead4u.freeserve.co.uk

ARMSTEAD, Paul Richard. b 63. Ox Poly BA85 ACA89 FCA99. St Steph Ho Ox 06. **d** 08 **p** 09. C Northampton St Matt *Pet* from 08. *89 Park Avenue North, Northampton NN3 2HX* Tel (01604) 710062 E-mail curate@stmatthews-northampton.org.uk

ARMSTRONG, Adrian Christopher. b 48. LSE BSc70 K Coll Lon PhD80. EAMTC 84. **d** 87 **p** 88. NSM Linton *Ely* 87-95; P-in-c N and S Muskham *S'well* 95-00; P-in-c Averham w Kelham 95-00; Perm to Offic *B & W* 01-02; Hon C Wiveliscombe w Chipstable, Huish Champflower etc 02-06; Hon C Lydeard St Lawrence w Brompton Ralph etc from 06. *Cridlands Barn, Brompton Ralph, Taunton TA4 2RU* Tel (01984) 632191 E-mail drmudpie@aol.com

ARMSTRONG, Alexander Milford. b 57. Local Minl Tr Course 87 96. **d** 95 **p** 95. NSM Livingston LEP *Edin* 95-97; C Cleator Moor w Cleator *Carl* 97-98; C Frizington and Arlecdon 97-98; C Crosslacon 98-99; V Westfield St Mary from 99. *St Mary's Vicarage, Salisbury Street, Workington CA14 3TA* Tel and fax (01900) 603227 E-mail amvarmstrong@hotmail.com

ARMSTRONG, The Very Revd Christopher John. b 47. Nottm Univ BTh75. Kelham Th Coll 72. **d** 75 **p** 76. C Maidstone All SS w St Phil and H Trin *Cant* 76-79; Chapl St Hild and St Bede Coll *Dur* 79-84; Abp's Dom Chapl and Dir of Ords *York* 85-91; V Scarborough St Martin 91-01; Dean Blackb from 01. *The Deanery, Preston New Road, Blackburn BB2 6PS* Tel (01254) 52502 *or* 51491 Fax 689666 E-mail dean@blackburn.anglican.org

ARMSTRONG, Christopher John Richard. b 35. Fribourg Univ LTh60 Ch Coll Cam BA64 MA68 PhD79. Edin Th Coll 74. **d** 59 **p** 59. In RC Ch 59-71; Lect Aber Univ 68-74; C Ledbury *Heref* 74-76; P in-c Bredenbury and Wacton w Grendon Bishop 76-79; P-in-c Edwyn Ralph and Collington w Thornbury 76-79; P-in-c Pencombe w Marston Stannett and Lt Cowarne 76-79; R Cherry Burton *York* 79-80; Tutor Westcott Ho Cam 80-85; V Bottisham *Ely* 85-89; P-in-c Lode and Longmeadow 85-89; P-in-c Cropthorne w Charlton *Worc* 89-93; Dioc Local Min Sec 89-93; R Aberdaron w Rhiw and Llanfaelrhys etc *Ban* 93-99; rtd 99; Perm to Offic *Heref* and *Ban* 99-06. *52 Bradford Road, Burley in Wharfedale, Ilkley LS29 7PU* Tel (01943) 864761

ARMSTRONG, Eileen. **d** 95 **p** 96. NSM *M & K* from 95. *Hennigan, Nobber, Co Meath, Republic of Ireland* Tel (00353) (46) 905 2314

ARMSTRONG, John Edwin. b 51. Leic Univ CertEd73 BEd74. Ridley Hall Cam 91. **d** 93 **p** 94. C Gt Wilbraham *Ely* 93-96; P-in-c Bassingbourn 96-02; V 02-04; P-in-c Whaddon 96-02; V 02-04; P-in-c Southam *Cov* from 04; P-in-c Ufton from 04; RD Southam from 08. *The Rectory, Park Lane, Southam, Leamington Spa CV47 0JA* Tel (01926) 812413 E-mail revarmstrong@yahoo.com

ARMSTRONG, John Gordon. b 64. Man Poly BSc86 MSc91 Man Univ MA03. Wycliffe Hall Ox 95. **d** 97 **p** 98. C Pennington *Man* 97-01; P-in-c Holcombe and Hawkshaw Lane 01-07; TV Deane from 07. *St Andrew's Vicarage, Crescent Avenue, Over Hulton, Bolton BL5 1EN* Tel (01204) 651851 E-mail armstrongfamily@ntlworld.com

ARMSTRONG, Mrs Margaret Betty. b 48. SRN70 RSCN71. Westcott Ho Cam 89. **d** 92 **p** 94. NSM Linton *Ely* 92-95; NSM Shudy Camps 92-95; NSM Castle Camps 92-95; NSM Bartlow 92-95; NSM N and S Muskham and Averham w Kelham *S'well* 95-00; P-in-c Lydeard St Lawrence w Brompton Ralph etc *B & W* from 01. *Cridlands Barn, Brompton Ralph, Taunton TA4 2RU* Tel (01984) 623191 E-mail wheelievicar@aol.com

ARMSTRONG, Maurice Alexander. b 62. Ulster Poly BA84. CITC 84. **d** 87 **p** 88. C Portadown St Mark *Arm* 87-90; I Sixmilecross w Termonmaguirke 90-95; I Richhill 95-01; I Tempo and Clabby *Clogh* from 01. *The Rectory, Clabby, Fivemiletown BT75 0RD* Tel (028) 8952 1697

ARMSTRONG, Nicholas Paul. b 58. Bris Univ BSc79. Trin Coll Bris 91. **d** 93 **p** 94. C Filey *York* 93-97; P-in-c Alveley and Quatt *Heref* 97-98; R from 98. *The Rectory, Alveley, Bridgnorth WV15 6ND* Tel and fax (01746) 780326 E-mail nicka@inbox.com

ARMSTRONG, Robert Charles (Robin). b 24. TCD BA46 HDipEd52 MA57. CITC 47. **d** 47 **p** 48. C Belfast St Luke *Conn* 48-50; Warden Gr Sch Dub 50-59; Succ St Patr Cathl Dublin 50-59; I Dublin Finglas *D & G* 59-67; I Dun Laoghaire 67-94; Dir of Ords (Dub) 74-84; USPG Area Sec 77-94; Can Ch Ch Cathl Dublin 84-88; Treas 88-94; rtd 94. *Brabazon House, 2 Gilford Road, Sandymount, Dublin 4, Republic of Ireland*

ARMSTRONG, Rosemary. *See* WYNN, Rosemary

ARMSTRONG, Samuel David. b 48. BD MTh. **d** 86 **p** 87. C Cambridge H Trin w St Andr Gt *Ely* 86-89; V Cambridge St Martin 89-00; I Carrigaline Union *C, C & R* from 00. *The Rectory, Church Road, Carrigaline, Co Cork, Republic of Ireland* Tel (00353) (21) 437 2224

ARMSTRONG, Samuel George. b 39. Ox Univ Inst of Educn TCert65 Open Univ BA72 Reading Univ MSc89. S Dios Minl Tr Scheme 90. **d** 93 **p** 94. NSM N Tadley St Mary *Win* 93-08; Perm to Offic from 08. *The Cedars, Blakes Lane, Tadley, Basingstoke RG26 3PU* Tel 0118-981 6531 E-mail sammie@armstrongsg.freeserve.co.uk

ARMSTRONG, Mrs Susan Elizabeth. b 45. **d** 05 **p** 06. OLM Tilstock, Edstaston and Whixall *Lich* 05-09; OLM Edstaston, Fauls, Prees, Tilstock and Whixall from 09. *Tarragon Cottage, Shrewsbury Street, Prees, Whitchurch SY13 2DH* Tel (01948) 840039 E-mail s.armstrong01@btinternet.com

ARMSTRONG, Mrs Valri. b 50. Man Univ BA73. **d** 04 **p** 05. OLM Stoke by Nayland w Leavenheath and Polstead *St E* from 04. *Orchid House, 38 Bramble Way, Leavenheath, Colchester CO6 4UN* Tel (01206) 262814
E-mail mrsvarmstrong@hotmail.co.uk

ARMSTRONG, William. b 29. Sarum Th Coll 52. **d** 54 **p** 55. C Hebburn St Cuth *Dur* 54-55; C Ferryhill 55-57; C Gateshead H Trin 57-60; V Cassop cum Quarrington 60-66; Australia 66-81; Asst Dir of Educn *Liv* 81-90; V Aintree St Pet 81-88; TV Speke St Aid 88-90; rtd 90. *3 Downing Court, Grenville Street, London WC1N 1LX* Tel (020) 7713 7847

ARMSTRONG-MacDONNELL, Mrs Vivienne Christine. b 42. Open Univ BA89 Ex Univ MEd01 Lambeth MA05. Ripon Coll Cuddesdon 88. **d** 90 **p** 94. C Crediton and Shobrooke *Ex* 90-93; Dioc Adv in Adult Tr 93-00; rtd 00; Perm to Offic *Ex* 00-07; Bp's Adv for Spirituality 07-09. *Strand House, Woodbury, Exeter EX5 1LZ* Tel and fax (01395) 232790
E-mail spiritualityadviser@exeter.anglican.org

ARNALL-CULLIFORD, Jane Margaret. *See* CULLIFORD, Jane Margaret

ARNESEN, Christopher Paul. b 48. Lon Univ BA70. Sarum & Wells Th Coll 78. **d** 80 **p** 81. C Dalton-in-Furness *Carl* 80-83; C Ranmoor *Sheff* 83-86; R Distington *Carl* 86-93; TV Sheff Manor 93-97; Mental Health Chapl Sheff Care Trust 98-04; Perm to Offic *Sheff* from 04; Bp's Adv in Past Care and Counselling from 08. *39 Greystones Crescent, Sheffield S11 7JN* Tel 0114-266 8836 E-mail paul.arnesen@arnies.org.uk

ARNESEN, Raymond Halfdan (Brother Ælred). b 25. Qu Coll Cam BA49 MA54. Linc Th Coll 50. **d** 52 **p** 53. C Newc St Fran 52-55; SSF 55-66; Cistercian Monk from 66; Ewell Monastery 66-04; rtd 95. *2 Brentmead Close, London W7 3EW*

ARNOLD, Adrian Paul. b 69. St Steph Ho Ox. **d** 01 **p** 02. C Staincliffe and Carlinghow *Wakef* 01-04; V New Cantley *Sheff* 04-08. *Address temp unknown* Tel 07951-873597 (mobile)
E-mail frarnold@orange.net

ARNOLD, Brother. *See* NODDER, Thomas Arthur

ARNOLD, David Alun. b 78. St Andr Univ MTheol00. Coll of Resurr Mirfield 01. **d** 03 **p** 04. C Ribbleton *Blackb* 03-05; C Hawes Side and Marton Moss 05-07; Bp's Dom Chapl from 07; Asst Dir of Ords from 06. *79 Ribchester Road, Clayton le Dale, Blackburn BB1 9HT* Tel (01254) 248612 *or* 248234 Fax 246668 Mobile 07786-168261
E-mail chaplain@bishopofblackburn.org.uk

ARNOLD, Derek John. b 59. Wycliffe Hall Ox 01. **d** 03 **p** 04. C St Jo in Bedwardine *Worc* 03-06; TV Kidderminster St Jo and H Innocents 06-09; TR from 09. *The Vicarage, 33 Lea Bank Avenue, Kidderminster DY11 6PA* Tel (01562) 60250 Mobile 07789-631346 E-mail vicar_kwtm@btinternet.com

ARNOLD, Elisabeth Anne Truyens. b 44. TCert66. **d** 91 **p** 94. OLM Ipswich St Thos *St E* 91-00; Chapl Dioc Min Course 00-01; OLM Tutor 01-06; rtd 06; Perm to Offic *St E* from 06. *66 Bromeswell Road, Ipswich IP4 3AT* Tel (01473) 257406

ARNOLD, Ernest Stephen. b 27. **d** 64 **p** 65. C Aberavon *Llan* 64-68; V Ferndale 68-74; Cyprus 81-85; rtd 94; Perm to Offic *Portsm* from 94. *Barn Cottage, Apse Manor Road, Shanklin PO37 7PN* Tel (01983) 866324

ARNOLD, Frances Mary. b 64. R Holloway Coll Lon BA86 Dur Univ PGCE90 Anglia Ruskin Univ MA07. Westcott Ho Cam 01. **d** 04 **p** 05. C Biggleswade *St Alb* 04-07; Exec Officer Abps' Coun from 07; Perm to Offic *Lon* from 08. *Central Secretariat, Church House, Great Smith Street, London SW1P 3AZ* Tel (020) 7898 1372 E-mail frances.arnold@c-of-e.org.uk

ARNOLD, Graham Thomas. b 62. Aston Tr Scheme 87 Ripon Coll Cuddesdon 89. **d** 92 **p** 93. C Margate St Jo *Cant* 92-95; TV Whitstable 95-00; Perm to Offic *S'wark* from 07. *62B Crawthew Grove, London SE22 9AB* Tel (020) 8693 2323 Mobile 07793-555017 E-mail grahamt62@btinternet.com

ARNOLD, Jennifer Anne. b 54. Univ Coll Lon BSc75 MB, BS78 FRCR83. Qu Coll Birm 00. **d** 02 **p** 03. C Aston SS Pet and Paul *Birm* 02-08; C Aston St Jas and Nechells 05-08; C Aston and Nechells from 08. *St Matthew's Vicarage, Duddeston Manor Road, Birmingham B7 4QD* Tel 0121-359 6965 Mobile 07754-449266 E-mail arnolds68@btopenworld.com

ARNOLD, The Very Revd John Robert. b 33. OBE02. SS Coll Cam BA57 MA61 Lambeth DD99. Westcott Ho Cam 58. **d** 60 **p** 61. C Millhouses H Trin *Sheff* 60-63; Chapl and Lect Southn Univ 63-72; Gen Sec Gen Syn Bd for Miss and Unity 72-78; Hon Can Win Cathl 74-78; Dean Roch 78-89; Dean Dur 89-02; rtd 03; Perm to Offic *Cant* from 02. *26 Hawks Lane, Canterbury CT1 2NU* Tel (01227) 764703

ARNOLD, Jonathan Allen. b 69. St Pet Coll Ox BA92 MA99 K Coll Lon PhD04 LTCL89 LRAM94. Ripon Coll Cuddesdon 03. **d** 05 **p** 06. NSM Chalgrove w Berrick Salome *Ox* 05-08; Chapl Worc Coll Ox from 08. *Worcester College, Oxford OX1 2HB, or Garsington Rectory, 17 Southend, Garsington, Oxford OX44 9DH* Tel (01865) 278371 Mobile 07939-093085 E-mail jonathan.arnold@worc.ox.ac.uk

✠**ARNOLD, The Rt Revd Keith Appleby.** b 26. Trin Coll Cam BA50 MA55. Westcott Ho Cam 50. **d** 52 **p** 53 **c** 80. C Haltwhistle *Newc* 52-55; C Edin St Jo 55-61; R 61-69; CF (TA) 58-62; V Kirkby Lonsdale w Mansergh *Carl* 69-73; RD Berkhamsted *St Alb* 73-80; TR Hemel Hempstead 73-80; Suff Bp Warw *Cov* 80-90; Hon Can Cov Cathl 80-90; rtd 90; Hon Asst Bp Ox from 97. *9 Dinglederry, Olney MK46 5ES* Tel (01234) 713044

ARNOLD, Michael John. b 44. Rhodes Univ BA68 St Edm Hall Ox BA72 MA77. St Jo Coll Nottm 93. **d** 98 **p** 98. Asst Chapl St Jo Coll Johannesburg S Africa 98-99; Chapl from 01; Chapl Clayesmore Sch Blandford 98-01. *St John's College, St David's Road, Houghton Estate, Johannesburg, 2198 South Africa* Tel (0027) (11) 648 9932 *or* 648 1350 Mobile (0) 72 3134315 Fax 487 2227 E-mail arnoldmj@hotmail.com

ARNOLD, Norman. *See* ARNOLD, Victor Norman

ARNOLD, Philip Robert. b 75. Qld Univ of Tech BN96. St Jo Coll Nottm 07. **d** 09. C Pudsey St Lawr and St Paul *Bradf* from 09; C Farsley from 09. *18 West Park, Pudsey LS28 7SN* Tel 07877-495111 (mobile) E-mail psarnold@tiscali.co.uk

ARNOLD, Richard Nicholas. b 54. AKC76. S'wark Ord Course 76. **d** 77 **p** 78. C Nunhead St Antony *S'wark* 77-80; C Walworth 80-82; P-in-c Streatham Hill St Marg 82-84; V 84-89; P-in-c Oseney Crescent St Luke *Lon* 89-93; P-in-c Kentish Town St Jo 89-93; P-in-c Kentish Town St Benet and All SS 89-93; V Kentish Town from 93; AD S Camden 00-05. *Kentish Town Vicarage, 43 Lady Margaret Road, London NW5 2NH* Tel (020) 7485 4231 Mobile 07802-730974 E-mail fr.arnold@lineone.net

ARNOLD, Canon Roy. b 36. St D Coll Lamp BA62. **d** 63 **p** 64. C Brislington St Luke 63-66; C Ches St Mary 67-70; V Brinnington w Portwood 71-75; V Sale St Paul 75-82; R Doddleston 82-84; V Sheff St Oswald 84-90; Dioc Communications Officer 84-97; Chapl w the Deaf 90-97; Hon Can Sheff Cathl 95-97; rtd 97; Perm to Offic *Ches* from 97. *49 Crossfield Road, Bollington, Macclesfield SK10 5EA* Tel (01625) 575472

ARNOLD, Ms Sonja Marie. b 63. Wycliffe Hall Ox BTh98. **d** 98 **p** 99. Assoc V Hammersmith St Simon *Lon* 98-06; Dean of Women's Min Kensington Area 02-06; Network Miss P *Bris* from 07. *6 Knole Court, Knole Lane, Bristol BS10 6TZ* Tel 0117-950 9352 Mobile 07809-636419
E-mail sonjaarnold@yahoo.com

ARNOLD, Victor Norman. b 45. Oak Hill Th Coll 91. **d** 94 **p** 95. NSM Chigwell and Chigwell Row *Chelmsf* 94-98; C W Ham 98-04; C Hornchurch St Andr from 04. *Spring Cottage, 6 Spring Grove, Loughton IG10 4QA* Tel (020) 8508 6572
E-mail standrews@f2s.com

ARNOTT, Preb David. b 44. Em Coll Cam BA66. Qu Coll Birm 68. **d** 69 **p** 70. C Charlton St Luke w St Paul *S'wark* 69-73; C S Beddington St Mich 73-78; Chapl Liv Poly 78-82; V Bridgwater St Fran *B & W* 86-02; Preb Wells Cathl 00-02; V Yealmpton and Brixton *Ex* from 02; RD Ivybridge from 03. *The Vicarage, Bowden Hill, Yealmpton, Plymouth PL8 2JX* Tel and fax (01752) 880979

ARORA, Arun. b 71. Birm Univ LLB93 St Jo Coll Dur BA06 Solicitor 96. Cranmer Hall Dur 04. **d** 07 **p** 08. NSM Harrogate St Mark *Ripon* from 07; Abp's Dir of Communications *York* from 06. *30 Halstead Road, Harrogate HG2 8BP* Tel 07738-354491 (mobile) E-mail arunarora1@yahoo.co.uk

ARRAND, The Ven Geoffrey William. b 44. K Coll Lon BD66 AKC66. **d** 67 **p** 68. C Washington *Dur* 67-70; C S Ormsby w Ketsby, Calceby and Driby *Linc* 70-73; TV Gt Grimsby St Mary and St Jas 73-79; TR Halesworth w Linstead and Chediston *St E* 79-80; TR Halesworth w Linstead, Chediston, Holton etc 80-85; R Hadleigh w Layham and Shelley 85-94; Dean Bocking 85-94; RD Hadleigh 86-94; Adn Suffolk 94-09; Hon Can St E Cathl 91-09; rtd 09; Perm to Offic *St E* from 09. *8 Elm Close, Saxilby, Lincoln LN1 2QH*

ARSCOTT, Barry James. b 36. AKC59. **d** 60 **p** 61. C Walthamstow St Andr *Chelmsf* 60-65; P-in-c Leyton St Luke 65-67; V 67-77; P-in-c Lt Ilford St Barn 77-86; V 86-01; rtd 01. *232 Fencepiece Road, Ilford IG6 2ST* Tel (020) 8502 6853

ARTHUR, Graeme Richard. b 52. Univ of NSW BCom78. Linc Th Coll 93. **d** 93 **p** 94. C Witney *Ox* 93-97; R Westcote Barton w Steeple Barton, Duns Tew etc from 97. *The Rectory, 29 Enstone Road, Westcote Barton, Chipping Norton OX7 7AA* Tel (01869) 340510 E-mail graeme@arfa.clara.net

ARTHUR, Canon Ian Willoughby. b 40. Lon Univ BA63 BA66 PGCE64 Lambeth STh94 Kent Univ MA98. Ripon Coll Cuddesdon 78. **d** 80 **p** 81. C Kempston Transfiguration *St Alb* 80-83; R Potton w Sutton and Cockayne Hatley 83-96; P-in-c Sharnbrook and Knotting w Souldrop 96-98; R 98-04; RD Sharnbrook 97-04; Hon Can St Alb 99-04; rtd 04; Perm to Offic *St Alb* from 04 and *Ox* from 05. *35 London Road, Chipping Norton OX7 5AX* Tel (01608) 646839
E-mail iwarthur@supanet.com

ARTHUR, Kenneth Paul. b 64. Univ of Wales (Cardiff) BScEcon86 Roehampton Inst PGCE87 Cardiff Univ LLM08. St Steph Ho Ox BTh05. **d** 00 **p** 01. C Bodmin w Lanhydrock and Lanivet *Truro* 00-02; P-in-c Treverbyn and Boscoppa 02-06; P-in-c St Dennis from 06; RD St Austell from 05; Warden of

Readers from 05; Dir Minl Tr from 06. *The Rectory, 16 Trelavour Road, St Dennis, St Austell PL26 8AH* Tel (01726) 822317

ARTHY, Ms Nicola Mary. b 64. St Jo Coll Ox BA85 MA93. SEITE. **d** 00 **p** 01. C Guildf H Trin w St Mary 00-01; C Farncombe 01-04; P-in-c Toddington, Stanton, Didbrook w Hailes etc *Glouc* 04-05; TV Winchcombe from 05; AD Tewkesbury and Winchcombe from 07. *St Martha's, 22 Delavale Road, Winchcombe, Cheltenham GL54 5HN* Tel (01242) 603109 Mobile 07944-721835 E-mail nikkiarthy@tesco.net

ARTLEY, Clive Mansell. b 30. St Jo Coll Dur BA56 Leeds Univ MA(Theol)01. Cranmer Hall Dur. **d** 58 **p** 59. C Eston *York* 58-61; R Burythorpe w E Acklam and Leavening 61-64; CF 64-73; Teacher 73-93; Perm to Offic *York* from 73; rtd 93. *56 High Street, Castleton, Whitby YO21 2DA* Tel (01287) 660470

ARTLEY, Miss Pamela Jean. b 47. Worc Coll of Educn CertEd68 Hull Univ MEd91 ALCM73. NEOC 99. **d** 02 **p** 03. NSM Bridlington Priory *York* 02-05; P-in-c Nafferton w Wansford from 05. *The Vicarage, 3 Middle Street, Nafferton, Driffield YO25 4JS* Tel (01377) 254372 E-mail pjartley@tiscali.co.uk

ARTUS, Stephen James. b 60. Man Poly BA82 W Midl Coll of Educn PGCE84. St Jo Coll Nottm MA95. **d** 95 **p** 96. C Altrincham St Geo *Ches* 95-99; P-in-c Norton 99-05; V 05-07. *Address temp unknown*

ARUNDEL, Canon Michael. b 36. Qu Coll Ox BA60 MA64. Linc Th Coll 60. **d** 62 **p** 63. C Hollinwood *Man* 62-65; C Leesfield 65-69; R Newton Heath All SS 69-80; RD N Man 75-80; P-in-c Eccles St Mary 80-81; TR Eccles 81-91; R Man St Ann 91-01; Hon Can Man Cathl 82-01; rtd 01. *20 Kiln Brow, Bromley Cross, Bolton BL7 9NR* Tel (01204) 591156

ARVIDSSON, Carl Fredrik. b 66. Regents Th Coll 88 Chich Th Coll 92. **d** 92 **p** 93. C Southsea H Spirit *Portsm* 92-94; C Botley, Curdridge and Durley 94-96; P-in-c Ringwould w Kingsdown *Cant* 96-97; R 97-01; Hon Min Can Cant Cathl from 01; Sen Chapl K Sch Cant from 01. *Broughton Lodge, Monastery Street, Canterbury CT1 1PB* Tel (01227) 595582 *or* 595613 E-mail cfa@kings-school.co.uk

ASBRIDGE, Preb John Hawell. b 26. Dur Univ BA47. Bps' Coll Cheshunt 47. **d** 49 **p** 50. C Barrow St Geo *Carl* 49-52; C Fort William *Arg* 52-54; C Lon Docks St Pet w Wapping St Jo 54-55; C Kilburn St Aug 55-59; V Northolt Park St Barn 59-66; V Shepherd's Bush St Steph w St Thos 66-96; Preb St Paul's Cathl 89-96; rtd 96; Perm to Offic *B & W* from 05. *Crystal Glen, The Old Mineral Line, Roadwater, Watchet TA23 0RL* Tel (01984) 640211

ASBRIDGE, Nigel Henry. b 58. Bris Univ BA80. Chich Th Coll 87. **d** 89 **p** 90. C Tottenham St Paul *Lon* 89; C W Hampstead St Jas 89-94; P-in-c Hornsey H Innocents 94-04; P-in-c Stroud Green H Trin 02-04; Nat Chapl-Missr Children's Soc from 04; NSM Edmonton St Alphege *Lon* from 06; NSM Ponders End St Matt from 06. *The Children's Society, Edward Rudolf House, Margery Street, London WC1X 0JL* Tel (020) 7841 4567 E-mail nigelasbridge@hotmail.com

ASH, Arthur Edwin. b 44. St Jo Coll Nottm 85. **d** 87 **p** 88. C Attleborough *Cov* 87-91; V Garretts Green *Birm* 91-02; rtd 02; Perm to Offic *Birm* from 02. *1 Margetts Close, Kenilworth CV8 1EN* Tel (01926) 853547 E-mail aash@tinyworld.co.uk

ASH, Brian John. b 32. ALCD62. **d** 62 **p** 63. C Plymouth St Andr *Ex* 62-66; Area Sec CMS *Cant* and *Roch* 66-73; V Bromley Common St Aug *Roch* 73-97; rtd 97; Perm to Offic *Chelmsf* 97-00. *The Vines, 95 Green Lane, Leigh-on-Sea SS9 5QU* Tel (01702) 523644 E-mail brian.ash@zen.co.uk

ASH, Christopher Brian Garton. b 53. Trin Hall Cam MA76. Wycliffe Hall Ox BA92. **d** 93 **p** 94. C Cambridge H Sepulchre *Ely* 93-97; P-in-c Lt Shelford 97-02; R 02-04; Dir Cornhill Tr Course from 04. *The Cornhill Training Course, 140-148 Borough High Street, London SE1 1LB* Tel (020) 7407 0562 E-mail cbga@proctrust.org.uk

ASH, David Nicholas. b 61. Southlands Coll Lon BA82. Wycliffe Hall Ox BTh03. **d** 03 **p** 04. C Walsall *Lich* 03-06; P-in-c Petton w Cockshutt, Welshampton and Lyneal etc from 06. *The Rectory, Cockshutt, Ellesmere SY12 0JQ* Tel (01939) 270211

ASH, Nicholas John. b 59. Bath Univ BSc81 Nottm Univ BTh88. Linc Th Coll 85. **d** 88 **p** 89. C Hersham *Guildf* 88-93; P-in-c Flookburgh *Carl* 93-97; Dioc Officer for Stewardship 94-97; TV Cartmel Peninsula 97-98; Dir of Ords 97-03; P-in-c Dalston 98-00; P-in-c Wreay 98-00; P-in-c Raughton Head w Gatesgill 98-00; V Dalston w Cumdivock, Raughton Head and Wreay 01-03; Can Res Portsm Cathl 03-09; TR Cartmel Peninsula *Carl* from 09. *The Rectory, Hampsfell Road, Grange-over-Sands LA11 6BE* Tel (01539) 532757 E-mail nickash405@hotmail.com

ASH, Nicholas Martin. b 62. Ch Ch Coll Cant BEd86. SEITE. 06. **d** 09. NSM Faversham *Cant* from 09; NSM Preston next Faversham, Goodnestone and Graveney from 09. *15 St Catherine's Drive, Faversham ME13 8LQ* Tel (01795) 536038 Mobile 07896-006282 E-mail n.ash@virgin.net

ASHBRIDGE, Clare Patricia Esther. *See* KAKURU, Mrs Clare Patricia Esther

ASHBRIDGE, Miss Kathleen Mary. b 30. Alnwick Tr Coll CertEd51. **d** 03 **p** 04. NSM Caldbeck, Castle Sowerby and Sebergham *Carl* from 03. *Sharpe House, Caldbeck, Wigton CA7 8EX* Tel (01697) 478205

ASHBURNER, David Barrington. b 26. Ch Coll Cam BA51 MA55. Wycliffe Hall Ox 51. **d** 53 **p** 54. C Coalville *Leic* 53-56; C Leic H Apostles 56-58; V Bucklebury w Marlston *Ox* 58-70; V Belton *Leic* 70-75; P-in-c Osgathorpe 73-75; R Belton and Osgathorpe 75-79; V Frisby-on-the-Wreake w Kirby Bellars 79-82; V Uffington w Woolstone and Baulking *Ox* 82-91; P-in-c Shellingford 83-91; RD Vale of White Horse 87-91; rtd 91; Perm to Offic *Glouc* and *Ox* from 91. *7 Stonefern Court, Stow Road, Moreton-in-Marsh GL56 0DW* Tel (01608) 650347

✠**ASHBY, The Rt Revd Godfrey William Ernest Candler.** b 30. Lon Univ AKC54 BD54 PhD69. **d** 55 **p** 56 **c** 80. C St Helier *S'wark* 55-57; P-in-c St Mark's Miss Cape Town *S Africa* 58-60; Sub-Warden St Paul's Th Coll Grahamstown 60-66; R Alice 66-68; Sen Lect Rhodes Univ 68-75; Can Grahamstown Cathl 69-75; Dean and Adn Grahamstown 75-80; Bp St John's 80-85; Prof Div Witwatersrand Univ 85-88; Asst Bp Johannesburg 85-88; Asst Bp Leic 88-95; P-in-c Newtown Linford 92-95; Hon Can Leic Cathl 93-95; rtd 95; Asst Bp George S Africa 95-08; Hon Asst Bp Portsm from 08. *12 Jay Close, Waterlooville PO8 9DJ* Tel (023) 9235 9914 Mobile 07968-396195 E-mail godfreyashby@gmail.com

ASHBY, Mrs Judith Anne Stuart. b 53. Man Univ BSc74 MSc76 Ox Brookes Univ PGCE99. STETS 96. **d** 99 **p** 00. NSM Swindon Ch Ch *Bris* 99-05; P-in-c Cricklade w Latton from 05; C Ashton Keynes, Leigh and Minety from 07. *Cricklade Vicarage, 14 Bath Road, Cricklade, Swindon SN6 6EY* Tel (01793) 750300 E-mail judith.ashby@tiscali.co.uk

ASHBY, Kevin Patrick. b 53. Jes Coll Ox BA76 MA80. Wycliffe Hall Ox 76. **d** 78 **p** 79. C Market Harborough *Leic* 78-82; C Horwich H Trin *Man* 82-84; C Horwich 84; TV 84-90; R Billing *Pet* 90-01; RD Northn 98-01; R Buckingham *Ox* 01-09; AD Buckingham 04-09; TR Melton Mowbray *Leic* from 09. *57 Burton Road, Melton Mowbray LE13 1DL* Tel (01664) 410393 E-mail kevinp.ashby@virgin.net

ASHBY, Mrs Linda. b 48. Dartford Coll of Educn CertEd70. **d** 03 **p** 04. OLM N w S Wootton *Nor* from 03. *4 Melford Close, South Wootton, King's Lynn PE30 3XH* Tel (01553) 672893 E-mail linda_ashby@tiscali.co.uk

ASHBY, Peter George. b 49. Univ of Wales (Cardiff) BSc(Econ)70. Linc Th Coll 70. **d** 73 **p** 74. C Bengeo *St Alb* 73-75; Chapl Hatf Poly 76-79; C Apsley End 80; TV Chambersbury 80-82; Adn N Harare Zimbabwe 82-87; V Eskdale, Irton, Muncaster and Waberthwaite *Carl* 87-93; TR Sedgley All SS *Worc* 93-99; TV Tettenhall Regis *Lich* 99-04; V W Bromwich St Jas w St Paul 04-06; R Bradeley, Church Eaton, Derrington and Haughton from 06. *The Rectory, Rectory Lane, Haughton, Stafford ST18 9HU* Tel (01785) 780201

ASHBY, Philip Charles. b 52. Bris Univ BSc73 Lon Univ MSc74 PhD03. WEMTC 05. **d** 08 **p** 09. NSM Stratton St Margaret w S Marston etc *Bris* from 08. *Cricklade Vicarage, 14 Bath Road, Cricklade, Swindon SN6 6EY* Tel (01793) 759008 E-mail phil.ashby@tiscali.co.uk

ASHCROFT, Canon Ann Christine. b 46. Cov Coll of Educn TCert68. NOC 82. **d** 87 **p** 94. Chapl Trin C of E High Sch Man 86-91; Burnage St Nic *Man* 86-95; Hon Par Dn 87-95; Dio Adv Man Coun for Educn 91-95; TV Wareham and Chapl Purbeck Sch *Sarum* 95-02; TR By Brook *Bris* from 02; P-in-c Colerne w N Wraxall from 06; Hon Can Bris Cathl from 08. *By Brook Rectory, 3 Church Farm, Yatton Keynell, Chippenham SN14 7FD* Tel (01249) 782663 E-mail bybrook.parishoffice@btopenworld.com

ASHCROFT, The Ven Mark David. b 54. Worc Coll Ox BA77 MA82 Fitzw Coll Cam BA81. Ridley Hall Cam 79. **d** 82 **p** 83. C Burnage St Marg *Man* 82-85; Tutor St Paul's Sch of Div Kapsabet Kenya 86-89; Prin St Paul's Th Coll Kapsabet 90-96; R Harpurhey Ch *Man* 96-09; R Harpurhey St Steph 96-06; AD N Man 00-06; Adn Man from 09; Hon Can Man Cathl from 04. *2 The Walled Gardens, Swinton, Manchester M27 0FR* Tel 0161-794 2401

ASHDOWN, Andrew William Harvey. b 64. K Coll Lon BD88 AKC88. Sarum & Wells Th Coll 88. **d** 90 **p** 91. C Cranleigh *Guildf* 90-94; V Ryhill *Wakef* 94-98; P-in-c Denmead *Portsm* 98-99; V 99-05; S Asia Regional Officer USPG 05-06; Hon C Tadley S and Silchester *Win* 05-06; P-in-c Knight's Enham and Smannell w Enham Alamein 06-09; TR from 09. *The Rectory, 1 Ryon Close, Andover SP10 4DG* Tel (01264) 357032 E-mail andrew@evib.net

ASHDOWN, Anthony Hughes. b 37. AKC63. **d** 64 **p** 65. C Tettenhall Regis *Lich* 64-67; P-in-c Bassaleg *Mon* 67-70; P-in-c Gatooma Rhodesia 70-77; P-in-c Longton St Jas *Lich* 77-78; P-in-c Longton St Jo 77-78; R Longton 78-80; TR Cove St Jo *Guildf* 80-87; Chapl Lisbon *Eur* 87-90; V Wanstead H Trin Hermon Hill *Chelmsf* 90-00; Perm to Offic *Chich* from 00; rtd 02. *1 Wharf House, Canal Wharf, Chichester PO19 8EW* Tel (01243) 532405

ASHDOWN, Barry Frederick. b 42. St Pet Coll Ox BA65 MA69. Ridley Hall Cam 66. **d** 68 **p** 69. C Shipley St Pet *Bradf* 68-71; C Rushden w Newton Bromswold *Pet* 71-74; R Haworth *Bradf* 74-82; V Ore Ch Ch *Chich* 82-87; C Southwick St Mich 91-93. *7 Nile Street, Cross Roads, Keighley BD22 9ED*

ASHDOWN, Ms Lucyann. b 64. LSE BSc95 RGN86 RM88. NTMTC BA08. **d** 08 **p** 09. C Stoke Newington St Mary *Lon* from 08; C Brownswood Park from 08. *Basement Flat, St Mary's Rectory, Stoke Newington Church Street, London N16 9ES* Tel (020) 7254 6072 E-mail lucyann.ashdown@gmail.com

ASHDOWN, Philip David. b 57. Imp Coll Lon BSc79 NW Univ Chicago MS80 Cranfield Inst of Tech PhD85 ARCS79 CMath MIMA87. Ripon Coll Cuddesdon 91. **d** 93 **p** 94. C Houghton le Spring *Dur* 93-96; C Stockton and Chapl Stockton Campus Dur Univ 96-02; V Stockton St Pet *Dur* from 02. *St Peter's Vicarage, 11 Lime Court, Stockton-on-Tees TS18 3UB* Tel (01642) 670981 E-mail philip.ashdown@durham.anglican.org

ASHE, The Ven Francis John. b 53. Sheff Univ BMet74. Ridley Hall Cam 77. **d** 79 **p** 80. C Ashtead *Guildf* 79-82; S Africa 82-87; R Wisley w Pyrford *Guildf* 87-93; V Godalming 93-01; TR 01-09; RD Godalming 96-02; Hon Can Guildf Cathl 03-09; Adn Lynn *Nor* from 09. *Holly Tree House, Whitwell Road, Sparham, Norwich NR9 5PN* Tel (01362) 688032 E-mail archdeacon.lynn@norwich.anglican.org

ASHENDEN, Canon Gavin Roy Pelham. b 54. Bris Univ LLB76 Oak Hill Th Coll BA80 Heythrop Coll Lon MTh89 Sussex Univ DPhil98. **d** 80 **p** 81. C Bermondsey St Jas w Ch Ch *S'wark* 80-83; TV Sanderstead All SS 83-89; Chapl and Lect Sussex Univ from 89; Can and Preb Chich Cathl from 03; Chapl to The Queen from 08. *The Meeting House, Sussex University, Southern Ring Road, Falmer, Brighton BN1 9RH* Tel (01273) 678217 Fax 678918 Mobile 07879-493491 E-mail g.ashenden@sussex.ac.uk *or* gavin@ashenden.org

ASHFORD-OKAI, Fred. b 57. NUI BA90 Lanc Univ MA92 TCD HDipEd93. St Pet Sem Ghana 79 NTMTC 06. **d** 84 **p** 85. NSM E Ham w Upton Park St Alb *Chelmsf* 07-09. *8 Bream Gardens, London E6 6HX* Tel (020) 8548 0647 Mobile 07940-984883 E-mail fashfordokai@googlemail.com

ASHFORTH, David Edward. b 37. Lon Univ BSc ARCS59. Qu Coll Birm. **d** 61 **p** 62. C Scarborough St Columba *York* 61-65; C Northallerton w Kirby Sigston 65-67; V Keyingham 67-73; Chapl Imp Coll *Lon* 73-89; V Balderstone *Blackb* 89-01; Dir Post-Ord Tr 89-01; rtd 01; Perm to Offic *Ripon* from 02. *Sunnyholme Cottage, Preston under Scar, Leyburn DL8 4AH* Tel (01969) 622438 E-mail d.ashforth@btinternet.com

ASHLEY, Brian. b 36. S'wark Ord Course 75. **d** 77 **p** 78. NSM Horsell *Guildf* 77-07; Perm to Offic from 07. *5 Birtley House, 38 Claremont Avenue, Woking GU22 7QB* Tel (01483) 761232 E-mail brianthebusiness@onetel.com

ASHLEY, Brian Christenson. b 33. Roch Th Coll 68. **d** 70 **p** 71. C New Sleaford *Linc* 70-72; Min Basegreen CD 72-74; TV Gleadless *Sheff* 74-77; R Dinnington 77-85; RD Laughton 82-85; V Mosbrough 85-88; P-in-c Curbar and Stoney Middleton *Derby* 88-91; rtd 91; Perm to Offic *Pet* from 95. *15 Eliot Close, Saxon Fields, Kettering NN16 9XR* Tel (01536) 524457

ASHLEY, Clive Ashley. b 54. Croydon Coll of Art and Design LSIAD75 Lon Hosp SRN80 E Ham Coll of Tech TCert82. Aston Tr Scheme 81 Cranmer Hall Dur 84. **d** 86 **p** 87. C Withington St Paul *Man* 86-89; Asst Chapl Freeman Hosp Newc 89-92; Chapl St Rich and Graylingwell Hosps Chich 92-98; Chapl Bognor Regis War Memorial Hosp 95-98; Chapl and Bereavement Cllr R W Sussex Trust 98-01; R New Fishbourne *Chich* from 01; P-in-c Appledram from 01. *The Rectory, 31 Caspian Close, Fishbourne, Chichester PO18 8AY* Tel (01243) 783364 Mobile 07747-155119 E-mail clive.ashley@tesco.net

ASHLEY, John Michael. b 28. Worc Coll Ox BA51 MA54. Linc Th Coll 50. **d** 54 **p** 55. Australia 54-60; C Anderby w Cumberworth *Linc* 60-66; P-in-c Huttoft 60-61; V 61-66; R Woolsthorpe 66-93; R W w E Allington and Sedgebrook 66-93; CF (TAVR) 79-93; rtd 93; Perm to Offic *Linc* 93-99. *35 Gregory Close, Harlaxton, Grantham NG32 1JG* Tel (01476) 561846

ASHLEY, Ms Rosemary Clare. b 60. Dur Univ BA82 Birkbeck Coll Lon MSc01 Brunel Univ MPhil05. Wycliffe Hall Ox 02. **d** 05 **p** 06. C Leyton St Cath and St Paul *Chelmsf* 05-09. *Address temp unknown* Tel 07984-618534 (mobile) E-mail rosyashley@hotmail.com

ASHLEY, Miss Victoria Lesley. St Mich Coll Llan. **d** 08 **p** 09. C Tredegar *Mon* from 08. *St James's Vicarage, Poplar Road, Tredegar NP24 4LH* Tel (01495) 722510 E-mail victoria.ashley151@btinternet.com

ASHLEY-ROBERTS, James. b 53. Lon Univ BD77. Oak Hill Th Coll 75 Wycliffe Hall Ox 79. **d** 80 **p** 81. C Gt Warley Ch Ch *Chelmsf* 80-83; C E Ham St Paul 83-85; TV Holyhead w Rhoscolyn w Llanfair-yn-Neubwll *Ban* 85-88; R 88-91; V Penrhyndeudraeth w Llanfrothen w Beddgelert 91-97; R Ffestiniog w Blaenau Ffestiniog 97-01. *5 Jones Street, Blaenau Ffestiniog LL41 3YF* Tel 07881-770437 (mobile)

ASHLING, Raymond Charles. b 32. Dur Univ BA58. Linc Th Coll 58. **d** 60 **p** 61. C Halifax St Aug *Wakef* 60-63; C Farlington *Portsm* 63-65; Rhodesia 65-71; Chapl Rishworth Sch Ripponden 71-75; Lesotho 75-85; V Somercotes *Linc* 85-88; Ethiopia 88-89; R Gt w Lt Snoring w Kettlestone and Pensthorpe *Nor* 89-94; rtd 94. *6 Wells Court, Morden College, 19 St Germans Place, London SE3 0PW*

ASHMAN, Paul Andrew. b 70. Wycliffe Hall Ox 05. **d** 07 **p** 08. C Portswood Ch Ch *Win* from 07. *6 Royston Close, Southampton SO17 1TB* Tel (023) 8059 5015 Mobile 07793-464721 E-mail ashmanpaul@gmail.com

ASHMAN, Peter Nicholas. b 52. CSS81 SEN73. Sarum & Wells Th Coll 87. **d** 89 **p** 90. C Stafford *Lich* 89-93; V Dymchurch w Burmarsh and Newchurch *Cant* 93-99; R Lyminge w Paddlesworth, Stanford w Postling etc from 99. *The Rectory, Rectory Lane, Lyminge, Folkestone CT18 8EG* Tel (01303) 862432 *or* tel and fax 862345 E-mail p.ashman@btinternet.com

ASHMAN, Mrs Vanessa Mary. b 53. Cant Ch Ch Univ BA07. **d** 03 **p** 04. NSM Lyminge w Paddlesworth, Stanford w Postling etc *Cant* from 03. *The Rectory, Rectory Lane, Lyminge, Folkestone CT18 8EG* Tel (01303) 862432 *or* tel and fax 862345 E-mail vanessa.ashman@btinternet.com

ASHTON, Anthony Joseph. b 37. Oak Hill Th Coll 62. **d** 65 **p** 66. C Crookes St Thos *Sheff* 65-68; C Heeley 68-73; V Bowling St Steph *Bradf* 73-78; R Chesterfield H Trin *Derby* 78-92; rtd 93; Perm to Offic *Derby* 93-00. *19 High Park, Stafford ST16 1BL* Tel (01785) 223943

✠**ASHTON, The Rt Revd Cyril Guy.** b 42. Lanc Univ MA86. Oak Hill Th Coll 64. **d** 67 **p** 68 **c** 00. C Blackpool St Thos *Blackb* 67-70; Voc Sec CPAS 70-74; V Lancaster St Thos *Blackb* 74-91; Lanc Almshouses 76-90; Dioc Dir of Tr *Blackb* 91-00; Hon Can Blackb Cathl 91-00; Suff Bp Doncaster *Sheff* from 00. *Bishop's House, 3 Farrington Court, Wickersley, Rotherham S66 1JQ* Tel (01709) 730130 Fax 730230 E-mail m.powell1@virgin.net

ASHTON, David. b 52. Sarum Th Coll 93. **d** 96 **p** 97. NSM St Leonards Ch Ch and St Mary *Chich* 96-98; NSM Upper St Leonards St Jo 98-99; C Uckfield 99-02; V Langney from 02. *St Richard's Rectory, 7 Priory Road, Eastbourne BN23 7AX* Tel (01323) 761158 E-mail frdavidashton@aol.com

ASHTON, David William. b 51. Reading Univ BA74 Lanc Univ PGCE75. Wycliffe Hall Ox 79. **d** 82 **p** 83. C Shipley St Pet *Bradf* 82-85; C Tadley St Pet *Win* 85-88; V Sinfin *Derby* 88-91; Chapl Sophia Antipolis *Eur* 91-94; P-in-c Swanwick and Pentrich *Derby* 95-00; V 00-02; RD Alfreton 95-02; Chapl Derby Hosps NHS Foundation Trust from 02. *Chaplaincy Services, Derby City General Hospital, Uttoxeter Road, Derby DE22 3NE* Tel (01332) 340131 E-mail david.ashton@derbyhospitals.nhs.uk

ASHTON, Grant. *See* ASHTON, William Grant

ASHTON, James Paul. b 75. UWE BA97. Wycliffe Hall Ox BTh06. **d** 06 **p** 07. C Horley *S'wark* 06-09; C S Merstham from 09. *The Vicarage, Battlebridge Lane, Redhill RH1 3LH*

ASHTON, Janet Heather Hephzibah. b 52. Westcott Ho Cam. **d** 07 **p** 08. C Wenlock *Heref* from 07. *3 Grenville Drive, Much Wenlock TF13 6HB* Tel (01952) 727344 Mobile 07737-916499 E-mail jan@janashton.co.uk

✠**ASHTON, The Rt Revd Jeremy Claude.** b 30. Trin Coll Cam BA53 MA57. Westcott Ho Cam 53. **d** 55 **p** 56 **c** 76. C Bury St Mary *Man* 55-60; CF (TA) 57-60; CF (TA - R of O) 60-70; Papua New Guinea 60-86; Asst Bp Papua 76-77; Bp Aipo Rongo 77-86; rtd 86; Australia from 86. *38 Urquhart Street, Castlemaine Vic 3540, Australia* Tel and fax (0061) (3) 5472 1074

ASHTON, Miss Joan Elizabeth. b 54. Eaton Hall Coll of Educn CertEd76. Cranmer Hall Dur 91. **d** 93 **p** 94. Par Dn Darnall-cum-Attercliffe *Sheff* 93-94; C Hillsborough and Wadsley Bridge 94-96; P-in-c Stainforth 96-98; P-in-c Arksey 98-03; Asst Chapl Doncaster R Infirmary and Montagu Hosp NHS Trust 98-01; Asst Chapl Doncaster and Bassetlaw Hosps NHS Trust 01-04; Co-ord Chapl Services Rotherham Gen Hosps NHS Trust from 04. *Rotherham District General Hospital, Moorgate Road, Rotherham S60 2UD* Tel (01709) 820000 E-mail joan.ashton@rothgen.nhs.uk

ASHTON, Kenneth. b 61. Ridley Hall Cam. **d** 08 **p** 09. C Walthamstow *Chelmsf* from 08. *17 Shernhall Street, London E17 3EU* Tel (020) 8520 1430 Mobile 07932-071715 E-mail ashtonken@gmail.com

ASHTON, Lesley June. b 49. York Univ BA89. NEOC 00. **d** 04 **p** 05. C Roundhay St Edm *Ripon* 04-08; P-in-c Hawksworth Wood from 08. *St Mary's Vicarage, 50 Cragside Walk, Leeds LS5 3QE* Tel 0113-258 2923 E-mail lesley.ashton1@ntlworld.com

ASHTON, Mrs Margaret Lucie. b 40. St Jo Coll Nottm 79. dss 83 **d** 87 **p** 94. Billericay and Lt Burstead *Chelmsf* 83-99; NSM 87-99; rtd 99; Hon C Fordingbridge and Breamore and Hale etc *Win* 01-05; Perm to Offic from 05. *3 Stephen Martin Gardens, Fordingbridge SP6 1RF* Tel (01425) 656205 E-mail peterdashton@onetel.com

ASHTON, Mrs Mary Isabel. b 57. Robert Gordon Inst of Tech Aber BSc78 Open Univ PGCE96. St Steph Ho Ox 07. **d** 09. C

Whitewater *Win* from 09. *The Rectory, Vicarage Lane, Hound Green, Basingstoke RG27 8LF*

ASHTON, Neville Anthony. b 45. Sarum & Wells Th Coll 78. **d** 80 **p** 81. C Hattersley *Ches* 80-82; C Lancaster Ch Ch w St Jo and St Anne *Blackb* 82-84; R Church Kirk from 84. *Church Kirk Rectory, 434 Blackburn Road, Accrington BB5 0DE* Tel (01254) 236946

ASHTON, Canon Peter Donald. b 34. Lon Univ BD62. ALCD61. **d** 62 **p** 63. C Walthamstow St Mary *Chelmsf* 62-68; V Girlington *Bradf* 68-73; Dir Past Studies St Jo Coll Nottm 73-80; TR Billericay and Lt Burstead *Chelmsf* 80-99; Chapl Mayflower Hosp Billericay 80-99; Chapl St Andr Hosp Billericay 80-93; Chapl Thameside Community Healthcare NHS Trust 93-99; RD Basildon *Chelmsf* 89-99; Hon Can Chelmsf Cathl 92-99; rtd 99; Hon C Fordingbridge and Breamore and Hale etc *Win* from 01. *3 Stephen Martin Gardens, Fordingbridge SP6 1RF* Tel (01425) 656205 E-mail peterdashton@onetel.com

ASHTON, Preb Samuel Rupert. b 42. Sarum & Wells Th Coll. **d** 83 **p** 84. C Ledbury w Eastnor *Heref* 83-86; R St Weonards w Orcop, Garway, Tretire etc 86-98; RD Ross and Archenfield 91-95 and 96-98; P-in-c Cradley w Mathon and Storridge 98-99; R 99-07; Preb Heref Cathl 97 07; rtd 07; Perm to Offic *Heref* from 08. *The Old Greyhound, Longtown, Hereford HR2 0LD* Tel (01873) 860492

ASHTON, Stephen Robert. b 55. BA BPhil Lon Univ MA99 FRSA03 FGMS03. Sarum & Wells Th Coll. **d** 84 **p** 85. C Penzance St Mary w St Paul *Truro* 84-86; C Tewkesbury w Walton Cardiff *Glouc* 86-89; P-in-c Newton Heath St Wilfrid and St Anne *Man* 89-92; V Breage w Germoe *Truro* 92-94. *5 Heron Close, Cheltenham GL51 6HA* E-mail sashton44@hotmail.com

ASHTON, William Grant. b 57. St Chad's Coll Dur BA79. Oak Hill Th Coll BA85. **d** 85 **p** 86. C Lancaster St Thos *Blackb* 85-89; CF from 89; Chapl R Memorial Chpl Sandhurst 06-07. *c/o MOD Chaplains (Army)* Tel (01980) 615804 Fax 615800

ASHURST, Mrs Judith Anne. b 57. St Aid Coll Dur BA80 St Jo Coll Dur BA08 ACIB83. Cranmer Hall Dur 06. **d** 08 **p** 09. C Belmont and Pittington *Dur* from 08. *Woodlea, Percy Lane, Durham DH1 4HE* Tel 0191-386 0794

ASHWELL, Anthony John. b 42. St Andr Univ BSc65. Sarum & Wells Th Coll 86. **d** 88 **p** 89. C Plymstock *Ex* 88-91; C Axminster, Chardstock, Combe Pyne and Rousdon 91-92; TV 92-95; C Crediton and Shobrooke 95-97; TV Bride Valley *Sarum* 97-07; P-in-c Symondsbury 05-07; RD Lyme Bay 03-06; rtd 07; Perm to Offic *Sarum* from 07. *Ven Cottage, Five Acres, Charmouth, Bridport DT6 6BE* Tel (01297) 560847 E-mail anthonyashwell@aol.com

ASHWIN, Canon Vincent George. b 42. Worc Coll Ox BA65. Coll of Resurr Mirfield 65. **d** 67 **p** 68. C Shildon *Dur* 67-70; C Newc St Fran 70-72; R Mhlosheni Swaziland 72-75; R Manzini 75-79; V Shildon *Dur* 79-85; V Fenham St Jas and St Basil *Newc* 85-97; RD Newc W 89-97; V Haydon Bridge and Beltingham w Henshaw 97-04; RD Hexham 97-02; Hon Can Newc Cathl 00-04; rtd 04; Perm to Offic *S'well* from 04. *83 Westgate, Southwell NG25 0LS* Tel (01636) 813975 E-mail vincentashwin@tiscali.co.uk

ASHWIN-SIEJKOWSKI, Piotr Jan. b 64. Warsaw Univ PhD97. Coll of Resurr Mirfield 98. **d** 91 **p** 92. Poland 92-98; C Tile Hill *Cov* 99-01; Chapl and Lect Univ Coll Chich 01-04; TV Richmond St Mary w St Matthias and St Jo *S'wark* from 04. *19 Deer Park Gardens, Richmond TW9 2TM* Tel (020) 8940 8359 E-mail piotrashwin@btinternet.com

ASHWORTH, Canon David. b 40. Nottm Univ BPharm62. Linc Th Coll 63. **d** 65 **p** 66. C Halliwell St Thos *Man* 65-72; C Heywood St Jas 69-72; C-in-c Heywood St Marg CD 72-78; V Hale *Ches* 78-87; V Hale and Ashley 87-96; V Prestbury 96-05; RD Bowdon 87-95; RD Macclesfield 98-03; Hon Can Ches Cathl 94-05; rtd 05; Perm to Offic *Ches* from 05. *12 Lime Close, Sandbach CW11 1BZ* Tel (01270) 529187 E-mail david@ashworth39.freeserve.co.uk

ASHWORTH, James Nigel. b 55. York Univ BA77. Cranmer Hall Dur 93. **d** 93 **p** 94. C Rothwell *Ripon* 93-96; Chapl Campsfield Ho Oxon 96-99; Hon C Akeman *Ox* 96-99; V Kemsing w Woodlands *Roch* 99-08; R Man St Ann from 08. *98 Rigby Street, Salford M7 4BQ* Tel 0161-792 1123 E-mail nigelashworth@btinternet.com

ASHWORTH, John Russell. b 33. Lich Th Coll 57. **d** 60 **p** 61. C Castleford All SS *Wakef* 60-62; C Luton St Sav *St Alb* 63-67; V Clipstone *S'well* 67-70; V Bolton-upon-Dearne *Sheff* 70-82; V Thornhill Lees *Wakef* 82-98; rtd 98; Perm to Offic *Wakef* from 99. *Walsingham, 2 Vicarage Road, Savile Town, Dewsbury WF12 9PD* Tel (01924) 461269

ASHWORTH, Keith Benjamin. b 33. NW Ord Course 76. **d** 79 **p** 80. C Pennington *Man* 79-83; P-in-c Bolton St Bede 83-88; V 88-95; V Hillock 95-01; rtd 01; Perm to Offic *Man* 01-06 and *Blackb* from 06. *3 Sandpiper Place, Thornton-Cleveleys FY5 3FE* Tel (01253) 855793

ASHWORTH, Martin. b 41. AKC63. **d** 64 **p** 65. C Wythenshawe

Wm Temple Ch CD *Man* 64-71; R Haughton St Anne 71-83; V Prestwich St Marg 83-06; rtd 06; Perm to Offic *Man* from 06. *Chiserley Stile Barn, 1 Chiserley Stile, Hebden Bridge HX7 8SB* Tel (01422) 843562

ASHWORTH, Nigel. See ASHWORTH, James Nigel

ASHWORTH, Timothy. b 52. Worc Coll of Educn CertEd74. Oak Hill Th Coll BA81. **d** 82 **p** 83. C Tonbridge St Steph *Roch* 82-85; C-in-c Whittle-le-Woods *Blackb* 85-90; Chapl Scargill Ho 90-96; V Ingleton w Chapel le Dale *Bradf* 96-03; TV Yate New Town *Bris* 03-08; NSM Lostock St Thos and St Jo *Man* from 09; NSM Bolton St Bede from 09. *St Bede's Vicarage, 92 Normanby Street, Bolton BL3 3QR* Tel (01204) 654016 E-mail timashworth52@tiscali.co.uk

ASHWORTH, Mrs Vivien. b 52. Worc Coll of Educn CertEd74. Trin Coll Bris 79 Oak Hill Th Coll BA82. **dss** 82 **d** 87 **p** 94. Tonbridge St Steph *Roch* 82-85; Whittle-le-Woods *Blackb* 85-90; Hon Par Dn 87-90; Chapl Scargill Ho 90-96; Hon C Ingleton w Chapel le Dale *Bradf* 96-03; Dioc Youth Adv 96-01; Hon C Yate New Town *Bris* 03-07; TV 07-08; Sub Chapl HM Pris Ashfield 04-09; P-in-c Lostock St Thos and St Jo *Man* from 09; P-in-c Bolton St Bede from 09. *St Bede's Vicarage, 92 Normanby Street, Bolton BL3 3QR* Tel (01204) 654016 E-mail viv.ashworth01@tiscali.co.uk

ASINUGO, Mrs Christiana Chidinma. NTMTC. **d** 09. NSM Becontree St Mary *Chelmsf* from 09. *187 Barley Lane, Romford RM6 4XU*

ASIR, Jebamani Sekar Anand. See ANAND, The Very Revd Sekar Anand Asir

ASKEW, Miss Alison Jane. b 57. Dur Univ BA78 PGCE79. S Dios Minl Tr Scheme 93. **d** 95 **p** 96. NSM Kingsclere *Win* 95-96; Asst Chapl N Hants Hosps NHS Trust 95-99; Chapl 99-04; Sen Chapl Basingstoke and N Hants NHS Foundation Trust from 04. *The Chaplaincy, Basingstoke and North Hampshire Hospital, Aldermaston Road, Basingstoke RG24 9NA* Tel (01256) 314901 E-mail alison.askew@bnhft.nhs.uk

ASKEW, Canon Dennis. b 34. Open Univ BA76. Kelham Th Coll 45 Lich Th Coll 55. **d** 58 **p** 59. C Garforth *Ripon* 58-61; C Seacroft 61-64; V Holland Fen *Linc* 64-69; R Folkingham w Laughton 69-77; V Aswarby w Swarby 69-77; R Osbournby w Scott Willoughby 69-77; R Pickworth w Walcot 69-77; V Threckingham 69-77; P-in-c Newton w Haceby 72-77; P-in-c Aunsby w Dembleby 72-77; R S Lafford 77-87; R Ruskington 87-96; Can and Preb Linc Cathl 86-05; rtd 96; Perm to Offic *Linc* 96-08. *c/o Mrs H R Pearce, 37 North Worple Way, London SW14 8QA*

ASKEW, Peter Timothy. b 68. Ridley Hall Cam 00. **d** 02 **p** 03. C Bilton *Ripon* 02-06; C Harrogate St Mark from 06; Chapl St Aid Sch Harrogate from 06. *59 Coppice Way, Harrogate HG1 2DJ* Tel (01423) 566983 Mobile 07754-046029 E-mail pete.askew2@ntlworld.com

ASKEW, Canon Reginald James Albert. b 28. CCC Cam BA51 MA55. Linc Th Coll 55. **d** 57 **p** 58. C Highgate St Mich *Lon* 57-61; Lect and Vice-Prin Wells Th Coll 61-69; PV Wells Cathl 61-69; V Paddington Ch Ch *Lon* 69-73; Member Corrymeela Community from 71; Prin Sarum & Wells Th Coll 73-87; Chmn S Dios Minl Tr Scheme 73-87; Can and Preb Sarum Cathl 75-87; Dean K Coll Lon 88-93; rtd 93; Perm to Offic *B & W* from 93 and *Lon* 93-96. *Carters Cottage, North Wootton, Shepton Mallet BA4 4AF* Tel (01749) 890728

ASKEW, Preb Richard George. b 35. BNC Ox BA59 MA63. Ridley Hall Cam 62. **d** 64 **p** 65. C Chesham St Mary *Ox* 64-66; C Mossley Hill St Matt and St Jas *Liv* 66-67; Chapl Ox Pastorate 67-72; Asst Chapl BNC Ox 67-71; R Ashtead *Guildf* 72-83; RD Leatherhead 80-83; Can Res and Treas Sarum Cathl 83-90; Dioc Adv on Miss and Min *B & W* 83-90; R Bath Abbey w St Jas 90-00; Preb Wells Cathl 92-00; Perm to Offic *Sarum* 00-01; TV Cley Hill Warminster 01-04; rtd 04. *Churchside, 3 Hindon Road, Monkton Deverill, Warminster BA12 7EZ* Tel (01985) 844587 E-mail askew.easter@btinternet.com

ASKEY, Gary Simon. b 64. K Coll Lon LLB99 Univ Coll Lon LLM00 Univ of S Qld MEd04. St Steph Ho Ox 88. **d** 91 **p** 92. SSM 87-99; Prior SSM Priory Kennington 96-98; C Middlesbrough All SS *York* 91-94; Sub-Chapl HM Pris Holme Ho 92-94; C Whitby 94-96; Missr Whitby Miss and Seafarer's Trust 94-96; Lic to Offic *S'wark* 96-03; Hon C Angell Town St Jo 98-03; Perm to Offic 05-07; Hon C Walworth St Jo from 07. *St John's Cottage, 16 Larcom Street, London SE17 1NQ* Tel (020) 7450 1530 E-mail simon@askey.gs

ASKEY, John Stuart. b 39. Chich Th Coll 63. **d** 66 **p** 67. C Feltham *Lon* 66-69; C Epsom Common Ch Ch *Guildf* 69-72; C Chesterton Gd Shep *Ely* 72-74; R Stretham w Thetford 74-93; Dioc Spirituality Officer 75-98; Dioc Youth Officer 80-99; P-in-c Brinkley, Burrough Green and Carlton 93-97; P-in-c Westley Waterless 93-97; P-in-c Dullingham 93-97; P-in-c Stetchworth 93-97; R Raddesley Gp 97-99; Chapl Gothenburg w Halmstad, Jönköping *Eur* 99-04; rtd 04. *165 Lewes Road, Brighton BN2 3LD*

ASKEY, Matthew. b 74. Loughb Coll BA96 Bretton Hall Coll

MA99 Leeds Univ BA09 Huddersfield Univ PGCE06. Coll of Resurr Mirfield 07. **d** 09. C Elland *Wakef* from 09. *50 Victoria Road, Elland HX5 0QA* Tel (01422) 370306 Mobile 07814-502034 E-mail maskey@mirfield.org.uk

ASKEY, Mrs Susan Mary. b 44. Leeds Univ MA00. NOC 99. **d** 99 **p** 00. C Golcar *Wakef* 99-02; P-in-c Drighlington from 02. *The Vicarage, Back Lane, Drighlington, Bradford BD11 1LS* Tel 0113-285 2402 E-mail susanaskey@virgin.net

ASKEY, Thomas Cyril. b 29. Sheff Univ BSc50 Man Univ MA(Theol)81 ACIPA58 MITMA76. NW Ord Course 70. **d** 73 **p** 74. NSM Gawsworth *Ches* 73-76; Perm to Offic 76-80; rtd 81; Perm to Offic *Derby* 99-05. *Park Cottage, Nether End, Baslow, Bakewell DE45 1SR* Tel (01246) 583780

ASKWITH, Mrs Helen Mary. b 57. Thames Valley Univ BSc00. ERMC 04. **d** 07 **p** 08. NSM Wembley St Jo *Lon* from 07. *21 Roxeth Green Avenue, Harrow HA2 8AE* Tel (020) 8422 3295 Mobile 07711-643220 E-mail hdaskwith@aol.com

ASMELASH, Berhane Tesfamariam. b 56. Addis Ababa Univ MD89 Lon Bible Coll MPhil04. SEITE BA08. **d** 08 **p** 09. C Upper Holloway *Lon* from 08. *6 Zoffany Street, London N19 3ER* Tel (020) 8424 8270 Mobile 07838-167198 E-mail berhanea@fastmail.fm

ASPDEN, Peter George. b 28. Univ of Wales (Lamp) BA50. Ely Th Coll 52. **d** 53 **p** 54. C Morecambe St Barn *Blackb* 53-55; C Marton 55-58; V Tockholes 58-63; P-in-c St Annes St Marg 63-66; V 66-75; V Lancaster Ch Ch 75-79; R Eccleston 79-94; rtd 94; Perm to Offic *Liv* from 94 and *Blackb* from 05. *21 Glencoyne Drive, Southport PR9 9TS* Tel (01704) 214066 E-mail pgandema@glencoyne.vispa.com

ASPINALL, Philip Norman. b 51. Cam Univ MA ATI. WMMTC 86. **d** 89 **p** 90. NSM Cov E 89-98. *139 Wiltshire Court, Nod Rise, Mount Nod, Coventry CV5 7JP* Tel (024) 7646 7509

✠**ASPINALL, The Most Revd Phillip John.** b 59. Univ of Tasmania BSc80 Trin Coll Melbourne BD88 Monash Univ PhD89 Deakin Univ MBA98. Melbourne Coll of Div. **d** 88 **p** 89 **c** 98. C S Launceston Australia 88-89; Asst P Brighton 89-91; P-in-c Bridgewater w Gagebrook 91-94; Dir Anglicare Tas 94-98; Adn for Ch and Soc 97-98; Asst Bp Adelaide 98-02; Abp Brisbane from 02; Primate of Australia from 05. *Bishopsbourne, GPO Box 421, Brisbane Qld 4001, Australia* Tel (0061) (7) 3835 2222 Fax 3832 5030 E-mail archbishops@anglicanbrisbane.org.au

ASQUITH, Barbara Rosemary. b 37. **d** 03 **p** 04. OLM S Ossett *Wakef* 03-06; OLM Batley All SS and Purlwell from 06. *115 Teall Street, Ossett WF5 0HS* Tel (01924) 271302 Mobile 07754-859247

ASQUITH, Michael John. b 60. St D Coll Lamp BA82 MPhil91 Ch Ch Coll Cant PGCE83. Cant Sch of Min 91. **d** 94 **p** 95. C S Ashford Ch Ch *Cant* 94-98; P-in-c Weldon w Deene *Pet* 98-00; P-in-c Corby Epiphany w St Jo 98-06; Dep Dioc Dir of Educn *Leic* from 06. *2 Rosebay Road, Desborough, Kettering NN14 2JS* Tel (01536) 760358 E-mail mikeasq@aol.com

ASQUITH, Rosemary. *See* ASQUITH, Barbara Rosemary

ASSON, Geoffrey Ormrod. b 34. Univ of Wales (Ban) BA54 St Cath Coll Ox BA56 MA61. St Steph Ho Ox 54. **d** 57 **p** 58. C Aberdare *Llan* 57-59; C Roath 59-61; R Hagworthingham w Asgarby and Lusby *Linc* 61-65; P-in-c Mavis Enderby w Raithby 62-65; V Friskney 65-69; R S Ormsby w Ketsby, Calceby and Driby 69-74, R Harrington w Brinkhill 69-74; R Oxcombe 69-74; R Ruckland w Farforth and Maidenwell 69-74; R Somersby w Bag Enderby 69-74; R Tetford and Salmonby 69-74; P-in-c Belchford 71-74; P-in-c W Ashby 71-74; V Riverhead w Dunton Green *Roch* 75-80; R Kington w Huntington *Heref* 80-82; R Kington and Weobley 80-86; P-in-c Almeley 81-82; P-in-c Knill 81-82; P-in-c Old Radnor 81-82; R Kington w Huntington, Old Radnor, Kinnerton etc 82-86; V Mathry w St Edren's and Grandston etc *St D* 86-97; Bp's Rural Adv and Tourist Officer 91-95; rtd 96. *Sincerity, St Dogmaels, Cardigan SA43 3JZ* Tel (01239) 615591

ASTBURY, Susan. b 61. St Hugh's Coll Ox BA82 MA85 DPhil85. SWMTC 05. **d** 08. C Teignmouth, Ideford w Luton, Ashcombe etc *Ex* from 08. *3 The Strand, Shaldon, Teignmouth TQ14 0DL* Tel (01626) 873807

ASTILL, Cyril John. b 33. Oak Hill Th Coll 62. **d** 65 **p** 66. C Carl St Jo 65-68; C St Helens St Helen *Liv* 68-71; V Blackb Sav 71-85; P-in-c Blackb Ch Ch w St Matt 81-83; TR N Ferriby *York* 85-97; V 97-99; rtd 99; P-in-c Burton Agnes w Harpham and Lowthorpe etc *York* 99-03. *18 Golden Vale, Churchdown, Gloucester GL3 2LU* Tel (01452) 859751

ASTIN, Alfred Ronald. b 18. St Pet Hall Ox BA43 MA45. Ridley Hall Cam. **d** 47 **p** 48. C Weaste *Man* 47-50; C Harpurhey Ch Ch 50-51; V Leesfield 51-57; V Earlham St Anne *Nor* 57-70; V Sheringham 70-84; rtd 84; Perm to Offic *Nor* 84-99. *c/o The Revd T R Astin, 23 Kingfisher Drive, Woodley, Reading RG5 3LG* Tel 0118-954 5669

ASTIN, Howard Keith. b 51. Warwick Univ LLB. Trin Coll Bris 83. **d** 83 **p** 84. C Kirkheaton *Wakef* 83-88; V Bowling St Jo *Bradf* from 88. *St John's Vicarage, 96 Lister Avenue, Bradford BD4 7QS* Tel (01274) 727355 E-mail howard.astin@bradford.anglican.org *or* h.astin@virgin.net

ASTIN, Mrs Moira Anne Elizabeth. b 65. Clare Coll Cam BA86 MA90. Wycliffe Hall Ox BA96. **d** 95 **p** 96. C Newbury *Ox* 95-99; C Thatcham 99-01; TV 01-05; TV Woodley 05-09; V Southlake from 09; Angl Ecum Officer (Berks) from 03. *23 Kingfisher Drive, Woodley, Reading RG5 3LG* Tel 0118-954 5669 E-mail moira.astin@btinternet.com

ASTIN, Timothy Robin. b 58. St Edm Hall Ox BA79 Darw Coll Cam PhD82 FGS. Ox Min Course 90. **d** 93 **p** 94. NSM Reading St Jo *Ox* 93-95; NSM Newbury 95-99; NSM Beedon and Peasemore w W Ilsley and Farnborough 99-05; NSM Woodley 05-09; NSM Woodley from 09. *23 Kingfisher Drive, Woodley, Reading RG5 3LG* Tel 0118-954 5669 E-mail t.r.astin@reading.ac.uk

ASTLEY, Prof Jeffrey. b 47. Down Coll Cam BA68 MA72 Dur Univ PhD79. Qu Coll Birm 68. **d** 70 **p** 71. C Cannock *Lich* 70-73; Lect and Chapl St Hild Coll Dur 73-75; Sen Lect and Chapl SS Hild and Bede Coll Dur 75-77; Prin Lect & Hd Relig Studies Bp Grosseteste Coll 77-81; Lic to Offic *Linc* 78-81; Dir N England Inst for Chr Educn from 81. *Carter House, Pelaw Leazes Lane, Durham DH1 1TB* Tel 0191-384 1034 *or* 374 7807 Fax 384 7529 E-mail jeff.astley@durham.ac.uk

ASTON, Glyn. b 29. Univ of Wales (Abth) BA54 TCert55. Sarum & Wells Th Coll 84. **d** 79 **p** 80. Hon C Maindee Newport *Mon* 79-85; C 85-86; V Llangwm Uchaf and Llangwm Isaf w Gwernesney etc 86-99; rtd 99; Lic to Offic *Mon* from 99. *Flat 4, 47 Caerau Road, Newport NP20 4HH*

ASTON, John Bernard. b 34. Leeds Univ BA55 PGCE56. Qu Coll Birm 72. **d** 75 **p** 76. NSM Shenstone *Lich* 75-05; NSM Stonnall 00-05; Chapl HM YOI Swinfen Hall 90-99; Perm to Offic *Lich* from 05. *4 Footherley Road, Shenstone, Lichfield WS14 0NJ* Tel (01543) 480388

ASTON, John Leslie. b 47. Open Univ BSc99 Win Univ MA07. Oak Hill Th Coll BA80. **d** 80 **p** 81. C Trentham *Lich* 80-83; C Meir Heath 83-85; V Upper Tean 85-91; CF 91-02; C Andover w Foxcott *Win* 02-05; P-in-c Felixstowe SS Pet and Paul *St E* from 05. *The Vicarage, 14 Picketts Road, Felixstowe IP11 7JT* Tel (01394) 284049 E-mail johnaston@oldfelixstoweparish.org

ASTON, Mrs Kim Elizabeth. b 57. Colchester Inst of Educn BA78 LRAM78. SEITE 00. **d** 03 **p** 04. C Croydon St Jo *S'wark* from 03. *61 Boundary Way, Croydon CR0 5AU* Tel (01689) 843669 *or* (020) 8688 8104 E-mail astonkim@hotmail.com

ASTON, Michael James. b 48. Loughb Univ BSc70 MBCS85. NTMTC 98. **d** 01 **p** 02. NSM Writtle w Highwood *Chelmsf* 01-07; P-in-c W Hanningfield from 07. *15 Weller Grove, Chelmsford CM1 4YJ* Tel (01245) 442547 Mobile 07940-417418 E-mail mikaston@globalnet.co.uk

ASTON, Roger. b 52. Ox Poly BEd83. SAOMC 96. **d** 99 **p** 00. OLM Eynsham and Cassington *Ox* from 99. *9 Bell Close, Cassington, Witney OX29 4EP* Tel (01865) 880757 E-mail rogera52@aol.com

ASTON SMITH, Anthony. b 29. Trin Coll Cam BA52 MA56 PhD56 CEng MIM FIDiagE MICorrST AMIMechE. Ox NSM Course 86. **d** 93 **p** 94. NSM Ox St Giles and SS Phil and Jas w St Marg 93-99; rtd 99; Perm to Offic *Ox* from 99. *32 Chalfont Road, Oxford OX2 6TH* Tel (01865) 557090 E-mail a.j.astonsmith@btinternet.com

ASTON, Archdeacon of. *See* RUSSELL, The Ven Brian Kenneth
ASTON, Suffragan Bishop of. *See* WATSON, The Rt Revd Andrew John

ATACK, John Philip. b 49. Lanc Univ MA91. Linc Th Coll 86. **d** 88 **p** 89. C Cleveleys *Blackb* 88-92; V Appley Bridge 92-96; P-in-c Mostyn w Ffynnongroyw *St As* 99-03; P-in-c Colwyn 03-08; R Colwyn and Llanelian from 08; AD Rhos from 09; Chapl Conwy and Denbighshire NHS Trust from 05; Hon Chapl Miss to Seafarers 01-03. *The Vicarage, 28 Bodelwyddan Avenue, Old Colwyn, Colwyn Bay LL29 9NP* Tel (01492) 518394 E-mail phil.atack@btopenworld.com

ATFIELD, Gladys. Univ Coll Lon BSc53. Gilmore Course. **dss** 79 **d** 87 **p** 94. Bexley St Mary *Roch* 79-01; Hon C 87-01; rtd 01; Perm to Offic *Roch* from 01. *7 Clarendon Mews, High Street, Bexley DA5 1JS* Tel (01322) 551741

ATHERFOLD, Mrs Evelyne Sara. b 43. Leeds Inst of Educn CertEd64. NOC 82. **dss** 85 **d** 92 **p** 94. Kirk Sandall and Edenthorpe *Sheff* 85-87; NSM Fishlake w Sykehouse and Kirk Bramwith etc 87-00; P-in-c 00-03; R from 03; Chapl HM YOI Hatfield 96-03. *The Vicarage, Church Street, Fishlake, Doncaster DN7 5JW* Tel (01302) 841396

ATHERSTONE, Andrew Castell. b 74. Ch Coll Cam BA95 MA98 Wycliffe Hall Ox MSt99 DPhil01 FRHistS08. **d** 01 **p** 02. C Abingdon *Ox* 01 05; NSM Eynsham and Cassington from 05; Research Fell Latimer Trust from 05; Tutor Wycliffe Hall Ox from 07. *44 Shakespeare Road, Eynsham, Witney OX29 4PY* Tel (01865) 731239 E-mail andrew.atherstone@wycliffe.ox.ac.uk

ATHERSTONE, Canon Castell Hugh. b 45. Natal Univ BA67. St

Chad's Coll Dur MA79. **d** 70 **p** 70. C Pietermaritzburg St Alphege S Africa 70-72; C Berea St Thos 72-74; C Kloor 74-77; R Hillcrest 77-80; R Newcastle 80-83; Dioc Stewardship Adv *Ely* 83-87; P-in-c Doddington w Benwick 83-87; R Frant w Eridge *Chich* 87-95; P-in-c Mark Cross 94-95; RD Rotherfield 90-94; V Seaford w Sutton from 95; RD Lewes and Seaford 97-07; Can and Preb Chich Cathl from 02. *The Vicarage, 46 Sutton Road, Seaford BN25 1SH* Tel and fax (01323) 893508 E-mail hugh@atherstoneweb.org

ATHERTON, Graham Bryson. b 47. FTCL68 GRSM69 ARMCM69 Man Univ CertEd70. Edin Th Coll 77. **d** 79 **p** 80. C Orford St Marg *Liv* 79-82; V Warrington St Barn 82-88; V Leeds Halton St Wilfrid *Ripon* 88-95; RD Whitkirk 92-95; TR Guiseley w Esholt *Bradf* from 95. *The Rectory, The Green, Guiseley, Leeds LS20 9BB* Tel (01943) 874321 E-mail graham.atherton@@bradford.anglican.org

ATHERTON, Henry Anthony. b 44. Univ of Wales BSc67 DipEd68 Fitzw Coll Cam BA72 MA75 Heythrop Coll Lon MTh00 FGS68. Westcott Ho Cam 70. **d** 72 **p** 73. C Leamington Priors All SS *Cov* 72-75; C Orpington All SS *Roch* 75-78; V Gravesend St Mary 78-87; Chapl St Jas Hosp Gravesend 82-87; V Bromley St Andr *Roch* from 87. *The Vicarage, 1 Lake Avenue, Bromley BR1 4EN* Tel and fax (020) 8460 0481

ATHERTON, Canon John Robert. b 39. Lon Univ BA60 Man Univ MA74 PhD79. Coll of Resurr Mirfield 60. **d** 62 **p** 63. C Aberdeen St Marg 62-64; C Bury St Mark *Man* 64-67; P-in-c Glas St Marg 67-68; R Hulme St Geo *Man* 68-74; Ind Chapl 68-74; Asst Dir Wm Temple Foundn 74-79; Dir from 79; Lic to Offic 74-84; Can Res Man Cathl 84-04; rtd 04. *102 Fairview Drive, Adlington, Chorley PR6 9SB* Tel (01257) 474882 Mobile 07989-969567

ATHERTON, Lionel Thomas. b 45. Univ of Wales (Ban) BA74 St Luke's Coll Ex. St Steph Ho Ox 74. **d** 76 **p** 77. C Chenies and Lt Chalfont *Ox* 76-79; C Fleet *Guildf* 79-84; V S Farnborough 84-89; TR Alston Team *Newc* 89-96; V Chorley St Pet *Blackb* from 96; Bp's Adv on New Relig Movements from 02. *St Peter's Vicarage, Harpers Lane, Chorley PR6 0HT* Tel and fax (01257) 263423 E-mail lionelatherton@hotmail.com

ATHERTON, Paul Christopher. b 56. Chich Th Coll. **d** 82 **p** 83. C Orford St Marg *Liv* 82-86; CR 86-88; Chapl Univ of Wales (Cardiff) *Llan* 88-89; TV Walton St Mary *Liv* 89-92; C Westmr St Matt *Lon* 92-96; C Somers Town 96-97; V Bush Hill Park St Mark from 97; Chapl N Middx Hosp NHS Trust from 97. *The Vicarage, St Mark's Road, Enfield EN1 1BE* Tel (020) 8363 2780 E-mail paul.atherton@blueyonder.co.uk

ATHERTON, Philip Gordon. b 47. NTMTC BA07. **d** 07 **p** 08. NSM Hornsey H Innocents *Lon* from 07; NSM Stroud Green H Trin from 07. *4 Pensilver Close, Barnet EN4 9BE* Tel (020) 8441 5524 Mobile 07901-355235 E-mail philipatherton@tiscali.co.uk

ATKIN, Arthur Courtney Qu'appelle. b 19. Dur Univ BA44. Lich Th Coll 59. **d** 59 **p** 60. Chapl Bromsgrove Jun Sch 59-64; C Kidderminster St Geo *Worc* 59-60; C Bromsgrove All SS 60-64; Chapl RN 64-69; Chapl R Hosp Sch Holbrook 69-72; P-in-c Brixham *Ex* 72-74; Chapl Colston's Sch Bris 74-79; P-in-c Pitcombe w Shepton Montague and Bratton St Maur *B & W* 79-85; rtd 86; Perm to Offic *B & W* 86-93; Perm to Offic *Heref* from 93. *6 Leadon Bank, Orchard Lane, Ledbury HR8 1BYD*

ATKINS, Austen Shaun (Shaun). b 55. St Pet Coll Ox MA82 Selw Coll Cam MA85. Ridley Hall Cam 79. **d** 82 **p** 83. C S Mimms Ch Ch *Lon* 82-86; C Fulham St Matt 86-91; P-in-c Fulham St Dionis Parson's Green 91-03; V 03-04; C Ox St Andr 05-09; Chapl Bedford Sch from 09. *The Chaplaincy, Bedford School, De Parys Avenue, Bedford MK40 2TU* Tel (01234) 362239 E-mail chaplain@bedfordschool.org.uk

ATKINS, Canon David John. b 43. Kelham Th Coll 64. **d** 68 **p** 69. C Lewisham St Mary S'wark 68-72; Min Motspur Park 72-77; P-in-c Mitcham Ascension 77-82; V 82-83; P-in-c Downham w S Hanningfield *Chelmsf* 83-88; R 88-01; P-in-c W Hanningfield 90-93; RD Chelmsf S 93-01; V Maldon All SS w St Pet from 01; Hon Can Chelmsf Cathl 00-09; rtd 09. *20 Bradford Crescent, Hadleigh, Ipswich IP7 5ET* E-mail atkins@dj@btinternet.com

ATKINS, Dean John. b 70. Univ of Wales (Cardiff) BD93. St Steph Ho Ox 93. **d** 95 **p** 96. C Merthyr Dyfan *Llan* 95-99; V Aberaman and Abercwmboi w Cwmaman 99-01; Dioc Youth Officer from 01; P-in-c Roath St Sav from 08. *St Anne's, 1 North Church Street, Cardiff CF10 5HB* Tel (029) 2049 9867

ATKINS, Mrs Diana. b 31. K Coll Lon BD54 DipEd55. Qu Coll Birm 81. **dss** 83 **d** 87. De Beauvoir Town St Pet *Lon* 83-85; Gleadless *Sheff* 85-93; Par Dn 87-93; rtd 93; Perm to Offic *Sheff* from 93. *27 Stannington Glen, Sheffield S6 6NA* Tel 0114-234 0543

ATKINS, Forrest William (Bill). b 59. Ch Coll Cam MA85 Lon Univ BD84. Ridley Hall Cam 83. **d** 86 **p** 87. C Normanton *Derby* 86-90; C Stratford St Jo and Ch Ch w Forest Gate St Jas *Chelmsf* 90-97; Asst Chapl Dubai and Sharjah w N Emirates 97-03; I Mohill w Farnaught, Aughavas, Oughteragh etc

K, E & A from 03. *St Mary's Rectory, Mohill, Co Leitrim, Republic of Ireland* Tel (00353) (71) 963 2959 E-mail fwatkins@eircom.net

ATKINS, Francis John. b 47. CEng MIStructE. S Dios Minl Tr Scheme. **d** 89 **p** 90. NSM Studley *Sarum* 89-92; Lic to RD Bradford from 92. *Church Cottage, 344 Frome Road, Trowbridge BA14 0EF* Tel (01225) 761757

ATKINS, Jane Elizabeth. b 51. EMMTC 98. **d** 01 **p** 02. NSM Fenn Lanes Gp *Leic* 01-05; Sub Chapl HM Pris Leic 03-05; P-in-c Ashill w Saham Toney *Nor* 05-07; V Ashill, Carbrooke, Ovington and Saham Toney from 07. *The Rectory, Swaffham Road, Ashill, Thetford IP25 7BT* Tel (01760) 441191

ATKINS, Joy Katherine. b 75. Lon Sch of Th BTh97 Dur Univ PGCE98. St Jo Coll Nottm MTh09. **d** 09. C Uxbridge *Lon* from 09. *St Andrew's Vicarage, 32A Greenway, Uxbridge UB8 2PJ* Tel (01895) 200252 Mobile 07799-835696 E-mail joy.atkins@uxbridgeparish.org

ATKINS, Nicholas Steven. b 60. Oak Hill Th Coll BA88. **d** 88 **p** 89. C Shepton Mallet w Doulting *B & W* 88-91; C Combe Down w Monkton Combe and S Stoke 91-93; TV N Wingfield, Clay Cross and Pilsley *Derby* 93-98; V Essington *Lich* 98-05; P-in-c Ipswich St Matt *St E* 05-06; R Triangle, St Matt and All SS from 06. *St Matthew's Rectory, 3 Portman Road, Ipswich IP1 2ES* Tel (01473) 251630

ATKINS, Canon Paul Henry. b 38. St Mich Coll Llan 62. **d** 65 **p** 66. C Sheringham *Nor* 65-68; V Southtown 68-84; RD Flegg (Gt Yarmouth) 78-84; R Aylmerton w Runton 84-99; P-in-c Beeston Regis 98-99; P-in-c Gresham 98-99; R Aylmerton, Runton, Beeston Regis and Gresham 99-03; RD Repps 86-95; Hon Can Nor Cathl 88-03; rtd 03; Perm to Offic *Nor* from 03. *34 Regis Avenue, Beeston Regis, Sheringham NR26 8SW* Tel (01263) 820147 E-mail amdd24@dial.pipex.com

ATKINS, Peter. b 29. Edin Univ MA52. Edin Th Coll 52. **d** 54 **p** 55. C Edin Old St Paul 54-59; P-in-c Edin St Dav 59-64; Chapl Fulbourn Hosp Cam 64-66; R Galashiels *Edin* 66-69; Perm to Offic 69-72; Divisional Dir Soc Services Brighton 72-83; Asst Dir Soc Services E Sussex from 83. *11 South Street, Lewes BN7 2BT* Tel (01273) 476230

ATKINS, Robert Brian. b 49. CIPFA78 Open Univ BA94. SAOMC 94. **d** 97 **p** 98. NSM Bicester w Bucknell, Caversfield and Launton *Ox* from 97. *8 Tubb Close, Bicester OX26 2BN* Tel (01869) 253448 Mobile 07973-713149

ATKINS, Roger Francis. b 30. AKC54. **d** 55 **p** 56. C Bromley All Hallows *Lon* 55-58; C Eastleigh *Win* 58-62; Missr The Murray Australia 62-65; R Mossman 65-69; Adn Carpentaria 69-71; V Wolverley *Worc* 71-76; V S Hackney St Mich w Haggerston St Paul *Lon* 76-85; TV Gleadless *Sheff* 85-93; rtd 93; Perm to Offic *Sheff* from 93. *27 Stannington Glen, Sheffield S6 6NA* Tel 0114-234 0543

ATKINS, Shaun. See ATKINS, Austen Shaun.

ATKINS, Timothy David. b 45. Ridley Hall Cam 71. **d** 74 **p** 75. C Stoughton *Guildf* 74-79; C Chilwell S'well 79-84; R Eastwood 84-91; V Finchley Ch Ch *Lon* from 91; Chapl Barnet Healthcare NHS Trust 92-01; Chapl Enfield Primary Care Trust from 01. *Christ Church Vicarage, 616 High Road, London N12 0AA* Tel (020) 8445 2377 or 8445 2532 Fax 8343 9406 or 8492 0278 E-mail christchurch@nfinchley.fsnet.co.uk

ATKINS, Timothy James. b 38. Worc Coll Ox BA62. Cuddesdon Coll 62. **d** 64 **p** 65. C Stafford St Mary *Lich* 64-67; C Loughborough St Pet *Leic* 67-69; C Usworth *Dur* 69-71; Lic to Offic *Newc* 71-76; P-in-c Slaley 76-87; P-in-c Shotley 87-05; Dioc Child Protection Adv 98-06. *5 Railway Terrace, Witton le Wear, Bishop Auckland DL14 0AL* Tel (01388) 488626

ATKINS, Timothy Samuel. b 22. DSC44. Em Coll Cam BA46 MA52. Ridley Hall Cam 47. **d** 49 **p** 50. C Melton Mowbray w Burton Lazars, Freeby etc *Leic* 49-51; C Preston St Jo *Blackb* 51-54; V Baxenden 54-58; R Mildenhall *St E* 58-63; V Bunbury *Ches* 63-87; RD Malpas 85-87; rtd 87; Perm to Offic *Ches* 87-01. *7 Fosbrooke House, 8 Clifton Drive, Lytham St Annes FY8 5RQ* Tel (01253) 667052

ATKINS, William. See ATKINS, Forrest William.

ATKINSON, Adam. b 70. Wycliffe Hall Ox. **d** 07 **p** 08. C Shadwell St Paul w Ratcliffe St Jas *Lon* from 07. *St Peter's Vicarage, St Peter's Close, London E2 7AE* Tel (020) 7739 2717 Mobile 07780-992112 E-mail a.atkinson@virgin.net

ATKINSON, Albert Edward. b 35. St Deiniol's Hawarden 79. **d** 79 **p** 80. C Ellesmere Port *Ches* 79-81; TV 81-84; P-in-c Kirkby Malzeard w Grewelthorpe and Mickley etc *Ripon* 84-88; P-in-c Fountains 88-90; R Fountains Gp 90-92; V Aysgarth and Bolton cum Redmire 92-96; rtd 96; Perm to Offic *Ripon* 96-07; Hon Min Can Ripon Cathl 01-07; Perm to Offic *Ches* from 07. *36 Forbes Road, Stockport SK1 4HN* Tel 0161-429 7180 E-mail albert.atkinson@tiscali.co.uk

ATKINSON, Ms Audrey. b 54. Univ of Wales (Lamp) BA97 Trin Coll Carmarthen PGCE98. Coll of Resurr Mirfield 06. **d** 08 **p** 09. C Beadnell *Newc* from 08; C N Sunderland from 08. *Gleneagles, 24 King Street, Seahouses NE68 7XR* Tel (01665) 720116 Mobile 07833-198968 E-mail audreyatkinson@hotmail.co.uk

ATKINSON, Brian Colin. b 49. Sarum & Wells Th Coll 85. **d** 87 **p** 88. C Up Hatherley *Glouc* 87-90; R Upper Stour *Sarum* 90-95; TR Trowbridge H Trin 95-04; P-in-c Fairford and Kempsford w Whelford *Glouc* 04-08; TR Fairford Deanery from 09; AD Fairford from 04. *The Vicarage, The Croft, Fairford GL7 4BB* Tel and fax (01285) 712467 E-mail katki01225@aol.com

ATKINSON, Christopher John. b 57. Man Univ BA80. Qu Coll Birm 82. **d** 85 **p** 86. C Stalybridge *Man* 85-88; P-in-c Westhall w Brampton and Stoven *St E* 88-89; P-in-c Sotterley, Willingham, Shadingfield, Ellough etc 88-90; P-in-c Hundred River Gp of Par 90-92; R Hundred River 92-97; P-in-c Eye w Braiseworth and Yaxley 97-00; P-in-c Occold 97-00; P-in-c Bedingfield 97-00; R Eye 00-03; RD Hartismere 97-03; V Bourne *Linc* from 03. *The Vicarage, Church Walk, Bourne PE10 9UQ* Tel (01778) 422412 E-mail chris_atk@yahoo.com

ATKINSON, Canon Christopher Lionel Varley. b 39. K Coll Lon 63. Chich Th Coll 65. **d** 67 **p** 68. C Sowerby Bridge w Norland *Wakef* 67-70; P-in-c Flushing *Truro* 70-73; Dioc Adv in RE 70-73; Perm to Offic *Worc* 74-78; TR Halesowen 78-88; RD Dudley 79-87; Hon Can Worc Cathl 83-88; V Cartmel *Carl* 88-97; TV Cartmel Peninsula 97-98; RD Windermere 94-98; Hon Can Carl Cathl 94-98; TR Bensham *Dur* 98-03; AD Gateshead 99-03; rtd 03; Bp's Adv Spiritual Development *Dur* 03-08; Hon Can Dur Cathl from 01. *4 Attwood Place, Tow Law, Bishop Auckland DL13 4ER* Tel (01388) 731749

ATKINSON, Clive James. b 68. QUB BSc90. CITC 90. **d** 93 **p** 94. C Belfast H Trin and Ardoyne *Conn* 93-97; I Belfast Upper Falls 97-02; Chapl Vevey w Château d'Oex and Villars *Eur* from 02. *The Parsonage, chemin de Champsavaux 1, 1807 Blonay, Vaud, Switzerland* Tel (0041) (21) 943 2239 E-mail info@allsaints.ch

ATKINSON, Prof David. b 44. Hull Univ BSc66 Newc Univ PhD69 CBiol FIBiol FRSA MIEEM. TISEC 03. **d** 05 **p** 06. C Aberdeen St Andr 05-07; P Bieldside 07-09; P Auchindoir from 09; P Inverurie from 09; P Kemnay from 09. *33 Norman Gray Park, Blackburn, Aberdeen AB21 0ZR* Tel (01224) 791163 E-mail atkinson390@btinternet.com

ATKINSON, David. b 64. St Cuth Soc Dur BA02. Cranmer Hall Dur 02. **d** 04 **p** 05. C Dunston *Dur* 04-07; C Pelton and W Pelton from 07. *The Vicarage, Church Road, Pelton, Chester le Street DH2 1XB* Tel 0191-370 2204 E-mail david@theatkinsons.co.uk

ATKINSON, Canon David James. b 41. K Coll Lon BD63 AKC63 Selw Coll Cam BA65 MA72. Linc Th Coll 65. **d** 66 **p** 67. C Linc St Giles 66-70; Asst Chapl Newc Univ 70-73; P-in-c Adbaston *Lich* 73-80; Adult Educn Officer 73-75; Dioc Dir of Educn 75-82; Preb Lich Cathl 79-82; Chapl Hull Univ 82-87; Dioc Dir of Educn *Linc* 87-94; P-in-c Bishop Norton, Wadingham and Snitterby 94-01; Perm to Offic from 01; Can and Preb Linc Cathl 89-06; rtd 06. *4 The Orchards, Middle Rasen, Market Rasen LN8 3TL* Tel (01673) 849979

✠**ATKINSON, The Rt Revd David John.** b 43. K Coll Lon BSc65 AKC65 PhD70 Bris Univ MLitt73 Ox Univ MA85 MSOSc. Trin Coll Bris and Tyndale Hall Bris 69. **d** 72 **p** 73 **c** 01. C Halliwell St Pet *Man* 72-74; C Harborne Heath *Birm* 74-77; Lib Latimer Ho Ox 77-80; Chapl CCC Ox 80-93; Fell 84-93; Visiting Lect Wycliffe Hall Ox 84-93; Can Res and Chan S'wark Cathl 93-96; Adn Lewisham 96-01; Suff Bp Thetford 01-09; rtd 09. *6 Bynes Road, South Croydon CR2 0PR* Tel (020) 8686 8815

ATKINSON, Derek Arthur. b 31. K Coll Lon BD39 AKC39. **d** 60 **p** 61. C Ashford *Cant* 60-64; C Deal St Leon 64-68; R E w W Ogwell *Ex* 68-81; Asst Dir of RE 68-78; Dep Dir and Children's Adv 78-88; R Ogwell and Denbury 81-84; R Kenton w Mamhead and Powderham 84-88; rtd 88; Perm to Offic *Ex* 88-98. *High Trees, Fulford Road, Fulford, Stoke-on-Trent ST11 9QT* Tel (01782) 397156 E-mail derek-atkinson@lineone.net

ATKINSON, Mrs Heather Dawn. b 69. Leeds Univ BA02. NOC 03. **d** 05 **p** 06. C Morley *Wakef* 05-08; P-in-c Moldgreen and Rawthorpe from 08. *The Vicarage, 35 Church Street, Huddersfield HD5 9DL* Tel (01484) 424432 Mobile 07766-575371 E-mail heatherwood19@yahoo.co.uk

ATKINSON, Ian. b 33. BNC Ox BA58 MA63. Coll of Resurr Mirfield 56. **d** 58 **p** 59. C Welling *S'wark* 58-62; C Camberwell St Giles 62-63; V Wandsworth Common St Mary 63-67; C Pretoria Cathl S Africa 67-68; C Oxted *S'wark* 68-69; Asst Chapl Ch Hosp Horsham 70-85; NSM Dalmahoy *Edin* 85-91; Asst Master Clifton Hall Sch 85-91; NSM Dunkeld *St And* from 92; rtd 98. *2 Pinel Lodge, Druids Park, Murthly, Perth PH1 4ES* Tel (01738) 710561

ATKINSON, Canon Prof James. b 14. St Jo Coll Dur BA36 MA39 MLitt50 Univ of Munster DTh55 Hull Univ Hon DD97. **d** 37 **p** 38. C Newc H Cross 37-41; Succ Sheff Cathl 41-42; Prec 42-44; V Shiregreen St Jas and St Chris 44-51; Fell Sheff Univ from 51; Can Th Leic Cathl 54-70; Lect Hull Univ 56-64; Reader 64-67; Prof Bibl Studies Sheff Univ 67-79; Lic to Offic *Sheff* 68-06; Perm to Offic from 07; Can Th Sheff Cathl 70-93; rtd 79; Latimer Ho Ox 81-84. *Leach House, Leadmill Bridge, Hathersage, Hope Valley S32 1BA* Tel (01433) 650570

ATKINSON, Canon John Dudley. b 38. ACA60 FCA71. Qu Coll Birm 63. **d** 66 **p** 67. C Bishop's Stortford St Mich *St Alb* 66-70; C

Norton 70-73; V Markyate Street 73-80; R Baldock w Bygrave 80-94; RD Stevenage 83-89; TR Bride Valley *Sarum* 94-03; RD Lyme Bay 98-03; Can and Preb Sarum Cathl 02-03; rtd 03; Perm to Offic *Heref* from 04. *48 Prince Rupert Road, Ledbury HR8 2FA* Tel (01531) 632014 E-mail canonjda@btinternet.com

ATKINSON, Ms Judith Angela. b 70. Leeds Univ BA92 Fitzw Coll Cam BA95 MA02. Ridley Hall Cam 93. **d** 96 **p** 97. C Chester le Street *Dur* 96-00; Community Employment Development Worker 00-01; NSM Dunston 01-02; Ch Partnership Co-ord N Tyneside 00-02; Lic to Offic *Birm* 03-06; Regional Manager KeyRing Living Support Networks 03-05; Dir (Research and Projects) 05-07; Perm to Offic Canberra and Goulburn Australia from 07. *United Theological College, 16 Masons Drive, North Parramatta, NSW 2151, Australia* E-mail juditha_stephenb@hotmail.com

ATKINSON, Mrs Kate Bigwood. b 56. Cranmer Hall Dur 94. **d** 96 **p** 97. C Woking St Jo *Guildf* 96-00; NSM Haslemere and Grayswood 00-03; Assoc P Incline Village USA from 03. *818 Barbara Street, Incline Village NV 89451-8514, USA*

ATKINSON, Canon Lewis Malcolm. b 34. St Jo Coll Dur. **d** 82 **p** 83. C Chapeltown *Sheff* 82-85; V Sheff St Paul 85-93; Ind Chapl 85-99; RD Ecclesfield 90-93; V Oughtibridge 93-99; RD Tankersley 96-99; Hon Can Sheff Cathl 98-99; rtd 99; Perm to Offic *Sheff* from 99. *14 Rowan Close, Chapeltown, Sheffield S35 1QE*

ATKINSON, Margaret Ann. **d** 07 **p** 08. OLM Fawdon *Newc* from 07. *48 Brotherlee Road, Newcastle upon Tyne NE3 2SL*

ATKINSON, Marianne Rose. b 39. Girton Coll Cam BA61 CertEd62 MA64. Linc Th Coll 86. **d** 88 **p** 94. C S w N Hayling *Portsm* 88-91; C Rainham *Roch* 91-92; Asst Chapl Salford R Hosps NHS Trust 92-97; Hon C Prestwich St Marg *Man* 94-97; Chapl R United Hosp Bath NHS Trust 97-00; rtd 00; Perm to Offic *B & W* 00-03 and *St E* from 03. *68 Barons Road, Bury St Edmunds IP33 2LW* Tel (01284) 752075 E-mail torrensatkinson@aol.com

ATKINSON, Megan Annice. b 37. SRN58. STETS 95. **d** 98 **p** 01. NSM Bridgemary *Portsm* 98-02; NSM Locks Heath 02-04; rtd 04; Perm to Offic *Portsm* from 05. *23 Home Rule Road, Locks Heath, Southampton SO31 6LH* Tel (01489) 575331 E-mail meganatkinson1@msn.com

ATKINSON, Michael Hubert. b 33. Qu Coll Ox BA57 MA60. Ripon Hall Ox 56. **d** 58 **p** 59. C Attercliffe w Carbrook *Sheff* 58-60; Ind Chapl 60-66; C Sharrow St Andr 60-66; Ind Chapl *Pet* 66-71; Sen Ind Chapl *Cant* 71-79; Research Officer Gen Syn Bd for Soc Resp 79-87; Representation Sec USPG 88-92; TV High Wycombe *Ox* 92-97; Chapl Bucks Coll of HE 94-97; rtd 97. *7 Birch Court, Old Bridge Rise, Ilkley LS29 9HH* Tel (01943) 609891

ATKINSON, Nigel Terence. b 60. Sheff Univ BA82 St Jo Coll Dur MA96. Westmr Th Sem (USA) MDiv87 Cranmer Hall Dur 87. **d** 89 **p** 90. C Oakwood St Thos *Lon* 89-92; P-in-c Dolton *Ex* 92-95; P-in-c Iddesleigh w Dowland 92-95; P-in-c Monkokehampton 92-95; Warden Latimer Ho Ox 95-98; V Knutsford St Jo and Toft *Ches* from 98. *The Vicarage, 11 Gough's Lane, Knutsford WA16 8QL* Tel (01565) 632834 Fax 755160 E-mail nigelatk@btopenworld.com

ATKINSON, Canon Patricia Anne. b 47. EAMTC 86. **d** 89 **p** 01. NSM Nor St Steph 89-94; Lic to Offic from 94; Chapl Norfolk Community Health and Care from 00; Chapl Norfolk and Nor Univ Hosp NHS Trust from 01; NSM Brundall w Braydeston and Postwick *Nor* 01-02; Hon Can Nor Cathl from 06. *32 Berryfields, Brundall, Norwich NR13 5QE* Tel (01603) 714720 E-mail pat.atkinson@nnuh.nhs.uk

ATKINSON, Paul William. b 64. St Steph Ho Ox 07. **d** 09. C Castleford *Wakef* from 09. *St Paul's Vicarage, Churchfield Lane, Castleford WF10 4BP* E-mail aldextra@sky.com

ATKINSON, Peter Duncan. b 41. Univ Coll Dur BA62. Linc Th Coll 63. **d** 65 **p** 66. C Beckenham St Geo *Roch* 65-69; C Caversham *Ox* 69-75; P-in-c Millfield St Mark *Dur* 76-86; V Dedworth *Ox* 86-93; TV Aylesbury w Bierton and Hulcott 93-05; rtd 05. *24 Grimbald Road, Knaresborough HG5 8HD* Tel (01423) 866593

ATKINSON, The Very Revd Peter Gordon. b 52. St Jo Coll Ox BA74 MA78 FRSA06. Westcott Ho Cam 77. **d** 79 **p** 80. C Clapham Old Town *S'wark* 79-83; P-in-c Tatsfield 83-90; R Bath H Trin *B & W* 90-91; Prin Chich Th Coll 91-94; Can and Preb Chich Cathl 91-97; R Lavant 94-97; Can Res and Chan Chich Cathl 97-07; Dean Worc from 07. *The Deanery, 10 College Green, Worcester WR1 2LH* Tel (01905) 732399 or 732900 Fax 732906 E-mail peteratkinson@worcestercathedral.org.uk

ATKINSON, Philip Charles. b 50. Hull Univ BA71 PhD76 Chorley Coll of Educn CertEd77. NOC 83. **d** 84 **p** 85. NSM Bolton SS Simon and Jude *Man* 84-87; Chapl R Wolv Sch 87-05; rtd 05. *22 Kirton Grove, Tettenhall, Wolverhampton WV6 8RX*

ATKINSON, Philip Stephen. b 58. K Coll Lon BD80 AKC80 Dur Univ MA97. Ridley Hall Cam 81. **d** 83 **p** 84. C Barrow St Matt *Carl* 83-86; C Kirkby Lonsdale 86-89; R Redmarshall *Dur* 89-95; V Bishopton w Gt Stainton 89-95; C Kirkby Lonsdale *Carl*

95-97; Chapl Casterton Sch Lancs from 95; NSM Kirkby Lonsdale *Carl* from 97. *Beckside, Casterton, Kirkby Lonsdale, Carnforth LA6 2SB* Tel (01524) 279248

ATKINSON, The Ven Richard William Bryant. b 58. OBE02. Magd Coll Cam MA. Ripon Coll Cuddesdon. **d** 84 **p** 85. C Abingdon w Shippon *Ox* 84-87; TV Sheff Manor 87-91; TR 91-96; Hon Tutor Ripon Coll Cuddesdon 87-92; V Rotherham *Sheff* 96-02; Hon Can Sheff Cathl 98-02; Adn Leic from 02. *46 Southernhay Road, Leicester LE2 3TJ* Tel and fax 0116-270 4441 *or* tel 0116-248 7419 E-mail richard.atkinson@leccofe.org

ATKINSON, Miss Ruth Irene. b 58. Worc Coll of Educn BEd80 Cant Ch Ch Univ MA08. Qu Coll Birm 06. **d** 09. C Old Swinford Stourbridge *Worc* from 09. *58 Arlington Court, Stourbridge DY8 1NN* Tel (01384) 373286 Mobile 07913-849532 E-mail home@riatkinson.plus.com

ATKINSON, Canon Samuel Charles Donald. b 30. TCD BA54. **d** 55 **p** 56. C Belfast St Simon *Conn* 55-62; I Ballynaclough *L & K* 62-68; I Cloughjordan w Modreeny 68-87; Dioc Youth Adv (Killaloe) 75-83; Dioc Info Officer 76-88; Can Killaloe Cathl 76-82; Chan 82-96; I Cloughjordan w Borrisokane etc 87-96; rtd 96. *Dromore Lodge, Rockcorry, Co Monaghan, Republic of Ireland* Tel (00353) (42) 42356

ATKINSON, Simon James. b 71. St Chad's Coll Dur BA93 Ustinov Coll Dur PGCE04 PGDE08. St Steph Ho Ox 93. **d** 95 **p** 96. C Norton St Mary *Dur* 95-96; C Hartlepool H Trin 96-99; TV Jarrow 99-01; V Chich St Wilfrid 01-03; Perm to Offic *Dur* 03-09 and *Lon* from 09; CMP from 98. *9 Pentland Close, London NW11 8SP* Tel (020) 8455 3290 E-mail simon@utopia101.plus.com

ATKINSON, Terence Harry. b 52. Coll of Resurr Mirfield 88. **d** 90 **p** 91. C Bottesford w Ashby *Linc* 90-93; TV Cleethorpes 93-98; C-in-c Cleethorpes St Fran CD 98-01; V Chapel St Leonards w Hogsthorpe 01-03; P-in-c Gt Grimsby St Andr w St Luke and All SS from 03. *St Andrew's Vicarage, 2A Albion Street, Grimsby DN32 7DY* Tel (01472) 348200

ATKINSON, Wendy Sybil. b 53. Man Univ BA95. NOC 95. **d** 97 **p** 98. NSM Brinnington w Portwood *Ches* 97-99; C 99-01; NSM Werneth from 01. *8 Freshfield Close, Marple Bridge, Stockport SK6 5ES* Tel 0161-427 5612

ATKINSON-JONES, Mrs Susan Florence. b 64. Univ of Wales (Cardiff) BD93. St Mich Coll Llan 96. **d** 98 **p** 99. C Bargoed and Deri w Brithdir *Llan* 98-05; TV Sanderstead *S'wark* from 05. *35 Audley Drive, Warlingham CR6 9AH* Tel (020) 8657 5505 E-mail susan@sanderstead-parish.org.uk

ATLING, Edwood Brian. b 46. ACIB FCMI. Westcott Ho Cam 00. **d** 02 **p** 03. NSM Godmanchester *Ely* 02-04; P-in-c Abbots Ripton w Wood Walton from 04; P-in-c Kings Ripton from 04; P-in-c Houghton w Wyton from 04; RD Huntingdon from 06. *Blue Cedars, 70 Common Lane, Hemingford Abbots, Huntingdon PE28 9AW* Tel (01480) 493975 Fax 496240 Mobile 07775-544679 E-mail atling@btopenworld.com

ATTA-BAFFOE, Victor Reginald. b 59. Trin Coll Toronto BTh88 Episc Div Sch Cambridge (USA) MA92 Yale Univ STM93. St Nic Th Coll Ghana LTh87. **d** 88 **p** 89. Ghana 88-90 and 93-98; USA 90-93; Lect St Nic Th Coll 88-90 and 93-98; NSM Finsbury Park St Thos *Lon* from 99. *20 Great Peter Street, London SW1P 2BU* Tel (020) 7222 3704 Fax 7233 0255

ATTAWAY, Mrs Elizabeth Ann. b 36. Herts Coll CertEd56. Cant Sch of Min 93 Bp Otter Coll 57. **d** 96 **p** 97. NSM Maidstone St Paul *Cant* 96-02; NSM Boxley w Detling from 02. *1 Staplers Court, Penenden Heath, Maidstone ME14 2XB* Tel (01622) 762656 E-mail glattaway@btinternet.com

ATTFIELD, David George. b 31. Magd Coll Ox BA54 MA58 BD61 K Coll Lon MPhil72 Dur Univ MA81. Westcott Ho Cam 57. **d** 58 **p** 59. C Edgbaston St Aug *Birm* 58-61; C Ward End 61-62; Lect Div St Kath Coll Tottenham 62-64; All SS Coll Tottenham 64-68; Sen Lect St Bede Coll Dur 68-75; St Hild and St Bede Coll 75-80; TV Drypool *York* 80-86; R Newton Heath All SS *Man* 86-96; rtd 97; Perm to Offic *Dur* from 97. *19 Laburnum Avenue, Durham DH1 4HA* Tel 0191-383 0509

ATTLEY, Ronald. b 46. Open Univ BA87. Brasted Th Coll 66 Chich Th Coll 68. **d** 70 **p** 71. C Heworth St Mary *Dur* 70-73; C Hulme Ascension *Man* 73-75; R Corozal and Orange Walk Belize 76-79; V Leadgate *Dur* 79-84; Chapl HM Rem Cen Ashford 84-87; Chapl HM Pris Ashwell and Stocken 87-89; Chapl HM Pris Frankland 89-92; Chapl HM YOI Deerbolt 92-96; V Bath St Barn w Englishcombe *B & W* 96-00; Belize 00; V Brinnington w Portwood *Ches* 01-06; P Narrogin Australia from 06. *The Rectory, 3 Park Street, PO Box 382, Narrogin WA 6312, Australia* Tel and fax (0061) (8) 9881 1041

ATTWATER, Mrs Sallyanne. b 48. Westmr Coll Ox MTh98. S Dios Minl Tr Scheme 86. **d** 94 **p** 95. Chapl Asst Eastbourne Distr Gen Hosp 94-95; Asst Chapl Princess Alice Hosp and All SS Hosp 94-95; C E Grinstead St Swithun *Chich* 95-98; P-in-c Bishop's Cannings, All Cannings etc *Sarum* from 98; RD Devizes from 07. *The Vicarage, The Street, Bishop's Cannings, Devizes SN10 2LD* Tel (01380) 860650 E-mail revsally@attwater.freeserve.co.uk

ATTWATER, Canon Stephen Philip. b 47. ALCM67. Linc Th Coll 85. **d** 87 **p** 88. C Warrington St Elphin *Liv* 87-90; P-in-c Eccleston St Thos 90-94; V 94-99; V Padgate from 99; AD Warrington from 05; Hon Can Liv Cathl from 05. *The Rectory, Station Road South, Padgate, Warrington WA2 0PD* Tel (01925) 821555 E-mail stephen@attwater1.freeserve.co.uk

ATTWOOD, Andrew Michael. b 66. Derby Coll of Educn BEd91. Trin Coll Bris BA02. **d** 02 **p** 03. C Leamington Priors St Mary *Cov* from 02. *12 Otters Rest, Leamington Spa CV31 1AD* Tel (01926) 315399 Mobile 07884-136816 E-mail a.attwood@talk21.com

ATTWOOD, Anthony Norman. b 47. Univ of Wales (Abth) BSc(Econ)69 Hull Univ MA82. Qu Coll Birm 69. **d** 72 **p** 73. C Greenhill *Sheff* 72-75; V Elsecar 76-81; Ind Missr 81-95; TV Maltby 81-86; Ind Chapl 86-95; RD Adwick 89-95; Teesside Ind Miss *Dur* 95-99; P-in-c Swindon St Aug *Bris* 99-03; Soc Resp Adv 99-03; P-in-c Dudley St Barn *Worc* 03-09; P-in-c Dudley St Thos and St Luke 04-09; TR Dudley TM from 09. *St Barnabas' Vicarage, Middlepark Road, Dudley DY1 2LD* Tel (01384) 252015 Mobile 07967-604435

ATTWOOD, Preb Carl Norman Harry. b 53. Bris Univ BA74. Cuddesdon Coll BA76 MA80. **d** 77 **p** 78. C Tupsley *Heref* 77-82; R Colwall w Upper Colwall and Coddington 82-08; Bp's Voc Officer 83-89; RD Ledbury 90-96; Chapl St Jas Sch Malvern 86-08; Preb Heref Cathl 97-08; rtd 08; Perm to Offic *Worc* from 82 and *Heref* from 08. *The Lodge, Old Colwall, Malvern WR13 6HF* Tel (01604) 540788 E-mail carl@attwoods.org

ATTWOOD, David John Edwin. b 51. Dur Univ BA76 Em Coll Cam BA73 MA77. Cranmer Hall Dur 74. **d** 77 **p** 78. C Rodbourne Cheney *Bris* 77-79; C Lydiard Millicent w Lydiard Tregoz 79-85; Dir and Lect Trin Coll Bris 85-97; V Prenton *Ches* 97-02; R Sundridge w Ide Hill and Toys Hill *Roch* from 02. *The Rectory, Chevening Road, Sundridge, Sevenoaks TN14 6AB* Tel (01959) 563749 E-mail david.attwood@diocese-rochester.org

ATTWOOD, Mrs Jennifer. **d** 08. NSM Lingfield and Crowhurst *S'wark* from 08. *28 Headland Way, Lingfield RH7 6BP* Tel (01342) 833100 E-mail jennyattwood@aol.com

ATTWOOD, Leslie Thomas. b 42. UWE MA94 Cranfield Univ MBA MCIPD76. St Steph Ho Ox. **d** 83 **p** 84. C Ascot Heath *Ox* 83-86; Dioc Tr Officer *Truro* 86-88; C Wallasey St Hilary *Ches* 98-00; C Devizes St Pet *Sarum* 00-02; TV Godrevy *Truro* 02-07; TR 07-09; rtd 09. *Chyrempter, Perranuthnoe, Penzance TR20 9NQ* Tel (01736) 710449 E-mail attwood99@lineone.net

ATTWOOD, Peter John. b 44. ACIB68. SEITE 00. **d** 03 **p** 04. NSM Langton Green *Roch* 03-06; C S Molton w Nymet St George, High Bray etc *Ex* from 06; RD S Molton from 09. *The Vicarage, East Street, North Molton, South Molton EX36 3HX* Tel (01598) 740325 E-mail rev@podlea.co.uk

ATTY, Norman Hughes. b 40. Dur Univ BA62. Cranmer Hall Dur 62. **d** 65 **p** 66. C Blackb St Gabr 65-67; Asst Master Billinge Sch Blackb 67-71; City of Leic Boys' Sch 71-73; P-in-c Elmley Lovett w Hampton Lovett *Worc* 73-78; P-in-c Elmbridge w Rushock 74-78; R Elmley Lovett w Hampton Lovett and Elmbridge etc 78-85; Hon Can Worc Cathl 81-85; rtd 05; Perm to Offic *Blackb* from 05. *The Dog Inn, King Street, Whalley, Clitheroe BB7 9SP* Tel (01254) 823009

ATWELL, The Very Revd James Edgar. b 46. Ex Coll Ox BA68 MA73 BD94 Harvard Univ ThM70. Cuddesdon Coll 68. **d** 70 **p** 71. C E Dulwich St Jo *S'wark* 70-74; C Cambridge Gt St Mary w St Mich *Ely* 74-77; Chapl Jes Coll Cam 77-81; V Towcester w Easton Neston *Pet* 81-95; RD Towcester 83-91; Provost St E 95-00; Dean St E 00-06; Dean Win from 06. *The Deanery, The Close, Winchester SO23 9LS* Tel (01962) 857203 E-mail the.dean@winchester-cathedral.org.uk

✠**ATWELL, The Rt Revd Robert Ronald.** b 54. St Jo Coll Dur BA75 Dur Univ MLitt79. Westcott Ho Cam 76. **d** 78 **p** c08. C Mill Hill Jo Keble CK *Lon* 78-81; Chapl Trin Coll Cam 81-87; OSB 87-98; Lic to Offic *Ox* 87-97; Perm to Offic *Ely* 97-98; V Primrose Hill St Mary w Avenue Road St Paul *Lon* 98-08; Suff Bp Stockport *Ches* from 08. *Bishop's Lodge, Back Lane, Dunham Town, Altrincham WA14 4SG* Tel 0161-928 5611 Fax 929 0692 E-mail bpstockport@chester.anglican.org

AUBREY-JONES, Adrian Frederick. b 51. ERMC 04. **d** 07 **p** 08. NSM Dersingham w Anmer and Shernborne *Nor* from 07. *23 Tudor Way, Dersingham, King's Lynn PE31 6LX* Tel (01485) 544689 Mobile 07775-514567 E-mail curate@stndersingham.co.uk

AUCHMUTY, John Robert. b 67. ACCA. CITC 89. **d** 92 **p** 93. C Dundela St Mark *D & D* 92-96; I Eglish w Killylea *Arm* 96-01; I Killaney w Carryduff *D & D* 01-07; I Knock from 07. *St Columba's Rectory, 29 King's Road, Knock, Belfast BT5 6JG* Tel (028) 9047 1514 E-mail johnauchmuty@btinternet.com

AUCKLAND, Bishop of. *See* PATERSON, The Rt Revd John Campbell

AUCKLAND, Archdeacon of. *See* BARKER, The Ven Nicholas John Willoughby

AUDEN, Lawson Philip. b 45. DL06. Qu Coll Birm 73. **d** 78 **p** 81. C Spalding *Linc* 78-81; TV Wordsley *Lich* 81-82; TV Kidderminster St Mary and All SS, Trimpley etc *Worc* 82-87;

Ind Chapl 82-87; Perm to Offic *Cov* and *Worc* 87-97; *Birm, Lich* and *Glouc* 94-97; Chapl Worcs Community Healthcare NHS Trust 91-97; P-in-c Pebworth w Dorsington and Honeybourne *Glouc* 97-99; Perm to Offic *Cov* 98-01; *B & W* 00-04; *Glouc* from 01; Chapl Miss to Seafarers from 99; Millennium Officer *Glouc* 99-01. *4 Penlea Court, Shirehampton, Bristol BS11 0BY* Tel 0117-982 7879 *or* (01275) 372926 E-mail philipauden@ukf.net

AUDIBERT, Mrs Janice Elizabeth. b 56. **d** 99 **p** 00. OLM Oakdale *Sarum* 99-02; C N Poole Ecum Team 02-06; TV from 06. *24 Blackbird Close, Poole BH17 7YA* Tel and fax (01202) 389751
E-mail janice.audibert@christ-church-creekmoor.org.uk

AULD, Jeremy Rodger. b 66. Edin Univ LLB87 Solicitor 89 Barrister 97. TISEC BD04. **d** 04 **p** 05. C Edin St Pet 04-06; Hon Chapl Edin Univ 04-06; R Dollar *St And* from 06. *St James's Rectory, 12 Harviestoun Road, Dollar FK14 7HF* Tel (01259) 742494 Mobile 07976-707253
E-mail jeremy.auld@btinternet.com

AULD, Mrs Sheila Edith. b 38. Newc Poly BA87 Univ of Northumbria at Newc MA99. NEOC 91. **d** 94 **p** 95. Project Worker Cedarwood Trust 88-02; NSM Newc St Gabr 94-02; rtd 02; Perm to Offic from 02. *5 Gibson Fields, Hexham NE46 1AS* Tel (01434) 602297

AUSSANT, Mrs Jill Amaryllis. MA LLB. Ripon Coll Cuddesdon. **d** 07 **p** 08. NSM Crawley and Littleton and Sparsholt w Lainston *Win* 07-08; NSM Downs Benefice from 08. *121 Hocombe Road, Chandler's Ford, Eastleigh SO53 5QD* Tel (023) 8026 9799

AUSTEN, Glyn Benedict. b 54. UEA BA77 MPhil80. Ripon Coll Cuddesdon BA81 MA85. **d** 82 **p** 83. C Newport w Longford and Chetwynd *Lich* 82-85; C Hawley H Trin *Guildf* 85-87; R Barnack w Ufford and Bainton *Pet* 87-03; Asst Master Stamford High Sch from 03. *31 Hill View Road, South Witham, Grantham NG33 5QW* Tel (01572) 767944 *or* (01780) 484200 Fax (01780) 484201 E-mail g.b.austen@ukf.net

AUSTEN, Canon John. b 46. St Cath Coll Cam BA69 MA72. Qu Coll Birm. **d** 71 **p** 72. C Thornaby on Tees *York* 71-74; C Aston St Jas *Birm* 74-82; Chapl Aston Univ 82-88; C Handsworth St Andr from 88; Hon Can Birm Cathl from 06. *151 Church Lane, Birmingham B20 2RU* Tel 0121-554 8882 Fax 551 8637
E-mail johnausten@iname.com

AUSTEN, Simon Neil. b 67. Warwick Univ BSc88. Wycliffe Hall Ox BA93 MA97. **d** 94 **p** 95. C Gt Chesham *Ox* 94-98; Chapl Stowe Sch 98-02; V Houghton *Carl* from 02. *12 Brunstock Close, Carlisle CA3 0HL* Tel (01228) 810076 *or* 515972
E-mail simon@hkchurch.org.uk

AUSTERBERRY, Preb David Naylor. b 35. Birm Univ BA58. Wells Th Coll 58. **d** 60 **p** 61. C Leek St Edw *Lich* 60-63; Iran 64-70; Chapl CMS Foxbury 70-73; V Walsall Pleck and Bescot *Lich* 73-82; R Brierley Hill 82-88; R Kinnerley w Melverley and Knockin w Maesbrook 88-99; RD Oswestry 92-95; Preb Lich Cathl 96-00; rtd 00; Perm to Offic *Heref* and *Lich* from 00. *Chad Cottage, Dovaston, Kinnerley, Oswestry SY10 8DT* Tel (01691) 682039

AUSTERBERRY, John Maurice. b 62. Birm Univ BA83. Sarum & Wells Th Coll 84. **d** 86 **p** 87. C Clayton *Lich* 86-89; Asst Chapl Withington Hosp Man 89-95; Chapl Tameside and Glossop NHS Trust 95-99; Chapl N Staffs Hosp NHS Trust from 99. *City General Hospital, Newcastle Road, Stoke-on-Trent ST4 6QG* Tel (01782) 715444 *or* 552252 Fax 552017
E-mail john.austerberry@uhns.nhs.uk

AUSTIN, Canon Alfred George. b 36. Ridley Coll Melbourne ThL61. **d** 61 **p** 62. C Bendigo All SS Australia 63-64; R W End 64-70; R Eaglehawk and Bp's Dom Chapl 70-77; C Dartford St Alb *Roch* 77-79; R Tatura Australia 79-84; R W Bendigo 84-90; R Kyneton 90-93; Can Bendigo Cathl 83-97; I Essendon Ch 97-00; rtd 01. *Brocklyn, 3 Alpina Place, Kangaroo Flat Vic 3555, Australia* Tel (0061) (3) 5447 0174

AUSTIN, Mrs Catherine Brenda. b 52. **d** 00 **p** 01. OLM Henley, Claydon and Barham *St E* from 00. *Fait Accompli, 7 Freeman Avenue, Henley, Ipswich IP6 0RZ* Tel (01473) 830100

AUSTIN, The Ven George Bernard. b 31. St D Coll Lamp BA53 Chich Th Coll 53. **d** 55 **p** 56. C Chorley St Pet *Blackb* 55-57; C Notting Hill St Clem *Lon* 57-60; Asst Chapl Lon Univ 60-61; C Dunstable *St Alb* 61-64; V Eaton Bray 64-70; V Bushey Heath 70-88; Hon Can St Alb 78-88; Adn York 88-99; Can and Preb York Minster 98-99; rtd 99; Perm to Offic *York* from 99. *North Back House, 3B Main Street, Wheldrake, York YO19 6AG* Tel (01904) 448509 Fax 448002 E-mail george.austin@virgin.net

AUSTIN, Glyn. *See* AUSTIN, Ronald Glyn

AUSTIN, Miss Jane. b 43. SRN64 SCM66. **dss** 81 **d** 87 **p** 94. Tonbridge SS Pet and Paul *Roch* 81-98; C 87-98; Hon Can Roch Cathl 96-98; P-in-c Meltham Wakef 98-01; V 01-07; P-in-c Helme 00-01; RD Almondbury 01-06; rtd 07. *177 Bourne View Road, Netherton, Huddersfield HD4 7JS* Tel (01484) 661212 E-mail j.austin.meltham@care4free.net

AUSTIN, Leslie Ernest. b 46. Trin Coll Bris 72. **d** 74 **p** 75. C Paddock Wood *Roch* 74-79; C Upper Armley *Ripon* 79-81; V Horton *Bradf* 81-85; V Long Preston w Tosside 85-97; TR

Shirwell, Loxhore, Kentisbury, Arlington, etc *Ex* from 97. *The Parsonage, 1 The Glebe, Bratton Fleming, Barnstaple EX31 4RE* Tel (01598) 710807 E-mail les@austin85.freeserve.co.uk

AUSTIN, Margaret Rose. b 41. Qu Coll Birm 01. **d** 03 **p** 04. NSM Farewell *Lich* from 03; NSM Gentleshaw from 03; NSM Hammerwich from 03. *137 Highfields Road, Chasetown, Burntwood WS7 4QT* Tel (01543) 686883

AUSTIN, Canon Michael Ridgwell. b 33. Lon Univ BD57 PhD69 Birm Univ MA66 FRHistS. Lon Coll of Div ALCD56. **d** 57 **p** 58. C Ward End *Birm* 57-60; PC Derby St Andr 60-66; Lect Th Derbyshire Coll of HE 66-73; Prin Lect 73-85; Chapl Derby Cathl 66-81; Can Res Derby Cathl 81-85; Bp's Adv on Tr *S'well* 85-88; Dir Post-Ord Tr 86-94; Can Res S'well Minster 88-94; Dioc Dir of Tr 88-94; Abps' Adv for Bps' Min 94-98; rtd 98; Perm to Offic *S'well* from 04. *7 Dudley Doy Road, Southwell NG25 0NJ* Tel (01636) 812604

AUSTIN, Ronald Glyn. b 52. Univ of Wales (Cardiff) BD90 Univ of Wales MPhil98. St Mich Coll Llan 88. **d** 90 **p** 91. C Llangynwyd w Maesteg 90-91; C Barry All SS 91-93; V Nantymoel w Wyndham 93-97; V Pontyclun w Talygarn 97-02; Tutor St Mich Coll Llan 02-04; V Llansantffraid, Bettws and Aberkenfig 04-06. *Address temp unknown*

AUSTIN, Mrs Susan Frances. b 47. Open Univ BA81. Cant Sch of Min 87. **d** 92 **p** 94. Chapl Ch Ch High Sch Ashford 90-94; C Gt Chart *Cant* 92-94; C Ashford 92-94; C Estover *Ex* 94-96; V Stevenage All SS Pin Green *St Alb* 96-98; P-in-c Bredgar w Bicknor and Frinsted w Wormshill etc *Cant* 00-04; rtd 04; Perm to Offic *Cant* from 04. *9 Pheasant Lane, Maidstone ME15 9QR* Tel (01622) 745276 E-mail susanandralphaustin@hotmail.com

AUSTRALIA, Primate of. *See* ASPINALL, The Most Revd Phillip John

AVANN, Canon Penelope Joyce. b 46. **dss** 83 **d** 87 **p** 98. Southborough St Pet w Ch Ch and St Matt *Roch* 83-89; Par Dn 87-89; Warden Past Assts from 89; Par Dn Beckenham St Jo 89-94; C 94-02; C Green Street Green and Pratts Bottom from 02; Hon Can Roch Cathl from 94. *9 Ringwood Avenue, Orpington BR6 7SY* Tel and fax (01689) 861742 Mobile 07710-418839 E-mail penny.avann@rochester.anglican.org

AVENT, Raymond John. b 28. St D Coll Lamp BA55 Coll of Resurr Mirfield 55. **d** 57 **p** 58. C Bury H Trin *Man* 57-60; C Holborn St Alb w Saffron Hill St Pet *Lon* 60-66; C Munster Square St Mary Magd 66-67; V Tottenham St Paul 67-77; RD E Haringey 73-77; V Kilburn St Aug w St Jo 77-87; AD Westmr Paddington 79-84; R St Vedast w St Mich-le-Querne etc 87-94; rtd 94; Perm to Offic *Lon* 94-00; *Glouc* from 00. *Maryvale House, Catbrook, Chipping Campden GL55 6DE* Tel (01386) 841323 E-mail avent@campadene.fsnet.co.uk

AVERY, Andrew James. b 58. Dudley Coll of Educn CertEd79 Open Univ BA81. St Jo Coll Nottm 06. **d** 08 **p** 09. C Brundall w Braydeston and Postwick *Nor* from 08. *47 Lackford Close, Brundall, Norwich NR13 5NL* Tel (01603) 713324 Mobile 07976-523554 E-mail crandajavery@hotmail.co.uk

AVERY, Mrs Lydia Dorothy Ann. b 57. Sheff Univ MA03 Bath Spa Univ Coll PGCE97. STETS BA08. **d** 08 **p** 09. C Pilton w Croscombe, N Wootton and Dinder *B & W* from 08. *Hill House, Fayre Way, Croscombe, Wells BA5 3RA* Tel (01749) 343427 E-mail lydiaavery@aol.com

AVERY, Richard Julian. b 52. Keble Coll Ox BA73. St Jo Coll Nottm 74. **d** 77 **p** 78. C Macclesfield St Mich *Ches* 77-80; Asst P Prince Albert St Dav Canada 82-83; C Becontree St Mary *Chelmsf* 84-87; R Hudson Bay Canada 87-90; R Duncan 90-97; TV Cheltenham St Mark *Glouc* 97-03; Perm to Offic 03-06; P-in-c Berkeley w Wick, Breadstone, Newport, Stone etc from 06. *The Vicarage, Church Lane, Berkeley GL13 9BN* E-mail averyfamily@yahoo.com

AVERY, Robert Edward. b 69. Magd Coll Cam BA90. Ripon Coll Cuddesdon 90. **d** 93 **p** 94. C Cen Telford *Lich* 93-96; C Cambridge Gt St Mary w St Mich *Ely* 96-99; V Tamerton Foliot *Ex* 99-03; V Tunbridge Wells K Chas *Roch* from 03. *The Vicarage, 5D Frant Road, Tunbridge Wells TN2 5SB* Tel (01892) 525455 E-mail robert.avery@diocese-rochester.org

AVERY, Canon Russel Harrold. b 46. JP74. Moore Th Coll Sydney 66. **d** 77 **p** 77. C Curtin Australia 79; C S Queanbeyan 77-78; C Prenton *Ches* 78-79; Chapl Tunis St Geo Tunisia 79-82; Chapl Maisons-Laffitte *Eur* 82-88; R Lane Cove Australia 88-98; Chapl Nord Pas de Calais *Eur* 98-00; Chapl Lille 00-02; Ind Chapl Australia 02-06; Chapl RAAF 04-09; Sen State Chapl NSW Police from 09; Hon Can Goulburn Cathl from 09. *1A Alliedale Close, Hornsby NSW 2077, Australia* Tel (0061) (2) 9487 5580 E-mail rhavery@cia.com.au

AVES, Peter Colin. b 57. Qu Mary Coll Lon BSc79 CertEd80 Lon Univ BD89. Wycliffe Hall Ox 85. **d** 88 **p** 89. C Thames Ditton *Guildf* 88-90; C Chertsey 90-93; R Stockbridge and Longstock and Leckford *Win* 93-00; Chapl to the Deaf *Sarum* 00-03; TV Beaminster Area 03 07. *Address temp unknown* E-mail peteraves@excite.co.uk

AVESON, Ian Henry. b 55. Jes Coll Ox BA77 MA81 Univ Coll Dur PGCE78 Birkbeck Coll Lon MSc85. St Mich Coll Llan BD97. **d** 97 **p** 98. C Penarth All SS *Llan* 97-99; TV Aberystwyth

St D 99-07; V Llandingat w Myddfai from 07. *The Vicarage, 42 Broad Street, Llandovery SA20 0AY* Tel (01550) 720524

AVEYARD, Ian. b 46. Liv Univ BSc68 Sheff Univ MEd00. ALCD72 St Jo Coll Nottm 71. **d** 71 **p** 72. C Bradley *Wakef* 71-74; C Knowle *Birm* 74-79; P-in-c Cofton Hackett 79; P-in-c Barnt Green 79; V Cofton Hackett w Barnt Green 80-94; Dioc Dir of Reader Tr 85-94; Warden of Readers 91-94; Course Leader St Jo Coll Nottm 96-99; P-in-c Thanington and Dioc Dir of Ords *Cant* 99-09. *19 The Damsells, Tetbury GL8 8JA* Tel (01666) 502278 E-mail ian.aveyard1@btinternet.com

AVIS, Canon Paul David Loup. b 47. Lon Univ BD70 PhD76. Westcott Ho Cam 73. **d** 75 **p** 76. C S Molton, Nymet St George, High Bray etc *Ex* 75-80; V Stoke Canon, Poltimore w Huxham and Rewe etc 80-98; Preb Ex Cathl 93-08; Sub Dean Ex Cathl 97-08; Can Th Ex Cathl from 08; Gen Sec Coun for Chr Unity from 98; Chapl to The Queen from 08. *Church House, Great Smith Street, London SW1P 3AZ,* or *Lea Hill, Membury, Axminster EX13 7AQ* Tel (020) 7898 1470 Fax 7898 1483 E-mail paul.avis@c-of-e.org.uk

AWRE, Richard William Esgar. b 56. Univ of Wales BA78. Wycliffe Hall Ox 78. **d** 81 **p** 82. C Blackpool St Jo *Blackb* 81-84; Asst Dir of Ords and Voc Adv 84-89; C Altham w Clayton le Moors 84-89; V Longridge 89-99; V Kenilworth St Nic *Cov* from 99; RD Kenilworth from 01. *The Vicarage, 7 Elmbank Road, Kenilworth CV8 1AL* Tel (01926) 854367 or 857509 E-mail stnicholasken@aol.com

AXFORD, Mrs Christine Ruth. b 53. Glam Coll of Educn BEd75. STETS BTh00. **d** 00 **p** 02. NSM Yeovil w Kingston Pitney *B & W* 00-01; NSM N Hartismere *St E* 02-08; NSM Wotton-under-Edge w Ozleworth, N Nibley etc *Glouc* from 08. *The Vicarage, Culverhay, Wotton-under-Edge GL12 7LS* Tel (01453) 842175 E-mail chris.axford@metronet.co.uk

AXFORD, Robert Henry. b 50. Univ of Wales BEng72 CEng85. Sarum & Wells Th Coll 89. **d** 91 **p** 92. C Castle Cary w Ansford *B & W* 91-95; P-in-c Queen Camel w W Camel, Corton Denham etc 95-01; R 01-02; R N Hartismere *St E* 02-08; RD Hartismere 04-08; P-in-c Wotton-under-Edge w Ozleworth, N Nibley etc *Glouc* from 08. *The Vicarage, Culverhay, Wotton-under-Edge GL12 7LS* Tel (01453) 842175 E-mail rob.axford@metronet.co.uk

AXON, Andrew John. b 76. Univ of Wales (Lamp) BTh97. Trin Coll Bris 99. **d** 01 **p** 02. C Sevenhampton w Charlton Abbots, Hawling etc *Glouc* 01-05; V Ruddington *S'well* from 05. *The Vicarage, Wilford Road, Ruddington, Nottingham NG11 6EL* Tel 0115-921 1505 E-mail andrew@ajaxon.freeserve.co.uk

AXTELL, Ronald Arthur John. b 33. Lon Univ BSc54 St Cath Soc Ox BA58 MA62. Wycliffe Hall Ox 56. **d** 58 **p** 59. C Walton Breck *Liv* 58-61; Iran 63-78; Chapl Tehran 63-67; Chapl Kerman 67-68; Chapl Shiraz 69-78; Chr Witness to Israel Miss in Man 78-82; Perm to Offic *Man* 79-82; TV Man Resurr 82; TV Man Gd Shep 82-88; R Levenshulme St Pet 88-98; rtd 98; Perm to Offic *Man* from 98. *15 Berwick Avenue, Stockport SK4 3AA* Tel 0161-432 5943 E-mail axtell@ntlworld.com

AXTELL, Stephen Geoffrey. b 57. Open Univ BSc96. St Jo Coll Nottm 00. **d** 02 **p** 03. C Coseley Ch Ch *Worc* 02-06; Chapl Rotterdam and Rotterdam Miss to Seafarers *Eur* from 06. *St Mary, Pieter de Hoochweg 133, 3024 BG Rotterdam-Delfshaven, The Netherlands* Tel (0031) (10) 476 4043 E-mail stmarys@hetnet.nl

AYERS, Canon John. b 40. FCollP Univ AFW BEd75 Newton Park Coll Bath MEd89 FRSA94. **d** 77 **p** 78. NSM Corsham *Bris* 77-79; NSM Gtr Corsham 79-88; NSM Ditteridge 88-92; NSM Box w Hazlebury and Ditteridge from 93; Hon Can Bris Cathl from 94. *Toad Hall, Middlehill, Box, Corsham SN13 8QP* Tel (01225) 742123 E-mail johnayers@middlehill.netlineuk.net

AYERS, Paul Nicholas. b 61. St Pet Coll Ox BA82 MA86. Trin Coll Bris 83. **d** 85 **p** 86. C Clayton *Bradf* 85-88; C Keighley St Andr 88-91; V Wrose 91-97; V Pudsey St Lawr and St Paul from 97. *The Vicarage, Vicarage Drive, Pudsey LS28 7RL* Tel 0113-256 4197 or 257 7843 E-mail paul.ayers@bradford.anglican.org

AYERS-HARRIS, Mrs Rebecca Theresa. b 70. Nottm Univ BA91 Birm Univ PGCE92. WEMTC 01. **d** 04 **p** 05. NSM Leominster *Heref* 04-08; Chapl Sherborne Sch for Girls from 08. *Sherborne School for Girls, Bradford Road, Sherborne DT9 3QN* Tel (01935) 812245

AYERST, Edward Richard. b 25. Leeds Univ BA51. Coll of Resurr Mirfield 51. **d** 53 **p** 54. C Bethnal Green St Jo w St Simon *Lon* 53-57; C Hayes St Mary 58-60; V Edmonton St Mary w St Jo 60-66; R Whippingham w E Cowes *Portsm* 66-77; V Bridgwater St Mary w Chilton Trinity *B & W* 77-84; V Durleigh 77-84; V Bridgwater St Mary, Chilton Trinity and Durleigh 84-90; Chapl to The Queen 87-95; rtd 90; Perm to Offic *B & W* 90-05. *56 Maple Drive, Burham-on-Sea TA8 1DH* Tel (01278) 780701

AYERST, Gabrielle Mary. b 52. St Luke's Coll Ex BEd74. SEITE 97. **d** 00 **p** 01. NSM Surbiton St Andr and St Mark *S'wark* 00-08. *Flat 3, 11 Claremont Gardens, Surbiton KT6 4TN* Tel (020) 8390 2166 E-mail gadrillea@paff.nsf.org.uk

AYKROYD, Harold Allan. b 22. DFC. Man Univ BA48. Qu Coll Birm 73. **d** 76 **p** 76. NSM Moseley St Agnes *Birm* 76-82; NSM Bournville 82-96; Perm to Offic from 96. *108 Middleton Hall Road, Birmingham B30 1DG* Tel 0121-451 1365 or 569 4687

AYLETT, Graham Peter. b 59. Qu Coll Cam BA81 MA84 PhD85 St Jo Coll Dur BA88. Cranmer Hall Dur 86 All Nations Chr Coll 96. **d** 90 **p** 91. C Wilton *B & W* 90-94; C Runcorn All SS *Ches* 94-96; C Thetford *Nor* 97-98; Mongolia from 98. *clo JCS, PO Box 49/532, Ulaanbaatar 210349, Mongolia*

AYLETT, Mrs Nicola Jane. b 63. St Anne's Coll Ox BA84 St Jo Coll Dur BA89. Cranmer Hall Dur 87 All Nations Chr Coll 96. **d** 90 **p** 94. C Wilton *B & W* 90-94; NSM Runcorn All SS *Ches* 94-96; Perm to Offic *Nor* 97-98; Mongolia from 98. *clo JCS, PO Box 49/532, Ulaanbaatar 210349, Mongolia*

AYLING, Miss Dallas Jane. b 53. Trin Coll Bris BA94. **d** 98 **p** 99. C Ellesmere Port *Ches* 98-02; TV Birkenhead Priory 02-06; TV 06-07; R from 07. *10 Cavendish Road, Birkenhead CH41 8AX* Tel 0151-653 6092 E-mail revdallasayling@yahoo.co.uk

AYLING, Canon John Michael. b 37. St Cath Coll Cam BA60 MA64. Linc Th Coll 60. **d** 62 **p** 63. C Stoke upon Trent *Lich* 62-66; C Codsall 66-67; Australia 67-71; Solomon Is 71-72; Lic to Offic *St Alb* 72-91; TR Boscastle w Davidstow *Truro* 91-98; R 98-02; RD Stratton 98-02; Hon Can Truro Cathl 01-02; rtd 02; Perm to Offic *Heref* from 03. *Woodstock House, Church Street, Leominster HR6 8ED* Tel (01568) 611523 E-mail john.ayling@virgin.net

AYLING, Mrs Susan Pamela. b 48. OBE03. SEITE 95. **d** 98 **p** 99. NSM Oxshott *Guildf* 98-02; NSM Cuddington from 02. *114 Edenfield Gardens, Worcester Park KT4 7DY* Tel (020) 8337 6347 or 7438 6589 E-mail sue.ayling@btinternet.com

AYLWARD, James Gareth. b 45. St Cath Coll Cam BA68 MA72. St As Minl Tr Course 94. **d** 97 **p** 98. NSM Wrexham *St As* 97-00; V Broughton 00-05; V Broughton and Berse Drelincourt from 05. *The Vicarage, Bryn-y-Gaer Road, Pentre Broughton, Wrexham LL11 6AT* Tel (01978) 756210

AYOK-LOEWENBERG, Joseph. b 60. DipEd91. Trin Coll Bris 85. **d** 88 **p** 89. C Swanage and Studland *Sarum* 88-90; Cam Univ Miss Bermondsey 90; Crowther Hall CMS Tr Coll Selly Oak 90-91; C Barnes St Mary *S'wark* 91-92; C Earlsfield St Jo 92; CMS Uganda 92-95; P-in-c Symondsbury and Chideock *Sarum* 96-98; TV Golden Cap Team 98-01; CMS Egypt 02-06; Hon C Barnes *S'wark* from 06. *52 Boileau Road, London SW13 9BL* E-mail ayokloewenberg@dataxprs.com.eg

✝**AYONG, The Most Revd James Simon.** b 44. Newton Th Coll Martin Luther Sem BTh. **d** 82 **p** 84 **c** 96. Papua New Guinea from 82; Asst P Popondetta Resurr 85-86; Lect Newton Th Coll 87-88; Prin 89-93; Par P Gerehu 94-95; Bp Aipo Rongo from 95; Abp Papua New Guinea from 96. *PO Box 893, Mount Hagen, Western Highlands Province, Papua New Guinea* Tel (00675) 542 1131 or 542 3727 Fax 542 1181 E-mail acpnphgn@global.net.pg

AYRE, Richard. b 40. Liv Inst of Educn CertEd61 Newc Univ BPhil(Ed)88. **d** 04 **p** 05. OLM Chapel House *Newc* from 04. *57 Grosvenor Court, Newcastle upon Tyne NE5 1RY* Tel 0191-267 2096

AYRES, Anthony Lawrence. b 47. Trin Coll Bris 69. **d** 73 **p** 74. C Plumstead All SS *S'wark* 73-77; Hon C 77-00; Member of Counselling Team CA from 83. *37 Donaldson Road, London SE18 4JZ* Tel (020) 8856 1542

AYRES, Dean Matthew. b 68. Bris Univ BSc89. Ridley Hall Cam 00. **d** 02 **p** 03. C Epsom Common Ch Ch *Guildf* 02-06; Chapl Thames Valley Univ from 06. *The Chaplaincy, Thames Valley University, St Mary's Road, London W5 5RF* Tel (020) 8231 2365 E-mail ayresnograces@yahoo.com

AZER, Ms Helen. b 77. Ch Ch Ox BA00 MA03. Wycliffe Hall Ox BTh04. **d** 04 **p** 05. C Ox St Aldate 04-07; C Cumnor from 07. *St Michael's Church Office, 1 Abingdon Road, Cumnor, Oxford OX2 9QN* Tel (01865) 861541 E-mail gryphius2000@hotmail.com

B

BABB, Ann Elizabeth. b 38. Battersea Coll of Educn TDip59. Qu Coll Newfoundland 96 St Steph Ho Ox 05. **d** 06. C Antwerp St Boniface *Eur* from 06. *Leo van Hullebuschstraat 37, 2900 Schoten, Belgium* Tel (0032) (3) 685 3420 E-mail ann.babb@skynet.be

BABB, Canon Geoffrey. b 42. Man Univ BSc64 MA74 Linacre Coll Ox BA67. Ripon Hall Ox 65. **d** 68 **p** 69. C Heywood St Luke *Man* 68-71; C-in-c Loundsley Green Ascension CD *Derby* 71-76; TV Old Brampton and Loundsley Green 76-77; TV

Stafford and Dioc Soc Resp Officer *Lich* 77-88; Preb Lich Cathl 87-88; P-in-c Salford Sacred Trin *Man* 88-99; Dir CME 88-99; TR Wythenshawe 99-06; TV 06-07; Hon Can Man Cathl 89-07; rtd 07; Perm to Offic *Man* 07-08 and *Newc* from 07. *St Peter's Vicarage, Druridge Drive, Newcastle upon Tyne NE5 3LP* Tel 0191-286 9913 E-mail gandjbabb@btinternet.com

BABB, Mrs Julia Bebbington. b 69. Man Univ BA98 St Jo Coll Dur MA00. Cranmer Hall Dur. **d** 00 **p** 01. C Langley and Parkfield *Man* 00-04; V Cowgate *Newc* from 04. *St Peter's Vicarage, Druridge Drive, Newcastle upon Tyne NE5 3LP* Tel 0191-286 9913 E-mail gandjbabb@btinternet.com

BABBAGE, Canon Stuart Barton. b 16. AM95. St Jo Coll Auckland 35 Univ of NZ BA35 MA36 K Coll Lon PhD42. Tyndale Hall Bris 37 ACT ThD50. **d** 39 **p** 40. C Havering-atte-Bower *Chelmsf* 39-41; Tutor and Lect Oak Hill Th Coll 39-41; Chapl-in-Chief RAF 42-46; Australia 46-63; Dean Sydney 47-53; Dean Melbourne 53-62; Prin Ridley Coll Melbourne 53-63; USA 63-73; V Atlanta and Austell 63-65; Visiting Prof Columbia Th Sem 63-67; Pres Conwell Th Sch Philadelphia 67-69; Vice-Pres and Dean Gordon-Conwell Th Sem 69-73; Australia from 73; Master New Coll Univ of NSW 73-82; Registrar ACT 77-92; rtd 83; Hon Can Sydney from 83. *46 St Thomas Street, Waverley NSW 2024, Australia* Tel (0061) (2) 9665 1882

BABINGTON, Canon Gervase Hamilton. b 30. Keble Coll Ox BA57 MA57. Wells Th Coll 55. **d** 57 **p** 58. C Sheff St Geo and St Steph 57-60; P-in-c Manor Park CD 60-65; R Waddington *Linc* 65-81; RD Graffoe 74-81; Can and Preb Linc Cathl 77-95; V Gainsborough All SS 81-90; RD Corringham 82-87; R Walesby 90-95; rtd 95; Perm to Offic *Linc* 95-98. *15 Highfields, Nettleham, Lincoln LN2 2ST* Tel (01522) 595702

BABINGTON, Peter Gervase. b 69. Aston Univ BSc91 Birm Univ MPhil03. Cuddesdon Coll BTh98. **d** 98 **p** 99. C Salter Street and Shirley *Birm* 98-02; V Bournville from 02; AD Moseley from 07. *The Vicarage, 61 Linden Road, Birmingham B30 1JT* Tel 0121-472 1209 *or* 472 7215 E-mail vicar@bournvilleparishchurch.org.uk

BACH, Mrs Frances Mary. b 48. Open Univ BA AIL. CITC BTh. **d** 94 **p** 95. NSM Ballynure and Ballyeaston *Conn* 94-96; C Larne and Inver 96-99; C Glynn w Raloo 96-99; I Armoy w Loughguile and Drumtullagh from 99. *The Rectory, 181 Glenshesk Road, Armoy, Ballymoney BT53 8RJ* Tel (028) 2075 1226 *or* 2082 3348 E-mail frances.bach@btinternet.com

BACH, John Edward Goulden. b 40. JP. Dur Univ BA66. Cranmer Hall Dur 66. **d** 69 **p** 70. C Bradf Cathl 69-72; Chapl and Lect NUU 73-84; Chapl and Lect Ulster Univ from 84. *The Anglican Chaplaincy, 70 Hopefield Avenue, Portrush BT56 8HE* Tel (028) 2075 1226, 2032 4549 *or* 2082 3348 Fax 2032 4904 E-mail revjegbach@hotmail.com *or* jeg.bach@ulst.ac.uk

BACHELL, Kenneth George. b 22. Lon Univ BD49. K Coll Lon 55. **d** 56 **p** 57. C Bitterne Park *Win* 56-60; C-in-c Andover St Mich CD 60-64; V Andover St Mich 64-68; V Southampton St Alb 68-76; Warden Dioc Conf Ho Crawshawbooth *Man* 76-79; P-in-c Crawshawbooth 76-79; V Holdenhurst *Win* 79-83; V Froyle and Holybourne 83-87; rtd 87; Perm to Offic *Blackb* 88-98. *18 Cherrylea, Auchterarder PH3 1QG* Tel (01764) 663824

BACHU, Jagjit. b 66. Man Univ BEd80 Leeds Univ MBA98 MA07. NOC 04. **d** 07 **p** 08. NSM Wales *Sheff* from 07. *11 Orchard Croft, Sheffield S26 5UA* Tel (01909) 772315 E-mail helen.bachu@tesco.net *or* jagjit.bachu@sheffield.anglican.org

BACK, Esther Elaine. *See* McCAFFERTY, Mrs Esther Elaine

BACKHOUSE, Alan Eric. b 37. Keble Coll Ox BA61 MA67. Tyndale Hall Bris 61. **d** 64 **p** 65. C Burnage St Marg *Man* 64-67; C Cheadle Hulme St Andr *Ches* 67-70; V Buglawton 70-80; V New Ferry 80-87; V Tarvin 87-92; V Knypersley *Lich* 93-99; Patr Sec Ch Soc Trust 99-00; C Watford *St Alb* 99-02; rtd 02. *Perelandra, Church Pitch, Llandyssil, Montgomery SY16 6LQ* Tel (01686) 669963

BACKHOUSE, Colin. b 41. Birm Coll of Art & Design BA67 MCSD82. Oak Hill Th Coll 85. **d** 87 **p** 88. C Branksome St Clem *Sarum* 87-91; P-in-c Bluntisham cum Earith w Colne and Woodhurst *Ely* 91-92; R 92-07; rtd 07. *13 Hillside View, Midsomer Norton, Bath BA3 2TB* Tel 07811-960048 (mobile) E-mail colin.backhouse@googlemail.com

BACKHOUSE, John. b 30. Univ Coll Southn BA50. Wycliffe Hall Ox 51. **d** 53 **p** 54. C Eccleston St Luke *Liv* 53-55; C Maghull 55-58; V Lathom 58-64; Area Sec CMS *Linc* and *Ely* 64-71; *Leic* 72-78; *Cov* 75-78; V Thorpe Acre w Dishley *Leic* 78-83; R Ab Kettleby Gp 83-89; P-in-c Bitteswell 89-94; RD Guthlaxton II 90-94; rtd 94; Perm to Offic *Leic* from 94. *29 Peashill Close, Sileby, Loughborough LE12 7PT* Tel (01509) 812016

BACKHOUSE, Jonathan Roland. b 60. Jes Coll Cam BA82 MA85. Trin Coll Bris 01. **d** 03 **p** 04. C Nailsea H Trin *B & W* 03-07; Chapl RN from 07. *Royal Naval Chaplaincy Service, Mail Point 1-2, Leach Building, Whale Island, Portsmouth PO2 8BY* Tel (023) 9262 5055 Fax 9262 5134 E-mail jcbackhouse@bigfoot.com

BACKHOUSE, Robert. b 35. ALCD70. **d** 70 **p** 71. C Harold Wood *Chelmsf* 70-74; Publicity Sec CPAS 74-78; rtd 00; Perm to Offic *Sarum* 01-05. *D143 Parliament View, 1 Albert Embankment, London SE1 7XQ*

BACON, David Gary. b 62. Leic Univ BA83 Southn Univ BTh88. Sarum & Wells Th Coll 85. **d** 88 **p** 89. C Bromley St Mark *Roch* 88-92; C Lynton, Brendon, Countisbury, Lynmouth etc *Ex* 92; TV 92-95; P-in-c Lapford, Nymet Rowland and Coldridge 95-99; P-in-c Dartford St Alb *Roch* 99-05; P-in-c Bramshaw and Landford w Plaitford *Sarum* 05-06; TV Forest and Avon from 06. *The Rectory, Bramshaw, Lyndhurst SO43 7JF* Tel (01794) 390256 E-mail david.bacon@tesco.net

BACON, Derek Robert Alexander. b 44. Birkbeck Coll Lon BA92 MSc94 Ulster Univ PhD04. TCD Div Sch 69. **d** 71 **p** 72. C Templemore *D & R* 71-73; V Choral Derry Cathl 72-73; C Heeley *Sheff* 74-76; V Sheff St Pet Abbeydale 76-82; Chapl Gt Ormond Street Hosp for Children NHS Trust 82-95; Visiting Fell Ulster Univ 95-97; Perm to Offic *Conn* from 04. *14A Heathmount, Portstewart BT55 7AP* Tel (028) 7083 4987 E-mail dra.bacon@btinternet.com

BACON, Eric Arthur. b 23. Qu Coll Birm 68. **d** 69 **p** 70. C Linc St Pet-at-Gowts and St Andr 69-71; C Asterby Gp 71-74; V Anwick 74-78; V S Kyme 74-78; P-in-c Kirkby Laythorpe w Asgarby 76-78; P-in-c Ewerby w Evedon 76-78; P-in-c Burton Pedwardine 76-78; V Messingham 78-89; rtd 89; Perm to Offic *Linc* 89-01. *2 Curtois Close, Branston, Lincoln LN4 1LJ* Tel (01522) 794265

BACON, Janet Ann. b 57. Man Univ LLB78. NTMTC 95. **d** 98 **p** 99. NSM Stifford *Chelmsf* 98-01; P-in-c Sandbach Heath w Wheelock *Ches* 01-03; V from 03. *Heath Vicarage, School Lane, Sandbach CW11 2LS* Tel (01270) 768826 E-mail j.bacon@virgin.net

BACON, John Martindale. b 22. St Aid Birkenhead 54. **d** 57 **p** 58. C Bury St Paul *Man* 57-59; C-in-c Clifton Green St Thos CD 59-71; V Astley Bridge 71-87; rtd 87; Perm to Offic *Man* from 87-00 and *Blackb* from 87. *21 Lichen Close, Charnock Richard, Chorley PR7 5TT* Tel (01257) 792535 E-mail johnandcon.bacon@tiscali.co.uk

BADDELEY, The Ven Martin James. b 36. Keble Coll Ox BA60 MA64. Linc Th Coll 60. **d** 62 **p** 63. C Stretford St Matt *Man* 62-64; Lect Linc Th Coll 65-66; Tutor 66-69; Chapl 68-69; Chapl Fitzw Coll and New Hall Cam 69-74; Can Res Roch Cathl 74-80; Hon Can 80-96; Prin S'wark Ord Course 80-94; Co-Prin SEITE 94-96; Adn Reigate *S'wark* 96-00; rtd 00; Perm to Offic *Heref* from 00 and *Worc* from 01. *2 Glendower, Fossil Bank, Upper Colwall, Malvern WR13 6PJ* Tel (01684) 569761

BADEN, Peter Michael. b 35. CCC Cam BA59 MA62. Cuddesdon Coll 58. **d** 60 **p** 61. C Hunslet St Mary and Stourton *Ripon* 60-63; Lic to Offic *Wakef* 63-64; C E Grinstead St Swithun *Chich* 65-68; V Brighton St Martin 68-74; TR Brighton Resurr 74-76; R Westbourne and V Stansted 76-84; V Copthorne 84-91; V Clifton and R Dean *Carl* 91-00; P-in-c Mosser 99-00; rtd 00; Perm to Offic *Pet* from 00; *Carl* from 01. *62 Springfield Avenue, Thrapston, Kettering NN14 4TN* Tel (01832) 733186 E-mail p.baden36@btinternet.com

BADGER, Mark. b 59. Qu Coll Birm BTh06. **d** 06 **p** 07. C Barbourne *Worc* 96-01; P-in-c Worc St Geo w St Mary Magd 01-05; Chapl R Gr Sch Worc 02-05; Chapl Thames Valley Police Force *Ox* 05-07. *Iris Cottage, Pershore Road, Little Comberton, Pershore WR10 3HF* Tel (01386) 710934 E-mail revmarkb@tiscali.co.uk

BADHAM, Prof Paul Brian Leslie. b 42. Jes Coll Ox BA65 MA69 Jes Coll Cam BA68 MA72 Birm Univ PhD73. Westcott Ho Cam 66. **d** 68 **p** 69. C Edgbaston St Bart *Birm* 68-69; C Rubery 69-73; Lic to Offic *St D* from 73; Lect Th Univ of Wales (Lamp) 73-83; Sen Lect 83-88; Reader 88-91; Prof Th 91-07; rtd 07; Dir Alister Hardy Relig Experience Research Cen from 02. *4 Coed y Bryn, Aberaeron SA46 0DW* Tel (01545) 571244 Mobile 07968-626902 E-mail pblbadham@hotmail.com

BAGE, Damon John. b 71. Teesside Univ BA95. St Steph Ho Ox 01. **d** 03 **p** 04. C Stockton St Jo *Dur* 03-07; P-in-c Norton St Mich from 07; Chapl John Snow Coll Dur from 06. *St Michael's Vicarage, 13 Imperial Avenue, Norton, Stockton-on-Tees TS20 2EW* Tel (01642) 553984 E-mail damon.bage1@ntlworld.com

BAGG, Marcus Christopher. b 75. Bath Univ BSc96. Trin Coll Bris BA07. **d** 07 **p** 08. C Stanmore *Win* from 07. *St Mark's House, Oliver's Battery Crescent, Winchester SO22 4EU* Tel (01962) 861970 E-mail rev_marcus_bagg@yahoo.co.uk

BAGGALEY, Mrs Patricia Anne. b 45. Open Univ BSc96 RGN68. ERMC 05. **d** 07 **p** 08. NSM Trunch *Nor* from 07. *Anglesea, Rosebery Road, West Runton, Cromer NR27 9QW* Tel (01263) 837490 E-mail baggaley157@btinternet.com

BAGLEY, Roy Victor. b 33. **d** 03 **p** 04. OLM Chasetown *Lich* from 03. *65 Oakdene Road, Burntwood WS7 4SA* Tel (01543) 686000 E-mail rv.bagley@btinternet.com

BAGNALL, Katherine Janet. b 67. Sunderland Univ BEd92. NEOC 02. **d** 05 **p** 06. NSM Monkwearmouth *Dur* 05-06; C

Darlington St Mark w St Paul from 06. *242 North Road, Darlington DL1 2EN* Tel (01325) 262034
E-mail katherine.bagnall@ntlworld.com

BAGOTT, Paul Andrew. b 61. Leeds Univ BA85. Westcott Ho Cam 86. **d** 88 **p** 89. C Chingford SS Pet and Paul *Chelmsf* 88-91; C Pimlico St Sav *Lon* 91-95; P-in-c Clerkenwell H Redeemer and St Mark 95-01; V Clerkenwell H Redeemer from 02; V Clerkenwell St Mark from 02. *Holy Redeemer Clergy House, 24 Exmouth Market, London EC1R 4QE* Tel and fax (020) 7837 1861 E-mail holyredeemerstmark@tiscali.co.uk

BAGSHAW, Paul Stanley. b 55. Selw Coll Cam BA78 MA81 CQSW80. NOC 85. **d** 88 **p** 89. Ind Missr *Sheff* 86-90; C Handsworth Woodhouse 88-90; NSM 91-93; C Newark *S'well* 93-96; P-in-c Ordsall 96-08. *12 Rosewood Crescent, Newcastle upon Tyne NE6 4PQ* Tel 0191-262 7158
E-mail paulbagshaw@gmail.com

BAGSHAWE, John Allen. b 45. St Jo Coll Dur BA70. Cranmer Hall Dur 67. **d** 71 **p** 72. C Bridlington Priory *York* 71-75; C N Ferriby 75-79; V Kingston upon Hull St Matt w St Barn from 79; AD W Hull from 00. *St Matthew's Vicarage, Boulevard, Hull HU3 2TA* Tel (01482) 326573
E-mail allen@stmatthews.karoo.co.uk

BAGULEY, Paul. b 36. NTMTC 94. **d** 98 **p** 99. NSM N Harrow St Alb *Lon* from 98. *86 Central Avenue, Pinner HA5 5BP* Tel (020) 8866 3454 E-mail paulbaguley@waitrose.com

BAILES, Kenneth. b 35. Dur Univ BA69 DPhil. **d** 71 **p** 72. C Redcar *York* 71-73; TV Redcar w Kirkleatham 73-74; P-in-c Appleton Roebuck w Acaster Selby 74-80; P-in-c Sutton on the Forest 80-82; R Stamford Bridge Gp 82-90; V Healaugh w Wighill, Bilbrough and Askham Richard 90-95; rtd 95; Perm to Offic *York* from 98. *The Peace Centre, Inholmes, Leeds Road, Tadcaster LS24 9LP* Tel (01937) 833752 Mobile 07764-614139 E-mail kb13@btinternet.com

BAILES, Mrs Rachel Jocelyn. b 60. Huddersfield Sch of Music BA81 Kingston Poly PGCE83 Leeds Univ MEd96 BA07. NOC 04. **d** 07 **p** 08. C Thornes St Jas w Ch Ch *Wakef* from 07; C Lupset from 07. *166 Horbury Road, Wakefield WF2 8BQ* Tel (01924) 382345 E-mail rjbailes@tiscali.co.uk

BAILEY, Adrian Richard. b 57. St Jo Coll Dur 89. **d** 91 **p** 92. C Oswestry St Oswald *Lich* 91-94; C Shobnall 94-99; C Burton 94-99; Town Cen Chapl 94-99; P-in-c Shobnall 99-01; P-in-c Hengoed w Gobowen 01-08; C Weston Rhyn and Selattyn 05-07; P-in-c Selattyn 07-08; P-in-c Selattyn and Hengoed w Gobowen from 08; Chapl Robert Jones/Agnes Hunt Orthopaedic NHS Trust from 01. *The Vicarage, Old Chirk Road, Gobowen, Oswestry SY11 3LL* Tel and fax (01691) 661226
E-mail arb2@totalise.co.uk

BAILEY, Alan George. b 40. Open Univ BA93. Ripon Hall Ox 62. **d** 64 **p** 65. C Formby H Trin *Liv* 64-67; C Upholland 67-70; P-in-c Edgehill St Dunstan 70-74; V 74-81; RD Toxteth 78-81; Perm to Offic 81-83; Asst Chapl Liv Cathl 83-85; C Liv Our Lady and St Nic w St Anne 85-89; V Waddington *Bradf* 89-03; rtd 03. *66 Woone Lane, Clitheroe BB7 1BJ* Tel (01200) 425699

BAILEY, Andrew Henley. b 57. AKC78. Sarum & Wells Th Coll 79. **d** 80 **p** 81. C Romsey *Win* 80-83; V Bournemouth St Alb 83-93; R Milton from 93. *The Rectory, Church Lane, New Milton BH25 6QN* Tel and fax (01425) 615150
E-mail andrew@miltonrectory.freeserve.co.uk

BAILEY, Andrew John. b 37. Trin Coll Cam BA61 MA. Ridley Hall Cam 60. **d** 63 **p** 64. C Drypool *York* 63-66; C Melton Mowbray w Thorpe Arnold *Leic* 66-69; C-in-c Skelmersdale Ecum Cen *Liv* 69-79; V Langley Mill *Derby* 79-90; V Gt Faringdon w Lt Coxwell *Ox* 90-02; AD Vale of White Horse 97-01; rtd 02; Perm to Offic *Ches* from 02. *58 Manor Road, Sandbach CW11 2ND* Tel (01270) 764076
E-mail baileyaj@talk21.com

BAILEY, Canon Angela. b 61. Kent Univ BA82. Qu Coll Birm 83. **dss** 85 **d** 87 **p** 94. Reculver and Herne Bay St Bart *Cant* 85-88; Par Dn 87-88; Asst Chapl Hull Univ 88-92; Sen Chapl 94-98; Perm to Offic 92-94; P-in-c Rowley w Skidby from 98; Sen Chapl E Riding Community Health Trust 98-04; Can and Preb York Minster from 03; Dioc Ecum Officer from 07; RD Beverley from 07. *The Rectory, 31 Old Village Road, Little Weighton, Cottingham HU20 3US* Tel (01482) 843317
E-mail angela@petermichael.karoo.co.uk

BAILEY, Anthony. b 27. Univ of Wales (Lamp) BA51. Ely Th Coll 51. **d** 53 **p** 54. C Barkingside H Trin *Chelmsf* 53-55; Chapl W Buckland Sch Barnstaple 55-59; R Machen *Mon* 59-66; Min Can Bris Cathl 66-84; Chapl Bris Cathl Sch 66-84; Succ Bris Cathl 68-82; P-in-c Maenclochog w Henry's Moat and Mynachlogddu etc *St D* 83-90; V 90-92; rtd 92; P-in-c Llanglydwen and Llanfyrnach *St D* 94-04. *Charing Cross, Llangolman, Clunderwen SA66 7XN* Tel(01437) 532430 Mobile 07974-557912 E-mail anthony_bailey@lineone.net

BAILEY, Bertram Arthur. b 20. Tyndale Hall Bris 65. **d** 67 **p** 68. C Bath St Luke *B & W* 67-72; C Bickenhill w Elmdon *Birm* 72-73; R N Tawton *Ex* 73-79; R N Tawton and Bondleigh 79-87; rtd 87; Perm to Offic *B & W* from 87; Clergy Retirement and Widows'

Officer 89-06. *4 Uphill Road South, Weston-super-Mare BS23 4SD* Tel (01934) 633552

BAILEY, Mrs Bethan. b 54. Univ of Wales CertEd93 MCSP75. St Jo Coll Nottm 04. **d** 06 **p** 07. C Dolgellau w Llanfachreth and Brithdir etc *Ban* from 06. *Ty'r Ficer, Ffordd Pen y Cefn, Dolgellau LL40 2ER* Tel (01341) 421362
E-mail bethbaileydol@tiscali.co.uk

BAILEY, Brendan John. b 61. Strathclyde Univ BSc83 K Coll Lon MA99. Ripon Coll Cuddesdon BTh93. **d** 94 **p** 95. C Purley *Ox* 94-99; R Nettlebed w Bix, Highmoor, Pishill etc from 99; P-in-c Nuffield from 06. *The Rectory, High Street, Nettlebed, Henley-on-Thames RG9 5DD* Tel (01491) 641575
E-mail baileybj@freeuk.com

BAILEY, Canon Brian Constable. b 36. K Coll Lon AKC62. **d** 63 **p** 64. C Mill Hill Jo Keble Ch *Lon* 63-66; C Gt Stanmore 66-69; C Gt Marlow *Ox* 69-72; R Burghfield 72-81; R Wokingham All SS 81-96; Hon Can Ch Ch 94-96; TV Pinhoe and Broadclyst *Ex* 96-00; rtd 00; V of Close Sarum Cathl 00-01. *2 Rose Cottages, Maudlin Road, Totnes TQ9 5TG* Tel (01803) 865992
E-mail bcbailey@ukonline.co.uk

BAILEY, The Ven David Charles. b 52. Linc Coll Ox BA75 MA78 MSc77. St Jo Coll Nottm BA79. **d** 80 **p** 81. C Worksop St Jo *S'well* 80-83; C Edgware *Lon* 83-87; V S Cave and Ellerker w Broomfleet *York* 87-97; RD Howden 91-97; V Beverley Minster 97-08; P-in-c Routh 97-08; Can and Preb York Minster 98-08; Adn Bolton *Man* from 08. *14 Springside Road, Bury BL9 5JE* Tel 0161-761 6117 Fax 763 7973
E-mail archdeaconbolton@manchester.anglican.org

BAILEY, David Ross. b 58. UNISA BTh82. St Bede's Coll Umtata 80. **d** 82 **p** 82. S Africa 82-08; C Somerset West S Africa 82-85; C Elgin 85-87; R Atlantis 87-95; R Salt River 95-08; P-in-c Honicknowle *Ex* from 08; C Ernesettle from 08; C Whitleigh from 08. *St Francis's Presbytery, 53 Little Dock Lane, Plymouth PL5 2LP* Tel and fax (01752) 773874 Mobile 07864-059302 E-mail fr.david@blueyonder.co.uk

BAILEY, Derek Gilbert. b 42. Div Hostel Dub 65. **d** 68 **p** 69. C Cork St Luke w St Ann *C, C & R* 68-72; CF 72-06; Rtd Officer Chapl RAChD from 06; Perm to Offic *York* from 98; *Sheff* 97-01 and from 03. *c/o MOD Chaplains (Army)* Tel (01980) 615804 Fax 615800

BAILEY, Derek William. b 39. Man Univ BA96. Cranmer Hall Dur 64. **d** 67 **p** 68. C Sutton *Liv* 67-69; C Chapel-en-le-Frith *Derby* 69-73; V Hadfield 73-90; R Collyhurst *Man* 90-95; V Chaddesden St Mary *Derby* 95-02; rtd 02; Perm to Offic *York* from 03. *187 Bishopthorpe Road, York YO23 1PD* Tel (01904) 628080

BAILEY, Canon Edward Ian. b 35. CCC Cam BA59 MA63 Bris Univ MA69 PhD77. United Th Coll Bangalore 59 Westcott Ho Cam 61. **d** 63 **p** 64. C Newc St Jo 63-65; Asst Chapl Marlborough Coll 65-68; Perm to Offic *Bris* 69-70; R Winterbourne 70-06; P-in-c Winterbourne Down 75-81; RD Stapleton 77-83; Chapl Frenchay Hosp Bris 79-84; Hon Can Bris Cathl 84-06; Warden of Readers 95-03; rtd 06; Visiting Prof Middx Univ from 97; Perm to Offic *Ox* from 07. *The Old School, Church Lane, Yarnton, Kidlington OX5 1PY* Tel (01865) 841772 E-mail eibailey@csircs.freeserve.co.uk

BAILEY, Edward Peter. b 35. Nottm Univ MA93. Qu Coll Birm. **d** 62 **p** 63. C Ordsall *S'well* 62-66; C Clifton w Glapton 66-71; V Lady Bay 71-83; Relig Affairs Adv to Radio Trent 83-85; C Gedling 86-89; C Bilborough St Jo 89-00; rtd 00; Perm to Offic *York* from 00. *Cragside Cottage, 18 Egton Road, Aislaby, Whitby YO21 1SU*

BAILEY, Elizabeth. b 47. **d** 03 **p** 04. OLM Bishop's Cannings, All Cannings etc *Sarum* 03-09; rtd 09. *Lynden, The Street, Bishop's Cannings, Devizes SN10 2LD* Tel (01380) 860400
E-mail liz@iftco.com

BAILEY, Mrs Elizabeth Carmen. b 45. EAMTC 89. **d** 93 **p** 94. NSM Roughton and Felbrigg, Metton, Sustead etc *Nor* 93-95 and 99-02; P-in-c 02-06; NSM Cromer and Gresham 95-99; C Buxton w Oxnead, Lammas and Brampton 06-07; C Bure Valley from 07. *5 Warren Road, Southrepps, Norwich NR11 8UN* Tel (01263) 834525 E-mail elizabeth.bailey2@btopenworld.com

BAILEY, Eric Arthur. b 14. AKC37. **d** 37 **p** 38. C S'wark St Geo 37-39; C Waltham Cross *St Alb* 39-41; C Diss *Nor* 41-42; Chapl CF (EC) 42-43; C Kingsbury *Birm* 44-45; V Dordon 45-52; R Londesborough *York* 52-60; P-in-c Nunburnholme 53-54; R 54-60; P-in-c Burnby 53-54; R 54-60; V Gt w Lt Ouseburn *Ripon* 60-65; V Stonegate *Chich* 65-79; rtd 79; Perm to Offic *St E* 81-88. *Hill End, Sapiston, Bury St Edmunds IP31 1RR* Tel (01359) 269638

BAILEY, Ian Arthur. b 53. **d** 01 **p** 02. NSM Clifton H Trin, St Andr and St Pet *Bris* from 01. *5 Queens Gate, Stoke Bishop, Bristol BS9 1TZ* Tel 0117-968 6251

BAILEY, Canon Ivan John. b 33. Keble Coll Ox BA57 MA65. St Steph Ho Ox 57. **d** 59 **p** 60. C Ipswich All Hallows *St E* 59-62; Clerical Sec CEMS 62-66; V Cringleford *Nor* 66-81; RD Humbleyard 73-81; R Colney 80-81; Relig Adv Anglia TV 81-91; P-in-c Kirby Bedon w Bixley and Whitlingham *Nor* 81-92; Hon

Can Nor Cathl 84-98; Chapl St Andr Hosp Norwich 92-94; Chapl Mental Health Unit Nor HA 92-94; Chapl Norfolk Mental Health Care NHS Trust 94-98; rtd 98; Perm to Offic *Nor* from 98. *21 Cranleigh Rise, Norwich NR4 6PQ* Tel (01603) 453565

BAILEY, Ms Jane Rome. b 50. Univ of Wales (Ban) BA99 BTh03. Ban Ord Course 00. **d** 03 **p** 04. C Llifon and Talybolion Deanery *Ban* 03-06; P-in-c Trefdraeth w Aberffraw, Llangadwaladr etc from 06. *The Rectory, 1 Maes Glas, Bethel, Bodorgan LL62 5NW* Tel (01407) 840190
E-mail jane.r.bailey@btinternet.com

BAILEY, Joyce Mary Josephine. *See* OUTEN, Mrs Joyce Mary Josephine

BAILEY, Judith Elizabeth Anne. b 61. RGN RSCN84. Trin Coll Carmarthen 96. **d** 99 **p** 00. OLM Blyth Valley *St E* 99-07. *13 Oak Way, Halesworth IP19 8EB* Tel (01986) 872747
E-mail judith.bailey@ntlworld.com

BAILEY, Justin Mark. b 55. Birm Univ BA77 Southn Univ MTh97 Wolv Poly PGCE78. Ripon Coll Cuddesdon 90. **d** 92 **p** 93. C Oakdale *Sarum* 92-96; P-in-c Milton Abbas, Hilton w Cheselbourne etc 96-05; P-in-c Piddletrenthide w Plush, Alton Pancras etc 02-05; V Piddle Valley, Hilton, Cheselbourne etc 05-06; P-in-c Bruton and Distr *B & W* from 06. *The Rectory, Plox, Bruton BA10 0EF* Tel (01749) 812616
E-mail frjustin@toucansurf.com

BAILEY, Mark David. b 62. Ripon Coll Cuddesdon 87. **d** 90 **p** 91. C Leigh Park *Portsm* 90-93; C Fleet *Guildf* 93-95; TV Basingstoke *Win* 95-00; P-in-c Twyford and Owslebury and Morestead 00-08; R Lower Dever from 08. *The Rectory, 6 Green Close, South Wonston, Winchester SO21 3EE* Tel (01962) 880650 E-mail revd.bailey@ukgateway.net

BAILEY, Canon Mark Robert. b 60. St Paul's Cheltenham BA81. Trin Coll Bris BA89. **d** 89 **p** 90. C Heigham H Trin *Nor* 89-94; Chapl UEA 92-93; TV Cheltenham St Mary, St Matt, St Paul and H Trin *Glouc* 94-07; TR Cheltenham H Trin and St Paul from 07; Hon Can Glouc Cathl from 04. *100 Hewlett Road, Cheltenham GL52 6AR* Tel (01242) 582398 *or* 262306
E-mail mark.bailey@trinityuk.org

BAILEY, Martin Tristram. b 57. Oak Hill Th Coll 89. **d** 91 **p** 92. C Brundall w Braydeston and Postwick *Nor* 91-95; TV Plymouth St Andr and Stonehouse *Ex* 95-06; Chapl St Dunstan's Abbey Sch Plymouth 02-05; V Riseley w Bletsoe *St Alb* from 06. *The Vicarage, 16 Church Lane, Riseley, Bedford MK44 1ER* Tel (01234) 708234 E-mail martin@7baileys.freeserve.co.uk

BAILEY, Nicholas Andrew. b 55. Open Univ BA84 Nottm Univ CertEd80. Ripon Coll Cuddesdon 88. **d** 90 **p** 91. C Guisborough *York* 90-92; Chapl Repton Prep Sch from 92. *Repton Preparatory School, Foremarke Hall, Milton, Derby DE65 6EJ* Tel (01283) 703269

BAILEY, Miss Patricia Laura. b 49. Wall Hall Coll Aldenham CertEd72. NTMTC 95. **d** 98 **p** 99. NSM Hackney Marsh *Lon* 98-01; NSM S Hackney St Jo w Ch Ch 01-04; NSM Cosby and Whetstone *Leic* from 04. *16 The Plantation, Countesthorpe, Leicester LE8 5ST* Tel 0116-277 4362

BAILEY, Peter. *See* BAILEY, Edward Peter

BAILEY, Canon Peter Robin. b 43. St Jo Coll Dur BA64. Trin Coll Bris 72. **d** 74 **p** 75. C Corby St Columba *Pet* 74-77; C Bishopsworth *Bris* 77-82; V Sea Mills 82-97; RD Westbury and Severnside 91-97; P-in-c Bishopston 97-98; P-in-c Bris St Andr w St Bart 97-98; TR Bishopston and St Andrews 98-09; Hon Can Bris Cathl 97-09; rtd 09. *4 The Croft, Backwell, Bristol BS48 3LY* Tel (01275) 790611 E-mail peterandheather@blueyonder.co.uk

BAILEY, Richard William. b 38. Man Univ BSc59. Ripon Hall Ox 63. **d** 65 **p** 66. C Tonge *Man* 65-68; C Stretford St Matt 68-71; R Abbey Hey 71-80; V E Crompton 80-86; V Chadderton St Matt 86-98; R Stand 98-04; rtd 04. *Address withheld by request*
E-mail bailey.ditchash@tesco.net

BAILEY, Richard William. b 47. Oak Hill Th Coll BA84. **d** 84 **p** 85. C Huyton St Geo *Liv* 84-87; V Wombridge *Lich* 87-97; P-in-c Shenstone and Stonnall 97-06; Chapl HM Pris Dovegate from 06. *HM Prison Dovegate, Uttoxeter ST14 8XR* Tel (01283) 829525 E-mail ricthevic@madasafish.com

BAILEY, Robert Henry. b 45. FCA69. NOC 99. **d** 02 **p** 03. NSM Dewsbury *Wakef* 02-05; Sub Chapl HM Pris Leeds 02-05; NSM Kinsley w Wragby *Wakef* from 05; P-in-c from 06. *The Vicarage, George Street, South Hiendley, Barnsley S72 9BX* Tel (01226) 715315 E-mail robertbailey.minster@btinternet.com

BAILEY, Canon Robert William. b 49. Open Univ BA91. Bernard Gilpin Soc Dur 68 Lich Th Coll 69. **d** 72 **p** 73. C Stoke *Cov* 72-75; Chapl RAF 75-99; RD Calne *Sarum* 97-98; TV Cartmel Peninsula *Carl* from 99; Hon Can Carl Cathl from 05. *The Vicarage, Priest Lane, Cartmel, Grange-over-Sands LA11 6PU* Tel and fax (01539) 536261 E-mail vicar.cartmel@virgin.net

BAILEY, Simon. b 56. Man Univ MusB Nottm Univ BCombStuds. Linc Th Coll. **d** 83 **p** 84. C Armley w New Wortley *Ripon* 83-86; C Harrogate St Wilfrid and St Luke 86-90; R Harby, Long Clawson and Hose *Leic* 90-94; V Woodhall *Bradf* 94-03; RD Calverley 98-01; R N Adelaide Ch Ch Australia 03-07; R Glen Osmond from 07. *2 Pridmore Road, Glen Osmond*

SA 5064, Australia Tel (0061) (8) 8379 1494 *or* 8379 4114 Fax 8338 3442 E-mail rector@stsavoursgo.net

BAILEY, Stella. b 76. Westhill Coll Birm BTheol98. Ripon Coll Cuddesdon 07. **d** 09. C Walsgrave on Sowe *Cov* from 09. *33 Brookshaw Way, Coventry CV2 2NJ*
E-mail chacethedog@sky.com

BAILEY, Stephen. b 39. Leic Univ BA61. Clifton Th Coll 61. **d** 62 **p** 63. C Wellington w Eyton *Lich* 62-66; C Rainham *Chelmsf* 66-69; V Ercall Magna *Lich* 69-75; V Rowton 69-75; RD Wrockwardine 72-75; V W Bromwich Gd Shep w St Jo 75-83; P-in-c W Bromwich St Phil 80-81; V 81-83; R Chadwell *Chelmsf* 83-96; RD Thurrock 92-96; V Galleywood Common 96-04; rtd 04; Perm to Offic *Chelmsf* from 04. *64 Bridport Way, Braintree CM7 9FJ* Tel (01376) 550859

BAILEY, Stephen Andrew. b 75. St Jo Coll Nottm 05. **d** 07 **p** 08. C Walton-on-Thames *Guildf* from 07. *1 Egmont Road, Walton-on-Thames KT12 2NW* Tel (01932) 225315
E-mail steveandangiebailey@tiscali.co.uk

BAILEY, Stephen John. b 57. Sarum & Wells Th Coll 88. **d** 90 **p** 91. C Redhill H Trin *S'wark* 90-95; Chapl E Surrey Coll 91-93; P-in-c Betchworth *S'wark* 95-00; V 00-06; P-in-c Buckland 95-00; R 00-06; R Hamilton H Trin Bermuda from 06. *PO Box CR 186, Hamilton Parish CR BX, Bermuda* Tel (001441) 293 1710 E-mail holytrinitychurch@logic.bm

BAILEY, Mrs Susan Mary. b 40. F L Calder Coll Liv CertEd61. EAMTC 89. **d** 92 **p** 94. NSM Chelmsf Cathl 92-93; NSM Needham Market w Badley *St E* 93-95; NSM Belper *Derby* 96-00; NSM Allestree St Nic and Quarndon 00-05; Chapl Morley Retreat and Conf Ho Derby 00-05; rtd 05. *28 Burleigh Way, Wickwar, Wotton-under-Edge GL12 8LR* Tel (01454) 294112 E-mail susan.m.bailey@gmail.com

BAILEY, Yvonne Mary. *See* HOBSON, Mrs Yvonne Mary

BAILIE, Alison Margaret. b 62. Leeds Univ LLB83. Trin Coll Bris BA98. **d** 98 **p** 99. C Halliwell St Pet *Man* 98-05; P-in-c Droylsden St Mary from 05. *St Mary's Rectory, Dunkirk Street, Droylsden, Manchester M43 7FB* Tel 0161-370 1569
E-mail alison@bailie.free-online.co.uk

BAILLIE, Canon Frederick Alexander. b 21. FRGS Open Univ BA75 QUB MA86 PhD87. CITC 53. **d** 55 **p** 56. C Belfast St Paul *Conn* 55-59; C Dunmurry 59-61; RAChD 57-84; I Eglantine *Conn* 61-69; I Belfast Whiterock 69-74; Hd of S Ch Miss Ballymacarrett 74-79; I Magheraculmoney *Clogh* 79-87; Dioc Communications Officer 80-86; Hon CF from 84; Can Clogh Cathl 85-87; rtd 87. *2 Raasay Court, Portree IV51 9TG* Tel (01478) 611376 E-mail fabmail@eidosnet.co.uk

BAILLIE, Terence John. b 46. New Coll Ox BA69 MA78 Man Univ MSc72. St Jo Coll Nottm 74. **d** 77 **p** 78. C Chadwell *Chelmsf* 77-80; C Bickenhill w Elmdon *Birm* 80-84; V Bedminster St Mich *Bris* 84-96; V Clevedon St Andr and Ch Ch *B & W* from 96. *The Vicarage, 10 Coleridge Road, Clevedon BS21 7TB* Tel (01275) 872982 E-mail terry.baillie@tesco.net

BAILY, Linda Rosemary. **d** 06 **p** 07. NSM Llanaber w Caerdeon *Ban* from 06. *Llwyn Gloddaeth, Abermaw, Barmouth LL42 1DX* Tel (01341) 280524

BAILY, Canon Robert Spencer Canning. b 21. G&C Coll Cam BA42 MA46. Westcott Ho Cam 42. **d** 44 **p** 45. C Sherborne w Castleton and Lillington *Sarum* 44-46; C Heacham *Nor* 46-47; C Bedford All SS *St Alb* 48-50, C-in-c Hayes St Edm CD *Lon* 50-56; R Blofield w Hemblington *Nor* 56-69; P-in-c Perlethorpe *S'well* 69-87; Dir of Educn 69-87; Hon Can S'well Minster 80-87; rtd 87; Perm to Offic *Linc* 87-02; *S'well* 87-00. *17 Ravendale Close, Grantham NG31 8BS* Tel (01476) 568614

BAIN, Alan. b 48. Thames Poly BSc72. St Jo Coll Nottm. **d** 77 **p** 78. C Wakef St Andr and St Mary 77-81; V Bath Odd Down *B & W* 81-82; P-in-c Combe Hay 81-82; V Bath Odd Down w Combe Hay from 82. *The Vicarage, 39 Frome Road, Bath BA2 2QF* Tel (01225) 832838 *or* tel and fax 835228
E-mail alanbain@stphilipstjames.org

BAIN, Andrew John. b 55. Newc Poly BA77 Edin Univ MTh89. Edin Th Coll 86. **d** 88 **p** 89. Chapl St Mary's Cathl 88-91; C Edin St Mary 88-91; R Edin St Jas 91-98; P-in-c Edin St Marg 93-98; R Haddington 98-06; P-in-c Edin St Ninian from 98; Dioc Dir of Ords 95-98 and 06-07. *Emmaus House, 14 Gilmore Place, Edinburgh EH3 9NQ* E-mail andrewbain99@hotmail.com

BAIN, David Roualeyn Findlater (Roly). b 54. Bris Univ BA75. Ripon Coll Cuddesdon 76. **d** 78 **p** 79. C Perry Hill St Geo *S'wark* 78-81; Chapl Asst Guy's Hosp Lon 81-84; Succ S'wark Cathl 81-84; V Streatham St Paul 84-90; Perm to Offic *Bris* 90-08; Hon C Almondsbury and Olveston from 08. *The Vicarage, The Street, Olveston, Bristol BS35 4DA* Tel and fax (01454) 616593

BAIN, The Ven John Stuart. b 55. Van Mildert Coll Dur BA77. Westcott Ho Cam 78. **d** 80 **p** 81. C Washington *Dur* 80-84; C Dunston 84-86; V Shiney Row 86-92; V Herrington 86-92; P-in-c Whitworth w Spennymoor 92-97; P-in-c Merrington 94-97; AD Auckland 96-02; V Spennymoor, Whitworth and Merrington 97-02; Hon Can Dur Cathl 98-02; Adn Sunderland from 02; P-in-c Hedworth from 02; P-in-c E Boldon from 09. *St Nicholas' Vicarage, Hedworth Lane, Boldon Colliery NE35 9JA* Tel 0191-536 2300 Fax 519 3369
E-mail archdeacon.of.sunderland@durham.anglican.org

BAIN, Lawrence John Weir. b 60. NTMTC BA05. **d** 05 **p** 06. C Stoughton *Guildf* 05-09; P-in-c Camberley Heatherside from 09. *30 Yockley Close, Camberley GU15 1QH* Tel (01276) 691127 Fax 678015 E-mail revlarrybain@aol.com

BAIN-DOODU, Canon Joseph Justice. b 56. Cape Coast Univ Ghana MEd09. St Nic Th Coll Ghana LTh86. **d** 86 **p** 86. Ghana 86-97 and 99-08; Hon C Sheldon *Birm* 97-98; Perm to Offic *Portsm* from 09. *The Rectory, 3A Wadham Road, Portsmouth PO2 9ED* Tel (023) 9234 2661 Mobile 07532-104795 E-mail josephbaindoodu@gmail.com

BAINBRIDGE, Mrs Christine Susan. b 48. St Aid Coll Dur BA70 K Coll Lon MA99. SEITE 93. **d** 96 **p** 97. C S'wark H Trin w St Matt 96-99; Asst to Bp Woolwich (Greenwich Area) 99-03; C Lee Gd Shep w St Pet 99-03; P-in-c Deptford St Jo w H Trin 03-06; TR Deptford St Jo w H Trin and Ascension from 06. *St John's Vicarage, St John's Vale, London SE8 4EA* Tel (020) 8692 2857 Fax 8318 1915 Mobile 07939-662980 E-mail bainbridge.c@tiscali.co.uk

BAINBRIDGE, David George. b 42. Wadh Coll Ox BA63 MA67 Lon Inst of Educn PGCE67. Ridley Hall Cam 84. **d** 86 **p** 87. C Downend *Bris* 86-90; TV Yate New Town 90-01; Warden Lee Abbey Internat Students' Club Kensington 01-07; rtd 07. *2 Kingsmead, Lechlade GL7 3BW* Tel (01367) 250347 E-mail bainbridge1973@yahoo.co.uk

BAINBRIDGE, John Richard. b 35. Pemb Coll Cam BA59 MA63. Clifton Th Coll 65. **d** 67 **p** 68. C Ex St Leon w H Trin 67-70; P-in-c Penge St Paul *Roch* 70-73; Chapl Uppingham Sch 73-87; V Stevenage St Nic and Graveley *St Alb* 87-98; rtd 98; Perm to Offic *Pet* from 99. *Willowdown Cottage, 8 Laxton, Corby NN17 3AT* Tel (01780) 450308

BAINBRIDGE, Richard Densham. b 49. Ch Coll Cam BA71 MA75 Edge Hill Coll of HE PGCE72. S'wark Ord Course 91. **d** 94 **p** 95. C Bermondsey St Jas w Ch Ch S'wark 94-99; V Lee Gd Shep w St Pet from 99; AD E Lewisham from 06. *The Vicarage, 47 Handen Road, London SE12 8NR* Tel (020) 8318 2363 Fax 8318 1915 E-mail revrdb@yahoo.com

BAINES, Alan William. b 50. S Bank Poly BSc72. Trin Coll Bris 92. **d** 94 **p** 95. C Chenies and Lt Chalfont, Latimer and Flaunden *Ox* 94-98; V Eye *Pet* 98-05; Post Ord Tr Co-ord 00-05; TV Duston Team from 05. *The Rectory, 3 Main Road, Duston, Northampton NN5 6JB* Tel (01604) 752591 E-mail a.baines93@ntlworld.com

BAINES, Derek Alfred. b 53. MCSP75. CBDTI 99. **d** 02 **p** 03. NSM Lostock Hall *Blackb* 02-09; NSM Lostock Hall and Farington Moss from 09. *16 Middlefield, Leyland PR26 7AE* Tel and fax (01772) 641521 Mobile 07774-200885

BAINES, Edward. *See* BAINES, Noel Edward

BAINES, John Charles. b 68. Ripon Coll Cuddesdon 00. **d** 02 **p** 03. C Morton and Stonebroom w Shirland *Derby* 02-06; P-in-c New Mills from 06. *St George's Vicarage, Church Lane, New Mills, High Peak SK22 4NP* Tel (01663) 743225 E-mail vicar@newmillschurch.co.uk

BAINES, John Edmund. b 22. Down Coll Cam BA47 MA50 Lon Univ BD51. New Coll Lon. **d** 58 **p** 59. C Penistone w Midhope *Wakef* 58-60; V Batley St Thos 60-69; V Cawthorne 69-89; rtd 89; Perm to Offic *Wakef* 90-04. *3 Huskar Close, Silkstone, Barnsley S75 4SX* Tel (01226) 791088

BAINES, Keith. b 46. **d** 99 **p** 00. OLM Atherton and Hindsford *Man* 99-02; OLM Atherton and Hindsford w Howe Bridge 02-05; TV from 05. *6 Marton Drive, Atherton, Manchester M46 9WA* Tel (01942) 897668 E-mail baines1@supanet.com

✠**BAINES, The Rt Revd Nicholas.** b 57. Bradf Univ BA80. Trin Coll Bris BA87. **d** 87 **p** 88 **c** 03. C Kendal St Thos *Carl* 87-91; C Leic H Trin w St Jo 91-92; V Rothley 92-00; RD Goscote 96-00; Adn Lambeth *S'wark* 00-03; Area Bp Croydon from 03. *53 Stanhope Road, Croydon CR0 5NS* Tel (020) 8686 1822 *or* 8256 9630 Fax 8686 2074 Mobile 07974-194735 E-mail bishop.nick@southwark.anglican.org

BAINES, Noel Edward (Ted). b 29. St Jo Coll Dur BSc52 MA62. **d** 54 **p** 55. C Rainham *Chelmsf* 54-58; C Surbiton Hill Ch Ch S'wark 58-61; V Southborough St Matt *Roch* 61-67; V Beckenham St Jo 67-74; Hd RE Taunton Manor High Sch Caterham 74-83; Keston Coll 85-91; Hon C Bromley Ch Ch *Roch* 91-98; Hon C New Beckenham St Paul from 98; rtd 94. *10 Bromley Avenue, Bromley BR1 4BQ* Tel and fax (020) 8460 8256 E-mail ted.baines@diocese-rochester.org

BAINES, Mrs Sharon June. b 52. Sheff Hallam Univ MSc05 MCSP74. LCTP 06. **d** 09. NSM Penwortham St Leon *Blackb* from 09. *16 Middlefield, Leyland PR26 7AE* Tel (01772) 641521 E-mail baines5253@btinternet.com

BAIRD, Agnes Murry (Nancy). Man Univ CertEd70. EAMTC 93. **d** 96 **p** 97. NSM Bramford *St E* 96-98; NSM Haughley w Wetherden and Stowupland 98-09; rtd 09; Perm to Offic *St E* from 09. *32 Maple Road, Stowupland, Stowmarket IP14 4DG* Tel (01449) 674734 E-mail nancy@ctlconnect.co.uk

BAIRD, Paul Drummond. b 48. N Co Coll Newc CertEd71 Open Univ BA85. Ripon Coll Cuddesdon 88. **d** 90 **p** 91. C Chandler's Ford *Win* 90-93; V Hythe 93-03; P-in-c Compton and

Otterbourne 03-06; rtd 08. *5 Kensington Close, Eastleigh SO50 6NS* Tel (023) 8064 7536 Mobile 07802-431012 E-mail paulbaird@aol.com

BAIRD, Robert Douglas. b 21. ERD56. Cam Univ MA64. Ripon Coll Cuddesdon. **d** 85 **p** 86. NSM Charlbury w Shorthampton *Ox* 85-87; Asst Chapl HM Pris Grendon and Spring Hill 85; Lic to Offic *Ox* 87-91; Perm to Offic 91-07. *Glebe House, Ibstone, High Wycombe HP14 3XZ* Tel (01491) 638642 E-mail robert@baird1921.freeserve.co.uk

BAIRD, Mrs Sally. b 53. St As Minl Tr Course 04. **d** 06. NSM Bistre *St As* from 06. *100 Park Avenue, Bryn-y-Baal, Mold CH7 6TP* Tel (01352) 758831 E-mail sally.baird@btinternet.com

BAIRD, Canon William Stanley. b 33. TCD BA54 Div Test. **d** 56 **p** 57. C Carlow *C & O* 56-59; I Dunganstown *D & G* 59-64; C Knock *D & D* 64-69; P-in-c Kilwarlin Upper w Kilwarlin Lower 69-71; I 71-72; Warden Ch Min of Healing (Ireland) 72-79; I Dublin Drumcondra w N Strand *D & G* 79-91; Dir of Ords (Dub) 84-99; Can Ch Ch Cathl Dublin 88-99; I Swords w Donabate and Kilsallaghan 91-99; rtd 99. *5 Weavers Way, Wheaton Hall, Dublin Road, Drogheda, Co Louth, Republic of Ireland* Tel (00353) (41) 984 6645 E-mail stanleybaird1@eircom.net

BAISLEY, George. b 45. Sarum & Wells Th Coll 78. **d** 80 **p** 81. C Glouc St Geo w Whaddon 80-83; R Welford w Weston and Clifford Chambers 83-87; Chapl Myton Hamlet Hospice 87-91; Chapl Warw Univ 87-91; R Berkswell 91-03; RD Kenilworth 96-01; Chapl Bromley Coll 03-04; P-in-c Doddington, Newnham and Wychling *Cant* 04-07; P-in-c Lynsted w Kingsdown 04-07; P-in-c Norton 04-07; rtd 07; Perm to Offic *Chelmsf* 07-08; P-in-c N Ockendon from 08. *52 Birch Crescent, South Ockendon RM15 6TZ* Tel (01708) 850525 Mobile 07974-151056 E-mail george@baisley45.co.uk

BAKER, Alan. b 42. Liv Univ BA64. Carl Dioc Tr Inst 93. **d** 96 **p** 97. NSM Flookburgh *Carl* 96-97; NSM Cartmel Peninsula 97-07; Perm to Offic *Blackb* from 98 and *Carl* from 08. *1 Church View, Priest Lane, Cartmel, Grange-over-Sands LA11 6PU* Tel (01539) 536551

BAKER, Albert George. b 30. Qu Coll Birm. **d** 61 **p** 62. C Merton St Mary *S'wark* 61-64; C Limpsfield and Titsey 64-65; C Chapel-en-le-Frith *Derby* 65-68; R Odd Rode *Ches* 68-76; V Holme Cultram St Mary *Carl* 76-78; R Blofield w Hemblington *Nor* 78-94; rtd 94. *240 Raedwald Drive, Bury St Edmunds IP32 7DN* Tel (01284) 701082

BAKER, Alicia Mary. b 63. Trin Coll Bris BA03. **d** 03 **p** 04. C E Ham St Paul *Chelmsf* 03-07; P-in-c Abercarn and Cwmcarn *Mon* from 07. *The Vicarage, Twyn Road, Abercarn, Newport NP11 5GU* Tel (01495) 243919 E-mail aliciabakeruk@btinternet.com

BAKER, Angela Mary. b 42. **d** 91. Par Dn Battersea St Sav and St Geo w St Andr *S'wark* 91-94; C 94-96; C Battersea Fields 96-02; rtd 02; Perm to Offic *Roch* from 03. *Finches, Ide Hill, Sevenoaks TN14 6JW* Tel (01732) 750470

BAKER, Mrs Ann Christine. b 49. Edin Univ BEd71. CBDTI 98. **d** 01 **p** 02. NSM St Bees *Carl* 01-04; P-in-c Eskdale, Irton, Muncaster and Waberthwaite from 04. *Eskdale Vicarage, Boot, Holmrook CA19 1TF* Tel (019467) 23242 E-mail j.baker@can-online.org.uk

BAKER, Anne-Marie Clare. *See* BIRD, Mrs Anne-Marie Clare

BAKER, Anthony Peter. b 38. Hertf Coll Ox BA59 MA63. Clifton Th Coll 60. **d** 63 **p** 64. C Ox St Ebbe w St Pet 63-66; C Welling *Roch* 66-70; V Redland *Bris* 70-79; Lect Tyndale Hall Bris 70-71; Lect Trin Coll Bris 71-77; V Beckenham Ch Ch *Roch* 79-94; Chapl Beckenham Hosp 79-94; V Hove Bp Hannington Memorial Ch *Chich* 94-03; rtd 03; Perm to Offic *Chich* from 04. *12 Paradise Close, Eastbourne BN20 8BT* Tel (01323) 438783

BAKER, Miss Barbara Ann. b 36. Linc Th Coll 85. **d** 87 **p** 94. Par Dn Hornchurch St Andr *Chelmsf* 87-94; C 94-97; rtd 97; Perm to Offic *Chelmsf* from 97. *120 Devonshire Road, Hornchurch RM12 4LN* Tel (01708) 477759

BAKER, Canon Bernard George Coleman. b 36. Lon Univ BD61. Oak Hill Th Coll 61. **d** 63 **p** 64. C Broadwater St Mary *Chich* 63-66; Tanzania 66-84 and 96-01; BCMS Miss P and Chapl Morogoro Em Ch 66-79; V Moshi St Marg 79-84; Hon Can Morogoro from 77; Hon Can Mt Kilimanjaro from 82; C-in-c Ryde St Jas Prop Chpl *Portsm* 84-96; Crosslinks 96-01; Asst P Ruaha Cathl and Teacher Amani Chr Tr Cen 96-01; rtd 01; Perm to Offic *Ex* from 02. *104 Merafield Road, Plympton, Plymouth PL7 1SJ* Tel (01752) 339879

BAKER (formerly BARTON), Mrs Caroline Janet. b 61. Ex Univ BA83. Westcott Ho Cam 93. **d** 96 **p** 97. C Ivybridge w Harford *Ex* 96-02; P-in-c Torquay St Luke and Dioc Adv in Adult Tr 02-05; rtd 05. *11 Arundel Close, Exeter EX2 8UG* Tel (01392) 426781

BAKER, Charles Edward. b 47. **d** 87 **p** 88. NSM Dublin Clontarf *D & G* 87-90; NSM Delgany 90-94; NSM Dublin Sandford w Milltown 94-97; NSM Dublin St Patr Cathl Gp from 97. *12 Aranleigh Vale, Rathfarnham, Dublin 14, Republic of Ireland* Tel (00353) (1) 494 6465

BAKER, Prof Christopher James. b 54. St Cath Coll Cam BA75 MA78 PhD78 CEng83 FICE96 FIHT95. EMMTC 85. **d** 88 **p** 89. NSM Matlock Bath *Derby* 88-95; NSM Matlock Bath and Cromford 95; NSM Beeston *S'well* 95-98; Perm to Offic *Lich* 98-00; NSM Lich St Mich w St Mary and Wall from 00. *28 Grosvenor Close, Lichfield WS14 9SR* Tel (01543) 256320 *or* 262211 E-mail cjsmbaker@btinternet.com

BAKER, Christopher Peter. b 64. St Cuth Soc Dur BA95 Greenwich Univ PGCE96. SEITE 99. **d** 02 **p** 03. C Kennington St Mark *S'wark* 02-06; Chapl Greenwich Univ from 07. *St Mark's Vicarage, 10 Church Road, Biggin Hill, Westerham TN16 3LB* Tel (01959) 540482

BAKER, Christopher Richard. b 61. Man Univ BA83 PhD02 Southn Univ BTh90 Heythrop Coll Lon MTh92. Sarum & Wells Th Coll 86. **d** 89 **p** 93. C Dulwich St Barn *S'wark* 89-92; Tutor Sarum & Wells Th Coll 92-94; Dir Chr Tr Milton Keynes *Ox* 94-98; Dir Tr OLM 98-99; Development Officer Wm Temple Foundn 01-04; Research Dir from 04. *Luther King House, Brighton Grove, Rusholme, Manchester M14 5JP* Tel 0161-249 2502 Mobile 07779-000021 E-mail temple@wtf.org.uk

BAKER, David. b 63. SWMTC 99. **d** 02 **p** 03. NSM Parkham, Alwington, Buckland Brewer etc *Ex* from 02. *4 Ashley Terrace, Bideford EX39 3AL* Tel (01237) 473453
E-mail bakerbuzz@hotmail.com

BAKER, David Ayshford. b 66. St Aid Coll Dur BA88. Wycliffe Hall Ox BTh97. **d** 97 **p** 98. C Chadwell Heath *Chelmsf* 97-01; C Surbiton Hill Ch Ch *S'wark* 01-09; R E Dean w Friston and Jevington *Chich* from 09. *The Rectory, Gilberts Drive, East Dean, Eastbourne BN20 0DL* Tel (01323) 423266

BAKER, David Clive. b 47. Sarum & Wells Th Coll 76. **d** 78 **p** 79. C Shirley *Birm* 78-82; R Wainfleet All SS w St Thos *Linc* 82-83; P-in-c Wainfleet St Mary 82-83; P-in-c Croft 82-83; R The Wainfleets and Croft 83-86; V Stirchley *Birm* 86-96; Perm to Offic 97-98; V Handsworth St Mich 98-02; Chapl Aston Univ 99-02; C Codsall *Lich* 02-05; P-in-c Coven 04-05; V Bilbrook and Coven from 05. *The New Vicarage, Church Lane, Coven, Wolverhampton WV9 5DE* Tel (01902) 790230 Mobile 07958-468819

BAKER, David Frederick. b 32. Clifton Th Coll 67. **d** 69 **p** 70. C Bilton *Ripon* 69-71; C Heworth w Peasholme St Cuth *York* 71-75; V Sand Hutton w Gate and Upper Helmsley 75-77; P-in-c Bossall w Buttercrambe 75-77; V Sand Hutton 77-80; R Preston in Holderness 80; P-in-c Sproatley 80; R Preston and Sproatley in Holderness 80-89; C Topcliffe w Dalton and Dishforth 89; V Baldersby w Dalton, Dishforth etc 89-96; rtd 96; Perm to Offic *York* and *Ripon* 96-08. *6 Mains Court, Westhill AB32 6QZ* Tel (01224) 743070

BAKER, David John. b 27. LRAM50 GRSM51. Ely Th Coll 53. **d** 55 **p** 56. C Swanley St Mary *Roch* 55-58; C Guildf St Nic 58-63; Prec St Alb Abbey 63-67; P-in-c Colney St Pet 67-68; V 68-73; V Tattenham Corner and Burgh Heath *Guildf* 73-84; R Fetcham 84-96; rtd 96; Perm to Offic *Guildf* from 96. *1 Terra Cotta Court, Quennels Hill, Wrecclesham, Farnham GU10 4SL* Tel (01252) 734202

BAKER, David Jordan. b 35. Univ of Wales (Lamp) BA59. Ely Th Coll 59. **d** 61 **p** 62. C Spalding *Linc* 61-66; C Gainsborough All SS 66-69; V Wrawby 69-78; V Melton Ross w New Barnetby 70-78; V Linc St Pet-at-Gowts and St Andr 78-94; rtd 98; Perm to Offic *Linc* from 01. *Fartherwell, The Paddock, Canwick, Lincoln LN4 2RX* Tel (01522) 526903

BAKER, Dilly. *See* BAKER, Ms Hilary Mary

BAKER, Mrs Elizabeth May Janet Margaret. b 51. Bretton Hall Coll CertEd73. Ox Min Course 04. **d** 07 **p** 08. NSM Watling Valley *Ox* from 07. *The Well, Newport Road, Willen, Milton Keynes MK15 9AA* Tel (01908) 662092
E-mail beth@willenbakers.co.uk

BAKER, Frank Thomas. b 36. Selw Coll Cam BA61. Coll of Resurr Mirfield. **d** 63 **p** 64. C Mackworth St Fran *Derby* 63-66; C Leeds St Pet *Ripon* 66-73; P-in-c Stanley *Dur* 73-74; R Crook 73-74; Chapl Bucharest *Eur* 74-75; C Tewkesbury w Walton Cardiff *Glouc* 75-81; Min Can Windsor 81-86; rtd 86. *15 Hartford Court, 33 Filey Road, Scarborough YO11 2TP* Tel (01723) 352466

BAKER, Frederick Peter. b 24. Bps' Coll Cheshunt 58. **d** 60 **p** 61. C Peckham St Jude *S'wark* 60-63; C Mitcham St Mark 63-66; C Northampton St Pet w Upton 66-69; P-in-c Northampton St Lawr 69-71; V Northampton St Edm 71-78; V Spratton 78-83; R Walgrave w Hannington and Wold 83-89; rtd 89; Perm to Offic *Win* 89-98 and *Ely* 00-08. *73 Five Arches, Orton Wistow, Peterborough PE2 6FQ* Tel (01733) 371349

BAKER, Canon Gerald Stothert. b 30. Univ of NZ MA54. St Jo Coll Auckland LTh56. **d** 56 **p** 57. C Morrinsville New Zealand 56-58; V Mokau 59-61; V Paeroa 61-65; V Huntly 65-70; V Stratford 70-73; V Karori 73-87; Hon Can Wellington 80-87; TV Kidderminster St Mary and All SS w Trimpley etc *Worc* 87-92; V S Wairarapa New Zealand 92-96; Adn Wairarapa 95-96; rtd 96. *47 Reading Street, Greytown 5712, New Zealand* Tel (0064) (6) 304 8367 Fax 304 8302

BAKER, Gillian Devonald. b 40. S Dios Minl Tr Scheme 88. **d** 91 **p** 94. NSM Redhorn *Sarum* 91-07; TV 02-07; Chapl HM Pris Erlestoke 94-01. *11 The Street, Chirton, Devizes SN10 3QS* Tel (01380) 848170 Fax 840152
E-mail davidb@atlanticbridge.co.uk

BAKER, The Very Revd Graham Brinkworth. b 26. AKC54. **d** 55 **p** 56. C Wandsworth St Anne *S'wark* 55-58; Canada from 58. *1280 Tracksell Avenue, Victoria BC V8P 2C9, Canada*

BAKER, Harry Hallas. b 16. Bps' Coll Cheshunt 51. **d** 53 **p** 54. C Killingworth *Newc* 53-58; V Mickley 58-63; V Howdon Panns 63-73; C Alnwick St Mich 73-74; C Alnwick 74-84; rtd 84; Perm to Offic *Newc* from 84. *clo Mrs J Woodcock, 60 Admirals Court, Sowerby, Thirsk YO7 1RR*

BAKER, Mrs Heather Elizabeth. b 48. WEMTC 94. **d** 97 **p** 98. NSM Ewyas Harold w Dulas, Kenderchurch etc *Heref* 97-98; C 98-00; C Burghill and Stretton Sugwas 00-01; P-in-c Glasbury and Llowes w Clyro and Betws *S & B* 02-08. *Park Lodge, Pontrilas, Hereford HR2 0HE*

BAKER, Ms Hilary Mary (Dilly). b 61. Man Univ BA83 CQSW86. Sarum & Wells Th Coll 86. **d** 89 **p** 94. Par Dn E Dulwich St Jo *S'wark* 89-92; Tutor Sarum & Wells Th Coll 92-94; TV Stantonbury and Willen *Ox* 94-01; Warden Scargill Ho 01-08; P-in-c Kirkby-in-Malhamdale w Coniston Cold *Bradf* 08-09; P-in-c Kirkby-in-Malhamdale from 09. *The Vicarage, Kirkby Malham, Skipton BD23 4BS* Tel (01729) 830144
E-mail dillybaker@gmail.com

BAKER, Hugh Crispin. b 58. Open Univ BA92. Linc Th Coll 95. **d** 95 **p** 96. C Birstall and Wanlip *Leic* 95-99; V Middlestown *Wakef* from 99; Dioc Rural Officer from 04. *The Vicarage, 2 Netherton Hall Gardens, Netherton, Wakefield WF4 4JA* Tel (01924) 278384 E-mail hugh.baker@tesco.net

BAKER, Hugh John. b 46. Birm Univ BSocSc68. Cuddesdon Coll 69. **d** 71 **p** 72. C Binley *Cov* 71-74; C Pemberton St Mark Newtown *Liv* 74-78; TV Sutton 78-90; V Hints *Lich* 90-05; V Fazeley from 90; V Canwell from 05; R Drayton Bassett from 05; Chapl S Staffs Healthcare NHS Trust from 00. *St Paul's Vicarage, 9 West Drive, Bonehill, Tamworth B78 3HR* Tel (01827) 287701 *or* 289414
E-mail elizabethatthevicarage@supanet.com

BAKER, Iain. b 70. St D Coll Lamp BA91. Oak Hill Th Coll BA99. **d** 99 **p** 00. C Gt Clacton *Chelmsf* 99-03; V Kidsgrove *Lich* from 03. *St Thomas's Vicarage, The Avenue, Kidsgrove, Stoke-on-Trent ST7 1AG* Tel (01782) 772895 *or* 771727
E-mail ib.ib@virgin.net

BAKER, Ivon Robert. b 28. St Aug Coll Cant 59. **d** 60 **p** 61. C Sutton in Ashfield St Mary *S'well* 60-62; V Gringley-on-the-Hill 62-94; Chapl HM YOI Gringley 82-91; RD Bawtry *S'well* 85-90; rtd 94; Perm to Offic *York* from 94. *2 Willowgate, Pickering YO18 7BE* Tel (01751) 472281

BAKER, Canon James Henry. b 39. MBE02. Kelham Th Coll 62. **d** 67 **p** 68. C Sheff Arbourthorne 67-70; C Pemberton St Jo *Liv* 70-71; Chapl and Prec St Mary's Cathl 71-74; R Lochgelly *St And* 74-84; P-in-c Rosyth and Inverkeithing 76-84; Can St Ninian's Cathl Perth 83-84; TR Whitehaven *Carl* 84-04; RD Calder 96-01; Hon Can Carl Cathl from 96; rtd 04. *Eskdale Vicarage, Boot, Holmrook CA19 1TF* Tel (019467) 23242
E-mail i.baker@can-online.org.uk

BAKER, James Roger. b 71. Bucks Chilterns Univ Coll BA99 RMN99. St Steph Ho Ox 05 Ripon Coll Cuddesdon 06. **d** 07 **p** 08. C Didcot St Pet *Ox* from 07. *25 Sovereign Close, Didcot OX11 81R* Tel (01235) 811995
E-mail jamesbaker_364@fsmail.net

BAKER, Jean Margaret. b 47. Sheff Univ BSc69 DipEd70 Lon Univ BD78. All Nations Chr Coll 75 Gilmore Course 81. **dss** 82 **d** 87 **p** 97. Liv Our Lady and St Nic w St Anne 82-87; Chapl Huyton Coll 87; Chapl St Mary and St Anne's Sch Abbots Bromley 87-91; Chapl Howell's Sch Denbigh 91-98; C Denbigh *St As* 97-08; rtd 08. *Lle Braf, 28 Abrams Lane, Denbigh LL16 3SS* Tel (01745) 812262
E-mail margaret@smallrev.demon.co.uk

BAKER, Jenifer Marlene. b 44. Bris Univ BSc65 Univ of Wales (Swansea) PhD71 York St Jo Coll BA05. **d** 05 **p** 06. OLM Ruyton XI Towns w Gt and Lt Ness *Lich* from 05. *Clock Cottage, Church Street, Ruyton XI Towns, Shrewsbury SY4 1LA* Tel (01939) 260910

BAKER, John Albert. b 29. St Edm Hall Ox BA52 MA56 Lon Univ BSc68 S Bank Poly MSc76. Cuddesdon Coll 52. **d** 54 **p** 55. C Battersea St Luke *S'wark* 54-58; C Richmond St Mary 58-62; V Battersea Park All SS 62-83; Tutor Roehampton Inst 83-91; rtd 94; Hon C Battersea St Luke *S'wark* 84-02. *44 Wroughton Road, London SW11 6BG* Tel (020) 7585 2492

BAKER, John Alfred. b 41. **d** 02 **p** 03. OLM Herne *Cant* 02-05; OLM St Nicholas at Wade w Sarre and Chislet w Hoath from 05; OLM Minster w Monkton from 05. *Oakfield, 219 Canterbury Road, Herne Bay CT6 7HB* Tel (01227) 362519 Mobile 07960-107169 E-mail john-baker@kent35.fslife.co.uk

✠**BAKER, The Rt Revd John Austin.** b 28. Oriel Coll Ox BA52 MA55 BLitt55 MLitt. Lambeth DD91 Cuddesdon Coll 52. **d** 54 **p** 55 **c** 82. C Cuddesdon *Ox* 54-57; Tutor Cuddesdon Coll 54-57;

C Hatch End St Anselm *Lon* 57-59; Lect K Coll Lon 57-59; Chapl CCC Ox 59-73; Lect Th Ox Univ 59-73; Can Westmr Abbey 73-82; Sub Dean Westmr 78-82; R Westmr St Marg 78-82; Chapl to Speaker of Ho of Commons 78-82; Bp SavaR 82-93; Can and Preb Sarum Cathl 82-93; rtd 93; Hon Asst Bp Win from 94. *4 Mede Villas, Kingsgate Road, Winchester SO23 9QQ* Tel (01962) 861388 Fax 843089

BAKER, John Carl. b 55. Chich Th Coll 77. **d** 80 **p** 81. C Wigan St Andr *Liv* 80-83; V Hollinfare 83-85; TV Seacroft *Ripon* 85-89; TV Bottesford w Ashby *Linc* 89-94; V Litt St Paul Stoneycroft 94-02; V Altcar and Hightown from 02. *St Stephen's Vicarage, St Stephen's Road, Liverpool L38 0BL* Tel 0151-926 2469
E-mail revjcb@btopenworld.com

BAKER, John Reginald. b 62. Hatf Coll Dur BSc83. Wycliffe Hall Ox 86. **d** 89 **p** 90. C Amersham *Ox* 89-92; C Greenford H Cross *Lon* 92-97. *11A Lakeside Road, London W14 0DX* Tel (020) 8574 3762

BAKER, Jonathan Mark Richard. b 66. St Jo Coll Ox BA88 MPhil90. St Steph Ho Ox BA92. **d** 93 **p** 94. C Ascot Heath *Ox* 93-96; C Reading St Mark 96; P-in-c 96-99; V 99-02; P-in-c Reading H Trin 96-99; V 99-02; Prin Pusey Ho from 03; Hon C Ox St Thos from 08. *Pusey House, Oxford OX1 3LZ* Tel (01865) 278415 Fax 278416 E-mail jonathan.baker@stx.ox.ac.uk

BAKER, Canon Jonathan William. b 61. SS Coll Cam MA85. Wycliffe Hall Ox BA91. **d** 92 **p** 93. C Sanderstead All SS *S'wark* 92-96; P-in-c Scalby w Ravenscar and Staintondale *York* 96-97; V Scalby 97-04; P-in-c Hackness w Harwood Dale 96-97; V 97-04; P-in-c Scarborough St Luke 03-04; Can Res Pet Cathl from 04. *The Chapter Office, Minster Precincts, Peterborough PE1 1XS* Tel (01733) 343342 *or* 355310 Fax 355316
E-mail jonathan.baker@peterborough-cathedral.org.uk

BAKER, Mrs Julie Ann Louise. b 77. Univ of Wales (Lamp) BA98. St Mich Coll Llan BTh06. **d** 06 **p** 07. C Barry All SS *Llan* from 06. *4 Alwen Drive, Barry CF62 7LH* Tel (01446) 733731
E-mail julie@treeherder.co.uk

BAKER, Canon Kenneth William. b 38. EMMTC 92. **d** 96 **p** 97. NSM Welford w Sibbertoft and Marston Trussell *Pet* 96-99; P-in-c 98-01; P-in-c N w S Kilworth and Misterton *Leic* 01-03; P-in-c Swinford w Catthorpe, Shawell and Stanford 01-03; TR Gilmorton, Peatling Parva, Kimcote etc from 03; RD Guthlaxton from 05; Hon Can Leic Cathl from 06. *Homestead, 9 The Green, Lilbourne, Rugby CV23 0SR* Tel (01788) 860409
E-mail kw.baker@btinternet.com

BAKER, Marc Crispin. b 75. Westmr Coll Ox BTh96. Oak Hill Th Coll 00. **d** 02 **p** 03. C Upton (Overchurch) *Ches* 02-06; TV Cheltenham St Mary, St Matt, St Paul and H Trin *Glouc* 06-07; C Cheltenham St Mary w St Matt from 07. *38 College Road, Cheltenham GL53 7HX* Tel (01242) 525994
E-mail marc.baker@virgin.net

BAKER, Margaret. b 55. **d** 08 **p** 09. C Herringthorpe *Sheff* from 08. *40 Flat Lane, Whiston, Rotherham S60 4EF* Tel (01709) 363959 E-mail margaret.baker@sheffield.anglican.org

BAKER, Canon Michael Robert Henry. b 39. Keele Univ MA88. Lich Th Coll 63. **d** 66 **p** 67. C Wellingborough All SS *Pet* 66-68; C Pet All SS 68-73; V Earls Barton 73-87; RD Wellingborough 76-87; P-in-c Gt Doddington 78-82; TR Kingsthorpe w Northampton St Dav 87-95; V Towcester w Easton Neston 95-04; RD Towcester 98-03; Can Pet Cathl 85-04; rtd 04; Perm to Offic *Pet* from 04. *Magdalene Cottage, 56 Queen Street, Geddington, Kettering NN14 1AZ* Tel (01536) 741091
E-mail mikemargbaker@aol.com

BAKER, Michael William. b 38. Roch Th Coll 68. **d** 70 **p** 71. C Woodmansterne *S'wark* 70-75; TV Danbury *Chelmsf* 75-78; P-in-c Barrington *Ely* 78-90; V 90-97; P-in-c Shepreth 78-90; V 90-97; rtd 97; Perm to Offic *Nor* from 98. *The White House, Church Street, Elsing, Dereham NR20 3EB* Tel (01362) 637370
E-mail hmb@waitrose.com

BAKER, Miles Anthony. b 71. Brunel Univ BA92. Ridley Hall Cam 99. **d** 02 **p** 03. C Paignton Ch Ch and Preston St Paul *Ex* 02-05; P-in-c Upton 05-08; Dioc Miss Enabler *Pet* from 08. *The Rectory, 32 West Street, Ecton, Northampton NN6 0QF* Tel (01604) 407899 E-mail dawnmiles@dbaker16.fsnet.co.uk

BAKER, Canon Neville Duff. b 35. St Aid Birkenhead 60. **d** 63 **p** 64. C Stranton *Dur* 63-66; C Houghton le Spring 66-68; V Tudhoe Grange 68-07; P-in-c Merrington 91-94; RD Auckland 83-94; Hon Can Dur Cathl 90-07; rtd 07. *2 The Bents, Sunderland SR6 7NX*

BAKER, Noel Edward Lloyd. b 37. Sarum & Wells Th Coll 73. **d** 75 **p** 76. C Charlton Kings St Mary *Glouc* 75-79; V Clearwell 79-81; R Eastington and Frocester 81-97; RD Stonehouse 90-94; P-in-c Eastington and Frocester 97-98; P-in-c Standish w Haresfield and Moreton Valence etc 97-98; rtd 98; Perm to Offic *Glouc* from 02. *46 Dozule Close, Leonard Stanley, Stonehouse GL10 3NL* Tel (01453) 823569
E-mail noel_brenda@yahoo.co.uk

BAKER, Mrs Pamela. Ox Min Course. **d** 08. NSM Blackbird Leys *Ox* from 08. *27 Exeter Road, Kidlington OX5 2DY*

BAKER, Paul Anthony. b 64. St Chad's Coll Dur BA85. St Steph Ho Ox BA88 MA98. **d** 89 **p** 90. C Hartlepool St Aid *Dur* 89-93;

TV Jarrow 93-98; V Sunderland Pennywell St Thos 98-04; V Darlington St Mark w St Paul from 04. *St Mark's Vicarage, 394 North Road, Darlington DL1 3BH* Tel (01325) 382400

BAKER, Peter Colin. b 43. Sarum & Wells Th Coll. **d** 82 **p** 83. C Bridgemary *Portsm* 82-86; V Ash Vale *Guildf* 86-99; P-in-c Earlham St Anne *Nor* 99-08; P-in-c Earlham St Mary 99-08; rtd 08. *15 Linden Close, Laverstock, Salisbury SP1 1PN* Tel 07710-844243 (mobile) E-mail peter.baker854@ntlworld.com

BAKER, Peter Graham. b 55. MA PhD. St Steph Ho Ox. **d** 82 **p** 83. C Cres H Trin 82-86; C Holborn St Alb w Saffron Hill St Pet *Lon* 86-91; V Golders Green 91-01; AD W Barnet 95-00; V Regent's Park St Mark from 01. *St Mark's Vicarage, 4 Regent's Park Road, London NW1 7TX* Tel (020) 7485 6340 *or* 7586 1694
E-mail petergbaker@freeuk.com

BAKER, Robert James. b 80. Oriel Coll Ox BA04 MA08. Wycliffe Hall Ox BA07. **d** 08 **p** 09. C Chesham Bois *Ox* from 08. *19 Milton Lawns, Amersham HP6 6BJ* Tel 07855-774384 (mobile) E-mail baker_robertj@hotmail.com

BAKER, Canon Robert John Kenneth. b 50. Southn Univ BSc71 MICE79. Oak Hill Th Coll 88. **d** 90 **p** 91. C Cromer *Nor* 90-94; R Pakefield from 94; Hon Can Nor Cathl from 07. *The Rectory, The Causeway, Pakefield, Lowestoft NR33 0JZ* Tel (01502) 574040

BAKER, Canon Robert Mark. b 50. Bris Univ BA73. St Jo Coll Nottm 74. **d** 76 **p** 77. C Portswood Ch Ch *Win* 76-80; R Witton w Brundall and Braydeston *Nor* 80-89; P-in-c Buckenham w Hassingham and Strumpshaw 80-86; R Brundall w Braydeston and Postwick 89-05; RD Blofield 89-94; TV Thetford from 05; Hon Can Nor Cathl from 93. *The Rectory, 6 Redcastle Road, Thetford IP24 3NF* Tel (01842) 762291
E-mail bob-baker@homecall.co.uk

BAKER, Ronald Kenneth. b 43. Open Univ BA80. St Jo Coll Nottm 85. **d** 87 **p** 88. C Paddock Wood *Roch* 87-90; V Ramsgate St Mark *Cant* 90-95; P-in-c Ewhurst and Bodiam *Chich* 95-98; V 98-03; rtd 03; Perm to Offic *Chich* from 03. *49 Coneyburrow Gardens, St Leonards-on-Sea TN38 9RZ* Tel (01424) 851870
E-mail revronbaker@talktalk.net

BAKER, Roy David. b 36. St Aid Birkenhead 59. **d** 62 **p** 63. C Garston *Liv* 62-64; C N Meols 64-68; V Newton-le-Willows 68-73; V Crossens 73-82; V Blundellsands St Nic 82-01; rtd 01; Perm to Offic *Liv* from 03. *18 Ennerdale Road, Formby, Liverpool L37 2EA* Tel (01704) 830622

BAKER, Sarah Jane. b 59. Lon Univ MB, BS82 Sheff Univ MPhil00 Coll of Ripon & York St Jo MA02. NOC 99. **d** 02 **p** 03. NSM Kinsley w Wragby *Wakef* 02-04; NSM Sandal St Cath 04-07; Perm to Offic from 07. *8 Talbot Avenue, Huddersfield HD3 3BH* Tel (01484) 559441 Mobile 07885-376182
E-mail sarah.baker17@btinternet.com

BAKER, Canon Simon Nicholas Hartland. b 57. K Coll Lon BD78. Qu Coll Birm 79. **d** 81 **p** 82. C Tupsley *Heref* 81-85; V Shinfield *Ox* 85-98; Prin Berks Chr Tr Scheme 93-98; Lay Min Adv and Warden of Readers *Win* 98-02; Dir of Min Development 02-07; Dir of Min and Past Planning from 07; Hon Can Win Cathl from 08. *The Rectory, Trinity Hill, Medstead, Alton GU34 5LT* Tel (01420) 568191

BAKER, Stuart. b 44. MATA63 AIAT65. Ripon Coll Cuddesdon 92. **d** 93 **p** 94. C Whitchurch *Bris* 93-97; R Brightling, Dallington, Mountfield etc *Chich* from 97. *The Rectory, Brightling, Robertsbridge TN32 5HE* Tel (01424) 838281

BAKER, Canon William John. b 45. FCII80. Cranmer Hall Dur 87. **d** 89 **p** 90. C Sale St Anne *Ches* 89-93; V Crewe St Andr w St Jo from 93; P-in-c Crewe Ch Ch from 07; RD Nantwich from 06; Hon Can Ches Cathl from 08. *St John's Vicarage, 14 Dane Bank Avenue, Crewe CW2 8AA* Tel (01270) 569000 Fax 650209
E-mail bill@revbaker.fsnet.co.uk

BAKKER, The Very Revd Ronald Duncan. b 35. TCD BA58 MA61 BD62 Ch Ch Ox MA66 FRSA68 FBIM79. **d** 59 **p** 60. C Knockbreda *D & D* 59-61; C Dublin Zion Ch *D & G* 61-63; Min Can St Patr Cathl Dublin 62-64; CF (TA) 65-67; Lect Plymouth Poly *Ex* 67-72; Prin Kuka Teachers' Coll Nigeria 73-77; Cen Org Red Cross *Ex* 78-81; Perm to Offic *Ex* 82-85; P-in-c Chew Magna w Dundry *B & W* 86-87; Hd RS Sir John Cass Foundn Lon 88-93; Dean Port Moresby Papua New Guinea 93-96; Visiting Prof H Spirit RC Sem 94-96; rtd 96; Perm to Offic *Lon* 96-04. *12 Dumbarton Road, London SW2 5LU* Tel (020) 8674 0283

BAKKER, Gregory Kendall. b 66. California State Univ BA89. Trin Episc Sch for Min Penn MDiv92 Trin Coll Bris 99. **d** 92 **p** 93. C Tariffville USA 92-96; Lect St Phil Coll Kongwa Tanzania 96-99; C Wroughton *Bris* 00-02; TV Stratton St Margaret w S Marston etc 02-08; V Sholing *Win* from 08. *The Vicarage, 41 Station Road, Southampton SO19 8FN* Tel (023) 8044 8337 E-mail gbakker@tiscali.co.uk
or sholingvicarage@googlemail.com

BAKKER (née CAMPBELL), Mrs Jane Judith. b 68. Trin Coll Bris BA01. **d** 01 **p** 02. NSM Lyddington and Wanborough and Bishopstone etc *Bris* 01-03; NSM Stratton St Margaret w S

Marston etc 03-08; NSM Sholing *Win* from 08. *The Vicarage, 41 Station Road, Southampton SO19 8FN* Tel (023) 8044 8337 E-mail jjbakker@tiscali.co.uk

BALCH, John Robin. b 37. Lon Univ BSc61 Bris Univ CertEd62. ALCD68. **d** 68 **p** 69. C Bath Walcot *B & W* 68-71; C Fulwood *Sheff* 71-76; V Erith St Paul *Roch* 76-93; RD Erith 90-93; P-in-c Fairlight *Chich* 93-94; R Fairlight, Guestling and Pett 94-01; rtd 01; Perm to Offic *Derby* from 01. *29 Whitecotes Park, Chesterfield S40 3RT* Tel (01246) 297099

BALCHIN, Michael John. b 38. Selw Coll Cam BA60 MA64. Wells Th Coll 60. **d** 62 **p** 63. C Bournemouth H Epiphany *Win* 62-65; C Bris St Mary Redcliffe w Temple etc 65-69; R Norton sub Hamdon *B & W* 69-70; P-in-c Chiselborough w W Chinnock 69-70; R Norton sub Hamdon w Chiselborough 70-77; P-in-c Chipstable w Huish Champflower and Clatworthy 77-82; R 82-88; Perm to Offic *Ban* from 88; rtd 03. *Gartheiniog, Aberangell, Machynlleth SY20 9QG* Tel (01650) 511659

BALDOCK, Andrew Robert. b 67. St Jo Coll Dur BA00. Cranmer Hall Dur 98. **d** 00 **p** 02. C Peterlee *Dur* 00-01; C Felling 01-03; C Dur St Nic 03-05; V Cheadle All Hallows *Ches* 05-08. *69 Waterloo Road, Uxbridge UB8 2RS* E-mail andrewr.baldock@virgin.net

BALDOCK, Charles William Martin. b 52. Nottm Univ BPharm73 York St Jo Coll MA07. St Jo Coll Nottm LTh. **d** 85 **p** 86. C Nailsea Ch Ch *B & W* 85-89; V Brampton Bierlow *Sheff* 89-00; RD Wath 95-00; Hon Can Sheff Cathl 98-00; V Dringhouses *York* from 00; RD City of York from 04; Chapl St Leon Hospice York from 02. *The Vicarage, Tadcaster Road, Dringhouses, York YO24 1QG* Tel (01904) 706120 *or* tel and fax 709111 E-mail ms@msbaldock.plus.com

BALDOCK, Canon Norman. b 29. K Coll Lon BD52 AKC52. **d** 53 **p** 54. C Cant St Pet w H Cross 53-54; C Thornton Heath St Jude 54-58; V Ash w W Marsh 58-67; V Sheerness H Trin w St Paul 67-75; V Margate St Jo 75-94; RD Thanet 80-86; Hon Can Cant Cathl 82-94; Chapl Margate Gen Hosp 82-94; rtd 94; Perm to Offic *Cant* from 94. *9 Beach Avenue, Birchington CT7 9VS* Tel (01843) 841173

BALDOCK, Reginald David. b 48. Oak Hill Th Coll 72. **d** 75 **p** 76. C Plymouth St Jude *Ex* 75-79; C Ardsley *Sheff* 79-85; V Rawthorpe *Wakef* 85-96; C Salterhebble All SS 96-98; P-in-c Bournemouth St Jo w St Mich *Win* from 98. *The Vicarage, 13 Durley Chine Road South, Bournemouth BH2 5JT* Tel (01202) 761962 E-mail r.baldock1@ntlworld.com

BALDRY, John Netherway. b 19. Lon Univ BA53. **d** 79 **p** 80. NSM Brighton St Paul *Chich* from 79. *81 Windsor Court, Tongdean Lane, Brighton BN1 5JS* Tel (01273) 501268

BALDWICK, Frank Eric. b 24. Ripon Hall Ox 54. **d** 55 **p** 56. C Newark Ch Ch and Hawton *S'well* 55-58; C W Bridgford 58-60; V Oldham St Barn *Man* 60-65; R Gt Lever 65-78; V Hindsford 78-81; TV Clifton *S'well* 81-89; rtd 89; Perm to Offic *S'well* from 89. *35 Lady Bay Road, West Bridgford, Nottingham NG2 5BJ* Tel 0115-982 1273

BALDWIN, Colin Steven. b 61. Brighton Poly BA85. St Jo Coll Nottm MTh01. **d** 01 **p** 02. C Billericay and Lt Burstead *Chelmsf* 01-05; P-in-c Prittlewell St Steph from 05. *26 Eastbourne Grove, Westcliff-on-Sea SS0 0QF* Tel (01702) 352448 Mobile 07714-048450 E-mail csbald@aol.com

BALDWIN, David Frederick Beresford. b 57. Ripon Coll Cuddesdon 93. **d** 95 **p** 96. C Uttoxeter w Bramshall *Lich* 95-97; C Uttoxeter Area 97-98; V Tilstock, Edstaston and Whixall 98-08; P-in-c Prees 03-08; P-in-c Fauls 03-08; Rural Chapl (Salop Adnry) 00-08; RD Wem and Whitchurch 06-08; P-in-c The Lulworths, Winfrith Newburgh and Chaldon *Sarum* from 08; C Wool and E Stoke from 09. *The Rectory, West Road, West Lulworth, Wareham BH20 5RY* Tel (01929) 400550 E-mail revddavidbaldwin@yahoo.co.uk

BALDWIN, Derek Wilfred Walter. b 23. Lon Univ LTh74. ALCD56. **d** 52 **p** 53. C Sharrow St Andr *Sheff* 52-54; C Woodlands 54-56; V Shepley *Wakef* 56-59; V Earl's Heaton 59-66; Org Sec CECS *B & W, Ex* and Truro 66-72; R Morchard Bishop *Ex* 72-73; Org Sec CECS *St Alb* and *Ox* 73-77; C Portishead *B & W* 77-79; R Wymondham w Edmondthorpe *Leic* 79-80; P-in-c St Mewan Truro 80-81; V Crowan w Godolphin 81-83; C Cockington Ex 83-87; rtd 87; Perm to Offic *Ex* from 90. *53 Higher Woolbrook Park, Sidmouth EX10 9ED*

BALDWIN, Mrs Frances Mary. b 49. SRN71. SEITE 99. **d** 02 **p** 03. NSM Caterham *S'well* from 02. *3 Hillhurst Gardens, Caterham CR3 5HX* Tel (020) 8660 7534 E-mail francesb3@btinternet.com

BALDWIN, John Charles. b 39. Bris Univ BSc61 Sussex Univ DPhil65 FBCS CEng. St Steph Ho Ox 82. **d** 83 **p** 84. C Llandaff w Capel Llanilltern 83-90; V Ewenny w St Brides Major 90-92; Lic to Offic from 92; Hon Chapl Llan Cathl from 96; rtd 04. *60 Llantrisant Road, Llandaff, Cardiff CF5 2PX* Tel (029) 2055 4457 Fax 2038 7835 E-mail johnbaldwin@rb.churchinwales.org.uk

BALDWIN, Jonathan Michael. b 58. Chich Th Coll 92. **d** 94 **p** 95. C Crawley *Chich* 94-96; C New Shoreham 96-02; C Old Shoreham 96-02; Chapl Gatwick Airport from 02; C Crawley

from 02. *18 Aldingbourne Close, Ifield, Crawley RH11 0QJ* Tel (01293) 406001 E-mail jonathan@theairport.wanadoo.co.uk

BALDWIN, Peter Alan. b 48. Bede Coll Dur BA70. Qu Coll Birm 72. **d** 73 **p** 74. C Hartlepool St Oswald *Dur* 73-75; C Darlington H Trin 75-78; OGS from 77; C-in-c Bishop Auckland Woodhouse Close CD *Dur* 78-82; V Ferryhill 82-88; V Pendleton St Thos *Man* 88-89; P-in-c Charlestown 88-89; TR Pendleton St Thos w Charlestown 89-90; TR Newton Aycliffe *Dur* 90-96; TR Gt Aycliffe 96-97; V The Trimdons 97-99; AD Sedgefield 96-99; P-in-c Bramley *Ripon* 99-00; TR 00-02; Hon C Harrogate St Wilfrid 02-03; Hon C Methley w Mickletown 03-04; Dom Chapl to Bp Horsham *Chich* 04-06; P-in-c Buncton and Wiston 05-06; P-in-c Brightlingsea *Chelmsf* from 06. *1 Love Lane, Brightlingsea, Colchester CO7 0QQ* Tel (01206) 302407 E-mail peterabaldwin5@aol.com

BALDWIN, Mrs Vivien Lindsay. b 50. SAOMC 97. **d** 98 **p** 99. NSM Westbury w Turweston, Shalstone and Biddlesden *Ox* 98-00; C W Buckingham 00-02; P-in-c Stoneleigh w Ashow *Cov* 02-07; Rural Life Officer 02-06; Chapl W Midl Police *Birm* 07-09; Perm to Offic *Pet* from 07. *20 Castle Road, Woodford Halse, Daventry NN11 3RS* Tel 07720-811477 (mobile) E-mail vivthevic@earthling.net

BALDWIN, William. b 48. RMN73 FRSH83. NW Ord Course 75. **d** 78 **p** 79. C Royton St Anne *Man* 78-82; V Halliwell St Thos 82-87; TR Atherton 87-99; TR Atherton and Hindsford 99-02; TV Atherton and Hindsford w Howe Bridge 02-08; AD Leigh 01-08; TV Turton Moorland Min from 08. *Walmsley Vicarage, Blackburn Road, Egerton, Bolton BL7 9RZ* Tel and fax (01204) 304283 E-mail frbill@fsmail.net

BALE, Edward William Carre. b 22. AKC55. **d** 55 **p** 56. C Mansfield SS Pet and Paul *S'well* 55-59; C Corby St Jo *Pet* 59-61; R Corby SS Pet and Andr 61-69; V Wollaston and Strixton 69-87; rtd 88; Perm to Offic *Pet* 89-94 and *Ox* from 88. *27 The Crescent, Haversham, Milton Keynes MK19 7AN* Tel (01234) 391443 E-mail tedcarrebale@lineone.net

BALE, Kenneth John. b 34. Univ of Wales (Lamp) BA58. Qu Coll Birm. **d** 60 **p** 61. C Mitcham St Olave *S'wark* 60-63; C Warlingham w Chelsham and Farleigh 63-67; V Battersea Rise St Mark 67-85; Perm to Offic 85-88; Hon C Balham St Mary and St Jo 88-90; V S Wimbledon All SS 90-01; Dioc Adv Min of Healing 91-01; rtd 01; Perm to Offic *Sheff* from 01. *23 Selhurst Crescent, Bessacarr, Doncaster DN4 6EF* Tel 07710-212263 (mobile) Fax (01302) 371850

BALE, Susannah. b 67. Univ of Wales (Cardiff) BA90 BTh06. St Mich Coll Llan 03. **d** 06 **p** 07. C Betws w Ammanford *St D* 06-08; C Bro Teifi Sarn Helen from 08. *Garthowen, 2 Kingsmead, Lampeter SA48 7AP* Tel (01570) 421922 E-mail suzybale@hotmail.com

BALFOUR, Andrew Crispin Roxburgh. b 49. Coll of Resurr Mirfield 93. **d** 95 **p** 96. C S Lafford *Linc* 95-99; P-in-c St Neot and Warleggan *Truro* 99-00; P-in-c Cardynham 99-00; R St Neot and Warleggan w Cardynham from 00. *The Vicarage, St Neot, Liskeard PL14 6NG* Tel (01579) 320472

BALFOUR, Hugh Rowlatt. b 54. SS Coll Cam BA76. Ridley Hall Cam 78. **d** 81 **p** 82. C Bedford Ch Ch *St Alb* 81-86; P-in-c Camberwell Ch Ch *S'wark* 86-90; V from 90. *Christ Church Vicarage, 79 Asylum Road, London SE15 2RJ* Tel (020) 7639 5662 E-mail hrbalfours@btinternet.com

BALFOUR, Mark Andrew. b 66. York Univ BA88 R Holloway Coll Lon PhD98 Trin Coll Bris BA01. **d** 02 **p** 03. C Churchdown *Glouc* 02-06; V Furze Platt *Ox* from 06. *The Vicarage, 259 Courthouse Road, Maidenhead SL6 6HF* Tel (01628) 621961 E-mail thebalfours@btinternet.com

BALFOUR, Mrs Penelope Mary. b 47. St Andr Univ MA69 St Jo Coll York DipEd72. Coates Hall Edin 89 St Jo Coll Nottm 84. **d** 88 **p** 95. C Dundee St Marg *Bre* 88-94; Dioc AIDS Officer 90-94; NSM Invergowrie 94-96; C 00-07; Chapl Abertay Univ 94-97; C Dundee St Marg 96-00. *10 Strathaird Place, Dundee DD2 4TN* Tel (01382) 643114 E-mail pennybalfour@btinternet.com

BALKWILL, Michael Robert. b 67. Univ of Wales (Lamp) BD89 Univ of Wales (Cardiff) MTh92. St Mich Coll Llan 89 Bp Tucker Coll Mukono 91. **d** 91 **p** 92. C Llanrhos *St As* 91-97; Dioc RE Adv from 94; R Llanfyllin and Bwlchycibau from 97; Perm to Offic *Ban* from 97; Dioc Co-ord Dept of Development and Tr for Miss *St As* from 99; AD Llanfyllin from 05. *The Rectory, Coed Llan Lane, Llanfyllin SY22 5BW* Tel (01691) 648306

BALKWILL, Roger Bruce. b 41. St Mich Coll Llan 61. **d** 64 **p** 65. C Llantrisant 64-68; C Caerphilly 68-73; Youth Chapl Dio Matabeleland Rhodesia 73-76; P-in-c Ilam w Blore Ray and Okeover *Lich* 76-81; P-in-c Albrighton 81-82; V 82-08; P-in-c Beckbury 89-90; P-in-c Badger 89-90; P-in-c Ryton 89-90; P-in-c Kemberton, Sutton Maddock and Stockton 89-90; RD Shifnal 89-98; P-ln-c Donington from 00; P-in-c Boningale 97-08; V Albrighton, Boningale and Donington from 08; RD Edgmond and Shifnal from 08. *The Vicarage, High Street, Albrighton, Wolverhampton WV7 3EQ* Tel (01902) 372701

BALL, Alan. b 26. Qu Coll Birm 72. **d** 75 **p** 75. NSM Hamstead St Paul *Birm* 75-93; rtd 93; Perm to Offic *Portsm* from 93. *25 Tebourba Drive, Alverstoke, Gosport PO12 2NT* Tel (023) 9260 1694

BALL, Andrew Thomas. b 54. K Coll Lon BD75 AKC75. Sarum & Wells Th Coll 76. **d** 77 **p** 78. C Ribbleton *Blackb* 77-80; C Sedgley All SS *Lich* 80-84; V Pheasey 84-90; Chapl Gd Hope Distr Gen Hosp Sutton Coldfield 90-94; Chapl Gd Hope Hosp NHS Trust Sutton Coldfield from 94. *Chaplain's Office, Good Hope Hospital, Rectory Road, Sutton Coldfield B75 7RR* Tel 0121-378 2211 ext 2676 or 243 1948

BALL, Anthony Charles. b 46. Lon Univ BD71. Chich Th Coll 72. **d** 73 **p** 74. C Heref St Martin 73-76; C Ealing St Pet Mt Park *Lon* 76-82; V Ruislip Manor St Paul from 82. *St Paul's Vicarage, Thurlstone Road, Ruislip HA4 0BP* Tel (01895) 633499

BALL, Canon Anthony James. b 68. St Chad's Coll Dur BA89. NTMTC 97. **d** 00 **p** 01. NSM Madrid *Eur* 00-03; Chapl Damascus 03-05; Abp's Asst Sec for Internat, Ecum and Angl Affairs *Cant* 05-08; Abp's Sec for Internat and Inter-Relig Relns from 08; Abp's Chapl from 09; Hon Can All SS Cathl Cairo from 07; Hon Can Madrid Cathl from 07; Lic Preacher *Lon* from 07; Perm to Offic *S'wark* from 09. *Lambeth Palace, London SE1 7JU* Tel (020) 7898 1220 Fax 7401 9886
E-mail anthony.ball@lambethpalace.org.uk

BALL, Anthony Michael. b 46. Kelham Th Coll 66. **d** 70 **p** 71. C Kingswinford St Mary *Lich* 70-74; C W Bromwich All SS 74-76; P-in-c Priorslee 76-80; V 80-82; Asst Chapl HM Pris Liv 82-83; Chapl 88-95; Chapl HM Pris Lewes 83-88; Featherstone 95-00; The Verne 00-06; rtd 06. *La Providence, 21 Portland Road, Weymouth DT4 9ES* Tel (01305) 787027

BALL, Mrs Carol Maureen. b 58. NTMTC BA08. **d** 08 **p** 09. C Danbury *Chelmsf* from 08. *40 Millfields, Danbury, Chelmsford CM3 4LE* Tel (01245) 227260 Mobile 07860-894139
E-mail revcarolball@googlemail.com

BALL, Christopher Jonathan. b 61. Ripon Coll Cuddesdon. **d** 07 **p** 08. C Bedford St Andr *St Alb* from 07. *5 St Minver Road, Bedford MK40 3DQ* Tel (01234) 217330

BALL, Christopher Rowland. b 40. Wycliffe Hall Ox. **d** 82 **p** 83. C Heysham *Blackb* 82-86; TV Swanborough *Sarum* 86-90; R Llanyblodwel and Trefonen *Lich* 90-99; rtd 99; Perm to Offic *Lich* 01-03. *27 Wallace Lane, Forton, Preston PR3 0BA* Tel (01524) 791619

BALL, Geoffrey Ernest. b 49. Ox Min Course 00. **d** 03. NSM Winslow w Gt Horwood and Addington *Ox* from 03. *4 Fledgelings Walk, Winslow, Buckingham MK18 3QU*
E-mail geoffball@btinternet.com

BALL, George Raymond. b 15. Univ of Wales (Lamp) BA40. St Mich Coll Llan 40. **d** 42 **p** 43. C Llansamlet *S & B* 42-46; C Swansea St Nic 46-50; R Bosherston w St Twynells *St D* 50-85; rtd 85. *1 Meadow Bank, St Twynnells, Pembroke SA71 5HZ* Tel (01646) 661432

BALL, Ian Raymond. b 45. CertEd Univ of Wales MPhil. Glouc Th Course 81. **d** 85 **p** 87. NSM Churchstoke w Hyssington and Sarn *Heref* from 85; Lic to Bp Ludlow from 87; Lic to Offic *St As* from 93. *Bachaethlon Cottage, Sarn, Newtown SY16 4HH* Tel (01686) 670505 Mobile 07966-022404
E-mail ian@pathways.plus.com

BALL, Mrs Jane. b 68. Charlotte Mason Coll of Educn BEd91. St Steph Ho Ox 01. **d** 03 **p** 04. C Bedale and Leeming *Ripon* 03-05; Hon C Devizes St Jo w St Mary *Sarum* 05-07; Chapl Godolphin Sch from 07. *The Godolphin School, Milford Hill, Salisbury SP1 2RA* Tel (01722) 430511 Mobile 07764-349957
E-mail jjball@onetel.com

BALL, John Kenneth. b 42. Lon Univ BSc64 AKC64. Linc Th Coll 69. **d** 71 **p** 72. C Garston *Liv* 71-74; C Eastham *Ches* 74-75; C Barnston 75-77; V Over St Jo 77-82; V Helsby and Dunham-on-the-Hill 82-94; RD Frodsham 88-94; P-in-c Alvanley 92-94; V Hoylake 94-98; rtd 98; P-in-c Downholme and Marske *Ripon* 00-05; C Richmond w Hudswell and Downholme and Marske 05-07; Perm to Offic *Blackb* from 06. *2 King Street, Longridge, Preston PR3 3RQ* Tel (01772) 783172

✠**BALL, The Rt Revd John Martin.** b 34. Univ of Wales BA55. Tyndale Hall Bris. **d** 59 **p** 60 **c** 95. C Blackb St Jude 59-63; Kenya 63-79; Dep Gen Sec BCMS 79-81; Gen Sec 81-93; Gen Sec Crosslinks 93-95; Hon C Sidcup Ch Ch *Roch* 81-95; Can Karamoja from 88; Asst Bp Tanzania 95-00; rtd 00; Hon Asst Bp Chelmsf from 00. *5 Hill View Road, Chelmsford CM1 7RS* Tel (01245) 268296 E-mail ball_john@onetel.com

BALL, John Roy. b 47. Fitzw Coll Cam MA71. Wycliffe Hall Ox 83. **d** 85 **p** 86. C Stockport St Mary *Ches* 85-88; C Fazeley *Lich* 88-94; Res Min Drayton Bassett 89-94; Chapl Grenoble *Eur* 94-00; P-in-c Lithuania 00-05; Asst Chapl Amsterdam w Den Helder and Heiloo from 05. *De Kuilenaar 60, 1851 RZ Heiloo, The Netherlands* Tel (0031) (72) 532 5720
E-mail jroyball@christchurch.nl

BALL, Jonathan. b 63. BNC Ox BA85 MA01 Leeds Univ BA87 Cardiff Univ MTh06. Coll of Resurr Mirfield 85. **d** 88 **p** 89. C

Blakenall Heath *Lich* 88-92; TV Rugeley 92-96; CF 96-08; Bp's Sen Chapl *Sarum* from 08. *68A The Close, Salisbury SP1 2EN* Tel (01722) 334031 Mobile 07787-758756
E-mail senior.chaplain@salisbury.anglican.org

BALL, Mrs Judith Anne. b 48. Nottm Univ BA70 Liv Univ PGCE71. NOC 98. **d** 01 **p** 02. C Upholland *Liv* from 01. *8 Beacon View Drive, Upholland, Skelmersdale WN8 0HL* Tel (01695) 622181

BALL, Kevin Harry. b 55. Linc Th Coll 92. **d** 94 **p** 95. C New Mills *Derby* 94-96; C Walthamstow St Sav *Chelmsf* 96-98; V Stocksbridge *Sheff* 98-00; C Barnsley St Mary *Wakef* 00-01; Chapl Barnsley Coll 00-01; P-in-c Sneinton St Cypr *S'well* 01-05; Chapl Notts Fire and Rescue Service 04-05; Sen Chapl Man Airport from 05. *8 Devoke Road, Wythenshawe, Manchester M22 1TY* Tel 0161-489 2838

BALL, Mrs Marion Elaine. b 62. Hertf Coll Ox BA90 St Jo Coll Dur BA99. Cranmer Hall Dur 97. **d** 02 **p** 03. C Kingston upon Hull H Trin *York* from 02. *67 Adelaide Street, Hull HU3 2EZ* Tel (01482) 329580 E-mail revpball@meandpj.karoo.co.uk

BALL, Mark Francis. b 72. St Jo Coll Dur BA94. St Steph Ho Ox BA00. **d** 01 **p** 02. C Poulton-le-Fylde *Blackb* 01-04; TV Loughton St Jo *Chelmsf* 04-08; P-in-c Cant St Pet w St Alphege and St Marg etc from 08. *83 St Peter's Lane, Canterbury CT1 2BO* E-mail thereverendmarkball@hotmail.com

BALL, Martin Francis. b 62. Wycliffe Hall Ox 06. **d** 08 **p** 09. C Woking Ch Ch *Guildf* from 08. *1 Tresillian Way, Woking GU21 3DL* Tel 07816-398459 (mobile)
E-mail martball@gmail.com
or martin.ball@christchurchwoking.org

✠**BALL, The Rt Revd Michael Thomas.** b 32. Qu Coll Cam BA55 MA59. **d** 71 **p** 71 **c** 80. CGA from 60; Prior Stroud Priory 64-76; C Whiteshill *Glouc* 71-76; Lic to Offic 76; P-in-c Stanmer w Falmer *Chich* 76-80; Chapl Sussex Univ 76-80; Suff Bp Jarrow *Dur* 80-90; Angl Adv Tyne Tees TV 84-90; Bp Truro 90-97; rtd 97; Perm to Offic *B & W* from 01. *Manor Lodge, Aller, Langport TA10 0QN* Tel (01458) 250495

BALL, Nicholas Edward. b 54. Man Univ BA75 Ox Univ MA85. Ripon Coll Cuddesdon 79. **d** 80 **p** 81. C Yardley Wood *Birm* 80-83; C Moseley St Mary 83-86; Chapl Cen 13 83-85; V Bartley Green 86-95; P-in-c Hall Green St Pet 95-97; Perm to Offic 00-03; Chapl Birm Children's Hosp NHS Trust from 03; Chapl Birm Heartlands and Solihull NHS Trust from 03. *5 Princethorpe Close, Shirley, Solihull B90 2LP* Tel 0121-243 1336 or 333 8526 E-mail n.ball@bch.nhs.uk

BALL, Norman. b 41. Liv Univ BA63 Ch Coll Liv CertEd72. Cuddesdon Coll 65. **d** 68 **p** 69. C Broseley w Benthall *Heref* 68-72; Hd RS Christleton High Sch 72-75; V Plemstall w Guilden Sutton *Ches* 75-79; Hd RS Neston Co High Sch 79-94; NSM Dodleston 86-91; NSM Buckley *St As* 91-94; TV Hawarden 94-00; rtd 00; Perm to Offic *St As* from 00. *White Cottage, Lower Mountain Road, Penyffordd, Chester CH4 0EX* Tel (01244) 661132

BALL, Peter Edwin. b 44. Lon Univ BD65 DipEd. Wycliffe Hall Ox 75. **d** 77 **p** 78. C Prescot *Liv* 77-80; R Lawford *Chelmsf* 80-99; RD Harwich 91-96; P-in-c Broomfield 99-04; V from 04. *Broomfield Vicarage, 10 Butlers Close, Chelmsford CM1 7BE* Tel (01245) 440318 E-mail brian@theworboys.freeserve.co.uk

✠**BALL, The Rt Revd Peter John.** b 32. Qu Coll Cam BA54 MA58. Wells Th Coll 54. **d** 56 **p** 57 **c** 77. C Rottingdean *Chich* 56-58; Novice SSM 58-60; CGA from 60; Prior CGA 60-77; Lic to Offic *Birm* 65-66; P-in-c Hoar Cross *Lich* 66-69; Lic to Offic *B & W* 69-77; Suff Bp Lewes *Chich* 77-84; Area Bp Lewes 84-92; Can and Preb Chich Cathl 78-92; Bp Glouc 92-93; rtd 93; Perm to Offic *B & W* from 01. *Manor Lodge, Aller, Langport TA10 0QN* Tel (01458) 250495

BALL, Peter Terence. b 49. **d** 07 **p** 08. OLM Hanborough and Freeland *Ox* from 07. *137 Wroslyn Road, Freeland, Witney OX29 8HP* Tel (01993) 882859 E-mail ptb49@yahoo.co.uk

BALL, Canon Peter William. b 30. Worc Coll Ox BA53 MA57. Cuddesdon Coll 53. **d** 55 **p** 56. C Poplar All SS w St Frideswide *Lon* 55-61; V Preston Ascension 61-68; R Shepperton 68-84; RD Staines 72-74; RD Spelthorne 74-83; Preb St Paul's Cathl 76-84; Can Res and Chan 84-90; Perm to Offic *Sarum* from 90; rtd 95. *Whittonedge, Whittonditch Road, Ramsbury, Marlborough SN8 2PX* Tel (01672) 520259

BALL, Philip John. b 52. Bris Univ BEd75 Ox Univ MTh98. Ripon Coll Cuddesdon 79. **d** 82 **p** 83. C Norton St Mich *Dur* 82-84; C Greenford H Cross *Lon* 84-88; V Hayes St Edm 88-97; AD Hillingdon 94-97; TR Bicester w Bucknell, Caversfield and Launton *Ox* 97-07; AD Bicester and Islip 00-05; R Abingdon *Pet* from 07. *The Rectory, 5 Abington Park Crescent, Northampton NN3 3AD* Tel (01604) 631041
E-mail philipjball@btinternet.com

BALL, Philip John. b 63. Coll of Ripon & York St Jo BA91. Cranmer Hall Dur 97. **d** 99 **p** 00. C Linthorpe *York* 99-02; C Kingston upon Hull H Trin 02-07; N Humberside Ind Chapl from 08. *67 Adelaide Street, Hull HU2 2EZ* Tel (01482) 329580

BALL, Phillip Eric. b 53. Open Univ BA91. Qu Coll Birm 07. **d** 09. NSM Walsall *Lich* from 09. *Dinglebank, 13 Bodmin Rise, Walsall WS5 3HY* Tel 07775-518879 (mobile) E-mail phillipball53@hotmail.com

BALL, Mrs Rita Enid. b 49. Sheff Univ LLB69. SAOMC 94. **d** 97 **p** 98. NSM Newbury *Ox* 97-03; R Wantage Downs 03-09; TR Hermitage from 09. *The Rectory, High Street, Hermitage, Thatcham RG18 9ST* Tel (01635) 202967 E-mail rita@ritaball.wanadoo.co.uk

BALL, Roy. *See* BALL, John Roy

BALL, Timothy William. b 60. Trin Coll Bris 96. **d** 96 **p** 97. C Harlow St Mary and St Hugh w St Jo the Bapt *Chelmsf* 96-99; V Springfield H Trin from 99; Ind Chapl from 00. *The Vicarage, 61 Hill Road, Chelmsford CM2 6HW* Tel (01245) 353389 E-mail timmyball@tesco.net

BALL, Vernon. b 34. Ox Min Course 87. **d** 90 **p** 91. NSM Banbury *Ox* 90-93. *20 Springfield Avenue, Banbury OX16 9HT* Tel (01295) 265740

BALLANTINE, Peter Sinclair. b 46. Nottm Univ MTh85. K Coll Lon BA68 AKC68 St Jo Coll Nottm 70 Lon Coll of Div ALCD71 BD73 LTh74. **d** 73 **p** 74. C Rainham *Chelmsf* 73-77; C Wennington 73-77; TV Barton Mills *St E* 77-80; TV Barton Mills, Beck Row w Kenny Hill etc 80-82; Chapl Liv Poly 83-86; Tr Officer Rugby Deanery *Cov* 86-97; P-in-c Churchover w Willey 86-97; P-in-c Clifton upon Dunsmore and Newton 86-97; Dir Buckingham Adnry Chr Tr Progr *Ox* 97-02; TV Stantonbury and Willen from 02. *The Rectory, The Green, Great Linford, Milton Keynes MK14 5BD* Tel (01908) 605892 Mobile 07984-902641 E-mail pballarev@aol.com

BALLANTINE, Roderic Keith. b 44. Chich Th Coll 66. **d** 69 **p** 70. C Nunhead St Antony *S'wark* 69-72; C S Hackney St Jo w Ch Ch *Lon* 72-75; P-in-c Kensal Town St Thos w St Andr and St Phil 75-79; V Stoke Newington St Andr 79-05; rtd 05; Perm to Offic *Lon* from 06. *67 Savernake Road, London NW3 2LA* Tel (020) 7267 2744

BALLANTYNE, Jane Elizabeth. *See* KENCHINGTON, Canon Jane Elizabeth Ballantyne

BALLARD, The Ven Andrew Edgar. b 44. Dur Univ BA66. Westcott Ho Cam 66. **d** 68 **p** 69. C St Marylebone St Mary *Lon* 68-72; C Portsea St Mary *Portsm* 72-76; V Haslingden w Haslingden Grane *Blackb* 76-82; V Walkden Moor *Man* 82-93; TR Walkden Moor w Lt Hulton 93-98; AD Farnworth 90-98; Chapl Salford Coll 82-92; P-in-c Rochdale *Man* 99-99; TR 00; Adn Rochdale 00-05; Adn Man 05-09; Hon Can Man Cathl 98-09; rtd 09. *30 Swift Drive, Scawby Brook, Brigg DN20 9FL* Tel (01652) 659560 E-mail ae.ballard@btinternet.com

BALLARD, Ann. **d** 09. NSM Norton in the Moors *Lich* from 09. *94 Chatterley Drive, Kidsgrove, Stoke-on-Trent ST7 4LL* Tel (01782) 785586

BALLARD, Miss Anne Christina. b 54. LRAM76 HonRCM93 ARAM94. Wycliffe Hall Ox 82. **dss** 85 **d** 87 **p** 94. Hon Bp Hannington Memorial *Ch Chich* 85-87; Chapl St Mich Sch Burton Park 87-89; Chapl RCM and Imp Coll *Lon* 89-93; Prec Ch Ch *Ox* 93-98; P-in-c Ivinghoe w Pitstone and Slapton 98-03; P-in-c Llanbadarn Fawr, Llandegley and Llanfihangel etc *S & B* 03-08; V Alstonfield, Butterton, Ilam etc *Lich* from 08. *The Vicarage, Alstonefield, Ashbourne DE6 2FX* Tel (01335) 310216 Mobile 07773-734201 E-mail annieballard@supanet.com

BALLARD, Charles Martin. b 29. Jes Coll Cam BA52 MA56. **d** 58 **p** 59. C Doncaster St Geo *Sheff* 58-61; V Balne 61-62; rtd 94; Perm to Offic *Ely* 95-00. *35 Abbey Road, Cambridge CB5 8HH*

BALLARD, Duncan Charles John. b 65. Sheff Univ BSc87. St Mich Coll Llan 00. **d** 02 **p** 03. C Worc St Barn w Ch Ch 02-06; TV Worc SE from 06. *11 Jasmine Close, Worcester WR5 3LU* Tel (01905) 350670 E-mail st.marys@virgin.net

BALLARD, Canon Michael Arthur. b 44. Lon Univ BA66. Westcott Ho Cam 68. **d** 70 **p** 71. C Harrow Weald All SS *Lon* 70-73; C Aylesbury *Ox* 73-78; V Eastwood *Chelmsf* 78-90; RD Hadleigh 83-90; R Southchurch H Trin from 90; RD Southend-on-Sea 94-00; Hon Can Chelmsf Cathl from 89. *The Rectory, 8 Pilgrims Close, Southend-on-Sea SS2 4XF* Tel (01702) 466423 E-mail michael@ballard4701.fsnet.co.uk

BALLARD, Nigel Humphrey. b 48. Linc Th Coll 92. **d** 94 **p** 95. C Old Brumby *Linc* 94; C Bottesford w Ashby 94-97; P-in-c Helpringham w Hale 97-01; rtd 02. *Tamarisk Cottage, 5 Homelands Avenue, East Preston, Littlehampton BN16 1PS*

BALLARD, The Ven Peter James. b 55. SS Hild & Bede Coll Dur BEd78. Sarum & Wells Th Coll 85. **d** 87 **p** 88. C Grantham *Linc* 87-90 and 91; Australia 90; V Lancaster Ch Ch *Blackb* 91-98; RD Lancaster 94-98; Can Res Blackb Cathl 98-06; Adn Lancaster from 06; Dioc Dir of Educn from 98. *Wheatfield, 7 Dallas Road, Lancaster LA1 1TN* Tel (01524) 32897 *or* (01254) 503070 Mobile 07970-923141 Fax (01524) 66095 *or* (01254) 699963 E-mail peter.j.ballard@btinternet.com

BALLARD, Steven Peter. b 52. Man Univ BA73 MA74 Philipps Univ Marburg DrTheol98. St Steph Ho Ox 76. **d** /8 **p** /9. C Lancaster St Mary *Blackb* 78-81; C Blackpool St Mich 81-84; V Brierfield 84-94; Perm to Offic *Carl* 95-07. *1 St Catherines Court, Drovers Lane, Penrith CA11 9EJ* Tel (01768) 890976

BALLENTINE, Ian Clarke. b 46. Aston Univ BSc71 CEng. BTh. **d** 91 **p** 92. C Lurgan St Jo *D & D* 91-95; I Mallusk *Conn* 95-07; Nat Dir (Ireland) SOMA UK from 07. *12 Gordonville, Coleraine BT52 1EF* Tel (028) 7035 8328 E-mail ian_ballentine@bigfoot.com

BALLENTYNE, Mrs Fiona Virginia Grace. b 61. ALAM80 R Holloway Coll Lon BA83 Dur Univ PGCE90. EAMTC 95. **d** 97 **p** 98. NSM Halesworth w Linstead, Chediston, Holton etc *St E* 97-98; C Sole Bay 98-00; Chapl St Felix Sch Southwold 99-00; Chapl HM YOI Castington 00-05; Chapl Northumbria Healthcare NHS Trust 00-05; Chapl HM Pris Sudbury from 05. *Chaplain's Office, HM Prison, Sudbury, Ashbourne DE6 5HW* Tel (01283) 584088 E-mail jvfb27@aol.com

BALLINGER, Francis James. b 43. AKC70. **d** 71 **p** 85. C Weston-super-Mare St Sav *B & W* 71-72; Dir Bd Soc Resp *Leic* 85-88; Hon C Bringhurst w Gt Easton 85-88; TV Melksham *Sarum* 88-93; P-in-c Coughton and Spernall, Morton Bagot and Oldberrow *Cov* 93-98; Dioc Rural Adv 93-98; R Kingstone w Clehonger, Eaton Bishop etc *Heref* 98-03; rtd 04. *4 Broxburn Road, Warminster BA12 8EX* Tel (01985) 300316 E-mail f.ballinger@midnet.com

BALLISTON THICKE, James. *See* THICKE, James Balliston

BALMER, Walter Owen. b 30. NOC 83. **d** 86 **p** 87. NSM Gateacre *Liv* 86-91; NSM Hale 91-00; Perm to Offic from 00. *38 Grangemeadow Road, Liverpool L25 4SU* Tel 0151-421 1189

BALOGUN, Olusegun Joseph. b 69. Ogun State Univ BSc91 Lagos Univ MSc96. Immanuel Coll Ibadan 96. **d** 98 **p** 99. Nigeria 98-02; C Mansfield St Jo *S'well* 04-06; V Beckton St Mark *Chelmsf* from 06. *10 Yarrow Crescent, London E6 5UH* Tel (020) 7473 6059 Mobile 07960-050923 E-mail vicar@stmarkscofebeckton.org.uk

BAMBER, Jeremy John. b 56. St Jo Coll Cam MA82. STETS 06. **d** 09. NSM Southover *Chich* from 09. *29 Montacute Road, Lewes BN7 1EN* Tel (01273) 474923 E-mail jjbj@bambers.net

BAMBER, Patrick Herbert. b 71. Dundee Univ MA93. Wycliffe Hall Ox BTh02. **d** 02 **p** 03. C St Austell *Truro* 02-09; I Calry *K, E & A* from 09. *Calry Rectory, The Mall, Sligo, Co Sligo, Republic of Ireland* Tel (00353) (71) 914 6513 E-mail patrick.bamber@talktalk.net

BAMBER, Canon Sheila Jane. b 54. Univ of Wales (Lamp) BA75 Sheff Univ MA77 Open Univ MBA94. Ripon Coll Cuddesdon 96. **d** 98 **p** 99. C Dur St Cuth 98-01; C Sacriston and Kimblesworth 01-02; TV Dur N 02-09; Hon C Lanchester from 09; Dioc Dir of Educn from 04; Adv for Women's Min from 09; Hon Can Dur Cathl from 06. *The Vicarage, 8 Woodland Close, Bearpark, Durham DH7 7EB* Tel 0191-373 3886 Mobile 07989-542565 E-mail sheila.bamber@durham.anglican.org

BAMBERG, Robert William. b 43. Chu Coll Cam BA65 PGCE66. SWMTC 98. **d** 01 **p** 02. NSM Kingsteignton and Teigngrace *Ex* from 01. *11 Portland Avenue, Teignmouth TQ14 8RR* Tel (01626) 773711 E-mail sllbmbrg@aol.com

BAMFORD, Geoffrey Belk. b 35. Lon Univ BA57 Leic Coll of Educn PGCE58. **d** 99 **p** 00. OLM Upper Holme Valley *Wakef* from 99. *11 Flushouse, Holmbridge, Holmfirth HD9 2QY* Tel (01484) 682532 E-mail jmgbbamford@tiscali.co.uk

BAMFORD, Mrs Marion. b 35. K Coll Lon BA56 AKC56. NOC 81. **dss** 84 **d** 90 **p** 94. Baildon *Bradf* 84-85; S Kirkby *Wakef* 85-90; Dn-in-c Brotherton 90-94; P-in-c 94-96; Chapl Pontefract Gen Infirmary 89-96; rtd 96; Perm to Offic *Bradf* and *Wakef* from 96. *170 Warren Lane, Eldwick, Bingley BD16 3BY* Tel (01274) 564925

BAMFORTH, Canon Marvin John. b 48. NOC 78. **d** 81 **p** 82. C Barnoldswick w Bracewell *Bradf* 81-84; V Cullingworth 84-88; V Mornington New Zealand 88-89; V Thornton in Lonsdale w Burton in Lonsdale *Bradf* 89-98; P-in-c Bentham St Jo 93-98; Dioc Chapl MU 91-94; Chapl Paphos Cyprus 98-05; rtd 06; Chapl Miss to Seafarers Limassol Cyprus from 06; Hon Can Kinkizi from 08. *PO Box 59358, Pissouri, 4610 Limassol, Cyprus* Tel (00357) (25) 222649 E-mail marvinandsue@cytanet.com.cy

BAMFORTH, Stuart Michael. b 35. Hertf Coll Ox BA58 MA61. Sarum Th Coll 60. **d** 62 **p** 63. C Adel *Ripon* 62-67; V Hempton and Pudding Norton 67-71; V Toftrees w Shereford 67-71; P-in-c Pensthorpe 67-71; P-in-c Colkirk 69-70; Lic to Offic *Derby* 72-77 and *Ripon* from 77; rtd 95; Perm to Offic *York* from 01. *52 Beverley Road, Market Weighton, York YO43 3JP* Tel (01430) 874105

BANBURY, David Paul. b 62. Coll of Ripon & York St Jo BA84. Ridley Hall Cam 85. **d** 88 **p** 89. C Blackb St Jas 88-90; C Preston St Cuth 90-95; P-in-c Bradf St Clem 95-00; V 00; CPAS Evang 01-08; Dir Miss and Faith Stratford-upon-Avon, Luddington etc *Cov* from 08. *3 Coopers Close, Stratford-upon-Avon CV37 0RS* Tel (01789) 415410 E-mail davidb@stratford-upon-avon.org

BANDAWE, Mrs Christine. b 57. NOC 01. **d** 04 **p** 05. C Middleton St Mary *Ripon* 04-08; TV Seacroft from 08. *30 Fearnville Road, Leeds LS8 3EA*

BANDS, Canon Leonard Michael. b 40. Rhodes Univ BA64. St Paul's Coll Grahamstown. **d** 69 **p** 70. C Uitenhage S Africa 69-72; R Alexandria 72-75; Chapl Rhodes Univ 75-80; Chapl Dioc Sch for Girls Grahamstown 80-86; Chapl Dioc Coll Cape

Town 87-94; Dean Bloemfontein 94-02; C Lockerbie *Glas* from 03; C Moffat from 03. *The Rectory, Ashgrove Terrace, Lockerbie DG11 2BQ* Tel and fax (01576) 202484 Mobile 07766-341094 E-mail michael.bands@btinternet.com

BANFIELD, Andrew Henry. b 48. AKC71. St Aug Coll Cant 72. **d** 73 **p** 74. C Crayford *Roch* 73-76; Youth Chapl *Glouc* 77-89; Soc Services Development Officer Glos Co Coun from 89. *18 East Approach Drive, Cheltenham GL52 3JE*

BANFIELD, The Ven David John. b 33. ALCD56. **d** 57 **p** 58. C Middleton *Man* 57-62; Chapl Scargill Ho 62-65; Asst Warden 65-67; V Addiscombe St Mary *Cant* 67-80; V Luton St Mary *St Alb* 80-90; Hon Can St Alb 89-90; RD Luton 89-90; Adn Bris 90-98; Hon Can Bris Cathl 90-98; rtd 98; Perm to Offic *Bris* from 98. *47 Avon Way, Stoke Bishop, Bristol BS9 1SL* Tel 0117-968 4227

BANGAY, Edward Newman. b 37. CQSW75. New Coll Lon BD60. **d** 98 **p** 98. NSM Yeovil w Kingston Pitney *B & W* 98-02; Chapl E Somerset NHS Trust 98-02; Perm to Offic *B & W* from 02. *Castle Cottage, Main Street, Mudford, Yeovil BA21 5TE* Tel (01935) 850452 E-mail edward@bangay.com

BANGAY (*formerly* **REAST), Mrs Eileen Joan.** b 40. Open Univ BA93. EMMTC 81. **dss** 84 **d** 87 **p** 94. Linc St Mary-le-Wigford w St Benedict etc 80-90; C 87-90; C Stamford All SS w St Jo 90-93; NSM Walesby 93-95; P-in-c Sutton Bridge 95-00; V 00; RD Elloe E 99-00; rtd 01; Perm to Offic *Linc* from 01. *35 Welland Mews, Stamford PE9 2LW* Tel (01780) 765115

BANGOR, Archdeacon of. *See* WILLIAMS, The Ven Meurig Llwyd

BANGOR, Bishop of. *See* JOHN, The Rt Revd Andrew Thomas Griffith

BANGOR, Dean of. *See* HAWKINS, The Very Revd Alun John

BANHAM, Richard Mark. b 69. Sheff City Poly BSc92. Trin Coll Bris 04. **d** 06 **p** 07. C Wroughton *Bris* from 06. *49 Perry's Lane, Wroughton, Swindon SN4 9AZ* Tel (01793) 813929 E-mail richard@banham.org

BANISTER, Desmond Peter. b 52. K Coll Lon BA75 AKC75. SAOMC 02. **dss** 05 **p** 06. Hd Master Quainton Hall Sch Harrow from 98; NSM Hatch End St Anselm *Lon* 05-09; V Hillingdon All SS from 09. *All Saints' Vicarage, Ryefield Avenue, Uxbridge UB10 9BT* Tel (01895) 234947 E-mail dpbanister@uk2.net

BANISTER, Jane Catherine. b 67. Man Univ BA90 Em Coll Cam BA96. Westcott Ho Cam 94. **d** 97 **p** 98. C Addington *S'wark* 97-00; C Wisley w Pyrford *Guildf* 00-02; Perm to Offic *St Alb* 03-08; NSM Tring from 08. *The Rectory, 2 The Limes, Station Road, Tring HP23 5NW* Tel (01442) 822170

BANISTER, Canon Martin John. b 39. Worc Coll Ox BA62 MA68. Chich Th Coll 62. **d** 64 **p** 65. C Wellingborough All Hallows *Pet* 64-67; C Heene Chich 67-70; V Denford w Ringstead *Pet* 70-78; P-in-c Wilshamstead *St Alb* 78-80; P-in-c Houghton Conquest 78-80; V Wilshamstead and Houghton Conquest 80-89; RD Elstow 86-89; V Waltham Cross 89-04; RD Cheshunt 00-04; Hon Can St Alb 03-04; rtd 04; Perm to Offic *St Alb* from 04. *35 Cottonmill Lane, St Albans AL1 2BT* Tel (01727) 847082

BANKS, Aleck George. b 18. Lon Univ BD42 AKC42. **d** 42 **p** 43. C Colchester St Jas, All SS, St Nic and St Runwald *Chelmsf* 42-45; C Leigh St Clem 45-51; V Bradfield 51-56; PC Becontree St Geo 56-61; V S Benfleet 61-83; rtd 83; Perm to Offic *Chelmsf* from 83 and *St E* from 85. *5 Gosford Close, Clare, Sudbury CO10 8PT* Tel (01787) 277088

BANKS, Allen James. b 48. CBDTI98. **d** 01 **p** 02. OLM Kells *Carl* from 01. *36 Basket Road, Whitehaven CA28 9AH* Tel (01946) 61470

BANKS, Brian William Eric. b 35. Lon Univ BD69 Open Univ BA94. Wycliffe Hall Ox 63. **d** 65 **p** 66. C Swindon Ch Ch *Bris* 65-68; C Halesowen *Worc* 68-71; R Wychbold and Upton Warren 71-77; V Bengeworth 77-87; RD Evesham 81-87; R Freshwater *Portsm* 87-00; R Yarmouth 95-00; rtd 00; Perm to Offic *Sarum* 01-09. *12 St Davids Road, Leyland PR25 4XX* Tel (01722) 935707

BANKS, Mrs Dawn. b 56. CBDTI 01. **d** 04 **p** 05. OLM Preesall *Blackb* 04-05; OLM Waterside Par 05-07; NSM from 07. *Squires Gate Farm, Head Dyke Lane, Pilling, Preston PR3 6SD* Tel (01253) 790250

BANKS, Geoffrey Alan. b 43. St Andr Univ MA66. NOC 84. **d** 87 **p** 88. NSM Shelley and Shepley *Wakef* 87-89; C Halifax 89-91; V Holmfield 91-98; TV Upper Holme Valley 98-09; rtd 09. *3 Brookside Fold, Oxenhope, Keighley BD22 9HQ* E-mail geoff@banksvicarage.fsnet.co.uk

BANKS, Helen. b 52. Yorks Min Course. **d** 09. NSM Garforth *Ripon* from 09. *Westfield Cottage, Carr Lane, Thorner, Leeds LS14 3HD* Tel 0113-289 2668 E-mail helen.banks@yahoo.co.uk

BANKS, John Alan. b 32. Hertf Coll Ox BA54 MA58. Westcott Ho Cam 56. **d** 58 **p** 59. C Warsop *S'well* 58-61; C Ox St Aldate w H Trin 61-64; V Ollerton *S'well* 64-75; V Boughton 64-75; R Wollaton 75-83; RD Beeston 77-81; Lic to Offic 83-85; C Bramcote 85-86; C Arnold 86-95; rtd 95; Perm to Offic *S'well*

from 95. *247 Oxclose Lane, Nottingham NG5 6FB* Tel 0115-926 6814

BANKS, Michael Lawrence. b 40. Open Univ BA72 Brunel Univ MA82. Westcott Ho Cam 84. **d** 86 **p** 87. C Cheshunt *St Alb* 86-89; Chapl HM Pris Blundeston 89-90; V Leagrave *St Alb* 90-94; V Hatfield Hyde 95-01; rtd 01; Perm to Offic *Nor* 01-03 and from 05; P-in-c Barningham w Matlaske w Baconsthorpe etc 03-05. *Quarndon, Post Office Lane, Saxthorpe, Norwich NR11 7BL* Tel (01263) 587319 E-mail mbanks@tiscali.co.uk

BANKS, Canon Michael Thomas Harvey. b 35. Ushaw Coll Dur 58 Open Univ BA75. **d** 63 **p** 64. In RC Ch 63-69; C Winlaton *Dur* 69-71; P-in-c Bishopwearmouth Gd Shep 71-75; TV Melton Mowbray w Thorpe Arnold *Leic* 75-80; TR Loughborough Em 80-88; Dir of Ords 83-97; Hon Can Leic Cathl 83-87; Can Res and Chan 87-03; Assoc P Christianity S 93-95; Hon C Leic H Spirit 01-03; rtd 03; Perm to Offic *Glouc* from 04. *Harvard House, 7 Harvard Close, Moreton-in-Marsh GL56 0JT* Tel (01608) 650706

BANKS, Norman. b 54. Oriel Coll Ox BA76 MA80. St Steph Ho Ox 79. **d** 82 **p** 83. C Newc Ch Ch w St Ann 82-87; P-in-c 87-90; V Tynemouth Cullercoats St Paul 90-00; V Walsingham, Houghton and Barsham *Nor* from 00; RD Burnham and Walsingham from 08. *The Vicarage, Church Street, Walsingham NR22 6BL* Tel (01328) 821316

BANKS, Philip Charles. b 61. NE Lon Poly BSc85 Nottm Univ BTh93 MRICS87. Linc Th Coll 90. **d** 93 **p** 94. C Chelmsf Ascension 93-94; C Brentwood St Thos 94-98; P-in-c Elmstead 98-03; V Coggeshall w Markshall from 03; Bp's Press Officer 97-05; Bp's Dom Chapl 01-04; RD Dedham and Tey from 08. *The Vicarage, 4 Church Green, Coggeshall, Colchester CO6 1UD* Tel (01376) 561234 Mobile 07798-681886 E-mail fr-philip@st-peter-ad-vincula.org.uk

BANKS, Stephen John. b 65. Newc Univ BSc87. St Jo Coll Nottm MA96. **d** 97 **p** 98. C Sheldon *Birm* 97-00; P-in-c Austrey and Warton 00-07; P-in-c Newton Regis w Seckington and Shuttington 06-07; R N Warks from 07; AD Polesworth 02-07. *The Vicarage, 132 Main Road, Austrey, Atherstone CV9 3EB* Tel (01827) 839022 E-mail sbanks4@sky.com

BANKS, Susan Angela. *See* GRIFFITHS, Mrs Susan Angela

BANKS, Mrs Susan June. b 60. NOC 03. **d** 06 **p** 07. C Medlock Head *Man* 06-09; TV Heywood from 09. *St Margaret's Vicarage, 27 Heys Lane, Heywood OL10 3RD* Tel (01706) 368053 E-mail sbanks4@sky.com

BANNARD-SMITH, Dennis Ronald. b 22. Birm Univ BSc42. St Alb Minl Tr Scheme 80. **d** 83 **p** 84. NSM Pavenham *St Alb* 83-88; NSM Odell and Pavenham 88-92; Perm to Offic from 92. *Goodly Heritage, 10 The Bury, Pavenham, Bedford MK43 7PX* Tel (01234) 822992

BANNER, John William. b 36. Open Univ BA78. Tyndale Hall Bris 61. **d** 64 **p** 65. C Bootle St Leon *Liv* 64-66; C Wigan St Jas 66-69; C Stapleton *Bris* 69-70; Gen Sec Scripture Union Australia 70-72; V Liv Ch Ch Norris Green 72-82; V Tunbridge Wells H Trin w Ch Ch *Roch* 82-05; rtd 05. *Kingsmead, Burwash Common, Etchingham TN19 7NA* Tel (01435) 882977 E-mail john@secondremake.plus.com

BANNER, Michael Charles. b 61. Ball Coll Ox BA83 MA86 DPhil87. **d** 86 **p** 87. Fell St Pet Coll Ox 85-88; Dean Peterho Cam 88-94; Prof Moral and Soc Th K Coll Lon 94-04; NSM Balsham, Weston Colville, W Wickham etc *Ely* 01-04; Prof Edin Univ 04-06; Dean Trin Coll Cam from 06. *Trinity College, Cambridge CB2 1TQ* Tel (01223) 338400

BANNISTER, Preb Anthony Peter. b 40. Ex Univ BA62. Clifton Th Coll 63. **d** 65 **p** 66. C Uphill *B & W* 65-69; C Hove Bp Hannington Memorial Ch *Chich* 69-74; V Wembdon *B & W* 74-91; Youth Chapl 80-83; RD Bridgwater 80-89; V Taunton St Jas 91-05; Preb Wells Cathl 97-05; rtd 05; Perm to Offic *B & W* from 05. *12 Mitre Court, Taunton TA1 3ER* Tel (01823) 259110 E-mail apbannister@ukonline.co.uk

BANNISTER, Clifford John. b 53. Hatf Coll Dur BA76. Ripon Coll Cuddesdon 84. **d** 86 **p** 87. C Weymouth H Trin *Sarum* 86-89; TV Basingstoke *Win* 89-94; V Hedge End St Jo from 94; AD Eastleigh 07-09; P-in-c Win St Bart from 09. *Hyde Vicarage, 1 Abbey Hill Close, Winchester SO23 7AZ* Tel (01962) 627253 E-mail cliffbannister@tiscali.co.uk

BANNISTER, John Leslie. b 55. Lanc Univ MA99. CBDTI 95. **d** 98 **p** 99. C Flimby and Netherton *Carl* 98-00; C Whitehaven 00-02; TV 02-04; TR from 04. *The Rectory, Autumn Garth, Harras Road, Harras Moor, Whitehaven CA28 6SG* Tel (01946) 693474 Mobile 07788-562488 E-mail johnlbannister@tiscali.co.uk

BANNISTER, Lesley. b 30. **d** 99 **p** 00. OLM Gt Cornard *St E* 99-07; Perm to Offic from 07. *58 Broom Street, Great Cornard, Sudbury CO10 0JT* Tel (01787) 372889

BANNISTER, Peter. *See* BANNISTER, Preb Anthony Peter

BANNISTER, Peter Edward. b 38. Leeds Univ BSc60. Linc Th Coll 72. **d** 74 **p** 75. C Norbury St Steph *Cant* 74-77; C Allington and Maidstone St Pet 77-80; R Temple Ewell w Lydden 80-86; TV Bracknell *Ox* 86-93; P-in-c Swallowfield 93-03; rtd 03.

15 Ryeland Street, Cross Hills, Keighley BD20 8SR Tel (01535) 636036 E-mail peter.bannister@virgin.net

BANNISTER-PARKER, Mrs Charlotte. b 63. Trevelyan Coll Dur BA84 Dur Univ MA92 Middx Univ BA05. Westmr Past Foundn 00. **d** 05 **p** 06. NSM Ox St Mary V w St Cross and St Pet from 05. *8 Belbroughton Road, Oxford OX2 6UZ* Tel (01865) 512252 E-mail charlotte@thegbps.co.uk

BANNON, Lyndon Russell. b 73. Ches Coll of HE BA95 Univ Coll Ches PGCE96 Leeds Univ MA06. NOC 04. **d** 06 **p** 07. NSM Leasowe *Ches* from 06. *7 Nelson's Croft, Wirral CH63 3DU* Tel 0151-334 9931
E-mail revlrbannon@talktalk.net

BANTING, Canon David Percy. b 51. Magd Coll Cam MA74. Wycliffe Hall Ox MA79. **d** 80 **p** 81. C Ox St Ebbe w H Trin and St Pet 80-83; Min St Jos Merry Hill CD *Lich* 83-90; V Chadderton Ch Ch *Man* 90-98; V Harold Wood *Chelmsf* from 98; Hon Can Chelmsf Cathl from 09. *The Vicarage, 15 Athelstan Road, Harold Wood, Romford RM3 0QB* Tel (01708) 376400 *or* 342080 E-mail david.banting@stpetersharoldwood.org

BANTING, The Ven Kenneth Mervyn Lancelot Hadfield. b 37. Pemb Coll Cam BA61 MA65. Cuddesdon Coll 64. **d** 65 **p** 66. Asst Chapl Win Coll 65-70; C Leigh Park *Portsm* 70-72; TV Hemel Hempstead *St Alb* 73-79; V Goldington 79-88; P-in-c Renhold 80-82; RD Bedford 84-87; V Portsea St Cuth *Portsm* 88-96; RD Portsm 94-96; Adn Is of Wight 96-03; Hon Can Portsm Cathl 95-96; rtd 03; Perm to Offic *Portsm* from 03 and *Chich* from 04; RD Westbourne *Chich* from 09. *Furzend, 38A Bosham Hoe, Bosham PO18 8ET* Tel (01243) 572340
E-mail merlinbanting@f2s.com

BANYARD, Douglas Edward. b 21. S'wark Ord Course 69. **d** 71 **p** 72. NSM Selsdon St Jo w St Fran *Cant* 71-77; Perm to Offic *Chich* 77-08 and *Portsm* from 77. *22 Lower Wardown, Petersfield GU31 4NY* Tel (01730) 261004

BANYARD, Michael George. b 47. Ch Ch Coll Cant CertEd69 Birm Univ BPhil79 Open Univ MA92. Westcott Ho Cam 01. **d** 03 **p** 04. NSM Chippenham *Ely* 03-08; NSM Fordham St Pet 07-08; NSM Isleham 07-08; NSM Kennett 07-08; NSM Snailwell 07-08; NSM Three Rivers Gp from 08. *The Vicarage, High Street, Chippenham, Ely CB7 5PP* Tel (01638) 721616
E-mail banyardmg1@yahoo.co.uk

BANYARD, Peter Vernon. b 35. Sarum Th Coll 57. **d** 59 **p** 60. C Southampton Maybush St Pet *Win* 59-63; C Tilbury Docks *Chelmsf* 63-65; Miss to Seamen 63-65; Namibia 65-68; V Chesterfield St Aug *Derby* 68-74; TV Grantham w Manthorpe *Linc* 74-78; TV Grantham 78-79; Chapl Warminster Sch 79-85; V Hykeham *Linc* 85-88; rtd 88; Perm to Offic *Linc* from 88. *56 Western Avenue, Lincoln LN6 7SY* Tel and fax (01522) 829026 E-mail ppbanyard@hotmail.com

BANYARD (or BRUNSKILL), Canon Sheila Kathryn. b 53. Univ of Wales (Ban) BA75 K Coll Lon MA83 Ox Univ MTh99. Cranmer Hall Dur 76. **dss** 82 **d** 92 **p** 94. Sunbury *Lon* 82-85; Asst Chapl Ch Hosp Horsham 85-90; Chapl Malvern Girls' Coll 90-95; TV Droitwich Spa *Worc* 95-00; TR from 00; RD Droitwich 99-02; Hon Can Worc Cathl from 03. *The Rectory, 205 Worcester Road, Droitwich WR9 8AS* Tel and fax (01905) 773134 *or* tel 794952 E-mail sk.banyard@virgin.net *or* droitwich.parish@virgin.net

✠**BARAHONA, The Most Revd Martin de Jesus.** c 92. Bp El Salvador from 92; Primate Cen America from 02. *47 Avenida Sur, 723 Col Flor Blanca, Apt Postal (01), 274 San Salvador, El Salvador* Tel (00503) 223 2252 *or* 224 6136 Fax 223 7952
E-mail anglican@saltel.net

BARBARA JUNE, Sister. *See* KIRBY, Barbara Anne June

BARBER, Ann. *See* BARBER, Mrs Margaret Ann

BARBER, Ms Annabel Ruth. b 58. Leeds Univ BSc80. NEOC 01. **d** 04 **p** 05. C Scawby, Redbourne and Hibaldstow *Linc* 04-07; Chapl N Lincs and Goole Hosps NHS Trust from 07. *Chaplains' Office, Diana Princess of Wales Hospital, Scartho Road, Grimsby DN33 2BA* Tel (01472) 874111

BARBER, Canon Christopher Albert. b 33. Ch Coll Cam BA53 MA57. Coll of Resurr Mirfield 56. **d** 58 **p** 59. C Cov St Pet 58-61; C Stokenchurch and Cadmore End *Ox* 61-64; V Royton St Paul *Man* 64-70; V Stapleford *Ely* 70-80; RD Shelford 76-80; V Cherry Hinton St Andr 80-88; Hon Can Ely Cathl 88-98; R Cottenham 88-92; RD N Stowe 90-92; V Terrington St John 92-98; V Tilney All Saints 92-98; rtd 98; Perm to Offic *Ely* from 98; Asst Rtd Clergy and Clergy Widow(er)s' Officer 00-07; Retired Clergy Officer from 07; PV Ely Cathl from 03. *20 King Edgar Close, Ely CB6 1DP* Tel (01353) 612338

BARBER, Craig John Francis. b 71. STETS 98. **d** 02 **p** 03. NSM Brighton St Bart *Chich* 02-03; C Brighton St Geo w St Anne and St Mark 03-06; TV Worth 06-08; C Worth, Pound Hill and Maidenbower from 08. *St Barnabas' Vicarage, 2 Crawley Lane, Crawley RH10 7EB* Tel (01293) 513398

BARBER, Garth Antony. b 48. Southn Univ BSc69 Lon Univ MSc79 FRAS MSOC. St Jo Coll Nottm. **d** 79 **p** 79. C Hounslow H Trin *Lon* 76-79; Chapl City of Lon Poly 79-86; P-in-c Twickenham All Hallows 86-97; Chapl Richmond Coll 87-97; Chapl UEA *Nor* 97-02; P-in-c Kingswood *S'wark* from

02; AD Reigate from 06. *The Vicarage, Woodland Way, Kingswood, Tadworth KT20 6NW* Tel (01737) 832164
E-mail garth.barber@virgin.net

BARBER, Hilary John. b 65. Aston Tr Scheme 92 Sarum Th Coll 94. **d** 96 **p** 97. C Moston St Jo *Man* 96-00; R Chorlton-cum-Hardy St Clem 00-07; P-in-c Chorlton-cum-Hardy St Werburgh 05-07; Adnry Liturg Adv 98-07; Dioc Music Adv 03-07; V Halifax *Wakef* from 07. *The Vicarage, Kensington Road, Halifax HX3 0HN* Tel (01422) 365477
E-mail barberhilary@hotmail.com

BARBER, John Eric Michael. b 30. Wycliffe Hall Ox 63. **d** 65 **p** 66. C Lupset *Wakef* 65-68; C Halifax St Jo Bapt 68-70; V Dewsbury St Matt and St Jo 70-80; V Perry Common *Birm* 80-95; rtd 95; Perm to Offic *Sarum* from 95. *21A Westhill Road, Weymouth DT4 9NB* Tel (01305) 786553

BARBER, Mrs Margaret Ann. b 31. GTCL52. Dalton Ho Bris 55 Sarum & Wells Th Coll 82. **dss** 83 **d** 87 **p** 94. Wimborne Minster and Holt *Sarum* 83-90; Par Dn 87-90; rtd 90; Hon Par Dn Hampreston *Sarum* 90-94; Hon C 94-02; Perm to Offic from 02. *1 Highbrow Place, 2 St Mary's Road, Ferndown BH22 9HB* Tel (01202) 873626

BARBER, Miss Marion. b 50. Birkbeck Coll Lon BSc97 K Coll Lon MSc03. **d** 07 **p** 08. NSM Lee St Mildred *S'wark* from 07. *12B Beechfield Road, London SE6 4NE* Tel (020) 8690 6035

BARBER, Martin John. b 35. Univ Coll Lon BA61. Linc Th Coll 61. **d** 63 **p** 64. C Stepney St Dunstan and All SS *Lon* 63-67; Chapl K Sch Bruton 67-93; rtd 93; Perm to Offic *B & W* from 93. *1 Plox Green, Bruton BA10 0EY* Tel (01749) 812290

BARBER, Michael. *See* BARBER, John Eric Michael

BARBER, Michael. b 40. Open Univ BA83. Oak Hill Th Coll 69. **d** 71 **p** 72. C Rothley *Leic* 71-74; C Leic Martyrs 74-76; V Queniborough 76-82; V Monkwearmouth All SS *Dur* 82-92; V Mirehouse *Carl* 92-05; rtd 05. *Allonby, 23 Victoria Park, Kirkcudbright DG6 4EN* Tel (01557) 339305

BARBER, Neil Andrew Austin. b 63. Ealing Coll of Educn BA85. NTMTC 94. **d** 98 **p** 98. St Mary's Chr Workers' Trust from 95; NSM Eastrop *Win* 98-01; V Normanton *Derby* from 01. *St Giles's Vicarage, 16 Browning Street, Derby DE23 8DN* Tel (01332) 767483 E-mail neil.barber@stgiles-derby.org

✠**BARBER, The Rt Revd Paul Everard.** b 35. St Jo Coll Cam BA58 MA66. Wells Th Coll 58. **d** 60 **p** 61 **c** 89. C Westborough *Guildf* 60-66; V York Town St Mich 66-73; V Bourne 73-80; RD Farnham 74-79; Hon Can Guildf Cathl 80-89; Adn Surrey 80-89; Suff Bp Brixworth *Pet* 89-01; Can Pet Cathl 89-01; rtd 01; Hon Asst Bp B & W from 01. *Hillside, 41 Somerton Road, Street BA16 0DR* Tel (01458) 442916

BARBER, Philip Kenneth. b 43. St Jo Coll Dur BA65 Sheff Univ DipEd66. NW Ord Course 74. **d** 76 **p** 77. NSM Burscough Bridge *Liv* 76-84; Asst Master Ormskirk Gr Sch 76-84; P-in-c Brigham *Carl* 84-85; V 85-89; P-in-c Mosser 84-85; 85-89; P-in-c Borrowdale 89-94; Chapl Keswick Sch 89-94; P-in-c Beetham and Educn Adv *Carl* 94-99; P-in-c Brampton and Farlam and Castle Carrock w Cumrew 99-02; P-in-c Irthington, Crosby-on-Eden and Scaleby 99-02; P-in-c Hayton w Cumwhitton 99-02; TR Eden, Gelt and Irthing 02-04; rtd 04; Perm to Offic *Carl* from 04 and *Blackb* from 05. *18 Holbeck Avenue, Morecambe LA4 6NP* Tel (01524) 401695
E-mail philipbarber326@btinternet.com

BARBER, Ralph Warwick. b 72. Lon Guildhall Univ BA94. Ripon Coll Cuddesdon 03. **d** 05 **p** 06. C Newquay *Truro* 05-08; Chapl RN from 08. *Royal Naval Chaplaincy Service, Mail Point 1-2, Leach Building, Whale Island, Portsmouth PO2 8BY* Tel (023) 9262 5055 Fax 9262 5134 E-mail ralphwbarber@aol.com

BARBER, Royston Henry. b 38. Univ of Wales (Abth) BD86. United Th Coll Abth 83. **d** 86 **p** 87. NSM Tywyn w Aberdyfi *Ban* 86-92; NSM Cannington, Otterhampton, Combwich and Stockland *B & W* 93-98; Perm to Offic *B & W* from 98 and *Ex* from 00. *Brambledown, Silver Street, Culmstock, Cullompton EX15 3JE* Tel (01884) 841041

BARBER, Sheila. b 50. NOC 96. **d** 99 **p** 00. C Dinnington *Sheff* 99-02; V Woodhouse St Jas 02-09; rtd 09. *5 Gannow Close, Killamarsh, Sheffield S21 2BB* Tel 0114-247 6537
E-mail sheilab@uwclub.net

BARBER, Thelma Naomi. b 53. Portsm Univ CertEd98. STETS 03. **d** 06 **p** 07. NSM Purbrook *Portsm* 06-07; C Carew *St D* 07-08; TV from 08. *9 Sageston Fields, Sageston, Tenby SA70 8TQ* Tel (01646) 650012 E-mail thelma.barber@ntlworld.com

BARBER, Mrs Jennifer Louise. b 32. JP67. Barrister-at-Law 55 St Hugh's Coll Ox BA54 MA57. Gilmore Course 80. **dss** 81 **d** 87 **p** 94. Bray and Braywood *Ox* 81-84; Hermitage and Hampstead Norreys, Cold Ash etc 84-87; Chapl Leeds Poly *Ripon* 87-92; Chapl Leeds Metrop Univ 92-95; rtd 95; NSM Shipton Moyne w Westonbirt and Lasborough *Glouc* 95-99; Perm to Offic *Bris* from 95; *Glouc* from 99; *Cov* and *Worc* from 00. *Cheriton, Aston Road, Chipping Campden GL55 6HR* Tel (01386) 840279

BARBOUR, Walter Iain. b 28. FICE65 Pemb Coll Cam BA48 MA53. Ox NSM Course 78. **d** 81 **p** 82. NSM Bray and Braywood *Ox* 81-84; NSM Thatcham 84-87; TV Moor Allerton *Ripon* 87-95; rtd 95; NSM Shipton Moyne w Westonbirt and

Lasborough *Glouc* 95-98; Perm to Offic *Bris* from 95; *Glouc* 98-01; *Cov* and *Worc* from 00. *Cheriton, Aston Road, Chipping Campden GL55 6HR* Tel (01386) 840279

BARBY, Canon Sheana Braidwood. b 38. Bedf Coll Lon BA59. EMMTC 81. **dss** 84 **d** 87 **p** 94. Derby St Paul 84-87; NSM Derby Cathl 87-03; Dioc Dir of Ords 90-97; Par Educn Adv 93-01; rtd 03; Hon Can Derby Cathl from 96; RD Derby N 00-05; Perm to Offic from 05. *2 Margaret Street, Derby DE1 3FE* Tel (01332) 383301 E-mail sheana@talktalk.net

BARCLAY, Mrs Christine Ann. b 54. TISEC. **d** 07. C St Andrews All SS *St And* from 07; NSM from 08. *12 Millfield, Cupar KY15 5UU* Tel (01334) 656154
E-mail christine.barclay1@btopenworld.com

BARCLAY, Ian Newton. b 33. Clifton Th Coll 58. **d** 61 **p** 62. C Cullompton *Ex* 61-63; C Ashill w Broadway *B & W* 63-66; V Chatham St Phil and St Jas *Roch* 66-67; C St Helen Bishopsgate w St Martin Outwich *Lon* 70-73; V Prestonville St Luke *Chich* 73-81; Lic to Offic 82-93; rtd 93; P-in-c Cannes *Eur* 98-02. *35 Marine Avenue, Hove BN3 4LH*
E-mail ibarclay692@btinternet.com

BARCLAY, Mrs Susan Molly. Wycliffe Hall Ox. **d** 87 **p** 99. Hon Par Dn March St Wendreda *Ely* 87-96; Tutor Past Studies Ridley Hall Cam 96-05; Perm to Offic *Ely* from 05. *42 Greystoke Road, Cambridge CB1 8DS* Tel (01223) 246877
E-mail sigb2@medschl.cam.ac.uk

BARCROFT, Ian David. b 60. UMIST BSc83 Edin Univ BD88 Glas Univ MTh01. Edin Th Coll 85. **d** 88 **p** 89. C Hamilton St Ninian's Cathl Perth 88-92; Min Perth St Ninian 88-92; P-in-c Aberdeen St Clem 92-97; R Hamilton *Glas* from 97. *The Rectory, 4C Auchingramont Road, Hamilton ML3 6JT* Tel and fax (01698) 429895 E-mail ian.barcroft@btinternet.com

BARDELL, Alan George. City Univ BSc. **d** 92 **p** 93. OLM Addlestone *Guildf* 92-06; rtd 06. *14 Dickens Drive, Addlestone KT15 1AW* Tel (01932) 847574

BARDELL, Terence Richard. b 53. EMMTC 04. **d** 01 **p** 02. OLM Coningsby w Tattershall *Linc* 01-05; C Gt Grimsby St Mary and St Jas 05-06; TV from 06. *62A Brighowgate, Grimsby DN32 0QW* Tel (01472) 345429

BARDSLEY, Warren Nigel Antony. b 52. AKC74. St Aug Coll Cant 74. **d** 75 **p** 76. C Leeds St Aid *Ripon* 75-78; C Cov St Jo 78-80; P-in-c Stoke Golding w Dadlington *Leic* 80-89; TV Swinton and Pendlebury *Man* 90-94. *Orchard House, 22 Upper Olland Street, Bungay NR35 1BH* Tel (01986) 895760

BARDWELL, Mrs Elaine Barbara. b 60. K Coll Lon BA81 AKC81. St Steph Ho Ox BA85 MA90. **dss** 86 **d** 87 **p** 95. Heref H Trin 86-89; C 87-89; Dir Past Studies St Steph Ho 89-96; V New Marston *Ox* from 96; AD Cowley 02-07. *The Vicarage, 8 Jack Straws Lane, Headington, Oxford OX3 0DL* Tel (01865) 434340 E-mail elaine.bardwell@virgin.net

BARDWELL, John Edward. b 53. Jes Coll Cam BA75 MA79 Ox Univ BA85 MA90. St Steph Ho Ox 83. **d** 86 **p** 87. C Heref H Trin 86-89; Perm to Offic *Ox* 90-96. *The Vicarage, 8 Jack Straws Lane, Headington, Oxford OX3 0DL* Tel (01865) 434340

BAREHAM, Miss Sylvia Alice. b 36. Hockerill Coll Cam CertEd59 Open Univ BA83 Ox Univ DipEd84. Ox Min Course 86. **d** 89 **p** 94. NSM N Leigh *Ox* 89-93; NSM Bampton w Clanfield 93-95; NSM Kedington *St E* 95-97; NSM Hundon w Barnardiston 95-97; NSM Haverhill w Withersfield, the Wrattings etc 95-97; NSM Stourhead 97-05; NSM Lark Valley 05-07; Perm to Offic *Chelmsf* from 05 and *St E* from 07. *Davaar, Old Hall Lane, Fornham St Martin, Bury St Edmunds IP31 1SS* Tel (01284) 724899

BARFF, John Robert. b 43. Ch Coll Cam BA66 MA70 K Coll Lon MTh69. ALCD68. **d** 69 **p** 70. C Fulham St Mary N End *Lon* 69-73; CMS 73-83; Sudan 75-83; P-in-c Pilning *Bris* 83-85; P-in-c Compton Greenfield 83-85; V Pilning w Compton Greenfield 85-92; rtd 92; Perm to Offic *Bris* from 92. *East View Cottage, Corton, Warminster BA12 0SZ* Tel (01985) 850593

BARFOOT, John Henry. b 38. **d** 08 **p** 09. NSM Tintagel *Truro* from 08. *Brambly Hedge, Castle Heights, Atlantic Road, Tintagel PL34 0DE* Tel (01840) 779047

BARFORD, Patricia Ann. b 47. Univ of Wales (Cardiff) BSc68 PhD73. WMMTC 95. **d** 98 **p** 99. NSM Stoke Prior, Wychbold and Upton Warren *Worc* 98-05; C Redditch H Trin 05-08; TV 08-09; rtd 09; Perm to Offic *Worc* from 09. *Greenfields, Church Road, Dodford, Bromsgrove B61 9BY* Tel (01527) 871614
E-mail thebarfords@hotmail.com

BARGE, Mrs Ann Marina. b 42. S'wark Ord Course 89. **d** 96 **p** 97. C Ludlow, Ludford, Ashford Carbonell etc *Heref* from 96. *8 Old Street, Ludlow SY8 1NP* Tel (01584) 877307

BARGE, David Robert. b 45. S Dios Minl Tr Scheme 92. **d** 95 **p** 96. NSM Westfield *B & W* 95-00; C Frome St Jo and St Mary 00; V Frome St Mary from 01; RD Frome from 08. *St Mary's House, 40 Innox Hill, Frome BA11 2LN* Tel (01373) 455996
E-mail barge@innox.fsnet.co.uk

BARGE, Marian. b 00. OLM Mynyddislwyn *Mon* from 00. *8 Pinewood Court, Pontllanfraith, Blackwood NP12 2PA* Tel (01495) 227208

BARGH, George Edward Norman. b 25. St Jo Coll Cam BA48

MA53 Leeds Univ LLB51. Carl Dioc Tr Course 80. **d** 83 **p** 84. NSM Ulverston St Mary w H Trin *Carl* 83-86; P-in-c Egton w Newland 86-87; P-in-c Blawith w Lowick 86-87; P-in-c Egton-cum-Newland and Lowick 87-89; rtd 90; Perm to Offic *Carl* from 90. *8 Highfield Road, Grange-over-Sands LA11 7JA* Tel (015395) 35755

BARHAM, Ian Harold. b 40. Clifton Th Coll 64. **d** 66 **p** 67. C Broadwater St Mary *Chich* 66-69 and 72-76; Burundi 71-72; R Beyton and Hessett *St E* 76-79; Perm to Offic 79-81; Hon C Bury St Edmunds St Mary 81-84; Chapl St Aubyn's Sch Tiverton 84-96; Chapl Lee Abbey 96-99; rtd 00; Perm to Offic *Ex* from 00. *53 Sylvan Road, Exeter EX4 6EY* Tel (01392) 251643

BARHAM, Mrs Jennifer Mary. b 43. RN65. Oak Hill Th Coll 92. **d** 95 **p** 96. NSM Leigh-on-Sea St Aid *Chelmsf* 95-02; NSM Gt Burstead 02-07; Chapl Basildon and Thurrock Gen Hosps NHS Trust 01-03; Perm to Offic *Chelmsf* 07-08; NSM Canvey Is from 08. *47 Walker Drive, Leigh-on-Sea SS9 3QT* Tel (01702) 558766
E-mail jen-john@barham47.freeserve.co.uk

✠**BARHAM, The Rt Revd Kenneth Lawrence.** b 36. OBE01. Clifton Th Coll BD63. **d** 63 **p** 64 **c** 93. C Worthing St Geo *Chich* 63-65; C Sevenoaks St Nic *Roch* 65-67; C Cheltenham St Mark *Glouc* 67-70; V Maidstone St Luke *Cant* 70-79; S Area Sec Rwanda Miss 79-84; P-in-c Ashburnham w Penhurst *Chich* 84-01; Asst Bp Cyangugu (Rwanda) 93-96; Bp 96-01; rtd 01; Hon Asst Bp Chich from 05. *Rosewood, Canadia Road, Battle TN33 0LR* Tel and fax (01424) 773073
E-mail bishopken@btinternet.com

BARHAM, Peter. b 62. Selw Coll Cam MA83. Linc Th Coll BTh94. **d** 94 **p** 95. C Fornham All SS and Fornham St Martin w Timworth *St E* 94-97; P-in-c Cockfield w Bradfield St Clare, Felsham etc 97-01; Min Can St E Cathl 98-03; Chapl 01-03; Can Res St E Cathl 03-08; V Ponteland *Newc* from 08. *The Vicarage, Thornhill Road, Ponteland, Newcastle upon Tyne NE20 9PZ* Tel (01661) 822140 E-mail revpeterbarham@aol.com

BARKER, Arthur John Willoughby. b 10. Lon Coll of Div 46. **d** 48 **p** 49. C Addiscombe St Mary *Cant* 48-53; V Westgate St Jas 53-58; Warden Scargill Ho 58-61; V Dent w Cowgill *Bradf* 61-76; rtd 76; Perm to Offic *Bradf* 76-99. *Manormead, Tilford Road, Hindhead GU26 6RA* Tel (01428) 602500

BARKER, Arundel Charles. b 24. Tyndale Hall Bris 54. **d** 56 **p** 57. C Rodbourne Cheney *Bris* 56-58; V Islington St Steph w St Bart and St Matt *Lon* 58-65; R Passenham *Pet* 65-90; P-in-c Cosgrove 65-66; rtd 90; Perm to Offic *Derby* from 90. *7 Bull Farm Mews, Bull Lane, Matlock DE4 5NB* Tel (01629) 580321

BARKER, Brian Wallwork. b 26. G&C Coll Cam BA50 MA55. Wells Th Coll 51. **d** 52 **p** 53. C Bradford cum Beswick *Man* 52-55; Singapore 55-61; Malaya 62-63; Malaysia 63-64; V Ashton St Jas *Man* 65-71; R Burnage St Nic 71-85; R Heaton Reddish 85-91; rtd 91; Perm to Offic *Man* and *Ches* from 91. *105 Crossfield Road, Cheadle Hulme, Cheadle SK8 5PD* Tel 0161-486 0334

BARKER, Cameron Timothy. b 62. Rhodes Univ BA83 Nottm Univ MA(TS)96. St Jo Coll Nottm 94. **d** 96 **p** 97. C W Streatham St Jas *S'wark* 96-00; V Herne Hill from 00. *The Vicarage, 1 Finsen Road, London SE5 9AX* Tel (020) 7771 0381
E-mail vicar@hernehillparish.org.uk

BARKER, Prof Charles Philip Geoffrey. b 50. Lon Univ MB, BS75 MS91 FRCS79 FICS92. S Dios Minl Tr Scheme 95. **d** 98 **p** 99. NSM Alverstoke *Portsm* 98-02; NSM The Lickey *Birm* 02-06; NSM Empangeni H Cross S Africa from 06. *PO Box 11032, Empangeni, 3880 South Africa* Tel and fax (0027) (35) 772 1211 E-mail barker@kznmail.co.za

✠**BARKER, The Rt Revd Clifford Conder.** b 26. TD71. Oriel Coll Ox BA50 MA55. St Chad's Coll Dur. **d** 52 **p** 53 **c** 76. C Falsgrave *York* 52-55; C Redcar 55-57; V Sculcoates 57-63; CF(TA) 58-74; P-in-c Sculcoates St Silas *York* 59-61; V Rudby in Cleveland w Middleton 63-70; RD Stokesley 65-70; V York St Olave w St Giles 70-76; RD City of York 71-75; Can and Preb York Minster 73-76; Suff Bp Whitby 76-83; Suff Bp Selby 83-91; rtd 91; Hon Asst Bp York from 95. *15 Oak Tree Close, Strensall, York YO32 5TE* Tel (01904) 490406

BARKER, David Robert. b 45. Worc Coll Ox BA67 MA70. Virginia Th Sem BD72. **d** 72 **p** 73. C Rowhampton H Trin *S'wark* 72-75; Chapl Goldsmiths' Coll Lon 75-79; Min Tr Officer *Cov* 79-85; Selection Sec and Sec for Continuing Minl Educn ACCM 85-90; V Sutton Valence w E Sutton and Chart Sutton *Cant* 90-08; rtd 09. *1 Colletts Close, Corfe Castle, Wareham BH20 5HG* Tel (01929) 481477
E-mail david_pennybarker@hotmail.com

BARKER, Edward. *See* BARKER, William Edward

BARKER, Gillian Ann. b 52. Portsm Univ MA02. Portsm Dioc Tr Course 91. **d** 92 **p** 98. NSM Alverstoke *Portsm* 92-95; NSM Bridgemary 95-96; Asst Chapl Portsm Hosps NHS Trust 96-98; Chapl 98-01; Chapl Ox Radcliffe Hosps NHS Trust 01-06; R Aynho and Croughton w Evenley etc *Pet* from 06. *The Rectory, Croughton Road, Aynho, Banbury OX17 3BD* Tel (01869) 810903

BARKER, Gordon Frank. b 43. Heriot-Watt Univ MSc75 Sheff Univ MA98. S & M Dioc Tr Inst 91. **d** 94 **p** 95. NSM Malew *S & M* 94-00; V Grain w Stoke *Roch* 00-04; Through Faith Miss Ev 00-04; P-in-c Andreas and Jurby *S & M* 04-08; P-in-c Lezayre

04-05; rtd 08. *The Harp Inn, Cross Four Ways, Ballasalla, Isle of Man IM9 3DH* Tel (01624) 824116

BARKER, Howard. See BARKER, Canon John Howard

BARKER, Canon Hugh Remington. b 19. Pemb Coll Cam BA41 MA45. Chich Th Coll 41. **d** 43 **p** 44. C Mill Hill St Mich *Lon* 43-48; C Welling *S'wark* 48-51; V Walworth All SS and St Steph 51-62; V Wisbech St Mary *Ely* 62-75; RD Wisbech 72-75; P-in-c Walpole St Andrew 75-77; V 77-84; P-in-c Walpole St Peter 75-77; R 77-84; RD Lynn Marshland 76-84; Hon Can Ely Cathl 81-84; rtd 84; Perm to Offic *Ely* from 84. *39 Dowgate Road, Leverington, Wisbech PE13 5DJ* Tel (01945) 585385

BARKER, Canon John Howard. b 36. Southn Univ BA58. Ripon Coll Cuddesdon 80. **d** 82 **p** 83. C W Leigh *Portsm* 82-84; V Cosham 84-88; Bp's Dom Chapl 88-96; Hon Can Portsm Cathl 93-02; V St Helens and Sea View 96-02; rtd 02; Perm to Offic *Portsm* from 02. *Coniston Lodge, 3 Coniston Drive, Ryde PO33 3AE* Tel (01983) 618674 Mobile 07802-281797 E-mail jhbarker@netcomuk.co.uk

BARKER, John Stuart. b 30. Keele Univ BA55. Wells Th Coll 55. **d** 57 **p** 58. C Oswestry St Oswald *Lich* 57-60; C Portishead *B & W* 60-63; V Englishcombe 63-69; R Priston 63-69; V Chew Magna w Dundry 70-85; rtd 94. *9 West Street, Axbridge BS26 2AA* Tel (01934) 732740

BARKER, Jonathan. b 55. Hull Univ BA79. Westcott Ho Cam 79. **d** 83 **p** 84. C Sketty *S & B* 83-86; Chapl Sport and Leisure 83-86; C Swansea St Mary w H Trin 85-86; Bermuda 86-90; TV Liv Our Lady and St Nic w St Anne 90-93; P-in-c S Shore St Pet *Blackb* 93-98; Chapl Blackpool Victoria Hosp NHS Trust 93-98; V Cleckheaton St Jo *Wakef* 98-08; Chapl St Pancras Internat and K Cross Stations *Lon* from 08. *3 Carleton Villas, Leighton Grove, London NW5 2QU* Tel (020) 7485 2472 E-mail jonathanbarker2004@tesco.net

BARKER, Julian Roland Palgrave. b 37. Magd Coll Cam BA61 MA65. Westcott Ho Cam 61. **d** 63 **p** 64. C Stafford St Mary *Lich* 63-66; Chapl Clare Hall Cam 66-69; Chapl Clare Coll Cam 66-70; Tutor St Aug Coll Cant 70-71; TV Raveningham *Nor* 71-78; TR 78-82; V Foremark *Derby* 82-02; V Repton 82-02; P-in-c Newton Solney 01-02; V Foremark and Repton w Newton Solney 02-03; RD Repton 91-95; rtd 03; Perm to Offic *St E* from 06. *Old Bank House, 12 Market Hill, Framlingham, Woodbridge IP13 9AN* Tel (01728) 621057

BARKER, Mark. b 62. ACIB90. St Jo Coll Nottm BTh95. **d** 95 **p** 96. C Barking St Marg w St Patr *Chelmsf* 95-98; C Cranham Park 98-04; V Tonbridge St Steph *Roch* from 04. *St Stephen's Vicarage, 6 Brook Street, Tonbridge TN9 2PJ* Tel (01732) 353079 E-mail mark.barker@diocese-rochester.org

BARKER, Neil Anthony. b 52. St Andr Univ BSc73. Ridley Hall Cam 74. **d** 77 **p** 78. C Leic H Apostles 77-81; C Camberley St Paul *Guildf* 81-86; R Bradfield *Ox* 86-88; R Bradfield and Stanford Dingley 88-92; R Woodmansterne *S'wark* 92-05; AD Reigate 05; Chapl MU 96-02; TR Modbury, Bigbury, Ringmore w Kingston etc *Ex* from 05; RD Woodleigh from 07. *The Vicarage, Church Lane, Modbury, Ivybridge PL21 0QN* Tel (01548) 830260 E-mail revneil@i.am

BARKER, The Ven Nicholas John Willoughby. b 49. Oriel Coll Ox BA73 BA75 MA77. Trin Coll Bris 75. **d** 77 **p** 78. C Watford St Alb 77-80; TV Didsbury St Jas and Em *Man* 80-86; TR Kidderminster St Geo *Worc* 86-07; RD Kidderminster 01-07; RD Kidderminster 01-07; Hon Can Worc Cathl 03-07; Adn Auckland and Can Dur Cathl from 07; P-in-c Darlington H Trin from 07. *Holy Trinity Vicarage, 45 Milbank Road, Darlington DL3 9NL* Tel (01325) 480444 E-mail archdeacon.of.auckland@durham.anglican.org

BARKER, Philip. See BARKER, Canon Charles Philip Geoffrey

BARKER, Canon Roy Thomas. b 33. K Coll Lon BD57 AKC57. **d** 58 **p** 59. C Headingley *Ripon* 58-62; C Hawksworth Wood 62-66; Chapl Cape Town Univ S Africa 66-72; Sub-Dean St Geo Cathl Cape Town 73-80; Can 74-80; Dean and Adn Grahamstown 80-92; Hon Can from 92; V Southmead *Bris* 92-98; rtd 98; Perm to Offic *Bris* from 98. *7 Cleeve Avenue, Downend, Bristol BS16 6BT* Tel 0117-956 9057 E-mail roy@cleeveave.freeserve.co.uk

BARKER, The Ven Timothy Reed. b 56. Qu Coll Cam BA79 MA82. Westcott Ho Cam 78. **d** 80 **p** 81. C Nantwich *Ches* 80-83; V Norton 83-88; V Runcorn All SS 88-94; Urban Officer 88-90; Dioc Communications Officer 91-98; Bp's Chapl 94-98; Hon P Asst Ches Cathl 94-98; V Spalding *Linc* 98-09; P-in-c Spalding St Paul 07-09; RD Elloe W 00-09; Can and Preb Linc Cathl from 03; Adn Linc from 09. *Archdeacon's House, 1A Northfield Road, Quarrington, Sleaford NG34 8RT* Tel (01529) 304348 Mobile 07775-833426 E-mail tim@tjkc.co.uk *or* archdeacon.lincoln@lincoln.anglican.org

BARKER, William Edward. b 28. Kelham Th Coll 49. **d** 54 **p** 55. C Warsop *S'well* 54-55; C Bawtry w Austerfield 55-57; V Frizington *Carl* 57-64; V Barrow St Jas 64-70; V Applethwaite 70-93; P-in-c Troutbeck 78-93; rtd 93; Perm to Offic *Carl* from 93. *114 Burneside Road, Kendal LA9 4RZ* Tel (01539) 734787

BARKING, Area Bishop of. See HAWKINS, The Rt Revd David John Leader

BARKS, Jeffrey Stephen. b 45. Cranmer Hall Dur 66. **d** 71 **p** 72. C

Wootton *St Alb* 71-74; C Boscombe St Jo *Win* 74-76; C Ringwood 76-80; P-in-c Spaxton w Charlynch *B & W* 80; P-in-c Enmore w Goathurst 80; P-in-c Spaxton w Goathurst, Enmore and Charlynch 80-81; R 81-92; RD Bridgwater 89-94; V Wembdon 92-07; rtd 07. *77 Alfoxton Road, Bridgwater TA6 7NW* Tel (01278) 423647 E-mail stephenbarks@dsl.pipex.com

BARLEY, Ann Christine. b 47. **d** 93 **p** 94. OLM Walton *St E* 93-00; OLM Walton and Trimley 00-08; rtd 08; Perm to Offic *St E* from 08. *13 New Road, Trimley St Mary, Felixstowe IP11 0TQ* Tel (01394) 283752 E-mail ann.carmel@lineone.net

BARLEY, Christopher James. b 56. St Steph Ho Ox BA90 MA93. **d** 93 **p** 94. C Upton cum Chalvey *Ox* 93-96; TV High Wycombe 96-01; V Swinton *Sheff* from 01; Dioc Chapl MU from 08. *The Vicarage, 50 Golden Smithies Lane, Swinton, Mexborough S64 8DL* Tel (01709) 582259 E-mail chris.barley@sheffield.anglican.org

BARLEY, Gordon Malcolm. b 59. Aston Tr Scheme 94 Oak Hill Th Coll 96. **d** 98 **p** 99. C Walthamstow St Jo *Chelmsf* 98-02; TV Barking St Marg w St Patr from 02. *St Patrick's Vicarage, 79 Sparsholt Road, Barking IG11 7YG* Tel (020) 8594 1960 E-mail revgbarley@eggconnect.net

BARLEY, Ivan William. b 48. Loughb Univ MA01 CEng74 MIET74. **d** 93 **p** 94. OLM Walton *St E* 93-00; OLM Walton and Trimley from 00; Dioc NSM/OLM Officer from 02. *13 New Road, Trimley St Mary, Felixstowe IP11 0TQ* Tel (01394) 283752 E-mail iwbarley@iee.org

BARLEY, Lynda Mary. b 53. York Univ BA74 PGCE75 Lon Univ MSc76 FSS77. S'wark Ord Course 93. **d** 96 **p** 97. NSM Lower Nutfield *S'wark* 96-97; NSM Littleham w Exmouth 97-98; NSM Tedburn St Mary, Whitestone, Oldridge etc 98-00; Hd Research and Statistics Abps' Coun from 00; NSM Cullompton, Willand, Uffculme, Kentisbeare etc *Ex* from 03. *Church House, Great Smith Street, London SW1P 3AZ* Tel (020) 7898 1542 Fax 7898 1532 E-mail lynda.barley@c-of-e.org.uk

BARLEY, Victor Laurence. b 41. St Jo Coll Cam MA66 Ch Ch Ox DPhil72 FRCSEd75 FRCR76. **d** 02 **p** 03. NSM Flax Bourton and Barrow Gurney *B & W* 02-06; NSM Clevedon St Jo 06-09; NSM Chew Stoke w Nempnett Thrubwell from 09. *1 Home Orchard, Chew Stoke, Bristol BS40 8UZ* Tel (01275) 333175 E-mail victor.barley@tiscali.co.uk

BARLING, Michael Keith. b 38. Oak Hill Th Coll 63. **d** 66 **p** 67. C Portman Square St Paul *Lon* 66-70; C Enfield Ch Ch Trent Park 70-74; V Sidcup St Andr *Roch* 74-78; Dir Fountain Trust 78-81; Chapl Bethany Fellowship and Roffey Place 81-88; Hon C Kennington St Mark *S'wark* 88-89; rtd 03. *10 Copper Beeches, Taunton TA1 5HS* Tel (01823) 272092 E-mail michael@kingdomfaithsw.com

BARLOW, Alan David. b 36. Worc Coll Ox BA59 MA65. Wycliffe Hall Ox 59. **d** 61 **p** 62. C Wealdstone H Trin *Lon* 61-67; V Neasden cum Kingsbury St Cath 67-73; Chapl Cranleigh Sch Surrey 73-81; Chapl Cheltenham Ladies' Coll 82-01; rtd 01; Perm to Offic *Glouc* from 02. *22 Moorend Road, Leckhampton, Cheltenham GL53 0EU* Tel and fax (01242) 584668 E-mail revdavid@globalnet.co.uk

BARLOW, Clive Christopher. b 42. Linc Th Coll 67. **d** 70 **p** 71. C Surbiton St Mark *S'wark* 70-74; C Spring Park *Cant* 74-77; V Ash w Westmarsh 77-92; R Chartham 92-08; RD E Bridge 86-92; RD W Bridge 95-01; rtd 08; Perm to Offic *Cant* from 08. *5 Barton Road, Canterbury CT1 1YG* Tel (01227) 784779 E-mail c.barlow@btinternet.com

BARLOW, Darren. b 65. Ridley Hall Cam 96. **d** 98 **p** 99. C Rayleigh *Chelmsf* 98-01; TV Billericay and Lt Burstead 01-06; TR Grays Thurrock from 06. *The Rectory, 10 High View Avenue, Grays RM17 6RU* Tel (01375) 377379 E-mail revbarlow@talktalk.net

BARLOW, David. See BARLOW, Alan David

BARLOW, David. b 50. Leeds Univ BA71 MA99. Wycliffe Hall Ox 71. **d** 73 **p** 74. C Horninglow *Lich* 73-75; C Wednesfield St Thos 75-77; C Bloxwich 77-78; Chapl RN 78-08; Prin Armed Forces Chapl Cen Amport Ho 05-08; P-in-c Baughurst, Ramsdell, Wolverton w Ewhurst etc *Win* from 08; QHC from 04. *The Rectory, Crabs Hill, Wolverton, Tadley RG26 5RU* Tel (01635) 297543 E-mail dbarlow@globalnet.co.uk

BARLOW, Canon Edward Burnley. b 29. St Aid Birkenhead 56. **d** 58 **p** 59. C Lenton Abbey *S'well* 58-61; C Ipswich All SS *St E* 61-63; R Fishtoft *Linc* 63-76; V Linc St Giles 76-96; Can and Preb Linc Cathl 92-05; rtd 96; Perm to Offic *Linc* 96-99. *8 Pynder Close, Washingborough, Lincoln LN4 1EX* Tel (01522) 793762

BARLOW, Paul Andrew. b 59. Imp Coll Lon BSc80 UMIST PhD84 Bolton Inst of HE PGCE85. Aston Tr Scheme 89 Chich Th Coll 91. **d** 93 **p** 94. C Hale *Guildf* 93-97; C Christchurch *Win* 97-01; P-in-c Alton All SS from 01. *All Saints' Vicarage, Queen's Road, Alton GU34 1HU* Tel (01420) 83458 E-mail paul@paulbarlow.plus.com

BARLOW, Paul Benson. b 31. Fitzw Coll Cam BA73 MA77 FRSA94. **d** 64 **p** 65. C Bath Abbey w St Jas *B & W* 64-74; Dep Hd Master Leys High Sch Redditch 74-81; Hd Master Jo Kyrle High Sch Ross-on-Wye 82-96; Perm to Offic *Heref* 82-85; Lic to

Offic 85-92; NSM Walford and St John w Bishopswood, Goodrich etc 92-97; Perm to Offic 97-08. *The Coach House, Hentland, Ross-on-Wye HR9 6LP*

BARLOW, Robert Mark. b 53. St Jo Coll Nottm 84. **d** 86 **p** 87. C Colwich w Gt Haywood *Lich* 86-91; R Crick and Yelvertoft w Clay Coton and Lilbourne *Pet* 91-04; Bp's Rural Officer 98-04; Chapl to Agric and Rural Life *Worc* from 04; C Worcs W from 05. *The White House, Ankerdine Hill, Knightwick, Worcester WR6 5PR* Tel (01886) 821339 Mobile 07947-600627 E-mail rbarlow@cofe-worcester.org.uk

BARLOW, Canon Timothy David. b 46. Univ Coll Ox BA67 MA71 Lon Univ BD71. Oak Hill Th Coll 71. **d** 71 **p** 72. C Marple All SS *Ches* 71-74; C Northwood Em *Lon* 74-78; Chapl Vevey w Château d'Oex and Villars *Eur* 78-84; Switzerland 84-89; V Chadkirk *Ches* from 89; Hon Can Ches Cathl from 08. *34 Church Lane, Romiley, Stockport SK6 4AA* Tel 0161-430 4841 E-mail timbarlow@romileylifecentre.co.uk

BARLOW, William George. b 40. Liv Univ BSc62 Univ of Wales BD65. St Mich Coll Llan 76. **d** 76 **p** 77. C Roath *Llan* 76-79; TV Cyncoed *Mon* 79-83; R Radyr *Llan* 83-05; RD Llan 95-04; rtd 05. *15 Cae Tymawr, Whitchurch, Cardiff CF14 2HB*

BARNARD, Canon Anthony Nevin. b 36. St Jo Coll Cam BA60 MA64. Wells Th Coll 61. **d** 63 **p** 64. C Cheshunt *St Alb* 63-65; Tutor Wells Th Coll 65-66; Chapl 66-69; Vice-Prin 69-71; Dep Prin Sarum & Wells Th Coll 71-77; Dir S Dios Minl Tr Scheme 74-77; Can Res and Chan Lich Cathl 77-06; Warden of Readers 77-91; Dir of Tr 86-91; rtd 06. *1 The Stables, The Knoll, Baron under Needwood, Burton-on-Trent DE13 8AB*

BARNARD, Catherine Elizabeth. b 54. York Univ BA76 Dur Univ BA79. Cranmer Hall Dur 77. **dss** 80 **d** 87 **p** 94. Mexborough *Sheff* 80-83; Sheff Manor 83-90; Hon Par Dn 87-90; Hon Par Dn Bolsterstone 90-94; C 94-08; P-in-c Stocksbridge from 08. *The Vicarage, Stone Moor Road, Bolsterstone, Sheffield S36 3ZN* Tel and fax 0114-288 2149

BARNARD, Jonathan Dixon. b 46. St Cath Coll Cam BA68. Cuddesdon Coll 69. **d** 71 **p** 72. C Silksworth *Dur* 71-74; C Hatfield Hyde *St Alb* 74-78; TV Hitchin 78-86; TR Penrith w Newton Reigny and Plumpton Wall *Carl* 86-91; rtd 91. *4 Hallin Croft, Penrith CA11 8AA* Tel (01768) 63000

BARNARD, Kevin James. b 52. Keble Coll Ox BA77 MA79. Cranmer Hall Dur 77. **d** 79 **p** 80. C Swinton *Sheff* 79-83; TV Sheff Manor 83-90; V Bolsterstone from 90; Bp's Adv on Issues Relating to Ageing from 94. *The Vicarage, Stone Moor Road, Bolsterstone, Sheffield S36 3ZN* Tel and fax 0114-288 2149

BARNARD, Leslie William. b 24. St Cath Coll Ox BA50 MA55 Southn Univ PhD70. Cuddesdon Coll 51. **d** 51 **p** 52. C Portswood Ch Ch *Win* 51-55; V Shaw and Whitley *Sarum* 55-61; R Chilcomb w Win All SS and Chesil 61-68; Sen Lect Leeds Univ 69-83; Dioc Dir of Tr *Ripon* 70-76; Chapl Harrogate Gen Hosp 83-89; rtd 89; Perm to Offic *Ripon* from 89. *10 All Saints Square, Low St Agnesgate, Ripon HG4 1FN* Tel (01765) 604420

BARNDEN, Saskia Gail. b 50. Waterloo Univ (Canada) BA70 Victoria Univ (BC) MA71 Indiana Univ PhD88 Westmr Coll Ox CertEd75. SAOMC 97. **d** 00 **p** 01. Asst Chapl Wycombe Abbey Sch 00-01; Chapl Haberdashers' Monmouth Sch for Girls from 01. *47 Eltham Road, Birmingham B15 2LY* Tel 0121-440 5677 *or* (01600) 711100 Mobile 07813-616574 E-mail headsec@hmsg.org

BARNES, Alan Dgerf. b 42. St Steph Ho Ox 75. **d** 77 **p** 78. C Wanstead H Trin Hermon Hill *Chelmsf* 77-80; C Clacton St Jas 80-82; R Cranham 82-89; V Calcot *Ox* 89-07; rtd 07; Perm to Offic *Ox* from 07. *18 Hartleys, Silchester, Reading RG7 2QE*

BARNES, Canon Brian. b 42. Sussex Univ MA82. Cant Sch of Min 79. **d** 82 **p** 83. NSM Maidstone All SS and St Phil w Tovil *Cant* 82-89; C 89-92; FE Adv Gen Syn Bd of Educn 86-92; R Staplehurst *Cant* 92-02; V Hythe 02-08; RD W Charing 95-99; AD Cranbrook 99-01; Hon Can Cant Cathl 01-08; rtd 08. *9 Egerton Road, Lincoln LN2 4PJ* Tel (01522) 569508 E-mail brian.barnes@virgin.net

BARNES, Brian. b 49. St Mich Coll Llan 93. **d** 93 **p** 94. C Betws w Ammanford *St D* 93-96; V Llanwnda, Goodwick w Manorowen and Llanstinan from 96. *The Vicarage, Dyffryn, Goodwick SA64 0AN* Tel (01348) 873758

BARNES, Canon Bryan Peter. b 24. Leeds Univ BA50. Coll of Resurr Mirfield 50. **d** 52 **p** 53. C Swindon New Town *Bris* 52-59; C Salisbury Cathl S Rhodesia 59-61; R Belvedere 63-66; V Moorfields *Bris* 66-71; P-in-c Winterbourne Down 71-75; V Fishponds St Mary 75-87; Hon Can Bris Cathl 84-87; rtd 87; NSM Duloe w Herodsfoot *Truro* 91-95; Warden Jes Hosp Cant 95-98. *St Katharine's House, Ormond Road, Wantage OX12 8EA* Tel (01235) 772798

BARNES, Canon Charles Peter Kentish. b 19. Ch Coll Cam BA40 MA44. Ridley Hall Cam 40. **d** 42 **p** 43. C Reading St Jo *Ox* 42-45; C Sutton Coldfield H Trin *Birm* 45-49; Sub-Dean Cairo Cathl Egypt 49-52; R Wavertree St Mary *Liv* 52-56; R Maghull 56-69; R Stratford-on-Avon w Bishopton *Cov* 69-75; TR 75-81; Hon Can Cov Cathl 75-84; C Priors Hardwick, Priors Marston and Wormleighton 81-84; rtd 84; Perm to Offic *Cov* 84-07 and *Glouc* from 84. *1 Capel Court, The Burgage, Prestbury, Cheltenham GL52 3EL* Tel (01242) 516591

BARNES, Christopher. **d** 06 **p** 07. NSM Bowling St Jo *Bradf* from 06. *257 Bowling Hall Road, Bradford BD4 7TJ* Tel (01274) 306230 E-mail chrisbarnes257@hotmail.co.uk

BARNES, Christopher Charles. b 51. Victoria Univ Wellington BA79 TDip79. Trin Coll Bris. **d** 00 **p** 01. C Langport Area *B & W* 00-03; P-in-c Burton and Rosemarket *St D* 03-07; Chapl Miss to Seafarers Milford Haven 03-07; Port Chapl Kobe Japan 07-09; Port Chapl Auckland New Zealand from 09. *PO Box 465, Shortland Street, Auckland 1140, New Zealand* Tel (0064) (9) 373 4352 Fax 373 4010 E-mail portchaplain1@gmail.com

BARNES, Colin. b 33. St Jo Coll York CertEd58. St Aid Birkenhead 61. **d** 64 **p** 65. C Eccles St Mary *Man* 64-66; C Barrow St Geo w St Luke *Carl* 66-68; V Goodshaw *Man* 68-80; P-in-c Wythenshawe St Martin 80-83; New Zealand 83-98; rtd 98; Perm to Offic *Man* from 98 and *Blackb* from 08. *5 Worston Close, Rawtenstall, Rossendale BB4 8UP* Tel (01706) 215199

BARNES, David John. b 37. Kent Univ MA96. Chich Th Coll 65. **d** 68 **p** 69. C Crayford *Roch* 68-71; Chapl RAF 71-75; Chapl Sutton Valence Sch Kent 75-87; C Minster-in-Sheppey *Cant* 87-93; V Ash w Westmarsh 93-01; RD E Bridge 98-01; rtd 01; Perm to Offic *Cant* and *Roch* from 02. *15 Meadow Lane, Edenbridge TN8 6HT* Tel and fax (01732) 300561 E-mail davidjbarnes@blueyonder.co.uk

BARNES, David Keith. b 53. Linc Th Coll. **d** 89 **p** 90. C E Crompton *Man* 89-93; V Belfield 93-99; V Honley *Wakef* from 99. *The Vicarage, St Mary's Road, Honley, Holmfirth HD9 6AZ* Tel (01484) 661178

BARNES, Derek Ian. b 44. Leeds Univ BA66. Westcott Ho Cam 66. **d** 68 **p** 69. C Far Headingley St Chad *Ripon* 68-71; Chapl Qu Eliz Coll *Lon* 72-77; Warden Lee Abbey Internat Students' Club Kensington 77-81; Hon C Willesden Green St Gabr *Lon* 81-83; P-in-c Southall H Trin 84-98; P-in-c Southall St Geo 89-92; Perm to Offic 89-02; Chapl W Lon Mental Health NHS Trust from 02. *West London Mental Health NHS Trust, Uxbridge Road, Southall UB1 3EU* Tel (020) 8354 8354 *or* 8354 8974 E-mail derekibarnes@gmail.com *or* derek.barnes@wlmht.nhs.uk

BARNES, Preb Donald Edward. b 26. K Coll Lon BD51 AKC51. **d** 52 **p** 53. C Willesden St Matt *Lon* 52-59; V Cricklewood St Pet 59-79; Lect Bays Coll Tottenham 63-68; V Belsize Park *Lon* 79-96; Preb St Paul's Cathl 84-96; AD N Camden 83-88; rtd 96; Perm to Offic *Lon* from 96. *94 Hamilton Road, London NW11 9DY* Tel (020) 8731 9860

BARNES, Duncan Christopher. b 64. Warwick Univ BA90. Trin Coll Bris BA93. **d** 93 **p** 94. C Hornchurch St Andr *Chelmsf* 93-98; V Bicker *Linc* 98-00; V Donington 98-00; Vineyard Ox 00-08. *Address temp unknown* E-mail dunc@classicfm.net

✠**BARNES, The Rt Revd Edwin Ronald.** b 35. Pemb Coll Ox BA58 MA62. Cuddesdon Coll 58. **d** 60 **p** 61 **c** 95. C Portsea N End St Mark *Portsm* 60-64; C Woodham *Guildf* 64-67; R Farncombe 67-78; V Hessle *York* 78-87; AD W Hull 85-87; Prin St Steph Ho Ox 87-95; Hon Can Ch Ch *Ox* 94-95; Suff Bp Richborough (PEV) *Cant* 95-01; Hon Asst Bp St Alb 96-01; Hon Asst Bp Chelmsf 99-01; rtd 01; Hon Asst Bp Win from 01. *1 Queen Elizabeth Avenue, Lymington SO41 9HN* Tel (01590) 610133 E-mail bishedwin@aol.com

BARNES, Mrs Enid Mabel. b 38. Homerton Coll Cam Dip Teaching58. WMMTC 87. **d** 90 **p** 94. Par Dn Walsall St Paul *Lich* 90-94; C 94-96; TV Cheli 96-02; rtd 02; Perm to Offic *Lich* 02-04. *10 Hind Avenue, Breaston, Derby DE72 3DG* Tel (01332) 873665 E-mail enidbarnes@hotmail.com

BARNES, Harvey Thomas. b 61. SWMTC 02. **d** 05 **p** 06. C Plympton St Mary *Ex* 05-08; P-in-c Whitchurch 08-09. *9 Dawlish Walk, Plymouth PL6 8PZ*

BARNES, Miss Heather Dawn. b 75. Liv Hope BA96 PGCE97. Ridley Hall Cam 03. **d** 05 **p** 06. C Luton Lewsey St Hugh *St Alb* from 05. *247 Leagrave High Street, Luton LU4 0NA* Tel (01582) 593402 Fax 472726

BARNES, Jennifer. b 45. Leeds Univ MA96. NOC 94. **d** 96 **p** 97. C Thorne *Sheff* 96-99; C Clifton St Jas 99-01; Chapl HM Pris Featherstone 01-04; Chapl HM YOI Swinfen Hall 04-05; P-in-c Barnsley St Edw *Wakef* 05-07; Chapl HM Pris and YOI New Hall 07-08; rtd 08; Perm to Offic *Wakef* from 07. *371 Hoylake Road, Wirral CH46 0RW* E-mail jcbjb7@aol.com

BARNES, Jeremy Paul Blissard. b 70. Southn Univ BSc92. Wycliffe Hall Ox BTh99. **d** 99 **p** 00. C Brompton H Trin w Onslow Square St Paul *Lon* 99-05; C Shadwell St Paul w Ratcliffe St Jas 05-09; V E Twickenham St Steph from 09. *St Stephen's Vicarage, 21 Cambridge Park, Twickenham TW1 2JE* Tel (020) 8607 9676 *or* 8892 5258

BARNES, Canon John Barwick. b 32. AKC58. **d** 59 **p** 60. C Brentwood St Thos *Chelmsf* 59-65; R Arkesden w Wicken Bonhunt 65-71; V Gt Ilford St Mary 71-99; Hon Can Chelmsf Cathl 95-99; rtd 99; Perm to Offic *Chelmsf* from 99. *352 Henley Road, Ilford IG1 1TJ* Tel (020) 8478 1954

BARNES, John Christopher. b 43. MA ATI. Linc Th Coll 78. **d** 80 **p** 81. C Guiseley *Bradf* 80-83; TV Guiseley w Esholt 83-86; V Rawdon 86-92; R Armthorpe *Sheff* 92-98; TR Maltby 98-01; RD Doncaster 96-98; Hon Can Sheff Cathl 00-01; TR Blakenall Heath *Lich* 01-05; P-in-c Gomersal *Wakef* 05-09; P-in-c

Cleckheaton St Jo 08-09; rtd 09. *371 Hoylake Road, Wirral CH46 0RW* E-mail jcbjb7@aol.com

BARNES, John Seymour. b 30. Qu Coll Birm 58. **d** 61 **p** 62. C Bromsgrove St Jo *Worc* 61-64; C Kingsthorpe *Pet* 64-66; C Styvechale *Cov* 66-69; P-in-c Avon Dassett w Farnborough 69-75; P-in-c Cov St Alb 75-84; R Weddington and Caldecote 84-89; P-in-c Wilnecote *Lich* 89-90; V Bentley 90-96; rtd 96; Perm to Offic *Lich* 96-04. *10 Hind Avenue, Breaston, Derby DE72 3DG* Tel (01332) 873665

BARNES, Canon Katrina Crawford. b 52. K Coll Lon BA98 AKC98. Oak Hill Th Coll 90. **d** 93 **p** 94. NSM Bromley H Trin *Roch* 93-98; C Meopham w Nurstead 98-00; Assoc Staff Tutor SEITE 99-03; R Longfield *Roch* 01-06; V Bromley Common St Aug from 06; Bp's Adv for Ord Women's Min from 05; Hon Can Roch Cathl from 05. *St Augustine's Vicarage, Southborough Lane, Bromley BR2 8AT* Tel (020) 8467 1351 E-mail katrina.barnes@diocese-rochester.org

BARNES, Lee. b 74. Trin Coll Bris BA03 MA09. **d** 09. C Malmesbury w Westport and Brokenborough *Bris* from 09; C Gt Somerford, Lt Somerford, Seagry, Corston etc from 09. *1 Park Close, Malmesbury SN16 0EB* Tel (01666) 823371 Mobile 07959-467359 E-mail mrleebarnes@gmail.com

BARNES, Mrs Mary Jane. b 48. St Jo Coll Nottm 97. **d** 99 **p** 00. C Harefield *Lon* 99-02; TV New Windsor *Ox* from 02. *The Vicarage, 73 Alma Road, Windsor SL4 3HD* Tel (01753) 861757 Mobile 07930-337407 E-mail mary@harefield9.fsnet.co.uk

BARNES, Matthew John. b 68. Leeds Univ MA99. St Jo Coll Nottm BA93. **d** 96 **p** 97. C Stanley *Wakef* 96-99; TV N Wingfield, Clay Cross and Pilsley *Derby* 99-08; R Brampton St Thos from 08. *The Rectory, 674 Chatsworth Road, Chesterfield S40 3NU* Tel (01246) 567634 Mobile 07797-976348

BARNES, Neal Duncan. b 63. Leeds Univ BSc84 Cranfield Inst of Tech PhD92. Oak Hill Th Coll 93. **d** 95 **p** 96. C Biggleswade *St Alb* 95-99; V Anlaby St Pet *York* from 99; Hon Chapl Ambulance Service Hull from 99. *The Vicarage, Church Street, Anlaby, Hull HU10 7DG* Tel (01482) 653024 E-mail neal@anvic.karoo.co.uk

BARNES, Canon Neil. b 42. Kelham Th Coll 61 Bps' Coll Cheshunt 65. **d** 68 **p** 69. C Poulton-le-Fylde *Blackb* 68-72; C Ribbleton 72-75; V Knuzden 75-81; Chapl Prestwich Hosp Man 81-88; Chapl Salford Mental Health Services NHS Trust 88-04; Manager Chapl Services 94-04; Hon Can Man Cathl 96-04; Perm to Offic *Blackb* and *Man* from 04. *Leads Cottage, Bacup Road, Cliviger, Burnley BB11 3QZ* Tel (01282) 451533 E-mail neilbarnes@bigfoot.com

BARNES, Paul. See BYLLAM-BARNES, Preb Paul William Marshall

BARNES, Paul Nicholas. b 58. Qu Coll Birm 89. **d** 91 **p** 92. C Weymouth H Trin *Sarum* 91-95; P-in-c Studley 95-07; P-in-c Mere w W Knoyle and Maiden Bradley from 07. *The Vicarage, Angel Lane, Mere, Warminster BA12 6DH* Tel (01747) 863313

BARNES, Peter. See BARNES, Canon Charles Peter Kentish

BARNES, Peter Frank. b 52. St Jo Coll Nottm LTh81. **d** 81 **p** 82. C Colne St Bart *Blackb* 81-83; C Melton Mowbray w Thorpe Arnold *Leic* 83-86; P-in-c Barlestone 86-89; V Broughton and Duddon *Carl* 89-98; V Shrewsbury St Geo w Greenfields *Lich* 98-08; P-in-c Bicton, Montford w Shrawardine and Fitz 98-00; P-in-c Myddle from 08; P-in-c Broughton from 08, P-in-c Loppington w Newtown from 08. *The Rectory, Myddle, Shrewsbury SY4 3RX* Tel (01939) 291801 E-mail peter.barnes@lineone.net

BARNES, Philip John. b 52. Cant Ch Ch Univ BA08. SEITE 01. **d** 04 **p** 05. NSM Gravesend St Mary *Roch* 04-06; C Gravesend St Aid 06-09; TV S Gillingham from 09. *58 Parkwood Green, Gillingham ME8 9PP* Tel (01634) 306806 Mobile 07764-151833 E-mail philip.barnes@diocese-rochester.org

BARNES, Philip Richard. b 73. Westmr Coll Ox BTh94 Heythrop Coll Lon MA99. St Steph Ho Ox 98. **d** 00 **p** 01. C Ruislip St Martin *Lon* 00-03; Shrine ₽ Shrine of Our Lady of Walsingham 03-08; V Northwood Hills St Edm *Lon* from 08. *St Edmund's Vicarage, 2 Pinner Road, Northwood HA6 1QS* Tel (020) 8866 9230 E-mail frphilipbarnes@btinternet.com

BARNES, Robin James. b 52. **d** 05 **p** 06. NSM Debenham and Helmingham *St E* from 05. *119 Gardeners Road, Debenham, Stowmarket IP14 6RZ* Tel (01728) 861498 E-mail robin@rbarnes.fsnet.co.uk

BARNES, Roland Peter. b 59. Ban Ord Course 01. **d** 03 **p** 04. NSM Bro Ddyfi Uchaf *Ban* from 03; P-in-c from 05. *Y Rheithordy, Mallwyd, Machynlleth SY20 9HJ* Tel (01650) 531650

BARNES, Stephen. b 46. Hull Univ BA69. Clifton Th Coll 69. **d** 72 **p** 73. C Girlington *Bradf* 72-74; TV Glyncorrwg w Afan Vale and Cymmer Afan *Llan* 74-79; R Aberavon 86-01; V Dulais Valley from 01. *The Vicarage, 86 Church Road, Seven Sisters, Neath SA10 9DT* Tel and fax (01639) 700286 E-mail sbarnes.cwmdulais@btinternet.com

BARNES, Stephen John. b 59. Univ of Wales (Cardiff) BSc80. Chich Th Coll 83. **d** 86 **p** 87. C Neath w Llantwit 86-89; C Coity w Nolton 89-95; V Troedyrhiw w Merthyr Vale from 95. *The Vicarage, Nixonville, Merthyr Vale, Merthyr Tydfil CF48 4RF* Tel (01443) 690249

BARNES, Stephen William. b 53. Man Univ BSc. St Jo Coll Nottm. **d** 83 **p** 84. C Chadwell Heath *Chelmsf* 83-87; C Becontree St Alb 88-89; Deanery Youth Chapl 88-91; C Becontree S 89-91; TV Worth *Chich* 91-98; Chapl Willen Hospice Milton Keynes from 99. *90 Bradwell Road, Bradville, Milton Keynes MK13 7AD* E-mail chaplain@willen-hospice.org.uk

BARNES, Mrs Sylvia Frances. b 43. Shoreditch Coll Lon CertEd75. S Tr Scheme 92. **d** 96 **p** 97. Hon C Cusop w Blakemere, Bredwardine w Brobury etc *Heref* from 96. *Pwll Cwm, Arthur's Stone Lane, Dorstone, Hereford HR3 6AY* Tel (01981) 500252

BARNES, Thomas. See BARNES, Canon William Thomas

BARNES, Timothy. b 56. Birm Univ BSc78. Westcott Ho Cam 96 Lon Bible Coll 82. **d** 98 **p** 99. C Shrub End *Chelmsf* 98-02; V Leigh-on-Sea St Aid from 02. *St Aidan's Vicarage, 78 Moor Park Gardens, Leigh-on-Sea SS9 4PY* Tel (01702) 512531 E-mail timbarnes@timbo7.fsnet.co.uk

BARNES, William Joseph Athanasius. b 57. St Andr Univ MTheol84 Newc Univ MA02 RGN89. Westcott Ho Cam 91. **d** 92 **p** 93. C S Bank *York* 92-95; C Northallerton w Kirby Sigston 95-97; V Dormanstown 97-01; P-in-c Netherton St Andr *Worc* 01-06; P-in-c Darby End 03-06. *20 Cropton Close, Redcar TS10 4HU* Tel (01642) 471772 E-mail bja.barnes@btopenworld.com

BARNES, Canon William Thomas. b 39. Dur Univ BA60. Wycliffe Hall Ox 60. **d** 62 **p** 63. C Scotforth *Blackb* 62-66; C Cleveleys 66-67; V Colne Ch Ch 67-74; V Bamber Bridge St Sav 74-04; Hon Can Blackb Cathl 00-04; rtd 04; Perm to Offic *Blackb* from 04. *12 Little Close, Farington Moss, Leyland PR26 6QU* Tel (01772) 457646

BARNES-CLAY, Peter John Granger. b 43. Cam Univ CertEd69 MCollP. Chich Th Coll 72. **d** 75 **p** 82. C Earlham St Anne *Nor* 75-76; Asst Master Hewett Sch Nor 76-83; Chapl Nor Cathl from 80; Hon C Eaton 81-83; C 83-87; R Winterton w E and W Somerton and Horsey 87-92; R Weybourne Gp 92-03; RD Holt 95-02; rtd 03; Perm to Offic *Nor* 03-05; C Smallburgh w Dilham w Honing and Crostwight 05-06; P-in-c 06-08; Perm to Offic from 08. *Hunters End, 1 Danby Close, Eaton Rise, Norwich NR4 6RH* Tel (01603) 501199 E-mail becketsthree1@aol.com

BARNES, Alec James Leon. b 44. Em Coll Cam BA66 MA70 PGCE71. Cuddesdon Coll 66. **d** 69 **p** 70. C Preston St Jo *Blackb* 69-72; Asst Master Hutton Grammar Sch 70-72; Asst Chapl Uppingham Sch 72-80; Hd of RE 73-80; Dir of Farmington/Ampleforth Project 79-83; C Witney *Ox* 80-84; P-in-c Lt Compton w Chastleton, Cornwell etc 84-88; Prin Ox Chr Tr Scheme 84-88; P-in-c St Michael Penkevil *Truro* 88-95; P-in-c Lamorran and Merther 88-95; Dioc Tr Officer 88-95; Chapl Strasbourg *Eur* 95-01; Abp Cant's Rep at Eur Inst from 95; Perm to Offic *Truro* from 95; rtd 01. *7 rue des Magnolias, La Croix, 17800 St Léger, France* Tel (0033) (5) 46 94 99 25 Fax 46 94 95 01 E-mail james.barnett@wanadoo.fr

BARNETT, Ann. See BARNETT, Miss Patricia Ann

BARNETT, David John. b 33. Magd Coll Ox BA56 MA61. St Steph Ho Ox BA58. **d** 59 **p** 60. C Styvechale *Cov* 59-62; Chapl Rhodes Univ S Africa 62-68; P-in-c Grahamstown St Bart 62-68; Lic to Offic Cape Town 68-69; Chapl and Lect Univ of Rhodesia 70-76; V Colindale St Matthias *Lon* 77-90; R Finchley St Mary 90 98; rtd 98; Perm to Offic *Ex* from 98. *2 Curlew Way, Exeter EX4 4SW* Tel (01392) 431486

BARNETT, Dudley Graham. b 36. Ch Ch Ox BA62 MA65. St Steph Ho Ox 62. **d** 64 **p** 65. C Abbey Hey *Man* 64-68; V Swinton H Rood 68-90; R Old Trafford St Hilda 90-01; R Firswood and Gorse Hill 01-02; rtd 02; Perm to Offic *Man* from 02. *6A Gilda Crescent Road, Eccles, Manchester M30 9AG* Tel 0161-707 9767

BARNETT, James. See BARNETT, Alec James Leon

BARNETT, James Andrew McWilliam. b 76. Leeds Univ BA99. Trin Coll Bris BA01. **d** 02 **p** 03. C Bolton St Paul w Em *Man* 02-05; TV Leeds St Geo *Ripon* from 05. *14 Parkside Green, Leeds LS6 4NY* Tel 0113-243 8498 Mobile 07747-892192 E-mail james.barnett@stgeorgesleeds.org.uk

BARNETT, John. See BARNETT, David John

BARNETT, John Raymond. b 51. Lon Univ LLB74 BD86 Birm Univ MA98. Westcott Ho Cam 74. **d** 77 **p** 78. C Northfield *Birm* 77-81; V Hamstead St Bernard 81-91; R The Quinton 91-03; AD Edgbaston 98-03; P-in-c Oldbury 03-07; P-in-c Langley St Jo 03-07; P-in-c Langley St Mich 03-07; P-in-c Londonderry 04-07; V Oldbury, Langley and Londonderry 07-09; Hon Can Birm Cathl 01-09; P-in-c Darlaston All SS *Lich* from 09; Inter-Faith Officer Wolverhampton Area from 09. *All Saints' Vicarage, 255 Walsall Road, Wednesbury WS10 9SQ* Tel 0121-552 6898 Mobile 07969-114132 E-mail barnett4@jajolohe.freeserve.co.uk

BARNETT, John Richard. b 28. Open Univ BA99, Portsm Dioc Tr Course 86. **d** 88 **p** 98. NSM Droxford and Meonstoke w Corhampton cum Exton *Portsm* 88-91; NSM W Meon and Warnford 91-01; rtd 01. *5 The Croft, 10 St Annes Road, Eastbourne BN21 2DL* Tel (01323) 731711

BARNETT, Michael. *See* BARNETT, Preb Raymond Michael
BARNETT, Canon Norman. b 19. Univ of Wales BA41. St Mich Coll Llan 41. **d** 43 **p** 44. C Roath St German *Llan* 43-49; Chapl Llan Cathl 49-53; R Liss *Portsm* 53-85; RD Petersfield 70-75; Hon Can Portsm Cathl 76-85; rtd 85; Perm to Offic *Portsm* and *Sarum* from 85. *8 Lovells Mead, Marnhull, Sturminster Newton DT10 1JL* Tel (01258) 820260
BARNETT, Miss Patricia <u>Ann</u>. b 38. Whitelands Coll Lon CertEd. St Jo Coll Dur 75. **dss** 78 **d** 87 **p** 94. Gateacre *Liv* 78-82; Litherland St Paul Hatton Hill 82-88; Par Dn 87-88; Par Dn Platt Bridge 88-94; C 94-95; V Skelmersdale Ch at Cen 95-98; rtd 98; Perm to Offic *Liv* from 00. *93 Alder Hey Road, St Helens WA10 4DW* Tel (01744) 607609
BARNETT, Peter Geoffrey. b 46. AKC71. St Aug Coll Cant 71. **d** 72 **p** 73. C Wolverhampton *Lich* 72-77; P-in-c Caldmore 77-83; TR Bris St Agnes and St Simon w St Werburgh 83-87; P-in-c Bris St Paul w St Barn 83-87; TR Bris St Paul's 87-94; Warden Pilsdon Community 94-04; Ewell Monastery from 04. *Ewell Monastery, Water Lane, West Malling, Maidstone ME19 6HH* Tel (01732) 843089 Fax 870279
E-mail community@ewell-monastery.co.uk
BARNETT, Preb Raymond <u>Michael</u>. b 31. Man Univ BA54. Wells Th Coll 54. **d** 56 **p** 57. C Fallowfield *Man* 56-59; Madagascar 59-60; V Blackrod *Man* 60-67; V Woolavington *B & W* 67-76; RD Bridgwater 72-76; V St Decumans 76-96; RD Quantock 78-86 and 93-95; Preb Wells Cathl 89-96; rtd 96; Perm to Offic *B & W* 96-08. *22 Fosbrooke House, Clifton Drive, Lytham St Annes FY8 5RQ*
BARNFATHER, Thomas Fenwick. b 52. Linc Th Coll 86. **d** 88 **p** 89. C Sedgefield *Dur* 88-91; TV E Darlington 91-92; CF 92-96; V Heybridge w Langford *Chelmsf* 96-98; Chapl HM YOI Dover 98-00; Chapl HM Pris Swaleside 00-01; P-in-c Aylesham w Adisham *Cant* 01-04; Asst Dir of Ords 02-05; Perm to Offic from 04. *54 Tothill Street, Minster, Ramsgate CT12 4AJ* Tel (01843) 822575 E-mail tom_barnfather@btinternet.com
BARNSHAW, Anthony James. b 72. Man Univ BA97. St Jo Coll Nottm 03. **d** 05 **p** 06. C Kersal Moor *Man* 05-08; TV Ramsbottom and Edenfield from 08. *The Vicarage, 16 Maple Grove, Ramsbottom, Bury BL0 0AN* Tel (01706) 821036
E-mail a.barnshaw@btopenworld.com
BARNSLEY, Mrs Angela Vera. b 47. St Hild Coll Dur BA70. St Alb Minl Tr Scheme 90. **d** 93. NSM Codicote *St Alb* 93-94. *Address temp unknown*
BARNSLEY, Anna. *See* BARNSLEY, Mrs Valerie Anne
BARNSLEY, David Edward. b 75. Ox Brookes Univ BSc97. Oak Hill Th Coll BA03. **d** 03 **p** 04. C Kilnhurst *Sheff* 03-06; C Duffield and Lt Eaton *Derby* from 06. *107 Duffield Road, Little Eaton, Derby DE21 5DT* Tel (01332) 843177
E-mail davidb@rnsley.freeserve.co.uk
BARNSLEY, Canon Melvyn. b 46. Dur Univ BA67 Lon Univ CertEd. St Chad's Coll Dur 64. **d** 71 **p** 72. C Cov St Thos 71-74; C Cov St Jo 71-75; V New Bilton 75-82; R Stevenage St Andr and St Geo *St Alb* from 82; RD Stevenage 89-99; Hon Can St Alb from 00. *The Rectory, Cuttys Lane, Stevenage SG1 1UP* Tel (01438) 351631
BARNSLEY, Mrs Valerie Anne (**Anna**). b 48. Sussex Univ BEd71. WMMTC 91. **d** 94 **p** 95. NSM Tettenhall Regis *Lich* 94-99; Perm to Offic from 99. *The Retreat, Clive Road, Pattingham, Wolverhampton WV6 7BU* Tel (01902) 701713
BARNSTAPLE, Archdeacon of. *See* GUNN-JOHNSON, The Ven David Allan
BARON, Thomas Michael. b 63. St Steph Ho Ox 85. **d** 88 **p** 89. C Hartlepool St Paul *Dur* 88-92; Chapl Asst Hartlepool Gen Hosp 89-92; Asst Chapl Whittington Hosp Lon 92-95; Chapl Enfield Community Care NHS Trust 95-01; Chapl Chase Farm Hosps NHS Trust 95-99; Chapl Barnet and Chase Farm Hosps NHS Trust from 99; Chapl Barnet, Enfield and Haringey Mental Health Trust from 01; Chapl Enfield Primary Care Trust from 01. *The Chaplaincy, Chase Farm Hospital, The Ridgeway, Enfield EN2 8JL* Tel (020) 8375 1078 *or* 8882 1195
E-mail frtom.baron@btinternet.com
BARON, Mrs Vanessa Lillian. b 57. City Univ BSc79 Fitzw Coll Cam BA84 MA85 Birkbeck Coll Lon MA06 SRN79. Ridley Hall Cam 83. **dss** 86 **d** 87 **p** 94. Roxbourne St Andr *Lon* 86-89; Par Dn 87-89; NSM Roxeth 92-95; Lic Preacher from 95; Asst Chapl Harrow Sch 95-04; Chapl St Paul's Girls' Sch Hammersmith from 04. *2 Kennet House, Harrow Park, Harrow HA1 3JE* Tel (020) 8872 8182 *or* 7603 2288
E-mail vbaron@spgs.org
BARR, Alan. b 59. TCD BTh07. **d** 07 **p** 08. C Bray *D & G* from 07. *14 Rosslyn Court, Kilarney Road, Bray, Co Wicklow, Republic of Ireland* Tel (00353) (1) 282 9044 Mobile 87-948 4408
E-mail alnbarr@gmail.com
BARR, John. *See* BARR, Michael John Alexander
BARR (*née* HAYTER), **Mary Elizabeth.** b 58. Jes Coll Ox BA80 CertEd81 MA84 Qu Coll Ox DPhil85. Ridley Hall Cam 84. **dss** 86 **d** 87 **p** 94. Chapl Cam Univ Pastorate 86-91; Cambridge H Trin w St Andr Gt *Ely* 86-87; Par Dn 87-91; Perm to Offic 91-92; Perm to Offic *Ex* 92-94; NSM Torquay St Luke 94-97;

NSM Gt Malvern St Mary *Worc* from 97; Chapl Worcs Community Healthcare NHS Trust 99-01; Chapl Worcs Community and Mental Health Trust from 01. *Priory Vicarage, Clarence Road, Malvern WR14 3EN* Tel and fax (01684) 563707 *or* 561020 E-mail jmbarr@ukonline.co.uk
or office@greatmalvernpriory.org.uk
BARR, Michael <u>John</u> **Alexander.** b 60. Qu Coll Ox BA82 MA86 Pemb Coll Cam BA86 MA90. Ridley Hall Cam 84. **d** 87 **p** 88. C Earley St Pet *Ox* 87-89; C Cambridge Gt St Mary w St Mich *Ely* 89-92; Chapl Girton Coll Cam 90-92; P-in-c Torquay St Luke *Ex* 92-97; Dioc Communications Officer 92-97; V from 99; RD Malvern 01-07. *Priory Vicarage, Clarence Road, Malvern WR14 3EN* Tel and fax (01684) 563707 *or* 561020 E-mail jmbarr@ukonline.co.uk
or office@greatmalvernpriory.org.uk
BARR, Norma Margaret. b 41. Trin Coll Bris BA99. **d** 00 **p** 01. C Aberdour *St And* 01-03; P-in-c Pontiac Grace Ch USA 03-05. *3300 W Kinnickinnic Rover Parkway, Apartment #2, Milwaukee WI 53215, USA* E-mail normabarr@gmail.com
BARR, The Very Revd William Norman Cochrane. b 20. TCD BA44 MA50 BD50. CITC 45. **d** 46 **p** 46. C Ballymena Conn 46-52; C Belf Cathl 52-54; R Duneane w Ballyscullion 54-58; Bp's Dom Chapl 56-71; P-in-c Belfast Whiterock 58-61; I Derriaghy w Colin 61-90; Can Conn Cathl 80-82; Dean Conn 82-90; rtd 90. *45 Killeaton Crescent, Dunmurry, Belfast BT17 9HB* Tel (028) 9062 1746
E-mail wncbarr@btinternet.com
BARR-HAMILTON, Nicholas James. b 74. Oak Hill Th Coll. **d** 08 **p** 09. C Linthorpe *York* from 08. *26 Emerson Avenue, Middlesbrough TS5 7QH*
BARRACLOUGH, Mrs Barbara <u>Amanda</u> **Juliet.** b 61. Stirling Univ BA83 Cees Coll of HE MA00. NOC 97. **d** 00 **p** 01. C Lupset *Wakef* 00-04; V W Ardsley from 04. *Woodkirk Vicarage, 1168 Dewsbury Road, Dewsbury WF12 7JL* Tel (01924) 472375 Fax 475758 Mobile 07808-382016
E-mail amanda.barraclough1@btinternet.com
BARRACLOUGH, Dennis. b 35. St Jo Coll York CertEd58 Lambeth STh68 LCP62 FCP74. Ripon Hall Ox 66. **d** 68 **p** 69. C Woodhouse *Wakef* 68-71; V Gildersome 71-83; V Kirkburton 83-00; RD Kirkburton 92-98; rtd 00; Perm to Offic *Wakef* from 00. *8 Clough Park, Fenay Bridge, Huddersfield HD8 0JH* Tel (01484) 325515
BARRACLOUGH, Canon Owen Conrad. b 32. Pemb Coll Cam BA55 MA59. Westcott Ho Cam 56. **d** 57 **p** 58. C Chippenham St Andr w Tytherton Lucas *Bris* 57-62; V Harringay St Paul *Lon* 62-70; Bp's Chapl for Community Relns *Cov* 70-77; P-in-c Baginton 72-77; V Swindon Ch Ch *Bris* 77-97; Chapl Princess Marg Hosp Swindon 77-89; Hon Can Bris Cathl 87-97; rtd 98; Perm to Offic *Bris* from 98 and *Glouc* 98-01; Jt P-in-c Staverton w Boddington and Tredington etc *Glouc* 01-04; Hon C Twigworth, Down Hatherley, Norton, The Leigh etc 04-06; Hon C Leckhampton SS Phil and Jas w Cheltenham St Jas from 06. *Robin Hollow, 10A Church Road, St Marks, Cheltenham GL51 7AN* Tel (01242) 230855
BARRALL, John Henry. b 31. BEd. Bps' Coll Cheshunt. **d** 61 **p** 62. C Digswell *St Alb* 61-65; C Aldershot St Mich *Guildf* 65-70; TV Hemel Hempstead *St Alb* 70-82; Perm to Offic 83-91; R Meppershall w Campton and Stondon 91-98; rtd 98; Perm to Offic *Ely* from 99 and *St Alb* from 01; OCF 97-03. *10 Caldecote Road, Ickwell, Biggleswade SG18 9EH* Tel (01767) 627407
E-mail john@barrall.fsnet.co.uk
BARRAND, George William (**Bill**). b 33. Lon Coll of Div 59. **d** 62 **p** 63. C Bucknall and Bagnall *Lich* 62-65; C Parr *Liv* 65-69; Australia from 70; rtd 98. *2/20 Riversdale Road, Yarra Junction Vic 3797, Australia* Tel (0061) (3) 5967 2592
BARRATT, The Ven Anthony John. b 19. Glas Univ MRCVS. Bible Churchmen's Coll Bris. **d** 49 **p** 50. C Slough *Ox* 49-52; SAMS Miss Cholchol Falkland Is 52-64; Hon Can Port Stanley 57-64; SAMS Miss Asunción Paraguay 64-70; Argentina 70-84; Adn Tucuman 73-84; rtd 84. *Couchill Villa, Couchill Farm Lane, Seaton EX12 3AL* Tel (01297) 21118
BARRATT, Mrs Elizabeth June. b 32. ACP65. Trin Coll Bris 75. **dss** 78 **d** 87 **p** 94. W Kilburn St Luke w St Simon and St Jude *Lon* 78-87; Par Dn 87-94; C 94-98; rtd 98; Hon C Kensal Rise St Mark and St Martin *Lon* from 99. *68A Bathhurst Gardens, London NW10 5HY* Tel (020) 8968 5951
BARRATT, Peter. b 29. Down Coll Cam BA53 MA57. Ridley Hall Cam 53. **d** 55 **p** 56. C Bebington *Ches* 55-58; C-in-c Cam St Martin CD *Ely* 58-61; V Cambridge St Martin 61-68; V Rawtenstall St Mary *Man* 68-83; AD Rossendale 80-83; V Bosley and N Rode w Wincle and Wildboarclough *Ches* 83-94; rtd 94; Perm to Offic *Ches* from 94. *10 Snab Wood Close, Little Neston, Neston CH64 0UP* Tel 0151-336 6641
BARRATT, Philip Norman. b 62. Aston Tr Scheme 87 St Steph Ho Ox 89 Coll of Resurr Mirfield 90. **d** 92 **p** 93. C Heywood St Luke w All So *Man* 92-96; V Thornham St Jas from 96. *St James's Vicarage, 120 Shaw Road, Rochdale OL16 4SQ* Tel (01706) 645256 Mobile 07775-646733
E-mail pn.barratt@zen.co.uk

BARRELL, Adrian Edward. b 36. Keble Coll Ox BA59. Ely Th Coll 59. **d** 62 **p** 63. C Plymouth St Jas Ham *Ex* 62-66; C Bideford 66-70; V Walkhampton 70-80; rtd 01. *Cartref, Dousland, Yelverton PL20 6PA* Tel (01822) 852612

BARRETT, Alan. b 48. Southn Univ BA69. Wycliffe Hall Ox 74. **d** 77 **p** 78. C Conisbrough *Sheff* 77-80; C Lower Homerton St Paul *Lon* 80-81; C-in-c Hounslow Gd Shep Beavers Lane CD 81-87; R Langdon Hills *Chelmsf* 87-97; P-in-c Tamworth *Lich* 97-03; V from 03; RD Tamworth 99-04. *The Vicarage, Hospital Street, Tamworth B79 7EE* Tel and fax (01827) 62446 *or* tel 68339 E-mail alan.barrett@breathemail.net

BARRETT, Alastair David. b 75. Fitzw Coll Cam BA97 MA01 Birm Univ BD00. Qu Coll Birm MA01. **d** 01 **p** 02. C Sutton Coldfield St Chad *Birm* 01-04; C Oldbury, Langley and Londonderry from 04. *St Mark's Vicarage, 15 St Mark's Road, Smethwick B67 6QF* Tel 0121-429 1149 E-mail alastair.barrett@btopenworld.com

BARRETT, Mrs Alexandra Mary. b 75. Clare Coll Cam BA96 MA99. Westcott Ho Cam 00. **d** 03 **p** 04. C Godmanchester *Ely* 03-07; R Buckden w the Offords from 07. *The Vicarage, Church Street, Buckden, St Neots PE19 5TL* Tel (01480) 810371 Mobile 07896-175631 E-mail ally.barrett@btopenworld.com

BARRETT, Arthur. *See* BARRETT, Kenneth Arthur Lambart

BARRETT, Christopher Paul. b 49. AKC71 St Aug Coll Cant 71. **d** 72 **p** 73. C Tupsley *Heref* 72-75; C Ex St Thos 75-79; R Atherington and High Bickington 79-83; V Burrington 79-83; Asst Dir of Educn 79-87; P-in-c Sticklepath 83-85; P-in-c Barnstaple 83-85; TV 85-90; V Whipton 90-99; TV Ex St Thos and Em 99-05; Chapl Burton Hosps NHS Trust from 05. *Queen's Hospital, Belvedere Road, Burton-on-Trent DE13 0RB* Tel (01283) 566333 *or* (01332) 516345 E-mail paul.barrett@burtonh-tr.wmids.nhs.uk

BARRETT, Clive. b 55. Ox Univ BA76 MA80 CertEd77 Leeds Univ PhD98. St Steph Ho Ox 80. **d** 83 **p** 84. C Wakef Cathl 83-87; Asst Chapl Leeds Univ 87-97; Dioc Development Rep 89-92; P-in-c Middleton St Cross 98-07; Co Ecum Development Officer W Yorks from 07; Hon C Headingley from 08. *West Yorkshire Ecumenical Council, Hinsley Hall, 62 Headingley Lane, Leeds LS6 2BX* Tel 0113-261 8053 Mobile 07966-540699 E-mail clivebarrett@wyec.co.uk

BARRETT, Canon Derek Leonard. b 25. St Fran Coll Brisbane ThL57. **d** 57 **p** 58. Australia 57-63; C Ramsgate St Geo *Cant* 64-65; C Putney St Mary *S'wark* 65-67; V Kidderminster St Jo *Worc* 67-77; V Stourbridge St Thos 77-90; RD Stourbridge 83-89; Hon Can Worc Cathl 87-90; rtd 90; Perm to Offic *Glouc* and *Worc* 90-02. *Lotty Leven, Crystal Waters, M/S 16, Maleny Qld 4552, Australia* Tel (0061) (7) 5494 4710

BARRETT, Gary John. b 46. Sarum & Wells Th Coll 87. **d** 90 **p** 91. NSM Guernsey St Peter Port *Win* 90-97; Chapl Eliz Coll Guernsey 93-97; P-in-c Westham *Chich* 97-98; V from 98. *The Vicarage, 6 Rattle Road, Westham, Pevensey BN24 5DE* Tel (01323) 762294

BARRETT, John Joseph James. b 38. Lon Univ BD65. Sarum & Wells Th Coll. **d** 78 **p** 78. C Danbury *Chelmsf* 78-80; Ind Chapl 80-89; C Dovercourt 80-83; TV Dovercourt and Parkeston 83-89; V Rubery *Birm* 89-04; rtd 04; Perm to Offic *Sheff* from 04. *4 Arran Hill, Thrybergh, Rotherham S65 4BH* Tel (01709) 850788 E-mail rev.barrett@btinternet.com

BARRETT, Jonathan Murray. b 68. Oak Hill Th Coll BA98. **d** 98 **p** 99. C Pennycross *Ex* 98-02; TV Plymouth Em, St Paul Efford and St Aug 02-08; V Thurnby w Stoughton *Leic* from 08. *The Vicarage, Thurnby, Leicester LE7 9PN* Tel 0116-241 2263

BARRETT, Canon Kenneth. b 42. Univ of Wales (Lamp) BA64. St Steph Ho Ox 65. **d** 67 **p** 68. C Poulton-le-Fylde *Blackb* 67-69; C S Shore H Trin 69-72; V Brierfield 72-83; V Chorley St Geo 83-07; Hon Can Blackb Cathl from 03; rtd 07; Perm to Offic *Blackb* from 07. *24 Astley Road, Chorley PR7 1RR* Tel (01257) 233421

BARRETT, Kenneth Arthur Lambart. b 60. CITC BTh94. **d** 97 **p** 98. C Seagoe *D & D* 97-00; I Dublin Booterstown *D & G* 00-04; I Dublin Mt Merrion 00-04; I Boyle and Elphin w Aghanagh, Kilbryan etc *K, E & A* 04-08; I Taunagh w Kilmactranny, Ballysumaghan etc 04-08; I Rossorry *Clogh* from 08. *Rossorry Rectory, Rossorry, Enniskillen BT74 7JZ* Tel (028) 6632 0239

BARRETT, Canon Kenneth Sydney. b 26. Roch Th Coll 60. **d** 62 **p** 63. C Wollaton *S'well* 62-65; C Hucknall Torkard 65-67; R Collie Australia 67-73; R Mandurah 73-92; Can Bunbury 76-92; rtd 92. *PO Box 818, 2 Loxton Street, Mandurah WA 6210, Australia* Tel and fax (0061) (8) 9581 2519 E-mail joykenb@westnet.com.au

BARRETT, Mrs Marion Lily. b 54. Ex Univ BA01 SRN75. SWMTC 91. **d** 94 **p** 95. C St Mawgan w St Ervan and St Eval *Truro* 94-97; C St Breoke and Egloshayle 97-98; Asst Chapl R Cornwall Hosps Trust 98-99; Chapl 00-05; R St Mewan w Mevagissey and St Ewe *Truro* from 05. *The Rectory, St Mewan Lane, St Mewan, St Austell PL26 7DP* Tel (01726) 72679 E-mail marionstmewan@btinternet.com

BARRETT, Paul. *See* BARRETT, Christopher Paul

✠**BARRETT, The Rt Revd Peter Francis.** b 56. TCD BA78 MA81 MPhil84. CITC 78. **d** 81 **p** 82 **c** 03. C Drumachose *D & R* 81-83; C Dublin St Ann *D & G* 83-85; I Conwal Union w Gartan *D & R* 85-90; I Belfast St Geo *Conn* 90-94; Chapl TCD 94-98; Min Can St Patr Cathl Dublin 94-96; Succ 96-98; Dean Waterford *C & O* 98-03; I Waterford w Killea, Drumcannon and Dunhill 98-03; Bp C & O 03-06. *Address temp unknown*

BARRETT, Mrs Rachel Jeanne Alexandra. b 56. Ex Univ BA78 PGCE79. SW Minl Tr Course 92. **d** 95 **p** 96. NSM Ex St Mark 95-96; NSM Ex St Mark, St Sidwell and St Matt 96-00; Chapl St Margaret's Sch Ex 00-05; Chapl Derby High Sch from 05. *Derby High School, Hillsway, Littleover, Derby DE23 3DT* Tel (01332) 514267 Fax 516085

BARRETT, Ronald Reginald. b 30. Roch Th Coll 61. **d** 64 **p** 65. C Spring Park *Cant* 64-66; C Thornton Heath St Jude 66-68; V Greengates *Bradf* 68-73; V Shelf 73-79; V Embsay w Eastby 79-87; V Farndon and Coddington *Ches* 87-92; rtd 92; Perm to Offic *Bradf* from 92. *12 Craigmore Drive, Ben Rhydding, Ilkley LS29 8PG* Tel (01943) 609713

BARRETT, Stephen David Norman. b 54. Aber Univ BSc75 Edin Univ BD78. Edin Th Coll 75. **d** 78 **p** 79. C Ardrossan *Glas* 78-80; R Peterhead *Ab* 80-81; Chapl HM Pris Peterhead 80-81; R Renfrew *Glas* 81-87; R Bishopbriggs 87-94; Chapl HM Pris Glas (Barlinnie) 87-94; Chapl Stobhill Gen Hosp 87-94; P-in-c Port Glas 94-99; R from 99. *St Mary's Rectory, Bardrainney Avenue, Port Glasgow PA14 6HB* Tel (01475) 707444

BARRETT, Mrs Susan Lesley. b 56. E Sussex Coll of HE CertEd77 BEd78. WMMTC 03. **d** 06. NSM Bowbrook N *Worc* 06-07; NSM Droitwich Spa from 07. *55-57 High Street, Feckenham, Redditch B96 6HU* Tel and fax (01527) 893866 Mobile 07717-412441 E-mail sue@artmetal.co.uk

BARRIBAL, Richard James Pitt. b 45. Trin Coll Bris. **d** 80 **p** 81. C Northampton St Giles *Pet* 80-82; V Long Buckby w Watford 82-86; Perm to Offic *Pet* 86-00 and *Leic* 00-08; P-in-c Welham, Glooston and Cranoe and Stonton Wyville *Leic* from 08. *45 Knights End Road, Great Bowden, Market Harborough LE16 7EY* Tel (01858) 431495 E-mail r.barribal@ntlworld.com

BARRIE, John Arthur. b 38. K Coll Lon 58 Bps' Coll Cheshunt 59. **d** 63 **p** 64. C Southgate St Mich *Lon* 63-66; CF 66-88; Sen CF 88-93; Chapl Guards Chpl Lon 88-92; QHC 91-93; P-in-c Heref H Trin 93-96; P-in-c Breinton 95-96; V St Marylebone St Mark Hamilton Terrace *Lon* from 96; Ecum Adv Two Cities Area from 99. *St Mark's Vicarage, 114 Hamilton Terrace, London NW8 9UT* Tel (020) 7328 4373 *or* 7624 4065 E-mail john.barrie1@btopenworld.com

BARRIE, Mrs Rosemary. **d** 07 **p** 08. NSM St Marylebone St Mark Hamilton Terrace *Lon* from 07. *St Mark's Vicarage, 114 Hamilton Terrace, London NW8 9UT* Tel (020) 7328 4373 E-mail rosybarrie1@btinternet.com

BARRINGTON, Dominic Matthew Jesse. b 62. Hatf Coll Dur BA84 MSc85 LTCL. Ripon Coll Cuddesdon BA94 MA98 Ch Div Sch of Pacific MTS95. **d** 95 **p** 96. C Mortlake w E Sheen *S'wark* 95-98; Chapl St Chad's Coll Dur 98-03; P-in-c Kettering SS Pet and Paul from 03. *The Rectory, Church Walk, Kettering NN16 0DJ* Tel and fax (01536) 513385 Mobile 07720-704953 E-mail dominic@peterandpaul.org.uk

✠**BARRINGTON-WARD, The Rt Revd Simon.** b 30. KCMG01. Magd Coll Cam BA53 MA57. Wycliffe Coll Toronto Hon DD Westcott Ho Cam 54. **d** 56 **p** 57 **c** 85. Chapl Magd Coll Cam 56-60; Nigeria 60 63; Fell and Dean of Chpl Magd Coll Cam 63-69; Prin Crowther Hall CMS Tr Coll Selly Oak 69-74; Gen Sec CMS 75-85; Hon Can Derby Cathl 75-85; Chapl to The Queen 84-85; Bp Cov 85-97; rtd 97; Hon Fell Magd Coll Cam from 87; Hon Asst Chapl from 98; Hon Asst Bp Ely from 97. *4 Searle Street, Cambridge CB4 3DB* Tel (01223) 740460 E-mail sb292@cam.ac.uk

BARRODALE, Canon George Bryan. b 44. St Mich Coll Llan 67. **d** 69 **p** 70. C Maindee Newport *Mon* 69-72; TV Merthyr Tydfil and Cyfarthfa *Llan* 72-76; R Cotgrave and P-in-c Owthorpe *S'well* 76-00; RD Bingham 94-00; CF (TA) 76-86; V Beeston *S'well* 00-06; Hon Can S'well Minster 97-06; rtd 06; Perm to Offic *S'well* from 06. *2 Daphne Close, Branston, Lincoln LN4 1PQ* Tel (01522) 826381 E-mail bbarrodale@aol.com

BARRON, Arthur Henry. b 45. Solicitor 72. SEITE 99. **d** 02 **p** 03. NSM Addiscombe St Mary Magd w St Martin *S'wark* 02-06; Perm to Offic 06-07; NSM Woodmansterne from 07; Chapl Asst St Mary's NHS Trust Paddington 05-09; Chapl Guy's and St Thos' NHS Foundn Trust from 09. *23 Little Woodcote Lane, Purley CR8 3PZ* Tel (020) 8660 1921 Mobile 07710-275977 E-mail art_barron@hotmail.com *or* art.barron@gstt.nhs.uk

BARRON, John William. b 66. Imp Coll Lon BSc88. Cranmer Hall Dur 06. **d** 08 **p** 09. C Whickham Dur from 08. *7A Coalway Drive, Whickham, Newcastle upon Tyne NE16 4BT* Tel 0191-488 6661 E-mail john.barron@ntlworld.com

BARRON, Kurt Karl. b 60. Chich Th Coll BTh92. **d** 92 **p** 93. C Bulwell St Mary *S'well* 92-97; TV Southend *Chelmsf* 97-01; P-in-c Mansfield St Lawr *S'well* 01-08. *Address temp unknown* E-mail kurt.barron@btopenworld.com

BARRON, Leslie Gill. b 44. ACII69. Lich Th Coll 67. **d** 70 **p** 71. C Bishopwearmouth Ch Ch *Dur* 70-72; C Bishopwearmouth St Mary V w St Pet CD 72-75; C Harton 75-77; V Lumley 77-88; P-in-c Hendon and Sunderland 88-90; R Hendon 90-94; P-in-c Ushaw Moor 94-95; V Bearpark and Ushaw Moor 95-04; rtd 08. *34 Brecongill Close, Hartlepool TS24 8PH* Tel (01429) 291197 E-mail l.barron@ntlworld.com

BARRON, Richard Davidson. b 51. Lon Univ BSc74. Trin Coll Bris 75. **d** 78 **p** 79. C Bradley *Wakef* 78-81; C Heworth H Trin *York* 81-82; TV 82-89; Chapl York Distr Hosp 82-86; R Greenhithe St Mary *Roch* from 89. *The Rectory, 131 Mounts Road, Greenhithe DA9 9ND* Tel (01322) 382031 E-mail richard.barron@diocese-rochester.org

BARRON, Canon Victor Robert. b 45. St Luke's Coll Ex CertEd70. Trin Coll Bris 76. **d** 78 **p** 79. C Rainham *Chelmsf* 78-81; V Easton H Trin w St Gabr and St Lawr and St Jude *Bris* 81-89; TR Kinson *Sarum* 89-00; RD Poole 94-00; Can and Preb Sarum Cathl 98-00; rtd 00; Perm to Offic *Sarum* 00-05; Hon C Witchampton, Stanbridge and Long Crichel etc 05-07. *159 Middlehill Road, Wimborne BH21 2HJ* Tel (01202) 885434 E-mail vicbarron@onetel.com

BARROW (*née* DONSON), Mrs Margaret Christine. b 44. Homerton Coll Cam CertEd65. Westcott Ho Cam 08. **d** 09. NSM Girton *Ely* from 09. *2 Cockerton Road, Girton, Cambridge CB3 0QW* Tel (01223) 575089 E-mail mcbarrow@mac.com

BARROW, Paul Beynon. b 48. Liv Univ LLB69 Man Univ MA01. St Steph Ho Ox 02. **d** 04 **p** 05. NSM Ches H Trin 04-05; P-in-c Hargrave from 05. *The Vicarage, Church Lane, Hargrave, Chester CH3 7RN* Tel (01829) 781378 Mobile 07792-154388 E-mail paul.barrow6@btopenworld.com

BARRY, Colin Lionel. b 49. Open Univ BSc94. Bp Attwell Tr Inst 85. **d** 96 **p** 97. NSM Arbory *S & M* from 96. *80 Ballanorris Crescent, Ballabeg, Castletown, Isle of Man IM9 4ER* Tel (01624) 823080

BARRY, Ms Jacqueline Françoise. b 44. Univ of Bordeaux II LSocEth86 MSoc87 York Univ PGCE91. Ridley Hall Cam. **d** 99 **p** 00. C Sydenham H Trin *S'wark* 99-03; C Paddington Em Harrow Road *Lon* from 03; C W Kilburn St Luke w St Simon and St Jude from 03. *Emmanuel Vicarage, 44C Fermoy Road, London W9 3NH* Tel (020) 8969 0438 E-mail jackie.barry@lineone.net

BARRY, Canon Jonathan Peter Oulton. b 47. TCD BA70 MA73 Hull Univ BA73 QUB PhD84. Ripon Hall Ox 73. **d** 74 **p** 75. C Dundela St Mark *D & D* 74-79; I Ballyphilip w Ardquin 79-85; Dioc Info Officer 80-90; I Comber from 85; Preb St Audoen St Patr Cathl Dublin from 01. *The Rectory, 12 Windmill Hill, Comber, Newtownards BT23 5WH* Tel (028) 9187 2283 E-mail comber@down.anglican.org

BARRY, Keith Gordon. b 67. TCD BA92 MA. CITC 92. **d** 94 **p** 95. C Templemore *D & R* 94-97; V Choral Derry Cathl 94-95; Dean's V 95-97; P-in-c 97; CF 97-07; Sen CF from 07. *c/o MOD Chaplains (Army)* Tel (01980) 615804 Fax 615800

BARRY, Nicholas Brian Paul. b 61. Leic Univ BA83. St Steph Ho Ox 84. **d** 87 **p** 88. C St John's Wood *Lon* 87-90; Chapl RAF from 90. *Chaplaincy Services, HQ Personnel and Training Command, RAF High Wycombe HP14 4UE* Tel (01494) 496800 Fax 496343 E-mail nicholas.barry247@mod.uk

BARSLEY, Canon Margaret Ann. b 39. Totley Hall Coll CertEd60. EMMTC 79. **dss** 83 **d** 87 **p** 94. Kirton in Holland *Linc* 83-89; NSM 87-89; NSM Skirbeck Quarter 89-96; P-in-c Swineshead 96-99; V 99-04; RD Holland W 97-04; Can and Preb Linc Cathl from 00; rtd 04. *44 Sentance Crescent, Kirton, Boston PE20 1XF* Tel (01205) 723824 E-mail margaret@churchlane8539.freeserve.co.uk

BARTER, Christopher Stuart. b 49. Chich Th Coll. **d** 84 **p** 85. C Margate St Jo *Cant* 84-88; V Whitwood and Chapl Castleford, Normanton and Distr Hosp 88-95; P-in-c Ravensthorpe and AIDS Cllr W Yorks HA 95-98; TV Gt Yarmouth *Nor* 98-02; R Somersham w Pidley and Oldhurst *Ely* from 02; P-in-c Holywell w Needingworth from 07; RD St Ives from 06. *The Rectory, Rectory Lane, Somersham, Huntingdon PE28 3EL* Tel (01487) 840676 E-mail christopher.barter@btopenworld.com

BARTER, The Very Revd Donald. b 34. St Fran Coll Brisbane ThL69 ACT ThSchol74. **d** 69 **p** 70. C Townsville Australia 69-72; R Mareeba 72-76; R Ingham 76-81; Adn of the W and R Mt Isa 81-86; Dean Townsville 86-90; Chapl Miss to Seamen 86-90; Chapl HM Police Service 88-90; Appeals Dir SPCK 90-93; Lic to Offic *Leic* 90-93; Australia from 93; Asst to Dean St Jas Cathl 94-00. *49 Macrossan Street, South Townsville Qld 4810, Australia* Tel and fax (0061) (7) 4772 7036 Mobile 414-989593 E-mail dba18613@bigpond.net.au

BARTER, Geoffrey Roger. b 41. Bris Univ BSc63. Clifton Th Coll 65. **d** 67 **p** 68. C Normanton *Derby* 67-70; C Rainham *Chelmsf* 70-75; V Plumstead St Jo w St Jas and St Paul *S'wark* 75-82; V Frogmore *St Alb* 82-01; rtd 01; Perm to Offic *Chich* from 02. *45 West Front Road, Pagham, Bognor Regis PO21 4SZ* Tel (01243) 262522

BARTER, Leonard Reginald Treseder. b 38. **d** 95. OLM St Stythians w Perranarworthal and Gwennap *Truro* from 95.

Vellandrucia Foundry, Stithians, Truro TR3 7BU Tel (01209) 860341

BARTER, Michael Christopher Charles. b 74. Coll of Resurr Mirfield 07. **d** 09. C Hangleton *Chich* from 09. *30 Bigwood Avenue, Hove BN3 6FQ* Tel (01273) 727125 E-mail mikeccbarter@hotmail.co.uk

BARTER, Susan Kathleen. b 53. Open Univ MBA97 Anglia Ruskin Univ MA09. Ridley Hall Cam 01. **d** 03 **p** 04. C Happisburgh, Walcott, Hempstead w Eccles etc *Nor* 03-06; C Bacton w Edingthorpe w Witton and Ridlington 04-06; C Ward End w Bordesley Green *Birm* from 06. *St Paul's Vicarage, 405 Belchers Lane, Birmingham B9 5SY* Tel 0121-772 0418 Mobile 07778-063644 E-mail susan@sbarter777.co.uk

BARTHOLOMEW, Craig Gerald. b 61. UNISA BTh82 Potchefstroom Univ MA92 Bris Univ PhD97. Wycliffe Hall Ox BA84 MA88. **d** 86 **p** 87. S Africa 86-92; C Pinetown Ch Ch 87-89; Lect Geo Whitefield Coll Cape Town 89-92; Research Fell Glos Univ 97-04; Perm to Offic *Glouc* 98-04; Canada from 04. *Redeemer University College, 777 Garner Road, Ancaster ON L9K 1J4, Canada* Tel (001) (905) 648 2139 ext 4270 E-mail cbartho@redeemer.ca

BARTHOLOMEW, David Grant. b 50. Univ of Wales (Lamp) BA77. Chich Th Coll 91. **d** 93 **p** 94. C Petersfield *Portsm* 93-96; R Etton w Helpston and Maxey Pet 96-98; R Burghclere w Newtown and Ecchinswell w Sydmonton *Win* from 98. *The Rectory, Well Street, Burghclere, Newbury RG20 9HS* Tel (01635) 278470 E-mail davidrectory@aol.com

BARTLAM, Alan Thomas. b 51. Bris Univ BEd74. Linc Th Coll 88. **d** 90 **p** 91. C Longdon-upon-Tern, Rodington, Uppington etc *Lich* 90-92; C Tilstock and Whixall 92-95; V Tilstock, Edstaston and Whixall 95-98; R Bewcastle, Stapleton and Kirklinton etc *Carl* 98-06; V Streetly *Lich* from 06. *All Saints' Vicarage, 2 Foley Church Close, Sutton Coldfield B74 3JX* Tel 0121-353 2392

BARTLE, Canon David Colin. b 29. Em Coll Cam BA53 MA57. Ridley Hall Cam 53. **d** 55 **p** 56. C Birm St Martin 55-57; C Boscombe St Jo *Win* 57-60; V Lowestoft St Jo *Nor* 60-70; P-in-c Thetford St Cuth w H Trin 70-72; P-in-c Thetford St Mary 70-72; P-in-c Thetford St Pet w St Nic 70-72; TR Thetford 72-75; P-in-c Kilverstone 70-75; P-in-c Croxton 70-75; Teacher Bournemouth Sch 75-83; R Brantham w Stutton *St E* 83-90; RD Samford 86-90; P-in-c Roxwell *Chelmsf* 90-93; Dioc Dir of Ords 90-93; Dioc Lay Min Adv 90-93; Hon Can Chelmsf Cathl 91-93; rtd 93; Perm to Offic *Win* 93-98; Chapl R Bournemouth and Christchurch Hosps NHS Trust 98-00. *40 Blue Waters Drive, Paignton TQ4 6JE* Tel (01803) 843456 E-mail dbartle8@aol.com

BARTLE, Canon Reginald Stephen. b 24. K Coll Lon AKC51 BD52. **d** 52 **p** 53. C Penge Ch Ch w H Trin *Roch* 52-55; SAMS 55-79; Chile 55-70; Adn Chile 64-70; Hon Can Chile from 64; NW Area Sec SAMS 70-73; Home Sec 73-79; C Tunbridge Wells St Jas 80-83; rtd 83; Perm to Offic *St D* 84-94; *Chelmsf* 94-00; *S'wark* 00-01; *Cant* 01-03. *24 Bromley College, London Road, Bromley BR1 1PE* Tel (020) 8460 7128

BARTLE-JENKINS, Canon Leonard Christmas. b 13. Univ of Wales (Lamp) BA35. Lich Th Coll 35. **d** 38 **p** 39. C Fleur-de-Lis *Mon* 38-41; C Trevethin 41-47; V Llangattock-vibon-Avel 47-55; V Bassaleg 55-74; Can St Woolos Cathl 64-82; RD Bassaleg 67-82; R Michaelston-y-Fedw and Rudry 74-82; rtd 82; Lic to Offic *Mon* from 82; Perm to Offic *Llan* from 82. *c/o Mrs C Judd, 13 Grove Road, Bridgend CF31 3EF*

BARTLE-JENKINS, Paul. b 43. Bris & Glouc Tr Course. **d** 84 **p** 86. NSM Bris St Agnes and St Simon w St Werburgh 84-87; NSM Bris St Paul's from 87; P-in-c from 07. *188A Henleaze Road, Westbury-on-Trym, Bristol BS9 4NE* Tel 0117-962 0286 E-mail fatherpaul00@hotmail.com

BARTLEM, Gregory John. b 68. Ox Brookes Univ BA05. Qu Coll Birm 07. **d** 09. NSM Cheylesmore *Cov* from 09. *17 Courtleet Road, Coventry CV3 5GS* Tel (024) 7650 5524 Mobile 07967-662184 E-mail greg.bartlem@covcofe.org

BARTLES-SMITH, The Ven Douglas Leslie. b 37. St Edm Hall Ox BA61 MA65. Wells Th Coll 61. **d** 63 **p** 64. C Westmr St Steph w St Jo *Lon* 63-68; P-in-c Camberwell St Mich w All So w Em *S'wark* 68-72; V 72-75; V Battersea St Luke 75-85; RD Battersea 81-85; Adn S'wark 85-04; rtd 04; Chapl to The Queen 96-07; Perm to Offic *Lich* from 04. *18 Vane Road, Shrewsbury SY3 7HB* Tel (01743) 363282

BARTLETT, Alan Bennett. b 58. G&C Coll Cam BA81 MA85 Birm Univ PhD87 St Jo Coll Dur BA90. Cranmer Hall Dur 88. **d** 91 **p** 92. C Newc H Cross 91-94; C Newburn 94-96; Tutor Cranmer Hall Dur 96-08; V Dur St Giles from 08; P-in-c Shadforth and Sherburn from 08. *St Giles's Vicarage, Gilesgate, Durham DH1 1QQ* Tel 0191-384 2452 E-mail vicarsgg@live.co.uk

BARTLETT, Anthony Martin. b 43. Cranmer Hall Dur 74. **d** 77 **p** 78. C Heworth St Mary *Dur* 77-80; V Cleadon 80-84; CF (TA) 81-90; Prec Dur Cathl 85-87; V Harton 87-95; P-in-c Hendon 95-96; R 96-97; V Greenlands *Blackb* from 01. *St Anne's House, Salmesbury Avenue, Blackpool FY2 0PR* Tel (01253) 353900 E-mail bcressell@aol.com

BARTLETT, David John. b 36. Pemb Coll Ox BA61. Linc Th Coll 63. **d** 65 **p** 66. C Wollaton *S'well* 65-70; V Woodthorpe 70-83; V Farnsfield 83-01; P-in-c Kirklington w Hockerton 83-01; RD S'well 83-93; Chapl Rodney Sch Kirklington 83-01; rtd 01; Perm to Offic *S'well* from 01. *6 De Havilland Way, Farndon Road, Newark NG24 4RF* Tel (01636) 651582

BARTLETT, David William. b 59. Trin Coll Bris 89. **d** 91 **p** 92. C Frinton *Chelmsf* 91-95; TV Eston w Normanby *York* 95-96; Assoc P Worksop St Jo *S'well* 96-01; TV Trunch *Nor* from 01. *The Rectory, Clipped Hedge Lane, Southrepps, Norwich NR11 8NS* Tel (01263) 833404

BARTLETT, George Frederick. b 34. Clifton Th Coll 61. **d** 64 **p** 65. C Branksome St Clem *Sarum* 64-71; V Gt Baddow *Chelmsf* 71-72; Perm to Offic *Win* 81-87; rtd 99. *8 Glencarron Way, Southampton SO16 7EF* Tel (023) 8032 5162
E-mail george.bartlett@cwcom.net

BARTLETT, Prof John Raymond. b 37. BNC Ox BA59 MA62 BLitt62 TCD MA70 LittD94. Linc Th Coll 61. **d** 63 **p** 64. C W Bridgford *S'well* 63-66; Lect Div TCD 66-86; Assoc Prof Bibl Studies 86-92; Fell 75-92; Prof Past Th 90-01; Prin CITC 89-01; Treas Ch Ch Cathl Dublin 86-88; Prec 88-01; rtd 01. *102 Sorrento Road, Dalkey, Co Dublin, Republic of Ireland* Tel (00353) (1) 284 7786 E-mail jrbartlett@eircom.net

BARTLETT, Kenneth Vincent John. b 36. OBE93. Oriel Coll Ox BA61 BTh63. Ripon Hall Ox 61. **d** 63 **p** 64. C Paddington St Jas *Lon* 63-67; Lic to Offic from 67; rtd 01. *25 Tudor Road, Kingston-upon-Thames KT2 6AS* Tel (020) 8541 0378
E-mail shaa4949@aol.com

BARTLETT, Canon Maurice Edward. b 33. G&C Coll Cam BA59 MA63. Wells Th Coll 59. **d** 60 **p** 61. C Batley All SS *Wakef* 60-64; Bp's Dom Chapl 64-66; Dir of Ords 64-66; Asst Chapl HM Pris Wakef 64-66; V Allerton *Liv* 66-81; V Lancaster St Mary *Blackb* 81-97; Chapl HM Pris Lanc 81-97; Hon Can Blackb Cathl 87-97; rtd 97. *Waverley House, West Common, Bowness-on-Solway, Carlisle CA7 5AG*

BARTLETT, Michael Fredrick. b 52. Ex Univ BA74 Liv Univ BPhil75. Ven English Coll Rome 78 Ripon Coll Cuddesdon BA79 MA. **d** 79 **p** 80. C Kirkby *Liv* 79-82; C Wordsley *Lich* 82-83; TV 83-88; Chapl Wordsley Hosp 82-88; TV Redditch, The Ridge *Worc* 88-05; TR Redditch Ch the K from 05. *St Peter's House, Littlewoods, Redditch B97 5LB* Tel (01527) 545709

BARTLETT, Preb Michael George. b 35. S Dios Minl Tr Scheme 84. **d** 87 **p** 88. NSM Wimborne Minster and Holt *Sarum* 87-90; C Charlestown *Truro* 90-91; R St Endellion w Port Isaac and St Kew 91-06; Preb St Endellion 91-06; rtd 06; Perm to Offic *Truro* from 07. *Chapel House, St Austell Road, Probus, Truro TR2 4LF* Tel (01726) 884310

✠**BARTLETT, The Rt Revd Peter.** b 54. **d** 96 **p** 97 **c** 08. SAMS Bolivia 96-05; TV Parr *Liv* 05-08; Bp Paraguay from 08. *Iglesia Anglicana Paraguaya, Casilla de Correo 1124, Asunción, Paraguay* Tel (00595) (21) 200933 *or* 214795 E-mail iapar@sce.cnc.una.py

BARTLETT, Canon Richard Charles. b 68. St Kath Coll Liv BA90 Surrey Univ MA01. Westcott Ho Cam 91. **d** 94 **p** 95. C Wareham *Sarum* 94-98; Assoc V Ealing All SS *Lon* 98-02; Chapl Twyford C of E High Sch Acton 98-02; USPG Brazil 02-05; Hon Can Brasilia Cathl from 05; V Northwood H Trin *Lon* from 05; AD Harrow from 07. *Holy Trinity Vicarage, Gateway Close, Northwood HA6 2RP* Tel (01923) 825732
E-mail richard.bartlett@london.anglican.org

BARTON, Allan Benjamin. b 77. Univ Coll Lon BA98 York Univ MA99 PhD04. Ripon Coll Cuddesdon 05. **d** 08 **p** 09. C Louth *Linc* from 08. *15 Grosvenor Crescent, Louth LN11 0BD* Tel (01507) 603635 E-mail vitrearum@googlemail.com

BARTON, Andrew Edward. b 53. St Jo Coll Ox MA77 DPhil80 Idaho Univ MTh06 MRSC. Ridley Hall Cam 87. **d** 90 **p** 91. C Ringwood *Win* 90-94; R Baughurst, Ramsdell, Wolverton w Ewhurst etc 95-07; Lect K Alfred's Coll Win 95-98; R Auchterarder *St And* from 07; R Muthill from 07. *St Kessog's Rectory, High Street, Auchterarder PH3 1AD* Tel (01764) 662525 Mobile 00778-771651 E-mail james.kessog@gmail.com

BARTON, Anne. *See* BARTON, Margaret Anne

BARTON, Canon Arthur Michael. b 33. CCC Cam BA57 MA61. Wycliffe Hall Ox 57. **d** 59 **p** 60. Min Can Bradf Cathl 59-61; C Maltby *Sheff* 61-63; V Silsden *Bradf* 63-70; V Moor Allerton *Ripon* 70-81; TR 81-82; V Wetherby 82-98; Chapl HM YOI Wetherby 82-89; RD Harrogate *Ripon* 88-95; Hon Can Ripon Cathl 89-98; rtd 98; Perm to Offic *Ripon* from 98. *22 Ash Road, Harrogate HG2 8EG* Tel (01423) 870799
E-mail teambarton@aol.com

BARTON, The Ven Charles John Greenwood. b 36. ALCD63. **d** 63 **p** 64. C Luton St Mary Bredin 63-66; V Whitfield w W Langdon 66-75; V S Kensington St Luke *Lon* 75-83; AD Chelsea 80-83; Chief Broadcasting Officer for C of E 83-90; Adn Aston *Birm* 90-03; Can Res Birm Cathl 90-02; P in o Bickenhill 02-03, rtd 03; Perm to Offic *Cant* from 03; Abp's Communications Adv York 05-06; Acting Prin Adv to Abp York 07; Abp's Chapl and Researcher 08. *10 Stuart Court, Puckle Lane, Canterbury CT1 3LA* Tel (01227) 379688 Mobile 07743-118544
E-mail johnbarton@waitrose.com

BARTON, Dale. b 49. Selw Coll Cam BA71 MA76. Linc Th Coll 71. **d** 73 **p** 74. C Gosforth All SS *Newc* 73-77; Lesotho 77-81; Dep Warden CA Hostel Cam 82-83; C Shepton Mallet w Doulting *B & W* 83-88; TV Preston St Steph *Blackb* 88-96; V 96-99; Bp's Adv on Inter-Faith Relns 99-07; P-in-c Bradf St Clem from 07; P-in-c Bradf St Aug Undercliffe from 07. *The Vicarage, 294A Barkerend Road, Bradford BD3 9DF* Tel (01274) 665109 E-mail st.barton@ukonline.co.uk

BARTON, David Gerald Story. b 38. Selw Coll Cam BA62 MA66. Cuddesdon Coll 63. **d** 65 **p** 66. C Cowley St Jas *Ox* 65-67; C Hambleden 67-70; Hon C Hammersmith St Jo *Lon* 72-77; Hon C Paddington St Jas 77-81; Hd Master Soho Par Sch 81-88; Hon C Westmr St Jas 81-92; RE Project Officer Lon Dioc Bd for Schs 88-92; Dioc Schs Adv Ox 93-99; rtd 00; Hon C Iffley *Ox* 93-06; Perm to Offic from 06. *254 Iffley Road, Oxford OX4 1SE* Tel (01865) 240059 E-mail daviebarton@aol.com

BARTON, Edward. b 23. **d** 75 **p** 76. C Budock *Truro* 75-79; P-in-c St Stithians w Perranarworthal 79-80; V St Stythians w Perranarworthal and Gwennap 80-82; rtd 88; Perm to Offic *Truro* from 98. *Riverside, 5 Riviera Terrace, Malpas, Truro TR1 1SR* Tel (01872) 271686

BARTON, Canon Geoffrey. b 27. Oriel Coll Ox BA48 MA52. Chich Th Coll 49. **d** 51 **p** 52. C Arnold *S'well* 51-53; C E Retford 53-54; V Mirfield Eastthorpe St Paul *Wakef* 54-60; V Boroughbridge w Roecliffe *Ripon* 60-73; V Aldborough w Boroughbridge and Roecliffe 73; P-in-c Farnham w Scotton and Staveley and Copgrove 73-74; R 74-77; Chapl Roundway Hosp Devizes 77-92; Can and Preb Sarum Cathl 86-92; rtd 92; Perm to Offic *Sarum* from 01. *4B Willow House, Downlands Road, Devizes SN10 5EA* Tel (01380) 725311

BARTON (née CRABB), Helen Maria. b 56. Lon Bible Coll BA83 St Jo Coll Dur MA04 St Mary's Coll Strawberry Hill PGCE98. Cranmer Hall Dur 01. **d** 03 **p** 04. C Wisley w Pyrford *Guildf* 03-04; C Lanchester *Dur* 04-06; C Hexham *Newc* 06-08; V Ulgham from 08; V Widdrington from 08. *The Vicarage, Grangemoor Road, Widdrington, Morpeth NE61 5PU* Tel (01670) 790389 E-mail hmbarton@fsmail.net

BARTON, Mrs Jean Valerie. b 42. Wycliffe Hall Ox BTh01. **d** 02 **p** 03. NSM Harwell w Chilton *Ox* 02-07; NSM Saddleworth *Man* from 07. *16 Sykes Close, Greenfield, Oldham OL3 7PT* Tel (01457) 878995 E-mail jeanbarton@onetel.com

BARTON, John. *See* BARTON, The Ven Charles John Greenwood

BARTON, Canon John. b 25. MBE91. Keble Coll Ox BA48 MA50. Ely Th Coll 48. **d** 50 **p** 51. C Worksop St Anne *S'well* 50-53; C Harrogate St Wilfrid *Ripon* 53-56; V Beeston Hill H Spirit 56-60; Chapl Stanley Royd and Pinderfields Hosps Wakef 60-72; RD Wakef 68-72; Chapl Jo Radcliffe Hosp and Radcliffe Infirmary 72-90; Chapl Chu Hosp Ox 72-89; Hon Can Ch Ch *Ox* 77-94; RD Cowley 89-94; rtd 90; Perm to Offic *Ox* 94-01 and *Roch* from 01. *150A Longlands Road, Sidcup DA15 7LF* Tel (020) 8300 7073

BARTON, Prof John. b 48. Keble Coll Ox BA69 MA73 Mert Coll Ox DPhil74 St Cross Coll Ox DLitt88. **d** 73 **p** 73. Jun Research Fell Mert Coll Ox 73-74; Lect St Cross Coll Ox 74-89; Fell 74-91; Chapl 79-91; Lect Th Ox Univ 74-89; Reader 89-91; Oriel and Laing Prof of Interp of HT Scrip from 91; Fell Oriel Coll Ox from 91; Can Th Win Cathl 91-03. *11 Withington Court, Abingdon OX14 3QA* Tel (01235) 525925
E-mail johnbarton@oriel.ox.ac.uk

BARTON, Canon John Christopher Peter. b 28. Trin Hall Cam BA51 MA56. Ridley Hall Cam 51. **d** 53 **p** 54. C Erith St Paul *Roch* 53-56; C Cockfosters Ch Ch CD *Lon* 56-64; V Welling *Roch* 64-75; P-in-c Malmesbury w Westport *Bris* 75-84; P-in-c Charlton w Brokenborough and Hankerton 80-84; V Malmesbury w Westport and Brokenborough 84-94; Hon Can Kigezi from 92; rtd 94; Perm to Offic *B & W* 94-07. *Orchard House, Orchard Road, Crewkerne TA18 7AF* Tel (01460) 72536

BARTON, John Michael. b 40. TCD BA62 Div Test. **d** 63 **p** 64. C Coleraine *Conn* 63-68; C Portadown St Mark *Arm* 68-71; I Carnteel and Crilly 71-83; I Derryloran 83-97; Bp's C Acton and Drumbanagher 97-99; Can Arm Cathl 94-09; Treas 98-01; Chan 01-09; rtd 09. *23 Strand Cottages, Sheskburn Avenue, Ballycastle BT54 6HR* Tel (028) 2076 9673

BARTON, Mrs Margaret Ann Edith. b 48. Newc Univ BA71. EMMTC 95. **d** 98 **p** 99. NSM Castle Bytham w Creeton *Linc* 98-04; P-in-c Corby Glen from 04. *Blanchland House, Swinstead Road, Corby Glen, Grantham NG33 4NU* Tel (01476) 550763

BARTON, Margaret Anne. b 54. St Anne's Coll Ox BA76 MA80 DPhil81 Selw Coll Cam BA89 MA94. Ridley Hall Cam 87. **d** 90 **p** 94. Par Dn Burley Ville *Win* 90-94; Chapl K Alfred Coll Win 98; Dioc Development and Research Officer for Liturg Matters 99-01; NSM Baughurst, Ramsdell, Wolverton w Ewhurst etc 99-01, Asst Chapl Gen Synod 99-00; rtd 01. *St Kessog's Rectory, High Street, Auchterarder FH3 1AD* Tel (01764) 662525
E-mail rev.anne.barton@ntlworld.com

BARTON, Michael. *See* BARTON, Canon Arthur Michael

BARTON, Patrick Michael. Huddersfield Univ BA. BTh. **d** 05 **p** 06. C Arm St Mark 05-08; I Ballintoy w Rathlin and

Dunseverick *Conn* from 08. *The Rectory, 2 Ballinlea Road, Ballintoy, Ballycastle BT54 6NQ* Tel (028) 2076 8155
E-mail patribart@aol.com

BARTON, Peter. *See* BARTON, Canon John Christopher Peter

BARTON, Canon Samuel David. b 45. d 84 p 85. C Ballywillan *Conn* 84-86; I Aghadowey w Kilrea *D & R* 86-92; Bp's C Fahan Lower and Upper from 92; Dioc Educn Co-ord from 94; Dioc Communications Officer from 98; Can Raphoe Cathl from 98. *The Rectory, Cahir O'Doherty Avenue, Buncrana, Co Donegal, Republic of Ireland* Tel (00353) (74) 936 1154 Fax 936 3726
E-mail dco@derry.anglican.org *or* sbarton@iol.ie

BARTON (née McVEIGH), Mrs Sandra. b 58. Reading Univ BA80. Cranmer Hall Dur 95. d 95 p 96. C Stranton *Dur* 95-98; P-in-c Blackhall, Castle Eden and Monkhesleden 98-99; R 99-02; Perm to Offic *St E* from 08. *The Old Village Stores, 6 The Street, Freckenham, Bury St Edmunds IP28 8HZ* Tel (01638) 720048 E-mail revsandiebarton@gmail.com

BARTON, Stephen Christian. b 52. Macquarie Univ (NSW) BA75 DipEd75 Lanc Univ MA78 K Coll Lon PhD92. Cranmer Hall Dur 91. d 93 p 94. NSM Neville's Cross St Jo CD *Dur* 93-00; NSM Dur St Marg and Neville's Cross St Jo 00-06; Perm to Offic *Newc* from 06. *The Vicarage, Grangemoor Road, Widdrington, Morpeth NE61 5PU* Tel (01670) 790389
E-mail s.c.barton@durham.ac.uk

BARTON, Stephen William. b 50. St Jo Coll Cam BA73 Leeds Univ MPhil81. Coll of Resurr Mirfield 75. d 77 p 78. C Horton *Bradf* 77-80; USPG 80-92; Presbyter Dhaka St Thos Bangladesh 81-88; St Andr Th Coll Dhaka 88-92; TV Southampton (City Cen) *Win* 92-98; Chapl Manager Birm Women's Healthcare NHS Trust 99-06; rtd 06. *290 City Road, Birmingham B16 0NE* Tel 0121-429 2176 E-mail notrabnehpets@yahoo.co.uk

BARTON, Timothy Charles. b 47. Sarum & Wells Th Coll 73. d 76 p 77. C Upholland *Liv* 76-80; V Dalton from 80. *88 Lyndhurst Avenue, Skelmersdale WN8 6UH* Tel (01695) 733148

BARTON, Trevor James. b 50. St Alb Minl Tr Scheme 79. d 87 p 88. NSM Hemel Hempstead *St Alb* from 87. *46 Crossfell Road, Hemel Hempstead HP3 8RQ* Tel and fax (01442) 251537
E-mail trevorbarton@hotmail.com

BARWELL, Brian Bernard Beale. b 30. Preston Poly CertEd79. AKC59 St Boniface Warminster 59. d 60 p 61. C Heywood St Jas *Man* 60-63; V Smallbridge 63-69; V Farington *Blackb* 69-72; C-in-c Blackb St Luke w St Phil 72-75; C Standish 75-76; Lic to Offic 76-92; rtd 92; Perm to Offic *Blackb* from 92. *70 Claytongate, Coppull, Chorley PR7 4PS* Tel (01257) 794251

BARZEY, Ms Michele Alison Lesley. b 63. Trin Coll Bris BA94. d 94. C Gravelly Hill *Birm* 94-96; Perm to Offic from 00. *6 Topcliffe House, Yatesbury Avenue, Birmingham B35 6DU* Tel 0121-730 3094

BASAVARAJ, Mrs Patricia Margaret. b 37. SRN61 SCM62. d 00. OLM Verwood *Sarum* 00-07; Perm to Offic 07-08. *Hope Cottage, Church Hill, Verwood BH31 6HT* Tel (01202) 822920

BASFORD HOLBROOK, Colin Eric. b 42. St Steph Ho Ox 73. d 75 p 76. C Dovecot *Liv* 75-78; V Hollinfare 79-83; CMS 83-88; Cyprus 83-91; Chapl Athens w Kifissia, Patras, Thessaloniki etc *Eur* 91-93; Chapl Athens w Patras, Thessaloniki and Voula 93-94; rtd 02. *7 St Catherine's Close, Uttoxeter ST14 8EF*

BASH, Anthony. b 52. Bris Univ LLB73 LLM76 Glas Univ BD88 Clare Hall Cam PhD96. Westcott Ho Cam 94. d 96 p 97. C Kingston upon Hull H Trin *York* 96-99; V N Ferriby 99-04; Chapl to Legal Profession 97-04; Hon Fell Hull Univ 97-04; Chapl and Fell Univ Coll Dur 05-06; TR Dur N 06-08; Chapl and Tutor Hatf Coll Dur from 08; Hon Research Fell Univ Coll Dur from 08. *Hatfield College, North Bailey, Durham DH1 3RQ* Tel 0191-334 2636 E-mail anthony.bash@durham.ac.uk

BASHFORD, Richard Frederick. b 36. Clifton Th Coll. d 68 p 69. C Bedworth *Cov* 68-71; C Lower Homerton St Paul *Lon* 71-75; V Bordesley Green *Birm* 75-81; R Birm Bp Latimer w St Alb 81-06; rtd 06. *244 Adams Hill, Birmingham B32 3PD* Tel 0121-421 1807 E-mail domusmariae@blueyonder.co.uk

BASHFORD, Robert Thomas. b 49. Ch Coll Cam BA70 CertEd72 MA74 Lon Univ BD84 MPhil89. Oak Hill Th Coll 86. d 88 p 89. C Frinton *Chelmsf* 88-91; C Galleywood Common 91-96; V Clapham *St Alb* 96-02; P-in-c Westgate St Jas *Cant* 02-06; V from 06. *St James's Vicarage, Orchard Gardens, Margate CT9 5JT* Tel (01843) 832380

BASHFORTH, Alan George. b 64. Ex Univ MA. Ripon Coll Cuddesdon BTh96. d 96 p 97. C Calstock *Truro* 96-98; C St Ives 98-01; V St Agnes and Mount Hawke w Mithian from 01; RD Powder from 04. *The Vicarage, 6 Penwinnick Parc, St Agnes TR5 0UQ* Tel (01872) 553391

BASINGSTOKE, Suffragan Bishop of. *See* WILLMOTT, The Rt Revd Trevor

BASKERVILLE, John. b 45. Open Univ BA78. Sarum & Wells Th Coll 92. d 93 p 94. C Wanstead St Mary w Ch Ch *Chelmsf* 93-96; C Chingford SS Pet and Paul 96-98; V Felkirk w Brierley *Wakef* 98-04; rtd 04. *131 Howard Road, Upminster RM14 2UQ* Tel (01708) 641242 Mobile 07710-209469

BASKERVILLE, Philip Duncan. b 58. St Chad's Coll Dur BSc79 Oriel Coll Ox PGCE80. Trin Coll Bris BA87. d 88 p 89. C Roby *Liv* 88-93; Tutor St Paul's Th Coll Kapsabet Kenya 93-98; C Barnston *Ches* 98-05; Chapl St Andr Sch Turi Kenya 05-08; P-in-c Guernsey St Sampson *Win* from 08. *The Rectory, Grandes Maisons Road, St Sampsons, Guernsey GY2 4JS* Tel (01481) 244710 Mobile 07839-213096
E-mail philbaskerville@cwgsy.net

BASON, Brian Vaudrey. b 27. Leeds Univ BA49 Lon Univ BD69 AMusTCL97. Coll of Resurr Mirfield 49. d 51 p 52. C Haggerston St Aug w St Steph *Lon* 51-55; C Bow w Bromley St Leon 55-56; V Audenshaw St Hilda *Man* 56-89; Audenshaw High Sch 89-92; rtd 92; Perm to Offic *Ches* from 89; *Man* 89-95 and from 99. *78 Windsor Road, Denton, Manchester M34 2HE* Tel 0161-320 4408

BASS, Colin Graham. b 41. Liv Univ BSc62 Fitzw Ho Cam BA64 MA68. Ox NSM Course 84. d 87 p 88. Dir of Studies Leighton Park Sch Reading 87-97; NSM Earley St Pet *Ox* 87-92; NSM Reading Deanery from 92. *9 Bramley Close, Reading RG6 7PL* Tel 0118-966 3732 E-mail colin.bass@lineone.net

BASS, George Michael. b 39. Ely Th Coll 62. d 65 p 66. C Romaldkirk *Ripon* 65-68; C Kenton Ascension *Newc* 68-71; CF 71-94; Chapl Northumbria Healthcare NHS Trust 95-02; rtd 02; Perm to Offic *Newc* from 02. *35 Kelso Drive, North Shields NE29 9NS* Tel 0191-258 2514

BASS, Mrs Marguerite Rowena. b 61. MA BD ARCM. St Jo Coll Nottm. d 05 p 06. C Wellingborough All SS *Pet* 05-08; Perm to Offic from 08; Chapl HM Pris Rye Hill 08; Chapl St Andr Hosp Northn from 08. *29 Northfield Avenue, Ringstead, Kettering NN14 4DX* Tel (01933) 460213
E-mail bassrowena@btopenworld.com

BASS, Mrs Rosemary Jane. b 38. Linc Th Coll 76. dss 79 d 87 p 94. Bedford All SS *St Alb* 79-84; Leavesden 84-94; Par Dn 87-94; C 94-95; V Luton St Andr 95-01; rtd 01; Perm to Offic *St Alb* from 01. *41 Darlow Drive, Biddenham, Bedford MK40 4AY* Tel and fax (01234) 219812

BASSETT, John Edmund. b 33. St Aid Birkenhead 63. d 66 p 67. C Guiseley *Bradf* 66-67; C Stechford *Birm* 67-71; C Ross *Heref* 71-72; P-in-c Brampton Abbotts 73-75; P-in-c Weston under Penyard 73-75; P-in-c Hope Mansell 73-75; TR Halesworth w Linstead and Chediston *St E* 75-78; R Laceby *Linc* 78-83; V Sale St Paul *Ches* 83-88; P-in-c Southport All SS *Liv* 88-94; P-in-c Southport All SS 88-94; V Southport All SS and All So 94-98; P-in-c Aspull 98-99; V Aspull and New Springs 99-02; rtd 02; Hon C Pool w Arthington *Ripon* 02-03; Hon C Lower Wharfedale from 03. *The Vicarage, Old Pool Bank, Pool in Wharfedale, Otley LS21 1EJ* Tel 0113-284 3706

BASSETT, Mrs Rosemary Louise. b 42. STETS. d 00 p 01. NSM The Winterbournes and Compton Valence *Sarum* 00-08; P-in-c 03-08; NSM Dorchester from 08. *12 Lime Close, Dorchester DT1 2HQ* E-mail trl@bassett-online.com

BASTABLE, Richard Michael. b 83. Ex Univ BA04 St Edm Coll Cam MPhil08. Westcott Ho Cam 06. d 08 p 09. C Ruislip St Martin *Lon* from 08. *5 Wytleaf Close, Ruislip HA4 7SP* Tel (01895) 672929 Mobile 07816-074597
E-mail rbastable@googlemail.com

BASTEN, Richard Henry. b 40. Codrington Coll Barbados 60. d 63 p 64. Br Honduras 63-67; Barbados 68-72; C Hartlepool H Trin *Dur* 72-73; Chapl Bedstone Coll 73-88; C Bow w Chapel Lawn *Heref* 73-77; P-in-c Clungunford 77-78; R Clungunford w Clunbury and Clunton, Bedstone etc 78-88; R Rowde and Poulshot *Sarum* 88-95; rtd 95; Perm to Offic *Glouc* from 95. *41 Bewley Way, Churchdown, Gloucester GL3 2DU* Tel (01452) 859738

BASTIDE, Derek. b 44. Dur Univ BA65 Reading Univ DipEd66 Sussex Univ MA77. Chich Th Coll 76. d 77 p 78. Hon C Lewes All SS, St Anne, St Mich and St Thos *Chich* 77-84; Prin Lect Brighton Poly 80-92; Prin Lect Brighton Univ from 92; P-in-c Hamsey *Chich* from 84. *The Rectory, Offham, Lewes BN7 3PX* Tel (01273) 474356 E-mail dandj@bastide8.wanadoo.co.uk

BASTOCK, Kenneth William. b 22. Launde Abbey 75. d 76 p 77. C Glen Parva and S Wigston *Leic* 76-80; V Orton-on-the-Hill w Twycross etc 80-92; rtd 92; Perm to Offic *Leic* from 92. *18 Beech Road, Oadby, Leicester LE2 5QL* Tel 0116-271 0454

BASTON, The Ven Caroline. b 56. Birm Univ BSc78 CertEd79. Ripon Coll Cuddesdon 81. d 89 p 94. Par Dn Southampton Thornhill St Chris *Win* 89-94; C 94-95; R Win All SS w Chilcomb and Chesil 95-06; Dioc Communications Officer 95-98; Dioc Dir of Ords 99-06; Hon Can Win Cathl 00-06; Adn Is of Wight *Portsm* from 06. *5 The Boltons, Wootton Bridge, Ryde PO33 4PB* Tel (01983) 884432
E-mail adiow@portsmouth.anglican.org

BATCHELOR, Alan Harold. b 30. Bris Univ BA54 Hull Univ MA63. Linc Th Coll 54. d 56 p 57. C Kingston upon Hull St Alb *York* 56-60; C Attercliffe w Darnall *Sheff* 60-62; India 63-87; Ind Chapl *Ripon* 87-95; C Kirkstall 92-95; rtd 95; Perm to Offic *Ripon* from 01. *16 Moor Grange Rise, Leeds LS16 5BP* Tel 0113-226 9671

BATCHELOR, Andrew George. b 59. St Jo Coll Nottm 07. **d** 09. C Ulverston St Mary w H Trin *Carl* from 09. *21 Victoria Park, Ulverston LA12 7TT* Tel 07934-483439 (mobile) E-mail andy.batchelor@yahoo.co.uk

BATCHELOR, John Millar. CITC 76. **d** 78 **p** 79. C Belfast All SS *Conn* 78-80; I Eglish w Killylea *Arm* 80-96; I Ballyhalbert w Ardkeen *D & D* 96-01; rtd 01. *Rhone Brae, 102 Eglish Road, Dungannon BT70 1LB* Tel (028) 8775 0177 E-mail jm_batchelor@lineone.net

BATCHELOR, Martin John. b 67. Plymouth Poly BSc91. St Jo Coll Nottm MA95. **d** 95 **p** 96. C Brecon St Mary and Battle w Llanddew *S & B* 95-97; Min Can Brecon Cathl 95-97; C Sketty 97-00; TV Hawarden *St As* 00-05; V Bistre from 05. *Bistre Vicarage, Mold Road, Buckley CH7 2NH* Tel (01244) 550947 E-mail martin_batchelor@bigfoot.com

BATCHFORD, Philip John. b 71. Sheff Univ BA99. Ridley Hall Cam 00. **d** 02 **p** 03. C Sheff St Mary Bramall Lane 02-05; V Netherthorpe St Steph from 05. *The Vicarage, 115 Upperthorpe Road, Sheffield S6 3EA* Tel 0114-276 7130

BATCOCK, Neil Gair. b 53. UEA BA74. Westcott Ho Cam 94. **d** 96 **p** 97. C Barton upon Humber *Linc* 96-99; TV Totnes w Bridgetown, Berry Pomeroy etc *Ex* 99-06; P-in-c Blakeney w Cley, Wiveton, Glandford etc *Nor* from 06. *The Rectory, Wiveton Road, Blakeney, Holt NR25 7NJ* Tel (01263) 740686 E-mail gair2@aol.com

BATE, Dylan Griffin. b 48. Mon Dioc Tr Scheme 91. **d** 94 **p** 95. NSM Fleur-de-Lis *Mon* 94-96; NSM Bedwellty 96-97; C Pontypool 97-99; C Tenby *St D* 99-02; R Begelly w Ludchurch and Crunwere 02-05; C Risca *Mon* from 05. *18 Commercial Street, Risca, Newport NP11 6AY* Tel (01633) 614084

BATE, Preb Lawrence Mark. b 40. Univ Coll Ox BA63. Coll of Resurr Mirfield 65. **d** 67 **p** 68. C Benwell St Jas *Newc* 67-69; C Monkseaton St Pet 69-72; TV Withycombe Raleigh *Ex* 72-84; RD Aylesbeare 81-84; R Alphington 84-00; RD Christianity 95-99; TV Heavitree w Ex St Paul 00-02; TV Heavitree and St Mary Steps 02-05; Preb Ex Cathl from 02; rtd 05. *Chapple Court, Kenn, Exeter EX6 7UR* Tel (01392) 833485 E-mail morleybate@freeuk.com

BATE, Michael Keith. b 42. Lich Th Coll 67. **d** 69 **p** 70. C W Bromwich St Jas *Lich* 69-73; C Thornhill *Wakef* 73-76; V Wrenthorpe 76-82; V Upper Gornal *Lich* 82-93; V Upper Gornal *Worc* 93-05; TV Gornal and Sedgley 05-08; Chapl Burton Road Hosp Dudley 82-94; Chapl Dudley Gp of Hosps NHS Trust 94-00; rtd 08; Perm to Offic *Lich* from 09. *44 Wentworth Road, Wolverhampton WV10 8EF* E-mail michael.bate@tesco.net

BATE, Stephen Donald. b 58. Sheff Univ BSc79 Cov Univ PhD92 CEng97 MIET97. **d** 05 **p** 06. OLM Whitnash *Cov* from 05. *73 Golf Lane, Whitnash, Leamington Spa CV31 2QB* Tel (01926) 334134 Mobile 07973-583356 E-mail sbate@aol.com

BATEMAN, James Edward. b 44. Univ Coll Lon BSc65. Trin Coll Bris 71. **d** 74 **p** 75. C Woodlands *Sheff* 74-77; C Rushden w Newton Bromswold *Pet* 77-84; R Vange *Chelmsf* 84-94; V Southminster 94-01; P-in-c Nazeing and Roydon 01-03; Warden Stacklands Retreat Ho W Kingsdown 03-05; C Rainham *Roch* from 05. *26 Beverley Close, Gillingham ME8 9HG* Tel and fax (01634) 230577

BATEMAN, Kenneth William. b 34. ACII58. NOC 85. **d** 88 **p** 89. Hon C Pilling *Blackb* 88-91; Chapl Lanc Moor Hosp 88-92; Chapl Lanc Priority Services NHS Trust 92-95; C Kirkby Lonsdale *Carl* 91-95; NSM 95-98; rtd 95; Perm to Offic *Carl* from 98. *Greenside, Barbon, Carnforth LA6 2LT* Tel (015242) 76318

BATEMAN, Martyn Henry. b 31. Jes Coll Cam BA54 MA58. Clifton Th Coll 54. **d** 56 **p** 57. C Heatherlands St Jo *Sarum* 56-59; C New Malden and Coombe *S'wark* 59-60; Iran 60-62; V Charsfield and R Monewden and Hoo *St E* 62-69; V Wickham Market 69-82; Hon Can St E Cathl 80-85; V Felixstowe SS Pet and Paul 82-85; TR Lydford, Brent Tor, Bridestowe and Sourton *Ex* 85-92; RD Tavistock 90-92; rtd 92; Lic to Offic *Mor* from 01. *Ardochy, Whitebridge, Inverness IV2 6UR* Tel (01456) 486273

BATEMAN, Mrs Nest Wynne. Univ of Wales (Cardiff) BA71 CQSW73. Westcott Ho Cam 08. **d** 09. NSM Lich Cathl from 09. *21 Christchurch Lane, Lichfield WS13 8BA* Tel (01543) 257681 Mobile 07729-256364 E-mail nestbateman@aol.com

BATEMAN, Patrick John. b 64. St Jo Coll Nottm 99. **d** 01 **p** 02. C Wallington *S'wark* 01-05; P-in-c Chipstead from 05. *The Rectory, Starrock Lane, Chipstead, Coulsdon CR5 3QD* Tel (01737) 552157 Mobile 07764-171400 E-mail patrick@batemannet.co.uk

BATES, Derek Alvin. b 27. St Mich Coll Llan 57. **d** 59 **p** 60. C Bishop's Cleeve *Glouc* 59-63; V Shebbear *Ex* 67-71; R Buckland Filleigh 67-71; R Coates *Ely* 71-80; R Clovelly *Ex* 80-92; V Woolfardisworthy and Buck Mills 80-92; rtd 92; Perm to Offic *Ex* 92-06. *1 Honeysuckle Close, Gosport PO13 0DY* Tel (01329) 825667

✠**BATES, The Rt Revd Gordon.** b 34. Kelham Th Coll 54. **d** 58 **p** 59 **c** 83. C New Eltham All SS *S'wark* 58-62; Asst Youth Chapl *Glouc* 62-64; Youth Chapl *Liv* 65-69; Chapl Liv Cathl 65-69; V

BATES, James. b 46. Linc Th Coll 73. **d** 75 **p** 76. C Ewell *Guildf* 75-77; C Farncombe 77-80; V Pet St Mary Boongate 80-92; V Kingston All SS w St Jo *S'wark* 92-05; P-in-c Win St Cross w St Faith 05-07; Master St Cross Hosp 05-07; V Offerton *Ches* from 07. *St Alban's Vicarage, 1A Salcombe Road, Stockport SK2 5AG* Tel 0161-480 3773

BATES, James Paul. QUB BSc PGCE Cranfield Univ MSc MPhil. **d** 06. NSM Bangor Abbey *D & D* 06-07. *16 Craigowen Road, Holywood BT18 0DL* Tel (028) 9042 2077 E-mail paul_tssf@hotmail.com

BATES, Miss Phyllis Edith. b 29. S'wark Ord Course 80. **dss** 83 **d** 87 **p** 94. Registrar S'wark Ord Course 83-89; Fulham St Dionis Parson's Green *Lon* 83-94; Hon Par Dn 87-94; rtd 89; NSM Hammersmith St Paul *Lon* 94-99; Perm to Offic *S'wark* 99 and *Lon* from 99. *26 St Dionis Road, London SW6 4TT* Tel (020) 7731 6935

BATES, Robert John. b 50. FRICS81. EAMTC 99. **d** 02 **p** 03. NSM Pet St Mary Boongate 02-05; C Ketton, Collyweston, Easton-on-the-Hill etc 05-09; Chapl Algarve *Eur* from 09. *Apartado 2135, Casa Sao Vincente, Boliqueime, Algarve 8100-170, Portugal* Tel (00351) (289) 366720 E-mail rev.bobbates@virgin.net or stvincentsbq@sapo.pt

BATES, Mrs Rosemary Eileen Hamilton. b 45. Ripon Coll Cuddesdon 87. **d** 89 **p** 94. Par Dn Brackley St Pet w St Jas 89-94; C 94-95; P-in-c N Hinksey and Wytham *Ox* 95-04; rtd 04; Perm to Offic *Ely* 04-08. *45 Spring Lane, Bottisham, Cambridge CB25 9BL* Tel (01223) 813902 E-mail revrosie@rosiebates.com

BATES, Stuart Geoffrey. b 61. Univ of Wales (Lamp) BA82. St Steph Ho Ox 83. **d** 85 **p** 86. C Bromley St Mark *Roch* 85-88; C Westmr St Matt *Lon* 88-89; C Gt Ilford St Mary *Chelmsf* 89-95; V Crofton Park St Hilda w St Cypr *S'wark* from 95. *St Hilda's Vicarage, 35 Buckthorne Road, London SE4 2DG* Tel (020) 8699 1277

BATES, William Frederic. b 49. St Jo Coll Dur BSc72 BA74 MA97. Cranmer Hall Dur. **d** 75 **p** 76. C Knutsford St Jo and Toft *Ches* 75-78; C Ripley *Derby* 78-80; R Nether and Over Seale 81-93; V Lullington 81-93; V Allestree St Nic from 93; Bp's Adv on New Relig Movements from 99; P-in-c Quarndon from 00. *The Vicarage, 4 Lawn Avenue, Allestree, Derby DE22 2PE* Tel (01332) 550224 E-mail williambates@btconnect.com

BATES, William Hugh. b 33. Keble Coll Ox BA56 MA59. Westcott Ho Cam 59. **d** 60 **p** 61. C Horsforth *Ripon* 60-63; Tutor St Chad's Coll Dur 63-70; V Bishop Wilton *York* 70-76; RD Pocklington 74-76; V Pickering 76-82; Prin NEOC 79-94; P-in-c Crayke w Brandsby and Yearsley 82-94; P-in-c Stillington and Marton w Moxby 82-94; rtd 94; Perm to Offic *York* from 94. *Jessbrook Cottage, Bugthorpe, York YO41 1QG* Tel (01759) 368402

BATESON, Canon Geoffrey Frederick. b 27. K Coll Lon BD51 AKC51. **d** 52 **p** 53. C Tynemouth Cullercoats St Paul *Newc* 52-56; C Gosforth All SS 56-60; V Monkseaton St Pet 60-68; V Newc St Geo 68-77; RD Newc 75-77; R Morpeth 77-89; Chapl St Geo and Cottage Hosp Morpeth 77-89; Hon Can Newc Cathl 80-89; rtd 89; Perm to Offic *York* from 91. *1 Netherby Close, Sleights, Whitby YO22 5HD* Tel (01947) 810997

BATESON, Canon James Howard. b 36. Qu Mary Coll Lon BSc57 MSOSc88. EMMTC 85. **d** 87 **p** 88. NSM W Bridgford *S'well* 87-88; NSM Wilford Hill 88-95; Dioc Officer for NSMs 94-04; P-in-c Kilvington and Staunton w Flawborough 96-04; Hon Can S'well Minster 99-04; rtd 04; Perm to Offic *S'well* from 04. *45 Musters Road, West Bridgford, Nottingham NG2 6GD* Tel and fax 0115-923 1820 E-mail h_bateson@primeuk.net

BATESON, Keith Nigel. b 43. **d** 00 **p** 01. OLM Wonersh w Blackheath *Guildf* from 00. *Advent Cottage, Blackheath Lane, Wonersh, Guildford GU5 0PN* Tel (01483) 892753 E-mail keith@batesonfamily.net

BATESON, Tracey Jane. b 74. St Mark & St Jo Coll Lon BEd96 MPhil04. Trin Coll Bris BA03. **d** 04 **p** 05. C Holdenhurst and Iford *Win* 04-07; CF from 07. *c/o MOD Chaplains (Army)* Tel (01980) 615804 Fax 615800 E-mail padretj@bateson.f2s.com

BATEY, Caroline. **d** 08. OLM Warrington H Trin *Liv* from 08. *22 Fairclough Avenue, Warrington WA1 2JS* E-mail cabethbatey@hotmail.com

BATEY, Canon Herbert Taylor. b 22. Qu Coll Ox BA46 MA48. Linc Th Coll 48. **d** 48 **p** 49. C Dalton-in-Furness *Carl* 48-50; C Egremont 50-52; V Cleator Moor w Cleator 52-59; Chapl St Bees Sch Cumbria 59-64; Chapl Culham Coll Abingdon 64-68; Prin Lect 68-75; P-in-c Culham *Ox* 68-75; Vice-Prin Coll of Ripon and York St Jo 75-92; Hon Can Ripon Cathl 85-92; rtd 87; Perm to Offic *Ripon* from 92. *Clova House Care Home, 2 Clotherholme Road, Ripon HG4 2DA* Tel (01765) 603678

BATH, David James William. b 43. Oak Hill NSM Course 87. **d** 89 **p** 90. NSM Henley *Ox* 89-90; Gen Manager Humberside Gd News Trust 90-96; NSM Anlaby St Pet *York* 96-04; P-in-c

Anlaby Common St Mark from 04. *St Mark's Vicarage, 1055 Anlaby Road, Hull HU4 7PP* Tel (01482) 351977 E-mail davidjwbath@hotmail.com

BATH AND WELLS, Bishop of. See PRICE, The Rt Revd Peter Bryan

BATH, Archdeacon of. See PIGGOTT, The Ven Andrew John

BATHURST, Bishop of. See HURFORD, The Rt Revd Richard Warwick

BATLEY-GLADDEN, Dane Christopher. b 68. St Steph Ho Ox 96. **d** 99 **p** 00. C Hendon St Alphage *Lon* 99-01; C-in-c Grahame Park St Aug CD from 01. *St Augustine's House, Great Field, London NW9 5SY* Tel (020) 8205 1979 Fax 8205 6127 E-mail frdane@dcbg.org.uk

BATSON, David Frederick Edward. b 38. K Coll Lon AKC61 BD69 FSAScot97. St Boniface Warminster. **d** 62 **p** 63. C Southport H Trin *Liv* 62-64; Asst Chapl Hurstpierpoint Coll 64-65; C Cleator Moor w Cleator *Carl* 65-66; Asst Master K Geo V Sch Southport 66-67; NSM Leigh w Bransford *Worc* 68-79; Hon Asst Chapl Convent of H Name Malvern Link 68-72; Prin Soc Work Tr Dept Dumfries and Galloway Coun 84-94; Lect and Tutor Langside Coll Glas 95-97; Lect Soc Studies Dumfries and Galloway Coll 96-04; Visiting Lect Paisley Univ 02-07; Perm to Offic *Glas* from 03. *Kindar House, New Abbey, Dumfries DG2 8DB* Tel (01387) 850514 Fax 850556

BATSON, Lee Paul. b 77. R Holloway Coll Lon BA99 MA00 Selw Coll Cam BA03. Westcott Ho Cam 01. **d** 04 **p** 05. C Saffron Walden w Wendens Ambo, Littlebury etc *Chelmsf* 04-08; P-in-c Boreham from 08; Co Ecum Officer from 08. *The Vicarage, Church Road, Boreham, Chelmsford CM3 3EG* Tel (01245) 451087 E-mail lbatson@chelmsford.anglican.org

BATSON, Paul Leonard. b 47. Southn Univ BTh79. Sarum & Wells Th Coll 73. **d** 75 **p** 76. C Chesham St Mary *Ox* 75-79; Dioc Youth Adv *Newc* 79-85; V Earley St Pet *Ox* 85-93; Perm to Offic *Sarum* 01-08. *Maple Cottage, 78 Murhill, Limpley Stoke, Bath BA2 7FB* Tel (01225) 722721 E-mail paul.and.linds@btinternet.com

BATSON, William Francis Robert. b 43. St Jo Coll Dur BA72. Cranmer Hall Dur. **d** 73 **p** 74. C Eastwood *S'well* 73-77; R Long Marton w Dufton and w Milburn *Carl* 77-79; V Flimby 79-85; TR Raveningham *Nor* 85-91; R Kinver and Enville *Lich* 91-00; V Ledsham w Fairburn *York* 00-08; rtd 08. *8 Langdale Avenue, Carlisle CA2 5QG* Tel (01228) 537798 E-mail bob@ledvic.fsnet.co.uk

BATSTONE, Bruce. b 70. Bris Univ BA92. St Steph Ho Ox 98. **d** 00 **p** 01. C Leigh-on-Sea St Marg *Chelmsf* 00-03; C Old St Pancras *Lon* 03-07; TV from 07; Chapl Camden and Islington Community Health NHS Trust from 03. *23 Albert Street, London NW1 7LU* Tel (020) 7387 4193 E-mail bruce.batstone@ic24.net

BATT, Canon Joseph William. b 39. Keele Univ BA62. Ripon Hall Ox 63. **d** 64 **p** 65. C Bushbury *Lich* 64-68; C Walsall 68-71; Tr Officer and Youth Chapl Dio Ibadan Nigeria 71-75; Hon Can Oke-Osun from 94; Area Sec CMS *Guildf* and *Chich* 75-84; V Ottershaw *Guildf* 84-04; rtd 04. *8 Parkwood Road, Shipley BD18 4SS* Tel (01274) 589775

BATT, Canon Kenneth Victor. b 41. Wycliffe Hall Ox 68. **d** 71 **p** 72. C Yateley *Win* 71-76; R The Candover Valley 76-82; R Durrington *Sarum* 82-89; V Kempshott *Win* 89-00; P-in-c Bournemouth H Epiphany 00-05; V 05-08; rtd 08; Hon Can Win Cathl from 07; Hon C Tadley S and Silchester from 08. *St Mary's House, 10 Romans Field, Silchester, Reading RG7 2QH* Tel 0118-970 2353

BATTE, Mrs Kathleen. b 44. Homerton Coll Cam TCert68. NEOC 91. **d** 94 **p** 95. NSM Newc St Gabr 94-96; NSM Wilford Hill *S'well* 96-99; P-in-c Cinderhill 99-05; Bp's Adv for Self-Supporting Min 05-07; Chapl Crowhurst Chr Healing Cen from 07. *The Old Rectory, Forewood Lane, Crowhurst, Battle TN33 9AD* Tel (01424) 830762 E-mail kath.batte@talk21.com

BATTEN, Stuart William. b 73. Univ of Wales (Abth) BD94 MTh96. Trin Coll Bris 96. **d** 98 **p** 99. C Northolt St Jos *Lon* 98-01; TV Hucknall Torkard *S'well* 01-06; P-in-c Wickham Bishops w Lt Braxted *Chelmsf* from 06; Asst Dir of Ords from 06. *The Rectory, 1 Church Road, Wickham Bishops, Witham CM8 3LA* Tel (01621) 891360 E-mail stuart.batten@btinternet.com

BATTERSBY, David George Sellers. b 32. AKC57. St Boniface Warminster 57 Lambeth STh80. **d** 58 **p** 59. C Glas St Marg 58-60; C Burnley St Pet *Blackb* 60-62; V Warton St Paul 62-71; Chapl K Wm's Coll Is of Man 71-91; C Ashchurch *Glouc* 91-97; rtd 97; Perm to Offic *Glouc* and *Worc* from 97, *Dio*c and 03. *Shill Brook Cottage, Buckland Road, Bampton OX18 2AA* Tel (01993) 851414 E-mail dgsb@fan.com

BATTERSBY, Simon Charles. b 64. Wycliffe Hall Ox BTh01. **d** 01 **p** 02. C Askern *Sheff* 01-03; Chapl Bethany Sch Goudhurst 03-07; Chapl Culford Sch Bury St Edmunds from 08. *Culford School, Bury St Edmunds IP28 6TX* Tel (01284) 728615 Mobile 07900-242757 E-mail chaplain@culford.co.uk

BATTERSHELL, Mrs Anne Marie. b 33. Ox Poly BEd83. SAOMC 95. **d** 98 **p** 99. NSM Goring w S Stoke *Ox* 98-01; NSM

Brafferton w Pilmoor, Myton-on-Swale etc *York* 01-03; rtd 03; Perm to Offic *Wakef* from 04 and *Man* from 07. *26 Winterbutlee Grove, Todmorden OL14 7QU* Tel (01706) 839848 E-mail revanne@battershell.fsnet.co.uk

BATTEY, Alexander Robert Fenwick. b 77. St Andr Univ MA99. Ripon Coll Cuddesdon BA05. **d** 05 **p** 06. C Whitby w Aislaby and Ruswarp *York* 05-08; CF from 08. *c/o MOD Chaplains (Army)* Tel (01980) 615804 Fax 615800 E-mail alexander.battey370@mod.uk *or* arfbattey@aol.com

BATTIN (*née* WEBB), Mrs Frances Mary. b 52. WEMTC 92. **d** 95 **p** 96. NSM Inkberrow w Cookhill and Kington w Dormston *Worc* 95-98; Asst Chapl HM Pris Brockhill 98-03; Perm to Offic *Worc* 03-07; NSM Church Lench w Rous Lench and Abbots Morton etc from 07. *2 The Rowans, Harvington, Evesham WR11 8SX*

BATTISON, David John. b 62. ACIB93. St Jo Coll Nottm 07. **d** 09. C Matlock Bath and Cromford *Derby* from 09. *Blossom House, 67 Morledge, Matlock DE4 3SB* Tel (01629) 580850 Mobile 07971-506088 E-mail davidbattison12@ntlworld.com

BATTISON, Mark Richard. b 62. EMMTC 01. **d** 04 **p** 05. NSM Leic St Jas 04-07; NSM Oadby 07-09; NSM Guilsborough w Hollowell and Cold Ashby *Pet* from 09; NSM Cottesbrooke w Gt Creaton and Thornby from 09; NSM Spratton from 09; NSM Ravensthorpe from 09. *The Vicarage, 2 Church Road, Spratton, Northampton NN6 8HR* Tel (01604) 846690 Mobile 07717-200777 E-mail markbattison@btinternet.com

BATTLE, Dean of. See EDMONDSON, The Very Revd John James William

BATTMAN, John Brian. b 37. ALCD61. **d** 61 **p** 62. C Fulham Ch Ch *Lon* 61-64; SAMS Argentina 64-69; Paraguay 69-76; Adn Paraguay 70-76; Ext Sec SAMS 77-80; V Romford Gd Shep *Chelmsf* 80-92; V Werrington *Pet* 92-02; rtd 02; Perm to Offic *St E* from 02. *57 Glencoe Road, Ipswich IP4 3PP* Tel (01473) 717902 E-mail john.battman@ntlworld.com

BATTY, John Ivan. b 35. Clifton Th Coll 59. **d** 62 **p** 63. C Clayton *Bradf* 62-67; V Toxteth Park St Clem *Liv* 67-73; R Darfield *Sheff* 73-90; Chapl Düsseldorf *Eur* 90-95; V The Marshland *Sheff* 95-00; rtd 00; Perm to Offic *Sheff* and *Linc* from 00. *4 St Lawrence Way, Tallington, Stamford PE9 4RH* Tel and fax (01780) 740151

BATTY, Mark Alan. b 56. BSc. Ripon Coll Cuddesdon. **d** 82 **p** 83. C Bottesford w Ashby *Linc* 82-86; V Scunthorpe All SS 86-95; P-in-c N Wolds Gp 95-97; V from 97. *The Vicarage, St Barnabas Road, Barnetby DN38 6JE* Tel (01652) 688182

BATTY, Stephen Roy. b 58. Chich Th Coll 88. **d** 90 **p** 91. C Wimborne Minster and Holt *Sarum* 90-94; P-in-c Yetminster w Ryme Intrinseca and High Stoy 94-02; V Branksome St Aldhelm from 02; Perm to Offic *Win* from 02. *The Vicarage, St Aldhelm's Road, Poole BH13 6BT* Tel (01202) 764420

BATTYE, John Noel. b 42. TCD BA64 MA73. CITC 66. **d** 66 **p** 67. C Drumglass *Arm* 66-69; C Ballynafeigh St Jude *D & D* 70-73; Chapl Pemb Coll Cam 73-78; Bp's C Knocknagoney *D & D* 78-80; I Cregagh 80-08; Preb Castleknock St Patr Cathl Dublin 94-08; rtd 08. *St Finnian's Rectory, 3 Upper Knockbreda Road, Belfast BT6 9QH* Tel (028) 9079 3822

BATTYE, Ms Lisa Katherine. b 55. Man Univ BN78 MA(Theol)96 Liv Univ MTh00 RM79. NOC 96. **d** 99 **p** 00. C Clifton *Man* 99-02; R Kersal Moor from 02. *St Paul's Rectory, 1 Moorside Road, Salford M7 3PJ* Tel 0161-792 5362 E-mail lisa@battye.fsbusiness.co.uk

BATY, Edward. b 30. Open Univ BA77 UEA PhD88 MRICS92. St Aid Birkenhead 60. **d** 62 **p** 63. C Acomb St Steph *York* 62-64; Succ Chelmsf Cathl 64-67; V Becontree St Cedd 67-71; R Hope Bowdler w Eaton-under-Heywood *Heref* 71-79; R Rushbury 71-79; P-in-c Cardington 71-79; R Fincham *Ely* 79-82; OCF 79-94; R Long Stanton w St Mich *Ely* 82-94; P-in-c Lolworth 85-88; CF(V) 86-95; rtd 95; Perm to Offic *Guildf* from 95. *25 Martindale Avenue, Camberley GU15 1BB* Tel (01276) 20315

BAUDAINS, Mrs Geraldine Louise. b 58. Ex Univ BTh07. SWMTC 02. **d** 05 **p** 06. NSM Jersey All SS *Win* from 05; NSM Jersey St Simon from 05. *Le Chataignier, La Rue du Flicquet, St Martin, Jersey JE3 6BP* Tel (01534) 855556 E-mail baudains@jerseymail.co.uk

✠**BAUERSCHMIDT, The Rt Revd John Crawford.** b 59. Kenyon Coll Ohio BA81. Gen Th Sem (NY) MDiv84. **d** 84 **p** 85 **c** 07. C Worcester All SS USA 84-87; Lib Pusey Ho 87-91; R Albemarle Ch Ch USA 92-97; R Covington Ch Ch 97-07; Bp Tennessee from 07. *50 Vantage Way, Suite 107, Nashville TN 37228-1524, USA* Tel (001) (615) 251 3322 Fax 251 8010 E-mail info@episcopaldiocese-tn.org

BAUGHAN, Emma Louise Langley. See LANGLEY, Ms Emma Louise

BAUGHEN, Andrew Jonathan. b 64. Lon Guildhall Univ BA87. Wycliffe Hall Ox BTh94. **d** 94 **p** 95. C Battersea Rise St Mark *S'wark* 94-97; P-in-c Clerkenwell St Jas and St Jo w St Pet *Lon* 97-00; V from 00. *St James's Church, Clerkenwell Close, London EC1R 0EA* Tel (020) 7251 1190 E-mail vicar@jc-church.org

✠**BAUGHEN, The Rt Revd Michael Alfred.** b 30. Lon Univ BD55. Oak Hill Th Coll 51. **d** 56 **p** 57 **c** 82. C Hyson Green

S'well 56-59; C Reigate St Mary S'wark 59-61; Ord Cand Sec CPAS 61-64; R Rusholme H Trin Man 64-70; TV St Marylebone All So w SS Pet and Jo Lon 70-75; R 75-82; AD Westmr St Marylebone 78-82; Preb St Paul's Cathl 79-82; Bp Ches 82-96; rtd 96; Hon Asst Bp Lon 96-06; Asst Bp Guildf from 06; Perm to Offic S'wark 97-02. 42 Rookwood Court, Guildford GU2 4EL Tel (01483) 457061 E-mail michaelmyrtle@tiscali.co.uk

BAULCOMB, Canon Geoffrey Gordon. b 46. K Coll Lon BD86. AKC68. **d** 69 **p** 70. C Crofton Park St Hilda w St Cypr S'wark 69-74; TV Padgate Liv 74-79; R Whitton and Thurleston w Akenham St E 79-03; Hon Can St E Cathl 03; rtd 03; Perm to Offic St E from 03 and Chich from 04. Greenlands, 39 Filching Road, Eastbourne BN20 8SE Tel (01323) 641746 Mobile 07880-731232 E-mail geoffreybaulcomb@hotmail.com

BAVERSTOCK, David John. b 76. K Coll Lon BA00 MA01. Westcott Ho Cam 07. **d** 09. C Mill End and Heronsgate w W Hyde St Alb from 09. St Thomas' House, 46 Chalfont Road, Maple Cross, Rickmansworth WD3 9TB Tel (01923) 771022 Mobile 07921-887513 E-mail curate@parishofmillend.org.uk

✠**BAVIN, The Rt Revd Timothy John.** b 35. Worc Coll Ox BA59 MA61. Cuddesdon Coll 59. **d** 61 **p** 62 **c** 74. S Africa 61-69 and 73-85; C Uckfield Chich 69-71; V Brighton Gd Shep Preston 71-73; Dean and Adn Johannesburg 73-74; Bp Johannesburg 74-85; Bp Portsm 85-95; OGS from 87; Community of Our Lady and St John from 96; Perm to Offic Win from 96; rtd 98. Alton Abbey, Abbey Road, Beech, Alton GU34 4AP Tel (01420) 562145 or 563575 Fax 561691

BAVINGTON, John Eduard. b 68. Loughb Univ BEng91. Trin Coll Bris BA99. **d** 99 **p** 00. C W Ealing St Jo w St Jas Lon 99-02; V Bradf St Clem 02-06; Chapl Giggleswick Sch from 06. Tems House, Tems Bank, Giggleswick, Settle BD24 0BP Tel (01729) 893000 Mobile 07704-854978 E-mail jebavington@giggleswick.org.uk

BAWTREE, Andrew James. b 66. Univ of Wales BD91 Ch Ch Coll Cant PGCE92. St Jo Coll Nottm MA95. **d** 96 **p** 97. C Hoddesdon St Alb 96-99; R S Boston Trin Ch USA 00-07; P-in-c River Cant from 07. The Vicarage, 23 Lewisham Road, Dover CT17 0QG Tel (01304) 822037 E-mail rockabillyrev@hotmail.com

BAWTREE, Canon Robert John. b 39. Oak Hill Th Coll 62. **d** 67 **p** 68. C Foord St Jo Cant 67-70; C Boscombe St Jo Win 70-73; C Kinson Sarum 73-75; TV Bramerton w Surlingham Nor 76-82; R Arborfield w Barkham Ox 82-91; V Hildenborough Roch 91-04; RD Tonbridge 95-01; Hon Can Roch Cathl 02-04; rtd 04; Hon C Camelot Par B & W 04-08. 47 Mount Pleasant Road, Weald, Sevenoaks TN14 6QB Tel (01732) 464427 E-mail robert.bawtree@virgin.net

BAXANDALL, Canon Peter. b 45. Tyndale Hall Bris 67. **d** 70 **p** 72. C Kidsgrove Lich 70-71; C St Helens St Mark Liv 71-75; C Ardsley Sheff 76-77; Rep Leprosy Miss E Anglia 77-86; P-in-c March St Wendreda Ely 86-87; R from 87; P-in-c March St Jo from 09; RD March 93-09; Hon Can Ely Cathl from 07. St Wendreda's Rectory, 21 Wimblington Road, March PE15 9QW Tel (01354) 653377 E-mail peter.baxandall@sky.com

BAXENDALE, John Richard. b 48. Cranmer Hall Dur 89. **d** 91 **p** 92. C Carl St Jo 91-94; C Dalston 94-95; P-in-c Monton Man 95-06; TV Eccles 06-04; V Clifton from 04. St Anne's Vicarage, 237 Manchester Road, Manchester M27 6PP Tel 0161-794 1939

BAXENDALE, Paul Gordon. b 70. Leeds Univ BA91. Ridley Hall Cam 93. **d** 96 **p** 97. C Kendal St Thos Carl 96-01, P-in-c Burton and Holme from 01. St James's Vicarage, Glebe Close, Burton, Carnforth LA6 1PL Tel (01524) 781391

BAXENDALE, Rodney Douglas. b 45. Ex Univ BA66. Linc Th Coll 78. **d** 80 **p** 81. C Maidstone All SS and St Phil w Tovil Cant 80-83; Chapl RN 83-03; Chapl Plymouth Hosps NHS Trust from 06. Derriford Hospital, Derriford Road, Plymouth PL6 8DH Tel 08451-558155 or (01752) 792022 E-mail thebaxendales@blueyonder.co.uk

BAXTER, Anthony. b 54. SEITE 99. **d** 02 **p** 08. NSM Romford Ascension Collier Row Chelmsf 02-07; NSM Hutton from 07. 44 Prower Close, Billericay CM11 2BU Tel (01277) 655514 Mobile 07909-984675 E-mail tonybaxter54@aol.com

BAXTER, Brian Raymond. b 31. Tyndale Hall Bris. **d** 58 **p** 59. C Heworth H Trin York 58-61; C Belper Derby 61-65; R Leverton Linc 65-67; C Mile Cross Nor 74-76; C Farnborough Guildf 76-79; Ldr Southgate Chr Project Bury St Edmunds 79-84; Chapl W Suffolk Hosp 79-81; R Ringsfield w Redisham, Barsham, Shipmeadow etc St E 82-88; V Nor Heartsease St Fran 88-91; rtd 91; Perm to Offic Nor from 91. 22A Gurney Close, Norwich NR5 0HB Tel (01603) 748588

BAXTEER, Carlton Edwin. **d** 07 **p** 08. NSM Lurgan Ch the Redeemer D & D from 07. 33 Charnwood Grange, Portadown, Craigavon BT63 5TU

BAXTER, David. See BAXTER, Canon Richard David

BAXTER, David Norman. b 39. Open Univ BA81. Kelham Th Coll 59. **d** 64 **p** 65. C Tonge Moor Man 64-68; Chapl RN 68-84; P-in-c Becontree St Pet Chelmsf 84-85; TV Becontree W 85-86; TR 86-94; Spain from 94; rtd 99. Cl Vidal i Barraquer, 10,

Escalera B, 1-2, 08870 Sitges (Barcelona), Spain Tel (0034) 938 946 151 Fax 938 943 800 E-mail dnbaxter@teleline.es

BAXTER, Dennis Alexander. b 56. Sheff Univ BA96. St Mich Coll Llan 03. **d** 05 **p** 06. C Tenby St D 05-09; P-in-c Llanedi w Tycroes and Saron from 09. The Vicarage, 37 Hendre Road, Tycroes, Ammanford SA18 3LA Tel (01269) 592315 Mobile 07963-467702 E-mail aarowkosky2@aol.com

BAXTER (née AVIS), **Elizabeth Mary.** b 49. Leeds Metrop Univ BA93 CYCW77. NOC 81. **dss** 84 **d** 87 **p** 94. Leeds St Marg and All Hallows Ripon 84-93; Par Dn 87-93; Chapl Abbey Grange High Sch 85-93; Par Dn Topcliffe York 93-94; C 94-96; C Thirsk 96-07; Jt Dir H Rood Ho Cen for Health and Past Care 93-07; Exec Dir from 07; Dir Miss from 93; Dur and Newc from 94; Bradf 97-04; Sheff from 95. 5 Glendale Road, Wooler NE71 6DN Tel (01668) 283125 or (01845) 522580 E-mail elizabeth.baxter@tiscali.co.uk

BAXTER, Harold Leslie. b 11. Roch Th Coll 62. **d** 64 **p** 65. C Corsham Bris 64-67; C Bath Lyncombe B & W 67-70; V Shapwick w Ashcott 70-88; P-in-c Burtle 75-88; V Shapwick w Ashcott and Burtle 88-95; rtd 96; Perm to Offic Truro from 97. Tredole, Prussia Cove Lane, Rosudgeon, Penzance TR20 9AX Tel (01736) 762133

BAXTER, Jane Elizabeth. b 51. EAMTC 98. **d** 01 **p** 02. C Clare w Poslingford, Cavendish etc St E 01-04; P-in-c Lyddington w Stoke Dry and Seaton etc Pet from 04; C Bulwick, Blatherwycke w Harringworth and Laxton from 04. The Rectory, 4 Windmill Way, Lyddington, Oakham LE15 9LY Tel (01572) 822717 E-mail revjanebaxter@tesco.net

BAXTER, John Richard. b 44. ACII66. STETS 96. **d** 99 **p** 00. NSM Banstead Guildf 99-03; TV Surrey Weald from 03. High Lea, 54 The Street, Capel, Dorking RH5 5LE Tel (01306) 711260 Mobile 07974-692334 E-mail johnbaxter@eastewell.freeserve.co.uk

BAXTER, Leslie. See BAXTER, Harold Leslie

BAXTER, Canon Richard David. b 33. Kelham Th Coll 53. **d** 57 **p** 58. C Carl St Barn 57-59; C Barrow St Matt 59-64; V Drighlington Wakef 64-73; V Penistone 73-80; V Carl St Aid and Ch Ch 80-86; Can Res Wakef Cathl 86-97; Prec from 86; Vice-Provost 92-97; rtd 97; Perm to Offic Carl from 97; Hon V Choral Carl Cathl from 04. 20 Summerfields, Dalston, Carlisle CA5 7NW Tel and fax (01228) 710496 E-mail canondavidbaxter@btinternet.com

BAXTER, Stanley Robert. b 31. Leeds Univ MA90 FRSA96 MICM96 MInstD97 FRSH99 FRSM02 FCIM07. Chich Th Coll 79. **d** 80 **p** 81. In Lutheran Ch 71-79; C Far Headingley St Chad Ripon 80-82; P-in-c Leeds St Marg 82-87; P-in-c Leeds All Hallows w Wrangthorn 85-87; P-in-c Leeds St Marg and All Hallows 87-93; P-in-c Topcliffe York 93-95; NSM 95-96; NSM Thirsk 96-07; Dir Leeds Cen for Urban Th Studies 88-93; Assoc Chapl Leeds Univ 91-93; Jt Dir H Rood Ho Cen for Health and Past Care 93-07; Dir Miss from 07; Perm to Offic Ripon from 93; Perm to Offic Dur and Newc from 94; Bradf and Sheff from 95; Chapl N Yorks and York Primary Care Trust 03-07; Chief Exec Hexthorpe Manor Community from 07. 5 Glendale Road, Wooler NE71 6DN Tel (01668) 283125 or (01845) 522580 E-mail stanleybaxter@holyroodhouse.org.uk

BAXTER, Stuart. b 42. Liv Univ BA65 Nottm Univ PGCE66. Cuddesdon Coll 66. **d** 70 **p** 71. C Kirkby Liv 70-73; C Ainsdale 73-76; CMS 76-77 and 83-84; Sierra Leone 77-83; V Nelson in Lt Marsden Blackb 84-92; V Lostock Hall 92-99; P-in-c Hatton Derby 99-04; Asst Chapl HM Pris Sudbury 99-03; Asst Chapl HM Pris Foston Hall 03-06; rtd 06; Perm to Offic Derby from 06. 11 Pingle Crescent, Belper DE56 1DY Tel (01773) 827309

BAXTER, Terence Hugh. b 48. Leeds Poly BSc74. NOC 89. **d** 92 **p** 93. NSM Guiseley w Esholt Bradf 92-04; NSM Weston w Denton 04-08; NSM Leathley w Farnley, Fewston and Blubberhouses 04-08; NSM Washburn and Mid-Wharfe from 08. The Rectory, Stainburn Lane, Leathley, Otley LS21 2LF Tel 0113-284 3744 Mobile 07985-391298 E-mail terry.baxter@bradford.anglican.org

BAYCOCK, Philip Louis. b 33. Wells Th Coll 64. **d** 66 **p** 67. C Kettering SS Pet and Paul 66-68; C St Peter-in-Thanet Cant 68-72; V Bobbing w Iwade 72-73; Perm to Offic 73-76; V Thanington w Milton 77-84; R Chagford w Gidleigh and Throwleigh Ex 84-01; rtd 01; Perm to Offic Ex from 01. 7 Grove Meadow, Sticklepath, Okehampton EX20 2NE Tel (01837) 840617 E-mail louisb@care4free.net

BAYES, Frederick Alan. b 60. Imp Coll Lon BSc81. St Jo Coll Dur BA92 Cranmer Hall Dur 93. **d** 93 **p** 94. C Talbot Village Sarum 93-97; Chapl St Hild and St Bede Coll Dur 97-03; Bp's Adv in Interfaith Matters 02-03; V Penllergaer St B from 03. The Vicarage, 16 Swansea Road, Penllergaer, Swansea SA4 9AQ Tel (01792) 892560

BAYES, Canon Paul. b 53. Birm Univ BA75. Qu Coll Birm 76. **d** 79 **p** 80. C Tynemouth Cullercoats St Paul Newc 79-82; Chapl Qu Eliz Coll Lon 82-87; Chapl Chelsea Coll 85-87; TV High Wycombe Ox 87-90; TR 90-94; TR Totton Win 95-04; AD Lyndhurst 00-04; Nat Miss and Evang Adv Abps' Coun from 04; Hon Can Worc Cathl from 07. Church House, Great Smith

Street, London SW1P 3AZ Tel (020) 7898 1502 Fax 7898 1431
E-mail paul.bayes@c-of-e.org.uk
BAYFORD, Terence Michael. b 48. Westmr Coll Ox MTh96.
Wilson Carlile Coll 70 NOC 97. **d** 99 **p** 00. Dep Chapl HM Pris
Wakef 99-01; NSM Alverthorpe *Wakef* 99-01; Chapl HM Pris
Moorland 01-05; Chapl HM Pris Wealstun from 05. *The
Chaplain's Office, HM Prison Wealstun, Thorp Arch, Wetherby
LS23 7AZ* Tel (01937) 844844
BAYLDON, Roger. b 38. MBE74 TD99. **d** 04 **p** 05. OLM
Parkstone St Pet and St Osmund w Branksea *Sarum* 04-08.
37 Blake Dene Road, Poole BH14 8HF Tel and fax (01202)
730683 Mobile 07831-272773
E-mail r.bayldon@btinternet.com *or* roger@bayldon.com
BAYLEY, Anne Christine. b 34. OBE86. Girton Coll Cam BA55
MB, ChB58 FRCS66 FRCSEd86. St Steph Ho Ox 90. **d** 91 **p** 94.
NSM Wembley Park St Aug *Lon* 91-97; Perm to Offic *York*
97-05 and *Heref* 05-08. *52 Frome Court, Bartestree, Hereford
HR1 4DX* Tel (01432) 850220
BAYLEY, David Francis. b 47. **d** 99 **p** 00. OLM Wriggle Valley
Sarum 99-04; NSM Weaverthorpe w Helperthorpe, Luttons
Ambo etc *York* 04-08; P-in-c 06-08; rtd 09; Perm to Offic *York*
from 09. *62 Newbiggin, Malton YO17 7JF* Tel 07817-023108
(mobile) E-mail revdavidbayley@tiscali.co.uk
BAYLEY, Canon John Benson. b 39. K Coll Cam BA60 MA64.
Qu Coll Birm 61. **d** 63 **p** 64. C Clee *Linc* 63-68; V Gainsborough
H Trin 68-73; P-in-c Linc St Mich 73-75; P-in-c Linc St Pet in
Eastgate w St Marg 73-75; P-in-c Linc St Mary Magd w St Paul
73-75; R Linc Minster Gp 75-02; Can and Preb Linc Cathl 75-02;
Hon PV 77-02; rtd 02. *16 Bexmore Drive, Streethay, Lichfield
WS13 8LB* Tel (01543) 417335
BAYLEY, Michael John. b 36. CCC Cam BA60 MA64 Sheff
Univ PhD73. Linc Th Coll 60. **d** 62 **p** 63. C Leeds Gipton
Epiphany *Ripon* 62-66; NSM Sheff St Mark Broomhill 67-93; C
Sheff St Mary w Highfield Trin 93-95; C Sheff St Mary Bramall
Lane 95-00; rtd 00. *27 Meadowbank Avenue, Sheffield S7 1PB*
Tel 0114-258 5248
BAYLEY, Oliver James Drummond. b 49. Mansf Coll Ox MA
PGCE. St Jo Coll Nottm 81. **d** 83 **p** 84. C Bath Weston St Jo w
Kelston *B & W* 83-88; P-in-c Bathampton 88-93; P-in-c
Claverton 92-93; R Bathampton w Claverton 93-96; Chapl
Dauntsey's Sch Devizes 96-02; rtd 02; Perm to Offic *Win* from
01. *19 Treeside Road, Southampton SO15 5FY* Tel (023) 8078
6498 E-mail ojdb80@hotmail.com
BAYLEY, Canon Raymond. b 46. Keble Coll Ox BA68 MA72 Ex
Univ PhD86. St Chad's Coll Dur 80. **d** 69 **p** 70. C Mold *St As*
69-74; Lay Tr Officer 71-74; C Llandaff w Capel Llanilltern 74;
PV Llan Cathl and Lay Tr Officer 74-77; V Cwmbach 77-80; Dir
Past Studies St Mich Coll Llan 80-84; Lect Univ of Wales
(Cardiff) *Llan* 80-84; V Ynysddu *Mon* 84-86; V Griffithstown
86-92; Tutor Dioc Minl Tr Course 84-92; V Rhosymedre *St As*
92-96; Warden and R Ruthin w Llanrhydd from 96; Tutor Dioc
Minl Tr Course 92-06; Dir CME 94-01; Warden of Readers from
02; Hon Can St As Cathl from 04. *The Cloisters, School Road,
Ruthin LL15 1BL* Tel (01824) 702068
E-mail raymond.bayley@virgin.net
BAYLIS (née LOFTS), Mrs Sally Anne. b 55. Kent Univ BA78 K
Coll Lon MA80 Nottm Univ PGCE93. St Jo Coll Nottm 01.
d 03 **p** 04. C Gedling *S'well* 03-07; P-in-c Daybrook from 07.
St Paul's Vicarage, 241 Oxclose Lane, Nottingham NG5 6FB Tel
0115-926 2686 E-mail k.baylis@ntlworld.com
BAYLISS, Geoffrey Brian Tudor. b 60. R Holloway Coll Lon
BSc83 Univ of Wales (Swansea) PGCE85. EAMTC 96. **d** 99
p 00. NSM Panfield and Rayne *Chelmsf* 99-04; TV Halstead
Area from 04; RD Hinckford from 08. *The Vicarage, Church
Road, Gosfield, Halstead CO9 1UD* Tel (01787) 273434
E-mail g.bayliss41@btinternet.com
BAYLISS, Grant David. b 75. Ex Univ BA96. Ripon Coll
Cuddesdon BA99. **d** 03 **p** 04. C Prestbury and All SS *Glouc*
03-07; Chapl St Jo Coll Cam from 07. *St John's College,
Cambridge CB2 3RF* Tel (01223) 338600
E-mail gdbayliss@ukonline.co.uk
BAYLOR, Nigel Peter. b 58. NUI BA80 TCD MPhil88. **d** 84 **p** 86.
C Carrickfergus *Conn* 84-87; C Dundela St Mark *D & D* 88-91; I
Galloon w Drummully *Clogh* 89-94; Adult Educn Adv 91-94; I
Carnmoney *Conn* 94-03; I Jordanstown from 03. *The Rectory,
120A Circular Road, Jordanstown, Newtownabbey BT37 0RH*
Tel (028) 9086 2119 E-mail revbaylor_munster@hotmail.co.uk
BAYLY, Mrs Janet. **d** 08. OLM Schorne *Ox* from 08. *Crandon
Farm, North Marston, Buckingham MK18 3PQ* Tel (01296)
670245 E-mail crancon@dial.pipex.com
BAYLY, Samuel Niall Maurice. b 36. TCD BA64 MA. CITC Div
Test65. **d** 65 **p** 66. C Belfast St Matt *Conn* 65-68; Miss to Seamen
68-69; C Belfast St Pet *Conn* 69-74; I Belfast Ch Ch 74-02.
81 Dunluce Avenue, Belfast BT9 7AW Tel (028) 9066 8732
BAYMAN, Ann Bernette. b 45. **d** 04 **p** 05. OLM Yoxmere *St E*
from 04. *Dove Cottage, 4 South Road, Beccles NR34 9NN*
Tel (01502) 471709 Mobile 07884-072944
E-mail annie@dovecottage.orangehome.co.uk

BAYNE, Canon David William. b 52. St Andr Univ MA75. Edin
Th Coll 88. **d** 90 **p** 91. C Dumfries *Glas* 90-92; P-in-c 92-93; R
93-99; Chapl Dumfries and Galloway Primary Care NHS Trust
92-99; Chapl Crichton R Hosp Dumfries 92-99; Chapl HM Pris
Dumfries 96-99; P-in-c Castle Douglas *Glas* from 99; Can
St Mary's Cathl from 99. *The Rectory, 68 St Andrew Street,
Castle Douglas DG7 1EN* Tel and fax (01556) 503818
E-mail dwbayne@aol.com
BAYNE, Mrs Felicity Meriel. b 47. WEMTC 91. **d** 94 **p** 95. NSM
Cheltenham Ch Ch *Glouc* 94-98; NSM Leckhampton St Pet
98-09; Chapl Glenfall Ho from 09. *Glenfall House, Mill Lane,
Charlton Kings, Cheltenham GL54 4EP* Tel (01242) 583654 Fax
251314 E-mail felicity.bayne@btinternet.com
BAYNE-JARDINE, Anthea Mary. *See* GRIGGS, Mrs Anthea
Mary
BAYNES, Mrs Clare. b 57. Reading Univ BA79. SAOMC 01. **d** 04
p 05. NSM Chambersbury *St Alb* 04-08; NSM St Alb St Steph
from 08. *4 Pilgrim Close, Park Street, St Albans AL2 2JD* Tel
(01727) 875524 E-mail clare@simonbaynes.fsnet.co.uk
BAYNES, Matthew Thomas Crispin. b 62. UEA BA83 Qu Coll
Cam BA86 MA91. Westcott Ho Cam 85. **d** 87 **p** 88. C Southgate
Ch Ch *Lon* 87-90; C Gt Berkhamsted *St Alb* 90-95; V Coseley
Ch Ch *Worc* 95-99; R Bredon w Bredon's Norton from 99; RD
Pershore from 05. *The Rectory, Bredon, Tewkesbury GL20 7LT*
Tel (01684) 772237 E-mail matthew@tcbaynes.fsnet.co.uk
BAYNES, Simon Hamilton. b 33. New Coll Ox BA57 MA62.
Wycliffe Hall Ox 57. **d** 59 **p** 60. C Rodbourne Cheney *Bris* 59-62;
Japan 63-80; C Keynsham *B & W* 80-84; P-in-c Winkfield *Ox*
84-85; V Winkfield and Cranbourne 85-99; rtd 99; Lic to Offic
Ox 99-02; Hon C Thame from 02. *23 Moorend Lane, Thame
OX9 3BQ* Tel (01844) 213673 E-mail baynes@psa-online.com
BAYNES, Timothy Francis de Brissac. b 29. Ely Th Coll 59. **d** 61
p 62. C Hockerill *St Alb* 61-65; C Mansfield Woodhouse *S'well*
65-67; Ind Chapl *Man* 67-94; P-in-c Miles Platting St Jo 67-72;
rtd 94; Perm to Offic *Man* 94-97. *46 Kirkbie Green, Kendal
LA9 7AJ* Tel (01539) 740605
BAYNES, William Hendrie. b 39. Adelaide Univ BA60. S'wark
Ord Course 77. **d** 79 **p** 80. C Notting Hill All SS w St Columb
Lon 79-85; Perm to Offic 86-87 and 99-00; Hon C Paddington
St Sav 88-98; Asst Chapl St Mary's NHS Trust Paddington
94-99; Hon C Paddington St Jas *Lon* from 00. *39E Westbourne
Gardens, London W2 5NR* Tel (020) 7727 9522
E-mail will.baynes@london.anglican.org
BAYNHAM, Matthew Fred. b 57. BNC Ox BA78 Birm Univ
MPhil00. Wycliffe Hall Ox 80. **d** 83 **p** 84. C Yardley St Edburgha
Birm 83-87; TV Bath Twerton-on-Avon *B & W* 87-93; V Reddal
Hill St Luke *Worc* 93-00; RD Dudley 98-00; Chapl Bp
Grosseteste Coll Linc 00-05; Assoc Chapl Liv Univ 05-07; Sen
Res Tutor from 07. *Fronnant, Nanternis, New Quay SA45 9RW*
Tel (01545) 560500 E-mail baynham@hope.ac.uk
BAYS, Mrs Helen Margaret. b 48. Kent Univ BA69 RGN71
RHV73. STETS 97. **d** 00 **p** 01. NSM Calne and Blackland
Sarum 00-02; NSM Dawlish *Ex* from 02. *14 Stockton Hill,
Dawlish EX7 9LP* Tel (01626) 862860
BAZELY, William Francis. b 53. Sheff Univ BEng75. St Jo Coll
Nottm 78. **d** 81 **p** 82. C Huyton St Geo *Liv* 81-84; TV
Netherthorpe *Sheff* 84-92; Chapl Lambeth Healthcare NHS
Trust 92-98; Chapl Guy's and St Thos' Hosps NHS Trust Lon
98-01; C Rotherham *Sheff* 01-03; Chapl Rotherham Gen Hosps
NHS Trust 01-03; Chapl Rotherham Priority Health Services
NHS Trust 01-03; Sen Chapl Norfolk & Waveney Mental Health
NHS Foundn Trust from 03. *34 Woodcock Road, Norwich
NR3 3TX* Tel (01603) 421345 Mobile 07786-734519
E-mail bill_bazely@hotmail.com
✠**BAZLEY, The Rt Revd Colin Frederick.** b 35. St Pet Coll Ox
BA57 MA61. Tyndale Hall Bris 57. **d** 59 **p** 60 **c** 69. C Bootle
St Leon *Liv* 59-62; SAMS Miss Chile 62-00; Adn Cautin and
Malleco 67-69; Asst Bp Cautin and Malleco 69-75; Asst Bp
Santiago 75-77; Bp Chile 77-00; Primate CASA 77-83; Primate
Iglesia Anglicana del Cono Sur 89-95; rtd 00; Hon Asst Bp Ches
from 00; Warden of Readers 00-05; RD Wallasey from 09.
121 Brackenwood Road, Higher Bebington, Wirral CH63 2LU
Tel 0151-608 1193 Mobile 07866-391333
E-mail colin@colbarb.fsnet.co.uk
BAZLINTON, Stephen Cecil. b 46. Lon Univ BDS RCS LDS.
Ridley Hall Cam 78. **d** 85 **p** 86. NSM Stebbing w Lindsell
Chelmsf 85-04; NSM Stebbing and Lindsell w Gt and Lt Saling
04-08; Perm to Offic from 08. *St Helens, High Street, Stebbing,
Dunmow CM6 3SE* Tel (01371) 856495
E-mail revbaz@care4free.co.uk
BEACH, Jonathan Mark. b 67. Essex Univ BSc89. Trin Coll
Bris BA94. **d** 94 **p** 95. C Oulton Broad *Nor* 94-97; Chapl RAF
from 97. *Chaplaincy Services, Valiant Block, HQ Air Command,
RAF High Wycombe HP14 4UE* Tel (01494) 496800
Fax 496343
BEACH, Mark Howard Francis. b 62. Kent Univ BA83 Nottm
Univ MA95. St Steph Ho Ox 85. **d** 87 **p** 88. C Beeston *S'well*
87-90; C Hucknall Torkard 90-93; R Gedling 93-01; R

Netherfield 96-01; Bp's Chapl *Wakef* 01-03; TR Rugby *Cov* from 03. *The Rectory, Church Street, Rugby CV21 3PH* Tel (01788) 542936 *or* 565609 Mobile 07930-577248
E-mail mark.beach@zetnet.co.uk *or* rector@rugbyteam.org.uk

BEACH, Stephen John. b 58. Man Univ BA81 BD88 Didsbury Coll of Educn PGCE82. NOC 92. **d** 93 **p** 94. C Harwood *Man* 93-97; TV Westhoughton and Wingates 97-01; P-in-c Devonport St Budeaux *Ex* 01-02; V from 02. *St Budeaux Vicarage, Agaton Road, Plymouth PL5 2EW* Tel (01752) 361019 *or* 351087
E-mail steph.beach@xalt.co.uk

BEACHAM, Peter Martyn. b 44. Ex Coll Ox BA65 MA70 Lon Univ MPhil67 FSA92 MRTPI69. Sarum Th Coll 70. **d** 73 **p** 74. NSM Ex St Martin, St Steph, St Laur etc 73-74; NSM Cen Ex 74-90; Perm to Offic from 99. *Bellever, Barrack Road, Exeter EX2 6AB* Tel (01392) 435074

BEACON, Canon Ralph Anthony. b 44. St Mich Coll Llan 70. **d** 71 **p** 72. C Neath w Llantwit 71-74; TV Holyhead w Rhoscolyn *Ban* 74-78; R Llanenddwyn w Llanddwywe, Llanbedr w Llandanwg 78-99; V Harlech and Llanfair-juxta-Harlech etc from 99; RD Ardudwy 89-02; AD from 02; Hon Can Ban Cathl 91-97; Can Cursal 97-03; Can and Preb Ban Cathl from 03. *The Rectory, Môn Dirion, Ffordd Uchaf, Harlech LL46 2SS* Tel (01766) 781336 Mobile 07713-421858

BEACON, Mrs Stephanie Kathleen Nora. b 49. Univ of Wales (Ban) BA70 PGCE71. NW Ord Course 94. **d** 96 **p** 97. NSM Llanenddwyn w Llanddwywe, Llanbedr w Llandanwg *Ban* 96-98; C Ardudwy 98-99; P-in-c Llanenddwyn w Llanddwywe, Llanbedr w Llandanwg 99-01; R from 01. *The Rectory, Môn Dirion, Ffordd Uchaf, Harlech LL46 2SS* Tel (01766) 781336 Mobile 07713-421858

BEADLE, David Alexander. b 37. St And Dioc Tr Course. **d** 88 **p** 89. NSM St Andrews St Andr *St And* from 88. *48 Clayton Caravan Park, St Andrews KY16 9YB* Tel (01334) 870001
E-mail dabeadle@lineone.net

BEADLE, Canon Janet Mary. b 52. Philippa Fawcett Coll CertEd74. EAMTC 91. **d** 94 **p** 95. C Kingston upon Hull H Trin *York* 94-98; V Ness Gp *Linc* from 98; Bp's Adv in Women's Min from 00; Can and Preb Linc Cathl from 03. *The Vicarage, 10 Church Street, Thurlby, Bourne PE10 0EH* Tel (01778) 422475
E-mail janet.beadle@talk21.com

BEADLE, Liam Paul. b 84. St Pet Coll Ox BA05 St Jo Coll Dur MA09. Cranmer Hall Dur 07. **d** 09. C Enfield St Andr *Lon* from 09. *159 Parsonage Lane, Enfield EN1 3UJ*
E-mail liam.beadle@gmail.com

BEADLE, Mrs Lorna. b 40. NEOC 92. **d** 95 **p** 96. NSM Ashington *Newc* from 95; Chapl MU from 02. *9 Arundel Square, Ashington NE63 8AW* Tel (01670) 816467

BEAHAN, Alan. b 64. Birm Univ BA87 York Univ PGCE89 St Jo Coll Dur BA07. Cranmer Hall Dur 05. **d** 07 **p** 08. C Warrington St Elphin *Liv* from 07. *5 Elliott Avenue, Warrington WA1 3SD* Tel (01925) 632176 E-mail hncsarmoss@hotmail.com

✠**BEAK, The Rt Revd Robert Michael Cawthorn.** b 25. OBE90. Lon Bible Coll. **d** 53 **p** 54 **c** 84. C Tunbridge Wells St Jo *Roch* 53-55; BCMS 55-56 and 84-89; Kenya 56-69 and 84-89; R Heanton Punchardon *Ex* 70-84; Offg Chapl RAF 70-80; RD Barnstaple *Ex* 77-81; R Heanton Punchardon w Marwood 79-84; Preb Ex Cathl 82-84; Asst Bp Mt Kenya E 84-89; rtd 90; Hon Asst Bp Derby from 91. *Ashcroft Cottage, Butts Road, Ashover, Chesterfield S45 0AX* Tel (01246) 590048

BEAK, Stephen Robert. b 64. City Univ BSc86. Wycliffe Hall Ox BTh94. **d** 94 **p** 95. C Lache cum Saltney *Ches* 94-97; C Howell Hill *Guildf* 97-01; NSM Woking St Mary 01-05; V from 05. *St Mary's Vicarage, Bethany House, West Hill Road, Woking GU22 7UJ* Tel (01483) 761269
E-mail stephen.beak@ntlworld.com

BEAKE, The Ven Stuart Alexander. b 49. Em Coll Cam BA72 MA76. Cuddesdon Coll 72. **d** 74 **p** 75. C Hitchin St Mary *St Alb* 74-76; C Hitchin 77-79; TV Hemel Hempstead 79-85; Bp's Dom Chapl *S'well* 85-87; V Shottery St Andr *Cov* 87-00; RD Fosse 93-99; Dioc Dir of Ords 96-00; Hon Can Cov Cathl 98-00; Can Res and Sub-Dean Cov Cathl 00-05; Adn Surrey *Guildf* from 05; Hon Can Guildf Cathl from 05; Warden CSP from 08. *Archdeacon's House, Lime Grove, West Clandon, Guildford GU4 7UT* Tel (01483) 211924 *or* 790352
E-mail stuart.beake@cofeguildford.org.uk
or sabeake@msn.com

BEAKEN, Robert William Frederick. b 62. SS Paul & Mary Coll Cheltenham BA83 Lambeth STh90 MA01 K Coll Lon PhD09 FSAScot01. Ripon Coll Cuddesdon 85 Ven English Coll & Pontifical Gregorian Univ Rome 87. **d** 88 **p** 89. C Forton *Portsm* 88-92; C Shepshed *Leic* 92-94; V Colchester St Barn *Chelmsf* 94-02; P-in-c Gt and Lt Bardfield from 02. *The Vicarage, Braintree Road, Great Bardfield, Braintree CM7 4RN* Tel (01371) 810267 E-mail robert@webform.com

BEAL, David Michael. b 61. St Jo Coll Nottm BTh89. **d** 89 **p** 90. C Marton *Blackb* 89-92; C Darwen St Pet w Hoddlesden 92-93; TV 93-97; R Itchingfield w Slinfold *Chich* 97-09; R W Chiltington from 09. *The Rectory, East Street, West Chiltington, Pulborough RH20 2JY* E-mail beals@tesco.net

BEAL, Malcolm. b 31. Bris Univ BA52. Ridley Hall Cam 57. **d** 59 **p** 60. C Keynsham w Queen Charlton *B & W* 59-62; C Speke All SS *Liv* 62-65; Uganda 65-74; V Salford Priors *Cov* 74-83; V Jersey St Clem *Win* 83-97; rtd 97; Perm to Offic *Ex* from 97 and *B & W* from 03. *3 Redwoods Close, Hemyock, Cullompton EX15 3QQ* Tel (01823) 680853 E-mail mmbeal@lineone.net

BEALES, Christopher Leader Day. b 51. St Jo Coll Dur BA72. Cranmer Hall Dur 72. **d** 76 **p** 77. C Upper Armley and Ind Chapl *Ripon* 76-79; Ind Chapl *Dur* 79-84; Sen Chapl 82-84; Sec Ind Cttee of Gen Syn Bd for Soc Resp 85-91; Sec Inner Cities Relig Coun (DOE) 92-94; Dir Churches' Regional Commn in the NE *Newc* and *Dur* 94-98; Consultant Dir 98; Chief Exec Employment Focus 99-07; C Thamesmead *S'wark* 99-01; Perm to Offic from 01; Chief Exec Afghan Action from 05; P-in-c Woburn Sands *St Alb* from 08. *The Vicarage, 30 Church Road, Woburn Sands, Milton Keynes MK17 8TR* Tel (01908) 582581
E-mail chrisbeales@afghanaction.com

BEALES, John David. b 55. SS Hild & Bede Coll Dur BA77 Univ of W Aus DipEd79. St Jo Coll Nottm 81. **d** 83 **p** 84. Australia 83-89 and 95-00; C Scarborough 83-86; Dioc Youth Chapl Perth 86-89; Dir Educn and Tr Philo Trust 89-90; NSM Nottingham St Nic *S'well* 89-95; Dir Evang Melbourne 95-00; Perm to Offic *Chelmsf* 99-01. *52 Wellesley Road, Colchester CO3 3HF* Tel (01206) 530934 E-mail davidbeales@ntlworld.com

BEALING, Andrew John. b 42. Sarum Th Coll 67. **d** 69 **p** 70. C Auckland St Andr and St Anne *Dur* 69-73; P-in-c Eastgate and Rookhope 73-76; V Frosterley 76-85; V Rekendyke 85-09; Chapl S Tyneside Distr Hosp 90-93; Chapl S Tyneside Healthcare Trust 93-09; Chapl Miss to Seafarers 02-09; rtd 09. *31 Cedar Drive, Jarrow NE32 4BF* Tel 0191-519 2588

BEALING, Mrs Patricia Ramsey. b 39. Lightfoot Ho Dur IDC63. dss 63 **d** 87 **p** 94. Rekendyke *Dur* 85-06; Par Dn 87-94; C 94-06; Chapl S Tyneside Distr Hosp 88-93; Chapl S Tyneside Healthcare Trust 93-06; rtd 06. *31 Cedar Drive, Jarrow NE32 4BF* Tel 0191-519 2588

BEAMENT, Canon Owen John. b 41. MBE01. Bps' Coll Cheshunt 61. **d** 64 **p** 65. C Deptford St Paul *S'wark* 64-68; C Peckham St Jo 69-73; C Vauxhall St Pet 73-74; V Hatcham Park All SS from 74; Hon Can S'wark Cathl from 97. *All Saints' Vicarage, 22 Erlanger Road, London SE14 5TG* Tel (020) 7639 3497 E-mail owenbeament@aol.com

BEAMER, Neville David. b 40. Univ of Wales (Lamp) BA62 Jes Coll Ox BA65 MA70. Wycliffe Hall Ox 64. **d** 65 **p** 66. C Hornchurch St Andr *Chelmsf* 65-68; C Warwick St Mary *Cov* 68-72; V Holton-le-Clay *Linc* 72-75; P-in-c Stoneleigh w Ashow *Cov* 75-79; P-in-c Baginton 77-79; V Fletchamstead 79-86; Warden Whatcombe Ho Blandford Forum 86-90; R Jersey St Lawr and V Jersey Millbrook St Matt *Win* 90-95; V Yateley 95-03; P-in-c Eversley 98-03; R Yateley and Eversley 03-05; RD Odiham 95-04; rtd 05; Perm to Offic *Cov* from 05. *8 Aintree Road, Stratford-upon-Avon CV37 9FL* Tel (01789) 263435
E-mail nevillebeamer@aol.com

BEAN, Douglas Jeyes Lendrum. b 25. Worc Coll Ox BA50 MA53. Ely Th Coll 50. **d** 51 **p** 52. C Croydon Woodside *Cant* 51-54; Min Can Windsor 54-59; V Reading St Laur *Ox* 59-68; Chapl HM Borstal Reading 61-68; RD Reading *Ox* 65-68; Min Can St Paul's Cathl 68-72; Hon Min Can from 72; V St Pancras w St Jas and Ch Ch 72-93; PV Westmr Abbey 75-80; rtd 93; Perm to Offic *Lon* from 99. *3 Bishop Street, London N1 8PH* Tel (020) 7226 8340

BEAN, James Corey. b 35. Centenary Coll New Jersey BA58 Long Is Univ MS74. Seabury-Western Th Sem LTh61. **d** 61 **p** 62. USA 61-79 and from 90; Chapl Wiesbaden *Eur* 79-90. *PO Box 490, Pomeroy WA 99347-0490, USA* Tel (001) (509) 843 1871

BEAN, Canon John Victor. b 25. Down Coll Cam BA47 MA51. Sarum Th Coll 48. **d** 50 **p** 51. C Milton *Portsm* 50-55; C Fareham SS Pet and Paul 55-59; V St Helens 59-66; V Cowes St Mary 66-91; RD W Wight 68-72; Hon Can Portsm Cathl 70-91; P-in-c Cowes St Faith 77-80; C-in-c Gurnard All SS CD 78-91; Chapl to The Queen 80-95; rtd 91; Perm to Offic *Portsm* from 91. *Heathercroft, 27 Salisbury Road, Ryde PO33 1BY* Tel (01983) 812516

BEANE, Andrew Mark. b 72. St Jo Coll Nottm BA02. **d** 02 **p** 03. C Thorpe St Matt *Nor* 02-05; P-in-c Horsham St Faith, Spixworth and Crostwick 05-06; R from 06. *The Rectory, Buxton Road, Spixworth, Norwich NR10 3PR* Tel (01603) 898258
E-mail andrewbeane@onetel.com

BEANEY, John. b 47. Trin Coll Bris 77. **d** 79 **p** 80. C Bromley Ch Ch *Roch* 79-84; V Broadheath *Ches* 84-08; Chapl Altrincham Gen Hosp 91-94; Chapl Trafford Healthcare NHS Trust 94-98; P-in-c Norton *Ches* from 08; Ecum Officer (Gtr Man) from 02. *The Vicarage, Windmill Hill, Runcorn WA7 6QE* Tel (01928) 715225

BEARCROFT, Bramwell Arthur. b 52. Homerton Coll Cam BEd82. EAMTC 87. **d** 90 **p** 91. Chapl and Hd RS Kimbolton Sch Cambs 88-94; NSM Tilbrook *Ely* 90-94; NSM Covington 90-94; NSM Catworth Magna 90-94; NSM Keyston and Bythorn 90-94; NSM Cary Deanery *B & W* 94-02; Hd Master

Hazlegrove Sch 94-02. *Clé de Tève, Devillac, 47210 Lot et Garonne, France* Tel (0033) (5) 53 71 46 24
E-mail jenniferbearcroft@hotmail.com

BEARD, Christopher Robert. b 47. Chich Th Coll 81. **d** 83 **p** 84. C Chich St Paul and St Pet 83-86; TV Ifield 86-91; V Haywards Heath St Rich 91-99; P-in-c Donnington from 99; Chapl St Wilfrid's Hospice Eastbourne from 99. *The Vicarage, 34 Graydon Avenue, Donnington, Chichester PO19 8RF* Tel (01243) 776395 Mobile 07845-482779

BEARD, Laurence Philip. b 45. Lon Univ BA68. Trin Coll Bris 88. **d** 90 **p** 91. C Trentham *Lich* 90-94; V Wolverhampton St Matt 94-01; P-in-c Hartshill *Cov* 01-08; rtd 08. *14 Beechcroft Avenue, Croxley Green, Rickmansworth WD3 3EQ* Tel (01923) 222312
E-mail lpbeard@talk21.com

BEARD, Robert John Hansley. b 61. St Andr Univ BD85. Ripon Coll Cuddesdon 86 Ch Div Sch of the Pacific (USA) 87. **d** 88 **p** 89. C Sheff Manor 88-91; C Rotherham 91-94; V Sheff St Pet Abbeydale 94-02; Assoc Chapl Sheff Hallam Univ 95-98; Bp's Adv on Interfaith Issues 96-02; Intercultural Regeneration Development Worker Simunye from 02. *18 Arnside Road, Sheffield S8 0UX* Tel 0114-255 6335
E-mail arjay61@hotmail.com

BEARDALL, Raymond. b 32. St Jo Coll Nottm 70. **d** 72 **p** 73. C Ilkley All SS *Bradf* 72-74; C Seasalter *Cant* 74-79; V Farndon *S'well* 79-84; R Thorpe 79-84; V Bloxham 84-97; rtd 97; Perm to Offic *S'well* from 03. *4 Winster Avenue, Ravenshead, Nottingham NG15 9DD* Tel (01623) 408205
E-mail ray@beardallhome.fsnet.co.uk

BEARDMORE, John Keith. b 42. FCP85 Bris Univ BEd74 K Coll Lon MA90. **d** 77 **p** 78. NSM Maindee Newport *Mon* from 77. *16 Hove Avenue, Newport NP19 7QP* Tel (01633) 263272

BEARDSHAW, David. b 37. JP. Wells Th Coll 65. **d** 67 **p** 68. C Wood End *Cov* 67-69; C Stoke 70-73; V Whitley 73-77; Dioc Educn Officer 77-87; P-in-c Offchurch and Warden Offa Retreat Ho 87-93; rtd 93. *188 Ashington Grove, Coventry CV3 4DB*

BEARDSLEY, Christina. b 51. Sussex Univ BA73 St Jo Coll Cam PhD99 Leeds Univ MA07. Westcott Ho Cam 76. **d** 78 **p** 79. C Portsea N End St Mark *Portsm* 78-85; V Catherington and Clanfield 85-00; Chapl Worthing and Southlands Hosps NHS Trust 00-01; Asst Chapl Chelsea and Westmr Hosp NHS Found Trust 01-04; Chapl 04-08; Hd Multi-Faith Chapl from 08. *Chaplains' Office, Chelsea and Westminster Hospital, 369 Fulham Road, London SW10 9NH* Tel (020) 8746 8083
E-mail christina.beardsley@chelwest.nhs.uk

BEARDSLEY, Nigel Andrew. b 61. Sheff Hallam Univ BSc88 Nottm Univ MA00. EMMTC 97. **d** 00 **p** 01. C Bath Bathwick *B & W* 00-05; Chapl RN from 05. *Royal Naval Chaplaincy Service, Mail Point 1-2, Leach Building, Whale Island, Portsmouth PO2 8BY* Tel (023) 9262 5055 Fax 9262 5134
E-mail beardsley@lanj.freeserve.co.uk

BEARDSMORE, John. b 19. Kelham Th Coll 46. **d** 51 **p** 51. C Caldmore *Lich* 51-53; C Otley *Bradf* 53-57; V Burley in Wharfedale 55-69; V Bromley H Trin *Roch* 69-70; V Buttershaw St Paul *Bradf* 70-88; rtd 88; Perm to Offic *Bradf* from 88. *41 Nab Wood Grove, Shipley BD18 4HR* Tel (01274) 596197

BEARE, William. b 33. TCD BA58. **d** 59 **p** 60. C Waterford St Patr *C & O* 59-62; C Cork H Trin w Shandon St Mary *C, C & R* 62-64; 1 Rathcormac 64-68; 1 Marmullane w Monkstown 68-76; Dioc C 76-82; I Stradbally w Ballintubbert, Coraclone etc *C & O* 82-99; Can Ossory and Leighlin Cathls 88-90; Chan 90-92; Prec 92-99; Dean Lismore and I Lismore w Cappoquin, Kilwatermoy, Dungarvan etc 99-08; Preb Stagonil St Patr Cathl Dublin 95-08; rtd 09. *24 Lapp's Court, Hartland's Avenue, Glasheen, Cork, Republic of Ireland* Tel (00353) 87-233 1508 (mobile)

BEARN, Hugh William. b 62. Man Univ BA84 MA98. Cranmer Hall Dur 86. **d** 89 **p** 90. C Heaton Ch Ch *Man* 89-92; Chapl RAF 92-96; V Tottington *Man* from 96; CF (TA) 96-02; Chapl Bury Hospice 99-03; CF (ACF) from 06; Chapl to The Queen from 06. *St Ann's Vicarage, Chapel Street, Tottington, Bury BL8 4AP* Tel (01204) 883713 E-mail hughbearn@aol.com

BEARPARK, Canon John Michael. b 36. Ex Coll Ox BA59 MA63. Linc Th Coll 59. **d** 61 **p** 62. C Bingley H Trin *Bradf* 61-64; C Baildon 64-67; V Fairweather Green 67-77; Chapl Airedale Gen Hosp 77-94; V Steeton 77-94; Hon Can Bradf Cathl 89-01; V Bentham St Marg 94-01; P-in-c Bentham St Jo 99-01; RD Ewecross 94-00; rtd 01; Perm to Offic *Bradf* from 01. *31 Northfields Crescent, Settle BD24 9JP* Tel (01729) 822522

BEASLEY, Noel Michael Roy. b 68. Imp Coll Lon BSc91 Oriel Coll Ox DPhil96 St Jo Coll Dur BA98. Cranmer Hall Dur. **d** 99 **p** 00. C Newport w Longford, Chetwynd and Forton *Lich* 99-03; Chapl Westcott Ho Cam 03-07; Tutor from 07. *Westcott House, Jesus Lane, Cambridge CB5 8BP* Tel (01223) 741000
E-mail nmrb2@cam.ac.uk

BEASLEY, Canon Walter Sydney. b 33. Nottm Univ BA57. Linc Th Coll 57. **d** 59 **p** 60. C Harworth *S'well* 59-64; V Forest Town 64-70; R Bulwell St Mary 70-97; Hon Can *S'well* Minster 85-97;

rtd 97; Perm to Offic *S'well* from 04. *3 Clayton's Drive, Nottingham NG7 2PF* Tel 0115-970 2717 Mobile 07889-350442

BEATER, David MacPherson. b 41. Chich Th Coll 66. **d** 69 **p** 70. C Withington St Crispin *Man* 69-72; C Lightbowne 72-74; V Prestwich St Hilda 74-81; V Northfleet *Roch* 81-85; C Bickley 86-90; TV Stanley *Dur* 90-97; CMP from 91; SSF 97-01; C Seaton Hirst *Newc* 01-05; rtd 05; Perm to Offic *Cant* from 07. *7 Ferndown, 146 Minnis Road, Birchington CT7 9QE* Tel (01843) 842166

BEATON, Mark Timothy. b 61. Univ of Wales (Ban) BA83. Trin Coll Bris 03. **d** 05 **p** 06. C Swindon St Jo and St Andr *Bris* 05-08; P-in-c New Radnor and Llanfihangel Nantmelan etc *S & B* from 08. *The Rectory, School Lane, New Radnor, Presteigne LD8 2SS* Tel (01544) 350342 E-mail mark.beaton@tesco.net

BEATTIE, David George. b 42. MIMechE76. CITC 01. **d** 04 **p** 05. Aux Min Belfast H Trin and St Silas *Conn* from 04. *6 Blackthorn Way, Newtownabbey BT37 0GW* Tel (028) 9086 3406 Mobile 07812-718080 E-mail beattie5@talktalk.net

BEATTIE, Ian David. b 36. Univ of NZ BA58. St Jo Coll Auckland LTh60. **d** 60 **p** 61. C Epsom St Andr New Zealand 60-64; C Shirley St Jo *Cant* 64-65; V S Wimbledon St Andr *S'wark* 65-71; C Napier St Aug New Zealand 71-73; V Onehunga 73-96; rtd 96. *11/148A Tasman Street, Nelson 7010, New Zealand* Tel (0064) (3) 546 7507

BEATTIE, Margaret. *See* BREWSTER, Margaret

BEATTIE, Canon Noel Christopher. b 41. TCD BTh65 Cranfield Inst of Tech MSc86. **d** 68 **p** 69. C Belfast H Trin *Conn* 68-70; C Belfast St Bart 70-73; C Doncaster St Mary *Sheff* 73-77; TV Northampton Em *Pet* 77-88; Ind Chapl 85-88; Ind Chapl *Linc* 88-92; Ind Chapl *Roch* 92-04; Ind Can Roch Cathl 00-04; rtd 04; Perm to Offic *Heref* from 05. *6 Oaks Road, Church Stretton SY6 7AX* Tel (01694) 725530 E-mail noelbt@globalnet.co.uk

BEAUCHAMP, Anthony Hazlerigg Proctor. b 40. Trin Coll Cam BA62 MA66 MICE68. St Jo Coll Nottm 73. **d** 75 **p** 76. C New Humberstone *Leic* 75-77; C-in-c Polegate *Chich* 77-80; Chapl Bethany Sch Goudhurst 80-86; Chapl Luckley-Oakfield Sch Wokingham 86-88; Chapl Clayesmore Sch Blandford 89-93; R Kirby-le-Soken w Gt Holland *Chelmsf* 93-00; Asst P Wetheral w Warwick *Carl* 00-01; rtd 01; Perm to Offic *Carl* 00-01 and Chich from 01. *2 Stelvio Cottages, 17 Beachy Head Road, Eastbourne BN20 7QP* Tel (01323) 732743

BEAUCHAMP, Gerald Charles. b 55. Hull Univ BA78 K Coll Lon MA96. Coll of Resurr Mirfield 78. **d** 80 **p** 81. C Hatcham St Cath *S'wark* 80-83; S Africa 83-86; C Ealing St Steph Castle Hill *Lon* 86-88; P-in-c Brondesbury St Anne w Kilburn H Trin 88-89; V 89-93; Chapl Kilburn Coll 88-93; C Chelsea St Luke and Ch Ch *Lon* 93-96; V W Brompton St Mary w St Pet 96-04; AD Chelsea 02-04; SSJE 04-07; C St Marylebone All SS *Lon* from 07. *6 Margaret Street, London W1W 8RQ* Tel (020) 7636 1788 Fax 7436 4470 E-mail geraldbeauchamp@msn.com

BEAUCHAMP, John Nicholas. b 57. Wycliffe Hall Ox 92. **d** 94 **p** 95. C Ipswich St Jo *St E* 94-97; TV Beccles St Mich 97-05; P-in-c Beccles St Mich and St Luke 05-08; R from 08. *44 Ringsfield Road, Beccles NR34 9PF* Tel (01502) 712317

BEAUCHAMP, Julian Thomas Proctor. b 68. Ex Univ BA91. Oak Hill Th Coll BA05. **d** 05 **p** 06. C Cheadle *Ches* 05-08; R Waverton w Aldford and Bruera from 08. *The Rectory, Village Road, Waverton, Chester CH3 7QN* Tel (01244) 336668 Mobile 07974-397022

BEAUMONT, Canon Brian Maxwell. b 34. Nottm Univ BA56. Wells Th Coll 58. **d** 59 **p** 60. C Clifton *S'well* 59-62; C E Stoke w Syerston 62; C Edgbaston St Geo *Birm* 62-65; V Smethwick St Alb 65-70; V Blackb H Trin 70-77; Asst Dir RE 70-73; Dir RE 73-92; Hon Can Blackb Cathl 73-77 and 92-99; Can Res 77-92; V Goosnargh w Whittingham 92-99; Bp's Adv for Rural Areas 92-99; rtd 99; Perm to Offic *Blackb* from 00. *14 Green Drive, Barton, Preston PR3 5AT* Tel (01772) 861131

BEAUMONT, Mrs Catherine Grace La Touche. b 60. SS Coll Cam MA83 Darw Coll Cam PGCE83 Solicitor 87. **d** 09. OLM Clopton w Otley, Swilland and Ashbocking *St E* from 09. *Otley Hall, Hall Lane, Otley, Ipswich IP6 9PA* Tel (01473) 890264 Mobile 07801-342336
E-mail catherine.beaumont@otleyhall.co.uk

BEAUMONT, Mrs Jane. b 56. Ches Coll of HE BTh. NOC 01. **d** 04 **p** 05. NSM Chadkirk *Ches* 04-08; NSM Ashton-upon-Mersey St Mary Magd from 08. *39 Kings Road, Sale M33 6QB* E-mail janebeaumont@romileylifecentre.co.uk

BEAUMONT, Canon John Philip. b 32. Leeds Univ BA55. Coll of Resurr Mirfield 55. **d** 57 **p** 58. C Leeds St Marg *Ripon* 57-60; C Wellingborough All Hallows *Pet* 60-64; V Wellingborough St Andr 64-70; Chapl HM Borstal Wellingborough 64-70; V Finedon *Pet* 70-96; Can Pet Cathl 80-96; RD Higham 83-87; rtd 96; Perm to Offic *Pet* from 96. *9 Warren Bridge, Oundle, Peterborough PE8 4DQ* Tel (01832) 273863
E-mail john@beaumont.plus.com

BEAUMONT, Stephen Martin. b 51. K Coll Lon BD73 AKC74. St Aug Coll Cant 73. **d** 74 **p** 75. C Benwell St Jas *Newc* 74-77; Asst Chapl Marlborough Coll 77-81; R Ideford, Luton and Ashcombe *Ex* 81-84; Bp's Dom Chapl 81-84; Chapl Taunton

Sch 85-91; Chapl Haileybury Coll 92-00; Second Chapl and Hd Div Tonbridge Sch 00-04; Sen Chapl from 04. *Tonbridge School, High Street, Tonbridge TN9 1JP* Tel (01732) 365555

BEAUMONT, Canon Terence Mayes. b 41. Lon Univ BA63. Linc Th Coll 68. **d** 71 **p** 72. C Hitchin St Mary *St Alb* 71-74; C Harpenden St Nic 75-79; V Stevenage St Pet Broadwater 79-87; V St Alb St Mich 87-06; Hon Can St Alb 05-06; rtd 06. *65 Weatherby, Dunstable LU6 1TP* Tel (01582) 661333
E-mail y.beaumont123@btinternet.com

BEAUMONT, Mrs Veronica Jean. b 38. Ox Min Course 90. **d** 93 **p** 94. NSM High Wycombe *Ox* 93-03; NSM W Wycombe w Bledlow Ridge, Bradenham and Radnage from 03; Fundraising Manager (Oxon) Children's Soc from 95. *Edgehill, Upper Stanley Road, High Wycombe HP12 4DB* Tel (01494) 523697
E-mail veronica.beaumont@virgin.net

BEAVAN, Canon Edward Hugh. b 43. Ex Coll Ox BA70 MA74 Solicitor 66. Cuddesdon Coll 69. **d** 71 **p** 72. C Ashford St Hilda *Lon* 71-74; C Newington St Mary *S'wark* 74-76; R Sandon *Chelmsf* 76-86; V Thorpe Bay 86-98; P-in-c Bradwell on Sea 98-05; P-in-c St Lawrence 98-05; V Burnham 05-09; Ind Chapl 98-05; RD Maldon and Dengie 00-05; Hon Can Chelmsf Cathl 02-09; rtd 09. *19 Wordsworth Road, Colchester CO3 4HR* Tel (01206) 564577 E-mail hugh@beavan.go-plus.net

BEAVER, William Carpenter. b 45. Colorado Coll BA Wolfs Coll Ox DPhil76. On NSM Course 79. **d** 82 **p** 83. NSM Kennington St Jo w St Jas *S'wark* 82-95; NSM Avonmouth St Andr *Bris* 96-97; NSM Bris St Mary Redcliffe w Temple etc 95-08; NSM St Andr Holborn *Lon* 01-04; Dir Communications for C of E 97-02; Dir Communications for Br Red Cross 02-04; Speech Writer to the Ld Mayor of Lon from 04; OCF from 09. *The Mansion House, Mansion House Street, London EC4N 8BH* Tel (020) 7626 2500 E-mail william.beaver@cityoflondon.gov.uk

BEAVIS, Adrian Neill. b 74. Worc Coll Ox BA97. Wycliffe Hall Ox MTh00. **d** 00 **p** 01. C E Twickenham St Steph *Lon* 04-08; V S Kensington St Luke from 08. *12 Wharfedale Street, London SW10 9AL* Tel (020) 7370 0338
E-mail adrian@stlukeschurch.co.uk

BEAVIS, Sandra Kathleen. b 51. Univ Coll Chich BA01. **d** 98 **p** 07. NSM Southbourne w W Thorney *Chich* 98-05; NSM Bedhampton *Portsm* from 05. *Lavande, 24A Gordon Road, Southbourne, Emsworth PO10 8AZ* Tel (01243) 371853
E-mail sandrabeavis@btinternet.com

BEAZLEY, Prof John Milner. b 32. Man Univ MB, ChB57 MRCOG62 FRCOG73 FACOG89 MD64. St Deiniol's Hawarden 83. **d** 86 **p** 87. NSM W Kirby St Bridget *Ches* 86-89; NSM Newton 89-92; NSM Hayton w Cumwhitton *Carl* 92-98; rtd 99; Perm to Offic *Carl* 99-07. *High Rigg, Faugh, Heads Nook, Carlisle CA8 9EA* Tel (01228) 70353

BEAZLEY, Miss Margaret Sheila Elizabeth Mary. b 32. Nor City Coll CertEd59. St Alb Minl Tr Scheme 86. **d** 89 **p** 94. NSM Ware St Mary *St Alb* from 89; Perm to Offic *St E* from 08. *38 Fanshawe Crescent, Ware SG12 0AS* Tel (01920) 462349

BEBB, Erica. STETS. **d** 09. NSM Sea Mills *Bris* from 09. *21 Bramble Drive, Bristol BS9 1RE*

BEBBINGTON, Julia. *See* BABB, Mrs Julia Bebbington

BECHTOLD, Bryant Coffin. b 51. Georgia Inst of Tech BCE73 MCE75 Univ of Utah PhD78 Univ of the S (USA) MDiv86. **d** 86 **p** 87. C Atlanta St Luke USA 86-87; C Deltona 87-89; V Price and E Carbon 90-97; V Fort Worth Ch the K 97-00; R 00-06; Perm to Offic *St Alb* 06-07; P-in-c The Wainfleet Gp *Linc* from 07. *The Rectory, Vicarage Lane, Wainfleet St Mary, Skegness PE24 4JJ* Tel (01754) 880401
E-mail frbryant@btinternet.com

BECK, Alan. b 28. AKC50. **d** 53 **p** 54. C N Harrow St Alb *Lon* 53-56; C Northolt St Mary 56-59; C Loughborough All SS *Leic* 59-61; V Crookham *Guildf* 61-69; V Puriton *B & W* 69-78; P-in-c Pawlett 74-78; V Puriton and Pawlett 78-79; P-in-c Staplegrove 79-84; R 84-88; rtd 88; Perm to Offic *B & W* 88-97 and 04-07. *Redwing, Creech Heathfield, Taunton TA3 5EG* Tel (01823) 443030

BECK, Amanda Ruth. b 68. Liv Univ BA91 Birm Univ BD93. Qu Coll Birm 91. **d** 94 **p** 95. C W Derby Gd Shep *Liv* 94-99; Asst Chapl Voorschoten *Eur* 99-02; P-in-c Kingston Vale St Jo *S'wark* from 03. *St John's Vicarage, Robin Hood Lane, London SW15 3PY* Tel (020) 8546 4079 E-mail mandy.beck@alty.org

BECK, Mrs Gillian Margaret. b 50. Sheff Univ CertEd71 Nottm Univ BTh78. Linc Th Coll 74. **dss** 78 **d** 87. Gt Grimsby St Mary and St Jas *Linc* 78-83; St Paul's Cathl 84-87; Hon Par Dn St Botolph Aldgate w H Trin Minories 87-88; Par Dn Monkwearmouth St Andr *Dur* 88-94; C 94-97; NSM Eppleton and Hetton le Hole 97-04; NSM E Rainton from 04; NSM W Rainton from 04. *The Rectory, South Street, West Rainton, Houghton le Spring DH4 6PA* Tel 0191-584 7595

BECK, John Edward. b 28. ARCM52 FRCO59 St Jo Coll Ox BA58 MA59. Wells Th Coll 56. **d** 58 **p** 59. C Dursley *Glouc* 58-61; C Glouc St Paul 61-63; S Rhodesia 63-65; Rhodesia 65-70; C Cheltenham Ch Ch *Glouc* 70-77; C Cirencester 77-93; rtd 93; Perm to Offic *Glouc* from 93. *25 Bowling Green Road, Cirencester GL7 2HD* Tel (01285) 653778

BECK, Ms Karen Maureen. b 53. R Holloway Coll Lon BA74. St Alb Minl Tr Scheme 88. **d** 92 **p** 94. Par Dn Royston *St Alb* 92-94; C 94-96; TV Chipping Barnet w Arkley 96-02; P-in-c Heddon-on-the-Wall *Newc* 02-07; Chapl Northumbria Police 02-07; P-in-c Didcot All SS *Ox* from 07. *The Rectory, 140 Lydalls Road, Didcot OX11 7EA* Tel (01235) 813244
E-mail karenandgod@yahoo.co.uk

BECK, Michael Leonard. b 50. K Coll Lon BD77 AKC77. Linc Th Coll 77. **d** 78 **p** 79. C Gt Grimsby St Mary and St Jas *Linc* 78-83; Min Can and Succ St Paul's Cathl 83-88; V Monkwearmouth St Andr *Dur* 88-96; TR Monkwearmouth 97; R Eppleton and Hetton le Hole 97-04; AD Houghton 97-04; P-in-c Lyons 00-04; P-in-c W Rainton from 04; P-in-c E Rainton from 04; Dir Reader Min from 04. *The Rectory, South Street, West Rainton, Houghton le Spring DH4 6PA* Tel 0191-584 7595

BECK, The Very Revd Peter John. b 48. Mert Coll Ox BA69 MA73. Sarum Th Coll 69. **d** 72 **p** 73. C Banbury *Ox* 72-75; TV 75-78; Dioc Youth and Community Officer 75-78; P-in-c Linc St Mary-le-Wigford w St Benedict etc 78-81; City Cen Chapl 78-81; New Zealand from 81; TV Glenfield 81-85; V Mt Albert St Luke 86-93; Adn Waitemata 87-93; V Auckland St Matt 93-00; Adn Auckland 98-00; Hon Asst P Wellington Cathl 00-02; Dir Vaughan Park Retreat Cen 02; Dean Christchurch from 02; V Gen from 03. *25 Springfield Road, St Albans, Christchurch, New Zealand* Tel (0064) (3) 377 6095 *or* 366 0046 Mobile 21-654445 E-mail peterbeck@xtra.co.nz

BECK, Roger William. b 48. Chich Th Coll 79. **d** 81 **p** 82. C St Marychurch *Ex* 81-85; TV Torre 85-88; V Torquay St Jo and Ellacombe 88-94; C Plympton St Mary from 94. *27 Pinewood Close, Plympton, Plymouth PL7 2DW* Tel (01752) 336393

BECK, Mrs Sandra Veronica. b 52. St Jo Coll Nottm 97. **d** 00 **p** 01. NSM Digswell and Panshanger *St Alb* 00-04; NSM Codicote 04-08; Perm to Offic from 08. *48 Grange Rise, Codicote, Hitchin SG4 8YR* Tel (01438) 820191
E-mail beck@colinsandie.freeserve.co.uk

BECKERLEG, Barzillai. b 20. Selw Coll Cam BA43 MA46. Westcott Ho Cam 42. **d** 44 **p** 45. C Golders Green St Alb *Lon* 44-48; Chapl St Jo Coll Dur 48-52; Lic to Offic *Dur* 49-52; V Battersea St Mary *S'wark* 52-58; V Wentworth *Sheff* 58-59; Hd Master Newc Cathl Choir Sch 59-62; Prec Newc Cathl 59-62; R Duncton *Chich* 62-64; R Burton w Coates 62-64; V Kippington *Roch* 64-75; R E Bergholt *St E* 75-79; Chapl St Mary's Sch Wantage 79-85; rtd 85; Perm to Offic *Truro* from 85; *Roch* 86-93; *Chich* from 93; *S'wark* and *Roch* from 00. *17 Ramsay Hall, 9-13 Byron Road, Worthing BN11 3HN*

BECKETT, George. b 26. Scawsby Coll of Educn CertEd76 Sheff Univ BEd77 Hull Univ MEd84. **d** 91 **p** 92. NSM Hatfield *Sheff* from 91. *10 Norman Drive, Hatfield, Doncaster DN7 6AQ* Tel (01302) 841091

BECKETT, Graham. b 49. St As Minl Tr Course 95. **d** 99 **p** 00. NSM Hawarden *St As* 99-01; C 01-07; V Gorsedd w Brynford, Ysgeifiog and Whitford from 07. *The Vicarage, Gorsedd, Holywell CH8 8QZ* Tel (01352) 711675

BECKETT, John Adrian. b 61. Bris Univ BVSc85. Trin Coll Bris. **d** 00 **p** 01. C Harrogate St Mark *Ripon* 00-04; P-in-c Sevenhampton w Charlton Abbots, Hawling etc *Glouc* from 04. *The Rectory, Station Road, Andoversford, Cheltenham GL54 4LA* Tel (01242) 820230

BECKETT, Michael Shaun. b 55. ACA79. Oak Hill Th Coll BA88. **d** 88 **p** 89. C Cambridge St Barn *Ely* 88-93, P-in-c Cambridge St Paul 93-94; V from 94. *St Paul's Vicarage, 15 St Paul's Road, Cambridge CB1 2EZ* Tel (01223) 354186 *or* 315832 Fax 471792 E-mail office@centrestpauls.org.uk

BECKETT, Mrs Patricia Anne. b 44. **d** 00 **p** 01. NSM Cheddleton *Lich* 00-06; NSM Upper Tean from 06. *The Vicarage, Vicarage Road, Tean, Stoke-on-Trent ST10 4LE* Tel (01538) 722227

BECKETT, Canon Stanley. b 20. Linc Th Coll. **d** 64 **p** 65. C Barnston *Ches* 64-71; V Daresbury 71-87; P-in-c Aston by Sutton 86-87; Hon C 87-90; Hon Can Ches Cathl 82-87; rtd 87; Hon C Grappenhall *Ches* 90-98; Perm to Offic *Linc* from 98. *82 Fairfields, Holbeach, Spalding PE12 7JE* Tel (01406) 490191

BECKHAM, John Francis. b 25. Bps' Coll Cheshunt 65. **d** 67 **p** 68. C Leytonstone St Jo *Chelmsf* 67-70; C Colchester St Mary V 70-73; R Lawford 73-80; V Gt w Lt Chesterford 80-90; rtd 90; Perm to Offic *St E* from 91. *North Barn, Reckford Road, Westleton, Saxmundham IP17 3BE* Tel (01728) 648969

BECKINSALE, Mrs Pamela Rachel. b 46. Man Univ BSc69. Cant Sch of Min 88. **d** 91 **p** 94. NSM Sittingbourne St Mich *Cant* 91-96; Hon Chapl N Kent Health Care NHS Trust 96-98; Chapl Thames Gateway NHS Trust from 98. *8 Glovers Crescent, Bell Road, Sittingbourne ME10 4DU* Tel (01795) 471632 *or* 418300

BECKLEY, Peter William (Pedr). b 52. Lon Univ BSc73 CertEd, Trin Coll Bris 76. **d** 79 **p** 80. C Plymouth St Jude *Ex* 79-83; C Ecclesall *Sheff* 83-88; V Greystones from 88. *The Vicarage, 1 Cliffe Farm Drive, Sheffield S11 7JW* Tel (0114) 266 6861

BECKLEY, Simon Richard. b 38. Lon Univ BA61. Oak Hill Th Coll 58. **d** 63 **p** 64. C Watford St Luke *St Alb* 63-67; C New Ferry *Ches* 67-70; C Chadderton Ch Ch *Man* 70-73; V Friarmere

73-80; V Tranmere St Cath *Ches* 80-03; Chapl Wirral Community Healthcare NHS Trust 80-97; Chapl Wirral and W Cheshire Community NHS Trust 97-03; rtd 03; Perm to Offic *Ches* from 04. *162 Heathbank Avenue, Wirral CH61 4YG* Tel 0151-648 7767

BECKWITH, Ian Stanley. b 36. Nottm Univ BA58 Selw Coll Cam CertEd59 Westmr Coll Ox MTh96. Linc Th Coll 78. **d** 79 **p** 80. NSM Linc Cathl 79-85; Sen Lect Bp Grosseteste Coll Linc 80-86; NSM Wallingford w Crowmarsh Gifford etc *Ox* 91-97; OLM Tr Officer (Berks) 96-02; P-in-c Gt Coxwell w Buscot, Coleshill etc 97-02; rtd 02; Perm to Offic *Heref* and *Lich* from 02. *2 Affcot Mill, Affcot, Church Stretton SY6 6RL* Tel (01694) 781667

BECKWITH, Canon John Douglas. b 33. AKC57. **d** 58 **p** 65. C Streatham St Leon *S'wark* 58-59; Lic to Offic *Ripon* 59-60; Tutor Ijebu-Igbo Gr Sch and Molusi Coll Nigeria 60-62; C Bedale *Ripon* 62-63; C Mottingham St Andr *S'wark* 64-69; Chapl Gothenburg w Halmstad and Jönköping *Eur* 69-70; Chapl to Suff Bp Edmonton 70-77; Dir of Ords *Lon* 77-88; V Brookfield St Anne, Highgate Rise 77-88; Can Gib Cathl 84-88; Hon Can Gib Cathl 88-05; P-in-c Bladon w Woodstock *Ox* 88-93; P-in-c Wootton and Kiddington w Asterleigh 88; C Kidlington w Hampton Poyle 93-94; Perm to Offic *Lon* from 94 and *Eur* from 98; rtd 98. *4 St James Close, Bishop Street, London N1 8PH* Tel and fax (020) 7226 6672 Mobile 07710-277124 E-mail malbis@dircon.co.uk

BECKWITH, James. b 53. UMIST BSc74 Newc Univ PGCE88. **d** 02 **p** 03. OLM Bothal and Pegswood w Longhirst *Newc* 02-04; C Morpeth 04-07; V Belford and Lucker from 07. *The Vicarage, North Bank, Belford NE70 7LY* Tel (01668) 213545 E-mail johnange@ne61yg.wanadoo.co.uk

BECKWITH, Roger Thomas. b 29. St Edm Hall Ox BA52 MA56 BD85 Lambeth DD92. Ripon Hall Ox 51 Tyndale Hall Bris 52 Cuddesdon Coll 54. **d** 54 **p** 55. C Harold Wood *Chelmsf* 54-57; C Bedminster St Luke w St Silas *Bris* 57-59; Tutor Tyndale Hall Bris 59-63; Lib Latimer Ho Ox 63-73 and from 94; Warden 73-94; Lect Wycliffe Hall Ox 71-94; Hon C Wytham *Ox* 88-90; Hon C N Hinksey and Wytham 90-96; rtd 94; Hon C Ox St Mich w St Martin and All SS 97-03; Perm to Offic from 03. *310 Woodstock Road, Oxford OX2 7NR* Tel (01865) 557340

BEDDINGTON, Peter Jon. b 36. ACP68 DipEd81. NW Ord Course 71. **d** 74 **p** 75. C Bury St Pet *Man* 74-77; Hon C Bury Ch King 77-82; Hon C Elton All SS 82-09; Hon C Kirklees Valley from 09. *9 Hebburn Drive, Bury BL8 1ED* Tel 0161-764 3292

BEDEAU (née MILLS), Mrs Melina. b 40. Local Minl Tr Course. **d** 00 **p** 04. NSM W Bromwich St Phil *Lich* 00-03; NSM W Bromwich Gd Shep w St Jo from 03. *4 Jervoise Street, West Bromwich B70 9LY* Tel 0121-553 6833

BEDELL, Anthony Charles John. b 59. Worc Coll Ox BA81 Univ Coll Chich PGCE05 ACA84 QTS05. Linc Th Coll BTh90. **d** 90 **p** 91. C Newbold w Dunston *Derby* 90-94; C Bedford Leigh *Man* 94-98; V Blackb St Luke w St Phil 98-03; Min Partnership Development Officer *Pet* 03; L'Arche Bognor Community 03-04; Perm to Offic *Chich* 03-04; Lic to Offic from 04; Teacher Bognor Regis Community Coll from 05. *3 Beaumont Park, Littlehampton BN17 6PE* Tel (01903) 714112 E-mail abedell@wsgfl.org.uk

BEDFORD, Christopher John. b 40. CEng68 MIStructE68. **d** 05 **p** 06. OLM Chobham w Valley End *Guildf* from 05. *23 Swallow Rise, Knaphill, Woking GU21 2LG* Tel (01483) 480127 E-mail ahbedford@hotmail.com

BEDFORD, The Ven Colin Michael. b 35. ALCD60. **d** 61 **p** 62. C Woking St Mary *Guildf* 61-63; C Guildf St Sav 63-65; C Morden *S'wark* 65-69; V Toxteth Park St Philemon *Liv* 69-75; P-in-c Toxteth Park St Gabr 69-75; P-in-c Toxteth Park St Jas and St Matt 69-75; P-in-c Prince's Park St Paul 70-75; P-in-c Toxteth Park St Cleopas 73-78; TR Toxteth St Philemon w St Gabr 75-89; TR Toxteth St Philemon w St Gabr and St Cleopas 89-91; R Edgware *Lon* 91-98; TR 98-00; Can Akoko from 96; Adn Ondo from 99; rtd 00; Perm to Offic *Liv* from 01. *44 Arbour Street, Southport PR8 6SQ* Tel (01704) 535811

BEDFORD, Mrs Linda. b 43. **d** 07. NSM Hanley Castle, Hanley Swan and Welland *Worc* from 06. *Linton, Roberts End, Hanley Swan, Worcester WR8 0DL* Tel (01684) 311324

BEDFORD, Michael Anthony. b 38. Reading Univ BSc59 Heythrop Coll Lon MA00. **d** 01 **p** 02. NSM Ruislip St Martin *Lon* from 01. *7 Chandos Road, Eastcote, Pinner HA5 1PR* Tel (020) 8866 4332 E-mail mabedford7cr@waitrose.com

BEDFORD, Richard Derek Warner. b 27. Clare Coll Cam BA52. ALCD54. **d** 54 **p** 55. C Wallington *S'wark* 54-57; C Sanderstead All SS 57; C Weybridge *Guildf* 57-59; C Addlestone 59-62; C-in-c New Haw CD 62-66; V Epsom Common Ch Ch 66-81; R Walton-on-the-Hill 81-87; Asst Chapl Burrswood Chr Cen 87-92; rtd 92; Perm to Offic *Chich* and *Roch* from 92. *2 Lealands Close, Groombridge, Tunbridge Wells TN3 9ND* Tel (01892) 864550

BEDFORD, Archdeacon of. See HUGHES, The Ven Paul Vernon

BEDFORD, Suffragan Bishop of. See INWOOD, The Rt Revd Richard Neil

BEDWELL, Stanley Frederick. b 20. MPS42. Ox NSM Course 77. **d** 80 **p** 81. NSM Farnham Royal w Hedgerley *Ox* 80-07; Perm to Offic from 07. *18 Ingleglen, Farnham Common, Slough SL2 3QA* Tel (01753) 644522

BEE, Mrs Judith Mary. b 52. STETS 03. **d** 06 **p** 07. NSM Hambledon *Portsm* from 06. *1 Hawkley Road, Liss GU33 6JJ* Tel (01730) 892144 E-mail judith.bee@clara.co.uk

BEEBEE, Meyrick Richard Legge. b 43. SAOMC 99. **d** 02 **p** 03. NSM Gerrards Cross and Fulmer *Ox* from 02. *Oak House, 86 Fulmer Road, Gerrards Cross SL9 7EG* Tel (01753) 882524 E-mail mbeebee@aol.com

BEEBY, Lawrence Clifford. b 28. S'wark Ord Course 70. **d** 73 **p** 74. C Notting Hill St Jo *Lon* 73-74; C Sunbury 74-76; C-in-c Hounslow Gd Shep Beavers Lane CD 76-80; Chapl Botleys Park Hosp Chertsey 80-96; rtd 96; Perm to Offic *Guildf* 96-99 and *Lon* from 96. *54 Bingley Road, Sunbury-on-Thames TW16 7RB* Tel (01932) 788922

BEECH, Miss Ailsa. b 44. N Co Coll Newc TDip65. Trin Coll Bris 78. **dss** 80 **d** 87 **p** 94. Pudsey St Lawr and St Paul *Bradf* 80-88; Par Dn 87-88; C Attleborough *Cov* 88-89; Par Dn Cumnor *Ox* 89-92; Asst Chapl Walsgrave Hosp Cov 92-94; Asst Chapl Walsgrave Hosps NHS Trust 94-96; Chapl 96-00; Chapl Univ Hosps Cov and Warks NHS Trust 00-04; rtd 04; Perm to Offic *York* from 04. *Oxenby, Whitby Road, Pickering YO18 7HL* Tel (01751) 472689 E-mail ailsab@btopenworld.com

BEECH, Mrs Charmian Patricia. b 45. RGN66 RHV70 TCert74. St As Minl Tr Course 99. **d** 02 **p** 03. C Connah's Quay *St As* 02-04; P-in-c Hodnet w Weston under Redcastle *Lich* from 04; Dioc Child Protection Officer from 04. *The Rectory, Abbots Way, Hodnet, Market Drayton TF9 3NQ* Tel (01630) 685491 E-mail charmian.beech@virgin.net

BEECH, Derek Charles. b 49. EMMTC 99. **d** 02 **p** 03. NSM Horsley and Denby *Derby* from 02. *39 Brook Street, Heage, Belper DE56 2AG* Tel (01773) 850168 Mobile 07967-582661

BEECH, Frank Thomas. b 36. Tyndale Hall Bris 64. **d** 66 **p** 67. C Penn Fields *Lich* 66-70; C Attenborough w Chilwell *S'well* 70-74; P-in-c 74-75; P-in-c Attenborough 75-76; V 76-84; V Worksop St Anne 84-03; Chapl Welbeck Coll 84-03; rtd 04; Perm to Offic *S'well* from 04. *43 Bescar Lane, Ollerton, Newark NG22 9BS* Tel 07743-592012 (mobile) E-mail frank.beech@lineone.net

BEECH, John. b 41. St Jo Coll Nottm. **d** 83 **p** 83. C York St Paul 83-84; P-in-c Bubwith w Ellerton and Aughton 84-85; P-in-c Thorganby w Skipwith and N Duffield 84-85; V Bubwith w Skipwith 85-87; V Acomb H Redeemer 87-00; P-in-c Westleigh St Pet *Man* 00-01; rtd 01. *32 Beech Avenue, Bishopthorpe, York YO23 2RJ*

BEECH, John Thomas. b 38. St Aid Birkenhead 64. **d** 67 **p** 68. C Burton St Paul *Lich* 67-70; Chapl RN 70-85; V Ellingham and Harbridge and Ibsley *Win* 85-94; Chapl Whiteley Village *Guildf* 94-03; rtd 03. *10 Friars Walk, Barton-on-Sea, New Milton BH25 7DA*

BEECH, Mrs Linda. **d** 06 **p** 07. NSM Lapley w Wheaton Aston *Lich* from 06; NSM Blymhill w Weston-under-Lizard from 06. *Blymhill Rectory, School Lane, Blymhill, Shifnal TF11 8LH* Tel (01952) 850149 E-mail beeches7@tiscali.co.uk

BEECH, Peter John. b 34. Bps' Coll Cheshunt 58. **d** 61 **p** 62. C Fulham All SS *Lon* 61-64; S Africa 64-67; V S Hackney St Mich *Lon* 68-71; P-in-c Haggerston St Paul 68-71; V S Hackney St Mich w Haggerston St Paul 71-75; V Wanstead H Trin Hermon Hill *Chelmsf* 75-89; P-in-c St Mary-at-Latton 89-90; V 90-99; rtd 99; Perm to Offic *Ely* from 99. *9 Fitzgerald Close, Ely CB7 4QB* Tel (01353) 666269

BEECH-GRÜNEBERG, Keith Nigel. b 72. CCC Ox BA93 MA96 St Jo Coll Dur BA97 PhD02. Cranmer Hall Dur 95. **d** 01 **p** 02. C Pangbourne w Tidmarsh and Sulham *Ox* 01-04; Dir Studies Dioc Bd Stewardship from 04. *47 Stockey End, Abingdon OX14 2NF* Tel (01235) 528661 E-mail keith.gruneberg@oxford.anglican.org

BEECHAM, Clarence Ralph. b 35. S'wark Ord Course. **d** 83 **p** 84. NSM Leigh-on-Sea St Jas *Chelmsf* 83-86. *27 Scarborough Drive, Leigh-on-Sea SS9 3ED* Tel (01702) 574923

BEECROFT, Benjamin Harold. b 77. Trin Coll Bris BA98. **d** 00 **p** 01. C Stapleford *S'well* 00-04; C Warfield *Ox* 04-07; V Addlestone *Guildf* from 07. *The Vicarage, 140 Church Road, Addlestone KT15 1SJ* Tel (01932) 842879 E-mail ben.beecroft@btinternet.com

BEECROFT, Mrs Christine Mary. b 62. RGN85. Trin Coll Bris BA97 MA99. **d** 98 **p** 99. C Roxeth *Lon* 98-00; Perm to Offic *S'well* 00-02; C Stapleford 02-04; NSM Warfield *Ox* 04-07. *The Vicarage, 140 Church Road, Addlestone KT15 1SJ* Tel (01932) 842879 E-mail christine.beecroft@ntlworld.com

BEEDELL, Trevor Francis. b 31. ALCD65. **d** 65 **p** 66. C Walton *St E* 65-68; R Hartshorne *Derby* 68-79; RD Repton 74-79; V Doveridge 79-86; Chapl HM Det Cen Foston Hall 79-80; Dioc Dir of Chr Stewardship *Derby* 79-97; rtd 97; Perm to Offic *Derby* from 97. *185 High Lane West, West Hallam, Ilkeston DE7 6HP* Tel 0115-932 5589

BEEDON, David Kirk. b 59. Birm Univ BA89 MPhil93. Qu Coll Birm 86. **d** 89 **p** 90. C Cannock *Lich* 89-92; V Wednesbury

St Bart 92-99; R Lich St Mich w St Mary and Wall from 99; P-in-c Lich Ch Ch 07-09. *St Michael's Rectory, St Michael Road, Lichfield WS13 6SN* Tel and fax (01543) 262420 *or* 262211 E-mail dkbeedon@aol.com

BEEK, Canon Michael Peter. b 27. Em Coll Cam BA50 MA55. Linc Th Coll 50. **d** 52 **p** 53. C Mitcham St Barn *S'wark* 52-55; C Talbot Village *Sarum* 55-58; V Higham and Merston *Roch* 58-66; R Gravesend St Geo and St Jas 66-74; RD Gravesend 70-74; Hon Can Roch Cathl 73-92; RD Tunbridge Wells 74-83; R Speldhurst w Groombridge 74-77; P-in-c Ashurst 77; R Speldhurst w Groombridge and Ashurst 77-83; V Bromley SS Pet and Paul 83-92; rtd 92; Perm to Offic *Nor* from 92 and *St E* from 97; RD Hartismere *St E* 93-97. *18 Henry Ward Road, Harleston IP20 9EZ* Tel (01379) 854003

BEER, Anthony. St Mich Coll Llan. **d** 09. NSM Caerau w Ely *Llan* from 09. *47 St Edwen Gardens, Cardiff CF14 4JZ* Tel (029) 2062 4348

BEER, Mrs Janet Margaret. b 43. Goldsmiths' Coll Lon CertEd64. Oak Hill Th Coll 83. **dss** 86 **d** 87 **p** 94. London Colney St Pet *St Alb* 86-97; Hon C 87-97; Chapl St Alb High Sch for Girls 87-89; Chapl Middx Univ 94-97; NSM Northaw and Cuffley *St Alb* 97-09; rtd 09. *15 Seymour Road, Lee-on-the-Solent PO13 9EG* E-mail janbeer@f2s.com

BEER, The Ven John Stuart. b 44. Pemb Coll Ox BA65 MA70 Fitzw Coll Cam MA78. Westcott Ho Cam 69. **d** 71 **p** 72. C Knaresborough St Jo *Ripon* 71-74; Chapl Fitzw Coll and New Hall Cam 74-80; Fell Fitzw Coll 77-80; Bye-Fell from 01; P-in-c Toft w Caldecote and Childerley *Ely* 80-83; R 83-87; P-in-c Hardwick 80-83; R 83-87; V Grantchester 87-97; Dir of Ords, Post-Ord Tr and Student Readers from 88; Hon Can Ely Cathl from 89; Adn Huntingdon 97-04; Acting Adn Wisbech 02-04; Adn Cam from 04. *St Botolph's Rectory, 1A Summerfield, Cambridge CB3 9HE* Tel and fax (01223) 350424 E-mail archdeacon.ely@ely.anglican.org

BEER, Michael Trevor. b 44. Chich Th Coll 66. **d** 69 **p** 70. C Leagrave *St Alb* 69-73; St Vincent 73-74; C Thorley w Bishop's Stortford H Trin *St Alb* 74-80; V London Colney St Pet 80-97; V Northaw and Cuffley 97-09; rtd 09. *15 Seymour Road, Lee-on-the-Solent PO13 9EG*

BEER, Nigel David. b 62. Portsm Poly BSc84. St Jo Coll Nottm MA93. **d** 93 **p** 94. C Rastrick St Matt *Wakef* 93-96; C Bilton *Ripon* 96-98; TV Moor Allerton from 98; Asst Dir of Ords from 05. *73 The Avenue, Leeds LS17 7NP* Tel 0113-267 8487 E-mail ndbeer@btinternet.com

BEER, William Barclay. b 43. ACT ThA68 St Steph Ho Ox. **d** 71 **p** 72. C St Marychurch *Ex* 71-76; V Pattishall w Cold Higham *Pet* 76-82; V Northampton St Benedict 82-85; V Chislehurst Annunciation *Roch* from 85. *The Vicarage, 2 Foxhome Close, Chislehurst BR7 5XT* Tel and fax (020) 8467 3606 E-mail williambbeer@tiscali.co.uk

BEESLEY, John Stanley. b 70. St Martin's Coll Lanc BSc92 QTS92. WEMTC 06. **d** 09. NSM Ludlow *Heref* from 09. *St Giles's Vicarage, Sheet Road, Ludlow SY8 1LR* E-mail john.beesley@lineone.net

BEESLEY, Michael Frederick. b 37. K Coll Cam BA59. Westcott Ho Cam 60. **d** 61 **p** 64. C Eastleigh *Win* 61-69; rtd 02. *24 Charmouth Grove, Poole BH14 0LP* Tel (01202) 773471

BEESLEY, Ramon John, b 27. Magd Coll Ox BA54 MA55. Wycliffe Hall Ox 51. **d** 53 **p** 56. C Gerrards Cross *Ox* 53-54; Asst Chapl Embley Park Sch Romsey 54-58; Perm to Offic *Win* 54-58; Asst Master Farnham Sch 58-62; Perm to Offic *Guildf* 58-62; Perm to Offic *Win* from 63; Hd Science Gore Sch New Milton 63-69; Dep Hd Applemore Sch Dibden Purlieu 69-74; Hd Master Bellemoor Sch Southn 74-84; rtd 84. *Wayfarers, Burley, Ringwood BH24 4HW* Tel (01425) 402284

BEESON, Christopher George. b 48. Man Univ BSc70. Qu Coll Birm 72. **d** 75 **p** 76. C Flixton St Mich *Man* 75-78; C Newton Heath All SS 78-80; R Gorton St Jas 80-90; Dioc Communications Officer *Blackb* 91-92; C Ribbleton 92-93; rtd 93; Perm to Offic *Blackb* from 93. *24 Arnold Close, Ribbleton, Preston PR2 6DX* Tel (01772) 702675 E-mail cbeeson@cix.co.uk

BEESON, The Very Revd Trevor Randall. b 26. OBE97. K Coll Lon MA76 FKC87 Southn Univ Hon DLitt99. **d** 51 **p** 52. C Leadgate *Dur* 51-54; C Norton St Mary 54-56; C-in-c Stockton St Chad CD 56-60; V Stockton St Chad 60-65; C St Martin-in-the-Fields *Lon* 65-71; V Ware St Mary *St Alb* 71-76; Can Westmr Abbey 76-87; Treas 78-82; R Westmr St Marg 82-87; Chapl to Speaker of Ho of Commons 82-87; Dean Win 87-96; rtd 96; Perm to Offic *Win* from 96. *69 Greatbridge Road, Romsey SO51 8FE* Tel (01794) 514627

BEESTON, Andrew Bernard. b 41. RMN64 RGN67. NEOC 99. **d** 01 **p** 02. NSM Cullercoats St Geo *Newc* 01-06; NSM Long Benton from 06. *21 Deepdale Road, Cullercoats, North Shields NE30 3AN* Tel 0191-259 0431 E-mail abeeston@ukf.net

BEET, Duncan Clive. b 65. LLB. Ridley Hall Cam 98. **d** 01 **p** 02. C Northampton Em *Pet* 01-04; P-in-c Mears Ashby and Hardwick

and Sywell etc from 04. *The Vicarage, 46 Wellingborough Road, Mears Ashby, Northampton NN6 0DZ* Tel (01604) 812907 E-mail avsy17@dsl.pipex.com

BEETHAM, Anthony. b 32. Lon Univ BSc53. Ox NSM Course. **d** 75 **p** 76. Dir Chr Enquiry Agency 88-97; NSM Ox St Clem 75-02; rtd 02; Perm to Offic *Ox* from 03. *44 Rose Hill, Oxford OX4 4HS* Tel (01865) 770923

BEETON, David Ambrose Moore. b 39. Chich Th Coll 62. **d** 65 **p** 66. C Forest Gate St Edm *Chelmsf* 65-71; V Rush Green 71-81; V Coggeshall w Markshall 81-02; rtd 02; Perm to Offic *Nor* from 03. *Le Strange Cottages, 2 Hunstanton Road, Heacham, King's Lynn PE31 7HH* Tel (01485) 572150

BEETY, Arthur Edward. b 38. Sheff Univ BA60. Cant Sch of Min 92. **d** 95 **p** 96. NSM Cobham w Luddesdowne and Dode *Roch* from 95. *The Old Forge, 4 The Street, Cobham, Gravesend DA12 3BN* Tel (01474) 816684 E-mail arthur.beety@diocese-rochester.org

BEEVER, Miss Alison Rosemary. b 59. Man Univ BA80. Linc Th Coll 88. **d** 90 **p** 94. Par Dn Watford Ch Ch *St Alb* 90-94; C 94-96; V Tilehurst St Cath *Ox* 96-01; P-in-c Cen Ex and Dioc Dir of Ords *Ex* 01-04; rtd 04. *7 Langridge Road, Paignton TQ3 3PT* Tel (01803) 553645

BEEVERS, Preb Colin Lionel. b 40. K Coll Lon BSc62 PhD66 CEng70 MIET70 MBIM73. Sarum & Wells Th Coll 87. **d** 89 **p** 90. C Ledbury w Eastnor *Heref* 89-93; C Lt Marcle 89-93; Asst Dir of Tr 92-96; P-in-c Kimbolton w Hamnish and Middleton-on-the-Hill 93-96; P-in-c Bockleton w Leysters 93-96; P-in-c Ledbury w Eastnor 96-98; P-in-c Much Marcle 96-98; TR Ledbury 98-05; RD Ledbury 96-02; Preb Heref Cathl 02-05; Chapl Herefordshire Primary Care Trust 96-05; rtd 05; Perm to Offic *Worc* from 06. *55 Lion Court, Worcester WR1 1UT* Tel (01905) 24132 E-mail annandcolin.beevers@virgin.net

BEGBIE, Jeremy Sutherland. b 57. Edin Univ BA77 Aber Univ BD80 PhD87 LRAM80 ARCM77 MSSTh. Ridley Hall Cam 80. **d** 82 **p** 83. C Egham *Guildf* 82-85; Chapl Ridley Hall Cam 85-87; Dir Studies 87-92; Vice-Prin 93-00; Assoc Prin 00-09; Hon Reader St Andr Univ 00-09; Research Prof Th Duke Div Sch USA from 09. *Duke University Divinity School, Box 90968, Durham NC 27708, USA* Tel (001) (919) 660 3591 E-mail jeremy.begbie@duke.edu

BEGGS, Norman Lindell. b 32. N Lon Poly CQSW77. S Dios Minl Tr Scheme 86. **d** 89 **p** 90. NSM Milborne St Andrew w Dewlish *Sarum* 89-92; C 92-95; C Piddletrenthide w Plush, Alton Pancras etc 92-95; C Puddletown and Tolpuddle 92-95; rtd 95; Perm to Offic *Sarum* from 95. *Wallingford House, Dewlish, Dorchester DT2 7LX* Tel (01258) 837320

BEGLEY, Mrs Helen. b 59. Kingston Poly BA81. NOC 87. **d** 89 **p** 94. Par Dn Leeds H Trin *Ripon* 89-90; Chapl to the Deaf 89-96; Par Dn Leeds City 91-94; C 94-96; Chapl to the Deaf (Wilts) *Sarum* 96-06; NSM Upper Wylye Valley from 03. *The Vicarage, Green Lane, Codford, Warminster BA12 0NY* Tel (01985) 850019 E-mail helenbegley@tiscali.co.uk

BEHENNA, Preb Gillian Eve. b 57. CertEd78. St Alb Minl Tr Scheme 82. **dss** 85 **d** 87 **p** 94. Chapl to the Deaf *Sarum* 85-90; Chapl w Deaf People *Ex* 90-04; Preb Ex Cathl 02-04; Chapl w Deaf Community *Bris* from 05. *1 Saxon Way, Bradley Stoke, Bristol BS32 9AR* Tel (01454) 202483 Mobile 07715-707137 E-mail gill@signsotgod.fsnet.co.uk

BEHREND, Michael Christopher. b 60. St Jo Coll Cam BA82 MA86 PGCE83. Oak Hill Th Coll 93. **d** 97 **p** 98. C Hensingham *Carl* 97-02; TV Horwich and Rivington *Man* from 02. *St Catherine's House, Richmond Street, Horwich, Bolton BL6 5QT* Tel (01204) 697162

BELCHER, Mrs Catherine Jane Allington. b 53. Charlotte Mason Coll of Educn CertEd75. EAMTC 02. **d** 05 **p** 06. NSM Norwich St Mary Magd w St Jas from 05. *70 Mill Hill Road, Norwich NR2 3DS* Tel (01603) 664779 E-mail revkatebelcher@yahoo.co.uk

BELCHER, David John. b 44. Ch Ch Ox BA65 MA69. Cuddesdon Coll 68. **d** 70 **p** 71. C Gateshead St Mary *Dur* 70-73; C Stockton St Pet 73-76; Lic to Offic *Lich* 76-81; P-in-c W Bromwich Ch Ch 81-85; P-in-c W Bromwich Gd Shep w St Jo 85-89; V 89-95; RD W Bromwich 90-94; R Bratton, Edington and Imber, Erlestoke etc *Sarum* 95-03; rtd 03; Hon C Smestow Vale *Lich* 03-07; Perm to Offic from 09. *81 The Lindens, Newbridge Crescent, Wolverhampton WV6 0LS* Tel (01902) 750903

BELCHER, Canon Derek George. b 50. Univ of Wales (Cardiff) MEd86 LLM04 Lon Univ PGCE82 MRSH73 MBIM82. Chich Th Coll 74. **d** 77 **p** 78. C Newton Nottage *Llan* 77-81; PV Llan Cathl 81-87; V Margam 87-01; RD Margam 99-01; TR Cowbridge from 01; Can Llan Cathl from 97; AD Vale of Glam from 08. *The Rectory, 85 Broadway, Llanblethian, Cowbridge CF71 7EY* Tel (01446) 771625 Mobile 07796-170671 E-mail derek@cowbridge.plus.com *or* rector@cowbridgeparish.com

BELCHER, Frederick William. b 30. Kelham Th Coll 50 Chich Th Coll 53. **d** 54 **p** 55. C Catford St Laur *S'wark* 54-58; C-in-c Plumstead Wm Temple Ch Abbey Wood CD 58-62; V Eltham

Park St Luke 62-64; Lic to Offic 65-81; NSM Charminster and Stinsford *Sarum* 88-94; Perm to Offic from 94; rtd 95. *Little Mead, North Street, Charminster, Dorchester DT2 9QZ* Tel (01305) 260688

BELFAST, Archdeacon of. *See* DODDS, The Ven Norman Barry
BELFAST, Dean of. *See* McKELVEY, The Very Revd Robert Samuel James Houston

BELHAM, John Edward. b 42. K Coll Lon BSc65 AKC65 PhD70. Oak Hill Th Coll 69. **d** 72 **p** 73. C Cheadle Hulme St Andr *Ches* 72-75; C Cheadle 75-83; R Gressenhall w Longham w Wendling etc *Nor* 83-08; P-in-c Mileham 07-08; rtd 08; Perm to Offic *Nor* from 08. *6 Brentwood, Norwich NR4 6PW* E-mail johnbelham@lords-prayer.co.uk

BELHAM, Michael. b 23. Lon Univ BScEng50. **d** 67 **p** 68. C Northwood Hills St Edm *Lon* 67-69; C Hendon St Mary 69-73; V Tottenham H Trin 73-78; V Hillingdon St Jo 78-85; P-in-c Broughton *Ox* 85; R Broughton w N Newington and Shutford 85-90; Chapl Horton Gen Hosp 90; rtd 90; Perm to Offic *Ox* and *Pet* 90-01; *B & W* from 01; Sec DBP *Ox* 95-01. *14 Holly Court, Frome BA11 2SQ* Tel (01373) 462941 E-mail michael-belham@supanet.com

BELING, David Gibson. b 30. Fitzw Ho Cam BA54 MA58. **d** 56 **p** 57. C Radipole *Sarum* 56-59; C Broadwater St Mary *Chich* 59-61; R W Knighton w Broadmayne *Sarum* 61-73; V Paignton St Paul Preston *Ex* 73-91; rtd 91; Perm to Offic *Ex* from 91. *51 Manor Road, Paignton TQ3 2HZ*

BELITHER, John Roland. b 36. Oak Hill Th Coll 83. **d** 86 **p** 87. NSM Bushey Heath *St Alb* 86-91; V Marsh Farm 91-06; rtd 06; Perm to Offic *St Alb* from 06. *43 Mallard Road, Abbots Langley WD5 0GE* Tel (01923) 494399

BELL, Adrian Christopher. b 48. AKC70. St Aug Coll Cant 70. **d** 71 **p** 72. C Sheff St Aid w St Luke 71-74; C Willesborough w Hinxhill *Cant* 74-78; P-in-c Wormshill 78; P-in-c Hollingbourne w Hucking 78-82; P-in-c Leeds w Broomfield 79-82; V Hollingbourne and Hucking w Leeds and Broomfield 82-84; V Herne Bay Ch Ch 84-91; R Washingborough w Heighington and Canwick *Linc* 91-01; R Fakenham w Alethorpe *Nor* from 01. *The Rectory, Gladstone Road, Fakenham NR21 9BZ* Tel and fax (01328) 862268 E-mail adrian.bell4@btopenworld.com

BELL, Canon Alan John. b 47. Liv Univ BA68. Ridley Hall Cam 69. **d** 72 **p** 73. C Speke St Aid *Liv* 72-77; P-in-c Halewood 77-81; R Wavertree St Mary 81-88; Chapl Mabel Fletcher Tech Coll and Olive Mt Hosp 81-88; R Fakenham w Alethorpe *Nor* 88-00; RD Burnham and Walsingham 92-00; TR Stockport SW *Ches* 00-07; V Stockport St Geo from 07; RD Stockport from 05; Hon Can Ches Cathl from 08. *St George's Vicarage, 7 Corbar Road, Stockport SK2 6EP* Tel and fax 0161-456 0918 *or* tel 480 2453 E-mail vicaralanbell@aol.com

BELL, Allan McRae. b 49. Moray Ho Teacher Tr Coll Edin CertEd80 E Lon Univ BA90. S'wark Ord Course 86. **d** 92 **p** 95. NSM Bow H Trin and All Hallows *Lon* 91-93; NSM R Foundn of St Kath in Ratcliffe 93-95; USA 95-97; Chapl Univ of California 95-96; P-in-c Bolinas St Aidan 96-97. *177 Well Street, London E9 6QU* Tel (020) 8985 1978

BELL, Andrew Thomas. b 58. Ripon Coll Cuddesdon 93. **d** 95 **p** 96. C Leighton Buzzard w Eggington, Hockliffe etc *St Alb* 95-98; TV Schorne *Ox* from 98. *The Vicarage, Church Street, North Marston, Buckingham MK18 3PH* Tel (01296) 670298

BELL, Anne Elizabeth. b 38. RGN60. SAOMC 98. **d** 08 **p** 08. NSM Shrivenham and Ashbury *Ox* from 08. *Whitcot, Shotover Corner, Uffington, Faringdon SN7 7RH* Tel (01367) 820091 E-mail anne@shotover.fsnet.co.uk

BELL, Anthony Lawson. b 47. AKC72. St Aug Coll Cant 71. **d** 72 **p** 73. C Peterlee *Dur* 72-77; C-in-c Stockton St Jas CD 82-89; P-in-c Byers Green 89-96; Ind Chapl Teesside 89-96; P-in-c Ault Hucknall *Derby* 96-99; V Ault Hucknall and Scarcliffe from 99. *The Vicarage, 59 The Hill, Glapwell, Chesterfield S44 5LX* Tel (01246) 850371 Fax 857530 E-mail tonybell@aulthucknall.org

BELL, Antony Fancourt. b 28. Sarum Th Coll BA51 MA58. Wells Th Coll 54. **d** 56 **p** 57. C Clapham H Trin *S'wark* 56-59; C Gillingham *Sarum* 59-61; R Stanway *Chelmsf* 61-94; RD Dedham and Tey 81-91; rtd 94. *7 Postern Close, Portchester, Fareham PO16 9NB* Tel (023) 9237 8272

BELL, Arthur James. b 33. Ch Coll Cam BA57 MA60. Coll of Resurr Mirfield 57. **d** 59 **p** 60. C New Cleethorpes *Linc* 59-63; C Upperby St Jo *Carl* 63-66; P-in-c Wabasca Canada 67-72 and 77-83; Perm to Offic *Ely* 73-75; Lic to Offic *Carl* 75-76; Warden Retreat of the Visitation Rhandirmwyn 83-99; Perm to Offic *Dur* from 00. *Burnside, 22 Rose Terrace, Stanhope, Bishop Auckland DL13 2PE* Tel (01388) 526514

BELL, Barnaby. *See* BELL, Simon Barnaby
BELL, Bede. *See* BELL, Canon William Wealands
BELL, Brian Thomas Benedict. b 64. Newc Poly BA87 Newc Univ PGCE88 Univ of Northumbria at Newc MA93 Leeds Univ BA97. Coll of Resurr Mirfield. **d** 97 **p** 98. C Tynemouth Cullercoats St Paul *Newc* 97-01; V Horton 01-08; V Norbury w Horbury Bridge *Wakef* from 08. *St Peter's Vicarage, Northgate, Horbury, Wakefield WF4 6AS* E-mail frbrian@ourladyandbenedict.fsnet.co.uk

BELL, Catherine Ann. *See* MOSS, Mrs Catherine Ann
BELL, Canon Charles William. b 43. TCD Div Test 66 BA66 MA69. CITC 64. **d** 67 **p** 68. C Newtownards *D & D* 67-70; C Larne and Inver *Conn* 70-74; C Ballymena w Ballyclug 74-80; Bp's C Belfast Ardoyne 80-88; Bp's C Belfast Ardoyne w H Redeemer 88-89; I Eglantine from 89; Dioc Info Officer (S Conn) from 89; Preb Conn Cathl from 04. *All Saints' Rectory, 16 Eglantine Road, Lisburn BT27 5RQ* Tel (028) 9266 2634 Fax 9266 8651 E-mail rector@eglantine.me.uk

BELL, Colin Ashworth. b 52. FCCA83. Westcott Ho Cam 89. **d** 91 **p** 92. C Lytham St Cuth *Blackb* 91-93; C Whittle-le-Woods 93-97; V Stalybridge H Trin and Ch Ch *Ches* 97-07. *Address temp unknown*

BELL, Colin Douglas. b 65. QUB BTh94 TCD MPhil96. CITC 94. **d** 96 **p** 97. C Dundonald *D & D* 96-98; C Knock 98-00; I Lack *Clogh* 00-02; I Rathcoole *Conn* 02-05; CF 05-07 and from 08; I Aghadrumsee w Clogh and Drumsnatt 07-08. *c/o MOD Chaplains (Army)* Tel (01980) 615804 Fax 615800

BELL, Cyril John. b 22. Lon Univ BA48. Wycliffe Hall Ox 52. **d** 53 **p** 54. C Monkwearmouth St Pet *Dur* 53-56; Asst Master Bede Gr Sch Sunderland 53-56; Lect and Chapl Union Chr Coll Alwaye S India 56-60; Lic to Offic *Ches* 62-87; Hon C Westlands St Andr *Lich* 66-71; Hd RE Marple Comp Sch 71-87; rtd 87; Perm to Offic *Lich* 87-96. *49 Delamere Road, Nantwich CW5 7DF* Tel (01270) 628910

BELL, David Bain. b 57. Bp Otter Coll BEd82. Ox Min Course 04. **d** 07 **p** 08. NSM Stantonbury and Willen *Ox* from 07. *6 Edgecote, Great Holm, Milton Keynes MK8 9ER* Tel (01908) 564434 E-mail fivebells@ukgateway.net

BELL, David James. b 62. QUB BSc84 BTh. **d** 91 **p** 92. C Ballyholme *D & D* 91-94; C Coleraine *Conn* 94-00; I Ardtrea w Desertcreat *Arm* from 00. *Tullyhogue Rectory, 50 Lower Grange Road, Cookstown BT80 8SL* Tel and fax (028) 8676 1163 E-mail bell.david@talk21.com

BELL, Canon David Owain. b 49. Dur Univ BA69 Fitzw Coll Cam BA72 MA80. Westcott Ho Cam 70. **d** 72 **p** 73. C Houghton le Spring *Dur* 72-76; C Norton St Mary 76-78; P-in-c Worc St Clem 78-84; R 84-85; R Old Swinford Stourbridge 85-97; RD Stourbridge 90-96; Hon Can Worc Cathl from 96; TR Kidderminster St Mary and All SS w Trimpley etc from 97. *The Vicarage, 22 Roden Avenue, Kidderminster DY10 2RF* Tel (01562) 823265 E-mail dowainbell@yahoo.co.uk

BELL, Canon Donald Jon. b 50. Sarum & Wells Th Coll 73. **d** 76 **p** 77. C Jarrow *Dur* 76-80; C Darlington St Cuth w St Hilda 80-83; V Wingate Grange 83-89; V Sherburn w Pittington 89-95; R Shadforth 94-95; P-in-c Dur St Cuth 95-97; V 97-02; R Witton Gilbert 97-02; TR Dur N 02-05; AD Dur 93-05; Chapl Dur and Darlington Fire and rescue Brigade 95-05; Bp's Sen Chapl and Exec Officer from 05; Hon Can Dur Cathl from 01. *Auckland Castle, Market Place, Bishop Auckland DL14 7NR* Tel (01388) 602576 Fax 605264 Mobile 07973-829491 E-mail chaplain@bishopdunelm.co.uk

BELL, Dorothy Jane. b 53. Teesside Univ BSc93. Cranmer Hall Dur 01. **d** 03 **p** 04. C Washington *Dur* 03-07; P-in-c Stockton St Jo from 07; P-in-c Stockton St Jas from 07. *St John the Baptist Vicarage, 190 Durham Road, Stockton-on-Tees TS19 0PS* Tel (01642) 674119

BELL, Evelyn Ruth. b 52. Univ of Wales (Cardiff) BSc(Econ). SAOMC 97. **d** 00 **p** 01. C Waltham Cross *St Alb* 00-03; Chapl HM Pris Edmunds Hill from 03. *HM Prison Edmunds Hill, Stradishall, Newmarket CB8 9YN* Tel (01440) 743595 E-mail eve.bell@hmps.gsi.gov.uk

BELL, Canon Francis William Albert. b 28. TCD BA52 MA57 BD57. **d** 53 **p** 54. C Belfast St Mich *Conn* 53-55; C Belfast All SS 55-61; C Ballynafeigh St Jude *D & D* 61-63; P-in-c Ballyhalbert 63-71; P-in-c Ardkeen 67-71; I Ballyhalbert w Ardkeen 71-95; Miss to Seamen 71-95; Can Belf Cathl 89-95; rtd 95. *Stationbanks, 18 Kilmore Road, Crossgar, Downpatrick BT30 9HJ* Tel (028) 4483 1665

BELL, Mrs Glynis Mary. b 44. Leeds Univ BA66. SAOMC 99. **d** 02 **p** 03. OLM Newport Pagnell w Lathbury and Moulsoe *Ox* from 02. *6 Kipling Drive, Newport Pagnell MK16 8EB* Tel (01908) 612971

BELL, Godfrey Bryan. b 44. Oak Hill Th Coll 72. **d** 75 **p** 76. C Penn Fields *Lich* 75-79; R Dolton *Ex* 79-89; R Iddesleigh w Dowland 79-89; R Monkokehampton 79-89; R Torland Royal w Farnham, Gussage St Michael etc *Sarum* 89-96; TV Washfield, Stoodleigh, Withleigh etc *Ex* 96-06; TR 06-09; rtd 09. *The Vicarage, 3 Court Gardens, Stoodleigh, Tiverton EX16 9PL* Tel (01398) 351373 E-mail gomar@stoodleigh.freeserve.co.uk

BELL, Graham Dennis Robert. b 42. K Coll Lon BSc63 AKC63 Nottm Univ MTh73 ALCM76 Lambeth STh01. Tyndale Hall Bris 65. **d** 68 **p** 69. C Stapleford *S'well* 68-71; C Barton Seagrave *Pet* 71-73; C Barton Seagrave w Warkton 73-76; Perm to Offic *Nor* 76-85; V Wickham Market *St E* 82-86; V Wickham Market w Pettistree and Easton 86-98; R Thrapston *Pet* 98-07; rtd 07. *22 Cottesmore Avenue, Barton Seagrave, Kettering NN15 6QX* Tel (01536) 725924 E-mail grahambellgood@talktalk.net

BELL, Canon Jack Gorman. b 23. Lon Univ BSc48. Oak Hill Th Coll 51. **d** 53 **p** 54. C Blackpool Ch Ch *Blackb* 53-55; C Chadderton Ch Ch *Man* 55-59; R Man St Jerome w Ardwick St Silas 59-69; V Mosley Common 69-89; Hon Can Man Cathl 87-89; rtd 89; Perm to Offic *Carl* from 89. *36 Sandgate, Kendal LA9 6HT* Tel (01539) 725807

✠**BELL, The Rt Revd James Harold.** b 50. St Jo Coll Dur BA72 St Pet Hall Ox BA74 MA78. Wycliffe Hall Ox 72. **d** 75 **p** 76 **c** 04. Hon C Ox St Mich w St Martin and All SS 75-76; Chapl and Lect BNC Ox 76-82; R Northolt St Mary *Lon* 82-93; AD Ealing 91-93; Adv for Min Willesden 93-97; Dioc Dir of Min and Tr *Ripon* 97-99; Dioc Dir of Miss 99-04; Can Res Ripon Cathl 97-99; Hon Can from 99; Suff Bp Knaresborough from 04. *Thistledown, Main Street, Exelby, Bedale DL8 2HD* Tel and fax (01677) 423525 E-mail bishop.knaresb@btinternet.com

BELL, James Samuel. b 40. MBE71. RMA 59 St Chad's Coll Dur BA69. Coll of Resurr Mirfield 71. **d** 72 **p** 73. C Lambeth St Phil *S'wark* 72-74; C N Lambeth 74; P-in-c Invergordon St Ninian *Mor* 74-77; P-in-c Dornoch 74-77; P-in-c Brora 74-77; V Pet H Spirit Bretton 77-83; P-in-c Marholm 82-83; Sen Chapl Tonbridge Sch 83-00; rtd 00. *Clocktower House, Edderton, Tain IV19 1LJ* Tel (01862) 821305

BELL, Jane. *See* BELL, Dorothy Jane

BELL, Canon Jeffrey William. b 37. Buckingham Univ MA94. Sarum Th Coll 60. **d** 63 **p** 64. C Northampton St Matt *Pet* 63-66; C Portishead *B & W* 66-68; C Digswell *St Alb* 68-72; V Pet St Jude 72-79; V Buckingham *Ox* 79-93; RD Buckingham 84-88 and 89-90; V Portsea N End St Mark *Portsm* 93-03; Hon Can Portsm Cathl 00-03; rtd 03; Hon C The Bourne and Tilford *Guildf* from 03. *All Saints' Vicarage, Tilford, Farnham GU10 2DA* Tel (01252) 792333

BELL, Jennifer Kathryn. b 77. Harper Adams Univ Coll BSc99. CITC BTh04. **d** 04 **p** 05. Asst Chapl R Group of Hosps Health and Soc Services Trust 04-06; Asst Chapl Belfast City Hosp Health and Soc Services Trust 04-06; Chapl Belfast Health and Soc Care Trust from 06; C Belfast St Anne *Conn* 04-06; C Belfast St Nic 06-08; I Templepatrick w Donegore from 08; Bp's Dom Chapl from 08. *The Vicarage, 926 Antrim Road, Templepatrick, Ballyclare BT39 0AT* Tel (028) 9443 2330 E-mail revjkbell@yahoo.co.uk

BELL, John. *See* BELL, Cyril John

BELL, John. *See* BELL, Canon Donald Jon

BELL, John Christopher. b 33. TCD BA56 MA66. TCD Div Sch Div Test. **d** 56 **p** 57. C Newtownards *D & D* 56-59; C Willowfield 59-62; I Carrowdore 62-70; I Drumbo 70-98; Chapl Young Offender Cen Belf 79-98; Can Down Cathl 87-98; Treas 91-98; rtd 98. *Ashwell House, 6 Ballywillin Road, Crossgar, Downpatrick BT30 9LE* Tel (028) 4483 1907

BELL, John Edward. b 34. Cranmer Hall Dur. **d** 67 **p** 68. C Harraby *Carl* 67-70; C Dalton-in-Furness 70-72; V Pennington 72-75; V Carl St Herbert w St Steph 75-84; V Wreay 84-85; rtd 99; Perm to Offic *Carl* from 01. *189 Brampton Road, Carlisle CA3 9AX* Tel (01228) 522746

BELL, John Holmes. b 50. Sheff City Coll of Educn CertEd71. Oak Hill Th Coll BA80. **d** 80 **p** 81. C Leic St Phil 80-83; C Portswood Ch Ch *Win* 83-86; TV S Molton w Nymet St George, High Bray etc *Ex* 86-01; V Stoke Fleming, Blackawton and Strete from 01. *The Rectory, Rectory Lane, Stoke Fleming, Dartmouth TQ6 0QB* Tel (01803) 771050 E-mail john@ding-dong.fsnet.co.uk

BELL, Karl Edwin. b 33. Minnesota Univ BA56, Seabury-Western Th Sem MDiv61. **d** 61 **p** 62. USA 61-71 and 76-92; Venezuela 71-76; Chapl Wiesbaden *Eur* from 92. *St Augustine of Canterbury, Frankfurterstrasse 3, 65189 Wiesbaden, Germany* Tel (0049) (611) 306674 Fax 372270 E-mail bell@wiesbaden.netsurf.de

BELL, Kenneth Murray. b 30. Sarum & Wells Th Coll 75. **d** 74 **p** 76. Perm to Offic *Guildf* 74-76; C Hartley Wintney and Elvetham 76-77; C Hartley Wintney, Elvetham, Winchfield etc 77-80; V Fair Oak 80-95; rtd 96; Perm to Offic *Win* from 96. *12 Hill Meadow, Overton, Basingstoke RG25 3JD* Tel (01256) 770890 E-mail keny12@talk21.com

BELL, Kevin David. b 58. Newc Univ MA93 Univ of Wales (Lamp) MA06. Aston Tr Scheme 78 Sarum & Wells Th Coll 80. **d** 83 **p** 84. C Weoley Castle *Birm* 83-87; C Acocks Green 87-89; CF 89-07; Asst Chapl Gen from 07; Dir of Ordds from 07. *c/o MOD Chaplains (Army)* Tel (01980) 615804 Fax 615800

BELL, Canon Nicholas Philip Johnson. b 46. St Jo Coll Dur BSc69. St Jo Coll Nottm 70. **d** 73 **p** 74. C Chadderton Ch Ch *Man* 73-77; C Frogmore St Alb 77-81; V Bricket Wood 81-91; RD Aldenham 87-91; V Luton St Mary from 91; Hon Can St Alb from 01. *The Vicarage, 48 Crawley Green Road, Luton LU2 0QX* Tel and fax (01582) 728925 E-mail nickbell@stmarysluton.org

BELL, Owain. *See* BELL, Canon David Owain

BELL, Paul Joseph. b 35. Dur Univ BA56 DipEd57. Trin Coll Bris 77. **d** 77 **p** 78. Burundi 77-81; C Highbury Ch Ch w St Jo and St Sav *Lon* 82-85; V Middleton w E Winch *Nor* 85-95; P-in-c Barningham w Matlaske w Baconsthorpe etc 95-99; R 99-02; rtd

02; Perm to Offic *Portsm* from 02. *21 Hurst Point View, Totland Bay PO39 0AQ* Tel (01983) 756180

BELL, Philip Harold. b 19. Leeds Univ BA45 K Alfred's Coll Win PGCE69. Coll of Resurr Mirfield 38. **d** 44 **p** 45. C Barrow St Matt *Carl* 44-49; C Lewisham St Jo Southend *S'wark* 50-56; Chapl Tristan da Cunha 56-61; R Crawley w Littleton *Win* 61-72; V Holdenhurst 72-78; P-in-c Hilperton w Whaddon *Sarum* 78-84; P-in-c Staverton 78-84; R Hilperton w Whaddon and Staverton etc 85-86; rtd 86; Perm to Offic *Sarum* from 86. *31 Duxford Close, Bowerhill, Melksham SN12 6XN* Tel (01225) 709732 E-mail phildil@talk21.com

BELL, Prof Richard Herbert. b 54. Univ Coll Lon BSc75 PhD79 Tubingen Univ DrTheol91. Wycliffe Hall Ox BA82 MA87. **d** 83 **p** 84. C Edgware *Lon* 83-86; W Germany 86-90; Lect Th Nottm Univ 90-97; Sen Lect 97-05; Reader 05-08; Prof from 08. *Department of Theology and Religious Studies, University Park, Nottingham NG7 2RD* Tel 0115-951 5858 Fax 951 5887 E-mail richard.bell@nottingham.ac.uk

BELL, Robert Clarke. b 30. Roch Th Coll 63. **d** 65 **p** 66. C Leeds All SS *Ripon* 65-67; C Claxby w Normanby-le-Wold *Linc* 67-69; R Newark St Leon *S'well* 69-71; V Gosberton Clough *Linc* 71-74; P-in-c Quadring 73-74; Chapl to the Deaf 74-85; V Harmston and Coleby 85-94; RD Graffoe 92-94; rtd 94; Perm to Offic *Blackb* 94-05 and *Carl* 94-98. *11A Bradway, Sturton by Stow, Lincoln LN1 2DU* Tel (01427) 788735

BELL, Robert Mason. b 35. Lon Coll of Div 66. **d** 68 **p** 69. C Burgess Hill St Andr *Chich* 68-78; R Lewes St Jo sub Castro 78-00; rtd 00. *10 Rufus Close, Lewes BN7 1BG* Tel (01273) 470561

BELL, Ross K. b 64. Bradf and Ilkley Coll BA87. Aston Tr Scheme 89 Westcott Ho Cam 91. **d** 94 **p** 95. C W Bromwich All SS *Lich* 94-98; TV Cen Wolverhampton 98-02; Chapl Bilston Street Police Station 04-06; Perm to Offic *Edin* from 06. *15/2 The Bond Building, Breadalbane Street, Edinburgh EH6 5JJ* Tel 07976-157022 (mobile) E-mail rotinkerbell@aol.com

BELL, Mrs Shena Margaret. b 49. EAMTC. **d** 00 **p** 01. C Earls Barton *Pet* 00-04; P-in-c Raunds 04-07; P-in-c Ringstead and Stanwick w Hargrave 04-07; R Raunds, Hargrave, Ringstead and Stanwick from 07. *The Vicarage, High Street, Raunds, Wellingborough NN9 6HS* Tel (01933) 461509 E-mail shena.bell@virgin.net

BELL, Simon Barnaby. b 48. Bris Univ CertEd70. Sarum & Wells Th Coll 87. **d** 89 **p** 90. C Ewyas Harold w Dulas *Heref* 89-90; C Ewyas Harold w Dulas, Kenderchurch etc 90-93; P-in-c Clungunford w Clunbury and Clunton, Bedstone etc 93-01; R from 01. *The Rectory, Clungunford, Craven Arms SY7 0PN* Tel (01588) 660342

BELL, Canon Stuart Rodney. b 46. Ex Univ BA67. Tyndale Hall Bris 69. **d** 71 **p** 72. C Henfynyw w Aberaeron and Llanddewi Aberarth *St D* 71-74; V 81-88; V Llangeler 74-80; TR Aberystwyth from 88; Chapl Univ of Wales (Abth) from 94; Ev St Teilo Trust from 95; Can St D Cathl from 01. *The Rectory, Laura Place, Aberystwyth SY23 2AU* Tel and fax (01970) 617184 *or* tel 625080

BELL, Terrance James. b 63. Toronto Univ BA92. Trin Coll Toronto MDiv97. **d** 97 **p** 98. C Wedmore w Theale and Blackford *B & W* 97-01; C Hampstead St Jo *Lon* 01-06; Chapl Eden Hall Marie Curie Hospice 01-06; P-in-c King's Walden and Offley w Lilley *St Alb* from 06. *Millstone Corner, Salusbury Lane, Offley, Hitchin SG5 3EG* Tel (01462) 768123 E-mail kwol@btinternet.com

BELL, Timothy John Keeton. b 59. Trin Coll Bris BA02. **d** 02 **p** 03. C Saltford w Corston and Newton St Loe *B & W* 02-06; Chapl Bath Spa Univ 04-06; P-in-c Wick w Doynton and Dyrham *Bris* from 06. *The Vicarage, 57 High Street, Wick, Bristol BS30 5QQ* Tel 0117-937 3581 E-mail tim.vicar@gmail.com

BELL, Canon William Wealands. b 63. York Univ BA86 Dur Univ PGCE87 Leeds Univ BA99. Coll of Resurr Mirfield 97. **d** 99 **p** 00. C Jarrow *Dur* 99-02; Novice CR 02-04; Chapl Aldenham Sch Herts 04-07; Can Res Lich Cathl from 07. *23 The Close, Lichfield WS13 7LD* E-mail wealands.bell@lichfield-cathedral.org

BELL-RICHARDS, Douglas Maurice. b 23. St Steph Ho Ox 59. **d** 61 **p** 62. C Chipping Campden *Glouc* 61-62; C Thornbury 62-67; V Dymock w Donnington 67-75; V Fairford 75-91; rtd 91. *21 Capel Court, The Burgage, Prestbury, Cheltenham GL52 3EL* Tel (01242) 578030

BELLAMY, David Quentin. b 62. Univ of Wales (Cardiff) BMus84 Univ of Wales (Ban) MA93. Ripon Coll Cuddesdon 87 Ch Div Sch of the Pacific (USA). **d** 90 **p** 91. C Rhyl w St Ann *St As* 90-94; V Llay 94-04; V Prestatyn from 04. *The Vicarage, 109 High Street, Prestatyn LL19 9AR* Tel (01745) 853780 E-mail vicar@parishofprestatyn.org.uk

BELLAMY, Mrs Dorothy Kathleen. b 33. Gilmore Course 74. **dss** 82 **d** 87 **p** 94. Feltham *Lon* 82-84; Twickenham St Mary 84; Hampton St Mary 84-85; Hampton Wick 85-87; Par Dn 87-88; Par Dn Teddington St Mark and Hampton Wick 88-90; Par Dn Westbury *Sarum* 90-94; C 94-96; rtd 97; NSM Freshwater

Portsm from 97; NSM Yarmouth from 97. *1 Meadows Close, Brighstone, Newport PO30 4BQ* Tel (01983) 740508

BELLAMY, Mrs Janet. d 09. NSM Hope Bowdler w Eaton-under-Heywood *Heref* from 09. *Orchard House, Diddlebury, Craven Arms SY7 9DH* Tel (01584) 841511
E-mail janetmbellamy@googlemail.com

BELLAMY, John Stephen. b 55. Jes Coll Ox BA77 MA81 Liv Univ PhD06. St Jo Coll Nottm. **d** 84 **p** 85. C Allerton *Liv* 84-87; C Southport Ch Ch 87-89; Bp's Dom Chapl 89-91; V Birkdale St Jas 91-08; V Dur St Nic from 08. *11 Beechways, Durham DH1 4LG* Tel 0191-384 6066 E-mail jsbellamy@onetel.com

BELLAMY, Canon Mervyn Roger Hunter. b 47. Sussex Univ CertEd Heythrop Coll Lon MA04. St Mich Coll Llan 81. **d** 81 **p** 82. C Frecheville and Hackenthorpe *Sheff* 81-85; V Shiregreen St Hilda 85-94; RD Ecclesfield 93-94; R Rawmarsh w Parkgate 94-01; P-in-c King's Sutton and Newbottle and Charlton *Pet* 01-09; V from 09; RD Brackley from 05; Can Pet Cathl from 09. *The Vicarage, Church Avenue, King's Sutton, Banbury OX17 3RJ* Tel (01295) 811364

BELLAMY, Peter Charles William. b 38. Birm Univ MA70 PhD79 AKC61. **d** 62 **p** 63. C Allestree *Derby* 62-65; Chapl All SS Hosp Birm 65-73; Chapl St Pet Coll of Educn Saltley 73-78; Chapl and Lect Qu Eliz Hosp Birm 78-90; Lect Past Psychology Birm Univ 79-92; Manager HIV Services Birm Cen HA 90-92; Commr for Public Health Cen and S Birm HA 92-96; Research Fell Birm Univ 97-02; Local Min Development Adv *Heref* 01-06; Dioc Co-ord for Min of Deliverance from 06. *Orchard House, Diddlebury, Craven Arms SY7 9DH* Tel (01584) 841511
E-mail peterchellamy@googlemail.com

BELLAMY, Robert John. b 40. Ripon Hall Ox 64. **d** 66 **p** 67. C Fishponds St Jo *Bris* 66-70; C Oldland 70-74; P-in-c Coalpit Heath 74-76; TV Cannock *Lich* 90-96; Perm to Offic 96-98 and 03-04; Hon C Longdon 98-03; Hon C Shareshill from 04. *10 Meadowlark Close, Hednesford, Cannock WS12 1UE* Tel (01543) 876809 E-mail robert.jbellamy@virgin.net

BELLAMY, Roger. *See* BELLAMY, Canon Mervyn Roger Hunter

BELLAMY, Stephen. *See* BELLAMY, John Stephen

BELLAMY-KNIGHTS, Peter George. b 41. Leic Univ BSc63 Man Univ MSc67 PhD70 Lon Univ BD03 CMath91 FIMA91 CEng94 FRAeS98. Man OLM Scheme 03. **d** 04 **p** 05. NSM Man Cathl from 04. *113 Old Hall Lane, Manchester M14 6HL* Tel 0161-224 2702

BELLENES, Peter Charles. b 49. Thurrock Coll Essex CQSW72. Linc Th Coll 79. **d** 81 **p** 90. C Penistone *Wakef* 81-82; Hon C Liskeard, St Keyne, St Pinnock, Morval etc *Truro* 89-91; Hon C Menheniot 91-99; P-in-c Marldon *Ex* 99-03; TV Totnes w Bridgetown, Berry Pomeroy etc from 03. *The Vicarage, 1 Love Lane, Marldon, Paignton TQ3 1TH* Tel and fax (01803) 557294 E-mail pbellenes@aol.com

BELLENGER, Peter John Russell. b 74. New Coll Ox BA96 MA02 St Jo Coll Dur BA03. Cranmer Hall Dur 01. **d** 04 **p** 05. C Tollington *Lon* 04-07. *Address temp unknown* Tel 07876-563698 (mobile)

BELLINGER, Canon Denys Gordon. b 29. Sheff Univ BA49. Westcott Ho Cam 51. **d** 53 **p** 54. C Ribbleton *Blackb* 53-56; C Lancaster St Mary 56-58; V Colne H Trin 58-68; V Scotforth 68-93; RD Lancaster 82-89; Hon Can Blackb Cathl 86-93; rtd 93; Perm to Offic *Blackb* from 93. *40 Yewlands Drive, Garstang, Preston PR3 1JP* Tel (01995) 601539

BELLINGER, Richard George. b 47. Univ of Wales (Abth) BSc(Econ)69. S Dios Minl Tr Scheme 91. **d** 94 **p** 95. NSM Guernsey St Steph *Win* 94-96; NSM Guernsey St Martin from 96. *La Maison des Vinaires, Rue des Vinaires, St Peter's, Guernsey GY7 9EZ* Tel (01481) 63203 Fax 66989

BELLIS, Huw. b 72. Univ of Wales (Lamp) BA94. Westcott Ho Cam 96. **d** 98 **p** 99. C Merrow *Guildf* 98-02; TV Tring *St Alb* 02-08; TR from 08. *The Rectory, 2 The Limes, Station Road, Tring HP23 5NW* Tel (01442) 822170
E-mail huwbellis@btinternet.com

BELOE, Mrs Jane. b 46. STETS. **d** 04 **p** 05. NSM Shedfield *Portsm* 04-06; NSM Bishop's Waltham from 06; NSM Upham from 06. *Roughay Cottage, Popes Lane, Upham, Southampton SO32 1JB* Tel (01489) 860452
E-mail janebeloe@btinternet.com

BELOE, Robert Francis. b 39. Sarum Th Coll. **d** 65 **p** 71. C Nor Heartsease St Fran 65-66; C Edmonton St Mary w St Jo *Lon* 68-70; C St Marylebone Ch Ch w St Paul 70-74; P-in-c Wicken *Ely* 74-76; V 76-00; rtd 00; Perm to Offic *Ely* 00-08 and *Carl* from 08. *20 Lakehead Court, Keswick CA12 5EU* Tel (01768?) 74796

BELSHAW, Patricia Anne. b 47. **d** 05 **p** 06. OLM Leyland St Jas *Blackb* 05-07; NSM from 07. *9 The Laund, Leyland, Preston PR26 7XX* Tel (01772) 453624

BEMAND, Matthew James. b 76. Mert Coll Ox MMath99 CCC Cam PGCE00. St Steph Ho Ox BA06. **d** 06 **p** 07. C Brentwood St Thos *Chelmsf* from 06. *Stokes House, 25 St Thomas Road, Brentwood CM14 4DF* Tel (01277) 210323 Mobile 07967-138277 E-mail curate@st-thomas.org.uk

BEMENT, Peter James. b 43. Univ of Wales (Cardiff) BA64 PhD69. Wycliffe Hall Ox 92. **d** 94 **p** 95. C Hubberston *St D* 94-97; V Llandeilo Fawr and Taliaris 97-08; rtd 08. *21 Chandler's Yard, Burry Port SA16 0FE* Tel (01554) 833905

BENCE, Helen Mary. b 44. Leic Univ BA65 PGCE66. EMMTC 93. **d** 97 **p** 98. NSM Humberstone *Leic* 97-02; NSM Thurnby Lodge 01-02; TV Oadby 03-08; NSM Thurnby w Stoughton from 08. *The Grange, 126 Shanklin Drive, Leicester LE2 3QB* Tel 0116-270 7820 E-mail helenbence@leicester.freeserve.co.uk

BENCE, Norman Murray. b 34. Ripon Hall Ox 63. **d** 63 **p** 64. C Eling *Win* 63-66; Australia 66 and 75; NSM Holdenhurst and Iford *Win* from 81. *72 Corhampton Road, Bournemouth BH6 5PB* Tel (01202) 421992 Fax 420154

BENDELL, David James. b 38. ACIB74. S'wark Ord Course 84. **d** 87 **p** 88. NSM Surbiton Hill Ch Ch *S'wark* 87-03. *3 Pine Walk, Surbiton KT5 8NJ* Tel (020) 8399 7143
E-mail bendell@talktalk.net

BENDING, Richard Clement. b 47. Southn Univ BSc68. Ridley Hall Cam 87. **d** 89 **p** 90. Par Dn St Neots *Ely* 89-92; V Buckden 92-99; P-in-c Hail Weston 97-99; P-in-c Terrington St John 99-02; P-in-c Tilney All Saints 99-02; P-in-c Wiggenhall St Germans and Islington 99-02; P-in-c Wiggenhall St Mary Magd 99-02; V E Marshland 02-05; rtd 05; Perm to Offic *Nor* from 05. *Dawn Cottage, Newgate Green, Cley, Holt NR25 7TT* Tel (01263) 741603 E-mail rcbending@hotmail.com

BENDREY (née BRIGNALL), Elizabeth Jane. b 69. St Mary's Coll Twickenham BA(QTS)91 Heythrop Coll Lon MA02 Cam Univ BTh06. Westcott Ho Cam 04. **d** 06 **p** 07. C Witham *Chelmsf* from 06. *23 Forest Road, Witham CM8 2PS* Tel (01375) 501902 Mobile 07940-516741
E-mail revbethbendrey@hotmail.co.uk

BENDREY, Iain Robert. b 73. Bp Grosseteste Coll BA96 Birm Univ MEd03. ERMC 06. **d** 08 **p** 09. NSM Wickham Bishops w Lt Braxted *Chelmsf* from 08. *23 Forest Road, Witham CM8 2PS* Tel (01375) 501902 Mobile 07960-810687

BENEDICT, Brother. *See* WINSPER, Arthur William

BENFIELD, Paul John. b 56. Newc Univ LLB77 Southn Univ BTh89 Barrister-at-Law (Lincoln's Inn) 78. Chich Th Coll 86. **d** 89 **p** 90. C Shiremoor *Newc* 89-92; C Hexham 92-93; TV Lewes All SS, St Anne, St Mich and St Thos *Chich* 93-97; R Pulborough 97-00; V Fleetwood St Nic *Blackb* from 00. *St Nicholas' Vicarage, Highbury Avenue, Fleetwood FY7 7DJ* Tel and fax (01253) 874402 E-mail benfield@btinternet.com

BENFORD, Steven Charles. b 61. Leic Univ MB, ChB86. NEOC 97. **d** 00 **p** 01. NSM Northallerton w Kirby Sigston *York* 00-04; P-in-c York St Luke from 04. *79 Burton Stone Lane, York YO30 6BZ* Tel (01904) 641058 E-mail benford@doctors.org.uk

BENGE, Charles David. b 40. Cranmer Hall Dur 63. **d** 68 **p** 69. C Millfield St Mark *Dur* 68-72; C Hensingham *Carl* 72-75; TV Maghull *Liv* 75-82; V Bootle St Leon 82-97; NSM Ormskirk 97-01; rtd 01; Perm to Offic *Liv* from 03. *26 Drummersdale Lane, Scarisbrick, Ormskirk L40 9RB* Tel (01704) 880956

BENHAM, Ms Sandra Rhys. b 59. Westcott Ho Cam 04. **d** 06 **p** 07. C Gainsborough and Morton *Linc* from 06. *St Paul's Vicarage, Morton Front, Gainsborough DN21 3AD* Tel (01427) 678873 E-mail sandra.benham@btopenworld.com

BENIAMS, Alec Charles. b 28. AKC52. **d** 53 **p** 54. C Gosforth All SS *Newc* 53-56; C Cullercoats St Geo 56-58; C Eltham St Jo *S'wark* 58-59; C-in-c Lynemouth St Aid CD *Newc* 59-61; CF (TA) 60-67; V Lynemouth *Newc* 61-63; V Whittingham 63-67; V Willington 67-71; CF (TA - R of O) from 67; V Haydon Bridge *Newc* 71-85; R Yardley Hastings, Denton and Grendon etc *Pet* 85-90; rtd 90; Perm to Offic *Newc* from 90. *12 Dixson Drive, Highford Park, Hexham NE46 2RB* Tel (01434) 600226

BENISON, Canon Brian. b 41. K Coll Lon 61. Bps' Coll Cheshunt 63. **d** 66 **p** 67. C Tynemouth Ch Ch *Newc* 66-70; C Gosforth All SS 70-72; TV Cullercoats St Geo 73-81; V Denton 81-93; V Blyth St Mary 93-04; RD Bedlington 98-03; Chapl Cheviot and Wansbeck NHS Trust 93-98; Chapl Northumbria Healthcare NHS Trust 98-04; Hon Can Newc Cathl from 01; rtd 04. *64 Monks Wood, North Shields NE30 2UA* Tel 0191-257 1631 E-mail brian.benison@btinternet.com

BENJAMIN, Adrian Victor. b 42. Wadh Coll Ox BA66 MA68. Cuddesdon Coll 66. **d** 68 **p** 69. C Gosforth All SS *Newc* 68-71; C Stepney St Dunstan and All SS *Lon* 71-75; V Friern Barnet All SS from 75; Relig Ed ITV Oracle from 83. *All Saints' Vicarage, 14 Oakleigh Park South, London N20 9JU* Tel (020) 8445 4654 *or* 8445 8388 Mobile 07889-83298 Fax 8445 6831
E-mail allsaints@mcmail.com

✠**BENN, The Rt Revd Wallace Parke. b** 47. UCD BA69. Trin Coll Bris 69. **d** 72 **p** 73 **c** 97. C New Ferry *Ches* 72-76; C Cheadle 76-82; V Audley *Lich* 82-87; V Harold Wood *Chelmsf* 87-97; Chapl Harold Wood Hosp *Chelmsf* 87-96; Area Bp Lewes *Chich* from 97; Can and Preb Chich Cathl from 97. *Bishop's Lodge, 16A Prideaux Road, Eastbourne BN21 2NB* Tel (01323) 648462 Fax 641514 E-mail bishlewes@diochi.org.uk

BENNELL, Canon Richard. b 25. Leeds Univ BA45 DipEd45. Coll of Resurr Mirfield 46. **d** 48 **p** 49. C Bedminster *Bris* 48-51; C Brislington St Anne 51-56; V Fishponds St Jo 56-68; V Knowle

St Martin 68-73; TR Knowle 73-80; RD Brislington 73-79; Hon Can Bris Cathl 76-91; Chapl St Monica Home Westbury-on-Trym 80-91; rtd 91; Perm to Offic *Bris* from 91. *1B Cooper Road, Bristol BS9 3QZ* Tel 0117-962 2364

BENNETT, Hadley Jane. b 66. **d** 09. NSM Grayshott *Guildf* from 09. *Landfall, Three Gates Lane, Haslemere GU27 2ET* Tel (01428) 658166 E-mail hadleybennet@yahoo.co.uk

BENNETT, Mark David. b 62. SS Coll Cam BA84 MA92 Anglia Poly Univ MA04 ACA89. Westcott Ho Cam 98. **d** 01 **p** 02. C Chapel Allerton *Ripon* 01-05; TV Gt Parndon *Chelmsf* 05-07; P-in-c 07-09; TR from 09. *Great Parndon Rectory, Perry Road, Harlow CM18 7NP* Tel (01279) 432626
E-mail markbennet@btinternet.com

BENNETT, Alan Robert. b 31. Roch Th Coll 62. **d** 64 **p** 65. C Asterby w Goulceby *Linc* 64-67; C St Alb St Pet *St Alb* 67-70; R Banham *Nor* 70-72; CF 72-77; P-in-c Colchester St Mary Magd *Chelmsf* 77; TV Colchester St Leon, St Mary Magd and St Steph 77-81; R Colne Engaine 81-88; P-in-c Stoke Ferry w Wretton *Ely* 88-89; V 89-96; V Whittington 88-96; rtd 96; Hon C Wimbotsham w Stow Bardolph and Stow Bridge etc *Ely* 96-00; Perm to Offic from 00. *34 West Way, Wimbotsham, King's Lynn PE34 3PZ* Tel (01366) 385958

BENNETT, Canon Alan William. b 42. Sarum Th Coll 65. **d** 68 **p** 69. C Fareham H Trin *Portsm* 68-71; C Brighton St Matthias *Chich* 71-73; C Stanmer w Falmer and Moulsecoomb 73-75; C Moulsecoomb 76; V Lower Sandown St Jo *Portsm* 76-80; V Soberton w Newtown 80-87; R Aston Clinton w Buckland and Drayton Beauchamp *Ox* 87-07; RD Wendover 94-04; Hon Can Ch Ch 03-07; rtd 07. *16 Boddington Road, Wendover, Aylesbury HP22 6HY* Tel (01296) 625614
E-mail canonbennett@hotmail.co.uk

BENNETT, Alexander Steven Frederick. b 69. Hull Univ BA91. Westcott Ho Cam 93. **d** 95 **p** 96. C Whitton and Thurleston w Akenham *St E* 95-99; OGS from 99; C Oswestry *Lich* 99-01; V Oswestry H Trin 01-04; CF from 04. *c/o MOD Chaplains (Army)* Tel (01980) 615804 Fax 615800
E-mail asfb@clara.co.uk

BENNETT, Mrs Alison. b 63. Open Univ BSc03 DipSW99. STETS 05. **d** 08 **p** 09. C Bramshott and Liphook *Portsm* from 08. *2 Meadow End, Liphook GU30 7UA* Tel (01428) 725390

BENNETT, Ms Anne Yvonn. b 62. Open Univ MSc95 Imp Coll Lon MBA00. Cranmer Hall Dur 06. **d** 08 **p** 09. C Harton *Dur* from 08. *218 Sunderland Road, South Shields NE34 6AT* Tel 0191-456 2875 E-mail timeshift@btinternet.com

BENNETT, Anton Wayne. b 69. SW Poly Plymouth BSc90. Westcott Ho Cam 00. **d** 02 **p** 03. C Pendleton *Man* 02-05; R Abberton, The Flyfords, Naunton Beauchamp etc *Worc* 05-07; rtd 07. *18 Churchway Piece, Inkberrow, Worcester WR7 4HB* Tel (01386) 791324 E-mail father.anton@virgin.net

BENNETT, Arnold Ernest. b 29. K Coll Lon BD59 AKC53. **d** 54 **p** 55. C S w N Hayling *Portsm* 54-59; C Stevenage *St Alb* 59-64; R N w S Wootton *Nor* 64-74; V Hykeham *Linc* 74-85; V Heckfield w Mattingley and Rotherwick *Win* 85-99; rtd 99; Perm to Offic *Win* from 99. *24 Cricket Green, Hartley Wintney, Basingstoke RG27 8PP* Tel (01252) 843147

BENNETT, Arthur Harling. b 22. Ripon Hall Ox 70. **d** 71 **p** 72. C Standish *Blackb* 71-74; TV Darwen St Pet w Hoddlesden 75-79; V Whitechapel 79-89; V Whitechapel w Admarsh-in-Bleasdale 89-90; rtd 90; Perm to Offic *Blackb* from 90. *1 Eden Gardens, Longridge, Preston PR3 3WF* Tel (01772) 784924

BENNETT, Avril Elizabeth Jean. b 63. BEd. **d** 00 **p** 01. NSM Dublin Crumlin w Chapelizod *D & G* 00-03; NSM Tallaght from 03. *17 Ardeevin Court, Lucan, Co Dublin, Republic of Ireland* Tel (00353) (1) 628 2353

BENNETT, Ben. *See* BENNETT, Stuart

BENNETT, Bernard Michael. b 27. Leeds Univ CertEd52. St Aid Birkenhead 55. **d** 58 **p** 59. C Hemsworth *Wakef* 58-60; C Chapelthorpe 60-62; V Birkenhead St Bede w All SS *Ches* 62-71; V Latchford St Jas 71-75; Chapl HM Pris Appleton Thorn 75-82; V Appleton Thorn and Antrobus *Ches* 75-86; Chapl HM Rem Cen Risley 81-84; rtd 86; Perm to Offic *Ches* from 86-01 and *Blackb* 91-03. *8 Hanover Close, Prenton CH43 1XR* Tel 0151-652 8968

BENNETT, Charles William. b 38. LTh. St Jo Coll Auckland 60. **d** 63 **p** 64. C Tauranga New Zealand 63-68; V Clive 68-71; C St Jo Cathl Napier 71-74; V Waipaoa 74-79; C N Walsham w Antingham *Nor* 80-81; V Waipaoa New Zealand 81-82; V Te Puke 82-87; V Dannevirke and P-in-c Woodville 87-91; V Westshore 91-93; Min Enabler 94-03; V Waipawa from 05. *59 McGrath Street, Napier South, Napier 4110, New Zealand* Tel (0064) (6) 835 9924 Fax 835 9920
E-mail bwbennett@inspire.net.nz

BENNETT, Mrs Christina Mary. b 45. **d** 07 **p** 08. NSM Henfield w Shermanbury and Woodmancote *Chich* from 07. *17 Gresham Place, Henfield BN5 9QJ* Tel (01273) 492222
E-mail christina@cmb45.wanadoo.co.uk

BENNETT, Christopher Ian. b 75. TCD BA98 BTh00. CITC 97. **d** 00 **p** 01. C Larne and Inver *Conn* 00-03; C Holywood *D & D*

from 03. *30 Abbots Wood, Holywood BT18 9PL* Tel (028) 9042 4319 or 9042 3622 Mobile 07980-885991
E-mail bennett@holywoodparishchurch.co.uk

BENNETT, Clifford Orford. b 32. St Mich Coll Llan 73. **d** 75 **p** 76. C Holywell *St As* 75-79; V Pontblyddyn 79-99; rtd 99. *4 Bryn Teg, Brynford, Holywell CH8 8AP* Tel (01352) 719028

BENNETT, David Edward. b 35. Fitzw Ho Cam BA56 MA60 Lon Univ PGCE. Wells Th Coll 58. **d** 60 **p** 61. C Lightcliffe *Wakef* 60-62; NE Area Sec Chr Educn Movement 62-68; Gen Insp RE Nottm Co Coun 68-00; Hon C Holme Pierrepont w Adbolton *S'well* 71-85; NSM Radcliffe-on-Trent and Shelford etc 85-00; rtd 00; Perm to Offic *S'well* from 04. *The Old Farmhouse, 65 Main Street, Gunthorpe, Nottingham NG14 7EY* Tel 0115-966 3451

BENNETT, Donovan Harry. b 27. Qu Mary Coll Lon BScEng52 FGS61 AMICE61 CEng61 FICE72. Moray Ord Course 88. **d** 92 **p** 93. Hon C Dingwall *Mor* 92-93; Hon C Strathpeffer 92-93; Hon C Inverness St Mich 93-95; Assoc Chapl Raigmore Hosp NHS Trust Inverness 94-96; P-in-c Grantown-on-Spey *Mor* 96-99; Can St Andr Cathl Inverness 98-00; Perm to Offic from 99. *8 Brewster Drive, Forres IV36 2JW* Tel (01309) 671478 E-mail donovan.bennett@btinternet.com

BENNETT, Edwin James. b 23. St Barn Coll Adelaide ThL47 STh52. **d** 47 **p** 48. Australia 47-74; V Oldham St Barn *Man* 74-78; V Alderney *Win* 78-84; R Hatherden w Tangley, Weyhill and Penton Mewsey 84-89; rtd 89; Perm to Offic *Win* from 89. *Kalgoorlie, 35 Hatherden Road, Charlton, Andover SP10 4AP* Tel (01264) 356358

BENNETT, Garry Raymond. b 46. K Coll Lon 66 St Aug Coll Cant 69. **d** 70 **p** 71. C Mitcham St Mark *S'wark* 70-73; C Mortlake w E Sheen 73-75; TV 76-78; V Herne Hill St Paul 78-88; P-in-c Ruskin Park St Sav and St Matt 82-88; V Herne Hill 89; Sen Dioc Stewardship Adv *Chelmsf* 89-94; TR Southend 94-98; Chapl Herne Hill Sch S'wark from 98; Perm to Offic *St D* from 00. *Hendre House, Llandeloy, Haverfordwest SA62 6LW* Tel (01348) 831160 Fax 837244

BENNETT, Geoffrey Kenneth. b 56. Ex Univ MA01. Oak Hill Th Coll. **d** 89 **p** 90. C Ipswich St Matt *St E* 89-92; R St Ruan w St Grade and Landewednack *Truro* 92-98; V Budock from 98; P-in-c Mawnan from 03. *The Vicarage, Merry Mit Meadow, Budock Water, Falmouth TR11 5DW* Tel (01326) 376422
E-mail g.k.bennett@amserve.net

BENNETT, Canon George Edward. b 51. Univ of Wales (Abth) BA72. St Steph Ho Ox 73. **d** 76 **p** 77. C Clifton All SS w Tyndalls Park *Bris* 76-78; C Clifton All SS w St Jo 78-82; Chapl Newbury and Sandleford Hosps 82-93; TV Newbury *Ox* 82-93; V Llwynderw *S & B* 93-06; V Newton St Pet from 06; AD Clyne from 98; Hon Can Brecon Cathl 00-02; Can Res Brecon Cathl from 02. *The Vicarage, Marytwill Lane, Mumbles, Swansea SA3 4RB* Tel (01792) 368348

BENNETT, Graham Eric Thomas. b 53. Sarum & Wells Th Coll 88. **d** 90 **p** 91. C Baswich *Lich* 90-94; C Codsall 94-00; P-in-c Willenhall St Steph 00-05; V from 05; AD Wolverhampton from 05. *St Stephen's Vicarage, 27 Wolverhampton Street, Willenhall WV13 2PS* Tel (01902) 605239
E-mail grahambennett.69@btinternet.com

BENNETT, Handel Henry Cecil. b 33. MCIM. Cant Sch of Min 79. **d** 82 **p** 83. NSM St Margarets-at-Cliffe w Westcliffe etc *Cant* 82-85; Dir Holy Land Chr Tours 85-94; Holy Land Consultant F T Tours 95-96; Sen Travel Consultant Raymond Cook Chr Tours from 96; Perm to Offic *St Alb* 85-99 and *Ex* from 99. *Camps Bay, 2 Victoria Road, Sidmouth EX10 8TZ* Tel and fax (01395) 514211 Mobile 07774-981569

BENNETT, Helen Anne. *See* EDWARDS, Helen Anne

BENNETT, Canon Ian Frederick. b 30. Ch Coll Cam BA54 MA62. Westcott Ho Cam 61. **d** 63 **p** 64. C Hemel Hempstead *St Alb* 63-68; Asst Chapl Man Univ 69-73; Sen Chapl 73-79; C Chorlton upon Medlock 69-73; P-in-c 73-79; TR Man Whitworth 79; Dioc Tr Officer *Birm* 79-88; Hon Can Birm Cathl 86-88; Can Res Newc Cathl 88-98; Dioc Dir of Min and Tr 90-98; Dir Post-Ord Tr 97-98; rtd 98; Perm to Offic *Newc* from 98. *21 Otterburn Avenue, Gosforth, Newcastle upon Tyne NE3 4RR* Tel 0191-285 1967

BENNETT, John David. b 58. Ox Univ BA79 MA83. Westcott Ho Cam 81. **d** 83 **p** 84. C Taunton St Andr *B & W* 83-86; Chapl Trowbridge Coll *Sarum* 86-90; Asst P Studley 86-90; V Yeovil H Trin *B & W* 90-95; R Yeovil H Trin w Barwick 95-02; R Sprowston w Beeston *Nor* from 02; RD Nor N from 05. *The Vicarage, 2 Wroxham Road, Norwich NR7 8TZ* Tel (01603) 426492 E-mail vicar@sprowston.org.uk

BENNETT, John Dudley. b 44. Open Univ BA87 Lanc Univ MA92 Huddersfield Univ PGCE04. Coll of Resurr Mirfield 08. **d** 09 **p** 09. NSM Bolton Abbey *Bradf* from 09. *Honeysuckle Cottage, The Green, Linton, Skipton BD23 5IJ* Tel (01756) 753763 E-mail brj.linton@virgin.net

BENNETT, John Seccombe. b 59. Wye Coll Lon BSc81 Leic Poly CertEd84. Trin Coll Bris. **d** 00 **p** 01. C Llanrhian w Llanhywel and Carnhedryn etc *St D* 00-01; C Dewisland 01-02; TV from

02; Chapl St D Cathl from 00. *The Vicarage, Llanrhian, Haverfordwest SA62 5BG* Tel (01348) 831354

BENNETT, Joyce Mary. b 23. OBE79. Westf Coll Lon BA44 DipEd45 Hong Kong Univ Hon DSocSc84. d 62 p 71. C Kowloon St Thos 62-66; C Hong Kong Crown of Thorns 67-68; C Kwun Tong St Barn 68-83; Lect Union Th Sem Hong Kong 63-66; Prin St Cath Girls Sch Kwun Tong 68-83; NSM St Martin-in-the-Fields *Lon* 84-87; Perm to Offic *Ox* 87-07. *The Cornerstone, 72 The Crescent, High Wycombe HP13 6JP* Tel (01494) 539016

BENNETT, Lee. b 70. Leeds Univ BA00 RGN93. Coll of Resurr Mirfield 97. d 00 p 01. C Hemsworth *Wakef* 00-03; V Huddersfield All SS and St Thos 03-04; Assoc P Athersley and Monk Bretton 04-07; V S Benfleet *Chelmsf* from 07. *St Mary's Vicarage, 105 Vicarage Hill, Benfleet SS7 1PD* Tel (01268) 792294 E-mail frlee.bennett@googlemail.com

BENNETT, Marian Joyce. b 53. BEd. EMMTC. d 06 p 07. NSM Castle Donington and Lockington cum Hemington *Leic* from 06. *174 Leicester Road, Loughborough LE11 2AH* Tel (01509) 263601 E-mail marian@bennett54.freeserve.co.uk

BENNETT, Mark Ian. b 61. K Coll Cam BA83 MA86. Trin Coll Bris BA94. d 94 p 95. C Selly Park St Steph and St Wulstan *Birm* 94-97; C Harrow Trin St Mich *Lon* 97-99; Hon C Redland *Bris* 99-00; TV Drypool York 00-06; V San Cross Cross *Ches* from 06. *The Vicarage, 16 Higham Lane, Hyde SK14 5LX* Tel 0161-368 2337 Mobile 07866-680535
E-mail mark@holytrinitychurch-gx.org.uk

BENNETT, Michael John. b 43. AKC66. St Boniface Warminster 66. d 67 p 68. C Chester le Street *Dur* 67-71; C Portland All SS w St Pet *Sarum* 71-74; V Portland St Jo 74-85; Chapl Portland Hosp Weymouth 74-85; R Alveley and Quatt *Heref* 85-92; Dep Chapl HM YOI Glen Parva 93-95; TV Wrexham *St As* 95-99; V Llansantffraid-ym-Mechain and Llanfechain 99-05; C Rhyl w St Ann 05-09; rtd 09. *122 Rhuddlan Road, Rhyl LL18 2RD* Tel (01745) 342949 E-mail smb@totalise.co.uk

BENNETT, Nigel John. b 47. Oak Hill Th Coll 66. d 71 p 72. C Tonbridge St Steph *Roch* 71-75; C Heatherlands St Jo *Sarum* 75-79; P-in-c Kingham w Churchill, Daylesford and Sarsden *Ox* 79; R 80-85; Chapl Blue Coat Sch Reading 85-08; rtd 08; Perm to Offic *Ox* from 08. *13 Wilmington Close, Woodley, Reading RG5 4LR* Tel 0118-969 9223
E-mail revnjb@nigel58.wanadoo.co.uk

BENNETT, Osmond Shirley. b 36. Oriel Coll Ox BA67. Ripon Hall Ox 64. d 68 p 69. C Stocking Farm *Leic* 68-71; C Thurcaston 71-72; V Leic St Marg 72-82; V Leic St Marg and All SS 83-89; R Houghton-on-the-Hill, Keyham and Hungarton 89-00; rtd 00. *48 Wide Lane, Hathern, Loughborough LE12 5LN* Tel (01509) 553644

BENNETT, Paul. b 55. Southn Univ BTh94. St Steph Ho Ox 95. d 97 p 98. C Willingdon *Chich* 97-00; C Hangleton 00-04; R Letchworth *St Alb* from 04. *St Michael's Rectory, 39 South View, Letchworth Garden City SG6 3JJ* Tel (01462) 684822 Fax 643592 E-mail revpaulbennett@ntlworld.com

BENNETT, Paul Jonathan. b 61. Ex Univ BA85. Ripon Coll Cuddesdon 85. d 87 p 88. C Henleaze *Bris* 87-91; P-in-c Swindon All SS 91-94; V Swindon All SS w St Barn 94-96; V Patrick, Foxdale and German St Jo *S & M* 96-00. *60 Teign View Road, Bishopsteignton, Teignmouth TQ14 9SZ* Tel (01626) 774474
E-mail pbennett1961@yahoo.co.uk

BENNETT, Paul William. b 61. Linc Th Coll 95. d 95 p 96. C Thornton-le-Fylde *Blackb* 95-00; V Wesham 00-03; P-in-c Treales 00-03; V Wesham and Treales 03-08; Chapl Dunkirk Miss to Seafarers *Eur* from 08. *Princess Alice House, 130 rue de l'Ecole Maternelle, 59140 Dunkerque, France* Tel (0033) (3) 28 59 04 20

BENNETT, Peter Hugh. b 22. K Coll Lon 46. d 50 p 51. C Newington Transfiguration *York* 50-53; C Bottesford *Linc* 53-57; V Tile Hill *Cov* 58-64; V Hillmorton 64-76; R Beaudesert w Henley-in-Arden 76-81; P-in-c Ullenhall cum Aspley 76-81; R Beaudesert and Henley-in-Arden w Ullenhall 81-87; rtd 87; Perm to Offic *Cov* from 87. *20 Avon Crescent, Stratford-upon-Avon CV37 7EY* Tel (01789) 296278

BENNETT, Miss Rachel Elizabeth. b 56. W Sussex Inst of HE CertEd79. d 04. NSM Littlehampton and Wick *Chich* 04-05; C Durrington 05-07; Chapl Worthing and Southlands Hosps NHS Trust from 08. *26 Vancouver Close, Worthing BN13 2SH* Tel (01903) 693075 *or* 205111 Mobile 07810-350098
E-mail rachel.bennett3@tesco.net

BENNETT, Robert Geoffrey. b 43. FCA. d 05 p 06. OLM Woking St Jo *Guildf* from 05. *10 Barricane, Woking GU21 7RB* Tel (01483) 722832 E-mail robgbennett@tiscali.co.uk

BENNETT, Roger Sherwood. b 35. Nottm Univ BA56. Wells Th Coll 58. d 59 p 60. C Mansfield Woodhouse *S'well* 59-60; C Spalding *Linc* 60-63; V Gedney 63-69; Chapl RNR 65-68; Chapl RN 69-90; V Amport, Grateley, Monxton and Quarley *Win* 90-95; rtd 96; Perm to Offic *Win* from 96. *Le Reduit, School Lane, Nether Wallop, Stockbridge SO20 8EH* Tel (01264) 782336

BENNETT, Roy Donald. b 40. Nottm Univ MA97. St Jo Coll Nottm 78. d 80 p 81. C Fletchamstead *Cov* 80-83; C Bedworth

83-87; P-in-c Studley 87-93; Chapl Univ Hosp Nottm 93-96; Chapl Qu Medical Cen Nottm 94-96; Chapl Bassetlaw Hosp and Community Services NHS Trust 96-01; Chapl Doncaster and Bassetlaw Hosps NHS Trust 01-02; rtd 02; Perm to Offic *Sarum* 03-08. *21 High Street, Puddletown, Dorchester DT2 8RT* Tel (01305) 848144

BENNETT, Shirley. *See* BENNETT, Osmond Shirley

BENNETT (née FORD), Ms Simone Louise. b 70. Warwick Univ BA92. Westcott Ho Cam 00. d 02 p 03. C Stockingford *Cov* 02-03; C Didsbury Ch Ch and Withington St Chris *Man* 03-05; Hon C Abberton, The Flyfords, Naunton Beauchamp etc *Worc* from 06. *18 Churchway Piece, Inkberrow, Worcester WR7 4HB* Tel (01386) 791324 Mobile 07946-548366
E-mail simone.bennett@virgin.net

BENNETT, Stuart (Ben). b 61. St Jo Coll Nottm BA02. d 02 p 03. C Consett *Dur* 02-06; P-in-c Castleside from 06. *The Vicarage, 6 Hillcrest, Castleside, Consett DH8 9EB* Tel (01207) 590086
E-mail stubennett@bigfoot.com

BENNETT, Ms Toni Elizabeth. b 56. Worc Coll of Educn BA81 Sheff Poly 87. St Jo Coll Nottm MA94. d 96 p 97. C Heanor *Derby* 96-00; TV Bedworth *Cov* 00-08; R Montgomery and Forden and Llandyssil *St As* from 08. *The Rectory, Lions Bank, Montgomery SY15 6PT* Tel (01686) 668539
E-mail toni.rev@tesco.net

BENNETT, William Leslie. b 52. TCD Div Sch. d 90 p 91. C Carrickfergus *Conn* 90-93; I Lisnaskea *Clogh* 93-00; I Newcastle w Newtownmountkennedy and Calary *D & G* from 00. *The Rectory, Church Lane, Newcastle, Greystones, Co Wicklow, Republic of Ireland* Tel (00353) (1) 281 9300
E-mail revwilliambennett@eircom.net

BENNETT-REES, Catherine Mary. b 77. LMH Ox BA99 Selw Coll Cam BA02. Ridley Hall Cam 02. d 04 p 05. NSM Cambridge H Trin *Ely* from 04. *Holy Trinity Church, Market Street, Cambridge CB2 3NZ* Tel (01223) 355397
E-mail catbennettrees@hotmail.com

BENNETT-SHAW, Miss Anne Elizabeth. b 38. d 02 p 03. OLM Upper Wylye Valley *Sarum* from 02. *5 Hospital of St John, Heytesbury, Warminster BA12 0HW* Tel (01985) 840339
E-mail revannebennettshaw@btinternet.com

✠**BENNETTS, The Rt Revd Colin James.** b 40. Jes Coll Cam BA63 MA67. Ridley Hall Cam 63. d 65 p 66 c 94. C Tonbridge St Steph *Roch* 65-69; Chapl Ox Pastorate 69-79; C Ox St Aldate w H Trin 69-73; Asst Chapl Jes Coll Ox 73-75; Chapl 75-78; P-in-c Ox St Andr 79; V 80-90; RD Ox 84-89; Can Res Ches Cathl and Dioc Dir of Ords 90-94; Area Bp Buckm *Ox* 94-98; Bp Cov 98-08; rtd 08; Asst Bp Guildf from 09. *23 Brox Road, Ottershaw, Chertsey KT16 0HG* Tel (01932) 875324
E-mail colinbennetts682@btinternet.com

BENNETTS, John Barrington. b 32. d 92 p 93. NSM Falmouth K Chas *Truro* 92; rtd 04; Perm to Offic *Truro* from 04. *39 Budock Terrace, Falmouth TR11 3NE* Tel (01326) 314961 *or* 312111 E-mail kcmvestry@onetel.com

BENNETTS, Ms Rachel Mary. b 69. Homerton Coll Cam BEd91. Trin Coll Bris BA01. d 02 p 03. C Wroughton *Bris* 02-06; TV N Farnborough *Guildf* from 06; Chapl Farnborough Sixth Form Coll from 07. *The Vicarage, 45 Sand Hill, Farnborough GU14 8ER* Tel (01252) 543789 Mobile 07749-045449
E-mail racheagle@yahoo.co.uk

BENNIE, Stanley James Gordon. b 43. Edin Univ MA65. Coll of Resurr Mirfield 66. d 68 p 69. C Ashington *Newc* 68-70; Prec St Andr Cathl Inverness 70-74; Itinerant Priest 74-81; R Portsoy *Ab* 81-84; R Buckie 81-84; R Stornoway *Arg* from 84; R Eorropaidh 84-95; Miss to Seafarers from 84. *St Peter's House, 10 Springfield Road, Stornoway HS1 2PT* Tel (01851) 703609 *or* 08453-458564 E-mail gm4ptq@btinternet.com
or stornoway@argyll.anglican.org

BENNISON, Philip Owen. b 42. Dur Univ BA64. Coll of Resurr Mirfield 64. d 66 p 67. C Guisborough *York* 66-67; C S Bank 67-71; C Thornaby on Tees St Paul 71-72; TV Thornaby on Tees 72-74; R Skelton in Cleveland 74-78; R Upleatham 75-78; Chapl Freeman Hosp Newc 78-84; V Ashington *Newc* 84-93; Chapl N Tees Health NHS Trust Stockton-on-Tees 93-02; P-in-c Newton Flowery Field *Ches* from 02; P-in-c Hyde St Thos from 02. *St Stephen's Vicarage, 154 Bennett Street, Hyde SK14 4SS* Tel and fax 0161-368 3333 E-mail philip_bennison@hotmail.com

BENNISON, Timothy Paul. b 63. Aber Univ BD94. Edin Th Coll 95. d 97 p 98. C St Andr Cathl 97-00; Asst Chapl Aberdeen Univ 97-00; P-in-c Glencarse *Bre* 05-08; R Dunfermline *St And* from 08. *The Rectory, 17 Ardeer Place, Dunfermline KY11 4YX* Tel (01383) 723901 Mobile 07707-353526

BENOY, Stephen Michael. b 66. Clare Coll Cam BA87 MA90. Trin Coll Bris BA93. d 96 p 97. C New Malden and Coombe *S'wark* 96-02; Kingston Borough Youth Project 00-02; V Kettering Ch the King *Pet* from 02. *The Vicarage, Deeble Road, Kettering NN15 7AA* Tel (01536) 512828
E-mail steve.benoy@virgin.net *or* vicar@ctk.org.uk

BENSON, Christopher Hugh. b 53. Bath Academy of Art BA75 Keble Coll Ox BA78 MA87. Chich Th Coll 78. d 80 p 81. C

Heavitree w Ex St Paul 80-83; P-in-c Broadclyst 83-85; TV Pinhoe and Broadclyst 85-90; V Kingsteignton and Teigngrace 90-08; Chapl Plymouth Univ 92-95; RD Newton Abbot and Ipplepen 01-07; C Baslow w Curbar and Stoney Middleton *Derby* from 08; C Ashford w Sheldon and Longstone from 08. *The Vicarage, Church Lane, Great Longstone, Bakewell DE45 1TB* Tel (01629) 640257
E-mail chrishbenson@hotmail.com

BENSON, David. *See* BENSON, John David

BENSON, Gareth Neil. b 47. Jordan Hill Coll Glas TCert80. St And NSM Tr Scheme 77. **d** 81 **p** 82. NSM Glenrothes *St And* 81-88; NSM Kirkcaldy from 88; NSM Kinghorn from 88; P-in-c from 04. *The Rectory, 1 Longbraes Gardens, Kirkcaldy KY2 5YJ* Tel (01592) 204208 *or* 568518
E-mail fathergareth@btinternet.com

BENSON, Canon George Patrick. b 49. Ch Ch Ox BA70 Lon Univ BD77 Open Univ MPhil94. All Nations Chr Coll 78 St Jo Coll Nottm 89. **d** 91 **p** 92. C Upton (Overchurch) *Ches* 91-95; V Barnston from 95; RD Wirral N 98-08; Hon Can Ches Cathl from 09. *The Vicarage, 87 Barnston Road, Heswall, Wirral CH61 1BW* Tel 0151-648 1776 *or* 648 2404 Fax 648 2407
E-mail paddy@kabare.freeserve.co.uk

BENSON, Mrs Hilary Christine. b 51. Man Univ BA72 Hughes Hall Cam PGCE73. Trin Coll Bris 81. **dss** 84 **d** 87 **p** 94. Starbeck *Ripon* 84-86; Birm St Martin w Bordesley St Andr 86-91; NSM 87-91; NSM Brandwood 91-97; Chapl Birm Univ 92-97; Chapl St Edw Sch Ox 97-00; Chapl Qu Anne's Sch Caversham from 00. *Queen Anne's School, Henley Road, Caversham, Reading RG4 6DX* Tel 0118-947 1582 *or* 954 5026
E-mail saintbede@ntlworld.com

BENSON, John David. b 36. St Aid Birkenhead 58. **d** 61 **p** 62. C Kingston upon Hull St Martin *York* 61-65; C Marfleet 65-68; V Ingleby Greenhow 68-72; P-in-c Kildale 68-72; Asst Youth Chapl 68-72; Dioc Youth Chapl *Sheff* 72-78; V Thorne 78-91; V Totley 91-98; rtd 98; Perm to Offic *Sheff* from 98. *14 Ash Hill Crescent, Hatfield, Doncaster DN7 6HY* Tel (01302) 846359

BENSON, John Patrick. b 51. Univ of Wales (Ban) BSc72. Trin Coll Bris 83. **d** 85 **p** 86. C Stoke Damerel *Ex* 85-88; P-in-c Petrockstowe, Petersmarland, Merton and Huish 88; TV Shebbear, Buckland Filleigh, Sheepwash etc 89-94; RD Torrington 93-94; P-in-c Newport, Bishops Tawton and Tawstock 94-97; TV Barnstaple 97-07; R Knockholt w Halstead *Roch* from 07. *The Rectory, Church Road, Halstead, Sevenoaks TN14 7HQ* Tel (01959) 532133
E-mail john.benson3@btinternet.com

BENSON, The Very Revd John Patrick. b 52. Ch Coll Cam BA73 MA76 PhD76. Trin Coll Bris 78. **d** 81 **p** 82. C Walmley *Birm* 81-84; C Chadkirk *Ches* 84-86; Singapore from 87; V St Geo Singapore 87-95; Dir of Tr from 95; Dean Cambodia from 95. *Anglican Retreat Centre, 41 Ceylon Road, Singapore 429630, Republic of Singapore* Tel (0065) 447 4416 Fax 447 0842

BENSON, Nicholas Henry. b 53. Man Univ BSc75 Leeds Univ MSc77. Trin Coll Bris 81. **d** 84 **p** 85. C Starbeck *Ripon* 84-86; C Birm St Martin w Bordesley St Andr 86-91; Chapl to the Markets 86-91; V Brandwood 91-97; Perm to Offic *Ox* 99-01; NSM Reading St Jo from 01. *Hillside, 2 Henley Road, Caversham, Reading RG4 6DS* Tel 0118-954 5026
E-mail saintbede@ntlworld.com

BENSON, Paddy. *See* BENSON, Canon George Patrick

BENSON, Peter Leslie. b 60. Leeds Univ BA81. Westcott Ho Cam 81. **d** 85 **p** 86. C Kippax w Allerton Bywater *Ripon* 85-88; C Potternewton 88-91; Asst Chapl St Jas Univ Hosp Leeds 91-94; Chapl Dewsbury Health Care NHS Trust 94-98; P-in-c Batley St Thos *Wakef* 98-99; V 99-08; V Brigham, Gt Broughton and Broughton Moor *Carl* from 08. *The Vicarage, Little Broughton, Cockermouth CA13 0YG* Tel (01900) 825317 Mobile 07985-054318 E-mail peterbenson@talktalk.net

BENSON, Philip Steven. b 59. ACertCM79 LLCM80 Ulster Univ BSc81. S Dios Minl Tr Scheme 88. **d** 92 **p** 93. Producer Relig Broadcasting Dept BBC 91-94; NSM W Ealing St Jo w St Jas *Lon* 92-94; Relig Progr Producer BBC Man from 94. *4 Cranford Avenue, Knutsford WA16 0EB* Tel (01565) 652513 Fax 641695

BENSON, Mrs Rachel Candia. b 43. JP76. TCD MA66 Lon Univ PGCE67. S'wark Ord Course 84. **d** 87 **p** 94. NSM Putney St Marg *S'wark* 87-97; NSM Sand Hutton and Whitwell w Crambe, Flaxton and Foston *York* 97; Perm to Offic from 07. *Grange Farm, Westow, York YO60 7NJ* Tel (01653) 658296 Fax 658456 E-mail rachelbenson4@btopenworld.com

BENSON, Richard John. b 55. Birm Coll of Educn CertEd78. Ripon Coll Cuddesdon 92. **d** 94 **p** 95. C Alford w Rigsby *Linc* 94-97; R Partney Gp from 97. *The Rectory, Partney, Spilsby PE23 4PG* Tel (01790) 753570

BENSON, Steven. *See* BENSON, Philip Steven

BENSON, Thomas Henry Frank. b 66. SWMTC 06. **d** 09. C Bideford, Northam, Westward Ho!, Appledore etc *Ex* from 09. *The Vicarage, Mines Road, Bideford EX39 4BZ*

BENT, David Michael. b 55. Leeds Univ BSc77. Trin Coll Bris BA94. **d** 96 **p** 97. C Gorleston St Andr *Nor* 96-00; TR

Brinsworth w Catcliffe and Treeton *Sheff* 00-03; TR Rivers Team from 03. *The Vicarage, 61 Whitehill Lane, Brinsworth, Rotherham S60 5JR* Tel (01709) 363850
E-mail david.bent@btinternet.com

BENT, Mrs Helen Margaret. b 56. Sheff Univ BMus77 Trent Poly PGCE78 Suffolk Poly BA00. EAMTC 97. **d** 98 **p** 99. C Gorleston St Mary *Nor* 98-00; C Brightside w Wincobank *Sheff* 00-04; Bp's Adv in Music and Worship from 05. *The Vicarage, 61 Whitehill Lane, Brinsworth, Rotherham S60 5JR* Tel (01709) 363850 E-mail helen@thebents.co.uk

BENT, Michael Charles. b 31. Kelham Th Coll 51. **d** 55 **p** 56. C Wellingborough St Mary *Pet* 55-60; New Zealand 60-85, 89-94 and from 96; Papua New Guinea 94-96; Adn Taranaki 76-85; Dean H Trin Cathl Suva Fiji 85-89; Can St Pet Cathl Hamilton 90-94. *34 Brooklands Road, New Plymouth 4601, New Zealand* Tel (0064) (6) 753 5507 E-mail miro@clear.net.nz

BENTALL, Mrs Jill Margaret. b 44. MCSP66. S Dios Minl Tr Scheme 91. **d** 94 **p** 95. NSM Knights Enham *Win* 94-02; C Andover w Foxcott 02-09; P-in-c Pastrow from 09; RD Andover from 06. *Old Farm Cottage, 102 Charlton, Andover SP10 4AN* Tel (01264) 365643

BENTHAM, John William. b 58. Loughb Univ BSc80 Nottm Univ LTh85. St Jo Coll Nottm 82. **d** 85 **p** 86. C Burmantofts St Steph and St Agnes *Ripon* 85-88; C Horsforth 88-90; P-in-c Nottingham St Sav *S'well* 90-92; V 92-98; Chapl Nottm Univ from 98; AD Nottingham W 06-08; AD W Bingham from 08. *51 Chaworth Road, West Bridgford, Nottingham NG2 7AE* Tel 0115-846 1054 *or* 846 6037
E-mail john.bentham@nottingham.ac.uk

BENTHAM, Philip John (Ben). b 55. Hull Univ BA83 PGCE85. Trin Coll Bris MA96. **d** 96 **p** 97. C Wrockwardine Deanery *Lich* 96-00; P-in-c Chipinge and Chimanimani Zimbabwe 00-03; Chapl Via del Mar St Pet Chile 03-07; Chapl Bethany Sch Goudhurst from 08. *1 Providence Cottages, Curtisden Green, Goudhurst, Cranbrook TN17 1LD* Tel (01580) 212994
E-mail benbentham@yahoo.co.uk

✠**BENTLEY, The Rt Revd David Edward.** b 35. Leeds Univ BA56. Westcott Ho Cam 58. **d** 60 **p** 61 **c** 86. C Bris St Ambrose Whitehall 60-62; C Guildf H Trin w St Mary 62-66; R Headley All SS 66-73; R Esher 73-86; RD Emly 77-82; Hon Can Guildf Cathl 80-86; Chmn Dioc Coun Soc Resp 80-86; Suff Bp Lynn *Nor* 86-93; Chmn Cand Cttee ACCM 87-91; ABM 91-93; Bp Glouc 93-03; rtd 04; Hon Asst Bp Lich from 04; Perm to Offic *Cov* from 04. *19 Gable Croft, Lichfield WS14 9RY* Tel (01543) 419376

BENTLEY, Frank Richard. b 41. K Coll Lon BD67 AKC67. **d** 68 **p** 69. C Feltham *Lon* 68-72; P-in-c Bethnal Green St Bart 72-77; R Bow w Bromley St Leon 77-88; P-in-c Mile End Old Town H Trin 77-88; P-in-c Bromley All Hallows 77-88; AD Tower Hamlets 83-88; TR E Ham w Upton Park St Alb *Chelmsf* 88-97; P-in-c Petersham *S'wark* 97-07; Chapl HM Pris Latchmere Ho 97-07; rtd 07; Perm to Offic *St E* from 08. *104 Cannon Street, Bury St Edmunds IP33 1JU* Tel (01284) 766063
E-mail richardbentley.41@virgin.net

BENTLEY, The Venr Frank William Henry. b 34. AKC57. **d** 58 **p** 59. C Shepton Mallet *B & W* 58-62; R Kingsdon w Podymore-Milton 62-66; P-in-c Yeovilton 62-66; P-in-c Babcary 64-66; V Wiveliscombe 66-76; RD Tone 73-76; V St Jo in Bedwardine *Worc* 76-84; P-in-c Worc St Mich 82-84; RD Martley and Worc W 80-84; Hon Can Worc Cathl 81-84; Adn Worc and Can Res Worc Cathl 84-99; rtd 99; Perm to Offic *Worc* from 04; Chapl to The Queen 94-04. *Willow Cottage, Station Road, Fladbury, Pershore WR10 2QW* Tel (01386) 861847
E-mail f.bentley@virgin.net

BENTLEY, Graham John. b 29. S'wark Ord Course 77. **d** 80 **p** 81. NSM Merton St Mary *S'wark* 80-83; C Balham St Mary 83-84; C Wimbledon 85-86; V Raynes Park St Sav 86-95; rtd 95; Perm to Offic *Guildf* from 95. *61 Clarence Road, Fleet, Aldershot GU51 3RY* Tel (01252) 682464

BENTLEY, Ian Robert. b 55. Sheff Univ BA76 Sheff City Poly PGCE78. Cranmer Hall Dur 93. **d** 95 **p** 96. C Mattishall w Mattishall Burgh, Welborne etc *Nor* 95-98; R Ditchingham, Hedenham, Broome, Earsham etc 98-06; V Oulton Broad from 06. *St Mark's Vicarage, 212 Bridge Road, Lowestoft NR33 9JX* Tel (01502) 572563 E-mail ian@revbentley.freeserve.co.uk

BENTLEY, Ian Ronald. b 51. BA79. Oak Hill Th Coll 76. **d** 79 **p** 80. C Northwood Em *Lon* 79-85; C St Marylebone All So w SS Pet and Jo 85-88; C Langham Place All So 88-91; V Eynsham and Cassington *Ox* 91-95; V Chineham *Win* from 95. *The Vicarage, 1 Hartswood, Chineham, Basingstoke RG24 8SJ* Tel (01256) 474285

BENTLEY, Lesley. b 55. Univ of Wales (Lamp) BA76 RMN80. St Jo Coll Nottm MTh82. **dss** 82 **d** 87 **p** 94. Mickleover St Jo *Derby* 82-84; Par Dn 84-89; Par Dn 87-89; Dir Diaconal Mins 89-92; Par Dn Farnworth 92-94; C 94-95; V Westbrook St Phil 95-01; Hon Can Liv Cathl 99-01; V Bilton *Ripon* 01-03; TR 03-09; Initial Minl Educn Officer 03-09; Dir Min

Development *Lich* from 09. *The Vicarage, Salt Lane, Salt, Stafford ST18 0BW* Tel (01889) 508066
E-mail lesley_bentley@btopenworld.com
BENTLEY, Paul. b 48. Sarum & Wells Th Coll. **d** 93 **p** 94. C Ex St Dav 93-96; P-in-c Marlpool *Derby* 96-01; V 01-02; Chapl Derbyshire Community Health Services 96-00; Chapl Amber Valley Primary Care Trust 00-02; Chapl Mansfield Distr Primary Care Trust from 02. *The Pilgrim Centre, Mansfield Community Hospital, Stockwell Gate, Mansfield NG18 5QJ* Tel (01623) 785011 E-mail paul.bentley@mansfield-pct.nhs.uk
or revpaulb@aol.com
BENTLEY, Richard. *See* BENTLEY, Frank Richard
BENTON, John Anthony. b 27. Ex Coll Ox BA48 MA52. Sarum Th Coll 49. **d** 50 **p** 51. C N Keyham *Ex* 50-52; C Tavistock and Gulworthy 52-55; C Heavitree 55-56; R Lower Gravenhurst *St Alb* 56-61; V Silsoe 56-61; V Upper Gravenhurst 56-61; C Port Elizabeth St Cuth S Africa 61-63; R Port Elizabeth St Sav 64-68; R Moretonhampstead *Ex* 68-74; RD Moreton 73-74; R Holsworthy w Cookbury and Hollacombe 74-80; TR Withycombe Raleigh 80-92; RD Aylesbeare 84-89; rtd 92; Perm to Offic *Ex* from 92. *38 Wreford's Close, Exeter EX4 5AY* Tel (01392) 211428
BENTON, Canon Michael John. b 38. Lon Univ BSc60 FRSA93 MSOSc. Sarum & Wells Th Coll 72. **d** 74 **p** 74. San Lect K Alfred Coll *Win* 74-76; NSM Weeke 74-76; C Bursledon 76-78; R Over Wallop w Nether Wallop 78-83; Dir of Educn 79-96; R Win St Lawr and St Maurice w St Swithun 83-90; Hon Can Win Cathl 89-03; P-in-c Kingsclere 96-03; Chapl to The Queen 98-08; rtd 03; Perm to Offic *Win* from 03. *South Lodge, Auchterarder House, Auchterarder PH3 1ER* Tel (01764) 662991
BENTON-EVANS, Martin James William. b 69. K Coll Lon BA90 Anglia Poly Univ PGCE97. Ripon Coll Cuddesdon BTh03. **d** 03 **p** 04. C Ivybridge w Harford *Ex* 03-06; P-in-c Lanteglos by Camelford w Advent *Truro* from 06; P-in-c St Teath from 06. *The Rectory, Trefrew Road, Camelford PL32 9TP* Tel (01840) 214877 Mobile 07915-650434
E-mail jim@benton-evans1.demon.co.uk
BENWELL, John Desmond. Jes Coll Cam BA54 MA58. St Jo Coll Nottm. **d** 89 **p** 89. Somalia 89-90; Chapl Fontainebleau *Eur* 91-93; Hon C Portswood Ch Ch *Win* 93-99; rtd 99; Perm to Offic *Win* from 04. *14 Furzedown Road, Southampton SO17 1PN* Tel (023) 8055 7622
BENWELL, Michael Patrick. b 55. Jes Coll Cam BA77 Glas Univ PhD80. Sarum & Wells Th Coll BTh92. **d** 92 **p** 93. C Eastleigh *Win* 92-95; Chapl Leeds Metrop Univ 95-99; TV Seacroft 99-06; TR from 06. *St Luke's Vicarage, Stanks Lane North, Leeds LS14 5AS* Tel 0113-273 1302
E-mail benwell@ndirect.co.uk
BENZIES, Neil Graham. Bede Coll Dur. Cranmer Hall Dur 93. **d** 95 **p** 96. NSM Stockton St Pet *Dur* 95-08. *62 Fairwell Road, Stockton-on-Tees TS19 7HX* Tel (01642) 582322
BERDINNER, Clifford. b 24. SS Mark & Jo Univ Coll Plymouth BA88 Ex Univ MPhil95. **d** 64 **p** 65. C Leic St Pet 64-67; R Heather 67-72; NSM Totnes and Berry Pomeroy *Ex* 86-91; NSM Totnes, Bridgetown and Berry Pomeroy etc 91-94; rtd 89; Perm to Offic *Ex* from 89. *Little Croft, 30 Droridge, Dartington, Totnes TQ9 6JQ* Tel (01803) 732518
BERESFORD, Charles Edward. b 45. St Jo Coll Nottm. **d** 86 **p** 87. C Bushbury *Lich* 86-90; TV Glascote and Stonydelph 90-98; TR N Wingfield, Clay Cross and Pilsley *Derby* from 98. *The Rectory, St Lawrence Road, North Wingfield, Chesterfield S42 5HX* Tel (01246) 851181
E-mail rev-ceb@north-wingfield.freeserve.co.uk
BERESFORD, David Charles. b 56. Leeds Univ BA09 ACIB93. Coll of Resurr Mirfield 07. **d** 09. C Lancing w Coombes *Chich* from 09. *30 Greenoaks, Lancing BN15 0HE* Tel (01903) 765385
E-mail davidberesford@gmail.com
BERESFORD, Canon Eric Brian. b 57. Liv Univ BSc78 Univ of K Coll Halifax NS Hon DD. Wycliffe Hall Ox BA82 MA86. **d** 82 **p** 83. C Upton (Overchurch) *Ches* 82-85; Canada from 85; Asst Prof Ethics McGill Univ Montreal 88-96; Consultant Ethics and Interfaith Relns Gen Syn 96-04; President Atlantic Sch of Th Halifax NS from 05; Consultant Ethics ACC 99-05; Hon Can Montreal from 99. *Atlantic School of Theology, 660 Francklyn Street, Halifax NS B3H 3B5, Canada* Tel (001) (902) 423 6801 E-mail eberesford@astheology.ns.ca
BERESFORD, Mrs Florence. b 33. Cranmer Hall Dur 75. dss 78 **d** 87 **p** 94. Eighton Banks *Dur* 78-86; Lobley Hill 86-87; Par Dn 87-90; Par Dn Chester le Street 90-91; rtd 91. *Gilead, 39 Picktree Lodge, Chester-le-Street DH3 4DH* Tel 0191-388 7425
BERESFORD, Peter Marcus de la Poer. b 49. Cranmer Hall Dur 74. **d** 77 **p** 78. C Walney Is *Carl* 77-80; C Netherton 80-83; TV Wednesfield *Lich* 83-88; TV Rugby *Cov* 88-97; Chapl Rugby Hosps 88-97; R Barby w Kilsby *Pet* from 97. *The Rectory, Rectory Lane, Barby, Rugby CV23 8TZ* Tel (01788) 890252
BERESFORD JONES, Gareth Martin. b 70. Ex Univ BA93 Fitzw Coll Cam BTh01. Westcott Ho Cam 98. **d** 01 **p** 02. C Sidcup St Jo *Roch* 01-05; Chapl Ealing Hosp NHS Trust 05-06; Perm to Offic *Ely* from 08. *40 Searle Street, Cambridge CB4 3DB*

Tel (01223) 697901 Mobile 07810-272076
E-mail gmbj27@mac.com
BERESFORD-PEIRSE, Mark de la Poer. b 45. Qu Coll Birm 73. **d** 76 **p** 77. C Garforth *Ripon* 76-79; C Beeston 79-83; V Barton and Manfield w Cleasby 83-90; V Pannal w Beckwithshaw 90-01; Dioc Chapl MU 91-98; R W Tanfield and Well w Snape and N Stainley from 01; rtd 09. *15 Eastfield Avenue, Richmond DL10 4NH*
BERG, John Russell. b 36. MBE78. Sarum Th Coll 57. **d** 60 **p** 61. C Ipswich St Aug *St E* 60-64; C Whitton and Thurleston w Akenham 64-65; Miss to Seafarers 65-04; Hong Kong 65-68; Japan 68-04; rtd 01; Perm to Offic *St E* from 04. *23 Old Maltings Court, Old Maltings Approach, Melton, Woodbridge IP12 1AE* Tel (01394) 383748 E-mail jrberg@tiscali.co.uk
BERGER, Otto. b 19. CEng FIMechE. Oak Hill Th Coll. **d** 83 **p** 84. NSM Dovercourt and Parkeston *Chelmsf* 83-93; Perm to Offic 93-03. *Nythle, Ffordd Uchaf, Gwynfryn, Wrexham LL11 5UN*
BERGQUIST, Anders Karim. b 58. Peterho Cam BA79 MA83 PhD90. St Steph Ho Ox BA85 MA90. **d** 86 **p** 87. C Abbots Langley *St Alb* 86-89; Hon C Cambridge St Mary Less *Ely* 89-97; Tutor Westcott Ho Cam 89-95; Vice-Prin 95-97; Can Res St Alb 97-02; Minl Development Officer 97-02; V St John's Wood Lon from 02. *St John's House, St John's Wood High Street, London NW8 7NE* Tel (020) 7722 4378 *or* 7586 3864
E-mail vicar.stjohnswood@london.anglican.org
BERKSHIRE, Archdeacon of. *See* RUSSELL, The Ven Norman Atkinson
BERMUDA, Archdeacon of. *See* DOUGHTY, The Ven Andrew William
BERMUDA, Bishop of. *See* WHITE, The Rt Revd Patrick George Hilliard
BERNARD, Miss Moina Suzanne. b 56. Cranmer Hall Dur 07. **d** 09. NSM Tong *Bradf* from 09; NSM Laisterdyke from 09. *36 Wenborough Lane, Bradford BD4 0PD* Tel 07967-709444 (mobile) E-mail moinab@googlemail.com
BERNARDI, Frederick John. b 33. JP75. Chich Th Coll 55. **d** 58 **p** 59. C Blackb St Luke 58-60; C Ribbleton 60-63; V Brinsley w Underwood *S'well* 63-66; V St Leon Barbados 67-71; V Sparkbrook St Agatha *Birm* 71-77; P-in-c Sparkbrook Ch Ch 73-75; V Haywards Heath St Wilfrid *Chich* 77-80; TR 80-87; Chapl Madrid *Eur* 87-90; NSM Tooting All SS *S'wark* 90-91; V Hanger Hill Ascension and W Twyford St Mary *Lon* 91-95; rtd 95; Perm to Offic *Chich* from 95. *42 Woodlands Way, Southwater, Horsham RH13 9HZ* Tel (01403) 733335
E-mail stella@knights-templar.org.uk *or* john@bernardi.co.uk
BERNERS-WILSON (*or* SILLETT), Preb Angela Veronica Isabel. b 54. St Andr Univ MTheol76. Cranmer Hall Dur 77. dss 79 **d** 87 **p** 94. Southgate Ch Ch *Lon* 79-82; St Marylebone Ch Ch 82-84; Ind Chapl 82-84; Chapl Thames Poly *S'wark* 84-91; Chapl Bris Univ 91-95; C Bris St Mich and St Paul 94-95; P-in-c Colerne w N Wraxall 95-01; R 01-04; Chapl Bath Univ from 04; Preb Wells Cathl from 09. *Chaplain's House, The Avenue, Claverton Down, Bath BA2 7AX* Tel (01225) 386193
E-mail a.berners-wilson@bath.ac.uk
or abw@colrec.freeserve.co.uk
BERNHARD, Peter James. b 55. Magd Coll Ox MA80. SAOMC 03. **d** 06 **p** 07. NSM Homerton St Luke *Lon* 06-08; Perm to Offic *Ox* from 08. *Spring House, Back Lane, Souldern, Bicester OX27 7JF* Tel (01869) 346965 Mobile 07970-855354
E-mail souldernspring@aol.com
BERRETT, Michael Vincent. b 56. St Chad's Coll Dur BA78. Ox Min Course 06. **d** 09. NSM Wantage *Ox* from 09. *Old Stock Cottage, Farnborough, Wantage OX12 8NT* Tel (01488) 639655
E-mail mvberrett@googlemail.com
BERRETT, Canon Paul Graham. b 49. St Chad's Coll Dur BA70. St Steph Ho Ox 71. **d** 74 **p** 75. C Hockerill *St Alb* 74-77; C Leighton Buzzard 77-81; C Leighton Buzzard w Eggington, Hockliffe etc 81-83; V Bournemouth St Fran *Win* from 83; Hon Can Win Cathl from 05. *St Francis's Vicarage, Charminster Road, Bournemouth BH8 9SH* Tel (01202) 529336 *or* tel and fax 511845 E-mail saintfrancis@ukonline.co.uk
BERRIDGE, Grahame Richard. b 38. S'wark Ord Course 71. **d** 72 **p** 73. NSM S Beddington St Mich *S'wark* 72-75; NSM Merton St Jas 75-81; Perm to Offic from 81. *11 Cedar Walk, Kingswood, Tadworth KT20 6HW* Tel (01737) 358882
BERRIMAN, Brinley John. b 50. Univ Coll Lon BSc71. SWMTC 95. **d** 98 **p** 99. NSM St Ives and Halsetown *Truro* 98-00; P-in-c Lanteglos by Camelford w Advent 00-05; P-in-c St Buryan, St Levan and Sennen from 05. *The Rectory, Rectory Road, St Buryan, Penzance TR19 6BB* Tel (01736) 810216
E-mail brin@dreckly.net
BERRIMAN, Gavin Anthony. b 60. S'wark Ord Course 87. **d** 90 **p** 91. C Greenwich St Alfege w St Pet and St Paul *S'wark* 90-94; V Lee St Aug from 94. *St Augustine's Vicarage, 336 Baring Road, London SE12 0DU* Tel (020) 8857 4941
BERRY, Canon Adrian Charles. b 50. Mert Coll Ox BA71 MA78. Cuddesdon Coll 72. **d** 75 **p** 76. C Prestbury *Glouc* 75-79; C Cirencester 79-83; V Cam w Stinchcombe 83-88; Dioc Ecum

Officer 83-95; P-in-c Twyning 88-95; R Leckhampton St Pet 95-02; Dioc Min Development Officer *Llan* from 02; P-in-c Wenvoe and St Lythans from 02; Can Llan Cathl from 02. *The Rectory, 2 Port Road, Wenvoe, Cardiff CF5 6DF* Tel (029) 2059 3392

BERRY, Alan Peter. b 36. NW Ord Course 74. **d** 77 **p** 78. NSM Headingley *Ripon* 77-78; NSM Chapel Allerton 78-91; Perm to Offic from 91. *17 High Street, Spofforth, Harrogate HG3 1BQ* Tel (01937) 590503 E-mail apeterberry@btinternet.com

BERRY, Anthony Nigel. b 53. Lon Bible Coll BA80. Sarum & Wells Th Coll 84. **d** 87 **p** 88. NSM Howell Hill *Guildf* 87-90; C 90; C Farnham 90-93; R Abinger cum Coldharbour from 93; Dioc Tr Officer for Past Assts from 94. *The Rectory, Abinger Lane, Abinger Common, Dorking RH5 6HZ* Tel (01306) 730746 E-mail revanberry@aol.com

BERRY, David Llewellyn Edward. b 39. St Jo Coll Cam BA61 MA65. Wells Th Coll 64. **d** 66 **p** 67. C Poplar All SS w St Frideswide *Lon* 66-69; C Ellesmere Port *Ches* 69-73; V Brafferton w Pilmoor and Myton-on-Swale *York* 73-79; P-in-c Thormanby 79-87; R Skelton w Upleatham 79-87; V Barrow St Aid *Carl* 87-97; Chapl Rotterdam *Eur* 97-99; rtd 99; Perm to Offic *Carl* from 04. *2 The Croft, Warcop, Appleby-in-Westmorland CA16 6PH* Tel (01768) 342175

BERRY, Mrs Eleanor Shields. b 48. Derby Univ BEd95. EMMTC 01. **d** 04 **p** 05. NSM Morley w Smalley and Horsley Woodhouse *Derby* 04-09; NSM Spondon from 09. *5 Gilbert Close, Spondon, Derby DE21 7GP* Tel (01332) 675265 E-mail es.berry@ukonline.co.uk

BERRY, Prof Frank John. b 47. Lon Univ BSc72 PhD75 DSc88 FRSC84. Qu Coll Birm 96. **d** 99 **p** 00. Prof Inorganic Chemistry Open Univ from 91; Hon Prof Chemistry Birm Univ from 07; NSM Rednal 99-04; NSM Birm St Martin w Bordesley St Andr 04-07; NSM Moseley St Mary and St Anne from 07. *44 Middle Park Road, Selly Oak, Birmingham B29 4BJ* Tel 0121-475 2718 E-mail frank@berry44.fsworld.co.uk

BERRY, Miss Heather Evelyn. b 45. Lon Univ BA67 Ex Univ PGCE68. **d** 00 **p** 01. OLM Gaywood *Nor* from 00. *12 Kent Road, King's Lynn PE30 4AF* Tel (01553) 764098 E-mail heberry@talktalk.net

BERRY, Ian Thomas Henry. b 73. QUB BSc94. CITC BTh98. **d** 98 **p** 99. C Bangor Abbey *D & D* 98-02; I Monaghan w Tydavnet and Kilmore *Clogh* from 02. *The Rectory, Clones Road, Monaghan, Republic of Ireland* Tel (00353) (47) 81136 E-mail monaghan@clogher.anglican.org

BERRY, John. b 41. Dur Univ BA62. Oak Hill Th Coll 63. **d** 65 **p** 66. C Burnage St Marg *Man* 65-68; C Middleton 68-70; Travelling Sec IVF 70-73; V Derby St Pet 73-76; P-in-c Derby Ch Ch and H Trin 73-76; V Derby St Pet and Ch Ch w H Trin 76-81; Bp's Officer for Evang *Carl* 81-86; P-in-c Bampton and Mardale 81-86; TR N Wingfield, Pilsley and Tupton *Derby* 86-89; Evang Sec Evang Alliance 89-92; V Guernsey H Trin *Win* 92-98; TR Broadwater *Chich* 98-07; rtd 07. *27 Blythe Close, Newport Pagnell MK16 9DN* Tel (01908) 217631 E-mail reverendjohn@sky.com

BERRY, Paul Edward. b 56. NOC 91. **d** 94 **p** 95. C Halliwell St Luke *Man* 94-98; TV Horwich and Rivington 98-08; TV Edgware *Lon* from 08. *1 Beulah Close, Edgware HA8 8SP* Tel (020) 8958 9730

BERRY, The Very Revd Peter Austin. b 35. Keble Coll Ox BA59 BTh61 MA63 Birm Univ Hon DD97. St Steph Ho Ox 59. **d** 62 **p** 63. C Cov St Mark 62-66; Dioc Community Relns Officer 64-70; C Cov Cathl 66-73; Can Res Cov Cathl 73-86; Vice-Provost Cov Cathl 77-86; Bp's Adv for Community Relns 77-86; Provost Birm 86-99; rtd 99; Perm to Offic *Cov* from 99 and *Birm* from 00. *Reed Lodge, D5 Kenilworth Court, Hagley Road, Birmingham B16 9NU* Tel 0121-454 0021

BERRY, Mrs Philippa Raines. b 51. Man Univ MA72 Univ of Wales (Cardiff) CertEd73. St Jo Coll Nottm 82. **d** 95 **p** 96. NSM Leic H Apostles 95-04; P-in-c from 04. *The Vicarage, 281 Fosse Road South, Leicester LE3 1AE* Tel 0116-282 4336 E-mail pipberry@hotmail.com

BERRY, Sister Susan Patricia (Sister Sue). b 49. Bris Univ BA70 Hughes Hall Cam PGCE72. Qu Coll Birm 77. **dss** 86 **d** 87 **p** 94. Chapl Barn Fellowship Whatcombe Ho 86-89; Chapl Lee Abbey 89-91; NSM Thatcham *Ox* 93-95; CSF from 95; Perm to Offic *B & W* 96-97 and from 98; Chapl Guy's and St Thos' Hosps NHS Trust Lon 97-98; Perm to Offic *S'wark* 97-98. *Community of St Francis, Compton Durville, South Petherton TA13 5ES* Tel (01460) 240473 Fax 242360 E-mail comptondurvillecsf@franciscans.org.uk

BERRY, Timothy Hugh. b 50. Reading Univ BA72. Oak Hill NSM Course 81. **d** 84 **p** 85. NSM Swanley St Paul *Roch* 84-88; C Gorleston St Andr *Nor* 88-93; V Grain w Stoke *Roch* 93-95; rtd 95; Perm to Offic *Roch* from 01. *26 Cyclamen Road, Swanley BR8 8HJ* Tel (01322) 613385

BERRY-DAVIES, Charles William Keith. b 48. MIOT71. Linc Th Coll. **d** 83 **p** 84. C Hythe *Cant* 83-86; Chapl RAF from 86; Perm to Offic *Linc* 93-96. *Chaplaincy Services, Valiant Block, HQ Air Command, RAF High Wycombe HP14 4UE* Tel (01494) 496800 Fax 496343

BERRYMAN, William Arthur David. b 47. Lon Univ BD69 St Pet Coll Ox CertEd71. Sarum & Wells Th Coll 75. **d** 76 **p** 77. Asst Master Preston Sch Yeovil 76-80; Hon C Yeovil St Mich *B & W* 76-80; C Ex St Dav and Chapl Ex Coll 80-83; Chapl RN 83-89; V Highertown and Baldhu *Truro* 89-95; TR Cov E 95-97; TR The Abbey and P-in-c Leic St Paul 97-01; R Banchory and P-in-c Kincardine O'Neil *Ab* 01-05; P-in-c Beeston *Ripon* from 05. *Beeston Vicarage, 16 Town Street, Beeston, Leeds LS11 8PN* Tel 0113-272 3337 E-mail davidberryman@hotmail.com

BERSON, Alan Charles. b 31. Univ of Michigan BA52 MA53 Lon Univ PhD62. St Steph Ho Ox 63. **d** 65 **p** 66. C Leeds St Pet *Ripon* 65-68; C St Giles-in-the-Fields *Lon* 68; Lic to Offic 69-80; Perm to Offic 80-88; rtd 96. *74 Ridgmount Gardens, London WC1E 7AX* Tel and fax (020) 7636 1990

BERSWEDEN, Judith Anne. b 63. St Jo Coll Dur BA84. Ripon Coll Cuddesdon BA91. **d** 92 **p** 94. Par Dn Mirfield *Wakef* 92-94; NSM Robert Town 94-97; NSM Roberttown w Hartshead 97-00; NSM Alderbury Deanery from 00; Chapl Bp Wordsworth Sch Salisbury from 01. *The Rectory, Winterslow, Salisbury SP5 1RE* Tel (01980) 862231 E-mail judith.bersweden@dsl.pipex.com

BERSWEDEN, Nils Herry Stephen. b 57. Newc Univ BSc78. Ripon Coll Cuddesdon 88. **d** 90 **p** 91. C Mirfield *Wakef* 90-93; P-in-c Purlwell 93-94; P-in-c Robert Town 94-97; V Roberttown w Hartshead 97-00; P-in-c Winterslow *Sarum* 00-01; TV Clarendon 01-08; TR from 08. *The Rectory, Winterslow, Salisbury SP5 1RE* Tel (01980) 862231 E-mail nils.bersweden@breathemail.net

BERTRAM, Canon Richard Henry. b 27. TCD BA50 MA64. CITC 50. **d** 53 **p** 54. C Sligo Cathl 53-56; C Dublin Booterstown *D & G* 56-58; I Stranorlar w Meenglas and Kilteevogue *D & R* 58-65; I Dublin St Cath w St Jas *D & G* 65-73; I Dublin Irishtown 73-74; I Dublin Irishtown w Donnybrook 74-02; Can Ch Ch Cathl Dublin 86-02; Treas 95-02; rtd 02. *Glencoe, The Harbour, North Beach, Greystones, Co Wicklow, Republic of Ireland* Tel (00353) (1) 287 5320

BESSANT, Brian Keith. b 32. Roch Th Coll 65. **d** 67 **p** 68. C Chatham St Wm *Roch* 67-70; C Cove St Jo *Guildf* 71-74; V Frimley Green 74-97; rtd 97; Perm to Offic *Guildf* from 97. *14 Tay Close, Farnborough GU14 9NB* Tel (01252) 376530

BESSANT, Christopher Dixon. b 69. Ridley Hall Cam 07. **d** 09. C Gt Bookham *Guildf* from 09. *19 The Lorne, Bookham, Leatherhead KT23 4JY* Tel (01372) 453729 Mobile 07800-719405 E-mail c.bessant@hotmail.com

BESSANT, Canon Idwal Brian. b 39. Cardiff Coll of Art ATD62. St Mich Coll Llan 65. **d** 68 **p** 69. C Llantwit Major and St Donat's 68-73; R Llangammarch w Garth, Llanlleonfel etc *S & B* 73-77; V Crickhowell 77-78; CMS Miss 78-83; Cyprus 80-83; V Crickhowell w Cwmdu and Tretower *S & B* 83-91; RD Crickhowell 86-91; V Llanwrtyd w Llanddulas in Tir abad etc 91-04; Can Res Brecon Cathl 98-04; RD Builth 02-04; rtd 04. *10 Bronant, Bronllys Road, Talgarth, Brecon LD3 0HF* Tel (01874) 712380

BESSANT, Simon David. b 56. Sheff Univ BMus77 MA00. St Jo Coll Nottm. **d** 81 **p** 82. C Litherland St Jo and St Jas *Liv* 81-84; C Holloway Em w Hornsey Road St Barn *Lon* 84-86; C Holloway St Mark w Em 86-91; V Blackb Redeemer 91-98; Acting RD Blackb 97-98; Dir Miss and Evang 98-07; Dir CMF 07-07; Hon Can Blackb Cathl 06-07; V Ecclesall *Sheff* from 07. *Ecclesall Vicarage, Ringinglow Road, Sheffield S11 7PQ* Tel 0114-236 0084 E-mail simon.bessant@sheffield.anglican.org

BESSENT, Stephen Lyn. b 53. Bris Univ BA75. Wycliffe Hall Ox 75. **d** 77 **p** 78. C Patchway *Bris* 77-80; TV Swindon St Jo and St Andr 80-83; TV Eston w Normanby *York* 83-90; V Cogges *Ox* 90-94; P-in-c S Leigh 90-94; V Cogges and S Leigh 94-01; P-in-c Alphington, Shillingford St George and Ide *Ex* from 01. *The Rectory, 6 Lovelace Gardens, Exeter EX2 8XQ* Tel (01392) 437662

BEST, Miss Karen Belinda. b 62. Qu Coll Birm 92. **d** 94 **p** 95. C Southall Green St Jo *Lon* 94-97; C Northolt Park St Barn 97-00; V Gillingham St Barn *Roch* 00-08; P-in-c Roxwell *Chelmsf* from 08; Lay Discipleship Adv (Bradwell Area) from 08. *The Vicarage, Vicarage Road, Roxwell, Chelmsford CM1 4NB* Tel (01245) 248157 E-mail revkbest@aol.com

BEST, Canon Raymond. b 42. Sarum & Wells Th Coll 71. **d** 74 **p** 75. C Whorlton *Newc* 74-78; C Seaton Hirst 78-83; C Benwell St Jas 83-85; TV Benwell 85-89; V Walker 89-00; P-in-c Byker St Martin 96-99; V Haltwhistle and Greenhead from 00; Hon Can Newc Cathl from 97; AD Hexham 02-06. *The Vicarage, Edens Lawn, Haltwhistle NE49 0AB* Tel (01434) 320215 E-mail canonbest@aol.com

BEST, Mrs Ruth Helen. b 54. **d** 05 **p** 06. NSM Ipswich St Matt *St E* 05-06; NSM Triangle, St Matt and All SS from 06. *2 Newson Street, Ipswich IP1 3NY* Tel (01473) 424121

BESTELINK, Canon William Meindert Croft. b 48. Hull Univ BA70 FRSA78. Cuddesdon Coll 71. **d** 73 **p** 74. C Holt *Nor* 73-74; C E Dereham w Hoe 74-76; C Thorpe St Andr 76-80; R

Colby w Banningham and Tuttington 80-90; R Felmingham 80-90; R Suffield 80-90; P-in-c Roydon St Remigius 90-04; P-in-c Scole, Brockdish, Billingford, Thorpe Abbots etc 02-04; P-in-c Gillingham w Geldeston, Stockton, Ellingham etc 04-09; RD Redenhall 00-03; Dioc Rural Officer 99-09; Hon Can Nor Cathl 02-09; rtd 09; Perm to Offic *Nor* from 09. *3 Linkside, 26 Park Road, Cromer NR27 0EA* Tel (01263) 511278 Mobile 07909-690073 E-mail wmcbestelink@hotmail.com

BESTLEY, Peter Mark. b 60. Qu Coll Cam MA Univ of Wales (Cardiff) MPhil92. St Mich Coll Llan 89. **d** 92 **p** 93. C Hampton All SS *Lon* 92-95; Chapl W Middx Univ Hosp NHS Trust 95-99; Hon C Bracknell *Ox* 04-06; C Easthampstead from 06. *4 Qualitas, Bracknell RG12 7QG* Tel (01344) 426741 E-mail peter.bestley@lineone.net

BESWETHERICK, Andrew Michael. b 55. Ex Univ BEd80. S'wark Ord Course 87. **d** 90 **p** 91. Dep Hd Master Sch Greenwich 88-98; NSM Blackheath St Jo *S'wark* from 90; Hd Sixth Form Rosemary Sch Islington from 98. *112 Charlton Road, London SE7 7EY* Tel (020) 8853 0853 E-mail aj@4bes.eclipse.co.uk

BESWICK, Canon Gary Lancelot. b 38. ALCD63. **d** 63 **p** 64. C Walthamstow St Mary *Chelmsf* 63-67; C Laisterdyke *Bradf* 67-70; V Idle 70-78; Area Sec (NW England) SAMS 78-92; Area Sec (N Thames) 92-97; Hon Can N Argentina from 87; R Gt Smeaton w Appleton Wiske and Birkby etc *Ripon* 97-03; rtd 03. *17 Gustory Road, Crantock, Newquay TR8 5RG* Tel (01637) 831361

BESWICK, Jane. See VOST, Mrs Jane

BESWICK, Joseph Hubert. b 25. Birm Univ MB, ChB48. **d** 59 **p** 60. Lic to Offic *S'well* 59-00. *38 Hallams Lane, Beeston, Nottingham NG9 5FH* Tel 0115-925 6719

BETSON, Christopher James. b 81. Writtle Agric Coll BSc03. Cranmer Hall Dur 06 St Jo Coll Dur BA09. **d** 09. C Anston *Sheff* from 09. *The Vicarage, 27 Skipton Road, Swallownest, Sheffield S26 4NQ* Tel 0114-287 2903 E-mail chrisbetson@hotmail.com

BETSON (née BIDDINGTON), Mrs Laura Claire. b 84. Trin Coll Cam BA05 St Jo Coll Dur MA08. Cranmer Hall Dur 06. **d** 08 **p** 09. C Aston cum Aughton w Swallownest and Ulley *Sheff* from 08. *The Vicarage, 27 Skipton Road, Swallownest, Sheffield S26 4NQ* Tel 0114-287 2903 Mobile 07984-960749 E-mail laura_biddington@yahoo.co.uk

BETSON, Mark John. b 77. Univ Coll Lon BSc99 Birkbeck Coll Lon PhD Cam Univ BA06. Westcott Ho Cam 04. **d** 07 **p** 08. C Southwick from 07. *1 Church House Close, Southwick, Brighton BN42 4WQ* Tel (01273) 592787 Mobile 07801-273074 E-mail m.betson@clara.co.uk

BETSON, Stephen. b 53. Sarum & Wells Th Coll 89. **d** 91 **p** 92. C Sittingbourne St Mich *Cant* 91-95; V Fairweather Green *Bradf* 95-01; R Hockwold w Wilton *Ely* 01-06; R Weeting 01-06; P-in-c Stanground from 06. *38 Riverside Mead, Peterborough PE2 8JN* Tel (01733) 772129 E-mail betson1@tesco.net

BETTELEY, John Richard. b 46. Sarum & Wells Th Coll 81. **d** 83 **p** 84. C Auchterarder *St And* 83-85; C Dunblane 83-85; Chapl RAF 85-89; R Callander *St And* 89-94; P-in-c Aberfoyle 89-94; P-in-c Doune 89-94; R Ballachulish *Arg* 94-04; R Glencoe 94-04; R Onich 94-04; Dioc Youth Officer 94-01; Syn Clerk 99-04; Can St Jo Cathl Oban 99-04; Can Cumbrae 99-04; R Aboyne 04-06; R Ballater 04-06; R Braemar 04-06. *3 School Street, Fearn, Tain IV20 1SX* Tel 07713-914602 (mobile) E-mail johnrbetteley@aol.com

BETTERIDGE, Simon Frank. b 66. St Jo Coll Nottm. **d** 00 **p** 01. C Studley *Cov* 00-02; C Leamington Priors St Paul 02-04; Chapl Univ Hosps Cov and Warks NHS Trust from 04. *17 Trinity Walk, Nuneaton CV11 4PH* Tel (024) 7634 4304 Mobile 07743-870601 E-mail simon.betty@yahoo.com *or* simon.betteridge@uhcw.nhs.uk

BETTIS, Canon Margaret Jean. b 42. Gilmore Ho 72. **dss** 77 **d** 87 **p** 94. Kenya 77-79; Tutor Crowther Hall CMS Tr Coll Selly Oak 79-82; Hodge Hill *Birm* 82-87; Par Dn 87; Par Dn Flitwick *St Alb* 87-93; P-in-c Westoning w Tingrith 93-94; V 94-04; Hon Can St Alb 97-04; rtd 04; Perm to Offic *St Alb* 04-05 and *Glouc* 05-06; Hon C Cirencester *Glouc* from 06. *19 Bathurst Road, Cirencester GL7 1SA* Tel (01285) 658695

BETTS, Alan John. b 55. Portsm Poly BSc77 St Martin's Coll Lanc PGCE81. St Jo Coll Nottm 93. **d** 93 **p** 94. C Cannock *Lich* 93-01; P-in-c Endon w Stanley 01-04; V Bagnall w Endon from 04. *St Luke's Vicarage, Leek Road, Endon, Stoke-on-Trent ST9 9BH* Tel (01782) 502166

BETTS, Canon Anthony Clive. b 40. Wells Th Coll 63. **d** 65 **p** 66. C Leeds All Hallows w St Simon *Ripon* 65-67; C Wetherby 67-70; C Adel 70-73; V Leeds All SS 73-79; V Leeds Richmond Hill 79-84; R Knaresborough 84-03; TR 03-05; RD Harrogate 95-03; Hon Can Ripon Cathl 04-05; rtd 05; Perm to Offic *York* from 06.

1 Bilsdale Close, Romanby, Northallerton DL7 8FT Tel (01609) 760378 E-mail tonybetts@bettst.freeserve.co.uk

BETTS, Canon Anthony Percy. b 26. Lon Univ BD52. ALCD52. **d** 52 **p** 53. C Guildf St Sav 52-56; C Hanworth St Geo *Lon* 56-59; V Derby St Aug 59-74; RD Derby 71-74; V Bracebridge *Linc* 74-83; R Fenny Bentley, Kniveton, Thorpe and Tissington *Derby* 83-91; RD Ashbourne 86-91; Hon Can Derby Cathl 87-91; rtd 91; Perm to Offic *Derby* from 91. *Otterbourne House, Windley, Belper DE56 2LP* Tel (01773) 550677

BETTS, David John. b 38. Lon Univ BSc61. Oak Hill Th Coll 63. **d** 65 **p** 66. C Slough *Ox* 65-70; C Welling *Roch* 70-75; V Swanley St Paul 75-93; R Nottingham St Nic *S'well* 93-98; TV Canford Magna *Sarum* 98-04; rtd 04. *290 Rempstone Road, Wimborne BH21 1SZ* Tel (01202) 840537

BETTS, Edmund John. b 51. St Chad's Coll Dur BA72 Lanc Univ MA81. Qu Coll Birm 73. **d** 76 **p** 77. C Leagrave *St Alb* 76-79; Asst Chapl R Albert Hosp Lanc 79-81; Chapl Lea Castle Hosp and Kidderminster Gen Hosp 81-86; Prov Officer Educn for Min Ch in Wales 86-88; Exec Sec for Min Ch in Wales 88-90; TR Haverhill w Withersfield, the Wrattings etc *St E* 90-97; V Haverhill w Withersfield 97-06; RD Clare 91-06; Hon Can St E Cathl 02-06; CUF Link Officer 02-06; V Altrincham St Geo *Ches* from 06; P-in-c Altrincham St Jo from 07. *St George's Vicarage, Townfield Road, Altrincham WA14 4DS* Tel 0161-928 4279 E-mail edmund.betts1@btinternet.com

BETTS, George William John. b 23. Ex Univ BA51. Westcott Ho Cam 51. **d** 53 **p** 54. C Wallsend St Luke *Newc* 53-54; C Benwell St Jas 54-56; C Plumstead St Jas w St Jo *S'wark* 56; C Peckham St Andr w All SS 56; C Eltham St Jo 57-60; C Findon *Chich* 60-67; Rhodesia 67-68; C Sherborne w Castleton and Lillington *Sarum* 68-69; C Brookfield St Anne, Highgate Rise *Lon* 69; rtd 88. *72 Westmount Road, London SE9 1JE* Tel (020) 8850 2116

BETTS, Ivan Ringland. b 38. TCD BA61 MA65. **d** 62 **p** 63. C Ballyholme *D & D* 62-65; C Dundela St Mark 65-69; Miss to Seamen 69-73; Sudan 69-71; Trinidad and Tobago 71-73; C Drumglass *Arm* 73-81; I Augher w Newtownsaville and Eskrahoole *Clogh* 81-86; Bp's C Ballymacarrett St Martin *D & D* 86-02; rtd 02. *56 Norwood Drive, Belfast BT4 2EB* Tel (028) 9065 0723 E-mail ivanbetts@btinternet.com

BETTS, Mrs Patricia Joyce. b 43. St Kath Coll Lon CertEd64 FRSA96. S Dios Minl Tr Scheme 90. **d** 96 **p** 97. NSM Bath Widcombe *B & W* 96-00; P-in-c 00-05; Perm to Offic from 05. *Hunters Lodge, North Road, Bath BA2 6HP* Tel (01225) 464918 E-mail candpbetts@talktalk.net

BETTS, Paul Robert. b 31. Lon Univ BSc51. Oak Hill Th Coll 53. **d** 56 **p** 57. C Plymouth St Jude *Ex* 56-59; C Cheltenham St Mark *Glouc* 59-63; V Finchley St Paul Long Lane 63-76; Warden St Columba Cen Cam 76-79; R Datchworth w Tewin *St Alb* 79-96; rtd 96; Perm to Offic *Ex* from 96. *2 Penny Close, Exminster, Exeter EX6 8SU* Tel (01392) 824403

BETTS, Richard Alan. b 56. ACA83 UEA BA77. Sarum & Wells Th Coll 93. **d** 93 **p** 94. C Mile Cross *Nor* 93-97; TV Dorchester *Sarum* from 97. *St George's Vicarage, 59 Fordington High Street, Dorchester DT1 1LB* Tel (01305) 262394 E-mail richard@betts39.fsnet.co.uk

BETTS, Canon Steven James. b 64. York Univ BSc86. Ripon Coll Cuddesdon 87. **d** 90 **p** 91. C Bearsted w Thurnham *Cant* 90-94; Bp's Chapl *Nor* 94-97; V Old Catton 97-05; RD Nor N 01-05; Bp's Officer for Ord and Initial Tr from 05; Hon Can Nor Cathl from 08. *Emmaus House, 65 The Close, Norwich NR1 4DH* Tel (01603) 628103 E-mail stevenbetts@norwich.anglican.org

BEVAN, Alan John. b 29. Bris Univ BA54. Oak Hill Th Coll 54. **d** 56 **p** 59. C Penn Fields *Lich* 56-57; C Corsham *Bris* 58-61; C Wath-upon-Dearne w Adwick-upon-Dearne *Sheff* 61-68; C Darfield 68-71; C Drypool St Columba w St Andr and St Pet *York* 71-79; Chapl HM Pris Wandsworth 79-83; Chapl HM Pris Kirkham 83-86; rtd 86; Perm to Offic *Ex* from 86. *c/o the Revd J Ancrum, 14 Merrivale Road, Dousland, Yelverton PL20 6NS*

BEVAN, Mrs Angela Ruth. b 56. Qu Coll Birm. **d** 07 **p** 08. NSM Shenley Green *Birm* from 07. *204 Shenley Fields Road, Birmingham B29 5BL* Tel 0121-477 9924

BEVAN, Bryan David. Lon Univ BD60 MA70 CertEd65 DipEd66 MPhil84 Lambeth STh62. St Aug Coll Cant 62. **d** 64 **p** 66. C E Dereham w Hoe *Nor* 64-65; C Hove All SS *Chich* 65-67; Lect St Mich Coll Salisbury 67-70; The Coll Bedf from 70. *Address temp unknown*

BEVAN, Canon Charles Joseph Godfrey. b 22. TCD BA44 MA52. **d** 45 **p** 46. C Dublin St Geo *D & G* 45-49; I Rathvilly *C & O* 49-59; I Carbury *M & K* 59-64; I Drogheda St Pet w Ballymakenny, Beaulieu etc *Arm* 64-90; I Drogheda w Ardee, Collon and Termonfeckin 90-95; Miss to Seamen 64-95; Can Arm Cathl 83-95; Chan 88-92; Prec 92-95; rtd 95. *13 St Peter's Place, Drogheda, Co Louth, Republic of Ireland* Tel (00353) (98) 414 4622

BEVAN, David Graham. b 34. Univ of Wales (Lamp) BA54 LTh56. Gen Th Sem (NY) MDiv57. **d** 57 **p** 58. C Llanelli *St D* 57-60; CF 60-76; rtd 99. *148 Bromley Heath Road, Bristol BS16 6JJ* Tel 0117-956 0946

BEVAN, Gordon Richard. b 26. NW Ord Course. **d** 75 **p** 76. C Spondon *Derby* 75-80; R Upper Langwith w Langwith Bassett etc 80-94; TV E Scarsdale 94-96; rtd 96; Perm to Offic *Derby* from 96. *8 Whaley Common, Langwith, Mansfield NG20 9HY* Tel (01623) 742413

BEVAN, Hubert Basil Henry. b 24. Univ of Wales (Lamp) BA52 LTh54 MTh75 PhD78. **d** 54 **p** 55. C Knighton and Heyope *S & B* 54-60; C Toxteth Park St Marg *Liv* 60-61; V Walsall St Mary and All SS Palfrey *Lich* 61-64; R Sunderland *Dur* 64-66; V Hendon St Paul 64-66; V Gilfach Goch w Llandyfodwg 66-73; R Cregina *S & B* 73-78; V Bettws Disserth w Llansantffraed in Elwell 73-78; V Glascwm and Rhulen 76-78; R Llanferres, Nercwys and Eryrys *St As* 78-80; Tutor St Deiniol's Lib Hawarden 79-89; V Treuddyn and Nercwys and Eryrys *St As* 80-85; R Llanfynydd 85-89; rtd 89. *Bryn Heulog, Bryniau Duon, Old Llandegfan, Menai Bridge LL59 5PP*

BEVAN, Janet Mary. *See* MOORE, Ms Janet Mary

BEVAN, Paul John. b 49. Bris Sch of Min 84. **d** 87. NSM Bishopsworth *Bris* 87-96. *10 Brookdale Road, Headley Park, Bristol BS13 7PZ* Tel 0117-964 6330

BEVAN, Peter John. b 54. K Coll Lon BA76 AKC76 MA86. St Steph Ho Ox BA79. **d** 80 **p** 81. C Brighouse *Wakef* 80-83; C Chapelthorpe 83-86; V Scholes 86-95; V Potters Bar *St Alb* from 95. *The Vicarage, 15 The Walk, Potters Bar EN6 1QN* Tel (01707) 644539 *or* 645080

BEVAN, Philip Frank. b 41. Brasted Th Coll 63 Chich Th Coll 65. **d** 67 **p** 68. C Walton St Mary *Liv* 67-71; P-in-c Long Is SS Pet and Paul Bahamas 71-73; R Nassau St Matt 73-78; Perm to Offic *S'wark* from 00. *5 Dunstable Road, Richmond TW9 1UH* Tel (020) 8940 3622 Mobile 07970-961539 E-mail fr.philip@btinternet.com

BEVAN, Mrs Rebecca Anne. b 64. Reading Univ BA86. Ox Min Course 04. **d** 07 **p** 08. NSM Thatcham *Ox* from 07. *47A Station Road, Thatcham RG19 4PU* Tel (01635) 871577 E-mail beckywinterbevan@aol.com

BEVAN, Canon Richard Justin William. b 22. LTh42 St Chad's Coll Dur BA45 DTh72 PhD80. St Aug Coll Cant 39. **d** 45 **p** 46. C Stoke upon Trent *Lich* 45-49; Chapl Aberlour Orphanage 49-51; Lic to Offic *Mor* 49-51; Lic to Offic *Blackb* 51-52; C Church Kirk 52-56; C Whalley 56-61; R Dur St Mary le Bow w St Mary the Less 61-64; Chapl Dur Univ 61-74; V Dur St Oswald 64-74; P-in-c Dur St Mary le Bow w St Mary the Less 64-67; R 67-74; R Grasmere *Carl* 74-82; Can Res, Lib and Treas Carl Cathl 82-89; Vice-Dean Carl 86-89; Chapl to The Queen 86-93; rtd 89; Perm to Offic *Carl* from 89. *Beck Cottage, West End, Burgh-by-Sands, Carlisle CA7 6BT* Tel (01228) 576781

BEVAN, Rodney. b 57. Leeds Univ BA80 Keele Univ PGCE81 Open Univ MA99. St Jo Coll Dur 97. **d** 99 **p** 00. C Ogley Hay *Lich* 99-03; TV Rossendale Middle Valley *Man* 03-04; TR from 04. *St Anne's Vicarage, Ashworth Road, Rossendale BB4 9JE* Tel (01706) 221889 E-mail rjdr@uk.packardbell.org

BEVER, Canon Michael Charles Stephen. b 44. Selw Coll Cam BA66 MA70. Cuddesdon Coll. **d** 69 **p** 70. C Steeton *Bradf* 69-72; C Northampton St Mary *Pet* 72-74; Niger 75-79; P-in-c Elmstead *Chelmsf* 80-83; V 83-85; V Bocking St Pet 85-96; P-in-c Odiham *Win* 96-07; rtd 07; Hon Can Awka from 93; Perm to Offic *Portsm* from 08. *68A Drift Road, Waterlooville PO8 0NX* Tel (023) 9259 6895 E-mail mcsb@ozala.reach.co.uk

BEVERIDGE, Mrs Freda Joy. b 38. Qu Mary Coll Lon BA59 Lon Inst of Educn PGCE60. Ripon Coll Cuddesdon 83. **dss** 85 **d** 87 **p** 94. Ox St Giles and SS Phil and Jas w St Marg 85-88; Par Dn 87-88; Par Dn Woughton 88-94; C 94-95; TR 95-97; C Woodham *Guildf* 97-00; rtd 00; Perm to Offic *Sarum* from 01. *Moonraker Cottage, 27 New Road, Chiseldon, Swindon SN4 0LY* Tel (01793) 741064

BEVERIDGE, Simon Alexander Ronald. b 61. Nottm Univ BA84. Chich Th Coll 84. **d** 87 **p** 88. C Braunton *Ex* 87-90; TV N Creedy 90-93; Chapl RN from 93. *Royal Naval Chaplaincy Service, Mail Point 1-2, Leach Building, Whale Island, Portsmouth PO2 8BY* Tel (023) 9262 5055 Fax 9262 5134

BEVERLEY, David John. b 46. Univ of Wales (Lamp) BA68. Linc Th Coll 71. **d** 73 **p** 74. C Cov E 73-76; C Immingham *Linc* 76-84; V Bracebridge Heath 84-86; Ind Chapl 86-97; P-in-c Scunthorpe Resurr 97-01; V 01-02; R Trentside E from 02. *The Vicarage, Mirfield Road, Scunthorpe DN15 8AN* Tel (01724) 842196 E-mail davejbev@aol.com

BEVERLEY, Suffragan Bishop of (Provincial Episcopal Visitor). *See* JARRETT, The Rt Revd Martyn William

BEVERLY, Mrs Susan Jane. b 53. Cardiff Univ BTh08. St Mich Coll Llan 05. **d** 07 **p** 08. NSM Coity, Nolton and Brackla *Llan* from 07. *17 Park Place, 92 Park Street, Bridgend CF31 4BB* Tel (01656) 651566 E-mail sue.beverly@zen.co.uk

BEVINGTON, Canon Colin Reginald. b 36. ALCD63. **d** 63 **p** 64. C Devonport St Budeaux *Ex* 63-65; C Attenborough w Chilwell *S'well* 65-68; R Benhall w Sternfield *St E* 68-74; P-in-c Snape w Friston 73-74; V Selly Hill St Steph *Birm* 74-81; P-in-c Selly Oak St Wulstan 80-81; V Selly Park St Steph and St Wulstan 81-88; Dioc Adv on Miss *St E* 88-95; Dioc and Co Ecum Officer 88-99; Hon Can St E Cathl 93-00; Bp's Dom Chapl and Personal Asst

95-99; R Holbrook, Freston, Woolverstone and Wherstead 99-00; RD Samford 99-00; rtd 01; Perm to Offic *St E* 01-05 and *Blackb* from 07. *4 Highgrove Road, Lancaster LA1 5FS* Tel (01524) 64851 E-mail bevington@capel19.freeserve.co.uk

BEVINGTON, David John. b 51. Ch Coll Cam BA72 MA76. Trin Coll Bris 73. **d** 76 **p** 77. C Tulse Hill H Trin *S'wark* 76-79; C Galleywood Common *Chelmsf* 79-82; TV Hanley H Ev *Lich* 82-90; TV Hemel Hempstead *St Alb* 90-99; V Calbourne w Newtown *Portsm* from 99; V Shalfleet from 99. *The Vicarage, 4 Manor Green, Shalfleet, Newport PO30 4QT* Tel (01983) 531238 E-mail dbevington@lineone.net

BEVIS, Anthony Richard. b 34. Chich Th Coll 87. **d** 87 **p** 89. NSM Hamble le Rice *Win* 87-94; NSM Woolston from 94; Chapl Southn Community Services NHS Trust 90-01; Chapl Southn City Primary Care Trust from 01. *Lynwood, High Street, Hamble, Southampton SO31 4HA* Tel (023) 8045 3102 *or* 8047 2258

BEWES, Anthony Charles Neill. b 71. Birm Univ BA93. Wycliffe Hall Ox 96. **d** 99 **p** 00. C Sevenoaks St Nic *Roch* 99-05; Team Ldr Titus Trust from 05. *45 Lonsdale Road, Oxford OX2 7ES* Tel (01865) 553625 E-mail anthony@bewes.com

BEWES, Helen Catherine. *See* SCAMMAN, Mrs Helen Catherine

BEWES, Preb Richard Thomas. b 34. OBE05. Em Coll Cam BA58 MA61. Ridley Hall Cam 57. **d** 59 **p** 60. C Beckenham Ch Ch *Roch* 59-65; V Harold Wood *Chelmsf* 65-74; V Northwood Em *Lon* 74-83; R St Marylebone All So w SS Pet and Jo 83-88; P-in-c Portman Square St Paul 87-88; R Langham Place All So 88-04; Preb St Paul's Cathl 88-04; rtd 04; Perm to Offic *Lon* from 05. *50 Curzon Road, London W5 1NF* Tel (020) 8998 1723

BEWLEY, Robin John. b 63. St Jo Coll Ox BA86 MA95 Fitzw Coll Cam BA99 PhD05. Ridley Hall Cam. **d** 00 **p** 01. NSM Histon and Impington *Ely* 00-04; C Harborne Heath *Birm* from 04. *55 Albert Road, Harborne, Birmingham B17 0AP* Tel 0121-426 2548 Mobile 07733-346631 E-mail rob@thebewleys.co.uk

BEXON, Mrs Valerie Joan. b 60. Chelt & Glouc Coll of HE BA96. Wycliffe Hall Ox 07. **d** 09. C Wotton-under-Edge w Ozleworth, N Nibley etc *Glouc* from 09. *9 Coombe Road, Wotton-under-Edge GL12 7LU* Tel (01453) 521417 Mobile 07882-882796 E-mail valeriebexon@onetel.com

BEYNON, Malcolm. b 36. Univ of Wales (Lamp) BA56 Univ of Wales (Cardiff) PGCE71. St Mich Coll Llan 56. **d** 59 **p** 60. C Aberavon *Llan* 59-62; C Whitchurch 63-68; V Llanwynno 68-73; Chapl Old Hall Sch Wellington Shropshire 74-75; Chapl Nevill Holt Sch Market Harborough 75-82; Chapl Denstone Coll Prep Sch Uttoxeter 82-93; V Dale and St Brides w Marloes *St D* 93-01; rtd 01. *22 Ostrey Bank, St Clears, Carmarthen SA33 4AH* Tel (01994) 231872

BEYNON, Nigel David. b 68. Collingwood Coll Dur BSc90 Fitzw Coll Cam BA94. Ridley Hall Cam 92. **d** 95 **p** 96. C Fulham St Matt *Lon* 95-98; Assoc V St Helen Bishopsgate w St Andr Undershaft etc 98-07; Student Team Ldr 01-07. *Address temp unknown*

BEYNON, Vincent Wyn. b 54. CertEd76 Lambeth STh97 Anglia Poly Univ MA04. St Mich Coll Llan 78. **d** 81 **p** 82. C Llantrisant 81-83; C Caerphilly 84-85; R Gelligaer 85-88; TV Gtn Corsham *Bris* 88-97; R Potton w Sutton and Cockayne Hatley *St Alb* 97-08; RD Biggleswade 01-06. *6 Minnis Green, Stelling Minnis, Canterbury CT4 6AA* Tel (01227) 709762 Mobile 07595-313035 E-mail wynbeynon@gmail.com

BIANCHI, Mrs Margaret Ruth. b 56. St Mary's Coll Dur BA77. Cranmer Hall Dur 78. **dss** 80 **d** 91 **p** 94. Chester le Street *Dur* 80-83; W Pelton 83-91; NSM 91-95; Perm to Offic from 95. *8 Lindisfarne, Washington NE38 7JR* Tel 0191-417 0852

BIANCHI, Frederick. b 56. St Jo Coll Dur BA77. Cranmer Hall Dur 78. **d** 80 **p** 81. C Chester le Street *Dur* 80-83; C W Pelton 83-86; P-in-c 86-95; Perm to Offic from 95. *8 Lindisfarne, Washington NE38 7JR* Tel 0191-417 0852

BIBBY, Canon Frank. b 37. ACP60 K Coll Lon BD64 AKC64. **d** 65 **p** 66. C Upholland *Liv* 65-67; Lect Birm Coll of Educn 67-72; V Prestwich St Gabr *Man* 72-76; Dir of Ords 72-76; V Hope St Jas 76-86; AD Salford 82-86; R Prestwich St Mary 86-02; Hon Can Man Cathl 96-02; AD Radcliffe and Prestwich 99-02; rtd 02; Perm to Offic *Man* from 02. *65 Leyton Drive, Bury BL9 9TS* Tel 0161-766 3123

BIBBY, Paul Benington. b 27. Magd Coll Cam BA51 MA56. Westcott Ho Cam 55. **d** 57 **p** 58. C Flixton St Mich *Man* 57-60; C Woolwich St Mary w H Trin *S'wark* 60-62; V Hurst *Man* 62-69; Hd of Cam Ho Camberwell 69-76; R Shepton Mallet *B & W* 76-81; P-in-c Doulting w E and W Cranmore and Downhead 78-81; R Shepton Mallet w Doulting 81-82; Sen Chapl Eton Coll 82-87; R Hambleden Valley *Ox* 87-93; rtd 93; Perm to Offic *Nor* from 94. *Vine Cottage, Cross Lane, Stanhoe, King's Lynn PE31 8PS* Tel (01485) 518291

BICK, David Jim. b 33. ALCD59 LTh74. **d** 59 **p** 60. C Glouc St Cath 59-61; C Coleford w Staunton 61-63; R Blaisdon w Flaxley 63-72; V Coaley 72-83; P-in-c Arlingham 80-83; P-in-c Frampton on Severn 80-83; Hon C Saul w Fretherne and

Framilode 83-84; Perm to Offic from 84; rtd 98. *St Joseph's, Prinknash Park, Cranham, Gloucester GL4 8EU* Tel (01452) 812973

BICK (*née* GRIFFITHS), Mrs Sarah. b 75. Ex Univ BA96 Homerton Coll Cam PGCE99. Qu Coll Birm 07. **d** 09. C Coleford, Staunton, Newland, Redbrook etc *Glouc* from 09. *28 Woodside Street, Cinderford GL14 2NS* Tel (01594) 825667 Mobile 07773-651893 E-mail sarahbick@enterprise.net

BICKERSTETH, David Craufurd. b 50. Wycliffe Hall Ox 71. **d** 75 **p** 76. C Beverley Minster *York* 75-79; C Farnborough *Guildf* 79-81; P-in-c Dearham *Carl* 81-85; V 85-86; R Gosforth w Nether Wasdale and Wasdale Head 86-93; P-in-c Harraby 93-97; V Maryport 98-04; TR Maryport, Netherton and Flimby 04-06; Dioc Chapl MU 94-97; R Draycott-le-Moors w Forsbrook *Lich* from 06; P-in-c Upper Tean from 08. *3 Willowcroft Rise, Blythe Bridge, Stoke-on-Trent ST11 9ST* Tel (01782) 397985 E-mail david.bickersteth@btinternet.com

BICKERSTETH, Edward Piers. b 56. MRICS80. Wycliffe Hall Ox 89. **d** 91 **p** 92. NSM Bebington *Ches* 91-92; C 92-94; Proclamation Trust 94-98; P-in-c Arborfield w Barkham *Ox* 98-02; R from 02. *The Rectory, Church Lane, Arborfield, Reading RG2 9HZ* Tel 0118-976 0285

✠**BICKERSTETH, The Rt Revd John Monier.** b 21. KCVO89. Ch Ch Ox BA49 MA53 Open Univ BA97. Wells Th Coll 48. **d** 50 **p** 51 **c** 70. C Moorfields *Bris* 50-54; C-in-c Hurst Green CD *S'wark* 54-62; V Chatham St Steph *Roch* 62-70; Hon Can Roch Cathl 68-70; Suff Bp Warrington *Liv* 70-75; Bp B & W 75-87; ChStJ and Sub-Prelate from 77; Clerk of the Closet 79-89; rtd 87. *Beckfords, Newtown, Tisbury, Salisbury SP3 6NY* Tel (01747) 870479

BICKERSTETH, Simon Craufurd. b 77. St Jo Coll Dur BA98. Wycliffe Hall Ox 99. **d** 01 **p** 02. C Windermere *Carl* 01-05; TV Walsall *Lich* from 05. *St Martin's House, 17 Daffodil Road, Walsall WS5 3DQ* Tel (01922) 611909 Mobile 07752-853148 E-mail simon.bickersteth@tiscali.co.uk

BICKLEY, Mrs Alice Elizabeth Ann. b 60. Qu Coll Birm 06. **d** 09. C Leagrave *St Alb* from 09. *39 Butely Road, Luton LU4 9EW* Tel (01582) 572054 Mobile 07977-601437 E-mail lizbickley@btinternet.com

BICKLEY, Mrs Pamela. b 59. Birm Univ BPhil99. WEMTC 06. **d** 09. NSM Minsterley *Heref* from 09. *High Ridge, Gorsty Bank, Snailbeach, Shrewsbury SY5 0LX* Tel (01743) 792824 E-mail shepherdstock@aol.com

BICKNELL, Jonathan Richard. b 62. Wycliffe Hall Ox. **d** 00 **p** 01. C Chesham Bois *Ox* 00-02. *210 High Street, Berkhamsted HP4 1AG* Tel (01442) 872447

BICKNELL (*née* RIDING), Mrs Pauline Alison. b 61. SEN82. Oak Hill Th Coll BA90. **d** 90 **p** 96. Par Dn Moor Allerton *Ripon* 90-93; Par Dn Leeds St Aid 93-94; C 94-96; C Rothwell 96-99; TV Drypool *York* 99-05; P-in-c Slyne w Hest *Blackb* 05-06; R Slyne w Hest and Halton w Aughton from 06. *The Vicarage, Summerfield Drive, Slyne, Lancaster LA2 6AQ* Tel (01524) 822128 E-mail pauline@bicknells.freeserve.co.uk

BIDDELL, Canon Christopher David. b 27. Ch Coll Cam BA48 MA52. Ridley Hall Cam 51. **d** 51 **p** 52. C Hornchurch St Andr *Chelmsf* 51-54; Succ S'wark Cathl 54-56; P-in-c Wroxall *Portsm* 56-61; R Bishop's Waltham 62-75; RD Bishop's Waltham 69-74; V Stockport St Geo *Ches* 75-86; Hon Can Ches Cathl 81-86; Can Res 86-93; RD Stockport 85-86; Vice-Dean Ches 91-93; rtd 93; P-in-c Duncton *Chich* 95-98; P-in-c Tillington 95-98; P-in-c Up Waltham 95-98; Perm to Offic from 98. *3 Park Terrace, Tillington, Petworth GU28 9AE* Tel (01798) 342008

BIDDINGTON, Laura Claire. See BETSON, Mrs Laura Claire

BIDDINGTON, Terence Eric. b 56. Hull Univ BA77 Trin & All SS Coll Leeds PGCE78 Leeds Univ PhD86 Nottm Univ BTh88 Man Univ MA(Theol)96 MCollP83. Linc Th Coll 85. **d** 88 **p** 89. C Harpenden St Jo *St Alb* 88-90; Chapl Keele Univ 90-93; Freelance Th Educator and Asst Lect Keele Univ 94-99; Assoc Min Betley and Keele 90-93; Asst Dir Cornerstone St Aug *Man* 95-96; Mental Health Advocate Stockport 96-98; Dir and Sen Advocate Stockport MIND from 99; Perm to Offic *Man* 99-01; P-in-c Heaton Norris Ch w All SS 01-02; C Heatons 02-03; Asst Chapl Man Mental Health Partnership 01-03; Chapl Man Univ from 03; Chapl Man Metrop Univ from 03. *St Peter's House, Oxford Road, Manchester M13 9GH* Tel 0161-275 2894 E-mail terry.biddington@manchester.ac.uk

BIDDINGTON, Mrs Wendy Elizabeth. b 51. Cov Univ BSc93 SRN73 SCM74. Qu Coll Birm 07. **d** 09. OLM Wellesbourne *Cov* from 09. *72 Mountford Close, Wellesbourne, Warwick CV35 9QQ* Tel (01789) 840953 E-mail nlb@biddington.spacomputers.com

BIDDLE, Nicholas Lawrence. b 71. K Coll Lon BA94 Leeds Univ MA98. Coll of Resurr Mirfield 96. **d** 98 **p** 99. C Bedford St Andr *St Alb* 98-01; Bp's Dom Chapl and Research Asst *Chich* 01-04; P-in-c Brighton Gd Shep Preston 04-05; TV Putney St Mary *S'wark* from 07. *21 Landford Road, London SW15 1AQ* Tel (020) 8789 0234 Mobile 07790-287280 E-mail nicklb@postmaster.co.uk

BIDDLE, Miss Rosemary. b 44. CertEd67. St Jo Coll Dur 76. **dss** 79 **d** 87 **p** 94. Sheldon *Birm* 79-83; Burntwood *Lich* 83-87;

Par Dn 87-89; Par Dn Gt Wyrley 89-94; C 94-99; rtd 99; Perm to Offic *Lich* from 00. *8 Brook Lane, Great Wyrley, Walsall WS6 6BQ* Tel (01922) 419032

BIDDLECOMBE, Francis William. b 30. St Mich Coll Llan 57. **d** 59 **p** 60. C Llangynwyd w Maesteg 59-62; C Roath 62-65; V Llanddewi Rhondda w Bryn Eirw 65-71; V Berse and Southsea *St As* 71-79; P-in-c Teme Valley S *Worc* 79-85; rtd 92; Perm to Offic *Heref* and *Worc* from 02. *Four Winds, New Road, Highley, Bridgnorth WV16 6NN* Tel (01746) 861746 E-mail francis@sagainternet.co.uk

BIDE, Mary Elizabeth. b 53. St Anne's Coll Ox BA74 MA78. S Dios Minl Tr Scheme 91. **d** 94 **p** 95. C Gt Bookham *Guildf* 94-98; Year Tutor Dioc Min Course 96-03; P-in-c Frimley Green 98-01; V Frimley Green and Mytchett 02-03; Prec Ch Ch *Ox* 03-07; TR Wimbledon *S'wark* from 07. *The Rectory, 14 Arthur Road, London SW19 7DZ* Tel (020) 8946 2830 or 8946 2605 Fax 8946 6293 E-mail rector.wimbledon@stmaryswimbledon.org

BIDEN, Neville Douglas. b 31. S'wark Ord Course 76. **d** 79 **p** 80. C Ash *Guildf* 79-82; NSM Surbiton St Andr and St Mark *S'wark* 87-91; Chapl Asst Long Grove Hosp Epsom 90-91; C Coulsdon St Jo *S'wark* 91-96; rtd 96; Perm to Offic *Heref* 95-97; *Guildf* from 97; *Win* from 01. *5 Taylor Drive, Bramley, Tadley RG26 5XB* Tel (01256) 880459 E-mail rev.nev@virgin.net

BIDGOOD, Julian Paul. b 71. Sussex Univ BA92. Oak Hill Th Coll BA03. **d** 03 **p** 04. C Ox St Ebbe w H Trin and St Pet 03-08; C Arborfield w Barkham from 08. *14 The Lilacs, Wokingham RG41 4UT* Tel 07779-296511 (mobile) E-mail julianbidgood@hotmail.com

BIELBY, Elaine Elizabeth. b 57. Surrey Univ MSc83. Ripon Coll Cuddesdon 96. **d** 98 **p** 99. C Marton-in-Cleveland *York* 98-01; P-in-c Welton w Melton from 01; Tr Officer E Riding from 01; Dean of Women's Min from 08. *St Helen's Vicarage, Cowgate, Welton, Brough HU15 1ND* Tel (01482) 666677 E-mail ebielby@ebielby.karoo.co.uk

BIENFAIT, Alexander. b 61. Hatf Poly BSc86. Sarum & Wells Th Coll BTh94. **d** 94 **p** 95. C Battersea St Luke *S'wark* 94-96; C Clapham Team 96-99; TV Whitstable *Cant* 99-07; P-in-c Biddenden and Smarden from 07. *The Rectory, High Street, Biddenden, Ashford TN27 8AH* Tel (01580) 291454 E-mail alex.bienfait@virgin.net

BIERBAUM, Ms Ruth Anne. b 67. RN89. Trin Coll Bris BA98. **d** 99 **p** 00. C Filey *York* 99-02; C Coxheath, E Farleigh, Hunton, Linton etc *Roch* 02-08; Lead Mental Health Chapl Kent & Medway NHS and Soc Care Partnership Trust from 08. *52 Stag Road, Chatham ME5 8LG* Tel (01634) 670715 or 838944 Mobile 017954-227184 E-mail ruth@bierbaumfreeserve.co.uk *or* ruth.bierbaum@kmpt.nhs.uk

BIGG, Howard Clive. b 40. Fitzw Coll Cam BA68 MA72. Ridley Hall Cam 73. **d** 74 **p** 75. C Worksop St Jo *S'well* 74-76; Min Can St Alb 76-77; Perm to Offic *Ches* 78-82; Ely 82-99 and 01-05; Vice-Prin Romsey Ho Cam 86-89; NSM Cambridge St Benedict *Ely* 99-01; rtd 05; Perm to Offic *Ely* from 08. *55 Hemingford Road, Cambridge CB1 3BY* Tel (01223) 514155

BIGGAR, Prof Nigel John. b 55. Worc Coll Ox BA76 MA88 Chicago Univ AM80 PhD86 Regent Coll Vancouver MCS81. **d** 90 **p** 91. Lib Latimer Ho Ox 85-91; Asst Lect Chr Ethics Wycliffe Hall Ox 87-94; Chapl Oriel Coll Ox 90-99; Prof Th Leeds Univ 99-04; Prof Th TCD 04-07; Can Ch Ch Cathl Dublin 05-07; Regius Prof Moral and Past Th Ox Univ from 07; Can Res Ch Ch *Ox* from 07. *Christ Church, Oxford OX1 1DP* Tel (01865) 276219 E-mail nigel.biggar@chch.ox.ac.uk

BIGGIN, Ronald. b 20. NW Ord Course 70. **d** 73 **p** 74. C Thelwall *Ches* 73-79; V 79-87; rtd 87; NSM Lt Leigh and Lower Whitley *Ches* 90-93; Perm to Offic from 93. *12 Wilmslow Crescent, Thelwall, Warrington WA4 2JE* Tel (01925) 261531

BIGGS, David James. b 55. St Jo Coll Auckland LTh82. **d** 81 **p** 82. New Zealand 81-86; C Stevenage St Andr and St Geo *St Alb* 86-89; TV Moulsecoomb *Chich* 89-99; C Brighton St Pet w Chpl Royal 99-02; P-in-c 02-09; P-in-c Brighton Chpl Royal from 09; Chapl St Mary's Hall Brighton from 03. *4 Parochial Mews, Princes Street, Brighton BN2 1WF* Tel (01273) 774492 E-mail david@crbtn.freeserve.co.uk

BIGGS, George Ramsay. b 45. Liv Univ BA67 Qu Coll Cam BA73. Westcott Ho Cam 72. **d** 74 **p** 75. C Lee St Aug *S'wark* 74-78; TV Eling, Testwood and Marchwood *Win* 78; TV Totton 78-93; V E and W Wellow 93-98; V E w W Wellow and Sherfield English from 98; Hosp Chapl Adv (Bournemouth Adnry) from 02. *Wellow Vicarage, 1 The Beeches, West Wellow, Romsey SO51 6RN* Tel (01794) 323562

BIGGS, Laurence James. b 60. Leeds Univ BSc81. Trin Coll Bris 92. **d** 94 **p** 95. C St Alb St Paul *St Alb* 94-99; V Codicote from 99. *The Vicarage, 4 Bury Lane, Codicote, Hitchin SG4 8XT* Tel (01438) 820266 Fax 822007 E-mail lbiggs@enterprise.net

BIGGS, Philip John. b 51. Ripon Coll Ox 74 Ripon Coll Cuddesdon 75. **d** 77 **p** 78. C Maidstone All SS w St Phil and H Trin *Cant* 77-80; Dioc Youth Officer *Truro* 80-84; Australia from 84; Hon Chapl Miss to Seafarers from 84; Chapl St Hilda's Angl Sch Perth 84-87; R Bicton 87-91; R Mosman Park from 92; AD Claremont 98-04. *20 Monument Street, Mosman Park WA 6012,*

Australia Tel (0061) (8) 9384 4279 *or* 9384 0108 Fax 9383 4260 E-mail stlukeau@bigpond.net.au

BIGGS, Stewart Richard. b 58. SEITE. **d** 01 **p** 02. C Tunbridge Wells St Jas w St Phil *Roch* 01-04; C Tunbridge Wells St Jas 04-05; V St Mary Cray and St Paul's Cray 05-06. *46 Watson Avenue, Chatham ME5 9SN* Tel 07967-979559 (mobile) E-mail revstewb@xalt.co.uk

BIGMORE, Graeme Paul. b 57. Univ of Wales (Cardiff) BTh95. St Mich Coll Llan 89. **d** 92 **p** 93. C Cardiff St Jo *Llan* 92-96; Cardiff City Cen Chapl 94-96; C Rhondda 96-98; V Tylorstown w Ynyshir 98-05; V Ynyshir from 05. *The Vicarage, Graig Road, Porth CF39 0NS* Tel (01443) 684148

BIGNELL, Alan Guy. b 39. Lon Univ BA64. Ox NSM Course 78. **d** 81 **p** 82. NSM Upton cum Chalvey *Ox* 81-90; NSM Burnham and Slough Deanery from 90. *Little Gidding, 2 Turners Road, Slough SL3 7AN* Tel (01753) 523005 E-mail abignell@waitrose.com

BIGNELL, David Charles. b 41. EMMTC 76. **d** 79 **p** 80. C Porchester *S'well* 79-82; V Awsworth w Cossall 82-86; V Edwalton 86-06; Bp's Ecum Officer 84-06; rtd 06; C Nottingham All SS, St Mary and St Pet *S'well* 08-09. *6 Allendale Avenue, Beeston, Nottingham NG9 6AN* Tel 0115-925 0060

BIGWOOD, Kate Elizabeth. *See* ATKINSON, Mrs Kate Bigwood

BILES, David George. b 35. AKC58 Open Univ BA75 Lambeth STh91 Leeds Univ MA96. **d** 59 **p** 60. C Cockerton *Dur* 59-62; C Winlaton 62-67; P-in-c Dipton 67-74; R Wolviston 74-89; P-in-c Thirkleby w Kilburn and Bagby *York* 89-90; V 90-00; RD Thirsk 90-91; RD Mowbray 91-00; rtd 00; Perm to Offic *York* from 00. *10 King Rudding Close, Riccall, York YO19 6RY* Tel and fax (01757) 248829

BILES, Mrs Kathleen Anne. b 52. Bradf Univ BA74. St Jo Coll Nottm 98. **d** 04 **p** 06. C Ch Ch Cathl Stanley Falkland Is from 04. *PO Box 166, 14 Kent Road, Stanley FIQQ 1ZZ, Falkland Islands* Tel and fax (00500) 21897 E-mail kbiles@horizon.co.fk

BILES, Canon Timothy Mark Frowde. b 35. St Mich Coll Llan 60. **d** 64 **p** 66. C Middleton St Cross *Ripon* 64-66; Chapl St Fran Sch Hooke 66-72; P-in-c Toller Porcorum w Hooke *Sarum* 72-79; P-in-c Melplash w Mapperton 74-79; P-in-c Beaminster 77-79; TR Beaminster Area 79-00; Can and Preb Sarum Cathl 83-00; RD Beaminster 84-89; rtd 00; Perm to Offic *Sarum* from 01. *36 Hound Street, Sherborne DT9 3AA* Tel (01935) 816247

BILL, Alan. b 29. K Coll Lon BD66 AKC66. **d** 67 **p** 68. C Gt Burstead *Chelmsf* 67-70; TV Thornaby on Tees *York* 71-76; R E Gilling 76-81; V Ormesby 81-91; rtd 91; Perm to Offic *Newc* from 91. *13 Wilmington Close, Tudor Grange, Newcastle upon Tyne NE3 2SF* Tel 0191-242 4467

BILL, Canon Thomas Andrew Graham. b 47. Dur Univ BA76. Cranmer Hall Dur. **d** 77 **p** 78. C Penwortham St Mary *Blackb* 77-80; C Torrisholme 80-82; P-in-c Accrington St Pet 82-89; P-in-c Haslingden St Jo Stonefold 82-89; V Skerton St Chad 89-03; R Burnley St Pet from 03; P-in-c Burnley St Steph from 08; Hon Can Blackb Cathl from 03. *St Peter's Rectory, 1 Ridge Court, Burnley BB10 3LN* Tel and fax (01282) 413599 E-mail tom.bill@lineone.net

BILLAM, John. b 38. St Aid Birkenhead 63. **d** 06 **p** 07. C Wellington Ch Ch *Lich* 66-70; P-in-c Colwyn *S & B* 03-08. *Melin y Cwm, Beulah, Llanwrtyd Wells LD5 4TT* Tel (01591) 620493

BILLETT, Anthony Charles. b 56. Bris Univ BEd. Wycliffe Hall Ox 82. **d** 85 **p** 86. C Waltham Abbey *Chelmsf* 85-88; C Nor St Pet Mancroft w St Jo Maddermarket 88-91; V Stalham and E Ruston w Brunstead 91-00; R Stalham, E Ruston, Brunstead, Sutton and Ingham 00-01; R Diss from 01; RD Redenhall from 06. *The Rectory, 26 Mount Street, Diss IP22 3QG* Tel (01379) 642072 E-mail billett@diss26.freeserve.co.uk

BILLETT (née RANDALL), Mrs Elizabeth Nicola. b 55. RGN75 SCM81. EAMTC 94. **d** 97 **p** 98. C Loddon, Sisland w Hales and Heckingham *Nor* 97-98; C Loddon, Sisland, Chedgrave, Hardley and Langley 98-01; TV Hempnall from 02. *The Flat, George's House, The Street, Woodton, Bungay NR35 1LZ* Tel (01508) 482366

BILLIN, David Robert. b 55. S Bank Poly BSc77 CEng82 MIET82 MIRSE86 EurIng89. **d** 06 **p** 07. NSM Carshalton *S'wark* from 06. *33 Beeches Avenue, Carshalton SM5 3LJ* Tel (020) 8647 5046 Mobile 07946-609387 E-mail davidbillin1955@btinternet.com

BILLIN, Mrs Susan Lynn. b 59. S Bank Univ BSc99 Greenwich Univ CertEd96 RGN82. SEITE 02. **d** 05 **p** 06. NSM S Beddington and Roundshaw *S'wark* from 05. *33 Beeches Avenue, Carshalton SM5 3LJ* Tel (020) 8647 5046 E-mail lynn_billin@lineone.net

BILLINGHURST, Richard George. b 48. St Jo Coll Cam BA70 MA74 FIA76. Ridley Hall Cam 76. **d** 79 **p** 80. C Caverswall *Lich* 79-81; C Cullompton *Ex* 81-84; R Redgrave cum Botesdale w Rickinghall *St E* 84-92; R Skellingthorpe w Doddington *Linc* from 92; RD Graffoe 94-02. *The Rectory, 50 Lincoln Road, Skellingthorpe, Lincoln LN6 5UY* Tel (01522) 682520 Fax 693330 Mobile 07971-590378 E-mail acorns@clara.co.uk

BILLINGS, Canon Alan Roy. b 42. Em Coll Cam BA65 MA69 Bris Univ PGCE66 Leic Univ MEd75 NY Th Sem DMin87. Linc Th Coll 66. **d** 68 **p** 69. C Knighton St Mary Magd *Leic* 68-72; P-in-c Sheff Gillcar St Silas 72-76; V Beighton 76-77; Hd RE Broadway Sch Barnsley 77-81; Perm to Offic 77-81; V Walkley 81-86; Dir Ox Inst for Ch and Soc 86-92; Perm to Offic *Ox* 86-92; Vice-Prin Ripon Coll Cuddesdon 88-92; Prin WMMTC 92-94; V Kendal St Geo *Carl* 94-07; C Grayrigg 06-07; Warden of Readers 96-03; Dir Cen for Ethics and Relig Lanc Univ 00-07; Hon Can Carl Cathl 05-07; rtd 07. *43 Northfield Court, Sheffield S10 1QR* Tel 0114-267 6549 E-mail alanbillingsuk@yahoo.co.uk

BILLINGS, Derek Donald. b 30. Fitzw Ho Cam BA54 MA59. Tyndale Hall Bris 55. **d** 56 **p** 57. C Attenborough w Bramcote and Chilwell *S'well* 56-58; R Ashley w Silverley *Ely* 59-66; V Bottisham 66-80; R Houghton w Wyton 80-97; rtd 97; Perm to Offic *Ely* from 97. *The Limes, 59 Cambridge Street, Godmanchester, Huntingdon PE29 2AY* Tel (01480) 414244

BILLINGS, Roger Key. b 41. ACIB. Oak Hill Th Coll BA80. **d** 80 **p** 81. C Tunbridge Wells St Jas *Roch* 80-84; V Chatham St Paul w All SS 84-95; V Carterton *Ox* 95-03; TR Brize Norton and Carterton 03-07; AD Witney 03-07; rtd 07; Perm to Offic *Nor* from 07. *Maudville, Norwich Road, Cromer NR27 9JU* Tel (01263) 519055 E-mail rogerb2006@tiscali.com

BILLINGS, Mrs Valerie Ann. b 52. Nottm Trent Univ CertEd02. EMMTC 07. **d** 09. NSM Ockbrook *Derby* from 09. *14 Conway Avenue, Borrowash, Derby DE72 3GT* Tel (01332) 726285 E-mail val-billings@excite.com

BILLINGSLEY, Raymond Philip. b 48. FCMA80 Open Univ BA98 DASS98. Qu Coll Birm 87. **d** 89 **p** 90. C Yardley St Edburgha *Birm* 89-92; V Ward End 92-96; V Brymbo *St As* 96-04; V Northop from 04. *The Vicarage, Sychdyn Road, Northop, Mold CH7 6AW* Tel (01352) 840235 Mobile 08315-39896 E-mail northopvicarage@hotmail.co.uk

BILLINGTON, Charles Alfred. b 30. Leeds Univ BA55. Coll of Resurr Mirfield 53. **d** 55 **p** 56. C Carl H Trin 55-59; CR 59-64; R Man St Aid 64-66; V Gt Crosby St Faith *Liv* 66-72; R Harrold and Carlton w Chellington *St Alb* 72-80; R Tintinhull w Chilthorne Domer, Yeovil Marsh etc *B & W* 80-81; Chapl Leybourne Grange Hosp W Malling 81-85; V Walsden *Wakef* 85-88; R Llanfair Talhaearn and Llansannan etc *St As* 88-97; rtd 97. *5 Sunningdale, Abergele LL22 7UB* Tel (01745) 824563

BILLINGTON, George. b 45. St Jo Coll Nottm 92. **d** 94 **p** 95. C Accrington St Jo w Huncoat *Blackb* 94-98; C Whittle-le-Woods 98-00; V Stalmine w Pilling from 00. *St John's Vicarage, Lancaster Road, Pilling, Preston PR3 6AE* Tel (01253) 799170 E-mail george.billington@ukonline.co.uk

BILLOWES, David. b 20. Chich Th Coll. **d** 76 **p** 77. NSM Cowes St Mary *Portsm* 76-91; Chapl St Mary's Hosp Newport 82-91; rtd 91; Perm to Offic *Portsm* 91-06. *3 Greenfields, Gosfield, Halstead CO9 1TR* Tel (01787) 472823

BILNEY, Kenneth Henry. b 25. FBCS. St Deiniol's Hawarden 75. **d** 75 **p** 76. Hon C Knighton St Mary Magd *Leic* 75-78; C Leic St Jas 78-80; R Leire w Ashby Parva and Dunton Bassett 80-90; rtd 90; Perm to Offic *Leic* from 90. *20 Ferndale Road, Leicester LE2 6GN* Tel 0116-257 0436

BILSTON, Barbara Bradley. b 35. Man Univ BA58 Essex Univ MA75. EAMTC 96. **d** 97 **p** 98. NSM Bacton w Wyverstone and Cotton *St E* 97-00; NSM Bacton w Wyverstone, Cotton and Old Newton etc 00-04; Asst to RD Stowmarket 04-05; RD from 05. *Boy's Hall, Ward Green, Old Newton, Stowmarket IP14 4EY* Tel and fax (01449) 781253 Mobile 07889-516674 E-mail b.b.bilston@open.ac.uk

BILTON, Canon Paul Michael. b 52. AKC74. St Aug Coll Cant 74. **d** 75 **p** 76. C Skipton Ch Ch *Bradf* 75-79; Ind Chapl *Worc* 79-81; V Greetland and W Vale *Wakef* 81-88; R Mablethorpe w Trusthorpe *Linc* 88-91; V Bradf St Wilfrid Lidget Green 91-04; P-in-c Bradf St Columba w St Andr 00-04; V Bradf St Wilfrid w St Columba from 04; RD Bowling and Horton from 02; Hon Can Bradf Cathl from 04. *St Wilfrid's Vicarage, St Wilfrid's Road, Bradford BD7 2LU* Tel (01274) 572504 E-mail paul.bilton@bradford.anglican.org

BIMSON, Sara Margaret. b 56. St Jo Coll Nottm BA. **d** 03 **p** 04. C Maidstone St Martin *Cant* 03-08; rtd 08; Voc Officer *Cant* from 08. *85 Loose Road, Maidstone ME15 7DA* Tel (01622) 679432 E-mail sara-mary@hotmail.co.uk *or* sbimson@diocant.org

BINDING, Ms Frances Mary. b 59. York Univ BA81 Newc Poly PGCE82. WEMTC 98. **d** 02 **p** 03. C Bromyard *Heref* 02-07; TV Worc SE from 07. *33 Aconbury Close, Worcester WR5 1JD* Tel (01905) 763378 E-mail franbinding@lineone.net

BINDOFF, Ms Anna. b 70. Leeds Univ BA94. Ripon Coll Cuddesdon BA97. **d** 98 **p** 99. Asst Chapl New Coll Ox 98-01; Hon C Blackbird Leys *Ox* 98-01; C 01-04. *23 Brook Street, Watlington OX49 5JH* Tel (01491) 613327

BING, Canon Alan Charles. b 56. St Edm Hall Ox BA78 MA91 Ex Univ MA96. Oak Hill Th Coll 89. **d** 91 **p** 92. C Fremington *Ex* 91-94; C-in-c Roundswell CD 94-97; TV Barnstaple 97-99; Chapl N Devon Coll Barnstaple 96-99; P-in-c Ulverston

St Mary w H Trin *Carl* 99-04; R from 04; Hon Can Carl Cathl from 09. *The Rectory, 15 Ford Park Crescent, Ulverston LA12 7JR* Tel and fax (01229) 584331

BINGHAM, Mrs Marie Joyce Phyllis. b 27. Glouc Sch of Min 80. **dss** 84 **d** 87 **p** 94. Glouc St Mary de Crypt w St Jo and Ch Ch 84-85; Glouc St Mary de Lode and St Nic 85-87; Hon C 87-95; Hon C Glouc St Mary de Crypt w St Jo and Ch Ch 94-95; Hon C Glouc St Mary de Crypt w St Jo, Ch Ch etc 95-98; Perm to Offic from 98. *Clematis Cottage, 1 Queenwood Grove, Prestbury, Cheltenham GL52 3NG* Tel (01452) 242252

BINGHAM, Norman James Frederick. b 26. Lon Univ BSc51. Tyndale Hall Bris 61. **d** 63 **p** 64. C Chell *Lich* 63-67; C Macclesfield St Mich *Ches* 67-71; P-in-c Macclesfield St Pet 71-73; V Leyton St Mary w St Edw *Chelmsf* 73-91; RD Waltham Forest 81-86; P-in-c Leyton St Luke 82-91; rtd 91; Perm to Offic *St Alb* from 91. *97 Monks Walk, Buntingford SG9 9DP* Tel (01763) 272275

BINKS, Andrew John. b 49. Open Univ BA Leeds Univ MA06. NOC 03. **d** 06 **p** 07. NSM Haslingden w Grane and Stonefold *Blackb* 06-09; NSM Accrington St Jo w Huncoat from 09. *18 Sandown Road, Haslingden, Rossendale BB4 6PL* Tel (01706) 229285 E-mail jmbinks@tiscali.co.uk

BINKS, Canon Edmund Vardy. b 36. K Coll Lon BD61 AKC61 Liv Univ Hon LLD98 FRSA89. **d** 62 **p** 63. C Selby Abbey *York* 62-65; Asst Chapl Univ Coll of Ripon and York St Jo 65-83; Hd St Kath Coll Liv 83-87; Prin Ches Coll of HE 87-98; Hon Can Ches Cathl 95-98; Perm to Offic *Chich* from 98; rtd 01. *2 Lodge Close, Lewes BN7 1AR* Tel (01273) 487136

BINLEY, Miss Teresa Mary. b 37. Dalton Ho Bris 61. **d** 87 **p** 94. Par Dn Ashton-upon-Mersey St Mary Magd *Ches* 87-92; Bp's Officer for Women in Min 87-92; C Chaddesden St Mary *Derby* 92-98; rtd 98; Perm to Offic *Derby* from 98. *27 Hindscarth Crescent, Mickleover, Derby DE3 9NN* Tel (01332) 511146

BINNEY, Mark James Gurney. b 58. K Coll Lon BD80. Qu Coll Birm 84. **d** 86 **p** 87. C Hornchurch St Andr *Chelmsf* 86-89; C Hutton 89-91; V Pheasey *Lich* 91-96; TV Wombourne w Trysull and Bobbington 96-99; V Hampton w Sedgeberrow and Hinton-on-the-Green *Worc* from 08. *St Andrew's Vicarage, 54 Pershore Road, Evesham WR11 2PQ* Tel (01386) 446381 E-mail reverend-mark-binney@hotmail.co.uk

BINNS, Miss Catherine Dorothy. b 70. Univ of Cen England in Birm BSc04 Leeds Univ BA07 RN99. NOC 04. **d** 07 **p** 08. NSM Stand *Man* from 07. *23 Scott Street, Radcliffe, Manchester M26 1EX* Tel (01204) 707922 E-mail cath@chazfrog.fsnet.co.uk

BINNS, David John. b 39. Moore Th Coll Sydney ThL64. **d** 64 **p** 65. Australia 64-67 and from 70; C Rainham *S'wark* 67-69; R Adelaide St Luke 80-98; Assoc Min 98-00; rtd 00. *Unit 4/2 Spence Avenue, Myrtle Bank SA 5064, Australia* Tel (0061) (8) 8338 5779 Mobile 0417-860560 E-mail djb29@ozemail.com.au

BINNS, Miss Elizabeth Ann. b 55. MBE06. Man Metrop Univ BA87 RGN77. **d** 05 **p** 06. OLM Bury St Jo w St Mark *Man* from 05. *36 Raymond Avenue, Bury BL9 6NN* Tel 0161-764 5071 Mobile 07976-818157 E-mail elizabethbinns@aol.com

BINNS, Mrs Janet Victoria. b 57. ACIB96. Ox Min Course 04. **d** 07 **p** 08. C Slough *Ox* from 07. *209 Stoke Road, Slough SL2 5AX* Tel (01753) 528672 E-mail janet.binns@talktalk.net

BINNS, Canon John Richard Elliott. b 51. St Jo Coll Cam MA76 K Coll Lon PhD89. Coll of Resurr Mirfield 74. **d** 76 **p** 77. C Clapham Old Town *S'wark* 76-80; TV Mortlake w E Sheen 80-87; V Upper Tooting H Trin 87-94; V Cambridge Gt St Mary w St Mich *Ely* from 94; RD Cambridge N from 07; Hon Can Ely Cathl from 07. *Great St Mary's Vicarage, 39 Madingley Road, Cambridge CB3 0EL* Tel (01223) 355285 or 741716 Fax 741775 E-mail jb344@cam.ac.uk

BINNS, Peter Rodney. b 44. St Andr Univ MA66. Ox NSM Course 72. **d** 75 **p** 76. NSM Amersham on the Hill *Ox* 75-90; NSM Wingrave w Rowsham, Aston Abbotts and Cublington 90-97; NSM Hawridge w Cholesbury and St Leonard 90-97; NSM Amersham on the Hill from 97. *16 Turnfurlong Row, Turnfurlong Lane, Aylesbury HP21 7FF* Tel (01296) 330836 Fax 337965

BINNY, John Wallace. b 46. Univ of Wales (Lamp) BA70. St Mich Coll Llan 69. **d** 71 **p** 72. C Llantrisant 71-77; V Troedyrhiw w Merthyr Vale 77-82; R Eglwysbrewis w St Athan, Flemingston, Gileston 82-95; R Eglwysbrewis w St Athan w Gileston 95-03; V Pentyrch w Capel Llanilltern from 03. *The Vicarage, Church Road, Pentyrch, Cardiff CF15 9QF* Tel (029) 2089 0318

BINSLEY, Michael. **d** 09. OLM Yoxall *Lich* from 09. *83 Lightwood Road, Yoxall, Burton-on-Trent DE13 8QE* Tel (01543) 472761

BIRBECK, Anthony Leng. b 33. MBE90. Linc Coll Ox BA59 MA61. Linc Th Coll 58. **d** 60 **p** 61. C Redcar *York* 60-74; Chapl Teesside Ind Miss 62-74; Can Res and Treas Wells Cathl 74-78; NSM Wells St Thos w Horrington 89-98; rtd 98; Perm to Offic *B & W* from 98; RD Shepton Mallet from 07. *Beeches, Cannard's Grave Road, Shepton Mallet BA4 4LX* Tel (01749) 330382 Mobile 07802-725024 E-mail tonybirbeck@hotmail.co.uk

BIRBECK, John Trevor. b 49. ACIB77. St Jo Coll Nottm 86. **d** 88 **p** 89. C Eccleshill *Bradf* 88-92; V Hurst Green and Mitton 92-03; R Rawmarsh w Parkgate *Sheff* from 03. *The Rectory, 2 High Street, Rawmarsh, Rotherham S62 6NE* Tel (01709) 527160 E-mail john.birbeck@ntlworld.com

BIRCH, Barry. b 46. Sheff Univ CertEd69 Lon Univ BA74 MIL84 MCollP85. **d** 06 **p** 07. NSM Cantley *Sheff* 06-08; NSM Eastchurch w Leysdown and Harty *Cant* from 08. *The Rectory, Warden Road, Eastchurch, Sheerness ME12 4EJ* Tel (01795) 880205 Mobile 07711-514671 E-mail barrybirch@hotmail.com

BIRCH, Derek. b 31. Univ of Wales (Lamp) BA58. Coll of Resurr Mirfield 58. **d** 60 **p** 61. C S Elmsall *Wakef* 60-62; C Penistone w Midhope 62-66; V Silkstone 66-89; Chapl Stainborough 76-89; P-in-c Hoyland Swaine 85-89; V Hoylandswaine and Silkstone w Stainborough 89-97; rtd 98; Perm to Offic *Wakef* from 98. *46 Pengeston Road, Penistone, Sheffield S36 6GW* Tel (01226) 761523

BIRCH, Mrs Elizabeth Ann Marie. b 65. Ball Coll Ox BA88 MA05. NTMTC BA06. **d** 06 **p** 07. NSM Pinner *Lon* 06-09; R Wantage Downs *Ox* from 09. *The Rectory, Church Street, East Hendred, Wantage OX12 8LA* Tel (01235) 833235

BIRCH, Graham James. b 62. NOC BTh94. **d** 97 **p** 98. C Southport St Phil and St Paul *Liv* 97-01; P-in-c Wigan St Cath 01-07; V Ainsdale from 07. *The Vicarage, 708 Liverpool Road, Southport PR8 3QE* Tel (01704) 577760 E-mail madrebgra@aol.com

BIRCH, Henry Arthur. b 24. St Jo Coll Dur BA48. Tyndale Hall Bris 48. **d** 49 **p** 50. C Edin St Thos 49-51; C Surbiton Hill Ch Ch *S'wark* 51-54; R Uphill *B & W* 54-69; Australia 69-81 and from 84; S Africa 81-84; rtd 90. *9/87 Yathong Road, Carringbah NSW 2229, Australia* Tel (0061) (2) 9525 1763

BIRCH, Janet Ann. St Alb Minl Tr Scheme 77. **dss** 80 **d** 87 **p** 94. Luton St Mary *St Alb* 80-87; Par Dn Streatley 87-91; rtd 91; NSM Aldeburgh w Hazlewood *St E* 91-01; Perm to Offic 01-03. *c/o Ms S J Clark, 13 West Bank, Carlton, Goole DN14 9PZ* Tel (01405) 860708

BIRCH, Mark Russell. b 70. Bris Univ BVSc93 Em Coll Cam BA99. Westcott Ho Cam 97. **d** 00 **p** 01. C Cirencester *Glouc* 00-03; Chapl and Fell Ex Coll Ox 03-06; Chapl Helen and Douglas Ho Ox from 06. *Helen and Douglas House, 14A Magdalen Road, Oxford OX4 1RW* Tel (01865) 794749 E-mail mbirch@helenanddouglas.org.uk

BIRCH, Richard Arthur. b 51. Brighton Poly BSc73 Chelsea Coll Lon MSc76. SEITE 98. **d** 01 **p** 02. NSM Foord St Jo *Cant* 01-04; NSM Hawkinge w Acrise and Swingfield 04-07; NSM Hythe 07-08; NSM Doddington, Newnham and Wychling from 08. *The Vicarage, The Street, Doddington, Sittingbourne ME9 0BH* Tel (01795) 886265 E-mail richarda.birch@btinternet.com

BIRCH, Shirley Anne. b 34. EMMTC 88. **d** 91 **p** 94. Hon Par Dn Melton Gt Framland *Leic* 91-93; NSM Melton Mowbray 93-01; NSM Minster-in-Sheppey *Cant* 02-09; rtd 09. *St Peter's House, 2 St Peter's Close, Minster on Sea, Sheerness ME12 3DD* Tel (01795) 662399 E-mail shirley@stpeters02.freeserve.co.uk

BIRCH, Thomas Reginald. b 33. AKC57. St Boniface Warminster 67. **d** 68. C Basildon St Andr CD *Chelmsf* 68-69; Ind Chapl 69-88; rtd 88. *29 Muspole Street, Norwich NR3 1DJ* Tel (01603) 631446

BIRCHALL, John Dearman. b 70. St Andr Univ MA93. Wycliffe Hall Ox BTh99. **d** 99 **p** 00. C Purley Ch Ch *S'wark* 99-02; C Fisherton Anger *Sarum* 02-08; V Surbiton Hill Ch Ch *S'wark* from 08. *Christ Church Vicarage, 7 Christ Church Road, Surbiton KT5 8JJ* Tel (020) 8399 3733 or 8390 7215 E-mail john.birchall@ccsurbiton.org

BIRCHALL, Robert Gary. b 59. Sheff Univ BA81. St Jo Coll Nottm 85. **d** 88 **p** 89. C Manston *Ripon* 88-91; C Leic Martyrs 91-94; C New Humberstone 94-95; V Burnopfield *Dur* from 95; AD Lanchester from 06. *The Vicarage, Front Street, Burnopfield, Newcastle upon Tyne NE16 6HQ* Tel (01207) 270261 E-mail gary.birchall@dsl.pipex.com

BIRCHARD, Canon Thaddeus Jude. b 45. Louisiana State Univ BA66. Kelham Th Coll 66. **d** 70 **p** 71. C Devonport St Mark Ford *Ex* 70-73; C Southend St Jo w St Mark, All SS w St Fran etc *Chelmsf* 73-76; TV Poplar *Lon* 76-80; V Paddington St Jo w St Mich 80-01; Hon Can Louisiana from 90; rtd 01; Perm to Offic *Lon* from 02. *142 Dibdin House, Maida Vale, London W9 1QG* Tel (020) 7328 2380 E-mail thaddeus@birchard.co.uk

BIRD, Mrs Ann Maud. b 39. **d** 00 **p** 01. OLM W Bromwich All SS *Lich* from 00. *16 Caldwell Street, West Bromwich B71 2DN* Tel 0121-588 4335

BIRD (née BAKER), Mrs Anne-Marie Clare. b 56. Wye Coll Lon BSc78 Glas Univ MSc80. St Jo Coll Nottm 88. **d** 90 **p** 94. Par Dn Levenshulme St Pet *Man* 90-94; C 94-95; P-in-c Crumpsall 95-03; TV Keynsham *B & W* 03-05; rtd 05; Perm to Offic *B & W* from 05. *26 Culvers Road, Keynsham, Bristol BS31 2DW* Tel 0117-904 8585 E-mail pjbird@blueyonder.co.uk

BIRD, Anthony Peter. b 31. St Jo Coll Ox BA54 BTh55 MA57 Birm Univ MB, ChB70. Cuddesdon Coll 55. **d** 57 **p** 58. C

Stafford St Mary *Lich* 57-60; Chapl Cuddesdon Coll 60-61; Vice-Prin 61-64; C Selly Oak St Wulstan *Birm* 64-68; Lic to Offic 68-79; Prin Qu Coll Birm 74-79; Perm to Offic *Birm* from 85. *93 Bournbrook Road, Birmingham B29 7BX*

BIRD, Brian Edward. b 37. Rhodes Univ BA. **d** 75. S Africa 75-99 and from 08; Bp's C Mt Merrion *D & D* 99-05; rtd 05. *17 Hillcrest, League Street, Telfin Heights, Knysna, 6570 South Africa* E-mail brian_bird23@hotmail.com

BIRD, The Ven Colin Richard Bateman. b 33. Selw Coll Cam BA56 MA61. Cuddesdon Coll 56. **d** 58 **p** 59. C St Mark's Cathl George S Africa 58-61; C Claremont St Sav 61-64; R N Suburbs Pretoria 64-66; R Tzaneen w Duiwelskloof and Phalaborwa 66-70; C Limpsfield and Titsey *S'wark* 70-75; V Hatcham St Cath 75-88; RD Deptford 80-85; Hon Can S'wark Cathl 82-88; Adn Lambeth 88-99; P-in-c Brixton Hill St Sav 91-94; rtd 00; Perm to Offic *St E* from 00; *Chelmsf* and *Nor* from 01; Min Prov (Eur) Third Order SSF 02-08. *32 Bristol Road, Bury St Edmunds IP33 2DL* Tel (01284) 723810 E-mail dickbird@btopenworld.com

BIRD, The Very Revd David John. b 46. St D Coll Lamp BA70 Duquesne Univ PhD87. Gen Th Sem (NY) STM74. **d** 70 **p** 71. C Kidderminster St Geo *Worc* 70-72; Univ Chapl New York 72-78; V Rochdale Ch Ch 78-79; R New Kensington St Andr 79-89; R Washington Grace Ch 89-03; Dean Trin Cathl San Jose from 03. *Trinity Cathedral, 81 North 2nd Street, San Jose, CA 95113-1205, USA* Tel (001) (408) 293 7953 Fax 293 4993 E-mail david3933@aol.com

BIRD, Canon David Ronald. b 55. York Univ BA76. St Jo Coll Nottm 83. **d** 86 **p** 87. C Kinson *Sarum* 86-90; R Thrapston *Pet* 90-97; P-in-c Islip 94-95; RD Higham 94-97; V Northampton St Giles from 97; Can Pet Cathl from 01. *St Giles's Vicarage, 2 Spring Gardens, Northampton NN1 1LX* Tel (01604) 634060 Fax 628623 E-mail david@dbird.freeserve.co.uk

BIRD, Douglas Norman. b 38. **d** 92 **p** 93. OLM New Bury *Man* 92-06; Perm to Offic *Blackb* from 06. *4 Oak Avenue, Horwich, Bolton BL6 6JE* Tel (01204) 695916

BIRD, Canon Frederick Hinton. b 38. St Edm Hall Ox BA62 MA66 Univ of Wales MEd81 PhD86. St D Coll Lamp BD65. **d** 65 **p** 66. C Mynyddislwyn *Mon* 65-67; Min Can St Woolos Cathl 67-70; Chapl Anglo-American Coll Farringdon 70-71; Perm to Offic *Ox* 70-78; *Cant* 72-78 and *Mon* 76-82; V Rushen *S & M* 82-03; Can St German's Cathl 93-03; rtd 03. *Conrhenny, 56 Selborne Drive, Douglas, Isle of Man IM2 3NL* Tel (01624) 621624

BIRD, Geoffrey. b 44. Dioc OLM tr scheme 97. **d** 99 **p** 00. Asst Chapl HM YOI and Remand Cen Brinsford 99; Sen Chapl 99-04; Chapl HM Pris Shepton Mallet 04-09; rtd 09. *2 Hosey Road, Sturminster Newton DT10 1QP* Tel (01258) 472904

BIRD, Canon Geoffrey Neville. b 22. AKC48. St Boniface Warminster 48. **d** 49 **p** 50. C Berkeley *Glouc* 49-53; C Malden St Jo *S'wark* 53-55; C Glouc St Aldate 54-56; R Edge w Pitchcombe 56-82; P-in-c Brookthorpe w Whaddon and Harescombe 76-82; R The Edge, Pitchcombe, Harescombe and Brookthorpe 82-90; Hon Can Glouc Cathl 83-90; RD Bisley 84-90; rtd 90; Perm to Offic *Glouc* from 90. *Ivycroft, Winstone, Cirencester GL7 7JZ* Tel (01285) 821664

BIRD, Graham Desmond. b 44. **d** 02. OLM Stalham, E Ruston, Brunstead, Sutton and Ingham *Nor* 02-06. *Address temp unknown*

BIRD, Henry John Joseph. b 37. ARCO58 Qu Coll Cam BA59 MA63. Linc Th Coll 62. **d** 64 **p** 65. C Harbledown *Cant* 64-68; C Skipton H Trin *Bradf* 68-70; V Oakworth 70-81; Chapl Abingdon Sch 81-82; P-in-c Doncaster St Geo *Sheff* 82-85; V 85-02; rtd 02. *332 Thorne Road, Doncaster DN2 5AL* Tel (01302) 326041

BIRD, Hinton. *See* BIRD, Canon Frederick Hinton

BIRD, Hugh Claud Handley. b 24. FRCGP SS Coll Cam MA MB BCh. Ridley Hall Cam. **d** 86 **p** 86. NSM Coxheath w E Farleigh, Hunton and Linton *Roch* 86-95; Perm to Offic *Cant* from 95. *The Slate Barn, Seamark Road, Brooksend, Birchington CT7 0JL* Tel (01843) 846610

BIRD, Ian Nicholas. b 62. Qu Eliz Coll Lon BSc83 Newc Univ PhD87. SAOMC 03. **d** 06 **p** 07. C Chandler's Ford *Win* from 06. *St Martin's House, 50 Randall Road, Chandler's Ford, Eastleigh SO53 5AL* Tel (023) 8025 4739 Mobile 07733-213535 E-mail ianbird@parishofchandlersford.org.uk

BIRD, Jeffrey David. b 54. Nottm Univ BCombStuds85. Linc Th Coll 82. **d** 85 **p** 86. C Frome St Jo *B & W* 85-88; Asst Chapl HM Pris Pentonville 88-89; Chapl HM Pris Dartmoor 89-95; Albany 95-03; Linc 03-07; Stafford from 07. *HM Prison, 54 Gaol Road, Stafford ST16 3AW* Tel (01785) 773000 Fax 773001

BIRD, Jeremy David. b 54. Ex Univ BSc77 Hull Univ MA88. Sarum Th Coll 78. **d** 80 **p** 81. C Tavistock and Gulworthy *Ex* 80-83; Chapl Teesside Poly *York* 83-88; R Chipstable w Huish Champflower and Clatworthy *B & W* 88-93; Rural Affairs Officer 88-93; V Uffculme *Ex* 93-01; P-in-c Dawlish 01-09; P-in-c Exwick from 09. *Exwick Vicarage, Exwick Hill, Exeter EX4 2AQ* E-mail jerry@credamus.freeserve.co.uk

BIRD, John. *See* BIRD, Henry John Joseph

BIRD, John Anthony. b 45. EMMTC 00. **d** 03 **p** 04. NSM Thringstone St Andr *Leic* from 03; NSM Whitwick and Swannington from 07. *8 Buckingham Drive, Loughborough LE11 4TE* Tel (01509) 234962 E-mail curate.thringstone@tiscali.co.uk

BIRD, Mrs Margaret Kathleen. b 48. SAOMC 04. **d** 06 **p** 07. NSM Cox Green *Ox* from 06. *33 Furrow Way, Maidenhead SL6 3NY* Tel (01638) 823321 Mobile 07881-712611 E-mail margaret.bird@talktalk.net

BIRD, Nicholas William Randle. b 70. Univ of Cen England in Birm BSc99 RGN92. NEOC 02. **d** 05 **p** 06. C Thirsk *York* 05-09; P-in-c Dunnington from 09; P-in-c Stockton-on-the-Forest w Holtby and Warthill from 09. *The Rectory, 30 Church Street, Dunnington, York YO19 5PW* Tel (01845) 523812

BIRD, Norman David. b 32. CQSW73. Coll of Resurr Mirfield 87. **d** 89 **p** 90. NSM Willesden Green St Andr and St Fran *Lon* 89-92; NSM Preston Ascension 93-98; rtd 98; Perm to Offic *Lon* from 99. *5 Oldfield Road, London NW10 9UD* Tel (020) 8451 4160

BIRD, Canon Peter Andrew. b 40. Wadh Coll Ox BA62 MA68. Ridley Hall Cam 63. **d** 65 **p** 66. C Keynsham w Queen Charlton *B & W* 65-68; C Strood St Nic *Roch* 68-72; TV Strood 72-79; V S Gillingham 79-89; V Westerham 89-02; Hon Can Roch Cathl 01-02; Perm to Offic *Roch* 02-05 and *Derby* from 05. *Iona, Prospect Terrace, Stanedge Road, Bakewell DE45 1DG* Tel (01629) 813087

BIRD, Richard. *See* BIRD, The Ven Colin Richard Bateman

BIRD, Canon Roger Alfred. b 49. AKC72. St Aug Coll Cant 72. **d** 73 **p** 74. C Prestatyn *St As* 73-78; R Llandysilio and Penrhos and Llandrinio etc 78-92; Dioc RE Adv from 84; Dioc Dir of Educn from 89; R Guilsfield 92-97; R Guilsfield w Pool Quay 97-02; V Guilsfield w Buttington from 02; Hon Can St As Cathl from 93; RD Pool 96-01 and from 07. *The New Vicarage, Guilsfield, Welshpool SY21 9NF* Tel and fax (01938) 554245 E-mail rogerb_790@fsmail.net

BIRDSEYE, Miss Jacqueline Ann. b 55. Sussex Univ BEd78 Southn Univ BTh88 K Coll Lon MTh93. Sarum & Wells Th Coll 85. **d** 88 **p** 94. C Egham Hythe *Guildf* 88-91; C Fleet 91-92; C Shottermill 92-95; C Leavesden St Alb 95-98; R Ashwell w Hinxworth and Newnham 98-05; R Moreton and Woodsford w Tincleton *Sarum* from 05. *The Rectory, 17 Warmwell Road, Crossways, Dorchester DT2 8BS* Tel (01305) 854046

BIRDWOOD, William Halhed. b 51. St Jo Coll Dur BA73. Sarum & Wells Th Coll 76. **d** 78 **p** 79. C Royston *St Alb* 78-82; C Thorley w Bishop's Stortford H Trin 82-89; Chapl HM Pris Ex 89-96; Chapl HM Pris Dartmoor from 96; Lic to Offic *Ex* from 89. *HM Prison Dartmoor, Princetown, Yelverton PL20 6RR* Tel (01822) 890261 Fax 890679

BIRKENHEAD, Suffragan Bishop of. *See* SINCLAIR, The Rt Revd Gordon Keith

BIRKETT, Christine Joy. b 53. Univ of Wales (Cardiff) BTheol99 PGCE02. Trin Coll Bris 07. **d** 08 **p** 09. NSM Berkeley w Wick, Breadstone, Newport, Stone etc *Glouc* from 08. *Stables Cottage, Wards Court, The Green, Frampton on Severn GL2 7DY* Tel (01452) 740422 E-mail chrisdne.birkett@virgin.net

BIRKETT, Mrs Joyce. b 38. WMMTC 84. **d** 87 **p** 94. Par Dn Hill *Birm* 87-91; Asst Chapl Highcroft Hosp Birm 87 91; Par Dn Rowley Regis *Birm* 91-94; C 94 96; V Londonderry 96-01; rtd 01; Perm to Offic *Birm* from 01. *83 Callowbrook Lane, Rubery, Rednal, Birmingham B45 9HP* Tel 0121-457 9759

BIRKETT, Neil Warren. b 45. Lanc Univ BEd74 Southn Univ MA84. Linc Th Coll 65. **d** 77 **p** 77. NSM Win St Matt from 77. *Corrymeela, 132 Teg Down Meads, Winchester SO22 5NS* Tel (01962) 864910

BIRKIN, Mrs Elspeth Joyce (Joy). b 36. CertEd58. WMMTC 95. **d** 96 **p** 97. NSM Hanley Castle, Hanley Swan and Welland *Worc* 96-01; NSM Berrow w Pendock, Eldersfield, Hollybush etc 01-04; Perm to Offic from 04. *9 Hastings Road, Malvern WR14 2SS* Tel (01684) 569493

BIRKINSHAW, Ian George. b 58. Pemb Coll Ox BA81 Leeds Univ MA97 Sheff Univ PGCE82. NOC 93. **d** 96 **p** 97. NSM Chapeltown *Sheff* 96-97; C Normanton *Wakef* 98-01; C York St Mich-le-Belfrey 01-08; TR Huntington from 08. *The Rectory, Chestnut Court, Huntington, York YO32 9RD* Tel (01904) 768160

BIRMINGHAM, Archdeacon of. *See* OSBORNE, The Ven Hayward John

BIRMINGHAM, Bishop of. *See* URQUHART, The Rt Revd David Andrew

BIRMINGHAM, Dean of. *See* WILKES, The Very Revd Robert Anthony

BIRNIE, Ms Ruth Burdett. b 41. Glas Univ MA64 Jordanhill Coll Glas PGCE65 Leeds Univ MA73. NEOC 02. **d** 04 **p** 05. NSM Gosforth All SS *Newc* from 04. *27 Delaval Terrace, Newcastle upon Tyne NE3 4RT* Tel 0191-284 1393 E-mail ruth@birnie27.fsnet.co.uk

BIRT, David Edward. b 26. St Steph Ho Ox 86. **d** 86 **p** 87. NSM Ealing Ch the Sav *Lon* 86-99; Perm to Offic from 99. *10 Manor Court Road, London W7 3EL* Tel (020) 8579 4871

BIRT, Patrick. b 34. Glouc Th Course 71. **d** 75 **p** 75. NSM Bisley *Glouc* 75-76; NSM Whiteshill 76-81; C Stroud H Trin 81; R Ruardean 81-86; V Newbridge-on-Wye and Llanfihangel Brynpabuan *S & B* 86-88; TV Gillingham *Sarum* 88-99; rtd 99; Perm to Offic *Sarum* from 01. *Hornbeam Cottage, Green Lane, Stour Row, Shaftesbury SP7 0QD* Tel (01747) 839716

BIRT, Richard Arthur. b 43. Ch Ch Ox BA66 MA69. Cuddesdon Coll 67. **d** 69 **p** 70. C Sutton St Mich *York* 69-71; C Wollaton *S'well* 71-75; R Kirkby in Ashfield 75-80; P-in-c Duxford *Ely* 80-87; R 87-88; P-in-c Hinxton 80-87; V 87-88; P-in-c Ickleton 80-87; V 87-88; V Weobley w Sarnesfield and Norton Canon *Heref* 88-00; P-in-c Letton w Staunton, Byford, Mansel Gamage etc 88-00; rtd 00; Perm to Offic *Heref* from 00. *Flat 2, 2 Cantilupe Street, Hereford HR1 2NU* Tel (01432) 360804

BIRTWISTLE, Canon James. b 33. FCA66. Ely Th Coll 57. **d** 59 **p** 60. C Southport St Luke *Liv* 59-63; V Cleator Moor w Cleator *Carl* 63-70; R Letchworth *St Alb* 70-73; P-in-c Wareside 73-80; Dep Dir of Educn 77-80; Dioc Dir of Educn 80-98; Hon Can St Alb 88-98; rtd 98; Perm to Offic *Ex* from 99. *9 Stoneborough Lane, Budleigh Salterton EX9 6HL* Tel (01395) 442517

BIRTWISTLE, Lesley Sutherland. b 44. LLB. EMMTC 00. **d** 00 **p** 01. NSM Appleby Gp *Leic* 00-07; NSM Measham 07-08; NSM Packington w Normanton-le-Heath 07-08; NSM Donisthorpe and Moira w Stretton-en-le-Field 07-08; NSM Woodfield Team from 08. *14 Nethercroft Drive, Packington, Ashby-de-la-Zouch LE65 1WT* Tel (01530) 413309
E-mail lesley@bwistle.f9.co.uk

BISASO-SEKITOLEKO, Capt Samuel. b 66. Cheltenham & Glouc Coll of HE BA99. St Paul's Coll Limuru. **d** 99 **p** 02. NSM Matson *Glouc* 99; NSM Ponders End St Matt *Lon* 01-02; NSM Brownswood Park 02-06; Chapl Miss to Seafarers from 06. *24 Victoria Road, Keelby, Grimsby DN41 8EH* Tel 07944-800605 (mobile) E-mail sambisaso@aol.com

BISCOE, Clive. b 45. St Deiniol's Hawarden 85. **d** 86 **p** 87. C Llansamlet *S & B* 86-90; V Landore 90-91. *6 Hazelwood Row, Cwmavon, Port Talbot SA12 9DP*

BISCOE, Ian Rowland. b 68. Ox Min Course 06. **d** 07 **p** 08. C Cherwell Valley *Ox* from 07. *9 Soden Road, Upper Heyford, Bicester OX25 5LR* Tel (01869) 232439 Mobile 07971-529234 E-mail ian.biscoe@googlemail.com

BISH, Donald. b 26. Ripon Hall Ox. **d** 75 **p** 75. C S Gillingham *Roch* 75-79; R Wateringbury w Teston and W Farleigh 79-92; rtd 92; Perm to Offic *Cant* 92-09; *Roch* 92-98 and 00-04. *5 Eynesford Road, Allington, Maidstone ME16 0TD* Tel (01622) 661847

BISHOP, Mrs Alice Margaret Marion. b 67. Newnham Coll Cam BA89 MA93 Lon Univ MTh92. St Steph Ho Ox 92. **d** 94. C Stepney St Dunstan and All SS *Lon* 94-99. *The Vicarage, Church Lane, Old Basing, Basingstoke RG24 7DJ* Tel (01256) 473762

BISHOP, Andrew Scott. b 70. Leeds Univ BA93 Heythrop Coll Lon MTh02. St Steph Ho Ox BTh93. **d** 96 **p** 97. C Westmr St Steph w St Jo *Lon* 96-99; C Kensington St Mary Abbots w St Geo 99-03; V Old Basing and Lychpit *Win* from 03; AD Basingstoke from 08. *The Vicarage, Church Lane, Old Basing, Basingstoke RG24 7DJ* Tel (01256) 473762
E-mail as.bishop@tiscali.co.uk

BISHOP, Canon Anthony John. b 43. G&C Coll Cam BA66 MA69 Lon Univ MTh69. ALCD67. **d** 69 **p** 70. C Eccleston St Luke *Liv* 69-73; C Gt Baddow *Chelmsf* 73-77; Nigeria 77-84; Lect Lon Bible Coll 84-85; TV Chigwell *Chelmsf* 85-93; P-in-c Walthamstow St Jo 93-98; V from 98; Hon Can Kano from 00. *St John's Vicarage, 18 Brookscroft Road, London E17 4LH* Tel (020) 8531 6249 E-mail tony_bishop@talktalk.net

BISHOP, The Ven Anthony Peter. b 46. CB01. Nottm Univ MPhil84 ALCD71 FRSA87. St Jo Coll Nottm 71. **d** 71 **p** 72. C Beckenham St Geo *Roch* 71-75; Chapl RAF 75-91; Command Chapl RAF 91-98; Chapl-in-Chief RAF 98-01; Can and Preb Linc Cathl 98-01; Hon C Tewkesbury w Walton Cardiff and Twyning *Glouc* 01-03; C 03-06; rtd 06. *La Croix Blanche, 50810 St Germain d'Elle, France*

BISHOP, Canon Christopher. b 48. St Aug Coll Cant 71. **d** 72 **p** 73. C Gt Ilford St Mary *Chelmsf* 72-75; C Upminster 75-78; Adn's Youth Chapl 77-80; Dioc Youth Officer 80-86; Chapl Stansted Airport from 86; P-in-c Manuden w Berden 86-03; P-in-c Manuden w Berden and Quendon w Rickling from 03; RD Newport and Stansted from 89; Hon Can Chelmsf Cathl from 99. *The Vicarage, 24 Mallows Green Road, Manuden, Bishops Stortford CM23 1DG* Tel (01279) 812228
E-mail chrismitre@hotmail.com

BISHOP, Craig. *See* BISHOP, Simon Craig

BISHOP, David. b 65. St Jo Coll Nottm 01. **d** 03 **p** 04. C Boulton *Derby* 03-07; V Ogley Hay *Lich* from 07. *St James's Vicarage, 37 New Road, Brownhills, Walsall WS8 6AT* Tel (01543) 372187 or 373251

BISHOP, Canon David Harold. b 28. ARIBA53 FRSA75. Westcott Ho Cam 55. **d** 57 **p** 58. C Cannock *Lich* 57-61; C Gt

Barr 61-67; V All Hallows Lon Wall 67-80; Architectural Adv CCC 67-80; Can Res Nor Cathl 80-92; Vice-Dean 84-92; rtd 92; Perm to Offic *Sarum* from 92; Chapl SW Dorset Primary Care Trust from 01. *Coneycote, 6 Coneygar Park, Bridport DT6 3BA* Tel (01308) 424673

BISHOP, David Henry Ryder. b 27. MRAC50. Tyndale Hall Bris 54. **d** 57 **p** 58. C Sevenoaks St Nic *Roch* 57-59; C Branksome St Clem *Sarum* 59-63; Chapl Jinja Uganda 64-67; Dep Sec CCCS 68; R Ox St Clem 69-91; Zimbabwe 91-93; rtd 93; Perm to Offic *Ox* from 99. *40 Old High Street, Headington, Oxford OX3 9HN* Tel (01865) 760099
E-mail david@bishox.go-plus.net

BISHOP, Donald. b 22. Lon Univ BSc48. Qu Coll Birm 56. **d** 57 **p** 58. C Trowbridge H Trin *Sarum* 57-60; CF (TA) 58-68; V Bodicote *Ox* 60-87; P-in-c Broughton 71-85; rtd 87; Perm to Offic *Cov* 87-01 and *Wakef* from 01. *17 Westminster Road, Halifax HX3 8DH* Tel (01422) 200844

BISHOP, Mrs Evelyn Joy. b 43. **d** 01 **p** 02. NSM Penkridge *Lich* 01-04; NSM Baswich from 04. *21 Farmdown Road, Stafford ST17 0AP* Tel (01785) 603074

BISHOP, Huw Daniel. b 49. Univ of Wales (Lamp) BA71. Bp Burgess Hall Lamp 71. **d** 73 **p** 74. C Carmarthen St Pet *St D* 73-77; Prov Youth Chapl Wales 77-79; V Llanybydder and Llanwenog w Llanwnnen 79-80; Youth and Community Officer 80-81; Hd RS Carre's Gr Sch Sleaford 81-85; Hd RS K Sch Pet 85-91; Assoc Hd Teacher St Pet Colleg Sch Wolv 91-98; Hd Teacher St Teilo's High Sch Cardiff 98-01; Prin St Pet Colleg Sch Wolv from 01; CF (TA) from 85. *St Peter's Collegiate School, Compton Road West, Wolverhampton WV3 9DU* Tel (01902) 558600

BISHOP, Ian Gregory. b 62. Portsm Poly BSc84 MRICS87. Oak Hill Th Coll BA91. **d** 91 **p** 92. C Purley Ch Ch *S'wark* 91-95; P-in-c Saxlingham Nethergate and Shotesham *Nor* 95-97; TR Newton Flotman, Swainsthorpe, Tasburgh, etc 98-01; V Middlewich w Byley *Ches* from 01; RD Middlewich from 05. *Poplar Fell, Nantwich Road, Middlewich CW10 9HG* Tel (01606) 833124 E-mail ian.bishop@live.com

BISHOP, Jeffrey Paul. b 67. Texas A&M Univ BA88 MD93 Dallas Univ MTh00. **d** 99 **p** 00. C Dallas Incarnation USA 99-05; Perm to Offic *Ex* 05-06; PV Ex Cathl 06-07; USA from 07. *1106 Lawrence Avenue, Nashville TN 37204, USA* Tel (001) (615) 942 7074

BISHOP, Jeremy Simon. b 54. Nottm Univ BSc75 Yonsei Univ S Korea 84. All Nations Chr Coll 82 Wycliffe Hall Ox 89. **d** 91 **p** 92. C Macclesfield Team *Ches* 91-98; R Carlton Colville w Mutford and Rushmere *Nor* 98-99; V Carlton Colville and Mutford from 99. *The Rectory, Rectory Road, Carlton Colville, Lowestoft NR33 8BB* Tel (01502) 565217
E-mail jbishop771@aol.com

BISHOP, John Charles Simeon. b 46. Chich Th Coll 77. **d** 79 **p** 79. SSF 66-86; P-in-c Edin St Dav 82-86; Chapl to the Deaf *Birm* 86-99; C Portsea N End St Mark *Portsm* 99-01; Chapl to the Deaf *Linc* from 01. *220 Boultham Park Road, Lincoln LN6 7SU* Tel and fax (01522) 787136 E-mail jcsbishop@btinternet.com

BISHOP, John David. b 36. Liv Univ BEng MIMechE. EMMTC. **d** 85 **p** 86. NSM Ockbrook *Derby* 85-07; Perm to Offic from 07. *143 Victoria Avenue, Borrowash, Derby DE7 3HF* Tel (01332) 663828

BISHOP, Kathleen Rachel. b 51. Open Univ BA88 Saffron Walden Coll CertEd76. ERMC 05. **d** 08 **p** 09. NSM Raddesley Gp *Ely* from 08. *4 The Woodlands, Linton, Cambridge CB21 4UF* Tel (01223) 892288 E-mail michael.bishop@virgin.net

BISHOP, Keith William. b 45. SEITE 00. **d** 03 **p** 04. NSM Balham St Mary and St Jo *S'wark* 03-07; NSM Clapham Common St Barn from 07. *43 Magdalen Road, London SW18 3ND* Tel (020) 8870 7267 E-mail keithwilliambishop@hotmail.com

BISHOP, Mark Andrew. b 58. Down Coll Cam BA80 MA83 Barrister 81. EAMTC 99. **d** 02 **p** 03. Dep Chan *Roch* from 01; NSM Cambridge St Mary Less *Ely* from 02. *10 Wordsworth Grove, Cambridge CB3 9HH* Tel (01223) 362281
E-mail markbishop@ukonline.co.uk

BISHOP, Mark Christopher. b 81. Sheff Hallam Univ BA03. **d** 08 **p** 09. C Oak Tree Angl Fellowship *Lon* from 08. *Flat 3, 25 Milton Road, London W3 6QA* Tel 07779-585105 (mobile)
E-mail bishop.mark@mac.com *or* markb@oaktree.org.uk

BISHOP, Philip Michael. b 47. Lon Univ BD69 AKC69. St Aug Coll Cant 70. **d** 71 **p** 72. C Mansfield Woodhouse *S'well* 71-76; C Liscard St Mary w St Columba *Ches* 76-78; V Thornton-le-Moors w Ince and Elton 78-90; V Sutton w Carlton and Normanton upon Trent etc *S'well* 90-96; P-in-c Ch Broughton w Barton Blount, Boylestone etc *Derby* 96-98; P-in-c Longford, Long Lane, Dalbury and Radbourne 96-98; R Boylestone, Church Broughton, Dalbury, etc from 98. *The Vicarage, Chapel Lane, Church Broughton, Derby DE65 5BB* Tel (01283) 585296
E-mail rev@michael.bishop.name

BISHOP, Phillip Leslie. b 44. K Coll Lon BD66 AKC66. **d** 67 **p** 68. C Albrighton *Lich* 67-70; C St Geo-in-the-East St Mary *Lon* 70-71; C Middlesbrough Ascension *York* 71-73; P-in-c Withernwick 73-77; Ind Chapl 73-82; V Gt Ayton w Easby and

Newton-in-Cleveland 82-89; RD Stokesley 85-89; R Guisborough 89-08; Chapl S Tees Community and Mental NHS Trust 90-99; Chapl Tees and NE Yorks NHS Trust 99-08; Chapl Langbaurgh Primary Care Trust 02-08; rtd 08; Perm to Offic *York* from 08. *2 Sunny Side Grove, Stockton-on-Tees TS18 5DH*

BISHOP, Roger John. b 49. SEITE 06. **d** 09. NSM Lamberhurst and Matfield *Roch* from 09. *Brambletye, Maidstone Road, Five Oak Green, Tonbridge TN12 6QR* Tel (01892) 833232
E-mail rogerjbishop@hotmail.com

BISHOP, Simeon. *See* BISHOP, John Charles Simeon

BISHOP, Stephen Craig. b 68. Wye Coll Lon BSc90 Man Univ MA92 Ex Univ MPhil97 Glos Univ PGCE98. Wycliffe Hall Ox 03. **d** 05 **p** 06. C Thornbury and Oldbury-on-Severn w Shepperdine *Glouc* 05-09; TV Fairford Deanery from 09. *The Vicarage, Coln St Aldwyns, Cirencester GL7 5AG* Tel (01285) 750013 E-mail scraigbishop@hotmail.com

BISHOP, Stephen John. b 62. Hull Univ BA84 PGCE86. Ripon Coll Cuddesdon 90 Ch Div Sch of the Pacific (USA) 90. **d** 92 **p** 93. C Syston *Leic* 92-95; C Market Harborough 95-97; TV Market Harborough and The Transfiguration etc 97-00; R Six Saints circa Holt from 00; Rural Officer (Leic Adnry) from 01. *The Rectory, Rectory Lane, Medbourne, Market Harborough LE16 8DZ* Tel (01858) 565933
E-mail stephenjbishop@btopenworld.com

BISHOP, Stephen Patrick. b 60. Dioc OLM tr scheme 99. **d** 02 **p** 03. OLM Purley Ch Ch *S'wark* from 02. *Elmwood, 117 Mitchley Avenue, South Croydon CR2 9HP* Tel (020) 8651 2840 *or* 7337 3135 E-mail elmwood@tinyonline.co.uk

BISHOP, Miss Waveney Joyce. b 38. Westf Coll Lon BSc60. Cranmer Hall Dur. **dss** 82 **d** 87 **p** 94. Leyton St Mary w St Edw *Chelmsf* 82-84; Bishopsworth *Bris* 84-96; Hon Par Dn 87-94; Hon C 94-96; rtd 96; Perm to Offic *Bris* 96-99 and *B &W* from 98. *14 Sayley Close, Clevedon BS21 7YF* Tel (01275) 343533

BISIG (née BOULNOIS), Linda Dianne. b 59. Trin Coll Bris 92. **d** 96 **p** 97. C Brampton Bierlow *Sheff* 96-99; Asst Chapl Berne w Neuchâtel *Eur* from 00. *Jubiläumsplatz 2, CH-3066 Bern, Switzerland* Tel (0041) (31) 352 8567 Fax 351 0548

BISSET, Michael Davidson. b 55. NTMTC 96. **d** 99 **p** 00. C Ickenham *Lon* 99-03; P-in-c Penn *Ox* 03-04; P-in-c Tyler's Green 03-04; V Penn and Tylers Green from 04. *The Vicarage, Church Road, Penn, High Wycombe HP10 8NU* Tel (01895) 676092
E-mail mike.bisset@talk21.com

BISSET, Canon Robert McBain. b 05. Glas Univ MA30. Edin Th Coll 30. **d** 32 **p** 33. C Glas St Cuth 32-37; I Glas St Luke 37-41; R Lanark 41-47; R Bearsden 47-73; R Milngavie 56-73; Can St Mary's Cathl 62-73; rtd 73; Hon Can St Mary's Cathl from 77. *Rannoch Lodge, Rannoch Drive, Cumbernauld, Glasgow G67 4EP* Tel (01236) 729273

BISSEX, Mrs Janet Christine Margaret. b 50. Westhill Coll Birm CertEd72. Trin Coll Bris 76. **dss** 86 **d** 87 **p** 94. Toxteth Park St Bede *Liv* 86-93; Par Dn 87-93; Dn-in-c Kirkdale St Mary and St Athanasius 93-94; P-in-c 94-03; C Litherland St Andr 03; TV Bootle from 04. *The Vicarage, 4 St Andrews Road, Bootle L20 5EX* Tel 0151-922 7916 Fax 944 1121

BISSON, Joyce Elaine. b 52. Liv Univ BTh98 Nottm Coll of Educn TCert73. NOC 06. **d** 08 **p** 09. NSM Gt Meols *Ches* from 08. *14 Howbeck Drive, Prenton CH43 6UY* Tel 0151-652 7888
E-mail elainebisson@yahoo.co.uk

BLACK, Canon Alexander Stevenson. b 28. Glas Univ MA53. Edin Th Coll 53. **d** 55 **p** 56. C Dumfries *Glas* 55-58; Chapl Glas Univ 58-61, C Glas St Mary 58-61; P-in-c E Kilbride 61-69; R Edin St Columba 69-79; TV Edin St Jo 79-83; R Haddington 83-93; R Dunbar 83-93; Can St Mary's Cathl from 88; rtd 93. *3 Bass Rock View, Canty Bay, North Berwick EH39 5PJ* Tel (01620) 894771 E-mail maags@tiscali.co.uk

BLACK, Dominic Paul. b 70. S Bank Univ BSc95 St Jo Coll Dur BA98. Cranmer Hall Dur 95. **d** 98 **p** 99. C N Hull St Mich *York* 98-04; V N Ormesby from 04. *The Vicarage, James Street, North Ormesby, Middlesbrough TS3 6LD* Tel (01642) 271814

BLACK, Douglas John. b 58. Middx Poly BA80. Ridley Hall Cam 89. **d** 91 **p** 92. C Wrexham *St As* 91-01; Chapl NE Wales Inst of HE 93-01; V Thelwall *Ches* from 01. *All Saints' Vicarage, Bell Lane, Thelwall, Warrington WA4 2SX* Tel (01925) 261166
E-mail revdouglasblack@aol.com

BLACK, Canon Ian Christopher. b 62. Kent Univ BA85 Nottm Univ MDiv93. Linc Th Coll 91. **d** 93 **p** 94. C Maidstone All SS and St Phil w Tovil *Cant* 93-96; P-in-c The Brents and Davington w Oare and Luddenham 96-02; Hon Min Can Cant Cathl 97-02; Asst Dir Post-Ord Tr 98-02; V Whitkirk *Ripon* from 02; Capitular Can Ripon Cathl from 08. *Whitkirk Vicarage, 386 Selby Road, Leeds LS15 0AA* Tel 0113-264 5790
E-mail vicar.whitkirk@btinternet.com

BLACK, Ian Forbes. b 29. St Aid Birkenhead 55. **d** 58 **p** 59. C Bramhall *Ches* 58-61; C Witton 61-63; P-in-c Prestonpans *Edin* 63-68; R Edin Ch Ch-St Jas 68-71; Asst Chapl HM Pris Liv *11-12*; Chapl HM Pris Haverigg 72-73; R Bootle w Corney *Carl* 73-75; P-in-c Whicham w Whitbeck 73-75; R Bootle, Corney, Whicham and Whitbeck 75-86; P-in-c Orton St Giles 86-89; R 89-94; P-in-c Aikton 86-89; R 89-94; rtd 94; Perm to Offic *Carl*

from 98. *Solwayside, Port Carlisle, Wigton CA7 5BU* Tel (01697) 351964

BLACK (formerly NAPIER), Jennifer Beryl. b 39. S Dios Minl Tr Scheme 89. **d** 93 **p** 96. NSM Itchen Valley *Win* 93-01; Perm to Offic 02-05; C Cupar *St And* from 05. *Edenwood, Cupar KY15 5NX* Tel (01334) 653159

BLACK, Canon Leonard Albert. b 49. Edin Th Coll 69. **d** 72 **p** 73. C Aberdeen St Marg 72-75; Chapl St Paul's Cathl Dundee 75-77; P-in-c Aberdeen St Ninian 77-80; N Area Chapl Miss to Seafarers 80-03; R Inverness St Mich *Mor* from 80; R Inverness St Jo 80-87; P-in-c Balloch New Town Distr 80-87; Relig Progr Producer Moray Firth Radio 87-03; Syn Clerk and Can St Andr Cathl Inverness 92-03; Hon Can from 03; Dean Mor 03-09; Perm to Offic The Murray Australia from 06. *St Michael's Rectory, 28 Abban Street, Inverness IV3 8HH* Tel and fax (01463) 233797 Mobile 07836-365719 E-mail fr.len@angelforce.co.uk

BLACK, Canon Neville. b 36. MBE97. Oak Hill Th Coll 61. **d** 64 **p** 65. C Everton St Ambrose w St Tim *Liv* 64-69; P-in-c Everton St Geo 69-71; V 71-81; P-in-c Everton St Benedict 70-72; P-in-c Everton St Chad w Ch Ch 70-72; Nat Project Officer Evang Urban Tr Project 74-81; TR St Luke in the City 81-04; Chapl Liv Women's Hosp 82-92; Chapl Liv Women's Hosp NHS Trust 92-04; Tutor NOC 82-89; Dir Gp for Urban Min and Leadership *Liv* 84-95; Hon Can Liv Cathl 87-04; P-in-c Edgehill St Dunstan 98-02; rtd 02. *445 Aigburth Road, Liverpool L19 3PA* Tel 0151-427 9803 Fax 494 0736 Pager 07699-727640
E-mail neville.black@btinternet.com

BLACK, Canon Robert John Edward Francis Butler. b 41. TCD BA65 HDipEd70 MA85. CITC 66. **d** 66 **p** 67. C Jordanstown *Conn* 66-68; C Dublin St Steph and St Ann *D & G* 68-73; C Stillorgan w Blackrock 73-85; Hd Master Dundalk Gr Sch *Arm* 85-96; Lic to Offic from 85; Hd Master Kilkenny Coll *C & O* from 96; Can Ossory Cathl from 96. *Kilkenny College, Kilkenny, Co Kilkenny, Republic of Ireland* Tel (00353) (56) 772 2213 *or* 776 1544 Fax 777 0918 E-mail robertblack05@eircom.net

BLACK, Samuel James. b 38. CITC. **d** 68 **p** 69. C Cloughfern *Conn* 68-72; C Lisburn St Paul 72-78; I Rasharkin w Finvoy 78-82; I Belfast Upper Malone (Epiphany) 82-95; I Ballymore *Arm* 95-05; rtd 05. *Toberhewny Hall, 22 Toberhewny Lane, Lurgan, Craigavon BT66 8JZ* Tel (028) 3834 3267

BLACK, William Henry. St Deiniol's Hawarden. **d** 88 **p** 89. NSM Malahide w Balgriffin *D & G* 88-89; NSM Dublin St Ann and St Steph 89-94; C 94-00; Hon Asst Chapl Miss to Seamen 89-00; I Dublin Drumcondra w N Strand *D & G* 00-07; rtd 07. *27 Greendale Avenue, Dublin 5, Republic of Ireland* Tel (00353) (1) 832 3141 Mobile 86-150 3747
E-mail willieblack@eircom.net

BLACKALL, Mrs Margaret Ivy. b 38. St Kath Coll Lon CertEd58. EAMTC 82. **dss** 86 **d** 87 **p** 94. NSM Wickham Market w Pettistree and Easton *St E* 86-88; Par Dn Leiston 88-92; Par Dn Gt and Lt Glemham, Blaxhall etc 92-94; P-in-c 94-96; R 96-02; P-in-c Sternfield w Benhall and Snape 98-02; rtd 03; Perm to Offic *St E* from 03. *6 Orchard Place, Wickham Market, Woodbridge IP13 0RU* Tel (01728) 747326 Mobile 07850-632900 E-mail mgtblack@globalnet.co.uk

BLACKALL, Robin Jeremy McRae. b 35. Ridley Hall Cam 67. **d** 69 **p** 70. C Stowmarket *St E* 69-72; R Stanstead w Shimplingthorne and Alpheton 72-77; R Bradwell on Sea *Chelmsf* 77-79; R St Lawrence 77-79; Warden Bede Ho Staplehurst 79-81; Chapl HM Det Cen Blantyre Ho 81-82; R Edith Weston w N Luffenham and Lyndon w Manton *Pet* 86-95; P-in-c Upwell St Pet *Ely* 95-99; Dioc Rural Miss Officer 95-01; P-in-c Barton Bendish w Beachamwell and Shingham 99-01; P-in-c Boughton 99-01; P-in-c Wereham 99-01; rtd 01; Perm to Offic *Ely* from 01 and *Nor* from 02. *The Pightle House, Eastmoor Road, Eastmoor, Oxborough, King's Lynn PE33 9PZ* Tel (01366) 328663 Fax 328163
E-mail rjmb@globalnet.co.uk

BLACKALL, Susan Elizabeth. b 52. Qu Univ Kingston Ontario BA74 MA75 CCC Ox DPhil82. SEITE 00. **d** 03 **p** 04. NSM Eltham St Barn *S'wark* from 03. *8 Park Place House, Park Vista, London SE10 9ND* Tel (020) 8853 3302 *or* 7656 5000
E-mail s.blackall@research-int.com

BLACKBURN, David James. b 45. Hull Univ BA67. Trin Coll Bris 85. **d** 87 **p** 88. C Bromsgrove St Jo *Worc* 87-90; V Cradley 90-01; R Kinver and Enville *Lich* from 01. *The Vicarage, Vicarage Drive, Kinver, Stourbridge DY7 6HJ* Tel (01384) 872556

BLACKBURN, Frederick John Barrie. b 28. TD73. Lich Th Coll 52. **d** 55 **p** 56. C Hebburn St Cuth *Dur* 55-58; C Bishopwearmouth St Mary V w St Pet CD 58-61; C Hunwick 61-64; CF (TA) 61-87; V Eighton Banks *Dur* 64-75; R Stella 75-87; TV Bellingham/Otterburn Gp *Newc* 87-89; rtd 89. *26 Kepier Chare, Ryton NE40 4UW* Tel and fax 0191-413 7365 Mobile 07745-028780

BLACKBURN, Helen Claire. b 55. Leeds Univ BA76 MA99 PGCE78 ARCM72. NOC 96. **d** 99 **p** 00. C Sheff Cathl 99-01; Asst Chapl Cen Sheff Univ Hosps NHS Trust 01-04; Chapl Sheff Teaching Hosps NHS Trust 04-06; C Ranmoor *Sheff*

06-07; P-in-c Abbeydale St Jo from 07. *34 Wilson Road, Sheffield S11 8RN* Tel 0114-266 6009
E-mail helen_blackburn@hotmail.co.uk

BLACKBURN, The Ven John. b 47. CB04. Open Univ BA88. St Mich Coll Llan 66. **d** 71 **p** 72. C Risca *Mon* 71-76; CF (TA) 73-76; CF 76-99; Dep Chapl Gen 99-00; Chapl Gen 00-04; Adn for the Army 99-04; QHC from 96; Hon Can Ripon Cathl 01-04; V Risca *Mon* from 04. *The Vicarage, 1 Gelli Crescent, Risca, Newport NP11 6QG* Tel (01633) 612307
E-mail northmanor@btinternet.com

BLACKBURN, Sister Judith Elizabeth. b 58. SEITE 99. **d** 02 **p** 03. NSM Old Ford St Paul and St Mark *Lon* 02-05; P-in-c Bethnal Green St Pet w St Thos from 05. *St Saviour's Priory, 18 Queensbridge Road, London E2 8NX* Tel (020) 7739 9976 Mobile 07855-510393 E-mail judithblackburn@aol.com

BLACKBURN, Keith Christopher. b 39. K Coll Lon BD63 AKC63. St Boniface Warminster 63. **d** 64 **p** 65. C Surbiton St Andr *S'wark* 64-66; C Battersea St Mary 67-70; Teacher Sir Walter St John Sch Battersea 67-70; Hon C Eltham H Trin 70-76; Hd of Ho Crown Woods Sch Eltham 70-76; Dep Hd Master Altwood C of E Sch 76-82; Chapl and Hd Master St Geo Sch Gravesend 83-93; Hon C Fawkham and Hartley *Roch* 83-93; V Seal St Pet 93-05; rtd 05; Perm to Offic *Heref* from 05. *The Tythe Barn, St Weonards, Hereford HR2 8NT* Tel (01981) 580389 E-mail revkcb@aol.com

BLACKBURN, Peter James Whittaker. b 47. Sydney Univ BA69. Coll of Resurr Mirfield. **d** 72 **p** 73. C Felixstowe St Jo *St E* 72-76; C Bournemouth St Pet w St Swithun, H Trin etc *Win* 76-79; R Burythorpe, Acklam and Leavening w Westow *York* 79-85; Chapl Naples Ch Ch *Eur* 85-91; Chapl Algarve 91-97; Perm to Offic *Lon* 07-09; Hon C Hampstead Ch Ch from 09. *8 Hampstead Square, London NW3 1AB* Tel (020) 7435 5818 E-mail peter.blackburn@virgilio.it

BLACKBURN, The Ven Richard Finn. b 52. St Jo Coll Dur BA74 Hull Univ MA97. Westcott Ho Cam 81. **d** 83 **p** 84. C Stepney St Dunstan and All SS *Lon* 83-87; P-in-c Isleworth St Jo 87-92; V Mosbrough *Sheff* 92-99; RD Attercliffe 96-99; Hon Can Sheff Cathl 98-99; Adn Sheff and Rotherham from 99; Can Res Sheff Cathl 99-05. *34 Wilson Road, Sheffield S11 8RN* Tel 0114-266 6009 *or* (01709) 309110 Fax (01709) 309107
E-mail archdeacons.office@sheffield.anglican.org

BLACKBURN, Archdeacon of. See HAWLEY, The Ven John Andrew

BLACKBURN, Bishop of. See READE, The Rt Revd Nicholas Stewart

BLACKBURN, Dean of. See ARMSTRONG, The Very Revd Christopher John

BLACKDEN, Mrs Diane Janice. b 40. **d** 06. NSM Buxted and Hadlow Down *Chich* from 06. *Oak Hill, Five Ashes, Mayfield TN20 6HL* Tel (01435) 872082

BLACKER, Herbert John. b 36. Bris Univ BSc59. Cranmer Hall Dur. **d** 61 **p** 62. C Wednesbury St Bart *Lich* 61-63; C Chasetown 63-65; C Chigwell *Chelmsf* 65-69; TV Barnham Broom w Kimberley, Bixton etc *Nor* 69-76; R Burgh Parva w Briston 76-92; P-in-c Melton Constable w Swanton Novers 86-92; R Briston w Burgh Parva and Melton Constable 92-01; rtd 01; Perm to Offic *Nor* from 01 and *St E* from 04. *8 Lloyds Avenue, Kessingland, Lowestoft NR33 7TP*

BLACKETT, James Gilbert. b 27. Tyndale Hall Bris 52. **d** 55 **p** 56. C Heworth H Trin *York* 55-57; C Newburn *Newc* 57-58; C Newc St Barn and St Jude 58-61; V Broomfleet *York* 61-67; V Ledsham 67-74; V Burton All SS *Lich* 74-82; V Burton All SS w Ch 82-92; rtd 92; Perm to Offic *Ox* and *Pet* from 92. *103 Milford Avenue, Stony Stratford, Milton Keynes MK11 1EZ* Tel (01908) 265149

BLACKETT, Robert Peter. b 63. Dur Univ BSc85 Open Univ BSc07. Ripon Coll Cuddesdon BTh95. **d** 95 **p** 96. C Wigton *Carl* 95-00; R Bowness-on-Solway, Kirkbride and Newton Arlosh from 00. *The Rectory, Church Road, Kirkbride, Carlisle CA7 5HY* Tel (01697) 351256

BLACKFORD, Barry Douglas. b 52. Southn Inst BSc96 MCMI00 MBCS04. STETS 05. **d** 08 **p** 09. C N Poole Ecum Team *Sarum* from 08. *6 Wingfield Avenue, Oakdale, Poole BH15 3DQ* Tel 07866-430428 (mobile)
E-mail bdblackford@hotmail.com

BLACKFORD, David Walker. b 25. **d** 70 **p** 71. C Holyhead w Rhoscolyn w Llanfair-yn-Neubwll *Ban* 70-72; Lic to Offic *Blackb* 72-80; Hon C Bassaleg *Mon* 80-85; V Treuddyn and Nercwys and Eryrys *St As* 85-90; Lic to Offic *Mon* from 99. *11 Whitechapel Walk, Undy, Caldicot NP26 3NS* Tel (01633) 880507

BLACKIE, Richard Footner (Brother Edmund). b 37. St Cath Coll Cam BA59 MA63 Worc Coll Ox BA59 BSc61. Ely Th Coll 60. **d** 62 **p** 63. C Saffron Walden *Chelmsf* 62-65; SSF from 66. *Society of St Francis, 42 Balaam Street, London E13 8AQ* Tel (020) 7476 5189

BLACKLEDGE, David John. b 51. Oak Hill Th Coll 89. **d** 92 **p** 93. NSM Woodford Wells *Chelmsf* from 92. *Hornbeam, 143 Monkhams Lane, Woodford Green IG8 0NW* Tel (020) 8262 7690
E-mail davidjblackledge@aol.com

BLACKLEDGE, Philip Vincent Patrick. b 74. Edin Univ BMus92 BD02. TISEC 99. **d** 02 **p** 03. C Edin St Mary 02-06; Chapl St Mary's Cathl 03-06; P-in-c Linlithgow from 06; P-in-c Bathgate from 06. *The Rectory, 85 Acredales, Linlithgow EH49 6JA* Tel (01506) 848726
E-mail philipblackledge@aol.com

BLACKLEY, Miles. b 69. Wycliffe Hall Ox. **d** 05 **p** 06. C Ches Square St Mich w St Phil *Lon* 05-08; C St Olave Hart Street w All Hallows Staining etc from 08; C St Kath Cree from 08. *Church Flat, All Hallows by the Tower, Byward Street, London EC3R 5BJ* Tel (020) 7488 4318 E-mail milesblackley@hotmail.com

BLACKMAN, Brian David Eric. b 38. Ox NSM Course 82. **d** 85 **p** 86. NSM Reading St Luke *Ox* 85-86; NSM Reading St Luke w St Bart 86-08; Perm to Offic from 08. *13 Avebury Square, Reading RG1 5JH* Tel 0118-926 0345

BLACKMAN (née PRATT), Christine Fiona. b 60. Reading Univ BSc81. Ox Min Course 88. **d** 91 **p** 94. NSM Reading St Luke w St Bart *Ox* 91-94; NSM Earley St Pet 94-95; NSM Reading St Luke w St Bart from 95. *13 Avebury Square, Reading RG1 5JH* Tel 0118-926 0345

BLACKMAN, Clive John. b 51. Hull Univ BSc73 MSc74. Qu Coll Birm 75. **d** 78 **p** 79. C Folkestone St Sav *Cant* 78-81; Chapl Birm Univ 81-86; V Thorpe St Matt *Nor* 86-94; R Cringleford w Colney and Bawburgh 94-98; Asst Dir Lay and Reader Tr 98-03; Chapl Nor City Coll of F&HE from 03. *13 Norvic Drive, Norwich NR4 7NN* Tel (01603) 505776
E-mail cliveblackman@norwich.anglican.org

BLACKMAN, John Franklyn. b 34. LRAM70. S'wark Ord Course 72. **d** 75 **p** 76. NSM Cov H Trin 75-81; Succ Cov Cathl 81-95; TV Cov E 88-95; rtd 98; Perm to Offic *Newc* 98-01. *1 Old Deanery Close, Minster Road, Ripon HG4 1LZ*

BLACKMAN, Michael Orville. b 46. Univ of W Ontario BMin80. Codrington Coll Barbados 67. **d** 71 **p** 71. C St Jo Cathl Antigua 71-73; R H Innocents w St Sav Barbados 73-78; Hon C Westminster St Jas Canada 78-80; P-in-c St Patr Barbados 80-86; TV E Ham w Upton Park St Alb *Chelmsf* 86-91; R St Pet Barbados 91-97; V Dalton *Sheff* 97-03; P-in-c S Wimbledon All SS *S'wark* from 03; P-in-c Raynes Park St Sav from 03. *St Saviour's Vicarage, Church Walk, London SW20 9DW* Tel (020) 8542 2787 E-mail michael.blackman1@btopenworld.com

BLACKMAN, Peter Richard. b 28. Sarum Th Coll 52. **d** 55 **p** 56. C Aylestone *Leic* 55-60; V Ratby cum Groby 60-84; TR 84-93; rtd 93; Perm to Offic *Chich* from 93. *25 Turnbull Road, Chichester PO19 7LY* Tel (01243) 787299

BLACKMORE, Frank Ellis. b 43. Univ of Wales (Lamp) BA66. Wells Th Coll 65. **d** 67 **p** 68. C S'wark St Geo 67-70; Hon C Camberwell St Giles 70-79; NSM Paddington St Sav *Lon* from 79. *37 Leith Mansions, Grantully Road, London W9 1LH* Tel (020) 7289 3020 E-mail ellisblackmore@btinternet.com

BLACKMORE, Robert Ivor. b 37. Univ of Wales (Lamp) 59 Open Univ BA78 Univ of Wales MTh94. **d** 62 **p** 63. C Llangynwyd w Maesteg 62-65; C Dowlais 65-67; C Neath w Llantwit 67-71; V Fochriw w Deri 71-73; V Troedrhiwgarth 73-80; V Seven Sisters 80-00; rtd 02. *Cefnforest, Bethlehem, Llandeilo SA19 6YL* Tel (01550) 777543

BLACKMORE, Vernon John. b 50. Southn Univ BSc Man Univ MSc K Coll Lon MTh. Oak Hill Th Coll. **d** 82 **p** 83. C Ecclesall *Sheff* 82-87; Bp's Adv on Youth 85-87; Ed Lion Publishing 87-90; Dir Publications, Tr and Sales CPAS 90-99. *6 Guy Street, Warwick CV34 4LN* Tel (01926) 498351

BLACKSHAW, Brian Martin. b 43. Lanc Univ MA74 Ch Ch Ox BA95 MA96. Ox NSM Course 87. **d** 90 **p** 91. NSM Amersham *Ox* 90-93; C Hatch End St Anselm *Lon* 93-95; V Cheshunt *St Alb* 96-07; rtd 07. *Holly Bush, Flaunden Lane, Flaunden, Hemel Hempstead HP3 0PQ* Tel (01442) 832254
E-mail brianblackshaw@f2s.com

BLACKSHAW, Trevor Roland. b 36. GIMechE59. Lon Coll of Div 67. **d** 69 **p** 70. C New Catton St Luke *Nor* 69-73; C Luton Lewsey St Hugh *St Alb* 73-78; V Llandinam w Trefeglwys w Penstrowed *Ban* 78-85; Dioc Dir of Adult Educn 83-85; Consultant Dir Wholeness Through Ch Min 86-92; Midl Regional Co-ord Crosslinks 92-97; Dir and Warden Divine Healing Miss Crowhurst 97-02; Perm to Offic *Lich* 04-06 and from 07; P-in-c Weston Rhyn and Selattyn 06-07. *Mayland, 2 Balmoral Crescent, Oswestry SY11 2XG* Tel (01691) 659645 E-mail trevor@blackshawt.freeserve.co.uk

BLACKTOP, Graham Leonard. b 33. St Alb Minl Tr Scheme 82. **d** 85 **p** 86. NSM Rickmansworth *St Alb* 85-92; Perm to Offic *Sarum* 92-08. *Dairy House, Wolfeton, Dorchester DT2 9QN* Tel and fax (01305) 262184

BLACKWALL, David d'Arcy Russell. b 35. Southn Univ BSc60. Wycliffe Hall Ox 63. **d** 65 **p** 66. C Southampton Thornhill St Chris *Win* 65-68; V Long Sutton 69-72; Chapl Ld Wandsworth Coll Hants 69-74; Hon C Odiham w S Warnborough *Win* 72-75; Chapl St Lawr Coll Ramsgate 75-95; Hd Jun Sch 95-97; rtd 97; Perm to Offic *Sarum* from 98. *Cookwell, Back Lane, Okeford Fitzpaine, Blandford Forum DT11 0RD* Tel (01258) 860157

BLACKWELL, Geoffrey Albert. b 27. Lon Coll of Div 62. **d** 65 **p** 66. C Clifton *York* 65-69; Chapl RN 69-73; Warden St Mich Home of Healing Cleadon 73-75; V S Hetton *Dur* 75-82; CSWG 83-94; P-in-c Burpham *Chich* 95-96; rtd 96; Perm to Offic *Chich* from 96. *1 Highfield Gardens, Rustington, Littlehampton BN16 2PZ* Tel (01903) 782219

BLACKWELL, Geoffrey David. b 34. Jes Coll Ox BA57 MA61. Chich Th Coll 57. **d** 59 **p** 60. C Romford St Edw *Chelmsf* 59-62; Chapl St Paul's Coll Grahamstown S Africa 62-68; Chapl Westcott Ho Cam 68-73; V Forest Gate St Edm *Chelmsf* 73-81; Pilsdon Community 83-95; rtd 94; Perm to Offic *Pet* from 94. *15 Chatsfield, Werrington, Peterborough PE4 5DJ* Tel (01733) 324278

BLACKWELL, Nicholas Alfred John. b 54. Warwick Univ MA97. St Jo Coll Nottm BTh85. **d** 85 **p** 86. C Birkenhead Priory *Ches* 85-88; C Stratford-on-Avon w Bishopton *Cov* 88-91; TV Cov E 91-98. *74 Brays Lane, Coventry CV2 4DW* Tel (024) 7626 1161

BLACKWELL-SMYTH, Charles Peter Bernard. b 42. TCD BA64 MA71 MB73. Gen Th Sem (NY) MDiv65. **d** 65 **p** 66. C Bangor Abbey *D & D* 65-67; C Dublin Ch Ch Leeson Park *D & G* 67-69; P-in-c Carbury *M & K* 73-75; Hon C St Stephen in Brannel *Truro* 87-94; Perm to Offic from 94. *Parcgwyn, Rectory Road, St Stephen, St Austell PL26 7RL* Tel (01726) 822465

BLACOE, Brian Thomas. b 36. Open Univ BA. Oak Hill Th Coll 63. **d** 66 **p** 67. C Dundonald *D & D* 66-69; C Drumcree *Arm* 69-74; I Ardtrea w Desertcreat 74-78; I Annalong *D & D* 78-95; I Knocknamuckley 95-08; Can Dromore Cathl 93-08; Prec 02-08; rtd 08. *91 Richmond Drive, Tandragee, Craigavon BT62 2JJ* Tel 07745-564056 (mobile) E-mail eablacoe@tiscali.co.uk

BLADE, Brian Alan. b 24. ACCS55 ASCA66. Roch Th Coll 67. **d** 69 **p** 70. C Barnehurst *Roch* 69-71; C Crayford 71-76; V Buttershaw St Aid *Bradf* 76-80; R Etton w Helpston *Pet* 80-86; V Hardingstone and Horton and Piddington 86-90; rtd 90; Perm to Offic *Cant* and *Roch* from 90. *25 Dan Drive, Faversham ME13 7SW* Tel (01795) 531842
E-mail revbrianblade@tesco.net

BLADE, Mrs Susan Joan. b 58. SEITE. **d** 00 **p** 01. NSM Wateringbury and Teston *Roch* 00-02; Asst Chapl Maidstone and Tunbridge Wells NHS Trust 00-02; Sen Chapl 02-06; Chapl Cant Ch Ch Univ from 07; Perm to Offic *Roch* from 03. *Eagle Lodge, Mill Lane, Wateringbury, Maidstone ME18 5PE* Tel (01622) 812581 E-mail sue@inwateringbury.fsnet.co.uk

BLAGDEN, Ms Susan. b 64. Ox Min Course 89 Ripon Coll Cuddesdon 97. **d** 99 **p** 00. C Grantham *Linc* 99-03; Asst Chapl Stoke Mandeville Hosp NHS Trust from 03. *Stoke Mandeville Hospital, Mandeville Road, Aylesbury HP21 8AL* Tel (01296) 315000

BLAGG, Colin. b 31. Leeds Univ BA57. Coll of Resurr Mirfield 57. **d** 59 **p** 60. C Edin Old St Paul 59-63; R Gourock *Glas* 63-68; Chapl to the Deaf RADD Lon 68-74; Hon C Stoke Newington St Olave *Lon* 73-74; Chapl to the Deaf *Chich* 74-80; V Shoreham Beach 80-96; rtd 97; Perm to Offic *Chich* from 97. *82 Buckingham Court, Shrubbs Drive, Bognor Regis PO22 7SF* Tel (01243) 855166

BLAIN, Anne Sharon. b 46. RGN89. Dioc OLM tr scheme 98. **d** 01 **p** 02. OLM Tadworth *S'wark* from 01. *Watts Cottage, Watts Lane, Tadworth KT20 5RW* Tel (01737) 355347 Fax 351546 Mobile 07811-267238 E-mail breusis@aol.com

BLAIR, Mrs Catherine Jill. b 62. Nottm Univ BA84 BArch87 RIBA88. St Jo Coll Nottm MA02. **d** 02 **p** 03. C Goldsworth Park *Guildf* 02-06; C Woking St Paul from 06. *St Paul's Vicarage, Pembroke Road, Woking GU22 7ED* Tel (01483) 772081 E-mail cathy.blair@tiscali.co.uk

BLAIR, Henry. See BLAIR, William Henry

BLAIR, Canon John Wallace. b 48. Lon Univ BSc70. Qu Coll Birm 79. **d** 81 **p** 82. C Chorlton-cum-Hardy St Werburgh *Man* 81-83; CF 83-97; I Faughanvale *D & R* from 97; Can Derry Cathl from 09. *21 Main Street, Eglinton, Londonderry BT47 3AB* Tel (028) 7181 0217

BLAIR, Jonathan Lewis. b 62. Nottm Univ BA84 ACA88. St Jo Coll Nottm. **d** 02 **p** 03. C Goldsworth Park *Guildf* 02-06; P-in-c Woking St Paul from 06. *St Paul's Vicarage, Pembroke Road, Woking GU22 7ED* Tel (01483) 772081 *or* 888611 E-mail jonny.blair@tiscali.co.uk

BLAIR, Patrick Allen. b 31. Trin Coll Cam BA54 MA58. Ridley Hall Cam 54. **d** 56 **p** 57. C Harwell *Ox* 56-59; Chapl Oundle Sch 59-64; Tutor St Geo Coll and Chapl to Abp in Jerusalem 64-66; Provost Khartoum Sudan 67-71; R Chester le Street *Dur* 71-77; TR Barking St Marg w St Patr *Chelmsf* 77-87; Chapl Barking Hosp 77-87; Chapl Tunis 87-91; Provost Nicosia Cyprus 91-96; rtd 96. *Grace Cottage, Pilley Green, Boldre, Lymington SO41 5QG* Tel (01590) 677015

BLAIR, Philip Hugh. b 39. St Edm Hall Ox BA62 MA67 Ex Univ DipEd75 PhD84. Ridley Hall Cam 62. **d** 64 **p** 65. C Camborne *Truro* 64-68; C Kenwyn 68-70; Sudan 70-73; P-in-c Probus *Truro* 73-74; P-in-c St Enoder 74-75; Perm to Offic Cyprus and the

Gulf 90-94; rtd 04. *St Martin's, 121 Newland, Sherborne DT9 3DU* Tel and fax (01935) 816022
E-mail philip@philipblair.net

BLAIR, William Henry. b 66. QUB BAgr89 TCD BTh04. CITC 01. **d** 04 **p** 05. C Monaghan w Tydavnet and Kilmore *Clogh* 04-06; C Magheraculmoney from 06. *The Rectory, 47 Main Street, Kesh, Enniskillen BT93 1TF* Tel (028) 6863 1820
E-mail henryblair@utvinternet.co.uk

BLAIR-CHAPPELL, Mrs Elcineide. b 47. Sao Paulo Univ Brazil 74 Birm Poly PGCE88. WMMTC 00. **d** 03 **p** 04. NSM Erdington *Birm* from 03; NSM Birm St Martin w Bordesley St Andr from 08; Hon Chapl Birm Children's Hosp NHS Trust from 07. *18 Kempson Avenue, Sutton Coldfield B72 1HJ* Tel 0121-682 5340

BLAIR-FISH, Canon John Christopher. b 20. Linc Coll Ox BA46 MA47. Cuddesdon Coll 48. **d** 49 **p** 50. C Mottingham St Andr *S'wark* 49-51; C Warlingham w Chelsham 51-55; V Surbiton St Mark 55-72; R Chipstead 73-89; Hon Can S'wark Cathl 79-88; rtd 89; Perm to Offic *Chich* from 93. *39 Beehive Lane, Ferring, Worthing BN12 5NR* Tel (01903) 241480

BLAKE, Colin David. b 52. Rolle Coll CertEd Ex Univ BEd Lon Univ BD. Trin Coll Bris 81. **d** 84 **p** 85. C Hucclecote *Glouc* 84-88; C Patchway and Min Bradley Stoke N CD *Bris* 88-00; TV Worle *B & W* from 00. *6 Gannet Road, Worle, Weston-super-Mare BS22 8UR* Tel (01934) 521765 E-mail colinblake1@aol.com

BLAKE, Ian Martyn. b 57. BA79. Oak Hill Th Coll 76. **d** 80 **p** 81. C Widford *Chelmsf* 80-84; C Barton Seagrave w Warkton *Pet* 84-90; V Sneinton St Chris w St Phil *S'well* 90-01; C Howell Hill w Burgh Heath *Guildf* 01-06; Perm to Offic *Guildf* from 06 and *S'wark* from 08. *87 Ambleside Gardens, Sutton SM2 5HN* Tel (020) 8643 2817 Mobile 07904-340783
E-mail ianneblake@yahoo.co.uk

BLAKE, Mrs Margaret. b 48. Open Univ BA87. S'wark Ord Course 92. **d** 95 **p** 96. C Farnham *Guildf* 95-01; P-in-c Farncombe 01-05; R 05-09; rtd 09. *Haul y Bryn, Llanfihangel Nant Bran, Brecon LD3 9NA* Tel (01874) 636390
E-mail revmargaretblake@aol.com

BLAKE, Preb Patrick John. b 30. Univ of Wales BA51 DipEd52 St Edm Hall Ox BA54 MA58. St Mich Coll Llan 54. **d** 55 **p** 56. C Buckley *St As* 55-59; C Oystermouth *S & B* 59-63; V Cleeve *B & W* 63-71; R Bruton w Lamyatt, Wyke and Redlynch 71-83; Dioc Ecum Officer 79-84; Preb Wells Cathl 79-03; TR Yeovil 83-88; P-in-c Backwell 88-89; R 89-92; R Backwell w Chelvey and Brockley 92-95; RD Portishead 92-95; rtd 95; Perm to Offic *B & W* from 95; Clergy Retirement and Widows' Officer 96-06. *The Firs, 47 Lower Street, Merriott TA16 5NN* Tel (01460) 78932

BLAKE, Peta Ruth. b 44. Lambeth STh89 Episc Div Sch Cam Mass MA89 DMin90. Trin Coll Bris 82. **dss** 83 **d** 87. New Swindon St Barn Gorse Hill *Bris* 83-88; Par Dn 87-88; Perm to Offic 88-93. *303 Beckett Condo, 220 Beckett Street, Arcadia, Pretoria, 0083 South Africa*

BLAKE, Philip Charles. b 29. Mitchell Coll of Adv Educn (NSW) BA80 Macquarie Univ (NSW) MA86 FAIWCW88 MACC88. Oak Hill Th Coll 54. **d** 57 **p** 58. C Slough *Ox* 57-60; C Uphill *B & W* 60-62; V Branston *Lich* 62-69; C-in-c Marsfield Australia 69-72; R Denistone E w Marsfield 72-75; Chal Long Bay Pris 75-80; Chapl W Metrop Pris 81-83; Sen Chapl Dept Corrective Services 81-85; Chapl Parramatta Hosp 86-91; Chapl Tas Univ 91-94; rtd 94. *Unit 23/144 Main Road, Exeter Tas 7275, Australia* Tel (0061) (3) 6394 3582 E-mail philipblake@bigpond.com

BLAKE, Steven Robert (Max). b 53. Furzedown Coll of Educn CertEd74 Brentwood Coll of Educn BEd91. NTMTC 98. **d** 01 **p** 02. NSM Orsett and Bulphan and Horndon on the Hill *Chelmsf* from 01. *Oakfield, Victoria Road, Horndon-on-the-Hill, Stanford-le-Hope SS17 8ND* Tel (01375) 360522
E-mail max@hobnob.org.uk

BLAKELEY, Julian Graham. b 60. Oak Hill Th Coll BA88. **d** 88 **p** 89. C Bedworth *Cov* 88-91; C Harlow St Mary and St Hugh w St Jo the Bapt *Chelmsf* 91-95; R Darfield *Sheff* 95-03; TR Eston w Normanby *York* from 03. *429 Normanby Road, Middlesbrough TS6 0ED* Tel (01642) 206264
E-mail julianandhelen@blakeley050682.freeserve.co.uk

BLAKELEY, Robert Daniel. b 29. Saskatchewan Univ BA63 St Pet Coll Ox BA66 MA70. Em Coll Saskatchewan 51. **d** 56 **p** 57. I Radisson Canada 56-59; USA 59-68 and 71-75; C New York St Alb 61-64; Asst P Brooklyn St Anne 66-68; C High Wycombe *Ox* 68-71; Chapl St Luke's Sch New Canaan 71-75; C St Marylebone St Mary *Lon* 75-82; Chapl Hill Ho Sch Knightsbridge 75-82; P-in-c Tasburgh *Nor* 82-85; P-in-c Tharston 82-85; P-in-c Forncett St Mary w St Pet 82-85; P-in-c Flordon 82-85; Hd Master and Chapl Corona Ravenscourt Sch Lon 85-92; rtd 92. *3841 Grace Crescent, Prince George BC V2N 4V9, Canada* Tel (001) (250) 564 1863

BLAKELY, Denise Irene. See CADDOO, Mrs Denise Irene
BLAKEMAN, Mrs Janet Mary. b 36. Man Univ BA57 CertEd58. Carl Dioc Tr Course 87. **d** 90 **p** 97. NSM Wetheral w Warwick *Carl* 90-97; NSM Thornthwaite cum Braithwaite, Newlands etc

97-01; Perm to Offic 01-07. *Langstrath, Greenfield Lane, Brampton CA8 1AU* Tel (01697) 72008

BLAKEMAN, Walter John. b 37. Qu Coll Birm 74. **d** 76 **p** 77. C Gnosall *Lich* 76-83; C Cheadle 83-86; Res Min Hednesford 86-90; Min Roundshaw LEP *S'wark* 90-94; TV E Scarsdale *Derby* 94-98; rtd 98. *10 Maes Madog, Pontfadog, Llangollen LL20 7BN* Tel (01691) 718173

BLAKESLEY, John. b 50. Keble Coll Ox BA72 MA76. St Steph Ho Ox 72. **d** 74 **p** 75. C Egremont *Carl* 74-77; C Doncaster Ch Ch *Sheff* 77-79; V Auckland St Helen *Dur* 79-94; Chapl Tindale Crescent Hosp Dur 90-94; Lect Th Dur Univ from 91; Tutor St Chad's Coll Dur 95-00; C Ch the King *Newc* 00-03; V Cambois and Sleekburn from 03. *St John's Vicarage, North View, Bedlington NE22 7ED* Tel (01670) 822309

BLAKEWAY-PHILLIPS, Richard John. b 19. St Chad's Coll Dur BA43. **d** 43 **p** 44. C Ledbury *Heref* 43-45; C Cirencester *Glouc* 45-50; C Lydney w Aylburton 50-52; R Dumbleton w Wormington 52-58; V Crawley Down All SS *Chich* 58-69; V Arrington *Ely* 69-77; R Orwell and Wimpole 69-77; P-in-c Hildersham and Gt w Lt Abington 77-86; rtd 86; Perm to Offic *Heref* 86-04 and *Ox* from 07. *Glanthus Cottage, 61 Long Row, Latchford Lane, Great Haseley, Oxford OX44 7LE* Tel (01844) 278035

BLAKEY, Canon Cedric Lambert. b 54. Fitzw Coll Cam BA76 MA80. St Jo Coll Nottm 77. **d** 79 **p** 80. C Cotmanhay *Derby* 79-83; C-in-c Blagreaves St Andr CD 83-89; P-in-c Sinfin Moor 84-89; V Heanor 89-97; RD Heanor 94-97; Bp's Dom Chapl 97-05; NSM Derby Cathl from 05; Hon Can from 02. *Derby Cathedral Office, 18/19 Irongate, Derby DE1 3GP* Tel (01332) 345848 E-mail c.blakey@btinternet.com

BLAKEY, William George. b 51. Southn Univ BSc72 PGCE73. Oak Hill Th Coll BA82. **d** 82 **p** 83. C Cheltenham St Mark *Glouc* 82-85; P-in-c Parkham, Alwington, Buckland Brewer etc *Ex* 85-86; R 86-94; TR 94-01; P-in-c Lundy Is 92-01; RD Hartland 89-96; TR Wareham *Sarum* 01-07; TR Brize Norton and Carterton *Ox* from 07; AD Witney from 08. *St John's Vicarage, 6 Burford Road, Carterton OX18 3AA* Tel (01993) 846996 E-mail rector@theblakeys.co.uk

BLAMEY, Mark Kendall. b 62. Bris Poly BSc84 MRICS86. Ripon Coll Cuddesdon 99. **d** 01 **p** 02. C Cowley St Jo *Ox* 01-04; P-in-c Goring w S Stoke 04-07; V Goring and Streatley w S Stoke from 07. *The Vicarage, Manor Road, Goring, Reading RG8 9DR* Tel (01491) 872196 E-mail mark@blamey.fslife.co.uk

BLAMIRE, Jean. *See* PROSSER, Jean

BLAMIRE, Philip Gray. b 50. St Pet Coll Birm CertEd71 Wall Hall Coll Aldenham BEd76 UEA MA91. EAMTC 00. **d** 03 **p** 04. C Swaffham *Nor* 03-07; P-in-c Weybourne Gp from 07. *The Rectory, The Street, Weybourne, Holt NR25 7SY* Tel (01263) 588268 E-mail philgb@lineone.net

BLAMIRE-BROWN, Charles Richard. b 21. St Cath Soc Ox BA49 MA53. Cuddesdon Coll 49. **d** 51 **p** 52. C Bedale *Ripon* 51-53; C Welwyn *St Alb* 53-58; P-in-c Tewin 58-67; R 67-75; RD Hatfield 71-75; V Chipperfield St Paul 75-86; rtd 86. *7 Willoughby Avenue, Kenilworth CV8 1DG* Tel (01926) 850808

BLANCH, Michael Dennis. b 46. TD and Bar 88. Birm Univ BSocSc69 PGCE70 PhD75. NOC 07. **d** 09. NSM Askrigg w Stallingbusk *Ripon* from 09. *Strands, Simonstone, Hawes DL8 3LY* Tel (01969) 667573 Mobile 07792-240684 E-mail mike@blanch.org

BLANCH, Paul Frederick. b 56. St Cuth Soc Dur BA97. Chich Th Coll 83. **d** 86 **p** 87. C Chaddesden St Phil *Derby* 86-88; C Auckland St Andr and St Anne *Dur* 88-91; P-in-c Hunwick 91-94; Chapl HM Pris Edin 98-02; P-in-c Edin St Salvador 98-00; R 00-02; P-in-c Wester Hailes St Luke 00-02; P-in-c Melton *St E* 02-03; P-in-c Ufford w Bredfield and Hasketon 02-03; R Melton and Ufford 03-05; V Meir Heath and Normacot *Lich* from 05. *St Francis's Vicarage, Sandon Road, Stoke-on-Trent ST3 7LH* Tel (01782) 393189 E-mail frpaul@meltuff.freeserve.co.uk

BLANCHARD, Christopher John. b 46. Univ of Wales (Lamp) BA70. St Mich Coll Llan 86. **d** 79 **p** 80. NSM Chepstow *Mon* 79-81; NSM Itton and St Arvans w Penterry and Kilgwrrwg etc 81-86; TV Ebbw Vale 87-89; R Llangenni and Llanbedr Ystrad Yw w Patricio *S & B* 89-98; V Chepstow *Mon* from 98. *The Vicarage, 25 Mount Way, Chepstow NP16 5NF* Tel (01291) 620980

BLANCHARD, Frank Hugh. b 30. St Jo Coll Dur BA54 MA62. **d** 55 **p** 56. C Bottesford *Linc* 55-58; CMS 58-65; C Kirby Grindalythe *York* 65-67; V 67-71; C N Grimston w Wharram Percy and Wharram-le-Street 65-67; V 67-71; P-in-c Thorpe Bassett 67-71; P-in-c Settrington 67-68; V Scarborough St Jas 71-79; P-in-c Scarborough H Trin 78-79; V Scarborough St Jas and H Trin 79-86; R Stockton-on-the-Forest w Holtby and Warthill 87-94; rtd 94; Perm to Offic *York* from 00. *23 Front Street, Sowerby, Thirsk YO7 1JG* Tel (01845) 574446

BLANCHARD, Mrs Jean Ann. b 43. St Alb Minl Tr Scheme 79. **dss** 85 **d** 87 **p** 94. Mill End and Heronsgate w W Hyde *St Alb* 85-92; Hon Par Dn 87-92; Par Dn Luton All SS w St Pet 92-94; C

94-95; P-in-c Skirbeck Quarter *Linc* 96-97; V 97-01; P-in-c Digby Gp 01-08; rtd 08. *92 High Street, Billingborough, Sleaford NG34 0QD* Tel (01529) 240536 E-mail jean.blanchard@btinternet.com

BLANCHARD, Canon Lawrence Gordon. b 36. Edin Univ MA60. Linc Th Coll 63. **d** 65 **p** 66. C Woodhouse *Wakef* 65-67; C Cannock *Lich* 67-70; Swaziland 70-76; TV Raveningham *Nor* 76-80; V Ancaster *Linc* 80-87; Dir LNSM 80-87; Can and Preb Linc Cathl 85-88; Dir of Tr CA 88-93; V Roxton w Gt Barford *St Alb* 93-98; rtd 98; Perm to Offic *St E* from 99. *2 Parkwood, Badingham Road, Framlingham, Woodbridge IP13 9JX* Tel (01728) 723373 E-mail laurie-blanchard@lineone.net

BLANCHARD, Hilary. STETS. **d** 09. NSM Horfield H Trin *Bris* from 09. *149 Abbey Road, Bristol BS9 3QH*

BLAND, Mrs Elizabeth Anne. b 63. Collingwood Coll Dur BA85. SAOMC 01. **d** 04 **p** 05. C N Shields *Newc* 04-08; V Ashington from 08. *Holy Sepulchre Vicarage, Wansbeck Road, Ashington NE63 8HZ* Tel (01670) 813358 Mobile 07903-044224 E-mail seat@seatbland.freeserve.co.uk

BLAND, Jean Elspeth. b 42. K Coll Lon BA63. Glouc Sch of Min 87. **d** 90 **p** 94. Par Dn Cen Telford *Lich* 90-94; Asst Chapl HM Pris Shrewsbury 92-94; Chapl HM Pris Onley 94-98; C Goole *Sheff* 99; P-in-c Purleigh, Cold Norton and Stow Maries *Chelmsf* 99-08; rtd 08. *38 Blythe Way, Maldon CM9 6UE3* Tel (01621) 855090 E-mail ebland@prowselyan.plus.com

BLANDFORD-BAKER, Neil James. b 64. Dundee Univ BSc86. St Jo Coll Nottm BTh92. **d** 93 **p** 94. C The Quinton *Birm* 93-96; V E Acton St Dunstan w St Thos *Lon* 96-06; Dir of Ords Willesden Area 02-06; V Histon *Ely* from 06; P-in-c Impington from 06; RD N Stowe from 07. *The Vicarage, 9A Church Street, Histon, Cambridge CB24 9EP* Tel (01223) 232255 or 233456 E-mail jamesbb@btinternet.com

BLANEY, Laurence. b 41. Open Univ BA85 Essex Univ MA88 PhD95. Oak Hill Th Coll 66. **d** 69 **p** 70. C Leyton St Mary w St Edw *Chelmsf* 69-73; P-in-c Wickham w Thunderley 73-77; P-in-c Mayland 77-82; P-in-c Steeple 77-82; R Pitsea 82-95; R Pitsea w Nevendon 95-96; P-in-c Mayland 96-06; P-in-c Steeple 96-06; rtd 06; Perm to Offic *Chelmsf* from 06. *14 Piercys, Basildon SS13 3HN* Tel (01268) 552254

BLANKENSHIP, Charles Everett. b 42. Santa Clara Univ BA64. Cuddesdon Coll 71. **d** 74 **p** 75. C Catford (Southend) and Downham *S'wark* 74-78; P-in-c Battersea St Phil w St Bart 78-83; V 83-85; TV Wimbledon 85-91; P-in-c Welling 91-92; V 92-99; P-in-c S Norwood St Alb 99-06; RD Croydon N 02-06; rtd 06; Perm to Offic *S'wark* from 06. *10 Bromley College, London Road, Bromley BR1 1PE* Tel (020) 8464 2443 E-mail charles.blankenship@btinternet.com

BLANKLEY, Roger Henry. b 32. MRICS60. Clifton Th Coll 62. **d** 66 **p** 67. C Peckham St Mary Magd *S'wark* 66-69; SAMS 70-74; Brazil 74-80; R Gillingham w Geldeston, Stockton, Ellingham etc *Nor* 80-91; P-in-c Charmouth and Catherston Leweston *Sarum* 91-97; rtd 97; Perm to Offic *Cov* 98-00 and 02-06; *Glouc* from 97, *Ox* from 00; Asst Area Sec SAMS 98-00. *12 Hubbard Close, Buckingham MK18 1YS* Tel (01280) 814710 E-mail mblankley@rblankley.freeserve.co.uk

BLANT, Edgar. b 18. St Chad's Coll Dur BA47. **d** 48 **p** 49. C Meir *Lich* 48-54; Antigua 55-85; St Kitts-Nevis 60-85; Adn St Kitts 78-85; rtd 86; Perm to Offic *Lich* 86-98. *326 Sandon Road, Stoke-on-Trent ST3 7EB* Tel (01782) 398300

BLATCHLEY, Ms Elizabeth. b 62. Wycliffe Hall Ox 01. **d** 03 **p** 04. C Northolt St Jos *Lon* 03-06; C Telford Park *S'wark* from 06. *12A Salford Road, London SW2 4BH* Tel (020) 8674 1466 E-mail betsyblatchley@btinternet.com

BLATCHLY, Owen Ronald Maxwell. b 30. Bps' Coll Cheshunt 62. **d** 64 **p** 65. C Boxmoor St Jo *St Alb* 64-67; C Boreham Wood All SS 67-69; C Frimley *Guildf* 69-77; V Manaccan w St Anthony-in-Meneage *Truro* 77-82; R Binfield *Ox* 82-97; rtd 97; Perm to Offic *Truro* from 97. *1 Rose Cottages, East Road, Stithians, Truro TR3 7BD* Tel (01209) 860845

BLATHERWICK, Mrs Jane Lesley. b 63. St Jo Coll Nottm. **d** 05 **p** 06. C Arnold *S'well* from 05. *3 Ashington Drive, Arnold, Nottingham NG5 8GH* Tel 0115-922 9085 E-mail janeblatherwick@aol.com

BLAY, Ian. b 65. Man Univ BA88. Westcott Ho Cam 89. **d** 91 **p** 92. C Withington St Paul *Man* 91-94; C Elton All SS 94-96; R Droylsden St Andr 96-05; Dioc Ecum Officer 98-05; R Mobberley *Ches* from 05. *The Rectory, Church Lane, Mobberley, Knutsford WA16 7RA* Tel (01565) 873218 Mobile 07879-004033 E-mail ianblay@btinternet.com

BLAY, Kenneth Neil. b 72. Leeds Univ BA07. Coll of Resurr Mirfield 05. **d** 07 **p** 08. C E Crompton *Man* 07-08; C Dearnley from 08. *94 Birch Road, Rochdale OL12 9QN* Tel (01706) 375338 E-mail nkblay@btinternet.com

BLEAKLEY, Melvyn Thomas. b 43. K Coll Lon BD66 AKC66 Reading Univ TCert78. **d** 67 **p** 68. C Cross Heath *Lich* 67-70; TV High Wycombe *Ox* 70-77; Perm to Offic 77-00; NSM Chalfont St Giles from 00. *294 Hughenden Road, High Wycombe HP13 5PE* Tel (01494) 529315 E-mail melvyn_bleakley@hotmail.com

BLEAZARD, John George. b 57. Univ of Wales (Abth) BA79 Qu Coll Birm MA06. Ripon Coll Cuddesdon 06. **d** 08 **p** 09. C Gt Cornard *St E* from 08. *58 Canhams Road, Great Cornard, Sudbury CO10 0ER* Tel (01787) 377397 E-mail johnbleazard@hotmail.com *or* john@standrews-gc.org.uk

BLEE, Peter Michael. b 64. St Jo Coll Cam BA86. St Steph Ho Ox BTh94. **d** 94 **p** 95. C Guildf St Nic 94-97; C Whipton *Ex* 97-03; P-in-c Berwick w Selmeston and Alciston *Chich* 03-07; R from 07. *The Parsonage, Berwick, Polegate BN26 6SR* Tel (01323) 870512 E-mail peterblee@btinternet.com

BLENKIN, Hugh Linton. b 16. Trin Coll Cam BA39 MA43. Lambeth STh56 Westcott Ho Cam 39. **d** 40 **p** 41. C Hitchin St Mary *St Alb* 40-43; Prec St Alb Abbey 43-48; Chapl and Lect Hockerill Coll Bishop's Stortford 48-66; Lect St Mich Coll Salisbury 66-78; Lect Sarum Th Coll 78-83; rtd 81. *Amesbury Abbey, Amesbury, Salisbury SP4 7EX* Tel (01980) 624813

BLEWETT, Martin Arthur. b 60. Keele Univ BA82 Glos Univ MA04. Trin Coll Bris 07. **d** 09. C Seaford w Sutton *Chich* from 09. *2 Benenden Close, Seaford BN25 3PG* Tel (01323) 891831 Mobile 07854-273489 E-mail prospero888@clara.co.uk

BLEWETT, Roy. b 32. K Coll Lon BSc54 MPhil74. Edin Th Coll 81. **d** 82 **p** 83. C Newc St Fran 82-85; P-in-c Branxton and Cornhill w Carham 85-91; rtd 92; Perm to Offic *Truro* 92-08. *37 Summerland Park, Upper Killay, Swansea SA2 7HU*

BLEWETT, Timothy John. b 67. Surrey Univ BA88 Cam Univ BA92 MA92 Coll of Ripon & York St Jo MA96. Westcott Ho Cam 89. **d** 92 **p** 93. C Knaresborough *Ripon* 92-95; V Hanmer, Bronington, Bettisfield, Tallarn Green *St As* 95-98; Can Res and Can Cursal St As Cathl 98-03; Asst Dioc Dir of Ords 98-00; Dioc Dir of Ords 00-03; Dioc Officer for Min and Adv for CME 98-03; CF 03-04; P-in-c Loddington *Leic* from 04; Warden Launde Abbey from 04. *The Warden's House, Launde Abbey, Launde Road, Launde, Leicester LE7 9XB* Tel (01572) 717254 E-mail tim.blewett@virgin.net

BLICK, John Harold Leslie. b 36. Univ of Wales (Lamp) BA61. Bps' Coll Cheshunt 61. **d** 63 **p** 64. C Radlett *St Alb* 63-66; Min St Cem Miss Labrador Canada 66-71; Min Marsh Farm CD *St Alb* 71-76; R Shaw cum Donnington *Ox* 76-89; rtd 96; Perm to Offic *Mon* from 99. *Springwood, Cleddon, Trelleck NP25 4PN* Tel (01600) 860094 Fax 869045 E-mail revdjblick@aol.com

BLIGH, Philip Hamilton. b 36. Lon Univ BSc57 PhD61 MEd79 St Cath Coll Ox BA63 MInstP75. S'wark Ord Course 86. **d** 88 **p** 89. C Abington *Pet* 88-90; V Bozeat w Easton Maudit 90-99; R Hackett Australia 99-01; rtd 01; Perm to Offic *Nor* from 02. *Harmony House, 40 Cromwell Road, Cromer NR27 0BE* Tel (01263) 511385 E-mail philaud@blighp.freeserve.co.uk

BLIGHT, Francis Charles. b 71. Newc Univ BA94. Oak Hill Th Coll BA08. **d** 08 **p** 09. C Virginia Water *Guildf* from 08. *6 Beechmont Avenue, Virginia Water GU25 4EY* E-mail francis@cc-vw.org

BLISS, Allan Ernest Newport. b 29. K Coll Lon AKC50. St Boniface Warminster 54. **d** 54 **p** 57. C Wooburn *Ox* 54-56; C Whitley Ch Ch 56-58; C Hatcham Park All SS *S'wark* 63-68; C Sundon w Streatley *St Alb* 68-73; P-in-c Caldecote All SS 74-78; V 78-91; V Old Warden 81-91; Perm to Offic 91-05; rtd 94. *6 Jubilee Gardens, Biggleswade SG18 0JW* Tel (01767) 313797

BLISS, Canon David Charles. b 52. Aston Univ BSc75 Cranfield Inst of Tech MSc82. St Jo Coll Nottm 87. **d** 89 **p** 90. C Burntwood *Lich* 89-93; TV Aston cum Aughton w Swallownest, Todwick etc *Sheff* 93-02; R Todwick 02-08; AD Laughton 03-08; Chapl among Deaf People 97-08; V Rotherham from 08; Hon Can Sheff Cathl from 06. *51 Hallam Road, Rotherham S60 3ED* Tel (01709) 364341 E-mail david.bliss@sheffield.anglican.org

BLISS, John Derek Clegg. b 40. Sarum Th Coll. **d** 68 **p** 69. C Wymondham *Nor* 68-73; V Easton 73-80; R Colton 73-80; R Madera H Trin USA 80-89; Human Outreach Agency Hayward 92-96; rtd 01; C Coconut Grove St Steph from 01. *4 Edgewater Hillside, Westport CT 06880-6101, USA* Tel (001) (203) 222 1879 E-mail jb106600@aol.com

BLISS, Mrs Lyn Elizabeth. b 54. SS Mark & Jo Univ Coll Plymouth CertEd76. Ox Min Course 06. **d** 09. NSM Bradfield and Stanford Dingley *Ox* from 09; NSM Bucklebury w Marlston from 09. *Holly Hedges, 2 Broad Lane, Upper Bucklebury, Reading RG7 6QJ* Tel (01635) 862281 Mobile 07824-741225 E-mail lyn.bliss@virgin.net

BLISS, Neil Humberstone. b 29. TCD BA54 MA59. Coll of Resurr Mirfield 55. **d** 57 **p** 58. C N Keyham *Ex* 57-60; C Usuthu Swaziland 61-65; P-in-c Piet Retief S Africa 65-66; R 66-67; Chapl St Chris Sch Swaziland 68-73; Chapl Waterford Kamhlaba Sch Mbabane 73-78; R Pigg's Peak 78-80; P-in-c Osmington w Poxwell *Sarum* 80-81; TV Preston w Sutton Poyntz and Osmington w Poxwell 81-84; V Ernesettle *Ex* 84-88; R S Tawton and Belstone 88-93; rtd 94. *4 Manor Gardens, Seaton EX12 2AL* Tel (01297) 23452

BLISSARD-BARNES, Christopher John. b 36. ARCO55 Linc Coll Ox BA61 MA64. Ridley Hall Cam 61. **d** 63 **p** 64. C Woking St Paul *Guildf* 63-67; C Orpington Ch Ch *Roch* 67-71; P-in-c Heref St Jas 71-78; Chapl Heref Gen Hosp 71-78; R

Hampreston *Sarum* 78-88; TR 88-89; RD Wimborne 80-85; P-in-c Hambledon *Guildf* 89-94; R Newdigate 94-01; Warden of Readers 93-99; rtd 01; Perm to Offic *Win* from 02. *148 Olivers Battery Road South, Winchester SO22 4LF* Tel and fax (01962) 862082 E-mail cf@blissard-barnes.freeserve.co.uk

BLOCK, Robert Allen. b 62. Univ of Wales (Lamp) BA84. Coll of Resurr Mirfield 86. **d** 88 **p** 89. C Hampton *Worc* 88-91; C Notting Hill St Mich and Ch Ch *Lon* 91-96; P-in-c Hammersmith St Luke 96-02; C-in-c Hammersmith SS Mich and Geo White City Estate CD 96-02. *Address temp unknown*

BLOCKLEY, Christopher John Hamilton. b 72. UWE LLB96 Rob Coll Cam BTh04 Barrister-at-Law (Gray's Inn) 98. Ridley Hall Cam 01. **d** 04 **p** 05. C Kingswood *Bris* 04-07; Chapl Bps' Coll Glouc from 07. *29 Wellesley Street, Gloucester GL1 4QP* Tel (01452) 539956 *or* 524879 ext 137 Mobile 07795-266674 E-mail chris_blockley@hotmail.com

BLODWELL, Ms Christine Maria. b 46. Open Univ BA Jo Dalton Coll Man CertEd71. NOC 04. **d** 05 **p** 06. NSM Marple All SS *Ches* from 05. *12 Ventura Court, Ollersett Avenue, New Mills, High Peak SK22 4LL* Tel (01663) 746523 Mobile 07931-714130 E-mail cmblodwell@aol.com

BLOFELD, Thomas Guest. *See* GUEST-BLOFELD, Thomas

BLOGG, Kevin Derek. b 55. Ch Ch Coll Cant BSc82 PGCE87. Franciscan Ho of Studies. **d** 84 **p** 85. NSM Eythorne and Elvington w Waldershare etc *Cant* 89-92; Orchard Sch Cant 89-90; Harbour Sch Dover 92-93; NSM Colkirk w Oxwick w Pattesley, Whissonsett etc *Nor* 95-02; NSM Gressenhall w Longham w Wendling etc from 02; Sidestrand Hall Sch Nor from 94. *The Rectory Barn, Rectory Road, Gressenhall, Dereham NR19 2QG* Tel (01362) 861084 E-mail bloggbarn@aol.com

BLOOD, David John. b 36. G&C Coll Cam BA60 MA64. Westcott Ho Cam 60. **d** 62 **p** 63. C Rushmere *St E* 62-66; C Harringay St Paul *Lon* 66-70; Lic to Offic 71-81; rtd 01. *42 Churston Gardens, London N11 2NL*

BLOOD, Canon Michael William. b 44. AKC67. **d** 69 **p** 70. C Moseley St Agnes *Birm* 69-75; V Cotteridge 75-09; Relig Progr Producer BBC Radio W Midl 76-06; Hon Can Birm Cathl 97-09; rtd 09; Perm to Offic *Birm* from 09. *19 Nursery Drive, Birmingham B30 1DR* Tel 0121-458 2815 E-mail michaelblood@blueyonder.co.uk

BLOOD, Stephen John. b 28. Keble Coll Ox BA53 MA58. Coll of Resurr Mirfield 53. **d** 55 **p** 56. C Greenford H Cross *Lon* 55-58; C Forest Gate St Edm *Chelmsf* 58-61; C-in-c Ashford St Hilda CD *Lon* 61-73; V Ashford St Hilda 73-00; rtd 00; Perm to Offic *St Alb* from 00. *69 Hampstead Road, Kings Langley WD4 8BS* Tel (01923) 268453

BLOOMER, Ms Sherry Lesley. b 50. TD91. Liv Jo Moores Univ BA91 Wolv Poly CertEd83 RN73 RM74 RHV78. Westcott Ho Cam 95. **d** 97 **p** 98. C Llangollen w Trevor and Llantysilio *St As* 97-00; R Cilcain and Nannerch and Rhydymwyn 00-04; V Worc St Clem and Lower Broadheath from 04; Chapl Worc Univ from 04. *St Clement's Rectory, 124 Laugherne Road, Worcester WR2 5LT* Tel (01905) 339455 E-mail sherry@sbloomer.freeserve.co.uk

BLOOMFIELD, Mrs Brenda Elizabeth. b 41. Gipsy Hill Coll of Educn TCert63. **d** 07 **p** 08. NSM Upper Weardale *Dur* from 07. *1 Broadwood View, Frosterley, Bishop Auckland DL13 2RT* Tel (01388) 527980

BLOOMFIELD, Mrs Christine Louise. b 52. ERMC 05. **d** 08 **p** 09. C Strasbourg *Eur* from 08. *28 rue Principale, 67270 Kienheim, France* Tel (0033) (3) 88 62 61 05 Fax (6) 67 45 20 56 E-mail bloomfieldhilaire@wanadoo.fr

BLOOMFIELD, John Michael. b 35. Univ of Wales (Lamp) BA57. Sarum Th Coll 59. **d** 61 **p** 62. C Fordington *Sarum* 61-64; C Branksome St Aldhelm 64-66; Youth Chapl *Win* 66-69; R Win All SS w Chilcomb and Chesil 71-79; P-in-c Corsley *Sarum* 79-81; P-in-c Studland 83-86; Chapl HM Pris Dorchester 87-89; C Dorchester *Sarum* 87-89; Chapl HM Pris The Verne 89-00; rtd 00; Perm to Offic *Sarum* from 01. *Green Acres, Valley Road, Corfe Castle, Wareham BH20 5HU* Tel (01929) 480234 Fax 481699 E-mail swanbeck@aol.com

BLOOMFIELD, John Stephen. b 56. Chich Th Coll 83. **d** 86 **p** 87. C Chich St Paul and St Pet 86-89; TV Littlehampton and Wick 89-98; V Hunstanton St Edm w Ringstead *Nor* from 98. *St Edmund's Vicarage, 53 Northgate, Hunstanton PE36 6DS* Tel (01485) 532157

BLOOR, Ms Amanda Elaine. b 62. Leic Univ BA83 Open Univ PGCE96 York Univ MA02. Ripon Coll Cuddesdon 02. **d** 04 **p** 05. C Hambleden Valley *Ox* 04-07; Bp's Dom Chapl from 07. *Diocesan Church House, North Hinksey, Oxford OX2 0NB* Tel (01865) 208221 E-mail amanda.bloor@oxford.anglican.org

BLOOR, Terence Bernard. b 62. Liv Univ BTh02. NOC 99. **d** 02 **p** 03. C Hadley *Lich* 02-06; P-in-c Basford from 06; Chapl N Staffs Hosp NHS Trust from 06. *211 Basford Park Road, Newcastle ST5 0FG* Tel (01782) 619045 Mobile 07890-980749 E-mail terry.bloor@btinternet.com

BLORE, Canon John Francis. b 49. Jes Coll Ox BA72 MA76. Wycliffe Hall Ox 73. **d** 75 **p** 76. C Waltham Abbey *Chelmsf* 75-78; C E Ham St Geo 78-81; R Colchester St Mich Myland

81-00; Chapl Oxley Parker Sch Colchester 81-00; P-in-c Halstead St Andr w H Trin and Greenstead Green *Chelmsf* 00-04; TR Halstead Area from 04; RD Hinckford 03-08; Hon Can Chelmsf Cathl from 09. *The Vicarage, Parsonage Street, Halstead CO9 2LD* Tel (01787) 472171
E-mail john@johnfblore.freeserve.co.uk

BLOUNT, Robin George. b 38. Lon Coll of Div 61 Wycliffe Hall Ox 67. **d** 68 **p** 69. C Bletchley *Ox* 68-71; C Washington *Dur* 71-74; TV Chelmsley Wood *Birm* 74-76; Ind Chapl *Worc* 76-89; Asst P Dudley St Jo 76-88; Asst P Dudley St Thos and St Luke 88-89; Ind Chapl (Eurotunnel Development) *Cant* 89-03; rtd 03; Perm to Offic *Cant* from 03. *6 Lyn Court, Shorncliffe Road, Folkestone CT20 2PE* Tel (01303) 250028
E-mail robin.blount@virgin.net

BLOWERS, Canon Ralph Barrie. b 28. Fitzw Ho Cam BA50 MA61. Ridley Hall Cam 51. **d** 53 **p** 54. C Higher Openshaw *Man* 53-56; R Man Albert Memorial Ch 56-68; RD Cheetham 63-69; R Man Albert Memorial Ch w Newton Heath 68-69; V Normanton *Derby* 69-93; RD Derby 74-79; RD Derby S 79-89; Hon Can Derby Cathl 85-93; rtd 93; Perm to Offic *Derby* from 93. *8 Portland Close, Mickleover, Derby DE3 9BQ* Tel (01332) 517114 E-mail canonblowers@onetel.com

BLOWS, Canon Derek Reeve. b 26. Linc Coll Ox BA50 MA52 SAP75. Cuddesdon Coll 50. **d** 52 **p** 53. C Cov St Mark 52-56; Lic to Offic *Sarum* 56-58; Chapl Warlingham Park Hosp Croydon 58-65; V Purley St Mark *S'wark* 65-70; Dir Past Care and Counselling 70-80; Hon Can S'wark Cathl 72-80; Dir Westmr Past Foundn 80-91; rtd 91; Perm to Offic *Roch* 91-09. *30 St James Street, Shaftesbury SP7 8HE* Tel (01747) 853088

BLOXAM-ROSE, Canon Simon Franklyn. b 61. Southn Univ BTh MA92 PhD99 HonFLCM88. Chich Th Coll 85. **d** 88 **p** 89. C Bassaleg *Mon* 88-89; Chapl Aldenham Sch Herts 89-94; Sen Chapl Millfield Sch Somerset 94-06; CF from 06; Can St Jo Pro-Cathl Katakwa from 95. *c/o MOD Chaplains (Army)* Tel (01980) 615804 Fax 615800

BLOXHAM, Oliver. b 27. Ely Th Coll 60. **d** 62 **p** 63. C Newc H Cross 62-65; C Ponteland 65-69; V Dudley 69-79; P-in-c Balkwell 79-81; V 81-92; rtd 92; Perm to Offic *Newc* from 92. *25 Dawson Place, Morpeth NE61 1AQ* Tel (01670) 514841

BLUNDELL, Catherine. b 62. SAOMC 96. **d** 99 **p** 00. C Furze Platt *Ox* 99-03; TV Bracknell 03-09; V Winkfield and Cranbourne from 09. *The Vicarage, Winkfield Street, Winkfield, Windsor SL4 4SW* Tel (01344) 884271
E-mail catherine.blundell@btinternet.com

BLUNDELL, Peter Grahame. b 61. Ealing Coll of Educn BA83. Oak Hill NSM Course 91. **d** 94 **p** 95. NSM Kensington St Barn *Lon* 94-97; Zimbabwe 97-99; Assoc Min Romford Gd Shep *Chelmsf* 99-04; I Oak Ridges Canada from 04. *19 Waldron Crescent, Richmond Hill ON L4E 4A3, Canada*

BLUNDEN, Jacqueline Ann. *See* MILLER, Mrs Jacqueline Ann

BLUNDEN, Jeremy Augustine. b 61. BSc CEng88 MIStructE88. SEITE 99. **d** 99 **p** 00. NSM Sydenham St Bart *S'wark* 99-01; C 01-03; V Clapham H Spirit from 03. *15 Elms Road, London SW4 9ER* Tel (020) 7622 8703
E-mail jeremy.blunden@btopenworld.com

BLUNSUM, Charles Michael. b 28. ACIB51 MBIM86. **d** 74 **p** 75. C Stoke Bishop *Bris* 74-79; Chapl Brunel Manor Chr Cen Torquay 79-94; rtd 94; Perm to Offic *Ex* from 94. *16A Hollywater Close, Torquay TQ1 3TN* Tel (01803) 214371

BLUNT, Jeremy William. b 49. Birm Univ MEd85 GRNCM73. **d** 07 **p** 08. OLM Streetly *Lich* from 07. *63 Lindrosa Road, Sutton Coldfield B74 3LB* Tel 0121-353 9712 Mobile 07849-689180
E-mail jeremy.blunt@virgin.net

BLYDE, Ian Hay. b 52. Liv Univ BSc74 Edin Univ BD80. Edin Th Coll 77. **d** 80 **p** 81. C Ainsdale *Liv* 80-83; Chapl Birkenhead Sch Merseyside 83-90; V Over St Chad *Ches* 90-93; Chapl Ex Sch and St Marg Sch 93-98; NSM Littleham w Exmouth 03-06; TV Brixham w Churston Ferrers and Kingswear from 06. *The Vicarage, 13 Warborough Road, Churston Ferrers, Brixham TQ5 0JY* Tel (01803) 844663

BLYTH, Andrew Kenneth Eric. b 63. Roehampton Inst BA86 Middx Univ PGCE87. Ridley Hall Cam 98. **d** 00 **p** 01. C Luton St Mary *St Alb* 00-04; P-in-c Walton H Trin from 04. *The Rectory, 42 Redwood Drive, Aylesbury HP21 7TN* Tel (01296) 394906 Mobile 07905-181002 E-mail hta_vicar@yahoo.co.uk

BLYTH, Bryan Edward Perceval. b 22. Linc Coll Ox BA49 MA52. Wells Th Coll 48. **d** 50 **p** 51. C Timperley *Ches* 50-52; C Talbot Village *Sarum* 52-55; C-in-c Weymouth St Edm 55; P-in-c 56-63; Asst Dir of Educn *Chelmsf* 64-67; Hon C Mountnessing 67-68; Hon C Ingatestone w Buttsbury 67-68; Teacher Ingatestone Sec Modern Sch 67-68; Teacher Westwood Co Jun Sch 68-72; Dep Hd 72-87; Hon C Thundersley 80-84; rtd 87; Perm to Offic *Sarum* and *Win* from 98. *Greenways, 19 Chiltern Drive, New Milton BH25 7JY* Tel (01425) 611140

BLYTH, Mrs Geraldine Anne. b 50. Llan Dioc Tr Scheme 90. **d** 94 **p** 97. C Llantrisant 94-01; P-in-c Llanharry 01-06; Chapl Pontypridd and Rhondda NHS Trust 01-06; V Llangynwyd w Maesteg from 06. *Yr Hen Ficerdy, Llangynwyd, Maesteg CF34 9SB* Tel (01656) 733194

BLYTH, Graham. *See* BLYTH, Canon Michael Graham

BLYTH, Ian John. b 40. Rhodes Univ BA66 Natal Univ BEd81 MEd96. **d** 82 **p** 83. S Africa 82-01; Dioc Educn Officer Natal 83-85; R Pietermaritzburg St Luke 85-87; Lic to Offic 88-01; NSM W Woodhay w Enborne, Hampstead Marshall etc *Ox* 02-09; NSM Kintbury w Avington 05-09; rtd 09; Hon C Burstwick w Thorngumbald *York* from 09. *The Rectory, Ottringham Road, Keyingham, Hull HU12 9RX* Tel (01964) 622907 Mobile 07900-857096 E-mail ian@blythkin.fsnet.co.uk

BLYTH, John Reddie. b 25. Wadh Coll Ox BA48 MA50. Ridley Hall Cam 48. **d** 50 **p** 51. C Southport Ch Ch *Liv* 50-52; C Enfield Ch Ch Trent Park *Lon* 52-55; V Plymouth St Jude *Ex* 55-63; E Midl Area Sec CPAS 63-70; V Parkstone St Luke *Sarum* 70-90; Chapl Uplands Sch Parkstone 70-73; rtd 90; Perm to Offic *Chich* from 90. *5 Powell Road, Newick, Lewes BN8 4LS* Tel (01825) 722011

BLYTH, Kenneth Henry. b 35. Oak Hill Th Coll 58. **d** 61 **p** 62. C St Alb St Paul *St Alb* 61-65; P-in-c Aspenden and Layston w Buntingford 65-66; R 66-72; R Washfield, Stoodleigh, Withleigh etc *Ex* 72-82; P-in-c Cruwys Morchard 72-74; RD Tiverton 76-82; V Eastbourne H Trin *Chich* 82-00; rtd 00; Perm to Offic *Ex* from 00. *Hamslade House, Bampton, Tiverton EX16 9JA*

BLYTH, Canon Michael Graham. b 53. Jes Coll Ox BA75 MA78 Dur Univ PhD79. Qu Coll Birm 82. **d** 84 **p** 85. C Nantwich *Ches* 84-86; C Coppenhall 86-88; TV Southend *Chelmsf* 88-95; P-in-c Danbury from 95; RD Chelmsf S 01-07; Hon Can Chelmsf Cathl from 07. *St John's Rectory, 55 Main Road, Danbury, Chelmsf CM3 4NG* Tel (01245) 223140
E-mail michaelg@canongate.org.uk

BOAG, David. b 46. Edin Th Coll 69. **d** 72 **p** 73. C Edin Old St Paul 72-75; P-in-c Edin St Andr and St Aid 75-88; Lic to Offic from 88. *7 Starch Mill, Ford Road, Haddington EH41 4AR* Tel (01620) 826839

BOAG, Michael John. b 61. Leeds Univ BA00. Coll of Resurr Mirfield 98. **d** 00 **p** 01. C Howden *York* 00-03; Min Can and Succ Windsor from 03; Chapl St Geo Sch Windsor 03-06; Dean's V from 06. *3 The Cloisters, Windsor Castle, Windsor SL4 1NJ* Tel (01753) 848737 E-mail succentor@stgeorges-windsor.org

BOAK, Canon Donald Kenneth. b 30. MBAOT53. S'wark Ord Course 82. **d** 85 **p** 86. C Tulse Hill H Trin and St Matthias *S'wark* 85-88; C Surbiton St Matt 88-91; Intercon Ch Soc, SAMS and Miss to Seamen 91-95; Peru 91-95; Dean Lima 93-95; rtd 95; Hon Can Peru from 95; Hon C Bournemouth St Andr *Win* 96-99; Perm to Offic *Sarum* 98-01 and *Win* from 99. *3 Hymans Way, Totton, Southampton SO40 3DL* Tel (023) 8086 8265

BOAKES, Norman. b 50. Univ of Wales (Swansea) BA71 Univ of Wales (Lamp) LTh73 Ox Univ MTh96. Bp Burgess Hall Lamp 71. **d** 73 **p** 74. C Swansea St Mary w H Trin *S & B* 73-78; Chapl Univ of Wales (Swansea) 76-78; Chapl K Alfred Coll *Win* 78-82; V Colbury 82-91; Chapl Ashurst Hosp 82-91; Chapl Mental Handicap Services Unit 82-91; V Southampton Maybush St Pet *Win* 91-06; P-in-c Southampton St Jude 04-06; V Maybush and Southampton St Jude 06-07; Bp's Adv for Hosp Chapl 87-00; AD Southampton 02-07; Continuing Min Development Officer from 08. *33 Shepherds Down, Alresford SO24 9PP* Tel (01962) 734599 E-mail norman.boakes@winchester.anglican.org

BOARDMAN, Frederick Henry. b 25. Liv Univ BSc46 St Cath Soc Ox BA49 MA54 Birm Univ MEd71 PhD77 Lon Univ PGCE68. Wycliffe Hall Ox 47. **d** 50 **p** 51. C Bootle Ch Ch *Liv* 50-52; C-in-c Netherton CD 52-57; V Stechford *Birm* 57-63; Lic to Offic *Birm* 63-69 and *Liv* 71-89; Hon C Sutton *Liv* 76-89; Hon C Burtonwood 89-02; rtd 90; Perm to Offic *Liv* from 92. *Woodside, Burtonwood Road, Great Sankey, Warrington WA5 3AN* Tel (01925) 635079

BOARDMAN, The Ven Jonathan. b 63. Magd Coll Cam BA89 Magd Coll Cam MA90. Westcott Ho Cam 87. **d** 90 **p** 91. C W Derby St Mary *Liv* 90-93; Prec St Alb Abbey 93-96; TR Catford (Southend) and Downham *S'wark* 96-99; RD E Lewisham 99; Chapl Rome *Eur* from 99; Sen Tutor Angl Cen Rome from 00; Can Gib Cathl from 07; Adn Italy and Malta from 09. *All Saints, via del Babuino 153, 00187 Rome, Italy* Tel (0039) (06) 3600 2171 *or* tel and fax 3600 1881 E-mail j.boardman@allsaintsrome.org *or* office@allsaintsrome.org

BOARDMAN, Preb Philippa Jane. b 63. Jes Coll Cam BA85 MA89. Ridley Hall Cam 87. **d** 90 **p** 94. Par Dn Walthamstow St Mary w St Steph *Chelmsf* 90-93; C Hackney Wick St Mary of Eton w St Aug *Lon* 93-96; P-in-c Old Ford St Paul and St Mark 96-03; V from 03; Dean of Women's Min Stepney Area 94-02; Preb St Paul's Cathl from 02. *The Vicarage, St Stephen's Road, London E3 5JL* Tel (020) 8980 9020

BOCKING (Essex), Dean of. *See* NEED, The Very Revd Philip Alan

BOCKING (Suffolk), Dean of. *See* THROWER, The Very Revd Martin Charles

BODDAM-WHETHAM, Tudor Alexander. b 76. St Aid Coll Dur BA97. Wycliffe Hall Ox 06. **d** 08 **p** 09. C Houghton *Carl* from 08. *167 Kingstown Road, Carlisle CA3 0AX* Tel 07910-754394 (mobile)

BODDINGTON, Canon Alan Charles Peter. b 37. Oak Hill Th Coll 63. **d** 66 **p** 67. C Bedworth *Cov* 66-69; Bp's Officer for Min 69-75; Bp's Chapl for Miss 69-73; P-in-c Wroxall and Honiley 72-75; V Westwood 75-85; Asst Chapl Warw Univ 78-85; TR N Farnborough 85-02; RD Aldershot 88-93; Hon Can Guildf Cathl 92-02; rtd 02; Perm to Offic *Cov* from 02. *Tremar, Hathaway Lane, Stratford-upon-Avon CV37 9BJ* Tel (01789) 263643 Mobile 07866-909092

BODDY, Alan Richard. b 47. Ripon Coll Cuddesdon. **d** 84 **p** 85. C Eastcote St Lawr *Lon* 84-87; C Kensington St Mary Abbots w St Geo 87-90; Chapl HM Pris Brixton 90-91; Chapl HM Pris Send and Downview 91-92; Chapl HM Pris High Down 92-98; Chapl HM Pris Wormwood Scrubs 98-02; rtd 02; Perm to Offic *Lon* and *S'wark* from 02; PV Westmr Abbey from 02. *105 Valiant House, Vicarage Crescent, London SW11 3LX* E-mail alanboddy@dsl.pipex.com

BODDY, David. b 57. Linc Th Coll 92. **d** 92 **p** 93. C Peterlee *Dur* 92-95; C Penshaw 95-97; P-in-c Shiney Row 95-98; P-in-c Herrington 95-98; TV S Shields All SS 98-04; V Haswell, Shotton and Thornley from 04. *The Vicarage, Shotton Colliery, Durham DH6 2JW* Tel 0191-526 1156 Mobile 07971-304622 E-mail davidboddy@lineone.net

BODLE, Richard Talbot. b 70. Southn Univ LLB91. Wycliffe Hall Ox BTh98. **d** 98 **p** 99. C S Mimms Ch Ch *Lon* 98-02; TV Edgware 02-08; V Churt and Hindhead *Guildf* from 08. *St Alban's Vicarage, Wood Road, Hindhead GU26 6PX* Tel (01428) 605305 E-mail richard@bodle.plus.com

BODMIN, Archdeacon of. *See* COHEN, The Ven Clive Ronald Franklin

BODY, Andrew. b 46. Pemb Coll Cam BA68 MA71. Ridley Hall Cam 68. **d** 70 **p** 71. C New Bury *Man* 70-73; TV Droylsden St Mary 73-78; V Low Harrogate St Mary *Ripon* 78-92; TR Redhorn *Sarum* 92-97; V Chobham w Valley End *Guildf* from 97; RD Surrey Heath from 06. *Chobham Vicarage, Bagshot Road, Chobham, Woking GU24 8BY* Tel (01276) 858197 E-mail ab@tasoma.orangehome.co.uk

BODY, Mrs Shuna Jane. b 67. SEITE 98. **d** 01 **p** 02. NSM Appledore w Brookland, Fairfield, Brenzett etc *Cant* from 01. *Hope Farm, Snargate, Romney Marsh TN29 9UQ* Tel (01797) 343977 Mobile 07977-981990 E-mail shunabody@hotmail.com

BODYCOMBE, Stephen John. b 58. Lanchester Poly Cov BA. St Mich Coll Llan. **d** 83 **p** 84. C Cardiff St Jo *Llan* 83-86; V Dinas and Penygraig w Williamstown 86-00; V Dyffryn from 00. *The Vicarage, Dyffryn, Neath SA10 7AZ* Tel (01792) 814237

BOFFEY, Ian. b 40. Glas Univ MA63. Glas NSM Course 75. **d** 75 **p** 78. NSM Dalry *Glas* 75-78; P-in-c 78-97; N Ayrshire TM from 97. *2 Kinloch Avenue, Stewarton, Kilmarnock KA3 3HF* Tel (01560) 482586 E-mail ian.boffey2@btinternet.com

BOGA, Bishop of. *See* NJOJO, The Rt Revd Patrice Byankya

BOGGUST, Mrs Patricia Anne. b 42. Portsm Dioc Tr Course. **d** 90 **p** 98. NSM Hook w Warsash *Portsm* 90-94; NSM Locks Heath 94-09; Chapl Southn Univ Hosps NHS Trust from 01. *21 Beverley Close, Park Gate, Southampton SO31 6QU* Tel (01489) 573586

BOGLE, Ms Elizabeth. b 47. York Univ BA68 Leeds Univ PGCE69. S'wark Ord Course 93. **d** 96 **p** 97. NSM E Greenwich *S'wark* 96-00; NSM Hatcham St Jas 00-06; NSM Newington St Paul from 06. *96 Grierson Road, London SE23 1NX* Tel (020) 8699 9996 E-mail elizabethbogle@hotmail.com

BOGLE, James Main Lindam Linton. b 33. Peterho Cam BA56 MA60. Wells Th Coll 59. **d** 61 **p** 62. C Bermondsey St Anne *S'wark* 61-65; Chapl York Univ 65-72; V Brayton 72-76; V Forest Hill St Aug *S'wark* 76-83; C Hatcham St Cath 83-85; Hon C 91-03; C Herne Hill St Paul 86-87; rtd 87; Perm to Offic *S'wark* from 04. *96 Grierson Road, London SE23 1NX* Tel (020) 8699 9996 E-mail jamesmllbogle@hotmail.com

BOHAN, Kimberley. b 50. St Andr Univ MA93 Smith Coll (USA) MAT94 St Andr Univ BD99 Edin Univ MTh03. **d** 03 **p** 04. C Glas St Ninian 03-06; R Dunoon *Arg* 06-09; P-in-c Rothesay 06-09; P-in-c Tighnabruaich 06-09; R Dunblane *St And* from 09. *The Rectory, Smith Loan, Dunblane FK15 0HQ* E-mail kbohan@btinternet.com

BOIT, Mervyn Hays. b 38. Univ of Wales (Lamp) BA59. St Mich Coll Llan 59. **d** 61 **p** 62. C Roath St German *Llan* 61-63; C Skewen 63-69; V Pontycymer and Blaengarw 69-03; rtd 03; P-in-c Biarritz *Eur* 06-07. *Maison Neuve, chemin d'la Poste, F-64780 Bidarray, France* Tel (0033) (5) 59 37 77 60

BOLAND, Christopher Paul. b 75. Hertf Coll Ox MPhys97. Ridley Hall Cam BTh01. **d** 01 **p** 02. C Skirbeck H Trin *Linc* 01-05; P-in-c Grantham, Harrowby w Londonthorpe from 05. *The Vicarage, Edinburgh Road, Grantham NG31 9QZ* Tel (01476) 564781 Mobile 07791-702537 E-mail cpboland@btinternet.com

BOLAND, Geoffrey. b 56. Open Univ BA03. Oak Hill Th Coll 87. **d** 89 **p** 90. C Ormskirk *Liv* 89-94; C Woodside Park St Barn *Lon* 94-99; TV Canford Magna *Sarum* from 99. *11 Plantagenet Crescent, Bournemouth BH11 9PL* Tel (01220) 573872

BOLD, Peter Edward. b 64. Sheff Univ BEng86 PhD90. Cranmer Hall Dur BA94. **d** 95 **p** 96. C Grenoside *Sheff* 95-97; C Rotherham and Dioc Communications Officer 97-01; P-in-c Brampton Bierlow 01-05; V from 05. *Brampton Vicarage, Christchurch Road, Wath-upon-Dearne, Rotherham S63 6NW* Tel (01709) 873210 E-mail pebold@talk21.com

BOLDING, Alan Frederick. b 40. NTMTC. **d** 07 **p** 07. NSM Woodford Bridge *Chelmsf* from 07. *21 Portman Drive, Woodford Green IG8 8QN* Tel (020) 8550 2070 Mobile 07932-797983 E-mail apbolding@onetel.com

BOLE, Malcolm Dennis. b 30. Oak Hill Th Coll 65. **d** 67 **p** 68. C Bridlington Priory *York* 67-70; Lect Stanley Smith Th Coll Gahini Rwanda 71; Prin 71-72; Lect École de Théologie Butare 72-73; P-in-c Combe Hay *B & W* 74-81; V Bath Odd Down 74-81; P-in-c Taunton St Jas 81-84; V 84-90; R Bicknoller w Crowcombe and Sampford Brett 90-98; rtd 98; Perm to Offic *B & W* from 01. *7 Putsham Mead, Kilve, Bridgwater TA5 1DZ* Tel (01278) 741297

BOLLARD, Canon Richard George. b 39. Fitzw Ho Cam BA61 MA65 K Coll Lon BD63 AKC63. **d** 64 **p** 65. C Southampton Maybush St Pet *Win* 64-68; Chapl Aston Univ 68-74; TR Chelmsley Wood 74-82; V Coleshill and Maxstoke 82-04; RD Coleshill 82-92; Hon Can Birm Cathl 85-04; Dioc Ecum Officer 97-02; rtd 04; Perm to Offic *Heref* from 05. *Moreton Cottage, 12 Prince Edward Road, Hereford HR4 0LG* Tel (01432) 267414

BOLLEY, Michael Francis. b 55. St Cath Coll Ox BA76 MSc77 MA92. Ripon Coll Cuddesdon 90. **d** 92 **p** 93. C Pinner *Lon* 92-95; C Eastcote St Lawr 95-99; P-in-c Southall H Trin 99-06; V from 06. *Holy Trinity Vicarage, Park View Road, Southall UB1 3HJ* Tel (020) 8574 3839 E-mail michael@bolley.freeserve.co.uk

BOLSTER, David Richard. b 50. BA. St Jo Coll Nottm. **d** 84 **p** 85. C Luton Lewsey St Hugh *St Alb* 84-87; V Woodside w E Hyde 87-01; V Edmonton St Aldhelm *Lon* from 01. *St Aldhelm's Vicarage, Windmill Road, London N18 1PA* Tel (020) 8807 5336 E-mail david.bolster@london.anglican.org

BOLT, George Henry. b 34. MInstP75 CPhys75 Lon Univ BSc60 Bath Univ MSc75. S Dios Minl Tr Scheme 85. **d** 88 **p** 89. NSM Oldbury *Sarum* 88-89; Chapl Chippenham Tech Coll 89-90; C Kington St Michael *Bris* 90-92; P-in-c Aldenham *St Alb* 92-98; rtd 98; Perm to Offic *Ban* from 98. *Ty Capel Ffrwd, Llanfachreth, Dolgellau LL40 2NR* Tel (01341) 422006

BOLT, Mrs Mary Veronica. b 36. S Dios Minl Tr Scheme 90. **d** 93 **p** 94. NSM Aldenham *St Alb* 93-98; Sub-Chapl HM Pris The Mount 93-98; rtd 98; Perm to Offic *Ban* 98-99; P-in-c Maentwrog w Trawsfynydd 99-03. *Ty Capel Ffrwd, Llanfachreth, Dolgellau LL40 2NR* Tel (01341) 422006 E-mail mary.bolt@care4free.net

BOLTON, Canon Christopher Leonard. b 60. St Mich Coll Llan. **d** 83 **p** 84. C Lampeter *St D* 83-86; P-in-c Llanarth and Capel Cynon w Talgarreg etc 86-87; V from 87; AD Glyn Aeron from 02; Hon Can St D Cathl from 09. *The Vicarage, Llanarth SA47 0NJ* Tel (01545) 580745

BOLTON, Mrs Jane Elizabeth. b 53. Leic Univ BA75. Ripon Coll Cuddesdon 95. **d** 97 **p** 98. C Sheff St Mark Broomhill 97-02; P-in-c Dinnington 02-04; P-in-c Laughton w Throapham 03-04; P-in-c Dinnington w Laughton and Throapham 04-05; R from 05; AD Laughton from 08. *The Rectory, 217 Nursery Road, Dinnington, Sheffield S25 2QU* Tel (01909) 562335 E-mail mail@janebolton.co.uk *or* jane.bolton@sheffield.anglican.org

BOLTON, John. b 43. SS Paul & Mary Coll Cheltenham DipEd64. Trin Coll Bris 83. **d** 85 **p** 86. C Minehead *B & W* 85-89; R Winford w Felton Common Hill 89-98; C-in-c Locking Castle CD 98-06; rtd 06; Perm to Offic *B & W* from 06. *The Poppies, 13 Cornlands, Sampford Peverell, Tiverton EX16 7UA* Tel (01884) 821445 E-mail john20011ccp@aol.com

BOLTON, Kelvin. b 53. Wilson Carlile Coll 88 Trin Coll Bris BA98. **d** 98 **p** 99. C Walton Breck Ch Ch *Liv* 98-01; V Goose Green 01-08; P-in-c Walton Breck from 08. *Christ Church Vicarage, 157 Hartnup Street, Liverpool L5 1UW* Tel 0151-263 2518 E-mail kelvb@uwclub.net

BOLTON, Paul Edward. b 71. St Jo Coll Ox BA94 MA98 Peterho Cam BA97. Ridley Hall Cam 95. **d** 98 **p** 99. C Lowestoft Ch Ch *Nor* 98-01; Titus Trust from 01. *93 Morrell Avenue, Oxford OX4 1NQ* Tel (01865) 248955 E-mail paul_bolton@lineone.net

BOLTON, Peter Richard Shawcross. b 58. Warwick Univ BA79. Sarum & Wells Th Coll 80. **d** 83 **p** 84. C Beckenham St Jas *Roch* 83-86; C Bedford Leigh *Man* 86-88; V Royton St Paul 88-94; AD Tandle 93-94; P-in-c Lower Broughton Ascension 95-01; P-in-c Salford Ordsall St Clem 98-01; P-in-c Ardwick St Benedict 99-01; V Leavesden *St Alb* 01-07; V Weston super Mare All SS and St Sav *B & W* from 07; CMP from 99. *The Vicarage, 46 Manor Road, Weston-super-Mare BS23 2SU* Tel (01934) 633910 E-mail fatherpeterbolton@yahoo.co.uk

BOLTON, Richard David Edward. b 52. MA. St Steph Ho Ox 79. **d** 81 **p** 82. C Rawmarsh w Parkgate *Sheff* 81-84; Chapl Wellingborough Sch 85-92; Chapl Merchant Taylors' Sch Northwood from 91; Perm to Offic *Lon* from 91; P in O from 96.

1 Askew Road, Sandy Lodge, Northwood HA6 2JE Tel (01923) 821136 *or* 820644

BOLTON, Archdeacon of. *See* BAILEY, The Ven David Charles

BOLTON, Suffragan Bishop of. *See* EDMONDSON, The Rt Revd Christopher Paul

BOMFORD, Canon Rodney William George. b 43. BNC Ox BA64 MA68. Coll of Resurr Mirfield 67 Union Th Sem (NY) STM69. **d** 69 **p** 70. C Deptford St Paul *S'wark* 69-77; V Camberwell St Giles w St Matt 77-01; RD Camberwell 87-97; Hon Can S'wark Cathl 93-01; rtd 01. *The Manor House, Modbury, Ivybridge PL21 0RA* Tel (01548) 831277

BOMYER, Julian Richard Nicholas Jeffrey. b 55. AKC78 Sarum & Wells Th Coll 78. **d** 79 **p** 80. C Rugby *Cov* 79-84; TV 85-88; P-in-c Clifton upon Dunsmore w Brownsover 84-85; Prec Ch Ch *Ox* 88-93; V Hampton *Worc* 93-01; P-in-c Sedgeberrow w Hinton-on-the-Green 00-01; R Hampton w Sedgeberrow and Hinton-on-the-Green 01-06; rtd 06. *52 Elmside, Evesham WR11 3DZ* Tel (01386) 421559 E-mail julian@bomyer.co.uk

BOND, Alan Richard. b 49. Lon Univ BSc71 Imp Coll Lon ARCS71 MCMI75 MIMA75 CMath98 CSci05. S Dios Minl Tr Scheme 80. **d** 83 **p** 84. NSM Westbourne *Chich* 83-86. *Southlyn, The Park, Castle Cary BA7 7EP*
E-mail alan.r.bond@btopenworld.com

✠**BOND, The Rt Revd Charles Derek.** b 27. AKC51. **d** 52 **p** 53 **c** 76. C Friern Barnet St Jas *Lon* 52-56; Lic to Offic *Birm* 56-58; Midl Sch Sec SCM 56-58; V Harringay St Paul *Lon* 58-62; V Harrow Weald All SS 62-72; P-in-c Pebmarsh *Chelmsf* 72-73; Adn Colchester 72-76; Suff Bp Bradwell 76-84; Area Bp Bradwell 84-92; rtd 92; Hon Asst Bp Glouc and Worc 92-06; Perm to Offic *Chelmsf* from 06; Hon Asst Bp Chelmsf from 07. *52 Horn Book, Saffron Walden CB11 3JW* Tel (01799) 521308 E-mail bondd46@aol.com

BOND, Daniel Michael. b 75. Bp Grosseteste Coll BA(QTS)97 Cam Univ BTh02. Ridley Hall Cam 99. **d** 02 **p** 03. C Ranworth w Panxworth, Woodbastwick etc *Nor* 02-05; R Acle w Fishley, N Burlingham, Beighton w Moulton 05-07; Chapl Aldenham Sch Herts from 07. *1 The Orchard, Aldenham School, Aldenham Road, Elstree, Borehamwood WD6 3AJ* Tel (01923) 858122 E-mail dmb40@cam.ac.uk

BOND, David. b 36. Oak Hill Th Coll 72. **d** 74 **p** 75. C Leyton St Mary w St Edw *Chelmsf* 74-78; C Slough *Ox* 78-80; V Selby St Jas *York* 80-93; P-in-c Wistow 80-82; V 82-93; RD Selby 89-93; P-in-c Northiam *Chich* 93-94; R 94-99; rtd 99; Perm to Offic *Chich* from 00. *32 Reginald Road, Bexhill-on-Sea TN39 3PH* Tel (01424) 731845

BOND, David Matthew. b 38. Leic Univ BA59 Leeds Univ PGCE67 Nottm Univ MA85. Sarum Th Coll 59. **d** 61 **p** 62. C Leic St Anne 61-64; E England Sec SCM 64-66; Hon C Nor St Pet Mancroft 64-67; Lect and Hd of Section Pet Regional Coll 67-96; Lect Pet Coll of Adult Educn from 96; Hon C Stamford All SS w St Pet *Linc* 74-81; Hon C Stamford All SS w St Jo from 81; Perm to Offic *Pet* from 85. *2 The Courtyard, Cotterstock, Peterborough PE8 5HD* Tel (01832) 226255

BOND, David Warner. b 32. MA BSc(Econ). Cant Sch of Min 79. **d** 82 **p** 83. NSM Otham w Langley *Cant* from 82. *6 Denton Close, Maidstone ME15 8ER* Tel (01622) 202239 Fax 205149 E-mail dwbond@blueyonder.co.uk *or* dwbond@bigfoot.com

BOND, Derek. *See* BOND, The Rt Revd Charles Derek

BOND, Douglas Gregory. b 39. FVCM. Edin Th Coll 74. **d** 76 **p** 77. NSM Edin St Paul and St Geo 76-83; P-in-c Abthorpe w Slapton *Pet* 83-84; R Silverstone and Abthorpe w Slapton 84-89; V Pet St Jude 89-95; R Kislingbury and Harpole 95-04; rtd 04; Perm to Offic *Pet* from 04. *2 Mews Cottages, Meeting Lane, Towcester NN12 6JX* Tel (01327) 358861 Mobile 07802-736409 E-mail father.d@highrev.fsnet.co.uk

BOND, Mrs Gita Devi. b 57. N Lon Poly BSc80 Chelsea Coll Lon PGCE81. Ridley Hall Cam 06. **d** 08 **p** 09. C The Ramseys and Upwood *Ely* from 08. *23 Signal Road, Ramsey, Huntingdon PE26 1NG* Tel (01487) 821105 Mobile 07977-555895 E-mail gita.bond@hotmail.com

BOND, Gordon. b 44. Chich Th Coll 68. **d** 71 **p** 72. C Wisbech St Aug *Ely* 71-74; C Wembley Park St Aug *Lon* 74-77; C York Town St Mich *Guildf* 77-80; TV Haywards Heath St Wilfrid *Chich* 80-82; V Lower Beeding 82-86; V E Grinstead St Mary 86-06; RD E Grinstead 98-04; rtd 06. *6 St Andrew's Close, Reigate RH2 7JF*

BOND, Mrs Jill Margaret. b 45. Newton Park Coll Bath TCert67. WEMTC 04. **d** 06 **p** 07. OLM Redmarley D'Abitot, Bromesberrow, Pauntley etc *Glouc* from 06. *Southfield, Hawcross, Redmarley, Gloucester GL19 3JQ* Tel (01452) 840202 E-mail rev.jbond@googlemail.com

BOND, Canon John Albert. b 35. LRAM55 GGSM56 St Cath Soc Ox BA61 MA65 MPhil75 Seabury-Western Th Sem BD62. Wycliffe Hall Ox 58. **d** 62 **p** 63. C Chelmsf Cathl 62-63; Succ 63-64; Prec 64-66; Lect St Osyth Coll Clacton-on-Sea 66-69; Lect Ch Ch Coll Cant 69-73; Sen Lect 73-85; Prin Lect and Hd RS Cant Ch Ch Univ Coll 85-00; Hon Min Can Cant Cathl 70-85; Hon Can 85-00; rtd 00; Perm to Offic *Cant* from 03. *1 St Lawrence Forstal, Canterbury CT1 3PA* Tel (01227) 765575

BOND, The Very Revd John Frederick Augustus. b 45. Open Univ BA75. CITC 64. **d** 67 **p** 69. C Lisburn St Paul *Conn* 67-70; C Finaghy 70-77; I Ballynure and Ballyeaston 77-99; I Skerry w Rathcavan and Newtowncrommelin from 99; Can Conn Cathl 96-98; Prec 98-01; Dean Conn from 01. *The Rectory, 49 Rectory Gardens, Broughshane, Ballymena BT42 4LF* Tel and fax (028) 2586 1215 Mobile 07711-285728
E-mail jfa.bond@btinternet.com *or* dean@connor.anglican.org

BOND, Kim Mary. *See* BURGESS, Mrs Kim Mary

BOND, Lawrence. b 53. ACIB77. Sarum & Wells Th Coll 92. **d** 92 **p** 93. C Saffron Walden w Wendens Ambo and Littlebury *Chelmsf* 92-95; TV 96-00; P-in-c Takeley w Lt Canfield 00-04; R from 04; RD Dunmow and Stansted from 02. *The Rectory, Parsonage Road, Takeley, Bishop's Stortford CM22 6QX* Tel and fax (01279) 870837 E-mail revlbond@hotmail.com

BOND, Linda. b 52. Nottm Univ BEd80 Lon Inst of Educn MA89 ACertCM87. EAMTC 96. **d** 99 **p** 00. C Brackley St Pet w St Jas 99-03; C Skegness Gp *Linc* 03-09; P-in-c Bromham w Oakley and Stagsden *St Alb* from 09. *The Vicarage, 47 Stagsden Road, Bromham, Bedford MK43 8PY* Tel (01234) 823268 E-mail lindabond@mypostoffice.co.uk

BOND, Mrs Marian Nancy Hamlyn. b 49. Univ of Wales (Cardiff) BSc(Econ)71 Westmr Coll Ox PGCE72 Ex Univ MEd77. SEITE BA06. **d** 06 **p** 07. NSM Marden *Cant* 06-09; NSM Len Valley from 09. *Vine House, East Street, Harrietsham, Maidstone ME17 1HJ* Tel (01622) 858251 Fax 08700-526044 Mobile 07966-442181 E-mail mnhbond@googlemail.com

BOND, Mark Francis Wilson. b 53. Sarum & Wells Th Coll 89. **d** 91 **p** 92. C Taunton Lyngford *B & W* 91-95; V Highbridge 95-02; R Jersey St Brelade *Win* from 02. *The Rectory, La Marquanderie Hill, St Brelade, Jersey JE3 8EP* Tel (01534) 742302 Fax 490878 E-mail rector@stbreladeschurch.com

BOND, Norman. b 23. Wycliffe Hall Ox. **d** 70 **p** 71. C Warrington St Ann *Liv* 70-73; P-in-c 73-77; P-in-c Warrington St Pet 73-77; V Wigan St Cath 77-88; rtd 88; Perm to Offic *Carl* 88-01; *Liv* 88-98; *S & M* 00-09. *10 Linstone Drive, Norton, Yarmouth PO41 0RL* Tel (01983) 760799

BOND, Paul Maxwell. b 36. TD73. Open Th Coll BA00 ACIB56. Oak Hill Th Coll 76. **d** 79 **p** 80. NSM Wisley w Pyrford *Guildf* 79-91; Org Children's Soc SW Lon 88-91; C Egham *Guildf* 91-93; C Horsell 93-94; V Rockfield and St Maughen's w Llangattock etc *Mon* 94-99; rtd 99; Hon C Islip w Charlton on Otmoor, Oddington, Noke etc *Ox* 99-01; Hon C Ray Valley 01-04; Nat Liaison Officer Ch Tourism Assn 94-99. *Fosters, Pyrford Heath, Pyrford, Woking GU22 8SS* Tel (01932) 351137
E-mail paul_bond@bigfoot.com

BOND, Mrs Susan Fraser. b 55. SS Hild & Bede Coll Dur BEd78 Leeds Univ MA00. NOC 96. **d** 99 **p** 00. C Tickhill w Stainton *Sheff* 99-02; R Warmsworth from 02; AD W Doncaster 06-07. *Warmsworth Rectory, 187 Warmsworth Road, Doncaster DN4 0TW* Tel (01302) 853324
E-mail sue@bond007.fslife.co.uk

BOND-THOMAS, David Harradence. b 23. Ch Coll Cam BA44 MA51. **d** 59 **p** 60. C Langley Marish *Ox* 59-62; C Earley St Pet 62-71; P-in-c Middleton Stoney 71-77; P-in-c Bucknell 71-76; P-in-c Weston on the Green 72-76; P-in-c Chesterton w Wendlebury 76-77; V Chesterton w Middleton Stoney and Wendlebury 77-89; rtd 89; Perm to Offic *Glouc* from 89. *35 Greet Road, Winchcombe, Cheltenham GL54 5JT* Tel (01242) 603150

BONE, David Hugh. b 39. Worc Coll Ox BA63 MA67. **d** 06 **p** 07. OLM Almondsbury and Olveston *Bris* from 06. *3 Hardy Lane, Tockington, Bristol BS32 4LJ* Tel (01454) 614601 Mobile 07958-411473 E-mail david.bone10@btinternet.com

BONE, Mrs Evelyn Mary. b 48. WEMTC 05. **d** 08 **p** 09. NSM Draycot *Bris* from 08. *Somerford House, 2 Fairleigh Rise, Kington Langley, Chippenham SN15 5QF* Tel (01249) 750519
E-mail langley@gebone.mail1.co.uk

BONE, Janet. **d** 05 **p** 06. NSM Trellech and Penallt *Mon* from 05. *Ty Ffynnon, The Narth, Monmouth NP25 4QJ* Tel (01600) 860466

✠**BONE, The Rt Revd John Frank Ewan.** b 30. St Pet Coll Ox BA54 MA59 Whitelands Coll Lon PGCE71. Ely Th Coll 54. **d** 56 **p** 57 **c** 89. C Pimlico St Gabr *Lon* 56-60; C Henley *Ox* 60-63; V Datchet 63-76; RD Burnham 74-77; R Upton cum Chalvey 76-78; Adn Buckingham 77-89; Area Bp Reading 89-96; rtd 97; Hon Asst Bp Ox from 97. *4 Grove Road, Henley-on-Thames RG9 1DH* Tel (01491) 413482 E-mail jfebone@onetel.com

BONE, Simon Adrian. b 78. Ripon Coll Cuddesdon BA09. **d** 09. C Newquay *Truro* from 09. *127 Penmere Drive, Newquay TR7 1NS* Tel (01637) 879419 Mobile 07971-270615 E-mail fathersimon@btinternet.com

BONHAM, Mrs Valerie. b 47. ALA94. SAOMC 94. **d** 97 **p** 98. NSM Newbury *Ox* 97-98; C Cookham 98-02; P-in-c Coleford w Holcombe *B & W* from 02. *The Vicarage, Church Street, Coleford, Radstock BA3 5NG* Tel (01373) 813382

BONHAM-CARTER, Gerard Edmund David. b 31. Lon Univ BSc53. S'wark Ord Course 84. **d** 87 **p** 88. NSM Wandsworth St Paul *S'wark* 87-04; Chapl R Hosp for Neuro-Disability 92-04; Perm to Offic *St E* from 87 and *S'wark* from 04. *7 Fleur Gates,*

Princes Way, London SW19 6QQ Tel and fax (020) 8788 1230 *or* 8780 5075 E-mail gerard.bonham-carter@ukgateway.net

BONIFACE, Lionel Ernest George. b 36. Lon Coll of Div ALCD63 BD64. **d** 64 **p** 65. C Attenborough w Chilwell *S'well* 64-69; C Farndon 69-71; C Thorpe 69-71; P-in-c Mansfield St Aug 71-77; V Oughtibridge *Sheff* 77-92; Ind Chapl 79-81; P-in-c Treeton 92-93; TV Brinsworth w Catcliffe and Treeton 93-98; rtd 98; Perm to Offic *Sheff* from 99. *30 Everard Avenue, Bradway, Sheffield S17 4LZ* Tel 0114-235 0415

BONIWELL, Timothy Richard. b 51. AKC73. St Aug Coll Cant 74. **d** 75 **p** 76. C Walthamstow St Mich *Chelmsf* 75-78; C Wigmore Abbey *Heref* 78-83; C Studley and Chapl Trowbridge Coll *Sarum* 83-86; V Bath St Barn w Englishcombe *B & W* 86-95; R Tintinhull w Chilthorne Domer, Yeovil Marsh etc 95-02; V Enfield St Geo *Lon* 02-05; Chapl Convent of St Mary at the Cross Edgware from 05. *St John's House, 27 Highview Avenue, Edgware HA8 9TX* Tel (020) 8958 8980 E-mail boniwell@btinternet.com

BONNER, David Robert. b 28. ASCA66 FCIS72 FCIB74. S'wark Ord Course 74. **d** 77 **p** 78. NSM Hampton All SS *Lon* 77-84; P-in-c Twickenham All SS 84-91; rtd 91; Perm to Offic *Lon* 91-05. *17 St James's Road, Hampton Hill, Hampton TW12 1DH* Tel (020) 8979 1565

BONNER, James Maxwell Campbell. b 28. Sydney Univ BSc48 DipEd49. Oak Hill Th Coll BD59. **d** 60 **p** 61. C Walthamstow St Mary *Chelmsf* 60-63; C Morden *S'wark* 63-65; Australia from 65; rtd 98. *1206/5 Albert Road, Strathfield NSW 2135, Australia* Tel (0061) (2) 9763 7535

BONNET, Tom. b 51. Univ of Wales (Cardiff) BTh90. St Mich Coll Llan 90. **d** 90 **p** 91. C Criccieth w Treflys *Ban* 90-91; C Denio w Abererch 91-93; R Llanfachraeth 93-94; R Valley w Llanfachraeth 94-98; R Valley w Llechylched and Caergeiliog 98-07; AD Llifon and Talybolion 04-07; V Caerhun w Llangelynin w Llanbedr-y-Cennin from 07. *Caerhun Vicarage, Tyn-y-Groes, Conwy LL32 8UG* Tel (01492) 650250 Mobile 07713-548941 E-mail rev@tbonnet.freeserve.co.uk

BONNEY, Canon Mark Philip John. b 57. St Cath Coll Cam BA78 MA82. St Steph Ho Ox BA84 MA89. **d** 85 **p** 86. C Stockton St Pet *Dur* 85-88; Chapl St Alb Abbey 88-90; Prec 90-92; V Eaton Bray w Edlesborough 92-96; R Gt Berkhamsted 96-04; RD Berkhamsted 02-04; Can Res and Treas Sarum Cathl from 04. *Loders, 23 The Close, Salisbury SP1 2EH* Tel (01722) 322172 E-mail treasurer@salcath.co.uk

BONNEY, Prof Richard John. b 47. Ox Univ DPhil73. **d** 96 **p** 97. NSM Knighton St Mary Magd *Leic* from 96. *7 Carisbrooke Park, Leicester LE2 3PQ* Tel 0116-212 5677 E-mail bon@leicester.anglican.org

BONNEY, Stuart Campbell. b 51. Edin Univ BD83. Edin Th Coll 81. **d** 83 **p** 84. C Edin St Luke 83-86; C Edin St Martin 83-86; P-in-c Auchterarder *St And* 86-90; P-in-c Muthill 86-90; Dep Chapl HM Pris Leeds 90-91; Chapl HM Pris Moorland 91-96; P-in-c Bathgate *Edin* 96-01; P-in-c Linlithgow 96-01. *Circlebay Cottage, 159 Main Street, Pathhead EH37 5SQ* Tel (01875) 320336

BONNEYWELL, Miss Christine Mary. b 57. Univ of Wales (Lamp) BA78 LTh80. Sarum & Wells Th Coll 80. **d** 81 **p** 94. C Swansea St Pet *S & B* 81-84; C Llangyfelach 84-86; Chapl Univ of Wales (Lamp) *St D* 86-90; Educn Officer Wells Cathl 90-95; C Yeovil H Trin w Barwick 95-97; Chapl Yeovil Distr Hosp 95-97; Chapl Pilgrim Health NHS Trust Boston 97 01; Chapl United Lincs Hosps NHS Trust from 01. *The Chaplaincy, Pilgrim Hospital, Sibsey Road, Boston PE21 9QT,* or *4 Hospital Lane, Boston PE21 9BY* Tel (01205) 364801 ext 2243 *or* 355151 Fax 354395

BONSALL, Charles Henry Brash. b 42. Ex Univ BA66. Ridley Hall Cam 66. **d** 68 **p** 69. C Cheltenham St Mary *Glouc* 68-72; Sudan 72-77 and 79-83; Perm to Offic *Nor* 78; Development and Miss Sec Intercon Ch Soc 83-93; rtd 93; Perm to Offic *Birm* from 91. *3 Pakenham Road, Birmingham B15 2NE* Tel 0121-440 6143

BONSEY, Hugh Richmond Lowry. b 49. Sarum & Wells Th Coll 74. **d** 76 **p** 77. C Bris St Mary Redcliffe w Temple etc 76-80; TV Sutton *Liv* 80-88; P-in-c Yatton Keynell *Bris* 88-89; P-in-c Biddestone w Slaughterford 88-89; P-in-c Castle Combe 88-89; P-in-c W Kington 88-89; P-in-c Nettleton w Littleton Drew 88-89; C Westbury-on-Trym H Trin 89-90; V Peasedown St John w Wellow *B & W* 90-04; TV Wylye and Till Valley *Sarum* from 04. *The Rectory, West Street, Great Wishford, Salisbury SP2 0PQ* Tel (01722) 790363 E-mail hbonsey@wylye.net

BONTING, Prof Sjoerd Lieuwe. b 24. Amsterdam Univ BSc44 MSc50 PhD52 Lon Univ BD58 SOSc. Washington Dioc Course 63. **d** 63 **p** 64. C Bethesda St Luke USA 63-65; Prof Biochemistry Nijmegen Univ 65-85; Chapl Nijmegen, Eindhoven, Arnhem and Twenthe *Eur* 80-85; Asst Sunnyvale St Thos USA 85-90; Asst Palo Alto St Mark 90-93; Perm to Offic *Eur* from 93. *Specreuse 12, 7471 TH Goor, The Netherlands* Tel (0031) (547) 260947 E-mail s.l.bonting@wxs.nl

BOOKER, Ms Alison Susan Wray. b 74. Worc Coll of Educn BA95 York St Jo Coll MA04. Westcott Ho Cam 06. **d** 08 **p** 09. C Countesthorpe w Foston *Leic* from 08. *7 Borrowcup Close, Countesthorpe, Leicester LE8 5XJ* E-mail abooker@leicester.anglican.org

BOOKER, Gerald Dennis. b 30. St Pet Coll Ox BA52 MA56. Ridley Hall Cam 53 Oak Hill Th Coll 80. **d** 81 **p** 82. Hon C Hertford All SS *St Alb* 81-83; R Bramfield w Stapleford and Waterford 83-96; Chapl Herts Univ 90-96; rtd 96; Perm to Offic *St Alb* from 96. *The Garden House, Churchfields, Hertford SG13 8AE*

BOOKER, Mrs Margaret Katharine. b 20. MCSP42. Westcott Ho Cam 82. dss 83 **d** 87 **p** 94. Stansted Mountfitchet *Chelmsf* 83-95; Par Dn 87-90; NSM 90-95; rtd 90; Perm to Offic *Ely* from 95. *49 Home Farm Road, Houghton, Huntingdon PE28 2BN* Tel (01480) 469167

BOOKER, Michael Charles. b 36. LLCM57 ARCO58. Lon Coll of Div LTh63. **d** 63 **p** 64. C Royston *St Alb* 63-66; C Mildenhall *St E* 66-68; Min Can St E Cathl 68-83; Prec 70-83; Chapl Framlingham Coll 84-99; rtd 99; Perm to Offic *St E* from 99. *29 The Mowbrays, Framlingham, Woodbridge IP13 9DL* Tel (01728) 723122

BOOKER, Michael Paul Montague. b 57. Jes Coll Ox BA79 Bris Univ PGCE80. Trin Coll Bris BA87. **d** 87 **p** 88. C Cant St Mary Bredin 87-91; V Leamington Priors St Mary *Cov* 91-96; Dir Miss and Past Studies Ridley Hall Cam 96-05; P-in-c Comberton *Ely* from 05; P-in-c Toft w Caldecote and Childerley from 05. *The Vicarage, 92 Swaynes Lane, Comberton, Cambridge CB23 7EF* Tel (01223) 260095 E-mail mpmb2@yahoo.co.uk

BOOKLESS, Andrew Pitcairn. b 63. Sheff Univ BA85. St Jo Coll Nottm 90. **d** 92 **p** 93. C Llantrisant 92-95; C Llangynwyd w Maesteg 95-97; V Bargoed and Deri w Brithdir from 97. *The Vicarage, Vicarage Lane, Bargoed CF81 8TR* Tel (01443) 831069 E-mail ahbookless@googlemail.com

BOOKLESS, David John Charles. b 62. Jes Coll Cam MA83 PGCE. Trin Coll Bris MA91. **d** 91 **p** 92. C Southall Green St Jo *Lon* 91-99; P-in-c Southall St Geo 99-01; Nat Dir A Rocha UK (Christians in Conservation) from 01; Hon C Southall Green St Jo from 03. *13 Avenue Road, Southall UB1 3BL* Tel (020) 8571 0981 E-mail dave.bookless@arocha.org *or* uk@arocha.org

BOOKLESS, Mrs Rosemary. b 26. Westf Coll Lon BA47 DipEd49 Serampore Univ BD72. St Mich Ho Ox 56. dss 80 **d** 91 **p** 94. Willoughby-on-the-Wolds w Wysall and Widmerpool *S'well* 80-85; rtd 85; Perm to Offic *Leic* 85-89; Loughborough Em 89-91; NSM 91-95; NSM Loughborough Em and St Mary in Charnwood 95-97; Perm to Offic 97-03. *7 Oakland Gardens, Bargoed CF81 8QF* Tel (01443) 832166 E-mail rosemary@rbookless.freeserve.co.uk

BOON, Marion. *See* SIMMONS, Ms Marion

BOON, Nigel Francis. b 39. St Jo Coll Nottm. **d** 83 **p** 84. C St Helens St Helen *Liv* 83-86; V Kirkdale St Lawr 86-92; V Huyton Quarry 92-99; rtd 01. *26 Montgomery Avenue, Belmont, North Shore, Auckland 0622, New Zealand* Tel (0064) (9) 445 7418 E-mail nigelfboon@hotmail.com

BOON, William John. b 54. Glouc Sch of Min 84. **d** 88 **p** 89. NSM Matson *Glouc* 88-91; C Gt Witcombe 91-95; C Brockworth 91-96; P-in-c Sharpness w Purton and Brookend 96-99; P-in-c Slimbridge 97-99; R Sharpness, Purton, Brookend and Slimbridge from 00; AD Dursley 02-07. *The Vicarage, Sanigar Lane, Newtown, Berkeley GL13 9NF* Tel (01453) 811360 E-mail bill_boon@lineone.net

BOORMAN, Hugh Ronald. b 58. Ox Min Course 07. **d** 08 **p** 08. C Didcot All SS *Ox* from 08. *Barnabus House, 12 Trent Road, Didcot OX11 7RB* Tel (01235) 819036 Mobile 07980-046162 E-mail hugh.boorman1@virgin.net

BOOT, Felicity Olivia. b 43. TCert64. STETS 94. **d** 97 **p** 98. NSM Lyndhurst and Emery Down and Minstead *Win* 97-04; Chapl Southn Univ Hosps NHS Trust 04-09; Perm to Offic *Win* from 09. *The Firs, Pikes Hill, Lyndhurst SO43 7AY* Tel (023) 8028 2616 E-mail felicityboot@hotmail.com

BOOTES, Michael Charles Edward. b 35. ACP70. Sarum Th Coll 58. **d** 61 **p** 62. C Winchmore Hill St Paul *Lon* 61-64; Switzerland 64-67; C St Marylebone All SS *Lon* 67-68; OGS from 68; Chapl Kingsley St Mich Sch W Sussex 69-75; V Brandon *Dur* 75-78; Chapl Shoreham Gr Sch 78-79; C Clayton w Keymer *Chich* 80-84; TV Ovingdean w Rottingdean and Woodingdean 84-85; R Ovingdean 85-88; V Lundwood *Wakef* 88-92; C Pontefract St Giles 92-95; P-in-c Kellington w Whitley 95-00; rtd 00; Hon C Castleford *Wakef* 00-05; Hon C Methley w Mickletown *Ripon* from 05. *The Rectory, Church Side, Methley, Leeds LS26 9BJ* Tel (01977) 557080 Mobile 07795-495222 E-mail mb@ogs.net

BOOTH, Charles. *See* BOOTH, Ewart Charles

BOOTH, Charles Robert. b 48. Leeds Univ CertEd75. NOC 79. **d** 82 **p** 83. C Eccleshill *Bradf* 82-84; C Jersey St Brelade *Win* 84-88; C Newman Australia 88-90; V Blurton *Lich* 90-93; Chapl Frederick Irwin Angl Communion Sch Mandurah Australia 94-98; R Spearwood 99-03; rtd 03. *PO Box 1474, Toodyay WA 6566, Australia* E-mail boothimages@hotmail.com

BOOTH, David. b 44. Coll of Resurr Mirfield 72. **d** 74 **p** 75. C Osmondthorpe St Phil *Ripon* 74-77; C Armley w New Wortley 77-79; V Leeds St Wilfrid 79-95; V Royton St Paul *Man* from 95.

St Paul's Vicarage, 2 Low Meadows, Royton, Oldham OL2 6YB Tel 0161-624 2388

BOOTH, Derek. b 36. LTCL ALCM AKC61. **d** 62 **p** 63. C Woodchurch *Ches* 62-65; C Penrith St Andr *Carl* 65-67; C Tranmere St Paul *Ches* 67-70; C Wilmslow 70-72; V Micklehurst 73-97; C Staveley and Barrow Hill *Derby* 97-01; rtd 01; Perm to Offic *Derby* from 01. *9 Ilam Close, Inkersall, Chesterfield S43 3EW* Tel (01246) 475421

BOOTH, Eric James. b 43. Open Univ BA84. NOC 86. **d** 89 **p** 90. NSM Nelson St Phil *Blackb* 89-93; NSM Fence and Newchurch-in-Pendle 93-97; NSM Padiham w Hapton and Padiham Green 97-03; rtd 03; Perm to Offic *Blackb* from 04. *5 Round Hill Place, Cliviger, Burnley BB10 4UA* Tel (01282) 450708

BOOTH, Ewart Charles. b 67. LTCL85 K Coll Lon LLB88. Sarum & Wells Th Coll BTh93. **d** 93 **p** 95. NSM Tadley St Pet *Win* 93-95; C Highcliffe w Hinton Admiral 95-00; R W Parley *Sarum* from 00. *The Rectory, 250 New Road, West Parley, Ferndown BH22 8EW* Tel (01202) 873561

BOOTH, Graham Richard. b 55. Birm Univ BSocSc75. St Jo Coll Nottm 89. **d** 91 **p** 92. C Woodthorpe *S'well* 91-96; P-in-c Trowell 96-02; P-in-c Awsworth w Cossall 00-02; R Trowell, Awsworth and Cossall 02-05; Community of Aid and Hilda from 05. *The Lifeboat House, Holy Island, Berwick-upon-Tweed TD15 2SQ* Tel and fax (01289) 389110 E-mail g.r.booth@ntlworld.com

BOOTH, Ian George. b 64. Chich Th Coll 85 Linc Th Coll 87. **d** 88 **p** 89. C Pet St Mary Boongate 88-90; C Hawley H Trin *Guildf* 90-94; V Willesden St Mary *Lon* 94-03; P-in-c Gosport H Trin *Portsm* 03-05; V 05-06; V Gosport Ch Ch 05-06; RD Gosport 03-06; V Leigh-on-Sea St Marg *Chelmsf* from 09. *St Margaret's Vicarage, 1465 London Road, Leigh-on-Sea SS9 2SB* Tel (01702) 471773 E-mail frianbooth@hotmail.com

BOOTH, Jon Alfred. b 42. Nottm Univ BA64 Lon Univ MPhil72. Coll of Resurr Mirfield 78. **d** 80 **p** 81. C Elland *Wakef* 80-84; C Royston 84-09; rtd 09; Perm to Offic *Wakef* from 09. *Millbank Cottage, Thorpe Bassett, Malton YO17 8LU* Tel (01944) 758518 E-mail jon.a.booth@uku.co.uk

BOOTH, Kenneth Neville. b 41. Otago Univ BA62 MA63 BD66 MTh69 St Andr Univ PhD74. St Jo Coll Auckland 63. **d** 65 **p** 66. C St Paul's Cathl Dunedin New Zealand 65-69; Perm to Offic *St And* 70-71; Lect St Andr Univ 70-71; Lect St Jo Coll Auckland 72-80; Asst P Tamaki St Thos 73-80; Warden Selwyn Coll Dunedin 81-85; Lect 85-97; V Roslyn 85-97; Adn Dunedin 86-95; V Gen 92-97; Dir Th Ho 97-06. *30 Church Lane, Merivale, Christchurch 8014, New Zealand* Tel (0064) (3) 355 9145 Fax 355 6140

BOOTH, Martin Allison. b 54. K Coll Lon MA06. SEITE. **d** 09. C Wimbledon *S'wark* from 09. *9 Thornton Road, London SW19 4NE* Tel (020) 8946 4494

BOOTH, Michael Kevin. b 47. Louvain Univ Belgium BA. St Jo Coll Nottm 88 Oscott Coll (RC) 65. **d** 71 **p** 72. In RC Ch 71-87; C N Reddish *Man* 88-89; R Heaton Norris Ch w All SS 89-99; rtd 99; Perm to Offic *Man* from 00 and *Derby* from 06. *3 Potter Road, Hadfield, Hyde SK13 2RA* Tel (01457) 853963

BOOTH, Paul Harris. b 49. St Jo Coll Nottm. **d** 79 **p** 80. C Thorpe Edge *Bradf* 79-82; P-in-c Frizinghall 82-83; TV Shipley St Paul and Frizinghall 83-97; rtd 97; Perm to Offic *Bradf* from 97. *3 Gilstead Court, Gilstead, Bingley BD16 3LA* Tel (01274) 551071 *or* (01535) 650526 Fax (01535) 650550 E-mail paul@gilcourt.freeserve.co.uk

BOOTH, Terrence Richard. b 44. Edith Cowan Univ (Aus) BA98. St Jo Coll Morpeth. **d** 69 **p** 70. Australia 69-79 and from 81; C Corowa 69-71; Asst Broken Hill 72-74; P-in-c Urana/Jerilderie 74-79; C Chesterfield St Mary and All SS *Derby* 79-81; Chapl Chesterfield R Hosp 79-81; R Coolamon/Ganmain 82; RD Murrumbidgee 83-84; Chapl Bunbury Cathl Gr Sch 85-93; Chapl Edith Cowan Univ 86-92; R Casino 94-98; R Ithaca-Ashgrove 98-01; AD from 01. *286 Waterworks Road, PO Box 31, Ashgrove Qld 4060, Australia* Tel (0061) (7) 3366 2320 Fax 3366 9793 E-mail stpaulsash@iprimus.com.au

BOOTHBY, Frank. b 29. St D Coll Lamp 56. **d** 58 **p** 59. C Maghull *Liv* 58-61; C N Meols 61-64; Miss to Seamen 64; rtd 94. *7 Belsfield Drive, Hesketh Bank, Preston PR4 6YB*

BOOTHBY, Mrs Julia. b 64. St Andr Univ MTheol87. SAOMC 02. **d** 04 **p** 05. C Welwyn *St Alb* 04-08; TV Ouzel Valley from 08. *St Michael's Vicarage, 4 Warneford Way, Leighton Buzzard LU7 4PX* Tel (01525) 370524 E-mail juliabby@aol.com

BOOTHMAN, Ms Olive. b 31. TCD BA. **d** 94 **p** 95. NSM Clondalkin w Rathcoole *D & G* from 94. *Miley Hall, Blessington, Co Wicklow, Republic of Ireland* Tel (00353) (45) 865119

BOOTS, Claude Donald Roy. b 26. Roch Th Coll 67. **d** 69 **p** 70. C Midsomer Norton *B & W* 69-73; V Westfield 73-80; R Ilton w Hambridge, Earnshill, Isle Brewers etc 80-91; rtd 91; Perm to Offic *B & W* from 91. *41 Furlong Close, Midsomer Norton, Bath BA3 2PR* Tel (01761) 419263 E-mail pairofboots@uwclub.net

BOOYS, Canon Susan Elizabeth. b 56. Bris Univ BA78 LMH Ox PGCE79. SAOMC 92. **d** 95 **p** 96. C Kidlington w Hampton Poyle *Ox* 95-99; TV Dorchester 99-05; TR from 05; TV Warborough 99-05; TR from 05; AD Aston and Cuddesdon

from 07; Hon Can Ch Ch from 08. *The Rectory, Manor Farm Road, Dorchester-on-Thames, Wallingford OX10 7HZ* Tel and fax (01865) 340007 E-mail sue@booys.fsnet.co.uk

BOREHAM, Harold Leslie. b 37. S'wark Ord Course. **d** 72 **p** 73. C Whitton and Thurleston w Akenham *St E* 72-77; R Saxmundham 77-85; V Felixstowe SS Pet and Paul 85-96; Chapl Felixstowe Hosp 85-96; Chapl Bartlet Hosp Felixstowe 95-96; P-in-c Ramsgate St Mark *Cant* 96-01; V 01-03; Chapl E Kent NHS and Soc Care Partnership Trust 98-03; rtd 03; Perm to Offic *St E* from 03. *313 St John's Road, Colchester CO4 0JR* Tel (01206) 853769 E-mail harry@borehamclan.fsnet.co.uk

BORLEY, Mark Letchford. b 61. Lon Univ BSc83 PhD87. St Jo Coll Nottm MTh03. **d** 04 **p** 05. C W Swindon and the Lydiards *Bris* 04-05; C Cricklade w Latton 05-07; C Cricklade w Latton and Maidstone St Pet *Cant* from 09. *The Rectory, 35 Poplar Grove, Allington, Maidstone ME16 0DE* Tel (01622) 758704 Mobile 07811-124237

BORROWDALE, Geoffrey Nigel. b 61. Southn Univ BSc83 W Sussex Inst of HE PGCE94. Chich Th Coll 87. **d** 90 **p** 99. C Tilehurst St Mich *Ox* 90-91; Perm to Offic *Chich* 93-97; NSM Sunninghill *Ox* 98-99; C Bracknell 99-01; P-in-c Theale and Englefield from 01. *The Rectory, Englefield Road, Theale, Reading RG7 5AS* Tel 0118-930 2739 E-mail priest@holytrinitytheale.org.uk

BORTHWICK, Alexander Heywood. b 36. Open Univ BA80 Surrey Univ MSc89 MBPsS90. Lich Th Coll 57. **d** 60 **p** 61. C Glas Ch Ch 60-62; C Landore *S & B* 62-64; C Swansea St Thos and Kilvey 64-65; Br Guiana 65-66; Guyana 66-70; C Oystermouth *S & B* 70-71; USPG 71-83; Area Sec *Man* and *Liv* 71-76; Area Sec *Blackb* and *S & M* 73-76; Sch and Children's Work Sec 76-83; Chapl Tooting Bec Hosp Lon 83-91; Chapl Charing Cross Hosp Lon 92-94; Chapl Hammersmith Hosps NHS Trust 94-00; TR Catford (Southend) and Downham *S'wark* 00-04; rtd 04. *Le Roc de Brolange, 5 Brolange, 17150 Soubran, France* Tel (0033) (5) 46 48 46 23

BOSHER, Philip Ross. b 61. Sarum & Wells Th Coll 84. **d** 87 **p** 88. C Warminster St Denys *Sarum* 87-90; P-in-c Farley w Pitton and W Dean w E Grimstead 90-91; TV Alderbury Team 91-96; CF from 96. *c/o MOD Chaplains (Army)* Tel (01980) 615804 Fax 615800

BOSS, Mrs Ann. b 42. Cen Lancs Univ BA93. CBDTI 99. **d** 02 **p** 03. NSM Scorton and Barnacre and Calder Vale *Blackb* 02-05; P-in-c Hanmer Springs New Zealand from 05. *The Vicarage, 31 Jollies Pass Road, Hanmer Springs 7334, New Zealand* Tel (0064) (3) 315 7221

BOSSCHAERT, Anthony John. b 34. St Fran Coll Brisbane 65 ACT ThL69. **d** 68 **p** 69. C Maryborough Australia 68-72; C Roath *Llan* 72-73; C Leamhampton SS Phil and Jas w Cheltenham St Jas *Glouc* 73-76; R Skipton Australia 76-80; C Westmr St Steph w St Jo *Lon* 80-82; TV Wood Green St Mich w Bounds Green St Gabr etc 82-89; In URC 89-03; rtd 03. *55 Willow Way, Potters Bar EN6 2PR* E-mail anton4.bosschaert@googlemail.com

BOSSWARD, Eric Paul. b 63. CQSW90. Trin Coll Bris BA99. **d** 99 **p** 00. C Ecclesall *Sheff* 99-01; C Netherthorpe St Steph 01-04; Co-ord Chapl HM YOI Castington from 04. *HM Young Offender Institution, Castington, Morpeth NE65 9XG* Tel (01670) 762100 E-mail eric.bossward@talktalk.net

BOSTOCK, Peter Anthony. b 64. Nottm Univ BA85 Fitzw Coll Cam BA89. Westcott Ho Cam 87. **d** 90 **p** 91. C Brighton St Matthias *Chich* 90-94; C Leytonstone St Marg w St Columba *Chelmsf* 94-98; P-in-c Bishopwearmouth Gd Shep *Dur* 98-02; V Monk Bretton *Wakef* 02-03; P-in-c Ryhill from 03; P-in-c Sharlston from 03; CMP from 99. *The Vicarage, 20 School Lane, Ryhill, Wakefield WF4 2DW* Tel (01226) 722363 Mobile 07752-886039 E-mail pbostock@tiscali.co.uk

BOSTON, Jonathan Bertram. b 40. Ely Th Coll 61. **d** 64 **p** 65. C Eaton *Nor* 64-70; Sen Chapl ACF Norfolk 65-05; Chapl Norfolk Constabulary from 94; V Horsham St Faith w Newton St Faith 70-90; V Horsford 71-90; V Horsford and Horsham w Newton St Faith 90-97; P-in-c Litcham w Kempston, E and W Lexham, Mileham etc 97-06; rtd 06; Perm to Offic *Nor* from 06. *Bevan House, Front Street, Litcham, King's Lynn PE32 2QG* Tel (01328) 701200

BOSWELL, Canon Colin John Luke. b 47. Sarum & Wells Th Coll 72. **d** 74 **p** 75. C Upper Tooting H Trin *S'wark* 74-78; C Sydenham St Phil 78-79; C St Helier 80-83; P-in-c Caterham 83-95; P-in-c Chaldon 85-95; RD Caterham 85-95; V Croydon St Jo from 95; RD Croydon Cen 00-06; Hon Can S'wark Cathl from 99. *Croydon Vicarage, 22 Bramley Hill, South Croydon CR2 6LT* Tel (020) 8688 1387 *or* 8688 8104 Fax 8688 5877 Mobile 07931-850905 E-mail croydon.parishchurch@lineone.net

BOTHAM, Arthur. b 53. St Jo Coll Nottm. **d** 00 **p** 01. C Hartley Wintney, Elvetham, Winchfield etc 00-04; TV Basingstoke from 04. *The Vicarage, 25 Tewkesbury Close, Popley, Basingstoke RG24 9DU* Tel (01256) 324734 E-mail arthur.botham@btinternet.com

BOTT, Graham Paul. b 49. Staffs Univ MBA95. NOC 00. **d** 03 **p** 04. NSM Rickerscote *Lich* from 03. *24 Wayfield Drive, Stafford ST16 1TR* Tel (01785) 255658
E-mail graham.pbott@btopenworld.com

BOTT, Theodore Reginald. b 27. MBE03. Birm Univ BSc52 PhD68 DSc84 CEng58 FIChemE68. WMMTC 85. **d** 86 **p** 87. NSM Harborne St Faith and St Laur *Birm* 86-97; Perm to Offic from 97. *17 Springavon Croft, Birmingham B17 9BJ* Tel 0121-427 4209

BOTTERILL, David Darrell. b 45. Open Univ BA. Sarum & Wells Th Coll. **d** 83 **p** 84. C Blandford Forum and Langton Long etc *Sarum* 83-86; TV Shaston 86-00; Chapl HM YOI Guys Marsh 89-91; P-in-c Portland St Jo *Sarum* from 00; Asst Chapl Dorset Community NHS Trust from 01; Hon Chapl Miss to Seafarers from 02. *St John's Vicarage, Ventnor Road, Portland DT5 1JE* Tel (01305) 820103
E-mail david.botterill45@btinternet.com

BOTTING, Canon Michael Hugh. b 25. K Coll Lon BSc51 AKC K Coll Lon PGCE52. Ridley Hall Cam 54. **d** 56 **p** 57. C Onslow Square St Paul *Lon* 56-61; V Fulham St Matt 61-72; RD Hammersmith 67; V Leeds St Geo *Ripon* 72-84; RD Headingley 81-84; Hon Can Ripon Cathl 82-84; R Aldford and Bruera *Ches* 84-90; rtd 90; Jt Dir Lay Tr *Ches* 90-95; Perm to Offic 95-07. *12 Hazelhurst, 24 Eldorado Road, Cheltenham GL50 2PT* Tel (01242) 541125 E-mail michael.botting@btinternet.com

BOTTING, Paul Lloyd. b 43. Brasted Th Coll 67 St Mich Coll Llan 69. **d** 71 **p** 72. C Hucknall Torkard *S'well* 71-74; C Cen Torquay *Ex* 74-76; P-in-c Sutton in Ashfield St Mich *S'well* 76; V 77-88; Chapl King's Mill Hosp Sutton-in-Ashfield 85-88; Perm to Offic *Leic* 95-97; NSM Vale of Belvoir Gp 95-97; C High Framland Par 97-01; C Waltham on the Wolds, Stonesby, Saxby etc 97-01; C Wymondham w Edmondthorpe, Buckminster etc 97-01; P-in-c High Framland Par from 01. *High Framland Rectory, 5 Croxton Lane, Harston, Grantham NG32 1PP* Tel (01476) 870188 E-mail plb@pixie-cat.fslife.co.uk

BOTTLEY, Mrs Kate. b 75. Trin & All SS Coll Leeds BA(QTS)97 Open Univ MTh08. St Jo Coll Nottm LTh08. **d** 08 **p** 09. C Skegby w Teversal *S'well* from 08. *64 Fackley Way, Stanton Hill, Sutton-in-Ashfield NG17 3HT* Tel (01623) 516160 Mobile 07910-242404 E-mail kate@skegbyparish.org.uk

BOTTOMLEY, Gordon. b 31. Oak Hill Th Coll 51. **d** 55 **p** 56. C Kinson *Sarum* 55-58; Lic to Offic *Man* 58-63; N Area Sec BCMS 58-63; V Hemswell w Harpswell *Linc* 63-72; V Glentworth 63-72; Chapl RAF 63-71; R Bucknall and Bagnall *Lich* 72-80; TR 80-82; P-in-c Worthing H Trin *Chich* 82-88; V Camelsdale 88-96; rtd 96; Perm to Offic *Portsm* from 98. *6 Jay Close, Fareham PO14 3TA*

BOTWRIGHT, Canon Adrian Paul. b 55. St Jo Coll Ox MA PGCE. Westcott Ho Cam 80. **d** 82 **p** 83. C Chapel Allerton *Ripon* 82-85; Chapl Chapel Allerton Hosp 82-85; C Bourne *Guildf* 85-88; V Weston 88-94; R Skipton H Trin *Bradf* from 94; P-in-c Embsay w Eastby from 05; Hon Can Bradf Cathl from 02. *The Rectory, Rectory Lane, Skipton BD23 1ER* Tel (01756) 793622 *or* 700773 E-mail rector@holytrinityskipton.org.uk

BOUCHER, Brian Albert. b 39. Univ of Wales (Lamp) BA61. Chich Th Coll 61. **d** 63 **p** 64. C Hoxton H Trin w St Mary *Lon* 63-67; Chapl RN 67-68; Asst Chapl Harrow Sch 68-73; Chapl 73 86; P in-c Clerkenwell H Redeemer w St Phil *Lon* 86-91; P-in-c Myddleton Square St Mark 86-91; Chapl Hurstpierpoint Coll 92-96; rtd 96; Perm to Offic *Chich* from 01. *20 Summervale Road, Tunbridge Wells TN4 8JB* Tel (01892) 530342

BOUCHER, Geoffrey John. b 61. Warwick Univ BA82 K Coll Lon 94. Ridley Hall Cam 94. **d** 96 **p** 97. C Tavistock and Gulworthy *Ex* 96-01; P-in-c W Monkton *B & W* from 01. *The Rectory, West Monkton, Taunton TA2 8QT* Tel (01823) 412226 E-mail geoffboucher@onetel.com

BOUGHEY, Richard Keith. b 26. Man Univ MEd71. Qu Coll Birm 77. **d** 80 **p** 82. NSM Upper Tean *Lich* 80-81; NSM Stoke-upon-Trent 80-81; NSM Uttoxeter w Bramshall 82-88; rtd 88; Perm to Offic *Lich* from 88. *Kontokali, The Old Lane, Deadman's Green, Checkley, Stoke-on-Trent ST10 4NQ* Tel (01538) 722013

BOUGHTON, Mrs Elisabeth Mary Victoria. b 66. St Anne's Coll Ox BA87 MA93. Ridley Hall Cam 89. **d** 91 **p** 94. C Guildf Ch Ch 91-95; Chapl St Cath Sch Bramley 92-97; NSM Fetcham *Guildf* from 97; Chapl Guildf YMCA from 97; Tutor CME *Guildf* from 08. *The Rectory, 10A The Ridgeway, Fetcham, Leatherhead KT22 9AZ* Tel (01372) 375000

BOUGHTON, Canon Michael John. b 37. Kelham Th Coll 57. **d** 62 **p** 63. C Grantham St Wulfram *Linc* 62-66; C Kingsthorpe *Pet* 66-68; C Linc St Nic w St Jo Newport 68-72; V Scunthorpe All SS 72-79; V Crowle 79-89; TR Bottesford w Ashby 89-02; Can and Preb Linc Cathl from 00; rtd 02; Perm to Offic *Linc* from 02. *45 Albion Crescent, Lincoln LN1 1EB* Tel (01552) 569653 E-mail mboughton@aol.com

BOUGHTON, Paul Henry. b 55. Imp Coll Lon BScEng77 ARSM77 ACA80. Ridley Hall Cam 89. **d** 91 **p** 92. C Guildf Ch Ch 91-96; R Fetcham from 96. *The Rectory, 10A The Ridgeway, Fetcham, Leatherhead KT22 9AZ* Tel (01372) 375000
E-mail boughtonfamily@yahoo.com

BOULCOTT, Thomas William. b 16. Bps' Coll Cheshunt 47. **d** 49 **p** 50. C Hitchin St Mary *St Alb* 49-51; C Kempston All SS 51-54; Chapl Bedf Gen Hosp 52-54; V Newfoundpool *Leic* 54-61; V N Evington 61-73; Chapl Leic Gen Hosp 62-73; V Loppington w Newtown *Lich* 73-85; RD Wem and Whitchurch 83-85; rtd 85; Perm to Offic *Lich* 85-94. *Silver Birch, Tilley Road, Wem, Shrewsbury SY4 5HA* Tel (01939) 233602

BOULD, Preb Arthur Roger. b 32. Selw Coll Cam BA54 MA58 Wadh Coll Ox BA55 DipEd57 MA58. St Steph Ho Ox 54. **d** 57 **p** 58. C Wednesfield St Thos *Lich* 57-64; V Wellington Ch Ch 64-71; R Cheadle 71-88; P-in-c Freehay 88-91; R Cheadle w Freehay 88-91; Chapl Cheadle Hosp 71-91; Chapl HM Pris Moorcourt 72-91; RD Cheadle 72-91; Preb Lich Cathl 83-99; Asst to Bp Wolv 91-97; Bp Lich's Past Aux 97-99; C Stafford 97-99; rtd 99; Perm to Offic *Lich* from 00. *4 Mansell Close, Castlefields, Stafford ST16 1AG* Tel and fax (01785) 220860

BOULD, Stephen Frederick. b 49. K Coll Lon BD78 AKC78. Sarum & Wells Th Coll 78. **d** 79 **p** 80. C Cantril Farm *Liv* 79-82; AV Hindley St Pet 82-85; Hon C Leic H Spirit 85-88; Chapl Leic Univ 85-88; V Leic Ch Sav 88-96; P-in-c New Humberstone 94-96; TR Leic Presentation 96-98; TR Bruton and Distr *B & W* 98-05; P-in-c Folkestone St Pet *Cant* from 05. *St Peter's Vicarage, North Street, Folkestone CT19 6AL* Tel (01303) 254472 E-mail boldini@btopenworld.com

BOULLIER, Kenneth John. b 51. Trin Coll Bris 82. **d** 84 **p** 85. C Heref St Pet w St Owen and St Jas 84-87; V Nutley *Chich* 88-93; R Maresfield 88-93; New Zealand 93-97; R Nailsea H Trin *B & W* 97-08; P-in-c St Just-in-Roseland and St Mawes *Truro* from 08. *16 Waterloo Close, St Mawes, Truro TR2 5BD* Tel (01326) 270248 E-mail revkjb@hotmail.co.uk

BOULNOIS, Linda Dianne. *See* BISIG, Linda Dianne

BOULT, David Ronald. b 51. Bris Univ BSc73. St Mich Coll Llan 04. **d** 07 **p** 08. NSM Llantwit Major from 07. *52 The Verlands, Cowbridge CF71 7BY* Tel and fax (01446) 772166 Mobile 07767-818257 E-mail daveboult@aol.com

BOULT, Geoffrey Michael. b 56. Southn Univ BTh88 Bris Univ MA90 Birm Univ MSc96. Sarum & Wells Th Coll 77. **d** 80 **p** 81. C Newark w Hawton, Cotham and Shelton *S'well* 80-83; TV Melksham *Sarum* 83-90; P-in-c Charminster and Stinsford 90-95; Perm to Offic *Birm* 95-96 and *Sarum* 95-98. *1 Chesterfield House, 123 Henbury Road, Bristol BS10 7AA* Tel 0117-950 4560 E-mail geoff@boultco.freeserve.co.uk

BOULTBEE, John Michael Godolphin. b 22. Oak Hill Th Coll 66. **d** 68 **p** 69. C Hawkwell *Chelmsf* 68-71; C St Keverne *Truro* 71-73; V Constantine 74-79; P-in-c St Merryn 79-81; V 81-87; rtd 87; Perm to Offic *Ex* from 87. *July Cottage, 8 Williams Close, Dawlish EX7 9SP* Tel (01626) 865761

BOULTER, Adam Charles. b 71. Bath Coll of HE BA93 Kingston Univ MA04 Fitzw Coll Cam BA07. Westcott Ho Cam 05. **d** 08 **p** 09. C Battersea St Mary *S'wark* from 08. *The Crypt, St Mary's Church, Battersea Church Road, London SW11 3NA* Tel and fax (020) 7228 9648 E-mail adamboulter@mac.com *or* office@stmarysbattersea.org.uk

BOULTER, Michael Geoffrey. b 32. Lon Univ BD56. Tyndale Hall Bris 53. **d** 57 **p** 58. C Tranmere St Cath *Ches* 57-60; R Cheetham Hill *Man* 60-65; R Tollard Royal w Farnham *Sarum* 65-66; Chapl Alderney Hosp Poole 66-96; V Branksome St Clem *Sarum* 66-96; rtd 96. *7 Temple Trees, 13 Portarlington Road, Bournemouth BH4 8BU* Tel (01202) 768718

BOULTER, Robert George. b 49. Man Univ BA90. St Aug Coll Cant 72. **d** 75 **p** 76. C Langley All SS and Martyrs *Man* 75-80; V Lower Kersal 80-84; Oman 84-86; Slough Community Chapl *Ox* 86-87; V Whalley Range St Marg *Man* 87-99; P-in-c Whalley Range St Marg from 99; Chapl Trin and All SS Coll Leeds from 07. *St Margaret's Rectory, Rufford Road, Manchester M16 8AE* Tel 0161-226 1289

BOULTON, Christopher David. b 50. Keble Coll Ox BA71 MA80. Cuddesdon Coll 71. **d** 74 **p** 75. C St Mary-at-Latton *Chelmsf* 74-77; C Shrub End 77-80; P-in-c Gt Bentley 80-83; V 83-89; V Cherry Hinton St Andr *Ely* 89-04; P-in-c Teversham 90-04; P-in-c Much Hadham *St Alb* 04-05; TR Albury, Braughing, Furneux Pelham, Lt Hadham etc from 06; RD Bishop's Stortford from 07. *The Rectory, High Street, Much Hadham SG10 6DA* Tel (01279) 842609
E-mail rectory@muchhadham.com

BOULTON, Ms Louise Jane. b 72. Goldsmiths' Coll Lon BA93 Heythrop Coll Lon MA98. SEITE 02. **d** 05 **p** 06. NSM Wandsworth St Anne *S'wark* 05-08; NSM Wandsworth St Anne w St Faith from 08. *17 Somers Road, London SW2 2AE* Tel (020) 7096 1646
E-mail louise.boulton@stanneswandsworth.org.uk

BOULTON, Wallace Dawson. b 31. MCIJ86. Lon Coll of Div 65. **d** 67 **p** 68. C Bramcote *S'well* 67-71; Dioc Public Relns Officer 69-71; Hon C St Bride Fleet Street w Bridewell etc *Lon* 71-86; Guild Chapl from 86; Publicity Sec CMS 71-79; Media Sec 79-86; Ed *C of E Newspaper* 86-88; Lic to Offic *Chich* 84-94; Perm to Offic 94-96; rtd 96; Hon C St Leonards St Leon *Chich*

96-01 and from 04; P-in-c 01-03. *44 Winterbourne Close, Hastings TN34 1XQ* Tel (01424) 713743
E-mail revw.boulton@talktalk.net

BOULTON-LEA, Peter John. b 46. St Jo Coll Dur BA68. Westcott Ho Cam 69. **d** 71 **p** 72. C Farlington *Portsm* 72-75; C Darlington St Jo *Dur* 75-77; R E and W Horndon w Lt Warley *Chelmsf* 77-82; V Hersham *Guildf* 82-91; R Kirk Sandall and Edenthorpe *Sheff* 91-96; RD Doncaster 95-96; V Campsall 96-97; R Burghwallis and Campsall 97-98; V Tattenham Corner and Burgh Heath *Guildf* 98-03; V Thorne *Sheff* 03-08; rtd 08; Perm to Offic *Ox* from 08. *25 Larkfields, Headington, Oxford OX3 8PF* Tel (01865) 744302

BOULTON-REYNOLDS, Mrs Jean. b 49. Sarum Th Coll 93. **d** 96 **p** 97. C Harnham *Sarum* 96-99; C Salisbury St Mark 99-01; TV Westborough *Guildf* 01-05; TV Barnes *S'wark* from 05. *The Vicarage, 162 Castelnau, London SW13 9ET* Tel (020) 8741 7330
E-mail revjbr@sarum26.freeserve.co.uk

BOUNDY, David. b 34. Kelham Th Coll 55. **d** 59 **p** 60. C Stirchley *Birm* 59-64; Chapl E Birm Hosp 64-74; V Bordesley St Oswald 64-70; V S Yardley St Mich 70-74; R Bideford *Ex* 74-82; RD Hartland 80-82; R Northfield *Birm* 82-88; P-in-c Penzance St Mary w St Paul *Truro* 88-90; V 90-94; rtd 94; Chapl Convent of St Mary at the Cross Edgware 94-99; Perm to Offic *Ex* 00-05. *34 Milford Hill, Salisbury SP1 2QX* Tel (01722) 410341
E-mail retreat5@btopenworld.com

BOUNDY, Canon Gerald Neville. b 36. BA. Linc Th Coll. **d** 65 **p** 66. C Bris St Mary Redcliffe w Temple etc 65-70; P-in-c Southmead 70-72; V 72-81; V Cotham St Sav w St Mary 81-99; Hon Can Bris Cathl 96-99; rtd 99; Perm to Offic *Bris* from 99. *10 Morley Road, Southville, Bristol BS3 1DT* Tel 0117-966 3337

BOURDEAUX, Canon Michael Alan. b 34. St Edm Hall Ox BA57 MA61 Lambeth DD96. Wycliffe Hall Ox BA59. **d** 60 **p** 61. C Enfield St Andr *Lon* 60-64; P-in-c Charlton St Luke w St Paul *S'wark* 64-65; Lic to Offic *Roch* 65-91 and *Ox* 91-04; Visiting Prof St Bernard's Inst Rochester NY 69; Gen Dir Keston Inst 69-99; Hon Can Roch Cathl 90-99; rtd 99; Perm to Offic *Ox* from 04. *101 Church Way, Iffley, Oxford OX4 4EG* Tel (01865) 777276
E-mail mbourdeaux@freenet.co.uk

✠**BOURKE, The Rt Revd Michael Gay.** b 41. CCC Cam BA63 MA67. Cuddesdon Coll 65. **d** 67 **p** 68 **c** 93. C Gt Grimsby St Jas *Linc* 67-71; C Digswell St Alb 71-73; C-in-c Panshanger CD 73-78; Course Dir St Alb Minl Tr Scheme 75-87; V Southill 78-86; Adn Bedford 86-93; Area Bp Wolverhampton *Lich* 93-06; rtd 07; Perm to Offic *Heref* from 07. *The Maltings, Little Stretton, Church Stretton SY6 6AP* Tel (01694) 722910

BOURKE, Peter Charles. b 80. Union Th Coll Belf BTh02. Oak Hill Th Coll. **d** 09. C Moreton *Ches* from 09. *9 Kinnerton Close, Wirral CH46 6HT* Tel 0151-605 1241 Mobile 07816-974454 E-mail peter_bourke@hotmail.com

BOURKE, Canon Ronald Samuel James. b 50. MA HDipEd. **d** 79 **p** 80. C Portadown St Mark *Arm* 79-83; I Carnteel and Crilly 83-90; I Mountmellick w Coolbanagher, Rosenallis etc *M & K* 90-97; I Kingscourt w Syddan 09-09; Chan Kildare Cathl 00-09; Can Meath 00-09; I Boyle and Elphin w Aghanagh, Kilbryan etc *K, E & A* from 09; Preb Tipper St Patr Cathl Dublin from 00. *The Rectory, Riverstown, Co Sligo, Republic of Ireland*

BOURKE, Canon Stanley Gordon. b 48. CITC 78. **d** 78 **p** 79. C Dundonald *D & D* 78-80; C Lurgan Ch the Redeemer 81-82; I Dungiven w Bovevagh *D & R* 82-89; I Lurgan St Jo *D & D* 89-03; I Inishmacsaint *Clogh* from 03; Preb Clogh Cathl from 06. *The Rectory, Main Street, Derrygonnelly, Enniskillen BT93 6HW* Tel (028) 6864 1638 E-mail sgbourke@hotmail.co.uk

BOURNE, Mrs Carole Sylvia. b 47. York Univ BA68 LSE MSc79 PhD85. SEITE 99. **d** 02 **p** 03. C Epsom St Martin *Guildf* 02-05; NSM E Molesey from 05. *The Vicarage, St Mary's Road, East Molesey KT8 0ST* Tel (020) 8979 0677 *or* 8783 1441 Mobile 07957-295842 E-mail cbmole@msn.com

BOURNE, Colin Douglas. b 56. Culham Coll of Educn CertEd77. Oak Hill Th Coll BA04. **d** 04 **p** 05. C Wellington All SS w Eyton *Lich* 04-08; P-in-c Toton *S'well* from 08. *95 Stapleford Lane, Beeston, Nottingham NG9 6FZ* Tel 0115-973 1138 Mobile 07821-967879
E-mail colin@bournesenf.supanet.com

BOURNE, David James. b 54. Reading Univ BA76. Trin Coll Bris 77. **d** 79 **p** 80. C W Bromwich Gd Shep w St Jo *Lich* 79-84; V Riseley w Bletsoe *St Alb* 84-05; V Hailsham *Chich* from 05. *St Mary's Vicarage, Vicarage Road, Hailsham BN27 1BL* Tel (01323) 842381 E-mail davidjbourne@googlemail.com

BOURNE, Canon Dennis John. b 32. Ridley Hall Cam 58. **d** 60 **p** 61. C Gorleston St Andr *Nor* 60-64; Min Gorleston St Mary CD 64-79; V Costessey 79-86; R Hingham w Wood Rising w Scoulton 86-97; RD Hingham and Mitford 90-95; Hon Can Nor Cathl 93-97; rtd 97; Perm to Offic *Nor* 97-06. *Amron, Star Lane, Long Stratton, Norwich NR15 2XH* Tel (01508) 530863
E-mail johnbourne@onetel.com

BOURNE, Mrs Diana Mary. b 46. St Jo Coll York BEd68. S Dios Minl Tr Scheme 92. **d** 95 **p** 96. C Pinner *Lon* 95-00; V Lamberhurst and Matfield *Roch* 00-06; rtd 07; Perm to Offic

Cant from 07. *The Pump House, Angley Road, Cranbrook TN17 2PN* Tel (01580) 712005
E-mail revdbourne@hotmail.com

BOURNE, Henry. b 34. Southampton's Coll 55. **d** 64 **p** 65. C Handsworth St Mary *Birm* 64-67; Chapl RAF 67-85; Asst Chapl-in-Chief RAF 85-87; P-in-c Bourn *Ely* 87-88; V 88-89; P-in-c Kingston 87-88; R 88-89; V Caxton 88-89; R Bourn and Kingston w Caxton and Longstowe 89-91; rtd 91; Perm to Offic *Truro* 95-00 and from 01; Hon C Sampford Peverell, Uplowman, Holcombe Rogus etc *Ex* 00-01. *13 The Bowjey Hill, Newlyn, Penzance TR18 5LW* Tel (01736) 330742

BOURNE, The Ven Ian Grant. b 32. Univ of NZ BA55 Otago Univ BD75. **d** 56 **p** 57. New Zealand 56-65 and from 67; Adn Wellington 78-86 and 90-95; C Epsom St Martin *Guildf* 65-67. *26 Annan Grove, Papakowhai, Porirua 5024, New Zealand* Tel (0064) (4) 233 0466 E-mail ian.marg@bourne.co.nz

BOURNE, John. See BOURNE, Canon Dennis John

BOURNE, John Mark. b 49. Cant Sch of Min 88. **d** 91 **p** 92. C Allington and Maidstone St Pet *Cant* 91-94; V Marden 94-03; Chapl HM Pris Blantyre Ho 94-02; rtd 03. *9 Eylesden Court, Bearsted, Maidstone ME14 4BF* Tel (01622) 734420
E-mail revjohnbourne@classicfm.net

BOURNE, Nigel Irvine. b 60. St Jo Coll Ox BA82 MA86. Trin Coll Bris BA92. **d** 92 **p** 93. C Bedhampton *Portsm* 92-94; C Newport St Jo 94-98; V Chalk *Roch* from 98. *The Vicarage, 2A Vicarage Lane, Gravesend DA12 4TF* Tel (01474) 567906 Fax 745147 E-mail nigel.bourne@diocese-rochester.org

BOURNE, Canon Philip John. b 61. Sussex Univ BEd83 Aber Univ MLitt86 Ex Univ MEd96 FRSA97. Cranmer Hall Dur 85. **d** 87 **p** 88. C Gildersome *Wakef* 87-89; Chapl Ex Univ 89-93; Assoc Chapl The Hague and Voorschoten *Eur* 94 and 95; Chapl Voorschoten 96-06; Can Brussels Cathl 04-06; Dir of fords *Chich* from 07. *6 Patcham Grange, Brighton BN1 8UR* Tel (01273) 564057 E-mail philipbourne@btinternet.com

BOURNEMOUTH, Archdeacon of. See HARBIDGE, The Ven Adrian Guy

BOURNER, Paul. b 48. CA Tr Coll. **d** 90 **p** 91. CA from 79; C Ipswich St Mary at Stoke w St Pet *St E* 90-93; R Ufford w Bredfield and Hasketon 93-01; V Ipswich St Thos from 01. *St Thomas's Vicarage, 102 Cromer Road, Ipswich IP1 5EP* Tel (01473) 741215 E-mail paul.bourner@ntlworld.com

BOUSFIELD, Andrew Michael. b 70. Middx Univ BA92. Oak Hill Th Coll BA00. **d** 00 **p** 01. C Beckenham Ch Ch *Roch* 00-03; C Surbiton Hill Ch Ch *S'wark* 03-07; C Patcham *Chich* from 07. *32 Fairview Rise, Brighton BN1 5GL* Tel (01273) 503926 Mobile 07866-434117 E-mail andybousfield@yahoo.co.uk

BOUSKILL, David Walter. b 72. Westcott Ho Cam 95. **d** 98 **p** 99. C Henley w Remenham *Ox* 98-02; TV Bicester w Bucknell, Caversfield and Launton 02-08; TV Horsham *Chich* from 08. *Holy Trinity House, Blunts Way, Horsham RH12 2BL* Tel (01403) 265401 E-mail rev.bouskill@virgin.net

BOUTAN, Marc Robert. b 53. Univ of Iowa BA74. Fuller Th Sem California MD87 Virginia Th Sem 90. **d** 91 **p** 92. USA 91-96 and from 99; Asst Chapl Brussels *Eur* 96-99. *St James Episcopal Church, 1872 Camp Road, Charleston, SC 29412, USA*

BOUTFLOWER, David Curtis. b 45. Man Univ BSc67 Linacre Coll Ox BA69. Ripon Hall Ox 67. **d** 70 **p** 71. C Shard End *Birm* 70-73; C Mortlake w E Sheen *S'wark* 73-74; C Caldicot *Mon* from 98. *29 Wentwood View, Caldicot NP26 4QG* Tel (01291) 423229

BOUTLE, David Francis. b 44. Leeds Univ BSc67. Cuddesdon Coll 69. **d** 72 **p** 73. C Boston *Linc* 72-77; C Waltham 77-80; P-in-c Morton 80-81; V 81-94; Chapl W Lindsey NHS Trust 80-94; Local Mental Health Chapl 88-94; P-in-c Heckington Gp *Linc* from 94. *The Vicarage, 10 Cameron Street, Heckington, Sleaford NG34 9RW* Tel (01529) 460302

BOVEY, Denis Philip. b 29. Ely Th Coll 50. **d** 53 **p** 54. C Southwick St Columba *Dur* 53-57; Perm to Offic *Ox* 57-59; Lic to Offic *Chich* 62-64; C W Hartlepool St Aid *Dur* 64-66; R Aberdeen St Jas 66-74; R Old Deer 74-89; R Longside 74-89; R Strichen 74-89; Can St Andr Cathl 75-88; Syn Clerk 78-83; Dean Ab 83-88; R Alford 89-94; R Auchindoir 89-94; R Inverurie 89-94; P-in-c Dufftown 89-94; P-in-c Kemnay 89-94; rtd 94. *15 Loskin Drive, Glasgow G22 7QW* Tel 0141-574 3603

BOVILL, Francis William. b 34. St Aid Birkenhead 55. **d** 58 **p** 59. C Bispham *Blackb* 58-61; C Crosthwaite Keswick *Carl* 61-64; V Radcliffe St Andr *Man* 64-68; P-in-c Woodside St Steph *Glouc* 68; V 69-73; V Scotby *Carl* 73-96; P-in-c Cotehill and Cumwhinton 94-96; rtd 96; Perm to Offic *Carl* from 96. *16 Summerfields, Dalston, Carlisle CA5 7NW* Tel (01228) 710682

BOWCOTT, Jonathan Michael William. b 67. Trin Coll Bris. **d** 01 **p** 02. C Cricklewood St Gabr and St Mich *Lon* 01-04. *Top Flat, 13 Florence Park, Bristol BS6 7LS*
E-mail jonathan@jonathanbowcott.com

BOWDEN, Andrew. See BOWDEN, Canon Robert Andrew

BOWDEN, Andrew David. b 59. Newc Univ BA80 BArch83. Cranmer Hall Dur 95. **d** 97 **p** 98. C Monkseaton St Pet *Newc* 97-01; V Whorlton from 01. *St John's Vicarage, Whorlton,*

Westerhope, Newcastle upon Tyne NE5 1NN Tel 0191-286 9648
E-mail abowden@tiscali.co.uk

BOWDEN, John Stephen. b 35. CCC Ox BA59 MA62 Edin Univ Hon DD81 Lambeth DD96. Linc Th Coll 59. **d** 61 **p** 62. C Nottingham St Mary *S'well* 61-64; Hon C 64-66; Lect Nottm Univ 64-66; Ed and Managing Dir SCM Press from 66; Hon C Highgate All SS *Lon* 66-00; Hon C Brentford St Faith 80-87; Perm to Offic from 87; rtd 00. *20 Southwood Avenue, London N6 5RZ* Tel and fax (020) 8340 7548 *or* tel 7359 8033

BOWDEN, John-Henry David. b 47. Magd Coll Cam BA69 MA73 MIL78. S Dios Minl Tr Scheme 81. **d** 84 **p** 85. NSM Redlynch and Morgan's Vale *Sarum* 84-88; NSM Cuckfield *Chich* 88-92; NSM St Mary le Bow w St Pancras Soper Lane etc *Lon* 92-98; NSM Chailey *Chich* 98-04; P-in-c Venice w Trieste *Eur* 04-09; rtd 09. *Dene House, South Chailey, Lewes BN8 4AB* Tel (01273) 401076

BOWDEN, Lynne. b 53. Bris Univ BA77 PGCE78. **d** 06 **p** 07. OLM Oatlands *Guildf* from 06. *Ulverstone House, Broom Way, Weybridge KT13 9TG* Tel (01932) 842218 Fax 842238 Mobile 07931-599045 E-mail a.curate@btinternet.com *or* lynne@bowden.freeserve.co.uk

BOWDEN, Mrs Mary Eiluned. b 53. St Anne's Coll Ox BA74 MA92. Dioc OLM tr scheme 04. **d** 07 **p** 08. NSM Gipsy Hill Ch Ch *S'wark* 07-09; C W Dulwich All SS from 09. *94 Auckland Hill, London SE27 9QQ* Tel 07921-315894 (mobile) E-mail mebowden@btinternet.com

BOWDEN, Canon Robert Andrew. b 38. Worc Coll Ox BA62 MA67 BDQ68. Cuddesdon Coll 63. **d** 65 **p** 66. C Wolverhampton St Geo *Lich* 65-69; C Duston *Pet* 69-72; R Byfield 72-79; Chapl R Agric Coll Cirencester 79-93; R Coates, Rodmarton and Sapperton etc *Glouc* 79-04; Bp's Adv on Rural Soc 81-93; Local Min Officer 93-04; rtd 04; Hon C Kemble, Poole Keynes, Somerford Keynes etc *Glouc* 04-08; Chapl to The Queen 02-08; Hon Can Glouc Cathl 90-08; Perm to Offic from 08. *Washbrook Cottage, Caudle Green, Cheltenham GL53 9PW* Tel (01285) 821067 E-mail bowdencoates@care4free.net

BOWEN, Canon Colin Wynford. b 48. St D Coll Lamp. **d** 71 **p** 72. C Hubberston *St D* 71-75; R Cosheston w Nash and Upton 75-77; V Carew and Cosheston w Nash and Upton 77-85; V Pembroke St Mary w St Mich 85-01; V Haverfordwest St Martin w Lambston from 01; P-in-c Camrose from 04; Can St D Cathl from 01. *St Martin's Vicarage, Barn Street, Haverfordwest SA61 1TD* Tel (01437) 762509 Mobile 07770-572464

BOWEN, Daniel Joseph George. b 51. St Mich Coll Llan 96. **d** 98 **p** 99. C Gorseinon *S & B* 98-00; C Cen Swansea 00-01; TV 01-02; V Birchfield *Birm* 02-07; rtd 07. *Dryslwyn, 41 Station Road, Ystradgynlais, Swansea SA9 1NX* Tel (01639) 843020 E-mail daniel@bowen4515.freeserve.co.uk

BOWEN, David Gregory. b 47. Lanchester Poly Cov BSc69. Cuddesdon Coll 70. **d** 74 **p** 75. C Rugby St Andr *Cov* 74-77; C Charlton St Luke w H Trin *S'wark* 78-80; TV Stantonbury *Ox* 80-82; Perm to Offic *B & W* 89-07 and *Ab* from 08. *Ebenezer Cottage, Lower Whitehall, Stronsay, Orkney KW17 2AS* Tel (01857) 616435 E-mail dbowenuk@btinternet.com

BOWEN, David John. b 46. Glouc Th Course 83. **d** 86 **p** 88. NSM Ross w Brampton Abbotts, Bridstow and Peterstow *Heref* 86-88; C Kingstone w Clehonger, Eaton Bishop etc 88-93; P-in-c Lugwardine w Bartestree and Weston Beggard 93-94; V Lugwardine w Bartestree, Weston Beggard etc from 94; P-in-c Withington w Westhide from 04; RD Heref Rural 99-05. *The Vicarage, Lugwardine, Hereford HR1 4AE* Tel and fax (01432) 850244 E-mail david@djbowen.demon.co.uk

BOWEN, Ms Delyth. b 54. St D Coll Lamp BA90. St Mich Coll Llan. **d** 91 **p** 97. C Llandybie *St D* 91-95; Dn-in-c Llanllwni 95-97; V Llanybydder and Llanwenog w Llanllwni 97-02; V Betws w Ammanford from 02. *The Rectory, 78 High Street, Ammanford SA18 2NB* Tel (01269) 592084 E-mail delyth.amman@btopenworld.com

BOWEN, Gareth James. b 60. Lon Guildhall Univ BA99 ARPS00. NTMTC 99. **d** 02 **p** 04. C Leyton St Cath and St Paul *Chelmsf* 02-05; C Upminster 05-07; V Barnehurst *Roch* from 07. *St Martin's Vicarage, 93 Pelham Road, Bexleyheath DA7 4LY* Tel (01322) 523344 Mobile 07775-674504 E-mail gareth@bowen.to

BOWEN, Canon Jennifer Ethel. b 46. Liv Univ BSc68 CertEd69. NOC 80. **dss** 83 **d** 87 **p** 94. Blundellsands St Nic *Liv* 83-86; W Derby St Mary 86-94; Par Dn 87-94; C 94-08; AD W Derby 01-08; Hon Can Liv Cathl 03-08; rtd 08. *6 Springhill Court, Liverpool L15 9EJ* Tel 0151-291 0845 E-mail jenny@happyserver.uk.com

BOWEN, John. b 39. **d** 68 **p** 69. C Aberavon *Llan* 68-73; Australia from 73. *3 Sculptor Street, Giralang ACT 2617, Australia* Tel (0061) (2) 6241 5317 *or* 6234 2263 E-mail john.bowen@radford.com.au

BOWEN, John Roger. b 34. St Jo Coll Ox BA59 MA62. Tyndale Hall Bris 59. **d** 61 **p** 62. C Cambridge St Paul *Ely* 61-65; Tanzania 65-76; Kenya 76-80; Dir Past Studies St Jo Coll Nottm 80-85; Tutor 85-95; Gen Sec Crosslinks 96-00; rtd 99; Perm to Offic *Ely* from 01; Asst Retired Clergy Officer from 09.

26 Lingholme Close, Cambridge CB4 3HW Tel (01223) 352592 E-mail bowenrw@onetel.com

BOWEN, Mark Franklin. b 61. Coll of H Cross (USA) BA79 Univ of S Florida MA89. **d** 93. Asst Chapl Univ of S Florida USA 93-96; C Tampa St Andr 96-97; Perm to Offic *S'wark* 07-09; Co-ord Inclusive Ch *Eur* from 09; Teacher Internat Sch of Basel from 09. *309 Guterstrasse, Basel 4053, Switzerland* Tel (0041) (61) 331 0961 E-mail markfbowen@hotmail.com

BOWEN, Canon Roger William. b 47. Magd Coll Cam BA69 MA73 Heythrop Coll Lon MA01 ALCD72. St Jo Coll Nottm 69. **d** 72 **p** 73. C Rusholme H Trin *Man* 72-75; Rwanda Miss (CMS) Burundi 75-84; Tutor and Lect All Nations Chr Coll Ware 85-91; Hon C Ware Ch Ch *St Alb* 86-91; Gen Sec Mid-Africa Min (CMS) 91-97; V Lt Amwell *St Alb* 97-04; RD Hertford and Ware 99-04; CMS Burundi 04-07; rtd 07. *The Outlook, Porteynon, Swansea SA3 1NL* Tel (01792) 391591

BOWEN, Canon Stephen Allan. b 51. Leic Univ BA72. Glouc Sch of Min 88. **d** 91 **p** 92. NSM Bream *Glouc* 91-92; NSM Tidenham w Beachley and Lancaut 91-94; C Glouc St Jas and All SS 94-97; P-in-c Woodchester and Brimscombe 97-00; R from 00; AD Stonehouse 07-08; AD Stroud from 08; Hon Can Glouc Cathl from 09. *The Vicarage, Walls Quarry, Brimscombe, Stroud GL5 2PA* Tel (01453) 882204 E-mail bowen_stephen@hotmail.com

BOWEN, Stephen Guy. b 47. Qu Coll Cam BA68 MA72 Bris Univ MA72. Clifton Th Coll 69. **d** 71 **p** 72. C Chelsea St Jo *Lon* 71-73; C Guildf St Sav 73-76; C Guildf St Sav w Stoke-next-Guildford 76-77; C Wallington *S'wark* 77-79; V Felbridge from 79. *The Vicarage, 8 The Glebe, Felbridge, East Grinstead RH19 2QT* Tel (01342) 321524 Fax 08701-629334 E-mail vicar@stjohnsfelbridge.co.uk

BOWEN, Thomas Raymond. b 20. Univ of Wales (Lamp) BA42. **d** 48 **p** 49. C Monkton *St D* 48-52; C Haverfordwest St Mary w St Thos 52; Chapl RAF 53-75; Chapl Gresham's Sch Holt 75-83; rtd 83; Perm to Offic *St D* from 83. *35 Gail Rise, Llangwm, Haverfordwest SA62 4HW* Tel (01437) 891179

BOWEN, Vincent Paul. b 26. Qu Coll Cam BA50 MA55. Ely Th Coll 51. **d** 53 **p** 54. C Cowley St Jo *Ox* 53-56; C Brentwood St Thos *Chelmsf* 56-61; R Cranham 61-71; R Wanstead St Mary 71-91; rtd 91; Perm to Offic *Cant* 92-09. *44 Nunnery Fields, Canterbury CT1 3JT* Tel (01227) 472036

BOWER, Brian Mark. b 60. QUB BA. **d** 85 **p** 86. C Orangefield w Moneyreagh *D & D* 85-87; I Inver w Mountcharles, Killaghtee and Killybegs *D & R* 87-93; Miss to Seafarers from 87; I Augher w Newtownsaville and Eskrahoole *Clogh* 93-03. *48 Campsie Road, Omagh BT79 0AG* Tel 07816-449399 (mobile)

BOWER, Jonathan James. b 72. Bp Grosseteste Coll BA96. Ripon Coll Cuddesdon 97. **d** 00 **p** 01. C Spalding *Linc* 00-02; C Sanderstead St Mary *S'wark* 02-03; P-in-c 03-05; TV Sanderstead 05-06; V E Crompton *Man* 06-09; R Broughty Ferry *Bre* from 09. *St Mary's Rectory, 46 Seafield Road, Broughty Ferry, Dundee DD5 3AN* Tel (01382) 805088 E-mail johnathanbower@clergy.net

BOWERING, John Anthony (Tony). b 34. SS Coll Cam BA57 MA. Wycliffe Hall Ox 57. **d** 59 **p** 60. C Hornchurch St Andr *Chelmsf* 59-62; Succ Chelmsf Cathl 62; Prec 63; V Brampton Blerlow *Sheff* 64 70; V Norton Woodseats St Paul 70-80; V Tickhill w Stainton 80-97; RD W Doncaster 87-92; rtd 97; Perm to Offic *S'well* and *Sheff* from 97. *Linthwaite Cottage, Main Street, Kirklington, Newark NG22 8ND* Tel (01636) 816995 E-mail john.bowering@which.net

BOWERING, The Ven Michael Ernest. b 35. Kelham Th Coll 55. **d** 59 **p** 60. C Middlesbrough St Oswald *York* 59-62; C Huntington 62-64; V Brayton 64-72; RD Selby 71-72; V Saltburn-by-the-Sea 72-81; Can Res York Minster 81-87; Sec for Miss and Evang 81-87; Adn Lindisfarne *Newc* 87-00; rtd 00; Perm to Offic *York* from 00. *Old Timbers, West Way, Crayke, York YO61 4TE* Tel (01347) 823682 E-mail mbwrng@aol.com

BOWERMAN, Andrew Mark. b 67. Southn Univ BSc88 Brunel Univ MSW91. Wycliffe Hall Ox 00. **d** 02 **p** 03. C Bradf St Aug Undercliffe 02-05; Miss P Bradf Adnry 05-09; P-in-c Wareham *Sarum* from 09. *The Rectory, 19 Pound Lane, Wareham BH20 4LQ* Tel (01929) 552684 Mobile 07720-398659 E-mail andy.bowerman@virgin.net

BOWERS, Dale Arthur. b 69. St Steph Ho Ox BTh04. **d** 04. C St Paul's St Helena from 04. *China Lane, Jamestown STHL 122, St Helena* Tel (00290) 2960 E-mail penelope19702000@yahoo.co.uk

BOWERS, David. b 56. Man Univ BA79. Wycliffe Hall Ox 82. **d** 84 **p** 85. C Lawton Moor *Man* 84-87; C Walmsley 87-93; V Milnrow 93-98; P-in-c Deerhurst and Apperley w Forthampton etc *Glouc* 98-04; V 04-08; Assoc Dir of Ords 98-05; V S Cerney w Cerney Wick, Siddington and Preston from 08. *The Vicarage, Silver Street, South Cerney, Cirencester GL7 5TP* Tel (01285) 860221 E-mail dbowers@btinternet.com

BOWERS, Canon Francis Malcolm. b 44. Chan Sch Truro 79. **d** 82 **p** 83. NSM Penzance St Mary w St Paul *Truro* 82-83; C 86-88; NSM Madron 83-86; TV Redruth w Lanner and Treleigh 88-91; V St Blazey from 91; P-in-c Lanlivery w Luxulyan 01-08;

P-in-c Luxulyan from 08; P-in-c Tywardreath w Tregaminion from 02; RD St Austell 96-05; Hon Can Truro Cathl from 01. *Church House, 2 Nursery Close, Tywardreath, Par PL24 2QW* Tel and fax (01726) 817665 Mobile 07974-818631
E-mail fathermalcolmorrightee@tiscali.co.uk

BOWERS, Canon John Edward. b 23. TD68. AKC50. **d** 51 **p** 52. C Leic St Pet 51-55; Sacr S'wark Cathl 55-57; CF (TA) 56-67; V Loughborough St Pet *Leic* 57-63; V Ashby-de-la-Zouch St Helen w Coleorton 63-88; CF (R of O) 67-78; RD Akeley W *Leic* 76-88; Hon Can Leic Cathl 78-88; rtd 88; Perm to Offic *Derby* and *Leic* 88-94; *Ely* 94-00. *19 Curtis Drive, Heighington, Lincoln LN4 1GF* Tel (01522) 791330

BOWERS, Canon John Edward William. b 32. St Aid Birkenhead 60. **d** 63 **p** 64. C Bromborough *Ches* 63-68; Ind Chapl 68-74; P-in-c Crewe St Pet 69-71; V Crewe St Mich 71-74; TR Ellesmere Port 74-79; V Hattersley 79-91; Hon Can Ches Cathl 80-02; RD Mottram 88-91; V Bunbury and Tilstone Fearnall 91-98; P-in-c Leasowe 98-02; rtd 02; Perm to Offic *Ches* from 02. *2 Shalford Grove, Wirral CH48 9XY* Tel 0151-625 4831

BOWERS, Julian Michael. b 48. Middx Univ BA97 Goldsmiths' Coll Lon MA00. Edin Th Coll 69. **d** 72 **p** 73. C Chippenham St Andr w Tytherton Lucas *Bris* 72-74; C Henbury 74-77; Chapl Kandy H Trin Sri Lanka 77-82; P-in-c Evercreech w Chesterblade and Milton Clevedon *B & W* 82-83; V 83-89; V Enfield St Jas *Lon* 89-04; Chapl St Andr Hosp Northn from 04. *The Chaplaincy, St Andrew's Hospital, Billing Road, Northampton NN1 5DG* Tel (01604) 616000
E-mail jbowers@standrew.co.uk

BOWERS, Michael Charles. b 52. Sarum & Wells Th Coll 89. **d** 91 **p** 92. C St Peter-in-Thanet *Cant* 91-95; V Reculver and Herne Bay St Bart 95-02; P-in-c Fen Ditton *Ely* from 02; P-in-c Horningsea from 02; P-in-c Teversham from 04. *The Rectory, 29 High Street, Fen Ditton, Cambridge CB5 8ST* Tel (01223) 295927

BOWERS, Preb Peter. b 47. Linc Th Coll 72. **d** 76 **p** 77. C Mackworth St Fran *Derby* 76-78; C Maidstone St Martin *Cant* 78-83; V Elmton *Derby* 83-89; R Swimbridge w W Buckland and Landkey *Ex* from 89; RD Shirwell from 01; Preb Ex Cathl from 07. *The Rectory, Barnstaple Hill, Swimbridge, Barnstaple EX32 0PH* Tel (01271) 830068 E-mail revpebo@hotmail.com

BOWERS, Peter William Albert. b 36. K Coll Lon BD61 AKC61. **d** 62 **p** 63. C Chorley St Pet *Blackb* 62-64; C New Sleaford *Linc* 64-67; C Folkestone H Trin w Ch Ch *Cant* 67-72; V Deal St Geo 72-80; Dir Galilee Community 80-85; R River 86-02; RD Dover 93-00; rtd 02; Perm to Offic *Cant* from 02. *7 River Street, River, Dover CT16 0RB* Tel (01304) 822808
E-mail pbowers4@aol.com

BOWERS, Mrs Rosemary Christine. b 49. Ripon Coll Cuddesdon 99. **d** 01 **p** 02. C Rossendale Middle Valley *Man* 01-04; P-in-c Micklehurst *Ches* 04-09; P-in-c Kinnerley w Melverley and Knockin w Maesbrook *Lich* from 09. *The Rectory, Vicarage Lane, Kinnerley, Oswestry SY10 8DE* Tel (01691) 682351 E-mail revrosie@btinternet.com

BOWERS, Stanley Percival. b 20. Lon Univ BD45 AKC45. Hartley Victoria Coll 40 Wells Th Coll 66. **d** 66 **p** 66. In Methodist Ch 45-66; C Lawrence Weston *Bris* 66-69; V Two Mile Hill St Mich 69-91; rtd 91; Perm to Offic *Bris* from 91; Perm to Offic *B & W* 91-95. *1 Windsor Road, Longwell Green, Bristol BS30 9AF* Tel 0117-932 4051

BOWES, Mrs Beryl Sylvia. b 48. Hull Univ BTh89 Leeds Univ MA06 SRN70 RSCN71. NEOC 89. **d** 91 **p** 94. NSM Kirk Ella *York* 91-99; Chapl R Hull Hosps NHS Trust 93-99; P-in-c Kexby w Wilberfoss *York* 99-04; R The Street Par from 04. *The Rectory, Church Street, Amotherby, Malton YO17 6TN* Tel (01653) 690663 E-mail rector@thestreetparishes.org.uk

BOWES, Canon John Anthony Hugh. b 39. Ch Ch Ox BA62 MA65. Westcott Ho Cam 63. **d** 65 **p** 66. C Langley All SS and Martyrs *Man* 65-68; Asst Chapl Bris Univ 68-73; TV Cramlington *Newc* 73-76; P-in-c Oldland *Bris* 76-80; TR 80-84; V Westbury-on-Trym St Alb 84-05; Hon Can Bris Cathl 02-05; rtd 05. *4 Royal Albert Road, Bristol BS6 7NY* Tel 0117-973 5844

BOWES, Peter Hugh. b 48. Hull Univ LLB69 Dur Univ MA05 Solicitor 72. Cranmer Hall Dur 02. **d** 03 **p** 04. NSM Pocklington and Owsthorpe and Kilnwick Percy etc *York* 03-04; NSM The Street Par 04-07; NSM New Malton 06-07; P-in-c from 07; Assoc Dir of Ords from 05. *The Rectory, Church Street, Amotherby, Malton YO17 6TN* Tel (01653) 690663 Mobile 07775-757723 E-mail vicar@stmichaelsmalton.org.uk

BOWES-SMITH, Edward Michael Crispin. b 67. K Coll Lon LLB89 AKC89 Solicitor 90 Selwy Coll Cam BA96. Ridley Hall Cam 94. **d** 97 **p** 98. C Combe Down w Monkton Combe and S Stoke *B & W* 97-00; C Enfield Ch Ch Trent Park *Lon* 00-03; P-in-c Linc Minster Gp from 03. *St Peter's Vicarage, Lee Road, Lincoln LN2 4BH* Tel (01522) 525741
E-mail bowessmith@waitrose.com

BOWETT, Canon Richard Julnes. b 45. EAMTC 86. **d** 89 **p** 90. C Hunstanton St Mary w Ringstead Parva, Holme etc *Nor* 89-93; C King's Lynn St Marg w St Nic 93-95; V Watton w Carbrooke and Ovington 95-02; RD Breckland 99-02; P-in-c Ashill w

Saham Toney 00-01; Dioc Sec 02-09; Hon Can Nor Cathl from 05; rtd 09. *Willow House, 6 Barnby Road, RAF Coltishall, Norwich NR10 5JN* Tel (01603) 882352
E-mail richardbowett@norwich.anglican.org

BOWIE, Michael Nicholas Roderick. b 59. Sydney Univ BA78 CCC Ox DPhil90. St Steph Ho Ox MA90. **d** 91 **p** 92. C Swanley St Mary *Roch* 91-93; C Penarth w Lavernock *Llan* 93-96; Australia 96-00; R Norton *Sheff* 00-05; TR Gt Berkhamsted, Gt and Lt Gaddesden etc *St Alb* from 05. *The Rectory, Rectory Lane, Berkhamsted HP4 2DH* Tel (01442) 864194
E-mail mnrbowie@hotmail.com

BOWIE, Sara. b 53. Open Univ BA83 Surrey Univ BA02. STETS 99. **d** 02 **p** 03. NSM Camberley St Mich Yorktown *Guildf* 02-07; C Coity, Nolton and Brackla *Llan* from 07. *Y Lletty, Heol-yr-Ysgol, Coity, Bridgend CF35 6BL* Tel (01656) 652540
E-mail sara@coitywithnolton.org.uk

BOWKER, Prof John Westerdale. b 35. Worc Coll Ox BA58. Ripon Hall Ox. **d** 61 **p** 62. C Endcliffe *Sheff* 61-62; Fell Lect and Dir of Studies CCC Cam 62-74; Lect Div Cam Univ 70-74; Prof RS Lanc Univ 74-86; Hon Prov Can Cant Cathl 85-03; Dean of Chpl Trin Coll Cam 86 91; rtd 91; Lic to Offic *Cant* 91-94; Perm to Offic *Ely* 94-00. *14 Bowers Croft, Cambridge CB1 8RP*

BOWKETT, Graham Philip. b 67. Open Univ BSc99. NEOC 06. **d** 09. C Thirsk *York* from 09. *3 Herriot Way, Thirsk YO7 1FL* E-mail bowkett520@hotmail.co.uk

✠**BOWLBY, The Rt Revd Ronald Oliver.** b 26. Trin Coll Ox BA50 MA54. Westcott Ho Cam 50. **d** 52 **p** 53. C Pallion *Dur* 52-56; C Billingham St Cuth 56-57; C-in-c Billingham St Aid CD 57-60; V Billingham St Aid 60-66; V Croydon St Jo *Cant* 66-73; Hon Can Cant Cathl 70-73; Bp Newc 73-80; Bp S'wark 80-91; rtd 91; Hon Asst Bp Lich from 91. *4 Uppington Avenue, Shrewsbury SY3 7JL* Tel (01743) 244192
E-mail rbowlby@phonecoop.coop

BOWLER, Christopher William. *See* JAGE-BOWLER, Christopher William

BOWLER, David Edward. b 53. Northumbria Univ BA04 RMN80. NEOC 05. **d** 08 **p** 09. NSM Cramlington *Newc* from 08. *1 Hickstead Grove, Cramlington NE23 2FF* Tel (01670) 716271 E-mail djbowler@sky.com

BOWLER, David Henderson. b 54. Kent Univ BA75. St Jo Coll Nottm 75. **d** 78 **p** 79. C Bramcote *S'well* 78-82; TV Kirby Muxloe *Leic* 82-88; V Quorndon from 88. *27 Mansfield Avenue, Quorn, Loughborough LE12 8BD* E-mail dhb300154@aol.com

BOWLER, Preb Kenneth Neville. b 37. K Coll Lon 61. **d** 61 **p** 62. C Buxton *Derby* 61-67; R Sandiacre 67-75; V E Bedfont *Lon* 75-87; AD Hounslow 82-87; V Fulham All SS 87-02; Preb St Paul's Cathl 85-02; rtd 02; Perm to Offic *St Alb* from 03. *The Coach House, 22 Brincliffe Crescent, Sheffield S11 9AW* Tel 0114-250 0043

BOWLER, Neil. b 70. Nottm Trent Univ LLB92 Leeds Univ BA05 Solicitor 93. Coll of Resurr Mirfield 03. **d** 05 **p** 06. C Doncaster St Jude *Sheff* 05-08; R Whiston from 09. *The Rectory, Doles Lane, Whiston, Rotherham S60 4JA* Tel (01709) 364430

BOWLES, Arthur William. b 36. **d** 96 **p** 97. OLM Gt Yarmouth *Nor* 96-06; Perm to Offic from 06. *4 Onslow Avenue, Great Yarmouth NR30 4DT* Tel (01493) 842360
E-mail revawb@talktalk.net

BOWLES, Preb Michael Hubert Venn. b 36. Selw Coll Cam BA59 MA63. Ridley Hall Cam 59. **d** 61 **p** 62. C Woodside Park St Barn *Lon* 61-64; C Swanage *Sarum* 64-67; Lect St Mich Coll Llan 67-72; Chapl 67-70; Lib 70-72; Lect Th Univ of Wales (Cardiff) 67-72; R Gt Stanmore *Lon* 72-01; Preb St Paul's Cathl 85-01; rtd 01; Perm to Offic *St Alb* from 02. *15 The Limes, St Albans AL1 4AT* Tel (01727) 832555

BOWLES, Peter John. b 39. Lon Univ BA60. Linc Th Coll 71. **d** 73 **p** 74. C Clay Cross *Derby* 73-76; C Boulton 76-79; R Brailsford w Shirley 79-85; P-in-c Osmaston w Edlaston 81-85; P-in-c Brailsford w Shirley and Osmaston w Edlaston 85-89; TR Old Brampton and Loundsley Green 89-98; V Hope, Castleton and Bradwell 98-04; rtd 04; Perm to Offic *Nor* from 04. *3 Blackhorse Yard, Wells-next-the-Sea NR23 1BN* Tel (01328) 711119

BOWLES, Ronald Leonard. b 24. K Coll Lon BD52 AKC52. **d** 53 **p** 54. C Berwick H Trin *Newc* 53-56; C Christchurch *Win* 56-60; R Nursling and Rownhams 60-66; V Woolston 66-75; V Moordown 75-89; rtd 89; Perm to Offic *Win* 89-99; *Portsm* from 89. *25 Cherry Tree Avenue, Cowplain, Waterlooville PO8 8BA* Tel (023) 9226 7376

BOWLEY, Canon John Richard Lyon. b 46. MRTPI76 Dur Univ BA68 QUB MSc72. CITC. **d** 79 **p** 80. C Knock *D & D* 79-81; Bp's C Knocknagoney 81-90; I Ballywalter w Inishargie from 90; Can Down Cathl from 03. *The Vicarage, 2 Whitechurch Road, Ballywalter, Newtownards BT22 2JY* Tel (028) 9175 8416

BOWMAN, Miss Alison Valentine. b 57. St Andr Univ MA79. St Steph Ho Ox 86. **d** 89 **p** 94. Par Dn Peacehaven *Chich* 89-94; C 94-95; Chapl to Bp Lewes 93-95; TV Rye 95-03; P-in-c Preston St Jo w Brighton St Aug and St Sav from 03. *33 Preston Drove, Brighton BN1 6LA* Tel (01273) 555033

BOWMAN, Clifford William. b 57. St Jo Coll Dur BA78 Nottm Univ MA96. Ridley Hall Cam 80. **d** 82 **p** 83. C Sawley *Derby*

82-85; C Hucknall Torkard *S'well* 85-89; R Warsop 89-00; Dioc Chapl amongst Deaf People 00-06; TV Uxbridge *Lon* from 06. *St Andrew's Vicarage, Nursery Waye, Uxbridge UB8 2BJ* Tel (01895) 239055 E-mail c.bowman@dunelm.org.uk

BOWMAN, Canon Ivelaw Alexander. b 46. **d** 97 **p** 98. OLM Stockwell Green St Andr *S'wark* 97-03; OLM Stockwell St Andr and St Mich from 03; Chapl S Lon and Maudsley NHS Foundn Trust 03-07; Hon Can S'wark Cathl from 05. *16 Horsford Road, London SW2 5BN* Tel (020) 7733 2309

BOWMAN, Prof John. b 16. Glas Univ MA38 BD41 Ch Ch Ox DPhil45. **d** 50 **p** 54. Hon C Leeds St Geo *Ripon* 51-53; Hon C Kirkstall 53-54; Perm to Offic *York* 54-59; Australia from 59; rtd 73. *15 Haines Street, North Melbourne Vic 3051, Australia* Tel and fax (0061) (3) 9329 0794 E-mail mbowman@vicnet.net.au

BOWMAN-EADIE, Canon Russell Ian. b 45. ACP68 K Coll Lon BD71 AKC71 FCP. St Aug Coll Cant 71. **d** 72 **p** 73. C Hammersmith St Pet *Lon* 72-74; V Leic St Nic 74-81; Chapl Leic Univ 74-81; Adult Educn Adv *Dur* 81-84; Dir of Tr *B & W* from 84; Preb Wells Cathl from 90; Can Res and Treas Wells Cathl from 02. *2 The Liberty, Wells BA5 2SU* Tel (01749) 674702 *or* 670777 Fax 674240
E-mail russell.bowman-eadie@bathwells.anglican.org

BOWNASS (*née* **FRYER), Alison Jane.** b 56. Univ Coll of Swansea BSc78 Birm Poly PGCE90. Qu Coll Birm 05. **d** 07 **p** 08. C The Quinton *Birm* from 07. *131 Glyn Farm Road, Birmingham B32 1NJ* Tel 0121-422 4949 Mobile 07958-911378
E-mail alison@bownass.co.uk

BOWNESS, William Gary. b 48. Warwick Univ BSc69 Chicago State Univ DMin98. Ripon Coll Cuddesdon 80. **d** 82 **p** 83. C Lancaster St Mary *Blackb* 82-86; V Lostock Hall 86-91; V Whittington w Arkholme and Gressingham 91-92; RD Tunstall 93-99; Dir Post-Ord Tr 00-02; R Alderley w Birtles *Ches* 02-07; P-in-c Henbury from 07. *St Thomas's Vicarage, Church Lane, Henbury, Macclesfield SK11 9NN* Tel (01625) 424113
E-mail gary@bowness1792.freeserve.co.uk

BOWRING, Stephen John. b 55. R Holloway Coll Lon BMus77 St Mary's Coll Twickenham PGCE78. EMMTC 89. **d** 92 **p** 93. C Thurmaston *Leic* 92-95; V Shepshed 95-02; R River *Cant* 02-06; P-in-c Charlton-in-Dover 05-06; AD Dover 03-06; Hon Min Can Cant Cathl 04-06; V Chesterton St Geo *Ely* from 06. *St George's Vicarage, 8 Chesterfield Road, Cambridge CB4 1LN* Tel (01223) 423374 E-mail vicar@riverparishchurch.co.uk

BOWRON, Hugh Mark. b 52. Cant Univ (NZ) BA74 MA76. Coll of Resurr Mirfield 76. **d** 79 **p** 80. C Northampton St Mary *Pet* 79-82; V Ellesmere New Zealand 82-86; V Addington St Mary 86-95; V Wellington St Pet 95-05; V Avonside H Trin from 05. *2/142 Avonside Drive, Christchurch, New Zealand* Tel (0064) (3) 389 3024 E-mail office@holytrinityavonside.co.nz

BOWSER, Alan. b 35. Univ of Wales (Lamp) BA60. **d** 63 **p** 64. C Gateshead St Chad Bensham *Dur* 63-67; C Owton Manor CD 67-72; V Horden 70-02; rtd 02. *Kengarth House, Coast Road, Blackhall Colliery, Hartlepool TS27 4HF* Tel 0191-586 1753

BOWSHER, Andrew Peter. b 59. Reading Univ BA81. St Jo Coll Nottm 83. **d** 86 **p** 87. C Grenoside *Sheff* 86-89; C Darfield 89-91; P-in-c Haley Hill *Wakef* 91-96; V Bradf St Aug Undercliffe 96-99; Chapl Bradf Univ and Bradf Coll 99-04; Perm to Offic *Dur* from 04; Tutor St Jo Coll Nottm from 07. *19 Willow Court, Ryton NE40 3PE* Tel 0191-413 1299 Mobile 07876-401339
E-mail a.bowsher@stjohns-nottm.ac.uk

BOWSKILL, Mrs Amanda. b 49. STETS 96. **d** 99 **p** 00. NSM Winklebury 99-03; NSM Tadley S and Silchester 03-04; NSM Kempshott from 05. *10 Portway Place, Basingstoke RG23 8DT* Tel (01256) 327301 E-mail mandy.bowskill@cwcom.net

BOWSKILL, Robert Preston. b 48. S Dios Minl Tr Scheme 88. **d** 91 **p** 92. NSM Eastrop *Win* 91-94; NSM Winklebury 94-05; NSM Kempshott from 05. *10 Portway Place, Basingstoke RG23 8DT* Tel (01256) 327301
E-mail bob.bowskill@cwcom.net

BOWTELL, Paul William. b 47. Lon Univ BSc68. St Jo Coll Nottm 80. **d** 82 **p** 83. C Gorleston St Andr *Nor* 82-85; TV Forest Gate St Sav w W Ham St Matt *Chelmsf* 85-91; R Spitalfields Ch Ch w All SS *Lon* 91-02; Co-ord Transform Newham 02-06; Chapl to Bp Barking *Chelmsf* from 06; C Leyton St Cath and St Paul from 07. *Barking Lodge, 35A Verulam Avenue, London E17 8ES* Tel (020) 8509 7377
E-mail pbowtell@chelmsford.anglican.org

BOWYER, Arthur Gustavus Frederick. b 36. **d** 00 **p** 01. NSM Kingswood *S'wark* from 00. *41 Tattenham Grove, Epsom KT18 5QT* Tel (01737) 357913 Mobile 07939-533506
E-mail abowyer@onetel.com

BOWYER, Frank. b 28. Man Univ BA49 BD56. Oak Hill Th Coll 53. **d** 55 **p** 56. C Halliwell St Paul *Man* 55-57; C Crosthwaite Keswick *Carl* 57-59; V Thornham w Gravel Hole *Man* 59-63, R Burnage St Marg 63-81; R Gosforth w Nether Wasdale and Wasdale Head *Carl* 81-85; R Holcombe *Man* 85-93; rtd 93; Perm to Offic *Man* from 93. *43 New Church Road, Bolton BL1 5QQ* Tel (01204) 844547

BOWYER, Geoffrey Charles. b 54. ACA79 ATII82 Lanc Univ BA76. St Jo Coll Nottm 85. **d** 87 **p** 88. C Walton *St E* 87-89; C

Macclesfield Team *Ches* 89-91; V Cinderford St Steph w Littledean *Glouc* 91-95; V Brockenhurst *Win* 95-98; Hon C Trull w Angersleigh *B & W* from 00. *36 Bakers Close, Bishops Hull, Taunton TA1 5HD* Tel (01823) 335289
E-mail us4bowyers@aol.com

BOX, David Norman. b 28. K Coll Lon BD48 AKC48. **d** 51 **p** 52. C Grays Thurrock *Chelmsf* 51-53; Hon C Aldershot St Mich *Guildf* 53-55; Asst Master St Benedict's Sch Aldershot 53-55; C Weston 55-58; C Camberley St Paul 58-61; V Blackheath and Chilworth 61-69; V Allerton *Bradf* 69-75; R Exford w Exmoor *B & W* 75-80; V Castle Cary w Ansford 80-90; P-in-c Childe Okeford, Manston, Hammoon and Hanford *Sarum* 90-91; R Childe Okeford, Okeford Fitzpaine, Manston etc 91-94; rtd 94; Perm to Offic *Carl* from 94. *Granary House, 1 Castle Street, Hilton, Appleby-in-Westmorland CA16 6LX* Tel (01768) 352689

BOX, Reginald Gilbert (Brother Reginald). b 20. Lon Univ BD41 AKC41 Em Coll Cam BA52 MA57 Lambeth STh91. Westcott Ho Cam 41. **d** 43 **p** 44. C Chingford SS Pet and Paul *Chelmsf* 43-47; Chapl Bps' Coll Cheshunt 47-50; SSF from 51; Lic to Offic *Ely* 51-55 and *Sarum* 55-61; C Cambridge St Benedict *Ely* 61-67; Chapl Coll of SS Mark and Jo Chelsea 67-69; New Zealand, Australia and Melanesia 69-84; Perm to Offic *Sarum* from 84 and *Ely* 85-97; rtd 90; Chapl Chich Th Coll 90-93; Perm to Offic *Cant* from 05. *The Friary, 6A Stour Street, Canterbury CT1 2NR* Tel (01227) 479364

BOXALL, David John. b 41. Dur Univ BA63. Sarum Th Coll 65. **d** 66 **p** 67. C Ipswich St Aug *St E* 66-69; C Bourne *Linc* 69-71; C Woodside Park St Barn *Lon* 71-72; C Thundersley *Chelmsf* 72-76; P-in-c Farcet *Ely* 76-77; TV Stanground and Farcet 77-85; V Guyhirn w Ring's End 85-90; V Southea w Murrow and Parson Drove 85-90; P-in-c Fletton 90-94; Perm to Offic 94-00 and 05-08; rtd 99. *11 Plover Drive, March PE15 9HY* Tel (01354) 659905

BOXALL, Keith Michael. b 37. Trin Coll Bris. **d** 82 **p** 83. C Staines St Pet *Lon* 82-83; C Staines St Mary and St Pet 83-85; C Lydiard Millicent w Lydiard Tregoz *Bris* 85-86; TV The Lydiards 86-93; V Mangotsfield 93-03; rtd 03; Perm to Offic *Bris* from 03. *25 Parc Plas, Blackwood NP12 1SJ* Tel (01495) 222572 Mobile 07745-016038 E-mail keith.boxall1@btinternet.com

BOXALL, Canon Martin Alleyne. b 37. Wells Th Coll 65. **d** 67 **p** 68. C Crowthorne *Ox* 67-70; C Tilehurst St Mich 70-76; V Tilehurst St Cath 76-78; V Padstow *Truro* 78-00; Miss to Seafarers from 78; RD Pydar *Truro* 93; Hon Can Truro Cathl from 93; rtd 01; Dioc Officer for Unity *Truro* from 01. *Goonhilland Farmhouse, Burnthouse, St Gluvias, Penryn TR10 9AS* Tel (01872) 863241 E-mail martinboxall@aol.com

BOXALL, Simon Roger. b 55. St Jo Coll Cam BA76 MA80. Ridley Hall Cam 77. **d** 79 **p** 80. C Eaton *Nor* 79-82; SAMS Brazil 82-04; P-in-c Belo Horizonte St Pet 84-88; P-in-c Santiago St Tim and Horizontina H Spirit 88-91; C Bagé Crucifixion 93-94; R Jaguarao Ch Ch 94-98; English Chapl Rio de Janeiro 99-04; TV Thamesmead *S'wark* from 05. *62-64 Battery Road, London SE28 0JT* Tel (020) 8836 9069

BOXLEY, Christopher. b 45. K Coll Lon BD68 AKC68 Southn Univ CertEd73 Reading Univ MA84. **d** 69 **p** 70. C Bitterne Park *Win* 69-73; Hd RS Midhurst Gr Sch from 73; Dir Midhurst and Petworth RS Cen from 78; Perm to Offic *Chich* 73-78; P-in-c Heyshott from 78. *The Rectory, Heyshott, Midhurst GU29 0DH* Tel (01730) 814405 E mail boxley@talktalk.net

BOYCE, Christopher Allan. b 44. ARIBA69. S Dios Minl Tr Scheme 84. **d** 87 **p** 88. NSM Eastbourne All SS *Chich* 87-93; C Upton (Overchurch) *Ches* 93-96; V New Brighton St Jas w Em 96-02; P-in-c New Brighton All SS 98-02; C Bicester w Bucknell, Caversfield and Launton *Ox* from 02. *4 Orpine Close, Bicester OX26 3ZJ* Tel (01869) 244918 Mobile 07989-269175
E-mail revcab@lineone.net

BOYCE, John Frederick. b 33. ALCD57. **d** 57 **p** 58. C Earlsfield St Andr *S'wark* 57-60; C Westerham *Roch* 60-63; C Farnborough 63-66; V Sutton at Hone 66-73; P-in-c Chiddingstone 73-74; R Chiddingstone w Chiddingstone Causeway 74-84; V Brenchley 84-98; rtd 98; Perm to Offic *Chich* from 99. *3 Orchard Rise, Groombridge, Tunbridge Wells TN3 9RU* Tel (01892) 864633

BOYCE, Joy. b 46. **d** 05 **p** 06. NSM Streatham Ch Ch w St Marg *S'wark* from 05. *60 Westover Road, London SW18 2RH* Tel (020) 8874 1905 Mobile 07867-830273
E-mail joy.boyce@fujitsu.com

BOYCE, Canon Kenneth Albert. b 51. St Edm Hall Ox BA72 MA76 Selw Coll Cam BA75 MA79. Westcott Ho Cam 73. **d** 75 **p** 76. C Evington *Leic* 75-78; P-in-c Gt Bowden w Welham 78-81; Dioc Stewardship Adv 78-81; Chapl Leic Poly 81-86; TV Leic H Spirit 82-86; P-in-c Astwood Bank and Chapl to the Deaf *Worc* 86-93; R Fladbury, Wyre Piddle and Moor 93-98; P in c Cropthorne w Charlton 94-98; R Fladbury w Wyre Piddle and Moor etc 98-00; RD Pershore 97-00; TR Worc SE from 00; RD Worc E from 05; Hon Can Worc Cathl from 07. *The Rectory, 6 St Catherine's Hill, Worcester WR5 2EA* Tel (01905) 355119
E-mail ken@kenboyce.fsnet.co.uk

BOYCE, Ms Susan. b 59. Ch Ch Coll Cant MA00 Birm Univ BPhil06. Ripon Coll Cuddesdon 05. **d** 06 **p** 07. NSM Rushall *Lich* from 06. *c/o the Lord Bishop of Lichfield, 22 The Close, Lichfield WS13 7LG* Tel 07941-927245 (mobile) E-mail sueboyceca@hotmail.com

BOYCE, William Alexander. d 03 **p** 04. C Willowfield *D & D* 03-04; C Bangor Abbey 04-07; I Mallusk *Conn* from 07. *The Rectory, 6 Carwood Drive, Newtownabbey BT36 5LP* Tel (028) 9087 9029 E-mail weebill@hotmail.com

BOYCE-TILLMAN, Prof June Barbara. b 43. St Hugh's Coll Ox BA65 Lon Inst of Educn PGCE66 PhD87 LRAM74. Dioc OLM tr scheme. **d** 06 **p** 07. NSM Streatham St Paul *S'wark* from 06. *108 Nimrod Road, London SW16 6TQ* Tel 07850-208721 (mobile) Fax (020) 8677 8752 E-mail junebt@globalnet.co.uk

BOYD, Alan McLean. b 50. St Jo Coll Nottm BTh79. **d** 79 **p** 80. C Bishop's Waltham *Portsm* 79-83; Chapl Reading Univ 83-88; Chapl E Birm Hosp 88-94; Chapl Birm Heartlands and Solihull NHS Trust from 94. *Solihull Hospital, Lode Lane, Solihull B91 2JL* Tel 0121-424 4099

BOYD, Alexander Jamieson. b 46. St Chad's Coll Dur BSc68 Nottm Univ PGCE69 MIBiol FSAScot. Coll of Resurr Mirfield 69. **d** 79 **p** 80. NSM Musselburgh *Edin* 79-83; CF 83-00; P-in-c Loddington *Leic* 00-03; Warden Launde Abbey 00-03; P-in-c Mareham-le-Fen and Revesby *Linc* 03-06; P-in-c Hameringham w Scrafield and Winceby 03-06; P-in-c Mareham on the Hill 03-06; R Fen and Hill Gp from 06; RD Horncastle from 06. *The Rectory, Fieldside, Mareham-le-Fen, Boston PE22 7QU* Tel (01507) 568215 E-mail alec@ajboyd.wanadoo.co.uk

BOYD, Allan Gray. b 41. St Jo Coll Nottm 84. **d** 87 **p** 88. Hon Chapl Miss to Seafarers from 87; NSM Glas St Gabr 87-93; NSM Greenock 93-96; NSM Paisley St Barn 96-00; NSM Paisley H Trin 96-00; NSM Alexandria 00-01; NSM Clydebank 02-08. *47 Holms Crescent, Erskine PA8 6DJ* Tel 0141-812 2754

BOYD, Canon David Anthony. b 42. Sarum & Wells Th Coll 72. **d** 75 **p** 76. C Ches H Trin 75-79; R 85-93; V Congleton St Jas 79-85; V Farndon and Coddington 93-07; RD Malpas 97-04; Hon Can Ches Cathl 02-07; rtd 07. *68 St James Avenue, Upton, Chester CH2 1NL* Tel (01244) 348800

BOYD, James. d 07 **p** 08. C Magheralin w Dollingstown *D & D* from 07. *43 Cottage Hill, Lurgan, Craigavon BT67 9NJ* Tel (028) 3832 4616 E-mail jamesthegrey@hotmail.com

BOYD, Michael Victor. b 33. St Chad's Coll Dur BA57 DipAdEd69 MEd77 PhD81. Coll of Resurr Mirfield 57. **d** 59 **p** 60. C Warsop *S'well* 59-61; Chapl St Geo Coll Quilmes Argen 62-63; Chapl Wolsingham Sch 63-67; Lect St Hild Coll Dur 67-75; Lect SS Hild and Bede Dur 75-79; Lect Dur Univ 79-84; rtd 98. *4 Aykley Green, Durham DH1 4LN* Tel 0191-384 9473

BOYD, Robert Henry. b 36. **d** 66 **p** 67. C Drumcree *Arm* 66-69; I Annaghmore 69-83; Bp's C Lissan 83-90; I 90-06; rtd 06. *Lillybank, 19 Killymaddy Knox, Dungannon BT70 1NL* Tel (028) 8772 2351

BOYD, Samuel Robert Thomas. b 62. **d** 90 **p** 91. NSM Derryloran *Arm* 90-95; C 95-97; I Woodschapel w Gracefield 97-05; I Killyman from 05. *St Andrew's Rectory, 85 Dungorman Road, Dungannon BT71 6SE* Tel and fax (028) 8772 2500 E-mail killyman@armagh.anglican.org

BOYD, Stephen William. b 71. Aston Tr Scheme 95 Ripon Coll Cuddesdon BTh00. **d** 00 **p** 01. C Walton-on-the-Hill *Liv* 00-04; V Westbrook St Jas 04-09; P-in-c Orford St Marg from 09. *St Margaret's Vicarage, 2 St Margaret's Avenue, Warrington WA2 8DT* Tel (01925) 631937

BOYD, Stuart Adrian. b 51. Open Univ BA99 UWE MA02. STETS 02. **d** 05 **p** 07. NSM Brent Knoll, E Brent and Lympsham *B & W* 05-06; NSM Knowle H Nativity *Bris* 06-09. *29 Stafford Road, Weston-super-Mare BS23 3BN* Tel (01934) 627897

BOYD, Canon William John Peter. b 28. Lon Univ BA48 BD53 PhD77 Birm Univ MA60. **d** 57 **p** 58. C Aston SS Pet and Paul *Birm* 57-60; V W Smethwick 60-63; V St Breward *Truro* 63-68; Adult Educn Chapl 64-85; Dioc Ecum Officer 65-83; R St Ewe 68-73; Preb St Endellion 73-85; V St Kew 73-77; R Falmouth K Chas 77-85; RD Carnmarth S 84-85; Dir of Tr 85-93; Prin SWMTC 85-93; Can Res and Chan Truro Cathl 85-93; rtd 93; Perm to Offic *Truro* from 93. *7 Chapel Crescent, Zelah, Truro TR4 9HN*

BOYD-WILLIAMS, Anthony Robert. b 46. St Mich Coll Llan 86. **d** 88 **p** 89. C Tonyrefail w Gilfach Goch *Llan* 88-91; V Treharris w Bedlinog 91-96; V Ocker Hill *Lich* 96-05; RD Wednesbury 03-05; rtd 05; Perm to Offic *Cov* from 05. *4 Beecham Walk, Stratford-upon-Avon CV37 9LW* Tel (01789) 290488

BOYDEN, Peter Frederick. b 41. Lon Univ BSc62 AKC62 Em Coll Cam BA64 MA68 MLitt69. Ridley Hall Cam 63. **d** 66 **p** 67. C Chesterton St Andr *Ely* 66-68; C Wimbledon *S'wark* 68-72; Chapl K Sch Cant 72-89; Asst Chapl Radley Coll 89-02; rtd 02; Perm to Offic *Derby* from 02. *30 Chesterfield Road, Shirland, Alfreton DE55 6BN* Tel (01773) 830552 E-mail pandjboyden@aol.com

BOYES, Canon David Arthur Stiles. b 30. Lon Coll of Div 62. **d** 63 **p** 64. C Islington St Mary *Lon* 63-71; V Canonbury

St Steph 71-75; V St Paul's Cray St Barn *Roch* 75-85; P-in-c Earl Soham w Cretingham and Ashfield *St E* 85-96; Dioc Development Officer 86-92; RD Loes 91-95; Hon Can St E Cathl 95-96; rtd 96; Perm to Offic *St E* from 96. *13 Magdalen Drive, Woodbridge IP12 4EF* Tel (01394) 383389

BOYES, Matthew John. b 70. Roehampton Inst BA91. Wycliffe Hall Ox BTh99. **d** 99 **p** 00. C Bury St Edmunds Ch Ch *St E* 99-02; P-in-c Penn Street *Ox* 02-06; V Turnham Green Ch Ch *Lon* from 06. *The Vicarage, 2 Wellesley Road, London W4 4BL* Tel (020) 8994 1617 E-mail matt_boyz@dsl.pipex.com

BOYES, Michael Charles. b 27. Lon Univ BA53 BD58. Wells Th Coll 53. **d** 55 **p** 56. C Heavitree *Ex* 55-61; C Exwick 61-68; V Broadclyst 68-83; RD Aylesbeare 77-81; TV Sampford Peverell, Uplowman, Holcombe Rogus etc 83-85; TR 85-92; rtd 92; Perm to Offic *Ex* from 92. *Southdown, Burlescombe, Tiverton EX16 7LB* Tel (01884) 840492

BOYLAND, Alice Teresa. b 41. **d** 99 **p** 05. NSM Llangybi and Coedypaen w Llanbadoc *Mon* 99-04; NSM Chard and Distr *B & W* 05-06; NSM Chaffcombe, Cricket Malherbie etc from 06. *62 Link Hay Orchard, South Chard, Chard TA20 2QS* Tel (01460) 221010 E-mail daveterri@waitrose.com

BOYLAND, David Henry. b 58. TCD BA79 TCD Div Sch BTh91. **d** 91 **p** 92. C Seapatrick *D & D* 91-94; I Celbridge w Straffan and Newcastle-Lyons *D & G* 94-98; I Kilmakee *Conn* from 98. *Kilmakee Rectory, 60 Killeaton Park, Dunmurry, Belfast BT17 9HE* Tel (028) 9061 0505 *or* 9061 1024

BOYLAND, Henry Hubert. b 23. CITC. **d** 84 **p** 85. NSM Dunboyne Union *M & K* 84-87; Bp's C Carrickmacross w Magheracloone *Clogh* 87-90; I 90-93; rtd 93. *2 Spring View, Wheaton Hall, Dublin Road, Drogheda, Co Louth, Republic of Ireland* Tel (00353) (41) 984 4724

BOYLAND, Peter James. b 68. TCD BA92 MA07. St Steph Ho Ox 07. **d** 09. C Towcester w Caldecote and Easton Neston etc *Pet* from 09. *35 Hazel Crescent, Towcester NN12 6UQ* Tel (01327) 323018 E-mail frboyland@gmail.com

BOYLE, Andrew McKenzie. b 45. Down Coll Cam BA67 MA71 CEng72 MICE72. WMMTC 82. **d** 85 **p** 86. NSM Woodthorpe *S'well* 85-87; Perm to Offic *Roch* 88-90; 91-96; Hon C Sevenoaks St Luke CD 90-91; NSM Sundridge w Ide Hill and Toys Hill from 96. *Greenridge, 35 Garth Road, Sevenoaks TN13 1RU* Tel (01732) 456546 Fax 450060 E-mail andrew.boyle@diocese-rochester.org

✠**BOYLE, The Rt Revd Christopher John.** b 51. AKC75. St Aug Coll Cant 75. **d** 76 **p** 77 **c** 01. C Wylde Green *Birm* 76-80; Bp's Dom Chapl 80-83; R Castle Bromwich SS Mary and Marg 83-01; AD Coleshill 92-99; P-in-c Shard End 96-97; Hon Can Birm Cathl 96-01; Bp N Malawi 01-09; Asst Bp Leic from 09. *32 Craighill Road, Leicester LE2 3FB* E-mail bishopboyle@googlemail.com

BOYLE, Mrs Lynn. b 58. Leeds Univ BEd79 BA07. NOC 04. **d** 07 **p** 08. NSM Stockport St Sav *Ches* from 07. *21 Cromley Road, Stockport SK2 7DT* Tel 0161-285 6558 E-mail lynnboyle1@aol.com

BOYLE, Paul. **d** 01 **p** 02. C Cen Cardiff *Llan* 01-03; C Barry All SS 03-05; P-in-c Pontypridd St Matt and Cilfynydd w Llanwynno 05-08; P-in-c Burton and Rosemarket *St D* from 08. *The Rectory, Burton, Milford Haven SA73 1NX* Tel (01646) 603622

BOYLE, Robert Leslie. b 52. EMMTC 97. **d** 00 **p** 01. NSM Derby St Anne and St Jo 00-08; C Paignton St Jo *Ex* from 08. *73 Dartmouth Road, Paignton TQ4 5AF* Tel (01803) 698412 E-mail robert.boyle7@btinternet.com

BOYLES, Peter John. b 59. Univ of Wales (Lamp) BA84. Sarum & Wells Th Coll 86. **d** 88 **p** 89. C Ches St Mary 88-91; C Neston 91-95; R Lavendon w Cold Brayfield, Clifton Reynes etc *Ox* 95-99; V Dent w Cowgill *Bradf* from 99. *The Vicarage, Flintergill, Dent, Sedbergh LA10 5QR* Tel (01539) 625226

BOYLING, Canon Denis Hudson. b 16. Keble Coll Ox BA38 MA42. Cuddesdon Coll 39. **d** 40 **p** 41. C Sheff St Cuth 40-46; Chapl K Coll Hosp Lon 46-49; Chapl United Sheff Hosps 49-57; V Endcliffe *Sheff* 57-68; Hon Can Sheff Cathl 58-68; V Almondbury *Wakef* 68-75; RD Almondbury 68-75; Hon Can Wakef Cathl 72-75; Can Res Wakef Cathl 75-82; rtd 82; Perm to Offic *Heref* from 82. *7 St Mary's Close, Tenbury Wells WR15 8ES* Tel (01584) 811633

BOYLING, The Very Revd Mark Christopher. b 52. Keble Coll Ox BA74 MA78. Cuddesdon Coll 74. **d** 77 **p** 78. C Kirkby *Liv* 77-79; P-in-c St Nic w St Mary 80-85; Bp's Dom Chapl 85-89; V Formby St Pet 89-94; Can Res and Prec Liv Cathl 94-04; Dean Carl from 04. *The Deanery, The Abbey, Carlisle CA3 8TZ* Tel (01228) 523335 Fax 548151 E-mail dean@carlislecathedral.org.uk

BOYNS, Martin Laurence Harley. b 36. St Jo Coll Cam BA49 MA51. Ridley Hall Cam 50. **d** 52 **p** 53. C Woodmansterne *S'wark* 52-55; C Folkestone H Trin w Ch Ch *Cant* 55-58; V Duffield *Derby* 58-71; V Rawdon *Bradf* 71-76; Chapl Woodlands Hosp Rawdon 71-76; R Melton *St E* 76-85; R Gerrans w St Anthony in Roseland *Truro* 85-92; Miss to Seamen 85-92; rtd 92; Perm to Offic *Truro* from 92. *Bojunda, Boscaswell Village, Pendeen, Penzance TR19 7EP* Tel (01736) 788390

BOYNS, Timothy Martin Harley. b 58. Warwick Univ BA80 Nottm Univ BCombStuds84. Linc Th Coll 81. **d** 84 **p** 85. C Oxhey St Matt *St Alb* 84-87; TV Solihull *Birm* 87-94; V Lillington *Cov* 94-06; RD Warwick and Leamington 99-06; V Hessle *York* from 06. *All Saints' Vicarage, 4 Chestnut Avenue, Hessle HU13 0RH* Tel (01482) 648555
E-mail tim.boyns@talk21.com

BOYS, Mrs Margaret Ann. b 34. Lon Univ TCert56. Oak Hill Th Coll 91. **d** 94 **p** 95. NSM Hadleigh St Barn *Chelmsf* 94-98; NSM Thundersley 98-04; rtd 04; Perm to Offic *Chelmsf* from 04. *10 Seymour Road, Westcliff-on-Sea SS0 8NJ* Tel (01702) 475997

BOYSE, Felix Vivian Allan. b 17. LVO78. CCC Cam BA39 MA42. Cuddesdon Coll 39. **d** 40 **p** 41. C New Mills *Derby* 40-43; P-in-c 43-45; Vice-Prin Cuddesdon Coll 46-51; V Kingswood *S'wark* 51-58; V St Mary Abchurch *Lon* 58-61; Prin St Geo Coll Jerusalem 61-64; Chapl Chpl Royal Hampton Court Palace 65-82; Preacher Lincoln's Inn 82-93; rtd 93; Perm to Offic *Chich* from 83. *Rose Cottage, Rookwood Road, West Wittering, Chichester PO20 8LT* Tel (01243) 514320

BRABIN-SMITH, Ms Lorna Daphne. b 54. Leeds Univ BSc75. Westcott Ho Cam 03. **d** 05 **p** 06. C Emmaus Par Team *Leic* 05-08; TV Syston from 08. *The Parsonage, 20 Hoby Road, Thrussington, Leicester LE7 4TH* Tel (01664) 424962

BRABY (*née* QUINTON), Rosemary Ruth. b 53. Univ Coll Lon BA75 Lon Inst of Educn PGCE79. **d** 06 **p** 07. OLM Old Catton *Nor* 06-09. *49 Woodland Drive, Norwich NR6 7AZ* Tel (01603) 427165 Fax 479556 E-mail rosemary.braby@ntlworld.com

BRACE, Alistair Andrew. b 53. Newc Univ MB, BS76. WMMTC 90. **d** 94. NSM Broseley w Benthall, Jackfield, Linley etc *Heref* 94-98. *58 Spout Lane, Benthall, Broseley TF12 1QY* Tel (01952) 884031

BRACE, Stuart. b 49. Open Univ BSc01. Bp Burgess Hall Lamp. **d** 74 **p** 75. C Llanelli Ch Ch *St D* 74-76; C Tenby w Gumfreston 76-77; V Ystradmeurig and Strata Florida 77-79; CF 79-86; CF(V) 86-93; Chapl HM Youth Cust Cen Everthorpe 86-88; Chapl HM Pris Stafford 88-93; Chapl HM Pris Long Lartin 93-95; Ecum Tr Officer HM Pris Service Chapl 95-99; Chapl HM Pris Glouc 99-03; Chapl HM Pris Leyhill from 03; Perm to Offic *Worc* from 95. *HM Prison Leyhill, 1 Tortworth Road, Wotton-under-Edge GL12 8BT* Tel (01454) 264000
E-mail brace3@chap0.freeserve.co.uk

BRACEGIRDLE, Canon Christopher Andrew. b 56. Dur Univ BEd79 St Edm Ho Cam BA84 MA89 Cov Univ PhD05. Ridley Hall Cam 82. **d** 85 **p** 86. C Livesey *Blackb* 85-88; TV E Farnworth and Kearsley *Man* 88-92; V Astley and Chapl Wigan and Leigh Health Services NHS Trust 92-98; P-in-c Walkden Moor w Lt Hulton *Man* 98-99; TR Walkden and Lt Hulton 99-03; V Heaton Ch Ch from 03; Tutor Dioc OLM and Reader Course 97-06; AD Bolton from 05; Hon Can Man Cathl from 07; Warden of Readers from 08. *The Vicarage, 2 Towncroft Lane, Heaton, Bolton BL1 5EW* Tel and fax (01204) 840430
E-mail chris@bracegirdles.co.uk

BRACEGIRDLE, Canon Cynthia Wendy Mary. b 52. LMH Ox BA73 MA77 Liv Univ DipAE82. NOC. **d** 87 **p** 94. Chapl Asst Man R Infirmary 85-88; Dir Dioc OLM Scheme *Man* 89-02, Hon Can Man Cathl 98-02; rtd 03; Perm to Offic *Carl* from 03. *The Vicarage, St George's Road, Millom LA18 4JA* Tel (01229) 772889 E-mail ignatius@globalnet.co.uk

BRACEGIRDLE, Robert Kevin Stewart. b 47. Univ Coll Ox BA69 MA73. St Steph Ho Ox 70. **d** 73 **p** 74. C Dorchester *Sarum* 73-75; C Woodchurch *Ches* 75-78; V Bidston 78-82; P-in-c Salford St Ignatius *Man* 82-86; R Salford St Ignatius and Stowell Memorial 86-02; P-in-c Salford Ordsall St Clem 99-02; P-in-c Millom *Carl* 02-06; V from 06. *The Vicarage, St George's Road, Millom LA18 4JA* Tel (01229) 772889
E-mail robert.bracegirdle@btinternet.com

BRACEWELL, Canon David John. b 44. Leeds Univ BA66 Man Univ MA82. Tyndale Hall Bris 67. **d** 69 **p** 70. C Tonbridge St Steph *Roch* 69-72; C Shipley St Pet *Bradf* 72-75; V Halliwell St Paul *Man* 75-84; R Guildf St Sav from 84; Hon Can Guildf Cathl from 05. *St Saviour's Rectory, Wharf Road, Guildford GU1 4RP* Tel (01483) 577811 *or* 455333 Fax 456895
E-mail st.saviours@dial.pipex.com

BRACEWELL, Howard Waring. b 35. FRGS73. Tyndale Hall Bris. **d** 63 **p** 63. Canada 63-72; Travel Missr World Radio Miss Fellowship 72-77; P-in-c Ashill *Nor* 72-74; Hon C Bris St Phil and St Jacob w Em 77-84; Perm to Offic *St Alb* 84-86; R Odell 86-88; V Pavenham 86-88; Lic to Offic *Man* 88-93; Assoc Min St Andrew's Street Bapt Ch Cambridge 94-99; Assoc Min Halliwell St Luke 99-01; rtd 01; Perm to Offic *Man* from 01. *10 Fairfields, Egerton, Bolton BL7 9EL* Tel (01204) 304028
E-mail howard@diglouvtl.fsnet.co.uk

BRACEY, David Harold. b 36. AKC63. **d** 64 **p** 65. C Westleigh St Pet *Man* 64-67; C Dunstable *St Alb* 67-76; V Benchill *Man* 70-76; V Elton St Steph 76-87; V Howe Bridge 87-00; rtd 00; Perm to Offic *Ban* from 06. *Rhiw Awel, Sarn, Pwllheli LL53 8EY* Tel (01758) 730381

BRACEY, Dexter Lee. b 70. Lanc Univ BA92. St Steph Ho Ox 07. **d** 09. C St Marychurch *Ex* from 09. *28 Barewell Road, Torquay TQ1 4PA* E-mail dexter_bracey@yahoo.co.uk

BRACHER, Paul Martin. b 59. Solicitor 84 Ex Univ LLB80. Trin Coll Bris BA90. **d** 90 **p** 91. C Sparkhill St Jo *Birm* 90; C Sparkhill w Greet and Sparkbrook 90-93; Chapl Birm Women's Hosp 92-93; P-in-c Lea Hall *Birm* 93-98; V from 98. *St Richard's Vicarage, Hallmoor Road, Birmingham B33 9QY* Tel 0121-783 2319 E-mail richard1552@aol.com

BRACKENBURY, The Ven Michael Palmer. b 30. Linc Th Coll 64. **d** 66 **p** 67. C S Ormsby w Ketsby, Calceby and Driby *Linc* 66-69; V Scothern w Sudbrooke 69-77; RD Lawres 73-78; Bp's Personal Asst 77-88; Dioc Dir of Ords 77-87; Can and Preb Linc Cathl 79-95; Dioc Lay Min Adv 86-87; Adn Linc 88-95; rtd 95. *18 Lea View, Ryhall, Stamford PE9 4HZ* Tel (01780) 752415

✠**BRACKLEY, The Rt Revd Ian James.** b 47. Keble Coll Ox BA69 MA73. Cuddesdon Coll 69. **d** 71 **p** 72 **c** 96. C Bris Lockleaze St Mary Magd w St Fran 71-74; Asst Chapl Bryanston Sch 77-87; Chapl 77-80; V E Preston w Kingston *Chich* 80-88; RD Arundel and Bognor 82-87; TR Haywards Heath St Wilfrid 88-96; RD Cuckfield 89-95; Suff Bp Dorking *Guildf* from 96; Hon Can Guildf Cathl from 96. *13 Pilgrim's Way, Guildford GU4 8AD* Tel (01483) 570829 Fax 567268
E-mail bishop.ian@cofeguildford.org.uk

BRACKLEY, Mark Ozanne. b 53. Boro Road Teacher Tr Coll CertEd75. S'wark Ord Course 90. **d** 93 **p** 94. C Hampstead St Steph w All Hallows *Lon* 93-97; V W Green Ch Ch w St Pet 97-04; Chapl Univ Coll Lon Hosps NHS Foundn Trust 04-08; Chapl Bolton Hospice from 08. *Bolton Hospice, Queens Park Street, Bolton BL1 4QT* Tel (01204) 663066 Fax 663060

BRACKNALL, Richard David Guy. b 43. Brasted Place Coll 71. Ripon Hall Ox 73. **d** 75 **p** 76. C Pocklington w Yapham-cum-Meltonby, Owsthorpe etc *York* 75-78; TV Thornaby on Tees 78-84; V New Marske 84-90; P-in-c Wilton 84-90; Ind Chapl 90-95; Perm to Offic from 05. *34 Margrove Park, Boosbeck, Saltburn-by-the-Sea TS12 3BX* Tel (01287) 653417

BRADBERRY, John Stephen. b 47. Hull Univ BSc70 Leeds Univ CertEd71 MEd86 Bradf Univ PhD91. NW Ord Course 76. **d** 79 **p** 80. NSM Warley *Wakef* from 79; Chapl H Trin Sch Holmfield 91-06; Chapl Rishworth Sch Ripponden from 06; Bp's Officer for NSMs *Wakef* 95-04; RD Halifax from 07. *129 Paddock Lane, Halifax HX2 0NT* Tel (01422) 358282

BRADBROOK, Mrs Averyl. b 46. Girton Coll Cam BA67 MA88 Man Univ PGCE69 MA(Theol)96. NOC 90. **d** 93 **p** 94. C Heaton Ch Ch *Man* 93-96; P-in-c Elton St Steph 96-02; Bp's Adv for Women's Min 01-02; V Moseley St Mary *Birm* 02-05; P-in-c Moseley St Anne 04-05; TR Eden, Gelt and Irthing *Carl* from 05. *St Martin's Vicarage, Main Street, Brampton CA8 1SH* Tel (01697) 742182 Mobile 07808-290817
E-mail abradbrook@onetel.com

BRADBROOK, Peter David. b 33. Kelham Th Coll 54. **d** 60 **p** 61. C Ches St Oswald St Thos 60-63; C Fulham St Etheldreda *Lon* 64-65; V Congleton St Jas *Ches* 65-79; V Wheelock 79-92; V Crewe All SS and St Paul 92-98; rtd 98; Perm to Offic *Ches* from 00. *20 Magdelen Court, College Fields, Dane Bank Avenue, Crewe CW2 8FF* Tel (01270) 669420

BRADBURY, Cedric. See BRADBURY, Canon Herbert Cedric

BRADBURY, George Graham. b 35. AKC58. **d** 59 **p** 60. C Portsea St Mary *Portsm* 59-62; C Melksham *Sarum* 62-64; R Winfrith Newburgh w Chaldon Herring 64-68; CF 68-71; rtd 99. *Wayside, Brook Street, Shipton Gorge, Bridport DT6 4NA* Tel (01308) 897714

BRADBURY, Canon Herbert Cedric. b 30. FPS Man Univ PhC53. Linc Th Coll 64. **d** 66 **p** 67. C Blackpool St Steph *Blackb* 66-71; TV Hempnall *Nor* 71-75; TR 75-81; R Fritton w Morningthorpe w Shelton and Hardwick 74-77; RD Depwade 77-81; R Wroxham w Hoveton and Belaugh 81-92; RD Tunstead 83-91; Hon Can Nor Cathl 90-97; R Gt and Lt Massingham and Harpley 92-97; P-in-c S Raynham, E w W Raynham, Helhoughton, etc 94-97; rtd 97; Perm to Offic *Nor* from 97; Bp's Officer for Rtd Clergy and Widows 99-08. *Morningthorpe, 66 Grove Lane, Holt NR25 6ED* Tel (01263) 712634

BRADBURY, Julian Nicholas Anstey. b 49. BNC Ox BA71 MA75 Birm Univ MA84 Cardiff Univ PhD07. Cuddesdon Coll 71. **d** 73 **p** 74. C S'wark H Trin 73-76; In RC Ch in USA 76-79; V Tottenham H Trin *Lon* 79-85; Dir Past Th Sarum & Wells Th Coll 85-90; P-in-c Yatton Keynell *Bris* 90-97; P-in-c Biddestone w Slaughterford 90-97; P-in-c Castle Combe 90-97; P-in-c W Kington 90-97; P-in-c Nettleton 90-97; R Horfield H Trin 97-02; Fell K Fund 02-07; Sen Fell from 07; Perm to Offic *Ox* from 02. *12 St Bernards Road, Oxford OX2 6EH* Tel (01865) 316825
E-mail n.bradbury@kingsfund.org.uk

BRADBURY, Justin Robert Grant. b 66. St Andr Univ MA92. Wycliffe Hall Ox 06. **d** 08 **p** 09. C Southbroom *Sarum* from 08. *73 Chivers Road, Devizes SN10 3FP* Tel (01380) 720149
E-mail justinrgbradbury@hotmail.com

BRADBURY, Nicholas. See BRADBURY, Julian Nicholas Anstey

BRADBURY, Paul. b 72. St Cath Coll Cam BA93 N Lon Univ MA99. Trin Coll Bris BA04. **d** 04 **p** 05. C Bitterne Park *Win* 04-08; C Pioneer Min Poole Old Town *Sarum* from 08. *67 Green Road, Poole BH1 1QH*

BRADBURY, Robert Douglas. b 50. Ripon Coll Cuddesdon 75. **d** 76 **p** 77. C Harlescott *Lich* 76-81; V Ruyton 81-88; P-in-c Gt w Lt Ness 84-88; V Ruyton XI Towns w Gt and Lt Ness 88-99. *Fairview, Holyhead Road, Froncysyllte, Llangollen LL20 7PU* Tel (01691) 777898

BRADDICK-SOUTHGATE, Charles Anthony Michael. b 70. K Coll Lon BD92. Chich Th Coll 92. **d** 94 **p** 95. C Catford St Laur *S'wark* 94-97; V Nunhead St Antony w St Silas from 97. *St Antony with St Silas Vicarage, Athenlay Road, London SE15 3EP* Tel (020) 7639 4261 Fax 7252 8152 E-mail cambs@aol.com

BRADDOCK, Andrew Jonathan. b 71. SS Coll Cam BA92 MA96. Ridley Hall Cam 95. **d** 98 **p** 99. C Ranworth w Panxworth, Woodbastwick etc *Nor* 98-01; R Cringleford and Colney 01-08; RD Humbleyard 04-08; Dioc Missr *Glouc* from 08. *Church House, College Green, Gloucester GL1 2LY* Tel (01452) 610346 E-mail abraddock@glosdioc.org.uk

BRADDOCK, Arthur Derek. b 25. Bolton Inst of Educn BA90 Bolton Univ MPhil05. Lich Th Coll 56. **d** 59 **p** 60. C Droylsden St Mary *Man* 59-61; C New Bury 61-65; V Kearsley Moor 65-79; C Ellesmere Port *Ches* 79-85; rtd 85; Perm to Offic *Man* from 85. *Room 35, Farnworth Care Home, Church Street, Farnworth, Bolton BL4 8AG* Tel (01204) 573355

BRADFORD, Alan. b 57. Southn Univ BSc79 Warwick Univ PGCE80. St Jo Coll Nottm MTh04. **d** 04 **p** 05. C Countesthorpe w Foston *Leic* 04-08; C Warfield *Ox* from 08. *2 Dorset Vale, Warfield, Bracknell RG42 3JL* Tel (01344) 425000 Mobile 07902-925826 E-mail abradford@hotmail.co.uk

BRADFORD, John. b 34. Lon Univ BA60 Birm Univ MEd81 FRSA FRGS. Oak Hill Th Coll 55. **d** 60 **p** 61. C Walcot *B & W* 60-64; Ass Master Wendover C of E Primary Sch 64-65; Hd RE Dr Challoner's High Sch Lt Chalfont 65-69; Perm to Offic *Ox* 66-70; Lect St Pet Coll of Educn Saltley 70-77; Perm to Offic *Birm* 70-71 and from 05; Lic to Offic 71-77; Perm to Offic *Cov* from 77; Nat Chapl-Missr Children's Soc 77-99; Gen Perm to Offic Ch in Wales from 89; rtd 99. *27 Marsh Lane, Solihull B91 2PG* Tel 0121-704 9895 *or* (020) 7837 4299 E-mail revjohnbradford@aol.com

BRADFORD, Peter. b 38. Sarum Th Coll 69. **d** 70 **p** 71. C Holdenhurst *Win* 70-73; C Stanmore 73-77; P-in-c Eling, Testwood and Marchwood 77-78; R Marchwood 78-86; C Christchurch 86-90; C Andover w Foxcott 90-92; V E and W Worldham, Hartley Mauditt w Kingsley etc 92-04; rtd 04. *23 Drummond Road, Bournemouth BH1 4DP* Tel (01202) 396451

BRADFORD, Steven John. b 59. Open Univ MBA01. St Jo Coll Nottm 06. **d** 08 **p** 09. C Bearsted w Thurnham *Cant* from 08. *66 Peverel Drive, Bearsted, Maidstone ME14 4PS* Tel 07909-560070 (mobile) E-mail stevejbradford@btinternet.com

BRADFORD, Archdeacon of. See LEE, The Ven David John

BRADFORD, Bishop of. See JAMES, The Rt Revd David Charles

BRADFORD, Dean of. See ISON, The Very Revd David John

BRADING, Jeremy Clive. b 74. Birm Univ BA95 MPhil98. Westcott Ho Cam 00. **d** 02 **p** 03. C Man Clayton St Cross w St Paul 02-05; TV Pendleton 05-07; P-in-c Daisy Hill from 07. *The Vicarage, 30 Lower Leigh Road, Westhoughton, Bolton BL5 2EH* Tel (01942) 857251 Mobile 07786-567140 E-mail jeremybrading@stjamesdaisyhill.co.uk

BRADISH, Paul Edward. b 61. Reading Univ LLB83. Ripon Coll Cuddesdon MA07. **d** 07 **p** 08. C Wokingham St Sebastian *Ox* 07-08; C Upper Kennet *Sarum* from 08. *The Rectory, High Street, Avebury, Marlborough SN8 1RF* Tel (01672) 539643 Mobile 07766-813661 E-mail revpaulbradish@googlemail.com

BRADLEY, Andrew Robert. b 65. Clare Coll Cam BA88. St Jo Coll Nottm MA94. **d** 94 **p** 95. C Burnage St Marg *Man* 94-98; TV Didsbury St Jas and Em 98-04; Nat Co-ord Acorn Chr Foundn from 04. *Acorn Christian Foundation, Whitehill Chase, Bordon GU35 0AP* Tel (01420) 478121 Fax 478122

BRADLEY, Anthony David. b 56. Wye Coll Lon BSc76. St Jo Coll Nottm 86. **d** 88 **p** 89. C Southchurch Ch Ch *Chelmsf* 88-91; C Cov H Trin 91-97; P-in-c Budbrooke 97-06; Dioc Lay Tr Adv 93-06; Development Dir Forward Vision 06-07; rtd 07; Perm to Offic *Carl* from 08. *187 Albert Street, Millom LA18 4AB* Tel (01229) 770535 E-mail tony.bradley@dial.pipex.com

BRADLEY, Anthony Edward. b 39. Perth Bible Coll 93. **d** 89 **p** 96. Dn-in-c Ravensthorpe Australia 95-96; P-in-c 96-99; C Wotton St Mary *Glouc* 00-04; rtd 04. *PO Box 1083, Bridgetown WA 6255, Australia* Tel (0061) (8) 9761 2917 E-mail tonychris@westnet.com.au

BRADLEY, Brian Hugh Granville. b 32. Univ Coll Ox 51. Lon Coll of Div 59. **d** 62 **p** 63. C E Twickenham St Steph *Lon* 62-65; C Herne Bay Ch Ch *Cant* 65-69; Miss to Seamen Teesside 69-71; Ceylon 71-72; Sri Lanka 72-74; Chapl Amsterdam w Haarlem and Den Helder *Eur* 75-79; Chapl Lyon w Grenoble and Aix-les-Bains 79-85; TV Bucknall and Bagnall *Lich* 87-93; Assoc Chapl

Dubai and Sharjah w N Emirates 93-97; rtd 97; Perm to Offic *Win* 97-03. *1 Maer Bay Court, Douglas Avenue, Exmouth EX8 2BX* Tel (01395) 263969

BRADLEY, Clifford David. b 36. Lon Univ BA60. St Aid Birkenhead 60. **d** 62 **p** 63. C Stoneycroft All SS *Liv* 62-65; C Chipping Sodbury and Old Sodbury *Glouc* 65-68; Br Honduras 68-70; C Leckhampton SS Phil and Jas *Glouc* 70-71; V Badgeworth w Shurdington 71-79; Dioc Missr *S & M* 79-84; V Santan 79-84; V Braddan 79-84; Bp's Dom Chapl 81-84; V Stroud and Uplands w Slad *Glouc* 84-89; C Shepshed *Leic* 90-92; R Leire w Ashby Parva and Dunton Bassett 92-99; rtd 99; P-in-c Renhold *St Alb* 99-06; Perm to Offic from 06. *47 Paddock Close, Clapham, Bedford MK41 6BD* Tel (01234) 305981

BRADLEY, Colin John. b 46. Edin Univ MA69. Sarum & Wells Th Coll 72. **d** 75 **p** 76. C Easthampstead *Ox* 75-79; V Shawbury *Lich* 79-90; R Moreton Corbet 80-90; P-in-c Stanton on Hine Heath 81-90; Can Res Portsm Cathl and Dir of Ords *Portsm* 90-98; C Chich 98-00; C Chich St Paul and Westhampnett 00-01; P-in-c Cocking, Bepton and W Lavington from 01. *The Rectory, Mill Lane, Cocking, Midhurst GU29 0HJ* Tel (01730) 817340 E-mail zen101842@zen.co.uk

BRADLEY (née DRAPER), Mrs Elizabeth Ann. b 38. Nottm Univ BTh75. Linc Th Coll 71. **dss** 84 **d** 87 **p** 94. Ind Chapl *Linc* 84-91; Bracebridge 84-91; Hon C 87-91; GFS Ind Chapl *Lon* 91-96; Hon Chapl GFS 96-98; Riverside Chapl *S'wark* 96; C Leighton Buzzard w Eggington, Hockliffe etc *St Alb* 98-01; Perm to Offic 01-02; Chapl Luton and Dunstable Hosp NHS Trust from 02. *26 Dew Pond Road, Flitwick, Bedford MK45 1RT* Tel (01525) 712369 E-mail elizabeth.bradley@ldh-tr.anglox.nhs.uk

BRADLEY, Gary Scott. b 53. Lon Univ LLB75. Ripon Coll Cuddesdon 75. **d** 78 **p** 79. C St John's Wood *Lon* 78-83; V Paddington St Sav from 83; P-in-c Paddington St Mary from 95; P-in-c Paddington St Mary Magd 98-03. *6 Park Place Villas, London W2 1SP* Tel (020) 7723 1968 Fax 7724 5332 Mobile 07957-140371 E-mail bottlerot@aol.com

BRADLEY, John Owen. b 30. Jes Coll Ox BA55 MA56. St Mich Coll Llan 52. **d** 56 **p** 57. C Cardiff St Mary *Llan* 56-59; Lect St Mich Coll Llan 59-61; C Caerau w Ely *Llan* 60; C Newton Nottage 61-64; V Aberavon H Trin 65-69; Lic to Offic *Cov* 70-76; C W Kirby St Bridget *Ches* 76-79; TV Knowle *Bris* 79-80; TR 80-91; RD Brislington 83-89; Chapl St Monica Home Westbury-on-Trym 91-00; Perm to Offic *Bris* from 00. *20 Home Ground, Bristol BS9 4UB* Tel and fax 0117-907 1503 E-mail bradley275@blueyonder.co.uk

BRADLEY, Joy Elizabeth. See COUSANS, Mrs Joy Elizabeth

BRADLEY, Mrs Julie Caroline. b 59. Ex Univ BSc80. WEMTC 00. **d** 03 **p** 04. NSM Stoke Gifford *Bris* from 03. *113 North Road, Stoke Gifford, Bristol BS34 8PE* Tel 0117-979 3418 E-mail cjcbradley@deltats.co.uk

BRADLEY, Michael Frederick John. b 44. Qu Coll Birm 76. **d** 77 **p** 78. C Sheff St Cuth 77-83; C Alford w Rigsby *Linc* 78-83; V Bracebridge 83-90; V Flitwick *St Alb* from 90; RD Ampthill from 08. *The Vicarage, 26 Dew Pond Road, Flitwick, Bedford MK45 1RT* Tel (01525) 712369 Fax 08701-259827 E-mail mfjbradley@btopenworld.com

BRADLEY, The Ven Peter David Douglas. b 49. Nottm Univ BTh79. Ian Ramsey Coll 74 Linc Th Coll 75. **d** 79 **p** 80. C Upholland *Liv* 79-83; TR 94-01; V Dovecot 83-94; Dir CME 89-02; Hon Can Liv Cathl from 00; Adn Warrington from 01; TR Upholland from 01. *The Rectory, 1A College Road, Upholland, Skelmersdale WN8 0PY* Tel (01695) 622936 Fax 625865 E-mail archdeacon@peterbradley.fsnet.co.uk

BRADLEY, The Very Revd Peter Edward. b 64. Trin Hall Cam BA86 MA90 FRSA02. Ripon Coll Cuddesdon 86. **d** 88 **p** 89. C Northampton St Mich w St Edm *Pet* 88-91; Chapl G&C Coll Cam 91-95; TV Abingdon *Ox* 95-98; TV High Wycombe 98-03; TR 03; Dean Sheff from 03. *Sheffield Cathedral, Church Street, Sheffield S1 1HA* Tel 0114-263 6063 Fax 263 6075 E-mail dean@sheffield-cathedral.org.uk

BRADLEY, Ronald Percival. b 25. ACP51 FRSA52 TCert49. Ex & Truro NSM Scheme 80. **d** 83 **p** 84. C Honiton, Gittisham, Combe Raleigh, Monkton etc *Ex* 83-86; P-in-c Halberton 86-87; rtd 90. *Abbeyfield Tamar House, 11 Brest Road, Plymouth PL6 5XN* Tel (01752) 721039

BRADLEY, Mrs Susan Kathleen. b 47. Hull Coll of Educn TCert68 Open Univ BA84 MA96. **d** 05 **p** 06. OLM S Lawres Gp *Linc* from 05. *17 Holly Close, Cherry Willingham, Lincoln LN3 4BH* Tel (01522) 750292 E-mail rev.s.bradley@gmail.com

BRADLEY (née NAYLOR), Ms Vivien Frances Damaris. b 55. New Hall Cam BA78 MA82 RGN86. Ripon Coll Cuddesdon. **d** 93 **p** 94. C Northampton St Jas *Pet* 93-95; Chapl Asst Southn Univ Hosps NHS Trust 95-98; Chapl 98-00; Chapl Addenbrooke's NHS Trust 00-03; Perm to Offic *Nor* from 03. *7 Station Road, Kimberley, Wymondham NR18 9HB* Tel (01603) 757807

BRADNUM, Canon Ella Margaret. b 41. CertEd64 St Hugh's Coll Ox MA65. **dss** 69 **d** 87 **p** 94. Illingworth *Wakef* 69-72; Batley All SS 72-73; Lay Tr Officer 77-82; Min Tr Officer 82-88; Sec

Dioc Bd of Min 88-06; Warden of Readers 88-02; Co-ord Lay Tr 88-02; Hon Can Wakef Cathl 94-06; Prin Wakef Min Scheme 97-06; rtd 06. *4 Southlands Drive, Huddersfield HD2 2LT* Tel (01484) 420721

BRADNUM, Richard James. b 39. Pemb Coll Ox BA62 MA67. Ridley Hall Cam 62. **d** 64 **p** 65. C Birm St Martin 64-68; C Sutton St Jas *York* 68-69; Perm to Offic *Wakef* 71-72; C Batley All SS 72-74; V Gawthorpe and Chickenley Heath 74-86; V Mixenden 86-97; rtd 97; Perm to Offic *Wakef* 97-99; Hon Retirement Officer from 99. *4 Southlands Drive, Huddersfield HD2 2LT* Tel (01484) 420721

BRADSHAW, Charles Anthony. b 44. Qu Coll Birm MA76. **d** 75 **p** 76. C Whickham *Dur* 75-78; C Bilton *Cov* 78-81; TV Coventry Caludon 81-89; V Birstall and Wanlip *Leic* 89-99; TR Vale of Belvoir Par 00-04; TV Caterham *S'wark* from 04. *The Rectory, Station Road, Woldingham, Caterham CR3 7DD* Tel (01883) 652192 E-mail cab@paxchristi.wanadoo.co.uk

BRADSHAW, Denis Matthew. b 52. Chich Th Coll 77. **d** 80 **p** 81. C Ruislip St Martin *Lon* 80-84; C Northolt Park St Barn 84-86; V Northolt St Jos 86-01; P-in-c Hayes St Nic CD 94-00; V Kennington St Jo w St Jas *S'wark* 01-09; V Burgess Hill St Edw *Chich* from 09. *St Edward's Vicarage, 7 Bramble Gardens, Burgess Hill RH15 8UQ* Tel (01444) 241300
E-mail denis.bradshaw1@btinternet.com

BRADSHAW, Graham. b 58. Edin Univ BD86. Edin Th Coll 83. **d** 86 **p** 87. C Thornton-le-Fylde *Blackb* 86-89; C Kirkby Lonsdale *Carl* 89-91; V Langford *St Alb* 91-97; Papua New Guinea 97-99; R Aspley Guise w Husborne Crawley and Ridgmont *St Alb* from 00. *The Rectory, Church Street, Aspley Guise, Milton Keynes MK17 8HN* Tel (01908) 583169
E-mail gbradshaw@tinyworld.co.uk

BRADSHAW, Miss Jennie McNeille. b 47. UEA BA69. Cranmer Hall Dur 85. **d** 90 **p** 94. Par Dn Herne *Cant* 90-94; C 94-95; P-in-c Claybrooke cum Wibtoft and Frolesworth *Leic* 95-96; R 96-06; P-in-c Burham and Wouldham *Roch* from 06. *The Rectory, 266 Rochester Road, Burham, Rochester ME1 3RJ* Tel (01634) 666862

BRADSHAW (née DAY), Mrs Jennifer Ann. b 67. Aber Univ BSc89. Wycliffe Hall Ox BTh95. **d** 95 **p** 96. C Whitburn *Dur* 95-98; C Monkwearmouth 98-99; TV 99-01; Hon C Silksworth from 02. *St Matthew's Vicarage, Silksworth Road, Sunderland SR3 2AA* Tel 0191-521 1167

BRADSHAW, Canon Malcolm McNeille. b 45. Kelham Th Coll 65. **d** 70 **p** 71. C New Addington *Cant* 70-76; Chapl Milan w Cadenabbia, Varese and Lugano *Eur* 77-82; V Boxley w Detling *Cant* 82-99; Sen Chapl Gtr Athens *Eur* from 99; Hon Can Malta Cathl from 01. *c/o the British Embassy, Plutarchou 1, 106-75 Athens, Greece* Tel and fax (0030) (210) 721 4906
E-mail anglican@otenet.gr

BRADSHAW, Canon Prof Paul Frederick. b 45. Clare Coll Cam BA66 MA70 K Coll Lon PhD71 Ox Univ DD94 FRHistS91. Westcott Ho Cam 67. **d** 69 **p** 70. C W Wickham St Jo *Cant* 69-71; C Cant St Martin and St Paul 71-73; Tutor Chich Th Coll 73-78; V Flamstead *St Alb* 78-82; Dir of Minl Tr Scheme 78-82; Vice-Prin Ripon Coll Cuddesdon 83-85; USA 85-95; Prof Th Notre Dame Univ from 85; Hon Can N Indiana from 90; PV Westmr Abbey from 95; Perm to Offic *Guildf* from 95; Dioc Liturg Officer *Eur* from 07. *Notre Dame London Centre, 1 Suffolk Street, London SW1Y 4HG* Tel (020) 7484 7811 Fax /484 7853
E-mail bradshaw.1@nd.edu

BRADSHAW, Philip Hugh. b 39. Qu Coll Ox BA64 MA67. S'wark Ord Course 88. **d** 91 **p** 92. NSM Bletchingley *S'wark* 91-98; Ldr Community of Celebration 91-98; NSM Redhill St Jo from 98. *35 Cavendish Road, Redhill RH1 4AL* Tel (01737) 778760

BRADSHAW, Richard Gordon Edward. b 66. Southn Univ LLB90. Wycliffe Hall Ox BTh94. **d** 97 **p** 98. C Bishopwearmouth St Gabr *Dur* 97-00; C Silksworth 00-01; P-in-c 01-03; V from 03; AD Wearmouth from 08. *St Matthew's Vicarage, Silksworth Road, Sunderland SR3 2AA* Tel 0191-521 1167

BRADSHAW, Roy John. b 49. Sarum & Wells Th Coll 85. **d** 87 **p** 88. C Gainsborough All SS *Linc* 87-90; V New Waltham 90-94; R Killamarsh *Derby* 94-06; C Barlborough and Renishaw 05-06; rtd 06; Perm to Offic *Derby* from 07. *22 St Peter's Close, Duckmanton, Chesterfield S44 5JJ* Tel (01246) 822280

BRADSHAW, Timothy. b 50. Keble Coll Ox BA72 MA78 PhD. St Jo Coll Nottm BA75. **d** 76 **p** 77. C Clapton Park All So *Lon* 76-79; Lect Trin Coll Bris 80-91; Hon C Sea Mills *Bris* 83-91; Tutor Regent's Park Coll Ox from 91; NSM Ox St Aldate w St Matt 91-94; NSM Ox St Matt 95-07. *54 St Giles, Oxford OX1 3LU* Tel (01865) 288147
E-mail timothy.bradshaw@regents.ox.ac.uk

BRADSHAW, Veronica. *See* CAROLAN, Mrs Veronica

BRADWELL, Area Bishop of. *See* GREEN, The Rt Revd Laurence Alexander

BRADY, Frederick Herbert James. b 33. Sydney Univ BSc55 DipEd56 Lon Univ BD65. Moore Th Coll Sydney ThL59. **d** 60 **p** 60. Australia 60-63 and from 69; Lic to Offic *Lon* 63-69; rtd 00.

18 Capel Street, West Melbourne Vic 3003, Australia Tel (0061) (3) 9328 8487 *or* 9650 3791 Fax 9650 4718
E-mail brady@ioville.net.au

BRADY, Ian. b 59. Ridley Hall Cam. **d** 01 **p** 02. C Cromer *Nor* 01-04; V Belmont *Lon* from 04; P-in-c Douglas All SS and St Thos *S & M* from 09. *St Thomas's Vicarage, Marathon Avenue, Douglas, Isle of Man IM2 4JA* Tel (01624) 611503
E-mail i.bradybunch@btopenworld.com

BRADY, Mrs Lynda. b 60. SRN83. SA Internat Tr Coll 87 Oak Hill Th Coll 07. **d** 07 **p** 08. NSM Belmont *Lon* 07-09; NSM Douglas All SS and St Thos *S & M* from 09. *St Thomas's Vicarage, Marathon Avenue, Douglas, Isle of Man IM2 4JA* Tel (01624) 611503 Mobile 07974-995561
E-mail revbrady@btopenworld.com

BRADY, Canon Madalaine Margaret. b 45. Univ of Wales (Ban) BD88 CertEd91 MA92. **d** 89 **p** 97. Asst Chapl Univ of Wales (Ban) 89-96; Dioc Communications Officer from 94; Dioc Lay Min Officer from 95; C Arllechwedd 96-97; P-in-c Llanfaelog 97-02; R Llanfaelog and Llangwyfan from 02; AD Llifon and Talybolion from 07. *The Rectory, Station Road, Rhosneigr LL64 5JX* Tel (01248) 354999 *or* tel and fax (01407) 810412 Fax (01248) 353882 E-mail dmbrady@lineone.net

BRAE, Mrs Yvonne Rosetta. b 45. WEMTC 05. **d** 08 **p** 09. NSM Cheltenham St Luke and St Jo *Glouc* from 08; NSM Cheltenham St Mich from 08. *86 Arle Road, Cheltenham GL51 8LB* Tel (01242) 519780 Mobile 07940-452211
E-mail jmyr@blueyonder.co.uk

BRAGG, Marie-Elsa Beatrice Roche. b 65. Ripon Coll Cuddesdon. **d** 07 **p** 08. NSM St Marylebone St Paul *Lon* 07-09; NSM Kilburn St Mary w All So and W Hampstead St Jas from 09. *12 Woodside, London NW11 6HH*
E-mail meboxford@hotmail.com

BRAGG, Mrs Rosemary Eileen. b 41. MRPharmS64. St Steph Ho Ox 99. **d** 00 **p** 01. NSM Boyne Hill *Ox* 00-06; NSM Golden Cap Team *Sarum* from 06. *Dove Inn Cottage, 48 Silver Street, Lyme Regis DT7 3HR* Tel (01297) 442403 E-mail rosie@brag.eu

BRAID, Simon. b 54. SS Coll Cam MA76 FCA79. SEITE 06. **d** 09. NSM Hildenborough *Roch* from 09. *Petresfield, Fordcombe Road, Penshurst, Tonbridge TN11 8DL* Tel (01892) 870480 Fax 871453 Mobile 07802-809849 E-mail simonbraid@aol.com

BRAILSFORD, Matthew Charles. b 64. Newc Univ BSc86 St Jo Coll Dur BA95. Cranmer Hall Dur 92. **d** 95 **p** 96. C Hull St Jo Newland *York* 95-06; P-in-c N Ferriby from 06. *The Vicarage, 20 Aston Hall Drive, North Ferriby HU14 3EB* Tel (01482) 631306
E-mail matthew.brailsford@ukgateway.net

BRAIN, Mrs Marina. b 52. **d** 01 **p** 02. OLM Wokingham St Sebastian *Ox* 01-05; Chapl HM Pris Reading, Grendon and Spring Hill 05-06; Chapl HM Pris High Down from 06. *The Chaplain's Office, HM Prison, High Down Lane, Sutton SM2 5PJ* Tel (020) 7147 6325
E-mail marina.brain@hmps.gsi.gov.uk

BRAIN, Michael Charles. b 39. Culham Coll Ox TCert61 ACP65. Lich Th Coll 68. **d** 70 **p** 71. C Stone St Mich *Lich* 70-73; C Harlescott 73-76; C Longton St Jas 76-77; P-in-c Dudley St Edm *Worc* 77-79; V 79-04; Chapl Dudley Coll of Tech 77-04; rtd 04; Perm to Offic *Worc* from 04. *33 Dibdale Road, Dudley DY1 2RX* Tel (01384) 232774

BRAITHWAITE, Albert Alfred. b 24. Clifton Th Coll. **d** 59 **p** 60. C Bestwood St Matt *S'well* 59-62; Chapl RN 62-81; QHC from 77; C Southsea St Jude *Portsm* 82-90; rtd 90; Perm to Offic *Portsm* from 90. *16 Charminster, 46 Craneswater Park, Southsea PO4 0NU*

BRAITHWAITE, Canon Michael Royce. b 34. Linc Th Coll 71. **d** 73 **p** 74. C Barrow St Geo w St Luke *Carl* 73-77; V Kells 77-88; RD Calder 84-88; V Lorton and Loweswater w Buttermere 88-99; Ldr Rural Life and Agric Team 93-96; Member Rural Life and Agric Team 96-99; RD Derwent 94-98; Hon Can Carl Cathl 94-99; rtd 99; Perm to Offic *Carl* from 00. *High Green Farm, Bothel, Carlisle CA7 2JA* Tel (01697) 32349

BRAITHWAITE, Canon Roy. b 34. Dur Univ BA56. Ridley Hall Cam 58. **d** 60 **p** 61. C Blackb St Gabr 60-63; C Burnley St Pet 63-66; V Accrington St Andr 66-74; V Blackb St Jas 74-95; RD Blackb 86-91; Hon Can Blackb Cathl 93-98; V Garstang St Helen Churchtown 95-98; Dioc Ecum Officer 95-98; rtd 98; Perm to Offic *Blackb* from 98. *9 Barker Lane, Mellor, Blackburn BB2 7ED* Tel (01254) 240724

BRALESFORD, Nicholas Robert. b 53. St Jo Coll Nottm LTh79 BTh79. **d** 79 **p** 80. C Leic St Chris 79-82; C Heeley *Sheff* 82-85; TV Kings Norton *Birm* 85-90; V Chapel-en-le-Frith *Derby* from 90. *The Vicarage, 71 Manchester Road, Chapel-en-le-Frith, High Peak SK23 9TH* Tel (01298) 812134

BRALEY, Robert James. *See* RILEY-BRALEY, Robert James

BRAMHALL, Eric. b 39. St Cath Coll Cam BA61 MA65. Tyndale Hall Bris 61. **d** 63 **p** 64. C Eccleston St Luke *Liv* 63-66; C Bolton Em *Man* 66-69; Perm to Offic *Ches* 70-74; V Aughton Ch Ch *Liv* 75-92; Chapl Ormskirk Children's Hosp 75-92; V Childwall All SS *Liv* 92-04; rtd 04. *Henfaes, Prior Street, Ruthin LL15 1LT* Tel (01824) 702757

BRAMHALL, John. d 08. NSM Greenham *Ox* from 08. *56 Greyberry Copse Road, Thatcham RG19 8XB* Tel (01635) 42348 E-mail johnbramuk@yahoo.co.uk

BRAMLEY, Thomas Anthony. b 44. BSc PhD. TISEC. d 96 p 97. NSM Penicuik *Edin* from 96; NSM W Linton from 96. *44 Bavelaw Crescent, Penicuik EH26 9AT*

BRAMMER, David John. b 62. d 99 p 00. C Acton St Mary *Lon* 99-02; C Ealing All SS and Chapl Twyford C of E High Sch Acton 02-09; R Acton St Mary *Lon* from 09. *The Rectory, 14 Cumberland Park, London W3 6SX* Tel (020) 8992 8876 E-mail rev.d.brammer@btinternet.com

BRAMPTON, Canon Fiona Elizabeth Gordon. b 56. St Jo Coll Dur BA78 BA83. Cranmer Hall Dur 81. dss 84 d 87 p 94. Bris St Andr Hartcliffe 84-90; Par Dn 87-90; C Orton Waterville *Ely* 90-96; C-in-c Orton Goldhay CD 90-96; TV The Ortons, Alwalton and Chesterton 96-00; V Haddenham from 00; V Wilburton from 00; P-in-c Witchford w Wentworth from 08; RD Ely 03-09; Hon Can Ely Cathl from 05. *The Vicarage, Church Lane, Haddenham, Ely CB6 3TB* Tel (01353) 740309 E-mail fiona.brampton@ely.anglican.org

BRANCHE, Brian Maurice. b 37. Chich Th Coll 73. d 75 p 76. C Brighton Resurr *Chich* 75-78; C Upper Norwood St Jo *Cant* 78-81; P-in-c Croydon St Martin 81-84; V Croydon St Martin *S'wark* 85-88; V St Helier 88-93; V New Malden All SS 93-97; V Barkingside H Trin *Chelmsf* 97-02; rtd 02. *113 Tong Road, Little Lever, Bolton BL3 1PU* E-mail bbranche@aol.com

BRAND, Frank Ronald Walter. b 25. ALCD56. d 56 p 57. C Brondesbury St Anne w Kilburn H Trin *Lon* 56-58; V Port Mourant Br Guiana 58-61; V Enmore 61-67; V N Greenford All Hallows *Lon* 67-91; rtd 91; Perm to Offic *B & W* 91-07. *11 Stuart Court, High Street, Kibworth, Leicester LE8 0LR* Tel 0116-279 3240

BRAND, Peter John. b 32. Lon Univ BSc54. Edin Dioc NSM Course 75. d 83 p 84. NSM Edin St Jo from 83. *24 Drum Brae Park, Edinburgh EH12 8TF* Tel 0131-339 4406

BRAND, Richard Harold Guthrie. b 65. Dur Univ BA87. Ripon Coll Cuddesdon 87. d 89 p 90. C N Lynn w St Marg and St Nic *Nor* 89-92; C King's Lynn St Marg w St Nic 92-93; C Croydon St Jo *S'wark* 93-95; TV Fendalton New Zealand 95-98; P-in-c Hambleton *Portsm* 98-06; Dir of Ords 98-06; P-in-c Market Harborough and The Transfiguration etc *Leic* 06-08; TR from 08. *The Rectory, Rectory Lane, Market Harborough LE16 8AS* Tel (01858) 462926 E-mail richard.brand@virgin.net

BRAND, Stuart William. b 30. Leeds Univ BSc53. Coll of Resurr Mirfield 53. d 55 p 56. C Stepney St Dunstan and All SS *Lon* 55-59; C Acton Green St Pet 59-60; C-in-c Godshill CD *Portsm* 60-63; Malawi 63-67; V Widley w Wymering *Portsm* 67-72; Chapl Fieldhead Hosp Wakef 72-80; Chapl Pinderfields & Stanley Royd Hosps Wakef 72-80; Chapl Brook Gen Hosp Lon 80-95; Chapl Greenwich Distr Hosp Lon 80-95; rtd 95; Perm to Offic *Ox* from 96. *17 Hayfield Road, Oxford OX2 6TX* Tel (01865) 316456

BRANDES, Simon Frank. b 62. Univ of Wales (Ban) BA83. Edin Th Coll 83. d 85 p 86. C Barton w Peel Green *Man* 85-88; C Longsight St Jo w St Cypr 88-90; R 90-94; Asst Dioc Youth Officer 88-94; V Lt Lever 94-02; P-in-c Lydgate w Friezland 02-03; TR Saddleworth 03-07; V Chiswick St Nic w St Mary *Lon* from 07. *Chiswick Vicarage, Chiswick Mall, London W4 2PJ* Tel (020) 8995 4717 Mobile 07775-526285

BRANDIE, Canon Beaumont Lauder. b 40. MBE07. K Coll Lon AKC64 BD66. d 65 p 66. C Whitton St Aug *Lon* 65-71; C Portsea St Mary *Portsm* 71-77; TR Brighton Resurr *Chich* 77-09; V Brighton St Martin w St Wilfrid and St Alban from 09; Can and Preb Chich Cathl from 87; RD Brighton 97. *St Martin's Rectory, Upper Wellington Road, Brighton BN2 3AN* Tel (01273) 604687 E-mail beaumont.brandie@btinternet.com

BRANDON, Mrs Helen Beatrice. b 53. Heythrop Coll Lon MA02. SAOMC 03. d 06 p 07. NSM Burton Latimer *Pet* 06-07; NSM Earls Barton 07-09; Abps' Adv for Healing Min from 07; Perm to Offic *Lon* from 07 and *Pet* from 09. *Clopton Manor, Clopton, Kettering NN14 3DZ* Tel (01832) 720346 Fax 720446 E-mail beatrice@healingministry.org.uk

BRANDON, Milesius. b 63. Heythrop Coll Lon BA92 MA07 City Univ MSc04 RMN97 PGCE98. St Steph Ho Ox MTh09. d 09. C Clerkenwell H Redeemer *Lon* from 09. *Most Holy Redeemer Church, 24 Exmouth Market, London EC1R 4QE* Tel (020) 7837 1861 E-mail mbrandon51@hotmail.com

BRANDRETH, Mrs Jacqueline. b 59. d 07 p 08. OLM Pendlebury St Jo *Man* from 07. *36 Asten Fold, Salford M6 7JH*

BRANSCOMBE, Michael Peter. b 65. Cranmer Hall Dur BA95. d 95 p 96. C Ogley Hay *Lich* 95-01; Dioc Voc Officer 99-01; Asst R Palm Harbor USA 01-04; Assoc R Clearwater Ascension from 04. *1010 Charles Street, Clearwater FL 33755-1008, USA* Tel (001) (727) 447 3469 E-mail mikeb@churchofascension.org

BRANSON, Robert David. b 46. Linc Th Coll 74. d 77 p 78. C Kempston Transfiguration *St Alb* 77-80; C Goldington 80-82; V Marsh Farm 82-91; V Aylsham *Nor* from 91; RD Ingworth from 00; Chapl Norfolk Community Health and Care from 99. *The Vicarage, 64 Holman Road, Aylsham, Norwich NR11 6BZ* Tel (01263) 733871

BRANT, Anthony William. b 31. TD67. Linc Th Coll 73. d 75 p 76. C Cove St Jo *Guildf* 75-79; P-in-c Puttenham and Wanborough 79-83; V Lightwater 83-93; rtd 93; Perm to Offic *Chich* from 93. *2 Southcourt Avenue, Bexhill-on-Sea TN39 3AR* Tel (01424) 217526

BRANT, Ms Karlyn Lee. b 72. Birm Univ BA99 MA01. Ripon Coll Cuddesdon 01. d 03 p 04. C Gaywood *Nor* 03-07; R Dunster, Carhampton, Withycombe w Rodhuish etc *B & W* from 07. *The Rectory, St George's Street, Dunster, Minehead TA24 6RS* Tel (01643) 821812 E-mail revd.lee@btinternet.com

BRANT, Leslie Harold. b 11. d 71 p 72. C Lower Sandown St Jo *Portsm* 71-74; P-in-c Newchurch 75-80; rtd 80; Perm to Offic *Portsm* from 82. *1 Dean's Court, 2 Dover Street, Ryde PO33 2AQ* Tel (01983) 564054

BRASIER, Ralph Henry (Jim). b 30. Cant Sch of Min 82. d 85 p 86. C S Ashford Ch Ch *Cant* 85-89; V Pembury *Roch* 89-95; rtd 95; Perm to Offic *Portsm* and *Win* from 95. *72 Jenkyns Close, Botley, Southampton SO30 2UU* Tel (01489) 788332

BRASSELL, Canon Kenneth William. b 23. Kelham Th Coll 46. d 50 p 51. C Woodbridge St Mary *St E* 50-53; C-in-c Bury St Edmunds All SS CD 53-57; V Ipswich St Thos 57-63; V Beckenham St Jas *Roch* 63-88; P-in-c Beckenham St Aug 66-77; P-in-c Beckenham St Mich w St Aug 77-78; Hon Can Roch Cathl 82-88; rtd 88; Perm to Offic *Glouc* from 88. *20 College Green, Gloucester GL1 2LR* Tel (01452) 309080

BRASSIL, Sen Adrian. b 56. Westf Coll Lon BSc79. STETS 97. d 00 p 01. NSM Westborough *Guildf* 00-04; NSM Woking St Jo 04-05; C Addlestone from 05. *17 Crockford Park Road, Addlestone KT15 2LF* Tel (01932) 821176 Mobile 07973-315423 E-mail sean.brassil@btinternet.com

BRATLEY, David Frederick. b 42. Linc Th Coll 80. d 82 p 83. C Holbeach *Linc* 82-85; R Fleet w Gedney 85-07; RD Elloe E 01-05; rtd 07. *1 Setts Green, Bourne PE10 0FZ* Tel (01778) 392567

BRATTON, Mark Quinn. b 62. Lon Univ BA84 K Coll Lon MA98 Barrister-at-Law (Middle Temple) 87. Wycliffe Hall Ox BA94. d 94 p 95. C W Ealing St Jo w St Jas *Lon* 94-98; Chapl Warw Univ 98-09; AD Cov S 02-09; P-in-c Berkswell from 09. *The Rectory, Meriden Road, Berkswell, Coventry CV7 7BE* Tel (01676) 533605 E-mail mark.bratton@talk21.com

BRAUN, Thomas Anthony. b 53. St Jo Coll Ox BA76 MA76 Univ Coll Lon PhD80. S'wark Ord Course 89. d 92 p 93. NSM Surbiton St Andr and St Mark *S'wark* 92-05. *8 Kings Drive, Surbiton KT5 8NG* Tel (020) 8399 6898

BRAVINER, William Edward. b 66. Leic Poly BSc88 St Jo Coll Dur BA94 ACA91. Cranmer Hall Dur 92. d 95 p 96. C Royton St Anne *Man* 95-99; R Lansallos and V Talland *Truro* 99-03; P-in-c Duloe, Herodsfoot, Morval and St Pinnock 01-03; TR Jarrow *Dur* from 03; AD Jarrow from 05. *St Peter's House, York Avenue, Jarrow NE32 5LP* Tel 0191-489 3279 E-mail bill.braviner@durham.anglican.org

BRAVINGTON, Timothy Frederick Desmond. b 34. Trin Coll Cam BA56 MA70. Cuddesdon Coll 56. d 58 p 59. C Caledon S Africa 58-61; Asst Chapl St Andr Coll Grahamstown 61-64; R Namaqualand 64-71; R Bellville Transfiguration 71-76; R Durban N St Martin-in-the-Fields 76-83; R Stellenbosch St Mary 84-88; R Elgin St Mich 88-98; rtd 98; Perm to Offic Cape Town 99-06; *Eur* 06-09; *Ox* from 08. *63 Cutteslowe House, Park Close, Oxford OX2 8NP* Tel (01865) 511416 E-mail timbrav@gmail.com

BRAY, Christopher Laurence. b 53. Leeds Univ BSc74 Qu Univ Kingston Ontario MSc76. St Jo Coll Nottm 78. d 81 p 82. C Aughton Ch Ch *Liv* 81-84; Hon C Scarborough St Mary w Ch Ch and H Apostles *York* 84-88; Chapl Scarborough Coll 84-88; V St Helens St Matt Thatto Heath *Liv* 88-98; V Southport All SS and All So 98-02; rtd 02; Perm to Offic *Liv* from 03. *9 Arbour Street, Southport PR8 6SB* Tel (01704) 530486 E-mail chrislbray@aol.com

BRAY, Gerald Lewis. b 48. McGill Univ Montreal BA69 Sorbonne Univ Paris LittD73. Ridley Hall Cam 76. d 78 p 79. C Canning Town St Cedd *Chelmsf* 78-80; Tutor Oak Hill Th Coll 80-92; Ed *Churchman* from 83; Angl Prof Div Beeson Div Sch Samford Univ Alabama from 93. *16 Manor Court, Cambridge CB3 9BE* Tel (01223) 311804 *or* (001) (205) 726 2585 Fax (01223) 566608 *or* (001) (205) 726 2234 E-mail glbray@samford.edu

BRAY, Jason Stephen. b 69. SS Hild & Bede Coll Dur BA90 MA91 Fitzw Coll Cam PhD96 MSOTS97. Westcott Ho Cam 95. d 97 p 98. C Abergavenny St Mary w Llanwenarth Citra *Mon* 97-99; Min Can St Woolos Cathl 99-02; V Blaenavon w Capel Newydd from 02; P-in-c Abersychan and Garndiffaith from 09. *The Vicarage, Llanover Road, Blaenavon, Pontypool NP4 9HR* Tel (01495) 790292

BRAY, Jeremy Grainger. b 40. Man Univ BA62. Wells Th Coll 62. d 64 p 65. C Bris St Andr w St Bart 64-67; C Bris H Cross Inns Court 67-71; C-in-c Stockwood CD 71-73; V Bris Ch the Servant Stockwood 73-83; RD Brislington 79-83; P-in-c Chippenham

St Pet 83-88; V 88-93; V Fishponds St Jo 93-04; rtd 04. *46 Charter Road, Chippenham SN15 2RA* Tel (01249) 655661 E-mail jg.bray@btinternet.com

BRAY, Joyce. b 32. CA Tr Coll. **dss** 80 **d** 87 **p** 94. Bloxwich *Lich* 80-84; Derringham Bank *York* 84-03; Par Dn 87-94; Hon C 94-03; rtd 94; Perm to Offic *York* from 03. *413 Willerby Road, Hull HU5 5JD* Tel (01482) 502193

BRAY, Kenneth John. b 31. St Mich Coll Llan 65. **d** 67 **p** 72. C Killay *S & B* 67-68; C S Harrow St Paul *Lon* 71-73; C Hillingdon St Jo 73-76; C Chipping Sodbury and Old Sodbury *Glouc* 76-79; C Worle *B & W* 79-80; Lic to Offic *Ches* 80-83; TV Wrexham *St As* 83-85; V Llay 85-94; rtd 94. *c/o M Bray Esq, 18 Springfield Road, Poole BH14 0LQ* Tel (01202) 741206

BRAY, Richard. b 29. Linc Th Coll 55. **d** 57 **p** 58. C Lt Ilford St Barn *Chelmsf* 57-62; R Tye Green w Netteswell 62-93; rtd 93; Perm to Offic *Chelmsf* from 93. *14 The Wayback, Saffron Walden CB10 2AX* Tel (01799) 526901

BRAY, Richard Antony. b 77. CCC Ox MA05. Oak Hill Th Coll BA09. **d** 09. C St Botolph without Aldersgate *Lon* from 09. *82 Saunders Ness Road, London E14 3EA* Tel 07798-940554 (mobile) E-mail brayra2001@yahoo.co.uk

BRAYBROOKE, Marcus Christopher Rossi. b 38. Magd Coll Cam BA62 MA65 Lon Univ MPhil68 Lambeth DD04. Wells Th Coll 63. **d** 64 **p** 65. C Highgate St Mich *Lon* 64-67; C Frindsbury w Upnor *Roch* 67-72; TV Frindsbury w Upnor 72-73; P-in-c Swainswick w Langridge and Woolley *B & W* 73-76; R 76-79; Dir of Tr 79-84; Hon C Bath Ch Ch Prop Chpl 84-91; Exec Dir Coun of Chrs and Jews 84-87; rtd 88; Perm to Offic *Bris* 88-93; Preb Wells Cathl 90-93; Chapl Bath St Mary Magd Holloway 92-93; Hon C Dorchester *Ox* 93-05. *17 Courtiers Green, Clifton Hampden, Abingdon OX14 3EN* Tel (01865) 407566 E-mail marcusbray@aol.com

BRAZELL, Denis Illtyd Anthony. b 42. Trin Coll Cam BA64 MA68. Wycliffe Hall Ox 78. **d** 80 **p** 81. C Cheltenham Ch Ch *Glouc* 80-84; V Reading St Agnes w St Paul *Ox* 84-96; Perm to Offic *Guildf* 96-97; Warden and Chapl Acorn Chr Healing Trust 97-99; rtd 99; Co-Dir Word for Life Trust from 99; Perm to Offic *Glouc* 02-09; Lead Chapl St Andr Healthcare Birm from 09. *32 Oakham Road, Harborne, Birmingham B17 9DG* Tel 0121-427 2934 *or* 432 2100 E-mail denisbrazell@mac.com

BRAZIER, Eric James Arthur. b 37. Qu Coll Birm 84. **d** 86 **p** 87. C Lighthorne *Cov* 86-89; P-in-c 89-92; P-in-c Chesterton 89-92; P-in-c Newbold Pacey w Moreton Morrell 89-92; R Astbury and Smallwood *Ches* 92-99; rtd 99; Perm to Offic *Ches* from 99; *Lich* and *Heref* from 00. *Wolf's Head Cottage, Chirbury, Montgomery SY15 6BP* Tel (01938) 561450

BRAZIER, Canon Raymond Venner. b 40. Wells Th Coll 68. **d** 71 **p** 72. C Horfield St Greg *Bris* 71-75; P-in-c Bris St Matt and St Nath 75-79; V 79-05; RD Horfield 85-91; P-in-c Bishopston 93-97; Hon Can Bris Cathl 94-05; rtd 05; Perm to Offic *Bris* from 05; Chapl to The Queen from 98. *51 Chalks Road, Bristol BS5 9EP* Tel 0117-952 3209 E-mail rayvb@tiscali.co.uk

BRAZIER-GIBBS, Samantha Elizabeth. b 78. Ridley Hall Cam 03. **d** 06 **p** 08. C Grays Thurrock *Chelmsf* from 06. *11 Conrad Gardens, Grays RM16 2TN* Tel (01375) 394338 Mobile 07876-301307 E-mail revsbg@mac.com

BREADEN, Robert William. b 37. Edin Th Coll 58. **d** 61 **p** 62. C Broughty Ferry *Bre* 61-65; R 72-07; R Carnoustie 65-72; Can St Paul's Cathl Dundee 77-07; Dean Bre 84-07; rtd 07; P-in-c Portree *Arg* from 07. *The Rectory, Somerled Square, Portree IV51 9EH* Tel (01478) 613135 E-mail ateallach@aol.com

BREADMORE, Martin Christopher. b 67. Lon Univ LLB89. Wycliffe Hall Ox BTh93. **d** 93 **p** 94. C Herne Bay Ch Ch *Cant* 93-97; C Camberley St Paul *Guildf* 97-01; Chapl Elmhurst Ballet Sch 97-98; C Wallington *S'wark* from 01. *47 Park Hill Road, Wallington SM6 0RU* Tel (020) 8395 9428 E-mail martin.breadmore@blueyonder.co.uk

BREADON, John Desmond. b 73. St Andr Univ BD96 Birm Univ PhD02. Westcott Ho Cam 99. **d** 01 **p** 02. C W Bromwich All SS *Lich* 01-05; Chapl St Geo Post 16 Cen *Birm* 05-08; Nat Adv for FE/Chapl Abps' Coun from 08. *Church House, Great Smith Street, London SW1P 3AZ* Tel (020) 7898 1513 E-mail john.breadon@c-of-e.org.uk *or* johnbreadon@hotmail.co.uk

BREAR, Alvin Douglas. b 43. **d** 87 **p** 96. NSM Leic H Spirit 87-88; NSM Leic Ch Sav 88-96; NSM Leic Presentation from 96; Finland from 98. *Sahurintie 44, SF28800 Pori, Finland* (00358) (2) 648 2060 E-mail douglas.brear@tukkk.fi

BREARLEY, Canon Janet Mary. b 48. Cranmer Hall Dur 88. **d** 90 **p** 94. C Prudhoe *Newc* 90-91; C Fenham St Jas and St Basil 91-95; Chapl MU 93-95; V Warkworth and Acklington *Newc* from 95; Hon Can Newc Cathl from 04; AD Alnwick from 05. *The Vicarage, 11 Dial Place, Warkworth, Morpeth NE65 0UR* Tel and fax (01665) 711217 E-mail jmbrearley@stlawrence-church.org.uk

BREBNER, Martin James. b 47. OBE02. ARCS68 Imp Coll Lon BSc68. St Alb Minl Tr Scheme 87. **d** 90 **p** 91. Hon C Letchworth St Paul w Willian *St Alb* 90-94; Hon C St Ippolyts 95-01; Perm

to Offic *St Alb* 01-02 and *Linc* from 02. *Willowcroft, Greatford, Stamford PE9 4QA* Tel (01778) 561145 Fax 561157 E-mail martin.brebner@yahoo.com

BRECH, Miss Suzy Zelda. b 73. Man Univ BSc95 Roehampton Inst PGCE97. SEITE 06. **d** 09. *St Michael's Church, Cobham Close, London SW11 6SP*

BRECHIN, Bishop of. See MANTLE, The Rt Revd John Ambrose Cyril

BRECHIN, Dean of. See MUMFORD, The Very Revd David Christopher

BRECKLES, Robert Wynford. b 48. St Edm Hall Ox BA72 MA74 CertEd. Cranmer Hall Dur. **d** 79 **p** 80. C Bulwell St Mary *S'well* 79-84; V Lady Bay 84-05; V Lady Bay w Holme Pierrepont and Adbolton from 06. *The Vicarage, 121 Holme Road, Nottingham NG2 5AG* Tel 0115-981 3565

BRECKNELL, David Jackson. b 32. Keble Coll Ox BA53 MA57. St Steph Ho Ox 56. **d** 58 **p** 59. C Streatham St Pet *S'wark* 58-62; C Sneinton St Steph w St Alb *S'well* 62-64; C Solihull *Birm* 64-68; V Streatham St Paul *S'wark* 68-75; R Rumboldswyke *Chich* 75-81; P-in-c Portfield 79-81; R Whyke w Rumboldswhyke and Portfield 81-95; rtd 95; Perm to Offic *Chich* from 95; P-in-c Boxgrove 98-99. *8 Priory Close, Boxgrove, Chichester PO18 0EA* Tel (01243) 784841 E-mail david.brecknell@tesco.net

BRECKWOLDT, Peter Hans. b 57. Man Poly BA79. Oak Hill Th Coll BA88. **d** 88 **p** 89. C Knutsford St Jo and Toft *Ches* 88-92; V Moulton *Pet* from 92. *The Vicarage, 30 Cross Street, Moulton, Northampton NN3 1RZ* Tel (01604) 491060 E-mail peterbreckwoldt@aol.com

BRECON, Archdeacon of. See THOMAS, The Ven Alfred James Randolph

BRECON, Dean of. See MARSHALL, The Very Revd Geoffrey Osborne

BREED, Kenneth Wilfred. b 11. Leeds Univ BA33. Coll of Resurr Mirfield 33. **d** 35 **p** 36. C Cov H Trin 35-37; C Parkstone St Pet w Branksea *Sarum* 37-43; Chapl RNVR 43-46; C Eastleigh *Win* 46-49; C Cheam *S'wark* 49-51; V Shirley *Birm* 51-77; rtd 77; Hon C St Andr Holborn *Lon* 77-79; Perm to Offic *Sarum* 80-03 and *B & W* 86-94. *4 Capel Court, The Burgage, Prestbury, Cheltenham GL52 3EL* Tel (01242) 582698

BREED, Mrs Verena. b 69. **d** 02 **p** 02. NSM Prestbury *Ches* 02-04; V Bosley and N Rode w Wincle and Wildboarclough from 04. *The Vicarage, Wincle, Macclesfield SK11 0QH* Tel (01260) 227234 E-mail verenabreed@onetel.com

BREEDS, Christopher Roger. b 51. Lon Univ CertEd73 LGSM83 ACertCM87. Chich Th Coll 84. **d** 87 **p** 88. C E Grinstead St Swithun *Chich* 87-90; TV Aldrington 90-92; P-in-c Hove St Andr Old Ch 92-93; TV Hove 93-99; V Wivelsfield from 99; RD Cuckfield from 06. *New Vicarage, Church Lane, Wivelsfield, Haywards Heath RH17 7RD* Tel (01444) 471783 E-mail christopher.breeds@virgin.net

BREENE, Timothy Patrick Brownell. b 59. Kent Univ BA81 CCC Cam BA89 MA90. Ridley Hall Cam 87. **d** 90 **p** 93. C Hadleigh w Layham and Shelley *St E* 90-95; C Martlesham w Brightwell 95-03; rtd 03. *85 Cliff Road, Felixstowe IP11 9SQ* Tel (01394) 283718

BREFFITT, Geoffrey Michael. b 46. CChem MRIC72 Trent Poly CertEd77. Qu Coll Birm 87. **d** 89 **p** 90. C Prenton *Ches* 89-92; V Frankby w Greasby 92-01; Dioc Ecum Officer 00-01; V German St Jo *S & M* 01-08; V Foxdale 01-08; V Patrick 01-08; RD Castletown and Peel 04-08; P-in-c Weston *Ches* from 08. *The Vicarage, 13 Cemetery Road, Weston, Crewe CW2 5LQ* Tel (01270) 582585

BRENCHLEY, Royston Harry Peter. b 32. Lon Inst of Educn CertEd73 BEd77. **d** 02 **p** 03. OLM Mitcham St Olave *S'wark* 02-05; Perm to Offic from 05. *74 Manor Way, Mitcham CR4 1EE* Tel (020) 8764 3797 E-mail roy.brenchley@ukgateway.net

BRENDON-COOK, John Lyndon. b 37. FRICS. SW Minl Tr Course. **d** 81 **p** 82. NSM Bodmin *Truro* 81-82; NSM St Breoke and Egloshayle 82-90; NSM Helland 90-94; P-in-c 94-98; NSM Cardynham 90-94; rtd 98; Perm to Offic *Truro* from 98. *Treworder Byre, 119 Egloshayle Road, Wadebridge PL27 6AG* Tel (01208) 812488

BRENNAN, John Lester. b 20. MRCP51 FRCPath77 Barrister-at-Law (Middle Temple) 71 Lon Univ MB, BS44 MD52 LLM86. St Aug Coll Cant 54. **d** 55 **p** 56. India 55-65; Hon C Woodside Park St Barn 65-69; Lic to Offic *Lich* 69-88; P-in-c Chrishall *Chelmsf* 88-89; Hon C 89-91; Hon C Heydon, Gt and Lt Chishill, Chrishall etc 91-93; Perm to Offic *St Alb* from 93. *16 Butterfield Road, Wheathampstead AL4 8PU* Tel (01582) 832230

BRENNAN, Samuel James. b 16. St Aid Birkenhead. **d** 57 **p** 58. C Magheralin *D & D* 57-60; C Down H Trin 60-63; Min Can Down Cathl 60-63; I Scarva 63-69; I Aghalee 69-84; rtd 84. *Mitchell Court, 50 West Street, Newtownards BT23 4EN* Tel (028) 9181 9139

BRENNAND (*née* PUNSHON), Ms Carol Mary. b 59. Liv Inst of Educn BEd83. Ridley Hall Cam 92. **d** 94 **p** 95. C Bushey *St Alb* 94-97; C Watford Ch Ch 97-00; P-in-c Ash Vale *Guildf*

00-06; V 06-07; P-in-c Claybrooke cum Wibtoft and Frolesworth *Leic* 07-08; P-in-c Leire w Ashby Parva and Dunton Bassett 07-08; C Upper Soar 08-09; R from 09. *The Vicarage, Main Road, Claybrooke Parva, Lutterworth LE17 5AE* Tel (01455) 208878 E-mail carolbrennand@btinternet.com

BRENNAND, Ian Peter. b 55. STETS 01. d 04 p 05. C Frimley *Guildf* 04-07; Chapl Univ Hosps Leic NHS Trust from 08. *The Vicarage, Main Road, Claybrooke Parva, Lutterworth LE17 5AE* Tel (01455) 202262 E-mail ianbrennand@btinternet.com

BRENNEN, Canon Colin. b 15. Lon Univ BA47 BD56 Dur Univ PhD88. Linc Th Coll 46. d 48 p 49. C Seaton Hirst *Newc* 48-50; C Bishopwearmouth Ch Ch *Dur* 50-52; V Grangetown 52-58; V Whitworth w Spennymoor 58-78; RD Auckland 74-82; Hon Can Dur Cathl 78-93; V Hamsterley 78-82; rtd 82. *1 Royton Close, Wrexham LL13 7EP* Tel (01978) 357747

BRENT, Prof Allen Leonard. b 40. Em Coll Cam BA66 Lon Univ MA72 Leeds Univ PhD78. N Queensland Coll of Min 82. d 84 p 85. Australia 84-95; Hon Can N Queensland 91-95; Sen Lect Coll of SS Mark and Jo Plymouth 95-01; Perm to Offic *Ex* 95-98; Lic to Offic 98-01; Perm to Offic *Ely* from 01. *18 St Albans Road, Cambridge CB4 2HG* Tel (01223) 362671

BRENT, Philip. b 68. K Coll Lon BD89. Cuddesdon Coll 94. d 96 p 97. C Sawbridgeworth *St Alb* 96-99; C Skegness and Winthorpe *Linc* 99-03; Chapl United Lincs Hosps NHS Trust 00-03; R Market Deeping *Linc* from 03. *The Rectory, 13 Church Street, Market Deeping, Peterborough PE6 8DA* Tel (01778) 342237 E-mail philip@candace.fsnet.co.uk

BRENTNALL, David John. b 53. UEA BA75 MPhil82. Ridley Hall Cam 84. d 86 p 87. C Eaton *Nor* 86-90; V Stevenage St Pet Broadwater *St Alb* 90-96; V St Alb St Pet 96-09. *Address temp unknown*

BRERETON, Catherine Louise. *See* WILLIAMS, Mrs Catherine Louise

BRETEL, Keith Michael. b 51. St Mich Coll Llan 79. d 81 p 82. C Thundersley *Chelmsf* 81-84; CF 84-06; Chapl Guards Chpl Lon 03-05. *Address temp unknown*

BRETHERTON, Canon Anthony Atkinson. b 51. Cant Univ (NZ) BA74 Waikato Univ (NZ) MMS97. St Jo Th Coll (NZ) LTh74 STh76. d 75 p 76. Asst C Ashburton New Zealand 75-79; Asst P St Geo-in-the-East w St Paul *Lon* 79-80; V Te Kauwhata New Zealand 80-85; V Cam 85-91; Can St Pet Cathl Waikato 88-90; Offg Min Waikato 91-01; Lic to Offic *L & K* 02-07; Perm to Offic *B & W* from 07. *18 Vicars Close, Wells BA5 2UJ* Tel 07738-993809 (mobile) E-mail tonybretherton@hotmail.com

BRETHERTON, Donald John. b 18. Lon Univ BD57. Handsworth Coll Birm 38 Headingley Coll Leeds 38 St Aug Coll Cant 59. d 60 p 61. In Methodist Ch 42-59; C Cant St Martin w St Paul 60-62; V Thornton Heath St Jude 62-70; V Herne 70-82; RD Reculver 74-80; rtd 82; Perm to Offic *Cant* from 84. *Martin's, The Green, Chartham, Canterbury CT4 7JW* Tel (01227) 730255

BRETT, Dennis Roy Anthony. b 46. Sarum & Wells Th Coll 86. d 88 p 89. C Bradford-on-Avon *Sarum* 88-92; P-in-c Bishopstrow and Boreham 92-01; R from 01; Chapl Warminster Hosp from 92. *The Rectory, 8 Rock Lane, Warminster BA12 9JZ* Tel (01985) 213000

BRETT, Canon Paul Gadsby. b 41. St Edm Hall Ox BA62 MA66. Wycliffe Hall Ox 64. d 65 p 66. C Bury St Pet *Man* 65-68; Asst Ind Chapl 68-72; Ind Chapl *Worc* 72-76; Sec Ind Cttee of Gen Syn Bd for Soc Resp 76-84; Dir Soc Resp *Chelmsf* 85-94; Can Res Chelmsf Cathl 85-94; R Shenfield 94-08; rtd 08. *Ore Cottage, Mill Road, Friston, Saxmundham IP17 1PH* Tel (01728) 687767 E-mail paul.brett@btinternet.com

BRETT, Canon Peter Graham Cecil. b 35. Em Coll Cam BA59 MA63. Cuddesdon Coll 59. d 61 p 62. C Tewkesbury w Walton Cardiff *Glouc* 61-64; C Bournemouth St Pet *Win* 64-66; Chapl Dur Univ 66-72; R Houghton le Spring 72-83; RD Houghton 80-83; Can Res Cant Cathl 83-01; rtd 01; Perm to Offic *Cant* from 01. *3 Appledore Road, Tenterden TN30 7AY* Tel (01580) 761794 E-mail pandgbrett@btinternet.com

BRETT YOUNG (née ROBIN), Ms Helen Mary Kathleen. b 67. St Martin's Coll Lanc BEd90. Cranmer Hall Dur BA98. d 98 p 99. C Gd Shep TM *Carl* 98-02; TV from 02. *The Rectory, Patterdale, Penrith CA11 0NL* Tel (01768) 482209 E-mail hmbrettyoung@hotmail.com

BREUILLY, Mrs Elizabeth Linda. b 48. York Univ BA70. WMMTC 02. d 05 p 06. NSM Bournville *Birm* from 05. *178 Bournville Lane, Birmingham B30 1LT* Tel 0121-458 2334 E-mail elizabeth.breuilly4@which.net

BREW, William Kevin Maddock. b 49. d 78 p 79. C Raheny w Coolock *D & G* 78-80; Bp's C Dublin Finglas 80-83; I Mountmellick w Coolbanagher, Rosenallis etc *M & K* 83-89; I Ahoghill w Portglenone *Conn* 89-05; I Howth *D & G* from 05. *The Rectory, 94 Howth Road, Howth, Co Dublin, Republic of Ireland* Tel (00353) (1) 832 3019 or tel and fax 832 6346 E-mail howth@dublin.anglican.org

BREW, William Philip. b 43. Derby Coll of Educn CertEd64 FCollP84. NOC 84. d 87 p 88. In Independent Methodist Ch 70-83; Hd Master Birtenshaw Sch 78-90; NSM Holcombe *Man* 87-90; TV Horwich 91-93; TV Horwich and Rivington 93-97; V

Lostock St Thos and St Jo 97-08; P-in-c Bolton St Bede 04-08; AD Deane 98-05; rtd 08; Perm to Offic *Wakef* from 08. *22 Deganwy Drive, Kirkheaton, Huddersfield HD5 0NG* Tel (01484) 301295 E-mail wp.brew@ntlworld.com

BREWER, Barry James. b 44. Oak Hill Th Coll 72. d 75 p 76. C Hove Bp Hannington Memorial Ch *Chich* 75-78; C Church Stretton *Heref* 78-81; TV Bishopsnympton, Rose Ash, Mariansleigh etc *Ex* 81-87; R Swynnerton and Tittensor *Lich* 87-07; RD Stone 01-07; rtd 07. *Les Nouhouds, 16500 Saint-Maurice-des-Lions, France* E-mail barry.brewer@orange.fr

BREWER, Mrs Susan Comport. b 55. LMH Ox MA76. SEITE 99. d 02 p 03. C Dartford St Edm *Roch* 02-07; V Milton next Gravesend Ch Ch from 07. *The Vicarage, 48 Old Road East, Gravesend DA12 1NR* Tel (01474) 352643 Mobile 07930-492323 E-mail suec@brewer86.plus.com

BREWER, Andrew Robert. b 70. Oak Hill Th Coll BA05. d 05 p 06. C Gt Clacton *Chelmsf* 05-09; V Kilnhurst *Sheff* from 09. *The Vicarage, Highthorn Road, Kilnhurst, Mexborough S64 5TX* Tel (01709) 589674 E-mail andy@brewerton.org

BREWIN, David Frederick. b 39. Leic Poly BSc PhD. Lich Th Coll 63. d 66 p 67. C Shrewsbury H Cross *Lich* 66-69; C Birstall *Leic* 69-73; V Eyres Monsell 73-79; V E Goscote 79-82; V E Goscote w Ratcliffe and Rearsby 82-90; R Thurcaston 90-91; R Thurcaston w Cropston 92-05; rtd 05; Perm to Offic *Leic* from 05 and *Pet* from 06. *28 Welland Way, Oakham LE15 6SL* Tel (01572) 720073

BREWIN, Donald Stewart. b 41. Ch Coll Cam BA62 MA66. Ridley Hall Cam 68. d 71 p 72. C Ecclesall *Sheff* 71-75; V Anston 75-81; V Walton H Trin *Ox* 81-89; TR 89-94; RD Aylesbury 90-94; Nat Dir SOMA UK 94-07; Perm to Offic *St Alb* from 94; rtd 07. *Wickham Cottage, Gaddesden Turn, Great Billington, Leighton Buzzard LU7 9BW* Tel (01525) 373644 Mobile 07816-362797 E-mail donbrewin@compuserve.com

BREWIN, Karan Rosemary. b 42. C Glas Coll 77 Glas NSM Course 80. dss 84 d 85. Clarkston *Glas* 84-89; Hon C 86-89 and 91-97; OHP 89 and 98-02; Perm to Offic *York* 01-02; Swaziland from 02. *St Hilda's House, PO Box 1272, Manzini, Swaziland* Tel (0026) (85) 053323 E-mail jdean@africaonline.co.sz

BREWIN, Wilfred Michael. b 45. Nottm Univ BA69. Cuddesdon Coll 69. d 70 p 71. C Walker *Newc* 70-73; C Alnwick St Paul 73-74; C Alnwick w Edlingham and Bolton Chpl 74-77; Fell Sheff Univ 77-79; C Greenhill *Sheff* 79; P-in-c Eggleston *Dur* 79-81; V Norton St Mich 81-87; V Headington *Ox* from 87. *The Vicarage, 33 St Andrew's Road, Oxford OX3 9DL* Tel (01865) 761094 E-mail michaelbrewin@btinternet.com

BREWSTER, Christine Elaine. b 45. Newc Univ BA67 CertEd68 Lon Univ DipEd62 MA84 Univ of Wales (Ban) PhD07 ALCM76 LTCL78. SAOMC 95. d 98 p 99. NSM Aylesbury w Bierton and Hulcott *Ox* 98-00; NSM Dacre w Hartwith and Darley w Thornthwaite *Ripon* 00-01; C Wetherby 01-04; Perm to Offic 04-08; P-in-c Llanwnnog and Caersws w Carno *Ban* from 08. *The Vicarage, Llanwnog, Caersws SY17 5JG* Tel (01686) 688318 E-mail cbholly@supanet.com

BREWSTER, David Pearson. b 30. Clare Coll Cam BA54 MA58 Lon Univ BA65 Oriel Coll Ox MA66 DPhil76. Ridley Hall Cam. d 58 p 59. C Southampton St Mary w H Trin *Win* 58-61; C N Audley Street St Mark *Lon* 61-62 and 63-65; Tunisia 62-63; Home Sec JEM 65-66; C Ox St Mary V w St Cross and St Pet 66-68; Lect Lady Spencer-Churchill Coll Ox 68-71; New Zealand 71-78; V Brockenhurst *Win* 78-95; rtd 95; Perm to Offic *Win* from 95. *4 Saxonford Road, Christchurch BH23 4ES* Tel (01425) 277860

BREWSTER, David Thomas. b 68. GLCM90 ALCM89. Cranmer Hall Dur BA99. d 99 p 00. C Bidston *Ches* 99-03; TV Stockport SW 03-07; V Edgeley and Cheadle Heath from 07. *St Mark's Vicarage, 66 Berlin Road, Stockport SK3 9QF* Tel 0161-480 5896

BREWSTER, Jonathan David. b 67. Bucks Coll of Educn BA89 Bris Univ BA94 K Coll Lon MA01. Trin Coll Bris 91. d 94 p 95. C Gt Horton *Bradf* 94-98; Chapl Univ of Westmr *Lon* 98-03; V Highbury Ch Ch w St Jo and St Sav from 03. *Christ Church Vicarage, 155 Highbury Grove, London N5 1SA* Tel (020) 7226 4544 Mobile 07977-127244 E-mail vicar@dsl.pipex.com

BREWSTER (née BEATTIE), Margaret. b 43. S'wark Ord Course 90. d 93 p 94. NSM S'wark H Trin w St Matt 93-97; NSM Newington St Paul 97-04; NSM Dunstable *St Alb* 04-07. *39 Glen Drive, Boston PE21 7QB* Tel (01205) 351298 E-mail brew95906@aol.com

BREWSTER, Mrs Susan Jacqueline. b 48. SEITE 94. d 97 p 98. NSM Goodmayes St Paul *Chelmsf* 97-01; TV Loughton St Jo 01-09; P-in-c Cranham from 09. *51 Courtenay Gardens, Upminster RM14 1DH* Tel (01708) 250854 E-mail suz@brewster6441.fsnet.co.uk

BRIAN, Brother. *See* HARLEY, Brother Brian Mortimer

BRIAN, Stephen Frederick. b 54. Sussex Univ BEd77 Open Univ MA90 Lanc Univ MPhil97 Surrey Univ PhD03. Qu Coll Birm 82. d 85 p 86. C Scotforth *Blackb* 85-88; V Freckleton 88-97; V Bagshot *Guildf* 97-06; Chapl Heathfield St Mary's Sch Wantage 06-07; P-in-c Mid Loes *St E* 07-08; R from 08. *The Rectory,*

Church Lane, Earl Soham, Woodbridge IP13 7SD   Tel (01728) 685308 E-mail sfb4510@aol.com

BRICE, Christopher John. b 48. St Edm Ho Cam MA80. Wycliffe Hall Ox 82. d 82 p 83. C N Hinksey Ox 82-86; Chapl Nuff Coll Ox 84-86; V S Hackney St Mich w Haggerston St Paul Lon 86-93; Dir Dioc Bd for Soc Resp 93-01; Adv for Soc Justice 01-08; Hon C De Beauvoir Town St Pet 93-08; P-in-c Kentish Town St Martin w St Andr from 08. 9 Beresford Road, London N5 2HS   Tel (020) 7226 3834 or 7932 1121
E-mail chris.brice@london.anglican.org

BRICE, Derek William Fred. b 39. Poly Cen Lon MA87 MCIM89 FCMI82. d 02 p 03. OLM Cheam S'wark from 02. Mallow, Parkside, Cheam, Sutton SM3 8BS   Tel (020) 8642 0241 or 8693 4324 E-mail derek.brice@ukgateway.net

BRICE, Jonathan Andrew William. b 61. d 92 p 93. C Buckhurst Hill Chelmsf 92-96; C Victoria Docks Ascension 96; P-in-c 96-98; V 98-06; Chapl Felsted Sch from 06. Felsted School, Felsted, Dunmow CM6 3LL   Tel (01371) 822600 Fax 822607

BRICE, Neil Alan. b 59. Man Univ BA81 Hughes Hall Cam CertEd87. Westcott Ho Cam 82. d 84 p 85. C Longton Lich 84-86; Hd of Relig Studies Coleridge Community Coll Cam 87-89; NSM Cherry Hinton St Andr Ely 88-89; C Fulbourn 89-92; C Gt Wilbraham 89-92; C Lt Wilbraham 89-92; V Arrington 92-00; R Orwell 92-00; R Wimpole 92-00; R Croydon w Clopton 92-00; P-in-c Barrington 98-00; R Orwell Gp from 00. The Rectory, Fishers Lane, Orwell, Royston SG8 5QX   Tel (01223) 208653 E-mail revnab@btinternet.com

BRICE, Paul Earl Philip. b 54. Bath Univ BSc77. Wycliffe Hall Ox 83. d 86 p 87. C Gt Baddow Chelmsf 86-89; Chapl Imp Coll Lon and St Mary's Hosp Med Sch 89-95; Chapl RCA 90-95; Sec HE/Chapl C of E Bd of Educn 95-02; Hon C S Kensington St Jude Lon 95-02; R Hartfield w Coleman's Hatch Chich from 02. The Rectory, Church Street, Hartfield TN7 4AG   Tel (01892) 770850

BRIDGE, John Jeremy. b 74. Ripon Coll Cuddesdon 07. d 09. C Four Oaks Birm from 09. 2 Knightsbridge Close, Sutton Coldfield B74 4UQ   Tel 0121-352 0441
E-mail john.100bridge@btinternet.com

BRIDGE, Martin. b 45. Lon Univ BA66 Linacre Coll Ox BA71 MA73. St Steph Ho Ox 69. d 72 p 73. C St Peter-in-Thanet Cant 72-77; New Zealand from 77. PO Box 87-145, Meadowbank, Auckland, New Zealand   Tel and fax (0064) (9) 521 5013 or 521 0636 E-mail martin.bridge@xtra.co.nz

BRIDGEN, Andrew Grahame. b 57. Aston Univ BSc81 Surrey Univ BA03 FCCA95. STETS 00. d 03 p 04. NSM Portchester Portsm 03-04; C Portsea St Luke 05-07; Perm to Offic from 08. 9 Campbell Road, Southsea PO5 1RH   Tel (023) 9234 8617
E-mail andrew.bridgen@ntlworld.com

BRIDGEN, John William. b 40. K Coll Cam BA62 MA66. Ripon Hall Ox 66. d 70 p 72. C Headstone St Geo Lon 70-71; C Hanwell St Mary 71-75; C Tolladine Worc 75; TV Worc St Barn w Ch Ch 76; R Barrow St E 76-83; V Denham St Mary 76-83; Perm to Offic Ely 84-88 and from 91; rtd 88; Perm to Offic Glas 89-91. 57 St Philip's Road, Cambridge CB1 3DA   Tel (01223) 571748

BRIDGEN, Mark Stephen. b 63. K Coll Lon BD85. Cranmer Hall Dur 86. d 88 p 89. C Kidderminster St Jo and H Innocents Worc 88-92; C Nor St Pet Mancroft w St Jo Maddermarket 92-94; V Longbridge Birm 94-00; V Wednesbury St Bart Lich 00-07; P-in-c Gnosall and Moreton from 08. The Vicarage, Glebe Lane, Gnosall, Stafford ST20 0ER   Tel (01785) 822213
E-mail mark.bridgen@btinternet.com

BRIDGER, Francis William. b 51. Pemb Coll Ox BA73 MA78 Bris Univ PhD81. Trin Coll Bris 74. d 78 p 79. C Islington St Jude Mildmay Park Lon 78-82; Lect St Jo Coll Nottm 82-90; V Woodthorpe S'well 90-99; Prin Trin Coll Bris 99-05; Prof Fuller Th Sem USA 05-08. 24 Watnall Road, Nuthall, Nottingham NG16 1DU   Tel 07507-885476 (mobile)
E-mail fbridger@yahoo.ie

BRIDGER, Canon Gordon Frederick. b 32. Selw Coll Cam BA53 MA58. Ridley Hall Cam 54. d 56 p 57. C Islington St Mary Lon 56-60; C Cambridge St Sepulchre Ely 60-64; V Fulham St Mary N End Lon 62-69; C Edin St Thos 69-76; R Heigham H Trin Nor 76-87; RD Nor S 79-86; Hon Can Nor Cathl 84-87; Prin Oak Hill Th Coll 87-96; rtd 96; Perm to Offic Nor from 96. The Elms, 4 Common Lane, Sheringham NR26 8PL   Tel (01263) 823522

BRIDGER, Mrs Helen Ruth. b 58. Bradf Univ BA91. Trin Coll Bris BA06. d 05 p 06. C Altadena USA 05-06; C Arcadia Transfiguration 06-08; C Nuthall S'well from 08; C Kimberley from 08. 24 Watnall Road, Nuthall, Nottingham NG16 1DU   Tel 0115-938 9725 E-mail helenbridger@yahoo.com

BRIDGES, The Rt Revd Dewi Morris. b 33. Univ of Wales (Lamp) BA54 CCC Cam BA56 MA60. Westcott Ho Cam 57. d 57 p 58 c 88. C Rhymney Mon 57-60; C Chepstow 60-63; V Tredegar St Jas 63-65; Lect Kidderminster Coll 65-69; Lic to Offic Worc 65-69; V Kempsey 69-79; RD Upton 74-79; RD Narberth St D 80-82; R Tenby 79-88; Adn St D 82-88; Bp S & B 88-98; rtd 98. Hafan Dawel, 4 St Mary's Hill, Heywood Lane, Tenby SA70 8BG   Tel (01834) 844087

BRIDGES, Mrs Gillian Mary. b 43. EAMTC 85. d 88 p 94. NSM Hellesdon Nor 88-96; NSM Lakenham St Jo 96-97; Assoc V Lakenham St Alb 97-99; Assoc V Sprowston w Beeston 99-08; rtd 08; Perm to Offic Nor from 08. 2 Vera Road, Norwich NR6 5HU   Tel (01603) 789634
E-mail sgbridges63v@talktalk.net

BRIDGES, John Malham. b 57. TD. Goldsmiths' Coll Lon BSc80. Ridley Hall Cam 03. d 05 p 06. C Cranleigh Guildf 05-08; Chapl RN from 08. Royal Naval Chaplaincy Service, Mail Point 1-2, Leach Building, Whale Island, Portsmouth PO2 8BY   Tel (023) 9262 5055 Fax 9262 5134 E-mail jmbridges@cantab.net

BRIDGES, The Ven Peter Sydney Godfrey. b 25. ARIBA51. Linc Th Coll 56. d 58 p 59. C Hemel Hempstead St Alb 58-64; Warden Angl Chapl Birm Univ 64-68; Perm to Offic Birm 65-72; Lect Aston Univ 68-72; Adn Southend Chelmsf 72-77; P-in-c Southend St Jo w St Mark, All SS w St Fran etc 72-73; Dir Dioc Research and Development Unit 73-77; Adn Cov 77-83; Can Th Cov Cathl 77-90; Adn Warwick 83-90; rtd 90; Dioc Adv for Chr Spirituality 90-93; Perm to Offic Win from 01. St Clare, 25 Rivermead Close, Romsey SO51 8HQ   Tel (01794) 512889

BRIDGES (née BANKS), Mrs Vivienne Philippa. b 46. Somerville Coll Ox BA69. SAOMC 02. d 05 p 06. NSM Wolvercote Ox from 05. 6 Haslemere Gardens, Oxford OX2 8EL   Tel (01865) 558705

BRIDGEWATER, Guy Stevenson. b 60. Ch Ch Ox BA83. Trin Coll Bris BA87. d 87 p 88. C Radipole and Melcombe Regis Sarum 87-90; Chapl Lee Abbey 90-93; V Cranbrook Cant 93-98; Dioc Officer for Par Resources (Miss and Lay Tr) Glouc 98-07; Dioc Can Res Glouc Cathl 02-07; TR Horsham Chich from 07. The Vicarage, Causeway, Horsham RH12 1HE   Tel (01403) 272919

BRIDGEWOOD, Bruce William. b 41. K Coll Lon BA02 Heythrop Coll Lon MA06. St Paul's Coll Grahamstown LTh67. d 67 p 68. C Plumstead S Africa 67-69; C Somerset W 70-71; Hon C Stanmer w Falmer Chich 81-86; Hon C Westmr St Matt Lon 90-93; Hon C Alexandra Park 93-04; P-in-c Friern Barnet St Pet le Poer from 04. 81 Warwick Road, London N11 2SP   Tel (020) 8211 9709 E-mail brucebridgewood@talktalk.net

BRIDGMAN, Canon Gerald Bernard. b 22. St Cath Coll Cam BA50 MA55. Bible Churchmen's Coll Bris 46 Wycliffe Hall Ox 50. d 51 p 52. C Broadwater St Mary Chich 51-54; C Ox St Aldate 54-56; C-in-c Southgate CD Chich 56-59; V Southgate 59-67; V Kingston upon Hull H Trin York 67-87; Chapl Hull R Infirmary 67-87; AD Cen and N Hull 81-86; Can and Preb York Minster 83-87; rtd 87; Perm to Offic Chich from 87. 129 The Welkin, Lindfield, Haywards Heath RH16 2PL   Tel (01444) 484563

BRIDGWATER, Philip Dudley. b 31. St Alb Minl Tr Scheme 88. d 91 p 92. NSM Buxton w Burbage and King Sterndale Derby 91-94 and 98-01; NSM Fairfield 94-98; Perm to Offic from 01. Millstone, 9 College Road, Buxton SK17 9DZ   Tel (01298) 72876

BRIDLE, Geoffrey Peter. b 52. CITC 87. d 87 p 88. C Lurgan Ch the Redeemer D & D 87-91; I Carnteel and Crilly Arm 91-99; I Cleenish w Mullaghdun Clogh from 99. Cleenish Rectory, Bellanaleck, Enniskillen BT92 2BA   Tel (028) 6634 8259 Fax 6634 8620 E-mail geoffreypbridle@email.com

BRIDSON, Canon Raymond Stephen. b 58. Southn Univ BTh82. Chich Th Coll. d 82 p 83. C St Luke in the City Liv 82-86; TV Ditton St Mich 86-98; V Anfield St Columba from 98; AD Walton from 02; Hon Can Liv Cathl from 03. St Columba's Vicarage, Pinehurst Avenue, Liverpool L4 2TZ   Tel 0151-474 7231
E-mail frray@busyyonder.co.uk

BRIDSTRUP, Juergen Walter. b 44. St Alb Minl Tr Scheme 84. d 87 p 88. C Leagrave St Alb 87-90; V Goff's Oak St Jas 90-08; TV Cheshunt 08-09; rtd 09. 4 The Vineyard, Lower Broad Street, Ludlow SY8 1PH   Tel (01584) 876992
E-mail juergen.bridstrup@btinternet.com

BRIEN, John Richard. b 57. Kingston Poly BSc80. EAMTC 98. d 01 p 02. NSM Mistley w Manningtree and Bradfield Chelmsf from 01. 1 East View, Crown Street, Dedham, Colchester CO7 6AN   Tel (01206) 322706 E-mail brienfamily@tiscali.co.uk

BRIERLEY, Charles Ian. b 46. MIMI69. S Dios Minl Tr Scheme 90. d 93 p 94. NSM Wellington and Distr B & W from 93. Shady Oak, 19 Immenstadt Drive, Wellington TA21 9PT   Tel (01823) 666101 E-mail brierley@aol.com

BRIERLEY, John Michael. b 32. Lon Univ BD71. Lich Th Coll 57. d 60 p 61. C Lower Mitton Worc 60-62; C-in-c Dines Green St Mich CD 62-68; V Worc St Mich 69-71; R Eastham w Rochford 71-79; P-in-c Knighton-on-Teme 79-79; P-in-c Reddal Hill St Luke 79-81; V 81-92; rtd 92; Perm to Offic Worc from 92. 10 Woodhouse Way, Cradley Heath, Warley B64 5EL   Tel (01384) 633527

BRIERLEY, Michael William. b 73. CCC Cam BA94 MA98 Birm Univ PhD07. Ripon Coll Cuddesdon 98. d 98 p 99. C Marnhull Sarum 98-01; C Okeford 98-01; Bp's Dom Chapl Ox 01-07; P-in-c Tavistock and Gulworthy Ex from 07. The Vicarage, 5A Plymouth Road, Tavistock PL19 8AU   Tel (01822) 617432 E-mail mwbrierley@aol.com

BRIERLEY, Philip. b 49. Salford Univ BSc74. **d** 92 **p** 93. OLM Stalybridge *Man* from 92. *Burnside, 30 Cranworth Street, Stalybridge SK15 2NW* Tel 0161-303 0809
E-mail irenephilipbrierley@yahoo.com
BRIERLEY, William David. b 64. Kent Univ BA87 New Coll Ox DPhil93. Ripon Coll Cuddesdon. **d** 93 **p** 94. C Amersham *Ox* 93-97; TV Wheatley 97-05. *37 Chessbury Road, Chesham HP5 1JT* E-mail william.brierley@tesco.net
BRIGGS, Christopher Ronald. b 58. K Coll Lon BD79 AKC79 PGCE80. Sarum & Wells Th Coll 87. **d** 89 **p** 90. C Horsell *Guildf* 89-93; Hong Kong 93-97; V Norton *St Alb* 97-00; Sen Chapl Haileybury Coll from 00. *Lawrence Cottage, 2 Hailey Lane, Hertford Heath, Hertford SG13 7NX* Tel and fax (01992) 462922 *or* tel 706314 E-mail chrisbriggs@freenet.co.uk
BRIGGS, Derek. b 26. St Aid Birkenhead 52. **d** 55 **p** 56. C Brownhill *Wakef* 55-57; C Trowbridge St Jas *Sarum* 57-60; R Levenshulme St Pet *Man* 60-67; V Farsley *Bradf* 67-90; rtd 90; Perm to Offic *Bradf* 90-99. *6 College Court, Bradley, Keighley BD20 9EA* Tel (01535) 630085
BRIGGS, Enid. b 50. CBDTI 03. **d** 06 **p** 07. NSM Walton-le-Dale St Leon w Samlesbury St Leon *Blackb* from 06. *85 Plantation Street, Accrington BB5 6RT* Tel (01254) 383568
E-mail enid_briggs@hotmail.com
BRIGGS, George William. b 76. Wadh Coll Ox BA98 Fitzw Coll Cam BA02. Ridley Hall Cam 00. **d** 03 **p** 04. C Old Trafford St Bride *Man* 03-06; P-in-c Clapham Park All SS *S'wark* from 06. *All Saints' Vicarage, 250 Lyham Road, London SW2 5NP* Tel (020) 8678 6020 E-mail george.briggs@bigfoot.com
BRIGGS, Gordon John. b 39. CIPFA. SAOMC 95. **d** 98 **p** 99. OLM Farnham Royal w Hedgerley *Ox* from 98. *52 Freemans Close, Stoke Poges, Slough SL2 4ER* Tel (01753) 662536
BRIGGS, Canon John. b 39. Edin Univ MA61. Ridley Hall Cam 61. **d** 63 **p** 64. C Jesmond Clayton Memorial *Newc* 63-66; Schs Sec Scripture Union 66-79; Tutor St Jo Coll Dur 67-74; Lic to Offic *Dur* 67-74 and *Edin* 74-79; V Chadkirk *Ches* 79-88; RD Chadkirk 85-88; TR Macclesfield Team 88-04; Hon Can Ches Cathl 96-04; Chapl W Park Hosp Macclesfield 90-99; rtd 04; Perm to Offic *Ches* from 04. *16 Lostock Hall Road, Poynton, Stockport SK12 1DP* Tel (01625) 267228
E-mail john.briggs20@ntlworld.com
BRIGGS, Michael Weston. b 40. Edin Th Coll 61. **d** 64 **p** 65. C Sneinton St Steph w St Alb *S'well* 64-67; C Beeston 67-70; P-in-c Kirkby Woodhouse 70-74; V Harworth 74-81; R Harby w Thorney and N and S Clifton 81-94; R N Wheatley, W Burton, Bole, Saundby, Sturton etc 94-05; P-in-c Clarborough w Hayton 03-05; CF (ACF) 74-97; rtd 05; Perm to Offic *S'well* from 06. *3 Monkwood Close, Collingham, Newark NG23 7SY* Tel (01636) 893344 E-mail m_w_briggs@lineone.net
BRIGGS, The Very Revd Roger Edward. b 36. ALCD61. **d** 61 **p** 61. Canada 61-71; C Upper Armley *Ripon* 71-72; Canada 72-99; Dean Arctic 96-99; rtd 99. *Apartment 1207, 415 Greenview Avenue, Ottawa ON K2B 8G5, Canada*
BRIGHAM, John Keith. b 48. Man Univ CertEd70 FSAScot. St Steph Ho Ox 71. **d** 74 **p** 75. C Ches H Trin 74-77; C Ealing Ch the Sav *Lon* 77-85; P-in-c Fulwell St Mich and St Geo 85-88; P-in-c Upper Teddington SS Pet and Paul 85-88; V Southport St Luke *Liv* 88-94; Dioc Chapl to the Deaf 88-94; V Lund *Blackb* 94-98. *17 South Meade, Timperley, Altrincham WA15 6QL* Tel 0161-973 6684 E-mail keebee@aol.com
BRIGHOUSE, George Alexander (Alex). b 46. NOC 87. **d** 90 **p** 91. NSM Ingrow cum Hainworth *Bradf* 90-91; NSM Keighley All SS 92; NSM Bradf St Wilfrid Lidget Green 92-04; NSM Bradf St Wilfrid w St Columba from 04. *38 Thirsk Grange, Clayton, Bradford BD14 6HS* Tel 07768-618562 (mobile)
BRIGHT, George Frank. b 50. Peterho Cam BA71 MA75 LSE MSc83 SAP99. Coll of Resurr Mirfield 71. **d** 74 **p** 75. C Notting Hill *Lon* 74-77; Perm to Offic 77-84; P-in-c Kentish Town St Benet and All SS 84-89; P-in-c Kensington St Jo 89-93; V 93-96. *The Vicarage, 176 Holland Road, London W14 8AH* Tel (020) 7602 4655 E-mail gfb@dircon.co.uk
BRIGHT, Reginald. b 26. Tyndale Hall Bris 57. **d** 60 **p** 61. C Toxteth Park St Philemon w St Silas *Liv* 60-63; P-in-c Everton St Polycarp 63-65; R Orton St Giles *Carl* 65-72; V Holme 72-79; P-in-c W Newton 79-81; V Bromfield w Waverton 79-81; R Bowness 81-93; rtd 93; Perm to Offic *Carl* from 95. *Spinney House, Cannonfield, Roadhead, Carlisle CA6 6NB* Tel (01697) 748645
BRIGHTMAN, Peter Arthur. b 30. ALCD61 LTh74. **d** 64 **p** 65. C Westgate St Jas *Cant* 64-67; C Lydd 67-70; C Lt Coates *Linc* 70; C Heaton Ch Ch *Man* 71-72; V Bolton SS Simon and Jude 72-77; R Bath St Sav *B & W* 77-85; R Farmborough, Marksbury and Stanton Prior 85-90; C Coney Hill *Glouc* 90-93; C Hardwicke, Quedgeley and Elmore w Longney 93-95; rtd 95; Perm to Offic *B & W* from 95. *2 Westmead Cottages, Dean Hill Lane, Weston, Bath BA1 4DT* Tel (01225) 315076
BRIGHTON, Margaret Elizabeth. b 53. Qu Coll Birm BA07. WMMTC 04. **d** 07 **p** 08. C Boldmere *Birm* from 07. *19 Southam Drive, Sutton Coldfield B73 5PD* Tel 0121-355 5430 *or* 373 0207 E-mail margaret.brighton@ntlworld.com

BRIGHTON, Terrence William. b 43. SWMTC 85. **d** 88 **p** 89. C Dawlish *Ex* 88-92; P-in-c Newton Poppleford w Harpford 92-94; V Newton Poppleford, Harpford and Colaton Raleigh 94-98; RD Ottery 96-98; P-in-c W Lavington and the Cheverells *Sarum* 98-02; Rural Officer (Ramsbury Area) 98-02; P-in-c Charleton w Buckland Tout Saints etc *Ex* 02-05; R 05-08; RD Woodleigh 03-07; rtd 08. *30 Millway, Chudleigh, Newton Abbot TQ13 0JN* Tel 07974-294044 (mobile) E-mail twb@madasafish.com
BRIGHTWELL, Johanna Clare. See CLARE, Ms Johanna Howard
BRIGNALL, Elizabeth Jane. See BENDREY, Elizabeth Jane
BRIGNALL, Simon Francis Lyon. b 54. St Jo Coll Dur BA78. Wycliffe Hall Ox 80. **d** 83 **p** 84. C Colne St Bart *Blackb* 83-86; SAMS 86-96; Peru 86-96; P-in-c Tetsworth, Adwell w S Weston, Lewknor etc *Ox* 96-98; TV Thame from 98. *The Rectory, 46 High Street, Tetsworth, Thame OX9 7AS* Tel (01844) 281267 Mobile 07718-627674 Fax 281827
BRIGNELL, Roger. b 39. CertEd65 ACP88 MCollP89. St Aid Birkenhead 60 St as Minl Tr Course 95. **d** 98 **p** 99. NSM Montgomery and Forden and Llandyssil *St As* from 98. *Minevia, Kerry Road, Montgomery SY15 6PD* Tel and fax (01686) 668539
BRIMACOMBE, Keith John. b 59. Open Univ BA92 Westmr Coll Ox MTh00. SWMTC 99. **d** 01 **p** 03. NSM Ottery St Mary, Alfington, W Hill, Tipton etc *Ex* from 01. *Banklea, Exeter Road, Newton Poppleford, Sidmouth EX10 0BJ* Tel (01395) 568404 E-mail brims@kjbrims.fsnet.co.uk
BRIMICOMBE, Mark. b 44. Nottm Univ BA66 CertEd. SWMTC 83. **d** 85 **p** 86. NSM Plympton St Mary *Ex* from 85. *4 David Close, Stoggy Lane, Plympton, Plymouth PL7 3BQ* Tel (01752) 338454 E-mail mark@thebrambles.eclipse.co.uk
BRIMSON, Mrs Dawn Diana. b 44. Ex Univ BTh08. SWMTC 02. **d** 05 **p** 06. NSM Quantoxhead *B & W* 05-07; NSM Quantock Coast from 07. *Ridges, Holford, Bridgwater TA5 1DU* Tel (01278) 741413 E-mail dawnbrimson@googlemail.com
BRINDLE, Peter John. b 47. MIStructE72 FLS05. NOC 78. **d** 81 **p** 82. NSM Bingley All SS *Bradf* 81-84; NSM Bingley H Trin 84-86; V Keighley All SS *Bradf* 86-96; V Kirkstall *Ripon* 91-96; V Beeston 96-02; TR 02-04; TR Leic Presentation from 04; P-in-c Leic St Chad 04-07; P-in-c N Evington from 07. *St Barnabas' Vicarage, 32 St Barnabas Road, Leicester LE5 6BD* Tel 0116-276 6054 Mobile 07860-157363
E-mail presentationrector@msm.com
BRINDLEY, Angela Mary. See SPEEDY, Mrs Angela Mary
BRINDLEY, The Very Revd David Charles. b 53. K Coll Lon BD75 AKC75 MTh76 MPhil81. St Aug Coll Cant 75. **d** 76 **p** 77. C Epping St Jo *Chelmsf* 76-79; Lect Coll of SS Paul and Mary Cheltenham 79-82; Dioc Dir of Tr *Leic* 82-86; V Quorndon 82-86; Prin Glouc Sch for Minl 87-92; Prin WEMTC 92-94; Dir of Minl Tr 87-94; Dioc Officer for NSM 88-94; Hon Can Glouc Cathl 92-94; TR Warwick *Cov* 94-02; Dean Portsm from 02. *The Deanery, 13 Pembroke Road, Portsmouth PO1 2NS* Tel (023) 9282 4400 *or* 9234 7605 Fax 9229 5480
E-mail david.brindley@portsmouthcathedral.org.uk
BRINDLEY, Canon Stuart Geoffrey Noel. b 30. St Jo Coll Dur BA53. **d** 55 **p** 56. C Newc St Anne 55-58; C Tynemouth Cullercoats St Paul 58-60; C Killingworth 60-63; V Newsham 63-69; W Germany 69-76; Asst Master Wyvern Sch Weston-super-Mare 76-80; V Stocksbridge *Sheff* 80-88; RD Tankersley 85-88; V Rotherham 88-96; Hon Can Sheff Cathl 95-96; rtd 96; Perm to Offic *Newc* from 96. *Hambury, Backcrofts, Rothbury, Morpeth NE65 7XY* Tel (01669) 621472
BRINKWORTH, Canon Christopher Michael Gibbs. b 41. Lanc Univ BA70. Kelham Th Coll 62. **d** 67 **p** 68. C Lancaster St Mary *Blackb* 67-70; C Milton *Portsm* 70-74; V Ault Hucknall *Derby* 74-84; V Derby St Anne and St Jo 84-06; Hon Can Derby Cathl 00-06; rtd 06; Perm to Offic *Derby* from 06. *3 Westfield Drive, Derby DE22 3SG* Tel (01332) 208478
E-mail michaelbrinkworth@btinternet.com
BRION, Martin Philip. b 33. Ex Univ BA55. Ridley Hall Cam 57. **d** 59 **p** 60. C Balderstone *Man* 59-62; C Morden *S'wark* 62-66; V Low Elswick *Newc* 66-73; P-in-c Giggleswick *Bradf* 73-77; V 77-80; V Camerton H Trin W Seaton *Carl* 80-86; V Dearham 86-95; rtd 95; Perm to Offic *Carl* from 95. *7 Falcon Place, Moresby Parks, Whitehaven CA28 8YF* Tel (01946) 691912
BRISBANE, Archbishop of. See ASPINALL, The Most Revd Phillip John
BRISCOE, Allen. b 42. Liv Univ BSc64 CertEd65. Coll of Resurr Mirfield 90. **d** 92 **p** 93. C Shiremoor *Newc* 92-95; V Barnsley St Pet and St Jo *Wakef* from 95; Asst Dioc Ecum Officer 01-03; Bp's Adv for Ecum Affairs from 03; RD Barnsley 04-09. *The Vicarage, 1 Osborne Mews, Barnsley S70 1UU* Tel (01226) 282220 E-mail abriscoe@talk21.com
BRISCOE, Canon Frances Amelia. b 35. Univ of Wales CertEd55 Man Univ BA71 MA74. Gilmore Course 74. **dss** 77 **d** 87 **p** 94. Gt Crosby St Luke *Liv* 77-81; Dioc Lay Min Adv 81-87; Chapl Liv Cathl 81-89; Dir Diaconal Mins 87-89; Lect St Deiniol's Minl Tr Scheme 88-00; Hon Can Liv Cathl 88-00; AD Sefton 89-00; Dir of Reader Studies 89-00; Dn-in-c Hightown 92-94;

P-in-c 94-00; rtd 00; Perm to Offic *Liv* from 01. *5 Derwent Avenue, Formby, Liverpool L37 2JT* Tel (01704) 830075

BRISCOE, Mark. b 71. Coll of Ripon & York St Jo BA(QTS)95. Ripon Coll Cuddesdon 05. **d** 07 **p** 08. C Saxilby Gp *Linc* from 07. *7 Vasey Close, Saxilby, Lincoln LN1 2WG* Tel (01522) 703918

BRISON, The Ven William Stanly. b 29. Alfred Univ NY BSc51 Connecticut Univ MDiv57 STM71. Berkeley Div Sch. **d** 57 **p** 57. USA 57-72; V Davyhulme Ch Ch *Man* 72-81; R Newton Heath All SS 81-85; AD N Man 81-85; Hon Can Man Cathl 82-85; Adn Bolton 85-92; TV E Farnworth and Kearsley 85-89; C Bolton St Thos 89-92; CMS 92-94; Nigeria 92-94; P-in-c Pendleton St Thos w Charlestown *Man* 94-95; TR Pendleton 95-98; rtd 98; Perm to Offic *Man* from 99. *2 Scott Avenue, Bury BL9 9RS* Tel 0161-764 3998

BRISTOL, Archdeacon of. *See* McCLURE, The Ven Timothy Elston

BRISTOL, Bishop of. *See* HILL, The Rt Revd Michael Arthur

BRISTOL, Dean of. *See* GRIMLEY, The Very Revd Robert William

BRISTOW, Keith Raymond Martin. b 56. Ex Univ BA78. Chich Th Coll 87. **d** 89 **p** 90. C Kirkby *Liv* 89-93; C Portsea St Mary *Portsm* 93-03; R Ash *Guildf* from 03. *The Rectory, Ash Church Road, Ash, Aldershot GU12 6LU* Tel (01252) 321517 E-mail frkeithbristow@ntlworld.com

BRISTOW, Peter Edmund. b 49. Pontificium Institutum Internationale Angelicum Rome JCL77 St Jos Coll Upholland 67. **d** 72 **p** 73. In RC Ch 72-87; C Poplar *Lon* 89-92; Lay Tr Officer 89-90; TV Droitwich Spa *Worc* 92-94; TR 94-00; V Boston Spa *York* from 00; P-in-c Thorp Arch w Walton from 00; P-in-c Bramham from 09; RD New Ainsty from 06. *The Vicarage, 86 High Street, Boston Spa, Wetherby LS23 6EA* Tel (01937) 842454

BRISTOW, Roger. b 60. Aston Tr Scheme 81 Ridley Hall Cam 83. **d** 86 **p** 87. C Leyton St Mary w St Edw *Chelmsf* 86-90; TV Kings Norton *Birm* 90-98; V Bromley H Trin *Roch* from 98. *Holy Trinity Vicarage, Church Lane, Bromley BR2 8LB* Tel and fax (020) 8462 1280 Mobile 07778-397224 E-mail roger.bristow@diocese-rochester.org

BRITT, Eric Stanley. b 47. St Jo Coll Nottm BTh75. **d** 74 **p** 75. C Chorleywood Ch Ch *St Alb* 74-78; C Frimley *Guildf* 78-80; P-in-c Alresford *Chelmsf* 80-88; R Takeley w Lt Canfield 88-93; Asst Chapl R Free Hosp Lon 93-96; Chapl Mid-Essex Hosp Services NHS Trust 96-00; Chapl Algarve *Eur* 01-06; rtd 06. *5 De Lisle Close, Papworth Everard, Cambridge CB23 3UT* E-mail e.britt@btinternet.com

BRITT, Sister Mary Stephen. b 44. Stockwell Coll of Educn TCert65 Open Univ BA76. SAOMC 02. **d** 05 **p** 06. CSJB from 05; NSM Hanborough and Freeland *Ox* from 05. *The Priory, 2 Spring Hill Road, Begbroke, Kidlington OX5 1RX* Tel (01865) 855324 E-mail marycsjb@csjb.org.uk

BRITTAIN, John. b 23. St Aug Coll Cant 59. **d** 60 **p** 61. C Heref St Martin 60-62; V Highley 62-88; rtd 88. *26 Stuart Court, High Street, Kibworth, Leicester LE8 0LR*

BRITTEN, Mrs Diana. **d** 07 **p** 08. OLM Cley Hill Villages *Sarum* from 07. *69 Lane End, Corsley, Warminster BA12 7PG* Tel (01373) 832515 E-mail dianabritten@ukonline.co.uk

BRITTLE, Miss Janice Lilian. b 50. Man Poly BA74 Open Univ BA84 Sheff Univ MMedSc00 RGN76. **d** 04 **p** 05. OLM Rugeley *Lich* 04-06; OLM Brereton and Rugeley from 06. *3 Norwood House, Peakes Road, Rugeley WS15 2ND* Tel (01889) 586138 E-mail janice.brittle@btinternet.com

BRITTON, Christine Mary. *See* BEECROFT, Mrs Christine Mary

BRITTON, John Anthony. b 39. Dur Univ BA60. Wycliffe Hall Ox 61. **d** 63 **p** 64. C Sheff St Swithun 63-64; C Sheff St Aid w St Luke 64-66; C Doncaster St Geo 66-68; C Grantham St Wulfram *Linc* 68-72; V Surfleet 72-76; V Bolsover *Derby* 76-86; V Harworth *S'well* 86-01; RD Bawtry 96-01; rtd 01; Perm to Offic *S'well* from 01 and *Sheff* from 02. *Beaver Lodge, 10 Weirside, Oldcotes, Worksop S81 8HW* Tel (01909) 540735 E-mail john.dorothy.britton@dunelm.org.uk

BRITTON, John Timothy Hugh. b 50. Dundee Univ BSc73. Trin Coll Bris 73. **d** 76 **p** 77. C Cromer *Nor* 76-79; P-in-c Freethorpe w Wickhampton 79-82; P-in-c Beighton and Moulton 79-82; P-in-c Halvergate w Tunstall 79-82; CMS 82-89; Uganda 83-89; R Allesley *Cov* 89-02; P-in-c Long Itchington and Marton from 02; P-in-c Wappenbury w Weston under Wetherley from 02; P-in-c Hunningham from 02; P-in-c Offchurch from 02. *The Vicarage, Leamington Road, Long Itchington, Southam CV47 9PL* Tel (01926) 812518 E-mail timbritton@myrealbox.com

BRITTON, Neil Bryan. b 35. Em Coll Cam BA59 MA63. Clifton Th Coll 61. **d** 63 **p** 64. C Eastbourne All SS *Chich* 63-67; C Ashtead *Guildf* 67-70; Chapl Scargill Ho 70-74; Chapl Aiglon Coll and Asst Chapl Villars *Eur* 74-78; In Reformed Ch of Switzerland 78-98; rtd 00; USA 01-05. *Rose Cottage, 7 Newbury Way, Kingsclere, Newbury RG20 5SP* Tel (01635) 297687 Mobile 07903-120368 E-mail britton.neil@googlemail.com

BRITTON, Canon Paul Anthony. b 29. SS Coll Cam BA52 MA57. Linc Th Coll 52. **d** 54 **p** 55. C Upper Norwood St Jo *Cant* 54-57; C Wantage *Ox* 57-61; V Stanmore *Win* 61-70; V Bitterne Park 70-80; Can Res Win Cathl 80-94; Lib 81-85; Treas 85-94; rtd 94; Perm to Offic *Sarum* from 94. *Pemberton, High Street, Hindon, Salisbury SP3 6DR* Tel (01747) 820406

BRITTON, Robert. b 37. Oak Hill Th Coll 78. **d** 79 **p** 80. C St Helens St Helen *Liv* 79-83; V Lowton St Mary 83-02; AD Winwick 89-01; rtd 02; Perm to Offic *Liv* and *Man* from 03. *15 Balmoral Avenue, Lowton, Warrington WA3 2ER* Tel (01942) 711135

BRITTON, Ronald George Adrian Michael (Robert). b 24. Univ of State of NY BSc78 Lambeth STh82. St D Coll Lamp 63. **d** 82 **p** 82. Arabia 82-85; Chapl Alassio *Eur* 85-90 and 92-93; Chapl San Remo 86; Hon C Southbourne St Kath *Win* 90-92; rtd 96; Perm to Offic *Bris* from 97. *2 Cherry Tree Road, Bristol BS16 4EY* Tel 0117-965 5734 E-mail robert@britton320.fsnet.co.uk

BRITTON, Timothy. *See* BRITTON, John Timothy Hugh

BRIXTON, Miss Corinne Jayne. b 63. Ex Univ BSc84. Wycliffe Hall Ox BTh95. **d** 95. C Leytonstone St Jo *Chelmsf* 95-00; C Buckhurst Hill from 00. *63 High Road, Buckhurst Hill IG9 5SR* Tel (020) 8504 6652 E-mail cbrixton@aol.com

BRIXWORTH, Suffragan Bishop of. *See* WHITE, The Rt Revd Francis

BROAD, Mrs Christine Jane. b 63. Leeds Univ BSc86 BA06. NOC 03. **d** 06 **p** 07. C Newchapel *Lich* from 06. *21 Powderham Close, Stoke-on-Trent ST6 6XN* Tel (01782) 871806 E-mail christine@broad1959.freeserve.co.uk

BROAD, David Nicholas Andrew. b 59. Man Univ BA. Edin Th Coll. **d** 87 **p** 88. C Fulham All SS *Lon* 87-90; TV Clare w Poslingford, Cavendish etc *St E* 90-93; TV Totton *Win* 93-99; R Abbotts Ann and Upper and Goodworth Clatford from 99. *The Rectory, Upper Clatford, Andover SP11 7QP* Tel and fax (01264) 352906 E-mail dna.broad@virgin.net

BROAD, Canon Hugh Duncan. b 37. Lich Th Coll 64. **d** 67 **p** 68. C Heref H Trin 67-72; Asst Master Bp's Sch Heref 72-73; C Fareham SS Pet and Paul *Portsm* 74-76; V Heref St Geo 76-90; R Matson *Glouc* 90-97; V Glouc St Geo w Whaddon 97-03; Hon Can Glouc Cathl 02-03; rtd 03; P-in-c Mojcar *Eur* from 03. *Apartado 617, 04638 Mojcar Playa (Almeria), Spain* Tel (0034) 950 478 432 Mobile 639 757 159 E-mail fr.hugh@hotmail.co.uk

BROAD, Hugh Robert. b 49. St Mich Coll Llan 67. **d** 72 **p** 73. C Tenby w Gumfreston *St D* 72-75; C Caerau w Ely *Llan* 75-79; V Llanharan w Peterston-super-Montem 79-89; RD Bridgend 88-89; Ex-Paroch Officer 90; V Whatborough Gp *Leic* 90-98; rtd 08. *12 Cooke Close, Thorpe Astley, Braunstone, Leicester LE3 3RG* E-mail hugh_broad@hotmail.com

BROAD, Canon William Ernest Lionel. b 40. Ridley Hall Cam 64. **d** 66 **p** 67. C Ecclesfield *Sheff* 66-69; Chapl HM Pris Wormwood Scrubs 69; Chapl HM Pris Albany 70-74; Chapl HM Rem Cen Risley 74-76; V Ditton St Mich *Liv* 76-81; TR 82-83; P-in-c Mayland and Steeple *Chelmsf* 83-91; V Blackhall *Dur* 91-97; TR Gt Aycliffe 97-03; P-in-c Chilton 03; TV Gt Aycliffe and Chilton 03-04; Hon Can Dur Cathl 02-04; rtd 04. *Moorcote, Thornley, Tow Law, Bishop Auckland DL13 4NU* Tel (01388) 731350 E-mail bill@deagol.fsnet.co.uk

BROADBENT, Mrs Doreen. b 36. **d** 94 **p** 95. OLM Stalybridge *Man* 94-02; Perm to Offic from 02. *37 Ladysmith Road, Ashton-under-Lyne OL6 9DJ* Tel 0161-330 9085

BROADBENT, Hugh Patrick Colin. b 53. Selw Coll Cam BA75 MA. **d** 78 **p** 79. C Chatham St Steph *Roch* 78-82; C Shortlands 82-84; C Crockham Hill H Trin 84-87; V Bromley H Trin 87-97; V Bromley St Jo from 97-09; Chapl St Olave's Gr Sch Orpington 95-09. R Snodland All SS w Ch Ch from 09. *The Vicarage, 11 St Katherine's Lane, Snodland ME6 5EN* Tel (01634) 240232 E-mail hugh.broadbent@diocese-rochester.org

BROADBENT, Neil Seton. b 53. Qu Coll Birm. **d** 81 **p** 82. C Knaresborough *Ripon* 81-84; C Leeds Gipton Epiphany 84-87; Lic to Offic 87-89; Chapl Minstead Community *Derby* 89; Perm to Offic from 89; Dir Sozein from 93. *The Old Vicarage, Church Lane, Horsley Woodhouse, Ilkeston DE7 6BB* Tel (01332) 780598 E-mail neil.broadbent@sozein.org.uk

BROADBENT, Paul John. b 41. Oak Hill Th Coll 83. **d** 85 **p** 86. C Duston *Pet* 85-88; TV Ross w Brampton Abbotts, Bridstow and Peterstow *Heref* 88-91; R Pattishall w Cold Higham and Gayton w Tiffield *Pet* from 91. *The Rectory, 17 Church Street, Pattishall, Towcester NN12 8NB* Tel and fax (01327) 830043 Mobile 07786-865015 E-mail pjbroadbent@aol.com

✚**BROADBENT, The Rt Revd Peter Alan.** b 52. Jes Coll Cam BA74 MA78. St Jo Coll Nottm 74. **d** 77 **p** 78 **c** 01. C Dur St Nic 77-80; C Holloway Em w Hornsey Road St Barn *Lon* 80-83; Chapl N Lon Poly 83-89; Hon C Islington St Mary 83-89; V Harrow Trin St Mich 89-94; AD Harrow 94; Adn Northolt 95-01; P-in-c Southall H Trin 98-99; Area Bp Willesden from 01. *173 Willesden Lane, London NW6 7YN* Tel (020) 8451 0189 Fax 8451 4606 Mobile 07957-144674 E-mail bishop.willesden@btinternet.com

BROADBENT, Ralph Andrew. b 55. K Coll Lon BD76 AKC76 Birm Univ PhD04. Chich Th Coll 77. **d** 78 **p** 79. C Prestwich St Mary *Man* 78-82; R Man Miles Platting 82-84; CF 84-87; TV Wordsley *Lich* 88-93; Chapl Wordsley and Ridge Hill Hosps 88-93; V Wollescote *Worc* from 93. *St Andrew's Vicarage, Oakfield Road, Wollescote, Stourbridge DY9 9DG* Tel (01384) 422695

BROADBENT, Thomas William. b 45. Chu Coll Cam BA66 MA70 PhD70. Ridley Hall Cam 75. **d** 78 **p** 79. C Allington and Maidstone St Pet *Cant* 78-82; Chapl Mid Kent Coll of H&FE 80-82; C Kings Heath *Birm* 82-84; Hon C Pendleton St Thos *Man* 84-89; TV Pendleton St Thos w Charlestown 89-92; Chapl Salford Univ 84-92; P-in-c Claydon and Barham *St E* 92-08; P-in-c Henley 99-08; P-in-c Gt Blakenham 02-08; Chapl Suffolk Coll 92-00; P-in-c Witham Gp *Linc* from 08. *The Rectory, 15 Hillview Road, South Witham, Grantham NG33 5QW* Tel (01572) 767240

BROADBERRY, Canon Richard St Lawrence. b 31. TCD BA53 BD59 MLitt66. **d** 54 **p** 55. C Dublin St Thos *D & G* 54-56; C Dublin Grangegorman 56-62; Min Can St Patr Cathl Dublin 58-62; Hon Clerical V Ch Ch Cathl Dublin 62-64; C Dublin Clontarf 62 64; C Thornton Heath St Jude *Cant* 64-66; V Norwood All SS 66-82; V Upper Norwood All SS w St Marg 82-84; RD Croydon N 81-84; Hon Can Cant Cathl 82-84; V Merton St Mary *S'wark* 85-92; RD Croydon N 85; Hon Can S'wark Cathl 85-01; V Riddlesdown 92-01; rtd 01; Perm to Offic *S'wark* from 01. *73 Court Avenue, Coulsdon CR5 1HG* Tel (01737) 551109

✠**BROADHURST, The Rt Revd John Charles.** b 42. AKC65 Lambeth STh82. **d** 66 **p** 67 **c** 96. C Southgate St Mich *Lon* 66-70; C Wembley Park St Aug 70-73; P-in-c 73-75; V 75-85; AD Brent 82-85; TR Wood Green St Mich w Bounds Green St Gabr etc 85-96; AD E Haringey 85-91; Suff Bp Fulham from 96. *26 Canonbury Park South, London N1 2FN* Tel (020) 7354 2334 Fax 7354 2335 E-mail bpfulham@aol.com

BROADHURST, Jonathan Robin. b 58. Univ Coll Ox BA81 MA86. Wycliffe Hall Ox 85. **d** 88 **p** 89. C Hull St Jo Newland *York* 88-91; P-in-c Burton Fleming w Fordon, Grindale etc 91-92; V 92-98; C Kingston upon Hull H Trin 98-01; P-in-c Rastrick St Jo *Wakef* 01-06; rtd 06. *1 Moravian Terrace, Halifax HX3 8AL* Tel (01422) 209549 Mobile 07790-899195 E-mail jonathan@broadhurst-jr.freeserve.co.uk

BROADLEY, Michael John. b 66. Roehampton Inst BA87. Trin Coll Bris 93. **d** 96 **p** 97. C Egham *Guildf* 96-01; TV Horsham *Chich* from 01. *St Mark's House, North Heath Lane, Horsham RH12 5PJ* Tel (01403) 254964 E-mail broadley@bigfoot.com

BROCK, Michael John. b 52. Birm Univ BSc74. St Jo Coll Nottm BA77. **d** 78 **p** 79. C Stapleford *S'well* 78-82; C Bestwood St Matt 82-86; TV Bestwood 86-90; R Epperstone and Gonalston and V Oxton 90-05; P-in-c Woodborough 02-05; RD S'well 93-96; Dioc Adv in Rural Affairs 97-02; R Dersingham w Anmer and Shernborne *Nor* from 05; RD Heacham and Rising from 08. *The Vicarage, Sherborne Road, Dersingham, King's Lynn PE31 6JA* Tel (01485) 540214 E-mail mjb65@btinternet.com

BROCKBANK, Arthur Ross. b 51. NOC 87. **d** 90 **p** 91. C Haughton St Mary *Man* 90-93; V Bircle from 93; P-in-c Walmersley 04; Chapl Bury Healthcare NHS Trust 93-02; Chapl Co-ord 02-03. *The Vicarage, 33 Castle Hill Road, Bury BL9 7RW* Tel 0161-764 3853

BROCKBANK, Donald Philip. b 56. Univ of Wales (Ban) BD78. Sarum & Wells Th Coll 79. **d** 81 **p** 82. C Prenton *Ches* 81-85; TV Birkenhead Priory 85-91; V Altrincham St Jo 91-96; Urban Officer 91-96; Dioc Ecum Officer *Lich* 96-98; C Lich St Mich w St Mary and Wall 96-98; V Acton and Worleston, Church Minshull etc *Ches* 98-06; rtd 07; Dioc Adv in Spirituality *Ches* from 07. *1 Plover Avenue, Winsford CW7 1LA* Tel (01606) 593651 E-mail donald@brockbankrev.freeserve.co.uk

BROCKBANK, John Keith. b 44. Dur Univ BA65. Wells Th Coll 66. **d** 68 **p** 69. C Preston St Matt *Blackb* 68-71; C Lancaster St Mary 71-73; V Habergham All SS 73-83; P-in-c Gannow 81-83; V W Burnley All SS 83-86; Dioc Stewardship Adv 86-92; P-in-c Shireshead 86-92; V Kirkham 92-09; rtd 09; Perm to Offic *Blackb* from 09. *44 Esthwaite Gardens, Lancaster LA1 3RG* Tel (01524) 847520 E-mail revjkb@talktalk.net

BROCKBANK, John Stanley. b 41. CBDTI 97. **d** 00 **p** 01. OLM Arnside *Carl* from 00. *Hough Close, 5 Ash Meadow Road, Arnside, Carnforth LA5 0AE* Tel (01524) 761634

BROCKHOUSE, Canon Grant Lindley. b 47. Adelaide Univ BA71 Ex Univ MA81. St Barn Coll Adelaide 70. **d** 73 **p** 74. C Edwardstown w Ascot Park Australia 73-74; Tutor St Barn Coll Belair 74-78; C Ex St Jas 78-80; Asst Chapl Ex Univ 80-83; V Marldon 83-98; Dep PV Ex Cathl 81-98; RD Torbay 95-98; V Higham Ferrers w Chelveston *Pet* from 98; RD Higham from 03; Can Pet Cathl from 07. *The Vicarage, Wood Street, Higham Ferrers, Rushden NN10 8DL* Tel (01933) 312433 E-mail grantbrockhouse@care4free.net

BROCKIE, Canon William James Thomson. b 36. Pemb Coll Ox BA58 MA62. Linc Th Coll 58. **d** 60 **p** 61. C Lin St Jo Bapt CD *Linc* 60-63; V Gt Staughton *Ely* 63-68; Chapl HM Borstal Gaynes Hall 63-68; TV Edin St Jo 68-76; Chapl Edin Univ 71-76; USA 76; R Edin St Martin 76-01; P-in-c Edin St Luke 79-90; Hon Can St Mary's Cathl from 98; rtd 00; Hon C Edin St Hilda and Edin St Fillan 02-03. *31 Holly Bank Terrace, Edinburgh EH11 1SP* Tel 0131-337 6482 E-mail billjennybrockie@hotmail.com

BROCKLEBANK, John. b 32. NOC 83. **d** 86 **p** 87. NSM Warrington St Barn *Liv* 86-93; NSM Orford St Marg 93-97; Perm to Offic from 97. *53 St Mary's Road, Penketh, Warrington WA5 2DT* Tel (01925) 722063

BROCKLEHURST, John Richard. b 51. Univ Coll Ox BA72 Lon Univ CertEd74. Oak Hill Th Coll BA81. **d** 81 **p** 82. C Harwood *Man* 81-85; V Hopwood 85-97; P-in-c Friarmere 97-03; TV Saddleworth 03-08; P-in-c Waddington *Bradf* from 08; Hon C Hurst Green and Mitton from 08; Hon C Bolton by Bowland w Grindleton from 08. *The Vicarage, Slaidburn Road, Waddington, Clitheroe BB7 3JQ* Tel (01200) 423589

BROCKLEHURST, Simon. b 63. Cranmer Hall Dur 86. **d** 89 **p** 90. C Clifton *S'well* 89-93; TV 93-96; P-in-c Mabe *Truro* 96-99; Miss to Seamen 96-99; V Ham St Andr *S'wark* from 99; Inland Hon Chapl Miss to Seafarers from 00. *St Andrew's Vicarage, Church Road, Ham, Richmond TW10 5HG* Tel and fax (020) 8940 9017 E-mail revsimonb@btinternet.com

BRODDLE, Christopher Stephen Thomas. b 57. **d** 87 **p** 88. C Lisburn St Paul *Conn* 87-90; CF 90-07; Sen CF from 07. *c/o MOD Chaplains (Army)* Tel (01980) 615804 Fax 615800

BRODIE, Miss Ann. b 55. Ex Univ BA76 PGCE77. St Jo Coll Nottm 03. **d** 05 **p** 06. C Putney St Marg *S'wark* 05-09; P-in-c from 09. *St Margaret's Vicarage, 46 Luttrell Avenue, London SW15 6PE* Tel (020) 8788 5522 E-mail vicar@stmargaretsputney.org.uk

BRODIE, Frederick. b 40. Leic Teacher Tr Coll TCert61. St Jo Coll Nottm 90. **d** 92 **p** 93. C Lutterworth w Cotesbach *Leic* 92-95; P-in-c Mountsorrel Ch Ch and St Pet 95-97; V 97-03; rtd 03; Perm to Offic *Leic* from 03. *11 Cooper Lane, Ratby, Leicester LE6 0QG* Tel 0116-238 7959

BRODRIBB, Carolyn Ann. b 48. Plymouth Univ MA CQSW. **d** 04 **p** 05. NSM Plymstock and Hooe *Ex* 04-06; C Dolton 06-07; P-in-c from 07; C Iddesleigh w Dowland 06-07; P-in-c from 07; C Monkokehampton 06-07; P-in-c from 07. *The Rectory, Cleave Hill, Dolton, Winkleigh EX19 8QT* Tel (01805) 804264 E-mail carolynbrodribb@aol.com

BRODY, Paul. b 40. NOC 85. **d** 88 **p** 89. C Leigh St Mary *Man* 88-90; C Peel 90-91; TR 91-97; TV Worsley 97-07; rtd 07; Perm to Offic *Man* from 07. *29 Parkfield Avenue, Tyldesley, Manchester M29 7BE* Tel (01942) 700102 E-mail brendabrody@blueyonder.co.uk

BROGGIO, Bernice Muriel Croager. b 35. Bedf Coll Lon BA57 K Coll Lon BD66. **dss** 84 **d** 87 **p** 94. Bris St Paul w St Barn 84-87; Hon Par Dn Bris St Paul's 87-88; C Charlton St Luke w H Trin *S'wark* 88-95; V Upper Tooting H Trin 95-03; Hon Can S'wark Cathl 95-03; RD Tooting 96-02; TV Bensham *Dur* 03-05; Hon C 06-07; rtd 06; Hon C Birtley *Dur* from 07. *86 Woodburn, Gateshead NE10 8LY* Tel 0191-495 0959 Mobile 07900-327316 E-mail berniebroggio@hotmail.com

BROMAGE, Kenneth Charles. b 51. EAMTC. **d** 90 **p** 91. NSM Woolpit w Drinkstone *St E* 90-92; Chapl RN from 92. *Royal Naval Chaplaincy Service, Mail Point 1-2, Leach Building, Whale Island, Portsmouth PO2 8BY* Tel (023) 9262 5055 Fax 9262 5134

BROMFIELD, Michael. b 32. Kelham Th Coll 54. Lich Th Coll 59. **d** 62 **p** 63. C Sedgley All SS *Lich* 62-64; C Tunstall Ch Ch 64-67; P-in-c Grindon 67-70; R 70-80; P-in-c Butterton 67-70; V 70-80; R Hope Bowdler w Eaton-under-Heywood *Heref* 80-97; R Rushbury 80-97; V Cardington 80-97; rtd 98; Perm to Offic *Lich* from 98. *11 Walklate Avenue, Newcastle ST5 0PR* Tel (01782) 630716 E-mail bromfield@stoke54.freeserve.co.uk

BROMFIELD, Nicholas Robert. b 60. St Jo Coll Cam MA82. WEMTC 98. **d** 02 **p** 03. C Tidenham w Beachley and Lancaut *Glouc* 02-07; C St Briavels w Hewelsfield 05-07; R Drybrook, Lydbrook and Ruardean from 07. *The Rectory, Oakland Road, Harrow Hill, Drybrook GL17 9JX* Tel (01594) 542232 E-mail bromfields@email.msn.com

BROMFIELD, Richard Allan. b 47. Sussex Univ MA96 LVCM85. Chich Th Coll 86. **d** 88 **p** 89. C Durrington *Chich* 88-95; V Woodingdean from 95; Chapl Nuffield Hosp Brighton from 96. *Woodingdean Vicarage, 2 Downsway, Brighton BN2 6BD* Tel (01273) 681582 E-mail r.a.bromfield@btinternet.com

BROMILEY, Paul Nigel. b 49. Univ of Wales (Cardiff) BSc71. Oak Hill Th Coll 88. **d** 90 **p** 91. C Gee Cross *Ches* 90-94; P-in-c Millbrook 94-03; Master Wyggeston's Hosp Leic from 03. *Master's House, Wyggeston's Hospital, Hinckley Road, Leicester LE3 0UX* Tel 0116-254 8682 or 255 9174 E-mail wyggeston.hospital@connectfree.co.uk

BROMILEY, Philip Arthur. b 73. Westmr Coll Ox BTh94 St Jo Coll Dur MA98. Cranmer Hall Dur 95. **d** 98 **p** 99. C Marton *Blackb* 98-01; Assoc P Calne and Blackland *Sarum* 01-06; P-in-c

Oldbury 06-08; R from 08. *The Rectory, The Street, Cherhill, Calne SN11 8XR* Tel (01249) 820062
E-mail philbromiley@cybermail.uk.com

BROMLEY, Mrs Janet Catherine Gay. b 45. Surrey Univ BSc68 Bradf Univ MSc72 Brunel Tech Coll Bris FE TCert86. S Dios Minl Tr Scheme 91. **d** 94 **p** 96. C Westbury-on-Trym H Trin *Bris* 94-96; C Wroughton 96-00; Dean of Women's Min 98-00; R Dursley *Glouc* from 00; AD Dursley 07-09. *The Rectory, Broadwell, Dursley GL11 4JE* Tel (01453) 542053
E-mail revjanet@dursleyparishchurch.freeserve.co.uk

BROMLEY, Richard. b 60. Birm Chr Coll MA02. **d** 08 **p** 09. NSM Binley *Cov* from 08. *22 Chaceley Close, Coventry CV2 2SF* Tel (024) 7660 4152 Mobile 07803-888257
E-mail richard@yehright.com

BROMLEY AND BEXLEY, Archdeacon of. *See* WRIGHT, The Ven Paul

BRONNERT, Preb David Llewellyn Edward. b 36. Ch Coll Cam BA57 MA61 PhD61 Lon Univ BD62. Tyndale Hall Bris 60. **d** 63 **p** 64. C Cheadle Hulme St Andr *Ches* 63-67; C Islington St Mary *Lon* 67-69; Chapl N Lon Poly 69-75; V Southall Green St Jo 75-01; Preb St Paul's Cathl 89-01; P-in-c Southall St Geo 92-99; AD Ealing W 84-90; rtd 01; Perm to Offic *Ox* from 04. *101 Walton Way, Aylesbury HP21 7JP* Tel (01296) 484048
E-mail david.bronnert@talk21.com

BRONNERT, John. b 33. Man Univ MA(Theol)84 Univ of Wales (Lamp) PhD98 ACA57 FCA68. Tyndale Hall Bris 65. **d** 68 **p** 69. C Hoole *Ches* 68-71; P-in-c Parr *Liv* 71-73; TV 73-85; V Runcorn St Jo Weston *Ches* 85-98; rtd 98; Perm to Offic *Liv* 85-04; *Man* from 98. *Tyndale, 15 Craig Avenue, Flixton, Urmston, Manchester M41 5RS* Tel 0161-748 7061
E-mail bronnert-revddrjohn@tyndale.freeserve.co.uk

BROOK, John Brendan Paul. b 79. CCC Ox MEng01. Oak Hill Th Coll BA06. **d** 06 **p** 07. C Hailsham *Chich* from 06. *19 St Wilfrid's Green, Hailsham BN27 1DR* Tel (01323) 442132
E-mail jbrook@gmail.com

BROOK, Jonathan Roger Wilson. b 67. St Jo Coll Nottm 05. **d** 07 **p** 08. C Ripley *Derby* from 07. *31 Porterhouse Road, Ripley DE5 3FL* Tel (01773) 743511 Mobile 07939-472799
E-mail jonathan-susie.brook@tiscali.co.uk

BROOK, Neville. *See* BROOK, William Neville

BROOK, Peter Geoffrey (Brother Simon). b 47. NOC 91. **d** 94 **p** 95. CGA from 71; NSM Heywood and Middleton Deanery 94-96; Perm to Offic *Ex* from 96. *The Priory, Lamacraft Farm, Start Point, Chivelstone, Kingsbridge TQ7 2NG* Tel (01548) 511474

BROOK, Priestly. b 42. CBDTI 04. **d** 07 **p** 08. NSM Colne and Villages *Blackb* from 07. *The Coach House, Foulds Road, Trawden, Colne BB8 8NT* Tel (01282) 869876
E-mail priestlybrook1@tiscali.co.uk

BROOK, Stephen Edward. b 44. Univ of Wales (Abth) BSc63 DipEd66. Wycliffe Hall Ox 71 All Nations Chr Coll 85. **d** 74 **p** 75. C Heworth H Trin *York* 74-77; C Linthorpe 77-80; TV Deane *Man* 80-85; Crosslinks 86-96; Portugal 88-96; P-in-c Bacup St Sav *Man* 96-03; P-in-c Tunstead 99-03; V Blackpool St Mark *Blackb* from 03. *St Mark's Vicarage, 163 Kingscote Drive, Blackpool FY3 8EH* Tel (01253) 392895

BROOK, William Neville. b 31. S'wark Ord Course 66. **d** 69 **p** 70. C Maidstone St Martin *Cant* 69-75; V Hartlip w Stockbury 75-80; R Willesborough w Hinxhill 80-87; R Willesborough 87-89; V Gt Staughton and Hail Weston *Ely* 89-96; rtd 96; Perm to Offic *Chich* from 96. *27 Middleton Drive, Eastbourne BN23 6HD* Tel (01323) 731243

BROOKE, Miss Bridget Cecilia. b 31. Coll of Resurr Mirfield 88. **d** 89 **p** 94. Hon Par Dn Ranmoor *Sheff* 89-94; Hon C 94-04; Bp's Adv for NSMs 94-01; Perm to Offic from 04. *166 Tom Lane, Sheffield S10 3PG* Tel 0114-230 2147

BROOKE, David Fewsdale. b 43. St Paul's Coll Grahamstown 80. **d** 90 **p** 90. Asst Chapl Dioc Coll Cape Town S Africa 90-92; NSM Crawford St Jo 93-97; NSM Sea Point St Jas 98-99; Perm to Offic *Newc* 00; C Norham and Duddo 01-04; C Cornhill w Carham 01-04; C Branxton 01-04; R Dunkeld *St And* from 04; R Strathtay from 04. *Spoutside, Snaigow, Dunkeld PH8 0RD* Tel (01738) 710726 E-mail stmarys.birnam@btinternet.com

BROOKE, David Martin. b 58. Selw Coll Cam BA80 MA83 Lon Inst of Educn PGCE81. SAOMC 96. **d** 98 **p** 00. C Luton Lewsey St Hugh *St Alb* 99-00; NSM Sunnyside w Bourne End 00-02; C 02-04; V Bishopton w Gt Stainton *Dur* from 04; R Redmarshall from 04; R Grindon, Stillington and Wolviston from 04; AD Stockton from 07. *The Rectory, Church Lane, Redmarshall, Stockton-on-Tees TS21 1ES* Tel (01740) 630810 Mobile 07967-326085 E-mail david@revd.co.uk

BROOKE, Katherine Margaret. b 58. GRSM79 LRAM80 ARCM80. SAOMC 01. **d** 04 **p** 05. C Auckland St Andr and St Anne *Dur* 04-07; C Stranton from 07. *The Rectory, Church Lane, Redmarshall, Stockton-on-Tees TS21 1ES* Tel (01740) 630810 Mobile 07973-539729 E-mail kate@revd.co.uk

BROOKE, Canon Robert. b 44. Qu Coll Birm 70. **d** 73 **p** 74. C Man Resurr 73-76; C Bournville *Birm* 76-77; Chapl Qu Eliz Coll *Lon* 77-82; C Bramley *Ripon* 82-85; TV 85-86; V Hunslet Moor St Pet and St Cuth 86-93; Chapl People w Learning Disabilities from 86; TV Seacroft 93-03; TV Beeston from 03; Chapl Leeds Mental Health Teaching NHS Trust 94-03; Hon Can Ripon Cathl from 01. *St David's House, Waincliffe Drive, Leeds LS11 8ET* Tel 0113-270 2829
E-mail bob.brooke@another.com

BROOKE, Rosemary Jane. b 53. Cam Univ BEd75 Open Univ BA83. NOC 86. **d** 89 **p** 94. NSM Poynton *Ches* 89-05; P-in-c Werneth from 05; Bp's Adv for Women in Min 96-05. *The Vicarage, Compstall Brow, Compstall, Stockport SK6 5HU* Tel 0161-427 1259 E-mail jane.brook@cheshire.gov.uk

BROOKE, Timothy Cyril. b 38. Jes Coll Cam BA60 MA70 Middx Poly CQSW76. Ripon Coll Cuddesdon 84. **d** 86 **p** 87. C Hillmorton *Cov* 86-90; V Earlsdon 90-98; V Cov St Fran N Radford 98-05; rtd 05; Perm to Offic *Cov* from 05. *80 Broadway, Coventry CV5 6NU* Tel (024) 7667 9126
E-mail brookenet@zetnet.co.uk

BROOKE, Vernon. b 41. St Aid Birkenhead 62. **d** 65 **p** 66. C Crofton Park St Hilda w St Cypr *S'wark* 65-68; C Eccleshill *Bradf* 68-70; Ind Chapl *Linc* 70-84; Ind Chapl *Derby* 84-97; Ind Chapl *Chich* 97-06; rtd 06; Perm to Offic *Pet* from 06. *5 Blakesley Close, Northampton NN2 8PA* Tel (01604) 845585
E-mail vernonbrooke@yahoo.co.uk

BROOKE, Canon William Edward. b 13. Birm Univ BA34 MA35. Westcott Ho Cam 35. **d** 37 **p** 38. C Wylde Green *Birm* 37-40; C Sparkbrook St Agatha 40-44; P-in-c Birm St Jude 44-50; V 50-60; R Castle Bromwich SS Mary and Marg 60-78; Hon Can Birm Cathl 61-78; rtd 78; Perm to Offic *Heref* from 78. *Ivy Cottage, Tarrington, Hereford HR1 4HZ*

BROOKER, Mrs Anna Lesley. b 56. York Univ BA78 MA79 Homerton Coll Cam PGCE80. Ridley Hall Cam 01. **d** 03 **p** 04. C Brentford *Lon* 03-06; P-in-c Isleworth All SS from 06. *Butterfield House, 61 Church Street, Isleworth TW7 6BE* Tel (020) 8560 6379 E-mail albrooker@email.com

BROOKER, Ruth Muriel. b 53. Wycliffe Hall Ox 96. **d** 98 **p** 99. C Beverley Minster *York* 98-02; R Haddlesey w Hambleton and Birkin 02-03; Perm to Offic *S'well* 03-04 and *Lich* from 05. *13 West Park Court, Connaught Road, Wolverhampton WV1 4SQ* Tel (01902) 711782 *or* (01384) 233511
E-mail ruth@christianvocations.org

BROOKER, Mrs Wendy Ann. b 41. St Alb Minl Tr Scheme 82. **dss** 85 **d** 87 **p** 94. Pinner *Lon* 85-87; Par Dn Greenhill St Jo 87-88; Ind Chapl 89-94; C Hayes St Edm 95-99; Chapl R Nat Orthopaedic Hosp NHS Trust from 99. *16 Rosecroft Walk, Pinner HA5 1LL* Tel (020) 8866 0795
E-mail wd.brooker@ukf.net

BROOKES, Arthur George. b 21. ACIB52. Worc Ord Coll 64. **d** 66 **p** 67. C Lower Mitton *Worc* 66-67; C Fladbury w Throckmorton, Wyre Piddle and Moor 67-70; C Abberton w Bishampton 67-70; R 70-73; V Cradley 73-78; P-in-c Castle Morton 78-79; P-in-c Holly Bush w Birtsmorton 78-79; P-in-c Castlemorton, Hollybush and Birtsmorton 79-80; P-in-c Norton w Whittington 80-81; TV Worc St Martin w St Pet, St Mark etc 81-86; rtd 86; Perm to Offic *Worc* from 86. *5 Capel Court, The Burgage, Prestbury, Cheltenham GL52 3EL* Tel (01242) 580523

BROOKES, Colin Stuart. b 70. Lon Bible Coll BA93. Ridley Hall Cam 00. **d** 02 **p** 03. C Cambridge St Barn *Ely* 02-06; C Woodside Park St Barn *Lon* from 06. *12 Courthouse Road, London N12 7PJ* Tel (020) 8446 1002 Mobile 07973-840340
E-mail colinbrookes@stbarnabas.co.uk

BROOKES, David Charles. b 45. St Mich Coll Llan 84. **d** 86 **p** 87. C Llanishen and Lisvane 86-89; TV Brighouse St Martin *Wakef* 89-92; TV Brighouse and Clifton 92-94; V Heddington and Hucking w Leeds and Broomfield *Cant* 94-03; rtd 03. *chemin de la Garenne, Le Vivier, 16240 Longre, France* Tel (0033) (1) 15 45 31 71 88 E-mail david@dcbrookes.freeserve.co.uk

BROOKES, Edwin William. b 39. St Mark & St Jo Coll Lon TCert63 Birm Univ BPhil(Ed)85 Open Univ BA73 BA93. OLM course 95. **d** 98 **p** 99. OLM Cen Wolverhampton *Lich* from 98. *23 Chetwynd Road, Blakenhall, Wolverhampton WV2 4NZ* Tel (01902) 654979 Fax 562616
E-mail ed.brookes@blueyonder.co.uk

BROOKES, Geoffrey John Denis. b 24. CMS Tr Coll Crowther Hall 78 Ridley Hall Cam 84. **d** 85 **p** 86. Bahrain 85-88; Project Officer Ch Action w the Unemployed 88-91; Hon C Hastings All So *Chich* 88-91; Asst Chapl Milan w Genoa and Varese *Eur* 91-94; Canada 94-97; Perm to Offic *Chich* 97-99 and 01-02; *Guildf* from 03. *50 Chapel Court, Church Street, Dorking RH4 1BT* Tel (01306) 884287

BROOKES, Keith Roy. b 37. JP74. Leeds Univ DipEd72 MHCIMA MRSH. St Aid Birkenhead 64. **d** 80 **p** 81. Hon C Stockport St Thos *Ches* 80-86; Hon C Stockport St Thos w St Pet 86-91; C 91-98; Hon C from 99. *42 Derby Road, Stockport SK4 4NE* Tel 0161-442 0301

BROOKES, Laurence. b 33. **d** 02 **p** 03. OLM Flockton cum Denby Grange *Wakef* 02-06; OLM Emley 02-06; Perm to Offic from 06. *Treetops, 6 Chessington Drive, Flockton, Wakefield WF4 4TJ* Tel (01924) 848238
E-mail lauriemarybrookes@supanet.com

BROOKES, Robin Keenan. b 47. Trin Coll Bris 72. **d** 75 **p** 76. C Livesey *Blackb* 75-78; C Burnley St Pet 78-80; P-in-c Bawdeswell w Foxley *Nor* 80-83; I Donagh w Tyholland and Errigal Truagh *Clogh* 83-91; Dioc Communications Officer 90-91; I Dublin Drumcondra w N Strand *D & G* 91-99; Chapl Ayia Napa Cyprus from 99. *PO Box 33873, 5318 Paralimni, Cyprus* Tel (00357) (23) 742955 *or* 742956 Fax 742957 Mobile 99-698049 E-mail angfam@spidernet.com.cy

BROOKES, Steven David. b 60. Lanc Univ BA81. Ripon Coll Cuddesdon 82. **d** 85 **p** 86. C Stanley Liv 85-88; C W Derby St Mary 88-90; Chapl RN 90-94; R Weybridge *Guildf* 94-03; P-in-c Liv Our Lady and St Nic w St Anne 03-07; R Liv Our Lady and St Nic from 07. *The Rector's Lodging, 233 South Ferry Quay, Liverpool L3 4EE* Tel 0151-709 2551 Mobile 07903-505639 E-mail rector@livpc.co.uk

BROOKFIELD, Alun John. b 50. Lon Univ BMus72 Spurgeon's Coll Lon BA82. **d** 00 **p** 01. NSM Stratton St Margaret w S Marston etc *Bris* 00-02; P-in-c Cwmtawe Uchaf *S & B* from 03. *The Vicarage, Heol Tawe, Abercrave, Swansea SA9 1TJ* Tel (01639) 730640 E-mail a.brookfield@ntlworld.com

BROOKFIELD, Patricia Anne. *See* HARDACRE, Mrs Patricia Anne

BROOKS, Alan Leslie. b 43. Nor City Coll TCert65. Dioc OLM tr scheme 98. **d** 01 **p** 02. OLM Waterloo Ch Ch and St Jo *Liv* from 01. *6 Kingsway, Waterloo, Liverpool L22 4RQ* Tel 0151-920 8770 E-mail alanbrooks@blueyonder.co.uk

BROOKS, Mrs Alison Margaret. b 46. EMMTC. **d** 03 **p** 04. Asst Chapl Qu Medical Cen Nottm Univ Hosp NHS Trust from 03. *12 Russell Avenue, Nottingham NG8 2BL*

BROOKS, Catherine Elizabeth. b 57. LCTP. **d** 08 **p** 09. C Blackb St Jas from 08. *4 Hawkshaw Bank Road, Blackburn BB1 8JS*

BROOKS, Mrs Christine. b 62. STETS. **d** 09. C N Poole Ecum Team *Sarum* from 09. *87 Verity Crescent, Poole BH17 8TT* E-mail christine.brooks3@ntlworld.com

BROOKS, Mrs Christine Ellen. b 43. Sheff Univ BA65 Lon Univ BD81 Lambeth STh81. EAMTC 86. **d** 88 **p** 94. NSM Palgrave w Wortham and Burgate *St E* 88-89; Par Dn Thorndon w Rishangles, Stoke Ash, Thwaite etc 89-94; P-in-c Aldringham w Thorpe, Knodishall w Buxlow etc 94-04; R Whinlands from 04; Asst P Sternfield w Benhall and Snape 98-03; P-in-c Alde River 03-06. *The Rectory, Aldeburgh Road, Friston, Saxmundham IP17 1NP* Tel (01728) 688972 Mobile 07752-652833 E-mail christine@brook7463.freeserve.co.uk

BROOKS, David Edward. b 73. **d** 09. OLM Middleton w Thornham *Man* from 09. *316 Windermere Road, Middleton, Manchester M24 4LA* Tel 0161-287 0448 Mobile 07904-520906 E-mail dbrooks@ntlworld.com

BROOKS, Dorothy Anne. *See* MOORE BROOKS, Dorothy Anne

BROOKS, Canon Francis Leslie. b 35. Kelham Th Coll 55. **d** 59 **p** 60. C Woodlands *Sheff* 59-61; Ind Missr S Yorkshire Coalfields 61-66; V Moorends 66-72; Chapl HM Borstal Hatfield 67-72; Chapl HM Pris Acklington 72-75; Chapl HM Borstal Wellingborough 75-79; Chapl HM Pris Wakef 79-83; Area Sec USPG *Wakef* and *Bradf* 83-88; V Carleton and E Hardwick *Wakef* 88-96; Can Mara (Tanzania) from 88; rtd 96; Perm to Offic *Wakef* 03-04; Hon C Chevington *Newc* from 04. *20 Robsons Way, Amble, Morpeth NE65 0GA* Tel (01665) 712765

BROOKS, Ian George. b 47. Selw Coll Cam BA68 MA72. Chich Th Coll 68. **d** 70 **p** 71. C Stoke Newington St Mary *Lon* 70-74; C Hoxton St Anne w St Sav and St Andr 74-75; C Hoxton St Anne w St Columba 75-80; P-in-c Croxteth St Paul CD *Liv* 80-81; V Croxteth from 81. *St Paul's Vicarage, Delabole Road, Liverpool L11 6LG* Tel and fax 0151-548 9009 E-mail frigb@blueyonder.co.uk

BROOKS, Jeremy Paul. b 67. Leic Univ LLB88 Clare Coll Cam BA96 MA01 K Coll Lon MA00. Ridley Hall Cam 94. **d** 97 **p** 98. C Highgate St Mich *Lon* 97-01; P-in-c Hoddesdon *St Alb* 01-07; V from 07. *11 Oxenden Drive, Hoddesdon EN11 8QF* Tel (01992) 464335 E-mail jpbrooks@ntlworld.com

BROOKS, Jonathan Thorburn. b 53. Solicitor 76 G&C Coll Cam BA75. Trin Coll Bris 84. **d** 86 **p** 87. C Dagenham *Chelmsf* 86-88; Perm to Offic *Glouc* 03; NSM Thornbury and Oldbury-on-Severn w Shepperdine 03-05. *12 Hyde Avenue, Thornbury, Bristol BS35 1JA* Tel (01454) 411853

BROOKS, Malcolm David. b 45. **d** 71 **p** 72. C Pontlottyn w Fochriw *Llan* 71-72; C Caerphilly 72-78; V Ferndale w Maerdy 78-81; C Port Talbot St Theodore 82-84; V Ystrad Mynach 84-85; V Ystrad Mynach w Llanbradach 85-06. *33 Heol y Gors, Whitchurch, Cardiff CF14 1HF*

BROOKS, Patrick John. b 27. Man Univ BA49 DipEd. Oak Hill Th Coll 78. **d** 77 **p** 79. Burundi 77-80; Perm to Offic *Ex* 80-83; P-in-c Phillack w Gwithian and Gwinear *Truro* 88-93; rtd 93; Perm to Offic *Chich* from 93. *Abbots, Claigmar Road, Rustington, Littlehampton BN16 2NL*

BROOKS, Paul John. b 59. Loughb Univ BSc81. St Jo Coll Nottm 88. **d** 90 **p** 91. C Long Eaton St Jo *Derby* 90-94; Min

Jersey St Paul Prop Chpl *Win* from 94. *5 Claremont Avenue, St Saviour, Jersey JE2 7SF* Tel (01534) 880393 E-mail pjbvic@aol.com

BROOKS, Peter. b 55. St Mich Coll Llan 97. **d** 99 **p** 00. C Morriston *S & B* 99-01; P-in-c Rhayader and Nantmel 01-02; P-in-c Cwmdauddwr w St Harmon and Llanwrthwl 02-05; P-in-c Llanwrthwl w St Harmon, Rhayader, Nantmel etc 05-08; P-in-c Gwastedyn from 08. *The Vicarage, Dark Lane, Rhayader LD6 5DA* Tel (01597) 810223 E-mail peter.rhayader1@tiscali.co.uk

BROOKS, Philip David. b 52. MA Cam Univ MTh. St Jo Coll Nottm 80. **d** 83 **p** 84. C Ipsley *Worc* 83-87; V Fulford w Hilderstone *Lich* 87-95; Chapl Stallington Hosp 87-95; P-in-c Crich *Derby* 95-01; V Crich and S Wingfield from 01; Dioc Adv Past Care and Counselling from 03. *The Vicarage, 19 Coasthill, Crich, Matlock DE4 5DS* Tel (01773) 852449 E-mail philipdbro@aol.com

BROOKS, Roger John. b 46. Nottm Univ PhD71 Liv Univ MTh05 MRPharmS70 FFARCS81. NOC 98. **d** 01 **p** 02. C Burley in Wharfedale *Bradf* 01-03; P-in-c Denholme 03-09; P-in-c Harden and Wilsden 03-09; P-in-c Chevington w Hargrave, Chedburgh w Depden etc *St E* from 09. *The Rectory, New Road, Chevington, Bury St Edmunds IP29 5QL*

BROOKS, Mrs Susan Margaret. b 50. Philippa Fawcett Coll CertEd71 Open Univ BA95. SEITE 00. **d** 03. NSM Chatham St Paul w All SS *Roch* 03-05. *189 Malling Road, Snodland ME6 5EE* Tel (01634) 241350 E-mail suebrooks@talk21.com

BROOKS, Mrs Susan Vera. b 51. NOC 87. **d** 90 **p** 94. Par Dn Carleton and E Hardwick *Wakef* 90-93; TV Almondbury w Farnley Tyas 93-98; Chapl Huddersfield NHS Trust 98-01; Chapl Calderdale and Huddersfield NHS Trust 01-03; Lead Chapl from 03. *Royal Infirmary, Acre Street, Huddersfield HD3 3EA* Tel (01484) 342092 *or* 323839 E-mail susan.brooks@cht.nhs.uk

BROOKS, Mrs Vivien June. b 47. Univ of Wales (Ban) BA68 Southn Univ MA70. Ridley Hall Cam 87. **d** 89 **p** 95. C Exning St Martin w Landwade *St E* 89-92; Par Dn Hermitage and Hampstead Norreys, Cold Ash etc *Ox* 92-94; C 94-95; P-in-c Cox Green 95-03; Co Ecum Officer (Berks) 00-03; P-in-c Earls Colne w White Colne and Colne Engaine *Chelmsf* 03-04; TV Halstead Area from 04. *St Andrew's Rectory, 5 Shut Lane, Earls Colne, Colchester CO6 2RE* Tel (01787) 220347 E-mail vbrooks@minnieb.com

BROOKS, Vivienne Christine. *See* ARMSTRONG-MacDONNELL, Mrs Vivienne Christine

BROOKSBANK, Alan Watson. b 43. Univ of Wales (Lamp) BA64 Edin Univ MEd76. Edin Th Coll 64. **d** 66 **p** 67. C Cleator Moor w Cleator *Carl* 66-70; V Dalston 70-80; P-in-c Greystoke, Matterdale and Mungrisdale 80-81; R 81-83; R Watermillock 81-83; R Hagley *Worc* 83-95; Bp's Officer for NSM 88-95; V Claines St Jo 95-98; rtd 98. *169 Northfields Lane, Brixham TQ5 8RD*

BROOKSHAW, Miss Janice Chitty. b 48. MCIPD90. Ripon Coll Cuddesdon 96. **d** 98 **p** 99. C Beaconsfield *Ox* 98-02; P-in-c The Stodden Churches *St Alb* 02-03; R from 03. *Stodden Rectory, High Street, Upper Dean, Huntingdon PE28 0ND* Tel and fax (01234) 708531 E-mail jan@revbrookshaw.freeserve.co.uk

BROOM, Andrew Clifford. b 65. Keele Univ BSocSc86. Trin Coll Bris BA92. **d** 92 **p** 93. C Wellington All SS w Eyton *Lich* 92-96; C Brampton St Thos *Derby* 96-00; V Walton St Jo from 00. *6 Medlock Road, Walton, Chesterfield S40 3NH* Tel (01246) 205993 E-mail andy@atdc.wanadoo.co.uk

BROOM, Jacqueline Anne. b 52. R Holloway Coll Lon BSc73. Trin Coll Bris 79. **dss** 82 **d** 95 **p** 95. Easton H Trin w St Gabr and St Lawr and St Jude *Bris* 82-86; OMF Internat 87-01; Hong Kong 87-95; Macao China 96-01; rtd 01; Perm to Offic *B & W* from 02. *31 Windermere Avenue, Weston-super-Mare BS23 3TN* Tel (01934) 629293

BROOME, David Curtis. b 36. Leeds Univ BA63. Coll of Resurr Mirfield. **d** 65 **p** 66. C Winshill *Derby* 65-69; C Leigh-on-Sea St Marg *Chelmsf* 69-74; V Leeds St Marg *Ripon* 74-81; V Stoke H Cross w Dunston *Nor* 81-93; P-in-c Arminghall 92-93; P-in-c Caistor w Markshall 92-93; R Stoke H Cross w Dunston, Arminghall etc 93-00; rtd 00; Perm to Offic *Nor* from 00. *13 Greenacres Drive, Poringland, Norwich NR14 7JG* Tel (01508) 493201

BROOME, Mildred Dorothy. b 43. **d** 00 **p** 01. NSM Malden St Jo *S'wark* from 00. *124 The Manor Drive, Worcester Park KT4 7LW* Tel (020) 8337 1572

BROOMFIELD, David John. b 37. Reading Univ BA59. Oak Hill Th Coll 64. **d** 66 **p** 67. C Gresley *Derby* 66-71; C Rainham *Chelmsf* 71-77; R High Ongar w Norton Mandeville 77-88; RD Ongar 83-88; P-in-c Stanford Rivers 84-86; P-in-c Loughton St Mary and St Mich 88-95; P-in-c Loughton St Mary 95-97; R 97-03; rtd 03; Perm to Offic *Glouc* from 03. *15 Oriel Grove, Moreton-in-Marsh GL56 0ED* Tel (01608) 651023 E-mail david@dabroomfield.freeserve.co.uk

BROOMFIELD, Iain Jonathan. b 57. Univ Coll Ox MA87. Wycliffe Hall Ox 80. **d** 83 **p** 84. C Beckenham Ch Ch *Roch* 83-87;

Sen Schs Worker Titus Trust 87-00; V Bromley Ch Ch *Roch* from 00. *Christ Church Vicarage, 18 Highland Road, Bromley BR1 4AD* Tel (020) 8313 9882 *or* 8464 1898 Fax 8464 5846 E-mail iain.broomfield@christchurchbromley.org

BROOMHEAD, Mark Roger. b 71. Nottm Univ BSc00. St Jo Coll Nottm 06. **d** 08 **p** 09. C N Wingfield, Clay Cross and Pilsley *Derby* from 08. *11 Pen Lane, Danesmoor, Chesterfield S45 9AD* Tel (01246) 250048 E-mail mark@claycross.org

BROSNAN, Mark. b 61. St Martin's Coll Lanc BA83 RMN88 Otley Agric Coll. EAMTC 92. **d** 95 **p** 96. C Rushmere *St E* 95-98; Perm to Offic *Chelmsf* 01-05; Hon C W w E Mersea 05-08; Hon C Peldon w Gt and Lt Wigborough 05-08; P-in-c Hadleigh St Barn from 08. *St Barnabas' Vicarage, 169 Church Road, Hadleigh, Benfleet SS7 2EJ* Tel (01702) 554658 E-mail gohiking@hotmail.co.uk

BROSTER, Godfrey David. b 52. Ealing Tech Coll BA75. Ripon Coll Cuddesdon 78. **d** 81 **p** 82. C Crayford *Roch* 81-82; C Brighton Resurr *Chich* 82-86; C-in-c The Hydneye CD 86-91; R Plumpton w E Chiltington 91-93; R Plumpton w E Chiltington cum Novington from 93. *The Rectory, Station Road, Plumpton Green, Lewes BN7 3BU* Tel (01273) 890570

BROTHERSTON, Miss Isabel Mary. b 42. Cranmer Hall Dur 81. **dss** 83 **d** 87 **p** 94. Coleshill *Birm* 83-87; Par Dn Duddeston w Nechells 87-92; Par Dn Harlescott *Lich* 92-94; C 94-04; R Llandulas and Llysfaen *St As* 04-08; rtd 08. *3 Marlow Terrace, Mold CH7 1HH* Tel (01352) 756011 E-mail mbrother@live.co.uk

BROTHERTON, The Ven John Michael. b 35. St Jo Coll Cam BA59 MA63. Cuddesdon Coll 59. **d** 61 **p** 62. C Chiswick St Nic w St Mary *Lon* 61-65; Chapl Trin Coll Port of Spain Trinidad 65-69; R Diego Martin 69-75; V Cowley St Jo and Chapl St Hilda's Coll Ox 76-81; RD Cowley 78-81; V Portsea St Mary *Portsm* 81-91; Hon Can Kobe Japan from 86; Adn Chich 91-02; rtd 02; Perm to Offic *Chich* and *Lon* from 03. *Flat 2, 23 Gledhow Gardens, London SW5 0AZ* Tel (020) 7373 5147 E-mail jmbrotherton@amserve.com

BROTHERTON, Michael. b 56. MBE93. Univ of Wales (Abth) BD80. Wycliffe Hall Ox 80. **d** 81 **p** 82. Hon Chapl Miss to Seamen 81-84; C Pembroke Dock *St D* 81-84; Chapl RN from 84. *Royal Naval Chaplaincy Service, Mail Point 1-2, Leach Building, Whale Island, Portsmouth PO2 8BY* Tel (023) 9262 5055 Fax 9262 5134

BROTHERWOOD, Nicholas Peter. b 50. Oak Hill Th Coll BA83. **d** 83 **p** 84. C Nottingham St Nic *S'well* 83-86; Canada from 86; Dir Quebec Lodge 86-89; Angl Chapl McGill Univ 89-91; Assoc R Westmount St Steph from 91. *3498 Harvard Avenue, Montreal QC H4A 2W3, Canada* Tel (001) (514) 489 4158 Fax 932 0550 E-mail st.stephens@qc.aira.com

BROTHWELL, Paul David. b 37. Lich Th Coll 62. **d** 65 **p** 66. C Honley *Wakef* 65-68; Min Can Wakef Cathl 68-71; V Whittington St Giles *Lich* 71-83; P-in-c Weeford 78-83; V Whittington w Weeford 83-92; Chapl Kidderminster Gen Hosp 92-94; Chapl Kidderminster Health Care NHS Trust 94-01; Chapl Worcs Community and Mental Health Trust 01-02; Hon Can Antananarivo 02; rtd 02; Perm to Offic *Worc* from 02. *8 Hillside Close, Stourport-on-Severn DY13 0JW* Tel (01299) 823495 *or* (01562) 823424 ext 3306

BROTHWOOD, Ian Sidney. b 56. K Coll Lon BD84. Linc Th Coll 87. **d** 89 **p** 90. C Selsdon St Jo w St Fran *S'wark* 89-93; P-in-c S Norwood St Alb 93-97; V 97-99; V Reigate St Mark 99-04; P-in-c Selsdon St Jo w St Fran 04-06; R from 06. *St John's Rectory, Upper Selsdon Road, South Croydon CR2 8DD* Tel (020) 8657 2343 E-mail iansb@aol.com

BROTHWOOD, John. b 31. Peterho Cam MA55 MB, BChir55. S'wark Ord Course 89. **d** 91 **p** 92. NSM Dulwich St Barn *S'wark* 91-04. *98 Woodwarde Road, London SE22 8UT* Tel (020) 8693 8273

BROUGH, Gerald William. b 32. Trin Coll Cam BA55 MA59. Ridley Hall Cam 55. **d** 57 **p** 58. C Westgate St Jas *Cant* 57-60; C New Addington 60-62; V Mancetter *Cov* 62-73; P-in-c Bourton w Frankton and Stretton on Dunsmore etc 73-74; R 74-93; rtd 93; Perm to Offic *Cov* from 93. *17 Brookhurst Court, Beverley Road, Leamington Spa CV32 6PB* Tel (01926) 430759 E-mail gwbrln@aol.com

BROUGH (née CROWLE), Mrs Sarah Ann. b 65. Ripon Coll Cuddesdon BTh99. **d** 99 **p** 00. C Godalming *Guildf* 99-03; Chapl Godalming Coll 01-03; R Chiddingfold *Guildf* from 03. *The Rectory, Coxcombe Lane, Chiddingfold, Godalming GU8 4QA* Tel (01428) 682008 Mobile 07747-031524 E-mail sarahbrough@btinternet.com

BROUGHALL, Rodney John. b 32. **d** 96 **p** 97. OLM Watton w Carbrooke and Ovington *Nor* 96-02; rtd 02; Perm to Offic *Nor* from 02. *15 Garden Close, Watton, Thetford IP25 6DP* Tel (01953) 881989 E-mail rodbroughall@hotmail.com

BROUGHTON, James Roger. b 48. Leeds Univ BA71 Nottm Univ CertEd72 Liv Univ MEd00. Wycliffe Hall Ox 87. **d** 89 **p** 90. C Stoneycroft All SS *Liv* 89-92; P-in-c Carr Mill 92-94; V 94-96; Chapl Duke of York's R Mil Sch Dover 96-08; rtd 08; Perm to

Offic *Cant* from 08. *Woodstock, St Vincent Road, St Margarets-at-Cliffe, Dover CT15 6ET* Tel (01304) 853840

BROUGHTON, Lynne Mary. b 46. Melbourne Univ BA67 PhD79. EAMTC 99. **d** 00 **p** 01. NSM Wood Ditton w Saxon Street *Ely* 00-07; NSM Kirtling 00-07; NSM Cheveley 00-07; NSM Ashley w Silverley 00-07; Perm to Offic from 07. *85 Richmond Road, Cambridge CB4 3PS* Tel (01223) 322014 E-mail lmb27@hermes.cam.ac.uk

BROUGHTON, Canon Stuart Roger. b 36. Wilson Carlile Coll 59 St Mich Coll Llan 61. **d** 64 **p** 65. C Bromley Ch Ch *Roch* 64-67; SAMS 67-79 and 86-95; Miss Paraguayan Chaco Paraguay 67-70; R Salvador Gd Shep Brazil 70-79; V Stoke sub Hamdon *B & W* 79-83; Hon CF 82-86; V Blackb Ch Ch w St Matt 83-86; R Alcacer do Sal Portugal 86-91; Chapl Rio de Janeiro Brazil 91-95; rtd 96; Chapl Agia Napa Cyprus 96; Chapl Ch Ch Cathl Falkland Is 97-98; P-in-c Corfu *Eur* 98-01; Hon C Jersey St Paul Prop Chpl *Win* 01-03; Chapl to Abp Congo from 03; Hon Can Bukavu from 04. *c/o P Broughton Esq, Point Cottage, 29 Fir Tree Lane, Littleton, Chester CH3 7DN* E-mail stuartrbroughton@hotmail.com

BROUN, Canon Claud Michael. b 30. BNC Ox BA55. Edin Th Coll 56. **d** 58 **p** 59. Chapl St Mary's Cathl 58-62; Can St Mary's Cathl 84-95; Hon Can from 95; P-in-c Cambuslang 62-70; R 70-75; R Hamilton 75-88; R Gatehouse of Fleet 88-95; R Kirkcudbright 88-95; rtd 95. *Martin Lodge, Ardross Place, Alness IV17 0PX* Tel (01349) 882442

BROWELL (née SHILLINGTON), Mrs Maureen Lesley. b 57. MIH89. NEOC 02. **d** 05 **p** 06. Soc Resp Officer *Ripon* 99-08; NSM Hoylandswaine and Silkstone w Stainborough *Wakef* 05-08; TV Almondbury w Farnley Tyas from 08; Dioc Co-ord for Soc Resp from 08. *The Vicarage, 150 Fleminghouse Lane, Huddersfield HD5 8UD* Tel (01484) 545085 Mobile 07930-194421 E-mail maureenbrowell@talktalk.net

BROWN, Canon Alan. b 37. Tyndale Hall Bris 59. **d** 63 **p** 64. C Braintree *Chelmsf* 63-66; C Tooting Graveney St Nic *S'wark* 66-68; C Chesham St Mary *Ox* 68-70; V Hornsey Rise St Mary *Lon* 70-75; V Sidcup Ch Ch *Roch* 75-88; V Newport St Jo *Portsm* 88-01; P-in-c Newport St Thos 96-99; V 99-01; RD W Wight 91-96; Hon Can Portsm Cathl 95-01; rtd 01. *65 Sherbourne Avenue, Ryde PO33 3PW* Tel (01983) 566956

BROWN, Alan George. b 51. Bradf Univ BSc84 Leeds Univ CertEd81 MBA92 SRN72 RMN75 RNT81. NOC 92. **d** 95 **p** 96. NSM Ilkley St Marg *Bradf* from 95; Hd of Division Applied Health Studies Leeds Univ from 98; Bp's Adv for Hosp Chapl from 03. *Waverley, Wheatley Road, Ilkley LS29 8TS* Tel and fax (01943) 601115 E-mail alan.brown@bradford.anglican.org

BROWN, Alan Michael Ernest. b 52. St Chad's Coll Dur BA74. St Jo Coll Nottm 81. **d** 83 **p** 84. C Bridlington Priory *York* 83-86; V Morton St Luke *Bradf* 86-02; Mental Health Worker Bradf City Primary Care Trust 02-07. *Address temp unknown*

BROWN, Albert Harry Alfred Victor. b 12. **d** 81 **p** 83. OLM Kennington Park St Agnes *S'wark* 81-92; Perm to Offic 92-00 and 05-07. *23/20 The Royal Hospital, London SW3 4SI* Tel (020) 7274 5982

BROWN, Alec George. b 53. Univ of Zimbabwe DipSW80 Univ of Wales (Cardiff) MSc(Econ)87. St Deiniol's Hawarden 88 NOC 90. **d** 93 **p** 94. C Stockton Heath *Ches* 93-96; C Thelwall 96-97; V 97-01; V Gt Budworth from 01. *The Vicarage, High Street, Great Budworth, Northwich CW9 6HF* Tel (01606) 891324 E-mail alec-brown@tiscali.co.uk

BROWN, Alexander Peter-Aidan. b 48. Sarum & Wells Th Coll. **d** 82 **p** 83. C Ifield *Chich* 82-86; TV 86-91; V St Leonards SS Pet and Paul from 91. *The Vicarage, 10 Blomfield Road, St Leonards-on-Sea TN37 6HH* Tel (01424) 445606 E-mail peter-aidan@lineone.net

BROWN, Mrs Alison Louise. b 60. RGN83. STETS 05. **d** 08 **p** 09. C Horsell *Guildf* from 08. *6 Waldens Park Road, Woking GU21 4RN* Tel (01483) 764094 E-mail alison@slbalb.co.uk

BROWN, Allan James. b 47. K Coll Lon BD69 AKC69 MTh70. St Aug Coll Cant 69. **d** 73 **p** 74. Chapl St Geo Sch Jerusalem 73-74; Chapl St Marg Sch Nazareth 74-75; C Clifton *S'well* 75-77; CF 77-99; Asst Chapl Gen 99-00; V Ilkeston St Mary *Derby* from 00; P-in-c Ilkeston St Jo from 05. *The Vicarage, 63B Manners Road, Ilkeston DE7 5HB* Tel 0115-932 4725 E-mail brown@lorisallan.freeserve.co.uk

BROWN, Canon Andrew. b 55. St Pet Hall Ox BA80 MA82. Ridley Hall Cam 79. **d** 80 **p** 81. C Burnley St Pet *Blackb* 80-82; C Elton All SS *Man* 82-86; P-in-c Ashton St Pet 86-93; V 94-96; V Halliwell St Luke 96-03; Can Th Derby Cathl from 03; Dioc CME Adv from 03. *149 Church Road, Quarndon, Derby DE22 5JA* Tel (01332) 553424 E-mail andie.brown@tiscali.co.uk

BROWN, Andrew. b 65. **d** 95 **p** 96. OLM Heywood *Man* 95-05. *24 Honiton Close, Heywood OL10 2PF* Tel (01706) 623091

BROWN, Andrew (Bod). b 66. Man Univ BSc87 Oak Hill Th Coll BA02. **d** 03 **p** 04. C Hyde St Geo *Ches* 03-06; V Weaverham from 06. *The Vicarage, Church Street, Weaverham, Northwich CW8 3NJ* Tel (01606) 852110

BROWN, Andrew James. b 60. Univ of Wales (Ban) BA81. Ripon Coll Cuddesdon 07. **d** 09. NSM Castle Bromwich SS Mary and Marg *Birm* from 09. *16 Oldington Grove, Solihull B91 3NF* Tel 05602-710769 Mobile 07974-947126
E-mail father.andrew@btinternet.com

BROWN, Anne Elizabeth. b 61. SWMTC 06. **d** 09. C Probus, Ladock and Grampound w Creed and St Erme *Truro* from 09. *The Rectory, Ladock, Truro TR2 4PL* Tel (01726) 883593
E-mail ladockrectory@btinternet.com

BROWN, Anthony Frank Palmer. b 31. Fitzw Ho Cam BA56 Fitzw Coll Cam MA84. Cuddesdon Coll 56. **d** 58 **p** 59. C Aldershot St Mich *Guildf* 58-61; C Chiswick St Nic w St Mary *Lon* 61-66; Asst Chapl Lon Univ 65-70; Lic to Offic 70-72; C-in-c Hammersmith SS Mich and Geo White City Estate CD 72-74; P-in-c Upper Sunbury St Sav 74-80; V 80-01; rtd 01; Perm to Offic *Chich* from 02. *6 Church Lane, Ditchling, Hassocks BN6 8TB* Tel (01273) 843847

BROWN, Anthony Paul. b 55. Reading Univ BSc75 MRICS87. Qu Coll Birm 77. **d** 80 **p** 81. C Pelsall *Lich* 80-83; C Leighton Buzzard w Eggington, Hockliffe etc *St Alb* 83-87; TV Langley Marish *Ox* 87-93; V Pet St Mary Boongate 93-98; TR Wombourne w Trysull and Bobbington *Lich* 98-02; TR Smestow Vale from 02. *The Vicarage, School Road, Wombourne, Wolverhampton WV5 9ED* Tel (01902) 892234 *or* 897700
E-mail revpbrown@aol.com

BROWN, Antony William Keith. b 26. RN Coll Dartmouth 43. Trin Coll Bris 86. **d** 87 **p** 88. NSM Lawrence Weston *Bris* 87-89; Chapl Casablanca *Eur* 89-93; Asst Chapl Paris St Mich 94-00; rtd 00; Perm to Offic *Bris* from 01. *13 Marklands, 37 Julian Road, Bristol BS9 1NP* Tel and fax 0117-377 6543
E-mail ansh.brown@blueyonder.co.uk

BROWN, Arthur Basil Etheredge. b 17. Reading Univ BA39. Wycliffe Hall Ox 46. **d** 47 **p** 48. C Camborne *Truro* 47-50; Org Sec (Midl) CPAS 50-53; PC Scarborough H Trin *York* 53-58; V Heworth H Trin 58-66; R Camborne *Truro* 66-82; rtd 82; Perm to Offic *Truro* from 82. *14 Tregenna Fields, Camborne TR14 7QS* Tel (01209) 716196

BROWN, Arthur William Stawell. b 26. St Jo Coll Ox BA50 MA51. Cuddesdon Coll 63. **d** 65 **p** 66. C Edin St Jo 65-66; C Petersfield w Sheet *Portsm* 67-75; V Portsea St Alb 75-79; R Smithfield St Bart *Lon* 79-91; R St Sepulchre w Ch Ch Greyfriars etc 81-91; Chapl Madeira *Eur* 90-93; rtd 91; Perm to Offic *Ex* from 93. *Clare Park, Crondall, Farnham GU10 5DT* Tel (01252) 851200

BROWN, Barry Ronald. b 48. Ridley Coll Melbourne ThL72. **d** 73 **p** 74. Australia 73-77 and 82-95; C Richmond St Mary *S'wark* 78-79; C Richmond St Mary w St Matthias and St Jo 79; C Edin Old St Paul 79-80; Chapl Belgrade w Zagreb *Eur* 81-82; Canada from 95. *46 Granby Street, Toronto ON M5B 2J5, Canada* Tel (001) (416) 979 6766

BROWN, Canon Bernard Herbert Vincent. b 26. Mert Coll Ox BA50 MA52. Westcott Ho Cam 50. **d** 52 **p** 53. C Rugby St Andr *Cov* 52-56; C Stoke Bishop *Bris* 56-59; Youth Chapl 56-62; Ind Chapl *Roch* 62-73; Bp's Dom Chapl 66-73; R Crawley *Chich* 73-79; TR 79-83; Ind Chapl *Bris* 83-92; Bp's Soc and Ind Adv 84-92; Hon Can Bris Cathl 85-92; RD Bris City 85-91; rtd 92; Perm to Offic *Sarum* from 92. *33B London Road, Dorchester DT1 1NF* Tel (01305) 260806

BROWN, Bernard Maurice Newall. b 26. Oak Hill Th Coll 47. **d** 51 **p** 52. C Penn Fields *Lich* 51-53; S Area Sec BCMS 53-55; Kenya 55-62; R Hartshorne *Derby* 62-68; V Stapenhill w Cauldwell 68-72; C Weston-super-Mare Ch Ch *B & W* 72-74; R Spaxton w Charlynch 74-80; rtd 80. *12 Ewart Road, Weston-super-Mare BS23 8NU* Tel (01934) 412170

BROWN, Bill Charles Balfour. b 44. Linc Th Coll 87. **d** 89 **p** 90. C Moulsham St Luke *Chelmsf* 89-91; C Prittlewell 91-94; V Worksop St Paul *S'well* from 95. *St Paul's Vicarage, Cavendish Road, Worksop S80 2ST* Tel (01909) 473289
E-mail fatherbill@btopenworld.com

BROWN, Bod. *See* BROWN, Andrew

BROWN, Brian Ernest. b 36. ALA64. Oak Hill NSM Course 82. **d** 85 **p** 86. NSM Wallington *S'wark* 85-91; C 91-00; rtd 00; Perm to Offic *Nor* from 00. *6 Burnside, Necton, Swaffham PE37 8ER* Tel (01760) 721292

BROWN, Charles Henry. b 48. Tulane Univ (USA) BA70 Ch Coll Cam BA75 MA81. Westcott Ho Cam. **d** 00 **p** 01. C Boston *Linc* 00-03; Lect 03-05; Lic Preacher 05-06; P-in-c Crowland from 06. *The Abbey Rectory, East Street, Crowland, Peterborough PE6 0EN* Tel (01733) 211763

BROWN, Charles Hubert. b 21. S'wark Ord Course 82. **d** 84 **p** 85. NSM Shortlands *Roch* 84-86; P-in-c Seal St Lawr 86-90; P-in-c Underriver 86-90; rtd 90; Perm to Offic *Roch* 90-02. *Barton Croft, 11 St Mary's Close, Sevenoaks TN15 8NH* Tel (01732) 882893

BROWN, Mrs Christine Lilian. b 54. Ex Univ BA75 Newc Univ MA93. NEOC 01. **d** 04 **p** 05. NSM Ponteland *Newc* from 04; Chapl St Oswald's Hospice Newc from 08. *4 Woodlands, Ponteland, Newcastle upon Tyne NE20 9EU* Tel (01661) 824196

BROWN, Christopher. b 38. AKC62 CQSW68. St Boniface Warminster 62. **d** 63 **p** 64. C Crofton Park St Hilda w St Cypr *S'wark* 63-64; C S Beddington St Mich 64-67; C Herne Hill St Paul 67-68; Lic to Offic *S'wark* 68-72; *Lich* 72-74; *Birm* 74-76; *Worc* 76-79; *Ox* 79-86; Perm to Offic *Chelmsf* from 86; Dir and Chief Exec NSPCC 89-95. *7 Baronia Croft, Colchester CO4 9EE* Tel (01206) 852904 E-mail chribrow@yahoo.co.uk

BROWN, Christopher. b 43. Linc Th Coll 79. **d** 81 **p** 82. C Stafford St Jo *Lich* 81-85; V Alton w Bradley-le-Moors and Oakamoor w Cotton 85-94; Chapl Asst Nottm City Hosp NHS Trust 94-05; Sen Chapl 05-06; rtd 06. *3 Kingsbury Drive, Nottingham NG8 3EP* Tel 0115-929 4821 E-mail revbrowncj@aol.com

BROWN, Christopher Charles. b 58. Univ of Wales (Cardiff) LLB79 Solicitor 82. Westcott Ho Cam 87. **d** 90 **p** 91. C Taunton St Mary *B & W* 90-94; R Timsbury and Priston 94-00; P-in-c Urmston *Man* from 00; AD Stretford from 05. *St Clement's Vicarage, 24 Stretford Road, Urmston, Manchester M41 9JZ* Tel 0161-748 3972
E-mail christopher56.brown@mypostoffice.co.uk

BROWN, Christopher David. b 49. Birm Univ BEd72. St Mich Coll Llan 92. **d** 94 **p** 95. C Swansea St Thos and Kilvey *S & B* 94-96; C Swansea St Jas 96-98; St Helena 99-01; Chapl and Hd RS Epsom Coll 01-03; Chapl Ellesmere Coll 03-05. *Flat 1, 13 Worcester Road, Malvern WR14 4QY*
E-mail kristophdavid@hotmail.com

BROWN, Christopher Edgar Newall. b 31. Oak Hill Th Coll 51. **d** 55 **p** 56. C Surbiton Hill Ch Ch *S'wark* 55-57; C Gipsy Hill Ch Ch 57-61; V Plumstead All SS 61-70; V Sissinghurst *Cant* 70-73; P-in-c Frittenden 72-73; V Sissinghurst w Frittenden 73-76; Perm to Offic *S & M* 84-91 and from 96; Bp's Dom Chapl 91-95; rtd 96. *21 College Green, Castletown, Isle of Man IM9 1BE* Tel (01624) 822364

BROWN, Canon Christopher Francis. b 44. Sarum Th Coll 68. **d** 71 **p** 72. C High Wycombe *Ox* 71-74; C Sherborne w Castleton and Lillington *Sarum* 74-77; P-in-c Wylye, Fisherton Delamere and the Langfords 77-79; R Yarnbury 79-82; R Portland All SS w St Pet 82-88; RD Weymouth 85-88; R Trowbridge St Jas 88-07; R Trowbridge St Jas and Keevil 07-09; Chapl Trowbridge and Distr Hosp 88-95; RD Bradford 94-01; Can and Preb Sarum Cathl 98-09; rtd 09; Perm to Offic *B & W* and *Sarum* from 09. *4 Alum Close, Trowbridge BA14 7HD* Tel (01225) 354811

BROWN, Christopher Howard. b 49. **d** 03 **p** 04. OLM Uttoxeter Area *Lich* from 03. *21 Carter Street, Uttoxeter ST14 8EY* Tel (01889) 567492 E-mail revchrishbrown@aol.co.uk

BROWN, Christopher James. b 50. Open Univ BA92. Trin Coll Bris 91. **d** 93 **p** 94. C Skelmersdale St Paul *Liv* 93-97; Chapl Asst Salford R Hosps NHS Trust 97-03; Chapl Trafford Healthcare NHS Trust from 03. *Trafford Healthcare NHS Trust, Moorside Road, Davyhulme, Manchester M41 5SL* Tel 0161-748 4022 *or* 746 2624

BROWN, Clive Lindsey. b 33. Southn Univ BA55. Oak Hill Th Coll 57. **d** 59 **p** 60. C Becontree St Mary *Chelmsf* 59-62; P-in-c Balgowlah w Manly Vale Australia 62-69; P-in-c Balgowlah Heights 66-69; R 69-72; R Roseville E 72-98; rtd 98. *80 Bower Street, Manly NSW 2095, Australia* Tel (0061) (2) 9977 2546

BROWN, Prof Colin. b 32. Liv Univ BA53 Lon Univ BD58 Nottm Univ MA61 DD94 Bris Univ PhD70. Tyndale Hall Bris 55. **d** 58 **p** 59. C Chilwell *S'well* 58-61; Lect Tyndale Hall Bris 61-78; Vice Prin 67-70; Dean Studies 70-71; Prof Systematic Th Fuller Th Sem California USA from 78; Assoc R Altadena St Mark from 80; Assoc Dean Adv Th Studies 88-97; rtd 00. *1024 Beverly Way, Altadena CA 91001-2516, USA* Tel (001) (626) 798 7180 E-mail colbrn@fuller.edu

BROWN, David Andrew. b 72. York Univ BA93. Wycliffe Hall Ox BTh04. **d** 04 **p** 05. C Rugby St Matt *Cov* 04-08; P-in-c Budbrooke from 08. *23 Robins Grove, Warwick CV34 6RF* Tel (01926) 497298

BROWN, David Charles Girdlestone. b 42. Solicitor 67. S'wark Ord Course 87. **d** 90 **p** 91. NSM Milford *Guildf* 90-92; NSM Haslemere 92-00; NSM Haslemere and Grayswood 00-01; Perm to Offic *Chich* 02-04; Lic to Offic 04-08; P-in-c Barlavington, Burton w Coates, Sutton and Bignor from 08. *The Rectory, The Street, Sutton, Pulborough RH20 1PS* Tel (01798) 869220
E-mail david.brown@bignor.net

BROWN, David Frederick. b 38. Illinois Univ BA60. Seabury-Western Th Sem MDiv67. **d** 67 **p** 67. C Evanston St Mark USA 67-68; C Camarillo St Columba 68-69; P-in-c 69-70; C San Francisco H Innocents and C Grace Cathl 70-75; Hon C Battersea Ch and St Steph *S'wark* 78-83; Sen Chapl R Marsden NHS Trust 83-00; rtd 00; Perm to Offic *Lon* from 02. *12 Caversham House, 21-25 Caversham Street, London SW3 4AE* Tel (020) 7352 3457

BROWN, Canon David Lloyd. b 44. TCD BTh90. **d** 86 **p** 87. C Cregagh *D & D* 86-91; Bp's C Knocknagoney from 91; Can Down Cathl from 07. *The Aslan Centre, 13A Knocknagoney Road, Belfast BT4 2NR* Tel and fax (028) 9076 0420
E-mail aslan@tesco.net

BROWN, David Mark. b 67. Bp Grosseteste Coll BSc93. Oak Hill Th Coll 05. **d** 07. C Sidmouth, Woolbrook, Salcombe Regis,

Sidbury etc *Ex* from 07. *25 Lymebourne Park, Sidmouth EX10 9HZ* Tel (01395) 579316 Mobile 07814-911937 E-mail daveandjudybrown@aol.com

BROWN, David Victor Arthur. b 44. Em Coll Cam BA66 MA70 CertEd. Linc Th Coll 72. **d** 74 **p** 75. C Bourne *Linc* 74-77; Chapl St Steph Coll Broadstairs 77-79; Chapl Asst N Gen Hosp Sheff 81-84; C Sheff St Cuth 81-84; Chapl Ridge Lea Hosp *Lanc* 84-92; Chapl Lanc Moor Hosp 84-92; Chapl Lanc Priority Services NHS Trust 92-98; Chapl Lanc R Infirmary 87-92; Chapl Lanc Acute Hosps NHS Trust 92-98; Chapl Morecambe Bay Hosps NHS Trust from 98; Chapl Morecambe Bay Primary Care Trust from 98; Hon C Scorton and Barnacre and Calder Vale *Blackb* from 06. *Chaplain's Office, Royal Lancaster Infirmary, Ashton Road, Lancaster LA1 4RP* Tel (01524) 583955, 762800 *or* 791229 E-mail dlgbrown@aol.com

BROWN, Prof David William. b 48. Edin Univ MA70 Oriel Coll Ox BA72 Clare Coll Cam PhD76 FBA02. Westcott Ho Cam 75. **d** 76 **p** 77. Chapl, Fell and Tutor Oriel Coll Ox 76-90; Van Mildert Prof Div Dur Univ 90-07; Can Res Dur Cathl 90-07; Wardlaw Prof St Andr Univ from 07. *St Mary's College, University of St Andrews, St Andrews KY16 9JU* E-mail dwb21@st-andrews.ac.uk

BROWN, Dennis Cockburn. b 27. Hatf Coll Dur BSc48 K Coll Dur PhD54. WMMTC 79. **d** 82 **p** 83. C Bilton *Cov* 82-84; V Wolford w Burmington 84-96; R Cherington w Stourton 84-96; R Barcheston 84-96; rtd 96; Perm to Offic *Cov* from 96; Dioc Rtd Clergy and Widows Officer from 98. *13 Cleveland Court, 41 Kenilworth Road, Leamington Spa CV32 6JA* Tel (01926) 423771

BROWN, Derek. *See* BROWN, John Derek

BROWN, Derek Henry Pridgeon. b 46. Cam Coll of Art and Tech BA67 Leeds Univ PGCE71. St Steph Ho Ox 90. **d** 92 **p** 93. C Finchley St Mary *Lon* 92-95; C W Hampstead St Jas 95-99; V Eyres Monsell *Leic* 99-08; TV Leic Presentation from 08. *11 Dixon Drive, Leicester LE2 1RA* Tel 0116-270 9750 E-mail dbrown@leicester.anglican.org

BROWN, Canon Donald Fryer. b 31. St Jo Coll Dur BA56. Cranmer Hall Dur 60. **d** 61 **p** 62. Min Can Bradf Cathl 61-64; C Bingley All SS 64-66; V Low Moor H Trin 66-97; Hon Can Bradf Cathl 85-97; RD Bowling and Horton 87-95; rtd 97; Perm to Offic *Bradf* from 98. *3 Northfield Gardens, Wibsey, Bradford BD6 1LQ* Tel (01274) 671869 E-mail don-brown@supanet.com

BROWN, Mrs Doreen Marion. b 39. Cam Univ CertEd67. NOC 85. **d** 88 **p** 94. Par Dn Axminster, Chardstock, Combe Pyne and Rousdon *Ex* 88-92; Ind Chapl *Linc* 92-98; TV Brumby 98-05; rtd 05. *7 Thorngarth Lane, Barrow-upon-Humber DN19 7AW* Tel (01469) 532102 E-mail doreen.bn@lineone.net

BROWN, Douglas Adrian Spencer. b 29. Univ of W Aus BA50 MA71 K Coll Lon MTh90. St Mich Th Coll Crafers 50. **d** 53 **p** 54. SSM 54-00; Chapl St Mich Th Coll Crafers Australia 54-60; Chapl Kelham Th Coll 60-66; Chapl Univ of W Aus 66-71; P-in-c Canberra St Alb 71-75; Warden St Mich Th Coll Crafers 75-82; P-in-c Adelaide St Jo 78-82; Academic Dean Adelaide Coll of Div 79-81; President 88; Visiting Scholar Union Th Sem NY 82; Perm to Offic *Lon* 88 90; Chapl Bucharest w Sofia *Eur* 90-91; Dir Angl Cen Rome 91-95; Chapl Palermo w Taormina *Eur* 95-96; Lect Newton Th Coll Papua New Guinea 97; Perm to Offic *Dur* 97-00 and *S'wark* 99-00; Dir Nor Cathl Inst and Hon PV Nor Cathl 00-02. *75/6 Manning Terrace, South Perth WA 6151, Australia* Tel (0061) (8) 9368 0014 E-mail douglasbrown01@dodo.com.au

BROWN, Mrs Elizabeth Alexandra Mary Gordon. b 67. Westcott Ho Cam 06. **d** 08 **p** 09. C Merrow *Guildf* from 08. *42 Finches Rise, Guildford GU1 2UW* Tel (01483) 560553 Mobile 07768-075803

BROWN, Ms Elizabeth Ann. b 43. **d** 00 **p** 01. OLM W Bromwich All SS *Lich* 01-08; OLM Wednesbury St Paul Wood Green from 08. *307 Beaconview Road, West Bromwich B71 3PS* Tel 0121-588 7530 E-mail e.a.brown@talktalk.net

BROWN, Miss Elizabeth Charlotte (Beth). b 54. Bris Univ BSc76 PGCE77. Trin Coll Bris 93. **d** 95 **p** 96. C Taunton Lyngford *B & W* 95-99; TV Bath Twerton-on-Avon 99-06; C N Swindon St Andr *Bris* from 06. *8 Figsbury Close, Swindon SN25 1UA* Tel (01793) 747493 E-mail revbethbrown@hotmail.com

BROWN, Eric. b 28. Leeds Univ BA98. NW Ord Course 73. **d** 76 **p** 77. NSM S Kirkby *Wakef* 76-83; NSM Knottingley 83-94; NSM Kellington w Whitley 89-94; Sub Chapl HM Pris Lindholme 90-94; Perm to Offic from 94. *Wynberg, Barnsley Road, South Kirby, Pontefract WF9 3BG* Tel (01977) 643683

BROWN, Canon Ernest George. b 23. Em Coll Cam BA51 MA56. Oak Hill Th Coll 52. **d** 53 **p** 54. C Darfield *Sheff* 53-56; V Ardsley 56-66; V Thurnby w Stoughton *Leic* 67-90; RD Gartree II 78-90; Hon Can Leic Cathl 82-90, rtd 90; Perm to Offic *Leic* 90-04. *16 Holbeck Drive, Broughton Astley, Leicester LE9 6UR* Tel (01455) 285458

BROWN, Ernest Harry. b 32. St Mich Coll Llan. **d** 59 **p** 60. C Swansea St Pet *S & B* 59-62; C Gowerton w Waunarlwydd 62-68; CF (TA) 62-68; Chapl to the Deaf *S & B* 68-98; rtd 98.

Montreaux, 30 Lon Cedwyn, Sketty, Swansea SA2 0TH Tel (01792) 207628

BROWN, Frank Seymour. b 10. S'wark Ord Course 62 St Aug Coll Cant 65. **d** 65 **p** 66. C Bexleyheath Ch Ch *Roch* 65-70; R Cratfield w Heveningham and Ubbeston *St E* 70-76; rtd 76; Perm to Offic *St E* 76-86 and *St Alb* 86-07; P-in-c Ixworth and Ixworth Thorpe *St E* 78; P-in-c Euston w Barnham and Fakenham 80. *3 Windsor Gardens, Bedford MK40 3BU* Tel (01234) 210999

BROWN, Geoffrey Alan. b 34. **d** 99 **p** 00. OLM Bury St Edmunds St Mary *St E* 99-07; rtd 07; Perm to Offic *St E* from 07. *Rodenkirchen, 12 Sharp Road, Bury St Edmunds IP33 2NB* Tel (01284) 769725

BROWN, Geoffrey Gilbert. b 38. Dur Univ BA62 DipEd63 Fitzw Coll Cam BA69 MA73 FBIS. Westcott Ho Cam 67. **d** 70 **p** 71. C Gosforth All SS *Newc* 70-73; Chapl Dauntsey's Sch Devizes 73-76; Chapl St Paul's Colleg Sch Hamilton NZ 76-78; V Barrow St Aid *Carl* 79-86; Chapl Ch Coll Canterbury NZ 86-90; C Digswell and Panshanger *St Alb* 91-93; Chapl E Herts Hospice Care 94-07; rtd 07. *32 Uplands, Welwyn Garden City AL8 7EW* Tel (01707) 327565

BROWN, Canon Geoffrey Harold. b 30. Trin Hall Cam BA54 MA58. Cuddesdon Coll 54. **d** 56 **p** 57. C Plaistow St Andr *Chelmsf* 56-60; C Birm St Pet 60-63; R Birm St Geo 63-73; TR Gt Grimsby St Mary and St Jas *Linc* 73-85; Can and Preb Linc Cathl 79-85; V St Martin-in-the-Fields *Lon* 85-95; rtd 95; Perm to Offic *Worc* from 95. *8 Worcester Close, Hagley, Stourbridge DY9 0NP* Tel (01562) 886921

BROWN, Graham Stanley. b 51. Sarum & Wells Th Coll 82. **d** 84 **p** 85. C Crediton and Shobrooke *Ex* 84-87; Chapl RAF 87-93 and 99-06; R Elgin w Lossiemouth *Mor* 93-98; R Castle Douglas *Glas* 98-99; Chapl Sherwood Forest Hosps NHS Trust 06-09; Chapl Univ Hosps Bris NHS Foundn Trust from 09. *Trust Headquarters, Marlborough Street, Bristol BS1 3NU* Tel 0117-342 0607 E-mail the.chaplaincy@uhbristol.nhs.uk

BROWN, Mrs Harriet Nina. b 37. Open Univ BA77 Lon Univ CertEd57. Gilmore Course 80 Oak Hill Th Coll 83. **dss** 83 **d** 87 **p** 94. Greenstead *Chelmsf* 83-90; Par Dn 87-90; Asst Chapl R Hosp Sch Holbrook 90-93; Perm to Offic *Chelmsf* from 93 and *St E* 93-96; P-in-c Gt and Lt Blakenham w Baylham and Nettlestead *St E* 96-01; rtd 01. *22 Gainsborough Road, Colchester CO3 4QN* Tel (01206) 523072

BROWN, Ian Barry. b 53. St Cuth Soc Dur BA80 PGCE81. Sarum & Wells Th Coll 84. **d** 86 **p** 87. C Winchmore Hill St Paul *Lon* 86-89; Hon Chapl Chase Farm Hosp Enfield 86-88; Hon Chapl Harley Street Area Hosps 88-90; Hon Chapl RAM 89; C St Marylebone w H Trin 89-94; rtd 94; Hon Chapl Regent's Coll Lon 96-05. *41 Allworth Drive, Davidson, Sydney NSW 2085, Australia* Tel and fax (0061) (2) 9975 3003

BROWN, Ian David. b 53. UEA BA76. Wycliffe Hall Ox BA80. **d** 81 **p** 82. C Southsea St Jude *Portsm* 81-84; Chapl Coll of SS Paul and Mary Cheltenham 84-89; V Lt Heath *St Alb* 89-05; V Frindsbury w Upnor and Chattenden *Roch* from 05. *Frindsbury Vicarage, 4 Parsonage Lane, Rochester ME2 4UR* Tel (01634) 717580

BROWN, Canon Jack Robin. b 44. Linc Th Coll 67. **d** 69 **p** 70. C Canning Town St Cedd *Chelmsf* 69-72; C Dunstable *St Alb* 72-78; V Luton St Andr 78-85; V Kempston Transfiguration 85-00; RD Bedford 92-95; Hon Can St Alb from 97; Dioc Officer for Local Min from 00. *St John's House, High Street, Markyate, St Albans AL3 8PD* Tel and fax (01582) 842151 E-mail lmo@stalbans.anglican.org

BROWN, Jacqueline. b 08. NSM Newton Longville and Mursley w Swanbourne etc *Ox* from 08. *Address temp unknown* E-mail jackie.br@tiscali.co.uk

BROWN, James Douglas. b 52. S'wark Ord Course 93. **d** 96 **p** 97. NSM Shooters Hill Ch Ch *S'wark* 96-01; P-in-c E Malling *Roch* 02-07; P-in-c Wateringbury and Teston 02-07; V E Malling, Wateringbury and Teston from 07; RD Malling from 07. *The Vicarage, 2 The Grange, East Malling, West Malling ME19 6AH* Tel and fax (01732) 843282 Mobile 07957-906297 E-mail james.brown@diocese-rochester.org

BROWN, Canon James Michael. b 49. Newc Univ Aus BA90. St Jo Coll Morpeth ThL78. **d** 77 **p** 78. Australia 77-81 and 02-05; C Gosford 77-79; C Cessnock 79-81; C Eyres Monsell *Leic* 81-83; C Entrance 83; P-in-c Windale 83-88; R Morpeth 88-97; Acting Registrar Wangaratta 98-02; Dom Chapl to Bp Wangaratta and Dir Min Tr 98-02; Adn The Hume 99-02; V Knowle H Nativity *Bris* from 02; P-in-c Easton All Hallows 02-03; Hon Can Wangaratta from 02. *Holy Nativity Vicarage, 41 Lilymead Avenue, Bristol BS4 2BY* Tel and fax 0117-977 4260 E-mail frjames@holynativity.org.uk

BROWN, Canon James Philip. b 30. Ex Coll Ox BA54 MA55. Westcott Ho Cam 54. **d** 56 **p** 57. C Hemel Hempstead *St Alb* 56-63; V Hellesdon *Nor* 63-71; P-in-c Kirkley w Lowestoft St Jo 71-79; TV Lowestoft St Marg 76-78; TV Lowestoft and Kirkley 79-81; P-in-c Northleach w Hampnett and Farmington *Glouc* 81-95; RD Northleach 83-92; P-in-c Cold Aston w Notgrove and Turkdean 86-95; Hon Can Glouc Cathl 91-95; rtd 95; Perm to

Offic *Ex* from 95. *The Priest's House, 1 St Scholastica's Abbey, Teignmouth TQ14 8FF* Tel (01626) 773623

BROWN, Jane Madeline. *See* SHARP, Mrs Jane Madeline

BROWN, Mrs Jean. b 49. WEMTC 05. **d** 08 **p** 09. NSM Lechlade *Glouc* 08; NSM Fairford Deanery from 09. *The Colt, Whelford, Fairford GL7 4EA* Tel (01285) 712503 Mobile 07957-657935 E-mail jeanbrown50@mail.com

BROWN, Jennifer. b 44. Guy's Hosp Medical Sch MSc91 Southn Univ BDS67 Open Univ BA81. Ripon Coll Cuddesdon 08. **d** 09. *18A Main Road, Littleton, Winchester SO22 6PS* Tel (01962) 888593 Mobile 07870-772905 E-mail jenniferandjosie@hotmail.com

BROWN, Mrs Jennifer Elizabeth. b 70. Geo Mason Univ Virginia BSc91. SAOMC 02. **d** 05 **p** 06. C Ox St Clem 05-08; Chapl Jes Coll Ox 09. *49 Laburnum Road, Oxford OX2 9EN* Tel (01865) 279757 E-mail chaplain@jesus.ox.ac.uk *or* chaplain@jenbrown.org.uk

BROWN, Jenny. b 78. St Martin's Coll Lanc BA99. Oak Hill Th Coll BA03. **d** 03 **p** 04. C Hyde St Geo *Ches* 03-06; C Weaverham from 06. *The Vicarage, Church Street, Weaverham, Northwich CW8 3NJ* Tel (01606) 852110 E-mail revjennybrown@yahoo.co.uk

BROWN, Mrs Joan Leslie. b 31. SS Hild & Bede Coll Dur CertEd55. Oak Hill Th Coll BA85. **dss** 85 **d** 87 **p** 94. Fulwood *Sheff* 85-88; Par Dn 87-88; TD Netherthorpe 88-93; NSM Ellesmere St Pet 93-99; rtd 99; Perm to Offic *Sheff* from 00. *15 Dover Gardens, Sheffield S3 7LB* Tel 0114-273 1364

BROWN, John. b 64. Kent Univ BA86. Westcott Ho Cam 87. **d** 90 **p** 91. C Lt Ilford St Mich *Chelmsf* 90-94; C E Ham w Upton Park St Alb 94; TV 94-01; P-in-c Gt Ilford St Luke from 01. *St Luke's Vicarage, Baxter Road, Ilford IG1 2HN* Tel (020) 8478 1248 *or* 8553 7606 E-mail livingfaith@stluke-ilford.org.uk

BROWN, Canon John Bruce. b 42. Nottm Univ BA64 MA68. Cuddesdon Coll 64. **d** 66 **p** 67. C Warwick St Nic *Cov* 66-71; C Bp's Hatfield *St Alb* 71-78; V Watford St Mich 78-08; RD Watford 94-99; Hon Can St Alb 02-08; rtd 08. *Broomfield Cottage, Poffley End, Hailey, Witney OX29 9US* Tel (01993) 703029 E-mail john.brown420@ntlworld.com

BROWN, John Derek. b 41. Linc Th Coll 71. **d** 73 **p** 74. C Rotherham *Sheff* 73-76; P-in-c V Pinchbeck *Linc* 76-78; V Surfleet 76-82; R Boultham 83-94; RD Christianity 85-92; P-in-c Epworth and Wroot 94-97; R Epworth Gp 97-05; RD Is of Axholme 96-05; Can and Preb Linc Cathl 88-05; rtd 05. *rue de l'École, Chille, 16140 Oradour, France* Tel (0033) (5) 45 25 39 06 E-mail jbrown@wanadoo.fr

BROWN, John Dixon. b 28. Pemb Coll Cam BA52. Oak Hill Th Coll 52. **d** 54 **p** 55. C Worthing St Geo *Chich* 54-57; C S w N Bersted 57-63; V W Hampnett 63-91; rtd 91; Perm to Offic *Chich* from 91. *3 Manor Way, Elmer, Bognor Regis PO22 6LA* Tel (01243) 583449

BROWN, Canon John Duncan. b 43. St Pet Coll Ox BA64 BA66 MA68 Lon Univ BSc. Wycliffe Hall Ox 65. **d** 67 **p** 68. C Kingston upon Hull H Trin *York* 67-69; C St Leonards St Leon *Chich* 69-72; Hon C Norbiton *S'wark* 72-75; C Kirkcaldy *St And* 75-78; Prec and Chapl Chelmsf Cathl 78-86; P-in-c Kelvedon Hatch 86-92; P-in-c Navestock 86-92; P-in-c Fryerning w Margaretting 92-99; Bp's ACORA Officer 92-99; Hon Can Chelmsf Cathl 93-03; rtd 99. *556 Galleywood Road, Chelmsford CM2 8BX* Tel (01245) 358185

BROWN, Canon John Roger. b 37. AKC60. **d** 61 **p** 62. C New Eltham All SS *S'wark* 61-64; C Bexhill St Pet *Chich* 64-68; V Eastbourne St Elisabeth 68-75; V E Grinstead St Swithun 75-97; Chapl Qu Victoria Hosp NHS Trust East Grinstead 75-97; Perm to Offic *Chich* 97-99; RD E Grinstead 82-93; Can and Preb Chich Cathl 89-98; TV Worth 00-04; rtd 05. *120 Malthouse Road, Crawley RH10 6BH* Tel (01293) 520454 E-mail jroger.brown@tesco.net

BROWN, John William Etheridge. b 13. St Pet Hall Ox BA35 MA39. Wycliffe Hall Ox 35. **d** 37 **p** 38. C Stratford New Town St Paul *Chelmsf* 37-40; C Rawtenstall St Mary *Man* 40-42; V Thame *Ox* 42-45; OCF 43-45; V St Keverne *Truro* 45-51; V Hoo All Hallows w Stoke *Roch* 51-55; V Crich *Derby* 55-61; V Leusden *Ex* 61-79; V Widecombe in the Moor 61-79; P-in-c Holne 70-74; P-in-c Princetown 74-79; RD Moreton 74-80; Asst Chapl HM Pris Dartmoor 75-82; V Widecombe, Leusden and Princetown etc *Ex* 79-82; rtd 82; Lic to Offic *Ex* from 82. *8 Emmetts Park, Ashburton, Newton Abbot TQ13 7DB* Tel (01364) 653072

BROWN, Jonathan. b 60. Univ Coll Dur BA83 MA85 Ex Univ CertEd86. Ripon Coll Cuddesdon 86 Ch Div Sch of the Pacific

(USA) 88. **d** 89 **p** 90. C Esher *Guildf* 89-97; TV Crawley *Chich* 97-04; Chapl St Cath Hospice 97-04; V Earlsfield St Andr *S'wark* from 04. *22 St Andrew's Court, Waynflete Street, London SW18 3QF* Tel (020) 8946 4214

BROWN, Prof Judith Margaret. b 44. Girton Coll Cam MA69 PhD68 Natal Univ Hon DSocSc01. Ripon Coll Cuddesdon 09. **d** 09. NSM N Hinksey and Wytham *Ox* from 09; Asst Chapl Ball Coll Ox from 09. *97 Victoria Road, Oxford OX2 7QG* Tel (01865) 514486

BROWN, Mrs Kathleen Margaret. b 40. MBE07. QUB BD BTh. **d** 88 **p** 90. C Carrickfergus *Conn* 88-92; I Belfast St Paul w St Barn 92-07; Can Belf Cathl 00-07; rtd 07. *3 The Avenue, Carrickfergus BT38 8LT* Tel (028) 9335 9273

BROWN, Keith Michael. b 42. **d** 07 **p** 08. OLM Earlham *Nor* from 07. *115 Colman Road, Norwich NR4 7HF* Tel (01603) 464707 E-mail keith.brown93@ntlworld.com

BROWN, Kenneth Arthur Charles. b 27. ACP65. **d** 84 **p** 85. OLM Ingoldsby *Linc* 84-97. *11 Ingoldsby Road, Lenton, Grantham NG33 4HB* Tel (01476) 85763

BROWN, Kenneth Roger. b 48. St Chad's Coll Dur BA69. Liturg Inst Trier 72. **d** 73 **p** 74. C Patchway *Bris* 73-77; C Fishponds St Jo 77-79; Chapl RAF 79-95; Chapl HM Pris Pentonville 95-96; Chapl HM Pris Wellingborough 96-98; Perm to Offic *B & W* 99-00; P-in-c Crook Peak from 00. *The Rectory, Sparrow Hill Way, Weare, Axbridge BS26 2LE* Tel (01934) 733140 E-mail rev_ken_brown@hotmail.com

BROWN (*née* BOWERS), Lady (Denise Frances). b 50. City Univ BSc72. SAOMC 99. **d** 02 **p** 03. NSM Beedon and Peasemore w W Ilsley and Farnborough *Ox* from 02; NSM Brightwalton w Catmore, Leckhampstead etc from 05. *Bridleway Cottage, Stanmore, Beedon, Newbury RG20 8SR* Tel and fax (01635) 281825 Mobile 07901-914975

BROWN, Miss Louise Margaret. b 53. MBE05. Trin Coll Bris 80. **dss** 83 **d** 87 **p** 94. Woodley St Jo the Ev *Ox* 84-87; Par Dn Woodley 87-92; Asst Chapl Reading Hosps 92-94; C Shinfield 93-94; P-in-c Dedworth from 94; P-in-c Clewer St Andr from 04. *3 Convent Court, Hatch Lane, Windsor SL4 3QR*

BROWN, Malcolm Arthur. b 54. Oriel Coll Ox BA76 MA82 Man Univ PhD00. Westcott Ho Cam 77. **d** 79 **p** 80. C Riverhead w Dunton Green *Roch* 79-83; TV Southampton (City Cen) *Win* 83-91; Assoc Dir Wm Temple Foundn 91-93; Exec Sec 93-00; Hon C Heaton Moor *Man* 95-00; Prin EAMTC *Ely* 00-05; Prin ERMC 05-07; Dir Miss and Public Affairs Abps' Coun from 07. *Church House, Great Smith Street, London SW1P 3AZ* Tel (020) 7898 1000 E-mail malcolm.brown@c-of-e.org.uk

BROWN (*née* PATTERSON), Mrs Marjorie Jean. b 54. Wooster Coll USA BA76 K Coll Lon MA04. S Dios Minl Tr Scheme 92. **d** 95 **p** 96. C Poplar *Lon* 95-99; P-in-c Stamford Hill St Thos 99-02; V 02-09; P-in-c Upper Clapton St Matt 06-08; Dean of Women's Min Stepney Area 02-07; V Primrose Hill St Mary w Avenue Road St Paul from 09. *St Mary's Vicarage, 44 King Henry's Road, London NW3 3RP* Tel (020) 7722 3062 Fax 07092-189271 E-mail revmarjorie@gmail.com

BROWN, Mark Edward. b 61. Southn Univ BSc83 Cam Univ PGCE84 Brunel Univ MTh98. Trin Coll Bris BA88. **d** 89 **p** 90. C Egham *Guildf* 88-92; C Northwood Em *Lon* 92-96; Assoc V 96-02; Bp's Officer for Evang 96-02; Can Missr *S'well* 02-07; Hon Can S'well Minster 02-07; P-in-c Tonbridge SS Pet and Paul *Roch* from 07. *The Vicarage, Church Street, Tonbridge TN9 1HD* Tel (01732) 770962 E-mail revmbrown@aol.com

BROWN, Martin Warwick. b 65. BSc MA. ERMC. **d** 07 **p** 08. NSM St Alb St Mary Marshalswick *St Alb* from 07. *Waterdell, Chequers Lane, Watford WD25 0GR* Tel (01923) 682763 *or* 672782

BROWN, Michael Brian. b 56. Trin Coll Bris BA97 Coll of Resurr Mirfield 98. **d** 99 **p** 00. C Trowbridge St Jas *Sarum* 99-02; C Bruton and Distr *B & W* 02-09; C Bickleigh and Shaugh Prior *Ex* from 09; Chapl Plymouth Hosps NHS Trust from 09. *The Vicarage, 2 Blackeven Close, Roborough, Plymouth PL5 7AX* Tel (01752) 782926 E-mail fr.michaelbrown@btopenworld.com

BROWN, Murray. *See* BROWN, Phillip Murray

BROWN, Nicholas Francis Palgrave. b 23. Fitzw Ho Cam BA51 MA54. **d** 53 **p** 54. C Warwick St Nic *Cov* 53-55; C Birm St Paul 55-60; V Temple Balsall 60-66; Gen Sec Ind Chr Fellowship 66-76; V St Kath Cree *Lon* 66-71; Chapl and Dir of Studies Holland Ho Cropthorne 76-80; P-in-c Cropthorne w Charlton *Worc* 76-88; Adult Educn Officer 80-85; rtd 88; Perm to Offic *Worc* from 88. *Bredon View, Rear of 40 Bridge Street, Pershore WR10 1AT* Tel (01386) 556816

BROWN, Nicholas James Watson. b 76. R Holloway Coll Lon BMus98 Lon Inst of Educn PGCE99 ACertCM97. Ripon Coll Cuddesdon 08. **d** 09. C Warminster St Denys and Upton Scudamore *Sarum* from 09. *22 Minster View, Warminster BA12 8TD* Tel (01985) 211049 Mobile 07901-852198 E-mail njwbrown@btinternet.com

BROWN, Nina. *See* BROWN, Mrs Harriet Nina

BROWN, Canon Norman Charles Harry. b 27. Univ of Wales BSc46. St Mich Coll Llan 48. **d** 50 **p** 51. C Canton St Jo *Llan* 50-57; C Llanishen and Lisvane 58-63; V Miskin 63-97; RD

Aberdare 82-97; Can Llan Cathl 86-97; rtd 97. *33 Bron y Deri, Mountain Ash CF45 4LL* Tel (01443) 476631

BROWN, Canon Norman John. b 34. Thames Poly MA90. Ripon Hall Ox 72. **d** 74 **p** 75. C High Wycombe *Ox* 74-78; V Tilehurst St Cath 78-82; V Boyne Hill 82-04; Chapl Windsor and Maidenhead Coll 87-89; Hon Can Ch Ch *Ox* 03-04; rtd 04; Perm to Offic *Ox* from 04. *Chantry House, Radley Road, Abingdon OX14 3SL* Tel (01235) 553454 E-mail revbrown@waitrose.com

BROWN, Patricia Valerie. b 37. CertEd58. STETS BTh95. **d** 98 **p** 99. NSM Tadley St Pet *Win* 98-02; NSM Tadley S and Silchester 02-07; rtd 07. *58 Bowmonts Road, Tadley, Basingstoke RG26 3SB* Tel 0118-981 6109

BROWN, Paul. *See* BROWN, Anthony Paul

BROWN, Paul David Christopher. b 50. Lon Univ LLB71. EMMTC 81. **d** 84 **p** 85. NSM Wollaton *S'well* from 84. *32 Benington Drive, Wollaton, Nottingham NG8 2TF* Tel 0115-928 4493

BROWN, Canon Penelope Jane. b 57. St Steph Ho Ox 94. **d** 96 **p** 97. C Croydon St Jo *S'wark* 96-99; V Croydon St Matt from 99; AD Croydon Cen from 07; Hon Can S'wark Cathl from 08. *The Vicarage, 7 Brownlow Road, Croydon CR0 5JT* Tel (020) 8688 5055 E-mail penny@st-matthews.fsnet.co.uk

BROWN, Peter. b 38. Leeds Univ BSc62 PhD65. Nashotah Ho 85. **d** 87 **p** 88. R Minneapolis St Andr USA 87-89; C Sprowston w Beeston *Nor* 89-92; P-in-c W Winch w Setchey and N Runcton 92-98; P-in-c Middleton w E Winch 96-98; P-in-c Nor St Andr and Nor St Geo Colegate 98-99; Chapl Norfolk and Nor Health Care NHS Trust 98-99; rtd 00; Perm to Offic *Leic* from 00. *41 Main Street, Cosby, Leicester LE9 1UW* Tel 0116-286 6184 E-mail peterbrown@tesco.net

BROWN, Canon Peter. b 47. RMN69. Kelham Th Coll 69. **d** 74 **p** 75. CMP from 75; C Hendon *Dur* 74-80; C Byker St Ant *Newc* 80-90; C Brandon and Ushaw Moor *Dur* 90-05; V from 05; Hon Can Dur Cathl from 01. *The Clergy House, Sawmill Lane, Brandon, Durham DH7 8NS* Tel 0191-378 0845

BROWN, Peter. b 53. St Chad's Coll Dur BA75. Sarum & Wells Th Coll 75. **d** 77 **p** 78. C Tunstall Ch Ch *Lich* 77-79; C Tunstall 79-80; C Willenhall H Trin 80-83; V Weston Rhyn 83-88; Australia 88-90; R Hubberston *St D* 90-01; V Chilvers Coton w Astley *Cov* from 01. *Chilvers Coton Vicarage, Coventry Road, Nuneaton CV11 4NJ* Tel (024) 7638 3010

BROWN, Peter Russell. b 43. Oak Hill Th Coll. **d** 71 **p** 72. C Gt Faringdon w Lt Coxwell *Ox* 71-73; C Reading Greyfriars 73-74; V Forty Hill Jes Ch *Lon* 74-81; V Laleham 81-09; rtd 09. *42A Tothill Street, Minster, Ramsgate CT12 4AJ* E-mail margaret.brown64@btinternet.com

BROWN, Peter Thomas. b 43. Leic Univ BSc64. WEMTC 00. **d** 03 **p** 04. OLM Prestbury and All SS *Glouc* 03-08; NSM N Cheltenham from 08. *32 Gallops Lane, Prestbury, Cheltenham GL52 5SD* Tel (01242) 529774 E-mail pete.brown@northchelt.org.uk

BROWN, Philip. *See* BROWN, Canon James Philip

BROWN, Philip Anthony. b 54. Oak Hill Th Coll BA91. **d** 91 **p** 92. C Rock Ferry *Ches* 91-95; V Hattersley 95-98; V Harold Hill St Geo *Chelmsf* 98-09; P-in-c Chartham *Cant* from 09. *The Rectory, The Green, Chartham, Canterbury CT4 7JW* Tel (01227) 738256 E-mail filbrown@btinternet.com

BROWN, Canon Philip Roy. b 41. St Steph Ho Ox 78. **d** 80 **p** 81. C Highters Heath *Birm* 80-83; P-in-c Washwood Heath 83-87; V Tysoe w Oxhill and Whatcote *Cov* 87-93; R Harbury and Ladbroke 93-07; RD Southam 95-97 and 99-02; Hon Can Cov Cathl 00-07; rtd 07. *3 Margetts Close, Kenilworth CV8 1EN* Tel (01926) 850638 E-mail canon.roybrown@lineone.net

BROWN, Phillip. b 75. WEMTC 05. **d** 08. NSM Heref S Wye from 08. *34 Pixley Walk, Hereford HR2 7TA* Tel (01432) 263433 E-mail pbrown777@aol.com

BROWN, Phillip Murray. b 59. Keele Univ BSc80. Trin Coll Bris. **d** 87 **p** 88. C Greasbrough *Sheff* 87-91; Ind Chapl 87-93; V Thorne 91-99; V Norton Lees St Paul *Sheff* from 99. *St Paul's Vicarage, 6 Angerford Avenue, Sheffield S8 9BG* Tel 0114-255 1945 E-mail murray.stpauls@btinternet.com

BROWN, Raymond John. b 49. Ox Univ BEd71. Wycliffe Hall Ox 72. **d** 75 **p** 76. C Barking St Marg w St Patr *Chelmsf* 75-78; C Walton H Trin *Ox* 78-82; V Enfield St Mich *Lon* 82-91; Chapl St Mich Hosp Enfield 82-91; R Springfield All SS *Chelmsf* from 91. *The Rectory, 4 Old School Field, Chelmsford CM1 7HU* Tel (01245) 356720 E-mail raymondjohnbrown@talktalk.net

BROWN, Richard George. b 38. Dur Univ BSc63. Wells Th Coll 63. **d** 65 **p** 66. C Norton St Mary *Dur* 65-69; C N Gosforth *Newc* 69-71; Chapl Wells Cathl Sch 71-81; P-in-c Dulverton and Brushford *B & W* 81-83; R 83-86; Chapl Millfield Jun Sch Somerset 86-89; Chapl Brighton Coll 89-92; Chapl Benenden Sch 92-94; Perm to Offic *Chich* 94-97; rtd 04. *4 Standean Farm Cottages, Standean Farm, Brighton BN1 8ZA* Tel (01273) 501469 E-mail richardgb@uk.gateway.net

BROWN, Richard Lessey. b 27. Keble Coll Ox BA51 MA55. Qu Coll Birm 51. **d** 53 **p** 54. C York St Lawr w St Nic 53-55; C Fulford 55-57; V Fridaythorpe w Fimber and Thixendale 57-61;

V York St Luke 61-75; V Barlby 75-92; rtd 92; Perm to Offic *York* from 92. *1 Kings Court, King Street, Cottingham HU16 5RW* Tel (01482) 845299

BROWN, Robert. b 47. Man Univ BSc72 Open Univ BA86 Dur Univ MA87. NEOC 95. **d** 98 **p** 99. C Yarm *York* 98-01; V Ormesby from 01. *The Vicarage, 54 Church Lane, Ormesby, Middlesbrough TS7 9AU* Tel (01642) 314445

BROWN, Robert Peter Cameron. b 63. K Coll Lon BSc84 Imp Coll Lon MSc87 Lon Bible Coll BA97. Cranmer Hall Dur 01. **d** 03 **p** 04. C Upper Weardale *Dur* 03-08. *Stapleton House, Roweltown, Carlisle CA6 6LD*

BROWN, Robin. *See* BROWN, Canon Jack Robin

BROWN, Robin. b 38. Leeds Univ BA60 MPhil69. Qu Coll Birm 89. **d** 91 **p** 92. C Far Headingley St Chad *Ripon* 91-94; V Hawksworth Wood 94-00; rtd 00; Perm to Offic *Ripon* from 00. *Dale Edge, 2A Harbour View, Bedale DL8 2DQ* Tel and fax (01677) 425483 Mobile 07960-277495 E-mail robin.stel@virgin.net

BROWN, Roger. *See* BROWN, Canon John Roger

BROWN, Roger George. b 37. CQSW. CA Tr Coll SEITE 92. **d** 95 **p** 96. C Maidstone St Martin *Cant* 95-97; C Oakham, Hambleton, Egleton, Braunston and Brooke *Pet* 97-04; Chapl Leics and Rutland Healthcare NHS Trust 97-04; rtd 04; Asst Chapl Kettering Gen Hosp NHS Trust from 04. *5 Valley Walk, Kettering NN16 0LY* Tel (01536) 524954

BROWN, Canon Roger Lee. b 42. Univ of Wales (Lamp) BA63 Univ Coll Lon MA73. Wycliffe Hall Ox 66. **d** 68 **p** 69. C Dinas w Penygraig *Llan* 68-70; C Bargoed and Deri w Brithdir 70-72; TV Glyncorrwg w Afan Vale and Cymmer Afan 72-74; R 74-79; V Tongwynlais 79-93; R Welshpool w Castle Caereinion *St As* 93-07; AD Pool 01-07; Can Cursal St As Cathl 02-07; rtd 07. *14 Berriew Road, Welshpool SY21 7SS* Tel (01938) 552161

✠**BROWN, The Rt Revd Ronald.** b 26. St Jo Coll Dur BA50. **d** 52 **p** 53 **c** 74. C Chorley St Laur *Blackb* 52-56; V Whittle-le-Woods 56-61; V Halliwell St Thos *Man* 61-69; R Ashton St Mich 69-74; RD Ashton-under-Lyne 69-74; Suff Bp Birkenhead *Ches* 74-92; rtd 92; Perm to Offic *Ches* 92-00. *16 Andrew Crescent, Chester CH4 7BQ* Tel (01244) 629955

BROWN, Canon Rosalind. b 53. Lon Univ BA74. Yale Div Sch MDiv97. **d** 97 **p** 97. V Canonsburg St Thos USA 97-99; Vice-Prin OLM Scheme *Sarum* 99-05; Tutor STETS 99-05; Can Res Dur Cathl from 05. *6A The College, Durham DH1 3EQ* Tel 0191-384 2415 Fax 386 4267 E-mail rosalind.brown@durhamcathedral.co.uk

BROWN, Mrs Rosémia. b 53. Ripon Coll Cuddesdon 97. **d** 99 **p** 00. C Shoreditch St Leon and Hoxton St Jo *Lon* 99-00; C Shoreditch St Leon w St Mich 00-02; TV Hackney 02-03; V Clapton St Jas from 03. *134 Rushmore Road, London E5 0EY* Tel (020) 8985 1750

BROWN, Roy. *See* BROWN, Canon Philip Roy

BROWN, Sandra Ann. b 51. **d** 04 **p** 05. OLM Linc St Geo Swallowbeck from 04. *10 Station Road, North Hykeham, Lincoln LN6 9AQ* Tel (01522) 870065 E-mail sandra.brown77@ntlworld.com

BROWN, Sarah. *See* DENNER-BROWN, Mrs Sarah

BROWN, Simon John. b 66. Birm Univ BSc87 PGCE88. St Jo Coll Nottm MA93. **d** 93 **p** 94. C Holbrooks *Cov* 93-97; C Leamington Priors All SS 97-00; C Leamington Spa H Trin and Old Milverton 97-00; P-in-c Woolavington w Cossington and Bawdrip *B & W* 00-01; V 01-05. *Address temp unknown* E-mail simon@vicar.plus.com

BROWN, Canon Simon Nicolas Danton. b 37. Clare Coll Cam BA61 MA65. S'wark Ord Course 61 Linc Th Coll 63. **d** 64 **p** 65. C Lambeth St Mary the Less *S'wark* 64-66; Chapl and Warden LMH Settlement 66-72; P-in-c Southampton St Mary w H Trin *Win* 72-73; TV Southampton (City Cen) 73-79; R Gt Brickhill w Bow Brickhill and Lt Brickhill *Ox* 79-84; TR Burnham w Dropmore, Hitcham and Taplow 84-04; RD Burnham and Slough 87-02; Hon Can Ch Ch 94-04; Dioc Consultant for Deanery Development 97-04; Sen Exec Asst to Bp Buckingham 02-04; rtd 04; Perm to Offic *St E* from 04. *Seagulls, Pin Mill Road, Chelmondiston, Ipswich IP9 1JN* Tel (01473) 780051 E-mail simon.brown1@orange.net

BROWN, Stephen Charles. b 60. Leeds Univ BA83 BA89 Reading Univ PGCE89. Coll of Resurr Mirfield 87. **d** 90 **p** 91. C Whitkirk *Ripon* 90-93; Asst Youth Chapl 92-95; C Chapel Allerton 93-95; R Stanningley St Thos 95-01; Chapl MU 98-01; V Laneside *Blackb* from 01; Hon Chapl ATC 03-07. *St Peter's Vicarage, Helmshore Road, Haslingden, Rossendale BB4 4BG* Tel (01706) 213838 E-mail highlow@talktalk.net

BROWN, Stephen James. b 44. Bradf Univ BTech Ho Cam 71. **d** 72 **p** 73. C Seaton Hirst *Newc* 72-75; C Marton-in-Cleveland *York* 75-77; Dioc Youth Adv *Dur* 77-82; V Thorner *Ripon* 82-92; Chapl Yorkshire TV from 89; Dioc Officer for Local Min 90-09; P-in-c Ripley w Burnt Yates from 92; rtd 09. *88 Prince Rupert Drive, Tockwith, York YO26 7QS* Tel 07929-606217 (mobile) E-mail stephen.brown83@hotmail.co.uk

BROWN, Susan Gertrude. b 48. Univ of Wales (Swansea) BA71 Roehampton Inst PGCE72. St Mich Coll Llan 98. **d** 02 **p** 03. NSM Gelligaer *Llan* 02-04; NSM Eglwysilan 04-07; Lic to Offic 07-08; NSM Caerphilly from 08. *27 Tenby Court, Hendredenny, Caerphilly CF83 2UE* Tel (029) 2086 2736
E-mail suebrown27_uk@yahoo.com

BROWN, Terence George Albert. b 49. SS Mark & Jo Univ Coll Plymouth BEd75. ERMC 04. **d** 06. NSM Langdon Hills *Chelmsf* from 06. *149 Great Berry Lane, Basildon SS16 6BP* Tel (01268) 415947 Mobile 07944-444675
E-mail tgabrown@hotmail.com

✠**BROWN, The Rt Revd Thomas John.** b 43. San Francisco Th Sem DMin84. St Jo Coll Auckland. **d** 72 **p** 73 **c** 91. C Christchurch St Alb New Zealand 72-74; C Leic St Jas 74-76; V Upper Clutha New Zealand 76-79; V Roslyn 79-85; V Lower Hutt St Jas 85-91; Adn Belmont 87-91; Asst Bp Wellington 91-97; Bp Wellington from 97. *20 Eccleston Hill, Wellington 6011, New Zealand* Tel (0064) (4) 472 3183 *or* 472 1057 Fax 499 1360
E-mail bishoptom@paradise.net.nz

BROWN, Mrs Verity Joy. b 68. Qu Mary Coll Lon BA89. Ripon Coll Cuddesdon BTh93. **d** 93 **p** 94. C Barnard Castle w Whorlton *Dur* 93-95; C Bensham 95-97; Perm to Offic from 97. *75 Eamont Gardens, Hartlepool TS26 9JE* Tel (01429) 423186

BROWN, Victor Charles. b 31. S'wark Ord Course 67. **d** 71 **p** 72. C Pinhoe *Ex* 71-73; C Egg Buckland 73-74; C Oakdale St Geo *Sarum* 74-77; R Old Trafford St Hilda *Man* 77-83; R Chigwell Row *Chelmsf* 83-92; R Fenny Bentley, Kniveton, Thorpe and Tissington *Derby* 92-96; rtd 96; Perm to Offic *Sarum* 96-08. *5 Gracey Court, Woodland Road, Broadclyst, Exeter EX5 3GA* Tel (01392) 462799

BROWN, Wallace. b 44. Oak Hill Th Coll 77. **d** 79 **p** 80. C Oadby *Leic* 79-85; V Quinton Road W St Boniface *Birm* 85-03; Hon Can Birm Cathl 01-03; TR Ipsley *Worc* 03-09; rtd 09. *2 Coppice Close, Withington, Hereford HR1 3PP*
E-mail wallace@rncb.ac.uk

BROWNBRIDGE, Bernard Alan. b 19. NW Ord Course 74. **d** 77 **p** 78. NSM Huntington *York* 77-80; V Sand Hutton 80-86; rtd 87; Hon C Birdsall w Langton *York* 87-92; Perm to Offic from 92. *2 Duncombe Close, Malton YO17 7YY* Tel (01653) 697626

BROWNE, Arnold Samuel. b 52. St Jo Coll Ox BA73 MA77 SS Coll Cam PhD87 Surrey Univ MSc89 MBPsS92. Westcott Ho Cam 76. **d** 78 **p** 79. C Esher *Guildf* 78-81; C Worplesdon 81-86; Chapl R Holloway and Bedf New Coll 86-92; Fell and Dean of Chpl Trin Coll Cam 92-06; Perm to Offic *Nor* from 06. *18 Riverside Road, Norwich NR1 1SN* Tel (01603) 629362
E-mail arnoldbrowne@btinternet.com

BROWNE, Aubrey Robert Caulfeild. b 31. Moore Th Coll Sydney 54. **d** 55 **p** 56. Australia 55-71; Producer of Relig Radio Progr USPG 72-84; Hon C S Kensington St Steph *Lon* 78-88; Hd of Area Sec Dept USPG 84-87; P-in-c Nunhead St Antony *S'wark* 88-90; V Nunhead St Antony w St Silas 90-96; rtd 97; Australia from 97. *15 Caroma Avenue, Kyeemagh NSW 2216, Australia* Tel (0061) (2) 9567 5371

BROWNE, Miss Christine Mary. b 53. Nottm Univ BEd75. EMMTC 87. **d** 90 **p** 94. C Bulwell St Mary *S'well* 90-95; TV Hucknall Torkard 95-00; Dep Chapl HM Pris Nor 00-01; Chapl HM YOI Swinfen Hall 01-03; Perm to Offic *Derby* 03-05; P-in-c Dudley St Aug Holly Hall *Worc* 05-09; TV Dudley TM from 09; Chapl Merry Hill Shopping Cen from 05. *St Augustine's Vicarage, 1 Hallchurch Road, Dudley DY2 0TG* Tel (01384) 261026

BROWNE, Herman Beseah. b 65. Cuttington Univ Coll BTh86 K Coll Lon BD90 AKC90 Heythrop Coll Lon PhD94. **d** 87 **p** 97. C N Lambeth *S'wark* 90-91; Tutor Simon of Cyrene Th Inst 90-96; Abp's Asst Sec for Ecum and Angl Affairs *Cant* 96-01; Abp's Officer for Angl Communion 01-05; Perm to Offic *S'wark* 96-04; Hon Prov Can Cant Cathl 01-04; Liberia from 05. *Trinity Cathedral, PO Box 10-0277, 1000 Monrovia 10, Liberia* Tel (00231) 224760 Fax 227519

BROWNE, Ian Cameron. b 51. St Cath Coll Ox BA74 MA78 Fitzw Coll Cam BA76 MA80. Ridley Hall Cam 74. **d** 77 **p** 78. C Cheltenham Ch Ch *Glouc* 77-80; Hon C Shrewsbury St Chad *Lich* 80-83; Asst Chapl Shrewsbury Sch 80-83; Chapl Bedford Sch 83-96; Sen Chapl Oundle Sch from 97. *The School, Oundle, Peterborough PE8 4EN* Tel (01832) 273372 *or* 273541
E-mail icb@oundleschool.org.uk

BROWNE, Mrs Karen. b 64. Ox Min Course 06. **d** 09. *94 Lakes Lane, Newport Pagnell MK16 8HR* Tel (01908) 217703
E-mail karen_browne@btopenworld.com

BROWNE, Leonard Joseph. b 58. St Cath Coll Cam BA81 MA84. Trin Coll Bris 87. **d** 89 **p** 90. C Reading Greyfriars *Ox* 89-92; V Cambridge St Barn *Ely* 92-00; Sen Chapl and Hd Div Dean Close Sch Cheltenham 00-03; Hd Master Dean Close Prep Sch from 03. *Dean Close Preparatory School, Lansdown Road, Cheltenham GL51 6QS* Tel (01242) 512217
E-mail hmdcps@deanclose.org.uk *or* lj-browne@supanet.com

BROWNE, Peter Clifford. b 59. Bris Univ BA80 SRN82. Ripon Coll Cuddesdon 88. **d** 90 **p** 91. C Southgate Ch Ch *Lon* 90-92; NSM Kemp Town St Mary *Chich* 93-95; Chapl United Bris Healthcare NHS Trust 96-98; NSM Southmead *Bris* 98-02; Chapl HM Pris Preston from 02. *HM Prison Preston, 2 Ribbleton Lane, Preston PR1 5AB* Tel (01772) 444725

BROWNE, Robert. *See* BROWNE, Aubrey Robert Caulfeild

BROWNHILL, Mrs Diane. b 56. Dioc OLM tr scheme 03. **d** 06 **p** 07. C Man Apostles w Miles Platting 06-09; TV Heatons from 09. *St Thomas' Rectory, 6 Heaton Moor Road, Stockport SK4 4NS* Tel 0161-432 1912 Mobile 07505-781530
E-mail gldbrownhill@aol.com

BROWNING, Derek. *See* BROWNING, Robert Derek

BROWNING, Edward Barrington Lee (Barry). b 42. St Pet Coll Saltley TCert65. Ripon Coll Cuddesdon 90. **d** 92 **p** 93. C Falmouth K Chas *Truro* 92-96; R Roche and Withiel 96-01; P-in-c Manaccan w St Anthony-in-Meneage and St Martin 01-06; P-in-c Cury and Gunwalloe w Mawgan 01-06; rtd 06. *73 Park Way, St Austell PL25 4HR* Tel (01726) 61319
E-mail barry@browningb.freeserve.co.uk

✠**BROWNING, The Rt Revd George Victor.** b 42. Chas Sturt Univ NSW DLitt07. St Jo Coll Morpeth ThL66. **d** 66 **p** 67 **c** 85. C Inverell Australia 66-68; C Armidale 68-69; V Warialda 69-73; Vice Prin St Jo Coll Morpeth 73-76; R Singleton and Adn Upper Hunter 76-84; R Woy Woy and Adn Cen Coast 84-85; Asst Bp Brisbane 85-93; Prin St Fran Th Coll 88-91; Bp Canberra and Goulburn 93-08; Dir Aus Cen Christianity and Culture 96-08; P-in-c Wriggle Valley *Sarum* from 08; rtd 09. *24 Henry Place, Long Beach NSW 2536, Australia* Tel (0061) (2) 4472 7470
E-mail gmbrowning@btconnect.com

BROWNING, Canon Jacqueline Ann. b 44. Sarum Th Coll 93. **d** 96 **p** 97. NSM New Alresford w Ovington and Itchen Stoke *Win* 96-02; Past Asst Win Cathl from 02. Can Man 06-09; Hon Can from 09. *1 Paddock Way, Alresford SO24 9PN* Tel (01962) 734372 *or* 857237
E-mail jackie.browning@winchester-cathedral.org.uk

BROWNING, Canon John William. b 36. Keele Univ BA61. Ripon Hall Ox 61. **d** 63 **p** 64. C Baswich *Lich* 63-66; Chapl Monyhull Hosp Birm 67-72; Chapl Wharncliffe Hosp Sheff 72-78; Chapl Middlewood Hosp Sheff 72-94; Hon Can Sheff Cathl 84-97; Chapl Sheff Mental Health Unit 85-94; Chapl Community Health Sheff NHS Trust 94-97; Chapl Sheff (South) Mental Health Centres 94-97; rtd 97; Perm to Offic *Sheff* from 97. *1 Anvil Close, Sheffield S6 5JN* Tel 0114-234 3740
E-mail johnpatbrowning@hotmail.com

BROWNING, Julian. b 51. St Jo Coll Cam BA72 MA76. Ripon Coll Cuddesdon 77. **d** 80 **p** 81. C Notting Hill *Lon* 80-81; C W Brompton St Mary w St Pet 81-84; Perm to Offic 84-91; NSM Paddington St Sav 99-06; NSM St Marylebone St Cypr from 06. *82 Ashworth Mansions, Grantully Road, London W9 1LN* Tel (020) 7286 6034

BROWNING, Kevin John. b 56. Ridley Hall Cam 96. **d** 98 **p** 99. C Northampton Em *Pet* 98-01; P-in-c Hardwick *Ely* from 01. *The Rectory, Main Street, Hardwick, Cambridge CB23 7QS* Tel (01954) 210695 E-mail kevin_browning@hotmail.co.uk

BROWNING, Robert Derek. b 42. Guildf Dioc Min Course 98. **d** 01 **p** 02. OLM Lightwater *Guildf* from 01. *16 Guildford Road, Lightwater GU18 5SN* Tel (01276) 474345
E-mail derekandcarol.b@tiscali.co.uk

BROWNING, Canon Wilfrid Robert Francis. b 18. Ch Ch Ox BA40 MA44 BD49. Cuddesdon Coll 40. **d** 41 **p** 42. C Towcester w Easton Neston *Pet* 41-44; C Woburn Square Ch Ch *Lon* 44-46; Chapl St Deiniol's Lib Hawarden 46-48; Chapl Heswall Nautical Sch 46-48; C-in-c Hove St Rich CD *Chich* 48-51; Lect Cuddesdon Coll 51-59; R Gt Haseley *Ox* 51-59; Ed *Bulletin Anglican* 55-60; Warden Whalley Abbey 59-63; Can Res Blackb Cathl 59-65; Dir Post-Ord Tr 62-65; Lect Cuddesdon Coll 65-70; Can Res Ch Ch *Ox* 65-87; Hon Can 87-89; Dir Post-Ord Tr 65-85; Dir of Ords 65-85; Dir Ox NSM Course 72-89; rtd 87; Tutor Westmr Coll Ox 93-99. *42 Alexandra Road, Oxford OX2 0DB* Tel (01865) 723464

BROWNLESS, Brian Paish. b 25. TD72. Keble Coll Ox BA50 MA50. Wells Th Coll 50. **d** 52 **p** 53. C Man St Aid 52-54; C Chorlton-cum-Hardy St Clem 54-56; C Swinton St Pet 56-58; V Elton St Steph 58-66; CF (TA) 60-66; Area Sec USPG *Lich* 66-77; Lic to Offic *Lich* 66-77; CF (TA - R of O) 66-72; R Yoxall *Lich* 77-82; V S Ramsey St Paul *S & M* 82-87; rtd 87; Perm to Offic *Heref* from 87. *10 Caple Avenue, Kings Caple, Hereford HR1 4UL* Tel (01432) 840246

BROWNLESS, Philip Paul Stanley. b 19. Selw Coll Cam BA41 MA45. Ridley Hall Cam 46. **d** 47 **p** 48. C Prittlewell St Mary *Chelmsf* 47-50; Min Prittlewell St Luke CD 50-54; Chapl and Hd Master Lambrook Sch Bracknell 54-71; V Heckfield cum Mattingley *Win* 71-74; V Heckfield w Mattingley and Rotherwick 74-87; RD Odiham 83-84; rtd 85; Perm to Offic *Chich* from 85. *The Hornpipe, Oak Meadow, Birdham, Chichester PO20 7BH* Tel (01243) 512177

BROWNLIE, Miss Caroline Heddon. b 47. CQSW75. Qu Coll Birm IDC81. **d** 87 **p** 94. Asst Chapl Fairfield Hosp Hitchin 87-91; NSM Ashwell w Hinxworth and Newnham *St Alb* 92-98; Chapl HM Rem Cen Low Newton 99-01; Perm to Offic *St Alb* 04-05; P-in-c Gilling and Kirkby Ravensworth *Ripon* 05-07; rtd

07; Perm to Offic *Ely* from 07. *9 Mount Pleasant, Cambridge CB3 0BL* Tel (01223) 350663

BROWNRIDGE, David Leonard Robert. b 76. Univ of Wales (Lamp) BA97. Trin Coll Bris 98. **d** 00 **p** 01. C Henfynyw w Aberaeron and Llanddewi Aberarth *St D* 00-04; V Laugharne w Llansadwrnen and Llandawke from 04. *The Vicarage, King Street, Laugharne, Carmarthen SA33 4QE* Tel (01994) 427218 E-mail davidbecky@brownridge97.freeserve.co.uk

BROWNRIGG, Canon Ronald Allen. b 19. Em Coll Cam BA47 MA50 FRSA91. Westcott Ho Cam 47. **d** 49 **p** 50. C Beverley Minster *York* 49-51; Dean Jerusalem 51-54; C Stanmore *Win* 54-60; R Bletchingley *S'wark* 60-74; V Petersham 74-85; Hon Can S'wark Cathl 78-85; Consultant Inter-Ch Travel from 83; rtd 85. *Marlborough Lodge, 13 Marlborough Lane, Bath BA1 2NQ* Tel (01225) 334831

BROWNSELL, Preb John Kenneth. b 48. Hertf Coll Ox BA69 BA72 MA89. Cuddesdon Coll 70. **d** 73 **p** 74. C Notting Hill All SS w St Columb *Lon* 73-74; C Notting Hill 74-76; TV 76-82; V Notting Hill All SS w St Columb from 82; AD Kensington 84-92; Preb St Paul's Cathl from 92; Dir of Ords from 95. *The Vicarage, Powis Gardens, London W11 1JG* Tel (020) 7727 5919 E-mail johbrwnsll@aol.com

BROXTON, Alan. b 40. UMIST BSc72 CEng MICE79 MIStructE77. **d** 96 **p** 97. OLM Rhodes *Man* from 96. *241 Heywood Old Road, Middleton, Manchester M24 4QR* Tel and fax 0161-643 6319

BRUCE, Miss Amanda Jane. b 67. Liv Univ BSc87 Southn Univ PGCE89 Chelt & Glouc Coll of HE AdDipEd01. Wycliffe Hall Ox 06. **d** 08. C Haydock St Mark *Liv* from 08. *303 Park Street, Haydock, St Helens WA11 0BG* Tel (01744) 634026 Mobile 07921-461381 E-mail mandylou@bluebottle.com

BRUCE, David Ian. b 47. St Mich Coll Llan 70. **d** 73 **p** 74. C Bordesley St Benedict *Birm* 73-74; C Llanishen and Lisvane 74-81; V Canley *Cov* 81-90; V Longford 90-97; rtd 97; Perm to Offic *Cov* from 97. *122 Hugh Road, Coventry CV3 1AF* Tel (024) 7644 5789

BRUCE, Francis Bernard. b 30. Trin Coll Ox BA52 MA56. Westcott Ho Cam 52. **d** 54 **p** 55. C Bury St Mary *Man* 54-59; C Sherborne w Castleton and Lillington *Sarum* 59-61; R Croston *Blackb* 61-86; V Bibury w Winson and Barnsley *Glouc* 86-95; rtd 95; Perm to Offic *Glouc* from 95. *6 Gloucester Street, Cirencester GL7 2DG* Tel (01285) 641954

BRUCE, James Hamilton. b 57. Dur Univ BSc78 Newc Univ MSc79 St Andr Univ PhD99. Trin Coll Bris 81. **d** 84 **p** 85. C Walmley *Birm* 84-86; Perm to Offic *Carl* 87-95; W Cumbria Sch Worker N Schs Chr Union 87-93; Nat Development Officer Wales Scripture Union 93-94; Chapl Turi St Andr Kenya 95-96; NSM St Andrews St Andr *St And* 96-99; R Penicuik and W Linton *Edin* 99-03; Perm to Offic *Win* 03-06; V Lyndhurst and Emery Down and Minstead from 06. *The Vicarage, 5 Forest Gardens, Lyndhurst SO43 7AF* Tel (023) 8028 2154 E-mail bruces@talktalk.net

BRUCE, John. b 26. **d** 50 **p** 51. Canada 50-62; V Broughton Moor *Carl* 63-66; V Carl St Herbert w St Steph 66-74; P-in-c Kendal St Geo 74-76; V 76 83; V Coundon *Dur* 83-86; rtd 86; Perm to Offic *Carl* 86-93. *9 Penton Close, Carlisle CA3 0PX*

BRUCE, John Cyril. b 41. EMMTC 95. **d** 98 **p** 99. NSM Spalding *Linc* 98-05; P-in-c Grantham, Manthorpe 05-08; rtd 09. *5 Welwyn Close, Grantham NG31 7JU* Tel (01476) 561546 Mobile 07947-156933 E-mail john@john-bruce.co.uk

BRUCE, Ms Kathrine Sarah. b 68. Leeds Univ BA89 St Jo Coll Dur BA01 Trin & All SS Coll Leeds MEd02. Cranmer Hall Dur 98. **d** 01 **p** 02. C Ripon H Trin 01-04; Chapl Trevelyan Coll *Dur* 04-08; Chapl Van Mildert Coll 04-08; NSM Dur St Oswald 04-08; Chapl St Jo Coll Dur from 08. *St John's College, 3 South Bailey, Durham DH1 3RJ* Tel 0191-334 3500

BRUCE, Leslie Barton. b 23. Liv Univ MB, ChB48. **d** 71 **p** 72. NSM Wavertree H Trin *Liv* 71-05. *3 Childwall Park Avenue, Liverpool L16 0JE* Tel 0151-722 7664

BRUCE, Mrs Susan Elizabeth. b 52. **d** 08 **p** 09. OLM Haughton le Skerne *Dur* from 08. *14 Haughton Green, Darlington DL1 2DF* Tel (01325) 281567 Mobile 07810-720490 E-mail s.bruce178@ntlworld.com

BRUECK, Ms Jutta. b 61. LSE MSc89 Heythrop Coll Lon MA92 Fitzw Coll Cam BA96 MA00. Westcott Ho Cam 94. **d** 97 **p** 98. C Is of Dogs Ch Ch and St Jo w St Luke *Lon* 97-01; Chapl Guildhall Sch of Music and Drama 01-06; Chapl Fitzw Coll Cam 06-08; P-in-c Cambridge St Jas *Ely* from 08. *St James's Vicarage, 110 Wulfstan Way, Cambridge CB1 8QJ* Tel (01223) 241791 E-mail jb200@cam.ac.uk

BRUNN, Steven. b 67. Ridley Hall Cam. **d** 05 **p** 06. C Chertsey, Lyne and Longcross *Guildf* 05-09. *Address temp unknown* E-mail steve.brunn@ntlworld.com

BRUNNING, Canon David George. b 32. St D Coll Lamp BA53. St Mich Coll Llan 53. **d** 55 **p** 56. C Llantwit Major and St Donat's 55-59; C Usk and Monkswood w Glascoed Chpl and Gwehelog 59-62; V Abercarn 62-71; V Pontnewydd 71-89; RD Pontypool 89-97; R Panteg 90-98; Can St Woolos Cathl from 94;

rtd 98; Lic to Offic *Mon* from 98. *6 Spitzkop, Llantwit Major CF61 1RD* Tel (01446) 792124

BRUNNING, Neil. b 29. NW Ord Course 73. **d** 76 **p** 77. C Cheadle Hulme All SS *Ches* 76-79; V 79-88; V Glentworth *Linc* 88-93; P-in-c Hemswell w Harpswell 88-93; V Glentworth Gp 93-94; rtd 94; Perm to Offic *Linc* from 94. *11 Cavendish Drive, Lea, Gainsborough DN21 5HU* Tel and fax (01427) 617938 E-mail neilbrun@aol.com

BRUNO, Canon Allan David. b 34. AKC59. St Boniface Warminster 59. **d** 60 **p** 61. C Darlington H Trin *Dur* 60-64; C Kimberley Cathl and Chapl Bp's Hostel S Africa 64-65; Asst Chapl Peterhouse Di Rhodesia 65-70; Overseas Chapl Scottish Episc Ch 70-75; C Edin Old St Paul 75-76; Dir of Miss Prov of S Africa 76-80; Namibia 80-86; Dean Windhoek 81-86; R Falkirk *Edin* 86-95; Hon Can Kinkizi from 95; Bp's Dom Chapl *Bradf* 96-99; Bp's Past Asst 99-01; rtd 01; Perm to Offic *Bradf* from 01 and *Blackb* from 02. *Pond House, 5 Twine Walk, Burton in Lonsdale, Carnforth LA6 3LR* Tel (015242) 61616 E-mail david@bruno81.freeserve.co.uk

BRUNSKILL, Mrs Sheila Kathryn. *See* BANYARD, Canon Sheila Kathryn

BRUNSWICK, Canon Robert John. b 38. TD86. St Aid Birkenhead 60. **d** 63 **p** 64. C Neston *Ches* 63-66; CF (TA - R of O) 65-96; C Warrington St Paul *Liv* 66-68; V Liv St Paul Stoneycroft 68-78; V Southport St Luke 78-87; R Croston *Blackb* 87-01; R Croston and Bretherton 01-05; Chapl Bp Rawstorne Sch Preston 88-05; Hon Can Koforidua from 94; rtd 05. *60 St Clements Avenue, Farington, Leyland PR25 4QU* Tel (01772) 426094

BRUNT, Prof Peter William. b 36. CVO01 OBE94. Liv Univ MB59 MD67 Lon Univ FRCP74 FRCPEd. Ab Dioc Tr Course. **d** 96 **p** 97. NSM Bieldside *Ab* 96-07. *Flat 4, 1 Hillpark Rise, Edinburgh EH4 7BB*

BRUNT, Mrs Philippa Ann. b 53. Leeds Univ BA74 Leeds and Carnegie Coll PGCE75. WEMTC 95. **d** 98 **p** 99. C Cinderford St Steph w Littledean *Glouc* 98-01; V Parkend and Viney Hill from 01; AD Forest S from 09. *The Vicarage, Lower Road, Yorkley, Lydney GL15 4TN* Tel (01594) 562828 E-mail pabrunt@ukonline.co.uk

BRUNYEE, Miss Hilary. b 46. Linc Th Coll 76. **dss** 81 **d** 87 **p** 94. Longsight St Jo w St Cypr *Man* 81-87; Par Dn Peel 87-94; TV 94-99; TV Walkden and Lt Hulton 99-00; rtd 00. *38 Holly Avenue, Worsley, Manchester M28 3DW* Tel 0161-790 7761

BRUSH, Canon Sally. b 47. Lon Univ BD75 Univ of Wales MPhil96. Trin Coll Bris 73. **dss** 76 **d** 80 **p** 97. Flint *St As* 76-83; C 80-83; C Cefn 83-87; C St As and Tremeirchion 83-87; Chapl St As Cathl 83-87; Dn-in-c Cerrigydrudion w Llanfihangel Glyn Myfyr etc 87-97; V 97-07; RD Edeirnion 98-04; Hon Can St As Cathl 01-07; rtd 07. *Persondy, 1 Tyddyn Terrace, Cerrigydrudion, Corwen LL21 9TN* Tel (01490) 420048

BRYAN, Cecil William. b 43. TCD BA66 MA73. CITC 66. **d** 68 **p** 69. C Dublin Zion Ch *D & G* 68-72; Chapl RAF 72-75; Dioc Info Officer *D & G* 75-90; I Castleknock w Mulhuddart, Clonsilla etc 75-89; Chapl K Hosp Dub 89-99; I Tullow *D & G* 99-07; Can Ch Ch Cathl Dublin 03-07; rtd 07. *2 Grange Heights, Green Road, Newbridge, Co Kildare, Republic of Ireland* Tel (00353) (45) 435572 Mobile 87-221 2004 E-mail c.bryan@iol.ie

BRYAN, Christopher Paul. b 75. Univ Coll Ox BA96 St Jo Coll Dur BA99. Cranmer Hall Dur 97. **d** 00 **p** 01. C Old Swinford Stourbridge *Worc* 00-04; P in c Lechlade *Glouc* 04-08; TV Fairford Deanery from 09. *The Vicarage, Sherbourne Street, Lechlade GL7 3AH* Tel (01367) 252262 E-mail cpbryan@hotmail.com

BRYAN, David John. b 56. Liv Univ BSc77 Hull Univ BTh85 Qu Coll Ox DPhil89. Ox Min Course 89. **d** 90 **p** 91. C Abingdon *Ox* 90-93; Tutor Qu Coll Birm 93-01; Dean of Studies 95-01; R Haughton le Skerne *Dur* from 01. *The Rectory, Haughton Green, Darlington DL1 2DD* Tel (01325) 468142 E-mail standrewshls.church@btinternet.com

BRYAN, Helen Ann. b 68. NTMTC BA07. **d** 07 **p** 08. NSM Laindon w Dunton *Chelmsf* from 07. *21 Ozonia Way, Wickford SS12 0PQ* Tel (01268) 562372 Mobile 07747-397973 E-mail hbryan@talktalk.net

BRYAN, Judith Claire. *See* STEPHENSON, Judith Claire

BRYAN, Michael John Christopher. b 35. Wadh Coll Ox BA58 BTh59 MA63 Ex Univ PhD83. Ripon Hall Ox 59. **d** 60 **p** 61. C Reigate St Mark *S'wark* 60-64; Tutor Sarum & Wells Th Coll 64-69; Vice-Prin 69-71; USA 71-74; Sen Officer Educn and Community Dept *Lon* 74-79; Chapl Ex Univ 79-83; USA from 83; rtd 96; Perm to Offic *Ex* from 95. *148 Proctors Hall Road, Sewanee TN 37383-1000, USA*

BRYAN, Nigel Arthur. b 39. Univ of Wales (Lamp) BA61. Burgess Hall Lamp 61. **d** 63 **p** 64. C Llanstadwel *St D* 63-69; Chapl RAF 69-94; R Gt w Lt Milton and Gt Haseley *Ox* 94-98; R Newport w Cilgwyn and Dinas w Llanllawer *St D* 98-05; rtd 05. *16 Grove Drive, Pembroke SA71 5QB* Tel (01646) 681894 Mobile 07773-456175

BRYAN, Canon Percival John Milward. b 19. St Pet Coll Ox BA40 MA46 BTh47. Wycliffe Hall Ox 46. **d** 48 **p** 49. C Belvedere All SS

Roch 48-51; C Hobart St Geo Australia 51-52; C Blindley Heath *S'wark* 53-54; R Warkton and Weekley *Pet* 54-56; R King's Cliffe 56-85; Can Pet Cathl 73-86; rtd 86; Perm to Offic *Linc* 91-00 and *Pet* from 86. *The College of St Barnabas, Blackberry Lane, Lingfield RH7 6NJ*

BRYAN, Canon Philip Richard. b 40. Dur Univ BA61. Wycliffe Hall Ox 72. **d** 74 **p** 75. C Macclesfield St Mich *Ches* 74-77; V St Bees *Carl* 77-06; Chapl St Bees Sch Cumbria 77-06; RD Calder *Carl* 88-96; Hon Can Carl Cathl 91-00; rtd 06. *18 Old Forde, Whitehead, Carrickfergus BT38 9XY* Tel (028) 9337 8438

BRYAN, Canon Sherry Lee. b 49. WMMTC 88. **d** 91 **p** 94. Par Dn St Columb Minor and St Colan *Truro* 91-94; C 94-96; P-in-c St Teath 96-05; P-in-c Blisland w St Breward from 05; P-in-c Helland from 05; Chapl Cornwall Healthcare NHS Trust 99-02; RD Trigg Minor and Bodmin from 02; Hon Can Truro Cathl from 03. *The Rectory, Green Briar, Coombe Lane, St Breward, Bodmin PL30 4LT* Tel (01208) 851829

BRYAN, Timothy Andrew. b 56. St Edm Hall Ox MA80. S'wark Ord Course 93. **d** 96 **p** 97. NSM Morden *S'wark* 96-99; NSM Carshalton Beeches 99-05; NSM Sutton 05-08; Resettlement Chapl HM Pris Wandsworth 07-08; Co-ord Chapl from 08. *HM Prison Wandsworth, PO Box 757, Heathfield Road, London SW18 3HS* Tel (020) 8588 4000 E-mail timbryan7@aol.com

BRYAN, William Terence. b 38. Dudley Coll of Educn CertEd68. Chich Th Coll 73. **d** 75 **p** 76. C Shrewsbury St Giles *Lich* 75-79; V Churchstoke w Hyssington and Sarn *Heref* 79-03; rtd 04; Hon C Betws Cedewain and Tregynon and Llanwyddelan *St As* from 07. *29 Llys Melyn, Tregynon, Newtown SY16 3EE* Tel (01686) 650899

BRYANS, Joseph. b 15. TCD BA39 MA43. CITC 40. **d** 42 **p** 43. C Kirby Moorside w Gillamoor *York* 42-45; C Thornaby on Tees St Luke 45-47; C Seapatrick *D & D* 47-54; I Gleneely w Culdaff *D & R* 54-60; I Tamlaghtard w Aghanloo 60-90; rtd 90. *23 Roe Fold, Main Street, Limavady BT49 0EL* Tel (028) 7776 2768

BRYANT, Andrew Watts. b 57. St Jo Coll Dur BA78 Birm Univ MA81. Qu Coll Birm 80. **d** 83 **p** 84. C Pelsall *Lich* 83-87; NSM 91-94; Perm to Offic 87-92; NSM Streetly 94-96; NSM Beckbury, Badger, Kemberton, Ryton, Stockton etc 96-99; R Worplesdon *Guildf* 99-09; Chapl Merrist Wood Coll of Agric and Horticulture 01-09; TR Portishead *B & W* from 09. *The Rectory, 2 Brambling Lane, Portishead, Bristol BS20 7NN* Tel and fax (01275) 848934 E-mail andybryant3@virgin.net

BRYANT, Canon Christopher. b 32. K Coll Lon AKC60. **d** 61 **p** 62. C Fareham H Trin *Portsm* 61-65; C Yatton Keynell *Bris* 65-71; C Biddestone w Slaughterford 65-71; C Castle Combe 65-71; V Chirton, Marden and Patney *Sarum* 71-76; V Chirton, Marden, Patney, Charlton and Wilsford 76-78; P-in-c Devizes St Jo w St Mary 78-79; R 79-97; RD Devizes 83-93; Can and Preb Sarum Cathl 87-04; rtd 97; Master St Nic Hosp Salisbury 97-04. *34 Mill Road, Salisbury SP2 7RZ* Tel (01722) 502336

BRYANT, David Henderson. b 37. K Coll Lon BD60 AKC60. **d** 61 **p** 62. C Trowbridge H Trin *Sarum* 61-63; C Ewell *Guildf* 63-67; V Leiston *St E* 67-73; Chapl RN 73; C Northam *Ex* 74-75; P-in-c Clavering w Langley *Chelmsf* 76-77; Teacher Mountview High Sch Harrow 77-85; P-in-c Boosbeck w Moorsholm *York* 85-89; V 89-90; V Sowerby 90-95; P-in-c Sessay 90-95; V Lastingham w Appleton-le-Moors, Rosedale etc 95-99; rtd 99. *35 West End, Kirkbymoorside, York YO62 6AD* Tel (01751) 430269

BRYANT, Donald Thomas. b 29. SE Essex Coll BSc56 Birkbeck Coll Lon BSc58 FSS59. S'wark Ord Course 85. **d** 88 **p** 89. NSM Redhill St Matt *S'wark* 88-99; Perm to Offic 99-04 and from 05; NSM Salfords 04-05. *21 Windermere Way, Reigate RH2 0LW* Tel (01737) 762382

BRYANT, Canon Edward Francis Paterson. b 43. S'wark Ord Course 75. **d** 78 **p** 79. NSM Hadlow *Roch* 78-84; C Dartford St Alb 84-87; R Hollington St Leon *Chich* 87-93; V Bexhill St Aug 93-99; TR Bexhill St Pet from 99; P-in-c Sedlescombe w Whatlington 02-05; RD Battle and Bexhill 98-04; Can and Preb Chich Cathl from 00. *The Rectory, Old Town, Bexhill-on-Sea TN40 2HE* Tel (01424) 211115 Fax 07970-991268 Mobile 07824-859044 E-mail bexhillrector@gmail.com

BRYANT, Graham Trevor. b 41. Keble Coll Ox BA63 MA67. Chich Th Coll 64. **d** 66 **p** 67. C Leeds St Wilfrid *Ripon* 66-69; C Haywards Heath St Wilfrid *Chich* 69-74; V Crawley Down All SS 74-79; V Bexhill St Aug 79-85; V Charlton Kings St Mary *Glouc* 85-02; rtd 02; Perm to Offic *Glouc* from 03. *6 The Close, Cheltenham GL53 0PQ* Tel (01242) 520313

✠**BRYANT, The Rt Revd Mark Watts.** b 49. St Jo Coll Dur BA72. Cuddesdon Coll 72. **d** 75 **p** 76 **c** 07. C Addlestone *Guildf* 75-79; C Studley *Sarum* 79-83; V 83-88; Chapl Trowbridge Coll 79-83; Voc Development Adv and Dioc Dir of Ords *Cov* 88-96; Hon Can Cov Cathl 93-01; TR Coventry Caludon 96-01; AD Cov E 99-01; Adn Cov 01-07; Can Res Cov Cathl 06-07; Suff Bp Jarrow *Dur* from 07. *Bishop's House, Ivy Lane, Gateshead NE9 6QD* Tel 0191-491 0917 Fax 491 5116 E-mail bishop.of.jarrow@durham.anglican.org

BRYANT, Patricia Ann. b 36. Qu Mary Coll Lon BA58. St Mich Coll Llan 94. **d** 91 **p** 97. NSM Llanbadoc *Mon* 91-93; NSM Llangybi and Coedypaen w Llanbadoc 93-94; C 94-98; Asst

Chapl Gwent Tertiary Coll 94-98; V Merthyr Cynog and Dyffryn Honddu etc *S & B* 98-02; rtd 03. *5 Trebarried Court, Llandefalle, Brecon LD3 0NB* Tel (01874) 754087 E-mail bryants@surfaid.org

BRYANT, Peter James. b 35. Jes Coll Cam BA58 MA64 UWIST 59 FInstM. St Deiniol's Hawarden 86 St Mich Coll Llan 96. **d** 97 **p** 98. NSM Raglan-Usk *Mon* 97-98; NSM Merthyr Cynog and Dyffryn Honddu etc *S & B* 98-02. *5 Trebarried Court, Llandefalle, Brecon LD3 0NB* Tel (01874) 754087 E-mail bryants@surfaid.org

BRYANT, Canon Richard Kirk. b 47. Ch Coll Cam BA68 MA72. Cuddesdon Coll 70. **d** 72 **p** 73. C Newc St Gabr 72-75; C Morpeth 75-78; C Benwell St Jas 78-82; V Earsdon and Backworth 82-93; V Wylam 93-97; Prin Local Min Scheme from 97; Prin Reader Tr from 97; Hon Can Newc Cathl from 97. *2 Burlington Court, Wallsend NE28 9YH* Tel 0191-270 4150 Fax 270 4101 *or* 263 7922 E-mail r.bryant@newcastle.anglican.org *or* rk.bryant@btinternet.com

BRYANT, Richard Maurice. b 46. MAAIS80. WMMTC 90. **d** 93 **p** 94. NSM The Stanleys *Glouc* 93-98; NSM Glouc St Geo w Whaddon 98-04; NSM Twigworth, Down Hatherley, Norton, The Leigh etc 04-08; NSM Bisley, Chalford, France Lynch, and Oakridge from 08. *6 Church Street, Kings Stanley, Stonehouse GL10 3HW* Tel (01453) 823172

BRYANT, Miss Sarah Elizabeth. b 82. Grey Coll Dur BA05 Wolfs Coll Cam MPhil07. Westcott Ho Cam 06. **d** 08 **p** 09. C Branksome St Aldhelm *Sarum* from 08. *St Francis House, 105A Winston Avenue, Poole BH12 1PB* Tel (01202) 764420 E-mail sarah.bryant82@googlemail.com

BRYARS, Peter John. b 54. BA MEd PhD. St Jo Coll Nottm. **d** 84 **p** 85. C Hull St Martin w Transfiguration *York* 84-87; TV Drypool 87-90; TV Glendale Gp *Newc* 90-94; P-in-c Heddon-on-the-Wall 94-01; Adult Educn Adv 94-01; V Delaval from 01; AD Bedlington from 03; Chapl MU from 02; Bp's Adv for Healing Min *Newc* from 06. *The Vicarage, The Avenue, Seaton Sluice, Whitley Bay NE26 4QW* Tel 0191-237 1982 E-mail pjbryars@btinternet.com

BRYCE, Michael Adrian Gilpin. b 47. TCD BA71 MA95. CITC 74. **d** 77 **p** 78. C Clondalkin w Tallaght *D & G* 77-79; C Ch Ch Cathl and Chapl Univ Coll Dub 79-82; I Ardamine w Kiltennel, Glascarrig etc *C & O* 82-84; CF 84-00; I Lisbellaw *Clogh* 00-05; R Bolam w Whalton and Hartburn w Meldon *Newc* from 05; V Nether Witton from 05. *The Rectory, Whalton, Morpeth NE61 3UX* Tel (01670) 775360

BRYCE, Paul Russell. b 79. SS Mark & Jo Univ Coll Plymouth BA00. Wycliffe Hall Ox MTh. **d** 06 **p** 07. C Paignton Ch Ch and Preston St Paul *Ex* from 06. *133 Torquay Road, Paignton TQ3 2AG* Tel (01803) 664227

BRYDON, Michael Andrew. b 73. St Chad's Coll Dur BA95 MA96 PhD00. St Steph Ho Ox BA01. **d** 02 **p** 03. C Bexhill St Pet *Chich* 02-06; C Brighton St Paul 06-08; C Brighton St Mich 06-08; Dioc Adv for Educn and Tr of Adults 06-08; R Catsfield and Crowhurst from 08. *The Rectory, Church Lane, Catsfield, Battle TN33 9DR* Tel (01424) 892319

BRYER, Anthony Colin. b 51. Qu Eliz Coll Lon BSc72. Trin Coll Bris 72. **d** 75 **p** 76. C Preston St Cuth *Blackb* 75-78; C Berontree St Mary *Chelmsf* 78-81; TV Loughton St Mary and St Mich 81-88; C Clifton St Paul *Bris* 88-91; P-in-c 91-94; R Bris St Mich and St Paul 94-96; In C of S and Lic to Offic *Edin* 96-04; C Towcester w Caldecote and Easton Neston *Pet* 04-07; C Greens Norton w Bradden and Lichborough 06-07; V Towcester w Caldecote and Easton Neston etc from 07. *The Vicarage, Chantry Lane, Towcester NN12 6YY* Tel (01327) 350459 Mobile 07814-832004 E-mail tsbryer@waitrose.com

BRYER, Paul Donald. b 58. Sussex Univ BEd80 Nottm Univ MA96. St Jo Coll Nottm. **d** 90 **p** 91. C Tonbridge St Steph *Roch* 90-94; TV Camberley St Paul *Guildf* 94-99; V Camberley St Mary 99-01; V Dorking St Paul from 01; RD Dorking from 09. *St Paul's Vicarage, South Terrace, Dorking RH4 2AB* Tel (01306) 881998 E-mail paul@stpaulsdorking.org.uk

BRYN-THOMAS, John. b 37. Lich Th Coll 63. **d** 66 **p** 67. C Stoke upon Trent *Lich* 66-71; R Wotton *Guildf* 71-79; P-in-c Holmbury St Mary 78-79; R Wotton and Holmbury St Mary 79-86; C Easthampstead *Ox* 86-88; TV Chambersbury *St Alb* 88-01; rtd 01; Perm to Offic *Guildf* from 02. *191 Peperharow Road, Godalming GU7 2PR* Tel (01483) 429782 E-mail jbrynthomas@tiscali.co.uk

BRYSON, James Ferguson. b 55. NE Lon Poly BSc RIBA. SEITE 04. **d** 07 **p** 08. C Old Ford St Paul and St Mark *Lon* from 07. *4 Vivian Road, London E3 5RF*

BUCHAN, Geoffrey Herbert. b 38. CEng MIMechE. NOC 91. **d** 94 **p** 95. NSM Barnton *Ches* 94-96; NSM Goostrey 96-99; C Stretton and Appleton Thorn from 99. *12 Hough Lane, Anderton, Northwich CW9 6AB* Tel (01606) 74512 E-mail gbuchan@tiscali.co.uk

BUCHAN, Matthew Alexander John. b 69. St Andr Univ MA92. Wycliffe Hall Ox BTh95. **d** 98 **p** 99. C Horninglow *Lich* 98-01; TV Moulsecoomb *Chich* 01-04; Bp's Chapl *Glouc* 04-06; P-in-c

Leybourne *Roch* from 06. *The Rectory, 73 Rectory Lane North, Leybourne, West Malling ME19 5HD* Tel (01732) 842187 E-mail frbuchan@frbuchan.force9.co.uk

BUCHANAN, Andrew Derek. b 64. Stirling Univ BA90. Wycliffe Hall Ox 98. **d** 01 **p** 02. C Plas Newton *Ches* 01-03; C Ches Ch Ch 03-06; C Plas Newton w Ches Ch Ch from 07; Asst Chapl Ches Univ from 03. *The Vicarage, Gloucester Street, Chester CH1 3HR* Tel (01244) 382217 E-mail rev_buchanan@hotmail.com

✠**BUCHANAN, The Rt Revd Colin Ogilvie.** b 34. Linc Coll Ox BA MA Lambeth DD93. Tyndale Hall Bris 59. **d** 61 **p** 62 **c** 85. C Cheadle *Ches* 61-64; Tutor St Jo Coll Nottm 64-85; Lib 64-69; Registrar 69-74; Dir of Studies 74-75; Vice-Prin 75-78; Prin 79-85; Hon Can S'well Minster 81-85; Suff Bp Aston *Birm* 85-89; Asst Bp Roch 89-96; Asst Bp S'wark 90-91; V Gillingham St Mark *Roch* 91-96; Area Bp Woolwich *S'wark* 96-04; rtd 04; Hon Asst Bp Bradf from 04; Hon Asst Bp Ripon and Leeds from 05. *21 The Drive, Alwoodley, Leeds LS17 7QB* Tel 0113-267 7721 E-mail colinbuchanan101@btinternet.com

BUCHANAN, Eoin George. b 59. Qu Coll Birm 98. **d** 00 **p** 01. C Dovercourt and Parkeston w Harwich *Chelmsf* 00-04; C Ramsey w Lt Oakley 02-04; TR N Hinckford from 04. *The Rectory, Gages Road, Belchamp St Paul, Sudbury CO10 7BT* Tel (01787) 277850 Mobile 07766-605489 E-mail belchamp@googlemail.com *or* rectory@vodafoneemail.co.uk

BUCHANAN, George Rowland. b 15. St Aug Coll Cant. **d** 59 **p** 60. C Sherborne w Castleton and Lillington *Sarum* 59-63; V Bradford Abbas w Clifton Maybank 63-67; R Gt Wishford 67-73; R Lt Langford 67-73; RD Wylye and Wilton 69-73; Org Sec CECS *Ex* and *B & W* 73-77; rtd 77; Perm to Offic *Sarum* from 77. *6 Pageant Drive, Sherborne DT9 3LP* Tel (01935) 812263

BUCHANAN, John Fraser Walter. b 32. Em Coll Cam BA55. **d** 93 **p** 94. OLM Wainford *St E* 93-07; rtd 07; Perm to Offic *St E* from 07. *The Hermitage, Bridge Street, Beccles NR34 9BA* Tel (01502) 712154

BUCHANAN, Stephanie Joan. b 65. Linc Coll Ox BA88 MA02 Selw Coll Cam BA01 Goldsmiths' Coll Lon PGCE93. Ridley Hall Cam 99. **d** 02 **p** 03. C Mirfield *Wakef* 02-06; TV Em TM from 06. *The Vicarage, 42 Beaumont Park Road, Huddersfield HD4 5JS* Tel (01484) 431163 E-mail stephanie.buchanan@btopenworld.com

BUCK, Ashley. *See* BUCK, William Ashley

BUCK, David Andrew. b 64. GMusRNCM88. Ripon Coll Cuddesdon 97. **d** 99 **p** 00. C Poulton-le-Sands w Morecambe St Laur *Blackb* 99-03; V Hednesford *Lich* from 03. *The Vicarage, Church Hill, Hednesford, Cannock WS12 1BD* Tel (01543) 426954

BUCK, Mrs Jacqueline Rosemary. b 66. ERMC 06. **d** 09. NSM Cople, Moggerhanger and Willington *St Alb* from 09. *54 Henderson Way, Kempston, Bedford MK42 8NP* Tel (01234) 407020 E-mail jackiebuck@hotmail.co.uk

BUCK (née JONES), Kathryn Mary. b 59. Birm Univ BA81 MEd91 Sheff Univ PGCE82. Ripon Coll Cuddesdon. **d** 99 **p** 00. C Uttoxeter Area *Lich* 99-00; C Scotforth *Blackb* 00-03; TV Cannock *Lich* from 03; C Hednesford from 05. *The Vicarage, Church Hill, Hednesford, Cannock WS12 1BD* Tel (01543) 879814

BUCK, Nicholas John. b 57. Leic Univ BScEng79. Ridley Hall Cam 81. **d** 84 **p** 85. C Oakwood St Thos *Lon* 84-87; C Darnall and Attercliffe *Sheff* 87-90; V Kimberworth 90-96; Chapl Scargill Ho 96-01; P-in-c Bassingham Gp *Linc* 01-06; R from 06. *The Rectory, 11 Torgate Lane, Bassingham, Lincoln LN5 9HF* Tel (01522) 788383 E-mail the-bucks@supanet.com

BUCK, Canon Richard Peter Holdron. b 37. AKC64. Lambeth Hon MA93. **d** 65 **p** 66. C Mill Hill Jo Keble *Lon* 65-68; C St Marylebone All SS 68-74; Can Res and Treas Truro Cathl 74-76; V Primrose Hill St Mary w Avenue Road St Paul *Lon* 76-84; Bp's Ecum Adv *S'wark* 84-91; P-in-c Dulwich Common St Pet 84-86; Hon Can S'wark Cathl 90-98; C Rotherhithe St Kath w St Barn 91-92; C Bermondsey St Kath w St Bart 92-94; C Greenwich St Alfege w St Pet and St Paul 94-98; rtd 98. *50 Viceroy Lodge, 143 Kingsway, Hove BN3 4RB* Tel (01273) 710155

BUCK, William Ashley. b 61. Man Univ BA82 Ox Univ BA86 MA91. Ripon Coll Cuddesdon 84. **d** 87 **p** 88. C Addington *S'wark* 87-91; C Pimlico St Pet w Westmr Ch Ch *Lon* 91-94; TV Wenlock *Heref* 94-03; RD Condover 00-03; R Cleobury Mortimer w Hopton Wafers etc from 03. *The Rectory, The Hurst, Cleobury Mortimer, Kidderminster DY14 8EG* Tel (01299) 270264

BUCKETT, Canon James Frederick. b 27. MBE97. ACP. Roch Th Coll 60. **d** 62 **p** 63. C Rowner *Portsm* 62-64; Lic to Offic 64-66; Chapl Highbury Tech Coll Portsm 64-66; V St Helens *Portsm* 66-72; CF (TA) 72-95; V Newport St Thos *Portsm* 72-95; Hon Can Portsm Cathl 81-95; rtd 95; Perm to Offic *Portsm* from 95.

The Coach House, 140A Staplers Road, Newport PO30 2DP Tel (01983) 521847 *or* 527298 Mobile 07889-784376 E-mail jamesbuckett@cs.com

BUCKINGHAM, The Ven Hugh Fletcher. b 32. Hertf Coll Ox BA57 MA60. Westcott Ho Cam 55. **d** 57 **p** 58. C Halliwell St Thos *Man* 57-60; C Sheff Gillcar St Silas 60-65; V Hindolveston *Nor* 65-70; V Guestwick 65-70; R Fakenham w Alethorpe 70-88; Chmn Dioc Bd Soc Resp 81-88; RD Burnham and Walsingham 81-87; Hon Can Nor Cathl 85-88; Adn E Riding *York* 88-98; Can and Preb York Minster 88-01; rtd 98; Perm to Offic *York* from 01. *2 Rectory Corner, Brandsby, York YO61 4RJ* Tel (01347) 888202

BUCKINGHAM, Paul John. b 63. Bris Univ BVSc87. WMMTC 94. **d** 98. NSM Kington w Huntington, Old Radnor, Kinnerton etc *Heref* from 98. *The Cottage, Prospect Lane, Kington HR5 3BE* Tel (01544) 231357

BUCKINGHAM, Richard Arthur John. b 49. Univ of Wales (Cardiff) BA71 PGCE72. Chich Th Coll 73. **d** 76 **p** 77. C Llantwit Major 76-80; C Leigh-on-Sea St Marg *Chelmsf* 80-84; C Westmr St Matt *Lon* 84-87; R Stock Harvard *Chelmsf* 87-02; Perm to Offic *Lon* from 02. *3 Priory Close, London N3 1BB* Tel (020) 8371 0178 E-mail rbuckingham@waitrose.com

BUCKINGHAM, Terence John. b 52. Aston Univ BSc73 MSc75 PhD78 FCOptom74. Coll of Resurr Mirfield 01. **d** 03 **p** 04. NSM Harrogate St Wilfrid *Ripon* 03-09; P-in-c Nidd from 09. *29 Dalesway, Guiseley, Leeds LS20 8JN* Tel (01943) 876066 Mobile 07815-994017 E-mail terry.j.buckingham@btopenworld.com

BUCKINGHAM, Archdeacon of. *See* GORHAM, The Ven Karen Marisa

BUCKINGHAM, Area Bishop of. *See* WILSON, The Rt Revd Alan Thomas Lawrence

BUCKLE, Graham Martin. b 62. Southn Univ BTh89 Sheff Univ MMinTheol04. Sarum & Wells Th Coll 85. **d** 89 **p** 90. C Paddington St Jas *Lon* 89-94; P-in-c Paddington St Pet 94-00; R St Marylebone St Paul from 00; Dir of Ords Two Cities Area from 99. *St Paul's House, 9 Rossmore Road, London NW1 6NJ* Tel and fax (020) 7262 9443 Pager 07654-327687 E-mail buckle@freeuk.com

BUCKLER, Andrew Jonathan Heslington. b 68. Trin Coll Ox BA89 MA96. Wycliffe Hall Ox BTh93. **d** 96 **p** 97. C Ox St Aldate 96-00; Crosslinks France from 00. *12 rue de Gassicourt, 78200 Mantes la Jolie, France* Tel (0033) (1) 30 33 07 95 E-mail bucklers@clara.net

BUCKLER, George Anthony (Tony). b 35. Open Univ BA74. Lich Th Coll 58. **d** 61 **p** 62. C Old Swinford *Worc* 61-65; C Droitwich St Nic w St Pet 65-67; C Droitwich St Andr w St Mary 65-67; Chapl Claybury Hosp Woodford Bridge 67-78; Chapl St Geo and Co Hosps Linc 78-87; Chapl Lawn Hosp Linc 78-81; Chapl Wexham Park Hosp Slough 87-90; Chapl Mapperley Hosp Nottm 90-94; Chapl Nottm Mental Illness and Psychiatric Unit 90-96; Chapl Wells Rd Cen Nottm 94-96; Chapl Qu Medical Cen Nottm 94-96; Chapl Highbury Hosp Nottm 94-96; rtd 96. *73 Westfield Drive, Lincoln LN2 4RE*

BUCKLER, Guy Ernest Warr. b 46. ACA69 FCA79. Linc Th Coll 71. **d** 74 **p** 75. C Dunstable *St Alb* 74-77; C Houghton Regis 77-86; TV Willington *Newc* 86-88; TR 88-95; Chapl N Tyneside Coll of FE 88-95; R Bedford St Pet w St Cuth *St Alb* 95-05; R Bushey from 05; RD Aldenham from 08. *The Rectory, High Street, Bushey WD23 1BD* Tel (020) 8950 1546 E-mail guybuckl@hotmail.com

BUCKLER, Kenneth Arthur. b 50. S Bank Univ MSc94. NTMTC 95. **d** 98 **p** 99. C Welwyn w Ayot St Peter *St Alb* 98-01; P-in-c Kimpton w Ayot St Lawrence 01-05; Asst Chapl E Herts NHS Trust 99-00; Asst Chapl E and N Herts NHS Trust 00-04; Chapl Team Ldr 04-05; V Hounslow W Gd Shep *Lon* from 05. *Good Shepherd House, 360 Beavers Lane, Hounslow TW4 6HJ* Tel (020) 8570 4035 Mobile 07909-970545 E-mail kenabuckler@yahoo.co.uk

BUCKLER, The Very Revd Philip John Warr. b 49. St Pet Coll Ox BA70 MA74. Cuddesdon Coll 70. **d** 72 **p** 73. C Bushey Heath *St Alb* 72-75; Chapl Trin Coll Cam 75-81; Min Can and Sacr St Paul's Cathl 81-87; V Hampstead St Jo 87-99; AD N Camden 93-98; Can Res St Paul's Cathl 99-07; Treas 00-07; Dean Linc from 07. *The Deanery, 11 Minster Yard, Lincoln LN2 1PJ* Tel (01522) 561611 E-mail dean@lincolncathedral.com

BUCKLES, Ms Jayne Elizabeth. **d** 07 **p** 08. NSM Penrhyndeudraeth and Llanfrothen w Maentwrog etc *Ban* from 07. *Tyddyn y Gwydd, Rhostryfan, Caernarfon LL54 7PN* Tel (01286) 650540 E-mail jaynebuckles@btinternet.com

BUCKLEY, Alexander Christopher Nolan. b 67. Univ of Wales (Abth) BD89 Man Univ MA06. St Mich Coll Llan. **d** 91 **p** 94. C Llandudno *Ban* 91-92; C Ynyscynhaearn w Penmorfa and Porthmadog 92-93 and 94-96; Jesuit Volunteer Community Manchester 93-94; C Caerau w Ely *Llan* 96-01; V Trowbridge Mawr *Mon* 01-03; Chapl ATC 96-05; Perm to Offic *Mon* 03-09 and *Man* 04-09; R Llanllyfni *Ban* from 09; CMP from 02. *Y Rheithordy, 2 Mor Awel, Penygroes, Caernarfon LL54 6RA* Tel (01286) 881124 E-mail rheithor@llanllyfni.plus.com

BUCKLEY

BUCKLEY, Anthony Graham. b 63. Keble Coll Ox BA84 MA90 PGCE85. Wycliffe Hall Ox 96. **d** 98 **p** 99. C Foord St Jo *Cant* 98-00; V 00-08; AD Elham 05-08; Hon Can Cant Cathl 08; Chapl Alleyn's Sch Dulwich from 08; Hon C Dulwich St Barn *S'wark* from 08. *40 Hillsborough Road, London SE22 8QE* Tel (020) 8557 1500 E-mail antmon64@hotmail.com

BUCKLEY, Christopher Ivor. b 48. Chich Th Coll. **d** 86 **p** 87. C Felpham w Middleton *Chich* 86-89; C Jersey St Brelade *Win* 89-93; V Jersey St Mark 93-06; Chapl Jersey Airport 00-06; V Knighton, Norton, Whitton, Pilleth and Cascob *S & B* from 06. *The Vicarage, Church Street, Knighton LD7 1AG* Tel (01547) 528566

BUCKLEY, David Rex. b 47. Ripon Coll Cuddesdon 75. **d** 77 **p** 78. C Witton *Ches* 77-81; V Backford 81-85; Youth Chapl from 81; V Barnton 85-93; P-in-c Bickerton w Bickley 93-97; P-in-c Harthill and Burwardsley 93-97; V Bickerton, Bickley, Harthill and Burwardsley 97-01; P-in-c Sandbach 01-03; V 03-07; rtd 08; Chapl Cheshire Constabulary from 08. *308 Swanlow Lane, Winsford CW7 4BN* Tel (01606) 559437 E-mail rex@chazandrex.freeserve.co.uk

BUCKLEY, Ernest Fairbank. b 25. Jes Coll Cam BA49 MA50 Jes Coll Ox BLitt53. Westcott Ho Cam 55. **d** 55 **p** 56. C Rochdale *Man* 55-58; V Hey 58-64; V Baguley 64-79; V Clun w Chapel Lawn, Bettws-y-Crwyn and Newcastle *Heref* 79-87; RD Clun Forest 82-87; rtd 88. *Hawthorn Bank, Clunton, Craven Arms SY7 0HP* Tel (01588) 660281

BUCKLEY, John. b 42. **d** 95 **p** 96. C Macclesfield Team *Ches* 95-01; P-in-c Pott Shrigley from 01; Chapl E Cheshire NHS Trust from 01. *The Vicarage, Spuley Lane, Pott Shrigley, Macclesfield SK10 5RS* Tel (01625) 573316

BUCKLEY, Michael. b 49. St Jo Coll Dur Cranmer Hall Dur 77. **d** 79 **p** 80. C Birkdale St Jo *Liv* 79-82; TV Maghull 82-88; V Earlestown 88-98; V Gt Sankey from 98. *The Parsonage, Parsonage Way, Great Sankey, Warrington WA5 1RP* Tel (01925) 723235

BUCKLEY, Rex. *See* BUCKLEY, David Rex

BUCKLEY, Richard Francis. b 44. Ripon Hall Ox 69. **d** 72 **p** 73. C Portsea St Cuth *Portsm* 72-75; C Portsea All SS w St Jo Rudmore 75-79; Chapl RN 79-00; Perm to Offic *B & W* from 00. *Ste Croix, Coryate Close, Higher Odcombe, Yeovil BA22 8UJ* Tel and fax (01935) 864039 Mobile 07810-123065 E-mail rfbuckley@onetel.com

BUCKLEY, Richard John. b 43. Hull Univ BSc(Econ)64 PhD87 Strathclyde Univ MSc69. Sarum Th Coll 64. **d** 66 **p** 67. C Huddersfield St Jo *Wakef* 66-68; C Sutton St Jas from 69-71; TV Sutton St Jas and Wawne 71-75; V Handsworth Woodhouse *Sheff* 75-85; R Adwick-le-Street 85-91; V Wentworth and Area Co-ord (S Yorks) Chr Aid 91-97; Area Co-ord (S and E Yorkshire) Chr Aid 97-07; rtd 07; Perm to Offic *York* 97-00 and *Sheff* from 97. *2 Kirkstead Abbey Mews, Thorpe Hesley, Rotherham S61 2UZ* Tel 0114-246 5064 E-mail richard@buckjley.wanadoo.co.uk

BUCKLEY, Richard Simon Fildes. b 53. WMMTC 97. **d** 00 **p** 01. NSM Moseley St Mary *Birm* 00-04; NSM Soho St Anne w St Thos and St Pet *Lon* from 05. *12 College Green Court, 55 Barrington Road, London SW9 7JG* Tel (020) 7095 1810 Mobile 07976-290351 E-mail puppet.buckley@virgin.net

BUCKLEY, Robert William. b 50. Grey Coll Dur BSc70 PhD73 DipEd73 CPhys75 MInstE91 FCollP92 FInstP97. NOC 85. **d** 87 **p** 88. NSM N Greenford All Hallows *Lon* 87-91; P-in-c 91-94; NSM W Acton St Martin 94-95; NSM Ealing All SS 94-95; C 95-97; P-in-c Preston Ascension 97-99; TR Wembley Park 99-03; AD Brent 00-03; TR Atherton and Hindsford w Howe Bridge *Man* from 03; AD Leigh from 08. *St Michael's Vicarage, Leigh Road, Atherton, Manchester M46 0PH* Tel (01942) 883359

BUCKLEY, Stephen Richard. b 45. Cranmer Hall Dur 82. **d** 84 **p** 85. C Iffley *Ox* 84-88; TV Halesowen *Worc* 88-00; TR Sedgley All SS 00-05; TR Gornal and Sedgley from 05. *All Saints' Vicarage, Vicar Street, Sedgley, Dudley DY3 3SD* Tel (01902) 883255 E-mail stephen@presbyter.freeserve.co.uk

BUCKLEY, Timothy Denys. b 57. BA. St Jo Coll Nottm. **d** 83 **p** 84. C S Westoe *Dur* 83-85; C Paddington Em Harrow Road *Lon* 85-88; C Binley *Cov* 88-98; Min Binley Woods LEP 88-98; V Belton Gp *Linc* from 98; P-in-c Crowle Gp from 09. *The Old Rectory, 118 High Street, Belton, Doncaster DN9 1NS* Tel (01427) 872207 E-mail timothybuckley@breathe.com

BUCKLEY, Timothy John. b 67. Jes Coll Cam BA90 MA94 ACA94. Wycliffe Hall Ox BTh99. **d** 99 **p** 00. C Langdon Hills *Chelmsf* 99-02; P-in-c Devonport St Mich and St Barn *Ex* from 02. *St Barnabas' Vicarage, 10 De la Hay Avenue, Plymouth PL3 4HU* Tel (01752) 666544 E-mail rev.tim@virgin.net

BUCKMAN, Rossly David. b 36. TCD BA64 MA67 St Pet Coll Ox BA65 MA98. Moore Th Coll Sydney. **d** 59 **p** 60. C Eastwood Australia 59-60; C Port Kembla 60-61; C Dublin Harold's Cross *D & G* 61-64; C Ox St Mich 64-65; C Leet Clifton Th Coll 65-69; CF 69-76; Tutor Canberra Coll of Min Australia 77-80; P-in-c Mid Marsh Gp *Linc* 81-82; R 82-89; P-in-c Blakehurst Australia 89-91; R 91-00; Chapl Düsseldorf *Eur* 00-05; rtd 05. *1/40*

Bundoran Parade, Mont Albert North Vic 3129, Australia Tel (0061) (3) 9890 4340 Fax 9899 9849 E-mail buckmen@bigpond.com

BUCKNALL, Ms Alison Mary. b 55. Leeds Univ BA76 Trin Coll Bris MA94. Qu Coll Birm 94. **d** 96 **p** 97. C The Quinton *Birm* 96-00; C Sutton Coldfield H Trin 00-01; Asst Chapl N Bris NHS Trust from 01. *North Bristol NHS Trust, Beckspool Road, Frenchay, Bristol BS16 1LE* Tel 0117-970 1070

BUCKNALL, Allan. b 35. St Matthias Coll Bris CertEd73. ALCD62. **d** 62 **p** 63. C Harlow New Town w Lt Parndon *Chelmsf* 62-69; Chapl W Somerset Miss to Deaf 69-71; Perm to Offic *Bris* 71-77; P-in-c Wisborough Green *Chich* 77-79; R Tillington 78-86; R Duncton 82-86; R Up Waltham 82-86; C Henfield w Shermanbury and Woodmancote 86-89; Asst Chapl Princess Marg Hosp Swindon 89-96; Angl Chapl Swindon and Marlborough NHS Trust 96-00; rtd 00; Perm to Offic *Bris* from 00. *5 The Willows, Highworth, Swindon SN6 7PG* Tel (01793) 762721

BUCKNALL, Miss Ann Gordon. b 32. K Coll Lon BSc53 Hughes Hall Cam DipEd54. Qu Coll Birm 80. **dss** 81 **d** 87 **p** 94. Birm St Aid Small Heath 81-85; Balsall Heath St Paul 85-92; Par Dn 87-92; C Handsworth St Jas 92-95; rtd 95; Perm to Offic *Lich* from 95. *20 St Margaret's Road, Lichfield WS13 7RA* Tel (01543) 257382

BUDD, John Christopher. b 51. QUB BA73. CITC. **d** 82 **p** 83. C Ballymena *Conn* 82-85; C Jordanstown w Monkstown 85-88; I Craigs w Dunaghy and Killagan 88-97; Dioc Info Officer 89-97; Bp's Dom Chapl from 94; I Derriaghy w Colin from 97. *Derriaghy Rectory, 20 Derriaghy Road, Magheralave, Lisburn BT28 3SH* Tel (028) 9061 0859

BUDD, John Victor. b 31. CCC Ox BA55 MA58 Open Univ BSc98. Bps' Coll Cheshunt 57. **d** 59 **p** 60. C Friern Barnet St Jas *Lon* 59-64; C Harrow Weald All SS 64-70; Lic to Offic *St Alb* 70-73; V Lt Amwell 73-96; RD Hertford 83-88; rtd 96; Perm to Offic *Worc* from 96. *37 Wykewane, Malvern WR14 2XD* Tel (01684) 566174

BUDD, Philip John. b 40. St Jo Coll Dur BA63 MLitt71 Bris Univ PhD78. Cranmer Hall Dur. **d** 66 **p** 67. C Attenborough w Chilwell *S'well* 66-69; Lect Clifton Th Coll 69-71; Lect Trin Coll Bris 72-80; Tutor Ripon Coll Cuddesdon 80-88; Asst Chapl and Tutor Westmr Coll Ox 80-00; Lect 88-00; Asst Chapl and Tutor Ox Brookes Univ 00-03; Lect 00-03; Hon C N Hinksey and Wytham 03-06; Perm to Offic from 06. *4 Clover Close, Oxford OX2 9JH* Tel (01865) 863682 E-mail budds@talk21.com

BUDDEN, Alexander Mark. b 60. UEA BA84. SEITE 01. **d** 04 **p** 05. NSM Mitcham St Barn *S'wark* 04-08; Perm to Offic from 09. *29 Dane Road, London SW19 2NB* Tel (020) 8542 0622 Mobile 07738-290534 E-mail markbudden@sky.com

BUDDEN, Clive John. b 39. Lon Univ DipEd Liv Univ BA. Chich Th Coll. **d** 84 **p** 86. C Gaywood, Bawsey and Mintlyn *Nor* 84-87; TV Brixham w Churston Ferrers and Kingswear *Ex* 87-90; R Exton and Winsford and Cutcombe w Luxborough *B & W* 90-99; Perm to Offic *Truro* 00-02; P-in-c Veryan w Ruan Lanihorne 02-07; rtd 07. *Carennac House, Polbreen Lane, St Agnes TR5 0UL* Tel (01872) 554313

BUDGELL, Peter Charles. b 50. Lon Univ BD74. **d** 83 **p** 84. C Goodmayes All SS *Chelmsf* 83-86; C Chipping Barnet w Arkley *St Alb* 86-88; V Luton St Anne 88-06; V Luton St Anne w St Chris from 06. *The Vicarage, 7 Blaydon Road, Luton LU2 0RP* Tel and fax (01582) 720052 E-mail pcbudgell@aol.com

BUDGETT, Preb Anthony Thomas. b 26. TD60. Oriel Coll Ox BA50 MA57. Wells Th Coll 52. **d** 59 **p** 60. C Hendford *B & W* 59-63; PC Lopen 63-68; R Seavington St Mich w St Mary 63-68; V Somerton 68-80; RD Ilchester 72-81; P-in-c Compton Dundon 76-80; R Somerton w Compton Dundon 80-81; R Somerton w Compton Dundon, the Charltons etc 81-84; Preb Wells Cathl 83-90; P-in-c Bruton w Lamyatt, Wyke and Redlynch 84-85; P-in-c Batcombe w Upton Noble 84-85; P-in-c S w N Brewham 84-85; TR Bruton and Distr 85-90; rtd 90; Perm to Offic *Ex* from 90 and *B & W* from 94. *Cornerways, White Ball, Wellington TA21 0LS* Tel (01823) 672321

BUFFREY, Canon Samuel John Thomas. b 28. Keble Coll Ox BA52 MA57. Cuddesdon Coll 52. **d** 54 **p** 55. C Lower Tuffley St Geo CD *Glouc* 54-56; C Branksome St Aldhelm *Sarum* 56-61; R Gussage St Michael and Gussage All Saints 61-69; V Amesbury 69-80; RD Avon 77-80; P-in-c Broadstone 80-82; V 82-93; Can and Preb Sarum Cathl 87-93; rtd 93; Perm to Offic *Sarum* from 93. *34 Woolslope Road, West Moors, Ferndown BH22 0PD* Tel (01202) 875522

BUFTON (née FORSHAW), Mrs Janet Elisabeth. b 41. Redland Coll of Educn CertEd61. **d** 99 **p** 00. OLM Debenham w Aspall and Kenton *St E* 99-04; OLM Helmingham w Framsden and Pettaugh w Winston 99-04; OLM Debenham and Helmingham 04-07; rtd 07. *Harkaway Cottage, 9 Fenn Street, Winston, Stowmarket IP14 6LD* Tel (01728) 860535

BUGBY, Timothy. b 53. AKC75. Chich Th Coll 76. **d** 77 **p** 78. C Hockerill *St Alb* 77-81; C Pimlico St Mary Graham-street *Lon* 81-87; V Highgate St Aug 87-03; Dir Educn, Min and Voc Confraternity of the Blessed Sacrament 00-03; Perm to Offic *Lon*

112

and *Nor* from 04; *St Alb* from 05. *Seaview Cottage, Cromer Road, East Runton, Cromer NR27 9NH* Tel and fax (01263) 512830 Mobile 07721-022626
E-mail timbugby1953@btinternet.com
BUGDEN, Ernest William. b 16. Lich Th Coll 56. **d** 58 **p** 59. C Esher *Guildf* 58-68; Hon C 68-81; rtd 81; Perm to Offic *Ely* 91-03. *32 French's Road, Cambridge CB4 3LA* Tel (01223) 311306
BUGG, Canon Peter Richard. b 33. Univ of BC BA62. Wells Th Coll 63. **d** 64 **p** 64. C Whitley Ch Ch *Ox* 64-67; C Ludlow *Heref* 67-69; Lic to Offic Zambia 69-72; P-in-c Brill w Boarstall *Ox* 72-78; P-in-c Chilton w Dorton 77-78; V Brill, Boarstall, Chilton and Dorton 78-97; Hon Can Ch Ch 92-97; rtd 97; Lic to Offic Kimberley and Kuruman S Africa 95-98; Perm to Offic *Ox* 04-09. *6 Woodward Parks, Fladbury, Pershore WR10 2RB* Tel (01386) 860531 E-mail pjbugg@btinternet.com
BUGLER, Canon Derek Leslie. b 25. Gen Th Sem NY 62. **d** 64 **p** 64. USA 64-90 and from 04; rtd 90; Lic to Offic *Win* 90-04. *51 Raymond Road, Brunswick ME 04011, USA*
E-mail dbugler@gwi.net
BUIK, Allan David. b 39. St Andr Univ BSc61. Coll of Resurr Mirfield 66. **d** 68 **p** 69. Perm to Offic *Win* 68-69; CMP from 69; C Eastleigh *Win* 69-72; C Brighton St Bart *Chich* 72-74; C Lavender Hill Ascension *S'wark* 74-78; V Kingstanding St Mark *Birm* 78-86; Guyana 86-91; V Tunstall *Lich* 91-07; rtd 07; P-in-c Hempton and Pudding Norton from 07; Chantry P Shrine of Our Lady of Walsingham from 06. *20 Cleaves Drive, Walsingham NR22 6EQ* Tel (01328) 820030 Mobile 07703-479715 E-mail allanbuik@googlemail.com
BUIKE, Desmond Mainwaring. b 32. Ex Coll Ox BA55 MA69 Leeds Univ CertEd72. **d** 57 **p** 58. C Man St Aid 57-60; C Ox SS Phil and Jas 60-63; V Queensbury *Bradf* 63-71; Perm to Offic *Bradf* 71-85 and *York* from 93; V Glaisdale *York* 85-93; rtd 93. *Wayside, 3 White Bridge Road, Whitby YO21 3JQ* Tel (01947) 821440
BULCOCK, Andrew Marcus. b 62. **d** 03 **p** 04. OLM Elton St Steph *Man* 03-06; Perm to Offic 06-08; OLM Turton Moorland Min from 08. *5 Fieldhead Avenue, Bury BL8 2LX* Tel 0161-761 6347
BULL, Andrew David. b 70. Hull Univ BSc91 Sheff Univ PGCE92. Regents Th Coll BA99. **d** 07 **p** 08. C Macclesfield Team *Ches* from 07. *7 Brocklehurst Way, Macclesfield SK10 2HY* Tel (01625) 617680 E-mail ukbulls@aol.com
BULL, Mrs Christine. b 45. Bedf Coll Lon BA67. NOC 91. **d** 94 **p** 95. NSM High Lane *Ches* 94-98; NSM Stockport SW 98-99; Perm to Offic *Derby* 98-04; *Ches* 99-04; *Man* from 00; C Hale and Ashley 04-07; NSM Wormhill, Peak Forest w Peak Dale and Dove Holes *Derby* 07-08; C Ches Cathl from 08. *Flat 4, 15 Abbey Street, Chester CH1 2JF* E-mail revchristinebull@yahoo.co.uk
BULL (née ADAMS), Mrs Christine Frances. b 53. Cam Inst of Educn CertEd74. NEOC 97. **d** 00 **p** 01. NSM St Oswald in Lee w Bingfield *Newc* from 00; P-in-c from 07. *East Side Lodge, Bingfield, Newcastle upon Tyne NE19 2LE* Tel (01434) 672303 E-mail pc.bull@ukonline.co.uk
BULL, Christopher Bertram. b 45. Lon Bible Coll BA87. Wycliffe Hall Ox 88. **d** 90 **p** 91. C Leominster *Heref* 90-95; P-in-c Westbury 95-02; R from 02; P-in-c Yockleton 95-02; R from 02; P-in-c Gt Wollaston 95-02; V from 02; P-in-c Worthen from 07. *The Rectory, Westbury, Shrewsbury SY5 9QX* Tel (01743) 884216 E-mail cbbull@fsmail.net
BULL, Christopher David. b 59. Univ of Wales MA08. St Jo Coll Nottm 89. **d** 91 **p** 92. C Bowbrook S *Worc* 91-95; P-in-c Flackwell Heath *Ox* 95-00; V from 00; RD Wycombe 97-05. *The Vicarage, 9 Chapel Road, Flackwell Heath, High Wycombe HP10 9AA* Tel (01628) 522795 or 533004
E-mail vicar@ccfh.org.uk
BULL, David. b 72. Worc Coll Ox BA94. Wycliffe Hall Ox BA07. **d** 08 **p** 09. C Reigate St Mary *S'wark* from 08. *3 St Clair Close, Reigate RH2 0QB* Tel (01737) 221100
BULL, George. *See* BULL, William George
BULL, John. *See* BULL, Michael John
BULL, Malcolm George. b 35. Portsm Dioc Tr Course 87. **d** 87 **p** 98. NSM Farlington *Portsm* 87-90; NSM Widley w Wymering 92-93; NSM S Hayling 93-97; NSM Hayling Is St Andr 97-00; Bp's Adv for Cults and New Relig Movements 99-00; rtd 00; Perm to Offic *Portsm* 00-01 and from 03; P-in-c Greatworth and Marston St Lawrence etc *Pet* 01-04. *20 Charleston Close, Hayling Island PO11 0JY* Tel (023) 9246 2025
E-mail bullmg@bushinternet.com
BULL, Martin Wells. b 37. Worc Coll Ox BA61 MA68. Ripon Hall Ox 61. **d** 63 **p** 64. C Blackley St Andr *Man* 63-67; C Horton *Bradf* 67-68; V Ingrow cum Hainworth 68-78; RD S Craven 74-77; V Bingley All SS 78-80; TR 80-92; P-in-c Gargrave 92-02; rtd 02; Perm to Offic *Ripon* from 03. *Mallard Cottage, Grewelthorpe, Ripon HG4 3BT* Tel (01765) 650473 Mobile 07870-138386
BULL, Michael John. b 35. Roch Th Coll 65. **d** 67 **p** 68. C N Wingfield *Derby* 67-69; C Skegness *Linc* 69-73; R Ingoldmells w Addlethorpe 72-79; Area Sec USPG *S'wark* 79-86; Area Org RNLI (Lon) 86-88; C Croydon St Jo *S'wark* 89-93; P-in-c

Mitcham Ch Ch 93-97; V Colliers Wood Ch Ch 97-00; rtd 00; Perm to Offic *Nor* 00-04; Hon C Guiltcross 04-08; P-in-c from 08. *The Rectory, Back Street, Garboldisham, Diss IP22 2SD* Tel (01953) 688347 E-mail mjbull@waitrose.com
BULL, Robert David. b 51. Westmr Coll Ox MTh03. Ripon Coll Cuddesdon 74. **d** 77 **p** 78. C Worsley *Man* 77-80; C Peel 80-81; TV 81-86; P-in-c Wisbech St Aug *Ely* 86-88; V 88-02; RD Wisbech 92-02; R Lich St Chad from 02; P-in-c Longdon from 08. *St Chad's Rectory, The Windings, Lichfield WS13 7EX* Tel (01543) 262254 E-mail robert.chad@tiscali.co.uk
BULL, Stephen Andrew. b 58. St Jo Coll Nottm 91. **d** 93 **p** 94. C Wroughton *Bris* 93-96; P-in-c Eyemouth *Edin* 96-98; Lic to Offic from 98. *12 Craigs Court, Torphichen, Bathgate EH48 4NU* Tel (01506) 650070 E-mail stvbull@btinternet.com
BULL, Miss Susan Helen. b 58. Qu Mary Coll Lon BSc79 ACIS84. STETS BTh98. **d** 98 **p** 99. NSM Epsom St Barn *Guildf* 98-04; Chapl Surrey and Borders Partnership NHS Trust from 04. *41 Stamford Green Road, Epsom KT18 7SR* Tel (01372) 742703 E-mail revd.sue@suebull.freeserve.co.uk
BULL, Timothy Martin. b 65. Worc Coll Ox BA87 MA93 Dur Univ PhD94 Fitzw Coll Cam BA98 MA07 FRSA96. Ridley Hall Cam 96. **d** 99 **p** 00. C Bath Walcot *B & W* 99-03; P-in-c Langham w Boxted *Chelmsf* from 03; Colchester Area CME Adv from 03. *The Rectory, Wick Road, Langham, Colchester CO4 5PG* Tel (01206) 230666
E-mail revdrtim@googlemail.com
BULL, William George. b 28. Sarum Th Coll 65. **d** 66 **p** 67. C Salisbury St Mich *Sarum* 66-69; V Swallowcliffe w Ansty 69-75; Dioc Youth Officer 69-71; P-in-c Laverstock 75-81; V 81-93; rtd 94; Perm to Offic *Sarum* from 94. *Bungalow 1, Boreham Field, Warminster BA12 9EB* Tel (01985) 847830
BULLAMORE, John Richard. b 41. Linc Coll Ox BA69 MA69. Wycliffe Hall Ox 74. **d** 95 **p** 95. NSM Eorropaidh *Arg* 95-98; NSM Bath St Sav w Swainswick and Woolley *B & W* 98-08; NSM Knaresborough *Ripon* from 08. *39 Birkdale Close, Knaresborough HG5 0LS* Tel (01423) 864484
E-mail john.bullamore@homecall.co.uk
BULLIMORE, Canon Christine Elizabeth. b 46. Nottm Univ BA67. St Jo Coll Nottm 96. **d** 96 **p** 97. Bp's Adv Past Care and Counselling *Wakef* 92-99 and from 01; NSM S Ossett 96-99; P-in-c Emley from 99; P-in-c Flockton cum Denby Grange from 99; RD Kirkburton from 05; Hon Can Wakef Cathl from 08. *The Rectory, 14 Grange Drive, Emley, Huddersfield HD8 9SF* Tel (01924) 849161 Fax 849219 Mobile 07778-022163
E-mail jcbullimor@aol.com
BULLIMORE, Matthew James. b 77. Em Coll Cam BA99 MA03 PhD07 Man Univ MPhil02. Harvard Div Sch 99 Westcott Ho Cam 01. **d** 05 **p** 06. C Roberttown w Hartshead *Wakef* 05-07; Bp's Dom Chapl from 07. *Bishop's Lodge, Woodthorpe Lane, Wakefield WF2 6JL* Tel (01924) 255349
E-mail mjb56@cantab.net
or mbullimore@bishopofwakefield.org.uk
BULLIVANT, Ronald. b 32. CertEd. St Mich Coll Llan. **d** 59 **p** 60. C Roath St German *Llan* 59-61; P-in-c Bradf H Trin 61-66; V Horbury *Wakef* 66-69; Lic to Offic *Ripon* 70-78; Perm to Offic *Nor* 78-81; Lic to Offic 81-98; Perm to Offic *Man* from 99. *14 St Albans Terrace, Manchester M8 8BZ* Tel 0161-832 2423
BULLOCH, William Gillespie. b 68. St Steph Ho Ox. **d** 01 **p** 02. C Bognor *Chich* 01-05; V Leigh-on-Sea St Jas *Chelmsf* from 05. *St James's Vicarage, 103 Blenheim Chase, Leigh-on-Sea SS9 3BY* Tel (01702) 471786 E-mail frbill.bulloch@gmail.com
BULLOCK, Andrew Belfrage. b 50. Univ of Wales (Ban) BSc73 MEd81 Westmr Coll Ox PGCE79. Wycliffe Hall Ox 94. **d** 97 **p** 98. C Sandhurst *Ox* 97-02; P-in-c Alfrick, Lulsley, Suckley, Leigh and Bransford *Worc* 02-08; TV Worcs W from 09. *The Rectory, Leigh, Worcester WR6 5LE* Tel (01886) 832355 Mobile 07958-654331 E-mail abullock@waitrose.com
BULLOCK, Andrew Timothy. b 56. Southn Univ BTh91. Sarum & Wells Th Coll 89. **d** 91 **p** 92. C Erdington St Barn *Birm* 91-94; TV Solihull 94-03; P-in-c Acocks Green 03-08; V from 08. *The Vicarage, 34 Dudley Park Road, Acocks Green, Birmingham B27 6QR* Tel and fax 0121-706 9764
E-mail andrewbullock2@blueyonder.co.uk
BULLOCK, Ian. b 74. Cranmer Hall Dur. **d** 08 **p** 09. C Pontefract St Giles *Wakef* from 08. *72A Eastbourne View, Pontefract WF8 2HG* E-mail ianb@mailshack.com
BULLOCK, Jude Ross. b 58. Heythrop Coll Lon BD89. Allen Hall 84. **d** 89 **p** 90. In RC Ch 89-97; C Lt Ilford St Mich *Chelmsf* 01-05; V Chingford St Anne from 05. *St Anne's Vicarage, 200A Larkshall Road, London E4 6NP* Tel (020) 8529 4740 Mobile 07976-395732 E-mail juderbullock1@yahoo.co.uk
BULLOCK, Kenneth Poyser. b 27. Down Coll Cam BA50 MA55. Ridley Hall Cam 50. **d** 52 **p** 53. C Aston SS Pet and Paul *Birm* 52-56; R Openshaw *Man* 56-63; V Ainsworth 63-91; rtd 91. *26 Plas Penrhyn, Penrhyn Bay, Llandudno LL30 3EH* Tel (01492) 543343
BULLOCK, Canon Michael. b 49. Hatf Coll Dur BA71. Coll of Resurr Mirfield 72. **d** 75 **p** 76. C Pet St Jo 75-79; Zambia 79-86; V Longthorpe *Pet* 86-91; Chapl Naples *Eur* 91-99; OGS from 93;

P-in-c Liguria *Eur* 99-00; Chapl Gtr Lisbon from 00; Can Malta Cathl from 98. *rua Joao de Deus 5, Alcoitão, 2645-128 Alcabideche, Portugal* Tel and fax (00351) (21) 469 2303 E-mail padre@lisbonanglicans.org

BULLOCK, Philip. b 59. Qu Coll Birm 05. **d** 08 **p** 09. C Cov E from 08. *129A London Road, Coventry CV1 2JQ* Tel 07831-147822 (mobile) E-mail philip.bullock00@btinternet.com

BULLOCK, Miss Rosemary Joy. b 59. Portsm Poly BA81 Southn Univ BTh94. Sarum & Wells Th Coll 89. **d** 91 **p** 94. Par Dn Warblington w Emsworth *Portsm* 91-94; C 94-95; C Gt Parndon *Chelmsf* 95-98; TV Beaminster Area *Sarum* 98-03; P-in-c Ridgeway 03-04. *82 Green Lane, Shanklin PO37 7HD* Tel (01983) 863345

BULLOCK (née WHEALE), Canon Sarah Ruth. b 64. Surrey Univ BA86 St Jo Coll Dur BA93. Cranmer Hall Dur 90. **d** 93 **p** 94. C Kersal Moor *Man* 93-98; P-in-c Whalley Range St Edm 98-04; P-in-c Moss Side St Jas w St Clem 99-04; R Whalley Range St Edm and Moss Side etc from 04; Dioc Voc Adv 98-05; Chapl MU 00-06; Hon Can Man Cathl from 07. *St Edmund's Rectory, 1 Range Road, Manchester M16 8FS* Tel 0161-226 1291 E-mail revsbullock@aol.com

BULLOCK, Stephanie Clair. b 46. St Mary's Hosp Medical Sch Lon MB, BS70. Ripon Coll Cuddesdon 90. **d** 92 **p** 94. Par Dn Cuddesdon *Ox* 92-94; Tutor Ripon Coll Cuddesdon 92-94; Asst Chapl Ox Radcliffe Hosp NHS Trust 94-97; Chapl Ox Radcliffe Hosps NHS Trust 97-03; Hon C Headington St Mary *Ox* from 03. *Church Farm, Church Lane, Old Marston, Oxford OX3 0PT* Tel (01865) 722926

BULLOCK, Victor James Allen. b 67. Southn Univ BTh90 St Mary's Coll Twickenham PGCE91. St Steph Ho Ox 92. **d** 94 **p** 95. C Cowley St Jas *Ox* 94-95; C Reading St Giles 95-99; V Fenny Stratford from 99. *The Vicarage, Manor Road, Milton Keynes MK2 2HW* Tel (01908) 372825

BULMAN, Madeline Judith. *See* STRONG, Ms Madeline Judith

BULMAN, Michael Thomas Andrew. b 34. Jes Coll Cam BA59 MA61. Ridley Hall Cam 58. **d** 60 **p** 61. C Blackpool St Mark *Blackb* 60-63; C Branksome St Clem *Sarum* 63-67; V York St Barn 67-84; CMJ Israel 84-93; R Jerusalem Ch 85-87; Can Jerusalem 87-93; R Maresfield and V Nutley *Chich* 94-00; rtd 00; Perm to Offic *Portsm* from 06. *Oate Villa, Western Road, Ivybridge PL21 9AT* Tel (01752) 691941 E-mail michael.bulman@btopenworld.com

BUNCE (née HOW), Gillian Carol. b 53. K Coll Lon MB, BS77 MRCGP82 MFHom96. STETS 04. **d** 07 **p** 08. NSM Worle *B & W* from 07. *85 Clevedon Road, Tickenham, Clevedon BS21 6RD* Tel (01275) 810610 E-mail gill.how@blueyonder.co.uk

BUNCE, Michael John. b 49. Westcott Ho Cam. **d** 80 **p** 81. C Grantham *Linc* 80-83; TV 83-85; R Tarfside *Bre* 85-92; R Brechin 85-92; R Auchmithie 91-92; Provost St Paul's Cathl Dundee 92-97; Chapl Menorca *Eur* from 00. *Apartado de Correos 102, 07720 Es Castell, Menorca, Spain* Tel (0034) 971 352 378 Fax 971 150 173

BUNCE, Raymond Frederick. b 28. Ely Th Coll 54. **d** 57 **p** 58. C Hillingdon St Andr *Lon* 57-62; C Greenford H Cross 62-67; V Ealing All SS 67-89; Chapl Ascot Priory 89-90; rtd 90; Perm to Offic *Portsm* from 91 and *Chich* from 99. *45 Guillards Oak, Midhurst GU29 9JZ* Tel (01730) 816282

BUNCH, Canon Andrew William Havard. b 53. Selw Coll Cam BA74 MA78 PhD79. Ox NSM Course 84. **d** 87 **p** 88. NSM Wantage *Ox* 87-91; C New Windsor 91-93; TV 93-97; V Ox St Giles and SS Phil and Jas w St Marg from 97; Hon Can Ch Ch from 09. *The Vicarage, Church Walk, Oxford OX2 6LY* Tel (01865) 510460 E-mail vicar@churchwalk.eclipse.co.uk

BUNDAY, Canon Paul. b 30. Wadh Coll Ox BA54 MA58. ALCD56. **d** 56 **p** 57. C Woking St Jo *Guildf* 56-60; Chapl Reed's Sch Cobham 60-66; R Landford w Plaitford *Sarum* 66-77; RD Alderbury 73-77; TR Radipole and Melcombe Regis 77-86; RD Weymouth 82-85; Can and Preb Sarum Cathl 83-95; TV Whitton 86-91; TR 91-95; Chapl Duchess of Somerset Hosp Froxfield 86-94; rtd 95; Perm to Offic *Sarum* from 95. *4 Springfield Park, Tisbury, Salisbury SP3 6QN* Tel (01747) 871530

BUNDAY, Richard William. b 76. Lanc Univ BA98 MA04. Cranmer Hall Dur 98. **d** 00 **p** 01. C Redcar *York* 00-01; C Marton *Blackb* 01-04; P-in-c Ashton-on-Ribble St Mich w Preston St Mark 04-06; TR W Preston from 06. *St Michael's Vicarage, 2 Edgerton Road, Ashton-on-Ribble, Preston PR2 1AJ* Tel (01772) 726157 E-mail bundays@blueyonder.co.uk

BUNDOCK, Canon Anthony Francis. b 49. Qu Coll Birm 81. **d** 83 **p** 84. C Stansted Mountfitchet *Chelmsf* 83-86; TV Borehamwood *St Alb* 86-94; TR Seacroft *Ripon* 94-05; AD Whitkirk 00-05; TR Leeds City from 05; Hon Can Ripon Cathl from 05. *Leeds Rectory, 1 Vicarage View, Leeds LS5 3HF* Tel 0113-278 6237 E-mail tony.pat.bundock@virgin.net

BUNDOCK, Edward Leigh. b 52. Keble Coll Ox BA73 Open Univ PhD94 MAAT. St Steph Ho Ox 74. **d** 76 **p** 77. C Malvern Link w Cowleigh *Worc* 76-80; C-in-c Portslade Gd Shep CD

Chich 80-88; V Wisborough Green 88-94; Perm to Offic *Guildf* 96-97; P-in-c E and W Rudham, Houghton-next-Harpley etc *Nor* 97-99; R E w W Rudham, Helhoughton etc from 99. *The Rectory, South Raynham Road, West Raynham, Fakenham NR21 7HH* Tel (01328) 838385

BUNDOCK, Canon John Nicholas Edward. b 45. Wells Th Coll 66. **d** 70 **p** 71. C Chingford SS Pet and Paul *Chelmsf* 70-74; P-in-c Gt Grimsby St Matt Fairfield CD *Linc* 74-81; V Hindhead *Guildf* 81-99; RD Farnham 91-96; V Bramley and Grafham from 99; RD Cranleigh from 04; Chapl Gosden Ho Sch from 99; Hon Can Guildf Cathl from 09. *The Vicarage, Birtley Rise, Bramley, Guildford GU5 0HZ* Tel (01483) 892109 E-mail jnebundock@tiscali.co.uk

BUNDOCK, Nicholas John. b 73. Sheff Univ BSc94 PhD98 Fitzw Coll Cam BA01. Ridley Hall Cam 99. **d** 02 **p** 03. C Mortomley St Sav High Green *Sheff* 02-05; TV Didsbury St Jas and Em *Man* from 05. *453 Parrs Wood Road, Manchester M20 5NE* Tel 0161-445 1310 E-mail nickbundock@stjamesandemmanuel.org

BUNDOCK, Ronald Michael. b 44. Leeds Univ BSc65. Ox NSM Course 87. **d** 90 **p** 91. NSM Buckingham *Ox* 90-98; NSM Stowe 98-03; P-in-c from 03. *1 Holton Road, Buckingham MK18 1PQ* Tel (01280) 813887 E-mail ron@bundock.com

BUNKER (née HARDING), Mrs Elizabeth. Chelsea Coll Lon BSc67 MSc69. SAOMC 04. **d** 06 **p** 07. NSM Baldock w Bygrave and Weston *St Alb* from 06. *Ariana, 6 Hinton Road, Letchworth Garden City SG6 3LL* Tel (01462) 686808 Fax 679276 Mobile 07850-413724 E-mail elizabethbunker@hotmail.com

BUNKER, Janet Constance. b 59. Qu Mary Coll Lon BSc81 R Holloway & Bedf New Coll Lon PhD85 Open Univ MA(Ed). Westcott Ho Cam 05. **d** 07 **p** 08. C Cambridge Ascension *Ely* from 07. *Ascension Rectory, 95 Richmond Road, Cambridge CB4 3PS* Tel (01223) 361919 Mobile 07811-357564 E-mail janetbunker@yahoo.com

BUNKER, John Herbert George. b 31. AKC56. **d** 57 **p** 58. C Newc St Jo 57-60; C Cullercoats St Geo 61-65; V Byker St Mich 65-74; V Ashington 74-84; V Halifax St Aug *Wakef* 84-93; rtd 93; Perm to Offic *Wakef* 93-98. *1 Hebble Dean, Hebble Lane, Halifax HX3 5JL*

BUNKER, The Very Revd Michael. b 37. Oak Hill Th Coll 59. **d** 63 **p** 64. C Alperton *Lon* 63-66; C St Helens St Helen *Liv* 66-70; V Muswell Hill St Matt *Lon* 70-79; V Muswell Hill St Jas 78-79; V Muswell Hill St Jas w St Matt 79-92; AD W Haringey 85-90; Preb St Paul's Cathl 90-92; Dean Pet 92-06; rtd 06. *21 Black Pot Lane, Oundle, Peterborough PE8 4AT* Tel (01832) 273032 E-mail mandmbbythesea@btinternet.com

BUNN, Mrs Rosemary Joan. b 60. EAMTC 94. **d** 97 **p** 98. NSM Sprowston w Beeston *Nor* 97-01; R Stoke H Cross w Dunston, Arminghall etc from 01. *Holy Cross Vicarage, Mill Road, Stoke Holy Cross, Norwich NR14 8PA* Tel (01508) 492305 E-mail rev.rosie@venta-group.org.uk

BUNNELL, Adrian. b 49. Univ of Wales (Abth) BSc72. St Mich Coll Llan 74. **d** 75 **p** 76. C Wrexham *St As* 75-78; C Rhyl w St Ann 78-79; CF 79-95; R Aberfoyle and Callander *St And* 95-03; R Newport-on-Tay 03-06; rtd 06. *Gauger Hall Cottage, Forneth, Blairgowrie PH10 6SP* Tel (01350) 724317 E-mail adrian.bunnell@tesco.net

BUNTING, Edward Garth. b 70. TCD BTh99. CITC 96. **d** 99 **p** 00. C Clooney w Strathfoyle *D & R* 99-02; I Leckpatrick w Dunnalong 02-06; I Belfast Upper Malone (Epiphany) *Conn* from 06; I Finaghy from 06. *The Rectory, 74 Locksley Park, Belfast BT10 0AS* Tel (028) 9060 1588 E-mail uppermalone@connor.anglican.org

BUNTING, Canon Ian David. b 33. Ex Coll Ox BA58 MA61. Tyndale Hall Bris 57 Princeton Th Sem ThM60. **d** 60 **p** 61. C Bootle St Leon *Liv* 60-63; V Waterloo St Jo 64-71; Dir Past Studies St Jo Coll Dur 71-78; R Chester le Street *Dur* 78-87; RD Chester-le-Street 79-84; Kingham Hill Fellow 87-89; Dioc Dir of Ords *S'well* 90-99; C Lenton 90-97; Hon Can S'well Minster 93-99; Bp's Research Officer 97-00; rtd 00; Perm to Offic *S'well* from 00. *8 Crafts Way, Southwell NG25 0BL* Tel (01636) 813868 E-mail ibunting@waitrose.com

BUNTING, Jeremy John. b 34. St Cath Coll Cam BA56 MA60 Worc Coll Ox BA58 MA60. St Steph Ho Ox 57. **d** 59 **p** 60. C Bickley *Roch* 59-62; C Cambridge St Mary Less *Ely* 62-66; Fell and Tutor Gen Th Sem New York USA 66-68; R Stock Harvard *Chelmsf* 68-87; RD Wickford 73-79; V Hampstead Garden Suburb *Lon* 87-94; rtd 99. *Fairview, 82 New Road, Haslingfield, Cambridge CB23 1LP* Tel (01223) 871602

BUNTING (née BYRNE), Mrs Lynda. b 47. STETS 06. **d** 08 **p** 09. NSM Chandler's Ford *Win* from 08. *18 Queen's Road, Chandler's Ford, Eastleigh SO53 5AH* Tel (023) 8026 9418 E-mail lyndabunting@aol.com

BUNYAN, David Richard. b 48. Edin Th Coll 93. **d** 96 **p** 97. NSM Musselburgh *Edin* 96-98; NSM Prestonpans 96-98; C Edin St Dav 98-00; R Grangemouth from 00; P-in-c Bo'ness from 00. *The Rectory, 33 Carronflats Road, Grangemouth FK3 9DG* Tel and fax (01324) 482438 E-mail drbdoe@blueyonder.co.uk

BUNYAN, Richard Charles. b 43. Oak Hill Th Coll 63 Ridley Hall Cam 69. **d** 71 **p** 72. C Luton Ch Ch *Roch* 71-74; C Bexleyheath

Ch Ch 74-76; C Bexley St Jo 76-79; TV Northampton Em *Pet* 79-81; V Erith St Jo *Roch* 81-86; V S Woodham Ferrers *Chelmsf* 86-89; Chapl Scargill Ho 89-90; Sub Chapl HM Pris Swaleside 91-94; Dep Chapl HM Pris Belmarsh 94-96; Chapl HM Pris Littlehey 96-08; rtd 08; Perm to Offic *Ely* from 08. *6 Swan End, Buckden, St Neots PE19 5SW* Tel (01480) 812950
E-mail rbunyan@btinternet.com

BUR, Patricia Margaret. *See* CAPRIELLO, Patricia Margaret

BURBERRY, Miss Frances Sheila. b 60. ACII83. TISEC 03. **d** 06 **p** 07. C Edin St Pet from 06; Hon Chapl Edin Univ from 06. *2F2 10 Hope Park Crescent, Edinburgh EH8 9NA* Tel 0131-667 4537

BURBERY, Ian Edward. b 37. Univ of Wales (Lamp) BA59. Coll of Resurr Mirfield 59. **d** 61 **p** 62. C Penarth w Lavernock *Llan* 61-68; V Porth 68-77; V Cainscross w Selsley *Glouc* 77-89; P-in-c Cheltenham Em 89-95; V Cheltenham Em w St Steph 95-98; rtd 98. *21 Fairy Grove, Killay, Swansea SA2 7BY* Tel (01792) 204460

BURBIDGE, Barry Desmond. b 52. STETS 94. **d** 97 **p** 98. NSM Fleet *Guildf* 97-03; NSM Crondall and Ewshot from 03; Chapl Frimley Park Hosp NHS Foundn Trust from 07. *34 Ashbury Drive, Hawley, Camberley GU17 9HH* Tel (01276) 32776
E-mail b.burbidge@ntlworld.com
or barry.burbidge@fph-tr.nhs.uk

BURBRIDGE, The Very Revd John Paul. b 32. K Coll Cam BA54 MA58 New Coll Ox BA54 MA58 FSA89. Wells Th Coll 58. **d** 59 **p** 60. C Eastbourne St Mary *Chich* 59-62; V Choral York Minster 62-66; Can Res and Prec 66-76; Adn Richmond *Ripon* 76-83; Can Res Ripon Cathl 76-83; Dean Nor 83-95; rtd 95; Perm to Offic *Ripon* 95-06. *The Clachan Bothy, Newtonairds, Dumfries DG2 0JL*

BURBRIDGE, Richard James. b 47. Univ of Wales (Ban) BSc68. Oak Hill Th Coll 68. **d** 72 **p** 73. C Rodbourne Cheney *Bris* 72-75; C Downend 75-78; P-in-c Bris H Cross Inns Court 78-83; P-in-c Fishponds All SS 83-86; V 86-97; RD Stapleton 89-95; C Bishopston 97-98; C Bris St Andr w St Bart 97-98; TV Bishopston and St Andrews from 98. *25 Morley Square, Bristol BS7 9DW* Tel 0117-942 4359

BURBURY, Janet. b 56. Sunderland Univ CertEd02. Cranmer Hall Dur 05. **d** 07 **p** 08. C Hart w Elwick Hall *Dur* from 07. *West Holling Carr, Trimdon, Trimdon Station, Durham TS29 6NN* Tel (01429) 880334 Mobile 07958-131271
E-mail janetb_231@hotmail.co.uk

BURCH, Charles Edward. b 57. Trin Coll Cam MA80 Lon Business Sch MBA87. ERMC 05. **d** 07 **p** 08. NSM Harpenden St Jo *St Alb* from 07. *12 Poynings Close, Harpenden AL5 1JD* Tel (01582) 712776 E-mail charlesburch37@hotmail.com

BURCH, Christopher. *See* BURCH, Canon John Christopher

BURCH, Canon John Christopher. b 50. Trin Coll Cam BA71 MA76 Leeds Univ MPhil95. St Jo Coll Nottm 73. **d** 76 **p** 77. C Sheff St Jo 76-79; C Holbeck *Ripon* 79-82; V Burmantofts St Steph and St Agnes 82-95; Can Res and Prec Cov Cathl 95-02; Chapl to Clergy of UPA 99-02; C-in-c Braunstone Park CD *Leic* 02-08; V Braunstone Park from 08; RD Christianity S 04-08; AD City of Leic from 08. *St Peter's Vicarage, Main Street, Leicester LE3 3AL* Tel 0116-289 3377 E-mail chris@burches.co.uk

BURCH, Paul Simon. b 75. St Jo Coll Dur MSc97 Man Metrop Univ PGCE98. St Steph Ho Ox BA03. **d** 04 **p** 05. C Carnforth *Blackb* 04-08; V Longford Cov from 08. *St Thomas's Vicarage, Hurst Road, Coventry CV6 6EL* Tel (024) 7636 4078
E-mail paulburch5@hotmail.com

BURCH, Canon Peter John. b 36. ACA60 FCA71. Ripon Hall Ox 62. **d** 64 **p** 65. C Brixton St Matt *S'wark* 64-67; Chapl Freetown St Aug Sierra Leone 68-72; P-in-c Chich St Pet 72-76; V Broadwater Down 76-85; V Steyning 85-94; R Ashurst 85-94; Hon Can Bauchi from 93; V Broadway *Worc* 94-96; V Broadway w Wickhamford 96-02; rtd 02; Perm to Offic *Glouc* from 03 and *Worc* from 04. *6 Jordan's Close, Willersey, Broadway WR12 7QD* Tel (01386) 853837 E-mail pj_pjburch@hotmail.com

BURCH, Stephen Roy. b 59. St Jo Coll Nottm 82. **d** 85 **p** 86. C Ipswich St Aug *St E* 85-89; Youth Chapl Cov 89-94; P-in-c Kinwarton w Gt Alne and Haselor 99-04; R 99-04; P-in-c Coughton 02-04; RD Alcester 99-04; V Fletchamstead from 04. *St James's Vicarage, 395 Tile Hill Lane, Coventry CV4 9DP* Tel (024) 7646 6262 E-mail stephen.burch@btinternet.com

BURCHELL, Mrs Elizabeth Susan. b 53. Sheff Univ BSc74. SAOMC 04. **d** 07 **p** 08. NSM Banbury St Leon *Ox* from 07. *11 Old Road, Great Tew, Chipping Norton OX7 4AN* Tel (01608) 683255 Mobile 07709-754914 E-mail burchellsue@aol.com

BURCHILL, Jane. b 31. Dalhousie Univ Canada BSc54 Aber Univ PhD81. Moray Ho Edin CertEd56 St Jo Coll Nottm 85. **d** 88 **p** 94. NSM Inverurie *Ab* from 88; NSM Auchindoir from 88; NSM Alford from 88; NSM Kemnay from 88. *5 Hopetoun Avenue, Bucksburn, Aberdeen AB21 9QU* Tel (01224) 712931

BURDEN, Miss Anne Margaret. b 47. Ex Univ BSc69 CQSW72. Linc Th Coll 89. **d** 91 **p** 94. Par Dn Mill Hill Jo Keble Ch *Lon* 91-94; C 94; TV Basingstoke *Win* 94-02; Dioc Adv for Women's Min 00-02; TV Brixham w Churston Ferrers and Kingswear *Ex* from 02. *6 Durleigh Road, Brixham TQ5 9JJ* Tel and fax (01803) 954924 E-mail anne-burden@virgin.com

BURDEN, Derek Ronald. b 37. Sarum Th Coll 59. **d** 62 **p** 63. C Cuddington *Guildf* 62-64; C Leamington Priors All SS *Cov* 64-66; C Stamford All SS w St Pet *Linc* 66-74; C-in-c Stamford Ch Ch CD 71-74; P-in-c Ashbury w Compton Beauchamp *Ox* 74-77; V 77-81; V Ashbury, Compton Beauchamp and Longcot w Fernham 81-84; V Wokingham St Sebastian 84-97; P-in-c Wooburn 97-02; rtd 02; Perm to Offic *Sarum* 03-05. *5 Cranford Park Drive, Yateley GU46 6JR* Tel (01276) 512343

BURDEN, Joanna Mary. *See* INGRAM, Mrs Joanna Mary

BURDEN, Michael Henry. b 36. Selw Coll Cam BA59 MA62 Hull Univ MEd79. Ridley Hall Cam 59. **d** 61 **p** 62. C Ashton-upon-Mersey St Mary Magd *Ches* 62-65; Chapl St Pet Sch York 65-70; Asst Master Beverley Gr Sch 70-74; R Walkington *York* 74-77; Chapl Asst Berwick R Infirmary 82-94; P-in-c Berwick H Trin *Newc* 82-87; V 87-89; P-in-c Berwick St Mary 82-87; V Berwick H Trin and St Mary 89-94; P-in-c Skirwith, Ousby and Melmerby w Kirkland *Carl* 94-98; Sec Guild of St Raphael 94-98; rtd 99; Perm to Offic *Newc* 99-09. *The College of St Barnabas, Blackberry Lane, Lingfield RH7 6NJ* Tel (01342) 872849

BURDEN, Paul. b 62. Rob Coll Cam BA84 MA88 AMIMechE87. Wycliffe Hall Ox BA91. **d** 92 **p** 93. C Clevedon St Andr and Ch Ch *B & W* 92-96; R Bathampton w Claverton from 96; Warden of Readers Bath Adnry from 06. *The Vicarage, Bathampton Lane, Bath BA2 6SW* Tel (01225) 463570
E-mail p.burden@talk21.com

BURDETT, John Fergusson. b 25. Pemb Coll Cam BA47 MA79. **d** 79 **p** 80. C Edin St Jo 79-87 and 90-95; Cyprus 87-90; rtd 95. *80/1 Barnton Park View, Edinburgh EH4 6HJ* Tel 0131-339 7226 Fax 317 1179 E-mail revjb@blueyonder.co.uk

BURDETT, Canon Stephen Martin. b 49. AKC72. St Aug Coll Cant 73. **d** 74 **p** 75. C Walworth St Pet *S'wark* 74-75; C Walworth 75-77; C Benhilton 77-80; P-in-c Earlsfield St Jo 80-83; V 83-89; V N Dulwich St Faith 89-99; Ldr Post Ord Tr Woolwich Area 96-99; TR Southend *Chelmsf* from 99; Hon Can Chelmsf Cathl from 09. *144 Alexandra Road, Southend-on-Sea SS1 1HB* Tel (01702) 342687 E-mail stephenburdett@btinternet.com

BURDON, Anthony James. b 46. Ex Univ LLB67 Lon Univ BD73. Oak Hill Th Coll 71. **d** 73 **p** 74. C Ox St Ebbe w St Pet 73-76; C Church Stretton *Heref* 76-78; Voc Sec CPAS and Hon C Bromley Ch Ch *Roch* 78-81; V Filkins w Broadwell, Broughton, Kelmscott etc *Ox* 81-84; R Broughton Poggs w Filkins, Broadwell etc 84-85; V Reading St Jo 85-96; C California and Adv for Spirituality (Berks) 96-98; Warden and P-in-c Cumbrae (or Millport) *Arg* 98-04; V Burstwick w Thorngumbald *York* from 04; P-in-c Roos and Garton w Tunstall, Grimston and Hilston from 08; RD S Holderness from 06. *The Vicarage, Main Road, Thorngumbald, Hull HU12 9NA* Tel (01964) 601381
E-mail tony@tonyburdon.karoo.co.uk

BURDON, Canon Christopher John. b 48. Jes Coll Cam BA70 MA74 Glas Univ PhD95. Coll of Resurr Mirfield 71. **d** 74 **p** 75. C Chelmsf All SS 74-78; TV High Wycombe *Ox* 78-84; P-in-c Olney w Emberton 84-90; R 90-92; Lic to Offic *Glas* 92-94; Lay Tr Officer *Chelmsf* 94-99; Prin NOC 00-07; Can Th and CME Adv *St E* from 07. *3 Crown Street, Bury St Edmunds IP33 1QX* Tel and fax (01284) 706813
E-mail chris@stedmundsbury.anglican.org

BURDON, Edward Arthur. b 11. Linc Th Coll 44. **d** 46 **p** 47. C Taunton H Trin *B & W* 46-48; C Mayfield *Chich* 48-54; V Gosfield *Chelmsf* 54-72; V Coggeshall w Markshall 72-80; rtd 80; Perm to Offic *St E* 81-02. *c/o the Revd Canon C J Burdon, 3 Crown Street, Bury St Edmunds IP33 1QX*

BURDON, Mrs Pamela Muriel. b 46. Ex Univ BA68 Reading Univ DipEd69. Wycliffe Hall Ox 88. **d** 90 **p** 94. Par Dn Reading St Jo 90-94; C 94-96; P-in-c California 96-98; NSM Cumbrae (or Millport) *Arg* 98-04; NSM Burstwick w Thorngumbald *York* from 04; C Preston and Sproatley in Holderness 05-06; P-in-c from 06; C Roos and Garton w Tunstall, Grimston and Hilston from 08. *The Vicarage, Main Road, Thorngumbald, Hull HU12 9NA* Tel (01964) 601464

BURFITT, Edward Ronald. b 42. MIMA64. Cranmer Hall Dur 91. **d** 93 **p** 94. C Monkseaton St Mary *Newc* 93-97; rtd 97. *Cragston Court, Cragston Close, Blakelaw, Newcastle upon Tyne NE5 3SR* Tel 0191-286 4443 Mobile 07870-762522
E-mail revburf@aol.com

BURFORD, Anthony Francis. b 55. Oak Hill Th Coll BA98. **d** 98 **p** 99. C Cov H Trin 98-02; P-in-c Rye Park St Cuth *St Alb* 02-07; V from 07. *The Vicarage, 8 Ogard Road, Hoddesdon EN11 0NU* Tel and fax (01992) 461866
E-mail revdtonyburford@ryepark.com

BURGE, Edward Charles Richard. b 70. Liv Univ BA92. Ridley Hall Cam 93. **d** 96 **p** 97. C Cayton w Eastfield *York* 96-99; P-in-c Lythe w Ugthorpe 99-03; Children's Officer (Cleveland Adnry) 99-03; Hon Chapl Miss to Seafarers 02-03; Dioc Youth and Children's Work Co-ord *Wakef* from 04. *37 Horton Street, Heckmondwike WF16 0LL* Tel (01924) 235216
E-mail richard.burge@wakefield.anglican.org

BURGE-THOMAS, Mrs Ruth. b 66. **d** 04 **p** 05. NSM Clapham H Spirit *S'wark* from 04. *86 Englewood Road, London SW12 9NY* Tel (020) 8675 6594
E-mail ruththomas@claphamhome.freeserve.co.uk

BURGER, David Joseph Cave. b 31. Selw Coll Cam BA58 MA62 Leic Univ 68. Coll of Resurr Mirfield 58. **d** 60 **p** 61. C Chiswick St Paul Grove Park *Lon* 60-63; C Charlton St Luke w H Trin *S'wark* 63-65; Warden St Luke Tr Ho Charlton 63-65; Chapl Moor Park Coll Farnham 66; Teacher Ysgol y Gader Dolgellau 68-85; Resettlement Officer Ches Aid to the Homeless 88-93; rtd 92; Perm to Offic *Ban* from 96. *Pwllygele Mawr, Llanfachreth, Dolgellau LL40 2DP* Tel (01341) 450350

BURGESS, Alan James. b 51. Ridley Hall Cam 87. **d** 89 **p** 90. C Glenfield *Leic* 89-92; V Donisthorpe and Moira w Stretton-en-le-Field 92-96; RD Akeley W 00-06; P-in-c Thringstone St Andr from 06; C Ravenstone and Swannington from 06; P-in-c Whitwick St Jo the Bapt from 07. *4 Badger's Croft, Thringstone, Coalville LE67 8JB* Tel (01530) 271456
E-mail sunergos@bigfoot.com

BURGESS, Mrs Anne. b 52. STETS 04, **d** 07 **p** 08. NSM Isleworth St Fran *Lon* from 07. *24 Penwerris Avenue, Isleworth TW7 4QX* Tel (020) 8570 4238 E-mail anne@ivanburgess.co.uk

BURGESS, Clive Brian. b 63. Trin Coll Bris BA00. **d** 00 **p** 01. C Oxton *Ches* 00-03; V Brewood and Bishopswood *Lich* 03-08; R Bentham *Bradf* from 08; Rural Miss Adv from 08. *1 Moons Acre, Bentham, Lancaster LA2 7BL* Tel (01524) 262119 Mobile 07894-637217 E-mail revdcliveburgess@btinternet.com

BURGESS, David James. b 58. Southn Univ BSc80. St Jo Coll Nottm. **d** 89 **p** 90. C S Mimms Ch Ch *Lon* 89-93; C Hanwell St Mary w St Chris 93-97; P-in-c Hawridge w Cholesbury and St Leonard *Ox* 97-08; R from 08; P-in-c The Lee 97-08; V from 08. *The Vicarage, The Lee, Great Missenden HP16 9LZ* Tel (01494) 837315 E-mail d.burgess@clara.net

BURGESS, Preb David John. b 39. Trin Hall Cam BA62 MA66 Univ Coll Ox MA66 FRSA91. Cuddesdon Coll 62. **d** 65 **p** 66. C Maidstone All SS w St Phil *Cant* 65; Asst Chapl Univ Coll Ox 66-70; Chapl 70-78; Can and Treas Windsor 78-87; V St Lawr Jewry *Lon* 87-08; Preb St Paul's Cathl 02-08; Chapl to The Queen 87-09; rtd 08. *62 Orbel Street, London SW11 3NZ* Tel (020) 7585 1572

BURGESS, Mrs Denise. b 49. **d** 00 **p** 01. OLM Glascote and Stonydelph *Lich* 00-06; NSM 06-07; NSM Elford from 07. *23 Croft Close, Elford, Tamworth B79 9BU* Tel 07818-890184 (mobile) E-mail burgess.denise@virgin.net

BURGESS, Edwin Michael. b 47. Ch Coll Cam BA69 MA73. Coll of Resurr Mirfield 70. **d** 72 **p** 73. C Beamish *Dur* 72-77; C Par *Truro* 77-80; P-in-c Duloe w Herodsfoot 80-83; R 83-86; Jt Dir SWMTC 80-86; Subwarden St Deiniol's Lib Hawarden 86-91; R Oughtrington *Ches* 91-05; P-in-c Warburton 93-05; R Oughtrington and Warburton from 05; CME Officer 99-03; Asst Chapl (Warrington) Ches Univ from 03; Dioc Chapl MU from 02. *The Rectory, Stage Lane, Lymm WA13 9JB* Tel (01925) 752388 E-mail m.e.burgess@tesco.com

BURGESS, Canon Henry Percival. b 21. Leeds Univ BA48. Coll of Resurr Mirfield 48. **d** 50 **p** 51. C Northfield *Birm* 50-54; V Shaw Hill 54-62; V Wylde Green 62-89; Hon Can Birm Cathl 75-90; RD Sutton Coldfield 76-88; rtd 90; Perm to Offic *Birm* from 90. *39 Chestnut Drive, Birmingham B36 9BH* Tel 0121-747 9926

BURGESS, Hugh Nigel. b 55. Edin Univ BSc76 Aber Univ MA79. St As Minl Tr Course. **d** 06 **p** 07. NSM Halkyn w Caerfallwch w Rhescyae *St As* from 06; P-in-c from 07. *The Chimneys, 7 Leete Park, Rhydymwyn, Mold CH7 5JJ* Tel (01352) 741646 E-mail hugh@halkynparish.wanadoo.co.uk

BURGESS, Jane Ellen. b 63. STETS. **d** 07 **p** 08. C Frome H Trin *B & W* from 07. *23 Westover, Frome BA11 4ET* Tel (01373) 469957

BURGESS, Mrs Jean Ann. b 62. Nottm Univ MA03. EMMTC 00. **d** 03 **p** 04. C Gresley *Derby* from 03. *The Vicarage, 25 Highfield Road, Derby DE22 1GX* Tel (01332) 332681

BURGESS, John. b 51. Ex Univ BSc73 Sussex Coll of Tech PGCE94. Trin Coll Bris 07. **d** 08 **p** 09. NSM Westfield *Chich* 08-09; NSM Fairlight, Guestling and Pett from 09. *25 Fairlight Gardens, Fairlight, Hastings TN35 4AY* Tel (01424) 812390 Mobile 07963-406854 E-mail jbtescom@hotmail.com

BURGESS, The Ven John Edward. b 30. Lon Univ BD57. ALCD56. **d** 57 **p** 58. C Bermondsey St Mary w St Olave and St Jo *S'wark* 57-60; C Southampton St Mary w H Trin *Win* 60-62; V Dunston w Coppenhall *Lich* 62-67; Chapl Stafford Coll of Tech 63-67; V Keynsham w Queen Charlton *B & W* 67-75; R Burnett 67-75; RD Keynsham 72-75; Adn Bath and Preb Wells Cathl 75-95; rtd 96; Perm to Offic *B & W* and *Sarum* from 96. *12 Berryfield Road, Bradford-on-Avon BA15 1SX* Tel (01225) 868905

BURGESS, John Henry William. b 35. Wells Th Coll 65. **d** 67 **p** 68. C Teddington St Alb *Lon* 67-72; C Northolt St Jos 72-74; Perm to Offic *B & W* 93-99 and 00-06; rtd 95; C Bruton and

Distr *B & W* 99-00; Perm to Offic *Nor* from 04. *9 Fairview Drive, Colkirk, Fakenham NR21 7NT* Tel (01328) 863410
E-mail burgess@walsingham9.wanadoo.co.uk

BURGESS, John Michael. b 36. ALCD61. **d** 61 **p** 62. C Eccleston St Luke *Liv* 61-64; S Rhodesia 64-65; Rhodesia 65-74; V Nottingham St Andr *S'well* 74-79; Bp's Adv on Community Relns 77-79; V Earlestown *Liv* 79-87; RD Warrington 82-87; TR Halewood 87-94; V Southport St Phil and St Paul 94-01; AD N Meols 95-00; rtd 01; Perm to Offic *Liv* from 03. *3 Glencoyne Drive, Southport PR9 9TS* Tel (01704) 506843

BURGESS, John Mulholland. b 32. Cranmer Hall Dur 58. **d** 61 **p** 62. C Frimley *Guildf* 61-67; C Cheltenham St Luke and St Jo *Glouc* 67-69; P-in-c Withington w Compton Abdale 69-74; R Woolstone w Gotherington and Oxenton 74-75; Chapl Rotterdam w Schiedam etc *Eur* 75-78; Chapl Sliema 78-80; C Nottingham All SS *S'well* 80; C Rolleston w Morton 80-83; C Rolleston w Fiskerton, Morton and Upton 83-84; V Mansfield St Aug 84-99; Asst RD Mansfield 88-92; RD 92-98; rtd 99; Perm to Offic *S'well* from 03. *278 Westfield Lane, Mansfield NG19 6NQ* Tel (01623) 421163

BURGESS, Kate Lamorna. b 64. Man Poly BA86 Leeds Univ MA97. NEOC 99. **d** 02 **p** 03. OHP 92-03; C Hessle *York* 02-06; TV Howden from 06. *The Vicarage, 3 Thimblehall Lane, Howden HU15 2PX* Tel (01430) 440546 E-mail kburgess1@tiscali.co.uk

BURGESS (née BOND), Mrs Kim Mary. b 58. SRN79. Trin Coll Bris BA87. **d** 87 **p** 94. Par Dn Cullompton *Ex* 87-91; Asst Chapl N Staffs R Infirmary Stoke-on-Trent 91-95; NSM Audley *Lich* 95-00. *6 Quarry Cottages, Nantwich Road, Audley, Stoke-on-Trent ST7 8DW* Tel (01782) 722961

BURGESS, Miss Laura Jane. b 74. Imp Coll Lon BSc95 ARSM95. Ripon Coll Cuddesdon BTh00. **d** 00 **p** 01. C St Alb Abbey 00-01; C Boxmoor St Jo 01-04; Min Can and Sacr St Paul's Cathl from 04. *7A Amen Court, London EC4M 7BU* Tel (020) 7248 6151 E-mail laura.burgess@telinco.co.uk

BURGESS, Michael. See BURGESS, Edwin Michael.

BURGESS, Michael Anglin. b 34. St Deiniol's Hawarden 81. **d** 83 **p** 84. C Habergham Eaves St Matt *Blackb* 83-85; C Burnley St Matt w H Trin 85-86; V Preston St Matt 86-93; V Nelson St Bede 93-99; rtd 99; Perm to Offic *Blackb* from 99. *39 Reedley Road, Reedley, Burnley BB10 2LU* Tel (01282) 449727
E-mail revmab1@ntlworld.com

BURGESS, Canon Michael James. b 42. Coll of Resurr Mirfield 74. **d** 76 **p** 77. C Leigh-on-Sea St Marg *Chelmsf* 76-79; C St Peter-in-Thanet *Cant* 79-82; Chapl Royal St Geo Coll Toronto Canada 82-89; R Toronto Epiphany and St Mark 89-04; R Toronto Transfiguration from 04; Can Toronto from 01. *318W-118 Montgomery Avenue, Toronto ON M4R 1E3, Canada* Tel (001) (416) 482 2462 *or* 489 7798 Fax 489 3272
E-mail michaelburgess@sympatico.ca

BURGESS, Neil. b 53. Univ of Wales (Lamp) BA75 Nottm Univ MTh87 PhD93. St Mich Coll Llan 75. **d** 77 **p** 78. C Cheadle *Lich* 77-79; C Longton 79-82; TV Hanley H Ev 82-86; C Uttoxeter w Bramshall 86-87; Lect Linc Th Coll 87-95; Hon C Linc Minster Gp 88-95; Dioc Dir of Clergy Tr *S'well* 95-00; C Newark 97-00; Perm to Offic *Linc* 00-06; Hon C Linc St Pet-at-Gowts and St Andr from 06; Hon C Linc St Botolph from 06; Hon C Linc St Mary-le-Wigford w St Benedict etc from 06; Hon C Linc St Faith and St Martin w St Pet from 06; Hon C Linc St Swithin from 06. *23 Drury Lane, Lincoln LN1 3BN* Tel (01522) 539408
E-mail ann.burgess@btinternet.com

BURGESS, Sister Patricia Jean. b 16. Edin Univ BSc38. New Coll Edin 65. **dss** 69 **d** 86. NSM Roslin (Rosslyn Chpl) *Edin* 69-73; Community of the Transfiguration Midlothian from 72. *Hermitage of the Transfiguration, 70E Clerk Street, Loanhead EH20 9RG*

BURGESS, Paul Christopher James. b 41. Qu Coll Cam BA63 MA67. Lon Coll of Div 66. **d** 68 **p** 69. C Islington St Mary *Lon* 68-72; C Church Stretton *Heref* 73-74; Lect Gujranwala Th Sem Pakistan 74-83; Warden Carberry Tower (Ch of Scotland) 84-86; Progr Co-ord 86-88; TV Livingston LEP *Edin* 88-92; Prof and Lib Gujranwala Th Sem from 94. *Gujranwala Theological Seminary, Civil Lines, Gujranwala, Pakistan* Tel (0092) (53) 254770 E-mail burgess@brain.net.pk

BURGESS, Peter Alan. b 40. St Edm Ho Cam BA86 MA89 MPhil86 St Jo Coll York MA99. Cranmer Hall Dur 02. **d** 03 **p** 04. NSM Wheldrake w Thorganby *York* 03-08; NSM Derwent Ings from 08. *2 Derwent Drive, Wheldrake, York YO19 6AL* Tel (01904) 448309 E-mail burgesspr@btinternet.com

BURGESS, Roy. b 32. S Dios Minl Tr Scheme 80. **d** 83 **p** 84. NSM Bentworth and Shalden and Lasham *Win* 83-89; R Ingoldsby *Linc* 89-97; RD Beltisloe 93-97; rtd 97; Perm to Offic *Nor* from 98. *4 Melton Gate, Wymondham NR18 0PQ* Tel (01953) 606449

BURGESS, Roy Graham. b 47. Birm Univ CertCYW72. Ox Min Course 91. **d** 94 **p** 95. C Easthampstead *Ox* 94-99; C Wokingham St Paul 99-04; P-in-c Owlsmoor 04-09; V from 09. *The Vicarage, 107 Owlsmoor Road, Owlsmoor, Sandhurst GU47 0SS* Tel (01344) 780110 *or* 771286
E-mail revroy@compriest.freeserve.co.uk

BURGHALL, Kenneth Miles. b 34. Selw Coll Cam BA57 MA61. Qu Coll Birm 57. **d** 59 **p** 60. C Macclesfield St Mich *Ches* 59-63; CF 63-66; P-in-c Birkenhead Priory *Ches* 67-71; V Macclesfield St Paul 71-87; V Lower Peover 87-04; P-in-c Over Peover 92-04; rtd 04; Perm to Offic *Ches* from 04. *45 Ullswater Road, Congleton CW12 4JE* Tel (01260) 289277

BURGON, Canon George Irvine. b 41. Open Univ BA92. Edin Th Coll 62. **d** 65 **p** 66. C Dundee St Mary Magd *Bre* 65-68; C Wellingborough All Hallows *Pet* 68-71; P-in-c Norton 71-73; TV Daventry w Norton 73-75; V Northampton St Mary 75-98; R Rothwell w Orton, Rushton w Glendon and Pipewell 98-08; Can Pet Cathl 95-08; rtd 08. *47 Woodlands Avenue, Barton Seagrave, Kettering NN15 6QS* Tel (01536) 722193
E-mail georgeburgon@yahoo.co.uk

BURGON, Mrs Lynne. b 58. RGN80 RM83. SWMTC 03. **d** 06 **p** 07. NSM Fremington *Ex* 06-07; C Okehampton w Inwardleigh, Bratton Clovelly etc from 07. *19 Fern Meadow, Okehampton EX20 1PB* Tel (01837) 54263
E-mail l.burgon@btinternet.com

BURKE, Charles Michael. b 28. Keble Coll Ox BA51 MA54 Ox Univ DipEd52. Glouc Th Course. **d** 84 **p** 85. C Colwall w Upper Colwall and Coddington *Heref* 84-88; V Canon Pyon w Kings Pyon and Birley 88-98; P-in-c Wellington 96-98; rtd 98; Perm to Offic *Heref* from 98. *Pyons, 7 Stretton Close, Fayre Oakes, Hereford HR4 0QN* Tel (01432) 270068

BURKE, Christopher Mark. b 65. Cov Poly LLB87 Heythrop Coll Lon MA06. Ripon Coll Cuddesdon 89. **d** 92 **p** 93. C Nunthorpe *York* 92-96; V S Bank 96-02; R Stepney St Dunstan and All SS *Lon* from 02. *St Dunstan and All Saints Rectory, Rectory Square, London E1 3NQ* Tel and fax (020) 7791 3545
E-mail christopher.burke@btinternet.com

BURKE, Colin Douglas. b 41. Bp Otter Coll CertEd64. **d** 92 **p** 93. OLM Fressingfield, Mendham etc *St E* 92-99; P-in-c Oare w Culbone *B & W* from 99. *The Rectory, Oare, Lynton EX35 6NX* Tel (01598) 741270

BURKE, Elisabeth Ann. b 44. St Matthias Coll Bris CertEd66. **d** 05 **p** 06. OLM E Horsley and Ockham w Hatchford and Downside *Guildf* from 05. *39 Copse Road, Cobham KT11 2TW* Tel (01932) 863886

BURKE, Eric John. b 44. Llan Dioc Tr Scheme 81. **d** 85 **p** 86. NSM Cardiff St Jo *Llan* 85-95; Chapl Asst Univ Hosp of Wales and Llandough NHS Trust 95-00; Chapl Asst Cardiff and Vale NHS Trust from 00. *Chaplaincy Department, University Hospital of Wales, Heath Park, Cardiff CF4 4XW* Tel (029) 2074 3230 *or* 2079 8147

BURKE, Jonathan. b 53. Lon Univ BEd. Westcott Ho Cam 79. **d** 82 **p** 83. C Weymouth H Trin *Sarum* 82-85; R Bere Regis and Affpuddle w Turnerspuddle 85-92; NSM Talbot Village 04-08; TR White Horse from 08. *The Vicarage, Bitham Lane, Westbury BA13 3BU* Tel (01373) 822209
E-mail jonathan.burke@whitehorseteam.org

BURKE, Kelvin Stephen. b 56. Man Univ BA77 FCA81. Cranmer Hall Dur. **d** 99 **p** 00. C Stanley *Wakef* 99-02; P-in-c Wakef St Andr and St Mary 02-06; Asst Chapl Leeds Teaching Hosps NHS Trust from 06. *The Chaplaincy, St James University Hospital, Beckett Street, Leeds LS9 7TF* Tel 0113-206 5935 Mobile 07793-979907 E-mail jburke@totalise.co.uk

BURKE, Michael Robert. b 61. Leeds Univ BA83. Trin Coll Bris BA89. **d** 89 **p** 90. C Anston *Sheff* 89-92; V Crosspool 92-00; V Hucclecote *Glouc* 00-09. *Address temp unknown*
E-mail mikburke@aol.com

BURKE, Patrick. CITC. **d** 09. C Douglas Union w Frankfield C, C & R from 09. *64 Willowbank, Church Road, Blackrock, Cork, Republic of Ireland* Tel (00353) (21) 435 8226
E-mail pathos@eircom.net

BURKE, Wayne Jackson. b 51. San Francisco State Univ BA76 MA78 Univ of Wales (Cardiff) PhD91. St Steph Ho Ox 01. **d** 02 **p** 03. Hon C Gtr Athens *Eur* from 02. *1 Iridos, Amarousion, 151-22 Athens, Greece* Tel and fax (0030) (210) 614 8198
E-mail paterw@hol.gr

BURKE, Canon William Spencer Dwerryhouse. b 46. Ripon Coll Cuddesdon 90. **d** 92 **p** 93. C Watford St Mich *St Alb* 92-95; R Castor w Sutton and Upton w Marholm *Pet* from 95; Can Pet Cathl from 07. *The Rectory, 5 Church Hill, Castor, Peterborough PE5 7AU* Tel (01733) 380244 E-mail wburke@btinternet.com

BURKETT, Canon Christopher Paul. b 52. Warwick Univ BA75 Westmr Coll Ox MTh93. Qu Coll Birm 75. **d** 78 **p** 79. C Streetly *Lich* 78-81; C Harlescott 81-83; TV Leek and Meerbrook 83-89; Chapl Leek Moorlands Hosp 83-89; Area Sec USPG *Ches* 89-92; V Whitegate w Lt Budworth *Ches* 92-00; Asst CME Officer 93-00; Can Res *Ches* Cathl from 00; Bp's Chapl from 00. *5 Abbey Green, Chester CH1 2JH* Tel (01244) 347500
E-mail bpchaplain@chester.anglican.org

BURKILL, Mark Edward. b 56. MA PhD. Trin Coll Bris. **d** 84 **p** 85. C Cheadle *Ches* 84-88; C Harold Wood *Chelmsf* 88-91; V Leyton Ch Ch from 91. *The Vicarage, 52 Elm Road, London E11 4DW* Tel (020) 8539 4980 E-mail m.burkill@ntlworld.com

BURKITT, Paul Adrian. b 49. RMN75 SRN77. St Steph Ho Ox 84. **d** 86 **p** 87. C Whitby *York* 86-90; V Egton w Grosmont 90-93;

V Newington w Dairycoates 93-96; P-in-c Kingston upon Hull St Mary 96-07; P-in-c Sculcoates 04-07; rtd 07; Perm to Offic *York* from 07. *2 Brookside, Iburndale, Whitby YO22 5DX* Tel (01947) 810035

BURKITT, Richard Francis. b 49. Leeds Univ BA71 CertEd72. Sarum & Wells Th Coll 82. **d** 90 **p** 90. R Fraserburgh w New Pitsligo *Ab* 90-95; R Fortrose *Mor* 95-08; R Cromarty 95-08; R Arpafeelie 95-08; C Inverness St Mich from 08. *Address temp unknown* E-mail rfburkitt@btopenworld.com

BURKITT-GRAY, Mrs Joan Katherine. b 47. Portsm Poly BSc68 Southn Univ MPhil74. SEITE 00. **d** 04 **p** 05. NSM Lee St Marg *S'wark* from 04; Hon Asst Chapl St Chris Hospice Lon from 08. *7 Foxes Dale, London SE3 9BD* Tel (020) 8463 0365 *or* 8768 4500 E-mail mail@burkitt-gray.com

BURLAND, Clive Beresford. b 37. Sarum & Wells Th Coll 81. **d** 85 **p** 86. C Warblington w Emsworth *Portsm* 85-87; C Cowes St Mary 87-92; V Gurnard 92-98; R Northwood 93-98; rtd 98; Perm to Offic *Portsm* from 98. *5A Orchard Close, Freshwater PO40 9BQ* Tel (01983) 753949

BURLEIGH, David John. b 42. FCII69. St Deiniol's Hawarden 84. **d** 87 **p** 88. NSM Lache cum Saltney *Ches* 87-88; NSM Eastham 89-92; C Birkenhead Priory 92-95; P-in-c Duloe w Herodsfoot *Truro* 95-99; TV Liskeard, St Keyne, St Pinnock, Morval etc 95-99; R Duloe, Herodsfoot, Morval and St Pinnock 99-01; V Bath St Barn w Englishcombe *B & W* from 01. *The Vicarage, Mount View, Southdown, Bath BA2 1JX* Tel (01225) 478952

BURLEIGH, Walter Coleridge. b 41. WMMTC 89. **d** 89 **p** 90. NSM N Evington *Leic* 90-96; Perm to Offic from 96. *20 Border Drive, Leicester LE4 2JH* Tel 0116-235 9230

BURLES, Canon Robert John. b 54. Bris Univ BSc75. St Jo Coll Nottm LTh86. **d** 88 **p** 89. C Mansfield SS Pet and Paul *S'well* 88-91; C The Lydiards *Bris* 91-92; TV W Swindon and the Lydiards 92-97; TR Swindon St Jo and St Andr from 97; AD Swindon from 06; Hon Can Bris Cathl from 04. *The Vicarage, Verwood Close, Swindon SN3 2LE* Tel (01793) 611473 Fax 574924 E-mail rob@burles.org.uk

BURLEY, John Roland James. b 46. St Jo Coll Cam BA67 MA70. Trin Episc Sch for Min Ambridge Penn MDiv88. **d** 81 **p** 82. SAMS Chile 81-90; TV Southgate *Chich* 90-99; R Alfold and Loxwood *Guildf* 99-07; P-in-c from 08. *The Rectory, Vicarage Hill, Loxwood, Billingshurst RH14 0RG* Tel and fax (01403) 752320 E-mail john@burleys.co.uk

BURLEY, Michael. b 58. Ridley Hall Cam 86. **d** 89 **p** 90. C Scarborough St Mary w Ch Ch and H Apostles *York* 89-92; C Drypool 93; TV 93-97; V Sutton St Mich 97-03; V Burley in Wharfedale *Bradf* from 03; Assoc Dioc Dir of Ords from 07. *The Vicarage, 21 Southfield Road, Burley in Wharfedale, Ilkley LS29 7PB* Tel (01943) 863216
E-mail burley@standrews.karoo.co.uk

BURLEY, Richard Alexander. b 80. Warwick Univ BA01 Fitzw Coll Cam BA07. Ridley Hall Cam 05. **d** 08 **p** 09. C Bilton *Cov* from 08. *10 Monks Close, Cawston, Rugby CV22 7FP* Tel 07875-123867 (mobile) E-mail rich@burley.biz

BURLTON, Aelred Harry. b 49. Sarum & Wells Th Coll 75. **d** 78 **p** 79. C Feltham *Lon* 78-82; Chapl Heathrow Airport 83-94; P-in-c Harmondsworth 92-94; R St Buryan, St Levan and Sennen *Truro* 94-05; rtd 05. *Farway Barn, Hellangove Farm, Gulval, Penzance TR20 8XD* Tel (01736) 330426

BURLTON, William Frank. b 12. K Coll Lon. **d** 43 **p** 44. C Glouc St Mark 43-46; C Northleach and Hampnett w Stowell and Yanworth 46-48; C St Briavels 48-51; R Cromhall 51-78; Chapl HM Pris Leyhill 54-89; R Cromhall w Tortworth *Glouc* 78-82; rtd 82; Perm to Offic *Glouc* 82-89 and *Truro* from 89. *24 Godolphin Terrace, Marazion TR17 0EX* Tel (01736) 710699

BURMAN, Philip Harvey. b 47. Kelham Th Coll 66. **d** 70 **p** 71. C Huyton St Mich *Liv* 70-75; C Farnworth 75-77; TV Kirkby 77-83; V Hindley All SS 83-93; V Middlesbrough St Martin *York* 93-97; V Middlesbrough St Martin w St Cuth 97-99; P-in-c Eccleston St Thos *Liv* 99-08; V Liv St Chris Norris Green from 08. *St Christopher's Vicarage, Lorenzo Drive, Liverpool L11 1BQ*

BURMAN, Thomas George. b 61. S'wark Ord Course 86. **d** 89 **p** 90. NSM Forest Hill *S'wark* 89-03; NSM Perry Hill St Geo w Ch Ch and St Paul 03-07; Perm to Offic from 07. *131 Como Road, London SE23 2JN* Tel (020) 8699 8929

BURMAN, William Guest. b 26. St Cath Coll Cam MA55 Worc Coll Ox MA63. St Steph Ho Ox 81. **d** 83 **p** 84. C Weymouth H Trin *Sarum* 83-86; R Exton and Winsford and Cutcombe w Luxborough *B & W* 86-89; TV Langport Area 89-91; rtd 91; Perm to Offic *B & W* 91-98 and from 02; Master Bath St Mary Magd Holloway from 94. *8 Stoneleigh Court, Lansdown Road, Bath BA1 5TL* Tel (01225) 312140

BURMESTER, Stephen John. b 66. Leeds Univ BSc87. Wycliffe Hall Ox 96. **d** 98 **p** 99. C Lenton *S'well* 98-02; C Bebington *Ches* 02-08; V Handforth from 08. *The Vicarage, 36 Sagars Road, Handforth, Wilmslow SK9 3EE* Tel (01625) 250559 *or* 532145
E-mail steve.burmester@gmail.com

BURN, Geoffrey Livingston. b 60. Sydney Univ BSc83 Imp Coll Lon PhD87 St Jo Coll Dur BA95. Cranmer Hall Dur 93. **d** 96

p 97. C St Austell *Truro* 96-03; Perm to Offic *Cant* 03-06; P Forest S Deanery *Glouc* from 06; Hon C Cinderford St Jo from 06; Chapl Glos Primary Care Trust from 06. *St John's Vicarage, 1 Abbots View, Buckshaft, Cinderford GL14 3EG* Tel (01594) 825446 E-mail geoffrey@burn.eclipse.co.uk

BURN, Mrs Helen Mary. b 64. Down Coll Cam BA86 Ox Univ PGCE88 Ex Univ MA02. SWMTC 00. **d** 03 **p** 04. C Eythorne and Elvington w Waldershare etc *Cant* 03-06; Tutor WEMTC *Glouc* from 06; Sen Lect Glos Univ from 09. *St John's Vicarage, 1 Abbots View, Buckshaft, Cinderford GL14 3EG* Tel (01594) 829602 E-mail helen@burn.eclipse.co.uk

BURN, Leonard Louis. b 44. K Coll Lon BD67 AKC67. **d** 68 **p** 69. C Kingswinford St Mary *Lich* 68-70; C S Ascot *Ox* 70-72; C Caversham 72-76; Chapl Selly Oak Hosp Birm 76-81; Bris City Hosp 81-82; P-in-c Bris St Mich 81-83; R Peopleton and White Ladies Aston w Churchill etc *Worc* 83-88; V Bengeworth 88-97; Chapl St Richard's Hospice Worc 88-97; Chapl Evesham Coll 90-97; rtd 97; Perm to Offic *Glouc* from 97 and *Worc* 97-98; Chapl Worcs Community and Mental Health Trust from 98. *Beckford Rise, Beckford, Tewkesbury GL20 7AN* Tel and fax (01386) 881160 Mobile 07734-505663

BURN, Richard James Southerden. b 34. Pemb Coll Cam BA56. Wells Th Coll 56. **d** 58 **p** 59. C Cheshunt *St Alb* 58-62; C Leighton Buzzard 65-66; C Glastonbury St Jo *B & W* 66-68; P-in-c Prestonpans *Edin* 68-71; P-in-c Stokesay *Heref* 71-75; P-in-c Dorrington 75-81; P-in-c Stapleton 75-81; P-in-c Leebotwood w Longnor 75-81; P-in-c Smethcott w Woolstaston 81; TR Melbury *Sarum* 81-87; P-in-c Quendon w Rickling and Wicken Bonhunt *Chelmsf* 87-92; R Quendon w Rickling and Wicken Bonhunt etc 92-95; rtd 95; V Isleworth St Fran *Lon* 95-00; Hon C Barcheston *Cov* 06-08; Hon C Cherington w Stourton 06-08; Hon C Long Compton, Whichford and Barton-on-the-Heath 06-08; Hon C Wolford w Burmington 06-08; Hon C S Warks Seven Gp 08-09. *The Vicarage, Great Wolford, Shipton-on-Stour CV36 5NQ* Tel (01608) 674909 E-mail richard.burn58@yahoo.co.uk

BURN, Robert Pemberton. b 34. Peterho Cam BA56 MA60 Lon Univ PhD68. CMS Tr Coll Chislehurst 60. **d** 63 **p** 81. India 63-71; Perm to Offic *Ely* 71-81; P-in-c Foxton 81-88; Perm to Offic *Ex* from 89. *Sunnyside, Barrack Road, Exeter EX2 6AB* Tel (01392) 430028

BURN-MURDOCH, Aidan Michael. b 35. Trin Coll Cam BA60 MA63. Ridley Hall Cam 59. **d** 61 **p** 62. C Bishopwearmouth St Gabr *Dur* 61-63; Tutor Ridley Hall Cam 63-67; CMS Miss 67-70; India 68-70; R Hawick *Edin* 70-77; Bp's Co-ord of Evang *S & B* 77-81; R Reynoldston w Penrice and Llangennith 77-83; R Port Eynon w Rhosili and Llanddewi and Knelston 83-89; R Uddingston and Cambuslang *Glas* 89-97; rtd 97; Missr Eyemouth *Edin* 98-00. *19 Blairston Avenue, Bothwell, Glasgow G71 8RZ* Tel (01698) 853377

BURNAGE, Arthur Gavin. b 63. **d** 07 **p** 08. C Aldridge *Lich* from 07. *5 Whetstone Lane, Aldridge, Walsall WS9 8PB* Tel (01922) 745738

BURNE, Sambrooke Roger. b 47. Lon Univ MB, BS70 MRCGP74. SAOMC 03. **d** 06 **p** 07. NSM Blackbird Leys *Ox* from 06. *5 Eleanor Close, Oxford OX4 3ND* E-mail roger.burne@ntlworld.com

BURNET, Norman Andrew Gray. b 32. Aber Univ BEd77 Cam Univ MLitt92. Edin Th Coll 53. **d** 55 **p** 56. C Ayr *Glas* 55-58; S Africa 58-69; C St Jo Cathl Umtata 58-63; R Mt Frere 63-69; R Leven *St And* 69-72; Perm to Offic *Ab, Bre* and *Ely* 73-81; P-in-c Brinkley, Burrough Green and Carlton *Ely* 82-83; P-in-c Westley Waterless 82-83; Australia 83-84; R Fraserburgh w New Pitsligo *Ab* 85-89; P-in-c Bicker *Linc* 89; V Bicker and Wigtoft 89-97; rtd 97; Perm to Offic *Nor* 97-99; *Linc* 97-00. *61 Westlode Street, Spalding PE11 2AE* Tel and fax (01775) 767429

BURNETT, Canon John Capenhurst. b 19. AKC49. **d** 49 **p** 50. C Shirehampton *Bris* 49-53; C Stoke Bishop 53-56; V Wroughton 56-76; RD Cricklade 70-76; Hon Can Bris Cathl 74-85; V Bris St Andr w St Bart 76-85; rtd 85; Perm to Offic *Bris* from 85. *57 Upper Cranbrook Road, Bristol BS6 7UR* Tel 0117-924 5284

BURNETT, Mrs Patricia Kay. b 38. Newnham Coll Cam MA60. Sarum Th Coll 94. **d** 97 **p** 98. NSM Jarvis Brook *Chich* 97-08; rtd 08. *20 St Richards Road, Crowborough TN6 3AT* Tel (01892) 655668

BURNETT, Susan Mary. b 50. Lon Univ BEd73. St Jo Coll Dur 76. **dss** 78 **d** 87 **p** 94. Welling *S'wark* 78-83; E Greenwich Ch Ch w St Andr and St Mich 83-91; Par Dn 87-91; Par Dn Sydenham All SS 91-94; C 94-95; C Lower Sydenham St Mich 91-95; V 95-09; rtd 09. *9 Grove Park, Chichester PO19 3HY* Tel (01243) 532248

BURNETT-HALL, Mrs Karen. b 46. Bp Grosseteste Coll CertEd68 Lon Univ BD82. Oak Hill Th Coll 86. **d** 89 **p** 94. Par Dn Norbury Ches 89-92; NSM York St Paul 93-95; NSM York St Barn 95-99; P-in-c from 00. *1 Centenary House, The Avenue, York YO30 6AU* Tel (01904) 638935 E-mail karen.bh@btinternet.com

✠**BURNHAM, The Rt Revd Andrew.** b 48. New Coll Ox BA69 BA71 MA73 Westmr Coll Ox CertEd72 ARCO(CHM).

St Steph Ho Ox 81. **d** 83 **p** 84 **c** 00. Hon C Clifton *S'well* 83-85; C Beeston 85-87; V Carrington 87-94; Vice-Prin St Steph Ho Ox 95-00; Suff Bp Ebbsfleet (PEV) *Cant* from 00; Hon Asst Bp B & W, Ex, Lich and Ox from 01. *Bishop's House, Church Lane, Dry Sandford, Abingdon OX13 6JP* Tel (01865) 390746 Fax 390611 E-mail bishop.andrew@ebbsfleet.org.uk

BURNHAM, Frank Leslie. b 23. Edin Th Coll 52. **d** 55 **p** 56. C York St Mary Bishophill Senior 55-58; C Marfleet 58-62; V 62-72; TR 72-74; V Acomb St Steph 74-85; C Fulford 85-88; rtd 88; Perm to Offic *York* from 88. *Dulverton Hall, Esplanade, Scarborough YO11 2AR* Tel (01723) 340101

BURNHAM, Stephen Patrick James. b 75. Ch Ch Ox BA97. Westcott Ho Cam 00. **d** 02 **p** 03. C Vale of Belvoir Par *Leic* 02-05; TV Leic Resurr from 05. *445A Loughborough Road, Birstall, Leicester LE4 4BH* Tel 0116-267 7074 Mobile 07905-882805

BURNIE, Judith. See SWEETMAN, Ms Judith

BURNINGHAM, Frederick George. b 34. ALCD60. **d** 60 **p** 61. C New Beckenham St Paul *Roch* 60-63; Canada 63-68 and 89-95; C Wisley w Pyrford *Guildf* 68-69; P-in-c Sydenham H Trin *S'wark* 69-71; C Broadwater St Mary *Chich* 72-77; R Sotterley, Willingham, Shadingfield, Ellough etc *St E* 77-82; R Ipswich St Clem w H Trin 82-89; P-in-c Thorndon w Rishangles, Stoke Ash, Thwaite etc 95-99; rtd 99; Perm to Offic *Bradf* from 99. *8 Meadow Rise, Skipton BD23 1BT* Tel (01756) 794440 E-mail f.burningham@btopenworld.com

BURNINGHAM, Richard Anthony. b 47. Keele Univ BA70 Aber Univ CQSW77 Roehampton Inst PGCE85. All Nations Chr Coll 82 Oak Hill Th Coll 94. **d** 96 **p** 97. C Reigate St Mary *S'wark* 96-00; V Weston *Win* from 00. *The Vicarage, Weston Lane, Southampton SO19 9HG* Tel (023) 8044 8421 E-mail richardb@ukonline.co.uk

BURNISTON, Aubrey John. b 53. St Jo Coll Dur BA92 Leeds Univ MA03. Cranmer Hall Dur 79. **d** 83 **p** 84. C Owton Manor *Dur* 83-86; TV Rugby *Cov* 86-93; V Heaton St Martin *Bradf* 93-09; Bp's Adv in Liturgy 00-09; V Islington St Jas w St Pet *Lon* from 09. *St James's Vicarage, 1A Arlington Square, London N1 7DS* Tel (020) 7226 4108 E-mail vicar@stjamesislington.org

BURNLEY, Suffragan Bishop of. See GODDARD, The Rt Revd John William

BURNS, Dane. b 51. **d** 85 **p** 86. C Enniskillen *Clogh* 85-87; I Augher w Newtownsaville and Eskrahoole 87-92; Dioc Communications Officer 91-92; I Camus-juxta-Bann *D & R* 92-96. *86 Donneybrewer Road, Eglinton, Londonderry BT47 3PD*

BURNS, Canon Edward Joseph. b 38. Liv Univ BSc58 St Cath Soc Ox BA61 MA64. Wycliffe Hall Ox 58. **d** 61 **p** 62. C Leyland St Andr *Blackb* 61-64; C Burnley St Pet 64-67; V Chorley St Jas 67-75; V Fulwood Ch Ch 75-03; RD Preston 79-86; Chapl Sharoe Green Hosp Preston 81-94; Hon Can Blackb Cathl 86-03; Bp's Adv on Hosp Chapls 89-94; rtd 03; Perm to Offic *Blackb* from 03. *17 Greenacres, Fulwood, Preston PR2 7DA* Tel (01772) 864741 E-mail eddieandsheila@ejburns.freeserve.co.uk

BURNS, Canon James Denis. b 43. Lich Th Coll 69. **d** 72 **p** 73. C Gt Wyrley *Lich* 72-75; C Atherton *Man* 75-76; Asst Chapl Sheff Ind Miss 76-79; C-in-c Masborough St Paul w St Jo 76-78; C-in-c Northfield St Mich 76-78; V Rotherham St Paul, St Mich and St Jo Ferham Park 78-79; V Lancaster Ch Ch *Blackb* 79-81; V Lancaster Ch Ch w St Jo and St Anne 81-86; V Chorley St Pet 86-96; R Rufford 96-07; Warden Past Assts 96-06; C Croston and Bretherton 06-07; rtd 07; Hon C Hesketh w Becconsall *Blackb* from 07; Hon Can Blackb Cathl from 99. *St Mary's Rectory, 17 Church Road, Rufford, Ormskirk L40 1TA* Tel (01704) 821261

BURNS, John Macdonald. See ODA-BURNS, John Macdonald

BURNS, Matthew. Leeds Univ BA. Coll of Resurr Mirfield. **d** 05 **p** 06. C Wrexham *St As* 05-08; V Towyn from 08. *The Rectory, 7 Parc Gwellyn, Kinmel Bay, Rhyl LL18 5HN* Tel (01745) 330390

BURNS, Michael John. b 53. AKC76. Chich Th Coll 76. **d** 77 **p** 78. C Broseley w Benthall *Heref* 77-81; C Stevenage All SS Pin Green *St Alb* 81-84; V Tattenham Corner and Burgh Heath *Guildf* 84-92; C and Chapl Younger People Milton Keynes *Ox* 92-00; P-in-c Potters Bar K Chas *St Alb* from 00. *The Vicarage, 8 Dugdale Hill Lane, Potters Bar EN6 2DW* Tel (01707) 661266

BURNS, Robert Joseph. b 34. Wycliffe Hall Ox 67. **d** 71 **p** 72. C Portswood Ch Ch *Win* 71-73; C Woking St Jo *Guildf* 73-77; C Glas St Mary 77; Bp's Dom Chapl 77-78; R Glas Gd Shep and Ascension 78-92; rtd 92. *The Vicarage, Church Street, Chipping Campden GL55 6JG* Tel (01386) 840671

BURNS, Stephen. b 70. Grey Coll Dur BA92 MA94 Clare Coll Cam MLitt96 Dur Univ PhD03. Ridley Hall Cam 93. **d** 96 **p** 97. C Houghton le Spring *Dur* 96-99; TV Gateshead 99-02; Dir Urban Miss Cen Cranmer Hall 99-02; Tutor Qu Coll Birm 03-06; Chapl and Lect St Jo Coll Dur 06-07; Fell Chas Sturt Univ Australia from 07. *United Theological College, 16 Masons Drive, North Parramatta, NSW 2151 Australia*

BURNS, Stuart Keith. b 54. Bp Grosseteste Coll BEd88 Lon Univ BD94 Leeds Univ MA95 PhD99. St Jo Coll Nottm. **d** 03 **p** 04. C Gt Bowden w Welham, Glooston and Cranoe etc *Leic* 03-06; Hd Sch for Min from 06. *The Rectory, 3 Stonton Road, Church*

Langton, Market Harborough LE16 7SZ Tel (01858) 540202
E-mail sburns@zetnet.co.uk

BURNS, The Rt Revd Stuart Maitland. b 46. Leeds Univ BA67. Coll of Resurr Mirfield 67. **d** 69 **p** 70. C Wyther *Ripon* 69-73; Asst Chapl Leeds Univ 73-77; Asst Chapl Leeds Poly 73-77; P-in-c Thornthwaite w Thruscross and Darley 77-84; V Leeds Gipton Epiphany 84-89; OSB from 89; Prior Burford Priory 96-01; Abbot from 01; Lic to Offic *Ox* 89-08. *St Benedict's Monastery, Broad Marston Manor, Broad Marston, Stratford-upon-Avon CV37 8XY* Tel (01789) 720252
E-mail abbot@burfordosb.org.uk

BURNS, Stuart Sandeman. b 62. Natal Univ BA85 Ball Coll Ox BA89 MA94. St Paul's Coll Grahamstown. **d** 89 **p** 90. S Africa 89-99; C Stanger 90-91; Dir Scripture Union Ind Schs 92-94; R Drakensberg 95-97; Chapl W Prov Prep Sch 98-99; I Kinneigh Union *C, C & R* 99-02; TV Bourne Valley *Sarum* 02-08; I Down H Trin w Hollymount *D & D* from 08. *The Rectory, 12 The Meadows, Strangford Road, Downpatrick BT30 6LN* Tel (028) 4461 2286 E-mail stuart.burns01@btinternet.com

BURR, Mrs Ann Pamela. b 39. S Dios Minl Tr Scheme 83. **dss** 86 **d** 87 **p** 94. Fareham H Trin *Portsm* 86-06; Hon C 87-06; Hon Asst Chapl Knowle Hosp Fareham 86-90; Asst Chapl Qu Alexandra Hosp Portsm 90-92; Chapl Portsm Hosps NHS Trust 92-00; rtd 06; Perm to Offic *Portsm* from 06. *3 Bruce Close, Fareham PO16 7QJ* Tel (01329) 281375 E-mail ann.burr@hotmail.co.uk

BURR, Mrs Anna Victoria. b 58. Southn Univ BA80 Leeds Univ MA07. NOC 04. **d** 07 **p** 08. NSM Fulford *York* from 07. *26 White House Gardens, York YO24 1EA* Tel (01904) 651508 E-mail burrs@tiscali.co.uk

BURR, Christopher Edward. b 68. Univ of Wales (Cardiff) BTh01. St Mich Coll Llan 98. **d** 01 **p** 02. C Llantrisant 01-04; P-in-c Pwllgwaun and Llanddewi Rhondda from 04. *The Vicarage, Lanelay Crescent, Pontypridd CF37 1JB* Tel and fax (01443) 402417 E-mail chris.burr1@ntlworld.com

BURR, Paul David. b 62. Birm Univ LLB83. St Jo Coll Nottm MA99. **d** 99 **p** 00. C Newark *S'well* 99-02; C Eaton *Nor* 02-05; P-in-c Swardeston w E Carleton, Intwood, Keswick etc 05-09; R from 09. *The Vicarage, The Common, Swardeston, Norwich NR14 8EB* Tel (01508) 570550 E-mail paul.burr@tiscali.co.uk

BURR, Raymond Leslie. b 43. NEOC 82 Edin Th Coll 84. **d** 85 **p** 86. C Hartlepool St Paul *Dur* 85-87; C Sherburn w Pittington 87-89; R Lyons 89-95; RD Houghton 94-96; V S Shields St Hilda w St Thos 95-08; rtd 08. *57 Pierremont Road, Darlington DL3 6DN* Tel (01325) 463666 E-mail ray@burr.org.uk

BURRELL, David Philip. b 56. Southn Univ BTh90. Sarum & Wells Th Coll 85. **d** 88 **p** 89. C Ixworth and Bardwell *St E* 88-91; P-in-c Haughley w Wetherden 91-96; P-in-c Culford, W Stow and Wordwell w Flempton etc 96-98; R Lark Valley from 98. *The Rectory, West Stow, Bury St Edmunds IP28 6ET* Tel (01284) 728556

BURRELL, Godfrey John. b 49. Reading Univ BSc70 Qu Coll Ox CertFd71. Wycliffe Hall Ox 84. **d** 86 **p** 87. C Didcot All SS *Ox* 86-89; Chapl St Alb Coll Pretoria 90-95; Chapl Pretoria Cen Prisn 90-94; R Lynnwood Trin Ch 96-01; Adn Pretoria E 00-01; R Lighthorne *Cov* from 01; V Chesterton from 01; V Newbold Pacey w Moreton Morrell from 01; RD Fosse from 07. *The Rectory, Church Lane, Lighthorne, Warwick CV35 0AR* Tel (01926) 651279 E-mail gjburrell@btinternet.com

BURRELL, Martin John. b 51. Cant Ch Ch Univ Coll MA00 ARCM71. Trin Coll Bris BA95. **d** 95 **p** 96. C Cant St Mary Bredin 95-99; V Cranbrook 99-09; Asst Dir of Ords 06-09; P-in-c Bushmead *St Alb* from 09. *Church House, 73 Hawkfields, Luton LU2 7NW* Tel (01582) 487327 Mobile 07791-536713 E-mail mburrell51@googlemail.com

BURRELL, Timothy Graham. b 43. JP83. St Steph Ho Ox 69. **d** 72 **p** 07. C Haltwhistle *Newc* 72-73; NSM Harrogate St Wilfrid *Ripon* from 06. *8 St Hilda's Road, Harrogate HG2 8JY* Tel (01423) 883832 Mobile 07885-681379
E-mail tim.burrell@virgin.net

BURRETT, Miss Gaynor Elizabeth. b 59. St Jo Coll Nottm 04. **d** 06 **p** 07. C Branksome St Clem *Sarum* from 06. *29 Croft Road, Poole BH12 3LB* Tel (01202) 733390

BURRIDGE, Matthew Guy. b 73. Univ Coll Lon BSc94 MB, BS97. NTMTC BA08. **d** 08 **p** 09. NSM Kentish Town St Silas and H Trin w St Barn *Lon* from 08. *Health E1 Homeless Medical Centre, 9-11 Brick Lane, London E1 6PU* Tel (020) 7247 0090 E-mail fr.matthew.burridge@googlemail.com

BURRIDGE, Richard Alan. b 55. Univ Coll Ox BA77 MA81 Nottm Univ CertEd78 PhD89. St Jo Coll Nottm 82 **d** 85 **p** 86. C Bromley SS Pet and Paul *Roch* 85-87; Chapl Fx Univ 87-94; Dean K Coll Lon from 94; Lic Preacher *Lon* from 94; Perm to Offic *S'wark* from 98 and *Chelmsf* from 05. *King's College, Strand, London WC2R 2LS* Tel (020) 7848 2333 Fax 7848 2344 E-mail dean@kcl.ac.uk

BURRIDGE-BUTLER, Paul David. See BUTLER, Paul David

BURROUGHS, Edward Graham. b 36. K Coll Lon BD AKC. **d** 60 **p** 61. C Walton St Mary *Liv* 60-63; Zimbabwe from 63. *Box 8045, Belmont, Bulawayo, Zimbabwe* Tel (00263) (9) 78711

BURROW, Miss Alison Sarah. b 59. Homerton Coll Cam BEd82. Westcott Ho Cam 84. **d** 87 **p** 03. Par Dn Hebden Bridge *Wakef* 87-88; Par Dn Prestwood and Gt Hampden *Ox* 88-90; Par Dn Olney w Emberton 90-92; rtd 92; Hon C Bedford St Pet w St Cuth *St Alb* 02-07; P-in-c Renhold from 07. *The Vicarage, Church Road, Renhold, Bedford MK41 0LU* Tel (01234) 771317 E-mail as.burrow@ntlworld.com

BURROW, Mrs Margaret Anne. b 46. Open Univ BA82 Leeds Univ MSc85 Lon Univ TCert68. Coll of Resurr Mirfield 06. **d** 07 **p** 08. NSM Douglas St Ninian *S & M* 07-08; NSM St German's Cathl from 08. *1 Thorny Road, Douglas, Isle of Man IM2 5EF* Tel (01624) 662173 Mobile 07624-235711 E-mail margaret.burrow@mcb.net

BURROW, Ronald. b 31. Univ Coll Dur BA55. St Steph Ho Ox 83. **d** 85 **p** 86. C Dawlish *Ex* 85-87; TV Ottery St Mary, Alfington, W Hill, Tipton etc 87-91; P-in-c Pyworthy, Pancrasweek and Bridgerule 91-95; rtd 95; Perm to Offic *Ex* from 95. *3 Riverside, Dolphin Street, Colyton EX24 6LU* Tel and fax (01297) 553882

BURROWS, Canon Brian Albert. b 34. Atlantic Sch of Th BTh83. St Aid Birkenhead 56. **d** 59 **p** 60. C Sutton St Geo *Ches* 59-62; Canada 62-69 and from 74; V Stratton St Margaret *Bris* 70-74; Hon Can Frobisher Bay 78-80; rtd 99. *334 Mary Street, Niagara on the Lake ON L0S 1J0, Canada*

BURROWS, Prof Clifford Robert. b 37. OBE05. Univ of Wales BSc62 Lon Univ PhD69 DSc(Eng)89 Aston Univ Hon DSc01 MIMechE68 FIMechE82 FIEE98 FREng98. Chich Th Coll 75. **d** 76 **p** 77. NSM Brighton St Pet *Chich* 76-78; NSM Brighton St Pet w Chpl Royal 78-80; NSM Brighton St Pet w Chpl Royal and St Jo 80-82; Perm to Offic *Glas* 82-85 and 86-89; NSM Clarkston 85-86; NSM Bath Ch Ch Prop Chpl *B & W* from 90. *Stonecroft, Entry Hill Drive, Bath BA2 5NL* Tel (01225) 334743 Fax 429990 E-mail c.r.burrows@bath.ac.uk

BURROWS, Clive Robert. b 60. Bath Coll of HE BEd82 Ches Coll of HE BA04. NOC 01. **d** 04 **p** 05. C N Wingfield, Clay Cross and Pilsley *Derby* from 04. *The Vicarage, Ankerbold Road, Tupton, Chesterfield S42 6BX* Tel (01246) 864524 E-mail clive@revburrows.plus.com

BURROWS, David. b 62. Leeds Univ BA85 MA03. Linc Th Coll 86. **d** 88 **p** 89. C Kippax w Allerton Bywater *Ripon* 88-91; C Manston 91-95; Chapl Killingbeck Hosp 94; V Halifax St Anne Southowram *Wakef* 95-00; P-in-c Charlestown 95-00; V Southowram and Claremount 00-02; TV Elland 02-05; TR from 05; rtd 03; RD Brighouse and Elland from 08; Chapl Overgate Hospice from 02. *All Saints' Vicarage, Charles Street, Elland HX5 0JF* Tel (01422) 373184 Mobile 07932-694555 E-mail rectorofelland@btinternet.com

BURROWS, David MacPherson. b 43. NOC. **d** 82 **p** 83. NSM Newburgh *Liv* 82-93; NSM Newburgh w Westhead from 93; Dioc Adv NSM from 03. *34 Woodrow Drive, Newburgh, Wigan WN8 7LB* Tel (01257) 462948 E-mail davidmacburrows@msn.com

BURROWS, Diane. b 48. **d** 05 **p** 06. NSM Saltash *Truro* from 05. *20 Andrews Way, Hatt, Saltash PL12 6PE* Tel (01752) 842540 E-mail di.burrows@connella.co.uk

BURROWS, Graham Charles. b 47. Leeds Univ CertEd69 Open Univ BA81. NOC 87. **d** 90 **p** 91. C Chorlton-cum-Hardy St Clem *Man* 90-93; TV Horwich 93; TV Horwich and Rivington 93-94. *29 Heaton Road, Lostock, Bolton BL6 4EE* Tel (01204) 494826

BURROWS, Graham John. b 63. Jes Coll Cam BA84 MA88 Goldsmiths' Coll Lon PGCE94. Oak Hill Th Coll 07. **d** 09. C Polegate *Chich* from 09. *99 Greenleaf Gardens, Polegate BN26 6PH* Tel (01323) 489666 Mobile 07740-622962 E-mail curate@polegate.org.uk

BURROWS, James. b 54. CertEd75. Trin Coll Bris 89. **d** 91 **p** 94. C Allesley *Cov* 91-95; C Thorley *St Alb* 95-99; P-in-c Harrold and Carlton w Chellington 99-06; R 06-07; P-in-c Boughton under Blean w Dunkirk and Hernhill *Cant* from 07. *The Vicarage, 101 The Street, Boughton-under-Blean, Faversham ME13 9BG* Tel (01227) 751410 E-mail jeanburrows@jeanius.me.uk

BURROWS, Canon John Edward. b 36. Leeds Univ BA60 PGCE63. Coll of Resurr Mirfield. **d** 63 **p** 65. C Much Hadham *St Alb* 63-65; Hon C Haggerston St Mary w St Chad *Lon* 65-73; P-in-c Finsbury St Clem w St Barn and St Matt 73-76; Chapl Woodbridge Sch 76-83; V Ipswich St Bart *St E* 83-03; Hon Can St E Cathl 01-03; Perm to Offic *St E* from 03. *55 Berners Street, Ipswich IP1 3LN* Tel (01473) 216629 E-mail burrows@freenetname.co.uk

BURROWS, Joseph Atkinson. b 32. St Aid Birkenhead 58. **d** 61 **p** 62. C Hoole *Ches* 61-67; Jamaica 67-68; C Ayr *Glas* 68-74; R Prestwick 74-78; Hon Chapl RAF 74-78; Hon Chapl RN 74-78; C Cronulla *Australia* 78-81; R Naremburn and Cammeray 81-87; Asst Min St Ives 87-02; Sen Asst Min from 02. *1/23 Ayres Road, St Ives NSW 2075, Australia* Tel (0061) (2) 0144 3019

✠**BURROWS, The Rt Revd Michael Andrew James.** b 61. TCD BA82 MA85 MLitt86. **d** 87 **p** 88 **c** 06. C Douglas Union w Frankfield *C, C & R* 87-91; Dean of Res TCD 91-94; Min Can St

Patr Cathl Dublin 91-94; I Bandon Union *C, C & R* 94-02; Can Cork and Cloyne Cathls 96-02; Dean Cork and I Cork St Fin Barre's Union 02-06; Bp C & O from 06. *Bishop's House, Troysgate, Kilkenny, Republic of Ireland* Tel (00353) (56) 778 6633 E-mail caselossorybishop@eircom.net

BURROWS, Canon Paul Anthony. b 55. Nottm Univ BA77 Gen Th Sem NY STM88. St Steph Ho Ox 77. **d** 79 **p** 80. C Camberwell St Giles *S'wark* 79-81; C St Helier 81-83; C Fareham SS Pet and Paul *Portsm* 83-85; V Union St Luke and All SS New Jersey USA 85-90; R Temple Hills St Barn Maryland 90-95; P-in-c Des Moines St Mark Iowa 95-01; Can Des Moines Cathl 98-01; R San Francisco Advent of Ch the K from 01. *162 Hickory Street, San Francisco CA 94102, USA* E-mail rector@advent-sf.org

BURROWS, The Ven Peter. b 55. BTh. Sarum & Wells Th Coll 80. **d** 83 **p** 84. C Baildon *Bradf* 83-87; R Broughton Astley *Leic* 87-95; TR Broughton Astley and Croft w Stoney Stanton 95-00; RD Guthlaxton I 94-00; Dir of Ords 97-03; Par Development Officer 00-03; Dir Min, Tr and Par Development 03-05; Hon Can Leic Cathl 98-05; Adn Leeds *Ripon* from 05. *Archdeacon's Lodge, 3 West Park Grove, Leeds LS8 2HQ* Tel and fax 0113-269 0594 E-mail archdeacon.leeds@riponleeds.anglican.org

BURROWS, Philip Geoffrey. b 59. Birm Univ BSc80. Oak Hill Th Coll 90. **d** 92 **p** 93. C Poynton *Ches* 92-96; Min Cheadle Hulme Em CD 96-03; V Mottram in Longdendale from 03. *30A Broadbottom Road, Mottram, Hyde SK14 6JB* Tel (01457) 762268 E-mail philipburrows@mottramparish.org.uk

BURROWS, Samuel Reginald. b 30. AKC57. **d** 58 **p** 59. C Shildon *Dur* 58-62; C Heworth St Mary 62-67; C-in-c Leam Lane CD 67-72; C-in-c Bishopwearmouth St Mary V w St Pet CD 72-77; R Bewcastle and Stapleton *Carl* 77-82; R Harrington 82-90; P-in-c Millom 90; V 90-95; rtd 95. *40 Lindisfarne Road, Durham DH1 5YQ*

✠**BURROWS, The Rt Revd Simon Hedley.** b 28. K Coll Cam BA52 MA56. Westcott Ho Cam 52. **d** 54 **p** 55 **c** 74. C St John's Wood *Lon* 54-57; Chapl Jes Coll Cam 57-60; V Hampstead Cov 60-67; V Fareham H Trin *Portsm* 67-71; TR 71-74; Suff Bp Buckingham *Ox* 74-87; Area Bp Buckm 87-94; rtd 94; Hon Asst Bp Win from 94. *8 Quarry Road, Winchester SO23 0JF* Tel (01962) 853332

BURROWS, Victoria Elizabeth. b 61. STETS 01. **d** 04 **p** 05. C The Bourne and Tilford *Guildf* 04-07; R Long Ditton from 07. *The Rectory, 5 Church Meadow, Surbiton KT6 5EP* Tel (020) 8398 1583 E-mail vicki@stmaryslongditton.org.uk *or* vicki@williamburrows.org

BURSELL, Michael Hingston McLaughlin. b 70. K Coll Cam MA96 Open Univ MBA02. ERMC 05. **d** 08 **p** 09. NSM Halstead Area *Chelmsf* from 08. *Bowyer's, North Road, Great Yeldham, Halstead CO9 4QD* Tel (01787) 237486 Mobile 07971-926937 Fax 08700-517360 E-mail mike.bursell@anglicanpriest.org

BURSELL, His Honour Judge Rupert David Hingston. b 42. QC86. Ex Univ LLB63 St Edm Hall Ox BA67 MA72 DPhil72. St Steph Ho Ox 67. **d** 68 **p** 69. NSM St Marylebone w H Trin *Lon* 68-69; NSM Almondsbury *Bris* 69-71; NSM Bedminster St Fran 71-75; NSM Bedminster 75-83; NSM Bris Ch Ch w St Ewen and All SS 83-88; NSM City of Bris 83-88; Lic to Offic 88-95; Lic to Offic *B & W* 92-92; Chan *Dur* from 89; Chan *B & W* 92; Chan *St Alb* from 92; NSM Cheddar *B & W* from 93; Hon Can St Alb 96-02; Hon CF from 97; Chan *Ox* from 02. *Brookside, 74 Church Road, Winscombe BS25 1BP*

BURSLEM, Christopher David Jeremy Grant. b 35. AKC58. **d** 59 **p** 60. C Bocking St Mary *Chelmsf* 59-63; C Glouc All SS 64-67; R Amberley 67-87; P-in-c Withington and Compton Abdale w Haselton 87-98; rtd 98; Perm to Offic *Derby* from 98. *44 Vestry Road, Oakwood, Derby DE21 2BL* Tel (01332) 830146

BURSON-THOMAS, Michael Edwin. b 52. Sarum & Wells Th Coll 84. **d** 86 **p** 87. C Bitterne Park *Win* 86-89; V Lockerley and E Dean w E and W Tytherley 89-95; P-in-c Fotherby *Linc* 95-99; Asst Local Min Officer 95-99; V Horncastle w Low Toynton 99-06; R Greetham w Ashby Puerorum 99-06; V High Toynton 99-06; R Horncastle Gp 06-07; RD Horncastle 01-06; P-in-c Scotton w Northorpe from 07. *The Rectory, Church Lane, Scotter, Gainsborough DN21 3RZ* Tel (01724) 762951 E-mail m.bursonthomas@btinternet.com

BURSTON, Richard John. b 46. MRICS70 MRTPI73. S Dios Minl Tr Scheme 89. **d** 93 **p** 94. Hon C Stratton St Margaret w S Marston etc *Bris* from 93. *17 Crawley Avenue, Swindon SN3 4LB* Tel (01793) 822403

BURSTON, Canon Robert Benjamin Stuart. b 45. St Chad's Coll Dur BA68. **d** 70 **p** 71. C Whorlton *Newc* 70-77; V Alwinton w Holystone and Alnham 77-83; TR Glendale Gp from 83; Hon Can Newc Cathl from 95. *The Rectory, 5 Fenton Drive, Wooler NE71 6DT* Tel and fax (01668) 281551

BURT, David Alan. b 44. Southn Univ BTh98. STETS 95. **d** 98 **p** 99. C Goring-by-Sea SM 98-06; P-in-c Lyminster from 06. *The Vicarage, 3 The Paddocks, Lyminster, Littlehampton BN17 7QH* Tel (01903) 885345 E-mail david.burt8@btopenworld.com

BURT, Leslie Reginald. b 22. ACIS49. St Aug Coll Cant 65. **d** 66 **p** 67. C Petersfield w Sheet *Portsm* 66-70; Perm to Offic from 82. *8 Ian Gibson Court, Carlisle Road, Southsea PO5 1DH* Tel (023) 9273 0989

BURT, Paul Andrew. b 52. Leeds Univ BA74 K Coll Lon MA02 Univ of Wales PhD09. Ridley Hall Cam 82. **d** 84 **p** 85. C Edin St Thos 84-88; CMS Bahrain 88-90; R Melrose *Edin* 91-00; Chapl Borders Gen Hosp NHS Trust 93-98; Ho Master Win Coll 00-04; Hd RS Pilgrims' Sch 00-04; Chapl and Hd RE K Coll Sch Cam 04-06; Sen Chapl Win Coll from 06. *Winchester College, College Street, Winchester SO23 9NA* Tel (01962) 862374 E-mail pab@wincoll.ac.uk

BURT, Roger Malcolm. b 45. MBE91. St Jo Coll Auckland. **d** 73 **p** 74. V Tinui New Zealand 73-80; P-in-c Colton *Nor* 80; P-in-c Easton 80; V Easton w Colton and Marlingford 80-88; CF 88-01; P-in-c E Coker w Sutton Bingham and Closworth *B & W* from 01. *The Vicarage, East Coker, Yeovil BA22 9JG* Tel (01935) 862125

BURTON, Andrew John. b 63. St Kath Coll Liv BA84. Cranmer Hall Dur 86. **d** 88 **p** 89. C Harlescott *Lich* 88-91; C Ches H Trin 91-94; P-in-c Congleton St Jas 94-01; R Calton, Cauldon, Grindon, Waterfall etc *Lich* 01-08; RD Alstonfield 03-08; V Bushey Heath St Alb from 08. *St Peter's Vicarage, 19 High Road, Bushey Heath, Bushey WD23 1EA* Tel (020) 8950 1424 E-mail ajburton63@btinternet.com

BURTON, Antony William James. b 29. Ch Coll Cam BA52 MA56. Cuddesdon Coll 52. **d** 54 **p** 55. C Linc St Nic w St Jo Newport 54-57; C Croydon St Jo *Cant* 57-62; V Winterton *Linc* 62-82; V Roxby w Risby 70-82; RD Manlake 76-82; V Nettleham 82-94; rtd 94; Perm to Offic *Linc* 94-02. *28 Eastfield Road, Messingham, Scunthorpe DN17 3PG* Tel (01724) 763916

BURTON, Miss Barbara Louise. b 57. Leic Univ LLB81 Solicitor 84. ERMC 03. **d** 06 **p** 07. NSM March St Jo *Ely* from 06. *1 Beech Grove, March PE15 8JS* Tel (01354) 652459 E-mail barbaraburton@btinternet.com

BURTON, Christopher Paul. b 38. FCA75 Bris Univ PhD00. Clifton Th Coll 67. **d** 69 **p** 70. C Wandsworth All SS *S'wark* 69-72; C York St Paul 72-75; V Castle Vale *Birm* 75-82; R Gt Parndon *Chelmsf* 82-99; TR 99-03; rtd 03; Perm to Offic *St E* 04-07. *Damson Cottage, 69B London Road North, Poynton, Stockport SK12 1AG* Tel (01625) 875266

BURTON, Daniel John Ashworth. b 63. Regent's Park Coll Ox BA88 MA93 Heythrop Coll Lon MTh93. St Mich Coll Llan 93. **d** 94 **p** 95. C Mountain Ash *Llan* 94-97; R St Brides Minor w Bettws 97-02; R St Brides Minor w Bettws w Aberkenfig 02-03; P-in-c Cheetham *Man* from 03. *The Vicarage, 105 Birdeoak Street, Manchester M8 0AY* Tel 0161-205 1734 E-mail daniel.burton2@virgin.net

BURTON, David Alan. b 53. St Jo Coll Dur BA75. Westcott Ho Cam 81. **d** 84 **p** 85. C Bedford St Andr *St Alb* 84-87; C Leighton Buzzard w Eggington, Hockliffe etc 87-91; V Kingsbury Episcopi w E Lambrook *B & W* 91-94; V Kingsbury Episcopi w E Lambrook, Hambridge etc 94-95; R Bishops Lydeard w Bagborough and Cothelstone 95-03; rtd 04; C Dawlish *Ex* from 06; C Kenton, Mamhead, Powderham, Cofton and Starcross from 06. *The Rectory, 1 Staplake Rise, Starcross, Exeter EX6 8SJ* Tel (01626) 891777 E-mail david_burton@dsl.pipex.com

BURTON, Desmond Jack. b 49. Sarum & Wells Th Coll 70. **d** 73 **p** 74. C Lakenham St Jo *Nor* 73-77; C Gt Yarmouth 77-80; R Tidworth *Sarum* 80-83; Chapl HM Pris Pentonville 83-84; Standford Hill 84-88; Swaleside 88-93; Roch 93-99; Whitemoor 99-05; Whatton from 05. *HM Prison Whatton, Nottingham NG13 9FQ* Tel (01949) 859200 Fax 859201

BURTON, Graham John. b 45. Bris Univ BA69. Tyndale Hall Bris 69. **d** 71 **p** 72. C Leic St Chris 71-75; C Southall Green St Jo *Lon* 75-79; CMS Pakistan 80-92; P-in-c Basford w Hyson Green *S'well* 92-99; P-in-c Hyson Green and Forest Fields 99-01; Assoc P 01-07; Dir Rainbow Project 01-07; rtd 07; Perm to Offic *S'well* from 07. *6 Meadow Brown Road, Nottingham NG7 5PH*

BURTON, Hugh Anthony. b 56. Edin Univ BD79. Cranmer Hall Dur 81. **d** 83 **p** 84. C Coalville and Bardon Hill *Leic* 83-87; P-in-c Packington w Normanton-le-Heath 87-92; V 92-96; TV Kidderminster St Geo *Worc* 96-08; P-in-c from 08. *The Rectory, 30 Leswell Street, Kidderminster DY10 1RP* Tel (01562) 824490 E-mail hburton@wfcsmail.com

BURTON, Leslie Samuel Bertram. b 23. **d** 91 **p** 92. NSM St Cleer *Truro* 91-93; Perm to Offic 93-00. *29 Vivian Court, Truro TR1 2TR*

BURTON, Michael John. b 55. Leeds Univ BSc76 Leeds Poly BSc80. St Jo Coll Nottm 86. **d** 88 **p** 89. C Charles w Plymouth St Matthias *Ex* 88-92; V Paignton St Paul Preston 92-99; TV Almondbury w Farnley Tyas *Wakef* 99-02; V Roade and Ashton w Hartwell *Pet* from 02; RD Towcester 03-09. *The Vicarage, 18 Hartwell Road, Roade, Northampton NN7 2NT* Tel (01604) 862284 E-mail michaelburton5@aol.com

BURTON, Nicholas Guy. b 69. Bris Univ BSc91 ACCA00. Ridley Hall Cam 03. **d** 05 **p** 06. C Ore St Helen and St Barn *Chich* from 05. *34 Fellows Road, Hastings TN34 3TY* Tel (01424) 440093 Mobile 07851-742049 E-mail 5.burton@tiscali.co.uk

BURTON, Nicholas John. b 52. St Steph Ho Ox 77. **d** 80 **p** 81. C Leic St Matt and St Geo 80-82; C Leic Resurr 82-83; TV 83-88; C Narborough and Huncote 88-90; R from 90. *All Saints' Rectory, 15 Church View, Narborough, Leicester LE19 2GY* Tel 0116-275 0388

BURTON, Norman George. b 30. NOC. **d** 83 **p** 84. C Rothwell w Lofthouse *Ripon* 83-86; C Rothwell 86-87; V Lofthouse 87-96; rtd 96; Perm to Offic *Ripon* from 96. *28 Temple Row Close, Leeds LS15 9HR* Tel 0113-260 1129

BURTON, Mrs Sarah Elizabeth. b 59. Nottm Univ BMedSci80 Dur Univ PGCE82. NOC 05. **d** 08 **p** 09. C Eastham *Ches* from 08. *6 Elizabeth Crescent, Chester CH4 7AZ* Tel (01244) 659874 E-mail seburton@fsmail.net

BURTON, Mrs Virginia Ann. b 55. St As Minl Tr Course 00. **d** 03 **p** 04. C Llanrhos *St As* 03-08; C Colwyn Bay w Brynymaen from 08. *The Rectory, 1 Rhodfa Sant Elian, Colwyn Bay LL29 8PY* Tel (01492) 512160

BURTON EVANS, David. *See* EVANS, David Burton

BURTON-JONES, Simon David. b 62. Em Coll Cam BA84 MA88. St Jo Coll Nottm BTh92 MA93. **d** 93 **p** 94. C Darwen St Pet w Hoddlesden *Blackb* 93-96; C Biggin Hill *Roch* 96-98; P-in-c Plaistow St Mary 98-00; V 00-05; R Chislehurst St Nic from 05; AD Bromley 01-06. *The Rectory, 2 Cardinal Close, Chislehurst BR7 6SA* Tel (020) 8467 4405 E-mail simon.burtonjones@diocese-rochester.org

BURTT, Andrew Keith. b 50. Massey Univ (NZ) BA72 MA74 DipEd76. St Jo Coll (NZ) LTh82. **d** 81 **p** 82. New Zealand 81-83; CF 84-92; Sen Chapl Brighton Coll 93-03; Chapl Portsm Gr Sch from 03. *8 Penny Street, Portsmouth PO1 2NH* Tel (023) 9268 1395

BURTWELL, Stanley Peter. b 32. Leeds Univ BA55. Coll of Resurr Mirfield 55. **d** 57 **p** 58. C Leeds St Hilda *Ripon* 57-61; S Africa 61-72; P-in-c Gt Hanwood *Heref* 72-78; R 78-83; RD Pontesbury 80-83; V Upper Norwood St Jo *Cant* 83-84; V Upper Norwood St Jo *S'wark* 85-90; RD Croydon N 85-90; TR Bourne Valley *Sarum* 90-97; rtd 97; Perm to Offic *Sarum* from 97. *Splinters, 116 High Street, Swanage BN19 2NY* Tel (01929) 421785

BURUNDI, Archbishop of. *See* NTAHOTURI, The Most Revd Bernard

BURY, Miss Dorothy Jane. b 53. Lanc Univ BA96 MA98 St Hild Coll Dur CertEd75. Ripon Coll Cuddesdon 00. **d** 02 **p** 03. C Thornton-le-Fylde *Blackb* 02-06; P-in-c Wigan St Anne *Liv* from 06; Chapl Deanery C of E High Sch Wigan from 06. *St Anne's Vicarage, 154 Beech Hill Avenue, Wigan WN6 7TA* Tel (01942) 241930 Mobile 07715-560031 E-mail tillybury@tiscali.co.uk

BURY, The Very Revd Nicholas Ayles Stillingfleet. b 43. Qu Coll Cam BA65 MA69 Ch Ch Ox MA71. Cuddesdon Coll. **d** 68 **p** 69. C Liv Our Lady and St Nic 68-71; Chapl Ch Ch Ox 71-75; V Stevenage St Mary Shephall *St Alb* 75-84; V St Peter-in-Thanet *Cant* 84-97; RD Thanet 93-97; Hon Can Cant Cathl 94-97; Dean Glouc from 97. *The Deanery, 1 Miller's Green, Gloucester GL1 2BP* Tel (01452) 524167 E-mail deanglos@uk.gateway.net

BUSBY, Ian Frederick Newman. b 32. Roch Th Coll 61. **d** 64 **p** 65. C Bedale *Ripon* 64-67; C Stevenage St Geo *St Alb* 67-71; V Stevenage St Mary Shephall 71-75; V Kildwick *Bradf* 75-92; rtd 93; Perm to Offic *Bradf* from 93. *65 Main Street, Farnhill, Keighley BD20 9BJ* Tel (01535) 633001

BUSBY, John. b 38. St Cath Coll Cam MA60 CEng. **d** 93 **p** 94. OLM Worplesdon *Guildf* 93-02; OLM Pirbright 02-04. *Iona, Fox Corner, Worplesdon, Guildford GU3 3PP* Tel (01483) 234562

BUSFIELD, Miss Lynn Maria. b 60. Trin Coll Bris BA99. **d** 99 **p** 00. C Scartho *Linc* 99-03; TV Marlborough *Sarum* 03-05; Chapl Mt Edgcumbe Hospice 05-08; P-in-c Fladbury w Wyre Piddle and Moor etc *Worc* from 09. *The Rectory, Station Road, Fladbury, Pershore WR10 2QW* Tel (01386) 860356 E-mail lynn.busfield@virgin.net

BUSH, Mrs Ann Kathleen. b 47. MATCA65. Ox Min Course 90. **d** 93 **p** 94. NSM Warfield *Ox* 93-96; Dep Chapl HM Pris Wormwood Scrubs 96-97; Chapl HM Pris Reading 97-99; Sen Chapl HM Pris Feltham 99-01; R Fort Smith Canada from 01. *PO Box 64, Fort Smith NT X0E 0P0, Canada* Tel (001) (867) 872 3438 E-mail abush@auroranet.nt.ca

BUSH, David. b 25. FRIBA47 Liv Univ BArch47. S'wark Ord Course 73. **d** 77 **p** 77. C Douglas St Geo and St Barn *S & M* 77-80; Chapl Ballamona Hosp and Cronk Grianagh 80-86; V Marown 80-87; R The Rissingtons *Glouc* 87-92; rtd 92; Perm to Offic *Glouc* 92-98 and *Ely* from 98. *12 Kentwell Place, Burwell, Cambridge CB25 0RT* Tel (01638) 741839 E-mail davdac.bush@care4free.net

BUSH, Esther Rachma Hartley. b 66. LMH Ox BA88 St Jo Coll Dur BA04. Cranmer Hall Dur 02. **d** 04 **p** 05. C Bethnal Green St Matt w St Jas the Gt *Lon* 04-07; C Staines from 07. *Christ Church Vicarage, Kenilworth Gardens, Staines TW18 1DR* Tel (01784) 455457 Mobile 07854-852806 E-mail rachmasaid@yahoo.co.uk

BUSH, George Raymond. b 57. St Jo Coll Cam BA81 MA84 Univ of Wales LLM95. Ripon Coll Cuddesdon BA84 MA88. **d** 85 **p** 86. C Leeds St Aid *Ripon* 85-89; Chapl St Jo Coll Cam 89-94;

V Hoxton St Anne w St Columba *Lon* 94-02; R St Mary le Bow w St Pancras Soper Lane etc from 02. *The Rector's Lodgings, Cheapside, London EC2V 6AU* Tel (020) 7248 5139 Fax 7248 0509 E-mail grbush@london.anglican.org

BUSH, Mrs Glenda. b 41. NOC 92. **d** 95 **p** 96. NSM Bolton St Phil *Man* 95-99; C 99-02; C Bolton SS Simon and Jude 99-02; P-in-c 02-06; rtd 06; Perm to Offic *Man* from 06. *46 Mary Street West, Horwich, Bolton BL6 7JU* Tel (01204) 691539

BUSH, Mrs Kathryn Ann. b 60. OLM course 95. **d** 99 **p** 00. OLM Mareham-le-Fen and Revesby *Linc* 99-06; OLM Mareham on the Hill 99-06; OLM Hameringham w Scrafield and Winceby 99-06; OLM Fen and Hill Gp from 06. *Wheatsheaf Farm, Chapel Lane, New Bolingbroke, Boston PE22 7LF* Tel (01205) 480631 Mobile 07775-736344

BUSH, Rachma. *See* BUSH, Esther Rachma Hartley

BUSH, The Ven Roger Charles. b 56. K Coll Lon BA78 Leeds Univ BA85. Coll of Resurr Mirfield 83. **d** 86 **p** 87. C Newbold w Dunston *Derby* 86-90; TV Leic Resurr 90-94; TR Redruth w Lanner and Treleigh *Truro* 94-04; RD Carnmarth N 96-03; Hon Can Truro Cathl 03-04; Can Res Truro Cathl from 04; Adn Cornwall from 06. *Westwood House, Tremorvah Crescent, Truro TR1 1NL* Tel (01872) 225630 E-mail roger@truro.anglican.org

BUSH, Lt Col Walter Patrick Anthony. b 39. **d** 07 **p** 08. OLM Watercombe *Sarum* from 07. *Holworth Farmhouse, Holworth, Dorchester DT2 8NH* Tel (01305) 852242 E-mail bushinarcadia@yahoo.co.uk

BUSHAU, Reginald Francis. b 49. Shimer Coll Illinois AB71. St Steph Ho Ox BA73 MA98. **d** 74 **p** 75. C Deptford St Paul *S'wark* 74-77; C Willesden St Andr and Gladstone Park St Fran *Lon* 77-82; P-in-c Brondesbury St Anne w Kilburn H Trin 83-88; V Paddington St Mary Magd 88-97; AD Westmr Paddington 92-97; P-in-c S Kensington St Steph 96-98; V from 98. *9 Eldon Road, London W8 5PU* Tel (020) 7937 5083 *or* 7370 3418 E-mail bushrf@aol.com

BUSHBY, Michael Reginald. b 42. LSE BSc70 Leeds Univ MA97. **d** 02 **p** 03. NSM S Cave and Ellerker w Broomfleet *York* 02-05; P-in-c Newbald from 05. *The Vicarage, 7 Dot Hill Close, North Newbald, York YO43 4TS* Tel (01430) 801088

BUSHELL, Anthony Colin. b 59. Pemb Coll Ox MA82 Barrister 83. S'wark Ord Course 93. **d** 96 **p** 97. NSM Felsted and Lt Dunmow *Chelmsf* 96-98; NSM Stanway 98-06; NSM Greenstead w Colchester St Anne from 06. *Pump Hall, Middle Green, Wakes Colne, Colchester CO6 2BJ* Tel (01787) 222487 Fax 222361 E-mail vicartone@aol.com

BUSHELL, Mrs Linda Mary. b 52. Bradf and Ilkley Coll BEd91. STETS 06. **d** 09. NSM Bembridge *Portsm* from 09. *2 Rowborough Cottages, Rowborough Lane, Brading, Sandown PO36 0AY* Tel (01983) 400261 E-mail linda.bushell1@btinternet.com

BUSHELL, Roy. b 32. NW Ord Course 75. **d** 79 **p** 80. NSM Croft w Southworth *Liv* 79-87; C Netherton 87-89; R Newton in Makerfield Em 89-97; rtd 97; Perm to Offic *Bradf* from 98. *34 Maple Avenue, Whitley Bay NE25 8JS* Tel (0191-251 9816

BUSHELL, Stephen Lionel. b 60. K Coll Lon BA84. Ripon Coll Cuddesdon 92. **d** 94 **p** 95. C Exhall *Cov* 94-97; Asst P Shelswell *Ox* 97-05; Asst Chapl Aylesbury Vale Community Healthcare NHS Trust 97-05; Chapl Oxon & Bucks Mental Health Partnership NHS Trust from 05. *6 Aris Way, Buckingham MK18 1FX* Tel (01280) 823772 E-mail tostephenbushell@hotmail.com *or* stephen.bushell@obmh.nhs.uk

BUSHYAGER, Ronald Robert. b 77. Belmont Univ Nashville BSc00. Wycliffe Hall Ox BTh04. **d** 04 **p** 05. C Gamston and Bridgford *S'well* 04-07; C Abingdon *Ox* from 07. *102 Gibson Close, Abingdon OX14 1XT* Tel (01235) 209145 E-mail ronbushyager@ntlworld.com

BUSHYAGER (née TWITCHEN), Mrs Ruth Kathleen Frances. b 77. Bris Univ MSci99. Wycliffe Hall Ox BA04. **d** 05 **p** 06. C Wilford *S'well* 05-07; NSM Abingdon *Ox* 08; Asst Chapl St Edw Sch Ox from 08. *102 Gibson Close, Abingdon OX14 1XT* Tel (01235) 209145 E-mail ruth.bushyager@ntlworld.com

BUSK, David Westly. b 60. Magd Coll Cam BA83 St Jo Coll Dur BA88. Cranmer Hall Dur 86. **d** 89 **p** 90. C Old Swinford Stourbridge *Worc* 89-93; USPG Japan 94-95; C Fukuoka Cathl 95-96; P-in-c Nagasaki H Trin 96-06; P-in-c Godmanchester *Ely* from 06. *The Vicarage, 59 Post Street, Godmanchester, Huntingdon PE29 2AQ* Tel and fax (01480) 436400 Mobile 07765-851757 E-mail dwbusk@hotmail.com

BUSK, Horace. b 34. Clifton Th Coll 56. **d** 60 **p** 61. C Burton All SS *Lich* 60-63; Paraguay 63-66; C Silverhill St Matt *Chich* 66-67; Lic to Offic *Sarum* 67-69; C W Kilburn St Luke w St Simon and St Jude *Lon* 69-74; TV Ashwellthorpe w Wreningham *Nor* 74-81; P-in-c Meysey Hampton w Marston Meysey and Castle Eaton *Glouc* 81-82, R 82-04; rtd 04; Perm to Offic *Glouc* from 04. *23 Eastcote Road, Cirencester GL7 2DB* Tel (01285) 650884

BUSS, Gerald Vere Austen. b 36. CCC Cam PhD87. St Steph Ho Ox 59. **d** 63 **p** 64. C Petersham *S'wark* 63-66; C Brompton H Trin *Lon* 66-69; Asst Chapl Hurstpierpoint Coll 70-73; Chapl 74-90; Ho Master 90-94; History teacher 94-96; rtd 96. *Souches,*

The Street, Albourne, Hassocks BN6 9DJ Tel and fax (01273) 832465

BUSSELL, Ian Paul. b 62. Reading Univ BA84 Kingston Poly PGCE85. Qu Coll Birm MA98. **d** 98 **p** 99. C Twickenham St Mary *Lon* 98-01; TV Godalming *Guildf* 01-07; P-in-c Leckhampton SS Phil and Jas w Cheltenham St Jas *Glouc* from 07. *The Vicarage, 80 Painswick Road, Cheltenham GL50 2EU* Tel (01242) 525460 E-mail ianbussell@googlemail.com

BUSSELL, Ronald William. b 34. CA Tr Coll 57 St Deiniol's Hawarden 81. **d** 83 **p** 84. C Claughton cum Grange *Ches* 83-85; P-in-c Preston St Oswald *Blackb* 85-87; V Fleetwood St Nic 87-93; Dioc Chapl MU 91-95; R Tarleton 93-95; rtd 95; Perm to Offic *Blackb* from 95. *4 Willoughby Avenue, Thornton-Cleveleys FY5 2BW* Tel (01253) 820067 E-mail ron.bussell@talk21.com

BUSSEY, Diane Jean. b 57. **d** 07 **p** 08. OLM Clifton upon Dunsmore w Newton and Brownsover *Cov* from 07. *2 Teasel Close, Rugby CV23 0TJ* Tel (01788) 339278 E-mail diane.bussey1@ntlworld.com

BUSSEY, Norman. b 22. Clifton Th Coll 63. **d** 65 **p** 66. C Upton (Overchurch) *Ches* 65-69; V Bradley *Wakef* 69-88; rtd 88; Perm to Offic *Glouc* from 88. *43 Crispin Road, Winchcombe, Cheltenham GL54 5JX* Tel (01242) 602754

BUSSEY, Rachel Anne. STETS 00. **d** 03 **p** 04. NSM Durrington *Sarum* from 03; NSM Avon Valley from 08. *3 Birchwood Drive, Durrington, Salisbury SP4 8ER* Tel 07899-926034 (mobile) E-mail rachel.bussey@ntlworld.com

BUSSMANN, Mrs Mary Elizabeth. b 52. Leeds Univ MA06. Trin Coll Bris. **d** 06 **p** 07. C Otham w Langley *Cant* from 06. *4 Kings Acre, Downswood, Maidstone ME15 8UP* Tel (01622) 862555 E-mail ebussmann@btinternet.com

BUSTARD, Guy Nicholas. b 51. K Coll Lon BD77 AKC77. St Steph Ho Ox 77. **d** 78 **p** 79. C Hythe *Cant* 78-81; Chapl RN 81-85; V Haddenham and Wilburton *Ely* 85-89; Chapl Qu Eliz Hosp Welwyn Garden City 89-92; Chapl E Herts NHS Trust 92-00; Chapl E and N Herts NHS Trust 00-02; Perm to Offic *St Alb* from 02. *2 Copper Beeches, Welwyn AL6 0SS* Tel (01438) 717916

BUSTIN, Canon Peter Ernest. b 32. Qu Coll Cam BA56 MA60. Tyndale Hall Bris 56. **d** 57 **p** 58. C Welling *Roch* 57-60; C Farnborough *Guildf* 60-62; V Hornsey Rise St Mary *Lon* 62-70; R Barnwell *Pet* 70-78; RD Oundle 76-84; P-in-c Luddington w Hemington and Thurning 77-78; R Barnwell w Thurning and Luddington 78-84; V Southwold *St E* 84-97; RD Halesworth 90-95; Hon Can St E Cathl 91-97; rtd 97; Perm to Offic *St E* from 97. *55 College Street, Bury St Edmunds IP33 1NH* Tel (01284) 767708 E-mail bustin@saintedmunds.vispa.com

BUSTIN, Peter Laurence. b 54. St Steph Ho Ox. **d** 83 **p** 84. C Northolt St Mary *Lon* 83-86; C Pimlico St Pet w Westmr Ch Ch 86-88; C Heston 88-91; P-in-c Twickenham All SS 91-98; V from 98. *All Saints' House, Church View Road, Twickenham TW2 5BX* Tel and fax (020) 8894 3580 E-mail peter@padova.fsnet.co.uk

BUSTIN, Timothy Mark. b 75. Wycliffe Hall Ox 05. **d** 07 **p** 08. C Bletchley *Ox* from 07. *14 Hamilton Lane, Bletchley, Milton Keynes MK3 5LU* Tel 07870-663861 (mobile) E-mail tim@freeserve.co.uk

BUTCHER, Andrew John. b 43. Trin Coll Cam BA66 MA69. Cuddesdon Coll 66. **d** 68 **p** 69. C Sheff St Mark Broomhall 68-70; P-in-c Louth H Trin *Linc* 70-72; Chapl RAF 72-87; Lic to Offic *Ox* 85-87; TR Cove St Jo *Guildf* 87-91; V Egham Hythe 91-98; V Docking, the Birchams, Stanhoe and Sedgeford *Nor* 98-08; rtd 08; Perm to Offic *Nor* from 08. *67 The Street, Hindringham, Fakenham NR21 0PR* Tel (01328) 878526 Mobile 07887-506876 E-mail andrewj.butcher@btinternet.com

BUTCHER, Miss Ann Lesley. b 46. Lon Coll of Printing BA67 Ex Univ BTh09. SWMTC 06. **d** 09. NSM St Michael Penkevil *Truro* from 09; NSM Tregony w St Cuby and Cornelly from 09; NSM Tresillian and Lamorran w Merther from 09. *Burnwithian House, Burnwithian, St Day, Redruth TR16 5LG* Tel (01209) 820788 E-mail mail@annbutcher.demon.co.uk

BUTCHER, Edwin William. b 39. Portsm Dioc Tr Course 91 STETS 04. **d** 92 **p** 05. NSM Ryde All SS *Portsm* from 92. *23 Quarry Road, Ryde PO33 2TX* Tel (01983) 616889

BUTCHER (née POTTS), Heather Dawn. b 52. **d** 98 **p** 99. C Attleborough w Besthorpe *Nor* 98-01; R Bunwell, Carleton Rode, Tibenham, Gt Moulton etc 01-09; RD Depwade 03-09; R Cringleford and Colney from 09. *The Vicarage, 7A Newmarket Road, Cringleford, Norwich NR4 6UE* Tel (01603) 458467 E-mail revheather@hpotts.wanadoo.co.uk

BUTCHER, Philip Warren. b 46. Trin Coll Cam BA68 MA70. Cuddesdon Coll 68. **d** 70 **p** 71. C Bris St Mary Redcliffe w Temple etc 70-73; Hon C W Wickham St Fran *Cant* 73-78; Chapl Abingdon Sch 78-85; Chapl Nor Sch 85-98; V Horsford and Horsham w Newton St Faith *Nor* 98-04; P-in-c Barningham w Matlaske w Baconsthorpe etc *Nor* 05-09; Perm to Offic from 09. *The Vicarage, 7A Newmarket Road, Cringleford, Norwich NR4 6UE* Tel (01603) 458467

BUTCHER, Richard Peter. b 50. St Chad's Coll Dur BA71. Chich Th Coll 73. **d** 74 **p** 75. C Yeovil St Mich *B & W* 74-77; Chapl Wellingborough Sch 77-83; R Gt w Lt Billing *Pet* 83-88; Chapl

Bp Stopford Sch Kettering 88-90; Perm to Offic *Pet* 90-01. *55 Field Street, Kettering NN16 8EN*

BUTCHERS, Mark Andrew. b 59. Trin Coll Cam BA81 K Coll Lon MTh90. Chich Th Coll BTh87. **d** 87 **p** 88. C Chelsea St Luke and Ch Ch *Lon* 87-90; C Mitcham SS Pet and Paul *S'wark* 90-93; R N Tawton, Bondleigh, Sampford Courtenay etc *Ex* 93-99; Chapl and Fell Keble Coll Ox 99-05; C Wolvercote w Summertown *Ox* 05-07; P-in-c Wolvercote from 07. *The Vicarage, 1 Mere Road, Oxford OX2 8AN* Tel (01865) 515640 E-mail mark.butchers@dsl.pipex.com

BUTLAND, Cameron James. b 58. BA. Ripon Coll Cuddesdon 81. **d** 84 **p** 85. C Tettenhall Regis *Lich* 84-88; V Bodicote *Ox* 88-95; TR Witney 95-04; RD Witney 97-02; R Grasmere *Carl* from 04; V Rydal from 04; Chapl Rydal Hall from 04. *The Rectory, Grasmere, Ambleside LA22 9SW* Tel (01539) 435326 E-mail cameron@butland555.fsnet.co.uk

BUTLAND, Godfrey John. b 51. Grey Coll Dur BA72. Wycliffe Hall Ox 73. **d** 75 **p** 76. C Much Woolton *Liv* 75-78; Bp's Dom Chapl 78-81; V Everton St Geo 81-94; AD Liv N 89-94; V Allerton 94-05; P-in-c Mossley Hill St Barn 04-05; TV Mossley Hill 05-06; TR from 06; AD Liv S 00-06; Hon Can Liv Cathl 03-06. *Allerton Vicarage, Harthill Road, Liverpool L18 3HU* Tel 0151-724 1561

BUTLER, Alan. b 53. Carl Dioc Tr Inst 89. **d** 89 **p** 90. NSM Flookburgh *Carl* 89-93; C Maryport 93-96; C Flimby 93-96; P-in-c St Saltash *Truro* 98-09; TR from 09. *The Vicarage, St Stephen by Saltash, Saltash PL12 4AB* Tel (01752) 842323

BUTLER, Alan. b 57. Leic Univ BA78. Coll of Resurr Mirfield 80. **d** 83 **p** 84. C Skerton St Luke *Blackb* 83-87; C Birch w Fallowfield *Man* 87-90; V Claremont H Angels 90-95; Chapl Pendleton Coll 95-99; TV Pendleton *Man* 95-99; P-in-c High Crompton from 99; AD Oldham E from 09. *St Mary's Vicarage, 18 Rushcroft Road, Shaw, Oldham OL2 7PR* Tel and fax (01706) 847455 E-mail alanbutler@freenetname.co.uk

BUTLER, Canon Alan John. b 30. Kelham Th Coll 51. **d** 56 **p** 57. S Africa 56-65 and 79-95; Bechuanaland 65-66; Botswana 66-70; V Fletchamstead *Cov* 71-79; Adn Griqualand W 79-85; Adn Kuruman 79-85; Dir Moffat Miss, Kuruman 81-95; TV Hanley H Ev *Lich* 95; rtd 95; Perm to Offic *Sarum* and *Win* from 95. *4 Osborne Road, Wimborne BH21 1BL* Tel (01202) 848859

BUTLER, Ms Angela Elizabeth. b 31. Gilmore Ho 60 Lambeth STh64. **dss** 81 **d** 87 **p** 94. Cookham *Ox* 81-86; Wheatley w Forest Hill and Stanton St John 86-97; Hon Par Dn 87-89; NSM 89-97; NSM Wheatley 97-01; Perm to Offic from 02. *10 River Gardens, Purley-on-Thames, Reading RG8 8BX* Tel 0118-942 2055

BUTLER, Angela Madeline. b 47. Oak Hill Th Coll Course 87. **d** 90 **p** 94. Hon Par Dn Chipperfield St Paul *St Alb* 90-93; Dn-in-c 93-94; P-in-c 94-01; Staff Oak Hill Th Coll 93-97; Springboard Missr 97-01; P-in-c Hempsted and Dioc Springboard Missr *Glouc* 01-07; rtd 07. *22 Esplanade Road, Newquay TR7 1QB* Tel (01637) 859238 E-mail angelambutler@btinternet.com

BUTLER, Betty. b 47. **d** 96. NSM Sully *Llan* 96-97; NSM Merthyr Dyfan 98-07. *Address temp unknown*

BUTLER, Catherine Elizabeth. b 46. **d** 06 **p** 07. NSM Waltham *Linc* from 06. *8 Danesfield Avenue, Waltham, Grimsby DN37 0QE* Tel (01472) 587692 E-mail elsiebutlerdane@msn.com

BUTLER, Christopher. b 67. St Jo Coll Nottm 99. **d** 01 **p** 02. C Retford *S'well* 01-05; P-in-c Holbeck *Ripon* from 05. *St Luke's Vicarage, Malvern View, Leeds LS11 8SG* Tel 0113-271 7996 E-mail vicar@stlukesholbeck.org.uk *or* crbutler@bigfoot.com

BUTLER, Christopher John. b 25. Leeds Univ BA50. Chich Th Coll 51. **d** 52 **p** 53. C Kensington St Mary Abbots w St Geo *Lon* 52-57; Australia 57-59; V Blackmoor *Portsm* 60-70; V Wellingborough St Andr *Pet* 70-79; P-in-c Garsington *Ox* 79-83; R Garsington and Horspath 83-95; rtd 95; Perm to Offic *Portsm*, *Chich*, *Guildf* and *Win* from 95. *33 Oak Tree Road, Whitehill, Bordon GU35 9DF* Tel (01420) 475311

BUTLER, Colin Sydney. b 59. Bradf Univ BSc81. Wycliffe Hall Ox 81. **d** 84 **p** 85. C Farsley *Bradf* 84-87; C Bradf Abbey Undercliffe 87-89; P-in-c Darlaston All SS *Lich* 89-95; Ind Missr 89-95; TR Chell 95-99; CF from 99. *c/o MOD Chaplains (Army)* Tel (01980) 615804 Fax 615800

BUTLER, David Edwin. b 56. ACA83 Jes Coll Ox BA79 BA86. St Steph Ho Ox MA87. **d** 87 **p** 88. C Hulme Ascension *Man* 87-90; V Patricroft 90-94; Perm to Offic *Liv* 97-03; *Man* and *Blackb* from 03; Hon C Prestwich St Hilda 00-01. *16 St George's Road, Nelson BB9 0YA*

BUTLER, Derek John. b 53. Aston Univ BSc74 St Jo Coll York PGCE75. St Jo Coll Dur 79. **d** 82 **p** 83. C Bramcote *S'well* 82-86; Perm to Offic *Roch* 86-88; Perm to Offic *Portsm* 86-92; Lic and SE Co-ord CPAS 86-88; NSM Bromley Ch Ch *Roch* 88-91; NSM Chesham Bois *Ox* from 92. *121 Woodside Road, Amersham HP6 6AL* Tel (01494) 724577

BUTLER, Donald Arthur. b 31. **d** 79 **p** 80. Hon C Apsley End *St Alb* 79-80; Hon C Chambersbury from 80. *143 Belswains Lane, Hemel Hempstead HP3 9UZ*

BUTLER, George James. b 53. AKC74 Kent Univ MA95. St Aug Coll Cant 75. **d** 76 **p** 77. C Ellesmere Port *Ches* 76-79; C Eastham 79-81; Chapl RAF 81-83; C W Kirby St Bridget *Ches* 83-84; V Newton 84-86; CF 86-91; V Folkestone St Sav *Cant* 91-99; P-in-c Wool and E Stoke *Sarum* 99-04; P-in-c Mansfield St Mark *S'well* from 04; AD Mansfield from 06. *St Mark's Vicarage, Nottingham Road, Mansfield NG18 1BP* Tel (01623) 655548 E-mail revgjb@btinternet.com

BUTLER, Canon George William. b 52. CITC. **d** 90 **p** 91. C Drung w Castleterra, Larah and Lavey etc *K, E & A* 90-93; I 93-95; I Castlemacadam w Ballinaclash, Aughrim etc *D & G* from 95; Can Ch Ch Cathl Dublin from 03. *The Rectory, Castlemacadam, Avoca, Co Wicklow, Republic of Ireland* Tel and fax (00353) (402) 35127 Mobile 87-679 5625 E-mail gwb2@hotmail.com

BUTLER, Mrs Helen Carole. b 66. Bath Coll of HE BEd87. Dioc OLM tr scheme 02. **d** 04 **p** 05. NSM Mirfield *Wakef* from 04. *1A Holmdene Drive, Mirfield WF14 9SZ* Tel (01924) 496189 E-mail curate-stmary@cofe-mirfield.org.uk

BUTLER, Henry. b 25. Ridley Hall Cam 73. **d** 75 **p** 76. C Cambridge St Paul *Ely* 75-77; P-in-c Stilton w Denton and Caldecote 77-83; P-in-c Folksworth w Morborne 77-83; V Histon 83-90; P-in-c Impington 84-90; rtd 90; Perm to Offic *Ely* from 90. *48 Church Road, Hauxton, Cambridge CB22 5HS* Tel (01223) 874184

BUTLER, Huw. b 63. Univ of Wales (Ban) BSc84. St Mich Coll Llan BTh95. **d** 95 **p** 96. C Llantwit Fardre 95-00; R Llangynhafal w Llanbedr DC and Llanychan *St As* 00-02; R Llanbedr DC w Llangynhafal, Llanychan etc from 02. *The Rectory, Llanbedr Dyffryn Clwyd, Ruthin LL15 1UP* Tel (01824) 704160 E-mail huw.butler@tesco.net

BUTLER, Ian Malcolm. b 39. Bris Univ BA67 BA69. Clifton Th Coll 67. **d** 69 **p** 70. C Clapham Common St Barn *S'wark* 69-73; C Reigate St Mary 73-78; V Sissinghurst w Frittenden *Cant* 78-91; Chapl Dulwich Prep Sch Cranbrook 90-05; rtd 92. *20 Kingsmead Road, Bognor Regis PO22 6NE* Tel 07786-935469 (mobile) E-mail ian@butler08.fsnet.co.uk

BUTLER, Jane. *See* BUTLER, Linda Jane

BUTLER, John. b 38. Gwent Coll Newport CertEd77. St Mich Coll Llan. **d** 68 **p** 69. C Ebbw Vale *Mon* 68-70; TV 70-75; Perm to Offic 76-77 and 79-88; P-in-c Crumlin 77-78; R Gt and Lt Casterton w Pickworth and Tickencote *Pet* 88-91; R Woolstone w Gotherington and Oxenton etc *Glouc* 91-97; Hon C Dawlish *Ex* 98-01; P-in-c Chevington w Hargrave, Chedburgh w Depden etc *St E* 01-03; R 02-03; rtd 03; C Shaldon, Stokeinteignhead, Combeinteignhead etc *Ex* 03-06. *3 Peak Coach House, Cotmaton Road, Sidmouth EX10 8SY* Tel (01395) 577248

BUTLER, John Philip. b 47. Leeds Univ BA70. Coll of Resurr Mirfield 70. **d** 72 **p** 73. C Elton All SS *Man* 72-75; C Bolton St Pet 75-78; Chapl Bolton Colls of H&FE 75-78; Asst Chapl Bris Univ 78-81; Hon C Clifton St Paul 78-81; V Llansawel w Briton Ferry 81-84; Warden Bp Mascall Cen *Heref* 84-88; Vice-Prin Glouc Sch for Mln 85-88; Chapl Univ of Wales (Ban) 88-07; rtd 07. *Cefn Engan, Llangybi, Pwllheli LL53 6LZ* Tel (01766) 810046

BUTLER, Mrs Linda. b 51. Liv Univ CertEd72. Cranmer Hall Dur 01. **d** 03 **p** 04. C Middlewich w Byley *Ches* 03-06; R Ditchingham, Hedenham, Broome, Earsham etc *Nor* from 06. *The Rectory, School Road, Earsham, Bungay NR35 2TF* Tel (01986) 892147 E-mail franandlinda@googlemail.com

BUTLER, Linda Jane. b 56. SRN77. St Jo Coll Nottm 85. **d** 88 **p** 94. C Burbage w Aston Flamville *Leic* 88-91; Asst Chapl Leic R Infirmary 91-93; Asst Chapl Towers Hosp Humberstone 93-95; Chapl 95-97; Chapl Leics and Rutland Healthcare NHS Trust 97-03; Chapl amongst Deaf People *Pet* from 03. *5 Kestrel Close, Northampton NN3 3JG* Tel and fax (01509) 812705 Mobile 07891-809767 E-mail janebutler01@tiscali.co.uk

BUTLER, Mrs Louise Gail Nesta. **d** 04 **p** 05. OLM Blewbury, Hagbourne and Upton *Ox* 04-06; OLM S w N Moreton, Aston Tirrold and Aston Upthorpe 05-06; OLM The Churn from 06. *Penridge, Church Road, Blewbury, Didcot OX11 9PY* Tel (01235) 851011 E-mail louisegbutler@aol.com

BUTLER, Malcolm. b 40. Linc Th Coll 76. **d** 78 **p** 79. C Whickham *Dur* 78-82; V Leam Lane 82-87; R Penshaw 87-90; rtd 90. *Lincoln Lodge, Front Street, Castleside, Consett DH8 9AR* Tel (01207) 507672

BUTLER, Canon Michael. b 41. St Mich Coll Llan 62 St Deiniol's Hawarden 63. **d** 64 **p** 65. C Welshpool *St As* 65; C Welshpool w Castle Caereinion 65-73; TV Aberystwyth *St D* 73-80; Chapl Univ of Wales (Abth) 73 80; V St Issell's and Amroth from 80; AD Narberth from 91; Can St D Cathl from 01. *St Issell's Vicarage, Saundersfoot SA69 9BD* Tel (01834) 812375

BUTLER, Canon Michael John. b 32. Keble Coll Ox BA58 MSW. Coll of Resurr Mirfield. **d** 59 **p** 60. C Poplar All SS w St Frideswide *Lon* 59-68; Hon C St Steph Walbrook and St Swithun etc 68-73; C Godalming *Guildf* 73-76; P-in-c Brighton St Anne *Chich* 77-79; Dioc Communications Officer and Dir Soc Resp 77-83; Dir Dioc Bd of Soc Resp 83-94; Soc Resp Adv 94-00; Hon C Brighton St Pet w Chpl Royal 94-00;

Can and Preb Chich Cathl 85-00; rtd 00; Perm to Offic *Nor* from 00. *Railway Cottage, 2 Buxton Road, Aylsham, Norwich NR11 6JD* Tel (01263) 734820

BUTLER, Canon Michael Weeden. b 38. Clare Coll Cam BA60 MA65. Westcott Ho Cam 63. **d** 65 **p** 66. C Bermondsey St Mary w St Olave, St Jo etc *S'wark* 65-68; Ind Chapl 68-72; Sierra Leone 73-77; Ind Chapl and R Gt Chart *Cant* 77-86; RD E Charing 81-86; V Glouc St Jas and All SS 86-04; RD Glouc City 94-99; Hon Can Glouc Cathl 96-04; rtd 04. *121 London Road, Gloucester GL2 0RR* Tel (01452) 421563 E-mail michael121@blueyonder.co.uk

BUTLER, Ms Pamela. b 53. Nottm Univ BTh86 CertEd74. Linc Th Coll 83. **dss** 86 **d** 87 **p** 94. Rotherhithe H Trin *S'wark* 86-87; Par Dn 87-88; Par Dn Old Trafford St Jo *Man* 88-89; Par Dn Claremont H Angels 90-94; C 94-95; C Pendleton 95-97; Chapl Asst S Man Univ Hosps NHS Trust from 96. *St Mary's Vicarage, 18 Rushcroft Road, Shaw, Oldham OL2 7PR* Tel (01706) 847455, 0161-291 2298 *or* 998 7070

BUTLER, Paul David. b 67. Sheff Univ BA88. Linc Th Coll 92. **d** 92 **p** 93. C Handsworth Woodhouse *Sheff* 92-96; V Bellingham St Dunstan *S'wark* 96-06; AD E Lewisham 99-06; R Deptford St Paul from 06. *St Paul's Rectory, Mary Ann Gardens, London SE8 3DP* Tel (020) 8692 7449 E-mail rector@paulsdeptford.org.uk

BUTLER, Paul Harnett. b 58. Perkins Sch of Th (USA) MTS95 Girton Coll Cam MPhil98. Ridley Hall Cam 05. **d** 07 **p** 08. C Histon *Ely* from 07; C Impington from 07. *The Vicarage, 60 Impington Lane, Impington, Cambridge CB24 9NJ* Tel (01223) 236887 Mobile 07903-904599 E-mail revpbutler@gmail.com

✠**BUTLER, The Rt Revd Paul Roger.** b 55. Nottm Univ BA77. Wycliffe Hall Ox BA82. **d** 83 **p** 84 **c** 04. C Wandsworth All SS *S'wark* 83-87; Inner Lon Ev Scripture Union 87-92; Dep Hd of Miss 92-94; NSM E Ham St Paul *Chelmsf* 87-94; P-in-c Walthamstow St Mary w St Steph 94-97; P-in-c Walthamstow St Luke 94-97; TR Walthamstow 97-04; AD Waltham Forest 00-04; Hon Can Byumba from 01; Suff Bp Southampton *Win* 04-09; Bp S'well and Nottm from 09. *Bishop's Manor, Bishop's Drive, Southwell NG25 0JP* Tel (01636) 812112 Fax 815401 E-mail bishop@southwell.anglican.org

BUTLER, Perry Andrew. b 49. York Univ BA70 Lon Univ PGCE75 Jes Coll Ox DPhil78 FRHistS. Linc Th Coll 78. **d** 80 **p** 81. C Chiswick St Nic w St Mary *Lon* 80-83; C S Kensington St Steph 83-87; V Bedford Park 87-95; Angl Adv Lon Weekend TV 87-99; P-in-c Bloomsbury St Geo w Woburn Square Ch Ch *Lon* 95-02; R from 02; Dioc Dir of Ords from 96. *The Rectory, 6 Gower Street, London WC1E 6DP* Tel (020) 7580 4010 *or* 7405 3044 E-mail stgeorgebloomsbury@hotmail.com *or* holmado@aol.com

BUTLER, Richard Charles Burr. b 34. St Pet Hall Ox BA59 MA62. Linc Th Coll 58. **d** 60 **p** 61. C St John's Wood *Lon* 60-63; V Kingstanding St Luke *Birm* 63-75; R Lee St Marg *S'wark* 75-00; rtd 00. *21 Defoe House, Barbican, London EC2Y 8DN* Tel (020) 7628 0527 E-mail eleanorandrichardbutler@btinternet.com

BUTLER, Robert Clifford. b 25. AKC54. **d** 55 **p** 56. C Gt Berkhamsted *St Alb* 55-59; C Dunstable 59-63; V Stanbridge w Tilsworth 63-73; R Maulden 73-80; R Oldbury *Sarum* 80-93; rtd 93; Perm to Offic *Sarum* from 93. *3 Mithras Close, Dorchester DT1 2RF* Tel (01305) 264817

BUTLER, Canon Robert Edwin. b 37. Ely Th Coll 60. **d** 62 **p** 63. C Lewisham St Jo Southend *S'wark* 62-65; C Eastbourne St Elisabeth *Chich* 65-69; V Langney 69-86; TR 86-96; Can and Preb Chich Cathl 94-97; rtd 96; Perm to Offic *Chich* from 97. *10 Langdale Close, Langney, Eastbourne BN23 8HS* Tel (01323) 461135

BUTLER, Sandra. *See* BARTON, Mrs Sandra

BUTLER, Canon Simon. b 64. UEA BSc86 RN Coll Dartmouth 86. St Jo Coll Nottm MA92. **d** 92 **p** 93. C Chandler's Ford *Win* 92-94; C Northolt St Jos *Lon* 94-97; V Streatham Immanuel and St Andr *S'wark* 97-04; RD Streatham 01-04; Lambeth Adnry Ecum Officer 99-02; P-in-c Sanderstead All SS 04-05; TR Sanderstead from 05; Hon Can S'wark Cathl from 06. *The Rectory, 1 Addington Road, South Croydon CR2 8RE* Tel (020) 8657 1366 *or* tel and fax 8657 0665 E-mail rector@sanderstead-parish.org.uk

BUTLER, Simon Richard. b 80. Oak Hill Th Coll BA03 Ripon Coll Cuddesdon MTh06. **d** 06 **p** 07. C W Bridgford *S'well* from 06. *9 Church Drive, West Bridgford, Nottingham NG2 6AY* Tel 07803-909284 (mobile) E-mail sib@christiansinmotorsport.org.uk

BUTLER, Stephen Ian. b 59. Edin Univ BA BSc80. Trin Coll Bris BA84. **d** 97 **p** 98. C Edin St Pet 97-99; R Edin St Jas 99-08. *Address temp unknown*

✠**BUTLER, The Rt Revd Thomas Frederick.** b 40. Leeds Univ BSc61 MSc62 PhD72. Coll of Resurr Mirfield 62. **d** 64 **p** 65 **c** 85. C Wisbech St Aug *Ely* 64-66; C Folkestone St Sav *Cant* 66-67; Lect Univ of Zambia 68-73; Chapl Kent Univ 73-80; Six Preacher Cant Cathl 79-84; Adn Northolt *Lon* 80-85; Area Bp Willesden 85-91; Bp Leic 91-98; Bp S'wark from 98. *Bishop's*

House, 38 Tooting Bec Gardens, London SW16 1QZ Tel (020) 8769 3256 Fax 8769 4126
E-mail bishop.tom@southwark.anglican.org

BUTLER, Valerie Joyce. b 58. EAMTC 99. **d** 02 **p** 03. NSM Southminster *Chelmsf* 02-06; Hon Chapl Miss to Seafarers Tilbury 05-06; C Bury St Edmunds All SS w St Jo and St Geo *St E* 06-08; TV Walton and Trimley from 08. *The Vicarage, Church Lane, Trimley St Martin, Felixstowe IP11 0SW* Tel (01394) 286388 E-mail valthevic@talktalk.net

BUTLER-SMITH, Basil George (Bob). b 30. Bps' Coll Cheshunt 66. **d** 67 **p** 68. C Bray and Braywood *Ox* 67-71; R Norton *St E* 71-74; P-in-c Tostock 71-74; R Rotherfield Peppard *Ox* 76-02; P-in-c Rotherfield Greys 79-80; R 80-02; rtd 02. *40 Westleigh Drive, Sonning Common, Reading RG4 9LB* Tel 0118-972 1871

BUTLIN, David Francis Grenville. b 55. Bris Univ BA77 Ox Univ CertEd78. Sarum & Wells Th Coll 85. **d** 87 **p** 88. C Bedford St Andr *St Alb* 87-90; C Milton *Portsm* 90-92; V Hurst Green *S'wark* from 92; RD Godstone 04-08. *The Vicarage, 14 Oast Road, Oxted RH8 9DU* Tel (01883) 712654
E-mail dfgbutlin@14oastroad.freeserve.co.uk

BUTLIN, Timothy Greer. b 53. St Jo Coll Dur BA75 Ox Univ CertEd76 Spurgeon's Coll MTh05. Wycliffe Hall Ox 85. **d** 87 **p** 88. C Eynsham and Cassington *Ox* 87-91; V Loudwater from 91. *The Vicarage, Treadaway Hill, Loudwater, High Wycombe HP10 9QL* Tel (01628) 526087 Fax 529354
E-mail vicar@loudwater.org

BUTT, Adrian. b 37. **d** 71 **p** 72. C Umtata Cathl S Africa 71-76; C Ilkeston St Mary *Derby* 76-79; R N and S Wheatley w W Burton *S'well* 79-84; P-in-c Bole w Saundby 79-84; P-in-c Sturton w Littleborough 79-84; R N Wheatley, W Burton, Bole, Saundby, Sturton etc 84-85; R Kirkby in Ashfield 85-05; rtd 05. *25 Searby Road, Sutton-in-Ashfield NG17 5JQ* Tel (01623) 555650
E-mail adrian@shopfront.freeserve.co.uk

BUTT, Mrs Catherine. b 76. St Hilda's Coll Ox BA99 MA02 St Jo Coll Dur BA02. Cranmer Hall Dur 00. **d** 03 **p** 04. C Bletchley *Ox* from 03. *1 Ashburnham Close, Bletchley, Milton Keynes MK3 7TR* Tel (01908) 631050 Mobile 07971-714223
E-mail butties01@yahoo.co.uk

BUTT, The Very Revd Christopher Martin. b 52. St Pet Coll Ox BA74 Fitzw Coll Cam BA77. Ridley Hall Cam 75. **d** 79 **p** 80. C Cambridge St Barn *Ely* 79-82; Hong Kong 82-89; P-in-c Windermere *Carl* 89-98; TR S Gillingham *Roch* from 98; Dean St Chris Cathl Bahrain from 09. *St Christopher's Cathedral, PO Box 36, Manama, Bahrain* Tel (00973) 253866 Fax 246436
E-mail revbutt@ymail.com

BUTT, Edward. b 46. CQSW80. Trin Coll Bris 86. **d** 88 **p** 89. C Erith St Paul *Roch* 88-92; C Shirley *Win* 92-99; V Stourbridge St Mich Norton *Worc* from 99. *St Michael's Vicarage, Westwood Avenue, Stourbridge DY8 3EN* Tel (01384) 376477

BUTT, Martin James. b 52. Sheff Univ LLB75. Trin Coll Bris 75. **d** 78 **p** 79. C Aldridge *Lich* 78-84; C Walsall 84-87; TV 87-94; P-in-c Farewell from 94; P-in-c Gentleshaw from 94; C Hammerwich 94-03; P-in-c from 03. *The Vicarage, Budds Road, Rugeley WS15 4NB* Tel (01543) 684329

BUTT, William Arthur. b 44. Kelham Th Coll 70 Linc Th Coll 71. **d** 71 **p** 72. C Mackworth St Fran *Derby* 71-75; C Aston cum Aughton *Sheff* 76-79; V Dalton 79-88; TR Staveley and Barrow Hill *Derby* from 88. *The Rectory, Staveley, Chesterfield S43 3XZ* Tel (01246) 472270

BUTTANSHAW, Graham Charles. b 59. TCD BA(Econ)80 BA85. St Jo Coll Nottm 88. **d** 91 **p** 92. C Toxteth St Cypr w Ch Ch *Liv* 91-94; CMS 94-99; Uganda 95-99; V Otley *Bradf* from 99. *The Vicarage, Vicarage Gardens, Otley LS21 3PD* Tel (01943) 462240
E-mail graham.buttanshaw@bradford.anglican.org

BUTTERFIELD, The Ven David John. b 52. Lon Univ BMus73. St Jo Coll Nottm 4. **d** 77 **p** 78. C Southport Ch Ch *Liv* 77-81; Min Aldridge St Thos CD *Lich* 81-91; V Lilleshall, Muxton and Sheriffhales 91-07; RD Edgmond 97-01; RD Shifnal 99-01; RD Edgmond and Shifnal 01-06; Adn E Riding *York* from 07; Can and Preb York Minster from 07. *Brimley Lodge, 27 Molescroft Road, Beverley HU17 7DX* Tel and fax (01482) 881659
E-mail archdeacon.of.eastriding@yorkdiocese.org

BUTTERFIELD, John Kenneth. b 52. Nottm Univ BCombStuds. Linc Th Coll 79. **d** 82 **p** 83. C Cantley *Sheff* 82-84; C Doncaster St Leon and St Jude 84-86; TV Ilfracombe, Lee, Woolacombe, Bittadon etc *Ex* 86-88; V Thurcroft *Sheff* 88-96; Chapl Chesterfield and N Derbyshire NHS Trust from 96. *Chesterfield and North Derbyshire Royal Hospital, Calow, Chesterfield S44 5BL* Tel (01246) 277271 ext 3398

BUTTERWORTH, Antony James. b 51. Hull Univ BSc73. Trin Coll Bris 73. **d** 76 **p** 77. C Halliwell St Pet *Man* 76-81; V Werneth 81-90; V Tonge Fold 90-06; V Pennington from 06. *Pennington Vicarage, Schofield Street, Leigh WN7 4HT* Tel (01942) 673619
E-mail tony@penningtonchurch.com

BUTTERWORTH, David Frederick. b 48. Oak Hill Th Coll BA88. **d** 88 **p** 89. R Telegraph Creek Canada 88-92; R Barrhead and Westlock 92-94; R Yellowknife 94-98; V Hanmer,

Bronington, Bettisfield, Tallarn Green *St As* 98-04. *Bettisfield Hall, Bettisfield, Whitchurch SY13 2LB* Tel (01948) 710525

BUTTERWORTH, Derek. b 27. Wells Th Coll 63. **d** 65 **p** 65. C Bottesford *Linc* 65-73; TV Bottesford w Ashby 73-83; Chapl St Hilda's Sch Whitby 83-85; V Derringham Bank *York* 85-90; rtd 90; Perm to Offic *Ripon* and *York* from 90. *26 St Mary's Gate, Ripon HG4 1LX* Tel (01765) 607827

BUTTERWORTH, Elsie. b 27. Linc Th Coll 81. **dss** 83 **d** 87 **p** 94. OHP 83-85; Derringham Bank *York* 85-87; Par Dn 87-88; Par Dn Filey 88-94; C 94-97; rtd 93; Perm to Offic *York* from 97. *3 Brooklands Close, Filey YO14 9BJ* Tel (01723) 515781

BUTTERWORTH, Frederick. *See* BUTTERWORTH, David Frederick

BUTTERWORTH, George John. b 58. Liv Univ BA85. Chich Th Coll 92. **d** 92 **p** 93. C Mayfield *Chich* 92-93; C Hastings St Clem and All SS 93-96; TV Brighton Resurr 96-02; P-in-c Saltdean 02-09; V from 09. *St Nicholas' Vicarage, Saltdean Vale, Saltdean, Brighton BN2 8HE* Tel (01273) 302345
E mail butt21158@aol.com

BUTTERWORTH, Canon George Michael. b 41. Man Univ BSc63 Lon Univ BD67 PhD89 Nottm Univ MPhil71. Tyndale Hall Bris. **d** 67 **p** 68. C S Normanton *Derby* 67-71; India 72-79; Lect United Th Coll Bangalore 72-77; Lect Oak Hill Th Coll 80-96; Prin SAOMC *Ox* 97-05; Prin Ox Min Course 05-06; Prin ERMC 05-06; Hon Can St Alb 02-06; Perm to Offic from 80; Hon C Walton H Trin *Ox* 06-09; Hon C Broughton from 09. *24 King Edward Avenue, Aylesbury HP21 7JD* Tel (01296) 481154 Mobile 07870-242250
E-mail mikebutterworth@waitrose.com

BUTTERWORTH, Mrs Gillian. b 49. Man Univ BA71 Dur Univ PGCE72. NOC 96. **d** 99. C Barnsley St Mary *Wakef* 99-03; Min Development Officer from 03; Hon Par Dn Outwood from 03; Asst Chapl Wakefield Hospice from 03. *Outwood Vicarage, 424 Leeds Road, Wakefield WF1 2JB* Tel (01924) 823150

BUTTERWORTH, Ian Eric. b 44. Aber Univ MA67 MTh79. Edin Th Coll 67. **d** 69 **p** 70. C Langley All SS and Martyrs *Man* 69-71; Prec St Andr Cathl 71-75; V Bolton St Matt w St Barn *Man* 75-85; C-in-c Lostock CD 85-92; Laity Development Officer (Bolton Adnry) 85-92; Teacher Fairfield High Sch Droylsden 92-99; Perm to Offic *Man* 96-99; Hon C Sudden St Aidan 00-05; P-in-c Castleton Moor 00-05; V from 05; AD Heywood and Middleton from 07. *St Martin's Vicarage, Vicarage Road North, Rochdale OL11 2TE* Tel and fax (01706) 632353 E-mail i.butterworth@tesco.net

BUTTERWORTH, James Frederick. b 49. St Chad's Coll Dur BA70 Birm Univ MA99. Cuddesdon Coll 70. **d** 72 **p** 73. C Kidderminster St Mary *Worc* 72-76; P-in-c Dudley St Barn 76-79; V 79-82; Prec and Min Can Worc Cathl 82-88; TR Bridgnorth, Tasley, Astley Abbotts, etc *Heref* 88-94; Can Res and Treas Heref Cathl 94-99; Preb 94-06; P-in-c Ewyas Harold w Dulas, Kenderchurch etc 99-06; RD Abbeydore 02-06; V Cirencester *Glouc* 06-08; rtd 08. *Meadows View, Orcop, Hereford HR2 8SF* Tel (01981) 540887

BUTTERWORTH, James Kent. b 49. Southn Univ BTh79. Chich Th Coll 75. **d** 79 **p** 80. C Heckmondwike *Wakef* 79-83; V Wrenthorpe 83-95; V Staincross from 95. *St John's Vicarage, 48 Greenside, Staincross, Barnsley S75 6GU* Tel (01226) 382261
E-mail jim@radiouk.com

BUTTERWORTH, John Walton. b 49. St Jo Coll Dur BSc70. Cranmer Hall Dur. **d** 74 **p** 75. C Todmorden *Wakef* 74-77; Chapl Wakef Cathl 77-78; C Wakef Cathl 77-78; V Outwood from 78. *Outwood Vicarage, 424 Leeds Road, Wakefield WF1 2JB* Tel (01924) 823150 E-mail johnbutterworth@blueyonder.co.uk

BUTTERWORTH, Canon Julia Kay. b 42. Edin Univ MA64 Bris Univ CertEd66. Linc Th Coll 73. **dss** 77 **d** 87 **p** 94. Cove E 77-79; Cant 77-79; Dioc Adv in Women's Min 82-92; Faversham 84-92; Par Dn 87-92; TD Whitstable 92-94; TV 94-97; P-in-c Tenterden St Mich 97-07; Dioc Adv in Spirituality 97-07; Hon Can Cant Cathl 96-07; rtd 07; Perm to Offic *Cant* from 07. *14 Cobham Close, Canterbury CT1 1YL* Tel (01227) 472806 E-mail jkbutterworth@btinternet.com

BUTTERWORTH, Michael. *See* BUTTERWORTH, Canon George Michael

BUTTERWORTH, Mildred Jean. b 42. Leeds Univ MB, ChB65 FRCOG84. St Jo Coll Nottm. **d** 00 **p** 01. NSM Moldgreen and Rawthorpe *Wakef* 00-03; NSM Almondbury w Farnley Tyas from 03. *1 Furnbrook Gardens, Kirkheaton, Huddersfield HD5 0DY* Tel (01484) 664455
E-mail mildred@mildredjb.plus.com

BUTTERWORTH, Roy. b 31. Selw Coll Cam BA55 MA59. Wells Th Coll 55. **d** 57 **p** 58. C Bathwick w Woolley *B & W* 57-61; Prec St Paul's Cathl Dundee 61-63; V Dearnley *Man* 63-81; V Tyldesley w Shakerley 81-83; V Healey 83-94; rtd 94. *102 Greenbank Road, Rochdale OL12 0EN* Tel (01706) 350808

BUTTERY, Bernard. b 36. Culham Coll Ox CertEd58 LCP75. OLM course 96. **d** 99 **p** 00. OLM Stafford *Lich* from 99. *7 Dearnsdale Close, Tillington, Stafford ST16 1SD* Tel (01785) 244771 E-mail bb.ngb@talktalk.net

BUTTERY, Graeme. b 62. York Univ BA84. St Steph Ho Ox 85. **d** 88 **p** 89. C Peterlee *Dur* 88-91; C Sunderland 91-92; TV 92-94; V Horsley Hill St Lawr 94-05; AD Jarrow 01-05; V Hartlepool St Oswald from 05. *St Oswald's Clergy House, Brougham Terrace, Hartlepool TS24 8EY* Tel (01429) 273201 E-mail buttery.stl@virgin.net

BUTTERY, Nathan James. b 72. Em Coll Cam BA94 MA97. Wycliffe Hall Ox BA98. **d** 00 **p** 01. C Hull St Jo Newland *York* 00-08; C Cambridge H Sepulchre *Ely* from 09. *1 Pretoria Road, Cambridge CB4 1HD* Tel (01223) 518299 E-mail nathan.debbie@ukgateway.net

BUTTIMER, Mrs Cynthia Margaret. b 45. STETS 07. **d** 08 **p** 09. OLM Clarendon *Sarum* from 08. *Willow Cottage, Gunville Road, Winterslow, Salisbury SP5 1PP* Tel (01980) 862017 E-mail cynthiabuttimer@hotmail.com

BUTTIMORE, Canon John Charles. b 27. St Mich Coll Llan 55. **d** 57 **p** 58. C Treherbert *Llan* 57-60; C Aberdare St Fagan *Llan* 60-64; V Williamstown 64-71; Chapl Ely Hosp Cardiff 71-98; V Caerau w Ely *Llan* 71-97; RD Cardiff 83-89; Can Llan Cathl 87-97; rtd 97; Perm to Offic *Llan* from 97. *3 Nant y Pepra, Cardiff CF5 4UB* Tel (029) 2065 9333

BUTTLE, Leslie Albert. b 32. Open Univ BA89. Edin Th Coll 61. **d** 64 **p** 65. C Sowerby Bridge w Norland *Wakef* 64-66; C Plymstock *Ex* 66-69; C Ilfracombe H Trin 69-71; V Woolfardisworthy and Buck Mills 71-76; C Sticklepath 76-77; Asst Chapl HM Pris Leeds 77-80; Lic to Offic *Ripon* 77-80; Chapl HM Youth Cust Cen Hindley 80-84; Perm to Offic *Ex* 86-93; Hon C Braunton from 93; rtd 97. *Church House, Saunton, Braunton EX33 1LG* Tel (01271) 817022

BUTTON, David Frederick. b 27. St Chad's Coll Dur BA53. **d** 54 **p** 55. C S Shields St Mary *Dur* 54-58; C Seacroft *Ripon* 58-60; V Holland Fen *Linc* 60-64; V Surfleet 64-71; R Belton SS Pet and Paul 71-78; V Barkston w Syston 72-78; V Honington 73-78; R Gunhouse w Burringham 78-82; P-in-c Gt w Lt Hockham w Wretham w Illington *Nor* 82-84; P-in-c Shropham w Larling and Snetterton 82-84; V Hockham w Shropham Gp of Par 84-91; rtd 91; Perm to Offic *Nor* 91-96. *6 Vallibus Close, Oulton, Lowestoft NR32 3DS*

BUXTON, Alyson Christina. b 65. Chelt & Glouc Coll of HE BA00 Nottm Univ MA03 RGN86. St Jo Coll Nottm MTh01. **d** 02 **p** 03. C New Sleaford *Linc* 02-05; Dioc Lay Min Co-ord and PV Linc Cathl 05-08; P-in-c Horncastle Gp from 08. *The Vicarage, 2 Millstone Close, Horncastle LN9 5SU* Tel (01507) 525974 E-mail alybux@mac.com

BUXTON, Canon Derek Major. b 31. Lon Univ BD63. Ripon Hall Ox 58. **d** 60 **p** 61. C Leic St Nic 60-64; Chapl Leic Univ 60-64; Chapl Leic Coll of Art and Tech 61-65; Min Can Leic Cathl 64-69; Prec 67; R Ibstock 69-76; R Ibstock w Heather 76-87; Chapl ATC from 78; OCF and Cen and E Regional Chapl from 87; RD Akeley S *Leic* 84-87; P-in-c Woodhouse Eaves 87-91; V Woodhouse and Woodhouse Eaves 91-98; Chapl Roecliffe Manor Cheshire Home from 87; Hon Can Leic Cathl from 88; rtd 98; Perm to Offic *Leic* from 99. *Shepherd's Hill, 74 Pitsford Drive, Loughborough LE11 4NY* Tel (01509) 216663

BUXTON, Francis Edmund. b 42. Trin Coll Cam MA68 Sheff Univ MA93. Linc Th Coll 65. **d** 67 **p** 68. C Wanstead St Mary *Chelmsf* 67-70; C Cambridge Gt St Mary w St Mich *Ely* 70-73; C Barking St Marg w St Paul *Chelmsf* 74-75; Chapl Vellore Hosp S India 75-79; Chapl Bath Univ 79-89; TR Willenhall H Trin *Lich* 89-96; Chapl Team Leader Univ Hosp Birm NHS Foundn Trust 96-07; rtd 07; Hon C St Briavels w Hewelsfield *Glouc* from 08. *3 St Anne's Way, St Briavels, Lydney GL15 6UE* Tel (01594) 531052 Mobile 07899-673096 E-mail fjbuxton@yahoo.co.uk

BUXTON, Graham. b 45. York Univ BA66 Bradf Univ MSc71. St Jo Coll Nottm 83 Melbourne Coll of Div MMin97. **d** 83 **p** 84. C Ealing Dean St Jo *Lon* 83-84; C W Ealing St Jo w St Jas 84-86; C S Harrow St Paul 86-89; P-in-c 89-91; Sen Lect Tabor Coll Australia from 91. *5 Heron Place, Flagstaff Hill SA 5159, Australia* Tel (0061) (8) 8370 6038 *or* 8373 8777 Fax 8373 1766 E-mail gbuxton@adelaide.tabor.edu.au

BUXTON, James Andrew Denis. b 64. Newc Univ BA86. Westcott Ho Cam 95. **d** 97 **p** 98. C Portsea St Mary *Portsm* 97-01; Succ S'wark Cathl 01-07; Chapl Guy's Campus K Coll Lon 01-07; Chapl CCC Cam from 07. *Corpus Christi College, Trumpington Street, Cambridge CB2 1RH* Tel (01223) 338002 E-mail jb225@cam.ac.uk

BUXTON, Nicholas. b 66. Wolfs Coll Cam BA02 Trin Hall Cam MPhil03 PhD07. St Steph Ho Ox MTh08. **d** 08 **p** 09. C Ripon Cathl from 08. *17 High St Agnesgate, Ripon HG4 1QR* Tel (01765) 602923 E-mail buxton.nicholas@googlemail.com

BUXTON, Richard Fowler. b 40. Univ of Wales BSc62 Linacre Coll Ox BA67 MA71 Ex Univ PhD73. St Steph Ho Ox 65. **d** 68 **p** 69. C Whitley Ch Ch *Ox* 68-70; C Pinhoe *Ex* 70-71; Asst Chapl Ex Univ 71-73; Tutor Sarum & Wells Th Coll 73-77; Vice-Prin 77; Perm to Offic *Ches* 77-97; Lect Liturgy Man Univ 80-94; Subwarden St Deiniol's Lib Hawarden 94-97; Perm to Offic *Ban* from 96; *St As* from 97; rtd 00. *Golygfa'r Orsaf, 6 Rhesdai Garth, Porthmadog LL49 9BE* Tel (01766) 514782

BUXTON, Canon Trevor George. b 57. Ex Univ BEd78. Chich Th

Coll 81. **d** 83 **p** 84. C Hove All SS *Chich* 83-87; C Burgess Hill St Jo 87-91; V Brighton St Aug and St Sav 91-03; P-in-c Sidley 02-04; V from 04; Can and Preb Chich Cathl from 01. *All Saints' Vicarage, All Saints Lane, Bexhill-on-Sea TN39 5HA* Tel (01424) 221071 Mobile 07885-942901 E-mail hojoe@waitrose.com

BUYERS, Stanley. b 39. Leeds Univ CertEd71 Sunderland Poly BEd78 Newc Univ MEd90. NEOC 97. **d** 00 **p** 01. NSM E Boldon *Dur* 00-03; P-in-c Boldon 03-09; rtd 09. *37 Tarragon Way, South Shields NE34 8TB* Tel 0191-519 0370 Mobile 07979-693153 E-mail stanbuyers@btinternet.com

BYATT, John William. b 55. St Jo Coll Nottm 99. **d** 01 **p** 02. C Heanor *Derby* 01-05; C Ilkeston St Jo 05-07; P-in-c Whipton *Ex* from 07. *The Vicarage, 9 Summer Lane, Exeter EX4 8BY* Tel (01392) 462206 Mobile 07773-906919

BYE, Canon Peter John. b 39. Lon Univ BD65. Clifton Th Coll 62. **d** 67 **p** 68. C Hyson Green *S'well* 67-70; C Dur St Nic 70-73; V Lowestoft Ch Ch *Nor* 73-80; V Carl St Jo 80-04; Hon Can Carl Cathl 98-04; RD Carl 00-04; Chapl Carl Gen Hosp 80-94; Chapl Carl Hosps NHS Trust 94-98; rtd 04. *21 McIlmoyle Way, Carlisle CA2 5GY* Tel (01228) 596256 E-mail peterbye@mcilmoyleway.plus.com

BYERS, Canon Christopher Martin. b 33. Jes Coll Ox BA59 MA62. Wycliffe Hall Ox 59. **d** 60 **p** 61. C Bermondsey St Mary w St Olave, St Jo etc *S'wark* 60-66; R Mottingham St Andr 66-86; TR Thamesmead 86-99; C 99-00; Hon Can S'wark Cathl 96-00; rtd 01; Perm to Offic *Cant* from 01. *36 Faversham Road, Whitstable CT5 4AR* Tel (01227) 272786

BYFIELD, Andrew Thornton Janes. b 77. St Pet Coll Ox MA99 Selw Coll Cam BTh09. Ridley Hall Cam 07. **d** 09. C Wimbledon Em Ridgway Prop Chpl *S'wark* from 09. *11 Preston Road, London SW20 0SS* Tel 07925-421085 (mobile) E-mail a.byfield@spc.oxon.org

BYFORD, Canon David Charles. b 30. Bps' Coll Cheshunt 58. **d** 61 **p** 62. C Short Heath *Birm* 61-63; C Londonderry 63-65; Chapl Selly Oak Hosp Birm 65-70; V Rowley Regis *Birm* 70-78; V Polesworth 78-95; RD Polesworth 84-91; Hon Can Birm Cathl 87-95; rtd 95; Perm to Offic *Sarum* from 95. *Rose Cottage, Stratford sub Castle, Salisbury SP1 3LB* Tel (01722) 322569

BYFORD, The Ven Edwin Charles. b 47. Aus Nat Univ BSc70 Melbourne Coll of Div BD73 Univ of Chicago MA76 Man Univ PhD85. Trin Coll Melbourne 70. **d** 73 **p** 73. C Qeanbeyan Ch Ch Australia 73-75; Chapl Univ of Chicago USA 75-76; Hon C Chorlton-cum-Hardy St Werburgh *Man* 76-79; Australia from 79; Chapl Woden Valley Hosp 80-83; Asst P Wagga Wagga 83-84; Asst P Ainslie All SS 84-87; Chapl Aus Nat Univ 87-91; R Binda 91-95; R Broken Hill St Pet and Adn The Darling from 95. *PO Box 185, Broken Hill NSW 2880, Australia* Tel and fax (0061) (8) 8087 3221 Mobile 409-467981 E-mail e-byford-4@alumni.uchicago.edu

BYLES, Canon Raymond Vincent. b 30. Univ of Wales (Lamp) BA52. St Mich Coll Llan 52. **d** 54 **p** 55. C Llanfairisgaer *Ban* 54-57; C Llandudno 57-59; V Carno 59-64; V Trefeglwys 63; V Newmarket and Gwaenysgor *St As* 64-72; R Llysfaen 72-80; V Bodelwyddan and St George 80-85; V Bodelwyddan 85-95; Hon Can St As Cathl from 89; rtd 95. *20 Lon Dderwen, Tan-y-Goppa Parc, Abergele LL22 7DW* Tel (01745) 833604

BYLLAM-BARNES, Preb Paul William Marshall. b 38. Birm Univ BCom Lon Univ MSc. Sarum & Wells Th Coll. **d** 84 **p** 85. C Gt Bookham *Guildf* 84-87; R Cusop w Blakemere, Bredwardine w Brobury etc *Heref* 87-03; RD Abbeydore 96-00; Preb Heref Cathl 99-03; rtd 03. *90 Granger Avenue, Maldon CM9 6AN* Tel (01621) 858978

BYNON, William. b 43. St Aid Birkenhead 63. **d** 66 **p** 67. C Huyton St Mich *Liv* 66-69; C Maghull 69-72; TV 72-75; V Highfield 75-82; V Southport All SS 82-88; P-in-c Southport All So 86-88; V Newton in Makerfield St Pet 88-94; V Caerhun w Llangelynin w Llanbedr-y-Cennin *Ban* 94-06; rtd 06. *Swn-y-Don, Maes Hyfryd, Moelfre LL72 8LR* Tel (01248) 410749 E-mail william@pontwgan.freeserve.co.uk

BYRNE, Bryn. *See* BYRNE, Ronald Brendan Anthony

BYRNE, David Patrick. b 48. PGCE96. St Jo Coll Nottm 74. **d** 77 **p** 78. C Bordesley Green *Birm* 77-79; C Weoley Castle 79-82; TV Kings Norton 82-92; TV Hodge Hill 92-94; Perm to Offic 94-97; Chapl Asst Birm Heartlands and Solihull NHS Trust 96-98; Chapl NW Lon Hosp NHS Trust 98-09; Chapl Harrow and Hillingdon Healthcare NHS Trust 98-09. *Address temp unknown*

BYRNE, David Rodney. b 47. St Jo Coll Cam BA70 MA73. Cranmer Hall Dur 71. **d** 73 **p** 74. C Maidstone St Luke *Cant* 73-77; C Patcham *Chich* 77-83; TV Stantonbury *Ox* 83-87; TV Stantonbury and Willen 87-92; TV Woodley 92-02; V Patchway *Bris* from 02. *St Chad's Vicarage, 1B Southsea Road, Patchway, Bristol BS34 5DP* Tel 0117-969 2935 *or* 979 3978 E-mail drbyrne@talktalk.net

BYRNE, Miss Georgina Ann. b 72. Trin Coll Ox BA92 MA96 CCC Cam MPhil98. Westcott Ho Cam. **d** 97 **p** 98. NSM W Bromwich All SS *Lich* 97-98; C 98-01; Hon Asst Chapl CCC Cam 97-98; Chapl to Bp Kensington *Lon* 01-04; Hon C Twickenham St Mary 01-04; TV Halas *Worc* from 04; Convenor for Women's Min from 05. *The Rectory, St Kenelm's Road, Romsley, Halesowen B62 0PH* Tel (01562) 710050

BYRNE, Ian Barclay. b 53. Ripon Coll Cuddesdon 01. **d** 03 **p** 04. C Blyth Valley *St E* 03-06; P-in-c Bungay H Trin w St Mary from 06; C Wainford from 06. *The Vicarage, 3 Trinity Gardens, Bungay NR35 1HH* Tel (01986) 892553
E-mail rev.ib@btinternet.com

BYRNE, Canon John Victor. b 47. FCA. St Jo Coll Nottm LTh73. **d** 73 **p** 74. C Gillingham St Mark *Roch* 73-76; C Cranham Park *Chelmsf* 76-80; V Balderstone *Man* 80-87; V Southsea St Jude *Portsm* 87-06; P-in-c Southsea St Pet 95-03; Hon Can Portsm Cathl 97-06; RD Portsm 01-06; V Branksome Park All SS *Sarum* from 06; Chapl to The Queen from 03. *The Vicarage, 28 Western Road, Poole BH13 7BP* Tel (01202) 708202
E-mail byrne.jv@gmail.com

BYRNE, The Very Revd Matthew. b 27. Man Univ MA69 TCD HDipEd81. Tyndale Hall Bris 47. **d** 51 **p** 52. C Rawtenstall St Mary *Man* 51-54; OCF 54-57; R Moss Side St Jas *Man* 57-62; R Whalley Range St Marg 62-80; P-in-c Chapelizod *D & G* 80-83; Chapl K Hosp Dub 83-89; Dean Kildare *M & K* 89-93; I Kildare w Kilmeague and Curragh 89-93; Producer Relig Dept RTE 83-92; Chapl Defence Forces 89-92; rtd 92. *5 Fairfield Park, Greystones, Co Wicklow, Republic of Ireland* Tel and fax (00353) (1) 287 3622

BYRNE, Miriam Alexandra Frances. b 46. Westcott Ho Cam. **d** 87 **p** 94. Par Dn Beoley *Worc* 87-90; C Ayr *Glas* 90-92; Dn-in-c Dumbarton 92-94; P-in-c 94-98; Provost St Paul's Cathl Dundee 98-06; R Dundee St Paul 98-06; rtd 06. *rue de la Bonnacherie, 16700 Salles-de-Villefagnan, France* Tel (0033) (6) 31 66 58 34

BYRNE, Rodney Edmund. b 18. **d** 84 **p** 84. Hon C Leckhampton SS Phil and Jas w Cheltenham St Jas *Glouc* 84-88; rtd 88; Perm to Offic *Glouc* 88-03. *39 Collum End Rise, Cheltenham GL53 0PA* Tel (01242) 526428

BYRNE, Ronald Brendan Anthony (Bryn). b 31. Reading Univ BA72. Westcott Ho Cam 86. **d** 64 **p** 65. Chapl Cov Cathl 87-91; Chapl Lanchester Poly 87-91; Lic to Offic 91-94; Chapl Limerick Univ 94-98; Chapl Villier's Sch Limerick 95-98; rtd 96; Chapl Lanzarote *Eur* 98-00; Perm to Offic *Lon* 02-07. *6 Newton Terrace, Crown Lane, Bromley BR2 9PH* Tel 07960-319294 (mobile) E-mail brynbyrne@aol.com *or* roybyrne@eircom.net

BYRNE, Roy Harold. b 71. Westmr Coll Ox BTh97 Irish Sch of Ecum MPhil00. CITC 97. **d** 99 **p** 00. C Dublin Ch Ch Cathl Gp 99-03; I Killeshin w Cloydagh and Killabban *C & O* 03-08; I Dublin Drumcondra w N Strand *D & G* from 08. *The Rectory, 74 Grace Park Road, Drumcondra, Dublin 9, Republic of Ireland* Tel (00353) (1) 837 2505 E-mail roybyrne@eircom.net

BYROM, Alan. b 51. Magd Coll Ox BA72 Leeds Univ PGCE73 Bris Univ MA85 Man Univ MPhil99. NOC 97. **d** 99 **p** 00. C Leyland St Andr *Blackb* 99-03; TV Solway Plain *Carl* from 03. *The Vicarage, Wigton Road, Silloth, Wigton CA7 4NR* Tel (016973) 31413 E-mail arm@abyrom.freeserve.co.uk

BYROM, Canon Malcolm Senior. b 37. Edin Th Coll 65. **d** 67 **p** 68. C Allerton *Bradf* 67-69; C Padstow *Truro* 69-72; V Hessenford 72-77; P-in-c St Martin by Looe 72-77; V Kenwyn 77-91; R Kenwyn w St Allen 91-99; Hon Can Truro Cathl 92-00; RD Powder 88-90; Sub-Warden Community of the Epiphany Truro 85-01; Warden from 01; rtd 99; Perm to Offic *Truro* from 00. *West Haven, Dobbin Lane, Trevone, Padstow PL28 8QP* Tel (01841) 520242 E-mail malcolmbyrom@supanet.com

BYRON, Terence Sherwood. b 26. Keble Coll Ox BA50 MA54. Linc Th Coll 50. **d** 52 **p** 53. C Melton Mowbray w Burton Lazars, Freeby etc *Leic* 52-55; C Whitwick St Jo the Bapt 55-60; India 60-76; C-in-c Beaumont Leys (Extra-paroch Distr) *Leic* 76-85; V Beaumont Leys 85-86; RD Christianity N 86-92; P-in-c Leic St Phil 86-88; V 88-92; rtd 93; Perm to Offic *Leic* from 93. *84 Flax Road, Leicester LE4 6QD* Tel 0116-266 1922

BYSOUTH, Paul Graham. b 55. Oak Hill Th Coll. **d** 84 **p** 85. C Gorleston St Andr *Nor* 84-87; C Ripley *Derby* 87-91; TV N Wingfield, Clay Cross and Pilsley 91-00; V Blagreaves from 00. *St Andrew's Vicarage, 5 Greenburn Close, Littleover, Derby DE23 1FF* Tel (01332) 773877
E-mail paulbysouth4@yahoo.co.uk

BYTHEWAY, Phillip James. b 35. MIIExE89 BA93. **d** 97. OLM Church Stretton *Heref* 97-00; rtd 00; Perm to Offic *Heref* from 00. *Ivy Glen, 55 Watling Street South, Church Stretton SY6 7BQ* Tel (01694) 723901 Mobile 07778-391088 Fax 724440

BYWORTH, Canon Christopher Henry Briault. b 39. Oriel Coll Ox BA61 MA65 Bris Univ BA63. Lon Coll of Div 64. **d** 65 **p** 66. C Low Leyton *Chelmsf* 65-68; C Rusholme H Trin *Man* 68-70; Lic to Offic *Lon* 71-75; TR Thetford *Nor* 75-79; Warden Cranmer Hall Dur 79-83; TR Fazakerley Em *Liv* 83-90; P-in-c St Helens St Helen 90-94; TR 94-04; AD St Helens 90-00; Hon Can Liv Cathl 99-04; rtd 04. *11 Oakleigh, Skelmersdale WN8 9QU* Tel (01744) 886481

BYWORTH, Mrs Ruth Angela. b 49. Cranmer Hall Dur BA82. **dss** 83 **d** 92 **p** 94. Kirkby *Liv* 83-89; Aintree St Pet 89-97; Dn-in-c 92-94; P-in-c 94-97; P-in-c St Helens St Mark 97-98; C Sutton 98-03; TV 03-04; rtd 04. *11 Oakleigh, Skelmersdale WN8 9QU* Tel (01744) 886481

C

CABLE, Kevin John. b 74. Ripon Coll Cuddesdon BA08. **d** 08 **p** 09. C Bromley Common St Aug *Roch* from 08. *40 Rolleston Avenue, Petts Wood, Orpington BR5 1AH* Tel (020) 8467 2937 Mobile 07739-539448 E-mail curate.st_aug@btopenworld.com

CABLE, Patrick John. b 50. AKC72. **d** 74 **p** 75. C Herne *Cant* 74-78; CF 78-06; Rtd Officer Chapl RAChD from 06. *c/o MOD Chaplains (Army)* Tel (01980) 615804 Fax 615800

CACKETT, Janice Susan. b 39. Goldsmiths' Coll Lon BA76 Surrey Univ MSc83. SWMTC 99. **d** 99 **p** 00. NSM Clyst St Mary, Clyst St George etc *Ex* 99-03; P-in-c E Budleigh w Bicton and Otterton from 03. *27 Elm Grove Road, Topsham, Exeter EX3 0EJ* Tel (01392) 877468 E-mail jcackett@ukgateway.net

CADDELL, Richard Allen. b 54. Auburn Univ Alabama BIE77. Trin Coll Bris BA88. **d** 88 **p** 89. C Uphill *B & W* 88-94; Perm to Offic 94-96; TV Beaconsfield *Ox* 96-07; P-in-c Lamp 07-09; R from 09. *The Rectory, High Street, Haversham, Milton Keynes MK19 7DT* Tel (01908) 312136
E-mail caddells@holtspur.plus.com

CADDEN, Brian Stuart. b 58. BSc BTh TCD. **d** 89 **p** 90. C Lecale Gp *D & D* 89-92; C Killowen *D & R* 92-95; I Muckamore *Conn* 95-06; I Castlewellan w Kilcoo *D & D* from 06. *5 Cedar Heights, Bryansford, Newcastle BT33 0PJ* Tel (028) 4372 3198
E-mail castlewellan@dromore.anglican.org

CADDEN, Terence John. b 60. TCD BTh89. CITC 86. **d** 89 **p** 90. C Coleraine *Conn* 89-92; C Lurgan Ch the Redeemer *D & D* 92-93; Past Dir 93-01; I Gilford 01-06; I Seagoe from 06. *Seagoe Rectory, 8 Upper Church Lane, Portadown, Craigavon BT63 5JE* Tel (028) 3833 2538 *or* 3835 0583 Fax 3833 0773 Mobile 07894-987702 E-mail cadden@talktalk.net
or seagoechurch@btinternet.com

CADDICK, Jeremy Lloyd. b 60. St Jo Coll Cam BA82 MA86 K Coll Lon MA93. Ripon Coll Cuddesdon BA86 MA91. **d** 87 **p** 88. C Kennington St Jo w St Jas *S'wark* 87-90; Chapl Lon Univ 90-94; Chapl R Free Medical Sch 90-94; Chapl R Veterinary Coll Lon 90-94; PV Westmr Abbey 92-94; Dean Em Coll Cam from 94. *Emmanuel College, Cambridge CB2 3AP* Tel (01223) 334264 *or* 330195 Fax 334426 E-mail jlc24@cam.ac.uk

CADDICK, Canon Lloyd Reginald. b 31. Bris Univ BA56 St Cath Coll Ox BA58 MA62 Nottm Univ MPhil73 K Coll Lon PhD78 Open Univ Hon MA79. St Steph Ho Ox 56. **d** 59 **p** 59. C N Lynn w St Marg and St Nic *Nor* 59-62; Chapl Oakham Sch 62-66; P-in-c Bulwick, Harringworth w Blatherwycke and Laxton *Pet* 66-67; R Bulwick, Blatherwycke w Harringworth and Laxton 67-77; V Oundle 77-96; Can Pet Cathl 94-96; rtd 96; Perm to Offic *Pet* from 96. *102 West Street, Kings Cliffe, Peterborough PE8 6XA* Tel (01780) 470332

CADDOO (née BLAKELY), Mrs Denise Irene. b 69. QUB BD91 PGCE92. CITC 93. **d** 95 **p** 96. C Holywood *D & D* 95-99; C Portadown St Columba *Arm* 99-00; I Carrowdore w Millisle *D & D* 00-04; C Holywood 04-06; I Gilford from 06. *The Vicarage, 18 Scarva Road, Gilford, Craigavon BT63 6BG* Tel (028) 3883 1130

CADDY, Canon Michael George Bruce Courtenay. b 45. K Coll Lon. **d** 71 **p** 72. C Walton St Mary *Liv* 71-76; C Solihull *Birm* 76-79; V Shard End 81-87; TR Shirley 87-00; P-in-c Tanworth St Patr Salter Street 97-00; TR Salter Street and Shirley from 00; AD Shirley 97-02; Hon Can Birm Cathl from 99. *The Vicarage, 2 Bishopton Close, Shirley, Solihull B90 4AH* Tel 0121-744 3123 *or* 745 8896
E-mail stjames@shirleyparishoffice.freeserve.co.uk

CADDY, Ms Susan. b 50. SWMTC 99. **d** 01 **p** 02. C Sutton in Ashfield St Mary *S'well* 01-05; P-in-c Shelton and Oxon *Lich* from 05. *Oxon Vicarage, 10A Shelton Gardens, Bicton Heath, Shrewsbury SY3 5AG* Tel (01743) 232774
E-mail sue.cee@talktalk.net

CADE, Mrs Margaret Elizabeth. b 34. Dioc OLM tr scheme 99. **d** 00. OLM Portland All SS w St Andr *Sarum* 00-07. *27 Avalanche Road, Portland DT5 2DJ* Tel (01305) 821317 Fax 826453 Mobile 07974-696892

CADE, Simon Peter Vincent. b 69. Univ of Wales BA90. Westcott Ho Cam 92. **d** 94 **p** 95. C Calne and Blackland *Sarum* 94-98; Chapl St Mary's Sch Calne 94-97; TV Basingstoke *Win* 98-05; TR Redruth w Lanner and Treleigh *Truro* from 05. *Chycarn, West Trewirgie Road, Redruth TR15 2TJ* Tel (01209) 215258
E-mail simon@simoncade.org.uk

CADMAN, Robert Hugh. b 49. St Jo Coll Nottm 77. **d** 78 **p** 79. C Ecclesall *Sheff* 78-82; C Worting *Win* 82-84; C-in-c Winklebury CD 84-87; R Widford *Chelmsf* 87-94; Chapl Anglia Poly Univ 94-95; NSM Brentwood St Thos 01-03; TV Southend 03-08; V Prittlewell St Pet w Westcliff St Cedd from 08. *The Vicarage, 122 Mendip Crescent, Westcliff-on-Sea SS0 0HN* Tel (01702) 525126 E-mail robcadman@blueyonder.co.uk

CADMORE, Albert Thomas. b 47. Open Univ BA81 UEA MA94 Lon Inst of Educn CertEd68. EAMTC 85. **d** 88 **p** 89.

NSM Gorleston St Andr *Nor* 88-96; NSM Winterton w E and W Somerton and Horsey 94-96; NSM Flegg Coastal Benefice from 96. *10 Upper Cliff Road, Gorleston, Great Yarmouth NR31 6AL* Tel (01493) 668762
E-mail acadmore@ntlworld.com

CADOGAN, Paul Anthony Cleveland. b 47. AKC74. **d** 75 **p** 76. C Fishponds St Jo *Bris* 75-79; C Swindon New Town 79-81; P-in-c Swindon All SS 81-82; V 82-90; R Lower Windrush *Ox* 90-94. *2 Malthouse Close, Ashbury SN6 8PB* Tel (01793) 710488

CADOGAN, Percil Lavine. b 41. WMMTC. **d** 01 **p** 02. NSM Bournville *Birm* 01-05; NSM Bordesley St Benedict from 05. *76 Highbury Road, Birmingham B14 7QW* Tel 0121-680 9595

CADWALLADER, Michael Godfrey. b 56. Bris Univ CertEd78 BEd79. Cranmer Hall Dur 05. **d** 07 **p** 08. C Kingston upon Hull St Aid Southcoates *York* from 07. *9 Lorenzo Way, Hull HU9 3HS* Tel (01482) 704517
E-mail cadwalladermg@waitrose.com

CAESAR, Canon Anthony Douglass. b 24. LVO87 CVO91. Magd Coll Cam BA47 MA49 MusB47 FRCO47. St Steph Ho Ox 59. **d** 61 **p** 62. C Kensington St Mary Abbots w St Geo *Lon* 61-65; Chapl RSCM Addington 65-70; Asst Sec CACTM 65-66; ACCM 65-70; Dep P in O 67-68; P-in-O 68-70; C Bournemouth St Pet *Win* 70-73; Prec and Sacr Win Cathl 74-79; Hon Can 75-76 and 79-91; Can Res 76-79; Dom Chapl to The Queen 79-91; Extra Chapl to The Queen from 91; Sub Almoner and Dep Clerk of the Closet 79-91; Sub Dean of HM Chpls Royal 79-91; rtd 91; Chapl St Cross Hosp Win 91-93; Perm to Offic *Portsm* 93-06. *26 Capel Court, The Burgage, Prestbury, Cheltenham GL52 3EL* Tel (01242) 577541

CAFFYN, Douglas John Morris. b 36. Peterho Cam MA60 Nairobi Univ MSc69 Westmr Coll Ox DipEd61 ACIS77. S Dios Minl Tr Scheme 87. **d** 90 **p** 91. NSM Hampden Park *Chich* 90-94; Chapl among Deaf People 94-97; Jt Sec Cttee for Min among Deaf People 95-97; Perm to Offic from 97; rtd 01. *255 King's Drive, Eastbourne BN21 2UR* Tel (01323) 500977

CAHILL, Canon Nigel. b 59. St Mich Coll Llan. **d** 82 **p** 83. C Whitchurch *Llan* 82-86; V Tonypandy w Clydach Vale 86-96; RD Rhondda 93-96; V Fairwater 96-03; V Caerau w Ely 03-08; AD Llan 06-08; TR Aberavon from 08. *The Rectory, Forge Road, Port Talbot SA13 1US* Tel (01639) 883630 E-mail ncahill@talktalk.net

CAHUSAC, Henry William James. b 73. Wycliffe Hall Ox BTh06. **d** 06 **p** 07. C Tollington *Lon* from 06. *St Saviour's Vicarage, Hanley Road, London N4 3DQ* Tel (020) 7561 5462 E-mail bill.cahusac@tollingtonpark.org

CAIN, Andrew David. b 63. Aber Univ BSc86. Ripon Coll Cuddesdon BA89. **d** 90 **p** 91. C Walworth St Jo *S'wark* 90-94; Bp's Dom Chapl *Ox* 94-98; P-in-c Kilburn St Mary w All So *Lon* 98-01; P-in-c W Hampstead St Jas 98-01; V Kilburn St Mary w All So and W Hampstead St Jas from 01; AD N Camden from 07. *St Mary's Vicarage, 134A Abbey Road, London NW6 4SN* Tel and fax (020) 7624 5434 E-mail acain@acain.screaming.net

CAIN, Andrew Paul. b 76. St Jo Coll Nottm. **d** 08 **p** 09. C Hinckley H Trin *Leic* from 08. *2 Brascote Road, Hinckley LE10 0YE*

CAIN, Frank Robert. b 56. Oak Hill Th Coll BA88. **d** 88 **p** 89. C Aughton Ch Ch *Liv* 88-91; P-in-c Toxteth Park St Clem 91-99, V Toxteth St Bede w St Clem 99-04; AD Toxteth and Wavertree 01-04; Hon Can Liv Cathl 03-04; Chapl N Mersey Community NHS Trust 96-04; V New Brighton St Jas w Em *Ches* from 04; RD Wallasey 07-09. *The Vicarage, 14 Albion Street, Wallasey CH45 9LF* Tel 0151-639 5844
E-mail frankandsuecain@ukgateway.net

CAIN, Michael Christopher. b 68. St Jo Coll Dur BA90 K Coll Lon MA92 Selw Coll Cam BA94. Ridley Hall Cam 92. **d** 95 **p** 96. C Wimbledon Em Ridgway Prop Chpl *S'wark* 95-99; Asst Chapl Leipzig *Eur* 99-02; C Clifton Ch Ch w Em *Bris* from 02. *60 Clifton Park Road, Bristol BS8 3HN* Tel 0117-973 3729

CAIN, Michael John Patrick. b 62. Chich Th Coll 88. **d** 91 **p** 92. C Cainscross w Selsley *Glouc* 91-94; C Mackworth St Fran *Derby* 94-97; V Derby St Luke 97-02; C Paignton St Jo *Ex* 02-07; rtd 07. *124 Forest Road, Torquay TQ1 4JY* Tel (01803) 316046 E-mail cainfamily@toucansurf.co.uk

CAINK, Richard David Somerville. b 37. Lich Th Coll 68. **d** 71 **p** 72. C Prittlewell St Mary *Chelmsf* 71-74; C Gt Yarmouth *Nor* 74-76; P-in-c Blickling w Ingworth 76-80; P-in-c Saxthorpe and Corpusty 76-80; P-in-c Oulton SS Pet and Paul 76-80; R Cheddington w Mentmore and Marsworth *Ox* 80-87; P-in-c Wooburn 87-90; V 90-96; P-in-c Lacey Green 96-98; TV Risborough 98-02; rtd 02. *1 Whitlock Drive, Great Yeldham, Halstead CO9 4EE* Tel (01787) 236091

CAIRD, The Rt Revd Prof Donald Arthur Richard. b 25. TCD BA49 MA55 BD55 HDipEd59 Hon DD88 Hon LLD93. TCD Div Sch 49. **d** 50 **p** 51 **c** 70. C Dundela St Mark *D & D* 50-53; Chapl and Asst Master Portora R Sch Enniskillen 53-57; Lect St D Coll Lamp 57-59; I Rathmichael *D & G* 60-69; Asst Master St Columba's Coll Dub 60-62; Lect TCD 62-64; Lect in Philosophy of Relig Div Hostel Dub 64-69; Dean Ossory *C & O*

69-70; Can Leighlin Cathl 69-70; I Kilkenny 69-70; Bp Limerick, Ardfert and Aghadoe *L & K* 70-76; Bp *M & K* 76-85; Abp Dublin *D & G* 85-96; Preb Cualaun St Patr Cathl Dublin 85-96; rtd 96; Visiting Prof Gen Th Sem New York from 97. *3 Crofton Avenue, Dun Laoghaire, Co Dublin, Republic of Ireland* Tel (00353) (1) 280 7869 Fax 230 1053

CAIRNS, Dorothy Elizabeth. b 66. Wilson Carlile Coll 87 CITC 07. **d** 09. CA from 90; C Portadown St Columba *Arm* from 09. *19 Derryvinney Road, Portadown, Craigavon BT62 1SX* Tel (028) 3885 1231 Mobile 07719-857187
E-mail ecairns@talk21.com

CAIRNS, Henry Alfred (Jim). Melbourne Univ BA49. ACT ThL43. **d** 42 **p** 43. Australia 42-81; Can Gippsland 59-60; Perm to Offic *Cant* 81-83; Perm to Offic *St Alb* 81-83 and from 85; Hon C Radlett 83-85. *47 Westminster Court, St Stephen's Hill, St Albans AL1 2DX* Tel (01727) 850949

CAISSIE, Mrs Elizabeth Anne. b 40. CBDTI 07. **d** 08 **p** 09. NSM Keighley St Andr *Bradf* from 08. *School House, Haworth Road, Cross Roads, Keighley BD22 9DL* Tel (01535) 645800

CAITHNESS, Mrs Joyce Marigold. b 45. **d** 06 **p** 07. OLM Bris St Matt and St Nath from 06. *383 Southmead Road, Westbury-on-Trym, Bristol BS10 5LT* Tel 0117-983 3755
E-mail jm.caithness@blueyonder.co.uk

CAKE, Nichola Carla. See CHATER, Nichola Carla

CALCOTT-JAMES, Colin Wilfrid. b 25. Bris Univ BSc48. S'wark Ord Course 77. **d** 80 **p** 81. NSM Barnes H Trin *S'wark* 80-85; C Hykeham *Linc* 85-88; R Barrowby 88-92; rtd 92; Perm to Offic *Lon* 93-94 and *S'wark* from 93. *23 Gwendolen Avenue, London SW15 6ET* Tel (020) 8788 6591

CALDECOURT, Ms Frances Ann. b 51. RGN72. Ridley Hall Cam 05. **d** 07 **p** 08. C Harlington Ch Ch CD *Lon* 07-08; C W Hayes from 08. *192 Waltham Avenue, Hayes UB3 1TF* E-mail francaldecourt@btinternet.com

CALDER, David Ainsley. b 60. NE Lon Poly BSc86 St Jo Coll Dur BA95. Cranmer Hall Dur 93. **d** 96 **p** 97. C Ireland Wood *Ripon* 96-00; V Woodhouse and Wrangthorn from 00; Chapl Leeds Metrop Univ from 02. *2 Halcyon Hill, Leeds LS7 3PU* Tel 0113-269 0448 Mobile 07947-535044
E-mail david.calder@lineone.net

CALDER, Canon Ian Fraser. b 47. York Univ BA68 CertEd69. Glouc Sch of Min 84. **d** 87 **p** 88. NSM Lydney w Aylburton *Glouc* 87-91; C Cirencester 91-95; V Coney Hill 95-01; RD Glouc City 99-01; R Bishop's Cleeve 01-08; AD Tewkesbury and Winchcombe 02-07; Hon Can Glouc Cathl 03-08; rtd 08. *11 Riversley Road, Elmbridge, Gloucester GL2 0QU* Tel (01452) 537845 E-mail revian@blueyonder.co.uk

CALDER, Roger Paul. b 53. Hatf Coll Dur BA75. Chich Th Coll 76. **d** 79 **p** 80. C Addlestone *Guildf* 79-82; C Grangetown *Dur* 82-84; TV Brighton Resurr *Chich* 84-87; CF 87-92; P-in-c Cocking, Bepton and W Lavington *Chich* 92-95; P-in-c Bognor 95-98; V 98-05; P-in-c Portsea St Sav *Portsm* 05-07; V from 07; P-in-c Portsea St Alb 05-07; V from 07. *St Saviour's Vicarage, Twyford Avenue, Portsmouth PO2 8PB* Tel (023) 9266 3664 E-mail fr.roger@stalban.org.uk

CALDERHEAD, Christopher Conrad. b 62. Princeton Univ AB84. Seabury Western Th Sem M Div98. **d** 98 **p** 99. C Chesterton Gd Shep *Ely* 98-02; USA from 02. *3075 Thirty-third Street Apt 4A, Astoria NY 11102, USA* Tel (001) (718) 278 3098 E-mail calderhead@yahoo.com

CALDERWOOD, Emma Louise. b 74. Derby Univ BSc96 Univ of Wales (Cardiff) MTh07. St Mich Coll Llan BTh05. **d** 06 **p** 07. C Stanley w Stoneycroft St Paul *Liv* from 06. *The Vicarage Flat, 8 Derwent Square, Liverpool L13 6QT* Tel 0151-252 1522 E-mail revdem1411@btinternet.com

CALDICOTT, Anthony. b 31. St Jo Coll Dur BA53 ARCO52 FRCO62. Ripon Hall Ox 55. **d** 57 **p** 58. C Finham *Cov* 57-61; C Bedford St Andr *St Alb* 61-64; Chapl Lindisfarne Coll 64-67; C W Bromwich All SS *Lich* 67-69; Lic to Offic *Cov* 69-75; Hon C Twickenham St Mary *Lon* 75-89; Perm to Offic from 91; rtd 96. *38 Lyndhurst Avenue, Twickenham TW2 6BX* Tel (020) 8894 6859

CALDWELL, Alan. b 29. Oak Hill Th Coll 65. **d** 67 **p** 68. C Aldershot H Trin *Guildf* 67-69; C New Malden and Coombe *S'wark* 69-73; C-in-c Edgware St Andr CD *Lon* 73-78; P-in-c Pettaugh and Winston *St E* 78; R Helmingham w Framsden and Pettaugh w Winston 78-87; R Cowden w Hammerwood *Chich* 87-94; rtd 94; Perm to Offic *Ban* from 94. *Ael-y-Bryn, Druid Road, Menai Bridge LL59 5BY* Tel (01248) 713550 E-mail alancaldwell3d@btinternet.com

CALDWELL, Alan Alfred. b 48. Loughb Univ BSc70 PhD83. Linc Th Coll 70. **d** 73 **p** 74. C Bulwell St Mary *S'well* 73-80; Chapl Nottm Univ 80-87; R Baxterley w Hurley and Wood End and Merevale etc *Birm* 87-91; Perm to Offic *S'well* from 06. *33 The Spinney, Bulcote, Nottingham NG14 5GY* Tel 0115-931 4556

CALDWELL, Ian Charles Reynolds. b 43. St Mich Coll Llan 68. **d** 70 **p** 71. C Oakham w Hambleton and Egleton *Pet* 70-74; C Swindon New Town *Bris* 74-78; P-in-c Honicknowle *Ex* 78-80; V

80-88; V Norton St Mich *Dur* 88-94; rtd 03. *Address withheld by request*

CALDWELL, Mrs Jill. b 47. Lon Univ BPharm69 MRPharmS70. S Dios Minl Tr Scheme 89. **d** 92 **p** 94. NSM Yiewsley *Lon* 92-97; NSM St Marylebone w H Trin 97-02; Chapl St Marylebone Girls' Sch Lon 97-98; Chapl R Academy of Music 97-98; Chapl Lon Sch of Pharmacy 97-98; Chapl Liv Cathl 03-04; Perm to Offic *Derby* 04-05; NSM Darley Abbey from 05. *3 Brick Row, Darley Abbey, Derby DE22 1DQ* Tel (01332) 550676 E-mail jill-caldwell@talk21.com

CALDWELL, Roger Fripp. b 31. Cranmer Hall Dur. **d** 64 **p** 65. C Gosforth St Nic *Newc* 64-67; C Sugley 67-74; R Greatworth and Helmdon w Stuchbury and Radstone *Pet* 74-91; rtd 91. *Silver House, Silver Street, Ditcheat, Shepton Mallet BA4 6QY* Tel (01749) 860239

CALE, Canon Clifford Roy Fenton. b 38. St Mich Coll Llan 65. **d** 67 **p** 68. C Griffithstown *Mon* 67-72; V Cwm 72-73; V Abersychan 73-79; V Abersychan and Garndiffaith 79-82; R Goetre w Llanover and Llanfair Kilgeddin 82-85; R Goetre w Llanover 85-01; RD Raglan-Usk 90-01; Can St Woolos Cathl 98-01; rtd 01. *3 Trelawny Close, Usk NP15 1SP* Tel (01291) 672252

CALE, Nicholas. b 66. St Mich Coll Llan. **d** 92 **p** 93. C Tenby *St D* 92-95; R Begelly w Ludchurch and Crunwere 95-01; V Wiston w Walton E and Clarbeston from 01. *The Vicarage, Wiston, Haverfordwest SA62 4PL* Tel (01437) 731266 E-mail cale@tinyonline.co.uk

CALITIS, Juris. Maryland Univ BA Latvia Univ DD. Harvard Div Sch STB. **d** 98 **p** 98. Chapl Riga, Latvia *Eur* from 98; Dean Faculty of Th Univ of Latvia from 99; Assoc Prof Bibl Studies from 99; Co-ord Bible Translation (Latvian Bible Soc) from 99. *Anglikanu iela 2A, Riga, LV1050, Latvia* Tel and fax (00371) 721 1390 *or* 721 1288 E-mail juris.calitis@lu.lv

CALLADINE, Joanne Elizabeth. b 71. Liv Inst of Educn BA93. Cranmer Hall Dur 95. **d** 97 **p** 98. NSM Blurton *Lich* 97-98; C Stoke-upon-Trent 98-01; Perm to Offic *Man* from 07. *St Mary's Rectory, 47 Nuthurst Road, Moston, Manchester M40 0EW* Tel 0161-681 1201 E-mail jo.calladine@lineone.net

CALLADINE, Matthew Robert Michael. b 65. St Jo Coll Dur BSc87 BA95 Reading Univ MSc89. Cranmer Hall Dur 93. **d** 96 **p** 97. C Blurton *Lich* 96-01; P-in-c Moston St Mary *Man* from 01. *St Mary's Rectory, 47 Nuthurst Road, Moston, Manchester M40 0EW* Tel 0161-681 1201 E-mail matthew.calladine@lineone.net

CALLAGHAN, Canon Harry. b 34. AKC59 Open Univ BA83. **d** 60 **p** 61. C Sheff St Cecilia Parson Cross 60-63; Br Guiana 63-66; Guyana 66-70; Barbados 70-74; Lic to Offic *Man* 74-84; Miss to Seamen 74-76; Area Sec USPG *Blackb, Man* and *S & M* 76-84; P-in-c Wythenshawe St Martin *Man* 84-85; V 85-91; V Bolton St Jo 91-98; Hon Can Massachusetts from 92; rtd 98; Perm to Offic *Man* from 98 and *Derby* from 99. *5 Manor Park View, Glossop SK13 7TL* Tel (01457) 868886 Mobile 07778-988523 E-mail harry@harrycallaghan.wanadoo.co.uk

CALLAGHAN, Martin Peter. b 57. Edin Th Coll 91. **d** 93 **p** 94. C Ayr *Glas* 93-96; C Girvan 93-96; C Maybole 93-96; P-in-c Gretna from 96; P-in-c Eastriggs from 96; P-in-c Annan from 97; P-in-c Lockerbie from 97; P-in-c Moffat from 97; Clergy Ldr Annandale Gp from 03. *South Annandale Rectory, 28 Northfield Park, Annan DG12 5EZ* Tel (01461) 202924 E-mail martinpcallaghan@btinternet.com

CALLAGHAN, Michael James. b 63. Clare Coll Cam BA85. SEITE 94. **d** 97 **p** 98. NSM Blackheath Park St Mich *S'wark* 97-08. *Address temp unknown*

CALLAGHAN, Robert Paul. b 59. K Coll Lon BD81 Kent Univ MA04. Linc Th Coll 81. **d** 83 **p** 85. C Winchmore Hill St Paul *Lon* 83-85; C Paddington St Jo w St Mich 85-91; V Dartford St Edm *Roch* from 91. *St Edmund's Vicarage, St Edmund's Road, Dartford DA1 5ND* Tel (01322) 225335 *or* 228984 E-mail bob.callaghan@diocese-rochester.org

CALLAGHAN, Yvonne Susan. b 58. St Jo Coll Nottm 06. **d** 08 **p** 09. C Middleham w Coverdale and E Witton etc *Ripon* from 08. *The Rectory, The Springs, Middleham, Leyburn DL8 4RB* Tel (01969) 620206 E-mail callaghans1992@ntlworld.com

CALLAN, Canon Terence Frederick. b 26. CITC 55. **d** 57 **p** 58. C Monaghan *Clogh* 57-58; I Clogh 58-64; C Derriaghy *Conn* 64-66; P-in-c Ballymacash 67-70; I Belfast St Aid 70-79; I Agherton 79-94; Can Conn Cathl from 86; Treas from 90; rtd 94. *18 Central Avenue, Portstewart BT55 7BS* Tel (028) 7083 2704

CALLAN, Ms Wendy Mary. b 52. Ox Brookes Univ BA93. SAOMC 96. **d** 99 **p** 00. C Bicester w Bucknell, Caversfield and Launton *Ox* 99-03; V Shipton-under-Wychwood w Milton, Fifield etc from 03. *The Vicarage, Church Street, Shipton-under-Wychwood, Chipping Norton OX7 6BP* Tel and fax (01993) 830257 Mobile 07788-442946

CALLAN-TRAVIS, Anthony. b 46. NOC 90. **d** 93 **p** 94. C Tong *Bradf* 93-97; C Harrogate St Wilfrid *Ripon* 97-03; TV Knaresborough 03-08; rtd 09. *3 Providence Terrace, Harrogate HG1 5EX* Tel (01423) 529266

CALLARD, Canon David Kingsley. b 37. St Pet Coll Ox BA61 MA65. Westcott Ho Cam 61. **d** 63 **p** 64. C Leamington Priors H Trin *Cov* 63-66; C Wyken 66-68; C Bp's Hatfield *St Alb* 68-73; R Bilton *Cov* 73-83; TR Swanage and Studland *Sarum* 83-93; TR Oakdale 93-02; Can and Preb Sarum Cathl 95-02; rtd 02; Perm to Offic *B & W* from 05. *Woodlands, 29 Folkestone Road, Salisbury SP2 8JP* Tel (01722) 501200

CALLENDER, Francis Charles. b 48. TCD BA70 DipEd71 MA73. TCD Div Sch 76. **d** 79 **p** 80. C Bandon *C, C & R* 79-82; New Zealand 82-88 and from 90; USA 88-90. *31 Grampian Street, Casebrook, Christchurch 8051, New Zealand* Tel (0064) (3) 359 4568 Fax 337 8236

CALLER, Laurence Edward Harrison. b 19. Lon Univ BMus77 MA82. Lich Th Coll 39. **d** 42 **p** 43. C Ipswich St Matt *St E* 42-45; C Walsall St Pet *Lich* 45-46; C Hednesford 46-48; R Stafford St Mary 48-55; Subchanter Lich Cathl 55-57; V Shrewsbury St Alkmund 57-63; V Harlescott 63-67; rtd 84. *103 Fronks Road, Dovercourt, Harwich CO12 4EG* Tel (01255) 504501

CALLIS, Gillian Ruth. *See* TURNER-CALLIS, Mrs Gillian Ruth

CALLON, Andrew McMillan. b 56. Chich Th Coll 77. **d** 80 **p** 81. C Wigan All SS *Liv* 80-85; V Abram 85-90; V Bickershaw 89-90; Chapl RN from 90. *Royal Naval Chaplaincy Service, Mail Point 1-2, Leach Building, Whale Island, Portsmouth PO2 8BY* Tel (023) 9262 5055 Fax 9262 5134

CALLWAY, Peter Stanley. b 55. SEITE 06. **d** 09. C Paddock Wood *Roch* from 09. *3 Ashcroft Road, Paddock Wood, Tonbridge TN12 6LG* Tel (01892) 833194 Mobile 07595-378715

CALVELEY, Mrs Susan. b 47. **d** 02 **p** 03. OLM Birkdale St Pet *Liv* 02-06; NSM from 06. *St Peter's Vicarage, 2 St Peter's Road, Southport PR8 4BY* Tel (01704) 562452 E-mail rev.sue@btconnect.com

CALVER, Canon Gillian Margaret. b 47. Qu Eliz Coll Lon BSc68. Cant Sch of Min 89. **d** 92 **p** 94. NSM Folkestone H Trin w Ch Ch *Cant* 92-95; P-in-c Alkham w Capel le Ferne and Hougham 95-01; V 01-02; Chapl Dover Coll 95-99; R Staplehurst *Cant* from 02; AD Weald from 06; Hon Can Cant Cathl from 08; Chapl to The Queen from 08. *The New Rectory, High Street, Staplehurst, Tonbridge TN12 0BJ* Tel (01580) 891258 E-mail revgc@ukonline.co.uk

CALVER, Nicholas James. b 58. Nottm Univ BTh83 Dur Univ MA90. Cranmer Hall Dur 86. **d** 88 **p** 89. C Forest Hill Ch Ch *S'wark* 88-91; C Forest Hill 91-92; P-in-c Mottingham St Edw 92-95; V 95-97; Voc Adv Lewisham Adnry 94-97; V Redhill St Jo from 97. *St John's Vicarage, Church Road, Redhill RH1 6QA* Tel (01737) 766562

CALVERT, Geoffrey Richard. b 58. Edin Univ BSc79 PhD84 Leeds Univ BA86. Coll of Resurr Mirfield 84. **d** 87 **p** 88. C Curdworth w Castle Vale *Birm* 87-90; C Barnsley St Mary *Wakef* 90-92; TV Halifax 92-94; V Halifax H Trin 95-99; V Luton St Aug Limbury *St Alb* from 99. *The Vicarage, 215 Icknield Way, Luton LU3 2JR* Tel and fax (01582) 572415 E-mail geoff.calver@dsl.pipex.com

CALVERT, Canon Jean. b 34. Lightfoot Ho Dur IDC63. **dss** 78 **d** 87 **p** 94. S Bank *York* 78-84; Chapl Asst Rampton Hosp Retford 84-88; Dn-in-c Dunham w Darlton, Ragnall, Fledborough etc *S'well* 88-94; P-in-c 94-04; Hon Can S'well Minster 93-04; rtd 04; Perm to Offic *S'well* from 06. *The Rafters, Lincoln Road, Darlton, Newark NG22 0TF* Tel (01777) 228758

CALVERT, John Raymond. b 42. Lon Coll of Div 64. **d** 67 **p** 68. C Kennington St Mark *S'wark* 67-70; C Southborough St Pet *Roch* 70-72; C Barton Seagrave *Pet* 72-75; Asst Master Shaftesbury High Sch 78-79; Dioc Children's Officer *Glouc* 79-87; P-in-c S Cerney w Cerney Wick and Down Ampney 87-89; V 89-07; P-in-c Siddington w Preston 02-07; rtd 07. *46 Penn Lane, Brixham TQ5 9NR*

CALVERT, John Stephen. b 27. Lon Univ BSc53. Wycliffe Coll Toronto BTh61. **d** 61 **p** 62. Canada 61-63; C Preston St Jo *Blackb* 63-70; rtd 92; Perm to Offic *Blackb* from 92. *17 Leyster Street, Morecambe LA4 5NF* Tel (01524) 424491

CALVERT, Mrs Judith. b 50. NOC 04. **d** 07 **p** 08. NSM Woodchurch *Ches* from 07. *33 Centurion Drive, Wirral CH47 7AL* Tel 0151-632 4729 E-mail rev.judithcalvert@btinternet.com

CALVERT, Canon Peter Noel. b 41. Ch Coll Cam BA63 MA67. Cuddesdon Coll 64. **d** 66 **p** 67. C Brighouse *Wakef* 66-71; V Heptonstall 71-82; V Todmorden 82-07; P-in-c Cross Stone 83-93; RD Calder Valley 84-06; Hon Can Wakef Cathl 92-07; rtd 07; P-in-c Leven Valley *Carl* from 07; Chapl to The Queen from 98. *Leven Valley Vicarage, Haverthwaite, Ulverston LA12 8AJ* Tel (01539) 531476 E-mail pncalvert@btinternet.com

CALVERT, Philip. b 62. St Steph Ho Ox 00. **d** 02 **p** 03. C Holbrooks *Cov* 02-06; P-in-c Kingstanding St Mark *Birm* from 06. *St Mark's Clergy House, Bandywood Crescent, Birmingham B44 9JX* Tel 0121-360 7288 Mobile 07969-362577 E-mail frphilipcarlvert@aol.com

CALVIN, Alison. CITC. **d** 09. C Killeshandra w Killegar and

Derrylane *K, E & A* from 09. *The Rectory, Killeshandra, Co Cavan, Republic of Ireland*

CALVIN-THOMAS, David Nigel. b 43. Univ of Wales (Cardiff) BSc64 Lon Univ BD77. St Mich Coll Llan 77. **d** 78 **p** 79. C Pontypridd St Cath *Llan* 78-80; Malawi 81-84; V Rastrick St Matt *Wakef* 84-88; V Birchencliffe 88-93; Chapl Huddersfield R Infirmary 88-93; R Aberdeen St Pet 93-01; P-in-c Cove Bay 93-01; TV Glenrothes *St And* 01-07; R 07-09; R Leven 07-09; R Lochgelly 07-09; rtd 09. *141 Napier Road, Glenrothes KY6 1AU* Tel (01592) 760210 Fax 07092-113255
E-mail davidct@blueyonder.co.uk

CALWAY, Geoffrey. b 45. Bris Sch of Min 84. **d** 87 **p** 88. NSM Cotham St Sav w St Mary *Bris* 87-94; NSM Horfield H Trin 94-97; P-in-c Publow w Pensford, Compton Dando and Chelwood *B & W* 97-07; P-in-c Instow *Ex* from 08; P-in-c Westleigh from 08. *10 South Road, Appledore, Bideford EX39 1QH* Tel (01237) 459729

CAM, Julian Howard. b 48. York Univ BA69 Man Univ MA99. Qu Coll Birm 73. **d** 75 **p** 76. C St Ives *Truro* 75-80; C Lelant 78-80; V Flookburgh *Carl* 80-82; V St Stephen by Saltash *Truro* 82-83; V Low Marple *Ches* 83-08; rtd 08; Perm to Offic *Derby* and *Ches* from 08. *14 High Lea Road, New Mills, High Peak SK22 3DP* Tel (01663) 744065
E-mail julian.angela.cam08@btinternet.com

CAMBODIA, Dean of. *See* BENSON, The Very Revd John Patrick

CAMBRIDGE, Benedict Howard. b 73. Westmr Coll Ox BTh95. Cranmer Hall Dur 99. **d** 02. C Chilwell *S'well* 01-05; Sen Chapl Staffs Univ from 05. *10 Fenton Hall Close, Stoke-on-Trent ST4 4PU* Tel (01782) 294974
E-mail b.h.cambridge@staffs.ac.uk

CAMBRIDGE, Archdeacon of. *See* BEER, The Ven John Stuart

✠**CAMERON, The Rt Revd Andrew Bruce.** b 41. Edin Th Coll 61. **d** 64 **p** 65 **c** 92. C Helensburgh *Glas* 64-67; C Edin H Cross 67-71; Prov and Dioc Youth Chapl 69-75; Chapl St Mary's Cathl 71-75; R Dalmahoy 75-82; Chapl Heriot-Watt Univ 75-82; TV Livingston LEP 82-88; R Perth St Jo *St And* 88-92; Convener Prov Miss Bd 88-92; Bp Ab 92-06; Primus 00-06; rtd 06. *2 Newbigging Grange, Coupar Angus, Blairgowrie PH13 9GA* Tel (01821) 650482 E-mail bruce2541@gmail.com

CAMERON, David Alan. b 59. Glas Univ MA81 DipEd82 PGCE82. Ripon Coll Cuddesdon 88. **d** 91 **p** 92. C Farncombe *Guildf* 91-93; C Guildf H Trin w St Mary 93-96; V Fenton *Lich* from 96. *The Vicarage, 65 Glebedale Road, Stoke-on-Trent ST4 3AQ* Tel and fax (01782) 412417

CAMERON, David Alexander. b 42. Reading Univ BA63 MRTPI. St And Dioc Tr Course 80. **d** 90 **p** 93. NSM Blairgowrie *St And* from 90; NSM Coupar Angus from 90; NSM Alyth from 90. *Firgrove, Golf Course Road, Blairgowrie PH10 6LF* Tel (01250) 873272 E-mail dacameron@talk21.com

CAMERON, Donald Eric Nelson. b 29. St Jo Coll Dur 68. **d** 70 **p** 71. C Kingston upon Hull H Trin *York* 70-73; V Eston 73-82; R Balerno *Edin* 82-87; rtd 94. *The Granary, Crauchie, East Linton EH40 3EB* Tel (01620) 860067

✠**CAMERON, The Rt Revd Douglas MacLean.** b 35. Edin Th Coll 59. **d** 62 **p** 63 **c** 93. C Falkirk *Edin* 62-65; Miss P Eiwo Papua New Guinea 66-67; Miss P Movi 67-72; R Goroka and Adn New Guinea Mainland 72-74; P-in-c Edin St Fillan 74-78; R 78-88; R Edin St Hilda 77-88; R Dalkeith 88-92; R Lasswade 88-92; Can St Mary's Cathl 90-91; Syn Clerk 90-91; Dean Edin 91-92; Bp Arg 93-03; rtd 03; Lic to Offic *Edin* from 04. *23 Craigs Way, Rumford, Falkirk FK2 0EU* Tel (01324) 714137

✠**CAMERON, The Rt Revd Gregory Kenneth.** b 59. Linc Coll Ox BA80 MA84 Down Coll Cam BA82 MA85 Univ of Wales (Cardiff) MPhil92 LLM95. St Mich Coll Llan 82. **d** 83 **p** 84 **c** 09. C Newport St Paul *Mon* 83-86; Tutor St Mich Coll Llan 86-89; C Llanmartin *Mon* 86-87; TV 87-88; Chapl Wycliffe Coll Glos 88-94; Dir Bloxham Project 94-00; Research Fell Cardiff Univ Cen for Law and Relig 98-00; Chapl to Abp Wales 00-03; Dir Ecum Relns ACC 03-04; Dep Sec 04-09; Hon Can St Woolos Cathl 03-09; Bp St As from 09. *Esgobty, St Asaph LL17 0TW* Tel (01745) 583503
E-mail bishop.stasaph@churchinwales.org.uk

CAMERON, James. *See* CAMERON, William James

CAMERON, Mrs Janice Irene. b 43. Reading Univ BA. TISEC 93. **d** 96 **p** 96. C Blairgowrie *St And* 96-98; C Coupar Angus 96-98; C Alyth 96-98; R Dunblane 99-08; Can St Ninian's Cathl Perth 05-08; rtd 08. *Firgrove, Golf Course Road, Blairgowrie PH10 6LF* Tel (01250) 873272
E-mail rector@stmarysdunblane.org

CAMERON, Preb Margaret Mary. b 48. Qu Mary Coll Lon BA69 Ex Univ MA95. SW Minl Tr Course 87. **d** 90 **p** 94. NSM Budleigh Salterton *Ex* 90-95; C Whipton 95-97; R Hennock w Culm Davy, Clayhidon and Culmstock 97-03; RD Cullompton 99-03; V Plympton St Mary from 03; Preb Ex Cathl from 05. *St Mary's Vicarage, 209 Ridgeway, Plymouth PL7 2HP* Tel (01752) 336157 or 348525 E-mail revd.cameron@tesco.net

CAMERON, Michael John. b 41. Linc Th Coll 91. **d** 92 **p** 93. C

Dinnington *Sheff* 92-96; V Beighton 96-06; AD Attercliffe 99-02; rtd 07. *17 Western Street, Barnsley S70 2BP* Tel (01226) 249573

CAMERON, Peter Scott. b 45. Edin Univ LLB67 BD76 Cam Univ PhD79 LRAM64. **d** 97 **p** 97. C Perth St Jo *St And* 97-98; R Dunkeld 98-04; R Strathtay 98-04; rtd 04. *Hope Cottage, Strathtay, Pithlochry PH9 0PG* Tel and fax (01887) 840212

CAMERON, Ms Sheila. b 34. TCert54. Gilmore Ho 65. **d** 98 **p** 99. NSM Catford St Laur *S'wark* 98-02; Perm to Offic from 02. *52 Engleheart Road, London SE6 2HW* Tel (020) 8698 9282 or 8698 9706

CAMERON, Sheila Helen MacLeod. b 46. St Andr Univ MA68 Stirling Univ MLitt83 Cam Univ MA96 Anglia Ruskin Univ MA06. ERMC 04. **d** 06 **p** 07. NSM Cherry Hinton St Andr *Ely* 06-07; NSM Chesterton St Geo from 07. *15 Grasmere Gardens, Cambridge CB4 3DR* Tel (01223) 314443
E-mail shc1001@cam.ac.uk

CAMERON, Thomas Edward. b 46. **d** 06. NSM St Paul's Cathl from 06. *26 Grove Road, London E17 9BN* Tel (020) 8925 9332
E-mail tomecam1@aol.com

CAMERON, William Hugh Macpherson. b 59. Edin Univ LLB82 BD86. Edin Th Coll 83. **d** 86 **p** 87. C Cheadle Hulme All SS *Ches* 86-89; Asst Chapl and Hd RS Wellington Coll Berks 89-93; Chapl K Sch Bruton 93-00; Perm to Offic *Chich* from 01. *Cranesden, West Street, Mayfield TN20 6DS* Tel (01435) 872991

CAMERON, William James. b 35. Brasted Th Coll 60 St Aid Birkenhead 62. **d** 64 **p** 65. C Halewood *Liv* 64-66; C-in-c Halewood St Mary CD 66-68; Asst Chapl Leeds Univ 68-71; Ind Chapl *Liv* 71-77; Tr Officer Gen Syn Bd of Educn 77-84; V Hickling and Waxham w Sea Palling *Nor* 89-95; P-in-c Ludham w Potter Heigham 94-95; V Ludham, Potter Heigham and Hickling 95-00; RD Waxham 93-96; rtd 00; Perm to Offic *Nor* 00-08. *Forge Bungalow, The Street, Lessingham, Norwich NR12 0DG* Tel (01692) 582790

CAMMELL, William John. b 36. Glouc Sch of Min 89. **d** 92 **p** 93. OLM Ruardean *Glouc* 92-07; OLM Drybrook, Lydbrook and Ruardean from 07. *The Beeches, High Beech Road, The Pludds, Ruardean GL17 9UD* Tel (01594) 860603

CAMP, Brian Arthur Leslie. b 50. St Jo Coll Nottm. **d** 83 **p** 84. C Blackheath *Birm* 83-86; TV Halesowen *Worc* 86-96; P-in-c Sheldon *Birm* 96-97; R from 97. *The Rectory, 165 Church Road, Sheldon, Birmingham B26 3TT* Tel 0121-743 2033
E-mail rector@stgilessheldon.org

CAMP, Mrs Carole Ann. b 48. Qu Coll Birm. **d** 08 **p** 09. NSM Chelmsley Wood *Birm* from 08. *The Rectory, 165 Church Road, Sheldon, Birmingham B26 3TT* Tel 0121-743 2033

CAMP, Frederick Walter. b 19. Sarum Th Coll 47. **d** 49 **p** 50. C Brookfield St Mary *Lon* 49-54; CF 54-58; V Brigham *Carl* 58-80; V Whittingham *Newc* 80-84; V Whittingham and Edlingham w Bolton Chapel 84-85; rtd 85; Perm to Offic *Carl* from 85. *2 Ellen Court, Church Terrace, Ellenborough, Maryport CA15 7PR* Tel (01900) 817936

CAMP, Michael Maurice. b 52. Southn Univ BTh83 K Coll Lon MA99 Brentwood Coll of Educn CertEd70. Sarum & Wells Th Coll 78. **d** 81 **p** 82. C Loughton St Jo *Chelmsf* 81-84; C Chingford SS Pet and Paul 84-87; V Northfleet *Roch* 87-94; V Hadlow 94-01; RD Paddock Wood 99-01; V Bromley SS Pet and Paul from 01; AD Bromley from 06. *The Vicarage, 9 St Paul's Square, Bromley BR2 0XH* Tel and fax (020) 8460 6275 Mobile 07734-424996 E-mail michael.mcamp@diocese-rochester.org

CAMPBELL, Mrs Brenda. b 47. St Jo Coll Nottm 92. **d** 94 **p** 95. C Rothley *Leic* 94-97; C Market Bosworth, Cadeby w Sutton Cheney etc 97-00; TV Bosworth and Sheepy Gp 00-07; rtd 07. *28 Ashfield Drive, Moira, Swandlincote DE12 6HQ* Tel (01530) 413534 E-mail brendajones101@tiscali.co.uk

CAMPBELL, David. b 70. St Andr Univ MTheol92 New Coll Edin MTh94. Edin Th Coll 92. **d** 94 **p** 95. C Perth St Jo *St And* 94-96; P-in-c Tayport and Newport-on-Tay 96-99; R Dunfermline 99-07; Dioc Youth Officer 96-07; Chapl Fettes Coll Edin from 07. *Fettes College, Carrington Road, Edinburgh EH4 1QX* Tel 0131-332 2281 E-mail d.campbell@fettes.com or frdavid.campbell@btinternet.com

CAMPBELL, Miss Elizabeth Hume. b 53. Glas Univ MA74 Hamilton Coll of Educn TCert75. St Jo Coll Nottm 01. **d** 02 **p** 03. NSM Alstonfield, Butterton, Ilam etc *Lich* 02-08; NSM Stonehaven *Bre* from 08; NSM Catterline from 08. *3 Ramsay Road, Stonehaven AB39 2HJ* Tel (01569) 764264
E-mail lizzie.campbell@virgin.net

CAMPBELL, Frederick David Gordon. b 15. Ex Coll Ox BA39. Wells Th Coll 39. **d** 40 **p** 41. C Portsea St Mary *Portsm* 40-45; Chapl RNVR 45-48; C Fareham SS Pet and Paul *Portsm* 48-49; Bp's Press Sec *Lon* 49-51; V Isleworth St Mary 51-54; SSJE from 57; Superior Gen SSJE 76-91; Lic to Offic *Lon* 69-97; Perm to Offic 99-02. *St John's Home, St Mary's Road, Oxford OX4 1QE* Tel (01865) 247725

CAMPBELL, George St Clair. b 32. Lon Univ BSc53. Clifton Th Coll 58. **d** 60 **p** 61. C Tunbridge Wells St Pet *Roch* 60-64; C Clitheroe St Jas *Blackb* 64-70; V Tibshelf *Derby* 70-86; V W Bromwich H Trin *Lich* 86-97; Chapl Heath Lane Hosp 87-97; rtd

97; Perm to Offic *Guildf* from 98. *2 Doreen Close, Farnborough GU14 9HB* Tel (01276) 31639

CAMPBELL, Mrs Hilary Anne. b 58. UMIST BSc80. SAOMC. **d** 01 **p** 02. C Goring w S Stoke *Ox* 01-05; TV Kidlington w Hampton Poyle from 05. *St John's Vicarage, 16 The Broadway, Kidlington OX5 1EF* Tel (01865) 375611
E-mail vicar@thecampbells.demon.co.uk

CAMPBELL, Ian George. b 47. FRICS74 FBEng93. SEITE 96. **d** 99 **p** 00. NSM Chilham w Challock and Molash *Cant* 99-01; P-in-c Crundale w Godmersham from 01. *The Forge, Godmersham Park, Godmersham, Canterbury CT4 7DT* Tel (01227) 730925 *or* (01622) 761605
E-mail campbellkent@fsmail.net

CAMPBELL, James Duncan. b 55. Qu Eliz Coll Lon BSc77. St Jo Coll Dur 85 Oak Hill Th Coll MA00. **d** 87 **p** 88. C Hendon St Paul Mill Hill *Lon* 87-92; V Stevenage St Hugh and St Jo *St Alb* from 92. *St Hugh's House, 4 Mobbsbury Way, Chells, Stevenage SG2 0HL* Tel (01438) 354307
E-mail shsj@nildram.co.uk

CAMPBELL, James Larry. b 46. Indiana Univ BSc69 E Kentucky Univ MA73 Hull Univ MA91. Linc Th Coll 86. **d** 88 **p** 89. C N Hull St Mich *York* 88-92; C Hessle 92-95; V Burton Pidsea and Humbleton w Elsternwick from 95. *The New Vicarage, Back Lane, Burton Pidsea, Hull HU12 9AN* Tel (01964) 671074 E-mail campbell822@aol.com

CAMPBELL, James Malcolm. b 55. MRICS81. Wycliffe Hall Ox 89. **d** 91 **p** 92. C Scole, Brockdish, Billingford, Thorpe Abbots etc *Nor* 91-95; R Bentley and Binsted *Win* 95-08; RD Alton 02-08; Hon Can Win Cathl 08; R The Lavingtons, Cheverells, and Easterton *Sarum* from 08. *The Vicarage, 14 Church Street, Market Lavington, Devizes SN10 4DT*

CAMPBELL, Canon James Norman Thompson. b 49. BTh MA. **d** 86 **p** 87. C Arm St Mark w Aghavilly 86-89; I Belfast H Trin and Ardoyne *Conn* 89-95; I Dundela St Mark *D & D* 95-01; I Portadown St Mark *Arm* from 01; Can Arm Cathl from 09. *The Rectory, Brownstown Road, Portadown, Craigavon BT62 3QA* Tel (028) 3833 2368 E-mail j.campbell147@btinternet.com

CAMPBELL, Jane Judith. See BAKKER, Mrs Jane Judith

CAMPBELL, Kenneth Scott. b 47. BA82. Oak Hill Th Coll. **d** 82 **p** 83. C Aughton St Mich *Liv* 82-85; V Brough w Stainmore *Carl* 85-90; R Brough w Stainmore, Musgrave and Warcop 90-92; rtd 92. *4 Quarry Close, Kirkby Stephen CA17 4SS* Tel (01768) 372390

CAMPBELL, Lawrence Henry. b 41. TCD BA63 MA66. **d** 63 **p** 65. C Larne and Inver *Conn* 63-66; C Finaghy 66-67; Chapl RN 67-83; R Brancaster w Burnham Deepdale and Titchwell *Nor* 83-95; P-in-c Hunstanton St Mary w Ringstead Parva, Holme etc 94-95; R Hunstanton St Mary w Ringstead Parva etc 95-08; RD Heacham and Rising 01-07; rtd 08; Perm to Offic *Nor* from 08. *5 Park Hill, Dersingham, King's Lynn PE31 6NE* Tel (01485) 543542 E-mail lawcor@talktalk.net

CAMPBELL, Mrs Margaret Ruth. b 62. Trin Coll Bris BA02. **d** 02 **p** 03. C Yeovil w Kingston Pitney *B & W* 02-06; TV Wellington and Distr from 06. *15 Cox Road, Wellington TA21 9RD* Tel (01823) 669446

CAMPBELL, Patrick Alistair. b 36. Qu Coll Birm 64. **d** 67 **p** 68. C Paston *Pet* 67-71; C Stockton Heath *Ches* 71-73; V Egremont St Jo 73-78; V Bredbury St Mark 78-85; R Astbury and Smallwood 85-91; V Wybunbury w Doddington 91-97; rtd 97; Perm to Offic *Ches* from 97; Warden Coll of St Barn Lingfield 01-07. *8 Brookside, Crawley Down, Crawley RH10 4UU* Tel (01342) 713667

CAMPBELL, Robin William. b 41. TCD BA63 MA67. Ridley Hall Cam 63. **d** 65 **p** 66. C Netherton *Liv* 65-68; C Liv Our Lady and St Nic w St Anne 68-70; V Hooton *Ches* 70-99; rtd 99. *77 Seaview Parade, Lakes Entrance Vic 3909, Australia* Tel (0061) (3) 5155 2157

CAMPBELL, Roger Stewart. b 40. Birm Univ BSc61 PhD65 St Jo Coll Dur BA71. Cranmer Hall Dur 68. **d** 71 **p** 72. C Jesmond Clayton Memorial *Newc* 71-77; V Singapore St Jo and St Marg 78-85; C Nottingham St Nic *S'well* 86-90; V Holloway St Mark w Em *Lon* 90-92; TR Tollington 92-97; Chapl Leeds Teaching Hosps NHS Trust 97-04; rtd 04; Perm to Offic *Carl* from 05. *Redesdale Cottage, Lazonby, Penrith CA10 1AJ* Tel (01768) 870695

CAMPBELL, Stephen James. b 60. TCD BTh91. CITC 88. **d** 91 **p** 92. C Lisburn Ch Ch *Conn* 91-95; I Kilcronaghan w Draperstown and Sixtowns *D & R* 95-00; I Dunluce *Conn* 00-03; Perm to Offic *Eur* from 04; C Kilkewen *D & R* from 06. *94A Mountsandel Road, Coleraine BT52 1TA*
E-mail sjmimc@yahoo.com

CAMPBELL, Stephen Lloyd. b 46. St Andr Univ LLB67 Solicitor 72. SEITE 95. **d** 98 **p** 99. NSM Quantoxhead *B & W* 98-07; NSM Quantock Coast from 07; RD Quantock from 06. *Hodderscombe Lodge, Holford, Bridgwater TA5 1SA* Tel and fax (01278) 741329 Mobile 07808-967046
E-mail stephencampbell0@tiscali.co.uk

CAMPBELL-SMITH, Robert Campbell. b 38. CCC Cam BA61

MA66 Ibadan Univ Nigeria 62. Linc Th Coll 61. **d** 63 **p** 64. C Norbury St Steph *Cant* 63-66; C W Wickham St Mary 66-71; Ind Chapl 65-76; V Croydon St Aug 71-81; Acting RD Croydon Cen 77-81; Spiritual Development Adv Nat Assn of Boys' Clubs 77-89; V Goudhurst *Cant* 81-87; Chapl Kent Assn of Boys' Clubs 81-97; RD W Charing *Cant* 82-89; P-in-c Kilndown 83-87; V Goudhurst w Kilndown 87-99; Hon Can Cant Cathl 94-99; Chapl Kent Youth Trust 97-99; TR Modbury, Bigbury, Ringmore w Kingston etc *Ex* 99-04; rtd 04. *Even Keel, Pillory Hill, Noss Mayo, Plymouth PL8 1ED* Tel (01752) 872559

CAMPBELL-TAYLOR, William Goodacre. b 65. Ox Univ BA87 Cam Univ BA93. Westcott Ho Cam 90. **d** 94 **p** 95. C Chingford SS Pet and Paul *Chelmsf* 94-97; Chapl Lon Guildhall Univ 97-02; Chapl Lon Metrop Univ 02-04; Hon C Hoxton St Anne w St Columba from 05. *203 Kings Wharf, 301 Kingsland Road, London E8 4DS* Tel (020) 7254 4159
E-mail enquiries@stethelburgas.org

CAMPBELL-WILSON, Allan. b 43. Dur Univ BEd74. NEOC 79. **d** 82 **p** 83. NSM Boosbeck w Moorsholm *York* 82-85; R Easington w Skeffling, Kilnsea and Holmpton 85-87; P-in-c Middlesbrough St Jo the Ev 89-95; V 95-99; V Cayton w Eastfield from 99. *The Vicarage, 90 Main Street, Cayton, Scarborough YO11 3RP* Tel (01723) 586569
E-mail frallancayton@aol.com

CAMPEN, William Geoffrey. b 50. Liv Univ CertEd71 Southn Univ BTh81 Lon Univ MA08. Sarum & Wells Th Coll 76. **d** 79 **p** 80. C Peckham St Jo w St Andr *S'wark* 79-83; P-in-c Mottingham St Edw 83-92; R Charlwood from 92; R Sidlow Bridge from 92. *The Rectory, The Street, Charlwood, Horley RH6 0EE* Tel (01293) 862343
E-mail w.g.campen@bigfoot.com

CAMPION, Keith Donald. b 52. S Dios Minl Tr Scheme. **d** 84 **p** 87. NSM Is of Scilly *Truro* 84-96. *20 Launceston Close, St Mary's TR21 0LN* Tel (01720) 422606

CAMPION (formerly HOUSEMAN), Mrs Patricia Adele. b 39. St Mich Coll Llan. **d** 93 **p** 97. C St Issell's and Amroth *St D* 93-95; C Llanegryn w Aberdyfi w Tywyn *Ban* 95-97; rtd 97. *3 Mariners Reach, The Strand, Saundersfoot SA69 9EX* Tel (01834) 811047

CAMPION, Canon Peter Robert. b 64. Bp's Univ Canada BA87 TCD BTh90 MA93 MPhil97 Homerton Coll Cam PGCE94. **d** 90 **p** 91. C Belfast H Trin and Ardoyne *Conn* 90-93; C Taney *D & G* 94-00; Dean's V St Patr Cathl Dublin 96-00; Chapl Netherwood Sch Rothesday Canada 00-05; Chapl K Hosp Dub from 05; Treas V St Patr Cathl Dublin from 05; Prec Ch Ch Cathl Dublin from 08. *The King's Hospital, Palmerstown, Dublin 20, Republic of Ireland* Tel (00353) (1) 626 5933 Fax 623 0349

CAMPLING, The Very Revd Christopher Russell. b 25. St Edm Hall Ox BA50 MA54. Cuddesdon Coll 50. **d** 51 **p** 52. C Basingstoke *Win* 51-55; Chapl K Sch and Min Can Ely Cathl 55-60; Chapl Lancing Coll 60-68; P-in-c Birlingham w Nafford *Worc* 68-75; V Pershore w Wick 68-75; V Pershore w Pinvin, Wick and Birlingham 75-76; RD Pershore 70-76; Hon Can Worc Cathl 74-84; Dioc Dir of Educn 76-84; Adn Dudley 76-84; P-in-c Dodderhill 76-84; Dean Ripon 84-95; Chmn CCC 88-94; rtd 95; Perm to Offic *Chich* from 95. *Pebble Ridge, Aglaia Road, Worthing BN11 5SW* Tel (01903) 246598

CAMPLING, Doreen Elizabeth. b 31. K Coll Lon BSc55. **d** 01 **p** 02. OLM Bridport *Sarum* 01-08. *Harbour Lights, Coneygar Park, Bridport DT6 3BA* Tel (01308) 425670

CAMPLING, Michael. b 27. Trin Coll Cam BA50 MA61. Wells Th Coll 51. **d** 53 **p** 54. C Calne *Sarum* 53-57; C Roehampton H Trin *S'wark* 57-61; V Crowthorne *Ox* 61-75; P-in-c Foleshill St Laur *Cov* 75-81; V 81-83; R Old Alresford and Bighton *Win* 83-92; rtd 92; Chapl St Marg Convent E Grinstead 92-99; Hon C Bexhill St Pet *Chich* 99-05. *9 Orchard Grove, Bloxham, Banbury OX15 4NZ* Tel (01295) 721599

CAMPLING-DENTON, Camilla Anne. b 76. St Andr Univ MA98 Jes Coll Cam MPhil04. Westcott Ho Cam 02. **d** 05 **p** 06. C Fountains Gp *Ripon* 05-07; C Caerleon w Llanhennock *Mon* from 07. *28 Roman Reach, Caerleon, Newport NP18 3SN* Tel (01633) 423930 Mobile 07779-429351

CANADA, Primate of. See HUTCHISON, The Most Revd Andrew Sandford

CANBERRA AND GOULBURN, Bishop of. See ROBINSON, The Rt Revd Stuart Peter

CANDELAND, Thomas Blyde. b 37. **d** 99 **p** 00. OLM Lyng, Sparham, Elsing, Bylaugh, Bawdeswell etc *Nor* 99-08; RD Sparham 05-08; Perm to Offic from 08. *2 Hammond Place, Lyng, Norwich NR9 5RQ* Tel (01603) 871674

CANDOW, Brian Gordon. b 58. Memorial Univ Newfoundland BComm82 BEd83. Qu Th Coll Newfoundland MDiv89. **d** 89 **p** 89. C Fogo Is Canada 89-91; R Botwood 91-95; R Summerside and St Eleanor 00-04; Hon C Skirbeck Quarter *Linc* 04-05; Assoc P Gander Canada from 05. *2 Lindberg Road, Gander NL A1V 2E7, Canada* Tel (001) (709) 256 3700
E-mail candows@bostonengland.freeserve.co.uk

CANE, Canon Anthony William Nicholas Strephon. b 61. Cape Town Univ BA81 Birm Univ MPhil93 PhD03. Westcott Ho Cam 87. **d** 90 **p** 91. C Kings Heath *Birm* 90-93; Chapl Brighton Univ 93-99; P-in-c Torquay St Luke *Ex* 99-01; Dioc Adv in Adult Tr 99-01; C Ringmer and Dioc Adv for Educn and Tr of Adults *Chich* 01-07; Can Res and Chan Chich Cathl from 07. *The Residentiary, 2 Canon Lane, Chichester PO19 1PX* Tel (01243) 813594 E-mail chancellor@chichestercathedral.org.uk

CANEY, Canon Robert Swinbank. b 37. St Jo Coll Cam 57. Lich Th Coll 58. **d** 61 **p** 62. C Kingswinford H Trin *Lich* 61-64; C Castle Church 64-67; V Bradwell *Derby* 67-73; V Fairfield 73-84; RD Buxton 78-84; P-in-c Peak Forest and Wormhill 79-83; R Wirksworth w Alderwasley, Carsington etc 84-92; TR Wirksworth 92-02; Hon Can Derby Cathl 93-02; rtd 02; Perm to Offic *Derby* from 02. *2 Erica Drive, South Normanton, Alfreton DE55 2ET* Tel (01773) 581106 E-mail randjcaney@aol.co.uk

CANHAM, Frances Elizabeth. b 55. MCIPD93. St Mich Coll Llan 05. **d** 07 **p** 08. NSM Thanington Canet from 07. *c/o Col T W Canham, Head C41SR, British Defence Staff, BFPO 2* Tel and fax (001) (703) 242 3782 E-mail frances.canham@cox.net

CANHAM, Francis. *See* CANHAM, Robert Edwin Francis

CANHAM, John Graham. b 33. Univ of Wales (Lamp) BA55. Chich Th Coll 55. **d** 57 **p** 58. C Hawarden *St As* 57-64; Asst Chapl Ellesmere Coll 64-66; Chapl Ches Cathl Choir Sch 66-73; Chapl Choral Ches Cathl 66-73; Asst Chapl Rossall Sch Fleetwood 73-76 and 83-93; Chapl 76-83; V Minera *St As* 93-05; V Bwlchgwyn and Minera 05-08; AD Minera 01-08; rtd 08. *2 Parkers Close, Wrexham LL11 2RR* Tel (01978) 291166

CANHAM, Robert Edwin Francis. b 24. FRCO59 ARCM. **d** 74 **p** 75. NSM Newlyn St Pet *Truro* 74-75; C Phillack w Gwithian 75-79; P-in-c Phillack w Gwithian and Gwinear 79-83; V Greenham *Ox* 83-93; rtd 93; Perm to Offic *Chich* from 93. *Cross Way, 1A Torton Hill Road, Arundel BN18 9HF* Tel (01903) 883614

CANHAM, William Alexander. b 26. Clare Coll Cam BA47 MA56. Roch Th Coll 65. **d** 67 **p** 68. C Orpington St Andr *Roch* 67-70; C Guernsey St Steph *Win* 70-75; Chapl Eliz Coll Guernsey 72-75; R Tadley St Pet *Win* 75-83; V Bournemouth St Luke 83-91; R Guernsey St Marguerite de la Foret 91-96; rtd 96; Perm to Offic *Win* from 96; Perm to Offic *Portsm* from 96. *56 The Causeway, Petersfield GU31 4JS* Tel (01730) 269413

CANN, Christopher James. b 64. St Andr Univ BA MA. St Steph Ho Ox. **d** 91 **p** 92. C Newport St Julian *Mon* 91-93; Chapl Smallwood Manor Sch Uttoxeter from 93; Hd Master from 97. *Smallwood Manor Preparatory School, Uttoxeter ST14 8NS* Tel (01889) 562083 E-mail headmaster@smallwoodmanor.co.uk

CANNAM, Martin Stafford John. b 68. Jes Coll Ox BA90 MA95. Wycliffe Hall Ox 93. **d** 96 **p** 97. C Childwall All SS *Liv* 96-00; V Biddulph *Lich* from 00. *The Vicarage, 7 Wrexham Close, Biddulph, Stoke-on-Trent ST8 6RZ* Tel (01782) 513247 or 513891 E-mail martin@cannam.fsnet.co.uk

CANNELL, Anthea Marjorie. b 45. UEA MA85. EAMTC 01. **d** 02 **p** 03. NSM Theydon Bois *Chelmsf* from 02. *118 High Street, Roydon, Harlow CM19 5EF* Tel (01279) 792543

CANNER, Canon Peter George. b 24. St Chad's Coll Dur BA49 MA55. **d** 51 **p** 52. C Stoke *Cov* 51-53; S Africa 53-63; R Piet Retief 53-56; R Eshowe 56-63; Can Eshowe 62-63; V Tynemouth Ch Ch *Newc* 63-77; V Ponteland 77-89; Hon Can Newc Cathl 80-89; rtd 89; Perm to Offic *Newc* from 89. *The Rigg, 4 Back Crofts, Rothbury, Morpeth NE65 7YB* Tel (01669) 621319

CANNING, Canon Arthur James. b 45. St Jo Coll Dur BA66 Linacre Coll Ox BA70 MA74 Lambeth STh90. Ripon Hall Ox 67. **d** 71 **p** 72. C Coleshill *Birm* 71-74; C Frome St Jo *B & W* 75-76; V Frizington and Arlecdon *Carl* 76-80; P-in-c Foleshill St Paul *Cov* 80-81; V from 81; Hon Can Cov Cathl from 00. *St Paul's Vicarage, 13 St Paul's Road, Coventry CV6 5DE* Tel (024) 7668 8283 E-mail jimcanningstpcov@aol.com

CANNING, Graham Gordon Blakeman. b 33. S'wark Ord Course 73. **d** 76 **p** 77. NSM Mill Hill Jo Keble Ch *Lon* 76-78; TV Dorchester *Ox* 78-85; V Shipton-under-Wychwood w Milton, Fifield etc 85-98; RD Chipping Norton 95-00; rtd 98; Perm to Offic *Ox* from 00. *Moredays, 36 The Slade, Oxford OX7 3SJ* Tel and fax (01608) 810421 E-mail gcanning@gcanning.u-net.com

CANNING, Peter Christopher. b 52. Birm Poly CQSW. St Jo Coll Nottm 87. **d** 89 **p** 90. C Cov St Mary 89-93; V Hartshill 93-96; rtd 96. *11 Thackeray Close, Galley Common, Nuneaton CV10 9RT* Tel (024) 7249 7639 8828

CANNON, Elizabeth Mary. b 50. EAMTC 94. **d** 97 **p** 98. NSM New Catton Ch Ch *Nor* 97-00; P-in-c Cross Roads cum Lees *Bradf* 00-06; TV Blyth Valley *St E* from 06. *The Vicarage, Beccles Road, Holton, Halesworth IP19 8NG* Tel (01986) 874548

CANNON, Mark Harrison. b 60. Keble Coll Ox BA82. Cranmer Hall Dur 83. **d** 85 **p** 86. C Skipton Ch Ch *Bradf* 85-88; Dioc Youth Officer 88-92; V Baildon 88-92; P-in-c Church Coniston *Carl* 92-00; P-in-c Torver 92-00, P-in-c Brindle *Blackb* from 00; Dioc Voc Adv 00-05. *The Rectory, Sandy Lane, Brindle, Chorley PR6 8NJ* Tel (01254) 854084 E-mail mhcannon@fsmail.net

CANNON, Tony Arthur. b 57. Oak Hill Th Coll 94. **d** 96 **p** 97. C Church Stretton *Heref* 96-00; P-in-c Kingham w Churchill,

---

Daylesford and Sarsden *Ox* 00-01; TV Chipping Norton from 01. *6 The Grange, Kingham, Chipping Norton OX7 6XY* Tel (01608) 658164 Fax 08700-940150 E-mail tonycannon@tiscali.co.uk

CANSDALE, George Graham. b 38. Mert Coll Ox BA60 MA64 DipEd61. Clifton Th Coll 62. **d** 64 **p** 65. C Heatherlands St Jo *Sarum* 64-67; BCMS Kenya 68-76; P-in-c Clapham *St Alb* 76-80; V 80-89; Asst Chapl Bedford Sch 89-97; Lic to Offic *St Alb* 93-01; Perm to Offic *Wakef* from 01; rtd 03. *7 Stubbins Close, Mytholmroyd, Hebden Bridge HX7 5HP* Tel (01422) 881693 E-mail graham.cansdale@virgin.net

CANSDALE, Michael Cranmer. b 70. Bradf Univ BA93 St Jo Coll Dur BA06. Cranmer Hall Dur 04. **d** 06 **p** 07. C Silsden *Bradf* 06-09; P-in-c Riddlesden from 09; P-in-c Morton St Luke from 09. *The Vicarage, St Mary's Road, Riddlesden, Keighley BD20 5PA* Tel (01535) 603419 Mobile 07545-566898 E-mail michael.cansdale@tesco.net

CANSDALE, Philip John. b 73. Keble Coll Ox BA95 MA99. Trin Coll Bris BA98 MA99. **d** 99 **p** 00. C Cant St Mary Bredin 99-03; C Penn Fields *Lich* 03-09; V Meole Brace from 09. *The Vicarage, Vicarage Road, Shrewsbury SY3 9EZ* Tel (01743) 231744

CANSDALE, Simon James Lee. b 68. Keble Coll Ox BA90. Wycliffe Hall Ox 93. **d** 95 **p** 96. C Bletchley *Ox* 95-98; C Cambridge H Trin *Ely* 98-01; R W Bridgford *S'well* 01-08; TR Gt Chesham *Ox* from 08. *The Rectory, Church Street, Chesham HP5 1HY* Tel and fax (01494) 783629 Mobile 07914-361911 E-mail rector@cheshamchurch.co.uk

CANT, Anthony David. b 59. Middx Univ BA04. NTMTC 01. **d** 04 **p** 05. C Walthamstow *Chelmsf* 04-07; TV from 07. *11 Sylvan Road, London E17 7QR* Tel (020) 8509 8792 Mobile 07980-291940 E-mail tonyc@walthamstowchurch.org.uk

CANT, Christopher Somerset Travers. b 51. Keble Coll Ox BA72 MA76 Ex Univ PGCE77. All Nations Chr Coll 80 Wycliffe Hall Ox 93. **d** 87 **p** 90. Pakistan 87-92; Lic to Offic *Cov* 92-93; Warden St Clem Family Cen Ox 93-95; C Gt Ilford St Andr *Chelmsf* 95-98; V Hainault from 98. *St Paul's Vicarage, 143 Arrowsmith Road, Chigwell IG7 4NZ* Tel (020) 8500 3366 E-mail chriscant@tiscali.co.uk

CANT, David Edward. b 49. Sheff Univ LLB70. Oak Hill Th Coll 87. **d** 89 **p** 90. C Newburn *Newc* 89-92; C N Shields 92-93; TV 93-98; Chapl Tynemouth Coll 94-98; P-in-c Wylam *Newc* from 98; Dioc Ecum Officer from 08. *The Vicarage, Church Road, Wylam NE41 8AT* Tel (01661) 853254 E-mail david@stoswin.totalserve.co.uk

CANT, Joseph Clifford. b 72. UEA BA94 MA98 DipSW98 Cam Univ BTh08. Westcott Ho Cam 06. **d** 08 **p** 09. C Hilton w Marston-on-Dove *Derby* from 08. *2A Eaton Close, Hatton, Derby DE65 5ED* Tel (01283) 815596 Mobile 07847-125341 E-mail cant740@btinternet.com

CANTACUZENE, Mrs Mary. b 52. **d** 05 **p** 06. NSM Bures w Assington and Lt Cornard *St E* from 05. *Peartree Barn, Peartree Hill, Mount Bures, Bures CO8 5BA* Tel (01787) 227616 Fax 227220 Mobile 07932-033019 E-mail mary@cantacuzene.co.uk

CANTERBURY, Archbishop of. *See* WILLIAMS, The Most Revd and Rt Hon Rowan Douglas

CANTERBURY, Archdeacon of. *See* WATSON, The Ven Sheila Anne

CANTERBURY, Dean of. *See* WILLIS, The Very Revd Robert Andrew

CANTI, Mrs Christine. b 24. St Alb Minl Tr Scheme 82. **dss** 85 **d** 87 **p** 94. Radlett *St Alb* 85-86; Hon C Pitminster w Corfe *B & W* 87-92; Perm to Offic from 90. *Tresawsen, Mill Lane, Corfe, Taunton TA3 7AH* Tel (01823) 421623

CANTRELL, David Grindon. b 59. Bris Univ BSc80 Nottm Univ PhD83 Pemb Coll Cam BA88. Ridley Hall Cam 86. **d** 89 **p** 90. C Low Harrogate St Mary *Ripon* 89-90; C Horsforth 90-94; Chapl Nottm Trent Univ 94-97; V Porchester 97-00; Chapl York Univ 00-04; Perm to Offic from 04. *52 Tranby Avenue, York YO10 3NJ* Tel (01904) 427146 E-mail david.cantrell@ukgateway.net

CANTRILL, Mark James. b 67. Lanc Univ BEd89. St Jo Coll Nottm 00. **d** 02 **p** 03. C Warsop *S'well* 02-07; TV Retford from 07. *Clarborough Vicarage, Church Lane, Clarborough, Retford DN22 9NA* Tel (01777) 711530 Mobile 07985-160694 E-mail revmark.cantrill@btinternet.com

CANTY, Mrs Katherine Anne. b 52. York Univ BA74 Coll of Ripon & York St Jo PGCE75. NOC 05. **d** 07 **p** 08. Asst Chapl HM Pris Altcourse 03-07; Chapl from 07; NSM Gateacre *Liv* from 07. *HM Prison Altcourse, Higher Lane, Liverpool L9 7LH* Tel 0151-522 2000 ext 2395

CAPE TOWN, Dean of. *See* SMITH, The Very Revd Rowan Quentin

CAPE TOWN, Archbishop of. *See* NDUNGANE, The Most Revd Winston Hugh Njongonkulu

CAPEL, Luke Thomas. *See* IRVINE-CAPEL, Luke Thomas

CAPEL-EDWARDS, Maureen. b 36. Southn Univ BSc60 Reading Univ PhD69. St Alb Minl Tr Scheme 84. **d** 87 **p** 94. NSM Ware St Mary *St Alb* 87-90; Chapl Hertf Regional Coll of FE 87-00; NSM Hertford All SS *St Alb* 90-94; NSM Aspenden and Layston w Buntingford 94-95; NSM Aspenden, Buntingford and Westmill 95-00; P-in-c Ardeley and Cottered w Broadfield and Throcking 00-05; rtd 05; Perm to Offic *Portsm* from 05. *Capeland, High Street, Soberton, Southampton SO32 3PN* Tel (01489) 878192 E-mail capeland@waitrose.com

CAPELIN-JONES, Kevin Stuart. b 73. Huddersfield Univ BMus96. Oak Hill Th Coll BA02. **d** 02 **p** 03. C Croglin and Holme Eden and Wetheral w Warwick *Carl* 02-06; Chapl RAF from 06. *Chaplaincy Services, Valiant Block, HQ Air Command, RAF High Wycombe HP14 4UE* Tel (01494) 496800 Fax 496343 E-mail rev.kev@virgin.net

CAPERON, John Philip. b 44. Bris Univ BA66 Open Univ MPhil80 Ox Univ MSc83 Kent Univ MA99. Ox NSM Course 80. **d** 83 **p** 84. NSM Hook Norton w Gt Rollright, Swerford etc *Ox* 83-86; NSM Knaresborough *Ripon* 86-92; Dep Hd St Aid Sch Harrogate 86-92; Hd and Chapl Bennett Memorial Dioc Sch Tunbridge Wells 92-04; rtd 04; Perm to Offic *Chich* 98-03; Hon C Mayfield from 03; Dir Bloxham Project from 06. *Sarum, 5 Twyfords, Beacon Road, Crowborough TN6 1YE* Tel (01892) 667207 E-mail johncaperon@btinternet.com

CAPES, Dennis Robert. b 34. Handsworth Coll Birm 55 Linc Th Coll 65. **d** 64 **p** 65. In Methodist Ch (Sarawak) 59-63; C Lt Coates *Linc* 64-66; R Miri Malaysia 66-69; V Gosberton Clough *Linc* 69-71; V Kirton in Holland 71-80; Area Sec USPG *Cov, Heref* and *Worc* 80-87; Chapl Copenhagen w Aarhus *Eur* 87-93; TV Liv Our Lady and St Nic w St Anne 93-99; rtd 99. *35 Hardwick Avenue, Newark NG24 4AW* Tel (01636) 672874

CAPIE, Fergus Bernard. b 47. Auckland Univ BA68 MA71. Wycliffe Hall Ox BA77. **d** 77 **p** 78. C Ox St Mich w St Martin and All SS 77-80; Chapl Summer Fields Sch Ox 80-91; Hon C Wolvercote w Summertown *Ox* 87-91; Perm to Offic *St E* 91; TV E Ham w Upton Park St Alb *Chelmsf* 91-95; P-in-c Brondesbury St Anne w Kilburn H Trin *Lon* 95-01; V from 01; Chapl NW Lon Coll from 95. *125 Salusbury Road, London NW6 6RG* Tel (020) 7625 7470, 7372 6864 or 7604 3053 Fax 7604 3052 E-mail fergus.capie@london.anglican.org

CAPITANCHIK, Sophie Rebecca. *See* JELLEY, Mrs Sophie Rebecca

CAPLE, Stephen Malcolm. b 55. Chich Th Coll 86. **d** 88 **p** 89. C Newington St Mary *S'wark* 88-92; V Eltham St Sav 92-97; V Salfords 97-07; P-in-c S Kensington St Aug *Lon* from 07; Dir Evang Kensington Area from 07. *St Augustine's Clergy Flat, 117A Queens Gate, London SW7 5LP* Tel (020) 7584 4496 E-mail stephencaple@blueyonder.co.uk

CAPON, Canon Anthony Charles. b 26. Trin Coll Cam BA51 MA55. Wycliffe Coll Toronto BD65 DD82 Oak Hill Th Coll 51. **d** 53 **p** 54. C Portman Square St Paul *Lon* 53-56; Canada from 56; Hon Can Montreal from 78; Prin Montreal Dioc Th Coll 78-91; rtd 91. *5 Landeau Crescent, Kingston ON K7K 6X9, Canada* Tel (001) (613) 545 9781 E-mail acapon@cgocable.net

CAPON, Gerwyn Huw. b 65. Liv Jo Moores Univ BSc92. St Steph Ho Ox 01. **d** 03 **p** 04. C W Derby St Mary *Liv* 03-07; Chapl to Abp Wales and Dir of Ords *Llan* 07-09; P-in-c Bolton-le-Sands *Blackb* from 09. *The Vicarage, 117 Main Road, Bolton-le-Sands, Carnforth LA5 8DX*

CAPPER, Alan. *See* CAPPER, William Alan

CAPPER, Mrs Elizabeth Margaret. b 31. St Chris Coll Blackheath 52. **dss** 79 **d** 87 **p** 94. The Dorothy Kerin Trust Burrswood 79; Whitstable *Cant* 80-96; Hon Par Dn 87-94; Hon C 94-96; rtd 91. *11 North Road, Loughor, Swansea SA4 6QE* Tel (01792) 892834

CAPPER, Canon Richard. b 49. Leeds Univ BSc70 Fitzw Coll Cam BA72 MA76. Westcott Ho Cam 70. **d** 73 **p** 74. C Wavertree H Trin *Liv* 73-76; P-in-c Ince St Mary 76-79; V 79-83; V Gt Crosby St Faith 83-97; AD Bootle 89-97; Can Res Wakef Cathl 97-05; Can Res Nor Cathl from 05; P-in-c Nor St Mary in the Marsh from 05. *52 The Close, Norwich NR1 4EG* Tel (01603) 665210

CAPPER, Robert Melville. b 52. Chu Coll Cam BA74 MA80. Wycliffe Hall Ox 74. **d** 77 **p** 78. C Maindee Newport *Mon* 77-81; TV Aberystwyth *St D* 81-87; Chapl Univ of Wales (Abth) 81-87; V Malpas *Mon* 87-00; V Gabalfa *Llan* from 00; P-in-c Tremorfa St Phil CD from 05. *St Mark's Vicarage, 208 North Road, Gabalfa, Cardiff CF14 3BL* Tel (029) 2061 3286

CAPPER, William Alan. QUB BTh. **d** 88 **p** 89. C Dundonald *D & D* 88-91; C Lisburn Ch Ch *Conn* 91-94; I Tamlaght O'Crilly Upper w Lower *D & R* 94-09; I Lack *Clogh* 03-09; I Lisnaskea from 09. *3 Castlebalfour Road, Lisnaskea, Enniskillen BT92 0LT* Tel (028) 6772 2413 *or* 6772 3977 E-mail lisnaskea@clogher.anglican.org

CAPPLEMAN, Graham Robert (Sam). b 56. Chelsea Coll Lon BSc79 Sheff Univ PhD83. SAOMC 94. **d** 97 **p** 98. NSM Bedf St Mark *St Alb* from 97. *107 Dover Crescent, Bedford MK41 8QR* Tel (01234) 266952 Fax 402624 Mobile 07836-784051 E-mail samc@tesco.net *or* nsm@thisischurch.com

CAPPLEMAN, Mrs Jennifer Margaret. b 53. Liv Univ CertEd74. SAOMC 97. **d** 00 **p** 01. NSM Bedford St Pet w St Cuth *St Alb* 00-03; C Goldington 03-07; TV Ouzel Valley from

07. *The Vicarage, 2 Reach Lane, Heath and Reach, Leighton Buzzard LU7 0AL* Tel (01525) 237633 Mobile 07714-701008 E-mail jennie.cappleman@ntlworld.com

CAPRIELLO (née BUR), Patricia Margaret. b 59. SEITE. **d** 99 **p** 01. C Clapham Team *S'wark* 99-01; C Nunhead St Antony w St Silas 01-03; P-in-c N Woolwich w Silvertown *Chelmsf* from 03; Ind Chapl from 04. *St John's Vicarage, Manwood Street, London E16 2JY* Tel (020) 7476 2388 E-mail stjohnse16@hotmail.co.uk

CAPRON, Canon David Cooper. b 45. Open Univ BA80. Sarum & Wells Th Coll 71. **d** 75 **p** 76. C Cov St Mary 75-79; V Shottery St Andr 79-86; TV Stratford-on-Avon w Bishopton 79-86; V Shottery St Andr 86; V Newton Aycliffe *Dur* 86-89; TR 89-90; P-in-c Alcester and Arrow w Oversley and Weethley *Cov* 90-95; R from 95; P-in-c Kinwarton w Gt Alne and Haselor from 06; P-in-c Coughton from 06; Hon Can Cov Cathl from 07; Chapl Warks Fire and Rescue Service from 93. *St Nicholas' Rectory, Old Rectory Garden, Alcester B49 5DB* Tel and fax (01789) 764261 Mobile 07780-707521 E-mail caprons@ntlworld.com

CAPRON, Ronald Beresford. b 35. Clifton Th Coll. **d** 62 **p** 63. Canada 62-65; C Evington *Leic* 65-67; R Gaddesby w S Croxton 67-71; R Beeby 67-71; Chapl RAF 71-83; rtd 95. *107 Coverside Road, Great Glen, Leicester LE8 9EB* Tel 0116-259 2809

CAPSTICK, John Nowell. b 30. AKC54. **d** 55 **p** 56. C Skipton Ch Ch *Bradf* 55-57; C Buxton *Derby* 57-61; V Codnor and Loscoe 61-63; C-in-c Rawthorpe CD *Wakef* 63-64; V Rawthorpe 64-70; V Netherthong 70-89; TV Upper Holme Valley 89-95; rtd 95; Perm to Offic *Wakef* from 96. *8 Town End Avenue, Holmfirth HD9 1QW* Tel (01484) 688708

CAPSTICK, William Richard Dacre. b 32. Pemb Coll Ox. Chich Th Coll 61. **d** 64 **p** 65. C Hunslet St Mary and Stourton St Andr *Ripon* 64-67; C Knaresborough H Trin 67-71; V Stratfield Mortimer *Ox* 71-76; P-in-c St Marylebone Ch Ch w St Paul *Lon* 76-78; TV St Marylebone Ch Ch 78-79; TR Newbury *Ox* 79-89; TV Brighton St Pet and St Nic w Chpl Royal *Chich* 89-97; rtd 97. *28 Bloomsbury Street, Brighton BN2 1HQ* Tel (01273) 681171

CARBERRY, Derek William. b 65. Leeds Univ BA03 SEN88. Coll of Resurr Mirfield 01. **d** 03 **p** 04. C Tynemouth Cullercoats St Paul *Newc* 03-08; P-in-c Horton from 08. *St Benedict's Vicarage, Brierley Road, Blyth NE24 5AU* Tel (01670) 367035 E-mail d_carberry@hotmail.com

CARBERRY, Leon Carter. b 54. Penn State Univ BSc76. St Steph Ho Ox 81. **d** 84 **p** 85. C Peterlee *Dur* 84-87; C Newton Aycliffe 87-89; V Choral York Minster 89-94; Chapl St Pet Sch York 94-95; V Fylingdales and Hawsker cum Stainsacre *York* 95-01; Chapl Burrswood Chr Cen *Roch* 01-03; V Beckenham St Jas from 03. *The Vicarage, 35 St James' Avenue, Beckenham BR3 4HF* Tel and fax (020) 8650 0420 E-mail leoncarberry@googlemail.com

CARBY, Stuart Graeme. b 51. CBiol77 MIBiol77 LRSC78 Man Univ BSc73 Leeds Univ PGCE74 Open Univ MA96. St Jo Coll Nottm 92. **d** 92 **p** 93. C Magor w Redwick and Undy *Mon* 92-96; TV Cyncoed from 96. *100 Hillrise, Llanederyn, Cardiff CF23 6UL* Tel (029) 2073 3915

CARD, Terence Leslie. b 37. K Coll Lon BD68 AKC68 Heythrop Coll Lon MTh84. **d** 69 **p** 70. C Thundersley *Chelmsf* 69-72; Lic to Offic *Bradf* 72-75; V Chingford St Anne *Chelmsf* 75-81; RD Waltham Forest 78-81; R Springfield All SS 81-83; C Becontree St Jo 85-87; rtd 87; Perm to Offic *Ely* 96-00. *11 Harvey Goodwin Gardens, Cambridge CB4 3EZ* Tel (01223) 367715

CARD, Thomas Ian. b 36. RD76. Master Mariner 61. Portsm Dioc Tr Course 88. **d** 89. NSM Binstead *Portsm* 89-95; Miss to Seafarers from 89; NSM Swanmore St Mich w Havenstreet *Portsm* 89-92; NSM Havenstreet St Pet 92-95; NSM Ryde All SS 95-06; Perm to Offic from 06. *Dolphins, 49 Mayfield Road, Ryde PO33 3PR* Tel (01983) 564749 E-mail deeptank@aol.com

CARD-REYNOLDS, Charles Leonard. b 67. Lon Univ BD92 Hughes Hall Cam BA94 MA98. St Steph Ho Ox 96. **d** 98 **p** 99. C Reading H Trin *Ox* 98-06; C Reading St Mark 98-06; V Stamford Hill St Bart *Lon* from 06. *St Bartholomew's Vicarage, 31 Craven Park Road, London N15 6AA* Tel (020) 8800 1554

CARDALE, Charles Anthony. b 21. St D Coll Lamp BA47 Lich Th Coll 55. **d** 56 **p** 57. C Honicknowle CD *Ex* 56-58; C Bideford 58-60; R Wembworthy w Eggesford 60-69; V Brushford 63-69; V Staverton w Landscove 69-87; R Broadhempston, Woodland, Staverton etc 88-95; Perm to Offic 89-06; rtd 90. *1 Barnetts Well, Draycott, Cheddar BS27 3TF*

CARDALE, Edward Charles. b 50. CCC Ox BA72 MA73. Cuddesdon Coll 72 Union Th Sem (NY) STM74. **d** 74 **p** 75. C E Dulwich St Jo *S'wark* 74-77; Asst P Bainbridge Is USA 77-80; V Ponders End St Matt *Lon* 80-84; V Lytchett Minster *Sarum* 84-98; Dir Past Studies Coll of the Resurr Mirfield 98-02; P-in-c Lemsford *St Alb* 02-05; TV Bp's Hatfield, Lemsford and N Mymms from 05; Tutor SAOMC 02-05; Dir Past Studies ERMC from 05. *7 High Oaks Road, Welwyn Garden City AL8 7BJ* Tel (01707) 327621 E-mail edward.cardale@btopenworld.com

CARDELL-OLIVER, John Anthony. b 43. Em Coll Cam BA67 MA72 Univ of W Aus BEd75 MEd85. Westcott Ho Cam 86. **d** 86 **p** 88. C Subiaco w Leederville Australia 86-88; Perm to Offic

Ely 88-89; C Stansted Mountfitchet *Chelmsf* 89-92; R Langham w Boxted 92-02; rtd 02. *40 Halesworth Road, Jolimont, Perth WA 6014, Australia* Tel and fax (0061) (8) 9383 7381
E-mail jco@graduate.uwa.edu.au

CARDEN, Edwin William. b 54. Cranmer Hall *Dur* 85. **d** 87 **p** 88. C Thundersley *Chelmsf* 87-91; CUF 91-93; NSM Poplar *Lon* 91-93; Chapl Pathfinder Mental Health Services NHS Trust 93-99; Chapl SW Lon and St George's Mental Health NHS Trust 99-00; Selection Sec Min Division 00-05; NSM Maldon St Mary w Mundon *Chelmsf* 00-02; Dioc Dep Chief Exec 03-08; Perm to Offic from 08; Chief Exec WHCM from 08. *21 Plume Avenue, Maldon CM9 6LB* Tel (01621) 854908
E-mail mudmonkeys4@btinternet.com

CARDEN, John Brumfitt. b 24. Lon Coll of Div 48. **d** 52 **p** 53. Pakistan 52-55, 57-60 and 65-69; C Leeds Halton St Wilfrid *Ripon* 56-57; Lit Sec CMS 60-65; Asia Sec CMS 70-76; Hon C Croydon St Sav *Cant* 75-76; C-in-c Bath St Steph *B & W* 76-82; V 82-84; CMS 84-89; Jerusalem 84-87; Exec Asst WCC Geneva 87-89; rtd 89; Miss Partner CMS from 89; Perm to Offic *York* from 89. *81 The Village, Haxby, York YO32 2JE* Tel (01904) 750035

CARDIGAN, Archdeacon of. *See* STRANGE, The Ven William Anthony

CARDINAL, Ian Ralph. b 57. Qu Coll Birm 81. **d** 84 **p** 85. C Whitkirk *Ripon* 84-87; C Knaresborough 87-89; R Ancaster Wilsford Gp *Linc* 89-94; P-in-c Wigginton *Lich* 94-07; Warden of Readers 96-03; P-in-c Stone St Mich and St Wulfad w Aston St Sav 07-08; R from 08. *11 Farrier Close, Stone ST15 8XP* Tel (01785) 812747 Mobile 07778-055993
E-mail ian.cardinal@ukonline.co.uk

CARDWELL, Edward Anthony Colin. b 42. Trin Coll Cam BA63 MA68. St Jo Coll Nottm 73. **d** 75 **p** 76. C Stapenhill w Cauldwell *Derby* 75-78; C Bramcote *S'well* 78-81; V S'well H Trin 81-92; R Eastwood 92-07; rtd 07. *49 Bramcote Road, Beeston, Nottingham NG9 1DW* Tel 0115-925 5866

CARDWELL, Joseph Robin. b 47. Qu Coll Cam BA68 MA77. Trin Coll Bris 73. **d** 76 **p** 77. C Bromley Ch Ch *Roch* 76-79; C Shirley *Win* 79-82; V Somborne w Ashley 82-90; V Derry Hill *Sarum* 90-94; V Derry Hill w Bremhill and Foxham 94-00; Community Affairs Chapl 90-94; V Lyddington and Wanborough and Bishopstone etc *Bris* from 00. *The Vicarage, 19 Church Road, Wanborough, Swindon SN4 0BZ* Tel (01793) 790242 E-mail robin@cardwell99.fsnet.co.uk

CARE, Canon Charles Richard. b 21. Univ of Wales (Lamp) BA42. St Mich Coll Llan 42. **d** 44 **p** 45. C Grangetown *Llan* 44-57; R St Brides Minor 57-88; RD Bridgend 75-88; Can Llan Cathl 83-88; Prec 87-88; rtd 88; Perm to Offic *Llan* from 88. *31 Laburnum Drive, Porthcawl CF36 5UA* Tel (01656) 785446

CAREW, Bryan Andrew. b 38. ACIB63. St D Coll Lamp. **d** 67 **p** 68. C Pembroke Dock *St D* 67-70; CF 70-74; P-in-c Gt and Lt Henny w Middleton *Chelmsf* 74-76; P-in-c Wickham St Paul w Twinstead 75-76; R Gt and Lt Henny w Middleton, Wickham St Paul etc 76-99; P-in-c Alphamstone w Lamarsh 99; V Alphamstone w Gt and Lt Henny, Lamarsh etc 99-03; rtd 03; Perm to Offic *Chelmsf* from 03. *The Hinckford Margin, 4 Raydon Way, Great Cornard, Sudbury CO10 0LE*

CAREW, Richard Clayton. b 72. York Univ BA94 PGCE96 St Jo Coll Dur BA04. Cranmer Hall Dur 02. **d** 05 **p** 06. C Beverley Minster from 05. *23 Outer Trinities, Beverley HU17 0HN* Tel (01482) 888249

CAREY, Alan Lawrence. b 29. K Coll Lon AKC53. **d** 54 **p** 55. C Radford *Cov* 54-57; C Burnham *Ox* 57-65; C-in-c Cippenham CD 65-77; rtd 94. *12 Ormsby Street, Reading RG1 7YR* Tel 0118-961 2309

CAREY, Charles John. b 29. K Coll Lon BD53 AKC53. St Aug Coll Cant 71. **d** 72 **p** 73. C Spring Park *Cant* 72-74; C Ifield *Chich* 74-78; C Burgess Hill St Jo 78-80; Chapl Rush Green Hosp Romford 80-94; Chapl Oldchurch Hosp Romford 80-94; rtd 94. *Address withheld by request*

CAREY, Christopher Lawrence John. b 38. St Andr Univ BSc61 Lon Univ BD64. Clifton Th Coll 61. **d** 64 **p** 65. C Battersea Park St Sav *S'wark* 64-67; CMS Kenya 68-79; Overseas Regional Sec for E and Cen Africa CMS 79-98; NSM Chislehurst Ch Ch *Roch* 79-98; R Stickney Gp *Linc* 99-04; RD Bolingbroke 02-03; rtd 04; Perm to Offic *Mon* from 04. *83 Wentwood View, Caldicot NP26 4QH* Tel (01291) 425010 E-mail crcandkili@tiscali.co.uk

CAREY, Donald Leslie. b 50. ACII78. CBDTI 01. **d** 04 **p** 05. OLM Ashton-on-Ribble St Mich w Preston St Mark *Blackb* 04-06; OLM W Preston 06-07; NSM 07-08; P-in-c Fairhaven from 08. *Fairhaven Vicarage, 83 Clifton Drive, Lytham St Annes FY8 1BZ* Tel (01253) 734562
E-mail fr.donaldcarey@tiscali.co.uk

CAREY, Mark Jonathan. b 65. St Jo Coll Nottm BTh94. **d** 94 **p** 95. C S Ossett *Wakef* 94-97; C Chapeltown *Sheff* 97-99; V Grenoside 99-07; P-in-c Low Harrogate St Mary *Ripon* from 07. *St Mary's Vicarage, 22 Harlow Oval, Harrogate HG2 0DS* Tel (01423) 701848 E-mail mpjcarey@aol.com
or mark@stmarysharrogate.org

CAREY, Canon Ronald Clive Adrian. b 21. K Coll Cam BA46 MA48. Chich Th Coll 47. **d** 48 **p** 49. C Harborne St Pet *Birm* 48-50; Bp's Dom Chapl *Chich* 50-52; C Keighley *Bradf* 52-55; V Illingworth *Wakef* 55-59; Asst in Relig Broadcasting BBC 59-68; Perm to Offic *S'wark* 59-68; V Claygate *Guildf* 68-78; RD Emly 72-77; Hon Can Guildf Cathl 78-86; R Guildf H Trin w St Mary 78-86; RD Guildf 84-86; rtd 86; Perm to Offic *Roch* 86-04 and *Linc* from 04. *23 Moores Court, Jermyn Street, Sleaford NG34 7UL* Tel (01529) 303698

CAREY, Mrs Wendy Marion. b 45. Bris Univ BA66 Lon Inst of Educn CertEd67. WMMTC 90. **d** 93 **p** 94. NSM Milton Keynes *Ox* 93-96; Sub Chapl HM Pris Woodhill 93-96; Chapl HM Pris Bullingdon 96-00; Ecum Tr Officer HM Pris Service Chapl 00-06; rtd 06; Perm to Offic *Ox* from 00. *46 Parklands, Great Linford, Milton Keynes MK14 5DZ* Tel (01908) 605997

✠**CAREY OF CLIFTON, The Rt Revd and Rt Hon Lord (George Leonard).** b 35. PC91. Lon Univ BD62 MTh65 PhD71 Dur Univ Hon DD93 Open Univ Hon DD95 FRSA91 FKC93. ALCD61. **d** 62 **p** 63 **c** 87. C Islington St Mary *Lon* 62-66; Lect Oak Hill Th Coll 66-70; Lect St Jo Coll Nottm 70-75; V Dur St Nic 75-82; Chapl HM Rem Cen Low Newton 77-81; Prin Trin Coll Bris 82-87; Hon Can Bris Cathl 84-87; Bp B & W 87-91; Abp Cant 91-02; rtd 02. *Rosemount, Garden Close Lane, Newbury RG14 6PR* E-mail carey.george01@googlemail.com

CARGILL THOMPSON, Edmund Alwyn James. b 72. St Jo Coll Ox BA94. Cranmer Hall Dur 98. **d** 00 **p** 01. C St Jo on Bethnal Green *Lon* 00-03; V Barkingside H Trin *Chelmsf* from 03. *Barkingside Vicarage, 36 Mossford Green, Ilford IG6 2BJ* Tel (020) 8550 2669 E-mail father.edmund@ntlworld.com

CARHART, John Richards. b 29. Bris Univ BA50 Salford Univ MSc77 Liv Univ MTh99 FRSA. St Deiniol's Hawarden 63. **d** 65 **p** 66. C Ches St Oswald w Lt St Jo 65-72; Lect Ches Coll of HE 63-72; Prin Lect from 72; Dean Academic Studies 88-94; C Ches 72; Lic to Offic 73-85; Hon C Ches St Mary 85-00; rtd 00; Perm to Offic Ches from 00. *29 Abbot's Grange, Chester CH2 1AJ* Tel (01244) 380923 E-mail jcarhart@nepc.co.uk

CARLESS, Canon Frank. b 22. Lon Univ BD56. St Aid Birkenhead 53. **d** 56 **p** 57. C Normanton *Wakef* 56-59; V Rashcliffe 59-64; V Warley 64-87; RD Halifax 82-86; Hon Can Wakef Cathl 86-87; rtd 87; Perm to Offic *Wakef* from 87. *8 Joseph Crossley Almshouses, Arden Road, Halifax HX1 3AA* Tel (01422) 348379

CARLILL, Adam Jonathan. b 66. Keble Coll Ox BA88. Linc Th Coll 88. **d** 90 **p** 91. C Romford St Edw *Chelmsf* 90-94; C Uckfield *Chich* 94-98; V Tilehurst St Geo *Ox* from 98; P-in-c Tilehurst St Mary from 02. *St George's Vicarage, 98 Grovelands Road, Reading RG3 2PD* Tel 0118-958 8354

CARLILL, Richard Edward. b 38. Westcott Ho Cam 77. **d** 79 **p** 80. C Prittlewell *Chelmsf* 79-83; TV Saffron Walden w Wendens Ambo and Littlebury 83-89; V Langtoft w Foxholes, Butterwick, Cottam etc *York* 89-94; V Gt and Lt Driffield 94-03; RD Harthill 99-02; rtd 03; Perm to Offic *Newc* from 03. *31 Riverdene, Tweedmouth, Berwick-upon-Tweed TD15 2JD* Tel (01289) 303701

CARLIN, Philip Charles. b 49. St Cath Coll Cam MA71 Didsbury Coll of Educn PGCE72. **d** 09. OLM Hurst *Man* from 09. *1 Sunderland Avenue, Ashton-under-Lyne OL6 8PF* Tel 0161-330 5530 Mobile 07708-398699
E-mail carlin@phonecoop.coop

CARLIN, William Patrick Bruce. b 53. St Steph Ho Ox 75. **d** 78 **p** 79. C Penistone *Wakef* 78-81; C Barnsley St Mary 81-83; V Stockton St Chad *Dur* 83-93; V Hedworth 93-01; TR Kippax w Allerton Bywater *Ripon* from 01. *The Rectory, Church Lane, Kippax, Leeds LS25 7HF* Tel 0113-286 2710 Fax 286 7339
E-mail brucecarlin@freeuk.com
or rector@stmarykippax.org.uk

CARLING, Mrs Bronwen Noël. b 43. SRN65 SCM73. Linc Th Coll 89. **d** 91 **p** 94. C Blakeney w Cley, Wiveton, Glandford etc *Nor* 91-94; C Trunch 94-96; TV 96-01; rtd 01; Perm to Offic *Nor* 01-04. *Meadowbank, Rathdermot, Bansha, Co Tipperary, Republic of Ireland* Tel (00353) (62) 54891
E-mail bncarling@sagainternet.co.uk

CARLISLE, Matthew David. b 74. Man Univ BA96. Westcott Ho Cam 99. **d** 02 **p** 03. C E Crompton *Man* 02-06; TV Heywood from 06. *St John's Vicarage, Manchester Road, Heywood OL10 2EQ* Tel (01706) 369324 Mobile 07870-760746
E-mail matthew.carlisle@ntlworld.com

CARLISLE, Archdeacon of. *See* ROBERTS, The Ven Kevin Thomas

CARLISLE, Bishop of. *See* NEWCOME, The Rt Revd James William Scobie

CARLISLE, Dean of. *See* BOYLING, The Very Revd Mark Christopher

CARLSON, Blair Truett. b 52. Wheaton Coll Illinois BA74. Cranmer Hall Dur 00. **d** 02 **p** 03. C Hailsham *Chich* 02-05; USA from 05. *4619 Arden Avenue, Edina MN 55424, USA* Tel (001) (952) 924 9062 E-mail btcarlson@gmail.com

CARLSSON, Miss Siw Ebba Christina. b 43. **d** 92 **p** 94. Par Dn Barnes St Mary *S'wark* 92-93; C Mitcham SS Pet and Paul

93-98; Asst Chapl SW Lon and St George's Mental Health NHS Trust 99-00; Chapl Ipswich Hosp NHS Trust 00-08; rtd 08; Perm to Offic *St E* from 08. *60 Bury Hill, Melton, Woodbridge IP12 1JD* Tel (01394) 384281

CARLTON, Preb Roger John. b 51. **d** 80 **p** 81. NSM Downend *Bris* 80-83; NSM Heavitree w Ex St Paul 83-87; Chapl Ex Sch and St Marg Sch 83-87; TV Bickleigh (Plymouth) *Ex* 87-91; TR 91-93; TR Bickleigh and Shaugh Prior from 94; RD Ivybridge 93-98; Preb Ex Cathl from 06. *The Vicarage, 2 Blackeven Close, Roborough, Plymouth PL6 7AX* Tel (01752) 702119 Fax 768882 E-mail roger.carlton@btinternet.com

CARLYON, Miss Catherine Rachel. b 67. RN89. Ripon Coll Cuddesdon BTh06. **d** 02 **p** 03. C Launceston *Truro* 02-06; C Crediton, Shobrooke and Sandford etc *Ex* from 06; Chapl w Deaf People from 06. *12 Linhay Park, Sandford, Crediton EX17 4LL* Tel (01363) 772163 E-mail catherinecarlyon@btopenworld.com

CARLYON (née ENGLAND), Mrs Jessie Marguerite Taric. b 44. Westf Coll Lon K Coll Lon PGCE67. WMMTC 92. **d** 95 **p** 97. C Pontypool *Mon* 95-97; TV Bedwellty w New Tredegar 05-07; rtd 07. *Address temp unknown*

CARMAN, Jill Youde. b 37. Cartrefle Coll of Educn CertEd69 Liv Univ DipEd86. SAOMC 97. **d** 99 **p** 00. NSM Markyate Street *St Alb* 99-02; NSM Quinton *Glouc* 02-05; NSM Quinton and Welford w Weston 05-06; NSM Bourton-on-the-Water w Clapton etc from 06. *6 De Havilland Road, Upper Rissington, Cheltenham GL54 2NZ* Tel (01451) 824389 E-mail jill.carman@virgin.net

CARMAN, Philip Gordon. b 80. York St Jo Coll BA01 St Jo Coll Dur BA07. Cranmer Hall Dur 04. **d** 07 **p** 08. C Acomb St Steph *York* from 07. *36 Fellbrook Avenue, York YO26 5PS* Tel (01904) 793240 E-mail philcarman3@gmail.com

CARMARTHEN, Archdeacon of. *See* EVANS, The Ven Alun Wyn

CARMICHAEL, Elizabeth Dorothea Harriet. b 46. MBE95. LMH Ox MA73 BM73 BCh73 Worc Coll Ox BA83 Ox Univ DPhil91. **d** 91 **p** 92. S Africa 91-96; Chapl and Tutor St Jo Coll Ox from 96. *St John's College, Oxford OX1 3JP* Tel (01865) 277300 Fax 277435 E-mail liz.carmichael@sjc.ox.ac.uk

CARMICHAEL, Peter Iain. b 28. Chich Th Coll 75. **d** 75 **p** 76. C Rye w Rye Harbour and Playden *Chich* 75-79; C Rye, Rye Harbour and Playden and Iden 79-80; R Earnley and E Wittering 80-94; rtd 94; Perm to Offic *Chich* from 94. *20 East Street, Selsey, Chichester PO20 0BJ* Tel (01243) 606197

CARMODY, Canon Dermot Patrick Roy. b 41. CITC 77. **d** 77 **p** 78. C Dublin Zion Ch *D & G* 77-79; I Dunganstown w Redcross 79-84; TV Dublin Ch Ch Cathl Gp 84-93; Can Ch Ch Cathl Dublin 84-92; Preb Ch Ch Cathl Dublin 92-93; I Mullingar, Portnashangan, Moyliscar, Kilbixy etc *M & K* 93-08; Dir of Ords (Meath) 97-08; Can Meath 98-08; Can Kildare Cathl 98-08; Treas 00-08; P-in-c Rathmolyon w Castlerickard, Rathcore and Agher 00-08; rtd 08. *15 Gleann Alain, Collinstown, Mullingar, Co Westmeath, Republic of Ireland* Tel and fax (00353) (44) 966 6232 Mobile 86-829 0183 E-mail patkcarmody@gmail.com

CARMYLLIE, Mrs Kathryn Ruth. b 61. Cov Poly BA84 CQSW84 Univ Coll Ches BTh04. NOC 01. **d** 04 **p** 05. C Leigh St Mary *Man* 04-07; TV Worsley from 07. *St Stephen's Vicarage, 7 Holbeck, Astley, Tyldesley, Manchester M29 7DU* Tel (01942) 883313

CARMYLLIE, Robert Jonathan. b 63. Cov Poly BSc85. St Jo Coll Dur 85. **d** 88 **p** 89. C Horwich *Man* 88-92; P-in-c Edgeside 92-99; P-in-c Astley 99-06; TR Astley, Tyldesley and Mosley Common from 06. *St Stephen's Vicarage, 7 Holbeck, Astley, Tyldesley, Manchester M29 7DU* Tel (01942) 883313

CARNALL, Mrs Nicola Jane. b 66. St Jo Coll Nottm 99. **d** 01 **p** 02. C Edwinstowe *S'well* 01-05; P-in-c Sowerby *York* from 05; P-in-c Sessay from 05. *The Vicarage, 5 The Close, Sowerby, Thirsk YO7 1JA* Tel (01845) 523546 E-mail njcarnall@aol.com

CARNE, Canon Brian George. b 29. Bris Univ BCom50. Qu Coll Birm 53. **d** 55 **p** 56. C Swindon St Aug *Bris* 55-58; C Bris St Andr w St Bart 58-60; R Lydiard Millicent w Lydiard Tregoz 60-68; V Bris St Andr Hartcliffe 68-74; V Almondsbury 74-91; RD Westbury and Severnside 80-86; Hon Can Bris Cathl 82-91; P-in-c Littleton on Severn w Elberton 83-91; P-in-c Olveston 83-91; rtd 91; Perm to Offic *Bris* from 92; *Glouc* 92-98 and from 01. *Whitehouse Farm, English Bicknor, Coleford GL16 7PA* Tel (01594) 860200

CARNE, Norman David John. b 27. Roch Th Coll 59. **d** 62 **p** 63. C Roch St Justus 62-66; C Strood St Mary 66-68; R Westcote Barton and Steeple Barton *Ox* 68-74; P-in-c Enstone and Heythrop 74-82; V 82-92; rtd 92; Perm to Offic *Leic* 93-98. *45 Beckingthorpe Drive, Bottesford, Nottingham NG13 0DN* Tel (01949) 843890

CARNEGIE, Ms Rachel Clare. b 62. New Hall Cam BA84 Sussex Univ MA94. SEITE 01. **d** 04 **p** 05. NSM Richmond St Mary w St Matthias and St Jo *S'wark* 04-09; Abp's Sec for Internat

Development *Cant* from 09. *Lambeth Palace, London SE1 7JU* Tel (020) 7898 1400 E-mail rachel.carnegie@gmail.com *or* rachel.carnegie@c-of-e.org.uk

CARNELL, Canon Geoffrey Gordon. b 18. St Jo Coll Cam BA40 MA44. Cuddesdon Coll 40. **d** 42 **p** 43. C Abington *Pet* 42-49; Chapl and Lect St Gabr Coll Camberwell 49-53; R Isham and V Gt w Lt Harrowden *Pet* 53-71; Dir of Post-Ord Tr and Dir of Ords 62-85; Can Pet Cathl 65-85; R Boughton 71-85; Dioc Lib Ecton Ho 67-93; Chapl to The Queen 81-88; rtd 85; Perm to Offic *Pet* from 86. *52 Walsingham Avenue, Kettering NN15 5ER* Tel (01536) 511415

CARNELLEY, The Ven Desmond. b 29. Open Univ BA77 Leeds Univ CertEd. Ripon Hall Ox 59. **d** 60 **p** 61. C Aston cum Aughton *Sheff* 60-63; C-in-c Ecclesfield St Paul CD 63-67; V Balby w Hexthorpe 67-73; P-in-c Mosbrough 73-74; V 74-85; RD Attercliffe 79-84; Adn Doncaster 85-94; Dioc Dir of Educn 91-94; rtd 94; Perm to Offic *Sheff* and *Derby* from 94. *7 Errwood Avenue, Buxton SK17 9BD* Tel (01298) 71460

CARNELLEY, Mrs Elizabeth Amy. b 64. St Aid Coll Dur BA85 Selw Coll Cam MPhil87. Ripon Coll Cuddesdon 88. **d** 90 **p** 94. Par Dn Sharrow St Andr *Sheff* 90-93; Par Dn Is of Dogs Ch Ch and St Jo w St Luke *Lon* 93-94; C 94-95; P-in-c Woolfold *Man* 95-99; TV Man Whitworth 99-02; Chapl Man Univ and Man Metrop Univ 99-02; Policy Officer Chs' Regional Commn for Yorks and the Humber 02-06; Chief Exec from 06; Perm to Offic *Ripon* from 02. *20 New Market Street, Leeds LS1 6DG* Tel 0113-244 3413 Mobile 07734-149725 E-mail liz.carnelley@crc-online.org.uk

CARNEY, David Anthony. b 42. Salford Univ BSc77. Linc Th Coll 77. **d** 79 **p** 80. C Wythenshawe St Martin *Man* 79-81; CF 81-84; Chapl Canadian Armed Forces 84-87; R Burford H Trin Ontario 87-91; P-in-c Whaplode *Linc* 91-97; V 97-02; P-in-c Holbeach Fen 91-97; V 97-02; R Colsterworth Gp 02-05; P-in-c Kirton in Holland 05-09; rtd 09. *The Vicarage, Penny Gardens, Kirton, Boston PE20 1HN* Tel (01205) 722380

CARNEY, Mrs Mary Patricia. b 42. Univ of Wales (Ban) BSc62. Wycliffe Hall Ox. **d** 90 **p** 94. Par Dn Carterton *Ox* 90-93; Par Dn Harwell w Chilton 93-94; C 94-01; P-in-c Ray Valley 01-07; rtd 07; Perm to Offic *Ox* from 07. *344B Woodstock Road, Oxford OX2 8BZ* Tel (01865) 515325 E-mail maryparcney@tiscali.co.uk

CARNEY, The Ven Richard Wayne. b 52. Lon Teachers' Coll Ontario TCert73 Toronto Univ BA79. Trin Coll Toronto MDiv84. **d** 84 **p** 85. Canada 84-95; C Scarborough St Andr 84-86; I Roche's Pt 86-91; P Asst Newmarket St Paul 91-93; Assoc P 93-95; I Clonfert Gp *L & K* 95-03; I Birr w Lorrha, Dorrha and Lockeen from 03; Adn Killaloe, Kilfenora, Clonfert etc from 02. *The Rectory, Birr, Co Offaly, Republic of Ireland* Tel (00353) (57) 912 0021 Mobile 87-677 3196 E-mail mapleire@eircom.net *or* archdeacon@killaloe.anglican.org

✠**CARNLEY, The Rt Revd Peter Frederick.** b 37. AO98. Melbourne Univ BA66 Cam Univ PhD69 Gen Th Sem NY Hon DD84 Newc Univ Aus Hon DLitt00 Univ of W Aus Hon DLitt00. St Jo Coll Morpeth. **d** 62 **p** 64 **c** 81. Lic to Offic Melbourne 63-65; C Parkes 66; Lic to Offic *Ely* 66-69; Chapl Mitchell Coll Bathurst 70-71; Research Fell St Jo Coll Cam 71-72; Warden St Jo Coll Brisbane 72-81; Can Res Brisbane 75-81; Abp Perth 81-05; Primate of Australia 00-05; rtd 05. *PO Box 221, Nannup WA 6275, Australia* Tel (0061) (8) 9756 0420

CAROLAN (née STUART-BLACK), Mrs Veronica. b 52. St Jo Coll Dur BA75. Cranmer Hall Dur. **dss** 82 **d** 87 **p** 08. Borehamwood *St Alb* 82-84; Watford Ch Ch 84-85; Stevenage St Mary Shephall 85-87; Par Dn Stevenage St Mary Shephall w Aston 87-88; Hon C from 08; Perm to Offic 98-08. *18 Randalls Hill, Shephall, Stevenage SG2 9YN* Tel (01438) 235597

CAROLAN-EVANS, Stewart James. b 65. Salford Univ BSc83 CEng95 MICE95. SEITE 04. **d** 06 **p** 07. NSM Dover St Mary *Cant* from 06. *Springfield, Eythorne Road, Shepherdswell, Dover CT15 7PW* Tel (01304) 832248 Fax 830641 Mobile 07940-544748 E-mail sjkgcarolan@tesco.net

CARPANI, Karl Augustus. b 50. St Jo Coll Nottm 96. **d** 98 **p** 99. C Biggin Hill *Roch* 98-01; V Green Street Green and Pratts Bottom from 01. *The Vicarage, 46 World's End Lane, Orpington BR6 6AG* Tel (01689) 852905 E-mail karl.carpani@diocese-rochester.org *or* karl@carpani.org

CARPENTER, Canon Bruce Leonard Henry. b 32. Lon Univ BA54. St Chad's Coll Dur. **d** 59 **p** 60. C Portsea N End St Mark *Portsm* 59-63; C Fareham SS Pet and Paul 63-67; V Locks Heath 67-74; TR Fareham H Trin 74-84; RD Alverstoke 71-76; Hon Can Portsm Cathl 79-84; V Richmond St Mary w St Matthias and St Jo *S'wark* 84-91; Chapl Ch Ch High Sch Ashford 91-93; P-in-c S Ashford Ch Ch Cant 94-97; rtd 97; Chapl Huggens Coll Northfleet 97-02; Perm to Offic *Portsm* from 02; Hon Chapl MU from 03. *Pistachio, 96 Festing Grove, Southsea PO4 9QF* Tel (023) 9229 4128

CARPENTER, Canon Derek George Edwin. b 40. K Coll Lon BD62 AKC62. **d** 63 **p** 64. C Friern Barnet All SS *Lon* 63-66; C Chingford SS Pet and Paul *Chelmsf* 66-70; V Dartford St Alb

Roch 70-79; R Crayford 79-90; RD Erith 82-90; R Beckenham St Geo 90-02; Hon Can Roch Cathl 97-02; rtd 02; Perm to Offic *Roch* from 04. *39 Chatfield Way, East Malling, West Malling ME19 6QD* Tel (01732) 874420

CARPENTER, Donald Arthur. b 35. Roch Th Coll 65. **d** 67 **p** 68. C Thornton Heath St Jude *Cant* 67-73; V Earby *Bradf* 73-78; V Skipton Ch Ch 78-88; V Baildon 88-91; P-in-c Perivale *Lon* 91-96; rtd 96; Perm to Offic *Lon* 96-05. *Le Moulin Verneau, 49390 Parcay-les-Pins, France* Tel (0033) (2) 41 51 42 22 Mobile (6) 77 98 48 07 E-mail carpenter.sue@wanadoo.fr

CARPENTER, Canon Judith Margaret. b 47. Bris Univ BA68 CertEd69. Trin Coll Bris BA95. **d** 95 **p** 96. C Warmley, Syston and Bitton *Bris* 95-99; V Withywood from 99; Hon Can Bris Cathl from 06. *Withywood Church House, 63 Turtlegate Avenue, Bristol BS13 8NN* Tel 0117-964 7763 E-mail judith.carpenter@btinternet.com

CARPENTER, Leonard Richard. b 32. EMMTC 82. **d** 85 **p** 86. NSM Leic H Apostles 85-90; P-in-c Barlestone 90-98; rtd 98; Perm to Offic *Leic* and *Derby* from 98. *10 Main Street, Albert Village, Swadlincote DE11 8EW* Tel (01283) 229335

CARPENTER, William Brodie. b 35. St Alb Minl Tr Scheme 76. **d** 79 **p** 80. NSM Hemel Hempstead *St Alb* 79-85; C Bp's Hatfield 85-88; C Caversham St Pet and Mapledurham etc *Ox* 88-89; V Caversham St Andr 89-99; rtd 99; Perm to Offic *St Alb* 00-02; P-in-c Wigginton 02-05; Perm to Offic *Ox* from 05. *33 Elm Tree Walk, Tring HP23 5EB* Tel (01442) 824585 E-mail billcarp@supanet.com

CARR, Alan Cobban. b 49. Nottm Univ BTh88. Linc Th Coll 85. **d** 88 **p** 89. C Rustington *Chich* 88-92; V Highbrook and W Hoathly from 92. *The Vicarage, North Lane, West Hoathly, East Grinstead RH19 4QF* Tel (01342) 810494 E-mail alancarr17@hotmail.com

CARR, Mrs Amanda Helen. b 70. Univ of Wales (Cardiff) BA91 Kent Univ MA97. SEITE 01. **d** 04 **p** 05. C Meopham w Nurstead *Roch* 04-07; P-in-c Lamberhurst and Matfield from 07. *The Vicarage, Old Town Hill, Lamberhurst, Tunbridge Wells TN3 8EL* Tel (01892) 891538 Mobile 07866-675015 E-mail mandy.carr@diocese-rochester.org

CARR, Anthony Howard. b 62. Ex Univ BA. **d** 92 **p** 93. C Taverham w Ringland *Nor* 92-97; P-in-c S Darley, Elton and Winster *Derby* 97-03; R E Peckham and Nettlestead *Roch* from 03. *The Rectory, Bush Road, East Peckham, Tonbridge TN12 5LL* Tel (01622) 871278

CARR, The Very Revd Arthur Wesley. b 41. KCVO06. Jes Coll Ox BA64 MA72 Jes Coll Cam BA66 MA70 Sheff Univ PhD75 Hon DLitt03 UWE Hon DLitt97. Ridley Hall Cam 65. **d** 67 **p** 68. C Luton w E Hyde *St Alb* 67-71; Tutor Ridley Hall Cam 71-74; Chapl 71-72; Hon C Ranmoor *Sheff* 72-74; Chapl Chelmsf Cathl 74-78; Can Res 78-87; Dep Dir Cathl Cen for Research and Tr 74-82; Dioc Dir of Tr 76-84; Dean Bris 87-97; Dean Westmr 97-06; rtd 06. *16 Church Road, Romsey SO51 8EY* E-mail wesley@wesleycarr.wanadoo.co.uk

CARR, David Scott. b 72. Derby Univ BA97 MCIM05. NEOC 06. **d** 09. NSM Horden *Dur* from 09. *Glen View, 26 Station Avenue, Brandon, Durham DH7 8QQ* Tel 07990-775054 (mobile) E-mail david@carrd.fsbusiness.co.uk

CARR, Derrick Charles. b 43. MCIPD. SAOMC 99. **d** 02 **p** 03. NSM Amersham *Ox* from 02; Ad Amersham from 09. *52 Warren Wood Drive, High Wycombe HP11 1EA* Tel and fax (01494) 452389 Mobile 07768-507391 E-mail dcarr@globalnet.co.uk

CARR, Mrs Elaine Susan. b 46. LTCL82. SAOMC 99. **d** 02 **p** 03. NSM High Wycombe *Ox* 02-09. *52 Warren Wood Drive, High Wycombe HP11 1EA* Tel and fax (01494) 452389 E-mail revcarr@btinternet.com

CARR, Miss Eveline. b 45. St Jo Coll Dur 91. **d** 93 **p** 95. NSM Eighton Banks *Dur* 93-98; NSM Gateshead from 98. *10 Lanchester Avenue, Gateshead NE9 7AJ* Tel 0191-482 1157 E-mail e-carr@supnet.com

CARR, John Henry Percy. b 52. NTMTC 95. **d** 98 **p** 99. C Hackney Wick St Mary of Eton w St Aug *Lon* 98-01; R Walesby *Linc* from 01. *The Rectory, Otby Lane, Walesby, Market Rasen LN8 3UT* Tel (01673) 838513 E-mail carr.ide@boltblue.com

CARR, John Robert. b 40. ACII62. Oak Hill Th Coll 63. **d** 66 **p** 67. C Tonbridge St Steph *Roch* 66-70; C Cheadle Hulme St Andr *Ches* 70-79; R Widford *Chelmsf* 79-87; TV Becontree W 87-93; V Basildon St Andr w H Cross 93-05; rtd 05; Perm to Offic *Chelmsf* from 06. *3 Windsor Way, Rayleigh SS6 8PE* Tel (01268) 741065 E-mail johnwendycarr@ukgateway.net

CARR, Miss Joy Vera. b 32. DipEd52. Dalton Ho Bris 56. **dss** 80 **d** 87 **p** 94. Scarborough St Jas and H Trin *York* 80-82; Kingston upon Hull St Matt w St Barn 82-87; Par Dn 87-89; Par Dn Elloughton and Brough w Brantingham 89-92; rtd 92; Perm to Offic *York* from 92. *15 Sea View Gardens, Scarborough YO11 3JD* Tel (01723) 376986

CARR, Leighton Westwood. b 60. Trin Coll Bris. **d** 09. NSM Kingswood *Bris* from 09. *19 Nutgrove Avenue, Bristol BS3 4QE* Tel 0117-983 2605

CARR, Mandy. *See* CARR, Mrs Amanda Helen

CARR, Paul Anthony. b 62. Aston Tr Scheme 93 Oak Hill Th Coll 95. **d** 97 **p** 98. C Handforth *Ches* 97-01; V Chadwell Heath *Chelmsf* 01-08; TR Billericay and Lt Burstead from 08. *The Rectory, 40 Laindon Road, Billericay CM12 9LD* Tel (01277) 658055 E-mail revpaulcarr@btinternet.com

CARR, Richard George. b 43. AKC65. St Boniface Warminster 65. **d** 66 **p** 67. C Fenham St Jas and St Basil *Newc* 66-69; C Alnwick St Mich 69-73; Ind Chapl *Llan* 73-77; Perm to Offic *Chelmsf* from 80. *Nelmes, Mill Lane, Birch, Colchester CO2 0NG* Tel (01206) 330521 E-mail richardcarr@nelmes.fsnet.co.uk

CARR, Wesley. *See* CARR, The Very Revd Arthur Wesley

CARRINGTON, David John. b 63. Trin Coll Bris. **d** 09. C Bovey Tracey SS Pet, Paul and Thos w Hennock *Ex* from 09. *Orchard Meadow, Coombe Cross, Bovey Tracey, Newton Abbot TQ13 9EP* Tel (01626) 830770

CARRINGTON, Mrs Elizabeth Ashby. b 46. EMMTC 86. **d** 90 **p** 94. NSM Nottingham St Ann w Em *S'well* 90-91; C Basford w Hyson Green 92-97; Lect Nottingham St Mary and St Cath 97-00; Assoc P W Bingham Deanery 00; Perm to Offic 00-01; Chapl Woodford Ho Sch New Zealand from 01; NSM Napier Cathl from 03. *Woodford House, Havelock North, Hastings 4201, New Zealand* Tel (0064) (6) 873 0722 Fax 873 0719 E-mail elizabeth.carrington@woodford.school.nz

CARRINGTON, Margaret Elizabeth. b 46. NSM York St Luke from 09. *202 Boroughbridge Road, York YO26 6BD* Tel (01904) 798916

CARRINGTON, Philip John. b 48. MBE03. Leeds Univ MA96 Leeds Poly CEng MCMI. Chich Th Coll 83. **d** 85 **p** 86. C W Acklam *York* 85-88; V Middlesbrough St Agnes 88-92; Chapl S Cleveland Hosp 88-92; Trust Chapl S Tees Hosps NHS Trust 92-06; V Guernsey St Steph *Win* from 06; Hd Chapl Services States of Guernsey Bd of Health from 07. *St Stephen's Vicarage, Les Gravees, St Peter Port, Guernsey GY1 1RN* Tel (01481) 720268 E-mail thecarringtons@cwgsy.net

CARRIVICK, Derek Roy. b 45. Birm Univ BSc66. Ripon Hall Ox 71. **d** 74 **p** 75. C Enfield St Jas *Lon* 74-78; C-in-c Woodgate Valley CD *Birm* 78-83; TR Chelmsley Wood 83-92; Dioc Ecum Officer 86-96; R Baxterley w Hurley and Wood End and Merevale etc 92-99; AD Polesworth 96-99; P-in-c Helland and Blisland w St Breward *Truro* 99-04; P-in-c Devoran from 04; Bp's Dom Chapl from 04. *The Vicarage, Devoran Lane, Devoran, Truro TR3 6PA* Tel (01872) 863116 E-mail pjc87@tutor.open.ac.uk

CARROLL, The Ven Charles William Desmond. b 19. TCD BA43 MA46. St Chad's Coll Dur. **d** 48 **p** 49. C Stanwix *Carl* 48-50; V 50-59; Hon Can Blackb Cathl 59-64; Dir RE 59-73; Can Res Blackb Cathl 64-75; Adn Blackb 73-86; V Balderstone 73-86; rtd 86; Perm to Offic *Blackb* from 86. *11 Assheton Road, Blackburn BB2 6SF* Tel (01254) 51915

CARROLL, Frederick Albert. b 16. Worc Coll Ox BA51 MA55. Ripon Hall Ox 46. **d** 51 **p** 52. C Oldbury *Birm* 51-56; V Cotteridge 56-65; C-in-c Castle Vale CD 65-68; V Castle Vale 68-74; V Coughton *Cov* 74-87; R Spernall, Morton Bagot and Oldberrow 74-87; RD Alcester 84-87; rtd 87. *8 Gracey Court, Woodland Road, Broadclyst, Exeter EX5 3GA* Tel (01392) 460788

CARROLL, James Thomas. b 41. Pittsburgh Univ MA85. St Deiniol's Hawarden 89 Oblate Fathers Sem Dub 59. **d** 63 **p** 64. C Dublin St Patr Cathl Gp 89-92; Min Can St Patr Cathl Dublin 90-96; I Raheny w Coolock *D & G* from 92; Chan V St Patr Cathl Dublin from 96. *403 Howth Road, Raheny, Dublin 5, Republic of Ireland* Tel (00353) (1) 831 3929 E-mail midnight@indigo.ie

CARROLL, John Hugh. b 31. Bris Univ BA57. Tyndale Hall Bris 54. **d** 58 **p** 59. C Slough *Ox* 58-61; V S Lambeth St Steph *S'wark* 61-72; V Norwood St Luke 72-81; P-in-c Purley Ch Ch 81-85; V 85-93; rtd 93; Perm to Offic *S'wark* from 93. *75 Court Avenue, Coulsdon CR5 1HJ* Tel (01737) 553471 E-mail jonthel.carroll@virgin.net

CARROLL, Laurence William. b 44. Birm Univ CertEd66 Open Univ BA73 Leic Univ BEd74 FRHS66 ACP67 LCP68. **d** 95 **p** 96. OLM Mid Marsh Gp *Linc* from 95. *15 Grantavon House, Brayford Wharf East, Lincoln LN5 7WA* Tel (01522) 522643

CARROLL WALLIS, Ms Joy Ann. b 59. SS Mark & Jo Univ Coll Plymouth BEd82. Cranmer Hall Dur 85. **d** 88 **p** 94. Par Dn Hatcham St Jas *S'wark* 88-93; Par Dn Streatham Immanuel and St Andr 93-94; C 94-97; USA from 97. *1305 Fairmont Street NW, Washington DC 20009, USA* Tel (001) (202) 483 0119 E-mail joycwallis@aol.com

CARRUTHERS, Arthur Christopher (Kester). b 35. Lon Coll of Div ALCD60 LTh73. **d** 60 **p** 61. C Addiscombe St Mary *Cant* 60-62; Prec Bradf Cathl 62-64; CF 64-92; R W Tanfield and Well w Snape and N Stainley *Ripon* 92-00; rtd 00; Perm to Offic *Guildf* from 00. *3 Park View Court, Woking GU22 7SE* Tel (01483) 721995

CARSON, Christopher John. b 69. QUB BA91 TCD BTh94. **d** 94 **p** 95. C Bangor St Comgall *D & D* 94-97; Bp's C Kilmegan w Maghera 97-98; I from 98. *The Rectory, 50 Main Street, Dundrum, Newcastle BT33 0LY* Tel (028) 4375 1225 Mobile 07905-660274

CARSON, Ms Claire. b 76. St Martin's Coll Lanc BA98 Birm Univ MA99. Qu Coll Birm 00. **d** 03 **p** 04. C Streetly *Lich* 03-04; C Stafford 04-05; C Lich St Mich w St Mary and Wall 05-07; Chapl R Free Hampstead NHS Trust from 07. *Royal Free Hospital, Pond Street, London NW3 2QG* Tel (020) 7794 0500
E-mail claire.carson3@btinternet.com

CARSON, Ernest. b 17. S'wark Ord Course 68. **d** 71 **p** 72. C Baldock w Bygrave and Clothall *St Alb* 71-75; R Hertingfordbury 75-86; rtd 86; Perm to Offic *Worc* from 86. *16 Woodward Close, Pershore WR10 1LP* Tel (01386) 553511

CARSON, Gerald James Alexander. b 24. TCD BA49 MA52. **d** 49 **p** 50. C Belfast St Phil *Conn* 49-51; C Derry Cathl 51-54; I Kilteevogue 54-57; I Dunfanaghy 57-68; Can Raphoe Cathl 67-81; I Urney w Sion Mills 68-85; Can Derry Cathl 81-85; I Clonallon w Warrenpoint *D & D* 85-90; rtd 90. *84 Avonbrook Gardens, Mountsandel, Coleraine BT52 1SS* Tel (028) 7035 6047

CARSON, James Irvine. b 59. TCD BA MTh. **d** 84 **p** 85. C Willowfield *D & D* 84-87; C Lecale Gp 87-89; I Devenish w Boho Clogh 89-95; Dioc Youth Adv 91-95; Dioc Communications Officer 93-95; I Belfast Upper Malone (Epiphany) *Conn* 95-99; I Lisburn St Paul from 99. *St Paul's Rectory, 3 Ballinderry Road, Lisburn BT28 1UD* Tel (028) 9266 3520
E-mail jamescarson203@btinternet.com

CARSON-FEATHAM, Lawrence William. b 53. AKC. **d** 78 **p** 79. SSM from 77; C Walton St Mary *Liv* 78-82; Chapl Bolton Colls of H&FE 82-87; C Bolton St Pet *Man* 82-87; TV Oldham 87-92; V Ashton St Jas 92-95; Perm to Offic *Liv* 95-97; C Leeds Belle Is St Jo and St Barn *Ripon* 97-01; TV Accrington Ch the King *Blackb* from 01. *St Mary Magdalen's Vicarage, 5 Queen's Road, Accrington BB5 6AR* Tel (01254) 233763

CARTER, Arthur. b 32. CITC. **d** 97 **p** 98. C Clonmel w Innislounagh, Tullaghmelan etc *C & O* from 97. *Suir Villa, Barnora, Cahir, Co Tipperary, Republic of Ireland* Tel (00353) (52) 41524 E-mail nacarter@eircom.net

CARTER, Barry Graham. b 54. K Coll Lon BD76 AKC76. St Steph Ho Ox 76. **d** 77 **p** 78. C Evesham *Worc* 77-81; C Amblecote 81-84; TV Ovingdean w Rottingdean and Woodingdean *Chich* 84-85; V Woodingdean 85-95; V Lancing St Mich from 95. *The Vicarage, 117 Penhill Road, Lancing BN15 8HD* Tel (01903) 753653
E-mail frbaz@saintmichaels.plus.com

CARTER, Celia. b 38. JP74. Glouc Sch of Min 86. **d** 89 **p** 94. NSM Avening w Cherington *Glouc* from 89; Asst Chapl Stroud Gen Hosp 89-93; Asst Chapl Severn NHS Trust from 93. *Avening Park, West End, Avening, Tetbury GL8 8NE* Tel (01453) 836390

CARTER (née SMITH), Mrs Christine Lydia. b 43. SRN64 SCM67. Trin Coll Bris 89. **d** 91 **p** 94. Par Dn Penkridge *Lich* 91-94; C 94-96; Perm to Offic *Blackb* 96-97; NSM Blackb Sav 97-01; Chapl Asst St Helens and Knowsley Hosps NHS Trust 97-01; NSM Elmdon St Nic *Birm* from 01. *Elmdon Rectory, Tanhouse Farm Road, Solihull B92 9EY* Tel 0121-743 6336
E-mail paul@tworevs.intml.net

CARTER, Christopher Franklin. b 37. Wadh Coll Ox BA59 MA63. Wycliffe Hall Ox 60. **d** 64 **p** 65. C Clifton St Jas *Sheff* 64-67; C Handsworth 67-70; C Clun w Chapel Lawn *Heref* 70-74; Lic to Offic 74-76; P-in-c Ironbridge 76-78; C Coalbrookdale, Iron-Bridge and Lt Wenlock 78-80; V Llansilin w Llangadwaladr and Llangedwyn *St As* 80-05; RD Llanfyllin 88-05; rtd 05. *Ysgubor Goch, Cefn Coch, Llanrhaeadr-ym-Mochnant, Oswestry SY10 0BQ* Tel (01691) 860577

CARTER, Christopher Paul. b 43. CCC Cam BA64. SAOMC 02. **d** 05 **p** 06. NSM W Buckingham *Ox* from 05. *The Mount, Upper Street, Tingewick, Buckingham MK18 4QN* Tel and fax (01280) 848291 E-mail lorraine.carter@btinternet.com

CARTER, Colin John. b 56. Fitzw Coll Cam BA77 MB, BChir80 MA81 FRCS86 FRCOphth89. Trin Coll Bris BA93. **d** 93 **p** 94. C Ripley *Derby* 93-97; TV Horsham *Chich* 97-00. *Duke Elder Eye Unit, Blackshaw Road, London SW17 0QT* Tel (020) 8266 6111

CARTER, David John. b 37. Chich Th Coll 64. **d** 67 **p** 68. C Plaistow St Andr *Chelmsf* 67-70; C Wickford 70-73; Chapl Asst Runwell Hosp Wickford 71-73; Chapl Basingstoke Distr Hosp 73-80; R E Woodhay and Woolton Hill *Win* 80-02; rtd 02; Perm to Offic *Win* from 02. *24 Sandford Close, Kingsclere, Newbury RG20 5LZ* Tel (01635) 299455

CARTER, Dudley Herbert. b 25. Peterho Cam BA49 MA51. Ridley Hall Cam 49. **d** 51 **p** 52. C Longfleet *Sarum* 51-53; C Rainham *Chelmsf* 54-56; R Tollard Royal w Farnham *Sarum* 60-64; Chapl Colston's Sch Bris 65-67; Lic to Offic *B & W* 67-85; Perm to Offic from 85; rtd 90. *18 Golf Links Road, Burnham-on-Sea TA8 2PW* Tel (01278) 789096

CARTER, Duncan Robert Bruton. b 58. Univ of Wales (Cardiff) BA79 Cam Univ BA83 MA89. Ridley Hall Cam 81. **d** 84 **p** 85. C Harold Wood *Chelmsf* 84-88; C S Kensington St Luke *Lon* 88-90; V Henley H Trin *Ox* from 90; AD Henley 02-06. *Holy Trinity Vicarage, Church Street, Henley-on-Thames RG9 1SE* Tel (01491) 574822 E-mail drbcarter@hotmail.com

CARTER, Edward John. b 67. Ex Univ BA88. Ripon Coll Cuddesdon BA96 MA01. **d** 97 **p** 98. C Thorpe St Matt *Nor* 97-00; Min Can and Dean's V Windsor 00-04; P-in-c Didcot St Pet *Ox* from 04; AD Wallingford from 07. *St Peter's Vicarage, Glebe Road, Didcot OX11 8PN* Tel (01235) 812114
E-mail revdedward.carter@ukgateway.net

CARTER, Eric. b 17. **d** 58 **p** 59. C S Shore H Trin *Blackb* 58-62; V Preesall 62-69; RD Garstang 68-69; V Adlington 69-75; V Garstang St Thos 75-84; rtd 84; Perm to Offic *Ripon* from 84. *16 Crystal Court, Pannal Green, Pannal, Harrogate HG3 1LH* Tel (01423) 810237

CARTER, Frank Howard James. b 23. Chich Th Coll 58. **d** 59 **p** 60. C Bethnal Green St Matt *Lon* 59-64; V Ipstones *Lich* 64-65; V Haggerston All SS *Lon* 65-75; V Alexandra Park St Andr 75-88; rtd 88; Perm to Offic *Lon* 91-98. *53 Naylor Road, London N20 0HE* Tel (020) 8445 0982

CARTER, Grayson Leigh. b 53. Univ of S California BSc76 Ch Ch Ox DPhil90. Fuller Th Sem California MA84 Wycliffe Hall Ox 89. **d** 90 **p** 91. C Bungay H Trin w St Mary *St E* 90-92; Chapl BNC Ox 92-96; Hon C Ox St Mary V w St Cross and St Pet 93-96; USA from 96; Assoc Prof Methodist Coll Fayetteville 96-03; Asst R Fayetteville H Trin 96-03; Assoc Prof Fuller Th Sem from 03. *1602 Palmcroft Drive SW, Phoenix AZ 85007-1738, USA* Tel (001) (602) 252 5582 or 220 0400 Fax 220 0444 E-mail gcarter10@yahoo.com or gcarter@fuller.edu

CARTER, Hazel June. b 48. Doncaster Coll of Educn CertEd72. Carl Dioc Tr Inst 89. **d** 92 **p** 94. C Wreay *Carl* 92-98; C Dalston and Raughton Head w Gatesgill 92-98; TV Carl H Trin and St Barn 98-02; TR 02-07; rtd 07. *4 Wandales Lane, Natland, Kendal LA9 7QY* Tel (01228) 526284

CARTER, Heather Ruth. b 62. SEN82. Trin Coll Bris 85. **d** 02 **p** 04. Dn Montevideo Cathl Uruguay 02-04; NSM Dalston w Cumdivock, Raughton Head and Wreay *Carl* from 04; Chapl to the Deaf and Hard of Hearing 05-08; Chapl N Cumbria Acute Hosps NHS Trust 05-07. *The Vicarage, Townhead Road, Dalston, Carlisle CA5 7JF* Tel (01228) 710215 Fax 710288
E-mail revhev@tiscali.co.uk

CARTER, Ian Sutherland. b 51. Trin Coll Ox BA73 MA77 DPhil77 Leeds Univ BA80. Coll of Resurr Mirfield 78. **d** 81 **p** 82. C Shildon *Dur* 81-84; C Darlington H Trin 84-87; Chapl Liv Univ 87-93; V Hindley St Pet 93-98; Chapl Oldham NHS Trust 98-03; Chapl Salford R Hosps NHS Foundn Trust from 03. *Hope Hospital, Stott Lane, Salford M6 8HD* Tel 0161-206 5167 or 789 7373 E-mail ian.carter@srht.nhs.uk

CARTER (née O'NEILL), Mrs Irene. b 44. Worc Coll of Educn CertEd65. EMMTC 92. **d** 93. NSM N and S Leverton *S'well* from 93. *25 Mill Close, North Leverton, Retford DN22 0AT* Tel (01427) 880451

CARTER, Mrs Jacqueline Ann. b 50. St Mich Coll Llan 01. **d** 03 **p** 04. C Ebbw Vale *Mon* 03-06; TV from 06. *1 Brecon Heights, Victoria, Ebbw Vale NP23 8WP* Tel (01495) 302708
E-mail jackiecarter16@hotmail.com

CARTER, John Howard Gregory. b 55. York Univ BA76 Leeds Univ CertEd77 Nottm Univ MA96. St Jo Coll Nottm LTh87. **d** 87 **p** 88. C Nailsea H Trin *B & W* 87-91; TV Camberley St Paul *Guildf* 91-97; Chapl Elmhurst Ballet Sch 91-97; Dioc Communications Officer *Ripon* from 97; Bp's Press Officer from 00. *7 Blenheim Court, Harrogate HG2 9DT* Tel (01423) 530369 Fax 382133778 Mobile 07798-652707
E-mail jhgcarter@aol.com

CARTER, Mrs Joy. **d** 09. OLM Didcot St Pet *Ox* from 09. *St Peter's Vicarage, Glebe Road, Didcot OX11 8PN* Tel (01235) 812114

CARTER, Leslie Alfred Arthur. b 27. K Coll Lon 50 St Boniface Warminster 53. **d** 54 **p** 55. C Northolt Park St Barn *Lon* 54-56; S Africa 57-62; C Wimbledon *S'wark* 63-68; Chapl Quainton Hall Sch Harrow 68-77; TV Brighton Resurr *Chich* 77-81; TV Southend *Chelmsf* 81-88; V Gt Waltham w Ford End 88-93; rtd 94; Perm to Offic *Sarum* from 94. *The Garden Flat, 11 Bathwick Street, Bath BA2 6NX*

CARTER, Marian. b 40. Whitelands Coll Lon TCert61 Lon Univ BD67 Nottm Univ MPhil79 Man Univ MA84 Ex Univ PhD05. Nor Bapt Coll 83. **d** 92 **p** 94. Par Dn Kempshott *Win* 92-93; Tutor SWMTC 92-96; Tutor Coll of SS Mark and Jo Plymouth 93-00; NSM Plymstock and Hooe *Ex* 94-98; NSM Widecombe-in-the-Moor, Leusdon, Princetown etc 98-00; Chapl St Eliz Hospice Ipswich 00-05; rtd 05; Perm to Offic *St E* from 06. *Shalom, 80 Woodlands, Chelmondiston, Ipswich IP9 1DU* Tel (01473) 780259

CARTER, Canon Michael John. b 32. St Alb Minl Tr Scheme 81. **d** 84 **p** 85. NSM Radlett *St Alb* 84-88; Chapl SW Herts HA 88-94; Chapl Watford Gen Hosp 88-94; Lic to Offic *St Alb* 88-99; Chapl Mt Vernon and Watford Hosps NHS Trust 94-99; Bp's Adv for Hosp Chapl *St Alb* 95-99; Hon Can St Alb 96-99; rtd 99; Perm to Offic *St Alb* from 99; Hon Chapl Peace Hospice Watford from 99. *4 Field View Rise, Bricket Wood, St Albans AL2 3RT* Tel (01923) 279870 E-mail mjc@mjcarter.com

CARTER, Michael William. b 33. Newland Park Teacher Tr Coll TCert56. Dioc OLM tr scheme 98. **d** 01 **p** 02. OLM Lingfield and Crowhurst *S'wark* 01-04; rtd 04; Perm to Offic *S'wark* from

04. *Redwood House, 76 Godstone Road, Lingfield RH7 6BT* Tel (01342) 833843

CARTER, Nicholas Adrian. b 47. Ripon Hall Ox 71. **d** 74 **p** 75. C Sowerby *Wakef* 74-79; V Hanging Heaton 79-83; CF 83-86; V Elton All SS *Man* 86-90; C Milton *Win* 90-94; P-in-c Boscombe St Andr 94-00; V 00-09; rtd 09; TV Winchcombe *Glouc* from 09. *The Vicarage, Church Road, Alderton, Tewkesbury GL20 8NR* Tel (01242) 620238 E-mail cdevildodger@aol.com

CARTER, Nigel John. b 53. Bolton Inst of Educn CertEd89. Sarum & Wells Th Coll 91. **d** 93 **p** 94. C Burntwood *Lich* 93-96; V Bentley 96-04; RD Wolverhampton 00-02; V Walsall Wood from 04. *The Vicarage, 2 St John's Close, Walsall Wood, Walsall WS9 9NH* Tel (01543) 360558 *or* 372284
E-mail nigel.carter@o2.co.uk

CARTER, Noel William. b 53. Birm Univ BSc75 Bris Univ CertEd76 Nottm Univ BSc83. Linc Th Coll. **d** 83 **p** 84. C Penrith w Newton Reigny and Plumpton Wall *Carl* 83-86; C Barrow St Matt 86-87; V Netherton 87-91; TR Penrith w Newton Reigny and Plumpton Wall 91-97; P-in-c Jersey St Brelade *Win* 97-98; R 98-01; Vice-Dean Jersey 00-01; P-in-c Brymbo and Southsea *St As* 05-07; P-in-c Brymbo, Southsea and Tanyfron from 07; AD Minera from 08. *The Bryn, Bryn Road, Moss, Wrexham LL11 6EL*

CARTER, Canon Norman. b 23. Leeds Univ BSc48. Coll of Resurr Mirfield 48. **d** 50 **p** 51. C Liv Our Lady and St Nic w St Anne 50-54; C Orford St Marg 54-56; V 56-71; PC Knotty Ash H Spirit 71-74; V Dovecot 74-83; RD W Derby 78-83; Hon Can Liv Cathl 82-88; V Formby St Pet 83-88; rtd 88; Perm to Offic *Liv* from 88. *34 Granby Close, Southport PR9 9QG* Tel (01704) 232821

CARTER, Canon Paul Brian. b 22. AKC49. **d** 50 **p** 51. C Scarborough St Columba *York* 50-53; C Pocklington w Yapham-cum-Meltonby, Owsthorpe etc 53-55; V Kingston upon Hull St Jo Newington 55-60; R Ainderby Steeple and Scruton *Ripon* 60-79; P-in-c Yafforth 76-79; R Ainderby Steeple w Yafforth and Scruton 79-87; Hon Can Ripon Cathl 86-87; rtd 87; Perm to Offic *Ripon* 87-09. *Cliffe Cottage, West Tanfield, Ripon HG4 5JR* Tel (01677) 470203

CARTER, Paul Joseph. b 67. St Chad's Coll Dur BA88. St Steph Ho Ox 89. **d** 91 **p** 92. C Ipswich All Hallows *St E* 91; C Newmarket St Mary w Exning St Agnes 91-94; V Thorpe-le-Soken *Chelmsf* 94-04; V Ipswich St Bart *St E* from 04. *St Bartholomew's Vicarage, Newton Road, Ipswich IP3 8HQ* Tel (01473) 727441 E-mail frpaul@stbarts.freeserve.co.uk

CARTER, Paul Mark. b 56. BA78 MA90 Cranfield Univ MBA95. Ridley Hall Cam 79. **d** 81 **p** 82. C Kidsgrove *Lich* 81-84; CF 84-00; Asst P Vancouver St Phil Canada 00-03. *1655 West 41st Avenue, Vancouver BC V6M 1X9 Canada* Tel (001) (604) 222 4497 E-mail paulcarter@acinw.org

CARTER, Paul Rowley. b 45. Lon Univ BD69 Lon Bible Coll ALBC69 Southn Univ PGCE70. Trin Coll Bris. **d** 91 **p** 92. C Penkridge *Lich* 91-96; V Blackb Sav 96-01; R Elmdon St Nic *Birm* from 01. *Elmdon Rectory, Tanhouse Farm Road, Solihull B92 9EY* Tel 0121-743 6336 E-mail paul@tworevs.intml.net

CARTER, Richard Anthony. b 59. Univ of Wales (Abth) BA80 Melbourne Coll of Div BD94 Leeds Univ MA02 Lon Inst of Educn PGCE87. Bp Patteson Th Coll (Solomon Is) 90. **d** 91 **p** 92. Lect Bp Patteson Th Coll 91-00; Miss and Tr Co-ord Melanesian Brotherhood 00-05; Chapl 94-00 and 02-05; Perm to Offic *Lon* 00-06, C St Martin-in-the-Fields from 06. *Flat 1, 6 St Martin's Place, London WC2N 4JJ* Tel (020) 7766 1100 Fax 7839 5163 E-mail richard.carter@smitf.org

CARTER, Richard William. b 75. Newc Univ BSc96. Westcott Ho Cam 04. **d** 07 **p** 08. C Llanbedr DC w Llangynhafal, Llanychan etc *St As* from 07. *7 Maes Celyn, Llanbedr Dyffryn Clwyd, Ruthin LL15 1YR* Tel (01824) 703867 Mobile 07769-727985 E-mail richardcarter1975@yahoo.co.uk

CARTER, Robert Desmond. b 35. Cranmer Hall Dur 62. **d** 65 **p** 66. C Otley *Bradf* 65-69; C Keighley 69-73; V Cowling 73-00; rtd 00; Perm to Offic *Bradf* from 00. *1 Quincy Close, Eccleshill, Bradford BD2 2EP* Tel (01274) 638385

CARTER, Robert Edward. b 44. Univ of Wales (Ban) BSc66. St Jo Coll Nottm 79. **d** 81 **p** 82. C Caverswall *Lich* 81-86; V Biddulph 86-94; V Wolverhampton St Jude from 94. *St Jude's Vicarage, St Jude's Road, Wolverhampton WV6 0EB* Tel (01902) 753360 E-mail stjudes@blueyonder.co.uk

CARTER, Robert Thomas. b 49. Moore Th Coll Sydney 72 Ridley Coll Melbourne ThL75. **d** 75 **p** 76. C Traralgon St Jas Australia 75-76; P-in-c Endeavour Hills St Matt 77-79; V 80-84; Assoc Min Kew St Hilary 85-91; V Blackburn N St Alfred 92-00; C Fisherton Anger *Sarum* 00-02; Australia from 02. *224 Maroondah Highway, Croydon, Melbourne Vic 3136, Australia*

CARTER, Robin. b 46. Cam Univ MSt02. Chich Th Coll 71. **d** 74 **p** 75. C Wortley de Leeds *Ripon* 74-76; C Hutton *Chelmsf* 76-78, C Wickford 78-81; TV Wickford and Runwell 81-83; Chapl HM Pris Leeds 83-85; Chapl HM Pris Reading 85-89; Chapl HM YOI Huntercombe and Finnamore 85-89; Chapl HM YOI Finnamore Wood Camp 86-89; Gov 5, Hd of Operations, HM

Pris Channings Wood 89-94; Gov 4, Hd of Operations/Régime and Throughcare, HM Pris Woodhill 94-99; Gov HM Pris E Sutton Park 99-05; Sen Operational Pris Service Manager 05-08; Chapl Costa Blanca *Eur* from 08. *Ptl 3 1G, Edif El Valle, Calle Nou de Octubre 2, 03520 Polop, Spain* Tel (0034) 695 321 866 E-mail robincarter@yahoo.com

CARTER, Ronald George. b 31. Leeds Univ BA58. Coll of Resurr Mirfield 58. **d** 60 **p** 61. C Wigan St Anne *Liv* 60-63; Prec Wakef Cathl 63-66; V Woodhall *Bradf* 66-77; Chapl Qu Marg Sch Escrick Park 77-83; Min Can, Prec and Sacr Pet Cathl 83-88; R Upper St Leonards St Jo *Chich* 88-94; rtd 94; Perm to Offic *York* from 95. *5 Greenwich Close, York YO30 5WN* Tel (01904) 610237

CARTER, Russell James Wigney. b 29. Chich Th Coll 80. **d** 82 **p** 83. C Aldwick *Chich* 82-86; R Buxted and Hadlow Down 86-90; rtd 90; Perm to Offic *Chich* from 90. *6 Lucerne Court, Aldwick, Bognor Regis PO21 4XL* Tel (01243) 862858

CARTER, Samuel. b 49. St Jo Coll Dur BA71. Cranmer Hall Dur 73. **d** 74 **p** 75. C Kingswinford St Mary *Lich* 74-77; C Shrewsbury H Cross 77-84; V Normacot 84-94. *Address withheld by request*

CARTER, Sarah Helen Buchanan. *See* GORTON, Sarah Helen Buchanan

CARTER, Stanley Reginald. b 24. St Jo Coll Dur BA49. **d** 50 **p** 51. C Stoughton *Guildf* 50-53; C Bucknall and Bagnall *Lich* 53-56; R Salford St Matthias w St Simon *Man* 56-62; V Highbury New Park St Aug *Lon* 62-69; V Sneinton St Chris w St Phil *S'well* 69-89; rtd 89; Perm to Offic *S'well* from 89. *31 Pateley Road, Nottingham NG3 5QF* Tel 0115-953 2122 E-mail stan.carter@dunelm.org.uk

CARTER, Canon Stephen. b 56. Univ of Wales (Lamp) BA77 Southn Univ BTh81. Sarum & Wells Th Coll 78. **d** 81 **p** 82. C Halstead St Andr w H Trin and Greenstead Green *Chelmsf* 81-84; C Loughton St Jo 84-89; V N Shoebury 89-95; R Lexden from 95; RD Colchester 01-06; Hon Can Chelmsf Cathl from 07. *The Rectory, 2 Wroxham Close, Colchester CO3 3RQ* Tel (01206) 575966 E-mail revscarter@googlemail.com

CARTER, Stephen Howard. b 47. City Univ BSc72. St Jo Coll Nottm 83. **d** 85 **p** 86. C Hellesdon *Nor* 85-88; Chapl Asst Birm Children's Hosp 88-91; Chapl Asst Birm Maternity Hosp 88-91; TV Tettenhall Wood *Lich* 91-98; Chapl Compton Hospice 91-98; P-in-c Coalbrookdale, Iron-Bridge and Lt Wenlock *Heref* 98-00; R 00-07; Asst Dioc Co-ord for Evang 00-01; P-in-c Netherton St Andr *Worc* 07-08; V from 08; P-in-c Darby End 07-08; V from 08. *St Andrew's Vicarage, Highbridge Road, Netherton, Dudley DY2 0HT* Tel and fax (01384) 257097 E-mail stevecarter@fastmail.net

CARTER, Stephen Paul. b 55. Cartrefle Coll of Educn CertEd76. Trin Coll Bris BA88. **d** 98 **p** 99. Dn-in-c Montevideo H Spirit Uruguay 98-99; P-in-c 00-04; V Dalston w Cumdivock, Raughton Head and Wreay *Carl* from 04. *The Vicarage, Townhead Road, Dalston, Carlisle CA5 7JF* Tel and fax (01228) 710215 E-mail spc55@tiscali.co.uk

CARTER, Stuart Conway. b 58. Lon Bible Coll 81 St Jo Coll Nottm 90. **d** 92 **p** 93. C Birm St Luke 92-96; C The Quinton from 96. *95 Oak Road, Quinton, Birmingham B68 0BH* Tel 0121-422 3621 E-mail stuwecarter@btinternet.com

CARTER, Terence John. b 31. K Coll Lon BD57 AKC57 Lon Univ BA68 PGCE69. **d** 58 **p** 59. C Woolwich St Jo *S'wark* 58-60; PV S'wark Cathl 60-63; Sacr S'wark Cathl 60-61; Succ S'wark Cathl 61-63; R Ockham w Hatchford *Guildf* 63-69; Lic to Offic *S'wark* 69-78 and *Portsm* 78-82; Perm to Offic *Portsm* from 82; rtd 91. *15 Balliol Road, Portsmouth PO2 7PP* Tel (023) 9269 9167 Mobile 07811-474020
E-mail terence.carter1@ntlworld.com

CARTER, Timothy Stephen. b 76. Somerville Coll Ox MEng99. St Jo Coll Nottm 06. **d** 08 **p** 09. C Hanley H Ev *Lich* from 08. *23 Mereside Close, Stoke-on-Trent ST1 5GH* Tel (01782) 208735 Mobile 07772-956146 E-mail tim@carterclan.me.uk

CARTER, Mrs Wendy Elise Grace. b 46. Battersea Coll of Educn TCert67. Qu Coll Birm 01. **d** 04 **p** 05. C Kingshurst *Birm* 04-07; P-in-c High Wych and Gilston w Eastwick *St Alb* from 07. *The Rectory, High Wych Road, High Wych, Sawbridgeworth CM21 0HX* Tel (01279) 600894
E-mail wegcarter@btinternet.com

CARTLEDGE, Margery. *See* TOLLER, Elizabeth Margery

CARTLEDGE, Mark John. b 62. Lon Bible Coll BA85 Univ of Wales PhD00. Oak Hill Th Coll MPhil89. **d** 88 **p** 89. C Formby H Trin *Liv* 88-91; Miss Partner CMS 91-93; Nigeria 91-93; Chapl Liv Univ 93-98; Chapl and Tutor St Jo Coll Dur 98-03; Lect Univ of Wales (Lamp) 03-06; Sen Lect Th Birm Univ from 08. *Department of Theology, University of Birmingham, Edgbaston, Birmingham B15 2TT* Tel 0121-414 7512
E-mail m.j.cartledge@bham.ac.uk

CARTMELL, Canon Richard Peter Watkinson. b 43. Cranmer Hall Dur 77. **d** 79 **p** 80. C Whittle-le-Woods *Blackb* 79-85; V Lower Darwen St Jas 85-03; RD Darwen 91-96; P-in-c S Shore H Trin 03-08; Hon Can Blackb Cathl 98-08; rtd 08; Perm to Offic

Blackb from 08. *4 Salwick Avenue, Blackpool FY2 9BT* Tel (01253) 590083

CARTMILL, Canon Ralph Arthur. b 40. St Jo Coll Dur BA62 Em Coll Cam MA64. Ridley Hall Cam 63. **d** 65 **p** 66. C Dukinfield St Jo *Ches* 65-68; C Wilmslow 68-69; Warden Walton Youth Cen Liv 69-70; Asst Master Aylesbury Gr Sch 70-74; Perm to Offic *Ox* 72-74; V Terriers 74-85; P-in-c Chinnor w Emmington and Sydenham 85-86; R Chinnor w Emmington and Sydenham etc 86-98; Hon Can Ch 97-98; rtd 98; Perm to Offic *Nor* from 00. *6 Longview Close, Snettisham, King's Lynn PE31 7RD* Tel (01485) 543357

CARTWRIGHT, Alan John. b 44. Liv Univ BEng66 Birm Univ MSc68 Warwick Univ PhD95 CEng72 MIMechE72. WMMTC 04. **d** 07 **p** 08. OLM Rugby W *Cov* from 07. *39 Buchanan Road, Rugby CV22 6AZ* Tel (01788) 574071 Mobile 07981-667534 E-mail alan@stmatthews.org.uk

CARTWRIGHT, Mrs Amanda Jane. b 58. St Jo Coll Nottm 00. **d** 02 **p** 03. C Beeston *S'well* 02-07; P-in-c Bilborough St Jo from 07; P-in-c Bilborough w Strelley from 07. *St John's Vicarage, Graylands Road, Nottingham NG8 4FD* Tel 0115-929 3320 E-mail revdmand@hotmail.com

CARTWRIGHT, Julia Ann. b 58. Nottm Univ BA80. Linc Th Coll 84. **dss** 86 **d** 87 **p** 94. Asst Chapl HM Pris Morton Hall 85-90; Linc St Jo 86-88; Hon C 87-88; Hon C Bardney 88-97; Chapl Linc Co Hosp 90-93; Chapl St Geo Hosp Linc 90-93; Chapl Linc Distr Health Services and Hosps NHS Trust 93-97; Chapl S Bucks NHS Trust 97-04; Lic to Offic *Ox* 97-04; Chapl S Warks Combined Care NHS Trust from 04. *St Michael's Hospital, St Michael's Road, Warwick CV34 5QW* Tel (01926) 496241 *or* 406789 Fax 406700

CARTWRIGHT, Michael. *See* CARTWRIGHT, William Michael

CARTWRIGHT, Michael John. b 42. Qu Coll Birm 67. **d** 70 **p** 71. C Astwood Bank w Crabbs Cross *Worc* 70-75; P-in-c Worc St Mich 75-77; R Linwood from 87; V Legsby from 87; RD W Wold 89-01; R Wickenby Gp 95-00; V Lissington from 00. *The Vicarage, 13 Lady Frances Drive, Market Rasen LN8 3JJ* Tel (01673) 843424

CARTWRIGHT, Paul. b 71. Leeds Metrop Univ BA99 Huddersfield Univ PGCE06 Leeds Univ BA08. Coll of Resurr Mirfield 06. **d** 08. C Athersley *Wakef* from 08. *Priory House, 24 Kirkland Gardens, Barnsley S71 2GD* Tel (01226) 285209 Mobile 07852-174303 E-mail fr.paul.cartwright@gmail.com

CARTWRIGHT, Samuel. b 27. Cuddesdon Coll 71. **d** 72 **p** 72. C Rochdale *Man* 72-76; V Roundthorn 76-83; V Ashton Ch Ch 83-93; rtd 93; Perm to Offic *Derby* from 93. *8 Wentworth Avenue, Walton, Chesterfield S40 3JB* Tel (01246) 232252

CARTWRIGHT, Sidney Victor. b 22. Launde Abbey 73. **d** 74 **p** 75. C Braunstone *Leic* 74-78; P-in-c Arnesby w Shearsby 78-86; R Arnesby w Shearsby and Bruntingthorpe 86-87; rtd 87; Perm to Offic *Leic* and *Pet* from 87. *32 Northleigh Grove, Market Harborough LE16 9QX* Tel (01858) 463915

CARTWRIGHT, Simon John. b 71. R Holloway Coll Lon BA93 Sheff Univ MA95. St Jo Coll Nottm MTh05. **d** 06 **p** 07. C Ward End w Bordesley Green *Birm* from 06. *The Vicarage, St Margarets Avenue, Birmingham B8 2BH* Tel 0121-327 9089 Mobile 07720-769631 E-mail simon@ccbl.org.uk

CARTWRIGHT, William Michael. b 44. Birm Univ CertEd67. Coll of Resurr Mirfield 83. **d** 83 **p** 84. Hd Master Chacombe Sch 83-85; Hon C Middleton Cheney w Chacombe *Pet* 83-85; Hd Master Chacombe Sch Banbury 83-85; C Kettering SS Pet and Paul 85-86; Perm to Offic 86-88; Chapl Northaw Prep Sch Win 89-92; P-in-c Altarnon w Bolventor, Laneast and St Clether *Truro* 92-97; V Treverbyn 97-01; V Bempton w Flamborough, Reighton w Speeton *York* 01-03; V Ampleforth w Oswaldkirk, Gilling E etc from 03. *The Vicarage, West End, Ampleforth, York YO62 4DU* Tel (01439) 788876

CARUANA, Mrs Rosemary Anne. b 38. St Alb Minl Tr Scheme 81. **dss** 84 **d** 87 **p** 94. Hertford St Andr *St Alb* 84-87; Par Dn Hertingfordbury 87-94; C Hw-Pet 98-05; rtd 05. *36 Holly Croft, Hertford SG14 2DR* Tel (01992) 306427 Mobile 07769-658756 E-mail r.caruana@ntlworld.com

CARVER, Miss Elizabeth Ann. b 36. ACIB73. Bp Otter Coll BA00. **d** 99. NSM Littlehampton and Wick *Chich* from 99. *13 Hearnfield Road, Littlehampton BN17 7PR* Tel (01903) 713169

CARVETH, Mrs Marlene. b 51. Ex Univ BA07. SWMTC 04. **d** 07 **p** 08. NSM Camborne *Truro* from 07. *Trelowarren, 5 Rosevale Crescent, Camborne TR14 7LU* Tel (01209) 713175 E-mail roseyvale@tiscali.co.uk

CARVOSSO, John Charles. b 45. ACA71 FCA79. Oak Hill Th Coll 75. **d** 78 **p** 79. C Chelsea St Jo w St Andr *Lon* 78-81; Chapl RAF 81-84; P-in-c Tawstock *Ex* 84-85; TV Newport, Bishops Tawton and Tawstock 85-96; TV Newton Tracey, Horwood, Alverdiscott etc from 96; RD Torrington 97-02. *The Rectory, Tawstock, Barnstaple EX31 3HZ* Tel (01271) 374963 E-mail devoncarvosso@classicfm.net

CASE, Preb Catherine Margaret. b 44. Ripon Coll Cuddesdon 86. **d** 88 **p** 94. C Blurton *Lich* 88-89; TD Hanley H Ev and Min to Hanley Care Agencies 92-94; P-in-c Wrockwardine Wood 95-98; R 98-00; V Gnosall 00-06; V Gnosall and Moreton 06-07; Preb Lich Cathl 02-07; rtd 07; Perm to Offic *Lich* from 07. *2 Fulmar Place, Stoke-on-Trent ST3 7QF* Tel (01782) 399291

CASE, Clive Anthony. b 70. St Andr Univ MTheol93 Surrey Univ BA05 St Jo Coll Dur PGCE94. STETS 02. **d** 05 **p** 06. NSM Epsom St Martin *Guildf* from 05; Asst Chapl Epsom Coll 05-07; Chapl St Jo Sch Leatherhead from 08. *St John's School, Epsom Road, Leatherhead KT22 8SP* Tel (01372) 385445 *or* 385487 Mobile 07801-288943 E-mail chaplain@stjohns.surrey.sch.uk

CASEBOW, Ronald Philip. b 31. Roch Th Coll 59. **d** 61 **p** 62. C Southgate Ch Ch *Lon* 61-64; C Oseney Crescent St Luke w Camden Square St Paul 64-70; Warden St Paul's Ho Student Hostel 64-70; V Colchester St Steph *Chelmsf* 70-74; V Burnham 74-89; rtd 89; Perm to Offic *Nor* from 95. *The Priory, Priory Road, Palgrave, Diss IP22 1AJ* Tel (01379) 651804

CASEY, Christopher Noel. b 61. Open Univ BA95. St Jo Coll Nottm BA01. **d** 01 **p** 02. C Penrith w Newton Reigny and Plumpton Wall *Carl* 01-06; P-in-c Mirehouse from 06. *The Vicarage, Hollins Close, Whitehaven CA28 8EX* Tel (01946) 693565 E-mail kc.family@btopenworld.com

CASH, Simon Andrew. b 62. St Jo Coll Nottm 99. **d** 01 **p** 02. C Aston cum Aughton w Swallownest and Ulley *Sheff* 01-04; P-in-c Worksop St Anne *S'well* from 04; P-in-c Norton Cuckney from 05. *The Vicarage, 11 Poplar Close, Worksop S80 3BZ* Tel (01909) 472069 E-mail s.cash@freenet.co.uk

CASHEL, Dean of. *See* KNOWLES, The Very Revd Philip John

CASHEL, WATERFORD AND LISMORE, Archdeacon of. *See* MURRAY, The Ven John Grainger

CASHEL, WATERFORD, LISMORE, OSSORY, FERNS AND LEIGHLIN, Bishop of. *See* BURROWS, The Rt Revd Michael Andrew James

CASIOT, David John. b 39. St Pet Coll Ox BA63 MA67. Clifton Th Coll 63. **d** 65 **p** 66. C Drypool St Columba w St Andr and St Pet *York* 65-67; C Barking St Marg *Chelmsf* 67-71; R Whalley Range St Edm *Man* 71-84; V Wandsworth St Mich *S'wark* 84-00; Perm to Offic *Roch* from 00; rtd 04. *52 High Street, Otford, Sevenoaks TN14 5PQ* Tel (01959) 522588 E-mail david@oakside.idps.co.uk

CASON, Preb Ronald Arthur. b 28. Kelham Th Coll 48. **d** 53 **p** 54. C Fenton *Lich* 53-56; V Brereton 56-63; V Hugglescote w Donington *Leic* 63-67; R Blakenall Heath *Lich* 67-74; R Stoke upon Trent 74-80; Preb Lich Cathl 75-93; RD Stoke 78-88; TR Stoke-upon-Trent 80-91; Lect Tettenhall Par 91-93; rtd 93; Perm to Offic *Lich* 93-00. *Talbot House Nursing Home, 28-30 Talbot Street, Rugeley WS15 2EG* Tel (01889) 570527

CASSAM, Victor Reginald. b 33. Chich Univ BA05. Chich Th Coll 59. **d** 62 **p** 63. C Portsea St Jo Rudmore *Portsm* 62-64; C W Leigh CD 64-66; C Torquay St Martin Barton *Ex* 66-69; C Stanmer w Falmer and Moulsecoomb *Chich* 69-73; P-in-c Catsfield 73-76; R Catsfield and Crowhurst 76-81; R Selsey 81-01; RD Chich 96-01; rtd 01; Perm to Offic *Chich* and *Portsm* from 01. *195 Oving Road, Chichester PO19 7ER* Tel and fax (01243) 783998 Mobile 07976-757451 E-mail vrc@vicas.demon.co.uk

CASSELTON, John Charles. b 43. Univ of Wales (Swansea) MA95. Oak Hill Th Coll 64. **d** 68 **p** 69. C Upton *Ex* 68-73; C Braintree *Chelmsf* 73-80; V Ipswich St Jo *St E* 80-92; RD Ipswich 86-92; Chapl St Clem Hosp Ipswich 92-98; Chapl St Eliz Hospice Ipswich 92-00; Dir Inspire Chr Counselling from 00; Perm to Offic *St E* from 00. *Rose Cottage, 41 North Hill Road, Ipswich IP4 2PN* Tel (01473) 401638 E-mail inspire.ipswich@btclick.com

CASSIDY, Brian Ross. b 31. Cape Town Univ. St Bede's Coll Umtata 88. **d** 89 **p** 91. S Africa 89-92; C Lymington *Win* 92-93; P-in-c Hyde Common 93-96; P-in-c Ellingham and Harbridge and Ibsley 95-96; V Ellingham and Harbridge and Hyde w Ibsley 96-03; rtd 03. *The Vicarage, Hyde, Fordingbridge SP6 2QJ* Tel (01425) 653216 E-mail cassidy@btinternet.com

✠**CASSIDY, The Rt Revd George Henry.** b 42. QUB BSc65 Lon Univ MPhil67. Oak Hill Th Coll 70. **d** 72 **p** 73 **c** 99. C Clifton Ch Ch w Em *Bris* 72-75; V Sea Mills 75-82; V Portman Square St Paul *Lon* 82-87; V London and Can Res St Paul's Cathl 87-99; P-in-c St Ethelburga Bishopgate 89-91; Bp S'well and Nottm 99-09; rtd 09. *Darch House, 17 St Andrew's Road, Stogursey, Bridgwater TA5 1TE* Tel (01278) 732625 E-mail georgecassidy123@btinternet.com

CASSIDY, Herbert. b 35. TCD BA57 MA65. CITC 58. **d** 58 **p** 59. C Belfast H Trin *Conn* 58-60; C Londonderry Ch Ch *D & R* 60-62; I Aghavilly w Derrynoose *Arm* 62-65; Hon V Choral Arm Cathl 63-85; C Portadown St Columba 65-67; I 67-85; Dean Kilmore *K, E & A* 85-89; I Kilmore w Ballintemple 85-86; I Kilmore w Ballintemple, Kildallan etc 86-89; Dir of Ords 89; Dean Arm and Keeper of Public Lib 89-06; rtd 06; Hon Sec Gen Syn from 90. *2 Kilmore Meadows, Kilmore, Armagh BT61 8PA* Tel (028) 3887 0825 Mobile 07759-323733 E-mail herbieandanncassidy@hotmail.co.uk

CASSIDY, Ian David. b 59. NOC 94. **d** 97 **p** 98. NSM Everton St Geo *Liv* from 97. *79 Gilroy Road, Liverpool L6 6BG* Tel 0151-263 9751 Mobile 0780-1933654

CASSIDY, Canon Joseph Patrick. b 54. Concordia Univ Montreal BA76 Detroit Univ MA80 Toronto Univ STB86 MDiv86 St Paul Univ Ottawa LTh89 DTh95 Ottawa Univ PhD95 FRSA. Toronto Bible Coll 82. **d** 85 **p** 86. Canada 85-96; NSM Laverstock *Sarum* 96-97; NSM Salisbury St Martin 96-97; Prin St Chad's Coll Dur from 97; Hon Can Dur Cathl from 01. *St Chad's College, University of Durham, 18 North Bailey, Durham DH1 3RH* Tel 0191-374 3364 *or* 374 3367 Fax 374 3309 E-mail j.p.cassidy@durham.ac.uk

CASSIDY, Patrick Nigel. b 40. TCD BA63 MA66. Sarum Th Coll 64. **d** 66 **p** 67. C Heaton St Barn *Bradf* 66-68; Asst Chapl Brussels *Eur* 68-70; Chapl SW France 70-72; V Oseney Crescent St Luke w Camden Square St Paul *Lon* 72-83; Chapl Strasbourg w Stuttgart and Heidelberg *Eur* 83-84; Perm to Offic *Chich* 86-90; Chapl Marseille w Aix-en-Provence *Eur* 90-05; Hon Chapl Miss to Seafarers 90-05; rtd 05. *73 La Canebière (Appt 83), 13001 Marseille, France* Tel (0033) (4) 91 90 18 81 E-mail palmeito@aol.com

CASSIDY, Canon Ronald. b 43. Lon Univ BD66 Man Univ MPhil85. Tyndale Hall Bris 63. **d** 68 **p** 69. C Kirkdale St Lawr *Liv* 68-70; C Bolton Em *Man* 70-74; V Roughtown 74-89; R Denton St Lawr 89-07; AD Ashton-under-Lyne 97-03; Hon Can Man Cathl 02-07; rtd 07; Perm to Offic *Man* from 07. *19 Broomfields, Denton, Manchester M34 3TH* Tel 0161-320 6955 E-mail roncass-99@yahoo.com

CASSON, David Christopher. b 41. Qu Coll Cam BA64 MA68. Ridley Hall Cam 65. **d** 67 **p** 68. C Birm St Martin 67-72; C Luton St Mary *St Alb* 72-77; P-in-c Luton St Fran 77; V 77-84; V Richmond H Trin and Ch Ch *S'wark* 84-97; R Acle w Fishley, N Burlingham, Beighton w Moulton *Nor* 97-04; rtd 04; Perm to Offic *Nor* from 04. *70 The Street, Brundall, Norwich NR13 5LH* Tel (01603) 712092

CASSON, Canon James Stuart. b 32. Liv Univ BA54 Nottm Univ MPhil70. Ridley Hall Cam. **d** 61 **p** 62. C Eccleston Ch Ch *Liv* 61-64; C Littleover Derby 64-67; V Dearham *Carl* 67-76; V Holme Eden 76-98; RD Brampton 91-96; Hon Can Carl Cathl 93-98; P-in-c Croglin 93-98; rtd 98; Perm to Offic *Carl* from 01. *5 High Woodbank, Brisco, Carlisle CA4 0QR* Tel (01228) 525962

CASSWELL, David Oriel. b 52. Loughb Coll of Educn DipEd74 CQSW79. Oak Hill Th Coll 85. **d** 87 **p** 88. C Acomb St Steph *York* 87-91; Dep Chapl HM Pris Leeds 91-92; Chapl HM Pris Everthorpe 92; Chapl HM Pris Wolds 92-98; V Clifton *York* from 98. *Clifton Vicarage, Clifton, York YO30 6BH* Tel (01904) 655071 Fax 654796 E-mail david.casswell@cliftonparish.org.uk

CASSWELL, Peter Joyce. b 22. Trin Coll Cam BA48 MA50. Ridley Hall Cam 48. **d** 50 **p** 51. C Addiscombe St Mildred *Cant* 50-53; C-in-c New Addington CD 53-55; V New Addington 55-64; R Buckhurst Hill *Chelmsf* 64-78; Hon Can Chelmsf Cathl 75-78; Chapl Forest Gate Hosp Lon 64-78; R Lutterworth w Cotesbach *Leic* 78-90; RD Guthlaxton II 89-90; rtd 90; Perm to Offic *Leic* from 90. *1 Spring Close, Lutterworth LE17 4DD* Tel (01455) 554197 *or* 282630

CASTER, John Forristall. b 71. Texas A&M Univ BA93. St Steph Ho Ox BTh05. **d** 05 **p** 06. C Hendon St Alphage *Lon* 05-09, TV Old St Pancras from 09. *St Mary's House, Eversholt Street, London NW1 1BN* Tel (020) 7267 8631

✠**CASTLE, The Rt Revd Brian Colin.** b 49. Lon Univ BA77 Ox Univ BA77 MA80 Birm Univ PhD89. Cuddesdon Coll 74. **d** 77 **p** 78 **c** 02. C Limpsfield and Titsey *S'wark* 77-81; USPG Zambia 81-84; Lect Locum Inst WCC Geneva 84-85; V N Petherton w Northmoor Green *B & W* 85-92; Dir Past Studies and Vice-Prin Cuddesdon Coll 92-01; Suff Bp Tonbridge *Roch* from 02; Hon Can Roch Cathl from 02. *Bishop's Lodge, 48 St Botolph's Road, Sevenoaks TN13 3AG* Tel (01732) 456070 Fax 741449 E-mail bishop.tonbridge@rochester.anglican.org

CASTLE, Brian Stanley. b 47. Oak Hill Th Coll 70. **d** 73 **p** 74. C Barnsbury St Andr w St Thos and St Matthias *Lon* 73-76; C Lower Homerton St Paul 76-79; P-in-c Bethnal Green St Jas Less 79-98; V Tile Cross *Birm* 98-08; P-in-c Garretts Green 03-08; V Garretts Green and Tile Cross from 08; AD Coleshill from 06. *The Vicarage, Haywood Road, Birmingham B33 0LH* Tel and fax 0121-779 2739 Mobile 07710-251790 E-mail revbcastle@aol.com

CASTLE, John Arthur. b 61. G&C Coll Cam BA83 St Jo Coll Dur BA95. Aston Tr Scheme 90 Cranmer Hall Dur 92. **d** 95 **p** 96. C Southborough St Pet w Ch Ch and St Matt *Roch* 95-99; Miss Partner CMS 99-04; P-in-c Sandhurst *Ox* from 04. *The Rectory, 155 High Street, Sandhurst GU47 8HR* Tel (01252) 872168

CASTLE, Martin Roger. b 69. Ridley Hall Cam. **d** 09. C Leic Martyrs from 09. *62 Ashleigh Road, Leicester LE3 0FB*

CASTLE, Michael David. b 38. Wells Th Coll 69. **d** 71 **p** 72. C Acocks Green *Birm* 71-75; C Weoley Castle 76-78, V 78-08; rtd 08. *12 West Pathway, Birmingham B17 9DU* Tel 0121-427 2914

CASTLE, Phillip Stanley. b 43. **d** 97 **p** 98. OLM E Farnworth and Kearsley *Man* from 97. *73 Bradford Street, Farnworth, Bolton BL4 9JY* Tel (01204) 571439

CASTLE, Roger James. b 39. St Jo Coll Cam BA62 MA66. Clifton Th Coll 63. **d** 65 **p** 66. C Rushden w Newton Bromswold *Pet* 65-68; C Stapenhill w Cauldwell *Derby* 68-72; V Hayfield 72-89; R Coxheath, E Farleigh, Hunton, Linton etc *Roch* 89-04; Chapl Invicta Community Care NHS Trust 91-04; rtd 04; Perm to Offic *Bris* from 04. *10 College Park Drive, Bristol BS10 7AN* Tel 0117-950 7028

CASTLETON, David Miles. b 39. Oak Hill Th Coll 66. **d** 72 **p** 73. C Canonbury St Steph *Lon* 72-76; C Guildf St Sav w Stoke-next-Guildford 76-89; rtd 04. *2 Lyne Place Manor, Bridge Lane, Virginia Water GU25 4ED*

CASTLETON, Mark. b 82. Bath Spa Univ BA04 Cam Univ BTh09. Ridley Hall Cam 06. **d** 09. C Salisbury St Mark *Sarum* from 09. *4 St Joseph's Close, Bishopdown, Salisbury SP1 3FX* E-mail castletonmark@yahoo.co.uk

CASWELL, Roger John. b 47. St Chad's Coll Dur BA70. St Steph Ho Ox 75. **d** 77 **p** 78. C Brighton Resurr *Chich* 77-83; TV Crawley 83-90; TR Littlehampton and Wick from 90; Chapl Littlehampton Hosp 90-93; Chapl Worthing Priority Care NHS Trust from 93. *St Mary's Vicarage, 34 Fitzalan Road, Littlehampton BN17 5ET* Tel (01903) 724410 *or* 726875

CASWELL, Thomas Hubert. b 55. Aston Tr Scheme 90 Coll of Resurr Mirfield 92. **d** 94 **p** 95. C Sheff St Leon Norwood 94-97; P-in-c Sheff St Cecilia Parson Cross 97-04; V Masbrough from 04. *St Paul's Vicarage, 256 Kimberworth Road, Rotherham S61 1HG* Tel (01709) 557810

CATCHPOLE, Geoffrey Alan. b 53. AKC. Westcott Ho Cam 76. **d** 77 **p** 78. C Camberwell St Luke *S'wark* 77-80; C Dulwich St Barn 80-82; TV Canvey Is *Chelmsf* 82-87; Ind Chapl 83-87; P-in-c Bradwell on Sea 87-92; P-in-c St Lawrence 87-92; V Holland-on-Sea 92-00; P-in-c Witchford w Wentworth *Ely* 00-02; Adult Educn and Tr Officer 00-02; R Colchester St Mich Myland *Chelmsf* 02-07; rtd 07. *Shobita's Ship, 21 Empire Road, Harwich CO12 3QA* Tel (01255) 508525 E-mail pole@pole97.fsnet.co.uk

CATCHPOLE, Guy St George. b 30. **d** 82 **p** 83. Kenya 82-89; C Woodford Wells *Chelmsf* 89-95; rtd 95; Perm to Offic *Cant* 95-08. *67 Trevor Drive, Allington, Maidstone ME16 0QW* Tel (01622) 761378

CATCHPOLE, Richard James Swinburne. b 65. St Steph Ho Ox 92. **d** 95 **p** 96. C Eastbourne St Andr *Chich* 95-98; C Eastbourne St Mary 98-00; C E Grinstead St Swithun 00-07. *23 Nineveh Shipyard, Arundel BN18 9SU* Tel 07951-427384 (mobile) E-mail rjscatchpole@hotmail.co.uk

CATCHPOLE, Roy. b 46. Sheff Univ MMinTheol95. St Jo Coll Nottm LTh74 ALCD74. **d** 74 **p** 75. C Rainham *Chelmsf* 74-76; C Hyson Green *S'well* 76-79; V Broxtowe 79-86; V Calverton 86-94; Hilfield Friary Dorchester 95-01; rtd 01; Perm to Offic *Sarum* from 06. *60 Gainsborough, Milborne Port, Sherborne DT9 5BB* Tel (01963) 250040 E-mail rev.catch@virgin.net

CATER, Lois May. b 37. S Dios Minl Tr Scheme 81. **dss** 84 **d** 87 **p** 94. Calne and Blackland *Sarum* 84-89; Hon Par Dn 87-89; Hon Par Dn Devizes St Jo w St Mary 89-94; Hon C 94-96; Hon TV Alderbury Team 96-01; Hon TV Clarendon 01-07. *18 St Margaret's Close, Calne SN11 0UQ* Tel (01249) 819432

CATERER, James Albert Leslie Blower. b 44. New Coll Ox BA67 MA81. Sarum & Wells Th Coll 79. **d** 81 **p** 82. C Cheltenham St Luke and St Jo *Glouc* 81-85; V Standish w Haresfield and Moreton Valence etc 85-96; P-in-c Glouc St Steph from 96. *Copelands, 180 Stroud Road, Gloucester GL1 5JX* Tel and fax (01452) 524694 E-mail jcaterer@atlas.co.uk

CATHCART, Adrian James. *See* MATTHEWS, Adrian James

CATHERALL, Mark Leslie. b 64. Chich Th Coll BTh93. **d** 93 **p** 94. C Lancing w Coombes *Chich* 93-95; C Selsey 95-98; Chapl RN 98-04; V S Thornaby *York* from 04. *St Peter's Rectory, White House Road, Thornaby, Stockton-on-Tees TS17 0AJ* Tel (01642) 888403

CATHERINE JOY, Sister. *See* MOON, Sister Catherine Joy

CATHIE, Sean Bewley. b 43. Dur Univ BA67 Birkbeck Coll Lon MSc04. Cuddesdon Coll 67. **d** 69 **p** 70. C Kensal Rise St Martin *Lon* 69-73; C Paddington H Trin w St Paul 73-75; P-in-c Bridstow w Peterstow *Heref* 75-79; Hon C Westmr St Jas *Lon* 85-97; Hon C St Marylebone w H Trin 99-06; Hon C St Marylebone St Cypr 99-06; rtd 06. *22 Southwood Park, Southwood Lawn Road, London N6 5SG* Tel (020) 8350 4372 *or* tel and fax 8347 7050 E-mail scathie@waitrose.com

CATLEY, John Howard. b 37. AKC60. K Coll Lon 57 St Boniface Warminster 60. **d** 61 **p** 62. C Sowerby Bridge w Norland *Wakef* 61-64; C Almondbury 64-67; V Earl's Heaton 67-75; V Brownhill 75-86; V Morley St Pet w Churwell 86-92; V St Annes St Marg *Blackb* 92-98; RD Kirkham 94-98; rtd 98; Perm to Offic *Blackb* from 98. *Flat 6, Herne Hill Lodge, 598 Lytham Road, Blackpool FY4 1RB* Tel (01253) 405483

CATLEY, Marc. b 59. Liv Univ BA82 Lon Bible Coll BA85 Man Poly PGCE90. St Jo Coll Nottm MTh06. **d** 07 **p** 08. C E Green Cov from 07. *27 Polperro Drive, Coventry CV5 7PT* Tel (024) 7640 5324 E-mail marc@marccatley.co.uk

CATLING, Michael David. b 56. Goldsmiths' Coll Lon CertEd77 DipEd84 Newc Univ MLitt06. Cranmer Hall Dur 88. **d** 90 **p** 91.

C Cullercoats St Geo *Newc* 90-94; TV Glendale Gp 94-01; V Whittingham and Edlingham w Bolton Chapel 01-09; R Wigmore Abbey *Heref* from 09. *The Rectory, Dark Lane, Leintwardine, Craven Arms SY7 0LJ* Tel (01547) 540235
E-mail mike@catlingfamily.fsnet.co.uk

CATLING, Canon Robert Mason. b 19. St Jo Coll Ox BA41 MA44. St Steph Ho Ox 41. **d** 43 **p** 44. C Falmouth All SS *Truro* 43-57; Lib Pusey Ho and Asst Chapl Univ Coll Ox 57-61; C Falmouth All SS 61-64; V Beckenham St Barn *Roch* 64-72; V Devoran *Truro* 72-87; Hon Can Truro Cathl 77-87; rtd 87; Perm to Offic *Ex* and Truro from 87. *Ground Floor Flat, 31 Cranford Avenue, Exmouth EX8 2QA* Tel (01395) 267896

CATO (*formerly* LEGGETT)**, Ms Vanessa Gisela.** b 51. St Osyth Coll of Educn TCert75. Westcott Ho Cam 93. **d** 93 **p** 94. C Southchurch H Trin *Chelmsf* 93-97; R Orsett and Bulphan and Horndon on the Hill 97-03; Chapl Basildon and Thurrock Gen Hosps NHS Trust 99-03; P-in-c Sandridge *St Alb* from 03; Herts Area Children's Work Adv from 03. *The Vicarage, 2 Anson Close, Sandridge, St Albans AL4 9EN* Tel (01727) 866089
E-mail vicarstleonards03@btinternet.com

CATON, David Arthur. b 25. Trin Coll Ox BA50 MA50. St Steph Ho Ox 49. **d** 51 **p** 52. C Seaton Hirst *Newc* 51-55; S Africa 55-61; V Stapleford *Ely* 61-69; V Hurst *Man* 69-75; V Hanwell St Thos *Lon* 75-84; AD Ealing W 82-84; V Staincross *Wakef* 84-95; rtd 95; Perm to Offic *Lon* from 95. *39 Beardsley Way, London W3 7YQ* Tel (020) 8743 2126

CATON, Philip Cooper. b 47. Oak Hill Th Coll 79. **d** 81 **p** 82. C Much Woolton *Liv* 81-85; TV Parr 85-98; V Birkdale St Jo from 98. *St John's Vicarage, 17 Kirkstall Road, Southport PR8 4RA* Tel (01704) 568318 E-mail caton@dircon.co.uk

CATT, Douglas Gordon. b 23. MCSP49 SRP67. Roch Th Coll 61. **d** 63 **p** 64. C Cant St Martin w St Paul 63-66; R Croughton and Hinton in the Hedges w Steane *Pet* 66-75; V Evenley 72-75; Chapl St Andr Hosp Northn 75-89; rtd 88; Perm to Offic *Pet* 88-07. *195 Billing Road, Northampton NN1 5RS* Tel (01604) 627710

CATTELL, The Ven Jack. b 15. Univ Coll Dur BA37 MA40 Lon Univ BD53. Sarum & Wells Th Coll 38. **d** 39 **p** 40. C Royston *Wakef* 39-41; Perm to Offic *Sarum* 41-42; CF (EC) 42-46; Lic to Offic *Ripon* 46-49; Chapl R Wanstead Sch 49-53; Bermuda 53-82; Adn Bermuda 61-82; Perm to Offic *Mon* 82-89. *39A Risca Road, Newport NP9 4HX* Tel (01633) 54529

CATTERALL, David Arnold. b 53. Lon Univ BSc74 ARCS74. Cranmer Hall Dur. **d** 78 **p** 79. C Swinton St Pet *Man* 78-81; C Wythenshawe St Martin 81-83; R Heaton Norris Ch w All SS 83-88; I Fanlobbus Union *C, C & R* 88-95; Can Cork and Ross Cathls 93-95; Warden Ch's Min of Healing in Ireland 95-02; I Templemichael w Clongish, Clooncumber etc *K, E & A* from 02. *Amberley, The Belfry, Co Longford, Republic of Ireland* Tel (00353) (43) 46442 E-mail djcatt@eircom.net

CATTERALL, Canon Janet Margaret. b 53. Univ of Wales (Ban) BA74. Cranmer Hall Dur 77. **dss** 81 **d** 87 **p** 90. Wythenshawe St Martin *Man* 81-83; Heaton Norris Ch w All SS 83-88; Par Dn 87-88; C Bandon Union *C, C & R* 88-89; Dioc Youth Adv (Cork) 89-94; Dioc Youth Chapl 94-95; I Drung w Castleterra, Larah and Lavey etc *K, E & A* 95-02; P-in-c Mostrim w Granard, Clonbroney, Killoe etc from 02; Preb Mulhuddart St Patr Cathl Dublin from 05. *Amberley, The Belfry, Co Longford, Republic of Ireland* Tel (00353) (43) 46442
E-mail djcatt@eircom.net

CATTERICK, Matthew John. b 68. W Sussex Inst of HE BA90. St Steph Ho Ox BTh95. **d** 95 **p** 96. C Colchester St Jas, All SS, St Nic and St Runwald *Chelmsf* 95-98; C Leic Resurr 98-99; TV 99-04; TR Wembley Park *Lon* from 04. *The Rectory, 319 Preston Road, Harrow HA3 0QQ* Tel (020) 8904 4062
E-mail ascension@ntlworld.com

CATTLE, David James. b 75. **d** 07 **p** 08. C Firswood and Gorse Hill *Man* from 07. *440 Kings Road, Stretford, Manchester M32 8QW* Tel 0161-865 2950
E-mail david_cattle@hotmail.com

CATTLE, Canon Richard John. b 40. WMMTC 88. **d** 90 **p** 91. NSM Brixworth Deanery *Pet* 90-91; NSM Welford w Sibbertoft and Marston Trussell 91-92; V 92-97; Bp's Dioc Chapl 97-00; Dioc Sec 98-00; Can Pet Cathl 98-02; rtd 01; Perm to Offic *Pet* from 02; Dean's Asst from 05. *18 Minster Precincts, Peterborough PE1 1XX* Tel (01733) 209275 *or* 355315
E-mail richard.cattle@peterborough-cathedral.org

CATTLEY, Richard Melville. b 49. Trin Coll Bris. **d** 73 **p** 74. C Kendal St Thos *Carl* 73-77; Nat Sec Pathfinders CPAS 77-82; Exec Sec 82-85; V Dalton-in-Furness *Carl* 85-90; V Dulwich St Barn *S'wark* 90-99; Chapl Alleyn's Foundn Dulwich 90-99; V Milton Keynes *Ox* 99-05; AD Milton Keynes 01-05; V Dorking w Ranmore *Guildf* from 05. *St Martin's Vicarage, Westcott Road, Dorking RH4 3DN* Tel (01306) 882875 *or* 884229
E-mail richardmcattley@aol.com

CATTON, Canon Cedric Trevor. b 36. JP. Lambeth STh94. Wells Th Coll 72. **d** 72 **p** 73. C Solihull *Birm* 72-74; R Whepstead w Brockley *St E* 74-75; R Hawstead and Nowton w Stanningfield etc 74-79; Dioc Stewardship Adv 77-83; P-in-c Cockfield 79-83; V

Exning St Martin w Landwade 83-99; Chapl Newmarket Gen Hosp 85-93; Chapl Mid Anglia Community Health NHS Trust 93-99; Hon Can St E Cathl 90-02; Dioc Par Resources and Stewardship Officer 99-02; Asst Can Past St E Cathl 02; Acting Can Past 03-05; rtd 02; Dioc Clergy Retirement Officer *St E* from 02. *60 Sextons Meadows, Bury St Edmunds IP33 2SB* Tel and fax (01284) 749429 E-mail moretee@vicar1.freeserve.co.uk

CATTON, Stanley Charles. b 44. **d** 99 **p** 00. OLM Bermondsey St Jas w Ch Ch and St Crispin *S'wark* from 99. *4 Reverdy Road, London SE1 5QE* Tel (020) 7237 7703 *or* 7274 0913
E-mail stan@pat-catton.freeserve.co.uk

CAUDWELL, Juliet Lesley. See STRAW, Mrs Juliet Lesley

CAUNT, Mrs Margaret. b 55. Coll of Ripon & York St Jo MA97. NOC 93. **d** 97 **p** 98. NSM Brightside w Wincobank *Sheff* 97-00; C Ecclesfield 00-02; TV Gleadless 02-07; V Anston from 07. *The Vicarage, 17 Rackford Road, Anston, Sheffield S25 4DE* Tel (01909) 563447 *or* 519459

CAVAGAN, Raymond. b 35. Hull Univ MA86 PhD87. **d** 63 **p** 64. C Upper Holloway St Pet *Lon* 63-66; C Hurworth *Dur* 66-68; V New Shildon 68-76; V Toxteth Park St Mich *Liv* 76-77; P-in-c Toxteth Park St Andr Aigburth Road 76-77; V Toxteth Park St Mich w St Andr 78-88; V Stamfordham w Matfen *Newc* 88-05; Hon CF from 90; rtd 05; Perm to Offic *Ches* from 05. *1 Leys Road, Timperley, Altrincham WA14 5AT* Tel 0161-969 5603

CAVAGHAN, Dennis Edgar. b 45. Ex Univ MA99. St Jo Coll Nottm BTh74. **d** 74 **p** 75. C Hartford *Ches* 74-77; C Plymouth St Andr w St Paul and St Geo *Ex* 77-80; V Cofton w Starcross 80-88; P-in-c W Exe 88-93; Perm to Offic *B & W* 93-02; Hon C Taunton St Mary from 02. *Combe House, Corfe, Taunton TA3 7BU* Tel (01823) 421013
E-mail dennis.cavaghan@btinternet.com

CAVALCANTI, Joabe Gomes. b 69. Federal Univ of Pernambuco BA97 Trin Coll Bris MA00. Nordeste Th Sem BA91. **d** 98 **p** 98. Perm to Offic *Bris* 99 and *S'wark* 01-05; Chapl St Sav and St Olave's Sch Newington *S'wark* 05-08; C Bermondsey St Hugh CD 05-08; V Mitcham St Barn from 08. *St Barnabas' Vicarage, 46 Thirsk Road, Mitcham CR4 2BD* Tel (020) 8648 2571 Mobile 07940-444241
E-mail joabec@gmail.com

CAVALIER, Mrs Sandra Jane. b 48. Guildf Dioc Min Course 98. **d** 00 **p** 01. OLM Guildf Ch Ch w St Martha-on-the-Hill 00-04; NSM Westborough 04-08; NSM Wrecclesham from 08. *107 Campbell Fields, Aldershot GU11 3TZ* Tel (01252) 325567 Mobile 07990-658445 E-mail revcav@hotmail.co.uk

CAVAN, Lawrence Noel. b 38. Trin Coll Bris 72. **d** 75 **p** 76. C Lurgan Ch the Redeemer *D & D* 75-78; C Chorleywood Ch Ch *St Alb* 78-82; I Durrus *C, C & R* 82-85; I Portarlington w Cloneyhurke and Lea *M & K* 85-90; TV Eston w Normanby York 90-03; rtd 03; Perm to Offic *Derby* from 05. *22 Wentworth Road, Dronfield Woodhouse, Dronfield S18 8ZU* Tel (01246) 418814

CAVANAGH, Anthony James. b 49. Ushaw Coll Dur 72. **d** 79 **p** 80. In RC Ch 79-95; C Goole *Sheff* 99-01; TV Cullercoats St Geo *Newc* 01-06; V Billy Mill from 06; V Marden w Preston Grange from 06. *St Aidan's Vicarage, 29 Billy Mill Lane, North Shields NE29 8BZ* Tel 0191-257 3616

CAVANAGH, Capt Kenneth Joseph. b 41. CA Tr Coll 60. **d** 77 **p** 77. CA 64; Paraguay 70-83; P-in-c Gt w Lt Snoring *Nor* 83-85; R Gt w Lt Snoring w Kettlestone and Pensthorpe 85-88; R Glencarse *Bre* 88-94; CA Co-ord (Scotland/Ireland) & Regional Voc Adv 90-95; R Dundee St Luke 95-06; rtd 06. *PD Barranquets, Calle 38 Casa 18, 03779 Els Poblets (Alicante), Spain* E-mail kscavanagh@tiscali.co.uk

CAVANAGH, Lorraine Marie. b 46. Lucy Cavendish Coll Cam BA97 MA01 PhD03. Ridley Hall Cam 00. **d** 01 **p** 02. Perm to Offic *Ely* 01-03; Chapl Fitzw Coll Cam 03; Chapl Cardiff Univ from 04. *The Anglican Chaplaincy, 61 Park Place, Cardiff CF10 3AT* Tel and fax (029) 2023 2550
E-mail cavanaghlm@cf.ac.uk

CAVANAGH, Michael Richard. b 49. Salford Univ MSc00. NOC 89. **d** 92 **p** 93. NSM Stalybridge H Trin and Ch Ch *Ches* 92-98; P-in-c Over Tabley and High Legh 98-03; V from 03. *The Vicarage, The Avenue, High Legh, Knutsford WA16 6ND* Tel (01925) 753612 Fax 753216 Mobile 07767-771599
E-mail michael@balmoralconsulting.com

CAVANAGH, Canon Peter Bernard. b 49. Sarum & Wells Th Coll 71. **d** 73 **p** 74. C Gt Crosby St Faith *Liv* 73-76; C Stanley 76-79; V Anfield St Columba 79-97; V Lancaster St Mary w St John and St Anne *Blackb* 97-09; P-in-c Scorton and Barnacre and Calder Vale 06-09; Hon Can Blackb Cathl 04-09; rtd 09; Perm to Offic *Blackb* from 09. *6 Lunesdale Court, Derwent Road, Lancaster LA1 3ET* Tel (01524) 62786
E-mail manderley552@btinternet.com

CAVE, Anthony Sidney. b 32. EMMTC. **d** 84 **p** 85. C Immingham *Linc* 84-88; V Keelby 88-89; V Riby 88-89; V Keelby w Riby and Aylesby 89-98; rtd 99; Perm to Offic *Linc* from 00. *Polruan, The Bungalow, Cherry Lane, Barrow-upon-Humber DN19 7AX* Tel (01469) 532350

CAVE, Bill. *See* CAVE-BROWNE-CAVE, Bernard James William

CAVE, Brian Malcolm. b 37. St Cath Soc Ox BA60 MA64. Oak Hill Th Coll. **d** 63 **p** 64. C Streatham Park St Alb *S'wark* 63-66; C Ruskin Park St Sav and St Matt 66-68; C Tunbridge Wells St Jas *Roch* 68-71; V Bootle St Leon *Liv* 71-75; Min St Mary w St John Bootle 73-75; Area Sec Leprosy Miss 75-81; V Hurst Green *Bradf* 81-82; P-in-c Mitton 81-82; V Hurst Green and Mitton 82-91; rtd 91; Perm to Offic *B & W* from 97. *63 Westway, Nailsea, Bristol BS48 2NB* Tel (01275) 854892

CAVE, Douglas Lionel. b 26. Lon Bible Coll 50 Lon Coll of Div 64. **d** 66 **p** 67. C Upper Holloway St Jo *Lon* 66-69; C Barking St Marg *Chelmsf* 69-73; V Blackb St Barn 73-81; Ind Chapl *Lon* 81-91; rtd 91; Perm to Offic *Lon* from 93. *8 Wood Rise, Pinner HA5 2JD* Tel (01895) 677426

CAVE, Mrs Rachel Mary. b 53. Warwick Univ BA75. NOC 98. **d** 01 **p** 02. NSM Gomersal *Wakef* 01-04; NSM Scholes from 04; NSM Cleckheaton St Luke and Whitechapel from 04. *Yew Tree Hall, 13 Leeds Road, Mirfield WF14 0BY* Tel (01924) 480666 E-mail rev_rachel_cave@hotmail.com

CAVE BERGQUIST, Julie Anastasia. b 59. St Jo Coll Dur BA80 Franciscan Univ Rome STL87. St Steph Ho Ox 85. **d** 87 **p** 98. Par Dn Kennington *Cant* 87-89; Chapl Trin Coll Cam 89-94; Chapl Westcott Ho Cam 94-97; C St Alb St Steph *St Alb* 98-02; P-in-c S Kensington H Trin w All SS *Lon* 02-06; Dir of Ords Two Cities Area 02-06; Selection Sec Min Division from 06. *Ministry Division, Church House, Great Smith Street, London SW1P 3AZ* Tel (020) 7898 1395 Fax 7898 1421 E-mail jules.cavebergquist@c-of-e.org.uk

CAVE-BROWNE-CAVE, Bernard James William (Bill). b 54. Trin Hall Cam BA76 MA80 Bradf Univ MA90. Westcott Ho Cam 77. **d** 79 **p** 80. C Chesterton Gd Shep *Ely* 79-83; Chapl Lanc Univ 83-95; Chapl HM Pris Service from 95. *Chaplaincy HQ, Room 410, Abell House, John Islip Street, London SW1P 4LH* Tel (020) 7217 5685 Fax 7217 5090 E-mail bill@cave_browne_cave.freeserve.co.uk

CAVEEN, David Francis. b 44. Univ of Wales (Cardiff) BSc63 DipEd67. STETS 95. **d** 98 **p** 99. C Swaythling *Win* 98-02; V Lord's Hill 02-09; rtd 09. *35A Bassett Row, Southampton SO16 7FT* E-mail davidcaveen@tinyworld.co.uk

✠**CAVELL, The Rt Revd John Kingsmill.** b 16. Qu Coll Cam BA39 MA44. Wycliffe Hall Ox 39. **d** 40 **p** 41 **c** 72. C Folkestone H Trin *Cant* 40; C Addington 40-44; Lic to Offic *Ox* 45-52; Area Sec (Dio Ox) CMS 44-52; Dio Pet 44-49; Tr Officer 49-52; V Cheltenham Ch Ch *Glouc* 52-62; V Plymouth St Andr *Ex* 62-72; RD Plymouth 67-72; Preb Ex Cathl 67-72; V E Stonehouse 68-72; Suff Bp Southampton *Win* 72-84; Hon Can Win Cathl 72-84; rtd 84; Perm to Offic *Win* from 84; Hon Asst Bp Sarum from 88; Can and Preb Sarum Cathl from 88. *143 The Close, Salisbury SP1 2EY* Tel (01722) 334782 Fax 413112

CAVELL-NORTHAM, Canon Cavell Herbert James. b 32. St Steph Ho Ox 53. **d** 56 **p** 57. C W Wycombe *Ox* 56-61; CF (TA) 60-63; V Lane End *Ox* 61-68; V Stony Stratford 68-97; P-in-c Calverton 69-72; R 72-97; Hon Can Ch Ch 91-97; rtd 97; Lic to Offic *Ox* 97-04; Perm to Offic from 04. *The Glebe House, Finings Road, Lane End, High Wycombe HP14 3EU* Tel (01494) 881552

CAW (née FINLAY), Alison Mary. b 40. Natal Univ BA62 Ox Univ PGCE64. Ox Min Course 90. **d** 93 **p** 94. NSM Beaconsfield *Ox* 93-04; NSM Penn and Tylers Green 04-08; Perm to Offic from 08. *1 Westway, Beaconsfield HP9 1DQ* Tel (01494) 674524

CAW, Hannah Mary. *See* JEFFERY, Mrs Hannah Mary

CAWDELL, Mrs Sarah Helen Louise. b 65. St Hugh's Coll Ox BA88 St Hugh's Coll Ox MA91 Trin Coll Cam BA94 MA99 K Coll Lon MA99. Ridley Hall Cam 92. **d** 95 **p** 96. C Belmont *S'wark* 95-98; Perm to Offic *Heref* 98-00; Hon C Claverley w Tuckhill from 00; CME Officer from 06. *The Vicarage, Lodge Park, Claverley, Wolverhampton WV5 7DP* Tel (01746) 710788 E-mail s.h.cawdell@btinternet.com

CAWDELL, Simon Howard. b 65. Univ Coll Dur BA86 K Coll Lon MA99. Ridley Hall Cam 91. **d** 94 **p** 95. C Cheam Common St Phil *S'wark* 94-98; V Claverley w Tuckhill *Heref* from 98; RD Bridgnorth from 09. *The Vicarage, Lodge Park, Claverley, Wolverhampton WV5 7DP* Tel (01746) 710268 E-mail s.h.cawdell@btinternet.com

CAWLEY, David Lewis. b 44. AKC71 FSA81. St Aug Coll Cant 71. **d** 72 **p** 73. C Sprowston *Nor* 72-75; Chapl HM Pris Nor 74-75; C Wymondham *Nor* 75-77; C Buckland in Dover w Buckland Valley *Cant* 77-83; V Eastville St Anne w St Mark and St Thos *Bris* 83-95; V Leic St Mary 95-97; TV Leic H Spirit 97-02; Chapl Trin Hosp Leic 96-09; rtd 09; Hon C Margate All SS *Cant* from 09. *All Saints' Vicarage, All Saints' Avenue, Margate CT9 5QL* Tel (01843) 290845

CAWRSE, Christopher William. b 60. Birkbeck Coll Lon BA97 Qu Mary and Westf Coll Lon MA00. Westcott Ho Cam 82. **d** 84 **p** 85. C Stoke Newington St Mary *Lon* 84-86; Chapl St Mark's Hosp Lon 86-90; C Islington St Jas w St Pet *Lon* 86-90; Chapl Asst Charing Cross Hosp Lon 90-93; Perm to Offic *Lon* 93-06; P-in-c St Pancras H Cross w St Jude and St Pet from 06. *Holy*

Cross Vicarage, 47 Argyle Square, London WC1H 8AL Tel (020) 7278 3706 E-mail chris@cawrse.freeserve.co.uk

CAWTE, Canon David John. b 30. St Mich Coll Llan. **d** 65 **p** 66. C Chorley St Laur *Blackb* 65-67; C Boyne Hill *Ox* 67-74; C-in-c Cox Green CD 75-78; V Cox Green 78-94; Hon Can Ch Ch 88-94; rtd 94; Perm to Offic *Win* from 94. *6 Broadfields Close, Milford on Sea, Lymington SO41 0SE* Tel (01590) 642793 E-mail david.cawte@tinyworld.co.uk

CAWTE, Martin Charles. b 51. Jes Coll Ox BA73 MA77 IPFA77. SEITE 97. **d** 00 **p** 01. NSM Sanderstead All SS *S'wark* 00-03; NSM Greenham *Ox* 03-06; NSM Hermitage from 06. *The Rectory, 8 Yew Tree Mews, High Street, Compton, Newbury RG20 6NQ* Tel 07775-706976 (mobile) E-mail martin_cawte@hotmail.com

CAWTHORNE, Jack. b 22. ATD50. Cuddesdon Coll 69. **d** 71 **p** 72. NSM Newchurch *Man* 71-86; NSM Garforth *Ripon* 87-88; Perm to Offic from 88. *15 Arran Drive, Garforth, Leeds LS25 2BU* Tel 0113-286 9527 Mobile 077451-325559

CAWTHORNE, Paul Howarth. b 66. St Hild Coll Dur BA88. Cuddesdon Coll 98. **d** 98 **p** 99. C Cen Telford *Lich* 98-01; TV Wrockwardine Deanery from 01. *The Vicarage, Eaton Constantine, Shrewsbury SY5 6RF* Tel (01952) 510333 E-mail paul@cawthorne52.fsnet.co.uk

CAYTON, John. b 32. Bps' Coll Cheshunt 54. **d** 57 **p** 58. C Hindley All SS *Liv* 57-59; C Littleham w Exmouth 59-63; V Burnley St Cath *Blackb* 63-72; V Marton 72-87; V Fleetwood St Pet 87-97; Miss to Seamen 87-97; rtd 97; Perm to Offic *Blackb* from 97. *19 Parkstone Avenue, Thornton-Cleveleys FY5 5AE* Tel (01253) 854088

CECIL, Kevin Vincent. b 54. BA PGCE. St Mich Coll Llan. **d** 82 **p** 83. C Llanilid w Pencoed 82-85; C Coity w Nolton 85-88; Area Co-ord CMS *St D, Llan, Mon* and *S & B* 88-05; P-in-c Dixton *Heref* 05-08; V Dixton, Wyesham, Bishopswood, Whitchurch etc from 08. *The Vicarage, 38 Hillcrest Road, Wyesham, Monmouth NP25 3LH* Tel (01600) 713459 E-mail vincent_cecil@yahoo.com

CECILE, Sister. *See* HARRISON, Sister Cécile

CENTRAL AFRICA, Archbishop of. *Vacant*

CENTRAL MELANESIA, Bishop of. *See* VUNAGI, The Most Revd David

CERMAKOVA, Ms Helena Maria Alija. b 43. **d** 88 **p** 95. NSM Roath *Llan* 88-91; Asst Chapl Univ Hosp of Wales Cardiff 92-95; Chapl United Bris Healthcare NHS Trust 95-99; Lead Chapl Jersey Gp of Hosps 99-06; Tutor St Mich Coll Llan from 06. *62A Heol Lewis, Cardiff CF14 6QB* Tel (029) 2061 2475 E-mail helenacermakova@talktalk.net

CERRATTI, Christa Elisabeth. *See* PUMFREY, Christa Elisabeth

CHADD, Jeremy Denis. b 55. Jes Coll Cam BA77 MA81. Coll of Resurr Mirfield 78. **d** 81 **p** 82. C Seaton Hirst *Newc* 81-84; C N Gosforth 84-88; V Sunderland St Chad *Dur* from 88. *St Chad's Vicarage, Charter Drive, Sunderland SR3 3PG* Tel 0191-528 2397

CHADD, Canon Leslie Frank. b 19. Leeds Univ BA41. Coll of Resurr Mirfield 41. **d** 43 **p** 44. C Portsea All SS w St Jo Rudmore *Portsm* 43-46; Chapl R NVR 46-48; C Greenford H Cross *Lon* 48-54; C Littlehampton St Mary *Chich* 54-58; V Hanworth All SS *Lon* 58-65; V Fareham SS Pet and Paul *Portsm* 65-92; Rellg Adv STV 72-81; Hon Can Portsm Cathl 81-92; rtd 92; Perm to Offic *Portsm* from 92. *Tree Tops, Hoads Hill, Wickham, Fareham PO17 5BX* Tel (01329) 834397

CHADDER, Philip Thomas James. b 66. Ex Univ BA88. Oak Hill Th Coll 01. **d** 03 **p** 04. C Gt Chesham *Ox* 03-07; Chapl HM Pris Brixton from 07. *HM Prison Brixton, Jebb Avenue, London SW2 5XF* Tel (020) 8588 6052 Mobile 07796-815285 E-mail philchadder@yahoo.co.uk

CHADWICK, Alan Michael. b 61. St Cath Coll Cam BA83 MA87. Wycliffe Hall Ox 96. **d** 98 **p** 99. C Hubberston *St D* 98-01; R from 01. *Hubberston Rectory, 35 Westaway Drive, Hubberston, Milford Haven SA73 3EQ* Tel (01646) 692251

CHADWICK, Arnold. *See* CHADWICK, Francis Arnold Edwin

CHADWICK, Carolyn Ann. b 52. Westhill Coll Birm CertEd73 Birm Univ BMus93 ABSM78. WMMTC 04. **d** 07 **p** 08. NSM Pontesbury I and II *Heref* from 07. *The Hermitage, Asterley, Minsterley, Shrewsbury SY5 0AW* Tel and fax (01743) 792421 Mobile 07766-832547 E-mail carolyn@thechadwickfamily.net

CHADWICK, Charles John Peter. b 59. Birm Univ BA81 Southn Univ BTh90. Sarum & Wells Th Coll 85. **d** 88 **p** 89. C Chalfont St Peter *Ox* 88-91; C Gt Marlow 91-93; TV Gt Marlow w Marlow Bottom, Lt Marlow and Bisham 93-95; P-in-c Stokenchurch and Ibstone 95-01; Asst Dir Chiltern Ch Tr Course 95-01; V Bridgwater St Mary and Chilton Trinity *B & W* from 01. *The Vicarage, 7 Durleigh Road, Bridgwater TA6 7HU* Tel (01278) 422437 *or* 424972 E-mail charles@chad0205.fsnet.co.uk

CHADWICK, David Emmerson. b 73. Lincs & Humberside Univ BA96. Ridley Hall Cam BTh00. **d** 00 **p** 01. C Whickham *Dur* 00-06; V Ryhope from 06. *St Paul's Vicarage, Ryhope Street North, Sunderland SR2 0HH* Tel 0191-523 7884

CHADWICK, David Guy Evelyn St Just. b 36. Bps' Coll Cheshunt 61. **d** 68 **p** 69. C Edmonton All SS *Lon* 68-71; C Edmonton St Mary w St Jo 71-72; C Greenhill St Jo 72-74; Bp's Dom Chapl *Truro* 74-79; Chapl Community of the Epiphany *Truro* 77-78; P-in-c Crantock *Truro* 79-83; R Clydebank *Glas* 83-87; R Renfrew 87-94; rtd 94. *Alverna, 1 Nithsdale Crescent, Bearsden, Glasgow G61 4DF*

CHADWICK, Francis Arnold Edwin. b 30. AKC54. **d** 55 **p** 56. C Chapel Allerton *Ripon* 55-58; C Hayes *Roch* 58-61; V Arreton *Portsm* 61-67; V Newchurch 61-67; V Kingshurst *Birm* 67-73; V York Town St Mich *Guildf* 73-83; P-in-c Long Sutton w Long Load *B & W* 83-87; R Stockbridge and Longstock and Leckford *Win* 87-93; rtd 93; Chapl Helsinki w Tallinn *Eur* 95-98; Perm to Offic *B & W* 98-02 and *Sarum* from 02. *Hillway, Wickfield, Devizes SN10 5DU* Tel (01380) 721489

CHADWICK, Helen Jane. *See* MARSHALL, Mrs Helen Jane

CHADWICK, Mark William Armstrong. Coll of Resurr Mirfield. **d** 05 **p** 06. C Colwyn Bay w Brynymaen *St As* 05-08; V Kerry, Llanmerewig, Dolfor and Mochdre from 08. *The Vicarage, 47 Willan's Drive, Kerry, Newtown SY16 4DB*

CHADWICK, Owen. *See* CHADWICK, Prof William Owen

CHADWICK, Peter MacKenzie. b 21. Lich Th Coll 63. **d** 65 **p** 66. C Buckhurst Hill *Chelmsf* 65-66; Jt Hd Master Forres Sch Swanage 56-81; Chapl 66-85; NSM Kingston, Langton Matravers and Worth Matravers *Sarum* 85-92; rtd 89; Perm to Offic *Sarum* from 92. *Flat 4, 18 Victoria Avenue, Swanage BH19 1AN* Tel (01929) 422258

CHADWICK, Philip Edward. b 41. AMICE63 IEng65. **d** 07 **p** 08. OLM Elland *Wakef* from 07. *26 Crestfield Avenue, Elland HX5 0LN* Tel (01422) 373298
E-mail pechadwick@hotmail.com

CHADWICK, Prof William Owen. b 16. OM83 KBE82. St Jo Coll Cam BA39 MA42 BD51 DD55 St Andr Univ Hon DD60 Ox Univ Hon DD73 Univ of Wales Hon DD93 FBA62. Cuddesdon Coll 39. **d** 40 **p** 41. C Huddersfield St Jo *Wakef* 40-42; Chapl Wellington Coll Berks 42-46; Fell Trin Hall Cam 47-56; Dean 49-56; Master Selw Coll Cam 56-83; Fell from 83; Dixie Prof Ecclesiastical Hist Cam 58-68; Regius Prof Modern Hist Cam 68-83; Pres Br Academy 81-85; Chan UEA 85-94; Perm to Offic *Ely* from 94. *67 Grantchester Street, Cambridge CB7 9HZ* Tel (01223) 314000

CHAFFEY, Jane Frances. b 59. Somerville Coll Ox BA80 MA84 St Jo Coll Dur BA86. Cranmer Hall Dur 84. **d** 88 **p** 94. Par Dn Roby *Liv* 88-90; NSM Finningley w Auckley *S'well* 95-96; Perm to Offic *Pet* 96-99 and *Linc* 98-01; Perm to Offic RAF from 98; Chapl Wycombe Abbey Sch from 08. *Wycombe Abbey School, Abbey Way, High Wycombe HP11 1PE* Tel (01494) 520381

CHAFFEY, Jonathan Paul Michael. b 62. St Chad's Coll Dur BA83. Cranmer Hall Dur 84. **d** 87 **p** 88. C Gateacre *Liv* 87-90; Chapl RAF from 90. *Chaplaincy Services, HQ Personnel and Training Command, RAF High Wycombe HP14 4UE* Tel (01494) 496800 Fax 496343

CHAFFEY, Michael Prosser. b 30. Lon Univ BA51. St Steph Ho Ox 53. **d** 55 **p** 56. C Victoria Docks Ascension *Chelmsf* 55-59; C Leytonstone H Trin Harrow Green 59-62; V Walthamstow St Mich 62-69; R Cov St Jo 69-85; P-in-c Cov St Thos 69-75; Hon C Bideford *Ex* 85; P-in-c Charlestown *Man* 85-88; V Sutton St Mich *York* 88-96; rtd 96; Perm to Offic *York* from 96. *7 Shirley Court, South Marine Drive, Bridlington YO15 3JJ* Tel (01262) 602758

CHALCRAFT, Christopher Warine Terrell (Kit). b 37. Oak Hill Th Coll. **d** 67 **p** 68. C Egham *Guildf* 67-70; P-in-c Slough *Ox* 70-73; TV Bramerton w Surlingham *Nor* 73-87; P-in-c Cockley Cley w Gooderstone 87-95; P-in-c Gt and Lt Cressingham w Threxton 87-95; P-in-c Didlington 87-95; P-in-c Hilborough w Bodney 87-95; P-in-c Oxborough w Foulden and Caldecote 87-95; Perm to Offic from 02. *The Malthouse, London Street, Swaffham PE37 7DD* Tel (01760) 724805
E-mail k.chalcraft@btinternet.com

CHALCRAFT, Mrs Sharon Anita. b 62. Ex Univ BTh09. SWMTC 05. **d** 08. NSM Carbis Bay w Lelant *Truro* from 08; NSM Towednack from 08; NSM Zennor from 08. *Summerhill Cottage, Nancledra, Penzance TR20 8AY* Tel (01736) 350779 Mobile 07889-406326 E-mail sharon@m8trix.ltd.uk

CHALK, Francis Harold. b 25. Lich Th Coll 61. **d** 62 **p** 63. C Linc St Nic w St Jo Newport 62-64; R Kirkby Laythorpe w Asgarby 64-69; V Ewerby w Evedon 65-69; R Gt Gonerby 69-89; rtd 89; Perm to Offic *Truro* from 90. *Chalkleigh, 3 Church Street, St Just, Penzance TR19 7HA* Tel (01736) 787925

CHALK, John Edward. b 33. St D Coll Lamp BA57. **d** 58 **p** 59. C Connah's Quay *St As* 58-61; C Abergele 61-65; V Cyfarthfa *Llan* 65-72; V Pyle w Kenfig 72-77; Lect in FE 84-92; NSM Mansfield Woodhouse *S'well* 92; Perm to Offic *Llan* 92-94; NSM Salt and Sandon w Burston 94-96; rtd 96. *Hendre Penprys, Pentre Uchaf, Pwllheli LL53 8EZ* Tel (01758) 750306

CHALKLEY, Andrew William Guy. b 64. Aston Tr Scheme 90 St Jo Coll Nottm BTh92. **d** 95 **p** 96. C Liskeard, St Keyne, St Pinnock, Morval etc *Truro* 95-99; TV Uphill *B & W* 99-07; P-in-c Beckington w Standerwick, Berkley, Rodden etc from 07.

8 Church Street, Beckington, Frome BA11 6TG Tel (01373) 830314

CHALLEN, Canon Peter Bernard. b 31. Clare Coll Cam BA56 MA60 FRSA94. Westcott Ho Cam 56. **d** 58 **p** 59. C Goole *Sheff* 58-61; V Dalton 61-67; Sen Ind Chapl *S'wark* 67-96; R S'wark Ch Ch 67-96; Hon Can S'wark Cathl 74-96; rtd 96; Perm to Offic *S'wark* from 96. *21 Bousfield Road, London SE14 5TP* Tel and fax (020) 7207 0509 E-mail peterchallen@gmail.com

CHALLENDER, John Clifford. b 32. CITC 67. **d** 67 **p** 68. C Belfast St Luke *Conn* 67-70; C Kilkenny w Aghour and Odagh *C & O* 70-71; Bp's V and Lib Kilkenny Cathl 70-71; Dioc Registrar (Ossory, Ferns and Leighlin) 70-71; I Fenagh w Myshall and Killeshin 72-76; I Fenagh w Myshall, Aghade and Ardoyne 76-79; I Crosspatrick Gp 79-95; Preb Ferns Cathl 85-88; Dioc Glebes Sec (Ferns) 86-91; Treas Ferns Cathl 88-91; Chan 91-95; I Killeshin w Cloydagh and Killabban 95-02; Can Ossory and Leighlin Cathls 00-02; rtd 02. *3 Adare Close, Killincarrig, Greystones, Co Wicklow, Republic of Ireland* Tel (00353) (1) 201 7268 or 287 6359 Mobile 86-243 3678
E-mail challen1@eircom.net

CHALLENGER, Ann. b 54. Leeds Univ BA09, NOC 06. **d** 09. NSM Bradf St Aug Undercliffe from 09; NSM Bradf St Clem from 09. *304 Undercliffe Street, Bradford BD3 0PH* Tel (01274) 640410 Mobile 07832-293751
E-mail ann_challenger@hotmail.co.uk

CHALLENGER, Peter Nelson. b 33. St Jo Coll Cam BA57 MA61. Ripon Hall Ox 57. **d** 59 **p** 60. C Bushbury *Lich* 59-62; V Horsley Woodhouse *Derby* 62-67; V Derby St Barn 67-75; Brazil 75-80; TV New Windsor *Ox* 80-89; V Wootton (Boars Hill) 89-98; rtd 99. *39 Moorland Road, Witney OX28 6LS* Tel (01993) 774630

CHALLICE, John Richard. b 34. ACP65. Sarum & Wells Th Coll 73. **d** 75 **p** 76. C Warminster St Denys *Sarum* 75-78; R Longfield *Roch* 78-00; rtd 00; Perm to Offic *Roch* from 00. *Magnolia, Allhallows Road, Lower Stoke, Rochester ME3 9SL* Tel (01634) 272468

CHALLIS, Douglas James. b 21. Selw Coll Cam BA48 MA55. Cuddesdon Coll 49. **d** 51 **p** 58. Kimbolton Sch 53-58; Chapl Summer Fields Sch Ox 58-60; Asst Chapl Stowe Sch 60-64; Chapl St Bees Sch Cumbria 64-67; Chapl Reed's Sch Cobham 67-80; rtd 80; Perm to Offic *Guildf* 84-07; Chapl Crowhurst Chr Healing Cen 05-06; Lic to Offic *Mor* from 07. *7 Milinclarin Way, Church Hill Road, Lairg IV27 4BL* Tel (01549) 402108

CHALLIS, Ian. b 46. St Jo Coll Nottm 82. **d** 84 **p** 85. C Heatherlands St Jo *Sarum* 84-86; C Lytchett Minster 86-88; Perm to Offic 88-95 and 00-08; NSM Canford Magna 95-00. *50 Constitution Hill Road, Poole BH14 0QD* Tel (01202) 691300

CHALLIS, John William Anthony. b 68. St Steph Ho Ox 98. **d** 00 **p** 01. C Ifield *Chich* 00-04; P-in-c Buxted and Hadlow Down 04-09; R Beeding and Bramber w Botolphs from 09. *The Rectory, Sele Priory Church, Church Lane, Upper Beeding BN44 3HP* Tel and fax (01903) 810265

CHALLIS, Terence Peter. b 40. St Aid Birkenhead 65. **d** 68 **p** 69. C Billericay St Mary *Chelmsf* 68-71; Admin Sec Dio Maseno S Kenya 72-75; Bp's Chapl 72-74; P-in-c Sparkbrook Ch Ch *Birm* 76-80; V Enfield St Jas *Lon* 80-89; V Astley Bridge *Man* 89-98; P-in-c Leigh St Mary and Leigh St Jo 99-02; rtd 02; Perm to Offic *Blackb* from 03. *48 Wilson Square, Thornton-Cleveleys FY5 1RF* Tel (01253) 864534

CHALLIS, William George. b 52. Keble Coll Ox BA73 K Coll Lon MTh75. Oak Hill Th Coll 73. **d** 75 **p** 76. C Islington St Mary *Lon* 75-79; Lect Trin Coll Bris 79-81; C Stoke Bishop *Bris* 79-81; Lect Oak Hill Th Coll 82; Burundi 82-85; P-in-c Bishopston *Bris* 86-89; TR 89-92; Vice-Prin Wycliffe Hall Ox 93-98; V Bitterne *Win* 98-03; Dir of Ords *Guildf* from 03. *80 York Road, Woking GU22 7XR* Tel (01483) 769759 or 790322
E-mail ddo@cofeguildford.org.uk

CHALMERS, Canon Brian. b 42. Oriel Coll Ox BA64 MA68 DPhil70 BA71. Wycliffe Hall Ox 71. **d** 72 **p** 73. C Luton St Mary *St Alb* 72-76; Chapl Cranfield Inst of Tech 76-81; Chapl Kent Univ 81-89; Six Preacher Cant Cathl 85-96; V Charing w Charing Heath and Lt Chart 89-05; AD Ashford 98-03; Hon Can Cant Cathl 97-05; rtd 05; Perm to Offic *Cant* from 05. *The Chantry, Pilgrims Lane, Chilham, Canterbury CT4 8AB* Tel (01227) 730669 E-mail brian.chalmers@tesco.net

CHAMBERLAIN, Allen Charles William. b 29. Lon Univ CertEd52 Birkbeck Coll Lon BSc56. **d** 96 **p** 97. OLM Gunton St Pet *Nor* 96-99; rtd 99; Perm to Offic *Nor* from 99. *28 Yarmouth Road, Lowestoft NR32 4AG* Tel (01502) 573637

CHAMBERLAIN, David (Bernard). b 28. Fitzw Ho Cam BA51. Linc Th Coll 52. **d** 54 **p** 55. C Brighouse *Wakef* 54-57; C Sheff St Cecilia Parson Cross 57-61; CR 63-85; S Africa 68-70; Bp's Adv on Community Relns *Wakef* 71-85; Bp's Adv Community Relns & Inter-Faith Dialogue *Bris* 86-93; V Easton All Hallows 86-93; rtd 93; Perm to Offic *B & W* from 94. *43 Bath Road, Wells BA5 3HR* Tel (01749) 679369

CHAMBERLAIN, David Murray. b 22. Cuddesdon Coll 55. **d** 57 **p** 58. C Barkingside H Trin *Chelmsf* 57-60; Japan 60-71 and 76-81; V Edgbaston St Germain *Birm* 71-76; Miss to Seamen N

Australia 81-88; rtd 88; Perm to Offic *Truro* from 88. *42 Tresawls Road, Truro TR1 3LE* Tel (01872) 272270

CHAMBERLAIN, Eric Edward. b 34. Tyndale Hall Bris 62. **d** 65 **p** 66. C Chell *Lich* 65-73; P-in-c Preston St Mary *Blackb* 73-76; V 76-89; P-in-c Preston St Luke 81-83; R S Normanton *Derby* 89-99; rtd 99; Perm to Offic *Ox* from 00. *1 The Closes, Haddenham, Aylesbury HP17 8JN* Tel (01844) 299303

CHAMBERLAIN, Frederick George. b 19. Univ of Wales (Lamp) BA50. Chich Th Coll 50. **d** 52 **p** 53. C Weybridge *Guildf* 52-54; C Bourne 54-57; V Blindley Heath *S'wark* 57-63; V Tilshead *Sarum* 63-71; R The Orchestons 66-71; V Chitterne 69-71; R Tilshead, Orcheston and Chitterne 71-80; P-in-c Handley w Pentridge 80-82; R 82-84; rtd 84; Perm to Offic *Sarum* 84-04. *22 Gracey Court, Woodland Road, Broadclyst, Exeter EX5 3GA* Tel (01392) 462633

CHAMBERLAIN, Jane Louise. b 62. Bedf Coll Lon BSc84. WEMTC 04. **d** 07 **p** 08. NSM Blagdon w Compton Martin and Ubley *B & W* from 07. *Grove House, The Street, Compton Martin, Bristol BS40 6JF* Tel (01761) 220070 Mobile 07949-037548 E-mail jlchamberlain@tiscali.co.uk

CHAMBERLAIN, Malcolm Leslie. b 69. York Univ BA92. Wycliffe Hall Ox 93. **d** 96 **p** 97. C Walsall Pleck and Bescot *Lich* 96-99; C Mossley Hill St Matt and St Jas *Liv* 99-02; Asst Chapl Liv Univ 99-02; Chapl Liv Univ and Dioc 18-30s Officer 02-08; P-in-c Wavertree St Mary from 08. *St Mary's Rectory, 1 South Drive, Wavertree, Liverpool L15 8JJ* Tel 0151-735 1615

✠**CHAMBERLAIN, The Rt Revd Neville.** b 39. Nottm Univ BA61 MA73 CQSW73. Ripon Hall Ox 61. **d** 63 **p** 64 **c** 97. C Balsall Heath St Paul *Birm* 63-64; C Hall Green Ascension 64-66; C-in-c Gospel Lane CD 66-69; V Gospel Lane St Mich 69-72; Lic to Offic *Linc* 73-74; Soc Resp Sec 74-82; Can and Preb Linc Cathl 79-98; R Edin St Jo 82-97; Bp Bre 97-05; rtd 05; Master Hugh Sexey's Hosp Bruton from 05. *The Master's House, Hugh Sexey's Hospital, Bruton BA10 0AS* Tel (01749) 813369

CHAMBERLAIN, Nicholas Alan. b 63. St Chad's Coll Dur BA85 PhD91 New Coll Edin BD91. Edin Th Coll 88. **d** 91 **p** 92. C Cockerton *Dur* 91-94; C Newton Aycliffe 94-95; TV 95-96; TV Gt Aycliffe 96-98; P-in-c Burnmoor 98-06; Bp's Adv for CME 98-06; V Newc St Geo and St Hilda from 06. *St George's Vicarage, St George's Close, Newcastle upon Tyne NE2 2TF* Tel 0191-281 1628

CHAMBERLAIN, Roger Edward. b 53. BEd76 BA87. Trin Coll Bris 84. **d** 87 **p** 88. C Plymouth Em w Efford *Ex* 87-90; C Selly Park St Steph and St Wulstan *Birm* 90-94; V Yardley St Cypr Hay Mill 94-96; Perm to Offic from 96. *22 Hanbury Croft, Acocks Green, Birmingham B27 6RX* Tel 0121-708 0998

CHAMBERLAIN, Roy Herbert. b 44. Oak Hill Th Coll 91 NOC 95. **d** 96 **p** 97. C Gee Cross *Ches* 96-98; Perm to Offic *Blackb* from 01. *125 Lancaster Road, Morecambe LA4 5QJ* Tel (01524) 409070

CHAMBERLAIN, Russell Charles. b 51. Univ of Wales (Cardiff) LLM00. Oak Hill Th Coll 76. **d** 78 **p** 79. C Harold Hill St Geo *Chelmsf* 78-80; C Uckfield *Chich* 80-83; R Balcombe 83-90; V Okehampton w Inwardleigh *Ex* 90-94; TR Okehampton w Inwardleigh, Bratton Clovelly etc 94-01; RD Okehampton 93-98; R Wolborough and Ogwell from 01. *The Rectory, 5 Coach Place, Newton Abbot TQ12 1ES* Tel (01626) 368889 E-mail russell@chamberlain70.fsnet.co.uk

CHAMBERLAIN, David John. b 56. St Jo Coll Nottm. **d** 94 **p** 95. C Chatham St Phil and St Jas *Roch* 94-97; R Swardeston w E Carleton, Intwood, Keswick etc *Nor* 97-04; RD Humbleyard 03-04; R Milton *Ely* from 04. *The Rectory, 24 Church Lane, Milton, Cambridge CB24 6AB* Tel (01223) 861511 Fax 441007 Mobile 07761-630775 E-mail rector@allsaintsmilton.org.uk

CHAMBERLIN, John Malcolm. b 38. Carl Dioc Tr Course 84. **d** 87 **p** 88. NSM Cockermouth w Embleton and Wythop *Carl* 87-97; Master St Mary Magd and H Jes Trust 97-05; Hon C Newc St Jo 98-05; rtd 05. *45 Wansbeck Avenue, North Shields NE30 3DU* Tel 0191-253 0022 E-mail johnchamberlin@btinternet.com

CHAMBERS, Canon Anthony Frederick John. b 40. ACII69. Sarum Th Coll 69. **d** 71 **p** 72. C Hall Green St Pet *Birm* 71-74; C Holdenhurst *Win* 74-77; P-in-c Ropley w W Tisted 77-79; R Bishop's Sutton and Ropley and W Tisted 79-83; V Pokesdown St Jas 83-99; RD Bournemouth 95-99; P-in-c Heckfield w Mattingley and Rotherwick 99-02; V 02-04; Chapl N Foreland Lodge Sch Basingstoke 99-04; Hon Can Win Cathl 03-04; rtd 05; Perm to Offic *Ex* from 05. *4 J H Taylor Drive, Northam, Bideford EX39 1TU* Tel (01237) 421306 E-mail anthony.chambers1@virgin.net

CHAMBERS, Miss Barbara Ada. b 51. **d** 98 **p** 99. OLM Gt Crosby St Luke *Liv* from 98. *12 Vale Road, Crosby, Liverpool L23 5RZ* Tel 0151-924 5851

CHAMBERS, Mrs Barbara Mary Sinnott. b 43. SRN65 RM67 HVCert75 Keele Univ TCert77. WMMTC 87. **d** 93 **p** 94. Par Dn Blurton *Lich* 93-94; C 94-96; Chapl Asst Qu Medical Cen Nottm Univ Hosp NHS Trust 96-03; Chapl 03-07; Chapl United Lincs

Hosps NHS Trust from 07. *51 Mill Lane, Woodhall Spa LN10 6QZ* Tel (01526) 354872 E-mail barbara.chambers@ulh.nhs.uk

CHAMBERS, Carl Michael. b 68. Pemb Coll Cam BA90 Oak Hill Th Coll BA00. **d** 01 **p** 02. C Hove Bp Hannington Memorial Ch *Chich* 01-05; C Preston St Jo w Brighton St Aug and St Sav from 05. *24 Stanford Avenue, Brighton BN1 6EA* Tel (01273) 553207

CHAMBERS, George William. b 24. TCD BA46 MA57. CITC 47. **d** 47 **p** 48. C Conwall *D & R* 47-50; Chapl Portora R Sch Enniskillen 50-51; I Tullyaughnish w Milford *D & R* 51-61; I Adare *L & K* 61-81; Dioc Registrar (Limerick etc) 62-81; Adn Limerick 69-81; Dean Limerick 81-86; I Limerick City 81-86; I Killeshin w Cloydagh and Killabban *C & O* 86-95; Can Ossory and Leighlin Cathls 90-92; Treas Ossory and Leighlin Cathls 92-95; rtd 95. *12 Rathdown Court, Greystones, Co Wicklow, Republic of Ireland* Tel (00353) (1) 287 1140

CHAMBERS, John Richard. b 50. EMMTC 01. **d** 04 **p** 05. C Farnsfield *S'well* 04-07; C Kirklington w Hockerton 04-07; C Bilsthorpe 04-07; C Eakring 04-07; C Maplebeck 04-07; C Winkburn 04-07; P-in-c E Bridgford and Kneeton from 07; P-in-c Flintham from 08; P-in-c Car Colston w Screveton from 08. *The Rectory, Kirk Hill, East Bridgford, Nottingham NG13 8PE* Tel (01949) 20218 Mobile 07875-348245 E-mail j_echambers@btinternet.com

CHAMBERS, Mrs Lynn. b 53. Northd Coll of Educn TCert74 Greenwich Univ MA96. St Mich Coll Llan 03. **d** 05 **p** 06. Dioc Children's Officer *St D* 01-06; NSM Carmarthen St Pet 05-08; P-in-c Brechfa w Abergorlech etc from 08. *Bromihangel, Gwernogle, Carmarthen SA32 7RP* Tel (01267) 223052 E-mail chambers@bromihangel.freserve.co.uk

CHAMBERS, Canon Peter Lewis. b 43. Imp Coll Lon BScEng64. St Steph Ho Ox 64. **d** 66 **p** 67. C Llandaff w Capel Llanilltern 66-70; Chapl Ch in Wales Youth Coun 70-73; Youth Chapl *Bris* 73-78; V Bedminster St Mich 78-84; RD Bedminster 81-84; Adv Ho of Bps Marriage Educn Panel Gen Syn 84-88; Dir Dioc Coun for Soc Resp *Guildf* 88-94; Hon Can Guildf Cathl 89-94; Dir Tr *Sheff* 95-00; P-in-c Harthill and Thorpe Salvin 00-07; Dioc Min Teams Officer 00-04; Hon Can Sheff Cathl 96-07; rtd 07. *5 Henley Grove, Bristol BS9 4EQ* Tel 0117-307 9427

CHAMBERS, Robert Anthony. b 46. **d** 05 **p** 06. OLM Kirkburton *Wakef* from 05. *4 Clough Park, Fenay Bridge, Huddersfield HD8 0JH* Tel (01484) 605920 Mobile 07968-279351 E-mail robert.chambers27@ntlworld.com

CHAMBERS, Simon Paul. b 65. Liv Univ BEng87 PhD91. Ripon Coll Cuddesdon 00. **d** 02 **p** 03. C Parkstone St Pet and St Osmund w Branksea *Sarum* 02-05; P-in-c Ashwell w Hinxworth and Newnham *St Alb* from 05. *The Rectory, Hodwell, Ashwell, Baldock SG7 5QQ* Tel (01462) 742277 E-mail simon@simonchambers.com

CHAMBEYRON, Mrs Julia Lynne. **d** 06 **p** 07. C La Côte *Eur* from 06. *1199 rue Guy de Maupassant, F-01220 Divonne les Bains, France* Tel (0033) (4) 50 20 19 37 E-mail pchambeyron@wanadoo.fr

CHAMP, Darren David. b 60. Kent Univ BA93. Linc Th Coll MA95. **d** 95 **p** 96. C Ashford *Cant* 95-97; Perm to Offic 02-03. *154 Beaver Road, Ashford TN23 7SS* Tel (01233) 663090 E-mail daz@dazchamp.co.uk

CHAMPION, Arthur. b 51. Loughb Univ BSc76 Aston Univ MSc77 CEng88 MIMechE88 FIOSH88. WEMTC 03. **d** 08 **p** 09. NSM Badgeworth, Shurdington and Witcombe w Bentham *Glouc* from 08. *21 Glynrosa Road, Charlton Kings, Cheltenham GL53 8QS* Tel (01242) 263081 Mobile 07768-658723 E-mail championarthur@gmail.com

CHAMPION, Canon John Oswald Cecil. b 27. St Chad's Coll Dur BA49. **d** 51 **p** 52. C Worc St Martin 51-53; Chapl RN 53-57; C Cant St Martin w St Paul 57-60; C-in-c Stourbridge St Mich Norton CD *Worc* 60-64; V Astwood Bank w Crabbs Cross 64-68; V Redditch St Steph 68-75; R Fladbury, Wyre Piddle and Moor 75-93; RD Pershore 79-85; Hon Can Worc Cathl 81-93; rtd 93; Perm to Offic *Worc* from 93. *Black Horse Cottage, 3 Church Row, Pershore WR10 1BL* Tel (01386) 552403

CHAMPNEYS, Michael Harold. b 46. LRAM66 GRSM67 ARCO67. Linc Th Coll 69. **d** 72 **p** 73. C Poplar *Lon* 72-75; C Bow w Bromley St Leon 73-75; P-in-c Bethnal Green St Barn 75-76; C Tewkesbury w Walton Cardiff *Glouc* 76-78; V Bedford Park *Lon* 78-83; V Shepshed *Leic* 84-87; Community Educn Tutor Bolsover 88-93; Perm to Offic *Derby* 90-92; NSM Bolsover 92-93; V Potterspury, Furtho, Yardley Gobion and Cosgrove *Pet* 93-98; RD Towcester 94-98; V Shap w Swindale and Bampton w Mardale *Carl* 98-01; R Calow and Sutton cum Duckmanton *Derby* from 01. *The Rectory, Top Road, Calow, Chesterfield S44 5AF* Tel (01246) 273486 E-mail michaelchampneys@yahoo.co.uk

CHANCE, David Newton. b 44. Univ of Wales (Lamp) BA68. St Steph Ho Ox 68. **d** 70 **p** 71. C Selsdon St Jo w St Fran *Cant* 70-73; C Plymstock *Ex* 73-77; P-in-c Northam 77-79; TR Northam w Westward Ho! and Appledore 79-93; V Banstead

Guildf from 93. *The Vicarage, 21 Court Road, Banstead SM7 2NQ* Tel (01737) 351134
E-mail david.chance93@ntlworld.com

CHAND, Richard. b 62. SAOMC 02. **d** 05 **p** 06. NSM Headington St Mary *Ox* from 05. *100 Bayswater Road, Headington, Oxford OX3 9NZ* Tel (01865) 741311 Mobile 07966-659270
E-mail richardchandrw@ministry.fsbusiness.co.uk

CHAND, Wazir. b 29. Punjab Univ BA56 BT59. Ox NSM Course. **d** 90 **p** 91. NSM Cowley St Jas *Ox* 90-04; Perm to Offic from 04. *38 Garsington Road, Oxford OX4 2LG* Tel (01865) 714160 *or* 433015

CHANDA, Daniel Khazan. b 28. Punjab Univ BA57 MA62 Saharanputh Coll. **d** 70 **p** 70. Hon C Handsworth St Jas *Birm* 70-83; Hon C Perry Barr 83-89; C Small Heath 89-98; rtd 98; Perm to Offic *Birm* 98-99 and from 00. *173 Wood Lane, Handsworth, Birmingham B20 2AG* Tel 0121-554 1093

CHANDLER, Anthony. b 43. Lon Inst of Educn CertEd65. EAMTC 94. **d** 97 **p** 98. Dioc Youth Officer *Ely* 96-00; NSM March St Mary 97-00; R from 00; NSM March St Pet 97-00; R from 00. *17 St Peter's Road, March PE15 9NA* Tel and fax (01354) 652894 E-mail anthony.chandler@ely.anglican.org

CHANDLER, Barbara Janet. b 58. Newc Univ BMedSci79 MB, BS82 MD93 FRCP00. NEOC 04. **d** 07 **p** 08. NSM Ponteland *Newc* from 07. *176 Darras Road, Ponteland, Newcastle upon Tyne NE20 9AF* Tel (01661) 823306 *or* 0191-287 5114
E-mail b.j.chandler@ncl.ac.uk

CHANDLER, Derek Edward. b 67. Southn Univ BTh91 Nottm Univ MDiv93. Linc Th Coll 91. **d** 93 **p** 94. C Bitterne Park *Win* 93-97; C Sholing 97-00; R Emmer Green w Caversham Park *Ox* from 00. *20 St Barnabas Road, Emmer Green, Reading RG4 8RA* Tel 0118-947 8239 E-mail rev.derek.chandler@virgin.net

CHANDLER, Ian Nigel. b 65. K Coll Lon BD89 AKC89. Chich Th Coll 92. **d** 92 **p** 93. C Hove *Chich* 92-96; Bp's Dom Chapl 96-00; V Haywards Heath St Rich from 00; RD Cuckfield 04-06. *St Richard's Vicarage, Queen's Road, Haywards Heath RH16 1EB* Tel (01444) 413621
E-mail ianchandler@hotmail.com

CHANDLER, John. b 49. ACIB73. NTMTC 05. **d** 07 **p** 08. NSM Colchester St Mich Myland *Chelmsf* from 07. *4 Longdryve, Wavell Avenue, Colchester CO2 7HH* Tel (01206) 249154 Mobile 07951-160558 E-mail john@mylandchurch.org.uk

CHANDLER, John Charles. b 46. Solicitor. Oak Hill Th Coll 91. **d** 94 **p** 95. C Tonbridge St Steph *Roch* 94-98; V Felsted and Lt Dunmow *Chelmsf* 98-05; V Hildenborough *Roch* from 05. *The Vicarage, 194 Tonbridge Road, Hildenborough, Tonbridge TN11 9HR* Tel (01732) 833569
E-mail jm@chandler464.freeserve.co.uk

CHANDLER, The Very Revd Michael John. b 45. Lambeth STh80 K Coll Lon PhD87. Linc Th Coll 70. **d** 72 **p** 73. C Cant St Dunstan w H Cross 72-75; C Margate St Jo 75-78; V Newington w Bobbing and Iwade 78-83; P-in-c Hartlip w Stockbury 80-83; V Newington w Hartlip and Stockbury 83-88; RD Sittingbourne 84-88; R Hackington 88-95; RD Cant 94-95; Can Res Cant Cathl 95-03; Dean Ely from 03. *The Deanery, The College, Ely CB7 4DN* Tel (01353) 667735 Fax 665668
E-mail dean@cathedral.ely.anglican.org

CHANDLER, Quentin David. b 62. Aston Tr Scheme 87 Trin Coll Bris BA92. **d** 92 **p** 93. C Goldington *St Alb* 92-96; TV Rushden w Newton Bromswold *Pet* 96-00; V Rushden St Pet 00-03; Dir Tr for Past Assts from 03; R Burton Latimer from 03. *The Rectory, Preston Court, Burton Latimer, Kettering NN15 5LR* Tel (01536) 722959 E-mail q.chandler@btopenworld.com

CHANDLER, Stephen Michael. NTMTC. **d** 09. NSM Victoria Docks St Luke *Chelmsf* from 09. *117 Atkinson Road, London E16 3LT*

CHANDLER, Mrs Susan May. b 54. WMMTC 06. **d** 09. NSM Olton *Birm* from 09. *14 Hollyberry Avenue, Solihull B91 3UA* Tel 0121-709 1512 Mobile 07970-791288
E-mail j14chand@aol.com

CHANDRA, Kevin Douglas Naresh. b 65. Lon Bible Coll BA91. Qu Coll Birm 94. **d** 96 **p** 97. C Walmley *Birm* 96-00; P-in-c Erdington St Chad 00-02; TV Erdington 02-05; Chapl St Pet Sch Ex from 06. *St Peter's C of E Aided School, Quarry Lane, Exeter EX2 5AP* Tel (01392) 204764 E-mail kc@chandra.plus.com

CHANDY, Sugu John Mathai. b 40. Kerala Univ BSc61 Serampore Univ BD66. Wycliffe Coll Toronto 67. **d** 66 **p** 68. India 66-74 and from 80; C Ormesby *York* 74-77; C Sutton St Jas and Wawne 78-80; rtd 90. *Matteethra, Muttambalam, Kottayam, Kerala 686 004, India* Tel (0091) (481) 572438 *or* 572590

✠**CHANG-HIM, The Rt Revd French Kitchener.** b 38. Lich Th Coll. **d** 62 **p** 63 **c** 79. C Goole *Sheff* 62-63; R Praslin Seychelles 63-67; C Sheff St Leon Norwood 67-68; C Mahé Cathl Mauritius 68-70; Missr Praslin 70-73; R Anse Royale St Sav and Adn Seychelles 73-79; Bp Seychelles 79-04; rtd 04. *PO Box 44, Victoria, Seychelles* Tel and fax (00248) 248151
E-mail changhim@seychelles.sc

CHANNER, Christopher Kendall. b 42. K Coll Lon BD64 AKC64. St Boniface Warminster 64. **d** 65 **p** 66. C Norbury St Steph *Cant* 65-68; C S Elmsall *Wakef* 68-70; V Dartford

St Edm *Roch* 70-75; Chapl Joyce Green Hosp Dartford 73-75; V Bromley St Andr *Roch* 75-81; V Langton Green 81-94; Chapl Holmewood Ho Sch Tunbridge Wells 94-98; P-in-c Lewes All SS, St Anne, St Mich and St Thos *Chich* 98-00; R Lewes St Mich and St Thos at Cliffe w All SS 00-08; rtd 08. *Willow Cottage, 3 Oakland Drive, Robertsbridge TN32 5EX* Tel (01580) 881478

CHANT, Edwin John. b 14. Lon Univ BA62. K Coll Lon 39 Clifton Th Coll 46. **d** 47 **p** 48. C Erith St Paul *Roch* 47-49; C Darfield *Sheff* 49-51; C Conisbrough 51-53; C Cliftonville *Cant* 53-56; V Gentleshaw *Lich* 56-80; V Farewell 56-80; rtd 80; Perm to Offic *Lich* from 80. *31 Huntsmans Gate, Burntwood WS7 9LL*

CHANT, Harry. b 40. Oak Hill Th Coll. **d** 78 **p** 79. C Heatherlands St Jo *Sarum* 78-81; P-in-c Bramshaw 81-83; P-in-c Landford w Plaitford 81-83; R Bramshaw and Landford w Plaitford 83-87; V Fareham St Jo *Portsm* 87-00; rtd 00; Perm to Offic *Truro* from 00. *Paradise Cottage, 34 Nanscober Place, Helston TR13 0SP* Tel and fax (01326) 561916 E-mail handrchant@aol.com

CHANT, Kenneth William. b 37. St Deiniol's Hawarden 67. **d** 70 **p** 71. C Ynyshir *Llan* 70-74; C Bargoed and Deri w Brithdir 74; P-in-c Aberpergwm and Blaengwrach 74-77; V 77-81; V Cwmavon 81-02; rtd 02. *22 Chalice Court, Port Talbot SA12 7DA* Tel (01639) 813456

CHANT, Maurice Ronald. b 26. Chich Th Coll 51. **d** 54 **p** 55. C Mitcham St Mark *S'wark* 54-57; C Surbiton St Matt 57-60; P-in-c Cookridge CD Ripon 60-64; V Cookridge H Trin 64-67; Chapl Miss to Seamen Tilbury 67-71; Gt Yarmouth 71-77; Australia 77-84 and from 85; Singapore 84-85; rtd 91. *Unit 2, 95 Charlotte Street, Wynnum Qld 4178, Australia* Tel (0061) (7) 3893 1251

CHANTER, Canon Anthony Roy. b 37. ACP60 Open Univ BA72 Lon Univ MA75. Sarum Th Coll 64. **d** 66 **p** 67. C W Tarring *Chich* 66-69; Chapl St Andr Sch Worthing 69-70; Hd Master Bp King Sch Linc 70-73; Hon PV Linc Cathl 70-73; Hd Master Grey Court Comp Sch Richmond 73-76; Hon C Kingston All SS *S'wark* 73-76; Hd Master Bp Reindorp Sch Guildf 77-84; Dir of Educn *Guildf* 84-01; Hon Can Guildf Cathl 84-01; rtd 02; Perm to Offic *Chich* from 02. *Thalassa, 62 Sea Avenue, Rustington, Littlehampton BN16 2DJ* Tel (01903) 774288
E-mail tonychanter@hotmail.com

CHANTREY, Preb David Frank. b 48. K Coll Cam BA70 PhD73 MA74. Westcott Ho Cam 83. **d** 86 **p** 87. C Wordsley *Lich* 86-89; C Beckbury 89-90; P-in-c 90-93; C Badger 89-90; P-in-c 90-93; C Kemberton, Sutton Maddock and Stockton 89-90; P-in-c 90-93; C Ryton 89-90; P-in-c 90-93; R Beckbury, Badger, Kemberton, Ryton, Stockton etc 93-08; TR Wrockwardine Deanery from 08; RD Wrockwardine from 08; Preb Lich Cathl from 99. *The Rectory, Wrockwardine, Telford TF6 5DD* Tel (01952) 251857 Mobile 07785-524495 E-mail david@wdtm.org.uk

CHANTRY, Ms Helen Fiona. b 59. Bradf Univ BSc82 Leeds Univ CertEd83. Trin Coll Bris BA89. **d** 89 **p** 94. NSM Hyde St Geo *Ches* 89-92; Dioc Youth Officer 92-00; NSM Barrow 94-99; C Acton and Worleston, Church Minshull etc 00-04; P-in-c Audlem from 04; Bp's Adv for Women in Min from 05. *The Rectory, Church Lane, Nantwich CW5 5RQ* Tel (01270) 625268 *or* 811543 E-mail helenchantry@btopenworld.com

CHANTRY, Peter Thomas. b 62. Bradf Univ BSc83. Trin Coll Bris BA89. **d** 89 **p** 90. C Hyde St Geo *Ches* 89-92; Dioc Youth Officer 91-99; P-in-c Barrow 94-99; R Nantwich from 99. *Rectory, Church Lane, Nantwich CW5 5RQ* Tel (01270) 625268 E-mail peterchantry@hotmail.com

CHANTRY, Mrs Sandra Mary. b 41. Cam Inst of Educn CertEd63. EMMTC 83. **dss** 86 **d** 87 **p** 94. Loughb Gd Shep *Leic* 86-87; Par Dn 87-89; Par Dn Belton and Osgathorpe 89-90; Par Dn Hathern, Long Whatton and Diseworth w Belton etc 90-94; C 94-97; P-in-c 97-01; rtd 01; Perm to Offic *Derby* from 07. *4 The Toft, Mill Lane, Belton, Loughborough LE12 9UL* Tel (01530) 222678 E-mail sandrachantry@aol.com

CHAPLIN, Ann. b 39. Em Coll Boston (USA) MA93 LRAM59 TCert75. WEMTC 95. **d** 98 **p** 99. NSM Heref S Wye 98-02; NSM St Weonards w Orcop, Garway, Tretire etc 02-05; P-in-c Belmont St Andr USA 06-09; Asst R Cambridge St Pet from 09. *St Peter's Church, PO Box 390390, Cambridge MA 02139, USA* Tel (001) (617) 547 7788

CHAPLIN, Colin. b 33. Edin Dioc NSM Course 74. **d** 76 **p** 77. NSM Penicuik *Edin* 76-91; P-in-c Peebles 89-90; NSM Bathgate 91-95; rtd 95; Asst P Edin St Mark 97-00; Asst P Innerleithen from 00; Asst P Peebles from 00. *26 Broomhill Road, Penicuik, Edinburgh EH26 9EE* Tel (01968) 672050

CHAPLIN, Douglas Archibald. b 59. Em Coll Cam BA81. St Jo Coll Nottm. **d** 86 **p** 87. C Glouc St Geo w Whaddon 86-89; C Lydney w Aylburton 89-93; R Worc St Clem 93-01; TV Droitwich Spa from 01. *The Vicarage, 29 Old Coach Road, Droitwich WR9 8BB* Tel (01905) 798929 Mobile 07905-842565
E-mail fatherdoug@actually.me.uk

CHAPLIN, Paul. b 57. Hull Univ BA80 CertEd81 K Coll Lon MA89. St Steph Ho Ox 85. **d** 87 **p** 88. C Ex St Jas 87-90; C Wokingham St Paul *Ox* 90-98; V Stratfield Mortimer 98-99; V Stratfield Mortimer and Mortimer W End etc from 99. *The*

Vicarage, 10 The Avenue, Mortimer, Reading RG7 3QY Tel 0118-933 2404 *or* 933 3704

CHAPMAN, Andrew John. b 81. Leeds Univ BA03 St Jo Coll Dur BA09. Cranmer Hall Dur 06. **d** 09. C Hykeham *Linc* from 09. *120A Station Road, Waddington, Lincoln LN5 9QS* Tel (01522) 723094 E-mail a.j.chapman@live.co.uk

CHAPMAN, Ms Ann Beatrice. b 53. Hull Coll of Educn BEd77 Leeds Univ BA87. St Jo Coll Nottm MA95. **d** 95 **p** 96. C Burley *Ripon* 95-98; TV Sheff Manor 98-01; P-in-c Askrigg w Stallingbusk *Ripon* from 01; Dir Practical Th NEOC from 04. *The Vicarage, Station Road, Askrigg, Leyburn DL8 3HZ* Tel (01969) 650301

CHAPMAN, Barry Frank. b 48. Trin Coll Bris 83. **d** 82 **p** 83. NSM Bradford-on-Avon Ch Ch *Sarum* from 82; Assoc Chapl Bath Univ from 83. *16 Church Acre, Bradford-on-Avon BA15 1RL* Tel (01225) 866861 *or* 461244 E-mail pysbfc@bath.ac.uk

CHAPMAN, Mrs Celia. b 32. Whitelands Coll Lon TCert53 Open Univ BA82. WMMTC 84. **d** 87 **p** 94. NSM Bilston *Lich* 87-93; Ind Chapl Black Country Urban Ind Miss 93-98; Chapl St Pet Colleg Sch Wolv 93-98; rtd 99; Perm to Offic *Glouc* and *Worc* from 99. *5 Tyne Drive, Evesham WR11 7FG* Tel (01386) 765878

CHAPMAN, Canon Christopher Robin. b 37. Ripon Hall Ox 72. **d** 73 **p** 74. C Kidbrooke St Jas *S'wark* 73-77; V Corton *Nor* 77-80; V Hopton 77-80; V Hopton w Corton 80-92; RD Lothingland 80-86; P-in-c Loddon w Sisland 92-93; P-in-c Loddon, Sisland w Hales and Heckingham 93-98; P-in-c Chedgrave w Hardley and Langley from 98; V Loddon, Sisland, Chedgrave, Hardley and Langley 98-03; Hon Can Nor Cathl 96-03; Chapl Langley Sch Nor 00-03; rtd 04; Perm to Offic *Chelmsf* 04-06 and *St E* from 06. *Preveli, 16 Riley Close, Ipswich IP1 5QD* Tel (01473) 462109

CHAPMAN, Colin Gilbert. b 38. St Andr Univ MA60 Lon Univ BD62 Birm Univ MPhil94. Ridley Hall Cam 62. **d** 64 **p** 65. C Edin St Jas 64-67; Asst Chapl Cairo Cathl Egypt 68-73; Tutor Crowther Hall CMS Tr Coll Selly Oak 73-75; Prin 90-97; Lebanon 75-82; Chapl Limassol St Barn 82-83; Lect Trin Coll Bris 83-90; Dir Faith to Faith Consultancy 97-99; Lect Near E Sch of Th Lebanon 99-03; rtd 04; Perm to Offic *Ely* from 07. *West Lodge, 17 Knights Way, Milton, Cambridge CB24 6DE* Tel (01223) 862169

CHAPMAN, Mrs Deborah Herath. b 55. Fort Lewis Coll (USA) BA76 Lon Bible Coll MA94. NTMTC 04. **d** 05 **p** 06. C Hanwell St Mellitus w St Mark *Lon* 05-08; C Northolt St Jos from 08. *St Hugh's House, 22 Gosling Close, Greenford UB6 9UE* Tel (020) 8813 0162 E-mail bee@rechord.com

CHAPMAN, Canon Derek. b 22. Westcott Ho Cam 52. **d** 53 **p** 54. C Earlsdon *Cov* 53-56; C Rugby St Andr 56-58; V E Malling *Roch* 58-79; CF (TA) 60-67; R Hever w Mark Beech *Roch* 79-89; P-in-c Four Elms 80-89; Hon Can Roch Cathl 84-89; rtd 89; Perm to Offic *Roch* 89-98 and *Chich* from 89. *1 Moat Lane, Sedlescombe, Battle TN33 0RZ* Tel (01424) 754455

CHAPMAN, Mrs Dorothy. b 38. EMMTC. **d** 89 **p** 94. Par Dn Bingham *S'well* 89-92; Sub-Chapl HM Pris Whatton 89-92; C Lenton 92-98, rtd 98; Perm to Offic *S'well* from 04. *86 Kenrick Road, Nottingham NG3 6FB* Tel 0115-950 3088

CHAPMAN, Drummond John. b 36. Cant Sch of Min 80. **d** 83 **p** 86. C Kington w Huntington, Old Radnor, Kinnerton etc *Heref* 83-84; C Llanidloes w Llangurig *Ban* 86-90; V Llanwnnog and Caersws w Carno 90-06; rtd 06. *Wgi Fawr, Carno, Caersws SY15 5LX*

CHAPMAN, Edwin Thomas. b 32. Man Univ BA60. St Mich Coll Llan 62. **d** 63 **p** 64. C Cleveleys *Blackb* 63-65; C Ox St Mary V w St Cross and St Pet 65-67; Chapl LMH Ox 67-68; Asst Dir of Educn *York* 68-75; R E Gilling 68-76; P-in-c Hockley *Chelmsf* 76-77; V 77-82; P-in-c Gosberton Clough and Quadring *Linc* 82-83; Chapl St Cath Sch Bramley 83-86; R Bulmer w Dalby, Terrington and Welburn *York* 86-97; RD Bulmer and Malton 91-97; rtd 97; Perm to Offic *York* from 97. *6 Undercroft, Dunnington, York YO19 5RP* Tel (01904) 488637

CHAPMAN, Mrs Elizabeth Ann. b 57. SEITE 05. **d** 09. NSM Gillingham St Mary *Roch* from 09. *93 Hempstead Road, Hempstead, Gillingham ME7 3RH* Tel (01634) 233477 Mobile 07961-337083 E-mail l.chapman431@btinternet.com

CHAPMAN, Canon Eric Ronald. b 19. Man Univ BA41 BD59. Bps' Coll Cheshunt 41. **d** 43 **p** 44. C Chorley St Pet *Blackb* 43-46; C Skerton St Luke 46-51; V Bolton St Mark *Man* 51-58; V Kells *Carl* 58-66; RD Whitehaven 66-70; R Egremont 66-81; Hon Can Carl Cathl 79-85; TR Egremont and Haile 81-85; rtd 85; Perm to Offic *Carl* from 86. *Bernaville, Highfield Road, Grange-over-Sands LA11 7JA* Tel (01539) 534351

CHAPMAN, Preb Gorran. b 55. Dur Univ BA. Westcott Ho Cam 78. **d** 80 **p** 81. C Par *Truro* 80-82, C Kenwyn 82 84; P-in-c Penwerris 84-89; V 89-92; V Torquay St Martin Barton *Ex* from 92; Perm to Offic *Truro* from 92; Preb Ex Cathl from 07. *St Martin's Vicarage, Beechfield Avenue, Barton, Torquay TQ2 8HU* Tel (01803) 327223

CHAPMAN, Guy Godfrey. b 33. Southn Univ BSc57. Clifton Th Coll 60. **d** 62 **p** 63. C Chadderton Ch Ch *Man* 62-67; V Edgeside 67-70; P-in-c Shipton Bellinger *Win* 70-72; V 72-83; RD Andover 75-85; Hon Can Win Cathl 79-91; R Over Wallop w Nether Wallop 83-91; V Ambrosden w Merton and Piddington *Ox* 91-00; RD Bicester and Islip 95-00; rtd 00; Perm to Offic *Sarum* and *Win* from 01. *65 St Ann Place, Salisbury SP1 2SU* Tel (01722) 335339

CHAPMAN, Henry Davison. b 31. Bris Univ BA55. Tyndale Hall Bris 52. **d** 56 **p** 57. C St Helens St Mark *Liv* 56-60; C Litherland St Jas *Blackb* 60-67; V Tipton St Martin *Lich* 67-68; SW Area Sec CPAS 68-72; V Eccleston St Luke *Liv* 72-78; P-in-c Ringshall w Battisford, Barking w Darmsden etc *St E* 78-80; R 80-93; RD Bosmere 87-91; rtd 93; Perm to Offic *Sarum* from 93. *Daracombe, 4 The Clays, Market Lavington, Devizes SN10 4AY* Tel (01380) 813774

CHAPMAN, Ian Martin. b 47. Oak Hill Th Coll BA94. **d** 94 **p** 95. C S Mimms Ch Ch *Lon* 94-99; Perm to Offic 02-08. *24 Vicars Close, Enfield EN1 3DN*

CHAPMAN (née CRAVEN), Canon Janet Elizabeth. b 58. St Jo Coll Dur BSc80 MA92. Cranmer Hall Dur 84. **d** 87 **p** 95. Par Dn Darlington St Cuth *Dur* 87-92; NSM Edin Gd Shep 93-95; NSM Long Marston and Rufforth w Moor Monkton and Hessay *York* 95-98; Chapl Qu Ethelburga's Coll York 97-99; Chapl Harrogate Ladies' Coll 00; P-in-c Banbury *Ox* 01-08; Can Res Birm Cathl from 08. *4 Nursery Drive, Handsworth, Birmingham B20 2SW* Tel 0121-262 1840 E-mail canonliturgist@birminghamcathedral.com

CHAPMAN, John Brown. b 54. Strathclyde Univ BSc76 Lon Bible Coll BA80. NTMTC 00. **d** 02 **p** 03. C W Ealing St Jo w St Jas *Lon* 02-05; C Northolt St Mary 05-08; Chapl for internat churches from 08. *St Hugh's House, 22 Gosling Close, Greenford UB6 9UE* Tel (020) 8813 0162 E-mail john@lchaimcommunity.com

CHAPMAN (née WHITFIELD), Mrs Joy Verity. b 46. SRN67 SCM71. Trin Coll Bris BA88. **d** 88 **p** 94. C Littleover *Derby* 88-92; Par Dn Bucknall and Bagnall *Lich* 92-94; TV Bucknall and Bagnall 94-97; Chapl LOROS Hospice 97-03; rtd 03; Perm to Offic *Leic* from 03. *15 Templar Way, Rothley, Leicester LE7 7RB* Tel 0116-230 1994 E-mail chapman@leicester.anglican.org

CHAPMAN, Mrs Lesley. b 61. NEOC 02. **d** 05 **p** 06. C Fenham St Jas and St Basil *Newc* 05-09; P-in-c Kenton Ascension from 09. *Kenton Vicarage, Creighton Avenue, Newcastle upon Tyne NE3 4UN* Tel 0191-285 7803 E-mail lesley.chapman414@btopenworld.com

CHAPMAN, Mrs Linda. b 46. Lon Univ BSc67 Lon Inst of Educn PGCE68. Guildf Dioc Min Course 98. **d** 00 **p** 01. NSM Ewell St Fran *Guildf* 00-04; NSM Cheswardine, Childs Ercall, Hales, Hinstock etc *Lich* from 04. *The Vicarage, High Street, Cheswardine, Market Drayton TF9 2RS* Tel (01630) 661204 E-mail rev.linda.chapman@dsl.pipex.com

CHAPMAN, Margaret. See FLINTOFT-CHAPMAN, Mrs Margaret

CHAPMAN, Mrs Margaret. b 34. Univ Coll Lon BA72 Qu Mary Coll Lon MA74. EAMTC 94. **d** 95 **p** 96. NSM Theydon Bois *Chelmsf* 95-01; P-in-c Gt Hallingbury and Lt Hallingbury 01-06; Perm to Offic from 06. *Broadacres, Cannons Lane, Hatfield Broad Oak, Bishop's Stortford CM22 7HJ* Tel (01279) 723341 E-mail revd.m.chapman@btinternet.com

CHAPMAN, Mark David. b 60. Trin Coll Ox MA83 DPhil89. Ox Min Course 93. **d** 94 **p** 95. Lect Ripon Coll Cuddesdon from 92; NSM Dorchester *Ox* 94-99; NSM Wheatley from 99. *Ripon College, Cuddesdon, Oxford OX44 9EX* Tel (01865) 874310 E-mail mchapman@ripon-cuddesdon.ac.uk

CHAPMAN, The Ven Michael Robin. b 39. Leeds Univ BA61. Coll of Resurr Mirfield 61. **d** 63 **p** 64. C Southwick St Columba *Dur* 63-68; Chapl RN 68-84; V Hale *Guildf* 84-91; RD Farnham 88-91; Adn Northn and Can Pet Cathl 91-04; rtd 04; Perm to Offic *Pet* from 04. *Dolphin House, High Street, Caenby, Market Rasen LN8 2EE* Tel (01673) 876190 E-mail chapmanhome@btinternet.com

CHAPMAN, Miss Patricia Ann. b 42. dss 84 **d** 87 **p** 94. Rainworth *S'well* 84-96; Par Dn 87-94; C 94-96; P-in-c Mansfield Oak Tree Lane 96-07; rtd 07. *28 St John's View, Mansfield NG18 1QP*

CHAPMAN, Peter Harold White. b 40. AKC64. **d** 65 **p** 66. C Havant *Portsm* 65-69; C Stanmer w Falmer and Moulsecoomb *Chich* 69-73; Chapl RN 73-86; Chapl Chigwell Sch Essex 86-90; P in c Stapleford Tawney w Theydon Mt *Chelmsf* 87-01. *12 Cova Boulevard, Hope Island Qld 4212, Australia* E-mail phwchapman@aol.com

CHAPMAN, Peter John. b 33. Dur Univ BA56. Cranmer Hall Dur. **d** 59 **p** 60. C Boulton *Derby* 59-62; Uganda 63-70; P-in-c Southampton St Matt *Win* 71-73; TV Southampton (City Cen)

73-78; V Bilston St Leon *Lich* 78-79; P-in-c Bilston St Mary 78-79; TR Bilston 80-98; RD Wolverhampton 89-98; rtd 99; Perm to Offic *Glouc* and *Worc* from 99. *5 Tyne Drive, Evesham WR11 6FG* Tel (01386) 765878

CHAPMAN, Peter John. b 50. ERMC 05. d 08 p 09. NSM Lt Barningham, Blickling, Edgefield etc *Nor* from 08. *Pump Cottage, The Street, Bessingham, Norwich NR11 7JR* Tel (01263) 577782 E-mail peternina@chapmansfarm.fsnet.co.uk

CHAPMAN, Prof Raymond. b 24. Jes Coll Ox BA45 MA59 Lon Univ MA47 BD75 PhD78. S'wark Ord Course 72. d 74 p 75. NSM St Mary le Strand w St Clem Danes *Lon* 74-82; NSM Barnes St Mary *S'wark* 82-94; Perm to Offic *Lon* 82-91 and *S'wark* from 94. *6 Kitson Road, London SW13 9HJ* Tel (020) 8748 9901

CHAPMAN, Raymond. b 41. Linc Th Coll 68. d 71 p 72. C Dronfield *Derby* 71-74; C Delaval *Newc* 75-76; TV Whorlton 76-79; V Newc St Hilda 79-83; V Blyth St Cuth 83-89; Hon C Fareham SS Pet and Paul *Portsm* 95-98; Perm to Offic 98-00 and from 05; C Purbrook 00-05. *170 White Hart Lane, Fareham PO16 9AX* Tel (023) 9232 4537 Fax 9264 4237 Mobile 07944-1245467

CHAPMAN, Canon Rex Anthony. b 38. Univ Coll Lon BA62 St Edm Hall Ox BA64 MA68. Wells Th Coll 64. d 65 p 66. C Stourbridge St Thos *Worc* 65-68; Chapl Aber Univ 68-78; Can St Andr Cathl 76-78; Bp's Adv for Educn *Carl* 78-85; Dir of Educn 85-04; Can Res Carl Cathl 78-04; rtd 04; Lic to Offic *Ab* from 06; Chapl to The Queen 97-08. *The Cottage, Myreside, Finzean, Banchory AB31 6NB* Tel (01330) 850645 E-mail rex.chapman@ukgateway.net

CHAPMAN, Robert Bertram. b 68. St Jo Coll Nottm BA00. d 00 p 01. C Daybrook *S'well* 00-03; P-in-c Colwick from 03; P-in-c Netherfield from 03. *St George's Rectory, 93 Victoria Road, Netherfield, Nottingham NG4 2NN* Tel 0115-961 5566 E-mail robertsarah@talktalk.net

CHAPMAN, Rodney Andrew. b 53. AKC75. St Aug Coll Cant 75. d 76 p 77. C Hartlepool St Aid *Dur* 76-81; Lic to Offic 81-83; C Owton Manor 83-87; P-in-c Kelloe 87-92; V Sharlston *Wakef* 92-01; V Stainland w Outlane from 01; C Elland from 06. *The Vicarage, 345 Stainland Road, Stainland, Halifax HX4 9HF* Tel (01422) 311848

CHAPMAN, Roger. b 60. Leic Univ BSc82. Westcott Ho Cam 04. d 06 p 07. C Norton St Alb from 06. *2 Common View, Letchworth SG6 1DA* Tel (01462) 672256 Mobile 07905-891890

CHAPMAN, Roger John. b 34. AKC58. d 59 p 60. C Guildf Ch Ch 59-61; Kenya 61-67; R S Milford *York* 68-77; RD Selby 72-77; V Beverley St Mary 77-88; RD Beverley 85-88; V Desborough *Pet* 88-95; R Brampton Ash w Dingley and Braybrooke 88-95; rtd 95; Perm to Offic *York* from 95. *14 Scrubwood Lane, Beverley HU17 7BE* Tel (01482) 881267

CHAPMAN, Sally Anne. b 55. Lanchester Poly Cov BSc76 Univ of Wales (Swansea) PGCE77. WMMTC 87. d 90 p 94. Par Dn Glascote and Stonydelph *Lich* 90-93; Par Dn Willenhall H Trin 93-94; C 94-96; TV 96-99; V Streetly 99-05; Dioc Adv for Women in Min 99-04; RD Walsall 04-05; Preb Lich Cathl 04-05; Lect Stourbridge Coll from 05. *41 Hunters Gate, Much Wenlock TF13 6BW* Tel (01952) 727569 E-mail robert@furzebank.freeserve.co.uk

CHAPMAN, Mrs Sarah Jean. b 55. Lon Univ DipCOT77. Sarum & Wells Th Coll 86. d 89 p 94. NSM Rogate w Terwick and Trotton w Chithurst *Chich* 89-94; NSM Easebourne 94-96; Perm to Offic *Portsm* 96-97; V Sheet 97-02; V Bitterne Park *Win* from 02. *Bitterne Park Vicarage, 7 Thorold Road, Southampton SO18 1HZ* Tel (023) 8055 1560 E-mail revsarah@sargil.co.uk

CHAPMAN, Simon Jon. b 75. Bris Bapt Coll 04 Trin Coll Bris 07. d 08 p 09. C Broxbourne w Wormley *St Alb* from 08. *11 Wharf Road, Broxbourne EN10 6HU* Tel (01992) 466834 E-mail simon@chapsters.org.uk

CHAPMAN (*formerly* WOOD), Canon Sylvia Marian. b 40. Univ of Wales (Lamp) BA09. Gilmore Ho 77. dss 80 d 87 p 94. Tolleshunt Knights w Tiptree *Chelmsf* 80-83; Leigh-on-Sea St Jas 83-86; Canvey Is 86-92; Par Dn 87-92; Miss to Seamen 87-92; Warden of Ords *Chelmsf* 89-92; C Hutton and CME Officer 92-97; Ind Chapl 97-99; V Moulsham St Luke 99-06; rtd 06; Hon Can Chelmsf Cathl 01-06; Perm to Offic *Nor* 00-05 and *St E* from 05. *Preveli, 16 Riley Close, Ipswich IP1 5QD* Tel (01473) 462109 E-mail canons.chapman@btinternet.com

CHAPMAN, Thomas Graham. b 33. Trin Coll Bris 73. d 75 p 76. C Branksome St Clem *Sarum* 75-81; V Quarry Bank *Lich* 81-93; V Quarry Bank *Worc* 93-99; rtd 99; Perm to Offic *Worc* from 99. *8 Somerset Drive, Wollaston, Stourbridge DY8 4RH* Tel (01384) 373921 E-mail thomas.chapman1@btinternet.com

CHAPMAN, Timothy Mark. b 69. Clare Coll Cam BA91. Oak Hill Th Coll BA02. d 02 p 03. C Lt Shelford *Ely* 02-08. *6 Wakelin Avenue, Sawston, Cambridge CB22 3DS* Tel (01223) 830169 *or* 843710 Mobile 07815-686072 E-mail timandlucychapman@btopenworld.com

CHAPMAN, Tristan David. b 79. K Alfred's Coll Win BA01. Ripon Coll Cuddesdon BTh07. d 07 p 08. C Bocking St Mary *Chelmsf* from 07. *3 Hadley Close, Braintree CM7 5LP* Tel (01376) 347357 E-mail fr.tristan@googlemail.com

CHAPMAN, Miss Yvonne Hazel. b 35. Serampore Th Coll BRE63 Brighton Coll of Educn CertEd55. EAMTC 95. d 96 p 97. NSM Duston Team *Pet* 96-02; NSM Officer 99-02; rtd 02; Perm to Offic *Pet* from 02. *18 Sundew Court, Northampton NN4 9XH* Tel (01604) 762091 E-mail rev.ychapman@virgin.net

CHAPPELL, Allan. b 27. Selw Coll Cam BA51 MA56. Coll of Resurr Mirfield 51. d 53 p 54. C Knowle *Bris* 53-57; Zanzibar 57-63; C Long Eaton St Laur *Derby* 64-67; C-in-c Broxtowe CD *S'well* 67-73; P-in-c Flintham 73-82; R Car Colston w Screveton 73-82; V Mansfield St Lawr 82-92; rtd 92; Perm to Offic *S'well* from '93 and *Derby* from 00. *43 Hillsway Crescent, Mansfield NG18 5DR* Tel (01623) 654155

CHAPPELL, Edward Michael. b 32. Glouc Sch of Min 84. d 87 p 88. NSM Wotton-under-Edge w Ozleworth and N Nibley *Glouc* 87-01; Perm to Offic from 01. *5 Parklands, Wotton-under-Edge GL12 7LT* Tel (01453) 844250

CHAPPELL, Frank Arnold. b 37. Dur Univ BA58. Bps' Coll Cheshunt. d 60 p 61. C Headingley *Ripon* 60-65; V Beeston Hill St Luke 65-73; R Garforth 73-91; V Dacre w Hartwith and Darley w Thornthwaite 91-02; rtd 02; Perm to Offic *York* and *Ripon* from 02. *14 Nelsons Lane, York YO24 1HD* Tel (01904) 709566

CHAPPELL, Michael. *See* CHAPPELL, Edward Michael

CHAPPELL, Michael Paul. b 35. Selw Coll Cam BA57 MA61 ACertCM65. Cuddesdon Coll 60. d 62 p 63. C Pershore w Pinvin, Wick and Birlingham *Worc* 62-65; Malaysia 65-67; V Choral and Chapl Heref Cathl 67-71; Min Can Dur Cathl 71-76; Prec 72-76; Chapl H Trin Sch Stockton 76-87; C-in-c Stockton Green Vale H Trin CD *Dur* 82-87; V Scarborough St Luke *York* 87-01; Chapl Scarborough Gen Hosp 87-97; rtd 01; Perm to Offic *York* from 01. *26 Dulverton Hall, Esplanade, Scarborough YO11 2AR* Tel (01723) 340126

CHARD, Reginald Jeffrey. b 40. Univ of Wales (Lamp) BA62 CQSW75. Coll of Resurr Mirfield 62. d 64 p 65. C Ystrad Mynach *Llan* 64-67; C Aberdare St Fagan 67-71; V Hirwaun 71-74; Hon C Stechford *Birm* 74-78; TV Banbury *Ox* 78-86; Ind Chapl 86-09; P-in-c Claydon w Mollington 86-96; R Ironstone 96-09; rtd 09. *15 The Glen, Yarmouth PO41 0PZ* Tel (01983) 760554 E-mail jeffreychard@btinternet.com

CHARING CROSS, Archdeacon of. *See* JACOB, The Ven William Mungo

CHARKHAM, Rupert Anthony. b 59. Ex Univ BA81. Wycliffe Hall Ox 83. d 89 p 89. C Ox St Aldate w St Matt 89-92; P-in-c Fisherton Anger *Sarum* 92-99; R 99-03; V Cambridge H Trin *Ely* from 03. *Holy Trinity Vicarage, 1 Selwyn Gardens, Cambridge CB3 9AX* Tel (01223) 354774 *or* 355397 E-mail rupert.charkham@htcambridge.org.uk

CHARLES, Cecilia. *See* CHARLES, Mary Cecilia

CHARLES, David Gordon. b 79. Ex Coll Ox BA01 MA04 CCC Cam BA05 MA09. Westcott Ho Cam 03. d 06 p 07. C Willingdon *Chich* from 06. *37 Church Street, Willingdon, Eastbourne BN20 9HT* Tel (01323) 502088 E-mail davidgcharles@hotmail.com

CHARLES, George Edward. b 41. St Jo Coll Morpeth 63. d 66 p 67. C Bentleigh St Jo Australia 66-67; C Broadmeadows 67-70; I Montmorency 70-74; I Mooroolbark 74-81; I Bacchus Marsh 81-86; I Sorrento 86-93; I Altona 93-98; I Inverleigh, Bannockburn and Meredith 98-01; TV Hanley H Ev *Lich* 02-06; rtd 06; Perm to Offic *Lich* from 06. *210 Junction Road, Leek ST13 5QT* Tel (01538) 399254 E-mail gpsecharles@ntlworld.com

CHARLES, James Richard. b 67. St Edm Hall Ox BA90 CertEd91. Oak Hill Th Coll BA03. d 03 p 04. C Throop *Win* 03-07; P-in-c Bexleyheath St Pet *Roch* from 07. *St Peter's Vicarage, 50 Bristow Road, Bexleyheath DA7 4QA* Tel (020) 8303 8713 E-mail jimrcharles@mac.com

CHARLES, Canon Jonathan. b 42. St Luke's Coll Ex CertEd64. Ripon Hall Ox 72 Ripon Coll Cuddesdon 78. d 79 p 80. C Leagrave *St Alb* 79-82; Chapl Denstone Coll Uttoxeter 82-86; Chapl Malvern Girls' Coll 86-89; Chapl K Sch Worc 89-95; Min Can Worc Cathl 89-95; R Burnham Gp of Par *Nor* 95-09; RD Burnham and Walsingham 00-08; Hon Can Nor Cathl 05-09; rtd 09. *Michaelmas Cottage, 8 Back Street, South Creak, Fakenham NR21 9PG* Tel (01328) 823072 E-mail revj.charles@virgin.net

CHARLES, Martin. *See* CHARLES, William Martin Darrell

CHARLES, Mary Cecilia. b 49. Univ of Wales BEd. Trin Coll Carmarthen. d 96 p 97. NSM Letterston w Llanfair Nant-y-Gof etc *St D* 96-08; C from 09; NSM Maenclochog and New Moat etc 08-09. *Hen Eglwys Farm, St David's Road, Letterston, Haverfordwest SA62 5SR* Tel (01348) 840452

CHARLES, Meedperdas Edward. b 28. Fitzw Ho Cam BA60 MA64. Bangalore Th Coll BD54. d 54 p 55. C Malacca Malaya 54-55; P-in-c Singapore St Paul and St Pet 55-58; Perm to Offic *Ely* 58-60; V Sheff St Bart Langsett Road 60-64; Chapl Univ of Singapore 64-66; V Gravelly Hill *Birm* 66-78; V Endcliffe *Sheff*

79-90; rtd 91; Perm to Offic *Sheff* from 91. *60 Ringinglow Road, Sheffield S11 7PQ* Tel 0114-266 4980

CHARLES, Robert Sidney James. b 40. Lon Univ CertEd77 Open Univ BA79 Univ of Wales LLM97. St Mich Coll Llan. **d** 65 **p** 66. C Merthyr Tydfil *Llan* 65-68; C Shotton *St As* 68-70; R Stock and Lydlinch *Sarum* 70-74; R Hubberston *St D* 74-76; Perm to Offic *Chelmsf* 81-83; V Crossens *Liv* 83-97; V Budleigh Salterton *Ex* from 97. *St Peter's Vicarage, 4A West Hill Lane, Budleigh Salterton EX9 6AA* Tel (01395) 443195

CHARLES, Robin. b 50. Sarum & Wells Th Coll. **d** 86 **p** 87. C Chesterton *Lich* 86-89; C Rugeley 89-90; TV 90-97; TV E Scarsdale *Derby* 97-01; C Chesterfield St Mary and All SS 01-04; V Worc Dines Green St Mich and Crown E, Rushwick from 04. *3 Grove Farm, Farmbrook Close, Worcester WR2 5UG* Tel and fax (01905) 749995 Mobile 07788-724581
E-mail robin@maize45.freeserve.co.uk

CHARLES, Mrs Susan Jane. b 67. SEITE 05. **d** 08. NSM Eltham H Trin *S'wark* from 08. *109 Tarnwood Park, London SE9 5PE* Tel (020) 8850 0189 E-mail susanjcharles@aol.com

CHARLES, William Martin Darrell. b 40. **d** 90 **p** 91. C Market Harborough *Leic* 90-91; P-in-c Higham-on-the-Hill w Fenny Drayton and Witherley 91-99; P-in-c Breedon cum Isley Walton and Worthington 99-02; rtd 02. *37 Whatton Road, Kegworth, Derby DE74 2EZ* Tel (01509) 672040

CHARLES-EDWARDS, David Mervyn. b 38. Trin Coll Cam BA61. Linc Th Coll 62. **d** 64 **p** 89. C Putney St Mary *S'wark* 64-65; Chief Exec Officer Br Assn for Counselling 82-87; Gen Manager Lon Lighthouse AIDS Project 87-88; Consultant in leadership and team building from 88; NSM Rugby *Cov* 89-99; P-in-c Clifton upon Dunsmore and Newton 99-03; Perm to Offic from 03. *236 Hillmorton Road, Rugby CV22 5BG* Tel (01788) 569212 E-mail cwa.david@btinternet.com

CHARLESWORTH, Eric Charlesworth. b 29. Kelham Th Coll 49. **d** 54 **p** 56. C Woodbridge St Mary *St E* 54-57; Asst Chapl Oslo St Edm *Eur* 57-59; Canada 60-66; R Huntingfield w Cookley *St E* 66-70; R Slimbridge *Glouc* 70-96; rtd 96; Perm to Offic *Glouc* from 96 and *Ox* from 04. *Gardener's Cottage, Fairford Park, Fairford GL7 4JQ* Tel (01285) 712411

CHARLESWORTH, Ian Peter. b 65. Lanc Univ BA87. St Mich Coll Llan 91. **d** 93 **p** 94. C Caereithin *S & B* 93-95; C Oystermouth 95-97; R Llandefalle and Llyswen w Boughrood etc from 97. *The Rectory, Church Lane, Llyswen, Brecon LD3 0UU* Tel (01874) 754255
E-mail ian.charlesworth@btinternet.com

CHARLESWORTH, Philip. b 55. Sheff City Poly BSc85 Anglia Poly MSc92. **d** 07 **p** 08. OLM Sprowston w Beeston *Nor* from 07. *63 Wroxham Road, Norwich NR7 8TN* Tel (01603) 411316 Mobile 07983-911958 E-mail pc111@tiscali.co.uk

CHARLEY, Canon Julian Whittard. b 30. New Coll Ox BA55 MA58. Ridley Hall Cam 55. **d** 57 **p** 58. C St Marylebone All So w SS Pet and Jo *Lon* 57-64; Lect Lon Coll of Div 64-70; Vice-Prin St Jo Coll Nottm 70-74; TR Everton St Pet *Liv* 74-87; Warden Shrewsbury Ho 74-87; P-in-c Gt Malvern St Mary *Worc* 87-97; Hon Can Worc Cathl 91-97; rtd 97; Perm to Offic *Heref* and *Worc* from 97. *155A Old Hollow, Malvern WR14 4NN* Tel (01684) 569801

CHARLTON, Canon Arthur David. b 23. Open Univ BA73 BPhil83. Chich Th Coll. **d** 66 **p** 67. C Rotherfield *Chich* 66-70; C Uckfield 70-72; C Isfield 70-72; C Lt Horsted 70-72; R Cocking w Bepton 72-79; P-in-c W Lavington 78-79; R Cocking, Bepton and W Lavington 79-90; Can and Preb Chich Cathl 88-90; rtd 90; Perm to Offic *Chich* from 91; Perm to Offic *Roch* 91-98. *33 High Cross Fields, Crowborough TN6 2SN* Tel (01892) 661351

CHARLTON, Mrs Elizabeth Anne. b 55. STETS BA08. **d** 08 **p** 09. C W Moors *Sarum* from 08. *22 Teasel Way, West Moors, Ferndown BH22 0PQ* Tel (01202) 854689 Mobile 07541-069078 E-mail eacharlton@btinternet.com

CHARMAN, Canon Jane Ellen Elizabeth. b 60. St Jo Coll Dur BA81 Selw Coll Cam BA84 MA88. Westcott Ho Cam 82. **d** 87 **p** 94. C Glouc St Geo w Whaddon 87-90; Chapl and Fell Clare Coll Cam 90-95; R Duxford *Ely* 95-04; V Hinxton 95-04; V Ickleton 95-04; RD Shelford 03-04; Dir of Min *Sarum* 04-07; Dir of Learning for Discipleship and Min from 07; Can and Preb Sarum Cathl from 07. *4 The Sidings, Downton, Salisbury SP5 3QZ* Tel (01722) 411944 Mobile 07867-146524
E-mail jane.charman@salisbury.anglican.org

CHARMLEY, Mark Richard. b 71. Ex Univ BA93. Qu Coll Birm MA01. **d** 01 **p** 02. C Blurton *Lich* 01-04; P-in-c Banbury St Leon *Ox* from 04. *St Leonard's Vicarage, Middleton Road, Banbury OX16 4RG* Tel (01295) 262120 E-mail charmley@totalise.co.uk

CHARNOCK, Deryck Ian. b 47. Oak Hill Th Coll 78. **d** 80 **p** 81. C Rowner *Portsm* 80-84; TV Southgate *Chich* 84-90; V Penge St Paul *Roch* 90-98; V Whitwick St Jo the Bapt *Leic* 98-06; R Hollington St Leon *Chich* from 06. *The Rectory, Tile Barn Road, St Leonards-on-Sea TN38 9PA* Tel (01424) 852257
E-mail deryck8@aol.com

CHARNOCK, Ms Tracy. b 75. Leeds Univ BA97 BA08. Coll of Resurr Mirfield 06. **d** 08 **p** 09. C Man Victoria Park from 08.

33 Tagore Close, Manchester M13 0YS Tel 0161-248 0741 Mobile 07778-163920 E-mail tracy.charnock@hotmail.co.uk

CHARRETT, Geoffrey Barton. b 36. ALCM Nottm Univ BSc57. Ridley Hall Cam 65. **d** 67 **p** 68. C Clifton *York* 67-68; Lic to Offic *Blackb* 69-80; C Walthamstow St Mary w St Steph *Chelmsf* 81-82; TV 82-87; Chapl Gordon's Sch Woking 87-94; P-in-c Hambledon *Guildf* 94-97; rtd 97; Perm to Offic *Linc* from 00. *2 Station Road, Sutton-on-Sea, Mablethorpe LN12 2HN* Tel (01507) 443525

CHARRINGTON, Nicholas John. b 36. MA. Cuddesdon Coll 60. **d** 62 **p** 63. C Shrewsbury St Chad *Lich* 62-65; C Gt Grimsby St Mary and St Jas *Linc* 65-72; P-in-c Wellington Ch Ch *Lich* 72-78; R Edgmond 78-79; R Edgmond w Kynnersley and Preston Wealdmoors 89-91; C Plymstock *Ex* 91-94; Chapl St Luke's Hospice Plymouth 91-94; P-in-c Longden and Annscroft w Pulverbatch *Heref* 94-00; rtd 00; Perm to Offic *Heref* from 00. *Domas Cottage, Harley, Shrewsbury SY5 6LX* Tel (01952) 510721 E-mail nick@charrington.enta.net

CHARTERIS, Hugo Arundale. b 64. Witwatersrand Univ BA88. Cranmer Hall Dur 90. **d** 93 **p** 94. C Byker St Mark and Walkergate St Oswald *Newc* 93-97; P-in-c New Ferry *Ches* 97-05; V 02-05. *26 Rothbury Terrace, Newcastle upon Tyne NE6 5XH* Tel 0191-209 2508 E-mail hugo@charteris.org.uk

CHARTERS, Alan Charles. b 35. Trin Hall Cam BA60 MA63 FCollP88. Linc Th Coll 60. **d** 62 **p** 63. C Gt Grimsby St Mary and St Jas *Linc* 62-65; Chapl and Hd RE Eliz Coll Guernsey 65-70; P-in-c Guernsey St Jas the Less 65-70; Dep Hd Master Park Sen High Sch Swindon 70-73; Chapl St Jo Sch Leatherhead 73-83; Dep Hd Master 76; Visiting Lect and Tutor Lon Univ Inst of Ed 76-80; Headmaster The K Sch Glouc 83-92; V Aberedw w Llandeilo Graban and Llanbadarn etc *S & B* 92-00; Bp's Visitor to Schs 92-00; rtd 00; Perm to Offic *Eur* 00-03; P-in-c Dinard 03-06. *Crescent House, Church Street, Talgarth, Brecon LD3 0BL* Tel (01874) 711135 E-mail alan@ccharterss.net.uk

✠**CHARTRES, The Rt Revd and Rt Hon Richard John Carew.** b 47. KCVO09 PC96. Trin Coll Cam BA68 MA73 BD83 Hon DLitt98 Hon DD99 FSA99 Hon FGCM97. Cuddesdon Coll 69 Linc Th Coll 72. **d** 73 **p** 74 **c** 92. C Bedford St Andr *St Alb* 73-75; Bp's Dom Chapl 75-80; Abp's Chapl *Cant* 80-84; P-in-c Westmr St Steph w St Jo *Lon* 84-85; V 86-92; Dir of Ords 85-92; Prof Div Gresham Coll 86-92; Six Preacher Cant Cathl 91-97; Area Bp Stepney *Lon* 92-95; Bp Lon from 95; Dean of HM Chpls Royal and Prelate of OBE from 95. *The Old Deanery, Dean's Court, London EC4V 5AA* Tel (020) 7248 6233 Fax 7248 9721
E-mail bishop@londin.clara.co.uk

CHASE, Mrs Elizabeth. Wycliffe Hall Ox. **d** 09. NSM Headbourne Worthy *Win* from 09; NSM King's Worthy from 09. *The Greetings, Grange Road, Winchester SO23 9RT*

CHATER, John Augustus. b 43. SEITE 99. **d** 04 **p** 05. NSM St Peter-in-Thanet *Cant* 04-07; Ramsgate Town Cen Missr from 07. *125 High Street, Ramsgate CT11 9UA* Tel (01843) 596175 E-mail johnchater@rya-online.net

CHATER, John Leathley. b 29. Qu Coll Cam BA54 MA58. Ridley Hall Cam 54. **d** 56 **p** 57. C Bath Abbey w St Jas *B & W* 56-60; V Bermondsey St Anne *S'wark* 60-64; Ind Chapl 60-64; V Heslington *York* 64-69; Chapl York Univ 64-69; V Lawrence Weston *Bris* 69-73; Perm to Offic 74-80; P-in-c Wraxall *B & W* 80-82; R 82-84; V Battle *Chich* 84-90; Dean Battle 84-90; RD Battle and Bexhill 86-90; R St Marylebone w H Trin *Lon* 90-96; rtd 96; Perm to Offic *Chich* from 96. *75 Braemore Road, Hove BN3 4HA* Tel (012/3) /48402

CHATER (née CAKE), Nichola Carla. b 58. Liv Univ BSc79 MB, ChB85 MRCGP FRCP08. Cranmer Hall Dur 05. **d** 07 **p** 08. NSM Dur St Marg and Neville's Cross St Jo from 07. *37 Hill Meadows, High Shincliffe, Durham DH1 2PE* Tel 0191-383 1869 E-mail nicky_chater@yahoo.co.uk

CHATFIELD, Adrian Francis. b 49. Leeds Univ BA71 MA72 MPhil89 PhD97. Coll of Resurr Mirfield 71. **d** 72 **p** 73. Trinidad and Tobago 72-83; TV Barnstaple, Goodleigh and Landkey *Ex* 83-85; TR Barnstaple 85-88; Lect St Jo Coll Nottm 88-98; S Africa 99-05; Tutor Wycliffe Hall Ox 05-07; Hon C Wallingford *Ox* 05-07; Dir Simeon Cen and Co-ord Mixed Mode Tr Ridley Hall Cam from 07. *12 Barrons Way, Comberton, Cambridge CB23 7EQ* Tel (01223) 263009 *or* 741080
E-mail adrian.chatfield@btinternet.com

CHATFIELD, Mrs Gillian. b 50. Leeds Univ BA71 PGCE72. St Jo Coll Nottm MA94. **d** 94 **p** 95. C Greasley *S'well* 94-98; S Africa 99-05; TV Wallingford *Ox* 05-07; Past Tutor Ridley Hall Cam from 07. *12 Barrons Way, Comberton, Cambridge CB23 7EQ* Tel (01223) 263009 Mobile 07758-591430
E-mail jill.chatfield@btinternet.com

CHATFIELD, Michael Francis. b 75. York Univ BSc96 Fitzw Coll Cam BA99 MA03. Ridley Hall Cam. **d** 00 **p** 01. C Attenborough *S'well* 00-03; P-in-c Chaguanas St Thos Trinidad and Tobago from 04. *Light Pole #65, #29 Serene Gardens, Longdenville, Trinidad, West Indies* Tel (001) (868) 754 4209 (mobile) E-mail thechatalots@hotmail.com

CHATFIELD, Neil Patrick. b 66. Nottm Univ BTh95. Linc Th Coll 93 Westcott Ho Cam 95. **d** 96 **p** 97. C Bexhill St Pet *Chich*

96-00; V Eastbourne Ch Ch and St Phil from 00; Chapl Eastbourne Hosps NHS Trust from 01. *Christ Church Vicarage, 18 Addingham Road, Eastbourne BN22 7DY* Tel (01323) 721952 E-mail vicar@xpeastbourne.org

CHATFIELD, Canon Norman. b 37. Fitzw Ho Cam BA59 MA68. Ripon Hall Ox 60. **d** 62 **p** 63. C Burgess Hill St Jo *Chich* 62-65; C Uckfield 65-69; V Lower Sandown St Jo *Portsm* 69-76; V Locks Heath 76-83; Bp's Chapl for Post-Ord Tr 78-85; R Alverstoke 83-91; Chapl HM Pris Haslar 83-90; Chapl Gosport War Memorial Hosp 83-91; Hon Can Portsm Cathl 85-91; Can Res Glouc Cathl 91-02; rtd 02; Perm to Offic *Portsm* from 03. *Ellwood, Garfield Road, Bishop's Waltham SO32 1AT* Tel (01489) 891995 E-mail chat.field@virgin.net

CHATFIELD, Thomas William. b 19. Chich Th Coll 44. **d** 46 **p** 47. C Hanworth All SS *Lon* 46-49; C Woolwich St Mich *S'wark* 49-51; C Eastbourne St Andr *Chich* 51-55; V Halton in Hastings St Clem 55-68; P-in-c Hastings St Mary Magd 68-71; R 71-78; P-in-c Bishopstone 78-84; rtd 84; Perm to Offic *Chich* from 84. *5 Leeds Close, Hastings TN35 5BX* Tel (01424) 437413

CHATTELL, David Malcolm. b 63. St Luke's Coll Ex BEd93. Wycliffe Hall Ox 03. **d** 05 **p** 06. C Bucklebury w Marlston *Ox* from 05. *The Rectory, Southend Road, Southend, Reading RG7 6EU* Tel 0118-974 4333 E-mail dchattell@tinyonline.co.uk

CHATTERLEY, Mrs Marion Frances. b 55. Edin Th Coll 95. **d** 98 **p** 99. C Edin Gd Shep 98-00; C Edin Ch Ch 00-05; Hon C Edin St Mich and All SS from 07; Chapl Napier Coll from 00; Dioc Dir of Ords from 06. *102 Relugas Road, Edinburgh EH9 2LZ* Tel 0131-667 6847 Mobile 07771-982163 E-mail marion.chatterley@blueyonder.co.uk

CHATTERTON, Thomas William. b 50. SEITE. **d** 99 **p** 00. OLM Blackheath All SS *S'wark* from 99. *44 Harland Road, London SE12 0JA* Tel (020) 8851 6813 *or* 7525 7912 ext 4482 E-mail trev2@amserve.com

CHATWIN, Ronald Ernest. b 34. St Aid Birkenhead 58. **d** 60 **p** 61. C Selsdon *Cant* 60-64; C Crawley *Chich* 64-68; V Coldwaltham 68-74; TV Ovingdean w Rottingdean and Woodingdean 74-83; V Saltdean 83-91; V Hellingly and Upper Dicker 91-02; rtd 02; Perm to Offic *Chich* from 03. *Cold Waltham, 29A New Road, Hellingly, Hailsham BN27 4EW* Tel (01323) 843346

CHAUDHARY, Jaisher Masih. b 56. Qu Coll Birm. **d** 08 **p** 09. NSM Handsworth St Mich *Birm* from 08. *29 George Street, Handsworth, Birmingham B21 0EG* Tel 0121-551 6279

CHAVE, Preb Brian Philip. b 51. Open Univ BA. Trin Coll Bris. **d** 84 **p** 85. C Cullompton *Ex* 84-87; TV Bishopsnympton, Rose Ash, Mariansleigh etc 87-93; Chapl for Agric *Heref* 93-96; Communications Adv and Bp's Staff Officer 97-01; Bp's Dom Chapl 97-01; TV W Heref from 01; Preb Heref Cathl from 97; Can 97-01; RD Heref City 04-07. *The Vicarage, Vowles Close, Hereford HR4 0DF* Tel (01432) 273086 E-mail chave@hfddiocesan.freeserve.co.uk

CHAVE-COX, Guy. b 56. St Andr Univ BSc79. Wycliffe Hall Ox 83. **d** 86 **p** 87. C Wigmore Abbey *Heref* 86-88; C Bideford *Ex* 88-91; TV Barnstaple from 91. *St Paul's Vicarage, Old Sticklepath Hill, Barnstaple EX31 2BG* Tel (01271) 344400 E-mail vicar@barnstaple-stpaul.org.uk

CHAVNER, Robert. b 59. ALCM82 AGSM85 FGMS00 FRSA05. Linc Th Coll 90. **d** 92 **p** 93. C Beckenham St Geo *Roch* 92-96; V Sevenoaks St Luke 96-06; P-in-c Brighton St Nic *Chich* from 06. *The Vicarage, 8 Prestonville Road, Brighton BN1 3TL* Tel (01273) 709045 E-mail robert.chavner@ntlworld.com

CHEADLE, Preb Robert. b 24. MBE71 TD66. Leeds Univ BA49. Coll of Resurr Mirfield 49. **d** 51 **p** 52. C Newbury St Jo *Ox* 51-55; C Tunstall Ch Ch *Lich* 55-57; TR Hanley H Ev 57-60; V Bloxwich 60-72; V Penkridge w Stretton 72-89; Preb Lich Cathl 79-89; P-in-c Dunston w Coppenhall 79-82; V 82-89; P-in-c Acton Trussell w Bednall 80-82; V 82-89; rtd 89; Perm to Offic *Lich* from 89. *26 Audley Place, Newcastle ST5 3RS* Tel (01782) 618685

CHEATLE, Adèle Patricia. b 46. York Univ BA73. Trin Coll Bris 76. **d** 87 **p** 98. Par Dn Harborne Heath *Birm* 87; NSM 92-93; Perm to Offic *Heref* 96-97; NSM Burghill 97-99; NSM Stretton Sugwas 97-99; NSM Heref St Pet w St Owen and St Jas 99-04; NSM Ches Square St Mich w St Phil *Lon* 04-07. *The Mews House, Mordiford, Hereford HR1 4LN* Tel (01432) 870888 E-mail adele@cheatle.fslife.co.uk

CHEDZEY, Derek Christopher. b 67. Trin Coll Bris BA93. **d** 93 **p** 94. C Bedgrove *Ox* 93-95; C Haddenham w Cuddington, Kingsey etc 95-98; TV High Wycombe 98-01; Deanery Tr Officer and C Washfield, Stoodleigh, Withleigh etc *Ex* 01-04; P-in-c Frenchay and Winterbourne Down *Bris* 04-06; Dioc Dir Lay Min 04-08; Adv for Initial Minl Educn from 08; Warden of Readers from 04. *The Rectory, Rectory Road, Frampton Cotterell, Bristol BS36 2BP* Tel 0117-906 0100 Mobile 07811-878774 E-mail derek.chedzey@bristoldiocese.org

CHEEK, Richard Alexander. b 35. Lon Univ LDS60 RCS 60. Ox NSM Course 72. **d** 75 **p** 76. NSM Maidenhead St Luke *Ox* 75-94; Asst Chapl Heatherwood and Wexham Park Hosp NHS

Trust from 94. *Windrush, 26 Sheephouse Road, Maidenhead SL6 8EX* Tel (01628) 628484 E-mail r.a.cheek@dialpipex.com

CHEESEMAN (née DUNHAM), Mrs Angela Mary. b 40. New Hall Cam MB, BChir66 MRCOG74 FRCSEd75 FRCOG96. **d** 05 **p** 06. OLM Eastling w Ospringe and Stalisfield w Otterden *Cant* from 05. *New House Farm, Otterden Road, Eastling, Faversham ME13 0BN* Tel (01795) 892124 E-mail angiecheeseman45@hotmail.com

CHEESEMAN, Colin Henry. b 47. Reading Univ BA69 Kent Univ PhD00. Sarum & Wells Th Coll 82. **d** 84 **p** 85. C Cranleigh *Guildf* 84-87; C Godalming 87-89; V Cuddington 89-96; Chapl HM Pris Wealstun 96-97; P-in-c Tockwith and Bilton w Bickerton *York* 97-01; RD New Ainsty 99-01; P-in-c Roundhay St Jo *Ripon* from 01. *The Vicarage, 2A Ryder Gardens, Leeds LS8 1JS* Tel 0113-266 9747 E-mail colin@stjohnsroundhay.co.uk

CHEESEMAN (née GOODAIR), Ms Janet. b 59. K Coll Lon BA81 Roehampton Inst PGCE82. NEOC 97. **d** 00 **p** 01. NSM Tockwith and Bilton w Bickerton *York* 00-01; NSM York St Olave w St Giles 00-01; Chapl Harrogate Ladies' Coll from 01. *Harrogate Ladies' College, Clarence Drive, Harrogate HG1 2QG* Tel (01423) 504543 Fax 568893 Mobile 07840-731137 E-mail revd.cheeseman@mail.hlc.org.uk

CHEESEMAN, John Anthony. b 50. Oriel Coll Ox BA73 MA75. Trin Coll Bris. **d** 76 **p** 77. C Sevenoaks St Nic *Roch* 76-79; C Egham *Guildf* 79-82; V Leyton Ch Ch *Chelmsf* 82-90; V Westgate St Jas *Cant* 90-01; V Eastbourne H Trin *Chich* from 01. *Holy Trinity Vicarage, 2 Hartington Place, Eastbourne BN21 3BE* Tel (01323) 729046 E-mail office@holytrinityeastbourne.co.uk

CHEESEMAN, Kenneth Raymond. b 29. Roch Th Coll 63. **d** 66 **p** 67. C Crayford *Roch* 66-69; C Beckenham St Jas 69-75; V Belvedere St Aug 75-83; V Thorley *Portsm* 83-94; R Yarmouth 83-94; rtd 94; Perm to Offic *Portsm* from 94. *10 St Catherine's View, Godshill, Ventnor PO38 3JJ* Tel (01983) 840700

CHEESEMAN, Nicholas James. b 72. Qu Mary and Westf Coll Lon BA94 Leeds Univ BA02. Coll of Resurr Mirfield 00. **d** 03 **p** 04. C Wantage *Ox* 03-07; V Reading All SS from 07. *All Saints' Vicarage, 14 Downshire Square, Reading RG1 6NH* Tel 0118-957 2000 Mobile 07732-252709

CHEESEMAN, Trevor Percival. b 38. Auckland Univ PhD64 Lon Univ BD67. K Coll Lon and St Boniface Warminster AKC67. **d** 68 **p** 69. C Warmsworth *Sheff* 68-71; New Zealand from 71. *49 Birdwood Avenue, Papatoetoe, Manukau 2025, New Zealand* Tel (0064) (9) 277 6145 E-mail tpandhmc@middleearth.net.nz

CHEESMAN, Canon Andrew Walford. b 36. St Mark's Coll Adelaide BA58. Cuddesdon Coll 59. **d** 61 **p** 62. C Man St Aid 61-63; P-in-c Keith Australia 64-68; Prec St Pet Cathl Adelaide 68-70; Chapl Flinders Univ 68-70; Asst Chapl St Pet Coll Adelaide 70-73; P-in-c Tea Tree Gully 73-76; R Mitcham Adelaide 76-01; Adn Torrens 85-93; Can Adelaide from 85. *1/4 Torrens Street, Mitcham SA 5062, Australia* Tel and fax (0061) (8) 8272 1864 E-mail mousal@bigbutton.com.au

CHEESMAN, Ashley Frederick Bruce. b 53. Oak Hill Th Coll. **d** 83 **p** 84. C Tranmere St Cath *Ches* 83-88; R Gaulby *Leic* 88-99; V from 99. *The Rectory, 1 Norton Lane, Gaulby, Leicester LE7 9BU* Tel 0116-259 6228

CHEESMAN, Peter. b 43. ACA65 FCA76 MCMI. Ridley Hall Cam 66. **d** 69 **p** 70. C Herne Bay Ch Ch *Cant* 69-74; TV Lowestoft St Marg *Nor* 75-78; TV Lowestoft and Kirkley 79-81; Ind Chapl *Glouc* 81-84; P-in-c Saul w Fretherne and Framilode 84-85; V Frampton on Severn, Arlingham, Saul etc 85-08; rtd 08. *Frampton Court, The Green, Frampton on Severn, Gloucester GL2 7EX* Tel (01452) 740533 E-mail peter@the-cheesman.net

CHEETHAM (née MUMFORD), Mrs Lesley Anne. b 51. Man Univ BA73. NOC 01. **d** 04 **p** 05. C Halifax *Wakef* 04-08; V Easby w Skeeby and Brompton on Swale etc *Ripon* from 08. *The Vicarage, St Paul's Drive, Brompton on Swale, Richmond DL10 7HQ* Tel (01748) 811748 Mobile 07963-620391 E-mail lesley.cheetham3@btinternet.com

✠**CHEETHAM, The Rt Revd Richard Ian.** b 55. CCC Ox BA77 CertEd78 MA82 Lon Univ PhD99. Ripon Coll Cuddesdon 85. **d** 87 **p** 88 **c** 02. C Newc H Cross 87-90; V Luton St Aug Limbury *St Alb* 90-99; RD Luton 95-98; Adn St Alb 99-02; Area Bp Kingston *S'wark* from 02. *Kingston Episcopal Area Office, 620 Kingston Road, London SW20 8DN* Tel (020) 8545 2440 *or* 8789 3218 Fax 8545 2441 E-mail bishop.richard@southwark.anglican.org

CHEEVERS, George Alexander. b 42. CITC 70. **d** 73 **p** 74. C Carrickfergus *Conn* 73-81; C Kilroot 78-81; I Kilmakee 82-91; I Magheragall 91-04; Can Belf Cathl 01-04; rtd 04. *1 Hampton Court, Dromore BT25 1SB* Tel (028) 9269 0701 E-mail bistokids@btinternet.com

CHEGE, James Gathioro. b 57. St Paul's Coll Limuru BD94. NTMTC. **d** 09. NSM Grays Thurrock *Chelmsf* from 09. *35 Oakley Close, Grays RM20 4AN* Tel (01375) 381513 Mobile 07983-607574 E-mail captjchege@aol.com

CHELMSFORD, Bishop of. *Vacant*

CHELMSFORD, Dean of. *See* JUDD, The Very Revd Peter Somerset Margesson

CHELTENHAM, Archdeacon of. *See* RINGROSE, The Ven Hedley Sidney

CHENERY, Mrs Janice Marienne. b 46. d 07 p 08. OLM Mid Loes *St E* from 07. *White House Cottage, Dallinghoo, Woodbridge IP13 0JP* Tel (01473) 737425

CHERRILL, John Oliver. b 33. Bath Univ MArch75. Sarum & Wells Th Coll 76. d 79 p 80. NSM Blackmoor *Portsm* 79-83; NSM Headley All SS *Guildf* 83-85; C 86-90; Perm to Offic *Portsm* from 95; rtd 98. *8 Londlandes, Church Crookham, Fleet GU52 6ZB* Tel (01252) 624508

CHERRIMAN, Colin Wilfred (Brother Colin Wilfred). b 37. Leeds Univ BA63. Coll of Resurr Mirfield 63. d 65 p 66. C Bournemouth St Fran *Win* 65-69; SSF from 69; Prov Min from 97; Lic to Offic *Chelmsf* 73-75; *Cant* 75-77; *Edin* 77-79; *Sarum* 79-82; *Newc* 82-88; Perm to Offic *Lon* 88-91; Adv HIV/AIDS Unit 91-92; HIV Support Worker St Botolph Aldgate *Lon* 92-96; New Zealand 96-02; rtd 02; Perm to Offic *Cant* from 03. *The Friary, 6A Stour Street, Canterbury CT1 2NR* Tel (01227) 479364

CHERRY, David. b 30. Roch Th Coll 59. d 61 p 62. C Seacroft *Ripon* 61-67; R Bamford *Derby* 67-75; Chapl Mlaga w Almunecar and Nerja *Eur* 83-91; rtd 91; NSM Waltham St Lawrence *Ox* 97-01; Perm to Offic *Leic* from 01. *2 Church Lane, Rearsby, Leicester LE7 4YE* Tel (01664) 424099

CHERRY, David Warwick. b 61. Cape Town Univ BMus86 Leeds Univ BA91. Coll of Resurr Mirfield 92. d 92 p 93. C Hammersmith SS Mich and Geo White City Estate CD *Lon* 92-01; C Hammersmith St Luke 94-01; Chapl Greenwich Univ 01-03; Chapl Univ of Westmr *Lon* from 03; Hon C St Marylebone St Cypr 06-08. *4A Luxborough Street, London W1U 5BF* Tel (020) 7911 5822 Mobile 07939-553547

CHERRY, Malcolm Stephen. b 28. Open Univ BA81. Sarum Th Coll 51. d 54 p 55. C Mill Hill Jo Keble Ch *Lon* 54-57; C Hendon All SS Childs Hill 57-59; Min Colchester St Anne CD *Chelmsf* 59-68; V Horndon on the Hill 68-79; Ind Chapl 69-79; Voc Officer Southend Adnry 74-79; R Lochgilphead *Arg* 79-82; V Mill End and Heronsgate w W Hyde *St Alb* 82-90; TV Chipping Barnet w Arkley 90-94; rtd 94; Perm to Offic *St E* from 94. *Nether Hankleys, Barrow Road, Higham, Bury St Edmunds IP28 6NN* Tel (01284) 810269

CHERRY, Canon Stephen Arthur. b 58. St Chad's Coll Dur BSc79 Fitzw Coll Cam BA85 MA90 K Coll Lon PhD95. Westcott Ho Cam 83. d 86 p 87. C Baguley and Asst Chapl Wythenshawe Hosp Man 86-89; Chapl K Coll Cam 89-94; R Loughborough All SS w H Trin *Leic* 94-06; RD Akeley E 96-99; Hon Can Leic Cathl 04-06; Dir Min and Tr *Dur* from 06; Can Res Dur Cathl from 06. *St Margaret's House, 30 South Street, Durham DH1 4QP* Tel 0191-384 3623 E-mail sacherry@btinternet.com

CHESHAM, William Gerald. b 23. MIMechE55. Wells Th Coll 61. d 63 p 64. C Ashford *Cant* 65-66; C Edgbaston St Bart *Birm* 66-68; V Smethwick 68-72; Lic to Offic *Heref* 72-78; TV Glendalc Gp *Newc* 78-84; rtd 84; Hon Asst Chapl Algarve *Eur* 84-97; Perm to Offic *Sarum* from 97. *Flat 10, Manormead, Tilford Road, Hindhead GU26 6RA*

CHESHER, Michael. b 52. Open Univ BA84. EAMTC. d 00 p 01. C Littleport *Ely* 00-03; V Chelmsf All SS 03-04; P-in-c Walpole St Peter w Walpole St Andrew *Ely* from 04; P-in-c W Walton from 04. *The Rectory, Church Road, Walpole St Peter, Wisbech PE14 7NS* Tel (01945) 780252 E-mail michael.chesher@tesco.net

CHESNEY, David Vince. b 69. UMIST BSc99. NTMTC BA08. d 08 p 09. C Springfield H Trin *Chelmsf* from 08. *49 Patching Hall Lane, Chelmsford CM1 4BU* Tel (01245) 352206 E-mail dave.chesney@btinternet.com

✠**CHESSUN, The Rt Revd Christopher Thomas James.** b 56. Univ Coll Ox BA78 MA82 Trin Hall Cam BA82. Westcott Ho Cam. d 83 p 84 c 05. C Sandhurst *Ox* 83-87; C Portsea St Mary *Portsm* 87-89; Min Can and Chapl St Paul's Cathl 89-93; Voc Adv 90-05; R Stepney St Dunstan and All SS 93-01; AD Tower Hamlets 97-01; Adn Northolt 01-05; Area Bp Woolwich *S'wark* from 05. *Trinity House, 4 Chapel Court, London SE1 1HW* Tel (020) 7939 9407 Fax 7939 9465 E-mail bishop.christopher@southwark.anglican.org

CHESTER, David Kenneth. b 50. Dur Univ BA73 Aber Univ PhD78 CGeol92 FGS88. NOC 93. d 96 p 97. NSM Hoylake *Ches* 96-04; NSM W Kirby St Bridget from 04. *Yenda, Grange Old Road, West Kirby, Wirral CH48 4ET* Tel 0151-625 8004 E-mail jg54@liv.ac.uk

CHESTER, Mark. b 55. Lanc Univ BA79. Wycliffe Hall Ox 86. d 88 p 89. C Plymouth St Andr w St Paul and St Geo *Ex* 88-94; V Burncy Lane *Birm* 94-99; V Camberley St Paul *Guildf* from 99; CF (TA) from 07. *The Vicarage, Sandy Lane, Camberley GU15 2AG* Tel (01276) 21100 *or* 700211 E-mail mark@stpaulscamb.co.uk

CHESTER, Maureen Olga. b 47. Univ of Wales (Swansea) BA70.

NEOC 94. d 97 p 98. NSM Morpeth *Newc* from 97. *10 Leland Place, Morpeth NE61 2AN* Tel (01670) 514569 E-mail mochester@classicfm.net

CHESTER, Philip Anthony Edwin. b 55. Birm Univ LLB76. Cranmer Hall Dur 77. d 80 p 81. C Shrewsbury St Chad *Lich* 80-85; C St Martin-in-the-Fields *Lon* 85-88; Chapl K Coll Lon 88-95; PV Westmr Abbey from 90; P-in-c Westmr St Matt *Lon* 95-03; V from 03; AD Westmr St Marg from 05. *St Matthew's House, 20 Great Peter Street, London SW1P 2BU* Tel (020) 7222 3704 Fax 7233 0255 E-mail office@stmw.org

CHESTER, Mrs Violet Grace. b 50. WEMTC 97. d 00 p 01. OLM Dymock w Donnington and Kempley *Glouc* 00; OLM Redmarley D'Abitot, Bromesberrow, Pauntley etc from 00. *1 Longbridge, Dymock GL18 2DA* Tel (01531) 890633 Fax 635919 E-mail vi@vichester.orangehome.co.uk

CHESTER, Archdeacon of. *See* ALLISTER, The Ven Donald Spargo

CHESTER, Bishop of. *See* FORSTER, The Rt Revd Peter Robert

CHESTER, Dean of. *See* McPHATE, The Very Revd Gordon Ferguson

CHESTERFIELD, Archdeacon of. *See* GARNETT, The Ven David Christopher

CHESTERMAN, Canon George Anthony (Tony). b 38. Man Univ BSc62 DipAdEd Nottm Univ PhD89. Coll of Resurr Mirfield 62. d 64 p 65. C Newbold w Dunston *Derby* 64-68; C Derby St Thos 68-70; Adult Educn Officer 70-79; R Mugginton and Kedleston 70-89; Vice-Prin EMMTC 79-86; Can Res Derby Cathl and Dioc Clergy In-Service Tr Adv *Derby* 89-03; rtd 03; Chapl to The Queen 98-08. *7 Hillside, Lesbury, Alnwick NE66 3NR* Tel (01665) 833124

✠**CHESTERS, The Rt Revd Alan David.** b 37. St Chad's Coll Dur BA59 St Cath Soc Ox BA61 MA65. St Steph Ho Ox 59. d 62 p 63 c 89. C Wandsworth St Anne *S'wark* 62-66; Hon C 66-68; Chapl Tiffin Sch Kingston 66-72; Hon C Ham St Rich *S'wark* 68-72; Dioc Dir of Educn *Dur* 72-85; R Brancepeth 72-85; Hon Can Dur Cathl 75-85; Adn Halifax *Wakef* 85-89; Bp Blackb 89-03; rtd 03; Hon Asst Bp Ches from 03; Hon Asst Bp Eur from 05. *64 Hallfields Road, Tarvin, Chester CH3 8ET* Tel (01829) 740825 E-mail alan@chesters1934.freeserve.co.uk

CHESTERS, David Nigel. b 45. d 04 p 05. NSM Wallasey St Hilary *Ches* 04-06; V Ches St Pet w St Jo from 06. *48 Elizabeth Crescent, Chester CH4 7AZ* Tel (01244) 676567 E-mail rectorofchester@btinternet.com

CHESTERS, Simon. b 66. Rob Coll Cam BA87 MA91. Wycliffe Hall Ox BA94. d 95 p 96. C Bidston *Ches* 95-99; P-in-c Runcorn St Jo Weston 99-03; Dioc Min Development Officer from 03; Hon C Lache cum Saltney from 03; Dir Reader Tr from 99. *46 Mount Pleasant, Chester CH4 8BW, or Church House, Lower Lane, Aldford, Chester CH3 6HP* Tel (01244) 679311 *or* 620444 E-mail simon.chesters@chester.anglican.org

CHESTERTON, Robert Eric. b 31. St Aid Birkenhead 63. d 65 p 66. C Kirby Muxloe *Leic* 65-67; Miss Cambridge Bay Canada 67-68; C St Annes St Thos *Blackb* 68-69; V Southminster *Chelmsf* 69-75; R Ashcroft and Savona Canada 75-78; V Wythenshawe Wm Temple Ch *Man* 78-82; TV Marfleet *York* 82-85; V Marshchapel *Linc* 85-88; R N Coates 85-88; V Grainthorpe w Conisholme 85-88; V Langtoft Gp 88-91; V Kingsbury *Birm* 91-94; rtd 94; Perm to Offic *Pet* 95-08; *Leic* 96-99 and from 03. *20 David Royce House, South Street, Oakham LE15 6IID* Tel (01572) 757262

CHESWORTH, Mrs Alison Louise. b 68. St Andr Univ MTheol97 Edin Univ MTh99. TISEC 98. d 00 p 01. C Ayr, Girvan and Maybole *Glas* 00-03; R Glas All SS from 03; P-in-c Glas H Cross from 03. *2 Skaterigg Drive, Glasgow G13 1SR* Tel 0141-959 3730 E-mail rector@allsaints-holycross.com

CHESWORTH, John Martin. b 44. Leeds Univ BSc67 PhD71 FRSC80. S Dios Minl Tr Scheme 90. d 92 p 93. Oman 92-95; Perm to Offic *Ab* 96-98 and *Ches* 98-03; C Egremont St Jo *Ches* 03-04; V Tranmere St Paul w St Luke from 04. *St Paul's Vicarage, 306 Old Chester Road, Birkenhead CH42 3XD* Tel 0151-645 3547 E-mail jchesworth44@tiscali.co.uk

CHEUNG, Anita Yen. b 40. d 98 p 99. OLM St Luke in the City *Liv* 98-06; rtd 06. *10 Pine Walks, Prenton, Birkenhead CH42 8LQ* Tel and fax 0151-609 1459

CHEVERTON, Miss Jill. b 48. Cranmer Hall Dur 93. d 93 p 94. Par Dn Bilton *Ripon* 93-94; C 94-96; V Burmantofts St Steph and St Agnes 96-03; Min Binley Woods LEP *Cov* from 03. *20 Daneswood Road, Binley Woods, Coventry CV3 2BJ* Tel (024) 7654 3003 E-mail revchev@email.com

CHEVILL, Elizabeth Jane. b 65. Colchester Inst of Educn BA86 K Coll Lon MMus87 PhD93 Warwick Univ BPhil00 AKC89 Lon Inst of Educn PGCE91. Wycliffe Hall Ox MSt04 MLitt08. d 08 p 09. C Blackheath St Jo *S'wark* from 08. *15A St John's Park, London SE3 7TD* Tel 07952-024571 (mobile) E-mail elizabethchevill@tiscali.co.uk

✠**CHEW, The Most Revd John Hiang Chea.** b 47. Nanyang Tech Univ Singapore BA69 MA77 Lon Univ BD77 Sheff Univ

PhD82. **d** 77 **p** 78 **c** 00. C St Andr Cathl Singapore 77-85; Hon Can 85-00; Lect Trin Th Coll Singapore 82-99; Dean of Studies 85-88; Prin 91-99; Bp Singapore from 00; Abp SE Asia from 06. *1 Francis Thomas Drive, #01-01 Singapore 359340, Republic of Singapore* Tel (0065) 6288 7585 Fax 6288 5574 E-mail bpoffice@anglican.org.sg

CHEW, Philip Vivian Frederick. b 62. St Martin's Coll Lanc BA96. Qu Coll Birm 96. **d** 98 **p** 99. C Chorley St Laur *Blackb* 98-02; V Burnley St Steph 02-08; P-in-c Blackb St Fran and St Aid from 08. *St Aidan's Vicarage, St Aidan's Avenue, Blackburn BB2 4EA* Tel (01254) 616570 E-mail revchew@fsmail.net

CHICHESTER, Caroline. STETS. **d** 09. NSM Winterborne Valley and Milton Abbas *Sarum* from 09. *Kingston Farmhouse, West Street, Winterborne Kingston, Blandford Forum DT11 9AX* E-mail cmchichester@tiscali.co.uk

CHICHESTER, Archdeacon of. See McKITTRICK, The Ven Douglas Henry

CHICHESTER, Bishop of. See HIND, The Rt Revd John William

CHICHESTER, Dean of. See FRAYLING, The Very Revd Nicholas Arthur

CHIDLAW, Richard Paul. b 49. St Cath Coll Cam BA71 MA. Ripon Hall Ox 72. **d** 74 **p** 81. C Ribbesford w Bewdley and Dowles *Worc* 74-76; NSM Coaley *Glouc* 81-83; NSM Frampton on Severn 81-83; NSM Arlingham 81-83; NSM Saul w Fretherne and Framilode 83-84; NSM Cam w Stinchcombe 85-90; Perm to Offic 90-91; NSM Berkeley w Wick, Breadstone and Newport 91-02; NSM Berkeley w Wick, Breadstone, Newport, Stone etc from 02. *38 May Lane, Dursley GL11 4HU* Tel (01453) 547838 E-mail richardandpauline@chidlaw.freeserve.co.uk

CHIDWICK, Alan Robert. b 49. MA MIL. Oak Hill NSM Course. **d** 84 **p** 85. NSM Pimlico St Pet w Westmr Ch Ch *Lon* 84-06; rtd 06; Perm to Offic *Nor* from 06. *The Croft House, The Croft, Costessey, Norwich NR8 5GY* Tel (01603) 745654 E-mail thecrofthouse@btinternet.com

CHIGUMIRA, Godfrey. St Mich Coll Llan. **d** 08. C Hawarden *St As* from 08. *3 Ffordd Tegid, Ewloe, Deeside CH5 3UJ*

CHIKE, Chigor. b 66. Glos Univ BA93. St Jo Coll Nottm 05. **d** 06 **p** 07. C Victoria Docks St Luke *Chelmsf* from 06. *26 Boreham Avenue, London E16 3AG* Tel (020) 7476 2077 Mobile 07905-155494 E-mail chigor@chike.fsbusiness.co.uk

CHILCOTT, Mark David. b 62. Ch Coll Cam BA83 MA87 PhD88. Ripon Coll Cuddesdon BA92. **d** 93 **p** 94. C Warrington St Elphin *Liv* 93-99; P-in-c Westbrook St Jas 99-01; V 01-02. *Estates Branch, Sedgley Park Centre, Sedgley Park Road, Prestwich, Manchester M25 0JT* Tel 0161-856 0505 Fax 856 0506

CHILD, Corin James. b 73. Man Univ BA95. Trin Coll Bris BA02 MA03. **d** 03 **p** 04. C Sanderstead *S'wark* 03-07; V King's Lynn St Jo the Ev *Nor* from 07; Chapl Coll of W Anglia from 07. *St John's Vicarage, Blackfriars Road, King's Lynn PE30 1NT* Tel (01553) 773034 E-mail corin@childfamily.wanadoo.co.uk

CHILD, David Francis. b 44. Birm Univ MB, ChB67 FRCP88. St As Minl Tr Course 02. **d** 04 **p** 05. NSM Gresford *St As* from 04. *Whitegate Farm, Gyfelia, Wrexham LL13 0YH* Tel (01978) 823396 E-mail d_f_child@yahoo.co.uk

CHILD, Margaret Mary. See MASLEN, Mrs Margaret Mary

CHILDS, Christopher. b 59. **d** 05 **p** 06. NSM Gt Finborough w Onehouse, Harleston, Buxhall etc *St E* from 05. *3 Chapel Close, Buxhall, Stowmarket IP14 3RY* Tel (01449) 736093

CHILDS, David Robert. b 64. Univ Coll Lon BSc86 Regent's Park Coll Ox MA95. Ripon Coll Cuddesdon 99. **d** 99 **p** 00. C Bloxham w Milcombe and S Newington *Ox* 99-02; TV Witney 02-06; TR 06-08; P-in-c Hadleigh St Jas *Chelmsf* from 08. *The Rectory, 50 Rectory Road, Hadleigh, Benfleet SS7 2ND* Tel (01702) 389532 E-mail dekm@sky.com

CHILDS, Emma Jane. See WESTERMANN-CHILDS, Miss Emma Jane

CHILDS, Ernest Edmund. b 23. Lich Th Coll 63. **d** 65 **p** 66. C Billesley Common *Birm* 65-68; C Elland *Wakef* 68-69; Clerical Org Sec CECS *Pet, Leic* and *Ely* 69-72; V Staverton w Helidon and Catesby *Pet* 72-76; rtd 77; Perm to Offic *Nor* 77-91; Hon C W Lynn *Ely* 92-94; P-in-c 94-95; Perm to Offic *Ely* from 95; *Nor* from 96. *4 Fieldview Court, Fakenham NR21 8PB* Tel (01328) 856595

CHILLINGTON, Barbara Ann. b 42. RGN84. WEMTC. **d** 00 **p** 01. NSM Madley w Tyberton, Peterchurch, Vowchurch etc *Heref* from 00. *Cephas House, 2 Princes Orchard, Peterchurch, Hereford HR2 0RW* Tel and fax (01981) 550979 Mobile 07891-248723 E-mail barbarathrv@aol.com

✠**CHILLINGWORTH, The Rt Revd David Robert.** b 51. TCD BA73 Oriel Coll Ox BA75 MA81. Ripon Coll Cuddesdon 75. **d** 76 **p** 77 **c** 05. C Belfast H Trin *Conn* 76-79; Ch of Ireland Youth Officer 79-83; C Bangor Abbey *D & D* 83-86; I Seagoe 86-05; Dean Dromore 95-02; Adn Dromore 02-05; Bp St And from 05; Primus from 09. *Perth Diocesan Centre, 28A Balhousie Street,*

Perth PH1 5HJ Tel (01738) 443173 *or* 564432 Fax 443174 Mobile 07921-168666 E-mail bishop@standrews.anglican.org

CHILLMAN, David James. b 59. Southn Univ BA82. Trin Coll Bris 93. **d** 95 **p** 96. C Yateley *Win* 95-99; V Halifax All So and St Aug *Wakef* 99-07; V Bagshot *Guildf* from 07. *The Vicarage, 43 Church Road, Bagshot GU19 5EQ* Tel (01276) 473348 E-mail david.chillman@virgin.net

CHILTON, Janice. **d** 08. NSM Wallingford *Ox* from 08. *2 Fairthorne Memorial, West End, Brightwell-cum-Sotwell, Wallingford OX10 0RY* Tel (01491) 836661 E-mail jchilton894@btinternet.com

CHIN, Michael Shoon Chion. b 41. Lon Univ BD71 Melbourne Univ BA76 DipEd79. Trin Th Coll Singapore BTh64 Melbourne Coll of Div. **d** 64 **p** 65. Malaysia 64-68; Australia 69-80, 87-91 and from 97; Miss to Seamen 72-81 and 83-89; USA 81-82; Gen Sec Internat Chr Maritime Assn 91-96. *711 Bouverie Street, Charlton Vic 3053, Australia* Tel and fax (0061) (3) 9347 0005 Mobile 40-859 7966 E-mail mschin22@goldenit.net.au

CHINERY, Simon Andrew. b 61. St Cath Coll Cam BA83 MA87. ERMC 06. **d** 08. C Plymouth St Pet and H Apostles *Ex* from 08. *261 North Road West, Plymouth PL1 5DH* Tel (01752) 223946 Mobile 07971-523008 E-mail fr.simon@chinerys.co.uk

CHING, Derek. b 37. St Cath Coll Cam BA58 MA Cam Inst of Educn CertEd59. Qu Coll Birm 81. **d** 83 **p** 84. C Finham *Cov* 83-87; V Butlers Marston and the Pillertons w Ettington 87-96; rtd 96; Perm to Offic *Ripon* from 96. *25 Kirkby Road, Ripon HG4 2EY* Tel (01765) 609419

CHIPLIN, Christopher Gerald. b 53. Lon Univ BSc75. St Steph Ho Ox BA77 MA81. **d** 78 **p** 79. C Chesterfield St Mary and All SS *Derby* 78-80; C Thorpe St Andr *Nor* 80-84; V Highbridge *B & W* 84-94; V Midsomer Norton w Clandown from 94. *The Vicarage, 42 Priory Close, Midsomer Norton, Radstock BA3 2HZ* Tel (01761) 412118 E-mail cchi759070@aol.com

CHIPLIN, Gareth Huw. b 50. Worc Coll Ox BA71 MA. Edin Th Coll 71. **d** 73 **p** 74. C Friern Barnet St Jas *Lon* 73-75; C Eastcote St Lawr 76-79; C Notting Hill St Mich and Ch 79-84; V Hammersmith St Matt from 84. *St Matthew's Vicarage, 1 Fielding Road, London W14 0LL* Tel (020) 7603 9769

CHIPLIN, Howard Alan. b 43. Sarum & Wells Th Coll 84. **d** 86 **p** 87. C Caerleon *Mon* 86-89; V Ferndale w Maerdy *Llan* 89-91; V Ysbyty Cynfyn w Llantrisant and Eglwys Newydd *St D* 91-95; R Narberth w Mounton w Robeston Wathen and Crinow 95-02; V Grwp Bro Ystwyth a Mynach 02-08; rtd 08. *Minffordd, 15 Hafren Terrace, Llanidloes SY18 6AT*

CHIPLIN, Malcolm Leonard. b 42. St Mich Coll Llan 86. **d** 88 **p** 89. C Newton Nottage *Llan* 88-91; V Pwllgwaun w Llanddewi Rhondda 91-03; V Mountain Ash and Miskin 03-08; rtd 08. *3 Maes y Ffynon Grove, Aberaman, Aberdare CF44 6PH* Tel (01685) 874720 E-mail malcolmchiplin@aol.com

CHIPPENDALE, Peter David. b 34. Dur Univ BA55. Linc Th Coll 57. **d** 59 **p** 60. C Claines St Jo *Worc* 59-63; V Defford w Besford 63-73; P-in-c Eckington 66-69; V 69-73; V Kidderminster St Geo 73-76; V The Lickey *Birm* 76-96; rtd 96. *1 Fairways, Pershore WR10 1HA* Tel (01386) 553478

CHIPPENDALE, Robert William. b 42. Ox Univ BA79 Dip Teaching84. St Fran Coll Brisbane 64. **d** 67 **p** 68. C Maryborough Australia 67-69; C Hollinwood 70-72; V Shaw *Man* 72-78; R Beaudesert Australia 79-84; Chapl St Hilda's Sch Southport 85-03; rtd 03. *31 Gladioli Court, PO Box 1124, Caboolture Qld 4510, Australia* Tel (0061) (7) 5495 4514

CHISHOLM, Canon Ian Keith. b 36. AKC62. **d** 63 **p** 64. C Lich St Chad 63-66; C Sedgley All SS 66-69; V Rough Hills 69-77; V Harrow Weald All SS *Lon* 77-88; V W Moors *Sarum* 88-01; Can and Preb Sarum Cathl 00-01; rtd 01; Perm to Offic *Sarum* from 02. *33 Meadoway, Shrewton, Salisbury SP3 4HE* Tel (01980) 620579

CHISHOLM, Ian Stuart. b 37. ALCD63. **d** 63 **p** 64. C Worksop St Jo *S'well* 63-66; Succ Sheff Cathl 66-68; Bp's Chapl for Soc Resp 68-72; C Ox St Andr 72-76; Tutor Wycliffe Hall Ox 72-76; V Conisbrough *Sheff* 76-94; Chapl Conisbrough Hosp 76-94; RD W Doncaster 82-87 and 93-94; V Chilwell *S'well* 94-99; rtd 99; Perm to Offic *Sheff* from 94; *Linc* from 00; *S'well* from 03. *72 Broadbank, Louth LN11 0EW* Tel (01605) 605970 E-mail ichisholm@waitrose.com

CHISHOLM, Canon Reginald Joseph. b 13. TCD BA40 MA51. TCD Div Sch 42. **d** 42 **p** 43. C Belfast St Donard *D & D* 42-45; C Bangor St Comgall 45-48; I Ardglass w Dunsford 48-51; I Newtownards 51-82; Min Can Belf Cathl 52-62; Treas Down Cathl 80-82; rtd 82. *20 Glendun Park, Bangor BT20 4UX* Tel (028) 9145 0100

CHISHOLM, Samuel James. b 20. Edin Th Coll 74 St Jo Coll Nottm 86. **d** 86 **p** 87. NSM Eastriggs *Glas* 87-92; NSM Gretna 90-91; rtd 92; Perm to Offic *Chich* from 95. *36 Peterhouse, Church Street, Bexhill-on-Sea TN40 2HF* Tel (01424) 219294

CHISLETT, David Norman Hilton. b 61. Kingston Poly BSc83 UEA PGCE84. Ridley Hall Cam 00. **d** 02 **p** 03. C Highley w Billingsley, Glazeley etc *Heref* 02-05; TV Eston w Normanby *York* 05-09; C Bridlington Quay Ch Ch from 09; C Bessingby from 09. *Bessingby Vicarage, West Hill, Bridlington YO16 4RU* Tel (01262) 400253 E-mail dave.chislett@btinternet.com

CHITHAM, Ernest John. b 57. LSE BSc79 Leeds Univ PGCE80 Dur Univ MA84. NEOC 88. **d** 91 **p** 92. C Swanborough *Sarum* 91-94; CMS Lebanon 95-98; TV Worthing Ch the King *Chich* 99-08; V Worthing St Matt from 08. *85 Heene Road, Worthing BN11 4PP* Tel (01903) 218026 E-mail john.chitham@tesco.net

CHITTENDEN, John Bertram d'Encer. b 24. ASCA. Lon Coll of Div 56. **d** 58 **p** 59. C St Mary-at-Lambeth *S'wark* 58-64; R Acrise *Cant* 64-82; R Hawkinge 64-82; R Hawkinge w Acrise and Swingfield 82-90; rtd 91; Perm to Offic *Cant* from 91. *19 Hasborough Road, Folkestone CT19 6BQ* Tel (01303) 241773

CHITTY, Lynne. b 64. **d** 06. NSM Glouc Cathl 06-08. *5 Millers Green, Gloucester GL1 2BN* Tel (01452) 414616 E-mail lynnechitty@gloucestercathedral.org.uk

CHITTY, Philip Crofts. b 27. Roch Th Coll 61. **d** 63 **p** 64. C Holbrooks *Cov* 63-68; V Long Itchington 68-77; R Ufton 69-77; P-in-c Cov St Marg 77-84; rtd 84. *17 Rotherham Road, Coventry CV6 4FF* Tel (024) 7668 5398

✠**CHIU, The Rt Revd Joshua Ban It.** b 18. K Coll Lon LLB41 AKC41 Barrister-at-Law (Inner Temple) 41. Westcott Ho Cam 43. **d** 45 **p** 46 c 66. C Bournville *Birm* 45-47; Malaya 47-50; Singapore 50-59 and 66-82; Hon Can St Andr Cathl Singapore 56-59; Australia 59-62; Service Laymen Abroad WCC Geneva 62-65; Fell St Aug Coll Cant 65-66; Bp Singapore and Malaya 66-70; Bp Singapore 70-82; Member Cen Cttee WCC 68-75; Member ACC 75-79; rtd 82; Perm to Offic *Sarum* 82-00 and *Chelmsf* from 02. *40 Beverley Crescent, Woodford Green IG8 9DD* Tel (020) 8924 6490

CHIUMBU, Esther Tamisa. See PRIOR, Esther Tamisa

CHIVERS, Canon Christopher Mark. b 67. Magd Coll Ox BA88 MA92 Selw Coll Cam BA96 MA00. Westcott Ho Cam 94. **d** 97 **p** 98. C Friern Barnet St Jas *Lon* 97-99; Can Prec St Geo Cathl Cape Town 99-01; Min Can and Prec Westmr Abbey 01-05; Can Res and Chan Blackb Cathl from 05. *1 St Francis Road, Blackburn BB2 2TZ* Tel (01254) 200720 or 51491 Mobile 07706-632508 E-mail chris.chivers@blackburn.anglican.org

CHIVERS, Ernest Alfred John. b 34. Bris & Glouc Tr Course. **d** 83 **p** 84. NSM Bedminster *Bris* 83-87; NSM Whitchurch 87-98; NSM Knowle St Martin 98-00; Sen Asst P Chard and Distr *B & W* 00-04; P-in-c 04-05; rtd 05; Perm to Offic *B & W* from 05. *40 Calcott Road, Bristol BS4 2HD* Tel 0117-977 7867

CHIVERS, Royston George. b 34. Glouc Th Course. **d** 83 **p** 84. NSM Gorsley w Cliffords Mesne *Glouc* 83-85; NSM Newent and Gorsley w Cliffords Mesne from 85. *Mayfield, Gorsley, Ross-on-Wye HR9 7SJ* Tel (01989) 720492

CHIVERTON, Dennis Lionel Dunbar. b 26. St D Coll Lamp BA51. **d** 53 **p** 54. C Cardiff St Mary *Llan* 53-54; C Dowlais 54-57; C Bargoed w Brithdir 57-61; P-in-c Cymmer and Abercregan 61-67; R Llanfabon 67-91; rtd 91; Perm to Offic *Llan* from 91. *3 Park Terrace, Trelewis, Treharris CF46 6BT* Tel (01443) 411237

CHO, Paul Hang-Sik. b 61. Kent Univ MA96 PhD04. Chr Th Sem & Div Sch of Korea BTh93. **d** 00 **p** 01. C Munster Square Ch Ch and St Mary Magd *Lon* 00-07; Chapl Angl Korean Community 00-07; Consultant for Institutional Advancement Ox Cen for Miss Studies from 08. *PO Box 70, Oxford OX2 6HB* Tel (01865) 517733 E-mail frpaulcho@hotmail.com

CHORLTON, John Samuel Woodard. b 45. Newc Univ BSc67. Wycliffe Hall Ox 89. **d** 89 **p** 91. Jerusalem 79-92; C Ox St Aldate w St Matt 92-94; C Ox St Aldate 95-04; Voc Adv from 98; AD Ox 99-04; TV W Slough 04-08; V Britwell from 08. *St George's House, Long Furlong Drive, Slough SL2 2LX* Tel (01753) 554684 Mobile 07709-873831 E-mail jsw@chorlton.org

CHOUFAR, Joseph Oriho Abulemoi. b 57. Nile Th Coll Khartoum BA95 ICI Univ Amman BA98. **d** 87 **p** 88. Sudan 87-96; All SS Cathl Khartoum 87-88 and 91-96; Torit Congregation Lologo Displaced Camp 88-90; NSM Ealing St Pet Mt Park *Lon* from 00. *11 Bromyard House, Bromyard Avenue, London W3 7BE* Tel (020) 8762 0714 E-mail abulemoi@hotmail.com

CHOW, Ting Suie Roy. b 46. Brasted Th Coll 68 Sarum & Wells Th Coll 70. **d** 72 **p** 73. C Weaste *Man* 72-74; C Swinton St Pet 74-78; R Blackley St Paul 78-85; Sec SPCK (Dio Man) from 80; R Burnage St Nic *Man* 85-95; P-in-c Man Gd Shep 95-97; P-in-c Openshaw 95-97; R Manchester Gd Shep and St Barn from 97. *All Soul's Rectory, Every Street, Ancoats, Manchester M4 7DQ* Tel 0161-273 6582

CHOW, Wai Meng. b 65. Bris Univ BSc89 ACA93. Trin Coll Bris BA97 MA02. **d** 02 **p** 03. NSM Westminster St Jas the Less *Lon* from 02. *29 Carillon Court, Oxford Road, London W5 3SX* Tel (020) 8810 1651 or 7630 6282 Mobile 07968-776557 E-mail waimeng.chow@sjtl.org

CHOWN, William Richard Bartlett. b 27. AKC54. **d** 55 **p** 56. C Egremont *Carl* 55-58; C Upminster *Chelmsf* 58-61; R Romford St Andr 61-78; R Newton Longville w Stoke Hammond, Whaddon etc *Ox* 78-83; P-in-c Kidmore End 83-85; V 85-90; rtd 90; NSM Harpsden *Ox* 93-94; Perm to Offic 94-03; Hon C

Shiplake w Dunsden and Harpsden 03-05. *3 Coniston Court, Weybridge KT13 9YR* Tel (01932) 821936

CHRICH, Andrew James. b 70. Girton Coll Cam BA92 MA96. Cranmer Hall Dur BA96. **d** 96 **p** 97. C Gerrards Cross and Fulmer *Ox* 96-99; Chapl Trin Coll Cam 99-04; R Linton in Craven *Bradf* 04-09; P-in-c Burnsall w Rylstone 04-09; V Trumpington *Ely* from 09. *28 Wingate Way, Trumpington, Cambridge CB2 9HD* E-mail andy@chrich.plus.com

CHRICH-SMITH, Joanne Elizabeth. b 71. Qu Coll Cam BA93 MA97. Cranmer Hall Dur BA96 Ripon Coll Cuddesdon 96. **d** 97 **p** 98. C Amersham on the Hill *Ox* 97-99; Perm to Offic *Ely* 99-04; Chapl Girton Coll Cam 00-02; Perm to Offic *Bradf* 04-09. *28 Wingate Way, Trumpington, Cambridge CB2 9HD*

CHRISMAN, John Aubrey. b 33. US Naval Academy BS58. Westcott Ho Cam 86. **d** 88 **p** 89. NSM Orwell *Ely* 88-89; NSM Wimpole 88-89; NSM Arrington 88-89; NSM Croydon w Clopton 88-89; Asst Chapl Oslo St Edm *Eur* 89-91; R Newport St Geo USA 91-01; rtd 01. *7118 Treymore Court, Sarasota FL 34243, USA* Tel (001) (941) 351 3177 E-mail fatherjack@comcast.net

CHRIST THE KING, Bishop of. See LEE, The Rt Revd Peter John

CHRISTCHURCH, Bishop of. See COLES, The Rt Revd David John

CHRISTENSEN, Mrs Carole Glenda. b 45. Qu Coll Birm 07. **d** 09. NSM Blackheath *Birm* from 09. *73 John Street, Rowley Regis B65 0EN* Tel 0121-561 5761 E-mail christensen_250@hotmail.com

CHRISTENSEN, Canon Norman Peter. b 37. St D Coll Lamp BA63. Ridley Hall Cam 63. **d** 65 **p** 66. C Barnston *Ches* 65-70; V Over St Jo 70-77; R Bromborough 77-92; RD Wirral S 86-92; Hon Can Ches Cathl 90-02; Chapl Arrowe Park Hosp Wirral 92-96; V Higher Bebington *Ches* 96-02; rtd 02; Perm to Offic *Ches* from 02. *13 Howbeck Close, Prenton CH43 6TH* Tel 0151-652 9869 E-mail canonpc@aol.com

CHRISTIAN, Mrs Alison Jean. b 51. S Dios Minl Tr Scheme 88. **d** 91 **p** 94. Par Dn Uxbridge *Lon* 91-94; C 94-95; Chapl Uxbridge Coll 91-95; V Sudbury St Andr *Lon* 95-02; R Gt Stanmore from 02. *St John's Rectory, Rectory Lane, Stanmore HA7 4AQ* Tel (020) 8954 0276 E-mail alison.christian1@btopenworld.com

CHRISTIAN, Anthony Clive Hammond. b 46. Kent Univ BA74 Sussex Univ MA95 DPhil99 FRSA01. K Coll Lon 74 St Aug Coll Cant 74. **d** 76 **p** 77. C Faversham *Cant* 76-79; C St Laur in Thanet 79-81; P-in-c 81-84; R Gt Mongeham w Ripple and Sutton by Dover 84-88; V Pevensey *Chich* 88-94; P-in-c 94-01; V from 01. *Marsh Hall, Church Lane, Pevensey BN24 5LD* Tel and fax (01323) 762247 Mobile 07711-170350

CHRISTIAN, Brother. See PEARSON, Christian David John

CHRISTIAN, Mark Robert. b 58. Linc Th Coll 95. **d** 95 **p** 96. C Stockport SW *Ches* 95-98; CF 98-08; Sen CF from 08. *c/o MOD Chaplains (Army)* Tel (01980) 615802 Fax 615800 E-mail mark@padre.me.uk

CHRISTIAN, Paul. b 49. Cam Sch of Min 84. **d** 87 **p** 88. C Folkestone St Sav *Cant* 87-91; R Temple Ewell w Lydden from 91. *The Rectory, Green Lane, Temple Ewell, Dover CT16 3AS* Tel (01304) 822865

CHRISTIAN, Richard. b 37. Nottm Univ DipEd74 Ox Univ MA81. AKC62. **d** 63 **p** 65. C Camberwell St Mich w All So w Em *S'wark* 63-66; C Woolwich St Mary w H Trin 66-70; Chapl and Lect Bp Lonsdale Coll Derby 70-74; P-in-c Hurley *Ox* 76-79; Chapl Lancing Coll 79-81; Chapl Harrow Sch 82-89; Chapl R W Sussex Hosp Chich 89-91; P-in-c Pulley *Lon* 91-95; Chapl Hillingdon Hosp NHS Trust from 91. *St John's Rectory, Rectory Lane, Stanmore HA7 4AQ* Tel (020) 8954 0276 or (01895) 279433 E-mail richard.christian@thh.nhs.uk

CHRISTIAN-EDWARDS, Canon Michael Thomas. b 36. Down Coll Cam BA60 MA64. Clifton Th Coll 60. **d** 62 **p** 63. C Ex St Leon w H Trin 62-67; V Trowbridge St Thos *Sarum* 67-75; R Wingfield w Rowley 67-75; P-in-c Fisherton Anger 75-81; R 81-92; Ind Chapl 85-92; RD Salisbury 85-90; Can and Preb Sarum Cathl 87-92; V Crofton *Portsm* 92-00; rtd 00; Perm to Offic *Win* from 02. *Rivendell, Westbeams Road, Sway, Lymington SO41 6AE* Tel (01590) 682353 E-mail mmce@cerivendell.freeserve.co.uk

CHRISTIAN-IWUAGWU, Canon Amatu Onundu. b 73. Port Harcourt Univ Nigeria BEng93. **d** 00 **p** 01. NSM Stonebridge St Mich *Lon* 00-03; NSM Welwyn *St Alb* 04-05; NSM Stonebridge St Mich 05-07; V Harmondsworth from 07; Can Ideato from 03. *St Mary's Vicarage, High Street, Harmondsworth, West Drayton UB7 0AQ* Tel (020) 8897 2385 Mobile 07961-593880 E-mail iwuagwuoa@yahoo.co.uk

CHRISTIANSON, Canon Rodney John (Bill). b 47. St Paul's Coll Grahamstown. **d** 72 **p** 73. C St Sav Cathl Pietermaritzburg S Africa 72-76; Miss to Seafarers 76-09; Min Sec 93-00; Sec Gen 00-09; Hon C Milton next Gravesend Ch Ch *Roch* 78-82; R Richard's Bay S Africa 82-91; Chapl Hull Miss to Seamen 91-93; Lic to Offic *Lon* 94-97; V St Mich Paternoster Royal 00-09; rtd 09; Perm to Offic *Lon* from 09; Hon Can Bloemfontein Cathl from 93. *45 Wimbledon Park Court, Wimbledon Park Road, London SW19 6NN* E-mail bill.christianson@mtsmail.org

CHRISTIE, Alexander Robert. b 58. Qu Coll Cam BA79 LLM80. Oak Hill Th Coll 92. **d** 94 **p** 95. C W Norwood St Luke *S'wark* 94-98; C Wandsworth All SS 98-03; V Blackheath Park St Mich from 03. *St Michael's Vicarage, 2 Pond Road, London SE3 9JL* Tel (020) 8852 5287 E-mail ar.christie@virgin.net

CHRISTIE, David James. b 58. York Univ BA80 MA83 PGCE81 Leeds Univ MPhil88. Cranmer Hall Dur 89. **d** 91 **p** 92. C Drypool *York* 91-95; V Patrick Brompton and Hunton *Ripon* 95-09; V Hornby 95-09; V Crakehall 95-09. *Address temp unknown* E-mail dc@christiepb.fsnet.co.uk

CHRISTIE, Canon Thomas Richard. b 31. CCC Cam BA53 MA57. Linc Th Coll 55. **d** 57 **p** 58. C Portsea N End St Mark *Portsm* 57-60; C Cherry Hinton St Andr *Ely* 60-62; C P-in-c Cherry Hinton St Jas CD 62-66; V Wisbech St Aug 66-73; V Whitstable All SS *Cant* 73-75; V Whitstable All SS w St Pet 75-80; Can Res and Treas Pet Cathl 80-01; Perm to Offic *Ely* from 80; RD Pet 87-96; Chapl to Rtd Clergy from 00; rtd 01; P-in-c Thornhaugh and Wansford *Pet* from 01. *16 College Park, Peterborough PE1 4AW* Tel (01733) 344228 E-mail thomas.christie@tinyworld.co.uk

CHRISTOPHER, Miss Barbara. b 58. Univ of Wales (Swansea) BA80. **d** 09. OLM Saddleworth Man from 09. *2 St Mary's Crest, Greenfield, Oldham OL3 7DS* Tel (01457) 876802 E-mail barbara.christopher@tiscali.co.uk

CHRISTOPHER, Richard. b 53. NTMTC 94. **d** 97 **p** 98. C Southall Green St Jo *Lon* 97-04; C Reading St Luke w St Bart *Ox* from 04. *107 Anderson Avenue, Earley, Reading RG6 1HA* Tel 0118-987 1495 E-mail rev.r.christopher@yahoo.com

CHRISTOU, Sotirios. b 51. St Jo Coll Nottm 84. **d** 88 **p** 92. C Berechurch St Marg w St Mich *Chelmsf* 88-89; C Goodmayes All SS 89-90; NSM Harston w Hauxton *Ely* 92-94; Lic to Offic 94-95; C Burgess Hill St Andr *Chich* 95-98; Perm to Offic *Ely* from 98. *18 Bullen Close, Cambridge CB1 8YU* Tel (01223) 246349 E-mail sotirioschristou@live.co.uk

CHUBB, John Nicholas. b 33. St Cath Soc Ox BA55 MA58. Qu Coll Birm 57. **d** 59 **p** 60. C Kirby Moorside w Gillamoor *York* 59-62; C Scarborough St Mary 62-64; V Potterspury w Furtho and Yardley Gobion *Pet* 64-69; V Brixworth 69-74; P-in-c Holcot 73-74; V Brixworth w Holcot 74-81; V Hampton Hill *Lon* 81-88; Chapl Pet Distr Hosp 88-97; Chapl Edith Cavell Hosp 88-97; rtd 97. *12 Alness Drive, York YO24 2XZ*

CHUBB, Richard Henry. b 45. Univ of Wales (Cardiff) BMus67 Bris Univ PGCE76. Linc Th Coll 67. **d** 70 **p** 71. C Chippenham St Andr w Tytherton Lucas *Bris* 71-72; C-in-c Stockwood CD 72-73; C Bris Ch the Servant Stockwood 73-76; Perm to Offic 76-79; Min Can and Succ Bris Cathl 79-88; Chapl w Deaf People 83-02; Chapl Qu Eliz Hosp Sch Bris 87-92; rtd 02. *17 Southmead Road, Westbury-on-Trym, Bristol BS10 5DL* Tel and fax 0117-962 9508 E-mail richard.chubb@lineonet.net

CHUDLEY, Cyril Raymond. b 29. Lon Univ BA53 DipEd. Wells Th Coll 70. **d** 72 **p** 73. C Newark St Mary *S'well* 72-75; C Egg Buckland *Ex* 75-77; P-in-c Plymouth St Aug 77-80; V 80-83; V Milton Abbot, Dunterton, Lamerton etc 83-91; TV Wickford and Runwell *Chelmsf* 91-95; rtd 95; Perm to Offic *Truro* from 95. *Ten Acres, Coxpark, Gunnislake PL18 9BB* Tel (01822) 832345

CHUMU MUTUKU, Norbert. b 68. Urbanian Univ Rome BA89 St Jo Fisher Coll USA MSc00. St Mathias Mulumba Sem Kenya 89. **d** 93 **p** 94. Ngong Kenya 93-98; Rochester USA 98-02; C Milton *Portsm* 03-06; C Pitsea w Nevendon *Chelmsf* from 06. *34 St Michael's Avenue, Basildon SS13 3DE* E-mail nchumu@yahoo.com

CHURCH, Mrs Annette Marie. b 56. **d** 09. C Caldicot *Mon* from 09. *Belle Grove, Manor Court, Rogiet, Caldicot NP26 3TU* Tel (01291) 431392 Mobile 07789-778312 E-mail anniechurch@hotmail.com

CHURCH, Linda Ann. b 51. MCSP73. EMMTC 88. **d** 91 **p** 94. NSM Kirkby in Ashfield St Thos *S'well* 91-95; NSM Skegby and Teversal 95-98; P-in-c Annesley w Newstead 98-03; TR Hucknall Torkard 03-09; Hon Can S'well Minster 07-09; R Fowlmere, Foxton, Shepreth and Thriplow *Ely* from 09. *The Rectory, High Street, Fowlmere, Royston SG8 7SU*

CHURCH, William John. b 41. Qu Coll Cam MA62 Solicitor. SAOMC 99. **d** 99 **p** 00. NSM Bengeo *St Alb* 99-01; NSM St Amwell w St Margaret's and Stanstead Abbots 01-05; NSM Hertford from 05. *115 Queen's Road, Hertford SG13 8BJ* Tel (01992) 410469 Fax 583079 E-mail bill.church@hertscc.gov.uk *or* churchwj@hotmail.com

CHURCHER, Ms Mandy. b 54. RN75 RM77 Surrey Univ PGCE87 Brunel Univ MEd92. NTMTC 96. **d** 99 **p** 00. C Wolverhampton St Matt *Lich* 99-02; Assoc Chapl Plymouth Hosps NHS Trust 02-06; Chapl S Devon Healthcare NHS Foundn Trust from 06. *Torbay Hospital Chaplaincy Service, Hengrave House, Lawes Bridge, Torbay TQ2 7AA* Tel (01803) 654186 E-mail mandy.churcher@nhs.net

CHURCHMAN, David Ernest Donald. b 21. Univ of Wales MTh01. Clifton Th Coll 45. **d** 48 **p** 49. C Preston All SS *Blackb* 48-49; C Braintree *Chelmsf* 50-52; V Harold Wood 52-59; V

Southsea St Jude *Portsm* 59-74; V Enfield Ch Ch Trent Park *Lon* 74-86; RD Enfield 75-82; rtd 86; Perm to Offic *Portsm* from 87. *23 Dilkusha Court, 124 Sea Front, Hayling Island PO11 9HW* E-mail don.churchman@btinternet.com

CHYNCHEN, John Howard. b 38. FRICS72. Sarum & Wells Th Coll 88. **d** 89 **p** 90. Bp's Dom Chapl *Sarum* from 89; Hon Chapl Hong Kong Cathl 90-07; Chapl from 07. *St John's Cathedral, 4-8 Garden Road, Hong Kong* Tel (00852) 2523 4157 Fax 2855 0420 E-mail chynchen@stjohnscathedral.org.hk

CIANCHI, Dalbert Peter. b 28. Lon Univ BSc57. Westcott Ho Cam 69. **d** 70 **p** 71. C Harpenden St Nic *St Alb* 70-74; TV Woughton *Ox* 74-80; P-in-c Wavendon w Walton 74-80; P-in-c Lavendon w Cold Brayfield 80-84; R Lavendon w Cold Brayfield, Clifton Reynes etc 84-94; rtd 94. *20 Fisken Crescent, Kambah ACT 2902, Australia* Tel (0061) (2) 6231 8556 E-mail pcianchi@cyberone.com.au

CIECHANOWICZ, Edward Leigh Bundock. *See* BUNDOCK, Edward Leigh

CINNAMOND, Andrew Victor. b 71. St Andr Univ MA94. Wycliffe Hall Ox BA00. **d** 01 **p** 02. C Clapham H Trin and St Pet *S'wark* 01-05; C Wandsworth All SS from 05. *74 Haldon Road, London SW18 1QG* Tel (020) 8870 2475 *or* 8788 4606 E-mail andrew_cinnamond@hotmail.com

CLABON, Ronald Oliver Edwin. b 30. **d** 97. NSM Pontnewydd *Mon* 97-03. *72 Anthony Drive, Caerleon, Newport NP18 3DX* Tel (01633) 420790

CLACEY, Derek Phillip. b 48. St Jo Coll Nottm 76. **d** 79 **p** 80. C Gt Parndon *Chelmsf* 79-82; C Walton H Trin *Ox* 82-88; P-in-c Bramshaw and Landford w Plaitford *Sarum* 88-04; P-in-c Redlynch and Morgan's Vale 03-04; TV E Greenwich *S'wark* from 04. *The Vicarage, 52 Earlswood Street, London SE10 9ES* Tel (020) 8853 5950 E-mail derekclacey@aol.com

CLACK (née JERWOOD), Mrs Eleanor Alice Jerwood. b 80. Bath Univ BSc03. St Jo Coll Nottm 05. **d** 08 **p** 09. C New Milverton *Cov* from 08. *37 Bridge Street, Warwick CV34 5PD* E-mail ellieclack@hotmail.co.uk

CLACK, Robert John Edmund. b 63. Lanc Univ BA85. Coll of Resurr Mirfield 89. **d** 92 **p** 93. C Bury St Pet *Man* 92-95; Chapl Bury Colls of FE 93-95; TV New Bury 95-97; R Ashton-upon-Mersey St Martin *Ches* from 97. *St Martin's Rectory, 367 Glebelands Road, Sale M33 5GG* Tel 0161-973 4204 E-mail rjec@fsmail.net

CLACKER, Martin Alexander. b 56. Trin Coll Bris 93. **d** 95 **p** 96. C Yate New Town *Bris* 95-98; V Southmead 98-00; C Portishead *B & W* 00-02; TV 02-03; Perm to Offic *Bris* 06-08; P-in-c Winterbourne from 08; C Frenchay and Winterbourne Down from 08; C Frampton Cotterell and Iron Acton from 08. *Orchard House, 70 High Street, Winterbourne, Bristol BS36 1JQ* E-mail martinclacker@hotmail.com

CLAMMER, Thomas Edward. b 80. Sussex Univ BA01 CCC Cam BA04. Westcott Ho Cam 02. **d** 05 **p** 06. C Wotton St Mary *Glouc* 05-08; P-in-c Deerhurst and Apperley w Forthampton etc from 08. *The Vicarage, 1 The Green, Apperley, Gloucester GL19 4DQ* Tel (01452) 780880 E-mail tomclammer@gmail.com

CLANCY, Michael. b 24. Kensington Univ (USA) BA82. Glas NSM Course 76. **d** 79 **p** 80. Hon C Glas St Silas 79-96; Perm to Offic from 96. *33 Highfield Drive, Clarkston, Glasgow G76 7SW* Tel 0141-638 4469

CLAPHAM, Christopher Charles. b 69. Man Univ BA91 St Jo Coll Dur BA96. Cranmer Hall Dur 94 Univ Tüb Sem (NY) STM98. **d** 99 **p** 00. NSM Withington St Chris *Man* 99-01; C Didsbury Ch Ch 01-03; P-in-c Swinton H Rood 03-08; Chapl Keele Univ from 08. *Berachah House, 51 Quarry Bank, Keele, Newcastle ST5 5AG* Tel (01782) 583393 E-mail charlesclapham@lineone.net

CLAPHAM, George Henry James. b 52. Trin Coll Bris. **d** 08 **p** 09. C Wellington and Distr *B & W* from 08. *15 Shuteleigh, Wellington TA21 8PG* Tel (01823) 660014 E-mail jamesclapham@talktalk.net

CLAPHAM, John. b 47. Open Univ BA76. Sarum & Wells Th Coll 77. **d** 80 **p** 81. Dep PV Ex Cathl from 80; C Lympstone 85-87; P-in-c 87-99; P-in-c Woodbury 97-99; RD Aylesbeare 96-01; R Lympstone and Woodbury w Exton 99-09; rtd 09. *The Rectory, Lympstone, Exmouth EX8 5HP* Tel (01395) 273343 E-mail johnclaphamuk@btinternet.com

CLAPHAM, Kenneth. b 47. Trin Coll Bris 76. **d** 78 **p** 79. C Pemberton St Mark Newtown *Liv* 78-81; C Darfield *Sheff* 81-83; P-in-c Over Kellet *Blackb* 83-88; V from 88. *The Vicarage, 3 Kirklands Road, Over Kellet, Carnforth LA6 1DJ* Tel and fax (01524) 734189 E-mail ukvicar@aol.com

CLAPHAM, Stephen James. b 61. Portsm Poly BSc84 Ches Coll of HE BTh04. NOC 01. **d** 04 **p** 05. C Nantwich *Ches* 04-06; V Crewe All SS and St Paul w St Pet from 07. *All Saints' Vicarage, 79 Stewart Street, Crewe CW2 8LX* Tel (01270) 560310 E-mail steve.clapham@dsl.pipex.com

CLAPPERTON, Mrs Carolin Beryl. b 43. Westcott Ho Cam 04. **d** 05 **p** 06. NSM Faversham *Cant* 05-08; NSM The Brents and Davington w Oare and Luddenham from 08. *5 Provender Walk,*

Belvedere Road, Faversham ME13 7NF Tel (01795) 538334 Mobile 07946-420745
E-mail carolinclapperton226@btinternet.com

CLAPSON, Clive Henry. b 55. Leeds Univ BA76. Trin Coll Toronto MDiv79. **d** 79 **p** 80. C Belleville St Thos Canada 79-80; R Loughborough 80-83; V Alpine Ch the K USA 83-88; C Hawley H Trin *Guildf* 88-90; R Invergordon St Ninian *Mor* 90-00; Prin Moray Ord and Lay Tr Course 90-94; Can St Andr Cathl Inverness 97-00; R Aberdeen St Mary 00-05; P-in-c Dundee St Salvador *Bre* from 05. *9 Minard Crescent, Dundee DD3 6LH* Tel (01382) 221785
E-mail father.clive@blueyonder.co.uk

CLAPTON, Timothy. b 59. Westmr Coll Ox MTh92. Westcott Ho Cam 96. **d** 98 **p** 99. C Wimborne Minster *Sarum* 98-02; Ecum Chapl Milton Keynes Gen NHS Trust 02-05; Milton Keynes Miss Partnership Development Chapl *Ox* from 05. *59 St Mary Street, New Bradwell, Milton Keynes MK13 0BD* Tel (01908) 314209 Mobile 07958-182077

CLARE, Christopher. b 52. Sheff Univ BSc73 Nottm Univ PGCE74. Ox Min Course 89. **d** 92 **p** 93. NSM Chesham Bois *Ox* from 92. *5 Lime Tree Walk, Amersham HP7 9HY* Tel (01494) 766513

CLARE, Ms Johanna Howard. b 64. Bris Univ BSc86 Heythrop Coll Lon MA98. Ridley Hall Cam 97. **d** 99 **p** 00. C Coulsdon St Jo *S'wark* 99-02; TV Morden 02-09; Dioc Continuing Professional Development Officer from 09. *5 Willows Avenue, Morden SM4 5SG* Tel and fax (020) 8646 2002 *or* tel 7939 9472
E-mail jcbrightwell@yahoo.com

CLARE, Lionel Philip. b 19. St Aid Birkenhead 46. **d** 49 **p** 50. C Far Headingley St Chad *Ripon* 49-52; C Low Harrogate St Mary 52-54; R Addingham *Bradf* 54-66; V Sunnyside w Bourne End *St Alb* 66-74; V Kirkbymoorside w Gillamoor, Farndale etc *York* 74-84; rtd 84; Perm to Offic *Bradf* from 84. *4 Abbeyfield Grove House, 12 Riddings Road, Ilkley LS29 9BF* Tel (01943) 886000

CLARE, Sister. *See* LOCKHART, Clare Patricia Anne

CLARIDGE, Antony Arthur John. b 37. Hull Univ MA LRAM. Bris & Glouc Tr Course. **d** 84 **p** 85. NSM Keynsham *B & W* 84-97; Bp's Officer for NSMs from 90; Min Bath Ch Ch Prop Chpl from 97. *62 Cranwells Park, Bath BA1 2YE* Tel (01225) 427462 E-mail antony.claridge@btinternet.com

CLARIDGE, Michael John. b 61. MCIEH. Qu Coll Birm 89 Bossey Ecum Inst Geneva 91. **d** 92 **p** 93. C Harlescott *Lich* 92-95; P-in-c Wellington Ch 95-97; V 97-03; V W Bromwich St Andr w Ch Ch from 03. *St Andrew's Vicarage, Oakwood Street, West Bromwich B70 9SN* Tel 0121-553 1871
E-mail mjclaridge@tiscali.co.uk

CLARINGBULL, Canon Denis Leslie. b 33. K Coll Lon BD57 AKC57 Univ of Cen England in Birm DUniv98 MCIPD85 FCIPD01. **d** 58 **p** 59. C Croydon St Aug *Cant* 58-62; Ind Chapl to Bp Croydon 62-71; Ind Chapl *Cov* 71-75; Chapl Cov Cathl 71-75; Succ 72-75; V Norbury St Phil *Cant* 75-80; Sen Ind Chapl *Birm* 80-98; P-in-c Birm St Paul 85-88; V 88-98; Hon Can Birm Cathl 87-98; rtd 98; Perm to Offic *Birm* and *Heref* from 98. *17 Merrivale Crescent, Ross-on-Wye HR9 5JU* Tel (01989) 567771 E-mail gms58@dial.pipex.com

CLARINGBULL, (née DAVID), Canon Faith Caroline. b 55. St Aid Coll Dur BA77. Ripon Coll Cuddesdon 87. **d** 89 **p** 94. Par Dn Is of Dogs Ch Ch and St Jo w St Luke *Lon* 89-93; Asst Chapl R Lon Hosps NHS Trust 93-98; NSM Wheatley *Ox* 98-00; Asst Dioc Dir of Ords *Worc* 00-04; Dioc CME Officer 02-04; Dioc Dir of Ords *Birm* from 04; Dean of Women's Min from 04; Hon Can Birm Cathl from 05. *175 Harborne Park Road, Birmingham B17 0BH* Tel 0121-426 0445
E-mail faith@birmingham.anglican.org

CLARINGBULL, Keith. b 49. Ripon Coll Cuddesdon 98. **d** 00 **p** 01. SSF 69-89; C Droitwich Spa *Worc* 00-04; P-in-c Hampton in Arden *Birm* from 04; P-in-c Bickenhill from 04. *The Vicarage, 1 High Street, Hampton-in-Arden, Solihull B92 0AE* Tel (01675) 442604 E-mail claring.bull@virgin.net

CLARK, Andrew. b 76. Anglia Poly Univ BA97. Oak Hill Th Coll BA08. **d** 08. C Heref St Pet w St Owen and St Jas from 08. *10 St Barnabas Close, Hereford HR1 1EY* Tel (01432) 266588
E-mail lurpak@aol.com

CLARK, Andrew James. b 50. ACIB72 ACIS76. EMMTC 91. **d** 94 **p** 95. NSM Allestree *Derby* 94-97; NSM Allenton and Shelton Lock 97-03; NSM Walbrook Epiphany 03-05. *Address temp unknown*

CLARK, Antony. b 61. York Univ BA83. Wycliffe Hall Ox 84. **d** 88 **p** 89. C Ashton-upon-Mersey St Mary Magd *Ches* 88-92; Chapl Lee Abbey 92-95; Lic to Offic *Ex* 95-95; Chapl Univ of Westmr *Lon* 95-98; C Bletchley *Ox* 98-00. *Address temp unknown*

CLARK, Arthur. b 30. MIBiol FRSC Sheff Univ BSc MCB. St D Dioc Tr Course. **d** 88 **p** 89. NSM Haverfordwest St Mary and St Thos w Haroldston *St D* 88-91; C 91-92; V Llawhaden w Bletherston and Llancefn 92-96; rtd 96. *84 Portfield, Haverfordwest SA61 1BT* Tel (01437) 762644

CLARK, Bernard Charles. b 34. Open Univ BA81. S'wark Ord Course 65. **d** 68 **p** 69. C Pemberton St Jo *Liv* 68-71; C Winwick 71-73; P-in-c Warrington St Barn 74-76; V 76-78; V Hindley All

SS 78-83; Perm to Offic 86-94; R Glazebury w Hollinfare 94-99; rtd 99; Perm to Offic *Man* from 00. *31 Linkfield Drive, Worsley, Manchester M28 1JU* Tel 0161-799 7998
E-mail bckathcain31@aol.com

CLARK, Brian John. b 48. Portsm Poly CQSW89 Portsm Univ MA94. STETS 97. **d** 00 **p** 01. NSM Titchfield *Portsm* 00-01; NSM Helston and Wendron *Truro* 01-02; Perm to Offic *Portsm* 02-06. *Address temp unknown*

CLARK, Cecil. b 44. Sarum Th Coll. **d** 98 **p** 99. OLM Canford Magna *Sarum* from 98. *Fermain Cottage, 133 Magna Road, Bearwood, Bournemouth BH11 9NE* Tel (01202) 577898 *or* 663275 E-mail firmain@ntlworld.com

CLARK, Mrs Christine Margaret. b 44. SAOMC 01. **d** 01 **p** 02. NSM Croxley Green St Oswald *St Alb* 01-06; P-in-c Odell from 06. *The Rectory, 3 Church Lane, Odell, Bedford MK43 7AA* Tel (01234) 720234 Mobile 07812-524992

CLARK, Daniel Alastair. b 74. St Jo Coll Dur BA96. Wycliffe Hall Ox BA99. **d** 00 **p** 01. C Rusholme H Trin *Man* 00-06; NSM 04-06; C Clifton Ch Ch w Em *Bris* from 06. *62 Clifton Park Road, Bristol BS8 3HN* Tel 0117-973 2128
E-mail dan@christchurchclifton.org.uk

CLARK, David. b 30. Nottm Univ BSc51. St Aid Birkenhead 55. **d** 57 **p** 58. C Tyldesley w Shakerley *Man* 57-60; V Ashton St Jas 60-64; rtd 93; Perm to Offic *Eur* from 07. *18 rue Neuve, 22160 Callac de Bretagne, France* Tel (0033) (2) 96 45 91 24
E-mail d2aclark@wanadoo.fr

CLARK, Canon David George Neville. b 25. Linc Coll Ox BA49 MA59. Wells Th Coll 49. **d** 51 **p** 52. C Sanderstead All SS *S'wark* 51-54; C Lewisham St Jo Southend 54-59; V Sutton New Town St Barn 59-72; R Charlwood 72-90; P-in-c Sidlow Bridge 76-77; R 77-90; P-in-c Buckland 85-87; P-in-c Leigh 87-90; Hon Can S'wark Cathl 88-90; rtd 90; Perm to Offic *Cov* from 90. *12 Marlborough Road, Coventry CV2 4EP* Tel (024) 7644 2400

CLARK, David Gordon. b 29. Clare Coll Cam BA52 MA57. Ridley Hall Cam 52. **d** 54 **p** 55. C Walthamstow St Jo *Chelmsf* 54-57; V 60-69; C Gt Ilford St Andr 57-60; R Stansted *Roch* 69-82; R Stansted w Fairseat and Vigo 82-94; rtd 94; Perm to Offic *Sarum* 94-06. *4 St Marys Close, Platt, Sevenoaks TN15 8NH* Tel (01732) 883191

CLARK, David Humphrey. b 39. G&C Coll Cam BA60. Wells Th Coll 62. **d** 64 **p** 65. C Leigh St Mary *Man* 64-68; Min Can and Prec Man Cathl 68-70; Ind Chapl *Nor* 70-85; P-in-c Nor St Clem and St Geo 70-76; P-in-c Nor St Sav w St Paul 70-76; V Norwich-over-the-Water Colegate St Geo 76-79; Hon Asst P Nor St Pet Mancroft 79-85; TR Oadby *Leic* 85-98; C Leic St Jas 98-04; rtd 04; Perm to Offic *Leic* from 04. *46 St James Road, Leicester LE2 1HQ* Tel 0116-255 8988
E-mail dhclark@leicester.anglican.org

CLARK, David John. b 40. Surrey Univ MPhil75 CEng MIStructE. Ridley Hall Cam 81. **d** 83 **p** 84. C Combe Down w Monkton Combe and S Stoke *B & W* 83-89; Voc Adv Bath Adnry 89-96; R Freshford, Limpley Stoke and Hinton Charterhouse 89-05; rtd 05; Perm to Offic *B & W* from 05. *14 Barn Close, Frome BA11 4ER* Tel (01373) 461073
E-mail david@freshford313.freeserve.co.uk

CLARK, Dennis Henry Graham. b 26. St Steph Ho Ox 52. **d** 55 **p** 56. C Southall St Geo *Lon* 55-58; C Barbourne *Worc* 58-61; Chapl RAF 61-78; Asst Chapl-in-Chief RAF 78-82; Chapl St Clem Danes (RAF Ch) 79-82; V Godmanchester *Ely* 82-91; rtd 91; Perm to Offic *Ely* from 91. *8 Arran Way, St Ives PE27 3DT* Tel (01480) 301951

CLARK, Diane Catherine. *See* FITZGERALD CLARK, Mrs Diane Catherine

CLARK, Edward Robert. b 39. Ex Coll Ox BA61 MA65. St Steph Ho Ox 61. **d** 63 **p** 64. C Solihull *Birm* 63-67; Perm to Offic *Bris* 67-69; *Leic* 69-71; *Ox* 71-80; *St Alb* 80-84; *Cant* from 84; rtd 96. *3 Hunters Bank, Old Road, Elham, Canterbury CT4 6SS* Tel (01303) 840134 E-mail edward.clark@virgin.net

CLARK, Ellen Jane. *See* CLARK-KING, Ellen Jane

CLARK, Frederick Albert George. b 15. MBE68. ACP66. **d** 67 **p** 68. Hon C Stroud *Glouc* 67-84; Hon C Stroud and Uplands w Slad 84-85; Perm to Offic 85-97. *2 Terrace Cottages, Thrupp, Stroud GL5 2BN* Tel (01453) 882060

CLARK, Harold Clive. b 28. Witwatersrand Univ LTh53. St Paul's Coll Grahamstown. **d** 54 **p** 55. C Orange Grove S Africa 54-56; R Mayfair 56-60; P-in-c Morden *S'wark* 60-62; R Verulam S Africa 62-68; Chapl Michaelhouse 68-77; V Green Island New Zealand 77-85; V Kaitaia 85-92; Chapl Kristin Sch Albany from 92. *351 East Coast Road, Mairangi Bay, North Shore City 0630, New Zealand* Tel (0064) (9) 479 3434
E-mail hr.clark@clear.net.nz

CLARK, Ian Duncan Lindsay. b 35. K Coll Cam BA59 MA63 PhD66. Ripon Hall Ox 62. **d** 64 **p** 65. C Willington *Newc* 64-66; India 66-76; Lect Bp's Coll Calcutta 66; Vice-Prin 69-74; Chapl St Cath Coll Cam 76; Fell 77-85; Tutor 78-85; Dean of Chpl and Lect 80-85; Select Preacher Cam Univ 82; Hon Asst P Kelso *Edin* 85-06. *4 Yewtree Lane, Yetholm, Kelso TD5 8RZ* Tel (01573) 420323

CLARK, Jacqueline Mary. b 58. **d** 08 **p** 09. OLM Canalside Benefice *Sarum* from 08. *3 Stonelea, Trowbridge Road, Hilperton, Trowbridge BA14 7QQ* Tel (01225) 769940 Mobile 07948-089865 E-mail revjclark@hotmail.co.uk

CLARK, Miss Janet Elizabeth. b 44. Derby Coll of Educn CertEd65 Open Univ BA75. Oak Hill Th Coll BA92. **d** 92 **p** 94. Par Dn Edmonton All SS w St Mich *Lon* 92-94; C 94-96; V Ealing St Steph Castle Hill 96-08; rtd 08; Perm to Offic *Ox* from 09. *55 Cranwells Lane, Farnham Common, Slough SL2 3GW* Tel (01753) 646546 E-mail jan@fortaguada.freeserve.co.uk

CLARK, Mrs Jean Robinson. b 32. K Coll Lon AKC BD79. dss 85 **d** 87 **p** 94. Cov E 85-88; C 87-88; NSM Upper Mole Valley Gp *S'wark* 89-90; Hon Par Dn Charlwood 89-90; Lic to Offic *Cov* 90-92; rtd 92; Perm to Offic *Cov* from 92. *12 Marlborough Road, Coventry CV2 4EP* Tel (024) 7644 2400

CLARK, Jeremy James. b 66. Cant Univ (NZ) BA88. St Jo Coll Auckland BTh97. **d** 94 **p** 95. C Shirley St Steph New Zealand 94-97; C Upton (Overchurch) *Ches* 97-01; P-in-c Ilfracombe SS Phil and Jas w W Down *Ex* 01-08; C Alphington, Shillingford St George and Ide from 08. *c/o Crockford, Church House, Great Smith Street, London SW1P 3AZ* E-mail pipjimcalix@aol.com *or* jemkiwi@aol.com

CLARK, John David Stanley. b 36. Dur Univ BA64. Ridley Hall Cam 64. **d** 66 **p** 67. C Benchill *Man* 66-69; C Beverley Minster *York* 69-74; Perm to Offic *S'well* 74-76; Lic to Offic 76-77; Miss to Seamen 77-80; Perm to Offic *York* 80-83; V Egton w Grosmont 83-89; R Thornton Dale w Ellerburne and Wilton 89-01; R Thornton Dale w Allerston, Ebberston etc 01-05; rtd 05; Perm to Offic *York* from 05. *22 Swainsea Lane, Pickering YO18 8AP* Tel (01751) 476118

CLARK, John Edward Goodband. b 49. Leeds Univ MA01. Chich Th Coll 70. **d** 73 **p** 74. C Thorpe St Andr *Nor* 73-76; C Earlham St Anne 76-78; Chapl RN 78-82; P-in-c Tittleshall w Godwick, Wellingham and Weasenham *Nor* 82-85; P-in-c Helhoughton w Raynham 82-85; R S Raynham, E w W Raynham, Helhoughton, etc 85-90; R Taverham w Ringland 90-96; V Eggleston and R Middleton-in-Teesdale w Forest and Frith *Dur* 96-03; AD Barnard Castle 00-03; R Caston, Griston, Merton, Thompson etc *Nor* 03-05; Perm to Offic from 07. *98 Norwich Road, Dereham NR20 3AR* Tel (01362) 698948

CLARK, John Michael. b 35. EMMTC 87. **d** 90 **p** 91. Chapl to the Deaf *Linc* 86-00; NSM Bracebridge Heath 90-00; rtd 00; Perm to Offic *Linc* from 00. *3 Hawthorn Road, Cherry Willingham, Lincoln LN3 4JU* Tel (01522) 751759

CLARK, John Patrick Hedley. b 37. St Cath Coll Cam BA61 MA65 Worc Coll Ox BA63 MA72 BD74 Lambeth Hon DD89. St Steph Ho Ox 61. **d** 64 **p** 65. C Highters Heath *Birm* 64-67; C Eglingham *Newc* 67-72; P-in-c Newc St Anne 72-77; V Longframlington w Brinkburn 77-95; V Chevington 95-02; rtd 02; Perm to Offic *Dur* from 02. *6 The Cottage, West Row, Greatham, Hartlepool TS25 2HW* Tel (01429) 870203

CLARK, Canon John Ronald Lyons. b 42. TCD BA69 MA72. Div Hostel Dub 67. **d** 70 **p** 71. C Dundela St Mark *D & D* 70-72; CF 72-75; C Belfast St Aid *Conn* 75-76; I Stranorlar w Meenglas and Kilteevogue *D & R* 76-81; Chapl Wythenshawe Hosp Man 81-95; I Kilgariffe Union *C, C & R* 95-96; Chapl Blackb, Hyndburn and Ribble Valley NHS Trust 96-03; Chapl Co-ord E Lancs Hosps NHS Trust 03-09; Chapl E Lancs Hospice 96-05; Hon Can Blackb Cathl 06-09; rtd 09. *Inishfree, Lefka Ori View, Xerosterni, 73008 Vamos, Chania, Crete, Greece* Tel (0030) (282) 502 2914 Mobile 6970-862858 E-mail rcronnieclark@googlemail.com

CLARK, Jonathan Dunnett. b 61. Ex Univ BA83 Bris Univ MLitt90 Southn Univ MA96. Trin Coll Bris 84. **d** 88 **p** 89. C Stanwix *Carl* 88-92; Chapl Bris Univ 92-93; Dir of Studies S Dios Minl Tr Scheme 94-97; Chapl Univ of N Lon 97-02; Chapl Lon Metrop Univ 02-03; AD Islington 99-03; R Stoke Newington St Mary from 03; P-in-c Brownswood Park from 04. *St Mary's Rectory, Stoke Newington Church Street, London N16 9ES* Tel (020) 7254 6072 Fax 7923 4135 Mobile 07968-845698 E-mail rectorofstokey@btinternet.com

CLARK, Jonathan Jackson. b 57. Linc Coll Ox 79 Down Coll Cam 83. Ridley Hall Cam 81. **d** 84 **p** 85. C W Derby St Luke *Liv* 84-87; C Gt Clacton *Chelmsf* 87-93; V Hammersmith St Simon *Lon* 93-03; AD Hammersmith and Fulham 96-01; TR Leeds St Geo *Ripon* from 03. *St George's Vicarage, 208 Kirkstall Lane, Leeds LS5 2AB* Tel 0113-274 4367 E-mail jonathan.clark@stgeorgesleeds.org.uk

CLARK, The Ven Kenneth James. b 22. DSC44. St Cath Soc Ox BA48 MA52. Cuddesdon Coll 52. **d** 52 **p** 53. C Brinkworth *Bris* 52-53; C Cricklade w Latton 53-56; C-in-c Filwood Park CD 56-59; V Bris H Cross Inns Court 59-61; V Westbury-on-Trym H Trin 61-72; V Bris St Mary Redcliffe w Temple etc 72-82; P-in-c Bedminster St Mich 73-78; RD Bedminster 73-79; Hon Can Bris Cathl 74-92; Adn Swindon 82-92; rtd 92; Perm to Offic *Sarum* 92-04. *25 Emmanuel Court, Guthrie Road, Bristol BS8 3EP* Tel 0117-923 9083

CLARK, Kenneth William. b 69. R Holloway Coll Lon BA92 Trin Coll Cam BA99 MA04. Westcott Ho Cam 97. **d** 00 **p** 01. C

Bromley St Mark *Roch* 00-04; R Stone from 04. *The Rectory, Church Road, Greenhithe DA9 9BE* Tel (01322) 382076 E-mail kenneth.clark@diocese-rochester.org

CLARK, Lance Edgar Dennis. b 52. MBE93. Linc Th Coll 74. **d** 77 **p** 78. C Arnold *S'well* 77-82; V Brinsley w Underwood 82-87; Chapl RAF 87-02; Chapl Cardiff and Vale NHS Trust from 02. *Chaplaincy Department, University Hospital of Wales, Heath Park, Cardiff CF14 4XW* Tel (029) 2074 3230

CLARK, Lynn. *See* PURVIS, Lynn

CLARK, Canon Martin Hudson. b 46. K Coll Lon BD68 AKC68 MTh91 Birm Univ PGCE89. **d** 71 **p** 72. C S'wark H Trin 71-74; C Parkstone St Pet w Branksea and St Osmund *Sarum* 74-77; V E Wickham *S'wark* 77-86; V Wandsworth St Anne 86-98; RD Wandsworth 90-95; V Angell Town St Jo 98-07; RD Brixton 01-05; Hon Can S'wark Cathl 05-07; rtd 07; Perm to Offic *Cant* 07-08; Hon C Deal St Leon w St Rich and Sholden etc from 08. *27 Century Walk, Deal CT14 6AL* Tel (01304) 366586 E-mail eveandmartin@hotmail.com

CLARK, Michael Arthur. b 46. S Dios Minl Tr Scheme. **d** 83 **p** 84. NSM Monkton Farleigh, S Wraxall and Winsley *Sarum* 83-05; Perm to Offic *Chich* from 05. *5 Park West, Southdowns Park, Haywards Heath RH16 4SG* Tel (01444) 440831 E-mail mike_clark55@hotmail.com

CLARK, Michael David. b 45. Ox Univ MA68. Trin Coll Bris. **d** 72 **p** 73. C Cheadle *Ches* 72-76; Brazil 77-86; Bolivia 86-88; C Wilton *B & W* 89-90; TV 90-99; C Tollington *Lon* 99-01; TR Edgware from 01. *The Rectory, Rectory Lane, Edgware HA8 7LG* Tel (020) 8952 1081 *or* tel and fax 8952 4066 E-mail mikeclark@wayfarer99.freeserve.co.uk

CLARK, Michael James. b 71. Univ of Wales (Cardiff) BSc92. Trin Coll Bris BA02. **d** 02 **p** 03. C Tiverton St Geo and St Paul *Ex* 02-07; TV Newton Tracey, Horwood, Alverdiscott etc from 07. *The Rectory, High Bickington, Umberleigh EX37 9AY* Tel (01769) 560870 E-mail revmikeclark@yahoo.co.uk

CLARK, Pamela Ann. b 45. Garnett Coll Lon CertEd72 Ch Ch Coll Cant PGCE93. SEITE 00 St Jo Coll Nottm 03. **d** 04 **p** 05. NSM Orlestone w Snave and Ruckinge w Warehorne etc *Cant* 04-06; NSM Hythe 06-09; Asst Chapl St Mich Hospice 06-07; Perm to Offic *Cant* from 09. *20 Wakefield Way, Hythe CT21 6HT* Tel (01303) 267564

CLARK, Miss Patricia Mary. b 36. Liv Univ BSc. **d** 88 **p** 94. Par Dn Leasowe *Ches* 88-92; Bp's Officer for Women in Min 89-97; Par Dn Davenham 92-94; C 94-97; rtd 97; Perm to Offic *Ches* from 97. *18 Farmstead Way, Great Sutton, Ellesmere Port CH66 2RU* Tel 0151-339 1450

CLARK, Canon Peter. b 39. Ch Coll Cam BA61 MA65. Chich Th Coll 61. **d** 63 **p** 64. C Huddersfield SS Pet and Paul *Wakef* 63-67; C Notting Hill St Jo *Lon* 67-74; Grenada 75-79; C Hove All SS *Chich* 79; P-in-c Hove St Patr 79-82; V Hove St Patr w Ch Ch and St Andr 82-83; V Battersea Ch Ch and St Steph *S'wark* 83-08; RD Battersea 90-01; Hon Can S'wark Cathl 96-08; rtd 08; Perm to Offic *S'wark* from 08. *46 Havil Street, London SE5 7RS* Tel 020-7708 8915 Mobile 07773-164134 E-mail peterclark263@btinternet.com

CLARK, Peter. b 45. Sarum & Wells Th Coll 87. **d** 89 **p** 90. C Portsea St Cuth *Portsm* 89-92; TV Rye *Chich* 92-96 and 04-08; P-in-c Chiddingly w E Hoathly 96-98; R 98-04; rtd 08. *44 Ingrams Way, Hailsham BN27 3NP* Tel (01323) 841809 E-mail clucksville@tiscali.co.uk

CLARK, Peter. b 47. DipCOT92. ERMC 04. **d** 07 **p** 08. NSM Vange *Chelmsf* from 07. *283 Church Road, Basildon SS14 2NE* Tel (01268) 527570 Mobile 07786-125795 E-mail pclark@blueyonder.co.uk

CLARK, Peter Norman. b 53. Qu Coll Cam BA79. Westcott Ho Cam 78. **d** 80 **p** 81. C Bris St Mary Redcliffe w Temple etc 80-83; C Potternewton *Ripon* 83-86; R Longsight St Luke *Man* from 86; AD Ardwick 00-03. *St Luke's Rectory, Stockport Road, Longsight, Manchester M13 9AB* Tel 0161-273 6662

CLARK, Peter Rodney. b 58. Oriel Coll Ox BA81 MCIH93. NOC 97. **d** 00 **p** 01. C Stone St Mich and St Wulfad w Aston St Sav *Lich* 00-03; TV Hanley H Ev from 03; RD Stoke N from 08. *Christ Church Vicarage, 10 Emery Street, Stoke-on-Trent ST6 2JJ* Tel (01782) 212639 E-mail rod@prclark.freeserve.co.uk

CLARK, Mrs Prudence Anne. b 44. Man Coll of Educn CertEd78. NOC 89. **d** 92 **p** 94. NSM Royton St Anne *Man* 92-94; Hon C 94-95; NSM Haughton St Anne 95-09; Perm to Offic from 09. *1 Hereford Way, Stalybridge SK15 2TD* Tel 0161-338 5275

CLARK, Richard Martin. b 60. Ch Coll Cam MA81 Nottm Univ MA99. Trin Coll Bris BA86. **d** 86 **p** 87. C Orpington Ch Ch *Roch* 86-89; C Marple All SS *Ches* 89-92; V Nottingham St Andr *S'well* from 92; AD Nottingham Cen from 08. *St Andrew's Vicarage, Chestnut Grove, Nottingham NG3 5AD* Tel 0115-912 0098 Mobile 07970-823462 E-mail standrews.office@ntlworld.com

CLARK, Robert Henry. b 32. Oak Hill Th Coll 61. **d** 64 **p** 65. C Haydock St Mark *Liv* 64-67; C Tranmere St Cath *Ches* 67-75; V Platt Bridge *Liv* 75-84; V Litherland St Paul Hatton Hill 84-94;

rtd 94; Perm to Offic *Liv* from 94. *9 Lime Vale, Ince, Wigan WN3 4PE* Tel (01942) 861751

CLARK, Rodney. *See* CLARK, Peter Rodney

CLARK, Preb Roland Mark Allison. b 21. St Cath Coll Cam BA48 MA53. Wells Th Coll 48. **d** 50 **p** 51. C Battersea St Paul *S'wark* 50-52; C Greenwich St Alfege w St Pet 52-56; Chapl RNVR 53-56; V Wilton *B & W* 56-79; RD Taunton S 60-65; Preb Wells Cathl from 63; R Backwell 79-88; RD Portishead 82-86; rtd 88; Perm to Offic *B & W* and *Chich* from 88; *Bris* from 95. *21 The Chimes, Nailsea, Bristol BS48 4NH* Tel (01275) 852670

CLARK, Ronald. *See* CLARK, Canon John Ronald Lyons

CLARK, Sarah Elizabeth. b 65. Loughb Univ BA86 Keele Univ MBA94. St Jo Coll Nottm MA97. **d** 98 **p** 99. C Porchester *S'well* 98-02; R Carlton-in-Lindrick and Langold w Oldcotes 02-09; AD Worksop 06-09; TR Clifton from 09. *The Rectory, 569 Farnborough Road, Nottingham NG11 9DG* Tel 0115-878 0541 E-mail saraheclark@ntlworld.com

CLARK, Simon Peter John. b 68. Westcott Ho Cam 95. **d** 98 **p** 99. C Bocking St Mary *Chelmsf* 98-02; C Edmonton St Alphege *Lon* 02-07; C Ponders End St Matt 02-07; P-in-c Noel Park St Mark from 07; Chapl NE Lon Coll from 07. *St Mark's Vicarage, Ashley Crescent, London N22 6LJ* Tel (020) 8888 3442 E-mail fr.simon@btinternet.com

CLARK, Stephen Kenneth. b 52. Bris Univ BEd74. Wycliffe Hall Ox 80. **d** 83 **p** 84. C Pitsea *Chelmsf* 83-86; Chapl Scargill Ho 86-89; R Elmley Castle w Bricklehampton and Combertons *Worc* 89-96; Chapl Burrswood Chr Cen *Roch* 96-01; Chapl Team Ldr 01-07; I Annagh w Drumaloor, Cloverhill and Drumlane *K, E & A* from 07. *The Rectory, 2 Creen, Belturbet, Co Cavan, Republic of Ireland* Tel (00353) (49) 952 4778 Mobile 86-382 6454 E-mail skclar@googlemail.com

CLARK, Terence Paul. b 62. Leeds Univ BSc85 PGCE94 St Jo Coll Ox DPhil91. Wycliffe Hall Ox 98. **d** 00 **p** 01. C Whitfield *Derby* from 00. *Church House, Fauvel Road, Glossop SK13 7AR* Tel and fax (01457) 860412 E-mail terry@glossop.org

CLARK-KING (née CLARK), Ellen Jane. b 62. Newnham Coll Cam BA85 MA89 Lon Univ MA99 Lanc Univ PhD03. Ripon Coll Cuddesdon 89. **d** 92 **p** 94. C Colwall w Upper Colwall and Coddington *Heref* 92-95; Chapl SS Coll Cam 95-00; NSM N Shields *Newc* 00-05; Asst Dioc Dir of Ords 01-05; Canada from 05. *195 East Windsor Road, North Vancouver BC V7N 1J9, Canada* Tel (001) (604) 985 5919 Fax 985 7667 E-mail ejck@lineone.net

CLARK-KING (formerly KING), Jeremy Norman. b 66. K Coll Lon BD88 AKC88 Lon Univ MA99. Ripon Coll Cuddesdon 88. **d** 90 **p** 91. C Ashby-de-la-Zouch St Helen w Coleorton *Leic* 90-93; C Ledbury w Eastnor *Heref* 93-96; C Cambridge Gt St Mary w St Mich *Ely* 96-00; Chapl Girton Coll Cam 96-99; Chapl Cam Univ 96-99; V Byker St Ant *Newc* 00-05; R N Vancouver St Martin Canada from 05. *195 East Windsor Road, North Vancouver BC V7N 1J9, Canada* Tel (001) (604) 985 5919 Fax 985 7667 E-mail anglican@uniserve.com

CLARKE, Alan John. b 55. St Jo Coll Dur BA77 MA85 PGCE. Westcott Ho Cam 78. **d** 80 **p** 81. C Heworth St Mary *Dur* 80-83; C Darlington St Jo 83-87; Asst Chapl Bryanston Sch 87-91; Chapl St Pet High Sch Ex 93-99; Lic to Offic *Ex* 93-99; Chapl and Hd RS Reed's Sch Cobham from 99. *Clover, Reed's School, Sandy Lane, Cobham KT11 2RL* Tel (01932) 869006 *or* 869080

CLARKE, Alexandra Naomi Mary. b 75. Trin Coll Cam BA96 MA99 MPhil97 SS Hild & Bede Coll Dur PhD02 Anglia Poly Univ BA04. Westcott Ho Cam 02. **d** 05 **p** 06. C Papworth *Ely* from 05; R Upper Itchen *Win* from 09. *Cheriton Rectory, The Goodens, Cheriton, Alresford SO24 0QH* Tel (01962) 771226 E-mail alexandra_clarke@btopenworld.com

CLARKE, Miss Alison Clare. b 33. MCST54 Open Univ BA85. EAMTC 90. **d** 93 **p** 94. NSM Lt Ilford St Mich *Chelmsf* 93-98; Asst Chapl Newham Healthcare NHS Trust *Lon* 93-98; Perm to Offic *Lon* 94-98; NSM Woodford St Mary w St Phil and St Jas *Chelmsf* 98-03; rtd 03; Perm to Offic *Chelmsf* 03-04. *29 Glengall Road, Woodford Green IG8 0DN* Tel (020) 8504 5106

CLARKE, Andrew John. b 58. Nene Coll BD82 Graduate Soc Dur PGCE89. Linc Th Coll 84. **d** 86 **p** 87. C High Harrogate Ch Ch *Ripon* 86-88; RE Teacher Royds Hall High Sch Huddersfield 89-91; C Thornbury *Bradf* 91-93; P-in-c Bingley H Trin 93-99; V from 99; RD Airedale 00-05. *6 Woodvale Crescent, Bingley BD16 4AL* Tel (01274) 562278 E-mail andrew.clarke@bradford.anglican.org

CLARKE, Ann. *See* CLARKE, Geraldine Ann

CLARKE, Anne. b 51. **d** 04 **p** 05. OLM E Dulwich St Jo *S'wark* from 04. *62 Oakhurst Grove, London SE22 9AQ* Tel (020) 8693 1276 E-mail apsy73@dsl.pipex.com

CLARKE, Arthur. b 34. Lon Univ BD66 Nottm Univ MPhil75 DipEd. Sarum & Wells Th Coll 75. **d** 76 **p** 77. C Wollaton *S'well* 76-79; R Sutton Bonington 79-91; P-in-c Normanton on Soar 79-91; R Sutton Bonington w Normanton-on-Soar 91-93; P-in-c Arnold 93-94; V 94-02; rtd 02; Perm to Offic *S'well* from 02 and

Leic from 03. *16 Kegworth Road, Kingston-on-Soar, Nottingham NG11 0DB* Tel (01509) 674545 E-mail aclarke@kos16.fsnet.co.uk

CLARKE, Miss Audrey May. b 35. Gilmore Ho 65. **dss** 75 **d** 87 **p** 94. Crofton Park St Hilda w St Cypr *S'wark* 75-79; Chapl Asst Middx Hosp Lon 80-84; Mottingham St Andr *S'wark* 84-87; Par Dn 87-89; C Westborough *Guildf* 89-95; rtd 95; Hon C St Mary's Bay w St Mary-in-the-Marsh etc *Cant* 95-98; Hon C New Romney w Old Romney and Midley 95-98; Perm to Offic *Pet* from 98. *47 Lindsay Street, Kettering NN16 8RG* Tel (01536) 410586

CLARKE, Barbara. b 51. Bradf Univ BA87 Leeds Univ PGCE89 MA07. NOC 04. **d** 07 **p** 08. NSM Addingham *Bradf* from 07. *8 Brighton Road, Ilkley LS29 8PS* Tel (01943) 605253 E-mail bclarke@talktalk.net

CLARKE, Bernard Ronald. b 53. FRGS. Ridley Hall Cam 74. **d** 77 **p** 78. C Leigh Park *Portsm* 77-78; C Petersfield w Sheet 78-81; Chapl RN from 81; Dir of Ords RN 93-03. *Royal Naval Chaplaincy Service, Mail Point 1-2, Leach Building, Whale Island, Portsmouth PO2 8BY* Tel (023) 9262 5055 Fax 9262 5134

CLARKE, Mrs Caroline Anne. b 49. Girton Coll Cam BA75 MA79 K Coll Lon PGCE76. SEITE 97. **d** 00 **p** 01. NSM Clapham H Trin and St Pet *S'wark* from 00; Chapl Trin Hospice Lon from 03. *42 The Chase, London SW4 0NH* Tel (020) 7622 0765 Fax 7652 4555 Mobile 07808-858674 E-mail clarkecaroline@hotmail.com

CLARKE, Charles David. b 37. Univ of Wales BA76 MA93 PhD98 Cam Univ DipEd77 MEd Lambeth MA95 LCP77. St Mich Coll Llan 88. **d** 90 **p** 91. C Whitchurch *Llan* 90-93; V Graig 93-96; P-in-c Cilfynydd 93-96; TV Cyncoed *Mon* 96-98; R Neath w Llantwit 98-01; TR Neath 01-02; rtd 02. *Lough Cutra, 11 Davies Andrews Road, Tonna, Neath SA11 1EU* Tel (01639) 638049

CLARKE, Canon Christopher George. b 43. Sarum Th Coll 67. **d** 68 **p** 69. C Sprowston *Nor* 68-72; V Hemsby 72-77; V Sutton Courtenay w Appleford *Ox* 77-84; TR Bracknell 84-97; RD Bracknell 90-96; Hon Can Ch Ch 95-08; P-in-c Sonning 97-98; V 98-08; rtd 08. *Oak Lodge, Upton Snodsbury, Worcester WR7 4NH* E-mail chrisclarke@vodafonemail.co.uk

CLARKE, Canon David James. b 55. Univ of Wales (Abth) BSc(Econ)77 Keele Univ MA78 PhD83. Trin Coll Bris. **d** 84 **p** 85. C Cardigan w Mwnt and Y Ferwig *St D* 84-87; P-in-c Llansantffraed and Llanbadarn Trefeglwys etc 87-88; V 88-91; Chapl Coll of SS Mark and Jo Plymouth 91-96; V Lindfield *Chich* from 96; Can and Preb Chich Cathl from 06. *The Vicarage, High Street, Lindfield, Haywards Heath RH16 2HR* Tel (01444) 482386

CLARKE, Dominic James. b 71. Surrey Univ BA07. STETS 04. **d** 07 **p** 08. C Petersfield *Portsm* from 07. *38 Larcombe Road, Petersfield GU32 3LS* Tel (01730) 260213

CLARKE, Douglas Charles. b 33. Bps' Coll Cheshunt 65. **d** 66 **p** 67. C Chingford SS Pet and Paul *Chelmsf* 66-72; V Romford Ascension Collier Row 72-79; V Bembridge *Portsm* 79-83; V Bournemouth St Mary *Win* 83-87; R High Wych and Gilston w Eastwick *St Alb* 87-00; rtd 00; Perm to Offic *Linc* and *St Alb* from 00. *36 Tennyson Drive, Bourne PE10 9WD* Tel (01778) 394840

CLARKE, Dudley Barrington. b 22. OBE. Em Coll Cam BA46 MA48 PhD. Ridley Hall Cam 46. **d** 48 **p** 49. C Aldershot H Trin *Guildf* 48-50; Chapl Monkton Combe Sch Bath 50-58; Australia from 59; rtd 87. *60 Duke Street, Sandy Bay Tas 7005, Australia* Tel (0061) (02) 6224 0784 *or* 6220 2385

CLARKE, Duncan James Edward. b 54. Wycliffe Hall Ox 75. **d** 78 **p** 79. C Newport St Andr *Mon* 78-80; C Griffithstown 80-82; Trinidad and Tobago 82-84 and 95-99; NSM Fleckney and Kilby *Leic* 92-95; USPG 95-99; C Wednesfield *Lich* 99; TV 99-01; Asst Chapl HM Pris Wormwood Scrubs 01-02; Chapl HM Pris Haverigg 02-07; Chapl HM Pris Garth 07-09; P-in-c Leyland St Ambrose *Blackb* from 09. *St Ambrose Vicarage, 85 Moss Lane, Leyland, Preston PR25 4XA* Tel (01772) 462204 Mobile 07946-668786

CLARKE, Mrs Elizabeth Hazel. b 55. Ridley Hall Cam 02. **d** 04 **p** 05. C Frankby w Greasby *Ches* 04-09; P-in-c Dodleston from 09. *St Mary's Rectory, Pulford Lane, Dodleston, Chester CH4 9NN* Tel (01244) 660257

CLARKE, Eric Samuel. b 26. Nottm Univ BSc51 St Cath Coll Ox BA69 MA69. Wycliffe Hall Ox 51. **d** 54 **p** 55. C Gedling *S'well* 54-57; C Nottingham St Pet and St Jas 57-69; Perm to Offic *Derby* 63-02; rtd 02. *Hillcrest, Cottington Mead, Sidmouth EX10 8HB*

CLARKE, Frank. b 21. St Jo Coll Nottm. **d** 85 **p** 87. NSM Farnsfield *S'well* 85-97; rtd 98; Perm to Offic *S'well* from 03. *Belvedere, Tippings Lane, Farnsfield, Newark NG22 8EP* Tel (01623) 882528 E-mail doreen@onetel.com

CLARKE, Frank Alfred. b 46. MCLIP67 MCMI82. **d** 08. OLM Weybourne Gp *Nor* from 08. *7 Alexandra Road, Sheringham NR26 8HU* Tel (01263) 825677 E-mail f.clarke46@tiscali.co.uk

CLARKE, Geoffrey. b 53. CA Tr Coll 84 Trin Coll Bris 94. **d** 97 **p** 98. C Belmont *Lon* 97-00; C Tonbridge SS Pet and Paul *Roch* 00-05; V Erith St Paul from 05. *The Vicarage, 44A Colyers Lane, Erith DA8 3NP* Tel (01322) 332809
E-mail geofftherev@ntlworld.com

CLARKE, Geraldine Ann. b 46. Hockerill Coll of Educn CertEd68 ACP81. NTMTC 93. **d** 96 **p** 97. NSM Aldersbrook *Chelmsf* 96-01; TR Becontree S from 01. *St Martin's Vicarage, Goresbrook Road, Dagenham RM9 6UX* Tel and fax (020) 8592 0967 E-mail ann.clarke@virgin.net

CLARKE, Canon Harold George. b 29. St D Coll Lamp 58. **d** 61 **p** 62. C Ebbw Vale Ch Ch *Mon* 61-64; C Roath St German *Llan* 64-73; Chapl Wales Poly 73-74; V Glyntaff 73-84; V Roath St Martin 84-00; RD Cardiff 89-99; Can Res Llan Cathl 91-99; rtd 00. *12 St Margaret's Crescent, Cardiff CF23 5AU* Tel (029) 2046 2280

CLARKE, Hazel. *See* CLARKE, Mrs Elizabeth Hazel

CLARKE, Hilary James. b 41. JP. Univ of Wales (Lamp) BA64 Ox Univ DipEd65. St Steph Ho Ox 64. **d** 66 **p** 67. C Kibworth Beauchamp *Leic* 66-68; Chapl to the Deaf 68-71; Prin Officer Co Miss for Deaf Walsall 71-73; Prin Officer & Sec Leic and Co Miss for the Deaf 73-89; Hon C Leic St Anne 73-98; TV Leic H Spirit 82-89; Hon Can Leic Cathl 88-96; Bp's Press Relns and Dio Communications Officer 95-96; Sec Gen Syn Coun for the Deaf 88-02; rtd 02. *The Gate House, Brough, Kirkby Stephen CA17 4DS* Tel 07730-002570 (mobile)

CLARKE, James. *See* CLARKE, Canon David James

CLARKE, Jason Philip. b 66. Lon Hosp BDS. Oak Hill Th Coll 99. **d** 01 **p** 02. C Fulwood *Sheff* 01-06; Dir Staff Tr UCCF from 06; Perm to Offic *Sheff* from 06. *469 Redmires Road, Sheffield S10 4LF* Tel 0114-230 9345

CLARKE, Jason Scott. b 65. Leeds Univ BA87. Coll of Resurr Mirfield 89. **d** 91 **p** 92. C Hendon St Mary *Lon* 91-95; V Enfield St Geo 95-01; V Ditchling *Chich* 01-06; CF from 06. *c/o MOD Chaplains (Army)* Tel (01980) 615804 Fax 615800

CLARKE, John Charles. b 31. St Jo Coll Nottm 91. **d** 92 **p** 93. NSM Winshill *Derby* 92-95; P-in-c Stanley 95-98; rtd 98. *5 The Tyleshades, Tadburn, Romsey SO51 5RJ* Tel (01794) 523945

CLARKE, Canon John David Maurice. b 60. **d** 89 **p** 90. C Dublin Whitechurch *D & G* 89-92; Asst Chapl St Vin Hosp Donnybrook 89-92; I Navan w Kentstown, Tara, Slane, Painestown etc *M & K* from 92; Can Meath from 00; Can Kildare Cathl from 00; Can St Patr Cathl Dublin from 09. *The Rectory, Boyne Road, Navan, Co Meath, Republic of Ireland* Tel and fax (00353) (46) 902 1172
E-mail johndmclarke@eircom.net

CLARKE, The Very Revd John Martin. b 52. Edin Univ BD76 Hertf Coll Ox BA89 MA89. Edin Th Coll 73. **d** 76 **p** 77. C Kenton Ascension *Newc* 76-79; Prec St Ninian's Cathl Perth 79-82; Info Officer to Gen Syn of Scottish Episc Ch 82-87; Greece 87-88; V Battersea St Mary *S'wark* 89-96; Prin Ripon Coll Cuddesdon 97-04; Can and Preb Linc Cathl 00-04; Dean Wells *B & W* from 04. *The Dean's Lodging, 25 The Liberty, Wells BA5 2SZ* Tel and fax (01749) 670278
E-mail dean@wellscathedral.uk.net

CLARKE, John Patrick Hatherley. b 46. Pemb Coll Ox BA68 Man Univ MBA73. St Jo Coll Nottm. **d** 83 **p** 84. C Leic H Trin w St Jo 83-87; C Selly Park St Steph and St Wulstan *Birm* 87-92; Hon C Woking St Mary *Guildf* 92-94; V Greenham *Ox* from 94. *Greenham Vicarage, New Road, Greenham, Thatcham RG19 8RZ* Tel (01635) 41075

CLARKE, Canon John Percival. b 44. TCD BA67 MA98. **d** 69 **p** 70. C Belfast St Simon *Conn* 69-72; C Monkstown *D & G* 72-76; Asst Chapl TCD 76-78; I Durrus *C, C & R* 79-82; I Carrigrohane Union 82-89; Tanzania 89-92; I Wicklow w Killiskey *D & G* from 92; Abp's Dom Chapl 95-97; Can Ch Ch Cathl Dublin from 97. *The Rectory, Wicklow, Republic of Ireland* Tel (00353) (404) 67132

CLARKE, John Philip. b 31. Trin Hall Cam BA54 MA62. Linc Th Coll. **d** 57 **p** 58. C Walworth Lady Marg w St Mary *S'wark* 57-59; C Warlingham w Chelsham and Farleigh 59-62; C Mottingham St Andr 62-67; C Eltham Park St Luke 67-72; Chapl Leeds Gen Infirmary 72-91; C Far Headingley St Chad *Ripon* 91-96; Bp's Adv on Chr Healing 91-96; rtd 96; Perm to Offic *Ripon* from 96. *13 Bishop Garth, Pateley Bridge, Harrogate HG3 5LL* Tel (01423) 711646

CLARKE, Mrs Joy Irene. b 44. **d** 98 **p** 02. OLM Ditton St Mich w St Thos *Liv* from 98. *55 Spinney Avenue, Widnes WA8 8LB* Tel 0151-424 8747

CLARKE, Judith Irene. b 46. SRN67 SCM69. EAMTC 97. **d** 00 **p** 01. NSM Shingay Gp *Ely* 00-02; P-in-c Gt Staughton 02-05; P-in-c Hail Weston and Southoe 04-05; R Gt Staughton w Hail Weston w Southoe from 05. *The Vicarage, Causeway, Great Staughton, St Neots PE19 5BF* Tel (01480) 861215

✠**CLARKE, The Rt Revd Kenneth Herbert.** b 49. TCD BA71. **d** 72 **p** 73 **c** 01. C Magheralin *D & D* 72-75; C Dundonald 75-78; Chile 78-81; I Crinken *D & G* 82-86; I Coleraine *Conn* 86-01; Chmn SAMS (Ireland) from 94; Can Conn Cathl 96-98; Adn

Dalriada 98-01; Bp K, E & A from 01. *48 Carrickfern, Cavan, Republic of Ireland* Tel (00353) (49) 437 2759 Fax 436 2829
E-mail ken@atnaf.freeserve.co.uk
or bishop@kilmore.anglican.org

CLARKE, Mrs Lynnette Jean. b 46. Qu Coll Birm 05. **d** 08 **p** 09. OLM Allesley Park and Whoberley *Cov* from 08. *14 High Park Close, Coventry CV5 7BE* Tel (024) 7646 7097 Mobile 07890-048210 E-mail lynnette@mountnod.co.uk

CLARKE, Canon Margaret Geraldine. b 33. Dalton Ho Bris 62. **dss** 68 **d** 87 **p** 94. Wells St Thos w Horrington *B & W* 68-74; Easthampstead *Ox* 74-94; Par Dn 87-94; C 94; Hon Can Ch Ch 90-94; rtd 94; Hon C Bracknell *Ox* from 97. *Hermon, London Road, Bracknell RG12 2XH* Tel (01344) 427451

CLARKE, Martin Howard. b 47. AKC70. St Aug Coll Cant 70. **d** 71 **p** 72. C Saffron Walden w Wendens Ambo *Chelmsf* 71-74; C Ely 74-78; V Messing w Inworth *Chelmsf* 78-90; V Layer de la Haye 90-02; R Layer de la Haye and Layer Breton w Birch etc from 03. *The Vicarage, 45 Malting Green Road, Layer-de-la-Haye, Colchester CO2 0JJ* Tel (01206) 734243
E-mail stationmaster@thelayers.fsnet.co.uk

CLARKE, Ms Mary Margaret. b 65. K Coll Lon BD86 AKC86. Linc Th Coll 89. **d** 89 **p** 94. Par Dn Northampton St Jas *Pet* 89-93; Chapl Nene Coll of HE Northn 92-93; TD Coventry Caludon 93-94; TV 94-01; Perm to Offic *Lon* 01-08. *1 Porchester Gardens, London W2 3LA* Tel (020) 7229 6359
E-mail mary-andrew@clarkewillson.fsnet.co.uk

CLARKE, Maurice Harold. b 30. K Alfred's Coll Win CertEd56 Sussex Univ MA79 LCP69. Cuddesdon Coll 65. **d** 67 **p** 68. Hd Master Co Sec Sch Cowplain (Lower Sch) 67-72; Dep Head Master Thamesview High Sch 72-80; Hd Master Eltham Green Comp Sch 80-83; Hon C Waterlooville *Portsm* 67-70; Hon C Fareham SS Pet and Paul 70-72; Hon C Higham and Merston *Roch* 72-83; V Hamble le Rice *Win* 83-90; rtd 91; Perm to Offic *Win* from 91 and *Chich* from 92. *10 Worcester Road, Chichester PO19 8DJ* Tel (01243) 775646

CLARKE, Michael. b 39. Ely Th Coll 60. **d** 62 **p** 63. C S Stoneham *Win* 62-64; C N Greenford All Hallows *Lon* 64-69; Hon C Milton *Portsm* 69-74; Chapl St Jas Hosp Portsm 69-91; Chapl Hurstpierpoint Coll 91-92; R Highnam, Lassington, Rudford, Tibberton etc *Glouc* 92-98; rtd 99; Perm to Offic *Glouc* 99-01 and *Portsm* from 02. *Little Barns, 77 Fishbourne Lane, Ryde PO33 4EX* Tel (01983) 883858

CLARKE, Canon Neil Malcolm. b 53. OBE05. Solicitor 79. WMMTC 89. **d** 92 **p** 93. NSM Desborough, Brampton Ash, Dingley and Braybrooke *Pet* from 92; Can Pet Cathl from 00. *53 Breakleys Road, Desborough, Kettering NN14 2PT* Tel (01536) 760667 E-mail revnclarke@aol.com

CLARKE, Nicholas John. b 57. Lon Univ BA78 Lon Inst of Educn PGCE80. Ridley Hall Cam 95. **d** 97 **p** 98. C Attleborough *Cov* 97-00; V Fillongley and Corley 00-07; Chapl Chantilly *Eur* from 07. *7A avenue du Bouteiller, 60500 Chantilly, France* Tel (0033) (3) 44 58 53 22 E-mail chaplain@stpeterschantilly.info

CLARKE, Norman. b 28. Keble Coll Ox BA52 MA58. St Steph Ho Ox 52. **d** 54 **p** 55. C Ellesmere Port *Ches* 54-57; C Kettering St Mary *Pet* 57-60; Chapl and Tutor St Monica Mampong Ghana 60-62; C Friern Barnet All SS *Lon* 62-63; Lic to Offic *Leic* 63-74; C Knighton St Mary Magd 74-81; Dioc Communications Officer 81-88; P-in-c Sproughton w Burstall *St E* 81-88; P-in-c Dunsford and Doddiscombsleigh *Ex* 88-95; P-in-c Cheriton Bishop 88-95; rtd 95; Perm to Offic *Ex* 95-08; RD Ottery 02-03; Perm to Offic St Helena from 96. *78 Malden Road, Sidmouth EX10 9NA* Tel (01395) 515849

CLARKE, Paul Wordsworth. b 74. Trevelyan Coll Dur LLB97. Oak Hill Th Coll BA06. **d** 07. C St Helen Bishopsgate w St Andr Undershaft etc *Lon* from 07. *4 Merrick Square, London SE1 4JB* Tel (020) 7283 2231 E-mail clarke@st-helens.org.uk

CLARKE, Canon Peter. b 25. Lon Univ BSc49. St Chad's Coll Dur. **d** 51 **p** 52. C Linc St Giles 51-53; C Gt Grimsby St Mary and St Jas 53-60; V Linc All SS 60-68; V Bardney 68-75; V Apley w Stainfeld 68-75; V Linc St Nic w St Jo Newport 75-88; RD Christianity 78-85; Can and Preb Linc Cathl 79-99; rtd 88; Perm to Offic *Linc* 88-00. *1 North Croft, Saxilby, Lincoln LN1 2PU* Tel (01522) 702795

CLARKE, Preb Peter Gerald. b 38. Cuddesdon Coll 74. **d** 76 **p** 77. NSM Marston Magna w Rimpton *B & W* 76-79; NSM Queen Camel, Marston Magna, W Camel, Rimpton etc 79-87; NSM Chilton Cantelo, Ashington, Mudford, Rimpton etc 87-88; R Tintinhull w Chilthorne Domer, Yeovil Marsh etc 88-94; TV Weston-super-Mare Cen Par 94-95; V Weston super Mare All SS and St Sav 96-06; Preb Wells Cathl 02-08; rtd 06; Perm to Offic *B & W* from 06. *6 West Camel Farm, West Camel, Yeovil BA22 7HH* Tel (01935) 850408 E-mail peter2117@lycos.com

CLARKE, Peter John. b 36. Qu Coll Ox BA60 MA64 Lon Univ BD79. Clifton Th Coll 62. **d** 62 **p** 63. C Upper Tulse Hill St Matthias *S'wark* 62-64; CMJ 64-96; Dir for S America 88-96; rtd 97. *Pedro Moran 4414, C 1419 HLH Buenos Aires, Argentina* Tel and fax (0054) (11) 4501 4629

CLARKE, Philip John. b 44. Bris Univ BA65 Univ of Wales (Abth) DipEd66. NOC 84. **d** 87 **p** 88. NSM Crewe Ch Ch and

St Pet *Ches* 87-88; NSM Coppenhall 88-90; Lic to Offic 90-91; C Altrincham St Geo 91-95; C Odd Rode 95-97; P-in-c Peterchurch w Vowchurch, Turnastone and Dorstone *Heref* 97-98; V Llansantffraid Glyn Ceirog and Llanarmon etc *St As* from 98. *The Vicarage, High Street, Glyn Ceiriog, Llangollen LL20 7EH* Tel (01691) 718245
E-mail revphilipjclarke@aol.com

CLARKE, Richard Leon. b 37. Sarum Th Coll 62. **d** 65 **p** 66. C Fordington *Sarum* 65-68; C Haywards Heath St Rich *Chich* 68-72; C Goring-by-Sea 72-76; P-in-c Southwick St Pet 76-77; P-in-c Portslade St Andr 76-77; V Portslade St Pet and St Andr 77-79; R Clayton w Keymer 79-02; RD Hurst 90-98; rtd 03; Perm to Offic *Chich* 03-05; Hon C Brighton Annunciation from 05. *107 Freshfield Road, Brighton BN2 0BL* Tel (01273) 628006

✠**CLARKE, The Most Revd Richard Lionel.** b 49. TCD BA71 MA79 PhD90 K Coll Lon BD75 AKC75. **d** 75 **p** 76 **c** 96. C Holywood *D & D* 75-77; C Dublin St Bart w Leeson Park *D & G* 77-79; Dean of Residence TCD 79-84; I Bandon Union *C, C & R* 84-93; Dir of Ords 85-93; Cen Dir of Ords 82-97; Can Cork and Ross Cathls 91-93; Dean Cork 93-96; I Cork St Fin Barre's Union 93-96; Chapl Univ Coll Cork 93-96; Bp M & K from 96; Hon Can St Ninian's Cathl Perth from 04. *Bishop's House, Moyglare, Maynooth, Co Kildare, Republic of Ireland* (00353) (1) 628 9354 E-mail bishop@meath.anglican.org

CLARKE, Canon Robert George. b 36. St Jo Coll Dur BA65 Natal Univ PhD83. Cranmer Hall Dur 65. **d** 67 **p** 68. C Basingstoke *Win* 67-70; R Ixopo 71-74; C Pietermaritzburg Cathl 75-80; Dir Pietermaritzburg Urban Min Project 77-83; R Grahamstown St Bart 84-87; Lect St Paul's Coll 84-87; Ecum Officer Albany Regional Coun of Chs 88-95; Hon Can Grahamstown from 05. *26 Somerset Street, Grahamstown, 6139 South Africa* Tel (0027) (046) 622 7803
E-mail bobandmaggy@imaginet.co.za

CLARKE, Robert Graham. b 28. S Dios Minl Tr Scheme 78. **d** 81 **p** 82. NSM Woolston *Win* 81-89; NSM Portswood St Denys 89-93; Chapl Torrevieja *Eur* 93-95; Perm to Offic *Win* 95-05 and *Eur* from 95. *10 River Green, Hamble, Southampton SO31 4JA* Tel (023) 8045 4230

CLARKE, Robert Michael. b 45. Oak Hill Th Coll BD71 Sarum & Wells Th Coll 78. **d** 78 **p** 79. Hon C Glastonbury St Jo w Godney *B & W* 78-81; Asst Hd Master Edington Sch 78-81; Chapl Felsted Sch 81-84; Asst Chapl and Ho Master 85-92; Hd Master Brocksford Hall 92-94; Hd Master The Park Sch Bath 94-96; Chapl Seaford Coll Petworth 96-99; Hd Master Bredon Sch 99-00; Perm to Offic *Lich* from 01. *17 Top Street, Whittington, Oswestry SY11 4DR* Tel (01691) 662548

CLARKE, Robert Sydney. b 35. OBE00. K Coll Lon AKC64 MA65. **d** 65 **p** 66. C Hendon St Mary *Lon* 65-69; C Langley Marish *Ox* 69-70; Chapl New Cross Hosp Wolv 70-74; Chapl Dorchester Hosps 74-79; Sen Chapl Westmr Hosp Lon 80-85; Sen Chapl Win Hosps 88-94; Sen Chapl Win and Eastleigh Healthcare NHS Trust 94-00; Chapl to The Queen 87-05; Sec and Dir Tr Gen Syn Hosp Chapl Coun 94-00; Perm to Offic *Lon* and *S'wark* 95-00; *Eur* from 00; *Win* from 05. *3 Brook Court, Middlebridge Street, Romsey SO51 8HR* Tel (01794) 524215

CLARKE, Canon Robert William. b 56. CITC. **d** 83 **p** 84. C Cloughfern *Conn* 83-85; C Drumragh w Mountfield *D & R* 85-87; I Edenderry w Clanabogan from 87; Can Derry Cathl from 05. *Edenderry Rectory, 91 Crevenagh Road, Omagh BT79 0EZ* Tel (028) 8224 5525

CLARKE, Roger David. b 58. Man Univ BA Ox Univ MA. Ripon Coll Cuddesdon 80. **d** 83 **p** 84. C Frodsham *Ches* 83-86; C Wilmslow 86-88; V High Lane 88-93; V Heald Green St Cath 93-99; R W Kirby St Bridget from 99. *St Bridget's Rectory, Rectory Road, Wirral CH48 7HL* Tel 0151-625 5229

CLARKE, Ronald George. b 31. Oak Hill Th Coll. **d** 64 **p** 65. C Carlton-in-the-Willows *S'well* 64-68; V Bestwood St Matt 68-76; V Barnsbury St Andr w St Thos and St Matthias *Lon* 76-77; V Barnsbury St Andr 77-78; V Barnsbury St Andr w H Trin 79-80; P-in-c Battle Bridge All SS w Pentonville St Jas 79-80; V Barnsbury St Andr and H Trin w All SS 81-86; TR Bath Twerton-on-Avon *B & W* 86-94; P-in-c Churchstanton, Buckland St Mary and Otterford *B & W* 94-97; Perm to Offic from 97. *Myrtle Cottage, 35 High Street, Chard TA20 1QL* Tel (01460) 65495

CLARKE, Steven Peter. b 61. Oak Hill Th Coll 93. **d** 97 **p** 98. C Frinton *Chelmsf* 97-01; C Woodford Wells from 01. *80 Montalt Road, Woodford Green IG8 9SS* Tel (020) 8505 1431

CLARKE (formerly **GARDNER), Mrs Susan Carol.** b 54. SRN75. St Jo Coll Nottm 02. **d** 04 **p** 05. C Abington *Pet* 04-07; P-in-c Woodhouse *Wakef* 07-08; V Birkby and Woodhouse from 08. *The Vicarage, 43 Ashbrow Road, Huddersfield HD2 1DX* Tel 07732-189485 (mobile)
E-mail sue.gardner1.wanadoo.co.uk

CLARKE (née **DAVIS), Susan Elizabeth Mary.** b 50. St Thos Hosp Lon MB, BS74 Univ Coll Lon MSc81 FRCP84 FRCR03. SEITE 03. **d** 06 **p** 07. NSM W Streatham St Jas *S'wark* from 06.

26 Abbotsleigh Road, London SW16 1SP Tel (020) 8769 5117 Mobile 07710-744006 E-mail sue.clarke@kcl.ac.uk

CLARKE, Timothy John. b 69. Jes Coll Cam BA91 MA95 Barrister 92. WMMTC 00. **d** 03 **p** 04. NSM Birm Cathl from 03. *The Rectory, St Kenelm's Road, Romsley, Halesowen B62 0PH* Tel (01562) 710057 E-mail timclarke@waitrose.com

CLARKE, Ms Valerie Diane. b 45. St Jo Coll Nottm BA00. NOC 91. **d** 95 **p** 96. C Sherburn in Elmet w Saxton *York* 95-97; C Brayton 97-99; Chapl Scargill Ho 00-03; P-in-c Barnburgh w Melton on the Hill etc *Sheff* from 03; rtd 09. *1 Arrunden Court, Holmfirth HD9 2AP* Tel (01484) 688609 Mobile 07974-698468

CLARKE, Mrs Yvonne Veronica. b 58. CA Tr Coll. **dss** 86 **d** 87 **p** 94. Nunhead St Silas *S'wark* 86-90; Par Dn 87-90; Par Dn Nunhead St Antony w St Silas 90-91; Par Dn Mottingham St Andr 91-94; C 94-98; V Spring Park All SS from 98. *All Saints' Vicarage, 1 Farm Drive, Croydon CR0 8HX* Tel (020) 8777 2775 Fax 8777 5228

CLARKSON, The Ven Alan Geoffrey. b 34. Ch Coll Cam BA57 MA61. Wycliffe Hall Ox 57. **d** 59 **p** 60. C Penn *Lich* 59-60; C Oswestry St Oswald 60-63; C Wrington *B & W* 63-65; V Chewton Mendip w Emborough 65-74; Dioc Ecum Officer 65-75; V Glastonbury St Jo w Godney 74-84; P-in-c W Pennard 80-84; P-in-c Meare 81-84; P-in-c Glastonbury St Benedict 82-84; V Glastonbury w Meare, W Pennard and Godney 84; Hon Can Win Cathl 84-99; Adn Win 84-99; V Burley Ville 84-99; rtd 99; Perm to Offic *Chelmsf*, *Ely* and *St E* from 99. *Cantilena, 4 Harefield Rise, Linton, Cambridge CB21 4LS* Tel (01223) 892988 E-mail a.clarkson@talktalk.net

CLARKSON, David James. b 42. St Andr Univ BSc66. NOC 85. **d** 88 **p** 89. NSM Slaithwaite w E Scammonden *Wakef* 88-89; C Morley St Pet w Churwell 89-91; R Cumberworth w Denby Dale 91-93; P-in-c Denby 91-93; R Cumberworth, Denby and Denby Dale 93-02; rtd 03; Lic to Offic *Glas* from 04. *Waulkmill Cottage, Westerkirk, Langholm DG13 0NJ* Tel (01387) 370279

CLARKSON, Eric George. b 22. St Jo Coll Dur BA48. **d** 50 **p** 51. C Birkdale St Jo *Liv* 50-52; C Grassendale 52-54; PC W Derby St Luke 54-66; V Blackb St Mich 66-75; V Blackb w Sale w St Jo 75; V Chapeltown *Sheff* 75-86; C Ranmoor 86-87; V Crosspool 87-92; rtd 92; Perm to Offic *York* from 92. *2 Harewood Drive, Filey YO14 0DE* Tel and fax (01723) 513957

CLARKSON, Geoffrey. b 35. AKC61. **d** 62 **p** 63. C Shildon *Dur* 62-65; Asst Chapl HM Pris Liv 65-66; Chapl HM Borstal Feltham 66-71; Development Officer Br Assn of Settlements 71-74; Dir Community Projects Foundn 74-87; Chapl HM Rem Cen Ashford 88-90; Chapl HM Pris Coldingley 90-99; Chapl HM Pris Send 92-94; rtd 00; Hon C Hampton St Mary *Lon* 71-05; Perm to Offic from 05. *109 Cambridge Road, Teddington TW11 8DF* Tel (020) 8977 1434 E-mail gfclarkson@aol.com

CLARKSON, Canon John Thomas. b 30. AKC53. St Boniface Warminster 54. **d** 54 **p** 55. C Luton St Sav *St Alb* 54-59; Australia 59-73 and from 77; Brotherhood of St Barn 59-64; R Mundingburra 64-72; V Dallington *Pet* 73-77; R W Wyalong St Barn 77-82; R Blayney Ch Ch 82-95; Hon Can Bathurst 95-96; rtd 96. *134 Mitre Street, Bathurst NSW 2795, Australia* Tel (0061) (2) 6332 6032 E-mail clarkson@netwit.net.au

CLARKSON, Michael. *See* CLARKSON, Richard Michael

CLARKSON, Michael Livingston. b 48. California Univ BA70 Loyola Univ JD73. Wycliffe Hall Ox 87. **d** 89 **p** 90. C Kensington St Barn *Lon* 89-93; Min Oak Tree Angl Fellowship 93-04; Oman 04-08; R Johns Island Our Sav USA from 08. *4416 Betsy Kerrison Parkway, Johns Island SC 29455-7125, USA* Tel (001) (843) 768 2046 Mobile 298 0003
E-mail mclarkson@our-saviour.net

CLARKSON, Canon Richard. b 33. Man Univ BSc54 Ball Coll Ox DPhil57. Oak Hill Th Coll 89. **d** 91 **p** 92. NSM Sunnyside w Bourne End *St Alb* from 91; RD Berkhamsted 97-02; Hon Can St Alb from 02. *Kingsmead, Gravel Path, Berkhamsted HP4 2PH* Tel (01442) 873014 E-mail r.sclarkson@btopenworld.com

CLARKSON, Richard Michael. b 38. St Jo Coll Dur BA60 Lanc Univ PGCE68. Cranmer Hall Dur 60. **d** 62 **p** 63. C Heyhouses on Sea *Blackb* 62-66; C Lancaster St Mary 66-68; Asst Master Kirkham Gr Sch 68-90; Asst Master Hurstpierpoint Coll 90-91; Asst Master St Mary's Hall Brighton 92-98; Chapl 96-98; rtd 93; Perm to Offic *Chich* from 93. *121 College Lane, Hurstpierpoint, Hassocks BN6 9AF* Tel (01273) 834117

CLARKSON, Robert Christopher. b 32. Dur Univ BA53 DipEd54. S Dios Minl Tr Scheme 85. **d** 87 **p** 88. NSM Lower Dever Valley *Win* 87-93; Perm to Offic from 03. *27 Wrights Way, South Wonston, Winchester SO21 3HE* Tel (01962) 881692

CLARRIDGE, Mrs Ann. b 44. Bournemouth Univ BSc89 S Bank Univ MSc94. SEITE 01. **d** 04 **p** 05. NSM Shepherd's Bush St Steph w St Thos *Lon* 04-07; NSM Whitton St Aug from 07. *80 Greenford Gardens, Greenford UB6 9NA* Tel (020) 8578 7025 E-mail clarria@lsbu.ac.uk

CLARRIDGE, Donald Michael. b 41. DipOT86. Oak Hill Th Coll 63. **d** 66 **p** 67. C Newc St Barn and St Jude 66-70; C Pennycross *Ex* 70-76; R Clayhanger 76-83; R Petton 76-83; R

Huntsham 76-83; V Bampton 76-83. *Winkley, Broad Road, Hambrook, Chichester PO18 8RF* Tel (01243) 573821
E-mail donclarridge@tiscali.co.uk

CLASBY, Michael Francis Theodore. b 37. Univ Coll Lon BA59. Chich Th Coll 59. **d** 61 **p** 62. C Leigh-on-Sea St Marg *Chelmsf* 61-64; C Forest Gate St Edm 64-69; V Walthamstow St Mich 69-70; Chapl Community of Sisters of the Love of God 87-89; Perm to Offic *St Alb* 87-89; NSM Hemel Hempstead 90-93; Perm to Offic 93-98; rtd 02. *14 Richmond Walk, St Albans AL4 9BA* Tel (01727) 853913

CLASPER, John. b 42. AKC67. **d** 68 **p** 69. C Leeds All Hallows w St Simon *Ripon* 68-71; C Hawksworth Wood 72-74; Ind Chapl *Dur* 74-97; TV Jarrow St Paul 75-77; TV Jarrow 77-91; Dioc Urban Development Officer 90-91; TR E Darlington 91-97; V Fenham St Jas and St Basil *Newc* 97-02; RD Newc W 98-02; rtd 03; Perm to Offic *Newc* from 03. *103 Warkworth Woods, Newcastle upon Tyne NE3 5RB* Tel 0191-217 1325 Mobile 07710-078945 E-mail john.clasper@virgin.net

CLASSON, Michael Campbell. b 32. TCD BA52 HDipEd54 MA55. CITC 87. **d** 89 **p** 91. NSM Conwal Union w Gartan *D & R* 89-90; NSM Ardara w Glencolumbkille, Inniskeel etc from 90. *Summy, Portnoo, Co Donegal, Republic of Ireland* Tel (00353) (74) 954 5242

CLATWORTHY, Jonathan Richard. b 48. Univ of Wales BA70. Sarum & Wells Th Coll 71. **d** 76 **p** 77. C Man Resurr 76-78; C Bolton St Pet 78-81; V Ashton St Pet 81-85; Chapl Sheff Univ 85-91; V Denstone w Ellastone and Stanton *Lich* 91-98; Chapl Liv Univ 98-02; rtd 02; Perm to Offic *Liv* from 04. *9 Westward View, Aigburth, Liverpool L17 7EE* Tel 0151-727 6291
E-mail jonathan@clatworthy.org

CLAUSEN, John Frederick. b 37. Sarum Th Coll 65. **d** 68 **p** 69. C Kentish Town St Jo *Lon* 68-71; C Rainham *Roch* 71-77; R Stone 77-89; Lic to Dartford RD 89-02; rtd 02. *24 Spring Vale North, Dartford DA1 2LL* Tel (01322) 279570

CLAWSON, Derek George. b 35. AMCST62. Qu Coll Birm 63. **d** 66 **p** 67. C Ditton St Mich *Liv* 66-70; C Speke All SS 70-72; V Hindley Green 72-85; V Wigan St Mich 85-00; rtd 00; Perm to Offic *Liv* from 01. *20 Parklands Drive, Aspull, Wigan WN2 1ZA* Tel (01942) 830769

CLAY, Canon Colin Peter. b 32. Ch Coll Cam BA55 MA59. Em Coll Saskatoon Hon DD91 Wells Th Coll 55. **d** 57 **p** 58. C Malden St Jas *S'wark* 57-59; Canada from 59; C Sudbury Epiphany 59-60; R Sudbury St Jas 60-69; R Sudbury St Geo 60-64; R French River St Thos 64-69; Asst Prof RS Laurentian Univ 69-72; R Capreol St Alb 70-77; Chapl Saskatchewan Univ 77-00; Hon Can Saskatoon from 97; Interim I St Jo Cathl 00-01; Hon Asst from 01. *812 Colony Street, Saskatoon SK SN7 0S1, Canada* Tel (001) (306) 664 4628 E-mail clay@sask.usask.ca

CLAY, Canon Elizabeth Jane. b 50. MBE06. Ridley Hall Cam. **dss** 86 **d** 87 **p** 94. Birstall *Wakef* 86-87; Hon Par Dn Lupset 87-90; Par Dn 90-94; C 94-96; Chapl HM Pris and YOI New Hall from 96; Hon Can Wakef Cathl from 00. *The Vicarage, 20A Station Road, Marsden, Huddersfield HD7 6DG* Tel and fax (01484) 847864

CLAY, Geoffrey. b 51. CertEd. Ridley Hall Cam. **d** 86 **p** 87. C Birstall *Wakef* 86-90; V Lupset 90-03; P-in-c Marsden from 03; Min Development Officer from 03. *The Vicarage, 20A Station Road, Marsden, Huddersfield HD7 6DG* Tel and fax (01484) 847864 E-mail geoff@ejclay.demon.co.uk

CLAY, Peter Herbert. b 31. Lich Th Coll 62. **d** 64 **p** 65. C Ross *Heref* 64-67; C Leamington Priors All SS *Cov* 67-70; P-in-c Temple Grafton w Binton 70-73; V 73-75; P-in-c Exhall w Wixford 70-73; R 73-75; TV Cen Telford *Lich* 75-86; USPG 86-90; V Loughb Gd Shep *Leic* 90-96; rtd 96; Perm to Offic *Cov* and *Leic* from 96. *78 Eastlands, Rugby CV21 3RR* Tel (01788) 569138

CLAY, Timothy Francis. b 61. St Mark & St Jo Coll Lon BA85 Ealing Coll of Educn 89. Linc Th Coll 95. **d** 95 **p** 96. C Wickford and Runwell *Chelmsf* 95-98; C S Ockendon 98-01; C S Ockendon and Belhus Park 01-02; P-in-c Ashingdon w S Fambridge from 02; P-in-c Canewdon w Paglesham from 03. *The Rectory, Church Road, Ashingdon SS4 3HY* Tel (01702) 549318
E-mail tim@tclay.fslife.co.uk

CLAYDEN, David Edward. b 42. Oak Hill Th Coll 74. **d** 76 **p** 77. C Worksop St Jo *S'well* 76-79; V Clarborough w Hayton 79-84; C Bloxwich *Lich* 87-90; TV 90-93; TV Tollington *Lon* 93-99; P-in-c Thorndon w Rishangles, Stoke Ash, Thwaite etc *St E* 99-00; P-in-c Thornhams Magna and Parva, Gislingham and Mellis 99-00; R S Hartismere 00-06; rtd 06. *151 Southview Road, Carlton, Nottingham NG4 3QT* Tel 0115-987 2690
E-mail david.clayden@boltblue.com

CLAYDON, Preb Graham Leonard. b 43. K Coll Lon BA65. Clifton Th Coll 66. **d** 68 **p** 69. C Walthamstow St Mary w St Steph *Chelmsf* 68-71; C St Marylebone All So w SS Pet and Jo *Lon* 71-73; Hon C 73-81; Warden All So Clubhouse 71-81; V Islington St Mary 81-99; Dioc Ev (Stepney) and C Highbury Ch Ch w St Jo and St Sav 99-03; TV Hackney Marsh 03-06; Preb

St Paul's Cathl 92-06; rtd 07. *Acre End, Tangmere Road, Tangmere, Chichester PO20 2HW* Tel (01243) 536789
E-mail graham@lclaydon.fsnet.co.uk

CLAYDON, John Richard. b 38. St Jo Coll Cam BA61 MA65. Trin Coll Bris 71. **d** 73 **p** 74. C Finchley Ch Ch *Lon* 73-76; Asst Chapl K Edw Sch Witley 76-77; C Macclesfield St Mich *Ches* 77-81; V Marple All SS 81-91; CMJ Israel 91-99; V Blackb Redeemer 99-02; rtd 02; Perm to Offic *Chelmsf* from 03. *54 Old Forge Road, Layer-de-la-Haye, Colchester CO2 0LH* Tel (01206) 734056 E-mail john@claydon4295.freeserve.co.uk

CLAYTON, Adam. b 78. Keble Coll Ox BA99. Westcott Ho Cam 00. **d** 02 **p** 03. C Far Headingley St Chad *Ripon* 02-06; TV Seacroft 06-08. *47 St James Approach, Leeds LS14 6JJ* Tel 0113-294 0414 Mobile 07834-827294
E-mail revdaclayton@aol.com

CLAYTON, Adam Jonathan Barnett. b 56. **d** 06 **p** 07. OLM Icknield *Ox* from 06. *5 Watlington Road, Shirburn, Watlington OX49 5DR* Tel (01491) 612210 E-mail adam@ajbc.fsnet.co.uk

CLAYTON, Canon Anthony Edwin Hay. b 36. Sarum Th Coll 61. **d** 63 **p** 64. C Tooting All SS *S'wark* 63-68; Perm to Offic *Leic* 69-74; Perm to Offic *S'well* 73-80; Hon C Lockington w Hemington *Leic* 74-80; P-in-c Eastwell 80-83; P-in-c Eaton 80-83; P-in-c Croxton Kerrial, Knipton, Harston, Branston etc 83-84; R 84-93; R High Framland Par 93-96; RD Framland 90-94; Hon Can Leic Cathl 92-96; rtd 97; Perm to Offic *Leic* 97-00. *18 Commerce Square, Nottingham NG1 1HS* Tel and fax 0115-988 1920

CLAYTON, Geoffrey Buckroyd. b 26. Newc Univ BA67. Roch Th Coll 62. **d** 64 **p** 65. C Newc St Geo 64-67; C Byker St Ant 67-68; Chapl Salonika *Eur* 68-69; C Cheddleton *Lich* 69-72; V Arbory *S & M* 72-97; RD Castletown 82-97; V Santan 88-97; rtd 97; Perm to Offic *St D* from 97. *Y Rheithordy, Llangeitho, Tregaron SY25 6TR* Tel (01974) 821388

CLAYTON, Canon John. b 11. Leeds Univ BA33 MA43. Wells Th Coll 34. **d** 35 **p** 36. C Dewsbury Moor *Wakef* 35-38; C Halifax St Jo Bapt 38-41; Lect 40-41; V Lupset 41-51; Chapl Snapethorpe Hosp 49-51; V Bolton St Jas *Bradf* 51-65; RD Calverley 56-65; V Otley 65-76; RD Otley 68-73; Hon Can Bradf Cathl 63-76; rtd 76; Perm to Offic *Bradf* and *Ripon* from 76. *10 Sandy Walk, Bramhope, Leeds LS16 9DW* Tel 0113-261 1388

CLAYTON, Melanie Yvonne. b 62. St Aid Coll Dur BA84 Victoria Univ (BC) MA85 Hertf Coll Ox DPhil89. WMMTC 91. **d** 94 **p** 95. C Penn *Lich* 94-97; TV Wolverhampton 97-98; TV Cen Wolverhampton from 98. *St Chad's Vicarage, Manlove Street, Wolverhampton WV3 0HG* Tel (01902) 426580
E-mail snap1@tinyworld.co.uk

CLAYTON, Norman James. b 24. AKC52. **d** 53 **p** 54. C Long Benton St Mary *Newc* 53-55; R Lomagundi S Rhodesia 55-60; Chapl St Geo Home Johannesburg 60-78; Dioc Communications Officer *Derby* 78-88; P-in-c Risley 78-87; R 87-89; rtd 89; Perm to Offic *Derby* and *S'well* 89-06. *Dulverton Hall, Esplanade, Scarborough YO11 2AR* Tel (01723) 340124

CLAYTON, Paul. b 47. Cranmer Hall Dur 03. **d** 04 **p** 05. NSM Elton and Preston-on-Tees and Longnewton *Dur* 04-06; NSM Bishopton w Gt Stainton from 06; NSM Redmarshall from 06; NSM Grindon, Stillington and Wolviston from 06. *144 Darlington Lane, Stockton-on-Tees TS19 0NG* Tel (01642) 607233 E-mail pclayton@tinyonline.co.uk

CLAYTON, Sydney Cecil Leigh. b 38. Pemb Coll Ox BA62 MA65 Lon Univ BD65. Linc Th Coll. **d** 65 **p** 66. C Birch St Jas *Man* 65-68; Lect Bolton Par Ch 68-77; V Denshaw 77-09; rtd 09. *The Vicarage, Huddersfield Road, Denshaw, Oldham OL3 5SB* Tel (01457) 874575

CLAYTON, William Alan. b 32. Liv Univ BSc54 Lon Univ BD60. **d** 63 **p** 64. C Wallasey St Hilary *Ches* 63-67; R Burton Agnes w Harpham *York* 67-69; V Batley St Thos *Wakef* 69-72; Lic to Offic *Ripon* 73-85; Hon C Grinton 75-85; R Barningham w Hutton Magna and Wycliffe 85-97; rtd 97; Perm to Offic *Newc* from 00. *Halidon View, 1 The Pastures, Tweedmouth, Berwick-upon-Tweed TD15 2NT*

CLEALL-HILL, Malcolm John. b 51. Salford Univ Man Metrop Univ. **d** 01 **p** 02. OLM Chorlton-cum-Hardy St Werburgh *Man* from 01. *62 Buckingham Road, Chorlton cum Hardy, Manchester M21 0RP* Tel 0161-881 7024 *or* 247 2288
E-mail m.cleall-hill@mmu.ac.uk

CLEATON, John. b 39. Open Univ BA86. S Dios Minl Tr Scheme 89. **d** 92 **p** 93. NSM Wareham *Sarum* 92-02. *1 Avon Drive, Wareham BH20 4EL* Tel (01929) 553149

CLEATON, Mrs Nancy. b 45. Lon Bible Coll BD67. WEMTC 05. **d** 07 **p** 08. NSM Church Stretton *Heref* from 07. *39 Swain's Meadow, Church Stretton SY6 6HT* Tel (01694) 723387
E-mail nancy.cleaton@tiscali.co.uk

CLEAVER, Gerald. b 20. Lon Univ BSc52. St Jo Coll Nottm 85. **d** 86 **p** 87. NSM W Bridgford *S'well* 86-96; NSM Clifton 96-02; rtd 02; Perm to Offic *S'well* from 02. *62 South Road, West Bridgford, Nottingham NG2 7AH* Tel 0115-914 3558
E-mail gerald.cleaver@ntlworld.com

CLEAVER, Gordon Philip. b 29. SW Minl Tr Course. **d** 78 **p** 79. NSM St Ruan w St Grade *Truro* 78-86; Perm to Offic from 86.

Bryn-Mor, Cadgwith, Ruan Minor, Helston TR12 7JZ Tel (01326) 290328

CLEAVER, John Martin. b 42. K Coll Lon BD64 AKC64. St Boniface Warminster 61. **d** 65 **p** 66. C Bexley St Mary *Roch* 65-69; C Ealing St Steph Castle Hill *Lon* 69-71; P-in-c Bostall Heath *Roch* 71-76; V Green Street Green 76-85; Primary Adv Lon Dioc Bd for Schs 85-92; V Teddington St Mary w St Alb 92-08; rtd 08. *5 Oaklands, Westham, Pevensey BN24 5AW* Tel (01323) 769964 E-mail jm.cleaver@amserve.net

CLEAVER, Stuart Douglas. b 46. ACIS. Oak Hill Th Coll. **d** 83 **p** 84. C Portsdown *Portsm* 83-86; C Blendworth w Chalton w Idsworth etc 86-88; P-in-c Whippingham w E Cowes 88-98; R 98-01; rtd 01. *The Crest, Soake Road, Waterlooville PO7 6HY* Tel (023) 9226 2277

CLEEVE, Admire William. b 43. Ox Univ MTh96 ACIS78 MBIM81. Sierra Leone Th Hall 78. **d** 82 **p** 83. Sierra Leone 82-86; NSM Douglas St Geo and St Barn *S & M* 87-91; TV Langley Marish *Ox* 91-97; P-in-c Tilehurst St Mary 97-02; rtd 02. *5346 Bressler Drive, Hilliard OH 43026-9401, USA* Tel (001) (614) 219 8407

CLEEVE, Martin. b 43. Bp Otter Coll TCert65 ACP67 Open Univ BA80. Oak Hill Th Coll 69. **d** 72 **p** 73. C Margate H Trin *Cant* 72-76; V Southminster *Chelmsf* 76-86; Teacher Castle View Sch Canvey Is 86-91; Hd RE Bromfords Sch Wickford 91-94; Hd RE Deanes Sch Thundersley 94-98; P-in-c St Mongeham w Ripple and Sutton by Dover *Cant* 99-04; rtd 04; Perm to Offic *Cant* from 04; Chapl Kent & Medway NHS and Soc Care Partnership Trust from 08. *Euphony, Waldershare Road, Ashley, Dover CT15 5JA* E-mail martincleeve@mcleeve.freeserve.co.uk

CLEEVES, David John. b 56. Univ of Wales (Lamp) BA Fitzw Coll Cam MA85. Westcott Ho Cam. **d** 82 **p** 83. C Cuddington *Guildf* 82-85; C Dorking w Ranmore 85-87; V Ewell St Fran 87-94; P-in-c Rotherfield w Mark Cross *Chich* 94-01; V Masham and Healey *Ripon* from 01; Jt AD Ripon 04-05; AD from 05. *The Vicarage, Rodney Terrace, Masham, Ripon HG4 4JA* Tel (01765) 689255 E-mail cleevesmasham@onetel.com

CLEGG, Anthony. *See* CLEGG, Canon John Anthony Holroyd

CLEGG, Herbert. b 24. Fitzw Ho Cam BA59 MA63 Bris Univ MA65. Sarum Th Coll 52. **d** 54 **p** 55. C Street *B & W* 54-56; Perm to Offic *Ely* 56-59; Tutor St Pet Th Coll Jamaica 59-61; R Newington Bagpath w Kingscote and Ozleworth *Glouc* 61-65; Prin Bp Willis Coll Uganda 65-69; P-in-c Aldsworth *Glouc* 70-75; P-in-c Sherborne w Windrush 70-75; V Marcham w Garford *Ox* 75-83; R Chipping Warden w Edgcote and Aston le Walls *Pet* 83-89; rtd 89. *C Ox St Giles and SS Phil and Jas w St Marg 90-94. 3 Case Gardens, Seaton EX12 2AP* Tel (01297) 23103

CLEGG, Jeffrey Thomas. *See* MIDDLEMISS, Jeffrey Thomas

CLEGG, Canon John Anthony Holroyd. b 44. Kelham Th Coll 65. **d** 70 **p** 71. C Heyhouses on Sea *Blackb* 70-74; C Lancaster St Mary 74-76; V Lower Darwen St Jas 76-80; TV Staxton *Sarum* 80-86; Chapl HM Youth Cust Cen Guys Marsh 80-86; R Poulton-le-Sands w Morecambe St Laur *Blackb* 86-97; RD Lancaster 89-94; TR Cartmel Peninsula *Carl* 97-04; RD Windermere 01-09; P-in-c Appleby 04-08; P-in-c Ormside 04-08; TR Heart of Eden 08-09; RD Appleby 04-09; Hon Can Carl Cathl 01-09; rtd 09. *33 Mayfield Road, Holme, Carnforth LA6 1PT CA16 6QW*
E-mail anthonyclegg@talktalk.net

CLEGG, John Lovell. b 48. Qu Coll Ox DA70 MA74. Trin Coll Bris. **d** 75 **p** 76. C Barrow St Mark *Carl* 75-79; R S Levenshulme *Man* 79-98; P-in-c Blackley St Paul from 98. *St Paul's Rectory, Erskine Road, Manchester M9 6RB* Tel 0161-740 1518

CLEGG, Patricia Ann. b 45. STETS 96. **d** 99 **p** 00. NSM Harnham *Sarum* 99-03; Perm to Offic 03-05; NSM Bemerton 05-07; NSM Arle Valley *Win* from 07. *24 Arle Close, Alresford SO24 9BG* Tel (01962) 736566
E-mail pat@wfarm.fsnet.co.uk

CLEGG, Peter Douglas. b 49. Sarum & Wells Th Coll 83. **d** 85 **p** 86. C Hangleton *Chich* 85-88; C-in-c Portslade Gd Shep CD 88-94; V Portslade Gd Shep from 94. *The Vicarage, 35 Stanley Avenue, Portslade, Brighton BN41 2WH* Tel (01273) 419518

CLEGG, Roger Alan. b 46. St Jo Coll Dur BA68 Nottm Univ CertEd69. St Jo Coll Nottm 75. **d** 78 **p** 79. C Harwood *Man* 78-81; TV Sutton St Jas and Wawne *York* 81-87; V Kirk Fenton w Kirkby Wharfe and Ulleskelfe 87-09; OCF from 87; Chapl HM Pris Askham Grange from 95. *HM Prison Askham Grange, Askham Richard, York YO23 3FT* Tel (01904) 772000
E-mail rogclegg@dunelm.org.uk

CLELAND, Miss Lucy Eleanor. b 74. Aston Univ BSc97 Anglia Poly Univ BTh05. Ridley Hall Cam 02. **d** 05 **p** 06. C Yaxley and Holme w Conington *Ely* 05-08; P-in-c Landbeach from 08; P-in-c Waterbeach from 08. *The Vicarage, 8 Chapel Street, Waterbeach, Cambridge CB25 9HR* Tel (01223) 440501 Mobile 07986-685792 E-mail lecleland@hotmail.com

CLELAND, Richard. b 26. Belf Coll of Tech MPS47. St Aid Birkenhead 58. **d** 60 **p** 61. C Lisburn Ch Ch *Conn* 60-63; C Ballynafeigh St Jude *D & D* 63-66; C Portman Square St Paul

Lon 66-67; V Ilkley All SS *Bradf* 67-83; Master Wyggeston's Hosp Leic 83-97; rtd 97; Perm to Offic *S'well* 97-02. *23 Stuart Court, High Street, Kibworth, Leicester LE8 0LR* Tel 0116-279 6245

CLELAND, Trevor. b 66. QUB BTh94 TCD MPhil97. CITC 94. **d** 96 **p** 97. C Lisburn Ch Ch *Conn* 96-99; C Carrickfergus 99-03; I Belfast Upper Falls from 03. *31 Dunmurry Lane, Belfast BT17 9RP* Tel (028) 9062 2400

CLEMAS, Nigel Antony. b 53. Wycliffe Hall Ox. **d** 83 **p** 84. C Bootle St Mary w St Paul *Liv* 83-87; V Kirkdale St Mary and St Athanasius 87-91; TV Netherthorpe *Sheff* 91-93; V Netherthorpe St Steph 93-98; R Chapel Chorlton, Maer and Whitmore *Lich* from 98; RD Eccleshall from 00. *The Rectory, Snape Hall Road, Whitmore, Newcastle ST5 5HS* Tel (01782) 680258 E-mail nclemas@hotmail.com

CLEMENCE, Paul Robert Fraser. b 50. St Edm Hall Ox MA90 MRTPI82. Wycliffe Hall Ox 88. **d** 90 **p** 91. C Lancaster St Mary *Blackb* 90-94; Chapl HM Pris Lanc Castle 90-94; V Lt Thornton *Blackb* from 94; AD Poulton 00-09. *St John's Vicarage, 35 Station Road, Thornton-Cleveleys FY5 5HY* Tel and fax (01253) 825107 E-mail p.clemence@tiscali.co.uk

CLEMENT, Miss Barbara Winifred. b 20. Gilmore Ho 49. **dss** 56 **d** 87. Frimley Green *Guildf* 53-66; Hd Dss 66-74; Dioc Adv Lay Min 74-82; Frimley 74-82; Frimley Hosp 74-87; rtd 82; Perm to Offic *Guildf* 82-99 and from 01. *9 Merlin Court, The Cloisters, Frimley, Camberley GU16 5JN* Tel (01276) 22527

CLEMENT, Geoffrey Paul. b 69. **d** 94 **p** 96. Jardines del Hipódromo St Aug Uruguay 94-96; Colon St Jas Miss 95-97; Barrio Fátima Salto St Luke w H Spirit 97-01; TV Wilford Peninsula *St E* 01-07; R Holbrook, Stutton, Freston, Woolverstone etc from 07. *The Rectory, 15 Denmark Gardens, Holbrook, Ipswich IP9 2BG* Tel (01473) 327141 Mobile 07766-601011 E-mail revgclement@btinternet.com

CLEMENT, Paskal. b 63. Punjab Univ BA92 Univ of Wales MA08. Nat Catholic Inst of Th Karachi 82. **d** 88 **p** 88. Pakistan 88-01; NSM Hounslow H Trin w St Paul *Lon* 04-08; C Oadby *Leic* from 08. *62 Fairstone Hill, Oadby, Leicester LE2 5RJ* Tel 0116-271 6474 Mobile 07727-286905
E-mail paskalm@yahoo.com

CLEMENT, Peter James. b 64. UMIST BSc88 Man Univ MA98. Qu Coll Birm 89. **d** 92 **p** 93. C Grange St Andr *Ches* 92-95; C Man Apostles w Miles Platting 95-97; TV Uggeshall w Sotherton, Wangford and Henham *St E* 97-99; TV Sole Bay 99-00; Dioc Youth Officer 01-02; V Fairweather Green *Bradf* 02-07; Assoc Dioc Dir of Ords 04-07; Dioc Dir of Ords *Ripon* from 07; C Ripon Cathl from 07. *16 Orchard Close, Sharow, Ripon HG4 5BE* Tel (01765) 607017

CLEMENT, Richard Percy. b 63. Bris Univ BA85. ERMC 04. **d** 06 **p** 08. C Framlingham w Saxtead *St E* 06-09; Chapl RAF from 09. *Chaplaincy Services, Valiant Block, HQ Air Command, RAF High Wycombe HP14 4UE* Tel (01494) 496800 Fax 496343 E-mail revd.richard@btinternet.com

CLEMENT, Thomas Gwyn. b 51. Lon Univ BMus73 Goldsmiths' Coll Lon PGCE74 LRAM73 LTCL74. St Steph Ho Ox. **d** 93 **p** 94. C Friern Barnet St Jas *Lon* 93-96; V Edmonton St Alphege 96-04; P-in-c Ponders End St Matt 02-04; AD Enfield 01-04; V Hendon St Mary and Ch Ch from 04; Warden of Readers Edmonton Area from 08. *The Vicarage, 34 Parson Street, London NW4 1QR* Tel (020) 8203 2884
E-mail fr.gwyn@btinternet.com

CLEMENT, Canon Timothy Gordon. b 54. Trin Coll Bris 92. **d** 94 **p** 95. C Chepstow *Mon* 94-97; R Bettws Newydd w Trostrey etc from 97; Rural Min Adv from 02; AD Raglan-Usk from 05; Can St Woolos Cathl from 08. *The Rectory, Bettws Newydd, Usk NP15 1JN* Tel (01873) 880258

CLEMENTS, Alan Austin. b 39. Newc Univ MA93 ACIB66 FCIE05. Linc Th Coll 74. **d** 76 **p** 77. C Woodley St Jo the Ev *Ox* 76-79; C Wokingham All SS 79-83; V Felton *Newc* 83-95; P-in-c Wallsend St Pet 95-01; rtd 01; Perm to Offic *Newc* 01-06; *Blackb* from 07; *Man* from 09. *15 Carleton Road, Chorley PR6 8TQ* Tel and fax (01257) 271782 E-mail fr_alan@btinternet.com

CLEMENTS, Andrew. b 48. K Coll Lon BD72 AKC72 Leeds Univ MA02. St Aug Coll Cant 72. **d** 73 **p** 74. C Langley All SS and Martyrs *Man* 73-76; C Westhoughton 76-81; R Thornton Dale w Ellerburne and Wilton *York* 81-89; Prec Leic Cathl 89-91; V Market Weighton *York* 91-97; R Goodmanham 91-97; V Osbaldwick w Murton from 97. *The Vicarage, 80 Osbaldwick Lane, York YO10 3AX* Tel (01904) 416763
E-mail andrew@ozmurt.freeserve.co.uk

CLEMENTS, Miss Christine Hilda. b 49. Ex Univ BTh04. SWMTC 99. **d** 02 **p** 03. C Halsetown *Truro* 02-05; Zambia 05-07; Perm to Offic *Nor* 07; TR Thamesmead *S'wark* from 07. *Thamesmead Rectory, 22 Manor Close, London SE28 8FY* Tel (020) 8312 0731 Mobile 07852-476805

CLEMENTS, Canon Doris Thomasina Sara. b 46. TCD BA68 MA90. CITC 92. **d** 95 **p** 96. NSM Killala w Dunfeeny, Crossmolina, Kilmoremoy etc *T, K & A* from 95; Can Achonry Cathl from 05. *Doobeg House, Bunninadden, Ballymote, Co Sligo,*

Republic of Ireland Tel (00353) (71) 918 5425 Fax 918 5255 Mobile 86-249 7806 E-mail dorisc.ias@eircom.net *or* dcolhoun@gofree.indigo.ie

CLEMENTS, Canon Edwin George. b 41. Chich Th Coll 77. **d** 79 **p** 80. C Didcot St Pet *Ox* 79-83; C Brixham w Churston Ferrers *Ex* 83; TV 84-86; TV Brixham w Churston Ferrers and Kingswear 86-88; P-in-c Hagbourne *Ox* 88; V 88-90; P-in-c Blewbury 89-90; P-in-c Upton 89-90; R Blewbury, Hagbourne and Upton 90-06; P-in-c S w N Moreton, Aston Tirrold and Aston Upthorpe 05-06; R The Churn 06-07; AD Wallingford 99-07; Hon Can Ch Ch 07; rtd 07; Hon C Uffington, Shellingford, Woolstone and Baulking *Ox* 07-09; Hon C Shrivenham and Ashbury from 09. *St Mary's House, Chapel Lane, Ashbury, Swindon SN6 8LS* Tel (01793) 710811 Mobile 07703-342950 E-mail revedwin@btinternet.com

CLEMENTS, Miss Mary Holmes. b 43. Bedf Coll Lon BA64 Lon Inst of Educn PGCE69. Ox Min Course 92. **d** 94 **p** 95. NSM High Wycombe *Ox* 94-01; C N Petherton w Northmoor Green *B & W* 01-03; C N Newton w St Michaelchurch, Thurloxton etc 01-03; C Alfred Jewel from 03. *8 Alder Close, North Petherton, Bridgwater TA6 6TT* Tel (01278) 662905 E-mail mary@holmesclements.freeserve.co.uk

CLEMENTS, Philip Christian. b 38. K Coll Lon BD64 AKC64. **d** 65 **p** 66. C S Norwood St Mark *Cant* 65-68; Chapl R Russell Sch Croydon 68-75; Asst Chapl Denstone Coll Uttoxeter 75-76; Chapl 76-81; Chapl Lancing Coll 82-90; R Ninfield *Chich* 90-99; V Hooe 90-99; rtd 99; Perm to Offic *Cant* from 95; Chapl St Bart Hosp Sandwich from 04. *21 Swaynes Way, Eastry, Sandwich CT13 0JP* Tel (01304) 617413 *or* 613982 E-mail philip@clements3739.freeserve.co.uk

CLEMENTS, Philip John Charles. b 42. Nottm Univ CertEd64. Ridley Hall Cam. **d** 85 **p** 86. C Aylestone St Andr w St Jas *Leic* 85-87; P-in-c Swinford w Catthorpe, Shawell and Stanford 87-91; V 91-99; Dioc Rural Officer 91-96; RD Guthlaxton II 94-99; P-in-c N w S Kilworth and Misterton 96-99; P-in-c Barrowden and Wakerley w S Luffenham *Pet* 99-02; R Barrowden and Wakerley w S Luffenham etc 03-06; RD Barnack 00-06; rtd 06; Perm to Offic *Pet* from 06. *Clementine Cottage, 51 Laughton Road, Lubenham, Market Harborough LE16 9TE* Tel and fax (01858) 432548 E-mail pipclements2@tiscali.co.uk

CLEMENTS, Canon Roy Adrian. b 44. St Chad's Coll Dur BA68 MA74. **d** 69 **p** 70. C Royston *Wakef* 69-73; V Clifton 73-77; V Rastrick St Matt 77-84; Dioc Communications Officer 84-98; V Horbury Junction 84-92; Bp's Chapl 92-00; V Battyeford 00-08; Hon Can Wakef Cathl 94-08; rtd 08; Perm to Offic *Wakef* from 08. *12 Castle Crescent, Sandal, Wakefield WF2 7HX* Tel (01924) 251834 E-mail royaclements@tiscali.co.uk

CLEMETT, Peter Thomas. b 33. Univ of Wales (Lamp) BA60. Sarum Th Coll 59. **d** 61 **p** 62. C Tredegar St Geo *Mon* 61-63; Chapl St Woolos Cathl 63-66; CF 66-99; Chapl R Memorial Chpl Sandhurst 84-88; rtd 88; OCF from 99. *Silver Birches, Gardeners Lane, East Wellow, Romsey SO51 6AD* Tel (023) 8081 4261

CLEMOW (née WINDER), Cynthia Frances. b 48. SWMTC 02. **d** 05 **p** 06. NSM Bodmin w Lanhydrock and Lanivet *Truro* from 05. *Denton, 2 Boxwell Park, Bodmin PL31 2BB* Tel (01208) 73306

CLENCH, Brian Henry Ross. b 31. Ripon Coll Cuddesdon. **d** 82 **p** 83. C Fulham All SS *Lon* 82-85; Ind Chapl *Truro* 85-92; P-in-c St Mewan 85-92; rtd 92; Perm to Offic *Sarum* from 96. *Tamworth Barn, Hampton Lane, Whitford, Axminster EX13 7NJ*

CLEPHANE, Alexander Honeyman. b 48. **d** 97 **p** 98. OLM Flixton St Mich *Man* from 97. *306 Church Road, Urmston, Manchester M41 6JJ* Tel 0161-747 8816 Mobile 07798-613291

CLEUGH, David Robert. b 80. New Coll Ox BA07. Ripon Coll Cuddesdon BTh09. **d** 09. C Dorchester *Ox* from 09. *26 Windrush Road, Berinsfield, Wallingford OX10 7PF* E-mail yellow3927@yahoo.co.uk

CLEUGH, Hannah Felicity. b 81. Worc Coll Ox MA08 MSt04 DPhil07. Ripon Coll Cuddesdon 07. **d** 09. C Dorchester *Ox* from 09. *26 Windrush Road, Berinsfield, Wallingford OX10 7PF* E-mail hannah.cleugh@theology.ox.ac.uk

CLEVELAND, Mrs Lorna Christina (Dickie). b 39. State Univ NY BSc60. SEITE 99. **d** 02 **p** 03. NSM Wye w Brook and Hastingleigh etc *Cant* from 02; NSM Mersham w Hinxhill and Sellindge from 08. *2 Church Street, Wye, Ashford TN25 5BJ* Tel (01233) 813051 E-mail dickie@clevelp.freeserve.co.uk

CLEVELAND, Michael Robin. b 64. Warwick Univ BA73. St Jo Coll Nottm 86 Serampore Th Coll BD88. **d** 88 **p** 89. C Bushbury *Lich* 88-92; V Foleshill St Laur *Cov* from 92. *St Laurence's Vicarage, 142 Old Church Road, Coventry CV6 7ED* Tel (024) 7668 8271

CLEVELAND, Archdeacon of. *See* FERGUSON, The Ven Paul John

CLEVERLEY, Michael Frank. b 36. Man Univ BScTech57. Wells Th Coll 61. **d** 63 **p** 64. C Halifax St Aug *Wakef* 63; C Huddersfield St Jo 63-66; C Brighouse 66-69; V Gomersal 69-83; P-in-c Clayton W w High Hoyland 83-89; P-in-c Scissett St Aug 83-89; R High Hoyland, Scissett and Clayton W 89-96; rtd 96;

NSM Leathley w Farnley, Fewston and Blubberhouses *Bradf* 96-08; NSM Washburn and Mid-Wharfe from 08. *86 Riverside Park, Otley LS21 2RW* E-mail michael.cleverley@bradford.anglican.org

CLEVERLY, Charles St George. b 51. St Jo Coll Ox MA75 Goldsmiths' Coll Lon PGCE76. Trin Coll Bris 79. **d** 82 **p** 83. C Cranham Park *Chelmsf* 82-89; V 89-92; Crosslinks Paris 92-02; R Ox St Aldate from 02. *Holy Trinity House, 19 Turn Again Lane, Oxford OX1 1QL* Tel (01865) 244713 Fax 201543 E-mail charlie.cleverly@staldates.org.uk

CLEWS, Nicholas. b 57. SS Coll Cam BA80 MA84 Leeds Univ BA87 CIPFA85. Coll of Resurr Mirfield 85. **d** 88 **p** 89. C S Elmsall *Wakef* 88-91; V Featherstone 91-97; P-in-c Purston cum S Featherstone 04-07; P-in-c Thornbury *Bradf* from 07; P-in-c Woodhall from 07. *St James's Vicarage, Galloway Lane, Pudsey LS28 8JR* Tel (01274) 662735 E-mail clewsclan@dsl.pipex.com

CLIFF, Frank Graham. b 38. St Paul's Cheltenham TCert60. Clifton Th Coll 63. **d** 66 **p** 67. C Leic St Chris 66-69; C Whitton and Thurleston w Akenham *St E* 69-71; USA from 71; Asst R Houston St Thos 71-72; Asst R Waco St Alb 72-74; Asst R Potomac St Jas 74-78; R Denton Ch Ch 78-85; V Pittsburgh St Phil 86-87; R Pittsburgh Advent Ch 87-94; R Honesdale Grace Ch 94-03. *15 Bede Circle, Honesdale PA 18431-7625, USA* Tel (001) (570) 253 4535 E-mail cliffam@ptd.net

CLIFF, Julian Arnold. b 41. Univ Coll Ches BEd86. Cranmer Hall Dur 63. **d** 66 **p** 67. C Bowdon *Ches* 66-69; C Poynton 69-73; P-in-c Crewe St Barn 73-74; V 74-79; Hon C Higher Bebington 98-00; Perm to Offic from 06. *15 Sandy Lane, Heswall, Wirral CH60 5SX* Tel 0151-342 3230 Mobile 07980-379699 E-mail julianann.cliff@talktalk.net

CLIFFE, Canon Christopher George. b 47. CITC 94. **d** 97 **p** 98. C Fiddown w Clonegam, Guilcagh and Kilmeaden *C & O* 97-00; I from 00; Bp's Dom Chapl from 97; Can Ossory Cathl from 07. *The Rectory, Piltown, Co Kilkenny, Republic of Ireland* Tel (00353) (51) 643275 Mobile 87-236 8682 E-mail fiddown@lismore.anglican.org *or* cgc2@eircom.net

CLIFFORD, Erin. b 77. **d** 08 **p** 09. C Ches Square St Mich w St Phil *Lon* from 08. *24 Sullivan Road, London SE11 4UH*

CLIFFORD, Raymond Augustine. b 45. Coll of Resurr Mirfield 91. **d** 93 **p** 94. C Saltdean *Chich* 93-96. *124 Arnold Estate, Druid Street, London SE1 2DT* Tel (020) 7232 2439

CLIFFORD, Miss Susan Frances. b 58. Qu Univ Kingston Ontario BA87. Westcott Ho Cam 02. **d** 04 **p** 05. C Winchmore Hill St Paul *Lon* 04-08; Canada from 08. *54 Kinsman Crescent, Arnprior ON K7S 1V6, Canada* E-mail susanclif@hotmail.com

CLIFTON, Canon Robert Walter. b 39. Solicitor. Westcott Ho Cam 82. **d** 84 **p** 85. C Bury St Edmunds St Geo *St E* 84-87; P-in-c Culford, W Stow and Wordwell 87-88; R Culford, W Stow and Wordwell w Flempton etc 88-95; P-in-c Fornham All SS and Fornham St Martin w Timworth 93-95; RD Thingoe 93-95; P-in-c Orford w Sudbourne, Chillesford, Butley and Iken 95-00; P-in-c Eyke w Bromeswell, Rendlesham, Tunstall etc 98-99; TR Wilford Peninsula 00-05; RD Woodbridge 96-04; Hon Can St E Cathl 00-05; rtd 05; Perm to Offic *Nor* and *St E* from 05. *12 Stan Petersen Close, Norwich NR1 4QJ* Tel (01603) 631758 Mobile 07713-237754

CLIFTON, Canon Roger Gerald. b 45. ACA70 FCA. Sarum & Wells Th Coll 70. **d** 73 **p** 74. C Winterbourne *Bris* 73-76; P-in-c Brislington St Cuth 76-83; P-in-c Colerne w N Wraxall 83-95; RD Chippenham 88-94; Hon Can Bris Cathl from 94; TR Gtr Corsham 95-01; TR Gtr Corsham and Lacock from 01. *The Rectory, Newlands Road, Corsham SN13 0BS* Tel and fax (01249) 713232 E-mail rogerclifton@btopenworld.com

CLIFTON, Sharon. b 66. **d** 07 **p** 08. C St Illogan *Truro* from 07. *Church House, 46 Bosmeor Park, Redruth TR15 3JN* Tel (01209) 218753

CLIFTON-SMITH, Gregory James. b 52. GGSM73 Lon Univ TCert74 Goldsmiths' Coll Lon BMus82. Sarum & Wells Th Coll 87. **d** 89 **p** 90. C Welling *S'wark* 89-93; V Tattenham Corner and Burgh Heath *Guildf* 93-97; Asst Chapl R Berks and Battle Hosps NHS Trust 97-99; Chapl Isle of Wight NHS Primary Care Trust from 99. *The Chaplaincy, St Mary's Hospital, Parkhurst Road, Newport PO30 5TG* Tel (01983) 534639 *or* 856781 Mobile 07790-089981 E-mail gregory.clifton-smith@iow.nhs.uk

CLINCH, Christopher James. b 60. Nottm Univ BEd82 BTh89. Linc Th Coll 86. **d** 89 **p** 90. C Newc St Geo 89-92; C Seaton Hirst 92-94; TV Ch the King 94-00; V Newc St Fran 00-09; Chapl K Sch Tynemouth from 09. *The King's School, Huntingdon Place, North Shields NE30 4RF* Tel 0191-258 5995 E-mail ccne12747@blueyonder.co.uk

CLINCH, Kenneth Wilfred. b 22. Bps' Coll Cheshunt 62. **d** 64 **p** 65. C Old Shoreham *Chich* 64-67; C Lancing St Mich 67-73; R Upper St Leonards St Jo 73-88; rtd 88; Perm to Offic *Chich* from 88. *7 The Leas, Essenden Road, St Leonards-on-Sea TN38 0PU* Tel and fax (01424) 438286 E-mail ken22@globalnet.co.uk

CLINES, Emma Christine. *See* LOUIS, Ms Emma Christine

CLINES, Jeremy Mark Sebastian. b 68. Cranmer Hall Dur. **d** 97 **p** 98. C Birm St Martin w Bordesley St Andr 97-99; Chapl York

St Jo Univ from 99. *York St John College, Lord Mayor's Walk, York YO31 7EX* Tel (01904) 716606 Fax 612512
E-mail j.clines@yorksj.ac.uk

CLITHEROW, Canon Andrew. b 50. St Chad's Coll Dur BA72 Ex Univ MPhil87. Sarum & Wells Th Coll 78. **d** 79 **p** 80. Hon C Bedford Ch Ch *St Alb* 79-84; Asst Chapl Bedford Sch 79-84; Chapl Caldicott Sch Farnham Royal 84-85; C Penkridge w Stretton *Lich* 85-88; Min Acton Trussell w Bednall 85-88; Chapl Rossall Sch Fleetwood 89-94; V Scotforth *Blackb* 94-00; Dioc Dir of Tr and Can Res Blackb Cathl 00-07; Hon Can from 07; P-in-c Lytham St Cuth from 08; P-in-c Lytham St Jo from 08; Chapl to The Queen from 08. *The Vicarage, Church Road, Lytham, Lytham St Annes FY8 5PX* Tel (01253) 736168
E-mail clitherow814@btinternet.com

CLOAKE, David Michael. b 72. Ripon Coll Cuddesdon 07. **d** 08 **p** 09. C Aylesbury w Bierton and Hulcott *Ox* from 08. *4 Cubb Field, Aylesbury HP19 7SH* Tel (01296) 582331 Mobile 07934-417897 E-mail fatherdavid@ntlworld.com

CLOCKSIN (née HOYLE), Mrs Pamela Margaret. b 61. Nottm Univ BA82. St Jo Coll Nottm 84. **d** 87 **p** 94. Par Dn Bulwell St Jo *S'well* 87-91; Cam Pastorate Chapl 91-95; C Cambridge H Trin *Ely* 91-95; Perm to Offic 95-01. *5 Stansfield Close, Oxford OX3 8TH* Tel (01865) 426022

CLOCKSIN, Prof William Frederick. b 55. BA76 St Cross Coll Ox MA81 Trin Hall Cam MA87 PhD93. EAMTC 91. **d** 94 **p** 95. Asst Chapl Trin Hall Cam 94-01; Acting Dean 00-01. *5 Stansfield Close, Oxford OX3 8TH* Tel (01865) 426022
E-mail wfc@brookes.ac.uk

CLODE, Arthur Raymond Thomas. b 35. Roch Th Coll 67. **d** 69 **p** 70. C Blackheath *Birm* 69-72; V Londonderry 73-75; R Kirkbride *S & M* 75-79; UAE 80-83; Min Stewartly LEP 86-90; C Wootton *St Alb* 86-90; C St Alb St Paul 90-94; rtd 94; Perm to Offic *Glouc* from 01. *60 Albemarle Gate, Cheltenham GL50 4PJ* Tel (01242) 577521

CLOETE, Richard James. b 47. AKC71. St Aug Coll Cant 72. **d** 72 **p** 73. C Redhill St Matt *S'wark* 72-76; V Streatham St Paul 76-84; P-in-c W Coker w Hardington Mandeville, E Chinnock etc *B & W* 84-88; R 88; R Wincanton and Pen Selwood 88-97; Sec and Treas Dioc Hosp Chapl Fellowship 91-97; Perm to Offic *Lon* 97-98 and *Ex* 99-02; C Sampford Peverell, Uplowman, Holcombe Rogus etc *Ex* from 02. *The Retreat, Gravel Walk, Cullompton EX15 1DA* Tel (01884) 38788 Mobile 07855-493868

CLOGHER, Archdeacon of. *See* PRINGLE, The Ven Cecil Thomas

CLOGHER, Bishop of. *See* JACKSON, The Rt Revd Michael Geoffrey St Aubyn

CLOGHER, Dean of. *Vacant*

CLONMACNOISE, Dean of. *See* JONES, The Very Revd Robert William

CLOSE, Brian Eric. b 49. St Chad's Coll Dur BA74 MA76. Ridley Hall Cam 74. **d** 76 **p** 77. C Far Headingley St Chad *Ripon* 76-79; C Harrogate St Wilfrid 79-80; C Harrogate St Wilfrid and St Luke 80-82; P-in-c Alconbury cum Weston 82-83; V 83-86; P-in-c Buckworth 82-83; R 83-86; P-in-c Upton and Copmanford 82-83; Chapl Reed's Sch Cobham 86-96; Chapl Malvern Coll 96-01; Chapl Uppingham Sch 01-04; R Easington, Easington Colliery and S Hetton *Dur* from 04. *The Rectory, 5 Tudor Grange, Easington Village, Peterlee SR8 3DF* Tel 0191-527 0287

CLOSE (née HITCHEN), Mrs Carol Ann. b 47. St Mary's Coll Ban CertEd69 St Martin's Coll Lanc DipEd91 Ches Coll of HE BTh02. NOC 99. **d** 02 **p** 03. NSM Hindley St Pet *Liv* 02-07. *271 Warrington Road, Abram, Wigan WN2 5RQ* Tel (01942) 861670

CLOSE, Mrs Jane. b 48. WMMTC 00. **d** 03 **p** 04. NSM Fillongley and Corley *Cov* 03-06; P-in-c Leam Valley from 06. *The Rectory, Lower Street, Willoughby, Rugby CV23 8BX* Tel (01926) 632455 Mobile 07957-233502
E-mail j-b.close@ntlworld.com

CLOSE, Canon Timothy John. b 68. QUB BA91 Leic Univ MSc95 TCD BTh00. CITC 97. **d** 00 **p** 01. C Glenageary *D & G* 00-03; Dean's V Belf Cathl 03-09; Can Belf Cathl from 07. *The Vicarage, 11 Woodfield, Newtownabbey BT37 0ZH* Tel (028) 9086 0023

CLOSS-PARRY, The Ven Selwyn. b 25. Univ of Wales (Lamp) BA50. St Mich Coll Llan 50. **d** 52 **p** 53. C Dwygyfylchi *Ban* 52-58; V Treuddyn *St As* 58-66; R Llangystennin 66-71; V Holywell 71-77; Can St As Cathl 76-82; Prec 82-84; Preb 82-90; V Colwyn 77-84; Adn St As 84-90; R Trefnant 84-90; rtd 91. *3 Llys Brompton, Brompton Avenue, Rhos-on-Sea LL28 4TB* Tel (01492) 545801

CLOTHIER, Gerald Harry. b 34. Oak Hill Th Coll 75. **d** 78 **p** 79. Hon C Highwood *Chelmsf* 78-79; Hon C Writtle w Highwood 79-83, P-in-c Westhall w Brampton and Stoven *St E* 83-86; TV Beccles St Mich 86-93; R Rougham, Beyton w Hessett and Rushbrooke 93-97; rtd 97; Perm to Offic *Nor* from 97; P-in-c Tenerife Sur *Eur* 01-02. *4 Wiggs Way, Corton, Lowestoft NR32 5JJ* Tel (01502) 733231

CLOUSTON, Eric Nicol. b 63. G&C Coll Cam BA85 MA88 PhD89. Ridley Hall Cam 03. **d** 05 **p** 06. C Chatham St Phil and St Jas *Roch* 05-08; CMS India from 09. *c/o V Duraikan Esq, 29 Aylesford Way, Stapleford, Cambridge CB22 5DP*
E-mail eclouston@btinternet.com

CLOVER, Brendan David. b 58. G&C Coll Cam BA79 MA83 LTCL74. Ripon Coll Cuddesdon 79. **d** 82 **p** 83. C Friern Barnet St Jas *Lon* 82-85; C W Hampstead St Jas 85-87; Chapl Em Coll Cam 87-92; Dean 92-94; P-in-c St Pancras w St Jas and Ch Ch *Lon* 94-99; P-in-c St Pancras H Cross w St Jude and St Pet 96-99; Can Res Bris Cathl 99-06; Sen Provost Woodard Corp from 06. *The Woodard Corporation, High Street, Abbots Bromley, Rugeley WS15 3BW* Tel (01283) 840670 *or* 840120
E-mail brendanclover@woodard.co.uk

CLOW, Laurie Stephen. b 65. Man Univ BA86 MA88. Wycliffe Hall Ox 96. **d** 98 **p** 99. C Trentham *Lich* 98-01; TV Hampreston *Sarum* from 01. *19 Canford Bottom, Wimborne Minster BH21 2HA* Tel (01202) 884796 E-mail w.m.clow@uclan.ac.uk *or* isclow@ccssite.freeserve.co.uk

CLOWES, John. b 45. AKC67. **d** 68 **p** 69. C Corby St Columba *Pet* 68-71; R Itchenstoke w Ovington and Abbotstone *Win* 71-74; V Acton w Gt and Lt Waldingfield *St E* 74-80; Asst Dioc Chr Stewardship Adv 75-80; TV Southend St Jo w St Mark, All SS w St Fran etc *Chelmsf* 80-82; TV Southend 82-85; Ind Chapl 80-85; R Ashwick w Oakhill and Binegar *B & W* 85-91; P-in-c Brompton Regis w Upton and Skilgate 91-97; rtd 98. *The Tythings, Tythings Court, Minehead TA24 5NT* Tel 07808-200619 (mobile)

CLOYNE, Dean of. *See* MARLEY, The Very Revd Alan Gordon

CLUCAS, Anthony John. b 56. Portsm Poly BA77. WMMTC 96. **d** 99 **p** 00. NSM Erdington *Birm* 99-04; NSM Nechells 04-05; P-in-c Shard End from 05. *Apartment 1, 11 York Crescent, Birmingham B34 7NS* Tel 0121-747 3299
E-mail clucas@btinternet.com

CLUCAS, Robert David. b 55. Cranmer Hall Dur. **d** 82 **p** 83. C Gateacre *Liv* 82-86; P-in-c Bishop's Itchington *Cov* 86-93; CPAS Staff 93-98; Freelance Tr GodStuff from 99; Perm to Offic *Cov* from 93. *1 Church Hill, Leamington Spa CV32 5AZ* Tel (01926) 887792 E-mail bob@godstuff.org.uk

CLUER, Donald Gordon. b 21. S'wark Ord Course 61. **d** 64 **p** 65. C Malden St Jas *S'wark* 64-68; C Bexhill St Pet *Chich* 68-73; V Shoreham Beach 73-77; V Heathfield St Rich 77-86; C Eastbourne St Mary 86-90; rtd 90; Perm to Offic *Ox* from 90. *St John's Home, St Mary's Road, Oxford OX4 1QE* Tel (01865) 241658

CLUES, David Charles. b 66. K Coll Lon BD87 Lon Univ PGCE95. St Steph Ho Ox 88. **d** 90 **p** 91. C Notting Hill All SS w St Columb *Lon* 90-94; NSM 94-96; NSM Notting Hill St Mich and Ch Ch 96-98; Asst Chapl HM Pris Wormwood Scrubs 97-98; C Paddington St Mary Magd *Lon* 98-03; C Paddington St Mary 98-03; C Paddington St Sav 98-03; V Willesden St Mary from 03. *St Mary's Vicarage, 18 Neasden Lane, London NW10 2TT* Tel (020) 8459 2167 E-mail transpontem@aol.com *or* stmarywillesden@aol.com

CLUETT, Michael Charles. b 53. Kingston Poly BSc78. St Steph Ho Ox 84. **d** 86 **p** 87. C Pontesbury I and II *Heref* 86-90; TV Wenlock 90-99; P-in-c Canon Pyon w Kings Pyon and Birley 99-04; V Canon Pyon w King's Pyon, Birley and Wellington from 04. *The Vicarage, Brookside, Canon Pyon, Hereford HR4 8NY* Tel (01432) 830802 E-mail mccluett@aol.com

CLUNE, David Julian. b 60. Open Univ BSc03. Wilson Carlile Coll 99 St Jo Coll Nottm LTh07. **d** 07 **p** 08. C Spalding *Linc* from 07. *The Chantry, 7 Church Street, Spalding PE11 2PB*
E-mail david@clune.org.uk

CLUNIE, Grace. b 60. Ulster Univ BA82 MA91. CITC BTh95. **d** 95 **p** 96. C Newtownards *D & D* 95-99; C Seagoe 99-01; I Belfast St Nic *Conn* 01-07; Dir Celtic Spirituality Arm Cathl from 07; Dom Chapl to Abp Arm from 09. *The Garden House, 23 Drumilly Road, Armagh BT61 8RG* Tel (028) 3887 0667
E-mail gclunie@gmail.com

CLUTTERBUCK, Herbert Ivan. b 16. Ch Coll Cam BA38 MA42. Chich Th Coll 38. **d** 39 **p** 40. C Lamorbey H Trin *Roch* 39-41; Hon CF 41-44; Chapl and Sen Classics Master Wellingborough Sch 44-47; Chapl RN 47-62; V Lanteglos by Fowey *Truro* 62-66; Org Sec Ch Union 66-74; Chapl Qu Marg Sch Escrick Park 74-76; Chapl and Dir Relig Studies Roedean Sch Brighton 76-81; rtd 82; Master St Jo Hosp Lich 82-91; Perm to Offic *Truro* 99-05 and *Roch* 00-05. *The College of St Barnabas, Blackberry Lane, Lingfield RH7 6NJ* Tel (01342) 872827

CLUTTERBUCK, Miss Marion Isobel. b 56. Oak Hill Th Coll BA91. **d** 94 **p** 95. C Lindfield *Chich* 92-96; TV Alderbury Team *Sarum* 96-01; TV Clarendon 01-05. *3 Hillside Close, West Dean, Salisbury SP5 1EX* Tel (01794) 342377
E-mail marion@mclutterbuck.fsnet.co.uk

CLUTTON, Mrs Barbara Carol. b 47. WMMTC 00. **d** 04 **p** 05. NSM Bourton w Frankton and Stretton on Dunsmore etc *Cov* from 04; P-in-c from 08; Rural Life Officer from 07. *Grange*

Farm, Sawbridge Road, Grandborough, Rugby CV23 8DN Tel (01788) 810372 Fax 521239 Mobile 07808-137550 E-mail barbaraclutton@gilberthouse.co.uk

CLYDE, John. b 39. Univ of Wales (Lamp) MA99 Greenwich Univ PhD. CITC. d 71 p 72. C Belfast St Aid *Conn* 71-74; I Belfast St Barn 74-80; I Belfast H Trin 80-89; Bp's C Acton and Drumbanagher *Arm* 89-94; I Desertlyn w Ballyeglish 94-02; rtd 02. *25 Castleoak, Castledawson, Magherafelt BT45 8RX* Tel (028) 7946 9153 E-mail jc@rclyde.freeserve.co.uk

CLYNES, William. b 33. Sarum & Wells Th Coll 78. d 79 p 80. C Winterbourne *Bris* 79-83; TV Swindon St Jo and St Andr 83-91; rtd 91. *34 Sandown Court, 22-62 Bromley Drive, Cardiff CF5 5EZ*

COAKLEY (née FURBER), Prof Sarah Anne. b 51. New Hall Cam BA73 PhD82. Harvard Div Sch ThM75. d 00 p 01. Edw Mallinckrodt Jr Prof Div Harvard Div Sch 95-07; Visiting Prof 07-08; Hon C Waban Th Gd Shep 00-08; Hon C Littlemore *Ox* 00-07; Norris-Hulse Prof Div Cam Univ from 07. *Faculty of Divinity, West Road, Cambridge CB3 9BS* Tel (01223) 763002

COATES, Alan Thomas. b 55. St Jo Coll Nottm 87. d 89 p 90. C Heeley *Sheff* 89-90; C Bramley and Ravenfield 90-92; V Askern 92-96; Chapl RAF from 96; Perm to Offic *Ripon* from 96. *Chaplaincy Services, Valiant Block, HQ Air Command, RAF High Wycombe HP14 4UE* Tel (01494) 496800 Fax 496343

COATES, Archie. See COATES, Richard Michael

COATES, Christopher Ian. b 59. Qu Coll Birm 81. d 84 p 85. C Cottingham *York* 84-87; TV Howden 87-91; V Sherburn in Elmet 91-94; V Sherburn in Elmet w Saxton 94-02; V Bishopthorpe from 02; V Acaster Malbis from 02; P-in-c Appleton Roebuck w Acaster Selby from 07. *The Vicarage, 48 Church Lane, Bishopthorpe, York YO23 2QG* Tel (01904) 707840

COATES, David Martin. b 57. Sheff Univ BSc78 Reading Univ MSc80 Birm Univ PhD83. STETS 04. d 07 p 08. NSM Salisbury St Mark *Sarum* from 07. *2 St Matthew's Close, Bishopdown, Salisbury SP1 3FJ* Tel (01980) 613207 E-mail dmc50@waitrose.com

COATES, Canon Jean Margaret. b 47. Sussex Univ BSc68 Reading Univ PhD77 MIBiol CBiol. SAOMC 93. d 96 p 97. C Wallingford *Ox* 96-99; P-in-c Watercombe *Sarum* 99-02; R from 02; Rural Officer (Dorset) from 99; Can and Preb Sarum Cathl from 05. *The Rectory, Main Street, Broadmayne, Dorchester DT2 8EB* Tel (01305) 852435 E-mail jeancoates@macunlimited.net

COATES, John David Spencer. b 41. St Jo Coll Dur BA64. Cranmer Hall Dur 64. d 66 p 67. C Chipping Campden w Ebrington *Glouc* 66-68; CF 69-96; rtd 96; Perm to Offic *B & W* from 96. *4 The Poplars, Hawkcombe, Porlock, Minehead TA24 8QN* Tel (01643) 862772

COATES, Canon Kenneth Will. b 17. St Jo Coll Dur LTh45 BA46. Bible Churchmen's Coll Bris 39. d 42 p 43. C Daubhill *Man* 42-44; Perm to Offic Bris 44-47; C Cheadle *Ches* 47-49; V Preston All SS *Blackb* 49-60; V St Helens St Helen *Liv* 60-88; Hon Can Liv Cathl 71-88; rtd 88; Perm to Offic *Liv* from 88. *122 Broadway, Eccleston, St Helens WA10 5DH* Tel (01744) 29629

COATES, Maxwell Gordon. b 49. Lon Univ CertEd70 Open Univ BA83 UEA MA86. Trin Coll Bris. d 77 p 78. C Blackheath Park St Mich *S'wark* 77-79; Chapl Greenwich Distr Hosp Lon 77-79; Asst Teacher Saintbridge Sch Glouc 79-81; Teacher Gaywood Park High Sch King's Lynn 81-85; NSM Lynn St Jo *Nor* 81-85; Dep Hd Teacher Winton Comp Sch Bournemouth 85-90; Hd Teacher St Mark's Comp Sch Bath 90-97; NSM Canford Magna *Sarum* 85-90 and 90-95; NSM Stoke Gifford *Bris* 93-96; Perm to Offic *B & W* 91-96; rtd 97. *3 Oakley Road, Wimborne BH21 1QJ* Tel (01202) 883162

COATES, Michael David. b 60. Ches Coll of HE BTh01. NOC 98. d 01 p 02. C Orrell Hey St Jo and St Jas *Liv* 01-07; P-in-c Edge Hill St Cypr w St Mary from 07. *The Vicarage, 48 John Lennon Drive, Liverpool L6 9HT* Tel 0151-260 6351 E-mail evertonmike@sky.com

COATES, Canon Nigel John. b 51. Reading Univ BSc MA. Trin Coll Bris. d 83 p 84. C Epsom St Martin *Guildf* 83-86; C Portswood Ch Ch *Win* 86-88; Chapl Southn Univ 89-97; Chapl Southn Inst of HE 89-95; P-in-c Freemantle 97-00; R 00-05; Can Res S'well Minster from 05. *3 Vicars Court, Southwell NG25 0HP* Tel (01636) 817296 E-mail nigelcoates@southwellminster.org

COATES, Canon Peter Frederick. b 50. K Coll Lon BD79 AKC79. St Steph Ho Ox 79. d 80 p 81. C Woodford St Barn *Chelmsf* 80-83; C E and W Keal *Linc* 83-86; R The Wainfleets and Croft 86-94; R The Wainfleet Gp 94-03; RD Calcewaithe and Candleshoe 92-03; P-in-c Spilsby Gp from 03; RD Bolingbroke from 03; Can and Preb Linc Cathl from 02. *The Vicarage, Church Street, Spilsby PE23 5DU* Tel (01790) 752526 E-mail peter.coates@onetel.net

COATES, Richard Michael (Archie). b 70. Birm Univ BA92. Wycliffe Hall Ox BA99. d 00 p 01. C Ashtead *Guildf* 00-03; C Brompton H Trin w Onslow Square St Paul *Lon* from 03. *3 Holy*

Trinity Church House, Brompton Road, London SW7 2RW Tel 08456-447533 E-mail coates@archieandson.co.uk *or* archie.coates@htb.org.uk

COATES, Robert. b 63. Aston Tr Scheme 87 St Steph Ho Ox 89. d 92 p 93. C Heavitree w Ex St Paul 92-95; Chapl RN 95-00; V Bexhill St Aug *Chich* from 00. *St Augustine's Vicarage, St Augustine's Close, Bexhill-on-Sea TN39 3AZ* Tel and fax (01424) 210785 E-mail ert@rcoates42.freeserve.co.uk

COATES, Robert Charles. b 44. Open Univ BA76. Cant Sch of Min 83. d 86 p 87. C Deal St Leon and St Rich and Sholden *Cant* 86-89; V Loose 89-00; V Barnwood *Glouc* 00-06; rtd 06; Perm to Offic *B & W* from 06. *70 Barrington Place, Shepton Mallet BA4 5GH* Tel (01749) 344698 E-mail robert.coates2@virgin.net

COATES, Stuart Murray. b 49. Lon Univ BA70 Edin Univ MTh91. Wycliffe Hall Ox 72. d 75 p 76. C Rainford *Liv* 75-78; C Orrell 78-79; V 79-86; Chapl Strathcarron Hospice Denny from 86; Hon C Stirling *Edin* 86-90; NSM Doune *St And* from 89; NSM Aberfoyle 89-94. *Westwood Smithy, Chalmerston Road, Stirling FK9 4AG* Tel (01786) 860531 *or* (01324) 826222 E-mail stuart@stuartcoates.wanadoo.co.uk

COATSWORTH, Nigel George. b 39. Trin Hall Cam BA61 MA. Cuddesdon Coll 61. d 63 p 64. C Hellesdon *Nor* 63-66; Ewell Monastery 66-80; TV Folkestone H Trin and St Geo w Ch Ch *Cant* 83-85; C Milton next Sittingbourne 85-86; P-in-c Selattyn *Lich* 86-91; P-in-c Weston Rhyn 88-91; R Weston Rhyn and Selattyn 91-05; rtd 05; Perm to Offic *Lich* from 05. *Oakmere House, 69 Hill Park, Dudleston Heath, Ellesmere SY12 9LB* Tel (01691) 690261 E-mail rev.coatsworth@micro-plus-web.net

COBB, George Reginald. b 50. Oak Hill Th Coll BA81. d 81 p 82. C Ware Ch Ch *St Alb* 81-84; C Uphill *B & W* 84-89; R Alresford *Chelmsf* 89-99; Chapl Mt Vernon and Watford Hosps NHS Trust 99-00; Chapl W Herts Hosps NHS Trust from 00. *Mount Vernon Hospital, Rickmansworth Road, Northwood HA6 2RN* Tel (01923) 844487 *or* (020) 8861 2720 E-mail gcobb83618@aol.com *or* george.cobb@whht.nhs.uk

COBB, Canon John Philip Andrew. b 43. Man Univ BSc65 New Coll Ox BA67 MA71. Wycliffe Hall Ox 66. d 68 p 69. C Reading St Jo *Ox* 68-71; C Romford Gd Shep *Chelmsf* 71-73; SAMS Chile 74-08; Can from 99; Dioc Ecum Officer 00-06; rtd 08; Lic to Offic Chile from 08. *Casilla 330, Correo Paine, Paine, Region Metropolitana, Chile* Tel (0056) (2) 259 4099 E-mail jn.cobb@yahoo.com

COBB, Miss Marjorie Alice. b 24. St Chris Coll Blackheath IDC52. dss 61 d 87. CSA 56-85; rtd 85; Perm to Offic *Cant* from 87; Chapl Jes Hosp Cant from 90. *2 John Boys Wing, Jesus Hospital, Sturry Road, Canterbury CT1 1BS* Tel (01227) 472615

COBB, Mark Robert. b 64. Lanc Univ BSc86 Keele Univ MA99. Ripon Coll Cuddesdon 88. d 91 p 92. C Hampstead St Jo *Lon* 91-94; Asst Chapl Derbyshire R Infirmary NHS Trust 94-96; Palliative & Health Care Chapl Derbyshire R Infirmary NHS Trust 96-98; Chapl Manager Cen Sheff Univ Hosps NHS Trust 98-02; Sen Chapl 98-04; Sen Chapl Sheff Teaching Hosps NHS Foundn Trust from 04. *Chaplaincy Services, Royal Hallamshire Hospital, Glossop Road, Sheffield S10 2JF* Tel 0114-271 2718 *or* 271 1900 E-mail mark.cobb@sth.nhs.uk

COBB, Canon Peter George. b 37. Ch Ch Ox BA59 MA63. St Steph Ho Ox 64. d 65 p 66. C Solihull *Birm* 65-69; Lib Pusey Ho 69-71; Sen Tutor St Steph Ho Ox 71-76; Cust Lib Pusey Ho 76-78; V Midsomer Norton *B & W* 78-83; V Clandown 78-83; V Midsomer Norton w Clandown 83-84; RD Midsomer Norton 83-84; V Clifton All SS w St Jo *Bris* 84-02; Hon Can Bris Cathl 92-02; rtd 02. *13 Knoll Court, Knoll Hill, Bristol BS9 1QX* Tel 0117-968 7460

COBB, Peter Graham. b 27. St Jo Coll Cam BA48 MA52. Ridley Hall Cam 66. d 68 p 69. C Porthkerry *Llan* 68-71; P-in-c Penmark 71-72; V Penmark w Porthkerry 72-81; V Magor w Redwick and Undy *Mon* 82-95; rtd 95. *2 Talycoed Court, Talycoed, Monmouth NP25 5HR* Tel (01600) 780309

COCHLIN, Maurice Reginald. b 19. TCert57 FVCM57 ACP60 FFChM Sussex Univ CertEd70 Lambeth STh74. Chich Th Coll 70. d 70 p 71. C Rowlands Castle *Portsm* 70-72; Chapl Paulsgrove Sch Cosham 71; C Warblington w Emsworth *Portsm* 72-75; C S w N Bersted *Chich* 76-78; Hd Littlemead Upper Sch Chich 78-79; C Saltdean *Chich* 79-83; V Kirdford 83-88; rtd 88; Perm to Offic *Chich* from 88. *56 Fairhurst Road, Barnham, Bognor Regis PO22 0JW* Tel (01243) 553584

COCHRANE, Alan George. b 28. S'wark Ord Course. d 82 p 83. NSM Clapham Old Town *S'wark* 82-85; C Spalding St Jo w Deeping St Nicholas *Linc* 85-87; R Southery and Hilgay *Ely* 87-98; V Fordham St Mary 87-91; rtd 98; Perm to Offic *Nor* from 99. *34 Pightle Way, Lyng, Norwich NR9 5RL* Tel (01603) 872795

COCHRANE, Mrs Anthea Mary. b 38. d 02 p 03. OLM Clarendon *Sarum* 02-07; Perm to Offic 07-08. *Old Timbers, Silver Street, Alderbury, Salisbury SP5 3AN* Tel (01722) 710503 E-mail anthea.cochrane@tiscali.co.uk

COCHRANE, Canon Kenneth Wilbur. b 27. TCD BA58 MA61. d 58 p 59. C Belfast St Aid *Conn* 58-61; C Belfast St Nic 61-62; C Lisburn Ch Ch 62-63; P-in-c Lisburn St Paul 63-65; I 65-98; Can Belf Cathl 86-90; Preb Clonmethan St Patr Cathl Dublin 90-98;

rtd 98. *3 Knockmore Park, Ballinderry Road, Lisburn BT28 2SJ* Tel (028) 9262 7934

COCHRANE, Philip Andrew. b 70. Reading Univ BA92. Trin Coll Bris BA07. **d** 07 **p** 08. C Fareham H Trin *Portsm* 07-09; TV from 09. *12 Greenwood Close, Fareham PO16 7UF* Tel (01329) 318665 E-mail philip@htscf.org.uk

COCHRANE, Canon Roy Alan. b 25. AKC53. **d** 54 **p** 55. C Linc St Faith 54-56; C Skegness 56-59; R Thurlby w Norton Disney 59-65; V Swinderby 59-65; Chapl HM Borstal Morton Hall 59-65; R N Coates *Linc* 65-69; Chapl RAF 65-69; V Marshchapel *Linc* 65-69; V Grainthorpe w Conisholme 65-69; V Glanford Bridge 69-89; Chapl Glanford Hosp 69-89; RD Yarborough 76-81; Can and Preb Linc Cathl 77-97; Chapl and Warden St Anne's Bedehouses 89-93; rtd 90. *4 Trinity Hospital, Hospital Road, Retford DN22 7BD* Tel (01777) 702882

COCKAYNE, Gordon. b 34. RMN73. **d** 92 **p** 93. NSM Owlerton *Sheff* 92-94; Ind Chapl 92-94; NSM Brightside w Wincobank 94-99; Perm to Offic from 99. *6 Austin Close, Loxley, Sheffield S6 6QD* Tel 0114-220 6626

COCKAYNE, Canon Mark Gary. b 61. UEA LLB82. St Jo Coll Nottm BTh92 MA93. **d** 93 **p** 94. C Armthorpe *Sheff* 93-96; V Malin Bridge 96-05; AD Hallam 02-05; C Haydock St Mark *Liv* 05-08; V from 08; AD St Helens from 06; Hon Can Liv Cathl from 06. *99 Springfield Park, Haydock, St Helens WA11 0XP* Tel (01744) 633104

COCKBILL, Douglas John. b 53. Chicago Univ BA75. Gen Th Sem (NY) MDiv78. **d** 78 **p** 79. Virgin Is 79-80; Bahamas 80-83; USA 84-90 and 05-06; P-in-c Roxbourne St Andr *Lon* 90-92; V 92-04; Chapl Larnaca St Helena Cyprus from 06. *16 Agiou Georgiou Makri, 6306 Larnaca, Cyprus* Tel (00357) (2) 465 1327 *or* (9) 965 8147 E-mail dcockbill22@yahoo.com

COCKBURN, Kathleen. b 50. NEOC 04. **d** 07 **p** 08. NSM Walker *Newc* from 07. *92 Paignton Avenue, Whitley Bay NE25 8SZ* Tel 0191-252 0710 E-mail kath.co@blueyonder.co.uk

COCKE, James Edmund. b 26. Wadh Coll Ox BA50 MA55. Wells Th Coll 50. **d** 52 **p** 53. C Christchurch *Win* 52-57; V Highfield *Ox* from 57; Chapl Wingfield-Morris Hosp Ox 57-90; Chapl Nuffield Orthopaedic Centre NHS Trust from 90. *All Saints' Vicarage, 85 Old Road, Oxford OX3 7LB* Tel (01865) 62536

COCKELL, Ms Helen Frances. b 69. Trin Hall Cam BA90 MA94. Qu Coll Birm BD94. **d** 95. C Bracknell *Ox* 95-98; Perm to Offic *Cov* from 00; Chapl S Warks Gen Hosps NHS Trust from 09. *The New Rectory, Pool Close, Rugby CV22 7RN* Tel (01788) 812613 E-mail nell.cockell@btinternet.com

COCKELL, Timothy David. b 66. Qu Coll Birm BTheol95. **d** 95 **p** 96. C Bracknell *Ox* 95-98; C Rugby *Cov* 98-99; TV 99-04; P-in-c Bilton 04-08; R from 08. *The New Rectory, Pool Close, Rugby CV22 7RN* Tel (01788) 812613 E-mail tim.cockell@btopenworld.com

COCKER (née BENTLEY), Mrs Frances Rymer (Sister Frances Anne). b 22. Man Univ BSc48 TDip49 PGCE49. **d** 95 **p** 95. Mother Superior CSD 87-00; Perm to Offic *Sarum* from 95. *7 St Nicholas Hospital, St Nicholas Road, Salisbury SP1 2SW* Tel (01722) 339761 Mobile 07702-659609

COCKERELL, David John. b 47. Univ of Wales (Cardiff) BA71 Univ of Wales (Swansea) MA74 Qu Coll Cam BA75. Westcott Ho Cam 73. **d** 76 **p** 77. C Chapel Allerton *Ripon* 76-79; C Farnley 79-81; TV Hitchin *St Alb* 81-89; TV Dorchester *Ox* 89-92; Adult Educn and Tr Officer *Ely* 92-00; R Raddesley Gp 00-06; rtd 06. *44 Humberley Close, Eynesbury, St Neots PE19 2SE* Tel (01480) 218225 E-mail david@cockerell.co.uk

COCKERTON, Canon John Clifford Penn. b 27. Liv Univ BA48 St Cath Soc Ox BA54 MA58. Wycliffe Hall Ox 51. **d** 54 **p** 55. C St Helens St Helen *Liv* 54-58; Tutor Cranmer Hall Dur 58-60; Chapl 60-63; Warden 68-70; Vice-Prin St Jo Coll Dur 63-70; Prin 70-78; R Wheldrake *York* 78-84; R Wheldrake w Thorganby 84-92; Can and Preb York Minster 87-92; rtd 92; Perm to Offic *York* from 98. *42 Lucombe Way, New Earswick, York YO32 4DS* Tel (01904) 765505

COCKETT, The Ven Elwin Wesley. b 59. Aston Tr Scheme 86 Oak Hill Th Coll BA91. **d** 91 **p** 92. C Chadwell Heath *Chelmsf* 91-94; Chapl W Ham United Football Club from 92; C Harold Hill St Paul 94-95; P-in-c 95-97; V 97-00; TR Billericay and Lt Burstead 00-07; RD Basildon 04-07; Adn W Ham from 07. *86 Aldersbrook Road, London E12 5DH* Tel (020) 8989 8557 E-mail a.westham@chelmsford.anglican.org

COCKFIELD, Mrs Myrtle Jacqueline. b 51. S Bank Univ BSc96. SEITE 05. **d** 08. NSM Mitcham SS Pet and Paul *S'wark* from 08. *28 Garden Avenue, Mitcham CR4 2EA* Tel (020) 8646 2333 Mobile 07722-568604 E-mail jackiecockfield@yahoo.co.uk

COCKING, Ann Louisa. b 44. **d** 03 **p** 04. OLM The Lavingtons, Cheverells, and Easterton *Sarum* from 03. *High Acre, Eastcott, Devizes SN10 4PH* Tel (01980) 812763

COCKING, Keith. b 59. Ripon Coll Cuddesdon 08. **d** 09. C Newbold w Dunston *Derby* from 09. *29 Bank Wood Close, Chesterfield S41 8XQ* Tel (01246) 238342 Mobile 07903-736791 E-mail k.cocking@raeuk.com

COCKING, Martyn Royston. b 53. Trin Coll Bris 83. **d** 85 **p** 86. C Weston-super-Mare Cen Par *B & W* 85-88; C Kingswood *Bris*

88-89; TV 89-93; V Pill w Easton in Gordano and Portbury *B & W* 93-96. *68 Friary Grange Park, Winterbourne, Bristol BS36 1NB* Tel (01454) 886771

COCKMAN, David Willie. b 32. Ex & Truro NSM Scheme 89. **d** 82 **p** 83. C Christow, Ashton, Trusham and Bridford *Ex* 82; NSM Exwick 83-84; Warden Mercer Ho 83-97; Lic to Offic from 83; rtd 97. *4 The Fairway, Pennsylvania, Exeter EX4 5DW* Tel (01392) 278590

COCKRAM, Anthony John. b 44. Leeds Univ BSc65 Birm Univ MEd83 Ex Univ BA04. SWMTC 98. **d** 01 **p** 02. NSM Seaton *Ex* 01-03; NSM Seaton and Beer 03-04; Asst Chapl R Devon and Ex NHS Foundn Trust 04-05; TV Aberavon *Llan* from 05. *The Vicarage, 44 Ynys y Gored, Port Talbot SA13 2EB* Tel (01639) 892306 E-mail ajcockram@hotmail.co.uk

COCKS, Canon Howard Alan Stewart. b 46. St Barn Coll Adelaide 78. **d** 80 **p** 81. C Portland Australia 80-82; C Prestbury *Glouc* 82-87; P-in-c Stratton w Baunton 87-94; P-in-c N Cerney w Bagendon 91-94; R Stratton, N Cerney, Baunton and Bagendon 95-98; V Leic St Aid 98-04; RD Christianity S 01-04; R Winchelsea and Icklesham *Chich* from 04; Can The Murray from 06. *The Rectory, St Thomas Street, Winchelsea TN36 4EB* Tel (01797) 226254

COCKS, Michael Dearden Somers. b 28. Univ of NZ MA50 St Cath Coll Ox BA53 MA57. Ripon Hall Ox. **d** 53 **p** 54. C Merivale New Zealand 53-56; V Geraldine 56-58; V Ross and S Westland 58-60; V Hinds 60-63; V St Martins 63-70; V Barrington Street w Speydon St Nic 70-79; V Hororata 79-93; Chapl Gothenburg w Halmstad, Jönköping etc *Eur* 93-98; rtd 98. *23 Fairfield Avenue, Addington, Christchurch 8020, New Zealand* Tel and fax (0064) (3) 377 7053 E-mail cocks@ihug.co.nz

COCKSEDGE, Hugh Francis. b 26. Magd Coll Cam BA50 MA52. **d** 88 **p** 89. NSM Alton All SS *Win* 88-89; Lic to Offic 89-91; Chapl Ankara *Eur* 91-96; rtd 96; Perm to Offic *Win* 96-01; *Eur* from 96; *Portsm* from 01; *Guildf* from 06. *Stancomb, Stancomb Lane, Medstead, Alton GU34 5QB* Tel (01420) 563624 E-mail hughcocksedge@talktalk.net

COCKSEDGE, Simon Hugh. b 56. Univ Coll Lon BSc78 New Coll Ox BM, BCh81 Man Univ MD03 FRCGP96. NOC 05. **d** 07 **p** 08. NSM Hayfield and Chinley w Buxworth *Derby* from 07. *Corrour, Hall Hill, Chapel-en-le-Frith, High Peak SK23 9RX*

COCKSHAW, Evan David. b 74. Sussex Univ BSc95. St Jo Coll Nottm MA99. **d** 00 **p** 01. C Horncastle w Low Toynton *Linc* 00-02; C Pennington *Man* 02-07; Pioneer Ldr Missional Community W Bromwich *Lich* from 07. *23 Rowley View, West Bromwich B70 8QR* Tel 07958-050009 (mobile)

✠**COCKSWORTH, The Rt Revd Christopher John.** b 59. Man Univ BA80 PhD89 PGCE81. St Jo Coll Nottm 84. **d** 88 **p** 89 **c** 08. C Epsom Common Ch Ch *Guildf* 88-97; Chapl R Holloway and Bedf New Coll 92-97; Dir STETS 97-01; Hon Can Guildf Cathl 99-01; Prin Ridley Hall Cam 01-08; Bp Cov from 08. *The Bishop's House, 23 Davenport Road, Coventry CV5 6PW* Tel (024) 7667 2244 Fax 7671 3271 E-mail bishcov@btconnect.com

CODLING, Timothy Michael. b 62. Trin Coll Ox BA84 MA91. St Steph Ho Ox 89. **d** 91 **p** 92. C N Shoebury *Chelmsf* 91-97; V Tilbury Docks from 97; Hon Chapl Miss to Seafarers from 97. *St John's Vicarage, Dock Road, Tilbury RM18 7PP* Tel (01375) 842417 E-mail tim@frcodling.fsnet.co.uk

CODRINGTON-MARSHALL, Louise. b 64. Westcott Ho Cam 06. **d** 08 **p** 09. C Mortlake w E Sheen *S'wark* from 08. *5 Vernon Road, London SW14 8NII* Tel (020) 8876 1630 E-mail office@mortlakeparish.org.uk

CODY, Paul James Luke. b 73. Westcott Ho Cam. **d** 08 **p** 09. C Cen Wolverhampton *Lich* from 08. *1B Claremont Road, Wolverhampton WV3 0EA* Tel 07834-345269 (mobile) E-mail paulcody@hotmail.co.uk

COE, Andrew Derek John. b 58. Nottm Univ BTh86. St Jo Coll Nottm 83. **d** 86 **p** 87. C Pype Hayes *Birm* 86-88; C Erddington St Barn 88-91; C Birm St Martin w Bordesley St Andr 91-96; P-in-c Hamstead St Bernard 96; V 96-02; P-in-c Newdigate *Guildf* 02-03; TR Surrey Weald from 03; RD Dorking 04-09. *The Rectory, Church Road, Newdigate, Dorking RH5 5DL* Tel (01306) 631469 E-mail revdandrewdj.coe@btinternet.com

COE, David. b 45. **d** 69 **p** 70. C Belfast St Matt *Conn* 69-72; C Belfast St Donard *D & D* 72-75; I Tullylish 75-81; I Lurgan St Jo 81-89; I Ballymacarrett St Patr 89-02; I Richhill *Arm* from 02. *The Rectory, 15 Annareagh Road, Richhill BT61 9JT* Tel (028) 3887 1232 E-mail davidcoe144@aol.com

COE, John Norris. b 31. Oak Hill Th Coll 57. **d** 59 **p** 60. C Stoughton *Guildf* 59-61; C Guernsey St Michel du Valle *Win* 61-63; C Norbiton *S'wark* 63-67; V Bath Widcombe *B & W* 67-84; R Publow w Pensford, Compton Dando and Chelwood 84-96; rtd 96; Perm to Offic *B & W* from 96. *12 Stirtingale Road, Bath BA2 2NF* Tel (01225) 789752

COE, Michael Stephen. b 63. Bath Univ BSc85. Wycliffe Hall Ox. **d** 00 **p** 01. C Moulton *Pet* 00-03; P-in-c Silverhill St Matt *Chich* 03-05; R from 05. *The Rectory, 9 St Matthew's Road, St Leonards-on-Sea TN38 0TN* Tel (01424) 430262 E-mail mikelisac@aol.com

COE, Noelle Elizabeth. b 60. **d** 08 **p** 09. NSM N Holmwood *Guildf* from 08. *The Rectory, Church Road, Newdigate, Dorking RH5 5DL* Tel (01306) 631469
E-mail noellecoe@btinternet.com

COE, Stephen David. b 49. Ch Coll Cam MA72 Oak Hill Th Coll MA99. Ox Min Course 90. **d** 93 **p** 94. NSM Abingdon *Ox* 93-97; Assoc Min Ox St Andr 97-05; V Wallington *S'wark* from 05. *Holy Trinity Vicarage, Maldon Road, Wallington SM6 8BL* Tel (020) 8401 8177 E-mail sdcoe@btinternet.com

COEKIN, Philip James. b 64. Wye Coll Lon BScAgr87. Oak Hill Th Coll BA93. **d** 96 **p** 97. C Eastbourne All SS *Chich* 96-00; V Hastings Em and St Mary in the Castle from 00. *Emmanuel Vicarage, Vicarage Road, Hastings TN34 3NA* Tel (01424) 421543 E-mail phil@pcoekin.freeserve.co.uk

COEKIN, Richard John. b 61. Solicitor 86 Jes Coll Cam BA83 MA87. Wycliffe Hall Ox 89. **d** 91 **p** 92. C Cheadle *Ches* 91-95; NSM Wimbledon Em Ridgway Prop Chpl *S'wark* from 95; Perm to Offic *Lon* from 02. *264 Worple Road, London SW20 8RG* Tel (020) 8545 2734
E-mail richard.coekin@dundonald.org

COFFEY, Hubert William (Bill). b 15. MBE46. TCD BA37 MA40, TCD Div Sch Div Test38. **d** 38 **p** 39. C Errigle Keerogue w Ballygawley and Killeshil *Arm* 38-41; Chapl RN 41-47; I Milltown *Arm* 47-52; Chapl Miss to Seamen 52-64; Australia from 53; V Melbourne S 64-80; rtd 80; Perm to Offic *Melbourne* from 80. *23 Hawthorn Avenue, Caulfield North Vic 3161, Australia* Tel (0061) (3) 9527 7875

COFFIN, Pamela. See PENNELL, Ms Pamela

COFFIN, Stephen. b 52. Pemb Coll Ox BA74 MA79. Trin Coll Bris 74. **d** 77 **p** 78. C Illogan *Truro* 77-80; C Liskeard w St Keyne and St Pinnock 80-82; CMS Burundi 82-86; V St Germans *Truro* 86-00; Chapl Grenoble *Eur* from 00. *14 rue Gérard Philippe, 38100 Grenoble, France* Tel (0033) (4) 76 25 33 79 E-mail chaplain@grenoble-church.org *or* coffin@onetelnet.fr

COGGINS, Glenn. b 60. Warwick Univ BA81. St Jo Coll Dur 93. **d** 95 **p** 96. C Cley Hill Warminster *Sarum* 95-99; R Doddington w Benwick and Wimblington *Ely* 99-06; V E Ardsley *Wakef* from 06; Bp's Adv for Ecum Affairs from 07. *The Vicarage, Church Lane, East Ardsley, Wakefield WF3 2LJ* Tel (01924) 822184

COGHLAN, Canon Patrick John. b 47. Down Coll Cam BA69. St Jo Coll Nottm MA73. **d** 73 **p** 74. C Crookes St Thos *Sheff* 73-78; Brazil 78-92; V Anston *Sheff* 92-06; V Malin Bridge from 06; Hon Can Sheff Cathl from 07. *St Polycarp's Vicarage, 33 Wisewood Lane, Sheffield S6 4WA* Tel 0114-234 3450
E-mail rev.patrick@btinternet.com

COHEN, The Ven Clive Ronald Franklin. b 46. ACIB71. Sarum & Wells Th Coll 79. **d** 81 **p** 82. C Esher *Guildf* 81-85; R Winterslow *Sarum* 85-00; RD Alderbury 89-93; Can and Preb Sarum Cathl 92-00; Adn Bodmin *Truro* from 00; Hon Can Truro Cathl from 00. *Archdeacon's House, Cardinham, Bodmin PL30 4BL* Tel and fax (01208) 821614 E-mail clive@truro.anglican.org

COHEN, Canon David Mervyn Stuart. b 42. Sydney Univ BA63 MA78. **d** 67 **p** 68. Exec Sec Bible Soc Mauritius 67-69; Dep Gen Sec Bible Soc New Zealand 70-72; Regional Sec (Africa) Bible Soc 73-75; C-in-c Sylvania Australia 75-77; R Manly St Matt 78-85; Gen Dir Scripture Union (England and Wales) 86-93; Tear Fund UK 93-96; Nat Dir Chr Nationals Evang Coun Australia from 96; Hon Can Antsiranana from 06. *1 Currawong Place, East Blaxland NSW 2774, Australia*
E-mail davidc@moringa-au.com

COHEN, Ian Geoffrey Holland. b 51. Nottm Univ BA74. Ripon Coll Cuddesdon 77. **d** 79 **p** 80. C Sprowston *Nor* 79-83; TV Wallingford w Crowmarsh Gifford etc *Ox* 83-88; V Chalgrove w Berrick Salome from 88. *The Vicarage, 58 Brinkinfield Road, Chalgrove, Oxford OX44 7QX* Tel (01865) 890392
E-mail ianghcohen@hotmail.com

COHEN, Malcolm Arthur. b 38. Canberra Coll of Min. **d** 78 **p** 79. Australia 79-84; C Moruya, Bega and Cootamundra 79-80; R Braidwood 82-83; R Stifford *Chelmsf* 84-92; Chapl Asst Thurrock Community Hosp Grays 84-86; Hon Chapl ATC from 86; P-in-c Mayland and Steeple *Chelmsf* 92-95; C Prittlewell 95-99; C Greenstead 99-00; TV Greenstead w Colchester St Anne 00-03; rtd 03. *177 Straight Road, Colchester CO3 5DG* Tel (01206) 573231

COKE, Canon William Robert Francis. b 46. St Edm Hall Ox BA68 MA79 Lon Univ BD78. Trin Coll Bris 75. **d** 79 **p** 80. C Blackb Sav 79-83; V Fence in Pendle 83-84; P-in-c Newchurch-in-Pendle 83-84; V Fence and Newchurch-in-Pendle 84-89; Switzerland 89-95; Chapl Ardingly Coll 95-96; V Ambleside w Brathay *Carl* from 96; P-in-c Langdale from 97; RD Windermere from 04; Hon Can Carl Cathl from 08. *The Vicarage, Millans Park, Ambleside LA22 9AD* Tel (01539) 433205
E-mail raphd.pcoke@cwcom.net

COKE-WOODS, Sylvia Jessie. b 47. Sheff Univ BA69. Qu Coll Birm 81 NOC 98. **d** 99 **p** 00. C Widnes St Mary *Liv* 99-03; Perm to Offic *B & W* from 04. *29 Southwoods, Yeovil BA20 2QQ* Tel (01935) 474542

COKER, Alexander Bryan. b 48. Fourah Bay Coll (Sierra Leone) LDiv73 K Coll Lon BD75 MTh76 Brunel Univ MA84 MEd89 AKC76 MCollP84. St Aug Coll Cant 75. **d** 86 **p** 87. NSM Belsize Park *Lon* 86-90; C Croydon Woodside *S'wark* 90-93; C Cheam Common St Phil 93-94; Perm to Offic *Lon* 02-04. *The Mission House, 19 Rosehill Park West, Sutton SM1 3LA* Tel (020) 8641 6690

COKER, Canon Barry Charles Ellis. b 46. K Coll Lon BD69 AKC69. **d** 70 **p** 71. C Newton Aycliffe *Dur* 70-74; Trinidad and Tobago 74-78; R Matson *Glouc* 78-90; V Stroud and Uplands w Slad from 90; RD Bisley 94-06; P-in-c The Edge, Pitchcombe, Harescombe and Brookthorpe 00-01; Hon Can Glouc Cathl from 98. *The Vicarage, Church Street, Stroud GL5 1JL* Tel (01453) 764555 Fax 751494
E-mail barrycoker@thevicarage.fsnet.co.uk

COLAM, (née TAVERNER), Mrs Lorraine Dawn. b 61. SRN82 RSCN86. **d** 07 **p** 08. OLM Tilehurst St Cath and Calcot *Ox* from 07. *120 Chapel Hill, Tilehurst, Reading RG31 5DH* Tel 0118-943 2001 Mobile 07790-076450
E-mail lorraine@colam.supanet.com

COLBOURN, John Martin Claris. b 30. Selw Coll Cam BA52 MA56. Ridley Hall Cam 52. **d** 54 **p** 55. C Cheadle *Ches* 54-58; V Trowbridge St Thos *Sarum* 59-65; V Fareham St Jo *Portsm* 65-87; V Crich *Derby* 87-95; RD Alfreton 88-95; rtd 95; Perm to Offic *Derby* from 95. *Stanton View Cottage, Dale Road North, Darley Dale, Matlock DE4 2HX* Tel (01629) 733284

COLBY, David Allan. b 33. Ox NSM Course 78. **d** 81 **p** 82. NSM Gt Faringdon w Lt Coxwell *Ox* 81-83; TV Ewyas Harold w Dulas, Kenderchurch etc *Heref* 83-91; V Westbury-on-Severn w Flaxley and Blaisdon *Glouc* 91-99; rtd 99; Perm to Offic *Ox* from 01. *Solway House, Faringdon Road, Kingston Bagpuize, Abingdon OX13 5AQ* Tel (01865) 820360

COLCHESTER, Archdeacon of. See COOPER, The Ven Annette Joy

COLCHESTER, Area Bishop of. See MORGAN, The Rt Revd Christopher Heudebourck

✠**COLCLOUGH, The Rt Revd Michael John.** b 44. Leeds Univ BA69. Cuddesdon Coll 69. **d** 71 **p** 72 **c** 96. C Burslem St Werburgh *Lich* 71-75; C Ruislip St Mary *Lon* 75-79; P-in-c Hayes St Anselm 79-85; V 85-86; AD Hillingdon 85-92; P-in-c Uxbridge St Marg 86-88; P-in-c Uxbridge St Andr w St Jo 86-88; TR Uxbridge 88-92; Adn Northolt 92-94; P-in-c St Vedast w St Mich-le-Querne etc 94-96; Bp's Sen Chapl 94-96; Dean of Univ Chapls from 94; Dep to V O 95-96; Area Bp Kensington *Lon* 96-08; Can Res St Paul's Cathl from 08. *2 Amen Court, London EC4M 7BU* Tel (020) 7236 0199
E-mail canonpastor@stpaulscathedral.org.uk

COLDERWOOD, Alfred Victor. b 26. Bps' Coll Cheshunt 58. **d** 60 **p** 61. C Oakwood St Thos *Lon* 60-63; C Enfield St Jas 63-66; V Edmonton St Aldhelm 66-91; rtd 91; Perm to Offic *Cant* 91-09. *15 The Bight, South Woodham Ferrers, Chelmsford CM3 5GJ*

COLDHAM, Miss Geraldine Elizabeth. b 35. FLA66 Trevelyan Coll Dur BA80. Cranmer Hall Dur 82. **dss** 83 **d** 87 **p** 94. S Normanton *Derby* 83-87; Par Dn 87-94; Par Dn Barking St Marg w St Patr *Chelmsf* 87-90; Par Dn Stifford 90-94; C 94-95; rtd 95; Perm to Offic *Glouc* from 01. *27 Capel Court, The Burgage, Prestbury, Cheltenham GL52 3EL* Tel (01242) 576425

COLDICOTT, Mrs Christine Mary. b 51. EMMTC 04. **d** 07 **p** 08. NSM Ascension TM *Leic* from 07. *5 Wayfarer Drive, East Goscote, Leicester LE7 3QZ* Tel 0116-260 2437
E-mail chris_grand2004@yahoo.co.uk

COLDICOTT, Richard Spencer. b 69. Leeds Univ BSc90 PhD93 PGCE94. Trin Coll Bris 06. **d** 08 **p** 09. C Aspley *S'well* from 08. *11 Robinswood Road, Nottingham NG8 3LA* Tel 0115-929 3113 Mobile 07742-014444

COLDWELL, John Philip. b 62. Trin Coll Bris 04. **d** 06 **p** 07. C Inglewood Gp *Carl* from 06. *The Rectory, Skelton, Penrith CA11 9SE* Tel (01768) 484797 E-mail j.coldwell@manx.net

COLDWELL, Rosemary Anne. b 52. Bretton Hall Coll CertEd75 Open Univ BA82 LTCL74 LLCM74. STETS 04. **d** 07 **p** 08. NSM Blandford Forum and Langton Long *Sarum* from 07. *12 Stileham Bank, Milborne St Andrew, Blandford Forum DT11 0LE* Tel (01258) 837600 Mobile 07929-090948
E-mail rosemarycoldwell@btinternet.com

COLE, Adrian Peter. See ROBBINS-COLE, Adrian Peter

COLE, Canon Alan John. b 35. Bps Coll Cheshunt 63. **d** 66 **p** 67. C Boreham Wood All SS *St Alb* 66-69; C St Alb St Mich 69-72; V Redbourn 72-80; R Thorley w Bishop's Stortford H Trin 80-87; Chapl St Edw K and Martyr Cam *Ely* 87-94; Chapl Arthur Rank Hospice Cam 87-94; P-in-c Gamlingay w Hatley St George and E Hatley *Ely* 94-99; Hon Can Ely Cathl 96-00; P-in-c Everton w Tetworth 98-99; R Gamlingay and Everton 99-00; rtd 01; Perm to Office *St E* and *Ely* from 01. *73 Finchams Close, Linton, Cambridge CB21 4ND* Tel (01223) 892286
E-mail alan73@waitrose.com

COLE, Alan Michael. b 40. Melbourne Univ DipEd74 BA74. ACT. **d** 66 **p** 67. Australia 66-75 and 90-97; Chapl Bp Otter Coll *Chich* 76-77; Chapl Ardingly Coll 77-82; Chapl Bonn w Cologne

Eur 82-86; Chapl Helsinki w Moscow 86-90; P-in-c Ilkeston H Trin *Derby* 97-01; V from 02. *Holy Trinity Vicarage, 1 Cotmanhay Road, Ilkeston DE7 8HR* Tel 0115-932 0833

COLE, Canon Brian Robert Arthur. b 35. Nottm Univ BA57. Ridley Hall Cam 59. **d** 61 **p** 62. C Tye Green w Netteswell *Chelmsf* 61-64; C Keighley *Bradf* 64-67; V Copley *Wakef* 67-73; Chapl Halifax Gen Hosp 67-73; R Gt w Lt Dunham *Nor* 73-82; R Gt w Lt Fransham 74-82; P-in-c Sporle w Gt and Lt Palgrave 81-82; R Gt and Lt Dunham w Gt and Lt Fransham and Sporle 83-03; P-in-c 03-06; rtd 06; Perm to Offic *Nor* from 06; RD Brisley and Elmham 93-08; Hon Can Nor Cathl 98-08. *Stone Cottage, The Street, Mileham, King's Lynn PE32 2RA* Tel (01328) 701466 E-mail brian@cole4235.freeserve.co.uk

COLE, Charles Vincent. b 26. Kelham Th Coll 47. **d** 51 **p** 52. C Harton *Dur* 51-54; C Gateshead St Jas 54-56; V Blackhall 56-91; rtd 91; Perm to Offic *Wakef* 91-06. *66 Scott Green Crescent, Gildersome, Morley, Leeds LS27 7DF* Tel 0113-253 0021

COLE, David Henry. *See* GIFFORD-COLE, David Henry

COLE, Mrs Elizabeth Marie. b 42. **d** 04 **p** 05. OLM Yoxmere *St E* from 04. *Middlegate Barn, High Street, Dunwich, Saxmundham IP17 3DP* Tel (01728) 648244 E-mail ecoledun@aol.com

COLE, Guy Spenser. b 63. Univ of Wales (Ban) BA84 Jes Coll Cam BA88 MA91. Westcott Ho Cam 85. **d** 88 **p** 89. C Eastville St Anne w St Mark and St Thos *Bris* 88-92; P-in-c Penhill 92-95; V 95-01; R Easthampstead *Ox* from 01. *The Rectory, Crowthorne Road, Easthampstead, Bracknell RG12 7ER* Tel (01344) 423253 *or* 425205 E-mail guycole@guycole.freeserve.co.uk

COLE, Jennifer Ann. b 52. Open Univ MBA04. STETS 07. **d** 09. NSM Radstock w Writhlington *B & W* from 09; NSM Kilmersdon w Babington from 09. *51 Under Knoll, Peasedown St John, Bath BA2 8TY* Tel (01761) 437768 Mobile 07749-079276 E-mail jennifer.cole@bathwells.anglican.org

COLE, John Gordon. b 43. Magd Coll Cam BA65 MA69. Cuddesdon Coll 66. **d** 68 **p** 69. C Leeds St Pet *Ripon* 68-71; C Moor Allerton 71-75; P-in-c Pendleton *Blackb* 75-86; Dioc Communications Officer 75-86; Dioc Missr *Linc* 86-98; Ecum Development Officer 98-02; Nat Adv for Unity in Miss 03-08; rtd 08. *Pelham House, Little Lane, Wrawby, Brigg DN20 8RW* Tel (01652) 657484 E-mail johngcole@btinternet.com

COLE, John Spensley. b 39. Clare Coll Cam BA62 MA66 FCA65. Linc Th Coll 78. **d** 80 **p** 81. C Cowes St Mary *Portsm* 80-83; C Portchester 83-87; V Modbury *Ex* 87-95; R Aveton Gifford 87-95; TR Modbury, Bigbury, Ringmore w Kingston etc 95-98; P-in-c Alne and Brafferton w Pilmoor, Myton-on-Swale etc *York* 98-05; rtd 05. *8 Honing Drive, Southwell NG25 0LB* Tel (01636) 819541 E-mail johnlzcole@firenet.uk.net

COLE, Michael Berkeley. b 44. Cuddesdon Coll. **d** 72 **p** 73. C Shepshed *Leic* 72-76; V Leic St Chad 76-79; Hon C Painswick w Sheepscombe *Glouc* 94-97; Hon C Painswick w Sheepscombe and Cranham 97-98; Hon C Fairford and Kempsford w Whelford 98-04; TR Redhorn *Sarum* 04-09; rtd 09. *Homestead, Church End, Twyning, Tewkesbury GL20 6DA* E-mail mbcole@btinternet.com

COLE, Michael George. b 35. CD75. Wesley Th Sem Washington DMin88. Kelham Th Coll 56 Lich Th Coll 57. **d** 60 **p** 61. C Doncaster Ch Ch *Sheff* 60 63; Chapl RAF 63-68: Canada 68-82; USA from 82; rtd 98. *1202 Stonegate Way, Crozet VA 22932-3150, USA* E-mail mvgrcr6@comcast.net

COLE, Canon Michael John. b 34. St Pet Hall Ox BA56 MA60. Ridley Hall Cam 56. **d** 58 **p** 59. C Finchley Ch Ch *Lon* 58; C Leeds St Geo *Ripon* 58-61; Travelling Sec IVF 61-64; V Crookes St Thos *Sheff* 64-71; R Rusholme H Trin *Man* 71-75; V Woodford Wells *Chelmsf* 75-00; Chapl Leytonstone Ho Hosp 85-00; Hon Can Chelmsf Cathl 89-00; RD Redbridge 95-00; rtd 00; Perm to Offic *Chelmsf* 00-06. *1 Paradise Drive, Eastbourne BN20 7SX* Tel (01323) 723425

COLE, Canon Norma Joan. b 46. EAMTC 93. **d** 96 **p** 97. C Ipswich St Mary at Stoke w St Pet *St E* 96-97; C Ipswich St Mary at Stoke w St Pet and St Fran 97-99; V Cornard 99-04; V Rushen *S & M* from 04; Hon Can St German's Cathl from 09. *Rushen Vicarage, Barracks Road, Port St Mary, Isle of Man IM9 5LP* Tel (01624) 832275

COLE, Canon Peter George Lamont. b 27. Pemb Coll Cam BA49 MA52. Cuddesdon Coll 50. **d** 52 **p** 53. C Aldershot St Mich *Guildf* 52-55; C St Jo Cathl Bulawayo S Rhodesia 55-59; P-in-c Riverside All SS 55-59; R 59-62; Chapl St Steph Coll Balla Balla 63-65; V Bromley St Andr *Roch* 65-72; V Folkestone St Mary and St Eanswythe *Cant* 72-87; Hon Can Cant Cathl 80-87; V E and W Worldham, Hartley Mauditt w Kingsley etc *Win* 87-92; RD Alton 89-92; rtd 92; RD Petworth *Chich* 94-95; Perm to Offic from 95. *29 Swan View, Pulborough RH20 2BF* Tel (01798) 873238

COLE, Stanley Westley Tom. b 28. **d** 97 **p** 98. NSM Chalke Valley *Sarum* from 97. *Cranborne Farm, Old Blandford Road, Coombe Bissett, Salisbury SP5 4LF* Tel and fax (01722) 718240 E-mail revcolecb@talktalk.net

COLE, Timothy Alexander Robertson. b 60. Aber Univ MA83 Edin Univ BD86. Edin Th Coll 83. **d** 86 **p** 87. C Dunfermline

St And 86-89; Vice-Provost St Andr Cathl Inverness 89-90; R Inverness St Andr 89-90; R Edin St Mich and All SS 90-95; CF from 95. *c/o MOD Chaplains (Army)* Tel (01980) 615804 Fax 615800

COLE, Mrs Vanessa Anne. b 73. K Alfred's Coll Win BA94. Trin Coll Bris BA03. **d** 04 **p** 05. C Congresbury w Puxton and Hewish St Ann *B & W* 04-09; TV Portway and Danebury *Win* from 09. *The Rectory, Over Wallop, Stockbridge SO20 8HT* Tel (01264) 782615 E-mail vanessa@cole.org.uk

COLE, William. b 45. Oak Hill Th Coll BA96. **d** 96 **p** 97. NSM St Keverne *Truro* 96-99; P-in-c St Ruan w St Grade and Landewednack from 99. *The Rectory, Church Cove, The Lizard, Helston TR12 7PQ* Tel (01326) 291011

COLE-BAKER, Peter Massey. b 58. New Univ of Ulster BSc80 TCD BTh98. CITC 95. **d** 98 **p** 99. C Ballywillan *Conn* 98-01; I Templemore w Thurles and Kilfithmone *C & O* from 01. *The Rectory, Roscrea Road, Templemore, Co Tipperary, Republic of Ireland* Tel and fax (00353) (504) 31175
E-mail pcolebaker@eircom.net

COLEBROOK, Canon Christopher John. b 36. Qu Mary Coll Lon BA60 BD69. St D Coll Lamp 60. **d** 62 **p** 63. C Llandeilo Tal-y-bont *S & B* 62-66; C Llansamlet 66-71; V Nantmel w St Harmon's and Llanwrthwl 71-76; V Glantawe 76-85; V Gowerton 85-01; RD Llwchwr 93-00; Hon Can Brecon Cathl 97-01; Prec 00-01; rtd 01. *79 Vivian Road, Sketty, Swansea SA2 0UN*

COLEBROOK, Peter Acland. b 29. Coates Hall Edin 52. **d** 55 **p** 56. C Northfield *Birm* 58-62; C Bideford *Ex* 62-66; rtd 89; Perm to Offic *Sarum* from 01. *Danes Lee, Ham Lane, Marnhull, Sturminster Newton DT10 1JN* Tel (01258) 820246

COLEBROOKE, Andrew. b 50. Imp Coll Lon BSc71 MSc72 PhD75. Ridley Hall Cam 92. **d** 94 **p** 95. C Shrub End *Chelmsf* 94-98; R Mistley w Manningtree and Bradfield 98-09; RD Harwich 04-09; R Heydon, Gt and Lt Chishill, Chrishall etc from 09. *The Rectory, 1 Hall Lane, Great Chishill, Royston SG8 8SG* Tel (01763) 838703
E-mail a.colebrooke@btinternet.com

COLEBY, Andrew Mark. b 59. Linc Coll Ox MA85 DPhil85 Dur Univ BA90 FRHistS88. Cranmer Hall Dur 88. **d** 91 **p** 92. C Heeley *Sheff* 91-93; TV Gleadless 94-97; Chapl Ox Brookes Univ 97-01; P-in-c Didcot All SS 01-06; Dioc FE Officer and Chapl Abingdon and Witney Coll 06-09; Soc Resp Adv *St Alb* from 09. *Silver Birches, Picklers Hill, Abingdon OX14 2BA* Tel (01235) 528374 E-mail amcoleby@btopenworld.com

COLEMAN, Aidan William. b 56. St Jo Coll Nottm 97. **d** 99 **p** 00. C Llandudno *Ban* 99-02; TV Bangor and P-in-c Llandygai and Maes y Groes 02-05; P-in-c Rhosymedre w Penycae *St As* from 05. *The Vicarage, Church Street, Rhosymedre, Wrexham LL14 3EA* Tel (01978) 810786

COLEMAN, Ann Valerie. b 51. K Coll Lon BD72 Heythrop Coll Lon MA03. St Aug Coll Cant. **dss** 80 **d** 87 **p** 94. Hampstead Garden Suburb *Lon* 80-84; Golders Green 85-87; Selection Sec and Voc Adv ACCM 87-91; Teacher Bp Ramsey Sch 92-93; Chapl 93-99; Dir of Ords Willesden Area *Lon* 96-99; Course Leader NTMTC 99-04; Hon C Eastcote St Lawr *Lon* 93-04; Dir Wydale Hall *York* 04-08; Dioc Moderator Reader Tr 05-08; Tutor St Mellitus Coll *Lon* from 08. *12 Craneswater Park, Southall UB2 5RP* Tel (020) 8574 8352
E-mail annvc@tiscali.co.uk

COLEMAN, Beverley Warren. b 20. Leeds Univ BA41. Coll of Resurr Mirfield 41. **d** 43 **p** 44. C Greenford H Cross *Lon* 43-46; C Stepney St Dunstan and All SS 46-47; CF 47-52; CF (TA) 52-87; PC Barrow Gurney *B & W* 52-54; Malaya 54-56; Indonesia 56-63; P-in-c Albrighton *Lich* 63-64; V 64-71; R Jersey St Sav *Win* 71-84; rtd 87; Perm to Offic *Worc* 87-99. *44 Walnut Crescent, Malvern WR14 4AX* Tel (01684) 563535

COLEMAN, Brian James. b 36. K Coll Cam BA58 MA61. Ripon Hall Ox 58. **d** 60 **p** 61. C Allestree *Derby* 60-65; V Allestree St Nic 65-69; Chapl and Lect St Mich Coll Salisbury 69-77; P-in-c Matlock Bank *Derby* 77-86; R Frimley *Guildf* 86-92; V Guildf All SS 92-02; rtd 02; Perm to Offic *Sarum* from 03. *6 Kingfisher Close, Salisbury SP2 8JE* Tel (01722) 410034

COLEMAN, Brian Ray. b 71. California State Univ Fullerton BPhil94. Seabury-Western Th Sem MDiv98. **d** 98 **p** 99. Assoc R Los Angeles St Jas USA 98-01; C Sheff St Leon Norwood 01-03; Chapl N Gen Hosp NHS Trust Sheff 01-03; P-in-c Sheff St Pet Abbeydale 03-08; P-in-c Sheff St Oswald 03-08; R Battle Creek St Thos USA from 08. *St Thomas's Rectory, 252 Chestnut Street, Battle Creek MI 49017-3348, USA*
E-mail frbrian@btopenworld.com

COLEMAN, David. b 49. K Coll Lon BD72 AKC72. St Aug Coll Cant 72. **d** 73 **p** 74. C Is of Dogs Ch Ch and St Jo w St Luke *Lon* 73-77; C Greenford H Cross 77-80; V Cricklewood St Pet 80-85; V Golders Green 85-90; V Eastcote St Lawr 90-04; P-in-c Upper Ryedale and CME Officer Cleveland Adnry *York* 04-08; V Heston *Lon* from 08. *12 Craneswater Park, Southall UB2 5RP* Tel (020) 8574 8352 E-mail frdavid.coleman@tiscali.co.uk

COLEMAN

COLEMAN, David Kenneth. b 60. SWMTC 06. **d** 09. *4 Torbridge Road, Horrabridge, Yelverton PL20 7SD* Tel (01822) 853311 E-mail deekaycee@hotmail.com

COLEMAN, Frank. b 58. Hull Univ BA79. St Steph Ho Ox BA83 MA87. **d** 83 **p** 84. C Brandon *Dur* 83-85; C Newton Aycliffe 85-88; V Denford w Ringstead *Pet* 88-00; P-in-c Islip 95-00; V Caldecote, Northill and Old Warden *St Alb* from 00. *The Vicarage, 2A Biggleswade Road, Upper Caldecote, Biggleswade SG18 9BL* Tel (01767) 315578 Fax 317988 Mobile 07840-646672 E-mail frankcoleman@ntlworld.com

COLEMAN, John Harold. b 38. Cant Sch of Min 83. **d** 86 **p** 87. NSM Dover St Martin *Cant* 86-92; V St Mary's Bay w St Mary-in-the-Marsh etc 92-03; P-in-c New Romney w Old Romney and Midley 95-03; rtd 03; Perm to Offic *Cant* from 03. *119 Canterbury Road, Hawkinge, Folkestone CT18 7BS* Tel (01303) 893952 E-mail john.coleman8@btinternet.com

COLEMAN, Jonathan Mark. b 59. Kent Univ BA81. Qu Coll Birm MA99. **d** 99 **p** 00. C Warrington St Elphin *Liv* 99-02; P-in-c Liv St Chris Norris Green 02-07; Area Dean W Derby and Hon Can Liv Cathl 06-07; P-in-c W Derby St Mary 07-09; P-in-c W Derby St Jas 07-09; V W Derby St Mary and St Jas from 09. *The Rectory, Meadow Lane, West Derby, Liverpool L12 5EA* Tel 0151-256 6600 E-mail markcoleman@bigfoot.com

COLEMAN, Michael. b 28. Nat Coll Div LTh90. **d** 95. NSM E Kilbride *Glas* 95-99; NSM Motherwell 99-01; NSM Wishaw 99-01; rtd 01; Lic to Offic *Glas* from 01. *51 Lammermoor, Calderwood, East Kilbride, Glasgow G74 3SE* Tel (01355) 902523

COLEMAN, Ms Nicola Jane. b 63. Goldsmiths' Coll Lon BA86. Ripon Coll Cuddesdon 99. **d** 01 **p** 02. C Croydon St Jo *S'wark* 01-05; P-in-c S Norwood H Innocents from 05. *Holy Innocents' Vicarage, 192A Selhurst Road, London SE25 6XX* Tel (020) 8653 2063 E-mail holyinnocents@btinternet.com

COLEMAN, Patrick Francis. b 58. Reading Univ Pontifical Univ Rome STL STB PhB. Ven English Coll Rome 77. **d** 82 **p** 83. In RC Ch 82-91; NSM Abergavenny St Mary w Llanwenarth Citra *Mon* 96-99; Asst Chapl Milan w Genoa and Varese *Eur* 99-01; R Goetre w Llanover *Mon* 01-06; P-in-c Abertillery w Cwmtillery from 06; Dir CME 02-06. *The Vicarage, Church Street, Abertillery NP13 1DA* Tel (01495) 212246

COLEMAN, Canon Peter Nicholas. b 42. St Mich Coll Llan 83. **d** 85 **p** 86. C Skewen *Llan* 85-88; R Ystradyfodwg 88-07; P-in-c Treorchy and Treherbert 04-07; RD Rhondda 96-04; Can Llan Cathl 04-07; rtd 07. *15 Pant Hendre, Pencoed, Bridgend CF35 6LN*

COLEMAN, Richard Ian. b 70. Open Univ BSc00. Wycliffe Hall Ox 05. **d** 07 **p** 08. C Peterlee *Dur* from 07. *59 O'Neill Drive, Peterlee SR8 5UD* Tel 0191-586 6490 E-mail coleman@orpheusmail.co.uk

COLEMAN, Canon Sybil Jean. b 30. St Deiniol's Hawarden 83. **d** 85 **p** 97. NSM Manselton *S & B* 85-90; C Swansea St Mark and St Jo 90-94; P-in-c 94-98; V 98-00; Hon Can Brecon Cathl 98-00; rtd 00. *Beckley, 25 Beverley Gardens, Fforestfach, Swansea SA5 5DR* Tel (01792) 584280

COLEMAN, Terence Norman. b 37. St Mich Coll Llan 83. **d** 85 **p** 86. C Machen *Mon* 85-87; C Penmaen and Crumlin 87-89; V 89-93; V Newbridge 93-02; rtd 02. *2 Fox Avenue, Newbridge, Newport NP11 4HP* Tel (01495) 243839

COLEMAN, Timothy. b 57. Southn Univ BSc79 CEng82 MIChemE86. Ridley Hall Cam 87. **d** 89 **p** 90. C Bisley and W End *Guildf* 89-93; C Hollington St Jo *Chich* 93-97; V Aldborough Hatch *Chelmsf* 97-02; Chapl Princess Alexandra Hosp NHS Trust 02-04; Chapl Barking Havering and Redbridge Hosps NHS Trust from 04. *The Chaplain's Office, Queen's Hospital, Rom Valley Way, Romford RM7 0AG* Tel (01708) 435000 E-mail tim.coleman@bhrhospitals.nhs.uk

COLERIDGE, William Paul Hugh. b 76. Newc Univ LLB98 Solicitor 01. Wycliffe Hall Ox 07. **d** 09. C Ches Square St Mich w St Phil *Lon* from 09. *24 Sullivan Road, London SE11 4UH* Tel 07968-078432 (mobile) E-mail william@coleridge129.freeserve.co.uk

COLES, Alasdair Charles. b 67. St Andr Univ BSc90 Homerton Coll Cam PGCE91 Ox Univ BTh96 Heythrop Coll Lon PhD03. Ripon Coll Cuddesdon 93. **d** 96 **p** 97. C Wymondham *Nor* 96-99; Min Can and Sacr St Paul's Cathl 99-04; P-in-c Pimlico St Mary Bourne Street 04-07; V from 07; P-in-c Pimlico St Barn 04-07; V from 07; PV Westmr Abbey from 04. *26 Graham Terrace, London SW1W 8JH* Tel (020) 7259 9425 E-mail alasdaircoles@btinternet.com

COLES, Alasdair John. b 66. Pemb Coll Ox BA87 Green Coll Ox BM, BCh90 CCC Cam PhD98 MRCP94. ERMC 05. **d** 08 **p** 09. NSM Chesterton St Andr *Ely* from 08. *Department of Neurology, Box 165, Addenbrooke's Hospital, Cambridge CB2 2QQ* Tel (01223) 216751 Fax 336941 E-mail ajc1020@medschl.cam.ac.uk

COLES, Miss Alison Elizabeth. b 60. St Mary's Coll Dur BA81. Ripon Coll Cuddesdon 95. **d** 97 **p** 98. C Leckhampton SS Phil and Jas w Cheltenham St Jas *Glouc* 97-00; Asst Chapl Dudley Gp of Hosps NHS Trust 00-04; Chapl Walsall Hosps NHS Trust from 04. *Walsall Hospitals NHS Trust, Manor Hospital, Moat Road, Walsall WS2 9PS* Tel (01922) 656216

COLES, Christopher Wayne. b 58. St Mich Coll Llan 97. **d** 99 **p** 00. C Coity w Nolton *Llan* 99-02; C Canton Cardiff 02-07; P-in-c Porth Newydd from 07. *St John's Vicarage, Cymmer, Porth CF39 9HW* Tel (01443) 682219

✠**COLES, The Rt Revd David John.** b 43. Auckland Univ MA67 Otago Univ BD69 MTh71 Man Univ PhD74. St Jo Coll Auckland 66. **d** 68 **p** 69 **c** 90. C Remuera New Zealand 68-70; Chapl Selwyn Coll Dunedin 70-71; Hon C Fallowfield *Man* 72-74; Chapl Hulme Hall 73-74; V Glenfield New Zealand 74-76; V Takapuna 76-80; Dean Napier 80-84; Dean Christchurch 84-90; Bp Christchurch from 90. *PO Box 4438, Christchurch 8140, New Zealand* Tel (0064) (3) 351 7711 *or* 363 0913 Fax 372 3357 E-mail bishop@chch.ang.org.nz

COLES, Preb Francis Herbert. b 35. Selw Coll Cam BA59 MA63. Coll of Resurr Mirfield 59. **d** 61 **p** 62. C Wolvercote *Ox* 61-65; C Farnham Royal 65-69; V Lynton and Brendon *Ex* 69-73; V Countisbury 70-73; TR Lynton, Brendon, Countisbury, Lynmouth etc 73-76; P-in-c Iffley *Ox* 76-88; V Ivybridge w Harford *Ex* 88-00; Preb Ex Cathl from 98; rtd 00; Perm to Offic *Ex* from 00. *8 Glenthorne Road, Exeter EX4 4QU* Tel (01392) 420238

COLES, Geoffrey Herbert. b 38. Nottm Univ CertEd59 TCert60. NOC 77. **d** 80 **p** 81. NSM Shelf *Bradf* 80-85; C Manningham 85-86; TV 86-92; P-in-c Wyke 92-97; P-in-c Riddlesden 97-04; rtd 04. *4 Ferndale Avenue, Clayton, Bradford BD14 6PG* Tel (01274) 427956 E-mail geoffandpamcoles@yahoo.com

COLES, Graham Robert. b 60. Qu Coll Birm 07. **d** 09. C Lillington *Cov* from 09. *10 Sandown Close, Leamington Spa CV32 7SX* Tel 07786-774881 (mobile)

COLES, John Spencer Halstaff. b 50. Hertf Coll Ox BA72 MA76. Wycliffe Hall Ox 72. **d** 75 **p** 76. C Reading Greyfriars *Ox* 75-79; C Clifton Ch Ch w Em *Bris* 79-82; V Woodside Park St Barn *Lon* 82-06; C from 06. *St Barnabas' Vicarage, 68 Westbury Road, London N12 7PD* Tel (020) 8349 8458 *or* 8446 7506 Fax 8343 9406 E-mail johncoles@stbarnabas.co.uk

COLES, Matthew Simon Robert. b 79. UEA BA02. Ridley Hall Cam 06. **d** 09. C Gt Chesham *Ox* from 09. *31 Chapmans Crescent, Chesham HP5 2QT* Tel 07736-464537 (mobile) E-mail mattsr7@yahoo.com

COLES, Mrs Pamela. b 39. Nottm Univ CertEd59. NOC 04. **d** 05 **p** 06. NSM Clayton *Bradf* from 05. *4 Ferndale Avenue, Clayton, Bradford BD14 6PG* Tel (01274) 427956 E-mail geoffandpamcoles@yahoo.com

COLES, Richard Keith Robert. b 62. K Coll Lon BA94 AKC94 Leeds Univ MA05. Coll of Resurr Mirfield 03. **d** 05 **p** 06. C Boston *Linc* 05-07; C Wilton Place St Paul *Lon* from 07; Chapl R Academy of Music 07-08. *Flat 7, 32 Wilton Place, London SW1X 8SH* Tel (020) 7201 9999 E-mail richard@stpaulsknightsbridge.org

COLES, Canon Robert Reginald. b 47. Surrey Univ BSc69. Cant Sch of Min 82. **d** 85 **p** 86. NSM Sittingbourne St Mich *Cant* 85-87; C St Laur in Thanet 87-93; P-in-c St Nicholas at Wade w Sarre and Chislet w Hoath from 93; P-in-c Minster w Monkton from 96; Hon Can Cant Cathl from 09. *The Vicarage, St Mildred's Road, Minster, Ramsgate CT12 4DE* Tel (01843) 821250

COLES, Stephen Richard. b 49. Univ Coll Ox BA70 MA74 Leeds Univ BA80. Coll of Resurr Mirfield 78. **d** 81 **p** 82. C Stoke Newington St Mary *Lon* 81-84; Chapl K Coll Cam 84-89; V Finsbury Park St Thos *Lon* from 89. *25 Romilly Road, London N4 2QY* Tel (020) 7359 5741 E-mail cardinal.jeoffry@btconnect.com

COLES, Mrs Sylvia Margaret. b 48. ERMC 04. **d** 07 **p** 08. NSM Northampton St Benedict *Pet* from 07. *37 Delapre Crescent Road, Northampton NN4 8NG* Tel (01604) 767305 E-mail lizziesgranny@talktalk.net

COLEY (*née* JOHNSON), **Mrs Emma Louise.** b 76. Ex Univ BA97 PGCE98. Wycliffe Hall Ox BTh04. **d** 04 **p** 05. C Wendover and Halton *Ox* 04-09. *1 Icknield Close, Wendover, Aylesbury HP22 6HG* E-mail rev.emcoley@ntlworld.com

COLEY, Peter Leonard. b 45. CEng MIMechE Bath Univ BSc67 City Univ MSc84. Oak Hill Th Coll 85. **d** 87 **p** 88. C Mile Cross *Nor* 87-92; R Stratton St Mary w Stratton St Michael etc 92-01; R Kirby-le-Soken w Gt Holland *Chelmsf* from 01. *The Rectory, 10 Thorpe Road, Kirby Cross, Frinton-on-Sea CO13 0LT* Tel and fax (01255) 675997 E-mail rev.petercoley@lineone.net

COLIN WILFRED, Brother. *see* CHERRIMAN, Colin Wilfred

COLLARD, Canon Harold. b 27. Wycliffe Hall Ox 51. **d** 53 **p** 54. C Rainham *Chelmsf* 53-56; C Kingston upon Hull H Trin *York* 56-59; V Upper Armley *Ripon* 59-68; R Chesterfield H Trin *Derby* 68-77; P-in-c Matlock Bath 77-83; V 83-92; Hon Can Derby Cathl 87-92; RD Wirksworth 88-92; rtd 92; Perm to Offic *Ripon* from 92. *10 Kirkby Avenue, Ripon HG4 2DR* Tel (01765) 606306

COLLARD, John Cedric. b 30. Pemb Coll Cam BA53 MA76. St Alb Minl Tr Scheme 77. **d** 80 **p** 81. NSM Roxton w Gt Barford

St Alb 80-84; C Liskeard w St Keyne, St Pinnock and Morval *Truro* 84-87; TV Liskeard, St Keyne, St Pinnock, Morval etc 87-93; rtd 93; Perm to Offic *Truro* from 93. *Curlew Cottage, Bohetherick, Saltash PL12 6SZ* Tel (01579) 350560

COLLARD, Norton Harvey. b 22. Open Univ BA80. Roch Th Coll 63. **d** 65 **p** 66. C Swanley St Mary *Roch* 65-67; C Dartford H Trin 67-70; V Grantham St Anne *Linc* 70-87; rtd 87; Perm to Offic *Linc* 87-02. *1 Kenwick Drive, Grantham NG31 9DP* Tel (01476) 577345

COLLAS, Canon Victor John. b 23. Pemb Coll Ox BA44 MA48. Wycliffe Hall Ox 49. **d** 51 **p** 52. C Milton *Win* 51-58; R Guernsey St Andr 58-81; Hon Can Win Cathl 78-81; Perm to Offic from 81; rtd 88. *Paradis, La Rue du Paradis, Vale, Guernsey GY3 5BL* Tel (01481) 44171

COLLEDGE, Christopher Richard. b 58. Chich Th Coll. **d** 82 **p** 83. C Deal St Leon *Cant* 82-83; C Deal St Leon and St Rich and Sholden 83-85; Bermuda 85-88; TV Wickford and Runwell *Chelmsf* 88-90; Chapl Runwell Hosp Wickford 88-90; Chapl RAD 90-03; rtd 04. *Address withheld by request* E-mail chriscolledge@aol.com

COLLESS, Mrs Salma. b 55. SRN77 RM80. EAMTC 89. **d** 92 **p** 94. NSM Chesterton St Andr *Ely* 92-93; Australia from 93; Hon Dn Chapman 93; C Curtin 94-96; Chapl Brindabella Gardens 96; P Worker Bernie Court 97; Asst P Woden 97-98. *12 Sollya Place, Rivett ACT 2611, Australia* Tel (0061) (2) 6288 7835 Mobile 414-755756

COLLETT, George Ernest. b 48. Cant Sch of Min 01. **d** 04 **p** 05. NSM Bromley H Trin *Roch* from 04. *Holy Trinity Cottage, 1 Church Lane, Bromley BR2 8LB* Tel (020) 8462 7561 E-mail george.collett@diocese-rochester.org

COLLETT-WHITE, Thomas Charles. b 36. Trin Coll Cam BA61 MA86. Ridley Hall Cam 60. **d** 62 **p** 63. C Gillingham St Mark *Roch* 62-66; V 79-90; C Normanton *Wakef* 66-69; V Highbury New Park St Aug *Lon* 69-76; R Huntingdon w Ormstown Canada 76-79; Chapl Medway Hosp Gillingham 79-85; P-in-c Clerkenwell St Jas and St Jo w St Pet *Lon* 90-96; rtd 01; Perm to Offic *Cant* from 06. *77 The Street, Boughton-under-Blean, Faversham ME13 9BE* Tel (01227) 750770

COLLICUTT McGRATH, Joanna Ruth. b 54. LMH Ox BA76 MA85 Lon Univ MPhil78 Ox Brookes Univ PhD98. Wycliffe Hall Ox 00 Ripon Coll Cuddesdon 05. **d** 06 **p** 07. NSM Witney *Ox* from 06. *Heythrop College, Kensington Square, London W8 5HQ* Tel (020) 7795 6600 E-mail jcollicutt@aol.com

COLLIE, Canon Bertie Harold Guy. b 28. Glas Univ MB, ChB56. Glas NSM Course 75. **d** 76 **p** 77. NSM Ayr *Glas* 76-84; NSM Maybole 76-04; NSM Girvan 84-04; NSM Pinmore 84-04; Dioc Supernumerary 91-99; Can St Mary's Cathl 96-99; Hon Can from 99. *4 Savoy Park, Ayr KA7 2XA* Tel (01292) 285889 E-mail b.collie@sky.com

COLLIE, Canon John Norman. b 25. Em Coll Cam BA51 MA56. Ridley Hall Cam 52. **d** 54 **p** 55. C Leic H Apostles 54-57; C Melton Mowbray w Thorpe Arnold 57-59; Chapl Lee Abbey 59-62; V Streatham Immanuel w St Anselm *S'wark* 62-68; V Ecclesall *Sheff* 68-90; Hon Can Sheff Cathl 83-90; RD Ecclesall 85-89; rtd 90; Perm to Offic *Sheff* from 90. *46 Sunnyvale Road, Sheffield S17 4FB* Tel 0114-235 2249

COLLIER, Anthony Charles. b 45. Peterho Cam BA68 MA72 Whitelands Coll Lon PGCE76. Cuddesdon Coll 68. **d** 71 **p** 72. C N Holmwood *Guildf* 71-75; Perm to Offic *S'wark* 75-79; Chapl Colfe's Sch Lon from 80; Hon C Shirley St Jo *Cant* 80-84; Hon C Shirley St Jo *S'wark* from 85. *56 Bennetts Way, Croydon CR0 8AB* Tel (020) 8777 6456 E-mail accollier@hotmail.com

COLLIER, Clive. *See* COLLIER, Paul Clive

COLLIER, Mrs Janice Margaret. b 57. MCSP79. Cam Th Federation 99. **d** 01 **p** 02. C Formby H Trin *Liv* 01-05; P-in-c Hale from 05. *The Vicarage, 24 Vicarage Close, Hale Village, Liverpool L24 4BH* Tel 0151-425 3195

COLLIER, Michael Francis. b 29. Wycliffe Hall Ox 71. **d** 73 **p** 74. C Hamstead St Paul *Birm* 73-75; P-in-c Castleton *Derby* 75-80; P-in-c Hope 78-80; V Hope and Castleton 80-97; RD Bakewell and Eyam 90-95; rtd 97; Perm to Offic *Derby* from 97. *Buffers Cottage, Station Road, Hope, Hope Valley S33 6RR* Tel (01433) 620915

COLLIER, Paul Clive. b 53. Trin Coll Bris 80. **d** 82 **p** 83. C Hazlemere *Ox* 82-90; V from 90. *The New Vicarage, 260 Amersham Road, High Wycombe HP15 7PZ* Tel (01494) 439404

COLLIER, Paul Edward. b 63. Mert Coll Ox BA85 Lon Univ PGCE87 Solicitor 93. S'wark Ord Course 91. **d** 94 **p** 95. C E Dulwich St Jo *S'wark* 94-97; C-in-c Bermondsey St Hugh CD 97-02; Chapl Goldsmiths' Coll Lon from 03. *5 Wickham Road, London SE4 1PF* Tel (020) 8692 1821 *or* 7717 2953 E-mail p.collier@gold.ac.uk

COLLIER, Richard John Millard. b 45. FRSA92. EAMTC 78. **d** 81 **p** 82. NSM Nor St Pet Mancroft w St Jo Maddermarket 81-97; NSM Thurton from 99. *Old Manor Farm, Fox Road, Framingham Pigot, Norwich NR14 7PZ* Tel (01508) 492916 E-mail rjsjc@yahoo.com

COLLIER, Stefan John. b 74. Man Univ BSc95 St Andr Univ PhD99 Cam Univ BTh09. Ridley Hall Cam 07. **d** 09. C E Win from 09. *28 Longfield Road, Winchester SO23 0NT* E-mail curateastwinchester@googlemail.com

COLLIER, Stephen John. b 46. St Pet Coll Ox MA68 Univ of Wales (Cardiff) DipSW74. Qu Coll Birm 92. **d** 94 **p** 95. C Thorpe St Andr *Nor* 94-98; C Nor St Pet Mancroft w St Jo Maddermarket 98-01; R Kessingland, Gisleham and Rushmere 01-05; rtd 05; Hon C N Greenford All Hallows *Lon* from 06. *9 Drew Gardens, Greenford UB6 7QF* Tel (020) 8903 9697

COLLIER, Susan Margaret. b 47. Cam Univ MB, BChir73. NOC 95. **d** 98 **p** 99. NSM Dringhouses *York* from 98. *12 St Helen's Road, York YO24 1HP* Tel (01904) 706064 Fax 708052

COLLIN, Terry. b 39. St Aid Birkenhead 65. **d** 67 **p** 68. C Bolton St Jas w St Chrys *Bradf* 67-71; C Keighley 71-74; V Greengates 74-04; rtd 04; Perm to Offic *Bradf* from 05. *275 Leeds Road, Eccleshill, Bradford BD2 3LD* Tel (01274) 200855

COLLING, Canon James Oliver (Joc). b 30. MBE95. Man Univ BA50. Cuddesdon Coll 52. **d** 54 **p** 55. C Wigan All SS *Liv* 54-59; V Padgate Ch Ch 59-71; R Padgate 71-73; RD Warrington 70-82 and 87-89; AD 89-95; R Warrington St Elphin 73-97; Hon Can Liv Cathl 76-97; Chapl to The Queen 90-00; rtd 97; Perm to Offic *Ches* from 99. *19 King Street, Chester CH1 2AH* Tel (01244) 317557

COLLING, Terence John. b 47. Linc Th Coll 84. **d** 86 **p** 87. C Wood End *Cov* 86-90; V Willenhall 90-02; V Wolvey w Burton Hastings, Copston Magna etc from 02. *St John's Vicarage, School Lane, Wolvey, Hinckley LE10 3LH* Tel (01455) 220385 Fax 221590 E-mail tc@vicwolvey.fsnet.co.uk

COLLINGBOURNE, David Edward. b 42. St D Coll Lamp. **d** 01. Treas Dioc Coun of Educn *Mon* from 94; NSM Bishton 01-06; NSM Newport Ch Ch 06-08; NSM Bedwas w Machen w Rudry from 08. *The Rectory, Rectory Gardens, Machen, Caerphilly CF83 8SU* Tel (01633) 440321 E-mail davidcollingbourne42@tiscali.co.uk

COLLINGBOURNE, Mrs Susan Lynne. b 48. Caerleon Coll of Educn TCert75 Univ of Wales (Cardiff) BEd82 MEd94. **d** 09. NSM Maesglas and Duffryn *Mon* from 09; Dioc Child Protection Officer from 98. *The Rectory, Rectory Gardens, Machen, Caerphilly CF83 8SU* Tel (01633) 440321 E-mail susan.collingbourne@tinyworld.co.uk

COLLINGE, Mrs Christine Elizabeth. b 47. Doncaster Coll of Educn CertEd68. SAOMC 95. **d** 98 **p** 99. NSM W Slough *Ox* 98-04; TV Stantonbury and Willen from 04. *29 Bradwell Road, Bradville, Milton Keynes MK13 7AX* Tel (01908) 314224 E-mail chriscollinge@hotmail.com

COLLINGRIDGE, Graham Ian. b 58. Pemb Coll Ox BA80 MA84 Bedf Coll Lon MSc84. Ridley Hall Cam 07. **d** 09. C Bitterne Park *Win* from 09. *24 Lacon Close, Southampton SO18 1JA* Tel (023) 8058 4640 E-mail g.collingridge@btinternet.com

COLLINGS, Ms Helen Mary. b 67. Warwick Univ BA88 St Jo Coll Dur BA06 Jes Coll Ox PGCE90. Cranmer Hall Dur 04. **d** 06 **p** 07. C Ossett and Gawthorpe *Wakef* from 06. *1C Westfield Drive, Ossett WF5 8HJ* Tel (01924) 276640 Mobile 07708-066063 E-mail helen@simoncollings.co.uk

COLLINGS, The Very Revd Neil. b 46. K Coll Lon BD69 AKC69. **d** 70 **p** 71. C Littleham w Exmouth 70-72; TV 72-74; Chapl Westm Abbey 74-79; Preb Heref Cathl 79-86; Dir of Ords and Post-Ord Tr 79-86; R Heref St Nic 79-86; Bp's Dom Chapl 82-86; R Harpenden St Nic *St Alb* 86-99; Hon Can St Alb 96-99; Can Res and Treas Ex Cathl 99-06; Chapl Devon and Cornwall Constabulary 99-06; Dean St E from 06. *The Deanery, Bury St Edmunds IP33 1RS* Tel (01284) 754933 Fax 768655 E-mail dean@burycathedral.fsnet.co.uk

COLLINGS, Robert Frank. b 26. Lon Univ BD53. ALCD52. **d** 52 **p** 53. C Bayswater *Lon* 52-55; Australia from 55; rtd 87. *Unit 5, 2 Wattle Street, Bunbury WA 6230, Australia* Tel (0061) (8) 9721 4520

COLLINGTON, Cameron James. b 68. Wycliffe Hall Ox BTh01. **d** 01 **p** 02. C Ealing St Paul *Lon* 01-05; V Hammersmith St Simon from 05. *153 Blythe Road, London W14 0HL* Tel (020) 7602 1043 E-mail bagpipes.collington@xalt.co.uk

COLLINGWOOD, Christopher Paul. b 54. Birm Univ BMus76 PGCE77 Ox Univ BA82 MA87 K Coll Lon MA01 PhD07 LRSM04. Ripon Coll Cuddesdon 80. **d** 83 **p** 84. C Tupsley *Heref* 83-86; Prec St Alb Abbey 86-90; V Bedford St Paul 90-97; Can Res and Prec Guildf Cathl 97-99; Hon C Loughton St Jo *Chelmsf* 99-09; Chapl Chigwell Sch Essex 99-09; Sen Tutor 01-09; R Minchinhampton *Glouc* from 09. *The Rectory, Butt Street, Minchinhampton, Stroud GL6 9JP* Tel (01453) 882289 E-mail rector@minchchurch.org.uk

COLLINGWOOD, Deryck Laurence. b 50. St Jo Coll Cam BA72. Edin Th Coll BD85. **d** 85 **p** 85. Chapl Napier Poly *Edin* 85-88; C Edin Ch Ch 85-88; TV 88-89; Tutor Edin Th Coll 89-94; Asst P Edin St Hilda and Edin St Fillan 94-03; Chapl Napier Univ 95-03; P-in-c Dalmahoy 03-06; R from 06. *St Mary's*

Rectory, Dalmahoy, Kirknewton EH27 8EB Tel 0131-333 1312
E-mail collingwoods@supanet.com

COLLINGWOOD, Graham Lewis. b 63. Open Univ BA92 Ex
Univ MA98. St Steph Ho Ox 92. **d** 95 **p** 96. C Heavitree w Ex
St Paul 95-97; CF 97-99; C St Marychurch *Ex* 99-00; C
Cottingham *York* 00-02; Chapl RAF from 02. *Chaplaincy
Services, Valiant Block, HQ Air Command, RAF High Wycombe
HP14 4UE* Tel (01494) 496800 Fax 496343

COLLINGWOOD, John Jeremy Raynham. b 37. Barrister 64
CCC Cam BA60 MA68 Lon Univ BD78. Trin Coll Bris 75. **d** 78
p 79. C Henleaze *Bris* 78-80; P-in-c Clifton H Trin, St Andr and
St Pet 80-81; V 81-91; RD Clifton 84-87; Bp's Officer for Miss
and Evang 87-91; V Guildf Ch H from 91-98; V Guildf Ch Ch w
St Martha-on-the-Hill 98-02; RD Guildf 95-00; rtd 02. *The Old
Manse, 55 Audley Road, Saffron Walden CB11 3HD* Tel (01799)
529055 E-mail mporokoso@aol.com

COLLINS, Adelbert Andrew. b 15. Lich Th Coll. **d** 61 **p** 62. C
Sedgley All SS *Lich* 61-77; P-in-c Enville 77-81 and 86-88; R
81-86; C Kinver and Enville 88-90; rtd 90; Perm to Offic *Lich* and
Worc from 90. *West Cottage, Bridgnorth Road, Enville,
Stourbridge DY7 5JA* Tel (01384) 873733

COLLINS, Anthony James. b 63. NEOC 04. **d** 07 **p** 08. NSM
Fountains Gp *Ripon* 07-08; NSM Dacre w Hartwith and Darley
w Thornthwaite from 08. *Harvest Cottage, Sawley, Ripon
HG4 3EQ* Tel (01765) 620393 Mobile 07971-245780

COLLINS, Barry Douglas. b 47. Kelham Th Coll 66. **d** 70 **p** 71. C
Peel Green *Man* 70-73; C Salford St Phil w St Steph 73-75; R
Blackley H Trin 75-79; Perm to Offic *Ripon* 80-82; *Pet* 83-93; Cov
85-93; *Ox* 93-97; P-in-c Bengeworth *Worc* 98-99; V from 99. *The
Vicarage, 1 Broadway Road, Evesham WR11 3NB* Tel and fax
(01386) 446164 E-mail barry.collins@tesco.net

COLLINS, Bruce Churton. b 47. BSc. Oak Hill Th Coll. **d** 83 **p** 84.
C Notting Hill St Jo *Lon* 83-87; C Notting Hill St Jo and St Pet
87-90; V Roxeth Ch Ch and Harrow St Pet 90-93; P-in-c S
Harrow St Paul 91-93; TR Roxeth 93-03; Overseer New Wine
Internat Min 03-07; Hon C Roxeth 03-07; Perm to Offic *St D*
from 07. *Medical Centre Flat, Llandovery College, Llandovery
SA20 0EE* Tel (01550) 720901 Mobile 07989-402012
E-mail bruce@collinsbruce.orangehome.co.uk

COLLINS, Ms Cheryl Anne. b 62. Rob Coll Cam BA85 MA89
MCA90. Ripon Coll Cuddesdon 91. **d** 93 **p** 94. C Sharrow St
Andr *Sheff* 93-95; Chapl Sheff Univ 95-01; Hon C Endcliffe
96-01; P-in-c Barton *Ely* from 01; P-in-c Coton from 01; P-in-c
Dry Drayton from 01; RD Bourn from 03. *St Peter's Parsonage,
70 High Street, Coton, Cambridge CB23 7PL* Tel (01954) 210287
E-mail revcherylc@aol.com

COLLINS, Christopher. b 46. K Coll Lon BSc67 AKC67 Pemb
Coll Ox BA70. St Steph Ho Ox 68. **d** 71 **p** 72. C Pennywell
St Thos and Grindon St Oswald CD *Dur* 71-74; C Pallion 74-76;
C Millfield St Mary 74-76; C Bishopwearmouth Gd Shep 74-76;
C Harton Colliery 76-78; TV Winlaton 78-85; V Grangetown
from 85. *St Aidan's Vicarage, Ryhope Road, Sunderland SR2 9RS*
Tel 0191-514 3485

COLLINS, Canon Christopher David. b 43. Sheff Univ
BA(Econ)64. Tyndale Hall Bris 65. **d** 68 **p** 69. C Rusholme H
Trin *Man* 68-71; C Bushbury *Lich* 71-74; V Fairfield *Liv* 74-81; V
Tunbridge Wells St Jo *Roch* 81-92; R Luton Ch Ch and Chapl
Thames Gateway NHS Trust 92-05; Chapl Medway NHS Trust
92-99; RD Roch 94-00; P-in-c Cobham w Luddesdowne and
Dode 05-08; Hon Can Roch Cathl 98-08; rtd 08. *2 Courtenay
Gardens, Alphington, Exeter EX2 8UH* Tel (01392) 203975
E-mail canonchris@blueyonder.co.uk

COLLINS, Darren Victor. b 69. NTMTC. **d** 05 **p** 06. C Chingford
SS Pet and Paul *Chelmsf* 05-07; Min Can St Alb Abbey from 07.
Deanery Barn, Sumpter Yard, St Albans AL1 1BY Tel (01727)
890206 E-mail mkyp@stalbanscathedral.org.uk

COLLINS, Donard Michael. b 55. Oak Hill Th Coll BA83. **d** 83
p 84. C Lurgan Ch the Redeemer *D & D* 83-87; I Ardmore w
Craigavon 87-98; I Killowen *D & R* from 98. *St John's Rectory, 4
Laurel Hill, Coleraine BT51 3AT* Tel (028) 7034 2629
E-mail revdonard@yahoo.co.uk

COLLINS, Canon Frederick Spencer. b 36. FCCA. Ripon Hall
Ox. **d** 67 **p** 68. C Evington *Leic* 67-71; C Hall Green Ascension
Birm 71-73; V Burney Lane 73-79; Dioc Stewardship Adv 79-84;
V Yardley St Edburgha 84-96; RD Yardley 86-92; Hon Can
Birm Cathl 89-97; rtd 96; Perm to Offic *Birm* 96-06; *Worc* 03-06;
Ox from 06. *31 Lunds Farm Road, Woodley, Reading RG5 4PZ*
Tel 0118-969 7790 E-mail fy.collins@virgin.net

COLLINS, Gavin Andrew. b 66. Trin Hall Cam BA89 MA93. Trin
Coll Bris BA96 MA97. **d** 97 **p** 98. C Cambridge St Barn *Ely*
97-02; V Chorleywood St Ch *St Alb* from 02; RD
Rickmansworth from 06. *Christ Church Vicarage, Chorleywood
Common, Rickmansworth WD3 5SG* Tel (01923) 284224 *or*
282149 E-mail gavin.collins@cccw.org.uk
or gavin-collins@supanet.com

COLLINS, Guy James Douglas. b 74. St Andr Univ MTheol96
Peterho Cam PhD00. Westcott Ho Cam 96. **d** 00 **p** 01. C Barnes
S'wark 00-03; R Huntington Valley USA from 03. *The Rectory,
2122 Washington Lane, Huntingdon Valley PA 19006-5824, USA*

COLLINS, Canon Ian Geoffrey. b 37. Hull Univ BA60 CertEd.
Sarum Th Coll 60. **d** 62 **p** 63. C Gainsborough All SS *Linc* 62-65;
Min Can Windsor 65-81; Succ Windsor 67-81; R Kirkby in
Ashfield *S'well* 81-85; Can Res S'well Minster 85-02; P-in-c
Edingley w Halam 91-00; rtd 02. *2 Marston Moor Road, Newark
NG24 2GN* Tel (01636) 702866

COLLINS, Miss Janet May. b 55. Qu Mary Coll Lon BA78 St Jo
Coll Dur BA84. Cranmer Hall Dur 82. dss 85 **d** 87 **p** 94.
Willington *Newc* 85-88; C 87-88; Par Dn Stevenage St Hugh
Chells *St Alb* 88-90; Par Dn Goldington 90-93; TD Witney *Ox*
93-94; TV 94-96; Tutor SAOMC 96-01; TV Langtree 99-01;
P-in-c Weldon w Deene *Pet* 01-08; P-in-c Gt and Lt Oakley
01-08; RD Corby 02-07; P-in-c Pet H Spirit Bretton from 08.
23 Westhawe, Bretton, Peterborough PE3 8BA Tel (01733)
267209 E-mail rev.jan@talktalk.net

COLLINS, John Gilbert. b 32. S'wark Ord Course 67. **d** 71 **p** 72.
C Coulsdon St Jo *S'wark* 71-75; Chapl St Fran Hosp Haywards
Heath 75-84; Chapl Hurstwood Park Hosp Haywards Heath
75-84; R Stedham w Iping, Elsted and Treyford-cum-Didling
Chich 84-92; rtd 92; Perm to Offic *Chich* 94-00. *12 Exeter Road,
Broyle, Chichester PO19 5EF* Tel (01243) 536861

COLLINS, Preb John Theodore Cameron Bucke. b 25. Clare Coll
Cam BA49 MA52. Ridley Hall Cam 49. **d** 51 **p** 52. C
St Marylebone All So w SS Pet and Jo *Lon* 51-57; V Gillingham
St Mark *Roch* 57-71; Chapl Medway Hosp Gillingham 70-71; V
Canford Magna *Sarum* 71-80; RD Wimborne 79-80; V
Brompton H Trin w Onslow Square St Paul *Lon* 80-85; C 85-89;
AD Chelsea 84-88; Preb St Paul's Cathl 85-89; rtd 89; Perm to
Offic *Lon* 89-90; Perm to Offic *Win* 89-97. *27 Woodstock Close,
Oxford OX2 8DB* Tel (01865) 556228

COLLINS, John William Michael. b 54. Bp Otter Coll 95. **d** 98
p 07. NSM S Patcham *Chich* 98-06; NSM Moulsecoomb from
06. *2 Buxted Rise, Brighton BN1 8FG* Tel (01273) 509388

COLLINS, Ms Kathryne Broncy. b 51. Portland State Univ BSc75
Lon Univ MSc76. Linc Th Coll 92. **d** 94 **p** 95. C Bishop's Castle
w Mainstone *Heref* 94-98; P-in-c 98-01; V Bishop's Castle w
Mainstone, Lydbury N etc 01-03; TV Wrexham *St As* 03-05;
NSM from 05; Chapl NE Wales NHS Trust from 03. *Chaplain's
Office, Wrexham Maelor Hospital, Croesnewydd Road, Wrexham
LL13 7TD* Tel (01978) 725590 E-mail kathy.collins@virgin.net

COLLINS, Ms Linda Kathleen. b 56. Girton Coll Cam BA77
MA80 Bris Univ PGCE78. WMMTC 99. **d** 02 **p** 03. C Harborne
St Pet *Birm* 02-05; C Cen Wolverhampton *Lich* 05-09; TV from
09; Chapl K Sch Wolv from 05; Chapl St Pet Colleg Sch Wolv
from 05. *9 Sanstone Road, Walsall WS3 3SJ* Tel (01922) 711225
Mobile 07985-033476 E-mail tobycol@aol.com

COLLINS, Mrs Lindsay Rosemary Faith. b 70. K Coll Lon BD91
AKC91 PGCE92. Ripon Coll Cuddesdon MTh95. **d** 97 **p** 98. C
Witney *Ox* 97-99; NSM 00-01; Chapl Cokethorpe Sch Witney
00-01; Chapl and Hd RE St Paul's Girls' Sch Hammersmith
01-04; Chapl K Coll Sch Wimbledon from 04; Hon C Barnes
S'wark from 04. *25 Glebe Road, London SW13 0DZ* Tel (020)
8878 6982

COLLINS, Louise Ridley. b 59. Lanc Univ BA81 LGSM83.
Cranmer Hall Dur 01. **d** 03 **p** 04. C Sheff St Cuth 03-07; V from
07. *St Cuthbert's Vicarage, 7 Horndean Road, Sheffield S5 6UJ*
Tel 0114-243 6506

COLLINS, Martin. *See* COLLINS, Canon William Francis
Martin

COLLINS, Canon Norman Hilary. b 33. Mert Coll Ox BA55
MA58. Wells Th Coll 58. **d** 60 **p** 61. C Ystrad Mynach *Llan*
60-62; C Gelligaer 62-67; V Maerdy 67-77; R Penarth w
Lavernock 77-98; RD Penarth and Barry 87-98; Can Llan Cathl
92-98; rtd 98. *4 Llys Steffan, Llantwit Major CF61 2UF* Tel
(01446) 794976

COLLINS, Paul David Arthur. b 50. Lanc Univ MSc91. K Coll
Lon BD72 AKC72 St Aug Coll Cant 73. **d** 73 **p** 74. C
Rotherhithe St Mary w All SS *S'wark* 73-76; C Stocking Farm
Leic 76-78; V 78-83; R Husbands Bosworth w Mowsley and
Knaptoft etc 83-87; Soc Resp Officer *Blackb* 87-94; R Worc City
St Paul and Old St Martin etc 94-03; Min Can Worc Cathl 95-03;
P-in-c Bishop's Castle w Mainstone, Lydbury N etc *Heref* from
03; RD Clun Forest 05-08. *The Vicarage, Church Lane, Bishops
Castle SY9 5AF* Tel (01588) 638095

COLLINS, Paul Michael. b 71. St Jo Coll Nottm 06. **d** 08 **p** 09. C
Chenies and Lt Chalfont, Latimer and Flaunden *Ox* from 08.
St George's Parsonage, White Lion Road, Amersham HP7 9LW
Tel (01494) 762229 Mobile 07973-838003
E-mail pmcollins2@yahoo.co.uk

COLLINS, Paul Myring. b 53. St Jo Coll Dur BA75 Ox Univ
BA78 MA83 K Coll Lon PhD95. St Steph Ho Ox 76. **d** 79 **p** 80.
C Meir *Lich* 79-82; C Fenton 82-83; TV Leek and Meerbrook
83-87; Tutor in Th and Liturgy Chich Th Coll 87-94; Dir of
Studies 90-94; V Brighton Gd Shep Preston *Chich* 94-96; Tutor
Qu Coll Birm 96-01; V Bournville *Birm* 01-02; Reader Chr Th
Chich Univ from 02. *University College, College Lane, Chichester
PO19 6PE* Tel (01243) 816000 E-mail p.collins@ucc.ac.uk

COLLINS, Peter Graham. b 60. Anglia Ruskin Univ MA07.
EMMTC 99 Westcott Ho Cam 05. **d** 07 **p** 08. C S Lawres Gp

Linc from 07. *The Rectory, Reepham Road, Fiskerton, Lincoln LN3 4EZ* Tel (01522) 750091 Mobile 07896-066302
E-mail revdpeter@msn.com

COLLINS, Peter John. b 33. Open Univ BA. Oak Hill Th Coll 64. **d** 66 **p** 67. C Low Leyton *Chelmsf* 66-69; C Portsdown *Portsm* 69-72; V Gatten St Paul 72-79; C-in-c Ingrave St Steph CD *Chelmsf* 79-85; V Roydon 85-98; rtd 98; Perm to Offic *S'wark* from 00. *14 Glyndale Grange, Mulgrave Road, Sutton SM2 6LP* Tel (020) 8770 7683

COLLINS, Philip Howard Norton. b 50. AKC73. St Aug Coll Cant 73. **d** 74 **p** 75. C Stamford Hill St Thos *Lon* 74-78; C Upwood w Gt and Lt Raveley *Ely* 78-81; C Ramsey 78-81; R Leverington 81-92; P-in-c Wisbech St Mary 89-92; RD Wisbech 90-92; TR Whittlesey and Pondersbridge 92-95; TR Whittlesey, Pondersbridge and Coates 95-02; R New Alresford w Ovington and Itchen Stoke *Win* 02-07; R Arle Valley from 07. *The Rectory, 37 Jacklyns Lane, Alresford SO24 9LF* Tel (01962) 732105
E-mail philip_nortoncollins@hotmail.com

COLLINS (née SHIRRAS), Rachel Joan. b 66. Univ of Wales (Abth) BSc88. St Jo Coll Nottm 88. **d** 91 **p** 94. Par Dn Ockbrook *Derby* 91-94; C Bris St Matt and St Nath 94-97; V Beckton St Mark *Chelmsf* 97-02; NSM Wandsworth St Steph *S'wark* 02-06; NSM Wandsworth St Mich 02-06; NSM Wandsworth St Mich w St Steph from 06. *11 Combemartin Road, London SW18 5PP* Tel (020) 8788 1851 E-mail rshirras@aol.com

COLLINS, Richard Andrew. b 65. K Coll Lon BD92 AKC92 Dur Univ MA00. St Steph Ho Ox 92. **d** 94 **p** 95. C Whickham *Dur* 94-97; C Bensham 97-98; TV 98-03; P-in-c Greatham and Chapl Greatham Hosp 03-09; Local Min Officer *Dur* 03-09; P-in-c Lumley from 09; Dir of Ords from 09. *Christ Church Vicarage, Great Lumley, Chester le Street DH3 4ER* Tel 0191-388 2228
E-mail richard.collins@durham.anglican.org

COLLINS, Roger Richardson. b 48. Birm Univ BPhil83. WMMTC 78. **d** 81 **p** 82. NSM Cotteridge *Birm* from 81. *6 Chesterfield Court, Middleton Hall Road, Birmingham B30 1AF* Tel 0121-459 4009
E-mail roger@rrcollins.freeserve.co.uk

COLLINS, Ross Nicoll Ferguson. b 64. Edin Univ MA87 Ven English Coll Rome 91 Pontifical Univ Rome 91. Ripon Coll Cuddesdon BA91. **d** 92 **p** 93. C Goring w S Stoke *Ox* 92-96; P-in-c N Leigh 96-01; TR Barnes *S'wark* from 01. *The Rectory, 25 Glebe Road, London SW13 0DZ* Tel and fax (020) 8404 3177 *or* tel and fax 8741 5422 E-mail ross@stmarybarnes.org *or* rosscollins@blueyonder.co.uk

COLLINS, Canon Stella Vivian. b 32. S Dios Minl Tr Scheme 74. **dss** 77 **d** 87 **p** 94. Harnham *Sarum* 77-88; Hon Par Dn 87-88; Dioc Lay Min Adv 82-97; Adv for Women's Min 82-97; Hon Par Dn Wilton w Netherhampton and Fugglestone 88-94; Hon C 94-97; RD Wylye and Wilton 89-94; Can and Preb Sarum Cathl 93-97; rtd 97; Perm to Offic *Sarum* 97-07. *1 Meadowside, Hanging Langford, Salisbury SP3 4NW* Tel (01722) 790743

COLLINS, Canon William Francis Martin. b 43. St Cath Coll Cam BA66 MA70. Cuddesdon Coll 68. **d** 70 **p** 71. C Man Victoria Park 70-73; P-in-c Ancoats 73-78; Chapl Abraham Moss Cen 78-91; Hon C Cheetham Hill 81-84; Chs' FE Officer for Gtr Man 84-91; V Norbury *Ches* 91-08; Hon Can Ches Cathl 05-08; rtd 08. *9 Milldale Avenue, Buxton SK17 9BE* Tel (01298) 74906 Mobile 07866-505589

COLLINS, Winfield St Clair. b 41. Univ of W Indies BA83 Man Univ BA88 MEd91. Codrington Coll Barbados. **d** 76 **p** 76. Asst Chapl HM Pris Wakef 76; Barbados 76-84; C St Jo 76; P-in-c St Mark and St Cath 77-84; Asst Chapl HM Pris Wandsworth 85; Chapl HM YOI Thorn Cross 85-91; Chapl HM Pris Pentonville 91-01; Can Res Barbados 01-02; rtd 02. *92 Barclay Road, London N18 1EQ* Tel (020) 8245 4145

COLLINSON, Mrs Amanda. b 74. Luton Univ BA96. Ripon Coll Cuddesdon 07. **d** 09. C Catherington and Clanfield *Portsm* from 09. *23 Piper's Mead, Clanfield, Waterlooville PO8 0ST* Tel (023) 9258 0806 E-mail amanda.collinson@ntlworld.com

COLLINSON, Ernest John. b 12. ALCD36. **d** 36 **p** 37. C Southall Green St Jo *Lon* 36-38; Sudan 38-46; R Graveley w Chivesfield *St Alb* 46-48; V Laleham *Lon* 48-52; Africa Inland Miss 52-54; V Penge St Jo *Roch* 54-63; Rwanda Miss 63-66; V Tiverton St Geo *Ex* 66-73; Perm to Offic from 74; rtd 77. *2 St Helens Court, Cotmaton Road, Sidmouth EX10 8SS* Tel (01395) 513878

COLLINSON, Leslie Roland. b 47. St Jo Coll Nottm 90. **d** 92 **p** 93. C Gorleston St Andr *Nor* 92-96; TV Banbury *Ox* 96-98; V Banbury St Fran 98-00; V Darwen St Barn *Blackb* from 00. *St Barnabas' Vicarage, 68 Park Road, Darwen BB3 2LD* Tel (01254) 702732 E-mail revles@ntlworld.com

COLLINSON, Mark Peter Charles. b 68. City Univ BSc90 Fitzw Coll Cam BA97 MA01. Ridley Hall Cam 95. **d** 98 **p** 99. C Ashton-upon-Mersey St Mary Magd *Ches* 98-01; Chapl Amsterdam w Den Helder and Heiloo *Eur* from 01. *Bouwmeester 2, 1188 DT Amstelveen, The Netherlands* Tel (0031) (20) 441 0355 Fax 453 7431
E-mail mark@christchurch.nl

COLLINSON, Roger Alfred. b 36. St Jo Coll Dur BA58 Cranmer Hall Dur 60. **d** 63 **p** 97. C Liv St Mich 63-64; NSM Ormside *Carl*

97-06; NSM Appleby 97-06; Perm to Offic from 06. *1 Caesar's View, Appleby-in-Westmorland CA16 6SH* Tel (01768) 352886

COLLIS, Jonathan. b 69. Selw Coll Cam BA91 MA94. Aston Tr Scheme 96 Westcott Ho Cam 97. **d** 99 **p** 00. C St Neots *Ely* 99-02; Chapl Jes Coll Cam 02-09; V Thorpe Bay *Chelmsf* from 09. *The Vicarage, 86 Tyrone Road, Southend-on-Sea SS1 3HB* Tel (01702) 587597 E-mail jonathan.collis@cantab.net

COLLIS, Michael Alan. b 35. K Coll Lon BD60 AKC60. **d** 61 **p** 62. C Worc St Martin 61-63; C Dudley St Thos 63-66; C St Peter-in-Thanet *Cant* 66-70; V Croydon H Trin 70-77; P-in-c Norbury St Steph 77-81; V 81-82; V Sutton Valence w E Sutton and Chart Sutton 82-89; R New Fishbourne *Chich* 89-00; P-in-c Appledram 89-00; rtd 00; Perm to Offic *Chich* from 00. *66 Orchard Way, Barnham, Bognor Regis PO22 0HY* Tel (01243) 552429

COLLIS, The Very Revd Stephen Thomas. b 47. MHCIMA94. Cranmer Hall Dur 80. **d** 82 **p** 83. C Crewe All SS and St Paul *Ches* 82-84; C Wilmslow 84-86 and 95-98; Chapl RAF 86-95; P-in-c Barthomley *Ches* 98-00; S Cheshire Ind Chapl 98-00; Chapl Abu Dhabi UAE 00-02; Dean St Paul's Cathl and Chapl Nicosia from 02; Adn Cyprus from 06. *2 Grigori Afxentiou Street, PO Box 22014, 1516 Nicosia, Cyprus* Tel (00357) (22) 677897 Fax 672241 Mobile 99-359813
E-mail stpauls@spidernet.com.cy

COLLISHAW, Ashley Stuart. b 66. Wycliffe Hall Ox 03. **d** 05 **p** 06. C Worc City from 05. *St Swithin's Institute, The Trinity, Worcester WR1 2PN* Tel (01905) 356266
E-mail crockfords@collishaw.net

COLLISON, Christopher John. b 48. Oak Hill Th Coll 68. **d** 72 **p** 73. C Cromer *Nor* 72-75; C Costessey 76-78; V 87-95; C Heckmondwike *Wakef* 78-79; P-in-c Shepley and Dioc Communications Officer 79-83; Chapl Flushing Miss to Seamen *Eur* 83-85; Asst Min Sec Miss to Seamen 85-87; C St Mich Paternoster Royal *Lon* 85-87; P-in-c Swainsthorpe w Newton Flotman *Nor* 95-97; TV Newton Flotman, Swainsthorpe, Tasburgh, etc 98-02; V Henfield w Shermanbury and Woodmancote *Chich* from 02; Dioc Evang Officer *Nor* 95-01; RD Hurst *Chich* 04-09. *The Vicarage, Church Lane, Henfield BN5 9NY* Tel and fax (01273) 492017
E-mail office@stpetershenfield.co.uk

COLLISON, Ms Elizabeth. b 38. Man Univ CertEd58. NOC 85. **d** 88 **p** 94. C Huyton St Mich *Liv* 88-94; C Rainhill 94-05; rtd 05. *25 Lowther Drive, Rainhill, Prescot L35 0NG* Tel 0151-426 3853
E-mail liz-collison@yahoo.co.uk

COLLYER, David John. b 38. JP. Keble Coll Ox BA61 MA86. Westcott Ho Cam 61. **d** 63 **p** 64. C Perry Beeches *Birm* 63-65; P-in-c Deritend 66-70; Bp's Chapl for Special Youth Work 65-70; Bp's Youth Chapl and Dioc Youth Officer 70-73; R Northfield 73-78; Hon Chapl Birm Cathl 78-81; Hon C Birm St Geo 81-86; V Handsworth St Andr 86-97; Dioc Development Officer 97-01; Hon Can Birm Cathl 95-06; Perm to Offic from 01. *19 Birch Close, Bournville, Birmingham B30 1NA*

COLLYER, Leon John. b 72. SS Hild & Bede Coll Dur BSc95 Leeds Univ BA00. Coll of Resurr Mirfield 98. **d** 01 **p** 02. C Airedale w Fryston *Wakef* 01-04; P-in-c Crofton from 04; P-in-c Warmfield from 04. *The Vicarage, 2A Ashdene Approach, Crofton, Wakefield WF4 1LZ* Tel 07714-986462 (mobile)
E-mail trleon@o2.co.uk

COLMAN, Geoffrey Hugh. b 29. Univ Coll Ox BA53 MA68. Wells Th Coll 67. **d** 68 **p** 69. C Wanstead St Mary *Chelmsf* 68-72; V Barking St Erkenwald 72-77; Youth Chapl 78-81; C Maidstone All SS and St Phil w Tovil *Cant* 85-88; P-in-c Norton 88-93; R 93-96; P-in-c Teynham 88-93; P-in-c Lynsted w Kingsdown 88-93; V Teynham w Lynsted and Kingsdown 93-96; rtd 96; Perm to Offic *Cant* 98-99. *c/o Mrs G H Fulcher, 87 Broyle Road, Chichester PO19 6BE* Tel (01243) 551448

COLMER, Andrew John. b 68. De Montfort Univ Leic BSc90. St Jo Coll Nottm MA96 LTh97. **d** 97 **p** 98. C Roby *Liv* 97-01; C Litherland St Andr 01-02; P-in-c Liv All So Springwood from 02. *Springwood Vicarage, 499 Mather Avenue, Liverpool L19 4TF* Tel and fax 0151-427 5699 E-mail andrew.colmer@virgin.net

COLMER, The Ven Malcolm John. b 45. Sussex Univ MSc67. St Jo Coll Nottm BA73. **d** 73 **p** 74. C Egham *Guildf* 73-76; C Chadwell *Chelmsf* 76-79; V S Malling *Chich* 79-85; V Hornsey Rise St Mary w St Steph *Lon* 85-87; TR Hornsey Rise Whitehall Park Team 87-96; Adn Islington 90-94; Adn Middx 96-05; Adn Heref from 05; Can Res Heref Cathl from 05. *The Palace, Palace Yard, Hereford HR4 9BL* Tel (01432) 373324
E-mail archdeacon@hereford.anglican.org

COLPUS (née EDWARDS), Mrs Anita Carolyn. b 71. Trin Coll Bris 01. **d** 03 **p** 04. C Notting Hill St Pet *Lon* 03-06; C Sittingbourne St Mary and St Mich *Cant* from 07. *2 Johnson Road, Sittingbourne ME10 1JS* Tel (01795) 471513
E-mail anitacolpus@tesco.net

COLSON, Ian Richard. b 65. Wolv Poly BSc86 Nottm Univ BTh89 Warwick Univ MA03. Linc Th Coll 86. **d** 89 **p** 90. C Nunthorpe *York* 89-92; C Thornaby on Tees 92-93; Chapl RAF 93-00; V Sunbury *Lon* 00-02; Chapl Ardingly Coll 02-09; Sen Chapl Ch Hosp Horsham from 09. *Christ's Hospital, Horsham RH13 0YP* Tel (01403) 252547 E-mail ianrcolson@aol.com

COLSTON, Canon John Edward. b 43. Open Univ BA91 Leeds Univ MA94. Lich Th Coll 65. **d** 68 **p** 69. C Bromsgrove All SS *Worc* 68-71; C Tettenhall Wood *Lich* 71-74; V Alrewas and Wychnor 74-88; R Ainderby Steeple w Yafforth and Kirby Wiske etc *Ripon* 88-95; V High Harrogate Ch Ch 95-07; Warden of Readers 90-96; AD Harrogate 01-05; Hon Can Ripon Cathl 06-07; rtd 08. *15 Sycamore Road, Ripon HG4 2LR* Tel (01765) 600747 E-mail john.colston@yahoo.co.uk

COLTON, Mrs Christine Ann. b 56. Univ of Wales (Cardiff) BA00 MTh06. St Mich Coll Llan 01. **d** 06 **p** 07. NSM Cen Cardiff *Llan* 06-07; NSM Radyr from 07. *Canton Vicarage, 3A Romilly Road, Cardiff CF5 1FH* Tel (029) 2022 9683

COLTON, Martin Philip. b 67. Sheff Univ BMus89 MMus92 FRCO92 Open Univ PGCE97. St Mich Coll Llan BA03. **d** 03 **p** 04. C Whitchurch *Llan* 03-06; TV Canton Cardiff from 06. *Canton Vicarage, 3A Romilly Road, Cardiff CF5 1FH* Tel (029) 2022 9683 E-mail martin.colton@which.net

✠**COLTON, The Rt Revd William Paul.** b 60. NUI BCL81 TCD MPhil87 Univ of Wales (Cardiff) LLM06. **d** 84 **p** 85 **c** 99. C Lisburn St Paul *Conn* 84-87; Bp's Dom Chapl 85-90; V Choral Belf Cathl 87-90; Min Can Belf Cathl 89-90; PV, Registrar and Chapter Clerk Ch Ch Cathl Dub 90-95; I Castleknock and Mulhuddart w Clonsilla 90-99; Co-ord Protestant Relig Progr RTE 93-99; Hon Chapl Actors' Ch Union 94-96; Area Chapl (Ireland) Actors' Ch Union 96-97; Can Ch Ch Cathl Dublin 97-99; Bp C, C & R from 99. *St Nicholas' House, 14 Cove Street, Cork, Republic of Ireland* Tel (00353) (21) 500 5080 Fax 432 0960 E-mail bishop@ccrd.ie

COLVILLE, Gary Stanley. b 59. Sarum & Wells Th Coll 90. **d** 92 **p** 94. C Plaistow St Mary *Roch* 92-94; P-in-c Foots Cray 94-96; R 96-00; P-in-c N Cray 97-00; R Pembroke Bermuda 01-04; V Roch from 04. *The Vicarage, 138 Delce Road, Rochester ME1 2EH* Tel (01634) 845122 E-mail moiracolville@hotmail.com

COLWELL, Ms Katherine Elizabeth. b 57. EMMTC. **d** 08. C Barton upon Humber *Linc* from 08. *82 West Acridge, Barton-upon-Humber DN18 5AN* Tel (01652) 632318

COLWILL, James Patrick (Jay). b 68. Man Poly BA91. St Jo Coll Nottm BTh93 MA94. **d** 94 **p** 95. C Reading St Agnes w St Paul *Ox* 94-97; C Easthampstead 97-03; V Orpington Ch Ch *Roch* from 03. *The Vicarage, 165 Charterhouse Road, Orpington BR6 9EP* Tel (01689) 870923 Mobile 07941-752513 E-mail jay.colwill@diocese-rochester.org

COMBE, The Very Revd John Charles. b 33. TCD BA53 MA56 BD57 MLitt65 PhD70. **d** 56 **p** 57. C Cork St Luke w St Ann *C, C & R* 56-58; C Ballynafeigh St Jude *D & D* 58-61; I Crinken *D & G* 61-66; Hon Clerical V Ch Ch Cathl Dublin 63-66; C Belfast St Bart *Conn* 66-70; I Belfast St Barn 70-74; I Portadown St Mark *Arm* 74-84; I Arm St Mark w Aghavilly 84-90; Can Arm Cathl 85-90; Dean Kilmore *K, E & A* 90-96; I Kilmore w Ballintemple, Kildallan etc 90-96; rtd 96. *24 Kensington Park, Maxwell Road, Bangor BT20 3RF* Tel (028) 9146 6123

COMBER, Mrs Alison. b 44. **d** 94 **p** 95. OLM New Bury *Man* 94-96; OLM New Bury w Gt Lever from 06. *12 Seymour Grove, Farnworth, Bolton BL4 0HF* Tel (01204) 397745

COMBER, The Ven Anthony James. b 27. Leeds Univ BSc49 MSc52. St Chad's Coll Dur 53. **d** 56 **p** 57. C Manston *Ripon* 56-60; V Oulton 60-69; V Hunslet St Mary 69-77; RD Armley 72-75 and 79-81; R Farnley 77-82; Hon Can Ripon Cathl 80-92; Adn Leeds 82-92; rtd 92; Perm to Offic *Ripon* from 92 and *Bradf* 93-99. *28 Blayds Garth, Woodlesford, Leeds LS26 8WN* Tel 0113-288 0489 Mobile 07840-763818 E-mail tony.comber@btinternet.com

COMBER, Michael. b 35. Carl Dioc Tr Inst. **d** 72 **p** 72. CA 59-72; C Carl H Trin and St Barn 72-73; C Upperby St Jo 73-76; V Dearham 76-81; V Harraby 81-84; R Orton and Tebay w Ravenstonedale etc 84-90; I Clonfert *Gp L & K* 90-94; I Convoy w Monellan and Donaghmore *D & R* 94-97; I Tamlaght O'Crilly Upper w Lower 97-02; rtd 02; Perm to Offic *Carl* from 03. *87 Pinecroft, Kingstown, Carlisle CA3 0DB* Tel (01228) 401428 Mobile 07742-392124 E-mail m.comber@talk21.com

COMBES, The Ven Roger Matthew. b 47. K Coll Lon LLB69. Ridley Hall Cam 72. **d** 74 **p** 75. C Onslow Square St Paul *Lon* 74-77; C Brompton H Trin 76-77; C Cambridge H Sepulchre w All SS *Ely* 77-86; R Silverhill St Matt *Chich* 86-03; RD Hastings 98-02; Adn Horsham from 03. *3 Danehurst Crescent, Horsham RH13 5HS* Tel (01403) 262710 Fax 210778 E-mail archhorsham@diochi.org.uk

COMER, Michael John. b 30. St Mich Coll Llan 79. **d** 81 **p** 82. C Bistre *St As* 81-84; R Llanfyllin and Bwlchycibau 84-91; V Hattersley *Ches* 91-94; rtd 94. *1B Trefnant Villas, Dolfor Road, Newtown SY16 1JD* Tel (01686) 624557

COMERFORD, Canon Patrick. b 52. Pontifical Univ Maynooth BD87 FRSAI87. CITC 99. **d** 00 **p** 01. NSM Dublin Whitechurch *D & G* from 00; Dir Spiritual Formation CITC from 06; Can Ch Ch Cathl Dublin from 07. *75 Glenvara Park, Knocklyon, Dublin 16, Republic of Ireland* Tel (00353) (1) 495 0934 Mobile 87-663 5116 E-mail patrickcomerford@citc.ie

COMERFORD, Mrs Suzanne Lyn. b 46. SAOMC 97. **d** 00 **p** 01. OLM Woodley *Ox* 00-08. *110 Lower Drayton Lane, Portsmouth PO6 2HE* Tel 07786-224247 (mobile)

COMFORT, Alan. b 64. Ridley Hall Cam 91. **d** 94 **p** 95. C Chadwell Heath *Chelmsf* 94-97; C Buckhurst Hill 97-98; TV 98-03; R Loughton St Mary 03-09; TR Gt Baddow from 09. *The Rectory, 12 Church Street, Great Baddow, Chelmsford CM2 7HZ* Tel (01245) 471740 E-mail alancomfort11@tiscali.co.uk

COMLEY, Thomas Hedges. b 36. Leeds Univ BA62. Coll of Resurr Mirfield 62. **d** 64 **p** 65. C Leadgate *Dur* 64-67; C Shirley *Birm* 67-71; V Smethwick St Alb 71-76; Perm to Offic 76-82; V N Wembley St Cuth *Lon* 82-92; V Taddington, Chelmorton and Flagg, and Monyash *Derby* 92-01; rtd 01; Perm to Offic *Derby* from 01. *19 Wentworth Avenue, Walton, Chesterfield S40 3JB* Tel (01246) 270911 E-mail tom_comley@lineone.net

COMMIN, Robert William. b 47. Cape Town Univ BA79. St Paul's Coll Grahamstown. **d** 70 **p** 71. S Africa 70-80 and from 89; Chapl Loretto Sch Musselburgh 80-84; TV Thetford *Nor* 84-89. *42 Earl Street, Woodstock, 7925 South Africa* Tel (0027) 82-202 5303 (mobile) E-mail bcommin@netactive.co.za

COMPTON, Barry Charles Chittenden. b 33. Linc Th Coll 60. **d** 62 **p** 63. C Beddington *S'wark* 62-65; C Limpsfield and Titsey 66-68; Hon C 71-94; R Ridley *Roch* 69-70; R Ash 69-70; Perm to Offic *S'wark* from 70; rtd 94. *14 Hallsland Way, Oxted RH8 9AL* Tel (01883) 714896 Fax 722842

COMPTON, Penelope. See GEORGE, Penelope

COMYNS, Clifford John. b 28. TCD BA50 HDipEd53 MA53 BD67. **d** 51 **p** 52. C Chapelizod *D & G* 51-55; CF 55-75; Asst Master Eastbourne Coll 75-06; Asst Chapl 85-06; rtd 06. *6 Nursery Way, Heathfield TN21 0UW* Tel (01435) 864941 E-mail helen@dormand.fsworld.co.uk

CONALTY, Julie Anne. b 63. SEITE. **d** 99 **p** 00. NSM E Wickham *S'wark* 99-04; Hon C Charlton from 04. *12 Littleheath, London SE7 8HU* Tel (020) 8855 6203 *or* 7740 8500

CONANT, Fane Charles. b 44. Oak Hill Th Coll 83. **d** 85 **p** 86. C Hoole *Ches* 85-89; V Kelsall 89-01; P-in-c Seer Green and Jordans *Ox* 01-06; rtd 06; Partner Evang Luis Palau Evang Assn from 06. *1 Spring Bank, Shrewsbury Road, Church Stretton SY6 6HA* Tel (01694) 722610 E-mail fanesue@aol.com

CONAWAY, Barry Raymond. b 41. CertEd69 Nottm Univ BEd70. Sarum & Wells Th Coll 86. **d** 88 **p** 89. C Ross w Brampton Abbotts, Bridstow and Peterstow *Heref* 88-91; R Bishop's Frome w Castle Frome and Fromes Hill 91-96; P-in-c Acton Beauchamp and Evesbatch 91-96; P-in-c Charminster and Stinsford *Sarum* 96-01; rtd 01; Perm to Offic *Glouc* 01-02 and *Sarum* from 03. *9 Constable Way, West Harnham, Salisbury SP2 8LN* Tel (01722) 334870

CONDER, Paul Collingwood Nelson. b 33. St Jo Coll Cam BA56 MA60. Ridley Hall Cam 56. **d** 58 **p** 59. C Grassendale *Liv* 58-61; Tutor St Jo Coll Dur 61-67; R Sutton *Liv* 67-74; TR 74-75; V Thames Ditton *Guildf* 75-86; RD Emly 82-86; V Blundellsands St Mich *Liv* 86-99; rtd 99; Perm to Offic *York* from 00. *112 Strensall Road, Earswick, York YO32 9SJ* Tel (01904) 763071

CONDRY, Canon Edward Francis. b 53. UEA BA74 Ex Coll Ox BLitt77 DPhil80 Open Univ MBA02. Linc Th Coll 80. **d** 82 **p** 83. C Weston Favell *Pet* 82-85; V Bloxham w Milcombe and S Newington *Ox* 85-93; TR Rugby *Cov* 93-02; Can Res Cant Cathl from 02; Dir Post-Ord Tr 02-06; Treas and Dir of Educn from 06. *15 The Precincts, Canterbury CT1 2EL* Tel (01227) 865228 E-mail edwardc@canterbury-cathedral.org

CONEY, Joanna Margery. b 39. Culham Coll of Educn CertEd75 Open Univ BA83. Ox Min Course 90. **d** 93 **p** 94. C Wolvercote w Summertown *Ox* 93-97; Hon C New Marston 97-06; Hon C Wolvercote w Summertown 06-07; Hon C Wolvercote from 07; OLM Tr Officer (Ox Adnry) 97-00; Dioc Portfolio Officer 00-04; rtd 04; Dioc Adv to Lic Lay Min *Ox* 02-09; NSM Voc Adv from 09. *4 Rowland Close, Wolvercote, Oxford OX2 8PW* Tel and fax (01865) 556456 E-mail joanna.coney@oxford.anglican.org

CONEY, Preb Peter Norman Harvey. b 28. Keble Coll Ox BA51 MA55. Cuddesdon Coll 51. **d** 53 **p** 54. C Northallerton w Deighton and Romanby *York* 53-56; C Wakef Cathl 56-59; V Milverton *B & W* 59-65; Chapl K Coll Taunton 65-70; V Martock *B & W* 70-72; V Martock w Ash 72-92; RD Martock 80-90; Dioc Press Officer 83-88; Preb Wells Cathl 85-92; rtd 93; Perm to Offic *Eur* from 92. *4 Wessex Rise, Somerton TA11 7BP* Tel (01458) 274193

CONEYS, Canon Stephen John. b 61. Sheff Univ LLB82. St Jo Coll Nottm 87. **d** 90 **p** 91. C Plymouth Em w Efford *Ex* 90-92; C Plymouth Em, Efford and Laira 93-94; TV Whitstable *Cant* 94-02; TR from 02; Hon Can Cant Cathl from 08. *The Vicarage, 11 Kimberley Grove, Seasalter, Whitstable CT5 4AY* Tel (01227) 276795 E-mail steveconeys@btinternet.com

CONGDON, John Jameson. b 30. St Edm Hall Ox BA53 MA57. Wycliffe Hall Ox 53. **d** 55 **p** 56. C Aspley *S'well* 55-58; C-in-c Woodthorpe CD 58-63; V Woodthorpe 63-69; V Spring Grove St Mary *Lon* 70-84; V Woodley St Jo the Ev *Ox* 84-89; Chapl W Middx Univ Hosp Isleworth 89-95; rtd 95; Perm to Offic *Lon* from 95 and *Ox* from 06. *23 Pates Manor Drive, Feltham TW14 8JJ* Tel (020) 8893 1823

CONGO, Archbishop of. *See* FIDÈLE, The Most Revd Dirokpa Balufuga

CONLEY, James Alan. b 29. Dur Univ BSc51. St Jo Coll Nottm. **d** 87 **p** 88. NSM Cropwell Bishop w Colston Bassett, Granby etc *S'well* 87-97; Perm to Offic *Sarum* 97-07. *30 The Waldrons, Thornford, Sherborne DT9 6PX* Tel (01935) 872672

CONLIN, Tiffany Jane Kate. b 71. K Coll Lon BA93 MA94 PhD00 AKC93. Westcott Ho Cam 03. **d** 05 **p** 06. C Wisbech St Aug and Wisbech SS Pet and Paul *Ely* 05-08; Chapl Fitzw Coll Cam from 08. *Fitzwilliam College, Cambridge CB3 0DG* Tel (01223) 332013 E-mail tiffanyjkconlin@yahoo.com

CONLON, Shaun. b 69. Birm Univ BA90. Ripon Coll Cuddesdon 91. **d** 93 **p** 94. C Castle Bromwich SS Mary and Marg *Birm* 93-97; C Hockerill *St Alb* 97-00; V St Mary-at-Latton *Chelmsf* 00-07; V Prittlewell from 07. *Prittlewell Vicarage, 489 Victoria Avenue, Southend-on-Sea SS2 6NL* Tel (01702) 343470 E-mail shaunconlon@tiscali.co.uk

CONN, Alistair Aberdein. b 37. Down Coll Cam BA60 MA64. Linc Th Coll 60. **d** 62 **p** 63. C W Hartlepool St Paul *Dur* 62-65; Uganda 65-66; Chapl Shrewsbury Sch 66-73; R Coupar Angus *St And* 73-78; V Ravenshead *S'well* 78-93; RD Newstead 90-93; R Collingham w S Scarle and Besthorpe and Girton 93-02; RD Newark 95-02; rtd 02; Perm to Offic *S'well* from 02. *17 Beacon Heights, Newark NG24 2JS* Tel (01636) 706291

CONNELL, Clare. *See* CONNELL, Mrs Penelope Clare

CONNELL, Frederick Philip Richard John. b 45. St Jo Coll Nottm MA98. **d** 99 **p** 00. Deacon Jos St Piran Nigeria 99-00; V 00-01; NSM Nottingham St Pet and All SS *S'well* 01-03; Perm to Offic 03-04; NSM Nottingham St Nic 04-07; C Leic Martyrs 07-09; TV Vale of Belvoir Par from 09. *4 Rutland Lane, Bottesford, Nottingham NG13 0DE* E-mail frederick.connell@tiscali.co.uk

CONNELL, Miss Heather Josephine. b 38. Open Univ BA93 SRN60 SCM61. S'wark Ord Course. **dss** 79 **d** 87 **p** 94. Heston *Lon* 79-84; Gillingham St Barn *Roch* 84-90; Par Dn 87-90; Distr Chapl Medway NHS Trust 91-96; NSM Gillingham H Trin *Roch* 94-07; rtd 98; Perm to Offic *Chelmsf* from 08. *27 Norman Close, St Osyth, Clacton-on-Sea CO16 8PN* Tel (01255) 820537 E-mail h.connell@tesco.net

CONNELL, John Richard. b 63. K Coll Lon BD84. St Mich Coll Llan 84. **d** 94 **p** 96. C Caldicot *Mon* 94-97; C Risca 97-00; V Llantilio Pertholey w Bettws Chpl etc 00-05; P-in-c Wokingham St Paul *Ox* from 05. *St Paul's Rectory, Holt Lane, Wokingham RG41 1ED* Tel 0118-978 0629 E-mail john@rectorystudy.wanadoo.co.uk

CONNELL, Julie. d 08. NSM Brixton Road Ch Ch *S'wark* from 08. *8 Helix Road, London SW2 2JS* Tel (020) 8671 0481 *or* 7587 0375 Fax 7582 7421

CONNELL, Mrs Penelope Clare. b 44. EMMTC. **d** 03 **p** 04. NSM Whatton w Aslockton, Hawksworth, Scarrington etc *S'well* 03-06; NSM Nottingham St Nic 06-07; NSM Ironstone Villages *Leic* from 07. *4 Rutland Lane, Bottesford, Nottingham NT13 0DG* Tel 07866-495720 (mobile) E mail clare.connell@tiscali.co.uk

CONNELL, Ms Sharon Margaret. b 65. St Jo Coll Nottm BA03. **d** 03 **p** 04. C S Hackney St Jo w Ch Ch *Lon* 03-06; C Stepney St Dunstan and All SS 06-08; Ecum Chapl Chelsea and Westmr Hosp NHS Found Trust from 08. *Chelsea and Westminster Hospital, 369 Fulham Road, London SW10 9NH* Tel (020) 8746 8083 E-mail sharon.connell@chelwest.nhs.uk

CONNER, Mrs Cathryn. b 42. Birm Univ BSc64. NEOC 91. **d** 94 **p** 95. NSM Bainton w N Dalton, Middleton-on-the-Wolds etc *York* 94-98; NSM Woldsburn 98-04; rtd 04. *Centre House, North Dalton, Driffield YO25 9XA* Tel (01377) 217265

CONNER, Charles Borthwick. b 20. Keble Coll Ox BA43 MA49. St Steph Ho Ox 48. **d** 50 **p** 51. C Saltburn-by-the-Sea *York* 50-52; Chapl Ely Th Coll 52-53; CF 53-70. *Angel Cottage, West Knighton, Dorchester DT2 8PE* Tel (01305) 852465

✠**CONNER, The Rt Revd David John.** b 47. Ex Coll Ox BA69 MA77. St Steph Ho Ox 69. **d** 71 **p** 72 **c** 94. Asst Chapl St Edw Sch Ox 71-73; Chapl 73-80; Hon C Summertown *Ox* 71-76; TV Wolvercote w Summertown 76-80; Chapl Win Coll 80-87; V Cambridge Gt St Mary w St Mich *Ely* 87-94; RD Cambridge 89-94; Suff Bp Lynn *Nor* 94-98; Dean Windsor and Dom Chapl to The Queen from 98; Bp HM Forces 01-09. *The Deanery, Windsor Castle, Windsor SL4 1NJ* Tel (01753) 865561 Fax 819002 E-mail david.conner@stgeorges-windsor.org

CONNING, Dowell Paul. b 64. Ripon Coll Cuddesdon BTh00. **d** 00 **p** 01. C Leckhampton St Pet *Glouc* 00-03; CF from 03; Hon Min Can Ripon Cathl from 05. *c/o MOD Chaplains (Army)* Tel (01980) 615804 Fax 615800 E-mail dowell@freenet.co.uk

CONNOLL, Miss Helen Dorothy. b 45. Oak Hill Th Coll BA86. **dss** 86 **d** 87 **p** 94. Leytonstone St Jo *Chelmsf* 86-90, Par Dn 87-90; Asst Chapl Grimsby Distr Gen Hosp 90-93; Chapl Kent and Cant Hosp 93-94; Chapl Kent and Cant Hosps NHS Trust 94-99; Chapl E Kent Hosps NHS Trust 99-01; Hon C Aylesham w Adisham and Nonington w Wymynswold and Goodnestone etc *Cant* 01-09; rtd 09; Perm to Offic *Cant* from 09. *5 White*

House, Farm Court, Easole Street, Nonington, Dover CT15 4NJ Tel (01304) 840271 E-mail helen.therev@virgin.net

CONNOLLY, Daniel. b 51. BEng. St Jo Coll Nottm 82. **d** 84 **p** 85. C Bedgrove *Ox* 84-87; C-in-c Crookhorn Ch Cen CD *Portsm* 87-88; V Crookhorn 88-97; R Sutton Coldfield H Trin *Birm* 97-98; V Reigate St Mary *S'wark* 98-05; RD Reigate 03-05; P-in-c Kenilworth St Jo *Cov* 05-08; Adnry Miss Enabler 08-09; P-in-c Blackpool St Jo *Blackb* from 09. *St John's Vicarage, 19 Leamington Road, Blackpool FY1 4HD* Tel (01253) 623190 E-mail dan@famcon.co.uk

CONNOLLY, Miss Lynne. b 53. Aston Tr Scheme 88 Linc Th Coll 92. **d** 92 **p** 94. Par Dn Hurst *Man* 92-94; C 94-96; R Burnage St Nic 96-02; V Spotland from 02. *10 Little Flatt, Rochdale OL12 7AU* Tel (01706) 648972

CONNOLLY, Canon Sydney Herbert. b 40. Leeds Univ BA66. Coll of Resurr Mirfield 66. **d** 68 **p** 69. C W Derby St Mary *Liv* 68-71; C Prescot 71-74; V Burtonwood 74-80; V Walker *Newc* 80-89; TR Whorlton 89-96; V Chapel House 96-99; TR N Shields 99-06; Hon Can Newc Cathl 04-06; rtd 06. *222 Brunton Walk, Newcastle upon Tyne NE3 2TL* Tel 0191-271 1473 E-mail sydandpat@blueyonder.co.uk

CONNOR, Ellis Jones. b 16. Univ of Wales BA38. St Mich Coll Llan 38. **d** 39 **p** 41. C Broughton *St As* 39-43; C Llandegfan and Beaumaris *Ban* 43-48; V Liv St Chris Norris Green 48-55; R Desford *Leic* 55-73; R N Hill *Truro* 73-75; V Lewannick 73-75; R Llanddewi Skirrid w Llanvetherine etc *Mon* 75-78; C Spalding St Jo *Linc* 79-82; rtd 82; Perm to Offic *Leic* 82-03. *35 Sycamore Street, Blaby, Leicester LE8 4FL* Tel 0116-277 7725

CONNOR, Geoffrey. b 46. K Coll Lon BD73 AKC73. St Aug Coll Cant. **d** 74 **p** 75. C Cockerton *Dur* 74-79; Dioc Recruitment Officer 79-87; Chapl St Chad's Coll 84-87; R Edin St Mary and Vice Provost St Mary's Cathl 87-90; Dioc Dir of Ords *Edin* and *Arg* 87-90; V Whitechapel w Admarsh-in-Bleasdale *Blackb* 90-00; Dir of Ords 90-00; TR Epping Distr *Chelmsf* from 00; RD Epping Forest from 04. *The Rectory, Hartland Road, Epping CM16 4PD* Tel and fax (01992) 572906 E-mail geoffrey_connor@priest.com

CONNOR, Archdeacon of. *See* McBRIDE, The Ven Stephen Richard

CONNOR, Bishop of. *See* ABERNETHY, The Rt Revd Alan Francis

CONNOR, Dean of. *See* BOND, The Very Revd John Frederick Augustus

CONRAD, Paul Derick. b 54. Worc Coll Ox BA76 MA82. St Steph Ho Ox 78. **d** 80 **p** 81. C Wanstead St Mary *Chelmsf* 80-83; C Somers Town *Lon* 83-85; P-in-c Kentish Town St Martin w St Andr 85-91; V 91-95; P-in-c Hampstead Ch Ch 95-97; V from 97; Chapl R Free Hampstead NHS Trust from 95. *Christ Church Vicarage, 10 Cannon Place, London NW3 1EJ* Tel and fax (020) 7435 6784

CONSTABLE, Douglas Brian. b 40. Lon Univ BA62 Southn Univ MPhil05. Linc Th Coll 63. **d** 65 **p** 66. C Stockwood CD *Bris* 65-70; Asst Chapl Bris Univ 70-72; Hon C Clifton St Paul 70-72; Chapl Lee Abbey 72-77; V Derby St Thos 77-85; TV Southampton (City Cen) *Win* 85-92; rtd 92; Perm to Offic *Win* 92-05. *Y Bwthyn, 9 Church Street, Llandeilo SA19 6BH* Tel (01558) 823518 E-mail douglasconstable@btinternet.com

CONSTABLE, Mrs Sybil Margaret. b 43. **d** 00 **p** 01. NSM Montgomery and Forden and Llandyssil *St As* 00-04; P-in-c Slindon, Eartham and Madehurst *Chich* 04-09; rtd 09. *Stubbs Oak, Straight Half Mile, Maresfield, Uckfield TN22 3DN* Tel (01825) 760715

CONSTANTINE, Miss Elaine Muriel. b 50. Univ of Wales (Swansea) BSc72 CertEd73 DipEd75 Lon Univ MEd78. St Alb Minl Tr Scheme. **dss** 86 **d** 87 **p** 94. Bedford St Martin *St Alb* 86-88; Par Dn 87-88; Par Dn Leighton Buzzard w Eggington, Hockliffe etc 88-94; C 94-98; TV Dunstable 98-04; P-in-c Earlham St Eliz *Nor* 04-08; R Earlham from 08. *St Elizabeth's Vicarage, 75 Cadge Road, Norwich NR5 8DG* Tel (01603) 250764 E-mail revd.elaine@virgin.net

CONSTANTINE, Leonard. b 30. AKC57. **d** 58 **p** 59. C W Hartlepool St Aid *Dur* 58-61; C Sheff St Geo and St Steph 61-62; Nyasaland 62-64; Malawi 64-69; V W Pelton *Dur* 69-73; V Shotton 73-78; V Stillington 78-80; V Grindon and Stillington 80-82; V Corbridge w Halton and Newton Hall *Newc* 82-95; Chapl Charlotte Straker Hosp 82-95; rtd 95; Perm to Offic *Wakef* from 95. *28 Tenterfield Road, Ossett WF5 0RU* Tel (01924) 276180

CONVERY, Canon Arthur Malcolm. b 42. Sheff Univ BSc63 DipEd64. NOC 79. **d** 82 **p** 83. NSM Parr *Liv* 82-87; V Marown *S & M* 87-04; V Onchan from 04; Can St German's Cathl from 99. *The Vicarage, Church Road, Onchan, Isle of Man IM3 1BF* Tel (01624) 675799

CONWAY, Alfred Sydney. b 22. Kelham Th Coll 40. **d** 45 **p** 46. C Fulham St Oswald w St Aug *Lon* 45-49; PC Allenton and Shelton Lock *Derby* 49-55; P-in-c Chaddesden St Phil 55-63; V Croxley Green All SS *St Alb* 63-81; V Walton St Jo *Liv* 81-89; rtd 89; Perm to Offic *Ex* from 89. *58 Millhead Road, Honiton EX14 1RA* Tel (01404) 46052

CONWAY, Canon Glyn Haydn. b 38. St Mich Coll Llan. **d** 65 **p** 66. C Wrexham *St As* 65-71; TV 71-77; V Holywell 77-83; V Upton Ascension *Ches* 83-05; rtd 05; Hon Can Accra from 03; Perm to Offic *St As* from 07. *15 Penygraig, Aberystwyth SY23 2JA* Tel (01970) 612637
E-mail glyn.conway@btinternet.com

CONWAY, John Arthur. b 67. Leeds Univ BEng90 Edin Univ BD97. Linc Th Coll 94 TISEC 95. **d** 97 **p** 98. C Edin St Mary 97-01; R Edin St Martin from 01; Chapl Edin Sick Children's NHS Trust 98-01. *15 Ardmillan Terrace, Edinburgh EH11 2JW* Tel 0131-337 5471 E-mail jaconway@talktalk.net

CONWAY, Philip James. b 66. Liv Inst of Educn BA91. St Steph Ho Ox 92. **d** 95 **p** 96. C High Harrogate Ch Ch *Ripon* 95-99; P-in-c Menheniot *Truro* 99-08; C St Ive and Pensilva w Quethiock 02-08; P-in-c Lostwithiel, St Winnow w St Nectan's Chpl etc from 08; P-in-c Lanlivery from 08. *The Rectory, 3 Springfield Close, Lostwithiel PL22 0ER*
E-mail lostwithielrectory@live.co.uk

CONWAY, Mrs Sandra Coralie. b 45. Bris Univ BA66. S'wark Ord Course 89. **d** 92 **p** 00. NSM Kenley *S'wark* 92-05; Perm to Offic 06-07; NSM E Horsley and Ockham w Hatchford and Downside *Guildf* from 09. *Rowan Tree Cottage, Norrels Drive, East Horsley, Leatherhead KT24 5DR* Tel (01483) 281497
E-mail sandyconway@btopenworld.com

✠**CONWAY, The Rt Revd Stephen David.** b 57. Keble Coll Ox BA80 MA84 CertEd81 Selw Coll Cam BA85. Westcott Ho Cam 83. **d** 86 **p** 87 **c** 06. C Heworth St Mary *Dur* 86-89; C Bishopwearmouth St Mich w St Hilda 89-90; Dir of Ords and Hon C Dur St Marg 90-94; P-in-c Cockerton 94-96; V 96-98; Bp's Sen Chapl and Communications Officer 98-02; Adn Dur and Can Res Dur Cathl 02-06; Area Bp Ramsbury *Sarum* from 06. *Ramsbury Office, Southborough House, London Road, Devizes SN10 1LT* Tel (01380) 729808
E-mail ramsbury.office@salisbury.anglican.org

CONWAY, Thomas Robertson. b 36. **d** 86 **p** 87. C Bangor Abbey *D & D* 86-95; I Dungiven w Bovevagh *D & R* 89-95; I Carrowdore w Millisle *D & D* 95-00; rtd 00. *6 Rosstulla Drive, Newtownabbey BT37 0QJ* Tel (028) 9086 0523

CONWAY-LEE, Stanley. b 17. Linc Th Coll 68. **d** 70 **p** 71. C Dedham *Chelmsf* 70-72; C Lt Ilford St Mich 72-74; V Tollesbury 74-75; V Tollesbury w Salcot Virley 75-79; V Bocking St Pet 79-85; rtd 85; Perm to Offic *Chelmsf* from 85. *10 Northumberland Close, Braintree CM7 9NL* Tel and fax (01376) 550117

COOGAN, The Ven Robert Arthur William. b 29. Univ of Tasmania BA51. St Jo Coll Dur 51. **d** 53 **p** 54. C Plaistow St Andr *Chelmsf* 53-56; R Bothwell Australia 56-62; V N Woolwich *Chelmsf* 62-73; P-in-c W Silvertown St Barn 62-73; V Hampstead St Steph *Lon* 73-77; P-in-c N St Pancras All Hallows 74-77; RD S Camden 75-81; P-in-c Old St Pancras w Bedford New Town St Matt 76-80; V Hampstead St Steph w All Hallows 77-85; P-in-c Kentish Town St Martin w St Andr 78-81; AD N Camden 78-83; Preb St Paul's Cathl 82-85; Adn Hampstead 85-94; rtd 94; Perm to Offic *Chich* 94-00 and *St E* from 03. *Salters Hall West, Stour Street, Sudbury CO10 2AX* Tel (01787) 370026

COOK, Alan. b 27. St Deiniol's Hawarden 79. **d** 80 **p** 81. Hon C Gatley *Ches* 80-83; Chapl Man R Eye Hosp 83-86; Chapl Asst Man R Infirmary 80-83 and 86-88; V Congleton St Jas *Ches* 89-93; rtd 93; Perm to Offic *Ches* from 93. *15 Buttermere Road, Gatley, Cheadle SK8 4RQ* Tel 0161-428 4350

COOK, Sister Anita Isabel. b 44. Whitelands Coll Lon CertEd66 Toronto Univ BA93. **d** 06 **p** 07. CSC from 67. *St Michael's Convent, 56 Ham Common, Richmond TW10 7JH* Tel (020) 8332 2926 Fax 8948 5525 Mobile 07803-928114
E-mail anita.csc@mac.com

COOK, Canon Brian Edwin. b 36. Sarum & Wells Th Coll 78. **d** 80 **p** 81. C E Wickham *S'wark* 80-83; C Petersfield w Sheet *Portsm* 83-86; R Liss 86-01; RD Petersfield 91-96 and 99; Hon Can Portsm Cathl 96-01; rtd 01; Perm to Offic *Chich* from 01. *Daubeney Cottage, Bersted Street, South Bersted, Bognor Regis PO22 9QE* Tel (01243) 828379 E-mail daubeney@tesco.net

COOK, Brian Robert. b 43. Chich Th Coll 83. **d** 85 **p** 86. C Whyke w Rumboldswhyke and Portfield *Chich* 85-87; C Worth 87-90; TV 90-94; P-in-c Chidham 94-99; V 99-04; RD Westbourne 99-04; P-in-c E Blatchington 04-08; R E Blatchington and Bishopstone from 08. *The Rectory, 86 Belgrave Road, Seaford BN25 2HE* Tel (01323) 892964 E-mail fbateastb@aol.com

COOK, Canon Charles Peter. b 32. St Jo Coll Dur BA54. Cranmer Hall Dur. **d** 58 **p** 59. C Kingston upon Hull H Trin *York* 58-64; V High Hawsk St Paul *Newc* 64-74; V Cheadle Hulme St Andr *Ches* 74-98; Hon Can Ches Cathl 91-98; rtd 98; Perm to Offic *Newc* 00-05; *Carl* 01-05; *Ches* from 05. *4 Moseley Grange, Cheadle Hulme, Cheadle SK8 5EZ* Tel 0161-485 1702

COOK, Christopher. *See* COOK, Canon James Christopher Donald

COOK, Christopher. b 44. Qu Coll Birm 68. **d** 69 **p** 70. C Gt Ilford St Mary *Chelmsf* 69-72; C Corringham 72-77; R E Donyland 77-84; R Pentlow, Foxearth, Liston and Borley 84-88; Chapl RAD Essex Area 88-89; rtd 89; Perm to Offic *Chelmsf* 89-04.

Oak Mill, Field View Drive, Little Totham, Maldon CM9 8ND Tel (01621) 893280

COOK, Canon Christopher Arthur. Edin Th Coll 53. **d** 56 **p** 58. C Motherwell *Glas* 56-59; S Africa 59-64 and from 70; Clydesdale Miss 59-60; Matatiele St Steph 60-61; Idutywa St Barn 61-64; Area Sec USPG *Wakef* and *Sheff* 65-70; R Grahamstown St Matt Miss 70-95; Adn Grahamstown 80-95; Hon Can Grahamstown from 96; rtd 96. *PO Box 7641, East London, 5200 South Africa* Tel (0027) (431) 385357

COOK, Christopher Charles Holland. b 56. K Coll Lon BSc77 MB, BS81 MD95 MRCPsych87. SEITE 97. **d** 00 **p** 01. Prof Psychiatry Alcohol Misuse Kent Inst of Medicine and Health Science 97-03; NSM Otham w Langley *Cant* 00-03; Chapl and Prof Fell St Chad's Coll Dur 03-05; Prof Research Fell Dur Univ from 05; Tutor and Lect Cranmer Hall Dur from 08. *Department of Theology and Religion, Abbey House, Palace Green, Durham DH1 3RS* Tel 0191-334 3885 E-mail c.c.h.cook@durham.ac.uk

COOK, David. b 46. Hertf Coll Ox BA MA72. Wycliffe Hall Ox 69. **d** 73 **p** 74. C Hartlepool All SS Stranton *Dur* 74-75; Lect Qu Coll Birm 75-81; Chapl Cranbrook Sch Kent from 81. *33 Oatfield Drive, Cranbrook TN17 3LA* Tel (01580) 713310

COOK, David Arthur. b 50. St Jo Coll Dur BA74. St Steph Ho Ox 86. **d** 88 **p** 89. C S Bank *York* 88-91; C Up Hatherley *Glouc* 91-93; P-in-c Cumbernauld *Glas* 93-04; P-in-c Helensburgh from 04. *The Rectory, 16 William Street, Helensburgh G84 8BD* Tel (01436) 672500 E-mail rector@stmichaelhelensburgh.org.uk

COOK, Canon David Charles Murray. b 41. MA. Wycliffe Hall Ox 65. **d** 67 **p** 68. C Chatham St Phil and St Jas *Roch* 67-71; S Africa 71-89; TR Newbury *Ox* 89-02; RD Newbury 98-02; Hon Can Ch Ch 02; P-in-c Chipping Campden w Ebrington *Glouc* from 02. *The Vicarage, Church Street, Chipping Campden GL55 6JG* Tel (01386) 840671

COOK, David Smith. b 47. Hull Univ BTh88 MA93. Lich Th Coll 68. **d** 71 **p** 72. C Tudhoe Grange *Dur* 71-75; C Bishopwearmouth St Mary V w St Pet CD 75-77; V Copley *Wakef* 77-80; V Birstall 80-83; V Holme upon Spalding Moor *York* 83-98; R Holme and Seaton Ross Gp 98-01; RD S Wold 96-01; V Copmanthorpe 01-07; P-in-c Askham Bryan 01-07; Chapl Askham Bryan Coll 01-04; P-in-c Eskdaleside w Ugglebarnby and Sneaton *York* 07-09; V Lower Esk from 09; RD Whitby from 08. *The Vicarage, 22 Eskdaleside, Sleights, Whitby YO22 5EP* Tel (01947) 810349
E-mail revcook@btinternet.com

COOK, Elspeth Jean. b 34. Edin Univ BSc56 PhD66. S Dios Minl Tr Scheme 85. **d** 88 **p** 94. C Yateley *Win* 88-91; Assoc Chapl Ld Mayor Treloar Hosp Alton 91-93; NSM Dunfermline *St And* 93-99; P-in-c Aberdour 96-01; rtd 01. *12 River View, Dalgety Bay, Dunfermline KY11 9YE* Tel (01383) 825222
E-mail andrewandjean.cook@tesco.net

COOK, Geoffrey John Anderson. b 64. St Steph Ho Ox. **d** 97 **p** 98. C St Leonards Ch Ch and St Mary *Chich* 97-99; Hon Asst P Brighton St Mich 00-02; Hon C Southwick St Mich 02-03; Asst Chapl Univ Coll Lon Hosps NHS Foundn Trust 03-05; Chapl W Herts Hosps NHS Trust 05-06; Chapl E Sussex Hosps NHS Trust from 06. *The Chaplain's Office, Eastbourne District General Hospital, King's Drive, Eastbourne BN21 2UD* Tel (01323) 417400

COOK, Ian. b 63. Trin Coll Bris. **d** 09. C Plymouth St Jude *Ex* from 09. *120 Salisbury Road, Plymouth PL4 8TB* Tel (01752) 665653

COOK, Ian Bell. b 38. NW Ord Course 70. **d** 73 **p** 74. C Oldham St Paul *Man* 73-75; Ind Chapl 76-79; P-in-c Newton Heath St Wilfrid and St Anne 76-79; V Middleton Junction 79-08; rtd 08; Perm to Offic *Man* from 09. *109 Hollin Lane, Middleton, Manchester M24 5LA* Tel 0161-654 0283
E-mail ian.cook13@btopenworld.com

COOK, Preb Ian Brian. b 38. Aston Univ MSc72 Birm Univ MA76 MBIM73. Kelham Th Coll 58. **d** 63 **p** 64. C Langley Marish *Ox* 63-66; C Stokenchurch and Cadmore End 66-68; V Lane End 68-72; P-in-c Ibstone w Fingest 68-72; Tutor W Bromwich Coll of Comm and Tech 72-74; Sen Tutor 74-80; NSM W Bromwich St Pet *Lich* 77-80; R Wednesbury St Jas and St Jo 80-03; Dir St Jas Tr Inst 81-03; RD Wednesbury 88-03; Preb Lich Cathl 94-03; rtd 03; Perm to Offic *Lich* from 03; RD Penkridge from 06. *4 Orams Lane, Brewood, Stafford ST19 9EA* Tel (01902) 850960

COOK, Canon James Christopher Donald. b 49. Ch Ch Ox BA70 MA74. St Steph Ho Ox 79. **d** 80 **p** 81. C Witney *Ox* 80-83; CF 83-04; P-in-c Toxteth Park St Agnes and St Pancras *Liv* 04-06; V from 06; Can Wiawso Ghana from 09. *St Agnes's Presbytery, 2 Buckingham Avenue, Liverpool L17 3BA* Tel and fax 0151-733 1742 E-mail leoclericus@aol.com

COOK, James Robert. b 45. ACCA68 FCCA73. Ox Min Course 05. **d** 08. NSM Newbury *Ox* from 08. *The Wyld, Forge Hill, Hampstead Norreys, Thatcham RG18 0TE* Tel (01635) 200428 E-mail jamesrobertcook@aol.com

COOK, Jean. *See* COOK, Elspeth Jean

COOK, Mrs Joan Lindsay. b 46. SRN70. St Jo Coll Dur 86. **d** 88 **p** 94. Par Dn Hartlepool St Hilda *Dur* 88-93; Dn-in-c 93-94;

P-in-c 94-96; rtd 96. *10 Peakston Close, Hartlepool TS26 0PN* Tel (01429) 231778

COOK, John. b 32. Linc Th Coll 87. **d** 89 **p** 90. C Bourne *Linc* 89-92; R Colsterworth Gp 92-02; rtd 02. *24 Portrush Drive, Grantham NG31 9GD* Tel (01476) 569063

COOK, John Edward. b 35. AKC61. **d** 62 **p** 63. C York Town St Mich *Guildf* 62-67; Singapore 67-77; P-in-c Beoley *Worc* 78-83; V 83-89; V Bromsgrove All SS 89-01; rtd 01; Perm to Offic *Cov* from 02. *61 Newport Drive, Alcester B49 5BJ* Tel (01789) 762553 Fax 400040 E-mail jcook120@btinternet.com

COOK, John Henry. b 11. Mert Coll Ox BA34 BSc35 MA39 MSc81. Clifton Th Coll 36. **d** 38 **p** 39. C Gt Faringdon w Lt Coxwell *Ox* 38-42; C Newbury St Nic 42-45; V Winkfield 45-52; V Furze Platt 52-68; R Witney 68-78; rtd 79; Hon C Witney *Ox* from 79. *7 Madley Park House, Madley Way, Witney OX28 1AT* Tel (01993) 704609

COOK, John Michael. b 48. Coll of Resurr Mirfield 72. **d** 74 **p** 75. C Weymouth H Trin *Sarum* 74-76; C Felixstowe St Jo *St E* 76-79; P-in-c Gt and Lt Whelnetham 79-84; P-in-c Cockfield 84-85; P-in-c Bradfield St George w Bradfield St Clare etc 84-85; R Cockfield w Bradfield St Clare, Felsham etc 85-87; V Workington St Jo *Carl* from 87. *St John's Vicarage, 59 Thorncroft Gardens, Workington CA14 4DP* Tel (01900) 602383

COOK, John Richard Millward. b 61. St Jo Coll Dur BA. Wycliffe Hall Ox 83. **d** 85 **p** 86. C Brampton St Thos *Derby* 85-89; C Farnborough *Guildf* 89-92; C Langham Place All So *Lon* 92-98; V Chelsea St Jo w St Andr 98-08; V Wargrave w Knowl Hill *Ox* from 08. *The Vicarage, Station Road, Wargrave, Reading RG10 8EU* Tel 0118-940 2202
E-mail johnrmcook@btinternet.com

COOK (née OBLESBY), Mrs Judith Mary. b 43. Cranmer Hall Dur 07. **d** 08 **p** 09. NSM Middlesbrough St Martin w St Cuth *York* from 08. *8 Windsor Crescent, Nunthorpe, Middlesbrough TS7 0AN* Tel (01642) 315482
E-mail judycook.nunthorpe@googlemail.com

COOK, Kenneth Hugh. b 30. ALAM. AKC55. **d** 56 **p** 57. C Netherfield *S'well* 56-59; C Newark w Coddington 59-61; V Basford St Aid 61-67; V Gargrave *Bradf* 67-77; Dir of Ords 77-89; Can Res Bradf Cathl 77-95; rtd 95; Perm to Offic *Ripon* from 95. *25 Hollins Close, Hampsthwaite, Harrogate HG3 2EH* Tel (01423) 772521

COOK (née McCLEAN), Mrs Lydia Margaret Sheelagh. b 72. Ball Coll Ox BA94 MA98. Cuddesdon Coll 94. **d** 96 **p** 97. C Brackley St Pet w St Jas 96-99; Chapl Cranford Ho Sch Ox 99-02; NSM Wallingford *Ox* 99-01; NSM Wallingford Deanery 01-04; NSM Sandford-on-Thames 04-06. *Tower View Farm, Kingston, Sturminster Newton DT10 2AR* Tel (01258) 817914
E-mail simonandlydia@towerviewfarm.co.uk

COOK, Marcus John Wyeth. b 41. Chich Th Coll 67. **d** 70 **p** 71. C Friern Barnet St Jas *Lon* 70-73; Hon C St Geo-in-the-East w St Paul 73-00; Perm to Offic 73-00. *St George-in-the-East Church, Cannon Street Road, London E1 0BH* Tel (020) 7481 1345

COOK, Matthew. b 78. Oak Hill Th Coll. **d** 06 **p** 07. C Bispham *Blackb* from 06. *88 All Hallows Road, Blackpool FY2 0AY* E-mail cook-matt@lycos.co.uk

COOK, Mrs Myrtle Bridget Weigela. b 47. BA LLM. EMMTC. **d** 04 **p** 05. NSM Kibworth and Smeeton Westerby and Saddington *Leic* 04-08; NSM Church Langton cum Tur Langton etc from 08. *1 Highcroft, Husbands Bosworth, Lutterworth LE17 6LF* Tel (01858) 880935
E-mail mchighcroft@aol.com

COOK, Neil John. b 70. Wolv Univ BA93. Wycliffe Hall Ox 05. **d** 06 **p** 07. C Roby *Liv* 06-07; C Huyton Quarry from 07. *28 Cedarwood Court, Liverpool L36 5YY* Tel 07733-296850 (mobile) E-mail cookrnj@googlemail.com

COOK, Nicholas Leonard. b 59. Nottm Univ BCombStuds84. Linc Th Coll 81. **d** 84 **p** 85. C Leic St Pet 84-85; C Knighton St Mich 85-86; Chapl Asst Towers Hosp Humberstone 86-89; Chapl Leics Mental Health Service Unit 89-91; Chapl Quainton Hall Sch Harrow 91-94; CF(V) 88-94; CF from 94. *c/o MOD Chaplains (Army)* Tel (01980) 615804 Fax 615800

COOK, Paul Raymond. *See* McLAREN-COOK, Paul Raymond

COOK, Peter John. b 57. Ridley Hall Cam 93. **d** 95 **p** 96. C Romford Gd Shep *Chelmsf* 95-98; C Colchester St Jo 98-06; V Bangkok Ch Ch Thailand from 06. *11 Convent Road, Bangkok 10500, Thailand* Tel (0066) (2) 266 2887
E-mail vicar@christchurchbangkok.org

COOK, Peter Ralph. b 69. Portsm Univ BA92 Kent Univ BA06. SEITE 03. **d** 06 **p** 07. C Hadlow *Roch* from 06; V Docking, the Birchams, Stanhoe and Sedgeford *Nor* from 09. *The Vicarage, Sedgeford Road, Docking, King's Lynn PE31 8PN* Tel (01485) 518247 E-mail t2andnor@supanet.com

COOK, Richard John Noel. b 49. Univ Coll Ox BA70 MA74 PGCE72. Wycliffe Hall Ox MA77. **d** 78 **p** 79. C Fulwood *Sheff* 78-80; C Bolton St Paul w Em *Man* 81-86; TV 86-93; V Goldsworth Park *Guildf* from 93; RD Woking 99-03. *St Andrew's Vicarage, 8 Cardingham, Woking GU21 3LN* Tel (01483) 764523 E-mail cookingwok@tiscali.co.uk

COOK, Canon Robert Bond. b 28. Dur Univ BSc54. Ripon Hall Ox 54. **d** 56 **p** 57. C Benwell St Jas *Newc* 56-60; C Sugley 60-64; V Denton 64-75; V Haltwhistle 75-88; P-in-c Greenhead 84-88; V Haltwhistle and Greenhead 88-93; RD Hexham 88-93; Hon Can Newc Cathl 92-93; rtd 93; Perm to Offic *St E* from 94; RD Lavenham 03-05. *Ashcroft, Heath Road, Woolpit, Bury St Edmunds IP30 9RN* Tel (01359) 240670

COOK, Mrs Ruth Anna Margaret. b 52. Bedf Coll of Educn CertEd74. **d** 08 **p** 09. OLM Smestow Vale *Lich* from 08. *10 Dowells Gardens, Stourbridge DY8 5QA* Tel (01384) 835311 Mobile 07796-615982
E-mail ruthfromstourbridge@googlemail.com

COOK, Simon David James. b 74. St Cath Coll Ox BA97 St Jo Coll Dur BA08. Cranmer Hall Dur 06. **d** 08 **p** 09. C Broughton *Man* from 08. *237 Great Clowes Street, Salford M7 2DZ* Tel 0161-792 9161 Mobile 07745-232662
E-mail simonandlizzie@aol.com

COOK, Stephen. b 62. JP05. Brunel Univ BSc(Econ)84. S'wark Ord Course 89. **d** 92 **p** 93. Hon C Forest Hill St Aug *S'wark* 92-98; P-in-c Eltham St Barn from 98; CF (TA) from 00. *St Barnabas' Vicarage, 449 Rochester Way, London SE9 6PH* Tel (020) 8856 8294 E-mail cooksca@aol.com

COOK, Stephen William. b 57. Bris Univ BA80 Lambeth STh86. Trin Coll Bris 82. **d** 85 **p** 86. C Heref St Pet w St Owen and St Jas 85-89; TV Keynsham *B & W* 89-95; V Hanham *Bris* 95-02; RD Bitton 98-99; AD Kingswood and S Glos 99-02; TR Okehampton w Inwardleigh, Bratton Clovelly etc *Ex* from 02; RD Okehampton from 05. *The Rectory, 1 Church Path, Okehampton EX20 1LW* Tel (01837) 659297

COOK, Timothy John. b 62. Cranmer Hall Dur 95. **d** 95 **p** 96. C Dorchester *Sarum* 95-99; TV Ilminster and Distr *B & W* 99-03; R Yeovil H Trin w Barwick from 03. *Holy Trinity Vicarage, 24 Turners Barn Lane, Yeovil BA20 2LM* Tel (01935) 423774
E-mail timcook@tesco.net

COOK, Trevor Vivian. b 43. Sarum Th Coll 67. **d** 69 **p** 70. C Lambeth St Phil *S'wark* 69-73; C St Buryan, St Levan and Sennen *Truro* 73-75; V The Ilketshalls *St E* 75-79; P-in-c Rumburgh w S Elmham 75-79; R Rumburgh w S Elmham w the Ilketshalls 79-84; TR Langport Area *B & W* 84-96; P-in-c Rode Major 96-02; C Hardington Vale 02-04; rtd 04; Perm to Offic *B & W* from 04. *Hedge End, 5 Queen Street, Keinton Mandeville, Somerton TA11 6EH* Tel (01458) 224448

COOKE, Alan. b 50. Nottm Univ BTh74 Lanc Univ PGCE75. Kelham Th Coll 69. **d** 75 **p** 76. C Tyldesley w Shakerley *Man* 75-78; C Langley All SS and Martyrs 80-82; TV Langley and Parkfield 82-83; P-in-c Chadderton St Mark 83-85; V from 85. *St Mark's Vicarage, Milne Street, Chadderton, Oldham OL9 0HR* Tel 0161-624 2005

COOKE, Angela Elizabeth. b 42. SRN65 SCM67. St Jo Coll Nottm 85. **d** 87 **p** 94. Par Dn Walton H Trin *Ox* 87-92; Par Dn Bexleyheath Ch Ch *Roch* 92-94; C 94-97; V St Mary Cray and St Paul's Cray 97-05; rtd 05. *7 Maytree Gardens, Bexhill-on-Sea TN40 2PE* Tel (01424) 213268
E-mail angelacooke@hotmail.com

COOKE (née LEA), Mrs Carolyn Jane. b 65. Nottm Univ BA88 PGCE90. St Jo Coll Nottm MTh02. **d** 02 **p** 03. C Hyson Green and Forest Fields *S'well* 02-06; TV Clifton from 06. *St Francis House, Southchurch Drive, Nottingham NG11 8AQ* Tel 0115-974 4190 E-mail d.cooke3@ntlworld.com

COOKE, Christopher Stephen. b 54. Lon Univ BA76 MA77 Ox Univ BA81 MA88. Ripon Coll Cuddesdon 79. **d** 82 **p** 83. C Cen Telford *Lich* 82-86; R Uffington, Upton Magna and Withington 86-95; RD Wrockwardine 92-01; TR Wrockwardine Deanery 95-01; P-in-c Wem from 01; P-in-c Lee Brockhurst from 01; P-in-c Loppington w Newtown 01-02. *The Rectory, Ellesmere Road, Wem, Shrewsbury SY4 5TU* Tel (01939) 232550
E-mail christopher@csc2000.f9.co.uk

COOKE, Daniel. b 84. Hull Univ BA06. St Jo Coll Nottm 06. **d** 08 **p** 09. C W Acklam *York* from 08. *41 Ambleside Grove, Middlesbrough TS5 7DQ* Tel (01642) 814568 Mobile 07840-319439 E-mail danielbcooke@hotmail.com

COOKE, David John. b 31. Linc Th Coll 60. **d** 62 **p** 63. C Brighton Gd Shep Preston *Chich* 62-65; C Clayton w Keymer 65-70; R Stone w Hartwell w Bishopstone *Ox* 70-77; R Stone w Dinton and Hartwell 77-07; rtd 07; Perm to Offic *Ox* from 08. *5 Astronomy Way, Aylesbury HP19 7WD* Tel (01296) 748215

COOKE, David Michael Randle. b 68. Newc Univ BA90. Wycliffe Hall Ox 05. **d** 07 **p** 08. C Richmond H Trin and Ch Ch *S'wark* from 07. *Holy Trinity Church, Sheen Park, Richmond TW9 1UP* Tel (020) 8404 1112 Mobile 07766-900267
E-mail davidcooke2003@hotmail.com

COOKE, Francis Theodore. b 34. Tyndale Hall Bris 53 Clifton Th Coll 58. **d** 62 **p** 03. Ind Missr Bentley Motors Ches from 02; NSM Woodford from 02; NSM Poynton 02-03. *13 Maple Avenue, Poynton, Stockport SK12 1PR* Tel (01625) 859246

COOKE, Frederic Ronald. b 35. Selw Coll Cam BA58 MA61. Ridley Hall Cam 59. **d** 61 **p** 62. C Flixton St Mich *Man* 61-64; C-in-c Flixton St Jo CD 64-67; V Flixton St Jo 68-74; R Ashton St Mich 74-77; Jerusalem 77-80; V Walmsley *Man* 80-85; AD

COOKE

Walmsley 81-85; Malaysia 85-90; Prin Ho of Epiphany Th Coll Borneo 85-90; P-in-c Accrington *Blackb* 90-91; TR 91-96; P-in-c Ringley w Prestolee *Man* 96-01; rtd 01. *314 Queens Court, St Pauls Square, Ramsey, Isle of Man IM8 1LF* Tel (01624) 816747

COOKE, Geoffrey. b 38. Sarum Th Coll 61. **d** 64 **p** 65. C Eastover *B & W* 64-67; Chapl RAF 67-71; C Bridgwater St Jo *B & W* 71-76; R N Newton w St Michaelchurch and Thurloxton 76-78; R N Newton w St Michaelchurch, Thurloxton etc 78-83; TV Yeovil 83-88; V Yeovil H Trin 83-89; R Staple Fitzpaine, Orchard Portman, Thurlbear etc 89-96; rtd 96; Perm to Offic *B & W* from 96. *34 Bluebell Close, Taunton TA1 3XQ* Tel (01823) 324235 E-mail endymion.99@virgin.net

COOKE (married name SHEARD), Ms Gillian Freda. b 39. Lon Univ BD73 Leeds Univ MA87. Linc Th Coll 74. **dss** 78 **d** 87 **p** 94. Cricklewood St Pet CD *Lon* 78-80; Chapl Middx Poly 78-80; Chapl Leeds Poly *Ripon* 80-87; N Humberside Ind Chapl *York* 87-90; Asst Chapl HM Pris Hull 90-94; Chapl Keele Univ 94-97; Assoc Min Betley and Keele 94-97; Chapl Rampton Hosp Retford 97-99; rtd 99; Perm to Offic *York* from 00; Chapl HM Pris Wolds from 05. *The Chaplain's Office, HM Prison Wolds, Everthorpe, Brough HU15 2JZ* Tel (01430) 428000 E-mail gilalsrd@gilalsrd.karoo.co.uk

COOKE (née MORRALL), Mrs Heather Lynne. b 55. LMH Ox BA76 MA80 MIPR88. Open Th Coll 94 Dioc OLM tr scheme 96. **d** 99 **p** 00. OLM Martlesham w Brightwell *St E* from 99. *9 Swan Close, Martlesham Heath, Ipswich IP5 3SD* Tel (01473) 623770 Mobile 07703-568051 E-mail hcookema@aol.com

COOKE, Canon Hereward Roger Gresham. b 39. FCA64. K Coll Lon BD69 AKC70. **d** 70 **p** 71. C Rugby St Andr *Cov* 70-76; P-in-c St Kath Cree *Lon* 76-82; P-in-c St Botolph without Aldersgate 82-89; AD The City 82-85; P-in-c St Edm the King and St Mary Woolnoth etc 82-89; TV Nor St Pet Parmentergate w St Jo 89-93; Ind Miss 89-05; Sen Ind Chapl 93-05; RD Nor E 93-02; rtd 05; Hon C Nor St Pet Mancroft w St Jo Maddermarket 93-08; P-in-c Nor St Steph 03-08; Hon Can Nor Cathl 97-08; Perm to Offic from 08; Dioc Environmental Officer from 09. *Friary Orchard, Mariners Hill, Blakeney, Holt NR25 7NB* Tel (01263) 740320 E-mail cookehd@paston.co.uk

COOKE, James Martin. b 46. Trin Coll Ox BA67 Ox Univ DipEd68. **d** 07 **p** 08. OLM Wonersh w Blackheath *Guildf* from 07. *7 Durnsford Way, Cranleigh GU6 7LN* Tel (01483) 276049 E-mail james.cooke20@ntlworld.com

COOKE, John Stephen. b 35. K Coll Lon BD58 AKC58. **d** 59 **p** 60. C W Bromwich St Fran *Lich* 59-62; C Chalfont St Peter *Ox* 62-66; V Cross Heath *Lich* 66-72; R Haughton 72-86; P-in-c Ellenhall w Ranton 72-80; V Eccleshall 86-00; Sub Chapl HM Pris Drake Hall 89-95; rtd 00; Perm to Offic *Lich* from 00. *50 High Street, Eccleshall, Stafford ST21 6BZ* Tel (01785) 850570

COOKE, Canon Kenneth John. b 29. Linc Coll Ox BA53 MA57. Ely Th Coll 53. **d** 55 **p** 56. C Nuneaton St Mary *Cov* 55-58; C Cov St Thos 58-61; V Willenhall 61-66; V Meriden 66-76; V Cov St Geo 76-84; V Leamington Spa H Trin and Old Milverton 84-94; Hon Can Cov Cathl 92-94; rtd 94; Perm to Offic *Cov* 94. *2 Chantry Crescent, Alcester B49 5BT* Tel (01789) 763460

COOKE, Michael David. b 46. New Coll Ox BA68 MA71 DPhil71. Ox NSM Course 75. **d** 78 **p** 79. NSM Newport Pagnell *Ox* 78-85; NSM Newport Pagnell w Lathbury and Moulsoe 85-88; NSM Beckenham Ch Ch *Roch* 90-96; P-in-c Seal St Lawr from 96; P-in-c Underriver from 96; Perm to Offic *Cant* 98-09. *St Lawrence Vicarage, Stone Street, Sevenoaks TN15 0LQ* Tel and fax (01732) 761766 E-mail michael.cooke@diocese-rochester.org

COOKE, Michael John. b 39. Ab Dioc Tr Course 78. **d** 80 **p** 81. NSM St Andr Cathl 80-81; Chapl Miss to Seamen 81-88; Miss to Seamen Tilbury 88-91; Hon C Immingham *Linc* 81-88; Ind Chapl Teesside *Dur* 91-97; V Kelloe and Coxhoe 97-06; rtd 06. *24 West Pasture, Kirkbymoorside, York YO62 6BR* E-mail mikecooke8@yahoo.co.uk

COOKE, Miss Priscilla Garland Hamel. b 24. Gilmore Ho 69. **dss** 80 **d** 87 **p** 94. Bromsgrove St Jo *Worc* 80-82; Lee Abbey 82-85; Torquay St Matthias, St Mark and H Trin *Ex* 86-87; NSM 87-92 and 94-98; Perm to Offic 92-94 and from 98. *7 Woodrow, Asheldon Road, Torquay TQ1 2QN* Tel (01803) 297366

COOKE, Raymond. b 34. Liv Univ BSc56. Wells Th Coll 58. **d** 60 **p** 61. C Newton Heath All SS *Man* 60-64; C-in-c Failsworth H Family CD 64-75; R Failsworth H Family 75-83; P-in-c Man Gd Shep 83-88; V Westleigh St Pet 88-99; rtd 99. *136 Victoria Avenue East, Manchester M9 6HF* Tel 0161-740 0664

COOKE, Richard James. b 60. Pemb Coll Ox BA82 MA88 Bris Univ PhD96. Trin Coll Bris 85. **d** 88 **p** 89. C Rugby St Matt *Cov* 88-92; V Fletchamstead 92-04; Dir Initial Tr for Readers 97-02; CME Adv 04-07; CME Lay Development and Local Min Adv 07-08; Dir of Discipleship Development from 09; C Warmington w Shotteswell and Radway w Ratley from 07; C Kineton from

07; C Combroke w Compton Verney from 07. *Diocesan Office, 1 Hill Top, Coventry CV1 5AB* Tel (024) 7652 1200 E-mail richard.cooke@covcofe.org

COOKE, Roger. b 68. Heriot-Watt Univ BA90 BArch91 Edin Univ MTh02. TISEC 98. **d** 99 **p** 00. C Prestonpans *Edin* 99-02; R 02-09; C Musselburgh 99-02; R 02-09; I Coleraine *Conn* from 09. *St Patrick's Rectory, 28 Mountsandel Road, Coleraine BT52 1JE* Tel (028) 7034 3429 E-mail carrington20@aol.com

COOKE, Stephen. *See* COOKE, John Stephen

COOKSON, Canon Diane Veronica. b 51. NOC 81. **dss** 84 **d** 87 **p** 94. Gt Sutton *Ches* 84-86; Neston 86-87; Par Dn 87-94; C 94-96; V Stockport St Sav from 96; Ecum Adv (Gtr Man) 00-02; Hon Can Ches Cathl from 04. *St Saviour's Vicarage, 22 St Saviour's Road, Great Moor, Stockport SK2 7QE* Tel 0161-483 2633 E-mail st.saviours@virgin.net

COOKSON, Canon Graham Leslie. b 37. Sarum Th Coll 64. **d** 67 **p** 68. C Upton Ascension *Ches* 67-69; C Timperley 69-75; V Godley cum Newton Green 75-83; R Tarporley 83-07; Hon Can Ches Cathl 04-07; rtd 07. *15 Dolphin Court, Chester CH4 8JX* Tel (01244) 671044

COOKSON, William. b 61. **d** 98 **p** 99. C Haydock St Mark *Liv* 98-02; Min Wallington Springfield Ch *S'wark* from 02. *49 Stanley Park Road, Carshalton SM5 3HT* Tel (020) 8404 6064 E-mail willcookson@blueyonder.co.uk

COOLING, Derrick William. b 35. AKC58 Heref Coll of Educn TCert68 Lon Univ BD69 DipEd71 Univ of Wales (Cardiff) MEd81. St Boniface Warminster 58. **d** 59 **p** 60. C Haydock St Jas *Liv* 59-61; C Hove St Barn *Chich* 61-63; V Llangattock w St Maughan's etc *Mon* 63-68; R Blaina 68-70; Perm to Offic *Sarum* 70-74; Chapl Windsor Girls' Sch Hamm 74-75; Asst Master Croesyceiliog Sch Cwmbran 75-81; Chapl Epsom Coll 81-84; V Bettws *Mon* 84-95; P-in-c Purleigh, Cold Norton and Stow Maries *Chelmsf* 95-98; rtd 98; Perm to Offic *Mon* from 98 and *Glouc* from 05. *St Thomas Cottage, The Fence, St Briavels, Lydney GL15 6QG* Tel and fax (01594) 530926 E-mail clericderrick@aol.com

COOLING (née YOUNG), Mrs Margaret Dorothy. b 37. K Coll Lon BA59 AKC Lon Univ BD69 DipEd71 Univ of Wales (Cardiff) MEd81. Mon Dioc Tr Scheme 89. **d** 90 **p** 95. NSM Bettws *Mon* 90-95; NSM Purleigh, Cold Norton and Stow Maries *Chelmsf* 95-98; rtd 98; Perm to Offic *Mon* from 98 and *Glouc* from 01; Warden, Lect and Preacher Newland Almshouses from 04. *St Thomas Cottage, The Fence, St Briavels, Lydney GL15 6QG* Tel and fax (01594) 530926 E-mail clericderrick@aol.com

COOMBE, James Anthony. b 31. Em Coll Cam BA53 MA57 Lon Univ BD60. Tyndale Hall Bris 57. **d** 60 **p** 61. C Chadderton Ch Ch *Man* 60-63; C Worthing St Geo *Chich* 63-65; V Wandsworth St Mich *S'wark* 65-76; P-in-c Warboys *Ely* 74-76; R 76-87; RD St Ives 83-87; P-in-c Broughton and Wistow 84-87; R Buckworth and V Alconbury cum Weston 87-96; rtd 96; Perm to Offic *Cant* from 06. *12 Nursery Fields, Hythe CT21 4DL* Tel (01303) 262151

COOMBE, John Morrell (Brother Martin). b 25. Chich Th Coll 56. **d** 57 **p** 58. SSF from 49; Lic to Offic *Sarum* 57-59; C-in-c Hillfield and Hermitage 59-66; Asst Chapl Ellesmere Coll 66-69; Chapl Ranby Ho Sch Retford 69-71; V Cambridge St Benedict *Ely* 71-85; Perm to Offic Jerusalem 85-86; Prov Sec SSF 86-94; Sec for Miss SSF from 99; Lic to Offic *Linc* 86-95; Perm to Offic *Ely* 97-05; *Lon* from 06; *Chelmsf* from 09. *The Vicarage, 11 St Mary's Road, London E13 9AE* Tel (020) 8552 4019 E-mail martin@stmarysssf.plus.com

COOMBE, Canon Michael Thomas. b 31. Lon Univ BA64. Ox NSM Course 73. **d** 75 **p** 76. Chapl St Piran's Sch Maidenhead 75-81; NSM Furze Platt *Ox* 75-81; C 86-88; Asst Chapl Oslo St Edm *Eur* 81-84; Chapl Belgrade w Zagreb 84-86; Chapl Marseille w St Raphaël, Aix-en-Provence etc 88-89; Chapl Reading Gp of Hosps 89-91; P-in-c Clewer St Andr *Ox* 91-92; C New Windsor 92-93; C Reading St Mark 93-95; C Reading H Trin 93-95; Prec Gib Cathl and Port Chapl 95-03; Can Gib Cathl 00-03; rtd 03. *28 Gipsy Lane, Exmouth EX8 3HN* Tel (01395) 272923

COOMBER, Ian Gladstone. b 47. Ch Ch Coll Cant CertEd68 Southn Univ BTh79. Sarum & Wells Th Coll 73. **d** 76 **p** 77. C Weeke *Win* 76-79; TV Saffron Walden w Wendens Ambo and Littlebury *Chelmsf* 79-82; V Weston *Win* 82-90; R Bedhampton *Portsm* 90-96; R Botley and Durley *Win* 96-05; V Curdridge 96-05; RD Bishop's Waltham 98-03; TR Cartmel Peninsula *Carl* 05-09; rtd 09. *Elder Cottage, Throop Road, Templecombe BA8 0HR* Tel (01963) 371205

COOMBER, Matthew James McKinnon. **d** 06. Perm to Offic *Sheff* from 06. *Flat 9, 36 Oakholme Road, Sheffield S10 3DF* Tel 0114-268 0707

COOMBES, Derek Fennessey. b 42. Edin Th Coll 61. **d** 65 **p** 66. Prec St Andr Cathl Inverness 65-68; Bp's Chapl 65-68; Perm to Offic *Nor* 76-79; V Happisburgh w Walcot 79-83; C Tewkesbury Abbey 84-85; Ind Chapl *S'wark* 85-89; R Asterby Gp *Linc* 89-95; Mental Health Chapl Louth 91-95; Perm to Offic *Lich* 95-97; TV Haywards Heath St Wilfrid *Chich* 97-07; rtd 07; Hon C

Haywards Heath St Rich *Chich* from 08. *Padua House, 33 Larch Way, Haywards Heath RH16 3TY* Tel and fax (01444) 411303 E-mail revcoombes@btopenworld.com

COOMBES, Frederick Brian John. b 34. Nottm Univ BA56 Plymouth Poly MPhil73 FRGS. SWMTC 85. **d** 88 **p** 89. NSM Bodmin w Lanhydrock and Lanivet *Truro* 88-07; Perm to Offic from 07. *191 Boslowick Road, Falmouth TR11 4QF* Tel (01326) 210788

COOMBS, Edward Neve. b 66. Bris Univ BSc88. Cranmer Hall Dur BA93. **d** 94 **p** 95. C Edin St Thos 94-96; C Dagenham *Chelmsf* 97-01; P-in-c Banbury St Paul *Ox* from 01. *St Paul's House, Bretch Hill, Banbury OX16 0LR* Tel (01295) 264003 E-mail encoombs@tesco.net

COOMBS, John Allen. b 46. Portsm Poly BSc70. Oak Hill Th Coll 86 Sarum & Wells Th Coll 89. **d** 89 **p** 90. C Leverington and Wisbech St Mary *Ely* 89-93; P-in-c Emneth 93-96; V Emneth and Marshland St James 96-99; P-in-c Papworth Everard 99-00; TV Papworth 00-02; Chapl Papworth Hosp NHS Foundn Trust 99-06; P-in-c Roche and Withiel *Truro* from 06. *The Rectory, Fore Street, Roche, St Austell PL26 8EP* Tel (01726) 890301 E-mail john@familycoombs.freeserve.co.uk

COOMBS, John Kendall. b 47. Culham Coll Ox BEd73. Sarum & Wells Th Coll 75. **d** 77 **p** 78. C Fareham H Trin *Portsm* 77-80; C Petersfield w Sheet 80-83; TV Beaminster Area *Sarum* 83-87; TR Preston w Sutton Poyntz and Osmington w Poxwell 87-97; TR Hermitage *Ox* 97-05; P-in-c Hurst from 05. *The Vicarage, Church Hill, Hurst, Reading RG10 0SJ* Tel 0118-934 0017 E-mail jkcoombs@yahoo.co.uk

COOMBS, Martin. *See* COOMBS, Canon Walter James Martin

COOMBS, The Ven Peter Bertram. b 28. Bris Univ BA58 MA61. Clifton Th Coll 55. **d** 60 **p** 61. C Beckenham Ch Ch *Roch* 60-63; R Nottingham St Nic *S'well* 63-68; V New Malden and Coombe *S'wark* 68-75; RD Kingston 71-75; Adn Wandsworth 75-88; Adn Reigate 88-95; rtd 95; Perm to Offic *Portsm* from 97. *92 Locks Heath Park Road, Locks Heath, Southampton SO31 6LZ* Tel (01489) 577288

COOMBS, Richard Murray. b 63. St Chad's Coll Dur BSc85 Rob Coll Cam BA89 MA90. Ridley Hall Cam 87. **d** 90 **p** 91. C Enfield Ch Ch Trent Park *Lon* 90-94; C St Helen Bishopsgate w St Andr Undershaft etc 94-98; P-in-c St Pet Cornhill 95-98; V Burford w Fulbrook, Taynton, Asthall etc *Ox* from 98. *The Vicarage, Church Lane, Burford OX18 4SD* Tel (01993) 822275 Fax 824699 E-mail rmcoombs@btinternet.com

COOMBS, Stephen John. b 54. Open Univ BA86. Trin Coll Bris 85. **d** 87 **p** 88. C Norton Canes *Lich* 87-90; Chapl Trowbridge Coll *Sarum* 90-94; C Studley 90-94. *48 Whitstone Rise, Shepton Mallet BA4 5QB* Tel (01749) 343750

COOMBS, Canon Walter James Martin. b 33. Keble Coll Ox BA57 MA61. Cuddesdon Coll 59. **d** 61 **p** 62. C Kennington St Jo *S'wark* 61-64; Chapl Em Coll Cam 64-68; Bp's Dom Chapl *S'wark* 68-70; V E Dulwich St Jo 70-77; V Pershore w Pinvin, Wick and Birlingham *Worc* 77-92; Hon Can Worc Cathl 84-92; RD Pershore 85-91; TV Dorchester *Ox* 92-98; rtd 98; Perm to Offic *Ox* from 01. *54 Divinity Road, Oxford OX4 1LJ* Tel (01865) 243865

COONEY, Craig Stephen. Ulster Univ BSc98 TCD BTh06. **d** 06 **p** 07. C Lurgan Ch the Redeemer *D & D* from 06. *136 Lough Road, Lurgan, Craigavon BT66 6JL* Tel (028) 3834 4402 Mobile 07708-905560 E-mail cooneycraig@hotmail.com

COONEY, Canon Michael Patrick. b 55. City of Lon Poly BA77. Ripon Coll Cuddesdon 77. **d** 80 **p** 81. C Cov E 80-83; C Old Brumby *Linc* 83-85; V Linc St Jo 85-90; V Frodingham 90-05; Ind Chapl from 05; RD Manlake from 99; RD Is of Axholme from 05; Can and Preb Linc Cathl from 04. *16 Neap House Road, Gunness, Scunthorpe DN15 8TT* Tel (01724) 784245 E-mail mike.cooney@btinternet.com

COONEY, William Barry. b 47. K Coll Lon 69. **d** 70 **p** 71. C W Bromwich All SS *Lich* 70-73; C Wolverhampton St Pet 73-75; C Rugeley 75-78; V Sneyd Green 78-87; R Sandiacre *Derby* from 87. *St Giles's Rectory, Church Drive, Sandiacre, Nottingham NG10 5EE* Tel 0115-939 7163

COOPER, Alexander James Goodenough. b 47. Bath Univ BSc69. WEMTC 04. **d** 06 **p** 07. NSM Soundwell *Bris* from 06. *1 Deerhurst, Bristol BS15 1XH* Tel 0117-973 9441 E-mail linsand@blueyonder.co.uk

COOPER, Alfred Philip. b 50. Bris Univ BA71. All Nations Chr Coll 72. **d** 77 **p** 78. Chile from 75; SAMS from 77. *Iglesia Anglicana del Chile, Casilla 50675, Correo Central, Santiago, Chile* Tel (0056) (2) 226 8794

COOPER, Mrs Alison. b 51. Ripon Coll Cuddesdon 03. **d** 04 **p** 05. NSM Ascot Heath *Ox* 04-07; NSM Sunninghill and S Ascot from 07. *2 Beaufort Gardens, Ascot SL5 8PG* Tel (01344) 624027 Mobile 07747-682139

COOPER, Andrew John. b 62. W Sussex Inst of HE BA87 Greenwich Univ PGCE03. St Steph Ho Ox 88. **d** 91 **p** 92. C Rawmarsh w Parkgate *Sheff* 91-93; C Mosbrough 93-95; P-in-c Donnington Wood *Lich* 95-96; CF from 96. *c/o MOD Chaplains (Army)* Tel (01980) 615804 Fax 615800

COOPER, Andrew John Gearing. b 48. Sir John Cass Coll Lon BSc70. Ripon Coll Cuddesdon 73. **d** 76 **p** 77. C Potternewton *Ripon* 76-79; Antigua 79-81; Anguilla 81-87; V W Bromwich St Andr w Ch Ch *Lich* 88-92. *45 Dimbles Lane, Lichfield WS13 7HW* Tel (01543) 416020 E-mail andrew.cooper@lichfield.anglican.org

COOPER, The Ven Annette Joy. b 53. Open Univ BA80 CQSW84. S'wark Ord Course 85. **d** 88 **p** 94. NSM Pembury *Roch* 88; Chapl Asst Kent and Sussex Hosp Tunbridge Wells 88-91; Chapl Asst Leybourne Grange Hosp W Malling 88-91; Chapl Bassetlaw Hosp and Community Services NHS Trust 91-96; P-in-c Edwinstowe *S'well* 96-04; Chapl Center Parcs Holiday Village 96-01; AD Worksop 99-04; Hon Can S'well Minster 02-04; Adn Colchester *Chelmsf* from 04. *63 Powers Hall End, Witham CM8 1NH* Tel (01376) 513130 Fax 500789 E-mail a.colchester@chelmsford.anglican.org

COOPER, Barrie Keith. b 56. Oak Hill Th Coll. **d** 85 **p** 86. C Partington and Carrington *Ches* 85-89; V Stockport St Mark 89-93; Chapl HM YOI Stoke Heath 93-01; Chapl HM Pris Acklington from 01. *HM Prison Acklington, Morpeth NE65 9XF* Tel (01670) 762300

COOPER, Barry Jack. Sarum Th Coll 59. **d** 61 **p** 62. C Norbury St Oswald *Cant* 61-64; C Crook *Dur* 64-68; R Cheriton St Martin *Cant* 68-84; V Cant All SS 84-00; rtd 00; Perm to Offic *Cant* from 01. *11 Wind Hill Lane, Charing Heath, Ashford TN27 0BG* Tel (01233) 714787

COOPER, Canon Bede Robert. b 42. Ex Univ BA69. Coll of Resurr Mirfield 69. **d** 71 **p** 72. C Weymouth H Trin *Sarum* 71-74; P-in-c Broad Town 74-79; V Wootton Bassett 74-86; R Wilton w Netherhampton and Fugglestone 86-07; Can and Preb Sarum Cathl 88-07; rtd 07. *205 High Street, Milborne Port, Sherborne DT9 5AG* Tel (01963) 250503

COOPER, Benedict Christopher. b 68. K Coll Cam BA90 Wolfs Coll Ox MPhil94 DPhil97. Oak Hill Th Coll BA03. **d** 03 **p** 04. C St Helen Bishopsgate w St Andr Undershaft etc *Lon* 03-07. *43 King Street, Newtown, Sydney NSW 2042, Australia*

COOPER, Bert. *See* COOPER, Herbert William

COOPER, Brian Hamilton. b 35. Keble Coll Ox BA58 MA67. Ripon Hall Ox 58. **d** 60 **p** 61. C Woolwich St Mary w H Trin *S'wark* 60-64; Canada 64-66; Vice-Prin Westcott Ho Cam 66-71; R Downham Market w Bexwell *Ely* 71-82; RD Fincham 80-82; V Chesterfield St Mary and All SS *Derby* 82-91; V Herringthorpe *Sheff* 91-00; RD Rotherham 93-98; rtd 00; Perm to Offic *Sheff* from 00. *51 Anston Avenue, Worksop S81 7HU* Tel (01909) 479306 E-mail m.y.cooper1723@aol.com

✠**COOPER, The Rt Revd Carl Norman.** b 60. Univ of Wales (Lamp) BA82 Trin Coll Carmarthen MPhil99. Wycliffe Hall Ox 82. **d** 85 **p** 86 **c** 02. C Llanelli *St D* 85-87; P-in-c Llanerch Aeron w Ciliau Aeron and Dihewyd etc 87-88; R 88-93; R Dolgellau w Llanfachreth and Brithdir etc *Ban* 93-02; Warden of Readers 88-02; Adn Meirionnydd 00-02; Bp St D 02-08. *Hafod Lon, 35 Llandeilo Road, Llandybie, Ammanford SA18 3JA*

COOPER, Cecil Clive. b 26. TD75. AKC52. **d** 53 **p** 54. C Chipping Campden *Glouc* 53-55; C Cheltenham St Mary 55-60; V Stroud 60-65; CF (TA) 63-75; R Woodmansterne *S'wark* 65-91; RD Sutton 80-90; rtd 91; Perm to Offic *Cov* and *Pet* from 91. *10 Mill Close, Braunston, Daventry NN11 7HY* Tel (01788) 890596

COOPER, Canon Cecil William Marcus. b 32. TCD BA58 MA66. CITC 57. **d** 59 **p** 60. C Cork St Fin Barre and St Nic *C, C & R* 59-62; Bp's V, Lib and Registrar Kilkenny Cathl 62-64; C Knockbreda *D & D* 65-67; Asst Ed *Church of Ireland Gazette* 66-82; Ed 82-00; I Magheradroll 67-82; Dioc Registrar 81-90; I Drumbeg 82-00; Can Down Cathl 86-00; Prec 90-91; Chan 91-00; rtd 00. *35 Manor Drive, Lisburn BT28 1JH* Tel (028) 9263 4425

COOPER, Clive Anthony Charles. b 38. Lon Univ BEd74. ALCD62. **d** 62 **p** 63. C Morden *S'wark* 62-65; SAMS Argentina 65-71; Asst Master St Nic Sch Cranleigh 74-92; Hon C Cranleigh *Guildf* 78-79; Hon C Ewhurst 80-82; Hon Chapl Duke of Kent Sch 83-92; Chapl Felixstowe Coll 92-93; Perm to Offic *Ex* 94-95; Chapl Puerto Pollensa *Eur* 95-02; P-in-c Instow and Westleigh *Ex* 03-07; rtd 08; Perm to Offic *Eur* from 08 and *Ex* from 09. *1 Stanbridge Park, Bideford EX39 3RS* Tel (01237) 424617 E-mail csa.cooper@hotmail.co.uk

COOPER, Colin. b 55. Open Univ BA. St Jo Coll Nottm 83. **d** 86 **p** 87. C Cheadle Hulme St Andr *Ches* 86-89; C Tunbridge Wells St Jo *Roch* 89-93; V Whitfield *Derby* from 93. *The Vicarage, 16 Scotty Brook Crescent, Glossop SK13 8KG* Tel (01457) 864938 E-mail colin@glossop.org

COOPER, Colin Charles. b 40. Middx Univ BA94. Oak Hill Th Coll 62. **d** 66 **p** 67. C Islington St Andr w St Thos and St Matthias *Lon* 66-69; C Bermuda 69-76; V Gorleston St Andr *Nor* 77-94; R Emporia Ch Ch w Purdy Grace USA from 94. *111 Battery Avenue, Emporia VA 23847-2001, USA* Tel (001) (434) 348 3863 E-mail christandgrace@cs.com

COOPER, Mrs Corynne Elizabeth. b 54. Kent Univ BA76 PGCE77 Nottm Univ MA98. EMMTC 95. **d** 98 **p** 99. NSM Kneesall w Laxton and Wellow *S'well* 98-01; C Widecombe-in-the-Moor, Leusdon, Princetown etc *Ex* 01-05; TV Ashburton, Bickington, Buckland in the Moor etc from 05. *The Vicarage, Holne, Newton Abbot TQ13 7RT* Tel (01364) 631522 E-mail corynne.cooper@virgin.net

COOPER, David Philip. b 65. York Univ BA86. Qu Coll Birm BTheol94. **d** 94 **p** 95. C Burslem *Lich* 94-98; TV Cen Wolverhampton and Dioc Inter-Faith Officer 98-05; P-in-c Arnside *Carl* from 05. *The Vicarage, 45 Church Hill, Arnside, Carnforth LA5 0DW* Tel (01524) 761319

COOPER, Derek Edward. b 30. Bps' Coll Cheshunt 61. **d** 62 **p** 63. C Bishop's Stortford St Mich *St Alb* 62-66; V Westcliff St Cedd *Chelmsf* 66-89; R Camerton w Dunkerton, Foxcote and Shoscombe *B & W* 89-95; rtd 95; Perm to Offic *Win* from 95. *6 Caerleon Drive, Andover SP10 4DE* Tel (01264) 362807

COOPER, Eric John. b 22. Cam Univ MA47. Chich Th Coll 52. **d** 53 **p** 54. C Tottenham St Paul *Lon* 53-55; C Hillingdon St Jo 55-62; C Knowle St Martin *Bris* 62-66; V Bedminster Down 66-72; rtd 87. *6 Deveron Grove, Keynsham, Bristol BS31 1UJ* Tel 0117-986 7339

COOPER, Frederick. b 30. Cranmer Hall Dur 68. **d** 70 **p** 71. C Preston All SS *Blackb* 70-72; C Preston St Jo 72-76; TV 76-78; V Higher Walton 78-91; P-in-c Preston All SS 91-95; rtd 95; Perm to Offic *Blackb* from 95. *10 Guardian Close, Fulwood, Preston PR2 8EX* Tel (01772) 713808

COOPER, Gordon William. b 54. Aston Tr Scheme 93 Ripon Coll Cuddesdon 95. **d** 97 **p** 98. C Kippax w Allerton Bywater *Ripon* 97-01; V Wyther 01-08; P-in-c Garforth from 08. *The Rectory, Church Lane, Garforth, Leeds LS25 1NR* Tel 0113-286 3737 E-mail gordon@williamcooper.freeserve.co.uk

COOPER, Graham Denbigh. b 48. Nottm Univ BTh75. St Jo Coll Nottm LTh75. **d** 75 **p** 76. C Collyhurst *Man* 75-78; C Stambermill *Worc* 78-80; V The Lye and Stambermill 80-90; P-in-c Frome H Trin *B & W* 90; V 91-95; Appeals Organiser Children's Soc 95-97; Area Manager Save the Children Fund from 97. *2 Coombe View, Shepton Mallet BA4 5YF* Tel (01749) 343157

COOPER, Herbert William. b 29. Chich Th Coll 77. **d** 79 **p** 80. C Leigh Park *Portsm* 79-82; C-in-c Hayling St Pet CD 82-85; V Whitwell and R St Lawrence 85-94; P-in-c Niton 89-94; rtd 94; Perm to Offic *Heref* 94-04 and *Chich* from 05. *10 Andrew Avenue, Felpham, Bognor Regis PO22 7QS* Tel (01243) 584212

COOPER, Ian. b 57. St Jo Coll Nottm 00. **d** 02 **p** 03. C Mildenhall *St E* 02-05; TV 05-06; V Blacklands Hastings Ch Ch and St Andr *Chich* from 06. *1 Henderson Close, Hastings TN34 2DU* Tel (01424) 422551 E-mail ian@rpmo.co.uk

COOPER, Ian Clive. b 48. Ex Univ BA76 K Coll Lon MTh94 FCA. Linc Th Coll 76. **d** 78 **p** 79. C Sunbury *Lon* 78-81; P-in-c Astwood Bank *Worc* 81-85; P-in-c Feckenham w Bradley 82-85; TV Hemel Hempstead *St Alb* 85-95; R Bushey 95-04; TV Witney *Ox* 04-06; TV Marlborough *Sarum* from 06. *Preshute Vicarage, 7 Golding Avenue, Marlborough SN8 1TH* Tel (01672) 513408 *or* 512357 E-mail iancoopermrlboro@aol.com

COOPER, Jack. b 44. St Jo Coll Nottm 76. **d** 78 **p** 79. C Roundhay St Edm *Ripon* 78-80; C Ripley *Derby* 81-82; V Willington 82-88; V Findern 82-88; P-in-c Parwich w Alsop-en-le-Dale 88-94; Perm to Offic *York* from 95; rtd 04. *3 Arundel Howe Court, Stakesbury Road, Whitby YO21 1YJ* Tel (01947) 604213 E-mail jackanann@btopenworld.com

COOPER, James Peter. b 61. Westf Coll Lon BSc82. Sarum & Wells Th Coll 82. **d** 85 **p** 86. C Durrington *Chich* 85-88; C Clayton w Keymer 88-95; TV Chich and Chapl Chich Coll of Tech 95-01; Chapl R W Sussex NHS Trust from 01. *St Richard's Hospital, Spitalfield Lane, Chichester PO19 6SE* Tel (01243) 788122 Fax 531269 Mobile 07989-741004 E-mail james.cooper@rws-tr.nhs.uk

COOPER, Mrs Jennifer Ann Lisbeth. b 45. MCSP67. **d** 04 **p** 05. OLM Ashwellthorpe, Forncett, Fundenhall, Hapton etc *Nor* from 04. *10 Boileau Avenue, Tacolneston, Norwich NR16 1DQ* Tel (01953) 789702

COOPER, Jennifer Elaine. b 62. Toronto Univ BA83 Ottawa Univ MA90 Keble Coll Ox DPhil05. Ripon Coll Cuddesdon 05. **d** 06 **p** 07. C Cotham St Sav w St Mary and Clifton St Paul *Bris* 06-09; Lect and Tutor Coll of Resurr Mirfield from 09; Visiting Lect Leeds Univ from 09. *College of the Resurrection, Stocks Bank Road, Mirfield WF14 0BW* Tel (01924) 481904 E-mail jcooper@mirfield.org.uk

COOPER, Jeremy John. b 45. Kelham Th Coll 65 Linc Th Coll 71. **d** 71 **p** 72. C Derby St Luke 71-76; TV Malvern Link w Cowleigh *Worc* 76-79; P-in-c Claypole *Linc* 79-80; P-in-c Westborough w Dry Doddington and Stubton 79-80; C Eye w Braiseworth and Yaxley *St E* 80-82; P-in-c Hundon w Barnardiston 82-83; R 83-97; V Hundon 97-99; Chapl St Marg Convent E Grinstead 99-03; Warden, Lect and Preacher Newland Almshouses 03-04. *The College of St Barnabas, Blackberry Lane, Lingfield RH7 6NJ* Tel (01342) 870260

COOPER, Jeremy Llewellyn John. b 51. Lanc Univ BA73 Sussex Univ PGCE74 York Univ MSc87. **d** 07 **p** 08. OLM Morpeth *Newc* from 07. *Southdown, 13 Curlew Hill, Morpeth NE61 3SH* E-mail jeremylcooper@aol.com

COOPER, John. b 34. BEd. NOC. **d** 83 **p** 84. C Tong *Bradf* 83-87; V Bingley H Trin 87-92; V Silsden 92-99; rtd 99; Perm to Offic *Bradf* 01-08. *15 Fosbrooke House, 8 Clifton Drive, Lytham St Annes FY8 5RQ* Tel (01253) 667052

COOPER, John. b 47. Sarum & Wells Th Coll 71. **d** 74 **p** 75. C Spring Grove St Mary *Lon* 74-77; C Shepherd's Bush St Steph w St Thos 77-82; V Paddington St Pet 82-89; V Darwen St Cuth w Tockholes St Steph *Blackb* 89-96; V Northampton St Mich w St Edm *Pet* 96-99; Perm to Offic *St Alb* from 99 and *Lon* from 02. *8B Hampstead Square, London NW3 1AB* Tel (020) 7209 4165 E-mail jco4328743@yahoo.co.uk

COOPER, John Edward. b 40. K Coll Lon BD63 AKC63. **d** 64 **p** 65. C Prittlewell St Mary *Chelmsf* 64-67; C Up Hatherley *Glouc* 67-69; C-in-c Dorridge CD *Birm* 69-71; V Longford and P-in-c Alkmonton w Yeaveley *Derby* 71-76; TV Canvey Is *Chelmsf* 76-82; R Spixworth w Crostwick *Nor* 82-91; R Frettenham w Stanninghall 82-91; V Gt w Lt Harrowden and Orlingbury *Pet* 91-01; rtd 01; Perm to Offic *Leic* and *Pet* from 01. *Staveley House, 30 Brooke Road, Braunston, Oakham LE15 8QR* Tel (01572) 770984

COOPER, Canon John Leslie. b 33. Lon Univ BD65 MPhil78. Chich Th Coll 59. **d** 62 **p** 63. C Kings Heath *Birm* 62-65; Asst Chapl HM Pris Wandsworth 65-66; Chapl HM Borstal Portland 66-68; Chapl HM Pris Bris 68-72; P-in-c Balsall Heath St Paul *Birm* 73-81; V 81-82; Adn Aston and Can Res Birm Cathl 82-90; Adn Coleshill 90-93; C Sutton Coldfield H Trin 93-97; Hon Can Birm Cathl 93-97; rtd 97; Perm to Offic *Derby* from 98. *4 Ireton Court, Kirk Ireton, Ashbourne, Derby DE6 3JP* Tel (01335) 370459

COOPER, John Northcott. b 44. Ox Min Course 89. **d** 92 **p** 93. NSM Burghfield *Ox* 92-99; P-in-c Wootton (Boars Hill) 99-00; V Wootton and Dry Sandford from 00; AD Abingdon 02-07. *The Vicarage, Wootton Village, Boars Hill, Oxford OX1 5JL* Tel (01865) 735661 E-mail cooper@woottonvic.freeserve.co.uk

COOPER, Jonathan Mark Eric. b 62. Man Univ BSc83 Edin Univ BD88. Edin Th Coll 85. **d** 88 **p** 89. C Stainton-in-Cleveland *York* 88-91; C W Bromwich All SS *Lich* 91-93; P-in-c Ingleby Barwick CD *York* 93-98; P-in-c Hinderwell w Roxby 98-03; R Kirby Misperton w Normanby, Edston and Salton from 03. *The Rectory, Normanby, Sinnington, York YO62 6RH* Tel (01751) 431288 E-mail jonathan@jmec.freeserve.co.uk

COOPER, Joseph Trevor. b 32. Linc Th Coll 65. **d** 67 **p** 68. C Fletchamstead *Cov* 67-69; Ind Chapl 69-90; rtd 92; Perm to Offic *Cov* 92-00. *16 Trevor Close, Tile Hill, Coventry CV4 9HP* Tel (024) 7646 2341

COOPER, Judith Mary. b 52. Leeds Univ BA09. NOC 06. **d** 09. C Prestwich St Mary *Man* from 09. *25 Rectory Lane, Prestwich, Manchester M25 1RB* Tel 07752-676007 (mobile) E-mail cooper_j@blueyonder.co.uk

COOPER, Ms Louise Helena. b 68. Leeds Univ BA90. Qu Coll Birm. **d** 93 **p** 94. Par Dn Dovecot *Liv* 93-94; C 94-96; Dep Chapl HM YOI Glen Parva 96-01; Chapl HM Pris Styal 01-02; Chapl HM Pris Man 02-09; Chapl HM Pris Nottm from 09. *The Chaplaincy, HM Prison Nottingham, Perry Road, Sherwood, Nottingham NG5 3AG* Tel 0115-872 3040 Fax 872 3001

COOPER, Malcolm Tydeman. b 37. Pemb Coll Ox BA61 MA64. Linc Th Coll 63. **d** 63 **p** 64. C Spennithorne *Ripon* 63-66; C Caversham *Ox* 66-71; Hon C Blackbird Leys *Ox* 71-75; Lic to Offic *Sarum* 75-78 and *B & W* 78-82; NSM Sutton and Witcham w Mepal *Ely* 82-97; P-in-c Coveney 97-06. *8 The Coppice, Merrington, Bomere Heath, Shrewsbury SY4 3QE* E-mail mtcm4@waitrose.com

COOPER, Marc Ashley Rex. b 62. Leeds Univ BA85 MA95. Linc Th Coll 92. **d** 92 **p** 93. C Bolton St Jas w St Chrys *Bradf* 92-96; P-in-c Fishtoft *Linc* 96-97; R from 97; RD Holland E from 03. *The Rectory, Rectory Close, Fishtoft, Boston PE21 0RZ* Tel and fax (01205) 363216 E-mail revmarccooper@dsl.pipex.com

COOPER, Sister Margery. b 26. CA Tr Coll 49. **dss** 79 **d** 87 **p** 94. CA from 52; Evang Family Miss *Dur, Newc* and *York* 79-86; Perm to Offic *York* 86-91 and from 00; NSM Fulford 91-00; rtd 00. *7 Grange Street, Fulford Road, York YO10 4BH* Tel (01904) 633990

COOPER, Mark Richard. b 69. Kent Univ BA98. St Jo Coll Morpeth. **d** 95 **p** 95. C Hamilton Australia 95-96; C Rainham *Roch* 96-98; Assoc P Kincumber Australia 98-02; P-in-c Blue Gum Hills from 02. *1 Jirra Way, Maryland NSW 2287, Australia* Tel (0061) (2) 4955 0370 *or* 4951 1391 Mobile 40-982 8006 E-mail markcooper1969@hotmail.com

COOPER, Canon Michael Leonard. b 30. St Jo Coll Cam BA53 MA58. Cuddesdon Coll 53. **d** 55 **p** 56. C Croydon St Jo *Cant* 55-61; V Spring Park 61-71; V Boxley 71-82; RD Sutton 74-80; V Cranbrook 82-92; Hon Chapl to Bp Dover 93-97; Asst Chapl Kent and Cant Hosps NHS Trust 94-97; Hon Can Cant Cathl 76-97; Perm to Offic *Roch* 97-06; rtd 00. *The Rectory, Bellingham, Hexham NE48 2JS* Tel (01434) 220019

COOPER, Canon Michael Sydney. b 41. Univ of Wales (Lamp) BA63. Westcott Ho Cam 63. **d** 65 **p** 66. C Farlington *Portsm* 65-69; Pakistan 70-71; Mauritius 71-73; C-in-c Hayling St Pet CD *Portsm* 74-81; V Carisbrooke St Mary 81-92; V Carisbrooke

St Nic 81-92; V Hartplain 92-98; V Portchester 98-06; RD Fareham 99-04; Hon Can Portsm Cathl 02-06; rtd 06; Perm to Offic *Portsm* from 06. *122 Paxton Road, Fareham PO14 1AE* Tel (01329) 822152

COOPER, Nicholas. b 62. Wycliffe Hall Ox. **d** 06 **p** 07. C Tenterden St Mildred w Smallhythe *Cant* 06-09; C Tenterden St Mich 07-09; P-in-c Saltwood from 09. *The Rectory, Rectory Lane, Saltwood, Hythe CT21 4QA* Tel (01303) 266932

COOPER, Nigel Scott. b 53. Qu Coll Cam BA75 MA79 PGCE76 CEnv MIEEM CBiol FIBiol FLS. Ripon Coll Cuddesdon BA83 MA88. **d** 83 **p** 84. C Moulsham St Jo *Chelmsf* 83-88; R Rivenhall 88-05; Chapl Anglia Ruskin Univ from 05; Bp's Adv on Further Educn from 08. *The Chaplaincy Office, Anglia Ruskin University, East Road, Cambridge CB1 1PT* Tel 08451-962398 E-mail nigel.cooper@anglia.ac.uk

COOPER, Noel. b 49. Oak Hill Th Coll. **d** 88 **p** 89. C Plymouth St Jude *Ex* 88-92; V Clapham Park All SS *S'wark* 92-99; R Bedford St Jo and St Leon *St Alb* from 99. *St John's Rectory, 36 St John's Street, Bedford MK42 0DH* Tel (01234) 354818 E-mail stjohns@nascr.net

COOPER, Peter. *See* COOPER, Wallace Peter

COOPER, Canon Peter David. b 48. Sarum & Wells Th Coll 70. **d** 73 **p** 74. C Yateley *Win* 73-78; C Christchurch 78-81; P-in-c Southampton St Mark 81-83; V 83-98; P-in-c Tadley St Pet 98-02; Hon Can Ife Nigeria from 00; R Tadley S and Silchester *Win* from 02. *The Rectory, The Green, Tadley RG26 3PB* Tel 0118-981 4860 E-mail peter.cooper@xaltmail.com

COOPER, Peter Timothy. b 65. Brunel Univ BSc95. Ridley Hall Cam 01. **d** 03 **p** 04. C Edgware *Lon* 03-07; China from 07. *4 Mount Orchard, Tenbury Wells WR15 8DW* E-mail pandmcooper@tiscali.co.uk

COOPER, Canon Richard Thomas. b 46. Leeds Univ BA69. Coll of Resurr Mirfield 69. **d** 71 **p** 72. C Rothwell *Ripon* 71-75; C Adel 75-78; C Knaresborough 78-81; P-in-c Croft 81-90; P-in-c Eryholme 81-90; P-in-c Middleton Tyas and Melsonby 81-90; RD Richmond 86-90; V Aldborough w Boroughbridge and Roecliffe 90-98; RD Ripon 93-96; R Richmond w Hudswell 98-05; R Richmond w Hudswell and Downholme and Marske from 05; Hon Can Ripon Cathl from 97; Chapl to The Queen from 03. *The Rectory, Church Wynd, Richmond DL10 7AQ* Tel (01748) 823398 E-mail richard@churchwynd.freeserve.co.uk

COOPER, Canon Robert Gerard. b 68. Univ of Wales (Abth) BD91. Linc Th Coll 93. **d** 93 **p** 94. C Whitkirk *Ripon* 93-96; C Leeds Richmond Hill 96-97; Chapl Agnes Stewart C of E High Sch Leeds 96-97; Chapl Chigwell Sch Essex 97-98; V Lightcliffe *Wakef* 98-05; V Pontefract St Giles from 05; RD Pontefract from 06; Hon Can Wakef Cathl from 08. *The Vicarage, 9 The Mount, Pontefract WF8 1NE* Tel (01977) 706803 Mobile 07931-565516 E-mail robert_cooper@msn.com

COOPER, Robert James. b 52. Bris Univ BA75. Ridley Hall Cam 76. **d** 78 **p** 79. C Street w Walton *B & W* 78-82; C Batheaston w St Cath 82-86; P-in-c Sadberge *Dur* 86-03; Asst Chapl Arts and Recreation 86-05; Chapl 05-08; Lic to AD Stockton from 08. *24 North Close, Thorpe Thewles, Stockton-on-Tees TS21 3JY* Tel (01740) 630015 E-mail robert@cooperphoto.co.uk

COOPER, Roger Charles. b 48. GRSM ARMCM69 PGCE70. Coll of Resurr Mirfield 79. **d** 81 **p** 82. C Monkseaton St Mary *Newc* 81-83; C Morpeth 83-87; Min Can and Prec Man Cathl 87-90; V Blackrod from 90; AD Deane from 05. *St Katharine's Vicarage, Blackhorse Street, Blackrod, Bolton BL6 5EN* Tel (01204) 468150

COOPER, Seth William. b 62. Westcott Ho Cam 94. **d** 96 **p** 97. C Golders Green *Lon* 96-00; TV Uxbridge 00-05; V Walmer *Cant* from 05. *Elizabeth House, 32 St Mary's Road, Walmer, Deal CT14 7QA* Tel (01304) 366605 E-mail sethandjen@tinyworld.co.uk

COOPER, Shirley Ann. *See* RUSSELL, Alexandra Blaise

COOPER, Stephen. b 54. Bernard Gilpin Soc Dur 73 Chich Th Coll 74. **d** 77 **p** 78. C Horbury *Wakef* 77-78; C Horbury w Horbury Bridge 78-81; C Barnsley St Mary 81-84; TV Elland 84-91; Hon C Huddersfield St Thos 93-94; P-in-c Middlesbrough St Columba w St Paul *York* 94-08; V from 09; P-in-c Middlesbrough St Jo the Ev 05-08; V from 09; Chapl S Tees Hosps NHS Trust 94-05. *St Columba's Vicarage, 115 Cambridge Road, Middlesbrough TS5 5HF* Tel (01642) 824779 E-mail fr_s_cooper@hotmail.com

COOPER, Stephen Paul Crossley. b 58. Trin Coll Bris 91. **d** 93 **p** 94. C Blackb Redeemer 93-95; C Altham w Clayton le Moors 95-98; V Langho Billington 98-03; Chapl Rossall Sch Fleetwood 03-09; TV Fellside Team *Blackb* from 09. *The Vicarage, Goosnargh Lane, Goosnargh, Preston PR3 2BN* Tel (01722) 865274 E-mail revscooper@googlemail.com

COOPER, Mrs Susan Mary. b 45. Westcott Ho Cam 01. **d** 04 **p** 04. C Syston *Leic* 03-06; R Chipping Ongar w Shelley *Chelmsf* from 06. *The Rectory, Shakletons, Ongar CM5 9AT* Tel (01277) 362173 E-mail scoople@btinternet.com

COOPER, Susan Mira. *See* RAMSARAN, Susan Mira

COOPER, Thomas Joseph Gerard Strickland. b 46. Lanc Univ PhD85. Ven English Coll & Pontifical Gregorian Univ Rome

PhB66 PhL67 STB69 STL71. **d** 70 **p** 70. In RC Ch 70-92; Chapl St Woolos Cathl 93-95; V Llandaff N 95-08; rtd 08. *Arwel, Cwmdegwel, St Dogmaels, Cardigan SA45 3JH* Tel (01239) 614156 E-mail teilo@woolos.supanet.com

COOPER, Trevor. *See* COOPER, Joseph Trevor

COOPER, Trevor John. b 51. Ex Univ MA95. Wycliffe Hall Ox 75. **d** 79 **p** 95. C Southsea St Pet *Portsm* 79-80; NSM Heavitree w Ex St Paul 93-96; C Standish *Blackb* 96-99; V Burnley St Cuth 99-03; P-in-c Lytham St Jo 03-06; rtd 06. *119 Emsworth Road, Portsmouth PO2 0BT* E-mail trevor.j.cooper@btinternet.com

COOPER, Wallace Peter. b 24. Kelham Th Coll 47. **d** 51 **p** 52. C Watford St Mich *St Alb* 51-52; C Ealing St Barn *Lon* 52-54; C New Brompton St Luke *Roch* 54-56; Perm to Offic *Ox* 62-81; Hon C Earley St Pet 81-83; Hon C Earley St Nic 83-92; rtd 90; Hon C Reading St Mark *Ox* 92-99; Perm to Offic *Ex* from 99. *7 Gracey Court, Woodland Road, Broadclyst, Exeter EX5 3GA* Tel (01392) 460612

COOPER, William Douglas. b 42. Open Univ BA83 St Andr Univ MA08 Aber Univ MA09. St Jo Coll Nottm 88 Qu Coll Birm 93. **d** 94 **p** 95. NSM Melbourne *Derby* 94-97; C Penwortham St Mary *Blackb* 97-00; P-in-c Smeeth w Monks Horton and Stowting and Brabourne *Cant* 00-04; rtd 04. *18A Market Street, St Andrews KY16 9NS* Tel (01334) 460678

COORE, Jonathan. b 71. Lon Inst of Educn PGCE97 GTCL94. Trin Coll Bris 05. **d** 07 **p** 08. C Heref St Pet w St Owen and St Jas from 07; Bp's Dom Chapl from 08. *61 Lichfield Avenue, Hereford HR1 2RL* Tel (01432) 270293 *or* 276320 E-mail jonathancoore@msn.com

COOTE, Anthony John. b 54. Qu Coll Birm 95. **d** 97 **p** 98. C Malvern H Trin and St Jas *Worc* 97-01; TV Heref S Wye 01-02; P-in-c Cradley *Worc* 02-04; rtd 04. *43 The Poplars, Stourbridge DY8 5SN* Tel (01384) 482446

COOTE, Bernard Albert Ernest. b 28. Lon Univ BD53. Chich Th Coll 54. **d** 55 **p** 56. C Addiscombe St Mary *Cant* 55-57; C Hawkhurst 57-59; C Sanderstead All SS *S'wark* 59-63; Chapl HM Borstal E Sutton Park 63-74; V Sutton Valence w E Sutton *Cant* 63-76; P-in-c Chart next Sutton Valence 71-76; Chapl and Dir R Sch for the Blind Leatherhead 76-91; rtd 91; Perm to Offic *Chich* and *Guildf* from 91. *6 Coxham Lane, Steyning BN44 3JG* Tel (01903) 813762

COPE, James Brian Andrew. b 58. Chich Th Coll 80. **d** 83 **p** 84. C Poulton-le-Fylde *Blackb* 83-86; C Fleetwood St Pet 86-87; V Fleetwood St Dav 87-94; P-in-c Somercotes *Derby* 94-99; V Watford St Jo *St Alb* 99-07; V Castle Vale w Minworth *Birm* from 07. *St Cuthbert's Vicarage, St Cuthbert's Place, Birmingham B35 7PL* Tel 0121-747 4041 E-mail fr.jamescopessc@sky.com

COPE, Judith Diane. b 50. St Hilda's Coll Ox BA72 Lon Univ MB, BS75 MRCGP80. SAOMC 00. **d** 03 **p** 04. NSM Lt Berkhamsted and Bayford, Essendon etc *St Alb* from 03. *18 Hatherleigh Gardens, Potters Bar EN6 5HZ* Tel (01707) 644391 E-mail m_cope@btinternet.com

COPE, Mrs Melia Lambrianos. b 53. Cape Town Univ BSocSc73. St Jo Coll Nottm 80 WMMTC 83. **dss** 86 **d** 93 **p** 94. W Bromwich All SS *Lich* 86-93; NSM 93-94; NSM W Bromwich St Mary Magd CD 93-94; TV Cen Telford 94-02; Chapl HM Pris Shrewsbury 95-98, P-in-c Stokesay *Heref* from 02; P-in-c Halford w Sibdon Carwood from 02; P-in-c Acton Scott from 02; P-in-c Wistanstow from 06. *Stokesay Vicarage, Clun Road, Craven Arms SY7 9QW* Tel (01588) 673463 E-mail meliacope@burwaynet.com

COPE, Miss Olive Rosemary. b 29. Gilmore Ho 63. **dss** 69 **d** 87 **p** 94. Kentish Town St Martin w St Andr *Lon* 69-72; Enfield St Andr 73-99; Par Dn 87-89; Hon Par Dn 89-94; Non C 94-99; Perm to Offic from 99. *7 Calder Close, Enfield EN1 3TS* Tel (020) 8363 8221 E-mail oliveclose2003@yahoo.co.uk

COPE, Peter John. b 42. Mert Coll Ox BA64 MA68 Lon Univ MSc74 Man Univ PhD91. Cuddesdon Coll 64. **d** 66 **p** 67. C Chapel Allerton *Ripon* 66-69; Ind Chapl *Lon* 69-76; Ind Chapl *Worc* 76-85; Min Can Worc Cathl 76-85; P-in-c Worc St Mark 76-81; Min W Bromwich St Mary Magd CD *Lich* 85-94; Ind Chapl 85-94; Telford Town Cen Chapl 94-07; W Midl FE Field Officer 94-97; Churches Ind Officer 97-07; rtd 07; Perm to Offic *Heref* from 96 and *Lich* from 07. *Stokesay Vicarage, Clun Road, Craven Arms SY7 9QW* Tel and fax (01588) 673463 E-mail peterjcope@hotmail.co.uk

COPE, Ralph Bruce. Sir Geo Williams Univ Montreal BA60 McGill Univ Montreal BD62. **d** 60 **p** 61. Canada 60-99 and from 00; P-in-c Sophia Antipolis *Eur* 99-00. *407-4701 Uplands Drive, Nanaimo BC V9T 5Y2, Canada* Tel (001) (250) 758 3296 E-mail ralglo@compuserve.com

COPE, Stephen Victor. b 60. St Jo Coll Ox BA81 MA87. Chich Th Coll 86. **d** 89 **p** 90. C Newmarket St Mary w Exning St Agnes *St E* 89-92; C Northampton St Matt *Pet* 92-94; V Rudston w Boynton and Kilham *York* 94-98; V Rudston w Boynton, Carnaby and Kilham 98-06; P-in-c Burton Fleming w Fordon, Grindale etc 00-06; RD Bridlington 98-03; P-in-c Owthorne and Rimswell w Withernsea 06-07; P-in-c Easington w Skeffling, Kilnsea and Holmpton 06-07; R Withernsea w Owthorne and

Easington etc from 07. *The Vicarage, 28 Park Avenue, Withernsea HU19 2JU* Tel (01964) 611462
E-mail stephenvcope@tiscali.co.uk

COPELAND, Annabel Susan Mary. b 64. Roehampton Inst BEd87. Wycliffe Hall Ox 03. **d** 05 **p** 06. C Billericay and Lt Burstead *Chelmsf* 05-08; TV Gt Baddow from 08. *124 Beehive Lane, Chelmsford CM2 9SH* Tel (01245) 269026
E-mail annabel.c@bun.com

COPELAND, Christopher Paul. b 38. AKC64. **d** 65 **p** 66. C Luton St Andr *St Alb* 65-67; C Droitwich St Nic w St Pet *Worc* 67-71; C Kings Norton *Birm* 71-72; TV 73-78; V Tyseley 78-88; P-in-c Grimley w Holt *Worc* 88-96; Dioc Stewardship Missr 88-96; P-in-c Forest of Dean Ch Ch w English Bicknor *Glouc* 96-03; rtd 03; Perm to Offic *Worc* from 03. *24 Players Avenue, Malvern WR14 1DU* Tel (01684) 563323

COPELAND, Derek Norman. b 38. Worc Coll Ox BA62 MA68. Westcott Ho Cam 63. **d** 64 **p** 65. C Portsea St Mary *Portsm* 64-71; P-in-c Avonmouth St Andr *Bris* 71-77; P-in-c Chippenham St Paul w Langley Burrell 78-79; 2nd Chapl from 78; TR Chippenham St Paul w Hardenhuish etc 79-89; V Kington St Michael 79-89; Perm to Offic *Bris*; *B & W* and *Sarum* from 89; rtd 03. *51B Lowden, Chippenham SN15 2BG* Tel (01249) 443879

COPELAND, Ian Trevor. b 51. FCA83. **d** 99 **p** 00. OLM Werrington *Lich* 99-09; OLM Werrington and Wetley Rocks from 09. *4 Heather Close, Werrington, Stoke-on-Trent ST9 0LB* Tel (01782) 303525 E-mail it.copeland@ntlworld.com

COPELAND, Trevor. b 57. St Jo Coll Nottm 04. **d** 07 **p** 08. C Westfield St Mary *Carl* from 07. *68 Rowe Terrace, Workington CA14 3SR* Tel (01900) 873303

COPLAND, Miss Carole Jean. b 37. Man Univ BA60. Wm Temple Coll Rugby 65. **d** 87 **p** 94. NSM Northallerton w Kirby Sigston *York* 88-90; Dioc Adv in Children's Work 81-90; Par Dn Dunnington 90-94; Faith in the City Link Officer 90-96; C Dunnington 94-96; V Ledsham w Fairburn 96-99; rtd 99; Perm to Offic *York* from 99. *4 Jedwell Close, New Earswick, York YO32 4DQ* Tel (01904) 767110
E-mail carolecopland@hotmail.com

COPLAND, Canon Charles McAlester. b 10. CCC Cam BA33 MA36. Cuddesdon Coll 33. **d** 34 **p** 35. C Pet St Jo 34-38; India 38-52; Can All SS Cathl Nagpur from 52; R Arbroath *Bre* 53-59; Can St Paul's Cathl Dundee 53-59; R Oban St Jo *Arg* 59-79; Provost St Jo Cathl Oban 59-79; Dean Arg 77-79; rtd 79; Hon Can St Jo Cathl Oban from 79. *3 West Hill Road, Kirriemuir DD8 4PR* Tel (01575) 575415

COPLETON, Roger Boyd. b 62. Edin Univ BD87. TISEC 97. **d** 97 **p** 98. NSM Haddington and Dunbar *Edin* 97-06. *30 Couston Drive, Dalgety Bay, Dunfermline KY11 9NX* Tel 07759-952618 (mobile)

COPLEY, Colin. b 30. FRSA85. Kelham Th Coll 51. **d** 55 **p** 56. C Linc St Swithin 55-58; C Bottesford 58-60; Chapl HM Borstal Hollesley Bay 60-66; Chapl HM Pris Liv 66-70; Chapl HM Pris Styal 70-73; N Regional Chapl HM Pris and Borstals 70-73; Midl Region 73-75; Chapl HM Pris Drake Hall 73-75; Asst Chapl Gen of Pris (Midl) 75-90; Chapl HM Pris Sudbury and Foston Hall 90-95; Chapl HM Pris Stafford 95-00; rtd 00; Perm to Offic *Lich* from 90; Lect Potchefstroom Univ from 98. *67 Porlock Avenue, Stafford ST17 0HT* Tel (01785) 663152
E-mail colincopley7@btinternet.com

COPLEY, Paul. b 58. NEOC 97. **d** 99 **p** 00. C Hessle *York* 99-02; TV Sutton St Jas and Wawne 02-07; P-in-c Kingston upon Hull St Nic from 07; P-in-c Newington w Dairycoates from 07. *St Nicholas' Vicarage, 898 Hessle High Road, Hull HU4 6SA* Tel (01482) 504088

COPPEN, Colin William. b 53. BCombStuds85. Linc Th Coll. **d** 85 **p** 86. C Tokyngton St Mich *Lon* 85-88; C Somers Town 88-90; P-in-c Edmonton St Alphege 90-92; V 92-95; P-in-c W Hampstead St Jas 95-97; P-in-c Kilburn St Mary w All So 95-97; TR Wood Green St Mich w Bounds Green St Gabr etc from 97. *St Michael's Rectory, 1A Selborne Road, London N22 7TL* Tel (020) 8888 1968 E-mail rector@woodgreenparish.com

COPPEN, George. *See* COPPEN, Robert George

COPPEN, Canon Martin Alan. b 48. Ex Univ BA69. St Jo Coll Nottm 83. **d** 85 **p** 86. C Bitterne *Win* 85-88; V St Mary Bourne and Woodcott 88-99; V Hurstbourne Priors, Longparish etc from 00; RD Whitchurch 98-03; Hon Can Win Cathl from 04. *The Vicarage, St Mary Bourne, Andover SP11 6AY* Tel and fax (01264) 738308 E-mail revd.coppen@dsl.pipex.com

COPPEN, Robert George. b 39. Cape Town Univ BA66. St Jo Coll Dur 79. **d** 81 **p** 82. C Douglas St Geo and St Barn *S & M* 81-84; TV Kidlington w Hampton Poyle *Ox* 84-05; Chapl HM YOI Campsfield Ho 84-91; rtd 05. *Taobh Mol, Kildary, Invergordon IV18 0NJ* Tel (01862) 842381
E-mail coppen@dunelm.org.uk

COPPIN, Canon Ronald Leonard. b 30. Birm Univ BA52. Ridley Hall Cam 54. **d** 56 **p** 57. C Harrow Weald All SS *Lon* 56-59; Bp's Dom Chapl *Man* 59-63; Chapl St Aid Birkenhead 63-65; Vice-Prin 65-68; Selection Sec ACCM 68-74; Sec Cttee for Th Educn 71-74; Can Res and Lib Dur Cathl 74-97; Dir of Clergy Tr 74-96;

Warden NEOC 76-84; Dir Post-Ord Tr 86-97; rtd 97; Perm to Offic *Lon* from 02. *157 Defoe House, London EC2Y 8ND* Tel (020) 7588 9228 E-mail ronald.coppin@virgin.net

COPPING, Adrian Walter Alexander. b 52. Ridley Hall Cam. **d** 00 **p** 01. C Royston *St Alb* 00-04; R Bangor Monachorum, Worthenbury and Marchwiel *St As* from 04; AD Bangor Isycoed from 05. *The Rectory, 8 Ludlow Road, Bangor-on-Dee, Wrexham LL13 0JG* Tel (01978) 780608
E-mail adriancopping@hotmail.com

COPPING, John Frank Walter Victor. b 34. K Coll Lon BD58 AKC58. **d** 59 **p** 60. C Hampstead St Jo *Lon* 59-62; C Bray and Braywood *Ox* 62-65; V Langley Mill *Derby* 65-71; V Cookham Dean *Ox* 71-03; RD Maidenhead 87-94; rtd 03; Perm to Offic *Ox* from 03. *41 Golden Ball Lane, Pinkneys Green, Maidenhead SL6 6NW* Tel (01628) 674433
E-mail johnfcopping@talktalk.net

COPPING, Raymond. b 36. St Mark & St Jo Coll Lon TCert59. Wycliffe Hall Ox 72. **d** 74 **p** 75. C High Wycombe *Ox* 74-77; TV 77-87; TV Digswell and Panshanger *St Alb* 87-95; P-in-c Charlton Kings H Apostles *Glouc* 95-00; rtd 00; Hon C Thame *Ox* from 04. *20 Friars Furlong, Long Crendon, Aylesbury HP18 9DQ* Tel (01844) 208509

COPSEY, Mrs Christine. b 51. Nottm Univ CertEd73. ERMC 04. **d** 07 **p** 08. NSM Fakenham w Alethorpe *Nor* 07-08; NSM King's Lynn St Marg w St Nic from 08. *5 Back Lane, Castle Acre, King's Lynn PE32 2AR* Tel (01760) 755558
E-mail g.copsey@btopenworld.com

COPSEY, Nigel John. b 52. K Coll Lon BD75 AKC75 Surrey Univ MSc88 Middx Univ DProf01. St Aug Coll Cant 72. **d** 76 **p** 77. C Barkingside St Fran *Chelmsf* 76-78; C Canning Town St Cedd 78-80; P-in-c Victoria Docks Ascension 80-87; Chapl E Surrey Mental Health Unit 87-90; Hd Past and Spiritual Care E Surrey Priority Care NHS Trust from 90; Co-ord Past Care Surrey Oaklands NHS Trust 99-05; Hd Past and Spiritual Care Surrey and Borders Partnership NHS Trust from 08; Co-ord Relig Care Newham Community Health Services NHS Trust 99-01; Co-ord Relig Care Newham Primary Care Trust from 01; Team Ldr Spiritual, Relig and Cultural Care E Lon NHS Foundation Trust from 08. *Newham Centre for Mental Health, Glen Road, London E13 8SP* Tel (020) 7540 4380 Fax 7540 2970
E-mail nigel.copsey@eastlondon.nhs.uk

COPUS, Brian George. b 36. AKC59. **d** 60 **p** 61. C Croydon St Mich *Cant* 60-63; C Swindon New Town *Bris* 63-69; V Colebrooke *Ex* 69-73; P-in-c Hittisleigh 69-73; R Perivale *Lon* 73-82; V Ruislip St Mary 82-01; rtd 01; Perm to Offic *Win* from 02. *Le Bec, 84 Carbery Avenue, Bournemouth BH6 3LQ* Tel (01202) 428943

COPUS, John Cecil. b 38. TCert64 Maria Grey Coll Lon DipEd71 Open Univ BA78. Cant Sch of Min. **d** 83 **p** 84. Hon C Folkestone H Trin and St Geo w Ch Ch *Cant* 83-85; Hon C Midsomer Norton w Clandown *B & W* 85-91; Dioc Adv for Children's Work *Ex* 91-98; Hon C Aylesbeare, Rockbeare, Farringdon etc 95-98; P-in-c 98-01; rtd 01; Perm to Offic *Ex* from 01; Clergy Widow(er)s Officer from 02; C N Creedy from 08. *The Sidings, Park Road, Lapford, Crediton EX17 6QJ* Tel (01363) 83408

COPUS, Jonathan Hugh Lambert. b 44. BNC Ox BA66 MA71 LGSM66 MInstPI94. S'wark Ord Course 68. **d** 71 **p** 72. C Horsell *Guildf* 71-73; Producer Relig Progr BBC Radio Solent 73-87; V Maenclochog and New Moat etc *St D* 06-07; V Martletwy w Lawrenny and Minwear etc 07; Perm to Offic from 07. *Llys Myrddin, Efailwen, Clynderwen SA66 7XG* Tel (01994) 419834 Mobile 07828-510283 E-mail revjc@dentron.co.uk

CORBAN-BANKS, Edrick Hale. b 53. Victoria Univ Wellington BMus74 LTCL79 FTCL81. St Jo Coll Auckland BTh91. **d** 91 **p** 92. New Zealand 91-99; P Asst Johnsonville St Jo 92-94; Ch Planter Churton Park 93-94; V Katikati 94-99; P Missr Alicante Spain 99; R Alicante St Paul 99-00; Chapl Ibiza *Eur* 00-03; V Stoke New Zealand from 04. *523 Main Road, Stoke, Nelson 7001, New Zealand* Tel (0064) (3) 547 3478
E-mail vicar.stbarnabas@paradise.net.nz

CORBETT, George. b 18. Bible Churchmen's Coll Bris 47. **d** 50 **p** 51. C Wednesfield Heath *Lich* 50-52; R Salford St Matthias w St Simon *Man* 52-55; N Area Sec BCMS 55-58; V S Lambeth St Steph *S'wark* 58-61; Assoc Home Sec BCMS 61-63; V Hatherleigh *Ex* 63-78; P-in-c Ringmore and Kingston 78-84; R Bigbury, Ringmore and Kingston 84-86; rtd 86; Perm to Offic *Heref* from 87. *2 Quantock Close, Hereford HR4 0TD* Tel (01432) 269211

CORBETT, Canon Henry. b 53. CCC Cam BA75. Wycliffe Hall Ox. **d** 78 **p** 79. C Everton St Pet *Liv* 78-84; TV 84-87; TR 87-02; R Everton St Pet w St Chrys from 02; AD Liv N from 03; Hon Can Liv Cathl from 03. *Shrewsbury House, Langrove Street, Liverpool L5 3LT* Tel 0151-207 1948
E-mail hjcorbett@shewsy.freeserve.co.uk

CORBETT, The Very Revd Ian Deighton. b 42. St Cath Coll Cam BA64 MA67 Cam Univ PGCE65. Westcott Ho Cam 67. **d** 69 **p** 70. C New Bury *Man* 69-72; C Bolton St Pet 72-75; Chapl Bolton Colls of H&FE 72-75; R Man Victoria Park 75-80;

Chapl Salford Univ 80-83; Dioc FE Officer 74-83; R Salford Sacred Trin 83-87; Dir CME and Hon Can Man Cathl 83-87; Warden Lelapa la Jesu Sem Lesotho 88-91; Can Missr Harare Zimbabwe 92-93; Can Missr Botswana 93-95; R Kuruman St Mary S Africa 95-97; Dean Tuam and I Tuam w Cong and Aasleagh *T, K & A* 97-99; R Whitesands Canada 99-01; V Utah Region USA 01-08; Hon C E Clevedon w Clapton in Gordano etc *B & W* from 09. *5 Chestnut Grove, Clevedon BS21 7LA* Tel (01275) 872723 E-mail iancorbett123@btinternet.com

CORBETT, Jocelyn Rory. d 05 **p** 06. Aux Min Aghalee *D & D* 05-06; Aux Min Donaghcloney w Waringstown from 06. *Badger Hill, 23 Magherabeg Road, Dromore BT25 1RS* Tel (028) 9269 2067 E-mail rory.corbett@ukonline.co.uk

CORBETT, John David. b 32. Oriel Coll Ox BA55 MA59. St Steph Ho Ox 55. **d** 57 **p** 58. C Plymouth St Pet *Ex* 57-64; V Marldon 64-74; TV Bournemouth St Pet w St Swithun, H Trin etc *Win* 74-83; V Beckenham St Barn *Roch* 83-88; V King's Sutton and Newbottle and Charlton *Pet* 88-97; rtd 97; Perm to Offic Portsm and *Win* from 98. *119 St Augustine Road, Southsea PO4 9AA* Tel (023) 9275 3212 E-mail jdc.augustine@virgin.net

CORBETT, Philip Peter. b 81. St Andr Univ MTheol03 Selw Univ STM04 Keble Coll Ox MPhil06. Coll of Resurr Mirfield 06. **d** 08 **p** 09. C Worksop Priory *S'well* from 08. *6 Conrad Close, Worksop S80 2EN* Tel (01909) 530860 E-mail philippetercorbett@googlemail.com

CORBETT, Miss Phyllis. b 34. Cranmer Hall Dur 76. **dss** 80 **d** 87 **p** 94. Walsall Wood *Lich* 80-87; Par Dn Baswich *Lich* 87-94; C 94-95; rtd 95; Perm to Offic *Lich* from 95. *9 Redhill Gorse, Crab Lane, Trinity Fields, Stafford ST16 1SW*

CORBETT, Rory. *See* CORBETT, Jocelyn Rory

CORBETT, Stephen Paul. b 57. BA80. St Jo Coll Nottm 83. **d** 85 **p** 86. C Tollington Park St Mark w St Anne *Lon* 85-86; C Holloway St Mark w Em 86-91; V Church Hill St Cuth 91-93; V Springfield *Birm* 93-04; AD Moseley 02-04; V Walmley from 04; P-in-c Blackb St Gabr from 09. *St Gabriel's Vicarage, 6 Charnwood Close, Blackburn BB2 7BT*

CORBIN, Frederick Athelston. b 42. S Dios Minl Tr Scheme 80. **d** 83 **p** 85. NSM Basingstoke *Win* 83-84; C Hulme Ascension *Man* 84-86; Lic to Hulme Deanery 86-87; C E Crompton 87-89; V Oldham St Barn 89-00; rtd 00; Grenada 00-01; Perm to Offic *Man* 01-07. *St Alban's and St Silas's Rectory, Lower Carlton, St James, Barbados* Tel (001) (246) 422 2913

CORBYN, John. b 58. Man Univ BA79 Ven English Coll & Pontifical Gregorian Univ Rome 83. Wycliffe Hall Ox BA83 MA87. **d** 84 **p** 85. C Deane *Man* 84-87; C Lancaster St Mary *Blackb* 87-90; Sub-Chapl HM Pris Lanc 89-90; V Blackb St Gabr 90-01; V Bearsted w Thurnham *Cant* from 01. *The Vicarage, Church Lane, Bearsted, Maidstone ME14 4EF* Tel (01622) 737135 E-mail vicar@holycrosschurch.co.uk

CORBYN, John Robert. b 54. Qu Coll Birm. **d** 82 **p** 83. C Northolt St Jos *Lon* 82-86; Urban Miss P *York* 86-88; C Sutton St Mich 86-88; V Dalton *Sheff* 88-96; R Cressing *Chelmsf* 96-99; R Cressing w Stisted and Bradwell etc from 99. *The House, Church Street, Bradwell, Braintree CM77 8EL* Tel (01376) 562398 E-mail frjohn@crestibrad.freeserve.co.uk

CORCORAN, Daniel Chad. b 71. Man Metrop Univ BA93. St Jo Coll Nottm 04. **d** 06 **p** 07. C Stapleford *S'well* from 06. *41 Perth Drive, Stapleford, Nottingham NG9 8PZ* Tel 0115-913 1436 Mobile 07963-332221 E-mail danchadcorcoran@hotmail.com

CORCORAN, Jennifer Miriam. b 78. Lanc Univ BA01 St Jo Coll Nottm MA(MM)07. **d** 07 **p** 08. C Chilwell *S'well* from 07. *41 Perth Drive, Stapleford, Nottingham NG9 8PZ* Tel 0115-913 1436

CORCORAN, Mrs Valerie A'Court. b 46. UEA BA68 Lon Inst of Educn PGCE69. STETS 99. **d** 02 **p** 03. NSM Boyatt Wood *Win* from 02. *Ashley, Finches Lane, Twyford, Winchester SO21 1QB* Tel (01962) 712951 Fax 715770 Mobile 07736-459500 E-mail v.corcoran@btinternet.com

CORDELL, Derek Harold. b 34. Chich Th Coll 57. **d** 60 **p** 61. C Whitstable All SS *Cant* 60-63; C Moulsecoomb *Chich* 63-69; Chapl Bucharest *Eur* 69-71; V Brighton St Wilfrid *Chich* 71-74; Chapl HM Borstal Roch 74-80; Asst Chapl HM Pris Man 80-81; Chapl HM Pris The Verne 81-89; Chapl HM Pris Channings Wood 89-90; Chapl Milan w Genoa and Varese *Eur* 90-91; Chapl Mojcar 91-94; Perm to Offic from 95; rtd 97. *27 Scalwell Mead, Seaton EX12 2DW* Tel (01297) 624182

CORDINER, Alan Dobson. b 61. Westmr Coll Ox BA87. **d** 92 **p** 93. C Upperby St Jo *Carl* 92-98; P-in-c Bootle, Corney, Whicham and Whitbeck 98-05; Asst Chapl HM Pris Haverigg 98-03. *32 Summer Hill, Bootle, Millom LA19 5UB* Tel (01229) 718605

CORDINGLEY, Canon Brian Lambert. b 30. St Aid Birkenhead 55. **d** 57 **p** 58. Ind Chapl *Sheff* 57-63; C Clifton St Jas 57-61; C Rotherham 61-63; Ind Chapl *Man* 63-92; R Old Trafford St Cuth 63-81; V Hamer 81-92; Hon Can Man Cathl 87-92, rtd 92; Perm to Offic *Man* from 99. *Wellsprings, 27 Fernthorpe Avenue, Uppermill, Oldham OL3 6EA* Tel (01457) 820130

CORE, Edward. b 54. Southn Univ BTh84 Westmr Coll Ox MTh96. Sarum & Wells Th Coll 79. **d** 82 **p** 83. C Newbold w

Dunston *Derby* 82-86; Chapl RAF 86-01; Command Chapl RAF 01-06; P-in-c Frodingham *Linc* from 06. *The Vicarage, Vicarage Gardens, Scunthorpe DN15 7AZ* Tel (01724) 842726 E-mail st.lawrence.frodingham@btinternet.com

CORFE, David Robert. b 35. Pemb Coll Cam BA58 MA60 Lambeth STh70. Cuddesdon Coll 58. **d** 60 **p** 61. C Wigan All SS *Liv* 60-63; SPG Miss India 63-68; V Lucknow Ch Ch w All SS and St Pet 70-75; C Northwood Em *Lon* 75; V Westwell and Eastwell w Boughton Aluph *Cant* 75-80; V Hildenborough *Roch* 80-91; Lic Preacher Stretford St Bride *Man* 91-98; Team Ldr Interserve 98-00; rtd 00; Perm to Offic from 03. *1 Hartley Court, 12 Winn Road, Southampton SO17 1EN* Tel (023) 8058 5557 E-mail drcorfe@freedomland.co.uk

CORK, Ronald Edward. b 43. Plymouth Poly CQSW72. NOC 89. **d** 92 **p** 93. Hon C Altrincham St Geo *Ches* 92-96; P-in-c Altrincham St Jo 96-01; rtd 01. *15 Emmasfield, Exmouth EX8 2LS* Tel (01395) 223489 E-mail roncork@aol.com

CORK, CLOYNE AND ROSS, Archdeacon of. *See* WHITE, The Ven Robin Edward Bantry

CORK, CLOYNE AND ROSS, Bishop of. *See* COLTON, The Rt Revd William Paul

CORK, Dean of. *See* DUNNE, The Very Revd Nigel Kenneth

CORKE, Andrew John. b 55. Bris Univ LLB77. **d** 98 **p** 00. OLM Canford Magna *Sarum* from 98. *2 Silverwood Close, Wimborne Minster BH21 1QZ* Tel (01202) 882449 Mobile 07711-898723 Fax 786140 E-mail a.corke@talk21.com

CORKE, Bryan Raymond. b 49. Westmr Coll Lon 81. **d** 95 **p** 96. OLM Flixton St Jo *Man* from 95. *40 Daresbury Avenue, Manchester M41 8GL* Tel 0161-748 1827

CORKE, Colin John. b 59. St Pet Coll Ox BA81. Cranmer Hall Dur 83. **d** 85 **p** 86. C Chapel Allerton *Ripon* 85-88; C Burmantofts St Steph and St Agnes 88-91; P-in-c Tatsfield *S'wark* 91-01; Reigate Adnry Ecum Officer 92-01; V Longbridge *Birm* from 01; Dioc Ecum Officer from 02; AD Kings Norton from 06. *St John's Vicarage, 220 Longbridge Lane, Birmingham B31 4JT* Tel 0121-475 3484 E-mail ado67@btinternet.com

CORKE, Francis Bonny. *See* RODRIGUEZ-VEGLIO, Francis Bonny

CORKE, John Harry. b 29. AKC55. **d** 56 **p** 57. C Stockingford *Cov* 56-58; C Nuneaton St Nic 58-60; V Hartshill 60-80; R Hampton Lucy w Charlecote and Loxley 80-94; rtd 94; Perm to Offic *Linc* from 95. *18 Haven Close, Fleet, Spalding PE12 8NS* Tel (01406) 426038

CORKE, Louise Dorothy. b 59. Southn Univ BSc80 PGCE81. Trin Coll Bris BA94. **d** 97 **p** 98. C Ipsley *Worc* 97-01; TV Bradgate Team *Leic* from 01. *The Rectory, 58 Pymm Ley Lane, Groby, Leicester LE6 0GZ* Tel 0116-231 3090 E-mail standstill@btopenworld.com

CORKE, Roderick Geoffrey. b 58. UEA BEd79 Open Univ MA96. St Jo Coll Nottm 90. **d** 92 **p** 93. C Trimley St *E* 92-95; C Walton 95-00; TR Walton and Trimley 00-05; P-in-c Taunton St Mary *B & W* from 05. V from 08. *St Mary's Vicarage, Church Square, Taunton TA1 1SA* Tel (01823) 272441 E-mail rodcorke@tiscali.co.uk

CORKER, Mrs Elizabeth Jane. b 42. **d** 99 **p** 00. OLM Martlesham w Brightwell *St E* from 99. *12 Fairfield Avenue, Felixstowe IP11 9JN* Tel (01394) 210793 E-mail e.corker@ntlworld.com

CORKER, John Anthony. b 37. TD93. ACIB75 AKC63. **d** 64 **p** 65. C Lindley *Wakef* 64-68; V Brotherton 68-72; Perm to Offic 72-82; CF (TA) 80-93; Hon C Askham Bryan *York* 82-91; TV York All SS Pavement w St Crux and St Martin etc 91-96; Chapl York Health Services NHS Trust 91-96; Chapl Dudley Gp of Hosps NHS Trust 96-99; Asst P Amblecote *Worc* 96-01; Asst P Dudley St Barn 01-02; rtd 02; Perm to Offic *Worc* from 02. *69 Lakeside Court, Brierley Hill DY5 3RQ* Tel (01384) 897378

CORKER, Canon Ronald. b 30. Ely Th Coll 51. **d** 54 **p** 55. C Whitworth w Spennymoor *Dur* 54-58; Min Dunstan St Nic ED 58-65; Chapl Dunston Hill Hosp Gateshead 58-68; V Dunston St Nic *Dur* 65-68; R Willington 68-75; P-in-c Sunnybrow 73-75; R Willington and Sunnybrow 75-80; V Billingham St Cuth 80-85; RD Stockton 83-85; TR Jarrow 85-95; Hon Can Dur Cathl 90-00; rtd 95. *195 Beaconsides, Cleadon Manor, South Shields NE34 7PT* Tel 0191-454 2987

CORLEY, Samuel Jon Clint. b 76. St Aid Coll Dur BA97 MA98 Hughes Hall Cam PGCE99. St Jo Coll Nottm MA04. **d** 04 **p** 05. C Lancaster St Thos *Blackb* 04-08; Asst Dioc Missr from 08; P-in-c Ellel w Shireshead from 08. *20 Highland Brow, Galgate, Lancaster LA2 0NB* Tel (01524) 752979 Mobile 07966-524683 E-mail samcorley@btinternet.com

CORMACK, Donald Stuart. b 45. Brock University Ontario TCert67 McMaster Univ Ontario BA71. Regent Coll Vancouver MTh85. **d** 92 **p** 93. C Singapore St Geo 92-93; P-in-c Phnom Penh Cambodia 93-96; Perm to Offic *Glouc* from 06. *305 Gloucester Road, Cheltenham GL51 7AR* Tel (01242) 699506 E-mail don.cormack@hotmail.co.uk

CORNE, Ronald Andrew. b 51. Sarum & Wells Th Coll 87. **d** 89 **p** 90. C Bitterne Park *Win* 89-93; R Headbourne Worthy and King's Worthy 93-01; P-in-c Broughton, Bossington, Houghton and Mottisfont 01-03; R from 03; RD Romsey from 06. *The Rectory, Rectory Lane, Broughton, Stockbridge SO20 8AB* Tel (01794) 301287 E-mail cronandrew@aol.com

CORNECK, Canon Warrington Graham. b 35. MBE05. ACA60 FCA62. Clifton Th Coll. **d** 65 **p** 66. C Islington St Jude Mildmay Park *Lon* 65-67; C Southgate *Chich* 67-73; P-in-c Deptford St Nic w Ch Ch *S'wark* 73-76; P-in-c Deptford St Luke 73-76; V Deptford St Nic and St Luke 76-05; RD Deptford 85-05; Hon Can S'wark Cathl 91-05; rtd 05. *42 Nadine Street, London SE7 7PG* Tel (020) 8465 5316
E-mail grahamcorneck@aol.com
Web corneck.freeserve.co.uk

CORNELIUS, Donald Eric. b 31. K Coll Lon BD52 AKC. Linc Th Coll 84. **d** 84 **p** 85. NSM Crowle *Linc* 84-97; NSM Crowle Gp 97-02; NSM Flixborough w Burton upon Stather 91-02; P-in-c Gunhouse w Burringham 91-02; Perm to Offic 02-04. *4 Mulberry Drive, Crowle, Scunthorpe DN17 4JF* Tel (01724) 710279

CORNELL, Miss Jean Cranston. b 36. Man Univ CertEd59 BA64 York Univ BPhil71. Ripon Coll Cuddesdon 87 MTh00. **d** 89 **p** 94. C Matson *Glouc* 89-92; C Bishop's Cleeve 92-96; rtd 96; NSM Winchcombe, Gretton, Sudeley Manor etc *Glouc* 96-01; Perm to Offic 01-02. *11 Willow Close, Woodmancote, Cheltenham GL52 9TU* Tel (01242) 662869
E-mail naej@chris47.freeserve.co.uk

CORNELL, Nicholas Simon. b 78. Trin Hall Cam BA00 MA03. Oak Hill Th Coll MTh08. **d** 08 **p** 09. C Eastbourne All SS *Chich* from 08. *1F Grassington Road, Eastbourne BN20 7BP* Tel (01323) 721231 Mobile 07946-220638
E-mail nscornell@gmail.com

CORNES, Alan Stuart. b 70. Open Univ BA98. St Jo Coll Nottm MA00. **d** 01 **p** 02. C Meole Brace *Lich* 01-04; P-in-c Halliwell St Luke *Man* from 04; P-in-c Halliwell from 06. *St Luke's Vicarage, Chorley Old Road, Bolton BL1 3BE* Tel (01204) 843060 Fax 848987 E-mail stuart.cornes@new-wine.net

CORNES, Canon Andrew Charles Julian. b 49. CCC Ox BA70 MA74. Wycliffe Hall Ox 70 Cranmer Hall Dur 72. **d** 73 **p** 74. C York St Mich-le-Belfrey 73-76; C St Marylebone All So w SS Pet and Jo *Lon* 76-85; R Pittsburgh Ascension USA 85-88; V Crowborough *Chich* from 89; RD Rotherfield 97-03; Can and Preb Chich Cathl from 00; Chapl Eastbourne and Co Healthcare NHS Trust 89-02; Chapl Sussex Downs and Weald Primary Care Trust from 02. *All Saints' Vicarage, Chapel Green, Crowborough TN6 1ED* Tel (01892) 667384 or 652081

CORNESS, Andrew Stuart. b 69. Bp Otter Coll Chich BA91 Westmr Coll Ox PGCE93. Wycliffe Hall Ox BA00 MA05. **d** 01 **p** 02. C Ewood *Blackb* 01-04; Chapl RN from 04. *Royal Naval Chaplaincy Service, Mail Point 1-2, Leach Building, Whale Island, Portsmouth PO2 8BY* Tel (023) 9262 5055 Fax 9262 5134
E-mail andrewcorness@hotmail.com

CORNFIELD, Richard James. b 67. St Jo Coll Nottm BA96. **d** 96 **p** 97. C Cheltenham Ch Ch *Glouc* 96-00; C Aldridge *Lich* 00-03; R from 03. *The Rectory, 14 The Green, Aldridge, Walsall WS9 8NH* Tel (01922) 452414
E-mail richard.cornfield@virgin.net

CORNISH, Anthony. b 30. Roch Th Coll 64. **d** 67 **p** 68. C Goodmayes All SS *Chelmsf* 67-71; C Buckhurst Hill 71-73; V Westcliff St Andr 73-83; R Rawreth w Rettendon 83-96; rtd 96; Perm to Offic *Chelmsf* from 99. *12 Fleetwood Avenue, Clacton-on-Sea CO15 5SE* Tel (01255) 813826

CORNISH, Dennis Henry Ronald. b 31. FCIB72 FCIS81. S'wark Ord Course 83. **d** 86 **p** 87. NSM Uxbridge *Lon* 86-89; R Lurgashall, Lodsworth and Selham *Chich* 89-96; rtd 96; Perm to Offic *Chich* from 96. *Peerley Lodge, 1 Peerley Road, East Wittering, Chichester PO20 8DW* Tel (01243) 672481

CORNISH, Gillian Lesley. b 45. ACIB77. **d** 96 **p** 97. OLM Moston St Mary *Man* 96-08; OLM Blackley St Pet from 08. *11 Rishworth Drive, New Moston, Manchester M40 3PS* Tel 0161-681 2839 E-mail gl.cornish@ntlworld.com

CORNISH, Graham Peter. b 42. Dur Univ BA67 FLA. NEOC 82. **d** 84 **p** 85. NSM Harrogate St Wilfrid and St Luke *Ripon* 84-96; Perm to Offic *York* from 84; NSM Bilton *Ripon* from 96. *33 Mayfield Grove, Harrogate HG1 5HD* Tel (01423) 562747 Fax 529928 E-mail gp-jm.cornish@virgin.net

CORNISH, Ivor. b 40. Reading Univ BSc61 DipEd62. Ox Min Course 86. **d** 89 **p** 90. NSM Aston Clinton w Buckland and Drayton Beauchamp *Ox* 89-97; NSM The Lee from 97; NSM Hawridge w Cholesbury and St Leonard from 97. *79 Weston Road, Aston Clinton, Aylesbury HP22 5EP* Tel (01296) 630345

CORNISH, John Douglas. b 42. Lich Th Coll 67. **d** 70 **p** 71. C Lt Stanmore St Lawr *Lon* 70-73; C Harefield 73-96; Perm to Offic from 96. *46 Arnos Grove, London N14 7AR*

CORNISH, Peter Andrew. b 55. Ch Ch Ox BA77 MA80 Ex Univ CertEd78. St Jo Coll Nottm 84. **d** 87 **p** 88. C Sanderstead All SS *S'wark* 87-92; TV Cen Telford *Lich* 92-98; R Sturry w Fordwich and Westbere w Hersden *Cant* from 98. *The Rectory, 2 The Hamels, Sturry, Canterbury CT2 0BL* Tel (01227) 710320
E-mail rector@sturrychurch.org.uk

CORNWALL, Archdeacon of. See BUSH, The Ven Roger Charles

CORNWELL, Christopher Richard. b 43. Dur Univ BA67. Cuddesdon Coll 67. **d** 69 **p** 70. C Cannock *Lich* 69-75; P-in-c Hadley 75-80; V 80-81; Bp's Dom Chapl 81-86; Subchanter Lich Cathl 81-86; V Ellesmere 86-89; V Welsh Frankton 86-89; V Ellesmere and Welsh Frankton 89-92; TV Leeds City *Ripon* 92-00; AD Allerton 94-97; V Ireland Wood 00-08; AD Headingley 01-07; Hon Min Can Ripon Cathl from 08. *The Vicarage, Knaresborough Road, Bishop Monkton, Harrogate HG3 3QQ* Tel (01765) 676367
E-mail christophercornwell08@btinternet.com

CORNWELL, Lisa Michele. b 70. Lon Bible Coll BA94 Westmr Coll Ox PGCE95 K Coll Lon MA99. Ridley Hall Cam 00. **d** 02 **p** 03. C Newport Pagnell w Lathbury and Moulsoe *Ox* 02-06; V Crowthorne from 06. *The Vicarage, 56 Duke's Ride, Crowthorne RG45 6NY* Tel (01344) 772413
E-mail revlisacornwell@aol.com

CORP, Ronald Geoffrey. b 51. Ch Ch Ox MA77. STETS. **d** 98 **p** 99. NSM Kilburn St Mary w All So and W Hampstead St Jas *Lon* 98-02; NSM Hendon St Mary and Ch Ch 02-07; NSM Holborn St Alb w Saffron Hill St Pet from 07. *The Clergy House, 18 Brooke Street, London EC1N 7RD* Tel 07956-847792 (mobile) E-mail ronald.corp@btconnect.com

CORRIE, Jennifer Sylvia. b 46. RMN68 SRN76. **d** 99 **p** 00. OLM Broughton *Man* from 99. *6 Briardene, Back Hilton Street, Salford M7 2GQ*

CORRIE, John. b 48. Imp Coll Lon BScEng69 MSc70 PhD73 Nottm Univ MTh86. Trin Coll Bris 74. **d** 77 **p** 78. C Kendal St Thos *Carl* 77-80; C Attenborough *S'well* 80-86; ICS Peru 86-91; Tutor and Lect All Nations Chr Coll Ware 91-02; Lect/Development Officer Cen for Angl Communion Studies Selly Oak 02-05; Abp's Internat Project Officer *Cant* 05-06; Tutor Trin Coll Bris from 07; Perm to Offic *Birm* from 03. *15 Woodfield Road, Kings Heath, Birmingham B13 9UL* Tel 0121-444 2767

CORRIE, Paul Allen. b 43. St Jo Coll Nottm 77. **d** 79 **p** 80. C Beverley Minster *York* 79-82; V Derby St Werburgh 82-84; V Derby St Alkmund and St Werburgh 84-95; Singapore 95-99; R Hawkwell *Chelmsf* 00-05; rtd 06. *4 Spindle Mill, Skipton BD23 1NY* Tel (01756) 795117
E-mail plcorrie@btopenworld.com

CORRIGAN, The Ven Thomas George. b 28. TCD BTh91. CITC 56. **d** 58 **p** 59. C Cavan and Drung *K, E & A* 58-60; I Drung 60-67; I Belfast St Mich *Conn* 67-70; I Kingscourt w Syddan *M & K* 70-96; Adn Meath 81-96; Dioc Registrar (Meath) 87-90; rtd 96. *The Beeches, Turner's Hill, Kingscourt, Co Cavan, Republic of Ireland* Tel (00353) (42) 966 8348
E-mail adngcorrigan@eircom.net

CORRY, Caroline Anne. b 58. St Hilda's Coll Ox BA79 Ox Univ MA97. S Tr Scheme 94. **d** 97 **p** 98. C Weston *Guildf* 97-01; P-in-c N Holmwood 01-05; V from 05. *The Vicarage, Willow Green, North Holmwood, Dorking RH5 4JB* Tel (01306) 882135
E-mail caroline_corry@hotmail.com

CORRY, Mrs Sarah. b 57. Sussex Univ BEd78. SEITE 06. **d** 09. NSM Crayford *Roch* from 09. *20 Glebelands, Dartford DA1 4RZ* Tel (01322) 523907 E-mail sarahcorry@aol.com

CORSIE, Andrew Russell. b 57. Middx Univ BA97. Trin Coll Bris 91. **d** 93 **p** 94. C Northolt Park St Barn *Lon* 93-97; C Perivale 97-01; P-in-c 01-06; R from 06; AD Ealing from 03. *Perivale Rectory, Federal Road, Perivale, Greenford UB6 7AP* Tel (020) 8997 1948 E-mail acorsie@aol.com
or andrew.corsie@perivalechurch.org.uk

CORSTORPHINE, Miss Margaret. b 34. SRN57 SCM59. Cranmer Hall Dur 70. **dss** 84 **d** 87 **p** 94. Colchester St Jo *Chelmsf* 84-94; Par Dn 87-94; C 94; rtd 94; Perm to Offic *Portsm* from 94. *12 Merrivale Court, Stein Road, Emsworth PO10 8LL* Tel (01243) 376867

CORWIN, Nigel Trevor. b 47. EAMTC 95. **d** 97 **p** 98. NSM Bury St Edmunds Ch Ch *St E* from 97. *121 Raedwald Drive, Bury St Edmunds IP32 7DG* Tel (01284) 725284 Fax 725391 Mobile 07713-769816 E-mail nigel@corwin.fsnet.co.uk

CORY, Valerie Ann. *See* DAWSON, Mrs Valerie Ann

COSBY, Ingrid St Clair. b 34. ACCM LLCM DipEd. **dss** 71 **d** 86 **p** 96. Cumbernauld *Glas* 71-73; Asst CF 73-78; Stromness *Ab* 83-86; NSM from 86. *Quarrybrae, Hillside Road, Stromness KW16 3HR* Tel and fax (01856) 850832

COSENS, William Edward Hyde. b 38. Lich Th Coll 61. **d** 64 **p** 65. C W Drayton *Lon* 64-68; C Roehampton H Trin *S'wark* 68-70; ILEA Youth Ldr 69-70; Miss to Seamen 70-94; Rotterdam 70-72; Tilbury 72-76; Dampier Seafarers' Cen Australia 76-81; Auckland New Zealand 81-89; Chapl Immingham Seafarers' Cen 89-94; Hon C Immingham *Linc* 89-94; Chapl Felixstowe Seafarers' Cen 94-97; Chapl Avonmouth Miss to Seamen 97-99; Sen Chapl Melbourne Miss to Seafarers Australia 99-03; Chapl State of Vic 99-03; rtd 03; Perm to Offic *Sarum* 04-05 and *Chich* from 05. *8 Barford Road, Chichester PO19 7DP* Tel (01243) 789698 Mobile 07963-093816 E-mail ted.caroline.cosens@virgin.net

COSGRAVE-HANLEY, Mirt Joseph. *See* HANLEY, Mirt Joseph

COSH, Roderick John. b 56. Lon Univ BSc78 Heythrop Coll Lon MA03. St Steph Ho Ox 78. **d** 81 **p** 82. C Swindon New Town

Bris 81-86; Chapl Asst R Marsden Hosp Lon and Surrey 86-91; V Whitton St Aug *Lon* 91-00; P-in-c Staines St Mary and St Pet 00-05; P-in-c Staines Ch Ch 04-05; V Staines from 06; AD Spelthorne from 04. *St Peter's Vicarage, 14 Thames Side, Staines TW18 2HA* Tel (01784) 453039 *or* 469155
E-mail rod@stainesparish.fsnet.co.uk

COSLETT, Anthony Allan. b 49. Cuddesdon Coll. **d** 84 **p** 85. C Notting Hill St Clem and St Mark *Lon* 84-85; C Brentford 85-87; C-in-c Hounslow Gd Shep Beavers Lane CD 87-90; V Hounslow W Gd Shep 90-92; CF 92-08; TR Leic Resurr from 08. *St Alban's House, Weymouth Street, Leicester LE4 6FN* Tel 0116-268 0255

COSLETT (née SLATER), Mrs Carol Ann. b 63. Univ of Wales (Ban) BD85 Jes Coll Cam PGCE86 Lon Inst of Educn MA92. Ripon Coll Cuddesdon 01. **d** 03 **p** 04. C Horsell *Guildf* 03-07; R Betchworth and Buckland *S'wark* from 07. *The Rectory, Old Reigate Road, Betchworth RH3 7DE* Tel (01737) 842102 Mobile 07803-671256 E-mail carolcoslett@tiscali.co.uk

COSS, Oliver James. b 82. Hull Univ BSc04 Leeds Univ BA06. Coll of Resurr Mirfield 04. **d** 07 **p** 08. C Cottingham *York* from 07. *10 Kingtree Avenue, Cottingham HU16 4DS*
E-mail oliver.coss@gmail.com

COSSAR, David Vyvyan. b 34. Lon Univ BA63. Chich Th Coll 63. **d** 65 **p** 66. C Upper Clapton St Matt *Lon* 65-68; C Withycombe Raleigh *Ex* 68-72; V Honicknowle 72-78; V Brixham w Churston Ferrers 78-86; P-in-c Kingswear 85-86; TR Brixham w Churston Ferrers and Kingswear 86-90; V Lamorbey H Trin *Roch* 90-03; rtd 03; Perm to Offic *Roch* from 03. *25 Bromley College, London Road, Bromley BR1 1PE* Tel (020) 8464 6911 E-mail dvanddlcossar@tiscali.co.uk

COSSAR, Canon Heather Jillian Mackenzie. b 27. dss 83 **d** 91 **p** 94. CMS Kenya 83-90; NSM Slindon, Eartham and Madehurst *Chich* 90-99; Perm to Offic from 99; Can Nyahururu from 03. *Gwitu, 38 Spinney Walk, Barnham, Bognor Regis PO22 0HT* Tel (01243) 552718

COSSINS, John Charles. b 43. Hull Univ BSc65. Oak Hill Th Coll 65. **d** 67 **p** 68. C Kenilworth St Jo *Cov* 67-70; C Huyton St Geo *Liv* 70-73; TV Maghull 73-79; Chapl Oakwood Hosp Maidstone 79-85; Maidstone Hosp 85-88; Chapl Park Lane Hosp Maghull 88-03; Chapl Moss Side Hosp Liv 88-03; Chapl Ashworth Hosp Maghull 88-03; rtd 03; Perm to Offic *Liv* from 03. *9 Longton Drive, Liverpool L37 7ET* Tel (01704) 833136 E-mail jcossins@jcossins.demon.co.uk

COSSINS, Roger Stanton. b 48. K Coll Lon BD67 AKC67. **d** 68 **p** 69. C Bramley *Ripon* 68-71; C W End *Win* 71-76; V Bramley 76-91; P-in-c Bournemouth H Epiphany 91-94; V 94-00; rtd 00. *5 Allen Court, Trumpington, Cambridge CB2 9LU* Tel (01223) 841726

COSSTICK, Mrs Helen Mary Vaux. b 47. K Alfred's Coll Win TCert69. NTMTC 06. **d** 09. NSM Hanwell St Mary w St Chris *Lon* from 09. *22 Shakespeare Road, London W7 1LR* Tel (020) 8579 6367 Mobile 07727-902309
E-mail helen.cosstick@btinternet.com

COSTER, Mrs Catherine Anne. b 47. Bris Poly BEd85. WEMTC 97. **d** 00 **p** 01. NSM Yate New Town *Bris* 00-04; NSM Warmley, Syston and Bitton from 04; Hon Min Can Bris Cathl from 04. *31 Vayre Close, Chipping Sodbury, Bristol BS37 6NT* Tel (01454) 314858 Fax 0117-927 7454
E-mail catherine.coster@bristoldiocese.org

COSTER, David John. b 65. Derby Univ BSc98. NTMTC BA09. **d** 09. NSM Leigh St Clem *Chelmsf* from 09. *33 Carlton Avenue, Westcliff-on-Sea SS0 0QN* Tel (01702) 307793 Fax (01268) 200129 Mobile 07747-391083 E-mail david@coster.ms

COSTERTON, Alan Stewart. b 40. Bris Univ BA67. Clifton Th Coll 67. **d** 69 **p** 70. C Peckham St Mary Magd *S'wark* 69-73; C Forest Gate St Sav w W Ham St Matt *Chelmsf* 73-76; TV 76-79; V Thornton cum Bagworth *Leic* 79-85; V Thornton, Bagworth and Stanton 85-95; TR Sileby, Cossington and Seagrave 95-04; R 04-05; rtd 05. *59 Station Road, Cropston, Leicester LE7 7HG* Tel 0116-234 1026 E-mail alan@costerton.freeserve.co.uk

COSTIGAN, Esther Rose. See FOSS, Esther Rose

COSTIN, Pamela Lindsay. b 49. Ridley Hall Cam 06. **d** 07 **p** 08. C Immingham, Habrough Gp and Keelby Gp *Linc* 07-09; C Scawby, Redbourne and Hibaldstow from 09; C Bishop Norton, Wadingham and Snitterby from 09; C Kirton in Lindsey w Manton from 09; C Grayingham from 09. *The Rectory, Church Road, Waddingham, Gainsborough DN21 4ST* Tel (01673) 818196 Mobile 07756-852907 E-mail pamcostin@yahoo.co.uk

COSTIN, Richard George Charles. b 38. Liv Univ CertEd59 Anglia Poly BEd85 ACP67 FCollP82. Coll of Resurr Mirfield 04. **d** 05 **p** 06. NSM Scarborough St Martin *York* from 05. *12 Lightfoots Close, Scarborough YO12 5NR* Tel (01723) 376141 Mobile 07768-856175 E-mail rcos38@hotmail.com

COTGROVE, Canon Edwin John. b 23. Kelham Th Coll 42. **d** 47 **p** 48. C Bris St Jude w St Matthias 47-50, C Southall St Geo *Lon* 50-52; S Africa 52-56; Swaziland 56-57; V Bromley St Mich *Lon* 57-64; V Hampton All SS 64-82; RD Hampton 72-82; R Bartlow *Ely* 82-91; V Linton 82-91; P-in-c Shudy Camps 85-91; P-in-c Castle Camps 85-91; RD Linton 88-93; Hon Can Ely Cathl

89-91; rtd 91; Perm to Offic *Ely* from 91. *96 The High Street, Great Abington, Cambridge CB21 6AE* Tel (01223) 893735

COTMAN, John Sell Granville (Jan). b 44. St Jo Coll Dur BA69. Wells Th Coll 70. **d** 73 **p** 74. C Leigh St Mary *Man* 73-76; P-in-c Coldhurst 76-78; TV Oldham 78-82; TV E Ham w Upton Park St Alb *Chelmsf* 82-85; C Hove All SS *Chich* 88-93; TV Hove 93-00; TV W Slough *Ox* 01-08; V Manor Park and Whitby Road from 08. *298 Stoke Poges Lane, Slough SL1 3LL* Tel (01753) 578503

COTSON, Tony Arthur. b 53. NEOC 00. **d** 03 **p** 04. C Kingston upon Hull St Nic *York* from 03; C Newington w Dairycoates from 08. *11 Kipling Walk, Summergroves Way, Hull HU4 6SX* Tel (01482) 504189 Mobile 07718-567675
E-mail tony@cotson.karoo.co.uk

COTTAM, Kenneth Michael David. b 46. St Mich Coll Llan 93. **d** 93 **p** 94. Lic to Offic Llangadog and Llandeilo Deanery *St D* 93-96; V Llangadog and Gwynfe w Llanddeusant from 96. *The Vicarage, Walters Road, Llangadog SA19 9AE* Tel (01550) 777604

COTTEE, Christopher Paul. b 54. Newc Univ BSc75. Wycliffe Hall Ox 77. **d** 80 **p** 81. C Much Woolton *Liv* 80-84; C Prescot 84-88; NSM Parr 89-91; V Watford St Pet *St Alb* from 91. *St Peter's Vicarage, 61 Westfield Avenue, Watford WD24 7HF* Tel (01923) 226717 E-mail chris.cottee1@ntlworld.com

COTTEE, Mary Jane. b 43. Open Univ BA81 CertEd64. Oak Hill Th Coll 87. **d** 90 **p** 94. NSM Gt Baddow *Chelmsf* 90-95; P-in-c Woodham Ferrers and Bicknacre from 95. *Church House, Main Road, Bicknacre, Chelmsford CM3 4HA* Tel (01245) 224895 E-mail marycottee@btinternet.com

COTTELL, Avril Jane. See GAUNT, Mrs Avril Jane

COTTER, Graham Michael. b 50. Univ of Wales (Ban) BA72. Ridley Hall Cam 75. **d** 78 **p** 79. C Headley All SS *Guildf* 78-81; C Plymouth St Andr w St Paul and St Geo *Ex* 81-84; V Buckland Monachorum from 84; RD Tavistock 93-98. *The Vicarage, Buckland Monachorum, Yelverton PL20 7LQ* Tel (01822) 852227 E-mail cotters@onetel.com

COTTER, James England. b 42. G&C Coll Cam BA64 MA67. Linc Th Coll 65. **d** 67 **p** 68. C Stretford St Matt *Man* 67-70; Lect Linc Th Coll 70-73; Perm to Offic *Lon* 73-74; Chapl G&C Coll Cam 74-77; C Leavesden *St Alb* 77-83; Asst Prin St Alb Minl Tr Scheme 77-83; Course Dir 83-86; Perm to Offic *Ex* 86-88; Lic to Offic *Sheff* 88-01; Perm to Offic *Ban* 99-08; P-in-c Aberdaron and Llanfaelrhys from 08. *Gernant, Aberdaron, Pwllheli LL53 8BG* Tel (01758) 760296 E-mail jim@cottercairns.co.uk

COTTER, Robert Edmund. **d** 05 **p** 06. NSM Mossley *Conn* 05-09; NSM Skerry w Rathcavan and Newtowncrommelin from 09. *33 Deerfin Road, Ballymena BT42 4HP* Tel (028) 2563 1303 E-mail robertcotter76@btinternet.com

COTTERELL, Michael Clifford. b 54. Oak Hill Th Coll 81. **d** 84 **p** 85. C Lutterworth w Cotesbach *Leic* 84-87; C Belper *Derby* 87-91; V Locking *B & W* 91-98; V Slough *Ox* from 98. *St Paul's Vicarage, 196 Stoke Road, Slough SL2 5AY* Tel (01753) 521497 E-mail mchtterell@toucansurf.com

COTTERILL, Joseph Charles. b 17. AMCT38 Lon Univ BD California Coll Peking MA46. Ox Min Course 92. **d** 93 **p** 94. NSM Marcham w Garford *Ox* 93-98; Perm to Offic from 98. *8 Draycott Road, Southmoor, Abingdon OX13 5BY* Tel (01865) 820436

COTTINGHAM, Peter John Garnet. b 24. Wadh Coll Ox BA48 MA50. Ridley Hall Cam 48. **d** 50 **p** 51. C Cheadle *Ches* 50-55; R Ox St Clem 55-68; V S Mimms Ch Ch *Lon* 68-81; V Derby St Pet and Ch Ch w H Trin 81-89; rtd 89; Perm to Offic *Ban* 89-07. *2 Sherwood Avenue, Potters Bar EN6 2LD*

COTTON, Charles Anthony. b 50. Linc Coll Ox BA72 MA77 PGCE73. Ridley Hall Cam 89. **d** 91 **p** 92. C Hendon St Paul Mill Hill *Lon* 91-96; C Wandsworth All SS *S'wark* 96-97; V Clapham St Jas 97-08; Perm to Offic from 08. *9 Woodcote Avenue, Wallington SM6 0QR* Tel (020) 8869 1143
E-mail revdcharlie@btinternet.com

COTTON, John Horace Brazel. b 28. MIMechE St Jo Coll Cam BA50 MA76. St Alb Minl Tr Scheme 78. **d** 81 **p** 82. NSM Lt Berkhamsted and Bayford, Essendon etc *St Alb* 81-87; P-in-c 87-96; rtd 96; Perm to Offic *St Alb* from 96. *49 Sherrardspark Road, Welwyn Garden City AL8 7LD* Tel (01707) 321815

COTTON, Canon John Wallis. b 31. Wells Th Coll 57. **d** 59 **p** 60. C Stepney St Dunstan and All SS *Lon* 59-64; C Hanworth All SS 64-67; V Hammersmith St Sav 67-74; R Lancing w Coombes *Chich* 75-86; RD Worthing 83-85; R Bexhill St Pet 86-90; TR 90-99; RD Battle and Bexhill 92-98; Can and Preb Chich Cathl 96-02; P-in-c Arlington, Folkington and Wilmington 99-02; rtd 02. *7 Jevington Close, Bexhill-on-Sea TN39 3BB* Tel (01424) 845273

COTTON, John William. b 53. Oak Hill Th Coll 86. **d** 86 **p** 87. C New Clee *Linc* 86-89; Chapl St Andr Hospice Grimsby 88-89; R Middle Rasen Gp 89-95; P-in-c Broughton 95-97; R from 97; Chapl Humberside Airport 99-00. *The Rectory, 22 Scawby Road, Broughton, Brigg DN20 0AF* Tel (01652) 652506

COTTON, Mrs Margaret Elizabeth. b 30. JP79. Newnham Coll Cam BA53 MA66. St Alb Minl Tr Scheme 78. dss 82 **d** 87 **p** 94.

Lt Berkhamsted and Bayford, Essendon etc *St Alb* 82-87; Hon Par Dn 87-94; Hon C 94-96; rtd 96; Perm to Offic *St Alb* from 96. *49 Sherrardspark Road, Welwyn Garden City AL8 7LD* Tel (01707) 321815

COTTON, Norman Joseph. b 39. Kelham Th Coll 59. **d** 64 **p** 65. C Auckland St Helen *Dur* 64-67; C Withington St Chris *Man* 67-68; C Hucknall Torkard *S'well* 69-71; TV 71-73; TV Fenny Stratford *Ox* 73-75; TV Fenny Stratford and Water Eaton 75-82; R Walton 82-90; TR Walton Milton Keynes 90-92; V Stewkley w Soulbury and Drayton Parslow 92-04; RD Mursley 94-01; rtd 04. *5 Whites Close, Steeple Claydon, Buckingham MK18 2HN* Tel (01296) 738602 E-mail nomo_uk@yahoo.co.uk

COTTON, Miss Patricia Constance. b 32. Gilmore Ho 54. **dss** 60 **d** 87 **p** 94. Forest Gate St Edm *Chelmsf* 60-64; Reading St Giles *Ox* 64-65; Basildon St Martin w H Cross and Laindon *Chelmsf* 65-79; Gt Burstead 79-87; Par Dn Maldon All SS w St Pet 87-91; rtd 92; NSM Holland-on-Sea *Chelmsf* 94-96; Perm to Offic from 96. *67 Copperfield Gardens, Brentwood CM14 4UD* Tel (01277) 224274

COTTON, Patrick Arthur William. b 46. Essex Univ BA67 Down Coll Cam MA73 Homerton Coll Cam PGCE96. Linc Th Coll 68. **d** 71 **p** 72. C Earlham St Anne *Nor* 71-73; Chapl Down Coll Cam 73-78; V Eaton Socon *St Alb* 78-84; TR Newc Epiphany 84-90; V Tunstall w Melling and Leck *Blackb* 90-95; Chapl Pet High Sch 01-05; P-in-c Debenham and Helmingham *St E* from 06. *The Vicarage, 6 Raedwald Way, Debenham, Stowmarket IP14 6SN* Tel (01728) 861073

COTTON, Peter John. b 45. BNC Ox BA66 CQSW76. Cuddesdon Coll 67. **d** 69 **p** 70. C Salford St Phil w St Steph *Man* 69-73; Asst Educn Officer *St Alb* 73-75; C Bris St Geo 75-76; C-in-c Portsea St Geo CD *Portsm* 76-80; Soc Resp Adv 78-88; Can Res Portsm Cathl 84-88; V St Laur in Thanet *Cant* 88-93; TR 93-97; Hon Min Can Cant Cathl 93-97; TR Hemel Hempstead *St Alb* 97-09; RD Hemel Hempstead 03-08; rtd 09. *45 Bepton Down, Petersfield GU31 4PR* Tel (01730) 233785 E-mail petercotton2@tiscali.co.uk

COTTON, Canon Richard William. b 35. Hertf Coll Ox BA58 MA62. Clifton Th Coll 58. **d** 60 **p** 61. C Harold Wood *Chelmsf* 60-64; C Higher Openshaw *Man* 64-67; Lic to Offic 67-71; Ch Youth Fellowships Assn and Pathfinders 67-71; Nat Sec Pathfinders CPAS 71-76; Lic to Offic *St Alb* 73-76; V Chislehurst Ch Ch *Roch* 76-92; V Herne Bay Ch Ch *Cant* 92-01; RD Reculver 93-01; Hon Can Cant Cathl 99-01; rtd 01; Perm to Offic *Cant* from 01. *16 Crundale Way, Cliftonville, Margate CT9 3YH* Tel (01843) 221970 E-mail rwcotton67@hotmail.com

COTTON, Canon Robert Lloyd. b 58. Mert Coll Ox MA79. Westcott Ho Cam 81. **d** 83 **p** 84. C Plaistow St Mary *Roch* 83-86; C Bisley and W End *Guildf* 87-89; P-in-c E Molesey St Paul 89-96; Dir of Reader Tr from 90; R Guildf H Trin w St Mary from 96; Hon Can Highveld S Africa from 06. *Holy Trinity Rectory, 9 Eastgate Gardens, Guildford GU1 4AZ* Tel (01483) 575489 E-mail rector@holytrinityguildford.org.uk

COTTON, Timothy. b 61. Ripon Coll Cuddesdon 97. **d** 99 **p** 00. C Godrevy *Truro* 99-02; P-in-c St Breoke and Egloshayle 02-06. *Address temp unknown*

COTTON-BETTERIDGE, Mrs Fiona Jane Marson. b 56. Nottm Univ MA05. EMMTC 02. **d** 05 **p** 06. NSM Burton Joyce w Bulcote and Stoke Bardolph *S'well* 05-08; P-in-c Old Leake w Wrangle *Linc* from 08; P-in-c Friskney from 08. *The Vicarage, 1 Giles Close, Old Leake, Boston PE22 9NN* Tel (01205) 872089 E-mail fionacb@aol.com

✠**COTTRELL, The Rt Revd Stephen Geoffrey.** b 58. Poly Cen Lon BA79. St Steph Ho Ox 81. **d** 84 **p** 85 **c** 04. C Forest Hill Ch Ch *S'wark* 84-88; C-in-c Parklands St Wilfrid CD *Chich* 88-93; Asst Dir Past Studies Chich Th Coll 88-93; Dioc Missr *Wakef* 93-98; Bp's Chapl for Evang 93-98; Springboard Missr and Consultant in Evang 98-01; Can Res Pet Cathl 01-04; Area Bp Reading *Ox* from 04. *Bishop's House, Tidmarsh Lane, Tidmarsh, Reading RG8 8HA* Tel 0118-984 1216 Fax 984 1218 E-mail bishopreading@oxford.anglican.org

COTTRILL, Derek John. b 43. MA. Qu Coll Birm. **d** 82 **p** 83. C Southampton Maybush St Pet *Win* 82-85; V Barton Stacey and Bullington etc 85-92; R Bishopstoke 92-06; Asst Chapl Win and Eastleigh Healthcare NHS Trust 92-06; rtd 06. *7 The Old Green, Sherborne DT9 3JY* Tel (01935) 816746

COUCH, Canon Andrew Nigel. b 48. K Coll Lon BD70 AKC70 Ex Coll Ox PGCE72. St Aug Coll Cant 70. **d** 71 **p** 72. C St Ives *Truro* 71-74; C St Martin-in-the-Fields *Lon* 74-78; USPG 78-91; Uruguay 79-84; Argentina 85-91; Chapl Qu Mary Coll *Lon* 91-94; V St Ives *Truro* 94-08; P-in-c Halsetown 98-08; RD Penwith 98-03; Chapl W of Cornwall Primary Care Trust 98-06; Chapl Cornwall and Is of Scilly Primary Care Trust 06-08; Hon Can Truro Cathl 06-08; rtd 08. *32 Cowling Gardens, Menheniot, Liskeard PL14 3QJ* Tel (01579) 340509 E-mail andycouch@bigfoot.com

COUCH, Ms Felicity Anne. b 59. CQSW85. SEITE 00. **d** 03 **p** 04. NSM Stockwell St Andr and St Mich *S'wark* 03-08; NSM Brocklesby Park *Linc* from 08; NSM Croxton from 08; NSM

Ulceby Gp from 08. *The Vicarage, Church Lane, Ulceby DN39 6TB* Tel (01469) 588239 Mobile 07745-905417 E-mail fcouch@tesco.net

COUCHMAN, Anthony Denis. b 37. Sarum Th Coll 66. **d** 69 **p** 70. C Barkingside St Fran *Chelmsf* 69-71; C Chingford SS Pet and Paul 71-76; P-in-c Walthamstow St Barn and St Jas 76-80; V 80-07; rtd 07; Perm to Offic *Nor* from 08. *Friarscot, Church Street, King's Lynn PE30 5EB* Tel (01553) 766643 E-mail anthony.couchman@yahoo.co.uk

COUCHMAN, Kathryn. b 60. Open Univ BA92 Coll of Ripon & York St Jo MA00. NOC 02. **d** 06 **p** 07. C Wetherby *Ripon* 06-08; C Spofforth w Kirk Deighton from 08. *Stonedale, 15 Barleyfields Terrace, Wetherby LS22 6PW* Tel (01937) 580902 E-mail kathycouchman@fsmail.net

COUGHLIN, Wayne Michael Timothy Vianney. b 77. Writtle Agric Coll BSc99 Leeds Univ BA03. Coll of Resurr Mirfield 00. **d** 03 **p** 04. C Neath *Llan* 03-06; C Port Talbot St Theodore from 06. *The Presbytery, 9 James Street, Port Talbot SA13 1AR* Tel (01639) 680585

COUGHTREY, Miss Sheila Frances. b 48. RSCN73 SRN73 S Bank Poly BSc79. Qu Coll Birm 79. **dss** 81 **d** 87 **p** 94. Sydenham St Bart *S'wark* 81-85; Roehampton H Trin 85-91; Par Dn 87-91; Par Dn Brixton Hill St Sav 91-94; P-in-c 94-01; Min King's Acre LEP 91-01; RD Brixton 99-01; P-in-c Pleshey *Chelmsf* from 01; Warden Dioc Retreat Ho from 01. *The Vicarage, The Street, Pleshey, Chelmsford CM3 1HA* Tel (01245) 237576 E-mail sheila@scoughtrey.fsnet.co.uk

COULDRIDGE, Janice Evelyn. See FOX, Mrs Janice Evelyn

COULING, Canon David Charles. b 36. Open Univ BA89. Qu Coll Birm 61. **d** 63 **p** 64. C Harborne St Faith and St Laur *Birm* 63-66; C E Grinstead St Mary *Chich* 66-70; V Copthorne 70-75; V Eastbourne St Mich 75-82; V Brighton St Matthias 82-83; C-in-c Harton St Lawr CD *Dur* 84-90; V Horsley Hill St Lawr 91-94; P-in-c Greatham 94-97; V 97-01; AD Hartlepool 95-01; Master Greatham Hosp 94-00; Hon Can Dur Cathl 99-01; rtd 01; P-in-c Brancepeth *Dur* 01-04; Chapl Dur Cathl from 04. *11 Shropshire Drive, Durham DH1 2LT* Tel 0191-375 7367

COULSON, Renée. b 45. **d** 03 **p** 04. OLM Potterne w Worton and Marston *Sarum* from 03. *40 Highlands, Potterne, Devizes SN10 5NS* Tel (01380) 726609 E-mail rcoulson@totalise.co.uk

COULSON, Canon Stephen Hugh. b 60. St Edm Hall Ox BA82 MA88 Lon Univ CertEd83. Wycliffe Hall Ox 85. **d** 88 **p** 89. C Summerfield *Birm* 88-91; Perm to Offic 91-92; CMS Uganda 92-01; Asst V Namirembe 92-96; Can from 99; Prin Uganda Martyrs Sem Namugongo 96-01; V Mitcham St Mark *S'wark* from 01. *St Mark's Vicarage, Locks Lane, Mitcham CR4 2JX* Tel (020) 8648 2397 E-mail steve@scoulson.freeserve.co.uk

COULSON, Thomas Stanley. b 32. TCD BA54 MA68. TCD Div Sch 55. **d** 55 **p** 56. C Maghera *D & R* 55-62; I Aghalurcher and Tattykeeran *Clogh* 62-63; I Woodschapel w Gracefield *Arm* 63-97; Preb Arm Cathl 88-97; Treas Arm Cathl 94-96; Chan Arm Cathl 96-97; rtd 97. *Lisadian, 84 Coleraine Road, Portrush BT56 8HN* Tel (028) 7082 4202 E-mail canoncoulson@btinternet.com

COULSON, Tony Erik Frank. b 32. St Edm Hall Ox BA55 MA59. Wycliffe Hall Ox 55. **d** 57 **p** 58. C Walthamstow St Mary *Chelmsf* 57-60; C Reading St Jo *Ox* 60-63; V Iver 63-86; R White Waltham w Shottesbrooke 86-97; rtd 97; Perm to Offic *Ox* from 98. *30 Ravensbourne Drive, Reading RG5 4LH* Tel 0118-969 3556

COULTER, Edmond James. b 60. QUB BSc82 BD96. **d** 87 **p** 88. C Ballymena w Ballyclug *Conn* 87-90; C Knockbreda *D & D* 90-92; I Belfast Upper Falls *Conn* 92-97; I Milltown *Arm* 97-03; Supt Dublin Irish Ch Miss *D & G* from 03. *38 Woodpark, Castleknock, Dublin 15, Republic of Ireland* Tel (00353) (1) 821 2336 or 873 0829 Fax 878 4049 E-mail ejcoulter@iolfree.ie or eddie@icm-online.ie

COULTER, Ian Herbert Young. b 54. TCD BA77 HDipEd78. **d** 99 **p** 00. Lic to Offic (Cashel, Waterford and Lismore) *C & O* from 99. *22 Rose Hill Court, Kilkenny, Co Kilkenny, Republic of Ireland* Tel and fax (00353) (56) 776 2675 E-mail coulters@gofree.indigo.ie

COULTER, Mrs Kirsten Ruth. b 43. Univ of Wales (Abth) BSc64 Homerton Coll Cam CertEd65 Lon Univ BD89 Newc Univ MA93. **d** 01 **p** 02. OLM Tweedmouth *Newc* from 01. *90 Shielfield Terrace, Tweedmouth, Berwick-upon-Tweed TD15 2EE* Tel (01289) 308485 E-mail timothy.coulter@btinternet.com

COULTER, (née REEVES), Mrs Maria Elizabeth Ann. b 72. Leeds Univ BA95 Heythrop Coll Lon MTh03. St Steph Ho Ox 96. **d** 98 **p** 99. C Newington St Mary *S'wark* 98-02; V Dulwich St Clem w St Pet from 02. *St Clement's Vicarage, 140 Friern Road, London SE22 0AY* Tel (020) 8693 1890 E-mail meareeves@hotmail.com

COULTER, Miss Marilyn Judith. b 48. City of Birm Coll BEd70 Qu Coll Birm BA05. WMMTC 02. **d** 05 **p** 06. NSM Brewood *Lich* from 05; NSM Bishopswood from 05; Chapl Mid Staffs

NHS Foundn Trust from 08. *14 St Chad's Close, Brewood, Stafford ST19 9DA* Tel (01902) 851168
E-mail coulter14@aol.com

COULTER, Stephen Paul. b 53. Nottm Univ BSc76 CEng MIMechE. **d** 92 **p** 93. C Oakwood St Thos *Lon* 92-95; V Grange Park St Pet 95-99; I Kells Union *M & K* 99-01; R Pimperne, Stourpaine, Durweston and Bryanston *Sarum* from 01. *The Vicarage, Shaston Road, Stourpaine, Blandford Forum DT11 8TA* Tel (01258) 480580

COULTHARD, Miss Nina Marion. b 50. CertEd71 Bp Lonsdale Coll BEd72. Trin Coll Bris 89. **d** 91 **p** 94. Par Dn Cant St Mary Bredin 91-94; C 94-95; C Bath Abbey w St Jas *B & W* 95-99; Chapl R Nat Hosp for Rheumatic Diseases NHS Trust 95-99; C Northwood Em *Lon* 99-06; V Loughton St Mich *Chelmsf* from 06. *St Michael's House, Roding Road, Loughton IG10 3EJ* Tel (020) 8508 1489

COULTHURST, Jeffrey Evans. b 38. Man Univ BA61 Leeds Univ PGCE62. **d** 84 **p** 85. OLM Ancaster *Linc* 84-89; OLM Ancaster Wilsford Gp 89-05. *5 North Drive, Ancaster, Grantham NG32 3RB* Tel (01400) 230280
E-mail jeff@jcoulthurst.fsnet.co.uk

COULTON, David. **d** 09. NSM Tewkesbury w Walton Cardiff and Twyning *Glouc* from 09. *4 Conigree Lane, Abbots Road, Tewkesbury GL20 5TF* Tel (01684) 293523

COULTON, David Stephen. b 41. Bernard Gilpin Soc Dur 63 Sarum Th Coll 64. **d** 67 **p** 68. C Guildf H Trin w St Mary 67-70; Asst Chapl St Luke's Hosp Guildf 67-70; Asst Chapl Radley Coll 70-83; Sen Chapl 83-01; Chapl Eton Coll 01-04; rtd 04. *20 The Oakbournes, Bishopdown, Salisbury SP1 3FZ* Tel (01722) 333928

COULTON, The Very Revd Nicholas Guy. b 40. Lon Univ BD72 Ox Univ MA07. Cuddesdon Coll 65. **d** 67 **p** 68. C Pershore w Wick *Worc* 67-70; Bp's Dom Chapl *St Alb* 71-75; P-in-c Bedford St Paul 75-79; V 79-90; Hon Can St Alb 89-90; Provost Newc 90-01; Dean Newc 01-03; Can Res and Sub-Dean Ch Ch *Ox* 03-08; rtd 08. *123 Merewood Avenue, Headington, Oxford OX3 8EQ* Tel (01865) 763790 E-mail ngc@proscenia.co.uk

COULTON, Philip Ernest. b 31. St Cath Coll Cam BA54 MA58 TCD BD68 Open Univ BA84. Ely Th Coll 55. **d** 57 **p** 58. Asst Master Perse Sch Cam 54-55; Asst Master Bradf Gr Sch 57; C Newark w Coddington *S'well* 57-61; Min Can and Sacr Cant Cathl 61-63; Min Can Ripon Cathl 63-68; Hd of RE Ashton-under-Lyne Gr Sch 69-84; V Ulceby Gp *Linc* 85-89; P-in-c Ingatestone w Buttsbury *Chelmsf* 89-99; P-in-c Fryerning w Margaretting 89-92; rtd 99; Perm to Offic *Sarum* from 01 and *B & W* 02-06. *90 Boreham Road, Warminster BA12 9JW* Tel (01985) 219353 E-mail pecoulton@talktalk.net

COUNSELL, Edwin Charles Robert. b 63. Univ of Wales (Cardiff) BA84 MTh97. St Steph Ho Ox 85. **d** 88 **p** 89. C Cardiff St Mary and St Steph w St Dyfrig etc *Llan* 88-94; Sub-Chapl HM Pris Cardiff from 90; V Pendoylan w Welsh St Donats from 94; Dioc Dir Statutory Educn from 00; Prov Adv on Educn Ch in Wales from 06. *The Vicarage, 9 Heol St Cattwg, Pendoylan, Cowbridge CF71 7UG* Tel (01446) 760195 *or* tel and fax 760210 E-mail post@llandaffschools.fs.net.co.uk

COUNSELL, Michael John Radford. b 35. Pemb Coll Cam BA59 MA63. Ripon Hall Ox 59. **d** 61 **p** 62. C Handsworth St Mary *Birm* 61-63; Singapore 64-68; Vietnam and Cambodia 68-71; Seychelles 72-76; Dean Mahé 73-76; V Harborne St Pet *Birm* 76-89; Relig Consultant Inter-Ch Travel Ltd 89-90; V Forest Hill St Aug *S'wark* 90-00; Perm to Offic *Cant* 91-00; rtd 00; Perm to Offic *Birm* and *Eur* from 05. *Flat 2, 340 Tessall Lane, Birmingham B31 5EN* Tel and fax 0121-628 2028 Mobile 07891-860473 E-mail mjrcounsell@hotmail.com

COUPAR, Thomas. b 50. BA71 ACE80. Edin Dioc NSM Course 77. **d** 80 **p** 81. NSM Dunbar *Edin* 80-86; NSM Haddington 80-86; Hd Master Pencaitland Primary Sch E Lothian 80-81; Hd Master K Meadow Sch E Lothian 81-87; Asst Dioc Supernumerary *Edin* 87-89; Primary Educn Adv Fife from 88; Dioc Supernumerary 90-96; Chapl Robin Chapel Edin from 06. *21/9 Rennie's Isle, Edinburgh EH6 6QB* Tel 0131-551 1800 E-mail tcoupar@hotmail.com

COUPER (*née* WOOD)**, Mrs Audrey Elizabeth.** b 54. Edin Univ BSc75 Westmr Coll of Educn PGCE76. ERMC 05. **d** 08 **p** 09. NSM Digswell and Panshanger *St Alb* from 08. *18 Netherfield Road, Harpenden AL5 2AG* Tel (01582) 346901
E-mail audrey@tizmoi.net

COUPER, Jeanette Emily (Jean). b 40. S'wark Ord Course 85. **d** 88. Par Dn Mitcham SS Pet and Paul *S'wark* 88-93; Chapl Asst Guy's Hosp Lon 93-94; Perm to Offic *S'wark* 93-04; rtd 00. *Rose Cottage, Wentnor, Bishops Castle SY9 5EE* Tel (01588) 650590

COUPER, Jonathan George. b 51. St Jo Coll Dur BA73. Wycliffe Hall Ox 73. **d** 75 **p** 76. C Clifton *York* 75-78; C Darfield *Sheff* 78-81; V Bridlington Quay Ch Ch *York* from 81. *21 Kingston Road, Bridlington YO15 3NF* Tel (01262) 673538

COUPLAND, Simon Charles. b 59. St Jo Coll Cam BA82 PGCE83 MA85 PhD87. Ridley Hall Cam 88. **d** 91 **p** 92. C Bath St Luke *B & W* 91-95; TV Broadwater *Chich* 95-04; V Kingston Hill St Paul *S'wark* from 04. *The Vicarage, 33 Queen's Road,*

Kingston upon Thames KT2 7SF Tel (020) 8549 8597 *or* 8549 5444 E-mail simon.coupland@stpaulskingston.org.uk

COURT, David Eric. b 58. Southn Univ BSc80 PhD83 PGCE84. Oak Hill Th Coll BA91. **d** 91 **p** 92. C Barton Seagrave w Warkton *Pet* 91-94; C Kinson *Sarum* 94-97; P-in-c Mile Cross *Nor* 97-99; V 99-03; V Cromer from 03. *The Vicarage, 30 Cromwell Road, Cromer NR27 0BE* Tel (01263) 512000
E-mail david@cromervicarage.fsnet.co.uk

COURT, Canon Kenneth Reginald. b 36. AKC60. **d** 61 **p** 62. C Garforth *Ripon* 61-63; C Harrogate St Wilfrid 63-65; V Thornbury *Bradf* 65-73; Prec Leic Cathl 73-76; V Douglas St Matt *S & M* 76-84; V Syston *Leic* 84-93; TR 93-98; RD Goscote 90-95; Hon Can Leic Cathl 92-98; rtd 98; Perm to Offic *Leic* from 99; *Linc* 01-03; *Pet* from 03. *12 Lord Burghley's Hospital, Station Road, Stamford PE9 2LD* Tel (01780) 754372 E-mail kenneth@kcourt.wanadoo.co.uk

COURT, Martin Jeremy. b 61. GRNCM84 Nottm Univ BTh89. Linc Th Coll 86. **d** 89 **p** 90. C Thurmaston *Leic* 89-92; C Leic St Jas 92-93; TV Leic Resurr 93-98; V Scraptoft from 98; P-in-c Leic St Chad from 98; Dioc Info Tech Co-ord from 96. *All Saints' Vicarage, 331 Scraptoft Lane, Scraptoft, Leicester LE5 2HU* Tel 0116-241 3205 Mobile 07798-876837
E-mail mcourt@leicester.anglican.org

COURT, Martin John. b 64. Ridley Hall Cam 03. **d** 05 **p** 06. C Blandford Forum and Langton Long *Sarum* 05-09; V Chadwell Heath *Chelmsf* from 09. *The Vicarage, 7 Chadwell Heath Lane, Romford RM6 4LS* Tel (020) 8590 2391 Mobile 07905-612542

COURT, Nicholas James Keble. b 56. Chich Th Coll 86. **d** 88 **p** 89. C Golders Green *Lon* 88-91; C Westbury-on-Trym H Trin *Bris* 91-94; PV Llan Cathl 94-96; V Graig 96-02; P-in-c Cilfynydd 96-01; Miss P *Mor* from 09. *Cair Paravel, Ardmuir, Ullapool IV26 2TN* Tel (01854) 612506

COURT, Richard Leonard. b 54. Univ of Wales (Ban) BTh04. EAMTC 94. **d** 97 **p** 98. NSM Framlingham w Saxtead *St E* 97-05; V Badsey w Aldington and Offenham and Bretforton *Worc* from 05. *The Vicarage, High Street, Badsey, Evesham WR11 7EW* Tel (01386) 834550 Mobile 07751-775917 E-mail richard.court@btinternet.com

COURTAULD, Augustine Christopher Caradoc. b 34. Trin Coll Cam BA58 MA61. Westcott Ho Cam 58. **d** 60 **p** 61. C Oldham St Mary *Man* 60-63; Chapl Trin Coll Cam 63-68; Chapl The Lon Hosp (Whitechapel) 68-78; V Wilton Place St Paul *Lon* 78-99; AD Westmr St Marg 92-97; rtd 99; Perm to Offic *St E* from 00. *Broke House, The Drift, Levington, Ipswich IP10 0LF* Tel (01473) 659773

COURTIE, John Malcolm. b 42. BNC Ox BA65 DPhil72 St Jo Coll Dur BA76. Cranmer Hall Dur 74. **d** 77 **p** 78. C Mossley Hill St Matt and St Jas *Liv* 77-80; V Litherland St Paul Hatton Hill 80-84; Wellingborough Sch 84-89; Hon C Wollaston and Strixton *Pet* 84-89; V Woodford Halse w Eydon 89-99; R Blisworth and Stoke Bruerne w Grafton Regis etc 99-02; rtd 02. *2 Flexford Close, Highclere, Newbury RG20 9PE*
E-mail thecourties@yahoo.co.uk

COURTNEY (*née* JORDAN)**, Mrs Avril Marilyn.** b 35. Lon Univ DipEd56. SW Minl Tr Course 79. **dss** 82 **d** 87 **p** 94. Highweek and Teigngrace *Ex* 82-88; Par Dn 87-88; Par Dn Ottery St Mary, Alfington, W Hill, Tipton etc 88-94; C 94-99; rtd 99; Perm to Offic *Ex* from 00. *Fairholme, Exeter Road, Newton Poppleford, Sidmouth EX10 0BJ* Tel (01395) 568691

COURTNEY, Canon Brian Joseph. b 44. BD92 MA97. CITC 70. **d** 73 **p** 74. C Willowfield *D & D* 73-75; P-in-c Knocknagoney 75-78; I Aghavea *Clogh* 78-83; I Carrickfergus *Conn* 83-95; I Enniskillen *Clogh* 95-09; Prec Clogh Cathl 95-09; rtd 09. *10 Berkeley Road, Carrickfergus BT38 9DS* Tel (028) 9335 5139 E-mail briancourtney@nireland.com

COURTNEY, Miss Louise Anita Hodd. b 48. Ex Univ BTh04. SWMTC 99. **d** 02 **p** 03. C St Keverne *Truro* 02-05; P-in-c Lanteglos by Fowey from 05. *The Vicarage, 4 Ocean View, Polruan, Fowey PL23 1QJ* Tel (01726) 870988
E-mail louisecourtney@tiscali.co.uk

COURTNEY, Martin Horace. b 34. SAOMC 95. **d** 98 **p** 99. OLM Flackwell Heath *Ox* from 98. *1 Green Crescent, Flackwell Heath, High Wycombe HP10 9JQ* Tel (01628) 526354

COURTNEY, Michael Monlas. b 19. Coll of Resurr Mirfield 58. **d** 60 **p** 61. C Shrewsbury St Chad *Lich* 60-63; P-in-c N Keyham *Ex* 63-68; V 68-73; TV Sidmouth, Woolbrook, Salcombe Regis etc 73-84; rtd 84; Perm to Offic *Ex* from 86. *Fairholme, Exeter Road, Newton Poppleford, Sidmouth EX10 0BJ* Tel (01395) 568691

COUSANS (*née* BRADLEY)**, Mrs Joy Elizabeth.** b 63. Sheff Univ BA85 Fitzw Coll Cam BA91 MA95. Ridley Hall Cam 89. **d** 92 **p** 94. Par Dn Wadsley *Sheff* 92-94; C 94-96; C Mosbrough 96-97; V Hillsborough and Wadsley Bridge 97-06; P-in-c High Hoyland, Scissett and Clayton W *Wakef* from 06; Asst Dioc Dir of Ords from 08. *The Rectory, Church Lane, Clayton West, Huddersfield HD8 9LY* Tel (01484) 862321
E-mail joy@daveandjoy.plus.com

COUSINS, Christopher William. b 44. Ox Univ MTh95. **d** 87 **p** 88. C Wallasey St Hilary *Ches* 87-90; R Rollesby w Burgh w

Billockby w Ashby w Oby etc *Nor* 90-94; P-in-c Ormesby w Scratby 92-94; V Ormesby St Marg w Scratby, Ormesby St Mich etc 94-98; RD Gt Yarmouth 94-98; V Altham w Clayton le Moors *Blackb* 98-03; P-in-c Rochford *Chelmsf* from 03; P-in-c Stambridge from 03; P-in-c Sutton w Shopland from 03; RD Rochford 04-08. *The Rectory, 36 Millview Meadows, Rochford SS4 1EF* Tel (01702) 530621 E-mail c4cousins@yahoo.com

COUSINS, Mrs Deborah Ann. b 52. LCST74. ERMC 06. d 09. C Earlham *Nor* from 09. *St Mary's Vicarage, Douglas Haig Road, Norwich NR5 8LD* Tel (01603) 457751 E-mail deb@madmotorbike.fsnet.co.uk

COUSINS, Graham John. b 55. Oak Hill Th Coll BA91. d 91 p 92. C Birkenhead St Jas w St Bede *Ches* 91-95; C Bebington 95-01; R Moreton from 01. *The Rectory, Dawpool Drive, Moreton, Wirral CH46 0PH* Tel 0151-641 0303 E-mail rector@christchurchmoreton.org.uk

COUSINS, Peter Gareth. b 37. d 95 p 96. NSM Cwmparc *Llan* 95-02. *15 Conway Road, Cwmparc, Treorchy CF42 6UW* Tel (01443) 773669

COUSINS, Canon Philip John. b 35. K Coll Cam BA58 MA62. Cuddesdon Coll 59. d 61 p 62. C Marton *Blackb* 61-63; PV Truro Cathl 63-67; USPG Ethiopia 67-75; V Henleaze *Bris* 75-84; RD Clifton 79-84; Provost All SS Cathl Cairo 84-89; Chan Malta Cathl 89-95; Chapl Valletta w Sliema *Eur* 89-94; R Llandudno *Ban* 95-04; rtd 04; Perm to Offic *York* from 04 and *Eur* from 05. *17 Chalfonts, York YO24 1EX* Tel (01904) 700316

COUSINS, Stephen Michael. b 53. SAOMC 98. d 01 p 02. OLM Caversham St Jo *Ox* 01-03; Perm to Offic 03-04; NSM Shiplake w Dunsden and Harpsden from 04; Chapl Shiplake Coll Henley from 09. *15 Champion Road, Caversham, Reading RG4 8EL* Tel 0118-948 1679 Mobile 07753-166687 E-mail stephen.cousins@btinternet.com

COUSLAND, Andrew Oliver. b 41. Goldsmiths' Coll Lon MA92. Edin Th Coll 62. d 65 p 66. C Broughty Ferry *Bre* 65-68; C Ayr *Glas* 68-70; R Renfrew 70-75; Perm to Offic *St E* 75-79; CF (TAVR) 76-82; Perm to Offic *Bre* 79-84 and *S'wark* 89-94; R Fraserburgh w New Pitsligo *Ab* 94-99; R Clogherny w Seskinore and Drumnakilly *Arm* 99-03; rtd 03; Perm to Offic *Carl* 03-06. *St Margarets, High Street, Ayton, Eyemouth TD14 5QP* Tel (01890) 781435

COUSSENS, Mervyn Haigh Wingfield. b 47. St Jo Coll Nottm BTh74. d 74 p 75. C Clifton Ch w Em *Bris* 74-77; C Morden *S'wark* 77-83; V Patchway *Bris* 83-91; R Lutterworth w Cotesbach *Leic* 91-98; P-in-c Bitteswell 95-98; R Lutterworth w Cotesbach and Bitteswell from 99; RD Guthlaxton II 01-05. *The Rectory, Coventry Road, Lutterworth LE17 4SH* Tel (01455) 552669 *or* 554780 E-mail rector.stmarys.lutterworth@care4free.net

COUSSMAKER, Canon Colin Richard Chad. b 34. OBE99. Worc Coll Ox BA57 BSc58 MA63 MSc85. Chich Th Coll 59. d 60 p 61. C Newtown St Luke *Win* 60-64; C Whitley Ch Ox 64-67; Chapl Istanbul *Eur* 67-72; Chapl Sliema 72-77; Chapl Antwerp St Boniface 77-93; Can Brussels Cathl 81-00; Chapl Moscow 93-99; rtd 99; Hon Asst Chapl Nice w Vence *Eur* 99-00; Perm to Offic from 00. *533 route des Vallettes Sud, 06140 Tourrettes-sur-Loup, France* Tel (0033) (4) 93 59 28 74

COUTTS, Diana. d 08 p 08. Chapl S Lon Healthcare NHS Trust from 08. *Queen Mary's Hospital, Frognal Avenue, Sidcup DA14 6LT* Tel (020) 8302 2678 ext 4399 E-mail diana.coutts@qms.nhs.uk

COUTTS, Canon Ian Alexander. b 56. Warwick Univ BA77 Jes Coll Ox MSc80 CQSW80. St Jo Coll Nottm 87. d 89 p 90. C Hamstead St Bernard *Birm* 89-92; C Warlingham w Chelsham and Farleigh *S'wark* 92-97; TV 97-00; Perm to Offic *S'wark* 00-03 and *Ox* from 03. *220 Headley Way, Headington, Oxford OX3 7TB* Tel (01865) 742655

COUTTS, James Allan. b 58. Fitzw Coll Cam MA. St Jo Coll Nottm MTh84. d 84 p 85. C Thorpe Acre w Dishley *Leic* 84-88; TV Kirby Muxloe 88-99; P-in-c Trowbridge St Thos and W Ashton *Sarum* 99-07; V from 07; Chapl Wilts and Swindon Healthcare NHS Trust from 99. *St Thomas's Vicarage, York Buildings, Trowbridge BA14 8SF* Tel (01225) 754826

COUTTS, Canon James Walter Cargill. b 35. Univ of Wales (Lamp) BA57 CCC Cam BA59. St Mich Coll Llan 59. d 60 p 61. C Cardiff St Mary *Llan* 60-63; C Greenford H Cross *Lon* 63-67; C Swansea St Gabr *S & B* 67-71; V Llanwrtyd w Llanddulas in Tir Abad etc 71-78; V Brecon St Dav 78-80; V Brecon St David w Llanspyddid and Llanilltyd 80-84; V Monmouth 84-02; Can St Woolos Cathl 94-02; RD Monmouth 99-01; rtd 02. *The Reynolds, Penallt, Monmouth NP25 4RX* Tel (01600) 860277

COUTTS, Mrs Mandy Rosalind. b 65. Ox Poly BSc87 Bath Univ PGCE88 St Jo Coll Dur BA06. Cranmer Hall Dur 04. d 06 p 07. C Chapel Allerton *Ripon* from 06. *21 Carr Manor Grove, Leeds LS17 5AH* Tel 0113-217 2102 E-mail mandy.coutts@virgin.net

COUTTS, Richard Ian Marcus. b 65. Bath Univ BSc87 PGCE88 St Jo Coll Dur BA06. Cranmer Hall Dur 04. d 06 p 07. C Leeds City *Ripon* from 06. *21 Carr Manor Grove, Leeds LS17 5AH* Tel 0113-217 2612 Mobile 07736-180461 E-mail curate@leedsparishchurch.com

COUTTS, Canon Robin Iain Philip. b 52. Portsm Univ MA00. Sarum & Wells Th Coll 80. d 83 p 84. C Alverstoke *Portsm* 83-86; Min Leigh Park St Clare CD 86-89; V Warren Park 89-91; V Purbrook 91-04; RD Havant 00-04; P-in-c Blendworth w Chalton w Idsworth 04-06; P-in-c Hambledon from 06; Dioc Dir NSM from 04; Dioc Dir of Ords from 06; Hon Can Portsm Cathl from 06. *The Vicarage, Church Lane, Hambledon, Waterlooville PO7 4RT* Tel (023) 9263 2717 E-mail robin.rocket@btinternet.com

COUTURE, *(née MAWBEY)*, Mrs Diane. b 55. Birm Univ MMedSc97. Cranmer Hall Dur. d 89 p 94. Par Dn Menston w Woodhead *Bradf* 89-92; C Barnoldswick w Bracewell 92-93; Chapl Asst Birm Children's Hosp 93-96; Chapl Asst Birm Maternity Hosp 93-96; Chapl Birm Women's Healthcare NHS Trust 96-98; R The Whitacres and Shustoke *Birm* from 98. *The Rectory, Dog Lane, Coleshill, Birmingham B46 2DU* Tel (01675) 481252 Mobile 07710-281648

COUVELA, Ms Stephanie Joy. b 68. Sheff City Poly BA89. Ridley Hall Cam 95. d 98 p 99. C Upper Holloway *Lon* 98-01; TV 01-04; C Busbridge and Hambledon *Guildf* from 04. *Mervil Bottom, Malthouse Lane, Hambledon, Godalming GU8 4HG* Tel (01428) 682753 E-mail stephanie.couvela@busbridgechurch.org

COVENTRY, Archdeacon of. *See* WATSON, The Ven Ian Leslie Stewart

COVENTRY, Bishop of. *See* COCKSWORTH, The Rt Revd Christopher John

COVENTRY, Dean of. *See* IRVINE, The Very Revd John Dudley

COVERLEY, Mrs Cheryl Joy. b 62. SS Hild & Bede Coll Dur BA83 PGCE84. St Jo Coll Nottm MA07. d 05 p 06. C Birkenhead St Jas w St Bede *Ches* 05-07; V Newton from 07; Asst Warden of Readers from 08. *St Michael's Vicarage, 56 Queensway, Wirral CH48 6EP* Tel 0151-625 8517

COVINGTON, Canon Michael William Rock. b 38. Open Univ BA78. Sarum Th Coll 60. d 63 p 64. C Daventry *Pet* 63-66; C Woolwich St Mary w H Trin *S'wark* 66-68; C Northampton All SS w St Kath *Pet* 68-71; V Longthorpe 71-86; Hon Min Can Pet Cathl 75-86; V Warmington, Tansor, Cotterstock and Fotheringhay 86-95; Warden of Readers 87-95; RD Oundle 89-95; V Oakham, Hambleton, Egleton, Braunston and Brooke 95-03; P-in-c Langham 97-03; RD Rutland 02-03; Can Pet Cathl 86-03; rtd 03; Perm to Offic *Leic* 05-06; C Burrough Hill Pars from 07. *Hall Farm House, Burroughs Road, Little Dalby, Melton Mowbray LE14 2UG* Tel (01664) 454015

COWAN, David John. b 47. Selw Coll Cam BA69 MA73. SEITE 06. d 09. NSM Dorking w Ranmore *Guildf* from 09. *Dolphin House, Harrow Road West, Dorking RH4 3BE* Tel (01306) 885341 Fax 740183 E-mail david@cowansdorking.co.uk

COWAN, Helen Jane. b 42. d 00 p 01. OLM Redhill H Trin *S'wark* from 00. *15 Westway Gardens, Redhill RH1 2JA* Tel (01737) 762543

COWAN, John Conway. b 71. Trin Coll Bris. d 03 p 04. C Redcar *York* 03-07; V Hull St Cuth from 07. *The Vicarage, 112 Marlborough Avenue, Hull HU5 3JX* Tel (01482) 342848

COWAN, Mrs Lynda Barbette. b 55. ALAM77. Ban Ord Course 02. d 05 p 06. C Arwystli Deanery *Ban* 05-08; P-in-c Llandinam w Trefeglwys w Penstrowed *Ban* from 08. *The Coach House, Old Hall Road, Llanidloes SY18 6PQ* Tel (01686) 413099

COWAN, Malcolm. b 45. CBDTI. d 00 p 01. NSM Keswick St Jo *Carl* 00-05; TV Whitehaven 05-07; P-in-c Kirkby Ireleth from 07; C Dalton-in-Furness and Ireleth-with-Askam from 07. *The Vicarage, School Road, Kirkby-in-Furness LA17 7UQ* Tel (01229) 889256

COWAN, Malcolm. b 60. Ches Coll of HE BTh04. NOC 01. d 04 p 05. C W Kirby St Bridget *Ches* 04-07; V Witton from 07. *The Vicarage, 61 Church Road, Northwich CW9 5PB* Tel (01606) 42943 E-mail jandmcowan@ukonline.co.uk

COWAN, Paul Hudson. b 69. Ripon Coll Cuddesdon BTh05. d 02 p 03. C Wokingham All SS *Ox* 02-05; C Kimberley Cathl S Africa 05-06; TV Newbury *Ox* from 06. *St George's Vicarage, 206 Andover Road, Newbury RG14 6NU* Tel (01635) 41249 E-mail vicar@st-george-newbury.org

COWARD, Colin Charles Malcolm. b 45. Kingston Poly DArch72. Westcott Ho Cam 75. d 78 p 79. C Camberwell St Geo *S'wark* 78-82; P-in-c Wandsworth St Faith 82-90; V 90-96; Chapl Richmond, Twickenham and Roehampton NHS Trust 96-97; Co-ord Changing Attitude 97-03; Dir from 03. *6 Norney Bridge, Mill Road, Worton, Devizes SN10 5SF* Tel (01380) 724908 E-mail colin@changingattitude.org

COWARD, Raymond. b 41. NW Ord Course 79. d 82 p 83. C Turton *Man* 82-84; C Heaton Ch Ch 84-86; V Rochdale St Geo w St Alb 86-92; V Daisy Hill 92-06; rtd 06; Perm to Offic *Man* from 06. *48 Eastbourne Grove, Bolton BL1 5LH* E-mail coward@tinyworld.co.uk

COWBURN, John Charles. b 48. Sarum & Wells Th Coll 88. d 90 p 91. C Andover w Foxcott *Win* 90-94; C Christchurch 94-96; Chapl to the Deaf *Lich* 96-09; P-in-c Church Aston 01-09; Chapl to the Deaf *Sarum* from 09. *The Vicarage, 25 White Street, West Lavington, Devizes SN10 4LW* Tel (01380) 816878

COWDREY, Herbert Edward John. b 26. Trin Coll Ox BA49 MA51. St Steph Ho Ox 50. **d** 52 **p** 53. Tutor St Steph Ho Ox 52-56; Chapl 54-56; Asst Chapl Ex Coll Ox 52-56; Fell St Edm Hall Ox from 56; Chapl 56-78; rtd 91; Perm to Offic *Ox* from 04. *19 Church Lane, Old Marston, Oxford OX3 0NZ* Tel (01865) 794486 Fax 279090

COWELL, Anthony. *See* COWELL, Neil Anthony

COWELL, Christopher Douglas. b 47. Ex Univ BA90 K Coll Lon PGCE92 Brunel Univ PGDE99. **d** 08 **p** 09. OLM Frimley Green and Mytchett *Guildf* from 08. *29 The Glade, Mytchett, Camberley GU16 6BG* Tel (01252) 513434

COWELL, Irene Christine. b 58. RGN80. Ridley Hall Cam 92. **d** 94 **p** 95. C Litherland St Phil *Liv* 94-98; R Sefton and Thornton from 98; Dioc Adv on HIV/AIDS and Sexual Health 97-06; Dioc Dir CME from 02; Dir Leadership and Management Tr from 05. *The Vicarage, Water Street, Liverpool L23 1TB* Tel 0151-931 4676
E-mail irene.cowell@btinternet.com

COWELL, Neil Anthony. b 61. **d** 98 **p** 99. OLM New Bury *Man* 98-06; OLM New Bury w Gt Lever from 06. *166 Harrowby Street, Farnworth, Bolton BL4 7DE* Tel (01204) 706957

COWELL, Peter James. b 58. Peterho Cam BA80 MA84. Coll of Resurr Mirfield 80. **d** 82 **p** 83. C Folkestone St Sav *Cant* 82-86; Chapl Asst St Thos Hosp Lon 86-90; Co-ord Chapl R Lon Hosp 90-94; Lead Trust Chapl Barts and The Lon NHS Trust from 94; Hospitaller from 05; V St Bart Less *Lon* from 05; PV Westmr Abbey from 94. *The Hospitaller, St Bartholomews Hospital, West Smithfield, London EC1A 7BE* Tel (020) 7601 8066
E-mail peter.cowell@bartsandthelondon.nhs.uk

COWEN, Canon Brian. b 45. Nottm Univ BTh77. Linc Th Coll 73. **d** 77 **p** 78. C Hexham *Newc* 77-80; C Eastnor *Heref* 80-81; C Ledbury 80-81; TV Glendale Gp *Newc* 81-90; V Lesbury w Alnmouth 90-08; V Longhoughton w Howick 98-08; AD Alnwick 93-05; Hon Can Newc Cathl 01-08; rtd 08. *13 Fenton Grange, Wooler NE71 6AW* Tel (01668) 281991
E-mail rev.cowan@btopenworld.com

COWGILL, Canon Michael. b 48. Linc Th Coll 84. **d** 86 **p** 87. C Bolton St Jas w St Chrys *Bradf* 86-89; V Buttershaw St Paul 89-93; P-in-c Cullingworth and Dir Dioc Foundn Course 93-97; V Sutton 97-07; V Sutton w Cowling and Lothersdale from 07; Hon Can Bradf Cathl from 07. *The Vicarage, Main Street, Sutton-in-Craven, Keighley BD20 7JS* Tel (01535) 633372
E-mail michael.cowgill@bradford.anglican.org

COWIE, Derek Edward. b 33. S'wark Ord Course 70. **d** 73 **p** 74. C Maldon All SS w St Pet *Chelmsf* 73-76; R Bowers Gifford w N Benfleet 76-79; V Chelmsf Ascension 79-84; V Shrub End 84-95; P-in-c Gosfield 95-03; RD Hinckford 01-03; rtd 03; Perm to Offic *Nor* from 03. *Bruar Cottage, 68 Wash Lane, Kessingland, Lowestoft NR33 7QY* Tel (01502) 740989 Mobile 07788-662211
E-mail decow@lineone.net *or* derekecowie@tiscali.co.uk

COWIE, John William Stephen. b 64. Wycliffe Hall Ox BTh97. **d** 97 **p** 98. C Shoreditch St Leon and Hoxton St Jo *Lon* 97-00. *Address withheld by request* E-mail williamcowie@onetel.com

COWLES, Richard Martin. b 53. Birm Univ BSc74. Ripon Coll Cuddesdon 91. **d** 93 **p** 94. C Iffley *Ox* 93-96; TV Wheatley 96-08; V Bray and Braywood from 08. *The Vicarage, High Street, Bray, Maidenhead SL6 2AB* Tel (01628) 621527
E-mail vicar@cowles.globalnet.co.uk

COWLEY, Anne. *See* COWLEY, Mrs Judith Anne

COWLEY, Charles Frederick. *See* HOWARD-COWLEY, Joseph Charles

COWLEY, Mrs Elizabeth Mary. b 47. Bris Univ PQCSW84. WMMTC 89. **d** 92 **p** 94. NSM Wolston and Church Lawford *Cov* 92-97; Soc Resp Officer 97-02; P-in-c Churchover w Willey 97-02; TV Daventry, Ashby St Ledgers, Braunston etc *Pet* from 02; Adv for Healing Min (Northn Adnry) from 06. *The Vicarage, 19 Church Street, Staverton, Daventry NN11 6JJ* Tel (01327) 702466 E-mail liz.cowley@btinternet.com

COWLEY, Herbert Kenneth. b 20. Glouc Sch of Min 75. **d** 79 **p** 80. Hon C Lydney w Aylburton *Glouc* 79-89; rtd 89; Perm to Offic *B & W* 89-98. *108 Waverley Court, Forth Avenue, Portishead BS20 7NY* Tel (01275) 856198

COWLEY, Ian Michael. b 51. Natal Univ BCom72 BA75 Sheff Univ MA83. Wycliffe Hall Ox 75. **d** 78 **p** 79. C Scottsville S Africa 78-81; C Norton Woodseats St Chad *Sheff* 81-83; R Hilton S Africa 83-94; R Milton *Ely* 94-03; RD Quy 00-02; V Yaxley and Holme w Conington 03-08; Co-ord of Voc and Spirituality *Sarum* from 08. *The Vicarage, Common Road, Whiteparish, Salisbury SP5 2SU* Tel (01794) 884315
E-mail iancowley@ukonline.co.uk

COWLEY, Mrs Judith Anne. b 59. Nottm Univ BSc80. Ox Min Course. **d** 08 **p** 09. NSM Shepherd's Bush St Steph w St Thos *Lon* from 08. *10 Barlby Road, London W10 6AR* Tel (020) 8960 9587 Mobile 07824-511029 E-mail anne.cowley@ntlworld.com

COWLEY, Kenneth. *See* COWLEY, Herbert Kenneth

COWLEY, Mrs Jean Louie Cameron. *See* HERRICK, Mrs Jean Louie Cameron

COWLEY, Paul William. b 55. Middx Univ BA02. NTMTC 99. **d** 02 **p** 03. C Brompton H Trin w Onslow Square St Paul *Lon*

from 02. *72 Archel Road, London W14 9QP* Tel (020) 7386 5140 *or* 08456-447544 Mobile 07860-146552
E-mail amanda.wilkie@htb.org.uk

COWLEY, Peter. b 53. NOC 06. **d** 08. NSM Prescot *Liv* from 08. *17 Kingsway, Prescot L35 5BG* Tel 0151-426 5441
E-mail petercowley@blueyonder.co.uk

COWLEY, Samuel Henry. b 44. St Jo Coll Nottm 85. **d** 87 **p** 88. C Hadleigh w Layham and Shelley *St E* 87-91; P-in-c Ipswich St Mich 91-99; P-in-c Westerfield and Tuddenham w Witnesham from 99. *The Rectory, Westerfield Road, Westerfield, Ipswich IP6 9AG* Tel (01473) 254483 Fax 236407
E-mail sam.cowley@stedmundsbury.anglican.org

COWLING, Canon Douglas Anderson. b 19. Leeds Univ BA40. Coll of Resurr Mirfield 40. **d** 42 **p** 43. C Linc St Andr 42-45; R Candlesby w Scremby 47-53; R Carlton Scroop w Normanton 53-61; V Spalding St Paul 61-84; Can and Preb Linc Cathl 77-93; rtd 84; Perm to Offic *Linc* from 84. *24 Campbell's Close, Spalding PE11 2UH* Tel (01775) 767044

COWLING, John Francis. b 32. K Coll Cam BA56. Linc Th Coll 56. **d** 58 **p** 59. C Leigh St Mary *Man* 58-61; Sec SCM in Schs Liv and Ches 61-65; V Bolton St Matt 65-71; V Bolton St Matt w St Barn 71-75; V Southport H Trin *Liv* 75-91; R St Olave Hart Street w All Hallows Staining etc *Lon* 91-05; P-in-c St Kath Cree 02-05; Dir of Ords 92-02; rtd 05; Perm to Offic *Cant* from 05. *Sankey Farm, Shear Way, Burmarsh, Romney Marsh TN29 0JJ* Tel (01303) 872312

COWLING, Canon Simon Charles. b 59. G&C Coll Cam BA80 MA88 K Coll Lon PGCE82. Linc Th Coll BTh91. **d** 91 **p** 92. C Potternewton *Ripon* 91-94; C Far Headingley St Chad 94-96; V Roundhay St Edm 96-07; AD Allerton 04-07; Can Res and Prec Sheff Cathl from 07. *62 Kingfield Road, Sheffield S11 9AU* Tel 0114-275 3434
E-mail simon.cowling@sheffield-cathedral.org.uk

COWMEADOW, Derek Lowe. b 28. Wells Th Coll 68. **d** 70 **p** 71. C Ledbury *Heref* 70-72; C Llanrhos *St As* 72-74; V Bringhurst w Gt Easton *Leic* 74-77; P-in-c Coln St Aldwyn w Hatherop and Quenington *Glouc* 77-82; V Coln St Aldwyns, Hatherop, Quenington etc 82-93; rtd 93; Perm to Offic *Glouc* from 93. *2 Hampton Grove, Meysey Hampton, Cirencester GL7 5JN* Tel (01285) 851645

COWPER, Christopher Herbert. b 44. AKC67 Open Univ BA76. **d** 68 **p** 69. C Pitsmoor *Sheff* 68-71; C Ulverston St Mary w H Trin *Carl* 71-74; R Kirklinton w Hethersgill and Scaleby 74-83; V Bridekirk 83-94; Chapl Dovenby Hall Hosp Cockermouth 83-94; P-in-c Wetheral w Warwick *Carl* 94-98; R Barningham w Hutton Magna and Wycliffe *Ripon* from 98; rtd 09. *6 Darnborough Gate, Ripon HG4 2TF*

COWPER, Peter James. *See* SELLICK, Peter James

COX, Alan John. b 34. Lon Coll of Div ALCD65 LTh. **d** 65 **p** 66. C Kirkheaton *Wakef* 65-67; C Keynsham w Queen Charlton *B & W* 67-71; R Chipstable w Huish Champflower and Clatworthy 71-76; TV Strood *Roch* 76-80; V Strood St Fran 80-83; R Keston 83-95; rtd 95; Perm to Offic *Roch* from 00. *12 Beech Court, 46 Copers Cope Road, Beckenham BR3 1LD* Tel (020) 8639 0082

COX, Albert Horace Montague. b 26. **d** 86 **p** 87. C Masvingo Zimbabwe 86-94; P-in-c Mucheke 91-94; Dean Gweru 95-02; V Gen Cen Zimbabwe 96-03; Hon C Winchelsea and Icklesham *Chich* from 03. *Pilgrim's End, Manor Close, Icklesham, Winchelsea TN36 4BT* Tel (01424) 815295

COX, Ms Alison Clare. b 63. MHort(RHS)89. Ripon Coll Cuddesdon 01. **d** 03 **p** 04. C Spalding *Linc* 03-07; P-in-c Dukinfield St Mark *Ches* from 07. *The Vicarage, 2 Church Square, Dukinfield SK16 4PX* Tel 0161-330 2783
E-mail alisoncox19@hotmail.com

COX, Alison Hilda. b 57. Coll of Ripon & York St Jo BEd79 Nottm Univ MA02. EMMTC 99. **d** 02 **p** 03. NSM Bakewell *Derby* 02-04; NSM Walton St Jo 04-05; TV Buxton w Burbage and King Sterndale 05-07; Lay Tr Officer *S'well* from 07. *7 Macclesfield Road, Buxton SK17 9AH* Tel (01298) 77699
E-mail alison.cox@southwell.anglican.org

COX, Canon Anthony James Stuart. b 46. BNC Ox BA68 MA74. Qu Coll Birm 69. **d** 71 **p** 72. C Smethwick St Matt w St Chad *Birm* 71-74; Chapl Liv Univ 74; Chapl Malosa Secondary Sch Malawi 75-79; Hd Master 80-87; Hon Can S Malawi from 80; Chapl Loughborough Gr Sch from 87; Perm to Offic *S'well* from 98. *Orchard House, 169 Main Street, Willoughby on the Wolds, Loughborough LE12 6SY* Tel (01509) 880861
E-mail tonycox169@googlemail.com

COX, Brian Leslie. b 49. S Dios Minl Tr Scheme 91. **d** 94 **p** 95. C Southampton Maybush St Pet *Win* 94-98; P-in-c Knights Enham 98-05; R Knight's Enham and Smannell w Enham Alamein 05-06; P-in-c Freemantle from 06. *The Rectory, 129 Paynes Road, Southampton SO15 3BW* Tel (023) 8022 1804

COX, David John. b 51. Lon Univ BD97 Man Univ MA04. Qu Coll Birm 76. **d** 79 **p** 80. C Brampton Bierlow *Sheff* 79-82; Miss Partner CMS 82-88; V N Perak W Malaysia 83-88; V Friarmere *Man* 88-96; P-in-c Denton Ch Ch 96-06; rtd 06; Perm to Offic

COX

Carl from 07. *5 Main Street, St Bees CA27 0DE* Tel (01946) 821601 E-mail cox.davidj@btinternet.com

COX (née FRANKLIN), Mrs Dianne Mary. b 48. UEA BA69 Univ Coll of Swansea PGCE70. NEOC 03. **d** 06 **p** 07. NSM Osbaldwick w Murton *York* 06-09; Chapl Aiglon Coll Switzerland from 09. *Aiglon College, CH-1885 Chesières-Villars, Switzerland* Tel (0041) (24) 496 6161 E-mail diannecoxuk@yahoo.co.uk

COX, Elizabeth Anne. b 55. SEITE 01. **d** 04 **p** 05. NSM Newington w Hartlip and Stockbury *Cant* from 04. *Appleden, 20 Pear Tree Walk, Newington, Sittingbourne ME9 7NG* Tel (01795) 844241 Mobile 07789-510499 E-mail lizapple@btopenworld.com

COX, Canon Eric William. b 30. Dur Univ BA54. Wells Th Coll 54. **d** 56 **p** 57. C Sutton in Ashfield St Mary *S'well* 56-59; Asst Chapl Brussels *Eur* 59-62; V Winningtons *Ches* 62-71; V Middlewich 71-76; Chapl Mid Cheshire Hosps Trust 73-95; P-in-c Biley *Ches* 73-76; V Middlewich w Byley 76-95; RD Middlewich 80-94; Hon Can Ches Cathl 84-95; rtd 95; Perm to Offic *Ches* from 95 and *Lich* from 96. *Lovel Hollow, Church Road, Baschurch, Shrewsbury SY4 2EE* Tel (01939) 261258 E-mail canoneric@lovelhollow.fsnet.co.uk

COX, Geoffrey Sidney Randel. b 33. Mert Coll Ox BA56 MA60. Tyndale Hall Bris. **d** 58 **p** 59. C St Paul's Cray St Barn CD *Roch* 58-61; C Bromley Ch 61-64; V Gorsley w Cliffords Mesne *Glouc* 64-79; V Hucclecote 79-89; V Wollaston and Strixton *Pet* 89-96; rtd 96; Perm to Offic *Glouc* from 96. *32 Murvagh Close, Cheltenham GL53 7QY* Tel (01242) 251604

COX, Hugh Teversham. b 42. Keble Coll Ox BA76 MA82 Trin Evang Div Sch (USA) DMin99. Moore Th Coll Sydney. **d** 69 **p** 70. C Manuka St Paul Australia 70-71; P-in-c Kameruka 71-74; Perm to Offic *Ox* 75-76; P-in-c Canberra Ch Ch Australia 76-82; Tutor and Lect St Mark's Nat Th Cen 77-82; R Lane Cove 82-87; R Castle Hill St Paul 87-01; Tervuren *Eur* 01-06; R E Sydney Australia from 06. *PO Box 465, Kings Cross NSW 1340, Australia* Tel (0061) (2) 9360 6844 Fax 9360 1759 E-mail rector@stjohnsanglican.org.au

COX, James David Robert. b 65. Lanc Univ BA88. Qu Coll Birm BD92. **d** 93 **p** 94. C Harborne St Pet *Birm* 93-96; C Chelmsley Wood 96-97; TV 97-00; V Smethwick Resurr 00-07; V Taunton St Andr *B & W* from 07. *St Andrew's Vicarage, 118 Kingston Road, Taunton TA2 7SR* Tel (01823) 365730

COX, Janet. b 48. CBDTI 04. **d** 05 **p** 06. NSM Long Marton w Dufton and w Milburn *Carl* 05-08; NSM Heart of Eden from 08. *Broom Cottage, Long Marton, Appleby-in-Westmorland CA16 6JP* Tel (017683) 62896 E-mail peter_janet_cox@hotmail.com

COX, John Anthony. b 45. Hull Univ BA67. Qu Coll Birm 71. **d** 73 **p** 74. C Buckingham *Ox* 73-76; C Whitley Ch Ch 76-81; V Reading St Agnes w St Paul 81-83; V Chaddesley Corbett and Stone *Worc* from 83. *The Vicarage, Butts Lane, Stone, Kidderminster DY10 4BH* Tel (01562) 69438

COX, John Edgar. b 26. Lon Univ BSc50 MSc69 CEng MIET56. Bps' Coll Cheshunt 67. **d** 68 **p** 69. NSM Harlow St Mary Magd *Chelmsf* 68-76; C S Petherwin w Trewen *Truro* 77-79; P-in-c 79-82; P-in-c Lawhitton 81-82; P-in-c Lezant 81-82; R Lezant w Lawhitton and S Petherwin w Trewen 82-83; V Breage w Germoe 83-91; rtd 91; Perm to Offic *Truro* from 91. *Manderley, 8 Trewartha Road, Praa Sands, Penzance TR20 9ST* Tel (01736) 762582

COX, The Ven John Stuart. b 40. Fitzw Ho Cam BA62 MA66 Linacre Coll Ox BA67. Wycliffe Hall Ox 64. **d** 68 **p** 69. C Prescot *Liv* 68-71; C Birm St Geo 71-73; R 73-78; Selection Sec ACCM 78-83; Hon C Orpington All SS *Roch* 78-83; Dioc Dir of Ords *S'wark* 83-91; Can Res and Treas S'wark Cathl 83-91; V Roehampton H Trin 91-95; Adn Sudbury *St E* 95-06; rtd 06; Perm to Offic *St E* from 06; Dioc Dir of Educn from 07. *2 Bullen Close, Bury St Edmunds IP33 3JP* Tel and fax (01284) 766796 E-mail archdeacon.john@stedmundsbury.anglican.org

COX, Jonathan James. b 63. Wollongong Univ BA85 Univ of NSW DipEd86. Ridley Hall Cam. **d** 00 **p** 01. C Tonbridge SS Pet and Paul *Roch* 00-03; R Oxley Vale Australia from 03. *95 Glengarvin Drive, Tamworth NSW 2340, Australia* Tel (0061) (2) 6761 7271

COX, Julie Margaret. b 55. SAOMC. **d** 00 **p** 01. NSM Luton St Chris Round Green *St Alb* 00-08; Perm to Offic from 08. *29 Maple Close, Pulloxhill, Bedford MK45 5EF* Tel (01525) 717002 E-mail revjuliecox@hotmail.com

COX, Martin Brian. b 64. Keele Univ BA91 CQSW91. St Jo Coll Nottm 01. **d** 03 **p** 04. C Sale St Anne *Ches* 03-05; V Sandiway from 05. *The Vicarage, 50 Norley Road, Sandiway, Northwich CW8 2JU* Tel (01606) 883286 E-mail martin_b_cox@btopenworld.com

COX, Martin Lloyd. b 57. Wilson Carlile Coll and Sarum & Wells Th Coll. **d** 88 **p** 89. C Risca *Mon* 88-91; TV Pontypool 91-96; V Monkton *St D* 96-04; TR from 04. *The Vicarage, Church Terrace, Monkton, Pembroke SA71 4LW* Tel (01646) 682723

COX, Ms Patricia Jean. b 44. WEMTC. **d** 00 **p** 01. NSM Coleford, Staunton, Newland, Redbrook etc *Glouc* 00-07; NSM

Lydney from 07. *67 Primrose Hill, Lydney GL15 5SW* Tel (01594) 843852 E-mail revp_cox@tiscali.co.uk

COX, Canon Paul Graham. b 40. Keele Univ BA62 DipEd62. Westcott Ho Cam 77. **d** 78 **p** 79. NSM Kemsing w Woodlands *Roch* 78-80; Hd Master and Chapl St Mich Sch Otford 81-90; C Petham and Waltham w Lower Hardres etc *Cant* 90-95; P-in-c 95-97; C Elmsted w Hastingleigh 90-95; P-in-c 95-97; R Biddenden and Smarden 97-06; Bp's Officer for NSM 91-98; Dioc Dir of Reader Selection and Tr 98-00; Bp's Officer for OLM 00-06; Hon Can Cant Cathl 01-06; rtd 06. *31 Waldron Thorns, Heathfield TN21 0AB* Tel (01435) 868814 Mobile 07766-545341 E-mail pgcox@tiscali.co.uk

COX, Peter Allard. b 55. Univ of Wales (Lamp) BA76. Wycliffe Hall Ox 77. **d** 79 **p** 80. C Penarth All SS *Llan* 79-82; V Aberpergwm and Blaengwrach 82-86; V Bargoed and Deri w Brithdir 86-97; V Penarth All SS from 97. *All Saints' Vicarage, 2 Lower Cwrt-y-Vil Road, Penarth CF64 3HQ* Tel (029) 2070 8952 E-mail petercox6@virgin.net

COX, Philip Gordon. b 36. St Jo Coll Cam MA62 Lon Univ PGCE71. Dioc OLM tr scheme 99. **d** 02 **p** 03. OLM Charing w Charing Heath and Lt Chart *Cant* from 02. *Home Meadow, Little Chart Forstal, Little Chart, Ashford TN27 0PU* Tel (01233) 840274 E-mail philip@homemeadow.plus.com

COX, Miss Rosemary Jennifer. b 54. Aber Coll of Dur BA75 Lon Bible Coll BTh97 Trin Coll Bris MA99. Cranmer Hall Dur 01. **d** 03 **p** 04. C Leeds All SS w Osmondthorpe *Ripon* 03-05; C Ireland Wood 05-07. *7 The Paddock, Waterhouses, Durham DH7 9AW* Tel 0191-373 1539 E-mail rosemaryjcox@aol.com

COX, Mrs Sheila Margaret. b 54. Nottm Univ BA76 Reading Univ PGCE77. SEITE 00. **d** 03 **p** 04. NSM Cranbrook *Cant* 03-08; NSM Mersham w Hinxhill and Sellindge from 08; NSM Smeeth w Monks Horton and Stowting and Brabourne from 08; Asst Dir of Ords from 08. *The Rectory, Bower Road, Mersham, Ashford TN25 6NN* Tel 07985-003095 (mobile) E-mail sheila.m.cox@btopenworld.com

COX, Mrs Sheila Susan. b 41. Aber Coll of Educn CertEd63. Edin Dioc NSM Course 85. **d** 88 **p** 94. NSM Livingston LEP *Edin* 88-93; Asst Chapl St Jo and Bangour Hosps W Lothian 89-93; Chapl 96-98; Hon C Edin St Mark 93-96; Missr Edin St Andr and St Aid 95-96; NSM Eyemouth 98-05; rtd 05; Lic to Offic *Edin* from 06. *5 Northfield Farm Cottages, St Abbs, Eyemouth TD14 5QF* Tel (01890) 771764

COX, Canon Simon John. b 53. Qu Mary Coll Lon BSc74 Liv Univ PhD81 Selw Coll Cam BA81 MA85 Lanc Univ MA87 MIBiol79 CBiol79. Ridley Hall Cam 79. **d** 82 **p** 83. C Livesey *Blackb* 82-85; C Cheadle Hulme St Andr *Ches* 85-89; V Disley 89-94; R Bispham *Blackb* from 94; P-in-c S Shore St Pet 05-07; AD Blackpool from 04; Hon Can Blackb Cathl from 07. *All Hallows Rectory, 86 All Hallows Road, Blackpool FY2 0AY* Tel (01253) 351886 E-mail drsjcox@yahoo.co.uk

COX, Stephen. b 38. Open Univ BA80. Bps' Coll Cheshunt 65. **d** 68 **p** 69. C Gaywood, Bawsey and Mintlyn *Nor* 68-72; Youth Chapl 72-82; C N Lynn w St Marg and St Nic 73-82; Chapl Guildf Coll of Tech 82-87; Chapl Surrey Univ 82-91; Tr and Development Manager Jas Paget Hosp Gorleston 91-93; Manager Medical Records 93-96; Consumer Relns and Litigation Manager 96-99; rtd 99. *56 Bately Avenue, Gorleston, Great Yarmouth NR31 6HN* Tel (01493) 662061

COX, Preb Stephen John Wormleighton. b 54. New Coll Ox MA79 Fitzw Coll Cam BA79. Ridley Hall Cam 77. **d** 80 **p** 81. C Clapton Park All So *Lon* 80-85; TV Hackney Marsh 85-87; V Holloway St Mary w St Jas 87-88; P-in-c Barnsbury St Dav w St Clem 87-88; V Holloway St Mary Magd 88-97; AD Islington 95-99; TR Upper Holloway from 97; Preb St Paul's Cathl from 07. *St Mary's Vicarage, 3 Highcroft Road, London N19 3AQ* Tel (020) 7272 9084 *or* 7272 1783 Fax 7272 9934 E-mail stephenj.cox@virgin.net

COX, Mrs Susan. b 55. WEMTC 05. **d** 08 **p** 09. NSM Bourton-on-the-Water w Clapton etc *Glouc* from 08. *30 Lamberts Field, Bourton-on-the-Water, Cheltenham GL51 8LB* Tel (01451) 821641 Mobile 07903-451932 E-mail suemcoxuk@yahoo.co.uk

COX, William John Francis. b 24. SW Minl Tr Course. **d** 77 **p** 78. NSM Liskeard w St Keyne and St Pinnock *Truro* 77-82; NSM Liskeard w St Keyne, St Pinnock and Morval 82-86; NSM N Hill w Altarnon, Bolventor and Lewannick 86-87; TV Bolventor 87-92; P-in-c North Hill and Lewannick 92-94; rtd 94; Perm to Offic *Truro* from 94. *9 Trelawney Rise, Callington PL17 7PT* Tel (01579) 384347

COXHEAD, Mrs Margaret. b 40. S Dios Minl Tr Scheme 91. **d** 94 **p** 95. NSM High Hurstwood *Chich* 94-00; P-in-c High Hurstwood and Fairwarp 00-05; rtd 05. *Rock Hall, Chillies Lane, High Hurstwood, Uckfield TN22 4AD* Tel (01825) 733833

COYNE, John Edward. b 55. Sheff Univ MA98. Oak Hill Th Coll BA79. **d** 79 **p** 80. C Cheadle Hulme St Andr *Ches* 79-81; C Macclesfield St Mich 81-83; V Stalybridge H Trin and Ch Ch 83-88; Chapl RAF 88-03; Command Chapl RAF 03-05; RAF Adv in Evangelism 93-98; Hon C Hemingford Grey *Ely* 96-98; Dean of Coll St Jo Coll Nottm 05-09; Dir Local and Regional

186

Delivery CPAS from 09. *CPAS, Athena Drive, Tachbrook Park, Warwick CV34 6NG* Tel (01926) 458458 Fax 458459
E-mail jcoyne@cpas.org.uk *or* j2scoyne@hotmail.com

COYNE, Terence Roland Harry. b 37. Chich Th Coll 64. **d** 66 **p** 67. C Meir *Lich* 66-69; C Horninglow 69-72; V Walsall St Gabr Fulbrook from 72; C Walsall St Mary and All SS Palfrey 97-02; C Caldmore w Palfrey from 02. *St Gabriel's Vicarage, Walstead Road, Walsall WS5 4LZ* Tel (01922) 622583

COZENS, Mrs Audrey Lilian. b 35. St Hugh's Coll Ox BA56 MA84. Gilmore Course 79. **dss** 82 **d** 87 **p** 94. Shenfield *Chelmsf* 82-87; Par Dn 87-89; Par Dn Westcliff St Andr 89-94; C 94-95; P-in-c Chelmsf St Andr 95-02; P-in-c The Chignals w Mashbury 95-02; rtd 02; Perm to Offic *Chelmsf* from 02. *56 Victoria Road, Writtle, Chelmsford CM1 3PA* Tel (01245) 420165
E-mail revacozens@supanet.com

COZENS, Daniel Harry. b 44. Oak Hill Th Coll. **d** 71 **p** 72. C St Paul's Cray St Barn *Roch* 71-74; C Deptford St Nic w Ch Ch *S'wark* 74-76; C Deptford St Nic and St Luke 76-78; Rees Missr *Ely* from 78; Six Preacher Cant Cathl from 94. *The Rectory, 73 High Street, Coton, Cambridge CB23 7PL* Tel (01954) 210239 Fax 211983 E-mail admin@through-faith-missions.org

COZENS, Michael Graeme. b 59. Chich Th Coll 91. **d** 93 **p** 94. C Emscote *Cov* 93-96; C Prestbury *Glouc* 96-03; TV Prestbury and All SS 03-06; P-in-c 06-08; TR N Cheltenham from 08. *The Vicarage, 66 All Saints' Road, Cheltenham GL52 2HA* Tel (01242) 523177 E-mail mg.cozens@8prestbury.fsnet.co.uk

CRABB, Paul Anthony. b 58. St Chad's Coll Dur BSc79 Leeds Univ PGCE80. Qu Coll Birm 90. **d** 91 **p** 92. C Gomersal *Wakef* 91-95; V Drighlington 95-01; TV Dewsbury 01-09; P-in-c Hanging Heaton from 09; P-in-c Batley St Thos from 09. *The Vicarage, 150 High Street, Hanging Heaton, Batley WF17 6DW* Tel (01924) 461917 Mobile 07946-530415
E-mail pauldewsteamvic@aol.com

CRABTREE, Derek. b 32. Leic Univ BSc(Econ)53. Cant Sch of Min 91. **d** 94 **p** 95. NSM Hackington *Cant* 94-02; Asst Chapl Kent Univ 94-02; rtd 02; Perm to Offic *Cant* from 02. *19 Monastery Street, Canterbury CT1 1NJ* Tel (01227) 471503

CRABTREE, Eric. b 30. Chelt & Glouc Coll of HE BA99 ACA55 FCA68. Premontre Community (RC) 58. **d** 64 **p** 64. In RC Ch 64-90; Perm to Offic *Glouc* 00-04 and *Ox* from 04. *St Katharine's House, Ormond Road, Wantage OX12 8EA* Tel (01235) 769279

CRABTREE, Hazel. b 40. SRN82 Yorks & Humberside Assn for F&HE TCert89. **d** 07 **p** 08. OLM Went Valley *Wakef* from 07. *11 Hillcroft Close, Darrington, Pontefract WF8 3BD* Tel (01977) 793268 E-mail hcrabtree453@btinternet.com

CRABTREE, Martine Charmaine. b 74. Glas Bible Coll BA96 St Jo Coll Nottm MTh02. **d** 02 **p** 03. C Kippax w Allerton Bywater *Ripon* 02-06; P-in-c Sowerby *Wakef* from 06; P-in-c Norland from 09. *The Vicarage, Towngate, Sowerby, Sowerby Bridge HX6 1JJ* Tel (01422) 834344 *or* 832830
E-mail martinecrabtree@aol.com

CRABTREE, Stephen. *See* JONES-CRABTREE, Stephen

CRABTREE, Stephen John. b 62. Roehampton Inst BEd85 Surrey Univ MA93. SEITE 93. **d** 96 **p** 97. NSM N Farnborough *Guildf* 96-08; NSM Rowledge and Frensham from 08. *40 West Street, Farnham GU9 7DX* Tel (01252) 541873
E-mail stephecrab@aol.com

CRADDOCK, Brian Arthur. b 40. Chich Th Coll 67. **d** 70 **p** 71. C Stoke-upon-Trent *Lich* 70-74; Bermuda 75-89; P-in-c Bury and Houghton *Chich* 89-95; Chapl St Mich Sch Burton Park 89-94; Chapl Mojcar *Eur* 95-99; rtd 99; Perm to Offic *Lich* from 04. *72 Pacific Road, Trentham, Stoke-on-Trent ST4 8UD* Tel (01782) 643602

CRADDOCK, Jeremy Graham. b 37. Lon Univ BSc64 Nottm Univ MPhil72. EAMTC 93. **d** 94 **p** 95. NSM Godmanchester *Ely* 94-99; Perm to Offic from 99. *8 Hall Close, Hartford, Huntingdon PE29 1XJ* Tel (01480) 458111

CRADDUCK, Martin Charles. b 50. Hull Univ BSc71. St Jo Coll Nottm. **d** 79 **p** 80. C W Kilburn St Luke w St Simon and St Jude *Lon* 79-83; C Oxhey All SS *St Alb* 83-86; Asst Chapl HM Pris Man 86-87; Dep Chapl HM Young Offender Inst Glen Parva 87-89; Chapl HM Pris Stocken 89-95. *35 Worcester Road, Grantham NG31 8SF* Tel (01476) 571351

CRADDUCK, Stuart William. b 74. Bp Otter Coll Chich BA97. Ripon Coll Cuddesdon BTh00. **d** 00 **p** 01. C W Leigh *Portsm* 00-03; Min Can St Alb Abbey 03-07; R Whyke w Rumboldswhyke and Portfield *Chich* from 07. *St George's Rectory, 199 Whyke Road, Chichester PO19 7HQ*
E-mail stuart@cradduckmail.freeserve.co.uk

CRAFER, Mrs Jeanette Angela. b 48. Keswick Hall Coll CertEd78. EAMTC 99. **d** 01 **p** 02. C Ashmanhaugh, Barton Turf etc *Nor* 01-05; P-in-c Martham and Repps with Bastwick, Thurne etc 05-07; V from 07. *The Rectory, 46 Black Street, Martham, Great Yarmouth NR29 4PR* Tel (01493) 740240
E-mail jeanette.crafer@tesco.net

CRAFT, William Newham. b 46. Lon Univ BSc68 MCIPD70. Oak Hill Th Coll 87. **d** 89 **p** 90. C Werrington *Pet* 90-93; C-in-c Norfolk Park St Leonard CD *Sheff* 93-02; Perm to Offic *Sheff* 99-02; V 02-03; V Stapleford *S'well* from 03; AD Beeston 07-09;

rtd 09. *435 Redmires Road, Sheffield S10 4LF* Tel 0114-230 2718
E-mail billncraft@gmail.com

✠**CRAGG, The Rt Revd Albert Kenneth.** b 13. Jes Coll Ox BA34 MA38 DPhil50 Huron Coll Hon DD63 Virginia Th Sem Hon DD85 Leeds Univ Hon DD93 Lambeth DD02. Tyndale Hall Bris 34. **d** 36 **p** 37 **c** 70. C Tranmere St Cath *Ches* 36-39; Lebanon 39-47; R Longworth *Ox* 47-51; USA 51-56; Can Res Jerusalem 56-59; St Aug Coll Cant 59-60; Sub-Warden 60-61; Warden 61-67; Hon Can Cant Cathl 61-80; Hon Can Jerusalem 65-73; Asst Bp Jerusalem 70-73; Bye-Fellow G&C Coll Cam 69-70; Asst Bp Chich 73-78; Asst Bp Wakef 78-81; V Helme 78-81; rtd 81; Hon Asst Bp Ox from 82. *3 Goring Lodge, White House Road, Oxford OX1 4QE* Tel (01865) 249895

CRAGG, Edward William Adrian. b 55. St Cath Coll Cam BA77 MA81. Cranmer Hall Dur 97. **d** 99 **p** 00. C Clifton *York* 99-02; R Skelton w Shipton and Newton on Ouse from 02; Chapl York Hosps NHS Foundn Trust from 02. *The Rectory, Church Lane, Skelton, York YO30 1XT* Tel (01904) 470045

CRAGG, Mrs Sandra Anne. b 45. St Hugh's Coll Ox BA67. SEITE 94. **d** 97 **p** 98. NSM Kingston All SS w St Jo *S'wark* from 97. *10 Lingfield Avenue, Kingston upon Thames KT1 2TN* Tel (020) 8546 1997 Fax 8541 5281 E-mail sandy@toadstool.co.uk

CRAGGS, Colin Frederick. b 41. Open Univ BA80. Sarum & Wells Th Coll 85. **d** 88 **p** 89. NSM Wilton *B & W* 88-90 and 93-06; NSM Taunton St Andr 90-93; Chapl Taunton and Somerset NHS Trust 90-06; rtd 06. *31 Highfield, Taunton TA1 5JG* Tel and fax (01823) 271989

CRAGGS, Michael Alfred. b 43. Open Univ BA79. St Mich Coll Llan 66. **d** 69 **p** 70. C Clee *Linc* 69-72; C Old Brumby 72-76; TV Kingsthorpe w Northampton St Dav *Pet* 76-83; P-in-c Gt w Lt Addington 83-89; RD Higham 88-89; TR Corby SS Pet and Andr w Gt and Lt Oakley 89-02; V Corby SS Pet and Andr 02-08; RD Corby 90-95; rtd 08. *1 Johnson Drive, Scotter, Gainsborough DN21 3HA* Tel (01724) 764200
E-mail mikeccorb@aol.com

CRAGO, Geoffrey Norman. b 44. Linc Th Coll 67. **d** 70 **p** 71. C Matson *Glouc* 70-75; V Dean Forest H Trin 75-80; Relig Progr Producer Radio Severn Sound 80-85; P-in-c Huntley 80-82; Perm to Offic 82-90; Dioc Communications Officer 84; Gen Syn Broadcasting Dept 85-88; Hon C Highnam, Lassington, Rudford, Tibberton etc 90-08; Relig Progr Producer BBC Radio Gloucestershire 94-03; Bp's Press Officer and Dioc Communications Officer 97-01; rtd 09. *Milestones, 2 Two Mile Lane, Highnam, Gloucester GL2 8DW* Tel (01452) 750575 Fax 08700-940404 E-mail g.crago@btinternet.com

CRAIG, Canon Alan Stuart. b 38. Leeds Univ BA59. Cranmer Hall Dur. **d** 61 **p** 62. C Newcastle w Butterton *Lich* 61-65; C Scarborough St Mary w Ch Ch, St Paul and St Thos *York* 65-67; V Werrington *Lich* 67-72; Asst Chapl HM Pris Man 72-73; Chapl HM Borstal Hindley 73-78; Chapl HM Pris Acklington 78-84; V Longhirst *Newc* 84-90; R Morpeth 90-99; RD Morpeth 84-95; Hon Can Newc Cathl 90-02; Chapl St Geo and Cottage Hosp Morpeth 90-93; Chapl Northd Mental Health NHS Trust 93-99; Dir of Ords and Bp's Chapl *Newc* 99-02; Chapl to The Queen 95-08; rtd 02; Perm to Offic *Newc* from 02. *5 Springfield Meadows, Alnwick NE66 2NY* Tel (01665) 602806 Mobile 07779-519040

CRAIG, Andrew John. b 54. Selw Coll Cam BA76 MA80 PhD80 Dur Univ MBA92. NEOC 00. **d** 03 **p** 04. NSM Stranton *Dur* from 03. *23 Egerton Road, Hartlepool TS26 0BW* Tel (01429) 422461 E-mail andrewj.craig@ntlworld.com

CRAIG, David Paul. b 46. Univ of K Coll Halifax NS Hon DD94. ACT. **d** 84 **p** 85. Australia 84-88; P-in-c Innisfail 85; C St Jas Cathl Townsville 85-88; Miss to Seamen Halifax Canada 88-94; Chapl Immingham Seafarers' Cen 94-05; Gen Preacher *Linc* 97-05; P-in-c Denman Australia from 05. *33 Palace Street, Denman NSW 2328, Australia* Tel (0061) (2) 6547 2243 *or* tel and fax 6547 1149 Fax 6547 2249 Mobile 41-083 8089
E-mail denmanap@bigpond.net.au

CRAIG, Eric. b 39. Birm Univ BA62. Qu Coll Birm 62. **d** 64 **p** 65. C Todmorden *Wakef* 64-68; C Hurstpierpoint *Chich* 68-70; C Cobham *Guildf* 70-73; V Dawley St Jerome *Lon* 73-76; V Stainland *Wakef* 76-87; R Yarnton w Begbroke and Shipton on Cherwell *Ox* 87-04; rtd 04. *17 Farmers Close, Witney OX28 1NN* Tel (01993) 704892

CRAIG, Gillean Weston. b 49. York Univ BA72 Qu Coll Cam BA76 MA80. Westcott Ho Cam 76. **d** 78 **p** 78. C St Marylebone Ch Ch *Lon* 77-82; C Ealing St Barn 82-88; P-in-c St Geo-in-the-East w St Paul 88-89; R 89-02; V Kensington St Mary Abbots w St George 02-06; V Kensington St Mary Abbots w Ch Ch and St Phil from 06. *St Mary Abbots Vicarage, Vicarage Gate, London W8 4HN* Tel (020) 7937 6032
E-mail gillean.craig@stmaryabbotschurch.org

CRAIG, James Owen Maxwell. b 72. Open Univ BA98. Cranmer Hall Dur 99. **d** 02 **p** 03. C The K *Dur* 02-05; Gateshead and Bensham Community Chapl to Arts from 05. *St Columba House, Peterborough Close, Gateshead NE8 1NL* Tel 07918-659088 (mobile) E-mail rev.jim@btopenworld.com

CRAIG, Canon John Newcome. b 39. Selw Coll Cam BA63 MA67. Linc Th Coll 63. **d** 65 **p** 66. C Cannock *Lich* 65-71; V Gt Wyrley 71-79; TR Wednesfield 79-91; Prec Leic Cathl 91-03; Hon Can 93-03; Can Res Leic Cathl 03-04; rtd 04; Perm to Offic *Birm* from 04. *109 Kingsbury Road, Erdington, Birmingham B24 8QH* Tel 0121-373 2809
E-mail john.olivia.craig@lineone.net
CRAIG, Judy Howard. See CRAIG PECK, Judy Howard
CRAIG, Julie Elizabeth. See LEAVES, Julie Elizabeth
CRAIG, Julie Elizabeth. See EATON, Mrs Julie Elizabeth
CRAIG, Patrick Thomas. b 36. BA. St D Coll Lamp 59 Bps' Coll Cheshunt 59. **d** 61 **p** 62. C Belfast St Mary *Conn* 61-65; C Belfast St Pet 65-69; CF 69-88; R Hartfield w Coleman's Hatch *Chich* 88-01; rtd 01; P-in-c Six Pilgrims *B & W* from 03. *Briars, Broadclose Way, Barton St David, Somerton TA11 6BS* Tel (01458) 850825 E-mail pat.craig092@btinternet.com
CRAIG, Richard Harvey. b 31. Em Coll Cam BA58. Linc Th Coll. **d** 60 **p** 61. C Bottesford *Linc* 60-65; Bp's Ind Chapl 65-69; Dioc Adv on Laity Tr *Bris* 69-74; V Whitchurch 74-86; TV N Lambeth *S'wark* 86-96; Bp's Ecum Adv 88-96; Ecum Officer 90-96; rtd 96; Perm to Offic *St Alb* 96-99 and *S'wark* from 01. *18 Holst Court, Westminster Bridge Road, London SE1 7JQ* Tel (020) 7928 0495
CRAIG, Robin Joseph. b 43. TCD BA65 Div Test66 Birm Univ CertEd70. **d** 66 **p** 67. C Carrickfergus *Conn* 66-69; Chapl Ld Wandsworth Coll Hants 75-85; Chapl K Sch Macclesfield 85-01; Lic to Offic *Ches* 85-01; rtd 01. *5 Winston Court, Lavant Road, Chichester PO19 5RG* Tel (01243) 778636
CRAIG PECK, Judy Howard. b 57. Lon Univ MB, BS81 MRCGP86. WMMTC 97. **d** 00 **p** 01. NSM Billing *Pet* 00-07; NSM Yardley Hastings, Denton and Grendon etc from 07; NSM Officer from 03. *Dreamstead, 10 Sharplands, Grendon, Northampton NN7 1JL* Tel (01933) 665965
E-mail judy@peckc.fsnet.co.uk
CRAIG-WILD, Ms Dorothy Elsie (Dhoe). b 54. Birm Univ BA77. Qu Coll Birm 79. **dss** 81 **d** 87 **p** 94. Middleton St Mary *Ripon* 81-87; Par Dn Chapeltown *Sheff* 88-94; C 94-96; P-in-c Bruntcliffe *Wakef* 96-02; RD Birstall 98-08; Jt P-in-c Morley St Paul 00-02; P-in-c Roberttown w Hartshead 02-08; V Heckmondwike 05-08; C Liversedge w Hightown 05-08; TV Maltby *Sheff* from 08; C Thurcroft from 09. *The Rectory, 69 Blyth Road, Maltby, Rotherham S66 7LF* Tel (01709) 812684
E-mail dhoe@craig-wild.me.uk
CRAIG-WILD, Peter John. b 55. Leeds Univ BA77. Qu Coll Birm 77. **d** 80 **p** 81. C Rothwell w Lofthouse *Ripon* 80-83; C Beeston 83-87; V Chapeltown *Sheff* 87-96; RD Tankersley 93-96; V Mirfield *Wakef* 96-08; P-in-c Eastthorpe and Upper Hopton 03-07; Hon Can Wakef Cathl 03-08; RD Dewsbury 06-08; TR Maltby *Sheff* from 08; P-in-c Thurcroft from 09. *The Rectory, 69 Blyth Road, Maltby, Rotherham S66 7LF* Tel (01709) 812684
E-mail peter@craig-wild.me.uk
CRAIGHEAD, Mrs Patricia Anne. b 60. Northumbria Univ BSc02. NEOC 05. **d** 08 **p** 09. C Monkseaton St Pet *Newc* from 08. *23 Airedale, Wallsend NE28 8TL* Tel 07967-316615 (mobile) E-mail patcraighead@hotmail.co.uk
CRAM, Mrs Ruth Frances Isobel. b 52. Kingston Poly BA87 Poly Cen Lon MA92. NOC 94. **d** 97 **p** 98. C E Crompton *Man* 97-99; C Cirencester *Glouc* 99-02; C Broad Blunsdon *Bris* 02; V N Swindon St Andr 02-05; rtd 05. *52 Hague Street, Glossop SK13 8NS* Tel (01457) 868107 E-mail rc.cram@btinternet.com
CRAMER, Mrs Mary Barbara. b 44. K Coll Lon BD65 AKC91 Lon Inst of Educn PGCE66. S Dios Minl Tr Scheme 86. **d** 88 **p** 94. C Whitton SS Phil and Jas *Lon* 88-91; Staff Member S Dios Minl Tr Scheme 91-97; Minl Development Officer STETS 97-98; Vice-Prin Sarum & Wells Th Coll 93-98; Par Dn Bemerton *Sarum* 91-92; TV Pewsey and Swanborough 98-00; TR Whitton 00-01; rtd 01; Perm to Offic *Sarum* 01-05; Hon C Chase *Ox* from 05. *The Vicarage, Church Enstone, Chipping Norton OX7 4NL* Tel and fax (01608) 678424
E-mail marymcrameri@freeserve.co.uk
CRAMP, Barry Leonard. b 46. St Luke's Coll Ex CertEd67 CChem76 MRSC76. **d** 04 **p** 05. OLM Ditchingham, Hedenham, Broome, Earsham etc *Nor* from 04. *Wyvern, The Street, Earsham, Bungay NR35 2TY* Tel (01986) 895535
E-mail sbcramp@waitrose.com
CRAMP, Susan Louise. b 53. Univ of Wales (Abth) BSc74 Leic Univ PGCE75. **d** 04 **p** 05. OLM Ditchingham, Hedenham, Broome, Earsham etc *Nor* from 04. *Wyvern, The Street, Earsham, Bungay NR35 2TY* Tel (01986) 895535
E-mail sbcramp@waitrose.com
CRAMPTON, John Leslie. b 41. CITC 64. **d** 67 **p** 68. C Lurgan Ch the Redeemer *D & D* 67-71; C Dundela St Mark 71-73; C Umtali Rhodesia 73-76; R Fort Victoria 73-76; I Kilanne w Killegney, Rossdroit and Templeshanbo *C & O* 82-88; Preb Ferns Cathl 85-88; Chapl Wilson's Hosp Sch Multyfarnham *M & K* 88-91; C Mullingar, Portnashangan, Moyliscar, Killucan etc 89-91; I Athy w Kilberry, Fontstown and Kilkea *D & G* 91-01; Can Ch Ch Cathl Dublin 95-01; I Geashill w Killeigh and Ballycommon *M & K* 01-06; rtd 06. *41 Beech Avenue, The*

Paddock, Enniscorthy, Co Wexford, Republic of Ireland Tel (00353) (53) 923 2589 Mobile 87-907 7981
E-mail cramptoj@gofree.indigo.ie
CRANE, John Walter. b 32. Chich Th Coll. **d** 58 **p** 59. C Forest Town *S'well* 58-60; C Primrose Hill St Mary w Avenue Road St Paul *Lon* 60-64; R Greenford H Cross 64-67; Min Can and Chapl Windsor 67-79; Chapl St Geo Sch Ascot 67-79; Warden Dioc Retreat Ho (Holland Ho) Cropthorne *Worc* 79-83; P-in-c Harvington and Norton and Lenchwick 84-87; rtd 87. *16 Allesborough Drive, Pershore WR10 1JH* Tel (01386) 556444
CRANE, Mrs Judith. b 53. Matlock Coll of Educn BCombStuds81. Cranmer Hall Dur 94. **d** 96 **p** 97. C Tadcaster w Newton Kyme *York* 96-99; TV Brayton 99-02; V Blackwell w Tibshelf *Derby* 02-08; Asst Dir of Ords from 06. *27 Highfield Road, Little Eaton, Derby DE21 5AG* Tel (01332) 833872
E-mail judithcrane@yahoo.co.uk
CRANE, Ronald Edward. b 48. Wilson Carlile Coll 73 St Steph Ho *Ox* 83. **d** 85 **p** 86. C Bicester w Bucknell, Caversfield and Launton *Ox* 85-88; P-in-c Washwood Heath *Birm* 88-92; V 92-01; V Wylde Green from 01. *Emmanuel Vicarage, 17 Greenhill Road, Sutton Coldfield B72 1DS* Tel and fax 0121-373 8348
E-mail fathercrane@btinternet.com
CRANFIELD, Nicholas William Stewart. b 56. Mert Coll Ox BA77 MA81 DPhil82 Leeds Univ BA81 Selw Coll Cam PhD95 FSA07. Coll of Resurr Mirfield 79 Union Th Sem (NY) STM84. **d** 86 **p** 87. C Ascot Heath *Ox* 86-89; Prin Berks Chr Tr Scheme 89-92; Hon C Reading St Mary w St Laur 89-92; Chapl and Fell Selw Coll Cam 92-99; V Blackheath All SS *S'wark* from 99; Chapl St Dunstan's Coll Catford 00-05. *All Saints' Vicarage, 10 Duke Humphrey Road, London SE3 0TY* Tel (020) 8852 4280
E-mail vicar@allsaintsblackheath.org
CRANIDGE, Mrs Wendy Ann. b 31. Sheff Univ CertEd52. Cant Sch of Min 81. **dss** 84 **d** 87 **p** 94. Roch 84-88; Hon Par Dn 87-88; Soc Resp Adv *Cant* and *Roch* 86-88; Hon C Washingborough w Heighington and Canwick *Linc* 88-92; Perm to Offic 92-93; C Farnborough *Roch* 94-96; rtd 96; Perm to Offic *Roch* 96-02 and *Wakef* from 04. *1 Fern Valley Chase, Todmorden OL14 7HB* Tel (01706) 815062
CRANKSHAW, Ronald. b 41. Coll of Resurr Mirfield 74. **d** 76 **p** 77. C Orford St Andr *Liv* 76; C N Meols 76-79; V Abram 79-85; V Wigan St Anne 85-99; AD Wigan W from 95; V Heston *Lon* 99-07; rtd 07. *Orchard House, Westlinton, Carlisle CA6 6AA* Tel (01228) 791434 E-mail roncrankshaw@sky.com
CRANMER, Ms Elaine. b 55. Hockerill Coll Cam CertEd77. SEITE 97. **d** 00 **p** 01. C Charlton *S'wark* 00-03; P-in-c Eltham Park St Luke from 03; AD Eltham and Mottingham from 06. *St Luke's Vicarage, 107 Westmount Road, London SE9 1XX* Tel (020) 8850 3030 E-mail rev.elaine@virgin.net
CRANMER, John Abery. b 33. K Alfred's Coll Win CertEd56 Southn Univ MPhil69. **d** 94 **p** 00. NSM Crawley and Littleton and Sparsholt w Lainston *Win* 94-02; rtd 02; Perm to Offic *Win* from 02. *The Coach House, Crawley, Winchester SO21 2PU* Tel (01962) 776214
CRANSHAW, Trevor Raymond. b 58. Trin Coll Bris 00. **d** 03 **p** 04. C Westbury-on-Trym H Trin *Bris* 03-07; P-in-c Wheathill Priory Gp *B & W* from 07. *The Rectory, Church Street, Keinton Mandeville, Somerton TA11 6ER* Tel (01485) 223216 Mobile 07734-304116
CRANSTON, Miss Margaret Elizabeth. b 56. Newnham Coll Cam BEd78. SWMTC 04. **d** 07. NSM Heanton Punchardon w Marwood *Ex* from 07. *Broom Cottage, Middle Marwood, Barnstaple EX31 4EG* Tel (01271) 372426
E-mail margaret@broomcottage.fsworld.co.uk
CRANSWICK, James Harvard. b 22. Melbourne Univ BA47 St Cath Coll Ox BA50 MA54 Birm Univ MA76. Wycliffe Hall Ox 49. **d** 50 **p** 51. C Werneth *Man* 50-51; C St Pancras H Cross w St Jude and St Pet *Lon* 52-54; P-in-c Dartford St Alb *Roch* 54-56; Australia 56-66 and from 70; C Raynes Park St Sav *S'wark* 68-70; rtd 88. *Rhodoglade Retirement Village, 3/1502 Mount Dandenong Tourist Road, Olinda Vic 3788 Australia* Tel (0061) (3) 9751 0021 Fax 9754 3518
E-mail jimcranswick@hotmail.com
CRANWELL, Brian Robert. b 32. Sheff Poly MSc Sheff Hallam Univ MPhil06. Cranmer Hall Dur. **d** 84 **p** 85. C Ecclesfield *Sheff* 84-86; V Handsworth Woodhouse 86-99; rtd 99; Perm to Offic *Sheff* from 99 and *Derby* from 00. *9 Westview Close, Totley, Sheffield S17 3LT* Tel 0114-262 1499
E-mail brian_cranwell@lineone.net
CRASKE, Leslie Gordon Hamilton. b 29. AKC54 Lambeth STh80. **d** 55 **p** 56. C Malden St Jo *S'wark* 55-58; C Streatham St Leon 58-60; S Rhodesia 60-65; Rhodesia 65-66; V Upper Norwood St Jo *Cant* 67-83; R Guernsey St Sav *Win* 83-97; rtd 97; Perm to Offic *Win* from 97. *La Gruterie, 3 Mount Row, St Peter Port, Guernsey GY1 1NS* Tel (01481) 716027
CRASTON (née FULLALOVE), Mrs Brenda Hurst. b 33. Open Univ BA75 Man Univ MPhil86. St Mich Ho Ox 58. **dss** 80 **d** 81 **p** 94. Bolton St Paul w Em *Man* 80-93; Par Dn 87-93; rtd 93;

Perm to Offic *Man* from 94. *12 Lever Park Avenue, Horwich, Bolton BL6 7LE* Tel (01204) 699972

CRASTON, Canon Richard Colin. b 22. Bris Univ BA49 Lon Univ BD51 Lambeth DD92. Tyndale Hall Bris 46. **d** 51 **p** 52. C Dur St Nic 51-54; V Bolton St Paul *Man* 54-76; P-in-c Bolton Em 64-66; V 66-76; Hon Can Man Cathl 68-95; RD Bolton 72-92; V Bolton St Paul w Em 77-86; TR 86-93; Chapl to The Queen 85-92; rtd 93; Perm to Offic *Man* from 93. *12 Lever Park Avenue, Horwich, Bolton BL6 7LE* Tel (01204) 699972

CRAVEN, Miss Alison Ruth Miranda. b 63. Cen Sch Speech & Drama BSc86. Westcott Ho Cam 05. **d** 07 **p** 08. C Chelsea St Luke and Ch Ch *Lon* from 07. *31 St Luke's Street, London SW3 3RP* E-mail alisoncraven@chelseaparish.org

CRAVEN, Canon Allan. b 35. LTCL77 Univ of Wales (Lamp) BA57 Lon Univ BD72. Chich Th Coll 57. **d** 59 **p** 60. C Blaenau Ffestiniog *Ban* 59-61; C Milford Haven *St D* 61-65; V Llwynhendy 65-68; R Nolton w Roch 68-00; RD Roose 85-99; Can St D Cathl from 91; rtd 00. *25 West Lane Close, Keeston, Haverfordwest SA62 6EW* Tel (01437) 710709

CRAVEN, Colin Peter. b 48. Dartmouth RN Coll. St Steph Ho Ox 83. **d** 85 **p** 86. C Holbeach *Linc* 85-88; Chapl Fleet Hosp 86-97; TV Grantham *Linc* 88-97; P-in-c Fairfield *Derby* 97-03; OCF 88-03; CF 03-06; Rtd Officer Chapl RAChD from 06. *c/o MOD Chaplains (Army)* Tel (01980) 615804 Fax 615800

CRAVEN, David Alex. b 80. Univ of Wales (Ban) BA01. Wycliffe Hall Ox BTh06. **d** 06 **p** 07. C Croglin *Carl* from 06; C Holme Eden and Wetheral w Warwick from 06. *The Rectory, Plains Road, Wetheral, Carlisle CA4 8LA* Tel (01228) 560216 E-mail dacraven@hotmail.com

CRAVEN, Janet Elizabeth. *See* CHAPMAN, Canon Janet Elizabeth

CRAVEN, Mrs Janet Mary. b 43. Bp Otter Coll TCert64. **d** 06 **p** 07. OLM Shelley and Shepley *Wakef* from 06. *70 Jenkyn Lane, Shepley, Huddersfield HD8 8AW* Tel (01484) 604107

CRAVEN, Rebecca Clare. b 58. Bris Univ BDS80 Glas Univ MPH90 Man Univ PhD97 RCPS FDS97. **d** 01 **p** 02. OLM Reddish *Man* 01-06; NSM 06-07; NSM Salford Sacred Trin and St Phil from 07. *201 Thornton Road, Fallowfield, Manchester M14 7NS* Tel 0161-225 7336 E-mail rebecca.c.craven@manchester.ac.uk

CRAVEN, Archdeacon of. *See* SLATER, The Ven Paul John

CRAWFORD, Mrs Anne Elizabeth. b 59. SAOMC 01. **d** 04 **p** 05. C Billington, Egginton, Hockliffe etc *St Alb* 04-08; R Toddington and Chalgrave from 08. *The Rectory, 41 Leighton Road, Toddington, Dunstable LU5 6AL* Tel (01525) 872298 E-mail annie.anselm@btinternet.com

CRAWFORD, Duncan Alexander. b 59. Newc Univ BA81 MA83 K Coll Lon CertEd83. St Jo Coll Nottm 86. **d** 89 **p** 90. C Hatcham St Jas *S'wark* 89-92; Perm to Offic 93-02. *Gortestraat 44, 2311 NM Leiden, The Netherlands*

CRAWFORD, Canon Ivy Elizabeth. b 50. Trin Coll Bris 83. **dss** 85 **d** 87 **p** 94. Collier Row St Jas *Chelmsf* 85; Collier Row St Jas and Havering-atte-Bower 86-89; Par Dn 87-89; Par Dn Harlow New Town w Lt Parndon 89-94; C Harlow Town Cen w Lt Parndon 94-95; V Blackmore and Stondon Massey 95-09; RD Ongar 06-09; P-in-c Doddinghurst w Mountnessing and Buttsbury from 09; CME Adv from 09; Hon Can Chelmsf Cathl from 98. *The Rectory, Park Road, Little Easton, Dunmow CM6 2JJ* Tel (01371) 872509 E-mail ivycrawford@btinternet.com

CRAWFORD, James Robert Harry. b 55. CBDTI 00. **d** 03 **p** 04. OLM Lower Darwen St Jas *Blackb* 03-07; NSM from 07. *10 Eastcott Close, Blackburn BB2 3WJ* Tel (01254) 693822

CRAWFORD, John William Rowland. b 53. Open Univ BA81 NUI MA95 PhD03 AKC75. CITC 75. **d** 76 **p** 77. C Dundela St Mark *D & D* 76-79; C Taney Ch Ch *D & D* 79-84; V Dublin St Patr Cathl Gp 84-09; Preb Tipperkevin St Patr Cathl Dublin 84-09; rtd 09. *9 Ashbrooke Manor, Moyne Hall, Cavan, Republic of Ireland* E-mail jwrcrawf@eircom.net

CRAWFORD, Kenneth Ian. b 48. Melbourne Univ BMus77 Columbia Univ MA79 MEd80 MACE84. Trin Coll Melbourne BD86. **d** 87 **p** 87. Australia 87-97; C Ringwood St Paul 87-89; C Cheltenham St Matt 89-90; P-in-c Vermont S H Name 90-93; Can Prec Melbourne Cathl 93-97; P-in-c Warndon St Nic *Worc* 97-03; V Pershore w Pinvin, Wick and Birlingham from 03. *The Abbey Vicarage, Church Street, Pershore WR10 1DT* Tel (01386) 552071 E-mail vicar@pershoreabbey.fsnet.co.uk

CRAWFORD, Louise Dorothy Anita. b 60. Oak Hill Th Coll BA91 Princeton Th Sem MDiv00. Irish Sch of Ecum MPhil02. **d** 02 **p** 03. C Drumragh w Mountfield *D & R* 02-05; I Aghadowey w Kilrea from 05. *The Rectory, 2 Moneygran Road, Kilrea, Coleraine BT51 5SJ* Tel (028) 2954 0257 E-mail anamchara00@yahoo.com

CRAWFORD, Michael Davis. b 45. Oak Hill Th Coll BA97 K Coll Lon PGCE98. **d** 00 **p** 01. NSM New Barnet St Jas *St Alb* 00-04; C Limassol St Barn Cyprus 04-08; Chapl SE Cyprus from 08. *39 Dionisou Street, Protaras, Paralimni 5296, Cyprus* Tel (00357) (2) 381 1045 Mobile 99-848164 E-mail rev.michael@cytanet.com.cy

CRAWFORD, Peter. b 22. Trin Coll Cam BA49 MA54. Wycliffe Hall Ox 49. **d** 51 **p** 52. C Ashton St Mich *Man* 51-54; V Pendlebury St Jo 54-60; Chapl R Man Children's Hosp 54-60; V Masham Ripon 60-75; RD Ripon 70-75; V Masham and Healey 75-79; R E Bergholt *St E* 79-87; RD Samford 82-86; rtd 87; Perm to Offic *St E* 87-02. *3 Burl's Yard, Crown Street, Needham Market, Ipswich IP6 8AJ* Tel (01449) 722343

CRAWFORD, Canon Robin. b 33. Pemb Coll Cam BA57 MA61. Roch Th Coll 66. **d** 67 **p** 80. Hd Master Navrongo Sch Ghana 67-69; Dep Sec Chrs Abroad 69-73; Dep Hd Priory Sch Lewes 74-76; Nigeria 77-79; Dep Sec Buttle Trust 79-86; Sec 86-90; Dir 90-92; Hon C Win H Trin 80-82; Hon C Notting Hill All SS w St Columb *Lon* 82-87; Hon C Westmr St Matt from 87; Hon Can Tamale from 01. *52 Dean Abbott House, 70 Vincent Street, London SW1P 4BS* Tel and fax (020) 7931 8013

CRAWFORD JONES, Neil. *See* JONES, Canon Neil Crawford

CRAWLEY, Alan John. b 58. Trin Coll Cam MA83. SAOMC 04. **d** 07 **p** 08. NSM Gt Marlow w Marlow Bottom, Lt Marlow and Bisham *Ox* 07-08; C Amersham on the Hill from 08. *23 Elm Close, Amersham HP6 5DD* Tel (01494) 433826 E-mail alan.crawley@btinternet.com

CRAWLEY, Canon David. b 47. TD. St Steph Ho Ox 75. **d** 78 **p** 79. C Solihull *Birm* 78-81; TV Newbury *Ox* 81-84; Lic to Offic 84-95; Chapl Stoke Mandeville Hosp Aylesbury 84-95; Distr Chapl 88-95; Hd Chapl Services W Suffolk Hosps NHS Trust from 95; Bp's Adv on Hosp Chapl *St E* from 00; Hon Can St E Cathl from 05. *22 Westbury Avenue, Bury St Edmunds IP33 3QE* Tel (01284) 750526 *or* 713486 Fax 701993 E-mail david.crawley@wsh.nhs.uk

CRAWLEY, John Lloyd Rochfort. b 22. Selw Coll Cam BA47 MA52. Cuddesdon Coll 47. **d** 49 **p** 50. C Newc H Cross 49-52; V Byker St Ant 52-59; V Longhoughton w Howick 59-69; Chapl Newc Univ 69-74; Master Newc St Thos Prop Chpl 69-74; P-in-c Cockermouth All SS w Ch Ch *Carl* 74-77; TR Cockermouth w Embleton and Wythop 77-86; Perm to Offic *Arg* from 86; rtd 87. *Flat 15, Manormead, Tilford Road, Hindhead GU26 6RA*

CRAWLEY, Nicholas Simon. b 58. Southn Univ BSc79 ACIB82 AIIM85. Wycliffe Hall Ox 85. **d** 88 **p** 89. C E Twickenham St Steph *Lon* 88-93; R Avondale Zimbabwe 93-99; P-in-c Netherthorpe St Steph *Sheff* 99-04; Network Miss P (Bris Adnry) from 04. *27 Carnarvon Road, Bristol BS6 7DU* Tel 0117-944 1980 E-mail nick.crawley@btopenworld.com

CRAWLEY, Simon Ewen. b 31. Em Coll Cam BA57 MA60. Ridley Hall Cam 56. **d** 58 **p** 59. C Denton Holme *Carl* 58-61; P-in-c Cinderford St Steph w Littledean *Glouc* 61-67; V Margate H Trin *Cant* 67-74; V Folkestone H Trin w Ch Ch 74-81; R Patterdale *Carl* 81-87; RD Penrith 83-86; R Culworth w Sulgrave and Thorpe Mandeville etc *Pet* 87-95; RD Brackley 89-95; rtd 95; Perm to Offic *Ex* from 96 and *York* from 03. *The Old Vicarage, Main Street, Healaugh, Tadcaster LS24 8DB* Tel (01937) 830160

CRAWSHAW, Clinton. b 70. St Steph Ho Ox. **d** 02 **p** 03. C Hendon St Alphage *Lon* 02-04; rtd 04. *Address temp unknown* E-mail revcrawshaw@yahoo.com

CRAWTE, William Richard. b 30. TCD BA54. **d** 55 **p** 56. C Belfast St Aid *Conn* 55-57; C Newcastle *D & D* 57-59; CF 59-79. *58 Heath Estate, Great Waldingfield, Sudbury CO10 0TZ* Tel (01787) 377356

✠**CRAY, The Rt Revd Graham Alan.** b 47. Leeds Univ BA68. St Jo Coll Nottm 69. **d** 71 **p** 72. **c** 01. C Gillingham St Mark *Roch* 71-75; N Area Co-ord CPAS Youth Dept 75-78; C York St Mich-le-Belfrey 78-82; V 82-92; Prin Ridley Hall Cam 92-01; Six Preacher Cant Cathl 97-01; Suff Bp Maidstone 01-09; Abps' Missr and Team Ldr Fresh Expressions from 09; Hon Asst Bp Cant from 09. *The Rectory, Church Road, Harrietsham, Maidstone ME17 1AP*

CRAY, Mrs Jacqueline. b 49. Glos Coll of Educn CertEd70. SEITE 01. **d** 04 **p** 05. NSM Gt Chart *Cant* 04-08; P-in-c Maidstone St Faith from 08. *The Rectory, Church Road, Harrietsham, Maidstone ME17 1AP* Tel (01622) 851822 Mobile 07889-742973 E-mail jackiecray@hotmail.com

CREAN, Patrick John Eugene. b 38. TCD BA81 MA84. Edin Th Coll 82. **d** 84 **p** 85. C Perth St Jo *St And* 84-86; P-in-c Liv St Phil w St Dav 86-87; V 87-90; R Cupar and Ladybank *St And* 90-92; P-in-c Sefton *Liv* 92-97; Dioc Children's Officer 92-03; V Aintree St Giles 97-98; V Aintree St Giles w St Pet 98-03; rtd 03; Perm to Offic *Liv* from 03. *36 Lingfield Close, Netherton, Bootle L30 1BB* Tel 0151-525 8838

CREASER, Canon David Edward. b 35. St Cath Coll Cam BA58 MA62. Clifton Th Coll 59. **d** 61 **p** 62. C Cheadle *Ches* 61-67; V Weston *Bradf* 67-69; P-in-c Denton 67-69; V Weston w Denton 69-74 and 82-02; Dir Educn 73-96; V Frizinghall 74-82; V Weston w Denton 82-02; Hon Can Bradf Cathl 90-02; P-in-c Leathley w Farnley, Fewston and Blubberhouses 96-02; rtd 02; Perm to Offic *Bradf* from 03. *Rose Cottage, Pant Lane, Austwick, Lancaster LA2 8BH* Tel (01542) 51536 E-mail david.creaser@bradford.anglican.org

CREASEY, David John. b 46. Univ of Wales (Abth) BSc69. **d** 06 **p** 07. OLM Ringstone in Aveland Gp *Linc* from 06. *Hanthorpe*

Farm, 22 Stainfield Road, Hanthorpe, Bourne PE10 0RE Tel (01778) 570553

CREASEY, Graham. *See* GOLDSTONE-CREASEY, Graham

CREBER, Preb Arthur Frederick. b 45. NOC 84. **d** 87 **p** 88. C Rickerscote *Lich* 87-91; V Gt Wyrley 91-99; RD Rugeley 94-98; P-in-c Newcastle w Butterton 99-07; R 07-08; Preb Lich Cathl 04-08; rtd 08. *22 Malvern Rise, Rhos-on-Sea, Colwyn Bay LL28 4RX* Tel (01492) 547761
E-mail arthur.creber@btinternet.com

CREDITON, Suffragan Bishop of. *See* EVENS, The Rt Revd Robert John Scott

CREE, John Richard. b 44. Open Univ BA74 Lanc Univ MA92. Coll of Resurr Mirfield. **d** 83 **p** 84. C Blackb St Jas 83-86; V Feniscowles 86-01; Chapl Blackb Coll 86-01; R Chorley St Laur *Blackb* 01-09; rtd 09; Perm to Offic *Bre* from 86 and *Blackb* from 09. *5 Bromley Green, Chorley PR6 8TX* Tel (01257) 263398
E-mail john.cree@tiscali.co.uk

CREER, Irene. *See* SHAW, Mrs Irene

CREES, David Paul. b 68. Southn Univ BSc89. Trin Coll Bris BA99 MA00. **d** 00 **p** 01. C Patcham *Chich* 00-04; CF from 04. *c/o MOD Chaplains (Army)* Tel (01980) 615804 Fax 615800

CREES, Geoffrey William. b 35. Open Univ BA85. Cranmer Hall Dur 65. **d** 67 **p** 68. C Hoddesdon *St Alb* 67-70; C Harwell and Chilton All SS *Ox* 70-73; V Greenham 73-82; TR Marfleet and AD E Hull *York* 82-88; TR Rodbourne Cheney *Bris* 88-99; rtd 99; Perm to Offic *Glouc* from 99. *The Thatch, New Road, Popes Hill, Newnham GL14 1JT* Tel (01452) 760843

CREGAN, Mark. b 59. Lon Bible Coll BA91. Wycliffe Hall Ox 95. **d** 97 **p** 98. C Chippenham St Pet *Bris* 97-01; P-in-c Stapleton 01-05; Asst Chapl Colston's Sch Bris 01-03; Chapl 03-05; Chapl Alexandria Egypt 05-07; P-in-c Casablanca *Eur* from 07. *7 Impasse Chasseur Jules Gros, Quartier Oasis, 20100 Casablanca, Morocco* Tel and fax (00212) (2) 257120
E-mail chaplain@stjohnscasablanca.org

CREGEEN, Gary Marshall. b 62. Oak Hill Th Coll BA00. **d** 00 **p** 01. C Carl St Jo 00-03; P-in-c Scotby and Cotehill w Cumwhinton 03-05; V from 06; RD Brampton from 09. *The Vicarage, Lambley Bank, Scotby, Carlisle CA4 8BX* Tel (01228) 513205 E-mail gary@gandjcregeen.co.uk

CREIGHTON, Canon Frederick David. b 50. TCD BTh88 ACII74. **d** 88 **p** 89. C Lisburn Ch Ch *Conn* 88-91; I Drumclamph w Lower and Upper Langfield *D & R* 91-00; I Glendermott from 00; Can Derry Cathl from 08. *Glendermott Rectory, Church Brae, Altnagelvin BT47 2LS* Tel (028) 7134 3001

CREIGHTON, Mrs Judith. b 36. Reading Univ BSc57. Trin Coll Bris 80 Edin Th Coll 81. **dss** 83 **d** 87 **p** 94. Greenock *Glas* 83-85; Lawrence Weston *Bris* 85-87; Par Dn Kingswood 87-90; Chapl Stoke Park and Purdown Hosps Stapleton 90-93; Hon C Marshfield w Cold Ashton and Tormarton etc *Bris* 93-97; rtd 96; Perm to Offic *Bris* from 97. *Rose Cottage, West Littleton, Marshfield, Chippenham SN14 8JE* Tel (01225) 891021

CREIGHTON, Ms Rachel Margaret Maxwell. b 64. Br Is Nazarene Coll BTh86 BD87 Lon Bible Coll MA89. Cranmer Hall Dur 92. **d** 94 **p** 95. C Basford w Hyson Green *S'well* 94-96; C Nottingham All SS 96-98; P-in-c Broxtowe 98-02; Chapl HM Pris Bedf 02-04; Chapl HM Pris Wellingborough 04-09; I Belfast H Trin and St Silas *Conn* from 09. *The Rectory, 313 Ballysillan Road, Belfast BT14 6RD* Tel (028) 9071 3046 Mobile 07748-063770 E-mail rachel.creighton64@btinternet.com

CRELLIN, Howard Joseph. b 30. Magd Coll Cam BA52 MA56 Magd Coll Ox BA54 MA56. Wycliffe Hall Ox 53. **d** 55 **p** 56. C Dovercourt *Chelmsf* 55-58; R Theydon Garnon 58-70; Select Preacher Ox Univ 68; Perm to Offic *Ox* 70-82; Hon C High Wycombe 72-77; Asst Master K Chas I Sch Kidderminster 74-80; Caldicott Sch Farnham 80-82; Perm to Offic *Chelmsf* 82-91; Asst Master Fryerns Sch Basildon 82-88; St Anselm's Sch Basildon 88-91; P-in-c Whatfield w Semer, Nedging and Naughton *St E* 91-98; rtd 98; Perm to Offic *St E* from 98 and *Eur* from 02. *10 Green Willows, Lavenham, Sudbury CO10 9SP* Tel (01787) 247588

CREMIN (*née* LAKE), Mrs Eileen Veronica. b 58. Aston Tr Scheme 83 Sarum & Wells Th Coll 85. **d** 88 **p** 94. Par Dn Islington St Mary *Lon* 88-92; Asst Chapl Homerton Hosp Lon and Hackney Hosp Gp 92-94; P-in-c Brondesbury Ch Ch and St Laur 94-01; C Douglas Union w Frankfield *C, C & R* 01-06; I Fermoy Union from 06. *The Rectory, Forglen Terrace, Fermoy, Co Cork, Republic of Ireland* Tel (00353) (25) 31016
E-mail evcremin@eircom.net *or* ecremin@hotmail.com

CRESSALL, Paul Richard. b 51. UEA BA74. Ripon Coll Cuddesdon 86. **d** 88 **p** 89. C Stevenage H Trin *St Alb* 88-91; V Caldecote All SS 91-95; V Old Warden 91-95; V Rothwell *Ripon* from 95. *The Vicarage, Beech Grove, Rothwell, Leeds LS26 0EF* Tel 0113-282 2369 Mobile 07801-582503
E-mail paul@cressall.fsnet.co.uk

CRESSEY, Canon Roger Wilson. b 35. Chich Th Coll 72. **d** 74 **p** 75. C Pontefract St Giles *Wakef* 74-77; Hon C Dewsbury All SS 77-80; Chapl Pinderfields Gen Hosp Wakef 80-94; Chapl Carr Gate Hosp Wakef 80-94; Chapl Fieldhead Hosp Wakef 80-94; Chapl Pinderfields and Pontefract Hosps NHS Trust 94-00; Hon Can Wakef Cathl 98-00; rtd 00. *1 Wellhead Mews, Chapelthorpe, Wakefield WF4 3JG* Tel (01924) 258972
E-mail roger-cressey@supanet.com

CRESSWELL, Howard Rex. b 31. Ely Th Coll 56. **d** 59 **p** 60. C Dovercourt *Chelmsf* 59-61; C Victoria Docks Ascension 61-64; V 64-71; R E w W Harling *Nor* 71-72; TV Quidenham w Eccles and Snetterton 72-75; V Arminghall 75-82; R Caistor w Markshall 75-82; V Trowse 75-82; V Heigham St Barn w St Bart 82-91; rtd 91; Perm to Offic *Nor* from 91. *28 Penryn Close, Norwich NR4 7LY* Tel (01603) 458591

CRESSWELL, Jane Stella. b 62. Bris Univ BA84. SEITE 04. **d** 07 **p** 08. C Sutton *S'wark* from 07. *The Vicarage, 37 St Barnabas Road, Sutton SM1 4NS*
E-mail janescresswell@hotmail.com

CRESSWELL, Canon Jeremy Peter. b 49. St Jo Coll Ox BA72 MA78 K Coll Lon MA83. Ridley Hall Cam 73. **d** 75 **p** 76. C Wisley w Pyrford *Guildf* 75-78; C Weybridge 78-82; P-in-c E Clandon 82-83; P-in-c W Clandon 82-83; R E and W Clandon 83-90; V Oxshott from 90; RD Leatherhead 03-08; Hon Can Owerri from 01. *The Vicarage, Steel's Lane, Oxshott, Leatherhead KT22 0QH* Tel (01372) 842071
E-mail vicar@oxshott.co.uk

CRETNEY, Mrs Antonia Lois. b 48. York Univ BA69 Bris Univ BA87 PGCE89. S Dios Minl Tr Scheme 92. **d** 94 **p** 95. NSM Bedminster *Bris* 94-96; C 96-97; P-in-c Beedon and Peasemore w W Ilsley and Farnborough *Ox* 97-99; R 99-04; Deanery P Wantage from 04; Bp's Adv for Women in Ord Min from 05. *8 Elm Farm Close, Grove, Wantage OX12 9FD* Tel (01235) 763192 E-mail antcret@aol.com

CRIBB, Robert John. b 22. Spurgeon's Coll 45. **d** 85 **p** 86. NSM Curry Rivel w Fivehead and Swell *B & W* 85-89; rtd 89; Perm to Offic *B & W* 89-94. *4 Heale Lane, Curry Rivel, Langport TA10 0PG* Tel (01458) 252333

CRICHTON, James Kenneth. b 35. Glouc Sch of Min 78. **d** 80 **p** 80. NSM Minchinhampton *Glouc* 80-83; NSM Nailsworth 83-86; Dep Chapl HM Pris Pentonville 86-87; Chapl HM Pris The Mount 87-97; rtd 97. *Pennant, Horeb, Llandysul SA44 4JG* Tel (01559) 362448

CRICK, Peter. b 39. Lon Univ BD68 NY Univ DMin84. Wells Th Coll 66. **d** 67 **p** 68. C Horsham *Chich* 67-71; Asst Dioc Youth Officer *Ox* 71-75; R Denham 75-88; Bp's Adv for CME *Dur* 88-97; P-in-c Coniscliffe 88-97; Hon Can Dur Cathl 93-97; R City of Bris 97-04; rtd 04. *7 Westfield Common, Hamble, Southampton SO31 4LB* Tel (023) 8045 7025
E-mail pandvcrick@btinternet.com

CRICK, Philip Benjamin Denton (Ben). b 33. Bris Univ BA63. Clifton Th Coll 60. **d** 64 **p** 65. C Clerkenwell St Jas and St Jo w St Pet *Lon* 64-67; CF 67-72; C Southall Green St Jo *Lon* 72-75; P-in-c Southall H Trin 75-83; P-in-c Kidbrooke St Jas *S'wark* 83-85; TV 85-92; C E Acton St Dunstan w St Thos *Lon* 92-95; Sub-Chapl HM Pris Wormwood Scrubs 92-95; rtd 95; Perm to Offic *Cant* from 95; Sub-Chapl HM Pris from 95. *232 Canterbury Road, Birchington CT7 9TD* Tel (01843) 846049 Mobile 07818-040651 E-mail ben.crick@argonet.co.uk

CRIDLAND, Clarissa Rosemary Dorothea. b 55. STETS 03. **d** 06 **p** 07. NSM Coleford w Holcombe *B & W* from 06. *4 Rock Terrace, Church Street, Coleford, Radstock BA3 5NF* Tel (01373) 812705 Mobile 07800-578967
E-mail clarissacridland@hotmail.co.uk

CRINKS, Kevin David. b 63. Aston Tr Scheme 86 Sarum & Wells Th Coll BTh91. **d** 93 **p** 94. C Aylesford *Roch* 93-96; C Hessle *York* 96-97; TV Upholland *Liv* 97-00; V Platt Bridge 00-09; P-in-c Leigh St Mary *Man* from 09. *The Vicarage, Westleigh Lane, Leigh WN7 5NW* Tel (01942) 882883 Mobile 07947-807767 E-mail kcrinks@btinternet.com

CRIPPS, Martyn Cyril Rowland. b 46. Birm Univ LLB68 Solicitor 71. Wycliffe Hall Ox 80. **d** 82 **p** 83. C Canford Magna *Sarum* 82-86; V Preston St Cuth *Blackb* 86-91; Warden Les Cotils *Win* 94-96; V Gipsy Hill Ch Ch *S'wark* 96-00; R Ashmanhaugh, Barton Turf etc *Nor* 00-04; P-in-c Davenham *Ches* 04-06; R from 06. *The Rectory, Church Street, Davenham, Northwich CW9 8NF* Tel (01606) 42450
E-mail mandmc@btopenworld.com

CRIPPS, Michael Frank Douglas. b 28. Ch Ch Ox BA50 MA53. Ridley Hall Cam 58. **d** 59 **p** 60. C Cambridge Gt St Mary w St Mich *Ely* 59-62; Ceylon 62-66; C-in-c Swindon Covingham CD *Bris* 66-72; V Swindon St Paul 72-73; P-in-c Aldbourne and Baydon *Sarum* 73; TV Whitton 73-81; C Marlborough 81-94; rtd 94; Chapl Pau *Eur* 94-96; Perm to Offic *Sarum* from 96. *1 Irving Way, Marlborough SN8 1UE* Tel (01672) 512748

CRITCHELL, Denise Eileen. b 49. SAOMC 96. **d** 99 **p** 00. C Flackwell Heath *Ox* 99-03; TV Risborough from 03. *The Vicarage, Church Lane, Lacey Green, Princes Risborough HP27 0QX* Tel (01844) 347741
E-mail denise@dncritchell.fsnet.co.uk

CRITCHLEY, Colin. b 41. Dur Univ BA63 Liv Univ MA69 AFBPsS94. NW Ord Course 75. **d** 78 **p** 79. NSM Halewood *Liv* 78-06; Dioc Child Protection Adv 96-06; rtd 06. *53 Elwyn Drive, Halewood, Liverpool L26 0UX* Tel 0151-487 5710 Fax 280 4937

CRITCHLEY, Mrs Patsy Eva. b 49. Reading Univ CertEd70. ERMC 04. **d** 07 **p** 08. NSM Meppershall and Shefford *St Alb* from 07. *39 Rooktree Way, Haynes, Bedford MK45 3PT* Tel (01234) 381510 E-mail patsy@critchley04.plus.com

CRITCHLOW, Mrs Anne-Louise. b 51. Westf Coll Lon BA73 Qu Mary Coll Lon MA75 Leeds Univ MA05 Grenoble Univ MèsL74 Cam Univ PGCE76. NOC 03. **d** 05 **p** 06. C Eccles *Man* 05-08; TV Eccles from 08. *St Andrew's Vicarage, 11 Abbey Grove, Eccles, Manchester M30 9QN* Tel 0161-707 9996
E-mail mmcritchlow@btinternet.com

CRITCHLOW (née KHARITONOVA), Natalia (Tasha). b 74. Westcott Ho Cam. **d** 09. C Brondesbury Ch Ch and St Laur *Lon* from 09. *The Vicarage, 13 Forty Avenue, Wembley HA9 8JL* Tel (020) 8908 5995 Mobile 07540-588860

CRITCHLOW, Trevor Francis. b 61. Lanc Univ BA83 K Coll Lon MA96. Westcott Ho Cam 88. **d** 90 **p** 91. C Croydon St Jo *S'wark* 90-92; C Lewisham St Mary 92-94; Perm to Offic *Ely* 94-05; Development Dir Westmr St Matt *Lon* 95-99; TV Wembley Park *Lon* from 05; CME Officer Willesden Area from 06. *The Vicarage, 13 Forty Avenue, Wembley HA9 8JL* Tel (020) 8908 5995 Mobile 07871-456322 Fax 07092-868327
E-mail trevor.critchlow@googlemail.com

CRITTALL, Richard Simon. b 47. Sussex Univ BA69 Linacre Coll Ox BA71. St Steph Ho Ox 69. **d** 72 **p** 73. C Oswestry H Trin *Lich* 72-75; C E Grinstead St Mary *Chich* 75-78; TV Brighton Resurr 78-83; R E Blatchington 83-95; V Heathfield St Rich 95-07; Dioc Ecum Officer *Ex* from 07; P-in-c Broadhembury, Payhembury and Plymtree from 07. *The Rectory, Broadhembury, Honiton EX14 3LT* Tel (01404) 841848
E-mail simoncrittall@breathmail.net

CROAD, Arthur Robert. b 35. Down Coll Cam BA58 MA61. Clifton Th Coll 58. **d** 61 **p** 62. C Sneinton St Chris w St Phil *S'well* 61-64; C Kinson *Sarum* 64-72; R Sherfield English *Win* 72-74; R Awbridge w Sherfield English 74-92; P-in-c Hinton Ampner w Bramdean and Kilmeston 92-01; rtd 01. *48 Woodfield Drive, Winchester SO22 5PU* Tel (01962) 851978

CROAD, David Richard. b 31. Reading Univ BSc55. Clifton Th Coll. **d** 57 **p** 58. C Iver *Ox* 57-60; C Rushden *Pet* 60-63; V Loudwater *Ox* 63-72; SW Area Sec CPAS 72-78; V Bovingdon *St Alb* 78-91; Min Hampstead St Jo Downshire Hill Prop Chpl *Lon* 91-94; rtd 94; Perm to Offic *Guildf* and *Win* from 97. *8 Compass Court, 42-44 Winn Road, Southampton SO17 1EZ*

CROCKER, Jeremy Robert. b 67. S Bank Univ MA94 Heythrop Coll Lon MA98 MCIM92. Westcott Ho Cam 94 CITC 96. **d** 97 **p** 98. C Stevenage H Trin *St Alb* 97-00; TV Bp's Hatfield 00-04; TR Elstow from 04. *The Abbey Vicarage, Church End, Elstow, Bedford MK42 9XT* Tel (01234) 261477
E-mail jeremy.crocker@tesco.net

CROCKER, Keith Gwillam. b 49. Lanchester Poly Cov BSc70. Oak Hill Th Coll 74. **d** 77 **p** 78. C Whitnash *Cov* 77-80; C Gt Horton *Bradf* 80-83; C Grays SS Pet and Paul, S Stifford and W Thurrock *Chelmsf* 83-84; TV Grays Thurrock 84-88; TR Wreningham *Nor* 88-95; P-in-c New Catton Ch Ch 95-99; V from 99. *Christ Church Vicarage, 65 Elm Grove Lane, Norwich NR3 3LF* Tel (01603) 408332 E-mail keith.crocker@which.net

CROCKER, Peter David. b 56. Lon Univ MB, BS80 MRCGP. Mon Dioc Tr Scheme 93. **d** 96 **p** 97. NSM Bassaleg *Mon* 96-02; TV 02-06; P-in-c Bedwas and Rudry 06-07; R Bedwas w Machen w Rudry from 07. *1A Navigation Street, Trethomas, Caerphilly CF83 8DJ* Tel (029) 2088 5220

CROCKER, Richard Campbell. b 54. Nottm Univ BSc76. Wycliffe Hall Ox BA81 MA85. **d** 82 **p** 83. C Summerfield *Birm* 82-84; Chapl K Edw Sch Birm 84-91; R Council Bluffs USA 91-99; Assoc R Truro Episc Ch from 99. *10520 Main Street, Fairfax VA 22030, USA* Tel (001) (703) 273 1300
E-mail rcrocker@trurochurch.org

CROCKETT, Peter James Sinclair. b 44. Sarum & Wells Th Coll 74. **d** 77 **p** 78. C Heavitree *Ex* 77; C Heavitree w Ex St Paul 78-80; TV Ex St Thos and Em 80-87; V Countess Wear from 87; Chapl St Loyes Tr Coll for the Disabled from 87; Chapl W of England Sch for those w little or no sight from 87; CF (TA) from 88. *The Vicarage, 375 Topsham Road, Exeter EX2 6HB* Tel (01392) 873263

CROFT, James Stuart. b 57. K Coll Lon BD80 Leeds Univ MA95 Ripon Coll Cuddesdon 83. **d** 85 **p** 86. C Friern Barnet St Jas *Lon* 85-88; R Lea *Linc* 88-93; V Knaith 88-93; V Upton 88-93; R Gate Burton 88-93; R Lea Gp 93-97; Chapl N Lincs Coll 90-93; V Froyle and Holybourne *Win* from 97. *The Vicarage, 7 Church Lane, Holybourne, Alton GU34 4HD* Tel (01420) 83240 E-mail jamescroft57@fsmail.net

CROFT, Jennifer Sara. b 69. Leeds Univ BSc94. Ripon Coll Cuddesdon 99. **d** 01 **p** 02. C Lillington *Cov* 01-05; Chapl Cov Univ from 05; Chapl amongst Deaf People 03-08. *St James's Vicarage, 171 Abbey Road, Coventry CV3 4BE* Tel (024) 7630 1960 E-mail j.croft@coventry.ac.uk

CROFT, Michael Peter. b 60. GradIPM MCIPD95 FCIPD08. Trin Coll Bris BA88. **d** 88 **p** 89. C Drypool *York* 88-91; P-in-c Sandal St Cath *Wakef* 91-95; V 95-07; Perm to Offic from 07. *5 College Terrace, Ackworth, Pontefract WF7 7LB* Tel (01977) 611251 Mobile 07793-820675 E-mail mike@caleb-group.co.uk

CROFT, Ronald. b 30. St Aid Birkenhead 61. **d** 63 **p** 64. C Lawton Moor *Man* 63-65; C Withington St Crispin 65-66; R 74-86; C Prestwich St Marg 66-67; V Oldham St Ambrose 67-71; P-in-c Oldham St Jas 67-68; V 68-71; V Prestwich St Hilda 71-74; P-in-c 96-00; R Heaton Norris St Thos 86-96; rtd 00. *St Hilda's Vicarage, 55 Whittaker Lane, Prestwich, Manchester M25 5ET* Tel 0161-773 1642

CROFT, Simon Edward Owen. b 51. Ch Ch Coll Cant CertEd73. St Steph Ho Ox 75. **d** 78 **p** 79. C Heavitree w Ex St Paul 78-83; V Seaton 83-93; P-in-c Ex St Mark 93-96; P-in-c Ex St Sidwell and St Matt 96; R Ex St Mark, St Sidwell and St Matt from 96. *St Mark's Rectory, 8 Lamacraft Drive, Exeter EX4 8QS* Tel (01392) 421050 E-mail simoncdevon@yahoo.co.uk

✠**CROFT, The Rt Revd Steven John Lindsey.** b 57. Worc Coll Ox BA80 MA83 St Jo Coll Dur PhD84. Cranmer Hall Dur 80. **d** 83 **p** 84 **c** 09. C Enfield St Andr *Lon* 83-87; V Ovenden *Wakef* 87-96; Dioc Miss Consultant 94-96; Warden Cranmer Hall Dur 96-04; Abps' Missr and Team Ldr Fresh Expressions 04-09; Bp Sheff from 09. *Bishopscroft, Snaithing Lane, Sheffield S10 3LG* Tel 0114-230 2170 Fax 263 0110
E-mail bishop@bishopofsheffield.org.uk

CROFT, Canon Warren David. b 36. ACT ThL62. **d** 61 **p** 62. Australia 61-69 and from 79; Papua New Guinea 69-77; C Mottingham St Andr *S'wark* 77-78; Hon Can Dogura 86; C Hunters Hill 87; R Kogarah 87-01; rtd 01. *43 Sierra Avenue, PO Box 3078, Bateau Bay NSW 2261, Australia* Tel (0061) (2) 4333 3967 Mobile 425-206621 Fax 9553 8594
E-mail isandwas@bigpond.com

CROFT, Canon William Stuart. b 53. Trin Hall Cam BA76 MA79 K Coll Lon MTh88. Ripon Coll Cuddesdon BA80. **d** 80 **p** 81. C Friern Barnet St Jas *Lon* 80-83; Tutor Chich Th Coll 83-92; Vice-Prin 88-92; V Fernhurst *Chich* 92-98; Dir of Ords *Pet* 98-03; Prec and Min Can Pet Cathl 98-01; Can Res and Prec 01-04; Non-res Can from 04; P-in-c Longthorpe from 04; Liturg Officer 03-04. *The Vicarage, 315 Thorpe Road, Longthorpe, Peterborough PE3 6LU* Tel (01733) 263016
E-mail williamsbill_croft@hotmail.com

CROFTON, Edwin Alan. b 46. Univ Coll Ox BA68 MA72. Cranmer Hall Dur. **d** 73 **p** 74. C Hull St Jo Newland *York* 73-77; C Worksop St Jo *S'well* 77-81; Chapl Kilton Hosp Worksop 80-81; V Scarborough St Mary w Ch Ch and H Apostles *York* 81-91; Miss to Seamen 81-91; Chapl St Mary's Hosp Scarborough 82-91; V Cheltenham Ch Ch *Glouc* 91-02; RD Cheltenham 95-00; Hon Can Glouc Cathl 01-02; TR Eccles *Man* from 02; P-in-c Hope St Jas 07-09; AD Eccles from 05. *The Rectory, 12B Westminster Road, Eccles, Manchester M30 9EB* Tel 0161-281 5739 E-mail ea_crofton@msn.com

CROFTON, Robert Edwin. b 75. UEA BSc98. Ridley Hall Cam 03. **d** 06 **p** 07. C Churchdown *Glouc* from 06. *11 Chapel Hay Lane, Churchdown, Gloucester GL3 2EY* Tel (01452) 713080

CROFTS, David Thomas. b 47. Cheshire Coll of Educn CertEd68 Open Univ BA76. Dioc OLM tr scheme. **d** 99 **p** 00. OLM Bury St Edmunds St Mary *St E* from 99. *8 Linton Gardens, Bury St Edmunds IP33 2DZ* Tel (01284) 761801 Fax 765501
E-mail david@pandda.co.uk

CROFTS, Ian Hamilton. b 55. BSc. St Jo Coll Nottm 79. **d** 82 **p** 83. C Leamington Priors St Paul *Cov* 82-86; C Oadby *Leic* 86; TV 86-91; V Maidstone St Faith *Cant* 91-07; V Forty Hill Jes Ch *Lon* from 07. *The Vicarage, Forty Hill, Enfield EN2 9EU* Tel (020) 8363 1935 E-mail ian.crofts@gmail.com

CROFTS, Stephen Andrew. b 76. Ch Ch Coll Cant BA98 Ox Brookes Univ MA09. Ripon Coll Cuddesdon 07. **d** 09. C Birstall and Wanlip *Leic* from 09. *22 Oakfield Avenue, Birstall, Leicester LE4 3DQ*

CROISDALE-APPLEBY, Mrs Carolynn Elizabeth. b 46. Ch Ch Coll Cant CertEd68. SAOMC 01. **d** 04 **p** 05. NSM Amersham and Gt Coxwell w Buscot, Coleshill etc *Ox* 04-07; NSM Beaconsfield from 07. *Abbotsholme, Hervines Road, Amersham HP6 5HS* Tel (01494) 725194 Fax 725474
E-mail croisdaleappleby@aol.com

CROMARTY, Andrew Robert McKean. b 63. Newc Univ MB, BS86 Homerton Coll Cam PGCE89 St Jo Coll Dur BA04. Cranmer Hall Dur 02. **d** 06 **p** 07. NSM Crook *Dur* from 06. *17 Silver Street, Wolsingham, Bishop Auckland DL13 3EJ* Tel (01388) 528676 E-mail andrew@cromarty4500.fsnet.co.uk

CROMPTON (née KILGOUR), Mrs Christine Mary. b 39. Newnham Coll Cam BA61 MA York Univ MA86 Lon Inst of Educn PGCE62. **d** 06 **p** 07. OLM Newc St Geo and St Hilda from 06. *11 South Bend, Newcastle upon Tyne NE3 5TR* Tel 0191-236 3679

CROMPTON, Canon Roger <u>Martyn</u> Francis. b 47. Sheff Univ BA69 PGCE73 St Jo Coll Dur BA84. Cranmer Hall Dur 82. **d** 85 **p** 86. C Woodford Wells *Chelmsf* 85-89; V Golcar *Wakef* from 89; RD Huddersfield 99-09; Hon Can Wakef Cathl from 06. *The Vicarage, Church Street, Golcar, Huddersfield HD7 4PX* Tel (01484) 654647
E-mail martyncrompton@stjohnsgolcar.freeserve.co.uk

CROMPTON-BATTERSBY, Holly Jo. b 74. Bath Coll of HE BA95. Wycliffe Hall Ox BTh01. **d** 01 **p** 02. C Luton Lewsey St Hugh *St Alb* 01-04; Chapl Bennett Memorial Dioc Sch Tunbridge Wells 04-07; Chapl Bedgebury Sch Kent 05-06. *Culford School, Bury St Edmunds IP28 6TX* Tel 07761-628335 (mobile) E-mail hollycrompton@hotmail.com

CRONIN, Mrs Linda Nancy. b 61. NTMTC BA08. **d** 08 **p** 09. C Barrow St Mark *Carl* from 08. *50 Furness Park Road, Barrow-in-Furness LA14 5PS* Tel (01229) 821510 Mobile 07817-678775 E-mail linda@thecronins.org

CRONK, Simon Nicholas. b 59. CQSW85 Poly of Wales BA82. Wycliffe Hall Ox 89. **d** 92 **p** 93. C Cheltenham Ch Ch *Glouc* 92-96; V Cinderford St Steph w Littledean 96-02; V Hughenden *Ox* from 02. *The Vicarage, Valley Road, Hughenden Valley, High Wycombe HP14 4PF* Tel (01494) 563439

CROOK, Colin. b 44. JP78. Lon Univ BSc(Econ)74 ALA67 FLA93. S'wark Ord Course 87. **d** 90 **p** 91. NSM Dartford Ch Ch *Roch* 90-97; P-in-c Crockenhill All So 97-05; Dioc Ecum Officer 96-04; rtd 05; Perm to Offic *Chich* from 06. *11 Fulbourne House, 56 Blackwater Road, Eastbourne BN20 7DN* Tel (01323) 728477 E-mail revcolincrook@yahoo.co.uk

CROOK, David Creighton. b 37. Trin Coll Cam BA61 MA68. Cuddesdon Coll 61. **d** 63 **p** 64. C Workington St Mich *Carl* 63-66; C Penrith St Andr 66-70; V Barrow St Jas 70-78; V Maryport 78-81; TV Greystoke, Matterdale and Mungrisdale 81-87; TV Watermillock 84-87; V Hesket-in-the-Forest and Armathwaite 87-98; rtd 98; Perm to Offic *Carl* from 01. *11 Lowther Street, Penrith CA11 7UW* Tel (01768) 866773

CROOK, Mrs Diana Elizabeth. b 47. Hull Univ BA73 Open Univ BSc93 City Univ MSc97 Middx Univ BA03 RGN70 CPsychol. NTMTC 00. **d** 03 **p** 04. NSM Waltham H Cross *Chelmsf* 03-07; P-in-c Uley w Owlpen and Nympsfield *Glouc* from 07. *The Rectory, 2 The Green, Uley, Dursley GL11 5SN* Tel (01453) 861363 *or* 860249 E-mail revdiana@dianacrook.org

CROOK, Graham Leslie. b 49. Chich Th Coll 74. **d** 76 **p** 77. C Withington St Crispin *Man* 76-79; C Prestwich St Marg 79-82; V Nelson St Bede *Blackb* 82-92; Chapl Southend Health Care NHS Trust from 92; Bp's Adv for Hosp Chapl (Bradwell Area) *Chelmsf* 98-04. *Ebenezer, 249 Woodgrange Drive, Southend-on-Sea SS1 2SQ* Tel (01702) 613429

✠**CROOK, The Rt Revd John Michael.** b 40. Univ of Wales (Lamp) BA62. Coll of Resurr Mirfield 62. **d** 64 **p** 65 **c** 99. C Horninglow *Lich* 64-66; C Bloxwich 66-70; R Inverness St Mich *Mor* 70-78; R Inverness St Jo 74-78; Dioc Youth Chapl *St And* 78-86; R Aberfoyle 78-87; R Doune 78-87; R Callander 78-87; Can St Ninian's Cathl Perth 85-99; R Bridge of Allan 87-99; Syn Clerk 97-99; Bp Mor 99-06; rtd 06; Lic to Offic *St And* from 07. *8 Buccleuch Court, Dunblane FK15 0AR* Tel (01786) 826872

CROOK, Malcolm Geoffrey. b 53. St Steph Ho Ox 88. **d** 90 **p** 91. C Pet St Jude 90-93; C Barrow St Matt *Carl* 93-96; TV Langley and Parkfield *Man* 96-97; P-in-c Sneinton St Steph w St Alb *S'well* 03-04; P-in-c Sneinton St Matthias 03-04; V Sneinton St Steph w St Matthias from 04. *The Vicarage, 4 Barnston Road, Nottingham NG2 4HW* Tel 0115-924 1917 E-mail malcrook@hotmail.com

CROOK, Marie Elizabeth. b 46. CBDTI 02. **d** 05 **p** 06. OLM Over Darwen St Jas *Blackb* 05-07; NSM from 07. *56 Roman Road, Darwen BB3 3BN* Tel (01254) 775820 Mobile 07742-029757 E-mail mariecrook500@hotmail.com

CROOK, Rowland William. b 39. Tyndale Hall Bris 61. **d** 64 **p** 65. C Penn Fields *Lich* 64-68; C Lower Broughton St Clem w St Matthias *Man* 68-70; C Bucknall and Bagnall *Lich* 70-76; V New Shildon *Dur* 76-86; V Northwich St Luke and H Trin *Ches* 86-99; P-in-c Helsby and Dunham-on-the-Hill 99-04; rtd 04; Perm to Offic *Ches* from 04. *14 Bollington Avenue, Northwich CW9 8SB* Tel (01606) 45177
E-mail rowland.crook@talktalk.net

CROOK, Timothy Mark. b 68. Oak Hill Th Coll BA00. **d** 00 **p** 01. C Charles w Plymouth St Matthias *Ex* 00-03; C Harold Wood *Chelmsf* 03-09; V S w N Bersted *Chich* from 09. *121 Victoria Drive, Bognor Regis PO21 2EH*

CROOKES, Keith John. b 54. Sheff Univ BA94 Leeds Univ PhD02. NOC 02. **d** 05 **p** 06. NSM Deepcar *Sheff* 05-09; NSM Sheff St Paul from 09. *219 High Greave, Sheffield S5 9GS* Tel 0114-240 3790 E-mail keith.crookes@sheffield.anglican.org

CROOKS, Canon Christopher John (<u>Kip</u>). b 53. St Bede's Coll Dur CertEd75. Trin Coll Bris BA90. **d** 90 **p** 91. C The Quinton *Birm* 90-93; V Ince Ch Ch *Liv* 93-03; R Much Woolton from 03; AD Liv S from 06; Hon Can Liv Cathl from 06. *The Rectory, 67 Church Road, Woolton, Liverpool L25 6DA* Tel 0151-428 1853

CROOKS, Canon David William Talbot. b 52. TCD BA75 MA78 BD83. **d** 77 **p** 78. C Glendermott *D & R* 77-81; C Edin Old St Paul 81-84; I Taughboyne, Craigadooish, Newtown-cunningham etc *D & R* from 84; Bp's Dom Chapl 88-07; Can Raphoe Cathl from 91. *Taughboyne Rectory, Churchtown, Carrigans, Lifford, Co Donegal, Republic of Ireland* Tel (00353) (74) 914 0135 Mobile 86-212 5670
E-mail dcrooks@eircom.net

CROOKS, Eric. b 34. Oak Hill Th Coll 68. **d** 70 **p** 71. C Chadderton Ch Ch *Man* 70-73; C Bolton St Paul 73-75; C Lurgan Ch the Redeemer *D & D* 75-77; I Aghaderg w Donaghmore 77-80; I Dundonald 80-01; rtd 01. *17 Cumberland Close, Dundonald, Belfast BT16 2AW* Tel (028) 9048 0443

CROOKS, Mrs Jayne Barbara. b 52. Birm Univ BSc73 Avery Hill Coll PGCE74. WMMTC 01. **d** 04 **p** 05. NSM Kings Norton *Birm* 04-08; C from 08. *15 Chalgrove Avenue, Birmingham B38 8YP* Tel 0121-459 3733
E-mail jayne.crooks@blueyonder.co.uk

CROOKS, Kenneth Robert. b 36. CEng FIEE FCMI. S'wark Ord Course 80. **d** 83 **p** 84. NSM Wisley w Pyrford *Guildf* 83-92; Perm to Offic *Ex* from 98. *Foxes Corner, Peak Hill Road, Sidmouth EX10 0NW* Tel (01395) 577578

CROOKS, Kip. *See* CROOKS, Canon Christopher John

CROOKS, Peter James. b 50. MBE09. St Jo Coll Cam BA72. Cranmer Hall Dur. **d** 76 **p** 77. C Onslow Square St Paul *Lon* 76-77; C Brompton H Trin w Onslow Square St Paul 77-79; C Wembley St Jo 79-82; CMS 82-92; Lebanon 83-89; Syria 85-89; Dean Jerusalem 89-92; P-in-c Hunningham and Wappenbury w Weston under Wetherley *Cov* 92-01; P-in-c Offchurch 96-01; V Long Itchington and Marton 96-01; CMS Iran 01-02; TV Dolgellau w Llanfachreth and Brithdir etc *Ban* 02-04; Chapl Aden Ch Ch Yemen 04-09; Dir Ras Morbat Clinics 04-09; P-in-c Arthog w Fairbourne w Llangelynnin w Rhoslefain *Ban* from 09; rtd 09. *Penbryn Croft, Cader Road, Dolgellau LL40 1RN* Tel (01341) 421155 Mobile 07866-276562
E-mail pncrooks@ukonline.co.uk

CROOS, John <u>Princely</u>. b 59. Madurai Univ BA82. Oak Hill Th Coll BA04. **d** 04 **p** 05. C Becontree St Mary *Chelmsf* 04-07; C E Ham St Paul 07-08; Chapl Lon City Miss from 08. *103 Browning Road, London E12 6RB* Tel (020) 8472 4143
E-mail sprincecroos@hotmail.com

CROSBIE, Andrew. b 62. St Steph Ho Ox 96. **d** 98 **p** 99. C St Paul's Cathl St Helena 98-00; CF 00-03; Perm to Offic *Blackb* from 03; Chantry P Shrine of Our Lady of Haddington from 08. *151 Ashley Gardens, London SW1P 1HW,* or *Oulcottis, Barjarg Tower, Auldgirth, Dumfries DG2 0TN* Tel (020) 7233 8240 Mobile 07791-540535 E-mail fathercrosbie@aol.com

CROSBIE, Timothy John. b 44. ACMA72. **d** 00 **p** 01. OLM Shotley *St E* 00-08. *27 Kitchener Way, Shotley Gate, Ipswich IP9 1RN* Tel (01473) 787316
E-mail tim@timcrosbie.fsnet.co.uk

CROSBY, Bernard Edward. b 47. Oak Hill Th Coll 86. **d** 88 **p** 89. C Springfield H Trin *Chelmsf* 88-91; C Penn Fields *Lich* 91-94; V St Leonards St Ethelburga *Chich* 94-02; R Fairlight, Guestling and Pett from 02. *The Rectory, 15 Battery Hill, Fairlight, Hastings TN35 4AP* Tel (01424) 812799
E-mail bernardcrosby@supanet.com

CROSBY, David Edward. b 48. SAOMC 96. **d** 99 **p** 00. NSM Newbury *Ox* 99-01; C The Bourne and Tilford *Guildf* 01-04; P-in-c Hurst Green and Mitton *Bradf* 04. *Address temp unknown*

CROSFIELD, Canon George <u>Philip</u> Chorley. b 24. OBE90. Selw Coll Cam BA50 MA55. Edin Th Coll 46. **d** 51 **p** 52. C Edin St Dav 51-53; C St Andrews St Andr *St And* 53-55; R Hawick *Edin* 55-60; Chapl Gordonstoun Sch 60-67; Can St Mary's Cathl 68-91; Vice-Provost 68-70; Provost 70-90; R Edin St Mary 70-90; rtd 90; Hon Can St Mary's Cathl from 91; Hon C Penicuik from 91; Hon C W Linton from 91. *21 Biggar Road, Silverburn, Penicuik EH26 9LQ* Tel (01968) 676607

CROSS, Alan. *See* CROSS, Thomas Alan

CROSS, Canon Alan. b 43. Chich Th Coll 68. **d** 70 **p** 71. C Bordesley St Oswald *Birm* 70; C S Yardley St Mich 70-73; C Colchester St Jas, All SS, St Nic and St Runwald *Chelmsf* 73-77; V Leigh-on-Sea St Jas 77-89; V Woodford St Barn 89-09; Hon Can Chelmsf Cathl 97-09; rtd 09; Perm to Offic *Chelmsf* from 09. *11 Grayling Drive, Colchester CO4 3EN* Tel (01206) 790984

CROSS, Preb Elizabeth Mary. b 46. Leeds Univ BA69 CertEd70. Sarum Th Coll 80. **dss** 83 **d** 87 **p** 94. Wootton Bassett *Sarum* 83-86; Westbury 86-87; Par Dn 87-89; C Glastonbury w Meare, W Pennard and Godney *B & W* 89-95; Asst Dir of Ords 89-95; Preb Wells Cathl 93-07; V Wedmore w Theale and Blackford 95-07; rtd 07. *7 Carpenters Close, Stratton, Dorchester DT2 9SR* Tel (01305) 260499

CROSS, Canon Greville Shelly. b 49. Sarum & Wells Th Coll 73. **d** 76 **p** 77. C Kidderminster St Mary *Worc* 76-80; P-in-c Worc St Mark 80-81; TV Worc St Martin w St Pet, St Mark etc 81-85; R Inkberrow w Cookhill and Kington w Dormston 85-98; RD Evesham 93-97; R Old Swinford Stourbridge from 98; RD Stourbridge 01-04; Hon Can Worc Cathl from 05. *The Rectory,*

Rectory Road, Stourbridge DY8 2HA Tel (01384) 395410 *or* 441003 E-mail canon.cross@btinternet.com

CROSS, James Stuart. b 36. Magd Coll Ox BA65 MA71. Ripon Hall Ox 62. **d** 65 **p** 66. C Leckhampton SS Phil and Jas *Glouc* 65-66; CF 66-92; QHC 89-92; R Stretford St Pet *Man* 92-00; rtd 00. *St Davids, Redbrook Road, Monmouth NP25 3LY* Tel and fax (01600) 715977 E-mail jimcross1@aol.com

CROSS, Jeremy Burkitt. b 45. St Pet Coll Ox BA68 MA71. Wycliffe Hall Ox 67. **d** 69 **p** 70. C Mildenhall *St E* 69-72; C Lindfield *Chich* 72-77; V Framfield 77-89; R St Leonards St Leon 89-01; R Birling, Addington, Ryarsh and Trottiscliffe *Roch* from 01. *The Vicarage, Birling Road, Ryarsh, West Malling ME19 5AW* Tel (01732) 842249
E-mail j-scross@81afilsham.freeserve.co.uk

CROSS, John Henry Laidlaw. b 30. Peterho Cam BA53 MA57. Ridley Hall Cam 53. **d** 55 **p** 56. C Ealing Dean St Jo *Lon* 55-58; C Gt Baddow *Chelmsf* 58-60; V Maidenhead St Andr and St Mary *Ox* 60-68; News Ed *C of E Newspaper* 68-71; Assoc Ed 71-72; Ed 72-75; Hon C St Pet Cornhill *Lon* 84-87; P-in-c 87-95; Hon C Chelsea All SS 76-93; rtd 95. *8 Pinetum Close, Devizes SN10 5EW* Tel (01380) 722997 E-mail revjhlcross@aol.com

CROSS, Kenneth James. b 69. Trin Coll Bris BA09. **d** 09. C Alcombe *B & W* from 09. *31 Manor Road, Minehead TA24 6EJ* Tel (01643) 706467 Mobile 07951-568703
E-mail kennethjcross@googlemail.com

CROSS, Canon Michael Anthony. b 45. Leeds Univ BA67 BA69. Coll of Resurr Mirfield 68. **d** 70 **p** 71. S Africa 70-73; C Adel *Ripon* 74-76; Chapl Birm Univ 76-81; V Chapel Allerton *Ripon* 81-92; V Headingley 92-04; AD Headingley 96-01; P-in-c Wetherby from 04; Hon Can Ripon Cathl from 06. *3 Lazenby Drive, Wetherby LS22 6WL* Tel (01937) 582423
E-mail mandacross@yahoo.co.uk

CROSS, Canon Michael Henry. b 28. Liv Univ BVSc50. Cuddesdon Coll 74. **d** 76 **p** 77. C Ledbury *Heref* 76-79; P-in-c Bosbury 79-82; P-in-c Coddington 79-82; P-in-c Wellington Heath 79-82; V Bosbury w Wellington Heath etc 82-83; V Bishop's Castle w Mainstone 83-84; P-in-c Snead 83-84; V Morland, Thrimby and Gt Strickland *Carl* 84-93; RD Appleby 91-93; Hon Can Carl Cathl 92-93; rtd 93; Perm to Offic *Carl* from 93. *Hollin Knowle, Kilmidyke Road, Grange-over-Sands LA11 7AQ* Tel (01539) 535908

CROSS, Mrs Rachel Beth. b 73. Ox Brookes Univ BA95. STETS 06. **d** 09. C Ponteland *Newc* from 09. *82 Dunsgreen, Ponteland, Newcastle upon Tyne NE20 9ES* Tel 07783-685901 (mobile)
E-mail rachelcross@bigfoot.com

CROSS, Stephanie. b 53. Essex Univ BSc74 Loughb Univ MSc76 Bris Univ BA01 Reading Univ PGCE93. Trin Coll Bris 99. **d** 01 **p** 02. C Lytchett Minster *Sarum* 01-05; TV Wheatley *Ox* from 05. *The New Vicarage, Cox Lane, Stanton St John, Oxford OX33 1HW* Tel (01865) 351142
E-mail crossstevie@hotmail.com

CROSS, Thomas Alan. b 58. CITC BTh05. **d** 05 **p** 06. C Drumglass w Moygashel *Arm* 05-08; I Lissan from 08; Dom Chapl to Abp Arm from 09. *Lissan Rectory, 150 Moneymore Road, Cookstown BT80 8PY*

CROSSE, Mrs Anne-Marie. b 48. **d** 99. NSM W Worthing St Jo *Chich* 99-02; NSM Arundel w Tortington and S Stoke 02-05; Perm to Offic from 05. *25 Strathmore Close, Worthing BN13 1PQ* Tel (01903) 247706 E-mail amcrosse@talktalk.net

CROSSEY, Nigel Nicholas. b 59. Cam Univ DA. **d** 84 **p** 85. C Drumglass w Moygashel *Arm* 84-87; I Magheraculmoney *Clogh* 87-93; CF 93-09; Chapl St Columba's Coll Dub from 09. *St Columba's College, Whitechurch, Dublin 16, Republic of Ireland* Tel (00353) (1) 4906791

CROSSLAND, Felix Parnell. b 20. CEng MIMechE57 Univ of Wales (Swansea) BSc49. St Deiniol's Hawarden 73. **d** 75 **p** 76. Hon C Skewen *Llan* 75-78; Hon C Neath w Llantwit 78-85; rtd 85; Perm to Offic from 85. *21 Cimla Road, Neath SA11 3PR* Tel (01639) 643560

CROSSLAND, June Marcia. b 44. **d** 01. OLM Monk Bretton *Wakef* from 01; OLM Staincross from 05. *16 Deacons Way, Barnsley S71 2HU* Tel (01226) 203895

CROSSLAND, Richard Henry. b 49. Ex Univ BA72. S'wark Ord Course 91. **d** 94 **p** 96. NSM Surbiton St Andr and St Mark *S'wark* 94-95; NSM Linc Cathl 95-98. *3 Vicars' Court, Minster Yard, Lincoln LN2 1PT* Tel (01522) 535225

CROSSLEY, Dennis Thomas. b 23. AKC52 St Boniface Warminster. **d** 53 **p** 54. C Crofton Park St Hilda *S'wark* 53-56; C Beddington 56-59; C Talbot Village *Sarum* 59-62; R Finchampstead *Ox* 62-97; rtd 97; Perm to Offic *Ox* from 97. *1 Larkswood Close, Sandhurst, Camberley GU47 8QJ*

CROSSLEY, George Alan. b 34. St Jo Coll Dur BA56. Cranmer Hall Dur. **d** 60 **p** 61. C Blackb St Steph 60-63; C Ashton-on-Ribble St Andr 63-65; V Oswaldtwistle St Paul 65-72; R Dufton *Carl* 72-73; P-in-c Milburn w Newbiggin 72-73; R Long Marton w Dufton and w Milburn 73-76; P-in-c Beckermet St Jo 76-78; V Beckermet St Jo and St Bridget w Ponsonby 78-84; Chapl Furness Gen Hosp 84-89; TV Newbarns w Hawcoat *Carl* 84-89; Chapl Princess R Hosp Telford 89-97; rtd 95; P-in-c Bilsborrow

Blackb 97-99; Perm to Offic from 00. *6 Eden Mount Way, Carnforth LA5 9XN* Tel (01524) 734568

CROSSLEY, George John. b 57. Bradf Univ BA81 PhD84. NOC 91. **d** 94 **p** 95. C Balderstone *Man* 94-98; V Branston w Tatenhill *Lich* 98-02; RD Tutbury 00-02; Chapl Burton Hosps NHS Trust from 04; P-in-c Burton St Chad *Lich* from 09. *St Chad's Vicarage, 113 Hunter Street, Burton-on-Trent DE14 2SS* Tel (01283) 564044 Mobile 07976-979755
E-mail george@gcrossley.wanadoo.co.uk

CROSSLEY, James Salter Baron. b 39. Linc Th Coll 70. **d** 72 **p** 74. C Chesterfield St Mary and All SS *Derby* 72-75; Chapl Doncaster R Infirmary 75-92; Chapl Doncaster R Infirmary and Montagu Hosp NHS Trust 92-95; Chapl Asst Tickhill Road and St Cath Hosps 75-92; Hon C Doncaster Intake *Sheff* 78-95; rtd 95; Perm to Offic *Sheff* 95-99 and *Ripon* from 00. *The Gables, Low Row, Richmond DL11 6NH* Tel (01748) 886429

CROSSLEY, Jeremy. *See* CROSSLEY, William Jeremy Hugh

CROSSLEY, Joan Winifred. b 57. Sussex Univ BA78 Leic Univ MA80 Univ Coll Lon PhD85. SAOMC 97. **d** 00 **p** 01. C Goldington *St Alb* 00-02; C Bedf St Mark 02-08; Asst Chapl Gt Ormond Street Hosp for Children NHS Trust 03-05; Asst Chapl Westmr Sch from 08. *Westminster School, Little Dean's Yard, London SW1P 3PF* Tel (020) 7963 1000 Fax 7963 1006
E-mail jwcrossley@aol.com

CROSSLEY, John Eric. b 51. St Martin's Coll Lanc BA92. Carl Dioc Tr Inst 92. **d** 94 **p** 95. C Westfield St Mary *Carl* 94-97; P-in-c Penrith w Newton Reigny and Plumpton Wall 97-02; Chapl Newton Rigg Coll of H&FE 97-02; TV Cartmel Peninsula *Carl* from 02. *The Vicarage, Station Road, Flookburgh, Grange-over-Sands LA11 7JY* Tel (01539) 558245 E-mail rjoncros@aol.com

CROSSLEY, Kenneth Ernest. b 38. NEOC 01. **d** 03 **p** 04. NSM Ripon Cathl from 03. *11 Station Drive, Ripon HG4 1JA* Tel (01765) 692499 E-mail kennethecrossley@aol.com

CROSSLEY, Canon Robert Scott. b 36. Lon Univ BSc61 BD68 PhD75. ALCD64. **d** 64 **p** 65. C Beckenham St Jo *Roch* 64-68; C Morden *S'wark* 68-72; Chapl Ridley Hall Cam 72-75; V Camberley St Paul *Guildf* 75-83; TR 83-98; RD Surrey Heath 81-84; Hon Can Guildf Cathl 89-98; rtd 98; Perm to Offic *Guildf* 98-01 and from 07; Hon C Camberley St Mich Yorktown 01-07. *20 Highbury Crescent, Camberley GU15 1JZ* Tel (01276) 500036 E-mail robertcrossley@ntlworld.com

CROSSLEY, Mrs Ruth Joy. b 54. Cranmer Hall Dur 00. **d** 02 **p** 03. C Cartmel Peninsula *Carl* 02-06; P-in-c Levens from 06; Bp's Adv for CME from 06. *The Vicarage, Vicarage Road, Levens, Kendal LA8 8PY* Tel (01539) 560223
E-mail rcross3357@aol.com

CROSSLEY, William Jeremy Hugh. b 55. St Jo Coll Dur BA76. Cranmer Hall Dur 81. **d** 84 **p** 85. C Gillingham St Mark *Roch* 84-87; C Ches Square St Mich w St Phil *Lon* 87-94; V Westminster St Jas the Less 94-00; R St Marg Lothbury and St Steph Coleman Street etc from 00; AD The City 06-09. *The Rectory, 1 St Olave's Court, London EC2V 8EX* Tel (020) 7600 2379 Fax 7606 1204 E-mail the.rector@stml.org.uk

CROSSMAN, Ms Sharon Margaret Joan. b 65. DipCOT87. Linc Th Coll BTh93. **d** 93 **p** 94. Par Dn Chippenham St Andr w Tytherton Lucas *Bris* 93-94; C 94-96; Chapl UWE 96-02; Hon C Almondsbury 97-98; Hon C Almondsbury and Olveston 98-02; Chapl Würzburg Univ Germany 02-03; TV Portishead *B & W* from 03; Chapl MU from 05. *25 Lambourne Way, Portishead, Bristol BS20 7LQ* Tel (01275) 840526
E-mail sharon.crossman@tdpenworld.com

CROSTHWAITE, George Roger. b 38. Dur Univ BSc62 Fuller Th Sem California DMin83. Ridley Hall Cam 62. **d** 65 **p** 66. C Bradf Cathl Par 65-67; C Ox St Aldate w H Trin 67-70; Youth Adv CMS 70-73; P-in-c Derby St Werburgh 73-78; V 78-82; C La Crescenta St Luke USA 77-78; V Anston *Sheff* 82-83; Registrar Ss Giles-in-the-Fields *Lon* 83-86; V Barnes St Mich *S'wark* 86-88; Perm to Offic *Guildf* 88-93; Dir Cen Essential Psychology from 92; Perm to Offic *Derby* 01-04 and *Chich* 04-07; P-in-c Findon w Clapham and Patching *Chich* 07-09; P-in-c Bexhill St Barn from 09; Hon C Bexhill St Pet from 09. *The Vicarage, Cantelupe Road, Bexhill-on-Sea TN40 1JG* Tel 07748-575592 (mobile) E-mail rogercrosthwaite@yahoo.com

CROSTHWAITE, Howard Wellesley. b 37. St Cuth Soc Dur BA59. St Steph Ho Ox 59. **d** 61 **p** 62. C Workington St Mich *Carl* 61-63; Grenada 63-64; C Barnsley St Mary *Wakef* 64-68; V Milnsbridge 68-70; V Thurgoland 70-79; rtd 99; Perm to Offic *Sheff* from 08. *50 Low Road West, Warmsworth, Doncaster DN4 9LE* Tel (01302) 859213 E-mail howard@yogadon.co.uk

CROUCH, Prof David Bruce. b 53. Univ of Wales (Cardiff) BA75 PhD84 FRHistS86. NEOC 95. **d** 98 **p** 99. NSM Scarborough St Martin *York* 98-01; NSM Scarborough St Columba 01-07. *Department of History, Hull University, Hull HU6 7RX* Tel (01482) 465613 E-mail d.crouch@hull.ac.uk

CROUCH, Keith Matheson. b 45. Whitelands Coll Lon CertEd71 Westhill Coll Birm BPhil00. K Coll Lon AKC70. **d** 72 **p** 73. C Hill *Birm* 72-75; C-in-c Woodgate Valley CD 75-77; V Bishop's Castle w Mainstone *Heref* 91-98; Vice-Prin WEMTC 98-04; TV Tenbury 98-02; Public Preacher 02-04; Chapl Dorothy House

Hospice Winsley from 05. *Dorothy House, Winsley, Bradford-on-Avon BA15 2LE* Tel (01225) 722988

CROUCHER, Jonathan Edward. b 68. Trin Coll Cam BA90 MA93. SEITE 01. **d** 04 **p** 05. NSM Lee Gd Shep w St Pet *S'wark* 04-08; NSM Blackheath Park St Mich from 08. *14 Southbrook Road, London SE12 8LQ* Tel (020) 8852 6913 *or* 7300 4758 Fax 7300 7100 Mobile 07956-649902
E-mail j.croucher@taylorwessing.com

CROUCHMAN, Eric Richard. b 30. Bps' Coll Cheshunt 64. **d** 66 **p** 67. C Ipswich H Trin *St E* 66-69; C Ipswich All Hallows 69-72; R Crowfield w Stonham Aspal and Mickfield 72-81; R Combs 81-90; RD Stowmarket 84-90; P-in-c Lydgate w Ousden and Cowlinge 90-95; R Wickhambrook w Lydgate, Ousden and Cowlinge 95-96; rtd 96; Perm to Offic *St E* from 97. *6 Mitre Close, Woolpit, Bury St Edmunds IP30 9SJ* Tel and fax (01359) 240070 E-mail ericthecleric@lineone.net

CROW, Arthur. b 26. St Chad's Coll Dur BA51. **d** 52 **p** 53. C Thornhill *Wakef* 52-54; C Holmfirth 54-57; V Shelley 57-63; V Flockton cum Denby Grange 63-91; rtd 91; Perm to Offic *York* from 91. *2 Thatchers Croft, Copmanthorpe, York YO23 3YD* Tel (01904) 709861

CROW, Michael John. b 35. AKC63. **d** 64 **p** 65. C Welwyn Garden City *St Alb* 64-67; C Sawbridgeworth 67-69; C Biscot 69-71; V Luton St Aug Limbury 71-79; TR Borehamwood 79-87; V Markyate Street 87-00; P-in-c Flamstead 00-00; rtd 00; Perm to Offic *Ex* from 00. *216 Pinhoe Road, Exeter EX4 7HH* Tel (01392) 424804

CROWDER, George Timothy. b 74. Liv Univ MEng96. Oak Hill Th Coll MTh07. **d** 07 **p** 08. C Hartford *Ches* from 07. *8 Woodlands Road, Hartford, Northwich CW8 1NS* E-mail gtcrowder@yahoo.co.uk

CROWDER, The Ven Norman Harry. b 26. St Jo Coll Cam BA48 MA52. Westcott Ho Cam 50. **d** 52 **p** 53. C Radcliffe-on-Trent *S'well* 52-55; Bp's Res Chapl *Portsm* 55-59; Asst Chapl Canford Sch Wimborne 59-64; Chapl 64-72; V Oakfield St Jo *Portsm* 72-75; Can Res Portsm Cathl 75-85; Dir RE 75-85; Adn Portsm 85-93; rtd 93; Perm to Offic *Portsm* and *Sarum* from 94. *37 Rectory Road, Salisbury SP2 7SD* Tel (01722) 320052 E-mail pauleen@pcrowder.freeserve.co.uk

CROWE, Anthony Murray. b 34. St Edm Hall Ox BA58 MA61. Westcott Ho Cam 57. **d** 59 **p** 60. C Stockingford *Cov* 59-62; C New Eltham All SS *S'wark* 62-66; V Clapham St Jo 66-73; R Charlton St Luke w H Trin 73-94; rtd 94; Sub-Chapl HM Pris Elmley 94-97; Sub-Chapl HM Pris Swaleside 94-99; Perm to Offic *Cant* from 94. *9 Park Avenue, Whitstable CT5 2DD* Tel (01227) 273046 E-mail ailsaandtonyc@aol.com

CROWE, Brian David. QUB BA92 PhD95 TCD BA98. **d** 98 **p** 99. C Ballynure and Ballyeaston *Conn* 98-01; I Galloon w Drummully *Clogh* 01-02. *Ulster Unionist Party, First Floor, 174 Albertbridge Road, Belfast BT5 4GS*
E-mail brian.crowe@uup.org

CROWE, Eric Anthony. b 29. St Jo Coll Dur BA53 MA98. Cuddesdon Coll 53. **d** 55 **p** 56. C Huddersfield St Jo *Wakef* 55-58; C Barnsley St Pet 58-60; R High Hoyland w Clayton W 60-68; V Battyeford 68-74; P-in-c Pitminster w Corfe *B & W* 75-76; V 76-90; rtd 90; Perm to Offic *Ex* 95-01 and *B & W* 02-08. *15 Gracey Court, Woodland Road, Broadclyst, Exeter EX5 3GA* Tel (01392) 460759

CROWE, Grant Norman. b 74. Keele Univ LLB96. Cranmer Hall Dur 00. **d** 03 **p** 04. C Burton All SS w Ch Ch *Lich* 03-07; TV Cen Telford from 07. *The Vicarage, 40 Church Road, Dawley, Telford TF4 2AS* Tel (01952) 501655

CROWE, Canon John Yeomans. b 39. Keble Coll Ox BA62 MA66. Linc Th Coll 62. **d** 64 **p** 65. C Tettenhall Regis *Lich* 64-67; C Caversham 67-71; V Hampton *Worc* 72-76; P-in-c Leek St Edw *Lich* 76-79; TR Leek 79-83; TR Leek and Meerbrook 83-87; RD Leek 82-87; TR Dorchester and V Warborough *Ox* 87-04; RD Aston and Cuddesdon 93-02; Hon Can Ch 94-04; rtd 04. *9 Pierrepont Road, Leominster HR6 8RB* Tel (01568) 611081 E-mail john.crowe90@ntlworld.com

CROWE, Leonard Charles. b 25. S Dios Minl Tr Scheme 80. **d** 82 **p** 83. NSM Buxted and Hadlow Down *Chich* 82-84; NSM Fairlight 84-86; P-in-c 86-89; V 89-92; RD Rye 93-95; Perm to Offic 95-98; Hon C Ashburnham w Penhurst 98-99; rtd 99; Perm to Offic *Chich* from 99. *34 Fair House, Church Street, Bexhill-on-Sea TN40 2HF* Tel (01424) 218676

CROWE, Canon Norman Charles. b 23. Launde Abbey. **d** 63 **p** 64. C Leic Martyrs 63-66; C-in-c Leic St Chad 66-68; V Leic St Chad 68-73; V Market Harborough 73-88; RD Gartree I 76-81; Hon Can Leic Cathl 80-88; rtd 88; Perm to Offic *Leic* 88-98 and *Pet* 88-06. *8 Wilton Close, Desborough, Kettering NN14 2QJ* Tel (01536) 760820

CROWE, Canon Philip Anthony. b 36. Selw Coll Cam BA60 MA64. Ridley Hall Cam 60. **d** 62 **p** 63. Tutor Oak Hill Th Coll 62-67; C Enfield Ch Ch Trent Park *Lon* 62-65; Ed *C of E Newspaper* 67-71; Lect Birm St Martin 71-76; R Breadsall *Derby* 77-88; Prin and Tutor Sarum & Wells Th Coll 88-95; Can and Preb Sarum Cathl 91-95; R Overton and Erbistock and Penley *St As* 95-97; Dir St As and Ban Minl Tr from 96; rtd 97; Perm to

Offic *Lich* from 01. *Alder Lea, Babbinswood, Whittington, Oswestry SY11 4PQ* Tel (01691) 671698

CROWE, Canon Sydney Ralph. b 32. Edin Th Coll 61. **d** 63 **p** 64. C Bingley H Trin *Bradf* 63-66; C Bierley 66-69; V Toller Lane St Chad from 69; Hon Can Bradf Cathl from 85; RD Airedale 95-99. *The Vicarage, St Chad's Road, Toller Lane, Bradford BD8 9DE* Tel (01274) 543957
E-mail ralph.crowe@bradford.anglican.org

CROWE, Toby Nicholas. b 70. Oriel Coll Ox BA94 Univ of Wales (Swansea) PGCE97 Cam Univ BTh09. Ridley Hall Cam 07. **d** 09. C Alperton *Lon* from 09. *19 Bowrons Avenue, Wembley HA0 4QS* E-mail toby.crowe@rocketmail.com

CROWHURST, Preb David Brian. b 40. Qu Coll Birm 77. **d** 80 **p** 81. NSM Ribbesford w Bewdley and Dowles *Worc* 80-82; Hon Chapl Birm Cathl 81-82; C Kidderminster St Jo *Worc* 82-83; C-in-c Wribbenhall 83-84; P-in-c 84-87; V Oswestry St Oswald *Lich* 87-94; P-in-c Oswestry H Trin 93-94; V Oswestry 94-08; P-in-c Rhydycroesau 90-91; R 91-08; RD Oswestry 95-01; Preb Lich Cathl 00-08; rtd 08; Perm to Offic *Heref* from 08. *The Old Coach House, Main Road, Dorrington, Shrewsbury SY5 7JD* Tel (01743) 718049 Mobile 07885-021878
E-mail d.crowhurst@btinternet.com

CROWIE, Hermon John. b 41. Kelham Th Coll 61. **d** 69 **p** 73. C Sneinton St Cypr *S'well* 69; C Balderton 72-75; V Basford St Aid 75-78; R Everton and Mattersey w Clayworth 78-84; St Helena 84-89; Chapl HM Pris Nor 89-91; Chapl HM Pris Cant 91-02; Bulgaria from 02. *Zora 23 (Profi Genchev Street), Nikolaevo 6190, Stara Zagora, Bulgaria* Tel (0035) (9) 4330 2450
E-mail j.crowie@yahoo.com

CROWLE, Sarah Ann. *See* BROUGH, Mrs Sarah Ann

CROWLEY, Mrs Jennifer Eileen. b 55. CITC 00. **d** 03 **p** 04. NSM Waterford w Killea, Drumcannon and Dunhill *C & O* 03-07; NSM New w Old Ross, Whitechurch, Fethard etc from 07. *Glen, Stradbally, Kilmacthomas, Co Waterford, Republic of Ireland* Tel (00353) (51) 293143 Mobile 087-780 0257

CROWN, Ola. b 06 **p** 07. NSM Walworth St Jo *S'wark* from 06. *23 Dawes House, Orb Street, London SE17 1RE*

✠**CROWTHER, The Rt Revd Clarence Edward.** b 29. Leeds Univ BA50 LLB52 LLM53 California Univ PhD75. Cuddesdon Coll 55. **d** 56 **p** 57 **c** 65. C Ox SS Phil and Jas 56-59; Episc Chapl California Univ USA 59-64; Dean Kimberley S Africa 64-65; Bp Kimberley and Kuruman 65-67; Asst Bp California 70-84; Asst Bp Los Angeles from 84. *289 Moreton Bay Lane Nr 2, Goleta CA 93117, USA* Tel (001) (805) 683 1016 E-mail cctravel@swsi.net

CROWTHER, Donald James. b 23. Oak Hill NSM Course 80. **d** 82 **p** 83. NSM Seal St Lawr *Roch* 82-85; NSM Sevenoaks St Nic 85-87; P-in-c Sevenoaks Weald 87-90; Perm to Offic 90-08. *2 Summerhill Court, 9-11 South Park, Sevenoaks TN13 1DR* Tel (01732) 461179
E-mail djcrowther@btinternet.com

CROWTHER, Frank. b 28. Qu Coll Birm 68. **d** 69 **p** 70. C Bulwell St Mary *S'well* 69-72; TV Clifton 72-77; V Kirkby in Ashfield St Thos 77-85; rtd 86; Perm to Offic *Derby* 86-00 and *S'well* from 86. *30 Bramley Court, Sutton-in-Ashfield NG17 4AT* Tel (01623) 443251

CROWTHER, Gordon Allan. b 63. Rhodes Univ BA85 LLB87. Spurgeon's Coll BD94 St Jo Coll Dur MA98. **d** 00 **p** 01. C Lancaster St Thos *Blackb* 00-03; Miss P Newcastle and Stake *Lich* 03-08; C Kirstenhof H Spirit S Africa from 09. *38 Raapkraal Road, Kirstenhof, Cape Town, 7945 South Africa* Tel (0027) (21) 701 201

CROWTHER, Mrs Hildred Anne. b 49. ERMC 05. **d** 08 **p** 09. NSM Oakham, Hambleton, Egleton, Braunston and Brooke *Pet* from 08. *6 The Limes, Market Overton, Oakham LE15 7PX* Tel (01572) 767779 E-mail hildred.c@btinternet.com

CROWTHER, Stephen Alfred. b 59. **d** 87 **p** 88. C Willowfield *D & D* 87-89; I Belfast St Chris 89-92; I Kiltegan w Hacketstown, Clonmore and Moyne *C & O* 93-99; Philippines 99-00; C Kill *D & G* 00-01; I Lisnaskea *Clogh* 01-07. *128 Newcourt Road, Bray, Co Wicklow, Republic of Ireland* E-mail crowther@oceanfree.net

CROWTHER-ALWYN, Benedict Mark. b 53. Kent Univ BA74. Qu Coll Birm 74. **d** 77 **p** 78. C Fenny Stratford and Water Eaton *Ox* 77-80; C Moulsecoomb *Chich* 80-81; TV 81-83; R Glas St Serf and Baillieston *Glas* 83-87; R Bassingham *Linc* 87-90; V Aubourn w Haddington 87-90; V Carlton-le-Moorland w Stapleford 87-90; R Thurlby w Norton Disney 87-90; V Elmton *Derby* 90-03; P-in-c Matlock 03-05; R from 05. *The Rectory, Church Street, Matlock DE4 3BZ* Tel (01629) 582199
E-mail mcrowther-alwyn@tiscali.co.uk

CROWTHER-GREEN, Michael Leonard. b 36. K Coll Lon 56. **d** 60 **p** 61. C Caterham *S'wark* 60-64; C Lewisham St Jo Southend 64-69; Chr Aid Area Sec (Berks, Oxon and Bucks) 69-78; Lic to Offic *Ox* 78-83; Dioc Stewardship Adv 83-92; rtd 92; Perm to Offic *Ox* from 92. *8 Egerton Road, Reading RG2 8HQ* Tel 0118-987 2502

CROYDON, Archdeacon of. *See* DAVIES, The Ven Vincent Anthony

CROYDON, Area Bishop of. *See* BAINES, The Rt Revd Nicholas

CRUDDAS, Mrs Valerie Mary. b 52. Univ of Wales (Swansea) BSc73 St Mark & St Jo Coll Lon PGCE75. St Jo Coll Nottm 05. **d** 07 **p** 08. NSM Leatherhead and Mickleham *Guildf* from 07. *11 Beechcroft, Ashtead KT21 2TY* Tel (01372) 272702
E-mail marycruddas@yahoo.co.uk

CRUICKSHANK, Ian Morison. QUB BTh. **d** 04 **p** 05. C Bray *D & G* 04-07; I Kilcooley w Littleon, Crohane and Fertagh *C & O* from 07. *The Rectory, Grange, Barna, Thurles, Co Tipperary, Republic of Ireland* Tel and fax (00353) (56) 883 4147 Mobile 87-948 4408
E-mail ian.mcruickshank@btopendoor.com

CRUICKSHANK, Jonathan Graham. b 52. K Coll Lon BD74 AKC74 Keble Coll Ox PGCE75. St Aug Coll Cant 75. **d** 76 **p** 77. C Stantonbury *Ox* 76-79; C Burnham 79-82; Chapl RNR 80-83; C Burnham w Dropmore, Hitcham and Taplow *Ox* 82-83; Chapl RN 83-89; TV New Windsor *Ox* 89-01; R Itchen Valley *Win* 01-09; RD Alresford 01-09; P-in-c Newton Ferrers w Revelstoke *Ex* from 09; P-in-c Holbeton from 09; Corps Chapl Sea Cadet Corps from 95. *The Rectory, Court Road, Newton Ferrers, Plymouth PL8 1DL* Tel and fax (01752) 872530
E-mail jcruickshank@btclick.com

CRUICKSHANKS, Mrs Arlene Elizabeth Henderson. b 42. **d** 06 **p** 07. OLM Gt Finborough w Onehouse, Harleston, Buxhall etc *St E* from 06. *23 Ash Road, Onehouse, Stowmarket IP14 3HA* Tel (01449) 676123

CRUISE, Brian John Alexander. Bris Univ BA86 TCD BTh88. **d** 88 **p** 89. C Lurgan Ch the Redeemer *D & D* 88-92; I Kildress w Altedesert *Arm* from 92. *Kildress Rectory, 6 Rectory Road, Cookstown BT80 9RX* Tel (028) 7965 1215
E-mail brian@aonet.org.uk

CRUMPTON, Colin. b 38. AKC61 Sheff Univ Dip Leadership, Renewal & Miss Studies 97. **d** 64 **p** 65. C Billingham St Cuth *Dur* 64-66; C Shirley *Birm* 66-69; V Mossley *Ches* 69-75; Miss to Seamen 75-77; V Burslem St Paul *Lich* 77-82; V Edensor 82-97; V Llanrhaeadr-ym-Mochnant etc *St As* 97-00; Dir Accra Retreat Cen Ghana 00-01; rtd 02; Hon C Redmarley D'Abitot, Bromesberrow, Pauntley etc *Glouc* 02-03; Perm to Offic *Lich* from 03 and *Ches* from 04. *60 Craig Walk, Alsager ST7 2RJ* Tel (01270) 882666 Mobile 07799-183971
E-mail colin.crumpton@virgin.net

CRUSE, Jack. b 35. ARIBA67. Sarum & Wells Th Coll 76. **d** 79 **p** 80. NSM W Teignmouth *Ex* 79-85; C Ideford, Luton and Ashcombe 85-89; C Bishopsteignton 85-89; R Broadhempston, Woodland, Staverton etc 90-98; RD Totnes 94-98; rtd 98; Perm to Offic *Ex* from 98. *41 Butts Close, Honiton EX14 2FS* Tel (01404) 46567 E-mail jack@jcruse.freeserve.co.uk

CRUSE, John Jeremy. b 58. Univ of Wales (Lamp) BA79 Hughes Hall Cam CertEd87. Sarum & Wells Th Coll 81. **d** 82 **p** 83. C Newton St Pet *S & B* 82-84; P-in-c Newbridge-on-Wye and Llanfihangel Brynpabuan 84-86; Perm to Offic *Heref* 88-89; C Waltham H Cross *Chelmsf* 89-91; TV Yatton Moor *B & W* 91-00; V Shalford *Guildf* from 00. *The Vicarage, East Shalford Lane, Shalford, Guildford GU4 8AE* Tel and fax (01483) 562396 Mobile 07889-919928
E-mail john_cruse@stmary-shalford.org.uk

CRUSE, Mrs Susan Elizabeth. b 51. Middx Univ BA04 RGN72 NTMTC 01. **d** 04 **p** 05. NSM Ingatestone w Fryerning *Chelmsf* from 04. *Silverstone, 10 Butts Way, Chelmsford CM2 8TJ* Tel (01245) 258083 Mobile 07885-909837
E-mail sue.cruse@sky.com

CRUTCHLEY, John Hamilton. b 62. Kingston Poly LLB85. Trin Coll Bris 99. **d** 01 **p** 02. C Barnstaple *Ex* 01-06; R Ardingly *Chich* from 06. *The Rectory, Church Lane, Ardingly, Haywards Heath RH17 6UR* Tel (01444) 892332 E-mail crutchleyfam@tesco.net

CRYER, Gordon David. b 34. St D Coll Lamp BA63. **d** 64 **p** 65. C Mortlake w E Sheen *S'wark* 64-67; C Godstone 67-70; Chapl St Dunstan's Abbey Sch Plymouth 71-02; R Stoke Damerel *Ex* 71-02; P-in-c Devonport St Aubyn 88-02; rtd 02; Perm to Offic *Truro* from 02. *9 St Stephens Road, Saltash PL12 4BG* Tel (01752) 510436

CRYER, Neville Barker. b 24. Hertf Coll Ox BA48 MA52. Ridley Hall Cam. **d** 50 **p** 51. C Derby St Werburgh 50-53; C Ilkeston St Mary 53-54; R Blackley St Pet *Man* 55-59; V Addiscombe St Mary *Cant* 59-67; Sec Conf Br Miss Socs 67-70; Gen Sec BFBS 70-86; rtd 86; Perm to Offic *York* from 90. *14 Carmires Road, Haxby, York YO32 3NN* Tel (01904) 763371

CUBA, Bishop of. See HURTADO, The Rt Revd Jorge A Perera

CUBITT, Paul. b 64. Sheff Univ BA86. Cranmer Hall Dur 95. **d** 97 **p** 98. C Bromyard *Heref* 97-01; V Elloughton and Brough w Brantingham *York* 01-07; R Blofield w Hemblington *Nor* from 07; RD Blofield from 08. *The Rectory, 10 Oak Wood, Blofield, Norwich NR13 4JQ* Tel (01603) 713160
E-mail revp@cubitt.karoo.co.uk

CUDDY, Paul Edward Frank. b 66. Hatf Poly BSc88. Ridley Hall Cam 99. **d** 02 **p** 03. C Bedford St Andr *St Alb* 02-06; V Tanworth *Birm* from 06. *The Vicarage, Vicarage Hill, Tanworth-in-Arden, Solihull B94 5EB* Tel (01564) 742565
E-mail paulcudby@ntlworld.com

CUFF, Gregor John. b 61. Keele Univ BSc82 LTCL07. Ridley Hall Cam 93. **d** 95 **p** 96. C Stanley *Liv* 95-99; V Waterloo Ch Ch and St Jo from 99; Hon Chapl Mersey Miss to Seafarers from 06. *The Vicarage, 22 Crosby Road South, Liverpool L22 1RQ* Tel and fax 0151-920 7791 E-mail gregor.cuff@btinternet.com

CUFF, Preb Pamela. b 47. MCSP68. S Dios Minl Tr Scheme 89. **d** 92 **p** 94. NSM Nether Stowey w Over Stowey *B & W* 92-93; NSM Quantoxhead 93-07; NSM Quantock Coast from 07; Asst Chapl Taunton Hosps 93-94; Asst Chapl Taunton and Somerset NHS Trust 94-05; Bp's Officer for Ord NSM (Taunton Adnry) *B & W* 06-09; Preb Wells Cathl from 08. *Millands, Kilve, Bridgwater TA5 1EA* Tel (01278) 741229
E-mail cuffings@hotmail.com

CULBERTSON, Eric Malcolm. b 54. Ch Ch Ox BA76 MA80 K Coll Lon PhD91. Edin Th Coll 78. **d** 80 **p** 81. C Edin St Thos 80-83; C Ealing St Mary *Lon* 83-87; R Clarkston *Glas* 87-89; Area Sec Crosslinks 89-94; I Tullaniskin w Clonoe *Arm* from 94. *215 Brackaville Road, Newmills, Dungannon BT71 4EJ* Tel (028) 8774 7154 E-mail ericmculbertson@yahoo.co.uk

CULL, John. b 31. Oak Hill Th Coll 56. **d** 59 **p** 60. C Radipole *Sarum* 59-66; Chapl Mariners' Ch Glouc 66-70; R Woodchester *Glouc* 70-90; RD Stonehouse 85-89; V Walton *St E* 90-94; rtd 94; Perm to Offic *Glouc* from 94. *Hillgrove Stables, Bear Hill, Woodchester, Stroud GL5 5DH* Tel (01453) 872145

CULLEN, Canon John Austin. b 43. Auckland Univ BA67 Otago Univ BD76 Keble Coll Ox DPhil86 FRSA89. St Jo Coll Auckland 66. **d** 69 **p** 70. C Papatoetoe New Zealand 69-73; Assoc P Mt Albert St Luke 73-75; P-in-c 74; Hon C Remuera St Aidan 75-78; Asst Chapl Keble Coll Ox 79-82; Perm to Offic *Lon* 82-84; Chapl and Lect Worc Coll Ox 84-86; Sec St Botolph Aldgate w H Trin Minories *Lon* 86-87; Dir Inst of Chr Studies 87-91; Hon C St Marylebone All SS 87-91; Dir of Tr *Win* 91-97; Dir of Min Development 97-01; Hon Can Win Cathl 96-02; Sen Asst to Bp Lon 02-04; P-in-c St Geo-in-the-East w St Paul 03-04; V Palmers Green St Jo from 05. *St John's Vicarage, 1 Bourne Hill, London N13 4DA* Tel (020) 8886 1348
E-mail john.cullen@ukgateway.net

CULLIFORD, Jane Margaret. b 48. Lon Univ MB, BS73. STETS 03. **d** 06 **p** 07. NSM Dorchester *Sarum* from 06. *8 Grosvenor Road, Dorchester DT1 2BB* Tel (01305) 264360
E-mail janeculliford@aol.com

CULLIMORE, Jeremy Stuart. b 53. TD. Westcott Ho Cam. **d** 06 **p** 07. C New Sleaford *Linc* from 06. *11 Covel Road, Sleaford NG34 8BP* Tel (01529) 300697 Mobile 07733-114280
E-mail jscullimore@btinternet.com

CULLING, Elizabeth Ann. See HOARE, Elizabeth Ann

CULLINGWORTH, Anthony Robert. b 42. BSc. Ox NSM Course. **d** 83 **p** 84. NSM Slough *Ox* 83-99; NSM Denham 99-02; NSM Morton St Luke *Bradf* 02-04; Perm to Offic from 04. *2 Thurleston Court, Great Morton, Keighley BD20 5RG* Tel (01535) 601187 E-mail thecullies@aol.com

CULLINGWORTH (née CHAPMAN), Mrs Claire Louise. b 74. St Anne's Coll Ox BA96 St Jo Coll Dur BA08. Cranmer Hall Dur 06. **d** 08 **p** 09. C Tadcaster w Newton Kyme *York* from 08. *83 Wighill Lane, Tadcaster LS24 8EY* Tel (01937) 830902
E-mail claire@secondmouse.co.uk

CULLIS, Andrew Stanley Weldon. b 48. Hertf Coll Ox BA69 LTh. St Jo Coll Nottm 70. **d** 73 **p** 74. C Reigate St Mary *S'wark* 73-78; C Yateley *Win* 78-82; V Dorking St Paul *Guildf* 82-00; RD Dorking 94-99; P-in-c Chilwell *S'well* 00-04; R Fisherton Anger *Sarum* from 04. *St Paul's Rectory, Fisherton Street, Salisbury SP2 7QW* Tel (01722) 334005

CULLWICK, Christopher John. b 53. Hull Univ BA75 Reading Univ Ox Univ BA80 MA85. Wycliffe Hall Ox 78. **d** 81 **p** 82. C Nottingham St Jude *S'well* 81-84; C York St Mich-le-Belfrey 84-87; TV Huntington 87-03; Ind Chapl from 02. *The Vicarage, 64 Strensall Road, Huntington, York YO32 9SH* Tel (01904) 764608

CULLY, Miss Elizabeth Faith. b 46. SRN67 SCM69 RGN72. Trin Coll Bris BA88. **d** 88 **p** 94. Par Dn Filton *Bris* 88-92; Par Dn Fishponds St Jo 92-94; C 94-95; P-in-c Brinsley w Underwood *S'well* 95-98; V 98-02; P-in-c Farnsfield 02-08; P-in-c Kirklington w Hockerton 02-08; P-in-c Bilsthorpe 02-08; P-in-c Eakring 02-08; P-in-c Maplebeck 02-08; P-in-c Winkburn 02-08; rtd 08; Hon C Salcombe and Malborough w S Huish *Ex* from 08. *26 Weymouth Park, Hope Cove, Kingsbridge TQ7 3HD* Tel (01548) 561081 E-mail faith.cully@btinternet.com

CULROSS, James Frank. b 17. Lon Univ BD51. Bps' Coll Cheshunt 47. **d** 50 **p** 51. C Pateley Bridge *Ripon* 50-54; C Romaldkirk 54-55; V Middleton St Cross 55-62; R Glas St Jas 62-65; C Bramley and Grafham *Guildf* 65-67; Chapl R Wanstead Sch 67-71; Chapl Sir Roger Manwood's Sch Sandwich 71-79; R Barrowden and Wakerley w S Luffenham *Pet* 79-82; rtd 82; Perm to Offic *Pet* from 77 and *B & W* from 82. *St Christopher's Home, Abington Park Crescent, Northampton NN3 3AE* Tel (01604) 234388

CULVERWELL, Martin Phillip. b 48. Sarum & Wells Th Coll 72. **d** 75 **p** 76. C Ashford St Hilda *Lon* 75-78; C Chelsea St Luke 78-80; Chapl RN 80-83; TV Yeovil *B & W* 83-87; P-in-c Sarratt

St Alb 87-90; NSM Bradford w Oake, Hillfarrance and Heathfield *B & W* 90-92; R Rode Major 92-96; Perm to Offic 07-09. *8 Sandisplatt, Fareham PO14 3AG* Tel (01329) 841358
E-mail martinculverwell@btinternet.com

CUMBERLAND, The Very Revd Barry John. b 44. Birm Univ BA67 Worc Coll Ox DipEd68. Trin Coll Singapore MDiv88. **d 88 p** 89. NSM Westmr St Matt *Lon* 88-90; Perm to Offic 90-96; Philippines 90-96, 98-01 and from 03; Dean Manila 92-96; Chapl Stockholm w Gävle and Västerås *Eur* 96-98; P-in-c Las Palmas 01-03; rtd 09. *4431 Immaculata Street, Italia 500, BFRV, Las Pinas 1740, Metro Manila, Philippines* Tel (0063) (2) 875 3528
E-mail barrycumberland@yahoo.co.uk

CUMBERLEGE, Francis Richard. b 41. AKC65. **d** 66 **p** 67. C Leigh Park St Fran CD *Portsm* 66-71; P-in-c Gona Papua New Guinea 71-75; Adn N Papua 74-81; R Popondetta 79-81; R Hastings St Clem and All SS *Chich* 81-86; V Broadwater Down 86-91; V Tunbridge Wells St Mark *Roch* 91-99; RD Tunbridge Wells 96-99; P-in-c Brockenhurst *Win* 99-03; V 03-06; rtd 06; P-in-c Ashburnham w Penhurst *Chich* from 09. *Faith Cottage, 5 The Byeway, Bexhill-on-Sea TN39 4PA* Tel (01424) 843728
E-mail cum.cum@littleoaks.net

CUMBERLIDGE, Anthony Wynne. b 49. ACIB75. Sarum & Wells Th Coll 79. **d** 82 **p** 83. C Llanrhos *St As* 82-85; R Llanfair Talhaearn and Llansannan etc 85-87; CF 87-04; P-in-c Lambourn *Ox* from 04; P-in-c Eastbury and E Garston from 04. *The Vicarage, Newbury Street, Lambourn, Hungerford RG17 8PD* Tel (01488) 71546
E-mail vicaratlambourn@aol.com

CUMBRAE, Provost of. *Vacant*

CUMINGS, Llewellyn Frank Beadnell. b 29. Natal Univ BA50 St Cath Coll Cam CertEd53. Ridley Hall Cam 65. **d** 67 **p** 68. C Leamington Priors St Mary *Cov* 67-70; V Lobley Hill *Dur* 70-74; R Denver *Ely* 74-82; V Roydon w Roxham 74-82; R St Leonards St Leon *Chich* 82-88; V Billinghay *Linc* 88-93; rtd 93. *Y Bwthyn, Coedllan, Llanfyllin SY22 5BP* Tel (01691) 648013

CUMMING, Canon Nigel Patrick. b 42. St Jo Coll Nottm 73. **d** 75 **p** 76. C Castle Hall *Ches* 75-77; C Stalybridge H Trin and Ch Ch 77-78; C Tadley St Pet *Win* 78-82; R Overton w Laverstoke and Freefolk 82-07; RD Whitchurch 89-98; Hon Can Win Cathl 99-07; rtd 07. *Pasture House, Whitsbury, Fordingbridge SP6 3QB* Tel (01725) 518248
E-mail nigel.cumming@btinternet.com

CUMMING, Ms Susan Margaret. b 47. Man Univ BSc68 Makerere Univ Kampala DipEd69. EMMTC 82. **dss** 82 **d** 87 **p** 95. Cinderhill *S'well* 82-85; Dioc Adv in Adult Educn 85-92; Par Dn Nottingham St Mary and St Cath 93-95; Lect 95-97; Asst Chapl Qu Medical Cen Nottm Univ Hosp NHS Trust 97-03; Sen Chapl 03-07; rtd 07. *33 Upton Close, Millers Reach, Castle Donington, Derby DE74 2GN* Tel (01332) 858267

CUMMING-LATTEY, Mrs Susan Mary Ruth. b 47. Open Univ BA77 SRN69. STETS 00. **d** 03 **p** 04. NSM Ash Vale *Guildf* 03-07; NSM Crondall and Ewshot from 07. *38A Elms Road, Fleet GU51 3EQ* Tel (01252) 621295 Fax 815882 Mobile 07761-126354 E-mail suelattey@btinternet.com

CUMMINGS, Mrs Elizabeth. b 45. St Jo Coll Dur BA84. NEOC 85. **d** 87 **p** 94. NSM Dur St Giles 87-89; Chapl HM Pris Dur 89-90; Chapl HM Rem Cen Low Newton 90-95; Chapl HM Pris Stocken 95-96; Chapl HM Pris Frankland 96-05; rtd 05. *8 Bridgemere Drive, Framwellgate Moor, Durham DH1 5FG* Tel 0191-383 0832

CUMMINGS, John Michael. b 53. Ex Univ BTh07 Solicitor 87. SWMTC 02. **d** 05 **p** 06. NSM Langport Area *B & W* from 05; Chapl Yeovil Distr Hosp NHS Foundn Trust from 09. *32 Bishops Drive, Langport TA10 9HW* Tel (01458) 250449 Mobile 07966-416675 E-mail headways1@waitrose.com

CUMMINGS, Canon William Alexander Vickery. b 38. Ch Ch Ox BA62 MA64. Wycliffe Hall Ox 61. **d** 64 **p** 65. C Leytonstone St Jo *Chelmsf* 64-67; C Writtle 67-71; R Stratton St Mary w Stratton St Michael *Nor* 71-73; R Wacton Magna w Parva 71-73; R Stratton St Mary w Stratton St Michael etc 73-91; RD Depwade 81-91; Hon Can Nor Cathl 90-91; V Battle *Chich* 91-04; Dean Battle 91-04; rtd 04. *80 Samber Close, Lymington SO41 9LF* Tel (01590) 610426

CUMMINS, Ashley Wighton. b 56. St Andr Univ BD83. Coates Hall Edin 82. **d** 84 **p** 85. C Broughty Ferry *Bre* 84-87; P-in-c Dundee St Ninian 87-92; P-in-c Invergowrie from 92; Chapl Angl Students Dundee Univ 92-07. *27 Errol Road, Invergowrie, Dundee DD2 5AG* Tel (01382) 562525

CUMMINS, Daphne Mary. *See* GREEN, Daphne Mary

CUMMINS, James Ernest. b 32. Brasted Th Coll 56 Westcott Ho Cam 57. **d** 60 **p** 61. C Baswich *Lich* 60-64; V Hales w Heckingham *Nor* 64-70; V Raveningham 70-76; Perm to Offic *Heref* and *S & B* 76-08; rtd 97. *Skyborry, Knighton LD7 1TW* Tel (01547) 528369 Fax 640677

CUMMINS, Nicholas Marshall. b 36. CITC 65. **d** 67 **p** 68. C Ballymena *Conn* 67-73; I Buttevant St Nic 70-73; I Buttevant Union *C, C & R* 73-78; I Mallow Union 78-83; I Kilmoe Union 83-96; Can Cork Cathl 90-96; Treas Cork Cathl 95-96; Preb Tymothan St Patr Cathl Dublin 95-01; Dean Killaloe and

Clonfert *L & K* 96-01; Dean Kilfenora and Provost Kilmacduagh 96-01; I Killaloe w Stradbally 96-01; rtd 01. *13 Borough Hill, Petersfield GU32 3LQ* Tel (01730) 269742

CUNDIFF, Mrs Margaret Joan. b 32. St Mich Ho Ox 51. **dss** 77 **d** 87 **p** 94. Broadcasting Officer *York* 75-99; Angl Adv Yorkshire TV 79-90; Selby St Jas *York* 77-01; Par Dn 87-94; Assoc Min 94-01; rtd 01; Perm to Offic *York* from 01. *37 Oaklands, Camblesforth, Selby YO8 8HH* Tel (01757) 618148

CUNDILL, David James. b 65. Leic Poly BEng88. St Jo Coll Nottm MTh05. **d** 05 **p** 06. C Leic Martyrs 05-09; Pioneer Min Leic City Cen from 09. *29 Holmfield Road, Leicester LE2 1SE* E-mail david.cundill@btinternet.com

CUNLIFFE, Anne. b 48. CBDTI 01. **d** 04 **p** 05. OLM Poulton-le-Sands w Morecambe St Laur *Blackb* 04-07; NSM from 04. *14 Coniston Road, Morecambe LA4 5PS* Tel (01524) 422509 E-mail revanne@gmail.com

CUNLIFFE, The Ven Christopher John. b 55. Ch Ch Ox BA77 MA81 DPhil81 Trin Coll Cam BA82 MA86 ARHistSc94. Westcott Ho Cam 80. **d** 83 **p** 84. C Chesterfield St Mary and All SS *Derby* 83-85; Chapl Linc Coll Ox 85-89; Chapl City Univ and Guildhall Sch of Music and Drama *Lon* 89-91; Voc Officer and Selection Sec ABM 91-97; Dir Professional Min *Lon* 97-03; Chapl to Bp Bradwell *Chelmsf* 04-06; Adn Derby from 06; Can Res Derby Cathl 06-08. *1 Thatch Close, Derby DE22 1EA* Tel (01332) 553455 *or* 382233 Fax 552322 *or* 292969
E-mail archderby@talk21.com

CUNLIFFE, Harold. b 28. St Aid Birkenhead 57. **d** 60 **p** 61. C Hindley All SS *Liv* 60-64; V Everton St Chad w Ch Ch 64-69; R Golborne 70-93; rtd 93; Perm to Offic *Liv* from 93. *51 Greenfields Crescent, Ashton-in-Makerfield, Wigan WN4 8QY* Tel (01942) 202956 E-mail cunliffe@cableinet.co.uk

CUNLIFFE, The Ven Helen Margaret. b 54. St Hilda's Coll Ox BA77 MA78. Westcott Ho Cam 81. **dss** 83 **d** 87 **p** 94. Chesterfield St Mary and All SS *Derby* 83-85; Ox St Mary V w St Cross and St Pet 86-89; Par Dn 87-89; Chapl Nuff Coll Ox 86-89; TD Clapham Team *S'wark* 89-94; TV 94-96; Can Res S'wark Cathl 96-03; Chapl Welcare 96-03; Adn St Alb 03-07; rtd 08. *1 Thatch Close, Derby DE22 1EA* Tel (01332) 553455

CUNLIFFE, Peter Henry. b 54. SRN77 RSCN79 RCNT83 Univ of Wales MA93. Trin Coll Bris 92. **d** 94 **p** 95. C Carshalton Beeches *S'wark* 94-95; C Reigate St Mary 95-02; P-in-c Hemingford Grey *Ely* 02-04; V from 04; P-in-c Hemingford Abbots from 04. *The Vicarage, 6 Braggs Lane, Hemingford Grey, Huntingdon PE28 9BW* Tel (01480) 394378
E-mail peter.cunliffe@sjhg.org.uk

CUNNINGHAM, Arthur. b 48. Man Univ PhD95 Oak Hill Th Coll BA88 Lon Bible Coll MA89. NOC 92. **d** 93 **p** 94. C Walkden Moor *Man* 93; C Walkden Moor w Lt Hulton 93-96; Chapl Salford 93-96; C Camelot Par *B & W* 96-98; Chapl Yeovil Coll 96-97; R Berrow w Pendock, Eldersfield, Hollybush etc *Worc* 98-03; Dioc Warden of Readers and Moderator of Reader Tr 98-03; P-in-c Leigh St Mary *Man* 03-08; rtd 08. *7 Milnes Avenue, Leigh WN7 3JU*
E-mail artcunningham@compuserve.com

CUNNINGHAM, Brian James. b 65. York Univ BA88. Ripon Coll Cuddesdon BA91. **d** 92 **p** 93. C Merrow *Guildf* 92-96; C Kennington St Jo w St Jas *S'wark* 96-99; Chapl Pangbourne Coll 99. *Sunbeam, Pangbourne College, Pangbourne, Reading RG8 8LA* Tel 0118-984 2101

CUNNINGHAM, John James. b 50. TCD Div Sch BTh98. **d** 98 **p** 99. C Drumachose *D & R* 98-01; I Camus-juxta-Bann 01-06; I Ballymoney w Finvoy and Rasharkin *Conn* from 06. *The Rectory, 4 Queen Street, Ballymoney BT53 6JA* Tel (028) 2766 2149 E-mail ballymoney@connor.anglican.org

CUNNINGHAM, Philip John. b 52. St Jo Coll Dur BA74 PGCE75 MA85. NOC 93. **d** 95 **p** 96. NSM York St Luke 95-97; NSM York St Olave w St Giles 97-99; TV Haxby w Wigginton 99-02; V Gosforth St Nic *Newc* from 02; AD Newc Cen from 05. *The Vicarage, Tr Rectory Road, Gosforth, Newcastle upon Tyne NE3 1XR* Tel 0191-285 1326
E-mail philipcunningham@hotmail.com

CUNNINGHAM, Richard Martin. b 61. Goldsmiths' Coll Lon BEd84. SAOMC 95. **d** 98 **p** 99. NSM Kingham w Churchill, Daylesford and Sarsden *Ox* 98-01; NSM Chipping Norton 01-02; NSM Ox St Andr from 01. *Churchill Mill, Sarsden Halt, Churchill, Chipping Norton OX7 6NT* Tel (01608) 659426 Fax 659134 E-mail richard.cunningham@standrewsoxford.org.uk

CUNNINGHAM, Wendy. b 42. SAOMC 01. **d** 04 **p** 05. NSM Hook Norton w Gt Rollright, Swerford etc *Ox* from 04. *Dewlands, Church End, Great Rollright, Chipping Norton OX7 5RX* Tel (01608) 737135

CUNNINGTON, Andrew Thomas. b 56. Southn Univ BTh86. Sarum & Wells Th Coll 82. **d** 85 **p** 86. C Ifield *Chich* 85-89; TV Haywards Heath St Wilfrid 89-94; V Midhurst 94-06; R Woolbeding 94-06; RD Midhurst 03-06; V Redhill St Matt *S'wark* from 06. *St Matthew's Vicarage, 27 Ridgeway Road, Redhill RH1 6PQ* Tel (01737) 761568

CUNNINGTON, Miss Averil. b 41. St Mary's Coll Chelt CertEd61 Man Univ BA68 MEd73. NOC 93. **d** 95 **p** 96. Hd

Mistress Counthill Sch Oldham 84-96; NSM Milnrow *Man* 95-98; NSM Hey 98-02; Lic Preacher 02-05; Tutor NOC 98-05; Perm to Offic *Heref* from 05. *6 Braemar Gardens, Hereford HR1 1SJ*

CUNNINGTON, Howard James. b 56. Southn Univ BA77 St Jo Coll Dur PGCE78. Trin Coll Bris 90. **d** 92 **p** 93. C Ex St Leon w H Trin 92-96; V Sandown Ch Ch and Lower Sandown St Jo *Portsm* 96-04; Perm to Offic from 04. *5 The Mall, Lake Hill, Sandown PO36 9ED* E-mail howard@cunnington.org.uk

CUPITT, Don. b 34. Trin Hall Cam BA55 MA58 Bris Univ Hon DLitt84. Westcott Ho Cam 57. **d** 59 **p** 60. C Salford St Phil w St Steph *Man* 59-62; Vice-Prin Westcott Ho Cam 62-66; Dean Em Coll Cam 66-91; Asst Lect Div Cam Univ 68-73; Lect 73-96; rtd 96; Life Fell Em Coll Cam from 96. *Emmanuel College, Cambridge CB2 3AP* Tel (01223) 334200

CURD, Preb Christine Veronica. b 51. Bris Univ BA. Oak Hill Th Coll 84 WMMTC 88. **d** 89 **p** 94. NSM Widecombe-in-the-Moor, Leusdon, Princetown etc *Ex* 89-93; NSM Bovey Tracey SS Pet, Paul and Thos w Hennock 94-97; Asst Chapl HM Pris Channings Wood 92-02; Chapl HM Pris Ex from 02; Preb Ex Cathl from 05. *HM Prison Exeter, New North Road, Exeter EX4 4EX* Tel (01392) 415700 Fax 422647
E-mail christine.curd@hmps.gsi.gov.uk

CURD, Clifford John Letsom. b 45. SRN RNT. Oak Hill Th Coll 84. **d** 86 **p** 87. C Stone Ch Ch *Lich* 86-89; TV Widecombe-in-the-Moor, Leusdon, Princetown etc *Ex* 89-93; P-in-c Ilsington 93-04; rtd 05. *c/o Crockford, Church House, Great Smith Street, London SW1P 3AZ* E-mail cliff-chris@ccurd.freeserve.co.uk

CURL, Roger William. b 50. BA BD DPhil. Oak Hill Th Coll. **d** 82 **p** 83. C Cromer *Nor* 82-86; C Sevenoaks St Nic *Roch* 86-88; V Fulham St Mary N End *Lon* from 88. *St Mary's Vicarage, 2 Edith Road, London W14 9BA* Tel (020) 7602 1996
E-mail stmarys.westken@london.anglican.org

CURNEW, Preb Brian Leslie. b 48. Qu Coll Ox BA69 DPhil77 MA77. Ripon Coll Cuddesdon 77. **d** 79 **p** 80. C Sandhurst *Ox* 79-82; Tutor St Steph Ho Ox 82-87; V Fishponds St Mary *Bris* 87-94; TR Ludlow *Heref* from 94; P-in-c Bitterley w Middleton, Stoke St Milborough etc from 09; Preb Heref Cathl from 02. *The Rectory, 4 College Street, Ludlow SY8 1AN* Tel (01584) 874988 *or* 872073 Fax 875138 E-mail rector@stlaurences.org.uk

CURNOCK, Canon Karen Susan. b 50. Nottm Univ BTh78. Linc Th Coll 74. **d** 95 **p** 97. NSM Graffoe Gp *Linc* 95-96; Dioc Sec *Sarum* 96-03; NSM Chalke Valley 96-03; V Buckland Newton, Cerne Abbas, Godmanstone etc from 03; Can and Preb Sarum Cathl from 02; RD Dorchester 06-09. *The Vicarage, 4 Back Lane, Cerne Abbas, Dorchester DT2 7LW* Tel (01300) 341251
E-mail kcurnock@dsl.pipex.com

CURNOW, Terence Peter. b 37. Univ of Wales (Lamp) BA62. **d** 63 **p** 64. C Llanishen and Lisvane 63-71; Youth Chapl 67-71; Asst Chapl K Coll Taunton 71-74; Chapl Taunton Sch 74-84; Ho Master 84-98; Perm to Offic *B & W* from 84; rtd 02. *19 Stonegallows, Taunton TA1 5JW* Tel (01823) 330003

CURRAH, Michael Ewart. b 31. Down Coll Cam BA54 MA58. Sarum Th Coll 54. **d** 56 **p** 57. C Calne *Sarum* 56-60; V Southbroom 60-69; Perm to Offic 70-88; Asst Master Woodroffe Sch Lyme Regis 71-83; Hon C Taunton H Trin *B & W* 88-96; rtd 96; Perm to Offic *B & W* 96-06 and *Leic* from 06. *14 Latimer Crescent, Market Harborough LE16 8AP* Tel (01858) 433706

CURRAN, John Henry. b 77. Nottm Univ BA00. Wycliffe Hall Ox 00. **d** 02 **p** 03. C W Bridgford *S'well* 02-05; Perm to Offic 05-07; P-in-c Wollaton Park from 07; Chapl Nottm Univ from 07. *St Mary's Vicarage, Wollaton Hall Drive, Nottingham NG8 1AF* Tel 0115-978 4914
E-mail henry@curransonline.co.uk

CURRAN, The Ven Patrick Martin Stanley. b 56. K Coll (NS) BA80 Southn Univ BTh84. Chich Th Coll 80. **d** 84 **p** 85. C Heavitree w Ex St Paul 84-87; Bp's Chapl to Students *Bradf* 87-93; Chapl Bonn w Cologne *Eur* 93-00; Chapl Vienna from 00; Can Malta Cathl from 00; Adn E Adnry from 02. *The British Embassy, Jaurèsgasse 12, A-1030 Vienna, Austria* Tel and fax (0043) (1) 714 8900 *or* 718 5902
E-mail office@christchurchvienna.org

CURRAN, Thomas Heinrich. b 49. Toronto Univ BA72 Dalhousie Univ Canada MA75 Hatf Coll Dur PhD91. Atlantic Sch of Th MTS80. **d** 78 **p** 79. Canada 77-81 and from 92; Chapl Hatf Coll Dur 88-92. *PO Box 28010 RPO Tacoma, Dartmouth NS B2W 6E2, Canada*

CURRELL, Linda Anne. *See* SCOTT, Mrs Linda Anne

CURRER, Caroline Mary. b 49. Keele Univ BA71 Warwick Univ PhD86 CQSW71. EAMTC 02. **d** 04 **p** 05. NSM Stansted Mountfitchet w Birchanger and Farnham *Chelmsf* 04-09; P-in-c Poynings w Edburton, Newtimber and Pyecombe *Chich* from 09. *The Rectory, The Street, Poynings, Brighton BN45 7AQ* Tel (01273) 857456 E-mail c.currer@ntlworld.com

CURRIE, Alan Richard. b 58. St Andr Univ MA82 Aber Univ DipEd83. NEOC 97. **d** 00 **p** 01. NSM Haydon Bridge and Beltingham w Henshaw *Newc* 00-05; NSM St John Lee and Warden w Newbrough 05-08; NSM Hexham from 08.

35 Dotland Close, Eastwood Grange, Hexham NE46 1UF Tel (01434) 607614

CURRIE, Daniel Robert. b 71. Trin Coll Bris 07. **d** 09. C Gorleston St Andr *Nor* from 09. *2 Elmgrove Road, Gorleston, Great Yarmouth NR31 7PP* E-mail revdcurrie@gmail.com

CURRIE, John Stuart. b 47. SEITE 94. **d** 97 **p** 98. C S Chatham H Trin *Roch* 97-01; TV from 01; Dioc Ecum Officer from 09. *The Team Vicarage, 18 Marion Close, Walderslade, Chatham ME5 9QA* Tel and fax (01634) 684888 Mobile 07803-283917
E-mail john.currie@diocese-rochester.org

CURRIE, Canon Stuart William. b 53. Hertf Coll Ox MA79 Fitzw Coll Cam BA85 CertEd. Westcott Ho Cam 82. **d** 85 **p** 86. C Whitley Ch Ch *Ox* 85-89; TV Banbury 89-94; V Barbourne *Worc* from 94; Hon Can Worc Cathl from 09. *St Stephen's Vicarage, 1 Beech Avenue, Worcester WR3 8PZ* Tel (01905) 452169 E-mail sw.currie@tiscali.co.uk

CURRIE, Walter. b 39. Tyndale Hall Bris 64. **d** 67 **p** 68. C Cromer *Nor* 67-70; C Macclesfield St Mich *Ches* 70-74; R Postwick *Nor* 74-87; Chapl Jas Paget Hosp Gorleston 87-94; Chapl Jas Paget Hosp NHS Trust Gorleston 94-01; rtd 01; Perm to Offic *Nor* from 01. *11 Langham Green, Blofield, Norwich NR13 4LD* Tel (01603) 713484 E-mail currie-w@tiscali.co.uk

CURRIN, John. b 56. Keele Univ CertEd78. St Jo Coll Nottm MA93. **d** 93 **p** 94. C Eastwood *S'well* 93-97; P-in-c Matlock Bath and Cromford *Derby* 97-02; V 02-06; R Dibden *Win* from 06. *The Rectory, Beaulieu Road, Dibden Purlieu, Southampton SO45 4PT* Tel (023) 8084 3204

CURRY, Anthony Bruce. b 31. St Edm Hall Ox BA53 MA56 ARCO49. Wells Th Coll 53. **d** 55 **p** 56. C Northfleet *Roch* 55-56; Chapl K Sch Cant 56-61; R Penshurst *Roch* 61-75; Dir Music Kelly Coll Tavistock 75-85; Hon C Calstock *Truro* 75-85; R Brasted *Roch* 85-93; rtd 93. *Monta Rosa, King Street, Gunnislake PL18 9JU* Tel and fax (01822) 834133

CURRY, Canon Bruce. b 39. Dur Univ BA61. Wells Th Coll 61. **d** 63 **p** 64. C Shepton Mallet *B & W* 63-67; C Cheam *S'wark* 67-71; R W Walton *Ely* 71-78; V St Neots 78-94; P-in-c Everton w Tetworth 94-98; P-in-c Abbotsley 94-99; P-in-c Waresley 94-99; P-in-c Gt w Lt Gransden 98-99; R Gt Gransden and Abbotsley and Lt Gransden etc 99-04; RD St Neots 90-02; Hon Can Ely Cathl 98-04; rtd 04; Perm to Offic *Ely* from 05. *10 Ravens Court, Ely CB6 3ED* Tel (01353) 661494
E-mail bruce@jcurry.fsnet.co.uk

CURRY, David John. b 24. St Cath Coll Cam BA48 MA58. Oak Hill Th Coll 73. **d** 74 **p** 75. C Watford *St Alb* 74-77; V Whitehall Park St Andr Hornsey Lane *Lon* 77-82; R Heydon w Gt and Lt Chishill *Chelmsf* 82-88; rtd 89; Perm to Offic *Chich* from 89. *40 Finches Gardens, Haywards Heath RH16 2PB* Tel (01444) 483670

CURRY, George Robert. b 51. JP90. Bede Coll Dur BA72 Newc Univ MA97. Cranmer Hall Dur Oak Hill Th Coll. **d** 76 **p** 77. C Denton Holme *Carl* 76-81; V Low Elswick *Newc* 81-96; P-in-c High Elswick St Paul 97-06; V Elswick from 06. *St Stephen's Vicarage, Clumber Street, Newcastle upon Tyne NE4 7ST* Tel 0191-273 4680 E-mail g.r.curry@btinternet.com

CURRY, James Sebastian. b 63. Hatf Coll Dur BA84. Ripon Coll Cuddesdon BTh93. **d** 93 **p** 94. C Four Oaks *Birm* 93-96; C Erdington St Barn 96-99; TV Jarrow *Dur* 99-06; R Aboyne from 06; R Ballater from 06; R Braemar from 06. *Glenmoriston, 7 Invercauld Road, Ballater AB35 5RP* Tel (01339) 755726
E-mail upper.deeside@virgin.net

CURRY, Thomas Christopher. b 47. Sarum & Wells Th Coll 71. **d** 74 **p** 75. C Bradford-on-Avon *Sarum* 74-78; Asst Chapl Hurstpierpoint Coll 78-82; P-in-c The Donheads *Sarum* 82-08; RD Chalke 87-92; rtd 08; Lic to Offic *Ex* 08-09; C Lifton, Broadwoodwidger, Stowford etc from 09. *The Rectory, Lewdown, Okehampton EX20 4DN*

CURTIS, Bert. b 20. Lon Univ BCom42 BA46. Ripon Hall Ox. **d** 46 **p** 47. C Moseley St Mary *Birm* 46-48; Perm to Offic *Carl* 74-07. *Greystones, Embleton, Cockermouth CA13 9YP* Tel (01768) 776503

CURTIS, Colin. b 47. Open Univ BA80 ALA69. St Jo Coll Nottm 83. **d** 93 **p** 94. NSM Clarkston *Glas* from 93. *78 Auldhouse Road, Glasgow G43 1UR* Tel 0141-569 4206
E-mail colin.curtis540@ntlworld.com

CURTIS, Canon Geoffrey John. b 35. Dur Univ BA57. Ripon Hall Ox 59. **d** 61 **p** 62. C Gosport Ch Ch *Portsm* 61-65; C Bedhampton 65-68; Producer Schs Broadcasting Dept BBC Lon 68-75; Dioc Communications Adv *Guildf* 75-00; P-in-c Grayswood 75-91; Dir Grayswood Studio 84-00; Hon Can Guildf Cathl 87-00; rtd 00; Perm to Offic *Guildf* from 00. *1 Clairville, Woodside Road, Chiddingfold, Godalming GU8 4QY* Tel (01428) 685943

CURTIS, Gerald Arthur. b 46. Lon Univ BA69. Sarum & Wells Th Coll 85. **d** 87 **p** 88. C Allington and Maidstone St Pet *Cant* 87-90; TV Gt Grimsby St Mary and St Jas *Linc* 90-95; P-in-c Morton w Hacconby 95-96; R Ringstone in Aveland Gp 96-02; rtd 03. *Le Val, 61560 Saint-Germain-de-Martigny, France* E-mail gacurt@btinternet.com

CURTIS, Mrs Jacqueline Elaine. b 60. Sarum & Wells Th Coll 87. **d** 90 **p** 94. Par Dn Bridport *Sarum* 90-94; C 94-95; TV Melbury 95-00; TV Maltby *Sheff* 00-02; TR 02-08; TR Crosslacon *Carl* from 08. *The Vicarage, Trumpet Road, Cleator CA23 3EF* Tel (01946) 810510 E-mail jacquelinecurtis@mac.com

CURTIS, Canon Jane Darwent. b 64. Leic Univ BA86. Linc Th Coll BTh93. **d** 93 **p** 94. Par Dn Oadby *Leic* 93-94; C 94-96; Chapl De Montfort Univ 96-03; C Leic H Spirit 96-97; TV 97-03; TV Gilmorton, Peatling Parva, Kimcote etc 03-09; Bp's Adv for Women's Min from 04; V Whatborough Gp from 09; Officer for IME 4-7 from 09; Hon Can Leic Cathl from 06. *The Vicarage, Oakham Road, Tilton on the Hill, Leicester LE7 9LB* Tel 0116-259 7244 E-mail jcurtis@leicester.anglican.org

CURTIS, John Durston. b 43. Lich Th Coll 65. **d** 68 **p** 69. C Coseley Ch Ch *Lich* 68-71; C Sedgley All SS 71-74; CF 74-79; P-in-c Newton Valence *Win* 79-82; P-in-c Selborne 79-82; R Newton Valence, Selborne and E Tisted w Colemore 82-87; R Marchwood 87-09; AD Lyndhurst 05-08; rtd 09. *7 Pearce Road, Diss IP22 4YF* Tel (01379) 640036 E-mail john.curtis@care4free.net

CURTIS, Layton Richard. b 61. Leic Univ BSc84 PGCE85. Linc Th Coll BTh93. **d** 93 **p** 94. C Knighton St Mary Magd *Leic* 93-96; C Leic St Phil 96-01; P-in-c Wigston Magna from 01. *The Vicarage, 5 Church Lane, Gilmorton, Lutterworth LE17 5LU* Tel (01455) 552119 Mobile 07855-746041 E-mail rcurtis@leicester.anglican.org

CURTIS, Mrs Marian Ruth. b 54. Nottm Univ BA75 CQSW80. Trin Coll Bris 03. **d** 05 **p** 06. C Blackheath Park St Mich *S'wark* 05-08; Chapl Salisbury Health Care NHS Trust from 08. Chaplaincy, *Salisbury District Hospital, Odstock Road, Salisbury SP2 8BJ* Tel (01722) 429271 E-mail mariancurtis@btinternet.com

CURTIS, Peter Bernard. b 35. St Pet Hall Ox BA60 MA64. Westcott Ho Cam 60. **d** 62 **p** 63. C Warsop *S'well* 62-65; Chapl Dur Univ 65-69; V Worle *B & W* 69-78; R Crewkerne w Wayford 78-00; rtd 00; Perm to Offic *B & W* from 01. *The Old Farmhouse, 28 Millstream Gardens, Wellington TA21 0AA* Tel (01823) 662638

CURTIS, Ronald Victor. b 47. SAOMC 98. **d** 01 **p** 02. NSM Shipton-under-Wychwood w Milton, Fifield etc *Ox* 01-05; P-in-c Stourbridge St Thos *Worc* from 05. *St Thomas's Vicarage, 34 South Road, Stourbridge DY8 3YB* Tel (01384) 392401

CURTIS, Mrs Susan Anne. b 51. Birm Univ CertEd72 Open Univ BA79. **d** 07 **p** 08. OLM Epsom Common Ch Ch *Guildf* from 07. *11 Epsom College, College Road, Epsom KT17 4JH* E-mail curtis-s@epsomcollege.org.uk

CURTIS, Thomas John. b 32. Pemb Coll Ox BA55 MA59 Lon Univ BD58. Clifton Th Coll 55. **d** 58 **p** 59. C Wandsworth All SS *S'wark* 58-61; Chile 61-71; R Saxmundham *St E* 71-77; V Cheltenham St Mark *Glouc* 77-84; TR 84-86; V Chipping Norton *Ox* 86-95; rtd 95; Hon Dioc Rep SAMS *St E* 95-01; Perm to Offic *Glouc* and *Worc* from 01. *60 Courtney Close, Tewkesbury GL20 5FB* Tel (01684) 295298 E-mail curtistomjon@aol.com

CURTIS, Timothy. **d** 08 **p** 09. NSM Cheltenham St Mary w St Matt *Glouc* from 08. *1 Benhall Avenue, Cheltenham GL51 6AF*

CURWEN, Canon David. b 38. St Cath Coll Cam BA62. Cuddesdon Coll 62. **d** 64 **p** 65. C Orford St Andr *Liv* 64-67; Ind Chapl *Cant* 67-77 and 83-84; C S'wark Ch Ch 78-83; Ind Chapl *S'wark* 78-83 and 88-93; Dioc Soc Resp Adv *St E* 88-93; Dioc Adv for CME 93-97; R Capel St Mary w Lt and Gt Wenham 97-03; Hon Can St E Cathl 97-03; rtd 03; Perm to Offic *St E* from 03. *41 Cuckfield Avenue, Ipswich IP3 8SA* Tel (01473) 272706

CURZEN, Prof Peter. b 31. Lon Univ BSc52 MB, BS55 MD66 MRCOG62 FRCOG70. Sarum & Wells Th Coll 93. **d** 94 **p** 95. NSM Bemerton *Sarum* 94-98; NSM Wylye and Till Valley 98-00; rtd 01; Perm to Offic *Sarum* 01-04. *The Meadows, Hindon Lane, Tisbury, Salisbury SP3 6PZ*

CUTCLIFFE, Canon Neil Robert. b 50. NUU BA72 TCD BA72. **d** 75 **p** 76. C Belfast St Mary *Conn* 75-78; C Lurgan Ch the Redeemer *D & D* 78-80; I Garrison w Slavin and Belleek *Clogh* 80-86; I Mossley *Conn* from 86; Can Belf Cathl from 07. *558 Doagh Road, Mossley, Newtownabbey BT36 6TA* Tel (028) 9083 2726 E-mail rathdune@hotmail.com

CUTHBERT, John. b 52. Edin Univ BSc76 PhD80. Coates Hall Edin BD92. **d** 92 **p** 93. Chapl St Mary's Cathl 92-98; C Edin St Mary 92-98; P-in-c Forres *Mor* 98-03; R Arbroath *Bre* from 04; R Auchmithie from 04. *St Mary's Rectory, 2 Springfield Terrace, Arbroath DD11 1EL* Tel (01241) 873392 E-mail john@cuth100.freeserve.co.uk

CUTHBERT, John Hamilton. b 34. Univ of Wales (Lamp) BA59. Coll of Resurr Mirfield 59. **d** 61 **p** 62. C Cov St Pet 61-64; Australia 64-69; C Willesden St Andr *Lon* 69-72; CMP from 72; C Sheff St Cecilia Parson Cross 72-74; V Lavender Hill Ascension *S'wark* 74-97; rtd 97; Perm to Offic *St Alb* from 97 and *Lon* from 99. *29 The Cloisters, Welwyn Garden City AL8 6DU* Tel (01707) 376748

CUTHBERT, Vernon John. b 66. Trin Coll Bris 02. **d** 04 **p** 05. C Alvaston *Derby* 04-08; P-in-c Cleadon *Dur* from 08. *The Vicarage, 5 Sunderland Road, Cleadon, Sunderland SR6 7UR* Tel 0191-536 7147

CUTHBERT, Victor. b 46. **d** 01 **p** 02. OLM Surbiton St Matt *S'wark* from 01. *4 St Thomas Close, Surbiton KT6 7TU* Tel (020) 8399 8722 E-mail victorcuthbert@btinternet.com

CUTHBERTSON, Mrs Amanda. b 54. K Coll Lon BD92 AKC92 Open Univ PGCE98 Loughb Univ MA00 ALCM85 LLCM87. EAMTC 98. **d** 00 **p** 01. C Northampton St Benedict *Pet* 00-03; V Wellingborough St Mark from 03. *St Mark's Vicarage, Queensway, Wellingborough NN8 3SD* Tel (01933) 673893 E-mail revacuthbertson@talk21.com

CUTHBERTSON, Raymond. b 52. AKC75. Coll of Resurr Mirfield 76. **d** 77 **p** 78. C Darlington St Mark w St Paul *Dur* 77-81; C Usworth 81-83; C Darlington St Cuth 83-86; V Shildon w Eldon 86-00; V Shildon 00-04; RD Auckland 94-96; Chapl N Tees and Hartlepool NHS Trust 04-07; Chapl Tees, Esk and Wear Valley NHS Trust from 07. *Tees, Esk and Wear Valley NHS Trust, County Hospital, North Road, Durham DH1 4ST* Tel 0191-333 3423 E-mail raymond.cuthbertson@cddps.nhs.uk

CUTHBERT, Robert Francis. b 37. Lon Univ BSc57. Clifton Th Coll 62. **d** 64 **p** 65. C Peckham St Mary Magd *S'wark* 64-68; C Redhill H Trin 68-70; Travel Sec Inter-Coll Chr Fellowship of IVF 70-74; Hon C Selly Hill St Steph *Birm* 70-74; Interserve Internat Bangladesh 74-93; Internat Fellowship Evang Students 74-85; Bible Students Fellowship of Bangladesh 85-93; V Rochdale Deeplish St Luke *Man* 94-99; TV S Rochdale 00-02; rtd 02; Perm to Offic *St Alb* from 03. *17 Woodlands, Park Street, St Albans AL2 2AD* Tel (01727) 872248 E-mail rfcutler@zetnet.co.uk

CUTLER, Roger Charles. b 49. Liv Univ BSc70 Glas Univ MPhil98. Coll of Resurr Mirfield 86. **d** 88 **p** 89. C Walney Is *Carl* 88-91; Chapl RN 91-98; Perm to Offic *Glas* 91-95; Hon C Challoch w Newton Stewart 95-98; V Gosforth St Nic *Newc* 98-01; P-in-c St John Lee 01-04; R 05-08; P-in-c Warden w Newbrough 01-04; V 05-08; R Kirkcudbright *Glas* from 08; R Gatehouse of Fleet from 08. *The Rectory, 9 St Mary Street, Kirkcudbright DG6 4AA* Tel (01557) 330146 E-mail therectory@dsl.pipex.com

CUTMORE, Simon Giles. b 72. Trin Coll Bris BA95 St Jo Coll Dur MA00. Cranmer Hall Dur 97. **d** 99 **p** 00. C Biggleswade *St Alb* 99-03; TV Chambersbury from 03. *The Rectory, 14 Pancake Lane, Laverstock Green, Hemel Hempstead HP2 4NB* Tel and fax (01442) 264860 E-mail simonandalexc@aol.com

CUTT, Canon Samuel Robert. b 25. Selw Coll Cam BA50 MA54. Cuddesdon Coll 51. **d** 53 **p** 54. C W Hartlepool St Aid *Dur* 53-56; Tutor St Boniface Coll Warminster 56-59; Sub Warden 59-65; Tutor Chich Th Coll 65-71; PV Chich Cathl 66-71; Min Can St Paul's Cathl 71-79; Lect K Coll Lon 73-79; P in O 75-79; Can Res Wells Cathl 79-93; Chan 79-93; Treas 85-93; Dir of Ords 79-86; Warden CSD 87-93; rtd 93. *c/o J C Cutt Esq, 37 Sallows Road, Peterborough PE1 4EX* Tel (01733) 562796

CUTTELL, The Very Revd Jeffrey Charles. b 59. Birm Univ BSc80 PhD83 Sheff Univ MA91. Trin Coll Bris 84. **d** 87 **p** 88. C Normanton *Wakef* 87-91; V 91-95; Producer Relig Progr BBC Radio Stoke 95-97; Presenter Relig Progr BBC 97-99; CF (TA) 97-06; R Astbury and Smallwood *Ches* 99-08; RD Congleton 04-08; Assoc Lect Th Univ of Wales (Cardiff) 01-06; Tutor St Mich Coll Llan 01-06; Dean Derby from 08. *Derby Cathedral Centre, 18-19 Iron Gate, Derby DE1 3GP* Tel (01332) 341201 E-mail dean@derbycathedral.org

CUTTER, John Douglas. b 31. Lon Univ BD61. Chich Th Coll 56. **d** 59 **p** 60. C Blyth St Mary *Newc* 59-62; C Rugeley *Lich* 62-65; V Rocester 65-73; V Shrewsbury St Giles 73-83; R Yoxall and Dean's V Lich Cathl 83-91; rtd 91; Perm to Offic *Win* from 91; Hon Chapl Win Cathl from 98. *Little Wykeham, 111 Teg Down Meads, Winchester SO22 5NN* Tel (01962) 852203

CUTTING, Alastair Murray. b 60. Westhill Coll Birm BEd83 Heythrop Coll Lon MA03. St Jo Coll Nottm 84. **d** 87 **p** 88. C Woodlands *Sheff* 87-88; C Wadsley 89-91; C Uxbridge *Lon* 91-96; Chapl to the Nave and Uxbridge Town Cen 91-96; V Copthorne *Chich* from 96. *The Vicarage, Church Road, Copthorne, Crawley RH10 3RD* Tel (01342) 712063 E-mail acutting@mac.com *or* vicar@copthorne.plus.com

CUTTS, Canon David. b 52. Van Mildert Coll Dur BSc73. St Jo Coll Nottm BA79. **d** 80 **p** 81. C Ipswich St Matt *St E* 80-82; Bp's Dom Chapl 82-85; R Coddenham w Gosbeck and Hemingstone w Henley 85-94; RD Bosmere 92-94; V Ipswich St Marg from 94; RD Ipswich 96-01; Hon Can St E Cathl from 00. *St Margaret's Vicarage, 32 Constable Road, Ipswich IP4 2UW* Tel (01473) 253906 Mobile 07733-406552 E-mail david.cutts3@ntlworld.com

CUTTS, Elizabeth Joan Gabrielle. *See* STRICKLAND, Mrs Elizabeth Joan Gabrielle

CUTTS, Nigel Leonard. b 57. Sheff Univ BA86 BTh. Linc Th Coll 83. **d** 87 **p** 88. C Old Brampton and Loundsley Green *Derby* 87-89; C Chesterfield St Mary and All SS 89-91; V Morecambe St Barn *Blackb* 91-99; V Colwyn *St As* 99-03; rtd 03. *2 Cwm Road, Dyserth, Rhyl LL18 6BB* Tel (01745) 571496

CZERNIAWSKA EDGCUMBE, Mrs Irena Christine. b 59. Trin Coll Ox BA82. Oak Hill Th Coll 93. **d** 95 **p** 96. NSM De Beauvoir Town St Pet *Lon* 95-99; Chapl Raines Foundn Sch Tower Hamlets 99-04; NSM Bow Common 00-04; P-in-c Hoxton St Anne w St Columba from 04; Min Development Adv Stepney Area 04-07; Dean of Women's Min Stepney Area from 07. *St Anne's Vicarage, 37 Hemsworth Street, London N1 5LF* Tel (020) 7729 1243
E-mail irenaczerniawskaedgcumbe@hotmail.com

D

DA SILVA, Carlos Alberto Tome. *See* TOME DA SILVA, Carlos Alberto

DABORN, Mark Henry. b 55. Magd Coll Cam BA76 MA80 Wolv Univ QTS01 MRICS82. WEMTC 99. **d** 05 **p** 06. NSM Cleobury Mortimer w Hopton Wafers etc *Heref* from 05. *Kinlet Hall, Kinlet, Bewdley DY12 3AY* Tel (01299) 841230 Fax 841444 Mobile 07808-840992 E-mail mhd@moffats.co.uk

DABORN, Robert Francis. b 53. Keble Coll Ox BA74 MA78 Fitzw Coll Cam BA77. Ridley Hall Cam 75. **d** 78 **p** 79. C Mortlake w E Sheen *S'wark* 78-81; Chapl Collingwood and Grey Coll *Dur* 82-86; V Lapley w Wheaton Aston *Lich* 86-91; P-in-c Blymhill w Weston-under-Lizard 89-91; P-in-c Tibberton w Bolas Magna and Waters Upton 91-99; Shropshire Local Min Adv 91-99; P-in-c Childs Ercall and Stoke upon Tern 92-95; Dir Local Min Development 99-05; Dir Past Studies WEMTC *Heref* 05-09; Vice-Prin from 09. *The Vicarage, Orleton, Ludlow SY8 4HN* Tel (01568) 780881
E-mail robert.daborn@btinternet.com

DACK, Miss Margaret Patricia. b 58. Offley Teacher Tr Coll TCert61. Oak Hill NSM Course 91. **d** 93 **p** 94. NSM Letchworth St Paul w Willian *St Alb* from 93. *91 Penn Way, Letchworth Garden City SG6 2SH* Tel (01462) 634956

DACK, Paul Marven. K Coll Lon AKC51 BD51. St Boniface Warminster. **d** 52 **p** 53. C Leckhampton St Pet *Glouc* 52-55; R Bourton on the Hill 55-61; R Quedgeley 61-82; P-in-c Hasfield w Tirley and Ashleworth 82-90; rtd 90; Perm to Offic *Glouc* 90-96; and from 01. *19 Arle Gardens, Cheltenham GL51 8HP* Tel (01242) 261627

DADD, Alan Edward. b 50. St Jo Coll Nottm 77. **d** 78 **p** 79. C Bishopsworth *Bris* 78-81; V Springfield *Birm* 81-85; Chapl Poly Cen Lon 85-86; V Hanger Lane St Ann 86-93; rtd 93. *C14 Elizabeth Court, Grove Road, Bournemouth BH1 3DU*

DADD, Canon Peter Wallace. b 38. Sheff Univ BA59. Qu Coll Birm 59. **d** 61 **p** 62. C Grays Thurrock *Chelmsf* 61-65; C Grantham St Wulfram *Linc* 65-70; C Grantham w Manthorpe 70-72; TV 72-73; V Haxey 73-90; RD Is of Axholme 82-90; V Gainsborough All SS 90-98; Can and Preb Linc Cathl 91-08; P-in-c Flixborough w Burton upon Stather 98-00; V 00-08; rtd 08. *15 Southfields Rise, North Leverton, Retford DN22 0AY* Tel (01427) 884191 E-mail peterdadd@tiscali.co.uk

DADSON, Lawrence Michael (Mike). b 29. G&C Coll Cam MA56 Lon Univ BSc(Econ)64. St Deiniol's Hawarden 80. **d** 92 **p** 92. NSM Bramhall *Ches* 92-95; Perm to Offic from 97. *14 Yew Tree Park Road, Cheadle Hulme, Cheadle SK8 7EP* Tel 0161-485 2482

DADSWELL, David Ian. b 58. New Coll Ox BA80 MA83 Brunel Univ MPhil97. Westcott Ho Cam 80. **d** 83 **p** 84. C W Derby St Mary *Liv* 83-87; Chapl Brunel Univ 87-96; Perm to Offic *Lon* 96-04 and *Ox* 98-04; Hon C New Windsor *Ox* from 04. *243 St Leonards Road, Windsor SL4 3DR* Tel (01753) 864827
E-mail d.dadswell@me.com

DADSWELL, The Ven Richard Edward. b 46. CITC BTh98. **d** 98 **p** 99. C Cork St Fin Barre's Union *C, C & R* 98-01; Min Can Cork Cathl 00-01; I Ballisodare w Collooney and Emlaghfad *T, K & A* 01-09; Dioc Dir of Ords 03-09; Adn Killala and Achonry 05-09; rtd 09. *8 Fox Ridge, Rathfriland, Newry BT34 5FR* Tel (028) 4063 1154

D'AETH, Mrs Emma Louise Alice. b 63. Portsm Univ BA03. STETS 04. **d** 07. NSM Portsea St Mary *Portsm* from 07. *52 Belmont Street, Southsea PO5 1ND* Tel (023) 9286 2108
E-mail emmadaeth@yahoo.co.uk

DAFFERN, Canon Adrian Mark. b 68. St Jo Coll Dur BA89 MA06 FRCO98 FRSA99. St Steph Ho Ox 90. **d** 92 **p** 93. C Lich St Chad 92-95; TV Stafford 95-00; V Walsall Wood 00-03; Treas V Lich Cathl 97-03; Can Res and Prec Cov Cathl from 03. *8 Priory Row, Coventry CV1 5EX* Tel (024) 7652 1200
E-mail adrian.daffern@coventrycathedral.org.uk

DAFFERN, Mrs Megan Isobel Jane. b 80. Ex Coll Ox BA02 MA06 SS Coll Cam BA05 MA09. Westcott Ho Cam 03. **d** 06 **p** 07. C Rugby *Cov* from 06; Chapl Jes Coll Ox from 09; Perm to Offic *Cov* from 09. *Jesus College, Oxford OX1 3DW* Tel (01865) 279757 E-mail chaplain@jesus.ox.ac.uk

DAGGETT, Michael Wayne. b 47. Portland State Univ BSc72. Ridley Hall Cam 84. **d** 86 **p** 87. C Tyldesley w Shakerley *Man* 86-90; V Swinton H Rood 90-02; Chapl Eccles Sixth Form Coll 90-02; rtd 02. *138 Elliott Street, Tyldesley, Manchester M29 8FJ* Tel (01942) 883437

DAGLEISH, John. b 38. Goldsmiths' Coll Lon MA01 ACIB74. S'wark Ord Course 75. **d** 78 **p** 79. NSM Riddlesdown *S'wark* 78-99; NSM All Hallows by the Tower etc *Lon* 79-89; Chapl Asst Guy's Hosp Lon 87-89. *42 Brancaster Lane, Purley CR8 1HF* Tel and fax (020) 8660 6060

DAGLISH, John David. b 44. RMCS BSc70. Cranmer Hall Dur 74. **d** 77 **p** 78. C Ormesby *York* 77-79; C Kirk Ella 79-82; V Hull St Cuth 82-97; NSM Beverley St Mary 00-01; P-in-c Thorpe Edge *Bradf* 01-05; V Gt Marsden w Nelson St Phil *Blackb* 05-09; rtd 09. *13 St Barnabas Close, Gloucester GL1 5LH* E-mail john.daglish2@ntlworld.com

DAGNALL, Canon Bernard. b 44. K Coll Lon BSc65 AKC65 Ox Univ BA75 MA78 CChem MRSC MSOSc88 CSci04. St Steph Ho Ox 72. **d** 75 **p** 76. C Stanningley St Thos *Ripon* 75-76; C Lightbowne *Man* 76-78; C-in-c Grahame Park St Aug CD *Lon* 78-84; V Earley St Nic *Ox* 84-91; Ind Chapl 85-91; TR N Huddersfield *Wakef* 91-93; TV Newbury *Ox* from 93; Chapl W Berks Priority Care Services NHS Trust 93-01; Chapl Newbury and Community Primary Care Trust 01-06; Chapl Berks W Primary Care Trust from 06; Superior Soc of Retreat Conductors 00-05; Hon Can Ho Ghana from 04. *The Vicarage, 1 Chesterfield Road, Newbury RG14 7QB* Tel (01635) 230216 Fax 230215 E-mail dagnall@boltblue.com *or* frbernard@saintjohn.co.uk

DAILEY, Douglas Grant. b 56. Nottm Univ BTh88. Linc Th Coll 85. **d** 88 **p** 89. C Leominster *Heref* 88-91; Assoc R Hickory Ascension USA 91-93; R Statesville 93-02; R Gainesville Grace Ch from 02. *3603 Tradition Drive, Gainesville GA 30506-3600, USA* Tel (001) (770) 536 0126
E-mail ddailey@gracechurchgainesville.org

DAIMOND, John Ellerbeck. b 39. St Cuth Soc Dur BA61. Ripon Hall Ox 61. **d** 63 **p** 64. C Caverswall *Lich* 63-66; Chapl RAF 66-85; Asst Chapl-in-Chief RAF 85-91; QHC 89-91; V Shawbury *Lich* 91-95; R Moreton Corbet 91-95; V Stanton on Hine Heath 91-95; rtd 99; P-in-c Pattingham w Patshull *Lich* 02-08; Perm to Offic from 08. *The Hollies, Church Street, Uffington, Shrewsbury SY4 4SN* Tel (01743) 709034

DAINTREE, Canon Geoffrey Thomas. b 54. Bris Univ BSc77. Trin Coll Bris 78. **d** 81 **p** 82. C Old Hill H Trin *Worc* 81-85; C Tunbridge Wells St Jo *Roch* 85-89; V Framfield *Chich* 89-00; RD Uckfield 96-00; V Eastbourne St Jo 00-09; Chs Relns Manager Chr Aid from 09; Perm to Offic *Chich* from 09; Hon Can Cyangugu (Rwanda) from 97. *5 Upper Wish Hill, Eastbourne BN20 9HB* Tel (01323) 501102
E-mail geoff.daintree@googlemail.com

DAINTY, James Ernest. b 46. Open Univ BA86 ALBC68. Cranmer Hall Dur 71. **d** 73 **p** 74. C Normanton *Wakef* 73-76; C Gillingham St Mark *Roch* 76-78; V Barnsley St Geo *Wakef* 78-88; Chapl Barnsley Distr Gen Hosp 78-88; Chapl Seacroft Hosp Leeds 88-94; Chapl Killingbeck and Meanwood Park Hosps Leeds 88-94; P-in-c Turnham Green Ch Ch *Lon* 94-97; V 97-06; rtd 06; Perm to Offic *Ches* from 06; Chapl Maranatha Community Flixton from 08. *10 Albion Street, Wallasey CH45 9LY* Tel 0151-638 4425
E-mail jimdainty@dunelm.org.uk

DAKIN (née HOLLETT), Mrs Catherine Elaine. b 53. Qu Eliz Coll Lon BSc73. St Jo Coll Nottm 88. **d** 90 **p** 05. Par Dn Horley *S'wark* 90-93; NSM Heydon, Gt and Lt Chishill, Chrishall etc *Chelmsf* 93-97; NSM Gt and Lt Maplestead w Gestingthorpe 97-99; NSM Knights and Hospitallers Par 99-01; NSM Fulford w Hilderstone *Lich* from 01. *20 Tudor Hollow, Fulford, Stoke-on-Trent ST11 9NP* Tel (01782) 397073

DAKIN, Peter David. b 57. Wye Coll Lon BSc79. St Jo Coll Nottm 91. **d** 91 **p** 92. NSM Southgate *Chich* 91-93; C Heydon, Gt and Lt Chishill, Chrishall etc *Chelmsf* 93-97; P-in-c Gt and Lt Maplestead w Gestingthorpe 97-99; P-in-c Pebmarsh 99; V Knights and Hospitallers Par 99-01; P-in-c Fulford w Hilderstone *Lich* from 01; Rural Officer for Staffs from 01; RD Stone from 07. *20 Tudor Hollow, Fulford, Stoke-on-Trent ST11 9NP* Tel (01782) 397073 Fax (01780) 761764
E-mail pdakin@waitrose.com

DAKIN, Reginald James Blanchard. b 25. S'wark Ord Course 66. **d** 70 **p** 71. C Preston Ascension *Lon* 70-74; C Greenhill St Jo 74-76; P-in-c Littleton 76-80; R 80-95; CF (ACF) 78-95; Warden for Readers (Kensington Episc Area) 88-95; rtd 95; Perm to Offic *Nor* 95-00 and from 01; Chapl Malta 97-99. *22 Heywood Avenue, Diss IP22 4DN* Tel (01379) 641167

DAKIN, Mrs Sally. b 58. SRN79 SCM82 RHV85 K Coll Lon MSc89 TCert92. SAOMC 02. **d** 04 **p** 05. NSM Ruscombe and

Twyford *Ox* from 04. *3 Highgrove Place, Ruscombe, Reading RG10 9LF* Tel 0118-934 3909 E-mail timsal@tinyworld.co.uk

DAKIN, Canon Stanley Frederick. b 30. CA52. Roch Th Coll 63. **d** 65 **p** 66. C Meole Brace *Lich* 65-68; V 68-72; R Sutton 68-72; Hosp Chapl Nairobi Kenya 72-75; P-in-c Nettlebed *Ox* 75-81; P-in-c Bix w Pishill 77-81; P-in-c Highmore 78-81; R Nettlebed w Bix and Highmore 81; V Ealing Dean St Jo *Lon* 81-84; V W Ealing St Jo w St Jas 84-92; Hon Can Mombasa from 89; Gen Sec CA Africa from 92; rtd 99; Perm to Offic *Lich* 99-02; *Ox* from 02. *71 Rectory Crescent, Middle Barton, Chipping Norton OX7 7BP* Tel (01869) 349983

DAKIN, Canon Timothy John. b 58. SS Mark & Jo Univ Coll Plymouth BA86 K Coll Lon MTh87. **d** 93 **p** 94. Prin Carlile Coll Kenya 93-00; C Nairobi Cathl 94-00; Gen Sec CMS from 00; Gen Sec SAMS from 09; Hon C Ruscombe and Twyford *Ox* from 00; Can Th Cov Cathl from 01. *3 Highgrove Place, Ruscombe, Reading RG10 9LF* Tel and fax 0118-934 3909 E-mail timsal@tinyworld.co.uk

DALAIS, Duncan John. b 56. St Paul's Coll Grahamstown. **d** 83 **p** 84. C Pinetown St Jo B S Africa 83-87; C Chingford SS Pet and Paul *Chelmsf* 87-92; V Aldersbrook 92-02; P-in-c Leytonstone St Andr from 02; Asst Chapl Forest Healthcare NHS Trust Lon from 02. *St Andrew's Vicarage, 7 Forest Glade, London E11 1LU* Tel (020) 8989 0942 *or* 8520 6328 Mobile 07714-760068 E-mail duncan.dalais@virgin.net

DALBY, The Ven John <u>Mark</u> Meredith. b 38. Ex Coll Ox BA61 MA65 Nottm Univ PhD77. Ripon Hall Ox 61. **d** 63 **p** 64. C Hambleden *Ox* 63-68; C Medmenham 66-68; V Birm St Pet 68-75; RD Birm City 73-75; Hon C Tottenham All Hallows *Lon* 75-80; Selection Sec and Sec Cttee for Th Educn ACCM 75-80; V Worsley *Man* 80-84; TR 84-91; AD Eccles 87-91; Adn Rochdale 91-00; rtd 00; Chapl Beauchamp Community 00-07. *St Christopher's, The Beauchamp Community, Newland, Malvern WR13 5AX* Tel and fax (01684) 899198 E-mail jmmdalby@btinternet.com

DALE, Miss Barbara. b 48. Cranmer Hall Dur 78. **dss** 81 **d** 87 **p** 94. N Wingfield, Pilsley and Tupton *Derby* 81-90; Par Dn 87-90; Par Dn N Wingfield, Clay Cross and Pilsley 90-94; TV 94-00; C Eckington and Ridgeway 00-04; TV E Scarsdale from 04. *The Vicarage, Main Street, Shirebrook, Mansfield NG20 8DN* Tel (01623) 740479

DALE, Charles William. b 49. **d** 02 **p** 03. OLM Uttoxeter Area *Lich* from 02. *Manor Court, Kingstone, Uttoxeter ST14 8QH* Tel (01889) 500428 E-mail charles.dale@tesco.net

DALE, Ms Christine. b 62. Trin Coll Bris BA94. **d** 94 **p** 95. C Thatcham *Ox* 94-98; TV Bracknell 98-02; R E Woodhay and Woolton Hill *Win* from 02; RD Whitchurch from 08. *The Rectory, The Mount, Woolton Hill, Newbury RG20 9QZ* Tel (01635) 253323 E-mail revdc@cdsm.wanadoo.co.uk

DALE, Eric <u>Stephen</u>. b 24. Roch Th Coll 63. **d** 65 **p** 66. C Kippax *Ripon* 65-67; C Fulford *York* 67-69; V Askham Bryan 69-70; V Askham Richard 69-70; V Askham Bryan w Askham Richard 70-78; Chapl HM Pris Askham Grange 69-78; Chapl HM Pris Wakef 78-79; Chapl HM Pris Gartree 79-82; Chapl HM Pris Leeds 82-89; rtd 89. *31 Kirkwood Lane, Leeds LS16 7EN* Tel 0113-230 0766

DALE, John Anthony. b 42. Open Univ BSc00. Qu Coll Birm 72. **d** 75 **p** 76. C Elmley Castle w Bricklehampton and Combertons *Worc* 75-81; P-in-c 81-83; R 83-88; Hon Can Worc Cathl 87-92; V Hallow 88-92; Dioc Registrar 92; P-in-c Michaelston-y-Fedw *Mon* 03-08; rtd 08. *Bron yr Aur, Pennal, Machynlleth SY20 8QA* E-mail jadale@onetel.com

DALE, Martin Nicholas. b 55. Chelsea Coll Lon BSc76 CPA83. Wycliffe Hall Ox 99. **d** 01 **p** 02. C Stiffkey and Cockthorpe w Morston, Langham etc *Nor* 01-03; C Stiffkey and Bale 03-04; P-in-c New Romney w Old Romney and Midley *Cant* 04-07; P-in-c St Mary's Bay w St Mary-in-the-Marsh etc 04-07; P-in-c Dymchurch w Burmarsh and Newchurch 05-07; P-in-c Upper Wreake *Leic* from 07; P-in-c S Croxton Gp from 07; P-in-c Burrough Hill Pars from 07. *The Rectory, 2 Carrfields Lane, Frisby on the Wreake, Melton Mowbray LE14 2NT* Tel (01664) 434878 Mobile 07887-554761 E-mail mndale@aol.com

DALE, Miss Olive Sylvia. b 44. Stockwell Coll of Educn TCert66. Faculté de Théologie Évangélique Vaux-sur-Seine France MScRel76 WMMTC 91. **d** 94 **p** 97. C Highley *Heref* 94-96; C Leominster 96-98; Chapl Asst Linc and Louth NHS Trust 98-00; rtd 00; Perm to Offic *Heref* from 00. *clo Miss V M Dale, 228 Whittern Way, Hereford HR1 1QP* Tel (01432) 352406

DALES, Douglas John. b 52. FRHistS90 Ch Ch Ox BA74 MA78 BD89. Cuddesdon Coll 74. **d** 77 **p** 78. C Shepperton *Lon* 77-81; C Ely 81-83; Chapl Marlborough Coll from 84; Hd of RE from 84. *Hillside, Bath Road, Marlborough SN8 1NN* Tel (01672) 514557

DALEY, David Michael. b 50. Oak Hill Th Coll BA90. **d** 92 **p** 92. C Enfield Ch Ch Trent Park *Lon* 92-94; V Chitts Hill St Cuth from 94. *St Cuthbert's Vicarage, 85 Wolves Lane, London N22 5JD* Tel (020) 8888 6178 E-mail ddaley@ukonline.co.uk *or* st.cuthbert@ukonline.co.uk

DALEY, Judith. b 54. Sheff Univ BA94 Leeds Univ PhD03. NOC 03. **d** 04 **p** 05. NSM Sheff St Leon Norwood from 04; Chapl Sheff Teaching Hosps NHS Foundn Trust from 02. *112 Broad Inge Crescent, Chapeltown, Sheffield S35 1RU* Tel 0114-246 8824 E-mail judith.daley@sth.nhs.uk

DALEY, Preb Victor Leonard. b 38. Chich Th Coll 76. **d** 78 **p** 79. C Durrington *Chich* 78-81; C Somerton w Compton Dundon, the Charltons etc *B & W* 81-87; P-in-c Cheddar 87-88; V 88-08; P-in-c Rodney Stoke w Draycott 02-03; RD Axbridge 91-03; rtd 08; Preb Wells Cathl from 97. *Barns, Cheddar Road, Wedmore BS28 4EJ* Tel (01934) 710404 E-mail victormrwoo@aol.com

DALGLISH, David John. b 45. Heriot-Watt Univ BSc70 Open Univ BA94 Edin Univ MBA97. TISEC 07. **d** 08. NSM Melrose *Edin* from 08. *The Birks, 14 Abbotsferry Road, Tweedbank, Galashiels TD1 3RX* Tel (01896) 758803 Mobile 07858-140200 E-mail david_dalglish@btinternet.com

DALLAWAY, Philip Alan. b 48. Chich Th Coll 80. **d** 81 **p** 82. C Newbury *Ox* 81-83; C Newport Pagnell w Lathbury 83-85; V Stewkley w Soulbury and Drayton Parslow 85-92; P-in-c Didcot All SS 92-97; R 97-00; V Caversham St Jo 00-07; rtd 07. *20 Applehaigh Close, Bradford BD10 9DW* Tel (01274) 614803 E-mail p.dallaway@btinternet.com

DALLEY, Gail Margaret. b 53. Cranmer Hall Dur 05. **d** 07 **p** 08. NSM Pocklington and Owsthorpe and Kilnwick Percy etc *York* from 07. *63 Algarth Rise, Pocklington, York YO42 2HX* Tel (01759) 301920

DALLING, Roger Charles. b 26. Lon Univ BSc53. S Dios Minl Tr Scheme 79. **d** 83 **p** 84. NSM Lewes St Jo sub Castro *Chich* 83-84; NSM Uckfield 84-98; NSM Isfield 84-98; NSM Lt Horsted 84-98; rtd 98; Perm to Offic *Chich* from 98. *1 Avis Close, Denton, Newhaven BN9 0DN* Tel (01273) 515970

DALLISTON, The Very Revd Christopher Charles. b 56. Ox Univ BA Cam Univ MA. St Steph Ho Ox 81. **d** 84 **p** 85. C Halstead St Andr w H Trin and Greenstead Green *Chelmsf* 84-87; Bp's Dom Chapl 87-91; V Forest Gate St Edm 91-95; P-in-c Boston *Linc* 95-97; V 97-03; RD Holland E 97-03; Dean Newc from 03. *The Cathedral Vicarage, 26 Mitchell Avenue, Jesmond, Newcastle upon Tyne NE2 3LA* Tel 0191-281 6554 *or* 232 1939 Fax 230 0735 E-mail dean@stnicnewcastle.co.uk

DALLOW, Gillian Margaret. b 45. Univ of Wales (Ban) BA66 DipEd67 Bris Univ MEd87. Oak Hill Th Coll 93. **d** 96 **p** 97. NSM W Ealing St Jo w St Jas *Lon* 96-99; P-in-c Barlestone and Dioc Children's Min Adv *Leic* 99-08; rtd 08; Perm to Offic *Lon* from 08. *57 The High Street, Northwood HA6 1EB* Tel (01923) 840111 Mobile 07801-650187 E-mail g.dallow@btinternet.com

DALLY, Keith Richard. b 47. FCCA77. St Jo Coll Nottm 80. **d** 82 **p** 83. C Southend St Sav Westcliff *Chelmsf* 82-85; Ind Chapl 85-93; C Southend 85-86; TV 86-92; C Harold Hill St Geo 92-93; Cen Co-ord Langham Place All So Clubhouse *Lon* 97-02; Perm to Offic *Ox* 02-05 and *Pet* from 05. *44 Findlay Avenue, Abington, Northampton NN3 2SJ* Tel (01604) 414453

DALRIADA, Archdeacon of. *See* FORDE, The Ven Stephen Bernard

DALRYMPLE, Wendy. b 75. Coll of Resurr Mirfield. **d** 07 **p** 08. C Mirfield *Wakef* from 07. *4 Hopton Hall Lane, Mirfield WF14 8EL* Tel 07939-513561 (mobile) E-mail priestwendy@btinternet.com

DALTON, Anthony Isaac. b 57. Em Coll Cam BA78 MA82 Leeds Univ BA82. Coll of Resurr Mirfield. **d** 82 **p** 83. C Carl St Aid and Ch Ch 82-86; C Caversham St Pet and Mapledurham etc *Ox* 86-88; P-in-c Accrington St Mary *Blackb* 88-91; V 91-92; Chapl Victoria Hosp Accrington 88-92; V Sheff St Cecilia Parson Cross 92-96; P-in-c Burnley St Cath w St Alb and St Paul *Blackb* 96-98; V 98-01; R Orton and Tebay w Ravenstonedale etc *Carl* 01-07; CF from 07. *clo MOD Chaplains (Army)* Tel (01980) 615804 Fax 615800 E-mail tonydaltonuk@yahoo.co.uk

DALTON, Bertram Jeremy (<u>Tod</u>). b 32. ACIB64. Sarum & Wells Th Coll 81. **d** 83 **p** 84. C Ringwood *Win* 83-86; R Norton sub Hamdon, W Chinnock, Chiselborough etc *B & W* 86-97; rtd 97; Perm to Offic *B & W* from 97. *Meadow Cottage, 8 Woodbarton, Milverton, Taunton TA4 1LU* Tel (01823) 400302

D'ALTON, Craig William. b 68. Melbourne Univ BA90 MA94 PhD99. Melbourne Coll of Div BTheol98. **d** 00 **p** 00. C S Yarra Ch Ch Australia 00-03; C Melbourne St Pet 03-07; C Ox St Mary V w St Cross and St Pet from 07. *22 Stratford Street, Oxford OX4 1SW* Tel (01865) 2279111 Mobile 07717-211252 E-mail craig.stmarys@gmail.com

DALTON, Derek. b 40. NOC. **d** 84 **p** 85. NSM Pool w Arthington *Ripon* 84-87; P-in-c Thornton Watlass w Thornton Steward 87-90; C Bedale 87-90; R Wensley 90-95; V W Witton 90-95; R Romaldkirk w Laithkirk 95-97; rtd 97; Perm to Offic *Ripon* from 98. *North Wing, Thornton Watlass Hall, Ripon HG4 4AS* Tel (01677) 425302

DALTON, Kevin. b 32. TCD BA65. Ch Div Sch of the Pacific (USA) BD67 CITC 66. **d** 66 **p** 67. C Stillorgan *D & G* 66-72; I Dublin Drumcondra w N Strand 72-79; I Monkstown 79-07; rtd 07. *Norwood Lodge, Shanganagh Road, Ballybrack, Co Dublin, Republic of Ireland* Tel (00353) (1) 282 2778 Mobile 87-122 4807 E-mail kevinthehumble@gmail.com

DALTON, Tod. *See* DALTON, Bertram Jeremy

DALTRY, Paul Richard. b 56. St Jo Coll Nottm 90. **d** 92 **p** 93. C Ipswich St Matt *St E* 92-96; P-in-c Needham Market w Badley 96-05; RD Bosmere 01-05; R Ipswich St Helen, H Trin, and St Luke 05-09; Min for Ch and Community Engagement from 09. *The Rectory, 42 Clapgate Lane, Ipswich IP3 0RD* Tel (01473) 723467 E-mail paul@daltry.co.uk

DALY, Ms Bernadette Theresa. b 45. TCD BTh94. **d** 97 **p** 98. C Taney *D & G* 97-00 and 05-06; Dir Past Studies CITC 00-04; rtd 06. *27 Southmede, Ballinteer Road, Ballinteer, Dublin 16, Republic of Ireland* Tel (00353) 86-241 9009 (mobile) E-mail berdaly@live.com

DALY, Miss Dorothy Isabel. b 40. Vancouver Sch of Th BTh74. **dss** 64 **d** 77. Stepney St Aug w St Phil *Lon* 65-66; Hanworth St Geo 66-71; Canada from 71; rtd 00. *26 Farquhar Place, Elliot Lake ON P5A 3J3, Canada* E-mail daly@onlink.net

DALY, Gary James. b 63. Wycliffe Hall Ox 07. **d** 09. C Muswell Hill St Jas w St Matt *Lon* from 09. *8 St James Lane, London N10 3DB* Tel (020) 8442 2902 Mobile 07957-154787 E-mail gazdaly@tinyonline.co.uk

DALY, Jeffrey. b 50. Bris Univ BA73 Jes Coll Cam PGCE74 Fitzw Coll Cam BA82 MA86 Westmr Coll Ox MTh03. Ridley Hall Cam 80. **d** 83 **p** 84. C Tilehurst St Mich *Ox* 83-89; P-in-c Steventon w Milton 89-92; Asst Chapl Sherborne Sch 92-96; Chapl St Pet Sch York from 96. *St Peter's School, Clifton, York YO30 6AB* Tel (01904) 527412 E-mail j.daly@st-peters.york.sch.uk

DALY, Martin Jonathan. b 48. Woolwich Poly BSc69. **d** 05 **p** 06. C Upton (Overchurch) *Ches* from 05. *Fairfield Lodge, 1 Columbia Road, Prenton CH43 6TU* Tel 0151-670 1461 Mobile 07710-242241 E-mail martin@stm-upton.org.uk

DAMIAN, Brother. *See* KIRKPATRICK, Roger James

DANBY, Shirley Elizabeth. b 49. St Hugh's Coll Ox BA72 Portsm Univ PhD76. STETS 07. **d** 09. NSM Cricklade w Latton *Bris* from 09; NSM Ashton Keynes, Leigh and Minety from 09. *The Old Manse, 21 High Street, Cricklade, Swindon SN6 6AP* Tel (01793) 751463 Mobile 07980-548844 E-mail shirleydanby@tiscali.co.uk

DANCE, Peter Patrick. b 31. Em Coll Saskatoon 66. **d** 69 **p** 69. Canada 69-71; C Hednesford *Lich* 71-75; P-in-c Westcote Barton and Steeple Barton *Ox* 76-77; P-in-c Sandford St Martin 76-77; R Westcote Barton w Steeple Barton, Duns Tew etc 77-89; R Castle Douglas *Glas* 89-97; rtd 97. *Mannville, High Street, Adderbury, Banbury OX17 3NA* Tel (01295) 811989

DAND, Mrs Angela Jane. b 49. St Andr Univ BSc70 Newc Univ PGCE71. **d** 98 **p** 99. OLM Astley *Man* 98-06; OLM Astley, Tyldesley and Mosley Common from 06. *20 Acresfield, Astley, Tyldesley, Manchester M29 7NL* Tel (01942) 879608

DANDO, Ms Elaine Vera. b 53. Coll of Resurr Mirfield 94 NOC 98. **d** 00 **p** 01. C Luddenden w Luddenden Foot *Wakef* 00-03; C Halifax 03-04; Lic to Offic 04-05; Chapl Univ Coll *Lon* 05-08; C St Pancras w St Jas and Ch Ch 05-08; C Northwood H Trin from 08. *St Lawrence's Vicarage, 2 Bridle Road, Pinner HA5 2SJ* Tel (020) 8866 1263 E-mail evd.macrina@btinternet.com

DANDO, Stephen. b 49. Goldsmiths' Coll Lon TCert70. Coll of Resurr Mirfield 81. **d** 83 **p** 84. C Wandsworth St Anne *S'wark* 83-87; V Stainland *Wakef* 87-99; V Illingworth 99-05; V Eastcote St Lawr *Lon* from 05. *St Lawrence's Vicarage, 2 Bridle Road, Pinner HA5 2SJ* Tel (020) 8866 1263 E-mail dandostephen@hotmail.com

DANE, John William. b 52. St Jo Coll Nottm 04. **d** 06 **p** 07. C Deddington w Barford, Clifton and Hempton *Ox* 06-09; Chapl Chich Univ from 09. *Chaplaincy, University of Chichester, Bishop Otter Campus, College Lane, Chichester PO19 6PE* Tel (01243) 816041 E-mail chaplain@chi.ac.uk *or* john@ausome.co.uk

DANES, Charles William. b 28. Chich Th Coll 54. **d** 56 **p** 57. C N Greenford All Hallows *Lon* 56-59; C Caversham *Ox* 59-63; V Walsgrave on Sowe *Cov* 63-65; P-in-c Hanworth All SS *Lon* 65-67; V 68-76; P-in-c Wick *Chich* 76-78; V Littlehampton St Jas 76-78; P-in-c Littlehampton St Mary 76-78; V W Worthing St Jo 78-87; Chapl Monte Carlo *Eur* 87-93; rtd 93; Perm to Offic *Chelmsf* and *Eur* from 93. *31 Oakley Road, Braintree CM7 5QS* Tel (01376) 324586

DANGERFIELD, Canon Andrew Keith. b 63. Univ of Wales (Ban) BD87. St Steph Ho Ox 87. **d** 89 **p** 90. C St Marychurch *Ex* 89-93; C-in-c Grahame Park St Aug CD *Lon* 93-96; V Tottenham St Paul 96-06; P-in-c Edmonton St Mary w St Jo 98-04; AD E Haringey 00-05; V Kensal Green St Jo from 06; Hon Can Cape Coast from 04. *St John's New Vicarage, Kilburn Lane, London W10 4AA* Tel (020) 8969 2615 Mobile 07767-687954

DANIEL, Arthur Guy St John. b 12. K Coll Cam BA33 MA37. Cuddesdon Coll 34. **d** 35 **p** 36. C Blandford Forum *Sarum* 35-38; C Reading St Jo 38-45; C Marlow 46-46; V Colnbrook 46-78; TV Riverside 78-80; rtd 80; Perm to Offic *Ox* 80-87. *45 Abbey View Nursing Home, Fairfield, Bristol Road, Sherborne DT9 4HG* Tel (01935) 389934

DANIEL, Gaynor Elizabeth. *See* DANIEL-LOWANS, Mrs Gaynor Elizabeth

DANIEL, Canon Herrick Haynes. b 38. Open Univ BA81. Trin Coll Bris 73. **d** 75 **p** 76. C Harlesden St Mark *Lon* 75-78; C Livesey *Blackb* 78-81; V Blackb St Barn 81-08; Hon Can Blackb Cathl 98-08; rtd 08; Perm to Offic *Blackb* from 08. *40 Appletree Drive, Lancaster LA1 4QY* Tel (01524) 389764 E-mail herrickdaniel@hotmail.co.uk

DANIEL, Mrs Joy. b 44. Gilmore Course 81 Oak Hill Th Coll 82. **dss** 84 **d** 87 **p** 94. Luton St Fran *St Alb* 84-02; Par Dn 87-94; C 94-02; P-in-c Woodside from 02. *St Andrew's Vicarage, Church Road, Slip End, Luton LU1 4BJ* Tel (01582) 424363 E-mail joy@daniel67.freeserve.co.uk

DANIEL, Philip Sharman. b 62. Man Univ BA83 Rob Coll Cam CertEd84. Wycliffe Hall Ox 84. **d** 86 **p** 87. C Macclesfield Team *Ches* 86-89; C Cheadle 89-94; V Disley 94-07; TR Mid Trent *Lich* from 07. *The Rectory, Stafford Road, Weston, Stafford ST18 0HX* Tel (01889) 271870 E-mail revpsdan@btinternet.com

DANIEL, Rajinder Kumar. b 34. St Steph Coll Delhi 55 Westcott Ho Cam 61. **d** 63 **p** 64. C Purley St Barn *S'wark* 63-66; C Battersea St Pet 66-67; C N Harrow St Alb *Lon* 67-72; TV Beaconsfield *Ox* 72-75; V Smethwick St Matt w St Chad *Birm* 75-87; Dioc Adv on Black Min 87-92; Chapl Birm Gen Hosp 91-92; TR Braunstone *Leic* 92-01; rtd 01; USPG and R Arima St Jude Trinidad and Tobago 03-04; Perm to Offic *Birm* from 04. *508 Chester Road, Kingshurst, Birmingham B36 0LG* Tel 0121-770 1066

DANIEL-LOWANS, Mrs Gaynor Elizabeth. b 46. Llan Ord Course 98. **d** 98 **p** 99. NSM St Brides Minor w Bettws *Llan* 98-01; C 01-02; C St Brides Minor w Bettws w Aberkenfig 02-04; C Llansantffraid, Bettws and Aberkenfig from 04. *5 Coronation Street, Bryn, Port Talbot SA13 2SE* Tel (01639) 891871

DANIELL, Robert. b 37. **d** 87 **p** 88. C Camberwell St Giles w St Matt *S'wark* 90-92; V Lewisham St Swithun 92-07; rtd 07. *4 Glenhouse Road, London SE9 1JQ* Tel (020) 8850 4594

DANIELS, Geoffrey Gregory. b 23. St Pet Coll Ox BA48 MA53 Lambeth STh60. Linc Th Coll 73. **d** 73 **p** 75. NSM Diss *Nor* 73-74; NSM Bexhill St Pet *Chich* 74-83; C Eastbourne St Andr 83-84; V Horam 84-88; rtd 88; Chapl Convent of Dudwell St Mary from 88; NSM Bexhill St Andr CD *Chich* 90-95; Perm to Offic from 95. *20 Richmond Grove, Bexhill-on-Sea TN39 3EQ* Tel (01424) 211719

DANIELS, John Wyn. b 60. Southn Univ BSc82 PhD87. Trin Coll Bris MA92. **d** 92 **p** 93. C Roundhay St Edm *Ripon* 92-95; India 96; C Ambleside w Brathay *Carl* 97-01; Chapl St Martin's Coll Lanc 97-01; Res Can Ban Cathl 01-05; Min Development Officer *Bradf* from 05; C Embsay w Eastby from 05; C Skipton H Trin from 05. *The Vicarage, 21 Shires Lane, Embsay, Skipton BD23 6SB* Tel (01756) 798057 E-mail john.daniels@bradford.anglican.org *or* jd001@supanet.com

DANIELS, Lee Martin. b 61. Coll of Resurr Mirfield 99. **d** 01 **p** 02. C Toxteth Park St Agnes and St Pancras *Liv* 01-05; TV Staveley and Barrow Hill *Derby* from 05. *30 Cedar Street, Hollingwood, Chesterfield S43 2LE* Tel (01246) 281489 E-mail mazdaz@fsmail.net

DANKS, Alan Adam. b 41. Essex Univ MA01. Edin Th Coll 61. **d** 64 **p** 65. C Dumfries *Glas* 64-67; C Earl's Court St Cuth w St Matthias *Lon* 68-71; C St Steph Walbrook and St Swithun etc 71-74; C Brookfield St Mary 75-76; C Hendon St Mary 76-85. *64 Lower Oldfield Park, Bath BA2 3HP* Tel (01225) 314064 E-mail luccas@btinternet.com

DANKS-FLOWER, Marilyn Clare. b 42. **d** 08. Chapl Barts and The Lon NHS Trust from 08. *The Chaplaincy, St Bartholomew's Hospital, West Smithfield, London EC1A 7BE* Tel (020) 7601 8066 Mobile 07967-369103 E-mail kajori@tiscali.co.uk

DANSIE, Bruce John. b 40. Woolwich Poly BSc67 Univ Coll Lon MSc71 CEng72. Linc Th Coll 92. **d** 92 **p** 93. C Ivybridge w Harford *Ex* 92-96; P-in-c Charleton w Buckland Tout Saints etc 96-01; rtd 01. *566 Ostrea Lake Road, Musquodoboit Harbour NS B0J 2L0, Canada*

DANSON, Mrs Mary Agatha. MPS48 Strathclyde Univ PhC48. St Jo Coll Nottm 82. **d** 88 **p** 94. NSM Uddingston *Glas* from 88; NSM Cambuslang from 88. *3 Golf Road, Rutherglen, Glasgow G73 4JW* Tel 0141-634 4330

DAPLYN, Timothy James. b 52. Ripon Coll Cuddesdon 92. **d** 94 **p** 95. C Southmead *Bris* 94-97; P-in-c Abbots Leigh w Leigh Woods 97-99; Dioc Communications Officer 97-99; R Clutton w Cameley *B & W* 99-04; RD Chew Magna 03-04; P-in-c E w W Harptree and Hinton Blewett 04-08. *Coillegillie, Applecross, Strathcarron IV54 8LZ* Tel 07747-464833 (mobile) E-mail coillegillie@tesco.net

DARBY, Canon Anthony Ernest. b 26. Linc Th Coll 74. **d** 76 **p** 77. C Chilvers Coton w Astley *Cov* 76-79; P-in-c Longford 79-81; V 81-84; V Cov St Mary 84-91; RD Cov S 88-91; rtd 91; Chapl Cov Cathl from 91; Hon Can Th 00; Perm to Offic *Cov* from 00. *53 Ivybridge Road, Coventry CV3 5PF* Tel (024) 7641 4174 E-mail darby@bushinternet.com

DARBY, George. b 48. SWMTC 06. **d** 09. NSM Egloskerry, N Petherwin, Tremaine and Tresmere *Truro* from 09; NSM Lezant

w Lawhitton and S Petherwin w Trewen from 09. *7 Culvers Meadow, Launceston PL15 8RR* Tel (01566) 774719
E-mail gdandpd@btinternet.com

DARBY, Michael Barwick. b 34. St D Coll Lamp BA61 Tyndale Hall Bris 61. **d** 63 **p** 64. C Islington St Andr w St Thos and St Matthias *Lon* 63-66; C Ealing Dean St Jo 66-68; V Broomfleet *York* 68-73; Area Sec CCCS *York* and *Sheff* 68-73; V Paddington Em Harrow Road *Lon* 73-78; Iran 78-79; Brazil 80-83; Perm to Offic *Cant* 80-84; from 01; V Maidstone St Faith 84-90; UAE 90-92; V Platt Bridge *Liv* 93-99; rtd 99. *Paqueta, 79 Sandwich Road, Cliffsend, Ramsgate CT12 5JA* Tel (01843) 597228 Mobile 07947-582469

DARBY, Nicholas Peter. b 50. Kent Univ BA82 Surrey Univ MSc02. Sarum & Wells Th Coll 71. **d** 74 **p** 75. C Walton-on-Thames *Guildf* 74-78; C Horsell 78-80; USA 82-84; Chapl Lon Univ 84-89; Chapl R Lon Hosp (Whitechapel) 90-91; V Kew St Phil and All SS w St Luke *S'wark* 91-04; Dean Gaborone Botswana 04-07; V Fenham St Jas and St Basil *Newc* from 09. *St James and St Basil Vicarage, Wingrove Road North, Newcastle upon Tyne NE4 9EJ* Tel 0191-274 5078

DARBY, Preb Philip William, b 44. Bede Coll Dur TCert66. Qu Coll Birm. **d** 70 **p** 71. C Kidderminster St Geo *Worc* 70-74; P-in-c Dudley St Jo 74-79; V 79-80; P-in-c Catshill 80-82; V Catshill and Dodford 82-88; V Ipplepen w Torbryan *Ex* 88-00; V Ipplepen, Torbryan and Denbury 01-02; RD Newton Abbot and Ipplepen 93-01; V Ashburton w Buckland in the Moor and Bickington 02-05; P-in-c Widecombe-in-the-Moor, Leusdon, Princetown etc 04-05; TR Ashburton, Bickington, Buckland in the Moor etc from 05; Preb Ex Cathl from 02. *The Vicarage, Copperwood Close, Ashburton, Newton Abbot TQ13 7JQ* Tel (01364) 652506 E-mail pwdarby@supanet.com

DARBYSHIRE, Brian. b 48. TD04. Oak Hill Th Coll BA83. **d** 83 **p** 84. C Enfield St Jas *Lon* 83-86; R Slaidburn *Bradf* 86-92; V Gt Harwood St Jo *Blackb* 92-02; V Douglas St Ninian *S & M* 02-08; CF (TA) 90-04; V Bingara Australia from 08. *St John's Vicaraage, 8 Frazer Street, Bingara NSW 2404, Australia* Tel (0061) (2) 7624 1668 E-mail darbyshirebrian@hotmail.com

DARCH, John Henry. b 52. Univ of Wales (Lamp) BA73 PhD97 Lon Univ PGCE73 MA77. Trin Coll Bris 80. **d** 82 **p** 83. C Meole Brace *Lich* 82-85; C Hoole *Ches* 85-88; V Hyde St Geo 88-99; P-in-c Godley cum Newton Green 89-93; RD Mottram 91-99; Lect St Jo Coll Nottm 99-06; Chapl 03-06; Public Preacher *S'well* 99-06; Perm to Offic *Derby* 03-06; Dir of Ords and Dir IME 4-7 *Blackb* from 06. *24 Bosburn Drive, Mellor Brook, Blackburn BB2 7PA* Tel (01254) 813544
E-mail j.darch248@btinternet.com

DARK, Nicholas John. b 62. Leic Univ BA83 ACIB92. CITC BTh98. **d** 98 **p** 99. C Ballyhome *D & D* 98-05; I Magheragall *Conn* from 05. *Magheragall Rectory, 70 Ballinderry Road, Lisburn BT28 2QS* Tel (028) 9262 1273
E-mail magheragall@aol.com

DARLEY, Canon Shaun Arthur Neilson. b 36. Dur Univ BA61 Reading Univ MSc75. Cranmer Hall Dur 61. **d** 63 **p** 64. C Luton w E Hyde *St Alb* 63-67; Chapl Bris Tech Coll 67-69; Chapl Bris Poly 69-92; Sen Chapl UWE 92-01; Sec Cher 75-01; Sen Lect 75-01; Dir Cen for Performing Arts 85-02; Bp's Cathl Chapl 69-76; Hon Can Bris Cathl 89-01; rtd 01; Perm to Offic *B & W* from 98 and *Bris* from 02. *Church Paddock, Winscombe Hill, Bristol BS25 1DE* Tel (01934) 843633

DARLING, David Francis. b 55. TISEC 93. **d** 96 **p** 97. SSF 88-05; Novice Guardian 99-05; NSM Edin St Ninian 96-98; Chapl W Gen Hosps NHS 96-98; Chapl Edin Sick Children's NHS Trust 96-98; Lic Preacher *Lon* 03-05. *8 Church Mead, 234 Camberwell Road, London SE5 0ET* Tel (020) 7703 9794

✠**DARLING, The Rt Revd Edward Flewett.** b 33. TCD BA55 MA58. CITC. **d** 56 **p** 57 **c** 85. C Belfast St Luke *Conn* 56-59; C Orangefield *D & D* 59-62; C-in-c Carnalea 62-72; Chapl Ban Hosp 63-72; I Belfast Malone St Jo *Conn* 72-85; Min Can Belf Cathl 78-85; Chapl Ulster Independent Clinic 81-85; Bp L & K 85-00. *15 Beechwood Park, Moira, Craigavon BT67 0LL* Tel (028) 9261 2982 E-mail darling-moira@utvinternet.com

DARLING, John. b 47. Sarum & Wells Th Coll 76. **d** 79 **p** 80. NSM Trowbridge St Thos *Sarum* 79-82; NSM Trowbridge St Thos and W Ashton 82-92; NSM Melksham from 01; NSM Atworth w Shaw and Whitley from 07; NSM Broughton Gifford, Gt Chalfield and Holt from 07. *43 Horse Road, Hilperton Marsh, Trowbridge BA14 7PF*

DARLINGTON, Paul Trevor. b 71. Imp Coll Lon BSc92 K Coll Lon PGCE93. Oak Hill Th Coll BA99 MPhil00. **d** 00 **p** 01. C Bispham *Blackb* 00-05; P-in-c Oswestry H Trin *Lich* from 05. *Holy Trinity Vicarage, 29 Balmoral Crescent, Oswestry SY11 2XQ* Tel (01691) 652184
E-mail paul.t.darlington@ntlworld.com

DARLISON, Geoffrey Stuart. b 49. MRTPI80. St Jo Coll Nottm 89. **d** 91 **p** 92. C Horncastle w Low Toynton *Linc* 91-95; P-in-c Welton and Dunholme w Scothern 95-97; V 97-08; RD Lawres 07-08; P-in-c Thorpe Edge *Bradf* from 08; P-in-c Greengates

from 08. *The Vicarage, Northwood Crescent, Bradford BD10 9HX* Tel (01274) 405421
E-mail s.darlison@googlemail.com

DARMODY, Canon Richard Arthur. b 52. Lon Univ BD90. Linc Th Coll MDiv94. **d** 94 **p** 95. C Cherry Hinton St Jo *Ely* 94-97; I Belfast St Aid *Conn* 97-99; TR The Ramseys and Upwood *Ely* from 99; RD St Ives 02-06; Hon Can Ely Cathl from 08. *The Rectory, Hollow Lane, Ramsey, Huntingdon PE26 1DE* Tel (01487) 813271 E-mail darmodyrichard@hotmail.com

DARRALL, Charles Geoffrey. b 32. Nottm Univ BA55 MA57. Qu Coll Birm 56. **d** 57 **p** 58. C Cockermouth All SS w Ch Ch *Carl* 57-63; Chapl Dioc Youth Cen 63-95; V St John's in the Vale w Wythburn 63-95; P-in-c Threlkeld 85-95; rtd 96; Perm to Offic *Carl* from 98. *Piper House, Naddle, Keswick CA12 4TF* Tel (01768) 774500

DARRALL, John Norman. b 34. Nottm Univ BA57. Ripon Hall Ox 57. **d** 60 **p** 61. C Nottingham St Mary *S'well* 60-65; Chapl Nottm Children's Hosp 64-65; V Bole w Saundby and Sturton w Littleborough *S'well* 65-66; Chapl Oakham Sch 89-99; rtd 99; Perm to Offic *Leic* from 01 and *Pet* from 05. *Grange Cottage, 69 Main Street, Cottesmore, Oakham LE15 7DH* Tel (01572) 812443

DARRANT, Louis Peter. b 77. Aber Univ BD00 Leeds Univ MA03. Coll of Resurr Mirfield 01. **d** 03 **p** 04. C Kennington St Jo w St Jas *S'wark* 03-07; R Mundon St Mary w Mundon *Chelmsf* from 07. *St Mary's Rectory, Park Drive, Maldon CM9 5JG* Tel (01621) 857191 Mobile 07949-765523
E-mail louis.darrant@btinternet.com

DARROCH, Ronald Humphrey. b 45. Trin Coll Cam BA67 MA71 Ch Ch Ox BA67 MA71. Ripon Hall Ox 67. **d** 70 **p** 71. C Kingston upon Hull St Nic *York* 70-73; Hon C 73-74; Hon C Perth St Jo *St And* from 74; Chapl Stancliffe Hall Derby 84-87; Perm to Offic *Worc* 87-98; Chapl Old Swinford Hosp Sch Worc 89-98. *17 Viewlands Terrace, Perth PH1 1BN* Tel (01738) 628880

DART, John Peter. b 40. St Jo Coll Ox BA62. Cuddesdon Coll 62. **d** 64 **p** 65. C W Hartlepool St Aid *Dur* 64-67; C Alverthorpe *Wakef* 67-70; Lic to Offic 70-79; rtd 05. *3 Springhill Avenue, Crofton, Wakefield WF4 1HA* Tel (01924) 860374
E-mail mail@dart.eclipse.co.uk

DARVILL, Christopher Mark. b 61. Ox Univ BA83. St Steph Ho Ox 84. **d** 86 **p** 87. C Tottenham St Paul *Lon* 86-88; C Oystermouth *S & B* 88-90; Chapl Univ of Wales (Swansea) 90-94; Asst Dioc Warden of Ords from 92; V Llansamlet from 94. *The Vicarage, 61 Church Road, Llansamlet, Swansea SA7 9RL* Tel (01792) 771420

DARVILL, Geoffrey. b 43. Oak Hill Th Coll 79. **d** 81 **p** 82. C Barking St Marg w St Patr *Chelmsf* 81-84; C Widford 84-86; P-in-c Ramsden Crays w Ramsden Bellhouse 86-90; Dep Chapl HM Pris Pentonville 90-91; Chapl HM YOI Onley 91-97; Chapl HM Pris Nor 97-01; Chapl HM Pris Man 01-02; P-in-c Chadderton Em *Man* 02-03; V 03-04; P-in-c Chevington w Hargrave, Chedburgh w Depden etc *St E* 04-07; rtd 07; Perm to Offic *Chelmsf* from 06. *2 Chase Lane, Harwich CO12 4NB* Tel (01255) 551794 E-mail geoffdarvill@hotmail.com

DARVILL, Canon George Collins. b 36. Kelham Th Coll 56. **d** 61 **p** 62. C Middlesbrough St Chad *York* 61-64; C Manston *Ripon* 64-66; V Kippax 66-79; V Catterick 79-88; RD Richmond 80-86; P-in-c Adel 88-89; R 89-01; RD Headingley 91-96; Hon Can Ripon Cathl 91-01; rtd 01; Perm to Offic *Ripon* from 01. *39 Woodlea Lane, Meanwood, Leeds LS6 4SX* Tel 0113-275 7973

✠**DARWENT, The Rt Revd Frederick Charles.** b 27. JP87. ACIB. Wells Th Coll 61. **d** 63 **p** 64 **c** 78. C Pemberton St Jo *Liv* 63-65; R Strichen *Ab* 65-71; R New Pitsligo 65-71; R Fraserburgh w New Pitsligo 71-78; Can St Andr Cathl 71-78; Dean Ab 73-78; Bp Ab 78-92; rtd 92; Lic to Offic *Ab* from 92. *107 Osborne Place, Aberdeen AB25 2DD* Tel (01224) 646497

DARWENT, Thomas James. b 74. Wycliffe Hall Ox. **d** 07 **p** 08. C Claygate *Guildf* from 07. *16 Claycorn Court, Station Way, Claygate, Esher KT10 0QR* Tel (01372) 462102
E-mail tomdarwent@holytrinityclaygate.org.uk

DASH, Mrs Janet Eleanor Gillian. b 47. SRN69. Cant Sch of Min 89. **d** 93 **p** 94. C Morden *S'wark* 93-96; C S Croydon Em 96-98; P-in-c Borstal and Chapl HM Pris Cookham Wood 98-05; P-in-c Darenth *Roch* from 05. *Darenth Vicarage, Lane End, Dartford DA2 7JR* Tel (01322) 227153 Mobile 07950-506257
E-mail jan.dash@diocese-rochester.org

DASHFIELD, Edward Maurice. b 26. LTh65. **d** 51 **p** 52. C Masterton New Zealand 51-55; C Cannock *Lich* 55-57; V Tinui New Zealand 57-64; P-in-c 83-88; V Carterton 64-69; Hd Master St Matt Sch Masterton 69-80; rtd 88. *Address temp unknown*

DATCHLER, Colin Neil. b 72. Univ Coll Chich BA01. Ripon Coll Cuddesdon 06. **d** 09. C Hythe *Cant* from 09. *2 Palmarsh Avenue, Hythe CT21 6NT* E-mail colindatchler@hotmail.com

DATE, Stephen James. b 69. LSE BA90 Dur Univ MA92. SEITE 99. **d** 02 **p** 03. NSM Brighton Gd Shep Preston *Chich* 02-08; C Uckfield from 08. *7 Park View Road, Uckfield TN22 1JP* Tel (01825) 762304 Mobile 07747-895213
E-mail heather.stephen@ntlworld.com

DATSON, Mrs Sheila Mary. b 24. CertEd67. S'wark Ord Course 76. **dss** 78 **d** 87 **p** 94. Bexleyheath Ch Ch *Roch* 78-91; Hon Par Dn 87-91; rtd 91; Perm to Offic *Worc* 91-94 and from 95; NSM Stourport and Wilden 94-95. *17 Moorhall Lane, Stourport-on-Severn DY13 8RB* Tel (01299) 823044

DAUBNEY, Howard. b 49. Woolwich Poly BA70. S'wark Ord Course 86. **d** 89 **p** 90. C Roch 89-04; V Strood St Fran from 04. *St Francis's Vicarage, Galahad Avenue, Rochester ME2 2YS* Tel and fax (01634) 717162 Mobile 07932-384823
E-mail howard.daubney@diocese-rochester.org

DAUGHTERY, Stephen John. b 61. Kent Univ BSc82. Trin Coll Bris BA94. **d** 96 **p** 97. C Guildf Ch Ch 96-98; C Guildf Ch Ch w St Martha-on-the-Hill 98-03; R Southover *Chich* from 03. *The Rectory, Southover High Street, Lewes BN7 1HT* Tel (01273) 472018 E-mail steve@daughtery.plus.com

DAULMAN, John Henry. b 33. Lich Th Coll 60. **d** 62 **p** 63. C Monkseaton St Mary *Newc* 62-65; Min Can Newc Cathl 65-67; Chapl Crumpsall and Springfield Hosp 67-73; V Tyldesley w Shakerley *Man* 73-81; V Turton 81-00; rtd 00; Perm to Offic *Blackb* from 01. *17 Higher Bank Street, Withnell, Chorley PR6 8SF* Tel (01254) 832597

DAUNTON-FEAR, Andrew. b 45. Univ of Tasmania BSc64 Qu Coll Cam BA67 MA72 St Andr Univ BPhil76 K Coll Lon PhD00. Ridley Hall Cam 67 ACT ThL68. **d** 68 **p** 70. C Thomastown Australia 68-71; P-in-c Islington H Trin Cloudesley Square *Lon* 71-75; Hon C Islington St Mary 71-75; C Stoke Bishop *Bris* 76-79; R Thrapston *Pet* 79-89; R Barming *Roch* 89-03; Lect St Andr Th Sem Philippines from 03. *PO Box 3167, 1099 Manila, Philippines* Tel (0063) (2) 722 2571
E-mail nothingdaunted@hotmail.com

DAVAGE, William Ernest Peter. b 50. MA94. St Steph Ho Ox 89. **d** 91 **p** 92. C Eyres Monsell *Leic* 91-94; P Lib Pusey Ho from 94. *Pusey House, St Giles, Oxford OX1 3LZ* Tel (01865) 278415

DAVENPORT (*née* HILL), **Elizabeth Jayne Louise.** b 55. St Hugh's Coll Ox BA77 MA81 Univ of S California PhD03. Fuller Th Sem California ThM89 NOC 79. **dss** 82 **d** 87 **p** 91. Halliwell St Pet *Man* 82-83; Paris St Mich *Eur* 83-85; Lic to Offic *St Alb* 85-87; Hon Par Dn Chorleywood St Andr 87-89; USA from 89. *University of Southern California, University Religious Center, Los Angeles, CA 90089-0751, USA* Tel (001) (213) 740 1366 E-mail ejld@usc.edu

DAVENPORT, Canon Ian Arthan. b 54. Linc Th Coll 85. **d** 87 **p** 88. C Ches H Trin 87-91; V Newton 91-97; V Oxton from 97; RD Birkenhead from 05; Hon Can Ches Cathl from 06. *Oxton Vicarage, 8 Wexford Road, Prenton CH43 9TB* Tel 0151-652 1194 Fax 653 7251 E-mail oxtonstsaviour@btinternet.com

DAVENPORT, Mrs Joy Gwyneth. b 46. Glam Coll of Educn TCert68. SEITE 01. **d** 04 **p** 01. NSM Rye *Chich* from 04; Asst Chapl E Sussex Hosps NHS Trust from 04. *2 The Oakfields, Rye Road, Rye TN31 7UA* Tel (01797) 224209

DAVENPORT, Ms Sally Elizabeth. b 59. Lon Bible Coll BA99. Ripon Coll Cuddesdon 99. **d** 01 **p** 02. C Bishop's Stortford St Mich *St Alb* 01-05; TV Bp's Hatfield, Lemsford and N Mymms from 05. *The Vicarage, North Mymms Park, North Mymms, Hatfield AL9 7TN* Tel (01727) 822062
E-mail sallydavenport@btinternet.com

DAVENPORT, Miss Sybil Ann. b 36. Nottm Univ CertEd57. EMMTC 85. **d** 89 **p** 94. NSM Thurgarton w Hoveringham and Bleasby etc *S'well* 89-94; NSM Collingham w S Scarle and Besthorpe and Girton 94-02; rtd 02; Perm to Offic *S'well* from 02. *Holmedale, North Muskham, Newark NG23 6HQ* Tel (01636) 701552

DAVEY, Andrew John. b 53. St Mich Coll Llan. **d** 77 **p** 78. C Gt Stanmore *Lon* 77-79; NSM Watford St Jo *St Alb* 87-92; C Potters Bar 92-95; P-in-c Clenchwarton *Ely* 95-96; P-in-c W Lynn 95-96; R Clenchwarton and W Lynn from 96. *The Rectory, Clenchwarton, King's Lynn PE34 4DT* Tel and fax (01553) 772089 E-mail postmaster@andrewdavey.plus.com

DAVEY, Andrew John. b 57. Magd Coll Ox BA78 MA83. Wycliffe Hall Ox 80. **d** 83 **p** 84. C Bermondsey St Jas w Ch Ch *S'wark* 83-87; Chapl Trin Coll Cam 87-92; Pilsdon Community 94-04. *Kingswood, North Street, Axminster EX13 5QF* Tel (01297) 33534

DAVEY, Andrew Paul. b 61. Southn Univ BA82 Sheff Univ DMinTh99. Westcott Ho Cam 85. **d** 87 **p** 88. C S'wark H Trin w St Matt 87-91; V Camberwell St Luke 91-96; Min Development Officer Woolwich Area Miss Team 96-98; Ho of Bps' Officer for UPAs 96-98; Asst Sec Abps' Coun Bd for Soc Resp from 98; Chapl S'wark Cathl from 01. *171 Waller Road, London SE14 5LX* Tel (020) 7277 9688 *or* 7898 1446
E-mail apd@clara.net *or* andrew.davey@c-of-e.org.uk

DAVEY, Christopher Mark. b 64. EN(G)84 RGN89. St Steph Ho Ox 92. **d** 95 **p** 96. C Leeds Belle Is St Jo and St Barn *Ripon* 95-97; C-in-c Grahame Park St Aug CD *Lon* 97-01; V St Alb St Mary Marshalswick *St Alb* 01-08; P-in-c Leavesden from 08. *All Saints' Vicarage, Horseshoe Lane, Watford WD25 7HJ* Tel (01923) 672375 E-mail cdavey2776@aol.com

DAVEY, Colin Hugh Lancaster. b 34. Em Coll Cam BA56 MA60 PhD89. Cuddesdon Coll 59. **d** 61 **p** 62. C Moseley St Agnes *Birm*
61-64; Lic to Offic *Eur* 64-65; Sub Warden St Boniface Coll Warminster 66-69; C Bath Weston St Jo *B & W* 69-70; Asst Chapl Abp Cant's Cllrs on Foreign Relns 70-74; Angl Sec ARCIC 70-74; Hon C St Dunstan in the West *Lon* 71-73; Hon C Kennington St Jo *S'wark* 73-74; V S Harrow St Paul *Lon* 74-80; V Paddington St Jas 80-83; Sec Ecum Affairs BCC 83-90; Ch Life Sec CCBI 90-99; Perm to Offic *St Alb* from 97; rtd 00. *20 Honeysuckle Way, Bedford MK41 0TF* Tel (01234) 360851
E-mail colinandjane@davey8.freeserve.co.uk

DAVEY, Canon Frederick Hutley David. b 14. Cranmer Hall Dur 58. **d** 60 **p** 62. C Bishopwearmouth St Nic *Dur* 60-62; C Dur St Giles 62-64; India 64-69; E Pakistan 69-71; Bangladesh 71-76; Chapl De Beer Miss to Seamen *Eur* 77-82; rtd 82; Perm to Offic *B & W* 82-95. *c/o Mrs Y J Lyons, 18 Viking Heights, Martlesham, Woodbridge IP12 4RT* Tel (01394) 385312

DAVEY, Mrs Hilary Margaret. b 49. Bris Univ BSc70. EAMTC 98. **d** 01 **p** 02. NSM Saffron Walden w Wendens Ambo, Littlebury etc *Chelmsf* 01-07; P-in-c Debden and Wimbish w Thunderley from 07. *3 Springhill Road, Saffron Walden CB11 4AH* Tel (01799) 522616
E-mail hilarydavey@btopenworld.com

DAVEY, James Garland. b 21. **d** 75 **p** 76. C Liskeard w St Keyne and St Pinnock *Truro* 75-77; Perm to Offic *B & W* 77-80; TV S Molton w Nymet St George, High Bray etc *Ex* 80-86; rtd 86; Perm to Offic *B & W* 86-05. *43 Tree Field Road, Clevedon BS21 6JD* Tel (01275) 540648

DAVEY, John. b 35. Birkbeck Coll Lon BSc84 MPhil87 PhD91 FRSH89 CPsychol92 AFBPsS92. Chich Th Coll 67. **d** 69 **p** 70. C Eastbourne St Elisabeth *Chich* 69-72; C Eastbourne St Mary 72-74; V W Wittering 74-77; Min Can and Chapl Windsor 77-81; R The Rissingtons *Glouc* 81-85; R Alfriston w Lullington, Litlington and W Dean *Chich* 85-92; Chapl Bramshill Police Coll *Win* 92-96; rtd 97; P-in-c Amberley w N Stoke and Parham, Wiggonholt etc *Chich* 97-98; Perm to Offic 98-08. *20 Holly Avenue, Wilford, Nottingham NG11 7AF*

DAVEY, John Michael. b 31. St Chad's Coll Dur BA54. **d** 56 **p** 61. C Southwick H Trin *Dur* 56-57; C Harton 60-64; C Bawtry w Austerfield *S'well* 64-67; V Stillington *Dur* 67-70; Lic to Offic 70-78; Perm to Offic *Sheff* 78-93; rtd 96. *11 Darfield Close, Owlthorpe, Sheffield S20 6SW* Tel 0114-248 0917

DAVEY, Julian Metherall. b 40. Jes Coll Ox BA62 MA65. Wells Th Coll 62. **d** 64 **p** 65. C Weston-super-Mare St Jo *B & W* 64-66; Perm to Offic *St Alb* 66-68; Chapl St Alb Sch 68-73; Chapl Merchant Taylors' Sch Crosby 73-82; Perm to Offic *Truro* 82-83; P-in-c Meavy w Sheepstor *Ex* 83-85; P-in-c Walkhampton 83-85; R Meavy, Sheepstor and Walkhampton 85; Chapl Warw Sch 86-89; P-in-c The Winterbournes and Compton Valence *Sarum* 89-94; TV Marshwood Vale 96-98; P-in-c St Gennys, Jacobstow w Warbstow and Treneglos *Truro* 98-02; rtd 02; Perm to Offic *Truro* from 02. *18 Pondfield Road, Latchbrook, Saltash PL12 4UA* Tel (01752) 840086

DAVEY, Julian Warwick. b 45. LRCPI70 LRCSI70. Qu Coll Birm 78. **d** 81 **p** 82. NSM Ipsley *Worc* 81-05; Perm to Offic *Cov* and *Worc* from 05. *The Field House, Allimore Lane, Alcester B49 5PR* Tel (01789) 764640 E-mail affgan1@yahoo.com

DAVEY, Kenneth William. b 41. Qu Coll Birm 84. **d** 86 **p** 87. C Baswich *Lich* 86-90; V Lostock Gralam *Ches* 90-96; P-in-c Thornton-le-Moors w Ince and Elton 96-07; rtd 07. *4 Firbank, Elton, Chester CH2 4LY* Tel (01928) 726166
E-mail kenzor@daveyk1.fsnet.co.uk

DAVEY, Nathan Paul. *See* PAINE DAVEY, Nathan Paul

DAVEY, Peter James. b 59. Bris Univ BSc81 Loughb Univ MBA91. Trin Coll Bris BA00. **d** 00 **p** 01. C Long Eaton St Jo *Derby* 00-04; V Cotmanhay from 04. *The Vicarage, 197 Heanor Road, Ilkeston DE7 8TA* Tel 0115-932 5670
E-mail petedavey@aol.com

DAVEY, Peter William. b 44. Culham Coll of Educn TCert65. Linc Th Coll 93. **d** 93 **p** 94. C Cheadle w Freehay *Lich* 93-96; P-in-c Calton, Cauldon, Grindon and Waterfall 96-99; R Calton, Cauldon, Grindon, Waterfall etc 99-00; R Norton in the Moors from 04; rtd 09. *24 rue des Vergers, Verdroux, 79120 St Coutant, France*

DAVEY, Piers Damer. b 57. Dur Univ BSc. Coll of Resurr Mirfield 80. **d** 83 **p** 84. C Heworth St Mary *Dur* 83-86; C Barnard Castle w Whorlton 86-89; V Aycliffe 89-95; V Chilton Moor 95-06; R Gawler St Geo Australia from 06. *26 Cowan Street, Gawler SA 5118, Australia* Tel (0061) (8) 8523 5677
E-mail stgeorgegawler@optusnet.com.au

DAVEY, Canon Richard Henry. b 66. Man Univ BA88 Nottm Univ PhD06. Linc Th Coll BTh93. **d** 93 **p** 94. C Parkstone St Pet w Branksea and St Osmund *Sarum* 93-96; Chapl and Min Can St E Cathl 96-04; Can Res S'well Minster 99-04; Chapl Nottm Trent Univ from 04; C Clifton from 04. *St Mary's Vicarage, 58 Village Road, Clifton, Nottingham NG11 8NE* Tel 0115 921 1856
E-mail rhdavey1175@aol.com

DAVID, Brother. *See* JARDINE, Canon David John

DAVID, Faith Caroline. *See* CLARINGBULL, Canon Faith Caroline

DAVID, Canon Kenith Andrew. b 39. Natal Univ BA(Theol)64. Coll of Resurr Mirfield 64. **d** 66 **p** 67. C Harpenden St Nic *St Alb* 66-69; R Chatsworth Epiphany S Africa 69-71; P-in-c Southwick St Mich *Chich* 71-72; Th Educn Sec Chr Aid 72-75; Project Officer India and Bangladesh 76-81; Hon C Kingston All SS *S'wark* 72-76; Hon C Kingston All SS w St Jo 76-81; Lic to Offic Botswana 81-83; Hon C Geneva *Eur* 83-95; Co-ord Urban Rural Miss WCC 83-94; Can Lundi Zimbabwe from 93; V Hessle *York* 95-05; rtd 05; Perm to Offic *Cant* from 05. *5 Randolph Close, Canterbury CT1 3AZ* Tel and fax (01227) 452009
DAVID, Michael Anthony Louis. b 29. AKC58. **d** 59 **p** 60. C Greenhill St Jo *Lon* 59-63; V Gravesend St Mary *Roch* 63-78; V Foremark *Derby* 78-81; V Repton 78-81; TV Buxton w Burbage and King Sterndale 81-85; R Warlingham w Chelsham and Farleigh *S'wark* 85-90; rtd 91; Perm to Offic *Sarum* from 91. *95 Lulworth Avenue, Hamworthy, Poole BH15 4DH* Tel (01202) 684475
DAVID, Philip Evan Nicholl. b 31. Jes Coll Ox BA53 MA57 Univ of Wales BA61 Nottm Univ MPhil86 Leic Univ MEd88. St Mich Coll Llan 56. **d** 57 **p** 58. C Llanblethian w Cowbridge 57-60; C Cardiff St Jo 60-64; Chapl Ch Coll Brecon 64-75; P-in-c Abcryscir and Llanfihangel Nantbran *S & B* 70-75; Chapl Loretto Sch Musselburgh 75-82; Chapl Trent Coll Nottm 83-91; R Llanfyllin and Bwlchycibau *St As* 91-96; P-in-c Llangynog 95-96; rtd 96; P-in-c Newbridge-on-Wye and Llanfihangel Brynpabuan etc *S & B* 98-00; P-in-c Llanwrtyd w Llanddulas in Tir Abad etc 05. *Woodside Cottage, The Bron, Cross Gates, Llandrindod Wells LD1 6RS* Tel (01597) 851401
DAVID, Wayne Aldwyn. b 74. Univ of Ccn England in Birm BA97. St Mich Coll Llan 04. **d** 07 **p** 08. NSM Merthyr Tydfil St Dav *Llan* from 07. *16 St Illtyd's Road, Church Village, Pontypridd CF38 1DA* Tel (01443) 203422 E-mail wayneadavid@hotmail.com
DAVID, William John. b 57. Ban Univ BTh07. **d** 04 **p** 05. OLM Eltham St Barn *S'wark* 04-07; NSM 07-09; C Toowoomba St Luke Australia from 09. *PO Box 2434, Toowoomba Qld 4350, Australia* E-mail stluke.tmba@bigpond.com.au *or* williamdavid10@aol.com
DAVID FRANCIS, Brother. *See* DARLING, David Francis
DAVIDGE-SMITH, Mrs Margaret Kathleen. b 53. CQSW77. STETS 99. **d** 02 **p** 03. NSM E Acton St Dunstan w St Thos *Lon* 02-06; Asst Chapl Ealing Hosp NHS Trust 04-06; Asst Chapl Meadow House Hospice 04-06; Asst Chapl W Middx Univ Hosp NHS Trust 05-06; Asst Chapl W Lon Mental Health NHS Trust 05-06; Chapl Ealing Hosp NHS Trust from 06. *36 Newburgh Road, London W3 6DQ* Tel and fax (020) 8993 0868 E-mail mdavidge_s@hotmail.com
DAVIDSON, Canon Charles Hilary. b 29. St Edm Hall Ox BA52 MA56 Leic Univ MPhil89. Lich Th Coll 52. **d** 54 **p** 55. C Abington *Pet* 54-59; C Pet St Jo 59-60; R Sywell w Overstone 60-66; P-in-c Lamport w Faxton 66-76; R Maidwell w Draughton and Scaldwell 67-76; R Maidwell w Draughton, Scaldwell, Lamport etc 77-80; RD Brixworth 77-79; V Roade 80-87; V Roade and Ashton w Hartwell 87-94; RD Towcester 91-94; Can Pet Cathl 79-94; rtd 94; Perm to Offic *Pet* from 94. *Croftside, Butlins Lane, Roade, Northampton NN7 2PU* Tel (01604) 863016
DAVIDSON, Christopher John. b 45. St Luke's Coll Ex CertEd67 St Martin's Coll Lanc BEd74. EAMTC. **d** 91 **p** 92. NSM Taverham w Ringland *Nor* 91-93; Dir of Educn 87-93; P-in-c Whixley w Green Hammerton *Ripon* 93-96; RE Adv 93-96; Dioc Dir of Educn *Ex* 97-01; Assoc P Exminster and Kenn 97-01; R Quidenham Gp *Nor* 01-08; P-in-c Guiltcross 04-08; rtd 08; P-in-c Pyworthy, Pancrasweek and Bridgerule *Ex* from 08. *The Rectory, Pyworthy, Holsworthy EX22 6SU* Tel (01409) 253547 E-mail chris.davidson@virgin.net
DAVIDSON, Donald. b 52. TISEC 00. **d** 05 **p** 06. C W Highland Region *Arg* from 05. *4 Kearan Road, Kinlochleven, Argyll PH50 4QU* Tel (01855) 831444 E-mail donaldd@btinternet.com
DAVIDSON, Graeme John. b 42. Victoria Univ Wellington BA64 BA66 Ox Univ MA70. St Steph Ho Ox 67. **d** 70 **p** 71. C Maidenhead St Luke *Ox* 70-73; New Zealand 73-77 and from 93; USA 77-88. *3 Tauroa Road, Havelock North, Hawke's Bay 4130, New Zealand* E-mail graeme.davidson@paradise.net.nz
DAVIDSON, Hilary. *See* DAVIDSON, Canon Charles Hilary
DAVIDSON, Ian George. b 32. LSE BSc(Econ)54. Linc Th Coll 55. **d** 58 **p** 59. C Waltham Cross *St Alb* 58-60; C St Alb Abbey 61-63; Hon PV S'wark Cathl 63-67; V Gt Cornard *St E* 67-72; R Lt Cornard 67-70; Lic to Offic 72-79; Student Counsellor Suffolk Coll 72-79; P-in-c Witnesham w Swilland and Ashbocking 79-83; Warden Scargill Ho 83-88; Chapl Chr Fellowship of Healing *Edin* 88-97; rtd 97. *28 Fox Spring Crescent, Edinburgh EH10 6NQ* Tel 0131-445 3381 E-mail iangill@foxspring.freeserve.co.uk
DAVIDSON, John Lindsay. b 27. LRCP51. St Steph Ho Ox. **d** 58 **p** 59. C Croydon St Mich *Cant* 58-61; P-in-c H Cross Miss 62-66; V Lewisham St Steph *S'wark* 67-70; V Croydon St Mich *Cant* 70-80; V Croydon St Mich w St Jas 80-81; TR N Creedy *Ex*

81-92; RD Cadbury 86-90; rtd 92; Perm to Offic *Ex* from 92. *12 Highfield, Lapford, Crediton EX17 6PY* Tel (01363) 83764
DAVIDSON, Ralph. b 38. **d** 01 **p** 02. OLM Birkenshaw w Hunsworth *Wakef* from 01. *Bedale, Moorhouse Lane, Birkenshaw, Bradford BD11 2BA* Tel (01274) 681955 E-mail ralphdavidson@bedale1938.wanadoo.co.uk
DAVIDSON, Trevor John. b 49. CertEd. Oak Hill Th Coll 80. **d** 85 **p** 86. C Drypool *York* 85-88; V Bessingby 88-97; V Carnaby 88-97; Chapl Bridlington and Distr Gen Hosp 88-94; Chapl E Yorks Community Healthcare NHS Trust 94-97; V Felling *Dur* from 97; CUF Projects Officer from 97. *The Vicarage, Carlisle Street, Felling, Gateshead NE10 0HQ* Tel 0191-420 3434 E-mail trevor@christchurch5.freeserve.co.uk
DAVIDSON, William Watkins. b 20. Wadh Coll Ox BA48 MA53. Westcott Ho Cam 49. **d** 50 **p** 51. C Radcliffe-on-Trent *S'well* 50-53; Chapl RN 53-57; R Esher *Guildf* 57-65; V Westmr St Steph w St Jo *Lon* 65-83; rtd 85. *62 Calmsden, Cirencester GL7 5ET* Tel (01285) 831823 E-mail sallyandbill62@talktalk.net
DAVIE (née JONES), Mrs Alyson Elizabeth. b 58. Ex Univ BA86. Wycliffe Hall Ox 86. **d** 88 **p** 94. Par Dn Ipswich St Fran *St E* 88-92; Perm to Offic *Ox* 92-93 and *St Alb* 93-94; NSM E Barnet *St Alb* 94-97; Asst Chapl Oak Hill Th Coll 94-96; P-in-c The Mundens w Sacombe *St Alb* 97-06; V St Paul's Cray St Barn *Roch* from 06. *The Vicarage, Rushet Road, Orpington BR5 2PU* Tel (01689) 825852 E-mail alyson.davie@btinternet.com
DAVIE, Peter Edward Sidney. b 36. LSE BSc57 Birm Univ MA73 K Coll Lon MPhil78 Kent Univ PhD90. Coll of Resurr Mirfield 57. **d** 60 **p** 61. C De Beauvoir Town St Pet *Lon* 60-63; C-in-c Godshill CD *Portsm* 63-67; R Upton St Leonards *Glouc* 67-73; Sen Lect Ch Ch Coll of HE Cant 73-98; Prin Lect Cant Ch Ch Univ Coll 98-01; Lic to Offic *Cant* from 73; Hon C Cant St Pet w St Alphege and St Marg etc from 79. *8 Brockenhurst Close, Canterbury CT2 7RX* Tel (01227) 451572 E-mail pedavie@dircon.co.uk
DAVIE, Stephen Peter. b 52. S Bank Poly BA75 MRTPI77. Oak Hill Th Coll BA93. **d** 93 **p** 94. C Luton Ch Ch *Roch* 93-97; R Cobham w Luddesdowne and Dode 97-04; P-in-c Horley *S'wark* 04-08; TR from 08. *4 Russells Crescent, Horley RH6 7DN* Tel (01293) 783509 E-mail steve.davie@btinternet.com
DAVIES, Adrian. *See* DAVIES, Glanmor Adrian
DAVIES, Adrian Paul. b 43. K Coll Lon. **d** 69 **p** 70. C Nottingham St Mary *S'well* 69-74; C Gt w Lt Billing *Pet* 74-75; P-in-c Marholm 75-82; R Castor 75; R Castor w Sutton and Upton 76-82; V Byker St Mich w St Lawr *Newc* 82-94; rtd 95. *27 Clougha Avenue, Halton, Lancaster LA2 6NR* Tel (01524) 811141
DAVIES, Alan. *See* DAVIES, James Alan
DAVIES, Alan Arthur. b 35. Sarum & Wells Th Coll 83. **d** 85 **p** 86. C Eastleigh *Win* 85-88; C Portsea N End St Mark *Portsm* 88-90; V Lydiate *Liv* 90-00; rtd 00; Perm to Offic *Sarum* from 01. *25 St Catherine's, Wimborne BH21 1BE* Tel (01202) 848233
DAVIES, Alastair John. b 56. Nottm Univ BA MTh. Westcott Ho Cam. **d** 84 **p** 85. C Eltham St Jo *S'wark* 84-87; C Dulwich St Barn 87-89; Chapl RAF 89-07; P-in-c Lyneham w Bradenstoke *Sarum* 01-03; Sen Chapl R United Hosp Bath NHS Trust from 07. *Royal United Hospital, Combe Park, Bath BA1 3NG* Tel (01225) 428331 E-mail alastair.davies@ruh-bath.swest.nhs.uk
DAVIES, Albert Brian. b 37. Worc Coll of Educn CertEd60. Wycliffe Hall Ox 03. **d** 04 **p** 05. C Poitou-Charentes *Eur* 04-07; P-in-c The Vendée from 07. *La Basse Coussaie, 85140 Les Essarts, France* Tel (0033) (2) 51 62 96 32 E-mail briandpam@free.fr
DAVIES, Mrs Alison Margaret. b 57. Nottm Univ BA78. STETS 96. **d** 99 **p** 00. NSM Win St Barn 99-04; Perm to Offic *Win* 04-07 and *Nor* from 07. *The Vicarage, Church Lane, Heacham, King's Lynn PE31 7HJ* Tel (01485) 570268
DAVIES, Alun Edwards. b 13. Univ of Wales BA40. St D Coll Lamp 45. **d** 46 **p** 47. C Treharris *Llan* 46-48; C Cardigan *St D* 48-50; CF 50-56; Hon CF 56; R Byford w Mansel Gamage *Heref* 56-58; P-in-c Preston-on-Wye w Blakemere 56-58; V Birch St Mary *Man* 58-62; R Lower Crumpsall 62-84; rtd 84; Perm to Offic *Man* from 84. *48 Ashtree Road, Crumpsall, Manchester M8 5AT* Tel 0161-720 8345
DAVIES, Andrew James. b 53. Univ of Wales (Cardiff) BD00. St Mich Coll Llan 01. **d** 03 **p** 04. C Caerphilly *Llan* 03-06; P-in-c Rhondda Fach Uchaf from 06. *Ty Nant, Margaret Street, Pontygwaith, Ferndale CF43 3EH* Tel (01443) 732321 Mobile 07931-370054 E-mail daviesaj8@yahoo.co.uk
DAVIES, Andrew John. b 54. Univ of Wales (Abth) BMus76 St Martin's Coll Lanc PGCE78 FRCO75 FTCL76 LRAM75. Sarum & Wells Th Coll 79. **d** 81 **p** 82. C Tenby w Gumfreston *St D* 81-84; C Llanelli 84-86; V Monkton 86-91; V Fairfield *Derby* 91-96; P-in-c Barlborough 96-01; R Barlborough and Renishaw 01-03; V Pembroke Dock *St D* 03-04; TR Carew 04-08; TR Tenby from 08. *The Rectory, Church Park, Tenby SA70 7EE* Tel (01834) 842068 E-mail andrewdavies19@aol.com

DAVIES, Anthony. *See* DAVIES, The Ven Vincent Anthony

DAVIES, Anthony. *See* DAVIES, David Anthony

DAVIES, Anthony Paul. b 56. JP02. Univ of Wales (Swansea) BSc76 CEng85. St Mich Coll Llan 03. **d** 06 **p** 07. NSM Penllergaer *S & B* 06-07; NSM Gorseinon from 07. *58 Dyffryn Road, Gorseinon, Swansea SA4 6BA* Tel (01792) 897218 Mobile 07855-237866 E-mail anthonypdavies@yahoo.com

DAVIES, Arthur Gerald Miles. b 29. Univ of Wales (Ban) BA51. St Mich Coll Llan 51. **d** 53 **p** 54. C Shotton *St As* 53-60; R Nannerch 60-63; V Llansilin and Llangadwaladr 63-68; V Llansilin w Llangadwaladr and Llangedwyn 68-71; V Llanfair Caereinion w Llanllugan 71-75; TV Wrexham 75-83; V Hanmer, Bronington, Bettisfield, Tallarn Green 83-94; rtd 94. *Elland, School Lane, Bronington, Whitchurch SY13 3HN* Tel (01948) 780296

DAVIES, Arthur Lloyd. *See* LLOYD-DAVIES, Arthur

DAVIES, Barry Lewis. b 46. Boro Road Teacher Tr Coll CertEd69 Lon Inst of Educn DipEd84 MA86. STETS 02. **d** 05 **p** 06. NSM Hardington Vale *B & W* 05-08; rtd 08; Perm to Offic *B & W* from 09. *3 The Lays, Goose Street, Beckington, Frome BA11 6RS* Tel (01373) 831344 E-mail bandkdavies@msn.com

DAVIES, Miss Belinda Jane. b 68. Ox Poly BSc91. STETS BA08. **d** 08. C Yateley *Win* 08–09. *Castle Close, Pound Lane, Wareham BH20 4LQ*

DAVIES, Benjamin John. b 27. Glouc Sch of Min 80 Trin Coll Bris 87. **d** 88 **p** 89. NSM Cinderford St Steph w Littledean *Glouc* 88-98; Perm to Offic 98-00. *22 Withy Park, Bishopston, Swansea SA3 3EY* Tel (01792) 232352

DAVIES, Canon Bernard. b 34. Lon Univ BD63. Oak Hill Th Coll 59. **d** 63 **p** 64. C Rawtenstall St Mary *Man* 63-69; Sec Rwanda Miss 69-71; R Wilford *Chelmsf* 71-78; V Braintree 78-00; RD Braintree 87-95; Hon Can Chelmsf Cathl 92-00; rtd 00; Perm to Offic *Nor* from 00 and *St E* from 01. *3 Brookwood Close, Worlingham, Beccles NR34 7RJ* Tel (01502) 719739

DAVIES, Brian. *See* DAVIES, Albert Brian

DAVIES, Carol Ann. b 52. Bp Otter Coll 94. **d** 96 **p** 98. NSM Oakfield St Jo *Portsm* 96-00; NSM Bonchurch 00-04; NSM Ventnor St Cath 00-04; NSM Ventnor H Trin 00-04; TR Upper Kennet *Sarum* 04; R 04-07; rtd 08. *La Salle, 16350 Le Bouchage, France* Tel (0033) (5) 45 85 58 94 E-mail caroldaviesfrance@yahoo.co.uk

DAVIES, Catharine Mary. *See* FURLONG, Mrs Catharine Mary

DAVIES, Mrs Catherine Olive Sarah Skeel. b 61. Univ of Wales (Cardiff) BA84. WMMTC 03. **d** 06 **p** 07. NSM Wootton Wawen and Claverdon w Preston Bagot *Cov* 06-09; NSM Barford w Wasperton and Sherbourne from 09; NSM Hampton Lucy w Charlecote and Loxley from 09. *3 Wilkins Close, Barford, Warwick CV35 8EX* E-mail davieshchl@aol.com

DAVIES, Ceri John. b 61. Univ of Wales (Lamp) BA91 Univ of Wales (Abth) PGCE92 Univ of Wales (Cardiff) BTh00. St Mich Coll Llan 97. **d** 00 **p** 01. C Carmarthen St Dav *St D* 00-03; TV Llanelli from 03. *Christ Church Vicarage, New Dock Road, Llanelli SA15 2HE* Tel (01554) 774710 E-mail ruth_ceri2000@coleg88.freeserve.co.uk

DAVIES, Chris. *See* DAVIES, Canon David Christopher

DAVIES, Christopher. b 51. NE Lon Poly BA72. SEITE 99. **d** 02 **p** 03. NSM Peckham St Sav *S'wark* 02-07. *Address temp unknown* E-mail christopherscott@tinyworld.co.uk

DAVIES, Christopher Edward. b 72. **d** 03 **p** 04. OLM Bilston *Lich* from 03. *10 Wroxham Glen, Willenhall WV13 3HU* Tel (01902) 655305 Mobile 07952-196204

DAVIES, Christopher John. b 55. St Alb Minl Tr Scheme 83. **d** 86 **p** 87. C Tooting All SS *S'wark* 86-90; V Malden St Jas 90-96; RD Kingston 92-96; TR Wimbledon 96-06; Hon Can S'wark Cathl 06; V Wymondham *Nor* from 06; RD Humbleyard from 08. *The Vicarage, 5 Vicar Street, Wymondham NR18 0PL* Tel (01953) 602269 E-mail revd@christopherdavies.fsnet.co.uk

DAVIES, Canon Clifford Thomas. b 41. Glouc Th Course. **d** 83 **p** 84. NSM Dean Forest H Trin *Glouc* 83-87; C Huntley and Longhope 87; R Ruardean 87-06; Hon Can Glouc Cathl 02-06; rtd 06. *Purbeck, 13 Park View, Ruardean GL17 9YW*

DAVIES, David Anthony (Tony). b 57. Thames Poly BSc81 MRICS84. Coll of Resurr Mirfield 85. **d** 88 **p** 89. C Stalybridge *Man* 88-91; C Swinton and Pendlebury 91-92 and 01-02; TV 92-01; V Tonge Moor from 02. *St Augustine's Vicarage, Redthorpe Close, Bolton BL2 2PQ* Tel and fax (01204) 523899 Mobile 07866-359864 E-mail tony@daviesses.co.uk

DAVIES, David Arthur Guy Hampton. b 27. St Jo Coll Ox BA50 MA55. Ely Th Coll 51. **d** 53 **p** 54. C Somers Town *Lon* 53-55; C Cranford 55-60; C Shrewsbury H Cross *Lich* 60-62; R Stamford St Mary and St Mich *Linc* 62-90; rtd 90; Perm to Offic *Lich* from 97. *8 Holywell Terrace, Shrewsbury SY2 5DF* Tel (01743) 245086

DAVIES, David Barry Grenville. b 38. St Jo Coll Dur BA60 MA77. Sarum Th Coll 61. **d** 63 **p** 64. C Aberystwyth St Mich *St D* 63-66; Min Can St D Cathl 66-72; R Stackpole Elidor w St Petrox 72-83; V Laugharne w Llansadwrnen and Llandawke 83-03; rtd 03. *3 Clos y Drindod, Buarth Road, Aberystwyth SY23 1LR* Tel (01970) 626289

DAVIES, David Berwyn. b 42. St Mich Coll Llan 95. **d** 96 **p** 97. C Llanelli *St D* 96-98; R Llanerch Aeron w Ciliau Aeron and Dihewyd etc 98-07; rtd 07; Perm to Offic *St D* from 07. *56 Tyisha Road, Llanelli SA15 1RW* Tel (01554) 774391 E-mail taddavid@aol.com

DAVIES, Canon David Christopher (Chris). b 52. Lon Univ BSc73. Coll of Resurr Mirfield 73. **d** 76 **p** 77. C Bethnal Green St Jo w St Simon *Lon* 76-78; C Bethnal Green St Jo w St Bart 78-80; C-in-c Portsea St Geo CD *Portsm* 80-81; V Portsea St Geo 81-87; Relig Affairs Producer Radio Victory 81-86; Chapl Ham Green Hosp Bris 87-94; Chapl Southmead Hosp Bris 87-94; Chapl Southmead Health Services NHS Trust 94-99; Chapl N Bris NHS Trust 99-05; Hd Spiritual and Past Care from 05; Hd Spiritual and Past Care Univ Hosps Bris NHS Foundn Trust from 05; Perm to Offic *B & W* from 94; Hon Can Bris Cathl from 99. *Southmead Hospital, Westbury-on-Trym, Bristol BS10 5NB* Tel 0117-342 0610 E-mail chris.davies@nbt.nhs.uk

DAVIES, David Geoffrey George. b 24. Univ of Wales (Ban) BA49 Lon Univ BD55 Chorley Coll of Educn PGCE75. St Mich Coll Llan 49. **d** 51 **p** 52. C Brecon St Mary w Battle and Llanhamlach *S & B* 51-55; Min Can Brecon Cathl 53-55; C Oystermouth 55-59; V Cwm *St As* 59-63; Warden of Ords 62-70; V Ruabon 63-70; Hon Can St As Cathl 66-69; Cursal Can 69-70; Hon C W Derby St Jo *Liv* 70-81; Chapl to Welsh Speaking Angl in Liv 74-81 and from 96; TV Bourne Valley *Sarum* 81-87; TR 87-89; Bp's Chapl to Schs 83-89; RD Alderbury 86-89; rtd 89; Hon Chapl Liv Cathl 89-04; Sub-Chapl HM Pris Risley 90-96. *55 Hattons Lane, Liverpool L16 7QR* Tel 0151-722 1415

DAVIES, Canon David Islwyn. b 42. St Deiniol's Hawarden 83. **d** 85 **p** 86. C Llangiwg *S & B* 85-87; C Swansea St Pet 87-89; Chapl Schiedam Miss w Seamen *Eur* 89-92; Chapl Milford Haven Miss to Seamen 92-94; V Pontyates and Llangyndeyrn *St D* 94-99; R Ystradgynlais *S & B* from 99; AD Cwmtawe from 06; Can Res Brecon Cathl from 06. *The Rectory, 2 Heol Eglwys, Ystradgynlais, Swansea SA9 1EY* Tel (01639) 843200

DAVIES, Canon David Jeremy Christopher. b 46. CCC Cam BA68 MA72. Westcott Ho Cam 68. **d** 71 **p** 72. C Stepney St Dunstan and All SS *Lon* 71-74; Chapl Qu Mary Coll 74-78; Chapl Univ of Wales (Cardiff) *Llan* 78-85; Can Res Sarum Cathl from 85. *Hungerford Chantry, 54 The Close, Salisbury SP1 2EL* Tel (01722) 555179 Fax 555117 E-mail jeremydavies@waitrose.com *or* precentor@salcath.co.uk

DAVIES, Canon David Michael Cole. b 44. St D Coll Lamp. **d** 68 **p** 69. C Carmarthen St Pet *St D* 68-72; R Dinas 72-77; V Ty-Croes w Saron 77-80; V Llanedi w Tycroes and Saron 80-90; RD Dyffryn Aman 85-90; V Dafen and Llwynhendy 90-94; V Dafen 94-08; Hon Can St D Cathl 00-08; rtd 08. *30 Bro'r Dderwen, Clynderwen SA66 7NR* E-mail dcmcd@aol.com

DAVIES, Prof David Protheroe. b 39. CCC Cam BA62 MA66 CCC Ox MA69 BD69. Ripon Hall Ox 62. **d** 64 **p** 65. C Swansea St Mary w H Trin *S & B* 64-67; Lect Th Univ of Wales (Lamp) 67-75; Sen Lect 75-86; Dean Faculty of Th 75-77 and from 81; Hd Th and Relig Studies from 84; Prof Th Univ of Wales (Lamp) from 86; Pro Vice-Chan from 88; Bp's Chapl for Th Educn *S & B* from 79. *University of Wales, Lampeter SA48 7ED* Tel (01570) 422351

DAVIES, David Vernon. b 14. AFBPsS68 Univ of Wales (Swansea) BA35 BD38 St Cath Coll Ox MA40 K Coll Lon PhD56. St D Coll Lamp 41. **d** 41 **p** 42. C Llanelli Ch Ch *St D* 41-46; Chapl St John's Coll Nassau Bahamas 46-50; Chapl Cane Hill Hosp Coulsdon 50-61; Lect St Luke's Coll Ex 61-65; Lic to Offic *Ex* 61-68; Sen Lect St Luke's Coll Ex 65-68; Lic to Offic *Llan* from 68; Prin Lect Llan Coll of Educn 68-77; Sen Lect Univ of Wales (Cardiff) 77-79; rtd 79. *41 Cefn Coed Avenue, Cyncoed, Cardiff CF23 6HF* Tel (029) 2075 7635

DAVIES, David William. b 64. **d** 90 **p** 91. C Newton St Pet *S & B* 90-93; V Llywel and Traean-glas w Llanulid 93-97; CF from 97. *c/o MOD Chaplains (Army)* Tel (01980) 615804 Fax 615800

DAVIES, Dennis William. b 24. Leeds Univ BA46 K Coll Lon AKC54 BD65 Open Univ BA92. **d** 54 **p** 55. C Aylesbury *Ox* 54-58; Lic to Offic 60-07; rtd 90. *45 Green End Street, Aston Clinton, Aylesbury HP22 5JE* Tel (01296) 631780

DAVIES, Derek George. b 47. UWIST BEng74 Univ of Wales (Lamp) BD03. St Mich Coll Llan 03. **d** 05 **p** 06. NSM Steynton *St D* from 05. *Ty Llosg, Clarbeston Road, Pembroke SA63 4SG* Tel (01437) 563560 E-mail derekgeorgedavies@hotmail.com

DAVIES, Dewi Gwynfor. b 56. Univ of Wales (Abth) BD92 MTh98 RIBA81. **d** 98 **p** 99. C Llangunnor w Cwmffrwd *St D* 98-99; P-in-c Elerch w Penrhyncoch w Capel Bangor and Goginan 99-00; P-in-c Cil-y-Cwm and Ystrad-ffin w Rhandir-mwyn etc 00-01; V 01-03; V Llanedi w Tycroes and Saron 03-09; V Pen-bre from 09. *The Vicarage, Ar-y-bryn, Pembrey, Burry Port SA16 0AJ* Tel (01554) 832403

DAVIES, Dillwyn. b 30. St Mich Coll Llan 52. **d** 54 **p** 55. C Laugharne w Llansadwrnen and Llandawke *St D* 54-57; Lic to Offic *Dur* 57-58; Miss to Seamen 57-58; Ceylon 58-62; R Winthorpe *S'well* 62-71; V Langford w Holme 62-71; V Mansfield Woodhouse 71-85; R Gedling 85-92; RD Gedling 85-90; Hon Can S'well Minster 90-92; rtd 92. *7 Norbury Drive, Mansfield NG18 4HT* Tel (01623) 458594

DAVIES, Canon Dorrien Paul. b 64. Univ of Wales (Lamp) BA95. Llan Dioc Tr Scheme 86. **d** 88 **p** 89. C Llanelli *St D* 88-91; V Llanfihangel Ystrad and Cilcennin w Trefilan etc 91-99; V St Dogmael's w Moylgrove and Monington from 99; Can St D Cathl from 07. *The Vicarage, St Dogmael's, Cardigan SA43 3DX* Tel (01239) 612030 E-mail dorriendavies@btinternet.com

DAVIES, Prof Douglas James. b 47. St Jo Coll Dur BA69 St Pet Coll Ox MLitt72 Nottm Univ PhD80 DLitt04 Uppsala Univ Hon DTh98. Cranmer Hall Dur 71. **d** 75 **p** 76. Lect Nottm Univ 75-97; Sen Lect 90-97; Hon C Wollaton *S'well* 75-83; Hon C Attenborough 83-85; Hon C E Leake 85-91; Hon C Daybrook 91-97; Prof RS Nottm Univ 93-97; Prin SS Hild and Bede Coll Dur 97-00; Prof Th Dur Univ from 97; Prof Study of Relig Dur Univ from 00. *Department of Theology and Religion, Abbey House, Palace Green, Durham DH1 3RS* Tel 0191-375 7697 E-mail douglas.davies@durham.ac.uk

DAVIES, Canon Douglas Tudor. b 20. Univ of Wales (Ban) BA44. Coll of Resurr Mirfield 44. **d** 46 **p** 47. C Swansea Ch Ch *S & B* 46-52; C Oystermouth 52-57; R Llangynllo and Bleddfa 57-63; C-in-c Treboeth CD 63-65; V Treboeth 65-90; RD Penderi 78-90; Hon Can Brecon Cathl 82-83; Can 83-90; rtd 90. *245A Swansea Road, Waunarlwydd, Swansea SA5 4SN* Tel (01792) 879587

DAVIES, Edward Earl. b 40. Llan Dioc Tr Scheme 88. **d** 90 **p** 91. C Pontypridd St Cath w St Matt *Llan* 90-93; V Ferndale w Maerdy 93-00; V Cardiff Ch Ch Roath Park 00-09; rtd 09. *4 St Augustine Road, Heath, Cardiff CF14 4BD*

DAVIES, Edward Trevor. b 37. MRSC62 MInstE74 CEng78. NOC 92. **d** 95 **p** 96. NSM Waverton *Ches* 95-99; NSM Hargrave 99-00; C Bunbury and Tilstone Fearnall 00-02; NSM 02-03; Hon Asst Chapl Countess of Chester Hosp NHS Foundn Trust from 95. *Athergreen, 5 Allansford Avenue, Waverton, Chester CH3 7QH* Tel and fax (01244) 332106 *or* 365000 E-mail e.trevordavies@virgin.net

DAVIES, Edward William Llewellyn. b 51. St Jo Coll Nottm BTh77. **d** 78 **p** 79. C Southsea St Jude *Portsm* 78-81; C Alverstoke 81-84; R Abbas and Templecombe w Horsington *B & W* 84-89; Perm to Offic *Ches* 89-99; V Sutton St Jas from 99; Asst Warden of Readers from 02; RD Macclesfield from 05. *St James's Vicarage, Church Lane, Sutton, Macclesfield SK11 0DS* Tel (01260) 252228 E-mail taffy@parishpump.co.uk

DAVIES, Eileen. *See* DAVIES, Mrs Rachel Hannah Eileen

DAVIES, Ms Elizabeth Jane. b 58. Man Univ BA97 RGN82 RSCN88. Qu Coll Birm MA01. **d** 01 **p** 02. C Spotland *Man* 01-04; Chapl Pennine Acute Hosps NHS Trust 04-05; Chapl Bolton Hospice 05-08; P-in-c Ladybarn *Man* from 08. *St Chad's Rectory, 1 St Chad's Road, Manchester M20 4WH* Tel 0161-445 1185

DAVIES, Mrs Elizabeth Jean. b 39. Lon Univ MB, BS63 MRCS63 LRCP63. Chich Th Coll 86. **d** 89 **p** 95. Par Dn Southwick St Mich *Chich* 89-91; Par Dn Littlehampton and Wick 91-95; C Seaford w Sutton 95-97; NSM E Preston w Kingston 97-04; rtd 99; P-in-c Everton and Mattersey w Clayworth *S'well* 04-05; Perm to Offic from 06. *Mayfield, Bone Mill Lane, Welham, Retford DN22 9NL* Tel (01777) 703727

DAVIES, Mrs Emma Louise. b 67. St Andr Univ MA89. Ripon Coll Cuddesdon 05. **d** 07 **p** 08. C Market Harborough and The Transfiguration etc *Leic* from 07. *69 Tymecrosse Gardens, Market Harborough LE16 7US* Tel (01858) 463062 E-mail emmydavies@aol.com

DAVIES, Eric Brian. b 36. St Jo Coll Nottm. **d** 87 **p** 89. NSM Castle Donington and Lockington cum Hemington *Leic* 87-88; Hon C Hathern, Long Whatton and Diseworth 89-90; Hon C Hathern, Long Whatton and Diseworth w Belton etc 90-93; C Minster-in-Sheppey *Cant* 93-00; rtd 00; NSM Walsall St Gabr Fulbrook *Lich* 00-03; NSM Caldmore 00-02; NSM Caldmore w Palfrey 02-03; NSM Kinver and Enville 03-08. *26 The Green, Castle Donington, Derby DE74 2JX* Tel (01332) 696869 E-mail reverend.ericdavies@kirion.net

DAVIES, Evelyn Dorothy. MBE99. BEd72 Liv Univ CertEd56. **d** 96 **p** 97. NSM Llangynog *St As* 96-00; P-in-c Aberdaron w Rhiw and Llanfaelrhys etc *Ban* 00-04; R 04-07; rtd 07. *Edmund V Bungalow, Lon Ednyfed, Criccieth LL52 0AG* E-mail melangell@pennant1.demon.co.uk

DAVIES, Frances Elizabeth. b 38. CertEd. Moray Ord Course. **d** 95. Hon C Thurso *Mor* from 95; Hon C Wick from 95. *22 Granville Crescent, Thurso, Caithness KW14 7NP* Tel (01847) 892386 E-mail reallyfed@yahoo.co.uk

✠**DAVIES, The Rt Revd Francis James Saunders.** b 37. Univ of Wales (Ban) BA60 Selw Coll Cam BA62 MA66 Bonn Univ 63. St Mich Coll Llan 62. **d** 63 **p** 64 **c** 00. C Holyhead w Rhoscolyn *Ban* 63-67; Chapl Ban Cathl 67-69; R Llanllyfni 69-75; Can Missr Ban Cathl 75-78; V Gorseinon *S & B* 78-86; RD Llwchwr 83-86; V Cardiff Dewi Sant *Llan* 86-93; R Criccieth w Treflys *Ban* 93-99; Adn Meirionnydd 93-99; Bp Ban 99-04; rtd 04. *Ger-y-Nant, 5 Maes-y-Coed, Cardigan SA43 1AP* Tel (01239) 615664

DAVIES, Gareth Rhys. b 51. Oak Hill Th Coll. **d** 83 **p** 84. C Gt Warley Ch Ch *Chelmsf* 83-86; C Oxhey All SS *St Alb* 86-90; V Aldridge *Lich* 90-99; V Colney Heath St Mark *St Alb* 99-00; V

Sneyd Green *Lich* from 00; Bp's Adv on Healing from 09. *St Andrew's Vicarage, 42 Granville Avenue, Sneyd Green, Stoke-on-Trent ST1 6BH* Tel (01782) 215139

DAVIES, Geoffrey. *See* DAVIES, David Geoffrey George

✠**DAVIES, The Rt Revd Geoffrey Francis.** b 41. Cape Town Univ BA62 Em Coll Cam BA67 MA71. Cuddesdon Coll 67. **d** 69 **p** 70 **c** 87. C W Brompton St Mary *Lon* 69-72; C Serowe St Aug Botswana 72-76; R Kalk Bay H Trin South Africa 77-80; Dir Dept of Miss 81-87; Suff Bp St John 88-91; Bp Umzimvubu 91-03; rtd 03. *Waterfall Cottage, 7 Upper Quarterdeck Road, Kalk Bay, 7990 South Africa* Tel and fax (0027) (21) 788 6591 E-mail geoffd@intermail.co.za

DAVIES, Canon Geoffrey Lovat. b 30. St Aid Birkenhead. **d** 62 **p** 63. C Davenham *Ches* 62-65; C Higher Bebington 65-67; V Witton 67-80; R Lymm 80-96; Dioc Clergy Widows and Retirement Officer 87-91; Hon Can Ches Cathl 88-96; RD Gt Budworth 91-96; rtd 96; Perm to Offic *Liv* and *Ches* from 96. *21 Howbeck Close, Prenton CH43 6TH* Tel 0151-653 2441

DAVIES, Geoffrey Michael. b 43. St D Coll Lamp. **d** 70 **p** 71. C Brynmawr *S & B* 70-73; Coll of Ascension Selly Oak 73-74; S Africa 74-91 and from 99; C Claremont St Sav 74-76; R Strand 76-82; R E London St Sav 82-84; Assoc R Constantia Ch Ch 90-91; C Roath *Llan* 91-95; V Llanishen w Trellech Grange and Llanfihangel etc *Mon* 95-99; R Graaff-Reinet St Jas from 03. *PO Box 473, Graaff-Reinet, 6280 South Africa* Tel (0027) (498) 922458

DAVIES, George Vivian. b 21. CCC Cam BA47 MA49. Ely Th Coll. **d** 49 **p** 50. C Maidstone St Martin *Cant* 49-51; C Folkestone St Mary and St Eanswythe 51-56; V Leysdown w Harty 56-59; R Warehorne w Kenardington 59-74; R Rounton w Welbury *York* 74-86; rtd 86; Perm to Offic *Derby* 86-99. *12 Rectory Drive, Wingerworth, Chesterfield S42 6RT* Tel (01246) 279222

DAVIES, George William. b 51. Open Univ BA74 MPhil89 MCIPD. Sarum & Wells Th Coll 83. **d** 85 **p** 86. C Mansfield SS Pet and Paul *S'well* 85-89; Chapl Cen Notts HA 86-89; P-in-c Fobbing and Ind Chapl *Chelmsf* 89-96; Chapl Thurrock Lakeside Shopping Cen 93-96; R Mottingham St Andr *S'wark* 96-04; V Lamorbey H Trin *Roch* from 04; Chapl Rose Bruford Coll from 04. *Holy Trinity Vicarage, 1 Hurst Road, Sidcup DA15 9AE* Tel (020) 8309 7886 *or* 8300 8231 E-mail george@daviesgeorge.wanadoo.co.uk

DAVIES, Glanmor Adrian. b 51. St D Coll Lamp. **d** 73 **p** 75. C Llanstadwel *St D* 73-78; R Dinas w Llanllawer and Pontfaen w Morfil etc 78-84; V Lamphey w Hodgeston 84-85; V Lamphey w Hodgeston and Carew 85-03; V Borth and Eglwys-fach w Llangynfelyn 03-06. *Bayford, Freshwater East Road, Lamphey, Pembroke SA71 5JX*

✠**DAVIES, The Rt Revd Glenn Naunton.** b 50. Sydney Univ BSc72 Sheff Univ PhD88. Westmr Th Sem (USA) BD78 ThM79. **d** 81 **p** 81 **c** 01. Australia 81-85; Hon C Fulwood *Sheff* 85-87; Hon C Lodge Moor St Luke 86-87; Australia from 87; Lect Moore Th Coll 83-95; R Miranda 95-01; Bp N Sydney from 01. *PO Box Q190, Queen Victoria Building, Sydney NSW 1230, Australia* Tel (0061) (2) 9265 1527 *or* 9419 6761 Fax 9265 1543

DAVIES, Glyn Richards. b 28. Solicitor 52. Mon Dioc Tr Scheme 76. **d** 79 **p** 80. NSM Michaelston-y-Fedw and Rudry *Mon* 79-88; NSM St Mellons and Michaelston-y-Fedw 88-96; NSM St Mellons 96-07. *Narnia, 4 Pilgrim's Way, Guildford GU4 8AB*

DAVIES, Glyndwr George. b 36. Glouc Sch of Min 88. **d** 91 **p** 92. NSM Clodock and Longtown w Craswall, Llanveynoe etc *Heref* 91-02; rtd 02; Perm to Offic *Heref* from 02. *White House Farm, Llanfihangel Crucorney, Abergavenny NP7 8HW* Tel (01873) 890251

DAVIES, The Ven Graham James. b 35. Univ of Wales BD72 St D Coll Lamp BA56. St Mich Coll Llan 56 Episc Th Sch Cam Mass 58. **d** 59 **p** 60. C Johnston w Steynton *St D* 59-62; C Llangathen w Llanfihangel Cilfargen 62-64; Min Can St D Cathl 64-66; R Burton 66-71; R Hubberston 71-74; Hon C Lenham w Boughton Malherbe *Cant* 74-80; V Cwmdauddwr w St Harmon and Llanwrthwl *S & B* 80-86; V Cydweli and Llandyfaelog *St D* 86-97; Can St D Cathl 92-02; Adn St D 96-02; V Steynton 97-02; rtd 02. *16 Freshwater East Road, Lamphey, Pembroke SA71 5JX*

DAVIES, Canon Henry Joseph. b 38. Univ of Wales (Cardiff) BSc61. St Mich Coll Llan 75. **d** 76 **p** 77. C Griffithstown *Mon* 76-79; TV Cwmbran 79-85; V Newport St Andr 85-03; Can St Woolos Cathl 98-03; rtd 03. *14 Morden Road, Newport NP19 7EU*

DAVIES, Herbert John. b 30. Cheltenham & Glouc Coll of HE BA97. Glouc Sch of Min 84. **d** 87 **p** 88. NSM Cheltenham St Mark *Glouc* 97-01; Perm to Offic from 01. *45 Farmington Road, Benhall, Cheltenham GL51 6AG* Tel (01242) 515996

✠**DAVIES, The Rt Revd Howell Haydn.** b 27. ARIBA52. Tyndale Hall Bris 56. **d** 59 **p** 60 **c** 81. C Heref St Pet w St Owen 59-61; Kenya 61-79; adn N Maseno 71-74; Provost Nairobi 74-79; V Woking St Pet *Guildf* 79-81; Bp Karamoja Uganda 81-87; V Wolverhampton St Jude *Lich* 87-93; rtd 93; Perm to Offic *Heref* 93-99. *2 Cherry Tree Close, Sheffield S11 9AF* Tel 0114-255 0233

DAVIES, Huw. *See* DAVIES, Philip Huw

DAVIES, Huw. *See* DAVIES, Peter Huw

DAVIES, Hywel John. b 45. Univ of Wales (Abth) BA67 Univ of Wales (Ban) DipEd68 Univ of Wales (Cardiff) MA90 Univ of Wales (Ban) BTh99. St Mich Coll Llan 94 Qu Coll Birm 96. **d** 97 **p** 98. Min Can Ban Cathl 97-98; C Llandudno 98-99; Lic to Offic *Llan* 99-03; NSM Canton Cardiff 03-04; P-in-c Llanarthne and Llanddarog *St D* 04-07; Chapl Coleg Sir Gâr 04-07; rtd 07; P-in-c Cardiff Dewi Sant *Llan* from 08. *The Vicarage, 51 Heath Park Avenue, Cardiff CF14 3RF* Tel (029) 2075 1418 E-mail hywel33@btinternet.com

DAVIES, Ian. b 45. Man Coll of Educn TCert74 Open Univ BA79. Carl Dioc Tr Inst 88. **d** 91 **p** 92. NSM Harraby *Carl* 91-95; C Barrow St Jo 95-96; P-in-c 96-00; P-in-c Beetham and Youth and Sch Support Officer 00-05; V Marown *S & M* from 05. *Marown Vicarage, Main Road, Crosby, Isle of Man IM4 4BH* Tel (01624) 851378 E-mail reviand@manx.net

DAVIES, Ian. b 54. Sheff Hallam Univ BA80 Univ of Wales (Cardiff) MSc(Econ)86 MBA92 Bris Univ PhD01 CQSW80. Wycliffe Hall Ox 02. **d** 04 **p** 05. C Swansea St Pet *S & B* 04-06; C Waunarllwydd 06-07; P-in-c from 07. *The Vicarage, 59 Victoria Road, Waunarlwydd, Swansea SA5 4SY* Tel (01792) 872251 Mobile 07779-145267 E-mail iandavies12@hotmail.com

DAVIES, Ian Charles. b 51. Sarum & Wells Th Coll 78. **d** 81 **p** 82. C E Bedfont *Lon* 81-84; C Cheam *S'wark* 84-87; V Merton St Jas 87-96; RD Merton 91-96; Chapl Tiffin Sch Kingston 96-97; P-in-c Kingston St Luke *S'wark* 96-98; V S Beddington St Mich 98-99. *111 Milton Road, London W7 1LG* Tel (020) 8621 4450

DAVIES, Ian Elliott. b 64. Univ of Wales (Ban) BD85. Ridley Hall Cam 86. **d** 88 **p** 89. C Baglan *Llan* 88-90; C Skewen 90-96; C St Marylebone All SS *Lon* 96-01; R Hollywood St Thos USA from 02. *St Thomas's Church, 7501 Hollywood Boulevard, Hollywood CA 90046, USA* Tel (001) (323) 876 2102 Fax 876 7738 E-mail frdavies@saintthomashollywood.org

DAVIES, Ion. *See* DAVIES, Johnston ap Llynfi

DAVIES, Islwyn. *See* DAVIES, Canon David Islwyn

DAVIES, Canon Ivor Llewellyn. b 35. Univ of Wales BA56 St Cath Soc Ox BA58 MA63. Wycliffe Hall Ox 56. **d** 62 **p** 63. C Wrexham *St As* 62-64; India 65-71; V Connah's Quay *St As* 71-79; P-in-c Gorsley w Cliffords Mesne *Glouc* 79-84; P-in-c Hempsted 84-90; Dir of Ords 84-90; Hon Can Glouc Cathl 89-01; V Parkend 90-01; P-in-c Viney Hill 97-01; rtd 01; Perm to Offic *Glouc* from 01 and *Heref* from 04. *Rose Cottage, Church Walk, Parkend, Lydney GL15 4HQ* Tel (01594) 564512

DAVIES, James Alan. b 38. Lambeth STh95. St Jo Coll Nottm. **d** 83 **p** 84. C Fletchamstead *Cov* 83-87; P-in-c Hartshill 87-89; V 89-93; V E Green 93-03; rtd 03; Hon C Mickleton, Willersey, Saintbury etc *Glouc* 04-05; Perm to Offic *Cov* from 05. *5 Margetts Close, Kenilworth CV8 1EN* Tel (01926) 854337 E-mail alan.davies@ukonline.co.uk

DAVIES, Canon James Trevor Eiddig. b 17. St D Coll Lamp BA39 AKC41. **d** 41 **p** 42. C Rhymney *Mon* 41-44; C Newport St Andr 44-47; P-in-c 47-51; P-in-c Nash 50-51; R Bettws Newydd w Trostrey and Kemeys Commander 51-58; V Blaenavon w Capel Newydd 58-68; V Llantarnam 68-71; TR Cwmbran 71-86; Hon Can St Woolos Cathl 83-86; rtd 86; Lic to Offic *Mon* from 86. *34 Rockfield Road, Monmouth NP25 5BA* Tel (01600) 716649

DAVIES, James William. b 51. Trin Hall Cam BA72 MA76 St Jo Coll Dur BA79. Cranmer Hall Dur 77. **d** 80 **p** 81. C Croydon Ch Ch Broad Green *Cant* 80-83; CMS 83-86; Chapl Bethany Sch Goudhurst 86-90; P-in-c Parkstone St Luke *Sarum* 90-00; Hon C Bournemouth St Andr *Win* from 05. *8 Newton Road, Swanage BH19 2DZ* Tel (01929) 475770 E-mail jameswdavies@btopenworld.com

DAVIES, Mrs Jane Ann. b 58. Coll of Ripon & York St Jo MA97. Aston Tr Scheme 91 WMMTC 93 NOC 94. **d** 96 **p** 97. NSM Heref S Wye 96-97; C 97-00; P-in-c Bishop's Frome w Castle Frome and Fromes Hill 00-08; P-in-c Acton Beauchamp and Evesbatch w Stanford Bishop 00-08; P-in-c Stoke Lacy, Moreton Jeffries w Much Cowarne etc 00-08; V Frome Valley from 09. *The Vicarage, Bishop's Frome, Worcester WR6 5AP* Tel (01885) 490204 E-mail jane@davies4771.fsnet.co.uk

DAVIES, Mrs Jaqueline Ann. b 42. Bris Univ BA64 CertEd65 Univ of Wales (Lamp) MA99. EMMTC 84 St As Minl Tr Course 97. **d** 98 **p** 99. NSM Llanfair DC, Derwen, Llanelidan and Efenechtyd *St As* 98-00; Perm to Offic from 00. *Sisial y Llyn, 3 Glannau Tegid, Bala LL23 7DZ* Tel (01678) 520636

DAVIES, Jeffrey William. b 45. St Cath Coll Cam BA66 MA69 LLM67 Liv Univ MTh07 Solicitor 69. NOC 01. **d** 04 **p** 05. NSM Ramsbottom St Andr *Man* 04-05; NSM Ramsbottom and Edenfield from 05. *44 Higher Dunscar, Egerton, Bolton BL7 9TF* Tel and fax (01204) 412503 E-mail jeffdavies1@ntlworld.com

DAVIES, Jeremy. *See* DAVIES, Canon David Jeremy Christopher

DAVIES, John. *See* DAVIES, Herbert John

DAVIES, John. *See* DAVIES, Benjamin John

DAVIES, John. *See* PAGE DAVIES, David John

DAVIES, John. *See* DAVIES, Kenneth John

DAVIES, John. b 62. Univ of Wales (Cardiff) BA88. Ridley Hall Cam 98. **d** 00 **p** 01. C Wavertree H Trin *Liv* 00-04; P-in-c W Derby Gd Shep 04-09; V from 09. *345 Utting Avenue East, Liverpool L11 1DF* Tel 0151-256 0510 E-mail johndavies.liverpool@blueyonder.co.uk

DAVIES, John Atcherley. b 27. St Jo Coll Dur BA55. Wycliffe Hall Ox 55. **d** 57 **p** 58. C Eastbourne St Jo *Chich* 57-61; Chapl RN 61-82; V Hyde Common *Win* 82-92; rtd 92; Perm to Offic *Win* from 98. *6 Durslton Crescent, Christchurch BH23 2ST* Tel (01202) 484398

DAVIES, John Barden. b 47. St D Coll Lamp 70. **d** 71 **p** 72. C Rhosllannerchrugog *St As* 71-75; R Llanbedr-y-Cennin *Ban* 75-86; Adult Educn Officer 86-93; V Betws-y-Coed and Capel Curig w Penmachno etc 86-93; R Llanfwrog and Clocaenog and Gyffylliog *St As* from 93; AD Dyffryn Clwyd from 95. *The Rectory, Mwrog Street, Ruthin LL15 1LE* Tel (01824) 704866 Fax 702724 Mobile 07850-152824 E-mail jbarden@btinternet.com

DAVIES, John Daniel Lee. b 55. Trin Coll Carmarthen BEd79. **d** 00 **p** 00. C Leverburgh *Arg* 00-01; P-in-c Harris Ch Ch from 01. *3A Cluer, Isle of Harris HS3 3EP* Tel (01859) 530344

✠**DAVIES, The Rt Revd John David Edward.** b 53. Southn Univ LLB74 Univ of Wales (Cardiff) LLM95. St Mich Coll Llan 82. **d** 84 **p** 85 **c** 08. C Chepstow *Mon* 84-86; C-in-c Michaelston-y-Fedw and Rudry 86-89; R Bedwas and Rudry 89-95; V Maindee Newport 95-00; Dean Brecon and V Brecon St Mary w Llanddew *S & B* 00-08; P-in-c Cynog Honddu 05-08; Bp S & B from 08. *Ely Tower, Castle Square, Brecon LD3 9DJ* Tel (01874) 622008 E-mail bishop.swansea&brecon@churchinwales.org.uk

✠**DAVIES, The Rt Revd John Dudley.** b 27. Trin Coll Cam BA51 MA63. Linc Th Coll 52. **d** 53 **p** 54 **c** 87. C Leeds Halton St Wilfrid *Ripon* 53-56; C Yeoville S Africa 57; R Evander 57-61; R Empangeni 61-63; Chapl Witwatersrand Univ 63-71; Sec Chapls in HE Gen Syn Bd of Educn 71-74; P-in-c Keele *Lich* 74-76; Chapl Keele Univ 74-76; Prin USPG Coll of the Ascension Selly Oak 76-81; Preb Lich Cathl 76-87; Can Res, Preb and Sacr St As Cathl 82-85; Dioc Missr 82-87; V Llanrhaeadr-ym-Mochnant, Llanarmon, Pennant etc 85-87; Suff Bp Shrewsbury *Lich* 87-92; Area Bp 92-94; rtd 94; Perm to Offic *Lich* from 05. *Nyddfa, By-Pass Road, Gobowen, Oswestry SY11 3NG* Tel and fax (01691) 653434 E-mail sddjdd@sddjdd.free-online.co.uk

DAVIES, John Edwards Gurnos. b 18. Ch Coll Cam BA41 MA45. Westcott Ho Cam 40. **d** 42 **p** 43. C Portwood St Paul *Ches* 42-44; CF (EC) 44-46; CF 46-73; Asst Chapl Gen 70; QHC 72; R Monk Sherborne and Pamber *Win* 73-76; P-in-c Sherborne 76; R The Sherbornes w Pamber 76-83; rtd 83. *3 Parsonage Lane, Edington, Westbury BA13 4QS* Tel (01380) 830479

DAVIES, John Gwylim. b 27. Ripon Hall Ox 67. **d** 70 **p** 71. C Ox St Mich 70-71; C Ox St Mich w St Martin and All SS 71-72; TV New Windsor 73-77; R Hagley *Worc* 77-83; TV Littleham w Exmouth 83-92; Asst Dioc Stewardship Adv 83-92; rtd 92; Perm to Offic *Ex* from 92. *5 The Retreat, The Retreat Drive, Topsham, Exeter EX3 0LS* Tel (01392) 876995

DAVIES, John Harverd. b 57. Keble Coll Ox BA80 MA84 CCC Cam MPhil82 Lanc Univ PhD. Westcott Ho Cam 82. **d** 84 **p** 85. C Liv Our Lady and St Nic w St Anne 84-87; C Pet St Jo 87-90; Min Can Pet Cathl 88-90; V Anfield St Marg *Liv* 90-94; Chapl, Fell and Lect Keble Coll Ox 94-99; V Melbourne *Derby* from 99; Dioc Dir of Ords 00-09; C Ticknall, Smisby and Stanton by Bridge etc from 07. *The Vicarage, Church Square, Melbourne, Derby DE73 8JH* Tel (01332) 862347 E-mail jhd@rdplus.net

DAVIES, Canon John Howard. b 29. St Jo Coll Cam BA50 MA54 Nottm Univ BD62. Westcott Ho Cam 54. **d** 55 **p** 56. Succ Derby Cathl 55-58; Chapl Westcott Ho Cam 58-63; Lect Th Southn Univ 63-81; Lic to Offic *Win* 63-81; Sen Lect 74-81; Dir Th and RS Southn Univ 81-94; Can Th Win Cathl 81-91; Hon C Southampton St Alb 88-91; Hon C Swaythling 91-94; rtd 94. *13 Glen Eyre Road, Southampton SO16 3GA* Tel (023) 8067 9359

DAVIES, Canon John Howard. b 35. Brasted Th Coll 60 Ely Th Coll 62. **d** 64 **p** 65. C Bromsgrove All SS *Worc* 64-67; C Astwood Bank w Crabbs Cross 67-70; R Worc St Martin 70-74; P-in-c Worc St Pet 72-74; R Worc St Martin w St Pet 74-79; RD Worc E 77-79; TR Malvern Link w Cowleigh 79-93; Hon Can Worc Cathl 81-00; RD Malvern 83-92; V Bromsgrove St Jo 93-00; rtd 00; Perm to Offic *Worc* from 00. *10 Baveney Road, Worcester WR2 6DS* Tel (01905) 428086 E-mail jjhd39@aol.com

DAVIES, John Howard. b 51. EAMTC 98. **d** 01 **p** 02. NSM Walsingham, Houghton and Barsham *Nor* 01-04; NSM Holt w High Kelling 04-06; P-in-c Lake *Portsm* from 06; P-in-c Shanklin St Sav from 06. *The Vicarage, 46 Sandown Road, Lake, Sandown PO36 9JT* Tel (01983) 401121 Mobile 07870-509439 E-mail john@apostle.co.uk

DAVIES, John Hugh Conwy. b 42. Bris Univ BSc64 PhD67 CEng72 MICE72. Linc Th Coll 84. **d** 86 **p** 87. C Limber Magna w Brocklesby *Linc* 86-89; R Wickenby Gp 89-94; R Denbigh and Nantglyn *St As* 94-99; R Denbigh 99-00; V Llanrhaeadr-ym-

Mochnant etc 01-07; rtd 07. *Sisial y Llyn, 3 Glannau Tegid, Bala LL23 7DZ* Tel (01678) 520636

DAVIES, Canon John Hywel Morgan. b 45. St D Coll Lamp BA71 LTh73. **d** 73 **p** 74. C Milford Haven *St D* 73-77; V from 89; R Castlemartin w Warren and Angle etc 77-82; R Walton W w Talbenny and Haroldston W 82-89; Can St D Cathl from 03. *St Katharine's Vicarage, 1 Sandhurst Road, Milford Haven SA73 3JU* Tel (01646) 693314
E-mail johnmorgandavies@talk21.com

DAVIES, John Ifor. b 20. ACP DipEd. **d** 80 **p** 81. Hon C Allerton *Liv* 80-84; Hon C Ffynnongroew *St As* 84-87; Hon C Whitford 87-88. *Hafan Deg, Ffordd-y-Graig, Lixwm, Holywell CH8 8LY* Tel (01352) 781151

DAVIES, John Keith. b 33. St Mich Coll Llan 80. **d** 82 **p** 83. C Llanbadarn Fawr w Capel Bangor and Goginan *St D* 82-84; V Llandygwydd and Cenarth w Cilrhedyn etc 84-89; V Abergwili w Llanfihangel-uwch-Gwili etc 89-98; RD Carmarthen 93-98; rtd 98. *Tanyfron, 81 Hafod Cwnin, Carmarthen SA31 2AS* Tel (01267) 223931

DAVIES, John Melvyn George. b 37. Wycliffe Hall Ox 68. **d** 71 **p** 72. C Nonynow *Ches* 71-75; C Heswall 76-78; V Claughton cum Grange 78-83; R Waverton 83-02; RD Malpas 90-97; rtd 02; Perm to Offic *Ches* from 03. *15 Tattenhall Road, Tattenhall, Chester CH3 9QQ* Tel (01829) 770184

DAVIES, Canon John Oswell. b 27. St D Coll Lamp 74. **d** 75 **p** 76. C Henfynyw w Aberaeron and Llanddewi Aberarth *St D* 75-76; P-in-c Eglwyswnewydd w Ysbyty Ystwyth 76-77; V 77-83; R Maenordeifi and Capel Colman w Llanfihangel etc 83-93; RD Cemais and Sub-Aeron 87-93; Hon Can St D Cathl 92-93; rtd 93. *Hafod, Carregwen, Llechryd, Cardigan SA43 2PJ* Tel (01239) 682568

✠**DAVIES, The Rt Revd John Stewart.** b 43. Univ of Wales BA72 Qu Coll Cam MLitt74. Westcott Ho Cam 72. **d** 74 **p** 75 **c** 99. C Hawarden *St As* 74-78; Tutor St Deiniol's Lib Hawarden 76-83; V Rhosymedre *St As* 78-87; Dir Dioc Minl Tr Course 83-93; Warden of Ords 83-91; Hon Can St As Cathl 86-91; V Mold 87-92; Adn St As 91-99; R Llandyrnog and Llangwyfan 92-99; Bp St As 99-08; rtd 09. *17 Pont y Bedol, Llanrhaeadr, Denbigh LL16 4NF*

DAVIES, Johnston ap Llynfi (Ion). b 28. St D Coll Lamp BA51 St Mich Coll Llan 51. **d** 53 **p** 54. C Swansea Ch Ch *S & B* 53-55; C Sketty 55-57; Nigeria 57-61; R Whittington *Derby* 61-64; Chapl Broadmoor Hosp Crowthorne 64-66; Perm to Offic *Ox* 67-72; Perm to Offic *York* 72-86; R Creeksea w Althorne, Latchingdon and N Fambridge *Chelmsf* 86-88; rtd 88; Asst Chapl Costa Blanca *Eur* 89-92; Chapl 92-93; Lic to Offic 93-95. *Calle Ponent 1, Apartamentos Esmeralda 41A, 03710 Calpe (Alicante), Spain* Tel (0034) 965 838 063

DAVIES, Jonathan Byron. b 69. Univ of Wales (Cardiff) BTh95. St Mich Coll Llan 94. **d** 96 **p** 97. C Betws w Ammanford and Dioc Youth Chapl *St D* 96-99; C Newton St Pet *S & B* 99-00; P-in-c Swansea St Luke 03-05; V Manselton w Swansea St Luke 05-08; V Manselton and Cwmbwrla from 08. *The Vicarage, Manor Road, Manselton, Swansea SA5 9PA* Tel (01792) 464595 Mobile 07760-210975 E-mail rev.jbd@sky.com

DAVIES, Judith. b 54. Man Univ BA75. WEMTC 97. **d** 00 **p** 01. C Harlescott *Lich* 00-04; Chapl Shrewsbury and Telford NHS Trust 04-05; Asst Chapl Severn Hospice Shrewsbury 05-06; Perm to Offic *Heref* 05-06; TV Wenlock from 06. *The Vicarage, Harley Road, Cressage, Shrewsbury SY5 6DF* Tel (01952) 510417

DAVIES, Prof Julia Mary. b 44. Ex Univ BA65 FCIPD00. **d** 04 **p** 05. OLM Deane *Man* from 04. *15 Newland Drive, Bolton BL5 1DS* Tel (01204) 660260 Mobile 07966-528877

DAVIES, Julian Edward. b 60. Jes Coll Ox BA82 MA86 DPhil87 Selw Coll Cam BA92 MA96. Ridley Hall Cam 90. **d** 94 **p** 95. C Hucknall Torkard *S'well* 94-96; C Eglwysilan *Llan* 96-99; Assoc R St Marylebone w H Trin *Lon* 99-03; Assoc R St Giles-in-the-Fields 03-08; TR Southampton (City Cen) *Win* from 08. *The Rectory, 32B Morris Road, Southampton SO15 2BR* Tel (023) 8023 5716 E-mail jed-ihs@o2.co.uk

DAVIES, Keith. *See* DAVIES, John Keith

DAVIES, Keith. *See* BERRY-DAVIES, Charles William Keith

DAVIES, Kenneth John. b 42. Ripon Coll Cuddesdon 79. **d** 80 **p** 81. C Buckingham *Ox* 80-83; V Birstall *Wakef* 83-91; TV Crookes St Thos *Sheff* 91-94; TR Huntington *York* 94-07; rtd 07. *18 Hall Rise, Haxby, York YO32 3LP* Tel (01904) 768211
E-mail johnsuedavies@aol.com

DAVIES, Leonard Hamblyn Kenneth. b 57. Birm Univ MA03 Dur Univ MA06. Sierra Leone Bible Coll 84. **d** 93 **p** 94. C St Geo Cathl Freetown Lierra Leone 93-96; C Freetown St Jo 96-98; P-in-c Freetown H Spirit 98-01; Perm to Offic *Worc* 01-02; *Birm* 02-03; *Chelmsf* 03-08; Lic to Offic 08; Asst Chapl Kingston and Wimbledon YMCA from 08. *52 Bolton Road, London E15 4JY* Tel (020) 8519 2774 Mobile 07834-971467
E-mail kendavies90@hotmail.com

DAVIES, The Ven Lorys Martin. b 36. JP78. Univ of Wales (Lamp) BA57 ALCM52. Wells Th Coll 57. **d** 59 **p** 60. C Tenby w Gumfreston *St D* 59-62; Asst Chapl Brentwood Sch Essex 62-66; Chapl Solihull Sch 66-68; V Moseley St Mary *Birm* 68-81; Can

Res Birm Cathl 81-92; Dioc Dir of Ords 82-90; Adn Bolton *Man* 92-01; Bp's Adv Hosp Chapl 92-01; Warden of Readers 94-01; rtd 02; Perm to Offic *Birm* and *Worc* from 04. *Heol Cerrig, 28 Penshurst Road, Bromsgrove B60 2SN* Tel (01527) 577337

DAVIES (née ROACH), Mrs Lynne Elisabeth. b 44. WMMTC 95. **d** 98 **p** 99. NSM Snitterfield w Bearley *Cov* 98-01; NSM Salford Priors from 01; NSM Exhall w Wixford from 01; NSM Temple Grafton w Binton from 01. *19 Garrard Close, Salford Priors, Evesham WR11 8XG* Tel (01789) 773711 Fax 490231

DAVIES, Malcolm. b 35. St Mich Coll Llan 82. **d** 84 **p** 85. C Roath *Llan* 84-88; C Pentre 88-94; V Llancarfan w Llantrithyd 94-02; rtd 02. *141 Fontygary Road, Rhoose, Barry CF62 3DU* Tel (01446) 710509

DAVIES, Malcolm Thomas. b 36. Open Univ BA81. St Mich Coll Llan 71. **d** 73 **p** 74. C Betws w Ammanford *St D* 73-76; V Cil-y-Cwm and Ystrad-ffin w Rhandir-mwyn etc 76-80; V Llangyfelach *S & B* 80-85; V Loughor 85-94; V Llanelli St Paul *St D* 94-95; V Llanelli St Pet 95-01; rtd 01. *25 Walters Road, Llanelli SA15 1LR* Tel (01554) 770295

DAVIES, Mrs Margaret Adelaide. b 45. Weymouth Coll of Educn CertEd67. S Dios Minl Tr Scheme 92. **d** 95 **p** 96. NSM Westbury *Sarum* 95-02; NSM White Horse from 02; TV from 07. *The Vicarage, The Hollow, Dilton Marsh, Westbury BA13 4BU* Tel (01373) 822560 E-mail margaret.davies@whitehorseteam.org

DAVIES, Mrs Margot Alison Jane. b 55. SWMTC 02. **d** 05 **p** 06. C St Ives *Truro* from 05; C Halsetown from 05. *The Vicarage, Hellesvean, St Ives TR26 2HG* Tel (01736) 797749

✠**DAVIES, The Rt Revd Mark.** b 62. Leeds Univ BA85. Coll of Resurr Mirfield 86. **d** 89 **p** 90 **c** 08. C Barnsley St Mary *Wakef* 89-95; R Hemsworth 95-06; Dioc Vocations Adv and Asst Dir of Ords 98-06; RD Pontefract 00-06; Hon Can Wakef Cathl 02-06; Adn Rochdale *Man* 06-08; Suff Bp Middleton from 08. *The Hollies, Manchester Road, Rochdale OL11 3QY* Tel (01706) 358550 Fax 354851 E-mail markdavies62@bigfoot.com

DAVIES, Martin. *See* DAVIES, William Martin

DAVIES, Martyn John. b 60. Chich Th Coll 82. **d** 85 **p** 86. C Llantrisant 85-87; C Whitchurch 87-90; V Porth w Trealaw 90-01; R Merthyr Tydfil St Dav from 01; AD Merthyr Tydfil from 04. *The Rectory, Bryntirion Road, Merthyr Tydfil CF47 0ER* Tel (01685) 722992 E-mail fr.martyn@sky.com

DAVIES, Melvyn. *See* DAVIES, John Melvyn George

DAVIES, Canon Mervyn Morgan. b 25. Univ of Wales BA49. Coll of Resurr Mirfield 49. **d** 51 **p** 52. C Penarth w Lavernock *Llan* 51-58; Lic to Offic *Wakef* 58-60; C Port Talbot St Theodore *Llan* 60-63; V Pontycymer and Blaengarw 63-69; V Fairwater 69-95; RD Llan 81-95; Jt Ed *Welsh Churchman* 82-95; Can Llan Cathl 84-89; Prec 89-95; rtd 95; Perm to Offic *Llan* from 95. *20 Palace Avenue, Llandaff, Cardiff CF5 2DW* Tel (029) 2057 5327

DAVIES, Michael. *See* DAVIES, Canon David Michael Cole

DAVIES, Miss Moira Kathleen. b 41. Cant Sch of Min. **d** 88 **p** 94. Par Dn Walmer *Cant* 88-94; C 94-96; P-in-c Somercotes and Grainthorpe w Conisholme *Linc* 96-99; R 99-06; rtd 06. *9 Amanda Drive, Louth LN11 0AZ* Tel (01507) 609960

DAVIES, Canon Mostyn David. b 37. AKC64. **d** 65 **p** 66. C Corby St Columba *Pet* 65-69; Ind Chapl 69-03; P-in-c Pet St Barn 80-03; Can Pet Cathl 95-03; rtd 03; Perm to Offic *Pet* from 03. *92 West End, Langtoft, Peterborough PE6 9LU* Tel (01778) 342838 E-mail mostyn@zetnet.co.uk

DAVIES, Canon Myles Cooper. b 50. Sarum & Wells Th Coll 71. **d** 74 **p** 75. C W Derby St Mary *Liv* 74-77; C Seaforth 77-80; V 80-84; V Stanley 84-07; P-in-c Liv St Paul Stoneycroft 05-07; V Stanley w Stoneycroft St Paul from 07; Chapl Rathbone Hosp Liv 84-92; Chapl N Mersey Community NHS Trust 92-05; Dir of Ords *Liv* 94-05; Hon Can Liv Cathl 01-05; Can Res Liv Cathl from 06; Prec from 08. *St Anne's Vicarage, 8 Derwent Square, Liverpool L13 6QT* Tel and fax 0151-228 5252
E-mail myles@saintanneslanley.co.uk

DAVIES, Neil Anthony Bowen. b 52. Ex Univ BSc74. Westcott Ho Cam 75. **d** 78 **p** 79. C Llanblethian w Cowbridge and Llandough etc 78-80; C Aberdare 80-82; V Troedyrhiw w Merthyr Vale 82-88; Min Lower Earley LEP *Ox* 88-92; V Earley Trin 92-95; P-in-c Reading St Luke w St Bart 95-99; Perm to Offic 99-02. *Address temp unknown*

DAVIES, Nicholas Duff. b 67. Sheff Univ BA88 Edin Univ MTh89 Anglia Ruskin Univ MA09 FRSA01. Westcott Ho Cam 06. **d** 08 **p** 09. C S Dulwich St Steph *S'wark* from 06. *18 Talisman Square, London SE26 6XY* Tel (020) 8768 4273 Mobile 07801-336144 E-mail nickduffdavies@gmail.com

DAVIES, Mrs Nicola Louise. b 55. Birm Univ BA77 Lon Inst of Educn PGCE78. STETS 02. **d** 05. NSM Rowledge and Frensham *Guildf* 05-06. *1 Little Austins, Farnham GU9 8JR* Tel (01252) 714640 E-mail nicoladavies27@hotmail.com

DAVIES, Canon Nigel Lawrence. b 55. Lanc Univ BEd77. Sarum & Wells Th Coll 84. **d** 87 **p** 88. C Heywood St Luke w All So *Man* 87-91; V Burneside *Carl* 91-07; P-in-c Crosscrake 04-06; P-in-c Skelsmergh w Selside and Longsleddale 06-07; V Beacon from 07; RD Kendal 03-08; Hon Can Carl Cathl from 06. *St Oswald's*

Vicarage, The Main Road, Burneside, Kendal LA9 6QX Tel (01539) 722015 Fax 07974-448370 E-mail vicar_stoswald@hotmail.com *or* ruraldean_kendal@hotmail.com

DAVIES, Noel Paul. b 47. Chich Th Coll 83. **d** 85 **p** 86. C Milford Haven *St D* 85-89; R Jeffreyston w Reynoldston and E Williamston etc from 89. *The Rectory, Jeffreyston, Kilgetty SA68 0SG* Tel (01646) 651269

DAVIES, Canon Patricia Elizabeth. b 36. Westf Coll Lon BA58 Hughes Hall Cam CertEd59 Leeds Univ MA74. NEOC 83. **dss** 86 **d** 87 **p** 94. Killingworth *Newc* 86-90; Hon C 87-90; Hon C Newc H Cross 91-96; NSM Newc Epiphany 96-99; NSM Gosforth St Hugh 99-00; P-in-c 00-01; Hon Can Newc Cathl 00-01; rtd 01; Perm to Offic *York* from 01. *Applegarth, Middlewood Lane, Fylingthorpe, Whitby YO22 4TT* Tel (01947) 881175

DAVIES, Patrick Charles Steven. b 59. RGN86 RMN92 RHV94 Leeds Univ BA99. Coll of Resurr Mirfield 97. **d** 99 **p** 00. C Reddish *Man* 99-04; P-in-c Withington St Crispin from 04. *St Crispin's Rectory, 2 Hart Road, Manchester M14 7LE* Tel 0161-224 3452 E-mail fatherpat@btinternet.com

DAVIES, Paul. *See* DAVIES, Richard Paul

DAVIES, Paul Lloyd. b 46. Bris Univ LLB68 Solicitor 71. Trin Coll Carmarthen 84. **d** 87 **p** 88. NSM Newport w Cilgwyn and Dinas w Llanllawer *St D* 87-97; P-in-c Mathry w St Edren's and Grandston etc 97-01; V 01-08; rtd 08. *Treetops, Osborn Park, Neyland, Milford Haven SA73 1SX*

DAVIES, Paul Martin. b 50. Lon Univ BD75. Sarum & Wells Th Coll 75. **d** 75 **p** 76. C Walthamstow St Mary w St Steph *Chelmsf* 75-79; Kenya 79-86; R Leven w Catwick *York* 86-95; RD N Holderness 90-95; rtd 95; Perm to Offic *York* from 95. *54 The Meadows, Cherry Burton, Beverley HU17 7SD* Tel (01964) 551739

DAVIES, Paul Scott. b 59. Cranmer Hall Dur 85. **d** 88 **p** 89. C New Addington *S'wark* 88-91; C Croydon H Sav 91-94; P-in-c Norton in the Moors *Lich* 94-99; R 99-03; V Sunbury *Lon* from 03. *The Vicarage, Thames Street, Sunbury-on-Thames TW16 6AA* Tel (01932) 779431 E-mail paul@zippor.com

DAVIES, Peter. b 67. Lon Bible Coll BA97. St Mich Coll Llan 06. **d** 07 **p** 08. C Llanelli *St D* from 07. *St Peter's Vicarage, St Peters Terrace, Llanelli SA15 2RT* Tel (01554) 752378

DAVIES, Peter Huw. b 57. Crewe & Alsager Coll BEd79. Wycliffe Hall Ox 87. **d** 89 **p** 90. C Moreton *Ches* 89-93; V Weston-super-Mare St Paul *B & W* 93-05; P-in-c Chesham Bois *Ox* 05-08; R from 08. *The Rectory, Glebe Way, Amersham HP6 5ND* Tel (01494) 726139 E-mail daviesp5@aol.com

DAVIES, Peter Richard. b 32. St Jo Coll Ox BA55 MA58. Westcott Ho Cam 56. **d** 58 **p** 59. C Cannock *Lich* 58-62; Kenya 63-76; Chapl Bedford Sch 76-85; V Dale and St Brides w Marloes *St D* 85-92; rtd 92. *Canthill Cottage, Dale, Haverfordwest SA62 3QZ* Tel (01646) 636535

DAVIES, Peter Timothy William. b 50. Leeds Univ BSc74. Oak Hill Th Coll 75. **d** 78 **p** 79. C Kingston Hill St Paul *S'wark* 78-81; C Hove Bp Hannington Memorial Ch *Chich* 81-88; V Audley *Lich* from 88; P-in-c Alsagers Bank from 06. *The Vicarage, 1 Wilbrahams Walk, Audley, Stoke-on-Trent ST7 8HL* Tel (01782) 720392

DAVIES, Philip Huw. b 64. Aston Univ BSc86 MRPharmS87. St Mich Coll Llan 00. **d** 02 **p** 03. C Llangynwyd w Maesteg 02-03; C Betws w Ammanford *St D* 03-07; P-in-c Slebech and Uzmaston w Boulston from 07; P-in-c Llawhaden w Bletherston and Llanycefn from 07. *The Vicarage, Maenclochog, Clynderwen SA66 7LD* Tel (01437) 532925

DAVIES, Philip James. b 58. UEA BA79 Keswick Hall Coll PGCE80 K Coll Lon MA92. Ridley Hall Cam 86. **d** 89 **p** 90. C Rainham *Roch* 89-90; C Gravesend St Geo and Rosherville 90-95; V Rosherville 95-98; P-in-c King's Cliffe *Pet* from 98; Dioc Schs Development Officer from 98; C Bulwick, Blatherwycke w Harringworth and Laxton from 07. *The Rectory, 3 Hall Yard, King's Cliffe, Peterborough PE8 6XQ* Tel (01780) 470314 E-mail p.j.davies@tesco.net

DAVIES, Philip Simon. b 65. Trin Coll Ox BA87 MA91. Aston Tr Scheme 93 Ridley Hall Cam 95. **d** 97 **p** 98. C Burntwood *Lich* 97-00; TV Cheswardine, Childs Ercall, Hales, Hinstock etc 00-03; TR 03-04; P-in-c Olney *Ox* 04-08; P-in-c Banbury St Hugh from 08. *St Hugh's Vicarage, 4 Longfellow Road, Banbury OX16 9LB* Tel (01295) 256513 E-mail davies1@ukonline.co.uk

DAVIES, Philip Wyn. b 50. Univ of Wales BA72 MA82. St D Dioc Tr Course 93 St Mich Coll Llan BD96. **d** 96 **p** 97. D Llandysul *St D* 96-98; V Tregaron w Ystrad Meurig and Strata Florida from 98; P-in-c Blaenpennal 01-07; V from 07; Dioc Archivist from 04. *The Vicarage, Tregaron SY25 6HL* Tel (01974) 299010

DAVIES, Mrs Rachel Hannah Eileen. b 64. St Mich Coll Llan 01. **d** 04 **p** 05. NSM Lampeter and Llanddewibrefi Gp *St D* 04-06; NSM Bro Teifi Sarn Helen 06-08; P-in-c Llanerch Aeron w Ciliau Aeron and Dihewyd etc from 08. *Gwndwn, New Inn,*

Pencader SA39 9BE Tel and fax (01559) 384248 Mobile 07814-272998

DAVIES, Raymond Emlyn Peter. b 25. St Mich Coll Llan 51. **d** 53 **p** 54. C Llangeinor 53-58; C Llanishen and Lisvane 58-62 and 65-68; R Glyncorrwg w Afan Vale and Cymmer Afan 62-65; V Penrhiwceiber w Matthewstown and Ynysboeth 68-72; C Whitchurch 72-73; V Childs Ercall *Lich* 73-81; R Stoke upon Tern 73-81; P-in-c Hamstall Ridware w Pipe Ridware 81-82; P-in-c Kings Bromley 81-82; P-in-c Mavesyn Ridware 81-82; R The Ridwares and Kings Bromley 83-90; rtd 90; Perm to Offic *B & W* from 95. *51 Vereland Road, Hutton, Weston-super-Mare BS24 9TH* Tel (01934) 814680

DAVIES, Rebecca Jane. b 75. Clare Coll Cam MA96. St Mich Coll Llan 01. **d** 03 **p** 04. C Llandeilo Fawr and Taliaris *St D* 03-05; C Llandybie 05-07; P-in-c Maenclochog and New Moat etc from 07. *The Vicarage, Maenclochog, Clynderwen SA66 7LD* Tel (01437) 532925

DAVIES, Reginald Charles. b 33. Tyndale Hall Bris 58. **d** 64 **p** 65. C Heywood St Jas *Man* 64-66; C Drypool St Columba w St Andr and St Pet *York* 66-69; V Denaby Main *Sheff* from 69. *The Vicarage, Church Road, Denaby Main, Doncaster DN12 4AD* Tel (01709) 862297

DAVIES, Rendle Leslie. b 29. St Chad's Coll Dur BA52. **d** 54 **p** 55. C Monmouth 54-58; V Llangwm Uchaf w Llangwm Isaf w Gwernesney etc 58-63; V Usk and Monkswood w Glascoed Chpl and Gwehelog 63-99; Chapl HM YOI Usk and Prescoed 63-94; rtd 99; Perm to Offic *Heref* from 08. *12 Ridgeway, Wyesham, Monmouth NP25 3JX* Tel (01600) 714189

DAVIES, Rhiannon Mary Morgan. *See* JOHNSON, Rhiannon Mary Morgan

DAVIES, Richard Paul. b 48. Wycliffe Hall Ox 72. **d** 75 **p** 76. C Everton St Sav w St Cuth *Liv* 75-78; Chapl Asst Basingstoke Distr Hosp 78-80; TV Basingstoke *Win* 80-85; V Southampton Thornhill St Chris 85-94; V Eastleigh from 94. *The Vicarage, 1 Cedar Road, Eastleigh SO50 9NR* Tel (023) 8061 2073

DAVIES, Richard Paul. b 73. Univ of Wales (Lamp) BA94 Ox Univ MTh98. Ripon Coll Cuddesdon 94. **d** 97 **p** 98. Min Can St D Cathl 97-00; Succ 00-06; TV Dewisland 01-06; V Burry Port and Pwll from 06; Dioc Ecum Officer 02-07; OCF 05-07. *The Vicarage, Cae Ffwrnes, Burry Port SA16 0FW* Tel (01554) 832936 E-mail plglldavies@btinternet.com

DAVIES, Robert Emlyn. b 56. N Staffs Poly BA79. Coll of Resurr Mirfield 83. **d** 86 **p** 87. C Cardiff St Jo *Llan* 86-90; V Cwmparc 90-97; V Aberdare from 97; AD Cynon Valley 02-08. *The Vicarage, 26 Abernant Road, Aberdare CF44 0PY* Tel (01685) 884769

DAVIES, Robert Gwynant. **d** 08 **p** 09. NSM Canwell *Lich* from 08; NSM Drayton Bassett from 08; NSM Fazeley from 08. *Middleton House Farm, Tamworth Road, Middleton, Tamworth B78 2BD* Tel (01827) 873474 E-mail rob.jane@tinyonline.co.uk

DAVIES, Roger Charles. b 46. Univ of Wales BD72. St Mich Coll Llan 67. **d** 73 **p** 74. C Llanfabon 73-75; C Llanblethian w Cowbridge and Llandough etc 75-78; CF 78-84; TV Halesworth w Linstead, Chediston, Holton etc *St E* 84-87; R Claydon and Barham 87-91; R Lavant and Chapl Lavant Ho Sch 91-94; TV Gt Aycliffe and Chilton *Dur* 04-08; P-in-c Wheatley Hill and Wingate w Hutton Henry from 08. *The Old Rectory, The Village, Castle Eden, Hartlepool TS27 4SL* Tel (01429) 836846 Mobile 07866-649300 E-mail r876davies@btinternet.com

✠**DAVIES, The Rt Revd Ross Owen.** b 55. Melbourne Univ BA77 LLB79. ACT ThL81. **d** 81 **p** 82 **c** 02. Australia 81-91 and from 97; P-in-c Mundford w Lynford *Nor* 91-94; P-in-c Ickburgh w Langford 91-94; P-in-c Cranwich 91-94; C Somerton w Compton Dundon, the Charltons etc *B & W* 94-97; R Hindmarsh 97-00; Vic Gen and Adn The Murray 00-02; Bp from 02. *23 Ellendale Avenue, PO Box 269, Murray Bridge SA 5253, Australia* Tel (0061) (8) 8532 2270 Fax 8532 5760 Mobile 42-889 1850 E-mail r.davies@murray.anglican.org

DAVIES, Miss Rowan. b 55. Univ of Wales (Swansea) BA78 PGCE79. WMMTC 00. **d** 03 **p** 04. NSM Wigginton *Lich* from 03. *16 Queen's Way, Tamworth B79 8QD* Tel (01827) 69651 E-mail rowan.davies1@ukonline.co.uk

DAVIES, Preb Roy Basil. b 34. Bris Univ BA55. Westcott Ho Cam 57. **d** 59 **p** 60. C Ipswich St Mary le Tower *St E* 59-63; C Clun w Chapel Lawn *Heref* 63-70; V Bishop's Castle w Mainstone 70-83; RD Clun Forest 72-83; Preb Heref Cathl 82-99; P-in-c Billingsley w Sidbury 83-86; P-in-c Chelmarsh 83-86; P-in-c Chetton w Deuxhill and Glazeley 83-86; P-in-c Middleton Scriven 83-86; R Billingsley w Sidbury, Middleton Scriven etc 86-89; RD Bridgnorth 87-89; TR Wenlock 89-99; rtd 99; Perm to Offic *Heref* from 00. *13 Courtnay Rise, Hereford HR1 1BP* Tel (01432) 341154

✠**DAVIES, The Rt Revd Roy Thomas.** b 34. St D Coll Lamp BA55 Jes Coll Ox BLitt59. St Steph Ho Ox 57. **d** 59 **p** 60 **c** 85. C Llanelli St Paul *St D* 59-64; V Llanafan y Trawscoed and Llanwnnws 64-67; Chapl Univ of Wales (Abth) 67-73; C Aberystwyth 67-69; TV 70-73; Sec Ch in Wales Prov Coun for Miss and Unity 73-79; V Carmarthen St Dav *St D* 79-83; Adn Carmarthen 82-85; V Llanegwad w Llanfynydd 83-85; Bp Llan

85-99; rtd 99. *25 Awel Tywi, Llangunnor, Carmarthen SA31 2NL* Tel (01267) 230654

DAVIES, Mrs Sally Jane. b 63. Linc Coll Ox BA86. Trin Coll Bris BA92. **d** 92 **p** 94. C E Molesey St Paul *Guildf* 92-96; C Chalfont St Peter *Ox* 96-99; Chapl RN Coll Greenwich and Trin Coll of Music 99-06; Hon C Greenwich St Alfege *S'wark* 99-06; P-in-c Shamley Green *Guildf* from 06. *The Vicarage, Church Hill, Shamley Green, Guildford GU5 0UD* Tel (01483) 892030 E-mail vicar@shamleygreen.net

DAVIES, Canon Sarah Isabella. b 39. Llan Dioc Tr Scheme 87. **d** 91 **p** 97. NSM Pontypridd St Cath w St Matt *Llan* 91-93; C Ferndale w Maerdy 93-00; Chapl Univ Hosp of Wales and Llandough NHS Trust 98-00; Chapl Pontypridd and Rhondda NHS Trust 98-00; C Cardiff Ch Ch Roath Park *Llan* 00-09; Dioc Child Protection Officer 02-09; Hon Can Llan Cathl 06-09; rtd 09. *4 St Augustine Road, Heath, Cardiff CF14 4BD*

DAVIES, Saunders. *See* DAVIES, The Rt Revd Francis James Saunders

DAVIES, Scott Lee. b 73. St Jo Coll Nottm. **d** 06 **p** 07. C Childwall All SS *Liv* from 06. *80 Green Lane North, Liverpool L16 8NL* Tel 0151-737 2214

DAVIES, Simon Stanley Miles. b 65. Cranfield Univ BEng88 MSc95 Greenwich Univ PGCE09. Seabury-Western Th Sem 97 Westcott Ho Cam 98. **d** 00 **p** 01. C Llanrhos *St As* 00-03; R Alberton Canada 03-05; Hon C Win St Cross w St Faith from 07. *7 St Cross Mede, Mead Road, Winchester SO23 9RF* Tel (01962) 843989

DAVIES, Stephen. b 56. Nottm Univ BSc77. Wycliffe Hall Ox 01. **d** 03 **p** 04. C Crawley and Littleton and Sparsholt w Lainston *Win* 03-07; V Heacham *Nor* from 07. *The Vicarage, Church Lane, Heacham, King's Lynn PE31 7HJ* Tel (01485) 570268 E-mail heacham.vicar@googlemail.com

DAVIES, Stephen John. b 55. Bp Otter Coll Chich BA01 IEng77. St Steph Ho Ox 96. **d** 98 **p** 99. C Leigh Park and Warren Park *Portsm* 98-02; C Durrington *Chich* 02-05; P-in-c Earnley and E Wittering 05-08; R from 08; Chapl Chich Cathl from 02. *The Rectory, Church Road, East Wittering, Chichester PO20 8PS* Tel (01243) 672260

DAVIES, Stephen John. b 65. Nottm Univ BA86 Reading Univ MPhil88 MRICS90. Wycliffe Hall Ox BTh97. **d** 97 **p** 98. C Barton Seagrave w Warkton *Pet* 97-01; P-in-c Enderby w Lubbesthorpe and Thurlaston *Leic* from 01. *The Rectory, 16A Desford Road, Leicester LE9 7TE* Tel (01455) 888488 E-mail steveandalidavies@btinternet.com

DAVIES, Stephen Walter. b 26. AKC54. **d** 55 **p** 56. C Plympton St Mary *Ex* 55-58; C Ex St Mark 58-61; Chapl RAF 61-77; R Feltwell *Ely* 78-84; R N Newton w St Michaelchurch, Thurloxton etc *B & W* 84-91; rtd 91. *5 Manchester Road, Exmouth EX8 1DE*

DAVIES, Mrs Susan Anne. b 48. N Co Coll Newc CertEd69. St Mich Coll Llan 98. **d** 01 **p** 02. NSM Monmouth w Overmonnow etc 01-05; NSM Goetre w Llanover 05; TV Rossendale Middle Valley *Man* from 07. *The Rectory, 539 Newchurch Road, Rossendale BB4 9HH* Tel (01706) 219768 E-mail susanannedavies@aol.com

DAVIES, Taffy. *See* DAVIES, Edward William Llewellyn

DAVIES, Canon Thomas Philip. b 27. Univ of Wales (Ban) BEd73. St Mich Coll Llan 55. **d** 56 **p** 57. C Ruabon *St As* 56-59; C Prestatyn 59-62; V Penley 62-69; V Bettisfield 66-69; V Holt and Isycoed 69-77; Dioc Dir of Educn 76-92; Dioc RE Adv 76-92; RD Wrexham 76-77; TR Hawarden 77-92; Can St As Cathl 79-92; rtd 93. *53 Muirfield Road, Buckley CH7 2NN* Tel (01244) 547099

DAVIES, Canon Timothy Robert. b 64. Bradf Univ BSc87. Wycliffe Hall Ox BTh93. **d** 93 **p** 94. C Eynsham and Cassington *Ox* 93-97; C Fulwood *Sheff* 97-03; Crosslinks Assoc Ch Ch Cen from 03; Hon Can Nairobi Cathl from 08. *Egerton Hall, Fitzwilliam Street, Sheffield S1 4JR* Tel 0114-273 9750 E-mail tim.davies@christchurchcentral.co.uk

DAVIES, Trevor. *See* DAVIES, Edward Trevor

DAVIES, Canon Trevor Gwesyn. b 28. Univ of Wales (Ban) BEd73. St Mich Coll Llan 55. **d** 56 **p** 57. C Holywell *St As* 56-63; V Cwm 63-74; V Colwyn Bay 74-95; Can St As Cathl from 79; rtd 95. *Dalkeith, 37 Brompton Avenue, Rhos on Sea, Colwyn Bay LL28 4TF* Tel (01492) 548044

DAVIES, The Ven Vincent Anthony (Tony). b 46. Brasted Th Coll 69 St Mich Coll Llan 71. **d** 73 **p** 74. C Owton Manor CD *Dur* 73-76; C Wandsworth St Faith *S'wark* 76-78; P-in-c 78-81; V Walworth St Jo 81-94; RD S'wark and Newington 88-93; Adn Croydon from 94; Bp's Adv for Hosp Chapl from 00; P-in-c Sutton New Town St Barn 04-06. *246 Pampisford Road, South Croydon CR2 6DD* Tel (020) 8688 2943 *or* 8681 5496 Fax 8686 2074 E-mail tony.davies@southwark.anglican.org

DAVIES, William Martin. b 56. Univ of Wales (Cardiff) BSc78. Wycliffe Hall Ox 78. **d** 81 **p** 82. C Gabalfa *Llan* 81-84; P-in-c Beguildy and Heyope *S & B* 84-85; V 85-87; V Swansea St Thos and Kilvey 87-93; V Belmont *Lon* 93-03; Asst Chapl Miss to Seafarers 89-03; Area Co-ord Leprosy Miss for Wales 04-07;

Area Co-ord Lon and Essex from 07. *24 Jacks Lane, Harefield, Uxbridge UB9 6HE* Tel (01895) 821237 E-mail martind@tlmwe.org.uk

DAVIES-COLE, Charles Sylester. b 38. New Coll Dur BA BD. Edin Th Coll 66. **d** 66. Hon C Edin Old St Paul from 66; Prin Teacher Jas Gillespie's High Sch 82-03. *121 Mayburn Avenue, Loanhead EH20 9ER* Tel 0131-440 4190

DAVIES-HANNEN, Robert John. b 65. W Glam Inst of HE BEd89. St Mich Coll Llan BTh92. **d** 92 **p** 93. C Gorseinon *S & B* 92-95; P-in-c Swansea St Luke 95-02; V Llangyfelach from 02. *The Vicarage, 64 Heol Pentrefelin, Morriston, Swansea SA6 6BY* Tel (01792) 774120

DAVIES-JAMES, Roxana. **d** 05 **p** 06. OLM Cusop w Blakemere, Bredwardine w Brobury etc *Heref* from 05. *12 Ridgeway, Wyesham, Monmouth NP25 3JX* Tel (01600) 714189 E-mail rana.james@virgin.net

DAVILL, Robin William. b 51. SS Paul & Mary Coll Cheltenham CertEd73 BEd74 Leic Univ MA79. Westcott Ho Cam 86. **d** 88 **p** 89. C Broughton *Blackb* 88-91; C Howden *York* 91-93; NSM Crayke w Brandsby and Yearsley 93-97; P-in-c 97-03; P-in-c Thirkleby w Kilburn and Bagby from 03. *Leyland House, 44 Uppleby, Easingwold, York YO61 3BB* Tel (01347) 823472

DAVINA, Sister. *See* WILBY, Mrs Jean

DAVIS, Alan. b 34. Birm Univ BSc56. Ox NSM Course. **d** 75 **p** 76. NSM Chesham St Mary *Ox* 75-80; NSM Gt Chesham 80-00; rtd 00; Perm to Offic *Ox* from 00. *18 Cheyne Walk, Chesham HP5 1AY* Tel (01494) 782124

DAVIS, Alan John. b 33. St Alb Minl Tr Scheme 77. **d** 80 **p** 81. NSM Goldington *St Alb* 80-84; C Benchill *Man* 84-86; R Gt Chart *Cant* 86-02; rtd 02; Perm to Offic *Cant* from 02. *8 Roberts Road, Greatstone, New Romney TN28 8RL* Tel (01797) 361917

DAVIS, The Ven Alan Norman. b 38. Open Univ BA75. Lich Th Coll 63. **d** 65 **p** 66. C Kingstanding St Luke *Birm* 65-68; C-in-c Ecclesfield St Paul CD *Sheff* 68-73; V Sheff St Paul 73-75; V Shiregreen St Jas and St Chris 75-80; R Maltby 80-81; TR 81-89; Abp's Officer for UPA 90-92; Dioc Communications Officer 92-96; Adn W Cumberland and Hon Can Carl Cathl 96-04; RD Solway 98-99; rtd 04; Perm to Offic *Cov* and *Leic* from 05; RD Sparkenhoe W *Leic* 07-08. *71 North Street, Atherstone CV9 1JW* Tel (01827) 718210 E-mail alannorman@aol.com

DAVIS, Preb Andrew Fisher. b 46. St Chad's Coll Dur BA67 K Coll Lon MA99 MPhil06. St Steph Ho Ox 68. **d** 70 **p** 71. C Beckenham St Jas *Roch* 70-74; C Kensington St Mary Abbots w St Geo *Lon* 74-80; V Sudbury St Andr 80-90; AD Brent 85-90; V Ealing Ch the Sav from 90; Preb St Paul's Cathl from 07. *The Clergy House, The Grove, London W5 5DX* Tel and fax (020) 8567 1288 E-mail fr.a@btopenworld.com

DAVIS, Andrew George. b 63. Bath Univ BSc Edin Univ BD. Edin Th Coll. **d** 89 **p** 90. C Alverstoke *Portsm* 89-92; C Portsea N End St Mark 92-96; Bp's Dom Chapl 96-98; R Bishop's Waltham and Upham 98-07; V Gosport H Trin from 07; V Gosport Ch Ch from 07. *9 Britannia Way, Gosport PO12 4FZ* Tel (023) 9258 0173

DAVIS, Anne. *See* DAVIS, Mrs Maureen Anne

DAVIS, Arthur Vivian. b 24. Clifton Th Coll 60. **d** 62 **p** 63. C Derby St Chad 62-65; C Cambridge St Andr Less *Ely* 65-68; V 68-75; V Kirtling 75-86; V Wood Ditton w Saxon Street 75-86; P-in-c Cheveley 83-86; P-in-c Ashley w Silverley 83-86; rtd 86; Perm to Offic *St E* from 93. *408 Studland Park, Newmarket CB8 7BB* Tel (01638) 661709

DAVIS, Canon Bernard Rex. b 33. OAM05. Sydney Univ BA55 Gen Th Sem (NY) MDiv60 Newc Univ MA67 FRSA87. Coll of Resurr Mirfield 55. **d** 57 **p** 58. C Guildf St Nic 57-59; USA 59-61; R Wickham Australia 62-66; Studies Sec ACC 66-68; Exec Sec Unit 3 WCC Geneva 68-77; Warden Edw K Ho 77-03; Can Res and Subdean Linc Cathl 77-03; rtd 03; Perm to Offic *Lon* and *Eur* from 06. *425 Bromyard House, Bromyard Avenue, London W3 7BY* Tel (020) 8743 0181 E-mail subdean@aol.com

DAVIS, Canon Brian. b 40. AKC69 BD69. St Aug Coll Cant 69. **d** 70 **p** 71. C Humberstone *Leic* 70-73; C Kirby Muxloe 73-74; V Countesthorpe w Foston 74-91; RD Guthlaxton I 90-91; V Hinckley St Mary from 91; RD Sparkenhoe W 92-02; Hon Can Leic Cathl from 94; Bp's Adv for Wholeness and Healing from 04. *St Mary's Vicarage, St Mary's Road, Hinckley LE10 1EQ* Tel (01455) 234241 E-mail revbdavis@aol.com

DAVIS, Mrs Bryony Elizabeth. b 64. DipCOT86. EAMTC 99. **d** 02 **p** 03. C Beccles St Mich *St E* 02-05; P-in-c Ottershaw *Guildf* 05-08; rtd 08. *2 Hammond Road, Woking GU21 4TQ* E-mail bryony.davis@tiscali.co.uk

DAVIS, Christopher James. b 63. Worc Coll Ox BA85. Cranmer Hall Dur 88. **d** 91 **p** 92. C Margate H Trin *Cant* 91-94; C Cambridge H Sepulchre *Ely* 94-00; C Wimbledon Em Ridgway Prop Chpl *S'wark* 00-04; R Tooting Graveney St Nic from 04. *The Rectory, 20A Rectory Lane, London SW17 9QJ* Tel (020) 8672 7691 E-mail cjd-stnicholas@ukonline.co.uk *or* cjandmary@ukonline.co.uk

DAVIS, Clinton Ernest Newman. b 46. Solicitor 71. Wycliffe Hall Ox 78. **d** 80 **p** 81. C Margate H Trin *Cant* 80-84; C St Laur in

Thanet 84-87; V Sandgate St Paul 87-92; P-in-c Folkestone St Geo 92; V Sandgate St Paul w Folkestone St Geo 92-97; Chapl HM Pris Standford Hill 97-08; rtd 08; Perm to Offic *Cant* from 08. *Springfield, 39 Ashford Road, Maidstone ME14 5DP* Tel (01622) 682330 E-mail clintonendavis@btinternet.com

DAVIS, Colin Anthony John. b 65. St Jo Coll Nottm. **d** 99 **p** 00. C Bletchley *Ox* 99-02; C S Molton w Nymet St George, High Bray etc *Ex* 02-03; TV from 03. *The Vicarage, Chittlehampton, Umberleigh EX37 9QL* Tel (01769) 540654 Mobile 07768-781357 E-mail revcol@chelseafc.net

DAVIS, David John. b 35. St Steph Ho Ox 79. **d** 81 **p** 82. C Reading St Mark *Ox* 81-84; C Gt Grimsby St Mary and St Jas *Linc* 84-85; TV 85-89; V Caistor w Clixby 89-94; TV Louth 98-01; rtd 01; Perm to Offic *Linc* from 03 and *Nor* from 04. *34 Park Road, Hunstanton PE36 5BY* Tel (01485) 534700

DAVIS, Donald Cyril. b 26. Open Univ BA79. NTMTC 94. **d** 96 **p** 97. NSM N Greenford All Hallows *Lon* from 96. *33 Sherwood Avenue, Greenford UB6 0PG* Tel (020) 8864 1060 E-mail donald.davis07@ntlworld.com

DAVIS, Donald Richard. b 59. Oak Hill Th Coll 92. **d** 94 **p** 95. C Plymouth St Jude *Ex* 94-99; C Devonport St Boniface and St Phil 99-08; V W Norwood St Luke *S'wark* from 08. *The Vicarage, 6 Chatsworth Way, London SE27 9HR* Tel (020) 8265 5139 E-mail dondavis@blueyonder.co.uk

DAVIS, Edward Gabriel Anastasius. b 75. R Holloway Coll Lon BA97. Trin Coll Bris BA02. **d** 03 **p** 04. C Boldmere *Birm* 03-06; Chapl Aston Univ 06; Chapl Bris Univ from 07; NSM Inner Ring Partnership from 07. *67 Waverley Road, Bristol BS6 6ET* Tel 0117-942 5390 E-mail ed.davis@bris.ac.uk

DAVIS, Edwin John Charles. b 36. Dur Univ BA60 St Cath Soc Ox BA62 MA66. Ripon Hall Ox 60. **d** 62 **p** 63. C Kington w Huntington *Heref* 62-65; Lect Lich Th Coll 65-66; Chapl Edin Th Coll 66-70; Hon Chapl St Mary's Cathl 66-70; P-in-c Hope w Shelve *Heref* 70-78; R 78-81; P-in-c Middleton 70-78; V 78-81; P-in-c Worthen 75-78; R 78-81; V S Hinksey *Ox* 81-01; Dep Dir Tr Scheme for NSM 84-92; rtd 01; Hon Lect Harris Manchester Coll Ox from 02. *13 Kennett Road, Headington, Oxford OX3 7BH* Tel (01865) 763383 E-mail ejcdavis@aol.com

DAVIS, Mrs Elizabeth Jane. b 42. S'wark Ord Course 91. **d** 94 **p** 95. NSM Plaistow St Mary *Roch* 94-99; NSM Bromley St Andr from 99. *11 Park Avenue, Bromley BR1 4EF* Tel (020) 8460 4672 E-mail elizabeth.davis@diocese-rochester.org

DAVIS, Felicity Ann. *See* SMITH, Felicity Ann

DAVIS, Geoffrey. *See* DAVIS, Ronald Geoffrey

DAVIS, Canon Herbert Roger. b 36. Kelham Th Coll 60. **d** 65 **p** 66. C Barkingside St Fran *Chelmsf* 65-69; C Harpenden St Nic *St Alb* 69-73; P-in-c Eaton Bray 73-75; V Eaton Bray w Edlesborough 75-81; RD Dunstable 77-81; R Gt Berkhamsted 81-95; Hon Can St Alb 93-95; rtd 99. *6 St Thomas Terrace, St Thomas Street, Wells BA5 2XG* Tel (01749) 677195

DAVIS, Ian Andrew. b 58. Sheff Univ BSc79 PGCE80 MIBiol85 CBiol85. St Jo Coll Nottm 87. **d** 90 **p** 91. C Hatfield *Sheff* 90-92; C Beighton 92-95; R Thurnscoe St Helen 95-99; P-in-c Chesterfield St Aug *Derby* 99-01; V 01-05; P-in-c Hope, Castleton and Bradwell from 05. *The Vicarage, Church Street, Bradwell, Hope Valley S33 9HJ* Tel (01433) 620485 E-mail reviandavis@aol.com

DAVIS, Jack. b 35. LRSC63 CChem80 MRSC80 Sheff Univ MSc88. Oak Hill Th Coll 86. **d** 88 **p** 89. C Owlerton *Sheff* 88-91; V Manea *Ely* 91-93; R Wimblington 91-93; P-in-c Walsoken 93-94; R 94-00; rtd 00; Perm to Offic *Sheff* from 00. *5 Pinfold Court, Barnby Dun, Doncaster DN3 1RQ* Tel and fax (01302) 888065 E-mail revjackdavis@aol.com

DAVIS, Mrs Jacqueline. b 47. Cant Ch Ch Univ Coll BA01. **d** 05 **p** 06. OLM Upchurch w Lower Halstow *Cant* from 05. *Mill House, The Street, Lower Halstow, Sittingbourne ME9 7DY* Tel (01795) 842557 E-mail jackytd@dsl.pipex.com

DAVIS, Jennifer Anne Stanway. b 38. SWMTC 04. **d** 05 **p** 06. NSM Cullompton, Willand, Uffculme, Kentisbeare etc *Ex* 06-08; rtd 08. *36 Church Acre, Bradford-on-Avon BA15 1RL* Tel (01225) 865777

DAVIS, John. *See* DAVIS, Edwin John Charles

DAVIS, John Brian. b 33. Linc Th Coll 72. **d** 75 **p** 76. Hon C Bungay H Trin w St Mary *St E* 75-84; P-in-c Barrow 84-85; P-in-c Denham St Mary 84-85; R Barrow w Denham St Mary and Higham Green 85-98; rtd 98; Perm to Offic *Nor* and *St E* from 98. *Cherry Tree House, 4 Outney Road, Bungay NR35 1DY* Tel (01986) 895574

DAVIS, John George. b 65. Roehampton Inst BSc87 S Glam Inst HE PGCE88. St Steph Ho Ox BTh96. **d** 96 **p** 97. C Newton Nottage *Llan* 96-00; V Tredegar *Mon* from 00. *St George's Vicarage, Church Street, Tredegar NP22 3DU* Tel (01495) 722672

DAVIS, John Harold. b 54. St Jo Coll Dur BSc76 MA86. Cranmer Hall Dur 76. **d** 79 **p** 80. C Marske in Cleveland *York* 79-82; C Pocklington w Pockthorpe, Owsthorpe etc 82-83; TV Pocklington Team 84-86; V Carlton and Drax 86-95; P-in-c Sessay 95-98; R 98-03; V Sowerby 95-03; Ind Chapl 88-95; Sen Chapl Selby Coalfield Ind Chapl from 03; Chapl Askham Bryan

Coll from 04. *The Vicarage, 25 Fox Lane, Thorpe Willoughby, Selby YO8 9NA* Tel (01757) 290840 *or* 704385 E-mail john@davishome.plus.com

DAVIS, John James. b 48. MBE08. Keele Univ MA93 Staffs Univ PGCE98. Qu Coll Birm BA05. **d** 05 **p** 06. NSM Baswich *Lich* 05-08; NSM Bradeley, Church Eaton, Derrington and Haughton 08-09; NSM Stafford from 09; CF (ACF) from 06. *Stockton Croft, 87 Weeping Cross, Stafford ST17 0DQ* Tel (01785) 661382 E-mail revjohndavis@talktalk.net

DAVIS, John Stephen. b 51. N Staffs Poly BSc75. Wycliffe Hall Ox 75. **d** 78 **p** 79. C Meole Brace *Lich* 78-81; C Bloxwich 81-85; V Walsall St Paul 85-96; Development Officer Prince's Trust 96-01; Hospice Development Manager Walsall Primary Care Trust 01-06; Hon C Halas *Worc* 98-07. *57 Moss Lane, Burscough, Ormskirk L40 4AL*

DAVIS, Mrs Kathleen Mary. b 37. Derby Coll of Educn TCert58. **d** 07 **p** 08. OLM Morley *Wakef* from 07. *13 New Park Street, Morley, Leeds LS27 0PT* Tel 0113-253 4521

DAVIS, Margaret Ann. b 59. Kingston Poly BA81 Liv Univ MSc93 RGN85. Westcott Ho Cam 06. **d** 08 **p** 09. C Abbots Langley *St Alb* from 08. *40 Kindersley Way, Abbots Langley WD5 0DQ* Tel (01923) 260353 Mobile 07941-691544 E-mail m.a.davis.merle@googlemail.com

DAVIS, Matthias. *See* DAVIS, Peter Langdon

DAVIS, Mrs Maureen Anne. b 59. St Hilda's Coll Ox BA80 MA84. NOC 96. **d** 99 **p** 00. NSM Plemstall w Guilden Sutton *Ches* 99-01; C Ches St Mary 01-03; R Woodchurch from 03. *The Rectory, Church Lane, Upton, Wirral CH49 7LS* Tel 0151-677 5352 Mobile 07974-816390 E-mail revannedavis@uwclub.net

DAVIS, Michael James Burrows. b 36. ED AJP87. St Deiniol's Hawarden Ridley Hall Cam. **d** 72 **p** 72. Bermuda from 72. *PO Box SN 74, Southampton SN BX, Bermuda* Tel (001441) 238 0236 Fax 238 3767

DAVIS, Nicholas Anthony Wylie. b 56. Univ of Wales (Lamp) BA80. Chich Th Coll 82. **d** 84 **p** 85. C N Lambeth *S'wark* 84-88; TV Catford (Southend) and Downham 88-94; V Camberwell St Phil and St Mark 94-04; V Shrub End *Chelmsf* from 04. *All Saints' Vicarage, 270 Shrub End Road, Colchester CO3 4RL* Tel (01206) 570922 E-mail nicholas_a.davis@virgin.net

DAVIS, Nicholas Edward. b 75. Univ of Wales (Ban) BD96. Coll of Resurr Mirfield 98. **d** 00 **p** 01. C Darwen St Cuth w Tockholes St Steph *Blackb* 00-05; P-in-c Tarleton from 05; P-in-c Rufford from 07; P-in-c Hesketh w Becconsall from 07. *The Rectory, 92 Blackgate Lane, Tarleton, Preston PR4 6UT* Tel and fax (01772) 812614

DAVIS, Canon Norman. b 38. FCII66. Oak Hill Th Coll 77. **d** 79 **p** 80. C Walton *St E* 79-82; P-in-c Grundisburgh w Burgh 82-91; P-in-c Bredfield w Boulge 86-91; R Boulge w Burgh and Grundisburgh 91-03; P-in-c Hasketon 01-03; R Boulge w Burgh, Grundisburgh and Hasketon 03-04; RD Woodbridge 90-96; Hon Can St E Cathl 01-04; rtd 04; Perm to Offic *St E* from 04. *The Randalls, Front Street, Orford, Woodbridge IP12 2LN* Tel (01394) 459469

DAVIS, Norman John. b 41. Oak Hill Th Coll 63. **d** 66 **p** 67. C Wellington w Eyton *Lich* 66-70; C Higher Openshaw *Man* 70-72; R S Levenshulme 72-79; P-in-c Bretforton w Pendock and Eldersfield *Worc* 79-81; V 81-87; R Churchill-in-Halfshire w Blakedown and Broome 87-07; rtd 07. *48 Waterside Grange, Kidderminster DY10 2LA* Tel (01562) 750079 E-mail n.davis@sky.com

DAVIS, Peter Langdon (Matthias). b 51. Univ of Wales (Cardiff) BD99 PGCE00. Westcott Ho Cam 03. **d** 05 **p** 06. C Daventry, Ashby St Ledgers, Braunston etc *Pet* 05-08; R Aylmerton, Runton, Beeston Regis and Gresham *Nor* from 08. *The Rectory, Cromer Road, West Runton, Cromer NR27 9QT* Tel (01263) 837279 E-mail plmd@hotmail.co.uk

DAVIS, Rex. *See* DAVIS, Canon Bernard Rex

DAVIS, Roger. *See* DAVIS, Canon Herbert Roger

DAVIS, Ronald Frank. b 26. Oak Hill Th Coll 62. **d** 64 **p** 65. C Bilton *Ripon* 64-67; V N and S Otterington *York* 67-77; C Rainham *Chelmsf* 77-82; V Hainault 82-88; rtd 88; Perm to Offic *Bradf* 90-04. *Home View, Westview Grove, Keighley BD20 6JJ* Tel (01535) 681294

DAVIS, Ronald Geoffrey (Geoff). b 47. St Jo Coll Nottm 79. **d** 81 **p** 81. C Maidstone St Luke *Cant* 81-84; P-in-c Lostwithiel *Truro* 84-86; P-in-c Lanhydrock 84-86; Asst Dioc Youth Officer 84-86; P-in-c Boughton Monchelsea *Cant* 86-88; V from 88; Six Preacher Cant Cathl 94-99; C-in-c Parkwood CD 95-98; AD N Downs 99-02. *The Vicarage, Church Hill, Boughton Monchelsea, Maidstone ME17 4BU* Tel and fax (01622) 743321 E-mail stpeters.church@btinternet.com

DAVIS, Ruth Elizabeth. *See* TAIT, Canon Ruth Elizabeth

DAVIS, Simon Charles. b 63. Plymouth Poly BSc86. Trin Coll Bris BA92. **d** 92 **p** 93. C Bollington St Jo *Ches* 92-96; P-in-c Abbots Bromley w Blithfield *Lich* from 96; P-in-c Colton, Colwich and Gt Haywood from 05; RD Rugeley from 07. *The Vicarage, Market Place, Abbots Bromley, Rugeley WS15 3BP* Tel (01283) 840242 E-mail simon.davis@freeuk.com

DAVIS, Stephen Charles. b 19. AKC48 St Cath Soc Ox BA50 MA54. Wycliffe Hall Ox 48. **d** 50 **p** 51. C Slough *Ox* 50-52; Chapl Witwatersrand Univ S Africa 53-57; R Brixton and Newlands 53-57; V Leic H Trin 58-64; Chapl HM Pris Leic 58-64; R Dur St Marg 64-87; rtd 87; Perm to Offic *Worc* from 87. *10 Spencer Avenue, Bewdley DY12 1DB* Tel (01299) 409014

DAVIS, Thomas Henry. b 60. Dioc OLM tr scheme 97 Coll of Resurr Mirfield 05. **d** 99 **p** 00. OLM Sudbury and Chilton *St E* 99-03; NSM Preston St Jo and St Geo *Blackb* 03-05; C Torrisholme 05-08; C Blackpool St Steph from 08. *16 Lowther Avenue, Blackpool FY2 9PA* Tel (01253) 351995 Mobile 07854-770360 E-mail vicarststephens@aol.com

DAVIS, Timothy Alwyn. b 74. Trin Coll Bris BTh. **d** 01 **p** 02. C Crich and S Wingfield *Derby* 01-05; V Leyton St Mary w St Edw and St Luke *Chelmsf* from 05. *St Mary's Vicarage, 4 Vicarage Road, London E10 5EA* Tel (020) 8539 7882 E-mail timdavis.tadhatter@virgin.net

DAVIS, Timothy Charles. b 59. Reading Univ BA81 Homerton Coll Cam PGCE82. Trin Coll Bris 89. **d** 91 **p** 92. C Normanton *Wakef* 91-95; C Fisherton Anger *Sarum* 95-99; TV Abingdon *Ox* from 99. *69 Northcourt Road, Abingdon OX14 1NR* Tel (01235) 520115 *or* 539172 Fax 539179 E-mail chch@clara.net

DAVIS, Trevor Lorenzo. b 45. Simon of Cyrene Th Inst 92. **d** 94 **p** 95. NSM Upper Norwood St Jo *S'wark* 94-00. *Address temp unknown*

DAVIS, Mrs Yvonne Annie. b 30. CQSW75. **d** 96 **p** 97. OLM Purley St Barn *S'wark* 96-00; Perm to Offic from 00. *1 Hurnford Close, South Croydon CR2 0AN* Tel (020) 8657 2097

DAVISON, Andrew Paul. b 74. Mert Coll Ox BA96 MA99 DPhil00 CCC Cam BA02 MA08. Westcott Ho Cam 00 Ven English Coll Rome 02. **d** 03 **p** 04. C Bellingham St Dunstan *S'wark* 03-06; Tutor St Steph Ho Ox from 06; Jun Chapl Mert Coll Ox from 06. *St Stephen's House, 16 Marston Street, Oxford OX4 1JX* Tel (01865) 432300 Fax 794338 E-mail andrew.davison@ssho.ox.ac.uk

DAVISON, George Thomas William. b 65. St Andr Univ BD88. Oak Hill Th Coll 88 CITC BTh92. **d** 92 **p** 93. C Portadown St Mark *Arm* 92-95; I Kinawley w H Trin *K, E & A* 95-09; Dir of Ords 97-09; Preb Kilmore Cathl 02-09; Adn Kilmore 04-09; I Carrickfergus *Conn* from 09. *The Rectory, 12 Harwood Gardens, Carrickfergus BT38 7US* Tel and fax (028) 9336 3244 *or* 9336 0061 Mobile 07771-812844 E-mail carrickfergus@connor.anglican.org

DAVISON, Philip Anthony. b 66. Magd Coll Cam BA88 MA93. Cuddesdon Coll BA98. **d** 98 **p** 99. C Lancaster St Mary w St John and St Anne *Blackb* 98-02; P-in-c Feniscowles 02-08; R Finchley St Mary *Lon* from 08. *St Mary's Rectory, Rectory Close, London N3 1TS* Tel (020) 8346 4600 *or* tel and fax 8248 3818 E-mail rector@stmaryatfinchley.org.uk

DAVISON, Canon Richard Ireland. b 42. St Chad's Coll Dur BSc63. Linc Th Coll 64. **d** 66 **p** 67. C Cockerton *Dur* 66-70; C Houghton le Spring 70-73; V Heworth St Alb 73-80; Ascension Is 80-82; V Dunston *Dur* 82-85; V Bishopwearmouth Ch Ch 85-98; AD Wearmouth 94-99; P-in-c Dur St Giles 99-00; V 00-08; P-in-c Shadforth and Sherburn 03-08; Hon Can Dur Cathl 97-08; AD Dur 06-08; rtd 08. *16 Loraine Crescent, Darlington DL1 5TF*

DAVISON, Canon Roger William. b 20. Kelham Th Coll 46. **d** 51 **p** 52. C Tonge Moor *Man* 51-55; V 55-65; Hon Can Man Cathl 63-65; V Higham Ferrers w Chelveston *Pet* 65-88; rtd 88; Perm to Offic *Roch* from 88. *The College of St Barnabas, Blackberry Lane, Lingfield RH7 6NJ* Tel (01342) 872819

DAVOLL, Ivan John (Snowy). b 33. LNSM course 87. **d** 88 **p** 90. NSM Bermondsey St Jas w Ch Ch *S'wark* 88-93; C 93-98; rtd 98; Perm to Offic *S'wark* 98-03 and *Heref* from 03. *42 Ecroyd Park, Credenhill, Hereford HR4 7EL*

DAVY, Mrs Helen Mary. b 44. **d** 05 **p** 06. NSM Kirton w Falkenham *St E* 05-06; NSM Nacton and Levington w Bucklesham etc from 06. *9 Roman Way, Felixstowe IP11 9NJ* Tel (01394) 270703

DAVY, Mrs Judith Ann. b 60. SRN82. STETS 01. **d** 04 **p** 05. NSM Jersey St Brelade *Win* from 04. *Brookvale House, Les Grupieaux, St Peter, Jersey JE3 7YW* Tel (01534) 507800 Mobile 07797-730983 E-mail judithdavy@jerseymail.com

DAVY, Peter Geoffrey. b 31. St Pet Coll Saltley TCert54. SWMTC 93. **d** 94 **p** 94. NSM St Columb Minor and St Colan *Truro* 94-99; rtd 99; Perm to Offic *Truro* from 00. *9 Tredour Road, Newquay TR7 2EY* Tel (01637) 872241

DAVYS, Mark Andrew. b 66. St Cath Coll Ox BA87 MA97 Keele Univ MA01 Qu Coll Birm BA04 Solicitor 90. WMMTC 01. **d** 04 **p** 05. NSM Colton, Colwich and St Haywood *Lich* from 04. *Deer's Leap, Meadow Lane, Little Haywood, Stafford ST18 0TT* Tel (01889) 882855 E-mail revmdavys@deersleap.org.uk

DAW, Geoffrey Martin. b 60. Oak Hill Th Coll 81. **d** 84 **p** 85. C Hollington St Leon *Chich* 84-87; C Seaford w Sutton 87-90; V Iford w Kingston and Rodmell from 90; RD Lewes and Seaford from 08. *The Rectory, 14 Lockitt Way, Kingston, Lewes BN7 3LG* Tel (01273) 473665 E-mail geoffrey.daw@btinternet.com

DAWE, David Fife Purchas. b 20. Keble Coll Ox BA41 MA45. Wells Th Coll 41. **d** 43 **p** 44. C Wolstanton *Lich* 43-46; C Meole Brace 46-47; C Leek All SS 47-50; C Tardebigge *Worc* 50-52; R Stoke Bliss w Kyre Wyard 52-54; R Jackfield *Heref* 54-61; V Criftins *Lich* 61-77; V Dudleston 63-77; P-in-c Alkmonton w Yeaveley *Derby* 77-81; P-in-c Cubley w Marston Montgomery 77-81; R Alkmonton, Cubley, Marston Montgomery etc 81-85; rtd 85; Perm to Offic *Derby* and *Lich* 85-94; *Pet* from 94. *11 Coaching Walk, Northampton NN3 3EU* Tel (01604) 414083

DAWES, Dori Katherine. b 37. ARCM. Oak Hill Th Coll 85. **d** 88 **p** 94. Par Dn Watford St Luke *St Alb* 88-90; Par Dn Watford 90-94; C 94-96; P-in-c Dunton w Wrestlingworth and Eyeworth 96-01; rtd 01; Perm to Offic *B & W* from 05. *Orchard House, Upway, Porlock, Minehead TA24 8QE* Tel (01643) 862474

DAWES, Mrs Helen Elizabeth. b 74. Trin Coll Cam BA96 MA00. Westcott Ho Cam 99. **d** 02 **p** 03. C Chesterton St Andr *Ely* 02-05; P-in-c Sandon, Wallington and Rushden w Clothall *St Alb* 05-09; Dep Public Affairs Sec to Abp Cant from 09. *Lambeth Palace, London SE1 7JU* Tel (020) 7898 1200 E-mail helen.dawes@c-of-e.org.uk

DAWES, Hugh William. b 48. Univ Coll Ox BA71 MA76. Cuddesdon Coll 71. **d** 74 **p** 75. C Purley St Mark *S'wark* 74-77; Chapl G&C Coll Cam 77-82; Chapl Em Coll Cam 82-87; V Cambridge St Jas *Ely* 87-00; Dir Focus Chr Inst Cambridge 87-00; V N Dulwich St Faith *S'wark* from 00. *St Faith's Vicarage, 62 Red Post Hill, London SE24 9JQ* Tel (020) 7274 1338 E-mail hugh@hughdawes.com

DAWES, Julian Edward. b 27. RAF Coll Cranwell 49. Bps' Coll Cheshunt 58. **d** 59 **p** 60. C Whitton St Aug *Lon* 59-62; Chapl RAF 62-65; V Overbury w Alstone, Teddington and Lt Washbourne *Worc* 65-70; V Cropthorne w Charlton 70-76; Chapl Dioc Conf Cen 70-76; Chapl Exe Vale Hosp Gp 76-84; Chapl Bromsgrove and Redditch Distr Gen Hosp 84-86; rtd 91; Perm to Offic *Ex* from 91. *Maranatha, Exeter Road, Rewe, Exeter EX5 4EU* Tel (01392) 841877 Fax 841577

✠**DAWES, The Rt Revd Peter Spencer.** b 28. Hatf Coll Dur BA52. Tyndale Hall Bris 53. **d** 54 **p** 55 **c** 88. C Whitehall Park St Andr Hornsey Lane *Lon* 54-57; C Ox St Ebbe 57-60; Tutor Clifton Th Coll 60-65; V Romford Gd Shep *Chelmsf* 65-80; Hon Can Chelmsf Cathl 78-80; Adn W Ham 80-88; Dioc Dir of Ords 80-86; Bp Derby 88-95; rtd 95; Hon Asst Bp Ely from 95. *45 Arundell, Ely CB6 1BQ* Tel (01353) 661241

DAWKES, Peter. b 31. Roch Th Coll 64. **d** 66 **p** 67. C Newbold w Dunston *Derby* 66-69; C Buxton 69-72; V Somercotes 72-93; rtd 93; Hon C Kenton, Mamhead, Powderham, Cofton and Starcross *Ex* from 93. *115 Exeter Road, Dawlish EX7 0AN* Tel (01626) 862593

DAWKIN, Peter William. b 60. Nottm Univ BTh88 Open Univ BA91. St Jo Coll Nottm 85. **d** 88 **p** 89. C Birkdale St Jo *Liv* 88-91; C Netherton 91-93; V Liv Ch Ch Norris Green 93-03; Assoc Min Wigan Deaneries 03-06; V Hough Green St Basil and All SS from 06. *339 Ditchfield Road, Widnes WA8 8XR* Tel 0151-420 4963 Mobile 07947-164207 E-mail peter.dawkin@blueyonder.co.uk

DAWKINS, Canon Alan Arthur Windsor. b 26. St Aid Birkenhead 53. **d** 55 **p** 56. C Preston Em *Blackb* 55-57; C S Shore H Trin 57-59; V Slade Green *Roch* 59-61; V St Mary Cray and St Paul's Cray 61-63; V White Colne *Chelmsf* 63-66; R Pebmarsh 63-66; P-in-c Mt Bures 65-66; V Westgate St Jas *Cant* 66-74; V Herne Bay Ch Ch 74-83; Hon Can Cant Cathl 79-91; P-in-c Chilham 83-85; Adv for Miss and Unity 85-91; rtd 91; Chapl St Jo Hosp Cant 96-07. *44 Columbia Avenue, Whitstable CT5 4EH*

DAWKINS, John Haswell. b 47. NEOC 98. **d** 01 **p** 02. NSM Barmby Moor Gp *York* from 01. *9 Fossbeck Close, Wilberfoss, York YO41 5PR* Tel (01759) 388144

DAWKINS, Michael Howard. b 46. Bris Univ BTh68 Man Univ MA96. Tyndale Hall Bris 67. **d** 69 **p** 69. C Drypool St Columba w St Andr and St Pet *York* 69-73; CF 74-80; P-in-c Bulford *Sarum* 80-81; P-in-c Figheldean w Milston 80-81; R Meriden Cov 85-09; rtd 09. *60 Wassell Road, Wollescoye, Stourbridge DY8 9DB* Tel (01384) 893299 E-mail mhdawkins@aol.com

DAWKINS, Nigel Jonathan. b 72. St Jo Coll Ox BA94 MA97 Univ Coll Lon MSc97 Peterho Cam BA05. Westcott Ho Cam 03. **d** 06 **p** 07. C Caterham *S'wark* 06-09; Chapl Aden Ch Ch and Yemen from 09. *PO Box 1319, Tawahi, Aden, Yemen* Tel (00967) (2) 201204 Mobile 73-376 2704 E-mail chaplain@christchurchaden.org

DAWN, Maggi Eleanor. b 59. Fitzw Coll Cam MA96 Selw Coll Cam PhD02. Ridley Hall Cam 96. **d** 99 **p** 00. C Ely 99-01; Chapl K Coll Cam 01-03; Chapl Rob Coll Cam from 03. *Robinson College, Cambridge CB3 9AN* Tel (01223) 339140 Mobile 07743-351467 E-mail med1000@cam.ac.uk

DAWSON, Alan. b 28. St Jo Coll Dur BA54 Liv Univ MA67. Clifton Th Coll 54. **d** 56 **p** 57. C Bowling St Steph *Bradf* 56-59; C Attenborough w Bramcote *S'well* 59-62; V Everton St Jo *Liv* 62-69; V Birkdale St Pet 69-91; rtd 91; NSM Kirkcudbright and Gatehouse of Fleet *Glas* 98-06; Perm to Offic *Ches* from 07. *The Bungalow, Church Lane, Guilden Sutton, Chester CH3 7EW* Tel (01244) 301685

DAWSON, Alan David Hough. b 67. Cranmer Hall Dur. **d** 09. C Hale and Ashley *Ches* from 09. *152 Hale Road, Hale, Altrincham WA15 8SQ* Tel 0161-941 2206

DAWSON, Andrew. *See* DAWSON, Canon William James Andrew

DAWSON, Andrew. *See* DAWSON, Francis Andrew Oliver Duff

DAWSON, Miss Anne. b 54. Nottm Univ BA76 Hull Coll of Educn PGCE77. NEOC 03. **d** 06 **p** 07. NSM Market Weighton *York* from 06. *23 Sloe Lane, Beverley HU17 8ND* Tel (01482) 862940 E-mail andaw@amaw.karoo.co.uk

DAWSON, Barry. b 38. Oak Hill Th Coll 63. **d** 66 **p** 67. C Fulham St Mary N End *Lon* 66-69; C St Marylebone All So w SS Pet and Jo 69-73; Bp's Chapl *Nor* 73-76; Gen Sec CEMS 76-81; V Rye Park St Cuth *St Alb* 81-89; V Attenborough *S'well* 89-98; rtd 98; Perm to Offic *S'well* from 98. *27 Orlando Drive, Carlton, Nottingham NG4 3FN*

DAWSON, Brian. b 33. Leeds Univ BA54 Man Univ MA84 Newc Univ MPhil01. Coll of Resurr Mirfield 56. **d** 58 **p** 59. C Hollinwood *Man* 58-62; C Rawmarsh w Parkgate *Sheff* 62-63; V Royton St Anne *Man* 63-75; V Urswick *Carl* 75-86; V Bardsea 75-86; R Skelton and Hutton-in-the-Forest w Ivegill 86-98; RD Penrith 91-96; Hon Can Carl Cathl 94-98; rtd 98; Perm to Offic *Carl* from 98. *Apple Croft, High Hesket, Carlisle CA4 0HS* Tel (01697) 473069

DAWSON, Christopher John Rowland. b 26. OBE QPM. S'wark Ord Course 82. **d** 86 **p** 87. NSM Sevenoaks St Jo *Roch* 86-98; Perm to Offic 98-99. *Craggan House, 58 Oak Hill Road, Sevenoaks TN13 1NT* Tel (01732) 458037

DAWSON, Miss Claire Louise. b 68. Nottm Poly BA92 CQSW92 Nottm Univ MA04. EMMTC 01. **d** 04 **p** 05. C Mansfield Woodhouse *S'well* 04-05; C Sutton in Ashfield St Mary 05-08; C Orrell Hey St Jo and St Jas *Liv* from 08. *20 Mount Avenue, Bootle L20 6DT* E-mail claire.dawson1@virgin.net

DAWSON, Canon Cyril. b 34. St Chad's Coll Dur BA58. **d** 59 **p** 60. C Honicknowle *Ex* 59-63; C Paignton St Jo 63-66; V Heptonstall *Wakef* 66-71; V Todmorden 71-82; RD Calder Valley 75-82; Can Res Wakef Cathl 82-92; Vice-Provost 86-92; Hon Can 92-99; V Darrington 92-99; rtd 99; Perm to Offic *York* and *Linc* from 00. *24 Beacon Road, Bridlington YO16 6UX* Tel (01262) 672911

DAWSON, David. b 57. TISEC 99. **d** 99 **p** 00. NSM Kirkwall *Ab* from 99; P-in-c from 05. St Olaf's Rectory, Dundas Crescent, Kirkwall, Orkney KW15 1JQ* Tel (01856) 872024 Mobile 07881-932657 E-mail frdave_473@hotmail.com

DAWSON, Edward. **d** 81 **p** 83. NSM Newington St Paul *S'wark* 81-85; NSM Walworth St Jo 85-00; Chapl Asst Maudsley Hosp Lon from 87. *3 Ethel Street, London SE17 1NH* Tel (020) 7701 8923

DAWSON, Francis Andrew Oliver Duff. b 48. Keble Coll Ox BA70 MA74. St Jo Coll Nottm 74. **d** 76 **p** 77. C Billericay St Mary *Chelmsf* 76-77; C Billericay and Lt Burstead 77-80; C Childwall All SS *Liv* 80-84; Chapl St Kath Coll 80-84; V Shevington *Blackb* 84-97; Internat Officer and Team Ldr for Evang Affairs *Man* 97-03; P-in-c Werneth from 03. *St Thomas's Vicarage, 3 Regency Close, Oldham OL8 1SS* Tel 0161-678 8926 Fax 832 2869 E-mail andrewdawson51@hotmail.com

DAWSON, Frederick William. b 44. St Chad's Coll Dur BA66 Nottm Univ MTh74. Linc Th Coll 67. **d** 69 **p** 70. C Caversham *Ox* 69-72; C Ranmoor *Sheff* 72-79; R Kibworth Beauchamp *Leic* 79 82; R Kibworth and Smeeton Westerby and Saddington 82-94; R Tilehurst St Mich *Ox* 94-07; P-in-c Mickleton, Willersey, Saintbury etc *Glouc* from 07. *The Rectory, Weston-sub-Edge, Chipping Campden GL55 6QH* Tel (01386) 840292

DAWSON, Hilary. b 64. Univ of Wales (Lamp) BA85 UWE PGCE89 Ex Univ MA08. SWMTC 05. **d** 08. C Thorverton, Cadbury, Upton Pyne etc *Ex* from 08. *The Vicarage, Stoke Canon, Exeter EX5 4AS* Tel (01392) 841240

DAWSON, Ian Douglas. b 52. Liv Univ BSc73. NOC 83. **d** 86 **p** 87. NSM Southport SS Simon and Jude *Liv* 86-93; NSM Birkdale St Jas 93-95; NSM Southport St Phil and St Paul 96-01; Perm to Offic *Linc* from 01. *18 Park View, Barton-upon-Humber DN18 6AX* Tel (01652) 637554

DAWSON, John William Arthur. b 43. EMMTC. **d** 95 **p** 96. NSM Breedon cum Isley Walton and Worthington *Leic* 95-05; NSM Ashby-de-la-Zouch and Breedon on the Hill from 05. *Orchard House, 2 Manor Drive, Worthington, Ashby-de-la-Zouch LE65 1RN* Tel (01530) 222673 E-mail johndawson@benefice.org.uk

DAWSON, Miss Mary. b 51. Loughb Coll ALA73. EMMTC 85. **d** 90 **p** 94. Par Dn Braunstone *Leic* 90-92; Par Dn Shrewsbury H Cross *Lich* 92-94; C 94-95; P-in-c Glentworth Gp *Linc* 95-97; V from 97. *The Vicarage, 1 Stoney Lane, Glentworth, Gainsborough DN21 5DF* Tel and fax (01427) 668203 E-mail mary.dawson@madasafish.com

DAWSON, Neil. b 49. Ripon Hall Ox 71. **d** 74 **p** 75. C Putney St Mary *S'wark* 74-78; C Camberwell St Giles 78-80; TV N Lambeth 84-86; V E Dulwich St Clem 86; V Dulwich St Clem w St Pet 86-89; Hon C Wilton Place St Paul *Lon* 92-06; P-in-c

Madeira *Eur* from 06. *The Parsonage, 18 rua do Quebra Costas, 9000 Funchal, Madeira* Tel (00351) (291) 220674 Fax 220161 E-mail neil.dawson6@btinternet.com *or* holytrinity@netmadeira.com

DAWSON, Nicholas Anthony. b 52. St Jo Coll Nottm 88. **d** 90 **p** 91. C Mortomley St Sav High Green *Sheff* 90-95; V Owlerton from 95; P-in-c Hillsborough and Wadsley Bridge 06-09. *Owlerton Vicarage, Forbes Road, Sheffield S6 2NW* Tel 0114-234 3560 E-mail nick.dawson@sheffield.anglican.org

DAWSON, Canon Norman William. b 41. MBE99. K Coll Lon BD63 AKC63. **d** 65 **p** 66. C Salford St Phil w St Steph *Man* 65-68; C Heaton Ch Ch 68-70; R Longsight St Jo 70-75; R Longsight St Jo w St Cypr 75-82; R Withington St Paul 82-99; Chapl Christie Hosp Man 81-91; AD Withington 91-99; P-in-c Davyhulme St Mary 99-04; Hon Can Man Cathl 98-04; rtd 04; Perm to Offic *Blackb* from 04. *Well House, Lowgill, Lancaster LA2 8RA* Tel (01524) 262936

DAWSON, Paul Christopher Owen. b 61. Leeds Univ BA82. Ripon Coll Cuddesdon 83. **d** 85 **p** 86. C Dovecot *Liv* 85-89; V Westbrook St Phil 89-94; Bp's Dom Chapl 94-98; V Witton *Ches* 98-06; R Ches St Mary from 06. *10 Lower Park Road, Chester CH4 7BB* Tel (01244) 675199 E-mail comet411@tiscali.co.uk

DAWSON, Paul Richard. b 67. Bris Univ BSc89. Oak Hill Th Coll 99. **d** 01 **p** 02. C Wimbledon Em Ridgway Prop Chpl *S'wark* from 01. *41 Circle Gardens, London SW19 3JX* Tel (020) 8404 3894 E-mail paul.dawson@dundonald.org

DAWSON, The Ven Peter. b 29. Keble Coll Ox BA52 MA56. Ridley Hall Cam 52. **d** 54 **p** 55. C Morden *S'wark* 54-59; R 68-77; V Barston *Birm* 59-63; R Harpur Openshaw *Man* 63-68; RD Merton *S'wark* 75-77; Adn Norfolk 77-93; rtd 93; Perm to Offic *Nor* from 93 and *Carl* from 98. *The Coach House, Harmony Hill, Milnthorpe LA7 7QA* Tel (01539) 562020

DAWSON, Peter John. b 44. Local Minl Tr Course. **d** 06 **p** 07. NSM Heckmondwike *Wakef* from 06; NSM Liversedge w Hightown from 06; NSM Roberttown w Hartshead from 06. *10 Meadow Drive, Liversedge WF15 7QF* Tel (01924) 404311

DAWSON, Peter Rodney. b 44. **d** 98 **p** 99. OLM Ashtead *Guildf* 98-05; Asst Chapl Pau *Eur* 05-06; Perm to Offic 06-08; P-in-c Biarritz from 08. *le Bosquet, 64400 Poey d'Oloron, France* Tel (0033) (5) 59 27 63 14 E-mail peter.dawson@free.fr

DAWSON, Ronald Eric John. b 27. St Mark & St Jo Coll Lon TCert54 Lon Univ BD64. Bps' Coll Cheshunt 62. **d** 62 **p** 63. C Dartford H Trin *Roch* 62-66; C Fulham St Etheldreda *Lon* 66-74; V Brentford St Faith 74-80; rtd 92. *13 Birkbeck Road, London W5 4ES* Tel (020) 8560 3564

DAWSON, Thomas Douglas. b 52. Newc Univ BA. St Steph Ho Ox. **d** 80 **p** 82. C N Gosforth *Newc* 80-81; C Leic St Chad 82-85; TV Catford (Southend) and Downham *S'wark* 85-88; V Chevington *Newc* 88-94; V Cowgate 94-96; P-in-c Cresswell and Lynemouth 96-98; V Blyth St Mary 98-01; rtd 01; Perm to Offic *Newc* from 02. *Iona, 2 Hillside, Lesbury, Alnwick NE66 3NR* Tel (01665) 830412 Mobile 07763-122259 E-mail fr_tom_dawson@hotmail.com

DAWSON (*formerly* CORY), **Mrs Valerie Ann.** b 44. CertEd65 Nottm Univ BEd85. EMMTC 85. **d** 88 **p** 94. Area Sec CMS *Linc* and *Pet* 87-91; NSM Grantham *Linc* 88-91; Par Dn Ealing St Mary *Lon* 91-94; Chapl NW Lon Poly 91-92; Chapl Thames Valley Univ 92-96; C Ealing St Mary 94-96; Chapl Birm Cathl 96-99; C Surbiton St Andr and St Mark *S'wark* 99-08; rtd 08. *15A Greengate Close, Chesterfield S40 3SJ* Tel (01246) 550445 E-mail valcory@blueyonder.co.uk

DAWSON, Canon William James Andrew. b 48. TCD MA72. CITC 88. **d** 88 **p** 89. NSM Killyman *Arm* 88-91; NSM Pomeroy from 91; Can Arm Cathl from 98; Preb 98-01. *Tamlaght, Coagh, Cookstown BT80 0AB* Tel (028) 8673 7151 *or* tel and fax 8676 2227

DAWSON-CAMPBELL, Olive Sheila. b 37. ACIB70. WEMTC 99. **d** 00 **p** 01. OLM Longden and Annscroft w Pulverbatch *Heref* from 00. *Sheaves, Lyth Bank, Lyth Hill, Shrewsbury SY3 0BE* Tel (01743) 872071

DAWSWELL, Jonathan Andrew. b 65. Jes Coll Cam BA86. Wycliffe Hall Ox BA91. **d** 92 **p** 93. C Childwall All SS *Liv* 92-96; C Leyland St Andr *Blackb* 96-99; V Knypersley *Lich* from 99; P-in-c Biddulph Moor from 05. *St John's Vicarage, 62 Park Lane, Knypersley, Stoke-on-Trent ST8 7AU* Tel (01782) 512240 E-mail andrew@dawswell.freeserve.co.uk

DAWTRY, Canon Anne Frances. b 57. Westf Coll Lon BA79 PhD85. Ripon Coll Cuddesdon 91. **d** 93 **p** 94. C Corfe Mullen *Sarum* 93-96; C Parkstone St Pet w Branksea and St Osmund 96-97; Chapl Bournemouth Univ 97-99; Prin OLM and Integrated Tr *Sarum* 99-03; Dir Tr and Prin Dioc OLM Scheme *Man* 03-06; Course Dir SNWTP 06-08; C Chorlton-cum-Hardy St Werburgh 06-08; P-in-c from 08; Hon Can Man Cathl from 06. *St Werburgh's Rectory, 388 Wilbraham Road, Manchester M21 0UH* Tel 0161-881 1642 Mobile 07834-390380 E-mail adawtry@aol.com

DAXTER, Preb Gregory. b 42. Chelmer Inst of HE PGCE76. Oak Hill Th Coll 64. **d** 68 **p** 69. C Paignton St Paul Preston *Ex* 68-72; C Woodford Wells *Chelmsf* 72-75; Hon C Harold Hill St Paul

75-77; Hon C Wilmington *Roch* 77-87; PV Ex Cathl and Chapl Ex Cathl Sch 87-03; Preb Ex Cathl from 02; rtd 03. *36 Lyncombe Crescent, Higher Lincombe Road, Torquay TQ1 2HP*

DAY, Audrey. b 30. CA Tr Coll IDC57. **d** 88 **p** 94. Par Dn Mildenhall *St E* 88-91; Dioc Officer for the Care of the Elderly 91-95; NSM Blackbourne 94-95; rtd 95; Perm to Offic *St E* 95-04 and *Glouc* from 04. *25 Capel Court, The Burgate, Prestbury, Cheltenham GL52 3EL* Tel (01242) 576494

DAY, Charles George. b 28. Keble Coll Ox BA51 MA63. Cuddesdon Coll 51. **d** 53 **p** 54. C Hythe *Cant* 53-56; C S Norwood St Alb 56-59; R Stisted *Chelmsf* 59-65; V Brenchley *Roch* 65-75; rtd 93. *Sparks Hall, Forsham Lane, Sutton Valence, Maidstone ME17 3EW* Tel (01622) 843248 Fax 844298

DAY, Charles Ian. b 48. Univ of Wales (Ban) BA72. St Mich Coll Llan 73. **d** 75 **p** 76. C Llanrhos *St As* 75-79; V Mochdre 79-83; CF 80-91; V Minera *St As* 83-92; Dioc Soc Resp Officer 89-94; V Mold from 92; AD Mold from 03. *The Vicarage, Church Lane, Mold CH7 1BW* Tel and fax (01352) 752960 Mobile 07977-001692 E-mail moldciw01@spamex.com

DAY, Christine Audrey. b 63. K Alfred's Coll Win BTh01 Univ of Wales (Lamp) MA(Theol)06. STETS 02. **d** 04 **p** 05. NSM N Stoneham *Win* 04-08; NSM Swaythling from 08. *86 Copperfield Road, Southampton SO16 3NY* Tel (023) 8058 2042 E-mail revchrisday@gmail.com

DAY, Canon Colin Michael. b 40. Lon Univ BSc62 AKC62 Em Coll Cam BA66 MA71. Ridley Hall Cam 65. **d** 67 **p** 68. C Heworth w Peasholme St Cuth York 67-70; C Ox St Clem 70-76; V Kidsgrove *Lich* 76-86; Exec Officer Angl Evang Assembly and C of E Coun 86-90; Adv on Miss and Evang *Sarum* 90-95; P-in-c Branksome Park All SS 95-01; V 01-05; Can and Preb Sarum Cathl 94-05; Dioc Tr in Evang 95-05; rtd 05. *113 Archery Grove, Southampton SO19 9ET* Tel (023) 8043 9854 E-mail colin.day1@tiscali.co.uk

DAY, David John. b 44. CEng72 MICE72. Trin Coll Bris. **d** 90 **p** 91. C Stratton St Margaret w S Marston etc *Bris* 90-94; Perm to Offic from 94; Manager SA Alcohol Rehabilitation Cen Highworth from 98. *56 Beechcroft Road, Swindon SN2 7PX* Tel (01793) 725721

DAY, David Vivian. b 36. Lon Univ BA57 Nottm Univ MEd73 MTh77. **d** 99 **p** 00. NSM Dur St Nic from 99. *35 Orchard Drive, Durham DH1 1LA* Tel 0191-386 6909 E-mail dv.day@virgin.net

DAY, Canon David William. b 37. St Andr Univ MA58 BD61 CertEd73. St And Dioc Tr Course 74. **d** 76 **p** 77. C St Andrews All SS *St And* 76-77; P-in-c Dundee St Ninian *Bre* 77-84; Itinerant Priest *Arg* 84-02; R Duror 84-02; P-in-c Gruline 84-02; P-in-c Kentallen 84-02; P-in-c Kinlochleven 84-02; P-in-c Kinlochmoidart 84-96; P-in-c Lochbuie 84-96; P-in-c Portnacrois 84-02; P-in-c Strontian 84-96; Can St Jo Cathl Oban 99-02; rtd 02; Hon Can Cumbrae *Arg* from 02; Hon C St Andrews All SS *St And* from 03. *10 Doocot Road, St Andrews KY16 8QP* Tel (01334) 476991 E-mail david@arkville.freeserve.co.uk

DAY, George Chester. b 45. Ex Univ BA66 Lon Univ BD70. Clifton Th Coll 67. **d** 71 **p** 72. C Reading St Jo *Ox* 71-75; C Morden S'wark 75-81; Sec for Voc and Min CPAS 81-86; Hon C Bromley Ch Ch *Roch* 83-86; V St Paul's Cray St Barn 86-05; RD Orpington 01-05; V Joydens Wood St Barn from 05. *The Vicarage, 6 Tile Kiln Lane, Bexley DA5 2BB* Tel (01322) 528923 E-mail george.day@diocese-rochester.org or georgeday@telco4u.net

DAY, Canon James Alfred. b 23. DFC44. AKC49. **d** 50 **p** 51. C Wembley Park St Aug *Lon* 50-52; Mauritius 52-57; V E and W Ravendale w Hatcliffe *Linc* 57-60; R Beelsby 57-60; PC Gt Grimsby St Paul 60-66; V Tattershall 66-80; R Coningsby 66-80; RD Horncastle 73-80; V Heckington 80-89; Can and Preb Linc Cathl 77-05; rtd 89. *22 Ancaster Drive, Sleaford NG34 7LY* Tel (01529) 305318

DAY, Prof James Meredith. b 55. Oberlin Coll (USA) AB77 Harvard Univ EdM81 Univ of Penn PhD87. Westcott Ho Cam 01. **d** 03 **p** 04. C Ostend and Antwerp St Boniface *Eur* 03-06; Asst Chapl Brussels from 06. *Mooiboslaan 20, 1170 St Pieters Woluwe, Belgium* Tel (0032) 486-141323 (mobile) E-mail james.day@psp.ucl.ac.be

DAY, Jennifer Ann. *See* BRADSHAW, Mrs Jennifer Ann

DAY, Canon John Alfred. b 25. TCD BA51. **d** 51 **p** 52. C Enniskillen and Trory *Clogh* 51-54; I Clontibret w Tullycorbet 54-58; I Drumkeeran 58-67; I Maguiresbridge w Derrybrusk 67-91; Can Clogh Cathl from 78; rtd 91. *Killeeninane Cottage, 40 Ballylucas Road, Tamlaght, Enniskillen BT74 4HD* Tel (028) 6638 7835

DAY, John Cuthbert. b 36. Sarum Th Coll 66. **d** 68 **p** 69. C Bedhampton *Portsm* 68-72; V Froxfield 72-73; V Froxfield w Privett 73-77; V Warminster Ch Ch *Sarum* 77-81; R Pewsey 81-90; Chapl Pewsey Hosp 81-90; P-in-c Sturminster Newton and Hinton St Mary *Sarum* 90-01; P-in-c Stock and Lydlinch 90-01; rtd 01; Perm to Offic *B & W* and *Sarum* from 01. *Kingfisher Cottage, Clements Lane, Mere, Warminster BA12 6DF* Tel (01347) 860984

DAY, John Kenneth. b 58. Hull Univ BA85. Cranmer Hall Dur 85. **d** 87 **p** 88. C Thornbury *Bradf* 87-90; V 90-96; V Whitkirk *Ripon* 96-01; V Fendalton New Zealand from 01. *7 Makora Street, Fendalton, Christchurch 8041, New Zealand* Tel (0064) (3) 351 7392 *or* 351 7064 E-mail thedays@clear.net.nz

DAY, Martyn John. b 69. Univ Coll Lon BSc90. St Jo Coll Nottm 07. **d** 09. C Horwich and Rivington *Man* from 09. *36 Greenstone Avenue, Horwich, Bolton BL6 5SJ* E-mail martyn.day9@btinternet.com

DAY, Canon Mary Elizabeth. b 57. Leic Poly BEd79. St Jo Coll Nottm 93. **d** 93 **p** 94. C Newbarns w Hawcoat *Carl* 93-98; P-in-c Allonby 98-03; P-in-c Cross Canonby 98-03; P-in-c Dearham 02-03; V Allonby, Cross Canonby and Dearham from 03; Adv for Women in Min from 07; RD Solway from 08; Hon Can Carl Cathl from 08. *The Vicarage, Crosscanonby, Maryport CA15 6SJ* Tel (01900) 814192 E-mail mary.day1@tesco.net

DAY, Michael. b 37. AKC61 RCA(Lon) MA75. **d** 62 **p** 63. C Hulme St Phil *Man* 62-65; Asst Chapl Newc Univ 65-70; Chapl Chelsea Coll *Lon* 70-85; Chapl R Coll of Art 70-90; Chapl Cen, Chelsea and St Martin's Schs of Art *Lon* 85-90; P-in-c Bloomsbury St Geo w Woburn Square Ch 91-95; C St Pancras w St Jas and Ch Ch 95-02; Chapl Lon Art Colls 95-02; rtd 02. *40 Thistlewaite Road, London E5 0QQ* Tel (020) 8985 8568

DAY, Paul Geoffrey. b 51. Dur Univ BEd75. Trin Coll Bris 76. **d** 78 **p** 79. C Roxeth Ch Ch *Lon* 78-82; TV Barking St Marg w St Patr *Chelmsf* 82-87; V Barrow St Mark *Carl* 87-00; V Eccleston St Luke *Liv* 00-07; TV Eccleston from 07. *St Luke's Vicarage, Mulberry Avenue, St Helens WA10 4DE* Tel (01744) 21173 E-mail paulgday@btinternet.com

DAY, Peter. b 50. BPharm71. Coll of Resurr Mirfield 85. **d** 87 **p** 88. C Eastcote St Lawr *Lon* 87-91; C Wembley Park St Aug 91-94; V Glen Parva and S Wigston *Leic* from 94. *9 Hindoostan Avenue, Wigston LE18 4UD* E-mail peterday@leicester.anglican.org

DAY, Peter Maurice. b 43. **d** 04 **p** 05. OLM Dover St Martin *Cant* from 04. *42 Elms Vale Road, Dover CT17 9NT* Tel (01304) 201966 E-mail peterm.day@ntlworld.com

DAY, Roy Frederick. b 24. S'wark Ord Course 63. **d** 67 **p** 68. C Newington St Paul *S'wark* 67-70; C Radlett *St Alb* 70-72; P-in-c Ponsbourne 72-76; R Campton 76-82; V Shefford 76-82; R Shenley 82-89; rtd 89; Perm to Offic *St Alb* from 89. *11 Hill End Lane, St Albans AL4 0TX* Tel (01727) 845782

DAY, Miss Sally Ann. b 43. **d** 07 **p** 08. OLM Shifnal and Sheriffhales *Lich* from 07. *11 Cherry Tree Hill, Coalbrookdale, Telford TF8 7EF* Tel and fax (01952) 433213 Mobile 07831-101361 E-mail sallyannday@hotmail.com

DAY, Stephen Michael. b 60. Down Coll Cam BA82 MA85 Open Univ BA00. Ridley Hall Cam 02. **d** 05 **p** 06. C Waltham H Cross *Chelmsf* 05-09; TV Papworth *Ely* from 09. *The Rectory, 1 Barons Way, Papworth Everard, Cambridge CB23 3QJ* Tel (01480) 831915 E-mail revdsmday@tesco.net

DAY, William Charles. b 47. Portsm Poly BEd86. Ripon Coll Cuddesdon 88. **d** 90 **p** 91. C Bishop's Waltham *Portsm* 90-93; P-in-c Greatham w Empshott and Hawkley w Prior's Dean 93-95; R 95-98; V Titchfield 98-09; RD Fareham 04-08; C-in-c Whiteley CD 08-09; rtd 09. *19 Peter's Road, Locks Heath, Southampton SO31 6EB* Tel (01489) 564035 E-mail caroldday@frmail.net

DAYKIN, Mrs Jean Elizabeth. b 43. **d** 04 **p** 05. NSM Cawthorne *Wakef* from 04. *13 Maltkiln Road, Cawthorne, Barnsley S75 4HH* Tel (01226) 793804 Mobile 07967-767839 E-mail daykin.jeantom@tiscali.co.uk

DAYKIN, Timothy Elwin. b 54. R Holloway Coll Lon BSc75 St Jo Coll Dur MA81 K Coll Lon MPhil93 MEHS89 FRSA02. Cranmer Hall Dur 75. **d** 78 **p** 79. C Bourne *Guildf* 78-81; Chapl K Alfred Coll *Win* 82-87; C-in-c Valley Park CD 87-91; V Valley Park 91-92; P-in-c Fordingbridge 92-98; V 98-01; P-in-c Hale w S Charford 94-01; P-in-c Breamore 99-01; TR Fordingbridge and Breamore and Hale etc 01-05; TV Southampton (City Cen) from 05; Producer/Presenter Relig Progr BBC Radio Solent from 05. *St Michael's Vicarage, 55 Bugle Street, Southampton SO14 2AG* E-mail vicar@buglestreet.co.uk

DAYNES, Andrew John. b 47. Jes Coll Cam BA69 MA73. Westcott Ho Cam 69. **d** 72 **p** 73. C Radlett *St Alb* 72-76; Chapl St Alb Abbey 76-80; Chapl Bryanston Sch 80-08; rtd 08. *20 Liddington Crescent, Blandford Forum DT11 7RP*

DAZELEY, Mrs Lorna. b 31. CertEd53 New Hall Cam BA82 MA86. EAMTC 82. **dss** 84 **d** 87 **p** 94. Chesterton St Andr *Ely* 84-87; C 87-97; rtd 97; Perm to Offic *Ely* from 01. *Chesterton House, Church Street, Chesterton, Cambridge CB4 1DT* Tel (01223) 356243

DE ALWIS, Anthony Clarence. b 39. Nottm Univ MA99. EAMTC 96. **d** 99 **p** 00. NSM Carrington *S'well* 99-04; NSM Basford St Leodegarius 04-06; rtd 06. *85 Marlborough Road, Beeston, Nottingham NG9 2HL* Tel 0115-967 8097 Mobile 07974-084514 E-mail tonydealwis270@hotmail.com

de BERRY, Andrew Piers. b 44. St Jo Coll Dur BA66. Ripon Hall Ox 70. **d** 74 **p** 75. C Aylesbury *Ox* 74-77; USA 78; TV Clyst St George, Aylesbeare, Clyst Honiton etc *Ex* 78-80; Asst Chapl

HM Pris Wormwood Scrubs 80-82; Chapl HM Pris Sudbury 82-84; V Blackwell *Derby* 84-91; V Thurgarton w Hoveringham and Bleasby etc *S'well* from 91. *The Vicarage, Southwell Road, Thurgarton, Nottingham NG14 7GP* Tel (01636) 830234 E-mail adeberry@tiscali.co.uk

de BERRY, Barnabas John de la Tour. b 75. Heythrop Coll Lon BA99. Wycliffe Hall Ox 99. **d** 01 **p** 02. C Derby St Alkmund and St Werburgh 01-04; C Cambridge H Trin *Ely* from 04. *42 Pretoria Road, Cambridge CB4 1HE* Tel (01223) 479473 Mobile 07968-728844 E-mail barneydeb@hotmail.com

DE BERRY, Robert Delatour. b 42. Qu Coll Cam BA64 MA68. Ridley Hall Cam 65. **d** 67 **p** 68. C Bradf Cathl 67-70; Youth Worker CMS Uganda 71-75; V Attercliffe *Sheff* 75-83; V W Kilburn St Luke w St Simon and St Jude *Lon* 83-97; Gen Sec Mid-Africa Min (CMS) 97-99; P-in-c Kennington St Mark *S'wark* 99-01; V 01-08; rtd 08. *27 Cossor Road, Pewsey SN9 5HX*

de BOWEN, Alfred William. b 24. St Paul's Coll Grahamstown 76. **d** 78 **p** 86. NSM Port Alfred S Africa 78-86; NSM Cil-y-Cwm and Ystrad-ffin w Rhandir-mwyn etc *St D* 86-88; Lic to Offic *Linc* 88-92; rtd 90. *Elmham House, Bay Hill, Ilminster TA19 0AT* Tel (01460) 52694

de BURGH-THOMAS, George Albert. b 30. Univ of Wales (Ban) BA50. St Mich Coll Llan 51. **d** 53 **p** 54. C Hawarden *St As* 53-56 and 60-63; C Roath St Martin *Llan* 56-58; C Llangeinor 58-60; V Bampton and Mardale *Carl* 63-70; V Fritwell *Ox* 70-83; R Souldern 70-83; R Fritwell w Souldern and Ardley w Fewcott 83-87; R Hawridge w Cholesbury and St Leonard 87-96; V The Lee 87-96; rtd 96; Perm to Offic *Ox* from 01. *6 Priory Orchard, Wantage OX12 9EI.* Tel (01235) 767780

DE CHAIR LADD, Anne. *See* LADD, Mrs Anne de Chair

de CHAZAL, Mrs Nancy Elizabeth. b 28. Bedf Coll Lon BA52 Lambeth STh90. Sarum & Wells Th Coll 81. dss 84 **d** 87 **p** 94. NSM Melbury *Sarum* 84-98. *Lavender Cottage, East Street, Sydling St Nicholas, Dorchester DT2 9NX* Tel (01300) 341693

de COSTOBADIE, James Palliser. b 72. G&C Coll Cam BA94 MA98. Oak Hill Th Coll BA01. **d** 02 **p** 03. C Mayfair Ch Ch and St Helen Bishopsgate w St Andr Undershaft etc *Lon* 02-05; P-in-c Sydenham w Beckenham New Zealand from 05. *8A Roxburgh Street, Sydenham, Christchurch 8023, New Zealand* Tel (0064) (3) 332 3432 E-mail jdecostabadie@hotmail.com

de GARIS, Jean Helier Thomson. b 60. K Alfred's Coll Win BA82 PGCE83. Sarum & Wells Th Coll BTh93. **d** 93 **p** 94. C Chandler's Ford *Win* 93-98; P-in-c Lytchett Minster *Sarum* from 98; RD Poole from 09. *The Vicarage, New Road, Lytchett Minster, Poole BH16 6JQ* Tel (01202) 622253 E-mail jean@degaris.freeserve.co.uk

de GAY, Sandra Jane. NOC. **d** 08 **p** 09. NSM Potternewton *Ripon* from 08. *48 Vesper Way, Leeds LS5 3LN* Tel 0113-258 2673 E-mail j.degay@leedstrinity.ac.uk

de GREY-WARTER, Philip. b 67. Leeds Univ BEng89. Ridley Hall Cam BA94. **d** 94 **p** 95. C Bromley Ch Ch *Roch* 94-97; C Sevenoaks St Nic 97-02; P-in-c Fowey *Truro* from 02; P-in-c St Sampson from 02; Chapl Cen Cornwall Primary Care Trust 02-07; Hon Chapl Miss to Seafarers 04-07. *The Vicarage, Church Avenue, Fowey PL23 1BU* Tel (01726) 833535 E-mail pdgw@btinternet.com

DE KEYSER, Nicholas David Llewellyn. b 49. Nottm Univ BTh75 MTh86. St Jo Coll Nottm 71. **d** 75 **p** 76. C Portswood Ch Ch *Win* 75-77; C Yateley 77-81; TV Grantham *Linc* 81-86; V Heyside *Man* 86-91; R Charlton-in-Dover *Cant* 91-03; R Stock Harvard *Chelmsf* from 03. *The Rectory, 61 High Street, Stock, Ingatestone CM4 9BN* Tel (01277) 840453 Fax 08701-249842 Mobile 07050-155481 E-mail nickdekeyser@btopenworld.com

de la BAT SMIT, Reynaud. b 50. St Edm Hall Ox BA80 MA86 Dur Univ PhD94 FRSA94. Ripon Coll Cuddesdon. **d** 82 **p** 83. C Headington *Ox* 82-85; Chapl St Hild and St Bede Coll *Dur* 85-96; Chapl Cheltenham Coll from 96; Sec Chs' Peace Forum CTBI from 97. *Cheltenham College, Bath Road, Cheltenham GL53 7LD* Tel (01242) 513540 or 230800 E-mail reynaud@ukonline.co.uk

de la HOYDE, Canon Denys Ralph Hart. b 33. G&C Coll Cam BA57 MA61. Westcott Ho Cam 57. **d** 59 **p** 60. C Moss Side Ch Ch *Man* 59-60; Chapl G&C Coll Cam 60-64; P-in-c Naini Tal etc India 64-68; C Eltham H Trin *S'wark* 68-69; Chapl Bromsgrove Sch 69-71; Asst Master Harrogate High Sch 71-78; Lic to Offic *Ripon* 71-78; V Pool w Arthington 86-98; Dioc Dir of Ords 86-98; Hon Can Ripon Cathl 92-98; rtd 98; Perm to Offic *Ripon* from 00. *36 Hookstone Chase, Harrogate HG2 7HS* Tel (01423) 548146 E-mail denys.delahoyde@ntlworld.com

de la MARE, Benedick James Hobart. b 38. Trin Coll Ox BA63 MA67. Cuddesdon Coll 63. **d** 65 **p** 66. C Gosforth All SS *Newc* 65-68; Chapl Trin Coll Cam 68-73; V Newc St Gabr 73-81; V Dur St Oswald 81-02; rtd 02; Chapl Collingwood Coll Dur 95-04; Hon Chapl from 04. *216 Gilesgate, Durham DH1 1QN* Tel 0191-383 2634

de la MOUETTE, Norman Harry. b 39. Southn Univ BEd73 MA98. Sarum & Wells Th Coll 76. **d** 79 **p** 80. NSM Win St Lawr and St Maurice w St Swithun 79-99; Deputation Appeals Org CECS *Win* and *Portsm* 83-96; Chapl St Jo Win Charity 96-99;

NSM Win St Lawr and St Maurice w St Swithun 99-04; rtd 04. *146 Greenhill Road, Winchester SO22 5DR* Tel (01962) 853191

DE MELLO, Mrs Bridget Dorothea Deuchar. SEITE. **d** 08 **p** 09. NSM Gt Ilford St Luke *Chelmsf* from 08. *3 Lennox Gardens, Ilford IG1 3LF* E-mail bridget@demello.co.uk

de MELLO, Gualter Rose. b 34. MBE96. Ridley Hall Cam 63. **d** 64 **p** 65. C S Hackney St Jo w Ch Ch *Lon* 64-66; Toc H Chapl (Hackney) 66-72; Hon C All Hallows by the Tower etc *Lon* from 73; Dir Friends Anonymous Service from 73; Dir Community of Reconciliation and Fellowship from 88; rtd 99. *Prideaux House, 10 Church Crescent, London E9 7DL*

de POMERAI, David Ian Morcamp. b 50. Edin Univ BSc72 Univ Coll Lon PhD75. EMMTC 90. **d** 93 **p** 94. NSM Sutton in Ashfield St Mary *S'well* 93-96; NSM Clifton 96-02; NSM Walton-on-Trent w Croxall, Rosliston etc *Derby* from 02. *The Rectory, 2 Station Lane, Walton-on-Trent, Swadlincote DE12 8NA* Tel (01283) 711350 E-mail david.depomerai@nottingham.ac.uk

de POMERAI, Mrs Lesley Anne. b 60. ACIPD82. St Jo Coll Nottm BTh90. **d** 92 **p** 94. Par Dn Sutton in Ashfield St Mary *S'well* 92-94; C 94-96; TV Clifton 96-02; R Walton-on-Trent w Croxall, Rosliston etc *Derby* from 02; RD Repton from 09. *The Rectory, 2 Station Lane, Walton-on-Trent, Swadlincote DE12 8NA* Tel (01283) 711350 E-mail ddepomerai@aol.com

DE PURY, Andrew Robert. b 28. K Coll Lon BD57 AKC57. **d** 58 **p** 59. C Epping St Jo *Chelmsf* 58-60; C Loughton St Jo 60-65; V Harold Hill St Geo 65-72; Missr Swan Par Gp *Ox* 72-76; TR Swan 76-85; R Worminghall w Ickford, Oakley and Shabbington 85-95; rtd 95; Perm to Offic *B & W* 95-06. *8 Russell Pope Avenue, Chard TA20 2JN* Tel (01460) 66714

de QUIDT, Mrs Fiona Margaret Munro. b 53. St Andr Univ MTheol76. NTMTC 97. **d** 00 **p** 01. NSM Kingston Hill St Paul *S'wark* from 00. *10 Norbiton Avenue, Kingston-upon-Thames KT1 3QS* Tel (020) 8549 4175

DE ROBECK, Fiona Caroline. *See* GIBBS, Mrs Fiona Caroline

DE SAUSMAREZ, Canon John Havilland Russell. b 26. Lambeth MA81 Wells Th Coll 54. **d** 56 **p** 57. C N Lynn w St Marg and St Nic *Nor* 56-58; C Hythe *Cant* 58-61; V Maidstone St Martin 61-68; V St Peter-in-Thanet 68-81; RD Thanet 74-81; Hon Can Cant Cathl 78-81; Can Res Cant Cathl 81-94; rtd 94; Perm to Offic *Cant* from 94. *9 St Peter's Court, Broadstairs CT10 2UU* Tel (01843) 867050

DE SILVA, David Ebenezer Sunil. b 48. **d** 72 **p** 73. Sri Lanka 72-84; C Elm Park St Nic Hornchurch *Chelmsf* 84-87; R Mistley w Manningtree and Bradfield 87-90; TR Stanground and Farcet *Ely* 90-01; V Stanground 01-05; rtd 05. *52 Spring Avenue, Hampton Vale, Peterborough PE7 8HW* Tel (01733) 240319

DE SMET, Andrew Charles. b 58. Ex Univ BSc79 Southn Univ BTh88. Sarum & Wells Th Coll 85. **d** 88 **p** 89. C Portsea St Mary *Portsm* 88-93; R Shipston-on-Stour w Honington and Idlicote *Cov* 93-00; Warden Offa Retreat Ho and Dioc Spirituality Adv 00-07; P-in-c Kirkdale w Harome, Nunnington and Pockley *York* from 07; Dioc Adv in Past Care from 07. *Kirkdale Vicarage, Main Road, Nawton, York YO62 7ST* Tel (01439) 770760

DE VERNY, David Dietrich Schuld. b 55. Trier Univ MTh81. **d** 83 **p** 83. Asst Chapl Bonn *Eur* 83; C Henfield w Shermanbury and Woodmancote *Chich* 84-86; C Westmr St Sav and St Jas Less *Lon* 86-88; P-in-c Cheddington w Mentmore and Marsworth *Ox* 88-90; Gen Sec Fellowship of St Alb and St Sergius 90-92; Chapl for Migrant Workers *Linc* 06-08; Dioc Link Person for Ethnic Minority Anglicans 06-08; Hon C Boston 05-08; Chapl Hull Univ from 08. *223 Cottingham Road, Hull HU5 4AU* Tel (01482) 343182 Mobile 07761-469456 E-mail ddeverny@gmx.net

de VIAL, Raymond Michael. b 39. Oak Hill Th Coll 77. **d** 80 **p** 81. NSM Beckenham St Jo *Roch* 80-84; C Morden *S'wark* 84-88; TV 88-94; V Kingston Hill St Paul 94-04; rtd 04; Perm to Offic *S'wark* 04-05 and *Carl* from 05. *39 Helme Drive, Kendal LA9 7JB* Tel (01539) 729396 E-mail revray@btinternet.com

de WAAL, Victor Alexander. b 29. Pemb Coll Cam BA49 MA53 Nottm Univ Hon DD83. Ely Th Coll 50. **d** 52 **p** 53. C Isleworth St Mary *Lon* 52-56; Chapl Ely Th Coll 56-59; Chapl K Coll Cam 59-63; Hon C Nottingham St Mary *S'well* 63-69; Chapl Nottm Univ 63-69; Can Res and Chan Linc Cathl 69-76; Dean Cant 76-86; Perm to Offic *Heref* 88-99; rtd 90; Chapl Soc of Sacred Cross Tymawr 90-00; Lic to Offic *Mon* 90-02; Perm to Offic from 02. *6 St James Close, Bishop Street, London N1 8PH* Tel (020) 7354 2741 E-mail victordewaal@aol.com

DE WIT, The Ven John. b 47. Oriel Coll Ox BA69 MA73 Clare Coll Cam BA78 MA84. Westcott Ho Cam 75. **d** 78 **p** 79. C The Quinton *Birm* 78-81; TV Solihull 81-85; V Kings Heath 85-94; RD Moseley 91-94; P-in-c Hampton in Arden 94-04; Chapl Utrecht w Zwolle *Eur* from 04; Adn NW Eur from 08. *Van Hogendorpstraat 26, 3581KE Utrecht, The Netherlands* Tel (0031) (30) 251 3424 Fax 254 1580 E-mail chaplain@holytrinityutrecht.nl

DE WOLF, Mark Anthony. b 32. BA55. Ely Th Coll 56. **d** 59 **p** 60. C Hackney Wick St Mary of Eton w St Aug *Lon* 59-64; USA from 64; rtd 97. *9 Weetamoe Farm Drive, Bristol RI 02809-5199, USA*

DEACON, Charles Edward. b 57. Westf Coll Lon BSc78. Ridley Hall Cam 92. **d** 94 **p** 95. C Ex St Jas 94-98; V Shiphay Collaton from 98. *St John's Vicarage, 83 Cadewell Lane, Torquay TQ2 7HP* Tel (01803) 401316

DEACON, Donald (Brother Angelo). Chich Th Coll 66. **d** 68 **p** 69. SSF from 63; Lic to Offic *Man* 69-70; USA 70-72; C Kennington St Jo *S'wark* 72-74; C Wilton Place St Paul *Lon* 74-75; Angl-Franciscan Rep Ecum Cen Assisi *Eur* 75; Franciscanum Sem 76-78; Perm to Offic *Sarum* 78-82; Lic to Offic *Chelmsf* 82-90; *Birm* 90-93; *Linc* 94-97; rtd 98; Lic to Offic *Lon* 98-07 and Chich from 07. *Bishop's House, 21 Guildford Road, Horsham RH12 1LU*

DEACON, Frederick George Raymond. b 15. Tyndale Hall Bris 63. **d** 65 **p** 66. C Kingswood *Bris* 65-69; C Leckhampton SS Phil and Jas *Glouc* 69-71; V Longcot *Ox* 71-72; V Longcot w Fernham and Bourton 72-77; Zambia 77-80; P-in-c Cressage w Sheinton *Heref* 80-81; P-in-c Harley w Kenley 80-81; TV Wenlock 81-85; rtd 85; Perm to Offic *Heref* 85-90; *Glouc* from 1986 and *Worc* from 90. *29 Robinson Meadow, Ledbury HR8 1SU* Tel (01531) 634500

DEACON, John. b 37. Arm Aux Min Course 87. **d** 90 **p** 91. NSM Enniscorthy w Clone, Clonmore, Monart etc *C & O* 90-05; rtd 05. *The Rectory, Creagh, Gorey, Co Wexford, Republic of Ireland* Tel (00353) (53) 942 0354

DEACON, Mrs Selina Frances. b 52. SRN74. Ripon Coll Cuddesdon 01. **d** 03 **p** 04. C White Horse *Sarum* 03-07; P-in-c Studley from 07. *The Vicarage, 340 Frome Road, Studley, Trowbridge BA14 0ED* Tel (01225) 753162 Mobile 07867-521909 E-mail selinadeacon@hotmail.com

DEACON, Timothy Randall. b 55. Ex Univ BA78. Chich Th Coll 79. **d** 80 **p** 81. C Whitleigh *Ex* 80-83; P-in-c Devonport St Aubyn 83-88; P-in-c Newton Ferrers w Revelstoke 88-94; R 94-07; P-in-c Holbeton 93-07; TR Brixham w Churston Ferrers and Kingswear from 07; RD Ivybridge 98-03. *The Rectory, 16 Holwell Road, Brixham TQ5 9NE* Tel and fax (01803) 851570 E-mail revtimdeacon@hotmail.co.uk

DEADMAN, Richard George Spencer. b 63. Ex Univ BA85. Coll of Resurr Mirfield 86. **d** 88 **p** 89. C Grangetown *York* 88-91; P-in-c 91-93; V 93-96; V Wallsend St Luke *Newc* 96-01; V Newc St Phil and St Aug and St Matt w St Mary from 01. *St Matthew's Vicarage, 10 Winchester Terrace, Newcastle upon Tyne NE4 6EY* Tel 0191-232 9039 E-mail richardgsd@aol.com

DEAKIN, Christopher Harold. b 49. ARMCM72. Qu Coll Birm 02. **d** 04 **p** 05. C Wrockwardine Deanery *Lich* 04-07; P-in-c Bicton, Montford w Shrawardine and Fitz from 07; P-in-c Leaton and Albrighton w Battlefield from 07. *The Rectory, 15 Brookside, Bicton, Shrewsbury SY3 8EP* Tel (01743) 851310 E-mail deaks@fsmail.net

DEAKIN, John David. b 58. Qu Coll Birm BA03. **d** 03 **p** 04. C Blakenall Heath *Lich* 03-07; TV Willenhall H Trin from 07. *129 Essington Road, Willenhall WV12 5DT* Tel (01922) 409460

DEAKIN, Preb John Hartley. b 27. K Coll Cam BA50 MA63. Cranmer Hall Dur. **d** 65 **p** 66. C Newcastle St Geo *Lich* 65-70; V Cotes Heath 70-84; RD Eccleshall 82-92; R Standon and Cotes Heath 84-95; Preb Lich Cathl 88-02; Sub-Chapl HM Pris Drake Hall 89-95; rtd 95; Hon C Kinver and Enville *Lich* 95-02; Perm to Offic *Heref* from 04. *8C Cliff Road, Bridgnorth WV16 4EY* Tel (01746) 762574

DEAMER, Mrs Carylle. b 40. SAOMC 96. **d** 99 **p** 00. OLM Riverside *Ox* 99-05; rtd 05; Perm to Offic *Ox* 05-08. *Address temp unknown*

DEAN, The Ven Alan. b 38. Hull Univ BA61. Qu Coll Birm. **d** 63 **p** 64. C Clitheroe St Mary *Blackb* 63-67; C Burnley St Pet 67-68; CF 68-93; Dep Chapl Gen and Adn for the Army 93-95; rtd 96; QHC from 93; Perm to Offic *York* from 95. *1 Midway Avenue, Nether Poppleton, York YO26 6NT* Tel (01904) 785305

DEAN, Andrew James. b 40. FCII ACIArb. WEMTC 92. **d** 95 **p** 96. NSM Rodbourne Cheney *Bris* 95-05; rtd 05; Perm to Offic *Bris* from 05. *Koinonia, 2 Wicks Close, Haydon Wick, Swindon SN25 1QH* Tel (01793) 725526

DEAN, Canon Arthur. b 32. Southn Univ CQSW80. Wesley Coll Leeds 55 S Dios Minl Tr Scheme 89. **d** 90 **p** 90. NSM Eastney *Portsm* 90-96; P-in-c Portsea St Alb 96-02; Hon Can Portsm Cathl from 02; rtd 02; Perm to Offic *Portsm* from 02. *9 Kingsley Road, Southsea PO4 8HJ* Tel (023) 9273 5773 Mobile 07855-146929 E-mail annenarthur.dean@btopenworld.com

DEAN, Benjamin Timothy Frederic. b 69. Bible Coll BA93 K Coll Lon MA94 Selw Coll Cam MPhil02 PhD06. Ridley Hall Cam 04. **d** 07. C Georgeham *Ex* 07-08; Lect Geo Whitefield Coll S Africa from 08. *George Whitefield College, PO Box 64, Muizenberg, 7950 South Africa* Tel (0027) (21) 788 1652 E-mail btfd@mac.com

DEAN, John Milner. b 27. S'wark Ord Course 69. **d** 72 **p** 73. C Lewisham St Mary *S'wark* 72-75; C Merton St Mary 75-77; V S Beddington St Mich 77-97; rtd 97. *69 Groveside Close, Carshalton SM5 2ER* Tel (020) 8669 9369

DEAN, Jonathan Charles. b 57. St Cath Coll Cam MA83. NEOC 04. **d** 07 **p** 08. NSM Gt Ayton w Easby and Newton under Roseberry *York* from 07. *The White House, 2 Dikes Lane, Great Ayton, Middlesbrough TS9 6HJ* Tel (01642) 722649

DEAN, Mrs Linda Louise. b 39. **d** 04 **p** 05. NSM Primrose Hill St Mary w Avenue Road St Paul *Lon* from 04. *52 Lanchester Road, London N6 4TA* Tel (020) 8883 5417 E-mail linda@lindadean52.wanadoo.co.uk

DEAN, Lucas John William. b 57. St Jo Coll Nottm 05. **d** 07 **p** 08. C St Laur in Thanet *Cant* from 07. *1 Warwick Drive, Ramsgate CT11 0JP* Tel (01843) 588385 Mobile 07712-834472 E-mail ljwdean@hotmail.com

DEAN, Malcolm. b 34. Tyndale Hall Bris 67. **d** 69 **p** 70. C Daubhill *Man* 69-73; P-in-c Constable Lee 73-74; V 74-79; P-in-c Everton St Sav w St Cuth *Liv* 79-86; P-in-c Anfield SS Simon and Jude 81-86; V Walton Breck Ch Ch 86-89; rtd 89; Perm to Offic *Man* from 89. *40 Grasmere Road, Haslingden, Rossendale BB4 4EB* Tel (01706) 215953

DEAN, Mrs Margaret Heath. b 50. Newton Park Coll Bris BEd72. STETS 05. **d** 07 **p** 08. C Farncombe *Guildf* from 07. *73 Binscombe Crescent, Godalming GU7 3RA* Tel (01483) 411909

DEAN, Preb Raymond Charles. b 27. Bris Univ BA51. Wycliffe Hall Ox 51. **d** 53 **p** 54. C Weston-super-Mare St Jo *B & W* 53-59; V Lyngford 59-70; V Burnham 70-93; Preb Wells Cathl from 73; RD Burnham 82-91; RD Axbridge 87-91; rtd 93; Perm to Offic *B & W* from 93. *258 Berrow Road, Berrow, Burnham-on-Sea TA8 2JH* Tel (01278) 780979

DEAN, Simon Timothy Michael Rex. b 62. Liv Univ BEng83. Ridley Hall Cam 86. **d** 89 **p** 90. C St German's Cathl 89-92; V Castletown 92-05; Perm to Offic *Cant* from 08. *11 Viking Court, St Stephen's Close, Canterbury CT2 7HZ*

DEAN, Stuart Peter. b 75. Cant Ch Ch Univ Coll BA97. Oak Hill Th Coll 03. **d** 06 **p** 07. C Lindfield *Chich* from 06. *All Saints' Office, 122-122A High Street, Lindfield, Haywards Heath RH16 2HS* Tel (01444) 482405 E-mail allsaints@lindfield.info

DEAN, Timothy Charles Painter. b 50. STETS MA08. **d** 07 **p** 08. NSM Godalming *Guildf* from 07. *73 Binscombe Crescent, Godalming GU7 3RA* Tel (01483) 429120 E-mail timdean@cnet.org

DEAN-REVILL, David Frank. b 68. Univ Coll Ches BA06. NOC 03. **d** 06 **p** 07. C Dinnington w Laughton and Throapham *Sheff* 06-09; P-in-c Shiregreen from 09. *The Vicarage, 510 Bellhouse Road, Sheffield S5 0RG* Tel 0114-245 6526 E-mail daviddeanrevill@hotmail.com

DEANE, Mrs Angela Christine. b 52. WEMTC 00. **d** 04 **p** 05. NSM Credenhill w Brinsop and Wormsley etc *Heref* from 04. *The Oak, Mansel Lacy, Hereford HR4 7HQ* Tel (01981) 590615 E-mail angiestutheoak@lineone.net

DEANE, John. b 02 **p** 03. NSM Stranorlar w Meenglas and Kilteevogue *D & R* 02-06; NSM Derg w Termonamongan 06-07; NSM Urney w Sion Mills 07-08; Bp's C Ardara w Glencolumbkille, Inniskeel etc from 08. *The Rectory, Ardara, Co Donegal, Republic of Ireland* Tel (00353) (74) 954 1124 E-mail revjohndeane@yahoo.ie

DEANE, Nicholas Talbot Bryan. b 46. Bris Univ BA69. Clifton Th Coll 70. **d** 72 **p** 73. C Accrington Ch Ch *Blackb* 72-75; OMF Korea 75-89; P-in-c Newburgh *Liv* 90-93; P-in-c Westhead 90-93; V Newburgh w Westhead 93-97; R Chadwell *Chelmsf* from 97. *The Rectory, 10 Rigby Gardens, Grays RM16 4JJ* Tel (01375) 842176 E-mail nic.deane@virgin.net

DEANE, Canon Robert William. b 52. CITC. **d** 85 **p** 86. C Raheny w Coolock *D & G* 85-88; I Clonsast w Rathangan, Thomastown etc *M & K* 88-00; Can Kildare Cathl 97-00; Can Meath Cathl 98-00; I Swords w Donabate and Kilsallaghan *D & G* from 00; Can Ch Ch Cathl Dublin from 05. *The Rectory, Church Road, Swords, Co Dublin, Republic of Ireland* Tel (00353) (1) 840 2308 E-mail rwdeane@eircom.net

DEANE, Stuart William. b 45. Sarum & Wells Th Coll 86. **d** 88 **p** 89. C Bromyard *Heref* 88-92; V Astley, Clive, Grinshill and Hadnall *Lich* 92-98; TV Cen Telford 98-00; TR 00-05; rtd 05; Perm to Offic *Heref* from 07. *38 Crest Court, Hereford HR4 9QD* Tel (01432) 351937

DEANS, Bruce Gibson. b 64. MCIBS86. Wycliffe Hall Ox 02. **d** 04 **p** 05. C Hartley Wintney, Elvetham, Winchfield etc 04-08; R Shedfield and Wickham *Portsm* from 08. *The Vicarage, 52 Brooklynn Close, Waltham Chase, Southampton SO32 2RZ* Tel (01489) 896637 E-mail brucedeans@thebearsden.fsnet.co.uk

DEAR, Graham Frederick. b 44. St Luke's Coll Ex CertEd66. Wycliffe Hall Ox 67. **d** 70 **p** 71. C Chigwell *Chelmsf* 70-73; C Chingford SS Pet and Paul 73-75; V Southchurch Ch Ch 75-82; CF 82-89; P-in-c The Cowtons *Ripon* 89-94; RE Adv 89-94; V Startforth and Bowes and Rokeby w Brignall 94-97; Chapl HM Pris Garth 97-01; rtd 09; Perm to Offic *Ripon* from 01. *1 The Old Wynd, Bellerby, Leyburn DL8 5QJ* Tel (01969) 623960

DEAR, Neil Douglas Gauntlett. b 35. Linc Th Coll 87. **d** 89 **p** 90. C Framlingham w Saxtead *St E* 89-92; P-in-c Eyke w Bromeswell, Rendlesham, Tunstall etc 92-98; Chapl Local Health Partnerships NHS Trust 98-02; Chapl Cen Suffolk

Primary Care Trust 02-05; P-in-c Worlingworth, Southolt, Tannington, Bedfield etc *St E* 02-05; rtd 05; Perm to Offic *St E* from 05. *Peacehaven, Duke Street, Stanton, Bury St Edmunds IP31 2AB* Tel (01359) 252001

DEARDEN, Geoffrey. b 36. Salford Univ MSc74. CBDTI 05. **d** 06 **p** 07. NSM Hurst Green and Mitton *Bradf* from 06; NSM Waddington from 06. *14 Church Close, Waddington, Clitheroe BB7 3HX* Tel (01200) 427380
E-mail elizabeth.dearden@virgin.net

DEARDEN, James Varley. b 22. Wycliffe Hall Ox 61. **d** 62 **p** 63. C Drypool St Columba w St Andr and St Pet *York* 62-66; V Newington Transfiguration 66-75; V Huddersfield H Trin *Wakef* 75-87; rtd 87; Perm to Offic *Wakef* from 87. *26 Sycamore Avenue, Meltham, Holmfirth HD9 4EE* Tel (01484) 852519

DEARDEN, Canon Philip Harold. b 43. AKC65. **d** 66 **p** 67. C Haslingden w Haslingden Grane *Blackb* 66-69; C Burnley St Pet 69-71; V Langho Billington 71-78; TR Darwen St Pet w Hoddlesden 78-91; RD Darwen 86-91; V Altham w Clayton le Moors 91-97; RD Accrington 95-97; V Clitheroe St Mary 97-08; Hon Can Blackb Cathl 96-08; rtd 08; Perm to Offic *Blackb* from 08. *16 Sun Street, Ulverston LA12 7BX* Tel (01229) 480155
E-mail philip.dearden@btinternet.com

DEARING, Henry Ernest. b 26. Lon Univ BD53. St Deiniol's Hawarden 55. **d** 55 **p** 56. C Skerton St Chad *Blackb* 55-57; V Huncoat 57-60; rtd 95. *St David's Rest Home, 49 Llandudno Road, Penrhyn Bay, Llandudno LL30 3EP* Tel (01492) 545402

DEARING, Trevor. b 33. Lon Univ BD58. Qu Coll Birm MA63. **d** 61 **p** 62. C Todmorden *Wakef* 61-63; V Silkstone 63-66; V Northowram 66-68; C Harlow New Town w Lt Parndon *Chelmsf* 68-70; V Hainault 70-75; Dir Healing Miss 75-79; Hon C Gt Ilford St Andr 75-79; Perm to Offic *Linc* 80-81; 99-02; USA 81-83; rtd 83. *4 Rock House Gardens, Radcliffe Road, Stamford PE9 1AS* Tel (01780) 751680

DEARNLEY, Miss Helen Elizabeth. b 77. De Montfort Univ LLB98 Cam Univ BTh02. Westcott Ho Cam 99. **d** 02 **p** 03. C Knighton St Mary Magd *Leic* 02-06; Co-ord Chapl HM Pris Leic from 06. *HM Prison, Welford Road, Leicester LE2 7AJ* Tel 0116-228 3000 Fax 228 3001
E-mail helen.dearnley@ukgateway.net

DEARNLEY, John Wright. b 37. Open Univ BA81. **d** 99 **p** 05. NSM Llandogo w Whitebrook Chpl and Tintern Parva *Mon* from 99; P-in-c from 07. *2 Greenbanks, Llandogo, Monmouth NP25 4TG* Tel (01594) 530080

DEARNLEY, Mark Christopher. b 59. Cranmer Hall Dur 84. **d** 87 **p** 88. C Purley Ch Ch *S'wark* 87-91; C Addiscombe St Mary 91-93; C Addiscombe St Mary Magd w St Martin 93-94; V Hook 94-02; R Wendover and Halton *Ox* from 02; AD Wendover from 04. *The Vicarage, 34 Dobbins Lane, Wendover, Aylesbury HP22 6DH* Tel (01296) 622230
E-mail dearnley@ukgateway.net

DEARNLEY, Preb Patrick Walter. b 34. Nottm Univ BA55 LTh75. ALCD64. **d** 64 **p** 65. C New Malden and Coombe *S'wark* 64-68; C Portswood Ch Ch *Win* 68-71; C Leeds St Geo *Ripon* 71-74; Hon C Nottingham St Nic *S'well* 74-77; P-in-c Holloway Em w Hornsey Road St Barn *Lon* 77-85; All Islington 80-85; Abp's Officer for UPA 85-90; Preb St Paul's Cathl 86-91; P-in-c Waterloo St Jo *Liv* 91-99; rtd 99; Perm to Offic *Bradf* from 00. *14 Beanlands Parade, Ilkley LS29 8EW* Tel (01943) 603927

DEAS, Leonard Stephen. b 52. New Coll Ox BA75 CertEd76 MA78. St Mich Coll Llan 81. **d** 82 **p** 83. C Dowlais *Llan* 82-84; Chapl St Mich Coll Llan 84-85; Chapl Univ of Wales (Cardiff) *Llan* 85-86; V Newbridge *Mon* 86-93; Can Res St Woolos Cathl 92-96; Master Charterhouse Hull from 96. *The Charterhouse, Charterhouse Lane, Hull HU2 8AF* Tel (01482) 329307

DEAVE, Mrs Gillian Mary. b 31. EMMTC 79. **dss** 82 **d** 87 **p** 94. Nottingham St Pet and St Jas *S'well* 82-87; Par Dn 87-91; rtd 91; Perm to Offic *Pet* and *S'well* from 91. *Greensmith Cottage, 8 City Road, Stathern, Melton Mowbray LE14 4HE* Tel (01949) 860340 E-mail g.deave@leicester.anglican.org

DEBENHAM, Peter Mark. b 68. Nottm Univ BSc89 PhD94. EAMTC 98. **d** 01 **p** 02. NSM Burwell *Ely* 01-02; NSM Swaffham Bulbeck and Swaffham Prior w Reach 01-02; Perm to Offic 02-03; NSM Fordham St Pet 03-08; NSM Kennett 03-08; NSM Three Rivers Gp from 08. *23 Burleigh Rise, Burwell, Cambridge CB25 0RS* Tel (01638) 603142
E-mail peter.debenham@ely.anglican.org

DEBNEY, Canon Wilfred Murray. b 26. ACA48 FCA60. Wycliffe Hall Ox 58. **d** 60 **p** 61. C Leic H Apostles 60-65; V Thorpe Edge *Bradf* 65-69; TV Wendy w Shingay *Ely* 69-75; R Brampton 75-94; Offg Chapl RAF 75-94; RD Huntingdon *Ely* 81-94; Hon Can Ely Cathl 85-94; rtd 94; Lic to Offic *Eur* 94-01; Chapl Lugano 98-02; Perm to Offic *Ely* from 02. *3 Hoo Close, Buckden, St Neots PE19 5TX* Tel (01480) 810652

DEBOO, Canon Alan John. b 45. Qu Coll Cam BA73 MA77. Westcott Ho Cam 72. **d** 74 **p** 75. C Brackley St Pet w St Jas 74-77; Perm to Offic *Sarum* 85-94; NSM Wexcombe 94-02; NSM Savernake from 02; Bp's Officer for NSMs from 03; Can and

Preb Sarum Cathl from 05. *Mayzells Cottage, Collingbourne Kingston, Marlborough SN8 3SD* Tel (01264) 850683
E-mail alandeboo@aol.com

DEBOYS, David Gordon. b 54. QUB BD76 Wolfs Coll Ox MLitt. Ridley Hall Cam 90. **d** 92 **p** 93. C Ipswich St Aug *St E* 92-93; C Whitton and Thurleston w Akenham 93-95; R Hardwick *Ely* 95-00; R Toft w Caldecote and Childerley 95-00; V Cambridge St Jas 00-07; Dir Focus Chr Inst Cambridge 00-07; V Ealing St Barn *Lon* from 07. *St Barnabas' Vicarage, 66 Woodfield Road, London W5 1SH* Tel (020) 8998 0826
E-mail daviddeboys@btinternet.com

DEDMAN, Canon Roger James. b 45. Oak Hill Th Coll 68. **d** 71 **p** 72. C Gresley *Derby* 71-74; C Ipswich St Fran *St E* 74-79; P-in-c Bildeston w Wattisham 79-92; P-in-c Bramford from 92; P-in-c Somersham w Flowton 94-02; P-in-c Lt Blakenham, Baylham and Nettlestead from 02; RD Bosmere 96-01 and 05-07; Hon Can St E Cathl from 01. *The Vicarage, Vicarage Lane, Bramford, Ipswich IP8 4AE* Tel (01473) 741105
E-mail roger.dedman@virgin.net

DEE, Clive Hayden. b 61. Ripon Coll Cuddesdon 86. **d** 89 **p** 90. C Bridgnorth, Tasley, Astley Abbotts, etc *Heref* 89-93; P-in-c Wellington w Pipe-cum-Lyde and Moreton-on-Lugg 93-96. *Ross Cottage, Crumpton Hill Road, Storridge, Malvern WR13 5HE* Tel (01886) 832639

DEED, Michael James. b 77. **d** 04 **p** 05. C Notting Dale St Clem w St Mark and St Jas *Lon* 04-07; C Burlington St Chris Canada from 07. *662 Guelph Line, Burlington ON L7R 3M8, Canada* Tel (001) (905) 320 6034 E-mail michael.deed@googlemail.com

DEEDES, Canon Arthur Colin Bouverie. b 27. Bede Coll Dur BA51. Wells Th Coll 51. **d** 53 **p** 54. C Milton *Portsm* 53-58; C Worplesdon *Guildf* 58-60; V Weston 60-66; V Fleet 66-73; RD Aldershot 69-73; TR Bournemouth St Pet w St Swithun, H Trin etc *Win* 73-80; RD Bournemouth 74-80; Hon Can Win Cathl 78-92; Master Win St Cross w St Faith 80-92; rtd 92; Perm to Offic *Win* from 92; Hon Chapl Win Cathl from 97. *Dolphins, 17 Chesil Street, Winchester SO23 0HU* Tel (01962) 861617

DEEDES, Ms Rosie Anne. b 66. Birm Univ BA87 City Univ 90. Westcott Ho Cam 94. **d** 96 **p** 97. C St Botolph Aldgate w H Trin Minories *Lon* 96-99; Asst Chapl HM Pris Holloway 99-02; Chapl HM Pris Downview from 02. *HM Prison Downview, Sutton Lane, Sutton SM2 5PD* Tel (020) 8196 6314
E-mail rosie.deedes@hmps.gsi.gov.uk

DEEGAN, Arthur Charles. b 49. CertEd71 Birm Univ BEd86. Qu Coll Birm 86. **d** 88 **p** 89. C Leic St Jas 88-91; C Melton Gt Framland 91-92; TV 92-93; TV Melton Mowbray 93-96; R Barwell w Potters Marston and Stapleton 96-08; P-in-c Braunstone Town from 08; CF (TA) from 95; Chapl ACF Leics, Northants, and Rutland from 95. *The Vicarage, 36 Woodcote Road, Leicester LE3 2WD* Tel 0116-224 8346
E-mail ac.deegan@ntlworld.com

DEELEY, Mrs Elke Christiane. b 58. Birm Univ BA81. SWMTC 99. **d** 02 **p** 03. NSM Roche and Withiel *Truro* from 02; NSM St Columb Major w St Wenn from 09. *44 Duporth Bay, St Austell PL26 6AQ* Tel (01726) 63083
E-mail elke1@tinyonline.co.uk

DEEMING, Paul Leyland. b 44. CA Tr Coll 65 CMS Tr Coll Selly Oak 70. **d** 80 **p** 80. CMS Pakistan 71-82; R E and W Horndon w Lt Warley *Chelmsf* 83-89; V Gt Ilford St Andr 89-01; Co-ord Chapl Heatherwood and Wexham Park Hosp NHS Trust 01-09; rtd 09. *10 Glenthorn Road, Bexhill-on-Sea TN39 3QH* Tel (01424) 222287 E-mail deeming346@btinternet.com

DEENY, David Anthony. b 61. Witwatersrand Univ BA81. ERMC 03. **d** 06 **p** 07. NSM Alresford *Chelmsf* from 06. *2 Church View, Ardleigh, Colchester CO7 7TG* Tel (01206) 231335 Mobile 07890-949062 E-mail davedeeny@aol.com

DEER, Diane Antonia. b 45. SEITE 97. **d** 00 **p** 01. C Hackington *Cant* 00-04; P-in-c Pitsea w Nevendon *Chelmsf* 04-06; R 06-09; RD Basildon 07-09; P-in-c Eastry and Northbourne w Tilmanstone *Cant* from 09; AD Sandwich from 09. *The Vicarage, Brook Street, Eastry, Sandwich CT13 0HR* Tel (01304) 611323 Mobile 07957-758721
E-mail revdiane@blueyonder.co.uk

DEES, Miss Marilyn Monica (Mandy). b 34. Nottm Univ BSc55 PGCE56. WEMTC 94. **d** 96 **p** 97. NSM Fownhope w Mordiford, Brockhampton etc *Heref* from 96. *Hazelbank, 24 Nover Wood Drive, Fownhope, Hereford HR1 4PN* Tel (01432) 860369

DEETH, William Stanley. b 38. St Pet Coll Ox BA59 MA67. St Steph Ho Ox 66. **d** 68 **p** 69. C Eastbourne St Mary *Chich* 68-71; C Benwell St Jas *Newc* 71-75; C-in-c Byker St Martin CD 75-76; P-in-c Byker St Martin 76; V 76-89; P-in-c Bothal 89-91; R Bothal and Pegswood w Longhirst 91-94; rtd 94; Perm to Offic *Newc* 94-08. *2 All Saints Square, Ripon HG4 1FN* Tel (01765) 690366

DEGG, Miss Jennifer Margaret. b 39. Open Univ BA85 Rolle Coll CertEd64. NOC. **d** 06 **p** 07. NSM Saddleworth *Man* from 06. *2 Lowerfields, Dobcross, Oldham OL3 5NW*
E-mail jennydegg@onetel.com

DEHOOP, Brother Thomas Anthony. b 38. Bp's Univ Lennox BA63 LTh63. **d** 68 **p** 69. Canada 68-79; C Fort George w Painthills 68-70; I Mistassini 70-72; R La Tuque 72-75; Assoc P Pierrefonds 75-79; SSF from 79; Perm to Offic *Sarum* 79-80; Hon C Toxteth St Marg *Liv* 80-85; Chapl Newsham Gen Hosp Liv 82-85; P-in-c Cambridge St Benedict *Ely* 85-88; V 88-92; Perm to Offic *Liv* 92-94 and *Eur* from 94. *Glasshampton Monastery, Shrawley, Worcester WR6 6TQ* Tel (01299) 896345
E-mail glasshamptonssf@franciscans.org.uk

DEIGHTON, Ian Armstrong. b 19. Glas Univ MA40. Edin Th Coll 40. **d** 43 **p** 44. C Paisley H Trin *Glas* 43-45; Bp's Dom Chapl *Arg* 45-47; P-in-c Nether Lochaber 45-47; P-in-c Kinlochleven 45-47; P-in-c Glas St Mark 47-52; R Clydebank *Glas* 52-57; R Musselburgh *Edin* 57-84; P-in-c Prestonpans 76-84; rtd 84. *6 Duddingston Park South, Edinburgh EH15 3PA* Tel 0131-669 5108

DEIGHTON, William John. b 44. Plymouth Poly CQSW74. K Coll Lon AKC68 St Boniface Warminster 68. **d** 69 **p** 70. C Kenwyn *Truro* 69-72; Hon C Winterbourne *Bris* 90-04. *22 Salem Road, Winterbourne, Bristol BS36 1QF* Tel (01454) 778847

DEIMEL, Margaret Mary. b 49. CertEd71. WMMTC 91. **d** 94 **p** 95. NSM Bidford-on-Avon *Cov* 94-97; NSM Studley from 97; NSM Spernall, Morton Bagot and Oldberrow from 07; Dioc Adv on New Relig Movements from 02. *The Vicarage, 3 Manor Mews, Manor Road, Studley B80 7NA* Tel (01527) 852830
E-mail studley.vic@virgin.net

DEIMEL, Richard Witold. b 49. Lon Univ BA84. Cranmer Hall Dur 86. **d** 88 **p** 89. C Bilton *Cov* 88-93; P-in-c Studley 93-97; V from 97; P-in-c Spernall, Morton Bagot and Oldberrow from 07; RD Alcester from 08; Dioc Adv on New Relig Movements from 02. *The Vicarage, 3 Manor Mews, Manor Road, Studley B80 7NA* Tel (01527) 852830 E-mail studley.vic@virgin.net

del RIO, Michael Paul Juan. b 73. Univ of Wales (Cardiff) BScEcon94 PGCE00. Oak Hill Th Coll MTh05. **d** 05 **p** 06. NSM Ealing St Mary *Lon* from 05. *12 St Mary's House, Church Gardens, London W5 4HL* Tel (020) 8840 2208
E-mail michael@didasko.org.uk

DELAFORCE, Stephen Robert. b 52. Middx Poly BSc80 Cranfield Inst of Tech MSc88 Nottm Univ MA03 CEng MIMechE83. EMMTC 04. **d** 07 **p** 08. NSM Woodhouse, Woodhouse Eaves and Swithland *Leic* from 07. *10 Silverbirch Way, Loughborough LE11 2DH* Tel (01509) 240496
E-mail steve.delaforce@googlemail.com

DELAMERE, Allen Stephen. BTh. **d** 90 **p** 91. C Bangor Abbey *D & D* 90-93; I Saintfield 93-03; P-in-c Cumbernauld *Glas* 05-07; I Killinchy w Kilmood and Tullynakill *D & D* from 07. *Killinchy Rectory, 11 Whiterock Road, Killinchy, Newtownards BT23 6PR* E-mail allen@sonow.com

DELAMERE, Isaac George. b 71. CITC BTh02. **d** 02 **p** 03. C Newtownards *D & D* 02-05; I Narraghmore and Timolin w Castledermot etc *D & G* from 05. *The Rectory, Timolin, Co Kildare, Republic of Ireland* Tel (00353) (59) 862 4278
E-mail delamereisaac@hotmail.com

DELANEY, Anthony. b 65. St Jo Coll Nottm BTh95. **d** 95 **p** 96. C Cullompton *Ex* 95-98; C Maidstone St Luke *Cant* 98-01; P-in-c W Horsley *Guildf* 01-03; R 03-08; Perm to Offic *Man* from 09. *97 Barlow Moor Road, Didsbury, Manchester M20 2GP* Tel 07881-902966 (mobile) E-mail antdel@tiscali.co.uk

DELANEY, Janet. b 50. STETS. **d** 07 **p** 08. C Wootton Bassett *Sarum* from 07. *2 Swallows Mead, Wootton Bassett, Swindon SN4 8QA* Tel (01793) 855158 E-mail reverendjan@tiscali.co.uk

DELANEY, The Ven Peter Anthony. b 39. MBE01. AKC65. **d** 66 **p** 67. C St Marylebone w H Trin *Lon* 66-70; Chapl Nat Heart Hosp Lon 66-70; Res Chapl Univ Ch Ch the K 70-73; Can Res and Prec S'wark Cathl 73-77; V All Hallows by the Tower etc *Lon* 77-04; P-in-c St Kath Cree 98-02; Can Cyprus and the Gulf from 88; Preb St Paul's Cathl 95-99; Adn Lon 99-09; P-in-c St Steph Walbrook and St Swithun etc from 04. *29 Portland Square, London E1W 2QR* Tel 07887 741786

DELANY, Michael Edward. b 34. Lon Univ BSc55 PhD58. S'wark Ord Course 80. **d** 83 **p** 84. NSM Hampton St Mary *Lon* 83-87; R Copythorne and Minstead *Win* 87-94; rtd 94; Perm to Offic *Win* 94-00. *Littlecott, Tytherley Road, Winterslow, Salisbury SP5 1PZ* Tel (01980) 862183

DELFGOU, John. b 35. Oak Hill Th Coll 81. **d** 84 **p** 85. NSM Loughton St Mary and St Mich *Chelmsf* 84-90; NSM Loughton St Jo 90-93; C 93-94; TV 94-00; Perm to Offic *Chelmsf* from 01. *20 Carroll Hill, Loughton IG10 1NN* Tel (020) 8508 6333 E-mail john@delfgou.freeserve.co.uk

DELFGOU, Jonathan Hawke. b 63. Aston Tr Scheme 89 Linc Th Coll BTh94. **d** 94 **p** 95. C Greenstead *Chelmsf* 94-98; TV Wickford and Runwell from 98; Chapl Southend Community Care Services NHS Trust 98-99; Chapl S Essex Mental Health & Community Care NHS Trust from 00. *St Mary's Vicarage, Church End Lane, Runwell, Wickford SS11 7JQ* Tel (01268) 732068

DELIGHT, The Ven John David. b 25. Liv Univ CSocSc48 Open Univ BA75. Oak Hill Th Coll 49. **d** 52 **p** 53. C Tooting Graveney St Nic *S'wark* 52-55; C Wallington 55-58; Lic to Offic *Man*

58-61; Travelling Sec IVF 58-61; C-in-c Leic St Chris CD 61-68; Chapl HM Pris Leic 64-67; V Leic St Chris 68-69; R Aldridge *Lich* 69-82; Preb Lich Cathl 80-90; RD Walsall 81-82; Adn Stoke 82-90; Dir Th Educn Machakos Kenya 90-94; Hon Can Machakos 90-94; Perm to Offic *Lich* 99-04 and *Ches* from 99. *Karibuni, 17 Hillside Drive, Macclesfield SK10 2PL* Tel (01625) 428117

DELINGER, Ian Michael. b 70. Truman State Univ (USA) BSc92 SS Coll Cam BTh04. Westcott Ho Cam 01. **d** 04 **p** 05. C Chorlton-cum-Hardy St Clem *Man* 04-07; Chapl Ches Univ from 08. *University of Chester, Warrington Campus, Crab Lane, Warrington WA2 0DB* Tel (01925) 534361
E-mail i.delinger@chester.ac.uk

DELL, Murray John. b 31. Cape Town Univ BA51 BSc54 Edin Univ MB, ChB59. Westcott Ho Cam 63. **d** 65 **p** 65. C Kloof S Africa 65-70; Dean Windhoek 71-80; V Lyme Regis *Sarum* 80-96; Chapl Lyme Regis Hosp 80-96; rtd 96. *2 Charles House, Ward Royal, Windsor SL4 1SR* Tel (01753) 832424

DELMEGE, Andrew Mark. b 68. Essex Univ BA91 Southn Univ MTh98. SWMTC 94. **d** 97 **p** 98. C Kings Heath *Birm* 97-01; V Brandwood from 01; Chapl to Deaf People from 01. *The Vicarage, 77 Doversley Road, Birmingham B14 6NN* Tel 0121-693 0217, 246 6100 *or* 456 1535 Fax 246 6125
E-mail andydelmege@blueyonder.co.uk

DELVE, Eric David. b 42. Trin Coll Bris. **d** 89 **p** 90. NSM Bris St Matt and St Nath 89-92; P-in-c Kirkdale St Lawr *Liv* 93-96; V Maidstone St Luke *Cant* from 96; AD Maidstone 99-03; Six Preacher Cant Cathl from 99. *The Vicarage, 24 Park Avenue, Maidstone ME14 5HN* Tel (01622) 754856
E-mail ericdelve@stlukes.org.uk

DELVES, Canon Anthony James. b 47. Birm Univ BSocSc70 Hull Univ PhD94. St Steph Ho Ox 83. **d** 85 **p** 86. C Cantley *Sheff* 85-90; V Goldthorpe w Hickleton 90-07; Hon Can Sheff Cathl 98-07; AD Wath 00-06; rtd 07; Perm to Offic *Sheff* and *Wakef* from 07. *4 Balmoral Street, Hebden Bridge HX7 8BJ* Tel (01422) 843948 E-mail ajd@delwood.plus.com

DELVES (formerly MANHOOD), Canon Phyllis. b 32. Aston Tr Scheme 78 Qu Coll Birm 79. **dss** 82 **d** 87 **p** 94. Harwich *Chelmsf* 82-83; Dovercourt and Parkeston 83-85; Fawley *Win* 85-87; Par Dn 87-92; P-in-c Bournemouth St Aug 92-99; Hon Can Win Cathl 96-99; rtd 99; Perm to Offic *Win* from 01. *11 Rhyme Hall Mews, Fawley, Southampton SO45 1FX* Tel (023) 8089 4450

DELVES BROUGHTON, Simon Brian Hugo. b 33. Ex Coll Ox BA56 MA64. Kelham Th Coll 56. **d** 59 **p** 60. Ox Miss to Calcutta 60-64; C Skirbeck St Nic *Linc* 64-67; E Pakistan/Bangladesh 67-74; Chapl Chittagong 67-69; V St Thos Cathl Dhaka 69-74; V Northampton Ch Ch *Pet* 74-95; Chapl Northn Gen Hosp 77-87; rtd 95; Perm to Offic *Ox* 95-00. *71A Observatory Street, Oxford OX2 6EP* Tel (01865) 515463

DEMERY, Rupert Edward Rodier. b 72. Trin Hall Cam BA94 MA01 BTh01. Ridley Hall Cam 98. **d** 01 **p** 02. C New Borough and Leigh *Sarum* 01-05; Lower Chapl Eton Coll from 05. *Top Flat, Corner House, Eton College, Windsor SL4 6DB* Tel (01753) 441629 Mobile 07801-825671
E-mail r.demery@etoncollege.org.uk

DEMPSTER, Adrian. b 49. Newc Univ BSc70. EMMTC 05. **d** 08 **p** 09. NSM Kirkby in Ashfield *S'well* from 08. *105 Nottingham Road, Selston, Nottingham NG16 6BU* Tel (01773) 811846 Fax 0115-950 4646 Mobile 07971-142829
E-mail adrian@dempstera.freeserve.co.uk

den HAAN, Peter Albert Percy. b 67. Wycliffe Hall Ox BA07. **d** 08 **p** 09. C Bedworth *Cov* from 08. *132 Heath Road, Bedworth CV12 0BH* Tel (024) 7664 4663 E-mail peter@denhaan.co.uk

DENBY, Canon Paul. b 47. NW Ord Course 73. **d** 76 **p** 77. C Stretford All SS *Man* 76-80; V Stalybridge 80-87; Chapl Tameside Distr Gen Hosp Ashton-under-Lyne 82-87; Dir of Ords *Man* 87-95; LNSM Officer 91-95; Hon Can Man Cathl 92-95; Bp's Dom Chapl 94-95; Can Admin and Prec Man Cathl 95-07; rtd 07; Perm to Offic *Man* from 07. *14 Cranberry Drive, Bolton BL3 3TB* Tel (01204) 655157
E-mail paul@denby94.wanadoo.co.uk

DENCH, Christopher David. b 62. RGN83. Aston Tr Scheme 86 Sarum & Wells Th Coll 88. **d** 91 **p** 92. C Crayford *Roch* 91-94; P-in-c Leybourne 94-98; R 98-05; Dioc Lay Tr Adv 01-05; Tr Officer for CME from 03; Min Development Officer from 05. *340 New Hythe Lane, Larkfield, Aylesford ME20 6RZ* Tel (01732) 220245 E-mail chris.dench@rochester.anglican.org

DENERLEY, John Keith Christopher. b 34. Qu Coll Ox BA58 MA61. St Steph Ho Ox 58. **d** 61 **p** 62. C Airedale w Fryston *Wakef* 61-64; Chapl Sarum Th Coll 64-68; Min Can Cov Cathl 68-76; Chapl Lanchester Poly 70-76; Chapl The Dorothy Kerin Trust Burrswood 76-85; V Trellech and Cwmcarvan *Mon* 85-87; V Penallt 85-87; V Penallt and Trellech 87-99; Chapl Ty Mawr Convent (Wales) 85-90; RD Monmouth 93-99; rtd 99; Perm to Offic *Glouc* from 00. *1 The Pales, English Bicknor, Coleford GL16 7PQ* Tel (01594) 860028

DENFORD, Keith Wilkie. b 35. AKC62. **d** 63 **p** 64. C Gunnersbury St Jas *Lon* 63-66; C Brighton St Pet *Chich* 66-71; Min Can Cant Cathl 71-75; R W Tarring *Chich* 75-85; V Burgess

Hill St Jo 85-90; R Pulborough 90-96; rtd 96; Perm to Offic *Chich* from 96. *31 John Street, Shoreham-by-Sea BN43 5DL* Tel (01273) 464251

DENGATE, Richard Henry. b 39. Cant Sch of Min 82. **d** 85 **p** 86. NSM Wittersham w Stone-in-Oxney and Ebony *Cant* 85; R Sandhurst w Newenden 90-01; rtd 01; Perm to Offic *Cant* from 01. *Apuldram, Main Street, Peasemarsh, Rye TN31 6UL* Tel (01797) 230980

DENHAM, Anthony Christopher. b 43. Keble Coll Ox BA65 MA70. Oak Hill Th Coll 91. **d** 93 **p** 94. C Hythe *Cant* 93-97; V Haddenham w Cuddington, Kingsey etc *Ox* 97-08; rtd 08; Perm to Offic *Guildf* from 08. *3 The Larches, Woking GU21 4RE* Tel (01483) 823310 E-mail a.chris.denham@googlemail.com

DENHAM, Nicholas Philip. b 50. Salford Univ BSc72 Birm Univ CertEd74. Wycliffe Hall Ox 87. **d** 89 **p** 90. C Bishopwearmouth St Gabr *Dur* 89-90; C Chester le Street 90-92; TV Rushden w Newton Bromswold *Pet* 92-95; R Teigh w Whissendine and Market Overton 95-02; P-in-c Thistleton 01-02; RD Rutland 01-02; TR Bedworth *Cov* 02-05; V Escomb *Dur* 05-08; R Etherley 05-08; V Witton Park 05-08; V Hamsterley and Witton-le-Wear 05-08; rtd 08. *13 Yarnton Court, Kidlington OX5 1AU* Tel (01865) 370294 E-mail nickden@btinternet.com

DENHOLM, Robert Jack. b 31. Edin Th Coll 53. **d** 56 **p** 57. C Dundee St Mary Magd *Bre* 56-59; C Edin St Pet 59-61; R Bridge of Allan *St And* 61-69; Chapl Stirling Univ 67-69; R N Berwick *Edin* 69-80; R Gullane 76-80; R Edin St Mark 80-90; Can St Mary's Cathl 88-90; rtd 90. *15 Silverknowes, Midway, Edinburgh EH4 5PP* Tel 0131-312 6462 E-mail jackdenholm@blueyonder.co.uk

DENIS LE SEVE, Hilary. *See* LE SEVE, Mrs Jane Hilary

DENISON, Canon Keith Malcolm. b 45. Down Coll Cam BA67 MA71 PhD70. Westcott Ho Cam 70. **d** 71 **p** 72. C Chepstow *Mon* 71-72; C Bassaleg 72-75; Post-Ord Tr Officer 75-85; V Mathern and Mounton 75-80; V Mathern and Mounton w St Pierre 80-85; RD Chepstow 82-85; V Risca 85-91; V Goldcliffe and Whitson and Nash 91-96; Dioc Dir of Educn from 91; Hon Can St Woolos Cathl 91-94; Can from 94; Can Res from 96. *Canon's House, Stow Hill, Newport NP20 4EA* Tel (01633) 264919

DENISON, Philip. b 55. York Univ BA77 CertEd. St Jo Coll Nottm 83. **d** 86 **p** 87. C Barnoldswick w Bracewell *Bradf* 86-88; P-in-c Basford St Leodegarius *S'well* 88-91; C Basford w Hyson Green 91-94; V Nether Stowey w Over Stowey *B & W* 94-04; R Aisholt, Enmore, Goathurst, Nether Stowey etc 05; RD Quantock 01-05; Perm to Offic from 06. *15 Sylvan Way, Monkton Heathfield, Taunton TA2 8PH* Tel (01823) 410021 E-mail denisonphil@hotmail.com

DENLEY, Trevor Maurice. b 47. **d** 06 **p** 07. OLM Bristol St Aid w St Geo from 06. *31 Dundridge Gardens, Bristol BS5 8SZ* Tel 0117-961 4468 Mobile 07960-329127

DENMAN, Frederick George. b 46. Chich Th Coll 67. **d** 70 **p** 71. C Stafford St Mary *Lich* 70-72; C Ascot Heath *Ox* 72-75; P-in-c Culham 75-77; P-in-c Sutton Courtenay w Appleford 75-77; TV Dorchester 78-81; Chapl Henley Memorial Hosp 81-82; P-in-c W Hill *Ex* 82; TV Ottery St Mary, Alfington and W Hill 82-87; V Sparkwell from 87; V Shaugh Prior 87-93; P-in-c Cornwood from 98. *The Vicarage, Sparkwell, Plymouth PL7 5DR* Tel (01752) 837218 E-mail freddie@sparkwell.fsnet.com

DENNEN, The Ven Lyle. b 42. Harvard Univ LLB67 Trin Coll Cam BA70 MA75. Cuddesdon Coll 70. **d** 72 **p** 73. C S Lambeth St Ann *S'wark* 72-75; C Richmond St Mary 75-78; P-in-c Kennington St Jo 78-79; V Kennington St Jo w St Jas 79-99; P-in-c Brixton Road Ch Ch 81-89; RD Brixton 90-99; Hon Can S'wark Cathl 99; Adn Hackney *Lon* from 99; V St Andr Holborn from 99. *St Andrew's Vicarage, 5 St Andrew's Street, London EC4A 3AB* Tel (020) 7353 3544 Fax 7583 2750 E-mail archdeacon.hackney@london.anglican.org

DENNER-BROWN, Mrs Sarah. ERMC. **d** 08 **p** 09. NSM Welford w Sibbertoft and Marston Trussell *Pet* from 08. *15 Wards Lane, Yelvertoft, Northampton NN6 6LY* Tel (01788) 823052

DENNESS, Mrs Linda Christine. b 51. Portsm Dioc Tr Course 88. **d** 89 **p** 01. NSM Milton *Portsm* 89-93; Chapl Asst Portsm Hosps NHS Trust 89-91; NSM Portsea St Mary *Portsm* 93-96; NSM Wymering 96-06; P-in-c Cosham 06-09; P-in-c Wymering 07-09; Perm to Offic from 09. *19 Fourth Avenue, Cosham, Portsmouth PO6 3HX* Tel (023) 9232 6885 E-mail linda@denness.wanadoo.co.uk

DENNETT, John Edward. b 36. Tyndale Hall Bris 66. **d** 68 **p** 69. C Chell *Lich* 68-71; C Bispham *Blackb* 71-73; C Cheltenham Ch Ch *Glouc* 73-75; V Coppull *Blackb* 75-79; P-in-c Parkham, Alwington and Buckland Brewer *Ex* 79-80; R 80-84; V Blackpool St Thos *Blackb* 84-92; rtd 92; Chapl Trin Hospice in the Fylde from 88; Perm to Offic *Blackb* from 92. *37 Village Way, Bispham, Blackpool FY2 0AH* Tel (01253) 358039 E-mail johned.dennett@virgin.net

DENNIS, Mrs Barbara Christine. b 56. NTMTC 94. **d** 97 **p** 98. NSM Romford St Edw *Chelmsf* 97-01; C from 01. *4 Oaklands Avenue, Romford RM1 4DB* Tel (01708) 739676

DENNIS, David Alan. b 46. St Luke's Coll Ex BSc90. **d** 05 **p** 06. OLM Alderholt *Sarum* from 05. *18 Oak Road, Alderholt, Fordingbridge SP6 3BL* Tel (01425) 655230 E-mail david@dennisd.fsnet.co.uk

DENNIS, Miss Drucilla Lyn. b 49. Culham Coll of Educn BEd71 Southn Univ MA82. S Dios Minl Tr Scheme 92. **d** 95 **p** 96. NSM Cowes H Trin and St Mary *Portsm* 95-01; TV Dorchester *Sarum* 01-08; Hon C Brighstone and Brooke w Mottistone *Portsm* from 08; Hon C Shorwell w Kingston from 08; Hon C Chale from 08; Chapl Isle of Wight NHS Primary Care Trust from 09. *The Vicarage, 5 Northcourt Close, Newport PO30 3LD* Tel (01983) 740522 E-mail d.dennis2008@btinternet.com

✠**DENNIS, The Rt Revd John.** b 31. St Cath Coll Cam BA54 MA59. Cuddesdon Coll 54. **d** 56 **p** 57 **c** 79. C Armley St Bart *Ripon* 56-60; C Kettering SS Pet and Paul 60-62; V Is of Dogs Ch Ch and St Jo w St Luke *Lon* 62-71; V Mill Hill Jo Keble Ch 71-79; RD W Barnet 73-79; Preb St Paul's Cathl 77-79; Suff Bp Knaresborough *Ripon* 79-86; Dioc Dir of Ords 80-86; Bp St E 86-96; rtd 96; Perm to Offic *St E* from 96; Hon Asst Bp Win from 99. *7 Conifer Close, Winchester SO22 6SH* Tel (01962) 868881 E-mail johndor_dennis@onetel.com

DENNIS, Keith Aubrey Lawrence. b 55. City of Lon Poly BA79. Cranmer Hall Dur 88. **d** 90 **p** 91. C Bushbury *Lich* 90-94; P-in-c Newcastle St Geo 94-99; TV Kirby Muxloe *Leic* 99-03; C Ashby-de-la-Zouch St Helen w Coleorton 03; C Breedon cum Isley Walton and Worthington 03; Chapl HM Pris Glouc from 04. *The Chaplaincy, HM Prison Gloucester, Barrack Square, Gloucester GL1 2JN* Tel (01452) 529551

DENNIS, Robert Franklin. b 51. St Paul's Coll Grahamstown 91. **d** 94 **p** 94. C Kuils River S Africa 94-96; C Matroosfontein 96-99; R Maitland 99-03; TR Bredasdorp 03-05; P-in-c Crumpsall *Man* 06-09; Min Can St Woolos Cathl from 09. *Hebron, 9 Clifton Road, Newport NP20 4EW* Tel (01633) 267191 E-mail r.dennis70@ntlworld.com

DENNIS, Canon Trevor John. b 45. St Jo Coll Cam BA68 MA71 PhD74. Westcott Ho Cam 71. **d** 72 **p** 73. C Newport Pagnell *Ox* 72-74; Chapl Eton Coll 75-82; Tutor Sarum & Wells Th Coll 82-94; Vice-Prin 89-94; Can Res Ches Cathl from 94. *13 Abbey Street, Chester CH1 2JF* Tel (01244) 314408 E-mail dennis@chestercathedral.com

DENNISON, Philip Ian. b 52. Nottm Univ BTh81. St Jo Coll Nottm 77. **d** 81 **p** 82. C Stalybridge H Trin and Ch Ch *Ches* 81-84; C Heswall 84-91; TV Bushbury *Lich* 91-04; V Shevington *Blackb* from 04. *St Anne's Vicarage, Gathurst Lane, Shevington, Wigan WN6 8HW* Tel (01257) 252136 E-mail revd.pidennison@tinyworld.co.uk

DENNISS, Mrs Amanda Jane. b 57. Univ Coll Lon LLB78. Oak Hill Th Coll 98 NTMTC 00. **d** 03 **p** 04. C Turnham Green Ch Ch *Lon* 03-06; Perm to Offic 06-08; C Westwood *Cov* from 08. *2 Follis Walk, Coventry CV4 8HP* Tel (024) 7646 1353 E-mail amandadenniss@aol.com

DENNISTON, James Keith Stuart. b 49. Barrister-at-Law 70 Down Coll Cam MA70. Oak Hill Th Coll DipEd92. **d** 93 **p** 94. C Harborne Heath *Birm* 93-97; Chapl Lee Abbey 97-02; Perm to Offic *Ex* 02-03; TV Chippenham St Paul w Hardenhuish etc *Bris* 03-07. *Orchard Cottage, Alswear, South Molton EX36 4LH* Tel (01769) 550600 E-mail james@lanhill.wanadoo.co.uk

DENNISTON, Robin Alastair. b 26. Ch Ch Ox MA48 Edin Univ MSc92 Univ Coll Lon PhD96. **d** 78 **p** 79. NSM Clifton upon Teme *Worc* 78-81; NSM Clifton-on-Teme, Lower Sapey and the Shelsleys 81-85; NSM S Hinksey *Ox* 85-87; NSM Gt w Lt Tew 87-90; NSM Aberdour *St And* 90-94; NSM W Fife Team Min 90-94; NSM St Marylebone St Mark Hamilton Terrace *Lon* 94-95; P-in-c Gt w Lt Tew and Over w Nether Worton *Ox* 95-02; rtd 02. *112 Randolph Avenue, London W9 1PQ* Tel (020) 7286 0880

DENNO, Basil. b 52. Dundee Univ BSc74, Oak Hill Th Coll BA81. **d** 81 **p** 83. C Chaddesden St Mary *Derby* 81-83; Hon C 83-84. *21 Parkside Road, Chaddesden, Derby DE21 6QR* Tel (01332) 672687

DENNO, Elizabeth (Skye). b 79. Derby Univ BA00. St Jo Coll Nottm BA08. **d** 08 **p** 09. C Dursley *Glouc* from 08. *1 Riversmill Walk, Dursley GL11 5GL* Tel (01453) 542404 Mobile 07720-768684 E-mail jaskso@yahoo.co.uk

DENNY, John Peter Sekeford. b 43. RIBA69. Chich Th Coll 90. **d** 91 **p** 92. C Aylmerton w Runton *Nor* 91-95; P-in-c Barney, Fulmodeston w Croxton, Hindringham etc 95-96; R 96-98; rtd 98; Perm to Offic *Truro* 98-04 and *Nor* 04-06. *Little Folly, Mutton Dingle, New Radnor, Presteigne LD8 2TL* Tel (01544) 350568

DENNY, Lorne Robert. b 58. Pemb Coll Ox MA84 Lon Inst of Educn PGCE84. SAOMC 98. **d** 01 **p** 02. NSM Ox St Barn and St Paul 01-04; NSM Cowley St Jo 04-07; P-in-c Milton next Sittingbourne *Cant* from 07. *The Vicarage, Vicarage Road, Sittingbourne ME10 2BL* Tel (01795) 472016

DENNY, Michael Thomas. b 47. Kelham Th Coll 68 St Jo Coll Nottm 71. **d** 73 **p** 74. C Gospel Lane St Mich *Birm* 73-77; P-in-c Frankley 77-82; R 82-07; rtd 07; Perm to Offic *Birm* from 07. *Orchard Cottage, Green Lane, Yarpole, Leominster HR6 0BE* Tel (01568) 780874 E-mail michael@revdenny1.freeserve.co.uk

DENNY, Peter Bond. b 17. Lon Univ BA41. Bps' Coll Cheshunt 41. **d** 43 **p** 44. C Bushey Heath *St Alb* 43-45; C Calstock *Truro* 52-56; V Newlyn St Newlyn 56-83; RD Pydar 61-64 and 74-81; rtd 83; Perm to Offic *Truro* from 83. *Tralee, The Crescent, Truro TR1 3ES* Tel (01872) 274492

DENT, Canon Christopher Mattinson. b 46. K Coll Lon BA68 AKC68 MTh69 Jes Coll Cam BA72 MA76 New Coll Ox MA76 DPhil80. Westcott Ho Cam 70. **d** 72 **p** 73. C Chelsea St Luke *Lon* 72-76; Asst Chapl New Coll Ox 76-79; Fell Chapl and Dean Div 79-84; V Hollingbourne and Hucking w Leeds and Broomfield *Cant* 84-93; V Bedford St Andr *St Alb* from 93; Hon Can St Alb from 01; RD Bedford from 05. *St Andrew's Vicarage, 1 St Edmond Road, Bedford MK40 2NQ* Tel (01234) 354234 *or* 216881 E-mail dent@tinyworld.co.uk

DENT, Joseph Michael. b 73. Jes Coll Cam BA94. Wycliffe Hall Ox 96. **d** 99 **p** 00. C Plymouth St Andr and Stonehouse *Ex* 99-03; Hon C Sevenoaks St Nic *Roch* from 03. *6 Sackville Close, Sevenoaks TN13 3QD* Tel (01732) 779140
E-mail joe.dent@diocese-rochester.org

DENT, Marie Penelope. b 46. K Coll Lon BA88. Westcott Ho Cam 02. **d** 04 **p** 05. C N Walsham and Edingthorpe *Nor* 04-08; TV Redditch H Trin *Worc* from 08. *The Vicarage, St Georges Road, Redditch B98 8EE* Tel (01527) 585446 Mobile 07799-220357 E-mail aviationresearch@tiscali.com

DENT, Michael Leslie. b 54. Leeds Univ BEd76. St Steph Ho Ox 93. **d** 95 **p** 96. C Cockerton *Dur* 95-98; V Escomb 98-03; R Etherley 98-03; V Witton Park 98-03; Chapl Dur Constabulary 02-03; TR E Darlington from 03. *30 Smithfield Road, Darlington DL1 4DD* Tel (01325) 244430

DENT, Raymond William. b 47. TD03. Open Univ BA84 Birm Coll of Educn CertEd68. Ridley Hall Cam 70. **d** 73 **p** 74. C Hyde St Geo *Ches* 73-76; C Eastham 76-79; TV E Runcorn w Halton 79-80; V Hallwood 80-83; V New Brighton Em 83-94; V Willaston from 94. *The Vicarage, 13 Hooton Road, Willaston, Neston CH64 1SE* Tel 0151-327 4737
E-mail raymond@raydent.freeserve.co.uk

DENT, Richard William. b 32. Down Coll Cam BA56 MA LLB59. Bris Sch of Min 73. **d** 77 **p** 78. NSM Southmead *Bris* 77-81; NSM Henleaze 81-85; V Highworth w Sevenhampton and Inglesham etc 85-88; TV Oldland 88-91; V Longwell Green 91-93; C Bedminster St Mich 93-94; C 94-97; Chapl Asst Frenchay Healthcare NHS Trust Bris 94-97; rtd 97; Perm to Offic *Bris* from 99 and *B & W* 03-06. *1 Bakers Buildings, Wrington, Bristol BS40 5LQ* Tel (01934) 861070

DENTON, Peter Brian. b 37. Kelham Th Coll 57. **d** 62 **p** 63. C Ellesmere Port *Ches* 62-66; Chapl HM Borstal Hollesley Bay 66-69; CF 69-90; Warden Bridge Cen 90-04; C Hounslow H Trin w St Paul *Lon* 90-92; V Northolt Park St Barn 92-94; P-in-c Perivale 97; P-in-c N Greenford All Hallows 00-04; rtd 04; Perm to Offic *Ely* and *Pet* from 05. *52 Lornas Field, Hampton Hargate, Peterborough PE7 8AY* Tel (01733) 552353
E-mail revddenton@aol.com

DENTON, Peter Charles. St Jo Coll Dur BA52. Oak Hill Th Coll 49. **d** 52 **p** 53. C Ushaw Moor *Dur* 52-54; C-in-c Throckley St Mary CD *Newc* 54-58; V Long Horsley 58-67; Lect City of Newc Coll of Educn 67-75; Sen Lect Newc Poly 75-90; rtd 90. *Avalon, High Street, Low Pittington, Durham DH6 1BE* Tel 0191-372 2494

DENYER, Alan Frederick. b 31. Wycliffe Hall Ox 80. **d** 82 **p** 83. C Rodbourne Cheney *Bris* 82-84; P-in-c Garsdon w Lea and Cleverton 84-87; R Garsdon, Lea and Cleverton and Charlton 87-91; R Lydbury N w Hopesay and Edgton *Heref* 91-97; Asst Dioc Soc Resp Officer 91-97; rtd 97; Hon C Long Preston w Tosside *Bradf* 97-02; Perm to Offic *Ripon* from 03. *25 Lupton Close, Glasshouses, Harrogate HG3 5QX* Tel (01423) 712307

DENYER, Canon Paul Hugh. b 46. Lon Univ BA68. Ripon Coll Cuddesdon 74. **d** 77 **p** 78. C Horfield H Trin *Bris* 77-82; TV Yate New Town 82-88; V Bris Lockleaze St Mary Magd w St Fran 88-95; Dioc Dir of Ords 95-02; Hon Can Bris Cathl from 99; R Warmley, Syston and Bitton from 02. *The Rectory, Church Avenue, Warmley, Bristol BS30 5JJ* Tel 0117-967 3965
E-mail paul@denyer03.freeserve.co.uk

DENYER, Samuel. b 74. Ripon Coll Cuddesdon 07. **d** 09. C Lostwithiel, St Winnow w St Nectan's Chpl etc *Truro* from 09; C Lanreath, Pelynt and Bradoc from 09; C Lanlivery from 09. *Woodpeckers, Cott Road, Lostwithiel PL22 0EU* Tel (01208) 871619 Mobile 07827-013808

DENZIL, Sister. *See* ONSLOW, Sister Denzil Octavia

DEO, Paul. b 60. Coll of Ripon & York St Jo CertEd81. St Jo Coll Nottm 95. **d** 97 **p** 98. C Tong *Bradf* 97-00; P-in-c Laisterdyke 00-02; V 02-07; C Baildon from 07. *93 Hoyle Court Road, Baildon, Shipley BD17 6EL* Tel (01274) 661449
E-mail paul.deo@bradford.anglican.org
or pauldeo@blueyonder.co.uk

DERBY, Archdeacon of. *See* CUNLIFFE, The Ven Christopher John

DERBY, Bishop of. *See* REDFERN, The Rt Revd Alastair Llewellyn John

DERBY, Dean of. *See* CUTTELL, The Very Revd Jeffrey Charles

DERBYSHIRE, Mrs Anne Margaret. b 31. Open Univ BA87 Lon Univ CertEd75. SW Minl Tr Course. **dss** 84 **d** 87 **p** 01. NSM Tiverton St Pet *Ex* 87-90; Perm to Offic 90-01 and 02-04; NSM Washfield, Stoodleigh, Withleigh etc 01-02. *6 Devenish Close, Weymouth DT4 8RU* Tel (01305) 750909

DERBYSHIRE, Douglas James. b 26. **d** 81 **p** 82. NSM Heald Green St Cath *Ches* 81-86; NSM Stockport St Geo 86-89; C 89-91; rtd 91; Perm to Offic *Man* 92-95 and 00-06; *Ches* from 92. *91 East Avenue, Heald Green, Cheadle SK8 3BR* Tel 0161-437 3748

DERBYSHIRE, Philip Damien. b 50. Leic Poly LLB71. Sarum & Wells Th Coll 80. **d** 82 **p** 83. C Chatham St Wm *Roch* 82-86; R Melfort Zimbabwe 86-88; TV Burnham w Dropmore, Hitcham and Taplow *Ox* 88-92; Chapl HM Pris Reading 92-97; Chapl HM Pris Holloway 97-00; Chapl HM Pris Bullingdon 00-04; C Buckingham *Ox* from 04. *The Rectory, Chapel Lane, Thornborough, Buckingham MK18 2DJ* Tel (01280) 812515
E-mail joydotphil@aol.com

DERHAM, Miss Hilary Kathlyn. b 50. Nottm Univ BPharm71 MRPharmS71. Chich Th Coll 89. **d** 91 **p** 95. Par Dn Stevenage H Trin *St Alb* 91-94; C 94-98; P-in-c London Colney St Pet 98-03; rtd 03; Perm to Offic *St Alb* from 03. *39 Brecken Close, St Albans AL4 9LF* Tel (01727) 842089
E-mail h.derham@btopenworld.com

DEROSAIRE, Leslie John. b 50. Univ of Wales BA85 Univ of Wales Coll Newport MA03. St Mich Coll Llan 01. **d** 04 **p** 05. NSM Govilon w Llanfoist w Llanelen *Mon* 04-07; NSM Llanddewi Rhydderch w Llangattock-juxta-Usk etc 07-09; P-in-c from 09. *Elmgrove, Hereford Road, Mardy, Abergavenny NP7 6HU* Tel (01873) 857256 E-mail derosaire@tiscali.co.uk

DEROY-JONES, Philip Antony (Tony). b 49. St Mich Coll Llan 92. **d** 92 **p** 93. C Neath w Llantwit 92-95; V Caerau St Cynfelin 95-98; V Pontlottyn w Fochriw from 98. *The Vicarage, Picton Street, Pontlottyn, Bargoed CF81 9PS* Tel and fax (01685) 841322 E-mail tony@deroy-jones.freeserve.co.uk

DERRICK, David John. b 46. S'wark Ord Course. **d** 84 **p** 85. NSM Angell Town St Jo *S'wark* 84-98; NSM St Mary le Strand w St Clem Danes *Lon* 86-93. *Weavers Cottage, 8 Bellvue Place, London E1 4UG* Tel (020) 7791 2943

DERRICK, Mrs Dorothy Margaret. b 41. St Mary's Coll Chelt CertEd63. Ox Min Course 89. **d** 92 **p** 94. NSM Gt Missenden w Ballinger and Lt Hampden *Ox* 92-98; P-in-c Drayton St Pet (Berks) 98-04; rtd 04. *33 Parkland Avenue, Carlisle CA1 3GN* Tel (01228) 593159 E-mail dorothyderrick@aol.com

DERRIMAN, Canon Graham Scott. b 39. Bps' Coll Cheshunt 63. **d** 66 **p** 67. C Wandsworth St Mich *S'wark* 66-70; C Merton St Mary 70-74; P-in-c Earlsfield St Andr 74-79; V 79-81; V Camberwell St Luke 81-90; V Croydon St Aug 90-04; Voc Adv Croydon Adnry 93-04; RD Croydon Cen 95-04; Hon Can S'wark Cathl 01-04; rtd 04; Perm to Offic *S'wark* from 05. *15 Goodwood Close, Morden SM4 5AW* Tel (020) 8648 1550 E-mail g.derriman@btinternet.com

DERRY AND RAPHOE, Bishop of. *See* GOOD, The Rt Revd Kenneth Raymond

DERRY, Archdeacon of. *See* McLEAN, The Ven Donald Stewart

DERRY, Dean of. *See* MORTON, The Very Revd William Wright

DESERT, Thomas Denis. b 31. Bps' Coll Cheshunt 54. **d** 56 **p** 57. C Goldington *St Alb* 56-60; C-in-c Luton St Hugh Lewsey CD 60-63; C St Alb St Sav 63-65; C Cheshunt 65-68; V Bedford All SS 68-89; R Northill w Moggerhanger 89-96; rtd 96; Perm to Offic *St Alb* from 96. *2 Phillpotts Avenue, Bedford MK40 3UJ* Tel (01234) 211413 E-mail denisdesert@ntlworld.com

DESHPANDE, Lakshmi Anant. *See* JEFFREYS, Mrs Lakshmi Anant

DESICS, Robert Anthony. b 77. Bp Grosseteste Coll BA99 Open Univ MA00. St Jo Coll Nottm 99. **d** 01 **p** 02. C Potters Bar *St Alb* 01-04; C Rainham w Wennington *Chelmsf* 04-05; V Hemlington *York* from 05. *St Timothy's House, 31 Coatham Close, Hemlington, Middlesbrough TS8 9JW* Tel (01642) 590496

DESMOND, Mrs Margaret Elspeth. b 49. S Dios Minl Tr Scheme 90. **d** 93 **p** 95. NSM Filton *Bris* from 93; Asst Chapl HM Pris Bris 98-09. *14 Kenmore Crescent, Bristol BS7 0TN* E-mail ian.desmond@lineone.net

DESON, Rolston Claudius. b 39. Qu Coll Birm 85. **d** 84 **p** 85. NSM Saltley *Birm* 84-86; C Edgbaston SS Mary and Ambrose 86-90; V W Bromwich St Phil *Lich* 90-08; rtd 08. *97 Cardington Avenue, Birmingham B42 2PB*

DESPARD, Canon Eric Herbert. b 17. TCD BA40 BD48. CITC 41. **d** 41 **p** 42. C Roscommon *K, E & A* 41-43; C Dublin St Pet *D & G* 43-51; I Blessington w Kilbride 51-65; I Lucan w Leixlip 65-92; Can Ch Ch Cathl Dublin 73-92; rtd 92. *59 Sweetmount Park, Dundrum, Dublin 14, Republic of Ireland* Tel (00353) (1) 298 2489

DESROSIERS, Jacques Thomas Maurice. b 55. Qu Univ Kingston Ontario BCom77. S'wark Ord Course 91. **d** 94 **p** 95. NSM Benenden *Cant* 94-97; C Maidstone All SS and St Phil w Tovil 97-01; TV Pewsey and Swanborough *Sarum* 01-04; P-in-c

Rolvenden *Cant* from 04; AD Tenterden from 07. *The Vicarage, Rolvenden, Cranbrook TN17 4ND* Tel (01580) 241235
E-mail vicarage1965@btinternet.com

d'ESTERRE, Mrs Jennifer Ann. b 48. Coll of St Matthias Bris BEd77. WEMTC 01. **d** 04 **p** 05. NSM Sharpness, Purton, Brookend and Slimbridge *Glouc* from 04. *Gossington Cottage, Gossington, Slimbridge GL2 7DN* Tel (01453) 890384 Mobile 07855-243264 E-mail reverend@slimbridge.wanadoo.co.uk

DETTMER, Douglas James. b 64. Univ of Kansas BA86 Yale Univ MDiv90. Berkeley Div Sch 90. **d** 90 **p** 91. C Ilfracombe, Lee, Woolacombe, Bittadon etc *Ex* 90-94; Bp's Dom Chapl 94-98; P-in-c Thorverton, Cadbury, Upton Pyne etc from 98; P-in-c Stoke Canon, Poltimore w Huxham and Rewe etc from 06. *The Rectory, School Lane, Thorverton, Exeter EX5 5NR* Tel (01392) 860332

DEUCHAR, Canon Andrew Gilchrist. b 55. Southn Univ BTh86. Sarum & Wells Th Coll 81. **d** 84 **p** 85. C Alnwick *Newc* 84-88; TV Heref St Martin w St Fran 88-90; Adv to Coun for Soc Resp *Roch* and Cant 90-94; Sec for Angl Communion Affairs 94-00; Hon Prov Can Cant Cathl from 95; R Nottingham St Pet and St Jas *S'well* 00-02; R Nottingham St Pet and All SS 02-07; P-in-c Nottingham St Mary and St Cath 04-07; P-in-c Nottingham All SS, St Mary and St Pet 07-08; Chapl to The Queen 03-08; Dioc Audit Officer *Mor* from 08. *Address temp unknown*

DEVADASON, Mrs Abraham Jasmine Jebakani. b 67. Kakatiya Univ India BA91 Tamilnadu Th Sem BD96 United Th Coll Bangalore MTh99. SNWTP. **d** 08 **p** 09. C W Didsbury and Withington St Chris *Man* from 08. *St Martin's Vicarage, 2 Blackcarr Road, Wythenshawe, Manchester M23 1LX* Tel 0161-998 3408 Mobile 07515-726923
E-mail jasdevadason@yahoo.co.uk

DEVAL, Mrs Joan Margaret. b 38. Southlands Coll Lon TDip58. SAOMC 95. **d** 98 **p** 99. OLM Chinnor, Sydenham, Aston Rowant and Crowell *Ox* from 98. *3 Orchard Way, Chinnor OX9 4UD* Tel (01844) 353404

DEVARAJ, Jacob Devadason. b 61. Madras Bible Sem BTh Serampore Univ BTh Annamalai Univ MA United Th Coll Bangalore MTh. Tamilnadu Th Sem BD NOC. **d** 06 **p** 07. C Man Clayton St Cross w St Paul 06-09; TV Wythenshawe from 09. *St Martin's Vicarage, 2 Blackcarr Road, Wythenshawe, Manchester M23 1LX* Tel 0161-998 3408
E-mail jacob_devadason@yahoo.co.uk

DEVENISH, Nicholas Edward. b 64. Ridley Hall Cam 02. **d** 04 **p** 05. C Huntingdon *Ely* 04-07; C Farcet Hampton from 07. *105 Eagle Way, Hampton Vale, Peterborough PE7 8EL* Tel (01733) 248764 E-mail nickdevenish@aol.com

DEVENNEY, Raymond Robert Wilmont. b 47. TCD BA69 MA73. CITC 70. **d** 70 **p** 71. C Ballymena *Conn* 70-75; C Ballyholme *D & D* 75-81; I Killinchy w Kilmood and Tullynakill 81-00; I Drumbeg from 00. *The Rectory, 64 Drumbeg Road, Dunmurry, Belfast BT17 9LE* Tel (028) 9061 0255
E-mail raydev@hotmail.com

✠**DEVENPORT, The Rt Revd Eric Nash.** b 26. Open Univ BA74. Kelham Th Coll 46. **d** 51 **p** 52 **c** 80. C Leic St Mark 51-54; C Barrow St Matt *Carl* 54-56; Succ Leic Cathl 56-59; V Shepshed 59-64; R Oadby 64-73; Hon Can Leic Cathl 73-80; Dioc Missr 73-80; Suff Bp Dunwich *St E* 80-92; rtd 92; Chapl Adn Italy and Malta *Eur* 92-97; Florence w Siena 92-97; Asst Bp Eur 93-97; Perm to Offic *Nor* from 97; Hon PV Nor Cathl from 98; Hon Asst Bp Nor from 00. *6 Damocles Court, Norwich NR2 1HN* Tel (01603) 664121

DEVER, Paul. b 71. BSc. Wycliffe Hall Ox. **d** 06 **p** 07. C Fair Oak *Win* from 06. *Windfall, Chapel Drove, Horton Heath, Eastleigh SO50 7DL* Tel (023) 8069 4577

DEVERELL, Clive David. b 61. Anglia Ruskin Univ BA09. CA Tr Coll 83 ERMC 04. **d** 07 **p** 08. C Paston *Pet* from 07. *1A Mead Close, Peterborough PE4 6BS* Tel (01733) 572991

DEVERELL, William Robert Henry. b 61. CITC 88 St Jo Coll Nottm 90. **d** 92 **p** 93. C Agherton *Conn* 92-95; I Sixmilecross w Termonmaguirke *Arm* 95-99; I Tallaght *D & G* from 99. *St Maelruain's Rectory, 6 Sally Park, Firhouse Road, Tallaght, Dublin 24, Republic of Ireland* Tel (00353) (1) 462 1044 *or* 462 6006 Fax 462 1044 Mobile 86-803 0239
E-mail tallaghtparish@ireland.com

DEVEREUX, Canon John Swinnerton. b 32. Lon Univ BSc53. Wells Th Coll. **d** 58 **p** 59. C Wigan St Mich *Liv* 58-60; C Goring-by-Sea *Chich* 60-69; Ind Chapl 69-97; Can and Preb Chich Cathl 90-97; rtd 97; Perm to Offic *Chich* from 97. *4 Pony Farm, Findon, Worthing BN14 0RS* Tel (01903) 873638

DEVERILL, Jennifer. b 40. Auckland Medical Sch MSR62. **d** 96 **p** 97. OLM Battersea St Luke *S'wark* 96-05; Chapl St Geo Healthcare NHS Trust Lon 96-05; P-in-c Le Gard *Eur* from 08. *8 rue de l'Eglise, 30140 Bagard, France* Tel (0033) (4) 66 25 17 63
E-mail jennifer.deverill@wanadoo.fr

DEVINE, Margaret Rose. b 50. Sunderland Poly BEd76. NEOC 00. **d** 03 **p** 04. NSM E Boldon *Dur* from 03. *13 Rectory Green, West Boldon NE36 0QD* Tel 0191-537 2129

DEVINE, Maureen Mary. b 37. Cheltenham & Glouc Coll of HE TCert74. SAOMC 95. **d** 98 **p** 99. NSM Reading St Jo *Ox* 98-01;

NSM Beech Hill, Grazeley and Spencers Wood 01-05; NSM Loddon Reach 05-08; Perm to Offic from 08. *33 Radstock Lane, Earley, Reading RG6 5RX* Tel 0118-921 2767
E-mail julmar99@aol.com

DEVONISH, Clive Wayne. b 51. Ridley Hall Cam. **d** 96 **p** 97. C Meole Brace *Lich* 96-05; V Greenside *Dur* from 05. *The Vicarage, Greenside, Ryton NE40 4AA* Tel 0191-413 8281
E-mail rev.cw.devo@cwcom.net

DEVONSHIRE, Canon Roger George. b 40. AKC62. **d** 63 **p** 64. C Rotherhithe St Mary w All SS *S'wark* 63-67; C Kingston Hill St Paul 67-71; Chapl RN 71-95; QHC 92-95; R Pitlochry and Kilmaveonaig *St And* 95-05; Syn Clerk and Can St Ninian's Cathl Perth 00-05; rtd 05; Perm to Offic *Portsm* 05-07; Chapl QinetiQ from 07. *4 Chiltern Court, 27 Florence Road, Southsea PO5 2NX* Tel (023) 9287 3397 Mobile 07769-680922
E-mail rdevonshire@btinternet.com

DEVONSHIRE JONES, Thomas Percy Norman. See JONES, Thomas Percy Norman Devonshire

DEW, Glyn. b 55. Worc Coll of Educn BEd90. St Jo Coll Nottm MA97. **d** 97 **p** 98. C Beoley *Worc* 97-01; TV Redditch, The Ridge 01-05; P-in-c Tardebigge 04-05. *St Luke's Rectory, 69 Evesham Road, Redditch B97 4JX* Tel (01527) 544987

DEW, Lindsay Charles. b 52. Wilson Carlile Coll 76 Cranmer Hall Dur 85. **d** 86 **p** 86. C Knottingley *Wakef* 86-89; V Batley St Thos 89-97; R Thornhill and Whitley Lower 97-09; RD Dewsbury 96-06; Hon Can Wakef Cathl 05-09; P-in-c Dunton w Wrestlingworth and Eyeworth *St Alb* from 09. *The Rectory, 7 Braggs Lane, Wrestlingworth, Sandy SG19 2ER* Tel (01767) 631596 Mobile 07917-807152 E-mail lindsaydew@aol.com

DEW, Martin John. b 49. CBDTI 00. **d** 04 **p** 05. NSM Natland *Carl* 04-09; NSM Shap w Swindale and Bampton w Mardale from 09. *The Vicarage, Shap, Penrith CA10 3LB* Tel (01931) 716232

DEW, Mrs Maureen. b 51. Univ of Wales MA98. Qu Coll Birm BA99. **d** 99 **p** 00. C Inkberrow w Cookhill and Kington w Dormston *Worc* 99-02; C Redditch, The Ridge 02-05; TV Redditch Ch the K from 05. *St Luke's Rectory, 69 Evesham Road, Redditch B97 4JX* Tel (01527) 545521
E-mail modew@thesharpend33.freeserve.co.uk

DEW, Robert David John. b 42. St Pet Coll Ox BA63. St Steph Ho Ox 63. **d** 65 **p** 66. C Abington *Pet* 65-69; Chapl Tiffield Sch Northants 69-71; Ind Chapl *Pet* 71-79; Ind Chapl *Liv* 79-87; Sen Ind Missr 88-91; V Skelsmergh w Selside and Longsleddale *Carl* 91-06; Bp's Research Officer 91-95; Bp's Adv for CME 95-06; rtd 06. *Tither Crag Barn, Crook, Kendal LA8 8LE* Tel (01539) 568680 E-mail bob.dew@virgin.net

DEWAR, Francis John Lindsay. b 33. Keble Coll Ox BA56 MA59. Cuddesdon Coll 58. **d** 60 **p** 61. C Hessle *York* 60-63; C Stockton St Chad *Dur* 63-66; V Sunderland St Chad 66-81; Org Journey Inward, Journey Outward Project 82-07; rtd 07; Perm to Offic *B & W* from 01. *Wellspring, Church Road, Wookey, Wells BA5 1JX* Tel (01749) 675365 E-mail dewar@avirose.com

DEWAR, Ian John James. b 61. Kingston Poly BA83. Cranmer Hall Dur 89. **d** 92 **p** 93. C Blackb St Gabr 92-95; C Darwen St Cuth w Tockholes St Steph 95-97; V Appley Bridge 97-05; Chapl St Cath Hospice Preston from 05. *St Catherine's Hospice, Lostock Lane, Lostock Hall, Preston PR5 5XU* Tel (01772) 629171 E-mail ijjdewar@hotmail.com

DEWAR, John. b 32. Chich Th Coll 58. **d** 61 **p** 62. C Leeds St Hilda *Ripon* 61-65; C Cullercoats St Geo *Newc* 65-69; V Newsham 69-76; V Kenton Ascension 76-86; R Wallsend St Pet 86-92; V Longhorsley and Hebron 92-96; rtd 96; Perm to Offic *S'well* from 04. *51 Bonner Lane, Calverton, Nottingham NG14 6FU* Tel 0115-965 2599
E-mail jandmedewar@ntlworld.com

DEWES, Ms Deborah Mary. b 59. Homerton Coll Cam BEd81 St Jo Coll Dur BA90 MA93. Cranmer Hall Dur 88. **d** 92 **p** 94. C Stockton St Pet *Dur* 92-96; C Knowle *Birm* 96-03; C Bath Abbey w St Jas *B & W* 03-08; Chapl R United Hosp Bath NHS Trust 03-08; P-in-c Brislington St Luke from 08. *The Vicarage, 9 St Luke's Gardens, Bristol BS4 4NW* Tel 0117-977 7633

DEWEY, David Malcolm. b 43. Lon Univ BA72 LSE MSc(Econ)87 Fitzw Coll Cam MPhil94. Westcott Ho Cam 76. **d** 78 **p** 79. Sen Lect Middx Poly 72-92; Sen Lect Middx Univ 92-01; Hon C Enfield St Mich *Lon* 78-79; Hon C Bush Hill Park St Steph 79-84; Hon C Palmers Green St Jo 84-90; Perm to Offic *Lon* 90-95 and *St Alb* 95-98; Hon C Hertford All SS *St Alb* 98-01; P-in-c St Paul's Walden 01-08; rtd 08; Perm to Offic *St Alb* from 09. *44 The Elms, Hertford SG13 7UX* Tel (01992) 551968 Mobile 07813-439463 E-mail daviddewey8566@fsmail.net

DEWEY, Peter Lewis. b 38. Wycliffe Hall Ox 69. **d** 71 **p** 72. C Hammersmith St Sav *Lon* 71-73; Chapl to Bp Kensington 73-75; C Isleworth All SS 75-81; TV Dorchester *Ox* 81-91; CF (TA) 86-91; Chapl Gordonstoun Sch 92-97; TR St Laur in Thanet *Cant* 97-03; rtd 03; P-in-c Sulhamstead Abbots and Bannister w Ufton Nervet *Ox* from 03. *The Rectory, Sulhamstead Road, Ufton Nervet, Reading RG7 4DH* Tel 0118-983 2328

DEWEY, Sanford Dayton. b 44. Syracuse Univ AB67 MA72. Gen Th Sem (NY) MDiv79. **d** 79 **p** 80. Assoc Chapl Roosevelt Hosp

New York USA 80-81; Assoc Dir Relig Services 81-86; C St Mary le Bow w St Pancras Soper Lane etc *Lon* 87-92; C Hampstead St Steph w All Hallows 92-94; Co-Dir Hampstead Counselling Service 94-00; Dir from 00; NSM Hampstead Ch Ch 94-96; Hon C Grosvenor Chpl from 96; Prov Past Consultant URC from 96; Perm to Offic from 97. *43 Shirlock Road, London NW3 2HR* Tel (020) 7482 1527 E-mail daytondewey@aol.com

DEWHIRST, Janice. b 50. EMMTC 99. **d** 02 **p** 03. NSM Forest Town *S'well* 02-04; NSM Mansfield SS Pet and Paul 04-06; P-in-c Ladybrook 06-09; rtd 09. *26 King Street, Mansfield Woodhouse, Mansfield NG19 9AU* Tel (01623) 454471 E-mail revd.jan.d@ntlworld.com

DEWHURST, Gabriel George. b 30. **d** 59 **p** 60. In RC Ch 60-69; C Darlington St Jo *Dur* 70; C Bishopwearmouth St Nic 71-73; C-in-c Stockton St Mark CD 73-81; V Harton 81-86; R Castle Eden w Monkhesleden 86-97; rtd 97; Perm to Offic *York* from 98. *9 Knott Lane, Easingwold, York YO61 3LX* Tel (01347) 823526

DEWHURST, Russell James Edward. b 77. Magd Coll Ox MPhys99 Selw Coll Cam BTh03. Westcott Ho Cam 00. **d** 03 **p** 04. C Blewbury, Hagbourne and Upton *Ox* 03-05; P-in-c Ox St Frideswide w Binsey from 05; Web Pastor i-church 05-07; Asst Chapl Ex Coll Ox from 06. *23 Botley Road, Oxford OX2 0BL* Tel (01865) 242680 E-mail russell_dewhurst@yahoo.co.uk

DEWICK, David Richard. b 36. SAOMC 96. **d** 99 **p** 00. NSM Risborough *Ox* from 99. *The Rectory, Church End, Bledlow, Princes Risborough HP27 9PD* Tel (01844) 344762

DEWING, Robert Mark Eastwood. b 68. Bris Univ BA90 PGCE91. Ridley Hall Cam BA98. **d** 99 **p** 00. C Alverstoke *Portsm* 99-03; V Sheet from 03; AD Petersfield from 09. *Sheet Vicarage, 2 Pulens Lane, Petersfield GU31 4DB* Tel (01730) 263673 E-mail robdewing@hotmail.com

DEWING, William Arthur. b 52. NEOC 99. **d** 02 **p** 03. NSM Middlesbrough St Oswald *York* 02-06; NSM Stainton w Hilton from 06. *19 Monarch Grove, Marton, Middlesbrough TS7 8QQ* Tel (01642) 321074 Fax 500661 Mobile 07966-191640 E-mail w.dewing@ntlworld.com

DEWIS, Harry Kenneth. b 19. NW Ord Course 75. **d** 78 **p** 79. NSM Bedale *Ripon* 78-89; Perm to Offic 89-99. *11 Masham Road, Bedale DL8 2AF* Tel (01677) 423588

DEWSBURY, Michael Owen. b 31. St Aid Birkenhead 54. **d** 57 **p** 58. C Hellesdon *Nor* 57-60; C Speke All SS *Liv* 60-62; R Gt and Lt Glemham *St E* 62-67; R W Lynn *Nor* 67-68; R Dongara Australia 69-71; R Nollamara 71-76; Chapl R Perth Hosp 76-79; Chapl Fremantle Hosp 79-99; rtd 99. *8 Thomas Street, South Fremantle WA 6162, Australia* Tel (0061) (8) 9335 6852 E-mail dewsbury@iinet.net.au

DEXTER, Canon Frank Robert. b 40. Cuddesdon Coll 66. **d** 68 **p** 69. C Newc H Cross 68-71; C Whorlton 71-73; V Pet Ch Carpenter 73-80; V High Elswick St Phil *Newc* 80-85; RD Newc W 81-85; V Newc St Geo 85-05; Hon Can Newc Cathl 94-05; P-in-c Newc St Hilda 95-98; rtd 05. *8 Tynedale Terrace, Hexham NE46 3JE* Tel (01434) 601759 E-mail frank.dexter@talk21.com

DEY, Canon Charles Gordon Norman. b 46. Lon Coll of Div. **d** 71 **p** 72. C Almondbury *Wakef* 71-76; V Mixenden 76-85; TR Tong *Bradf* from 85; Hon Can Bradf Cathl from 00. *The Rectory, Holmewood Road, Tong, Bradford BD4 9EJ* Tel (01274) 682100 E-mail gordon@thedeyteam.freeserve.co.uk

DEY, John Alfred. b 33. ALCD57 ALCM57. **d** 57 **p** 58. C Man Albert Memorial Ch 57-60; C Pennington 60-62; V Mosley Common 62-69; V Chadderton Em 69-79; V Flixton St Jo 79-96; rtd 96; Perm to Offic *Man* from 96. *8 Woodlands Avenue, Urmston, Manchester M41 6NE*

DI CASTIGLIONE, James Alexander. b 81. St Jo Coll Nottm. **d** 08 **p** 09. C Mid-Sussex Network Ch *Chich* from 08. *22 Marchants Road, Hurstpierpoint, Hassocks BN6 9UU* Tel (01273) 835262 Mobile 07796-945662

DI CASTIGLIONE, Nigel Austin. b 57. St Jo Coll Dur BA78. St Jo Coll Nottm MA94. **d** 94 **p** 95. C Tamworth *Lich* 94-97; P-in-c Trentham 97-01; V from 02; V Hanford from 02. *The Vicarage, Trentham Park, Stoke-on-Trent ST4 8AE* Tel (01782) 658194 E-mail nigel.dicastiglione@googlemail.com

DI CHIARA, Miss Alessandra Maddalena. b 59. Univ of Wales (Swansea) BA80. Wycliffe Hall Ox 00. **d** 02 **p** 03. C Hooton *Ches* 02-05; P-in-c Millbrook from 05. *11 Standrick Hill Rise, Stalybridge SK15 3RT* Tel 0161-304 0281 E-mail rev.alessandra@stjamesmillbrook.org.uk

DIALI, The Ven Daniel Chukwuma. b 47. Portsm Univ BA80 Surrey Univ MA04. Basic Ord Course by Ext 85. **d** 84 **p** 86. Nigeria 84-01; V Lagos St Bart 86-92; V Bp Tugwell Ch 92-96; Can Lagos W 96-99; Adn St Paul's 00-01; Perm to Offic *S'wark* from 02. *9 Springall Street, London SE15 2TY* Tel (020) 7732 6639 E-mail dcdvnd@yahoo.com

DIAMOND, Canon Michael Lawrence. b 37. St Jo Coll Dur BA60 MA74 Sussex Univ DPhil84. ALCD62. **d** 62 **p** 63. C Wandsworth St Mich *S'wark* 62-64; C Patcham *Chich* 64-69; R Hamsey 70-75; P-in-c Cambridge St Andr Less *Ely* 75-86; V 86-04; Hon Can Ely Cathl 94-04; RD Cambridge 96-04; rtd 04;

Perm to Offic *S'well* from 04. *16 St Michael's Square, Beeston, Nottingham NG9 3HG* Tel 0115-925 4452

DIAMOND, Capt Richard Geoffrey Colin. b 49. MBE00. CA Tr Coll. **d** 93 **p** 93. Miss to Seafarers Kenya 90-01; rtd 01; Perm to Offic *Win* from 02. *209A Priory Road, Southampton SO17 2LR* Tel (02380) 678558 E-mail rgcdiamond@ic24.net

DIANA, Sister. *See* MORRISON, Diana Mary

DIAPER, James Robert. b 30. Portsm Dioc Tr Course 84. **d** 85. NSM Portsea St Sav *Portsm* 85-89 and 91-95; NSM Milton 89-91; rtd 95; Perm to Offic *Portsm* from 95. *48 Wallington Road, Portsmouth PO2 0HB* Tel (023) 9269 1372

DIAPER, Trevor Charles. b 51. Anglia Poly Univ MA05 ALA79. Coll of Resurr Mirfield 88. **d** 90 **p** 91. C N Walsham w Antingham *Nor* 90-94; P-in-c Ardleigh *Chelmsf* 94-95; P-in-c The Bromleys 94-95; R Ardleigh and The Bromleys 95-97; V Bocking St Pet from 97. *The Vicarage, 6 St Peter's in the Fields, Bocking, Braintree CM7 9AR* E-mail father.trevor@btinternet.com

DIAZ BUTRON, Marcos Mximo. b 72. St Steph Ho Ox 06. **d** 08. V Wantage *Ox* from 08. *5 Barnards Way, Wantage OX12 7EA* Tel (01235) 763309 E-mail maxdiazbutron@yahoo.es

DIBB SMITH, John. b 29. Ex & Truro NSM Scheme 78. **d** 81 **p** 82. NSM Carbis Bay *Truro* 81-82; NSM Carbis Bay w Lelant 82-84; Warden Trelowarren Fellowship Helston 84-89; Chapl 89-91; NSM Halsetown *Truro* 91-97; rtd 98; Perm to Offic *Truro* from 00. *Cargease Cottage, Cockwells, Penzance TR20 8DG* Tel (01736) 740707

DIBBENS, Canon Hugh Richard. b 39. Lon Univ BA63 MTh67 St Pet Coll Ox BA65 MA74. Oak Hill Th Coll 60. **d** 67 **p** 68. C Holborn St Geo w H Trin and St Bart *Lon* 67-72; CMS 73-74; Japan 74-77; TR Chigwell *Chelmsf* 78-92; V Hornchurch St Andr 92-06; RD Havering 98-04; Hon Can Chelmsf Cathl 01-06; rtd 06; Perm to Offic *Chelmsf* from 07. *9 Stonehill Road, Roxwell, Chelmsford CM1 4PF* Tel (01245) 248173 E-mail hughandruth@dibbens10.freeserve.co.uk

DIBDEN, Alan Cyril. b 49. Hull Univ LLB70 Fitzw Coll Cam BA72 MA76. Westcott Ho Cam 70 Virginia Th Sem 73. **d** 73 **p** 74. C Camberwell St Luke *S'wark* 73-77; TV Walworth 77-79; TV Langley Marish *Ox* 79-90; C Chalfont St Peter 84-90; TV Burnham w Dropmore, Hitcham and Taplow 90-08; V Taplow and Dropmore from 08. *The Rectory, Rectory Road, Taplow, Maidenhead SL6 0ET* Tel (01628) 661182 E-mail alan.dibden@btinternet.com

DICK, Miss Angela. b 62. Sheff Univ BA92. St Jo Coll Nottm MA94. **d** 96 **p** 97. C Mixenden *Wakef* 96-97; C Mount Pellon 97-99; P-in-c Bradshaw 99-00; P-in-c Holmfield 99-00; V Bradshaw and Holmfield from 00. *The Vicarage, Pavement Lane, Bradshaw, Halifax HX2 9JJ* Tel (01422) 244330 E-mail angedix@onetel.net

DICK, Canon Caroline Ann. b 61. Nottm Univ BTh88. Linc Th Coll 85. **d** 88 **p** 94. Par Dn Houghton le Spring *Dur* 88-93; Par Dn Hetton le Hole 93-94; C 94-96; Asst Chapl Sunderland Univ 96-99; Development Officer Dioc Bd of Soc Resp 98-09; Adv for Women's Min 02-09; TV Dur N from 09; Hon Can Dur Cathl from 03. *Harton Vicarage, 182 Sunderland Road, South Shields NE34 6AH* Tel 0191-454 3804 E-mail bsr.development.officer@durham.anglican.org

DICK, Cecil Bates. b 42. TD97. Selw Coll Cam BA68 MA72. EMMTC 73. **d** 76 **p** 78. NSM Cinderhill *S'well* 76-79; Chapl Dame Allan's Schs Newc 79-85; CF (TA) 84-99; C Gosforth All SS *Newc* 85-87; Chapl HM Pris Dur 88-89; Chapl HM Pris Hull 89-04; rtd 04; Perm to Offic *Newc* from 01 and *York* from 04. *11 Juniper Chase, Beverley HU17 8GD* Tel (01482) 862985

DICK, Norman MacDonald. b 32. ACIB. Ox NSM Course 87. **d** 90 **p** 91. NSM Bedgrove *Ox* 90-95; NSM Ellesborough, The Kimbles and Stoke Mandeville 95-01; Perm to Offic from 01. *21 Camborne Avenue, Aylesbury HP21 7UH* Tel (01296) 485530 E-mail norman.dick@care4free.net

DICK, Raymond Owen. b 53. Edin Univ BD77. Edin Th Coll 73. **d** 77 **p** 78. C Glas St Mary 77-84; Perm to Offic *St Alb* 84-85; P-in-c Edin St Paul and St Geo 85; Edin St Phil 85-86; P-in-c Edin St Marg 85-87; TV Edin Old St Paul 87-88; R Hetton le Hole *Dur* 88-96; V Harton from 96. *Harton Vicarage, 182 Sunderland Road, South Shields NE34 6AH* Tel and fax 0191-427 5538 E-mail rodick182@aol.com *or* raymond.dick@durham.anglican.org

DICKENS, Adam Paul. b 65. Man Univ BA89 Nottm Univ MDiv93. Linc Th Coll 91. **d** 93 **p** 94. C Pershore w Pinvin, Wick and Birlingham *Worc* 93-98; C Fortune Bay Canada *Newfld* 98-04; Pilsdon Community from 04. *Pilsdon Manor, Pilsdon, Bridport DT6 5NZ* Tel (01308) 868308

DICKENS, Timothy Richard John. b 45. Leeds Univ BSc68. Westcott Ho Cam 68. **d** 71 **p** 72. C Meole Brace *Lich* 71-74; C-in-c Stamford Ch Ch CD *Linc* 74-80; V Anlaby St Pet *York* 80-91; V Egg Buckland *Ex* from 91; P-in-c Estover from 04; RD Plymouth Moorside 03-09. *The Vicarage, 100 Church Hill, Eggbuckland, Plymouth PL6 5RD* Tel (01752) 701399 E-mail tim.dickens@lineone.net

DICKENSON, Charles Gordon. b 29. Bps' Coll Cheshunt 53. **d** 56 **p** 57. C Ellesmere Port *Ches* 56-61; R Egremont St Columba 61-68; V Latchford Ch Ch 68-74; P-in-c Hargrave 74-79; Bp's Chapl 75-79; V Birkenhead St Jas w St Bede 79-83; R Tilston and Shocklach 83-94; rtd 94; Perm to Offic *Ches* from 94. *58 Kingsway, Crewe CW2 7ND* Tel (01270) 560722
E-mail cg.dickenson@talktalk.net

DICKINSON, Canon Robin Christopher Wildish. b 44. Lon Univ CertEd67 Ex Univ BPhil81 MA98. SWMTC 94. **d** 97 **p** 98. NSM Week St Mary w Poundstock and Whitstone *Truro* 97-98; P-in-c 98-06; P-in-c St Gennys, Jacobstow w Warbstow and Treneglos 02-06; R Week St Mary Circle of Par from 06; RD Stratton from 05; Hon Can Truro Cathl from 07. *The Rectory, The Glebe, Week St Mary, Holsworthy EX22 6UY* Tel and fax (01288) 341134 E-mail parsonrob@aol.com

DICKER, Ms Jane Elizabeth. b 64. Whitelands Coll Lon BA87 Anglia Ruskin Univ MA08. Linc Th Coll 87. **d** 89 **p** 94. Par Dn Merton St Jas *S'wark* 89-93; C Littleham w Exmouth 93-97; Chapl Plymouth Univ 93-97; Ecum Chapl for F&HE Grimsby *Linc* 97-02; Chapl Univ of Greenwich *Roch* 02-05; Chapl Kent Inst of Art and Design 02-05; Hon PV Roch Cathl 03-05; P-in-c Waltham Cross *St Alb* 05-08; TV Cheshunt from 08. *The Vicarage, 5 Longlands Close, Cheshunt, Waltham Cross EN8 8LW* Tel (01992) 633243 Mobile 07843-667971
E-mail mthr_jane@yahoo.co.uk

DICKER, Miss Mary Elizabeth. b 45. Girton Coll Cam BA66 MA70 Sheff Univ MSc78. Cranmer Hall Dur 83. **dss** 85 **d** 87 **p** 94. Hinde St Sheen *S'wark* 85-88; Par Dn 87-88; Par Dn Irlam *Man* 88-92; Par Dn Ashton Ch Ch 92-94; C 94-97; P-in-c Hopwood 97-98; TV Heywood 98-05; rtd 05; Perm to Offic *Man* from 05. *32 Souchay Court, 1 Clothorn Road, Manchester M20 6BR* Tel 0161-434 7634

DICKERSON, Richard Keith. b 31. Sir Geo Williams Univ Montreal BA60 McGill Univ Montreal BD60. Montreal Dioc Th Coll. **d** 60 **p** 60. Canada 60-69 and from 78; C Hampstead St Matt 60-63; R Waterloo St Luke 63-69; Perm to Offic *Cant* 72; C Canvey Is *Chelmsf* 73-75; Perm to Offic Montreal 75-78; C Georgeville St Geo 78-82; P-in-c 82-91; R Lennoxville St Geo 91-01; rtd 96. *172 McGowan Road, Georgeville QC J0B 1T0, Canada* E-mail keithdi@globetrotter.net

DICKIE, James Graham Wallace. b 50. Worc Coll Ox BA72 MA BLitt77. Westcott Ho Cam 78. **d** 81 **p** 82. C Bracknell *Ox* 81-84; Lic to Offic *Ely* 84-89; Chapl Trin Coll Cam 84-89; Chapl Clifton Coll Bris 89-96; Sen Chapl Marlborough Coll from 96. *Marlborough College, Marlborough SN8 1PA* Tel (01672) 892204 E-mail chaplain@marlboroughcollege.wilts.sch.uk

DICKIN (née LENTON), Mrs Patricia Margarita. b 72. STETS MA08. **d** 08 **p** 09. C Epsom Common Ch Ch *Guildf* from 08. *278 The Greenway, Epsom KT18 7JF*

DICKINSON, Albert Hugh. b 34. Trin Coll Connecticut AB55. Episc Th Sch Harvard STB58. **d** 58 **p** 59. USA 58-97; C Portarlington w Cloneyhurke and Lea *M & K* 97-99; USA from 99. *807 Seashore Road, Cold Spring NJ 08204, USA*
E-mail husan@avaloninternet.com

DICKINSON, Canon Anthony William. b 48. New Coll Ox BA71 MA74. Linc Th Coll 80. **d** 82 **p** 83. C Leavesden *St Alb* 82-86; TV Upton cum Chalvey *Ox* 86-94; P-in-c Terriers 94-99; V from 99; Chapl Bucks New Univ from 03; Hon Can Ch Ch *Ox* from 05. *St Francis's Vicarage, Amersham Road, High Wycombe HP13 5AB* Tel (01494) 520676
E-mail tony.dickinson@ukonline.co.uk *or* sainsw01@bcuc.ac.uk

DICKINSON, David Charles. b 58. BA79 Lanc Univ MA97. CBDTI. **d** 99 **p** 00. NSM Ewood *Blackb* 99-04; NSM Blackb Redeemer 04-05; P-in-c Hoghton from 05. *The Vicarage, Chapel Lane, Hoghton, Preston PR5 0RY* Tel (01254) 852026

DICKINSON, Dyllis Annie. b 52. **d** 01 **p** 02. OLM Stalmine w Pilling *Blackb* 01-07; NSM from 07. *Springfield, Moss Side Lane, Stalmine, Poulton-le-Fylde FY6 0JP* Tel (01253) 700011
E-mail dyljohn@lineone.net

DICKINSON, Gareth Lee. b 69. Ridley Hall Cam 06. **d** 08 **p** 09. C Bryanston Square St Mary w St Marylebone St Mark *Lon* from 08. *39B Donaldson Road, London NW6 6NE* Tel (020) 7258 5040 Mobile 07788-742700 E-mail gareth@stmaryslondon.com

DICKINSON, Henry. b 59. St Deiniol's Hawarden 84. **d** 86 **p** 87. NSM Blackb St Mich w St Jo and H Trin 86-89; NSM Burnley St Cath w St Alb and St Paul 89-95; Perm to Offic from 95. *22 Notre Dame Gardens, Blackburn BB1 5EF* Tel (01254) 693414

DICKINSON, The Very Revd the Hon Hugh Geoffrey. b 29. Trin Coll Ox BA53 MA56. Cuddesdon Coll 54. **d** 56 **p** 57. C Melksham *Sarum* 56-58; Chapl Trin Coll Cam 58-63; Chapl Win Coll 63-69; P-in-c Milverton *Cov* 69-77; V St Alb St Mich *St Alb* 77-86; Dean Sarum 86-96; rtd 96; Perm to Offic *Glouc* from 96. *5 St Peter's Road, Cirencester GL7 1RE* Tel (01285) 657710
E-mail hughanjean@aol.com

DICKINSON, Canon Robert Edward. b 47. Nottm Univ BTh74. St Jo Coll Nottm 70. **d** 74 **p** 75. C Birm St Martin 74-78; P-in-c Liv St Bride w St Sav 78-81; TV St Luke in the City 81-86; Chapl Liv Poly 86-92; Chapl Liv Jo Moores Univ 92-08; Hon Can Liv

Cathl 03-08; rtd 08. *3 Wightman Avenue, Newton-Le-Willows WA12 0LS* Tel (01925) 271124
E-mail bobdicko@blueyonder.co.uk

DICKINSON, Simon Braithwaite Vincent. b 34. SAOMC 94. **d** 97 **p** 98. OLM Waddesdon w Over Winchendon and Fleet Marston *Ox* 97-02; OLM Schorne 02-04; Perm to Offic from 04. *12A Croft Road, Thame OX9 3JF* Tel (01844) 212408
E-mail dickinson@whitehousewaddesdon.freeserve.co.uk

DICKINSON, Stephen Paul. b 54. SRN75. NOC 85. **d** 88 **p** 89. NSM Purston cum S Featherstone *Wakef* 88-91; C Goldthorpe w Hickleton *Sheff* 91-94; V New Bentley 94-05; P-in-c Arksey 04-05; V New Bentley w Arksey from 05. *The Vicarage, Victoria Road, Bentley, Doncaster DN5 0EZ* Tel (01302) 875266

DICKINSON, Victor Tester. b 48. Univ of Wales (Cardiff) BSc70. St Steph Ho Ox 70. **d** 73 **p** 74. C Neath w Llantwit 73-76; Asst Chapl Univ of Wales (Cardiff) 76-79; TV Willington *Newc* 79-86; V Kenton Ascension 86-97; V Lowick and Kyloe w Ancroft from 97; R Ford and Etal from 97. *The Vicarage, 1 Main Street, Lowick, Berwick-upon-Tweed TD15 2UD* Tel (01289) 388229

DICKSON, Brian John. b 19. Reading Univ BSc41. Qu Coll Birm 49. **d** 51 **p** 52. C S Wimbledon H Trin *S'wark* 51-53; C Golders Green St Alb *Lon* 53-55; Sec SCM Th Colls Dept 53-55; Chapl Hulme Gr Sch Oldham 55-59; Chapl K Sch Worc 60-67; Min Can Worc Cathl 60-67; Chapl Colston's Sch Bris 67-74; V Bishopston *Bris* 74-85; RD Horfield 80-85; rtd 85; Perm to Offic *Worc* 85-05 and *Heref* from 05. *2 Coach House Fields, Livesey Road, Ludlow SY8 1EZ* Tel (01584) 874018

DICKSON, Colin James. b 74. St Andr Univ MA96 MPhil00 Leeds Univ BA01. Coll of Resurr Mirfield 99. **d** 02 **p** 03. C Tottenham St Paul *Lon* 02-05; C Croydon St Mich w St Jas *S'wark* from 05. *3 St Michael's Court, 5 Poplar Walk, Croydon CR0 1UA* Tel (020) 8633 1817

DICKSON, Colin Patrick Gavin. b 56. **d** 96 **p** 97. C Grays Thurrock *Chelmsf* 96-00; V Glantawe *S & B* from 00. *The Vicarage, 122 Mansel Road, Bonymaen, Swansea SA1 7JR* Tel (01792) 652839

DICKSON, Samuel Mervyn James. b 41. CITC. **d** 66 **p** 67. C Ballyholme *D & D* 66-70; C Knockbreda 70-75; I Clonallon w Warrenpoint 75-84; I Down H Trin w Hollymount 84-06; Bp's C Rathmullan 00-05; Bp's C Tyrella 00-06; Bp's C Loughinisland 01-06; Can Down Cathl 91-06; Treas 98-00; Prec 00-01; Chan 01-06; rtd 06. *1 Moneycarragh, 40 Main Street, Dundrum, Newcastle BT33 0LY* Tel (028) 4375 1112

DIETZ, Matthew Paul Richard. b 70. Magd Coll Cam MA95. Wycliffe Hall Ox 05. **d** 07 **p** 08. C Win Ch Ch 07-08; C Throop from 08. *Epiphany House, 81 Castle Lane West, Bournemouth BH9 3LH* Tel (01202) 512481 Mobile 07751-454993
E-mail matthew.dietz@btinternet.com

DIFFEY, Margaret Elsie. b 39. MCSP. **d** 02 **p** 03. OLM Nor St Geo Tombland from 02. *45 Welsford Road, Norwich NR4 6QB* Tel and fax (01603) 457248
E-mail maggiediffey@tiscali.co.uk

DIGGLE, Judith Margaret. *See* BROWN, Prof Judith Margaret

DIGGLE, Richard James. b 47. Lon Inst BA69 Man Poly CertEd73. **d** 01 **p** 02. OLM Chorlton-cum-Hardy St Werburgh *Man* 01-05; NSM Bickerton, Bickley, Harthill and Burwardsley *Ches* 05-08; V Antrobus, Aston by Sutton, Lt Leigh etc from 08. *The Vicarage, Street Lane, Lower Whitley, Warrington WA4 4EN* Tel (01925) 730158 Mobile 07749-849783
E-mail diggle163@btinternet.com

DIGGORY, Mrs Susan. b 51. SEITE BA09. **d** 09. NSM Tunbridge Wells St Mark *Roch* from 09. *Oakdene, 8 Glenmore Park, Tunbridge Wells TN2 5NZ* Tel (01892) 531941
E-mail sue.diggory@oakdene.eclipse.co.uk

DIGMAN (née BUTTERFIELD), Mrs Amanda Helen. b 73. Derby Univ BA96. St Jo Coll Nottm 07. **d** 09. C Sutton in Ashfield St Mary *S'well* from 09. *10 Huthwaite Road, Sutton-in-Ashfield NG17 2GW* Tel 07803-625049 (mobile) E-mail amanda.digman@ntlworld.com

DILKES, Nigel Bruce. b 58. Univ of Wales (Ban) BSc97 Lanc Univ PhD01. Ridley Hall Cam 03. **d** 05 **p** 06. C Llandudno *Ban* 05-07; C Holyhead from 07. *St Seiriol's House, 25 Gors Avenue, Holyhead LL65 1PB* Tel (01407) 764780
E-mail nigeldilkes@aol.com

DILL, Nicholas Bayard Botolf. b 63. Toronto Univ BA86 Lon Univ LLB89 Barrister 91. Wycliffe Hall Ox 96. **d** 98 **p** 99. C Lindfield *Chich* 98-05; R Pembroke St Jo Bermuda from 05. *St John's Rectory, 15 Langton Hill, Pembroke HM 13, Bermuda* Tel (001) (441) 292 5308 Fax 296 9173 E-mail nickdill@logic.bm

DILL, Peter Winston. b 41. ACP66 K Coll Lon BD72 AKC72. St Aug Coll Cant 72. **d** 73 **p** 74. C Warsop *S'well* 73-75; C Rhyl w St Ann *St As* 75-77; C Oxton *Ches* 77-78; V Newton in Mottram 78-82; P-in-c Shelton and Oxon *Lich* 82-84; V 84-87; Chapl Clifton Coll Bris 87-00; C Thorverton, Cadbury, Upton Pyne etc *Ex* 00-01; Perm to Offic *Bris* 02-03; Past Co-ord St Monica Trust Westbury Fields 03-06; rtd 06. *85B Pembroke Road, Clifton, Bristol BS8 3EB* Tel 0117-973 9769

DILNOT, Canon John William. b 36. Selw Coll Cam BA60 MA64. Cuddesdon Coll 60. **d** 62 **p** 63. C Stafford St Mary *Lich* 62-66; C Stoke upon Trent 66-67; V Leek All SS 67-74; V Leeds w Broomfield *Cant* 74-79; P-in-c Aldington 79-81; P-in-c Bonnington w Bilsington 79-81; P-in-c Fawkenhurst 79-81; R Aldington w Bonnington and Bilsington 81-87; RD N Lympne 82-87; Hon Can Cant Cathl 85-99; V Folkestone St Mary and St Eanswythe 87-99; rtd 99; Perm to Offic *Cant* from 99. *Underhill Cottage, The Undercliff, Sandgate, Folkestone CT20 3AT* Tel (01303) 248000

DILWORTH, Anthony. b 41. St Deiniol's Hawarden 87. **d** 90 **p** 91. NSM Gt Saughall *Ches* 90-93; P-in-c Cwmcarn *Mon* 93-95; V 95-99; V Abercarn and Cwmcarn 99-01; TV Upholland *Liv* 01-06; rtd 06. *4 Maes Owain, Glyndyfrdwy, Corwen LL21 9HF* Tel (01490) 430821 Mobile 07773-389179
E-mail tony@dilworth4.wanadoo.co.uk

DIMERY, Richard James. b 76. CCC Cam MA98 Leeds Univ MA99. Wycliffe Hall Ox MA03. **d** 04 **p** 05. C Upper Armley *Ripon* 04-08; P-in-c Woodside from 08. *11 Bedford View, Leeds LS16 6DL* E-mail richard@dimery.com

DIMES, Stuart Christopher Laurence. b 60. Warwick Univ BSc01. St Jo Coll Nottm 99. **d** 01 **p** 02. C Branksome St Clem *Sarum* 01-05; P-in-c W Heath *Birm* from 05. *The Vicarage, 54A Lilley Lane, Birmingham B31 3JT* Tel 0121-476 7776
E-mail revsdimes@live.com

DIMMICK, Kenneth Ray. b 55. Texas A&M Univ BA77. Nashotah Ho MDiv84. **d** 84 **p** 84. C Shreveport St Matthias USA 84-86; P-in-c 86-87; R St Francisville Grace Ch 87-00; Assoc R Houston Palmer Memorial Ch 00-05; V Anahuac Trin 05-06; P-in-c Stuttgart *Eur* from 06. *Lorenzstaffel 8, 70182 Stuttgart, Germany* Tel (0049) (711) 787 8783 Mobile 151-5798 9140 E-mail vicar@stcatherines-stuttgart.de

DIMMICK, Mrs Margaret Louisa. b 44. Keswick Hall Coll TCert66 Open Univ BA75. SAOMC 97. **d** 00 **p** 02. OLM Caversham St Pet and Mapledurham etc *Ox* 00-03; OLM Emmer Green w Caversham Park from 03. *12 Lowfield Road, Caversham, Reading RG4 6PA* Tel 0118-947 0258
E-mail margaret@dimmick33.freeserve.co.uk

DIMOLINE, Keith Frederick. b 22. Clifton Th Coll 48. **d** 51 **p** 52. C Watford Ch Ch *St Alb* 51-54; C Corsham *Bris* 54-59; C-in-c Swindon St Jo Park CD 59-62; V Swindon St Jo 62-65; V Coalpit Heath 65-74; V Hanham 74-83; C Cudworth w Chillington *B & W* 83-84; P-in-c Dowlishwake w Chaffcombe, Knowle St Giles etc 83-84; R Dowlishwake w Chaffcombe, Knowle St Giles etc 84-88; rtd 88; Perm to Offic *B & W* from 88. *16 Exeter Road, Weston-super-Mare BS23 4DB* Tel (01934) 635006

DINES, The Very Revd Philip Joseph (Griff). b 59. Univ Coll Lon BScEng80 Clare Coll Cam PhD84 Man Univ MA(Theol)93. Westcott Ho Cam 83. **d** 86 **p** 87. C Northolt St Mary *Lon* 86-89; C Withington St Paul *Man* 89-91; V Wythenshawe St Martin 91-98; P-in-c Newall Green St Fran 95-98; R Glas St Mary and Provost St Mary's Cathl 98-05; Lic to Offic 05-08. *Address temp unknown* Tel 07974-611438 (mobile) E-mail griff@dines.org

DINNEN, John Frederick. b 42. TCD BA65 BD72 QUB MTh91. CITC. **d** 66 **p** 67. C Belfast All SS *Conn* 66-68; ICM Dub 69-71; C Carnmoney 71-73; Asst Dean of Residences QUB 73-74; Dean 74-84; I Hillsborough *D & D* 84-07; Preb Down Cathl 93-96; Dir of Ords 96-98; Dean Down 96-06; rtd 06. *74 Demesne Road, Ballynahinch BT24 8NS* Tel (028) 4481 1148
E-mail jdinnen@btinternet.com

DINNEN, Mrs Judith Margaret. b 48. Open Univ BA87 Univ of Wales (Cardiff) MA00 Goldsmiths' Coll Lon TCert71. WEMTC 01. **d** 05 **p** 06. NSM Madley w Tyberton, Peterchurch, Vowchurch etc *Heref* from 05. *Minstercote, Much Birch, Hereford HR2 8HT* Tel (01981) 540730
E-mail judy@dinnen5.fsnet.co.uk

DINSMORE, Ivan Ernest. b 71. TCD BTh01. CITC 98. **d** 01 **p** 02. C Glendermott *D & R* 01-04; I Balteagh w Carrick from 04; I Tamlaghtard w Aghanloo from 04. *Balteagh Rectory, 115 Drumsurn Road, Limavady BT49 0PD* Tel (028) 7776 3069
E-mail ivandinsmore@hotmail.com

DINSMORE, Stephen Ralph. b 56. Wye Coll Lon BSc78. Cranmer Hall Dur 82. **d** 85 **p** 86. C Haughton le Skerne *Dur* 85-88; C Edgware *Lon* 88-93; V Plymouth St Jude *Ex* 93-05; RD Plymouth Sutton 96-01; Dioc Adv for Miss and Par Development *Chelmsf* 05-07; Hon C Cranham Park 05-07; Nat Dir SOMA from 07. *SOMA UK, PO Box 69, Merriott TA18 9AP* Tel (01460) 279737
E-mail stephen.dinsmore@somauk.org

DISLEY, Mrs Edith Jennifer. b 51. Sheff Univ BSc72 Man Univ BD79. NOC 99. **d** 01 **p** 02. NSM Man Victoria Park from 01. *49 Broadstone Hall Road North, Heaton Chapel, Stockport SK4 5LA* Tel 0161-432 5114 E-mail sisteredith@priest.com

DISS, Canon Ronald George. b 31. Sarum Th Coll 58. **d** 61 **p** 62. C Greenwich St Alfege w St Pet *S'wark* 64-67; C-in-c 65-80; Lic to Offic *Lon* 68-77; Chapl Lon Univ 68-71; Bp's Dom Chapl *Win* 78-80; V Southampton Maybush St Pet 80-91; Hon Can Win Cathl 85-96; R Freemantle 91-96; rtd 96; Hon Chapl to Bp

Dover *Cant* from 97. *35 Castle Row, Canterbury CT1 2QY* Tel (01227) 462410

DITCH, David John. b 45. St Cath Coll Cam BA67 MA70 Leeds Univ PGCE68. WMMTC 88. **d** 91 **p** 92. C Biddulph *Lich* 91-94; V Hednesford 94-02; V Chasetown 02-08; rtd 09. *6 Redwing Croft, Derby DE23 1WF*

DITCHBURN, Hazel. b 44. NEOC 82. **dss** 84 **d** 87 **p** 94. Scotswood *Newc* 84-86; Ind Chapl *Dur* 86-95; TV Gateshead 95-98; AD Gateshead 92-98; P-in-c Stella 98-04; P-in-c Swalwell 01-04; R Blaydon and Swalwell 04-06; AD Gateshead W 98-00; Hon Can Dur Cathl 94-06; P-in-c Freshwater Australia 06-09. *2 Woburn Way, Westerhope, Newcastle upon Tyne NE5 5JD* Tel 0191-286 0553

DITCHFIELD, Timothy Frederick. b 61. CCC Cam BA83. Cranmer Hall Dur 85. **d** 88 **p** 89. C Accrington St Jo *Blackb* 88-89; C Accrington St Jo w Huncoat 89-91; C Whittle-le-Woods 91-95; Chapl K Coll Lon from 95. *19 Maunsel Street, London SW1P 2QN*, or *King's College, Strand, London WC2R 2LS* Tel (020) 7828 1772 *or* 7848 2373 Fax 7848 2344
E-mail tim.ditchfield@kcl.ac.uk

DIVALL, David Robert. b 40. New Coll Ox BA64 Sussex Univ DPhil74. Sarum & Wells Th Coll 73. **d** 77 **p** 78. Hon C Catherington and Clanfield *Portsm* 77-92; Hon C Rowlands Castle 92-93; Perm to Offic from 01. *17 Pipers Mead, Clanfield, Waterlooville PO8 0ST* Tel (023) 9259 4845

DIVALL, Stephen Robert. b 70. Pemb Coll Ox MA92. Ridley Hall Cam 95. **d** 98 **p** 99. C Cheadle *Ches* 98-01; Team Ldr UCCF 01-06; V Kensington St Helen w H Trin *Lon* from 06. *St Helen's Vicarage, St Helen's Gardens, London W10 6LP* Tel (020) 8968 7807

DIX, Edward Joseph. b 77. Goldsmiths' Coll Lon BMus00. Wycliffe Hall Ox BTh09. **d** 09. C Shadwell St Paul w Ratcliffe St Jas *Lon* from 09. *53 Prospect Place, Wapping Wall, London E1W 3TJ* Tel 07899-075935 (mobile)
E-mail edjdix@gmail.com

DIXON, Ms Anne Elizabeth. b 56. Leeds Univ LLB77 Solicitor 80. Westcott Ho Cam. **d** 01 **p** 02. C Guildf H Trin w St Mary 01-05; Chapl HM Pris Bullwood Hall from 06. *HM Prison Bullwood Hall, High Road, Hockley SS5 4TE* Tel (01702) 562800 E-mail annie.dixon@hmps.gsi.gov.uk

DIXON, Bruce Richard. b 42. Lon Univ BScEng63. Sarum Th Coll 66. **d** 68 **p** 69. C Walton St Mary *Liv* 68-70; C Harnham *Sarum* 70-73; C Streatham St Leon *S'wark* 73-77; R Thurcaston *Leic* 77-83; R Cranborne w Boveridge, Edmondsham etc *Sarum* 83-02; rtd 07. *East Heddon, Filleigh, Barnstaple EX32 0RY* Tel (01598) 760513 E-mail bandk2d@hotmail.com

DIXON, Bryan Stanley. b 61. St Jo Coll Nottm BTh93. **d** 93 **p** 94. C Beverley Minster *York* 93-96; C Kingston upon Hull St Aid Southcoates 96-97; Asst Chapl HM Pris Dur 97-98; R Mid Marsh Gp *Linc* 98-03; R Brandesburton and Leven w Catwick *York* from 03. *The Rectory, West Street, Leven, Beverley HU17 5LR* Tel (01964) 503731

DIXON, Campbell Boyd. d 07 **p** 08. NSM Jordanstown *Conn* from 07. *10 Meadowbank, Newtownabbey BT37 0UP*
E-mail campbellbdixon@hotmail.co.uk

DIXON, Charles William. b 41. NW Ord Course 78. **d** 81 **p** 82. C Almondbury *Wakef* 81-82; C Almondbury w Farnley Tyas 82-84; P-in-c Shelley 84-88; P-in-c Shepley 84-88; V Shelley and Shepley 88-89; V Ripponden 89-94; V Barkisland w W Scammonden 89-94; P-in-c Thornes St Jas w Ch Ch 94-98; Chapl among Deaf People *Chelmsf* 98-06; rtd 06; Chapl among Deaf People *Ely* from 06. *83 Wertheim Way, Huntingdon PE29 6UH* Tel (01480) 434075 E-mail cdixon41@msn.com

DIXON, Canon David. b 19. Lich Th Coll 57. **d** 58 **p** 59. C Barrow St Luke *Carl* 58-61; V Westfield St Mary 61-68; Warden Rydal Hall 68-84; P-in-c Rydal 78-84; rtd 84; Perm to Offic *Carl* from 84; Hon Can Carl Cathl 84-85. *Rheda, The Green, Millom LA18 5JA* Tel (01229) 774300

DIXON, David Hugh. b 40. Chich Th Coll 90. **d** 92 **p** 93. C Launceston *Truro* 92-95; TV Probus, Ladock and Grampound w Creed and St Erme 95-06; rtd 06. *1 Rectory Close, Old Village, Willand, Cullompton EX15 2RH* Tel (01884) 839984

DIXON, David Michael. b 58. Preston Poly BA82 Barrister 83. Coll of Resurr Mirfield BA98. **d** 98 **p** 99. C Goldthorpe w Hickleton *Sheff* 98-01; P-in-c W Kirby St Andr *Ches* 01-07; V from 07. *St Andrew's Vicarage, 2 Lingdale Road, West Kirby, Wirral CH48 5DQ* Tel 0151-632 4728
E-mail standvic@aol.com

DIXON, Edward Michael. b 42. St Chad's Coll Dur BA64 Newc Univ MA93. **d** 66 **p** 67. C Hartlepool H Trin *Dur* 66-70; C Howden *York* 70-73; Chapl HM Pris *Liv* 73; Chapl HM Pris Onley 74-82; Chapl HM Pris Frankland 82-87; Chapl HM Pris Dur 87-97; Chapl HM Pris Acklington 97-98; Asst Chapl 98-02; P-in-c Shilbottle *Newc* 98-07; P-in-c Chevington 03-07; rtd 07. *2 Crowley Place, Newton Aycliffe DL5 4JH* Tel (01325) 312872

DIXON, Eric. b 31. MPS. EMMTC 78. **d** 81 **p** 82. NSM Kirk Langley *Derby* 81-96; NSM Mackworth All SS 81-96; Perm to Offic from 96. *5 Wentworth Close, Mickleover, Derby DE3 9YE* Tel (01332) 516546

DIXON, Mrs Francesca Dorothy. b 52. Cam Univ MA73. Qu Coll Birm 81. dss 84 d 87 p 94. W Bromwich All SS *Lich* 84-94; Par Dn 87-94; C 94; Chapl Burrswood Chr Cen *Roch* 95; Perm to Offic *Chich* 97-04; Lic to Offic from 04. *46 Arun Vale, Coldwaltham, Pulborough RH20 1LP* Tel (01798) 872177

DIXON, John Kenneth. b 40. Linc Th Coll 79. d 81 p 82. C Goldington *St Alb* 81-85; V Cardington 85-94; RD Elstow 89-94; R Clifton 94-95; P-in-c Southill 94-95; R Clifton and Southill 95-05; RD Shefford 95-01; rtd 05. *7 Milton Fields, Brixham TQ5 0BH* Tel (01803) 854396
E-mail eidyn@cainnech.fsworld.co.uk

DIXON, John Scarth. b 69. Aber Univ MA92. Westcott Ho Cam 95. d 98 p 99. C Walney Is *Carl* 98-01; R Harrington 01-06; V Hawkshead and Low Wray w Sawrey and Rusland etc from 06. *The Vicarage, Vicarage Lane, Hawkshead, Ambleside LA22 0PD* Tel (01539) 530375 E-mail jjcdixon@btinternet.com

DIXON, Karen Belinda. See BEST, Miss Karen Belinda

DIXON, Kenneth. See DIXON, John Kenneth

DIXON, Lorraine. b 65. Leeds Univ BA96. Qu Coll Birm BD98. d 98 p 99. C Potternewton *Ripon* 98-01; Chapl Ches Univ 01-05; Min Can Ches Cathl 04-05; Deanery Missr to Young Adults Yardley & Bordsley *Birm* from 05. *288A Ladypool Road, Birmingham B12 8JU* Tel 0121-449 2790
E-mail l.dixon65@btopenworld.com

DIXON, Michael. See DIXON, Edward Michael

DIXON, Nicholas Scarth. b 30. G&C Coll Cam BA54 MA63. Westcott Ho Cam 54. d 56 p 57. C Walney Is *Carl* 56-59; CF 59-62; V Whitehaven Ch Ch w H Trin *Carl* 62-70; R Blofield w Hemblington *Nor* 70-77; P-in-c Bowness *Carl* 77-79; R 79-81; V Frizington and Arlecdon 81-87; V Barton, Pooley Bridge and Martindale 87-95; rtd 95; Perm to Offic *Carl* from 95. *7 Mayburgh Avenue, Penrith CA11 8PA* Tel (01768) 892864

DIXON, Canon Peter. b 36. Qu Coll Ox BA58 MA62 Birm Univ BD65 PhD75. Qu Coll Birm. d 60 p 61. C Mountain Ash *Llan* 60-63; C Penrhiwceiber w Matthewstown and Ynysboeth 63-68; P-in-c 68-70; V Bronllys w Llanfilo *S & B* 70-02; Bp's Chapl for Readers 80-02; Bp's Chapl for Th Educn 83-02; Warden of Readers 92-02; RD Hay 90-02; Can Res Brecon Cathl 98-02; rtd 02. *22 The Caerpound, Hay-on-Wye, Hereford HR3 5DU* Tel (01497) 820775

DIXON, Peter. b 70. Ex Univ BTh08. SWMTC 04. d 07 p 08. C Redruth w Lanner and Treleigh *Truro* from 07. *11 Park Road, Redruth TR15 2JF* Tel (01209) 216441
E-mail peter_dixon@btinternet.com

DIXON, Peter David. b 48. Edin Univ BSc71 MIMechE. Edin Dioc NSM Course 75. d 79 p 80. NSM Prestonpans *Edin* 79-89; NSM Musselburgh 79-89; NSM Edin St Luke 90; P-in-c Edin St Barn from 91. *8 Oswald Terrace, Prestonpans EH32 9EG* Tel (01875) 812985

DIXON, Philip. b 48. Leeds Univ BSc69 Open Univ BA91. St Jo Coll Nottm 77. d 80 p 81. C Soundwell *Bris* 80-82; C Stoke Bishop 82-84; TV Hemel Hempstead *St Alb* 84-85; Chapl Westonbirt Sch from 85; Perm to Offic *Bris* from 86. *East Lodge, Westonbirt School, Tetbury GL8 8QG* Tel (01666) 880333

DIXON, Philip Roger. b 54. CCC Ox BA77 MA80. Oak Hill Th Coll BA80. d 80 p 81. C Droylsden St Mary *Man* 80-84; TV Rochdale 84-91; V Audenshaw St Steph from 91; AD Ashton-under-Lyne 03-08. *St Stephen's Vicarage, 176 Stamford Road, Audenshaw, Manchester M34 5WW* Tel 0161-370 1863
E-mail ssaudenshaw@aol.com

DIXON, Robert. b 50. Univ of Wales (Lamp) BA80 Sussex Univ MA04. Chich Th Coll 80. d 81 p 82. C Maidstone St Martin *Cant* 81-84; Chapl HM Youth Cust Cen Dover 84-88; C All Hallows by the Tower etc *Lon* 88-90; P-in-c Southwick H Trin *Dur* 90-97; R 97; R Etchingham *Chich* from 97; V Hurst Green from 97. *9 McMichaels Way, Hurst Green, Etchingham TN19 7HJ* Tel (01580) 860105 Mobile 07779-121169
E-mail sussexrob@aol.com

DIXON, Roger John. b 33. Magd Coll Cam BA58 MA61. EAMTC 78. d 79 p 80. NSM Fakenham w Alethorpe *Nor* 79-82; C Brandeston w Kettleburgh *St E* 82-84; P-in-c 84-99; Asst Chapl Framlingham Coll 82-99; RD Loes *St E* 97-98; rtd 99; Perm to Offic *Nor* 99-05 and *Llan* from 05. *9 The Crescent, Fairwater, Cardiff CF5 3DF* Tel (029) 2056 6031

DIXON, Ms Sheila. b 46. Open Univ BA78 Trent Poly CertEd79. St Jo Coll Nottm 93. d 93 p 94. Par Dn Ordsall *S'well* 93-94; C 94-97; P-in-c Sutton w Carlton and Normanton upon Trent etc from 97; P-in-c Norwell w Ossington, Cromwell and Caunton from 05. *The Vicarage, Main Street, Norwell, Newark NG23 6JT* Tel (01636) 636329 E-mail sdixonrev@btinternet.com

DIXON, Stephen William. b 53. Nottm Univ BA75 Man Metrop Univ PGCE88 Liv Univ MTh00. NOC 96. d 99 p 00. NSM Meltham *Wakef* 99-02; NSM Upper Holme Valley from 02; Lic Preacher *Man* from 01. *83 Totties, Holmfirth HD9 1UJ* Tel (01484) 687376

DIXON, Mrs Teresa Mary. b 61. Southn Univ BSc82 Ball Coll Ox PGCE83. EAMTC 99. d 02 p 03. NSM Sutton and Witcham w Mepal *Ely* 02-04; C Littleport 04-06; NSM Witchford w Wentworth from 06. *Ash Tree Farm, A Furlong Drove, Little Downham, Ely CB6 2EW* Tel (01353) 699552
E-mail teresa.dixon@ely.anglican.org

DNISTRIANSKYJ, Stefan Mykola. b 61. Leic Univ BSc82 Ches Coll of HE BTh02. NOC 99. d 02 p 03. C Halliwell St Luke *Man* 02-06; TV New Bury w Gt Lever 06-09; P-in-c Anchorsholme *Blackb* from 09. *The Vicarage, 36 Valeway Avenue, Thornton-Cleveleys FY5 3RN* Tel (01253) 823904 Mobile 07931-785598
E-mail dnists@gmail.com

DOBB, Canon Arthur Joseph. b 31. ARIBA54 ACertCM80 Hon FGCM93. Oak Hill Th Coll 56. d 58 p 59. C Bolton St Paul *Man* 58-60; C Rawtenstall St Mary 60-62; V Bircle 62-72; V Harwood 72-84; Hon Can Man Cathl 81-96; V Wingates 84-96; rtd 96; Perm to Offic *Man* from 96. *97 Turton Heights, Bromley Cross, Bolton BL2 3DU* Tel (01204) 308419

DOBB, Christopher. b 46. Dur Univ BA68. Cuddesdon Coll 68. d 70 p 71. C Portsea St Mary *Portsm* 70-73; Lic to Offic *S'wark* 73-77; Perm to Offic *Bris* 77-79; Lic to Offic 79-81; V Swindon St Aug 81-98; rtd 98. *Kingsbury Hall, The Green, Calne SN11 8DG* Tel (01249) 821521 Fax 817246
E-mail kingsburyhallcd@aol.com

DOBBIE, Charles William Granville. b 49. OBE92. Wycliffe Hall Ox 94. d 96 p 97. C Morriston *S & B* 96-00; Asst Chapl Morriston Hosp/Ysbyty Treforys NHS Trust 97-00; V Lyonsdown H Trin *St Alb* from 00. *Holy Trinity Vicarage, 18 Lyonsdown Road, Barnet EN5 1JE* Tel (020) 8216 3786
E-mail charles@holytrinitylyonsdown.org.uk

DOBBIE, Gary William. b 51. St Andr Univ MA75 BD77 Magd Coll Cam CertEd80 FRSA98 FSAScot. Coll of Resurr Mirfield 83. d 83 p 83. C Kimbolton Sch 83-84; Hon C Kimbolton *Ely* 83-84; Sen Chapl Ch Hosp Horsham 86-96; Asst Chapl 96-03; Housemaster 93-03; Chapl Shrewsbury Sch from 03. *Shrewsbury School, Kingsland, Shrewsbury SY3 7BA* Tel (01743) 280550 Mobile 07879-426056 E-mail chaplain@shrewsbury.org.uk

DOBBIN, Canon Charles Philip. b 51. Jes Coll Cam BA73 MA77 Oriel Coll Ox BA75 MA88. St Steph Ho Ox 74. d 76 p 77. C New Addington *Cant* 76-79; C Melton Mowbray w Thorpe Arnold *Leic* 79-83; V Loughb Gd Shep 83-89; V Ashby-de-la-Zouch St Helen w Coleorton 89-00; RD Akeley W 93-00; Hon Can Leic Cathl 94-00; TR Moor Allerton *Ripon* from 00; Dioc Interfaith Relns Officer from 09. *St John's Rectory, 1 Fir Tree Lane, Leeds LS17 7BZ* Tel 0113-268 4598
E-mail cdobbin@aol.com

DOBBIN, Harold John. b 47. Liv Univ BSc69. St Steph Ho Ox 70. d 73 p 74. C Newbold w Dunston *Derby* 73-77; C Leckhampton SS Phil and Jas w Cheltenham St Jas *Glouc* 77-80; V Hebburn St Cuth *Dur* 80-86; R Barlborough *Derby* 86-95; P-in-c Alfreton 95-00; V 00-04; RD Alfreton 02-04; P-in-c Clifton 04-08; P-in-c Norbury w Snelston 04-08; rtd 08. *21 Dale Close, Fritchley, Belper DE56 2HZ* E-mail harolddobbin@yahoo.co.uk

DOBBIN, Miss Penelope Jane. b 59. Slough Coll GRSC88. SAOMC 96. d 99 p 00. C Bideford, Northam, Westward Ho!, Appledore etc *Ex* 99-05; TV from 05. *The Rectory, Weare Gifford, Bideford EX39 4QP* Tel (01237) 429468
E-mail penelopedobbin@btinternet.com

DOBBINS, Lorraine Sharon. b 72. Ripon Coll Cuddesdon BTh01. d 01 p 02. C Talbot Village *Sarum* 01-05; TV Preston w Sutton Poyntz and Osmington w Poxwell from 05. *2 Primula Close, Weymouth DT3 6SL*
E-mail lorrainedobbins@hotmail.com

DOBBS, George Christopher. b 43. Linc Th Coll 66. d 68 p 69. C Hykeham *Linc* 68-71; Asst Master Heneage Sch Grimsby 71-78; Perm to Offic *S'well* 78-80; TV Chelmsley Wood *Birm* 80-84; TV Rochdale *Man* 84-99; V Sudden St Aidan and C Castleton Moor 00-08; rtd 08. *9 Highlands, Littleborough OL15 0DS* Tel (01706) 377688 E-mail g3rjy@gqpr.demon.co.uk

DOBBS, Matthew Joseph. b 62. St Mich Coll Llan BTh04. d 04 p 05. C Llantwit Major 04-08; TV Monkton *St D* from 08. *Limestone Cottage, St Twynnells, Pembroke SA71 5HX* Tel (01646) 661236 E-mail matthew@mdobbs.freeserve.co.uk

DOBBS, Michael John. b 48. Linc Th Coll 74. d 77 p 78. C Warsop *S'well* 77-82; V Worksop St Paul 82-89; P-in-c Mansfield St Mark 89-03; V Kirk Hallam *Derby* 03-05; rtd 05; Perm to Offic *S'well* from 06. *30 Waverley Road, Mansfield NG18 5AG* E-mail mjdmjd@ntlworld.com

DOBELL (née PRICE), Mrs Alison Jane. b 63. Aston Tr Scheme 91 Westcott Ho Cam 93. d 95 p 96. C Upper Norwood All SS *S'wark* 95-99; V Mitcham St Barn 99-07. *74 Radway Road, Southampton SO15 7PJ* Tel (023) 8077 3631
E-mail alisonjane.price@btinternet.com

DOBLE, Mrs Maureen Mary Thompson. b 44. RGN65. S Dios Minl Tr Scheme 90. d 93 p 94. NSM Kingston St Mary w Broomfield etc *B & W* 93-07; Chapl Taunton and Somerset NHS Trust 03-07; rtd 07; Perm to Offic *B & W* from 07. *Rosebank, Lyngford Lane, Taunton TA2 7LL* Tel (01823) 286727

DOBLE, Peter. b 29. Univ of Wales (Cardiff) BA51 Fitzw Coll Cam BA54 MA58 St Edm Hall Ox MA68 Leeds Univ PhD92. Wesley Ho Cam 52. d 55 p 58. In Ch of S India 55-60; In Meth Ch 60-64; Hd of RE Qu Mary Sch Lytham St Annes *Blackb*

64-67; Lect RS Culham Coll Abingdon *Ox* 67-69; Sen Lect 69-74; Prin Lect and Hd Relig Studies 74-80; Perm to Offic *York* from 80; Dir York RE Cen 80-94; Sen Fell Th and RS Leeds Univ 95-98; Hon Lect from 98. *6 Witham Drive, Huntington, York YO32 9YD* Tel (01904) 761288
E-mail peter.doble@btinternet.com

DOBSON, Catherine Heather. b 71. ERMC. **d** 09. NSM Broughton w Loddington and Cransley etc *Pet* from 09. *72 Northampton Road, Broughton, Kettering NN14 1NS* Tel (01536) 790648 E-mail catherine.dobson2@virgin.net

DOBSON, Christopher John. b 62. Univ of Wales (Abth) BA83. Wycliffe Hall Ox BA88. **d** 89 **p** 90. C Biggin Hill *Roch* 89-92; C Tunbridge Wells St Jas w St Phil 92-95; USPG Zimbabwe 95-99; V Paddock Wood *Roch* 00-08; Dioc Ecum and Global Partnership Officer *Bris* from 08; C Downend from 09. *St John's Vicarage, Mayfield Park, Bristol BS16 3NW* Tel 0117-965 0878 Mobile 07904-831829 E-mail chris.j.dobson@gmail.com *or* chris.dobson@bristoldiocese.org

DOBSON, Geoffrey Norman. b 46. Leeds Univ CertEd68 Open Univ BA77 MA05 ACP70. Wells Th Coll 71. **d** 74 **p** 75. C Wanstead H Trin Hermon Hill *Chelmsf* 74-76; Colchester Adnry Youth Chapl 76-78; C Halstead St Andr w H Trin and Greenstead Green 76-78; Asst Dir Educn (Youth) *Carl* 78-82; P-in-c Kirkandrews-on-Eden w Beaumont and Grinsdale 78-82; V Illingworth *Wakef* 82-86; V Roxton w Gt Barford *St Alb* 86-93; Chapl N Man Health Care NHS Trust 93-98; P-in-c Newton Heath St Wilfrid and St Anne *Man* 93-97; C Newton Heath 97-98; P-in-c Alconbury cum Weston *Ely* 98-00; P-in-c Buckworth 98-00; P-in-c Gt w Lt Stukeley 98-00; Perm to Offic from 02. *30 Lees Lane, Southoe, St Neots PE19 5YG* Tel (01480) 475474 E-mail geoffreyndobson@aol.com

DOBSON, Mrs Joanna Jane Louise. b 61. Coll of Ripon & York St Jo BEd83. NEOC 98. **d** 01 **p** 02. NSM Scalby *York* 01-04; V Bridlington Em 04-08; P-in-c Skipsea w Ulrome and Barmston w Fraisthorpe 04-08; Fresh Expressions Min Retford Deanery *S'well* from 08. *The Rectory, Main Street, Rampton, Retford DN22 0HR* Tel (01777) 248143 Mobile 07828-181506 E-mail revjoannadobson@yahoo.co.uk

DOBSON, Canon John Richard. b 64. Van Mildert Coll Dur BA87. Ripon Coll Cuddesdon 87. **d** 89 **p** 90. C Benfieldside *Dur* 89-92; C Darlington St Cuth 92-96; C-in-c Blackwell All SS and Salutation CD 96-98; V Blackwell All SS and Salutation from 98; P-in-c Coniscliffe from 04; AD Darlington from 01; Hon Can Dur Cathl from 08. *104 Blackwell Lane, Darlington DL3 8QQ* Tel (01325) 354503 E-mail john.dobson@durham.anglican.org

DOBSON, Philip Albert. b 52. Lanc Univ BA73 CertEd74. Trin Coll Bris 89. **d** 89 **p** 90. C Grenoside *Sheff* 89-92; C Cove St Jo *Guildf* 92-93; TV 93-96; V Camberley St Martin Old Dean 96-07; TR Bushbury *Lich* from 07. *The Rectory, 382 Bushbury Lane, Wolverhampton WV10 8JP* Tel (01902) 787688
E-mail philipdobson1@tiscali.co.uk

DOBSON, Stuart Joseph. b 51. Westmr Coll Ox BA85. Chich Th Coll 86. **d** 88 **p** 89. C Costessey *Nor* 88-90; C Chaddesden St Phil *Derby* 90-92; C Friern Barnet St Jas *Lon* 92-93; TV Plymouth Em, Efford and Laira *Ex* 93-96; P-in-c Laira 96; R Withington St Crispin *Man* 96-98; P-in-c Beguildy and Heyope *S & B* 98-00; P-in-c Llangynllo and Bleddfa 99-00; TV Bruton and Distr *B & W* 00-01; Community Chapl *Linc* from 09. *The Vicarage, Station Road, Sutterton, Boston PE20 2JH* Tel (01205) 461294 E-mail stuart.dobson@btinternet.com

DOCHERTY, William Sales Hill. b 54. Callendar Park Coll of Educn Falkirk DipEd75 Open Univ BA96. TISEC 98. **d** 05 **p** 06. C Broughty Ferry *Bre* from 05. *27 Seafield Road, Broughty Ferry, Dundee DD5 3AH* Tel (01382) 731914
E-mail therevdoc@btinternet.com

✠**DOCKER, The Rt Revd Ivor Colin.** b 25. Birm Univ BA46 St Cath Soc Ox BA49 MA52. Wycliffe Hall Ox 46. **d** 49 **p** 50 **c** 75. C Normanton *Wakef* 49-52; C Halifax St Jo Bapt 52-54; Area Sec (Dios Derby Linc and S'well) CMS 54-58; Metrop Sec (S) 58-59; V Midhurst *Chich* 59-64; RD Midhurst 61-64; R Woolbeding 61-64; V Seaford w Sutton 64-71; RD Seaford 64-71; Can and Preb Chich Cathl 66-91; V Eastbourne St Mary 71-75; RD Eastbourne 71-75; Suff Bp Horsham 75-84; Area Bp Horsham 84-91; rtd 91; Asst Bp Ex from 91. *Braemar, Bradley Road, Bovey Tracey, Newton Abbot TQ13 9EU* Tel (01626) 832468

DODD, Alan Henry. b 42. Man Univ BA70 MA79. Chich Th Coll 82. **d** 82 **p** 83. C Fareham H Trin *Portsm* 82-84; TV 84-89; V Osmotherley w Harlsey and Ingleby Arncliffe *York* 89-05; RD Mowbray 02-04; Chapl Northallerton Health Services NHS Trust 92-05; rtd 06; Perm to Offic *Ripon* from 06. *3 Nightingale Close, Brompton on Swale, Richmond DL10 7TR* Tel (01748) 810147 E-mail thedodds178@btinternet.com

DODD, Andrew Patrick. b 68. Hatf Poly BEng91 Selw Coll Cam BTh00. Westcott Ho Cam 97. **d** 00 **p** 01. C New Addington *S'wark* 00-04; R Newington St Mary from 04; AD S'wark and Newington from 07. *The Rectory, 57 Kennington Park Road, London SE11 4JQ* Tel (020) 7735 2807 *or* 7735 1894 E-mail rector@stmarynewington.org.uk

DODD, Miss Denise Kate. b 72. Cranmer Hall Dur 07. **d** 09. C Porchester *S'well* from 09. *127A Digby Avenue, Nottingham NG3 6DT* Tel 0115-987 7938
E-mail denisekdodd@yahoo.co.uk

DODD, James Henry Birchenough. b 25. CPsychol AFBPsS Ox Univ MA. Westcott Ho Cam 85. **d** 85 **p** 86. NSM Epping Upland *Chelmsf* 85-95; NSM Epping Distr 95-96; Perm to Offic from 96. *The Chequers, Epping Upland, Epping CM16 6PH* Tel (01992) 572561

DODD, Jane. b 33. Loughb Univ ALA51 FLA51. **d** 98 **p** 99. OLM Wroxham w Hoveton and Belaugh *Nor* 98-08; Perm to Offic from 08. *Locheil, Tunstead Road, Hoveton, Norwich NR12 8QN* Tel (01603) 782509

DODD, Mrs Jean. b 47. **d** 98 **p** 99. OLM Irlam *Man* from 98; OLM Cadishead from 09. *75 Harewood Road, Manchester M44 6DL* Tel 0161-775 9125

DODD, John Dudley. b 15. Liv Univ BA36 Lon Univ BD51 DipEd54. Westcott Ho Cam 54. **d** 54 **p** 55. C Jersey St Helier *Win* 54-78; rtd 78; P-in-c Jersey Gouray St Martin *Win* 78-93; NSM Jersey St Luke 94-96; Perm to Offic from 96. *Lakeside Nursing Home, La Rue de la Commune, St Peter, Jersey JE3 7BN*

DODD, John Stanley. b 24. Huron Coll Ontario 46. **d** 50 **p** 51. C Kitchener Canada 50-52; Leeds St Jo Ev *Ripon* 52-54; C High Harrogate Ch Ch 54-58; V Stainton 58-65; V Weeton 58-64; V Meanwood 65-89; rtd 89; Perm to Offic *Ripon* from 89. *3 Shawdene, Burton Crescent, Leeds LS6 4DN* Tel 0113-278 9069

DODD, Malcolm Ogilvie. b 46. Dur Univ BSc67 Loughb Univ MSc90. Edin Th Coll 67. **d** 70 **p** 71. C Hove All SS *Chich* 70-73; C Crawley 73-78; P-in-c Rusper 79-83; Chapl Brighton Coll Jun Sch 83; Chapl Stancliffe Hall Sch 84-97; rtd 01. *210 chemin des Villecrozes, 26170 Buis-les-Baronnies, France* Tel (0033) (4) 75 28 05 99 E-mail m.et.j.dodd@wanadoo.fr

DODD, Michael Christopher. b 33. Ch Coll Cam BA55 MA59. Ridley Hall Cam 57. **d** 59 **p** 60. C Stechford *Birm* 59-62; V Quinton Road W St Boniface 62-72; TV Paston *Pet* 72-77; TR Hodge Hill *Birm* 77-89; rtd 90; Perm to Offic *Birm* from 90. *39 Regency Gardens, Birmingham B14 4JS* Tel 0121-474 6945

DODD, Canon Peter Curwen. b 33. St Jo Coll Cam BA57 FRSA93. Linc Th Coll 58 Wm Temple Coll Rugby 59. **d** 60 **p** 61. C Eastwood *Sheff* 60-63; Ind Chapl 63-67; Ind Chapl *Newc* 67-98; RD Newc E 78-83 and 92-95; Hon Can Newc Cathl 82-98; rtd 98; Perm to Offic *Newc* from 98. *Glenesk, 26 The Oval, Benton, Newcastle upon Tyne NE12 9PP* Tel 0191-266 1293

DODDS, Alan Richard. b 46. Greenwich Univ BA92 K Coll Lon MA94. **d** 95 **p** 96. C Deal St Geo *Cant* 95-99; C-in-c Deal, The Carpenter's Arms 98-99; Prin OLM Course 99-01; TV Cullompton, Willand, Uffculme, Kentisbeare etc *Ex* 02-07; rtd 07. *Green Pastures, Smithincott Farm, Uffculme, Cullompton EX15 3EF* Tel (01884) 841801 E-mail alan.and.chris@tesco.net

DODDS, Brian Martin. b 37. AKC62. **d** 63 **p** 64. C Morpeth *Newc* 63-67; C Georgetown Cathl Guyana 67-69; V Morawhanna 69-71; V Willington 71-74; TV Brayton *York* 75-79; V Gravelly Hill *Birm* 79-83; V Winterton *Linc* 83-85; V Winterton Gp 85-90; V Gainsborough St Jo 90-96; V Morton 95-96; R Walesby 96-00; rtd 00; Perm to Offic *Linc* from 01. *69 Pennell Street, Lincoln LN5 7TD* Tel (01522) 512593 E-mail bmdodds@talk21.com

DODDS, Preb Graham Michael. b 58. York Univ PGCE81 Liv Univ MA01 LTCL80 GTCL80. Trin Coll Bris 84. **d** 84 **p** 85. C Reigate St Mary *S'wark* 84-91; P-in-c Bath Walcot *B & W* 91-93; R 93-96; Lay Tr Adv from 96; Dir Reader Studies from 96; Asst Dir Min Development from 01; Preb Wells Cathl from 03. *25 Wood Close, Wells BA5 2GA* Tel (01749) 677531 *or* 670777 Fax 674240 E-mail general@bathwells.anglican.org

DODDS, Linda. b 54. **d** 08 **p** 09. OLM Bishop Auckland Woodhouse Close CD *Dur* from 08. *30 Low Etherley, Bishop Auckland DL14 0EU* Tel (01388) 832756
E-mail linda_dodds@yahoo.co.uk

DODDS, Canon Neil Sutherland. b 35. Keble Coll Ox BA59 MA63 ARCO59. Linc Th Coll 60. **d** 62 **p** 63. C Handsworth St Jas *Birm* 62-65; V Highters Heath 65-75; V Olton 75-00; RD Solihull 79-89; Hon Can Birm Cathl 82-00; rtd 00; Perm to Offic *Birm* and *Cov* from 00. *29 Stuart Close, Warwick CV34 6AQ* Tel (01926) 402909 E-mail neil.jean.dodds@talk21.com

DODDS, The Ven Norman Barry. b 43. Open Univ BA. CITC 73. **d** 76 **p** 77. C Ballynafeigh St Jude *D & D* 76-80; I Belfast St Mich *Conn* from 80; Chapl HM Pris Belfast from 84; Can Belf Cathl from 98; Adn Belfast *Conn* from 07. *5 Sunningdale Park, Belfast BT14 6RU* Tel and fax (028) 9071 5463 Mobile 07763-935160 E-mail doddscavehill@yahoo.com

DODDS, Peter. b 35. WMMTC 88 Qu Coll Birm 88. **d** 91 **p** 92. NSM Hartshill *Cov* 91-93; NSM Nuneaton St Mary 94-95; Hon Chapl Geo Eliot Hosp NHS Trust Nuneaton from 95; Hon Chapl Mary Ann Evans Hospice from 95; NSM Camp Hill w Galley Common *Cov* 99-01; Perm to Offic from 02. *Wem House, 51 Magyar Crescent, Nuneaton CV11 4SQ* Tel (024) 7638 4061

DODGE, Robin Dennis. b 58. Cornell Univ NY BA80 Boston Univ JD83. Virginia Th Sem MDiv99. **d** 98 **p** 99. C Arlington St Mary USA 98-02; C Bris St Mary Redcliffe w Temple etc

DODGE — continued
02-05; R Washington St Dav USA from 05. *5150 Macomb Street NW, Washington DC 20016, USA* Tel (001) (202) 966 2093 Fax 966 3437 E-mail robindodge@starpower.net

DODHIA, Hitesh Kishorilal. b 57. Cranmer Hall Dur 85. **d** 88 **p** 89. C Leamington Priors All SS *Cov* 88-91; Chapl HM YOI Glen Parva 91-92; Asst Chapl 94-98; Chapl HM Pris Roch 92-94; Chapl HM Pris The Mount 98-01; Chapl HM Pris Wormwood Scrubs from 01; Perm to Offic *St Alb* from 02. *HM Prison Wormwood Scrubs, Du Cane Road, London W12 0TU* Tel (020) 8588 3331 E-mail dodhias@hotmail.com

DODSON, Canon Gordon. b 31. Em Coll Cam BA54 MA58 LLB55 LLM01 Barrister 56. Ridley Hall Cam 57. **d** 59 **p** 60. C Belhus Park *Chelmsf* 59-60; C Barking St Marg 60-63; CMS 63-67; C New Malden and Coombe *S'wark* 67-69; V Snettisham *Nor* 69-81; RD Heacham and Rising 76-81; P-in-c Reepham and Hackford w Whitwell and Kerdiston 81-83; P-in-c Salle 81-83; P-in-c Thurning w Wood Dalling 81-83; R Reepham, Hackford w Whitwell, Kerdiston etc 83-94; Hon Can Nor Cathl 85-94; rtd 94; Perm to Offic *Nor* from 94. *Poppygate, 2 The Loke, Cromer NR27 9DH* Tel (01263) 511811

DODSON, James Peter. b 32. Lich Th Coll 58. **d** 61 **p** 62. C Chasetown *Lich* 61-63; C Hednesford 63-68; V Halifax St Hilda *Wakef* 68-76; V Upperthong 76-85; TV York All SS Pavement w St Crux and St Martin etc 85-90; rtd 92; Perm to Offic *Ripon* from 92. *Roseville, Studley Road, Ripon HG4 2QH* Tel (01765) 602053

DODSWORTH, George Brian Knowles. b 34. Open Univ BSc94. St Mich Coll Llan 59. **d** 62 **p** 63. C Kidderminster St Mary *Worc* 62-67; Asst Chapl HM Pris Man 67-68; Chapl HM Pris Eastchurch 68-70; Chapl HM Pris Wakef 70-74; Chapl HM Pris Wormwood Scrubs 74-83; Asst Chapl Gen of Pris (SE) 83-90; Asst Chapl Gen of Pris (HQ) 90-94; Chapl HM Pris Brixton 94-95; rtd 95; Perm to Offic *S'wark* from 95. *19 Farnsworth Court, West Parkside, London SE10 0QF* Tel and fax (020) 8305 0283 E-mail briandodsworth611@btinternet.com

DODWELL, Andrew. b 75. Man Univ BSc96 MSc98. SWMTC 06. **d** 08. C Barnstaple *Ex* from 08. *28 Old School Road, Barnstaple EX32 9DP* Tel (01271) 371068

DOE, Martin Charles. b 54. Lon Univ BSc(Econ)75 PGCE87 MA95. St Steph Ho Ox 89. **d** 91 **p** 92. C Portsea St Mary *Portsm* 91-94; Chapl Abbey Grange High Sch Leeds 94-00; Sen Angl Chapl Scarborough and NE Yorks Healthcare NHS Trust from 00. *Scarborough Hospital, Woodlands Drive, Scarborough YO12 6QL* Tel (01723) 342500
E-mail martin.doe@acute.sney.nhs.uk

✠**DOE, The Rt Revd Michael David.** b 47. St Jo Coll Dur BA69 Bath Univ Hon LLD02. Ripon Hall Ox 69. **d** 72 **p** 73 **c** 94. C St Helier *S'wark* 72-76; Youth Sec BCC 76-81; C-in-c Blackbird Leys CD Ox 81-88; V Blackbird Leys 88-89; RD Cowley 86-89; Soc Resp Adv *Portsm* 89-94; Can Res Portsm Cathl 89-94; Suff Bp Swindon *Bris* 94-04; Gen Sec USPG from 04; Hon Asst Bp S'wark from 04. *USPG, 200 Dover Street, London SE1 4YB* Tel (020) 7378 5678 E-mail michaeld@uspg.org.uk

DOE, Mrs Priscilla Sophia. b 41. LRAM62. SEITE 97. **d** 00 **p** 01. NSM Maidstone All SS and St Phil w Tovil *Cant* from 00. *Mount St Laurence, High Street, Cranbrook TN17 3EW* Tel (01580) 712330

DOEL, Patrick Stephen. b 71. Peterho Cam BA92 MA97. Wycliffe Hall Ox BA01 MA06 MSt03. **d** 03 **p** 04. C Blackheath St Jo *S'wark* 03-06; P-in-c Deptford St Nic and St Luke 06-08; V from 08. *11 Evelyn Street, London SE8 5RQ* Tel (020) 8692 2749 E-mail steve@deptfordchurch.org *or* steve@doel.org

DOERR, Mrs Anne. b 55. Man Univ BA76. SEITE 06. **d** 09. NSM Belmont *S'wark* from 09. *14 Central Way, Carshalton SM5 3NF* Tel (020) 8669 2494 Mobile 07811-908731 E-mail aedoerr@btinternet.com

DOGGETT, Margaret Ann. b 36. Open Univ BA78 Homerton Coll Cam PGCE79. **d** 96 **p** 97. OLM Pulham Market, Pulham St Mary and Starston *Nor* 96-99; OLM Dickleburgh and The Pulhams 99-01; rtd 02; Perm to Offic *Nor* from 02. *Antares, Station Road, Pulham St Mary, Diss IP21 4QT* Tel and fax (01379) 676662 Mobile 07710-621547
E-mail john.doggett@btinternet.com

DOHERTY, Mrs Christine. b 46. SEN72. STETS 97. **d** 00 **p** 01. NSM Framfield *Chich* 00-03; C Seaford w Sutton from 03. *St Luke's House, 16 Saltwood Road, Seaford BN25 3SP* Tel (01323) 892969 E-mail chris.doh@virgin.net

DOHERTY, Deana Rosina Mercy. b 21. St Aid Coll Dur BA55. **dss** 82 **d** 87 **p** 94. Sutton St Jas and Wawne *York* 82-95; Par Dn 87-94; C 94-95; Perm to Offic 95-99; rtd 98. *Alana, Chapel Street, Lismore, Co Waterford, Republic of Ireland* Tel (00353) (58) 54418

DOHERTY, Sean William. d 07 **p** 08. C Cricklewood St Gabr and St Mich *Lon* from 07. *31 Olive Road, London NW2 6TY* Tel (020) 8450 8707 E-mail sean.doherty@st-gabriels.org

DOHERTY, Thomas Alexander. b 48. Chich Th Coll 73. **d** 76 **p** 77. V Choral Derry Cathl 76-79; C Llandaff w Capel Llanilltern 79-80; PV Llan Cathl 80-84; V Penmark w Porthkerry 84-90; R Merthyr Dyfan 90-02; V Margam from 02. *Margam Vicarage, 59A Bertha Road, Margam, Port Talbot SA13 2AP* Tel (01639) 891067

DOICK, Paul Stephen James. b 70. Ripon Coll Cuddesdon 03. **d** 05 **p** 06. C Hove *Chich* from 05. *The Vicarage, 119 Holland Road, Hove BN3 1JS* Tel 07742-868602 (mobile)
E-mail p.doick@btinternet.com

DOIDGE, Charles William. b 44. Univ Coll Lon BSc65 MSc67 PhD72. EMMTC 93. **d** 93 **p** 94. NSM Blaby *Leic* 93-96; P-in-c Willoughby Waterleys, Peatling Magna etc 96-04; rtd 04. *21 Brunel Mews, Solsbro Road, Torquay TQ2 6QA* Tel (01803) 690548 E-mail doidge@dmu.ac.uk

DOIDGE, Valerie Gladys. b 49. STETS 98. **d** 01 **p** 02. C St Leonards St Ethelburga *Chich* 01-07; C Hollington St Leon from 07. *6 Collinswood Drive, St Leonards-on-Sea TN38 0NU* Tel (01424) 425651 E-mail valrod@rdoidge.freeserve.co.uk

DOIG, Allan George. b 51. Univ of BC BA69 K Coll Cam BA73 MA80 PhD82 FSA98. Ripon Coll Cuddesdon 86. **d** 88 **p** 89. C Abingdon *Ox* 88-91; Chapl LMH Ox from 91; Fell from 96; Select Preacher *Ox* 95-96. *Lady Margaret Hall, Oxford OX2 6QA* Tel (01865) 274300 Fax 511069
E-mail allan.doig@lmh.ox.ac.uk

DOLAN, Miss Louise. b 68. St Paul's Cheltenham BA89 Reading Univ PGCE90. Aston Tr Scheme 92 Linc Th Coll 94 Westcott Ho Cam MA95. **d** 96 **p** 97. C N Stoneham *Win* 96-99. *19 Ipswich Grove, Norwich NR2 2LU* Tel (01603) 469865

DOLBY, Mrs Christine Teresa. b 54. Nottm Univ MA01 SRN80. EMMTC 98. **d** 01 **p** 02. C Cropwell Bishop w Colston Bassett, Granby etc *S'well* 01-05; P-in-c Ancaster Wilsford Gp *Linc* 05-08; Chapl Qu Medical Cen Nottm Univ Hosp NHS Trust from 08. *16 Morley's Close, Lowdham, Nottingham NG14 7HN* Tel 0115-966 5890 Mobile 07738-851181
E-mail c.dolby263@btinternet.com

DOLL, Canon Peter Michael. b 62. Yale Univ BA84 Ch Ch Ox DPhil89. Cuddesdon Coll BA94. **d** 95 **p** 96. C Cowley St Jo *Ox* 95-99; Chapl Worc Coll Ox 98-02; TV Abingdon *Ox* 02-09; Can Res Nor Cathl from 09. *56 The Close, Norwich NR1 4EG* Tel (01603) 218405 E-mail canonlibrarian@cathedral.org.uk

DOLLERY, Anne Mary Elizabeth. b 55. Hull Univ BA78. Ridley Hall Cam 02. **d** 04. C Thundersley *Chelmsf* 04-09; Perm to Offic from 09. *14 Grangeway, Benfleet SS7 3RP* Tel (01268) 771047
E-mail anne@thundersley.org

DOLMAN, Derek Alfred George Gerrit. b 40. ALCD64. **d** 65 **p** 66. C St Alb St Paul *St Alb* 65-68; C Bishopwearmouth St Gabr *Dur* 68-72; R Jarrow Grange 72-80; V New Catton St Luke *Nor* 80-98; V New Catton St Luke w St Aug 98-00; R S Croxton Gp *Leic* 00-06; rtd 06; Perm to Offic *Derby* and *Lich* from 07. *17 Kestrel Way, Burton-on-Trent DE15 0DJ* Tel (01283) 845330 E-mail derekdolman@uwclub.net

DOLMAN, William Frederick Gerrit. b 42. JP. K Coll Lon MB, BS65 Lon Univ LLB87 MRCS65 LRCP65. SEITE 04. **d** 06 **p** 07. NSM Beckley and Peasmarsh *Chich* from 06. *Little Bellhurst Cottage, Hobbs Lane, Beckley, Rye TN31 6TT*
E-mail hmcwd@aol.com

DOLPHIN, Mark Patrick (Pads). b 58. Man Univ BSc81. St Jo Coll Nottm 06. **d** 08 **p** 09. C Reading Greyfriars *Ox* from 08. *3 Auclum Close, Burghfield Common, Reading RG7 3DY* Tel 0118-983 2916 Mobile 07866-754770
E-mail pads.dolphin@greyfriars.org.uk

DOMINIAK, Paul Anthony. b 78. Univ of the S (USA) BA05 SS Coll Cam BA07 MPhil08. Westcott Ho Cam 05. **d** 08 **p** 09. C Ingleby Barwick *York* from 08. *27 Berrington Gardens, Ingleby Barwick, Stockton-on-Tees TS17 0UH* Tel 07972-761831 (mobile) E-mail pdominiak@gmail.com

DOMINIC MARK, Brother. *See* IND, Dominic Mark

DOMINY, Canon Peter John. b 36. Qu Coll Ox BA60 MA64 Aber Univ MLitt83. Oak Hill Th Coll 60. **d** 62 **p** 63. C Bedworth *Cov* 62-66; Nigeria 67-84; Sudan United Miss 67-72; V Jos St Piran 72-84; R Broadwater St Mary *Chich* 84-92; TR Broadwater 92-98; P-in-c Danehill 98-99; V 99-03; Can and Preb Chich Cathl 93-03; RD Uckfield 00-03; rtd 03; Perm to Offic *Sarum* from 03. *5 St Nicholas Gardens, Durweston, Blandford Forum DT11 0QH* Tel (01258) 450975

DOMMETT, Canon Richard Radmore. b 19. St Jo Coll Ox BA41 MA45. Wells Th Coll 41. **d** 43 **p** 44. C E Dulwich St Jo *S'wark* 43-48; C Peckham St Jo 48-52; V Clapham St Pet 52-60; R Caister *Nor* 60-81; P-in-c Saxthorpe and Corpusty 81-85; P-in-c Oulton SS Pet and Paul 81-85; P-in-c Blickling w Ingworth 81-85; P-in-c Heydon w Irmingland 82-85; Hon Can Nor Cathl 77-85; rtd 85; Perm to Offic *Nor* and *St E* from 85. *14 Norwich Road, Halesworth IP19 8HN* Tel (01986) 873778

DOMMETT, Simon Paul. b 58. Warwick Univ BSc79. St Jo Coll Nottm MA99. **d** 99 **p** 00. C Weston Favell 99-02; P-in-c Gt w Lt Harrowden and Orlingbury 02-06; P-in-c Isham w Pytchley 05-06; R Gt w Lt Harrowden and Orlingbury and Isham etc from 06. *The Vicarage, 18 Kings Lane, Little Harrowden, Wellingborough NN9 5BL* Tel (01933) 678225
E-mail rev.simon@virgin.net

DOMONEY, Canon Lynette May (Lyndy). b 44. Th Ext Educn Coll 90. **d** 92 **p** 93. S Africa 92-06; P-in-c Kessingland, Gisleham and Rushmere *Nor* 06-08; R from 08. *The Rectory, 1 Wash Lane, Kessingland, Lowestoft NR33 7QZ* Tel (01502) 740256 E-mail l.domoney@btinternet.com

DONAGHEY, Thomas Alfred. b 67. Trin Coll Bris 06. **d** 08 **p** 09. C Whittle-le-Woods *Blackb* from 08. *16 Carr Meadow, Bamber Bridge, Preston PR5 8HS* Tel (01772) 497687 Mobile 07974-457544 E-mail tdonaghey@hotmail.com

DONAGHY, Paul Robert Blount. b 56. **d** 00 **p** 01. OLM Goldsworth Park *Guildf* from 00. *5 Knightswood, Woking GU21 3PU* Tel (01483) 835503 E-mail p.donaghy@hotmail.co.uk

DONALD, Andrew William. b 19. St Jo Coll Morpeth 47 ACT ThL50. **d** 49 **p** 50. C Claremont Australia 49-50; C Perth Cathl 50-52; R Wyalkatchem 52-56; Perm to Offic *Lon* 57-58; Chapl Gothenburg *Eur* 58-65; Chapl Lausanne 65-68; Asst P Mt Lawley Australia 68-70; R Bellevue and Darlington 70-79; R Toodyay and Goomalling 79-84; rtd 84. *Eriswell, 18A Cobham Way, Westfield Park WA6111, Australia* Tel (0061) (8) 9390 8425

DONALD, Brother. *See* GREEN, Donald Pentney

DONALD, Dennis Curzon. b 38. Oak Hill Th Coll 68. **d** 70 **p** 71. C Carl St Jo 70-73; Lic to Offic 73-77; Warden Blaithwaite Ho Chr Conf Cen Wigton 73-90; Chapl Cumberland Infirmary 85-92; Chapl Eden Valley Hospice Carl 92-98; rtd 98; Perm to Offic *Carl* from 77. *5 The Old Bakery, Gretna DG16 5FZ* Tel (01461) 338053

DONALD, Robert Francis. b 49. St Jo Coll Nottm BTh75 LTh. **d** 75 **p** 76. C New Barnet St Jas *St Alb* 75-79; C St Alb St Paul 79-86; C St Alb St Mary Marshalswick 86-87; Lic to Offic from 87; Dir Chr Alliance Housing Assn Ltd 89-98. *24 Meadowcroft, St Albans AL1 1UD* Tel (01727) 841647 Mobile 07973-208289

DONALD, Rosemary Anne. b 52. STETS 99. **d** 02 **p** 03. NSM Blendworth w Chalton w Idsworth *Portsm* 02-07; P-in-c from 07. *1A Havant Road, Horndean, Waterlooville PO8 0DB* Tel (023) 9259 1719 E-mail rosemary.donald@virgin.net

DONALD, Steven. b 55. CertEd76 Hull Univ MA99. Oak Hill Th Coll BA88. **d** 88 **p** 89. C Cheadle All Hallows *Ches* 88-91; C Ardsley *Sheff* 91; V Kendray 92-99; P-in-c Chadderton Ch Ch *Man* 99-03; V 03-05; V Carl St Jo from 05. *St John's Vicarage, London Road, Carlisle CA1 2QQ* Tel (01228) 521601 E-mail stevedon1@aol.com

DONALD, William. b 30. Tyndale Hall Bris 58. **d** 61 **p** 62. C Stapenhill w Cauldwell *Derby* 61-63; Perm to Offic *Ox* 63-66; Lic to Offic *Bris* 66-70; C Cheltenham St Mark *Glouc* 70-77; C Glouc St Jas 77-82; Lic to Offic 82-95; rtd 95; Perm to Offic *Glouc* from 95. *82 Forest View Road, Gloucester GL4 0BY* Tel (01452) 506993

DONALDSON, Miss Elizabeth Anne. b 55. Univ of Wales (Ban) BSc76 Surrey Univ MSc80 Nottm Univ BA82. St Jo Coll Nottm 80. **dss** 83 **d** 87 **p** 94. Guildf Ch Ch 83-86; Cuddington 86-90; C 87-90; C Keresley and Coundon *Cov* 90-99; V Gt Amwell w St Margaret's and Stanstead Abbots *St Alb* from 00. *The Vicarage, 25 Hoddesdon Road, Stanstead Abbotts, Ware SG12 8EG* Tel (01920) 870115 Pager 07666-545248 E-mail vicar@3churches.net *or* anne.donaldson@ntlworld.com

DONALDSON, Mrs Janet Elizabeth. b 53. GTCL74 Whitelands Coll Lon CertEd75. EAMTC 95. **d** 98 **p** 99. NSM Tolleshunt Knights w Tiptree and Gt Braxted *Chelmsf* 98-02; V Knights and Hospitallers Par from 02. *The Rectory, Church Street, Great Maplestead, Halstead CO9 2RG* Tel (01787) 463106 E-mail janet@amdonaldson.freeserve.co.uk

DONALDSON, Malcolm Alexander. b 48. Cranmer Hall Dur 84. **d** 86 **p** 87. C Heworth H Trin *York* 86-89; Chapl York Distr Hosp 86-89; C Marfleet *York* 89-90; TV 90-96; R Collyhurst *Man* 96-05; rtd 05. *12 Clove Court, Tweedmouth, Berwick-upon-Tweed TD15 2FJ*

DONALDSON, Canon Roger Francis. b 50. Jes Coll Ox BA71 MA75. Westcott Ho Cam 72. **d** 74 **p** 75. C Mold *St As* 74-78; V Denio w Abererch *Ban* 78-95; TR Llanbeblig w Caernarfon and Betws Garmon etc from 95; AD Arfon from 04; Hon Can Ban Cathl from 04. *The Rectory, 4 Ffordd Menai, Caernarfon LL55 1LF* Tel (01286) 673750

DONALDSON, William Richard. b 56. St Cath Coll Cam BA78 MA81. Ridley Hall Cam 79. **d** 82 **p** 83. C Everton St Sav w St Cuth *Liv* 82-85; C Reigate St Mary *S'wark* 85-89; V Easton H Trin w St Gabr and St Lawr and St Jude *Bris* 89-99; V Ealing St Jo w St Jas *Lon* 99-07; Dir of Ords Willesden Area 06-07; Dir Chr Leadership Wycliffe Hall Ox from 07. *Wycliffe Hall, 54 Banbury Road, Oxford OX2 6PW* Tel (01865) 274200 E-mail will.donaldson@lineone.net

DONCASTER, Archdeacon of. *See* FITZHARRIS, The Ven Robert Aidan

DONCASTER, Suffragan Bishop of. *See* ASHTON, The Rt Revd Cyril Guy

DONE, Mrs Margaret. b 43. LNSM course 84 Linc Th Coll 91. **d** 92 **p** 94. OLM Saxilby w Tattershall *Linc* 92-06; OLM Bain Valley Gp from 06. *43 Park Lane, Coningsby, Lincoln LN4 4SW* Tel (01526) 343013

DONE, Nigel Anthony. b 68. Wye Coll Lon BSc89. St Jo Coll Dur BA98. **d** 98 **p** 99. C Pilton w Croscombe, N Wootton and Dinder

B & W 98-02; R Hardington Vale from 02. *The Rectory, Vicarage Lane, Norton St Philip, Bath BA2 7LY* Tel (01373) 834447 E-mail nigel.done@btinternet.com

DONEGAN-CROSS, Guy William. b 68. St Aid Coll Dur BA90. Trin Coll Bris BA98. **d** 99 **p** 00. C Swindon Ch Ch *Bris* 99-03; V Saltburn-by-the-Sea *York* from 03. *The Vicarage, Greta Street, Saltburn-by-the-Sea TS12 1LS* Tel (01287) 622007 E-mail guy@donegan-cross.freeserve.co.uk

DONELLA, Sister. *See* MATHIE, Patricia Jean

DONEY, Malcolm Charles. b 50. Lon Univ BA71 Middx Univ BA05. NTMTC 02. **d** 05 **p** 06. NSM Tufnell Park St Geo and All SS *Lon* 05-07; NSM W Holloway St Luke 07; NSM All Hallows Lon Wall from 07. *26 Womersley Road, London N8 9AN* Tel (020) 8340 2060 Mobile 07812-566520 E-mail malcolmdoney@blueyonder.co.uk

DONKERSLEY, Mrs Christine Mary. b 44. K Alfred's Coll Win CertEd65. STETS 98. **d** 01 **p** 02. NSM Baltonsborough w Butleigh, W Bradley etc *B & W* 01-06; P-in-c Fosse Trinity from 06. *The Rectory, Folly Drive, Ditcheat, Shepton Mallet BA4 6QH* Tel (01749) 860345 E-mail cm.donkersley@route56.co.uk

DONKIN, Canon Robert. b 50. St Mich Coll Llan 71. **d** 74 **p** 75. C Mountain Ash *Llan* 74-77; C Coity w Nolton 77-79; V Oakwood 79-84; V Aberaman and Abercwmboi 84-91; V Aberaman and Abercwmboi w Cwmaman 91-99; R Penarth w Lavernock 99-04; R Penarth and Llandough 04-08; AD Penarth and Barry 04-08; R Caerphilly from 08; Hon Can Llan Cathl from 06. *2 Clos Cae'r Wern, Caerphilly CF83 1SQ* Tel (029) 2088 8442 E-mail robert.donkin@sky.com

DONNE, Miranda. b 44. **d** 04 **p** 05. NSM Whitchurch *Ex* from 04. *Whitchurch House, Whitchurch, Tavistock PL19 9EL* Tel (01822) 614552

DONNELLY, Ms Juliet Ann. b 70. K Coll Lon BD92 AKC92 PGCE93. Ripon Coll Cuddesdon 01. **d** 05 **p** 06. C Bexley St Jo *Roch* 05-07; C Sidcup St Jo 07-08; Chapl Bp Justus C of E Sch Bromley from 09. *The Vicarage, 40 Dartmouth Row, London SE10 8AP* Tel 07910-166491 (mobile) E-mail juliet.blessed@virgin.net

DONNELLY, Trevor Alfred. b 71. K Coll Lon BA93 AKC93. Cuddesdon Coll 94. **d** 97 **p** 98. C Southgate Ch Ch *Lon* 97-01; V Hinchley Wood *Guildf* 01-05; Sen Chapl Medway Secure Tr Cen 06-09; TV Deptford St Jo w H Trin and Ascension *S'wark* from 09. *The Vicarage, 40 Dartmouth Row, London SE10 8AP* E-mail trevordonnelly@mac.com

DONOHOE, Olive Mary Rose. b 58. TCD BA79 BTh94 MA95 CPA83. CITC 91. **d** 95 **p** 96. C Bandon Union *C, C & R* 95-98; I Mountmellick w Coolbanagher, Rosenallis etc *M & K* from 98. *The Rectory, Mountmellick, Portlaoise, Co Laois, Republic of Ireland* Tel and fax (00353) (57) 862 4143 E-mail revol@elive.ie

DONOVAN, Mrs Rosalind Margaret. b 48. Birm Univ LLB69 Bedf Coll Lon DASS73. SAOMC 95. **d** 98 **p** 99. NSM Stone Green and Jordans *Ox* 98-03; P-in-c Wexham from 03. *The Rectory, 7 Grangewood, Wexham, Slough SL3 6LP* Tel (01753) 523852 E-mail rosdonovan@tiscali.co.uk

DONOVAN, Mrs Rosemary Ann. b 71. La Sainte Union Coll BTh92 Birm Univ PGCE93. Qu Coll Birm MA01. **d** 04. C Kings Heath *Birm* 01-04; C Moseley St Mary and St Anne from 04. *The Vicarage, 15 Park Hill, Birmingham B13 8DU* Tel 0121-449 1071 E-mail rosemary@donovan123.freeserve.co.uk

DONSON, Miss Helen Cripps. b 32. Somerville Coll Ox DipEd55 MA58. Dalton Ho Bris 58 Gilmore Ho 69. **dss** 79 **d** 87. Staines St Pet *Lon* 80-83; Staines St Mary and St Pet 83-90; Par Dn 87-90; Par Dn Herne Bay Ch Ch *Cant* 90-92; rtd 93; Hon Par Dn Bexhill St Aug *Chich* 93-97; Perm to Offic 97-07. *Flat 27, Manormead, Tilford Road, Hindhead GU26 6RA* Tel (01428) 601527

DOODES, Peter John. b 45. STETS 98. **d** 01. NSM Ninfield and Hooe *Chich* 01-02; NSM Hastings H Trin 02-07. *Catslide, The Common, Hooe, Battle TN33 9ET* Tel (01424) 892329 Mobile 07718-302115 E-mail pjdoodes@hotmail.com

DOOGAN, Simon Edward. b 70. Univ of Wales (Abth) LLB92 Univ of Wales (Cardiff) LLM01 TCD BTh97. CITC 94. **d** 97 **p** 98. C Cregagh *D & D* 97-01; Dom Chapl to Bp Horsham *Chich* 01-04; I Aghalee *D & D* 04-08; I Ballyholme from 08; Dioc Registrar from 07. *Ballyholme Rectory, 3 Ward Avenue, Bangor BT20 5JW* Tel (028) 9127 4901 *or* 9127 4912 Fax 9146 6357 E-mail simon_doogan@hotmail.com

DOOLAN, Leonard Wallace. b 57. St Andr Univ MA79 Ox Univ BA82 MA88. Ripon Coll Cuddesdon 80. **d** 83 **p** 84. C High Wycombe *Ox* 83-85; C Bladon w Woodstock 85-88; C Wootton by Woodstock 85-88; P-in-c 88-90; C Kiddington w Asterleigh 85-88; P-in-c 88-90; P-in-c Glympton 88-90; R Wootton w Glympton and Kiddington 90-91; TR Halesworth w Linstead, Chediston, Holton etc *St E* 91-98; RD Halesworth 95-98; TR Ifield *Chich* 98-08; V Cirencester *Glouc* from 08. *The Vicarage, 1 Dollar Street, Cirencester GL7 2AJ* Tel (01285) 653142 E-mail vicarcirencester@hotmail.com

DOOR, Hazel Lesley. b 48. Open Univ BSc99. EAMTC 01. **d** 04 **p** 05. C Poitou-Charentes *Eur* 05-07; P-in-c Brittany from 07. *79 rue Glatinier, 56120 Josselin, France* Tel (0033) (2) 97 22 31 38

DOORES, Miss Jennifer Mary. b 78. Hull Univ BA99 St Jo Coll Dur BA03. Cranmer Hall Dur 01. **d** 04 **p** 05. C Old Swinford Stourbridge *Worc* 04-08; V Cam w Stinchcombe *Glouc* from 08. *The Vicarage, Church Road, Cam, Dursley GL11 5PQ* Tel (01453) 542084 E-mail jenniferdoores@btinternet.com

DOORES, Canon Peter George Herbert. b 46. Hull Univ BSc67 Birm Univ PGCE68. Linc Th Coll 92. **d** 92 **p** 93. C N Stoneham *Win* 92-96; V St Leonards and St Ives 96-03; P-in-c Alton St Lawr from 03; Hon Can Win Cathl from 09. *St Lawrence's Vicarage, Church Street, Alton GU34 2BW* Tel (01420) 83234

DORAN, Clive. b 58. St Jo Coll Nottm 99. **d** 01 **p** 02. C Maghull *Liv* 01-05; V Huyton St Geo from 05; Bp's Adv on Children and Communion from 06. *St George's Vicarage, 46 Primrose Drive, Liverpool L36 8DW* Tel 0151-489 1997 E-mail revclivedoran@yahoo.co.uk

DORAN, Edward Roy. b 47. St Jo Coll Nottm. **d** 85 **p** 86. C Roby *Liv* 85-88; V Ravenhead 88-07; TV Eccleston 07-09; V Knotty Ash St Jo from 09. *St John's Vicarage, Thomas Lane, Liverpool L14 5NR* Tel 0151-228 2396

DORANS, Robert Marshall. b 47. Open Univ BA82 Ex Univ MEd85 Dur Univ MA96. **d** 01 **p** 02. OLM Longhorsley and Hebron *Newc* 01-05. *25 Green Close, Stannington, Morpeth NE61 6PE* E-mail bdorans@tiscali.co.uk

DORBER, The Very Revd Adrian John. b 52. St Jo Coll Dur BA74 K Coll Lon MTh91. Westcott Ho Cam 76. **d** 79 **p** 80. C Easthampstead *Ox* 79-85; P-in-c Emmer Green 85-88; Chapl Portsm Poly 88-92; Chapl Portsm Univ 92-97; Lect 91-97; Public Orator 92-97; Hon Chapl Portsm Cathl 92-97; P-in-c Brancepeth *Dur* 97-01; Dir Min and Tr 97-05; Hon Can Dur Cathl 97-05; Dean Lich from 05. *The Deanery, 16 The Close, Lichfield WS13 7LD* Tel (01543) 306250 Fax 306109 E-mail adrian.dorber@lichfield-cathedral.org

DORCHESTER, Area Bishop of. *See* FLETCHER, The Rt Revd Colin William

DORÉ, Eric George. b 47. S Dios Minl Tr Scheme 87. **d** 90 **p** 91. NSM Hove Bp Hannington Memorial Ch *Chich* 90-92; C Burgess Hill St Andr 92-95; R Frant w Eridge 95-00; V Framfield 00-07; rtd 07; Perm to Offic *St E* from 08. *Oak House, 86A Southwold Road, Wrentham, Beccles NR34 7JF* Tel (01502) 675777 E-mail ericdore@onetel.com

DOREY, Miss Alison. b 77. Sheff Univ BA98 Sheff Hallam Univ PGCE01 St Jo Coll Dur MA08. Cranmer Hall Dur 05. **d** 07 **p** 08. C Askern *Sheff* from 07. *46 Eastfield Drive, Askern, Doncaster DN6 0NU* Tel (01302) 708549 E-mail ali.dorey@sheffield.anglican.org

DOREY, Trevor Eric. b 30. ACIS53. S Dios Minl Tr Scheme 87. **d** 90 **p** 91. NSM E Woodhay and Woolton Hill *Win* 90-96; P-in-c Manaccan w St Anthony-in-Meneage and St Martin *Truro* 96-99; rtd 99; Perm to Offic *Sarum* 01-05 and *Ox* from 07. *12 Speen Place, Speen, Newbury RG14 1RX* Tel (01635) 551956 E-mail tandvdorey@btinternet.com

DORGU, Woyin Karowei. b 58. MB, BS85. Lon Bible Coll BA93 Oak Hill Th Coll 93. **d** 95 **p** 96. C Tollington *Lon* 95-98; C Upper Holloway 98-00; TV from 00. *St John's Vicarage, 51 Tytherton Road, London N19 4PZ* Tel and fax (020) 7272 5309 E-mail karmos.timsim@virgin.net

DORKING, Archdeacon of. *See* HENDERSON, The Ven Julian Tudor

DORKING, Suffragan Bishop of. *See* BRACKLEY, The Rt Revd Ian James

DORLING, Philip Julian. b 69. Edin Univ BSc90. Ripon Coll Cuddesdon 03. **d** 05 **p** 06. C Ulverston St Mary w H Trin *Carl* from 05. *Greety Gate Cottage, Foxfield, Broughton-in-Furness LA20 6BY* Tel (01229) 715166

DORMANDY, Richard Paul. b 59. Univ Coll Lon BA81 St Edm Ho Cam BA88. Ridley Hall Cam 86. **d** 89 **p** 90. C Sydenham H Trin *S'wark* 89-93; V 93-01; V Westminster St Jas the Less *Lon* 01-09; V Tulse Hill H Trin and St Matthias *S'wark* from 09. *Holy Trinity Vicarage, 49 Trinity Rise, London SW2 2QP* Tel (020) 8674 6721 E-mail richard@dormandy.co.uk

DORMER, Christopher Robert. b 39. Bris Univ BA61. Lich Th Coll 61. **d** 63 **p** 64. C Sheff St Cecilia Parson Cross 63-67; C Greenford H Cross *Lon* 67-69; Brotherhood of St Barn Australia 69-74; Area Sec (Ireland) USPG 74-75; R Catton *York* 75-78; R Stamford Bridge Gp 78-81; RD Pocklington 80-81; Itinerant Priest *Mor* 81-98; P-in-c Lochalsh 81-98; P-in-c Poolewe 81-98; P-in-c Ullapool 81-98; P-in-c Kishorn 81-98; Miss to Seamen 81-98; Can St Andr Cathl Inverness 94-98; R Kelso *Edin* 98-04; Lic to Offic *Mor* from 04. *1 Fraser Place, Ullapool IV26 2UX* Tel (01854) 613373

DORMOR, Duncan James. b 67. Magd Coll Ox BA88 Lon Univ MSc89. Ripon Coll Cuddesdon BA94. **d** 95 **p** 96. C Wolverhampton *Lich* 95-98; Chapl St Jo Coll Cam 98-02; Fell and Dean from 02. *St John's College, Cambridge CB2 1TP* Tel (01223) 338633 E-mail djd28@cam.ac.uk

DORMOR, Preb Duncan Stephen. b 36. St Edm Hall Ox BA60. Cuddesdon Coll 60. **d** 62 **p** 63. C Headington *Ox* 62-66; USA 66-72; R Hertford St Andr *St Alb* 72-88; RD Hertford 77-83; TR

Tenbury *Heref* 88-01; R Burford I 88-01; R Burford II w Greete and Hope Bagot 88-01; R Burford III w Lt Heref 88-01; V Tenbury St Mich 94-01; RD Ludlow 96-01; Preb Heref Cathl 99-02; C Tenbury 01-02; C Burford I 01-02; C Burford II w Greete and Hope Bagot 01-02; C Burford III w Lt Heref 01-02; C Tenbury St Mich 01-02; rtd 02; Perm to Offic *Heref* from 02. *Brantwood, Hereford Road, Leominster HR6 8JU* Tel (01568) 610897

DORNAN, Michael. CITC. **d** 09. C Hillsborough *D & D* from 09. *2 Beechgrove, Ballynahinch BT24 8NQ* Tel (028) 9756 5685 E-mail mikedornan@gmail.com

DORRELL, Martin Christopher. STETS. **d** 09. NSM Portsea St Alb *Portsm* from 09; NSM Portsea St Sav from 09. *284B Allaway Avenue, Portsmouth PO6 4QR* Tel (023) 9238 8689

DORRIAN, Adrian Terence Warren. b 82. QUB BA03 TCD BTh06. CITC 04. **d** 06 **p** 07. C Newtownards *D & D* 06-09; I Belfast St Pet and St Jas *Conn* from 09. *St Peter's Rectory, 17 Waterloo Park South, Belfast BT15 5HX* Tel (028) 9077 7053 Mobile 07946-398027 E-mail adriandorrian@gmail.com

DORRINGTON, Brian Goodwin. b 32. Leeds Univ CertEd55. St Deiniol's Hawarden 65. **d** 66 **p** 67. C Poynton *Ches* 66-71; Perm to Offic *Truro* 71-78; Hd Master Veryan Sch Truro 71-84; Hon C Veryan *Truro* 78-84; C N Petherwin 84-87; C Boyton w N Tamerton 84-87; TV Bolventor 87-90; R Kilkhampton w Morwenstow 90-97; RD Stratton 92-97; rtd 97; Perm to Offic *Truro* from 00. *Southcroft, 18 Elm Drive, Bude EX23 8EZ* Tel (01288) 352467

DORRINGTON, Richard Bryan. b 48. Linc Th Coll 79. **d** 81 **p** 82. C Streetly *Lich* 81-84; C Badger 84-85; R 85-88; C Ryton 84-85; R 85-88; C Beckbury 84-85; R 85-88; V Geddington w Weekley *Pet* 88-98; P-in-c Bradworthy *Ex* 98-00; P-in-c Abbots Bickington and Bulkworthy 98-00; R Bradworthy, Sutcombe, Putford etc from 00; RD Holsworthy from 99. *The Rectory, St Peterswell Lane, Bradworthy EX22 7TQ* Tel (01409) 241411 E-mail therector@bradworthy.co.uk

DORSET, Archdeacon of. *Vacant*

DORSETT, Mark Richard. b 63. Univ of Wales (Lamp) BA84 MTh86 Birm Univ PhD90. Ripon Coll Cuddesdon 91. **d** 93 **p** 94. C Yardley St Edburgha *Birm* 93-96; Chapl K Sch Worc from 96; Min Can Worc Cathl from 96. *12A College Green, Worcester WR1 2LH* Tel (01905) 25837

DOSE, Lara Ellen. b 70. De Pauw Univ USA BA92 Trin Hall Cam BTh08. Westcott Ho Cam 06. **d** 09. C Birch-in-Rusholme St Agnes w Longsight St Jo etc *Man* from 09. *58 Reynell Road, Manchester M13 0PT* Tel 07801-789802 (mobile) E-mail lara@stagneslongsight.org

DOSSOR, John Haley. b 41. Leeds Univ BA62. EAMTC 87. **d** 90 **p** 91. NSM Hadleigh *St E* 90-01; P-in-c Ipswich St Mary at the Elms 01-07; rtd 07; Perm to Offic *Chelmsf* and *St E* from 07. *Butley Barn, 1 Struston Mead, Kirton, Felixstowe IP10 0QH* Tel (01394) 448188 E-mail haley@dossor.org

DOSSOR, Timothy Charles. b 70. Birm Univ BEng94. Ridley Hall Cam BTh99. **d** 99 **p** 00. C Ipswich St Jo *St E* 99-03; Asst Ldr Iwerne Holidays Titus Trust from 03; Perm to Offic *Ox* from 08. *31 Southdale Road, Oxford OX2 7SE* Tel (01865) 553226 *or* 310513 Mobile 07748-184503 E-mail tim@dossor.org

DOTCHIN, Andrew Steward. b 56. Federal Th Coll S Africa. **d** 84 **p** 85. S Africa 84-01; C Standerton w Evender 84-87; Asst P St Martin's-in-the-Veld 87-89; R Belgravia St Jo the Divine 89-94; Chapl St Martin's Sch Rosettenville 94-01; TV Blyth Valley *St E* 01-04; P-in-c Whitton and Thurleston w Akenham 04-09; R from 09. *The Rectory, 176 Fircroft Road, Ipswich IP1 6PS* Tel (01473) 741389 Mobile 07814-949828 E-mail andrew.dotchin@ntlworld.com

DOTCHIN, Canon Joan Marie. b 47. NEOC 84. **d** 87 **p** 94. C Newc St Gabr 87-92; TD Willington 92-94; TV 94-95; TR 95-03; V Fenham St Jas and St Basil 03-08; Hon Can Newc Cathl 01-08; rtd 08. *22 Astley Gardens, Seaton Sluice, Whitley Bay NE26 4JJ* Tel 0191-237 3030 E-mail revj.dotchin@goldserve.net

DOUBLE, Richard Sydney (Brother Samuel). b 47. K Coll Lon BD69 AKC69. St Aug Coll Cant 69. **d** 70 **p** 71. C Walton St Mary *Liv* 70-74; SSF from 75; Guardian Hilfield Friary Dorchester 92-01; Can and Preb Sarum Cathl 95-01; V Cambridge St Benedict *Ely* 01-05. *The Friary, Hilfield, Dorchester DT2 7BE* Tel (01300) 341345

DOUBTFIRE, Canon Barbara. b 39. LMH Ox BA61 MA65. **d** 91 **p** 94. Par Development Adv *Ox* 88-04; NSM Kidlington w Hampton Poyle 91-04; Hon Can Ch Ch 98-04; rtd 04. *6 Meadow Walk, Woodstock OX20 1NR* Tel (01993) 812095 E-mail spidir@oxford.anglican.org

DOUBTFIRE, Samuel. b 33. Edin Th Coll 63. **d** 66 **p** 66. C Knottingley *Wakef* 66-68; V Ripponden 68-76; V Crosthwaite Keswick *Carl* 76-81; V Barrow St Matt 81-87; R N Reddish *Man* 87-92; rtd 92; Perm to Offic *Bradf* 92-06. *21 Lichfield Lane, Mansfield NG18 4RA* Tel (01623) 633266

DOUGAL, Stephen George. b 62. FICS. **d** 06 **p** 07. OLM Lyminge w Paddlesworth, Stanford w Postling etc *Cant* from 06.

Bereforstal Farm Bungalow, Canterbury Road, Elham, Canterbury CT4 6UE Tel (01303) 840750

DOUGHTY, The Ven Andrew William. b 56. K Coll Lon BD AKC. Westcott Ho Cam 80. **d** 82 **p** 83. C Alton St Lawr *Win* 82-85; TV Basingstoke 85-91; V Chilworth w N Baddesley 91-95; R Warwick St Mary V Bermuda from 95; Adn Bermuda from 04. *PO Box WK 530, Warwick WK BX, Bermuda* Tel (001) (441) 236 5744 Fax 236 3667 E-mail adoughty@ibl.bm

DOUGLAS, Ann Patricia. b 49. Lon Univ CertEd71. Oak Hill NSM Course 85. **d** 88 **p** 94. Par Dn Chorleywood Ch Ch *St Alb* 88-94; V Oxhey All SS 94-02; TR Woodley *Ox* 02-06; rtd 06; Perm to Offic *Sarum* from 07; Development Officer Li Tim-Oi Foundn from 06. *Heather Cottage, 9A Cauldron Crescent, Swanage BH19 1QL* Tel (01929) 421691 Mobile 07885-022155 E-mail annidouglas@btopenworld.com

DOUGLAS, Anthony Victor. b 51. St Jo Coll Nottm 74. **d** 76 **p** 77. C Gt Crosby St Luke *Liv* 76-79; TV Fazakerley Em 79-84; TR Speke St Aid 84-90; TR Gt and Lt Coates w Bradley *Linc* 90-97; TR E Ham w Upton Park St Alb *Chelmsf* 97-02; R Holkham w Egmere w Warham, Wells and Wighton *Nor* from 02. *The Rectory, Church Street, Wells-next-the-Sea NR23 1JB* Tel (01328) 710107

DOUGLAS, Gavin Allan. b 52. OBE00. Cardiff Univ BTh08. St Mich Coll Llan 03. **d** 05 **p** 06. C Week St Mary Circle of Par *Truro* 05-08; R Castle Bromwich SS Mary and Marg *Birm* from 08. *67 Chester Road, Castle Bromwich, Birmingham B36 9DP* Tel 0121-747 8546 E-mail gavinadouglas@yahoo.co.uk

DOUGLAS, Miss Janet Elizabeth. b 60. SS Paul & Mary Coll Cheltenham BEd83. Cranmer Hall Dur 88. **d** 90 **p** 94. Par Dn Yardley St Edburgha *Birm* 90-93; Par Dn Hamstead St Paul 93-94; C 94-00; Perm to Offic 00-04; C Birm St Martin w Bordesley St Andr from 04. *6 Baxter Court, 96 School Road, Moseley, Birmingham B13 9TP* Tel 0121-449 3763

DOUGLAS, Michael Williamson. b 51. Birm Univ BSc72 Liv Univ PGCE74. Trin Coll Bris 00. **d** 02 **p** 03. C Macclesfield Team *Ches* 02-06; TV Hawarden *St As* from 06. *St Mary's Vicarage, Church Road, Broughton, Chester CH4 0QB* Tel (01244) 520148 E-mail mikedouglas@yahoo.co.uk

DOUGLAS, Pamela Jean. See WELCH, Pamela Jean

DOUGLAS, Peter Melvyn. b 47. **d** 96 **p** 97. NSM Prestwick *Glas* 96-01; Chapl HM Pris Dovegate 01-03; P-in-c Kilmarnock *Glas* from 07. *The Parsonage, 1 Dundonald Road, Kilmarnock KA1 1EQ* Tel (01563) 523577

DOUGLAS, Richard Norman Henry. b 37. SAOMC 94. **d** 97 **p** 98. NSM Watercombe *Sarum* 97-02; Perm to Offic *Sarum* 02-04 and *Ox* 04-06; NSM Grove *Ox* 06-07; rtd 07; Perm to Offic *Ox* from 07. *6 Vale Avenue, Grove, Wantage OX12 7LU* Tel (01235) 767753 E-mail dickandnan@talktalk.net

DOUGLAS LANE, Charles Simon Pellew. b 47. BNC Ox MA71 MCIPD79. Oak Hill Th Coll 91. **d** 94 **p** 95. C Whitton St Aug *Lon* 94-97; P-in-c Hounslow W Gd Shep 97-02; V 02-05; TV Riverside *Ox* 05-08; V Horton and Wraysbury from 08. *The Vicarage, 55 Welley Road, Wraysbury, Staines TW19 5ER* Tel (01784) 481258 E-mail simondouglaslane@tiscali.co.uk

DOUGLASS, Michael Crone. b 49. Open Univ BA96. NEOC 02. **d** 05 **p** 06. NSM Gosforth St Nic *Newc* from 05. *44 Regent Road, Newcastle upon Tyne NE3 1ED* Tel and fax 0191-285 0977 E-mail m.douglass@blueyonder.co.uk

DOUGLASS, Preb Philip. b 48. Open Univ BA88. St Steph Ho Ox 87. **d** 89 **p** 90. C Peterlee *Dur* 89-92; V Crowan w Godolphin *Truro* 92-97; V Crowan and Treslothan from 98; P-in-c Penponds from 01; Preb St Endellion from 02. *Crowan Vicarage, 37 Trethannas Gardens, Praze, Camborne TR14 0LL* Tel and fax (01209) 831009 E-mail philip@thedouglasses.freeserve.co.uk

DOULL, Iain Sinclair. b 43. St Mich Coll Llan 86. **d** 88 **p** 89. C Malpas *Mon* 88-91; P-in-c Newport All SS 91-98; V 98-02; V Newport Ch H from 02. *The Vicarage, Christchurch, Newport NP18 1JJ* Tel (01633) 420701

DOULTON, Dick. b 32. St Cath Coll Cam BA60 MA64. Ridley Hall Cam 61. **d** 63 **p** 64. C Gedling *S'well* 63-65; C Danbury *Chelmsf* 65; Lic to Offic *Ox* 88-90; Lic to Offic *L & K* from 90. *Ballygriffin, Kenmare, Killarney, Co Kerry, Republic of Ireland* Tel (00353) (64) 41743

DOULTON, Roderick John. b 55. Oak Hill Th Coll 91. **d** 93 **p** 94. C Hoddesdon *St Alb* 93-96; P-in-c Caldecote All SS 96-98; P-in-c Old Warden 97-98; V Caldecote, Northill and Old Warden 98-99; TV Macclesfield Team *Ches* 99-07; Chapl W Park Hosp Macclesfield 99-07; P-in-c Heydon, Gt and Lt Chishill, Chrishall etc *Chelmsf* 07-08. *2 Stockbridge Meadows, Melbourn, Royston SG8 6FG*

DOVE, Giles Wilfred. b 62. St Andr Univ MA85 MPhil88 FSAScot FRSA. TISEC 03. **d** 05 **p** 06. NSM Dunblane *St And* 05-07; Chapl Glenalmond Coll from 07. *The Chaplain's House, Glenalmond College, Glenalmond, Perth PH1 3RY* Tel (01738) 880479 E-mail gilesdove@glenalmondcollege.co.uk

DOVE, Lionel John. b 38. **d** 06 **p** 07. OLM N Bradley, Southwick, Heywood and Steeple Ashton *Sarum* from 06. *Chobham Cottage, Acreshot Lane, Steeple Ashton, Trowbridge BA14 6HD* Tel (01380) 870013 E-mail lionel@dove8569.freeserve.co.uk

DOVE, Richard. b 54. EMMTC. **d** 99 **p** 00. NSM Dronfield w Holmesfield *Derby* from 99. *29 Hollins Spring Avenue, Dronfield S18 1RN* Tel (01246) 412502 E-mail rdove1553@aol.com *or* dick.dove@dwhparish.org.uk

DOVER, Suffragan Bishop of. See VENNER, The Rt Revd Stephen Squires

DOVEY, Andrew Michael Stanley. b 59. SEITE 00. **d** 06 **p** 07. NSM Selsdon St Jo w St Fran *S'wark* from 06. *6 Stokes Road, Croydon CR0 7SD* Tel (020) 8656 9911 E-mail kdoveys@tiscali.co.uk

DOW, Canon Andrew John Morrison. b 46. Univ Coll Ox BA67 MA71. Oak Hill Th Coll 69. **d** 71 **p** 72. C Watford St Luke *St Alb* 71-74; C Chadderton Ch Ch *Man* 75-78; V Leamington Priors St Paul *Cov* 78-88; V Knowle *Birm* 88-97; RD Solihull 95-97; V Clifton Ch Ch w Em *Bris* 97-04; P-in-c Cheltenham St Mary, St Matt, St Paul and H Trin *Glouc* 04-07; R Cheltenham St Mary w St Matt from 07; AD Cheltenham from 06; Hon Can Glouc Cathl from 08. *The Rectory, Windrush Cottage, Thorncliffe Drive, Cheltenham GL51 6PY* Tel (01242) 701580 E-mail andrewdow@blueyonder.co.uk

✠**DOW, The Rt Revd Geoffrey Graham.** b 42. Qu Coll Ox BA63 MA68 BSc65 MSc81 Nottm Univ MPhil82. Clifton Th Coll 66. **d** 67 **p** 68 **c** 92. C Tonbridge SS Pet and Paul *Roch* 67-72; Chapl St Jo Coll Ox 72-75; Lect St Jo Coll Nottm 75-81; V Cov H Trin 81-92; Can Th Cov Cathl 88-92; Area Bp Willesden *Lon* 92-00; Bp Carl 00-09; rtd 09; Hon Asst Bp Ches from 09. *34 Kimberley Avenue, Romiley, Stockport SK6 4AB* Tel 0161-494 9148 E-mail graham@gdow.co.uk

DOWD, Garfield George. b 60. QUB BSc. **d** 86 **p** 87. C Monkstown *D & G* 86-90; I Carlow w Urglin and Staplestown *C & O* 90-05; Can Ossory Cathl 96-05; I Glenageary *D & G* from 05. *St Paul's Vicarage, Silchester Road, Glenageary, Co Dublin, Republic of Ireland* Tel and fax (00353) (1) 280 1616 Mobile 87-926 6558 E-mail glenageary@dublin.anglican.org

DOWDESWELL, Anne Marjory. b 68. **d** 06 **p** 07. C Leckhampton St Pet *Glouc* from 06. *55 Church Road, Leckhampton, Cheltenham GL53 0PF* Tel (01242) 539169

DOWDING, Ms Clare Alice Elizabeth. b 74. Ch Ch Coll Cant BA98 Greenwich Univ PGCE99. Westcott Ho Cam BA02. **d** 03 **p** 05. USA 03-04; C Longsight St Luke *Man* 04-07; Chapl Man HE Institutions from 07. *St Peter's House, Precinct Centre, Oxford Road, Manchester M13 9GH* Tel 0161-275 2894 Fax 275 0890 Mobile 07903-553113 E-mail caedowding@hotmail.com

DOWDING, Edward Brinley. b 47. St Mich Coll Llan 70 St D Coll Lamp BA71. **d** 72 **p** 73. C Canton St Cath *Llan* 72-75; C Aberdare 75-78; V Aberavon H Trin 78-85; R Sully from 85; RD Penarth and Barry 98-04. *The Rectory, 26 South Road, Sully, Penarth CF64 5TG* Tel (029) 2053 0221

DOWDING, Mrs Elizabeth Jean. b 43. Bath Coll of HE TCert67. SAOMC 00. **d** 04 **p** 05. NSM Goring w S Stoke *Ox* 04-07; NSM Goring and Streatley w S Stoke from 07. *30 Milldown Avenue, Goring, Reading RG8 0AS* Tel (01491) 873140 E-mail elizdowding@aol.com

DOWDING, Jeremy Charles. b 51. St Steph Ho Ox 89. **d** 91 **p** 92. C Newport St Steph and H Trin *Mon* 91-94; C Risca 94-96; P-in-c Whitleigh *Ex* 96-05; P-in-c Thorpe-le-Soken *Chelmsf* from 05. *The Vicarage, Mill Lane, Thorpe-le-Soken, Clacton-on-Sea CO16 0ED* Tel (01255) 861234

DOWDING, Stanley Frederick. b 10. ALCD32 St Jo Coll Dur BA33 LTh33. **d** 34 **p** 35. C Bris St Silas 34-37; C Downend 37-39; C Portland All SS w St Pet *Sarum* 39-42; OCF 39-42; P-in-c Weston Mill *Ex* 42-46; V Preston St Luke *Blackb* 46-55; Chapl HM Pris Preston 51-52; V Nelson in Lt Marsden *Blackb* 55-75; Chapl Reedyford Hosp 64; RD Burnley 68-70; RD Pendle 70-75; rtd 75; Lic to Offic *Blackb* 76-93; Perm to Offic from 93. *Hilton Rest Home, Quarry Street, Padiham, Burnley BB12 8PH* Tel (01282) 775016

DOWDLE, Canon Cynthia. b 48. Cranmer Hall Dur 88. **d** 90 **p** 94. C Allerton *Liv* 90-94; TR Halewood 94-00; V Knowsley from 00; Dean of Women's Min from 01; Hon Can Liv Cathl from 01. *The Vicarage, Tithebarn Road, Prescot L34 0JA* Tel 0151-546 4266 Fax 546 3897 E-mail cynthiadowdle@hotmail.com

DOWDY, Simon Mark Christopher. b 67. Trin Hall Cam BA89 MA93. Wycliffe Hall Ox 93. **d** 96 **p** 97. C Beckenham Ch Ch *Roch* 96-00; C St Helen Bishopsgate w St Andr Undershaft etc *Lon* 00-05; P-in-c St Botolph without Aldersgate from 02. *45 Woodwarde Road, London SE22 8UN* Tel (020) 8299 1631 E-mail mail@stbotolphsaldersgate.org.uk

DOWER, Frances Helen. b 45. Lon Univ MB, BS69. **d** 09. OLM Kirkwhelpington, Kirkharle, Kirkheaton and Cambo *Newc* from 09. *Cambo House, Front Row, Cambo, Morpeth NE61 4AY* Tel (01670) 774297 E-mail frances.dower@dower.org.uk

DOWIE, Canon Winifred Brenda McIntosh. b 57. Callendar Park Coll of Educn Falkirk DipEd78. Trin Coll Bris BA91. **d** 92 **p** 94. Par Dn Downend *Bris* 92-94; C 94-95; Chapl Asst Southmead Health Services NHS Trust 95-98; Chapl St Pet Hospice Bris from 98; Hon Can Bris Cathl from 02. *St Peter's Hospice,*

St Agnes Avenue, Knowle, Bristol BS4 2DU   Tel 0117-977 4605 *or* 915 9462 Fax 915 9473

DOWLAND, Martin John. b 48. Lon Univ BD70 Southn Univ PGCE71. Wycliffe Hall Ox 75. **d** 77 **p** 78. C Jesmond Clayton Memorial *Newc* 77-80; C Chadderton Ch Ch *Man* 80-85; R Haughton St Mary from 85. *Haughton Green Rectory, Meadow Lane, Denton, Manchester M34 7GD*   Tel and fax 0161-336 4529 E-mail m.dowland@ntlworld.com

DOWLAND-OWEN, Edward Farrington. b 73. St D Coll Lamp BA95 Trin Coll Carmarthen PGCE96 FVCM99. S Wales Ord Course 00 St Mich Coll Llan 03. **d** 04 **p** 05. C Llandaff 04-08; P-in-c Llandyfodwg and Cwm Ogwr from 08. *The Vicarage, Coronation Street, Ogmore Vale, Bridgend CF32 7HE*   Tel (01656) 840248 *or* 759561   Mobile 07853-154604 E-mail vicarcwmogwr@hotmail.co.uk

DOWLAND-PILLINGER, Catherine Louise. b 60. New Hall Cam BA82 MA86 PhD89. SEITE 03. **d** 08. C Addington *S'wark* from 08. *56 Viney Bank, Courtwood Lane, Croydon CR0 9JT*   Tel (020) 8657 4603   Mobile 07768-065301 E-mail rev.catherine1@googlemail.com

DOWLEN, Isabella McBeath. b 45. Man Univ CertEd86 Edin Univ MTh06 RGN67 SCM68 HVCert69. STETS 96. **d** 99 **p** 01. NSM Branksome St Clem *Sarum* 99-04; NSM Clarkston *Glas* 04-06; P-in-c Glas St Oswald 06-08. *Address temp unknown*   Tel 07974-084657 (mobile) E-mail isabel.dowlen@tesco.net

DOWLER, Robert Edward Mackenzie. b 67. Ch Ch Ox BA89 Selw Coll Cam BA93 Dur Univ PhD07. Westcott Ho Cam 91. **d** 94 **p** 95. C Southgate Ch Ch *Lon* 94-97; C Somers Town 97-01; Tutor and Dir Past Th St Steph Ho Ox 01-09; Vice Prin 03-09; Asst Chapl Malvern Coll from 09. *Malvern College, College Road, Malvern WR14 3DF*   Tel (01684) 581500

DOWLING, Donald Edward. b 43. St Andr Univ MA66. Cranmer Hall Dur. **d** 74 **p** 75. C Thame w Towersey *Ox* 74-77; C Norton *St Alb* 77-80; V Wilbury 81-99; V Stevenage St Nic and Graveley from 99. *St Nicholas House, 2A North Road, Stevenage SG1 4AT*   Tel (01438) 354355 E-mail don.dowling@ntlworld.com

DOWLING, Graham Paul. b 62. NTMTC BA09. **d** 09. C Rainham w Wennington *Chelmsf* from 09. *260 Upminster Road North, Rainham RM13 9JL*   Tel 07889-286308 (mobile) E-mail graham@pdowling.freeserve.co.uk

DOWLING, Kingsley Avery Paul. b 60. Open Univ BA. Aston Tr Scheme 93 Ripon Coll Cuddesdon 95. **d** 97 **p** 99. C Headingley *Ripon* 97-99; C Far Headingley St Chad 99-01; V Wortley de Leeds from 01; AD Armley from 08. *Wortley Vicarage, Dixon Lane Road, Leeds LS12 4RU*   Tel 0113-263 8867 E-mail kingsleydowling@talktalk.net

DOWLING, Paul Martin. b 55. ACA G&C Coll Cam MA79. Cranmer Hall Dur 88. **d** 90 **p** 91. C Redhill St Jo *S'wark* 90-94; V Wakef St Jo from 94. *St John's Vicarage, 65 Bradford Road, Wakefield WF1 2AA*   Tel and fax (01924) 371029 E-mail the.dowlings@tiscali.co.uk

DOWMAN, Jonathan Robert. b 76. Westmr Coll Ox BEd00. Trin Coll Bris 04. **d** 07 **p** 08. C Anglesey Gp *Ely* from 07. *25 Spring Lane, Bottisham, Cambridge CB25 9BL* E-mail dowman@tiscali.co.uk

DOWMAN, Peter Robert. b 52. City Univ BSc76 Wycliffe Hall Ox 82. **d** 84 **p** 85. C Cheltenham Ch Ch *Glouc* 84-87; C Danbury *Chelmsf* 87-90; R Woodham Ferrers and Bicknacre 90-95; Consultant E England CPAS 95-03; R Warboys w Broughton and Bury w Wistow *Ely* from 03. *The Rectory, 15 Church Road, Warboys, Huntingdon PE28 2RJ*   Tel (01487) 824612 E-mail pdowman@bigfoot.com

DOWN, Martin John. b 40. Jes Coll Cam BA62 MA68. Westcott Ho Cam 63. **d** 65 **p** 66. C Bury St Mary *Man* 65-68; C Leigh St Mary 68-70; R Fiskerton *Linc* 70-75; V Irnham w Corby 75-79; RD Beltisloe 76-84; P-in-c Swayfield and Creeton w Swinstead 78-79; V Corby Glen 79-84; Good News Trust 84-88; Perm to Offic *Linc* 84-88 and *Pet* 86-88; P-in-c Ashill w Saham Toney *Nor* 88-94; R 94-00; C Watton w Carbrooke and Ovington 00-05; rtd 05; Perm to Offic *Nor* from 05. *22 Lee Warner Road, Swaffham PE37 7GD*   Tel and fax (01760) 336492

DOWN, Peter Michael. b 54. K Coll Lon BD78 AKC. Coll of Resurr Mirfield 78. **d** 79 **p** 80. C Swindon Ch Ch *Bris* 79-82; C Southmead 82-84; TV Cannock *Lich* 84-92; V Coleford w Holcombe *B & W* 92-01; Hon C Westfield 01-02; Perm to Offic from 07. *35 Beaconsfield Way, Frome BA11 2UD*   Tel (01373) 469885

DOWN, The Ven Philip Roy. b 53. Hull Univ MA93. Melbourne Coll of Div BTh82 MTh88. **d** 89 **p** 89. C Gt Grimsby St Mary and St Jas *Linc* 89-91; TV 91-95; R Hackington *Cant* 95-02; AD Cant 99-02; Adn Maidstone from 02. *The Old Rectory, The Street, Pluckley, Ashford TN27 0QT*   Tel (01233) 840291 Fax 840759 E-mail pdown@archdeaconmaid.org

✠**DOWN, The Rt Revd William John Denbigh.** b 34. St Jo Coll Cam BA57 MA61 FNI91. Ridley Hall Cam 57. **d** 59 **p** 60 **c** 90. C Fisherton Anger *Sarum* 59-63; Miss to Seamen 63-90; Australia 71-74; Dep Gen Sec Miss to Seamen 75; Gen Sec 76-90; Hon C Gt Stanmore *Lon* 75-90; Chapl St Mich Paternoster Royal 76-90;

Perm to Offic *St Alb* 78-90; Hon Can Gib Cathl 85-90; Hon Can Kobe Japan from 87; Bp Bermuda 90-95; Asst Bp Leic 95-01; P-in-c Humberstone 95-01; P-in-c Thurnby Lodge 01; rtd 01; Hon Asst Bp Ox from 01. *54 Dark Lane, Witney OX28 6LX*   Tel (01993) 706615 E-mail bishbill@aol.com

DOWN AND DROMORE, Bishop of. *See* MILLER, The Rt Revd Harold Creeth

DOWN, Archdeacon of. *See* PATTERSON, The Ven Philip Fredrick

DOWN, Dean of. *See* HULL, The Very Revd Thomas Henry

DOWNER, Barry Michael. b 58. STETS 99. **d** 02 **p** 07. NSM Lake and Shanklin St Sav *Portsm* 02-05; NSM Bonchurch 05-08; NSM Ventnor H Trin 05-08; NSM Ventnor St Cath 05-08; NSM Oakfield St Jo from 09. *1 Rocklands Cottages, Woolverton Road, Ventnor PO38 1XW*   Tel and fax (01983) 855970

DOWNER, Cuthbert John. b 18. S'wark Ord Course 60. **d** 74 **p** 75. Hon C Kirdford *Chich* 74-76; C Halesworth w Linstead and Chediston *St E* 76-79; P-in-c Knodishall w Buxlow 79-80; P-in-c Friston 79-80; R Bacton w Wyverstone 80-83; P-in-c Cotton and Wickham Skeith 80-83; R Bacton w Wyverstone and Cotton 83-84; rtd 84; Perm to Offic *St Alb* 84-87; *B & W* 88-95 and from 97. *6 The Maples, Princes Road, Shepton Mallet BA4 5HL*   Tel (01749) 344102

DOWNES, Gregory Charles. b 69. Roehampton Inst BSc91 Hughes Hall Cam PGCE92. Wycliffe Hall Ox BA95. **d** 96 **p** 97. C Hazlemere *Ox* 96-99; Chapl HM Pris Ashfield 99-01; Lect Lon Sch of Th 01-04; Chapl Pemb Coll Ox 04-05; Chapl Ox Pastorate 05-06. *Address temp unknown*

DOWNES, Richard John. b 63. Cranmer Hall Dur 91. **d** 94 **p** 95. C Bishopwearmouth St Gabr *Dur* 94-97; CF from 97. *c/o MOD Chaplains (Army)*   Tel (01980) 615804 Fax 615800

DOWNEY, Canon John Stewart. b 38. QUB CertEd60 Open Univ BA76. Oak Hill Th Coll 63. **d** 66 **p** 67. C Londonderry St Aug *D & R* 66-71; I Dungiven w Bovevagh 71-82; Bp's Dom Chapl 75-82; V Bishopwearmouth St Gabr *Dur* 82-91; V New Malden and Coombe *S'wark* 91-06; Hon Can S'wark Cathl 97-06; rtd 06; Perm to Offic *S'wark* from 08. *33A Queen's Road, Kingston upon Thames KT2 7SF*   Tel (020) 8974 5074

DOWNHAM, Canon Peter Norwell. b 31. Man Univ BA52. Ridley Hall Cam 54. **d** 56 **p** 57. C Cheadle *Ches* 56-62; V Rawtenstall St Mary *Man* 62-68; Chapl Rossendale Gen Hosp 62-68; V Denton Holme *Carl* 68-79; V Reading Greyfriars *Ox* 79-95; Hon Can Ch Ch 90-95; rtd 95; Hon C Cotehill and Cumwhinton *Carl* 95-00; Perm to Offic *Carl* 98-07 and *Ox* from 07. *17 Grange Close, Goring, Reading RG8 9DY*   Tel (01491) 875983

DOWNHAM, Simon Garrod. b 61. K Coll Lon LLB84 Solicitor 87. Wycliffe Hall Ox BA93. **d** 94 **p** 95. C Brompton H Trin w Onslow Square St Paul *Lon* 94-99; C Hammersmith St Paul 00-06; V from 06. *14 Lena Gardens, London W6 7PZ*   Tel (020) 7603 9662 *or* 8748 3855 E-mail simon.downham@sph.org.uk

DOWNING, Francis Gerald. b 35. Qu Coll Ox BA56 MA60. Linc Th Coll. **d** 58 **p** 59. C Filwood Park CD *Bris* 58-60; Tutor Linc Th Coll 60-64; V Unsworth *Man* 64-80; Tutor NOC 80-82; Vice-Prin 82-90; V Bolton SS Simon and Jude *Man* 90-97; rtd 97; Perm to Offic *Blackb* from 97. *33 Westhoughton Road, Chorley PR7 4EU*   Tel (01257) 474240

DOWNS, Caroline Rebecca. b 58. UWIST BA80 Univ of Wales (Cardiff) PGCE81. St Mich Coll Llan 98. **d** 02 **p** 03. C Roath *Llan* 02-07; P-in-c Cathays from 07. *6 Newminster Road, Roath, Cardiff CF23 5AP*   Tel (029) 2049 5699 E-mail carolinerebecca.downs@btinternet.com

DOWNS, Miss Geinor. b 47. UEA BA72 Southn Univ BTh89 Birm Univ MA05. Chich Th Coll 85. **d** 87 **p** 94. Par Dn Wellingborough All SS *Pet* 87-89; Development Officer Chich Th Coll 89-92; C Durrington *Chich* 92-95; Chapl City Hosp NHS Trust Birm 95-02; Chapl Sandwell and W Birm Hosps NHS Trust 02-06. *35 Fairmead Rise, Northampton NN2 8PP*   Tel (01604) 842554

DOWNS, John Alfred. b 58. Leic Univ BSc79 PGCE80 CBiol80 MIBiol80. EMMTC 90. **d** 93 **p** 94. NSM Barlestone *Leic* 93-96; NSM Markfield, Thornton, Bagworth and Stanton etc from 96. *29 Meadow Road, Barlestone, Nuneaton CV13 0JG*   Tel (01455) 290195

DOWNS, Mrs Lynsay Marie. b 75. Hull Univ BA98. Ripon Coll Cuddesdon BTh05. **d** 05 **p** 06. C Tettenhall Wood and Perton *Lich* 05-09; TV Brereton and Rugeley from 09. *The Vicarage, 14 Peakes Road, Rugeley ES15 2LY*   Tel (01889) 582809

DOWSE, Edgar. b 10. Dur Univ LTh35 Lon Univ BD37 Fitzw Coll Cam BA72 MA74 Lon Univ MPhil90 Lon Sch of Th PhD04. Clifton Th Coll 32. **d** 35 **p** 36. Asst Chapl and Tutor Clifton Th Coll 35-36; C Chippenham St Andr w Tytherton Lucas *Bris* 36-40; Tutor St Andr Th Coll Whittlesford 40-41; C Bournemouth St Mich *Win* 41-45; P-in-c Bournemouth H Epiphany 45-51; R Freemantle 51-57; V Bethnal Green St Bart *Lon* 57-71; Lect Lon Bible Coll 60-61; Lect St Mich Cornhill 60-63; St Steph Walbrook 65-68; P-in-c Acton Green St Alb *Lon* 71-72; V 72-75; rtd 75; Perm to Offic *Lon* 75-96 and from 00. *87 College Road, Isleworth TW7 5DP*   Tel (020) 8568 2548

DOWSE, Ivor Roy. b 35. ARHistS MRSL. St Deiniol's Hawarden 66. **d** 68 **p** 70. C Harrow St Pet *Lon* 68-69; C Sudbury St Andr 69-71; C Weeke *Win* 71-73; Min Can Ban Cathl 73-78; V Hollym w Welwick and Holmpton *York* 78-81; R Bearwood *Ox* 81-82; P-in-c Rothesay *Arg* 83-86; C Boxmoor St Jo *St Alb* 86-92; Hon C Cowes H Trin and St Mary *Portsm* 92-94; Perm to Offic 94-98; P-in-c St Hilary w Perranuthnoe *Truro* 98-00; rtd 01; Perm to Offic *Win* from 06; Hon Chapl Win Cathl from 06; Hon Asst Chapl St Jo Win Charity from 09. *10 St Mary Magdalen Almshouses, Colebrook Street, Winchester SO23 9LR* Tel (01962) 890877

DOWSETT, Alan Charles. b 27. Selw Coll Cam BA51 MA55 Bris Poly CQSW76. Cuddesdon Coll 51. **d** 53 **p** 54. C Portsea St Mary *Portsm* 53-57; C Wokingham All SS *Ox* 57-60; V Water Orton *Birm* 60-64; Chapl Coalston's Sch Bris 64-65; C Stoke Bishop *Bris* 65-68; Lic to Offic 69-89; rtd 89. *23 Upper Cranbrook Road, Bristol BS6 7UW* Tel 0117-924 3227

DOWSETT, Andrew Christopher. b 72. Sheff Univ BA95 PhD99. St Jo Coll Nottm 07. **d** 09. C Clubmoor Liv from 09. *88 Lisburn Lane, Liverpool L13 9AQ* Tel 07783-760012 (mobile) E-mail andrew@dowsetts.net

DOWSETT, Ian Peter. b 71. Liv Univ BA95 Lon Inst of Educn PGCE96. Wycliffe Hall Ox BA01. **d** 02. C Kensington St Helen w H Trin *Lon* 02-09; V S Harrow St Paul from 09. *St Paul's Vicarage, Findon Close, Harrow HA2 8NJ* Tel (020) 8864 0362 Mobile 07985-726465 E-mail irdowsett@talk21.com

DOWSETT, Marian Ivy Rose. b 40. **d** 88 **p** 97. NSM Rumney *Mon* 88-94; C St Mellons and Michaelston-y-Fedw 94-96; C St Mellons 96-03; V Llanrumney from 03. *114 Ridgeway Road, Rumney, Cardiff CF3 4AB* Tel (029) 2079 2635

DOWSON, Roger Christopher. b 32. Clifton Th Coll 60. **d** 63 **p** 64. C Virginia Water *Guildf* 63-66; C Darfield *Sheff* 66-68; V Thorpe Edge *Bradf* 68-80; V Wyke 80-91; rtd 91; Hon C Coley *Wakef* 91-01; Perm to Offic *Bradf* 93-99 and from 03; Perm to Offic *Wakef* 01-08. *1 Windsor Villas, Norwood Green, Halifax HX3 8QS* Tel (01274) 674557

DOWSON, Simon Paul. b 63. Bris Univ BSc85 Cam Univ PGCE89. Cranmer Hall Dur 95. **d** 97 **p** 98. C Bradf St Aug Undercliffe 97-99; C Werrington *Pet* 99-04; V Skirbeck H Trin *Linc* from 04. *Holy Trinity Vicarage, 64 Spilsby Road, Boston PE21 9NS* Tel (01205) 363657 E-mail sid@dowzim.fsnet.co.uk

DOXSEY, Canon Roy Desmond. b 41. St D Coll Lamp 64. **d** 67 **p** 68. C Pembroke St Mary w St Mich *St D* 67-70; C Milford Haven 70-73; C Loughton *Ox* 73-75; Chapl Llandovery Coll 75-81 and 92-96; Zambia 81-86; Chapl Epsom Coll 86-92; V Roath St German *Llan* from 96; Hon Can Llan Cathl from 09. *St German's Clergy House, Metal Street, Cardiff CF24 0LA* Tel (029) 2049 4488

DOYE, Andrew Peter Charles. b 64. BNC Ox BA85. Trin Coll Bris BA93. **d** 93 **p** 94. C Surbiton St Matt *S'wark* 93-96; C Bourne *Guildf* 96-99; C The Bourne and Tilford 99-00; R Wheathampstead *St Alb* 00-09; RD Wheathampstead 07-09. *Address temp unknown* E-mail andrewdoye@hotmail.com

DOYLE, Canon Alan Holland. b 22. JP72. Lon Univ BD55 Birm Univ MA86 Buckingham Univ DPhil93. Wycliffe Hall Ox 52. **d** 52 **p** 53. C Braddan *S & M* 52-54; C Douglas St Geo 54-55; R Oldham St Andr *Man* 55-59; Chapl Ruzawi Prep Sch S Rhodesia 59-62; V Chaddesley Corbett *Worc* 62-66; CF (TA) 63-67; V Kidderminster St Jo *Worc* 66-67; R Salwarpe 67-74; RD Droitwich 69-78; P-in-c Himbleton w Huddington 74-78; Hon Can Worc Cathl 74-87; P-in-c Ombersley w Doverdale 78-83; R 83-87; rtd 87; Perm to Offic *Worc* from 87. *3 Graham Court, Graham Road, Malvern WR14 2HX* Tel (01684) 891816

DOYLE, Andrew Michael. b 63. K Coll Lon BD85 AKC85. Ripon Coll Cuddesdon 86. **d** 88 **p** 89. C Lytchett Minster *Sarum* 88-92; TV Kirkby *Liv* 92-97; V Rotherhithe H Trin *S'wark* from 97; AD Bermondsey 00-08. *Holy Trinity Vicarage, Bryan Road, London SE16 5HF* Tel (020) 7237 4098

DOYLE, Edward Michael. b 70. St Mich Coll Llan BTh93. **d** 94 **p** 95. C Sketty *S & B* 94-96; C Llwynderw 96-00; R Rogate w Terwick and Trotton w Chithurst *Chich* from 00. *The Vicarage, Fyning Lane, Rogate, Petersfield GU31 5EE* Tel (01730) 821576 E-mail edwarddoyle@freenet5.freeserve.co.uk

DOYLE, Graham Thomas. b 48. St Barn Coll Adelaide ThL73 ThSchol77 Worc Coll Ox BA85 MA90. **d** 73 **p** 74. Australia 73-83; Perm to Offic *Ox* 83-85; C Cobbold Road St Sav w St Mary *Lon* 86; P-in-c Bradf St Oswald Chapel Green 86-91; Chapl Belgrade w Zagreb *Eur* 91-93; Chapl Belgrade 93-97; Taiwan 97-00; I Killeshandra w Killegar and Derrylane *K, E & A* 00-03; I Athlone w Benown, Kiltoom and Forgney *M & K* from 03. *St Mary's Rectory, Killion Hill Street, Bonavalley, Athlone, Co Westmeath, Republic of Ireland* Tel and fax (00353) (90) 647 8350 E-mail gtdoyleathlone@eircom.net

DOYLE, Michael Christopher. b 64. St Jo Coll Nottm 06. **d** 08 **p** 09. C Ashbourne w Mapleton *Derby* from 08. *12 Meynell Rise, Ashbourne DE6 1RU* Tel (01335) 346474 E-mail mike_c_doyle@hotmail.co.uk

DOYLE, Nigel Paul. b 55. MHort(RHS)82. St Mich Coll Llan 00. **d** 03 **p** 04. NSM Treboeth *S & B* from 03; NSM Landore from 03. *3 Ael-y-Bryn, Penclawdd, Swansea SA4 3LF* Tel (01792) 850659 E-mail tadnigel@yahoo.co.uk

DOYLE, Robin Alfred. b 43. Dur Univ BA65. Westcott Ho Cam 66. **d** 68 **p** 69. C Edgbaston St Geo *Birm* 68-70; C Erdington St Barn 70-73; P-in-c Oldbury 73-81; R Maker w Rame *Truro* from 81. *The Vicarage, Fore Street, Kingsand, Torpoint PL10 1NB* Tel (01752) 822302

DOYLE, Mrs Tracey Elizabeth. b 58. Open Univ BA00. SAOMC 94. **d** 97 **p** 98. OLM Winslow w Gt Horwood and Addington *Ox* 97-99; C 00-04; P-in-c Ivinghoe w Pitstone and Slapton 04-08; V Ivinghoe w Pitstone and Slapton and Marsworth from 08. *The Vicarage, Station Road, Ivinghoe, Leighton Buzzard LU7 9EB* Tel (01296) 668260 Mobile 07814-538208 E-mail mick.doyle@virgin.net

DRACKLEY, John Oldham. b 36. Em Coll Cam BA57 MA61. Wells Th Coll 57. **d** 59 **p** 60. C Eckington *Derby* 59-62; C Lee Gd Shep w St Pet *S'wark* 62-63; C Derby St Thos 63-67; C Matlock and Tansley 67-77; P-in-c Radbourne 77-82; P-in-c Dalbury, Long Lane and Trusley 77-82; P-in-c Longford 77-82; Sec Dioc Cttee for Care of Chs 82-98; rtd 95; Perm to Offic *Derby* from 98. *26 Highfield Drive, Matlock DE4 3FZ* Tel (01629) 55902

DRAFFAN, Canon Ian William. b 42. Aston Univ BSc65 MSc66 FBCS77 CEng88. NOC 83. **d** 86 **p** 87. NSM Millhouses H Trin *Sheff* 86-04; NSM Endcliffe from 04; P-in-c from 08; Hon Can Sheff Cathl from 05. *13 Bocking Lane, Sheffield S8 7BG* Tel 0114-236 4523 E-mail ian.draffan@sheffield.anglican.org

DRAIN, Wayne. b 39. JP75. Open Univ BA76 ACP66. NW Ord Course 76. **d** 79 **p** 80. NSM Cheadle *Ches* 79-81; C 81-84; V Chatburn *Blackb* 84-02; Sub Chapl HM Pris Preston 94-02; rtd 02; Perm to Offic *Blackb* from 02. *Angels, 28 The Croft, Euxton, Chorley PR7 6LH* Tel (01257) 249646

DRAKE, Frances Maud. b 43. Brentwood Coll of Educn TCert67 Sussex Univ BEd74. S'wark Ord Course 90. **d** 93 **p** 94. NSM Fryerning w Margaretting *Chelmsf* 93-01; P-in-c Margaretting w Mountnessing and Buttsbury 01-07; rtd 07; Perm to Offic *Chelmsf* from 07. *Little Pump House, Ongar Road, Kelvedon Hatch, Brentwood CM15 0LA* Tel and fax (01277) 364383 E-mail revfrances.drake@tiscali.co.uk

DRAKE, Graham. b 46. Linc Th Coll 81. **d** 83 **p** 85. C Alford w Rigsby *Linc* 83-84; Perm to Offic *Wakef* 84-85; Hon C Purston cum S Featherstone 85-89; NSM Castleford All SS 89-92; C Cudworth 92-95. *Flat 3, Woodland House, 5 Mill Hill, Pontefract WF8 4HR* Tel (01977) 708713 *or* 683324

DRAKE, Canon Graham Rae. b 45. Fitzw Coll Cam BA68 MA72. Qu Coll Birm 70. **d** 73 **p** 74. C New Windsor *Ox* 73-77; TV 77-78; P-in-c Bath Ascension *B & W* 78-81; TV Bath Twerton-on-Avon 81-86; P-in-c Buxton w Oxnead *Nor* 86-90; P-in-c Lammas w Lt Hautbois 86-90; R Buxton w Oxnead, Lammas and Brampton 90-95; RD Ingworth 88-94; P-in-c Cockley Cley w Gooderstone 95-01; P-in-c Gt and Lt Cressingham w Threxton 95-01; P-in-c Didlington 95-01; P-in-c Hilborough w Bodney 95-01; P-in-c Oxborough w Foulden and Caldecote 95-01; P-in-c Mundford w Lynford 99-01; P-in-c Ickburgh w Langford 99-01; P-in-c Cranwich 99-01; V Thorpe St Matt from 01; Hon Can Nor Cathl from 99. *St Matthew's Vicarage, Albert Place, Norwich NR1 4JL* Tel (01603) 620820 E-mail grahamrdrake@btinternet.com

DRAKE, John Paul. b 19. Qu Coll Ox BA41 MA44. Cuddesdon Coll 46. **d** 47 **p** 48. C Stepney St Dunstan and All SS *Lon* 47-54; V Brighton All So *Chich* 54-59; Chapl St Edw Sch Ox 59-69; V Stewkley *Ox* 69-75; V Stewkley w Soulbury and Drayton Parslow 75-85; RD Mursley 77-83; rtd 85; Perm to Offic *St Alb* from 85. *c/o Mrs C E Grace, Tythe Cottage, 1 School Lane, Stewkley, Leighton Buzzard LU7 0HL*

DRAKE, Leslie Sargent. b 47. Boston Univ BA69 MTh72 Hull Univ BPhil74 Anglia Poly Univ MSc93. Coll of Resurr Mirfield 78. **d** 78 **p** 79. C Oldham *Man* 78-81; TV Rochdale 81-83; V Palmers Green St Jo *Lon* 83-89; St Mary's Sch Cheshunt 89-91; Hd RE St Mary's Sch Hendon 91-99; TV Wimbledon *S'wark* 99-03; V Clay Hill St Jo and St Luke *Lon* 03-09; V Aiken St Aug USA from 09. *184 Kline Street, Aiken SC 29801, USA* Tel (001) (803) 514 2486

DRAKELEY, Stephen Richard Francis. b 51. Aston Univ BSc73. Chich Th Coll 76. **d** 76 **p** 77. C Yardley Wood *Birm* 76-79; V Rednal 79-89; TV Bodmin w Lanhydrock and Lanivet *Truro* 89-99; P-in-c Falmouth All SS from 99. *All Saints' Vicarage, 72 Dracaena Avenue, Falmouth TR11 2EN* Tel and fax (01326) 317474 E-mail srfd@compuserve.com

DRAPER, Canon Alfred James. b 23. Natal Univ BA50. St Aug Coll Cant St Paul's Coll Grahamstown. **d** 54 **p** 54. C Durban St Paul 54-58; V Umkomaas 60-63; V Tile Cross *Birm* 63-72; V Olton 72-75; R Durban St Paul 75-87; Adn Durban 79-87; R S Ferriby *Linc* 87-93; V Horkstow 87-93; R Saxby All Saints 87-93; rtd 93; Perm to Offic *Ches* from 93. *13 St James Avenue, Gawsworth, Macclesfield SK11 9RY* Tel (01625) 619033

DRAPER, Charles James. b 59. Dur Univ BSc80 Cam Univ BA86. Ridley Hall Cam 84. **d** 87 **p** 88. C Wareham *Sarum* 87-90; C Maltby *Sheff* 90-93; R The Claydons *Ox* 93-99; R Chinnor w Emmington and Sydenham etc 99-02; P-in-c Gt Faringdon w Lt

Coxwell 02-07; V from 07. *The Vicarage, Coach Lane, Faringdon SN7 8AB* Tel (01367) 240106
E-mail 6drapers@cdraper.fslife.co.uk

DRAPER, Christine. b 46. **d** 06 **p** 07. OLM Newburgh w Westhead *Liv* from 06. *Arenal, 38 Hoscar Moss Road, Lathom, Ormskirk L40 4BQ* Tel (01704) 893081

DRAPER, Derek Vincent. b 38. Linc Th Coll 65. **d** 68 **p** 69. C Orpington All SS *Roch* 68-72; C Bramley *Guildf* 72-74; P-in-c Kempston All SS *St Alb* 74-76; Min Kempston Transfiguration CD 77-79; V Kempston Transfiguration 79-84; RD Bedford 79-84; V Bromham w Oakley 84-88; P-in-c Stagsden 84-88; V Bromham w Oakley and Stagsden 88-03; RD Elstow 00-03; Chapl Bromham Hosp 84-03; rtd 03; Perm to Offic *Ely* and *St Alb* from 03. *24 Wilkinson Close, Eaton Socon, St Neots PE19 8HJ* Tel (01480) 384031

DRAPER, Elizabeth Ann. *See* BRADLEY, Mrs Elizabeth Ann

DRAPER, Ivan Thomas. b 32. Aber Univ MB, ChB56 FRCP FRCPGlas. St Jo Coll Nottm 87. **d** 90 **p** 91. NSM Glas St Bride from 90; P-in-c 96-99. *13/1 Whistlefield Court, 2 Canniesburn Road, Bearsden, Glasgow G61 1PX* Tel 0141-943 0954

DRAPER, James. *See* DRAPER, Canon Alfred James

DRAPER, Jean Margaret. b 31. **d** 80 **p** 97. NSM Pontnewydd *Mon* 80-83; BRF 82-83; NSM Llantilio Pertholey w Bettws Chpl etc *Mon* 83-94; NSM Newport St Andr 94-03. *Govilon House, Merthyr Road, Govilon, Abergavenny NP7 9PT* Tel (01873) 830380

DRAPER, John William. b 54. Qu Coll Birm 88. **d** 90 **p** 91. C Stepney St Dunstan and All SS *Lon* 90-94; C Leigh Park and Warren Park *Portsm* 94-96; R Rowner from 96; V Bridgemary 04-08. *The Rectory, 174 Rowner Lane, Gosport PO13 9SU* Tel (023) 9258 1834 Fax 9258 7934 Mobile 07966-559970
E-mail stmrowner@aol.com

DRAPER, Canon Jonathan Lee. b 52. Gordon Coll Mass BA76 St Jo Coll Dur BA78 PhD84. Ripon Coll Cuddesdon 83. **d** 83 **p** 84. C Baguley *Man* 83-85; Dir Academic Studies Ripon Coll Cuddesdon 85-92; V Putney St Mary *S'wark* 92-00; Can Res York Minster from 00. *3 Minster Court, York YO1 7JJ* Tel (01904) 625599 *or* 557211 Fax 672022 *or* 557215
E-mail jonathan.draper3@btinternet.com

DRAPER, Canon Martin Paul. b 50. OBE98. Birm Univ BA72 Southn Univ BTh79. Chich Th Coll 72. **d** 75 **p** 76. C Primrose Hill St Mary w Avenue Road St Paul *Lon* 75-78; C Westmr St Matt 79-84; Chapl Paris St Geo *Eur* 84-02; Adn France 94-02; Can Gib Cathl 94-02. *25 rue Vicq D'azir, 75010 Paris, France*

DRAPER, Patrick Hugh. b 43. S Dios Minl Tr Scheme 91. **d** 94 **p** 95. NSM Boscombe St Jo *Win* 94-99; P-in-c Southbourne St Chris 99-02; rtd 02; Perm to Offic *Win* from 02. *82 Tuckton Road, Bournemouth BH6 3HT* Tel (01202) 420190

DRAPER, The Very Revd Paul Richard. b 64. Glas Univ MA87 TCD BTh90. **d** 90 **p** 91. C Drumragh w Mountfield *D & R* 90-94; I Ballydehob w Aghadown *C, C & R* 94-09; Can Cork and Ross Cathls 98-09; Bp's Dom Chapl 99-09; Dean Lismore *C & O* from 09; I Lismore w Cappoquin, Kilwatermoy, Dungarvan etc from 09. *The Deanery, The Mall, Lismore, Co Waterford, Republic of Ireland* Tel (00353) (58) 54105

DRAPER, Peter Raymond. b 57. Leeds Poly BSc86 Leeds Univ CertEd88 Hull Univ PhD94 SRN80. NEOC 01. **d** 04 **p** 05. NSM S Cave and Ellerker w Broomfleet *York* from 04. *2 East Dale Road, Melton, North Ferriby HU14 3HS* Tel (01482) 632470 Mobile 07956-531002 E-mail p.r.draper@hull.ac.uk

DRAPER, Raymond James. b 48. Ex Coll Ox BA70 MA75 Em Coll Cam BA73 MA78. Ridley Hall Cam 71. **d** 74 **p** 75. C Sheff Manor 74-78; Ind Chapl 78-82; R Wickersley 82-00; V Leytonstone St Jo *Chelmsf* from 00. *St John's Vicarage, 44 Hartley Road, London E11 3BL* Tel (020) 8257 2792

DRAPER, Mrs Sylvia Edith. b 39. ARCM60. NOC 86. **d** 89 **p** 94. C Aughton St Mich *Liv* 89-92; Par Dn Wigan St Jas w St Thos 92-94; Asst Chapl Wigan and Leigh Health Services NHS Trust 92-97; C Wigan St Jas w St Thos *Liv* 94-97; TV Walton-on-the-Hill 97-02; rtd 02; Perm to Offic *Liv* from 03. *6 Brookfield Lane, Aughton, Ormskirk L39 6SP* Tel (01695) 422138

DRAX, Elizabeth Margaret. *See* ANSON, Mrs Elizabeth Margaret

DRAY, John. b 66. St Chad's Coll Dur BSc87. St Steph Ho Ox BTh95. **d** 95 **p** 96. C Bushey St Ant *Newc* 95-98; C Cullercoats St Geo 98-01; P-in-c Platt *Roch* 01-05; Chapl to the Deaf 01-05. *51 Widmore Lodge Road, Bromley BR1 2QE*
E-mail john.dray@bigfoot.com

DRAYCOTT, John. b 53. Sheff Univ BA84. Linc Th Coll 85. **d** 85 **p** 86. In Wesleyan Reform Union 77-82; C Wombwell *Sheff* 85-87; V W Bessacarr 87-92; V Erith Ch Ch *Roch* from 92; P-in-c Erith St Jo 92-95. *Christ Church Vicarage, Victoria Road, Erith DA8 3AN* Tel and fax (01322) 334729

DRAYCOTT, John Edward. b 54. EMMTC 99. **d** 01 **p** 02. C Calverton, Epperstone, Gonalston etc *S'well* 01-05; TV Purr *Liv* from 05. *St Philip's Vicarage, 459 Fleet Lane, St Helens WA9 2NQ* Tel (01744) 21213

DRAYCOTT, Philip John. b 27. Sarum & Wells Th Coll. **d** 83 **p** 84. C Bishop's Cleeve *Glouc* 83-86; V Chedworth, Yanworth

and Stowell, Coln Rogers etc 86-93; rtd 94; Perm to Offic *B & W* from 94. *April Cottage, Newton Road, North Petherton, Bridgwater TA6 6NA* Tel (01278) 662487

✠**DRAYSON, The Rt Revd Nicholas James Quested.** b 53. Keble Coll Ox BA75 MA82. Wycliffe Hall Ox 82. **d** 79 **p** 79 **c** 09. SAMS Argentina 79-82 and 92-00; Pastor Tartagal and Chapl to Chorote Indians 79-82; P-in-c Seville Ascension Spain 83-91; Adn Andalucia 89-91; Translations Co-ord 92-98; Pastor Salta St Andr 98-00; C Beverley Minster *York* 00-09; Suff Bp N Argentina from 09. *Casilla 187, 4400 Salta, Argentina* Tel (0054) (387) 431 1718 E-mail diaan.epi@gmail.com
or nicobispo@gmail.com

DRAYTON, James Edward. b 30. St Deiniol's Hawarden 81. **d** 84 **p** 86. Hon C Heald Green St Cath *Ches* 84-88; C Bollington St Jo 88-92; P-in-c Lt Leigh and Lower Whitley 92-96; P-in-c Aston by Sutton 92-96; P-in-c Antrobus 92-96; rtd 96; Perm to Offic *York* from 96. *87 Wharfedale, Filey YO14 0DP*

DREDGE, David John. b 32. Cranmer Hall Dur 69. **d** 71 **p** 72. C Goole *Sheff* 71-74; P-in-c Eastoft 74-77; V Whitgift w Adlingfleet 74-77; V Whitgift w Adlingfleet and Eastoft 77-78; V Walkley 78-81; TV Bicester w Bucknell, Caversfield and Launton *Ox* 81-86; V N Brickhill and Putnoe *St Alb* 86-90; P-in-c Sarratt 90-95; rtd 95; Perm to Offic *Lich* from 95. *19 Waterdale, Wombourne, Wolverhampton WV5 0DH* Tel (01902) 897467

DREDGE, David Julian. b 36. ALA74 Sheff Univ BA59. Cranmer Hall Dur 61 Ban Ord Course 85. **d** 87 **p** 88. NSM Dwygyfylchi *Ban* 87-92; R Llanllechid 92-97; rtd 97; Perm to Offic *Ban* from 97. *Westfield, Treforris Road, Penmaenmawr LL34 6RH* Tel (01492) 623439 Mobile 07721-941861 Fax 0870-056 7258 E-mail david@djdredge.plus.com

DREW, Gerald Arthur. b 36. Bps' Coll Cheshunt 59. **d** 61 **p** 62. C Lyonsdown H Trin *St Alb* 61-67; C Tring 67-71; R Bramfield w Stapleford and Waterford 71-78; V Langleybury St Paul 78-90; P-in-c Hormead, Wyddial, Anstey, Brent Pelham etc 90-95; V 95-01; rtd 01; Perm to Offic *St Alb* and *St E* from 01. *33 The Glebe, Lavenham, Sudbury CO10 9SN* Tel (01787) 248133

DREW (née ROY), Mrs Jennifer Pearl. b 53. SRN75 CSS91. Cranmer Hall Dur. **d** 01 **p** 02. C Hebburn St Jo and Jarrow Grange *Dur* 01-05; NSM Broom Leys *Leic* 05-08; Perm to Offic from 08. *5 Balmoral Road, Coalville LE67 4RF* Tel (01530) 836329 E-mail revjen@dudrop.clara.co.uk

DREW, Michael Edgar Cecil. b 31. Oriel Coll Ox BA55 MA59. St Steph Ho Ox 55. **d** 57 **p** 58. C Plymouth St Pet *Ex* 57-63; Missr Pemb Coll Cam Miss Walworth 63-67; Asst Chapl All Hallows Sch Rousdon 67-75; Chapl 80-81; Chapl Ex Sch 81-83; V Scraptoft *Leic* 83-97; V Hungarton 83-87; P-in-c Leic St Eliz Nether Hall 87-97; rtd 97. *28 St Mary's Paddock, Wellingborough NN8 1HJ* Tel (01933) 277407

DREW, Canon Rosemary. b 43. SRN64. EAMTC 90. **d** 93 **p** 94. NSM Gt Dunmow *Chelmsf* 93-96; NSM Gt Dunmow and Barnston from 96; Hon Can Chelmsf Cathl from 01; Area Adv for Healing and Deliverance Min from 04. *The Bowling Green, 8 The Downs, Dunmow CM6 1DT* Tel and fax (01371) 872662
E-mail bruce.drew@btinternet.com

DREW, Simon Mark. b 68. Liv Univ BEng89 CEng94 MICE94. St Jo Coll Nottm MA98. **d** 99 **p** 00. C Torquay St Matthias, St Mark and H Trin *Ex* 99-03; V Marshfield w Cold Ashton and Tormarton etc *Bris* from 03. *The Vicarage, Church Lane, Marshfield, Chippenham SN14 8NT* Tel (01225) 891850
E-mail simon@smdrew.freeserve.co.uk

DREWERY, Graeme Robert. b 66. St Jo Coll Cam BA88 MA92 PhD94 FRCO89. Linc Th Coll MDiv94. **d** 94 **p** 95. C Paston *Pet* 94-97; C Cottingham *York* 97-00; V Middlesbrough St Jo the Ev 00-05; R Brotton Parva from 05. *St Margaret's Rectory, 9 Crispin Court, Brotton, Saltburn-by-the-Sea TS12 2XL* Tel (01287) 676275

DREWETT, Canon Mervyn Henry. b 27. Wadh Coll Ox BA50 MA53. Linc Th Coll 52. **d** 54 **p** 55. C Filwood Park CD *Bris* 54-58; C Bishopston 58-61; V Brislington St Chris 61-67; V Henbury 67-80; RD Westbury and Severnside 79-80; TR Gtr Corsham 80-94; Hon Can Bris Cathl 80-94; RD Chippenham 82-88; rtd 94; Perm to Offic *Bris* and *Sarum* from 94. *14 The Beeches, Shaw, Melksham SN12 8EP* Tel (01225) 702726

DREWETT, Mrs Susan. **d** 06 **p** 07. NSM Bemerton *Sarum* from 06. *Melford House, 36 Bulford Road, Durrington, Salisbury SP4 8DJ* Tel (01980) 652751 E-mail susandrewett@fsmail.net

DREYER, Rodney Granville. b 55. Lon Univ MPhil91 AKC91. St Paul's Coll Grahamstown 79. **d** 81 **p** 82. S Africa 81-84 and 94-98; NSM Headstone St Geo *Lon* 84-86; NSM Northolt St Mary 86-87; C Portsea St Mary *Portsm* 87-90; V Sudbury St Andr *Lon* 90-94; Adn W and S Free State 94-95; V Hawkhurst *Cant* from 98. *The Vicarage, Moor Hill Road, Hawkhurst, Cranbrook TN18 4QB* Tel (01580) 753397
E-mail rodneydreyer@sky.com

DRISCOLL, Canon David. b 42. Lon Univ BSc64. Linc Th Coll 68. **d** 71 **p** 72. C Walthamstow St Jo *Chelmsf* 71-76; Chapl NE Lon Poly 71-79; C-in-c Plaistow St Mary 76-79; P-in-c Stratford St Jo and Ch Ch w Forest Gate St Jas 79-89; V Theydon Bois

89-01; RD Epping Forest 92-00; Hon Can Chelmsf Cathl 01; C All Hallows by the Tower etc *Lon* 01-07; rtd 07; Educn Tutor R Foundn of St Kath in Ratcliffe from 05; Exec Officer Miss in London's Economy from 07; Perm to Offic *Chelmsf* and *Lon* from 07. *281 Central Park Road, London E6 3AF* Tel (020) 7791 9873 *or* 8548 1522 Fax 7702 7603 E-mail ddriscoll@rfsk.org.uk

DRIVER, Arthur John Roberts. b 44. SS Coll Cam MA70 FCIPA73. Linc Th Coll 73. d 76 p 77. C S'wark H Trin w St Matt 76-80; TV N Lambeth 80-85; CMS Sri Lanka 86-92; V Putney St Marg *S'wark* 92-97; V Streatham St Paul 97-09; rtd 09. *91 Ernest Road, Wivenhoe, Colchester CO7 9LJ* Tel (01206) 822135 E-mail ajrdriver@aol.com

DRIVER, Bruce Leslie. b 42. Lon Univ LLB73. Linc Th Coll 76. d 78 p 79. C Dunstable *St Alb* 78-81; TV 81-86; V Rickmansworth 86-98; RD Rickmansworth 91-98; V Northwood Hills St Edm *Lon* 98-08; rtd 08. *7 Bromley College, London Road, Bromley BR1 1PE* Tel (020) 8290 0366 E-mail bldriver@tiscali.co.uk

DRIVER, Geoffrey. b 41. Chich Th Coll 86. d 88 p 89. C Pontefract St Giles *Wakef* 88-91; V Glass Houghton 91-97; Chapl Pontefract Hosps NHS Trust 97-99; R Southwick H Trin *Dur* 99-03; TR N Wearside from 03. *The Team Rectory, Rotherham Road, Sunderland SR5 5QS* Tel 0191-549 1261 E-mail fathergeoff@lineone.net

DRIVER, Geoffrey Lester. b 59. Liv Poly BA83. Chich Th Coll 86. d 89 p 90. C Walton St Mary *Liv* 89-92; C Selsey *Chich* 92-95; V Cowfold 95-07; Lic to Offic from 07; Chapl St Mich Hospice from 08. *1 Belvedere Court, 12 St Anne's Road, Eastbourne BN21 2HH* Tel (01323) 439669 Mobile 07871-488224

DRIVER, Gordon Geoffrey. b 32. Garnett Coll Lon Dip Teaching59. Trin Coll Bris. d 95 p 96. NSM Radipole and Melcombe Regis *Sarum* 95-03; rtd 03; Perm to Offic *Sarum* from 03. *11 Greenway Close, Weymouth DT3 5BQ* Tel (01305) 812784

DRIVER (*née* FRENCH), Janet Mary. b 43. Leeds Univ BA65 PGCE66 Surrey Univ BA98. Linc Th Coll 74. dss 80 d 92 p 94. St Paul's Cathl 80-82; N Lambeth *S'wark* 80-85; CMS Sri Lanka 86-92; NSM Putney St Marg *S'wark* 92-97; Hon C Streatham St Paul 97-09; rtd 09. *91 Ernest Road, Wivenhoe, Colchester CO7 9LJ* Tel (01206) 822135 E-mail janet@janetdriver.co.uk

DRIVER, Jennifer. b 63. SEITE 05. d 08 p 09. NSM Farnborough *Roch* from 08. *3 Starts Hill Road, Orpington BR6 7AR* Tel (01689) 858766 Mobile 07974-722736 E-mail driverjen1@aol.com

DRIVER, John. *See* DRIVER, Arthur John Roberts

DRIVER, The Ven Penelope May. b 52. NOC. d 87 p 94. Dioc Youth Adv *Newc* 86-88; C Cullercoats St Geo 87-88; Youth Chapl *Ripon* 88-96; Dioc Adv Women's Min 91-06; Asst Dir of Ords 96-98; Dioc Dir of Ords 98-06; Min Can Ripon Cathl 96-06; Hon Can 98-06; Adn Ex from 06. *Emmanuel House, Station Road, Ide, Exeter EX2 9RS* Tel (01392) 420972 *or* 425577 E-mail archdeacon.of.exeter@exeter.anglican.org

DRIVER, Canon Roger John. b 64. Liv Univ MA08. Trin Coll Bris BA88. d 90 p 91. C Much Woolton *Liv* 90-93; C Fazakerley Em 93-94; TV 94-00; P-in-c Bootle St Matt 00-03; P-in-c Bootle St Leon 00-03; P-in-c Litherland St Andr 00-03; TR Bootle from 04; AD Bootle from 07; Hon Can Liv Cathl from 07. *The Vicarage, 70 Merton Road, Bootle L20 7AT* Tel 0151-922 3316 E-mail rogerdriver@btinternet.com

DROBIG, Marion. b 76. Hannover Univ MA01 Pemb Coll Ox DPhil05. ERMC 04. d 06 p 07. C Newmarket All SS *St E* 06-09; R Shaw cum Donnington *Ox* from 09. *The Rectory, Well Meadow, Shaw, Newbury RG14 2DS* Tel (01635) 600532 Mobile 07979-534948 E-mail mariondrobig@hotmail.com

DROMORE, Archdeacon of. *See* SCOTT, The Ven William John

DROMORE, Dean of. *See* LOWRY, The Very Revd Stephen Harold

DROWLEY, Arthur. b 28. Oak Hill Th Coll 54. d 56 p 57. C Longfleet *Sarum* 56-59; C Wallington *S'wark* 59-62; V Taunton St Jas *B & W* 62-73; RD Taunton N 72-73; V Rodbourne Cheney *Bris* 73-87; R Bigbury, Ringmore and Kingston *Ex* 87-94; rtd 94; Perm to Offic *Ex* 94-02; *Man* from 03; *Lich* from 05. *4 Inglis Road, Park Hall, Oswestry SY11 4AN* Tel (01691) 671994

DROWN, Richard. b 19. BNC Ox BA41 MA43. Wycliffe Hall Ox 41. d 42 p 43. C St Helens St Helen *Liv* 42-45; Chapl K Coll Budo Uganda 46-65; Hd Master St Andr Sch Turi Kenya 65-73; Hd Master Edin Ho Sch New Milton 73-84; rtd 84; Hon C Brockenhurst *Win* from 85. *3 Waters Green Court, Brockenhurst SO42 7QR* Tel (01590) 624038

DRUCE, Brian Lemuel. b 31. MRICS55. Bps' Coll Cheshunt 58. d 60 p 61. C Whitton St Aug *Lon* 60-63; C Minehead *B & W* 63-66; R Birch St Agnes *Man* 66-70; V Overbury w Alstone, Teddington and Lt Washbourne *Worc* 70-81; Ind Chapl 81-91; rtd 91; Perm to Offic *Worc* from 91. *Park Cottage, Elmley Castle, Pershore WR10 3HU* Tel (01386) 710577 E-mail brian.druce@talk21.com

DRUCE, John Perry. b 34. Em Coll Cam BA57 MA61 Lambeth STh97 ALCM86. Wycliffe Hall Ox 57. d 59 p 60. C Wednesbury St Bart *Lich* 59-62; C Bushbury 62-64; V Walsall Wood 64-74; R

Farnborough *Roch* 74-87; R E Bergholt *St E* 87-99; P-in-c Bentley w Tattingstone 95-99; rtd 99. *9 Fullers Close, Hadleigh, Ipswich IP7 5AS* Tel (01473) 827242 E-mail jgdruce@realemail.co.uk

DRUMMOND, Canon Christopher John Vaughan. b 26. Magd Coll Ox MA51 Magd Coll Cam MA56. Ridley Hall Cam 51. d 53 p 54. C Barking St Marg *Chelmsf* 53-56; Tutor Ridley Hall Cam 56-59; Lic to Offic *Ely* 57-62; Chapl Clare Coll Cam 59-62; Nigeria 63-69; V Walthamstow St Jo *Chelmsf* 69-74; P-in-c Stantonbury *Ox* 74-75; R 75-84; P-in-c Ducklington 84-88; Dioc Ecum Officer 84-88; Can Ibadan from 87; Home Sec Gen Syn Bd for Miss and Unity 88-91; rtd 91; P-in-c Colton *Lich* 91-94; Perm to Offic *Lich* 94-99 and *Guildf* from 97. *77 Markham Road, Capel, Dorking RH5 5JT* Tel (01306) 712637 Mobile 07966-518681

DRUMMOND, John Malcolm. b 44. Nottm Univ CertEd65. Edin Th Coll 68. d 71 p 72. C Kirkholt *Man* 71-74; C Westleigh St Pet 74-76; Hd of RE Leigh High Sch from 76; Lic Preacher from 76; Hon C Leigh St Jo 84-90; Hon C Tonge Moor from 90. *14 Bull's Head Cottages, Turton, Bolton BL7 0HS* Tel (01204) 852232 E-mail rev.m.drummond@btinternet.com

DRUMMOND, Josceline Maurice Vaughan. b 29. Lon Univ BD70. Wycliffe Hall Ox 55. d 58 p 59. C Tunbridge Wells St Jo *Roch* 58-60; C Walthamstow St Mary *Chelmsf* 60-62; V Oulton *Lich* 62-68; V Leyton St Cath *Chelmsf* 71-85; Gen Dir CMJ 85-94; Public Preacher *St Alb* 88-94; rtd 94; Perm to Offic *St Alb* from 94. *3 Fryth Mead, St Albans AL3 4TN* Tel (01727) 857620

DRUMMOND, Ms Judi. Cranmer Hall Dur. d 06 p 07. C Kirkby *Liv* from 06. *18 Askern Road, Liverpool L32 9QH* Tel 0151-546 5487 Fax 167 3589

DRURY, Anthony Desmond. b 42. NOC. d 99 p 00. NSM New Ferry *Ches* from 99. *61 Church Road, Bebington, Wirral CH63 3DZ* Tel 0151-334 4797 E-mail des@stmarksnewferry.org.uk

DRURY, Mrs Carol. b 61. SRN83. Trin Coll Bris BA02. d 01 p 02. NSM Soundwell *Bris* 01-03; CMS Uganda 04-05; C Motueka New Zealand from 06. *St Thomas's Church, 101 High Street, Motueka, New Zealand* Tel (0064) (3) 528 8825

DRURY, Mrs Caroline Nora. b 60. SAOMC 00. d 03 p 04. C Leavesden *St Alb* from 03. *49 Ross Crescent, Watford WD25 0DA* Tel (01923) 673129 E-mail caroline.drury@btinternet.com

DRURY, Desmond. *See* DRURY, Anthony Desmond

DRURY, The Very Revd John Henry. b 36. Trin Hall Cam MA66. Westcott Ho Cam 61. d 63 p 64. C St John's Wood *Lon* 63-66; Chapl Down Coll Cam 66-69; Chapl Ex Coll Ox 69-73; Can Res Nor Cathl 73-79; Vice-Dean 78-79; Lect Sussex Univ 79-81; Dean K Coll Cam 81-91; Dean Ch Ch *Ox* 91-03; rtd 03; Chapl and Fell All So Coll Ox from 03. *All Souls College, Oxford OX1 4AL* Tel (01865) 279379 Fax 279299

DRURY, Michael Dru. b 31. Trin Coll Ox BA55 MA59. Wycliffe Hall Ox. d 58 p 59. C Fulham St Mary N End *Lon* 58-62; C Blackheath St Jo *S'wark* 62-64; Chapl and Asst Master Canford Sch Wimborne 64-80; Chapl and Teacher Fernhill Manor Sch New Milton 80-81; P-in-c Stowe *Ox* 82-92; Asst Master Stowe Sch Bucks 82-92; R Rampton w Laneham, Treswell, Cottam and Stokeham *S'well* 92-96; rtd 96; Perm to Offic *Sarum* from 96. *Tanfield, Giddylake, Wimborne BH21 2QT* Tel (01202) 881246

DRURY, Richard Alexander. b 63. Lon Univ BD85 Avery Hill Coll PGCE86 ACII91. Trin Coll Bris MA00. d 00 p 01. C Kingswood *Bris* 00-03; CMS Uganda 04-05; V Motueka New Zealand from 06. *St Thomas's Church, 101 High Street, Motueka, New Zealand* Tel (0064) (3) 528 8825

DRURY, Stephen Roger. b 45. Univ Coll Lon LLB66 Solicitor 70. Coll of Resurr Mirfield 06. d 07 p 08. NSM Seamer w East Ayton *York* from 07. *74 Racecourse Road, West Ayton, Scarborough YO13 9JH* Tel (01723) 862044 E-mail stephen_drury@hotmail.com

DRURY, Valerie Doreen. b 40. Univ of Wales (Cardiff) BA62 K Coll Lon PGCE63 Lon Inst of Educn ADEDC80 MBATOD80. Oak Hill Th Coll 85. d 87 p 94. NSM Becontree St Alb *Chelmsf* 87-89; NSM Becontree S 89-02; rtd 02; Perm to Offic *Chelmsf* from 02. *37 Blunts Hall Road, Witham CM8 1ES* Tel (01376) 517330 E-mail vdrury@tiscali.co.uk

DRYDEN, Barry Frederick. b 44. Ches Coll of HE BTh00. NOC 97. d 00 p 01. C Formby St Pet *Liv* 00-03; V Woolston from 03. *The Vicarage, 20 Warren Lane, Woolston, Warrington WA1 4ES* Tel (01925) 813083

DRYDEN, Martin John. b 57. Loughb Univ BA80 Univ of Wales (Lamp) MA09. STETS 07. d 09. NSM Jersey St Clem *Win* from 09. *Mont Ubé House, La rue de la Blinerie, St Clement, Jersey JE2 6QT* Tel (01534) 874468 Mobile 07797-729525 E-mail martin@mont-ube.net

DRYE, Douglas John. b 37. Man Univ BSc61. Clifton Th Coll. d 63 p 64. C Whalley Range St Edm *Man* 63-66; C Drypool St Columba w St Andr and St Pet *York* 66-68; V Worsbrough Common *Sheff* 68-86; R Armthorpe 86-92; rtd 92; Perm to Offic *Pet* from 92. *25 Willow Crescent, Oakham LE15 6EQ* Tel (01572) 770429

D'SOUZA, Derek Emile. b 54. Trin Coll Bris. **d** 07 **p** 08. C Edgbaston St Germain *Birm* from 07. *410 Gillott Road, Birmingham B16 9LP* Tel 0121-242 3059 *or* 429 3431
E-mail helennderek@yahoo.co.uk

du SAIRE, Ms Michele Marie. b 55. Leeds Poly BSc78. ERMC 06. **d** 09. C Leavesden *St Alb* from 09. *49 Ross Crescent, Watford WD25 0DA* Tel (01923) 673129
E-mail micheledusaire@googlemail.com

DUBLIN (Christ Church), Dean of. *See* DUNNE, The Very Revd Dermot Patrick Martin

DUBLIN (St Patrick's), Dean of. *See* MacCARTHY, The Very Revd Robert Brian

DUBLIN, Archbishop of, and Bishop of Glendalough. *See* NEILL, The Most Revd John Robert Winder

DUBLIN, Archdeacon of. *See* PIERPOINT, The Ven David Alfred

DUBREUIL, Yann. b 70. Birm Univ BA04. Wycliffe Hall Ox 05. **d** 07 **p** 08. C Four Marks *Win* from 07. *25 Badger Close, Four Marks, Alton GU34 5HB* Tel (01420) 562933 Mobile 07984-213083 E-mail yann@handydubreuil.plus.com

DUCK, Mrs Jacqueline. b 44. Ches Coll of HE BTh00 ACMA70. NOC 97. **d** 00 **p** 01. NSM Ormskirk *Liv* 00-04; C Sutton 04-06; P-in-c Brington w Molesworth and Old Weston *Ely* from 06; P-in-c Leighton Bromswold from 06; P-in-c Gt w Lt Gidding and Steeple Gidding from 06; P-in-c Winwick from 06; P-in-c Hamerton from 06. *The Rectory, Church Lane, Brington, Huntingdon PE28 5AE* Tel (01832) 710207
E-mail revjackieduck@btinternet.com

DUCKERS, Miss Linda Jean. b 62. Univ of Wales (Abth) BSc84 PGCE85 Rob Coll Cam BTh06. Ridley Hall Cam 04. **d** 06 **p** 07. C Leek and Meerbrook *Lich* from 06. *Old Timbers, 5 Stockwell Street, Leek ST13 6DH* Tel (01538) 383590
E-mail linda.duckers@googlemail.com

DUCKERS, Paul Gerrard. b 42. Qu Coll Birm 07. **d** 09. NSM Sutton Coldfield H Trin *Birm* from 09. *5 Moor Meadow Road, Sutton Coldfield B75 6BU* Tel 0121-378 1835
E-mail paulduckers@talktalk.net

DUCKETT, Canon Brian John. b 45. ALCD70. **d** 70 **p** 71. C S Lambeth St Steph *S'wark* 70-73; C Norwood St Luke 73-75; C Bushbury *Lich* 75-77; TV 77-79; V Dover St Martin *Cant* 79-92; TR Swindon Dorcan *Bris* 92-00; R Highworth 95-99; V Clifton H Trin, St Andr and St Pet 00-09; Vulnerable Adults Policy Officer 07-09; Hon Can Bris Cathl 98-09; rtd 09. *Holy Trinity Vicarage, 6 Goldney Avenue, Bristol BS8 4RA* Tel 0117-973 4751 E-mail office@hthotwells.fsnet.co.uk

DUCKETT, Mrs Helen Lorraine. b 71. Keble Coll Ox BA92 Sheff Univ MA94 Birm Univ MPhil98. Qu Coll Birm 95. **d** 98 **p** 99. C Cannock *Lich* 98-01; TV Wednesfield from 01. *167 Colman Avenue, Wolverhampton WV11 3RU* Tel (01902) 630094
E-mail duckett.h@tinyworld.co.uk

DUCKETT, John Dollings. b 41. Nottm Univ BA62 BTh81. Linc Th Coll 79. **d** 81 **p** 82. C Boston *Linc* 81-84; V Baston 84-86; V Langtoft Gp 86-88; V Sutterton and Wigtoft 88-89; R Sutterton w Fosdyke and Algarkirk 89-92; P-in-c Chapel St Leonards w Hogsthorpe 92-97; V 97-00; V Bracebridge 00-06; rtd 06. *Old Post Office, Faldingworth Road, Spridlington, Market Rasen LN8 2DF* Tel (01673) 860116

DUCKETT, Keith Alexander. b 69. Worc Coll of Educn BA93. Qu Coll Birm BD97 MA98. **d** 98 **p** 99. C Willenhall H Trin *Lich* 98-01; TV Blakenall Heath 01-03; Asst Chapl Sandwell and W Birm Hosps NHS Trust 03-06; Chapl from 06. *Sandwell General Hospital, Lyndon, West Bromwich B71 4HJ* Tel 0121-553 1831 *or* (01902) 732763 E-mail keith.duckett@swbh.nhs.uk *or* duckettk@fish.co.uk

DUCKETT, Lee Christopher James. b 67. Wycliffe Hall Ox BTh04. **d** 04 **p** 05. C Cranham Park *Chelmsf* 04-08; C Purley Ch Ch *S'wark* from 08. *72 Riddlesdown Road, Purley CR8 1DB* Tel 07782-171320 (mobile) E-mail leeduckett@ymail.com

DUCKETT, Matthew Robert. b 64. UEA BSc85 PGCE88. NTMTC BA09. **d** 09. NSM Old St Pancras *Lon* from 09. *Little Ilford Rectory, 124 Church Road, London E12 6HA* Tel (020) 8478 2182 E-mail m.duckett@ucl.ac.uk

DUCKETT, Raphael Thomas Marie James. b 65. N Staffs Poly BA87. Cranmer Hall Dur 01. **d** 03 **p** 04. C Madeley *Heref* 03-06; V Bradley St Martin *Lich* from 06. *St Martin's Vicarage, 7 King Street, Bradley, Bilston WV14 8PQ* Tel (01902) 650101
E-mail revraphael@blueyonder.co.uk

DUCKWORTH, Mrs Angela Denise. b 58. SRN95 RM98. Ripon Coll Cuddesdon 05. **d** 07 **p** 08. C Malvern H Trin and St Jas *Worc* from 07. *4 Malus Close, Malvern WR14 2WD* Tel (01684) 563856 E-mail angie@duckworthonline.net

DUCKWORTH, Annette Jacqueline. b 54. Univ of Wales (Ban) BSc75 PGCE76. **d** 00 **p** 01. OLM Moxley *Lich* from 00; Chapl Blue Coat Comp Sch Walsall from 07. *1 Sutton Road, Wednesbury WS10 8SG*
E-mail annette.duckworth@hotmail.co.uk

DUCKWORTH, Brian George. b 47. Edin Th Coll 85. **d** 87 **p** 88. C Sutton in Ashfield St Mary *S'well* 87-95; C Sutton in Ashfield St Mich 89-95; P-in-c 95-98; TV Hucknall Torkard 98-03; R S

DUDDING, Edward Leslie (Father Gregory). b 30. Auckland Univ MSc52. St Jo Coll Auckland. **d** 57 **p** 57. C Takapuna New Zealand 57-58; Asst Missr Dio Auckland 58-60; Lic to Offic *Chich* from 62; CSWG from 62; Father Superior from 73. *Monastery of The Holy Trinity, Crawley Down, Crawley RH10 4LH* Tel (01342) 712074

DUDLEY, Mrs Janet Carr. b 36. EMMTC 86. **d** 89 **p** 94. NSM Countesthorpe w Foston *Leic* 89-94; NSM Arnesby w Shearsby and Bruntingthorpe 94-01; rtd 01; Perm to Offic *Leic* 01-02; NSM Market Harborough and The Transfiguration etc from 02. *13 The Broadway, Market Harborough LE16 7LZ* Tel (01858) 467619

DUDLEY, John Donald Swanborough. b 34. Ox Univ BTh95. SAOMC 96. **d** 97 **p** 98. NSM Emmer Green *Ox* 97-02; Perm to Offic from 02. *26 Russet Glade, Emmer Green, Reading RG4 8UJ* Tel and fax 0118-954 6664

DUDLEY, Ms Josephine. b 52. ACertCM89. ERMC 04. **d** 06 **p** 07. NSM Tolleshunt Knights w Tiptree and Gt Braxted *Chelmsf* from 06. *112 London Road, Copford, Colchester CO6 1BJ* Tel (01206) 210209 Mobile 07778-735410
E-mail jo@jdudley.plus.com

DUDLEY, Martin Raymond. b 53. K Coll Lon BD77 AKC77 MTh78 PhD94 City Univ MSc07 FRHistS95 FSA97 FRSA06. St Mich Coll Llan 78. **d** 79 **p** 80. C Whitchurch *Llan* 79-83; V Weston *St Alb* 83-88; P-in-c Ardeley 87-88; V Owlsmoor *Ox* 88-95; Lect Simon of Cyrene Th Inst 92-95; R Smithfield St Bart Gt *Lon* from 95. *The Parish Office, 6 Kinghorn Street, London EC1A 7HW* Tel (020) 7606 5171 *or* 7628 3644 Fax 7600 6909
E-mail rector@greatstbarts.com

DUDLEY, Miss Wendy Elizabeth. b 46. City of Sheff Coll CertEd68. Cranmer Hall Dur 79. **dss** 81 **d** 87 **p** 94. Cumnor *Ox* 81-89; Par Dn 87-89; Par Dn Hodge Hill *Birm* 89-94; C 94-95; TV 95-98; TV Bucknall *Lich* 98-06; rtd 06; Perm to Offic *Lich* from 08. *26 Swallow Croft, Lichfield WS13 7HF* Tel (01543) 306509 E-mail wed.btm@tinyworld.co.uk

DUDLEY-SMITH, James. b 66. Fitzw Coll Cam BA89 MA92. Wycliffe Hall Ox BTh94. **d** 97 **p** 98. C New Borough and Leigh *Sarum* 97-01; C Hove Bp Hannington Memorial Ch *Chich* 01-06; R Yeovil w Kingston Pitney *B & W* from 06. *The Rectory, 41 The Park, Yeovil BA20 1DG* Tel (01935) 475352

✠**DUDLEY-SMITH, The Rt Revd Timothy.** b 26. OBE03. Pemb Coll Cam BA47 MA51 Lambeth MLitt91 Dur Univ Hon DD09. Ridley Hall Cam 48. **d** 50 **p** 51 **c** 81. C Erith St Paul *Roch* 50-53; Lic to Offic *S'wark* 53-62; Hd of Cam Univ Miss Bermondsey 55-55; Chapl 55-60; Ed Sec Evang Alliance and Ed *Crusade* 55-59; Asst Sec CPAS 59-65; Gen Sec 65-73; Adn Nor 73-81; Suff Bp Thetford 81-91; rtd 92. *9 Ashlands, Ford, Salisbury SP4 6DY* Tel (01722) 326417

DUDLEY, Archdeacon of. *See* TRETHEWEY, The Ven Frederick Martyn

DUDLEY, Suffragan Bishop of. *See* WALKER, The Rt Revd David Stuart

DUERDEN, Martin James. b 55. Liv Poly BA77. Oak Hill Th Coll 86. **d** 88 **p** 89. C Tunbridge Wells St Jas *Roch* 88-92; V Southport SS Simon and Jude *Liv* 92-98; P-in-c Maghull 98-02; TR 02-07; P-in-c Marsh Green w Newtown 07; V from 08. *65 Planc Avenue, Wigan WN5 9PT* Tel (01942) 211545
E-mail martinmduerden@hotmail.com

DUERR, Robert Kenneth. b 54. Univ of S California BMus77 MMus80. Ridley Hall Cam 99. **d** 04 **p** 06. NSM Cambridge Gt St Mary w St Mich *Ely* 04-05; C Marton-in-Cleveland *York* 06-07; C Scarborough St Martin from 07; C Scarborough St Sav w All SS from 07. *136 Filey Road, Scarborough YO11 3AA* Tel (01723) 378105 E-mail robert@robertduerr.com

DUFF, Alison. *See* FINCH, Mrs Alison

DUFF, Andrew John. b 57. Open Univ BSc07. Sarum & Wells Th Coll 92. **d** 92 **p** 93. C Banbury *Ox* 92-95; C Bracknell 95-96; TV 96-98; CF 98-04; Chapl RN from 04. *Royal Naval Chaplaincy Service, Mail Point 1-2, Leach Building, Whale Island, Portsmouth PO2 8BY* Tel (023) 9262 5055 Fax 9262 5134

DUFF, Garden Ian. b 34. Imp Coll Lon BScEng56. Sarum & Wells Th Coll 92. **d** 93 **p** 94. NSM Ashton Gifford *Sarum* 93-97; TV Upper Wylye Valley 97-03; rtd 03. *Trinity Trees Cottage, 58 Upton Lovell, Warminster BA12 0JP* Tel and fax (01985) 850291

DUFF, Canon Jeremy. b 71. MA DPhil. **d** 97 **p** 97. NSM Toxteth St Philemon w St Gabr and St Cleopas *Liv* from 06; Dir Lifelong Learning and Can Liv Cathl from 04. *20 Lady Chapel Close, Liverpool L1 7BZ* Tel 0151-702 7243
E-mail jeremy.duff@liverpool.anglican.org

DUFF, Jillian Louise Calland. b 72. Ch Coll Cam BA93 MA97 Worc Coll Ox DPhil96. Wycliffe Hall Ox BA04. **d** 03. C Litherland St Phil *Liv* 03-05; Lic to Adn Liv from 05. *20 Lady Chapel Close, Liverpool L1 7BZ* Tel 0151-709 4454

DUFF, John Alexander. b 57. York Univ BA78. EMMTC 91. **d** 94 **p** 95. NSM Linc St Geo Swallowbeck 94-00; Perm to Offic *Ripon*

from 02. *37 Mornington Crescent, Harrogate HG1 5DL* Tel (01423) 549987 Mobile 07788-432009 E-mail ffudnhoj@hotmail.com

DUFF, Michael Ian. b 63. Ox Univ BA85. Trin Coll Bris BA98 MA99. **d** 99 **p** 00. C Southsea St Jude *Portsm* 99-03; CMS Bandung Indonesia 03-07; V Southsea St Jude *Portsm* from 07. *St Jude's Vicarage, 7 Hereford Road, Southsea PO5 2DH* Tel (023) 9234 9622 E-mail all@theduffs.me.uk

DUFF, Timothy Cameron. b 40. G&C Coll Cam BA62 LLM63 MA66 Solicitor 65. NEOC 90. **d** 93 **p** 94. NSM Tynemouth Priory *Newc* 93-96; NSM N Shields 96-00; Hon TV 00-05; rtd 05; Perm to Offic *Newc* from 05. *24A Percy Gardens, Tynemouth, North Shields NE30 4HQ* Tel 0191-257 1463 E-mail timothy@timothyduff.co.uk

DUFFETT, Canon Paul Stanton. b 33. Keble Coll Ox BA55 MA59. Ripon Hall Ox. **d** 59 **p** 60. C Portsea St Cuth *Portsm* 59-63; S Africa 63-80; Hon Can Zululand from 87; Accredited Rep Zululand and Swaziland Assn from 89; P-in-c Greatham w Empshott *Portsm* 80-85; R 85-88; R Papworth Everard *Ely* 88-98; Chapl Papworth Hosps 88-98; rtd 98; Hon Chapl MU from 97; Perm to Offic *Ely* from 99. *11 Roman Hill, Barton, Cambridge CB23 7AX* Tel (01223) 262831

DUFFETT-SMITH (née RUSHTON), Ms Patricia Mary. b 54. Lon Univ BPharm76 Anglia Poly Univ MA99 MRPharmS77. EAMTC 94. **d** 97 **p** 98. NSM Haddenham and Wilburton *Ely* 97-00; Asst Chapl Hinchingbrooke Health Care NHS Trust from 99. *41 Denmark Road, Cottenham, Cambridge CB24 8QS* Tel 07788-668900 (mobile) E-mail trishads@hotmail.com

DUFFIELD, Ian Keith. b 47. K Coll Lon BD71 AKC71 MTh73. NY Th Sem DMin84. **d** 73 **p** 74. C Broxbourne *St Alb* 73-77; C Harpenden St Nic 77-81; TV Sheff Manor 81-87; V Walkley 87-02; V Sheff St Leon Norwood from 02. *St Leonard's Vicarage, 93 Everingham Road, Sheffield S5 7LE* Tel 0114-243 6689

DUFFIELD, John Ernest. b 55. BA86. Oak Hill Th Coll 83. **d** 86 **p** 87. C Walton Breck Ch Ch *Liv* 86-89; TV Fazakerley Em 89-00; Chapl N Cheshire Hosps NHS Trust from 00. *Warrington Hospital, Lovely Lane, Warrington WA5 1QG* Tel (01925) 662146 Fax 662048 E-mail john.duffield@nch.nhs.uk

DUFFIELD, Ronald Bertram Charles. b 26. Hull Univ Coll BA49 TCert50. Sarum & Wells Th Coll 91. **d** 92 **p** 93. NSM E Knoyle, Semley and Sedgehill *Sarum* 92-94; P-in-c 94-95; rtd 95; Perm to Offic *York* 95-99 and from 01; P-in-c Isfield *Chich* 99-01. *16 Wylies Road, Beverley HU17 7AP* Tel (01482) 880983

DUFFUS, Barbara Rose. *See* HOBBS, Mrs Barbara Rose

DUGDALE, Angela Marion. b 33. MBE06 DL92. ARCM52 GRSM54 UEA Hon MA89. **d** 97 **p** 98. OLM Weybourne Gp *Nor* 97-03; rtd 03; Perm to Offic *Nor* from 03. *The Old Carpenter's Shop, Kelling, Holt NR25 7EL* Tel (01263) 588389 Fax 588594 E-mail dugdale@freeuk.com

DUGMORE, Barry John. b 61. STETS. **d** 01 **p** 02. C Cowplain *Portsm* 01-04; C-in-c Whiteley CD and Dioc Ecum Officer 04-07; P-in-c Tiverton St Geo and St Paul *Ex* from 07. *St Paul's Vicarage, Bakers Hill, Tiverton EX16 5NE* Tel (01884) 255705 E-mail b.dugmore@ukgateway.net

DUGUID, Alison Audrey. b 52. STETS 99. **d** 02 **p** 03. C Appledore w Brookland, Fairfield, Brenzett etc *Cant* 02-06; P-in-c The Brents and Davington w Oare and Luddenham from 06; P-in-c Ospringe from 06; Dir Dioc Poverty and Hope Appeal from 07. *The Vicarage, Brent Hill, Faversham ME13 7EF* Tel (01795) 533272 Mobile 07880-711202 E-mail ali@dogooders.co.uk

DUGUID, Reginald Erskine. b 29. S'wark Ord Course. **d** 88 **p** 89. NSM Notting Hill All SS w St Columb *Lon* 88-99; Perm to Offic from 99. *53 Sandbourne, Dartmouth Close, London W11 1DS* Tel (020) 7221 4436

DUKE, Canon Alan Arthur. b 38. Tyndale Hall Bris 59. **d** 64 **p** 65. C Whalley Range St Marg *Man* 64-67; C Folkestone H Trin w Ch Ch *Cant* 67-71; V Queenborough 71-76; V Bearsted w Thurnham 76-86; P-in-c Torquay St Luke *Ex* 86-91; R Barham w Bishopsbourne and Kingston *Cant* 91-00; Dioc Communications Officer 91-95; Hon Can Cant Cathl 99-03; Chapl to Bp Dover 00-03; Bp's Media Link Officer 00-03; rtd 03; Perm to Offic *Cant* from 03. *Roundways, Derringstone Hill, Barham, Canterbury CT4 6QD* Tel (01227) 831817 Fax 784985 Mobile 07751-833670

DUKE, David Malcolm. b 40. Ch Ch Ox BA61 MA65 Newc Poly MPhil80 CQSW81. Cuddesdon Coll 63. **d** 65 **p** 66. C Sunderland Pennywell St Thos *Dur* 65-68; C Dur St Oswald 68-70; C Harton 70-74; Perm to Offic 85-96; Hon C Hedworth from 96. *43 Coquet Street, Jarrow NE32 5SW* Tel 0191-430 1200 Fax 537 4409 Mobile 07979-036977

DUKE, Mrs Judith Mary. b 47. Leeds Univ LLB68. Cranmer Hall Dur 03. **d** 04 **p** 05. NSM Buckrose Carrs *York* 04-07; R from 07. *2 High Street, Rillington, Malton YO17 8LA* Tel (01944) 758305

DULFER, John Guidi. b 37. Lich Th Coll 62. **d** 64 **p** 65. C Fenny Stratford and Water Eaton *Ox* 64-67; C Cheshunt *St Alb* 67-68; C Kennington Cross St Anselm *S'wark* 68-74; C N Lambeth 74-76; P-in-c Kensington St Phil Earl's Court *Lon* 76-79; V

79-84; V Jersey City St Jo and Jersey City St Matt USA 84-85; R New York Resurr 00-01; P-in-c Castleton 02-06. *110 West 15 Street, Apartment 1, New York NY 10011-6724, USA* E-mail johndulfer@hotmail.com

DULLEY, Arthur John Franklyn. b 32. Mert Coll Ox BA54 MA57. St Jo Coll Nottm 69. **d** 71 **p** 72. Lect St Jo Coll Nottm 71-96; Hon C Attenborough w Chilwell *S'well* 71-73; C Penn Fields *Lich* 73-74; Chapl Aldenham Sch Herts 74-79; Chapl HM Pris Ashwell 79-87; V Langham *Pet* 79-96; rtd 96; Perm to Offic *Ely* 96-98. *2 St Augustines Close, Bexhill-on-Sea TN39 3AZ* Tel (01424) 733020

DUMAT, Mrs Jennifer. b 42. ARCM62. Qu Coll Birm 80 EMMTC 82. **dss** 83 **d** 87 **p** 94. Chapl Asst Pilgrim Hosp Boston 83-94; P-in-c Friskney *Linc* 94-04; rtd 04. *11 Sea Lane, Butterwick, Boston PE22 0EY* Tel (01205) 760883

✠**DUMPER, The Rt Revd Anthony Charles.** b 23. Ch Coll Cam BA45 MA48. Westcott Ho Cam. **d** 47 **p** 48 **c** 77. C E Greenwich Ch Ch w St Andr and St Mich *S'wark* 47-49; Malaya 49-63; Malaysia 63-64; Dean Singapore 64-70; V Stockton St Pet *Dur* 70-77; P-in-c Stockton H Trin 76-77; RD Stockton 70-77; Suff Bp Dudley *Worc* 77-93; rtd 93; Hon Asst Bp Birm from 93. *117 Berberry Close, Birmingham B30 1TB* Tel 0121-458 3011

DUNBAR, Peter Lamb. b 46. Bede Coll Dur DipEd68. Lambeth STh77 NOC 78. **d** 81 **p** 82. NSM Knaresborough *Ripon* 81-82; C Knaresborough 82-84; R Farnham w Scotton, Staveley, Copgrove etc 84-92; V Upper Nidderdale from 92; Chapl St Aid Sch Harrogate 86-94. *The Vicarage, Church Street, Pateley Bridge, Harrogate HG3 5LQ* Tel (01423) 711414 E-mail lion.lamb@virgin.net

DUNCAN, Canon Bruce. b 38. MBE93. Leeds Univ BA60 FRSA. Cuddesdon Coll 65. **d** 67 **p** 68. C Armley St Bart *Ripon* 67-69; Dir Children's Relief Internat 69-71; Hon C Cambridge St Mary Less *Ely* 69-70; Chapl OHP and St Hilda's Sch Whitby 70-71; Chapl Vienna w Budapest and Prague *Eur* 71-75; V Crediton *Ex* 75-82; R Crediton and Shobrooke 82-86; RD Cadbury 76-81 and 84-86; Can Res Man Cathl 86-95; Prin Sarum Coll 95-02; Can and Preb Sarum Cathl 95-02; rtd 02; Perm to Offic *Ex* 02-08 and *Sarum* from 08; Chapl Ex Univ 03-04. *92 Harnham Road, Salisbury SP2 8JW* Tel (01722) 502227 Mobile 07851-737230 E-mail churchpath1@ntlworld.com

DUNCAN, Christopher Robin. b 41. AKC71. **d** 72 **p** 73. C Allington *Cant* 72-77; P-in-c Wittersham 77-82; R Wittersham w Stone-in-Oxney and Ebony 82-85; V Chilham 85-92; P-in-c Challock w Molash 87-92; RD W Bridge 92-95 and 02-03; V Chilham w Challock and Molash from 92. *The Vicarage, 3 Hambrook Close, Chilham, Canterbury CT4 8EJ* Tel (01227) 730235 E-mail chris.duncan@chil-vic.co.uk

DUNCAN, Colin Richard. b 34. SS Coll Cam BA58 MA60. Ripon Coll Cuddesdon 83. **d** 85 **p** 86. C Stafford *Lich* 85-89; C Wednesfield 89-90; TV 90-99; rtd 99; Perm to Offic *Glouc* from 99. *Fir Tree Cottage, Union Road, Bakers Hill, Coleford GL16 7QB*

DUNCAN, Graham Charles Dewar. b 65. Sheff Univ BSc87. NTMTC 95. **d** 98 **p** 99. NSM Dawley St Jerome *Lon* 98-00; NSM Sheff St Mary Bramall Lane from 00; Manager St Mary's Ch Community Cen from 00. *11 Coverdale Road, Sheffield S7 2DD* Tel 0114-258 7275 *or* 272 5596 Fax 275 3892

DUNCAN, The Very Revd Gregor Duthie. b 50. Glas Univ MA72 Clare Coll Cam PhD77 Oriel Coll Ox BA83. Ripon Coll Cuddesdon 81. **d** 83 **p** 84. C Oakham, Hambleton, Egleton, Braunston and Brooke *Pet* 83-86; Edin Th Coll 87-89; R Largs *Glas* 89-99; Dean Glas from 96; R Glas St Ninian from 99. *St Ninian's Rectory, 32 Glencairn Drive, Glasgow G41 4PW* Tel 0141-423 1247 Fax 424 3332 E-mail dean@glasgow.anglican.org

DUNCAN, James Montgomerie. b 29. Edin Th Coll 53. **d** 56 **p** 57. C Edin St Pet 56-59; C Edin Old St Paul 59-60; S Africa 60-65; Prov Youth Org Scotland 65-69; R Edin St Salvador 69-86; Chapl HM Pris Saughton 69-86; R Aberlour *Mor* 86-98; R Fochabers 86-98; rtd 98. *Address temp unknown* E-mail heduncan@onetel.net.uk

DUNCAN, John. b 22. Open Univ BA. Roch Th Coll 64. **d** 66 **p** 67. C Gainsborough All SS *Linc* 66-68; C Boultham 68-71; V W Pinchbeck 72-76; Canada 76-81; R Ridgewell w Ashen, Birdbrook and Sturmer *Chelmsf* 81-88; rtd 88; Perm to Offic *Pet* from 91. *20 Westcott Way, Northampton NN3 3BE* Tel (01604) 630797

DUNCAN, The Ven John Finch. b 33. Univ Coll Ox BA57 MA63. Cuddesdon Coll 58. **d** 59 **p** 60. C S Bank *York* 59-61; SSF 61-62; C Birm St Pet 62-65; Chapl Birm Univ 65-76; V Kings Heath 76-85; Hon Can Birm Cathl 83-85; Adn Birm 85-01; rtd 01; Perm to Offic *Birm* and *Pet* from 01. *66 Glebe Rise, King's Sutton, Banbury OX17 3PH* Tel (01295) 812641 E-mail stevekingssutton@aol.com

DUNCAN, Peter Harold Furlong. b 25. AKC52 Lon Univ BA54 Goldsmiths' Coll Lon BA71 MPhil79. **d** 53 **p** 54. C Sheff St Geo and St Steph 53-56; C Wealdstone H Trin *Lon* 56-57; V Battersea St Pet *S'wark* 57-64; Nigeria 64-66; Hon C All Hallows by the Tower etc *Lon* 67-73; Ind Chapl Lon Docks 67-73; Sen Lect in

Sociology City of Lon Poly 73-87; Hon C Gt Ilford St Andr *Chelmsf* 73-80; P-in-c Gt Canfield 80-87; P-in-c N Woolwich w Silverdown 87-93; rtd 93; Perm to Offic *York* from 93. *179 Windsor Drive, Haxby, York YO32 2YD* Tel and fax (01904) 769888 E-mail duncanpeteing@aol.com

DUNCAN, Thomas James. b 37. **d** 97 **p** 98. NSM Poplar *Lon* from 97. *1 Chardwell Close, London E6 5RR* Tel (020) 7474 9965 *or* 7538 9198 Mobile 07732-666434

DUNCAN, The Ven William Albert. b 30. TCD BA53 MA61 BD66. CITC 54. **d** 54 **p** 55. C Bangor Abbey *D & D* 54-57; C Larne and Inver *Conn* 57-61; Hd of Trin Coll Miss Belf 61-66; I Rasharkin w Finvoy 66-78; I Ramoan w Ballycastle and Culfeightrin 78-96; Adn Dalriada 93-96; rtd 96. *8 Beech Hill, Ballymoney BT53 6DB* Tel (028) 7066 4285

DUNCANSON, Derek James. b 47. TD93. AKC69 Open Univ BA80 Lon Univ MA(Ed)93 FCollP94. St Aug Coll Cant 69. **d** 70 **p** 71. C Norbury St Oswald *Cant* 70-72; CF (TAVR) 71-76 and 79-95; C Woodham *Guildf* 72-76; CF 76-79; V Burneside *Carl* 79-84; R Coppull St Jo *Blackb* 84-86; Chapl Bloxham Sch 86-99; V Pet St Mary Boongate 99-04; RD Pet 01-04; Chapl Pet Regional Coll 00-04; Chapl Heathfield St Mary's Sch Ascot 04-08; rtd 08; Perm to Offic *Cant* from 08; rtd 08. *Old Forge Cottage, 235 Canterbury Road, Birchington CT7 9TB* Tel (01843) 843289 E-mail dmduncanson@btinternet.com

DUNCOMBE, Maureen Barbara. *See* WHITE, Mrs Maureen Barbara

DUNDAS, Edward Paul. b 67. NUU BSc88. TCD Div Sch BTh91. **d** 91 **p** 92. C Portadown St Mark *Arm* 91-95; I Ardtrea w Desertcreat 95-00; Dioc Youth Adv to Abp Armagh 99-00; I Belfast St Aid *Conn* 00-05; I Lisburn Ch Ch from 05. *Christ Church Rectory, 27 Hillsborough Road, Lisburn BT28 1JL* Tel (028) 9266 2163 *or* 9267 3271 Mobile 07740-589465 E-mail paul_dundas@yahoo.com

DUNDAS, Edward Thompson. b 36. TCD BA63. **d** 64 **p** 65. C Conwall *D & R* 64-67; I Kilbarron 67-78; I Donagheady 78-84; I Kilmore St Aid w St Sav *Arm* 84-04; rtd 04. *114 Brownstown Road, Portadown, Craigavon BT62 3PZ* Tel (028) 3833 4474 Mobile 07989-842709

DUNDAS, Gary Walter. b 56. EMMTC 04. **d** 07 **p** 08. NSM Stanton-by-Dale w Dale Abbey and Risley *Derby* from 07. *17-19 Victoria Road, Draycott, Derby DE72 3PS* Tel (01332) 872893 Fax 875371 Mobile 07971-783083 E-mail gwdundas@aol.com

DUNDEE, Provost of. *Vacant*

DUNFORD, Malcolm. b 34. FCA74. EMMTC 73. **d** 76 **p** 77. NSM Frodingham *Linc* from 76. *57 Rowland Road, Scunthorpe DN16 1SP* Tel (01724) 840879

DUNGAN, Hilary Anne. b 46. TCD BA98 ARCM68. CITC 98. **d** 00 **p** 01. C Arm St Mark 00-03; I Maryborough w Dysart Enos and Ballyfin *C & O* from 03; Chapl Midlands Portlaoise Pris from 03. *The Rectory, Coote Street, Portlaoise, Co Laois, Republic of Ireland* Tel (00353) (57) 862 1154 E-mail portlaoise@leighlin.anglican.org

DUNGAN, Ivan. CITC. **d** 09. NSM Bunclody w Kildavin, Clonegal and Kilrush *C & O* from 09. *Address temp unknown*

DUNHAM, Angela Mary. *See* CHEESEMAN, Mrs Angela Mary

DUNK, Carolyn Margaret. b 55. Wycliffe Hall Ox 04. **d** 06 **p** 07. C Uxbridge *Lon* 06-09; C W Ealing St Jo w St Jas from 09. *23A Culmington Road, London W13 9NJ* Tel (020) 8566 3459 E-mail cazdunk@yahoo.co.uk *or* caz.dunk@stjamesealing.org.uk

DUNK, Michael Robin. b 43. Oak Hill Th Coll BA82. **d** 82 **p** 83. C Northampton All SS *Pet* 82-86; Ind Chapl *Birm* 86-96; P-in-c Warley Woods 96; V 96-08; AD Warley 01-06; rtd 08; Hon C Shepshed and Oaks in Charnwood *Leic* from 08. *4 Wortley Close, Shepshed, Loughborough LE12 9QU* Tel (01509) 501939 E-mail michael.dunk@talk21.com

DUNK, Peter Norman. b 43. Sarum Th Coll 67. **d** 69 **p** 70. C Sheff St Mary w St Simon w St Matthias 69-71; C Margate St Jo *Cant* 71-74; Dioc Youth Officer *Birm* 74-78; R Hulme Ascension *Man* 78-83; V E Farleigh and Coxheath *Roch* 83; P-in-c Linton w Hunton 83; R Coxheath w E Farleigh, Hunton and Linton 83-88; R Swanbourne Australia 88-99; rtd 00. *7 Raffan View, Gwelup WA 6018, Australia* Tel and fax (0061) (8) 9447 8877

DUNKERLEY, James Hobson. b 39. Seabury-Western Th Sem BD69 STh70. **d** 64 **p** 65. C Stirchley *Birm* 64-66; C Perry Barr 66-70; R Chicago St Pet USA from 70. *6033 N Sheridan Road, Unit 44B, Chicago IL 60660-3059, USA* Tel (001) (772) 275 2773

DUNKLEY, Canon Christopher. b 52. Edin Univ MA74 Ox Univ BA77 MA81. St Steph Ho Ox 75. **d** 78 **p** 79. C Newbold w Dunston *Derby* 78-82; C Chesterfield St Mary and All SS 82; Chapl Leic Univ 82-85; TV Leic Ascension 85-92; Chapl Leics Hospice 85-87; V Leic St Aid 92-97; V Holbrooks *Cov* from 97; Hon Can Cov Cathl from 07. *St Luke's Vicarage, Rotherham Road, Coventry CV6 4FE* Tel (024) 7668 8604 E-mail kitdunkley@tiscali.co.uk

DUNKLING, Miss Judith Mary. b 77. Westcott Ho Cam 01 Bossey Ecum Inst Geneva 03. **d** 04 **p** 05. C Holbeach *Linc* 04-07; TV Maryport, Netherton and Flimby *Carl* 07-08; TV Tenbury

Heref from 08. *The Rectory, Burford, Tenbury Wells WR15 8HG* Tel (01584) 819119 E-mail j.dunkling@btinternet.com

DUNLOP, Andrew James. b 76. Collingwood Coll Dur BSc97 PGCE98. Wycliffe Hall Ox BTh07. **d** 07. C Plymouth St Andr and Stonehouse *Ex* from 07. *117 Lipson Road, Plymouth PL4 7NQ* Tel (01752) 221913 E-mail ajdunlop@tiscali.co.uk

DUNLOP, Mrs Frances Jane. b 57. New Hall Cam MA82 ACA84. STETS 06. **d** 09. *Little Paddock, Romsey Road, Whiteparish, Salisbury SP5 2SD* Tel (01794) 884793 Mobile 07795-836653 E-mail fjdunlop@hotmail.com

DUNLOP, Canon Ian Geoffrey David. b 25. New Coll Ox BA48 MA56 FSA65. Linc Th Coll 54. **d** 56 **p** 57. C Bp's Hatfield *St Alb* 56-60; Chapl Westmr Sch 60-62; C Bures *St E* 62-72; Can Res and Chan Sarum Cathl 72-92; Dir Post-Ord Tr 72-92; Dir of Ords 73-92; Lect Sarum & Wells Th Coll 76-92; rtd 92; Hon C Selkirk *Edin* 99-04; Lic to Offic from 04. *Gowanbrae, The Glebe, Selkirk TD7 5AB* Tel (01750) 20706

DUNLOP, Peter John. b 44. TCD BA68 MA72 Dur Univ CertEd71. Cranmer Hall Dur. **d** 71 **p** 72. C Barking St Marg w St Patr *Chelmsf* 71-75; C Gt Malvern Ch Ch *Worc* 75-78; Chapl K Sch Tynemouth 78-89; V Monkseaton St Pet *Newc* 90-96; rtd 96; Perm to Offic *Newc* from 96. *19 Cliftonville Gardens, Whitley Bay NE26 1QJ* Tel 0191-251 0983

DUNN, Canon Alastair Matthew Crusoe. b 40. Lon Univ LLB64 AKC64. Wycliffe Hall Ox 78. **d** 80 **p** 81. C Yardley St Edburgha *Birm* 80-83; R Bishop's Sutton and Ropley and W Tisted *Win* 83-90; V Milford 90-04; Hon Can Win Cathl 03-04; C Harrogate St Mark *Ripon* 04-05; Hon C 05-07; rtd 05. *13 Littlefield Close, Nether Poppleton, York YO26 6HX* Tel (01904) 798487 E-mail asdunn@talk21.com

DUNN, Mrs Anne. b 36. **d** 03 **p** 04. OLM Weymouth H Trin *Sarum* from 03. *6 Ilchester Road, Weymouth DT4 0AW* Tel (01305) 770066 E-mail annedunn@uk2.net

DUNN, Mrs Barbara Anne. b 42. Man Univ BA72 Sheff Univ CQSW76. NOC 92. **d** 95 **p** 96. NSM Stretford St Matt *Man* 95-02; Perm to Offic from 02. *36 Alcester Road, Sale M33 3QP* E-mail bnsdunn@btinternet.com

DUNN, Brian. b 40. St Aid Birkenhead 66. **d** 69 **p** 70. C Over Darwen H Trin *Blackb* 69-71; C Burnley St Pet 71-74; V Darwen St Barn 74-84; V S Shore H Trin 84-02; Chapl Arnold Sch Blackpool 84-02; rtd 02; Perm to Offic *Blackb* from 02. *11 Kingsway, Blackpool FY4 2DF*

DUNN, Christopher George Hunter. b 28. Pemb Coll Cam BA49 MA53. Oak Hill Th Coll 51. **d** 53 **p** 54. C Tunbridge Wells H Trin *Roch* 53-54; C Broadwater St Mary *Chich* 54-58; R Garsdon w Lea and Cleverton *Bris* 59-74; Chapl Marie Curie Foundn (Tidcombe Hall) 74-95; V Tiverton St Geo *Ex* 74-01; RD Tiverton 84-91; rtd 01; Perm to Offic *Sarum* from 02. *8 Counter Close, Blandford Forum DT11 7XJ* Tel (01258) 456843

DUNN, David James. b 47. Leeds Univ CertEd79 BA82. Trin Coll Bris 88. **d** 90 **p** 91. C Magor w Redwick and Undy *Mon* 90-92; Chapl Toc H from 90; C St Mellons and Michaelston-y-Fedw *Mon* 92-93; V Pontnewydd from 93. *The Vicarage, 44 Church Road, Pontnewydd, Cwmbran NP44 1AT* Tel (01633) 482300

DUNN, David Michael. b 47. AKC70. St Aug Coll Cant 70. **d** 71 **p** 72. C Padgate *Liv* 71-74; C Halliwell St Marg *Man* 74-76; V Lever Bridge 76-84; V Bradshaw 84-01; TR Turton Moorland Min from 01. *St Maxentius Rectory, Bolton Road, Bolton BL2 3EU* Tel and fax (01204) 304240

DUNN, Derek William Robert. b 48. Open Univ BA81 MA01 Stranmillis Coll CertEd70 AMusTCL74 LTCL75. **d** 85 **p** 87. Aux Min Carnalea *D & D* 85-97; Aux Min Bangor Abbey 97-05; C Ballymena w Ballyclug *Conn* from 05. *38 Ballee Road East, Ballymena BT42 3DH* Tel (028) 2564 7049 E-mail derek@mambolo.freeserve.co.uk

DUNN, Florence Patricia. b 37. Ches Coll of HE BTh02. NOC 99. **d** 02 **p** 03. NSM Basford *Lich* from 02. *213 Newcastle Road, Trent Vale, Stoke-on-Trent ST4 6PU* Tel (01782) 846417 E-mail rev.patdunn@tesco.net

DUNN, John Frederick. b 44. Trin Coll Bris 71. **d** 74 **p** 75. C Carl St Jo 74-77; C Tooting Graveney St Nic *S'wark* 77-82; V Attleborough *Cov* 85; Perm to Offic *Cant* 86-02; V Tipton St Martin and St Paul *Lich* from 02. *St Martin's Vicarage, 1 Dudley Port, Tipton DY4 7PR* Tel 0121-557 1902

DUNN, Julian. b 46. Open Univ BA84. K Coll Lon 67 St Aug Coll Cant 70. **d** 71 **p** 72. C Hanworth All SS *Lon* 71-74; C Kidlington Ox 74-76; C-in-c Cleethorpes St Fran CD *Linc* 76-77; TV Cleethorpes 77-85; Chapl Friarage and Distr Hosp Northallerton 85-88; Chapl Broadmoor Hosp Crowthorne 88; Ind Chapl *York* 88-99; P-in-c Micklefield 88-89; Perm to Offic Ox from 99. *timbles brewery* (sic*), 1 Lewington Close, Great Haseley, Oxford OX44 7LS* Tel (01844) 279687 E-mail eisendora@aol.com

DUNN, Kevin Lancelot. b 62. Newc Univ BSc83. St Steph Ho Ox 89. **d** 92 **p** 93. C Tynemouth Cullercoats St Paul *Newc* 92-95; C Newc St Matt w St Mary 95-97; P-in-c Kirkholt *Man* 97-00; Chapl Rochdale Healthcare NHS Trust 00-02; Chapl Pennine Acute Hosps NHS Trust 02-07; Chapl Christie Hosp NHS Trust

Man from 07. *Christie Hospital, Wilmslow Road, Manchester M20 4BX* Tel 0161-446 3000

DUNN (*née* **LEE**), **Mrs Mary Elizabeth.** b 49. Open Univ BA81 Bp Grosseteste Coll CertEd78. St Mich Coll Llan 08. **d** 09. NSM Malpas *Mon* from 09. *The Vicarage, 44 Church Road, Pontnewydd, Cwmbran NP44 1AT* Tel (01633) 482300 E-mail ourmarylou@googlemail.com

DUNN, Michael Henry James. b 34. Em Coll Cam BA56 MA62. Cuddesdon Coll 57 and 62. **d** 62 **p** 63. C Chatham St Steph *Roch* 62-66; C Bromley SS Pet and Paul 66-70; V Roch St Justus 70-83; P-in-c Malvern Wells and Wyche *Worc* 83-85; P-in-c Lt Malvern, Malvern Wells and Wyche 85-97; rtd 97; Perm to Offic *Worc* from 97. *253 Oldbury Road, Worcester WR2 6JT* Tel (01905) 429938

DUNN, Pat. *See* DUNN, Florence Patricia

DUNN, Paul James Hugh. b 55. Dur Univ PhD93. Ripon Coll Cuddesdon. **d** 83 **p** 84. C Wandsworth St Paul *S'wark* 83-87; C Richmond St Mary w St Matthias and St Jo 88-92; TV Wimbledon 92-98; V Ham St Rich from 98. *The Vicarage, Ashburnham Road, Ham, Richmond TW10 7NL* Tel (020) 8948 3758 E-mail revpdunn@aol.com

DUNN, Reginald Hallan. b 31. Oak Hill NSM Course 79. **d** 82 **p** 83. NSM Enfield St Andr *Lon* 82-88; NSM Forty Hill Jes Ch 88-92; NSM Enfield Chase St Mary 92-97; rtd 97; Perm to Offic *Lon* from 97. *3 Conway Gardens, Enfield EN2 9AD* Tel (020) 8366 3982

DUNN, Sharon Louise. *See* GOBLE, Mrs Sharon Louise

DUNN, Simon David. b 69. Trin Coll Bris BA08. **d** 08 **p** 09. C Stoke Gifford *Bris* from 08. *18 Marjoram Place, Bradley Stoke, Bristol BS32 0DQ* Tel (01454) 616864 Mobile 07904-733141 E-mail dunnsimonann@aol.com

DUNN, Canon Struan Huthwaite. b 43. Ch Coll Hobart 66 Moore Th Coll Sydney 67 Clifton Th Coll 68. **d** 70 **p** 71. C Orpington Ch Ch *Roch* 70-74; C Cheltenham St Mary *Glouc* 74-76; C Welling *Roch* 76-79; Chapl Barcelona w Casteldefels *Eur* 79-83; R Addington w Trottiscliffe *Roch* 83-89; P-in-c Ryarsh w Birling 83-89; P-in-c S Gillingham 89-90; TR 90-96; RD Gillingham 91-96; R Meopham w Nurstead 96-08; Hon Can Roch Cathl 97-08; rtd 08; Perm to Offic *Cant* and *Roch* from 08. *18 Blenheim Avenue, Faversham ME13 8NR* Tel (01795) 531700

DUNNAN, Donald Stuart. b 59. Harvard Univ AB80 AM81 Ch Ch Ox BA85 MA90 DPhil91. Gen Th Sem (NY) 86. **d** 86 **p** 87. USA 86-87; Lib Pusey Ho 87-89; Lic to Offic *Ox* 87-92; Perm to Offic *Cant* 87-92; Chapl Linc Coll Ox 90-92; USA from 92. *St James School, 17641 College Road, St James MD 21781-9900, USA* E-mail dsdunnan@stjames.edu

DUNNE, The Very Revd Dermot Patrick Martin. b 59. Dub City Univ BA04. St Patr Coll Maynooth 78 CITC 98. **d** 83 **p** 84. In RC Ch 83-95; Dean's V Ch Ch Cathl Dublin 99-01; I Crosspatrick Gp *C & O* 01-08; Prec Ferns Cathl 04-08; Adn Ferns 07-08; Dean Ch Ch Cathl Dublin from 08. *19 Mountainview Road, Ranelagh, Dublin 6, Republic of Ireland* Tel (00353) (1) 499 1571 *or* 677 8099 Fax 679 8991 Mobile 87-137 1955 E-mail revdunne@eircom.net

DUNNE, Kevin Headley. b 43. Cranmer Hall Dur 85. **d** 87 **p** 88. C Chester le Street *Dur* 87-90; V S Hetton w Haswell 90-94; P-in-c Oxclose 94-02; R Chester le Street 02-08; AD Chester-le-Street 97-02 and 04-08; rtd 08; Chapl Sherburn Hosp Dur from 09. *Shincliffe House, Sherburn Hospital, Durham DH1 2SE* Tel 0191-372 4993 E-mail revdunne@btopenworld.com

DUNNE, The Very Revd Nigel Kenneth. b 66. TCD BA88 BTh90 MA00 MPhil00. **d** 90 **p** 91. C Dublin St Bart w Leeson Park *D & G* 90-93; C Taney 93-95; I Blessington w Kilbride, Ballymore Eustace etc 95-03; Can Ch Ch Cathl Dublin 01-03; I Bandon Union *C, C & R* 03-07; Dean Cork from 07; I Cork St Fin Barre's Union from 07. *The Deanery, Gilabbey Street, Cork, Republic of Ireland* Tel (00353) (21) 431 8073 E-mail nidunne@oceanfree.net

DUNNETT, John Frederick. b 58. SS Coll Cam MA84 Worc Coll Ox MSc83 CQSW82. Trin Coll Bris BA87. **d** 88 **p** 89. C Kirkheaton *Wakef* 88-93; V Cranham Park *Chelmsf* 93-06; Gen Dir CPAS from 06. *201 Front Lane, Upminster RM14 1LD* Tel (01708) 222122 E-mail jd@johndunnett.co.uk *or* jdunnett@cpas.org.uk

DUNNETT, Keith Owen. b 66. Cranfield Inst of Tech BSc87. Trin Coll Bris BA00. **d** 00 **p** 01. C Walton and Trimley *St E* 00-03; V Clayton *Bradf* from 03. *The Vicarage, Clayton Lane, Clayton, Bradford BD14 6AX* Tel (01274) 880373 Mobile 07779-832286 E-mail keith.dunnett@bradford.anglican.org

DUNNETT, Nigella. *See* YOUNGS-DUNNETT, Elizabeth Nigella

DUNNETT, Robert Curtis. b 31. SS Coll Cam BA54 MA58. Oak Hill Th Coll 56. **d** 58 **p** 59. C Markfield *Leic* 58-60; C Bucknall and Bagnall *Lich* 60-73; Perm to Offic *Birm* from 72; Chapl and Tutor Birm Bible Inst 72-79; Vice-Prin 84-92; Hon Vice-Prin 92-05; rtd 96. *30 Station Road, Harborne, Birmingham B17 9LY* Tel 0121-428 3945 Fax 428 3370

DUNNILL, Canon John David Stewart. b 50. UEA BA72 Ox Univ CertEd76 Birm Univ PhD88. Ripon Coll Cuddesdon 86.

d 88 **p** 89. C Tupsley *Heref* 88-92; Lect Glouc Sch for Min 89-91; Sen Lect Murdoch Univ Australia from 92; Dir Bibl and Th Studies Angl Inst of Th from 92; Can Perth from 99. *School of Social Inquiry, Murdoch University, Murdoch WA 6150, Australia* Tel (0061) (8) 9360 6369 *or* 9383 4403 Fax 9360 6480 E-mail j.dunnill@murdoch.edu.au

DUNNING, Adam Jonathan. b 73. Regent's Park Coll Ox BA95 MA99 Birm Univ PhD00 Wolv Univ CertEd05. Westcott Ho Cam 97. **d** 99 **p** 00. C Evesham w Norton and Lenchwick *Worc* 99-02; C Hamstead St Paul *Birm* 02-03; Hon C Moseley St Mary and Moseley St Anne 03-05; P-in-c The Ortons, Alwalton and Chesterton *Ely* from 06. *The Rectory, The Village, Orton Longueville, Peterborough PE2 7DN* Tel (01733) 371071 E-mail a.dunning@ukonline.co.uk

DUNNING, Martyn Philip. b 51. Reading Univ MSc79 Dur Univ MA95 MRTPI77. St Jo Coll Dur 89. **d** 92 **p** 93. C Beverley Minster *York* 92-96; P-in-c Brandesburton 96-97; P-in-c Leven w Catwick 96-97; R Brandesburton and Leven w Catwick 97-02; RD N Holderness 97-02; P-in-c Scarborough St Mary w Ch Ch and H Apostles 02-04; V from 04; RD Scarborough from 04. *St Mary's Vicarage, 1 North Cliff Gardens, Scarborough YO12 6PR* Tel (01723) 371354

DUNNINGS, Reuben Edward. b 36. Clifton Th Coll 62. **d** 66 **p** 67. C Longfleet *Sarum* 66-70; C Melksham 70-73; TV 73-78; R Broughton Gifford w Gt Chalfield 78-84; V Holt St Kath 78-84; R Broughton Gifford, Gt Chalfield and Holt 85-86; V Salisbury St Fran 86-99; P-in-c Stratford sub Castle 98-99; V Salisbury St Fran and Stratford sub Castle 99-01; rtd 01; Perm to Offic *Sarum* from 01. *11 Cornbrash Rise, Hilperton, Trowbridge BA14 7TS* Tel (01225) 768834

DUNSETH, George William. b 52. Multnomah Sch of the Bible Oregon BRE79. Oak Hill Th Coll BA85. **d** 85 **p** 86. C Cheadle All Hallows *Ches* 85-88; C New Borough and Leigh *Sarum* 88-91; V Thurnby w Stoughton *Leic* 91-06; Perm to Offic 07-08; P-in-c Leic St Leon CD from 08. *46 Brading Road, Leicester LE3 9BG* E-mail g52e0@btinternet.com

DUNSTAN, Canon Gregory John Orchard. b 50. Cam Univ MA75 TCD BTh90. CITC 87. **d** 90 **p** 91. C Ballymena w Ballyclug *Conn* 90-93; I Belfast St Matt from 93; Preb Swords St Patr Cathl Dublin from 07. *Shankill Rectory, 51 Ballygomartin Road, Belfast BT13 3LA* Tel and fax (028) 9071 4325

DUNSTAN, Kenneth Ian. b 40. Goldsmiths' Coll Lon BEd71 ACP. Oak Hill NSM Course 86. **d** 88 **p** 89. NSM Creeksea w Althorne, Latchingdon and N Fambridge *Chelmsf* 88-94; P-in-c Woodham Mortimer w Hazeleigh 94-98; P-in-c Woodham Walter 94-98; NSM Bradwell on Sea 99-05; rtd 05; Perm to Offic *Chelmsf* from 05. *35 Ely Close, Southminster CM0 7AQ* Tel (01621) 772199 E-mail kandk@wclub.net

DUNSTAN, Mark Philip. b 70. Middx Univ BSc93. Oak Hill Th Coll BA03. **d** 03 **p** 04. C Stranton *Dur* 03-06; P-in-c Hunsdon w Widford and Wareside *St Alb* from 06. *The Rectory, Acorn Street, Hunsdon, Ware SG12 8PB* Tel (01920) 877276 E-mail dunstan_mark@hotmail.com

DUNSTAN-MEADOWS, Victor Richard. b 63. Chich Th Coll BTh90. **d** 90 **p** 91. C Clacton St Jas *Chelmsf* 90-93; C Stansted Mountfitchet 93-95; CF 95-00; Chapl RAF from 00. *Chaplaincy Services, Valiant Block, HQ Air Command, RAF High Wycombe HP14 4UE* Tel (01494) 496800 Fax 496343

DUNTHORNE, Paul. b 63. K Coll Lon LLB85 St Jo Coll Dur BA90 Dur Univ MA98. Cranmer Hall Dur 88. **d** 91 **p** 92. C Heacham and Sedgeford *Nor* 91-95; C Eastbourne H Trin *Chich* 95-98; P-in-c Preston and Ridlington w Wing and Pilton *Pet* 98-00; Local Min Officer 98-00; CME Officer *Heref* 00-06; TR Ledbury from 06. *The Rectory, Worcester Road, Ledbury HR8 1PL* Tel (01531) 632571 E-mail p.dunthorne@btinternet.com

DUNWICH, Suffragan Bishop of. *See* YOUNG, The Rt Revd Clive

DUNWOODY, Stephen John Herbert. b 71. Glam Univ BA92. St Steph Ho Ox BTh96. **d** 96 **p** 97. C Skewen *Llan* 96-98; C Roath 98-99; C Stanley *Liv* 99-02; TV Colyton, Southleigh, Offwell, Widworthy etc *Ex* 02-03; V Offwell, Northleigh, Farway, Cotleigh etc 03-05; CF from 05. *c/o MOD Chaplains (Army)* Tel (01980) 615804 Fax 615809 E-mail stephendunwoody@hotmail.com

DUNWOODY, Thomas Herbert Williamson. b 35. TCD BA58 MA64. TCD Div Sch Div Test59. **d** 59 **p** 60. C Newcastle *D & D* 59-61; Asst Missr Ballymacarrett St Martin 61-63; C Lurgan Ch the Redeemer 63-66; I Ardglass w Dunsford 66-74; Offg Chapl RAF 66-74; V Urmston *Man* 74-85; I Wexford w Ardcolm and Killurin *C & O* 85-93; Can Ferns Cathl 88-93; I Newry *D & D* 93-02; rtd 02. *36 Godfrey Avenue, Bangor BT20 5LS* Tel (028) 9145 3918 E-mail thw_dunwoody@tiscali.co.uk

DUPLOCK, Canon Peter Montgomery. b 16. OBE76. Qu Coll Cam BA38 MA42. Ridley Hall Cam 38. **d** 40 **p** 41. C Hoddesdon *S'wark* 40-43; CF (EC) 43-47; R Nottingham St Nic *S'well* 47-52; R Loddington w Harrington *Pet* 52-55; V Kettering St Andr 55-64; Chapl Geneva *Eur* 64-71; Chapl Brussels w Charleroi, Liège and Waterloo 71-81; Chan Brussels Cathl 81; Adn NW

Eur 81; rtd 81; Hon Can Brussels Cathl from 81; R Breamore *Win* 81-86; Perm to Offic 86-95; Perm to Offic *Sarum* 86-98. *9 Capel Court, The Burgage, Prestbury, Cheltenham GL52 3EL* Tel (01242) 580518

DUPREE, Hugh Douglas. b 50. Univ of the South (USA) BA72 Virginia Th Sem MDiv75 Ch Ch Ox MA86 Ball Coll Ox DPhil88. **d** 75 **p** 76. USA 75-80; Hon C Ox St Mich w St Martin and All SS 80-87; Asst Chapl Ball Coll Ox 84-87; Chapl from 87; Dean from 07; Chapl HM Pris Ox 88-97. *Balliol College, Oxford OX1 3BJ* Tel (01865) 277777
E-mail douglas.dupree@balliol.ox.ac.uk

DUPUY, Alan Douglas William. b 48. SEITE 98. **d** 00 **p** 01. NSM Forest Hill St Aug *S'wark* 00-01; NSM S Dulwich St Steph 01-04; NSM Perry Hill St Geo w Ch Ch and St Paul from 04. *16 Dominic Court, 43 The Gardens, London SE22 9QR* Tel (020) 8695 5769 Fax 8693 4175 Mobile 07960-226518
E-mail alandupuy1@aol.com

DURAND, Noel Douglas. b 33. Jes Coll Cam BA57 MA61 BD76. Westcott Ho Cam 72. **d** 74 **p** 75. C Eaton *Nor* 74-78; V Cumnor *Ox* 78-01; rtd 01; Perm to Offic *Nor* from 01. *21 Nelson Road, Sheringham NR26 8BU* Tel (01263) 822388

DURAND, Stella Evelyn Brigid, Lady. b 42. TCD BA64 Sorbonne Univ Paris DèS65. CITC BTh99. **d** 00. C Kiltegan w Hacketstown, Clonmore and Moyne *C & O* 00-03; I from 03. *The Rectory, Kiltegan, Co Wicklow, Republic of Ireland* Tel and fax (00353) (59) 647 3368 E-mail stelladurand@eircom.net

DURANT, Robert-Ashton. b 23. St D Coll Lamp BA47. Bp Burgess Hall Lamp. **d** 48 **p** 49. C Brynmawr *S & B* 48-49; C Fleur-de-Lis *Mon* 49-51; C Bassaleg 51-56; CF (TA) 53-55; V Trelleck and Cwmcarvan *Mon* 56-69; Priest Tymawr Convent 56-69; V Slapton *Ex* 69-81; V Strete 69-81; R E Allington, Slapton and Strete 81-92; rtd 92; Perm to Offic *Ex* from 92. *Fairfield, Hynetown Road, Strete, Dartmouth TQ6 0RS*

DURANT, William John Nicholls. b 55. K Coll Lon BA76. St Jo Coll Nottm 77. **d** 80 **p** 81. C Norwood St Luke *S'wark* 80-83; C Morden 83-88; TV 88-92; V Frindsbury w Upnor *Roch* 92-00; CF from 00. *c/o MOD Chaplains (Army)* Tel (01980) 615804 Fax 615800

DURANT-STEVENSEN, Mrs Helen Mary. b 53. Saffron Walden Coll Cam TCert74. Trin Coll Bris BA04. **d** 04 **p** 05. C S Croydon Em *S'wark* 04-08; C New Malden and Coombe from 08. *2 California Road, New Malden KT3 3RU* Tel (020) 8942 0544

DURBIN, Roger. b 41. Bris Sch of Min 83. **d** 85 **p** 86. NSM Bedminster *Bris* 85-91; NSM Henbury 91-94; NSM Clifton All SS w St Jo from 94. *13 Charbury Walk, Bristol BS11 9UU* Tel 0117-985 8404

DURELL, Miss Jane Vavasor. b 32. Bedf Coll Lon BSc55 Lambeth STh64. Gilmore Ho 61. **dss** 86 **d** 87 **p** 94. Banbury *Ox* 86-92; Par Dn 87-92; rtd 92; Perm to Offic *Nor* 92-94 and from 02; NSM Norwich St Mary Magd w St Jas 94-02. *38 Brakendon Close, Norwich NR1 3BX* Tel (01603) 627949

DURHAM, Miss Bethany Helen. b 58. Cranmer Hall Dur 86. **d** 89 **p** 94. C Newark *S'well* 89-93; rtd 93; Perm to Offic *S'well* from 93. *c/o Crockford, Church House, Great Smith Street, London SW1P 3AZ*

DURHAM, Mrs Eleanore Jane. b 62. St Andr Univ MTheol84. Trin Coll Bris BA01. **d** 01 **p** 02. C Childwall All SS *Liv* 01-05; P-in-c Hunts Cross from 05. *The Vicarage, 7 Kingsmead Drive, Liverpool L25 0NG* Tel 0151-486 1220
E-mail jane.durham@dsl.pipex.com

DURHAM, Archdeacon of. See JAGGER, The Ven Ian

DURHAM, Bishop of. See WRIGHT, The Rt Revd Nicholas Thomas

DURHAM, Dean of. See SADGROVE, The Very Revd Michael

DURIE, Mrs Patricia James. b 63. Cen Lancs Univ BA93 St Martin's Coll Lanc MA99. CBDTI 97. **d** 99 **p** 00. C Briercliffe *Blackb* 99-01; P-in-c Edin St Dav from 02. *33 Lamberton Shiels, Lamberton, Berwick-upon-Tweed TD15 1XB* Tel (01890) 781542
E-mail patricia.durie@btinternet.com

DURING, Arthur Christopher. b 59. Sierra Leone Th Hall 80. **d** 83 **p** 85. C Freetown H Trin Sierra Leone 83-85; C St Geo Cathl 85-86; Perm to Offic *S'wark* 00-05. *22 Challice Way, London SW2 3RD* Tel (020) 8671 7678

DURKAN, Barbara Isobel Mary. b 43. Kent Univ BSc71 MPhil00 Ch Ch Coll Cant MA95 Sarum Dioc Tr Coll CertEd65. SEITE 99. **d** 01 **p** 02. Aux Chapl HM Pris Standford Hill 01-08; rtd 08; Perm to Offic Cant 08-09; Hon C Minster-in-Sheppey from 09. *69 Darlington Drive, Minster-on-Sea, Sheerness ME12 3LG*

DURKIN, Anthony Michael. b 45. Sarum & Wells Th Coll 87. **d** 89 **p** 90. C Faversham *Cant* 89-92; V St Margarets-at-Cliffe w Westcliffe etc 92-09; rtd 09. *Church Cottage, Leigh, Sherborne DT9 6HL* Tel (01935) 872117
E-mail tony@durkin6595.freeserve.co.uk

DURKIN, Mrs Derath May. b 52. N Staffs Poly LLB87. SAOMC 01. **d** 02 **p** 03. C Harlington Ch Ch CD *Lon* 02-06; 1 V Brentford from 06. *St Faith's Vicarage, 122 Windmill Road, Brentford TW8 9NA* Tel (020) 8560 3782 Mobile 07962-168440
E-mail derath.durkin@parishofbrentford.org.uk

DURLEY, Jonathan Richard Hall. b 66. Wolv Univ BA97 Ch Ch Coll Cant MA01. S Wales Ord Course 04. **d** 05 **p** 06. C Canton Cardiff *Llan* 05-07; C Newton Nottage from 07. *Ty Dewi Sant, 5B West End Avenue, Porthcawl CF36 3NE* Tel (01656) 772504
E-mail fatherjon@btinternet.com

DURNDELL, Miss Irene Frances. b 43. Trin Coll Bris 84. **dss** 86 **d** 87 **p** 94. Erith Ch Ch *Roch* 86-93; Par Dn 87-93; Par Dn Erith St Paul 93-94; C 94-98; Asst Dir of Tr 93-98; V Falconwood 98-07; rtd 07. *17A Buxton Drive, Bexhill-on-Sea TN39 4BA* Tel (01424) 810477
E-mail renee.durndell@btinternet.com

DURNELL, John. b 32. St Aid Birkenhead 64. **d** 66 **p** 67. C Newport w Longford *Lich* 66-69; P-in-c Church Aston 69-72; R 72-77; V Weston Rhyn 77-82; P-in-c Petton w Cockshutt and Weston Lullingfield etc 82-83; R Petton w Cockshutt, Welshampton and Lyneal etc 83-97; rtd 97; Perm to Offic *Lich* from 97. *Fronlwyd, Hirnant, Penybontfawr, Oswestry SY10 0HP* Tel (01691) 870686

DURNFORD, Canon Catherine Margaret. b 36. St Mary's Coll Dur BA57. Gilmore Course 78 NW Ord Course 77. **d** 87 **p** 94. Area Sec USPG *York* and *Ripon* 82-89; Par Dn Whitby *York* 89-92; Par Dn Redcar 92-94; C Selby Abbey 94-97; V New Marske and Wilton 97-03; Can and Preb York Minster 01-03; rtd 03; Perm to Offic *York* from 03. *18 Canongate, Cottingham HU16 4DG* Tel (01482) 844868

DURNFORD, John Edward. b 30. CCC Cam BA53 MA61. Linc Th Coll 53. **d** 55 **p** 56. C Selby Abbey *York* 55-58; C Newland St Jo 58-62; C Umtali S Rhodesia 62-64; R Mazoe Valley 64-76; V Hebden Bridge *Wakef* 76-84; RD Calder Valley 82-84; P-in-c Blanchland w Hunstanworth *Newc* 84-90; P-in-c Edmundbyers w Muggleswick *Dur* 84-90; R Blanchland w Hunstanworth and Edmundbyers etc *Newc* 90-94; RD Corbridge 88-93; rtd 94; Perm to Offic *Newc* 94-05 and *Cant* 06-09. *19 Sunburst Close, Marden, Tonbridge TN12 9TS*

DURNFORD, Comdr Peter Jeffrey. b 20. Bps' Coll Cheshunt 63. **d** 65 **p** 66. C Edmonton St Alphege *Lon* 65-67; Chapl Bonn w Cologne *Eur* 67-69; R St Just in Roseland *Truro* 70-82; P-in-c Ruan Lanihorne w Philleigh 70-82; P-in-c St Mewan 82-85; Chapl Mount Edgcumbe Hospice 82-88; rtd 85; Perm to Offic *Truro* from 85. *8 Tredenham Road, St Mawes, Truro TR2 5AN* Tel (01326) 270793

DURRAN, Ms Margaret. b 47. Surrey Univ MSc96 Lady Spencer Chu Coll of Educn CertEd70. S'wark Ord Course 88. **d** 91 **p** 94. Par Dn Brixton St Matt *S'wark* 91-94; C Streatham St Leon 94-95; V Walworth St Chris 95-99; Hon C S'wark St Geo w St Alphege and St Jude from 99; Hist Churches Project Officer *Lon* from 99; rtd 08. *2 St Alphege House, Pocock Street, London SE1 0BJ* Tel and fax (020) 7401 8808 Mobile 07739-988742
E-mail maggie.durran@virgin.net

DURRANT, Melvyn Richard Bloomfield. b 59. Leeds Univ BA82 St Luke's Coll Ex PGCE86. Trin Coll Bris 01. **d** 03 **p** 04. C Watercombe *Sarum* 03-06; C Moreton and Woodsford w Tincleton 03-06; P-in-c Sixpenny Handley w Gussage St Andrew etc from 06; C Chase from 06. *The Vicarage, 60 High Street, Sixpenny Handley, Salisbury SP5 5ND* Tel (01725) 552608
E-mail durrant@talktalk.net

DURSTON, Canon David Michael Karl. b 36. Em Coll Cam BA60 MA64. Clifton Th Coll 61. **d** 63 **p** 64. C Wednesfield Heath *Lich* 63-66; Project Officer Grubb Inst 67-78; Ind Chapl *Lich* 78-84; P in-c W Bromwich St Paul 78-82; V 82-84; Adult Educn Officer 84-92; Preb Lich Cathl 89-92; Can Res and Chan Sarum Cathl 92-03; Can and Preb 03-06; TR Wylye and Till Valley 03-06; rtd 06. *26 Mill Road, Salisbury SP2 7RZ* Tel (01722) 334017

DUSSEK, Jeremy Neil James Christopher. b 70. St Jo Coll Dur BA92. Westcott Ho Cam 96. **d** 97 **p** 98. C Whickham *Dur* 97-00; C Fareham H Trin *Portsm* 00-01; TV 01-07; V Moseley St Mary and St Anne *Birm* from 07. *St Mary's Vicarage, 18 Oxford Road, Moseley, Birmingham B13 9EH* Tel 0121-449 1459 Fax 449 2243
E-mail jeremy@dussek.fsnet.co.uk

DUST, Simon Philip. b 63. Oak Hill Th Coll BA95. **d** 95 **p** 96. C Chesham Bois *Ox* 95-00; C-in-c Bushmead CD *St Alb* 00-04; V Bushmead 04-08; TV High Wycombe *Ox* from 08. *15 The Brackens, High Wycombe HP11 1EB* Tel (01494) 529668
E-mail simon@sac-hw.org.uk

DUTFIELD, Canon Alan. b 20. Linc Th Coll 54. **d** 55 **p** 56. C Kimberworth *Sheff* 55-60; V New Rossington 60-71; R Old Brumby *Linc* 71-77; TR 77-86; Can and Preb Linc Cathl 81-86; RD Manlake 82-86; rtd 86; Perm to Offic *Linc* 89-94 and from 01; Perm to Offic *S'well* from 03. *30 Barnes Green, Scotter, Gainsborough DN21 3RW* Tel (01724) 764220

DUTHIE, Elliot Malcolm. b 31. Clifton Th Coll 63. **d** 66 **p** 67. C Eccleston St Luke *Liv* 66-69; Malaysia 70-75; P-in-c Bootle St Leon *I iv* 76-78; V 78-81, V Charlton Kings H Apostles *Glouc* 81-94; Perm to Offic *Glouc* 94-00; *Ex* 02-05; *Derby* from 07. *11 Fairisle Close, Oakwood, Derby DE21 2SJ* Tel (01332) 668238 E-mail m.duthie@tesco.net

DUTHIE, John. b 39. **d** 04 **p** 05. NSM Aberdeen St Pet 04-07; Chapl Grampian Healthcare NHS Trust from 06. *Moraine, Inchmarlo, Banchory AB31 4BR* Tel (01330) 824108
E-mail johnduthie@nhs.net

DUTTON, Andrew Rivers George. b 49. Bris Univ BSc71 PGCE72 Reading Univ MSc79. EAMTC 98. **d** 98 **p** 99. NSM Kettering SS Pet and Paul 98-03; NSM Broughton w Loddington and Cransley etc from 04; Chapl Bp Stopford Sch from 99. *10 Beardsley Gardens, Kettering NN15 5UB* Tel (01536) 392401 E-mail adutton@bishopstopford.com

DUTTON, Leonard Arthur. b 35. Bps' Coll Cheshunt 63. **d** 66 **p** 67. C Knighton St Jo *Leic* 66-70; C Chilvers Coton w Astley *Cov* 70-73; R Hathern *Leic* 73-79; V Ashby-de-la-Zouch H Trin 79-04; rtd 04; Perm to Offic *Leic* from 04. *8 Merganser Way, Coalville LE67 4QA* Tel (01530) 815420
E-mail lenmeg@dutton8.wanadoo.co.uk

DUTTON, Sandra Rosemary. b 50. Ripon Coll Cuddesdon 03. **d** 04 **p** 05. NSM Chatham St Steph *Roch* 04-08; TV Hartshill, Penkhull and Trent Vale *Lich* from 08. *The Vicarage, 214 Queens Road, Penkhull, Stoke-on-Trent ST4 7LG* Tel (01782) 744224 E-mail sandydutton@hotmail.com

DUVAL, Canon Philip Ernest. b 18. MBE45. Mert Coll Ox BA45 MA45. Westcott Ho Cam 47. **d** 47 **p** 48. C Tooting All SS *S'wark* 47-51; C Raynes Park St Sav 51-55; V Balham St Mary 55-66; R Merstham and Gatton 66-86; Hon Can S'wark Cathl 78-86; rtd 86; Perm to Offic *Cant* 88-06 and *B & W* from 07. *7 George & Crown Cottages, Hinton St George TA17 8SD* Tel (01460) 75369

DUVALL, Michael James. b 31. **d** 79 **p** 80. Hon C Kings Langley *St Alb* 79-89; Hon C Selworthy and Timberscombe and Wootton Courtenay *B & W* 89-95; Hon C Luccombe 89-95; Hon C Selworthy, Timberscombe, Wootton Courtenay etc 95-97; rtd 97; Perm to Offic *B & W* from 97. *Dovery Edge, 19 Hawkcombe View, Porlock, Minehead TA24 8NB* Tel (01634) 862834

DUXBURY, Clive Robert. b 49. Open Univ BA(ThM)06. St Jo Coll Nottm 90. **d** 92 **p** 93. C Horwich and Rivington *Man* 92-96; P-in-c Bury St Paul and Bury St King 98-00; P-in-c Freethorpe, Wickhampton, Halvergate w Tunstall *Nor* 00-02; P-in-c Reedham w Cantley w Limpenhoe and Southwood 00-02; R Freethorpe, Wickhampton, Halvergate etc 02-05; RD Blofield 04-05; R High Ongar w Norton Mandeville *Chelmsf* 05-08; Chapl HM Pris Everthorpe from 08. *HM Prison Everthorpe, Beck Road, Everthorpe, Brough HU15 1RB* Tel (01430) 426500 Mobile 07777-602980 E-mail duxbury@duxbury.karoo.co.uk

DUXBURY, Canon James Campbell. b 33. Tyndale Hall Bris 58. **d** 61 **p** 62. C Southport SS Simon and Jude *Liv* 61-65; V Tittensor *Lich* 65-70; V W Bromwich Gd Shep w St Jo 70-75; P-in-c Wellington w Eyton 75-80; V 80-85; V Padiham *Blackb* 85-01; Hon Can Blackb Cathl 97-01; rtd 01; Can Emer Blackb Cathl from 01; Perm to Offic from 01. *1 Gills Croft, Clitheroe BB7 1LJ* Tel (01200) 429261
E-mail duxbury@ribble-valley.co.uk

DUXBURY, Miss Margaret Joan. b 30. JP81. DipEd52. St Jo Coll Nottm 83. **dss** 84 **d** 87 **p** 94. Thornthwaite w Thruscross and Darley *Ripon* 84-86; Middleton St Cross 86-90; C 87-90; Par Dn Dacre w Hartwith and Darley w Thornthwaite 90-94; C 94-96; rtd 97; NSM Bishop Monkton and Burton Leonard *Ripon* 97-02; Perm to Offic from 01. *Scot Beck House, Low Lane, Darley, Harrogate HG3 2QN* Tel (01423) 780451

DYAS, Stuart Edwin. b 46. Lon Univ BSc67. Ridley Hall Cam 78. **d** 80 **p** 81. C Bath Weston St Jo w Kelston *B & W* 80-83; C Tunbridge Wells St Jas *Roch* 83-90; V Nottingham St Jude *S'well* 90-99; AD Nottingham Cen 93-98; V Long Eaton St Jo *Derby* 99-05; rtd 05; Perm to Offic *Derby* from 05. *179 Bye Pass Road, Beeston, Nottingham NG9 5HR* Tel 0115-922 5844

DYAS, Sylvia Denise (Dee). b 51. Bedf Coll Lon BA72 Nottm Univ PhD99. St Jo Coll Nottm 98. **d** 00 **p** 01. Tutor St Jo Coll Nottm from 00; Perm to Offic *Derby* from 00. *179 Bye Pass Road, Beeston, Nottingham NG9 5HR* Tel 0115-922 5844
E-mail d.dyas@stjohns-nottm.ac.uk

DYE, Mrs Margaret Mary. b 48. NOC 95. **d** 98 **p** 99. C Morley St Pet w Churwell *Wakef* 98-02; TV Morley 02-08; TR from 08. *St Andrew's Vicarage, 4 Lewisham Street, Morley, Leeds LS27 0LA* Tel 0113-252 3783 E-mail rev.m.dye@ntlworld.com

DYE, Stephen. b 49. NOC 01. **d** 04 **p** 05. C Gildersome *Wakef* 04-08; Chapl St Geo Crypt Leeds *Ripon* from 08. *St Andrew's Vicarage, 4 Lewisham Street, Morley, Leeds LS27 0LA* Tel 0113-252 3783 E-mail rev.s.dye@ntlworld.com

DYER, Canon Anne Catherine. b 57. St Anne's Coll Ox MA80 Lon Univ MTh89. Wycliffe Hall Ox 84. **d** 87 **p** 94. NSM Beckenham St Jo *Roch* 87-88; NSM Beckenham St Geo 88-89; Hon Par Dn Luton Ch Ch 89-94; Chapl for Evang 93-98; NSM Istead Rise 94-98; Min Development Officer 98-04; Hon Can Roch Cathl 00-04; Warden Cranmer Hall Dur from 05; Hon Can Dur Cathl from 04. *16 Briardene, Durham DH1 4QU* Tel 0191-384 0048 E-mail adyer82120@aol.com

DYER, Ms Catherine Jane. b 46. Westf Coll Lon BA68. Ox NSM Course 85. **d** 88 **p** 94. NSM Wokingham All SS *Ox* 88-90; C 90-95; TV W Slough 95-01; P-in-c Linslade 01-07; AD Mursley 03-06; rtd 07. *45 Shady Bower, Salisbury SP1 2RG* E-mail catherine.dyer46@hotmail.co.uk

DYER, Canon Christine Anne. b 53. Nottm Univ BEd75 MA97. EMMTC 81. **dss** 84 **d** 87 **p** 94. Mickleover St Jo *Derby* 85-90; Par Dn 87-90; Dioc Voc Adv 86-90; Par Educn Adv 90-98; Dioc Youth Officer 91-98; P-in-c Morton and Stonebroom 98-99; P-in-c Shirland 98-99; R Morton and Stonebroom w Shirland 99-06; P-in-c Allestree from 06; P-in-c Darley Abbey from 06; Hon Can Derby Cathl from 02. *The Vicarage, Kings Croft, Allestree, Derby DE22 2FN* Tel (01332) 551404
E-mail c.a.dyer.t21@btinternet.com *or* c.a.dyer@talk21.com

DYER, Fraser Colin. b 65. SEITE. **d** 09. C De Beauvoir Town St Pet *Lon* from 09. *Studio 3, 96 De Beauvoir Road, London N1 4EN* Tel (020) 7683 1609
E-mail fraserdyer@mac.com

DYER, Mrs Gillian Marie. b 50. Sheff Univ BA71 Leic Univ PGCE72. S Dios Minl Tr Scheme 81. **dss** 84 **d** 87 **p** 94. Witney *Ox* 84-85; Carl St Cuth w St Mary 86-89; Par Dn 87-89; Dioc Communications Officer 86-89; Par Dn Kirkbride w Newton Arlosh 89-91; Par Dn Carl H Trin and St Barn 91-94; TV 94-97; P-in-c Arbroath *Bre* 01-03; P-in-c Lower Darwen St Jas *Blackb* from 03. *The Vicarage, Stopes Brow, Lower Darwen, Darwen BB3 0QP* Tel (01254) 677903 E-mail tergill@aol.com

DYER, Canon James Henry. b 14. ALCD39. **d** 39 **p** 40. C S Hackney St Jo w Ch Ch *Lon* 39-43; C New Malden and Coombe *S'wark* 43-50; New Zealand from 50; V Murchison 50-56; V Collingwood 56-59; V Spring Creek 59-67; V Amuri 67-70; V Motupiko 70-77; Hon Can Nelson Cathl 85. *7 Talbot Street, Richmond, Nelson, New Zealand* Tel (0064) (3) 554 8638 E-mail james.dyer@xtra.co.nz

DYER, Janet. b 35. LNSM course 77. **dss** 85 **d** 86 **p** 94. Balerno *Edin* 85-86; NSM 86-93; Chapl Edin R Infirmary 88-93; Dn-in-c Roslin (Rosslyn Chpl) *Edin* 93-94; P-in-c 94-97; NSM Livingston LEP 97-00; Angl Chapl Livingstone St Jo Hosp 97-00; NSM Dalmahoy from 02. *499 Lanark Road West, Balerno EH14 7AL* Tel 0131-449 3767 E-mail adrian@dyer499.freeserve.co.uk

DYER, Ronald Whitfield. b 29. Solicitor 51. Guildf Dioc Min Course 91. **d** 95 **p** 96. NSM Fleet *Guildf* 95-99; rtd 99; Perm to Offic *Guildf* from 99. *7 Dukes Mead, Fleet GU51 4HA* Tel (01252) 621457

DYER, Stephen Roger. b 57. Brunel Univ BSc. Wycliffe Hall Ox 83. **d** 86 **p** 91. C Beckenham St Jo *Roch* 86-89; C Luton Ch Ch 89-94; V Istead Rise 94-01; V Frindsbury w Upnor 01-04; Hon C Easington, Easington Colliery and S Hetton *Dur* from 05. *16 Briardene, Durham DH1 4QU* Tel 0191-384 0048
E-mail revrogdyer@aol.com

DYER, Miss Sylvia Mary. b 30. Westf Coll Lon BA66. Ab Dioc Tr Course 90. **d** 95 **p** 98. NSM Turriff *Ab* 95-06; NSM Cuminestown 95-06; rtd 06; Perm to Offic *Bre* from 07. *Lily Cottage, 19 Long Row, Westhaven, Carnoustie DD7 6BE* Tel (01241) 856652 E-mail sylviadyer@blueyonder.co.uk

DYER, Terence Neville. b 50. Sheff Univ BEng71 Leic Univ PGCE72. Carl Dioc Tr Course 86. **d** 89 **p** 90. NSM Kirkbride w Newton Arlosh *Carl* 89-91; NSM Carl H Trin and St Barn 91-97; NSM Arbroath *Bre* 01-03; P-in-c Monifieth 01-03; P-in-c Over Darwen St Jas *Blackb* from 03; C Darwen St Pet w Hoddlesden from 08. *The Vicarage, Stopes Brow, Lower Darwen, Darwen BB3 0QP* Tel (01254) 677903 E-mail tergill@aol.com

DYKE, Mrs Elizabeth Muriel. b 55. St Mary's Coll Dur BSc77 St Martin's Coll Lanc PGCE78. Oak Hill Th Coll 92. **d** 94 **p** 95. C High Wycombe *Ox* 94-95; C W Wycombe w Bledlow Ridge, Bradenham and Radnage 95-97; TV Bedworth *Cov* 97-02; V Dunchurch 02-09; R Kidman Park and Mile End Australia from 09. *2 Elgar Court, Fulham Gardens SA 5024, Australia* Tel (0061) (8) 8353 0049 E-mail elizabeth@dykefamily.plus.com

DYKE, George Edward. b 22. TCD BA65 BCom65 MA80. CITC. **d** 79 **p** 80. NSM Dublin St Geo *D & G* 79-82; NSM Tallaght 83-89; NSM Killiney Ballybrack 89-90; Bp's C Dublin St Geo and St Thos and Finglas 90-95; Bp's C Dublin St Geo and St Thos 95-96; Chapl Mountjoy Pris 90-96; Chapl Arbour Hill Pris 90-96; rtd 96. *45 Thornhill Road, Mount Merrion, Co Dublin, Republic of Ireland* Tel (00353) (1) 288 3376

DYKES, John Edward. b 33. Trin Coll Bris 82. **d** 84 **p** 85. C Rushden w Newton Bromswold *Pet* 84-87; R Heanton Punchardon w Marwood *Ex* 87-97; rtd 97; Perm to Offic *Guildf* 98-01 and *B & W* from 02. *42 Ashley Road, Taunton TA1 5BP* Tel (01823) 282507 E-mail johnandvickyd@tiscali.co.uk

DYKES, Mrs Katrina Mary. b 66. Trin Coll Bris BA90. Guildf Dioc Min Course 03. **d** 04 **p** 05. NSM Windlesham *Guildf* 04-07; Chapl St Swithun's Sch Win from 08. *St Swithun's School, Alresford Road, Winchester SO21 1HA* Tel (01962) 835700 E-mail dykesk@stswithuns.com

DYKES, Michael David Allan. b 42. Chich Th Coll 68. **d** 71 **p** 72. C Pocklington w Yapham-cum-Meltonby, Owsthorpe etc *York* 72-75; C Howden 75-77; V Eskdaleside w Ugglebarnby and Sneaton 77-85; R Stokesley 85-04; P-in-c Seamer in Cleveland 85-04; P-in-c Hilton in Cleveland 85-95; R Stokesley w Seamer

05-08; rtd 08; Perm to Offic *York* from 09. *21 Wreyfield Drive, Scarborough YO12 6NN* Tel (01723) 378576
E-mail michael@dykes41.wanadoo.co.uk

DYKES, Philip John. b 61. Loughb Univ BSc83. Trin Coll Bris 88. **d** 91 **p** 92. C Morden *S'wark* 91-95; C St Helier 95-98; TV Camberley St Paul *Guildf* 98-99; V Camberley Heatherside 99-08; Chapl Win Univ from 08. *University of Winchester, Sparkford Road, Winchester SO22 4NR* Tel (01962) 827063
E-mail phil.dykes@ntlworld.com

DYMOND, Rosemary Carmen. b 70. Ox Univ MEng94 Aber Univ MSc95 Bremen Univ Dr rer nat 99. Wycliffe Hall Ox BA02. **d** 03 **p** 04. C The Hague *Eur* 03-06; Asst Chapl 06-07; V Bedwellty w New Tredegar *Mon* from 07. *The Rectory, Church Street, Aberbargoed, Bargoed CF81 9FF* Tel (01443) 829555
E-mail rosiedymond@yahoo.com

DYSON, Mrs Clare Louise. b 63. WMMTC 02. **d** 05 **p** 06. C Tupsley w Hampton Bishop *Heref* 05-08; P-in-c Kingstone w Clehonger, Eaton Bishop etc from 08. *The Rectory, Kingstone, Hereford HR2 9EY* Tel (01981) 250350

DYSON, Mrs Debra Anne. b 62. **d** 08 **p** 09. C Lich St Mich w St Mary and Wall from 08. *19 Mawgan Drive, Lichfield WS14 9SD* Tel (01543) 411694 E-mail debdyson@btinternet.com

DYSON, Frank. b 28. Oak Hill Th Coll 60. **d** 62 **p** 63. C Parr *Liv* 62-65; V Newchapel *Lich* 65-77; R Bunwell w Carleton Rode *Nor* 77-79; P-in-c Tibenham 78-80; R Bunwell w Carleton Rode and Tibenham 80-81; R Pakefield 81-93; rtd 93; Perm to Offic *Nor* from 93. *12 Viburnum Green, Lowestoft NR32 2SN* Tel (01502) 574898

DYSON, Peter Whiteley. b 51. Man Univ BA73 LLB75. Qu Coll Birm 77. **d** 81 **p** 82. C Swindon Ch Ch *Bris* 81-84; P-in-c Brislington St Luke 84-91; V Bourne *Guildf* 91-92; Perm to Offic 02-04; P-in-c Herriard w Winslade and Long Sutton etc 04-08; P-in-c Newnham w Nately Scures w Mapledurwell etc 04-08; R N Hants Downs from 08. *The Vicarage, Church Street, Upton Grey, Basingstoke RG25 2RB* Tel (01256) 861750
E-mail pwdyson@onetel.com

DYTHAM, Linda Alison. b 52. STETS 02. **d** 05 **p** 06. NSM Savernake *Sarum* 05-07; Chapl Fitzwarren Ho and Standon Lodge from 07. *Fitzwarren House, Kingsdown Road, Swindon SN3 4TD* Tel (01793) 836920 Mobile 07921-123422
E-mail ladytham@btinternet.com

E

EADE, John Christopher. b 45. Ch Coll Cam BA68 MA72. Linc Th Coll 68. **d** 70 **p** 71. C Portsea N End St Mark *Portsm* 70-73; C Henleaze *Bris* 73-77; V Slad *Glouc* 77-82; V N Bradley, Southwick and Heywood *Sarum* 82-91; R Fovant, Sutton Mandeville and Teffont Evias etc 91-08; C Nadder Valley 06-08; TR from 08. *The Rectory, Brookwood House, Fovant, Salisbury SP3 5JA* Tel (01722) 714826
E-mail john@cade47.freeserve.co.uk

EADES, David Julian John. b 74. Univ of Wales BA95 St Jo Coll Dur BA99. Cranmer Hall Dur. **d** 00 **p** 01. C Walbrook Epiphany *Derby* 00-04; Chapl Essex Univ 04-06. *Address temp unknown*
E-mail julian_eades@yahoo.co.uk

EADES, Preb Jonathan Peter. b 51. Dundee Univ MA74 Edin Univ BD77. Coates Hall Edin 74. **d** 77 **p** 78. Chapl St Paul's Cathl Dundee 77-88; Chapl Dundee Univ 79-88; TV Leek and Meerbrook *Lich* 88-96; RD Leek 93-96; TR Wolstanton 96-08; P-in-c Ashley and Mucklestone from 08; C Broughton w Croxton and Cotes Heath w Standon from 08; Preb Lich Cathl from 08. *The Rectory, Charnes Road, Ashley, Market Drayton TF9 4LQ* Tel (01630) 672210

EADY, David Robert. b 43. Salford Univ BSc. Glouc Th Course 82. **d** 85 **p** 86. NSM Highnam, Lassington, Rudford, Tibberton etc *Glouc* 85-95; NSM Stratton, N Cerney, Baunton and Bagendon 95-99; P-in-c Swindon and Elmstone Hardwicke w Uckington 99-08; P-in-c N Cheltenham from 08. *The Rectory, Rectory Lane, Swindon, Cheltenham GL51 9RD* Tel (01242) 239069 E-mail davideady@hotmail.com

EADY, Timothy William. b 57. Open Univ BA. Cranmer Hall Dur 82. **d** 85 **p** 86. C Boulton *Derby* 85-88; C Portchester *Portsm* 88-92; R Brighstone and Brooke w Mottistone 92-07; Relig Progr Adv Ocean Sound Radio 88-07; V Iver *Ox* from 07. *The Vicarage, Delaford Close, Iver SL0 9JX* Tel (01753) 653131
E-mail timothy_eady@yahoo.co.uk

EAGER, Ms Rosemary Anne McDowall. b 65. St Andr Univ MA87 Strathclyde Univ 88. Ridley Hall Cam 92. **d** 95 **p** 96. C Walthamstow St Mary w St Steph *Chelmsf* 95-98; C Walthamstow 98-01; TV Bushbury *Lich* 01-05; Perm to Offic 05-07. *37 Park Dale East, Wolverhampton WV1 4TD* Tel (01902) 710340 *or* 553945 E-mail revdrosie@yahoo.co.uk

EAGGER, Mrs Christine Mary. b 32. **d** 94 **p** 95. NSM Upper w Lower Gravenhurst *St Alb* 94-03; Perm to Offic *St Alb* 03-05 and *S'well from 05. 27 Lancaster Road, Coddington, Newark NG24 2TA* Tel (01636) 643885

EAGLE, Canon Julian Charles. b 32. Qu Coll Cam BA56 MA60. Westcott Ho Cam. **d** 58 **p** 59. C Billingham St Aid *Dur* 58-61; C Eastleigh *Win* 61-65; Ind Chapl 65-97; Hon Can Win Cathl 83-97; rtd 97; Perm to Offic *Win* from 97. *123 Cranleigh Road, Bournemouth BH6 5JY* Tel (01202) 429639

EAGLES, Peter Andrew. b 59. K Coll Lon BA82 AKC82 Ox Univ BA88. St Steph Ho Ox 86. **d** 89 **p** 90. C Ruislip St Martin *Lon* 89-92; CF from 92; Chapl Guards Chpl Lon 07-08; Asst Chapl Gen from 08. *c/o MOD Chaplains (Army)* Tel (01980) 615804 Fax 615800

EALES, Geoffrey Pellew. b 50. Trin Coll Bris 95. **d** 97 **p** 98. C Uphill *B & W* 97-00; C Weston super Mare w Milton 00-05; Chapl Weston Area Health Trust 00-05; V Milton *B & W* from 05; P-in-c Kewstoke w Wick St Lawrence from 08. *St Peter's Vicarage, Baytree Road, Weston-super-Mare BS22 8HG* Tel (01934) 624247 E-mail geoffeales@aol.com

EALES, Canon Howard Bernard. b 46. Sarum & Wells Th Coll 73. **d** 76 **p** 77. C Timperley *Ches* 76-78; C Stockport St Thos 78-82; V Wythenshawe Wm Temple Ch *Man* 82-95; V Cheadle Hulme All SS *Ches* from 95; RD Cheadle from 02; Hon Can Ches Cathl from 06. *All Saints' Vicarage, 27 Church Road, Cheadle Hulme, Cheadle SK8 7JL* Tel 0161-485 3455

EAMAN, Michael Leslie. b 47. Ridley Hall Cam 87. **d** 89 **p** 90. C Wharton *Ches* 89-93; V Buglawton 93-98; TV Congleton from 98. *St John's Vicarage, Buxton Road, Congleton CW12 2DT* Tel (01260) 273294 E-mail revmike@btopenworld.com

EAMES, Charles George. b 69. CITC 05. **d** 08 **p** 09. NSM Magheracross *Clogh* from 08. *79 The Limes, Drumlyon, Enniskillen BT74 5NB* Tel 07792-191565 (mobile)
E-mail charles@charleseames.orangehome.co.uk

EAMES, David John. b 80. Liv Hope Univ Coll BA01 MA04 St Jo Coll Dur MA08. Cranmer Hall Dur 06. **d** 08 **p** 09. C Brigg, Wrawby and Cadney cum Howsham *Linc* from 08. *5 Winston Way, Brigg DN20 8UA* Tel (01652) 652396

⛪**EAMES, The Most Revd and Rt Hon Lord (Robert Henry Alexander).** b 37. OM07. QUB LLB60 PhD63 Hon LLD89 TCD Hon LLD92 Cam Univ Hon DD94 Lanc Univ Hon LLD94 Aber Univ Hon DD97 Ex Univ Hon DD99 Hon FGCM88. TCD Div Sch Div Test 60. **d** 63 **p** 64 **c** 75. C Bangor St Comgall *D & D* 63-66; I Gilnahirk 66-74; Bp's Dom Chapl 70-72; I Dundela St Mark 74-75; Bp D & R 75-80; Bp D & D 80-86; Abp Arm 86-06; rtd 06. *3 Downshire Crescent, Hillsborough BT26 6DD* Tel (028) 9268 9913

EARDLEY, John. b 38. Ch Coll Cam BA61. Ridley Hall Cam 60. **d** 62 **p** 63. C Barnston *Ches* 62-65; C Wilmslow 65-67; V Hollingworth 67-75; V Leasowe 75-91; Chapl Leasowe Hosp 75-82; RD Wallasey 86-91; V Church Hulme and Chapl Cranage Hall Hosp 91-03; rtd 03; Perm to Offic *Ches* from 03. *7 Banks Road, Heswall, Wirral CH60 9JS* Tel 0151-342 9537

EARDLEY, Canon John Barry. b 35. MBE97. MEd87. AKC62. **d** 63 **p** 64. C Merton St Jas *S'wark* 63-66; C St Helier 66-69; C Bilton *Cov* 69-70; C Canley CD 70-74; P-in-c Church Lawford w Newnham Regis 74-80; P-in-c Leamington Hastings and Birdingbury 82-88; Dioc Educn Officer 82-00; Hon Can Cov Cathl 87-00; rtd 01; Perm to Offic *Cov* from 01. *8 Margetts Close, Kenilworth CV8 1EN* Tel 024-7630 2345 *or* 7667 3467
E-mail johnbarry.eardley@ntlworld.com

EARDLEY, Robert Bradford. b 44. St Alb Minl Tr Scheme 90. **d** 93 **p** 94. NSM Digswell and Panshanger *St Alb* 93-96; NSM Wheathampstead 97-98; NSM Tewin 98-05; P-in-c 98-04; rtd 05; Perm to Offic *St Alb* 05-07. *Bridge Cottage, Martin, Fordingbridge SP6 3LD* Tel (01725) 519423 Mobile 07941-345895 E-mail rob.eardley@virgin.net

EARDLEY, William Robert. b 56. Oak Hill Th Coll 94. **d** 96 **p** 97. C Whitfield *Derby* 96-99; TV Dronfield w Holmesfield from 99. *The Vicarage, Vicarage Close, Holmesfield, Dronfield S18 7WZ* Tel 0114-289 1425 E-mail william.eardley@dwhparish.org.uk

EAREY, Mark Robert. b 65. Loughb Univ BSc87 St Jo Coll Dur BA91. Cranmer Hall Dur 88. **d** 91 **p** 92. C Glen Parva and S Wigston *Leic* 91-94; C Luton Ch Ch *Roch* 94-97; Praxis Nat Educn Officer Sarum Coll 97-02; TR Morley *Wakef* 02-07; Tutor Qu Foundn Birm from 07. *The Queen's Foundation, Somerset Road, Edgbaston, Birmingham B15 2QH* Tel 0121-452 2667
E-mail m.earey@queens.ac.uk

EARIS, Stanley Derek. b 50. Univ Coll Dur BA71 BCL80. Ripon Hall Ox MA80. **d** 74 **p** 75. C Sutton St Jas and Wawne *York* 74-77; C Acomb St Steph 77-81; V Skelmanthorpe *Wakef* 81-87; R Market Deeping *Linc* 87-02; V N Walsham and Edingthorpe *Nor* from 02; C Bacton w Edingthorpe w Witton and Ridlington 04-07. *The Vicarage, 28A Yarmouth Road, North Walsham NR28 9AT* Tel (01692) 406380
E-mail derek.earis@ntlworld.com

EARL, Andrew John. b 61. Huddersfield Univ CertEd01 Ches Coll of HE BTh04. NOC. **d** 04 **p** 05. NSM Barnsley St Mary *Wakef* from 04; Chapl W Yorks Police from 04. *The Chines, 22 Faith Street, South Kirkby, Pontefract WF9 3AL* Tel (01977) 658925 Mobile 07919-048689 E-mail aj-sc-earl@hotmail.com

EARL, David Arthur. b 34. Hartley Victoria Coll 63 Coll of Resurr Mirfield. **d** 83 **p** 83. In Meth Ch 67-83; P-in-c Paddock *Wakef* 83-84; C Huddersfield St Pet and All SS 84-99; rtd 99; Perm to Offic *Wakef* from 99. *2 Clifton Court, Cleveland Road, Huddersfield HD1 4PU* Tel (01484) 535608

EARL, The Very Revd David Kaye Lee. b 28. TCD BA54. **d** 55 **p** 56. C Chapelizod *D & G* 55-58; I Rathkeale *L & K* 58-65; I Killarney 65-79; Prec Limerick Cathl 77-79; Dean Ferns *C & O* 79-94; I Ferns w Kilbride, Toombe, Kilcormack etc 79-94; rtd 94. *Random, Seafield, Tramore, Co Waterford, Republic of Ireland* Tel (00353) (51) 390503

EARL, Simon Robert. b 50. Culham Coll of Educn CertEd71 Open Univ BA82. Linc Th Coll 94. **d** 96 **p** 97. C Bexhill St Aug *Chich* 96-99; R Ninfield from 99; V Hooe from 99. *The Rectory, Church Lane, Ninfield, Battle TN33 9JW* Tel and fax (01424) 892308 E-mail srearl@btopenworld.com

EARL, Canon Stephen Geoffrey Franklyn. b 53. Lon Univ BA76 Goldsmiths' Coll Lon PGCE77. Ridley Hall Cam 91. **d** 93 **p** 94. C Sawston *Ely* 93-96; V Burwell w Reach from 96; RD Fordham and Quy from 02; Hon Can Ely Cathl from 07. *The Vicarage, High Street, Burwell, Cambridge CB25 0HB* Tel and fax (01638) 741262 E-mail searl@toucansurf.com

EARLE, Mrs Sylvia. b 51. St Aid Coll Dur BA72. Cranmer Hall Dur 05. **d** 07 **p** 08. C Whitkirk *Ripon* from 07. *12 Darnley Lane, Leeds LS15 9EX* Tel 0113-260 0382 E-mail sylvia.earle@tesco.net

EARLEY, Stephen John. b 48. Trin Coll Bris 91. **d** 93 **p** 94. C Stroud H Trin *Glouc* 93-98; C Leckhampton SS Phil and Jas w Cheltenham St Jas 98-02; V Nailsworth w Shortwood, Horsley etc from 02. *The Vicarage, Avening Road, Nailsworth, Stroud GL6 0BS* Tel (01453) 832181 E-mail stevearl@earleys.f9.co.uk

EARNEY, Preb Graham Howard. b 45. AKC67. **d** 68 **p** 69. C Auckland St Helen *Dur* 68-72; C Corsenside *Newc* 72-76; P-in-c 76-79; TV Willington 79-83; TR 83-87; Dioc Soc Resp Officer *B & W* 87-95; Dir Bp Mascall Cen *Heref* 95-02; Hon TV Ludlow, Ludford, Ashford Carbonell etc 95-02; Dioc Development Rep 96-02; Local Min Officer from 02; Preb Heref Cathl from 02; RD Condover 03-06. *The Rectory, Wistanstow, Craven Arms SY7 8DG* Tel (01588) 672067

EARNSHAW, Alan Mark. b 36. CQSW81. Lon Coll of Div LTh60. **d** 60 **p** 61. C Fazakerley Em *Liv* 60-65; V Ovenden *Wakef* 65-79; NSM Halifax St Jude 79-90; V Coley 90-99; rtd 99; Perm to Offic *Wakef* from 00. *67 Smithy Clough Lane, Ripponden, Sowerby Bridge HX6 4LG* Tel (01422) 822833

EARNSHAW, Robert Richard. b 42. NOC 78. **d** 81 **p** 82. NW Area Sec Bible Soc 78-85; NSM Liv All So Springwood 81-85; R Hinton Ampner w Bramdean and Kilmeston *Win* 85-87; Chapl HM YOI Huntercombe and Finnamore 87-92; Chapl HM YOI Finnamore Wood Camp 87-92; R Spaxton w Charlynch, Goathurst, Enmore etc *B & W* 92-98; R Old Cleeve, Leighland and Treborough 98-03; rtd 03; Perm to Offic *Cov* from 03. *33 Westhill Road, Coventry CV6 2AD* Tel (024) 7659 1256 E-mail bobjen@sagainternet.co.uk

EARP, John William. b 19. Jes Coll Cam BA42 MA45. Ridley Hall Cam 42. **d** 43 **p** 44. C Portman Square St Paul *Lon* 43-46; Tutor Ridley Hall Cam 46-48; Chapl 48-51; Vice-Prin 51-56; Chapl Eton Coll 56-62; V Hartley Wintney and Elvetham 62-77; RD Odiham 76-83; V Hartley Wintney, Elvetham, Winchfield etc 77-88; rtd 88; Perm to Offic *Nor* from 89. *3 The Driftway, Sheringham NR26 8LD* Tel (01263) 825487

EARWAKER, John Clifford. b 36. Keble Coll Ox BA59 MA63 Man Univ MEd71. Linc Th Coll 59. **d** 61 **p** 62. C Ecclesall *Sheff* 61-64; Succ St Mary's Cathl 64-65; Lic to Offic *Man* 65-69 and *Sheff* 69-93; Chapl and Lect Sheff Poly 81-92; Chapl and Lect Sheff Hallam Univ 92-93; rtd 93; Perm to Offic *Sheff* from 93. *89 Dransfield Road, Crosspool, Sheffield S10 5RP* Tel 0114-230 3487

EASEMAN, Robert Leslie. b 44. **d** 00 **p** 01. OLM Hunstanton St Mary w Ringstead Parva etc *Nor* 00-09; rtd 09; Perm to Offic *Nor* from 09. *5 Lighthouse Close, Hunstanton PE36 6EL* Tel and fax (01485) 535258 Mobile 07941-323218 E-mail robert.easeman@virgin.net

EASON, Canon Cyril Edward. b 21. Leeds Univ BA43 MA67. Coll of Resurr Mirfield 43. **d** 45 **p** 46. C Tonge Moor *Man* 45-51; C Blackpool H Cross *Blackb* 51-53; V Lever Bridge *Man* 53-65; Area Sec USPG *B & W* 65-86; Area Sec USPG *Ex* and *Truro* 75-86; Perm to Offic *Truro* 75-86; Hon Can Mufulira from 85; rtd 86; P-in-c Tilshead, Orcheston and Chitterne *Sarum* 86-92; Perm to Offic *Truro* from 92 and *Ripon* from 95. *11 Bishop's Court, Williamson Drive, Ripon HG4 1AY* Tel (01765) 608300 E-mail edward.eason1@virgin.net

EAST, Bryan Victor. b 46. Oak Hill Th Coll 91. **d** 93 **p** 94. C Waltham Cross *St Alb* 93-96; C Wotton St Mary *Glouc* 96-99; V

Humberston *Linc* from 99. *The Vicarage, 34 Tetney Road, Humberston, Grimsby DN36 4JF* Tel (01472) 813158 E-mail bryan.east@ntlworld.com

EAST, Mark Richard. b 57. Trin Coll Bris BA89. **d** 89 **p** 90. C Dalton-in-Furness *Carl* 89-93; TV Bucknall and Bagnall *Lich* 93-00; P-in-c Church Coniston *Carl* from 00; P-in-c Torver from 00. *St Andrew's Vicarage, Yewdale Road, Coniston LA21 8DX* Tel (01539) 441262 E-mail mark.east@lineone.net

EAST, Peter Alan. *See* OSTLI-EAST, Peter Alan

EAST, Richard Kenneth. b 47. Oak Hill Th Coll 86. **d** 88 **p** 89. C Necton w Holme Hale *Nor* 88-92; R Garsdon, Lea and Cleverton and Charlton *Bris* from 92; RD Malmesbury 93-99. *The Rectory, The Street, Lea, Malmesbury SN16 9PG* Tel (01666) 823861 E-mail lea.rectory@btinternet.com

EAST, Stuart Michael. b 50. Chich Th Coll 86. **d** 88 **p** 89. C Middlesbrough St Martin *York* 88-92; R Upper Ryedale 92-97; V Macclesfield St Paul *Ches* 97-01; C Maidstone St Luke *Cant* 01-03; R Peopleton and White Ladies Aston w Churchill etc *Worc* from 03. *The Rectory, Peopleton, Pershore WR10 2EE* Tel (01905) 840243 Mobile 07754-244929 E-mail stuart@the-rectory.fsnet.co.uk

EAST KERALA, Bishop of. *See* SAMUEL, The Most Revd Kunnumpurathu Joseph

EAST RIDING, Archdeacon of. *See* BUTTERFIELD, The Ven David John

EASTELL, Jane Rosamund. b 47. Sheff Univ BA68 Bris Univ BA99 Univ of Wales (Lamp) MA07 RIBA73. Trin Coll Bris 97. **d** 99 **p** 00. C Backwell w Chelvey and Brockley *B & W* 99-03; NSM 99-00; C Chew Stoke w Nempnett Thrubwell 03-08; C Chew Magna w Dundry and Norton Malreward 03-08; Dioc Adv in Prayer and Spirituality from 04; Hon C Taunton St Jo from 09. *Meadowside, Wild Oak Lane, Trull, Taunton TA3 7JT* Tel (01823) 321069 E-mail jane.eastell@btclick.com

EASTER, Canon Ann Rosemarie. SRN68 Univ of E Lon MBA94. Gilmore Ho 78. **dss** 80 **d** 87 **p** 94. Stratford St Jo and Ch Ch w Forest Gate St Jas *Chelmsf* 80-89; Par Dn 87-89; Chapl Asst Newham Gen Hosp 80-89; Perm to Offic *Chelmsf* from 89; Chief Exec Officer The Renewal Programme from 95; AD Newham 97-07; NSM W Ham from 08; Hon Can Chelmsf Cathl from 00; Chapl to The Queen from 07. *The Renewal Programme, 66B Sebert Road, London E7 0NJ* Tel (020) 8221 4420 Mobile 07889-799290 E-mail ann@renewalprogramme.org.uk

EASTERN ARCHDEACONRY, Archdeacon of the. *See* CURRAN, The Ven Patrick Martin Stanley

EASTGATE, Canon John. b 30. Kelham Th Coll 47. **d** 54 **p** 55. C Ealing St Pet Mt Park *Lon* 54-58; C-in-c Leic St Gabr CD 58-64; V Leic St Gabr 64-69; V Glen Parva and S Wigston 69-74; V Woodley St Jo the Ev *Ox* 74-83; V Hughenden 83-94; RD Wycombe 87-90; Hon Can Ch Ch 90-94; rtd 94; Perm to Offic *Sarum* from 05. *12A Mowlem Court, Rempstone Road, Swanage BH19 1DR* Tel (01929) 421558 E-mail john@eastgate1702.fsnet.co.uk

EASTOE, Canon Robin Howard Spenser. b 53. Lon Univ BD75 AKC75. Coll of Resurr Mirfield 77. **d** 78 **p** 79. C Gt Ilford St Mary *Chelmsf* 78-81; C Walthamstow St Sav 81-84; V Barkingside St Fran 84-92; V Leigh-on-Sea St Marg 92-08; RD Hadleigh 00-08; Chapl Southend Health Care NHS Trust 96-08; Hon Can Chelmsf Cathl 06-08; P-in-c Heavitree and St Mary Steps *Ex* from 08. *The Rectory, 10 Victoria Park Road, Exeter EX2 4NT* Tel (01392) 677150 E-mail theeastoes@btinternet.com

EASTON, Christopher Richard Alexander. b 60. TCD BA81. **d** 84 **p** 85. C Belfast St Donard *D & D* 84-89; I Inishmacsaint *Clogh* 89-95; I Magheralin w Dollingstown *D & D* 95-01; I Coleraine *Conn* 01-09; P-in-c Belfast Whiterock from 09. *1 Knockbracken Court, Coleraine BT52 1WS* Tel (028) 7034 3855 E-mail stpat@btinternet.com

EASTON, Donald Fyfe. b 48. St Edm Hall Ox BA69 MA85 Nottm Univ CertEd70 Univ Coll Lon MA76 PhD90 Clare Hall Cam MA85. Westcott Ho Cam 89. **d** 90 **p** 91. NSM Fulham St Andr Fulham Fields *Lon* 90-97; Lic Preacher from 97. *12 Weltje Road, London W6 9TG* Tel (020) 8741 0233

EASTON, John. b 34. St Cath Soc Ox BA59 MA63. Chich Th Coll 59. **d** 61 **p** 62. C Rugeley *Lich* 61-64; TR 72-87; C Shrewsbury All SS 64-66; Ind Chapl *Sheff* 66-72; V Bolsover *Derby* 87-99; RD Bolsover and Staveley 93-98; rtd 99; Perm to Offic *Derby* from 99. *71 Wythburn Road, Chesterfield S41 8DP* Tel (01246) 555610

EASTON, John. b 41. Nor City Coll 71. **d** 97. OLM New Catton Ch Ch *Nor* from 97. *14 Carteford Drive, Norwich NR3 4DW* Tel (01603) 412589 E-mail jejo@waitrose.com

EASTON, Robert Paul Stephen. b 62. Bris Univ BA84. St Steph Ho Ox BTh00. **d** 00 **p** 01. C Stoke Newington St Mary *Lon* 00-03; Chapl Brighton Coll from 03. *The Chaplaincy, Brighton College, Eastern Road, Brighton BN2 2AL* Tel (01273) 606524 E-mail roberteaston1@onetel.com

EASTON-CROUCH, Jonathan Brian. b 65. SEITE 96. **d** 99 **p** 00. C Mitcham SS Pet and Paul *S'wark* 99-02; Hon C S Wimbledon H Trin and St Pet 03-06; C New Addington 06-09; P-in-c

Merton St Jas from 09. *St James's Vicarage, Beaford Grove, London SW20 9LB* Tel 07939-121252 (mobile) E-mail jonathan.ec@virgin.net

EASTWOOD, Colin Foster. b 34. Leeds Univ BA56 MA66. Linc Th Coll 65. **d** 67 **p** 68. C Cottingham *York* 67-70; C Darlington St Cuth *Dur* 70-75; V Eighton Banks 75-81; V Sutton St Jas *Ches* 81-99; rtd 99; Perm to Offic *Glouc* from 00. *14 Ross Close, Chipping Sodbury, Bristol BS37 6RS* Tel (01454) 317594

EASTWOOD, David. b 54. Newc Univ LLB77. Ridley Hall Cam 06. **d** 08 **p** 09. C Westbrook St Phil *Liv* from 08. *36 Raleigh Close, Old Hall, Warrington WA5 9QS* Tel 07785-542594 (mobile) E-mail davideastwood86@googlemail.com

EASTWOOD, Harry. b 26. Man Univ BSc48. Ridley Hall Cam 81. **d** 82 **p** 83. NSM Barton Seagrave w Warkton *Pet* 82-00; Perm to Offic from 00. *22 Poplars Farm Road, Kettering NN15 5AF* Tel (01536) 513271

EASTWOOD, Canon Janet. b 54. Wycliffe Hall Ox 83. **dss** 86 **d** 87 **p** 94. Ainsdale *Liv* 86-90; Par Dn 87-90; TD Kirkby Lonsdale *Carl* 90-94; TV 94-95; Dioc Youth Officer 90-94; R Wavertree H Trin *Liv* from 95; P-in-c Wavertree St Thos 95-97; Hon Can Liv Cathl from 06; Chapl Blue Coat Sch Liv from 96. *Wavertree Rectory, Hunters Lane, Liverpool L15 8HL* Tel 0151-733 2172 E-mail janet@holytrinitywavertree.co.uk

EASTWOOD, Martin Russell. b 66. Edin Univ BMus88 LRSM02. Ripon Coll Cuddesdon BTh05. **d** 03 **p** 04. C Wymondham *Nor* 03-06; P-in-c Fulham St Andr Fulham Fields *Lon* 06-07; V from 07. *The Vicarage, 10 St Andrew's Road, London W14 9SX* Tel (020) 7385 5023 E-mail fathermartin@hotmail.co.uk

EATOCK, John. b 45. Lanc Univ MA82. Lich Th Coll 67. **d** 70 **p** 71. C Crumpsall St Mary *Man* 70-73; C Atherton 73-74; C Ribbleton *Blackb* 74-77; V Ingol 77-83; V Laneside 83-92; RD Accrington 90-92; Perm to Offic *Blackb* 92-08 and *Truro* from 08. *29 Wellington Road, Camborne TR14 7LH* Tel (01209) 714899 E-mail john.eatock@tiscali.co.uk

EATON, Barry Anthony. b 50. St Martin's Coll Lanc MA98. CBDTI 94. **d** 97 **p** 98. C W Burnley All SS *Blackb* 97-99; Dep Chapl HM Pris Leeds 99-00; Chapl HM Pris Buckley Hall 00-07; Chapl HM Pris Styal from 07. *HM Prison Styal, Styal Road, Styal, Wilmslow SK9 4HR* Tel (01625) 553000 Fax 553001

EATON, Benjamin. *See* EATON, Canon Oscar Benjamin

EATON, David Andrew. b 58. MBE06. Man Univ BSc79 ACA83 FCA. Trin Coll Bris BA89. **d** 89 **p** 90. C Barking St Marg w St Patr *Chelmsf* 89-92; C Billericay and Lt Burstead 92-95; P-in-c Vange 95-05; TV Sole Bay *St E* from 05; CF (TA) from 94. *The Vicarage, Parkgate, High Street, Wangford, Beccles NR34 8RL* Tel and fax (01502) 578827 E-mail davidaeaton@lineone.net

EATON, Canon David John. b 45. Nottm Univ LTh BTh74. St Jo Coll Nottm 70. **d** 74 **p** 75. C Headley All SS *Guildf* 74-77; Ind Chapl *Worc* 77-82; TV Halesowen 80-82; V Rowledge *Guildf* 82-89; V Leatherhead 89-01; R Leatherhead and Mickleham 01-09; RD Leatherhead 93-98; Hon Can Guildf Cathl 02-09; rtd 09. *Two Way House, Wheelers Lane, Brockham, Betchworth RH3 7LA* Tel (01737) 843915 E-mail rev_davideaton@hotmail.com

✠**EATON, The Rt Revd Derek Lionel.** b 41. MA78. Trin Coll Bris. **d** 71 **p** 71 **c** 90. C Barton Hill St Luke w Ch Ch *Bris* 71-72; Chapl Br Emb Tunisia 72-78; Provost All SS Cathl Cairo and Chapl Br Emb 78-83; Hon Can 85; Assoc P Papanui St Paul New Zealand 84; V Sumner-Redcliffs 85-90; Bp Nelson 90-06; rtd 06. *728 Cable Bay Road, Cable Bay, Nelson 7071, New Zealand* Tel (0064) (5) 451573

EATON (*née* CRAIG), **Mrs Julie Elizabeth.** b 57. Open Univ BA08 SEN81. Trin Coll Bris 87. **d** 89 **p** 94. Par Dn GT Ilford St Andr *Chelmsf* 89-92; NSM Billericay and Lt Burstead 92-95; C 95-96; TV 96-01; Chapl Thameside Community Healthcare NHS Trust 92-95; Perm to Offic *Chelmsf* 01-05; TV Sole Bay *St E* from 05. *The Vicarage, Parkgate, High Street, Wangford, Beccles NR34 8RL* Tel (01502) 578827 E-mail juliecraigeaton@tiscali.co.uk

EATON, Mrs Margaret Anne. b 44. Ab Dioc Tr Course 82. **dss** 84 **d** 86 **p** 94. NSM Ellon and Cruden Bay *Ab* 84-95; C Bridge of Don 95-00; Co-ord Scottish Episc Renewal Fellowship 00-04; C Ellon 01-03; C Elgin w Lossiemouth *Mor* 03-04 and 06-09; C Aberlour 06-09; C Dufftown 06-09. *Address temp unknown* E-mail maggie-e@hotmail.co.uk

EATON, Canon Oscar Benjamin (Ben). b 37. Puerto Rico Th Coll STB66. **d** 66 **p** 67. Ecuador 66-69; C Wandsworth St Anne S'wark 69-71; C Aldrington *Chich* 71-73; TV Littleham w Exmouth 74-79; R Alphington 79-84; Chapl Barcelona w Casteldefels *Eur* 84-88; Chapl Maisons-Laffitte 88-02; Can Malta Cathl from 96; rtd 02; P-in-c St Raphaël *Eur* from 02. *62 Hameau de Valescure, 83600 Fréjus, France* Tel (0033) (4) 94 40 48 61 *or* tel and fax (4) 94 95 45 78 E-mail revbeaton@aol.com

EATON, The Very Revd Peter David. b 58. K Coll Lon BA82 AKC82 Qu Coll Cam BA85 MA89 Magd Coll Ox MA90. Westcott Ho Cam 83. **d** 86 **p** 87. C Maidstone All SS and St Phil w Tovil *Cant* 86-89; Fells' Chapl Magd Coll Ox 89-91; Lic to

Offic *Ox* 89-06; Assoc R Salt Lake City St Paul USA 91-95; Hon Can Th Utah 91-01; R Lancaster St Jas Penn 95-01; Dean St Jo Cathl Denver from 02. *St John's Cathedral, 1350 Washington Street, Denver CO 80203-2008, USA* Tel (001) (303) 831 7115 *or* 295 0956 Fax 831 7119 E-mail deansadmin@sjc-den.org

EATON, Miss Phyllis Mary. b 42. SRD Qu Eliz Coll Lon BSc63 UNISA BA79. WMMTC 87. **d** 90 **p** 94. NSM Washwood Heath *Birm* 90-91; NSM Edgbaston SS Mary and Ambrose 91-95; Perm to Offic 95-05; NSM Oldbury, Langley and Londonderry from 05. *26 Blackthorne Road, Smethwick, Warley B67 6PZ* Tel 0121-552 4904 *or* 507 4085

EAVES, Alan Charles. b 37. Tyndale Hall Bris 62. **d** 65 **p** 66. C Southport SS Simon and Jude *Liv* 65-66; C Eccleston Ch Ch 66-70; V Earlestown 70-79; V Orpington Ch Ch *Roch* 79-02; rtd 02; Perm to Offic *Ely* from 03. *4 Chervil Close, Folksworth, Peterborough PE7 3SZ* Tel (01733) 241644 Mobile 07904-357476

EAVES, Brian Maxwell. b 40. Tyndale Hall Bris 66. **d** 69 **p** 70. C Wolverhampton St Jude *Lich* 69-72; C Fazeley 72-75; TV Ipsley *Worc* 75-79; Chapl Amsterdam *Eur* 79-86; Chapl Bordeaux w Riberac, Cahors, Duras etc 86-91; Monaco 91-93; TV Buckhurst Hill *Chelmsf* 93-96; R Culworth w Sulgrave and Thorpe Mandeville etc *Pet* 96-03; rtd 03. *17 Browning Road, Ledbury HR8 2GA* Tel (01531) 631582

EBBSFLEET, Suffragan Bishop of (Provincial Episcopal Visitor). *See* BURNHAM, The Rt Revd Andrew

EBELING, Mrs Barbara. b 44. Hull Univ BA67. St Alb Minl Tr Scheme 87. **d** 94 **p** 95. C Stevenage St Hugh and St Jo *St Alb* 94-99; R Riversmeet 99-08; rtd 08; Perm to Offic *St Alb* from 08 and *Chelmsf* from 09. *7 Wicklands Road, Hunsdon, Ware SG12 8PD* Tel (01279) 842086 E-mail chris.ebeling@sky.com

ECCLES, James Henry. b 30. DipEd. Wycliffe Hall Ox 86. **d** 87 **p** 88. NSM Llandudno *Ban* 87-91; rtd 91; NSM Llanrhos *St As* 94-00; Perm to Offic *Ban* from 97. *Lowlands, 7 St Seiriol's Road, Llandudno LL30 2YY* Tel (01492) 878524

ECCLES, Mrs Vivien Madeline. **d** 92 **p** 94. OLM Old Trafford St Bride *Man* from 92. *479 Barton Road, Stretford, Manchester M32 9TA* Tel 0161-748 9795

ECCLESTON, Mrs Frances Mary. b 61. Jes Coll Cam BA83 York St Jo Coll MA05 CQSW88. NOC 00. **d** 03 **p** 04. C Ranmoor *Sheff* 03-06; C Sheff St Leon Norwood 06-09; P-in-c Crosspool from 09. *The Vicarage, 1 Barnfield Road, Sheffield S10 5TD* Tel 0114-230 2531 E-mail frances.eccleston@sheffield.anglican.org

ECCLESTONE, Gary Edward. b 73. Ex Univ BA95 PGCE96. Cuddesdon Coll BTh99. **d** 99 **p** 00. C Salisbury St Martin and Laverstock *Sarum* 99-03; P-in-c Hanslope w Castlethorpe *Ox* from 03. *The Vicarage, Park Road, Hanslope, Milton Keynes MK19 7LT* Tel (01908) 337936

ECHOLS, Mrs Janet Lyn Roberts. b 58. Coll of Charleston (USA) BA. Trin Episc Sch for Min Penn MDiv. **d** 95 **p** 96. Asst R Mt Pleasant Ch Ch USA 95-02; P-in-c Stapleford *Ely* 02-07; Tutor Past Studies Ridley Hall Cam 05-07. *Address temp unknown* E-mail janetechols@yahoo.com

ECKERSLEY, Mrs Nancy Elizabeth. b 50. York Univ BA72 Leeds Univ CertEd73. NEOC 86. **d** 89 **p** 94. C Clifton *York* 89-00; Chapl York Distr Hosp 90-93; Lay Tr Officer *York* 93-00, V Heslington from 00. *The Vicarage, School Lane, Heslington, York YO10 5EE* Tel (01904) 410389

ECKERSLEY, Canon Richard Hugh. b 25. Trin Coll Cam BA48 MA50. Chich Th Coll 49. **d** 51 **p** 52. C Portsea St Jo Rudmore *Portsm* 51-57; C Portsea N End St Mark 57-62; V Paulsgrove 62-73; V Brighton St Nic *Chich* 73-84; Can Res Portsm Cathl 84-92; rtd 92; Perm to Offic *Portsm* from 92. *136 Kensington Road, Portsmouth PO2 0QY* Tel (023) 9265 3512

ECKHARD, Robert Leo Michael. b 60. Middx Poly BA87 Open Univ MA96 La Sainte Union Coll PGCE88. NTMTC BA05. **d** 05 **p** 06. C Ealing St Paul *Lon* 05-08; C Hounslow H Trin w St Paul from 08. *183 Bath Road, Hounslow TW3 3BU* Tel (020) 8570 9401 E-mail bob.eckhard@ukonline.co.uk

EDDISON, Robert John Buchanan. b 16. Trin Coll Cam BA38 MA42. Ridley Hall Cam 38. **d** 39 **p** 40. C Tunbridge Wells St Jo *Roch* 39-43; Travelling Sec Scripture Union 42-80; rtd 81; Perm to Offic *Chich* 81-08. *The College of St Barnabas, Blackberry Lane, Lingfield RH7 6NJ* Tel (01342) 872877

EDDY, Paul Anthony. b 67. St Jo Coll Nottm 07. **d** 09. C Grove *Ox* from 09. *2 Edington Place, Grove, Wantage OX12 0BX* Tel 07958-905716 (mobile) E-mail paul@pauleddy.org

EDE, The Ven Dennis. b 31. Nottm Univ BA55 Birm Univ MSocSc73. Ripon Hall Ox 55. **d** 57 **p** 58. C Sheldon *Birm* 57-60; C Castle Bromwich SS Mary and Marg 60-64; Chapl E Birm Hosp 60-76; C-in-c Hodge Hill CD *Birm* 64-70; V Hodge Hill 70-72; TR 72-76; Chapl Sandwell Distr Gen Hosp 76-90; V W Bromwich All SS *Lich* 76-90; P-in-c W Bromwich Ch Ch 76-79; RD W Bromwich 76-90; Preb Lich Cathl 83-90; Adn Stoke 90-97; rtd 97; Hon C Tilford *Guildf* 97-99; Hon C The Bourne and Tilford 99-02; Perm to Offic *Guildf* and *S'wark* from 03. *Tilford, 13 Park Close, Carshalton SM5 3EU* Tel (020) 8647 5891 E-mail dennisangelaede@aol.co.uk

EDEN, Grenville Mervyn. b 37. Bris Univ BA58 Lon Univ MPhil78. Ox Min Course 88. **d** 95 **p** 96. NSM Burnham w Dropmore, Hitcham and Taplow *Ox* 95-06; Perm to Offic from 06. *Langdale, Grays Park Road, Stoke Poges, Slough SL2 4JG* Tel (01753) 525962

EDEN, Henry. b 36. G&C Coll Cam BA59 MA64. Ox NSM Course. **d** 87 **p** 88. NSM Abingdon w Shippon *Ox* 87-88; Chapl Brentwood Sch Essex 88-95; TV Beaconsfield *Ox* 95-00; Perm to Offic *St E* from 01 and *Ely* from 03. *Ely Cottage, Denham, Bury St Edmunds IP29 5EQ* Tel (01284) 811884
E-mail heden@btinternet.com

EDEN, Mrs Lesley Patricia. b 54. Liv Univ MTh99. NOC 93. **d** 96 **p** 97. C Wallasey St Hilary *Ches* 96-98; C Oxton 98-01; V Whitegate w Lt Budworth from 01; Min Review Officer 01-07. *The Vicarage, Cinder Hill, Whitegate, Northwich CW8 2BH* Tel and fax (01606) 882151 E-mail lesley_eden88@hotmail.com

EDEN, Leslie Thomas Ernest. b 19. ACII55. S'wark Ord Course. **d** 69 **p** 70. NSM Kidbrooke St Jas *S'wark* 69-94; rtd 94; Perm to Offic *S'wark* from 94. *47 Begbie Road, London SE3 8DA* Tel (020) 8856 3088

EDEN, Mervyn. *See* EDEN, Grenville Mervyn

EDEN, Michael William. b 57. Nottm Univ BTh86. Linc Th Coll 83. **d** 86 **p** 87. C Daventry *Pet* 86-89; TV Northampton Em 89-92; V Corby St Columba 92-03; P-in-c Stowmarket *St E* from 03. *The Vicarage, 7 Lockington Road, Stowmarket IP14 1BQ* Tel (01449) 678623 *or* 774652 Fax 774652
E-mail theedens@talk21.com

EDGAR, David. b 59. Newc Univ BA81. Linc Th Coll BTh86. **d** 86 **p** 87. C Wednesbury St Paul Wood Green *Lich* 86-91; V Winterton Gp *Linc* 91-00; C Linc St Swithin 00-01; P-in-c from 01; P-in-c Linc All SS from 06; Chapl N Lincs Coll from 00. *1 St Giles Avenue, Lincoln LN2 4PE* Tel (01522) 528199
E-mail david.edgar1@tesco.net

EDGCUMBE, Irena Christine. *See* CZERNIAWSKA EDGCUMBE, Mrs Irena Christine

EDGE, Canon John Francis. b 32. Ex Coll Ox BA54 MA56. St Steph Ho Ox 54. **d** 58 **p** 59. C Oswestry H Trin *Lich* 58-62; V 64-79; Tutor Lich Th Coll 62-64; Malaysia 79-87; Hon Can Kuching from 88; TV Wolverhampton *Lich* 88-91; Chapl R Hosp Wolv 88-91; Subwarden St Deiniol's Lib Hawarden 91-93; C Briercliffe *Blackb* 93-96; C W Felton *Lich* 96-97; Res Min 97-01; rtd 97; Perm to Offic *Blackb* from 01. *24 Talbot Street, Briercliffe, Burnley BB10 2HW* Tel (01282) 429287

EDGE, John Nicholson. b 53. **d** 99 **p** 00. OLM Flixton St Jo *Man* from 99. *5 Devon Road, Flixton, Manchester M41 6PN* Tel 0161-748 4736

EDGE, Michael MacLeod. b 45. St Andr Univ BSc68 Qu Coll Cam BA70 MA74. Westcott Ho Cam 68. **d** 72 **p** 73. C Allerton *Liv* 72-76; R Bretherton *Blackb* 76-82; P-in-c Kilpeck *Heref* 82-84; P-in-c St Devereux w Wormbridge 82-84; TR Ewyas Harold w Dulas, Kenderchurch etc 82-93; RD Abbeydore 84-90; V Enfield St Andr *Lon* from 93. *Enfield Vicarage, Silver Street, Enfield EN1 3EG* Tel (020) 8363 8676

EDGE, Philip John. b 54. Ripon Coll Cuddesdon 77. **d** 80 **p** 81. C N Harrow St Alb *Lon* 80-83; C St Giles Cripplegate w St Bart Moor Lane etc 83-86; P-in-c Belmont 86-88; V 88-92; V Ellesmere and Welsh Frankton *Lich* 92-97; V Ellesmere from 97. *The Vicarage, Church Hill, Ellesmere SY12 0HB* Tel (01691) 622571

EDGE, Ms Renate Erika. b 50. Cranmer Hall Dur 86. **d** 88. Par Dn Leic Spiritual Centre 88-89; Asst Chapl for the Deaf 88-89; Par Dn Leic H Apostles 89-94. *10F Millhill Lane, Musselburgh EH21 7RD* Tel 0131-665 9651
E-mail renata.edge@hotmail.co.uk

EDGE, Timothy Peter. b 55. Brighton Poly BSc80 CEng85 MIET85 FRAS80. Westcott Ho Cam 85. **d** 88 **p** 89. C Norton *Ches* 88-91; C Bedworth *Cov* 91-96; TV Witney *Ox* 96-02; Asst Chapl HM Pris Bullingdon 02-04; Chapl 04-09; NSM Cogges and S Leigh *Ox* from 03. *27 Burford Road, Witney OX28 6DP* Tel (01993) 773438 E-mail tim.edge@talk21.com

EDGELL, Hugh Anthony Richard. b 31. ARHistS84. AKC57. **d** 58 **p** 59. C N Lynn w St Marg and St Nic *Nor* 58-64; R S Walsham 64-74; V Upton w Fishley 64-74; R Hingham 74-81; R Hingham w Woodrising w Scoulton 81-85; V Horning 85-89; P-in-c Beeston St Laurence w Ashmanhaugh 85-89; R Horning w Beeston St Laurence and Ashmanhaugh 89-95; Prior St Benet's Abbey Horning 87-95; rtd 95; Perm to Offic *Nor* from 95. *Brambles, Brimbelow Road, Hoveton, Norwich NR12 8UJ* Tel (01604) 782206

EDGERTON, Ms Hilary Ann. b 66. R Holloway & Bedf New Coll Lon BSc88. Wycliffe Hall Ox BTh93. **d** 93 **p** 94. Par Dn S Cave and Ellerker w Broomfleet *York* 93-94; C 94-97; TV Howden 97-00; V Hayfield and Chinley w Buxworth *Derby* from 00. *8 Bluebell Close, Hayfield, High Peak SK22 2PG* Tel (01663) 743350 E-mail hilaryedgerton@freeola.net

EDIE, Jennifer Mary. b 40. Edin Univ MA62 Hong Kong Univ PGCE77. **d** 03 **p** 04. NSM Eyemouth *Edin* 03-09; P-in-c 06-09; rtd 09. *Burnbank House, Foulden, Berwick-upon-Tweed TD15 1UH* Tel (01289) 386338 E-mail rev.jennifer@gmail.com

EDINBOROUGH, David. b 36. Nottm Univ BA58 MEd74. EMMTC 79. **d** 82 **p** 83. NSM Bramcote *S'well* 82-01; P-in-c 94-01; Dioc Officer for NSMs 89-94; rtd 01; Perm to Offic *S'well* 01-02; P-in-c Radford St Pet from 02. *105A Derby Road, Beeston, Nottingham NG9 3GZ* Tel 0115-925 1066
E-mail david.edinborough@btopenworld.com

EDINBURGH, Bishop of. *See* SMITH, The Rt Revd Brian Arthur

EDINBURGH, Dean of. *See* PEARSON, The Very Revd Kevin

EDINBURGH, Provost of. *See* FORBES, The Very Revd Graham John Thompson

EDIS, John Oram. b 26. Open Univ BA81 ACIS50 ACP52 FCollP89. Ox NSM Course 85. **d** 88 **p** 89. Hon Warden and Chapl E Ivor Hughes Educn Foundn from 88; NSM Gt Chesham *Ox* 88-96; Perm to Offic *Lon* 96-03 and *Ox* from 96. *2 Meades Lane, Chesham HP5 1ND* Tel (01494) 774242

EDMEADS, Andrew. b 53. Linc Th Coll 84. **d** 86 **p** 87. C Sholing *Win* 86-89; R Knights Enham 89-97; rtd 97; Perm to Offic *Win* 97-99; Chapl St Mich Hospice Basingstoke from 00. *10 Altona Gardens, Andover SP10 4LG* Tel (01264) 391464

EDMONDS (née HARRIS), Mrs Catherine Elizabeth. b 52. Leic Coll of Educn CertEd73 ACP79. S Dios Minl Tr Scheme 91. **d** 95 **p** 96. NSM Basing *Win* 95-99; C Yeovil H Trin w Barwick B & W 99-01; Chapl Coll of SS Mark and Jo Plymouth *Ex* 01-06; TV Ottery St Mary, Alfington, W Hill, Tipton etc from 06; C Broadhembury, Payhembury and Plymtree from 09; Dioc Youth Adv from 06. *The Rectory, Station Road, Feniton, Honiton EX14 3DF* Tel (01404) 851401
E-mail pauledmonds@lineone.net

EDMONDS, Clive Alway. b 42. ACII. S'wark Ord Course 78. **d** 81 **p** 82. C Horsell *Guildf* 81-85; R Bisley and W End 85-92; RD Surrey Heath 90-92; R Haslemere 92-00; Chapl Wispers Sch Haslemere 92-00; P-in-c Westbury-on-Severn w Flaxley and Blaisdon *Glouc* 00-02; V Westbury-on-Severn w Flaxley, Blaisdon etc 03-06; rtd 06; Perm to Offic *Heref* from 07. *3 Church Road, Longhope GL17 0LH* Tel (01452) 831545
E-mail alwayedmonds@hotmail.com

EDMONDS, Michelle Kay. b 70. S Bank Univ BSc98. Ripon Coll Cuddesdon BTh08. **d** 06 **p** 07. C Croydon St Matt *S'wark* 06-09; TV Warlingham w Chelsham and Farleigh from 09. *The Vicarage, 2 Chelsham Road, Warlingham CR6 9EQ* Tel (01883) 623011 Mobile 07799-713957
E-mail revmichelle@btinternet.com

EDMONDS (née MAGUIRE), Mrs Sarah Alison. b 65. Univ Coll Lon BSc87 Southn Univ MSc93. STETS 95. **d** 98 **p** 99. C Warwick St Paul *Cov* 98-02; P-in-c Hampton Lucy w Charlecote and Loxley 02-06. *39 Hammond Green, Wellesbourne, Warwick CV35 9EY* E-mail sedmonds@informs.co.uk

EDMONDS, Stephen Harry James. b 77. SS Hild & Bede Coll Dur BA99 Leeds Univ MA08. Coll of Resurr Mirfield 06. **d** 08 **p** 09. C Hendon *Dur* from 08. *2 Bennett Court, Sunderland SR2 9QZ* Tel 07882-443025 (mobile)
E-mail sedmonds@mirfield.org.uk

EDMONDS, Tony Ernest. b 50. BSc MA MSc PhD. EMMTC. **d** 05 **p** 06. NSM Barrow upon Soar w Walton le Wolds *Leic* from 05. *Mulberry Lodge, 8 Melton Road, Burton-on-the-Wolds, Loughborough LE12 5AG* Tel (01509) 881369
E-mail t.e.edmonds@btconnect.com

EDMONDS-SEAL, John. b 37. FFARCS63 Lon Univ MB, BS58. Ox NSM Course. **d** 90 **p** 91. NSM Ox St Aldate w St Matt 90-94; NSM Wheatley from 95. *Otway, Woodperry Road, Oxford OX3 9UY* Tel (01865) 351582
E-mail edmondsseal@doctors.org.uk

✠**EDMONDSON, The Rt Revd Christopher Paul.** b 50. St Jo Coll Dur BA71 MA81. Cranmer Hall Dur 71. **d** 73 **p** 74. **c** 08. C Kirkheaton *Wakef* 73-79; V Ovenden 79-86; Bp's Adv on Evang 81-86; Dioc Officer for Evang *Carl* 86-92; P-in-c Bampton w Mardale 86-92; V Shipley St Pet *Brad* 92-02; Warden Lee Abbey 02-08; Suff Bp Bolton *Man* from 08. *Bishop's Lodge, Walkden Road, Worsley, Manchester M28 2WH* Tel 0161-790 8289 Fax 703 9157
E-mail bishopchrisedmondson@manchester.anglican.org

EDMONDSON, The Very Revd John James William. b 55. St Jo Coll Dur BA83 MA91 PhD04. Cranmer Hall Dur 80. **d** 83 **p** 84. C Gee Cross *Ches* 83-86; C Camberley St Paul *Guildf* 86-88; TV 88-90; Chapl Elmhurst Ballet Sch 86-90; V Foxton w Gumley and Laughton and Lubenham *Leic* 90-94; R Bexhill St Mark *Chich* 94-05; V Battle from 05; Dean Battle from 05; P-in-c Sedlescombe w Whatlington from 05; Dioc Voc Adv 98-02; Asst Dir of Ords from 02. *The Deanery, Caldbec Hill, Battle TN33 0JY* Tel and fax (01424) 772693
E-mail dean@johnedmondson.org.uk

EDMONTON, Area Bishop of. *See* WHEATLEY, The Rt Revd Peter William

EDMUND, Brother. *See* BLACKIE, Richard Footner

EDMUNDS, Andrew Charles. b 57. Whitelands Coll Lon BEd80 Croydon Coll CQSW83. Oak Hill NSM Course 87. **d** 89 **p** 90. NSM Hawkwell *Chelmsf* 89-95; C Torquay St Matthias,

St Mark and H Trin *Ex* 95-97; V Ripley *Derby* 97-09; RD
Heanor 06-09. *Address temp unknown*
E-mail acedmunds@dsl.pipex.com

EDMUNDS, Eric John. b 39. Univ of Wales TCert60. WMMTC
87. **d** 90 **p** 91. NSM Brewood *Lich* 90-93; Chapl St Pet Colleg Sch
Wolv 91-93; R Llanerch Aeron w Ciliau Aeron and Dihewyd etc
St D 93-97; R Aberporth w Tremain w Blaenporth and Betws
Ifan 97-02; Bp's Adv on Tourism 95-02; Asst Dioc Dir of Educn
95-97 and 97-02; rtd 02. *15 Cwrt y Gloch, Peniel, Carmarthen
SA32 7HW* Tel (01267) 221426

EDSON, John Benedict (Ben). b 73. Wolv Univ BSc95 York St Jo
Coll MA02. NOC 06. **d** 08 **p** 09. C Brunswick *Man* from 08.
12 Roseleigh Avenue, Manchester M19 2NP Tel 07951-170511
(mobile) E-mail ben@sanctus1.co.uk

EDSON, The Ven Michael. b 42. Birm Univ BSc64 Leeds Univ
BA71. Coll of Resurr Mirfield 69. **d** 72 **p** 73. C Barnstaple St Pet
w H Trin *Ex* 72-77; TV Barnstaple and Goodleigh 77-79; TV
Barnstaple, Goodleigh and Landkey 79-82; V Roxbourne
St Andr *Lon* 82-89; AD Harrow 85-89; P-in-c S Harrow St Paul
86-89; Warden Lee Abbey 89-94; Lic to Offic *Ex* 89-94; Adn Leic
94-02; Bp's Insp of Par Registers and Records 94-02; TR
Bideford, Northam, Westward Ho!, Appledore etc *Ex* from 02.
The Rectory, Abbotsham Road, Bideford EX39 3AB Tel (01237)
470228 *or* 474078 E-mail st.marys@easynet.co.uk

EDWARD, Brother. *See* LEES-SMITH, Christopher John

EDWARDS, Aled. b 55. OBE06. Univ of Wales (Lamp) BA77.
Trin Coll Bris 77. **d** 79 **p** 80. C Glanogwen *Ban* 79-82; V
Llandinorwig w Penisa'r-waen 82-85; R Botwnnog 85-93; V
Cardiff Dewi Sant *Llan* 93-99; Nat Assembly Liaison Officer
from 99; Hon Chapl Llan Cathl from 99. *20 Hilltop Avenue,
Cilfynydd, Pontypridd CF37 4HZ* Tel (01443) 407310
E-mail aled@globalnet.co.uk

EDWARDS, Allen John. b 50. Univ of Wales (Cardiff) BSc72 Imp
Coll Lon PhD81 CEng81 EurIng88 FIMechE93 FINucE95
MCMI95. SAOMC 00. **d** 02 **p** 03. NSM Didcot All SS *Ox* from
02. *23 North Bush Furlong, Didcot OX11 9DY* Tel (01235)
519090

EDWARDS, Andrew Colin. b 55. ACA81 Pemb Coll Cam BA77
MA80. St Mich Coll Llan BD89. **d** 89 **p** 90. C Newport St Paul
Mon 89-91; C Newport St Woolos 91-93; Min Can St Woolos
Cathl 91-93; P-in-c Ynysddu 93-95; TV Mynyddislwyn 95-97; rtd
97. *197 Heritage Park, St Mellons, Cardiff CF3 0DU* Tel (029)
2079 2715

EDWARDS, Canon Andrew David. b 42. Tyndale Hall Bris 67.
d 70 **p** 71. C Blackpool Ch Ch *Blackb* 70-73; C W Teignmouth
Ex 73-76; P-in-c Ilfracombe SS Phil and Jas 76-85; C-in-c Lundy
Is 79-89; V Ilfracombe SS Phil and Jas w W Down 85-89; TV
Canford Magna *Sarum* 89-98; R Moresby *Carl* 98-07; RD
Calder 02-07; Hon Can Carl Cathl 05-07; rtd 07; Perm to Offic
Carl from 07. *Kiln Brow Cottage, High Ireby, Wigton CA7 1HF*
Tel (01697) 371618 E-mail a.edwards432@btinternet.com

EDWARDS, Andrew James. b 54. York Univ BA76. Wycliffe Hall
Ox 77. **d** 80 **p** 81. C Beckenham St Jo *Roch* 80-83; C Luton Ch
Ch 83-87; V Skelmersdale Ch at Cen *Liv* 87-95; V Netherton
95-02; V Southport St Phil and St Paul from 02; C Southport All
SS from 03. *37 Lethbridge Road, Southport PR8 6JA* Tel (01704)
531615 E-mail andrew@ajedwards.freeserve.co.uk

EDWARDS, Andrew Jonathan Hugo. b 56. Ex Univ BA78. Sarum
& Wells Th Coll BTh93. **d** 93 **p** 94. C Honiton, Gittisham,
Combe Raleigh, Monkton etc *Ex* 93-97; P-in-c Queen Thorne
Sarum 97-01; Chapl Clayesmore Sch Blandford from 01.
*Hambledon, Clayesmore School, Iwerne Minster, Blandford
Forum DT11 8LJ* Tel (01747) 813064
E-mail joe.edwards@btinternet.com

EDWARDS, Anita Carolyn. *See* COLPUS, Mrs Anita Carolyn

EDWARDS, Mrs Anne Joan. b 67. Lanc Univ BA89. NOC 97.
d 00 **p** 01. C Elton All SS *Man* 00-04; Chapl Bolton Hosps NHS
Trust 02-04; Chapl Team Ldr Wrightington Wigan and Leigh
NHS Trust from 04. *St Paul's Vicarage, 10 Old Vicarage Gardens,
Worsley, Manchester M28 3JR* Tel 0161-790 2483
E-mail anna.edwards@dsl.pipex.com

EDWARDS, Canon Arthur John. b 42. Qu Mary Coll Lon BA64
MPhil66. St Mich Coll Llan 66. **d** 68 **p** 69. C Newport St Woolos
Mon 68-71; V Llantarnam 71-74; Chapl Bp of Llan High Sch
74-78; V Griffithstown *Mon* 78-86; Dioc Dir RE 86-91; TR
Cwmbran 86-95; Hon Can St Woolos Cathl 88-91; Can from 91;
V Caerleon 95-02; V Caerleon w Llanhennock from 02; AD
Newport from 98. *The Vicarage, Caerleon, Newport NP18 1AZ*
Tel (01633) 420248

EDWARDS, Carl Flynn. b 63. Cranmer Hall Dur 03. **d** 05 **p** 06. C
Scartho *Linc* 05-09; P-in-c Fairfield *Derby* from 09; C Buxton w
Burbage and King Sterndale from 09. *The Vicarage, North Road,
Fairfield, Buxton SK17 7EA* Tel (01298) 23629
E-mail carl.mara@tiscali.co.uk

EDWARDS, Miss Carol Rosemary. b 46. Trin Coll Bris 74. dss 81
d 87 **p** 94. Hengrove *Bris* 81-82; Filton 82-85; Brislington
St Chris 85-99; Dn-in-c 87-94; P-in-c 94-99; P-in-c Brislington
St Chris and St Cuth 99-00; Hon Can Bris Cathl 93-00; P-in-c

California *Ox* from 00. *California Vicarage, Vicarage Close,
Finchampstead, Wokingham RG11 4JW* Tel 0118-973 0030

EDWARDS, Charles Grayson. b 37. Macalester Coll (USA)
BSc59. Ripon Hall Ox 64. **d** 66 **p** 67. C Bletchley *Ox* 66-68; C
Ware St Mary *St Alb* 68-73; TV Basingstoke *Win* 73-80; P-in-c
Sandford w Upton Hellions *Ex* 80-82; R 82-94; Perm to Offic
from 95; rtd 97. *The Peak, Higher Road, Crediton EX17 2EU* Tel
(01363) 772530

EDWARDS, Christopher. b 61. ACT BTh92. Moore Th Coll
Sydney 90. **d** 94 **p** 94. C Engandine Australia 94-95; C Adelaide
H Trin 95-07; Chapl Tervuren *Eur* from 07. *Parklaan 49, 3080
Tervuren, Belgium* Tel (0032) (2) 767 3435 Fax 688 0989

EDWARDS, Christopher Alban. b 29. Hertf Coll Ox. Th Ext
Educn Coll. **d** 89 **p** 92. C Pietersburg Ch Ch S Africa 89; C
Montagu 90-96; C Harare Cathl Zimbabwe 96-01; Perm to Offic
Ripon 01 and *York* from 01. *1 Hastings House, Holyrood Lane,
Ledsham, South Milford, Leeds LS25 5LL* Tel (01977) 682117
Mobile 07780-543114 E-mail chrisalban@btopenworld.com

EDWARDS, David Arthur. b 26. Wadh Coll Ox BA50 MA51.
Wycliffe Hall Ox 50. **d** 52 **p** 53. C Didsbury St Jas and Em *Man*
52-55; Liv Sec SCM 55-58; Chapl Liv Univ 55-58; R Burnage
St Nic *Man* 58-65; V Yardley St Edburgha *Birm* 65-73; Org Sec
CECS *Blackb, Carl* and *Man* 73-78; R Man Resurr 78-81; V
Lorton and Loweswater w Buttermere *Carl* 81-87; USPG 87-92;
Malaysia 87-92; rtd 92; Perm to Offic *Carl* from 00. *Wood Close,
11 Springs Road, Keswick CA12 4AQ* Tel (01768) 780274

EDWARDS, David John. b 60. Loughb Univ BA81 Homerton
Coll Cam PGCE82 Kent Univ MA95. CA Tr Coll 86 EAMTC
94. **d** 95 **p** 96. C High Ongar w Norton Mandeville *Chelmsf*
95-98; Prin Taylor Coll Saint John Canada 98-05; P-in-c Saint
John St Jas 98-00; R Saint John St Mark (Stone Ch) from 00.
31 Carlile Crescent, Saint John NB E2J 5C3, Canada Tel (001)
(506) 634 1474 E-mail david.edwards@anglican.nb.ca

EDWARDS, The Very Revd David Lawrence. b 29. OBE95. Magd
Coll Ox BA52 MA56 Lambeth DD90. Westcott Ho Cam 53.
d 54 **p** 55. Fell All So Coll Ox 52-59; Tutor Westcott Ho Cam
54-55; SCM Sec 55-58; C Hampstead St Jo *Lon* 55-58; C
St Martin-in-the-Fields 58-66; Ed SCM Press 59-66; Gen Sec
SCM 65-66; Dean K Coll Cam 66-70; Six Preacher Cant Cathl
69-76; Can Westmr Abbey 70-78; R Westmr St Marg 70-78;
Chapl to Speaker of Ho of Commons 72-78; Sub Dean Westmr
74-78; Chmn Chr Aid 71-78; Dean Nor 78-83; Provost S'wark
83-94; rtd 94; Perm to Offic *Win* from 95; Hon Chapl Win Cathl
from 95. *Flat 18, Manormead, Tilford Road, Hindhead
GU26 6RA*

EDWARDS, Canon Diana Clare. b 56. Nottm Univ BTh86
SRN77 RSCN81. Linc Th Coll 83. dss 86 **d** 87 **p** 94. S
Wimbledon H Trin and St Pet *S'wark* 86-90; Par Dn 87-90; Par
Dn Lingfield and Crowhurst 90-94; C 94-95; Chapl St Piers
Hosp Sch Lingfield 90-95; R Bletchingley *S'wark* 95-04; RD
Godstone 98-04; Hon Can S'wark Cathl 01-04; Dean of
Women's Min 03-04; Can Res Cant Cathl from 04. *22 The
Precincts, Canterbury CT1 2EP* Tel (01227) 865227
E-mail canonclare@canterbury-cathedral.org

EDWARDS, Erwyd. *See* EDWARDS, The Very Revd Thomas
Erwyd Pryse

EDWARDS (née DALLISON), Canon Frances Mary. b 39.
RSCN61 SRN64. Cranmer Hall Dur IDC71. **d** 92 **p** 94. NSM
Skerton St Chad *Blackb* 92-97; Asst Chapl R Albert Hosp Lanc
92-94; Chapl 94-96; Regional Co-ord (NW) Ch Action on
Disability 96-04; Hon Can Blackb Cathl 00-04; rtd 04; Perm to
Offic *Blackb* from 04. *9 Rochester Avenue, Morecambe LA4 4RH*
Tel (01524) 421224 Fax 413661
E-mail frances@floray.fsnet.co.uk

EDWARDS, Canon Geraint Wyn. b 47. Univ of Wales (Ban)
BTh93. St D Coll Lamp. **d** 71 **p** 72. C Llandudno *Ban* 71-73; C
Ban St Mary 73-74; V Penisarwaen and Llanddeiniolen 74-77; V
Llandinorwig w Penisarwaen and Llanddeiniolen 77-78; R
Llanfechell w Bodewryd w Rhosbeirio etc from 78; RD Twrcelyn
94-01; AD from 01; Hon Can Ban Cathl 97-99; Prec from 99.
*The Rectory, Penbodeistedd Estate, Llanfechell, Amlwch
LL68 0RE* Tel (01407) 710356
E-mail geraintedwards@fsmail.net

EDWARDS, Canon Gerald Lalande. b 30. Bris Univ MEd72.
Glouc Th Course 75. **d** 76 **p** 76. NSM Pittville All SS *Glouc*
76-79; NSM Cheltenham St Mich 79-96; Hon Can Glouc Cathl
91-96; rtd 96; Perm to Offic *Glouc* 96-97. *26 Monica Drive,
Cheltenham GL50 4NQ* Tel (01242) 516863

EDWARDS, Canon Graham Arthur. b 32. St D Coll Lamp 56.
d 61 **p** 62. C Betws w Ammanford *St D* 61-65; V Castlemartin
and Warren 65-69; R Castlemartin w Warren and Angle etc
69-77; V St Clears w Llangynin and Llanddowror 77-83; CF
(TAVR) 78-96; V St Clears w Llangynin and Llanddowror etc
St D 83-94; Can St D Cathl 90 94; rtd 94. *Caswell, Station Road,
St Clears, Carmarthen SA33 4BX* Tel (01994) 230342

EDWARDS, Graham Charles. b 40. Qu Coll Birm 80. **d** 82 **p** 83. C
Baswich *Lich* 82-86; C Tamworth 86-88; R Hertford St Andr
St Alb 88-05; RD Hertford and Ware 96-99; rtd 05; Perm to Offic

Lich from 06. *2 The Old Forge, Main Road, Great Haywood, Stafford ST18 0RZ* Tel (01889) 882868

EDWARDS, Guy. See EDWARDS, Jonathan Guy

EDWARDS, Harold James. b 50. Lon Univ CertEd72. Ridley Hall Cam 84 Qu Coll Birm 78. **d** 81 **p** 82. NSM The Quinton *Birm* 81-84; C Highters Heath 84-85; V Llanwddyn and Llanfihangel-yng-Nghwynfa etc *St As* 85-88; V Ford *Heref* 88-97; V Alberbury w Cardeston 88-97; Chapl Team Ldr Severn Hospice from 96. *Severn Hospice, Bicton Heath, Shrewsbury SY3 8HS* Tel (01743) 236565 Mobile 07713-639447
E-mail harrye@severnhospice.org.uk

EDWARDS, Harry Steadman. b 37. St Aid Birkenhead 64. **d** 66 **p** 67. Hon C Handsworth St Jas *Birm* 66-83; Hon C Curdworth w Castle Vale 83-85; P-in-c Small Heath St Greg 85-88; V High Crompton *Man* 88-98; rtd 98; Perm to Offic *Man* from 99. *42 Manor Road, Shaw, Oldham OL2 7JJ* Tel (01706) 672820

EDWARDS, Helen. See HINGLEY, Mrs Helen

EDWARDS (née BENNETT), Helen Anne. b 69. Coll of Ripon & York St Jo BEd91 Bris Univ BA01. Trin Coll Bris 99. **d** 01 **p** 02. C Beverley Minster *York* 01-05; P-in-c Liv Ch Ch Norris Green 05-09; V from 09. *9 Kingsland Crescent, Liverpool L11 7AN* Tel 0151-474 1444 E-mail helenedwards@ymail.com

EDWARDS, Helen Glynne. See WEBB, Mrs Helen Glynne

EDWARDS, The Ven Henry St John. b 30. Southn Univ DipEd. Ripon Hall Ox. **d** 59 **p** 60. C Wickford *Chelmsf* 59-62; R Woodburn Australia 62-65; Educn Officer Dio Grafton 65-69; Dean Grafton 69-78; V Mt Waverley St Steph 78-83; R Chelmer 83-89; Adn Moreton 85-89; Abp's Chapl 89-90; R Tamborine Mountain 90-95; Adn W Moreton 91-93; Adn Gold Coast 93-95; rtd 95. *24 Kooya Road, Mitchelton Qld 4053, Australia* E-mail stjohne@bigpond.com

EDWARDS, Canon Henry Victor. b 48. AKC71 Open Univ BA85 Middx Univ MSc00. St Aug Coll Cant 72. **d** 73 **p** 74. C W Leigh CD *Portsm* 73-77; V Cosham 77-84; V Reydon *St E* 84-86; V Blythburgh w Reydon 86-96; Chapl St Felix Sch Southwold 86-96; Chapl Blythburgh Hosp 86-96; P-in-c Campsea Ashe w Marlesford, Parham and Hacheston *St E* 96-00; R from 00; P-in-c Brandeston w Kettleburgh and Easton from 07; Dioc Adv for Counselling and Past Care from 96; Hon Can St E Cathl from 00. *The Rectory, Marlesford, Woodbridge IP13 0AT* Tel (01728) 746747 Fax 748175 Mobile 07710-417071
E-mail harry@psalm23.demon.co.uk

EDWARDS, Herbert Joseph. b 29. Nottm Univ BA51. Wells Th Coll 54. **d** 56 **p** 57. C Leic St Pet 56-61; C-in-c Broom Leys CD 61-65; V Broom Leys 65-68; Lect Lich Th Coll 68-71; Rhodesia 71-79; Botswana 74-75; V Bloxwich *Lich* 80-84; R Asfordby *Leic* 84-92; R N w S Kilworth and Misterton 92-96; rtd 96; Perm to Offic *Leic* from 97 and *Lich* from 00. *Beechfields Nursing Home, 1 Wissage Road, Lichfield WS13 6EJ* Tel (01543) 418351 or 418354

EDWARDS, Canon James Frederick. b 36. ALCD62. **d** 62 **p** 63. C Kenwyn *Truro* 62-68; V Tuckingmill 68-76; V St Columb Minor and St Colan 76-01; RD Pydar 84-93; Hon Can Truro Cathl 92-01; rtd 01; Perm to Offic *Truro* from 01. *45 Tretherras Road, Newquay TR7 2TF* Tel (01637) 870967

EDWARDS, Jane. See EDWARDS, Wendy Jane

EDWARDS, Janet Margaret. b 41. TCert62 Lon Bible Coll BD73. WEMTC 98. **d** 01 **p** 02. NSM Coalbrookdale, Iron-Bridge and Lt Wenlock *Heref* from 01. *2 Madeley Wood View, Madeley, Telford TF7 5TF* Tel (01952) 583254

EDWARDS, Mrs Jill Kathleen. b 48. Man Univ BA69 CQSW72. S'wark Ord Course 90. **d** 93 **p** 95. NSM Grays Thurrock and Ind Chapl *Chelmsf* 93-07; Asst Dioc Soc Resp Officer *Truro* from 07; Public Preacher 07-08; P-in-c Gerrans w St Anthony-in-Roseland and Philleigh from 08. *Trelowen, Rosevine, Portscatho, Truro TR2 5EW* Tel (01872) 580117
E-mail jill@jilledwards.com

EDWARDS, John Ralph. b 50. Bris Univ BSc71 FCA74. SAOMC 98. **d** 01 **p** 02. NSM California *Ox* 01-06; NSM Finchampstead from 06. *Green Hedges, 25 St John's Street, Crowthorne RG45 7NJ* Tel (01344) 774586 Fax 774056 Mobile 07850-602488

EDWARDS, Jonathan. See EDWARDS, Andrew Jonathan Hugo

EDWARDS, Jonathan Guy. b 63. Bris Univ BA85. Ridley Hall Cam BA93 MA96. **d** 94 **p** 95. C Preston Plucknett *B & W* 94-98; C Clevedon St Andr and Ch 98-02; V Farrington Gurney 02-06; V Paulton 02-06; P-in-c High Littleton 05-06; V Paulton w Farrington Gurney and High Littleton from 07. *The Vicarage, Church Street, Paulton, Bristol BS39 7LG* Tel (01761) 416581
E-mail guyedwards455@btinternet.com

EDWARDS, Joseph. See EDWARDS, Herbert Joseph

EDWARDS, Judith Sarah. See McARTHUR-EDWARDS, Mrs Judith Sarah

EDWARDS (née EVANS), Mrs Linda Mary. b 49. Univ of Wales (Cardiff) BA71 K Coll Lon BD74 AKC74. Yale Div Sch STM76. **dss** 76 **d** 80 **p** 99. Llanishen and Lisvane 76-78; Wrexham *St As* 78-80; C 80-82; Chapl Maudsley Hosp Lon 82-84; Chapl Bethlem R Hosp Beckenham 82-84; Chapl Lon Univ 84-87; NSM Llanfair-pwll and Llanddaniel-fab etc *Ban*

99-03; P-in-c Llangynog *St As* 03-06; C 07; C Llanrhaeadr ym Mochnant etc from 07. *Maes-y-Llan, Pennant Melangell, Llangynog, Oswestry SY10 0HQ* Tel (01691) 860455 *or* tel and fax 860408

EDWARDS, Malcolm Ralph. b 27. Man Univ 49. Cranmer Hall Dur 57. **d** 59 **p** 60. C Withington St Paul *Man* 59-62; C Chadderton Em 62-64; R Longsight St Jo 64-70; V Halliwell St Thos 70-81; V Milnrow 81-92; rtd 92; Perm to Offic *Man* from 92. *20 Upper Lees Drive, Westhoughton, Bolton BL5 3UE* Tel (01942) 813279

EDWARDS, Mrs Marie. b 73. NEOC 06. **d** 09. NSM Middlesbrough St Agnes *York* from 09. *76 Hesleden Avenue, Middlesbrough TS5 8RN* Tel (01642) 509381 Mobile 07908-608605 E-mail paul.edwards170@ntlworld.com

EDWARDS, Mark Anthony. b 61. Cranmer Hall Dur 91. **d** 95 **p** 97. C Ulverston St Mary w H Trin *Carl* 95-97; C Barrow St Jo 97-00; TV Barrow St Matt 00-08; TV Ch the King *Newc* from 08; Chapl Northumbria Police from 08. *The Vicarage, 2 East Acres, Dinnington, Newcastle upon Tyne NE13 7NA*
E-mail hayden@fox9411.freeserve.co.uk

EDWARDS, Mrs Mary. b 47. St Jo Coll York CertEd69 Birkbeck Coll Lon BSc74 New Coll Edin BD93. S Dios Minl Tr Scheme 96. **d** 96 **p** 97. NSM Avon Valley *Sarum* 96-00; TV Wexcombe 00-02; TV Savernake from 02. *The Vicarage, Church Street, Collingbourne Ducis, Marlborough SN8 3EL* Tel (01264) 852692
E-mail mary_avonvalley@hotmail.com

EDWARDS, Michael Norman William. b 34. Bp Gray Coll Cape Town 61 St Paul's Coll Grahamstown 62. **d** 63 **p** 65. S Africa 63-81; C Woodstock 63-66; C Plumstead 66-69; P-in-c Lansdowne All SS 69-72; R Hoetjes Bay 73-78; R Parow St Marg 78-80; Chaplain Tristan da Cunha 81-83; R Aston-on-Trent and Weston-on-Trent *Derby* 84-87; V Derby St Thos 87-95; P-in-c Blackwell 95-01; rtd 01; Perm to Offic *Win* from 02. *16 Ridley Close, Holbury, Southampton SO45 2NR* Tel (023) 8089 2924 E-mail mnwedwards.novaforest@googlemail.com

EDWARDS, Nicholas John. b 53. UEA BA75 Fitzw Coll Cam BA77 MA80. Westcott Ho Cam 75. **d** 78 **p** 79. C Kirkby *Liv* 78-81; V Cantril Farm 81-87; V Hale 87-94; R Chingford SS Pet and Paul *Chelmsf* 94-04; R Colyton, Musbury, Southleigh and Branscombe *Ex* from 04. *The Vicarage, Vicarage Street, Colyton EX24 6LJ* Tel (01297) 552307
E-mail nicholas_edwards@ntlworld.com

EDWARDS, Mrs Nita Mary. b 50. Univ of Wales (Ban) BD72 Nottm Univ PGCE73. Cranmer Hall Dur 93. **d** 93 **p** 94. C Ormesby *York* 93-95; C Billingham St Aid *Dur* 95-97; V 97-02; V Clayton *Lich* from 02. *The Vicarage, Clayton Lane, Newcastle ST5 3DW* Tel and fax (01782) 614500
E-mail nita.edwards@ntlworld.com

EDWARDS, Mrs Patricia Anne. b 52. EMMTC 76. **dss** 79 **d** 87 **p** 94. Hon Par Dn Clifton *S'well* 87-91; NSM Edwalton from 91. *Le Petit Champ, Widmerpool Road, Wysall, Nottingham NG12 5QW* Tel (01509) 880385

EDWARDS, Peter Clive. b 50. Lon Univ BA72. St Steph Ho Ox 83. **d** 85 **p** 86. C Lee St Aug *S'wark* 85-90; V Salfords 90-97; R Newington St Mary 97-03; Chapl Costa Blanca *Eur* 04-09; Sen Chapl from 09. *Apdo Correos 158, 03420 Castalla, Alicante, Spain* Tel (0034) 966 560 716 E-mail pce11@yahoo.com

EDWARDS, Peter Richard Henderson. b 65. Nottm Univ BA86. St Steph Ho Ox 03. **d** 05 **p** 06. C Uppingham w Ayston and Wardley w Belton *Pet* 05-08; TV Bridport *Sarum* from 08. *Allington Vicarage, Parsonage Road, Bridport DT6 5ET* Tel (01308) 424698 E-mail edwards.peter@tesco.net

EDWARDS, Canon Philip John. b 28. Lon Univ MRCS51 LRCP51. Chich Th Coll 58. **d** 60 **p** 61. C Orpington St Andr *Roch* 60-67; C Mayfield *Chich* 67-71; V Haywards Heath St Rich 71-91; Can and Preb Chich Cathl 84-91; rtd 91; Perm to Offic *Chich* from 91. *22 Hamsey Road, Sharpthorne, East Grinstead RH19 4PA* Tel (01342) 810210

EDWARDS, Phillip Gregory. b 52. Lon Univ BSc73 Imp Coll Lon ARCS73 MSOSc90. Qu Coll Birm 78. **d** 81 **p** 82. C Lillington *Cov* 81-85; P-in-c Cov St Alb 85-86; TV Cov E 86-01; C Bury St Paul and Bury Ch King *Man* 01-03; Chapl Bolton Univ from 03; C Westhoughton and Wingates 04-05; C Leverhulme 05-07. *St Stephen and All Martyrs Vicarage, Radcliffe Road, Bolton BL2 1NZ* Tel (01204) 528300 E-mail phil@edwards.clara.co.uk

EDWARDS, Raymond Lewis. Keble Coll Ox BA46 MA47 TCert48. St Deiniol's Hawarden 69. **d** 70 **p** 71. Prin Educn Cen Penmaenmawr 56-81; Hon C Dwygyfylchi *Ban* 70-81; P-in-c Llandwrog 81-82; R 82-90; Dioc Dir of Educn 84-92; rtd 90; Perm to Offic *Ban* from 90. *Bryn Llwyd, St Davids Road, Caernarfon LL55 1EL* Tel 07789-566370 (mobile)

EDWARDS, Richard John. b 47. Univ of Qld BA85. St Fran Coll Brisbane 83. **d** 85 **p** 85. C St Lucia Australia 85-87; C Olveston *Bris* 87-88; R N Pine Australia 88-96; R Kingston St Mary w Broomfield etc *B & W* from 96. *The Rectory, Kingston St Mary, Taunton TA2 8HW* Tel (01823) 451257 Fax 451933
E-mail roberted@supanet.com

EDWARDS, Robert James. b 52. Cranmer Hall Dur 01. **d** 03 **p** 04. C Broadwater *Chich* 03-08; TV Southgate from 08. *Holy Trinity*

House, Titmus Drive, Crawley RH10 5EU Tel (01293) 618214
E-mail roberted@supanet.com

EDWARDS, Roger Brian. b 41. Sarum & Wells Th Coll 87. **d** 89 **p** 90. C Wellington and Distr *B & W* 89-92; V Hursley and Ampfield *Win* 92-06; rtd 06. *34 Heatherstone Avenue, Dibden Purlieu, Southampton SO45 4LH* Tel (023) 8087 9689

EDWARDS, Canon Rowland Thomas. b 62. Univ of Wales BTh91. St Mich Coll Llan 85. **d** 88 **p** 89. C Llangiwg *S & B* 88-90; C Morriston 90-91; V Llangorse, Cathedine, Llanfihangel Talyllyn etc 91-01; V Llyn Safaddan 01-06; V Talgarth w Bronllys w Llanfilo from 06; AD Hay from 02; Can Res Brecon Cathl from 08. *The Vicarage, Bronllys, Brecon LD3 0HS* Tel (01874) 711200

EDWARDS, Rupert Quintin. b 67. Bris Univ LLB89. Wycliffe Hall Ox BTh94. **d** 97 **p** 98. C Bromley Ch Ch *Roch* 97-00; C Hammersmith St Paul *Lon* 00-02; Hon C from 06. *342 Bluewater House, Smugglers Way, London SW18 1ED*
E-mail rupert.edwards@arqiva.com

EDWARDS, Canon Ruth Blanche. b 39. Girton Coll Cam BA61 MA65 PhD68 Aber Coll of Educn PGCE75. Ab Dioc Tr Course 77. **d** 87 **p** 94. Lect Aber Univ 77-90; Sen Lect 90-96; NSM Aberdeen St Jas 87-88; NSM Aberdeen St Jo 88-96; Lect Ripon Coll Cuddesdon 96-99; Hon Can St Andr Cathl from 97; rtd 00; NSM Aberdeen St Jas from 00. *99 Queen's Den, Aberdeen AB15 8BN* Tel (01224) 312688

EDWARDS, Mrs Sandra May. b 48. STETS 96. **d** 99 **p** 01. NSM Denmead *Portsm* 99-05; P-in-c 05-06; V from 06. *The Vicarage, Ludcombe, Waterlooville PO7 6TL* Tel (023) 9225 5490
E-mail sandra@pinoy.fsnet.co.uk

EDWARDS, Scott. b 71. Wolv Univ LLB93 St Jo Coll Dur BA00. Cranmer Hall Dur 97. **d** 00 **p** 01. C Halas *Worc* 00-03; V Frimley Green and Mytchett *Guildf* from 03. *The Vicarage, 37 Sturt Road, Frimley Green, Camberley GU16 6HY* Tel (01252) 835179
E-mail scott.edwards@btopenworld.com

EDWARDS, Stephen. b 44. S'wark Ord Course. **d** 82 **p** 83. C Benhilton *S'wark* 82-86; P-in-c Clapham Ch Ch and St Jo 86-87; TV Clapham Team 87-94; Chapl HM Pris Wormwood Scrubs 94-96; Chapl HM Pris Maidstone 96-01; Chapl HM Pris Wandsworth 01-04; rtd 04; Perm to Offic *S'wark* from 04. *12 Bucharest Road, London SW18 3AR* Tel (020) 8870 1991

EDWARDS, Stephen Michael. b 72. Lanc Univ BSc93 Anglia Poly Univ MA99. Westcott Ho Cam 93. **d** 96 **p** 97. C Colwyn Bay *St As* 96-02; P-in-c Brynymaen 99-02; P-in-c Birch-in-Rusholme St Agnes w Longsight St Jo etc *Man* from 02. *St Agnes's Rectory, Slade Lane, Manchester M13 0GN* Tel 0161-224 2596 E-mail stephen@stagneslongsight.org

EDWARDS, Steven Charles. b 58. Lanc Univ BSc82 PhD86. Linc Th Coll 94. **d** 94 **p** 95. C Bradshaw *Man* 94-98; P-in-c Bolton Breightmet St Jas 98-04; TR Walkden and Lt Hulton from 04. *St Paul's Vicarage, 10 Old Vicarage Gardens, Worsley, Manchester M28 3JR* Tel 0161-790 2483
E-mail steve.edwards@dsl.pipex.com

EDWARDS, Stuart. b 46. Lanc Univ BA73. Kelham Th Coll 66. **d** 71 **p** 72. C Skerton St Luke *Blackb* 71-76; C Ribbleton 76-80; TV 80-82; V Blackb St Mich w St Jo and H Trin 82-91; V Blackpool H Cross from 91; RD Blackpool 93-94, P-in-c S Shore St Pet 00-05. *Holy Cross Vicarage, Central Drive, Blackpool FY1 6LA* Tel (01253) 341263

EDWARDS, Mrs Susan. b 54. R Holloway Coll Lon BSc75 SS Hild & Bede Coll Dur PGCE76. Qu Coll Birm 78. **dss** 81 **d** 87 **p** 94. Lillington *Cov* 81-85; Cov E 85-01; Par Dn 87-94; C 94-01; P-in-c Woolfold *Man* 01-07; TV Leverhulme from 07. *St Stephen and All Martyrs Vicarage, Radcliffe Road, Bolton BL2 1NZ* Tel (01204) 528300 E-mail sue@edwards.clara.co.uk

EDWARDS, Mrs Susan Diane. b 48. St Alb Minl Tr Scheme 86 Cranmer Hall Dur 91. **d** 92 **p** 94. Par Dn Borehamwood *St Alb* 92-94; C 94-96; V Arlesey w Astwick from 96. *The Vicarage, 77 Church Lane, Arlesey SG15 6UX* Tel (01462) 731227
E-mail susan.d.edwards@ntlworld.com

EDWARDS, The Very Revd Thomas Erwyd Pryse. b 33. Univ of Wales (Lamp) BA56. St Mich Coll Llan 56. **d** 58 **p** 59. C Llanbeblig w Caernarfon *Ban* 58-63; Chapl Asst St Geo Hosp Lon 63-66; Lic to Offic *S'wark* 63-72; Chapl K Coll Hosp Lon 66-72; R Penmon and Llangoed w Llanfihangel Dinsilwy *Ban* 72-75; V Llandysilio 75-81; V Llanallgo 81-84; Chapl Gwynedd Hosp Ban 84-86; V Ban St D and St Jas 86-88; Dean Ban 88-98; Hon Can Ban Cathl from 88; TR Bangor 88-93; rtd 98; Perm to Offic *Ban* from 98. *61 Ffriddoedd Road, Bangor LL57 2TT* Tel (01248) 362108

EDWARDS, Wendy Jane. b 49. Bingley Coll of Educn CertEd71. SEITE 03. **d** 06 **p** 07. C Riverhead w Dunton Green *Roch* from 06. *c/o Crockford, Church House, Great Smith Street, London SW1P 3AZ* Tel (01732) 455736
E-mail edwards23@supanet.com

EDWARDSON, David Roger Hately. b 54. Stirling Univ BSc79 DipEd79 Edin Univ BD91. Edin Th Coll 88. **d** 91 **p** 92. C Edin St Jo 91-93; R Kelso 93-98; Asst Chapl Oundle Sch from 98.

Crosby House, Milton Road, Oundle, Peterborough PE8 2AG Tel and fax (01832) 274405 E-mail david.edwardson@lineone.net

EDWARDSON, Joseph Philip. b 28. Dur Univ BA52 Leeds Univ PGCE53. Wells Th Coll 61. **d** 63 **p** 64. C Macclesfield St Mich *Ches* 63-66; V Egremont St Jo 66-72; V Eastham 72-81; V Poulton 81-94; rtd 94; Perm to Offic *Ches* from 94. *Keppler, 38 Hazel Grove, Irby, Wirral CH61 4UZ* Tel 0151-648 2661

EDY, Robert James. b 48. Southn Univ BA70 CertEd71. Ox Min Course 90. **d** 93 **p** 94. Dep Hd Master Henry Box Sch Witney from 90; NSM Ducklington *Ox* 93-99; P-in-c from 99. *The Rectory, 6 Standlake Road, Ducklington, Witney OX29 7XG* Tel (01993) 776625 E-mail bobedy21@hotmail.com

EDYE, Ian Murray. b 21. K Coll Lon BD AKC. S'wark Ord Course 66. **d** 69 **p** 70. NSM E Grinstead St Swithun *Chich* 69-00; Perm to Offic 00-02. *Bramcote House, Town Street, Beeston, Nottingham NG9 3DP* Tel 0115-925 7316

EFEMEY, Raymond Frederick. b 28. Ball Coll Ox BA51 MA64. Cuddesdon Coll 51. **d** 53 **p** 54. C Croydon St Mich *Cant* 53-57; C Hendford *B & W* 57-60; V Upper Arley *Worc* 60-66; Ind Chapl 60-66; P-in-c Dudley St Jas 66-69; V Dudley St Thos 66-69; V Dudley St Thos and St Luke 69-75; Hon C Stretford All SS *Man* 76-82; SSF from 81; P-in-c Weaste *Man* 82-87; V 87-93; rtd 93. *20 Groby Road, Chorlton-cum-Hardy, Manchester M21 1DD* Tel 0161-860 5416

EGAR, Miss Judith Anne. b 57. Somerville Coll Ox BA79 MA84 Solicitor 83. STETS 01. **d** 04 **p** 05. NSM Brighton St Nic *Chich* 04-07; Lic to Offic from 09; Perm to Offic *Lon* from 08. *15 St Peter's Place, Lewes BN7 1YP* Tel (020) 7898 1722
E-mail judith.egar@c-of-e.org.uk

EGERTON, George. b 28. S'wark Ord Course 70. **d** 73 **p** 74. NSM Shere *Guildf* 73-94; Perm to Offic from 94. *Weyside, Lower Street, Shere, Guildford GU5 9HX* Tel (01483) 202549

EGERTON, Mrs Susan Doreen. b 52. MCSP75. **d** 09. OLM Surrey Weald *Guildf* from 09. *Hollington, Horsham Road, Capel, Dorking RH5 5LF* Tel (01306) 711299

EGGERT, Max Alexander. b 43. AKC67 Birkbeck Coll Lon BSc74 Poly Cen Lon MA87 CPsychol90. **d** 67 **p** 68. C Whitton St Aug *Lon* 67-69; Hon C Hackney 72-74; Hon C Llantwit Major 74-76; NSM Haywards Heath St Rich *Chich* 78-93. *94 High Street, Lindfield, Haywards Heath RH16 2HP* Tel (01444) 483057

EGGLETON, Michael John. b 50. SAOMC 96 ERMC 06. **d** 07 **p** 08. NSM Northchurch and Wigginton *St Alb* from 07. *St Bartholomew's Vicarage, Vicarage Road, Wigginton, Tring HP23 6DZ* Tel (01442) 823273 Mobile 07962-145398 E-mail mikeeggleton7@btopenworld.com

EGLIN, Ian Charles. b 55. St Jo Coll Dur BA76. Coll of Resurr Mirfield 77. **d** 79 **p** 80. C Cov St Mary 79-83; TV Kingsthorpe w Northampton St Dav *Pet* 83-87; P-in-c Pitsford w Boughton 85-87; Chapl RN 87-03; V Ipplepen, Torbryan and Denbury *Ex* from 03; RD Newton Abbot and Ipplepen from 07. *The Rectory, Paternoster Lane, Ipplepen, Newton Abbot TQ12 5RY* Tel and fax (01803) 812215 E-mail ianeglin@talktalk.net

EJIAKU, Sebastian Chidozie. b 58. Herts Univ MSc95. NTMTC 02. **d** 05 **p** 06. NSM Hoxton St Jo w Ch Ch *Lon* from 05. *116 Cann Hall Road, London E11 3NH* Tel (020) 8519 2555 Mobile 07952-950681 E-mail ejiakuo@aol.com

EJINKONYE, Prorenata Emeka. d 08 **p** 09. OLM Victoria Docks St Luke *Chelmsf* from 08. *46 Willrose Crescent, London SE2 0LG*

EKIN, Tom Croker. b 29. Linc Th Coll 59. **d** 60 **p** 61. C Leamington Priors All SS *Cov* 60-63; R Ilmington w Stretton-on-Fosse 63-72; S Africa 72-77; R Moreton-in-Marsh w Batsford *Glouc* 77-83; R Moreton-in-Marsh w Batsford, Todenham etc 83-94; rtd 96; Hon C Theale and Englefield *Ox* 96-04; Perm to Offic *B & W* from 04. *The Parsonage, Redcroft, Redhill, Bristol BS40 5SL* Tel and fax (01934) 862398

ELBOURNE, Keith Marshall. b 46. Nottm Univ BTh74 Lon Univ BD76. St Jo Coll Nottm 70. **d** 74 **p** 75. C Romford Gd Shep *Chelmsf* 74-78; C Victoria Docks St Luke 78-81; P-in-c 81-92; V Walthamstow St Pet 92-02; TR Tettenhall Wood and Perton *Lich* from 02. *Christ Church Rectory, 7 Broxwood Park, Tettenhall Wood, Wolverhampton WV6 8LZ* Tel (01902) 751116 E-mail petros2@surfaid.org

ELBOURNE, Canon Raymond Nigel Wilson. b 43. Dur Univ BA66. Linc Th Coll 67. **d** 69 **p** 70. C Liscard St Mary *Ches* 69-72; V Hattersley 72-77; R Odd Rode 77-02; P-in-c Congleton St Jas 02-03; V 03-08; RD Congleton 97-04; Hon Can Ches Cathl 99-08; rtd 08; Perm to Offic *Eur* from 08. *La Petite Mortrée, 61570 Mortrée, France* Tel (0033) (2) 33 36 95 70 E-mail elbourne@europe.com

ELBOURNE, Canon Timothy. b 60. Selw Coll Cam BA81 MA85 PGCE82. Westcott Ho Cam 84. **d** 86 **p** 87. C Tottenham H Trin *Lon* 86-88; Chapl York Univ 88-94; P-in-c Thorp Arch w Walton 94-98; Dir of Educn *Ely* from 98; Hon Can Ely Cathl from 99. *19 The Oaks, Soham, Ely CB7 5FF* Tel and fax (01353) 723867 *or* tel 652711 Fax 652745 Pager (04325) 320796
E-mail tim.elbourne@ely.anglican.org

ELCOCK, Jonathan. b 64. Westcott Ho Cam 07. d 09. C Aberavon *Llan* from 09. *Holy Trinity House, Fairway, Port Talbot SA12 7HG* Tel (01639) 893972
E-mail curate@parishofaberavon.org

ELDER, Andrew John. b 49. Sunderland Poly BSc72 MSc76. NEOC 91. d 94 p 95. NSM Wallsend St Luke *Newc* 94-02; NSM Wallsend St Pet and St Luke 02-03; C Monkseaton St Pet 03-06; V Blyth St Mary from 06. *St Mary's Vicarage, 51 Marine Terrace, Blyth NE24 2JP* Tel (01670) 353417
E-mail andy.elder@btinternet.com

ELDER, David. b 28. Brechin NSM Ord Course 75. d 79 p 80. NSM Dundee St Salvador *Bre* 79-93; rtd 93; P-in-c Dundee St Martin *Bre* from 93. *Thistlemount, 21 Law Road, Dundee DD3 6PZ* Tel (01382) 827844

ELDER, Nicholas John. b 51. Hatf Poly BA73. Cuddesdon Coll 73. d 76 p 77. C Mill End and Heronsgate w W Hyde *St Alb* 76-79; TV Borehamwood 79-85; V Bedford St Mich 85-90; V Bedford All SS 90-00; V Camberwell St Geo *S'wark* from 00; Warden Trin Coll Cen Camberwell from 00. *St George's Vicarage, 115 Wells Way, London SE5 7SZ* Tel (020) 7703 2895 or 7703 9855 E-mail nicholas.elder@virgin.net

ELDRID, John Gisborne Charteris. b 25. OBE97. AKC52. d 53 p 54. C St Geo-in-the-East w Ch Ch w St Jo *Lon* 53-56; C E Grinstead St Mary *Chich* 56-58; C St Steph Walbrook and St Swithun etc *Lon* 58-64 and 72-81; V Portsea All SS *Portsm* 64-71; P-in-c Portsea St Jo Rudmore 69-71; V Portsea All SS w St Jo Rudmore 71-72; Gen Consultant Cen Lon Samaritans 72-74; Dir The Samaritans 74-87; Gen Consultant-Dir 87-99; Consultant from 99; Lic to Offic *Lon* from 82; rtd 90; Perm to Offic *Portsm* from 90. *46 Marshall Street, London W1V 1LR* Tel (020) 7439 1406 Fax 7439 1233

ELDRIDGE, John Frederick. b 48. Loughb Univ BSc70 Golden Gate Sem (USA) MDiv83 Fuller Th Sem California DMin96. Oak Hill Th Coll 90. d 92 p 93. C Maidstone St Luke *Cant* 92-97; Min Prince's Park CD *Roch* 97-02; P-in-c Wickham Market w Pettistree *St E* 02-07; V from 07. *The Vicarage, Crown Lane, Wickham Market, Woodbridge IP13 0SA* Tel (01728) 746026
E-mail jeldridge@supanet.com

ELDRIDGE, John Kenneth Tristan. b 59. St Steph Ho Ox 90. d 92 p 93. C Brighton Resurr *Chich* 92-96; C Hangleton 96-98; TR Moulsecoomb 98-05; V W Worthing St Jo from 05; Chapl Sussex Beacon Hospice from 00. *St John's Vicarage, 15 Reigate Road, Worthing BN11 5NF* Tel (01903) 247340

ELDRIDGE, Stephen William. b 50. Open Univ BA98. Chich Th Coll 87. d 89 p 90. C Stroud and Uplands w Slad *Glouc* 89-92; C Glouc St Mary de Crypt w St Jo and Ch Ch 92-95; C Glouc St Mary de Lode and St Nic 92-95; Bp's Chapl 92-93; P-in-c Kingswood w Alderley and Hillesley 95-00; P-in-c Cheltenham St Pet 00-08; TV N Cheltenham from 08. *St Peter's Vicarage, 375 Swindon Road, Cheltenham GL51 9LB* Tel and fax (01242) 524369 E-mail stephen.eldridge@northchelt.org.uk

ELEY, John Edward. b 49. Sarum & Wells Th Coll 74. d 77 p 78. C Sherborne w Castleton and Lillington *Sarum* 77-80; Min Can Carl Cathl 80-84; V Bromsgrove All SS *Worc* 84-88; Perm to Offic *St E* 90-98; V Stourhead from 98. *The Rectory, Mill Road, Kedington, Haverhill CB9 7NN* Tel and fax (01440) 710216 Mobile 07785-575230 E-mail john.eley5@btopenworld.com

ELFICK, Brian Richard. b 76. Ex Coll Ox BA98 Selw Coll Cam BA04 MPhil05. Ridley Hall Cam 02. d 06 p 07. C Cambridge H Sepulchre *Ely* from 06. *9 Victoria Street, Cambridge CB1 1JP* Tel (01223) 518218

ELFORD, Keith Anthony. b 59. Em Coll Cam BA80 MA84. Wycliffe Hall Ox 87. d 90 p 91. C Chertsey *Guildf* 90-94; P-in-c Ockham w Hatchford 94-98; Bp's Chapl 94-98; Perm to Offic 98-00; Lic to Offic from 01. *15 Canford Drive, Addlestone KT15 2HH* Tel (01932) 885137
E-mail keith.elford@lineone.net

ELFORD, Canon Robert John. b 39. Man Univ MA71 Ex Univ PhD74. Brasted Th Coll 64 Ridley Hall Cam 66. d 68 p 69. C Denton St Lawr *Man* 68-71; P-in-c Gwinear *Truro* 71-74; R Phillack w Gwithian and Gwinear 74-78; Lect Man Univ 78-87; Hon C Withington St Paul *Man* 79-83; Warden St Anselm Hall 82-87; Lic to Offic 84-87; Pro-R Liv Inst of HE 88-99; Can Th Liv Cathl 92-04; rtd 04. *1 North Quay, Wapping Quay, Liverpool L3 4BU* Tel 0151-709 0461

ELFRED, Michael William. b 48. BA76 MPhil. Linc Th Coll 77. d 79 p 80. C Boultham *Linc* 79-82; C Croydon H Sav *Cant* 82-84; C Upper Norwood All SS *S'wark* 84-88; V Sanderstead St Mary 88-01; P-in-c Tadworth from 01. *The Vicarage, 1 The Avenue, Tadworth KT20 5AS* Tel (01737) 813152 Mobile 07931-463661 E-mail michael.elfred@talk21.com

ELGAR, Richard John. b 50. Charing Cross Hosp Medical Sch MB, BS73 LRCP73 MRCS73 MRCGP80. St Jo Coll Nottm 92. d 92 p 93. NSM Derby St Alkmund and St Werburgh 92-96; P-in-c Derby St Barn 96-01; V 01-08; RD Derby N 05-06; rtd 08. *38 Holborn Drive, Derby DE22 4DX* Tel (01332) 342553
E-mail relgar1015@aol.com

ELIZABETH, Danny Rollan Henry. b 67. Seychelles Poly DipEd87 Edith Cowan Univ (Aus) BEd93 Rhodes Univ BTh00.

Coll of Transfiguration Grahamstown 97. d 99 p 00. R St Paul's Cathl Seychelles 00-05; Perm to Offic *Lon* 05-06; NSM Hanwell St Mellitus w St Mark 06-08; V Hayes St Anselm from 08. *St Anselm's Vicarage, 101 Nield Road, Hayes UB3 1SQ* Tel (020) 8573 0958 Mobile 07880-971585
E-mail dannyelizabeth@btinternet.com

ELIZABETH, Sister. *See* WEBB, Marjorie Valentine

ELIZABETH MARY, Sister. *See* NOLLER, Hilda Elizabeth Mary

ELKINGTON, Canon Audrey Anne. b 57. St Cath Coll Ox BA80 UEA PhD83. St Jo Coll Nottm 85 EAMTC 86. dss 88 d 92 p 94. Monkseaton St Mary *Newc* 88-91; Ponteland 91-93; Par Dn 92-93; C Prudhoe 93-02; RD Corbridge 99-02; Bp's Adv for Women in Min from 01; Bp's Chapl from 02; Dir of Ords from 02; Hon Can Newc Cathl from 06. *16 Towers Avenue, Jesmond, Newcastle upon Tyne NE2 3QE* Tel 0191-281 0714 or 285 2220 Fax 284 6933 E-mail a.elkington@newcastle.anglican.org

ELKINGTON, Canon David John. b 51. Nottm Univ BTh76 Leic Univ MEd81 Dur Univ MATM05. St Jo Coll Nottm 73. d 76 p 77. C Leic Martyrs 76-78; C Kirby Muxloe 78-80; Asst Chapl Leic Univ 80-82; Hon C Leic H Spirit 82; Chapl UEA *Nor* 82-88; TV Newc Epiphany 88-91; TR 91-93; P-in-c Prudhoe 93-98; V 98-02; Can Res Newc Cathl from 02. *16 Towers Avenue, Jesmond, Newcastle upon Tyne NE2 3QE* Tel 0191-281 0714
E-mail djelk@tiscali.co.uk

ELKINGTON-SLYFIELD, John David. *See* SLYFIELD, John David

ELKINS, Alan Bernard. b 47. Sarum & Wells Th Coll 70. d 73 p 74. C Wareham *Sarum* 73-77; P-in-c Codford, Upton Lovell and Stockton 77-79; P-in-c Boyton w Sherrington 77-79; C Ashton Gifford 79; R Bishopstrow and Boreham 79-92; R Corfe Mullen 92-03; V W Byfleet *Guildf* 03-08; P-in-c from 08; Bp's Adv for Spirituality from 08. *The Vicarage, 5 Dartnell Avenue, West Byfleet KT14 6PJ* Tel (01932) 345270
E-mail alan-elkins@lineone.net

ELKINS, Mrs Joy Kathleen. b 45. S Tr Scheme 93. d 96 p 97. NSM Corfe Mullen *Sarum* 96-03; NSM W Byfleet *Guildf* 03-08; C from 08. *The Vicarage, 5 Dartnell Avenue, West Byfleet KT14 6PJ* Tel (01932) 345270 E-mail joy-elkins@lineone.net

ELKINS, Canon Patrick Charles. b 34. St Chad's Coll Dur BA57 DipEd58. d 60 p 61. C Moordown *Win* 60-63; C Basingstoke 64-67; V Bransgore 67-04; Hon Can Win Cathl 89-04; rtd 04; Perm to Offic *Win* from 04. *1 Tyrrells Court, Bransgore, Christchurch BH23 8BU* Tel (01425) 673103

ELKS, Roger Mark. b 60. Imp Coll Lon BSc83. Wycliffe Hall Ox 89. d 92 p 93. C St Austell *Truro* 92-95; V Carbis Bay w Lelant 95-01; I Holywood *D & D* from 01. *The Vicarage, 156 High Street, Holywood BT18 9HT* Tel (028) 9042 2069 or 9042 3622 E-mail vicarroger@ntlworld.com

ELLACOTT, Alan Gren. b 58. Ripon Coll Cuddesdon 02. d 04 p 05. C Crewkerne w Wayford *B & W* 04-07; C Wulfric Benefice 07-09; R Llandysilio and Penrhos and Llandrinio etc *St As* from 09. *The Rectory, Rhos Common, Four Crosses, Llanymynech SY22 6RW* Tel (01691) 830533 Mobile 07989-299063
E-mail alkatch@tiscali.co.uk

ELLACOTT, David Alfred. b 35. SWMTC 95. d 97 p 98. NSM Fremington *Ex* 97-02; Perm to Offic from 02. *2 Coppice Close, Fremington, Barnstaple EX31 2QE* Tel (01271) 373270

ELLAM, Stuart William. b 53. Westcott Ho Cam. d 85 p 86. C Ditton St Mich *Liv* 85-88; C Greenford H Cross *Lon* 88-91; Perm to Offic 91-94. *26 Church Road, Cowley, Uxbridge UB8 3NA* Tel (01895) 238815

ELLEM, Peter Keith. b 58. Nottm Univ BTh90 Leeds Univ MA99 CQSW. St Jo Coll Nottm 87. d 90 p 91. C Islington St Mary *Lon* 90-94; C Leeds St Geo *Ripon* 94-99; Australia from 99; R Yagoona from 00. *211 Auburn Road, Yagoona NSW 2199, Australia* Tel (0061) (2) 9790 6281 Fax 9796 6201
E-mail prellem@bigfoot.com

ELLENS, Gordon Frederick Stewart. b 26. Columbia Univ (NY) MPhil62 PhD68 FRAS. K Coll Lon BD52 AKC52 St Boniface Warminster 52. d 53 p 54. C Old Street St Luke w St Mary Charterhouse etc *Lon* 53-55; C Chiswick St Mich 55-57; Canada 57-60; USA 62-66 and from 88; Japan 70-88; Asst Prof Relig St Sophia Univ Tokyo 70-75; Rikkyo Women's Univ 75-84; Prof Humanities Ueno Gakueu 84-88; rtd 92. *4 Bennetts Close, West Wittering, Chichester PO20 8EP* Tel (01243) 671313

ELLERTON, Mrs Mary Diane. b 45. RGN67 Southn Univ RHV68. NOC 90. d 93 p 94. NSM Upper Holme Valley *Wakef* from 93; Chapl Calderdale and Huddersfield NHS Trust from 01. *13 Liphill Bank Road, Holmfirth, Huddersfield HD9 2LQ* Tel (01484) 684207, 482266 or 343437
E-mail diane.ellerton@btopenworld.com

ELLERY, Arthur James Gabriel. b 28. St Jo Coll Dur BSc49. Linc Th Coll 51. d 53 p 54. C Milton next Sittingbourne *Cant* 53-56; C St Laur in Thanet 56-58; C Darlington St Cuth *Dur* 58-62; V Tanfield 62-70; Chapl St Olave's Sch York 70-78; V Gt Ayton w Easby and Newton-in-Cleveland *York* 78-81; Chapl Bancroft's Sch Woodford Green 81-86; V Chipperfield St Paul *St Alb* 86-93;

rtd 93; Perm to Offic *Pet* from 93. *7 Church Drive, Orton Waterville, Peterborough PE2 5EX* Tel (01733) 231800

ELLERY, Ian Martyn William. b 56. K Coll Lon BD AKC. Chich Th Coll. **d** 82 **p** 83. C Hornsey St Mary w St Geo *Lon* 82-85; V Choral York Minster 85-89; Subchanter 86-89; R Patrington w Hollym, Welwick and Winestead 89-97; TR Howden 97-05; RD Howden 97-02; P-in-c Cawood w Ryther and Wistow from 05. *Cawood Vicarage, Rythergate, Cawood, Selby YO8 3TP* Tel (01757) 268273 E-mail jeimwe@aol.com

ELLIN, Lindsey Jane. *See* GOODHEW, Mrs Lindsey Jane Ellin

ELLINGTON, David John. b 39. Oriel Coll Ox BA63 MA. Cuddesdon Coll 63. **d** 65 **p** 66. C Sheff St Mark Broomhall 65-68; C Timperley *Ches* 68-72; P-in-c Altrincham St Jo 72-74; V 74-80; P-in-c Ashley 82-86; rtd 86; Perm to Offic *Ches* 87-00. *34 Cockpit Close, Woodstock OX20 1UH* Tel (01993) 815808

ELLIOT, Neil Robert Minto. b 63. Hatf Poly BEng87 Herts Univ CertEd93. St Jo Coll Nottm 94. **d** 96 **p** 97. C Walbrook Epiphany *Derby* 96-00; Chapl Univ of Cen England in Birm 00-05; V Trail SS Andr and Geo Canada from 05. *St Andrew's Church, 1347 Pine Avenue, Trail BC V1R 4E7, Canada* Tel (001) (250) 368 5581 E-mail rev.nelli@virgin.net

ELLIOT, William. b 33. Glouc Sch of Min 84. **d** 87 **p** 88. C Kington w Huntington, Old Radnor, Kinnerton etc *Heref* 87-90; C Heref H Trin 90-92; Chapl Corfu *Eur* 92-98; rtd 98; P-in-c Barlavington, Burton w Coates, Sutton and Bignor *Chich* 98-06. *2 Lawn Road, Guildford GU2 4DE* Tel (01483) 574540

ELLIOT, William Brunton. b 41. Edin Dioc NSM Course 81. **d** 84 **p** 85. Hon C Edin St Mark Dalkeith 84-92; NSM Dalkeith 84-92; NSM Lasswade *Edin* 84-92; NSM Dalkeith 84-92; Assoc P Edin St Pet 92-94; R Selkirk 94-06; rtd 06; Lic to Offic *Edin* from 06. *157 Newbattle Abbey Crescent, Dalkeith EH22 3LR* Tel 0131-663 1369 E-mail bille157@aol.com

ELLIOT-NEWMAN, Christopher Guy. b 43. Bede Coll Dur TCert67 Hull Univ BTh83 MEd87. Westcott Ho Cam 67. **d** 70 **p** 71. C Ditton St Mich *Liv* 70-73; C Hazlemere *Ox* 73-77; R Stockton-on-the-Forest w Holtby and Warthill *York* 77-87; Dir of Educn *Cant* 87-94; P-in-c Warden w Newbrough *Newc* 99-01; Perm to Offic 95-99 and from 02. *15 Hextol Terrace, Hexham NE46 2DF* Tel (01434) 600547 Mobile 07951-471189 E-mail christopher@firststandardltd.co.uk

ELLIOTT, Ben. *See* ELLIOTT, William Henry Venn

ELLIOTT, Brian. b 49. Dur Univ BA73. Coll of Resurr Mirfield 73. **d** 75 **p** 76. C Nunthorpe *York* 75-77; CF from 77. *c/o MOD Chaplains (Army)* Tel (01980) 615804 Fax 615800 E-mail brian@newpost.org

ELLIOTT, Christopher John. b 44. Sarum Th Coll 66. **d** 69 **p** 70. C Walthamstow St Pet *Chelmsf* 69-71; C Witham 71-74; P-in-c Gt and Lt Bentley 74-80; R Colchester Ch Ch w St Mary V 80-85; R Sible Hedingham 85-93; V Leigh-on-Sea St Aid 93-98; P-in-c Thornton Gp *Linc* 98-01; RD Horncastle 98-01; P-in-c Gt Leighs *Chelmsf* 01-05; P-in-c Lt Leighs 01-05; P-in-c Lt Waltham 01-05; R Gt and Lt Leighs and Lt Waltham 05-06; RD Chelmsf N 04-06; rtd 06; Perm to Offic *Chelmsf* from 06. *2 Park Cottages, Chelmsford Road, Great Waltham, Chelmsford CM3 1AQ* Tel (01245) 361888 E-mail christopher@celliott1.wanadoo.co.uk

ELLIOTT, Christopher John. b 67. Southn Univ 93. Chich Th Coll 94. **d** 94 **p** 95. C Alton St Lawr *Win* 94-97; Perm to Offic *Guildf* 99-02. *77 Wickham Place, Church Crookham, Fleet GU52 6NQ* Tel 07788-195548 (mobile)

ELLIOTT, Colin David. b 32. AKC55. **d** 56 **p** 57. C W Wickham St Jo *Cant* 56-59; C Dover St Mary 59-64; V Linton 64-66; V Gillingham H Trin *Roch* 66-81; V Belvedere All SS 81-88; V Bromley St Jo 88-97; rtd 97; Perm to Offic *S'wark* from 98 and *Roch* 99-03. *Flat 3, 160 George Lane, London SE13 6JF* Tel (020) 8698 4901

ELLIOTT, David John Henry Gregory. b 75. Mansf Coll Ox BA96 MA00 MSt98. St Steph Ho Ox MTh06. **d** 06 **p** 07. C Small Heath *Birm* from 06. *1 Waterside Close, Bordesley Green, Birmingham B9 4QJ* Tel 0121-771 1337 Mobile 07973-241424 E-mail frdavidelliott@hotmail.co.uk

ELLIOTT, David Reed. b 62. Lon Bible Coll BA91. Oak Hill Th Coll 91. **d** 93 **p** 94. C Luton Lewsey St Hugh *St Alb* 93-98; Dioc Communications Dept 98-00; Chapl W Herts Hosps NHS Trust from 07. *Chaplaincy Department, General Hospital, Hillfield Road, Hemel Hempstead HP2 4AD* Tel (01442) 287600 E-mail david.elliott@whht.nhs.uk

ELLIOTT, Derek John. b 26. Pemb Coll Cam BA50 MA55. Oak Hill Th Coll 48. **d** 51 **p** 53. C Ealing Dean St Jo *Lon* 51-53; C New Milverton *Cov* 53-55; C Boscombe St Jo *Win* 55-57; V Biddulph *Lich* 57-63; R Rushden w Newton Bromswold *Pet* 63-68; RD Higham 66-68; Chapl Bedford Modern Sch 68-83; V Potten End w Nettleden *St Alb* 83-91; Hon C Twickenham St Mary *Lon* from 91; Perm to Offic *Guildf* from 99. *Westwinds, Ridgeway Road, Dorking RH4 3AT* Tel (01306) 876655

ELLIOTT, Miss Eveline Mary. b 39. Bedf Coll Lon BA60 Cam Univ 92 ALA63. EAMTC 92. **d** 95 **p** 96. NSM Bury St Edmunds St Mary *St E* 95-97; NSM Lark Valley 97-07; rtd

07; Perm to Offic *St E* from 07. *4 St Michael's Close, Northgate Street, Bury St Edmunds IP33 1HT* Tel (01284) 753592 E-mail me@larkvalley57.fsnet.co.uk

ELLIOTT, George Evan. b 17. Sarum Th Coll. **d** 58 **p** 59. C Padiham *Blackb* 58-61; C Cleveleys 61-63; V Kimblesworth *Dur* 63-71; V Sutton St James *Linc* 71-77; V Sutton St Edmund 71-77; R Wadingham w Snitterby 77-80; P-in-c Bishop Norton 77-80; R Bishop Norton, Wadingham and Snitterby 80-82; rtd 82; Perm to Offic *Nor* 82-98. *10 Ramsay Hall, 11-13 Byron Road, Worthing BN11 3HN* Tel (01903) 215480

ELLIOTT, Gordon. b 25. St Aid Birkenhead 63. **d** 65 **p** 66. C Latchford St Jas *Ches* 65-68; C Bollington St Jo 68-70; V Dukingfield St Mark 70-73; TV Tenbury *Heref* 74-78; V Bromfield 78-82; R Culmington w Onibury 78-82; V Stanton Lacy 78-82; P-in-c Withybrook w Copston Magna *Cov* 82-83; P-in-c Wolvey, Burton Hastings and Stretton Baskerville 82-83; V Wolvey w Burton Hastings, Copston Magna etc 83-90; rtd 90; Perm to Offic *Worc* from 90; Perm to Offic *Heref* 90-95. *12 Handbury Road, Malvern WR14 1NN* Tel (01684) 569388

ELLIOTT, Ian David. b 40. Qu Coll Cam BA61 MA65. Tyndale Hall Bris 64. **d** 66 **p** 67. C Halewood *Liv* 66-71; C Gt Crosby St Luke 71-74; C-in-c Dallam CD 74-80; V Dallam 80-83; TV Fazakerley Em 83-92; V Warrington H Trin 92-05; rtd 05. *High Bank, 1 West End Road, Orton, Penrith CA10 3RT* Tel (015396) 24441 E-mail ian.andronelliott.freeserve.co.uk

ELLIOTT, Jane. **d** 08. NSM Hatcham St Cath *S'wark* from 08. *13 Seymour Gardens, London SE4 2DN* Tel (020) 7277 7968 E-mail jane.elliott@kcl.ac.uk

ELLIOTT, Mrs Joanna Margaret. b 64. Bris Univ BA85. STETS 03. **d** 06 **p** 07. NSM Haywards Heath St Wilfrid *Chich* from 06. *20 Courtlands, Haywards Heath RH16 4JD* Tel (01444) 413799 Mobile 07710-273299 E-mail joanna@ctsn.co.uk

ELLIOTT, John Andrew. b 44. ACIB68. SAOMC 95. **d** 98 **p** 99. NSM Bedgrove *Ox* 98-01; C Modbury, Bigbury, Ringmore w Kingston etc *Ex* from 01. *Little Cunery, Aveton Gifford, Kingsbridge TQ7 4NN* Tel (01548) 830688 E-mail johnaelliott@compuserve.com

ELLIOTT, John Philip. b 37. MIChemE61 MBIM Salford Univ CEng. Glouc Th Course 79. **d** 80 **p** 80. NSM Brimscombe *Glouc* 80-86; C Caverswall *Lich* 86-91; R Tredington and Darlingscott w Newbold on Stour *Cov* 91-97; rtd 97; Perm to Offic *Glouc* from 97. *Pipers Barn, 69 Bownham Park, Stroud GL5 5BZ*

ELLIOTT, Kathryn Georgina. b 50. **d** 08. NSM Manston *Ripon* from 08. *19 Roper Avenue, Leeds LS8 1LG* Tel 0113-217 7805 Mobile 07979-954472 E-mail kelliott@ntlworld.com

ELLIOTT, Capt Keith Alcock. b 51. CA Tr Coll 83 Cranmer Hall Dur 94. **d** 95 **p** 96. C Chulmleigh, Chawleigh w Cheldon, Wembworthy etc *Ex* 95-99; TV Barnstaple and C-in-c Roundswell CD 99-08; V Thorpe Acre w Dishley *Leic* from 08. *The Vicarage, Thorpe Acre Road, Loughborough LE11 4LF* Tel (01509) 211656 E-mail elliottkeith@btinternet.com

ELLIOTT (*née* JUTSUM), **Mrs Linda Mary.** b 56. St Pet Coll Birm CertEd77. WMMTC 92. **d** 95 **p** 96. NSM Longthorpe *Pet* 95-99; P-in-c Etton w Helpston and Maxey 99-04; Chapl Thorpe Hall Hospice 04-09; Perm to Offic *Pet* from 09. *68 Bradwell Road, Peterborough PE3 9PZ* Tel (01733) 261793 E-mail rev_linda@lycos.co.uk

ELLIOTT, Mrs Marilyn Elizabeth. b 53. SWMTC 05. **d** 08 **p** 09. C Stoke Climsland *Truro* from 08; C Linkinhorne from 08. *23 Woodland Rise, Rilla Mill, Callington PL17 7NZ* Tel (01579) 363307

ELLIOTT, Mary. *See* ELLIOTT, Miss Eveline Mary

ELLIOTT, Maurice John. b 65. St Andr Univ MA87 TCD BTh92 MPhil93 QUB PhD01. CITC 89. **d** 93 **p** 94. C Coleraine *Conn* 93-98; I Greenisland 98-02; I Lurgan Ch the Redeemer *D & D* 02-08; Dir Ch of Ireland Th Inst from 08. *7 Coolgraney, Nutgrove Park, Clonskeagh, Dublin 14, Republic of Ireland* Tel (00353) (1) 260 5737 or 492 3506 Fax 492 3508 Mobile 87-968 5218 E-mail mauriceelliott@theologicalinstitute.ie

ELLIOTT, Canon Michael Cowan. b 38. Auckland Univ BA63 Episc Th Sch Mass MDiv66 Massey Univ (NZ) MPhil82. St Jo Coll Auckland LTh61. **d** 61 **p** 62. New Zealand 61-65; C New Lynn 61-64; C Thames 65; USA 65-66; Warden Pemb Coll Miss Walworth *S'wark* 66-70; Dir St Luke's Cen Haifa Jerusalem 70-74; BCC 74-75; C Amersham *Ox* 74-75; Ecum Secretariat on Development NZ 76-84; Dir Chr Action NZ 84-87; Chapl City of Lon Poly 87-89; Dir Inner City Aid 89-91; Tutor Westmr Coll Ox 91-98; Dir Studies 00-02; Dir Min and Can Res Brecon Cathl 02-03; rtd 03; Lect Univ of Wales (Lamp) from 03. *Orchard House, Chapel Road, Llanfihangel Talyllyn, Brecon LD3 7TH* Tel (01874) 658194 E-mail canonmelliott@aol.com

ELLIOTT, Michael James. b 58. St Jo Coll Nottm 80. **d** 83 **p** 84. C Pontypridd St Cath *Llan* 83-86; C Leamington Priors St Paul *Cov* 86-89; Chapl RAF 89-06 and from 07; Chapl Kimbolton Sch 06-07. *Chaplaincy Services, HQ Air Command, RAF High Wycombe HP14 4UE* Tel (01494) 496800 Fax 496343 E-mail rev@kimbolton.cambs.sch.uk

ELLIOTT, Nigel Harvey. b 55. St Jo Coll Nottm 90. **d** 92 **p** 93. C Radcliffe *Man* 92-95; V Kilnhurst *Sheff* 95-08; R Wombwell from 08; AD Wath from 06. *The Rectory, 1 Rectory Close, Wombwell, Barnsley S73 8EY* Tel (01226) 211100
E-mail nell199076@aol.com

ELLIOTT, The Ven Peter. b 41. Hertf Coll Ox BA63 MA68. Linc Th Coll 63. **d** 65 **p** 66. C Gosforth All SS *Newc* 65-68; C Balkwell 68-72; V High Elswick St Phil 72-80; V N Gosforth 80-87; V Embleton w Rennington and Rock 87-93; RD Alnwick 89-93; Hon Can Newc Cathl 93-05; Adn Northld and Can Res Newc Cathl 93-05; rtd 05. *56 King Street, Seahouses NE68 7XS* Tel (01665) 721133

ELLIOTT, Peter Wolstenholme. b 31. CChem MRSC. NEOC 78. **d** 81 **p** 82. NSM Yarm *York* 81-02; Perm to Offic from 02. *48 Butterfield Drive, Eaglescliffe, Stockton-on-Tees TS16 0EZ* Tel (01642) 652698 E-mail revdpeter@hotmail.com

ELLIOTT, Philip. See ELLIOTT, John Philip

ELLIOTT, Richard David Clive. b 53. Portsm Poly BSc74 MICE79 MIStructE. STETS 03. **d** 06 **p** 07. NSM Sway *Win* from 06. *19 Heron Close, Sway, Lymington SO41 6ET* Tel (01590) 683778 Mobile 07836-760150
E-mail richard.elliott3@tesco.net

ELLIOTT, Mrs Rosemary Miriam. b 37. Toronto Univ BPaed62 Birm Univ BPhil86. **d** 04 **p** 05. Asst Chapl Birm Specialist Community Health NHS Trust 04-05; rtd 06. *10 Homethwaite House, Erskin Street, Keswick CA12 4DG* Tel (017687) 72513 Mobile 07721-855007 E-mail rosemary.elliott@btinternet.com

ELLIOTT, Simon Mark. b 76. Liv Hope Univ Coll BA97. Ridley Hall Cam 05. **d** 08. C Gt Crosby St Luke *Liv* from 08. *69 York Road, Crosby, Liverpool L23 5TT*
E-mail sielliott76@btinternet.com

ELLIOTT, Simon Richard James. b 66. Lon Univ BSc88. Cranmer Hall Dur BA95. **d** 95 **p** 96. C Hendon St Paul Mill Hill *Lon* 95-99; V Hull St Martin w Transfiguration *York* from 99. *St Martin's Vicarage, 942 Anlaby Road, Hull HU4 6AH* Tel (01482) 352995

ELLIOTT, Stuart. b 75. Univ of Wales (Ban) BTh98 MTh00. St Mich Coll Llan 05. **d** 07 **p** 08. C Holywell *St As* from 07. *4 Yr Aber, Holywell CH8 7RN* Tel (01352) 714243
E-mail stu@stubiedoo.co.uk

ELLIOTT, William. b 20. Lon Univ BA56. Ripon Hall Ox 60. **d** 61 **p** 62. C Kidderminster St Mary *Worc* 61-70; V Bewdley Far Forest 70-78; V Rock w Heightington w Far Forest 78-82; V Mamble w Bayton, Rock w Heightington etc 82-85; rtd 85; Perm to Offic *Heref* and *Worc* from 85. *8 Lea View, Cleobury Mortimer, Kidderminster DY14 8EE* Tel (01299) 270993

ELLIOTT, William Henry Venn (Ben). b 34. K Coll Cam BA55 MA59. Wells Th Coll 59. **d** 61 **p** 62. C Almondbury *Wakef* 61-66; V Bramshaw *Sarum* 66-81; P-in-c Landford w Plaitford 77-81; V Mere w W Knoyle and Maiden Bradley 81-99; rtd 99. *3 St George's Close, Salisbury SP2 8HA* Tel (01722) 338409

ELLIOTT, William James. b 38. Jes Coll Cam BA62 MA66 Birm Univ MA69 PhD74. Qu Coll Birm 62. **d** 64 **p** 65. C Hendon St Paul Mill Hill *Lon* 64-67; C St Pancras w St Jas and Ch Ch 67-69; P-in-c Preston St Paul *Blackb* 69-74; Chapl Preston R Infirmary 69-74; R Elstree *St Alb* 74-00; Research Fell Birm Univ 00-03; rtd 03; Perm to Offic *Nor* from 00. *23 Neil Avenue, Holt NR25 6TG* Tel and fax (01263) 713853
E-mail bbillholt@aol.com

ELLIOTT SMITH, Mark Charles. b 59. Lon Univ MA96 LRAM85 GRSM86 ARCO88. St Steph Ho Ox 92. **d** 94 **p** 97. C W Hampstead St Jas *Lon* 94-95; In RC Ch 95-96; C Tottenham St Paul 96-01; P-in-c New Southgate St Paul 01-03; V 03-07; V Tottenham St Paul from 07; CMP from 97. *St Paul's Vicarage, 60 Park Lane, London N17 0JR* Tel (020) 8808 7297
E-mail frmarkelliottsmith@blueyonder.co.uk

ELLIS, Anthony. See ELLIS, Canon John Anthony

ELLIS, Anthony Colin. b 56. Keble Coll Ox BA77 Man Univ PhD80. Linc Th Coll 80. **d** 81 **p** 82. C Mill Hill Jo Keble Ch *Lon* 81-83; Staff Tutor in RS Man Univ from 83; Dir Cen for Continuing Educn from 99; C Stretford St Pet *Man* 83-87; NSM Shore 87-89; Lic Preacher from 88. *2 Crowther Terrace, Blackshaw, Hebden Bridge HX7 6DE* Tel (01422) 844242 *or* 0161-275 3302

ELLIS, Brian Eric James. b 50. STETS 05. **d** 08 **p** 09. NSM Preston w Sutton Poyntz and Osmington w Poxwell *Sarum* from 08. *27 Fisherbridge Road, Preston, Weymouth DT3 6BT* Tel (01305) 832427 Mobile 07533-941686
E-mail brian-ellis@talktalk.net

ELLIS, Canon Bryan Stuart. b 31. Qu Coll Cam BA54 MA58. Ridley Hall Cam 55. **d** 57 **p** 58. C Ramsgate St Luke *Cant* 57-59; C Herne Bay Ch Ch 59-62; V Burmantofts St Steph and St Agnes *Ripon* 62-81; V Wakef 81-96; V Wakef St Andr and St Mary 81-00; Hon Can Wakef Cathl 89-00; rtd 00; Perm to Offic *Ripon* from 01. *302 Oakwood Lane, Leeds LS8 3LE* Tel 0113-240 3122

ELLIS, Charles Harold. b 50. NOC 78. **d** 81 **p** 82. C Davyhulme St Mary *Man* 81-85; V Tonge w Alkrington 85-91; P-in-c Radcliffe St Thos and St Jo 91; P-in-c Radcliffe St Mary 91; TR

Radcliffe 91-99; AD Radcliffe and Prestwich 96-99; P-in-c Newchurch 99-00; TR Rossendale Middle Valley 00-04; AD Rossendale 00-04; V Ingleton w Chapel le Dale *Bradf* from 04. *St Mary's Vicarage, Main Street, Ingleton, Carnforth LA6 3HF* Tel (01524) 241440 E-mail charlesandsue@compuserve.com

ELLIS, Christopher Charles. b 55. Edin Univ BD78 Hull Univ MA80. Edin Th Coll 76 Irish Sch of Ecum 78. **d** 79 **p** 80. C Selby Abbey *York* 79-82; C Fulford 82-85; Dioc Ecum Officer 81-98; Dioc Ecum Adv 90-98; Lect Ecum Th Hull Univ from 84; P-in-c Kexby w Wilberfoss *York* 85-90; Ecum Officer S Cleveland and N Yorks Ecum Coun 88-98; P-in-c Bulmer w Dalby, Terrington and Welburn 98-01; R Howardian Gp 01-05; P-in-c Sheriff Hutton, Farlington, Stillington etc 05-06; V Forest of Galtres from 06. *The Vicarage, Main Street, Sutton-on-the-Forest, York YO61 1DW* Tel (01347) 870336

ELLIS, Christopher Duncan. b 67. Anglia Ruskin Univ BA09. ERMC 08. **d** 08 **p** 09. C Thorpe St Andr *Nor* from 08. *9 Pine Road, Norwich NR7 9LE* Tel (01603) 436675

ELLIS, Canon David Craven. b 34. Man Univ BA56 MA57. St Aid Birkenhead 59. **d** 61 **p** 62. C Gt Crosby St Luke *Liv* 61-65; Hong Kong 65-69; P-in-c Sawrey *Carl* 69-74; Dioc Youth Officer 69-74; V Halifax St Aug *Wakef* 74-84; R Greystoke, Matterdale and Mungrisdale *Carl* 84-87; R Watermillock 84-87; TR Greystoke, Matterdale, Mungrisdale etc 88-91; RD Penrith 87-91; TR Carl H Trin and St Barn 91-96; Hon Can Carl Cathl 91-96; rtd 96; Perm to Offic *Carl* 97-02 and from 04; NSM Cartmel Peninsula 02-04. *Calderstones, 5 Fellside, Allithwaite, Grange-over-Sands LA11 7RN* Tel (01539) 533974

ELLIS, Dorothy Pearson. b 43. Sheff Univ BA66 MA67. Dioc OLM tr scheme 05. **d** 07 **p** 08. NSM Oakenshaw, Wyke and Low Moor *Bradf* from 07. *2 Woodrow Drive, Low Moor, Bradford BD12 0JU* Tel (01274) 679048

ELLIS, Mrs Emma Louise. b 79. Coll of Ripon & York St Jo BA00 Heythrop Coll Lon MTh03. Ridley Hall Cam 05. **d** 07 **p** 08. C Addiscombe St Mary Magd w St Martin *S'wark* from 07. *68 Elgin Road, Croydon CR0 6XA* Tel 07949-697075 (mobile) E-mail ele24@hotmail.com

ELLIS, Gay Winifred. b 48. Oak Hill Th Coll 94. **d** 96 **p** 97. NSM Nazeing *Chelmsf* 96-99; C 99-00; P-in-c Chingford St Anne 00-02; V 02-04; P-in-c Lambourne w Abridge and Stapleford Abbotts from 04; Ind Chapl from 04. *The Rectory, 39 Hoe Lane, Abridge, Romford RM4 1AU* Tel (01992) 814390
E-mail gayellis@aol.com

ELLIS, Gillian Patricia. **d** 99 **p** 00. OLM Blymhill w Weston-under-Lizard *Lich* 99-00; OLM Lapley w Wheaton Aston from 00. *18 Ashleigh Crescent, Wheaton Aston, Stafford ST19 9PN* Tel (01785) 840925 E-mail gellis3011@toucansurf.com

ELLIS, Hugh William. b 54. Sussex Univ BSc76. Ridley Hall Cam 88. **d** 90 **p** 91. C Reading St Jo *Ox* 90-93; P-in-c Bradfield and Stanford Dingley 93-97; R 97-03; TR Langport Area *B & W* from 03. *The Rectory, Huish Episcopi, Langport TA10 9QR* Tel (01458) 250480 E-mail hughelli@aol.com

ELLIS, Canon Ian Morton. b 52. QUB BD75 MTh82 TCD PhD89. CITC. **d** 77 **p** 78. C Portadown St Columba *Arm* 77-79; C Arm St Mark 79-85; Chapl Arm R Sch 79-85; Hon V Choral Arm Cathl 82-93; I Mullavilly 85-93; Dom Chapl to Abp Arm 86-93; Tutor for Aux Min (Arm) 90-93; Dioc Adv on Ecum 92-93; I Newcastle *D & D* from 93; Can Belf Cathl from 00; Ed *The Church of Ireland Gazette* from 01; Preb Newcastle St Patr Cathl Dublin from 01. *The Rectory, 1 King Street, Newcastle BT33 0HD* Tel (028) 4372 2439 Fax 4372 5977
E-mail ian.m.ellis@btinternet.com

ELLIS, Ian William. b 57. QUB BSc78 CertEd79 TCD BTh89. CITC 86. **d** 89 **p** 90. C Arm St Mark w Aghavilly 89-91; I Loughgall w Grange 91-02; Sec Gen Syn Bd of Educn from 02. *Church of Ireland House, 61-67 Donegall Street, Belfast BT1 2QH* Tel (028) 9023 1202 Fax 9023 7802
E-mail edunorth@ireland.anglican.org

ELLIS, Jean Miriam. b 35. St Mich Coll Llan 92. **d** 95 **p** 97. NSM Llanelli *S & B* 95-98; NSM Rockfield and St Maughen's w Llangattock etc *Mon* 99-04; NSM Rockfield and Dingestow Gp from 05. *2 Watery Lane, Monmouth NP25 5AT* Tel (01600) 719562

ELLIS, Canon John Anthony. b 47. Open Univ BA80. Coll of Resurr Mirfield 70. **d** 72 **p** 73. C Sketty *S & B* 72-75; C Duston *Pet* 75-80; R Lichborough w Maidford and Farthingstone 80-85; V Stratford Mortimer *Ox* 85-98; P-in-c Mortimer W End w Padworth 85-98; TR Kidlington w Hampton Poyle from 98; AD Ox from 04; Hon Can Ch Ch from 07. *St Mary's Rectory, 19 Mill Street, Kidlington OX5 2EE* Tel and fax (01865) 372230
E-mail churchkid@tesco.net

ELLIS, John Beaumont. b 45. Univ of Wales (Lamp) BA67 LTh69. Bp Burgess Hall Lamp. **d** 69 **p** 70. C Abergavenny St Mary w Llanwenarth Citra *Mon* 69-72; C Swansea St Gabr *S & B* 72-75; V Llanbister and Llanbadarn Fynydd w Llananno 75-77; V Newport St Andr *Mon* 77-80; V Risca 80-84; V Cheadle Heath *Ches* 84-94. *12 Upper Hibbert Lane, Marple, Stockport SK6 7HX* Tel 0161-427 1963

ELLIS, John Franklyn. b 34. Leeds Univ BA58. Linc Th Coll 58. **d** 60 **p** 61. C Ladybarn *Man* 60-63; C Stockport St Geo *Ches* 63-66; V High Lane 66-81; V Chelford w Lower Withington 81-99; rtd 99; Perm to Offic *Ches* from 00. *3 Millers Croft, Adlington Street, Macclesfield SK10 1BD*

ELLIS, John Keith Randolph. b 44. Univ of Wales MEd Man Univ CertEd. Westcott Ho Cam 98. **d** 01 **p** 02. C Glanogwen w St Ann's w Llanllechid *Ban* 01-04; Min Can Ban Cathl from 04. *Glan Arthur, Penisarwaun, Caernarfon LL55 3PW* Tel (01286) 873623 E-mail randolph@afoncegin.freeserve.co.uk

ELLIS, John Raymond. b 63. St Steph Ho Ox 95. **d** 97 **p** 98. C Clare w Poslingford, Cavendish etc *St E* 97-00; P-in-c Bury St Edmunds St Jo 00-02; P-in-c Bury St Edmunds St Geo 00-02; TV Bury St Edmunds All SS w St Jo and St Geo 02-04; Chapl RAF from 04. *Chaplaincy Services, Valiant Block, HQ Air Command, RAF High Wycombe HP14 4UE* Tel (01494) 496800 Fax 496343

ELLIS, John Roland. b 32. Wells Th Coll 67. **d** 69 **p** 70. C Kettering SS Pet and Paul 69-71; C Kingsthorpe 71-73; TV 73-74; TV Ebbw Vale *Mon* 74-76; V Llanddewi Rhydderch w Llanvapley etc 76-83; Miss to Seamen 79-86; V New Tredegar *Mon* 83-86; V Llanelli *S & B* 86-98; RD Crickhowell 91-98; rtd 99; P-in-c Rockfield and St Maughen's w Llangattock etc *Mon* 99-05; Hon C Rockfield and Dingestow Gp 05-07. *2 Watery Lane, Monmouth NP25 5AT* Tel (01600) 719562

ELLIS, Canon John Wadsworth. b 42. MBE98. TCD BA64. **d** 66 **p** 67. C Lisburn Ch Ch Cathl 66-69; C Norbiton *S'wark* 69-72; C New Clee *Linc* 72-85; V from 85; RD Grimsby and Cleethorpes 94-99; Can and Preb Linc Cathl from 98. *120 Queen Mary Avenue, Cleethorpes DN35 7SZ* Tel and fax (01472) 696521 or 329922 E-mail jwellis@ntlworld.com

ELLIS, Keith. b 39. Univ of Wales (Swansea) BSc60 Birm Poly BSc(Econ)74 Liv Univ CertEd61. St Jo Coll Nottm 95. **d** 96 **p** 97. NSM Marple All SS *Ches* 96-99; NSM Camelot Par *B & W* 99-03. *Address temp unknown*

ELLIS, Kevin Stuart. b 67. Newc Univ BA91 Lon Bible Coll PhD97. Qu Coll Birm 99. **d** 01 **p** 02. C Matson *Glouc* 01-04; TV Maryport, Netherton and Flimby *Carl* 04-07; TR from 07. *The Vicarage, Church Terrace, Maryport CA15 7PS* Tel (01900) 819886

ELLIS, Sister Lilian. b 44. Keswick Hall Coll TCert66. Oak Hill Th Coll 95. **d** 96 **p** 97. C Vange *Chelmsf* 96-00; C Pitsea w Nevendon 00-02; rtd 02; Perm to Offic *Chelmsf* from 02. *9 The Poplars, Basildon SS13 2ER* Tel (01268) 551018 E-mail lilian.ellis@tesco.net

ELLIS, Malcolm Railton. b 35. LTCL71 Univ of Wales (Lamp) BA56. Sarum Th Coll 56. **d** 58 **p** 59. C Llangynwyd w Maesteg 58-61; C Llantrisant 61-67; V Troedrhiwgarth 67-70; PV Truro Cathl 70-73; V Eglosshayle 73-81; V Margam *Llan* 81-87; V Cardiff St Jo 87-00; TR Cen Cardiff 00-02; Prec and Can Llan Cathl 96-02; rtd 02. *41 Wendron Street, Helston TR13 8PT* Tel (01326) 574000

ELLIS, Preb Mark Durant. b 39. Ex Univ BA62. Cuddesdon Coll 62. **d** 64 **p** 65. C Lyngford *B & W* 64-67; V Weston-super-Mare St Andr Bournville 67-76; TV Yeovil 76-88; V Yeovil St Mich from 88; Preb Wells Cathl from 90; RD Yeovil 94-04. *St Michael's Vicarage, St Michael's Avenue, Yeovil BA21 4LH* Tel and fax (01935) 475732

ELLIS, Paul. b 49. **d** 07 **p** 08. NSM Wakef St Jo from 07. *98 Bradford Road, Wakefield WF1 2AH* Tel (01924) 367976

ELLIS, Paul. b 56. Aston Tr Scheme 88 Trin Coll Bris 92. **d** 92 **p** 93. C Pennington *Man* 92-96; TV Deane 96-06; P-in-c Grassendale *Liv* from 06. *St Mary's Vicarage, 22 Eaton Road, Cressington, Liverpool L19 0PW* Tel 0151-427 1474

ELLIS, Peter Andrew. b 46. St D Coll Lamp 65. **d** 69 **p** 70. C Milford Haven *St D* 69-71; R Walwyn's Castle w Robeston W 71-74; Miss to Seafarers from 74; Hong Kong 74-75 and from 92; Singapore 75-82; The Tees and Hartlepool 82-92. *The Mariner's Club, 11 Middle Road, Kowloon, Hong Kong* Tel (00852) 2368 8261 Fax 2366 0928

ELLIS, Randolph. *See* ELLIS, John Keith Randolph

ELLIS, Richard. b 47. **d** 02 **p** 03. OLM Leiston *St E* from 02. *9 Kings Road, Leiston IP16 4DA* Tel (01728) 832168 Mobile 07759-349057 E-mail us@rellis41.freeserve.co.uk

ELLIS, Robert Albert. b 48. K Coll Lon BD70 AKC70. St Aug Coll Cant 70. **d** 72 **p** 73. C Liv Our Lady and St Nic w St Anne 72-76; P-in-c Meerbrook *Lich* 76-80; Producer Relig Progr BBC Radio Stoke 76-80; V Highgate All SS *Lon* 80-81; P-in-c Longdon *Lich* 81-87; Dioc Communications Officer 81-01; Chapl Palma de Mallorca *Eur* from 01. *Nuez de Balboa 6, Son Armadans, 07014 Palma de Mallorca, Spain* Tel (0034) 971 737 279 Fax 971 454 492 E-mail anglicanpalma@terra.es

ELLIS, The Ven Robin Gareth. b 35. Pemb Coll Ox BA57 BCL58 MA62. Chich Th Coll 58. **d** 60 **p** 61. C Swinton St Pet *Man* 60-63; Asst Chapl Worksop Coll Notts 63-66; V Swaffham Prior *Ely* 66-74; Asst Dir Educn 66-74; V Wisbech St Aug 74-82; V Yelverton *Ex* 82-86; Adn Plymouth 82-00; rtd 00; Perm to Offic *Ex* from 00. *24 Lyndhurst Road, Exmouth EX8 3DT* Tel (01395) 272891

ELLIS, Roger Henry. b 40. Natal Univ BA61 Selw Coll Cam BA64 MA68 Linacre Coll Ox BLitt69. **d** 66 **p** 67. C Ox St Mich 66-68; Sen Lect Univ of Natal S Africa 68-76; Hon C Pietermaritzburg Cathl 68-76; P-in-c Wortham *St E* 77; V Wheatley Hills *Sheff* 77-84; Chapl St Edm Sch Cant 84-00; P-in-c Dymchurch w Burmarsh and Newchurch *Cant* 00-04; AD Romney 01-03; rtd 05. *5 Bishops Reach, Wyndham Lane, Allington, Salisbury SP4 0BB* Tel (01980) 610797 E-mail ellisrhdm@yahoo.co.uk

ELLIS, Simon David. b 68. Univ of Wales (Cardiff) BSc89 Bris Univ PGCE90 MA00. St Steph Ho Ox BTh94. **d** 97 **p** 98. C Knowle H Nativity *Bris* 97-01; V Long Eaton St Laur *Derby* from 01. *The Vicarage, Regent Street, Long Eaton, Nottingham NG10 1JX* Tel 0115-973 3154 E-mail stlaurencechurch@live.co.uk

ELLIS, Susannah Margaret. b 44. Open Univ BA82 New Coll Dur CertEd88. EAMTC 93. **d** 96 **p** 97. NSM S Elmham and Ilketshall *St E* 96-98; Warden Quiet Waters Chr Retreat Ho 96-98; C Worlingham w Barnby and N Cove *St E* 98-01; C Beccles St Mich 98-01; P-in-c Worlingham w Barnby and N Cove 01-03; R from 03. *27 Lowestoft Road, Worlingham, Beccles NR34 7DZ* Tel (01502) 715403

✠**ELLIS, The Rt Revd Timothy William.** b 53. AKC75 York Univ DPhil98. St Aug Coll Cant 75. **d** 76 **p** 77 **c** 06. C Old Trafford St Jo *Man* 76-80; V Pendleton St Thos 80-87; Chapl Salford Coll of Tech 80-87; V Sheff St Leon Norwood 87-01; P-in-c Shiregreen St Hilda 94-01; RD Ecclesfield 94-99; Hon Can Sheff Cathl 00-01; Adn Stow *Linc* 01-06; Suff Bp Grantham from 06; Can and Preb Linc Cathl from 01. *Saxonwell Vicarage, Church Street, Long Bennington, Newark NG23 5ES* Tel (01400) 283344 Fax 283321 E-mail bishop.grantham@lincoln.anglican.org

ELLISDON, Patrick Leon Shane. b 61. St Jo Coll Nottm 99. **d** 01 **p** 02. C Margate St Phil *Cant* 01-04; P-in-c Cliftonville from 04. *St Paul's Vicarage, 18 Devonshire Gardens, Margate CT9 3AF* Tel (01843) 226832 Mobile 07932-734932 E-mail panddellisdon@tesco.net

ELLISON, John. b 37. FCA64. Qu Coll Birm. **d** 04 **p** 05. NSM Northanger *Win* from 04. *High Candovers, Hartley Mauditt, Alton GU34 3BP* Tel (01420) 511346 E-mail revjohnellison@hotmail.com

✠**ELLISON, The Rt Revd John Alexander.** b 40. ALCD67. **d** 67 **p** 68 **c** 88. C Woking St Paul *Guildf* 67-70; SAMS from 71; C Belgrano St Sav Argentina 80-83; R Aldridge *Lich* 83-88; Bp Paraguay 88-07; rtd 07. *The Furrow, Evingar Road, Whitchurch RG28 7EU* Tel (01256) 892126

ELLISON, Mrs Margaret Helen. b 50. Edin Univ BSc77 RN72. Yorks Min Course 07. **d** 09. NSM York St Hilda from 09; NSM York St Lawr w St Nic from 09. *17 Foresters Walk, Stamford Bridge, York YO41 1BB* Tel (01759) 372696 E-mail maggs.ellison@googlemail.com

ELLISON, Ms Sandra Anne. b 53. Anglia Poly Univ BA96 RMN74. EAMTC 99. **d** 02 **p** 03. C Hunstanton St Mary w Ringstead Parva etc *Nor* 02-05; R Ashmanhaugh, Barton Turf etc from 05. *11 Pinewood Drive, Horning, Norwich NR12 8LZ* Tel (01692) 630216

ELLISON, Simon John. b 51. SEITE 99. **d** 02 **p** 03. NSM Caterham *S'wark* 02-08; Asst Chapl Newcastle upon Tyne Hosps NHS Foundn Trust 08-09; Chapl Epsom and St Helier Univ Hosps NHS Trust from 09. *Trust Headquarters, St Helier Hospital, Wrythe Lane, Carshalton SM5 1AA* Tel (020) 8296 2000 E-mail simon.ellison@epsom-sthelier.nhs.uk

ELLISTON, John Ernest Nicholas. b 42. ALCD61. **d** 61 **p** 62. C Gipsy Hill Ch Ch *S'wark* 61-64; C Whitton and Thurleston w Akenham *St E* 64-68; P-in-c New Clee *Linc* 68-71; V 75-76; V Grimsby St Steph 71-75; P-in-c Mildenhall *St E* 77-79; RD Mildenhall 81-84; R Barton Mills, Beck Row w Kenny Hill etc 80-84; V Ipswich St Aug 84-96; R Guernsey St Peter Port *Win* 96-02; Chapl Princess Eliz Hosp Guernsey 96-02; rtd 02; Perm to Offic *St E* from 03. *27 Wyvern Road, Ipswich IP3 9TJ* Tel (01473) 726617 or 720036

ELLMORE, Peter Robert. b 44. Portsm Univ MA. Sarum & Wells Th Coll 84. **d** 86 **p** 87. C Bridgemary *Portsm* 86-89; C Portsea N End St Mark 89-91; Asst Chapl St Mary's Hosp Portsm 91-92; Chapl Qu Alexandra Hosp Portsm 91-93; Chapl Team Ldr Portsm Hosps NHS Trust 93-97; P-in-c Cosham *Portsm* 97-99; angl Chapl Univ Coll Lon Hosps NHS Trust 99-01; Chapl Team Ldr United Bris Healthcare NHS Trust 01-04; Lead Chapl (S) *Caring for the Spirit* NHS Project 04-07; Chapl St Pet Hospice Bris 07-09; rtd 09. *2 Westover Drive, Bristol BS9 3LX* Tel 0117-950 2927 E-mail peter.ellmore@lineone.net

ELLOR, Michael Keith. b 52. St Jo Coll Nottm 92. **d** 94 **p** 95. C Stafford St Jo and Tixall w Ingestre *Lich* 94-97; TV Bucknall and Bagnall 97-03; TR Bucknall from 03; RD Stoke 02-06. *The Rectory, 151 Werrington Road, Bucknall, Stoke-on-Trent ST2 9AQ* Tel (01782) 280667 or 279300 E-mail ellors@bucknall12.fsnet.co.uk

ELLSON, Montague Edward. b 33. Birm Univ BA56 Cam Univ CertEd67 Univ of Wales (Lamp) MA08. EAMTC 84. **d** 87 **p** 88.

Hon C Freethorpe w Wickhampton, Halvergate etc *Nor* 87-90; C Gaywood, Bawsey and Mintlyn 90-92; Miss to Seafarers from 90; R Pulham *Nor* 92-94; P-in-c Starston 93-94; Dioc NSM Officer 94-97; R Pulham Market, Pulham St Mary and Starston 94-97; RD Redenhall 95-97; rtd 97; Perm to Offic *Nor* from 97. *Barn Cottage, Neatishead Road, Horning, Norwich NR12 8LB* Tel (01692) 630251

ELLSWORTH, Lida Elizabeth. b 48. Columbia Univ (NY) BA70 Girton Coll Cam PhD76. EMMTC 85. **d** 88 **p** 94. NSM Bakewell *Derby* 88-07; Perm to Offic from 07. *Apple Croft, Granby Gardens, Bakewell DE45 1ET* Tel and fax (01629) 814255

ELLWOOD, Mrs Ethney. **d** 06 **p** 07. OLM Uttoxeter Area *Lich* from 06. *42 Jacks Lane, Marchington, Uttoxeter ST14 8LW* Tel (01283) 820459 E-mail revethneyellwood@hotmail.co.uk

ELLWOOD, Keith Brian. b 36. Curwen Coll Lon BA58 MMus65 Bede Coll Dur CertEd59 Hon DD99 AIGCM58 FRSA64 ACP66 FCollP83. Bps' Coll Cheshunt 64. **d** 64 **p** 65. Asst Master R Wanstead Sch 60-66; Chapl 64-66; C Wanstead St Mary *Chelmsf* 64-66; CF 66-70; OCF 70-71 and 76-79; Chapl St Paul's Coll Hong Kong 70-71; P-in-c Bicknoller *B & W* 71-73; Chapl Roedean Sch Brighton 73-76; Chapl Windsor Boys' Sch Hamm W Germany 76-79; Chapl Trin Coll Glenalmond 79-81; Hd Master St Chris Sch Burnham-on-Sea 82-86; Hon C Burnham *B & W* 82-86; R Staple Fitzpaine, Orchard Portman, Thurlbear etc 86-89; P-in-c Hugill and Dioc Educn Adv *Carl* 89-93; P-in-c Coldwaltham and Hardham *Chich* 93-95; rtd 96; Perm to Offic *Chich* 96-04 and *Sheff* from 04. *21 Fiddlers Drive, Armthorpe, Doncaster DN3 3TS* Tel (01302) 834031
E-mail k.b.e@btinternet.com

ELMAN, Simon Laurie. b 57. NTMTC. **d** 99 **p** 00. C Loughton St Jo *Chelmsf* 99-01; C Tye Green w Netteswell 01-07; Perm to Offic from 08. *26 Pakes Way, Theydon Bois, Epping CM16 7NA* Tel (01992) 813057 E-mail simon.elman@btinternet.com

ELMES, Amanda Jane. b 53. Lon Univ BDS76 RCS LDS77 Herts Univ PhD04. ERMC 06. **d** 08 **p** 09. NSM W w E Mersea *Chelmsf* from 08. *Deoban, 171 Lexden Road, Colchester CO3 3TE* Tel (01206) 543516
E-mail amanda.elmes@deoban.co.uk

ELMES, Sister Evelyn Sandra. b 61. **d** 97 **p** 98. CA from 89; C Southchurch H Trin *Chelmsf* 97-00; Perm to Offic *Win* 01-08. *Address temp unknown* E-mail eveelmes@tesco.net

ELMES, Ruth Katherine. CITC. **d** 09. C Stillorgan w Blackrock *D & G* from 09. *97 Wedgewood, Sandyford, Dublin 16, Republic of Ireland* Tel (00353) (1) 295 4870 E-mail relmes@eircom.net

ELMQVIST, Gunilla. *See* AQUILON-ELMQVIST, Mrs Gunilla

ELMS, Christian Grant. b 71. Salford Univ BSc04. Trin Coll Bris 07. **d** 09. C Pennington *Man* from 09. *11 Ruby Grove, Leigh WN7 4JW* Tel (01942) 607695 Mobile 07796-988907
E-mail christian.elms@virgin.net

ELPHICK, Robin Howard. b 37. ALCD63. **d** 64 **p** 65. C Clapham Common St Barn *S'wark* 64-67; C Woking St Pet *Guildf* 67-71; R Rollesby w Burgh w Billockby *Nor* 71-80; P-in-c Ashby w Oby, Thurne and Clippesby 79-80; R Rollesby w Burgh w Billockby w Ashby w Oby etc 80-84; R Frinton *Chelmsf* 84-94; P-in-c W w E Mersea and Peldon w Gt and Lt Wigborough 94-02; rtd 02; Perm to Offic *Nor* from 02. *1 Barn Cottages, Dodma Road, Weasenham, King's Lynn PE32 2TJ* Tel (01328) 838340
E-mail robin@relphick.fsnet.co.uk

ELPHICK, Canon Vivien Margaret. b 53. Kent Univ BA74 Solicitor 77. Trin Coll Bris BA90. **d** 90 **p** 94. C Oulton Broad *Nor* 90-94; P-in-c Burlingham St Edmund w Lingwood, Strumpshaw etc 94-06; RD Blofield 98-04; Hon Can Nor Cathl 03-06; P-in-c Measham *Leic* 06-08; P-in-c Packington w Normanton-le-Heath 06-08; P-in-c Donisthorpe and Moira w Stretton-en-le-Field 06-08; TR Woodfield Team from 08. *The Vicarage, High Street, Measham, Swadlincote DE12 7HZ* Tel (01530) 270354
E-mail vivien@rectorybarn.wanadoo.co.uk

ELPHIN AND ARDAGH, Archdeacon of. *Vacant*

ELPHIN AND ARDAGH, Dean of. *See* WILLIAMS, The Very Revd Arfon

ELSDON, Bernard Robert. b 29. Roch Th Coll 65. **d** 67 **p** 68. C Wallasey St Hilary *Ches* 67-71; C Liv Our Lady and St Nic w St Anne 71-72; V Anfield St Marg 73-89; Dioc Exec Dir for Chr Resp 80-83; rtd 89; Perm to Offic *Man* and *Ches* from 89. *31 Douglas Road, Hazel Grove, Stockport SK7 4JE* Tel 0161-292 1858 E-mail bernard.hillcrest@ntlworld.com

ELSDON, Mrs Janice Margaret. b 49. CITC 92. **d** 95 **p** 96. NSM Cloughfern *Conn* 95-99; NSM Ahoghill w Portglenone 99-02; NSM Belfast St Thos from 02. *St Bartholomew's Rectory, 16 Mount Pleasant, Belfast BT9 5DS* Tel (028) 9066 9995

ELSDON, Ronald. b 44. St Jo Coll Cam BA66 Trin Hall Cam PhD69 K Coll Lon BD86 Milltown Inst Dub PhD. CITC 97. **d** 99 **p** 00. C Ballymena w Ballyclug *Conn* 99-02; I Belfast St Bart from 02. *St Bartholomew's Rectory, 16 Mount Pleasant, Belfast BT9 5DS* Tel (028) 9066 9995 E-mail elsdon.rj@nireland.com *or* stbartholomew@connor.anglican.org

ELSMORE, Guy Charles. b 66. Edin Univ BSc88. Ridley Hall Cam 93. **d** 93 **p** 94. C Huyton St Mich *Liv* 93-98; V Hough

Green St Basil and All SS 98-05; AD Widnes and Hon Can Liv Cathl 03-05; P-in-c St Luke in the City from 05. *31 Mount Street, Liverpool L1 9HD* Tel 0151-709 2788 Mobile 07787-848229

ELSMORE, (née HANOVA), Ms Petra. b 70. Chas Univ Prague BA97. Ridley Hall Cam 00. **d** 03 **p** 04. C Toxteth St Philemon w St Gabr and St Cleopas *Liv* 03-06; P-in-c Everton St Geo 06-09. *31 Mount Street, Liverpool L1 9HD* Tel 0151-709 2788
E-mail petra.elsmore@yahoo.co.uk

ELSON, Christopher John. b 52. K Coll Lon BD75 AKC75. St Aug Coll Cant. **d** 76 **p** 77. C New Haw *Guildf* 76-79; C Guildf H Trin w St Mary 79-82; C Hale 85-87; V Ripley from 87; Sub Chapl HM Pris Send 88-92. *The Vicarage, 8 Grove Heath North, Ripley, Woking GU23 6EN* Tel (01483) 211798 Mobile 07956-103289 E-mail chris@elsons.org.uk

ELSON, John Frederick. Roch Th Coll 62. **d** 64 **p** 65. C Tenterden St Mildred w Smallhythe *Cant* 64-68; P-in-c Chart next Sutton Valence 68-71; V Fletching *Chich* 71-93; Chapl Wivelsfield Green Hospice 91-93; rtd 93; Perm to Offic *Chich* from 93. *Fernbank, 36 Olive Meadow, Uckfield TN22 1QY* Tel (01825) 760663

ELSON, Sharon Anne. b 50. WEMTC 99. **d** 00 **p** 01. OLM Heref St Pet w St Owen and St Jas from 00. *26 Craig House, Sudbury Avenue, Hereford HR1 1XU* Tel (01432) 370417 Mobile 07718-481318

ELSTOB, Stephen William. b 57. Sarum & Wells Th Coll. **d** 86 **p** 87. C Sunderland Springwell w Thorney Close *Dur* 86-88; C Upholland *Liv* 88-89; TV 89-96; V Cinnamon Brow 96-07; TV N Wearside *Dur* from 07. *The Vicarage, Bootle Street, Sunderland SR5 4EY* Tel 0191-537 3744

ELSTON, James Ian. b 70. City Univ BSc95. SEITE 01. **d** 04 **p** 05. NSM Old St Pancras *Lon* from 04. *8 Mansfield Road, London NW3 2HN* Tel (020) 7482 4056 E-mail jamesielston@aol.com

ELSTON, Philip Herbert. b 35. RD80 and Bar 90. Leeds Univ MA76 K Coll Lon AKC63 Leic Coll of Educn CertEd67. St Boniface Warminster 63. **d** 64 **p** 65. C Thurnby Lodge *Leic* 64-66; Hon C 66-67; Chapl RNR 67-90; Chapl Malosa Sch Malawi 68-75; Hon C Far Headingley St Chad *Ripon* 75-79; V Knowl Hill w Littlewick *Ox* 79-84; Chapl RN Sch Haslemere 85-89; C Felpham w Middleton *Chich* 89-90; Asst S Regional Dir Miss to Seamen 91-93; Dep S Regional Dir 93-97; S Regional Dir 97-00; Perm to Offic *Win* from 93; *Cant* 94-00; *Chich* from 97; Corps Chapl Sea Cadet Corps 83-95; rtd 00; Hon C Witchampton, Stanbridge and Long Crichel etc *Sarum* 00-04; Hon Chapl Miss to Seafarers from 00. *East Farm Cottage, Dinton Road, Wylye, Warminster BA12 0RE* Tel (01985) 248598

ELSWORTH, Mrs Teresa Karen. b 60. Cape Town Univ BSc82. SEITE 03. **d** 06 **p** 07. NSM Yalding w Collier Street *Roch* from 06; Perm to Offic *Cant* from 07. *10 Lurkins Rise, Goudhurst, Cranbrook TN17 1ED* Tel (01580) 211550
E-mail karenelsworth@hotmail.com

ELTON, Canon Derek Hurley. b 31. Lon Univ BSc52. Wycliffe Hall Ox 53. **d** 55 **p** 56. C Ashton-on-Ribble St Andr *Blackb* 55-57; India 58-70; R Wickmere w Lt Barningham and Itteringham *Nor* 71-79; R Lt w Gt Ellingham 79-83; P-in-c Rockland All SS and St Andr w St Pet 81-83; R Lt w Gt Ellingham w Rockland 83-88; Chapl Wayland Hosp Norfolk 84-88; Miss to Seamen 89-98; Algeria 89-94; Eritrea 94-98; rtd 96; Perm to Offic *Nor* from 00. *22 Alfred Road, Cromer NR27 9AN* Tel (01263) 511730 E-mail jedclef@paston.co.uk

ELTRINGHAM, Anna. b 74. St Jo Coll Dur BA96. SEITE 05. **d** 08. C S Norwood H Innocents *S'wark* from 08. *2 Mount Pleasant View, Dalmally Road, Croydon CR0 6LU* Tel (020) 8656 4548 E-mail revd.anna@gmail.com

ELTRINGHAM, Mrs Fiona Ann. b 48. Bp Grosseteste Coll CertEd69. NEOC 86. **d** 89 **p** 94. Par Dn Willington *Newc* 89-92; Chapl HM YOI Castington 92-95; Chapl HM Pris Dur 95-07; rtd 07; Perm to Offic *Dur* from 07. *Granary Cottage, Stockley House Farm, Oakenshaw, Crook DL15 0TJ* Tel (01388) 746058 E-mail davefi@tiscali.co.uk

ELVERSON, Ronald Peter Charles. b 50. St Edm Hall Ox BA73 MA86. St Jo Coll Nottm 84. **d** 86 **p** 87. C Whitnash *Cov* 86-90; V Dunchurch 90-01; R Dersingham w Anmer and Shernborne *Nor* 01-05; P-in-c Ore Ch Ch *Chich* 05-08; V from 08. *103 Fairlight Road, Hastings TN35 5EJ* Tel (01424) 715193
E-mail ronelverson@theelversons.fsnet.co.uk

ELVEY, Ms Charlotte Evanthia. b 44. St Anne's Coll Ox BA66 Bris Univ CertEd67. S'wark Ord Course 91. **d** 94 **p** 95. C Sydenham St Bart *S'wark* 94-98; P-in-c Worcester Park Ch Ch w St Phil 98-03; V from 03. *The Vicarage, 1E Lindsay Road, Worcester Park KT4 8LF* Tel (020) 8337 1327
E-mail c.elvey@btinternet.com

ELVIDGE, Joanna. b 55. FCIPD84. STETS BA06. **d** 06 **p** 07. NSM Horsham *Chich* from 06. *2 Garden Cottages, Forest Grange, Horsham RH13 6HX* Tel (01293) 852105 Fax 852187 E-mail joanna.elvidge@ukonline.co.uk

ELVIN, Jonathan Paul Alistair. b 65. Bris Univ BSc90 Fitzw Coll Cam BA94. Ridley Hall Cam 92. **d** 95 **p** 96. C Gravesend St Geo *Roch* 95-98; C Ex St Leon w H Trin 98-07; Min Ex Trin CD from 07. *23 Couper Meadows, Exeter EX2 7TF* Tel (01392) 363627 E-mail jonny@trinityexeter.com

ELVY, Canon Peter David. b 38. Lon Univ BA62 Fitzw Ho Cam BA64 MA68 Edin Univ PhD95. Ridley Hall Cam. d 65 p 66. C Herne Cant 65-66; C New Addington 66-68; C Addiscombe St Mildred 69-71; Youth Chapl Chelmsf 71-80; V Gt Burstead 75-92; Can Chelmsf Cathl 80-92; V Chelsea All SS Lon 92-05; Can Ughelli from 98; Preb St Paul's Cathl from 05; rtd 05; Perm to Offic Lon from 05. 2 Honiton Mansions, Flood Street, London SW3 5TU Tel (020) 7795 0084
E-mail peterelvy@googlemail.com

ELWIN, Ernest John. b 31. Selw Coll Cam BA54 MA58. Ridley Hall Cam 54. d 56 p 57. C Wandsworth All SS S'wark 56-59; C Harlow New Town w Lt Parndon Chelmsf 59-61; Asst Teacher Tidworth Down Sch Dorset 61-63; V Soundwell Bris 63-66; Asst Teacher Seldown Sch Dorset 66-68; Wareham Modern Sch 68-69; Perm to Offic Sarum from 67; Lect S Dorset Tech Coll Weymouth 70-85; Weymouth Coll 85-88; Sub Chapl HM Youth Cust Cen Portland from 93. 4 Portesham Hill, Portesham, Weymouth DT3 4EU Tel (01305) 871358

ELWIS, Malcolm John. b 42. Melbourne Univ DipEd74. St Jo Coll Morpeth 69. d 70 p 72. C Bentleigh St Jo Australia 70-72; C St Paul's Cathl Sale 72-73; Perm to Offic Brisbane 73-80; Perm to Offic Chich from 80; Chapl Hellingly and Amberstone Hosps 88-93; Chapl Eastbourne and Co Healthcare NHS Trust 93-02; Chapl E Sussex Co Healthcare NHS Trust from 02; Sub Chapl HM Pris Lewes 92-04; Chapl 04-06. Puddledock, Boreham Lane, Wartling, Hailsham BN27 1RS Tel (01323) 833233
E-mail malcolmelwis21@yahoo.co.uk

ELWOOD, Alan Roy. b 54. Sarum & Wells Th Coll 90. d 92 p 93. C Street w Walton B & W 92-96; V Kingsbury Episcopi w E Lambrook, Hambridge etc from 96. The Vicarage, Folly Road, Kingsbury Episcopi, Martock TA12 6BH Tel (01935) 824605

ELY, Nigel Patrick. b 62. Thames Poly BA83 Southn Univ BTh92. Chich Th Coll 89. d 92 p 93. C Rustington Chich 92-93; C Bexhill St Pet 93-96; Chapl St Geo Post 16 Cen Birm 96-99; Perm to Offic from 02. 57 Cherry Orchard Road, Birmingham B20 2LD Tel 0121-554 6340

ELY, Bishop of. See RUSSELL, The Rt Revd Anthony John

ELY, Dean of. See CHANDLER, The Very Revd Michael John

EMBLETON, Harold. b 21. Ch Coll Cam BA47 MA52. Qu Coll Birm 47. d 49 p 50. C Kidderminster St Mary Worc 49-52; CF (TA) 50-52; C Wimbledon S'wark 52-53; Chapl RN 53-76; QHC 74-76; V Bognor Chich 76-84; RD Arundel and Bognor 77-82; V Skirwith, Ousby and Melmerby w Kirkland Carl 84-87; rtd 87; Perm to Offic Carl 87-93 and Chich from 93. Flat 3, 7 Chatsworth Gardens, Eastbourne BN20 7JP Tel (01323) 411426

EMBLIN, Canon Richard John. b 48. BEd71 MA81. S Dios Minl Tr Scheme 83. d 86 p 87. C S w N Hayling Portsm 86-89; P-in-c Wootton 89-95; V Cowes H Trin and St Mary from 95; RD W Wight 01-07; Hon Can Portsm Cathl from 05. The Vicarage, Church Road, Cowes PO31 8HA Tel (01983) 292509
E-mail cowesvic@yahoo.com

EMERSON, Arthur Edward Richard. b 24. Lich Th Coll 69. d 72 p 73. C Barton upon Humber Linc 72-74; V Chapel St Leonards 75-88; V Hogsthorpe 77-88; V Chapel St Leonards w Hogsthorpe 88-91; rtd 91; Perm to Offic Linc from 91. 47 Highfields, Nettleham, Lincoln LN2 2SZ Tel (01522) 754175

EMERSON, Miss Jan Vivien. b 44. S Dios Minl Tr Scheme 89. d 92 p 95. NSM Chich St Paul and St Pet 92-94; NSM Bosham 94-02; Asst Chapl R W Sussex NHS Trust from 02. Lea-Rig, 3 Elm Park, Bosham, Chichester PO18 8PD Tel (01243) 574948
E-mail janvemerson@aol.com

EMERTON, Andrew Neil. b 72. York Univ BSc93 Qu Coll Ox DPhil96 Down Coll Cam BTh05. Ridley Hall Cam 02. d 05 p 06. C Brompton H Trin w Onslow Square St Paul Lon 05-07; Dir St Paul's Th Cen from 08. 70 Archel Road, London W14 9QP Tel (020) 7052 0755 or 7381 0506 Mobile 07815-498162
E-mail andy.emerton@htb.org.uk

EMERTON, Prof John Adney. b 28. CCC Ox BA50 MA54 CCC Cam MA55 BD60 St Jo Coll Cam DD73 Edin Univ Hon DD77 FBA79. Wycliffe Hall Ox 50. d 52 p 53. C Birm Cathl 52-53; Asst Lect Th Birm Univ 52-53; Lect Hebrew and Aramaic Dur Univ 53-55; Lect Div Cam Univ 55-62; Fell St Pet Coll Ox 62-68; Reader in Semitic Philology Ox Univ 62-68; Regius Prof Hebrew Cam Univ 68-95; Fell St Jo Coll Cam from 70; Hon Can Jerusalem from 84; Perm to Offic Ely from 98. 34 Gough Way, Cambridge CB3 9LN Tel (01223) 363219

EMERY, Karen Maureen. See BECK, Ms Karen Maureen

EMINSON, Mark Franklin. b 79. Merton Coll Ox BA01 MSt03 MA06 Trin Coll Cam BA07. Westcott Ho Cam 05. d 08 p 09. C E Grinstead St Swithun Chich from 08. 21 Bourg de Peage Avenue, East Grinstead RH19 3YD Tel (01342) 311021 Mobile 07816-273452 E-mail eminsons@btinternet.com

EMM, Robert Kenneth. b 46. K Coll Lon BD68 AKC68. d 69 p 70. C Hammersmith SS Mich and Geo White City Estate CD Lon 69-72; C Keynsham B & W 72-75; C Yeovil 75-80; TV Gt Grimsby St Mary and St Jas Linc 80-85; R N Thoresby 85-94; R Grainsby 85-94; V Waithe 85-94; R The North-Chapel Parishes

from 94. The Rectory, Church Lane, North Thoresby, Grimsby DN36 5QG Tel and fax (01472) 840029
E-mail bob@bobemm.demon.co.uk

EMMEL, Canon Malcolm David. b 32. Qu Coll Birm. d 58 p 59. C Hessle York 58-62; Canada 62-66; V Catterick Ripon 66-73; V Pateley Bridge and Greenhow Hill 73-77; P-in-c Middlesmoor w Ramsgill 76-77; V Upper Nidderdale 77-88; RD Ripon 79-86; Hon Can Ripon Cathl 84-97; R Bedale 88-97; P-in-c Leeming 88-97; rtd 97; Perm to Offic Bradf from 98. 29 Greystone Close, Burley in Wharfedale, Ilkley LS29 7RS Tel (01943) 865047

EMMETT, Kerry Charles. b 46. St Jo Coll Dur BA68. St Jo Coll Nottm 71. d 73 p 74. C Attenborough w Chilwell S'well 73-75; C Chilwell 75-76; C Wembley St Jo Lon 76-79; V Hanworth St Rich 79-89; R Ravenstone and Swannington Leic 89-04; RD Akeley S 97-03; P-in-c Mountsorrel Ch Ch and St Pet from 04. Christ Church Vicarage, 4 Rothley Road, Mountsorrel, Loughborough LE12 7JU Tel 0116-230 2235

EMMOTT, David Eugene. b 41. St Chad's Coll Dur BA63. d 66 p 67. C Bingley H Trin Bradf 66-69; C Anfield St Marg Liv 69-70; C Kirkby 70-75; Chapl Newc Poly 75-78; Hon C Toxteth Park St Marg Liv 78-80; TV Upholland 80-88; V Southfields St Barn S'wark 88-99; TV Liv Our Lady and St Nic w St Anne 99-06; rtd 06. 6A Eastern Drive, Liverpool L19 0NB Tel 0151-281 5493
E-mail davidemmott@mac.com

EMMOTT, Douglas Brenton. b 45. K Coll Lon BD78 AKC78 York Univ MA97. Linc Th Coll 79. d 80 p 81. C Kingston upon Hull St Alb York 80-83; V Scarborough St Sav w All SS 83-91; V York St Chad 91-99; V Leeds All So Ripon 99-07; rtd 07. Le Moulin de Vernay, 72500 Dissay-sous-Courcillon, France Tel (0033) (2) 43 46 53 82 Mobile (6) 37 79 26 45
E-mail douglas.emmott@mac.com

EMMOTT, John Charles Lionel. b 32. SEITE 96. d 96 p 97. NSM Tenterden St Mich Cant 96-02; rtd 02; Perm to Offic Cant from 02. 58 Grange Crescent, St Michaels, Tenterden TN30 6DZ Tel (01580) 762092 E-mail emmott@connectfree.co.uk

EMPEY, Clement Adrian. b 42. TCD BA64 MA68 PhD71. CITC. d 74 p 75. C Dublin St Ann D & G 75-76; I Kells-Inistioge Gp C & O 76-84; I Clane w Donadea and Coolcarrigan M & K 84-88; Hon Chapl Miss to Seafarers from 88; Sen Chapl Miss to Seamen (Irish Republic) 97-08; I Dublin St Ann and St Steph D & G 88-01; Preb Tassagard St Patr Cathl Dublin 82-89; Treas 89-91; Chan 91-96; Prec 96-01; Chapl Rotunda Hosp 98-08; Prin CITC 01-08; Prec Ch Ch Cathl Dublin 01-08; rtd 08. Address temp unknown Tel (00353) 87-902 2169 (mobile)
E-mail adrianempey@gmail.com

✠EMPEY, The Rt Revd Walton Newcome Francis. b 34. TCD BA57 Hon FGCM02. K Coll (NS) BD68. d 58 p 59 c 81. C Glenageary D & G 58-60; Canada 60-66; Bp's C Grand Falls New Brunswick 60-63; I Madawaska 63-66; I Stradbally C & O 66-71; Dean Limerick L & K 71-81; I Limerick St Mich 71-81; Preb Taney St Patr Cathl Dublin 73-81; Bp L & K 81-85; Bp M & K 85-96; Abp Dublin D & G 96-02; Preb Cualaun St Patr Cathl Dublin 96-02; rtd 02. Rathmore Lodge, Rathmore, Tullow, Co Carlow, Republic of Ireland Tel (00353) (59) 916 1891
E-mail louempey@hotmail.com

EMSON, Stanley George. b 26. Glouc Sch of Min. d 89 p 90. NSM Cirencester Glouc 89-02; NSM Coates, Rodmarton and Sapperton etc 91-96; Perm to Offic 96-04; C-in-c Rodmarton CD 04-06; rtd 06. The School House, 31 Rodmarton, Cirencester GL7 6PE Tel (01285) 841348

EMTAGE, Miss Susan Raymond. b 34. St Mich Ho Ox 63. dss 79 d 87 p 94. SW Area Sec CPAS Women's Action 75-82; Leic St Chris 82-86; Bramerton w Surlingham Nor 86-88; C 87-88; C Rockland St Mary w Hellington, Bramerton etc 88-89; Par Dn W Bromwich St Jas and St Paul 89-94; C 94; rtd 94; Hon C Stapleton Bris 96-04. 23 Capel Court, The Burgage, Prestbury, Cheltenham GL52 3EL Tel (01242) 577535
E-mail sue.emtage@ukonline.co.uk

ENDALL, Peter John. b 38. Linc Th Coll 83. d 85 p 86. C Burley in Wharfedale Bradf 85-88; V Thwaites Brow 88-03; RD S Craven 96-02; rtd 03; Hon C Tamworth Lich 04-08; Perm to Offic from 08. 19 Cordwell Close, Castle Donington, Derby DE74 2JL Tel (01332) 390863

ENDEAN, Michael George Devereux. b 33. Ox NSM Course. d 84 p 85. NSM Wantage Downs Ox 84-93. 87 Brookmead Drive, Wallingford OX10 9BH Tel (01491) 824231

ENDICOTT, Michael John. b 45. d 97. NSM Pontnewydd Mon 97; NSM The Well Cen from 97. The Well Centre, Station Road, Pontnewydd, Cwmbran NP44 1NZ Tel (01633) 483660

ENEVER, John William. b 44. MBE92. Open Univ BA80. NTMTC 94. d 97 p 98. NSM Waltham H Cross Chelmsf 97-02; NSM Gt Ilford St Andr 02-08; Asst Chapl Gt Ormond Street Hosp for Children NHS Trust from 08. St Andrew's Vicarage, St Andrew's Road, Ilford IG1 3PE Tel (020) 8554 3858
E-mail johnenever@gmail.com

ENEVER, Canon Rosemary Alice Delande. b 45. Oak Hill Th Coll 86. d 88 p 94. NSM Gt Ilford St Jo Chelmsf 88-94; TV Waltham H Cross 94-02; Asst Area Dean Epping Forest 00-01; V Gt Ilford St Andr from 02; RD Redbridge 06-08; Hon Can

Chelmsf Cathl from 06. *St Andrew's Vicarage, St Andrew's Road, Ilford IG1 3PE* Tel (020) 8554 3858
E-mail rosemaryenever@googlemail.com

ENEVER, Mrs Susan Elizabeth. b 33. WMMTC 87. **d** 92 **p** 94. NSM Rugby *Cov* 92-97; Perm to Offic 97-05; *Pet* 98-05; *Worc* from 00. *7 Rocheberie Way, Rugby CV22 6EG* Tel (01788) 813135

ENEVER, Vivian John. b 61. Collingwood Coll Dur BA82 Cam Univ PGCE85 Man Univ BPhil97. Westcott Ho Cam 88. **d** 91 **p** 92. C Gt Crosby St Faith *Liv* 91-95; C Cantril Farm 95-97; TV Halas *Worc* 97-03; TR Newark *S'well* from 03. *The Rectory, 6 Bede House Lane, Newark NG24 1PY* Tel (01636) 704513

ENGEL, Jeffrey Davis. b 38. Man Univ BA59 Liv Univ PGCE60 Aston Univ MSc82 FCP83. St Deiniol's Hawarden 86. **d** 89 **p** 90. NSM Formby St Pet *Liv* 89-92; C Prescot 92-94; P-in-c Hale 94-03; Dioc Adv for Past Care and Counselling 94-03; rtd 04; Chapl MU from 05. *Church View, West Street, Prescot L34 1LQ*

ENGELSEN, Christopher James. b 57. Nottm Univ BTh86. Linc Th Coll 83. **d** 86 **p** 87. C Sprowston *Nor* 86-89; C High Harrogate Ch Ch *Ripon* 89-92; TV Seacroft 92-95; P-in-c Foulsham w Hindolveston and Guestwick *Nor* 95-01; P-in-c Hevingham w Hainford and Stratton Strawless 01-05; R Coltishall w Gt Hautbois, Frettenham etc from 05. *The Rectory, Rectory Road, Coltishall, Norwich NR12 7HL* Tel (01603) 737255
E-mail christopher.engelsen@btinternet.com

ENGLAND (formerly LEFROY), Mrs Kathleen Christine. b 33. Newton Park Coll Bris TCert53. St Mich Ho Ox 56 Trin Coll Bris 90. **d** 90 **p** 02. Personnel Sec SAMS 83-91; Asst Gen Sec 87-92; rtd 92; NSM Eastbourne H Trin *Chich* 90-02; NSM Eastbourne St Jo 02-08; Perm to Offic from 08. *11 Holywell Close, Eastbourne BN20 7RX* Tel (01323) 640294
E-mail katieengland8@gmail.com

ENGLAND, Richard Alan. b 74. Sheff Univ BA97 Dur Univ MA07. Wycliffe Hall Ox 06. **d** 08 **p** 09. C Whitfield *Derby* from 08. *12 Rushmere, Glossop SK13 8TH* Tel (01457) 855993
E-mail richard@glossop.org

ENGLAND, Tarie. *See* CARLYON, Mrs Jessie Marguerite Tarie

ENGLAND-SIMON, Haydn Henry. b 57. Llan Dioc Tr Scheme 92. **d** 96 **p** 97. NSM Penydarren *Llan* 96-97; C Caerphilly 97-01; V Pentre 01-07; V Ystradyfodwg from 07. *The Vicarage, 7 Llewellyn Street, Pentre CF41 7BY* Tel (01443) 433651

ENGLER, Mrs Margaret Dorothy. b 44. Lon Univ TCert77. S'wark Ord Course 90. **d** 93 **p** 94. NSM Harlesden All So *Lon* 93-97; Dep Chapl HM Pris Wandsworth 97; Acting Chapl HM Pris Wormwood Scrubs 97-98; Chapl HM Pris High Down 98-04; rtd 04; Perm to Offic *Lon* 04-07; NSM Harlesden All So from 07. *22A Langton Road, London NW2 6QA* Tel (020) 8450 2395 E-mail margaret@homechoice.co.uk

ENGLISH, Peter Gordon. b 31. Edin Univ MA55. Ripon Hall Ox 59. **d** 61 **p** 62. C Bingley All SS *Bradf* 61-64; V Cottingley 64-66; Uganda 66-72; rtd 86; Perm to Offic *Sarum* from 96. *9 Carlton Row, Trowbridge BA14 0RJ* Tel (01225) 752243

ENGLISH, Philip Trevor. b 37. Dur Univ BSc60 FLIA81 MITPA84. Cranmer Hall Dur 60. **d** 62 **p** 63. C Hall Green Ascension *Birm* 62-66; Chapl St Jo Cathl Hong Kong 66-67; V Dorridge *Birm* 67-72; Perm to Offic *Ox* from 04. *Churchlands, Appletree Road, Chipping Warden, Banbury OX17 1LN* Tel (01295) 660222 Fax 660725 Mobile 07831-446421
E-mail pteifs@aol.com

ENNION, Peter. b 56. Aston Tr Scheme 85 Coll of Resurr Mirfield 87. **d** 89 **p** 90. C Middlewich w Byley *Ches* 89-91; C Aylestone St Andr w St Jas *Leic* 91-92; C Coppenhall *Ches* 92-94; P-in-c Newton in Mottram 94-99; P-in-c Tranmere St Paul w St Luke 99-04; V Torrisholme *Blackb* from 04. *The Ascension Vicarage, 63 Michaelson Avenue, Morecambe LA4 6SF* Tel (01524) 413144

ENNIS, Mrs Lesley. b 47. Bp Lonsdale Coll CertEd68 Open Univ BA84. OLM course 97. **d** 99 **p** 00. NSM Sowerby *Wakef* from 99; NSM Norland from 09. *26 Springfield, Sowerby Bridge HX6 1AD* Tel (01422) 832747 Mobile 07703-628897 Fax 842747 E-mail lesleyennis@hotmail.co.uk

ENNIS, Martin Michael. b 58. Man Univ BSc80 MCollP84. Sarum & Wells Th Coll 87. **d** 89 **p** 90. C Newquay *Truro* 89-92; C Tewkesbury w Walton Cardiff *Glouc* 92-95; P-in-c Brockworth 95-96; V 96-03; Hon C Wotton St Mary from 09. *61 Howard Street, Gloucester GL1 4UU*
E-mail martinennis@blueyonder.co.uk

ENOCH, William Frederick Palmer. b 30. EMMTC 76. **d** 79 **p** 80. NSM Ilkeston St Mary *Derby* 79-85; P-in-c Ilkeston H Trin 85-95; rtd 95; Perm to Offic *Derby* from 95. *82 Derby Road, Ilkeston DE7 5EZ* Tel 0115-944 3003

ENSOR, Paul George. b 56. Ripon Coll Cuddesdon. **d** 82 **p** 83. C Newington St Mary *S'wark* 82-87; TV Croydon St Jo 87-91; P-in-c Brandon and Santon Downham *St E* 91-92; R Brandon and Santon Downham w Elveden 92-95; V Mitcham St Olave *S'wark* from 95. *St Olave's Vicarage, 22 Church Walk, London SW16 5JH* Tel (020) 8764 2048
E-mail pedrazzini@ukgateway.net

ENSOR, Canon Terence Bryan. b 45. K Coll Lon BD78 AKC78. Westcott Ho Cam 78. **d** 79 **p** 80. C Bermondsey St Hugh CD *S'wark* 79-82; Seychelles 82-85; V Northampton St Benedict *Pet* 85-90; Uruguay 90-93; Fieldworker USPG *Blackb, Bradf, Carl* and *Wakef* 93-96; V Blackb St Jas 96-02; Assoc P Caracas Venezuela 02-03; Hon Can Venezuela and Curazao from 02; TV Ribbleton *Blackb* 03-06; C Standish from 06. *St Wilfrid's House, 7 Rectory Lane, Standish, Wigan WN6 0XA* Tel (01257) 425806

ENTICOTT, Ian Peter. b 59. Sheff Univ BA82 St Jo Coll Dur MA00. Cranmer Hall Dur 97. **d** 99 **p** 00. C Higher Bebington *Ches* 99-02; P-in-c Kelsall from 02. *St Philip's Vicarage, Chester Road, Kelsall, Tarporley CW6 0SA* Tel (01829) 751472
E-mail ian.enticott@tiscali.co.uk

ENTWISLE, George Barry. b 43. St Jo Coll Ox BA66 MA72 Massey Univ (NZ) MEd99. Linc Th Coll 73. **d** 75 **p** 76. C Rawmarsh w Parkgate *Sheff* 75-78; C Ashburton New Zealand 78-80; V Upper Clutha 80-84; V Gore 84-94; Can St Paul's Cathl Dunedin 87-94; Hon C Upper Clutha 01-06; rtd 08. *5 Bruce Street, Cromwell 9310, New Zealand* Tel and fax (0064) (3) 445 1797 Mobile 27-426 5539 E-mail b.entwistle@xtra.co.nz

ENTWISTLE, Christopher John. b 47. NOC 79. **d** 82 **p** 83. NSM Colne H Trin *Blackb* 82-84; C Poulton-le-Fylde 84-87; V Blackpool St Paul 87-96; RD Blackpool 94-96; P-in-c Overton 96-01; V Ashton-on-Ribble St Andr 01-06; TV W Preston from 06; AD Preston 04-09. *The Vicarage, 240 Tulketh Road, Ashton-on-Ribble, Preston PR2 1ES* Tel (01772) 726848
E-mail revcjentwistle@yahoo.co.uk

ENTWISTLE, Frank Roland. b 37. Dur Univ BA59. Cranmer Hall Dur 59. **d** 61 **p** 62. C Harborne Heath *Birm* 61-65; S Area Sec BCMS 65-66; Educn Sec 66-73; Hon C Wallington *S'wark* 68-73; UCCF 73-02; Hon C Ware Ch Ch *St Alb* 73-76; Hon C Leic H Trin w St Jo 76-02; rtd 02. *Three Gables, Tews Lane, Bickington, Barnstaple EX31 2JU* Tel (01271) 321861
E-mail entwistles@cwcom.net

ENTWISTLE, Howard Rodney. b 36. Ball Coll Ox BA61. Linc Th Coll 61. **d** 63 **p** 64. C Langley St Aid CD *Man* 63-64; C Langley All SS and Martyrs 64-66; V Wythenshawe St Martin 66-73; R Stretford St Matt 73-99; rtd 99; Perm to Offic *Ches* from 03. *3 Coombes Avenue, Marple, Stockport SK6 7BW* Tel 0161-427-6294

ENWUCHOLA, Canon Benjamin Ameh. b 56. Lon Bible Coll BA94. **d** 95 **p** 98. NSM S Tottenham St Ann *Lon* 96-99; NSM W Kilburn St Luke w St Simon and St Jude from 99; Chapl Nigerian Congregation from 99; Hon Can Ondo from 02. *St Marylebone Church, 17 Marylebone Road, London NW1 5LR* Tel (020) 7935 9478 Fax 7486 5493 *or* Tel and fax 8969 2379
E-mail benwuchola@yahoo.co.uk
or nigerianchaplaincy@yahoo.co.uk

EPPS, Christopher Derek. b 54. ACII79. Linc Th Coll 95. **d** 95 **p** 96. C Clevedon St Jo *B & W* 95-98; R St John w Millbrook *Truro* 98-03; P-in-c Truro St Geo and St Jo from 03; P-in-c Truro St Paul and St Clem from 03. *St George's Vicarage, St George's Road, Truro TR1 3NR* Tel (01872) 272630 Fax 823559
E-mail frcdepps@btinternet.com

EPPS, Gerald Ralph. b 31. Open Univ BA79. Oak Hill Th Coll 52 K Coll Lon 54. **d** 57 **p** 58. C Slade Green *Roch* 57-60; V Freethorpe w Wickhampton *Nor* 60-70; P-in-c Halvergate w Tunstall 62-67; V 67-70; R Pulham St Mary Magd 70-80; P-in-c Alburgh 76-77; P-in-c Denton 76-77; P-in-c Pulham St Mary V 76-80; R Pulham 80-91; rtd 91; Perm to Offic *Nor* from 91. *10 Lime Close, Harleston IP20 9DG* Tel (01379) 854532

EQUEALL, Canon David Edward Royston. b 41. Open Univ BA. St Mich Coll Llan 68. **d** 71 **p** 72. C Mountain Ash *Llan* 71-74; C Gabalfa and Chapl Asst Univ Hosp of Wales Cardiff 74-77; Chapl 77-79; Chapl N Gen Hosp Sheff 79-94; Chapl N Gen Hosp NHS Trust Sheff 94-02; Chapl Manager Sheff Teaching Hosps NHS Trust 02-06; Hon Can Sheff Cathl 98-06; rtd 06. *4 Riverside Court, Dinnington, Sheffield S25 3PH* Tel (01909) 655355

ERIKSSON, Olaf Lennart. b 62. Ridley Hall Cam 03. **d** 05 **p** 06. C Cockerton *Dur* 05-09; P-in-c Millfield St Mark and Pallion St Luke from 09. *The Vicarage, St Mark's Terrace, Sunderland SR4 7BN* Tel 0191-565 1789

ERLEBACH, Jonathan Bartholomew (Bart). b 77. York Univ BSc99. Oak Hill Th Coll BA05. **d** 05 **p** 06. C Hove Bp Hannington Memorial Ch Church from 05. *47 Nevill Avenue, Hove BN3 7NB* Tel (01273) 739144 Mobile 07714-379836
E-mail bartbev@erlebach.org.uk

✠**ERNEST, The Most Revd Gerald James Ian.** b 54. **p** 85 **c** 01. Bp Mauritius from 01; Abp Indian Ocean from 08. *Bishop's House, Nalletamby Avenue, Phoenix, Mauritius* Tel (00230) 686 5158 Fax 697 1096 E-mail dioang@intnet.mu

ERRIDGE, David John. b 45. Tyndale Hall Bris 66. **d** 69 **p** 70. C Bootle St Matt *Liv* 69-72; C Horwich H Trin *Man* 72-77; R Blackley St Andr 77-00; AD N Man 85-94; V Acomb St Steph *York* from 00. *The Vicarage, 32 Carr Lane, York YO26 5HX* Tel (01904) 798106

ERRINGTON, Mrs Sarah. b 67. UEA BA90. Wycliffe Hall Ox BTh94. **d** 97 **p** 98. C Gateacre *Liv* 97-02; TV Halewood from 02. *22 Kenton Road, Liverpool L26 9TS* Tel 0151-486 1159

ESAU, John Owen. b 39. St Mich Coll Llan 93. **d** 95 **p** 96. Min Can St D Cathl 95-97; V Llanpumsaint w Llanllawddog 97-01; V Cydweli and Llandyfaelog 01-03; R Aberporth w Tremain w Blaenporth and Betws Ifan 03-04; rtd 04. *28 Cwrt y Gloch, Peniel, Carmarthen SA32 7HW* Tel (01267) 220549

ESCOLME, Miss Doreen. b 29. St Jo Coll Nottm 82. **dss** 83 **d** 87 **p** 94. Hunslet Moor St Pet and St Cuth *Ripon* 83-87; C 87-88; Par Dn Wyther 88-94; C 94; rtd 94; Perm to Offic *Ripon* from 94. *6 Heather Gardens, Leeds LS13 4LF* Tel 0113-257 9055

ESCRITT, Canon Margaret Ruth. b 37. Selly Oak Coll IDC62. **d** 87 **p** 94. Dioc Adv for Diaconal Mins *York* 85-91; Hon C Selby Abbey 87-90; C Kexby w Wilberfoss 93-94; Asst Chapl HM Pris Full Sutton 92-94; Chapl HM Pris Everthorpe 95-98; Can and Preb York Minster 95-01; rtd 97; Perm to Offic *York* from 01. *73 Heslington Lane, York YO10 4HN* Tel (01904) 639444

ESCRITT, Michael William. b 35. Qu Coll Birm 64. **d** 67 **p** 68. C Huntington *York* 67-69; Abp's Dom Chapl 69-72; V Bishopthorpe 72-83; V Acaster Malbis 73-83; V Selby Abbey 83-90; TR Haxby w Wigginton 90-98; rtd 98; Perm to Offic *York* from 98. *73 Heslington Lane, York YO10 4HN* Tel (01904) 639444

ESDAILE, Canon Adrian George Kennedy. b 35. Mert Coll Ox BA57 MA61. Wells Th Coll 59. **d** 61 **p** 62. C St Helier *S'wark* 61-64; C Wimbledon 64-68; V Hackbridge and N Beddington 68-80; RD Sutton 76-80; TR Chipping Barnet w Arkley *St Alb* 80-01; RD Barnet 89-94; Hon Can St Alb 94-01; rtd 01; Perm to Offic *S'wark* from 01 and *Guildf* from 02. *29 Hereford Close, Epsom KT18 5DZ* Tel (01372) 723770
E-mail esdaileadrian@yahoo.co.uk

ESHUN, Daniel Justice. b 69. Cape Coast Univ Ghana BA93 K Coll Lon MA97 PhD00 St Jo Coll Dur MA03. Cranmer Hall Dur 00. **d** 03 **p** 04. C Staines *Lon* 03-06; C Kensal Town St Thos w St Andr and St Phil 06-07; Chapl Surrey Univ Roehampton from 07. *Whitelands College, Holybourne Avenue, London SW15 4JD* Tel (020) 8392 3500
E-mail daniel.eshun@yahoo.co.uk

ESPIN-BRADLEY, Richard John. b 61. Lanc Univ BSc84. Oak Hill Th Coll 93. **d** 95 **p** 96. C Brundall w Braydeston and Postwick *Nor* 95-98; C St Helier *S'wark* 98-02; V Wolverhampton St Luke *Lich* from 02. *St Luke's Vicarage, 122 Goldthorn Hill, Wolverhampton WV2 3HU* Tel (01902) 340261
E-mail richardeb@blueyonder.co.uk

ESSER, Lindsay Percy David. b 53. BA. Oak Hill Th Coll. **d** 84 **p** 85. C Barnsbury St Andr and H Trin w All SS *Lon* 84-87; Chapl Paris St Mich *Eur* 87-90; C Spring Grove St Mary *Lon* 90-95; Mauritius from 95. *The Rectory, St Barnabas Church, Royal Road, Pamplemousses, Mauritius* Tel (00230) 243 3549
E-mail st.barnabas@intnet.mu

ESSEX, Mary Rose. b 50. **d** 02 **p** 03. NSM E and W Leake, Stanford-on-Soar, Rempstone etc *S'well* 02-08; P-in-c Kirkby Woodhouse from 08. *The Vicarage, 57 Skegby Road, Kirkby-in-Ashfield, Nottingham NG17 9JE* Tel (01623) 759094
E-mail rev.maryessex@btopenworld.com

ETCHELLS, Peter. b 26. Kelham Th Coll 48. **d** 52 **p** 53. C Chesterton St Geo *Ely* 52-55; C Leic St Marg 55-58; R Willoughby Waterleys, Peatling Magna etc 58-96; rtd 96. *29 Upperfield Drive, Felixstowe IP11 9LS*

ETCHES, Haigh David. b 45. St Jo Coll Dur BA71. Cranmer Hall Dur. **d** 73 **p** 74. C Whitnash *Cov* 73-77; C Wallingford *Ox* 77-79; C Wallingford w Crowmarsh Gifford etc 79-83; P-in-c Bearwood 83-86; R from 86. *The Rectory, 6 St Catherine's Close, Sindlesham, Wokingham RG41 5BZ* Tel 0118-979 4364

ETHERIDGE, Canon Richard Thomas. b 32. Lon Univ BD62. ALCD61. **d** 62 **p** 63. C Wilmington *Roch* 62-65; C Rainham 65-69; V Langley St Jo *Birm* 69-01; P-in-c Oldbury 83-01; P-in-c Langley St Mich 95-01; Hon Can Birm Cathl 97-01; rtd 01; Perm to Offic *Birm* from 01 and *Worc* from 02. *23 Scobell Close, Pershore, Worcester WR10 1QJ* Tel (01386) 554745

ETHERIDGE, Terry. b 44. Wells Th Coll 68. **d** 70 **p** 71. C Barrow St Jo *Carl* 70-73; C Wilmslow *Ches* 73-76; V Knutsford St Cross 76-85; R Malpas and Threapwood from 85. *The Rectory, Church Street, Malpas SY14 8PP* Tel (01948) 860209

ETHERINGTON (née SMITH), Mrs Elizabeth Anne. b 68. Keele Univ BA95. Ridley Hall Cam 04. **d** 06 **p** 07. C E Twickenham St Steph *Lon* from 06. *61 Elizabeth Gardens, Isleworth TW7 7BD* Tel 07903-112082 (mobile)
E-mail libbyjesha@hotmail.com

ETHERINGTON, Mrs Ferial Mary Gould. b 44. Open Univ BA. St Alb Minl Tr Scheme 86. **d** 93 **p** 94. NSM Luton St Chris Round Green *St Alb* 93-04; Selection Sec and Co-ord for OLM Min Division 97-04; rtd 04; Perm to Offic *Carl* from 04; Dioc Min Review Officer from 05. *Northview, Durdar, Carlisle CA2 4TX* Tel (01228) 537676
E-mail ferial.etherington@talktalk.net

ETHERINGTON, Robert Barry. b 37. Man Univ BA62. Linc Th Coll 62. **d** 64 **p** 65. C Linc St Jo 64-67; C Frodingham 67-69; V Reepham 69-78; Ind Chapl 70-78; Ind Chapl *St Alb* 78-88; V Luton St Chris Round Green 88-04; RD Luton 98-02; rtd 04; Perm to Offic *Carl* from 05. *Northview, Durdar, Carlisle CA2 4TX* Tel (01228) 537676

ETHERTON, Christopher Charles. b 47. UMIST BSc68. STETS 04. **d** 07 **p** 08. NSM Lower Sandown St Jo *Portsm* from 07; NSM Sandown Ch Ch from 07. *19 Station Avenue, Sandown PO36 9BW* Tel (01983) 407088 Mobile 07906-238368
E-mail chrisetherton@tiscali.co.uk

ETHERTON, Geoffrey Robert. b 74. Univ of Cen England in Birm BMus96. Trin Coll Bris BA01. **d** 02 **p** 03. C Trentham and Hanford *Lich* 02-03; C Hanley H Ev 03-06; Pioneer Min 04-06. *c/o Crockford, Church House, Great Smith Street, London SW1P 3AZ*

ETHIOPIA AND THE HORN OF AFRICA, Area Bishop of.
See PROUD, The Rt Revd Andrew John

ETTERLEY, Peter Anthony Gordon. b 39. Kelham Th Coll 63 Wells Th Coll 66. **d** 68 **p** 69. C Gillingham St Aug *Roch* 68-71; Papua New Guinea 71-80; V Cleeve w Chelvey and Brockley *B & W* 80-84; V Seaton Hirst *Newc* 84-86; TR 86-96; P-in-c Longframlington w Brinkburn 96-00; V 00-04; P-in-c Felton 96-00; V 00-04; rtd 04. *4 Clive Terrace, Alnwick NE66 1LQ* Tel (01665) 606252 E-mail peter.etterley@tiscali.co.uk

EUNSON, Ms Lisa Kei. b 54. San Francisco State Univ BA78. Ch Div Sch of the Pacific (USA) MDiv01. **d** 01 **p** 02. C Burlingame USA 01-06; R Banchory *Ab* from 06; R Kincardine O'Neil from 06. *The Rectory, High Street, Banchory AB31 5TB* Tel (01330) 826045 Mobile 07917-886672
E-mail rev_lisa_eunson@yahoo.com

EUROPE, Bishop of Gibraltar in. *See* ROWELL, The Rt Revd Douglas Geoffrey

EUROPE, Suffragan Bishop in. *See* HAMID, The Rt Revd David

EUSTICE, Peter Lafevre. b 32. AKC56. **d** 57 **p** 58. C Finsbury Park St Thos *Lon* 57-60; C Redruth *Truro* 60-63; V Treslothan 63-71; V Falmouth All SS 71-76; R St Stephen in Brannel 76-97; rtd 97; Perm to Offic *Truro* from 97. *21 Gloucester Avenue, Carlyon Bay, St Austell PL25 3PT* Tel (01726) 817343

EVANS, Miss Alison Jane. b 66. Sheff Univ BSc87 Bris Univ PGCE93. Trin Coll Bris BA04. **d** 04 **p** 05. C Finham *Cov* 04-08; V Cov St Geo from 08. *St George's Vicarage, 101 Moseley Avenue, Coventry CV6 1HR* Tel (024) 7659 1994
E-mail aevans@talktalk.net

EVANS, The Ven Alun Wyn. b 47. Down Coll Cam BA70 MA73. Cuddesdon Coll 70. **d** 72 **p** 73. C Bargoed w Brithdir *Llan* 72-74; C Bargoed and Deri w Brithdir 74-75; C Coity w Nolton 75-77; V Cwmavon 77-81; Warden of Ords 80-81; V Llangynwyd w Maesteg 81-86; Prov Officer for Soc Resp 86-93; V Cardiff Ch Ch 93-99; V Swansea St Mary w H Trin *S & B* 99-00; TR Cen Swansea 00-04; Can Res Brecon Cathl 00-04; V Cynwil Elfed and Newchurch *St D* 04-07; V Cynwyl Elfed w Newchurch and Trelech a'r Betws from 07; Adn Carmarthen from 04. *The Vicarage, Cynwyl Elfed, Carmarthen SA33 6TU* Tel (01267) 281605

EVANS, Mrs Amanda Jane. b 49. Rachel McMillan Teacher Tr Coll Lon CertEd70 Cant Ch Ch Univ Coll MA01. STETS 94. **d** 97 **p** 98. C Faversham *Cant* 97-01; TV Whitstable 01-06; Dioc Co-ord for Healing and Wholeness from 07. *The Vicarage, Vicarage Lane, Nonington, Dover CT15 4JT* Tel (01304) 842847
E-mail amanda.livingwell@btinternet.com

EVANS, Andrew. *See* EVANS, John Andrew

EVANS, Canon Andrew. b 57. Southn Univ BEd80. S Dios Minl Tr Scheme 88. **d** 91 **p** 92. NSM Cricklade w Latton *Bris* 91-97; C Yatton Keynell 97-99; TV By Brook 99-00; R Hullavington, Norton and Stanton St Quintin from 00; P-in-c Sherston Magna, Easton Grey, Luckington etc from 06; Bp's Adv for Rural Min from 00; Hon Can Bris Cathl from 05; AD N Wilts from 06; OCF from 00. *The Rectory, 1 Rectory Close, Stanton St Quintin, Chippenham SN14 6DT* Tel and fax (01666) 837187 Mobile 07931-616329 E-mail andrew@evans63.fsnet.co.uk

EVANS, Andrew Eric. b 58. Sheff Univ LLB80 Solicitor 83. Trin Coll Bris 01. **d** 03 **p** 04. C Gt Bookham *Guildf* 03-06; P-in-c Broughton Gifford, Gt Chalfield and Holt *Sarum* from 06; C Atworth w Shaw and Whitley from 07; C Melksham from 07; RD Bradford from 08. *The Rectory, Ham Green, Holt, Trowbridge BA14 7PZ* Tel (01225) 782289
E-mail goodevansitsandrew@tiscali.co.uk

EVANS, Anne. b 47. Ches Coll of HE MTh99. **d** 05 **p** 06. Broughton *Lich* from 05; OLM Myddle from 05; OLM Loppington w Newtown from 05. *The Fields, Welshampton, Ellesmere SY12 0NP* Tel (01948) 710206

EVANS, Canon Anthony Nigel. b 53. Nottm Univ BA74 Fitzw Coll Cam BA76. Westcott Ho Cam 74. **d** 77 **p** 78. C Sneinton St Cypr *S'well* 77-80; C Worksop Priory 80-83; V Nottingham St Geo w St Jo 83-88; R Ordsall 88-95; P-in-c Sutton in Ashfield St Mary 95-07; AD Newstead 01-05; Bp's Dom Chapl from 07; Hon Can S'well Minster from 04. *8 Raysmith Close, Southwell NG25 0BG* Tel (01636) 816764 E-mail frtony@care4free.net

EVANS, Ashley Francis. b 58. Birm Univ BA79. WEMTC 00. **d** 03 **p** 04. C Kington w Huntington, Old Radnor, Kinnerton etc *Heref* 03-07; P-in-c Ewyas Harold w Dulas, Kenderchurch etc from 07; RD Abbeydore from 09. *The Rectory, Ewyas Harold, Hereford HR2 0EZ* Tel (01981) 240079 Mobile 07763-070177
E-mail ashley@castlefrome.freeserve.co.uk

EVANS, Aylmer. See EVANS, David Aylmer

EVANS, Barrie. See EVANS, The Ven John Barrie

EVANS, Brian. b 34. Open Univ BA86. St Deiniol's Hawarden 70. **d** 71 **p** 72. C Porthkerry *Llan* 71-72; C Barry All SS 72-75; V Abercynon 75-82; V Pendoylan w Welsh St Donats 82-87; R Maentwrog w Trawsfynydd *Ban* 87-99; rtd 99; Perm to Offic *Ban* from 99. *Madryn, 46 Glan Ysgethin, Talybont LL43 2BB* Tel (01341) 247965

EVANS, Caroline Mary. b 46. Ban Coll CertEd69. St Jo Coll Nottm. **d** 86 **p** 97. C Llanbedig w Caernarfon and Betws Garmon etc *Ban* 86-88; Dn-in-c Bodedern w Llechgynfarwy and Llechylched etc 88-97; V 97; RD Llifon and Talybolion 96-97; R Llanfairfechan w Aber from 97. *The Rectory, Aber Road, Llanfairfechan LL33 0HN* Tel (01248) 680591

EVANS, Prof Christopher Francis. b 09. CCC Cam BA32 MA38 Ox Univ MA48 Southn Univ Hon DLitt77 Glas Univ Hon DD85 FBA91 FKC70. Linc Th Coll 33. **d** 34 **p** 35. C Southampton St Barn *Win* 34-38; Tutor Linc Th Coll 38-44; Chapl and Lect Linc Dioc Tr Coll 44-48; Chapl and Fell CCC Ox 48-58; Select Preacher Ox Univ 55-57; Select Preacher Cam Univ 59-60; Lightfoot Prof Div Dur Univ 58-62; Can Res Dur Cathl 58-62; Prof NT Studies K Coll Lon 62-77; rtd 77. *23 The Court, Fen End Road West, Knowle, Solihull B93 0AN* Tel (01564) 776233

EVANS, Christopher Idris. b 51. Chich Th Coll 74. **d** 77 **p** 78. C Gelligaer *Llan* 77-80; C St Andrews Major w Michaelston-le-Pit 80-81; V Llangeinor 81-87; V Watlington w Pyrton and Shirburn Ox 87-97; R Icknield from 97. *The Vicarage, Hill Road, Watlington OX49 5AD* Tel (01491) 612494
E-mail icknield@aol.com

EVANS, Christopher Jonathan. b 43. AKC67 and 88. **d** 68 **p** 69. C Wednesfield St Thos *Lich* 68-71; C Dorridge *Birm* 71-74; V Marston Green 74-81; V Acocks Green 81-86; RD Yardley 84-86; V Hill 86-88; Area Officer COPEC Housing Trust 88-91; V Harborne St Pet 91-08; rtd 08; Perm to Offic *Heref* from 08. *5 The Square, Clun, Craven Arms SY7 9EY* Tel (01588) 640439
E-mail jo@evansj84.fsnet.co.uk

EVANS, Clive Richard. b 44. WEMTC 99. **d** 00 **p** 01. OLM Heref S Wye from 00. *14 St Vincents Cross, Lower Bullingham, Hereford HR2 6EL* Tel (01432) 270838 *or* 353717
E-mail clivelinda@clivevans11.wanadoo.co.uk

EVANS, Canon Clive Roger. b 59. Worc Coll Ox BA80 MA84. St Jo Coll Nottm 94. **d** 94 **p** 95. C Barton Seagrave w Warkton *Pet* 94-97; V Long Buckby w Watford from 97; P-in-c W Haddon w Winwick and Ravensthorpe from 03; RD Brixworth 01-09; Can Pet Cathl from 09. *The Vicarage, 10 Hall Drive, Long Buckby, Northampton NN6 7QU* Tel and fax (01327) 842909
E-mail clivevans@tiscali.co.uk

EVANS, Canon Colin Rex. b 24. Reading Univ BA49. Linc Th Coll. **d** 57 **p** 58. C Boultham *Linc* 57-59; C Linc St Nic w St Jo Newport 59-62; V Linc St Mary-le-Wigford w St Martin 62-66; P-in-c Linc St Faith 63-66; R Bassingham 66-74; V Aubourn w Haddington 66-74; V Carlton-le-Moorland w Stapleford 66-74; R Skinnand 66-74; R Thurlby w Norton Disney 66-74; RD Graffoe 69-74; RD Elloe E 74-89; Can and Preb Linc Cathl 74-89; V Holbeach 74-89; rtd 90; Hon C Dawlish *Ex* 90-97; RD Kenn 95-97; Perm to Offic from 97. *87 West Cliff Park Drive, Dawlish EX7 9EL* Tel (01626) 865191

EVANS, Daniel Barri. b 70. St Steph Ho Ox 01. **d** 03 **p** 04. C Weymouth H Trin *Sarum* 03-07; V Llwynderw *S & B* from 07. *Llwynderw Vicarage, Fairwood Road, West Cross, Swansea SA3 5JP* Tel (01792) 401903 Mobile 07952-679760
E-mail vicar.llwynderw@virgin.net

EVANS, Miss Daphne Gillian. b 41. Bible Tr Inst Glas 67 Trin Coll Bris IDC75. **dss** 83 **d** 87. Wenlock *Heref* 83-88; TD 87-88; rtd 88. *33 Light Oaks Avenue, Light Oaks, Stoke-on-Trent ST2 7NF* Tel (01782) 541218

EVANS, Canon David. b 37. Keble Coll Ox BA60 MA65 Lon Univ BD64. Wells Th Coll 62. **d** 64 **p** 65. Min Can Brecon Cathl 64-68; C Brecon w Battle 64-68; C Swansea St Mary and H Trin 68-71; Chapl Univ of Wales (Swansea) 68-71; Bp's Chapl for Samaritan and Soc Work *Birm* 71-75; Jt Gen Sec Samaritans 75-84; Gen Sec 84-89; R Heyford w Stowe Nine Churches *Pet* 89-96; R Heyford w Stowe Nine Churches and Flore etc 96-01; Chapl Northants Police 89-01; RD Daventry 96-00; Can Pet Cathl 97-01; rtd 01; Perm to Offic *Ex* from 01. *Curlew River, The Strand, Starcross, Exeter EX6 8PA* Tel (01626) 891712

EVANS, David. b 37. Open Univ BA73 FRSA95. St Mich Coll Llan 65. **d** 67 **p** 68. C Swansea St Pet *S & B* 67-70; C St Austell *Truro* 70-75; R Purley *Ox* 75-90; RD Bradfield 85-90; R Bryanston Square St Mary w St Marylebone St Mark *Lon* 90-99; P-in-c St Marylebone Ch Ch 90-91; R Nuthurst and Mannings Heath *Chich* 99-07; P-in-c from 07. *The Rectory, Nuthurst Street, Nuthurst, Horsham RH13 6LH* Tel (01403) 891449 E-mail rector.nuthurst@tiscali.co.uk

EVANS, David Aylmer. b 28. Lon Univ CertEd62. St D Coll Lamp BA49 LTh51. **d** 51 **p** 52. C Brecon St David w Llanspyddid and Llanilltyd *S & B* 51-53; C Colwyn Bay *St As* 53-54; C Macclesfield St Mich *Ches* 54-56; V Lostock Gralam

56-59; Chapl Endsleigh Sch 59-65; Wokingham Gr Sch 65-72; Cllr S Molton Sch and Community Coll 73-87; V Middlezoy and Othery and Moorlinch *B & W* 87-93; rtd 93; Perm to Offic *B & W* 94-02 and *Ex* from 94. *2 Higher Mead, Hemyock, Cullompton EX15 3QH* Tel (01823) 680974

EVANS (or BURTON EVANS), David Burton. b 35. Open Univ BA87 Goldsmiths' Coll Lon BMus93. K Coll Lon 58 Edin Th Coll 60. **d** 62 **p** 63. C Leeds St Hilda *Ripon* 62-63; C Cross Green St Sav and St Hilda 63-67; Min Can Dur Cathl 67-71; PV Chich Cathl and Chapl Prebendal Sch 71-74; R Lynch w Iping Marsh *Chich* 74-79; V Easebourne 79-86; Chapl K Edw VII Hosp Midhurst 77-86; R St Mich Cornhill w St Pet le Poer etc *Lon* 86-96; rtd 96; Pau *Eur* 96-01; Perm to Offic from 05. *128 Little Breach, Chichester PO19 5UA* Tel (01243) 773266 Mobile 07795-662991 E-mail evtherev7@btinternet.com

EVANS, David Elwyn. b 43. St Mich Coll Llan 71. **d** 73 **p** 74. C Llandybie *St D* 73-75; C Llanelli 75-78; V Tre-lech a'r Betws w Abernant and Llanwinio 78-02; rtd 02. *8 Ger y Llan, The Parade, Carmarthen SA31 1LY*

EVANS, David Frederick Francis. b 35. Univ of Wales BSc59. Wells Th Coll 59. **d** 61 **p** 62. C Eltham St Jo *S'wark* 61-64; C Banbury *Ox* 64-69; V Brize Norton and Carterton 69-73; V Tilehurst St Geo 73-84; V Lydney w Aylburton *Glouc* 84-95; V Lydney 95-02; RD Forest S 90-95; Chapl Severn NHS Trust 94-02; rtd 02. *2 Bodforis, Braichmelyn, Bethesda, Bangor LL57 3PU* Tel (01248) 601994

EVANS, David John. b 49. Univ of Wales (Ban) BSc72 Bath Univ CertEd73. Coll of Resurr Mirfield 75. **d** 78 **p** 79. C Wandsworth St Anne *S'wark* 78-81; C Angell Town St Jo 81-82; TV Catford (Southend) and Downham 82-90; P-in-c Broughton *Ely* 90-91; P-in-c Somersham w Pidley and Oldhurst 90-91; R 91-98; R Hilgay from 98; R Southery from 98. *The Rectory, Church Road, Hilgay, Downham Market PE38 0JL* Tel (01366) 384418
E-mail david.evans@ely.anglican.org

EVANS, David Julian James. b 65. Rob Coll Cam BA87. Westcott Ho Cam 03. **d** 05 **p** 06. C W Hackney St Barn *Lon* 05-08; C St John-at-Hackney from 08. *21B Blurton Road, London E5 0NL* Tel (020) 8986 4456 E-mail davidjjevans@mac.com

EVANS, David Leslie Bowen. b 28. Univ of Wales (Lamp) BA52 LTh54. **d** 54 **p** 55. C Cardigan *St D* 54-57; C Llangathen w Llanfihangel Cilfargen 57-58; C Betws w Ammanford 58-60; V Betws Ifan 60-64; V Burry Port and Pwll 64-76; V Cardiff Dewi Sant *Llan* 76-86; Asst Chapl HM Pris Cardiff 76-86; V Llan-llwch w Llangain and Llangynog *St D* 86-95; Can St D Cathl 89-90; rtd 95. *35 Ger y Capel, Llangain, Carmarthen SA33 5AQ* Tel (01267) 241916

EVANS, David Richard. b 47. St Steph Ho Ox 68. **d** 72 **p** 73. C Cardiff St Jo *Llan* 72-76; PV Llan Cathl 76-80; V Cleeve Prior and The Littletons *Worc* from 80. *The Vicarage, South Littleton, Evesham WR11 8TJ* Tel and fax (01386) 830397
E-mail father.richard@tesco.net

✠**EVANS, The Rt Revd David Richard John.** b 38. G&C Coll Cam BA63 MA66. Clifton Th Coll 63. **d** 65 **p** 66 **c** 78. C Enfield Ch Ch Trent Park Lon 65-68; SAMS Argentina 69-77; Peru 77-88; Bp Peru 78-88; Bp Bolivia 82-88; Asst Bp Bradf 88-93; Gen Sec SAMS 93-03; Hon Asst Bp Chich 94-97; Hon Asst Bp Roch 95-97; Hon Asst Bp Birm 97-03; rtd 03; Hon Asst Bp Cov from 03; Hon C Alderminster and Halford 03-07; Hon C Butlers Marston and the Pillertons w Ettington 03-07; Hon C Stourdene Gp from 07. *The Vicarage, Alderminster, Stratford-upon-Avon CV37 8PE* Tel (01789) 450198
E-mail bishop.drjevans@virgin.net

EVANS, David Russell. b 36. St As Univ BA57. Ripon Hall Ox 59. **d** 61 **p** 62. C Netherton CD *Liv* 61-65; Chapl Canon Slade Sch Bolton 65-93; Lic Preacher *Man* from 65; Perm to Offic *Liv* 76-03; rtd 00. *2 Rushford Grove, Bolton BL1 8TD* Tel (01204) 592981

EVANS, Derek. b 38. St As Minl Tr Course 93. **d** 97 **p** 98. NSM Llangollen w Trevor and Llantysilio *St As* 97-00; NSM Corwen and Llangar w Gwyddelwern and Llawrybetws 00-02; NSM Betws Gwerful Goch w Llangwm, Gwyddelwern etc 02-05; P-in-c Gwyddelwern 05-08; rtd 09. *Fern Mount, 68 Berwyn Street, Llangollen LL20 8NA* Tel (01978) 861893

EVANS, Canon Derek. b 45. St D Coll Lamp. **d** 68 **p** 69. C Pembroke Dock *St D* 68-74; V Ambleston, St Dogwells, Walton E and Llysyfran 74-78; V Wiston w Ambleston, St Dogwells and Walton E 78-81; V Wiston w Ambleston, St Dogwells, Walton E etc 81-85; R Haverfordwest St Mary and St Thos w Haroldston 85-09; Dep Dioc Dir of Educn 92-97; Dir 97-09; Can St D Cathl 99-09; RD Roose 00-04; rtd 09. *Address temp unknown*
E-mail derek.evans0@talk21.com

EVANS, Desmond. b 26. Univ of Wales (Lamp) BA48 St Cath Soc Ox BA50 MA54. St Steph Ho Ox 48. **d** 52 **p** 53. C Clydach *S & B* 51-54; V 82-87; Chapl Cranleigh Sch Surrey 54-59; Lic to Offic *Ban* 59-78; St Mary's Coll Ban 59-78; V Llanwrtyd w Llanddulas in Tir Abad etc *S & B* 78-82; RD Builth 79-82; V Abercraf and Callwen 87-95; rtd 95. *26 Palleg Road, Lower Cwmtwrch, Swansea SA9 2QE* Tel (01639) 845389

EVANS, Canon Edward John. b 47. St Mich Coll Llan 67. **d** 71

p 72. C Llantwit Fardre 71-77; R Eglwysilan 77-88; V Laleston w Tythegston and Merthyr Mawr 88-09; V Laleston and Merthyr Mawr from 09; RD Bridgend 94-04; Hon Can Llan Cathl from 07. *The Vicarage, Rogers Lane, Laleston, Bridgend CF32 0LB* Tel and fax (01656) 654254   Mobile 07968-044583
E-mail edward@laleston.org.uk

EVANS, Elaine. *See* EVANS, Jennifer Elaine

EVANS, Ms Elaine. b 63. St Mich Coll Llan BTh02. **d** 02 **p** 03. C Llantwit Major 02-05; C Penarth All SS 05-09; P-in-c Pontypridd St Matt and Cilfynydd w Llanwynno from 09. *The Vicarage, 40 Heol-y-Plwyf, Ynysybwl, Pontypridd CF37 3HU* Tel (01443) 790340

EVANS, Elwyn David. b 36. Keble Coll Ox BA58 MA62. St Steph Ho Ox 58 St Mich Coll Llan 60. **d** 61 **p** 62. C Aberystwyth H Trin *St D* 61-63; C Llanelli St Paul 63-66; C Roath St German *Llan* 66-69; V Crynant 69-78; R Llanilid w Pencoed 79-95; rtd 95; Perm to Offic *Llan* and *S & B* from 95. *23 Christopher Rise, Pontlliw, Swansea SA4 9EN* Tel (01792) 891961

EVANS, Ernest Maurice. b 28. JP70. MIMechE66. St As Minl Tr Course 84. **d** 86 **p** 87. NSM Hope *St As* 86-89; P-in-c Corwen and Llangar w Gwyddelwern and Llawrybetws 89-90; R 90-95; rtd 95; Perm to Offic *Ban* from 97. *43 Cil-y-Graig, Llanfairpwllgwyngyll LL61 5NZ* Tel (01248) 712169
E-mail e.mauriceevans@btinternet.com

EVANS, Ms Freda Christine. b 48. MBE89. NTMTC 96. **d** 99 **p** 00. C Hampton Hill *Lon* 99-02; V Kingshurst *Birm* 02-08; TR Erdington from 08. *The Vicarage, 26 Church Road, Birmingham B24 9AX* Tel 0121-373 0884

EVANS, Mrs Freda Mary Ann (Frieda). b 54. St D Coll Lamp 95. **d** 00 **p** 05. OLM Malpas *Mon* from 00. *3 The Firs, Malpas, Newport NP20 6YD* Tel (01633) 850600   Mobile 0411-650088
E-mail frieda@evafirs.freeserve.co.uk

EVANS, Frederick James Stephens. b 21. Qu Coll Cam BA42 MA46. St D Coll Lamp LTh44. **d** 44 **p** 45. C Shirley *Birm* 44-47; R Scotter w E Ferry *Linc* 47-65; CF (TA) 48-51; R Chalfont St Peter *Ox* 65-78; V Rustington *Chich* 78-86; rtd 86; Perm to Offic *Chich* from 86. *45 Falmer Avenue, Goring-by-Sea, Worthing BN12 4SY* Tel (01903) 503905

EVANS, Canon Frederick John Margam. b 31. Magd Coll Ox BA53 MA57. St Mich Coll Llan 53. **d** 54 **p** 55. C New Tredegar *Mon* 54-58; C Chepstow 58-60; Asst Chapl United Sheff Hosps 60-62; Chapl Brookwood Hosp Woking 62-70; V Crookham *Guildf* 70-98; RD Aldershot 78-83; Hon Can Guildf Cathl 89-98; rtd 98; Perm to Offic *Guildf* from 98. *4 Radford Close, Farnham GU9 9AB* Tel and fax (01252) 710594
E-mail johnjunee@btinternet.com

EVANS, Gareth Milton. b 39. Bris Univ LLB60 St Cath Coll Ox BA62 MA66. Ripon Hall Ox 60. **d** 63 **p** 64. C Hengrove *Bris* 63-65; Min Can Bris Cathl 65-68; C Bishopston 68-71; C Notting Hill *Lon* 71-83; V Bayswater from 83. *St Matthew's Vicarage, 27 St Petersburgh Place, London W2 4LA* Tel (020) 7229 2192

EVANS, Gareth Rae. b 48. MCIPD. Ripon Coll Cuddesdon 96. **d** 98 **p** 99. C Chepstow *Mon* 98-00; TV Cwmbran 00-07; Hon C Torquay St Martin Barton *Ex* from 07. *4 Froude Avenue, Torquay TQ2 8RU*

EVANS, Genevieve Sarah. b 62. Univ of Wales (Cardiff) BA04. St Mich Coll Llan 02. **d** 04 **p** 05. C Whalley Range St Edm and Moss Side etc *Man* 04-08; V Walsall Pleck and Bescot *Lich* from 08; C Walsall from 00, C Walsall St Paul from 08. *St John's Vicarage, Vicarage Terrace, Walsall WS2 9HB* Tel (01922) 639805   E-mail rev.gen@tiscali.co.uk

EVANS, Canon Geoffrey Bainbridge. b 34. Lambeth MA94. St Mich Coll Llan 56. **d** 58 **p** 59. C Llan All SS CD 58-60; C Llandaff N 60-67; Guyana 67-73; Chapl Izmir (Smyrna) w Bornova *Eur* 73-94; Adn Aegean 78-94; Can Malta Cathl 78-00; Chapl Ankara 85-91; Chapl Istanbul 87-89; Chapl Rome 94-99; Chapl Moscow 99; P-in-c Ankara from 00. *Sehit Ersan Caddesi 32/12, Cankaya, Ankara 06680, Turkey* Tel (0090) (312) 467 8276 *or* 455 3285 Fax 455 3352   E-mail gb_evans@hotmail.com

EVANS, Geoffrey David. b 44. Ex Univ PGCE74. K Coll Lon BD69 AKC69 St Aug Coll Cant 69. **d** 70 **p** 71. C Lawrence Weston *Bris* 70-73; Chapl Grenville Coll Bideford 74-79; Chapl Eastbourne Coll 79-82; Chapl Taunton and Somerset Hosp 83-91; Chapl Musgrove Park Hosp 83-91; Chapl Taunton Sch 92-04; rtd 09. *Milton House, 75 Wellsway, Bath BA2 4RU* Tel (01225) 335632   E-mail bidabid@yahoo.co.uk

EVANS, Gerald Arthur. b 35. Univ of Wales (Swansea) BA57. S'wark Ord Course 74. **d** 77 **p** 78. NSM Balcombe *Chich* 77-81; NSM Cuckfield 81-87; R Tillington, Duncton and Up Waltham 87-93; R W Chiltington and Dioc Ecum Officer 93-98; RD Storrington 93-98; rtd 98; Perm to Offic *Chich* 98-00. *19 Crawford Close, Earley, Reading RG6 7PE* Tel 0118-926 8901

EVANS, Mrs Gillian. b 39. Imp Coll Lon BSc61. Mon Dioc Tr Scheme 88. **d** 88 **p** 94. NSM Penallt and Trellech *Mon* 88-89; NSM Overmonnow w Wonastow and Michel Troy 89-92; Dioc Ecum Officer and C Ludlow, Ludford, Ashford Carbonell etc *Heref* 92-95; Pakistan 95-96; Perm to Offic *Heref* 96-06; Hon C Dawlish *Ex* 97-98; TV Golden Cap Team *Sarum* 98-01; rtd 01; Perm to Offic *Cov* and *Mon* 01-06; Hon C Wolford w

Burmington *Cov* 06-08; Hon C Cherington w Stourton 06-08; Hon C Barcheston 06-08; Hon C Long Compton, Whichford and Barton-on-the-Heath 06-08; Hon C S Warks Seven Gp from 08. *16 The Long Close, Stourton, Shipston-on-Stour CV36 5HT* Tel (01608) 685773

EVANS, Glyn. b 59. Nene Coll Northn BA80 Leic Univ BA80 Ch Ch Coll Cant CertEd82 Kent Univ PGCE82. Qu Coll Birm 85. **d** 88 **p** 89. C Denton *Newc* 88-92; V Choppington 92-97; P-in-c Longhorsley and Hebron 97-01; Chapl HM Pris Acklington 97-01; P-in-c Newc St Andr and St Luke from 01; City Cen Chapl from 01. *12 The Glebe, Stannington, Morpeth NE61 6HW* Tel 0191-232 7935 *or* 222 0259

EVANS, Canon Glyn Peter. b 54. Leeds Univ BA75. Ripon Coll Cuddesdon 76. **d** 77 **p** 78. C Binley *Cov* 77-80; C Clifton upon Dunsmore w Brownsover 80-84; P-in-c Lacock w Bowden Hill *Bris* 84-89; P-in-c Lt Compton w Chastleton, Cornwell etc *Ox* 89-00; Agric Chapl 89-00; Dioc Rural Officer from 00; Hon Can Ch Ch from 05. *Stonewalls, Sibford Gower, Banbury OX15 5RT* Tel (01295) 280664   Mobile 07870-405241
E-mail glynevansrro@tiscali.co.uk *or* glynevans@goldserve.net

EVANS, Godfrey. *See* EVANS, Joseph Henry Godfrey

EVANS, Canon Gwyneth Mary. b 43. Gilmore Ho 69 Linc Th Coll 70. **dss** 74 **d** 87 **p** 94. Stamford Hill St Thos *Lon* 74-79; Chapl Asst R Free Hosp Lon 79-89; Chapl Salisbury Health Care NHS Trust 89-01; Can and Preb Sarum Cathl 96-01; rtd 01; Perm to Offic *Sarum* from 01. *39 The Close, Salisbury SP1 2EL* Tel (01722) 412546

EVANS, Canon Henry Thomas Platt. b 28. Selw Coll Cam BA51 MA55. Linc Th Coll 51. **d** 53 **p** 54. C Lt Ilford St Barn *Chelmsf* 53-56; C-in-c Stocking Farm CD *Leic* 56-58; V Stocking Farm 58-67; R Stretford St Matt *Man* 67-73; V Knighton St Mary Magd *Leic* 73-83; Hon Can Leic Cathl 76-93; RD Christianity S 81-83; Warden Launde Abbey 83-93; P-in-c Loddington 83-92; rtd 93; Perm to Offic *Leic* from 93. *24 Central Avenue, Leicester LE2 1TB* Tel 0116-270 2169

EVANS (née TAYLOR), Mrs Hilary Elizabeth. b 57. **d** 03 **p** 04. OLM Reddish *Man* from 03. *13 Lindfield Road, Stockport SK5 6SD* Tel 0161-442 3023
E-mail hilary@mojomusica.freeserve.co.uk

EVANS, Hilary Margaret. b 49. Redland Coll of Educn TDip71 Ches Coll of HE BTh97. NOC 94. **d** 97 **p** 98. C Heald Green St Cath *Ches* 97-00; P-in-c Davyhulme Ch Ch *Man* 00-03; P-in-c Blackley St Pet 03-09; AD N Man 06-08; rtd 09; Hon C SW Gower *S & B* from 09. *The Rectory, Church Meadow, Reynoldston, Swansea SA3 1AF* Tel (01792) 392963
E-mail hilary@evanses.plus.com

EVANS, Huw David. b 68. Sheff Univ BEng90 PGCE91. Trin Coll Bris BA98. **d** 98 **p** 02. C Sherborne w Castleton and Lillington *Sarum* 98-99; NSM Martock w Ash *B & W* 01-04; CF from 04. *c/o MOD Chaplains (Army)* Tel (01980) 615804 Fax 615800

EVANS, Mrs Jane. b 59. W Midl Coll of Educn BEd81. **d** 03 **p** 04. OLM Lilleshall and Muxton *Lich* from 03. *5 Collett Way, Priorslee, Telford TF2 9SL* Tel (01952) 291340
E-mail revjane@talktalk.net

EVANS, Mrs Jennifer. b 41. Ilkley Coll DipEd62. Sarum Th Coll 88. **d** 88. Par Dn Bramshott *Portsm* 88-91; Par Dn Bramshott and Liphook 91-92; Par Dn Whippingham w E Cowes 92-95; Par Dn Sarisbury 95-05; Hon C Llawhaden w Bletherston and Llancefn *St D* from 08; Hon C Slebech and Uzmaston w Boulston from 08. *Hermons Hook, Clarbeston Road SA63 4SG* Tel (01437) 731749   E-mail jennie.honeycombs@virgin.net

EVANS, Mrs Jennifer. b 43. **d** 01. NSM New Tredegar *Mon* 01-05; NSM Bedwellty w New Tredegar from 05. *26 Glynsifi, Elliots Town, New Tredegar NP24 6DE* Tel (01443) 836798

EVANS, Jennifer Elaine. b 59. Wolv Univ BA92. Qu Coll Birm 00. **d** 02 **p** 03. C Stafford St Jo and Tixall w Ingestre *Lich* 02-06; TV Stafford from 06. *St Bertelin's Vicarage, 36 Holmcroft Road, Stafford ST16 1JF* Tel (01785) 252874

EVANS, Jill. *See* EVANS, Mrs Gillian

EVANS, Mrs Joan. b 36. Nor Tr Coll TCert57 UEA BEd94. **d** 02 **p** 03. OLM Loddon, Sisland, Chedgrave, Hardley and Langley *Nor* 02-06; rtd 06; Perm to Offic *Nor* from 06. *13 Drury Lane, Loddon, Norwich NR14 6LB* Tel (01508) 528656
E-mail jevansolm@tiscali.co.uk

EVANS, John. *See* EVANS, Canon Frederick John Margam

EVANS, John Andrew. b 53. Hull Univ BSc74 Univ of Wales MSc75 Bris Univ BA96. Trin Coll Bris 94. **d** 96 **p** 97. C Walton H Trin *Ox* 96-98; C Caversham St Pet and Mapledurham etc 98-01; R Bradford Abbas and Thornford w Beer Hackett *Sarum* 01-09; V N Hayes St Nic *Lon* from 09. *St Nicholas' Vicarage, Raynton Drive, Hayes UB3 2LR* Tel (020) 8573 4122   Mobile 07725-805437 E-mail j_andrew_evans@btconnect.com

EVANS, The Ven John Barrie. b 23. Univ of Wales (Lamp) BA47 St Edm Hall Ox BA49 MA54. St Mich Coll Llan 50. **d** 51 **p** 52. C Trevethin *Mon* 51-57; V Caerwent w Dinham and Llanfair Discoed 57-64; V Chepstow 64-79; Can St Woolos Cathl 71-77; Adn Mon 77-86; R Llanmartin w Wilcrick and Langstone 79-83; R Llanmartin 83-86; Adn Newport 86-93; rtd 93; Lic to Offic *Mon* from 93; Perm to Offic *Glouc* 93-06. *Rockfield, Coleford Road, Tutshill, Chepstow NP16 7BU* Tel (01291) 626147

EVANS, John David Vincent. b 41. CQSW78. Lich Th Coll 66. **d** 68 **p** 70. C Kingsthorpe *Pet* 68-69; C Corby Epiphany w St Jo 69-72; Bp's Adv in Children's Work 72-74; Probation Officer 74-90; Perm to Offic 88-90; R Green's Norton w Bradden 90-91; R Greens Norton w Bradden and Lichborough 91-96; V Northampton Ch Ch 96-06; rtd 06; Perm to Offic *Pet* from 06. *Ivy Cottage, Creaton Road, Hollowell, Northampton NN6 8RP* Tel (01604) 743878 E-mail revjohnwenevans@yahoo.co.uk

EVANS, Canon John Griffiths. b 37. Glouc Th Course 76. **d** 77 **p** 77. Hd Master Corse Sch Glos from 70; C Hartpury w Corse and Staunton *Glouc* 77-79; P-in-c from 79; Hon Can Glouc Cathl from 96; P-in-c Maisemore from 01. *Elm House, Gadfield Elms, Staunton, Gloucester GL19 3PA* Tel (01452) 840302

EVANS, John Laurie. b 34. Pretoria Univ BSc54 Imp Coll Lon BSc55 Rhodes Univ BA59. Ripon Coll Cuddesdon 84. **d** 86 **p** 87. C Bruton and Distr *B & W* 86-89; P-in-c Ambrosden w Merton and Piddington *Ox* 89-91; C Pet St Mary Boongate 91-93; V Michael *S & M* 93-96; R Ballaugh 93-96; rtd 96; Chapl Allnutt's Hosp Goring Heath 96-99; P-in-c Fochabers *Mor* 00; P-in-c Strathnairn St Paul 00-03; TV Langtree *Ox* 03-07; Hon C Kelso *Edin* from 07; Hon C Coldstream from 07. *The Cottage, Pressen Farm, Cornhill-on-Tweed TD12 4RS* Tel (01890) 850309 Mobile 07909-986369 E-mail jonevansscotland@btinternet.com

EVANS, John Miles. b 39. Yale Univ BA61 JD67 St Cath Coll Cam BA64 MA68. NY Th Sem MDiv93. **d** 95 **p** 95. Chapl St Jo Cathl Oban 95-97; USA from 97; Interim R Lynbrook Ch Ch 98-99; R Davidsonville All Hallows 99-05. *Address temp unknown*

EVANS, John Rhys. b 45. Hull Univ BSc66. Sarum & Wells Th Coll 77. **d** 79 **p** 80. C Alton St Lawr *Win* 79-82; C Tadley St Pet 82-85; V Colden 85-91; V Bitterne Park 91-01; C Ringwood from 01; Chapl R Bournemouth and Christchurch Hosps NHS Trust from 01. *3 Waterside Close, Poulner, Ringwood BH24 1SB* Tel (01425) 483370

EVANS, John Ronald. b 16. Univ of Wales BA40. St Mich Coll Llan 41. **d** 42 **p** 44. C Rhosllannerchrugog *St As* 42-45; C Holywell 45-54; V Glyndyfrdwy 54-81; RD Edeyrnion 64-81; Dioc Sec SPCK 66-81; rtd 81. *22 Glebe Avenue, Hardingstone, Northampton NN4 6DG*

EVANS, John Stuart. b 57. Univ of Wales (Abth) BA78 Bretton Hall Coll PGCE82. Trin Coll Bris BA98. **d** 98 **p** 99. C Connah's Quay *St As* 98-02; V Rhosllannerchrugog from 02; AD Llangollen from 05. *16 Delyn, Johnstown, Wrexham LL14 1UY* Tel (01978) 840809 E-mail jsevans@surfaid.org

EVANS, Canon John Thomas. b 43. St Mich Coll Llan 66. **d** 67 **p** 68. C Connah's Quay *St As* 67-71; C Llanrhos 71-74; Chapl Rainhill Hosp Liv 74-78; TV Wrexham *St As* 78-83; V Holywell 83-96; RD Holywell 95-96; V Colwyn Bay 96-99; V Colwyn Bay w Brynymaen 99-02; RD Rhos 00-02; R Caerwys and Bodfari 02-08; Can Cursal St As Cathl 96-08; rtd 08. *26 Everard Road, Rhos-on-Sea, Colwyn Bay LL28 4EY* Tel (01492) 540506 Mobile 07905-861174 E-mail johnbethevans@btinternet.com

✠**EVANS, The Rt Revd John Wyn.** b 46. FSA88 FRHistS94 Univ of Wales (Cardiff) BA68 BD71. St Mich Coll Llan 68. **d** 71 **p** 72 **c** 08. C St D Cathl 71-72; Min Can St D Cathl 72-75; Perm to Offic *Ox* 75-77; Dioc Archivist *St D* 76-82; R Llanfallteg w Clunderwen and Castell Dwyran etc 77-82; Warden of Ords 78-83; Dioc Dir of Educn 82-92; Chapl Trin Coll Carmarthen 82-90; Dean of Chpl 90-94; Hd Th and RS 91-94; Dioc Can St D Cathl 88-90; Can St D Cathl 90-94; Dean St D 94-08; V St D Cathl 94-01; TR Dewisland 01-08; Bp St D from 08. *Llys Esgob, Abergwili, Carmarthen SA31 2JG* Tel (01267) 236597 E-mail bishop.stdavids@churchinwales.org.uk

EVANS, Jonathan Alan. b 53. Fitzw Coll Cam BA75 PGCE77 MA79. St Jo Coll Nottm MA95. **d** 95 **p** 96. C Drypool *York* 95-98; V Beverley St Nic from 98. *St Nicholas' Vicarage, 72 Grovehill Road, Beverley HU17 0ER* Tel (01482) 881458 E-mail evansfamily@macunlimited.net

EVANS, Joseph Henry Godfrey. b 31. Univ of Wales (Lamp) BA50 St Mary's Coll Chelt CertEd75 Kingston Poly 89. Qu Coll Birm 53. **d** 55 **p** 56. C Hackney St Jo *Lon* 55-58; C Stonehouse *Glouc* 58-60; V Selsley 60-65; V Cheltenham St Pet 65-74; R Willersey w Saintbury 74-77; Chapl Tiffin Sch Kingston 77-94; rtd 95; Perm to Offic *S'wark* from 01. *300 Raeburn Avenue, Surbiton KT5 9EF* Tel (020) 8390 0936

EVANS, Mrs Judith Ann. b 55. SEITE 99. **d** 02 **p** 03. C Crayford *Roch* 02-06; P-in-c Kells *Carl* from 06; Chapl N Cumbria Acute Hosps NHS Trust from 06. *St Peter's Vicarage, Cliff Road, Whitehaven CA28 9ET* Tel (01946) 692496 Mobile 07929-978523 E-mail revdjudyevans@btopenworld.com

EVANS, Canon Keith. b 57. Trin Coll Carmarthen CertEd81 BEd82. St D Coll Lamp BA84 Sarum & Wells Th Coll 84. **d** 85 **p** 86. C Swansea St Thos and Kilvey *S & B* 85-87; C Gorseinon 87-89; V Oxwich w Penmaen and Nicholaston 89-94; Dir Post-Ord Tr from 93; R Ystradgynlais 94-98; V Oystermouth from 98; Hon Can Brecon Cathl from 04. *The Vicarage, 9 Western Close, Mumbles, Swansea SA3 4HF* Tel (01792) 369971

EVANS, Kenneth. b 50. Bp Burgess Hall Lamp. **d** 74 **p** 75. C Llanaber w Caerdeon *Ban* 74-79; C Upper Clapton St Matt *Lon*

79-82; P-in-c Tottenham St Phil 82-95; V from 95. *St Philip's Vicarage, 226 Philip Lane, London N15 4HH* Tel and fax (020) 8808 4235 E-mail fr_kenmjd@tiscali.co.uk

EVANS, Kenneth Roy. b 47. Lon Univ BSc FRSA96. Ridley Hall Cam 79. **d** 81 **p** 81. C Stratford-on-Avon w Bishopton *Cov* 81-82; C Trunch *Nor* 82-85; Chapl Mapperley Hosp Nottm 85-89; Chapl Nottm Mental Illness and Psychiatric Unit 85-94; Chapl Notts Healthcare NHS Trust from 94; Lic to Offic *S'well* from 85; Dir Scarborough Psychotherapy Tr Inst from 03. *117 Columbus Ravine, Scarborough YO12 7QU* Tel (01723) 376246 E-mail ken@kenevans.fsnet.co.uk

EVANS, Kevin Stuart. b 56. Bris Poly CQSW80. Qu Coll Birm 93. **d** 95 **p** 96. C Madeley *Heref* 95-98; P-in-c Wombridge *Lich* from 98; TV Cen Telford from 05. *Wombridge Vicarage, Wombridge Road, Telford TF2 6HT* Tel (01952) 613334

EVANS, Mrs Linda Joyce. b 54. Trin Coll Bris BA06. **d** 06 **p** 07. NSM Weston super Mare Ch Ch and Em *B & W* from 06. *16 The Drive, Weston-super-Mare BS23 2SR* Tel (01934) 612534 E-mail landevans79@aol.com

EVANS, Linda Mary. *See* EDWARDS, Mrs Linda Mary

EVANS, Miss Madeleine Thelma Bodenham. b 30. K Coll Lon BD76 AKC76. Gilmore Course 80. **dss** 85 **d** 87 **p** 94. Chapl Pipers Corner Sch 85-91; Par Dn Calne and Blackland *Sarum* 91-94; C 94-00; Chapl St Mary's Sch Calne 91-99; rtd 00; Perm to Offic *Sarum* from 00. *11 Fairway, Rookery Park, Calne SN11 0LB* Tel and fax (01249) 814755

EVANS, Ms Margaret Elizabeth. b 48. Leeds Univ BA69 Lon Inst of Educn CertEd70. Oak Hill Th Coll 91. **d** 94 **p** 95. NSM Canonbury St Steph *Lon* from 94. *St Stephen's Canonbury, 17 Canonbury Road, London N1 2DF* Tel (020) 7226 7526 *or* 7359 4343 E-mail margareteevans@hotmail.com

EVANS, Mark Roland John. b 55. St Cath Coll Cam MA81 Bris Univ PGCE78. WEMTC 01. **d** 04 **p** 05. NSM Frenchay and Winterbourne Down *Bris* 04-08; NSM Frampton Cotterell and Iron Acton 08; NSM Winterbourne 08. *60 High Street, Thornbury, Bristol BS35 2AN* Tel (01454) 414101 Mobile 07702-289385 E-mail mark.evans@bathwells.anglican.org

EVANS, Martin Lonsdale. b 69. Man Univ BA91. Ripon Coll Cuddesdon 93. **d** 95 **p** 96. C Morpeth *Newc* 95-98; Chapl RN from 98. *Royal Naval Chaplaincy Service, Mail Point 1-2, Leach Building, Whale Island, Portsmouth PO2 8BY* Tel (023) 9262 5055 Fax 9262 5134 E-mail ml.evans@virgin.com

EVANS, Matthew Scott. b 72. Grey Coll Dur BA93. Cranmer Hall Dur 96. **d** 98 **p** 99. C Fountains Gp *Ripon* 98-03; P-in-c Dacre w Hartwith and Darley w Thornthwaite from 03. *The Vicarage, Dacre Banks, Harrogate HG3 4ED* Tel (01423) 780262

EVANS, Michael. b 49. St Jo Coll Nottm 88. **d** 90 **p** 91. C Beeston *S'well* 90-93; P-in-c Kirkby in Ashfield St Thos 93-97; V 97-08; Chapl Notts Healthcare NHS Trust 93-08; rtd 08. *26 Farm View Road, Kirkby-in-Ashfield, Nottingham NG17 7HF* Tel (01623) 750558 Mobile 07825-223189 E-mail munnamonk@aol.com

EVANS, Michael John. b 53. **d** 00 **p** 01. OLM Longnor, Quarnford and Sheen *Lich* 00-04; OLM Ipstones w Berkhamsytch and Onecote w Bradnop from 04. *Lower Marnshaw Head, Barrowmoor, Longnor, Buxton SK17 0QR* Tel (01298) 83293

EVANS, Neil Robert. b 54. Lon Univ MA93. Coll of Resurr Mirfield. **d** 84 **p** 85. C Bethnal Green St Jo w St Bart *Lon* 84-86; C St Jo on Bethnal Green 87-88; P-in-c Stoke Newington Common St Mich 88-95; V 95-98; V Twickenham All Hallows 98-05; Kensington Area CME Officer 98-05; Par Min Development Adv Willesden Area 05-07; Dir Tr and Development from 07. *23 St Albans Avenue, London W4 5LL* Tel (020) 8987 7332 E-mail neil.evans@london.anglican.org

EVANS, Nicholas Anthony Paul. b 60. Sheff Univ BA81 Liv Univ PGCE86. Qu Coll Birm 81. **d** 84 **p** 87. C Ludlow *Heref* 84-85; C Sunbury *Lon* 86-92; Hd RE Guildf Co Sch 93-99; NSM Crookham *Guildf* 94-99; CF 99-02; V Shenley Green *Birm* from 02. *St David's Vicarage, 49 Shenley Green, Birmingham B29 4HH* Tel 0121-475 4874 Mobile 07769-550204 E-mail evansnick@aol.com

EVANS, Nigel William Reid. b 70. Sheff Hallam Univ BEd96. Ridley Hall Cam BTh01. **d** 01 **p** 02. C Ossett and Gawthorpe *Wakef* 01-05; V Loddon, Sisland, Chedgrave, Hardley and Langley *Nor* from 05; RD Loddon from 06. *The Vicarage, 4 Market Place, Loddon, Norwich NR14 6EY* Tel (01508) 520251 E-mail nigel.evans4@tesco.net

EVANS, Norman Cassienet. b 30. Keble Coll Ox MA54. Guildf Dioc Min Course 91. **d** 95 **p** 96. OLM Seale, Puttenham and Wanborough *Guildf* 95-00; Perm to Offic from 00. *Hoplands, Riversmeet, Tilford, Farnham GU10 2BW* Tel (01252) 782933 E-mail norman@thereverend.fsnet.co.uk

EVANS, Mrs Patricia Rosemary. b 47. **d** 01 **p** 05. Par Dn Panteg *Mon* 01-03; Par Dn Panteg w Llanfihangel Pontymoile from 03. *Pentwyn Farm, Glascoed, Pontypool NP4 0TX* Tel and fax (01495) 785285 Mobile 07814-783714

EVANS, The Ven Patrick Alexander Sidney. b 43. Linc Th Coll 70. **d** 73 **p** 74. C Lyonsdown H Trin *St Alb* 73-76; C Royston 76-78; V Gt Gaddesden 78-82; V Tenterden St Mildred w Smallhythe

Cant 82-89; Adn Maidstone 89-02; Hon Can Cant Cathl 89-02; Dir of Ords 89-93; Adn Cant and Can Res Cant Cathl 02-07; rtd 07. *1 Streamside, Main Road, Tolpuddle, Dorchester DT2 7FD* Tel (01305) 849484 E-mail patrickevans120@hotmail.co.uk

EVANS, Peter. b 35. St Aid Birkenhead 57. **d** 60 **p** 61. C Higher Bebington *Ches* 60-63; C W Kirby St Bridget 63-66; P-in-c Lower Tranmere 66-68; V Flimby *Carl* 68-74; V Kirkby Ireleth 74-79; P-in-c Kirkbride w Newton Arlosh 79-80; R 80-85; V Beckermet St Jo and St Bridget w Ponsonby 85-97; rtd 97; Perm to Offic *Carl* from 98. *26 Gelt Close, Carlisle CA3 0HJ*

EVANS, Peter. b 40. S'wark Ord Course 75. **d** 75 **p** 76. C Welling *S'wark* 75-78; C Sutton New Town St Barn 78-81; C Kingston All SS w St Jo 81-87; V Croydon Woodside 87-99; TV Sanderstead All SS 99-03; rtd 03. *174 Main Street, Stanton-under-Bardon, Markfield LE67 9TP* Tel (01530) 245470

EVANS, Peter Anthony. b 36. Imp Coll Lon BScEng57. St Steph Ho Ox 58. **d** 60 **p** 61. C Surbiton St Mark *S'wark* 60-63; Asst Chapl Lon Univ 63-64; C S Kensington St Luke 64-68; C Surbiton St Andr and St Mark *S'wark* 68-69; C Loughton St Jo *Chelmsf* 69-74; P-in-c Becontree St Geo 74-82; Perm to Offic 82-89; NSM Romford St Alb 89-93; NSM Coopersale 93-95; NSM Epping Distr 95-96; rtd 97; Perm to Offic *Chelmsf* from 97. *6 Woodhall Crescent, Hornchurch RM11 3NN* Tel (01708) 509399

EVANS, Peter Gerald. b 41. Man Univ BA71. AKC65. **d** 65 **p** 66. C Kidbrooke St Jas *S'wark* 65-68; C Fallowfield *Man* 68-71; C Brockley Hill St Sav *S'wark* 71-73; P-in-c Colchester St Botolph w H Trin and St Giles *Chelmsf* 74-79; V 79-92; Perm to Offic from 93. *97 Northgate Street, Colchester CO1 1EY* Tel (01206) 543297

EVANS, Peter Kenneth Dunlop. b 38. Ch Coll Cam BA60. St D Coll Lamp 72. **d** 74 **p** 75. C Roath *Llan* 74-77; V Buttington and Pool Quay *St As* 77-87; V Llanfair Caereinion w Llanllugan 87-03; rtd 03. *Stepaside, Llanfair Caereinion, Welshpool SY21 0HU* Tel (01686) 627076

EVANS, Richard. *See* EVANS, David Richard

EVANS, Richard Edward Hughes. b 14. Univ of Wales BA44. St Mich Coll Llan. **d** 45 **p** 46. C Nantymoel *Llan* 45-48; C Pontyberem *St D* 48-50; C Llandeilo Fawr 50-53; V Ysbyty Cynfyn 53-64; V Llanybydder and Llanwenog w Llanwnnen 64-72; V Llanychaiarn 72-79; rtd 79. *23 Gwarfelin, Llanilar, Aberystwyth SY23 4PE* Tel (01974) 241357

EVANS, Richard Edward Victor. b 21. Linc Th Coll 66. **d** 68 **p** 69. C Aston cum Aughton *Sheff* 68-71; C Prestwich St Mary *Man* 71-74; R Moston St Jo 74-83; R Failsworth H Family 83-91; rtd 91; Perm to Offic *Man* from 91. *2 Tarnside House, Counthill Drive, Manchester M48 4JP* Tel 0161-720 8111

EVANS, Richard Gregory. b 50. St Mich Coll Llan 69. **d** 73 **p** 74. C Oystermouth *S & B* 73-76; C Clydach 76-79; CF 78-81; V Llanddew and Talachddu *S & B* 79-83; Youth Chapl 79-83; Hon Min Can Brecon Cathl 79-83; Chapl Huntley Sch New Zealand 83-87; Chapl Nga Tawa Sch 83-90; Chapl Wanganui Sch from 90. *Wanganui Collegiate School, Private Bag 3002, Wanganui 4540, New Zealand* Tel (0064) (6) 349 0281 ext 8750 Fax 348 8302 E-mail rgevans@collegiate.school.nz

EVANS, Richard Trevor. b 33. Jes Coll Ox MA58 DipEd58. St And Dioc Tr Course 73. **d** 76 **p** 76. NSM Leven *St And* 76-95; NSM St Andrews St Andr from 95. *33 Huntingtower Park, Whinnyknowe, Glenrothes KY6 3QF* Tel and fax (01592) 741670 E-mail revans9973@blueyonder.co.uk

EVANS, Robert. *See* EVANS, Simon Robert

EVANS, Canon Robert Arthur. b 24. Univ of Wales (Cardiff) BA48. St Mich Coll Llan 48. **d** 50 **p** 51. C Aberdare St Fagan *Llan* 50-52; C Roath 52-57; C Llandaff w Capel Llanillterm 57-61; Asst Chapl Mersey Miss to Seamen 61-62; Chapl Supt Mersey Miss to Seamen 62-74 and 79-89; Chapl RNR 67-89; V Rainhill *Liv* 74-79; Perm to Offic *Ches* 79-91; Hon Can Liv Cathl 88-89; rtd 89; Perm to Offic *Liv* 89-05. *1 Floral Wood, Riverside Gardens, Liverpool L17 7HR* Tel 0151-727 3608

EVANS, Robert Charles. b 55. K Coll Lon BA77 AKC77 MA78 MTh89 Qu Coll Cam BA80 MA83 CertEd85. Westcott Ho Cam 79. **d** 81 **p** 87. C St Breoke *Truro* 81-83; C St Columb Minor and St Colan 83-84; Chapl Rob Coll Cam 87-92; Lect Ches Univ from 92. *University of Chester, Parkgate Road, Chester CH1 4BJ* Tel (01244) 510000

EVANS, Robert George Roger. b 49. Cam Univ MA. Trin Coll Bris 74 St Jo Coll Nottm 94. **d** 77 **p** 78. C Bispham *Blackb* 77-80; C Chadwell *Chelmsf* 80-84; V Ardsley *Sheff* 84-09; P-in-c Kendray 04-09; Chapl Barnsley Community & Priority Services NHS Trust 98-00; rtd 09. *The Vicarage, Doncaster Road, Barnsley S71 5EF* Tel (01226) 203784 E-mail rgrevans@gmail.com

EVANS, Robert Stanley. b 51. Univ of Wales (Lamp) BA72 Univ of Wales (Cardiff) PGCE73. St Mich Coll Llan 90. **d** 92 **p** 93. V Penarth All SS *Llan* 92-95; R Gelligaer 95-99; V Roath 99-04; R Coychurch, Llangan and St Mary Hill 04-06; rtd 06. *13 Priory Gardens, Barry CF63 1FH* Tel (01446) 407606

EVANS, Ronald. b 47. St Mich Coll Llan 85. **d** 87 **p** 88. C Flint *St As* 87-91; TV Wrexham 91-97; V Rhosymedre 97-99; V

Rhosymedre w Penycae 99-05; PV Connah's Quay from 05. *8 Eurgain Avenue, Connah's Quay, Deeside CH5 4PW* Tel (01244) 812101 E-mail godshelp2002@yahoo.com

EVANS, Ronald Wilson. b 47. Windsor Univ Ontario BA69 Dalhousie Univ MA83. Trin Coll Toronto MDiv73. **d** 72 **p** 73. Canada 72-98; R Springhill 73-76; Chapl Univ of Prince Edw Is 76-79; Lect 82-85; Chapl King's-Edgehill Sch 85-87; R Clements 87-98; Lect Bilgi Univ Istanbul 98-00; Asst Chapl Izmir (Smyrna) w Bornova *Eur* 00-03; P-in-c 03-04; Chapl from 04. *PK 1005, Pasaport, Izmir 35120, Turkey* Tel (0090) (232) 463 7263 *or* tel and fax 464 5753 E-mail seljuk85@hotmail.com

EVANS, Roy Clifford. b 39. Qu Coll Birm 04. **d** 05. Chapl Univ Hosp Birm NHS Foundn Trust 05-07; NSM Billesley Common *Birm* 05-07. *Hawthorn Cottage, Llandrinio, Llanymynech SY22 6SB* Tel 07791-398923 (mobile) E-mail brother.evans@tesco.co.net

EVANS, Mrs Sarah Rosemary. b 64. Trevelyan Coll Dur BA85. STETS 05. **d** 08 **p** 09. NSM Hullavington, Norton and Stanton St Quintin *Bris* from 08; NSM Sherston Magna, Easton Grey, Luckington etc from 08. *The Deanery Office, The Old Squash Court, Holloway, Malmesbury SN16 9BA* Tel (01666) 818228 E-mail sarah.evans@deanery.org.uk

EVANS, Sheila Jean. *See* ROBERTSON, Mrs Sheila Jean

EVANS, Canon Simon. b 55. Newc Univ BA77 Heythrop Coll Lon MA06. St Steph Ho Ox 78. **d** 80 **p** 81. C Pet St Jude 80-84; Chapl Asst Pet Distr Hosp 80-84; C Wantage *Ox* 84-87; V W Leigh *Portsm* 87-96; Chapl E Hants Primary Care Trust 88-96; V Ruislip St Martin *Lon* from 96; AD Hillingdon from 08; Can Wiawso Ghana from 08. *The Vicarage, 13 Eastcote Road, Ruislip HA4 8BE* Tel (01895) 633040 *or* 625456 E-mail frsimon@waitrose.com

EVANS, Simon Andrew. b 59. Sarum & Wells Th Coll 81. **d** 84 **p** 85. C Norbury St Steph and Thornton Heath *S'wark* 84-88; C Putney St Mary 88-92; P-in-c Telford Park St Thos 92-94; V 94-04; V Ensbury Park *Sarum* from 04. *St Thomas's Vicarage, 42 Coombe Avenue, Bournemouth BH10 5AE* Tel (01202) 519735 E-mail simon@evansonline.info

EVANS, Simon Robert. b 58. Reading Univ BSc79. NOC 99. **d** 02 **p** 03. C Pudsey St Lawr and St Paul *Bradf* 02-04; P-in-c Low Moor 04-05; TV Oakenshaw, Wyke and Low Moor 06-07; TR from 07. *St Mary's Vicarage, 6 Vicarage Close, Wyke, Bradford BD12 8QW* Tel (01274) 678216 E-mail bob.evans@bradford.anglican.org *or* bob@wyke.me.uk

EVANS, Stanley George. b 43. CITC 00. **d** 03 **p** 04. Aux Min Killaloe w Stradbally *L & K* 03-04; P-in-c Killarney w Aghadoe and Muckross 04-05; Aux Min Leighlin w Grange Sylvae, Shankill etc *C & O* from 05. *Pallas, Tynagh, Co Galway, Republic of Ireland* Tel (00353) 87-636 9473 (mobile) E-mail stanevans@eircom.net

EVANS, Stanley Munro. b 30. AKC53. **d** 54 **p** 55. C Norbury St Oswald *Cant* 54-57; C St Laur in Thanet 57-63; V Bredgar 63-71; V Bredgar w Bicknor and Huckinge 71-72; V Westgate St Sav 72-01; rtd 01; Perm to Offic *Cant* from 01. *40 Queen Bertha Road, Ramsgate CT11 0ED* Tel (01843) 594459

EVANS, Canon Stephen John. b 60. Dartmouth RN Coll 81 St Steph Ho Ox BA85 MA89 Aber Univ MPhil94. **d** 86 **p** 87. Prec St Andr Cathl Inverness 86-89; R Montrose and P-in-c Inverbervie *Bre* 89-91; Miss to Seamen 89-91; V Northampton St Paul *Pet* 91-98; Continuing Minl Educn Officer 94-00; Liturg Officer 96-03; P-in-c Ecton and Warden Ecton Ho 98-00; R Uppingham w Ayston and Wardley w Belton *Pet* from 00; Can Pet Cathl from 03; RD Rutland from 03. *The Rectory, London Road, Uppingham, Oakham LE15 9TJ* Tel and fax (01572) 823381 E-mail stephen@stephenjevans.wanadoo.co.uk

EVANS, Steven Edward. b 52. CBDTI 97. **d** 00 **p** 01. NSM Caton w Littledale *Blackb* 00-05; NSM Hornby w Claughton and Whittington etc 05-06; NSM Slyne w Hest and Halton w Aughton 06-08; Perm to Offic from 08. *Brookhouse Hall, Brookhouse Road, Brookhouse, Lancaster LA2 9PA* Tel (01524) 771827

EVANS, Stuart. *See* EVANS, John Stuart

EVANS, Ms Susan Mary. b 55. St Jo Coll Dur BA76 CertEd77 Nottm Univ BCombStuds84. Linc Th Coll 81. **dss** 84 **d** 87 **p** 94. Weaste *Man* 84-88; Par Dn 87-88; Par Dn Longsight St Luke 88-92; Par Dn Claydon and Barham *St E* 92-94; C 94-99; P-in-c Henley 95-99; Chapl HM YOI Hollesley Bay Colony 99-02; NSM Henley, Claydon and Barham *St E* 02-06; Chapl HM Pris Whatton 06-09. *The Rectory, 15 Hillview Road, South Witham, Grantham NG33 5QW* Tel (01572) 767240

EVANS, Terence. b 55. St Mich Coll Llan 67. **d** 69 **p** 70. C Loughor *S & B* 69-73; C Gowerton w Waunarlwydd 73-77; V Llanbister and Llanbadarn Fynydd w Llananno 77-82; V Llanyrnewydd 82-01; rtd 01. *28 Orchard Court, New Orchard Street, Swansea SA1 5EN*

EVANS, Terence Robert. b 45. NOC 82. **d** 85 **p** 86. C Warrington St Elphin *Liv* 85-88; V Cantril Farm 88-94; V Rainhill 94-03; R Odd Rode *Ches* from 03. *Odd Rode Rectory, Church Lane, Scholar Green, Stoke-on-Trent ST7 3QN* Tel and fax (01270) 882195 E-mail evans338@btinternet.com

EVANS, Thomas Norman. b 30. K Coll Lon BA51 BD53 AKC56. d 56 p 57. C Handsworth *Sheff* 56-59; C Mexborough 59-61; V Denaby Main 61-65; V Wythenshawe Wm Temple Ch *Man* 65-78; RD Withington 72-78; R Prestwich St Mary 78-85; AD Radcliffe and Prestwich 78-85; Hon Can Man Cathl 79-85; R Skelton w Upleatham *York* 87-99; RD Guisborough 91-99; rtd 99; Perm to Offic *York* from 00. *4 Castelo Grove, Pickering YO18 7JV* Tel (01751) 476628

EVANS, Timothy Simon. b 57. York Univ BA79 Sussex Univ MA81 Fitzw Coll Cam BA85 MA88. Ridley Hall Cam 83. d 87 p 88. C Whitton St Aug *Lon* 87-90; C Ealing St Steph Castle Hill 90-93; P-in-c Shireshead *Blackb* 93-97; Asst Chapl Lanc Univ 93-97; Dep Prin LCTP 97-09; P-in-c Natland *Carl* 97-09; C Old Hutton and New Hutton 06-09; RD Kendal 00-03; Hon Can Carl Cathl 00-09; Dir Past Studies and Tutor Yorks Min Course from 09. *The Yorkshire Ministry Course, The Mirfield Centre, Stocks Bank Road, Mirfield WF14 0BW* Tel (01924) 481925 E-mail tim@ymc.org.uk

EVANS, Trevor Owen. b 37. Univ of Wales BSc59. Coll of Resurr Mirfield 59. d 61 p 62. C Llanaber w Caerdeon *Ban* 61-64; C Llandudno 64-70; TV 70-75; V Llanidloes w Llangurig 75-89; RD Arwystli 75-89; Can and Preb Ban Cathl 82-98; Dioc Adv on Spirituality 84-03; R Trefdraeth 89-90; Dir of Min 89-98; R Llanfairpwll w Penmynydd 90-98; Dean Ban 98-03; RD Ogwen 99-00; rtd 03. *Hafan, 3 Coed y Castell, Bangor LL57 1PH* Tel (01248) 352855

EVANS, William James Lynn. b 30. St D Coll Lamp 73. d 75 p 76. P-in-c Penbryn and Blaenporth *St D* 75-77; V Penbryn and Betws Ifan w Bryngwyn 77-79; V Penrhyncoch and Elerch 79-83; V Cynwil Elfed and Newchurch 83-87; V Llandybie 87-95; rtd 95. *5 Dolau Tywi, Manordeilo, Llandeilo SA19 7BL* Tel (01550) 777944

EVANS, Wyn. *See* EVANS, The Rt Revd John Wyn

EVANS-HILLS, Ms Bonnie Jean. b 57. Westcott Ho Cam. d 09. C Leic Resurr from 09. *St Gabriel's House, 20 Kerrysdale Avenue, Leicester LE4 7GH* Tel 0116-266 6844

EVANS-PUGHE, Thomas Goronwy. b 29. TCD. Wycliffe Hall Ox 59. d 61 p 62. C Grassendale *Liv* 61-63; P-in-c Mossley Hill St Matt and St Jas 63-64; C 64-65; Prec Chelmsf Cathl 65-69; R Birchanger 69-94; rtd 94; Perm to Offic *Glouc* from 94. *Bath Orchard, Blockley, Moreton-in-Marsh GL56 9HU* Tel (01386) 701223

EVANS-SMITH, Brian George. b 49. d 02 p 03. OLM S Ramsey St Paul *S & M* 02-06; P-in-c Lezayre from 06. *41 Barrule Park, Ramsey, Isle of Man IM8 2BR* Tel (01624) 817322

EVASON, Stuart Anthony. b 44. Salford Univ BSc. Chich Th Coll 79. d 81 p 82. C Heref St Martin 81-85; TV Cleethorpes *Linc* 85-87; TV Howden *York* 87-92; V Heywood St Jas *Man* 92-03; P-in-c Barrow St Jas *Carl* from 03; TR Barrow St Matt 06-09. *St James's Vicarage, 36 Thorncliffe Road, Barrow-in-Furness LA14 5PZ* Tel (01229) 821475 E-mail stuart_evason@bigfoot.com

EVE, David Charles Leonard. b 45. AKC74. St Aug Coll Cant 74. d 75 p 76. C Hall Green Ascension *Birm* 75-79; TV Kings Norton 79-84; V Rowley Regis 84-93; Perm to Offic *Heref* 94-98 and from 01; *Worc* from 05; NSM Hallow and Grimley w Holt *Worc* 98-05. *14 Orchard End, Cleobury Mortimer, Kidderminster DY14 8BA* Tel (01299) 270510 E-mail gabrielle.davideve@btinternet.com

EVE, Hilary Anne. *See* FIFE, Hilary Anne

EVE, Canon Ian Halliday. b 33. St Paul's Coll Grahamstown LTh59. d 59 p 60. S Africa 59-80 and from 81; P-in-c Salcombe *Ex* 80-81; Can Cape Town from 86. *Christ Church Rectory, Main Road, Constantia, 7800 South Africa* Tel (0027) (21) 794 6352 *or* 794 5051 Fax 794 1065

EVELEIGH, Raymond. b 36. Univ of Wales (Cardiff) BSc58. NW Ord Course 73. d 76 p 77. NSM S Cave and Ellerker w Broomfleet *York* 76-79; P-in-c Kingston upon Hull St Mary 79-82; Chapl Hull Coll of FE 79-01; V Anlaby Common St Mark *York* 82-94; V Langtoft w Foxholes, Butterwick, Cottam etc 94-01; rtd 01; Perm to Offic *York* from 04. *Pasture Lodge, West End, Kilham, Driffield YO25 4RR* Tel (01262) 420060 E-mail rev@revray.co.uk

EVENS, Jonathan Adrian Harvey. b 63. Middx Poly BA84 Middx Univ BA03 ACIPD90. NTMTC 00. d 03 p 04. C Barking St Marg w St Patr *Chelmsf* 03-06; V Gt Ilford St Jo from 06. *St John's Vicarage, 2 Regent Gardens, Ilford IG3 8UL* Tel (020) 8590 5884 E-mail jonathan.evens@btinternet.com

EVENS, Robert Alan. b 51. d 00 p 01. NSM Sharnbrook and Knotting w Souldrop *St Alb* 00-03; P-in-c Wymington w Podington 03-05; R Sharnbrook, Felmersham and Knotting w Souldrop from 05. *The Rectory, 81 High Street, Sharnbrook, Bedford MK44 1PE* Tel (01234) 782000 E-mail robert.evens@lineone.net

✠EVENS, The Rt Revd Robert John Scott. b 47. ACIB74. Trin Coll Bris 74. d 77 p 78 c 04. C Southsea St Simon *Portsm* 77-79; C Portchester 79-83; V Locks Heath 83-96; RD Fareham 93-96; Adn Bath and Preb Wells Cathl 96-04; Suff Bp Crediton *Ex* from

04. *32 The Avenue, Tiverton EX16 4HW* Tel (01884) 250002 Fax 258454 E-mail bishop.of.crediton@exeter.anglican.org

EVEREST, Prof Graham Robert. b 57. Bedf Coll Lon BSc80 K Coll Lon PhD83. EAMTC 02. d 05 p 06. NSM Cringleford and Colney *Nor* from 05. *1 Thistle Close, Norwich NR5 9HR* Tel (01603) 744475 E-mail graham.everest@googlemail.com

EVEREST, Canon John Cleland. b 45. Sarum Th Coll 66. d 68 p 69. C Moulsecoomb *Chich* 68-71; C Easthampstead *Ox* 71-74; C Southwick St Mich *Chich* 74-77; Dioc Soc Services Adv *Worc* 77-84; Ind Chapl 84-93; R Worc City St Paul and Old St Martin etc 84-93; RD Worc E 89-93; Hon Can Worc Cathl from 90; TR Halas from 93; RD Dudley 95-98. *The Rectory, Bundle Hill, Halesowen B63 4AR* Tel and fax 0121-550 1158 E-mail parishoffice@halasteam.org.uk

EVERETT, Alan Neil. b 57. St Cath Coll Ox BA79 DPhil96 SS Coll Cam BA84. Westcott Ho Cam 82. d 85 p 86. C Hindley All SS *Liv* 85-88; Chapl Qu Mary Coll *Lon* 88-91; V S Hackney St Mich w Haggerston St Paul from 94. *97 Lavender Grove, London E8 3LR* Tel (020) 7249 4440 *or* 7249 2627 E-mail alan@n16.org.uk

EVERETT, Anthony William. b 60. S Bank Poly BA82. Oak Hill Th Coll BA89. d 89 p 90. C Hailsham *Chich* 89-92; C New Malden and Coombe *S'wark* 92-97; V Streatham Park St Alb 97-02; V Herne Bay Ch Ch *Cant* from 02; Asst Dir of Ords from 05. *Christ Church Vicarage, 38 Beltinge Road, Herne Bay CT6 6BU* Tel (01227) 374906 *or* 366640 E-mail anthony@fayland.freeserve.co.uk

EVERETT, Mrs Christine Mary. b 46. St Osyth Coll of Educn CertEd67. Westcott Ho Cam 90. d 92 p 94. Par Dn Ipswich St Fran *St E* 92-94; C 94-95; C Gt and Lt Bealings w Playford and Culpho 96; P-in-c 96-02; P-in-c Creeting St Mary, Creeting St Peter etc from 02. *35 Chainhouse Road, Needham Market, Ipswich IP6 8TB* Tel (01449) 720319 Mobile 07980-023236 E-mail chrstevr@aol.com

EVERETT, Colin Gerald Grant. b 44. Open Univ BA77 Keswick Hall Coll CertEd. Ripon Coll Cuddesdon 79. d 81 p 82. C Aston cum Aughton *Sheff* 81-84; R Fornham All SS and Fornham St Martin w Timworth *St E* 84-92; P-in-c Old Newton w Stowupland 92-94; C Ipswich All Hallows 94-95; TV Ipswich St Fran 95-97; TV Ipswich St Mary at Stoke w St Pet and St Fran 97-09; rtd 09; Perm to Offic *St E* from 09. *35 Chainhouse Road, Needham Market, Ipswich IP6 8TB* Tel (01449) 720319 E-mail revcolin@btinternet.com

EVERETT, David Gordon. b 45. Pemb Coll Ox BA67 MA. Lon Coll of Div 68. d 70 p 71. C Hatcham St Jas *S'wark* 70-73; C Reading St Jo *Ox* 73-77; TV Fenny Stratford and Water Eaton 77-82; Hon C Bletchley 82-87; C Loughton 84-85; NSM Stantonbury and Willen 87-92; Chapl Ox Brookes Univ 92-96; NSM Iffley 93-96; C Treslothan *Truro* 96-97; C Crowan and Treslothan 98-02; Chapl Camborne Pool Redruth Coll 98-02; R Ketton, Collyweston, Easton-on-the-Hill etc *Pet* from 03. *The Vicarage, 4 Edmonds Drive, Ketton, Stamford PE9 3TH* Tel (01780) 720228

EVERETT, David John. b 51. Leeds Univ BA07. NOC 04. d 07 p 08. NSM Moor Allerton *Ripon* from 07. *2 Church Farm Garth, Leeds LS17 8HD* Tel 0113-273 7035 E-mail david.everett@talktalk.net

EVERETT, Canon John Wilfred. b 37. Qu Coll Cam BA61 MA65. Cuddesdon Coll 64. d 66 p 67. C St Helier *S'wark* 66-69; C Yeovil St Jo w Preston Plucknett *B & W* 69-73; R Wincanton 73-82; R Pen Selwood 80-82; V Ashford *Cant* 82-02; Hon Can Cant Cathl 90-02; rtd 02; Perm to Offic *Cant* from 02. *Stream Cottage, 17 Gladstone Road, Willesborough, Ashford TN24 0BY* Tel (01233) 640736

EVERETT, Robert Henry. b 60. Em Coll Cam BA82 MA86 Ox Univ BA85 MA90 Ex Univ MPhil95. St Steph Ho Ox 83. d 86 p 87. C Ex St Thos and Em 86-88; C Plymstock 88-91; R St Dominic, Landulph and St Mellion w Pillaton *Truro* 91-96; P-in-c Reading All SS *Ox* 96-98; V 98-07; P-in-c Paddington St Mary Magd *Lon* from 07; P-in-c Paddington St Pet from 07. *The Vicarage, 2 Rowington Close, London W2 5TF* Tel (020) 7289 1818 *or* 7289 2011 E-mail frhenry@btinternet.com

EVERETT, Robin Nigel. b 34. Dur Univ BA55. Cranmer Hall Dur 57. d 59 p 60. C New Humberstone *Leic* 59-62; C Humberstone 62-66; V Quorndon 66-74; V Castle Donington 74-82; P-in-c Lockington w Hemington 81-82; V Castle Donington and Lockington cum Hemington 82-86; Antigua 86-87; R Ibstock w Heather *Leic* 87-98; rtd 98; Perm to Offic *Derby* 98-01 and *Leic* 99-01. *90 Sevenlands Drive, Boulton Moor, Derby DE24 5AQ* Tel (01332) 751879

EVERETT, Canon Simon Francis. b 58. Oak Hill Th Coll BA89. d 89 p 90. C Wroughton *Bris* 89-93; TV Wexcombe *Sarum* 93-98; P-in-c The Iwernes, Sutton Waldron and Fontmell Magna 98-01; V Iwerne Valley from 01; RD Milton and Blandford from 01; Can and Preb Sarum Cathl from 09. *The Vicarage, Iwerne Minster, Blandford Forum DT11 8NF* Tel and fax (01747) 811291 E-mail reveverett@btinternet.com

EVERETT-ALLEN, Canon Clive. b 47. AKC70. St Aug Coll Cant 69. d 70 p 71. C Minera *St As* 70-72; C Hatcham St Cath

S'wark 72-75; TV Beaconsfield Ox 75-83; R Southwick St Mich Chich 83-98; V E Grinstead St Swithun from 98; Can and Preb Chich Cathl from 98; RD E Grinstead from 05; Chapl Qu Victoria Hosp NHS Trust East Grinstead from 98. St Swithun's Vicarage, Church Lane, East Grinstead RH19 3AZ Tel (01342) 323307 E-mail revclive@aol.com

EVERINGHAM, Georgina Wendy (formerly WALLACE, Godfrey Everingham). b 32. Tyndale Hall Bris BA57. d 58 p 59. C Broadwater St Mary Chich 58-61; V Shipton Bellinger w S Tidworth Win 61-70; V Bournemouth St Paul 70-84; V Throop 84-95; rtd 95; Perm to Offic Worc from 96. 3 Harlech Close, Berkeley Alford, Worcester WR4 0JU Tel (01905) 754394 E-mail gina@wordoflife.uk.com

EVERITT, Mark. b 34. Linc Coll Ox BA58 MA62. Wells Th Coll. d 60 p 61. C Hangleton Chich 60-63; Chapl Mert Coll Ox 63-02; rtd 02. 48 Annandale Avenue, Bognor Regis PO21 2EX Tel (01243) 823852

EVERITT, Michael John. b 68. K Coll Lon BD90 AKC90. Qu Coll Birm 90 English Coll Rome 91. d 92 p 93. C Cleveleys Blackb 92-95; S Africa 95-98; Succ Bloemfontein Cathl 95-98; Prec 96-98; Chapl and Asst Lect Univ of Orange Free State 96-98; Sen Chapl St Martin's Coll Blackb 98-02; Asst Dir of Ords 00-02; R Standish from 02; P-in-c Appley Bridge from 06; AD Chorley from 04. The Rectory, 13 Rectory Lane, Standish, Wigan WN6 0XA Tel (01257) 421396 E-mail rector@standish.org.uk

EVERITT, William Frank James. b 38. Dur Univ BA68 FCA63. Cranmer Hall Dur 65. d 69 p 70. C Leic St Phil 69-73; P-in-c Prestwold w Hoton 73-77; R Settrington w N Grimston and Wharram York 77-84; RD Buckrose 80-84; V Cheltenham St Pet Glouc 84-99; rtd 99; Perm to Offic Ripon from 03. 27 Lark Hill Crescent, Ripon HG4 2HN Tel (01765) 603683 E-mail reveveritt@yahoo.com

EVES, Barry. b 51. Cranmer Hall Dur 86. d 88 p 89. C Tadcaster w Newton Kyme York 88-91; C York St Paul 91-93; V Bubwith w Skipwith 93-04. 8 Marina Avenue, Sunderland SR6 9AL Tel 0191-549 1742

EVETTS-SECKER, Ms Josephine. b 42. Univ Coll Lon BA63 MPhil65. Coll of Resurr Mirfield 06. d 07 p 08. NSM Hinderwell, Roxby and Staithes etc York from 07. Lidgate, Victoria Square, Lythe, Whitby YO21 3RW Tel and fax (01947) 893338 Mobile 07717-061343 E-mail josephine@evetts-secker.co.uk

EWART, John. b 66. QUB BA89. CITC BTh02. d 02 p 03. C Derryloran Arm 02-05; China 05-07; I Bright w Ballee and Killough D & D from 07. Bright Rectory, 126 Killough Road, Downpatrick BT30 8LL Tel (028) 4484 2229 E-mail ewartj@btinternet.com

EWBANK, Mark Robert. b 59. Qu Coll Ox MA86 Heythrop Coll Lon MTh05. Westcott Ho Cam 84. d 86 p 87. Zimbabwe 86-00; Asst P N End St Marg Bulawayo 87-88; P-in-c Pumula St Luke 88-96; R Famona St Mary 96-00; C Chalfont St Peter Ox 00-06; V Englefield Green Guildf from 06; CF (ACF) from 01; CF (TA) from 05. The Vicarage, 21 Willow Walk, Englefield Green, Egham TW20 0DQ Tel (01784) 432553 E-mail v.ewbank@btinternet.com

EWBANK, Canon Robin Alan. b 42. Ex Coll Ox BA64 MA88 Lon Univ BD68. Clifton Th Coll 66. d 69 p 70. C Woodford Wells Chelmsf 69-72; Warden Cam Univ Miss Bermondsey 72-76; TV Sutton St Jas and Wawne York 76-82; R Bramshott Portsm 82-91; R Bramshott and Liphook 91-99; Hon Can Koforidua from 96; P-in-c Hartley Wintney, Elvetham, Winchfield etc 99-02; V from 02; RD Odiham from 04. The Vicarage, Church Lane, Hartley Wintney, Basingstoke RG27 8DZ Tel (01252) 842670 Fax 08707-052123 E-mail robin_ewbank@lineone.net or robin.ewbank@stjohnshw.co.uk

EWBANK, The Very Revd Robert Arthur Benson. b 22. Qu Coll Ox BA45 MA48. Cuddesdon Coll 46. d 48 p 49. C Boston Linc 48-52; Chapl Uppingham Sch 52-56; Zimbabwe 57-00; Prin Cyrene Secondary Sch Bulawayo 57-82; P-in-c Figtree CD 60-82; Can Bulawayo 64-80; Can Th 80-82; Dean Bulawayo 82-96; rtd 97; Perm to Offic Ely 01-05. 15 Egremont Street, Ely CB6 1AE Tel (01353) 645981

EWBANK, Canon Robin Alan. b 42. Ex Coll Ox BA64 MA88 Lon Univ BD68. Clifton Th Coll 66. d 69 p 70. C Woodford Wells

EWBANK, The Ven Walter Frederick. b 18. Ball Coll Ox BA45 MA45 BD52. Bps' Coll Cheshunt. d 46 p 47. C Windermere St Martin Carl 46-49; V Hugill 49-52; V Casterton H Trin 52-62; V Raughton Head w Gatesgill 62-66; Hon Can Carl Cathl 66-78 and 83-84; V Carl St Cuth 66-71; Adn Westmorland and Furness 71-77; V Winster 71-78; Adn Carl 78-84; Can Res Carl Cathl 78-82; rtd 84; Perm to Offic Carl 84-94. 10 Castle Court, Castle Street, Carlisle CA3 8TP Tel (01228) 810293

EWEN, Keith John McGregor. b 43. Sarum & Wells Th Coll 77. d 79 p 80. C Kington w Huntington Heref 79-82; C Kington w Huntington, Old Radnor, Kinnerton etc 82-83; P-in-c Culmington w Onibury 83-89; P-in-c Bromfield 83-89; P-in-c Stanton Lacy 83 89; R Culmington w Onibury, Bromfield etc 90-01; R Llangenni and Llanbedr Ystrad Yw w Patricio S & B 01-08; rtd 08. Ty Goleuddydd, 5 Goylands Close, Llandrindod Wells LD1 5RB Tel (01597) 825183

EWER, Edward Sydney John (Jonathan). b 36. Univ of New England BA69 Lanc Univ MPhil91 Ch Div Sch of the Pacific (USA) DMin02. St Mich Th Coll Crafers ThL63. d 62 p 63. Australia 62-83; SSM from 68; Perm to Offic Blackb 83-84; Lic to Offic Dur 84-98; Prior SSM Priory Dur 85-98; Dioc Dir of Ords 94-98; Perm to Offic S'wark 00-05; Hon C Pimlico St Mary Bourne Street Lon 05-06; Perm to Offic from 06. The Well, Newport Road, Willen, Milton Keynes MK15 9AA Tel (01908) 242741 Mobile 07915377554 E-mail j_ewer@yahoo.com

EWINGTON, John. b 43. MRICS65. Chich Th Coll 74. d 78 p 79. C Walthamstow St Jo Chelmsf 78-81; Papua New Guinea 81-87; V Southend St Sav Westcliff Chelmsf 87-96; TV Bideford, Northam, Westward Ho!, Appledore etc Ex from 96. The Vicarage, Meeting Street, Appledore, Bideford EX39 1RJ Tel (01237) 470469 E-mail john@vicars.co.uk

EXCELL, Robin Stanley. b 41. AKC64. St Boniface Warminster 64. d 65 p 66. C Ipswich St Mary Stoke St E 65-68; C Melton Mowbray w Thorpe Arnold Leic 68-70; TV 70-71; R Gt and Lt Blakenham w Baylham St E 71-76; R Gt and Lt Blakenham w Baylham and Nettlestead 76-86; RD Bosmere 84-86; NSM Sproughton w Burstall 91-94; R Rattlesden w Thorpe Morieux, Brettenham etc 94-05; rtd 05; Perm to Offic St E from 05. Hollywater, Upper Street, Baylham, Ipswich IP6 8JR Tel (01473) 830228 E-mail robin.excell@tesco.net

EXELL, Ernest William Carter. b 28. Qu Coll Cam BA52 MA53. Tyndale Hall Bris 49. d 52 p 53. C Sydenham H Trin S'wark 52-54; C E Ham St Paul Chelmsf 54-57; Uganda 57-65; Tanzania 66-70; R Abbess and Beauchamp Roding Chelmsf 70-71; P-in-c White Roding w Morrell Roding 70-71; R Abbess Roding, Beauchamp Roding and White Roding 71-94; RD Roding 75-79; rtd 94; Perm to Offic St E from 94. 8 Ickworth Drive, Bury St Edmunds IP33 3PX Tel (01284) 724726

EXELL, Michael Andrew John. b 45. FHCIMA MRIPHH67 MICA70. Sarum & Wells Th Coll 87. d 89 p 90. C Ryde H Trin Portsm 89-93; C Swanmore St Mich w Havenstreet 89-92; C Swanmore St Mich 92-93; P-in-c Carisbrooke St Mary 93-99; V from 99; P-in-c Carisbrooke St Nic 93-99; V from 99. The Vicarage, 56 Castle Road, Carisbrooke, Newport PO30 1DT Tel (01983) 522095

EXETER, Archdeacon of. See DRIVER, The Ven Penelope May

EXETER, Bishop of. See LANGRISH, The Rt Revd Michael Laurence

EXETER, Dean of. See MEYRICK, The Very Revd Cyril Jonathan

EXLEY, Malcolm. b 33. Cranmer Hall Dur. d 67 p 68. C Sutton St Jas York 67-73; V Mappleton w Goxhill 73-77; V Market Weighton 77-90; P-in-c Goodmanham 77-78; R 78-90; V Bridlington Em 90-98; rtd 98; Perm to Offic York from 00. 11 The Chase, Driffield YO25 7FJ Tel (01377) 272312

EXLEY-STIEGLER, Canon George Ebdon. b 16. Syracuse Univ BS51. Berkeley Div Sch STM53. d 53 p 54. R Camden Trin USA 53-57; R Brockport St Luke 57-64; R Rochester Calvary-St Andr 64-79; rtd 79; Hon C Knowsley Liv 80-81; Hon C Upholland 81-89; Lect Upholland N Inst 80-84; USA from 89. 168 Dalaker Drive, Rochester NY 14624, USA E-mail geoes@frontiernet.net

EXON, Heller John Philip. b 44. MBE87. BSc70 CEng87 MIET87. STETS 96. d 99 p 00. NSM Milton Abbas, Hilton w Cheselbourne etc Sarum 99-05; NSM Piddletrenthide w Plush, Alton Pancras etc 02-05; NSM Piddle Valley, Hilton, Cheselbourne etc from 05. The Monk's House, Hilton, Blandford Forum DT11 0DG Tel (01258) 880396 E-mail helier@exon.demon.co.uk

EYDEN, Christopher David. b 59. RSAMD BA81. St Steph Ho Ox 88. d 91 p 92. C Tottenham St Paul Lon 91-93; C Ealing St Pet Mt Park 93-96; TV Wimbledon S'wark 96-04; Perm to Offic 04-05; C Putney St Mary from 05. All Saints' Vicarage, 70 Fulham High Street, London SW6 3LG Tel (020) 7384 0115 Mobile 07951-600924 E-mail chriseyden@talk21.com

EYEONS, Keith James. b 70. Clare Coll Cam BA92 MA96 Lon Inst of Educn PGCE95. St Jo Coll Nottm MA(MM)03. d 01 p 02. C Iffley Ox 01-03; Chapl Down Coll Cam from 03. Downing College, Cambridge CB2 1DQ Tel (01223) 334800 E-mail kje11@cam.ac.uk

EYERS, Frederick Thomas Laurence. b 12. Ridley Coll Melbourne LTh39. d 39 p 40. Australia 39-46, 50-73 and from 82; Perm to Offic York 46-50; SSM from 50. Broughton Hall, 2 Berwick Street, Camberwell Vic 3124, Australia Tel (0061) (3) 9813 4053

EYLES, Anthony John. b 34. Bris Univ BSc57. Sarum Th Coll 61. d 63 p 64. C Wellington w W Buckland B & W 63-67; C Wilton 67-74; Ind Chapl Dur 74-85; Ind Chapl Worc 85-90; P-in-c Bickenhill w Elmdon Birm 90; P-in-c Bickenhill 90-00; Chapl Birm Airport 90-00; rtd 00; Perm to Offic Ex from 00. 5 Kersbrook Lane, Kersbrook, Budleigh Salterton EX9 7AD Tel (01395) 446084

EYNON, John Kenneth. b 56. Nottm Univ BA77 BArch80. d 96 p 97. OLM Croydon Ch Ch S'wark 96-05. 21 Rye Close,

Saltdean, Brighton BN2 8PP Tel (01273) 308397 Mobile 07789-877541 E-mail johneynon@btinternet.com

EYNSTONE, Ms Sarah Francesca Louise. b 75. Univ Coll Lon BA96 Fitzw Coll Cam BA04. Westcott Ho Cam 02. **d** 05 **p** 06. C Hampstead St Jo *Lon* from 05. *10A Dennington Park Mansions, 267-279 West End Lane, London NW3 6TX* Tel (020) 7794 5808 E-mail sarah.eynstone@cantab.net

EYRE, The Very Revd Richard Montague Stephens. b 29. Oriel Coll Ox BA53 MA56. St Steph Ho Ox 53. **d** 56 **p** 57. C Portsea N End St Mark *Portsm* 56-59; Tutor Chich Th Coll 59-61; Chapl 61-62; Chapl Eastbourne Coll 62-65; V Arundel w Tortington and S Stoke *Chich* 65-73; V Brighton Gd Shep Preston 73-75; Dir of Ords 75-79; Adn Chich 75-81; Can Res and Treas Chich Cathl 78-81; Dean Ex 81-95; rtd 95; Perm to Offic *B & W* 95-00 and from 04; P-in-c Pau *Eur* 01-03. *Hathersage, Enmore, Bridgwater TA5 2DP* Tel (01278) 671790

EYRE, Canon Richard Stuart. b 48. Bris Univ BEd81 Nottm Univ MTh86. Linc Th Coll 74. **d** 77 **p** 78. C Henbury *Bris* 77-81; C Bedminster 81-82; TV 82-84; Chapl Bp Grosseteste Coll Linc 84-95; Sen Tutor 89-95; P-in-c Long Bennington w Foston *Linc* 95; P-in-c Saxonwell 95-97; R 97-01; RD Grantham 96-01; TR Hykeham from 01; RD Graffoe from 02; Can and Preb Linc Cathl from 03. *The Rectory, Mill Lane, North Hykeham, Lincoln LN6 9PA* Tel (01522) 882880 Fax 883100 E-mail richard.eyre3@ntlworld.com

EZE, Geoffrey Ejike. b 73. Trin Coll Bris 06. **d** 08 **p** 09. C Gt Ilford St Jo *Chelmsf* from 08. *53 Friars Close, Ilford IG1 4AZ* Tel (020) 8553 9898 E-mail geoffj-e-eze@yahoo.fr

F

FACCINI (née LEGG), Sandra Christine. b 55. Surrey Univ BSc78 PhD82 Univ of Wales (Ban) BTh07. **d** 04 **p** 05. OLM Howell Hill w Burgh Heath *Guildf* 04-09; P-in-c Ottershaw from 09. *50 Slade Road, Ottershaw, Chertsey KT16 0HZ* Tel (01932) 873160 Mobile 07743-675633 E-mail sandra@faccinis.freeserve.co.uk

FACER, Miss Rosemary Jane. b 44. Hull Univ BA65 Reading Univ CertEd66 LTCL72. Trin Coll Bris 78. **dss** 80 **d** 87 **p** 98. St Paul's Cray St Barn *Roch* 80-88; Par Dn 87-88; C Cheltenham St Mark *Glouc* 88-01; C Clifton *York* 01-09; rtd 09. *16 Garborough Close, Crosby, Maryport CA15 6RZ* Tel (01900) 810776 E-mail r.rj.facer@talk21.com

FACEY, Andrew John. b 57. Trin Coll Cam BA79 MA83 Barrister-at-Law 80. Trin Coll Bris BA92. **d** 92 **p** 93. C Egham *Guildf* 92-96; P-in-c E Molesey St Paul 96-01; P-in-c Epsom Common Ch Ch 01-02; V from 02; Dioc Inter Faith Adv from 96. *Christ Church Vicarage, 20 Christ Church Road, Epsom KT19 8NE* Tel and fax (01372) 720302 E-mail andrew.facey@virgin.net

FACEY, Jane (BJ). b 54. EMMTC 05. **d** 07 **p** 08. NSM W Hallam and Mapperley w Stanley *Derby* from 07. *2 George Street, Langley Mill, Nottingham NG16 4DJ* Tel (01773) 531057

FAGAN, Jeremy David. b 75. Qu Coll Ox BA98. Wycliffe Hall Ox 99. **d** 01 **p** 02. C Chell *Lich* 01-04; TV Kirkby *Liv* from 04. *27 Shakespeare Avenue, Liverpool L32 9SH* Tel 0151-547 2133 E-mail faganj@mac.com

FAGAN, John Raymond. b 32. Lon Univ BD69. Ripon Hall Ox 71. **d** 72 **p** 73. C Stalybridge *Man* 72-74; C Madeley *Heref* 74-79; V Amington *Birm* 79-91; P-in-c Stonnall *Lich* 91-97; Chapl HM YOI Swinfen Hall 91-97; rtd 97; C Stonnall *Lich* 97; Res Min Elford 98-07. *19 Homewelland House, Leicester Road, Market Harborough LE16 7BT* Tel (01858) 419988

FAGAN, Thomas. b 27. MCIOB67 Man Univ CertEd70. NW Ord Course 78. **d** 81 **p** 82. NSM Rainhill *Liv* 81-90; NSM Prescot 90-97; rtd 97; Perm to Offic *Liv* 97-03. *4 Wensleydale Avenue, Prescot L35 4NR* Tel 0151-426 4788

FAGBEMI, Olubunmi Ayobami (Bunmi). b 57. Lagos Univ LLB78 LSE LLM81 Qu Mary Coll Lon PhD91 Solicitor 79. Ripon Coll Cuddesdon 95. **d** 97 **p** 98. C Enfield St Andr *Lon* 97-01; V Tottenham H Trin from 01. *Holy Trinity Vicarage, Philip Lane, London N15 4GZ* Tel (020) 8801 3021 E-mail bunmif@btinternet.com

FAGBEMI, Canon Stephen Ayodeji Akinwale. b 67. St Jo Coll Nottm BTh96 Kent Univ PhD04. Immanuel Coll Ibadan 87. **d** 90 **p** 91. C Iyere St Jo Nigeria 90-91; C Owo St Patr 91-92; P-in-c Wakajaye-Etile Ch 92-93; V Emure-Ile St Sav 96-00; Can Owo from 99; Perm to Offic *Cant* 00-03; Hon C Murston w Bapchild and Tonge 03-05; Co-ord Chapl Sunderland Univ and

Assoc Chapl Sunderland Minster from 05. *The Chaplaincy, The Gateway, 1st Floor Edinburgh Building, Chester Road, Sunderland SR1 3SD* Tel 0191-515 3482 Fax 515 2949 Mobile 07796-643468 E-mail saaf95@hotmail.com *or* saaf90@yahoo.co.uk

FAGERSON, Joseph Leonard Ladd. b 35. Harvard Univ BA57. Ridley Hall Cam 61. **d** 63 **p** 64. C Tonbridge SS Pet and Paul *Roch* 63-67; Afghanistan 67-74; P-in-c Marbury *Ches* 74-75; P-in-c Kinloch Rannoch *St And* 75-00; Chapl Rannoch Sch Perthshire 75-00; rtd 00; Hon C Killin *St And* from 00. *Westgarth, Tomnacroich, Fortingall, Aberfeldy PH15 2LJ* Tel (01887) 830569

FAHIE, Mrs Stephanie Bridget. b 48. St Jo Coll Nottm 85. **d** 87 **p** 94. Par Dn Leic St Chris 87-90; Chapl Scargill Ho 90-95; P-in-c Hickling w Kinoulton and Broughton Sulney *S'well* 95-00; R from 00. *The Rectory, 41 Main Street, Kinoulton, Nottingham NG12 3EA* Tel (01949) 81657 E-mail kinoulton.rectory@virgin.net

FAINT, Paul Edward. b 38. Qu Coll Birm 85. **d** 87 **p** 88. C Cradley *Worc* 87-90; V Hanley Castle, Hanley Swan and Welland 90-94; V Northwood H Trin *Lon* 94-97; Miss to Seafarers from 97; Chapl Larnaca Cyprus 97-01; rtd 01; Perm to Offic *Ox* from 01; Hon Chapl Miss to Seafarers from 02. *17 Priory Orchard, Wantage OX12 9EL* Tel (01235) 772297 E-mail thefaints@lineone.net

FAIRALL, Hannah Marie. *See* MEARS, Mrs Hannah Marie

FAIRALL, Michael John. b 55. SW Minl Tr Course 88. **d** 90 **p** 91. NSM Southway *Ex* from 90. *132 Lakeview Close, Tamerton Foliot, Plymouth PL5 4LX* Tel (01752) 707694 E-mail m.j.fairall@talk21.com

FAIRBAIRN, Andrew Graham. b 48. SEITE 06. **d** 09. NSM Surbiton Hill Ch Ch *S'wark* from 09. *Christ Church, 8 Christ Church Road, Surbiton KT5 8JL* Tel (020) 8390 7215 Mobile 07789-992843 E-mail graham.fairbairn@ccsurbiton.org

FAIRBAIRN, Francis Stephen. b 41. **d** 98 **p** 99. OLM Orrell *Liv* from 98. *27 Greenslate Road, Billinge, Wigan WN5 7BQ* Tel (01695) 623127 *or* (01722) 812176 Fax (01722) 815398

FAIRBAIRN, John Alan. b 46. Trin Coll Cam BA67 MA72. Wycliffe Hall Ox 84. **d** 86 **p** 87. C Boscombe St Jo *Win* 86-89; C Edgware *Lon* 89-95; R Gunton St Pet *Nor* from 95; Chapl Jas Paget Healthcare NHS Trust 96-08. *The Rectory, 36 Gunton Church Lane, Lowestoft NR32 4LF* Tel (01502) 580707

FAIRBAIRN, Stella Rosamund. **d** 87 **p** 94. NSM Banbury *Ox* 87-99; Perm to Offic *Pet* 88-94. *Hillside, Overthorpe, Banbury OX17 2AF* Tel (01295) 710648

FAIRBAIRN, Stephen. *See* FAIRBAIRN, Francis Stephen

FAIRBANK, Brian Douglas Seeley. b 53. AKC75. St Steph Ho Ox 77. **d** 78 **p** 79. C Newton Aycliffe *Dur* 78-81; C Stocking Farm *Leic* 81-84; TV Ratby cum Groby 84-91; Chapl RN 91-04; R Bramfield, Stapleford, Waterford etc *St Alb* from 04. *The Rectory, Church Lane, Watton-at-Stone, Hertford SG14 3RD* Tel (01920) 830575

FAIRBROTHER, Robin Harry. b 44. Ho of Resurr Mirfield 64 Wells Th Coll 68. **d** 69 **p** 70. C Wrexham *St As* 69-74; C Welshpool w Castle Caereinion 74-77; V Bettws Cedewain and Tregynon 77-80; V Betws Cedewain and Tregynon and Llanwyddelan 80-92; TR Marshwood Vale *Sarum* 92-98; TR Golden Cap Team 98-05; rtd 06. *14 Mannington Way, West Moors, Ferndown BH22 0JE* Tel (01202) 870895 E-mail robin.fairbrother2356@freeserve.co.uk

FAIRCLOUGH, Clive Anthony. b 54. TISEC 01. **d** 04 **p** 05. C Nadder Valley *Sarum* 04-08; R Abberton, The Flyfords, Naunton Beauchamp etc *Worc* from 08. *The Rectory, Church End, Bishampton, Pershore WR10 2LT* Tel (01386) 462648 Mobile 07962-023882

FAIRCLOUGH, John Frederick. b 40. St Jo Coll Dur BA63 MA68 MBIM. Coll of Resurr Mirfield 81. **d** 83 **p** 84. C Horninglow *Lich* 83-87; V Skerton St Luke *Blackb* 87-94; V Thornton-le-Fylde 94-00; rtd 00; Perm to Offic *Blackb* from 01. *18 Crossfield Avenue, Bury BL9 5NX* Tel (01706) 825664

FAIREY, Michael. b 51. NEOC. **d** 08. NSM York St Hilda from 08. *Boston Gates, Whinns Lane, Thorp Arch, Wetherby LS23 7AL* Tel (01937) 844794

FAIRHURST, John Graham. b 39. Linc Th Coll 86. **d** 88 **p** 89. C Whiston *Sheff* 88-91; V Elsecar 91-04; AD Tankersley 01-04; Chapl Barnsley Community & Priority Services NHS Trust 98-04; rtd 04; Perm to Offic *Sheff* from 04. *30 Barberry Way, Ravenfield, Rotherham S65 4RE* Tel (01709) 548206

FAIRHURST, Ms Rosemary Anne. b 63. Newnham Coll Cam BA85 MA85 Lon Inst of Educn PGCE86. Wycliffe Hall Ox BA92. **d** 93 **p** 94. C Hackney Marsh *Lon* 93-97; C Islington St Mary 97-02; Dir Miss and Min Ripon Coll Cuddesdon 02-06; Organizational Analyst Grubb Inst from 07; Perm to Offic *Lon* from 07. *The Grubb Institute, Cloudesley Street, London N1 0HU* Tel (020) 7278 8061 E-mail r.fairhurst@grubb.org.uk

FAIRLAMB, Neil. b 49. Univ of Wales (Ban) BA71 Jes Coll Ox BPhil73 Pemb Coll Cam CertEd74 Univ of Wales (Abth) MTh00. S'wark Ord Course 90. **d** 93 **p** 94. Hon C Dulwich St Barn *S'wark* 93-95; P-in-c Elerch w Penrhyncoch w Capel

Bangor and Goginan *St D* 95-96; V 96-98; R Arthog w Fairbourne w Llangelynnin w Rhoslefain *Ban* 98-03; R Beaumaris from 03. *The Rectory, 5 Tros yr Afon, Beaumaris LL58 8BN* Tel and fax (01248) 811402
E-mail rheithor@aol.com

FAIRLESS (née CARTER), Mrs Elizabeth Jane. b 57. Derby Univ BSc00. St Jo Coll Nottm MTh02. **d** 02 **p** 03. C Leek and Meerbrook *Lich* 02-05; C Harlescott from 05; Chapl Shropshire Co Primary Care Trust from 05. *Emmanuel Vicarage, Mount Pleasant Road, Shrewsbury SY1 3HY* Tel (01743) 350907 Mobile 07968-033489 E-mail liz.fairless@btinternet.com

FAIRWEATHER, David James. b 35. Keele Univ BEd79. Wycliffe Hall Ox 70. **d** 72 **p** 73. C Trentham *Lich* 72-76; C Cheddleton 76; C Hanley H Ev 77-79; C Rugeley 79-86; V Brown Edge 86-03; rtd 03; Perm to Offic *Lich* from 09. *The Spinney, Bellamour Way, Colton, Rugeley WS15 3LL* Tel (01889) 582847 E-mail father.david@btinternet.com

FAIRWEATHER, John. b 39. K Coll Lon AKC66 BD72. **d** 67 **p** 68. C Plymouth St Jas Ham *Ex* 67-69; C Townstal w St Sav and St Petrox w St Barn 69-73; R Corringham w Springthorpe *Linc* 73-78; P-in-c Blyborough 76-78; P-in-c Heapham 76-78; P-in-c Willoughton 76-78; V Pinchbeck 78-82; V Exwick 82-04; rtd 04. *52 Woodman's Crescent, Honiton EX14 2DY* Tel (01404) 549711

FAIRWEATHER, Sally Helen. *See* ROSS, Mrs Sally Helen

FALASCHI-RAY, Sonia Ofelia. Surrey Univ BSc79 Wolfs Coll Cam BA02 MA06 CEng86. Ridley Hall Cam 03. **d** 05 **p** 06. NSM Fowlmere, Foxton, Shepreth and Thriplow *Ely* 05-09; Perm to Offic *St Alb* from 09. *27 Church Lane, Barkway, Royston SG8 8EJ* Tel (01763) 849057 Mobile 07747-844265
E-mail sonia.falaschi-ray@virgin.net

FALCONER, Ian Geoffrey. b 40. BNC Ox BA62 Newc Univ MA93. Cuddesdon Coll 62. **d** 64 **p** 65. C Chiswick St Nic w St Mary *Lon* 64-68; C-in-c Hounslow Gd Shep Beavers Lane CD 68-76; P-in-c Hammersmith St Matt 76-84; P-in-c Byker St Silas *Newc* 84-93; V 93-95; P-in-c Newc St Phil and St Aug 95-98; P-in-c Newc St Matt w St Mary 95-98; P-in-c Newc St Phil and St Aug and St Matt w St Mary 98-00; V Seghill 00-06; rtd 06. *70 Lowgates, Staveley, Chesterfield S43 3TU* Tel (01246) 471913 E-mail frianfalc@yahoo.co.uk

FALKINGHAM (née MOORE), Mrs Caroline Judith. b 57. Coll of Ripon & York St Jo BA78 Leeds Univ MA07. NOC 05. **d** 07 **p** 08. C Bilton *Ripon* from 07. *64 Knox Lane, Harrogate HG1 3DA* Tel (01423) 505372
E-mail caroline@falkingham.fslife.co.uk

FALKNER, Jonathan Michael Shepherd. b 47. Open Univ BA74. Cranmer Hall Dur. **d** 79 **p** 80. C Penrith w Newton Reigny *Carl* 79-81; C Penrith w Newton Reigny and Plumpton Wall 81-82; C Dalton-in-Furness 82-84; V Clifton 84-90; P-in-c Dean 85-89; R 89-90; P-in-c Rumburgh w S Elmham w the Ilketshalls *St E* 90-92; R S Elmham and Ilketshall 92-99; RD Beccles and S Elmham 94-99; Hon Can St E Cathl 98-99; P-in-c W Newton and Bromfield w Waverton *Carl* 99-02; P-in-c Holme Cultram St Mary and St Cuth 00-02; TR Solway Plain 02-05; P-in-c Gosforth w Nether Wasdale and Wasdale Head from 05. *The Rectory, Gosforth, Seascale CA20 1AZ* Tel (01946) 725251 E-mail jonathan.falkner@talk21.com

FALLA, Miles. b 43. MCIM. EAMTC 93. **d** 96 **p** 97. NSM Buckden *Ely* 96-98; P-in-c Gretton w Rockingham *Pet* 98-99· V Gretton w Rockingham and Cottingham w E Carlton 99-04; RD Corby 01-02; rtd 04; Perm to Offic *Ely* from 05. *Bowlings, Silver Street, Buckden, St Neots PE19 5TS* Tel (01480) 811335

FALLONE, Christopher. b 55. Aston Tr Scheme 85 Oak Hill Th Coll 87. **d** 90 **p** 91. C Rochdale *Man* 90-93; P-in-c Thornham w Gravel Hole 93-94; TV Middleton w Thornham 94-08; P-in-c Collyhurst from 08. *The Rectory, Eggington Street, Collyhurst, Manchester M10 7RN* Tel 0161-205 2808 Mobile 07976-624124 E-mail chrisfallone@bigfoot.com

FALLOWS, Stuart Adrian. b 50. Moray Ho Edin 75. **d** 78 **p** 79. Hon C Forres w Nairn *Mor* 78-81; Hon C Elgin w Lossiemouth 81-86; Hon Dioc Chapl 86; C Brighton St Geo w St Anne and St Mark *Chich* 86-89; V Wivelsfield 89-98; P-in-c Kieth, Huntly and Aberchirder *Mor* 98-02; P-in-c Ringwould w Kingsdown *Cant* 02-04; R Ringwould w Kingsdown and Ripple etc 05-09; R W Highland Region *Arg* from 09. *The Rectory, Carnoch, Glencoe, Ballachulish PH49 4HP* Tel (01855) 811212 E-mail afallows222@aol.co.uk

FALSHAW, Simon Meriadoc. b 60. Leeds Univ BSc82. Oak Hill Th Coll BA93. **d** 93 **p** 94. C Stapleford *S'well* 93-99; Miss Partner Crosslinks 99-00; P-in-c The Lye and Stambermill *Worc* from 01; RD Stourbridge 04-07. *Christ Church Vicarage, High Street, Lye, Stourbridge DY9 8LF* Tel (01384) 423142 or 894948
E-mail christchurchlye@classicfm.net

FALUDY, Alexander Raban Spencer. b 83. Peterho Cam BA01 MA05 Linc Coll Ox MSt04. Coll of Resurr Mirfield 05. **d** 08 **p** 09. C Tynemouth Cullercoats St Paul *Newc* from 08. *14 Naters Street, Whitley Bay NE26 2PQ* Tel 0191-289 5135 Mobile 07806-459374 E-mail alexander.faludy@lincoln.oxon.net

FANE, Clifford Charles. b 39. Kelham Th Coll 62. **d** 67 **p** 68. C Heston *Lon* 67-73; C Bedminster St Mich *Bris* 73-76; P-in-c

76-77; C Gaywood, Bawsey and Mintlyn *Nor* 77-81; V Bolton St Jo *Man* 81-90; rtd 90. *10 Booth Road, Little Lever, Bolton BL3 1JY* Tel (01204) 709420

FANTHORPE, Robert Lionel. b 35. Open Univ BA80 CertEd63 FCMI81 FCP90. Llan Dioc Tr Scheme. **d** 87 **p** 88. NSM Roath St German *Llan* 87-00; Lic to Offic from 00. *Rivendell, 48 Claude Road, Roath, Cardiff CF24 3QA* Tel (029) 2049 8368 Fax 2049 6832 Mobile 07767-207289 E-mail fanthorpe@aol.com

FARADAY, John. b 49. Leeds Univ BSc71 MICE78. Oak Hill Th Coll 81. **d** 83 **p** 84. C Sutton *Liv* 83-86; C Rainhill and Chapl Whiston Hosp 86-89; V Over Darwen St Jas *Blackb* 89-02; TR S Rochdale *Man* 02-08; TR Gorton and Abbey Hey from 08. *Emmanuel Rectory, 35 Blackwin Street, Manchester M12 5LD* Tel 0116-223 3510 E-mail john.faraday@sky.com

FARAH, Mones Anton. b 64. Trin Coll Bris BA88. **d** 88 **p** 89. C Aberystwyth *St D* 88-91; Chapl St D Coll Lamp 91-98; TV Gt Baddow *Chelmsf* from 98. *The Vicarage, 42 Riffhams Drive, Great Baddow, Chelmsford CM2 7DD* Tel (01245) 471516 E-mail monesf@yahoo.com

FARBRIDGE, Nicholas Brisco. b 33. FCA. Sarum & Wells Th Coll 75. **d** 77 **p** 78. C Gt Bookham *Guildf* 77-80; C Ewell 80-83; V Addlestone 83-89; R Shere 89-95; rtd 96; Perm to Offic *Guildf* from 96. *55 Curling Vale, Guildford GU2 7PH* Tel (01483) 531140

FARDON, Raymond George Warren. b 30. St Pet Hall Ox BA52 MA56. Ridley Hall Cam 54. **d** 59 **p** 60. C High Wycombe All SS *Ox* 59-63; Chapl Bedford Secondary Modern Sch 63-68; Dep Hd Dunstable Secondary Modern Sch 68-72; Hd Master K Sch Grantham 72-82; Travelling Ev from 82; Hon C Longfleet *Sarum* 82-83; Perm to Offic *Sarum* 83-05 and *S'well* from 05; rtd 95. *9 Somerby Court, Bramcote, Nottingham NG9 3NB* Tel 0115-928 0810

FAREY, David Mark. b 56. St Jo Coll Dur BA85. Cranmer Hall Dur 82. **d** 86 **p** 87. C Brackley St Pet w St Jas 86-89; TV Kingsthorpe w Northampton St Dav 89-96; R Laughton w Ripe and Chalvington *Chich* from 96; Chapl to Bp Lewes from 96. *The Rectory, Church Lane, Laughton, Lewes BN8 6AH* Tel and fax (01323) 811642 E-mail david@dfarey.fsnet.co.uk

FARGUS, Gavin James Frederick. b 30. AKC54. K Coll Lon. **d** 55 **p** 57. C Salisbury St Mark *Sarum* 55-57; C Wareham w Arne 57-60; C Marlborough 60-63; P-in-c Davidstow w Otterham *Truro* 63-65; R Nether Lochaber *Arg* 65-81; R Kinlochleven 65-81; rtd 81; Lic to Offic *Arg* 82-94. *61 Loan Fearn, Ballachulish, Argyll PH49 4JB* Tel (01855) 811851

FARGUS, Maxwell Stuart. b 34. Linc Coll Ox BA57 MA61 Leeds Univ DipAdEd79. Cuddesdon Coll 57. **d** 59 **p** 60. C Newc St Fran 59-62; C Rothbury 62-64; Dioc Youth Officer *Ripon* 64-76; R Kirkby Wiske 64-76; Community Educn Officer Barnsley MBC 76-88; Perm to Offic *Sheff, Wakef* and *York* 77-88; V Rudston w Boynton and Kilham *York* 88-93; rtd 93; Perm to Offic *York* from 93. *56 Fir Tree Drive, Filey YO14 9NR* Tel and fax (01723) 513511

FARISH, Alan John. b 58. Lanc Univ BA. St Jo Coll Nottm 83. **d** 86 **p** 87. C Bishopwearmouth St Gabr *Dur* 86-89; C Fatfield 89-98; P-in-c Preston on Tees 98-03; V Preston-on-Tees and Longnewton 03; P-in-c Stockton from 03. *17 Pennypot Lane Eaglescliff, Stockton-on-Tees TS16 0BN* Tel (01642) 782961

FARLEY, Claire Louise. *See* MADDOCK, Mrs Claire Louise

FARLEY, David Stuart. b 53. Univ Coll Dur BA75 Westmr Coll Ox MTh00. St Jo Coll Nottm. **d** 84 **p** 85. C Bath Weston All SS w N Stoke *B & W* 84-87; Chapl Scargill Ho 87-90; Min Hedge End N CD *Win* 90-94; V Hedge End St Luke 94-00; Dep Chapl HM Pris Belmarsh 00-01; Chapl HM Pris Shrewsbury from 01. *HM Prison, The Dana, Shrewsbury SY1 2HR* Tel (01743) 352511 ext 325

FARLEY, Ian David. b 56. Linc Coll Ox BA78 MA87 Dur Univ PhD88. Cranmer Hall Dur 84. **d** 87 **p** 88. C Thorpe Acre w Dishley *Leic* 87-92; V S Lambeth St Steph *S'wark* 92-99; V Bacton w Edingthorpe w Witton and Ridlington *Nor* 99-03; Ind Chapl 99-03; TR Buckhurst Hill *Chelmsf* from 03. *St John's Rectory, High Road, Buckhurst Hill IG9 5RX* Tel (020) 8504 1931 E-mail parish-office@buckhursthill.free-online.co.uk

FARLEY, James Trevor. b 37. IEng MIET FRSA. EMMTC 80. **d** 82 **p** 83. NSM Grantham *Linc* from 82. *Highfield Cottage, Station Road, Bottesford, Nottingham NG13 0EN* Tel (01949) 843646 Fax 843860
E-mail jimandroma@highfield40.fsnet.co.uk

FARLEY, Ronald Alexander. b 30. Oak Hill NSM Course. **d** 79 **p** 80. NSM Stoke Newington St Faith, St Matthias and All SS *Lon* 79-97; NSM Upper Clapton St Matt 99-04; rtd 04; Perm to Offic *Lon* from 04. *2 St James Close, Bishop Street, London N1 8PH* Tel (020) 7354 2231

FARLEY-MOORE, Peter James, b 72. Sheff Univ BA94 UEA MA00. Ridley Hall Cam. **d** 00 **p** 01. C Chapeltown *Sheff* 00-03; Miss Cell Adv CMS 04-05; Asst Min Kowloon St Andr Hong Kong 05-07; V Blackheath St Jo *S'wark* from 07. *146 Langton Way, London SE3 7JS* E-mail peter@stjohnsblackheath.org.uk

FARMAN, Joanne Margaret. b 46. Birkbeck Coll Lon BA81 Southlands Coll Lon PGCE82. SEITE 97. **d** 00 **p** 01. NSM Limpsfield and Titsey *S'wark* 00-04; Chapl St Geo Healthcare NHS Trust Lon from 00; Lead Chapl R Hosp for Neuro-Disability from 04. *10 Detillens Lane, Limpsfield, Oxted RH8 0DJ* Tel (01883) 713086 *or* (020) 8725 3070 E-mail joanne.farman@stgeorges.nhs.uk

FARMAN, Robert Joseph. b 54. Ridley Hall Cam 86. **d** 88 **p** 89. C Sutton St Nic *S'wark* 88-90; C Cheam Common St Phil 90-92; R Wootton w Glympton and Kiddington *Ox* 92-00; TV Kings Norton *Birm* 00-04; Chapl St Mary's Hospice from 04; Chapl R Orthopaedic Hosp NHS Trust 05-06; Chapl Birm and Solihull Mental Health Trust from 06. *58 Station Road, Kings Norton, Birmingham B30 1DA* Tel 0121-451 1234, 472 1191 *or* 678 2000 Mobile 07766-054137 E-mail robfarman@evemail.net

FARMAN, Mrs Roberta. b 48. Aber Univ MA70 Cam Univ CertEd72. Qu Coll Birm 78. **dss** 82 **d** 87 **p** 01. Ovenden *Wakef* 80-82; Scargill Ho 83-84; Coulsdon St Jo *S'wark* 85-86; Hon Par Dn Cambridge St Mark *Ely* 86-88; Hon Par Dn Sutton St Nic *S'wark* 88-92; Hon Par Dn Wootton w Glympton and Kiddington *Ox* 92-00; NSM Kings Norton *Birm* 01-04; Chapl Univ Hosp Birm NHS Foundn Trust from 01. *58 Station Road, Kings Norton, Birmingham B30 1DA* Tel 0121-451 1234 *or* 627 1627 E-mail bj@robfarman.evesham.net

FARMBOROUGH, James Laird McLelland (Mac). b 22. MBE90. Magd Coll Cam BA49 MA54. Tyndale Hall Bris. **d** 52 **p** 53. C Wolverhampton St Luke *Lich* 52-55; C Holloway St Mary w St Jas *Lon* 55-56; C Broadwater St Mary *Chich* 56-58; Chapl All SS Niteroi Brazil 58-64; Org Sec SAMS 65-70; V Marple All SS *Ches* 70-80; Chapl Vina del Mar St Pet Chile 80-92; Miss to Seamen 80-92; rtd 92. *Flat 8, Manormead, Tilford Road, Hindhead GU26 6RA*

✠**FARMBROUGH, The Rt Revd David John.** b 29. Linc Coll Ox BA51 MA53. Westcott Ho Cam 51. **d** 53 **p** 54 **c** 81. C Bp's Hatfield *St Alb* 53-57; P-in-c 57-63; V Bishop's Stortford St Mich 63-74; RD Bishop's Stortford 73-74; Adn St Alb 74-81; Suff Bp Bedford 81-93; rtd 94; Hon Asst Bp St Alb from 94. *St Michael Mead, 110 Village Road, Bromham, Bedford MK43 8HU* Tel (01234) 825042 E-mail david@farmbrough.com

FARMER, Mrs Anne. b 61. Warwick Univ BEd84. Trin Coll Bris 04. **d** 06 **p** 07. NSM Stoke Bishop *Bris* from 06. *42 Cote Park, Bristol BS9 2AD* Tel 0117-949 2407 E-mail alfarmer@blueyonder.co.uk

FARMER, Diane Marcia (Diana). b 61. Warwick Univ BSc82 PGCE83. WMMTC 97 Cranmer Hall Dur 00. **d** 01 **p** 02. C Allesley Park and Whoberley *Cov* 01-05; Hd Tr and Development Rethink from 05; Hon C Pennsett *Worc* 05-07; Perm to Offic 07-09; Hon C Wollaston from 09. *13 Rectory Street, Stourbridge DY8 5QT* Tel (01384) 295205 E-mail diana@farmerfamilyuk.fsnet.co.uk *or* diana.farmer@rethink.org

FARMER, Lorelie Joy. Southn Univ BA65 MA68 Univ of Mass EdD88. Cranmer Hall Dur 97. **d** 99 **p** 00. C Newbury *Ox* 99-03; C Stratford-upon-Avon, Luddington etc *Cov* 03-05; C Warmington w Shotteswell and Radway w Ratley 05-06; rtd 08; Hon C Witchampton, Stanbridge and Long Crichel etc *Sarum* from 08. *The Vicarage, Witchampton, Wimborne BH21 5AP* Tel (01258) 840422 E-mail loreliefarmer@dunelm.org.uk

FARMER, Robert James. b 65. WMMTC 03. **d** 06 **p** 07. C Lich St Chad from 06; C Longdon from 08. *The Vicarage, Longdon, Rugeley WS15 4PS* Tel (01543) 492871 E-mail robert@farmer2181.freeserve.co.uk

FARMER, Robert John Thayer. b 62. Kent Univ BA84. St Steph Ho Ox 91. **d** 93 **p** 94. C Leigh St Clem *Chelmsf* 93-96; P-in-c Wellingborough St Mary *Pet* 96-00; V from 00; Chapl Northants Healthcare NHS Trust from 00. *St Mary's Vicarage, 193 Midland Road, Wellingborough NN8 1NG* Tel (01933) 225626 E-mail robert@farmer17.freeserve.co.uk

FARMER, Simon John. b 60. Birm Univ BSc82. St Jo Coll Nottm 86. **d** 89 **p** 90. C Ulverston St Mary w H Trin *Carl* 89-92; CF 92-97; Chapl HM Pris Lowdham Grange 97-00; CF (TA) from 99; Perm to Offic *S'well* from 00; Operations Dir (Africa) ACCTS Mil Min Internat from 00. *26 Haloughton Road, Southwell NG25 0LR* Tel (01636) 813599 E-mail farmer@f2s.com

FARMILOE, Preb Trevor James. b 42. Sarum & Wells Th Coll. **d** 82 **p** 82. C S Petherton w the Seavingtons *B & W* 82-85; R Norton St Philip w Hemington, Hardington etc 85-93; Chapl Rural Affairs Wells Adnry 87-92; RD Frome 89-93; V Martock w Ash 93-07; RD Ivelchester 95-01 and 04-07; Preb Wells Cathl 96-07; rtd 07; Perm to Offic *B & W* from 07. *38 Ashmead, Yeovil BA20 2SQ* Tel (01935) 428952

FARNHAM, Douglas John. b 30. SS Mark & Jo Univ Coll Plymouth TCert52 Ex Univ MEd75. S Dios Minl Tr Scheme 80. **d** 83 **p** 84. Lect Bp Otter Coll Chich 70-78; Sen Lect W Sussex Inst of HE 78-92; NSM Barnham and Eastergate *Chich* 83-85; NSM Aldingbourne, Barnham and Eastergate 85-92; R 92-96; rtd 96; Perm to Offic *Chich* from 96. *12 Summersdale Court, The Drive, Chichester PO19 5RF* Tel (01243) 532251

FARNWORTH, Ms Joanna Helen. b 66. Jes Coll Cam BA88 MA92. St Jo Coll Nottm BTh98 MA99. **d** 99 **p** 00. C Middleton w Thornham *Man* 99-03; C Ashton 03-05; TV from 05. *St James's Vicarage, Union Street, Ashton-under-Lyne OL6 9NQ* Tel 0161-330 4925 E-mail joannafarnworth@aol.com

FARNWORTH, Roger. b 60. Man Univ BSc81. St Jo Coll Nottm MA99. **d** 99 **p** 00. C Tonge w Alkrington *Man* 99-03; TV Ashton 03-05; TR from 05; AD Ashton-under-Lyne from 08. *St James's Vicarage, Union Street, Ashton-under-Lyne OL6 9NQ* Tel 0161-330 2771 E-mail rogerfarnworth@aol.com

FARQUHAR, Iain. b 45. **d** 05 **p** 06. OLM Catford St Laur *S'wark* from 05. *18 Birkhall Road, London SE6 1TE* Tel (020) 8698 7438 E-mail iain@thefarquhars.freeserve.co.uk

FARQUHAR, Preb Patricia Ann. b 42. **dss** 78 **d** 87 **p** 94. S Hackney St Jo w Ch Ch *Lon* 80-01; Par Dn 87-94; C 94-01; Preb St Paul's Cathl 97-01; rtd 01. *5A Coronation Close, Norwich NR6 5HF* Tel (01603) 417554

FARQUHARSON, The Very Revd Hunter Buchanan. b 58. ALAM LLAM. Edin Th Coll 85. **d** 88 **p** 89. C Dunfermline *St And* 88-91; R Glenrothes 91-97; R Leven 95-97; R Dunfermline 97-99; Provost St Ninian's Cathl Perth from 99. *St Ninian's Cathedral, North Methven Street, Perth PH1 5PP* Tel and fax (01738) 850987 *or* tel 632053 E-mail huntfar@gmail.com *or* stninians.cathedral@btinternet.com

FARR, Arthur Ronald. b 24. JP77. Llan Dioc Tr Scheme 77. **d** 80 **p** 81. NSM Penarth All SS *Llan* 80-90; rtd 90; Perm to Offic *Llan* from 90. *3 Cymric Close, Ely, Cardiff CF5 4GR* Tel (029) 2056 1765

FARR, John. See FARR, William John

FARR, John. b 44. ACIOB68. NOC 04. **d** 06 **p** 07. C Wallasey St Hilary *Ches* from 06. *41 Knaresborough Road, Wallasey CH44 2BQ* Tel 0151-639 1367 Fax 637 1777 Mobile 07966-665402 E-mail johnfarr@talktalk.net

FARR (née ROSE), Margaret. b 37. Man Univ BDS, LDS60 Birm Univ MB, ChB69 MD85. WMMTC 99. **d** 02 **p** 03. NSM Handsworth St Jas *Birm* from 02; Hon Chapl Sandwell and W Birm Hosps NHS Trust from 07. *35 West Drive, Handsworth, Birmingham B20 3ST* Tel 0121-554 0909

FARR, Richard William. b 55. Ridley Hall Cam. **d** 83 **p** 84. C Enfield Ch Ch Trent Park *Lon* 83-87; C Eastbourne H Trin *Chich* 87-90; P-in-c Henham and Elsenham w Ugley *Chelmsf* 90-91; V 91-09; C Tunbridge Wells St Jo *Roch* from 09. *112 Stephens Road, Tunbridge Wells TN4 9QA* Tel (01892) 521767 E-mail dickthevic@btopenworld.com

FARR, William John. b 66. QUB BTh05 MTh07. **d** 08 **p** 09. NSM Muckamore *Conn* from 08; NSM Killead w Gartree from 08. *1 Ballyvannon Road, Ballinderry Upper, Lisburn BT28 2LB* Tel (028) 9442 2158 Mobile 07808-399579 E-mail j20far@hotmail.com

FARRAN, Canon George Orman. b 35. Worc Coll Ox BA58 MA62. Wycliffe Hall Ox 58. **d** 60 **p** 61. C Tyldesley w Shakerley *Man* 60-62; Tutor Wycliffe Hall Ox 62-64; V Netherton *Liv* 64-73; R Sefton 69-73; R Credenhill w Brinsop, Mansel Lacey, Yazor etc *Heref* 73-83; RD Heref Rural 81-83; R Ditcheat w E Pennard and Pylle *B & W* 83-94; Dir of Ords 86-89; Can and Chan Wells Cathl 85-97; rtd 97; Perm to Offic *B & W* 97-00 and from 01. *Bethany, Ashton Hill, Corston, Bath BA2 9EY* Tel (01225) 872348

FARRANT, David Stuart. b 38. Ripon Coll Cuddesdon 82. **d** 84 **p** 85. C Woodford St Mary w St Phil and St Jas *Chelmsf* 84-87; R Clymping and Yapton w Ford *Chich* 87-92; Dioc Schs Admin Officer 92-95; Chapl Qu Alexandra Hosp Home Worthing 95-04; P-in-c Amberley w N Stoke and Parham, Wiggonholt etc *Chich* from 04. *The New Vicarage, School Road, Amberley, Arundel BN18 9NA* Tel (01798) 831500

FARRANT, Canon John Frederick Ames. b 30. Aber Univ MA51 BD58 MTh80. Edin Th Coll 51. **d** 53 **p** 54. C Dundee St Mary Magd *Bre* 53-58; R Clydebank *Glas* 58-65; R Motherwell 65-70; Papua New Guinea 70-73 and 81-84; R Glas St Bride 73-81; Can St Mary's Cathl 77-81; Provost Rabaul 81-84; R Penicuik *Edin* 85-96; R W Linton 85-96; Can St Mary's Cathl 92-96; Chapl Madeira *Eur* 96-98; rtd 98; Hon Asst P St Mary le Strand w St Clem Danes *Lon* from 98; Perm to Offic from 01. *20 Defoe House, London EC2Y 8DN* Tel (020) 7638 3963 E-mail marjoryfarrant@hotmail.com

FARRANT, Canon Martyn John. b 38. AKC61. **d** 62 **p** 63. C Hampton St Mary *Lon* 62-65; C Shere *Guildf* 65-67; V Stoneleigh 67-75; V Addlestone 75-83; V Dorking w Ranmore 83-98; RD Dorking 89-94; Hon Can Guildf Cathl 96-98; rtd 98; Perm to Offic *Guildf* from 98; Chapl Phyllis Tuckwell Hospice Farnham 98-01. *42 Hampstead Road, Dorking RH4 3AE* Tel (01306) 740916

FARRAR, Canon James Albert. b 27. TCD BA55 MA57. CITC 56. **d** 56 **p** 57. C Dublin Drumcondra w N Strand *D & G* 56-59; C Dublin Rathmines 59-61; I Ballinaclash 61-72; I Dunganstown w Redcross 72-79; Warden Ch Min of Healing 79-95; Hon Clerical V Ch Ch Cathl Dublin 79-92; Can Ch Ch Cathl Dublin from 92; rtd 95. *15 Hillside, Greystones, Co Wicklow, Republic of Ireland* Tel (00353) (1) 287 2706

FARRAR, Prof Roy Alfred. b 39. Imp Coll Lon BSc60 PhD67 FWeldI85. Wycliffe Hall Ox 99. **d** 00 **p** 01. NSM Portswood St Denys *Win* 00-04; P-in-c Lille *Eur* 04-06; Perm to Offic *Bris* from 07. *20 Orchard Court, Arches Lane, Malmesbury SN16 0ED* Tel (01666) 826700

FARRAR, Ruth. b 43. Matlock Coll of Educn CertEd64. **d** 04 **p** 05. OLM Leesfield *Man* from 04. *Belvoir, 43 Coverhill Road, Grotton, Oldham OL4 5RE* Tel 0161-633 0374

FARRELL, Mrs Joanna Susan Elizabeth. b 53. Southn Univ LLB95. STETS 03. **d** 06 **p** 07. NSM Steep and Froxfield w Privett *Portsm* from 06. *Hurst Farm Cottage, Hurst Lane, Privett, Alton GU34 3PL* Tel (01730) 828450
E-mail joanna@hurstfarmcottage.co.uk

FARRELL, Miss Katherine Lucy Anne. b 61. Westcott Ho Cam 00. **d** 02 **p** 03. C Forest Gate Em w Upton Cross *Chelmsf* 02-03; C Lt Ilford St Mich 03-07; V Bellingham St Dunstan *S'wark* from 07. *St Dunstan's Vicarage, 5 Gramsci Way, London SE6 3HA* Tel (020) 8698 3291
E-mail k.farrell916@btinternet.com

FARRELL, Stephen Andrew. b 57. Linc Inst Melbourne BAppSc(OT)78. **d** 02 **p** 03. C Bury St Edmunds All SS w St Jo and St Geo *St E* 02-06; P-in-c Woolpit w Drinkstone 06-08; R from 08. *The Rectory, Rectory Lane, Woolpit, Bury St Edmunds IP30 9QP* Tel (01359) 242244

FARRELL, Peter Godfrey Paul. b 39. Sarum & Wells Th Coll 72. **d** 74 **p** 75. C St Just in Roseland *Truro* 74-77; C Kenwyn 77-80; V Knighton St Jo *Leic* 80-86; TR Clarendon Park St Jo w Knighton St Mich 86-89; V Woodham *Guildf* 89-99; V Wells St Cuth w Wookey Hole *B & W* 99-09; rtd 09. *The Rectory, Bath Road, West Harptree, Bristol BS40 6HB* Tel (01761) 221239
E-mail peter.farrell2@tiscali.co.uk

FARRELL, Robert Edward. b 54. Univ of Wales (Abth) BA74 Jes Coll Ox BA77 MA81. Qu Coll Birm 85. **d** 86 **p** 87. C Llanrhos *St As* 86-88; C Prestwich St Marg *Man* 89-91; V Moulsham St Luke *Chelmsf* 91-98; V Thorpe Bay 98-08; R Ardleigh and The Bromleys from 08. *The Rectory, Hall Road, Great Bromley, Colchester CO7 7TS* Tel (01206) 230344
E-mail robert_farrell21@hotmail.com

FARRELL, Ronald Anthony. b 57. Edin Univ BD84 Birm Univ MA86. Qu Coll Birm 84. **d** 86 **p** 87. C Shard End *Birm* 86-87; C Shirley 87-89; Bp's Officer for Schs and Young People 89-93; V Kingstanding St Mark 93-01; TR Swinton and Pendlebury *Man* 01-05; P-in-c Lower Broughton Ascension 02-05; V W Bromwich St Fran *Lich* from 05. *Friar Park Vicarage, Freeman Road, Wednesbury WS10 0HJ* Tel 0121-556 5823

FARRELL, Stephen Andrew. b 84. Jes Coll Ox BA05. CITC BTh08. **d** 08 **p** 09. C Taney *D & G* from 08. *Church Cottage, 19 Taney Road, Dundrum, Dublin 14, Republic of Ireland* Tel (00353) (1) 296 0736 E-mail curate2.taney@dublin.anglican.org

FARRELL, Thomas Stanley. b 32. Lon Univ BD71. Ridley Hall Cam 69. **d** 71 **p** 72. C Much Woolton *Liv* 71-73; C Gt Sankey 73-74; Asst Chapl Dulwich Coll 74-76; Chapl 76-81; P-in-c Wonersh *Guildf* 81-86; V 86-90; RD Cranleigh 87-90; R St Marg Lothbury and St Steph Coleman Street etc *Lon* 90-00; P-in-c St Botolph without Aldersgate 90-97; rtd 00; Hon C Burford w Fulbrook, Taynton, Asthall etc *Ox* 00-04; Perm to Offic from 04. *Candle Cottage, 23 Frogmore Lane, Long Crendon, Aylesbury HP18 9DZ*

FARRER, Canon Carol Elizabeth. b 47. Open Univ BA88. Cranmer Hall Dur 81. **dss** 83 **d** 87 **p** 94. Newbarns w Hawcoat *Carl* 83-86; Egremont and Haile 86-91; Par Dn 87-91; TD Penrith w Newton Reigny and Plumpton Wall 91-94; TV 94-01; Dioc Lay Min Adv 87-88; Assoc Dir of Ords 88-97; Dir of Ords 97-00; Dioc OLM Officer 00-05; TV S Barrow 01-07; Hon Can Carl Cathl 01-07; rtd 08. *3 Marlow Terrace, Mold CH7 1HH* Tel (01352) 756011

FARRER, Canon Michael Robert Wedlake. b 22. St Pet Hall Ox BA52 MA57. Tyndale Hall Bris 47. **d** 52 **p** 53. C Ox St Ebbe 52-56; Tutor Clifton Th Coll 56-65; R Barton Seagrave *Pet* 65-73; R Barton Seagrave w Warkton 73-78; V Cambridge St Paul *Ely* 78-92; RD Cambridge 84-89; Hon Can Ely Cathl 88-92; rtd 92; Bp's Sen Chapl *Ely* 92-95; Perm to Offic 92-03. *2 Houghton Gardens, Ely CB7 4JN* Tel (01353) 665654

✠**FARRER, The Rt Revd Ralph David.** b 44. St Barn Coll Adelaide ThL68. **d** 68 **p** 69 **c** 98. C Plympton w Richmond Australia 68-71; P-in-c Hillcrest 71-73; C Melbourne St Pet 73-75; V Brunswick 75-90; V Melbourne St Pet 90-98; Can La Trobe 85-98; Adn La Trobe 94-96; Adn Melbourne 96-98; Bp Wangaratta 98-08; V Arundel w Tortington and S Stoke *Chich* from 08; Hon Asst Bp Chich from 09. *The Vicarage, 26 Maltravers Street, Arundel BN18 9BU* Tel (01903) 885209
E-mail stnicholasvicar@tiscali.co.uk

FARRINGTON, Ann Christine Marion b 42. Birkbeck Coll Lon BA65 Nottm Univ DASS66 Middx Poly MA75. St Alb Minl Tr Scheme 79. **dss** 82 **d** 87 **p** 94. Redbourn *St Alb* 82-87; Dir Past Studies Linc Th Coll 86-87; HM Pris Linc 86-87; Dir Sarum

Chr Cen 87-93; Dn Sarum Cathl 87-93; Co-Dir of Ords and Dir of Women's Min *Ely* 93-02; Hon Can Ely Cathl 93-02; C Cambridge Gt St Mary w St Mich 93-96; V Cambridge St Mark 96-02; Chapl Wolfs Coll Cam 97-02; Perm to Offic *St Alb* 97-04; Chapl to The Queen from 98; rtd 02; RD Wheathampstead *St Alb* 04-07. *30 Lybury Lane, Redbourn, St Albans AL3 7HY* Tel (01582) 793409

FARRINGTON, Mrs Lynda June. b 59. WMMTC. **d** 01 **p** 02. NSM Cannock *Lich* 01-07; NSM Abbots Bromley w Blithfield from 07; Officer for NSMs 06-08. *Blithford Farm, Blithbury, Rugeley WS15 3JB* Tel (01283) 840253 *or* 502131
E-mail revmumlynda@aol.com

FARROW, Edward. b 38. Sarum Th Coll 69. **d** 71 **p** 72. C Parkstone St Pet w Branksea *Sarum* 71-74; R Tidworth 74-79; P-in-c W and E Lulworth 79-80; P-in-c Winfrith Newburgh w Chaldon Herring 79-80; R The Lulworths, Winfrith Newburgh and Chaldon 80-83; V Ensbury Park 83-03; Chapl Talbot Heath Sch Bournemouth 83-97; rtd 03; P-in-c Marseille w Aix-en-Provence *Eur* 05-08. *21 Avenue de Bourgogne, 13600 La Ciotat, France* Tel (0033) (4) 42 83 03 20

FARROW, Elizabeth Maura. b 43. Edin Th Coll. **d** 91 **p** 96. NSM Glas H Cross 91-96; TV Bearsden w Milngavie 96-00 and 03-05. *5 Campsie Road, Strathblane G63 9AB* Tel (01360) 770936

FARROW, Ian Edmund Dennett. b 38. S'wark Ord Course 70. **d** 72 **p** 73. C Tunbridge Wells St Jo *Roch* 72-78; Chapl N Cambs Gen Hosp Gp 78-92; P-in-c Walsoken *Ely* 78-80; R 80-92; V Bisley, Oakridge, Miserden and Edgeworth *Glouc* 92-04; rtd 04. *Wellspring, Brook Lane, Stonesfield, Witney OX29 8PR* Tel (01993) 891293

FARROW, Keith. b 59. Leeds Univ BA05. NOC 02. **d** 05 **p** 06. C Sprotbrough *Sheff* 05-07; C Hillsborough and Wadsley Bridge 07-09; P-in-c from 09. *Christ Church Vicarage, 218 Fox Hill Road, Sheffield S6 1HJ* Tel 0114-231 1576
E-mail keith.farrow@sheffield.anglican.org

FARROW, Peter Maurice. b 44. St Chad's Coll Dur BSc65. **d** 68 **p** 69. C Gt Yarmouth *Nor* 68-71; C N Lynn w St Marg and St Nic 71-75; P-in-c Sculthorpe w Dunton and Doughton 75-77; Perm to Offic 78-89; TV Lowestoft and Kirkley 89-94; Ind Miss 89-94; Sen Ind Chapl 94-99; TV Gaywood 95-02; P-in-c Mundford w Lynford, Cranwich and Ickburgh w Langford 02-09; rtd 09; Perm to Offic *Nor* from 09. *129 Carlton Road, Lowestoft NR33 0LZ* Tel (01502) 521817
E-mail farrpm@dialstart.net

FARROW, Robin Thomas Adrian. b 72. K Coll Lon BA93 AKC93 MA01 Heythrop Coll Lon MA06. St Steph Ho Ox 94. **d** 96 **p** 97. C Lancing w Coombes *Chich* 96-00; R W Blatchington from 00. *St Peter's Rectory, 23 Windmill Close, Hove BN3 7LJ* Tel (01273) 732459

FARTHING, Michael Thomas. b 28. St Cuth Soc Dur 48 Lambeth STh81 CertHE08. St Steph Ho Ox. **d** 58 **p** 59. C St Marylebone St Mark w St Luke *Lon* 58-63; C Newport Pagnell *Ox* 63-69; R Standlake 69-76; R Yelford 69-76; R Lower Windrush 76-82; V Wheatley w Forest Hill and Stanton St John 82-95; rtd 95; Perm to Offic *Ox* from 95. *32 Falstaff Close, Eynsham, Oxford OX29 4QA* Tel (01865) 883805

FARTHING, Paul Andrew. b 58. McGill Univ Montreal BA80 STM82. Montreal Dioc Th Coll. **d** 83 **p** 84. C Montreal W St Phil Canada 83-85; R Montreal St Jo Divine 85-96; R Montreal St Jo Ev 96-99; P-in-c Burton *Lich* 99-05; V Burton St Aid and St Paul from 05. *The Vicarage, Rangemore Street, Burton-on-Trent DE14 2ED* Tel (01283) 544054
E-mail paul@pafarthing.clara.co.uk

FARTHING, Ronald Edward. b 27. Oak Hill Th Coll. **d** 58 **p** 59. C Tollington Park St Anne *Lon* 58-61; C Tollington Park St Mark 58-61; V Clodock and Longtown w Craswell and Llanveyno *Heref* 61-67; R Langley *Cant* 67-72; V Bapchild w Tonge and Rodmersham 72-80; TV Widecombe, Leusden and Princetown etc *Ex* 80-84; P-in-c Riddlesworth w Gasthorpe and Knettishall *Nor* 84-87; P-in-c Garboldisham w Blo' Norton 84-87; P-in-c Brettenham w Rushford 84-87; R Garboldisham w Blo' Norton, Riddlesworth etc 88-92; rtd 92; Perm to Offic *Nor* and *St E* from 92. *23 Home Close, Great Ellingham, Attleborough NR17 1HW* Tel (01953) 456750

FASS, Michael John. b 44. Trin Coll Cam MA75. Edin Dioc NSM Course 89. **d** 95 **p** 95. NSM Penicuik *Edin* 95-97; NSM W Linton 95-97; NSM Roslin (Rosslyn Chpl) 97-06; Bp's Officer for Min from 03. *Royal Scots Club, 29 Abercomby Place, Edinburgh EH3 6QE* E-mail michael.fass@btinternet.com

FATHERS, Jeremy Mark. b 54. Crewe & Alsager Coll BEd78. WMMTC 93. **d** 96 **p** 97. NSM Baxterley w Hurley and Wood End and Merevale etc *Birm* 96-00; C Sheldon 00-03; Chapl N Warks NHS Trust 00-02; R Chelmsley Wood *Birm* from 03. *The Vicarage, Pike Drive, Birmingham B37 7US* Tel 0121-770 5155 *or* 770 1511 Mobile 07769-780306 E-mail j.fathers@virgin.net

FAUCHON-JONES, Susan Gurmito. b 61. **d** 06 **p** 07. NSM Eynsford w Farningham and Lullingstone *Roch* 06-08; NSM Southborough St Pet w Ch Ch and St Matt etc from 08. *1 Springfield Cottages, Glebe Road, Weald, Sevenoaks TN14 6RD* Tel (01732) 463289

FAULDS, Ian Craig. b 48. **d** 03 **p** 04. NSM Maughold *S & M* from 03. *The Lynague, Ramsey Road, Lynague, Peel, Isle of Man IM5 2AQ* Tel (01624) 842045

FAULDS, John Parker. b 33. Edin Th Coll 55. **d** 57 **p** 58. C Edin St Dav 57-58; C Edin St Jo 58-60; Chapl Dundee Hosps 60-63; Chapl Qu Coll Dundee 60-63; Dioc Supernumerary *Bre* 60-63; Lic to Offic *Birm* 65-66; P-in-c Aston Brook 66-69; V Handsworth St Pet 69-87; Perm to Offic 87-98; rtd 99. *Address withheld by request*

FAULKES, Edmund Marquis. *See* MARQUIS-FAULKES, Edmund

FAULKNER, Mrs Anne Elizabeth. b 38. Bp Otter Coll BA58. **d** 00 **p** 01. NSM Aylesbury w Bierton and Hulcott *Ox* 00-04; Chapl to Bp Buckingham 02-04; rtd 04; Hon C Wroxall *Portsm* 04-05; P-in-c from 05; P-in-c St Lawrence from 08. *13 Western Road, Shanklin PO37 7NF* Tel and fax (01983) 862291 E-mail anne.faulkner@dsl.pipex.com

FAULKNER, Brian Thomas. b 48. S Dios Minl Tr Scheme. **d** 84 **p** 85. C W Leigh *Portsm* 84-88; R Foulsham w Hindolveston and Guestwick *Nor* 88-93; P-in-c Erpingham w Calthorpe, Ingworth, Aldborough etc 93-94; R from 94. *The Rectory, School Road, Erpingham, Norwich NR11 7QX* Tel (01263) 768073 E-mail brian-faulkner@lineone.net

FAULKNER, Bruce Stephen. b 63. Trin Coll Bris BA97 St Jo Coll Dur MA08. Cranmer Hall Dur 06. **d** 08 **p** 09. C Somerton w Compton Dundon, the Charltons etc *B & W* from 08. *6 Northfield Way, Somerton TA11 6ST* Tel 07796-283766 (mobile) E-mail bsfaulkner@aol.com

FAULKNER, Mrs Catherine Evelyn. b 43. Man Poly RHV43. **d** 01 **p** 02. OLM Urmston *Man* from 01. *5 Barnfield, Urmston, Manchester M41 9EW* Tel 0161-748 3226 E-mail cath@northwood1.freeserve.co.uk

FAULKNER, David Ernest. b 43. St Mich Coll Llan 65. **d** 66 **p** 67. C Aberystwyth St Mich *St D* 66-68; C Tenby and Gumfreston 68-69; C Burry Port and Pwll 69-73; R Jeffreyston w Reynalton and E Williamston 73-79; R Jeffreyston w Reynoldston and E Williamston etc 79-89; V Whitland w Cyffig and Henllan Amgoed etc 89-96; V Llawhaden w Bletherston and Llanycefn 96-06; rtd 06. *Daveann, Broadmoor, Kilgetty SA68 0RH*

FAULKNER, Henry Odin. b 35. G&C Coll Cam BA56 MA59. St Jo Coll Nottm 70. **d** 74 **p** 75. C Heigham H Trin *Nor* 74-76; C Heeley *Sheff* 76-80; TV Netherthorpe 80-84; Perm to Offic *St Alb* from 84; rtd 00. *69 Holywell Hill, St Albans AL1 1HF* Tel (01727) 854177 Mobile 07719-642479

FAULKNER (née RITCHIE), Mrs June. b 41. UCD BA64. **d** 05 **p** 06. OLM New Windsor *Ox* from 05. *69 Springfield Road, Windsor SL4 3PR* Tel (01753) 622808

FAULKNER, Margaret Evelyn. *See* WHITFORD, Mrs Margaret Evelyn

FAULKNER, Peter Graham. b 47. Lon Univ CertEd69. Oak Hill Th Coll BA87. **d** 82 **p** 83. C Crofton *Portsm* 87-89; R Mid Marsh Gp *Linc* 89-98; V S Cave and Ellerker w Broomfleet *York* from 98; P-in-c N Cave w Cliffe from 09; P-in-c Hotham from 09; RD Howden from 05. *The Vicarage, 10 Station Road, South Cave, Brough HU15 2AA* Tel (01430) 423693 E-mail peter@faulknerzp.karoo.co.uk

FAULKNER, Canon Roger Kearton. b 36. AKC62. **d** 63 **p** 64. C Oxton *Ches* 63-67; C Ellesmere Port 67-69; V Runcorn H Trin 69-73; TV E Runcorn w Halton 73-76; V Altrincham St Geo 76-90; Chapl Altrincham Gen Hosp 80-96; Hon Can Ches Cathl 88-96; V Higher Bebington 90-96; rtd 96; Perm to Offic *Ches* 96-98. *58 Albermarle Road, Wallasey, Wirral CH44 6LX*

FAULKNER, Ms Susan Ann. b 70. Lanc Univ BA96. Ripon Coll Cuddesdon 97. **d** 99 **p** 00. C Scotswood *Newc* 99-03; P-in-c Byker St Silas from 03. *St Wilfrid's House, Trevelyan Drive, Newcastle upon Tyne NE5 4DA* Tel 0191-271 1866 Mobile 07786-265422 E-mail revsuefaulkner@aol.com

FAULKS, David William. b 45. EMMTC 82. **d** 86 **p** 87. C Market Harborough *Leic* 86-88; C Wootton Bassett *Sarum* 88-90; R Clipston w Naseby and Haselbech w Kelmarsh *Pet* from 90. *The Rectory, 18 Church Lane, Clipston, Market Harborough LE16 9RW* Tel and fax (01858) 525342 E-mail david.faulks@btinternet.com

FAULL, The Very Revd Cecil Albert. b 30. TCD BA52 MA87. **d** 54 **p** 55. C Dublin Zion Ch *D & G* 54-57; C Dublin St Geo 57-59; Hon Clerical V Ch Ch Cathl Dublin 58-63; C Dun Laoghaire 59-63; I Portarlington w Cloneyhurke and Lea *M & K* 63-71; I Dublin St Geo and St Thos *D & G* 71-80; I Clondalkin w Rathcoole 81-91; Can Ch Ch Cathl Dublin 90-91; I Dunleckney w Nurney, Lorum and Kiltennel *C & O* 91-96; Dean Leighlin 91-96; P-in-c Leighlin w Grange Sylvae, Shankill etc 91-96; rtd 96. *1 Mageough Home, Cowper Road, Rathmines, Dublin 6, Republic of Ireland* Tel (00353) (1) 497 2377

FAULL, Mrs Janet. b 60. SS Paul & Mary Coll Cheltenham PGCE86 LGSM82. WEMTC 05. **d** 08 **p** 09. C Cheltenham Ch Ch *Glouc* from 08. *26 Eldorado Road, Cheltenham GL50 2PT* Tel (01242) 519183 Mobile 07986-650459 E-mail martin.faull@btinternet.com

FAULL, The Very Revd Vivienne Frances. b 55. St Hilda's Coll Ox BA77 MA82 Clare Coll Cam MA90. St Jo Coll Nottm BA81. **dss** 82 **d** 87 **p** 94. Mossley Hill St Matt and St Jas *Liv* 82-85; Chapl Clare Coll Cam 85-90; Chapl Glouc Cathl 90-94; Can Res Cov Cathl 94-00; Vice-Provost 95-00; Provost Leic 00-02; Dean Leic from 02. *The Cathedral Centre, 21 St Martin's, Leicester LE1 5DE* Tel 0116-248 7456 Fax 248 7470 E-mail viv.faull@leccofe.org

FAULL, William Baines. b 29. FRCVS70 Lon Univ BSc51. NW Ord Course 77. **d** 79 **p** 80. NSM Willaston *Ches* 79-80; NSM Neston 80-82; P-in-c Harthill and Burwardsley 82-86; Perm to Offic 87-91; from 96; Sen Fell Liv Univ from 89; V Ashton Hayes *Ches* 91-96; Chapl Hospice of the Good Shepherd Backford 99-06. *Tioman, Briardale Road, Willaston, Neston CH64 1TD* Tel 0151-327 4424

FAULTLESS, Mrs Patricia Doreen. b 53. **d** 05 **p** 06. OLM Glascote and Stonydelph *Lich* from 05. *40 Stephenson Close, Glascote, Tamworth B77 2DQ* Tel (01827) 287171 Mobile 07980-434897 E-mail patfaultless@hotmail.com

FAURE WALKER, Edward William. b 46. DL01. SAOMC 01. **d** 04 **p** 05. NSM Stevenage All SS Pin Green *St Alb* from 04. *Sandon Bury, Sandon, Buntingford SG9 0QY* Tel and fax (01763) 287753 Mobile 07801-175009 E-mail e.faure.walker@farming.me.uk

FAUX, Steven Paul. b 58. UEA BA79. Trin Coll Bris BA07. **d** 07 **p** 08. C Bath St Mich w St Paul *B & W* from 07. *Fleetlands, Weston Park, Bath BA1 4AL* Tel (01225) 313145 E-mail steven@stevenfaux.plus.com

FAWCETT, Mrs Diane Elizabeth. b 49. Cant Univ (NZ) BA72 Kent Univ MA03. Westcott Ho Cam 03. **d** 04 **p** 05. C Egerton w Pluckley *Cant* 04-08; Perm to Offic from 08. *8 Luxmore House, 75 New Dover Road, Canterbury CT1 3DZ* Tel (01227) 760593 E-mail fawcett38@hotmail.com

FAWCETT, Canon Frederick William. TCD BA49 MA52. CITC 50. **d** 50 **p** 51. C Belfast St Aid *Conn* 50-52; C-in-c Draperstown *D & R* 52-59; I 59-60; I Cumber Upper w Learmount 60-87; Can Derry Cathl 86-99; I Camus-juxta-Mourne 87-99; rtd 99. *Springbank, 73 Moneysallin Road, Kilrea, Coleraine BT51 5SR* Tel (028) 2954 1744

FAWCETT, Mrs Joanna Mary. b 45. SRN67 SCM69. EAMTC 01. **d** 04 **p** 05. NSM Blakeney w Cley, Wiveton, Glandford etc *Nor* from 04. *14 The Cornfields, Langham, Holt NR25 7DQ* Tel (01328) 830415 Mobile 07979-070562 E-mail jofawcett@btinternet.com

FAWCETT, Canon Pamela Margaret. b 29. Univ Coll Lon BA51 DipEd75. EAMTC 83. **dss** 86 **d** 87 **p** 94. Stiffkey and Cockthorpe w Morston, Langham etc *Nor* 86-90; Hon C 87-90; Hon Asst Min Repps Deanery 91-92; Hon C Trunch 92-01; Asst Dir of Ords 93-99; Bp's Consultant for Women's Min 93-01; Hon Can Nor Cathl 94-01; Perm to Offic from 01. *Seekings, 47A High Street, Mundesley, Norwich NR11 8JL* Tel (01263) 721752 E-mail pam.seekings@tinyworld.co.uk

FAWCETT, Timothy John. b 44. K Coll Lon BD66 AKC67 PhD71. St Boniface Warminster 66. **d** 67 **p** 68. C Blackpool St Steph *Blackb* 67-70; Hon C St Marylebone All SS *Lon* 68-70; C Southgate St Mich 70-72; Sacr Dur Cathl 72-75; V Wheatley Hill 75-79; V Torrisholme *Blackb* 79-84; V Thaxted *Chelmsf* 84-89; NSM Holt Deanery *Nor* 89-06; C Stiffkey and Bale 06-09; rtd 09. *Dowitchers, 14 The Cornfield, Langham, Holt NR25 7DQ* Tel (01328) 830415 E-mail tjfawcett@btinternet.com

FAWNS, Lynne. b 56. Thames Valley Univ BA95. NTMTC 97. **d** 00 **p** 01. C Hillingdon All SS *Lon* 00-03; V London Colney St Pet *St Alb* from 03. *The Vicarage, Riverside, London Colney, St Albans AL2 1QT* Tel (01727) 769797 E-mail lynne@ffamily.freeserve.co.uk

FAYERS, Robert Stanley. b 48. St Steph Ho Ox 82. **d** 84 **p** 85. C Deptford St Paul *S'wark* 84-88; V Beckenham St Mich w St Aug *Roch* 88-00; V Brighton St Mich *Chich* from 00; P-in-c Brighton St Paul from 06. *St Michael's Vicarage, 6 Montpelier Villas, Brighton BN1 3DH* Tel (01273) 727362 E-mail smb@supanet.com

FAYLE, David Charles Wilfred. b 51. Sarum & Wells Th Coll. **d** 83 **p** 84. C Parkstone St Pet w Branksea and St Osmund *Sarum* 83-87; TV Dorchester 87-96; P-in-c Taunton All SS *B & W* 96-97; V from 97. *All Saints' Vicarage, Roman Road, Taunton TA1 2DE* Tel (01823) 324730 E-mail dfayle@freeserve.co.uk

FAZZANI, Keith. b 47. Portsm Poly BSc70. Cant Sch of Min 93. **d** 96 **p** 97. NSM Appledore w Brookland, Fairfield, Brenzett etc *Cant* 96-01 and from 05; Chapl Team Ldr E Kent Hosps NHS Trust from 01. *Oakhouse Farm, Appledore, Ashford TN26 2BB* Tel (01233) 758322 *or* (01227) 766877 ext 74212 E-mail kfazzani@btinternet.com

FEAK, Christopher Martin. b 52. Keele Univ BA75. Trin Coll Bris 92. **d** 94 **p** 95. C Handsworth St Mary *Birm* 94-97; P-in-c Perry Common 97-00; V 00-05; AD Aston 01-05; P-in-c Sandown Ch Ch *Portsm* from 05; P-in-c Lower Sandown St Jo from 05. *10 Elmbank Gardens, Sandown PO36 9SA* Tel (01983) 402548 E-mail chris.feak@ukonline.co.uk

FEARN, Anthony John. b 34. Lich Th Coll 58. **d** 61 **p** 62. C Redditch St Steph *Worc* 61-64; C Bladon w Woodstock *Ox* 64-66; V Ruscombe and Twyford 67-85; P-in-c Westmill w Gt Munden *St Alb* 85-87; Asst Dioc Stewardship Adv 85-87; Chr Giving Adv *Heref* 87-99; rtd 99; Perm to Offic *Heref* from 99. *8 St Mary's Close, Madley, Hereford HR2 9DP* Tel and fax (01981) 250320 E-mail john_fearn@bigfoot.com

FEARN, Michael Wilfred. b 47. Sarum & Wells Th Coll 92. **d** 94 **p** 95. C Blandford Forum and Langton Long *Sarum* 94-98; TV Wylye and Till Valley 98-04; R Flint *St As* 04-08; rtd 09. *22 Hesketh Road, Old Colwyn, Colwyn Bay LL29 8AT* Tel (01492) 512723 E-mail fearn_m@sky.com

FEARNLEY, Jeffrey Malcolm. b 46. Newc Univ BSc69. St Jo Coll Nottm 90. **d** 92 **p** 93. C Bispham *Blackb* 92-95; C Bolton w Ireby and Uldale *Carl* 95-00; TV Binsey 00-02; C 02-07; rtd 07; Perm to Offic *Blackb* from 07. *32 Chestnut Court, Leyland PR25 3GN* Tel (01772) 458696

FEARNSIDE, Mary Ingrid. b 44. OLM course 98. **d** 98 **p** 99. OLM Shelton and Oxon *Lich* from 98; Chapl R Shrewsbury Hosps NHS Trust 98-04; Chapl Shrewsbury and Telford NHS Trust from 04. *23 Eastwood Road, Shrewsbury SY3 8YJ* Tel (01743) 353290 Pager 01743-261000 E-mail mary.fearnside@fsmail.net

FEARON, Mrs Doris Ethel Elizabeth. b 26. Gilmore Ho 66. **dss** 72 **d** 87. Lingfield *S'wark* 68-75; Farnborough *Roch* 75-77; Bitterne *Win* 78-86; rtd 86; Bexhill St Pet *Chich* 86-87; Hon Par Dn 87-89; Perm to Offic 89-95; New Zealand from 96; Hon Asst Dn One Tree Hill St Oswald 99-02. *Waiatarua Mercy Parklands, 12 Umere Crescent, Ellerslie, Auckland 1051, New Zealand*

FEARON, Mrs Irene. b 51. CBDTI 00. **d** 03 **p** 04. NSM Maryport, Netherton and Flimby *Carl* 03-08; NSM Camerton, Seaton and W Seaton from 08. *Kirkborough Lodge, Ellenborough, Maryport CA15 7RD* Tel (01900) 813108 E-mail irene@kirklodge.com

FEATHERSTONE, Margery. *See* GRANGE, Mrs Alice Margery

FEATHERSTONE, Canon Andrew. b 53. St Chad's Coll Dur BA74 MA93. Sarum & Wells Th Coll 78. **d** 80 **p** 81. C Newc H Cross 80-83; C Seaton Hirst 83-86; TV 86-87; R Crook *Dur* 87-99; V Stanley 87-99; AD Stanhope 94-99; V Stockton 99-05; Can and Chan Wells Cathl from 05. *8 The Liberty, Wells BA5 2SU* Tel (01749) 679587 E-mail andrew.featherstone@btinternet.com

FEATHERSTONE, Gray. b 42. Stellenbosch Univ BA62 LLB64. Cuddesdon Coll 65. **d** 67 **p** 68. C Woodstock S Africa 67-70; Asst Master Waterford Sch Swaziland 70-72; P-in-c Maputo St Steph and St Lawr Mozambique 73-76; Miss to Seamen 73-80; V Upper Clapton St Matt *Lon* 80-83; V Stamford Hill St Thos 80-89; Chr Aid Area Sec (N & W Lon) 89-06; (Lon) 06-07; rtd 07; Perm to Offic *Lon* from 97. *137 Leslie Road, London N2 8BH* Tel (020) 8444 1975

FEATHERSTONE, John. b 32. Man Univ BA53 St Cath Soc Ox MTh59 Dur Univ DipEd66. Wycliffe Hall Ox 57. **d** 60 **p** 61. C Newland St Aug *York* 60-62; C Kidderminster St Jo and H Innocents *Worc* 62-65; Hd RE Co Gr Sch Pet 66-70; Hd RE Qu Anne Gr Sch *York* 70-85; Chapl Tangier *Eur* 86-87 and 90-93; Chapl Pau w Biarritz 87-88; C Mexborough *Sheff* 88-90; rtd 93; Perm to Offic *York* from 93. *39 Cambridge Avenue, Marton-in-Cleveland, Middlesbrough TS7 8EH* Tel (01642) 318181

FEATHERSTONE, Robert Leslie. b 54. Leeds Univ MA04 LLCM74 Lon Univ GradL75. Chich Th Coll 84. **d** 86 **p** 87. C Crayford *Roch* 86-89; V Belvedere St Aug 89-94; V Crowborough St Jo *Chich* 94-01; P-in-c New Brompton St Luke *Roch* 01-06; Hon Succ Roch Cathl 03-06; Perm to Offic 07-08; P-in-c Hastings St Clem and All SS *Chich* from 09. *The Rectory, 7 High Street, Hastings TN34 3EY* Tel (01424) 422023 Mobile 07878-237312 E-mail frrobertf@live.co.uk

FEAVER, Nigel Conway McDonald. b 51. Leeds Univ BA73 Brunel Univ MA76 CQSW76. Ripon Coll Cuddesdon 03. **d** 05 **p** 06. C Oxton *Ches* 05-08; R Wincanton *B & W* from 08; R Pen Selwood from 08. *The Oaks, 3 Bayford Court, Bayford Hill, Wincanton BA9 9GY* Tel (01963) 31507 E-mail revnigelfeaver@googlemail.com

FEENEY, Damian Prescott Anthony. b 62. Grey Coll Dur BA83 PGCE84 ALCM81. Chich Th Coll BTh94. **d** 94 **p** 95. C Harrogate St Wilfrid *Ripon* 94-96; C Preston St Jo and St Geo *Blackb* 96-99; Bp's Miss P to Longsands 99-01; TR Ribbleton 01-04; V Woodplumpton from 04; Vice Prin St Steph Ho Ox from 09. *St Stephen's House, 16 Marston Street, Oxford OX4 1JX* Tel (01865) 613500 E-mail frdfeeney@aol.com

FEIST, Canon Nicholas James. b 45. Solicitor 70. St Jo Coll Nottm. **d** 76 **p** 77. C Didsbury St Jas *Man* 76-80; TV Didsbury St Jas and Em 80; V Friarmere 80-88; R Middleton 88-94; TR Middleton w Thornham from 94; Hon Can Man Cathl from 98; AD Heywood and Middleton 99-07. *St Leonard's Rectory, Mellalieu Street, Middleton, Manchester M24 3DN* Tel 0161-643 2693 E-mail nickjfeist@ntlworld.com

FEIT, Michael John. b 24. FICE68 FIStructE68. S'wark Ord Course. **d** 69 **p** 71. C Feltham *Lon* 69-76; C Ashford St Matt 76-78; C Hykeham *Linc* 78-81; V Cranwell 81-85; R Leasingham

81-85; R Bishop Norton, Wadingham and Snitterby 85-90; rtd 90; Hon C Surrey Epiphany Canada from 91. *162-10659 150th Street, Surrey BC V3R 4B9, Canada* Tel (001) (604) 582 5889

FELCE, Brian George. b 30. Jes Coll Ox BA54 MA57. Oak Hill Th Coll. **d** 58 **p** 59. C E Twickenham St Steph *Lon* 58-60; C Ramsgate St Luke *Cant* 60-64; R Bedingfield w Southolt *St E* 64-73; V Preston All SS *Blackb* 73-86; rtd 86. *11 St Barnabas Road, Sutton SM1 4NL* Tel (020) 8642 7885

FELIX, Canon David Rhys. b 55. Univ of Wales (Cardiff) LLB76 Solicitor 81. Ripon Coll Cuddesdon 83. **d** 86 **p** 87. C Bromborough *Ches* 86-89; V Grange St Andr 89-99; Chapl Halton Gen Hosp NHS Trust 95-99; P-in-c Runcorn H Trin *Ches* 96-99; RD Frodsham 98-99; V Daresbury from 99; Sen Ind Chapl from 00; Hon Can Ches Cathl from 06. *All Saints' Vicarage, Daresbury Lane, Daresbury, Warrington WA4 4AE* Tel (01925) 740348 Fax 740799 E-mail david.felix@btinternet.com

FELL, Canon Alan William. b 46. Ball Coll Ox BA69. Coll of Resurr Mirfield 68. **d** 71 **p** 72. C Woodchurch *Ches* 71-74; C Man Clayton St Cross w St Paul 74-75; C Prestwich St Marg 75-77; V Hyde St Thos *Ches* 77-80; R Tattenhall and Handley 80-86; V Sedbergh, Cautley and Garsdale *Bradf* from 86; Hon C Firbank, Howgill and Killington 86-06; P-in-c from 06; Hon Can Bradf Cathl from 96; RD Ewecross 00-05. *The Vicarage, Loftus Hill, Sedbergh LA10 5SQ* Tel (01539) 620283 E-mail alan.fell@bradford.anglican.org or vixed@btopenworld.com

FELL, David Edward. b 61. Bradf Univ BSc84 Brunel Univ BA05. ERMC 05. **d** 07 **p** 08. C Wootton *St Alb* from 07. *9 Studley Road, Wootton, Bedford MK43 9DL* Tel (01234) 767294 Mobile 07989-203429 E-mail ted_fell@hotmail.com

FELLINGHAM, Wendy Margaret. b 48. St Mich Coll Sarum BEd70. STETS 03. **d** 06 **p** 07. NSM Swanage and Studland *Sarum* from 06. *47 Bay Crescent, Swanage BH19 1RB* Tel (01929) 426454 E-mail wendy.fellingham@btinternet.com

FELLOWS, Grant. b 56. K Coll Lon BD77 AKC77. Coll of Resurr Mirfield 79. **d** 80 **p** 81. C Addington *Cant* 80-84; C S Gillingham *Roch* 84-86; V Heath and Reach *St Alb* 86-94; V Radlett 94-03; RD Aldenham 98-03; V Leighton Buzzard w Eggington, Hockliffe etc 03-05; TR Billington, Egginton, Hockliffe etc 06-08; TR Ouzel Valley from 08. *The Vicarage, Pulford Road, Leighton Buzzard LU7 1AB* Tel (01525) 373217 E-mail grantfellows@btinternet.com

FELLOWS, Ian Christopher. b 73. Univ Coll Ox BA94 MA98 St Jo Coll Dur BA99. Cranmer Hall Dur 96. **d** 99 **p** 00. C Bucknall and Bagnall *Lich* 99-03; TV Broughton *Man* 03-07; P-in-c Blackley St Andr from 07. *St Andrew's Vicarage, Churchdale Road, Higher Blackley, Manchester M9 8NE* Tel 0161-740 2961 E-mail ianfellows@yahoo.co.uk

FELLOWS, John Lambert. b 35. LTCL67 SS Mark & Jo Coll Chelsea CertEd58. Portsm Dioc Tr Course 86. **d** 88. NSM Portsea St Cuth *Portsm* 88-94; NSM Farlington 94-05; Perm to Offic from 05. *7 Court Lane, Portsmouth PO6 2LG* Tel (023) 9237 7270

FELLOWS, John Michael. b 46. Oriel Coll Ox MA77. Coll of Resurr Mirfield 74. **d** 77 **p** 78. C Kings Heath *Birm* 77-80; TV E Ham w Upton Park St Alb *Chelmsf* 80-85; P-in-c Wormingford 85-90; P-in-c Mt Bures 85-90; P-in-c Lt Horkesley 85-90; V Wormingford, Mt Bures and Lt Horkesley 90; R Compton w Shackleford and Peper Harow *Guildf* from 90; RD Godalming from 07; Chapl Prior's Field Sch from 90. *The Rectory, The Street, Compton, Guildford GU3 1ED* Tel (01483) 810328 E-mail johnfellows@comptonrec.fslife.co.uk

FELLOWS, Lesley June. b 70. Salford Univ BEng91 New Coll Ox DPhil01. Ox Min Course 04. **d** 07 **p** 08. C Bernwode *Ox* from 07. *Westfields, Church Lane, Ludgershall, Aylesbury HP18 9NU* Tel (01844) 239268 E-mail lesley.fellows@hotmail.co.uk

FELLOWS, Peter William. b 48. CertEd70 DipEd79. Chich Th Coll 86. **d** 88 **p** 89. C Westmr St Steph w St Jo *Lon* 88-93; R Deptford St Paul *S'wark* from 05; TV Redruth w Lanner and Treleigh *Truro* from 05. *The Vicarage, Pencoys, Four Lanes, Redruth TR16 6LR* Tel (01209) 215835

FELLOWS, Mrs Susan Elizabeth. b 46. ATCL65 LTCL66 GTCL67. SAOMC 99. **d** 02 **p** 03. NSM Weston Turville *Ox* from 02. *65 Craigwell Avenue, Aylesbury HP21 7AG* Tel (01296) 424982 Mobile 07712-226999 E-mail susan@sefellows.freeserve.co.uk

FELTHAM, Keith. b 40. **d** 75 **p** 76. In Bapt Ch 66-75; C Plympton St Mary *Ex* 75-79; TV Northam w Westward Ho! and Appledore 79-82; TR Lynton, Brendon, Countisbury, Lynmouth etc 82-85; P-in-c Bickleigh (Plymouth) 85-86; TR 86-91; Chapl R Bournemouth Gen Hosp 91-95; P-in-c Whimple, Talaton and Clyst St Lawr *Ex* 95-00; rtd 00; Perm to Offic *Ex* from 00. *16 Jefferson Walk, Plymouth PL3 4HN* Tel (01792) 254383

FELTHAM-WHITE, Antony James. b 67. Ox Brookes Univ BSc92 Reading Univ MA94. Wycliffe Hall Ox 99. **d** 01 **p** 02. C Bernwode *Ox* 01-05; CF from 05. *c/o MOD Chaplains (Army)* Tel (01980) 615804 Fax 615800 E-mail antony@revelation-racing.org.uk

FENBY, Andrew Robert. b 66. Loughb Univ BSc88. St Steph Ho Ox 03. **d** 05 **p** 06. C Leigh-on-Sea St Marg *Chelmsf* 05-09; V Barkingside St Fran from 09. *St Francis's Vicarage, 144 Fencepiece Road, Ilford IG6 2LA* Tel (020) 8500 2970 E-mail frandrew@mac.com

FENBY, Mrs Sarah Louise. b 66. Kent Univ BA88 Lon Bible Coll BA96. Trin Coll Bris MA00. **d** 00 **p** 01. C Stoke Gifford *Bris* 00-04; C S Croydon Em *S'wark* from 04; Min Selsdon St Fran CD from 07. *St Francis House, 146 Tedder Road, South Croydon CR2 8AH* Tel (020) 8657 7864 E-mail sarahfenby@fsmail.net

FENN, Norman Alexander. b 20. Kelham Th Coll 37. **d** 43 **p** 44. C Tunstall Ch Ch *Lich* 43-47; C Leek St Edw 47-51; V Tilstock 51-55; V Milton 55-61; V Ellesmere 61-85; V Welsh Frankton 62-85; RD Ellesmere 70-85; rtd 85; Perm to Offic *Lich* from 85. *1 Larkhill Road, Oswestry SY11 4AW* Tel (01691) 659411

FENN, Roy William Dearnley. b 33. FRHistS70 FCP86 FSA88 Jes Coll Ox BA54 MA59 BD68. St Mich Coll Llan 54. **d** 56 **p** 57. C Swansea St Mary and H Trin *S & B* 57-59; C Cardiff St Jo *Llan* 59-60; C Coity w Nolton 60-63; V Glascombe w Rhulen and Gregrina *S & B* 63-68; V Glascwm and Rhulen 68-74; P-in-c Letton w Staunton, Byford, Mansel Gamage etc *Heref* 75-79; Perm to Offic *S & B* 00-85; Perm to Offic *Heref* 85-95; rtd 98. *9 Victoria Road, Kington HR5 3BX* Tel (01544) 230018

FENNELL, Anthony Frederick Rivers. b 26. Pemb Coll Cam BA50 MA55 York Univ BPhil76 Leic Univ PGCE51. Ab Dioc Tr Course 90. **d** 90 **p** 91. NSM Braemar *Ab* 90-96; NSM Ballater 90-96; NSM Aboyne 90-96; rtd 96; Lic to Offic *Ab* from 01. *19 Craigendarroch Circle, Ballater AB35 5ZA* Tel (01339) 755048

FENNELL, Julian. b 56. **d** 08 **p** 09. NSM Ipswich St Mary at Stoke w St Pet and St Fran *St E* from 08. *70 Wellesley Road, Ipswich IP4 1PH* Tel (01473) 212818 E-mail julianfennell@hotmail.co.uk

FENNEMORE, Canon Nicholas Paul. b 53. Wycliffe Hall Ox 76. **d** 79 **p** 80. C N Mymms *St Alb* 79-82; C Chipping Barnet w Arkley 82-83; TV 83-84; TV Preston w Sutton Poyntz and Osmington w Poxwell *Sarum* 84-86; Chapl St Helier Hosp Carshalton 86-90; Chapl Jo Radcliffe Hosp Ox 90-94; Chapl Ox Radcliffe Hosp NHS Trust 94-96; Sen Chapl Ox Radcliffe Hosps NHS Trust 96-06; Hon Can Ch Ch *Ox* 03-06; Hd Chapl Services Portsm Hosps NHS Trust from 06. *Queen Alexandra Hospital, Southwick Hill Road, Cosham, Portsmouth PO6 3LY* Tel (023) 9232 1554 E-mail nick@npfennemore.fsnet.co.uk

FENSOME, Canon Anthony David. b 49. Open Univ BA89. Sarum & Wells Th Coll 82. **d** 84 **p** 85. C Gtr Corsham *Bris* 84-88; P-in-c Lyddington w Wanborough 88-91; P-in-c Bishopstone w Hinton Parva 88-91; V Lyddington and Wanborough and Bishopstone etc 91-93; V Chippenham St Pet 93-08; RD Chippenham 94-99; AD 06-08; Hon Can Bris Cathl 98-08; rtd 08. *42 Francis Crescent, Tiverton EX16 4EP* E-mail tonyfens@aol.com

FENTIMAN, David Frank. b 43. RIBA74 Roehampton Inst PGCE94. S Dios Minl Tr Scheme 90. **d** 93 **p** 94. NSM Hastings St Clem and All SS *Chich* 93-98; P-in-c Blacklands Hastings Ch Ch and St Andr 98-01; V 01-05; rtd 05. *4 Barnfield Close, Hastings TN34 1TS* Tel (01424) 421821 E-mail xxblacklands@tiscali.co.uk

FENTON, Ms Allison Jane. b 66. Grey Coll Dur BA87 Dur Univ PGCE90 St Jo Coll Dur MATM08. Cranmer Hall Dur 06. **d** 08 **p** 09. C Newc St Geo and St Hilda from 08. *63 Rosebery Crescent, Newcastle upon Tyne NE2 1EX* Tel 0191-281 5639 E-mail allison@fentonius.net

FENTON, Barry Dominic. b 59. Leeds Univ BA85. Coll of Resurr Mirfield 85. **d** 87 **p** 88. C Leigh Park *Portsm* 87-90; Chapl and Prec Portsm Cathl 90-95; Min Can and Prec Westmr Abbey 95-02; Chapl N Middx Hosp NHS Trust from 02; PV Westmr Abbey from 04. *North Middlesex Hospital, Sterling Way, London N18 1QX* Tel (020) 8887 2000 or 8887 2724 E-mail dominic.fenton@nmh.nhs.uk

FENTON, Christopher Miles Tempest. b 28. Qu Coll Cam BA50 LLB51 MA55 LLM. Ridley Hall Cam 52. **d** 54 **p** 55. C Welling *Roch* 54-57; Chapl Malsis Prep Sch Keighley 57-63; C Hove Bp Hannington Memorial Ch *Chich* 63-65; V Ramsgate Ch Ch *Cant* 65-71; Hd Dept of Gp Studies Westmr Past Foundn 71-83; P-in-c Mottingham St Andr *S'wark* 71-73; Sen Tutor Cambs Consultancy in Counselling 73-85; Co-ord of Tr St Alb Past Foundn 80-88; Dir St Anne's Trust for Psychotherapy Ledbury from 85; Perm to Offic *Heref* from 85; rtd 93. *The Leys, Aston, Kingsland, Leominster HR6 9PU* Tel (01568) 708632

FENTON, David Frank. b 43. Open Univ BA79 Matlock Coll of Educn CertEd67. Wycliffe Hall Ox 07. **d** 08 **p** 09. NSM Win Ch Ch from 08. *5 Glenwood Avenue, Southampton SO16 3PY* Tel (023) 8076 9574 Mobile 07967-419169 E-mail dave.fenton1@btinternet.com

FENTON, Geoffrey Eric Crosland. b 54. St Jo Coll Ox BA75 MSc76. WEMTC 98. **d** 01 **p** 02. NSM Wedmore w Theale and Blackford *B & W* 01-05; NSM Greinton and W Poldens 05-08; C Mark w Allerton from 08. *Grove Cottage, Redmans Hill,*

Blackford, Wedmore BS28 4NG Tel (01934) 713083 *or* 710224 E-mail geoffrey.fenton@wildyeast.co.uk

FENTON, Heather. b 48. Trin Coll Bris. **d** 87 **p** 97. C Corwen and Llangar *St As* 87-89; C Corwen and Llangar w Gwyddelwern and Llawrybetws 89-98; Dioc Rural Min Co-ord 87-98; Lic to Offic from 98; Asst P Penllyn Deanery 01-03; P-in-c Bryneglwys from 03; P-in-c Gwyddelwern from 09. *Coleg y Groes, The College, Corwen LL21 0AU* Tel (01490) 412169 E-mail colegygroes@btconnect.com

FENTON, Ian Christopher Stuart. b 40. AKC62. **d** 63 **p** 64. C Banstead *Guildf* 63-67; V N Holmwood 67-84; RD Dorking 80-84; V Witley 84-00; Perm to Offic *Ex* from 00; rtd 05. *The Barn, Kingsford Farm, Longdown, Exeter EX6 7SB* Tel (01392) 811887

FENTON, Keith John. b 54. Coll of Resurr Mirfield 01. **d** 03 **p** 04. C St Annes St Anne *Blackb* 03-07; TV Ribbleton from 07. *140 Teil Green, Fulwood, Preston PR2 9PE* Tel (01772) 468009 Mobile 07773-630784

FENTON, Michael John. b 42. Linc Th Coll 67. **d** 69 **p** 70. C Guiseley *Bradf* 69-72; C Heswall *Ches* 72-75; TV Birkenhead Priory 75-81; V Alvanley 81-91; Chapl Crossley Hosp Cheshire 82-91; V Holbrook and Lt Eaton *Derby* 91-03; V Allenton and Shelton Lock 03-07; rtd 07; Perm to Offic *Derby* from 07. *11 Nethercroft Lane, Donesmoor, Chesterfield S45 9DE* Tel (01246) 250071 E-mail michaeljfenton@yahoo.co.uk

FENTON, Miss Penelope Ann. b 41. Leic Univ BSc64. Cant Sch of Min 92. **d** 95 **p** 96. NSM Eastling w Ospringe and Stalisfield w Otterden *Cant* 95-00; P-in-c 00-05; Asst to Bp's Officer for NSM 99-05; rtd 05; Perm to Offic *Cant* from 05. *9 Brogdale Road, Faversham ME13 8SX* Tel (01795) 536366 E-mail penny.fenton@lineone.net

FENTON, Vincent Thompson. b 52. Cranmer Hall Dur 94. **d** 96 **p** 97. C Heworth St Mary *Dur* 96-99; C-in-c Bishop Auckland Woodhouse Close CD 99-06; Chapl S Durham Healthcare NHS Trust 01-05; P-in-c Crook *Dur* from 06; AD Stanhope from 07. *The Rectory, 14 Hartside Close, Crook DL15 9NH* Tel (01388) 766129 E-mail vincent.fenton@durham.anglican.org

FENTON, Canon Wallace. b 32. TCD. **d** 64 **p** 65. C Glenavy *Conn* 64-67; I Tullaniskin w Clonoe *Arm* 67-87; Bp's C Sallaghy *Clogh* 87-96; Warden of Readers 91-96; Preb Clogh Cathl 95-96; I Kilwarlin Upper w Kilwarlin Lower *D & D* 96-99; rtd 99. *2 Beech Green, Doagh, Ballyclare BT39 0QB* Tel (028) 9334 0576

FENWICK, The Very Revd Jeffrey Robert. b 30. Pemb Coll Cam BA53 MA57. Linc Th Coll 53. **d** 55 **p** 56. C Upholland *Liv* 55-58; P-in-c Daramombe S Rhodesia 58-64; Area Sec USPG *Ox* 64-65; R Gatooma All SS Rhodesia 65-67; R Salisbury E 67-75; P-in-c Mabvuku 68-70; Adn Charter 73-75; Dean and Adn Bulawayo 75-78; Can Res Worc Cathl 78-89; R Guernsey St Peter Port *Win* 89-95; Dean Guernsey 89-95; Hon Can Win Cathl 89-95; Pres Guernsey Miss to Seamen 89-95; rtd 95; Zimbabwe 95-04; S Africa from 04. *3 Suid Street, Alexandria, 6185 South Africa*

FENWICK, Canon Malcolm Frank. b 38. Cranmer Hall Dur 62. **d** 65 **p** 66. C Tynemouth Cullercoats St Paul *Newc* 65-68; C Bywell 68-73; V Alnmouth 73-75; CF (TAVR) 75-83; V Lesbury w Alnmouth *Newc* 75-80; V Delaval 80-91; RD Bedlington 83-88; V Riding Mill 91-01; P-in-c Whittonstall 91-01; Chapl Shepherd's Dene Retreat Ho from 91; RD Corbridge 93-99; P-in-c Slaley 97-99; P-in-c Healey 99-01; Hon Can Newc Cathl 97-01; rtd 01; Perm to Offic *Newc* from 01. *21 Welburn Close, Ovingham, Prudhoe NE42 6BD* Tel (01661) 835565

FENWICK, The Very Revd Richard David. b 43. Univ of Wales (Lamp) BA66 MA68 TCD MusB79 MA92 Univ of Wales (Lamp) PhD95 FLCM68 FTCL76 Hon FGCM04. Ridley Hall Cam 66. **d** 68 **p** 69. C Skewen *Llan* 68-72; C Penarth w Lavernock 72-74; PV, Succ and Sacr Roch Cathl 74-78; Min Can St Paul's Cathl 78-79; Min Can and Succ 79-83; Warden Coll Min Cans 81-83; PV Westmr Abbey 83-90; V Ruislip St Martin *Lon* 83-90; Can Res and Prec Guildf Cathl 90-97; Sub-Dean 96-97; Dean Mon from 97; V Newport St Woolos from 97; Warden Guild of Ch Musicians from 98. *The Deanery, Stow Hill, Newport NP20 4ED* Tel and fax (01633) 263338

FEREDAY, Harold James Rodney. b 46. St Jo Coll Nottm 87. **d** 89 **p** 90. C Rastrick St Matt *Wakef* 89-92; V Siddal 92-99; Dir Chr Care from 99; rtd 01; Perm to Offic *Wakef* and *York* from 01. *311 Filey Road, Scarborough YO11 3AF*

FERGUS, David. b 52. Imp Coll Lon BSc74. St Jo Coll Nottm 00. **d** 02 **p** 03. C Ilkeston St Mary *Derby* 02-06; P-in-c Kirk Hallam from 06. *The Vicarage, 71 Ladywood Road, Ilkeston DE7 4NF* Tel 0115-932 2402 E-mail revdave.fergus@ntlworld.com

FERGUSON, Aean Michael O'Shaun. b 39. CITC 87. **d** 90 **p** 91. NSM Kilmallock w Kilflynn, Kilfinane, Knockaney etc *L & K* 90; NSM Killaloe w Stradbally 90-94; NSM Adare and Kilmallock w Kilpeacon, Croom etc 94-97; C Killala w Dunfeeny, Crossmolina, Kilmoremoy etc *T, K & A* 97-00; I Skreen w Kilmacshalgan and Dromard 00-08; Can Killala Cathl 05-08; rtd 08; Dioc Information Officer *T, K & A* from 04. *Rathlee, Easkey, Co Sligo, Republic of Ireland* Tel (00353) (96) 49865 Mobile 87-812 1020 E-mail amferguson@iol.ie

FERGUSON, Alastair Stuart. b 45. Lon Univ MB, BS69 Ball Coll Ox BA78 MA82 LRCP69 MRCS69. St Steph Ho Ox 80. **d** 82 **p** 83. NSM Dengie w Asheldham *Chelmsf* 82-86; NSM Mayland 86-89; NSM Steeple 86-89; Perm to Offic 89-91; R Mvurwi St Andr Zimbabwe 91-00; V Lastingham w Appleton-le-Moors, Rosedale etc *York* from 00. *The Vicarage, Lastingham, York YO62 6TN* Tel (01751) 417344 Mobile 07967-588776
E-mail vicarage@lastinghamchurch.org.uk

FERGUSON, David Edward. d 04 **p** 05. Aux Min Antrim All SS *Conn* from 04. *7 Three Trees Manor, Broughshane, Ballymena BT43 7GY* Tel (028) 2586 2994

FERGUSON, Edith Constance May (Joy). b 37. Ch of Ireland Tr Coll DipEd60. CITC 99. **d** 02 **p** 03. NSM Bandon Union *C, C & R* from 02. *Telkador, Kinure, Oysterhaven, Co Cork, Republic of Ireland* Tel (00353) (21) 477 0663 Mobile 86-350 3138

FERGUSON, Canon Ian John. b 51. Aber Univ BD77. Trin Coll Bris 77. **d** 78 **p** 79. C Foord St Jo *Cant* 78-82; C Bieldside *Ab* 82-86; Dioc Youth Chapl 82-86; P-in-c Westhill 86-96; R from 96; Can St Andr Cathl from 01. *1 Westwood Drive, Westhill, Skeene AB32 6WW* Tel (01224) 740007
E-mail ianferguson@freenet.co.uk

FERGUSON, John Aitken. b 40. Glas Univ BSc64 Strathclyde Univ PhD74 CEng MICE ARCST64. Linc Th Coll 79. **d** 81 **p** 82. C Morpeth *Newc* 81-85; V Whittingham and Edlingham w Bolton Chapel 85-96; rtd 00. *Cold Harbour Cottage, Cold Harbour, Berwick-upon-Tweed TD15 2TQ*

FERGUSON, Joy. See FERGUSON, Edith Constance May

FERGUSON, Mrs Kathleen. b 46. LMH Ox BA68 MA72 ALA76. St as Minl Tr Course 86. **d** 88 **p** 97. NSM Llanidloes w Llangurig *Ban* 88-01; P-in-c Llandinam w Trefeglwys w Penstrowed 01-02; V 02-04; AD Arwystli 02-04; NSM Shelswell *Ox* 04-07; rtd 07; Perm to Offic *Ban* from 07. *Oerle, Trefeglwys, Caersws SY17 5QX* Tel (01686) 430666
E-mail kathy@oerle.co.uk

FERGUSON, Michelle Dorothy Marie. b 58. Ottawa Univ BA78. Cranmer Hall Dur 93. **d** 95 **p** 96. NSM Gt Aycliffe *Dur* 95-97; Chapl Asst HM Pris Holme Ho 97-98; NSM Heighington *Dur* 99-04; R Hurworth from 04; R Dinsdale w Sockburn from 04. *The Rectory, 3 Croft Road, Hurworth, Darlington DL2 2HD* Tel (01325) 720362

FERGUSON, The Ven Paul John. b 55. New Coll Ox BA76 MA80 K Coll Cam BA84 MA88 FRCO75. Westcott Ho Cam 82. **d** 85 **p** 86. C Ches St Mary 85-88; Sacr and Chapl Westmr Abbey 88-92; Prec 92-95; Can Res and Prec York Minster 95-01; Adn Cleveland from 01; Can and Preb York Minster from 01; Warden of Readers from 04. *48 Langbaurgh Road, Hutton Rudby, Yarm TS15 0HL* Tel (01642) 706095 Fax 706097
E-mail archdeacon.of.cleveland@yorkdiocese.org

FERGUSON, Richard Archie. b 39. Dur Univ BA62. Linc Th Coll 62. **d** 64 **p** 65. C Stretford St Matt *Man* 64-68; Bp's Dom Chapl *Dur* 68-69; C Newc St Geo 69-71; V Glodwick *Man* 71-77; V Tynemouth Ch Ch *Newc* 77-82; V Tynemouth Ch Ch w H Trin 82-87; P-in-c Tynemouth St Aug 82-87; TR N Shields 87-90; TR Upton cum Chalvey *Ox* 90-95; V Kirkwhelpington, Kirkharle, Kirkheaton and Cambo *Newc* 95-04; AD Morpeth 95-04; rtd 04. *6 Green Close, Stannington, Morpeth NE61 6PE* Tel (01670) 789795 E-mail frgsno@aol.com

FERGUSON, Robert Garnett Allen. b 48. Leeds Univ LLB70 Clare Coll Cam. Cuddesdon Coll 71. **d** 73 **p** 74. C Wakef Cathl 73-76; V Lupset 76-83; Chapl Cheltenham Coll 83-87; Sen Chapl Win Coll 87-05. *Follaton, Highfield Drive, Baldrine, Isle of Man IM4 6EE*

FERGUSON, Robin Sinclair. b 31. Worc Coll Ox BA53 MA57 Lon Univ CertEd63. ALCD55 Wycliffe Coll Toronto 55. **d** 57 **p** 58. C Brompton H Trin *Lon* 57-60; C Brixton St Matt *S'wark* 60-63; Hon C Framlingham w Saxtead *St E* 63-65; Hon C Haverhill 65-67; Chapl St Mary's Sch Richmond 67-75; C Richmond St Mary *S'wark* 68-76; P-in-c Shilling Okeford *Sarum* 76-87; Chapl Croft Ho Sch Shillingstone 76-87; R Milton Abbas, Hilton w Cheselbourne etc *Sarum* 87-96; rtd 96; Perm to Offic *Sarum* from 96. *7 Durnovria, East Walls, Wareham BH20 4NJ* Tel (01929) 551340

FERGUSON, Ronald Leslie. b 36. Open Univ BA86 BA89. Chich Th Coll 65. **d** 68 **p** 69. C Toxteth Park St Marg *Liv* 68-72; C Oakham w Hambleton and Egleton *Pet* 72-74; Asst Chapl The Dorothy Kerin Trust Burrswood 74-76; V Castleside *Dur* 76-96; C Washington 96-99; P-in-c Eighton Banks 99-06; Chapl Gateshead Health NHS Trust 96-06; rtd 06. *2 Lapwing Court, Burnopfield, Newcastle upon Tyne NE16 6LP* Tel (01207) 271559

FERGUSON, (née PAMPLIN), Mrs Samantha Jane. b 71. St Andr Univ MTheol06. TISEC 06. **d** 08 **p** 09. C Aberdeen St Pet from 08; C Aberdeen St Jo from 08. *15 Corse Wynd, Kingswells, Aberdeen AB15 8TP* Tel (01224) 743955 Mobile 07971-231709
E-mail samferguson@fsmail.net

FERGUSON, The Very Revd Wallace Raymond. b 47. Qu Coll Birm B1heol CITC 76. **d** 78 **p** 79. C Lurgan Ch the Redeemer *D & D* 78-80; I Newtownards w Movilla Abbey 80-84; I Mullabrack w Markethill and Kilcluney *Arm* 84-00; I Carnteel

and Crilly 00-05; Hon V Choral Arm Cathl 86-05; Dioc Chapl to Rtd Clergy 92-05; Dean Kilmore *K, E & A* from 05; I Kilmore w Ballintemple from 05. *The Deanery, Danesfort, Kilmore, Cavan, Republic of Ireland* Tel and fax (00353) (49) 433 1918
E-mail dean@kilmore.anglican.org

FERGUSON FLATT, Roy Francis. See FLATT, Canon Roy Francis Ferguson

FERGUSON-STUART, Hamish. b 51. Open Univ BA92 RGN. **d** 99 **p** 00. OLM Burton St Chad *Lich* 99-05; Asst Chapl Rotherham NHS Foundn Trust from 05. *13 Oakwood Hall Drive, Rotherham S60 3AQ* Tel (01709) 837503
E-mail hamish.ferguson-stuart@rothgen.nhs.uk

FERMER, Michael Thorpe. b 30. Lon Univ BSc52 ARCS52 St Cath Soc Ox BA54. Wycliffe Hall Ox 52. **d** 54 **p** 55. C Upper Holloway All SS *Lon* 54-57; C Plymouth St Andr *Ex* 57-59; V Tamerton Foliot 59-63; Asst Chapl United Sheff Hosps 63-64; Chapl 64-66; Lic to Offic *Sheff* 66-73; V Holmesfield *Derby* 73-79; TR Old Brampton and Loundsley Green 79-83; V Brightside St Thos and St Marg *Sheff* 83; V Brightside w Wincobank 83-89; V Loscoe *Derby* 89-94; rtd 94; Perm to Offic *Derby* from 94. *123 Bacons Lane, Chesterfield S40 2TN* Tel (01246) 555793

FERMER, Richard Malcolm. b 71. St Pet Coll Ox BA94 K Coll Lon MA95 PhD02 Surrey Univ PGCE96. Coll of Resurr Mirfield 00. **d** 02 **p** 03. C Palmers Green St Jo *Lon* 02-05; USPG Brazil 05-09; Asst Chapl Paris St Geo *Eur* from 09. *St George, 7 rue Auguste-Vacquerie, 75116 Paris, France* Tel (0033) (1) 47 20 22 51 E-mail richard.fermer@tiscali.co.uk

FERN, John. b 36. Nottm Univ BA57 MA88. Coll of Resurr Mirfield 57. **d** 59 **p** 60. C Carlton *S'well* 59-61; C Hucknall Torkard 61-68; V Rainworth 68-97; rtd 97; Perm to Offic *S'well* from 03. *17 Wharfedale Gardens, Mansfield NG18 3GZ* Tel (01623) 420165

FERNANDES, Sheila Maud. Punjab Univ MB, BS69. NTMTC 05. **d** 08 **p** 09. NSM Leyton Em *Chelmsf* from 08. *33 Markmanor Avenue, London E17 8HJ* E-mail fernandesgideon@aol.com

FERNANDEZ, Mrs Valerie Anne. b 48. WMMTC 03. **d** 05 **p** 06. C Mile Cross *Nor* 05-08; P-in-c Doddington w Benwick and Wimblington *Ely* from 08. *The Rectory, Ingle's Lane, Doddington, March PE15 0TE* Tel (01354) 742715
E-mail revval@btinternet.com

FERNANDEZ-VICENTE, Lorenzo Michel Manuel. b 68. Louvain Univ BA92 MA97 STL97. **d** 97 **p** 97. C Battersea St Mary *S'wark* 04-08; V Malden St Jas from 08. *St James's Vicarage, 7 Bodley Road, New Malden KT3 5QD* Tel (020) 8942 5070 Mobile 07780-914434
E-mail lorenzo.fernandez@mac.com

FERNANDO, Percy Sriyananda. b 49. St And Dioc Tr Course 85. **d** 88 **p** 89. NSM Blairgowrie *St And* 88-93; NSM Alyth and Coupar Angus 89-93. *Gowrie Cottage, Perth Road, Blairgowrie PH10 6QB*

FERNELEY, Alastair John. b 69. Roehampton Inst BA93 K Coll Lon MA94 Birm Univ MPhil98 St Jo Coll Dur MA02. Cranmer Hall Dur 00. **d** 02 **p** 03. C Skipton Ch Ch *Bradf* 02-05; P-in-c Scalby *York* from 05; P-in-c Scarborough St Luke from 05. *The Vicarage, 48 High Street, Scalby, Scarborough YO13 0PS* Tel (01723) 362740

FERNS, Stephen Antony Dunbar. b 61. St Chad's Coll Dur BA84 MA94. Ripon Coll Cuddesdon BA87 MA91. **d** 88 **p** 89. C Billingham St Cuth *Dur* 88-90; Chapl Dur Univ 91; Chapl Van Mildert and Trevelyan Colls Dur 91-95; V Norton St Mary 95-97; Bp's Dom Chapl *Blackb* 97-01; Voc Officer and Selection Sec Min Division 01-06; Sen Selection Sec from 06. *Ministry Division, Church House, Great Smith Street, London SW1P 3AZ* Tel (020) 7898 1399 Fax 7898 1421
E-mail stephen.ferns@c-of-e.org.uk

FERNS, Archdeacon of. See LONG, The Ven Christopher William

FERNS, Dean of. See FORREST, The Very Revd Leslie David Arthur

FERNYHOUGH, Timothy John Edward. b 60. Leeds Univ BA81. Linc Th Coll 81. **d** 83 **p** 84. C Daventry *Pet* 83-86; Chapl Tonbridge Sch 86-92; Chapl Dur Sch 92-02; Hd RS and Asst Chapl Radley Coll from 02. *Radley College, Radley, Abingdon OX14 2HR* Tel (01235) 543000 Fax 543106

FERRAR, Andrew Nicholas. b 46. Em Coll Cam MA70 Liv Univ PhD70. **d** 06 **p** 07. NSM St Alb St Sav *St Alb* from 06. *The Jolly Gardener, 2 Church End, Redbourn, St Albans AL3 7DU* Tel (01582) 794265 Mobile 07818-446720
E-mail andrewferrar@btinternet.com

FERRIS, Amanda Jane. b 61. RGN83. SAOMC 00. **d** 03 **p** 04. NSM Letchworth St Paul w Willian *St Alb* from 03; Chapl E and N Herts NHS Trust from 07. *Rivendell, 33B Gosmore Road, Arlesey SG15 6XI* Tel (01462) 834627 *or* (01438) /81518 Mobile 07780-670651 E-mail amanda.ferris@btinternet.com

FERRIS, Robert Joseph. b 82. Ulster Univ BSc05 QUB PGCE06. CITC BTh09. **d** 09. C Knock *D & D* from 09. *3 Sandown Park South, Belfast BT5 6HE* Tel (028) 9065 3370
E-mail rferris281@gmail.com

FERRIS, Samuel Albert. b 41. Open Univ BA80. S & M Dioc Tr Inst 98. **d** 99 **p** 00. OLM Douglas All SS and St Thos *S & M* from 99. *27 Hillberry Meadows, Governors Hill, Douglas, Isle of Man IM2 7BJ* Tel and fax (01624) 619631

FERRIS, Samuel Christopher. b 77. Univ of Wales (Lamp) BA98. Trin Coll Bris 02. **d** 04 **p** 05. C Tunbridge Wells St Mark *Roch* 04-07; TV S Gillingham from 07. *26 Pear Tree Lane, Hempstead, Gillingham ME7 3PT* Tel (01634) 322711 Mobile 07910-077885 E-mail chris.ferris@diocese-rochester.org

FERRITER, Felicity Eunicé Myfanwy. b 54. Sheff Univ BA76 Nottm Univ MA98. EMMTC 95. **d** 98 **p** 99. NSM Retford S'well 98-03; Asst Chapl Rampton Hosp Retford 99-01; Asst Chapl Notts Healthcare NHS Trust 01-02; Chapl 02-03; Asst to AD Retford 03-04; NSM Rampton w Laneham, Treswell, Cottam and Stokeham *S'well* from 04; NSM N and S Leverton from 04. *The Gables, Treswell Road, Rampton, Retford DN22 0HU* Tel (01777) 248580 E-mail felicityferriter@yahoo.com

FERRY, Canon David Henry John. b 53. TCD BTh88. **d** 88 **p** 89. C Enniskillen *Clogh* 88-90; I Leckpatrick w Dunnalong *D & R* 90-01; Bp's Dom Chapl from 96; I Donagheady from 01; Can Derry Cathl from 05. *Earlsgift Rectory, 33 Longland Road, Dunamanagh, Strabane BT82 0PH* Tel (028) 7139 8017

FERRY, Malcolm Ronald Keith. b 66. QUB BEd88. CITC BTh96. **d** 96 **p** 97. C Agherton *Conn* 96-99; I Kilwaughter w Cairncastle and Craigy Hill 99-03; I Castlerock w Dunboe and Fermoyle *D & R* 03-08; I Clooney w Strathfoyle from 08. *All Saints' Rectory, 20 Limavady Road, Londonderry BT47 6JD* Tel (028) 7134 4306 *or* 7134 9348 E-mail allsaintsclooney@btinternet.com

FESSEY, Mrs Annis Irene. b 40. St Mary's Coll Chelt CertEd60. Ripon Coll Cuddesdon 88. **d** 90 **p** 94. Par Dn Bris St Andr Hartcliffe 90-94; C The Lydiards 94-95; C Penhill 95-00; rtd 00; Perm to Offic *Bris* 00-03 and *Portsm* from 03. *Tintern, 17 Mayfield Road, Ryde PO33 3PR* Tel (01983) 616466

FESSEY, Canon Brian Alan. b 39. Bris Univ CertEd61 Leeds Univ DipEd71. Ripon Coll Cuddesdon 88. **d** 90 **p** 91. Hon C Bishopsworth *Bris* 90; C Withywood CD 91-94; V Purton 94-03; Hon Can Bris Cathl 01-03; rtd 03; Perm to Offic *Portsm* from 03. *Tintern, 17 Mayfield Road, Ryde PO33 3PR* Tel (01983) 616466

FEWKES, Jeffrey Preston. b 47. Derby Univ MA99 DMin04. Wycliffe Hall Ox 72. **d** 75 **p** 76. C Chester le Street *Dur* 75-78; C Kennington St Mark *S'wark* 78-81; V Bulwell St Jo *S'well* 81-98; V Stapleford 98-02; Victim Support Nottinghamshire from 02; Perm to Offic *Derby* from 06. *3 Monks Close, Ilkeston DE7 5EY* Tel 0115-930 2482 E-mail j.fewkes@btopenworld.com

FFRENCH (née WILLIAMS), Mrs Janet Patricia (Trish). b 59. Bradf Univ BTech81. Trin Coll Bris BA02. **d** 02 **p** 03. C Quinton Road W St Boniface *Birm* 02-05; C Mamble w Bayton, Rock w Heightington etc *Worc* 05-07; C Elmsett w Aldham, Hintlesham, Chattisham etc *St E* from 07. *The Rectory, Hadleigh Road, Elmsett, Ipswich IP7 6ND* Tel (01473) 658803 Mobile 07801-257959 E-mail revsff@btinternet.com

FFRENCH, Timothy Edward. b 58. Ball Coll Ox MA86. Trin Coll Bris BA01 MA03. **d** 03 **p** 04. C Pedmore *Worc* 03-07; R Elmsett w Aldham, Hintlesham, Chattisham etc *St E* from 07. *The Rectory, Hadleigh Road, Elmsett, Ipswich IP7 6ND* Tel (01473) 658803 Mobile 07801-492126 E-mail revsff@btinternet.com

FICKE, Michael John. b 46. **d** 97 **p** 98. OLM Marnhull *Sarum* 97-07; rtd 07; Perm to Offic *Sarum* from 07. *13 Plowman Close, Marnhull, Sturminster Newton DT10 1LB* Tel (01258) 820509

FIDDIAN-GREEN, Anthony Brian. *See* GREEN, Anthony Brian

FIDDYMENT, Alan John. b 40. Cant Sch of Min 91. **d** 94 **p** 95. NSM Chatham St Wm *Roch* 94-96; NSM Spalding *Linc* 96-99; R Barkston and Hough Gp 99-07; rtd 07. *5 Ascot Close, Spalding PE11 3BZ* Tel (01775) 712837 Mobile 07930-434106 E-mail alan.fiddyment@tiscali.co.uk

FIDLER, John Harvey. b 49. Hatf Poly BSc72. St Alb Minl Tr Scheme 84. **d** 87 **p** 88. NSM Royston *St Alb* from 87; Perm to Offic *Ely* from 00. *8 Stamford Avenue, Royston SG8 7DD* Tel (01763) 241886

FIELD, Brian Hedley. b 31. St Jo Coll York CertEd53 ACP66 FCP84. **d** 99 **p** 00. NSM Maidstone St Luke *Cant* 99-04; Hon C from 06; Perm to Offic 04-05. *Shebri, 21 Fauchons Close, Bearsted, Maidstone ME14 4BB* Tel (01622) 730117 Fax 663109 Mobile 07785-156606

FIELD, David Hibberd. b 36. K Coll Cam BA58. Oak Hill Th Coll 58. **d** 60 **p** 61. C Aldershot H Trin *Guildf* 60-63; C Margate H Trin *Cant* 63-66; Sec Th Students Fellowship 66-68; Tutor Oak Hill Th Coll 68-93; Vice Prin 79-93; Dean Minl Tr Course 88-93; Dir Professional Min Div CPAS 94-00; Perm to Offic *Cov* from 94; rtd 00. *25 Field Barn Road, Hampton Magna, Warwick CV35 8RX* Tel (01926) 410291

FIELD, Geoffrey Alder. b 18. Ely Th Coll. **d** 47 **p** 48. C King Cross *Wakef* 47-50; C Ely 50-54; V Whittlesey St Andr 54-75; V Foxton 75-80; rtd 81; Perm to Offic *Ely* 81-02. *14 Poplar Close, Great Shelford, Cambridge CB22 5LX* Tel (01223) 842099

FIELD, Gerald Gordon. b 54. K Coll Lon BD75 AKC75. Coll of Resurr Mirfield 76. **d** 77 **p** 78. C Broughton *Blackb* 77-79; C Blackpool St Steph 79-82; V Skerton St Luke 82-86; NSM Westleigh St Pet *Man* 92-93; V Shap w Swindale and Bampton w Mardale *Carl* 93-97; P-in-c Netherton 97; V 98-01; I Tullamore w Durrow, Newtownfertullagh, Rahan etc *M & K* from 01. *St Catherine's Rectory, Church Avenue, Tullamore, Co Offaly, Republic of Ireland* Tel and fax (00353) (57) 932 1731 E-mail tullamore@meath.anglican.org

FIELD, James Lewis. b 46. Open Univ BSc96. SEITE 94. **d** 97 **p** 98. NSM Chatham St Mary w St Jo *Roch* 97-00; R Gravesend H Family w Ifield 00-08; P-in-c New Romney w Old Romney and Midley *Cant* from 08. *The Vicarage, North Street, New Romney TN28 8DR* Tel (01797) 362308 Mobile 07749-591496 E-mail revjimfield@googlemail.com

FIELD, Martin Richard. b 55. Keswick Hall Coll CertEd76 Leic Univ MA87. St Jo Coll Nottm BTh82. **d** 82 **p** 83. C Gaywood, Bawsey and Mintlyn *Nor* 82-85; Perm to Offic *Leic* 85-87; Hon C S'well Minster 87-88; Hon C Stand *Man* 88-89; Dioc Press and Communications Officer 88-91; CUF 91-95; Perm to Offic *Cant* 96-99; Fundraising and Campaigns Dir Children's Soc from 04. *40 Elm Grove Road, Salisbury SP1 1JW* Tel (01722) 502910 E-mail mrf@childsoc.org.uk

FIELD, Miss Olwen Joyce. b 53. St Jo Coll Nottm 86. **d** 88 **p** 94. Par Dn Kensal Rise St Mark and St Martin *Lon* 88-91; Par Dn Northwood H Trin 91-94; C 94-95; Chapl Mt Vernon Hosp 91-99; P-in-c W Drayton 99-03; V from 03; Dean of Women's Min Willesden Area from 01; AD Hillingdon 03-08. *The Vicarage, 4 Beaudesert Mews, West Drayton UB7 7PE* Tel (01895) 442194 E-mail olwen@swanroad.go-plus.net

FIELD, Richard Colin. b 33. St Cath Soc Ox BA54 MA63. Clifton Th Coll 63. **d** 65 **p** 66. C Highbury Ch Ch Lon 65-70; V Hanger Lane St Ann 70-85; V Leytonstone St Jo *Chelmsf* 85-98; rtd 98; Perm to Offic *Chich* from 99. *21 Rufus Close, Lewes BN7 1BG* Tel (01273) 472884

FIELD, Canon Susan Elizabeth. b 59. York Univ BA80 Birm Univ CertEd81 Ox Univ MTh98. Qu Coll Birm 84. **d** 87 **p** 94. C Coleshill *Birm* 87-90; Chapl Loughb Univ 91-98; TV Loughborough Em and St Mary in Charnwood from 98; Dir Post-Ord Tr 95-04; Bp's Adv for Women's Min 97-04; Dir of Ords from 04; Hon Can Leic Cathl from 04. *134 Valley Road, Loughborough LE11 3QA* Tel (01509) 234472 E-mail sue.field1@tesco.net

FIELD, William Jenkin. b 25. St Deiniol's Hawarden. **d** 66 **p** 67. C Cardiff St Jo *Llan* 66-72; V Llancarfan w Llantrithyd 72-94; rtd 94; Perm to Offic *Llan* from 94. *20 Whitmore Park Drive, Barry CF62 8JL* Tel (01446) 701027

FIELDEN, Elizabeth Ann. b 42. TCert63. **d** 99 **p** 00. OLM Broughton Gifford, Gt Chalfield and Holt *Sarum* from 99; OLM Atworth w Shaw and Whitley from 07; OLM Melksham from 07. *393 Ham Green, Holt, Trowbridge BA14 6PX* Tel (01225) 782509 Fax 783152 E-mail winesource@saqnet.co.uk

FIELDEN, Hugh. b 66. BNC Ox BA88 Birm Univ PGCE90. Qu Coll Birm 91. **d** 93 **p** 94. C Sholing *Win* 93-97; TV Bramley *Ripon* 97-02; TV Bingley All SS *Bradf* 02-07; P-in-c Earby 07; P-in-c Kelbrook 07; V Earby w Kelbrook from 08. *The Vicarage, 40 Brookfield Way, Earby, Barnoldswick BB18 6YQ* Tel (01282) 844877 E-mail hugh.fielden@bradford.anglican.org

FIELDEN, Mrs Janice. b 46. Warwick Univ BEd82 MEd89. SAOMC 99. **d** 02 **p** 03. NSM Chipping Norton *Ox* 02-05; NSM Charlbury w Shorthampton from 05. *The Vicarage, Church Lane, Charlbury, Chipping Norton OX7 3PX* Tel and fax (01608) 810286 E-mail jan@cnfogies.co.uk

FIELDEN, Robert. b 32. Linc Th Coll 65. **d** 67 **p** 68. C Bassingham *Linc* 67-72; R Anderby w Cumberworth 72-88; P-in-c Huttoft 72-88; P-in-c Mumby 77-88; R Fiskerton 88-90; rtd 90; Perm to Offic *Carl* 91-99 and *Linc* from 91. *Woodlands, 8 Fiskerton Road, Reepham, Lincoln LN3 4EB* Tel (01522) 750480 E-mail robert@rfielden.freeserve.co.uk

FIELDER, Joseph Neil. b 67. Univ of Wales BSc89. Wycliffe Hall Ox 93. **d** 96 **p** 97. C Cheadle All Hallows *Ches* 96-00; V Preston St Steph *Blackb* 00-09; P-in-c Baxenden from 09. *The Vicarage, Langford Street, Baxenden, Accrington BB5 2RF* Tel (01254) 232471

FIELDGATE, John William Sheridan. b 44. St Jo Coll Dur BA68. Ox NSM Course 75. **d** 79 **p** 80. NSM Haddenham w Cuddington, Kingsey etc *Ox* 79-90; C Northleach w Hampnett and Farmington *Glouc* 90-92; C Cold Aston w Notgrove and Turkdean 90-92; P-in-c Upper and Lower Slaughter w Eyford and Naunton 92-01; P-in-c The Guitings, Cutsdean and Farmcote 92-01; V Acton w Gt Waldingfield *St E* 01-09; rtd 09; Perm to Offic *St E* from 09. *Patmos, 23 Woodfield Drive, West Mersea, Colchester CO5 8PX* Tel (01206) 386851 E-mail jandjfieldgate@tiscali.co.uk

FIELDING, John Joseph. b 29. TCD BA53 MA65 QUB DipEd57. TCD Div Sch Div Test 54. **d** 54 **p** 55. C Belfast St Luke *Conn* 54-57; C Belfast St Mary Magd 57-60; Chapl Windsor Boys' Sch Hamm W Germany 61-69; Chapl St Edw Sch Ox 69-73; V Highgate St Mich *Lon* 73-95; rtd 95; Perm to Offic

Guildf from 95 and *S'wark* from 06. *30 Sackville Mews, Sackville Road, Sutton SM2 6HS* E-mail j.j.fielding@btinternet.com

FIELDING, Robert David. b 67. Liv Univ BA89 St Jo Coll Dur BA08. Cranmer Hall Dur 07. **d** 08. C Formby St Pet *Liv* from 08. *3 Kenton Close, Formby, Liverpool L37 7EA* Tel 07951-173434 (mobile) E-mail rfielding@homecall.co.uk

FIELDING, Stephen Aubrey. b 67. Ulster Univ BSc89 TCD BTh93. CITC 90. **d** 93 **p** 94. C Bangor Abbey *D & D* 93-97; I Templepatrick w Donegore *Conn* 97-07; I Agherton from 07. *The Rectory, 59 Strand Road, Portstewart BT55 7LU* Tel (028) 7083 2538 *or* 7083 3277 E-mail agherton@connor.anglican.org

FIELDING, Stephen Lister. b 52. Ch Ch Ox BA73 MA77 Barrister 74. SAOMC 04. **d** 07 **p** 08. NSM Welwyn *St Alb* from 07. *Holly Hall, 13 Church Street, Welwyn AL6 9LN* Tel (01438) 718028 Mobile 07760-287614 E-mail slfielding@hotmail.com

FIELDSEND, John Henry. b 31. Nottm Univ BSc54 Lon Univ BD61. Lon Coll of Div ALCD59. **d** 61 **p** 62. C Pennington *Man* 61-64; C Didsbury Ch Ch 64-66; P-in-c Bayston Hill *Lich* 66-67; V 67-88; UK Dir CMJ 89-91; Dir and Min at Large CMJ 91-96; rtd 96; Perm to Offic *St Alb* 96-00; Hon C Thame *Ox* from 01. *58 Cedar Crescent, Thame OX9 2AU* Tel (01844) 212559 E-mail john@tehillah.freeserve.co.uk

FIELDSON, Robert Steven. b 56. Qu Coll Cam BA78 MA81 Wye Coll Lon MSc79. St Jo Coll Nottm BA86. **d** 87 **p** 88. C Walmley *Birm* 87-90; Chapl Protestant Ch in Oman 90-95; P-in-c Cofton Hackett w Barnt Green *Birm* 95-98; V from 98; AD Kings Norton 00-06. *The Vicarage, 8 Cofton Church Lane, Barnt Green, Birmingham B45 8PT* Tel 0121-445 1269 E-mail rob@fieldson.co.uk

FIENNES, The Very Revd the Hon Oliver William. b 26. New Coll Ox BA54 MA55. Cuddesdon Coll 52. **d** 54 **p** 55. C Milton *Win* 54-58; Chapl Clifton Coll Bris 58-63; R St Mary-at-Lambeth *S'wark* 63-68; RD Lambeth 68; Can and Preb Linc Cathl 69-97; Dean Linc 69-89; rtd 89. *3A Vicars Court, Lincoln LN2 1PT* Tel (01522) 526036

FIFE (née EVE), Hilary Anne. b 57. Lon Univ BEd80. Ripon Coll Cuddesdon 89. **d** 91 **p** 94. Par Dn Coulsdon St Andr *S'wark* 91-94; C 94-95; Chapl Croydon Coll 92-94; Asst Chapl Mayday Healthcare NHS Trust Thornton Heath 94-02; Sen Chapl from 02; Chapl Harestone Marie Curie Cen Caterham 94-98; Hon C Shirley St Geo *S'wark* from 08. *19 Greenview Avenue, Croydon CR0 7QW* Tel (020) 8654 8685 *or* 8401 3105

FIFE, Janet Heather. b 53. Sussex Univ BA77 Man Univ MPhil98. Wycliffe Hall Ox 84. **d** 87 **p** 94. Chapl Bradf Cathl 87-89; Par Dn York St Mich-le-Belfrey 89-92; Chapl Salford Univ 92-00; Hon TV Pendleton St Thos w Charlestown 92-95; Hon TV Pendleton 95-96; V Upton Priory *Ches* from 00. *The Vicarage, Churchway, Macclesfield SK10 3HT* Tel (01625) 827761 E-mail j.fife@virgin.net

FIGG, Robin Arthur Rex. b 62. RN Eng Coll Plymouth BScEng84. Westcott Ho Cam 91. **d** 94 **p** 95. C Old Cleeve, Leighland and Treborough *B & W* 94-97; C Gt Berkhamsted *St Alb* 97-01; V Kildwick *Bradf* from 01. *The Vicarage, Kildwick, Keighley BD20 9BB* Tel (01535) 633307 E-mail robin.figg@bradford.anglican.org

FILBERT-ULLMANN, Mrs Clair. b 44. Leuven Univ Belgium BTh94 MA94. Virginia Th Sem 95. **d** 94 **p** 96. USA 94-95; Asst Chapl Charleroi *Eur* 95-00; P-in-c Leuven 99-02; Asst Chapl Tervuren w Liège 99-01; Perm to Offic from 02. *Muhlbach am Hochkönig 437, A-5505, Austria* Tel (0043) (6467) 20107 E-mail crullmann2001@yahoo.com

FILBY, The Ven William Charles Leonard. b 33. Lon Univ BA58. Oak Hill Th Coll 53. **d** 59 **p** 60. C Eastbourne All SS *Chich* 59-62; C Woking St Jo *Guildf* 62-65; V Richmond H Trin *S'wark* 65-71; V Hove Bp Hannington Memorial Ch *Chich* 71-79; R Broadwater St Mary 79-83; RD Worthing 80-83; Can and Preb Chich Cathl 81-83; Adn Horsham 83-02; rtd 02; Perm to Offic *Chich* from 03. *Kymber Cottage, Hale Hill, Westburton, Pulborough RH20 1HE* Tel (01798) 831269 E-mail williamfilby@btopenworld.com

FILLERY, William Robert. b 42. Univ of Wales (Swansea) BA65 St D Coll Lamp BD69 PGCE72 Surrey Univ MA96. Bp Burgess Hall Lamp 65. **d** 68 **p** 69. C Llangyfelach and Morriston *S & B* 68-71; C Morriston 71-72; Lic to Offic *Ox* 73-76; Chapl Windsor Girls' Sch Hamm W Germany 76-81; OCF 79-81; Chapl Reed's Sch Cobham 81-86; V Oxshott *Guildf* 86-89; P-in-c Seale 89-91; P-in-c Puttenham and Wanborough 89-91; Hd RE Streatham Hill & Clapham Sch for Girls 91-03; V Llanybydder and Llanwenog w Llanllwni *St D* from 03. *The Vicarage, Llanllwni, Pencader SA39 9DR* Tel (01559) 395413 Mobile 07971-007336 E-mail billfill@btinternet.com

FILLINGHAM, Richard James. b 58. Man Univ BA80 Sheff Univ MA03 ACA83. All Nations Chr Coll Wycliffe Hall Ox. **d** 98 **p** 99. C Brinsworth w Catcliffe and Treeton *Sheff* 98-01; C Ecclesall 01-05. *92 Greystones Road, Sheffield S11 7BQ* Tel 0114-266 1804

FILMER, Paul James. b 58. Open Univ BA88. Aston Tr Scheme 93 Oak Hill Th Coll 95. **d** 97 **p** 98. C Petham and Waltham w Lower Hardres etc *Cant* 97-00; P-in-c Patrixbourne w Bridge and Bekesbourne 00-06; P-in-c Lower Hardres w Nackington 00-06; Chapl Univ of Greenwich *Roch* 06-09; Chapl Univ for the Creative Arts 06-09; V Yalding w Collier Street from 09. *The Vicarage, Vicarage Road, Yalding, Maidstone NE18 6DR* Tel (01622) 814182 Mobile 07595-176797 E-mail revpfilmer@mac.com

FILTNESS, Trevor Moshe. b 50. MNI MInstD. STETS 05. **d** 08 **p** 09. NSM Farlington *Portsm* from 08. *Manor Cottage, 1 Lower Road, Havant PO9 3LH* Tel 07785-568056 (mobile) E-mail trevor@filtness.org *or* trevor@farlingtonparish.co.uk

FINCH, Alan James. b 51. **d** 06 **p** 07. OLM Orrell Hey St Jo and St Jas *Liv* from 06. *1 Kirkstone Road North, Liverpool L21 7NP* Tel 0151-928 3919 E-mail alan@chesed.freeserve.co.uk

FINCH, Mrs Alison. b 59. SEN79. Sarum & Wells Th Coll 90. **d** 92 **p** 94. Par Dn Banbury *Ox* 92-94; C 94-95; C Wokingham All SS 95-98; C Binfield 98-99; C St Peter-in-Thanet *Cant* 99-02; R Kirkwall and P-in-c Stromness *Ab* 02-05; Ind Chapl *Chelmsf* from 05; C Colchester St Pet and St Botolph from 05. *St Botolph's Vicarage, 50B Priory Street, Colchester CO1 2QB* Tel (01206) 868043 Mobile 07762-744977

FINCH, Barry Marshall. *See* PALMER FINCH, Barry Marshall

FINCH, Christopher. b 41. Lon Univ BA63 AKC63 BD69. Sarum Th Coll 63. **d** 65 **p** 66. C High Wycombe *Ox* 65-69; Prec Leic Cathl 69-73; R Lt Bowden St Nic 73-81; V Evington 81-99; P-in-c Leic St Phil 95-99; P-in-c Lower Dever Valley *Win* 99-00; R 00-07; rtd 07; Perm to Offic *Portsm* from 07. *7 Arundel Drive, Fareham PO16 7NP* Tel (01329) 829015

FINCH, Canon David Walter. b 40. Cam Univ MA74 FIBMS69. Ridley Hall Cam. **d** 91 **p** 92. C Ixworth and Bardwell *St E* 91-92; C Blackbourne 92-94; P-in-c Stoke by Nayland w Leavenheath 94-00; P-in-c Polstead 95-00; P-in-c Fressingfield, Mendham etc 00-08; C Hoxne w Denham, Syleham and Wingfield 06-08; RD Hoxne 00-07; Hon Can St E Cathl 05-08; rtd 08; Perm to Offic *St E* from 08; Lic to Offic *Ab* from 08. *Mayfield House, Seafield Place, Cullen, Buckie AB56 4TE* Tel (01542) 840098

FINCH, Frank. b 33. Qu Coll Birm 72. **d** 74 **p** 75. C Bilston St Leon *Lich* 74-78; R Sudbury and Somersal Herbert *Derby* 78-87; Chapl HM Pris Sudbury 78-87; HM Det Cen Foston Hall 80-87; V Lilleshall and Sheriffhales *Lich* 87-90; R The Ridwares and Kings Bromley 90-98; rtd 98; Perm to Offic *Lich* from 00. *11 Ferrers Road, Yoxall, Burton-on-Trent DE13 8PS* Tel (01543) 472065

FINCH, Jeffrey Walter. b 45. Man Univ BA(Econ)66 Liv Univ DASE80. Linc Th Coll 82. **d** 84 **p** 85. C Brierscliffe *Blackb* 84-87; P-in-c Brindle and Asst Dir of Educn 87-93; V Laneside 93-00; TV Fellside Team 00-08; TR from 08. *The Vicarage, Church Lane, Bilsborrow, Preston PR3 0RL* Tel (01995) 640269

FINCH, John. b 20. Bps' Coll Cheshunt 59. **d** 61 **p** 62. C Middlesbrough St Paul *York* 61-64; V Easington w Skeffling and Kilnsea 64-68; V Habergham Eaves St Matt *Blackb* 68-75; V Garstang St Helen Churchtown 75-86; rtd 86; Perm to Offic *Blackb* from 86. *55 Worcester Avenue, Garstang, Preston PR3 1FJ* Tel (01995) 602386

FINCH, Morag Anne Hamilton. b 64. EAMTC 97. **d** 00 **p** 01. C Cranham *Chelmsf* 00-05; V Gidea Park from 05. *St Andrew's Vicarage, Main Road, Romford RM2 5EL* Tel (01708) 741084 E-mail thefinches@ntlworld.com

FINCH, Paul William. b 50. Oak Hill Th Coll Lon Bible Coll. **d** 75 **p** 76. C Hoole *Ches* 75-78; C Charlesworth *Derby* 78-87; C Charlesworth and Dinting Vale 87-88; TV Radipole and Melcombe Regis *Sarum* 88-01; V Malvern St Andr and Malvern Wells and Wyche *Worc* from 01. *St Andrew's Vicarage, 48 Longridge Road, Malvern WR14 3JB* Tel (01684) 573912 E-mail paul@finchnest.freeserve.co.uk

FINCH, Richard William. b 62. Westcott Ho Cam 95. **d** 97 **p** 98. C Saffron Walden w Wendens Ambo and Littlebury *Chelmsf* 97-00; C Elm Park St Nic Hornchurch 00-01; V from 01. *St Michael's Vicarage, Main Road, Romford RM2 5EL* Tel (01708) 741084 E-mail finches@aic.co.uk

FINCH, Ronald. b 15. Qu Coll Birm 79. **d** 80 **p** 80. Hon C Welford w Weston and Clifford Chambers *Glouc* 80-85; Perm to Offic *Ches* 85-03 and *Sheff* from 03. *55 Folds Crescent, Sheffield S8 0EP* Tel 0114-249 9029

FINCH, Miss Rosemary Ann. b 39. Leeds Univ CertEd60. **d** 93 **p** 94. OLM S Elmham and Ilketshall *St E* 93-00; Asst Chapl Ipswich Hosp NHS Trust from 00. *Ipswich Hospital, Heath Road, Ipswich IP4 5PD* Tel (01473) 712233 E-mail rosiestmse@aol.com

FINCH, Canon Stanley James. b 31. Mert Coll Ox BA55 MA58. Wells Th Coll 55. **d** 57 **p** 58. C Lancaster St Mary *Blackb* 57-61; C Leeds St Pet *Ripon* 61-65; V Habergham All SS *Blackb* 65-73; V S Shore H Trin 73-84; V Broughton 84-98; RD Preston 86-92; Hon Can Blackb Cathl 91-98; rtd 98; P-in-c Alderton, Gt Washbourne, Dumbleton etc *Glouc* 98-02; Perm to Offic from 02. *14 Belltower Road, Walton Cardiff, Tewkesbury GL20 7SB* Tel (01684) 850544

FINCH, Thomas. b 20. Lon Univ BD57. Edin Th Coll 48. **d** 51 **p** 51. Chapl St Andr Cathl 51-55; C St Marylebone St Cypr *Lon* 55-58; V Warmington *Pet* 58-67; RD Oundle 62-67; V

Wellingborough St Mary 67-88; rtd 88; Perm to Offic *Blackb* from 88. *18 Royal Avenue, Leyland, Preston PR25 1BQ* Tel (01772) 433780

FINCHAM, Nicholas Charles. b 56. St Jo Coll Dur BA78 MA80. Westcott Ho Cam 80 Bossey Ecum Inst Geneva 81. **d** 82 **p** 83. C Seaham w Seaham Harbour *Dur* 82-85; C Lydney w Aylburton *Glouc* 85-87; C Isleworth All SS *Lon* 87-95; P-in-c Chiswick St Mich from 95. *St Michael's Vicarage, 60 Elmwood Road, London W4 3DZ* Tel (020) 8994 3173
E-mail nicholas.fincham@talk21.com

FINDLAY, Brian James. b 42. Wellington Univ (NZ) BA62 MA63 BMus66 Magd Coll Ox MA75. Qu Coll Birm. **d** 72 **p** 73. C Deptford St Paul *S'wark* 72-75; Chapl and Dean of Div Magd Coll Ox 75-84; V Tonge Moor *Man* 84-02; Hon Can Man Cathl 00-03; R Monks Eleigh w Chelsworth and Brent Eleigh etc *St E* from 03. *The Rectory, The Street, Monks Eleigh, Ipswich IP7 7AU* Tel (01449) 740244

FINDLAY, James. b 68. Bp Otter Coll BA90 Westmr Coll Ox PGCE92. Wycliffe Hall Ox 02. **d** 04 **p** 05. C Gillingham St Mark *Roch* 04-07; P-in-c Salisbury St Mark *Sarum* from 07. *St Mark's Vicarage, 62 Barrington Road, Salisbury SP1 3JD* Tel (01722) 323767 Mobile 07854-510569
E-mail jim.magsfindlay@btinternet.com

FINDLAYSON, Roy. b 44. Man Univ MA89 CQSW69. Sarum & Wells Th Coll 80. **d** 82 **p** 83. C Benwell St Jas *Newc* 82-83; Hon C 83-85; C Morpeth 85-88; C N Gosforth 88; TV Ch the King 88-94; V Newc St Fran 94-98; Asst Chapl Newcastle upon Tyne Hosps NHS Trust 98-06; Chapl Marie Curie Cen Newc 98-06; rtd 06. *6A Hawthorn Mews, Newcastle upon Tyne NE3 4DA* Tel 0191-284 4166

FINDLEY, Peter. b 55. Trin Coll Ox BA77 MA80 Barrister-at-Law (Gray's Inn) 78. Trin Coll Bris 90. **d** 92 **p** 93. C Yateley *Win* 92-97; V Westwood *Cov* from 97; P-in-c Canley from 09. *St John's Vicarage, Featherbed Lane, Coventry CV4 7DD* Tel (024) 7647 0515 *or* 7669 5026
E-mail peterfindley@stjohnswestwood.freeserve.co.uk

FINDON, John Charles. b 50. Keble Coll Ox BA71 MA75 DPhil79. Ripon Coll Cuddesdon. **d** 77 **p** 78. C Middleton *Man* 77-80; Lect Bolton St Pet 80-83; V Astley 83-91; V Baguley 91-98; P-in-c Bury St Mary 98-05; R from 05. *St Mary's Rectory, Tithebarn Street, Bury BL9 0JR* Tel 0161-764 2452

FINKENSTAEDT, Harry Seymour. b 23. Yale Univ BA49 Univ of Mass MA68. Episc Th Sch Cam Mass BD50. **d** 53 **p** 54. USA 53-71; C Hazlemere *Ox* 71-73; C Huntingdon St Mary w St Benedict *Ely* 73-75; R Castle Camps 75-84; R Shudy Camps 75-84; P-in-c W Wickham 79-84; P-in-c Horseheath 79-81; P-in-c Gt w Lt Stukeley 84-88; rtd 88; Perm to Offic *Ely* 88-01. *13761 Charismatic Way, Gainesville VA 20155-3119, USA* Tel (001) (703) 743 5787

FINLAY, Alison Mary. *See* CAW, Alison Mary

FINLAY, Christopher John. b 46. FCII71. WMMTC 95. **d** 98 **p** 99. NSM Coln St Aldwyns, Hatherop, Quenington etc *Glouc* 98-08; NSM Fairford Deanery from 09. *Coombe House, Calcot, Cheltenham GL54 3JZ* Tel (01285) 720806
E-mail coombehousecalcol@tiscali.co.uk

FINLAY, Canon Hueston Edward. b 64. TCD BA85 BAI85 BTh89 MA92 Cam Univ MA98 Lon Univ PhD98. CITC 86. **d** 89 **p** 90. C Kilkenny w Aghour and Kilmanagh *C & O* 89-92; Bp's Dom Chapl 89-92; Lib and Registrar Kilkenny Cathl 89-92; Bp's V Ossory Cathl 90-92; Chapl Girton Coll Cam 92-95; C Cambridge Gt St Mary w St Mich *Ely* 92-95; Chapl and Fell Magd Coll Cam 95-99; Dean of Chpl 99-04; Can Windsor from 04. *8 The Cloisters, Windsor Castle, Windsor SL4 1NJ* Tel (01753) 867094 Fax 833806
E-mail hueston.finlay@stgeorges-windsor.org

FINLAY, Canon Michael Stanley. b 45. NOC 78. **d** 81 **p** 82. C Padgate *Liv* 81-85; V Newton-le-Willows 85-90; V Orford St Marg 90-98; P-in-c Warrington St Elphin 98-00; R from 00; Hon Can Liv Cathl from 07. *The Rectory, Church Street, Warrington WA1 2TL* Tel (01925) 635020

FINLAY, Nicholas. b 47. Regent Coll Vancouver MCS00. St Jo Coll Nottm 01. **d** 02 **p** 03. C Haydock St Mark *Liv* 02-03; C Bootle 03-04; Lic to Adn Warrington 04-05; V Sittingbourne St Mary and St Mich *Cant* from 05. *The Vicarage, 26 Valenciennes Road, Sittingbourne ME10 1EN* Tel (01795) 472874 E-mail nickfinlay@blueyonder.co.uk

FINLAYSON, Duncan. b 24. **d** 76 **p** 76. NSM Bridge of Allan *St And* 76-94; NSM Alloa 77-94; NSM Dollar 77-94; Hon AP Hillfoots Team 80-87; rtd 94. *29 Cawder Road, Bridge of Allan, Stirling FK9 4JJ* Tel (01786) 833074

FINLAYSON, Mrs Gladys Victoria. b 49. TCert67. ERMC 05. **d** 09. NSM Luton St Anne w St Chris *St Alb* from 09. *St Andrew's Vicarage, 11 Blenheim Crescent, Luton LU3 1HA* Tel (01582) 732380 E-mail gladysfinlayson@sky.com

FINLAYSON, Grantley Adrian. b 55. Wilson Carlile Coll 74 Chich Th Coll 87. **d** 89 **p** 90. C Watford St Mich *St Alb* 89-92; TV W Slough *Ox* 92-97; Dioc Officer for Race Relations *Glouc* 97-02; V Luton St Andr *St Alb* from 02. *St Andrew's Vicarage,*

11 Blenheim Crescent, Luton LU3 1HA Tel and fax (01582) 481711 E-mail grantley@gfinlayson.fsworld.co.uk

FINLINSON, Paul. b 58. St Chad's Coll Dur BA79 St Martin's Coll Lanc PGCE81. Carl Dioc Tr Course 86. **d** 89 **p** 90. NSM Kirkby Lonsdale *Carl* 89-99; Chapl Worksop Coll Notts from 99. *Worksop College, Sparken Hill, Worksop S80 3AP* Tel (01909) 537109 *or* (01524) 69652

FINN, Gordon Frederick. b 33. Dur Univ BA60. Ely Th Coll 60. **d** 62 **p** 63. C Kingswinford St Mary *Lich* 62-65; C Northampton St Mary *Pet* 65-67; Chapl Barnsley Hall Hosp and Lea Hosp Bromsgrove 67-71; C Swanage *Sarum* 71-73; P-in-c Ford End *Chelmsf* 73-79; V S Shields St Oswin *Dur* 79-98; rtd 98. *58 Hutton Lane, Guisborough TS14 8AW* Tel (01287) 619132

FINN, Ian Michael. b 58. AKC. Chich Th Coll 81. **d** 82 **p** 83. C Habergham All SS *Blackb* 82-83; C W Burnley All SS 83-85; C Torrisholme 85-87; V Lancaster Ch Ch w St Jo and St Anne 87-91; P-in-c Tillingham and Dengie w Asheldham *Chelmsf* 91-97; Chapl R Gr Sch Worc 97-99; P-in-c Denston w Stradishall and Stansfield *St E* 99-01; P-in-c Wickhambrook w Lydgate, Ousden and Cowlinge 00-01; R Bansfield 02-07; V Haverhill w Withersfield from 07; RD Clare from 06. *The Rectory, 10 Hopton Rise, Haverhill CB9 7FS* Tel (01440) 708768
E-mail ian.finn1@btinternet.com

FINN, Miss Sheila. b 30. LMH Ox BA68 MA69. Gilmore Ho 68. **dss** 78 **d** 87 **p** 94. Tettenhall Wood *Lich* 78-86; Dioc Ecum Officer 86-95; The Ridwares and Kings Bromley 86-87; Par Dn 87-94; C 94-95; rtd 95; Perm to Offic *Lich* from 97. *15 Leacroft Road, Penkridge, Stafford ST19 5BU* Tel (01785) 716018

FINNEMORE, James Christopher. b 59. Pemb Coll Cam BA81 MA85. Coll of Resurr Mirfield. **d** 85 **p** 86. C Manston *Ripon* 85-88; C Hessle *York* 88-92; R Bishop Wilton w Full Sutton, Kirby Underdale etc 92-99; R Garrowby Hill from 99; RD S Wold from 07. *The Rectory, Bishop Wilton, York YO42 1SA* Tel (01759) 368230

FINNEMORE, Thomas John. b 79. Hull Univ BA01. Wycliffe Hall Ox 05. **d** 07 **p** 08. C Crookes St Thos *Sheff* from 07. *St Thomas's Church Office, Nairn Street, Sheffield S10 1UL* Tel 0114-267 1090 E-mail tom.finnemore@stthomascrookes.org

FINNERTY, Cynthia Ann. b 46. **d** 05 **p** 06. OLM E Greenwich *S'wark* from 05. *33 Ruthin Road, London SE3 7SJ* Tel (020) 8858 2883 E-mail cynthiafin@hotmail.com

FINNEY, Canon David. b 41. St Mich Coll Llan 68. **d** 70 **p** 71. C Wythenshawe Wm Temple Ch *Man* 70-73; C Bedford Leigh 73-75; V Royton St Anne 75-81; V Dearnley 81-94; TV Rochdale 94-07; Hon Can Man Cathl 04-07; rtd 07; Perm to Offic *Man* from 09. *59 Knowl Road, Rochdale OL1 4BB* Tel (01706) 346384

FINNEY, Canon Fred. b 17. Bris Univ BA38 DipEd39. Wycliffe Hall Ox 61. **d** 62 **p** 63. C Gt Crosby St Luke *Liv* 62-66; V Ashton-in-Makerfield St Thos 66-86; Hon Can Liv Cathl 83-86; rtd 86; Perm to Offic *Blackb* and *Liv* 86-08. *clo Mrs B J Nuttall, 2 Barelees Farm Cottages, Cornhill-on-Tweed TD12 4SF*

FINNEY, Canon John Thomas. b 27. Sheff Univ BA51 DipEd52. Ripon Hall Ox 60. **d** 62 **p** 63. C Leigh St Mary *Man* 62-65; V 83-97; V Peel 65-69; Chapl Hockerill Coll Bishop's Stortford 69-74; V Astley *Man* 74-83; AD Leigh 85-93; Hon Can Man Cathl 87-97; rtd 97; Perm to Offic *Man* from 97. *36 Station Road, Blackrod, Bolton BL6 5BW* Tel (01204) 698010

✠**FINNEY, The Rt Revd John Thornley.** b 32. Hertf Coll Ox BA55. Wycliffe Hall Ox 56. **d** 58 **p** 59 **c** 93. C Highfield *Ox* 58-61; C Weston Turville 61-65; R Tollerton *S'well* 65-71; V Aspley 71-80; Bp's Adv on Evang 80-89; Bp's Research Officer 88-89; Hon Can S'well Minster 84-89; Officer for Decade of Evang in C of E 90-93; Suff Bp Pontefract *Wakef* 93-98; rtd 98; Hon Asst Bp S'well and Nottm from 98. *Greenacre, Crow Lane, South Muskham, Newark NG23 6DZ* Tel and fax (01636) 679791
E-mail john.finney2@ntlworld.com

FINNEY, Ms Melva Kathleen. b 24. LTh76. St Jo Coll Auckland 47 Gilmore Ho 56. **dss** 57 **d** 78. E Dulwich St Jo *S'wark* 56-59; Community of Sisters of the Love of God Ox 59-61; New Zealand from 61; Asst Chapl Christchurch 61-62; Fendalton St Barn 62-63; Asst Chapl Womens and Templeton Hosp 63-72; Asst Chapl Princess Marg Hosp Christchurch 63-72; Chapl 72-86; rtd 86. *22 Gunns Crescent, Cashmere, Christchurch 8022, New Zealand* Tel (0064) (3) 332 7100

FINNIE, Canon Robert. b 20. **d** 84 **p** 84. NSM Aberdeen St Andr from 84; NSM Aberdeen St Ninian 84-97; Hon Can St Andr Cathl from 97. *10 Cairngorm Crescent, Aberdeen AB12 5BL* Tel (01224) 874669

FINNIMORE, Keith Anthony. b 36. AKC59. **d** 60 **p** 61. C Wanstead H Trin Hermon Hill *Chelmsf* 60-63; C Kingswood *S'wark* 63-65; V Bolney *Chich* 65-67; V Elmstead *Chelmsf* 67-73; R Pentlow, Foxearth, Liston and Borley 73-77; NSM Cockfield w Bradfield St Clare, Felsham etc *St E* 89-91; R Hawstead and Nowton w Stanningfield etc 91-96; P-in-c 96-01; rtd 96; Perm to Offic *St E* from 01. *Larkhill, Rede Road, Whepstead, Bury St Edmunds IP29 4SS* Tel (01284) 735291

FIRBANK, Michael John. b 73. R Holloway Coll Lon BA94 St Mary's Coll Twickenham PGCE94. St Jo Coll Nottm MTh05. **d** 05 **p** 06. C St Illogan *Truro* 05-07; P-in-c Camborne from 07.

The Rectory, Rectory Gardens, Camborne TR14 7DN Tel (01209) 613020 Mobile 07888-711645 E-mail mjfirbank@hotmail.com

FIRMIN, Canon Dorrie Eleanor Frances. b 19. LNSM course. **d** 88 **p** 94. NSM Ellon *Ab* 88-99; NSM Cruden Bay 88-99; Hon Can St Andr Cathl from 97; rtd 99. *Airdlin Croft, Ythanbank, Ellon AB41 7TS* Tel (01358) 761344

FIRMIN, Paul Gregory. b 57. ACIB80. Trin Coll Bris BA87. **d** 87 **p** 88. C Swindon Ch Ch *Bris* 87-91; V Shrewsbury H Trin w St Julian *Lich* 91-99; V Astley, Clive, Grinshill and Hadnall 99-01; V Southampton St Mary Extra *Win* from 01. *The Vicarage, 65 Peartree Avenue, Bitterne, Southampton SO19 7JN* Tel (023) 8043 7192 E-mail nimrifs@btinternet.com

FIRMSTONE, Ian Harry. b 44. Qu Coll Birm. **d** 82 **p** 83. C Warminster St Denys *Sarum* 82-84; C N Stoneham *Win* 84-88; R Freemantle 88-90; V Littleport *Ely* 90-91; TV Stanground and Farcet 91-97; P-in-c Holme w Conington 95-96; rtd 97. *Cotswold Cottage, School Lane, Alvechurch, Birmingham B48 7SA* Tel 0121-445 1318

FIRTH, Mrs Ann Neswyn. b 40. St As Minl Tr Course 95. **d** 98 **p** 99. NSM Llanidloes w Llangurig *Ban* 98-05; Perm to Offic from 05. *Springfield, Westgate Street, Llanidloes SY18 6HJ* Tel (01686) 413098 E-mail davidandneswyn@firth19.freeserve.co.uk

FIRTH, Christopher John Kingsley. b 37. St Mich Coll Llan. **d** 66 **p** 67. C Sutton in Ashfield St Mary *S'well* 66-70; V Langold 70-74; C Falmouth K Chas *Truro* 74-77; P-in-c Mabe 77-81; V 81-95; RD Carnmarth S 90-94; rtd 99. *1 Boscawen, Cliff Road, Falmouth TR11 4AW* Tel (01326) 316734

FIRTH, Geoffrey David. b 74. Lincs & Humberside Univ BA96. Oak Hill Th Coll BA06. **d** 06 **p** 07. C Poynton *Ches* from 06. *18 Ivy Road, Poynton, Stockport SK12 1PE* Tel (01625) 872048 E-mail geoffreyfirth@gmail.com *or* poyntoncurate@googlemail.com

FIRTH, Graham Alfred. b 38. Man Univ BA60. Ripon Hall Ox. **d** 62 **p** 63. C Norton Woodseats St Paul *Sheff* 62-65; C-in-c Kimberworth Park CD 65-69; V Kimberworth Park 69-71; P-in-c Egmanton and Laxton *S'well* 71-77; V Sibthorpe 77-04; R Elston w Elston Chapelry 77-04; R E Stoke w Syerston 77-04; R Shelton 91-04; rtd 04; Perm to Offic *S'well* 04-08. *Cherry Tree Cottage, 2 Fulmodeston Road, Stibbard, Fakenham NR21 0LT*

FIRTH, Mrs Jennifer Anne. b 52. Goldsmiths' Coll Lon BMus75 Kingston Poly PGCE83. **d** 07 **p** 08. OLM Dorking St Paul *Guildf* from 07. *33 Downsview Gardens, Dorking RH4 2DX* Tel (01306) 887189 Mobile 07970-102987 E-mail jennyafirth@aol.com

FIRTH, Matthew Paul. b 83. Magd Coll Cam BA04 MA08. Wycliffe Hall Ox BTh09. **d** 09. C Triangle, St Matt and All SS *St E* from 09. *43 Clarkson Street, Ipswich IP1 2JN* Tel 07932-482929 (mobile) E-mail matthewfirth@cantab.net

FIRTH, Neswyn. *See* FIRTH, Mrs Ann Neswyn

✠**FIRTH, The Rt Revd Peter James.** b 29. Em Coll Cam BA52 MA63. St Steph Ho Ox 53. **d** 55 **p** 56 **c** 83. C Barbourne *Worc* 55-58; C Malvern Link St Matthias 58-62; R Abbey Hey *Man* 62-66; Asst Network Relig Broadcasting BBC Man 66-67; Sen Producer/Org Relig Progr TV & Radio BBC Bris 67-83; Hon Can Bris Cathl 74-83; Suff Bp Malmesbury 83-94; Angl Adv HTV West 84-94; rtd 94; Hon Asst Bp Glouc from 03. *Mill House, High Lane, Winchcombe, Cheltenham GL54 5HZ* Tel (01242) 603669 E-mail peter@firth7.fsbusiness.co.uk

FIRTH, Mrs Rachel Naomi. b 73. Huddersfield Univ BA97 Leeds Univ BA08. NOC 05. **d** 08 **p** 09. C Halifax *Wakef* from 08. *27 Central Park, Halifax HX1 2BT* Tel (01422) 361942 Mobile 07793-709988 E-mail rnfirth@hotmail.com

FIRTH, Richard Geoffrey. b 48. **d** 06 **p** 07. OLM Dur St Marg and Neville's Cross St Jo 06-08; Perm to Offic *York* from 08. *6 Vicarage Close, Seamer, Scarborough YO12 4QS* Tel (01723) 867957 E-mail afirth9819@aol.com

FISH, Mrs Jacqueline Wendy. b 42. NTMTC 02. **d** 04 **p** 05. NSM Enfield Chase St Mary *Lon* from 04. *41 Churchbury Lane, Enfield EN1 3TX* Tel (020) 8366 2235 E-mail jacquiefishie@aol.com

FISH, Michael. b 61. Lanc Univ BA05. CBDTI 01. **d** 04 **p** 05. NSM Blackb St Mich w St Jo and H Trin 04-07; NSM Blackb St Thos w St Jude 04-07; P-in-c Cen Buchan *Ab* 07-08; P-in-c Shrewsbury All SS w St Mich *Lich* from 08. *All Saints' Vicarage, 5 Lingen Close, Shrewsbury SY1 2UN* Tel (01743) 244879 Mobile 07867-760110 E-mail fr.michaelfish@btinternet.com

FISH, Winthrop. b 40. Dalhousie Univ Canada BA63 BEd Birm Univ BPhil76 MEd78. K Coll (NS) 62. **d** 64 **p** 65. I Arichat Canada 64-66; I Neil's Harbour and Baddock 66-67; I Cut Knife 68-70; Perm to Offic Nova Scotia 70-74; Perm to Offic *Birm* 74-77; Asst Chapl Solihull Sch 77-79; Chapl Wroxall Abbey Sch 79-82; C Newquay *Truro* 82-84; V Highertown and Baldhu 84-89; P-in-c Newlyn St Newlyn 89-97; Dioc Children's Adv 89-97; Dioc Adv in RE 95-97; rtd 98; Perm to Offic *Ex* from 98. *4 Dukes Close, Otterton, Budleigh Salterton EX9 7EY* Tel (01395) 568331

FISHER, Adrian Charles Proctor. b 24. TCD BA48 MA62. TCD Div Sch Div Test47. **d** 49 **p** 50. C Carlow *C & O* 49-52; C Tintern and Killesk 49-52; CF 52-57 and 62-69; I Fethard w Killesk, Tintern and Templetown *C & O* 57-62; P-in-c N Stoke w Mongewell and Ipsden *Ox* 70-83; V 83-92; Chapl Oratory Prep Sch 73-80; rtd 92; Perm to Offic *Ox* from 99. *Pitt House, 25 New Street, Henley-on-Thames RG9 2BP* Tel (01491) 636 008

FISHER, Mrs Alison. b 48. Cranmer Hall Dur 04. **d** 05 **p** 06. NSM The Thorntons and The Otteringtons *York* from 05. *The Vicarage, 4 Endican Lane, Thorton le Moor, Northallerton DL7 9FB* Tel (01609) 761806 E-mail ali@endican.gotadsl.co.uk

FISHER, Andrew John. b 72. St Jo Coll Nottm BA02. **d** 02 **p** 03. C Ilkeston St Jo *Derby* 02-05; P-in-c Hodge Hill *Birm* 05-08; Chapl Worcs Acute Hosps NHS Trust from 08. *Department of Spiritual and Pastoral Care, The Alexandra Hospital, Woodrow Drive, Redditch B98 7UB* Tel (01527) 505723 E-mail andrew.fisher@worcsacute.nhs.uk

FISHER, Brian Robert. b 36. **d** 02 **p** 03. OLM Sole Bay *St E* 02-07; rtd 07; Perm to Offic *St E* from 07. *Green Gates, The Street, Walberswick, Southwold IP18 6UH* Tel (01502) 723023 Mobile 07766-216111 E-mail fishell@btopenworld.com

FISHER, David Stephen. b 66. Ripon Coll Cuddesdon BTh98. **d** 98 **p** 99. C Stockport SW *Ches* 98-01; V Gatley 01-06; V Gt Sutton from 06. *St John's Vicarage, 1 Church Lane, Great Sutton, Ellesmere Port CH66 4RE* Tel 0151-339 9916 E-mail daifisher@aol.com

FISHER, Mrs Diana Margaret. b 44. EMMTC 91. **d** 94 **p** 95. NSM E and W Leake, Stanford-on-Soar, Rempstone etc *S'well* 94-97; NSM W Bridgford 97-98; NSM Aberfoyle and Callander *St And* 99; C Spalding St Jo w Deeping St Nicholas *Linc* 99-01; R Hallaton and Allexton, w Horninghold, Tugby etc *Leic* 01-07; rtd 07. *17 St John's Drive, Melton Mowbray LE13 1JX* Tel (01664) 500278 E-mail fisher983@aol.com

FISHER, Eric Henry George. b 48. NTMTC 94. **d** 97 **p** 98. NSM Heydon, Gt and Lt Chishill, Chrishall etc *Chelmsf* 97-03; P-in-c Gt Oakley w Wix and Wrabness 03-08; rtd 08. *Sheldon, 12 Joseph Close, Hadleigh, Ipswich IP7 5FH* E-mail revd_efisher@btinternet.com

FISHER, Eric William. b 30. Birm Univ BA53. Coll of Resurr Mirfield 70. **d** 72 **p** 73. C Styvechale *Cov* 72-75; C Chesterfield St Mary and All SS *Derby* 75-78; Chapl Buxton Hosps 78-84; TV Buxton w Burbage and King Sterndale *Derby* 78-84; R Shirland 84-89; V Sheff St Matt 89-95; rtd 95; Perm to Offic *Lich* from 95. *6 Wickstead Row, Main Road, Betley, Crewe CW3 9AB* Tel (01270) 820653

FISHER, Frank. *See* FISHER, Canon Kenneth Francis McConnell

FISHER, George Arnold. b 54. Lon Univ BD75. NOC 81. **d** 84 **p** 85. C Conisbrough *Sheff* 84-92; V Blackpool St Thos *Blackb* 92-07; Dir Par Miss *Lich* from 07; Hon C Walsall from 07. *14 Gorway Gardens, Walsall WS1 3BJ* Tel (01922) 650063 Mobile 07814-166951 E-mail george.fisher@lichfield.anglican.org

FISHER, Gordon. b 44. NW Ord Course 74. **d** 77 **p** 78. NSM Airedale w Fryston *Wakef* 77-81; C Barkisland w W Scammonden 81-84; C Ripponden 81-84; V Sutton St Mich *York* 84-87; V Marton-ln-Cleveland 87-96; R Kettering SS Pet and Paul 96-02; rtd 02. *8 Mount Pleasant Avenue, Marske-by-the-Sea, Redcar TS11 7BW* Tel (01642) 489489 E-mail rector@sspp.co.uk

FISHER, Humphrey John. b 33. Harvard Univ AB55 Ox Univ DPhil59. Heythrop Coll Lon MA. **d** 92. NSM Bryngwyn and Newchurch and Llanbedr etc *S & B* 91-06; Perm to Offic from 06. *Rose Cottage, Newchurch, Kington, Hereford HR5 3QF* Tel (01544) 370632

FISHER, Ian St John. b 59. Down Coll Cam BA80 MA84 Leic Univ PhD84. St Steph Ho Ox BA88. **d** 88 **p** 89. C Colwall w Upper Colwall and Coddington *Heref* 88-91; Chapl Surrey Univ 92-97; V Hurst *Man* 97-04; V N Shoebury *Chelmsf* from 04. *The Vicarage, 2 Weare Gifford, Shoeburyness, Southend-on-Sea SS3 8AB* Tel (01702) 584053 E-mail ian.fisher@btclick.com

FISHER, Mrs Joan. b 52. **d** 00 **p** 01. NSM Blackpool St Mark *Blackb* 00-04; NSM Blackpool St Thos 04-07; C Aldridge *Lich* from 08. *14 Gorway Gardens, Walsall WS1 3BJ* Tel (01922) 650063

FISHER, John Andrew. b 63. Bath Univ BSc85 MA97. Wycliffe Hall Ox BA93. **d** 94 **p** 95. C Rayleigh *Chelmsf* 94-98; V Burton Joyce w Bulcote and Stoke Bardolph *S'well* from 98; AD Gedling 00-05. *The Vicarage, 9 Chestnut Grove, Burton Joyce, Nottingham NG14 5DP* Tel 0115-931 2109 E-mail john.a.fisher@btinternet.com

FISHER, Canon Kenneth Francis McConnell (Frank). b 36. K Coll Lon 57. **d** 61 **p** 62. C Sheff St Geo and St Steph 61-63; Chapl Sheff Univ 64-69; Chapl Lon Univ 69-75; P-in-c Dean Carl 75-80; Soc Resp Officer 75-80; TR Melksham *Sarum* 80-90; P-in-c Stapleford *Ely* 90-01; Dioc Ecum Officer 90-01; RD Shelford 94-03; Hon Can Ely Cathl 98-06; rtd 01; P-in-c Grantchester *Ely* 01-06; Perm to Offic *B & W* from 06.

Hollybrook, Station Road, Castle Cary BA7 7BU Tel (01963) 351304 E-mail frankfisher@waitrose.com

FISHER, Mark Simon. b 52. K Coll Lon BD76 AKC76 Trin Coll Ox MA82 DPhil83. Kelham Th Coll 70 Perkins Sch of Th (USA) 76. **d** 78 **p** 78. SSF 78-80; Hon C Victoria Docks Ascension *Chelmsf* 78-79; Lic to Offic *Eur* and *Lon* 78-80; *Ox* 78-87; Chapl LMH Ox 80-86; R Glas St Matt 87-89; Hon Asst P W Derby St Jo *Liv* 97-05. *29A Rodney Street, Liverpool L1 9EH* Tel 0151-707 9748

FISHER, Mary Christine. b 43. Bris Univ BA64. LCTP 07. **d** 08 **p** 09. NSM Heaton St Barn *Bradf* from 08. *423 Toller Lane, Bradford BD9 5NN* Tel (01274) 541238

FISHER, Canon Michael Harry. b 39. Ex Univ BA61. St Steph Ho Ox 61. **d** 63 **p** 64. C Wolverhampton St Pet *Lich* 63-67; C Newquay *Truro* 67-70; V Newlyn St Pet 70-75; P-in-c Launceston St Steph w St Thos 75-82; V Carbis Bay w Lelant 82-95; V Newquay 95-99; Hon Can Truro Cathl 85-99; RD Penwith 88-93; Chapl Costa del Sol W *Eur* 99-00; rtd 00; Perm to Offic *Truro* from 00 and *Eur* from 04. *Chymedda, Southway, Windmill, Padstow PL28 8RN* Tel (01841) 521544 Mobile 07970-865049 E-mail mfisher39@aol.com

FISHER, Michael John. b 43. Leic Univ BA64 Keele Univ MA67. Qu Coll Birm 75. **d** 78 **p** 79. NSM Stafford St Mary and St Chad *Lich* 78-79; NSM Stafford from 79. *35 Newland Avenue, Stafford ST16 1NL* Tel (01785) 245069

FISHER, Nicholas. **d** 08. NSM Northleach w Hampnett and Farmington etc *Glouc* from 08. *Address temp unknown*

FISHER, Paul Vincent. b 43. Worc Coll Ox BA66 MA70 ARCM73. Qu Coll Birm. **d** 70 **p** 71. C Redditch St Steph *Worc* 70-73; C Chorlton upon Medlock *Man* 73-79; Chapl Man Univ 73-79; Exec Sec Community Affairs Division BCC 79-81; Asst Dir of Tr and Dir of Lay Tr *Carl* 81-86; P-in-c Raughton Head w Gatesgill 81-85; Lay Tr Team Ldr *S'wark* 86-90; Dir of Tr 90-94; V Kingswood 94-00; rtd 00; Perm to Offic *Bradf* from 01. *3 Buxton Park, Langcliffe, Settle BD24 9NQ* Tel (01729) 824058 E-mail paul.fisher@ukonline.co.uk

FISHER, Peter Francis Templar. b 36. CCC Cam BA60 MA. Wells Th Coll 62. **d** 63 **p** 64. C Gt Ilford St Mary *Chelmsf* 63-67; C Colchester St Mary V 67-70; C-in-c Basildon St Andr CD 70-72; P-in-c Edstaston *Lich* 83-87; P-in-c Whixall 83-87; P-in-c Tilstock 84-87; V Shelton and Oxon 87-97; rtd 97; Perm to Offic *Derby* from 07. *8 Cecil Road, Dronfield S18 2GU* Tel 0114-258 1455

FISHER, Canon Peter Timothy. b 44. Dur Univ BA68 MA75. Cuddesdon Coll 68. **d** 70 **p** 71. C Bedford St Andr *St Alb* 70-74; Chapl Surrey Univ 74-78; Sub-Warden Linc Th Coll 78-83; R Houghton le Spring *Dur* 83-94; RD Houghton 87-92; Prin Qu Coll Birm 94-02; V Maney *Birm* from 02; Hon Can Birm Cathl from 00. *The Vicarage, Maney Hill Road, Sutton Coldfield B72 1JJ* Tel 0121-354 2426

FISHER, Richard John. b 60. K Coll Lon BA82 AKC82 Selw Coll Cam BA87 MA95. Ridley Hall Cam 85. **d** 88 **p** 89. C Woodley St Jo the Ev *Ox* 88-91; C Acomb St Steph *York* 91-95; Chapl Preston Acute Hosps NHS Trust 98-02; Chapl Lancs Teaching Hosps NHS Trust 02-06; Perm to Offic *Blackb* 08-09; NSM Tarleton from 09; NSM Rufford from 09. *13 Colman Court, Broadgate, Preston PR1 8DL* Tel (01772) 464707 E-mail richardfisher@blueyonder.co.uk

FISHER, Roy Percy. b 22. SS Mark & Jo Coll Chelsea TCert50 Univ of Wales MTh00. Linc Th Coll 51. **d** 53 **p** 54. C Lewisham St Jo Southend *S'wark* 53-56; Clare Coll Miss Rotherhithe 56-59; V Boughton under Blean *Cant* 59-66; V Westgate St Sav 66-71; R Staplegrove *B & W* 71-79; TR Eckington w Handley and Ridgeway *Derby* 79-87; rtd 87; Perm to Offic *Llan* from 87. *258 New Road, Porthcawl CF36 5BA* Tel (01656) 788682

FISHER, Mrs Sheila Janet. b 50. WEMTC 01. **d** 04 **p** 05. NSM Cam w Stinchcombe *Glouc* from 04. *1 Ashmead Court, Ashmead, Cam, Dursley GL11 5EN* Tel (01453) 544656 E-mail ashmead.fishers@btinternet.com

FISHER, Simon John Plumley. b 80. St Jo Coll Dur BA01. Ripon Coll Cuddesdon BA04. **d** 05 **p** 06. C Bath Bathwick *B & W* 05-09; P-in-c Brigstock w Stanion and Lowick and Sudborough *Pet* from 09; P-in-c Weldon w Deene from 09. *The Rectory, 12 Church Street, Brigstock, Kettering NN14 3EX* Tel (01536) 373798 Mobile 07525-617067 E-mail frsimon@brigstockrectory.com

FISHER, Stephen Newson. b 46. Univ of Wales (Swansea) BSc63 CEng82 MIET82. Linc Th Coll 84. **d** 86 **p** 87. C Nunthorpe *York* 86-89; P-in-c Middlesbrough St Oswald 89-90; V 90-94; V Redcar 94-02; P-in-c The Thorntons and The Otteringtons from 02. *The Vicarage, 4 Endican Lane, Thornton le Moor, Northallerton DL7 9FB* Tel (01609) 761806 E-mail stephen@endican.gotadsl.co.uk

FISHER, Thomas Andrew. b 35. Sarum & Wells Th Coll 84. **d** 86 **p** 87. C Win Ch Ch 86-89; Chapl Salisbury Coll of Tech *Sarum* 89-94; Chapl Salisbury Coll of FE 89-94; Perm to Offic *Sarum* 94-99; rtd 00; NSM Salisbury St Mark *Sarum* from 99. *Mombasa, Manor Farm Road, Salisbury SP1 2RR* Tel (01722) 335155

FISHER, Thomas Ruggles. b 20. Cranmer Hall Dur 58. **d** 60 **p** 61. C Melton Mowbray w Thorpe Arnold *Leic* 60-63; R Husbands Bosworth 63-74; R Husbands Bosworth w Mowsley and Knaptoft etc 74-82; Perm to Offic *Leic* 82-96 and *Pet* 83-04; rtd 85. *12 The Dell, Oakham LE15 6JG* Tel (01572) 757630

FISHER-BAILEY, Mrs Carol. b 56. **d** 96 **p** 97. C Eccleshill *Bradf* 96-99; TV Sutton St Jas and Wawne *York* from 99. *Wawne Vicarage, 50 Main Street, Wawne, Hull HU7 5XH* Tel (01482) 370414 E-mail ladyvicar@googlemail.com

FISHLOCK, Christopher Douglas. b 70. Anglia Poly BA91. Oak Hill Th Coll BA06. **d** 07. C St Helen Bishopsgate w St Andr Undershaft etc *Lon* from 07. *St Helen's Church Office, Great St Helens, London EC3A 6AT* E-mail c.fishlock@st-helens.org.uk

FISHLOCK, Mrs Margaret Winifred (Peggy). b 28. Cant Sch of Min 87. **d** 97 **p** 98. NSM Deal St Leon and St Rich and Sholden *Cant* 97-04; Perm to Offic from 04. *58 Gilford Road, Deal CT14 7DQ* Tel (01304) 365841

FISHWICK, Alan. b 48. Chich Th Coll 87. **d** 89 **p** 90. C Laneside *Blackb* 89-92; C Accrington 92-93; TV 93-96; V Blackb St Aid 96-02; V Scorton and Barnacre and Calder Vale 02-05; P-in-c Coppull St Jo from 05. *St John's Vicarage, Darlington Street, Coppull, Chorley PR7 5AB* Tel (01257) 791258

FISHWICK, Mrs Ann. b 40. St Barn Coll Adelaide 91 Trin Coll Melbourne 93. **d** 91 **p** 94. Chapl Charters Towers Hosp and Home Australia 91-94; Dn Charters Towers St Paul 91-94; Asst P 94-97; Perm to Offic *Heref* 98-99; NSM Worthen 99-02; NSM Hope w Shelve 99-02; NSM Middleton 99-02; Asst P Weipa Australia 02-04; Asst P Innisfail 04-08. *217 Edward Road, Meru WA 6530, Australia* E-mail rayannf@bigpond.com

FISHWICK, Ian Norman. b 54. Lanc Univ BEd E Lon Univ MA99. **d** 82 **p** 83. C High Wycombe *Ox* 82-87; V Walshaw Ch Ch *Man* 87-93; Area Voc Adv 88-93; V W Ealing St Jo w St Jas *Lon* 93-98; Dir of Ords Willesden Area 94-98; E Region Area Co-ord for CA 98-99; Operations Dir 99-04; Par Development Adv *Ox* 05-07; Lead Org Consultant S Lon and Maudsley NHS Foundn Trust from 07. *89 Carver Hill Road, High Wycombe HP11 2UB* Tel (01494) 538775

FISHWICK, Raymond Allen. b 42. St Fran Coll Brisbane 93 N Queensland Coll of Min ACP96. **d** 91 **p** 92. P-in-c Charters Towers Australia 92-94; R 94-97; P-in-c Worthen *Heref* 98-02; P-in-c Hope w Shelve 98-02; P-in-c Middleton 98-02; P-in-c Weipa Australia 02-04; P-in-c Innisfail 04-08; CF 02-08; rtd 08. *217 Edward Road, Meru WA 6530, Australia* E-mail rfi64412@bigpond.net.au

FISKE, Paul Francis Brading. b 45. St Jo Coll Dur BA68 PhD72. Wycliffe Hall Ox 72. **d** 73 **p** 74. C Sutton *Liv* 73-76; TV Cheltenham St Mary, St Matt, St Paul and H Trin *Glouc* 76-80; C-in-c Hartplain CD *Portsm* 80-84; Hd of Miss UK CMJ 84-86; Hon C Edgware *Lon* 84-86; R Broughton Gifford, Gt Chalfield and Holt *Sarum* 86-95; TV Bourne Valley 95-97; Adv Chr Action 95-97; P-in-c Princes Risborough w Ilmer *Ox* 97-98; TR Risborough 98-08; rtd 08. *30 Elmdene Road, Kenilworth CV8 2BX* Tel (01926) 857118 E-mail paulfiske@live.co.uk

FISON, Geoffrey Robert Martius. b 34. Dur Univ BA59. Ely Th Coll 59. **d** 61 **p** 62. C Heavitree *Ex* 61-64; Australia 64-69; BSB 64-69; C Southampton Maybush St Pet *Win* 70-73; TV Strood *Roch* 73-79; TV Swindon Dorcan *Bris* 79-83; P-in-c Brislington St Cuth 83-99; rtd 99; Perm to Offic *Glouc* and *Bris* from 99. *88 Oakleaze Road, Thornbury, Bristol BS35 2LP* Tel (01454) 850678

FITCH, Capt Alan John. b 45. Open Univ BA82 Warwick Univ MA84. Wilson Carlile Coll 64 Qu Coll Birm 92. **d** 92 **p** 93. CA from 66; C Glouc St Jas and All SS 92-97; NSM Wotton St Mary 93-97; V Douglas All SS and St Thos *S & M* 97-02; Chapl HM Pris Is of Man 97-02; TR Walbrook Epiphany *Derby* 02-09; Dioc Adv on Racial Justice from 02; rtd 09. *8 The Crescent, Stanley Common, Ilkeston DE7 6GH* E-mail a.fitch@virgin.net

FITCH, Canon John Ambrose. b 22. CCC Cam BA44 MA48. Wells Th Coll 45. **d** 47 **p** 48. C Newmarket All SS *St E* 47-50; Chapl St Felix Sch Southwold 51-69; V Reydon *St E* 51-70; R Brandon and Santon Downham 70-80; Hon Can St E Cathl 75-87; RD Mildenhall 78-80; R Monks Eleigh w Chelsworth and Brent Eleigh etc 80-87; rtd 87; Perm to Offic *St E* and *Chelmsf* from 87. *The Oak House, High Street, Great Yeldham, Halstead CO9 4EX* Tel (01787) 237058

FITTER, Matthew Douglas. b 59. City of Lon Poly BSc81. Trin Coll Bris MA03. **d** 03 **p** 04. C Purley Ch Ch *S'wark* 03-07; C Beckenham Ch Ch *Roch* from 07. *5 Thornton Dene, Beckenham BR3 3ND* Tel (020) 8249 5330 E-mail matthewfitter@hotmail.com

FITZGERALD, John Edward. b 44. Leic Univ MSc98. Oak Hill Th Coll. **d** 76 **p** 77. C Rainham *Chelmsf* 76-79; C Cambridge St Andr Less *Ely* 79-86; Min Cambridge St Steph CD 79-86; V Holmesfield *Derby* 86-88; Chapl HM Pris Wakef 88-90; Whatton 90-93; Nottm 90-98; Chapl HM YOI Glen Parva 98-05; Chapl Leic Constabulary from 05. *Police Headquarters, St Johns, Leicester LE19 2BX* Tel 0116-248 2448 E-mail john.fitzgerald@leicestershire.pnn.police.uk

FITZGERALD, Miss Melanie Anne. b 52. Sheff Univ BMus75. Westcott Ho Cam 96. **d** 98 **p** 99. C Rotherham *Sheff* 98-01; C Stannington 01-02; P-in-c Walkley 02-05; V from 05. *St Mary's Vicarage, 150 Walkley Road, Sheffield S6 2XQ* Tel 0114-234 5029 E-mail mfitzg@tesco.net

FITZGERALD, Sarah. b 65. DipCOT87. St Jo Coll Nottm 06. **d** 08 **p** 09. C Folkestone Trin *Cant* from 08. *St George's Vicarage, 133 Shorncliffe Road, Folkestone CT20 3PB* Tel (01303) 248675 E-mail sarah.vicar@googlemail.com

FITZGERALD CLARK, Mrs Diane Catherine. b 54. Rhode Is Univ BA76. Gen Th Sem NY MDiv86. **d** 86 **p** 87. USA 86-95; NSM Hampstead Em W End *Lon* 96-99; Chapl St Alb High Sch for Girls from 98; Assoc Min St Alb Abbey from 98. *13 Eleanor Avenue, St Albans AL3 5TA* Tel (01727) 860099

FITZGIBBON, Kevin Peter. b 49. St Jo Coll Nottm BTh81. **d** 81 **p** 82. C Corby St Columba *Pet* 81-85; V Newborough 85-99; V Eaton Socon *St Alb* 99-07; P-in-c Christchurch and Manea and Welney *Ely* from 07; Min Consultant CPAS from 07. *The Rectory, 49 Charlemont Drive, Manea, March PE15 0GD* Tel (01354) 680969 E-mail k.fitzgibbon@care4free.net

FITZHARRIS, Barry. b 47. Lon Univ BA69 W Ontario Univ MA70 K Coll Lon BD72 AKC72. St Aug Coll Cant 72. **d** 73 **p** 74. C Whitstable All SS *Cant* 73-75; C Whitstable All SS w St Pet 75-76; Hon C Clapham Old Town *S'wark* 77-79; Asst Chapl Abp Tenison's Sch Kennington 78-84; Chapl and Hd RS 87-89; Hon C Streatham Ch Ch *S'wark* 80-84; R Radwinter w Hempstead *Chelmsf* 84-87; Hon C Streatham St Pet *S'wark* 87-89 and 97-98. *8 Holmlea Court, Chatsworth Road, Croydon CR0 1HA*

FITZHARRIS, The Ven Robert Aidan. b 46. Sheff Univ BDS71. Linc Th Coll 87. **d** 89 **p** 90. C Dinnington *Sheff* 89-92; V Bentley 92-01; RD Adwick 95-01; Hon Can Sheff Cathl 98-01; Adn Doncaster from 01. *Fairview House, 14 Armthorpe Lane, Doncaster DN2 5LZ* Tel (01302) 325787 *or* (01709) 309110 Mobile 07767-355357 Fax (01709) 309107 E-mail archdeacons.office@sheffield.anglican.org

FITZMAURICE, Arthur William John. b 65. AGSM89 Lon Inst of Educn PGCE92 Leeds Univ BA99 Heythrop Coll Lon MA04. Coll of Resurr Mirfield 97. **d** 99 **p** 00. C Spondon *Derby* 99-02; P-in-c Emscote *Cov* 02-03; TV Warwick from 03. *All Saints' Vicarage, Vicarage Fields, Warwick CV34 5NJ* Tel (01926) 492073 E-mail john@fmaurice.freeserve.co.uk

FITZPATRICK, Paul Kevin. b 60. Open Univ BA99 Univ of Wales (Lamp) MTh05 Plymouth Univ PGCE07. Cuddesdon Coll 96. **d** 98 **p** 99. C Okehampton w Inwardleigh, Bratton Clovelly etc *Ex* 98-02; P-in-c Whipton 02-04; V 04-07; RD Christianity 05-06; Chapl Univ of Wales Inst Cardiff *Llan* from 07. *The Student Centre, UWIC, Western Avenue, Cardiff CF5 2YB* Tel (029) 2041 7252

FITZPATRICK, Victor Robert Andrew. b 75. Milltown Inst Dub BA00 Pontifical Univ Maynooth BD03 Cant Ch Ch Univ MA04. CITC 08. **d** 03 **p** 04. Chapl Cork Univ Hosp 03; C Bray *D & G* 04-07; C Dublin St Ann and St Steph from 09. *The Curatage, St Ann's Parish Centre, Molesworth Place, Dublin 2, Republic of Ireland* Tel (00353) (1) 676 8111 Mobile 86-397 4035 E-mail prayspot@live.ie

FITZSIMONS, Canon Kathryn Anne. b 57. Bedf Coll of Educn CertEd78. NEOC 87. **d** 90. NSM Bilton *Ripon* 90-01; Soc Resp Development Officer Richmond Adnry 02-09; Urban Min Officer from 99; Hon Can Ripon Cathl from 04. *52 Newton Court, Leeds LS8 2PM* Tel 0113-248 5011 E-mail kathrynfitzsimons@hotmail.com

FLACH (*née* ROLLINS), Canon Deborah Mary Rollins. b 54. Sarum & Wells Th Coll 88. **d** 94 **p** 97. C Chantilly *Eur* 94-96; C Maisons-Laffitte 96-04; Asst Chapl 04-07; P-in-c Lille from 07; Can Gib Cathl from 07. *Christ Church, 14 rue Lyderic, 59000 Lille, France* Tel and fax (0033) (3) 28 52 66 36 E-mail debbieflach@gmail.com

FLACK, Miss Heather Margaret. b 47. **d** 95 **p** 96. C Shenley Green *Birm* 95-00; TV Kings Norton 00-07; rtd 07; Perm to Offic *Birm* from 07. *23 Stourport Road, Bewdley DY12 1BB*

FLACK, The Rt Revd John Robert. b 42. Leeds Univ BA64. Coll of Resurr Mirfield 64. **d** 66 **p** 67 **c** 97. C Armley St Bart *Ripon* 66-69; C Northampton St Mary *Pet* 69-72; V Chapelthorpe *Wakef* 72-81; V Ripponden and Barkisland w W Scammonden 81-85; Chapl Rishworth Sch Ripponden 81-85; V Brighouse *Wakef* 85-88; TR Brighouse St Martin 88-92; RD Brighouse and Elland 86-92; Hon Can Wakef Cathl 89-92; Adn Pontefract 92-97; Suff Bp Huntingdon and Hon Can Ely Cathl 97-03; Abp's Rep H See and Dir Angl Cen Rome 03-08; P-in-c Nassington w Yarwell and Woodnewton w Apethorpe *Pet* from 08; Hon Asst Bp Pet and Eur from 03; Can Pet Cathl from 04. *The Vicarage, 34 Station Road, Nassington, Peterborough PE8 6QB* Tel (01780) 782271 E-mail johnrobertflack@hotmail.com

FLAGG, David Michael. b 50. CCC Cam BA71 MA75. St Jo Coll Nottm BA76. **d** 77 **p** 78. C Hollington St Leon *Chich* 77-80; C Woodley St Jo the Ev *Ox* 80-86; Chapl The Dorothy Kerin Trust Burrswood 86-94; R Knockholt w Halstead *Roch* 94-99; Dir Chapl Services Mildmay UK 99-02; Hd Chapl Services Qu Eliz Hosp NHS Trust from 02. *Queen Elizabeth Hospital, Stadium Road, London SE18 4QH* Tel (020) 8836 6831 *or* 8836 6000 bleep 370 E-mail david.flagg@nhs.net

FLAHERTY, Jane Venitia. *See* ANDERSON, Mrs Jane Venitia

FLAHERTY, Ms Mandy Carol. b 63. Ches Coll of HE BA86 Leic Univ PGCE87. St Jo Coll Nottm MTh04. **d** 04 **p** 05. C Oadby *Leic* 04-08; Perm to Offic *Ely* from 09. *15 Highfield Avenue, Alconbury Weston, Huntingdon PE28 4JS*

FLANAGAN, Kevin Joseph. b 60. Middx Poly BA87 Newman Coll Birm PGCE80. St Jo Coll Nottm 04. **d** 06 **p** 07. C Allesley Park and Whoberley *Cov* from 06. *14 Harewood Road, Coventry CV5 8BQ* Tel (024) 7667 6839 E-mail kevandjayne@yahoo.co.uk

FLANAGAN, Miss Vivienne Lesley. b 66. Liv Poly BA89 Nottm Univ PGCE98. St Jo Coll Nottm MA98. **d** 98 **p** 99. C Huthwaite *S'well* 98-02; P-in-c Lenton Abbey 02-08; Chapl Bp Bell Sch from 08. *Bishop Bell Church of England School, 16 Priory Road, Eastbourne BN23 7EJ* Tel (01323) 465400 E-mail vflanagan@bishopbell.e-sussex.sch.uk

FLATHER, Peter George. b 29. Sarum Th Coll. **d** 59 **p** 60. C Fordingbridge w Ibsley *Win* 59-63; C Lyndhurst 63-65; R E w W Bradenham *Nor* 65-72; P-in-c Speke All SS *Liv* 72-73; R Gunthorpe w Bale *Nor* 73-87; P-in-c Sharrington 73-87; P-in-c Gt w Lt Snoring 77-83; R Gunthorpe w Bale w Field Dalling, Saxlingham etc 87-89; rtd 89; Perm to Offic *Nor* 89-99. *9 Lloyd Court, High Kelling, Holt NR25 6AE* Tel (01263) 713936

FLATT, Canon Roy Francis Ferguson. b 47. Edin Th Coll 78. **d** 80 **p** 81. C St Andrews St Andr *St And* 80-82; C Elie and Earlsferry 80-82; C Pittenweem 80-82; Dioc Supernumerary 82-83; Dioc Sec *Arg* 83-87; Dioc Youth Chapl 83-94; R Lochgilphead from 83; R Kilmartin from 83; P-in-c Inveraray from 83; Dean Arg 99-05; Hon Can St Jo Cathl Oban from 06. *Bishopton House, Bishopton Road, Lochgilphead PA31 8PY* Tel (01546) 602315 Fax 602519 Mobile 07775-852115 E-mail lochgilphead@argyll.anglican.org

FLATT, Stephen Joseph. b 57. SRN79 RSCN81. Sarum & Wells Th Coll 92. **d** 92 **p** 93. C Limpsfield and Titsey *S'wark* 92-96; TV Pewsey *Sarum* 96-97; Staff Nurse R Free Hampstead NHS Trust 97-99; Charge Nurse 99-00; Asst Chapl Univ Coll Lon Hosps NHS Trust 00-01; Chapl 01-03; Perm to Offic *S'wark* 98-99; NSM Clapham H Trin and St Pet 99-02; Lead Chapl St Mary's NHS Trust Paddington from 03. *Chaplain's Office, St Mary's Hospital, Praed Street, London W2 1NY* Tel (020) 7886 1508 E-mail stephen.flatt@st-marys.nhs.uk

FLATTERS, Clive Andrew. b 56. Sarum & Wells Th Coll 83. **d** 86 **p** 88. C Weston Favell *Pet* 86-87; C Old Brumby *Linc* 88-91; C Syston *Leic* 91-93; TV 93-99; V Knottingley *Wakef* 99-02; TR Knottingley and Kellington w Whitley from 02. *The Vicarage, Chapel Street, Knottingley WF11 9AN* Tel (01977) 672267

FLAVELL, Paul William Deran. b 44. St Mich Coll Llan 67. **d** 68 **p** 69. C W Cairns Australia 68-71; C Blaenavon w Capel Newydd *Mon* 71-74; V Ynysddu 74-84; R Llanaber w Caerdeon *Ban* 84-00; V Llanstadwel *St D* from 00. *The Vicarage, 68 Church Road, Llanstadwel, Milford Haven SA73 1EB* Tel (01646) 600227

FLEET, Daniel James Russell. b 60. Wye Coll Lon BSc84 Keele Univ PGCE02. St Jo Coll Nottm 86. **d** 89 **p** 90. C Boldmere *Birm* 89-92; C Caverswall and Weston Coyney w Dilhorne *Lich* 92-95; V Alton w Bradley-le-Moors and Oakamoor w Cotton 95-01; rtd 01; Perm to Offic *Lich* from 01. *124 Byrds Lane, Uttoxeter ST14 7NB* Tel (01889) 560214 E-mail byrdfleet@tiscali.co.uk

FLEMING (*formerly* LOOKER), Miss Clare Margaret. b 55. Liv Univ CertEd78. Westcott Ho Cam 85. **d** 87 **p** 02. Par Dn Prestwood and Gt Hampden *Ox* 87-90; Hon C Olney w Emberton 90-92; Hon C Blunham, Gt Barford, Roxton and Tempsford etc *St Alb* 01-03; P-in-c Welford w Sibbertoft and Marston Trussell *Pet* 03-04; Perm to Offic *St Alb* 04-05; Hon C Wilden w Colmworth and Ravensden 05-08. *17 Crosshall Road, Eaton Ford, St Neots PE19 7AA*

FLEMING, The Ven David. b 37. Kelham Th Coll 58. **d** 63 **p** 64. C Walton St Marg Belmont Road *Liv* 63-67; Chapl HM Borstal Gaynes Hall 68-76; V Gt Staughton *Ely* 68-76; RD St Neots 72-76; V Whittlesey 76-85; RD March 77-82; Hon Can Ely Cathl 82-01; P-in-c Ponds Bridge 83-85; Adn Wisbech 84-93; V Wisbech St Mary 85-89; Chapl Gen of Pris 93-01; Chapl to The Queen 95-07; Perm to Offic *Ely* from 01. *Fair Haven, 123 Wisbech Road, Littleport, Ely CB6 1JJ* Tel (01353) 862498

FLEMING, Elizabeth Julie. b 57. Westhill Coll Birm CertEd79 Ches Coll of HE BTh00. NOC 97. **d** 00 **p** 01. C Widnes St Jo *Liv* 00-03; P-in-c Walton Breck Ch Ch 03-04; V Walton Breck 04-08; V Becontree St Mary *Chelmsf* from 08. *The Vicarage, 191 Valence Wood Road, Dagenham RM8 3AH* Tel (020) 8592 2822 E-mail jooolz57@hotmail.com

FLEMING, George. b 39. CITC. **d** 78 **p** 79. C Donaghcloney w Waringstown *D & D* 78-80; C Newtownards 80; I Movilla 80; C Heref St Pet w St Owen and St Jas 80-85; V Holmer w Huntington 85-96; P-in-c Worfield 96-98; V 98-04; rtd 04; Perm to Offic *Truro* 05-08. *The Vicarage, South Marston, Swindon SN3 4SR* Tel (01793) 827021

FLEMING, Mrs Kathryn Claire. b 60. Trin Coll Cam BA82 MA91 Montessori TDip92. WEMTC 01. **d** 04 **p** 05. C Charlton Kings St Mary *Glouc* 04-08; P-in-c Cainscross w Selsley from 08. *The Vicarage, 58 Cashes Green Road, Stroud GL5 4RA* Tel (01453) 750949 Mobile 07775-630922 E-mail revkathryn@googlemail.com

FLEMING, Mrs Penelope Rawling. b 43. Glas Univ MA63. Westcott Ho Cam 87. **d** 89 **p** 94. C Bourne *Guildf* 89-94; R Wotton and Holmbury St Mary 94-01; RD Dorking 99-01; Dioc Voc Adv 94-01; R Gt Bookham 01-07; rtd 07. *Westrip Farm House, Redhouse Lane, Westrip, Stroud GL6 6HA* Tel (01453) 757296 E-mail pennyflem@aol.com

FLEMING, Ronald Thorpe. b 29. Codrington Coll Barbados 52. **d** 56 **p** 57. Barbados 56-61; C Delaval *Newc* 61-64; V Cambois 64-69; V Ancroft w Scremerston 69-81; V Tartaghan 81-84; Chapl Preston Hosp N Shields 84-94; Chapl N Tyneside Hosps 84-94; rtd 94; Perm to Offic *Newc* 94-04; Lic to Offic *Mor* from 04. *49 Woodside Drive, Forres IV36 2UF* Tel (01309) 671101

FLEMING, Victoria Rosalie. b 58. WEMTC 01. **d** 04 **p** 05. NSM St Breoke and Egloshayle *Truro* 04-08; TV Stratton St Margaret w S Marston etc *Bris* from 08. *The Vicarage, South Marston, Swindon SN3 4SR* Tel (01793) 827021 E-mail revs.fleming@tiscali.co.uk

FLEMING, William Edward Charlton. b 29. TCD BA51 MA65. CITC 52. **d** 52 **p** 53. C Dublin Santry *D & G* 52-56; C Arm St Mark 56-61; I Tartaraghan 61-80; Prov Registrar 79-96; I Tartaraghan w Diamond 80-96; Can Arm Cathl 86-96; Treas Arm Cathl 88-92; Chan Arm Cathl 92-96; rtd 96. *65 Annareagh Road, Drumorgan, Richhill, Armagh BT61 9JT* Tel (028) 3887 9612

FLENLEY, Benjamin Robert Glanville. b 50. Sarum & Wells Th Coll 86. **d** 88 **p** 89. C Eastleigh *Win* 88-92; V Micheldever and E Stratton, Woodmancote etc 92-03; R Bentworth, Lasham, Medstead and Shalden from 03. *The Rectory, Bentworth, Alton GU34 5RB* Tel and fax (01420) 563218 E-mail flenbenley@aol.com

FLETCHER, Mrs Angela. b 59. EMMTC 04. **d** 07 **p** 08. C Edwinstowe *S'well* from 07; C Perlethorpe from 07. *46 Occupation Lane, Edwinstowe, Mansfield NG21 9HU* Tel (01623) 820274 E-mail angela_fletcher43@hotmail.com

FLETCHER, Anthony. *See* FLETCHER, James Anthony

FLETCHER, Anthony Peter Reeves. b 46. Bede Coll Dur CertEd Nottm Univ BTh78. Ridley Hall Cam 71. **d** 74 **p** 75. C Luton St Mary *St Alb* 74-78; Chapl RAF 78-00; P-in-c Lyneham w Bradenstoke *Sarum* 98-99; P-in-c Kyrenia St Andr and Chapl N Cyprus 00-04; P-in-c Lyneham w Bradenstoke *Sarum* 04-07; rtd 07. *Glentworth House, Giles Avenue, Cricklade, Swindon SN6 6HS* Tel (01793) 751333

FLETCHER, Barbara. b 41. ALAM79. WMMTC 93. **d** 96 **p** 97. NSM Smethwick *Birm* 96-97; C 97-02; rtd 02; Perm to Offic *Birm* from 02. *231 Abbey Road, Smethwick B67 5NN* Tel 0121-429 9354

FLETCHER, Bryce Clifford. ACIB. Cranmer Hall Dur. **d** 08 **p** 09. NSM Arle Valley *Win* from 08. *Robinia House, 23 Rosebery Road, Alresford SO24 9HQ*

FLETCHER, Colin John. b 46. Chich Th Coll. **d** 83 **p** 84. C Lt Ilford St Mich *Chelmsf* 83-86; C Hockerill *St Alb* 86-89; V New Cantley *Sheff* 89-95; C Kenton *Lon* 95-01; C Heavitree w Ex St Paul 01-02; C Heavitree and St Mary Steps 02-09; C Exwick 05-09; rtd 09. *8 Belvedere Court, High Street, Dawlish EX7 9ST* E-mail abcon@kenton62.freeserve.co.uk

✠**FLETCHER, The Rt Revd Colin William.** b 50. OBE00. Trin Coll Ox BA72 MA76. Wycliffe Hall Ox 72. **d** 75 **p** 76 **c** 00. C Shipley St Pet *Bradf* 75-79; Tutor Wycliffe Hall Ox 79-84; Hon C Ox St Andr 79-84; V Margate H Trin *Cant* 84-93; RD Thanet 88-93; Abp's Chapl 93-00; Hon Can Dallas from 93; Area Bp Dorchester *Ox* from 00. *Arran House, Sandy Lane, Yarnton, Kidlington OX5 1PB* Tel (01865) 375541 Fax 379890 E-mail bishopdorchester@oxford.anglican.org

FLETCHER, David Clare Molyneux. b 32. Worc Coll Ox BA55 MA59. Wycliffe Hall Ox 56. **d** 58 **p** 59. C Islington St Mary *Lon* 58-62; Hon C 62-83; Field Worker Scripture Union 62-86; R Ox St Ebbe w H Trin and St Pet 86-98; rtd 98; Perm to Offic *Ox* from 06. *32 Linkside Avenue, Oxford OX2 8JB* Tel (01865) 552420

FLETCHER, David Ernest. b 53. Worc Coll of Educn BEd76 Open Univ MTh01. St Jo Coll Nottm 99. **d** 01 **p** 02. C Mixenden *Wakef* 01-04; P-in-c from 04; Dioc Urban Officer from 08. *37 Hops Lane, Halifax HX3 5FB* Tel (01422) 349844 Mobile 07702-385885 E-mail de.fletcher@btopenworld.com

FLETCHER, David Mark. b 56. Chich Th Coll 84. **d** 87 **p** 88. C Taunton St Andr *B & W* 87-91; P-in-c Chard, Furnham w Chaffcombe, Knowle St Giles etc 91-95; P-in-c Tiverton St Andr *Ex* from 95; RD Tiverton from 02; Chapl Mid Devon Primary Care Trust from 95. *St Andrew's Vicarage, Blackmore Road, Tiverton EX16 4AR* Tel (01884) 257865 E-mail dj.fletcher@tiscali.co.uk

FLETCHER, Douglas. b 40. Coll of Resurr Mirfield 67. **d** 68 **p** 69. C Notting Hill St Jo *Lon* 68-73; C Cambridge St Mary Less *Ely*

73-74; C Fulham St Jo Walham Green *Lon* 74-76; C Walham Green St Jo w St Jas 76-84; P-in-c Kensal Town St Thos w St Andr and St Phil 84-92; V 92-06; rtd 06; Perm to Offic *Lon* from 07. *68 Clarendon Road, London W11 2HW* Tel (020) 7229 8146

FLETCHER, Capt Frank. b 40. Wilson Carlile Coll 71 EAMTC 94. **d** 96 **p** 96. Asst Chapl HM Pris Highpoint 90-97; Chapl HM Pris Wealstun 97-05; rtd 05; Perm to Offic *York* from 05. *6 Kingsclere, Huntington, York YO32 9SF*

FLETCHER, Gordon Wolfe (Robin). b 31. Edin Th Coll. **d** 62 **p** 63. C Eston *York* 62-65; C Harton Colliery *Dur* 65-68; V Pelton 68-81; V Ryhope 81-96; rtd 96. *23 Swinburne Road, Darlington DL3 7TD* Tel (01325) 265994 E-mail gordon.fletcher@btinternet.com

FLETCHER, James Anthony. b 36. St Edm Hall Ox BA60 MA66. St Steph Ho Ox 60. **d** 62 **p** 63. C Streatham St Pet *S'wark* 62-65; C Hobs Moat CD *Birm* 65-68; C Cowley St Jo *Ox* 68-77; V Hanworth All SS *Lon* 77-02; P-in-c Hanworth St Geo 89-91; rtd 02; Perm to Offic *Cant* from 02. *19 Strand Street, Sandwich, Kent CT13 9OX* Tel (01304) 620506

FLETCHER, James Arthur. b 71. Reading Univ BA99. Trin Coll Bris 03. **d** 05 **p** 06. C Bexleyheath Ch Ch *Roch* 05-08; R Fawkham and Hartley from 08. *The Rectory, 3 St John's Lane, Hartley, Longfield DA3 8ET* Tel (01474) 703819 E-mail rector@fawkhamandhartley.org.uk

FLETCHER, James John Gareth. b 79. Aber Univ MA02 Cam Univ BA08. Ridley Hall Cam 06. **d** 09. C Tooting Graveney St Nic *S'wark* from 09. *48 Ashvale Road, London SW17 8PW* Tel 07880-552660 (mobile) E-mail james.fletcher@cantab.net

FLETCHER, Miss Janet. b 59. Lanc Univ MA07. Cranmer Hall Dur. **d** 00 **p** 01. C Ainsdale *Liv* 00-04; TV Walton-on-the-Hill from 04; Hon Chapl Liv Cathl from 04. *St Nathanael's Vicarage, 65 Fazakerley Road, Liverpool L9 2AJ* Tel 0151-525 7720 E-mail jan.f.nathanael@btinternet.com

FLETCHER, Canon Jeremy James. b 60. Dur Univ BA81. St Jo Coll Nottm 85. **d** 88 **p** 89. C Stranton *Dur* 88-91; C Nottingham St Nic *S'well* 91-94; P-in-c Skegby 94-00; P-in-c Teversal 96-00; Bp's Dom Chapl 00-02; Can Res and Prec York Minster 02-09; V Beverley Minster from 09; P-in-c Routh from 09. *The Minster Vicarage, Highgate, Beverley HU17 0DN* Tel (01482) 868540 E-mail jeremyf@tiscali.co.uk

FLETCHER, Canon John Alan Alfred. b 33. Oak Hill Th Coll 58. **d** 61 **p** 62. C Erith St Paul *Roch* 61-64; C Rushden *Pet* 64-67; R Hollington St Leon *Chich* 67-86; V Chadwell Heath *Chelmsf* 86-00; RD Barking and Dagenham 91-00; Chapl Chadwell Heath Hosp Romford 86-93; Chapl Redbridge Health Care NHS Trust 93-00; Hon Can Chelmsf Cathl 99-00; rtd 00; Perm to Offic *Chich* from 01. *87 Hoads Wood Road, Hastings TN34 2BB* Tel (01424) 712345 Mobile 07860-128912 E-mail jaaf@btinternet.com

FLETCHER, Jonathan James Molyneux. b 42. Hertf Coll Ox BA66 MA68. Wycliffe Hall Ox 66. **d** 68 **p** 69. C Enfield Ch Ch Trent Park *Lon* 68-72; C Cambridge St Sepulchre *Ely* 72-76; St Helen Bishopsgate w St Martin Outwich *Lon* 76-81; Min Wimbledon Em Ridgway Prop Chpl *S'wark* from 82. *Emmanuel Parsonage, 8 Sheep Walk Mews, London SW19 4QL* Tel (020) 8946 4728

FLETCHER, Keith. b 47. Chich Th Coll 79. **d** 80 **p** 81. C Hartlepool St Paul *Dur* 80-82; V Eighton Banks 82-85; V Haydon Bridge *Newc* 85-96; P-in-c Beltingham w Henshaw 93-96; R Ashmanhaugh, Barton Turf etc *Nor* 96-99; rtd 99. *2 Churchill Terrace, Sherburn Hill, Durham DH6 1PF* Tel 0191-372 0362

FLETCHER, Ms Linda. b 72. Man Univ BA93. Trin Coll Bris BA09. **d** 09. C Coulsdon St Jo *S'wark* from 09. *8 Waddington Avenue, Coulsdon CR5 1QE* Tel 07852-911598 (mobile) E-mail lindaandarun@tiscali.co.uk

FLETCHER, Linden Elisabeth. b 50. Lon Univ BEd73 MA80. St Jo Coll Nottm 87. **d** 89 **p** 94. C Fakenham w Alethorpe *Nor* 89-93; C Cumnor *Ox* 93-02; P-in-c Ringshall w Battisford, Barking w Darmsden etc *St E* 02-08; P-in-c Somersham w Flowton and Offton w Willisham 02-08; V Llanfair Caereinion, Llanllugan and Manafon *St As* from 08. *5 Lon Cafnant, Llanfair Caereinion, Welshpool SY21 0RA* Tel (01938) 811232

FLETCHER, Mrs Margaret. b 44. **d** 04 **p** 05. NSM Thurstaston *Ches* 04-07; V Thornton-le-Moors w Ince and Elton from 07. *The Vicarage, Ince Lane, Elton, Chester CH2 4QB* Tel (01928) 724028

FLETCHER, Mark. b 72. Staffs Poly BSc93. Oak Hill Th Coll BA00. **d** 00 **p** 01. C Paddington Em Harrow Road *Lon* 00-03; C W Kilburn St Luke w St Simon and St Jude 00-03; C Barnsbury from 04. *43 Matilda Street, London N1 0LA* Tel (020) 7278 5208 E-mail mark@midwinter.org.uk

FLETCHER, Martin. b 60. Bradf Univ BEng83 CEng MIMechE. Ripon Coll Cuddesdon. **d** 00 **p** 01. C Oatlands *Guildf* 00-04; R Tolleshunt Knights w Tiptree and Gt Braxted *Chelmsf* from 04. *The Rectory, Rectory Road, Tiptree, Colchester CO5 0SX* Tel (01621) 815260 E-mail fletcher_martin@yahoo.co.uk

FLETCHER, Maurice. *See* FLETCHER, Ralph Henry Maurice

FLETCHER, Mrs Patricia. b 34. K Alfred's Coll Win CertEd74. Chich Th Coll 94. **d** 94. NSM Droxford *Portsm* 94-97; NSM Meonstoke w Corhampton cum Exton 94-97; Perm to Offic 97-00; NSM Blendworth w Chalton w Idsworth 00-04; rtd 04; Perm to Offic *Portsm* from 04. *17 Maylings Farm Road, Fareham PO16 7QU* Tel (01329) 311489 E-mail patfletch2004@yahoo.co.uk

FLETCHER, Paul Gordon MacGregor. b 61. St Andr Univ MTheol84. Edin Th Coll 84. **d** 86 **p** 87. C Cumbernauld *Glas* 86-89; C-in-c Glas H Cross 89-93; P-in-c Milngavie 93-99; R Clarkston 99-07; Lic to Offic *Arg* from 08. *Corriecravie Moor Farm, Sliddery, Isle of Arran KA27 8PE* Tel (01770) 870234 E-mail paulmcgregorfletcher@hotmail.com

FLETCHER, Ralph Henry Maurice. b 43. St Luke's Coll Ex CertEd65. St Steph Ho Ox 71. **d** 74 **p** 75. C Chislehurst Annunciation *Roch* 74-77; Chapl Quainton Hall Sch Harrow 77-87 and 94-00; Hon C Hillingdon All SS *Lon* 87-94; Perm to Offic *Lon* 94-00; *Roch* 00-02; *Wakef* from 05. *6 Joseph Court, Joseph Street, Barnsley S70 1LJ* Tel (01226) 779928

FLETCHER, Robert Alexander. b 52. Ridley Hall Cam. **d** 84 **p** 85. C Churchill St Peter *Ox* 84-88; C Bushey *St Alb* 88-93; TV Digswell and Panshanger 93-00; P-in-c Aldenham 00-05; TV Aldenham, Radlett and Shenley from 05. *The Vicarage, Church Lane, Aldenham, Watford WD25 8BE* Tel and fax (01923) 854209 E-mail r.a.fletcher@btinternet.com

FLETCHER, Robin. *See* FLETCHER, Gordon Wolfe

FLETCHER, Canon Robin Geoffrey. b 32. Nottm Univ BA57. Ridley Hall Cam 57. **d** 59 **p** 60. C S Mimms Ch Ch *Lon* 59-64; V Wollaton Park *S'well* 64-71; V Clifton *York* 71-97; Chapl Clifton Hosp York 71-88; RD City of York 86-97; Can and Preb York Minster 89-00; rtd 98; Perm to Offic *York* from 00 and *Wakef* from 04. *14 South Avenue, Fartown, Huddersfield HD2 1BY* Tel (01484) 510266 E-mail rgfletcher@tiscali.co.uk

FLETCHER, Mrs Sheila Elizabeth. b 35. Nottm Univ BA57 CertEd58. NEOC 84. **d** 87 **p** 94. NSM Dringhouses 87-90; Par Dn 90-94; C 94-97; P-in-c Sutton on the Forest 97-02; rtd 02; Perm to Offic *York* from 02. *68 Huntsman's Walk, York YO24 3LA* Tel (01904) 796876 E-mail rgeoff@soo.co.uk

FLETCHER, Stephen. b 57. Man Univ BA79 MA84. St Jo Coll Nottm 82. **d** 84 **p** 85. C Didsbury St Jas and Em *Man* 84-88; R Kersal Moor 88-01; TR Horwich and Rivington from 01. *The Rectory, Chorley Old Road, Horwich, Bolton BL6 6AX* Tel and fax (01204) 468263 E-mail stephen@fletchers.freeserve.co.uk

FLETCHER, Stephen William. b 62. Wolv Poly BA84. Qu Coll Birm 85. **d** 88 **p** 89. C Rainham *Roch* 88-91; C Shottery St Andr *Cov* 91-97; Min Bishopton St Pet 91-97; V Llanrumney *Mon* 97-02; V Adderbury w Milton *Ox* from 02. *11 Walton Avenue, Adderbury, Banbury OX17 3JY*

FLETCHER, Timothy John. b 63. Sheff Univ BA88 St Jo Coll Dur MA04. Cranmer Hall Dur 01. **d** 03 **p** 04. C Four Marks *Win* 03-06; V Walton le Soken *Chelmsf* from 06. *The Vicarage, Martello Road, Walton on the Naze CO14 8BP* Tel (01255) 675452 E-mail tim@fletcherchester.fsnet.co.uk

FLEWKER, David William. b 53. Birm Univ BA75. Wycliffe Hall Ox 76. **d** 78 **p** 79. C Netherton *Liv* 78-82; C Prescot 82-84; V Seaforth 84-88; TV Whitstable *Cant* 88-96; Miss to Seamen 88-96; V Bethersden w High Halden *Cant* 96-08; Asst Dir of Ords 02-06; P in c Deal St Leon w St Rich and Sholden etc from 08. *St Leonard's Rectory, Addelam Road, Deal CT14 9BZ* Tel (01304) 374076 E-mail d.flewker@btinternet.com

FLEWKER-BARKER, Miss Linda. b 68. Redcliffe Coll BA02 St Jo Coll Dur MA04. Cranmer Hall Dur 02. **d** 04 **p** 05. C Cheltenham Ch Ch *Glouc* 04-07; Chapl RAF from 07. *Chaplaincy Services, Valiant Block, HQ Air Command, RAF High Wycombe HP14 4UE* Tel (01494) 496800 Fax 496343 E-mail lindafbarker@yahoo.com

FLIGHT, Michael John. b 41. Sarum Th Coll 68. **d** 71 **p** 72. C Wimborne Minster *Sarum* 71-75; R Tarrant Gunville, Tarrant Hinton etc 75-78; P-in-c Tarrant Rushton, Tarrant Rawston etc 77-78; R Tarrant Valley 78-80; V Westbury 80-00; RD Heytesbury 83-87 and 96-00; R Broad Town, Clyffe Pypard, Hilmarton etc 00-07; RD Calne 03-06; rtd 07. *11 Nursteed Close, Devizes SN10 3EU* Tel (01380) 738493 E-mail flightvic@aol.com

FLINN, Canon John Robert Patrick. b 30. CITC. **d** 65 **p** 66. C Dublin Rathfarnham *D & G* 65-67; I Baltinglass w Ballynure etc *C & O* 67-76; I Castlepollard and Oldcastle w Loughcrew etc *M & K* 76-84; rtd 84; Treas Ossory and Leighlin Cathls 90-92; Chan Ossory and Leighlin Cathls 96-01. *The Old School House, Kells, Co Kilkenny, Republic of Ireland* Tel (00353) (56) 772 8297

FLINT, Howard Michael. b 59. Edge Hill Coll of HE BEd81. Cranmer Hall Dur 95. **d** 97 **p** 98. C Chipping Campden w Ebrington *Glouc* 97-00; V Upper Wreake *Leic* 00-06; RD Framland 02-06; V Tunbridge Wells H Trin w Ch Ch *Roch* from 06. *The Vicarage, 63 Claremont Road, Tunbridge Wells TN1 11E* Tel (01892) 526644 *or* 522323 Fax 529100 E-mail rev4howard@hotmail.com

FLINT, Nicholas Angus. b 60. Chich Th Coll 84. **d** 87 **p** 88. C Aldwick *Chich* 87-91; Bp's Asst Chapl for the Homeless *Lon* 91-92; TV Ifield *Chich* 92-96; R Rusper w Colgate from 96. *The Rectory, High Street, Rusper, Horsham RH12 4PX* Tel (01293) 871251 E-mail nick.flint@totalise.co.uk

FLINT, Toby. b 76. Wycliffe Hall Ox BA08. **d** 08 **p** 09. C Brompton H Trin w Onslow Square St Paul *Lon* from 08. *Holy Trinity Brompton, Brompton Road, London SW7 1JA* Tel 08456-447533 E-mail tobyflint@hotmail.co.uk

FLINTHAM, Alan Jenkinson. b 45. Leeds Univ BSc66 PGCE67 MEd74. EMMTC 98. **d** 00 **p** 01. NSM Melbourne *Derby* from 00. *50 Burlington Way, Mickleover, Derby DE3 9BD* Tel (01332) 512293 E-mail flintham@flinthams.org.uk

FLINTOFT, Ian Hugh. b 74. Pemb Coll Cam BA97 MA99 MPhil98. Westcott Ho Cam 01. **d** 04 **p** 05. C Newc St Geo 04-06; C Newc St Geo and St Hilda 06-07; C Ch the King 07-08; TV from 08. *North Gosforth Vicarage, West View, Wideopen, Newcastle upon Tyne NE13 6NH* Tel 0191-236 2280 E-mail ianflintoft@hotmail.com

FLINTOFT-CHAPMAN, Margaret. *See* CHAPMAN, Mrs Margaret

FLINTOFT-CHAPMAN, Mrs Margaret. b 47. Leeds Univ BA68. NTMTC 03. **d** 05 **p** 06. NSM Barkingside St Cedd *Chelmsf* from 05. *84 Roding Lane North, Woodford Green IG8 8NG* Tel (020) 8504 6750

FLIPPANCE, Kim Sheelagh May. *See* STEPHENS, Mrs Kim Sheelagh May

FLIPSE, Miss Adriana Maria (Marja). b 82. Leiden Univ MA05. St Mich Coll Llan 07. **d** 08 **p** 09. C Roath *Llan* from 08. *3 Snipe Street, Cardiff CF24 3RB* Tel (029) 2049 3940 E-mail marjaflipse@btinternet.com

FLOATE, Herbert Frederick Giraud. b 25. Keble Coll Ox BA50 MA54. Qu Coll Birm 50. **d** 61 **p** 62. Seychelles 61; Hon C Quarrington w Old Sleaford *Linc* 63-65; P-in-c Mareham le Fen 65-66; Australia 66-72; R Stroxton *Linc* 72-74; R Harlaxton w Wyville and Hungerton 72-74; Lect Shenston New Coll Worcs 74-78; P-in-c Redditch St Geo *Worc* 78-79; Lic to Offic 80-84; R Upton Snodsbury and Broughton Hackett etc 84-89; Chapl Mojcar *Eur* 89-91; rtd 91; Perm to Offic *Heref* from 97. *15 Progress Close, Ledbury HR8 2QZ* Tel (01531) 635509

FLOATE, Miss Rhona Cameron. b 59. Univ of Wales (Cardiff) BA80. Trin Coll Bris 01. **d** 03 **p** 04. C Lighthorne *Cov* 03-07; C Chesterton 03-07; C Newbold Pacey w Moreton Morrell 03-07; P-in-c Wool and E Stoke *Sarum* from 07. *The Vicarage, Vicarage Close, Wool, Wareham BH20 6EB* Tel (01929) 462215 E-mail vicar@holyroodwool.org.uk

FLOCKHART, Mrs Ruth. b 56. TISEC 96. **d** 99 **p** 00. NSM Strathpeffer *Mor* from 99; NSM Dingwall from 99. *Kilmuir Farm Cottage, North Kessock, Inverness IV1 3ZG* Tel (01463) 731580 E-mail kilmuirseabreeze@btinternet.com

FLOOD, Mrs Jean Anne. b 51. Liv Hope Univ MEd00 Liv Univ CertEd95. NOC 06. **d** 08. NSM Fazakerley Em *Liv* from 08. *19 Palm Close, Liverpool L9 1JD* Tel 0151-525 0304 E-mail floods@merseymail.com

FLOOD, Kenneth. b 75. St Chad's Coll Dur BSc96. St Steph Ho Ox BTh01. **d** 01 **p** 02. C Hulme Ascension *Man* 01-05; C Wokingham St Paul *Ox* 05-08; P-in-c Chorlton-cum-Hardy St Clem *Man* from 08. *The Rectory, 6 Edge Lane, Manchester M21 9JF* Tel 0161-881 3063 E-mail ken@mightyflood.org.uk

FLOOD, Nicholas Roger. b 47. FCA. Ripon Hall Ox 71. **d** 92 **p** 93. NSM Romsey *Win* 92-94; Chapl Win and Eastleigh Healthcare NHS Trust 94-08; rtd 08. *Forest View, Salisbury Road, Plaitford, Romsey SO51 6EE* Tel (01794) 323731

FLORANCE, James Andrew Vernon. b 44. MCIOB. Linc Th Coll 84. **d** 86 **p** 87. C Lt Ilford St Mich *Chelmsf* 86-90; TV Becontree S 90-93; R Orsett and Bulphan and Horndon on the Hill 93-97; P-in-c Liscard St Mary w St Columba *Ches* 97-02; RD Wallasey 99-02; Chapl St D Foundn Hospice Care Newport 02-03; P-in-c Abersychan and Garndiffaith *Mon* 03-08; rtd 08; Perm to Offic *Heref* and *Mon* from 08. *24 Radnor View, Leominster HR6 8TF* Tel (01568) 612617 E-mail jandp.florance@tiscali.co.uk

FLORANCE (née WAINWRIGHT), Mrs Pauline Barbara. b 40. St Deiniol's Hawarden 83. **dss** 84 **d** 87 **p** 94. New Ferry *Ches* 84-90; Par Dn 87-90; Par Dn Hallwood 90-94; C 94-00; rtd 00; Perm to Offic *Ches* 00-03; *Mon* 04-08; *Heref* from 08; Bp's Adv in Past Care and Counselling *Mon* from 07. *24 Radnor View, Leominster HR6 8TF* Tel (01568) 612617 E-mail jandp.florance@tiscali.co.uk

FLORENTINUS, Erik. ERMC. **d** 09. C Amsterdam w Den Helder and Heiloo *Eur* from 09. *0Z Achterburgwal 100, NL-1012 DS Amsterdam, The Netherlands*

FLORY, John Richard. b 35. Clare Coll Cam BA59 MA63. Westcott Ho Cam 69. **d** 71 **p** 72. C Shirehampton *Bris* 71-74; V Patchway 74-82; R Lydiard Millicent w Lydiard Tregoz 82-86; TR The Lydiards 86-93; R Box w Hazlebury and Ditteridge 93-01; rtd 01; Perm to Offic *Derby* from 02. *Beechbank, 3 Ivonbrook Close, Darley Bridge, Matlock DE4 2JX* Tel (01629) 734707

FLOWERDAY, Andrew Leslie. b 53. Imp Coll Lon BSc75. St Jo Coll Nottm. **d** 90 **p** 91. C Farnborough *Guildf* 90-95; TV Morden *S'wark* from 95. *140 Stonecot Hill, Sutton SM3 9HQ* Tel (020) 8330 6566 *or* 8337 6421

FLOWERDEW, Martin James. b 56. Herts Coll CertEd78 Pemb Coll Cam BEd79. Sarum & Wells Th Coll 89. **d** 91 **p** 92. C Leagrave *St Alb* 91-95; C Radlett 95-99; TV Wilford Peninsula *St E* 99-01; V St Osyth *Chelmsf* 01-09; V Hoylake *Ches* from 09. *The Vicarage, 1 Stanley Road, Hoylake, Wirral CH47 1HL* Tel 0151-632 3897 E-mail theblacksheep@tinyworld.co.uk

FLOWERS, John Henry. b 33. Qu Coll Birm 63. **d** 65 **p** 66. C Aberdare St Fagan *Llan* 65-68; C Llantrisant 68-72; V Nantymoel w Wyndham 72-76; Asst Chapl HM Pris Wormwood Scrubs 76-78; Chapl HM Pris Birm 78-80; Chapl HM Pris Albany 80-93; rtd 93; Perm to Offic *Portsm* from 93. *1 Ulster Crescent, Newport PO30 5RU* Tel (01983) 525493

FLUX, Brian George. b 39. Oak Hill Th Coll 68. **d** 71 **p** 72. C Chadderton Ch Ch *Man* 71-74; C Preston All SS *Blackb* 74-76; Min Preston St Luke 76-81; CF (TA) from 78; R Higher Openshaw *Man* 81-88; Chapl HM Pris Haverigg 88-92; rtd 92. *65 Crosby Street, Maryport CA15 6DR* Tel (01900) 810635

FLYNN, Alexander Victor George. b 45. **d** 90 **p** 91. C Kilsaran w Drumcar, Dunleer and Dunany *Arm* 90-91; P-in-c 91-94; I 94-98; I Clonenagh w Offerlane, Borris-in-Ossory etc *C & O* 98-00; I Aughrim w Ballinasloe etc *L & K* from 08. *The Rectory, Aughrim, Ballinasloe, Co Galway, Republic of Ireland* Tel (00353) (90) 967 3735 Mobile 87-2074739 E-mail georgeandgwyn@eircom.net

FLYNN, Mrs Diane. b 62. Yorks Min Course. **d** 09. C Roundhay St Edm *Ripon* from 09. *15 Talbot Court, Leeds LS8 1LT* Tel 0113-266 9243 E-mail dianeflynn888@btinternet.com

FLYNN, Peter Murray. b 35. Oak Hill Th Coll 76. **d** 79 **p** 80. NSM Finchley St Mary *Lon* 79-83; NSM Mill Hill Jo Keble Ch 84-86; C Mill End and Heronsgate w W Hyde *St Alb* 86-92; V Chessington *Guildf* 92-05; rtd 05; Perm to Offic *Roch* from 05. *16 The Street, Plaxtol, Sevenoaks TN15 0QQ* Tel (01732) 811304 E-mail revpeterflynn@yahoo.co.uk

FOALE, Rosemary. See MASON, Sheila Rosemary

FOBISTER, Mrs Wendy Irene. b 44. Lon Inst of Educn TCert65. **d** 07 **p** 08. OLM Charminster and Stinsford *Sarum* from 07. *44 Meadow View, Charminster, Dorchester DT2 9RE* Tel (01305) 251681 E-mail wenfob@gmail.com

FODEN, Eric. Local Min Tr Course. **d** 93 **p** 94. OLM New Bury *Man* 93-96. *45 Stetchworth Drive, Worsley, Manchester M28 1FU* Tel 0161-790 4627

FODEN, Mrs Janice Margaret. b 54. Sheff Univ BA76 Sheff City Poly PGCE77. NOC 98. **d** 01 **p** 02. NSM Kimberworth *Sheff* 01-05; P-in-c Barnby Dun from 05. *The Vicarage, Stainforth Road, Barnby Dun, Doncaster DN3 1AA* Tel (01302) 882835 E-mail janfoden@hotmail.com

FODEN-CURRIE, Mary Agnes. b 43. Bp Grosseteste Coll BEd64. St Jo Coll Nottm MA97. **d** 98 **p** 99. NSM Skegby *S'well* 98-02; NSM Skegby w Teversal 02-03; rtd 03; Perm to Offic *S'well* from 03. *40 Harvey Road, Mansfield NG18 4ES* Tel (01623) 479838

FOGDEN, Canon Elizabeth Sally. b 40. MBE04. MCSP61. Qu Coll Birm 76. **dss** 78 **d** 87 **p** 94. Chevington w Hargrave and Whepstead w Brockley *St E* 78-84; Honington w Sapiston and Troston 84-92; Par Dn 87-92; Par Dn Euston w Barnham, Elvedon and Fakenham Magna 90-92; TD Blackbourne 92-94; TV 94-06; Chapl Center Parc Elvedon from 90; Dioc Adv Women's Min 90-06; Hon Can St E Cathl 92-06; rtd 06; Perm to Offic *St E* from 06. *Meadow Farm, Coney Weston Road, Sapiston, Bury St Edmunds IP31 1RX* Tel (01359) 268923 Mobile 07860-101980

FOGDEN, Mrs Patricia Lily Margaret. b 51. SRN73. **d** 03 **p** 04. OLM Orlestone w Snave and Ruckinge w Warehorne etc *Cant* from 03. *Harewood, Wey Street, Snave, Ashford TN26 2QH* Tel (01233) 733862 Mobile 07885-285636

FOGG, Cynthia Mary (Sister Mary Clare). b 34. Bp Grosseteste Coll TCert54. LNSM course 94. **d** 95 **p** 96. NSM Westgate Common *Wakef* from 95. *St Peter's Convent, Dovecote Lane, Horbury, Wakefield WF4 6BD* Tel (01924) 272181 Fax 261225

FOGG, Mrs Margaret. b 37. CBDTI 04. **d** 05 **p** 06. NSM Allonby, Cross Canonby and Dearham *Carl* from 05. *Green Pastures, 59 Sycamore Road, Maryport CA15 7AE* Tel (01900) 816203 E-mail margaret.fogg@btinternet.com

FOLEY, Geoffrey Evan. b 30. Univ of New England BA71 DipEd73 MEd79. St Jo Coll Morpeth 51. **d** 53 **p** 54. C Murwillumbah Australia 53-59; R Mallanganee 59-65; R Woodburn 65-72; P-in-c Lismore 84-85; P-in-c Bangalow 87-88; P-in-c Alstonville 88-89; Perm to Offic *S'wark* 90-91; Chapl Hamburg w Kiel *Eur* 91; C Stoke-upon-Trent *Lich* 91; rtd 93; Perm to Offic Grafton from 93; Dioc Archivist from 97. *198 Dawson Street, Lismore NSW 2480, Australia* Tel (0061) (2) 6621 4684 E-mail gefoley@bigpond.net.au

FOLEY, James Frank. b 50. MBE91. Reading Univ BSc72. STETS 95. **d** 99 **p** 00. C St Illogan *Truro* 99-03; P-in-c Droxford and Meonstoke w Corhampton cum Exton *Portsm* 03-08; C

Balham Hill Ascension *S'wark* from 09. *22 Rochelle Close, London SW11 2RX* Tel 07545-831961 (mobile) E-mail jim.ffoley@yahoo.co.uk

✠**FOLEY, The Rt Revd Ronald Graham Gregory.** b 23. St Jo Coll Dur BA49. **d** 50 **p** 51 **c** 82. C S Shore H Trin *Blackb* 50-54; V Blackb St Luke 54-60; Dir RE *Dur* 60-71; R Brancepeth 60-71; Hon Can Dur Cathl 65-71; Hon Can Ripon Cathl 71-82; V Leeds St Pet 71-82; Chapl to The Queen 77-82; Suff Bp Reading *Ox* 82-87; Area Bp Reading 87-89; rtd 89; Hon Asst Bp York from 95. *2 Poplar Avenue, Kirkbymoorside, York YO62 6ES* Tel (01751) 432439

FOLKARD, Oliver Goring. b 41. Nottm Univ BA63. Lich Th Coll 64. **d** 66 **p** 67. C Carlton *S'well* 66-67; C Worksop Priory 67-68; C Brewood *Lich* 68-71; C Folkingham w Laughton *Linc* 72-75; P-in-c Gedney Hill 76-77; V 77-84; V Whaplode Drove 76-84; V Sutton St Mary 84-94; RD Elloe E 89-94; P-in-c Scotter w E Ferry 94-99; R 99-06; R Scotton w Northorpe 99-06; rtd 06; Perm to Offic *Nor* from 06. *1 Barons Close, Fakenham NR21 8BE* Tel (01328) 851468

FOLKS, Andrew John. b 42. St Jo Coll Dur BA65. Cranmer Hall Dur. **d** 69 **p** 70. C Stranton *Dur* 69-72; Chapl Sandbach Sch 73-80; Chapl Casterton Sch Lancs 80-85; Hd Master Fernhill Manor Sch New Milton 85-97; NSM Langdale *Carl* 97-07; rtd 07. *10 Winfield Road, Sedbergh LA10 5AZ* Tel (01539) 621314

FOLKS, Peter William John. b 30. FRCO56 ARCM. Launde Abbey 72. **d** 72 **p** 73. C Leic St Aid 72-76; V Newfoundpool 76-84; V Whetstone 84-94; rtd 94; Perm to Offic *Leic* from 94. *4 Beaufort Close, Desford, Leicester LE9 9HS* Tel (01455) 828090 E-mail peterfolks@hotmail.com

FOLLETT, Jeremy Mark. b 60. Jes Coll Cam BA82. St Jo Coll Nottm 90. **d** 91 **p** 92. C Newark *S'well* 91-95; C Hellesdon *Nor* 95-01; V St Alb Ch Ch *St Alb* from 01. *Christ Church Vicarage, 5 High Oaks, St Albans AL3 6DJ* Tel (01727) 857592

FOLLETT, Neil Robert Thomas. b 50. RMCS BSc75 Open Univ BA85. EAMTC 86. **d** 89 **p** 90. C Godmanchester *Ely* 89-92; V 92-00; V Wilton Place St Paul *Lon* 00; rtd 00. *Address withheld by request*

FOLLIN, Michael Stuart. b 62. UMIST BSc84. St Jo Coll Nottm MTh02. **d** 02 **p** 03. C Aughton Ch Ch *Liv* 02-06; TV Maghull 06-09; TV Maghull and Melling from 09. *St Peter's Vicarage, 1 St Peter's Row, Liverpool L31 5LU* Tel 0151-526 3434 Mobile 07813-794252 E-mail michael.follin@tiscali.co.uk

FOLLIS, Bryan Andrew. b 61. Ulster Poly BA83 QUB PhD90 TCD BA98. CITC 95. **d** 98 **p** 99. C Portadown St Mark *Arm* 98-01; I Belfast All SS *Conn* from 01. *All Saints' Rectory, 25 Rugby Road, Belfast BT7 1PT* Tel (028) 9032 3327 E-mail b.a.follis@hotmail.co.uk

FOLLIS, Raymond George Carlile. b 23. DFC45. Lich Th Coll 63. **d** 65 **p** 66. C Walsall Wood *Lich* 65-69; R New Fishbourne *Chich* 69-88; P-in-c Appledram 84-88; rtd 88; Perm to Offic *Chich* from 88. *8 Old Rectory Gardens, Felpham, Bognor Regis PO22 7EP* Tel (01243) 825388

FONTAINE, Mrs Marion Elizabeth. b 39. RN61 RM62. SAOMC 96. **d** 99 **p** 00. OLM Thatcham *Ox* from 99. *33 Druce Way, Thatcham RG19 3PF* Tel (01635) 827746

FOOKES, Roger Mortimer. b 24. VRD63 and Bar 73. Ch Ch Ox BA49 MA53. Wells Th Coll 48. **d** 50 **p** 51. C Westbury-on-Trym H Trin *Bris* 50-53; Chapl RNVR 51-58; Chapl RNR 58-74; C Frome St Jo *B & W* 53-55; R Barwick and Closworth 55-62; V Midsomer Norton 62-78; RD Midsomer Norton 72-78; P-in-c Stratton on the Fosse 74-78; P-in-c Clandown 75-78; V Wotton-under-Edge w Ozleworth and N Nibley *Glouc* 78-89; RD Dursley 85-89; rtd 89; Perm to Offic *B & W* 90-99 and *Ex* 90-05. *c/o R L Fookes Esq, 408 Wimbledon Park Road, London SW19 6PN* Tel (020) 8788 7584

FOOKS, George Edwin. b 25. Trin Hall Cam BA49 MA53 Reading Univ AdDipEd70. Linc Th Coll 49. **d** 51 **p** 52. C Portsea St Cuth *Portsm* 51-53; C Fareham SS Pet and Paul 53-55; Chapl Earnseat Sch Carl 55-59; V Sheff St Cuth 59-64; Hd Careers Fairfax Gr Sch Bradf 64-66; Hd RE/Careers Buttershaw Comp Sch Bradf 66-70; Counsellor Ifield Sch Crawley 70-73; Hd Guidance Hengrove Sch Bris 73-78; Counsellor w Hearing Impaired Children (Avon) 78-89; Perm to Offic *Bris* from 83; Chapl Southmead Hosp Bris 89-90; Chapl Qu Eliz Hosp Bris 90-96; Chapl Thornbury Hosp from 90; rtd 90; Perm to Offic *Glouc* 90-95. *26 Rudgeway Park, Rudgeway, Bristol BS35 3RU* Tel (01454) 614072

FOOT, Adam Julian David. b 58. Thames Poly BSc80 Garnett Coll Lon CertEd87. Trin Coll Bris 93. **d** 97 **p** 98. C Luton Ch Ch *Roch* 97-00; V Welling from 00. *St John's Vicarage, Danson Lane, Welling DA16 2BQ* Tel (020) 8303 1107 E-mail adam.foot@diocese-rochester.org

FOOT, Daniel Henry Paris. b 46. Peterho Cam BA67 MA74. Ridley Hall Cam 77. **d** 79 **p** 80. C Werrington *Pet* 79-82; P-in-c Cranford w Grafton Underwood 82; R Cranford w Grafton Underwood and Twywell from 83; P-in-c Slipton from 94. *The Rectory, Rectory Hill, Cranford, Kettering NN14 4AH* Tel (01536) 330231

FOOT, Elizabeth Victoria Anne. b 55. St Mich Coll Sarum BEd77. Trin Coll Bris BA04. **d** 04 **p** 05. C Linkinhorne and Stoke Climsland *Truro* 04-07; C Godrevy 07-08; TV from 08. *Godrevy House, Penpol Avenue, Hayle TR27 4NQ* Tel (01736) 757151 E-mail godrevyvic@hotmail.co.uk

FOOT, Keith George. b 45. Surrey Univ BSc70 Lon Univ PhD73 MRSC CChem. NTMTC 96. **d** 99 **p** 00. C New Thundersley *Chelmsf* 99-03; Min Prince's Park CD *Roch* 03-07; V Prince's Park from 07. *6 Thrush Close, Chatham ME5 7TG* Tel (01634) 685828 E-mail keith.foot@diocese-rochester.org

FOOT, Lynda. b 43. Reading Univ BEd75 Loughb Univ MSc82 Nottm Univ MA00. EMMTC 97. **d** 00 **p** 01. NSM Coalville and Bardon Hill *Leic* 00-03; NSM Hickling w Kinoulton and Broughton Sulney *S'well* 04-05; NSM Bingham 05-08; rtd 08. *34 White Furrows, Cotgrave, Nottingham NG12 3LD* Tel 0115-989 9724 Mobile 07799-662852 E-mail lyndafoot@btinternet.com

FOOT, Paul. b 41. Lon Univ BA64. Chich Th Coll 65. **d** 67 **p** 68. C Portsea N End St Mark *Portsm* 67-72; C Grimsbury *Ox* 72-74; V Cury w Gunwalloe *Truro* 74-80; P-in-c Port Isaac 80-83; P-in-c St Kew 80-83; V St Day 83-91; rtd 95. *Aeaea, 39 New Road, Llandovery SA20 0EA* Tel (01550) 720140

FOOTE, Desmond. b 46. S Dios Minl Tr Scheme. **d** 82 **p** 83. NSM Furze Platt *Ox* 82-88; NSM Ruscombe and Twyford 88-05; NSM Woolhampton w Midgham and Beenham Valance 05-08; NSM Aldermaston w Wasing and Brimpton 05-08; NSM Aldermaston and Woolhampton from 08. *The Rectory, Birds Lane, Midgham, Reading RG7 5UL* Tel 0118-971 2186 E-mail des@foote52fsnet.co.uk

FOOTE, John Bruce. b 18. G&C Coll Cam BA39 MA43 MD51 FRCPath. St Jo Coll Nottm 78. **d** 79 **p** 80. NSM Crookes St Thos *Sheff* 79-88; rtd 88; Perm to Offic *Sheff* from 88 and *Derby* 79-07. *67 St Thomas Road, Sheffield S10 1UW* Tel 0114-266 5021 E-mail feete@feete.org

✠**FOOTTIT, The Rt Revd Anthony Charles.** b 35. K Coll Cam BA57 MA70. Cuddesdon Coll 59. **d** 61 **p** 62 **c** 99. C Wymondham *Nor* 61-64; C Blakeney w Lt Langham 64-67; P-in-c Hindringham w Binham and Cockthorpe 67-71; P-in-c Yarlington *B & W* 71-76; R N Cadbury 71-75; P-in-c S Cadbury w Sutton Montis 75-76; TR Camelot Par 76-81; RD Cary 79-81; Dioc Missr *Linc* 81-87; Can and Preb Linc Cathl 86-87; Dioc Rural Officer *Nor* 87; Adn Lynn 87-99; Suff Bp Lynn 99-03; rtd 03; Hon Asst Bp Nor from 04; Dioc Environmental Officer 04-09. *Ivy House, Whitwell Street, Reepham, Norwich NR10 4RA* Tel (01603) 870340

FORAN, Andrew John. b 55. Aston Tr Scheme 84 Linc Th Coll 86. **d** 88 **p** 89. C Epping St Jo *Chelmsf* 88-92; TV Canvey Is 92-97; C Dorking w Ranmore *Guildf* 97-99; Chapl HM Pris Send 97-09; Chapl HM Pris Bullingdon from 09. *HM Prison Bullingdon, PO Box 50, Bicester OX25 1PZ* Tel (01869) 353100 E-mail andrew.foran@hmps.gsi.gov.uk

FORBES, Mrs Angela Laura. b 47. Ox Min Course 91. **d** 94 **p** 96. NSM Cowley St Jo *Ox* 94-04; Perm to Offic from 04. *6 Elm Crescent, Charlbury, Chipping Norton OX7 3PZ* Tel (01608) 819121

FORBES, The Very Revd Graham John Thompson. b 51. CBE04. Aber Univ MA73 Edin Univ BD76. Edin Th Coll 73. **d** 76 **p** 77. C Edin Old St Paul 76-82; Can St Ninian's Cathl Perth 82-90; R Stanley 82-88; Provost St Ninian's Cathl Perth 82-90; R Perth St Ninian 82-90; Provost St Mary's Cathl from 90; R Edin St Mary from 90. *8 Lansdowne Crescent, Edinburgh EH12 5EQ* Tel 0131-225 2978 or 225 6293 Mobile 07711-199297 Fax 0131 226 1482 or 225 3181 E-mail provost@cathedral.net

FORBES, Iain William. b 56. Ex Univ BA81 Chich Th Coll 83. **d** 85 **p** 86. C Upper Norwood St Jo *S'wark* 85-88; C Lewisham St Mary 88-90; Chapl St Martin's Coll of Educn *Blackb* 90-94; P-in-c Woodplumpton 94-99; Dioc Voc Adv 94-99; V Woodham *Guildf* from 99. *The Vicarage, 25 Woodham Waye, Woking GU21 5SW* Tel (01483) 762857 E-mail fatheriainforbes@aol.com

FORBES, Canon John Francis. b 29. CITC 85. **d** 88 **p** 90. Aux Min Ferns w Kilbride, Toombe, Kilcormack etc *C & O* 88-04; Treas Ferns Cathl 98-03; rtd 04. *Ballinabarna House, Enniscorthy, Co Wexford, Republic of Ireland* Tel (00353) (53) 923 3353 Mobile 87-237 9319

FORBES, Canon John Franey. b 33. AKC57. **d** 58 **p** 59. C Darlington H Trin *Dur* 58-62; C St Geo Cathl Cape Town S Africa 62-65; R Hoedjies Bay 65-69; Warden Zonnebloem Coll Cape Town 69-75; Dean Pietermaritzburg 76-03; rtd 03. *PO Box 481, Noordhoek, 7979 South Africa* Tel and fax (0027) (21) 789 2227

FORBES, Joyce Brinella. b 52. **d** 03 **p** 04. OLM Norbury St Steph and Thornton Heath *S'wark* from 03. *36 Dalmeny Avenue, London SW16 4RT* Tel (020) 8240 0283 or 7525 7982 E-mail petnard36@aol.com

FORBES, Patrick. b 38. Open Univ BA82. Linc Th Coll 64. **d** 66 **p** 67. C Yeovil *B & W* 66-69; C Plumstead Wm Temple Ch Abbey Wood CD *S'wark* 69-70; Thamesmead Ecum Gp 70-73; TV Thamesmead 73-78; Dioc Communications Officer *St Alb*

78-90; P-in-c Offley w Lilley 78-82; Info Officer Communications Dept Ch Ho Lon 91-95; Press Officer Miss to Seamen 95-99; rtd 99; Perm to Offic *St Alb* from 04. *18 Francis Road, Hinxworth, Baldock SG7 5HL* Tel (01462) 742015 E-mail fool1@tiscali.co.uk

FORBES, Raymond John. b 34. ALCD58. **d** 58 **p** 59. C Wandsworth St Steph *S'wark* 58-61; C Kewstoke *B & W* 61-63; V Fordcombe *Roch* 63-73; R Ashurst 64-73; P-in-c Morden w Almer and Charborough *Sarum* 73-76; P-in-c Bloxworth 73-76; V Red Post 76-84; P-in-c Hamworthy 84-92; P-in-c Symondsbury and Chideock 92-96; rtd 96; Perm to Offic *Sarum* from 96. *65A Millmans Road, Bournemouth BH10 7LJ* Tel (01202) 582966

FORBES, Stuart. b 33. Lon Univ BD59. Oak Hill Th Coll 56. **d** 61 **p** 62. C Halliwell St Pet *Man* 61-64; P-in-c Wicker w Neepsend *Sheff* 64-69; V Stainforth 69-77; V Salterhebble All SS *Wakef* 77-89; V Toxteth Park St Mich w St Andr *Liv* 89-98; rtd 98; Perm to Offic *Lich* from 00. *29 Firbeck Gardens, Wildwood, Stafford ST17 4QR* Tel (01785) 663658

FORBES, Susan Margaret. *See* VAN BEVEREN, Mrs Susan Margaret

FORBES ADAM, Stephen Timothy Beilby. b 23. Ball Coll Ox. Chich Th Coll 59. **d** 61 **p** 62. C Guisborough *York* 61-64; R Barton in Fabis *S'well* 64-70; V Thrumpton 65-70; P-in-c S Stoke *B & W* 74-81; C Combe Down w Monkton Combe and S Stoke 81-83; Perm to Offic *B & W* 83-86; *Ox* 86-87; *York* from 88; NSM Epwell w Sibford, Swalcliffe and Tadmarton *Ox* 87-92; rtd 88. *Woodhouse Farm, Escrick, York YO19 6HT* Tel (01904) 878827

FORBES STONE, Elizabeth Karen. b 61. Birm Univ MB, BCh85 MRCGP89. Ridley Hall Cam BA99. **d** 00 **p** 01. C Brentford *Lon* 00-02; C Shaw cum Donnington *Ox* from 02. *The Rectory, 64 Northcroft Lane, Newbury RG14 1BN* Tel (01635) 35320 Mobile 07980-431710 E-mail buff@dandb.org.uk

FORCE-JONES, Graham Roland John. b 41. Sarum Th Coll 65. **d** 68 **p** 69. C Calne and Blackland *Sarum* 68-73; TV Oldbury 73-78; R 78-80; TR Upper Kennet 80-94; RD Marlborough 90-94; P-in-c Atworth w Shaw and Whitley 94-06; Chapl Stonar Sch Melksham 01-06; rtd 06. *Le Petit Cormy, 86700 Vaux-en-Couche, France*

FORD, Adam. b 40. Lanc Univ MA72 K Coll Lon BD63 AKC63. **d** 65 **p** 65. C Cirencester *Glouc* 65-70; V Hebden Bridge *Wakef* 70-76; Chapl St Paul's Girls' Sch Hammersmith 77-01; Lic to Offic *Lon* 77-98; P in O 84-91; rtd 05. *3 Paddock View, Sloe Lane, Alfriston, Polegate BN26 5UR* E-mail adamfordspgs@hotmail.com

FORD, Ms Amanda Kirstine. b 61. Middx Univ BA83 Open Univ MA97. St Steph Ho Ox 98. **d** 00 **p** 01. C Leic Resurr 00-05; P-in-c Beaumont Leys 05-09; V from 09; Dioc CUF Officer from 04. *The Vicarage, 10 Parkside Close, Leicester LE4 1EP* Tel 0116-235 2667 E-mail mandyford@btinternet.com

FORD, Anthony. b 60. Oak Hill Th Coll 06. **d** 08 **p** 09. C Chadderton Ch Ch *Man* from 08. *23 Lindale Avenue, Chadderton, Oldham OL9 9DW* Tel 0161-628 2299 Mobile 07816-596878 E-mail tony@chad46.fsnet.co.uk *or* tonyford227@btinternet.com

FORD, Mrs Avril Celia. b 43. St Mary's Coll Dur D3c04 Chelsea Coll Lon PGCE65. **d** 92 **p** 04. OLM Horncastle w Low Toynton *Linc* 92-98, NSM 98-06; OLM High Toynton 92-98; NSM 98-06; OLM Greetham w Ashby Puerorum 92-98; NSM 98 06, NSM Horncastle Gp from 06. *Frolic, Reindeer Close, Horncastle LN9 5AA* Tel (01507) 526234 or 525600

FORD, Brian. b 40. OBE89. Imp Coll Lon BSc62 Nottm Univ MSc66 PhD74 Ox Univ MA74 CMath FIMA ARCS. SAOMC 96. **d** 99 **p** 00. NSM Witney *Ox* 99-02; NSM Forest Edge from 02. *Ramsden Farmhouse, Ramsden, Oxford OX7 3AU* Tel (01993) 868343 Fax 868322 E-mail brian@nag.co.uk

FORD (née HARRISON-WATSON), Mrs Carole. b 44. Reading Univ BSc66 St Martin's Coll Lanc PGCE79. Carl Dioc Tr Inst 92. **d** 95 **p** 96. NSM Windermere *Carl* 95-98; NSM Borrowdale 98-01; NSM Thornthwaite cum Braithwaite, Newlands etc 01-05; rtd 05; Perm to Offic *Carl* from 05. *Croft View, Low Lorton, Cockermouth CA13 9UW* Tel (01900) 85519

FORD, Canon Christopher Simon. b 51. Leeds Univ MPhil86 PhD91. AKC74. **d** 75 **p** 76. C Wythenshawe Wm Temple Ch *Man* 75-77; C New Bury 77-80; R Old Trafford St Jo 80-94; R Moston St Jo 94-05; P-in-c Davyhulme St Mary from 05; Bp's Adv on Archives from 93; AD N Man 94-00; Hon Can Man Cathl from 04. *St Mary's Vicarage, 13 Vicarage Road, Urmston, Manchester M41 5TP* Tel 0161-748 2210 E-mail christopher.ford5@btinternet.com

FORD, David John. b 38. Lon Coll of Div BD68. **d** 69 **p** 70. C Blackheath St Jo *S'wark* 69-71; C Westlands St Andr *Lich* 71-75; V Sheff St Steph w St Phil and St Ann 75-77; R Netherthorpe 77-80; TR 80-84; R Thrybergh 82-84; R Thrybergh w Hooton Roberts 84 94, Ind Chapl 86-87; TV Parkham, Alwington, Buckland Brewer etc *Ex* 94-01; rtd 03; Hon C Knaresborough *Ripon* 01-05; Perm to Offic *York* from 07. *10 Grove Hill Road, Filey YO14 9NL* Tel (01723) 518292

FORD, David Stuart. b 61. City of Lon Poly BA82 Qu Coll Birm MA09. WMMTC 06. **d** 09. C Bramhope *Ripon* from 09; C Ireland Wood from 09; Chapl Abbey Grange High Sch from 09. *St Paul's Vicarage, Raynel Drive, Leeds LS16 6BS* Tel 0113-267 2907 Mobile 07973-412625
E-mail davidford09@googlemail.com

FORD, Mrs Deborah Perrin. b 59. Leeds Univ BA81 Birm Univ MSocSc85 Univ of Wales (Ban) BTh CQSW85. EAMTC 00. **d** 03 **p** 04. NSM Cambridge St Benedict *Ely* from 03; Chapl Cam Univ Hosps NHS Foundn Trust from 03. *102 Millington Lane, Cambridge CB3 9HA* Tel (01223) 329321
E-mail deborahford@myrealbox.com

FORD, Derek Ernest. b 32. St Mich Coll Llan 56. **d** 58 **p** 59. C Roath St Martin *Llan* 58-61; C Newton Nottage 61-67; V Abercanaid 67-70; Perm to Offic *Win* 70-80; SSF from 72; Lic to Offic *Sarum* 73-80 and *Newc* 75-80; USA from 80; Min Prov American Province SSF 02-05; P-in-c Siparia Trinidad and Tobago 06-09. *PO Box 399, Mount Sinai NY 11766-0399, USA* E-mail broderekssf@aol.com

FORD, Eric Copeland. b 20. Linc Th Coll 68. **d** 70 **p** 71. C Lupset *Wakef* 70-73; V Cornholme 73-78; V Wragby w Sharlston 78-85; P-in-c Hightown 85-87; V 87-88; V Hartshead and Hightown 88-90; rtd 90; P-in-c Halifax St Jo *Wakef* 90-91; Chapl Las Palmas *Eur* 91-97; Perm to Offic *Blackb* 98-03. *Le Grand Nursing Home, 103 Preston Old Road, Freckleton, Preston PR4 1HD* Tel (01772) 679300

FORD, Canon Henry Malcolm. b 33. Em Coll Cam BA54 MA58. Ely Th Coll 58. **d** 59 **p** 69. C Ipswich St Matt *St E* 59-61; Hon C Bury St Edmunds St Jo 66-76; Hon C Hawstead and Newton w Stanningfield etc 76-89; Hon Can St E Cathl 86-97; NSM Cockfield w Bradfield St Clare, Felsham etc 89-98. *Thatch on the Green, Cross Green, Cockfield, Bury St Edmunds IP30 0LG* Tel (01284) 828479

FORD, John. See FORD, William John

✠**FORD, The Rt Revd John Frank.** b 52. Chich Univ MA04. Chich Th Coll 76. **d** 79 **p** 80 **c** 05. C Forest Hill Ch Ch *S'wark* 79-82; V Lee St Aug 82-91; V Lower Beeding and Dom Chapl to Bp Horsham *Chich* 91-94; Dioc Missr 94-00; Can and Preb Chich Cathl 97-00; Can Res and Prec 00-05; Suff Bp Plymouth *Ex* from 05. *31 Riverside Walk, Tamerton Foliot, Plymouth PL5 4AQ* Tel (01752) 769836 Fax 769818
E-mail bishop.of.plymouth@exeter.anglican.org

FORD, Jonathan Laurence. See ALDERTON-FORD, Canon Jonathan Laurence

FORD, Joyce. b 42. Qu Coll Birm 97. **d** 00 **p** 01. NSM Bentley *Lich* 00-04; NSM Wednesfield 04-06; Perm to Offic from 07. *33 Bowness Grove, Willenhall WV12 5DB* Tel (01922) 408420

FORD, Nancy Celia. b 48. Open Univ BA02 FCIPD00. STETS 98. **d** 01 **p** 02. NSM Crookham *Guildf* 01-04; NSM Aldershot St Mich 04-07; Asst Dioc Dir of Ords 04-05; Bp's Chapl from 05. *34 Rowhill Avenue, Aldershot GU11 3LS* Tel (01252) 677995
E-mail nancy.ford@ntlworld.com

FORD, Peter. b 46. York Univ MA96 Bede Coll Dur TCert72 ACP75. Linc Th Coll 76. **d** 78 **p** 79. OGS from 72; C Hartlepool H Trin *Dur* 78-81; Dioc Youth Officer *Wakef* 81-84; C Mirfield Eastthorpe St Paul 82-84; C Upper Hopton 82-84; V Dodworth 84-88; Chapl and Hd RS Rishworth Sch Ripponden 88-97; Ho Master 97-99; P-in-c Accrington St Mary *Blackb* 97-99; C Torrisholme 99-01; V Warton St Paul 01-08; Dioc Ecum Officer 01-08; Germany 08-09; P-in-c Las Palmas *Eur* from 09. *Calle Montevideo 2-7, 35007 Las Palmas de Gran Canaria, (Las Palmas), Spain* Tel (0034) 928 267 202 E-mail pford@ogs.net

FORD, Canon Peter Hugh. b 43. St Cath Coll Cam BA65 MA69. Cuddesdon Coll 65. **d** 67 **p** 68. C Is of Dogs Ch Ch and St Jo w St Luke *Lon* 67-70; C Tillsonburg St Jo Canada 70-71; St Catharine's St Thos 71-73; P-in-c Thorold South Resurr 71-73; R Port Colborne St Brendan 73-78; R Milton Grace Ch 78-80; Can Pastor Ch Ch Cathl Hamilton 80-86; Adn Lincoln 86-91; R Niagara-on-the-Lake St Mark 86-91; Hon Can Niagara from 91; Hon C Montserrat Ste Gen 91; R Saba 92-98; Perm to Offic *Chich* 98-99; V Newchurch and Arreton *Portsm* 99-07; rtd 07. *11 Vokins Rise, Esplanade, Ryde PO33 2AX* Tel (01983) 568286 E-mail islandpeter@btinternet.com

FORD, Richard. b 47. Grey Coll Dur BA69 PGCE70 FRSA94. SEITE 04. **d** 09. *7 Sylvan Way, West Wickham BR4 9HA* Tel (020) 8289 2432 Mobile 07706-998272
E-mail richard.ford73@ntlworld.com

FORD, Richard Graham. b 39. AKC65 Open Univ BA96. **d** 66 **p** 67. C Morpeth *Newc* 66-71; C Fordingbridge w Ibsley *Win* 71-73; TV Whorlton *Newc* 73-80; Chapl RNR 75-92; V Choppington *Newc* 80-92; V Tynemouth Priory 92-04; rtd 04. *43 Farriers Rise, Shilbottle, Alnwick NE66 2EN* Tel (01665) 581115

FORD, Roger James. b 33. Sarum & Wells Th Coll 81. **d** 83 **p** 84. C Sidcup St Jo *Roch* 83-86; V Darenth 86-98; rtd 98; Perm to Offic *Cov* 02-04. *21 Hawthorn Way, Shipston-on-Stour CV36 4FD* Tel (01608) 664875 E-mail margaretandroger@hotmail.com

FORD, Roger Lindsay. b 47. Ex Univ LLB68. Llan Dioc Tr Scheme 87. **d** 91 **p** 92. NSM Fairwater *Llan* 91-96; NSM

Llandaff 96-01. *93 Cardiff Road, Caerphilly CF83 1WS* Tel (029) 2088 2441

FORD, Mrs Shirley Elsworth. b 40. AIMLS67. Sarum & Wells Th Coll 89. **d** 91 **p** 94. C Farnham *Guildf* 91-96; V Wrecclesham 96-04; rtd 04; Perm to Offic *Chich* from 05. *North House, Queen's Park Mews, Queen's Park Rise, Brighton BN2 9YY* Tel (01273) 674061

FORD, Simone Louise. See BENNETT, Ms Simone Louise

FORD, William John. b 50. Linc Th Coll 89. **d** 91 **p** 92. C Marton-in-Cleveland *York* 91-94; V Whorlton w Carlton and Faceby 94-02; P-in-c Stainton w Hilton from 02; RD Stokesley from 03. *The Vicarage, 21 Thornton Road, Stainton, Middlesbrough TS8 9DS* Tel (01642) 288131
E-mail revjohn.ford@ntlworld.com

FORD-WHITCOMBE, William. See WHITCOMBE, William Ashley

FORDE, Barry George. d 07 **p** 08. C Coleraine *Conn* from 07. *18 Avonbrook Gardens, Coleraine BT52 1SS* Tel (028) 7035 9753 E-mail barry.claire@btinternet.com

FORDE, The Ven Stephen Bernard. b 61. Edin Univ BSc. TCD Div Sch. **d** 86 **p** 87. C Belfast St Mary *Conn* 86-89; Chapl QUB 89-95; Min Can Belf Cathl 89-91; Bp's Dom Chapl *Conn* 90-95; I Dublin Booterstown *D & G* 95-99; Dean of Res UCD 95-99; I Larne and Inver *Conn* from 99; I Glynn w Raloo from 99; Adn Dalriada from 06. *The Rectory, 8 Lower Cairncastle Road, Larne BT40 1PQ* Tel (028) 2827 2788 or 2827 4633
E-mail stephenforde@btinternet.com

FORDHAM, Mrs June Erica. b 28. Oak Hill Th Coll 83. dss 86 **d** 87 **p** 94. Digswell and Panshanger *St Alb* 86-87; Par Dn 87-90; TD 91-93; rtd 93; NSM Lemsford *St Alb* 93-01; Perm to Offic from 01. *22 Crossway, Welwyn Garden City AL8 7EE* Tel (01707) 326997

FORDHAM, Richard George. b 34. AIMarE60 TEng(CEI)71 FBIM74. **d** 91 **p** 92. NSM Cookham *Ox* 91-94; NSM Hedsor and Bourne End 94-01; Perm to Offic *Ox* 01-03 and *Ely* from 03. *6 Sorrel Way, Downham Market PE38 9UD* Tel (01366) 384696

FORDYCE, Andrew Ian. b 70. K Alfred's Coll Win BA94 Southn Univ PGCE96. Trin Coll Bris BA03. **d** 03 **p** 04. C Bramshott and Liphook *Portsm* 03-07; V Berechurch St Marg w St Mich *Chelmsf* from 07. *The Vicarage, 348 Mersea Road, Colchester CO2 8RA* Tel (01206) 576859 Mobile 07884-010376
E-mail andrew.fordyce@tiscali.co.uk

FOREMAN, Joseph Arthur. b 26. ACIB. S Dios Minl Tr Scheme 83. **d** 86 **p** 87. NSM Win St Bart 86-96; Perm to Offic from 96. *4 Denham Close, Winchester SO23 7BL* Tel (01962) 852138

FOREMAN, Canon Patrick Brian. b 41. CertEd. St Jo Coll Nottm 77. **d** 79 **p** 80. C Gainsborough All SS *Linc* 79-83; V Thornton St Jas *Bradf* 83-91; R Hevingham w Hainford and Stratton Strawless *Nor* 91-99; RD Ingworth 94-99; V Heacham 99-06; Hon Can Nor Cathl 03-06; rtd 06; Perm to Offic *Nor* from 06; Bp's Officer for Rtd Clergy and Widows from 08. *Seorah, 7 Mallard Close, Fakenham NR21 8PU* Tel (01328) 853691
E-mail patrick@pandmforeman.eclipse.co.uk

FOREMAN, Mrs Penelope. b 47. Lon Inst of Educn TCert68 Ch Ch Coll Cant BEd90 MA93. SEITE 04. **d** 06 **p** 07. NSM Roch St Justus from 06. *28 Kingsway, Chatham ME5 7HT* Tel (01634) 571220 E-mail penny.foreman@btinternet.com

FOREMAN, Roy Geoffrey Victor. b 31. Oak Hill Th Coll 62. **d** 64 **p** 65. C Chitts Hill St Cuth *Lon* 64-67; C Rodbourne Cheney *Bris* 67-70; C Walthamstow St Mary w St Steph *Chelmsf* 71-92; TV 92-96; rtd 96; Perm to Offic *S'wark* 97-05. *c/o E C Foreman Esq, 7 Netherne Lane, Coulsdon CR5 1NR* Tel (01737) 557456

FOREMAN, Timothy. b 56. K Coll Lon BD77. SEITE 97. **d** 99 **p** 00. C Camberwell St Giles w St Matt *S'wark* 99-02; R Buckland in Dover w Buckland Valley *Cant* from 02; Hon Min Can Cant Cathl from 04. *St Andrew's Rectory, London Road, Dover CT17 0TF* Tel (01304) 201324
E-mail fr.tim@ntlworld.com

FOREMAN, Vanessa Jane. See LAWRENCE, Mrs Vanessa Jane

FORGAN, Eleanor. b 44. St Andr Univ MA66 Aber Univ DipEd67. St And Dioc Tr Course. **d** 89 **p** 95. NSM Alloa *St And* from 89. *18 Alexandra Drive, Alloa FK10 2DQ* Tel (01259) 212836

FORMAN, Alastair Gordon. b 48. St Jo Coll Nottm 78. **d** 80 **p** 81. C Pennycross *Ex* 80-83; C Woking St Jo *Guildf* 83-88; V Luton Lewsey St Hugh *St Alb* 88-95; P-in-c Jersey Millbrook St Matt *Win* 95-01; P-in-c Jersey St Lawr 95-01. *Address temp unknown*

FORMAN, Carolyn Dawn. b 45. SEITE. **d** 07 **p** 08. NSM Meopham w Nurstead *Roch* from 07. *Aysgarth, White Hill Road, Meopham, Gravesend DA13 0NZ* Tel (01474) 812373
E-mail acform@btinternet.com

FORMAN, Deborah Jayne. b 56. LMH Ox BA78 MA83 PGCE79 Lambeth STh07. STETS 05. **d** 08 **p** 09. C Churchdown St Jo and Innsworth *Glouc* from 08. *15 Luke Lane, Innsworth, Gloucester GL3 1HJ* Tel (01452) 730935 Mobile 07985-943371
E-mail deborah.forman@tesco.net

FORMAN, Miss Diana Blanche Grant. b 19. Edin Dioc NSM Course 79. dss 83 **d** 86 **p** 94. Edin St Jo 83-91; NSM 86-91; rtd

91. *Strathmore House, 4/3 Church Hill, Edinburgh EH10 4BQ* Tel 0131-447 4463

FORRER, Michael Dennett Cuthbert. b 34. St Pet Hall Ox BA59 MA63. Wycliffe Hall Ox 59. **d** 60 **p** 61. C Westwood *Cov* 60-63; C Cov Cathl 63-71; Ind Chapl 63-69; Sen Ind Chapl 69-71; Hon C All Hallows by the Tower etc *Lon* 76-99; Asst P Bangkok Ch Ch Thailand 81-89; Perm to Offic *Sarum* from 99 and *Ox* 01-02; Hon C Sonning *Ox* from 02; rtd 04. *6 Park View Drive South, Charvil, Reading RG10 9QX* Tel 0118-934 1989

FORREST, The Very Revd Leslie David Arthur. b 46. TCD BA68 MA86. CITC 70. **d** 70 **p** 71. C Conwall *D & R* 70-73; I Tullyaughnish 73-80; I Galway w Kilcummin *T, K & A* 80-95; Dir of Ords 84-95; Can Tuam Cathl 86-95; Provost Tuam 91-95; Preb Tassagard St Patr Cathl Dublin from 91; Dean Ferns *C & O* from 95; I Ferns w Kilbride, Toombe, Kilcormack etc from 95. *The Deanery, Ferns, Enniscorthy, Co Wexford, Republic of Ireland* Tel (00353) (53) 936 6124 E-mail dean@ferns.anglican.org

FORREST, Michael Barry Eric. b 38. Lon Univ BA87 MA89. NZ Bd of Th Studies LTh62 Chich Th Coll 64. **d** 66 **p** 67. C Beckenham St Jas *Roch* 66-70; P-in-c Cape Vogel Papua New Guinea 70-73; P-in-c Alotau 74; R Lae 74-76; C Altarnon and Bolventor *Truro* 76-78; TV N Hill w Altarnon, Bolventor and Lewannick 78-79; R St Martin w E and W Looe 79-84; V Kensington St Phil Earl's Court *Lon* 84-04; rtd 04; Perm to Offic *Chich* from 04. *12 Riley Road, Brighton BN2 4AH* Tel (01273) 690231

FORREST, Canon Robin Whyte. b 33. Edin Th Coll 58. **d** 61 **p** 62. C Glas St Mary 61-66; R Renfrew 66-70; R Motherwell 70-79; R Wishaw 75-79; R Forres *Mor* 79-98; R Nairn 79-92; Can St Andr Cathl Inverness 88-98; Hon Can from 98; Syn Clerk 91-92; Dean Mor 92-98; rtd 98. *Landeck, Cunmingston, Elgin IV30 5XY* Tel and fax (01343) 835539

FORREST-REDFERN, Mrs Susan Michéle. b 57. S Bank Poly BEd86. St Jo Coll Nottm 01. **d** 03 **p** 04. C Lostock St Thos and St Jo *Man* 03-06; C Bolton St Bede 05-06; Ch/Sch Missr in E Bolton from 06; C Tonge Fold from 07. *St Chad's Vicarage, 9 Tonge Fold Road, Bolton BL2 6AW* Tel (01204) 528159 E-mail revsuefr@yahoo.co.uk

FORRESTER, Ian Michael. b 56. Chich Th Coll. **d** 82 **p** 83. C Leigh-on-Sea St Marg *Chelmsf* 82-84; Min Can, Succ and Dean's V Windsor 84-86; Prec and Chapl Chelmsf Cathl 86-91; Chapl Lancing Coll 91-99; P-in-c Boxgrove *Chich* from 99; Dioc Liturgy and Music Consultant from 95. *The Vicarage, Boxgrove, Chichester PO18 0ED* Tel (01243) 774045 E-mail iforrester@hotmail.com

FORRESTER, James Oliphant. b 50. SS Coll Cam BA72 MA76. Wycliffe Hall Ox 73. **d** 76 **p** 77. C Hull St Jo Newland *York* 76-80; C Fulwood *Sheff* 80-87; V Lodge Moor St Luke 87-90; V Ecclesfield 90-01; AD Ecclesfield 90-01; P-in-c Kingston upon Hull H Trin *York* 01-02; V and Lect from 02. *Holy Trinity Vicarage, 66 Pearson Park, Hull HU5 2TQ* Tel (01482) 342292

FORRESTER, Mrs Joyce. b 33. Thornbridge Hall Coll of Educn TCert53 ACP84 DACE85 Crewe & Alsager Coll MSc88. St Jo Coll Nottm 94. **d** 94 **p** 95. NSM Endon w Stanley *Lich* 94-00; NSM Stonnall 00-06; rtd 06; Perm to Offic *Lich* from 06. *Daisybank Bungalow, The Village, Endon, Stoke-on-Trent ST9 9EY* Tel (01782) 504990

FORRESTER, Matthew Agnew. b 31. Univ of Wales (Cardiff) BA64. Trin Coll Bris 70. **d** 72 **p** 73. C Tonbridge SS Pet and Paul *Roch* 72-77; Chapl Elstree Sch Woolhampton 77-78; Chapl Duke of York's R Mil Sch Dover 78-96; rtd 96; Perm to Offic *Cant* from 96. *4 Abbots Place, Canterbury CT1 2AH* Tel (01227) 458882

FORRESTER, Robin William. b 43. Kent Univ MA84 Aston Univ MSc90. All Nations Chr Coll 64. **d** 04 **p** 05. NSM Wharton *Ches* 04-06; P-in-c Moulton from 06. *The Vicarage, 66 Jack Lane, Moulton, Northwich CW9 8NR* Tel (01606) 593355 E-mail robin.forrester@tiscali.co.uk

FORRYAN, Canon John Edward. b 31. Wells Th Coll 58. **d** 60 **p** 61. C Leckhampton SS Phil and Jas *Glouc* 60-63; C Cirencester 63-68; V Glouc St Paul 68-78; R Rodborough 78-91; P-in-c Deerhurst, Apperley w Forthampton and Chaceley 91-95; V 95-97; Hon Can Glouc Cathl 94-97; rtd 97; Perm to Offic *Glouc* from 97. *26 Wye Road, Brockworth, Gloucester GL5 4PP* Tel (01452) 863578

FORRYAN, Thomas Quested. b 64. Pemb Coll Cam BA85. Wycliffe Hall Ox 87. **d** 90 **p** 91. C Cheadle Hulme St Andr *Ches* 90-93; C Aberavon *Llan* 93-94; UCCF 94-98. *1 Grosvenor Road, Watford WD1 2QS*

FORSDIKE, Alan William. b 55. **d** 05 **p** 06. NSM Westerfield and Tuddenham w Witnesham *St E* from 05. *Hill House, 2 Henley Road, Ipswich IP1 3SF* Tel (01473) 252904 E-mail alan.forsdike@btinternet.com

FORSE, Reginald Austin. b 43. Oak Hill Th Coll 77. **d** 79 **p** 80. C Crofton *Portsm* 79-84; NSM Gosport Ch Ch 91-96; NSM Alverstoke from 96. *40 Osprey Gardens, Lee-on-the-Solent PO13 8LJ* Tel (023) 9255 3395 E-mail regforse@yahoo.co.uk

FORSHAW, David Oliver. b 27. Trin Coll Cam BA50 MA52. Qu Coll Birm. **d** 53 **p** 54. C Glen Parva and S Wigston *Leic* 53-55;

Singapore 55-59; V Heptonstall *Wakef* 59-66; V Whitehaven St Nic *Carl* 66-76; P-in-c Whitehaven Ch Ch w H Trin 73-76; V Benchill *Man* 76-89; C Elton All SS 89-92; rtd 92; Perm to Offic *Carl* from 92. *Tynashee, Church Street, Broughton-in-Furness LA20 6HJ* Tel (01229) 716068

FORSHAW, Mrs Frances Ann. b 52. Edin Univ BSc74 Glas Univ MN91 RGN76 SCM78. Moray Ord Course 91. **d** 98 **p** 02. NSM Elgin w Lossiemouth *Mor* 98-01; NSM Perth St Jo *St And* 01-05; P-in-c Pitlochry and Kilmaveonaig 05-09. *1 Cairnies House, Glenalmond College, Glenalmond, Perth PH1 3RY* Tel (01738) 880777 E-mail jandfforshaw@tiscali.co.uk

FORSTER, Andrew James. QUB BA89. CITC BTh92. **d** 92 **p** 93. C Willowfield *D & D* 92-95; Dean of Res QUB 95-02; C of I Adv Downtown Radio Newtownards 96-02; I Drumcliffe w Lissadell and Munninane *K, E & A* 02-07; Adn Elphin and Ardagh 02-07; I Drumglass w Moygashel *Arm* from 07. *The Rectory, 26 Circular Road, Dungannon BT71 6BE* Tel (028) 8772 2614 E-mail drumglass@armagh.anglican.org

FORSTER, Gregory Stuart. b 47. Worc Coll Ox BA69 MA73. Wycliffe Hall Ox 69. **d** 72 **p** 73. C Bath Walcot *B & W* 72-74; C Bolton Em *Man* 74-76; C Bolton St Paul w Em 77-79; R Northenden from 79. *The Rectory, Ford Lane, Northenden, Manchester M22 4NQ* Tel 0161-998 2615 E-mail gsf.m22@amserve.com

FORSTER, Ian Duncan. b 51. St Mich Coll Llan 95. **d** 97 **p** 98. C Lampeter Pont Steffan w Silian *St D* 97-00; C Llandysul w Bangor Teifi w Henllan etc 00-03; V Llangrannog w Llandysiliogogo w Penbryn from 03. *The Vicarage, Pontgarreg, Llandysul SA44 6AJ* Tel (01239) 654943

FORSTER, Kenneth. b 27. St Jo Coll Cam BA50 MA52 Salford Univ MSc77 PhD80. NEOC 83. **d** 86 **p** 87. NSM Hessle *York* 86-92; Chapl Humberside Univ 87-92; rtd 92; NSM Hull St Mary Sculcoates *York* 92-95; Perm to Offic *York* from 95 and *Ox* 04-09. *3 Ventnor Way, Fareham PO16 8RU*

✠**FORSTER, The Rt Revd Peter Robert.** b 50. Mert Coll Ox MA73 Edin Univ BD77 PhD85. Edin Th Coll 78. **d** 80 **p** 81 **c** 96. C Mossley Hill St Matt and St Jas *Liv* 80-82; Sen Tutor St Jo Coll Dur 83-91; V Beverley Minster *York* 91-96; C Routh 91-96; Bp Ches from 96. *Bishop's House, 1 Abbey Street, Chester CH1 2JD* Tel (01244) 350864 Fax 314187 E-mail bpchester@chester.anglican.org

FORSTER, Thomas Shane. b 72. QUB BA93. CITC BTh93. **d** 96 **p** 97. C Drumglass w Moygashel *Arm* 96-99; Hon V Choral Arm Cathl 97-99; I Donaghmore w Upper Donaghmore 99-06; I Ballymore from 06; Sen Dom Chapl to Abp Arm from 06; Dioc Communications Officer 02-09; Asst Dioc and Prov Registrar from 09. *Ballymore Rectory, 10 Glebe Hill Road, Tandragee, Craigavon BT62 2DP* Tel (028) 3884 0234 E-mail ballymore@armagh.anglican.org *or* dco@armagh.anglican.org

FORSTER, The Ven Victor Henry. b 17. TCD BA45 MA49. **d** 45 **p** 46. C Magheralin *D & D* 45-47; C-in-c Garrison w Slavin *Clogh* 47-51; Bp's C Ballybay 51-52; I Killeevan 52-59; I Rathgraffe *M & K* 59-67; I Aghalurcher w Tattykeeran, Cooneen etc *Clogh* 67-89; Preb Clogh Cathl 80-83; Adn Clogh 83-89; rtd 89; Lic to Offic *D & D* 89-96; V 4 Ard-Na-Ree, Groomsport, Bangor BT19 6JL Tel (028) 9146 4548

FORSTER, William. b 50. NOC 92. **d** 95 **p** 96. C Ashton-in-Makerfield St Thos *Liv* 95-00; TR Fazakerley Em 00-08; TV Eccleston from 08. *The Vicarage, Chapel Lane, Eccleston, St Helens WA10 5DA* Tel (01744) 22698 E-mail william.forster1@btopenworld.com

FORSYTH, Jeanette Mary Shaw. b 48. Aber Coll of Educn ACE78. St Jo Coll Nottm 85. **d** 89. NSM Old Deer *Ab* 89-92; NSM Longside 89-92; NSM Strichen 89-92; NSM Fraserburgh 92-94; Tanzania 95-96, 97-98 and 99-00. *Moss-side of Strichen, Bogensouzie, Strichen AB43 7TU* Tel (01771) 637230 E-mail jeanetteforsyth@hotmail.com

FORSYTH, John Warren. b 38. Univ of W Aus BA62 Princeton Th Sem DMin98. St Mich Th Coll Crafers 65. **d** 65 **p** 66. C Busselton Australia 65-68; R Kondinin 68-72; C Warwick St Mary *Cov* 72-74; C Edin St Pet 74-76; R E Fremantle and Palmyra Australia 76-79; Chapl Abp Perth and Warden Wollaston 79-82; R Midland 82-89; Sen Angl Chapl R Perth Hosp 89-06; rtd 06; Perm to Offic Dio Perth from 06. *40B Cookham Road, Lathlain WA 6100, Australia* Tel (08) 9472 1893 Mobile 89-472 1893 E-mail forsyth@iinet.net.au

FORSYTHE, John Leslie. b 27. CITC. **d** 65 **p** 66. C Cloughfern *Conn* 65-67; C Carnmoney 67-71; I Mossley 71-80; I Antrim All SS 80-95; Preb Conn Cathl 94-95; rtd 95. *96 Hopefield Road, Portrush BT56 8HF* Tel (028) 7082 2623

FORTNUM, Brian Charles Henry. b 48. Hertf Coll Ox MA Imp Coll Lon MSc. Wycliffe Hall Ox 82. **d** 84 **p** 85. C Tonbridge St Steph *Roch* 84-87; V Shorne 87-94; P-in-c Speldhurst w Groombridge and Ashurst 94-98; R 98-01; V Tunbridge Wells St Mark from 01. *The Vicarage, 1 St Mark's Road, Tunbridge Wells TN2 5LT* Tel (01892) 526069 E-mail brian.fortnum@diocese-rochester.org

FORWARD, Canon Eric Toby. b 50. Nottm Univ BEd72 Hull Univ MA93. Cuddesdon Coll 74. **d** 77 **p** 78. C Forest Hill Ch Ch *S'wark* 77-80; Chapl Goldsmiths' Coll Lon 80-84; Chapl Westwood Ho Sch Pet 84-86; V Brighton St Aug and St Sav *Chich* 86-90; Perm to Offic *York* 90-95; V Kingston upon Hull St Alb 95-05; Can Res and Prec Liv Cathl 05-07; rtd 07. *2 Kingsway, Liverpool L22 4RQ* Tel 0151-928 0681
FORWARD, Miss Frances Mary. b 43. Bp Otter Coll Chich TCert64. SEITE 96. **d** 99 **p** 00. NSM Ham St Andr *S'wark* 99-09; NSM Ham St Rich from 09; NSM Petersham from 09. *66 Tudor Drive, Kingston upon Thames KT2 5QF* Tel (020) 8546 1833
FORWARD, Canon Ronald George. b 25. Selw Coll Cam BA50 MA54. Ridley Hall Cam 50. **d** 52 **p** 53. C Denton Holme *Carl* 52-55; C-in-c Mirehouse St Andr CD 55-61; V Mirehouse 61-66; V Kendal St Thos 66-90; V Crook 78-90; Hon Can Carl Cathl 79-90; rtd 90; Perm to Offic *Carl* from 90. *51 Mayo Park, Cockermouth CA13 0BJ* Tel (01900) 824359
FORWARD, Toby. See FORWARD, Canon Eric Toby
FOSBUARY, David Frank. b 32. Leeds Univ BA63. Coll of Resurr Mirfield 63. **d** 65 **p** 66. C Fleetwood St Pet *Blackb* 65-68; Lesotho 69-76; C Dovercourt *Chelmsf* 76-78; TV 78-79; TV Basildon St Martin w H Cross and Laindon etc 79-82; R Colsterworth *Linc* 82-84; R Colsterworth Gp 84-90; RD Beltisloe 89-90; R Lawshall w Shimplingthorne and Alpheton *St E* 90-96; rtd 96; Perm to Offic *St E* from 96. *56 Lindisfarne Road, Bury St Edmunds IP33 2EH* Tel (01284) 767687
FOSDIKE, Lewis Bertram. b 23. Keble Coll Ox BA52 MA56. Wells Th Coll 52. **d** 54 **p** 55. C Westbury-on-Trym H Trin *Bris* 54-58; V Bedminster St Fran 58-64; V Summertown *Ox* 64-76; TR Wolvercote w Summertown 76-89; rtd 89; Chapl St Hugh's Coll Ox 89-97. *18 Osberton Road, Oxford OX2 7NU* Tel (01865) 515817
FOSKETT, Canon John Herbert. b 39. St Cath Coll Cam BA62 Lambeth MA04. Chich Th Coll 62. **d** 64 **p** 65. C Malden St Jo *S'wark* 64-70; P-in-c Kingston St Jo 70-76; Chapl Maudsley Hosp Lon 76-94; Chapl Bethlem R Hosp Beckenham 76-94; Hon Can S'wark Cathl 88-94; rtd 94; Perm to Offic *B & W* 95-01 and from 06. *Victoria Cottage, 8 Cornwall Road, Dorchester DT1 1RT* Tel (01305) 751572
FOSS, David Blair. b 44. Bris Univ BA65 Dur Univ MA66 Fitzw Coll Cam BA68 MA72 K Coll Lon PhD86. St Chad's Coll Dur 68. **d** 69 **p** 70. C Barnard Castle *Dur* 69-72; Sierra Leone 72-74; Chapl St Jo Coll York 74-75; Chapl Ch Ch Coll of HE Cant 75-80; Chapl Elmslie Girls' Sch Blackpool 80-83; Tutor Coll of Resurr Mirfield 83-88; V Battyeford *Wakef* 88-99; TR Wyke All SS *Portsm* 99-01; TR Rochdale *Man* 01-09; R from 09. *The Vicarage, Sparrow Hill, Rochdale OL16 1QT* Tel (01706) 645014
FOSS, Esther Rose. b 79. Regent's Park Coll Ox BA00 MA04 Clare Hall Cam MPhil04. Westcott Ho Cam 03. **d** 05 **p** 06. C Altrincham St Geo *Ches* 05-07; C Bramhall from 07. *2 Hillside Close, Bramhall, Stockport SK7 2LP* Tel 0161-440 7689 E-mail estherfoss@yahoo.co.uk
FOSSETT, Michael Charles Sinclair. b 30. Dur Univ BSc54 CEng59 MIMechE59. NEOC 82. **d** 90 **p** 91. NSM Nether w Upper Poppleton *York* from 90. *20 Fairway Drive, Upper Poppleton, York YO26 6HE* Tel (01904) 794712
FOSSEY (*née* HIRST), **Margaret.** b 52. Huddersfield Univ BA96. NOC 06. **d** 09. NSM Birkby and Birchencliffe *Wakef* from 09. *103 Kirkstone Avenue, Dalton, Huddersfield HD5 9ES* Tel (01484) 301242
FOSTEKEW, Dean James Benedict. b 63. Bulmershe Coll of HE BEd86. Chich Th Coll 89. **d** 92 **p** 93. C Boyne Hill *Ox* 92-95; P-in-c Lockerbie and Annan *Glas* 95-97; P-in-c Dalmahoy *Edin* 97-02; TV Edin St Mary 02-09; R Edin Gd Shep from 09; Dioc Miss 21 Co-ord from 97; Prov Miss 21 Co-ord from 01. *9 Upper Coltbridge Terrace, Edinburgh EH12 6AD* Tel 0131-346 4127 Mobile 07968-099470 E-mail therector@uwclub.net *or* mission21@edinburgh.anglican.org
FOSTER, Anthony Stuart. b 47. K Coll Lon BD69 Peterho Cam BA72 MA74 Lon Inst of Educn PGCE70. Pontifical Beda Coll Rome 82. **d** 85 **p** 86. In RC Ch 85-98; NSM Leighton-cum-Minshull Vernon *Ches* 05-07; rtd 07; Perm to Offic *Ches* from 07. *10 Uppergate Street, Conwy LL32 8RF* Tel (01492) 562658 E-mail revtonyfoster@btinternet.com
FOSTER, Antony John. b 39. Down Coll Cam BA61 MA65. Ridley Hall Cam 65. **d** 66 **p** 67. C Sandal St Helen *Wakef* 66-69; Uganda 69-74; V Mount Pellon *Wakef* 74-92; rtd 92; Perm to Offic *Wakef* from 92. *32 Savile Drive, Halifax HX1 2EU* Tel (01422) 344152
✠**FOSTER, The Rt Revd Christopher Richard James.** b 53. Univ Coll Dur BA75 Man Univ MA77 Trin Hall Cam BA79 MA83 Wadh Coll Ox MA83. Westcott Ho Cam 78. **d** 80 **p** 81 **c** 01. C Tettenhall Regis *Lich* 80-82; Chapl Wadh Coll Ox 82-86; C Ox St Mary V w St Cross and St Pet 82-86; V Southgate Ch Ch *Lon* 86-94; CME Officer 88-94; Can Res and Sub-Dean St Alb 94-01; Suff Bp Hertford from 01. *Hertford House, Abbey Mill Lane, St Albans AL3 4HE* Tel (01727) 866420 Fax 811426 E-mail bishophertford@stalbans.anglican.org

FOSTER, David Brereton. b 55. Selw Coll Cam BA77 MA81 Ox Univ BA80. Wycliffe Hall Ox 78. **d** 81 **p** 82. C Luton St Mary *St Alb* 81-84; C Douglas St Geo and St Barn *S & M* 84-87; V S Ramsey St Paul 87-91; Dir Dioc Tr Inst 88-91; Asst Dir Buckingham Adnry Chr Tr Progr *Ox* 91-95; Dir 95-97; C W Wycombe w Bledlow Ridge, Bradenham and Radnage 91-97; TV High Wycombe 97-07; Tr Officer CME and Laity Development *Man* from 07. *109 Ascot Avenue, Sale M33 4GT* Tel 0161-976 1693 E-mail rev.dbf@ntlworld.com
FOSTER, Edward James Graham. b 12. St Jo Coll Cam BA34 MusBac35 MA38. Wells Th Coll 35. **d** 37 **p** 38. C Kidderminster St Mary *Worc* 37-43; C Feckenham w Astwood Bank 43-45; Chapl and Lect Dioc Tr Coll Chester 45-51; V Balby w Hexthorpe *Sheff* 51-67; V Ashford w Sheldon *Derby* 67-78; rtd 78; Perm to Offic *Derby* from 78. *Beckside, Baslow Road, Ashford-in-the-Water, Bakewell DE45 1QA* Tel (01629) 812868
FOSTER, Edward Philip John. b 49. Trin Hall Cam BA70 MA74. Ridley Hall Cam 76. **d** 79 **p** 80. C Finchley Ch Ch *Lon* 79-82; C Marple All SS *Ches* 82-86; P-in-c Cambridge St Matt *Ely* 86-90; V 90-07; rtd 07. *1 Barnfield, Common Lane, Hemingford Abbots, Huntingdon PE28 9AX* Tel (01480) 399098
FOSTER, Frances Elizabeth. See TYLER, Mrs Frances Elizabeth
FOSTER, Canon Gareth Glynne. b 44. Open Univ BA. Chich Th Coll 66. **d** 69 **p** 70. C Fairwater *Llan* 69-71; C Merthyr Tydfil 71-72; C Merthyr Tydfil and Cyfarthfa 72-76; TV 76-87; Dioc Soc Resp Officer from 87; P-in-c Abercanaid from 87; Exec Officer Dioc Bd Soc Resp from 95; Can Llan Cathl from 05. *19 The Walk, Merthyr Tydfil CF47 8RU,* or *Diocesan Office, The Court, Coychurch, Bridgend CF35 5EH* Tel (01685) 722354 *or* (01656) 868853 Fax (01656) 868869 Mobile 07753-823038 E-mail garethfoster@churchinwales.org.uk
FOSTER, Gavin Richard. b 76. Regent's Park Coll Ox BA97 MA01 Barrister-at-Law (Gray's Inn) 98. Wycliffe Hall Ox BTh09. **d** 09. C Radipole and Melcombe Regis *Sarum* from 09. *130B Belgrave, Southill Garden Drive, Weymouth DT4 9SN*
FOSTER, Mrs Geraldine. b 55. RGN77. SAOMC 00. **d** 03 **p** 04. C Flackwell Heath *Ox* 03-07; C Ashton-upon-Mersey St Mary Magd *Ches* from 07. *109 Ascot Avenue, Sale M33 4GT* Tel 0161-976 1693 E-mail rev.gf@virgin.net
FOSTER, Mrs Gillian Susan. b 62. Leeds Univ BA09. NOC 06. **d** 09. C Frankby w Greasby *Ches* from 09. *35 Hillfield Drive, Wirral CH61 6UJ* Tel 0151-342 8412 Mobile 07970-522365 E-mail stephen@foster5344.fsnet.co.uk
FOSTER, Graham Paul. b 66. Univ of W Aus BSc86 DipEd87 BEd88 Murdoch Univ Aus BD99 Qu Coll Ox MSt00 DPhil02. **d** 04 **p** 05. Lect NT Edin Univ from 03; NSM Edin St Mary from 04. *University of Edinburgh, Mound Place, Edinburgh EH1 2LX*
FOSTER, James. b 29. Man Univ BA52 MA55 Lon Univ CertEd53 Leeds Univ MEd74. NEOC 82. **d** 85 **p** 86. NSM Aldborough w Boroughbridge and Roecliffe *Ripon* 85-91; P-in-c Kirby-on-the-Moor, Cundall w Norton-le-Clay etc 91-97; rtd 97; Perm to Offic *Ripon* from 97. *Bishopen Bower, Marton, Marton cum Grafton, York YO51 9QY* Tel (01423) 323133
FOSTER, Mrs Joan Alison. b 46. ARMCM67. NOC 95. **d** 98 **p** 99. NSM Blundellsands St Nic *Liv* 98-02; Asst Chapl Southport and Ormskirk NHS Trust 98-02; V N Harrow St Alb *Lon* from 02. *St Alban's Vicarage, Church Drive, Harrow HA2 7NS* Tel (020) 8868 6567 Mobile 07713-819012 E-mail revjoanfoster@yahoo.co.uk
FOSTER, Jonathan Guy Vere. b 56. Goldsmiths' Coll Lon BA78. Wycliffe Hall Ox 83. **d** 86 **p** 87. C Hampreston *Sarum* 86-90; Chapl Chantilly *Eur* 90-97; V Branksome St Clem *Sarum* from 97. *The Vicarage, 7 Parkstone Heights, Branksome, Poole BH14 0QE* Tel (01202) 748058
FOSTER, Joseph James Frederick. b 22. SS Paul & Mary Coll Cheltenham CertEd42 Birm Univ DipEd59. **d** 88 **p** 88. NSM Elstead *Guildf* 88-94; Perm to Offic 94-03. *2 The Oakhurst, 21 The Knoll, Beckenham BR3 5UD* Tel (020) 8658 4559
FOSTER, Mrs Julia. b 58. RGN RSCN. STETS 03. **d** 06 **p** 07. NSM Chilworth w N Baddesley *Win* from 06; NSM Ampfield from 07. *11 West Lane, North Baddesley, Southampton SO52 9GB* Tel (023) 8041 0682 E-mail juliafoster58@hotmail.com
FOSTER, Leslie. b 49. Linc Th Coll 89. **d** 91 **p** 92. C Coseley Ch Ch *Lich* 91-93; C Coseley Ch Ch *Worc* 93-95; V Firbank, Howgill and Killington *Bradf* 95-00; Hon C Sedbergh, Cautley and Garsdale 95-00; Dioc Rural Adv 96-00; P-in-c Ruyton XI Towns w Gt and Lt Ness *Lich* from 00; RD Ellesmere from 08. *The Vicarage, The Village, Ruyton Eleven Towns, Shrewsbury SY4 1LQ* Tel (01939) 261234 E-mail lesfoster@lunevic.freeserve.co.uk
FOSTER, Michael John. b 52. St Steph Ho Ox 76. **d** 79 **p** 80. C Wood Green St Mich *Lon* 79-82; TV Clifton *S'well* 82-85; P-in-c Aylesbury *Ox* 85-87; Dep Warden Durning Hall Chr Community Cen 87-89; V Lydbrook *Glouc* 89-97; R Hemsby, Winterton, E and W Somerton and Horsey *Nor* 97-99; P-in-c Tarrant Valley *Sarum* 99-01; P-in-c Tollard Royal w Farnham, Gussage St Michael etc 99-01; R Chase from 01; C Sixpenny Handley w Gussage St Andrew etc from 06. *The Rectory, Church*

Hill, Tarrant Hinton, Blandford Forum DT11 8JB Tel (01258) 830764 E-mail drmike@church.prestel.co.uk

FOSTER, Paul. *See* FOSTER, Graham Paul

FOSTER, Paul. b 60. MAAT80. Oak Hill Th Coll 91. **d** 93 **p** 94. C New Clee *Linc* 93-96; P-in-c Aldington w Bonnington and Bilsington *Cant* 96-02; P-in-c Lympne w W Hythe 00-02; Chapl HM Pris Aldington 96-02; Chapl HM YOI Feltham from 02. *HM Young Offender Institution, Bedfont Road, Feltham TW13 4ND* Tel (020) 8890 0061 *or* 8844 5325
E-mail pfozzy@hotmail.com *or* paul.foster01@hmps.gsi.gov.uk

FOSTER, Philip. *See* FOSTER, Edward Philip John

FOSTER, Ronald George. b 25. Bris Univ BSc51 AKC51. **d** 52 **p** 53. C Lydney w Aylburton *Glouc* 52-54; C Leighton Buzzard *St Alb* 54-60; Chapl Bearwood Coll Wokingham 60-83; R Wantage Downs *Ox* 83-91; rtd 91; RD Wantage *Ox* 92-95; Perm to Offic from 92. *Ascension Cottage, Horn Lane, East Hendred, Wantage OX12 8LD* Tel (01235) 820790
E-mail ronfos@ukgateway.uk

FOSTER, Miss Samantha. b 80. Sunderland Univ BA01 St Jo Coll Dur BA04. Cranmer Hall Dur 01. **d** 04 **p** 05. C Fulford *York* 04-08; Pioneer Miss Worker from 08. *9 Green Lane, Scarborough YO12 6HL* Tel (01723) 378205

FOSTER, Simon John Darby. b 57. Qu Mary Coll Lon BSc78. Wycliffe Hall Ox 85. **d** 88 **p** 89. C Bedgrove *Ox* 88-92; C Glyncorrwg w Afan Vale and Cymmer Afan *Llan* 92-94; R Breedon cum Isley Walton and Worthington *Leic* 94-98; R Anstey 98-06; R Anstey and Thurcaston w Cropston from 06. *The Rectory, 1 Hurd's Close, Anstey, Leicester LE7 7GH* Tel 0116-236 2176 E-mail revsimonfoster@ntlworld.com

FOSTER, Stephen. b 47. Leeds Univ CertEd69. NEOC 83. **d** 86 **p** 87. NSM Kingston upon Hull St Nic *York* 86-87; NSM Aldbrough, Mappleton w Goxhill and Withernwick 87-98; TV Howden 98-05; RD Howden 02-05; Chapl HM Pris Wolds 03-05; rtd 05; Perm to Offic *York* from 05. *Wycliffe, 6 Victoria Terrace, Robin Hoods Bay, Whitby YO22 4RJ* Tel (01947) 880055

FOSTER, Stephen. b 52. **d** 06 **p** 07. OLM Halliwell *Man* from 06; Chapl Bolton Hosps NHS Trust from 07. *68 Adrian Road, Bolton BL1 3LQ* Tel (01204) 841382

FOSTER, Canon Stephen Arthur. b 54. Lon Univ BMus75 BA78 Potchefstroom Univ PhD98. Coll of Resurr Mirfield 75. **d** 78 **p** 79. C Ches H Trin 78-82; C Tranmere St Paul w St Luke 82-83; V Grange St Andr 83-88; V Cheadle Hulme All SS 88-94; P-in-c Stockport St Matt 94-00; Asst Dir of Ords 96-04; V Sale St Anne 00-04; Can Res Leic Cathl from 04; Prec Leic Cathl from 04. *15 Rockery Close, Leicester LE5 4DQ* Tel 0116-246 1230 *or* 248 7472 Fax 248 7470 Mobile 07715-560669
E-mail stephen.foster@leccofe.org

FOSTER, Steven. b 52. Wadh Coll Ox BA75 MA80. Ridley Hall Cam 76. **d** 79 **p** 80. C Ipsley *Worc* 79-83; TV Woughton *Ox* 83-94; V Walshaw Ch Ch *Man* from 94. *Christ Church Vicarage, 37 Gisburn Drive, Walshaw, Bury BL8 3DH* Tel 0161-763 1193 Fax 08707-052490 E-mail mail@alimus.plus.com

FOSTER, Steven Francis. b 55. Lon Univ BD76 AKC76 Open Univ BA91 FRSA90. Coll of Resurr Mirfield 77. **d** 78 **p** 79. C Romford St Edw *Chelmsf* 78-80; C Leigh St Clem 80-83; Ed Mayhew McCrimmon Publishers 04-06; Hon C Southend 83-86; P-in-c Sandon 86-90; R 90-91; R Wanstead St Mary 91-93; R Wanstead St Mary w Ch Ch 93-00; Perm to Offic 00-05; Asst to Master R Foundn of St Kath in Ratcliffe 00-04; P-in-c Brighton Annunciation *Chich* from 05. *Annunciation Vicarage, 89 Washington Street, Brighton BN2 9SR* Tel (01273) 681341 Mobile 07901-554866 E-mail stevenfoster@aol.com

FOSTER, Stuart Jack. b 47. Oak Hill Th Coll BA80 Lambeth STh86. **d** 80 **p** 81. C Worting *Win* 80-84; C-in-c Kempshott CD 84-88; R Hook 88-95; Chapl and Warden Bp Grosseteste Coll Linc 95-99; R Grayingham and Kirton in Lindsey w Manton *Linc* 99-05; P-in-c Vale of Belvoir Par *Leic* 05-09; OCF 99-04; Chapl ATC 04-09; rtd 09. *Sans Souci, 1 The Garage Flat, Belvoir, Grantham NG32 1PF* Tel (01476) 870567 Mobile 07885-701876

FOSTER, Susan. b 58. Nottm Univ BMedSci80 BM, BS82. WEMTC 00. **d** 03 **p** 05. NSM Tenbury *Heref* from 03. *Little Oaks Cottage, Hope Bagot, Ludlow SY8 3AE* Tel (01584) 891092 E-mail thefosters@littleoakshb.fsnet.uk

FOSTER, Susan Anne. b 53. Trin Coll Bris BA97. **d** 98 **p** 99. C Watton w Carbrooke and Ovington *Nor* 98-02; Min S Wonston CD *Win* 02-07; P-in-c Micheldever and E Stratton, Woodmancote etc 05-07; V Upper Dever from 07. *The Rectory, Micheldever, Winchester SO21 3DA* Tel (01962) 774379

FOSTER, Thomas Andrew Hayden. b 43. CITC 70. **d** 73 **p** 74. C Dublin Clontarf *D & G* 73-78; I Drumcliffe w Clare Abbey and Kildysart *L & K* 78-80; P-in-c Polstead *St E* 78; I Kilscoran w Killinick and Mulrankin *C & O* 80-85; I Fanlobbus Union *C, C & R* 85-86; R Lasswade and Dalkeith *Edin* 86-87; C Woodford St Mary w St Phil and St Jas *Chelmsf* 87-88; I New w Old Ross, Whitechurch, Fethard etc *C & O* 89-91; Dioc Info Officer (Ferns) 90-91; I Whitehouse *Conn* from 03. *The Rectory, 283 Shore Road, Newtownabbey BT37 9SR* Tel (028) 9085 1622 E-mail hfoster@ireland.com

FOSTER, Thomas Arthur. b 23. St D Coll Lamp BA47. Cuddesdon Coll 47. **d** 49 **p** 50. C Risca *Mon* 49-52; C Win H Trin 52-55; C Rumney *Mon* 55-56; V Cwmtillery 56-59; R Llanfoist and Llanellen 59-92; rtd 92; Perm to Offic *Mon* from 98. *The Bungalow, 5 The Bryn, Llangattock-juxta-Usk, Abergavenny NP7 9AG* Tel (01873) 840516

FOSTER-CLARK, Mrs Sarah Hazel. b 75. Man Univ BA97 Heythrop Coll Lon MA99. Wycliffe Hall Ox 98. **d** 00 **p** 01. C Walmsley *Man* 00-01; C Turton Moorland Min 01; C Horwich and Rivington 01-04; C Halliwell 04-07; Perm to Offic from 07. *Address temp unknown* Tel 07909-916741 (mobile)
E-mail revdf-c@xalt.co.uk

FOTHERBY, Miss Doreen. b 41. **d** 05 **p** 06. OLM Shipdham w E and W Bradenham *Nor* from 05. *6 Pound Green Lane, Shipdham, Thetford IP25 7LF* Tel (01362) 821481
E-mail d.fotherby@btinternet.com

FOTHERGILL, Richard Patrick. b 61. Newc Univ BA83. Trin Coll Bris 91. **d** 95 **p** 96. C E Twickenham St Steph *Lon* 95-97; Assoc R Kirstenhof S Africa 97-04; Network Miss P *Bris* 04-06; Hon C Peasedown St John w Wellow *B & W* from 09. *Flossie Cottage, South Stoke, Bath BA2 7ED* Tel (01225) 832804

FOUGNER, Tor Even. b 65. Lutheran Sch of Th Oslo 84. **p** 92. Norway 92-01; NSM Walkley *Sheff* 02-03; C Sheff St Leon Norwood 03-06. *Address temp unknown* Tel 07966-670207 (mobile) E-mail fougner@online.no

FOUHY, Giles. b 71. Oak Hill Th Coll. **d** 07 **p** 08. C Shoreditch St Leon w St Mich *Lon* from 07. *16 Albion Drive, London E8 4ET* E-mail gilesfouhy@hotmail.com

FOULDS, John Stuart. b 64. Lanc Univ BA87 Southn Univ BTh91. Chich Th Coll 88. **d** 91 **p** 92. C Eastcote St Lawr *Lon* 91-95; C Wembley Park 95-99; P-in-c Meir *Lich* 99-07. *Address temp unknown*

FOULGER, Bernard Darwin. b 28. Cant Sch of Min 86. **d** 89 **p** 90. OLM Sittingbourne H Trin w Bobbing *Cant* 89-97; rtd 97; Perm to Offic *Cant* from 97. *30 Frederick Street, Sittingbourne ME10 1AU* Tel (01795) 422724

FOULIS BROWN, Graham Douglas. b 50. JP87. St Steph Ho Ox 80. **d** 82 **p** 83. C Hungerford and Denford *Ox* 82-84; Chapl Hungerford Hosp 83-84; C Bicester w Bucknell, Caversfield and Launton *Ox* 84-85; TV 85-90; V Kidmore End and Sonning Common 90-03; P-in-c Rotherfield Peppard 02-03; R Rotherfield Peppard and Kidmore End etc from 03; AD Henley from 06. *The Rectory, Kidmore End, Reading RG4 9AY* Tel 0118-972 3987 Fax 972 4202 E-mail gdfb.vicarage@lineone.net

FOULKES, Chan Meurig. b 21. St D Coll Lamp BA46. St Mich Coll Llan 46. **d** 47 **p** 48. C Llanbeblig w Caernarfon *Ban* 47-55; Bp's Private Chapl 55-58; V Harlech and Llanfair juxta Harlech 58-66; RD Ardudwy 64-76; R Llanaber w Caerdeon 66-76; Can Ban Cathl 71-89; Treas 74-83; Chan 83-89; R Llandegfan and Beaumaris w Llanfaes w Penmon etc 76-89; rtd 90; Perm to Offic *Ban* from 90. *Llanaber, 11 Gogarth Avenue, Penmaenmawr LL34 6PY* Tel (01492) 623011

FOULKES, Simon. b 58. Ox Poly BA81. Oak Hill Th Coll BA89. **d** 89 **p** 90. C St Austell *Truro* 89-92; C Boscombe St Jo *Win* 92-94; P-in-c Portswood St Denys 94-99; Par Evang Adv *Wakef* 99-01; TR Almondbury w Farnley Tyas 02-03; Perm to Offic *Cant* 07-09; P-in-c Bethersden w High Halden from 09. *The Vicarage, Bull Lane, Bethersden, Ashford TN26 3HA* Tel (01233) 820764 E-mail vicar@idnet.com

FOUNTAIN, David Roy (Brother Malcolm). b 48. Qu Coll Birm 85. **d** 87 **p** 88. SSF from 72; NSM Handsworth St Mich *Birm* 87-92; Lic to Offic *Sarum* 92-95; Perm to Offic *Worc* 95-00, *Newc* 00-02, *Lon* 02-03; V Bentley *Sheff* from 03. *The Vicarage, 3A High Street, Bentley, Doncaster DN5 0AA* Tel (01302) 876272

FOUNTAIN, John Stephen. b 43. RAF Coll Cranwell 65 Solicitor 80. LNSM course 91. **d** 93 **p** 94. NSM Nacton and Levington w Bucklesham and Foxhall *St E* 93-03; NSM Taddington, Chelmorton and Flagg, and Monyash *Derby* from 03. *The Old School, Chelmorton, Buxton SK17 9SG* Tel (01298) 85009

FOUNTAIN, Miss Stephanie Ann Cecilia. b 58. Lon Univ BMus81 Roehampton Inst PGCE88. Westcott Ho Cam 00. **d** 02 **p** 03. C Tadworth *S'wark* 02-06; TV Boston *Linc* from 07. *St Thomas's Vicarage, 2 Linley Drive, Boston PE21 7EJ* Tel (01205) 352381 E-mail stephaniefountain@yahoo.co.uk

FOUTS, Arthur Guy. b 44. Washington Univ BA72 Seabury-Western Th Sem DMin89. Ridley Hall Cam 78. **d** 81 **p** 82. C Alperton *Lon* 81-84; R Pinxton *Derby* 84-87; R Dublin St Patr USA 88-89; Pastor Warren St Mark 90-91; R Silver Spring St Mary Magd 91-99; Chapl St Andr Sch 99-00; P-in-c Point of Rocks St Paul 01-08. *12304 Guinevere Road, Glenn Dale MD 20769-8938, USA* Tel (001) (301) 860 1551
E-mail rubberduck301@yahoo.com

FOWELL, Preb Graham Charles. b 48. Southn Univ BTh85. Chich Th Coll. **d** 82 **p** 83. C Clayton *Lich* 82-86; C Uttoxeter w Bramshall 86-90; V Oxley 90-95; P-in-c Shifnal 95-07; V Shifnal and Sheriffhales 07-08; RD Edgmond and Shifnal 06-08; TR Stafford from 08; Preb Lich Cathl from 08. *The Rectory, 32 Rowley Avenue, Stafford ST17 9AG* Tel (01785) 258511

FOWLER, Anthony Lewis. b 57. Oak Hill Th Coll BA93. **d** 93 **p** 94. C Walton *St E* 93-96; P-in-c Combs 96-00; P-in-c Hitcham w Lt Finborough 98-00; R Combs and Lt Finborough 00-04; Chapl Suffolk Coll 00-04; Chapl HM Pris Coldingley 04-05; Chapl HM Pris Blundeston 05-07; Chapl HM Pris Swinfen Hall from 07. *HM Prison Swinfen Hall, Swinfen, Lichfield WS14 9QS* Tel (01543) 484125 E-mail tony.fowler@hmps.gsi.gov.uk *or* alfowler@supanet.com

FOWLER, Canon Colin. b 40. Linc Th Coll 80. **d** 82 **p** 83. C Barbourne *Worc* 82-85; TV Worc St Martin w St Pet, St Mark etc 85-86; TV Worc SE 86-92; P-in-c Moulton *Linc* 92-95; Chapl Puerto de la Cruz Tenerife *Eur* 95-01; Hon Can Madrid Cathl from 99; R Tangmere and Oving *Chich* 01-05; rtd 05; Perm to Offic *Nor* from 07. *10 Drakes Heath, Lowestoft NR32 2QQ* Tel (01502) 564707

FOWLER, Canon David Mallory. b 51. Ian Ramsey Coll 74 Trin Coll Bris 75. **d** 78 **p** 79. C Rainhill *Liv* 78-81; C Houghton *Carl* 81-84; P-in-c Grayrigg 84-89; P-in-c Old Hutton w New Hutton 84-89; V Kirkoswald, Renwick and Ainstable 89-99; P-in-c Gt Salkeld w Lazonby 98-99; R Kirkoswald, Renwick, Gt Salkeld and Lazonby from 00; RD Penrith 99-06; Hon Can Carl Cathl from 99. *The Vicarage, Kirkoswald, Penrith CA10 1DQ* Tel (01768) 898176 E-mail revdmf@aol.com

FOWLER, Mrs Carole Karen Brenda. b 56. Middx Univ BA97. Oak Hill Th Coll 91. **d** 93 **p** 94. NSM Walton *St E* 93-96; Chapl Ipswich Hosp NHS Trust 94-00; NSM Combs *St E* 96-00; NSM Combs and Lt Finborough 98-00; C 00-04; P-in-c 04; C S Hartismere 04-07; Perm to Offic *Lich* 08-09; C Lich St Chad from 09. *45 Giles Road, Lichfield WS13 7JY* Tel (01543) 415850 Mobile 07709-921385 E-mail jan.fowler@lichfield.anglican.org

FOWLER, John Ronald. b 30. Ely Th Coll 55. **d** 58 **p** 59. C Surbiton St Andr *S'wark* 58-61; C St Sidwell Lodge Guyana 61-62; V Morawhanna 62-65; R Plaisance 65-70 and 83-89; V Sydenham All SS 70-81; V Wood End *Cov* 81-83; Adn Demerara and Can St Geo Cathl 86-89; V Bedford St Mich *St Alb* 90-95; rtd 95. *12 St Marys Paddock, Wellingborough NN8 1HL* Tel (01933) 228691

FOWLER, John Thomas. b 42. EAMTC. **d** 01 **p** 02. NSM Stoke by Nayland w Leavenheath and Polstead *St E* from 01. *Warners, Thorington Street, Stoke by Nayland, Colchester CO6 4SP* Tel and fax (01206) 337229 E-mail jm@albys2.freeserve.co.uk

FOWLES, Canon Christopher John. b 31. Lich Th Coll 54. **d** 58 **p** 59. C Englefield Green *Guildf* 58-63; C Worplesdon 63-69; V Chessington 69-77; V Horsell 77-95; RD Woking 92-94; Hon Can Guildf Cathl 94-95; rtd 95; Perm to Offic *Guildf* from 95. *78 St Jude's Road, Egham TW20 0DF* Tel (01784) 439457

FOX, Mrs Carole Ann. b 36. TISEC 98. **d** 99 **p** 00. NSM Ellon *Ab* from 99. *4 Mavis Bank, Newburgh, Ellon AB41 6FB* Tel (01358) 789693 E-mail charlesandcarole@btinternet.com

FOX, Charles Edward. b 36. Lich Th Coll 62. **d** 66 **p** 67. C S Bank *York* 66-69; C Stokesley 69-72; V Egton w Grosmont 72-82; P-in-c Ugthorpe 72-82; P-in-c Newbold Verdon *Leic* 82-83; R Newbold de Verdun and Kirkby Mallory 84-04; rtd 04; Perm to Offic *Leic* from 04. *White Rose Cottage, 6 Brascote Lane, Newbold Verdon, Leicester LE9 9LF* Tel (01455) 822103

FOX, Colin George. b 46. TD. Sarum & Wells Th Coll 73. **d** 75 **p** 76. C N Hammersmith St Kath *Lon* 75-79; CF (TA) 76-90; C Heston *Lon* 79-81; TV Marlborough *Sarum* 81-90; P-in-c Pewsey 90-91; TR 91-98; TR Pewsey and Swanborough 98-03; Chapl Pewsey Hosp 90-95; P-in-c Avon Valley *Sarum* from 03; C Durrington from 08. *The Vicarage, High Street, Netheravon, Salisbury SP4 9QP* Tel (01980) 670326 E-mail foxy.col@talk21.com

FOX, Cynthia. b 39. Ripon Coll of Educn CertEd59 Man Univ MEd72 Sheff Univ PhD81 Bradf Univ MSc83 Leeds Univ MA87 Westmr Coll Ox BTh98. NOC 03. **d** 04 **p** 05. NSM Battyeford *Wakef* 04-05; NSM Brighouse and Clifton from 05. *Foxdene, 134 Nab Lane, Mirfield WF14 9QJ* Tel (01924) 499112 Fax 499799 E-mail cynthia@nablane.fsnet.co.uk

FOX, Harvey Harold. b 27. Lich Th Coll 58. **d** 60 **p** 61. C Birchfield *Birm* 60-62; C Boldmere 62-65; V Sparkbrook Em 65-71; V Dordon 71-77; V Four Oaks 77-82; V Packwood w Hockley Heath 82-90; rtd 90; Perm to Offic *Cov* from 90. *37 Meadow Road, Henley-in-Arden B95 5LB* Tel (01564) 795302

FOX, Canon Herbert Frederick. b 26. Leeds Univ BA50. Coll of Resurr Mirfield 50. **d** 52 **p** 53. C Bury St Thos *Man* 52-55; V Unsworth 55-61; V Turton 61-72; V Farnworth and Kearsley 72-78; RD Farnworth 77-84; TR E Farnworth and Kearsley 78-84; Hon Can Man Cathl 81-84; V Ashford Hill w Headley Win 84-91; rtd 91; Perm to Offic *Man* from 91. *9 Highfield Road, Blackrod, Bolton BL6 5BP* Tel (01204) 698368

FOX, Canon Ian James. b 44. Selw Coll Cam BA66 MA70. Linc Th Coll 66. **d** 68 **p** 69. C Salford St Phil w St Steph *Man* 68-71; C Kirkleatham *York* 71-73; TV Redcar w Kirkleatham 73-77; V Bury St Pet *Man* 77-85; V Northallerton w Kirby Sigston *York* 85-03; RD Northallerton 85-91; Chapl Friarage and Distr Hosp Northallerton 88-92; Chapl Northallerton Health Services NHS Trust 92-03; P-in-c Barlby w Riccall *York* 03-09; P-in-c

Hemingbrough 06-09; Can and Preb York Minster 95-09; rtd 09. *21 Springfield Close, Thirsk YO7 1FH* Tel (01845) 523154 E-mail ianfox321@btinternet.com

FOX, Preb Jacqueline Frederica. b 43. Ripon Coll of Educn CertEd66 Leeds Univ BEd74 MEd84 HonRCM85. S Dios Minl Tr Scheme 83. **dss** 85 **d** 87 **p** 94. RCM *Lon* 85-86; Dioc FE Officer 87-96; Hon C Acton St Mary 87-96; R 96-08; Dean of Women's Min 96-08; Dir of Ords Willesden Area 01-08; Preb St Paul's Cathl 01-08; rtd 08. *52 North Street, Ripon HG4 1EN* Tel (01765) 603698 E-mail jackie@actonfox.co.uk

FOX, Mrs Jane. b 47. Open Univ BA91 Bp Otter Coll Chich CertEd75 ALA70. S Dios Minl Tr Scheme 92. **d** 95 **p** 96. NSM W Blatchington *Chich* 95-98; C Peacehaven and Telscombe Cliffs 98-01; C Telscombe w Piddinghoe and Southease 98-01; TV Hitchin *St Alb* 01-08; P-in-c Harrold and Carlton w Chellington from 08. *Church House, 3 The Moor, Carlton, Bedford MK43 7JR* Tel (01234) 720262 E-mail janefox_1@btinternet.com

FOX *(née* **COULDRIDGE), Mrs Janice Evelyn.** b 49. Bognor Regis Coll of Educn CertEd71. Glouc Sch of Min 89. **d** 92 **p** 94. C Tupsley w Hampton Bishop *Heref* 92-96; P-in-c Orleton w Brimfield 96-01; Dioc Ecum Officer 96-01; TV Worc SE 01-05; rtd 05. *4 McIntyre Road, Worcester WR2 5LG* Tel (01905) 423637 E-mail janfox7@netscape.net

FOX, Jeremy Robin. b 68. St Chad's Coll Dur BA89 MA92 Leeds Univ BA94. Coll of Resurr Mirfield 92. **d** 95 **p** 96. C S Shields All SS *Dur* 95-99; C Tottenham St Paul *Lon* 99-04; C Edmonton St Mary w St Jo 99-04; Chapl Belgrade *Eur* from 04. *clo FCO (Belgrade), King Charles Street, London SW1A 2AH* Tel (00381) (11) 402315 E-mail robin.fox@sbb.co.yu

FOX, John Brian. b 38. **d** 94 **p** 95. NSM Phillack w Gwithian and Gwinear *Truro* 94-96; NSM Godrevy 96-03; Chapl St Mich Mt from 04. *Abbeydale, 26 Tresdale Parc, Connor Downs, Hayle TR27 5DX* Tel (01736) 753935

FOX, Jonathan Alexander. b 56. St Jo Coll Nottm LTh77 BTh78. **d** 81 **p** 82. C Chasetown *Lich* 81-85; TV Fazakerley Em *Liv* 85-89; NSM Swanwick and Pentrich *Derby* 89-92; Miss Aviation Fellowship Kenya 92-96; TV Madeley *Heref* 97-02; Co-ord Chapl HM Pris Onley from 04. *HM Prison Onley, Willoughby, Rugby CV23 8AP* Tel (01788) 523530 E-mail jonathan.fox@hmps.gsi.gov.uk

FOX, Leonard. b 41. AKC66. **d** 67 **p** 68. C Salford Stowell Memorial *Man* 67-68; C Hulme St Phil 68-72; C Portsea All SS w St Jo Rudmore *Portsm* 72-75; V Oakfield St Jo 75-92; P-in-c Portsea All SS 92-06; V 06; Dir All SS Urban Miss Cen 92-06; rtd 06; Perm to Offic *Portsm* from 07. *Middle Reach, Ashlake Farm Lane, Wootton Bridge, Ryde PO33 4LF* Tel (01983) 880138

FOX, Linda Margaret. b 58. **d** 08. NSM S Croydon St Pet and St Aug *S'wark* from 08. *67 Kingsdown Avenue, South Croydon CR2 6QJ*

FOX, Maurice Henry George. b 24. Lon Univ BD58. St Aid Birkenhead 47. **d** 49 **p** 50. C Eccleshill *Bradf* 49-52; C Bingley All SS 52-56; V Cross Roads cum Lees 56-62; V Sutton 62-79; V Grange-over-Sands *Carl* 79-88; rtd 89. *7 Manor Close, Topcliffe, Thirsk YO7 3RH* Tel (01845) 578322

FOX, Michael Adrian Orme. b 47. Bris Univ BSc68 PhD72. WMMTC 01. **d** 04 **p** 05. NSM Codsall *Lich* from 04; Ind Chapl Black Country Urban Ind Miss from 04. *30 Bromley Gardens, Codsall, Wolverhampton WV8 1BE* Tel (01902) 843442 E-mail mike@maofox.me.uk

FOX, The Ven Michael John. b 42. Hull Univ BSc63. Coll of Resurr Mirfield 64. **d** 66 **p** 67. C Becontree St Elisabeth *Chelmsf* 66-70; C Wanstead H Trin Hermon Hill 70-72; V Victoria Docks Ascension 72-76; V Chelmsf All SS 76-88; P-in-c Chelmsf Ascension 85-88; RD Chelmsf 86-88; R Colchester St Jas, All SS, St Nic and St Runwald 88-93; Hon Can Chelmsf Cathl 91-93; Adn Harlow 93-95; Adn W Ham 95-07; rtd 07; Perm to Offic *Chelmsf* from 08. *17A Northgate Street, Colchester CO1 1EZ* Tel (01206) 710701

FOX, Michael John Holland. b 41. Lon Univ BD68. Oak Hill Th Coll 64. **d** 69 **p** 70. C Reigate St Mary *S'wark* 69-73; NSM 76-01; C Guildf St Sav 73-76; Asst Chapl Reigate Gr Sch 76-81; Chapl 81-01; NSM Reigate St Pet CD *S'wark* 96-01; P-in-c Reigate St Luke w Doversgreen 01-09; rtd 09; Hon C Reigate St Mary *S'wark* from 09. *31 Blackborough Road, Reigate RH2 7BU* Tel (01737) 226616 E-mail mikejh.fox@virgin.net

FOX, Norman Stanley. b 39. Wolv Univ LLB97 Birm Univ LLM09. St Mich Coll Llan 61. **d** 64 **p** 65. C Brierley Hill *Lich* 64-67; C Tettenhall Regis 67-70; V Cradley *Worc* 70-73; Asst Chapl HM Pris Wakef 73-74; Chapl HM Pris The Verne 74-76; R Clayton W w High Hoyland *Wakef* 76-81; R Cumberworth 81-84; C Tettenhall Wood *Lich* 85-89; TV 89-91; V Pensnett 91-93; rtd 99. *54 Lyndon Road, Solihull B92 7RQ* Tel 0121-707 8216 E-mail normanfox@blueyonder.co.uk

✠**FOX, The Rt Revd Peter John.** b 52. AKC74. St Aug Coll Cant 74. **d** 75 **p** 76 **c** 02. C Wymondham *Nor* 75-79; Miss P Papua New Guinea 79-85; R Gerehu 80-85; Dioc Sec Port Moresby 84-85; P-in-c E w W Rudham *Nor* 85-88; P-in-c Syderstone w Barmer and Bagthorpe 85-88; P-in-c Tatterford 85-88; P-in-c Tattersett 85-88; P-in-c Houghton 85-88; R Coxford Gp 88-89;

TR Lynton, Brendon, Countisbury, Lynmouth etc *Ex* 89-95; RD Shirwell 92-95; P-in-c Harpsden *Ox* 95-02; Gen Sec Melanesian Miss 95-02; Bp Port Moresby Papua New Guinea 02-06; Hon Asst Bp Nor from 06; P-in-c Nor Lakenham St Jo and All SS and Tuckswood 06-07; V from 07. *The Vicarage, Harwood Road, Norwich NR1 2NG* Tel (01603) 625679
E-mail peterandangiefox@yahoo.co.uk

FOX, Canon Raymond. b 46. QUB BSc69. CITC 71. **d** 71 **p** 72. C Holywood *D & D* 71-75; C Min Can Down Cathl 75-78; I Killinchy w Kilmood and Tullynakill 78-81; I Belfast St Mary *Conn* 81-88; I Killaney w Carryduff *D & D* 88-02; Can Down Cathl 98-02; Chapter Clerk and V Choral Belf Cathl 00-02; I Donegal w Killymard, Lough Eske and Laghey *D & R* from 02. *The Rectory, Ballyshannon Road, Donegal, Republic of Ireland* Tel (00353) (73) 972 1075 E-mail donegal@raphoe.anglican.org

FOX, Robert. b 54. Man Univ BEd76. NOC 89. **d** 91 **p** 92. NSM Stalybridge *Man* 91; NSM Ashton 91-08; NSM Ashton from 08. *36 Norman Road, Stalybridge SK15 1LY* Tel 0161-338 8481
E-mail rob.foxesbridge@tiscali.co.uk

FOX, Robin. *See* FOX, Jeremy Robin

FOX, Sidney. b 47. Nottm Univ BTh79 PhD93. Linc Th Coll 75. **d** 79 **p** 80. C Middlesbrough St Oswald *York* 79-81; P-in-c 81-86; V 86-87; V Newby 87-92; R Brechin and Tarfside *Bre* 92-05; P-in-c Auchmithie 92-00; Can St Paul's Cathl Dundee 98-05; V Broughton *Blackb* from 05. *The Vicarage, 410 Garstang Road, Broughton, Preston PR3 5JB* Tel (01772) 862330
E-mail revsfox@tiscali.co.uk

FOX, Timothy William Bertram. b 37. CCC Cam BA61. Qu Coll Birm 66. **d** 68 **p** 69. C Cannock *Lich* 68-72; C Bilston St Leon 72-75; V Essington 75-81; R Buildwas and Leighton w Eaton Constantine etc 81-92; RD Wrockwardine 88-92; R Bradeley, Church Eaton and Moreton 92-04; rtd 04; Hon C Hanbury, Newborough, Rangemore and Tutbury *Lich* 04-08. *40 Lakebar Avenue, High Bentham, Lancaster LA2 7JN* Tel (01524) 262575

FOX-WILSON, Francis James. b 46. Nottm Univ BTh73. Linc Th Coll 69. **d** 73 **p** 74. C Eastbourne St Elisabeth *Chich* 73-76; C Seaford w Sutton 76-78; P-in-c Hellingly 78-79; P-in-c Upper Dicker 78-79; V Hellingly and Upper Dicker 79-85; V Goring-by-Sea 85-93; R Alfriston w Lullington, Litlington and W Dean 93-08; rtd 08; Hon C Isfield *Chich* from 08. *The Parsonage, Station Road, Isfield, Uckfield TN22 5EY* Tel (01825) 750247

FOXWELL, Rupert Edward Theodore. b 54. Magd Coll Cam BA76 MA80 Solicitor 79. Wycliffe Hall Ox 91. **d** 93 **p** 94. C Tonbridge SS Pet and Paul *Roch* 93-98. *24 Cheviot Close, Tonbridge TN9 1NH* Tel and fax (01732) 358555
E-mail foxwell@harvester.org.uk

FOY, Malcolm Stuart. b 48. ACP80 FCollP FRSA Univ of Wales (Lamp) BA71 Magd Coll Cam CertEd72 K Coll Lon MA89. Ox NSM Course 84. **d** 87 **p** 88. NSM Tilehurst St Mich *Ox* 87-90; C Ireland Wood *Ripon* 90-96; Adv RE Leeds Adnry 90-96; Dir Educn *Bradf* 96-99; C Otley 99; Perm to Offic from 00. *45 The Chase, Keighley BD20 6HU* Tel (01535) 665112

FOY, Peter James. b 59. **d** 08 **p** 09. NSM Warminster Ch Ch *Sarum* from 08. *122 High Street, Chapmanslade, Westbury BA13 4AW* Tel (01373) 832088

FRAIS, Jonathan Jeremy. b 65. Kingston Poly LLB87. Oak Hill Th Coll BA92. **d** 92 **p** 93. C Orpington Ch Ch *Roch* 92-96; Asst Chapl Moscow *Eur* 96-99; Chapl Kiev 99-05; R Bexhill St Mark *Chich* from 05. *St Mark's Rectory, 11 Coverdale Avenue, Bexhill-on-Sea TN39 4TY* Tel and fax (01424) 843733
E-mail frais@tiscali.co.uk

FRAMPTON, John Marcia Ellen. b 36. SRN65 SCM66. Ripon Coll Cuddesdon 86. **d** 88 **p** 95. Par Dn Paston *Pet* 88-89; Par Dn Burford w Fulbrook and Taynton *Ox* 90-92; Par Dn Witney 92-93; NSM Heref S Wye 94-01; rtd 01; Perm to Offic *Heref* from 02. *15 Waterfield Road, Hereford HR2 7DD* Tel (01432) 278955

FRAMPTON-MORGAN, Anthony Paul George. *See* MORGAN, Anthony Paul George

FRANCE, Alistair. *See* FRANCE, Robert Alistair

FRANCE, Andrew. *See* FRANCE, John Andrew

FRANCE, Charles Malcolm. b 48. ACA71 FCA76. EAMTC 94. **d** 97 **p** 98. C Gt Grimsby St Mary and St Jas *Linc* 97-02; P-in-c Skegness and Winthorpe 02-04; P-in-c Ingoldmells w Addlethorpe 02-04; R Skegness Gp from 04. *20 Drake Road, Skegness PE25 3BH* Tel (01754) 612079
E-mail malcolmfrance@aol.com

FRANCE (née PIERCY), Mrs Elizabeth Claire. b 66. Qu Mary Coll Lon BSc83. Wycliffe Hall Ox 97. **d** 99 **p** 00. C Dronfield w Holmesfield *Derby* 99-03; V Allestree 03-05. *The Rectory, Rectory Close, Etchingham Road, Burwash, Etchingham TN19 7BH* Tel (01435) 882301 E-mail lizcfrance@tiscali.co.uk

FRANCE, Evan Norman Lougher. b 52. Jes Coll Cam BA74 MA78. Wycliffe Hall Ox 76. **d** 79 **p** 80. C Hall Green Ascension *Birm* 79-82; CMS 82-84; C Bexhill St Pet *Chich* 84-87; V Westfield from 87. *The Vicarage, Vicarage Lane, Westfield, Hastings TN35 4SD* Tel (01424) 751029
E-mail evanfrance@tiscali.co.uk

FRANCE, Geoffrey. b 37. S Dios Minl Tr Scheme 87. **d** 90 **p** 91. NSM Uckfield *Chich* 90-92; C 92-94; R Warbleton and Bodle Street Green 94-02; rtd 02. *Little Croft, 19 James Avenue, Herstmonceux, Hailsham BN27 4PB* Tel (01323) 831840

FRANCE, John Andrew. b 68. Edin Univ MA90 Leeds Univ BA00 Dur Univ MA09. Coll of Resurr Mirfield 98. **d** 00 **p** 01. C Hartlepool H Trin *Dur* 00-04; Co-ord Chapl HM Pris Low Newton 04-05; V Earsdon and Backworth *Newc* from 05. *The Vicarage, 5 Front Street, Earsdon, Whitley Bay NE25 9JU* Tel 0191-252 9393 E-mail andrewfrance1968@hotmail.com

FRANCE, Malcolm. *See* FRANCE, Charles Malcolm

FRANCE, Malcolm Norris. b 28. Ch Ch Ox BA53 MA57 Essex Univ PhD75. Westcott Ho Cam 53. **d** 55 **p** 56. C Ipswich St Mary le Tower *St E* 55-58; V Esholt *Bradf* 58-64; Chapl Essex Univ 64-73; Perm to Offic *Chich* 77-87; P-in-c Starston *Nor* 87-93; rtd 93; Perm to Offic *Nor* from 93. *The Old Swan, Townsend, Wylye, Warminster BA12 0RZ* Tel (01985) 248189

FRANCE, Canon Richard Thomas. b 38. Ball Coll Ox BA60 MA63 Lon Univ BD62 Bris Univ PhD67. Tyndale Hall Bris 60. **d** 66 **p** 67. C Cambridge St Matt *Ely* 66-69; Nigeria 69-73 and 76-77; Hon Can Ibadan from 94; Lib Tyndale Ho Cam 73-76; Warden 78-81; Vice-Prin Lon Bible Coll 81-88; Prin Wycliffe Hall Ox 89-95; R Wentnor w Ratlinghope, Myndtown, Norbury etc *Heref* 95-99; rtd 99; Perm to Offic *Ban* from 00. *Tyn-y-twll, Llwyngwril LL37 2QL* Tel (01341) 250596
E-mail dick@tynytwll.co.uk

FRANCE, Robert Alistair. b 71. Ox Poly BA92. Oak Hill Th Coll BA97. **d** 97 **p** 98. C Hartford *Ches* 97-02; P-in-c Stokenchurch and Ibstone *Ox* from 02. *The Vicarage, Wycombe Road, Stokenchurch, High Wycombe HP14 3RG* Tel (01494) 483384
E-mail revalistair@aol.com

FRANCE, Stephen Mark. b 66. Wycliffe Hall Ox BTh00. **d** 00 **p** 01. C Newbold w Dunston *Derby* 00-03; P-in-c Darley Abbey 03-05; Dioc Duty Press Officer 03-04; P-in-c Burwash *Chich* 05-06; R from 06. *The Rectory, Rectory Close, Etchingham Road, Burwash, Etchingham TN19 7BH* Tel (01435) 882301
E-mail revfrance@tiscali.co.uk

FRANCE, William Michael. b 43. Sydney Univ BA68 Lon Univ BD72 Chas Sturt Univ NSW MEd96. Moore Th Coll Sydney LTh70. **d** 73 **p** 73. C Turramurra Australia 73-75; C Barton Seagrave w Warkton *Pet* 76-78; R Dundas Australia 79-82; Chapl The K Sch 83-94; Chapl Syndey C of E Girls' Gr Sch 94-99; Assoc Chapl St Andr Cathl Sch 99-04; R Murchison 04-08; rtd 08. *6 Wesson Road, West Pennant Hills NSW 2125, Australia* Tel (0061) (2) 9945 0939
E-mail billandjackie@optusnet.com.au
or wfrance@sacs.nsw.edu.au

FRANCE, Archdeacon of. *See* LETTS, The Ven Kenneth John

FRANCES, Nicolas Francis. b 61. MBE98. NOC 92. **d** 95 **p** 96. NSM Anfield St Columba *Liv* 95-98; Australia from 98; Acting Dir Health and Welfare Chapls Melbourne 98-99; Exec Dir Brotherhood of St Laur from 99. *15 Traill Street, Northcote Vic 3070, Australia* Tel (0061) (3) 9481 7373 *or* 9483 1347 Fax 9486 9724 E-mail nic@bsl.org.au

FRANCES ANNE, Sister. *See* COCKER, Mrs Frances Rymer

FRANCIS, Miss Annette. b 44. Trin Coll Bris 91. **d** 93 **p** 94. NSM Belmont *Lon* 93; C 94-97; C Swansea St Pet *S & B* 97-99; V Llanelli from 99. *Llanelly Rectory, Abergavenny Road, Gilwern, Abergavenny NP7 0AD* Tel (01873) 830280

FRANCIS, Claude Vernon Eastwood. b 15. Univ of Wales BA38. Ripon Hall Ox 38. **d** 40 **p** 41. C Cilybebyll *Llan* 40-44; C Treorchy 44-46; C Whitchurch 46-49; C Winscombe *B & W* 49-55; R E Pennard w Pylle 55-75; R Ditcheat w E Pennard and Pylle 75-81; rtd 81; Perm to Offic *B & W* from 81. *The Garden Flat, Sexey's Hospital, Bruton BA10 0AS* Tel (01749) 812147

FRANCIS, David Carpenter. b 45. Southn Univ BSc66 Loughb Univ MSc71 Sussex Univ MA83. Westcott Ho Cam 85. **d** 87 **p** 88. C Ealing St Mary *Lon* 87-90; Chapl Ealing Coll of HE 87-90; Chapl Clayponds Hosp Ealing 88-90; P-in-c Wembley St Jo *Lon* 90-93; Chapl Wembley Hosp 90-93; V Platt *Roch* 93-01; Post Ord Tr Officer 93-98; RD Shoreham 99-01; R Stow on the Wold, Condicote and The Swells *Glouc* from 01; AD Stow from 04. *The Rectory, Sheep Street, Stow on the Wold, Cheltenham GL54 1AA* Tel (01451) 830607 Fax 830903 Mobile 07799-410370

FRANCIS, David Everton Baxter. b 45. St Deiniol's Hawarden 76. **d** 77 **p** 78. C Llangyfelach *S & B* 77-78; C Llansamlet 78-80; V Llanrhaeadr-ym-Mochnant, Llanarmon, Pennant etc *St As* 80-85; V Penrhyncoch and Elerch *St D* 85-93; V Borth and Eglwys-fach w Llangynfelyn 93-02; V Garthbeibio w Llanerfyl w Llangadfan etc *St As* from 02; AD Caereinion from 02. *Ty'r Eglwys, Pont Robert, Meifod SY22 6HY* Tel (01938) 500361

FRANCIS, Miss Gillian Cartwright. b 40. CertFd61. Dalton Ho Bris 69. **dss** 85 **d** 87 **p** 94. Blackheath *Birm* 86-94; Par Dn 87-94; P-in-c Stechford 94-03; rtd 03; Perm to Offic *Glouc* from 03. *22 Ince Castle Way, Gloucester GL1 4DT* Tel (01452) 503059

FRANCIS, Canon Graham John. b 45. St Mich Coll Llan 66. **d** 70 **p** 71. C Llanblethian w Cowbridge and Llandough etc 70-76; V Penrhiwceiber w Matthewstown and Ynysboeth 76-02; V

285

Cardiff St Mary and St Steph w St Dyfrig etc from 02; V Grangetown from 05; Can Llan Cathl from 02. *St Mary's Vicarage, 2 North Church Street, Cardiff CF10 5HB* Tel and fax (029) 2048 7777 E-mail fathergraham@aol.com

FRANCIS, Canon James More MacLeod. b 44. Edin Univ MA65 BD68 PhD74 Yale Univ STM69. New Coll Edin 65. **d** 87 **p** 87. Sen Lect RS Sunderland Univ from 82; NSM Sunderland St Chad 87-98; TV Sunderland 98-07; NSM Sunderland Minster from 07; Tutor NEOC 89-98; Bp's Adv for NSM *Dur* from 99; Prin Dioc OLM Course from 02; Hon Can Dur Cathl from 00. *Woodside, David Terrace, Bowburn, Durham DH6 5EF* 0191-377 9215 E-mail jamesfrancis@mac.com

FRANCIS, James Stephen. b 66. FInstD97 FRSA99. SEITE 95. **d** 99 **p** 07. NSM St Botolph Aldgate w H Trin Minories *Lon* 99-02; NSM Soho St Anne w St Thos and St Pet 02-05; Chapl RNR 05-07; NSM St Mary le Strand w St Clem Danes *Lon* 07; Chapl RN from 07. *Royal Naval Chaplaincy Service, Mail Point 1-2, Leach Building, Whale Island, Portsmouth PO2 8BY* Tel (023) 9262 5055 Fax 9262 5134 Mobile 07961-123811 E-mail james.francis118@hotmail.co.uk

FRANCIS, Canon James Woodcock. b 28. OBE97. Wilberforce Univ Ohio AB57 Payne Th Sem Ohio BD58. Bexley Hall Div Sch Ohio 59. **d** 59 **p** 60. USA 59-84; Bermuda from 85; Can Res Bermuda 85-99; R Devonshire Ch Ch from 99. *PO Box HM 627, Hamilton HM CX, Bermuda* Tel (001809) 295 1125 Fax 292 5421

FRANCIS, Jeffrey Merrick. b 46. Bris Univ BSc69. Qu Coll Birm 72. **d** 76 **p** 77. C Bris Ch the Servant Stockwood 76-79; C Bishopston 79-82; V Bris St Andr Hartcliffe 82-93; TV Bris St Paul's 93-00; P-in-c Barton Hill St Luke w Ch Ch and Moorfields 00-02; Perm to Offic from 02. *32 Burfoot Gardens, Stockwood, Bristol BS14 8TE* Tel (01275) 831020

FRANCIS, Jennifer Anne Harrison. b 45. JP. Southn Univ BSc67 Brunel Univ MA74 CQSW73. WEMTC 07. **d** 07 **p** 08. NSM Stow on the Wold, Condicote and The Swells *Glouc* from 07. *The Rectory, Sheep Street, Stow on the Wold, Cheltenham GL54 1AA* Tel (01451) 830607 Fax 830903 Mobile 07881-953769 E-mail jennyfrancis1@btinternet.com

FRANCIS, Jeremy Montgomery. b 31. BNC Ox BA53 MA56. Glouc Sch of Min 84. **d** 87 **p** 88. NSM Chedworth, Yanworth and Stowell, Coln Rogers etc *Glouc* 87-90; NSM Coates, Rodmarton and Sapperton etc 90-01; NSM Daglingworth w the Duntisbournes and Winstone 95-97; NSM Brimpsfield w Birdlip, Syde, Daglingworth etc 97-00; Perm to Offic from 01. *Old Barnfield, Duntisbourne Leer, Cirencester GL7 7AS* Tel (01285) 821370

FRANCIS, John. b 56. Bris Poly BA78 MCIH81. **d** 98 **p** 99. OLM Hatcham Park All SS *S'wark* from 98. *Flat 2, 133 Deptford High Street, London SE8 4NS* Tel (020) 8691 3145 *or* 8875 5942 E-mail franci@threshold.org.uk

FRANCIS, John Sims. b 25. Fitzw Ho Cam BA54 MA58. St D Coll Lamp BA47 LTh49. **d** 49 **p** 50. C Swansea St Barn *S & B* 49-52; C Chesterton St Andr *Ely* 52-54; C Swansea St Mary and H Trin *S & B* 54-58; V Newbridge-on-Wye and Llanfihangel Brynpabuan 58-65; R Willingham *Ely* 65-82; RD N Stowe 78-82; R Rampton 82; P-in-c Buckden 82-85; V 85-91; rtd 91; Perm to Offic *Linc* 92-01. *3 The Brambles, Bourne PE10 9TF* Tel (01778) 426396

FRANCIS, Julian Montgomery. b 60. Selw Coll Cam BA83 MA83. S'wark Ord Course 88. **d** 91 **p** 92. C S Wimbledon H Trin and St Pet *S'wark* 91-95; V Cottingley *Bradf* 95-99; Minority Ethnic Angl Concerns Officer *Lich* 99-02; Assoc Min W Bromwich St Andr w Ch Ch 99-02; TR Coventry Caludon 02-08; Nat Tr Co-ord for Minority Ethnic Anglicans from 08. *The Queen's College, Somerset Road, Edgbaston, Birmingham B15 2QH* Tel 0121-454 1527 E-mail j.francis@queens.ac.uk

FRANCIS, Miss Katherine Jane. b 67. St Jo Coll Dur BA08 RGN88 RM92. Cranmer Hall Dur 06. **d** 08 **p** 09. C Sprotbrough *Sheff* from 08. *31 Ambleside Crescent, Sprotbrough, Doncaster DN5 7PR* Tel (01302) 851414 E-mail katynana@msn.com

FRANCIS, Kenneth. b 30. Em Coll Cam BA56 MA60. Coll of Resurr Mirfield. **d** 58 **p** 59. C De Beauvoir Town St Pet *Lon* 58-61; Zambia 62-70; V Harlow St Mary Magd *Chelmsf* 70-76; V Felixstowe St Jo *St E* 76-97; rtd 98. *33 Cordy's Lane, Trimley, Felixstowe IP10 0UD*

FRANCIS, Kenneth Charles. b 22. Oak Hill Th Coll 46. **d** 50 **p** 51. C Wandsworth All SS *S'wark* 50-53; V Deptford St Nic w Ch Ch 53-61; V Summerstown 61-77; R Cratfield w Heveningham and Ubbeston etc *St E* 77-87; rtd 87; Perm to Offic *Truro* from 87. *Wheal Alfred, Chapel Hill, Bolingey, Perranporth TR6 0DQ* Tel (01872) 571317

FRANCIS, Canon Leslie John. b 47. Pemb Coll Ox BA70 MA74 BD90 Nottm Univ MTh76 Qu Coll Cam PhD76 ScD97 Lon Univ MSc77 FBPsS88 FCP94. Westcott Ho Cam 70. **d** 73 **p** 74. C Haverhill *St E* 73-77; P-in-c St Bradley 78-82; P-in-c Lt Wratting 79-82; Research Officer Culham Coll Inst 82-88; P-in-c N Cerney w Bagendon *Glouc* 82-85; Perm to Offic 85-95; Fell Trin Coll Carmarthen 89-99; Dean of Chpl 95-99; Prof Th Univ

of Wales (Lamp) 92-99; Prof Practical Th Univ of Wales (Ban) 99-07; Prof Religions and Educn Warw Univ from 07; Perm to Offic *Ox* 95-01 and *Ban* 99-06; Hon C Llanfair-pwll and Llanddaniel-fab etc *Ban* from 06; Hon Can St D Cathl 98-99; Hon Can and Can Th Ban Cathl from 06. *Llys Onnen, Abergwyngregyn, Llanfairfechan LL33 0LD* Tel (01248) 681877

FRANCIS, Martin Rufus. b 37. Pemb Coll Ox BA60 MA64. Linc Th Coll. **d** 63 **p** 64. C W Hartlepool St Paul *Dur* 63-67; C Yeovil St Jo w Preston Plucknett *B & W* 67-69; Chapl Tonbridge Sch 69-83; Chapl and Dep Hd St Jo Sch Leatherhead 83-94; R Herstmonceux and Wartling *Chich* 94-01; rtd 01; Perm to Offic *Sarum* from 02. *50 Lower Bryanston, Blandford Forum DT11 0DR* Tel (01258) 488619

FRANCIS, Paul Edward. b 52. Southn Univ BTh84. Sarum & Wells Th Coll 78. **d** 81 **p** 82. C Biggin Hill *Roch* 81-85; R Fawkham and Hartley 85-90; V Aylesford 90-99; V Riverhead w Dunton Green from 99; Chapl Dioc Assn of Readers from 01; RD Sevenoaks from 05. *St Mary's Vicarage, The Glebe Field, Shoreham Lane, Sevenoaks TN13 3DR* Tel (01732) 455736 E-mail paul.francis@diocese-rochester.org

FRANCIS, Peter Alan. b 73. Wycliffe Hall Ox. **d** 09. C Horsham *Chich* from 09. *18 Queensway, Horsham RH13 5AY* Tel (01403) 250329

FRANCIS, Peter Brereton. b 53. St Andr Univ MTheol77. Qu Coll Birm 77. **d** 78 **p** 79. C Hagley *Worc* 78-81; Chapl Qu Mary Coll *Lon* 81-87; R Ayr *Glas* 87-92; Miss to Seamen 87-92; Provost St Mary's Cathl 92-96; R Glas St Mary 92-96; Warden and Lib St Deiniol's Lib Hawarden from 97. *St Deiniol's Library, Church Lane, Hawarden, Deeside CH5 3DF* Tel (01244) 532350 E-mail deiniol.visitors@btinternet.com

FRANCIS, Peter Philip. b 48. St Jo Coll Dur BA73. Wycliffe Hall Ox 73. **d** 75 **p** 76. C Foord St Jo *Cant* 75-78; C Morden *S'wark* 78-83; P-in-c Barford St Martin, Dinton, Baverstock etc *Sarum* 83-88; P-in-c Fovant, Sutton Mandeville and Teffont Evias etc 83-86; R Newick *Chich* from 88. *The Rectory, Church Road, Newick, Lewes BN8 4JX* Tel (01825) 722692 E-mail pnfrancis@btinternet.com

FRANCIS, Philip Thomas. b 58. TD03. St D Coll Lamp BA81 Regent's Park Coll Ox MTh99. Chich Th Coll 81. **d** 82 **p** 83. C Llanelli St Paul *St D* 82-84; C Barnsley St Mary *Wakef* 84-87; V Burton Dassett *Cov* from 87; V Gaydon w Chadshunt from 87; P-in-c Avon Dassett w Farnborough and Fenny Compton from 07; CF (TA) from 88. *Burton Dassett Vicarage, Northend, Southam CV47 2TH* Tel (01295) 770400 E-mail philip.francis@regents.ox.ac.uk

FRANCIS, Mrs Sharon. b 57. Westmr Coll Ox BTh99. SEITE 98. **d** 08 **p** 09. NSM Langton Green *Roch* from 08. *Mill Cottage, Mill Lane, Lamberhurst, Tunbridge Wells TN3 8EG* Tel (01892) 890109 E-mail sharon.francis@ukonline.co.uk

FRANCIS, Younis. b 66. **d** 95 **p** 95. C Addington *S'wark* 05-07; TV Cheam from 07. *49 Brocks Drive, Sutton SM3 9UW* E-mail younis_francis@hotmail.com

FRANCIS-DEHQANI, Gulnar Eleanor (Guli). b 66. Nottm Univ BA89 Bris Univ MA94 PhD99. SEITE 95. **d** 98 **p** 99. C Mortlake w E Sheen *S'wark* 98-02; Chapl R Academy of Music *Lon* 02-04; Chapl St Marylebone C of E Sch 02-04; Perm to Offic *Pet* from 04. *The Vicarage, Vicarage Road, Oakham LE15 6EG* Tel and fax (01572) 722108 Mobile 07771-948190 E-mail guli@uwclub.net

FRANCIS-DEHQANI, Lee Thomas. b 67. Nottm Univ BA89. Sarum & Wells Th Coll 92 Trin Coll Bris BA95. **d** 95 **p** 96. C Putney St Mary *S'wark* 95-98; TV Richmond St Mary w St Matthias and St Jo 98-04; P-in-c Oakham, Hambleton, Egleton, Braunston and Brooke *Pet* from 04; P-in-c Langham from 04; C Teigh w Whissendine and Market Overton from 04; C Cottesmore and Barrow w Ashwell and Burley from 04. *The Vicarage, Vicarage Road, Oakham LE15 6EG* Tel and fax (01572) 722108 Mobile 07867-503059 E-mail oakhamvicarage@uwclub.net

FRANK, Derek John. b 49. Imp Coll Lon BScEng70 Warwick Univ MSc71. Cranmer Hall Dur 83. **d** 85 **p** 86. C Clay Cross *Derby* 85-87; C Crookes St Thos *Sheff* 87-90; TV 90-93; Chapl Vevey w Château d'Oex and Villars *Eur* 93-02; rtd 07. *702 rue des Allobroges, 74140 Saint-Cergues, France* Tel (0033) (4) 50 94 26 22 E-mail derek@ebeg.ch

FRANK, Penelope Edith. b 45. WMMTC 96. **d** 99 **p** 00. NSM Edgbaston St Geo *Birm* 99-02; Perm to Offic *Cov* 03-04; NSM Stoneleigh w Ashow from 04; CPAS 87-06; rtd 06. *23 Hall Close, Stoneleigh, Coventry CV8 3DG* Tel (024) 7641 3730 E-mail pennyfrank@mail.com

FRANK, Canon Richard Patrick Harry. b 40. St Chad's Coll Dur BA66. **d** 68 **p** 69. C Darlington H Trin *Dur* 68-72; C Monkwearmouth St Andr 72-74; C-in-c Harlow Green CD 74-79; R Skelton and Hutton-in-the-Forest w Ivegill *Carl* 79-86; V Carl St Luke Morton 86-92; RD Carl 88-89; P-in-c Thursby 89-90; P-in-c Kirkbride w Newton Arlosh 89-92; TR Greystoke, Matterdale, Mungrisdale etc 92-98; P-in-c Patterdale 95-98; TR Gd Shep TM 98-99; RD Penrith 96-99; Hon Can Carl Cathl

97-99; rtd 99; Perm to Offic *Carl* 00-02; *York* from 02. *11 Risby Place, Beverley HU17 8NT* Tel (01482) 679540
E-mail richardandann.frank@virgin.net

FRANK, Richard Stephen. b 70. Keble Coll Ox MEng93 Fitzw Coll Cam MA98. Ridley Hall Cam 96. **d** 99 **p** 00. C Cranham Park *Chelmsf* 99-04; P-in-c St Margaret's-on-Thames *Lon* from 05. *295 St Margarets Road, Twickenham TW1 1PN* Tel (020) 8891 3504 Mobile 07973-719730
E-mail richardfrank@allsoulschurch.org.uk

FRANKLAND, Angela Tara. b 69. Lon Bible Coll BA96 MA98. EAMTC 97. **d** 99 **p** 00. C Hornchurch St Andr *Chelmsf* 99-03; TV Wickford and Runwell from 03. *8 Friern Walk, Wickford SS12 0HZ* Tel (01268) 734077
E-mail tfrankland@btinternet.com

FRANKLIN, David John. b 67. Selw Coll Cam BA88 MA92. St Jo Coll Nottm MTh06. **d** 06 **p** 07. C Windermere *Carl* from 06. *Burnthwaite, Kendal Road, Bowness-on-Windermere, Windermere LA23 3EW* Tel (015394) 44301
E-mail david@franklind.freeserve.co.uk

FRANKLIN, Hector Aloysius. b 32. NOC 94. **d** 97 **p** 98. NSM Chapeltown *Sheff* 97-99; P-in-c Sheff St Paul 99-02; rtd 02; Perm to Offic *Sheff* from 04. *108 Mackenzie Crescent, Burncross, Sheffield S35 1US* Tel 0114-245 7160

FRANKLIN, Canon Lewis Owen. b 46. Natal Univ BSc67. S'wark Ord Course 68. **d** 73 **p** 74. C Durban St Paul S Africa 74-75; R Newcastle H Trin 76-79; Dir St Geo Cathl Cen Cape Town 80-83; Chapl St Geo Gr Sch 84-86; R Sea Pt H Redeemer 87-89; R Cape Town St Paul 89-90; Subdean and Prec Kimberley Cathl 91-94 and 96-99; Hon Can from 93; Dioc Sec Kimberley and Kuruman 94-96; C Altrincham St Geo *Ches* 99-00; P-in-c Newcastle St Paul *Lich* 00-05; R Bryanston St Mich S Africa 05-09; rtd 08. *258 Shingara Sands, 20 Petroy Drive, Magalies View, Fourways, 2191 South Africa* Tel (0027) (11) 465 1262
E-mail fr.owen@gmail.com

FRANKLIN, Miss Ola. b 55. Balls Park Coll Hertford CertEd76 Open Univ BA92 Birkbeck Coll Lon MA95. NTMTC BA09. **d** 09. C Harlow St Mary and St Hugh w St Jo the Bapt *Chelmsf* from 09. *9 Longacre, Harlow CM17 0TA* Tel (01279) 426209
E-mail ofrank@ukonline.co.uk

FRANKLIN, Richard Charles Henry. b 48. Ch Ch Coll Cant CertEd70 Heythrop Coll Lon MA08. Sarum & Wells Th Coll 75. **d** 78 **p** 79. C Pershore w Pinvin, Wick and Birlingham *Worc* 78-80; Educn Chapl 80-85; V Wollescote 85-92; V Fareham SS Pet and Paul *Portsm* 92-98; V Luton All SS w St Pet *St Alb* from 98; RD Luton 07-12. *All Saints' Vicarage, Shaftesbury Road, Luton LU4 8AH* Tel (01582) 720129
E-mail richardfranklin@mail2world.com

FRANKLIN, Canon Richard Heighway. b 54. Southn Univ BA75 MPhil83. Sarum & Wells Th Coll 75. **d** 78 **p** 79. C Thame w Towersey *Ox* 78-81; Asst Chapl Southn Univ 81-83; Dir of Studies Chich Th Coll 83-89; P-in-c Stalbridge *Sarum* 89-94; V Weymouth H Trin from 94; Can and Preb Sarum Cathl from 02; RD Weymouth 04-08. *Holy Trinity Vicarage, 7 Glebe Close, Weymouth DT4 9RL* Tel (01305) 760354 *or* 774597
E-mail richardfranklin@iname.com

FRANKLIN (née WESTMACOTT), Mrs Rosemary Margaret. b 41. WEMTC 03. **d** 05 **p** 06. NSM Cirencester *Glouc* from 05. *Waterton Farm House, Ampney Crucis, Cirencester GL7 5RR* Tel (01285) 654282 E-mail revrmf@btinternet.com

FRANKLIN, Preb Simon George. b 54. Bris Univ BA75. Ridley Hall Cam 77. **d** 79 **p** 80. C Woodmansterne *S'wark* 79-83; C St Peter-in-Thanet *Cant* 83-86; R Woodchurch 86-96; P-in-c Ottery St Mary, Alfington, W Hill, Tipton etc *Ex* 96-99; TR from 99; P-in-c Feniton and Escot from 07; Preb Ex Cathl from 07. *The Vicar's House, 7 College Road, Ottery St Mary EX11 1DQ* Tel (01404) 812062
E-mail stpaul_church@lineone.net
or safranklin@btopenworld.com

FRANKLIN, Stephen Alaric. b 58. Lon Univ BD87. Sarum & Wells Th Coll 87. **d** 89 **p** 90. C Chenies and Lt Chalfont, Latimer and Flaunden *Ox* 89-93; CF from 93. *c/o MOD Chaplains (Army)* Tel (01980) 615804 Fax 615800

FRANKS, John Edward. b 29. **d** 61 **p** 62. C Plymouth St Matthias *Ex* 61-66; V Upton Grey w Weston Patrick and Tunworth *Win* 66-77; V Upton Grey, Weston Patrick, Tunworth etc 77-79; P-in-c Wolverton cum Ewhurst and Hannington 79-80; R Baughurst, Ramsdell, Wolverton w Ewhurst etc 81-94; rtd 94. *57 Victoria, Santa Lucija, Naxxar, NXR 02, Malta GC* Tel (00356) 2143 7006

FRANKS, John William. b 45. K Alfred's Coll Win BEd87 DAES94 MISM89. STETS 97. **d** 00 **p** 01. NSM Fareham H Trin *Portsm* 00-03; Hon Chapl Pitmore Sch Chandler's Ford 00; Hon Chapl Fareham Coll of F&HE 01-03; C Rowner *Portsm* 03-07; C Bridgemary 05-07; P in c Banwell *B & W* from 08. *Park House, East Street, Banwell BS29 6BW* Tel (01934) 822320

FRANKUM, Matthew David Hyatt. b 65. Leic Poly BSc87. Trin Coll Bris 94. **d** 99 **p** 00. C Bath St Luke *B & W* 99-03; TV Worle 03-08; P-in-c Bath St Luke from 08. *St Luke's Vicarage, Hatfield Road, Bath BA2 2BD* Tel (01225) 311904

FRANSELLA, Cortland Lucas. b 48. Trin Hall Cam BA70 MA74 Heythrop Coll Lon MA00 Open Univ BSc05. NTMTC 95. **d** 98 **p** 99. NSM Palmers Green St Jo *Lon* 98-03; NSM Hornsey St Mary w St Geo 03-08; Perm to Offic from 08. *17 Warner Road, London N8 7HB* Tel (020) 8340 7706
E-mail fransella@btinternet.com

FRANZ, Canon Kevin Gerhard. b 53. Edin Univ MA74 BD79 PhD92. Edin Th Coll 76. **d** 79 **p** 80. C Edin St Martin 79-83; R Selkirk 83-90; Provost St Ninian's Cathl Perth 90-99; R Perth St Ninian 90-99; Gen Sec Action of Churches Together in Scotland from 99; Hon Can St Ninian's Cathl Perth from 00. *7 Forrester Lodge, Inglewood, Alloa FK10 2HU* Tel (01259) 216980 Fax 215964 E-mail kevinfranz@acts-scotland.org

FRASER, Alan Richard. b 69. Leeds Univ BA91 MA94. WMMTC 04. **d** 07 **p** 08. NSM Gravelly Hill *Birm* from 07. *41 Hobhouse Close, Birmingham B42 1HB*
E-mail alan-fraser@blueyonder.co.uk

FRASER, Alister Douglas. b 26. Qu Coll Cam BA49 MA55. Tyndale Hall Bris 50. **d** 68 **p** 69. C Weymouth St Jo *Sarum* 68-72; R Kingswood *Glouc* 72-80; V Woodside St Steph 80-84; RD Forest S 84-88; V Cinderford St Steph w Littledean 84-90; rtd 90; Perm to Offic *Ex* from 91. *4 Stevens Cross Close, Sidmouth EX10 9QJ* Tel (01395) 579568

FRASER, Andrew Thomas. b 52. Newc Univ Aus BA81. St Jo Coll (NSW) ThL79. **d** 81 **p** 82. Australia 81-87; C Prestbury *Glouc* 87-91; C Wotton St Mary 91-92. *79 Victoria Street, Gloucester GL1 4EP* Tel (01452) 381082

FRASER, Christine Nancy. b 61. TISEC 98. **d** 02 **p** 03. NSM St Ninian's Cathl Perth from 02. *9 Balvaird Place, Perth PH1 5EA* Tel (01738) 623827 E-mail cnfraser@btinternet.com

FRASER, Darren Anthony. b 71. Wilson Carlile Coll 02. **d** 08 **p** 09. C Bucknall *Lich* from 08. *The Vicarage, 161A Dawlish Drive, Stoke-on-Trent ST2 0ET* Tel (01782) 260876 Mobile 07766-198455

FRASER, David Ian. b 32. Em Coll Cam BA54 MA58. Oak Hill Th Coll 56. **d** 58 **p** 59. C Bedford St Jo *St Alb* 58-61; C Cheadle Hulme St Andr *Ches* 61-64; R Fringford w Hethe and Newton Purcell *Ox* 64-67; V Preston St Luke *Blackb* 67-71; V Surbiton Hill Ch Ch *S'wark* 71-91; rtd 91; Perm to Offic *Ox* from 97. *7 Godwyn Close, Abingdon OX14 1BU* Tel (01235) 532049
E-mail david@ab-frasers.freeserve.co.uk

FRASER, Mrs Elizabeth Ann. b 44. **d** 07 **p** 08. OLM Witley *Guildf* from 07. *Oakwood, Petworth Road, Milford, Godalming GU8 5BS* Tel (01483) 417190 Mobile 07966-513450
E-mail ann.fraser@btinternet.com

FRASER, Geoffrey Michael. b 29. Sarum Th Coll. **d** 59 **p** 60. C Thames Ditton *Guildf* 59-63; C Shere 63-65; C Dunsford and Doddiscombsleigh *Ex* 65-70; V Uffculme 70-92; rtd 92; Perm to Offic *Worc* from 92. *46 Priory Road, Malvern WR14 3DB* Tel (01684) 576302

FRASER, Canon Giles Anthony. b 64. Newc Univ BA84 Ox Univ BA92 MA97 Lanc Univ PhD99. Ripon Coll Cuddesdon. **d** 93 **p** 94. C Streetly *Lich* 93-97; C Ox St Mary V w St Cross and St Pet 97-00; Chapl Wadh Coll Ox 97-00; V Putney St Mary *S'wark* 00-04; TR 04-09; Hon Can Sefwi-Wiawso Ghana from 09; Can Res and Chan St Paul's Cathl from 09. *6 Amen Court, London EC4M 7BU* E-mail giles.fraser@btinternet.com

FRASER, Canon Jane Alicia. b 44. Man Univ BA. Glouc Sch of Min 86. **d** 89 **p** 94. NSM Upton on Severn *Worc* 89-00; NSM Ripple, Earls Croome w Hill Croome and Strensham 97-00; Faith Adv Dept of Health's Adv Gp on Teenage Pregnancy from 00; NSM Upton-on-Severn, Ripple, Earls Croome etc *Worc* from 00; Hon Can Worc Cathl from 05. *The Rectory, Ryelands Lane, Elmley Lovett, Droitwich WR9 0PU* Tel (01299) 251798
E-mail ministry@revjane.demon.co.uk

FRASER, Jeremy Stuart. b 58. **d** 08 **p** 09. NSM E Greenwich *S'wark* 08-09; C from 09. *185 Charlton Church Lane, London SE7 7AA* Tel (020) 8293 3245 Mobile 07970-139881
E-mail jeremy.fraser@fourcommunications.com

FRASER, Leslie. b 34. ALCD62. **d** 62 **p** 63. C St Helens St Matt Thatto Heath *Liv* 62-64; C Fazakerley Em 64-67; R Collyhurst St Oswald and St Cath *Man* 67-72; P-in-c Collyhurst St Jas 67-72; R Collyhurst 72-74; RNLI 75-92; rtd 95; Hon C Bispham *Blackb* 95-98; Perm to Offic 98-00; P-in-c Bridekirk *Carl* 99-04. *Bridesbeck Cottage, Dovenby, Cockermouth CA13 0PG* Tel (01900) 821282

FRASER, Leslie John. b 60. **d** 99 **p** 00. NSM Thamesmead *S'wark* 99-04; Perm to Offic 05-07. *4 Goldcrest Close, London SE28 8JA* Tel (020) 8473 4736 E-mail les.fraser@virgin.net

FRASER, Mark Adrian. b 69. Warwick Univ BSc90 Birm Univ MSc91. St Jo Coll Nottm MTh04. **d** 05 **p** 06. C Astley Bridge *Man* 05-08; P-in-c Gamston and Bridgford *S'well* from 08. *10 Scafell Close, West Bridgford, Nottingham NG2 6RT* Tel 0?/963-397688 (mobile) E-mail mark.fraser@tiscali.co.uk

FRASER-SMITH, Keith Montague. b 48. St Jo Coll Dur BA70. Trin Coll Bris. **d** 73 **p** 74. C Bishopsworth *Bris* 73-75; CMS 76-84; Egypt 76-80; Jerusalem 80-84; Asst Chapl Marseille w St Raphaël, Aix-en-Provence etc *Eur* 84-90; Media Dir Arab World Min 84-92; E Area Dir 92-97; Dep Internat Dir 97-98;

NSM Worthing Ch the King *Chich* 90-93; Cyprus 93-97; NSM Tranmere St Cath *Ches* 97-98; P-in-c Barnton 98-03; Dir Global Mobilisation Arab World Min from 03; Perm to Offic *Ches* from 03. *33 Lord Street, Crewe CW2 7DH* Tel (01270) 214212
E-mail kieth.fraser-smith@tiscali.co.uk

FRAY, Bernard Herbert. b 44. Worc Coll of Educn CertEd65 Open Univ BA73 LTCL67. Cranmer Hall Dur 02. **d** 03 **p** 04. NSM Long Marston *York* 03-06; NSM Rufforth w Moor Monkton and Hessay 03-06; NSM Healaugh w Wighill, Bilbrough and Askham Richard 03-06; NSM Tockwith and Bilton w Bickerton 03-06; P-in-c Aberford w Micklefield from 06. *The Vicarage, Great North Road, Micklefield, Leeds LS25 4AG* Tel 0113-232 0975
E-mail bernardfray@hotmail.com

FRAY, Vernon Francis. b 41. FCIOB79. S'wark Ord Course 91. **d** 94 **p** 95. NSM Heston *Lon* 94-96; NSM Twickenham All Hallows 96-02; NSM Teddington St Mark and Hampton Wick 02-08; NSM Whitton SS Phil and Jas from 08. *198 Broom Road, Teddington TW11 9PQ* Tel (020) 8977 2068
E-mail vfray@btinternet.com

FRAY, Vivienne Jane. *See* KERNER, Vivienne Jane

FRAYLING, The Very Revd Nicholas Arthur. b 44. Ex Univ BA69 Liv Univ Hon LLD01. Cuddesdon Coll 69. **d** 71 **p** 72. C Peckham St Jo *S'wark* 71-74; V Tooting All SS 74-83; Can Res and Prec Liv Cathl 83-87; R Liv Our Lady and St Nic w St Anne 87-90; TR 90-02; Hon Can Liv Cathl 89-02; Dean Chich from 02. *The Deanery, Canon Lane, Chichester PO19 1PX* Tel (01243) 812485 *or* 812494 Fax 812499
E-mail dean@chichestercathedral.org.uk

FRAYNE, The Very Revd David. b 34. St Edm Hall Ox BA58 MA62. Qu Coll Birm 58. **d** 60 **p** 61. C E Wickham *S'wark* 60-63; C Lewisham St Jo Southend 63-67; V N Sheen St Phil and All SS 67-73; R Caterham 73-83; RD Caterham 80-83; Hon Can S'wark Cathl 82-83; V Bris St Mary Redcliffe w Temple etc 83-92; RD Bedminster 86-92; Hon Can Bris Cathl 91-92; Provost Blackb 92-00; Dean Blackb 00-01; rtd 01; Perm to Offic *Sarum* from 02. *Newlands Cottage, Peacemarsh, Gillingham SP8 4HD* Tel (01747) 824065

FRAZER, David. b 60. QUB BSSc. TCD Div Sch. **d** 84 **p** 85. C Taney *D & G* 84-87; C Dublin Ch Ch Cathl Gp 87-88; I Clane w Donadea and Coolcarrigan *M & K* 88-05; Dioc P and Soc Officer from 05. *3 The Glen, Inse Bay, Laytown, Co Meath, Republic of Ireland* Tel (00353) (41) 981 3897 Mobile 87-383 6215 E-mail dublinblackdog@yahoo.ie

FRAZER, Deborah. b 58. Open Univ BA90 PGCE96. Th Ext Educn Coll 89. **d** 92 **p** 95. C Pretoria St Fran S Africa 92-93; Perm to Offic *S'wark* 93-94; NSM Merton St Mary 94-96; Asst Chapl HM Pris Brixton 96-97; P-in-c Barton Hill St Luke w Ch Ch and Moorfields *Bris* from 02; AD City from 06. *287 North Street, Bedminster, Bristol BS3 1JP* Tel 0117-955 5947 Mobile 07817-567215 E-mail rev.d.frazer@btinternet.com

FRAZER, Ian Martin. b 44. QUB BTh. **d** 91 **p** 93. Lic to Offic *D & D* 91-92; Aux Min Orangefield w Moneyreagh 98-04; Aux Min Ballymacarrett from 04. *The Stacks, Deramore Park South, Belfast BT9 5JY* Tel (028) 9066 7100

FRAZER, Canon James Stewart. b 27. TCD Div Sch. **d** 57 **p** 58. C Belfast Whiterock *Conn* 57-59; C Belfast St Matt 59-61; I Lack *Clogh* 61-64; I Mullaglass *Arm* 64-65; I Milltown 65-70; Australia 70-74; I Heathcote w Axedale 70-72; I Kangaroo Par w Marong, Lockwood and Ravenswood 72-74; I Dromore *Clogh* 74-82; Bp Dom Chapl 82; I Derryvullen S w Garvary 82-90; Can Clogh Cathl 83-85; Preb 85-94; I Clogh w Errigal Portclare 90-94; Glebes Sec 91-94; Chan Clogh Cathl 93-94; rtd 94. *8 Carsons Avenue, Ballygowan, Newtownards BT23 5GD* Tel (028) 9752 1562

FREAR, Canon Philip Scott. b 45. Univ of Wales (Lamp) BA66. Bris & Glouc Tr Course 77. **d** 80 **p** 81. Hon C Purton *Bris* 80-81; C Rodbourne Cheney 81-85; V Hengrove 85-95; V Braddan *S & M* from 95; Chapl Isle of Man Dept of Health and Social Security from 98; Can St German's Cathl from 04. *The Vicarage, Saddle Road, Braddan, Isle of Man IM4 4LB* Tel (01624) 675523

FREARSON, Andrew Richard. b 57. Wolv Univ BA80. Wycliffe Hall Ox. **d** 83 **p** 84. C Acocks Green *Birm* 83-86; C Moseley St Mary 86-89; P-in-c Holme *Blackb* 89-96; P-in-c Norcross Ch Ch USA 97-06; TV Bracknell *Ox* from 06. *St Andrew's Vicarage, 25 Stoney Road, Bracknell RG42 1XY* Tel (01344) 425229
E-mail andrewfrearsontron@hotmail.co.uk

FREATHY, Nigel Howard. b 46. Lon Univ BA68 CertEd. Sarum & Wells Th Coll 79. **d** 81 **p** 82. C Crediton *Ex* 81-82; C Crediton and Shobrooke 82-84; TV Ex St Thos and Em 84-86; V Beer and Branscombe 86-01; P-in-c Stockland, Dalwood, Kilmington and Shute 01-03; V Kilmington, Stockland, Dalwood, Yarcombe etc 03-08; RD Honiton 96-99; rtd 08. *5 Mill Lane, Branscombe, Seaton EX12 3DS* Tel (01297) 680424
E-mail nigelfreathy@hotmail.com

FREDERICK, John Bassett Moore. b 30. Princeton Univ BA51 Birm Univ PhD73. Gen Th Sem (NY) MDiv54. **d** 54 **p** 55. C Cheshire St Pet USA 54-56; C All Hallows Barking *Lon* 56-58; C Ox SS Phil and Jas 58-60; R New Haven St Jo USA 61-71; R

Bletchingley *S'wark* 74-95; Reigate Adnry Ecum Officer 90-95; RD Godstone 92-95; rtd 95. *32 Chestnut Street, Princeton NJ 08542-3806, USA* Tel (001) (609) 924 7590 Fax 924 1694
E-mail jf9642@netscape.net

FREDERICK, Warren Charles. b 47. Illinois Univ BSc. Qu Coll Birm 86. **d** 88 **p** 89. C W Leigh *Portsm* 88-91; V N Holmwood *Guildf* 91-00; R Cumberland H Cross USA from 00. *612 Brookfield Avenue, Cumberland 21502-3712, USA* Tel (001) (301) 759 2688

FREDRIKSEN, Martin. b 47. St Chad's Coll Dur BA69 Univ of Wales (Lamp) MA03. **d** 70 **p** 71. C Bideford *Ex* 70-73; C Guildf St Nic 73-76; R Cossington *B & W* 76-82; V Woolavington 76-82; Asst Chapl K Coll Taunton 82-84; C Bp's Hatfield *St Alb* 84-94; P-in-c Broadstone *Sarum* 94; V from 94. *St John's Vicarage, Macaulay Road, Broadstone BH18 8AR* Tel (01202) 694109 E-mail fr.martin1@eggconnect.net

FREE, Canon James Michael. b 25. K Coll Lon BD50 AKC50. **d** 51 **p** 52. C Corsham *Bris* 51-54; Trinidad and Tobago 54-62; PC Knowle St Barn *Bris* 62-67; V Pilning 67-75; P-in-c Lydiard Millicent w Lydiard Tregoz 75-82; Hon Can Bris Cathl 76-82; Can Res, Prec and Sacr Bris Cathl 82-83; Can Treas 83-90; Bp's Adv for Miss 82-87; Bp's Officer for Miss and Evang 87-89; rtd 90; Perm to Offic *B & W* 90-03 and from 06; *Bris* from 90; P-in-c Haselbury Plucknett, Misterton and N Perrott 03-05. *Well House, Silver Street, Misterton, Crewkerne TA18 8NG* Tel (01460) 271133 E-mail jamesfree05@aol.com

FREEBAIRN-SMITH, Canon Jane. b 36. St Chris Coll Blackheath IDC60. **d** 88 **p** 94. NSM Uddingston *Glas* 88-91; NSM Cambuslang 88-91; Dioc Missr 88-92; Dioc Past Cllr 92-95; NSM Baillieston 91-92; C St Mary's Cathl 92-95; TV Hykeham *Linc* 95-03; Can and Preb Linc Cathl 02-03; rtd 04. *12 Bell Grove, Lincoln LN6 7PL* Tel (01522) 705421

FREEBORN, John Charles Kingon. b 30. G&C Coll Cam BA52 MA56. Ridley Hall Cam 53. **d** 55 **p** 56. C Doncaster St Geo *Sheff* 55-57; Tutor Wycliffe Hall Ox 57-61; R Flixton St Mich *Man* 61-72; C Leic H Apostles 72-73; C E Crompton *Man* 73-74; Teacher Greenacres Sch Oldham 73-75; Hon C Ashton St Mich 74-76; Teacher St Jo Sch Ellesmere 75-79; Perm to Offic 77-80; Hd Master H Trin Sch Halifax 80-88; Hon C Sowerby Wakef 83-94; Teacher St Chad's Sch Hove Edge Wakef 88-91; NSM Halifax All SS from 94; Perm to Offic *Bradf* from 01. *27 Crossley Hill, Halifax HX3 0PL* Tel (01422) 342489

FREEMAN, Canon Alan John Samuel. b 27. SS Coll Cam BA48 MA52. Sarum Th Coll 50. **d** 52 **p** 53. C Tottenham Ch Ch W Green *Lon* 52-55; C Harpenden St Nic *St Alb* 55-60; R Aspley Guise 60-75; RD Fleete 67-70; RD Ampthill 70-75; Hon Can St Alb 74-92; V Boxmoor St Jo 75-92; Chapl Hemel Hempstead Gen Hosp (W Herts Wing) 75-92; RD Berkhamsted *St Alb* 85-92; rtd 92; Perm to Offic *St Alb* from 00. *3A Queen Street, Leighton Buzzard LU7 1BZ* Tel (01525) 384799

FREEMAN, Anthony John Curtis. b 46. Ex Coll Ox BA68 MA72. Cuddesdon Coll 70. **d** 72 **p** 73. C Worc St Martin 72-74; C Worc St Martin w St Pet 74-75; Bp's Dom Chapl *Chich* 75-78; C-in-c Parklands St Wilfrid CD 78-82; V Durrington 82-89; P-in-c Staplefield Common 89-94; Bp's Adv on CME 89-93; Asst Dir of Ords 89-93. *4 Godolphin Close, Newton St Cyres, Exeter EX5 5BZ* Tel and fax (01392) 851453
E-mail anthony@imprint.co.uk

FREEMAN, Mrs Dorothy Lloyd (Dee). b 54. Lon Inst of Educn BEd76. EMMTC 06. **d** 09. NSM Linc St Geo Swallowbeck from 09. *Bethany, 69 Lincoln Road, Bassingham, Lincoln LN5 9JR* Tel (01522) 788942 E-mail freemen@btinternet.com

FREEMAN, Douglas James. b 20. Ox NSM Course 80. **d** 83 **p** 84. NSM Ellesborough *Ox* 83-91; NSM Ellesborough, The Kimbles and Stoke Mandeville 91-00 and 04-05; Perm to Offic 05-06. *29 Chadley, Chalkshire Road, Butlers Cross, Aylesbury HP17 0TS* Tel (01296) 623240

FREEMAN, Gordon Bertie. b 37. CITC BTh95. **d** 95 **p** 96. C Lecale Gp *D & D* 95-98; I Ardara w Glencolumbkille, Inniskeel etc *D & R* 98-07; Bp's Dom Chapl 06-07; rtd 07. *3 Leyland Meadow, Ballycastle BT54 6JX* Tel (028) 2076 8458

FREEMAN, Canon Jane. b 54. Dur Univ BA75 PhD80. Qu Coll Birm BD00. **d** 00 **p** 01. C Waterloo St Jo w St Andr *S'wark* 00-03; TV E Ham w Upton Park St Alb *Chelmsf* from 03; Hon Can Chelmsf Cathl from 09. *The Rectory, Navarre Road, London E6 3AQ* Tel (020) 8470 8703 Mobile 07702-922818
E-mail email@janefreeman.org.uk

FREEMAN, Mrs Karen Lynn. b 62. San Diego State Univ USA BS86 Leeds Univ BA09. NOC 06. **d** 09. C New Brighton St Jas w Em *Ches* from 09. *86 Bayswater Road, Wallasey CH45 8ND* Tel 0151-638 8672 E-mail k.freeman62@gmail.com

FREEMAN, Karl Fredrick. b 57. St Luke's Coll Ex BEd80. **d** 90 **p** 91. C Plymouth St Andr w St Paul and St Geo *Ex* 90-95; TV Plymouth St Andr and Stonehouse 95-96; Chapl Coll of SS Mark and Jo Plymouth 96-01; TR Plymouth Em, St Paul Efford and St Aug from 01. *The Rectory, 9 Seymour Drive, Plymouth PL3 5BG* Tel (01752) 248601 *or* 260317
E-mail revkarl@aol.com

FREEMAN (*formerly* **MARSHALL**)**, Kirstin Heather.** b 64. St Jo Coll Nottm 90 TISEC 95. **d** 93 **p** 95. NSM Glas St Marg 93-96; Hon Asst P Glas St Mary 96-99; P-in-c E Kilbride from 99. *6 Kelvin Crescent, East Kilbride, Glasgow G75 0TY* Tel (01355) 261232 E-mail revkirstin@freemanhome.co.uk

FREEMAN, Malcolm Robin. b 48. Master Mariner 78. St And NSM Tr Scheme 85. **d** 88 **p** 89. NSM Kirkcaldy *St And* 88-94; NSM Westbury *Sarum* 99-02; R Tidworth, Ludgershall and Faberstown from 02. *The Rectory, 10 St James's Street, Ludgershall, Andover SP11 9QF* Tel (01264) 791202 Mobile 07810-862740 E-mail fgmastermariner@aol.com

FREEMAN (*née* **ADAMS**)**, Mrs Margaret Anne.** b 27. AKC48. Gilmore Ho. **dss** 82 **d** 87 **p** 94. Gt Yarmouth *Nor* 80-87; rtd 87; Hon Par Dn Malborough w S Huish, W Alvington and Churchstow *Ex* 87-94; Hon C 94-96; Perm to Offic *Nor* 97-04 and *Portsm* from 07. *4 Beamond Court, Lindisfarne Close, Portsmouth PO6 2SB*

FREEMAN, Martin. *See* FREEMAN, Philip Martin

FREEMAN, Michael. *See* FREEMAN, Philip Michael

FREEMAN, Michael Charles. b 36. Magd Coll Cam BA61 MA68 Lon Univ BD69 PhD93. Clifton Th Coll 67. **d** 69 **p** 70. C Bedworth *Cov* 69-72; C Morden *S'wark* 72-77; P-in-c Westcombe Park St Geo 77-85; V Kingston Vale St Jo 85-94; rtd 99. *6 Wristland Road, Watchet TA23 0DH* Tel (01984) 634378 E-mail FreemMic@aol.com

FREEMAN, Michael Curtis. b 51. Lanc Univ BA72 Liv Hope Univ Coll MA96 PhD05. Cuddesdon Coll 72. **d** 75 **p** 76. C Walton St Mary *Liv* 75-78; C Hednesford *Lich* 78-81; TV Solihull *Birm* 81-86; V Yardley Wood 86-90; V Farnworth *Liv* 90-03; AD Widnes 02-03; P-in-c Blundellsands St Mich from 03; P-in-c Gt Crosby All SS from 05. *St Michael's Vicarage, 41 Dowhills Road, Liverpool L23 8SJ* Tel 0151-924 9905 E-mail mcfreeman@btinternet.com

FREEMAN, Michael Raymond. b 58. Chu Coll Cam BA80 MA84 Ox Univ BA87. St Steph Ho Ox 85. **d** 88 **p** 89. C Clifton All SS w St Jo *Bris* 88-92; TV Elland *Wakef* 92-01; V Horninglow *Lich* from 01. *Horninglow Vicarage, 14 Rolleston Road, Burton-on-Trent DE13 0JZ* Tel (01283) 568613 E-mail cft-rfreeman@supanet.com

FREEMAN, Preb Pamela Mary. b 45. WMMTC 83. **dss** 86 **d** 87 **p** 94. Cannock *Lich* 86-88; Par Dn 87-88; Min for Deaf (Salop Adnry) 88-95; Par Dn Shelton and Oxon 88-94; C 94-95; TV Stafford 95-00; P-in-c High Offley and Norbury 00-02; R Adbaston, High Offley, Knightley, Norbury etc from 02; Preb Lich Cathl from 07. *The Rectory, Newport Road, Woodseaves, Stafford ST20 0NP* Tel (01785) 284747

FREEMAN, Peter Cameron Jessett. b 41. **d** 05 **p** 06. OLM Sturry w Fordwich and Westbere w Hersden *Cant* from 05. *29 Cedar Road, Sturry, Canterbury CT2 0HZ*

FREEMAN, Philip Martin. b 54. Westcott Ho Cam 76. **d** 79 **p** 80. C Stanley *Liv* 79-82; C Bromborough *Ches* 82-84; V Runcorn H Trin and Chapl Halton Gen Hosp 84-91; R Ashton-upon-Mersey St Martin 91-96; SSF 96-06; Perm to Offic *Sarum* 96-99; *Birm* 98-99; Perm to Offic *Ely* 02-05; *S'wark* 05-07; Asst Chapl HM Pris Birm 98-99; Chapl Barts and The Lon NHS Trust 00-03 and 05-08; Chapl Guy's and St Thos' NHS Foundn Trust 05-08; Chapl Univ Coll Lon Hosps NHS Foundn Trust from 08; Hon C Smithfield St Bart Gt Lon from 06. *Flat 1, 48 Huntley Street, London WC1E 6DD* Tel (020) 7419 9095 Mobile 07985-512436 E-mail martin.freeman@uclh.nhs.uk

FREEMAN, Philip Michael. b 25. Jes Coll Cam BA50 MA54. Qu Coll Birm 50. **d** 52 **p** 53. C Gainsborough All SS *Linc* 52-58; V Messingham 58-65; V Goxhill 65-66; P-in-c Brocklesby w Ashby 66-73; TR 73-75; P-in-c Warwick St Nic *Cov* 75-76; TV Warwick 77-87; P-in-c Claverdon w Preston Bagot 87-90; rtd 90; Perm to Offic *Cov* from 90. *38 Cocksparrow Street, Warwick CV34 4ED* Tel (01926) 411431

FREEMAN, Richard Alan. b 52. Ripon Coll Cuddesdon. **d** 83 **p** 84. C Crayford *Roch* 83-86; V Slade Green 86-94; R Eynsford w Farningham and Lullingstone 94-01; P-in-c Shoreham from 01; Chapl St Mich Sch Otford from 01. *The Vicarage, Station Road, Shoreham, Sevenoaks TN14 7SA* Tel (01959) 522363 E-mail richard.freeman@diocese-rochester.org

FREEMAN, The Ven Robert John. b 52. St Jo Coll Dur BSc74 Fitzw Coll Cam BA76 MA. Ridley Hall Cam 74. **d** 77 **p** 78. C Blackpool St Jo *Blackb* 77-81; TV Chigwell *Chelmsf* 81-85; V Leic Martyrs 85-99; Hon Can Leic Cathl 94-03; RD Christianity S 95-98; Nat Adv in Evang 99-03; Lic to Offic *Leic* 99-03; Adn Halifax *Wakef* from 03. *2 Vicarage Gardens, Brighouse HD6 3HD* Tel (01484) 714553 Fax 711897 E-mail archdeacon.halifax@wakefield.anglican.org

FREEMAN, Rodney. *See* FREEMAN, William Rodney

FREEMAN, Rosemary. b 47. **d** 03 **p** 04. NSM Madeley *Heref* from 03. *5 Rowley Close, Madeley, Telford TF7 5RR* Tel (01952) 583460

FREEMAN, Terence. b 40. Wells Th Coll 67. **d** 70 **p** 71. C Hanham *Bris* 70-75; C Cockington *Ex* 75-77; R Sampford

Spiney w Horrabridge 77-89; V Wembury 89-08; rtd 08. *85 Blackstone Close, Plymouth PL9 8UW* E-mail revkarl.freeman@lineone.net

FREEMAN, William Rodney. b 35. Ch Coll Cam MA63 FCA73. **d** 95 **p** 96. OLM Chelmondiston and Erwarton w Harkstead *St E* 95-05; rtd 05; Perm to Offic *St E* from 05. *Lavender Cottage, Harkstead, Ipswich IP9 1BN* Tel (01473) 328381 E-mail revrod@lavcot.freeserve.co.uk

FREESTONE, Anne Elizabeth. b 52. Bp Otter Coll Chich CertEd73 Coll of Ripon & York St Jo MA00. NEOC 04. **d** 07 **p** 08. NSM Middleton-in-Teesdale w Forest and Frith *Dur* from 07. *22 Birch Road, Barnard Castle DL12 8JR* Tel (01833) 631018 Mobile 07939-964011 E-mail silverbirch22@hotmail.com

FREETH, Barry James. b 35. Birm Univ BA60. Tyndale Hall Bris 60. **d** 62 **p** 64. C Selly Hill St Steph *Birm* 62-63; C Birm St Jo Ladywood 63-71; Chapl RAF 71-75; P-in-c Crudwell w Ashley *Bris* 75-81; P-in-c Lanreath *Truro* 81-84; R 84-87; P-in-c Pelynt 81-84; V 84-87; R Harvington and Norton and Lenchwick *Worc* 87-93; V Ramsden, Finstock and Fawler, Leafield etc *Ox* 93-99; rtd 99; Perm to Offic *Derby* 99-03 and *Ox* from 08. *The Vicarage, High Street, Cropredy, Banbury OX17 1NG* Tel (01295) 750980

FREETH, John Stanton. b 40. Selw Coll Cam BA62 MA66. Ridley Hall Cam 64. **d** 66 **p** 67. C Gillingham St Mark *Roch* 66-72; TV Heslington *York* 72-80; Chapl Yurk Univ 72-80; TR Wynberg St Jo S Africa 80-93; Adn Athlone 88-93. *15 Wellington Road, Wynberg, 7800 South Africa* Tel (0027) (21) 761 0908 E-mail jill@pdg.co.za

FREETH, Mrs Patricia. b 48. Wycliffe Hall Ox BTh95. **d** 95 **p** 96. NSM Ramsden, Finstock and Fawler, Leafield etc *Ox* 95-99; TV Buxton w Burbage and King Sterndale *Derby* 99-03; V Shires' Edge *Ox* from 03. *The Vicarage, High Street, Cropredy, Banbury OX17 1NG* Tel (01295) 750980 Mobile 07947-436751 E-mail patfreeth@objn.freeserve.co.uk

FREMMER, Ludger. b 56. Ridley Hall Cam 02. **d** 04 **p** 05. C Mattishall w Mattishall Burgh, Welborne etc *Nor* 04-07; P-in-c Kibworth and Smeeton Westerby and Saddington *Leic* from 07. *The Rectory, 25 Church Road, Kibworth, Leicester LE8 0NB* Tel 0116-279 2294 Mobile 07753-213145 E-mail ludger.fremmer@tesco.net

FRENCH, Basil Charles Elwell. b 19. Edin Th Coll LTh44. **d** 45 **p** 46. C Falkirk *Edin* 45-46; C Bris St Aid 46-49; C Hendford *B & W* 49-51; V Ash S1-58; P-in-c Long Load 57-58; C Ndola N Rhodesia 59-60; Chapl Rhodesia and Nyasaland Railway Miss 60-61; P-in-c Arcadia and Cranbourne S Rhodesia 61-69; R Umvukwes 69-85; Adn Gt Dyke 80-85; rtd 85; Hon C Wrington w Butcombe *B & W* 85-88; Perm to Offic *B & W* 88-92 and *Ex* from 92. *9 Elmbridge Gardens, Exeter EX4 4AE* Tel (01392) 215933

FRENCH, Mrs Christine. b 68. Nottm Trent Univ PGCE05. EMMTC MA08 Qu Coll Birm MPhil09. **d** 09. C Keyworth and Stanton-on-the-Wolds and Bunny etc *S'well* from 09. *The Vicarage, 10 Moor Lane, Bunny, Nottingham NG11 6QX* Tel 0115-984 2407 E-mail clayton-french@live.com

FRENCH, Canon Clive Anthony. b 43. AKC70. St Aug Coll Cant 70. **d** 71 **p** 72. C Monkseaton St Mary *Newc* 71-73; Dioc Youth Adv 73-76; Chapl RN 76-97; Dir of Ords RN 87-90; Chapl RN Coll Greenwich 95-97; R Cheam *S'wark* 97-06; TR Catford (Southend) and Downham 06-09; Hon Can S'wark Cathl 08 09; rtd 09. *17 Kingslea, Leatherhead KT22 7SN*

FRENCH, Daniel Alain. b 68. Kent Univ BSc91. St Jo Sem Wonersh BTh97. **d** 97 **p** 98. In RC Ch 97-01; P-in-c Aberdeen St Clem 03-08; V Salcombe and Malborough w S Huish *Ex* from 08. *The Vicarage, Devon Road, Salcombe TQ8 8HJ* Tel (01548) 842853

FRENCH, Canon Dendle Charles. b 29. Lon Univ BD56. ALCD55. **d** 56 **p** 57. C Gt Yarmouth *Nor* 56-63; Jamaica 63-66; V Sedgeford w Southmere *Nor* 66-71; P-in-c Gt Ringstead 66-67; R 67-71; TV Thetford 71-74; Chapl Hockerill Coll Bishop's Stortford 74-78; P-in-c St Paul's Walden *St Alb* 78-85; V 85-94; RD Hitchin 84-89; Hon Can St Alb 91-94; rtd 94; Chapl Glamis Castle from 94. *Woodfaulds, 7 Braehead Road, Glamis, Angus DD8 1RW* Tel and fax (01307) 840485 E-mail dendle.french@talk21.com

FRENCH, Derek John. b 47. Man Univ BA03. Ripon Coll Cuddesdon 93. **d** 95 **p** 96. C Stand *Man* 95-98; TV E Farnworth and Kearsley 98-00; P-in-c Halliwell St Marg from 00; P-in-c Ringley w Prestolee 06-09. *St Margaret's Vicarage, 1 Somerset Road, Bolton BL1 4NE* Tel (01204) 840850 E-mail rev.djf@btinternet.com

FRENCH, George Leslie. b 47. AIFST NE Lon Poly BSc70. S'wark Ord Course 86. **d** 89 **p** 90. NSM Reading St Barn *Ox* 89-99. *Hawthorne House, 2 Cutbush Close, Lower Earley, Reading RG6 4XA* Tel 0118-986 1886

FRENCH, Janet. b 54. Anglia Poly Univ MA05. EAMTC 99. **d** 02 **p** 03. C Thetford *Nor* 02-06; R Thrybergh *Sheff* from 06. *The Rectory, 14 Manor Farm Court, Thrybergh, Rotherham S65 4NZ* Tel (01709) 850336 E-mail frenchrevj@hotmail.com

FRENCH, Janet Mary. *See* DRIVER, Janet Mary

FRENCH, Jonathan David Seabrook. b 60. Westcott Ho Cam 84. **d** 87 **p** 88. C Loughton St Jo *Chelmsf* 87-90; Chapl St Bede's Ch for the Deaf Clapham 90-92; C Richmond St Mary w St Matthias and St Jo *S'wark* 92-95; TV 96-03; V Downham St Barn from 03; Chapl RAD 92-03; Dioc Adv for Min of Deaf and Disabled People *S'wark* from 03. *St Barnabas' Vicarage, 1 Churchdown, Bromley BR1 5PS* Tel (020) 8698 4851 E-mail jo.nathan@btinternet.com

FRENCH, Ms Judith Karen. b 60. St D Coll Lamp BA89. St Steph Ho Ox 89. **d** 91 **p** 94. Par Dn Botley *Portsm* 91-94; C Bilton *Cov* 94-97; V Charlbury w Shorthampton *Ox* from 97; AD Chipping Norton from 07. *The Vicarage, Church Lane, Charlbury, Chipping Norton OX7 3PX* Tel and fax (01608) 810286 E-mail vicar@stmaryscharlbury.co.uk

FRENCH, Julia. d 06 **p** 07. NSM Plympton St Maurice *Ex* from 06. *45 Lotherton Close, Plymouth PL7 1QQ*

FRENCH, Michael Anders. b 61. Ch Coll Cam BA83 MA87 Ridley Hall Cam BA91 Man Univ MA(Econ)96. **d** 92 **p** 93. C Norbury *Ches* 92-96; Chapl Univ Coll Ches 96-01; Chapl Geneva *Eur* 01-08; Dir Advocacy World Vision UK from 08; Perm to Offic *Ox* and *St Alb* from 09. *47 Leighton Street, Woburn, Milton Keynes MK17 9PH* Tel (01908) 244524 E-mail michael.french@worldvision.org.uk *or* m.french@bluewin.ch

FRENCH, Michael John. b 37. WEMTC 92. **d** 95 **p** 96. OLM Cheltenham St Pet *Glouc* 95-01; NSM 01-08; NSM N Cheltenham from 08. *8 Alexandria Walk, Cheltenham GL52 5LG* Tel (01242) 236661

FRENCH, Peter Robert. b 65. Man Univ BTh87. Qu Coll Birm 88. **d** 90 **p** 91. C Unsworth *Man* 90-93; C Bury Ch King w H Trin 93-95; V Bury Ch King 95-98; V Handsworth St Andr *Birm* 98-06; Sch Support Officer from 06. *Diocesan Office, 175 Harborne Park Road, Birmingham B17 0BH* Tel 0121-426 0400 E-mail pfrench@birmingham.anglican.org *or* peterfrench55@aol.com

FRENCH, Philip Colin. b 50. Sarum & Wells Th Coll 81. **d** 83 **p** 84. C Llansamlet *S & B* 83-86; P-in-c Waunarllwydd 86-87; V 87-97; P-in-c Swansea St Barn 97-98; V 98-07; rtd 08. *17 Corrymore Mansions, Sketty Road, Swansea SA2 0LQ* Tel (01792) 423984

FRENCH, Richard John. b 34. Open Univ BA82. Tyndale Hall Bris 62. **d** 64 **p** 65. C Rustington *Chich* 64-68; C Walton H Trin *Ox* 68-72; V Grove 72-99; rtd 99; Perm to Offic *Chich* from 01. *5 Green Meadows, The Welkin, Haywards Heath RH16 2PE* Tel (01444) 487842

FRENCH, Stephen Robert James. b 52. St Jo Coll Nottm. **d** 87 **p** 88. C Chell *Lich* 87-91; TV 91-94; V Wednesfield Heath 94-01; TV Hemel Hempstead *St Alb* 01-06; P-in-c Bugbrooke w Rothersthorpe *Pet* from 06; P-in-c Kislingbury and Harpole from 06. *The Rectory, Church Lane, Bugbrooke, Northampton NN7 3PB* Tel (01604) 830373 E-mail srjfrench@hotmail.co.uk

FRERE, Christopher Michael Hanbury. b 21. Roch Th Coll 65. **d** 67 **p** 68. C Spilsby w Hundleby *Linc* 67-71; V N Kelsey 71-76; V Cadney 71-76; P-in-c Aisthorpe w W Thorpe and Scampton 75-79; P-in-c Brattleby 75-79; R Fillingham 76-78; V Ingham w Cammeringham 76-78; RD Lawres 78-84; V Ingham w Cammeringham w Fillingham 79-86; R Aisthorpe w Scampton w Thorpe le Fallows etc 79-86; rtd 86; Perm to Offic *Linc* from 86. *164 Newark Road, North Hykeham, Lincoln LN6 8LZ* Tel (01522) 806326 E-mail cmh.frere@ntlworld.com

FRESHNEY, June. b 46. EMMTC 95. **d** 98 **p** 99. NSM Washingborough w Heighington and Canwick *Linc* 98-05; Asst Chapl St Barn Hospice Linc 03-05; P-in-c Caythorpe *Linc* from 05. *The Rectory, 45B Old Lincoln Road, Caythorpe, Grantham NG32 3EJ* Tel (01400) 272728 Mobile 07798-840015 E-mail revjune@supanet.com

FRESTON, John Samuel Kern. b 28. Lich Th Coll 70. **d** 72 **p** 73. C Walsall *Lich* 72-75; TV Trunch w Swafield *Nor* 75-77; TV Trunch 77-82; R W Winch 82-91; Chapl St Jas Hosp King's Lynn 82-85; Chapl Qu Eliz Hosp King's Lynn 85-90; rtd 91; Perm to Offic *Ely* and *Nor* from 91. *71 Howdale Road, Downham Market PE38 9AH* Tel (01366) 385936

FRETT, Daniel Calvin. b 60. Univ of S Carolina 85. NTMTC 95 Oak Hill Th Coll BA99. **d** 98 **p** 99. NSM Clerkenwell St Jas and St Jo w St Pet *Lon* 98-00; NSM Chelsea St Jo w St Andr 00-05; NSM Tulse Hill H Trin and St Matthias *S'wark* 05-08; NSM Cranleigh *Guildf* from 09. *3 Edgefield Close, Cranleigh GU6 8PX* Tel (01483) 275861 E-mail frettd@netscape.net

FRETWELL, Brian George. b 34. TD. CEng MIMechE. Chich Th Coll 79. **d** 81 **p** 82. C Bude Haven *Truro* 81-82; C Saltash 82-85; C Walthamstow St Sav *Chelmsf* 85-87; V Doncaster Intake *Sheff* 87-97; rtd 99. *55 Bankside, Woking GU21 3DZ* Tel (01483) 721182

FRETWELL, Cynthia Mary. b 37. EMMTC 90. **d** 91 **p** 94. Chapl Asst Doncaster R Infirmary 91-92; Chapl Asst Tickhill Road and St Cath Hosps 91-92; Chapl Asst Doncaster R Infirmary and Montagu Hosp NHS Trust 92-95; Chapl 95-96; rtd 96. *55 Bankside, Woking GU21 3DZ* Tel (01483) 721182

FREWIN, William Charles. b 46. Trin Coll Bris 84. **d** 86 **p** 87. C Southchurch H Trin *Chelmsf* 86-89; C Shrub End 89-91; R W Bergholt 91-00; P-in-c Gt Wakering w Foulness 00-07; P-in-c Barling w Lt Wakering 06-07; rtd 07. *95 Windermere Avenue, Ramsgate CT11 0QD*

FREY, Christopher Ronald. b 44. AKC69 Uppsala Univ BD73 MTh77. St Aug Coll Cant 69. **d** 70 **p** 71. C Addington *Ox* 70-72; Lic to Offic *Eur* 73-78; Chapl Stockholm w Uppsala 78-85; Can Brussels Cathl 81-85; Chapl Casterton Sch Lancs 85-89; Chapl Epsom Coll 89-91; Chapl Worksop Coll Notts 91-94; rtd 96. *Koriandergatan 42, 261 61 Landskrona, Sweden* Tel (0046) (418) 20953

FRIARS, Ian Malcolm George. b 50. Sarum & Wells Th Coll 83. **d** 85 **p** 86. C Norton *St Alb* 85-88; C Ramsey *Ely* 88-90; TV The Ramseys and Upwood 90-93; P-in-c Cottenham 93-94; R 94-01; P-in-c Long Melford *St E* 01-02; R Chadbrook from 02. *The Rectory, The Green, Long Melford, Sudbury CO10 9DT* Tel (01787) 310845 E-mail ianfriars@btinternet.com

FRICKER, Canon David Duncan. b 27. Lon Univ BA53. Ridley Hall Cam 53. **d** 55 **p** 56. C Ecclesfield *Sheff* 55-58; C Luton St Mary *St Alb* 58-61; V Luton St Paul 61-64; R Bedford St Pet 64-75; RD Bedford 69-79; Hon Can St Alb 74-88; P-in-c Bedford St Paul 75-79; R Bedford St Pet w St Cuth 75-88; R Brightling, Dallington, Mountfield etc *Chich* 88-97; RD Dallington 88-95; rtd 97; Perm to Offic *Chich* from 97. *Merton, Langham Road, Robertsbridge TN32 5EP* Tel (01580) 880064

FRIDD, Nicholas Timothy. b 53. Ch Ch Ox BA74 MA78. STETS 05. **d** 08 **p** 09. NSM Wells St Thos w Horrington *B & W* from 08. *Manor Farm, East Horrington, Wells BA5 3EA* Tel (01749) 679832 Mobile 07831-209240

FRIEND, Adam Lyndon David. b 76. St Martin's Coll Lanc BA98. Cranmer Hall Dur 99. **d** 02 **p** 03. C Witton *Ches* 02-05; V Over St Chad from 05; Chapl St Luke's Hospice Cheshire from 06. *The Vicarage, 1 Over Hall Drive, Winsford CW7 1EY* Tel (01606) 593222 E-mail vicarofstchad@yahoo.co.uk

FRIEND, Frederick James. b 41. BA. Oak Hill NSM Course. **d** 82 **p** 83. NSM Hughenden *Ox* from 82. *The Chimes, Cryers Hill Road, High Wycombe HP15 6JS* Tel (01494) 563168

FRIENDSHIP, Roger Geoffrey (John-Francis). b 46. ACII72. WMMTC 90. **d** 93 **p** 94. SSF 76-02; NSM Harborne St Faith and St Laur *Birm* 93-94; Asst Novice Guardian Hilfield Friary 94-97; Novice Guardian 97-99; Gen Sec SSF 99-01; C Clerkenwell H Redeemer and St Mark *Lon* 00-01; R Romford St Andr *Chelmsf* from 01. *The Rectory, 119 London Road, Romford RM7 9QD* Tel and fax (01708) 741256 Mobile 07808-500717 E-mail francis.jon@btinternet.com

FRIGGENS, Canon Maurice Anthony. b 40. Sheff Univ BA65. Westcott Ho Cam 65. **d** 67 **p** 68. C Stocksbridge *Sheff* 67-70; C St Buryan, St Levan and Sennen *Truro* 70-72; R 72-84; RD Penwith 82-84; R St Columb Major w St Wenn 84-91; Dioc Dir of Ords 87-93; Hon Can Truro Cathl 87-00; V St Cleer 91-00; rtd 00; Perm to Offic *Ban* from 00; *Eur* from 01. *Tŷ Cernyw, Rhiw, Pwllheli LL53 8AF* Tel (01758) 780365

FRISWELL, Caroline Anne. b 52. St Mary's Coll Chelt BEd78 Sunderland Poly MA90 Dur Univ PhD99. Cranmer Hall Dur 06. **d** 09. NSM Greenside *Dur* from 09. *Westholme, Durham Moor, Durham DH1 5AH* Tel 0191-384 0191 E-mail caroline.friswell@btinternet.com

FRITH, Canon Christopher John Cokayne. b 44. Ex Coll Ox BA65 MA69. Ridley Hall Cam 66. **d** 68 **p** 69. C Crookes St Thos *Sheff* 68-71; C Rusholme H Trin *Man* 71-74; R Haughton St Mary 74-85; R Brampton St Thos *Derby* 85-02; V Alvaston 02-09; Hon Can Derby Cathl 99-09; rtd 09. *Cover Point, Back Lane, Bredon, Tewkesbury GL20 7LH* E-mail cjcfrith@gmail.com

FRITH, Mrs Gillian. b 43. EAMTC 99. **d** 02 **p** 03. NSM Chipping Ongar w Shelley *Chelmsf* 02-06; P-in-c Doddinghurst from 06. *The Rectory, Church Lane, Doddinghurst, Brentwood CM15 0NJ* Tel (01277) 821366 Mobile 07890-376779 E-mail g.frith@waitrose.com

FRITH, Jonathan Paul (Jonty). b 72. Jes Coll Cam BA94 MA97. Wycliffe Hall Ox 95. **d** 97 **p** 98. C Houghton *Carl* 97-00; Chapl Cranleigh Sch Surrey 00-04; C Crowborough *Chich* from 04. *1 Croft Cottages, Church Road, Crowborough TN6 1ED* Tel (01892) 662909 E-mail jp@jpfrith.freeserve.co.uk

✠**FRITH, The Rt Revd Richard Michael Cokayne.** b 49. Fitzw Coll Cam BA72 MA76. St Jo Coll Nottm 72. **d** 74 **p** 75 **c** 98. C Mortlake w E Sheen *S'wark* 74-78; TV Thamesmead 78-83; TR Keynsham *B & W* 83-92; Preb Wells Cathl 91-98; Adn Taunton 92-98; Suff Bp Hull York from 98. *Hullen House, Woodfield Lane, Hessle HU13 0ES* Tel (01482) 649019 Fax 647449 E-mail richard@bishop.karoo.co.uk

FRITZE-SHANKS, Miss Annette. Sydney Univ BA86 DipEd87 LLB89 Solicitor. SEITE 01. **d** 04 **p** 05. NSM Kilburn St Mary w All So and W Hampstead St Jas *Lon* 04-08; Perm to Offic from 08. *21A Kylemore Close, London NW6 2PS* Tel 07771-544201 (mobile) E-mail annettefritze-shanks@campbellhooper.com

FROGGATT, Mrs Alison. b 35. Dur Univ BA56 Bradf Univ MA79. NOC 96. **d** 98 **p** 98. NSM Bingley H Trin *Bradf* 98-02;

rtd 02; Perm to Offic *Bradf* from 02. *2 Gilstead Hall, Bingley BD16 3NP* Tel (01274) 565716
E-mail alison.froggatt@bradford.anglican.org

FROGGATT, Mrs Elaine Muriel. b 43. **d** 00 **p** 01. OLM Skirwith, Ousby and Melmerby w Kirkland *Carl* 00-04; OLM Cross Fell Gp from 04. *The Old Corn Mill, Blencarn, Penrith CA10 1TX* Tel (01768) 88757

FROGGATT, Peter Michael. b 65. St Hild Coll Dur BA86 PGCE88. Wycliffe Hall Ox BTh95. **d** 95 **p** 96. C Bebington *Ches* 95-00; V Rock Ferry from 00. *The Vicarage, St Peter's Road, Birkenhead CH42 1PY* Tel 0151-645 1622 *or* 643 1042
E-mail peter@froggatt.org.uk

FRONDIGOUN, Mrs Marjorie Elizabeth. b 46. Open Univ BA87 MSc94. **d** 08 **p** 09. OLM Cannock *Lich* from 08. *12 Adamson Close, Cannock WS11 1TJ* Tel (01543) 571199 Mobile 07889-359358
E-mail elizabeth.frondigoun@btinternet.com

FROOM, Ian Leonard John. b 42. Sarum Th Coll 69. **d** 71 **p** 72. C Gillingham and Fifehead Magdalen *Sarum* 71-75; C Parkstone St Pet w Branksea and St Osmund 75-78; V Sedgley St Mary *Lich* 78-85; TV Weston-super-Mare Cen Par *B & W* 85-94; Perm to Offic 94-97; V Truro St Geo and St Jo 97-03; rtd 03; Perm to Offic *Truro* from 03. *11 Marlborough Crescent, Falmouth TR11 2RJ* Tel (01326) 311760

FROST, Alan Sydney. b 26. K Coll Lon BD50 AKC50. **d** 51 **p** 52. C Folkestone St Sav *Cant* 51-56; C Sneinton St Steph *S'well* 56-59; C Croydon Woodside *Cant* 60-63; Asst Chapl Mersey Miss to Seamen 63-66; rtd 91. *Address withheld by request*

FROST, David J. b 48. **d** 86 **p** 87. Hon C Upper Norwood All SS *S'wark* 86-89; C Battersea St Luke 90-94; V Shirley St Geo from 94. *St George's Vicarage, The Glade, Croydon CR0 7QJ* Tel (020) 8654 8747 Fax 8654 1102
E-mail revdavid@stgeorgeschurch.co.uk

FROST, David Richard. b 54. Ridley Hall Cam 84. **d** 86 **p** 87. C Burgess Hill St Andr *Chich* 86-90; TV Rye 90-94; V Bexhill St Steph from 94; RD Battle and Bexhill from 06. *The Vicarage, 67 Woodsgate Park, Bexhill-on-Sea TN39 4DL* Tel and fax (01424) 211186 E-mail david@drfrost.org.uk

FROST, Derek Charles. b 47. Lich Th Coll 69. **d** 71 **p** 72. C Woodley St Jo the Ev *Ox* 71-76; V Bampton w Clanfield 76-81; V Minster Lovell and Brize Norton 81-88; TV Upper Kennet *Sarum* 88-92; P-in-c Seend and Bulkington 92-97; P-in-c Poulshot 95-97; V Seend, Bulkington and Poulshot 97-01; V Derry Hill w Bremhill and Foxham from 01. *The New Vicarage, Church Road, Derry Hill, Calne SN11 9NN* Tel (01249) 812172

FROST, The Ven George. b 35. Dur Univ BA56 MA61. Linc Th Coll 57. **d** 60 **p** 61. C Barking St Marg *Chelmsf* 60-64; C-in-c Marks Gate CD 64-70; V Tipton St Matt *Lich* 70-77; V Penn 77-87; RD Trysull 84-87; Preb Lich Cathl 85-87; Adn Salop 87-98; V Tong 87-98; P-in-c Donington 97-98; Adn Lich and Can Res and Treas Lich Cathl 98-00; rtd 00; Perm to Offic *Lich* from 00. *23 Darnford Lane, Lichfield WS14 9RW* Tel (01543) 415109 E-mail frost151@btinternet.com

FROST, Jeremy James. b 74. New Coll Ox BA96 MA99. Wycliffe Hall Ox BA99. **d** 00 **p** 01. C Wellington All SS w Eyton *Lich* 00-04; Min Can and Prec Cant Cathl 04-09; Chapl Greenwich Univ from 09; Chapl RN Coll Greenwich from 09; Chapl Trin Coll of Mus from 09. *40 Vanburgh Park, London SE3 7AA* Tel (020) 8853 1969 E-mail jeremy@jamesfrost.fsnet.co.uk

FROST, Canon Jonathan Hugh. b 64. Aber Univ BD88 Nottm Univ MTh99 MSSTh91 FRSA06. Ridley Hall Cam 91. **d** 93 **p** 94. C W Bridgford *S'well* 93-97; Police Chapl Trent Division 94-97; R Ash Guildf 97-02; Tutor Local Min Progr from 99; Can Res Guildf Cathl from 02; Chapl Surrey Univ from 02; Co-ord Chapl from 08; Bp's Adv Inter-Faith Relns from 07. *6 Cathedral Close, Guildford GU2 7TL* Tel (01483) 576380 Mobile 07870-277709 E-mail j.frost@surrey.ac.uk

FROST, Canon Julian. b 36. Bris Univ BA61 MA65 Lon Univ CertEd62 MIL Solicitor 57. Clifton Th Coll 64. **d** 65 **p** 66. C Welling *Roch* 65-69; Hon C 70-73; Dep Dir Schs Coun RE Project Lanc Univ 73-78; V New Beckenham St Paul 78-01; Hon Can Roch Cathl 00-01; rtd 01; Perm to Offic *Blackb* from 01. *93 Scotforth Road, Lancaster LA1 4JN* Tel (01524) 841967

FROST, Michael John. b 42. Westmr Coll Ox TCert64. **d** 95 **p** 96. OLM Harwood *Man* from 95. *86 Harden Drive, Harwood, Bolton BL2 5BX* Tel (01204) 418596

FROST, Paul William. b 75. Sheff Univ BA97 Ox Univ PGCE98. Wycliffe Hall Ox MTh08. **d** 08 **p** 09. C Kettering Ch the King *Pet* from 08. *9 Churchill Way, Kettering NN15 5DP* Tel (01536) 485772 Mobile 07979-547329 E-mail p-frost@bigfoot.com

FROST, Richard John. b 49. Ch Ch Coll Cant CertEd71 BA00. SWMTC 95. **d** 97 **p** 98. NSM Bideford, Northam, Westward Ho!, Appledore etc *Ex* 97-03; C from 03. *The Rectory, Fore Street, Northam, Bideford EX39 1AW* Tel (01237) 476749

FROST, Ronald Andrew. b 48. Univ of S Carolina BTh81 Ridley Hall Cam 86. **d** 87 **p** 88. C St Gilbrahan *Ely* 87-89; P-in-c Stow Longa 89-91; V from 91; P-in-c Kimbolton 89-91; V from 91. *The Vicarage, 3 St Andrew's Court, Kimbolton, Huntingdon PE28 0BF* Tel (01480) 860279 Mobile 07866-648493

FROST, Stanley. b 37. Univ of Wales BSc61 Liv Univ MSc65 PhD68 MIBiol66 CBiol66 FAEB82. NOC 79. **d** 82 **p** 83. NSM Lower Kersal *Man* 82-87; NSM Patricroft 87-89; NSM Convenor *Man* 87-95; Lic Preacher 89-03; P-in-c Pittenweem and Elie and Earlsferry *St And* 03-04; rtd 04; Perm to Offic *Derby* from 04. *25 Somersall Park Road, Chesterfield S40 3LD* Tel (01246) 567184 E-mail stan.trost@homecall.co.uk

FROST, Preb William Selwyn. b 29. Wells Th Coll 61. **d** 62 **p** 63. C Cheddleton *Lich* 62-67; V Longdon-upon-Tern 67-81; R Rodington 67-81; RD Wrockwardine 77-84; Preb Lich Cathl 81-96; R Longdon-upon-Tern, Rodington, Uppington etc 81-84; R Whittington St Jo 84-86; C Trysull 86-89; TV Wombourne w Trysull and Bobbington 89-96; rtd 96; Perm to Offic *Heref* from 96. *Ty Ffos, Dilwyn, Hereford HR4 8HZ* Tel (01544) 318703

FROSTICK, Canon John George. b 23. Wells Th Coll 52. **d** 54 **p** 55. C Loughborough St Pet *Leic* 54-57; C Knighton St Mary Magd 57-58; V Frisby-on-the-Wreake w Kirby Bellars 58-71; V Shepshed 71-83; R Kirton w Falkenham *St E* 83-90; Hon Can Leic Cathl 80-83; rtd 90; Perm to Offic *Leic* from 91. *68 Melton Road, Barrow-upon-Soar, Loughborough LE12 8NX* Tel (01509) 620110

FROSTICK, Paul Andrew. b 52. Stockwell Coll of Educn CertEd73. Ripon Hall Ox 74. **d** 77 **p** 78. C Shepton Mallet *B & W* 77-80; TV Barton Mills, Beck Row w Kenny Hill etc *St E* 80-85; TV Mildenhall 85-86; TV Raveningham *Nor* 86-89; V Bottisham and P-in-c Lode and Longmeadow *Ely* 89-90; V Bottisham and Lode w Long Meadow 90-94; Hd RE Brittons Sch Romford 94-97; Hd RE The Grove Sch St Leonards 97-00; rtd 00; Assoc P Bexhill St Aug *Chich* from 99. *18 The Ridings, Bexhill-on-Sea TN39 5HU* Tel (01424) 218126
E-mail paul@frostickrev.freeserve.co.uk

FROUD, Andrew William. b 65. Mansf Coll Ox BA87 St Cath Coll Cam MPhil92. Westcott Ho Cam 90. **d** 93 **p** 94. C Almondbury w Farnley Tyas *Wakef* 93-96; P-in-c Wootton *Portsm* 96-00; R 00-01; V Thornton-le-Fylde *Blackb* 01-05; Chapl St Geo C of E Sch Blackpool 05-09; P-in-c Clitheroe St Mary from 09. *The Vicarage, Church Street, Clitheroe BB7 2DD* E-mail froud.family@virgin.net

FROUDE (née WOOLCOCK), Canon Christine Ann. b 47. ACIB73. S Dios Minl Tr Scheme 92. **d** 95 **p** 96. NSM Stoke Bishop *Bris* 95-99; Chapl United Bris Healthcare NHS Trust 99-01; P-in-c Shirehampton *Bris* from 01; Dean Women's Min from 00; Hon Can Bris Cathl from 01. *St Mary's Vicarage, 8 Priory Gardens, Bristol BS11 0BZ* Tel and fax 0117-985 5450
E-mail christinefroude@lineone.net

FROWLEY, Peter Austin. b 32. CEng61 MIMechE61. WMMTC 82. **d** 84 **p** 85. NSM Tardebigge *Worc* 84-87; P-in-c 87-88; NSM Redditch St Steph 84-87; Hong Kong 88-92; V St Minver *Truro* 92-96; rtd 96; Perm to Offic *Ex* 96-07. *40 Sandhills Lane, Barnt Green, Birmingham B45 8NX* E-mail peter.frowley@virgin.net

FRY, Alison Jacquelyn. b 65. Newnham Coll Cam BA86 MA90 Hertf Coll Ox DPhil90 St Jo Coll Dur BA95. Cranmer Hall Dur 93. **d** 96 **p** 97. C Milton *B & W* 96-00; V Batheaston w St Cath from 00. *Batheaston Vicarage, Bannerdown Road, Batheaston, Bath BA1 7ND* Tel (01225) 858192
E-mail revajfry@tiscali.co.uk

FRY, Canon Barry James. b 49. K Alfred's Coll Win MA03 ACIB. Ripon Coll Cuddesdon 81. **d** 83 **p** 84. C Highcliffe w Hinton Admiral *Win* 83-87; V Southampton St Barn from 87; Hon Can Ruvuma Cathl Tanzania from 02. *St Barnabas' Vicarage, 12 Rose Road, Southampton SO14 6TE* Tel (023) 8022 3107

FRY, David William. b 51. St Jo Coll Nottm. **d** 08 **p** 09. C Heeley and Gleadless Valley *Sheff* from 08. *The Vicarage, 5 Blackstock Close, Sheffield S14 1AE* Tel 0114-239 3897
E-mail davefry@talktalk.net

FRY, Mrs Florence Marion. b 24. WMMTC 87. **d** 88 **p** 94. Chapl and Welfare Officer for the Deaf 70-94; Chapl Cov Cathl 88-94; Chmn Cov Coun of Chs 88-91; rtd 94; Perm to Offic *St Alb* from 96. *37 Grace Gardens, Bishop's Stortford CM23 3EU* Tel (01279) 652315

FRY, Canon James Reinhold. b 30. St Cath Soc Dur BSc53 MA70 Kent Univ MA04 Lambeth STh90. Oak Hill Th Coll 55. **d** 57 **p** 58. C Bromley St Jo *Roch* 57-60; V Deptford St Luke *S'wark* 60-66; V Chalk *Roch* 66-97; RD Gravesend 81-91; Hon Can Roch Cathl 87-97; rtd 97; Perm to Offic *Roch* from 99 and *Cant* from 00. *67 Park Lane, Birchington CT7 0AU* Tel (01843) 843423 Fax 845376 E-mail j.fry3@btinternet.com

FRY, Lynn Jane. b 60. **d** 03 **p** 04. OLM E w W Harling, Bridgham w Roudham, Larling etc *Nor* from 03. *40 White Hart Street, East Harling, Norwich NR16 2NE* Tel (01953) 717423
E-mail fryfam@talktalk.net

FRY, Marion. See FRY, Mrs Florence Marion

FRY, Michael John. b 59. Nottm Univ BA80 Sheff Univ CQSW83 Cam Univ BA85. Westcott Ho Cam 83. **d** 86 **p** 87. C Upholland *Liv* 86-89; C Dovecot 89-91; TV St Luke in the City from 91. *2 Minster Court, Liverpool L7 3QB* Tel 0151-709 9665

FRY, Nigel. b 49. Kent Univ BA95 Cant Ch Ch Univ MA06. SEITE 97. **d** 00 **p** 01. NSM Len Valley *Cant* 00-03; C Hollingbourne and Hucking w Leeds and Broomfield from 03;

Chapl HM Pris E Sutton Park from 02. *The Vicarage, Upper Street, Hollingbourne, Maidstone ME17 1UJ* Tel (01622) 880243 Mobile 07768-053400 E-mail nigel.fry1@btinternet.com

FRY, Nigel Edward. b 57. St Jo Coll Nottm 91. **d** 93 **p** 94. C Wellingborough All Hallows *Pet* 93-96; R Peakirk w Glinton and Northborough 96-05; V Pet Ch Carpenter from 05. *The Vicarage, Chestnut Avenue, Peterborough PE1 4PE* Tel (01733) 567140 E-mail enfrys@gmail.com

FRY, Roger Joseph Hamilton. b 29. Em Coll Cam BA52 MA56. Clifton Th Coll 52. **d** 54 **p** 55. C Walcot *B & W* 54-57; C Gresley *Derby* 57-61; P-in-c Bowling St Bart and St Luke *Bradf* 61-65; V Bowling St Jo 61-87; V Ingleton w Chapel le Dale 87-95; rtd 95; Perm to Offic *Bradf* from 95. *5 Margerison Crescent, Ilkley LS29 8QZ* Tel (01943) 608738

FRY, Roger Owen. b 30. Sarum Th Coll 58. **d** 60 **p** 61. C Yeovil St Mich *B & W* 60-63; P-in-c Weston-in-Gordano 64-70; R Clapton-in-Gordano 64-70; R Portishead 64-80; V Weston Zoyland w Chedzoy 80-94; rtd 94; Perm to Offic *B & W* 95-07. *14 Lewmond Avenue, Wells BA5 2TS*

FRYDAY, Canon Barbara Yvonne. b 47. Ch of Ireland Tr Coll TCert67. CITC 90. **d** 92 **p** 93. NSM Cashel w Magorban, Tipperary, Clonbeg etc *C & O* 93-96; C Kilcooley w Littleon, Crohane and Fertagh 96-99; I 99-07; I Clonmel w Innislounagh, Tullaghmelan etc from 07; Can Ossory Cathl from 03; Warden of Readers from 08. *The Rectory, 7 Linden Lea, Silversprings, Clonmel, Co Tipperary, Republic of Ireland* Tel and fax (00353) (52) 618 7464 Mobile 86-275 0735 E-mail frydayb@eircom.net

FRYER, Alison Jane. See BOWNASS, Alison Jane

FRYER, Mrs Jenifer Anne. b 43. NOC 89. **d** 92 **p** 94. Par Dn Ecclesfield *Sheff* 92-94; C 94-95; Asst Chapl Cen Sheff Univ Hosps NHS Trust 93-96; Chapl Weston Park Hosp Sheff 94-96; Chapl Asst N Gen Hosp NHS Trust Sheff 96-04; Chapl Asst Sheff Teaching Hosps NHS Foundn Trust 04-07; rtd 07; Perm to Offic *Sheff* from 07. *5 Nursery Drive, Ecclesfield, Sheffield S35 9XU* Tel 0114-246 1027 E-mail jeni_fryer@talktalk.net

FRYER, Michael Andrew. b 56. St Jo Coll Nottm 88. **d** 90 **p** 91. C Hull St Martin w Transfiguration *York* 90-95; V Kingston upon Hull St Aid Southcoates from 95; AD E Hull from 06. *St Aidan's Vicarage, 139 Southcoates Avenue, Hull HU9 3HF* Tel (01482) 374403 E-mail mick@staidans.org.uk

FRYER-SPEDDING, Mrs Clare Caroline. b 47. St Aid Coll Dur BA69. LCTP 06. **d** 09. NSM Binsey Carl from 09. *West Mirehouse, Underskiddaw, Keswick CA12 4QE* E-mail cfs@mirehouse.com

FUDGE, Prof Erik Charles. b 33. Ch Coll Cam BA55 MA59 Southn Univ CertEd58 Cam Univ PhD68. Ox Min Course 91. **d** 93 **p** 94. NSM Wokingham St Sebastian *Ox* from 93. *4 South Close, Wokingham RG40 2DJ* Tel 0118-978 6081

FUDGER, David John. b 53. Sheff Univ MMin96. K Coll Lon 73 Coll of Resurr Mirfield 76. **d** 77 **p** 78. C Sutton in Ashfield St Mary *S'well* 77-80; P-in-c Duston *Pet* 80-82; V Radford All So w Ch Ch and St Mich *S'well* 82-91; Min Bermondsey St Hugh CD *S'wark* 91-97; P-in-c Blackheath Ascension 97-04; Hon PV S'wark Cathl 91-01; P-in-c Mansfield SS Pet and Paul *S'well* from 04. *The Vicarage, Lindhurst Lane, Mansfield NG18 4JE* Tel (01623) 642546 *or* tel and fax 640250 E-mail revfudger@mistral.co.uk

FUDGER, Michael Lloyd. b 55. K Coll Lon BD77 AKC77. Coll of Resurr Mirfield 77. **d** 78 **p** 79. C Weston Favell *Pet* 78-82; C Pet H Spirit Bretton 82-84; V Irchester 84-90; TV Darnall-cum-Attercliffe *Sheff* 90-96; TV Attercliffe, Darnall and Tinsley 96-97; TR 97-03; TR Attercliffe and Darnall 03-05; V 05-06; Chapl Nine o'Clock Community 04-06; RD Attercliffe 91-96; Hon Can Sheff Cathl 00-06; R Bedford St Pet w St Cuth *St Alb* from 06. *St Peter's Rectory, 36 De Parys Avenue, Bedford MK40 2TP* Tel (01234) 354543 E-mail fudgerml@yahoo.co.uk

FULFORD, Alison Jane. b 79. CCC Cam BA00 MA04. Ridley Hall Cam 01. **d** 04 **p** 05. C Old Catton *Nor* 04-07; NSM Lenton Abbey *S'well* from 08. *1 Peache Way, Chilwell Lane, Bramcote, Nottingham NG9 3DX* Tel 0115-922 0064 E-mail alisonfulford_1@hotmail.com

FULFORD, Susan Yvonne. b 61. **d** 03. OLM Pemberton St Mark Newtown *Liv* 03-07; OLM Marsh Green w Newtown from 08. *13 Mitchell Street, Wigan WN5 9BY* Tel (01942) 242369 E-mail sueandmike2003@yahoo.co.uk

FULHAM, Suffragan Bishop of. See BROADHURST, The Rt Revd John Charles

FULKER, Lois Valerie. b 42. Keele Univ BA64. Cranmer Hall Dur 03. **d** 04 **p** 05. NSM Egremont and Haile *Carl* from 04. *3 Mill Farm, Calderbridge, Seascale CA20 1DN* Tel (01946) 841475 E-mail m.l.fulker@btinternet.com

FULLAGAR, Michael Nelson. b 35. SS Coll Cam BA57 MA61. Chich Th Coll 57. **d** 59 **p** 60. C Camberwell St Giles *S'wark* 59-61; C Northolt Park St Barn Lon 61-64; C Hythe *Cant* 64-66; R Chipata Zambia 66-70; P-in-c Livingstone 70-75; P-in-c Chingola 75-78; R Freemantle *Win* 78-87; P-in-c Westbury w Turweston, Shalstone and Biddlesden *Ox* 87-94; Chapl S Bucks NHS Trust 94-96; rtd 96; P-in-c Burwash Weald *Chich* 97-04;

Perm to Offic from 04. *1 Roffrey Avenue, Eastbourne BN22 0AE* Tel (01323) 503212 E-mail fullagar1662@aol.com

FULLALOVE, Brenda Hurst. See CRASTON, Mrs Brenda Hurst

FULLARTON, Mrs Heather Mary. b 42. Whitelands Coll Lon TCert63. Qu Coll Birm 90. **d** 92 **p** 94. Par Dn Colwich w Gt Haywood *Lich* 92-94; C 94-97; P-in-c Swindon and Himley 97-01; V Prees and Fauls 01-02; rtd 02; Perm to Offic *Sarum* from 03. *3 Rivers Arms Close, Sturminster Newton DT10 1DL* Tel (01258) 471895 Mobile 07703-379684 E-mail hfullarton@aol.com

FULLER, Alison Jane. b 61. St Andr Univ MTheol84. Edin Th Coll 85. **d** 87 **p** 94. C Selkirk *Edin* 87-89; C Melrose 87-89; C Galashiels 87-89; C Edin H Cross 89-92; Dn-in-c Edin St Columba 92-94; R from 94; Chapl Edin Univ 96-00. *28 Castle Terrace, Edinburgh EH1 2EL* Tel and fax 0131-228 6470 E-mail rector.stcs@blueyonder.co.uk

FULLER, Alistair James. b 66. Univ of Wales (Lamp) BA87. Ripon Coll Cuddesdon 88. **d** 90 **p** 91. C Thornton-le-Fylde *Blackb* 90-95; V Skerton St Luke 95-01; R Bowbrook N *Worc* 01-07; RD Droitwich 04-07. *Address temp unknown* E-mail alistair@alistairfuller.fsnet.co.uk

FULLER, Christopher John. b 53. Chich Th Coll 85. **d** 87 **p** 88. C Swinton and Pendlebury *Man* 87-90; C Chiswick St Nic w St Mary *Lon* 90-92; V Hounslow W Gd Shep 92-96; V Stoke Newington St Faith, St Matthias and All SS 96-05; V Enfield St Geo from 05. *St George's Vicarage, 706 Hertford Road, Enfield EN3 6NR* Tel (01992) 762581

FULLER, Canon Graham Drowley. b 33. AKC58. **d** 59 **p** 60. C E Grinstead St Swithun *Chich* 59-62; C Coulsdon St Andr *S'wark* 62-64; Chapl RN 64-68; V Battersea St Luke *S'wark* 68-75; V S Stoneham *Win* 75-90; R Eversley 90-96; Bp's Ecum Officer 84-95; Hon Can Win Cathl 93-96; rtd 96; Perm to Offic *Portsm* from 03. *Brookside Dairy, Nunnery Lane, Newport PO30 1YR* Tel (01983) 525976 E-mail teazle@metronet.co.uk

FULLER, Canon John James. b 38. SS Coll Cam BA63 SS Coll Cam MA66. Chich Th Coll 63 Union Th Sem (NY) STM64. **d** 65 **p** 66. C Westmr St Steph w St Jo Lon 65-71; Tutor Cuddesdon Coll 71-75; Tutor Ripon Coll Cuddesdon 75-77; Prin S Dios Minl Tr Scheme 77-96; Can and Preb Sarum Cathl 83-96; V Wheatley w Forest Hill and Stanton St John 96-97; TR Wheatley 97-03; rtd 03. *11 Ratcliffs Garden, Shaftesbury SP7 8HJ* Tel (01747) 850079

FULLER, Matthew John. b 74. Birm Univ BA95 PGCE96. Oak Hill Th Coll BA05. **d** 05 **p** 06. C St Helen Bishopsgate w St Andr Undershaft etc *Lon* from 05. *61 Monkton Street, London SE11 4TX* Tel (020) 7735 2494 Mobile 07903-045667 E-mail matt@thebibletalks.com

FULLER, Michael George. b 66. Chich Th Coll 90. **d** 92 **p** 93. C Fulham All SS *Lon* 92-94; C Kensington St Mary Abbots w St Geo 94-06; V Holland Park from 06; Dir Post-Ord Tr Kensington Area 94-99; Bp Kensington's Liaison Officer to Metrop Police from 99. *32A Campden Hill Gardens, London W8 7AZ* Tel (020) 7727 9486 Mobile 07980-932403 E-mail frmichael@stgeorgescampdenhill.co.uk

FULLER, Canon Michael Jeremy. b 63. Worc Coll Ox BA85 MA89 DPhil89 Qu Coll Cam BA91. Westcott Ho Cam 89. **d** 92 **p** 93. C High Wycombe *Ox* 92-95; C Edin St Jo 95-00; Prin TISEC 00-02; Min Development Officer from 02; Can St Mary's Cathl from 06. *28 Blackford Avenue, Edinburgh EH9 2PH* Tel 0131-667 7273 *or* 220 2272 Fax 220 2294 E-mail michaelf@scotland.anglican.org

FULLER, Robert Peter. b 49. Bernard Gilpin Soc Dur 71 Trin Coll Bris 72. **d** 75 **p** 76. C Tonbridge SS Pet and Paul *Roch* 75-79; C Welling 79-83; V Nottingham St Sav *S'well* 83-89; V Ripley *Derby* 89-97; Chapl Ripley Hosp 89-93; Chapl S Derbyshire Community Health Services NHS Trust 93-97; V Colchester St Jo *Chelmsf* from 97. *St John's Vicarage, Evergreen Drive, Colchester CO4 0HU* Tel (01206) 843232 E-mail stjohnschurch.col@talk21.com

FULLER, Canon Terence James. b 30. Bris Univ BA55. Clifton Th Coll 55. **d** 56 **p** 57. C Uphill *B & W* 56-60; V Islington St Jude Mildmay Park *Lon* 60-67; V Southgate *Chich* 67-80; R Stoke Climsland *Truro* 80-95; RD Trigg Major 85-91; P-in-c Lezant w Lawhitton and S Petherwin w Trewen 93-95; Hon Can Truro Cathl 94-96; rtd 96; Perm to Offic *Truro* from 96. *9 Westover Road, Callington PL17 7EW* Tel (01579) 384958

FULLERTON, Hamish John Neville. b 45. Ball Coll Ox BA68 MA73. S'wark Ord Course 76. **d** 79 **p** 80. Hd English Abp Tenison's Sch Kennington 79-88; Hon C Clapham Old Town S'wark 79-82; Perm to Offic 82-89; Hon C Brixton Road Ch Ch 89-91; C Streatham Ch Ch 91-96; C Purley St Mark 96-98; Asst P Tooting St Aug 98-01; Perm to Offic from 03. *Flat 4, 21 Offerton Road, London SW4 0DJ* Tel (020) 7622 7890

FULLJAMES, Mrs Janet Kathleen Doris. b 43. Open Univ BA79 Birm Univ MA93. Qu Coll Birm 85. **d** 87 **p** 94. Par Dn Harborne St Pet *Birm* 87-93; Par Dn Smethwick SS Steph and Mich 93-94; C 94-95; C Smethwick Resurr 95-98; P-in-c Dudley St Thos and St Luke *Worc* 98-04; P-in-c Dudley St Jo 98-04; rtd 04; Perm to

Offic *B & W* from 04. *12 Obridge Road, Taunton TA2 7PX* Tel (01823) 333585

FULLJAMES, Michael William. b 36. OBE94. K Coll Lon AKC60. St Boniface Warminster 60. **d** 61 **p** 62. C Armley St Bart *Ripon* 61-64; C E Wells *B & W* 64-67; Chapl Mendip Hosp Wells 64-67; R Stanningley St Thos *Ripon* 67-73; Chapl St Aug Hosp Cant 73-88; St Martin's Hosp 82-88; RD W Bridge *Cant* 87-88; Chapl Rotterdam *Eur* 88-94; Sen Chapl Rotterdam Miss to Seamen 88-94; Sen Chapl Burrswood Chr Cen *Roch* 94-01; rtd 01; Perm to Office *Cant* and *Roch* from 01. *40 Somner Close, Canterbury CT2 8LJ* Tel (01227) 766950
E-mail m.fulljames@gmail.com

FULLJAMES, Peter Godfrey. b 38. BNC Ox BA60 MA64 Birm Univ PhD91. Qu Coll Birm. **d** 62 **p** 63. C Mexborough *Sheff* 62-65; Chapl Union Chr Coll India 65-69; Asst Master Wednesfield High Sch Wolverhampton 69-71; Asst Master Moorside High Sch Werrington 71-79; NSM Nairobi St Mark Kenya 80-85; Asst Master Nairobi High Sch 80-85; Research Fell Qu Coll Birm 85-87; Tutor WMMTC 87-90; Vice-Prin 90-93; Tutor Qu Coll Birm 93-94; Tutor Crowther Hall CMS Tr Coll Selly Oak 94-00; Hon Lect Th Birm Univ 97-03; rtd 00; Perm to Offic *B & W* from 04. *12 Obridge Road, Taunton TA2 7PX* Tel (01823) 333585

FULTON, Miss Ann Elizabeth. b 47. SWMTC 01. **d** 04 **p** 05. NSM Kingston St Mary w Broomfield etc *B & W* from 04. *105 Stoke Road, Taunton TA1 3EL* Tel (01823) 282544
E-mail annfulton@tiscali.co.uk

FULTON, John William. b 49. Ex Coll Ox BA71 BPhil72 MA75 MPhil79. Wycliffe Hall Ox 72. **d** 76 **p** 77. C Bexleyheath Ch Ch *Roch* 76-79; C Ealing Dean St Jo *Lon* 79-83; V Aldborough Hatch *Chelmsf* 83-87; Chapl Chantilly *Eur* 87-90; R Hepworth, Hinderclay, Wattisfield and Thelnetham *St E* from 90; RD Ixworth from 09. *The Rectory, Church Lane, Hepworth, Diss IP22 2PU* Tel and fax (01359) 250285

FUNNELL, Preb Norman Richard James. b 40. Univ of Wales (Lamp) BA64. Ripon Hall Ox 64. **d** 66 **p** 67. C Hackney *Lon* 66-70; Hon C 71-85; TV 85-93; R S Hackney St Jo w Ch Ch 93-08; Chapl St Joseph's Hospice 93-08; Preb St Paul's Cathl 05-08; rtd 08. *37 Brunel Quays, Great Western Village, Lostwithiel PL22 0JB* Tel (01208) 873867 Mobile 07966-238934
E-mail jamesfunnell@btinternet.com

FURBER, Mrs Jennifer Margaret. b 50. WEMTC 98. **d** 01 **p** 02. NSM Malvern Link w Cowleigh *Worc* 01-08; rtd 09. *8 Eden Court, 28 Grove Road, Bournemouth BH1 3AZ* Tel (01202) 296886 E-mail jenny@furber.me.uk

FURBER, Peter. b 43. Ex Univ BA. Sarum & Wells Th Coll 83. **d** 85 **p** 86. C Stanmore *Win* 85-88; TV Basingstoke 88-95; C Ringwood 95-98; P-in-c Gt Malvern Ch Ch *Worc* 98-99; V 99-08; rtd 09. *8 Eden Court, 28 Grove Road, Bournemouth BH1 3AZ* Tel (01202) 296886 E-mail peter@furber.me.uk

FURBEY, Mrs Linda Alice. b 49. Hockerill Coll of Educn CertEd70 Wolfs Coll Cam BEd71 Coll of Ripon & York St Jo MA03. NOC 00. **d** 03 **p** 04. NSM Crosspool *Sheff* 03-07 and from 08; Perm to Offic 07-08; Chapl Sheff Children's NHS Foundn Trust from 08. *20 Crimicar Avenue, Sheffield S10 4EQ* Tel 0114-230 6356

FURBY, Penelope. b 51. Middx Univ 06. NTMTC BA03. **d** 06 **p** 07. NSM Leigh-on-Sea St Aid *Chelmsf* from 06. *72A Cliffsea Grove, Leigh-on-Sea SS9 1NQ* Tel (01702) 711067 Mobile 07817-766513 E-mail penny.furby@btinternet.com

FURLONG, Andrew William Ussher. b 47. TCD BA69 Jes Coll Cam BA71. Westcott Ho Cam 70 CITC 72. **d** 72 **p** 73. C Dundela St Mark *D & D* 72-76; C Dublin St Ann w St Mark and St Steph *D & G* 76-83; Zimbabwe 83-94; Adn W Harare 88-89; Can Harare 89-94; Asst Chapl Leeds Teaching Hosps NHS Trust 94-97; Dean Clonmacnoise *M & K* 97-02; I Trim and Athboy Gp 97-02; Prec Kildare Cathl 98-02. *12 Tubbermore Road, Dalkey, Co Dublin, Republic of Ireland* Tel (00353) (1) 285 9817 E-mail tiripo@gofree.indigo.ie

FURLONG (née DAVIES), Mrs Catharine Mary. b 48. Philippa Fawcett Coll CertEd73. EMMTC 85. **d** 88 **p** 95. C Spalding *Linc* 88-92; Zimbabwe 92-94; C Gt w Lt Gidding and Steeple Gidding *Ely* 94-96; P-in-c 96-06; P-in-c Brington w Molesworth and Old Weston 96-06; P-in-c Leighton Bromswold 96-06; P-in-c Winwick 96-06; P-in-c Gt Gransden and Abbotsley and Lt Gransden etc from 06; Asst Chapl Hinchingbrooke Health Care NHS Trust from 06. *The Vicarage, 4 Webb's Meadow, Great Gransden, Sandy SG19 3BL* Tel (01767) 677227

FURNESS, Barry Keith. b 47. Open Univ BSc93. **d** 04 **p** 05. OLM High Oak, Hingham and Scoulton w Wood Rising *Nor* 04-09; P-in-c Smallburgh w Dilham w Honing and Crostwight from 09. *The Rectory, The Street, Honing, North Walsham NR28 9AB* Tel (01692) 536693 E-mail barry.furness@norwich.anglican.org

FURNESS, Christine Anne. b 51. Leic Coll of Educn CertEd73 Open Univ BA76 Man Univ MEd84 PhD91 Ches Coll of HE MTh02. NOC 99. **d** 02 **p** 03. C Offerton *Ches* 02-06; V Brinnington w Portwood from 06. *St Luke's Vicarage, Brinnington Road, Stockport SK5 8BS* Tel 0161-430 4164 Mobile 07771-601615 E-mail anne@afurness.co.uk

FURNESS, Colin. b 43. Lich Th Coll 65. **d** 68 **p** 69. C New Bentley *Sheff* 68; C Sheff St Cecilia Parson Cross 68-74; V Edlington 74-78; C Heavitree w Ex St Paul 78-81; TV 81-89; R Sampford Spiney w Horrabridge 89-03; TV Chard and Distr *B & W* 03-06; V Chard Gd Shep and Cricket St Thomas from 06. *The Rectory, Furnham Road, Chard TA20 1AE* Tel (01460) 61012
E-mail fr.colin@yahoo.co.uk

FURNESS, Dominic John. b 53. Bris Univ BA76. Ridley Hall Cam 82. **d** 84 **p** 85. C Downend *Bris* 84-88; V Stoke Hill *Guildf* 88-05; V Milford *Win* from 05; AD Lyndhurst from 08. *The Vicarage, Lymington Road, Milford on Sea, Lymington SO41 0QN* Tel (01590) 643289
E-mail dominic.furness@tiscali.co.uk

FURNESS, Edward Joseph. b 41. S'wark Ord Course 74. **d** 77 **p** 78. NSM S Lambeth St Steph *S'wark* 77-81; Warden Mayflower Family Cen Canning Town *Chelmsf* 82-96; P-in-c Aston St Jas *Birm* 96-00; V 00-05; rtd 05; Perm to Offic *Birm* from 05. *83 Pype Hayes Road, Birmingham B24 0LU* Tel 0121-382 1218

FURNESS, John Alfred. b 31. Chich Th Coll 60. **d** 62 **p** 63. C Leeds St Aid *Ripon* 62-66; C Rickmansworth *St Alb* 66-73; R Wymington 73-75; P-in-c Podington w Farndish 74-75; R Wymington w Podington 75-79; V Waltham Cross 79-89; RD Cheshunt 84-89; R Swyncombe w Britwell Salome *Ox* 89-97; rtd 97; Perm to Offic *St Alb* from 97; Perm to Offic *S'wark* from 00. *9 The Quadrangle, Morden College, 19 St German's Place, London SE3 0PW* Tel (020) 8858 2838
E-mail johnfurness@amserve.com

FURST, John William. b 41. Bris Sch of Min 81 Ripon Coll Cuddesdon. **d** 84 **p** 85. C Bris Ch the Servant Stockwood 84-88; V Hanham 88-94; Perm to Offic *Llan* 98-99; V Gosberton, Gosberton Clough and Quadring *Linc* 99-05; P-in-c Hasfield w Tirley and Ashleworth *Glouc* 05-06; rtd 06. *10 Wetherby Crescent, Lincoln LN6 8SX* Tel (01522) 684910
E-mail sandjifurst@btinternet.com

FUTCHER, Christopher David. b 58. Edin Univ BD80 Lon Univ MTh04. Westcott Ho Cam 80. **d** 82 **p** 83. C Borehamwood *St Alb* 82-85; C Stevenage All SS Pin Green 85-88; V St Alb St Steph 96-00; R Harpenden St Nic from 00. *The Rectory, 9 Rothamsted Avenue, Harpenden AL5 2DD* Tel (01582) 712202 or 765524 Fax 713646 E-mail cfutcher@toucansurf.com

FUTERS, Michael Roger. b 58. Trin & All SS Coll Leeds BEd80. St Jo Coll Nottm 82. **d** 85 **p** 86. C Narborough and Huncote *Leic* 85-87; C Spondon *Derby* 87-90; P-in-c Derby St Jas 90-95; TV Walbrook Epiphany 95-99; Hon C Derby St Mark from 99; Community Development Officer Home Housing from 99. *3 St Pancras Way, Derby DE1 3TH* Tel (01332) 203075
E-mail michaelf@derwentliving.com

FYFE, Mrs Deirdre Bettina. b 44. STETS 05. **d** 07 **p** 08. NSM S Petherton w the Seavingtons *B & W* from 07. *The Beeches, Water Street, Seavington, Ilminster TA19 0QH* Tel (01460) 241977
E-mail d.alastairf@virgin.net

FYFE, Gordon Boyd. b 63. Aber Univ BD93 Edin Univ MTh95. TISEC 94. **d** 96 **p** 97. C Ayr *Glas* 96-99; C Maybole 96-99; C Girvan 96-99; R Airdrie from 99; R Coatbridge from 99. *The Rectory, 24 Etive Drive, Airdrie ML6 9QQ* Tel and fax (01236) 756330 E-mail gordonfyfe@blueyonder.co.uk

FYFE, Stewart John. b 69. City Univ BSc91. Ridley Hall Cam 03. **d** 05 **p** 06. C Barony of Burgh *Carl* 05-07 and from 08. *7 Cross House Gardens, Great Orton, Carlisle CA5 6NW* Tel (01228) 712139 Mobile 07895-900477
E-mail stewart.fyfe@btinternet.com

FYFFE, Robert Clark. b 56. Edin Univ BD78 Napier Univ Edin MBA98. Edin Th Coll 74. **d** 79 **p** 80. C Edin St Jo 79-83; Youth Chapl *B & W* 83-87; Prov Youth Officer Scottish Episc Ch 87-92; R Perth St Jo *St And* 93-06; Co-ord Internat Angl Youth Network 88-92; Can St Ninian's Cathl Perth 06-06; Gen Sec CTBI from 06. *Bastille Court, 2 Paris Garden, London SE1 8ND* Tel 7654 7254 Fax 7654 7222
E-mail gensec@ctbi.org.uk

FYFFE, Timothy Bruce. b 25. New Coll Ox MA54. Westcott Ho Cam 54. **d** 56 **p** 57. C Lewisham St Mary *S'wark* 56-60; Nigeria 60-68; TV Lowestoft St Marg *Nor* 69-80; Chapl HM Pris Blundeston 70-78; TV Tettenhall Regis *Lich* 80-85; Chapl Compton Hospice 85-87; NSM Wolverhampton St Andr *Lich* from 88; rtd 90. *40 Glentworth Gardens, Wolverhampton WV6 0SG* Tel (01902) 716510
E-mail tim@timfyffe.plus.com

FYLES, Gordon. b 39. Trin Coll Bris 76. **d** 77 **p** 78. C Islington St Mary *Lon* 77-81; Ext Sec BCMS 81-88; C Wimbledon Em Ridgway Prop Chpl *S'wark* 88-97; I Crinken *D & G* 97-04; rtd 04. *7 Shore Street, Hilton, Tain IV20 1XD* Tel (01862) 832131 E-mail gordonandyvonne@yahoo.co.uk

FYSH, Leslie David. b 35. Glouc Sch of Min 88. **d** 91 **p** 92. NSM Stonehouse *Glouc* 91-93; Asst Chapl Wycliffe Coll Glos 91-95; NSM W Walton *Ely* 95-00; Perm to Offic *Ely* from 00 and *Nor* from 06; PV Ely Cathl 03-06. *2 Waldens Barn, Chapel Road, Dersingham, King's Lynn PE31 6PN* Tel (01485) 542785

G

GABB-JONES, Adrian William Douglas. b 43. MRICS. Ripon Coll Cuddesdon 79. **d** 81 **p** 82. C Northolt Park St Barn *Lon* 81-84; C Ruislip St Martin 84-89; V Minster Lovell and Brize Norton *Ox* 89-03; V Minster Lovell from 03. *The Vicarage, Burford Road, Minster Lovell, Oxford OX29 0RA* Tel (01993) 776492

GABBADON, Kenneth Fitz Arthur. b 53. Elim Bible Coll 77 NOC 97. **d** 99 **p** 00. C Burnage St Marg *Man* 99-01; C Bury St Jo w St Mark 01-03; P-in-c Newton Heath 03-08; R 08-09; Chapl HM Pris Leeds from 09; P-in-c Clifford *York* from 09. *HM Prison Armley, 2 Gloucester Terrace, Stanningley Road, Leeds LS12 2TJ* Tel 0113-203 2704 *or* 203 2705
E-mail ken.gabbadon@hmps.gsi.gov.uk
or kgabba7036@aol.com

GABLE, Michael David. b 70. Poly of Wales BEng92. St Mich Coll Llan BTh95. **d** 95 **p** 96. C Newton Nottage *Llan* 95-99; V Aberavon H Trin 99-01; TV Aberavon 01-05; P-in-c Rhydyfelin w Graig from 05. *St John's Vicarage, 28 Llantrisant Road, Graig, Pontypridd CF37 1LW* Tel (01443) 651810
E-mail michaelgable@hotmail.com

GABRIEL, Michael Hunt. b 29. BA. **d** 57 **p** 58. C Waterford Ch Ch *C & O* 57-60; C New Windsor H Trin *Ox* 60-62; C Albany Street Ch Ch *Lon* 62-63; R W and E Shefford *Ox* 63-67; C Hillingdon St Jo *Lon* 67-86; C Kingston Buci *Chich* 86-94; rtd 94. *Flat 1, 6 Dittons Road, Eastbourne BN21 1DN*

GADD, Alan John. b 44. Imp Coll Lon BSc65 PhD69 FRMetS67. S'wark Ord Course 68. **d** 71 **p** 72. Asst Chapl Lon Univ 71-72; Perm to Offic *S'wark* 73-91; C Battersea Park All SS 91-95; P-in-c 95-96; C Battersea Fields 96-05; rtd 05; Perm to Offic *S'wark* from 05. *24 Holmewood Gardens, London SW2 3RS* Tel (020) 8678 8977

GADD, Brian Hayward. b 33. Hatf Coll Dur BA54 DipEd55. Glouc Sch of Min 82. **d** 85 **p** 87. NSM Cleobury Mortimer w Hopton Wafers etc *Heref* 85-98; rtd 98; Perm to Offic *Heref* from 99. *34 Lower Street, Cleobury Mortimer, Kidderminster DY14 8AB* Tel (01299) 270758

GADD, Bryan Stephen Andrew. b 56. Dur Univ BA Ox Univ CertEd. Chich Th Coll. **d** 81 **p** 82. C Newlyn St Pet *Truro* 81-86; R St Mawgan w St Ervan and St Eval 86-90; Chapl Summer Fields Sch Ox 90-02; Perm to Offic *Truro* 90-00; Chapl Southport Sen Sch Australia from 02. *Southport School, Winchester Street, Southport Qld 4215, Australia* Tel (0061) (7) 5531 9956 *or* 5531 9935 E-mail bsag@tss.qld.edu.au

GADEN, Timothy John. b 64. Melbourne Univ BA86 Monash Univ Aus PhD96. Melbourne Coll of Div BD90. **d** 91 **p** 91. Australia 91-96 and from 01; C Battersea St Mary *S'wark* 97; V 97-01; Dir Post-Ord Tr Kingston Area 99-01; R Camberwell St Jo from 01. *15 The Grove, Camberwell Vic 3124, Australia* Tel (0061) (3) 9889 6456 *or* 9882 4851 Fax 9882 0086 Mobile 41-911 4697 E-mail gaden@stjohnscamberwell.org.au

GADSBY, Julian Timothy David Moritz. b 74. K Coll Lon BA96 AKC96. Oak Hill Th Coll 02. **d** 04 **p** 05. C Chadwell *Chelmsf* 04-09; P-in-c Bucklebury w Marlston *Ox* from 09. *The Vicarage, Burdens Heath, Upper Bucklebury, Reading RG7 6SX* Tel (01635) 874441 E-mail j_gadsby@tiscali.co.uk

GAFFIN, Jennifer Clare. b 78. Mansf Coll Ox BA99 Man Univ MA00 Win Univ PhD06. Ripon Coll Cuddesdon 07. **d** 09. C Talbot Village *Sarum* from 09. *St Saviour's House, 18 Hillside Road, Poole BH12 5DY* Tel (01202) 518176 Mobile 07855-024789 E-mail jennygaffin@hotmail.com

GAGE, Alan William. b 52. Univ of Wales (Cardiff) BMus72 PGCE73 Bris Univ MEd90. WEMTC 98. **d** 00 **p** 01. NSM Tuffley *Glouc* 00-08; NSM Hardwicke and Elmore w Longney 08-09. *Chadburn, 83 Dinglewell, Hucclecote, Gloucester GL3 3HT* Tel (01452) 614892
E-mail curatealan@blueyonder.co.uk

GAGE, Aëlla Rupert Fitzehardinge Berkeley. b 66. Reading Univ BEd92. Oak Hill Th Coll 98. **d** 00. C Muswell Hill St Jas w St Matt *Lon* 00-05; C Hadley Wood St Paul Prop Chpl 05-08; Australia from 08. *391 Crawford Road, Dianella, Perth WA 6059, Australia* E-mail aella@stalbans.org.au

GAGE, Jennifer Anne. b 50. Girton Coll Cam MA75 Open Univ BA85 PhD05 Keele Univ PGCE86. ERMC 07. **d** 09. NSM Three Rivers Gp *Ely* from 09. *51 Henley Way, Ely CB7 4YH* Tel (01353) 666426 E-mail jennygage3@talktalk.net

GAGE, Canon Robert Edward. b 47. Whitman Coll Washington BA69. Cuddesdon Coll BA75 MA81. **d** 76 **p** 77. C Cheshunt *St Alb* 76-79; C Harpenden St Nic 79-81; V S Mymms 81-82; P-in-c Ridge 81-82; V S Mymms and Ridge 82-97; Prec and Can Res Wakef Cathl 97-05; Can Res Newc Cathl 05-09; rtd 09. *44 Warkworth Avenue, Whitley Bay NE26 3PS*
E-mail robert@rtage8.wanadoo.co.uk

GAINER, Jeffrey. b 51. Jes Coll Ox BA73 MA77 Univ of Wales

LLM94. Wycliffe Hall Ox 74. **d** 77 **p** 78. C Baglan *Llan* 77-81; V Cwmbach 81-85; V Tonyrefail w Gilfach Goch and Llandyfodwg 85-87; Dir NT Studies and Dir Past Studies St Mich Coll Llan 87-92; V Meidrim and Llanboidy and Merthyr *St D* from 92; AD St Clears from 03; P-in-c Abernant from 07. *The Vicarage, Meidrim, Carmarthen SA33 5QF* Tel (01994) 231378

GAIR, Andrew Kennon. b 62. Westcott Ho Cam 88. **d** 91 **p** 92. C Clare w Poslingford, Cavendish etc *St E* 91-95; R Debden and Wimbish w Thunderley *Chelmsf* 95-06. *18-20 High Street, Wrentham, Beccles NR34 7HB*
E-mail andrew.gair@btinternet.com

✠**GAISFORD, The Rt Revd John Scott.** b 34. St Chad's Coll Dur BA59 MA76. **d** 60 **p** 61 **c** 94. C Audenshaw St Hilda *Man* 60-62; C Bramhall *Ches* 62-65; V Crewe St Andr 65-86; RD Nantwich 74-85; Hon Can Ches Cathl 80-86; Adn Macclesfield 86-94; Suff Bp Beverley (PEV) *York* 94-00; Asst Bp Ripon and Leeds 96-00; rtd 00; Perm to Offic *Ches* from 00. *5 Trevone Close, Knutsford WA16 9EJ* Tel (01565) 633531 Mobile 07855-615469
E-mail jandg.gaisford@tiscali.co.uk

GAIT, Canon David James. b 48. BNC Ox BA71 BSc72 MA77 MSc83. Ridley Hall Cam 71. **d** 74 **p** 75. C Litherland St Paul Hatton Hill *Liv* 74-77; C Farnworth 77-80; V Widnes St Jo from 80; Chapl Widnes Maternity Hosp 86-90; Hon Can Liv Cathl from 05; AD Widnes from 07. *St John's House, Greenway Road, Widnes WA8 6HA* Tel 0151-424 3134
E-mail dave.gait@btinternet.com

GALBRAITH, Alexander Peter James. b 65. Qu Coll Ox BA86 MA90. Wycliffe Hall Ox 87. **d** 90 **p** 91. C Southport Em *Liv* 90-94; C Mossley Hill St Matt and St Jas 94-97; V Kew from 97; Chapl Southport and Ormskirk NHS Trust from 97. *20 Markham Drive, Kew, Southport PR8 6XR* Tel (01704) 547758

GALBRAITH, Jane Alexandra. **d** 95 **p** 96. NSM Kildare w Kilmeague and Curragh *M & K* 95-97; NSM Newbridge w Carnalway and Kilcullen 97-99; C Limerick *L & K* from 03. *50 Ballinvoher, Father Russell Road, Dooradoyle, Limerick, Republic of Ireland* Tel and fax (00353) (61) 302038

GALBRAITH, John Angus Frame. b 44. Sarum Th Coll 68. **d** 71 **p** 72. C Richmond St Mary *S'wark* 71-74; Chapl W Lon Colls 74-79; R S'wark H Trin w St Matt 79-95; V New Addington 95-02; Asst Chapl HM Pris Wandsworth 02-04; Chapl 04-09; rtd 09. *35 Joseph Hardcastle Close, London SE14 5RN* Tel (020) 7635 3607 E-mail angus.galbraith@talktalk.net

GALBRAITH, Peter John. b 59. QUB BA MTh. CITC. **d** 85 **p** 86. C Knockbreda *D & D* 85-88; C Ballynafeigh St Jude 88-91; I Broomhedge *Conn* from 91. *Broomhedge Rectory, 30 Lurganure Road, Broughmore, Lisburn BT28 2TR* Tel (028) 9262 1229

GALE, Ms Charlotte. b 70. Leeds Univ BEng92 Nottm Univ MA00. St Jo Coll Nottm 98. **d** 01 **p** 02. C Whitnash *Cov* 01-05; P-in-c Potters Green 05-08; P-in-c Lillington from 08; C Leamington Spa H Trin and Old Milverton from 08. *The Vicarage, Vicarage Road, Lillington, Leamington Spa CV32 7RH* Tel (01926) 424674 *or* 470449
E-mail charlotte.gale@tiscali.co.uk

GALE, Canon Christopher. b 44. ALCD67. **d** 68 **p** 69. C Balderton *S'well* 68-72; C Bilborough St Jo 72-75; P-in-c Colwick 75-78; V Radford St Pet 78-84; V Sherwood 84-98; AD Nottingham N 90-98; P-in-c Bulwell St Mary 98-02; R 02-07; Hon Can S'well Minster 03-07; rtd 08. *11 Cliff Road, Carlton, Nottingham NG4 1BS* Tel 0115-844 0209
E-mail rev.chrisgale@gmail.com

GALE, Colin Edward. b 49. Lon Univ PGCE74. St Jo Coll Nottm BTh73. **d** 79 **p** 80. C Hoole *Ches* 79-82; C Woodley St Jo the Ev *Ox* 83-87; V Clapham St Jas *S'wark* 87-96; V Sutton Ch Ch 96-05; R Burstow w Horne from 05. *The Rectory, 5 The Acorns, Smallfield, Horley RH6 9QJ* Tel (01342) 842224
E-mail revceg@aol.com

GALE, The Ven John. b 34. Univ of Wales (Lamp) 67. **d** 69 **p** 70. C Aberdare *Llan* 69-71; C Merthyr Dyfan 71-74; S Africa 74-00; R Walmer St Sav 74-82; R Knysna St Geo 82-00; Adn Knysna 93-00; Lic to Offic *St D* from 00. *3 Connacht Way, Pembroke Dock SA72 6FB* Tel and fax (01646) 622219

GALE, Keith George. b 44. St Jo Coll Lusaka 68 Sarum Th Coll 69. **d** 70 **p** 71. C Sheff St Cuth 70-77; P-in-c Brightside All SS 72-77; C Birm St Martin 77-81; C Dwangwa Malawi 81-83; R Lilongwe St Pet 83-93; Adn Lilongwe 89-92; TV Sampford Peverell, Uplowman, Holcombe Rogus etc *Ex* 94-09; rtd 09. *101 Chapel Street, Tiverton EX16 6BU* Tel (01884) 821879
E-mail keith@gale5.eclipse.co.uk

GALE, Ms Lucille Catherine. b 67. Sarum & Wells Th Coll 92. **d** 94 **p** 95. C Welling *S'wark* 94-97; Chapl Greenwich Univ 97-00; V Welling 00-09; Officer Lay Min and Miss from 09. *The Vicarage, 2 The Grove, West Wickham BR4 9JS*

GALE, Peter Simon. b 56. Welsh Coll of Music & Drama 73 K Alfred's Coll Win PGCE78. St Mich Coll Llan BD83. **d** 83 **p** 84. C Caerphilly *Llan* 83-89; Chapl RN 89-93; V Ystrad Rhondda w Ynyscynon *Llan* 93-07; V Pont Rhondda from 07. *St Stephen's Vicarage, Ystrad, Pentre CF41 7RR* Tel (01443) 434426

GALES, Alan. b 29. Sarum Th Coll 56. **d** 59 **p** 60. C Greenside *Dur* 59-60; C Peterlee 60-63; Ind Chapl 60-70; V Marley Hill 63-94; Asst Chapl HM Pris Dur 74-81; rtd 94. *46 Corsair, Whickham, Newcastle upon Tyne NE16 5YA* Tel 0191-488 7352

GALES, Bernard Henry. b 27. Lon Univ BSc(Econ)51 Open Univ BA02. Wells Th Coll 62. **d** 64 **p** 65. C Sholing *Win* 64-67; C Fordingbridge w Ibsley 67-71; C S Molton w Nymet St George *Ex* 71-73; C Thelbridge 73-77; P-in-c 77-78; P-in-c Creacombe 77-78; P-in-c W w E Worlington 77-78; P-in-c Meshaw 77-78; P-in-c Witheridge 77-78; C Witheridge, Thelbridge, Creacombe, Meshaw etc 79-80; R Bow w Broad Nymet 80-93; V Colebrooke 80-93; R Zeal Monachorum 80-93; RD Cadbury 90-93; rtd 93; Perm to Offic *Ex* from 93. *8 Old Rectory Gardens, Morchard Bishop, Crediton EX17 6PF* Tel (01363) 877601

GALES, Simon Richard. b 59. CEng87 MICE87 Jes Coll Cam BA81 MA84. Wycliffe Hall Ox 91. **d** 93 **p** 94. C Houghton *Carl* 93-97; V Lindow *Ches* from 97. *St John's Vicarage, 137 Knutsford Road, Wilmslow SK9 6EL* Tel (01625) 583251 *or* 586329 E-mail simon@srgales.freeserve.co.uk

GALILEE, Canon George David Surtees. b 37. Oriel Coll Ox BA60 MA64. Westcott Ho Cam 61. **d** 62 **p** 63. C Knighton St Mary Magd *Leic* 62-67; V Stocking Farm 67-69; Tutor Westcott Ho Cam and Homerton Coll 69-71; V Sutton *Ely* 71-80; P-in-c Addiscombe St Mildred *Cant* 80-81; V 81-84; V Addiscombe St Mildred *S'wark* 85-95; Can Res and Chan Blackb Cathl 95-04; rtd 04; Perm to Offic *Blackb* from 04. *Ivy Hatch, 25 Ryburn Avenue, Blackburn BB2 7AU* Tel (01254) 671540 Fax 689666

GALLAGHER, Adrian Ian. b 43. CITC 89. **d** 92 **p** 93. C Drumachose *D & R* 92-96; I Camus-juxta-Bann 96-00; TV Langley and Parkfield *Man* 00-09; rtd 09. *12 Ashness Drive, Middleton, Manchester M24 5PJ* Tel 0161-654 9470 Mobile 07749-719028

GALLAGHER, Mrs Barbara Jean. b 53. Ex Univ BA73 Coll of Ripon & York St Jo PGCE76 Open Univ MA99. **d** 08 **p** 09. OLM Creeting St Mary, Creeting St Peter etc *St E* from 08. *Primrose Cottage, Forward Green, Stowmarket IP14 5HJ* Tel (01449) 711337 E-mail barbarajg@btopenworld.com

GALLAGHER, Canon Ian. BTh. **d** 90 **p** 91. C Annagh w Drumgoon, Ashfield etc *K, E & A* 90-93; I Drumcliffe w Lissadell and Munninane 93-01; Can Elphin Cathl 97-01; Dioc Sec (Elphin and Ardagh) 97-01; Preb Mulhuddart St Patr Cathl Dublin 98-01; I Stillorgan w Blackrock *D & G* from 01. *The Rectory, St Brigid's Church Road, Stillorgan, Blackrock, Co Dublin, Republic of Ireland* Tel (00353) (1) 288 1091 Fax 278 1833 Mobile 86-811 9544 E-mail stillorgan@dublin.anglican.org

GALLAGHER, Ian Mcel. b 71. Oberlin Coll (USA) BMus93 Duke Univ (USA) MA95. Westcott Ho Cam 06. **d** 08. C Walton-on-the-Hill *Liv* from 08. *Curate's House, 7 Walton Village, Liverpool L4 6TJ* Tel 0151-523 0683 E-mail imgall@gmx.net

GALLAGHER, Matthew Edward. b 51. Glas Univ BSc75. EAMTC. **d** 00 **p** 01. NSM Northampton St Jas *Pet* 00-02. *11 Penfold Gardens, Great Billing, Northampton NN3 9PG* Tel (01604) 416972 E-mail me.gallagher@virgin.net

GALLAGHER, Michael Collins. b 48. St Jo Coll Dur BA70 Sarum Th Coll 79. **d** 82 **p** 83. C Bridport *Sarum* 82-86; V Downton 86-01; RD Alderbury 93-99; R Crewkerne w Wayford *B & W* 01-07; R Wulfric Benefice from 07. *The Rectory, Gouldsbrook Terrace, Crewkerne TA18 7JA* Tel (01460) 271188 Fax 271194 E-mail mcfgallagher@lineone.net

GALLAGHER, Neville Roy. b 45. Birm Univ CertEd66 K Coll Lon AKC70 BD76 Open Univ BA97. **d** 71 **p** 72. C Folkestone St Mary and St Eanswythe *Cant* 71-74; Hon C Sutton Valence w E Sutton and Chart Sutton 74-76; TV Cen Telford *Lich* 76-78; P-in-c Gt Mongeham *Cant* 78-80; P-in-c Ripple 78-80; R Gt Mongeham w Ripple and Sutton by Dover 80-83; V Kennington 83-88; Chapl and Dep Hd Bedgebury Sch Kent 88-05; P-in-c Appledore w Brookland, Fairfield, Brenzett etc *Cant* from 05; P-in-c Woodchurch from 06; AD Romney from 08. *The Vicarage, Appledore, Ashford TN26 2DB* Tel (01233) 758250 E-mail nrwg45@aol.com

GALLAGHER, Robert. b 43. St Chad's Coll Dur BSc65. **d** 67 **p** 68. C Crosland Moor *Wakef* 67-69; C Huddersfield SS Pet and Paul 69-71; Chapl Huddersfield Poly 72-79; Min Coulby Newham LEP *York* 79-90; V Toxteth St Marg *Liv* from 90. *St Margaret's Vicarage, 3 Princes Road, Liverpool L8 1TG* Tel 0151-709 1526

GALLAGHER, Stephen. b 58. Southn Univ BTh89. Chich Th Coll 86. **d** 89 **p** 90. C S Shields All SS *Dur* 89-92; C Hartlepool St Paul and Chapl Hartlepool Gen Hosp 92-94; R Loftus and Carlin How w Skinningrove *York* 94-97; P-in-c Lower Beeding *Chich* from 97; Dioc Youth Officer from 97. *The Vicarage, Plummers Plain, Lower Beeding, Horsham RH13 6NU* Tel (01403) 891367 Mobile 07740-196675 E-mail fatherstephen@plummersplain.freeserve.co.uk

GALLANT, Mrs Joanna-Sue Sheena. b 62. SAOMC 99. **d** 02 **p** 03. C Amersham on the Hill *Ox* 02-05; NSM Gt Missenden w

Ballinger and Lt Hampden from 06. *50 Frances Street, Chesham HP5 3ER* Tel (01494) 580077 Mobile 07813-886805

GALLETLY, Thomas. b 23. St Chad's Coll Dur BA50. **d** 52 **p** 53. C Woodhorn w Newbiggin *Newc* 52-55; Chapl Aycliffe Approved Sch Co Dur 56-57; Chapl Chailey Heritage Hosp and Sch Lewes 57-88; rtd 88; Perm to Offic *Chich* from 88. *The Glen, Lewes Road, Scaynes Hill, Haywards Heath RH17 7PG* Tel (01444) 831510

GALLEY, Giles Christopher. b 32. Qu Coll Cam BA56 MA60. Linc Th Coll 56. **d** 58 **p** 59. C Gt Yarmouth *Nor* 58-62; C N Lynn w St Marg and St Nic 62-66; C Leeds St Pet *Ripon* 66-69; V N Hull St Mich *York* 70-79; V Strensall 79-00; RD Easingwold 82-97; rtd 00; Perm to Offic *York* from 00. *19 St John's Road, Stamford Bridge, York YO41 1PH* Tel (01759) 371592

✠**GALLIFORD, The Rt Revd David George.** b 25. Clare Coll Cam BA49 MA51. Westcott Ho Cam. **d** 51 **p** 52 **c** 75. C Newland St Jo *York* 51-54; C Eton w Boveney *Ox* 54-56; Min Can Windsor 54-56; V Middlesbrough St Oswald *York* 56-61; R Bolton Percy 61-71; Dioc Adult Tr Officer 61-71; Can and Preb York Minster 69-70; Can Res and Treas 70-75; Suff Bp Hulme *Man* 75-84; Suff Bp Bolton 84-91; rtd 91; Hon Asst Bp York from 95. *10 St Mary's Mews, Greenshaw Drive, Wigginton, York YO32 2SE* Tel (01904) 761489

GALLIGAN, Ms Adrienne. TCD BA81 HDipEd82. CITC BTh03. **d** 03 **p** 04. C Seapatrick *D & D* 03-08; I Dublin Crumlin w Chapelizod *D & G* from 08. *St Mary's Rectory, 118 Kimmage Road West, Dublin 12, Republic of Ireland* Tel (00353) (1) 455 5639 Fax 456 0006

GALLON, Mrs Audrey Kay. b 41. SEITE 94. **d** 97 **p** 98. NSM Gt Mongeham w Ripple and Sutton by Dover *Cant* 97-98; NSM Eastry and Northbourne w Tilmanstone etc 97-98; NSM Walmer 98-04; Perm to Offic *Cant* 04-05 and *Roch* from 07. *12 Arne Close, Tonbridge TN10 4DH* Tel (01732) 355633

GALLOWAY, Canon Charles Bertram. b 41. Lon Univ BA62. Qu Coll Birm 64. **d** 64 **p** 65. C Darlington H Trin *Dur* 64-68; Ind Chapl Teesside 68-77; Sen Ind Chapl *Liv* 77-87; Team Ldr and Convener Lon Ind Chapl 87-93; P-in-c Gosforth w Nether Wasdale and Wasdale Head *Carl* 93-98; R 98-04; Chapl Sellafield 94-04; Hon Can Carl Cathl from 03; rtd 04. *27 Oakfield Close, Sunderland SR3 3RT* Tel 0191-528 8459 E-mail bert.galloway@btinternet.com

GALLOWAY, Michael Edward. b 41. Chich Th Coll 72. **d** 74 **p** 75. C Aldwick *Chich* 74-77; C Bournemouth St Clem w St Mary *Win* 78-82; V S Benfleet *Chelmsf* 83-06; rtd 06; Perm to Offic *B & W* from 06. *3 Church Street, Chard TA20 2DW* Tel (01460) 65026 E-mail ceag@dialstart.net

GALLOWAY, Prof Peter John. b 54. OBE96 JP89. Goldsmiths' Coll Lon BA76 K Coll Lon PhD87 Brunel Univ Hon DLitt09 FRSA88 FSA00. St Steph Ho Ox 80. **d** 83 **p** 84. C St John's Wood *Lon* 83-86; C St Giles-in-the-Fields 86-90; Warden of Readers (Lon Episc Area) 87-92; P-in-c Hampstead Em W End 90-95; V 95-08; AD N Camden 02-07; Chapl to RVO and Qu Chpl of the Savoy from 08; Hon Fell Goldsmiths' Coll Lon from 99; Visiting Prof Brunel Univ from 08. *The Queen's Chapel of the Savoy, Savoy Hill, London WC2R 0DA* Tel (020) 7379 8088 E-mail peter.galloway@sja.org.uk

GALSWORTHY, Colin. b 44. St Mich Coll Llan 95. **d** 00 **p** 01. NSM Skewen *Llan* 00-01; NSM Resolven w Tonna 01-04; NSM Tonna and Cadoxton-juxta-Neath 04-08; rtd 08. *29 Woodlands Park Drive, Cadoxton, Neath SA10 8DE* Tel (01639) 636128

GALT, Ian Ross. b 34. Leeds Univ BSc56. **d** 76 **p** 77. NSM Newport St Julian *Mon* 76-87; NSM Newport St Teilo 87-98. *47 Brynglas Avenue, Newport NP20 5LR* Tel (01633) 821499

GALWAY, Gary Ford. **d** 04 **p** 05. C Donaghadee *D & D* 04-06; C Portadown St Mark *Arm* 06-08; I Drumcree from 08. *78 Drumcree Road, Portadown, Craigavon BT62 1PE* Tel (028) 3833 2503 E-mail galwayhome@aol.com

GAMBLE, Bronwen. *See* GAMBLE, Mrs Edana Bronwen

GAMBLE, David Lawrence. b 34. AKC61. **d** 62 **p** 63. C-in-c Shrub End All SS CD *Chelmsf* 62-65; C Colchester St Jas, All SS, St Nic and St Runwald 65-69; V Chelmsf St Andr 69-73; P-in-c Hatfield Heath 69-73; C 74-77; TV Hemel Hempstead *St Alb* 77-82; P-in-c Renhold 82-90; Chapl HM Pris Bedf 82-90; P-in-c Petersham *S'wark* 90-96; Chapl HM Pris Latchmere Ho 90-96; P-in-c Portsea St Geo *Portsm* 96-99; rtd 99; Hon C Yarmouth and Freshwater *Portsm* 99-04. *35 Kings Chase, Andover SP10 3TH* Tel (01264) 338017

GAMBLE, Diane Mary. b 36. BSc. **d** 00 **p** 01. NSM Sanderstead *S'wark* 00-07; Perm to Offic from 07. *14 Barnfield Road, Sanderstead CR2 0EY* Tel (020) 8651 0700

GAMBLE, Donald William. b 67. NUU BSc88. TCD Div Sch BTh91. **d** 91 **p** 92. C Belfast St Mich *Conn* 91-95; I Dromore *Clogh* 95-00; P-in-c Renewal and Outreach in the City *Conn* from 00; Chapl Belfast Health and Soc Care Trust from 09. *5 Fernridge Road, Newtownabbey BT36 5SP* Tel (028) 9084 2171 *or* 9074 1099 Mobile 07876-361653 E-mail don.gamble@rocbelfast.com

GAMBLE, Mrs Edana Bronwen. b 56. Hull Univ BSc(Econ)78

Nottm Univ MA02 FCA82. EMMTC 99. **d** 02 **p** 03. NSM Nuthall *S'well* 02-06; R Cropwell Bishop w Colston Bassett, Granby etc from 06. *The Rectory, 2 Dobbin Close, Cropwell Bishop, Nottingham NG12 3GR* Tel 0115-989 3172

GAMBLE, Ian Robert. b 66. Ulster Univ BA90 MA98 TCD BTh93. CITC 90. **d** 93 **p** 94. C Bangor St Comgall *D & D* 93-96; C Bangor Primacy 93-96; Bp's C Belfast Whiterock *Conn* 96-99; R Donaghadee *D & D* from 99. *The Rectory, 3 The Trees, New Road, Donaghadee BT21 0EJ* Tel (028) 9188 2594

GAMBLE, Kenneth Wesley. b 52. Ulster Univ BA81. CITC 04. **d** 07 **p** 08. NSM Ballymacash *Conn* from 07. *21 Dalboyne Park, Lisburn BT28 3BU* Tel (028) 9267 7498
E-mail ken_gamble@talktalk.net

GAMBLE, Norman Edward Charles. b 50. TCD BA72 HDipEd73 PhD78. CITC 76. **d** 79 **p** 80. C Bangor St Comgall *D & D* 79-83; I Dunleckney w Nurney, Lorum and Kiltennel *C & O* 83-90; Warden of Readers 84-90; P-in-c Leighlin w Grange Sylvae, Shankill etc 89-90; Can Leighlin Cathl 89-90; Preb Ossory Cathl 89-90; I Malahide w Balgriffin *D & G* from 90; Abp's Dom Chapl 95-03. *The Rectory, Church Road, Malahide, Co Dublin, Republic of Ireland* Tel and fax (00353) (1) 845 4770 Mobile 86-815 3277 E-mail normanegamble@iol.ie

GAMBLE, Robin Philip. b 53. Oak Hill Th Coll 74. **d** 77 **p** 78. C Kildwick *Bradf* 77-78; C Laisterdyke 78-80; C York St Paul 80-82; V Bradf St Aug Undercliffe 82-95; Dioc Adv in Evang 93-01; Can Ev Man Cathl 01-08; P-in-c Idle *Bradf* from 08; Dioc Ev from 08. *The Vicarage, 470 Leeds Road, Idle, Bradford BD10 9AA* Tel (01274) 419754 Mobile 07748-943541
E-mail robinp.gamble@virgin.net

GAMBLE, Ronald George. b 41. Cant Sch of Min 92. **d** 95 **p** 96. NSM Loose *Cant* 95-00; P-in-c Boxley w Detling 00-07; Chapl NHS Ambulance Trust 99-07; rtd 07; Perm to Offic *Cant* from 07. *18 Copper Tree Court, Maidstone ME15 9RW* Tel (01622) 744455 E-mail r-gamble@sky.com

GAMBLE, Stanley Thomas Robert. b 82. QUB BA03 MTh05. CITC 05. **d** 07 **p** 08. C Knockbreda *D & D* from 07. *28 Church Road, Newtownbreda, Belfast BT8 7AQ* Tel (028) 9064 1339
E-mail stanleygamble@gmail.com

GAMBLE, Stephen Robert. b 69. York Univ BA91. Cranmer Hall Dur 07. **d** 08 **p** 09. C Loughborough All SS w H Trin *Leic* from 08. *60 Brush Drive, Loughborough LE11 1LT* Tel (01509) 219545

GAMBLES, Una Beryl. b 33. Man Univ BEd78. St Chris Coll Blackheath 59. **d** 87 **p** 94. NSM Upton Priory *Ches* 87-01; Chapl Parkside Hosp Ches 87-93; Chapl E Cheshire NHS Trust 93-01; Chapl HM Pris Styal 94-98; Perm to Offic *Ches* from 01. *23 Grangelands, Upton, Macclesfield SK10 4AB* Tel (01625) 421691

GAMBLING, Paul Anthony. b 62. Middx Univ BA06. NTMTC 03. **d** 06 **p** 07. C Warley Ch Ch and Gt Warley St Mary *Chelmsf* from 06. *4 Thorndales, St John's Avenue, Warley, Brentwood CM14 5DE* Tel (01277) 203559
E-mail paul.gambling@btinternet.com

GAMESTER, Sidney Peter. b 27. SS Coll Cam BA51 MA55. Oak Hill Th Coll 56. **d** 58 **p** 59. C Surbiton Hill Ch Ch *S'wark* 58-61; C Worthing H Trin *Chich* 61-69; R Silverhill St Matt 69-86; R Bexhill St Mark 86-93; rtd 93; Perm to Offic *Chich* from 93. *18 Crofton Park Avenue, Bexhill-on-Sea TN39 3SE* Tel (01424) 842276

GAMLEN, Laurence William. b 59. STETS BA07. **d** 07 **p** 08. NSM Chertsey, Lyne and Longcross *Guildf* from 07. *9 Redwood, Egham TW20 8SU* Tel (01932) 561503 Fax 570299 Mobile 07939-094851 E-mail lgamlen@cpas.org.uk

GAMMON, Elizabeth Angela Myfanwy. b 47. SWMTC 06. **d** 09. *Tracey Mill, Tracey Road, Honiton EX14 3SL* Tel (01404) 45114
E-mail angiegammon@hotmail.com

GAMMON, William Paul Lachlan. b 60. SS Hild & Bede Coll Dur BA82. St Steph Ho Ox 89. **d** 91 **p** 92. C Chalfont St Peter *Ox* 91-94; Lect Bolton St Pet *Man* 94-98; R Woodston *Ely* from 98; P-in-c Fletton from 98. *The Rectory, 2 Rectory Gardens, Peterborough PE2 8HN* Tel (01733) 562786

✠**GANDIYA, The Rt Revd Chad Nicholas.** b 53. Nottm Univ BTh80 Univ of Zimbabwe MA84 DPhil06 Michigan State Univ MA95. St Jo Coll Nottm 77. **d** 80 **p** 81 **c** 09. C Avondale Zimbabwe 80-83; R Mabelreigh St Pet 83-85; Chapl Michigan Univ USA 86-87; Asst P Harare Cathl 88; Warden Bp Gaul Coll 88-91; USA 92-95; R Marlborough St Paul 95-96; Prin Bp Gaul Coll 96-01; Tutor Internat Coll of Ascension Selly Oak 01-05; Regional Desk Officer USPG 05-09; Tanzania and Cen Africa 05-06; Africa and Indian Ocean 06-09; Bp Harare from 09. *Bishopsmount Close, PO Box UA7, Harare, Zimbabwe* Tel (00263) (4) 702253 *or* 702254 Fax 700419

GANDIYA, Leonard Farirayi (Lee). b 64. Boston Coll (USA) MA92. Gordon-Conwell Th Sem 90 Ridley Hall Cam 92. **d** 94 **p** 95. NSM Camberwell St Luke *S'wark* 94-95; C Lowestoft St Marg *Nor* 95-98; Dioc Rep for Black Anglican Concerns 96-98; CF from 98. *c/o MOD Chaplains (Army)* Tel (01980) 615804 Fax 615800

GANDON, Andrew James Robson. b 54. St Jo Coll Dur BA76.

Ridley Hall Cam 76. **d** 78 **p** 79. C Aston SS Pet and Paul *Birm* 78-82; CMS 82-95; Zaïre 82-88; Kenya 89-94; V Harefield *Lon* from 95; Chapl R Brompton and Harefield NHS Trust 95-05. *The Vicarage, 28 Countess Close, Harefield, Uxbridge UB9 6DL* Tel (01895) 825960 Fax 820705
E-mail andrew.gandon@london.anglican.org

GANDON, James Philip. b 31. ALCD56. **d** 56 **p** 57. C Westcliff St Mich *Chelmsf* 56-58; Canada from 58; rtd 92. *62 Cambria Road North, Goderich ON N7A 2P3, Canada*
E-mail phil.gandon@odyssey.on.ca

GANDY, Nicholas John. b 53. Westf Coll Lon BSc75 Reading Univ MSc76 Ex Coll Ox CertEd78 CBiol79 MIBiol. St Steph Ho Ox 86. **d** 88 **p** 89. C Crowthorne *Ox* 88-89; C Tilehurst St Mary 89-93; P-in-c Didcot St Pet 93-97; V 97-03; V Brackley St Pet w St Jas from 03; OGS from 96. *The Vicarage, Old Town, Brackley NN13 7BZ* Tel (01280) 702767
E-mail nicholas@ngandy.fsnet.co.uk

GANE, Canon Christopher Paul. b 33. Qu Coll Cam BA57 MA61. Ridley Hall Cam 57. **d** 59 **p** 60. C Rainham *Chelmsf* 59-62; C Farnborough *Guildf* 62-64; V Erith St Paul *Roch* 64-71; V Ipswich St Marg *St E* 71-88; Hon Can St E Cathl 82-98; R Hopton, Market Weston, Barningham etc 88-98; rtd 98; Perm to Offic *St E* from 98. *1 Post Office Lane, Thurston, Bury St Edmunds IP31 3RW* Tel (01359) 271152

GANE, Nicholas. b 57. St Jo Coll Nottm 93. **d** 95 **p** 96. C Keynsham *B & W* 95-99; TV 99-02. *10 Ludlow Court, Willsbridge, Bristol BS30 6HB* E-mail nick.gane@virgin.net

GANGA, Jeremy Franklin. b 62. Cape Town Univ BSocSc86 Lon Bible Coll BA92 St Jo Coll Nottm MA93. Ridley Hall Cam 93. **d** 95 **p** 96. C St Peter-in-Thanet *Cant* 95-98; Chapl Felsted Sch 98-00; Past Chapl St Paul's Sch Barnes 00-02; NSM Fulham St Pet *Lon* 00-02; P-in-c Fulham St Pet 02-06; Tutor Reader Min Tr from 03; Tutor and Registrar NTMTC from 06. *The Crypt, St George-in-the-East, 16 Cannon Street Road, London E1 0BH* Tel (020) 7481 9477 Fax 7481 8907
E-mail jeremy.ganga@btinternet.com
or admissions@ntmtc.org.uk

GANJAVI, John Farhad. b 57. Imp Coll Lon BSc79. Ridley Hall Cam 79. **d** 82 **p** 83. C Yardley St Edburgha *Birm* 82-85; C Knowle 85-89; P-in-c Beaudesert and Henley-in-Arden w Ullenhall *Cov* 89-92; R from 92; RD Alcester 92-99. *The Rectory, Beaudesert Lane, Henley-in-Arden B95 5JY* Tel (01564) 792570
E-mail bdesert@btinternet.com

GANN, Canon Anthony Michael. b 37. TCD BA60 MA64 BD64. **d** 62 **p** 63. V Choral Derry Cathl 62-66; Lesotho 66-74; Dioc Officer for Miss and Unity *Carl* 75-80; P-in-c Bampton and Mardale 75-80; TV Cen Telford *Lich* 80-89; TR Wolvercote w Summertown *Ox* 89-02; RD Ox 95-99; rtd 02; Perm to Offic *Worc* from 02. *2 Avalon, 84 Pickersleigh Road, Malvern WR14 2RS* Tel (01684) 568114

GANN, John West. b 29. Ex Coll Ox BA55 MA59. Wells Th Coll 55. **d** 57 **p** 58. C Wendover *Ox* 57-59; C Walton St Mary *Liv* 59-62; R Didcot *Ox* 62-70; R Newbury St Nic 70-78; TR Newbury 73-78; V Twickenham St Mary *Lon* 78-87; Dir of Ords 81-87; TR Bridport *Sarum* 87-94; RD Lyme Bay 89-92; rtd 94; Perm to Offic *Glouc* from 94 and *Bris* from 96. *3 Buttercross Lane, Prestbury, Cheltenham GL52 5SF* Tel (01242) 220787
E-mail jandhgann@btinternet.com

GANNEY (née CHAMBERS), Mrs Rachel Jill. b 73. Hull Univ BSc94 MSc96 Selw Coll Cam BTh04. Ridley Hall Cam 01. **d** 04 **p** 05. C Sutton St Jas and Wawne *York* from 04. *7 Corinthian Way, Hull HU9 1UF* Tel (01482) 212216
E-mail rachel@ganney.net

GANT, Canon Brian Leonard. b 45. Ox Univ MTh01. K Coll Lon 72. **d** 73 **p** 74. C Hillmorton *Cov* 73-75; C Cov St Geo 76; P-in-c Maldon St Mary *Chelmsf* 76-79; R Muthill, Crieff and Comrie *St And* 79-81; V Walsall St Paul *Lich* 81-84; Chapl K Sch Worc and Min Can Worc Cathl 84-89; V Tunbridge Wells K Chas *Roch* 89-95; P-in-c Han Kumasi from 94; V Wymondham *Nor* 95-01; P-in-c York All SS N Street 01-03; TV Haxby and Wigginton 03-09; CME Officer York Adnry 01-07; rtd 09. *7 Slessor Road, York YO24 3JJ* Tel (01904) 790799 Mobile 07800-922985 E-mail brianlgant@aol.com

GANT, Peter Robert. b 38. BNC Ox BA60 MA64 G&C Coll Cam BA62 MA67. Ridley Hall Cam 61. **d** 63 **p** 64. C Portsea St Mary *Portsm* 63-67; V Blackheath *Birm* 67-73; Asst Master Harold Malley Gr Sch Solihull 73-75; Perm to Offic *Birm* 73-75 and *Guildf* from 75; rtd 93. *8 Sandon Close, Esher KT10 8JE* Tel (020) 8398 5107

GANT, Trevor Malcolm. b 56. Leeds Univ BSc97. NEOC 05. **d** 08 **p** 09. NSM York St Luke from 08. *6 Lumley Road, York YO30 6DB* Tel (01904) 654784

GANZ, Timothy Jon. b 36. Univ Coll Ox BA58 MA62 ARCM63. St Steph Ho Ox 58. **d** 61 **p** 62. C Shrewsbury H Cross *Lich* 61-65; Asst Chapl Hurstpierpoint Coll 65-69; Chapl 69-73; Chapl Univ of Wales (Swansea) *St & B* 74-75; P-in-c Hanley All SS *Lich* 75-80; TV Stoke-upon-Trent 80-81; V Tutbury 81-04; rtd 04. *3 Warren Close, Stretton, Burton-on-Trent DE13 0DD* Tel (01283) 749171

GARBETT, Capt Phillip Ronald. b 52. EAMTC 95. **d** 97 **p** 98. CA from 80; C Ipswich St Mary at Stoke w St Pet and St Fran *St E* 97-00; TV Walton and Trimley 00-09; TR Blackbourne from 09. *The Vicarage, Commister Lane, Ixworth, Bury St Edmunds IP31 2HE* Tel (01359) 234415 Mobile 07884-212218 E-mail philip.garbett@ntlworld.com

GARBUTT, Gerald. b 41. St Aid Birkenhead 65. **d** 67 **p** 68. C Stretford All SS *Man* 67-70; Lic to Offic 70-72; R Salford St Bart 72-74; V Lower Kersal 74-79; TR Bethnal Green St Jo w St Bart *Lon* 79-90; P-in-c Stepney St Pet w St Benet 85-87; Chapl Furness Gen Hosp 90-94; Chapl S Cumbria HA 90-94; Hosp Services Chapl Furness Hosps NHS Trust 94-98; Chapl Westmorland Hosps NHS Trust 94-98; Chapl Morecambe Bay Hosps NHS Trust 98-06; rtd 03; P-in-c Beetham *Carl* 06-07. *20 Highbury Road, Stockport SK4 5AZ* Tel 0161-975 9110

GARBUTT, Mrs Mary Yvonne. b 45. Ridley Hall Cam 00. **d** 02 **p** 03. C Desborough, Brampton Ash, Dingley and Braybrooke *Pet* 02-05; P-in-c Arthingworth, Harrington w Oxendon and E Farndon 05-07; R from 07; P-in-c Maidwell w Draughton, Lamport w Faxton 05-07; R from 07; RD Brixworth from 09. *The Rectory, 35 Main Street, Great Oxendon, Market Harborough LE16 8NE* Tel (01858) 461992 E-mail mary@familygarbutt.plus.com

GARDEN, Robert Andrew (Robin). b 26. Edin Univ BSc49 Kent Univ MA95 MInstP58 FIMA72. Cant Sch of Min 87. **d** 90 **p** 91. NSM Sandwich *Cant* 90-97; Chapl St Bart Hosp Sandwich 91-00; Perm to Offic *Cant* from 97. *Naini, 164 St George's Road, Sandwich CT13 9LD* Tel (01304) 612116

GARDHAM, Mrs Linda Elizabeth. b 49. Leeds Univ BA70 Warwick Univ PGCE71. Cranmer Hall Dur 04. **d** 05 **p** 06. NSM Monkseaton St Pet *Newc* 05-08; NSM Cornhill w Carham from 08; NSM Branxton from 08. *The Vicarage, Old School House, Branxton, Cornhill-on-Tweed TD12 4SW* Tel (01890) 820308 E-mail leg@lgardham.freeserve.co.uk

GARDINER, Anthony Reade. b 35. Univ of NZ BA59. Cuddesdon Coll 60. **d** 62 **p** 63. C Gosforth All SS *Newc* 62-65; V Waikohu New Zealand 65-69; V Edgecumbe 69-74; V Eltham 74-78; V Trentham 78-81; V Waipukurau 81-88; Chapl Nelson Cathl 88-92; C Highcliffe w Hinton Admiral *Win* 93-94; TV N Creedy *Ex* 94-00; rtd 00; Perm to Offic Wellington from 00. *1 Puriri Street, Eastbourne, Lower Hutt 5013, New Zealand* Tel (0064) (4) 562 6177 E-mail nantony2@paradise.net.nz

GARDINER, Mrs Cathrine Leigh. b 64. STETS 05. **d** 08 **p** 09. C Bedminster *Bris* from 08. *St Dunstan's Vicarage, 66 Bedminster Down Road, Bristol BS13 7AA* Tel 0117-939 4688 E-mail cathrinegardiner@googlemail.com

GARDINER, Charles Graham. b 18. AKC49. St Boniface Warminster. **d** 50 **p** 51. C Clapham H Trin *S'wark* 50-54; S Africa from 54. *55 Weltevreden Avenue, Rondebosch, 7700 South Africa* Tel (0027) (21) 689 1111

GARDINER, David Andrew. b 81. Surrey Univ BA03 Fitzw Coll Cam BTh08. Westcott Ho Cam 05. **d** 08 **p** 09. C N Cheltenham *Glouc* from 08. *8 Boulton Road, Cheltenham GL50 4RZ* Tel (01242) 238601 E-mail david.gardiner@northchelt.org.uk

GARDINER, Gerald. *See* GARDINER, Preb William Gerald Henry

GARDINER, James Carlisle. b 10. Tyndale Hall Bris. **d** 49 **p** 50. C Blackpool Ch Ch *Blackb* 49-52; C Rushen *S & M* 52-56; R Ditton *Roch* 56-83; rtd 83; Perm to Offic *Roch* 83-04. *Rosset Holt Care Home, Pembury Road, Tunbridge Wells TN2 3RB* Tel (01892) 526077

GARDINER (née SAYERS), Mrs Karen Jane. b 69. Sheff Univ BMus92. Ripon Coll Cuddesdon 00. **d** 02 **p** 03. C Dunstable *St Alb* 02-05; TV Elstree and Borehamwood from 05. *The Rectory, St Nicholas Close, Elstree, Borehamwood WD6 3EW* Tel (020) 8953 1411 E-mail revdkarengardiner@googlemail.com

GARDINER, Canon Kenneth Ashton. b 27. S'wark Ord Course 60. **d** 63 **p** 64. C Sydenham H Trin *S'wark* 63-67; C Macclesfield St Mich 67-70; V Chatham St Phil and St Jas *Roch* 70-93; RD Roch 88-93; Hon Can Roch Cathl 88-93; rtd 93; Perm to Offic *Roch* from 93. *44 Trevale Road, Rochester ME1 3PA* Tel (01634) 844524 E-mail ken.gardiner@diocese-rochester.org

GARDINER, Preb William Gerald Henry. b 46. Lon Univ BD72. Oak Hill Th Coll 68. **d** 72 **p** 73. C Beckenham St Jo *Roch* 72-75; C Cheadle *Ches* 75-81; P-in-c Swynnerton *Lich* 81-83; P-in-c Swynnerton and Tittensor 81-83; R Swynnerton and Tittensor 83-86; V Westlands St Andr from 86; RD Newcastle from 97; Preb Lich Cathl from 05. *St Andrew's Vicarage, 50 Kingsway West, Westlands, Newcastle ST5 3PU* Tel (01782) 619594

GARDINER, Canon Anthony Brian. b 32. Lon Coll of Div 62. **d** 64 **p** 65. C Stoke *Cov* 64-68; R Whitnash 68-98; RD Leamington 78-79; RD Warwick and Leamington 79-87; Hon Can Cov Cathl 83-98; rtd 98; Perm to Offic *Cov* from 99. *4 Mark Antony Drive, Heathcote, Warwick CV34 6XA* Tel (01926) 832690

GARDINER, Brian Charles. b 46. FIBMS71. **d** 04 **p** 05. OLM Bodicote from 04. *11 Farm Way, Banbury OX16 9TB* Tel (01295) 253309 Mobile 07967-859457 E-mail bri.jen@btopenworld.com

GARDNER, Christine. *See* GARDNER, Mary Christine

GARDNER, Clive Bruce. b 67. Selw Coll Cam BA89 MA92 Wycliffe Hall Ox BA93. **d** 96 **p** 97. C Beverley Minster *York* 96-98; Bp's Dom Chapl *Liv* 98-01; V Cumnor *Ox* 01-06. *Flat 9, 24-25 Broad Street, Brighton BN2 1TJ* Tel (01273) 681200 E-mail clivegardner@tesco.net

GARDNER, David. b 57. Oak Hill Th Coll BA87. **d** 87 **p** 88. C Ogley Hay *Lich* 87-91; TV Mildenhall *St E* 91-98; P-in-c Woodbridge St Jo 98-00; V 00-03; P-in-c Bredfield 01-03; V Woodbridge St Jo and Bredfield from 03. *St John's Vicarage, St John's Hill, Woodbridge IP12 1HS* Tel (01394) 382083 *or* tel and fax 383162 E-mail stjohns.woodbridge@btinternet.com

GARDNER, Elizabeth Mary. b 47. Nottm Univ BA01. Trin Coll Bris 72 St Jo Coll Nottm 00. **d** 01 **p** 02. C Swindon Dorcan *Bris* 01-04; P-in-c Runcorn St Jo Weston *Ches* 04-09; V from 09; Dioc Clergy Widows and Retirement Officer from 07. *The Vicarage, 225 Heath Road South, Weston, Runcorn WA7 4LY* Tel (01928) 573798 E-mail beth47@btopenworld.com

GARDNER, Geoffrey Maurice. b 28. K Coll Lon BA51 Lon Inst of Educn PGCE52 Bris Univ DipEd74. Cranmer Hall Dur. **d** 59 **p** 60. C Bowling St Jo *Bradf* 59-62; Nigeria 62-72; Hon C Bath St Luke *B & W* 72-73; Perm to Offic 73-90; and 94-99; NSM Bath Widcombe 90-94; rtd 94; Perm to Offic *Ex* from 99. *15 Bramley Gardens, Whimple, Exeter EX5 2SJ* Tel (01404) 823235

GARDNER, Mrs Helen Elizabeth. b 56. ERMC 05. **d** 08 **p** 09. C Sunnyside w Bourne End *St Alb* from 08. *3 Broadwater, Berkhamsted HP4 2AH* Tel (01442) 862512 E-mail helerevg@aol.com

GARDNER, Helen Jane. b 39. Man Univ BSc61 PGCE62. WMMTC 93. **d** 96 **p** 97. NSM Stow on the Wold *Glouc* 96-00; NSM Stow on the Wold, Condicote and The Swells 00-03; NSM Upper and Lower Slaughter w Eyford and Naunton from 03; NSM The Guitings, Cutsdean, Farmcote etc from 03. *6 St Mary's Close, Lower Swell, Cheltenham GL54 1LJ* Tel (01451) 832553 E-mail jane.gardner@dsl.pipex.com

GARDNER, Ian Douglas. b 34. St Pet Hall Ox BA58 MA62. Oak Hill Th Coll 58. **d** 60 **p** 61. C Biddulph *Lich* 60-63; C Weston St Jo *B & W* 64; Nigeria 65-76; P-in-c Hurstbourne Tarrant and Faccombe *Win* 77-79; V Hurstbourne Tarrant, Faccombe, Vernham Dean etc 79-85; R Nursling and Rownhams 85-99; rtd 99. *Wilderness Cottage, Haroldston Hill, Broad Haven, Haverfordwest SA62 3JP* Tel (01437) 781592

GARDNER, Ian Norman. b 52. Open Univ BSc96. WEMTC 03. **d** 05 **p** 06. NSM Dursley *Glouc* from 05. *9 Chestal Lodge, Chestal, Dursley GL11 5AA* Tel (01453) 546895 Mobile 07960-287403 E-mail ian@chestal.freeserve.co.uk

GARDNER, Mrs Jacqueline Anne. b 49. WEMTC 95. **d** 98 **p** 99. NSM Fairford and Kempsford w Whelford *Glouc* 98-02; NSM Cirencester 02-05; Perm to Offic *Ox* 05-07; NSM Hanborough and Freeland from 07. *15 Oakdale Road, Witney OX28 1AX* Tel (01993) 866110

GARDNER, Jane. *See* GARDNER, Helen Jane

GARDNER, Canon John Phillip Backhouse. b 21. St Aid Birkenhead 49. **d** 52 **p** 53. C Ashtead *Guildf* 52-55; C Bromley SS Pet and Paul *Roch* 55-57; V New Hythe 57-63; V Roch St Justus 63-69; R Wisley w Pyrford *Guildf* 70-87; RD Woking 82-87; Hon Can Guildf Cathl 86-87; rtd 87; Perm to Offic *Pet* 87-98 and *Guildf* from 98. *42 Godley Road, Byfleet, West Byfleet KT14 7ER* Tel (01932) 347431

GARDNER, Mrs Marian Elizabeth. b 50. Ripon Coll of Educn DipEd71. WMMTC 00. **d** 03 **p** 04. NSM Kirkleatham *York* 03-07; P-in-c Easington w Liverton from 07. *The Rectory, Grinkle Lane, Easington, Saltburn-by-the-Sea TS13 4NT* Tel (01287) 641348 Mobile 07736-350643 E-mail marian@thegardners.org.uk

GARDNER, Canon Mark Douglas. b 58. TCD BA80 MA83. **d** 83 **p** 84. C Ballymacarrett St Patr *D & D* 83-87; C Belfast St Steph w St Luke *Conn* 87-89; C Hendon and Sunderland *Dur* 89-90; TV Sunderland 90-95; I Dublin Santry w Glasnevin and Finglas *D & G* 95-01; PV and Chapter Clerk Ch Ch Cathl Dublin from 96; Min Can St Patr Cathl Dublin 96; Treas V 96-01; Can Ch Ch Cathl Dublin from 08. *67 Brookfield Green, Kimmage, Dublin 12, Republic of Ireland* Tel (00353) (1) 478 1797 *or* 677 8099 Fax 679 8991 Mobile 87-266 0228 E-mail deansvicar@cccdub.ie

GARDNER, Mary Christine. b 42. SRN64 SCM66. St Jo Coll Nottm 80. **dss** 82 **d** 85 **p** 94. Ches St Paul 82-87; Macclesfield St Mich 84-85; Macclesfield Team 85-87; Par Dn 87; Chapl Asst Nottm City Hosp 87-93; Chapl St Chris Hospice Lon 93-01; V Over St Jo *Ches* 01-03; rtd 03. *Pot Shop Cottage, Main Street, Farnsfield, Newark NG22 8EF* Tel (01623) 884116

GARDNER, Michael Ronald. b 53. Trin Coll Bris 95. **d** 97 **p** 98. CA 86-00; C Stanmore *Win* 97-01; V from 01. *St Luke's Vicarage, Mildmay Street, Winchester SO22 4BX* Tel (01962) 865240

GARDNER, Neil Kenneth. b 65. Univ of Wales (Swansea) BA92 Peterho Cam BA00 Univ of Wales (Cardiff) PhD01. Westcott Ho Cam 98. **d** 01 **p** 02. C Wisbech SS Pet and Paul *Ely* from 01;

C Wisbech St Aug 03-04; P-in-c from 04. *The Rectory, 35 Gorefield Road, Leverington, Wisbech PE13 5AS* Tel and fax (01945) 581486 Mobile 07855-111794
E-mail n.gardner952@btinternet.com

GARDNER, Richard Beverley Twynam. b 11. Chich Th Coll 33. **d** 36 **p** 37. C Gainsborough St Jo *Linc* 36-38; C Linc St Giles 38-39; C Horsell *Guildf* 39-42; Chapl RNVR 42-47; C York Town St Mich *Guildf* 47-48; V E Molesey St Paul 48-54; V Botleys and Lyne 54-71; V Long Cross 56-71; V Ewshott 71-76; rtd 76; Perm to Offic *Guildf* 81-03. *Manormead, Tilford Road, Hindhead GU26 6RA* Tel (01428) 602500

GARDNER (née JAMES), Mrs Sandra Kay. b 66. Westcott Ho Cam 97. **d** 99 **p** 00. C Whittlesey, Pondersbridge and Coates *Ely* 99-02; R Leverington 02-04; V Southea w Murrow and Parson Drove 02-04; R Leverington, Newton and Tydd St Giles from 05. *The Rectory, 35 Gorefield Road, Leverington, Wisbech PE13 5AS* Tel (01945) 585850
E-mail sandra.gardner@ely.anglican.org

GARDNER, Stephen John. b 70. Southn Univ MEng92. St Jo Coll Nottm 00. **d** 02 **p** 03. C Brinsworth w Catcliffe and Treeton *Sheff* 02-03; C Rivers Team 03-05; V Woodlands from 05. *All Saints' Vicarage, 9 Great North Road, Woodlands, Doncaster DN6 7RB* Tel (01302) 339618 Mobile 07740-200942
E-mail stephen@gardnerfamily.co.uk

GARDNER, Susan Carol. See CLARKE, Mrs Susan Carol

GARDNER, Vincent Lyndon. b 62. K Coll Lon MA98 Robert Gordon Univ Aber BFA90. St Steph Ho Ox 02. **d** 04 **p** 05. C Carew *St D* 04-07; V Reading St Jo *Ox* from 08. *The Vicarage, 5A Alexandra Road, Reading RG1 5PE* Tel 07901-737649 (mobile) E-mail vincent_gardner@hotmail.com

GARDOM, Francis Douglas. b 34. Trin Coll Ox BA55 MA59. Wells Th Coll 58. **d** 60 **p** 61. C Greenwich St Alfege w St Pet *S'wark* 60-68; C Lewisham St Steph and St Mark 68-76; Hon C from 76. *79 Maze Hill, London SE10 8XQ* Tel (020) 8858 7052 *or* 8852 1474 E-mail francisgardom@aol.com

GARDOM, James Theodore Douglas. b 61. St Anne's Coll Ox BA83 K Coll Lon PhD92. Ripon Coll Cuddesdon 88. **d** 90 **p** 91. C Witney *Ox* 90-92; Zimbabwe 92-97; Dean of Studies Bp Gaul Coll Harare 93-97; V Chesterton St Andr *Ely* 97-06; Dean and Chapl Pemb Coll Cam from 06. *Pembroke College, Cambridge CB2 1RF* Tel (01223) 338147 Fax 338163
E-mail dea@pem.cam.ac.uk

GARLAND, Christopher John. b 47. Ex Univ BA69 PhD72. Qu Coll Birm 78. **d** 80 **p** 81. C Beckenham St Jas *Roch* 80-82; C Roch 82-84; Papua New Guinea 85-93; Australia 94-95; R Copford w Easthorpe and Messing w Inworth *Chelmsf* from 95. *The Vicarage, Kelvedon Road, Messing, Colchester CO5 9TN* Tel (01621) 815434 E-mail garlandc79@aol.com

GARLAND, Michael. b 50. Sarum & Wells Th Coll 72. **d** 73 **p** 74. C Swansea St Thos and Kilvey *S & B* 73-76; C Boldmere Birm 76-79; V Kingshurst 79-88; P-in-c Curdworth w Castle Vale 88-90; R Curdworth 90-03; P-in-c Wishaw 99-00; V Charlton Kings St Mary *Glouc* from 03. *The Vicarage, 63 Church Street, Charlton Kings, Cheltenham GL53 8AT* Tel (01242) 253402 Mobile 07974-066929
E-mail michaelgarland@compuserve.com

GARLAND, Peter Stephen John. b 52. Univ Coll Lon BA73 Univ of W Ontario MA74 St Jo Coll Dur MA09 Dur Univ PGCE75 ALA79. Ripon Coll Cuddesdon 88. **d** 90 **p** 91. C Crookham *Guildf* 90-94; V Tongham 94-99; Chapl Farnborough Coll of Tech 94-99; V Spalding St Jo w Deeping St Nicholas *Linc* from 99; Chapl Lincs Teaching Primary Care Trust from 07. *St John's Vicarage, 66A Hawthorn Bank, Spalding PE11 1JQ* Tel and fax (01775) 722816 E-mail peter@stjohnsspalding.org

GARLICK, Canon David. b 37. Nottm Univ BA62. St Steph Ho Ox 62. **d** 64 **p** 65. C Kennington St Jo *S'wark* 64-66; Hon C Newington St Paul 66-68; P-in-c Vauxhall St Pet 68-79; V Lewisham St Mary 79-07; RD E Lewisham 92-99; Hon Can S'wark Cathl 93-07; rtd 07. *Limekilns Farmhouse, Braidley, Horsehouse, Leyburn DL8 4TX* Tel (01969) 640280
E-mail limekilnsfarm@yahoo.co.uk

GARLICK, Preb Kathleen Beatrice. b 49. Leeds Univ BA71 Birm Univ PGCE72. Glouc Sch of Min 87. **d** 90 **p** 94. NSM Much Birch w Lt Birch, Much Dewchurch etc *Heref* 90-03; P-in-c 03-07; R Wormelow Hundred 07-09; Chapl Heref Sixth Form Coll 96-03; Chapl Heref Cathl from 99; Preb Heref Cathl from 99. *Birch Lodge, Much Birch, Hereford HR2 8HT* Tel (01981) 540666 Mobile 07812-995442 E-mail kaygarlick@hotmail.com

GARLICK, Canon Peter. b 34. AKC57. **d** 58 **p** 59. C Swindon New Town *Bris* 58-63; St Kitts-Nevis 63-66; V Heyside *Man* 66-73; R Stretford All SS 73-79; RD Wootton *Pet* 79-88; V Duston 79-91; TR Duston Team 91-94; Can Pet Cathl 85-94; rtd 94; Perm to Offic *Pet* from 94. *120 Worcester Close, Northampton NN3 9GD* Tel (01604) 416511
E-mail pandcgarlick@tiscali.co.uk

GARLICK, William Frederick. b 51. **d** 98 **p** 99. OLM Bermondsey St Jas w Ch Ch and St Crispin *S'wark* 98-06. *33 Penfolds Place, Arundel BN18 9SA*

GARNER, Alistair Ross. b 58. Pemb Coll Ox BA81 MA86. St Jo Coll Nottm 90. **d** 92 **p** 93. C Ashton-upon-Mersey St Mary Magd *Ches* 92-96; P-in-c Bredbury St Mark 96-01; V 01-09; Miss Growth Team Ldr *Roch* from 09. *St Barnabas Vicarage, 1 St Barnabas Close, Gillingham ME7 4BU*
E-mail revrossgarner@hotmail.com

GARNER, Canon Carl. b 42. Rhodes Univ BA62 Keble Coll Ox BA65 MA70. St Paul's Coll Grahamstown 66. **d** 67 **p** 68. C Pietersburg S Africa 67-71; R Louis Trichardt 71-75; Chapl St Paul's Coll Grahamstown 75-84; Dioc Missr *St Alb* 84-98; Can Res St Alb 84-98; P-in-c Digswell and Panshanger 98-06; TR from 06; Hon Can St Alb from 99; Jt RD Welwyn Hatfield from 01. *The Rectory, 354 Knightsfield, Welwyn Garden City AL8 7NG* Tel (01707) 326677
E-mail carl@stjohnsdigswell.freeserve.co.uk

GARNER, David Henry. b 40. Trin Coll Bris 70. **d** 73 **p** 74. C Tunstead *Man* 73-75; C Fazeley *Lich* 76-78; V Sparkhill St Jo *Birm* 78-85; V Blackheath 85-01; Deanery P Warley Deanery 01-05; rtd 05; Perm to Offic *Birm* from 05; Chapl Sandwell and W Birm Hosps NHS Trust from 06. *94 Honeybourne Road, Halesowen B63 3HD* Tel 0121-550 2498 Mobile 07779-948333

GARNER, Geoffrey Walter. b 40. Ripon Hall Ox 69. **d** 71 **p** 72. C Stoke *Cov* 71-76; V Tile Hill 76-80; TV Hackney *Lon* 80-89; R Bow w Bromley St Leon 89-06; rtd 06. *98 Wordsworth Road, Plymouth PL2 2JQ*

GARNER, John David. b 47. **d** 03. OLM Kirkdale St Lawr *Liv* from 03. *10 Doon Close, Liverpool L4 1XW* Tel 0151-284 0388

GARNER, John Howard. b 45. Univ of Wales (Swansea) BSc67 Univ of Wales (Ban) PhD75. SWMTC 95. **d** 98 **p** 99. NSM Upton *Ex* from 98; Sen Chapl S Devon Healthcare NHS Foundn Trust from 06. *Highgrove Lodge, Sunbury Hill, Upton, Torquay TQ1 3ED* Tel (01803) 293640 *or* 654186
E-mail johngarner@onetel.net.uk

GARNER, Canon Peter. b 35. Lon Univ BSc56 Leeds Univ MEd91. Wycliffe Hall Ox 56. **d** 58 **p** 59. C Walthamstow St Jo *Chelmsf* 58-61; V Hainault 61-70; R Theydon Garnon 70-73; P-in-c Kirby-le-Soken 73-74; V 74-82; P-in-c Fountains *Ripon* 82-88; P-in-c Kirkby Malzeard w Grewelthorpe and Mickley etc 82-88; Par Development Adv 88-93; P-in-c Birstwith 91-93; R Walkingham Hill 93-01; Hon Can Ripon Cathl 99-01; rtd 01; Perm to Offic *Ripon* from 02. *Laver House, 29 Hell Wath Grove, Ripon HG4 2JT* Tel (01765) 601543 Mobile 07734-088521
E-mail peter@hellwath29.fsnet.co.uk

GARNER, Canon Rodney George. b 48. Lon Univ BA87 Hull Univ MPhil96 Man Univ PhD01 MCIPD75. Qu Coll Birm 75. **d** 78 **p** 79. C Tranmere St Paul w St Luke *Ches* 78-81; V Eccleston St Thos *Liv* 81-90; P-in-c Sculcoates St Paul w Ch Ch and St Silas *York* 90-95; Lay Tr Officer (E Riding Adnry) 90-95; P-in-c Southport H Trin *Liv* 95-96; V from 96; Dioc Th Consultant from 95; Hon Can Liv Cathl from 07. *24 Roe Lane, Southport PR9 9DX* Tel and fax (01704) 538560
E-mail anglican@garnerr.freeserve.co.uk

GARNER, Ross. See GARNER, Alistair Ross

GARNER, Mrs Selina Clare. b 69. Newnham Coll Cam BA90 K Coll Lon PGCE93. EAMTC 00. **d** 06 **p** 07. C Fulbourn *Ely* 06-09; C Gt Wilbraham 06-09; C Lt Wilbraham 06-09; C Cullompton, Willand, Uffculme, Kentisbeare etc *Ex* from 09; Pioneer Youth Min Cullompton Deanery from 09. *The Vicarage, Bridge Street, Uffculme, Cullompton EX15 3AX* Tel (01884) 841001 E-mail selina@thegarners.me.uk

GARNER, Thomas Richard. b 28. Cuddesdon Coll 58. **d** 60 **p** 61. C Broseley w Benthall *Heref* 60-64; V Leintwardine 64-69; P-in-c Downton w Burrington and Aston and Elton 66-69; RD Ludlow 72-75; R Burford II w Greete and Hope Bagot 69-87; R Burford III w Lt Heref 69-87; P-in-c Burford I 72-74; R 74-87; V Tenbury 69-74; TR 74-87; Preb Heref Cathl 82-93; P-in-c Fownhope 87-93; P-in-c Brockhampton w Fawley 87-93; RD Heref Rural 92-93; rtd 93; Perm to Offic *Heref* from 93. *5 Hampton Manor Close, Hereford HR1 1TG* Tel (01432) 274985

GARNER, Canon Peter. b 35. Lon Univ BSc56 Leeds Univ MEd91. [...]

GARNETT, James Arthur. b 42. NOC 77. **d** 80 **p** 81. C Kirkby *Liv* 80-91; P-in-c Liv St Phil w St Dav 91-07; rtd 07. *19 Nicholas Road, Widnes WA8 8ST* Tel 0151-257 9885

GARNETT, Preb Ralph Henry. b 28. [...]

GARNETT, The Ven David Christopher. b 45. Nottm Univ BA67 Fitzw Coll Cam BA69 MA73. Westcott Ho Cam 67. **d** 69 **p** 70. C Cottingham *York* 69-72; Chapl Selw Coll Cam 72-77; P-in-c Patterdale *Carl* 77-80; Dir of Ords 78-80; V Heald Green St Cath *Ches* 80-87; R Christleton 87-92; TR Ellesmere Port 92-96; Adn Chesterfield *Derby* from 96; Hon Can Derby Cathl from 96; P-in-c Beeley and Edensor from 07. *The Vicarage, Edensor, Bakewell DE45 1PH* Tel (01246) 582130
E-mail davidcgarnett@yahoo.co.uk

GARNSEY, George Christopher. b 36. Qu Coll Ox BA63. **d** 60 **p** 60. Lic to Offic *Wakef* 78-79; C Lupset 80; Australia from 80; Prin St Jo Coll Morpeth 80-91; R Gresford w Paterson 93-01; rtd 01; Lect St Jo Coll Morpeth from 01. *17 James Street, Morpeth NSW 2321, Australia* Tel (0061) (2) 4934 2658 Fax 4921 6898
E-mail jan@maths.newcastle.edu.au

GARRARD, Mrs Christine Ann. b 51. Open Univ BA86 LCST75. EAMTC 87. **d** 90 **p** 94. Par Dn Kesgrave *St E* 90-94; C 94-96; V Ipswich All Hallows 96-02; R Higham, Holton St Mary, Raydon and Stratford 02-08; Asst Dioc Dir of Ords 03-08; Sen Chapl Burrswood Chr Hosp from 08. *May Cottage, Burrswood, Groombridge, Tunbridge Wells TN3 9PY* Tel (01892) 860433
E-mail revdchris@aol.com

GARRARD, Canon James Richard. b 65. Dur Univ BA88 Keble Coll Ox DPhil92 Leeds Univ MA01. Westcott Ho Cam. **d** 94 **p** 95. C Elland *Wakef* 94-97; TV Brighouse and Clifton 98-01; P-in-c Balderstone *Blackb* 01-08; Warden of Readers 01-08; Can Res Ely Cathl from 08. *The Precentor's House, 32 High Street, Ely CB7 4JU* Tel (01353) 660335 Fax 665658

GARRARD, Nicholas James Havelock. b 62. Leeds Univ BA83. Westcott Ho Cam 86. **d** 88 **p** 89. C Scotforth *Blackb* 88-91; C Eaton *Nor* 91-95; V Heigham St Thos 95-06; RD Nor S 03-06; R Ranworth w Panxworth, Woodbastwick etc from 06. *The Rectory, The Street, South Walsham, Norwich NR13 6DQ* Tel (01603) 270769 E-mail nickgarr39@aol.com

✠**GARRARD, The Rt Revd Richard.** b 37. K Coll Lon BD60 AKC60. **d** 61 **p** 62 **c** 94. C Woolwich St Mary w H Trin *S'wark* 61-66; C Cambridge Gt St Mary w St Mich *Ely* 66-68; Chapl Keswick Hall Coll of Educn 68-74; Prin Wilson Carlile Coll of Evang 74-79; Can Res and Chan S'wark Cathl 79-87; Dir of Tr 79-87; Can Res St E Cathl 87-94; Dioc Adv for CME 87-91; Adn Sudbury 91-94; Suff Bp Penrith *Carl* 94-01; Hon Can Carl Cathl 94-01; Abp's Rep H See and Dir Angl Cen Rome 01-03; Hon Asst Bp Eur from 01; rtd 03; Perm to Offic *Nor* from 03; Hon Asst Bp Nor from 03. *26 Carol Close, Stoke Holy Cross, Norwich NR14 8NN* Tel (01508) 494165
E-mail garrard.r-a@tiscali.co.uk

GARRARD, Miss Valerie Mary. b 48. K Alfred's Coll Win TCert69 St Paul's Cheltenham BEd84. **d** 03 **p** 04. OLM Wylye and Till Valley *Sarum* from 03. *Cowslip Cottage, Wylye Road, Hanging Langford, Salisbury SP3 4NW* Tel (01722) 790739
E-mail vmgarrard@btinternet.com

GARRATT, Alan. b 54. **d** 04 **p** 05. NSM Hazlemere *Ox* 04-08; TR Thame from 08. *The Rectory, 3 Fish Ponds Lane, Thame OX9 2BA* Tel (01844) 212225
E-mail alan.garratt@hazlemere.org

GARRATT, Bernard John. b 43. Lon Univ BA65 Linacre Coll Ox BA67 MA71. St Steph Ho Ox 65. **d** 68 **p** 69. C Notting Hill St Jo *Lon* 68-71; C Fareham SS Pet and Paul *Portsm* 71-73; Chapl City of Lon Poly 73-79; R Trowbridge H Trin *Sarum* 79-81; TR 81-87; V Wootton Bassett 87-05; RD Calne 88-90; rtd 05. *66 Rowell Way, Chipping Norton OX7 5BD* Tel (01608) 644560

GARRATT, David John. b 66. Leic Poly BA98. Wycliffe Hall Ox 05. **d** 07 **p** 08. C Southover *Chich* from 07. *6 Verralls Walk, Southover, Lewes BN7 1LP* Tel (01273) 480114 Mobile 07963-988618 E-mail david.garratt@macmail.com

GARRATT, Malcolm John. b 52. Nottm Univ BSc73. Trin Coll Bris 97. **d** 99 **p** 00. C Bawtry w Austerfield and Misson *S'well* 99-00; C Hucknall Torkard 00-03; P-in-c Clipstone from 03. *The Vicarage, Church Road, Clipstone, Mansfield NG21 9DG* Tel and fax (01623) 623916 E-mail malcolm.garratt@ntlworld.com

GARRATT, Peter James. b 37. ALCD64. **d** 64 **p** 65. C Bingham *S'well* 64-67; C Mansfield SS Pet and Paul 67-69; V Purlwell *Wakef* 69-73; R Kirk Sandall and Edenthorpe *Sheff* 73-82; R Whippingham w E Cowes *Portsm* 82-87; V Soberton w Newtown 87-01; rtd 02; Perm to Offic *Portsm* from 02. *35 Fair Isle Close, Fareham PO14 3RT* Tel (01329) 661162

GARRATT, Roger Charles. b 50. St Jo Coll Dur BA72. Cranmer Hall Dur 72. **d** 74 **p** 75. C Leamington Priors St Paul *Cov* 74-77; Chapl Emscote Lawn Sch Warw 77-00; Chapl and Dep Hd Arden Lawn Sch 77-00; TV Warwick *Cov* 02-08; rtd 08. *8 Wasdale Close, Leamington Spa CV32 6NF* Tel (01926) 335474 E-mail roger.garratt@btinternet.com

GARRETT, Ms Celia Joy. b 60. RGN81 RM85. Cant Sch of Min 92. **d** 95. C S Ashford St Fran *Cant* 95-98; NSM 98-05. *Address withheld by request*

GARRETT, Christopher Hugh Ahlan. b 35. Sarum & Wells Th Coll 72. **d** 75 **p** 76. C Addiscombe St Mildred *Cant* 75-81; V Thornton Heath St Jude w St Aid *S'wark* 81-00; rtd 00; Perm to Offic *Glouc* from 01. *Edge View, 18 Gloucester Road, Painswick GL6 6RA* Tel (01452) 813688

GARRETT, Clive Robert. b 54. Sheff Univ BA75 PhD80 Ex Univ PGCE88. St Jo Coll Nottm MA98. **d** 98 **p** 99. C Bath Weston St Jo w Kelston *B & W* 98-02; R from 02. *The Rectory, 8 Ashley Avenue, Bath BA1 3DR* Tel (01225) 427206
E-mail crg@cix.co.uk

GARRETT, Miss Elizabeth Clare. b 46. Trin Coll Bris. **d** 94 **p** 95. C Ewyas Harold w Dulas, Kenderchurch etc *Heref* 94-96; C

Tupsley w Hampton Bishop 96-00; TV Uttoxeter Area *Lich* 00-05; P-in-c Gt Canfield w High Roding and Aythorpe Roding *Chelmsf* from 05. *The Rectory, 3 Old Vicarage Close, High Easter, Chelmsford CM1 4RW* Tel (01245) 231429
E-mail claregarrett@aol.com

GARRETT, Geoffrey David. b 57. Oak Hill Th Coll 83. **d** 86 **p** 87. C Trentham *Lich* 86-90; V Rhodes *Man* 90-00; P-in-c Bardsley 00-05; V 05-08; V Watton *Nor* from 08. *St Mary's Vicarage, Norwich Road, Watton, Thetford IP25 6DB* Tel (01953) 881439
E-mail garretts@talktalk.net

GARRETT, Ian Lee. b 60. MCSP81. Sarum & Wells Th Coll 86. **d** 89 **p** 90. C Maidstone St Martin *Cant* 89-95; P-in-c S Ashford St Fran 95-07; TV Bishopsworth and Bedminster Down *Bris* from 07; C Brislington St Chris and St Cuth 07-08; P-in-c Brislington St Cuth from 08. *St Oswald's Vicarage, Cheddar Grove, Bristol BS13 7EN* Tel 0117-964 2649
E-mail ian@ilgarrett.fsnet.co.uk

GARRETT, John Watkins. b 09. St Chad's Coll Dur BA35 LTh36. **d** 36 **p** 37. C Leic St Mary 36-38; C Win H Trin 38-42; C Staveley *Derby* 42-44; C Derby St Barn 44-48; R Aylestone Park *Leic* 48-59; Chapl Carlton Hayes Psychiatric Hosp Narborough 54-90; R Narborough 59-75; rtd 75; Lic to Offic *Leic* 75-81; Perm to Offic 81-95. *4 Walcot Lane, Folkingham, Sleaford NG34 0TP* Tel (01529) 497385

GARRETT, Kevin George. b 48. Oak Hill Th Coll BA86. **d** 86 **p** 87. C Hoddesdon *St Alb* 86-89; C Loughton St Mary and St Mich *Chelmsf* 89-90; TV 90-95; P-in-c Loughton St Mary 95-96; Public Preacher 97; V Dover St Martin *Cant* from 97. *St Martin's Vicarage, 339 Folkestone Road, Dover CT17 9JG* Tel (01304) 205391 Fax 332353
E-mail kevingarrett48@hotmail.com

GARRETT (née KIRK), Natalie Roberta. b 71. Leeds Univ BA93. Wycliffe Hall Ox 03. **d** 05 **p** 06. C Gipsy Hill Ch Ch *S'wark* 05-06; Hon C Burford w Fulbrook, Taynton, Asthall etc *Ox* from 06. *Westfarthing Cottage, Lawrence Lane, Burford OX18 4RP* Tel (01993) 823951

GARRETT, Timothy Michael. b 70. Univ of Wales (Abth) BA91. Wycliffe Hall Ox BA01. **d** 02 **p** 03. C Ox St Andr 02-06; C Burford w Fulbrook, Taynton, Asthall etc from 06. *Westfarthing Cottage, Lawrence Lane, Burford OX18 4RP* Tel (01993) 823951
E-mail revgaz@hotmail.com

GARRISH (née SMITH), Elaine Joan. b 46. NTMTC BA07. **d** 07 **p** 08. NSM Roxbourne St Andr *Lon* from 07. *37 Farthings Close, Pinner HA5 2QR* Tel (020) 8429 0659 Mobile 07780-904402 E-mail elainegarrish@blueyonder.co.uk

GARROD, Mrs Christine Anne. b 49. EAMTC. **d** 00 **p** 01. C N w S Wootton *Nor* 00-04; P-in-c Brinklow *Cov* 04-09; P-in-c Harborough Magna 04-09; P-in-c Monks Kirby w Pailton and Stretton-under-Fosse 04-09; P-in-c Churchover w Willey 04-09; R Gt and Lt Plumstead w Thorpe End and Witton *Nor* from 09. *The Rectory, 9 Lawn Crescent, Thorpe End, Norwich NR13 5BP* Tel (01603) 434778 E-mail cagarrod@hotmail.com

GARROW, Alan John Philip. b 67. Lon Bible Coll BA90 Wycliffe Hall Ox MPhil94 Jes Coll Ox DPhil00. **d** 93 **p** 94. C Waltham H Cross *Chelmsf* 93-97; C Akeman *Ox* 00-04; Tutor SAOMC 00-04; Dir Studies 00-05; Dir Studies Ox Min Course 05 06; C Bath Abbey w St Jas *B & W* from 06. *48 Devonshire Buildings, Bath BA2 4SU* Tel (01225) 464172
E-mail alan.garrow@ctrt.net

GARRUD, Christopher Charles. b 54. Cranmer Hall Dur. **d** 85 **p** 86. C Watford *St Alb* 85-89; C Ireland Wood *Ripon* 89-95; Chapl Cookridge Hosp Leeds 93-95; R Farnley 95-02. *75 Hill Court Drive, Leeds LS13 2AN*

GARSIDE, Geoffrey Malcolm. b 43. Huddersfield Poly CertEd Huddersfield Univ BEd. **d** 05 **p** 06. OLM Almondbury w Farnley Tyas *Wakef* from 05. *16 Mountfield Avenue, Huddersfield HD5 8RD* Tel (01484) 516364 E-mail ggarside@aol.com

GARSIDE, Canon Howard. b 24. Leeds Univ BA49. Coll of Resurr Mirfield 49. **d** 51 **p** 52. C Barnsley St Pet *Wakef* 51-53; C Linthorpe *York* 53-56; V Middlesbrough St Aid 56-64; V Manston *Ripon* 64-78; RD Whitkirk 70-78; Hon Can Ripon Cathl 78-89; V Harrogate St Wilfrid 78-80; P-in-c Harrogate St Luke 78-80; V Harrogate St Wilfrid and St Luke 80-89; RD Harrogate 83-88; rtd 89; Perm to Offic *Ripon* from 89. *73 Kirkby Road, Ripon HG4 2HH* Tel (01765) 690625 Mobile 07714-454829 E-mail hjgarside@aol.com

GARSIDE, Melvin. b 42. NOC 85. **d** 88 **p** 89. C Lindley *Wakef* 88-91; C Shelf *Bradf* 91-93; V Lundwood *Wakef* 93-97; V Hanging Heaton 97-01; V Woodhouse and Bp's Adv in Racial Justice 01-05; rtd 05. *45 Osgodby Hall Road, Scarborough YO11 3PX* Tel (01723) 583523 Mobile 07803-250258
E-mail melgarside@melgarside.demon.co.uk

GARTLAND, Christopher Michael. b 49. Man Univ BA78 Leeds Univ MEd99 Univ Coll Lon MSc04. Coll of Resurr Mirfield 82. **d** 84 **p** 85. C Almondbury w Farnley Tyas *Wakef* 84-87; P-in-c Upperthong 87-89; TV Upper Holme Valley 89-91; Chapl Stanley Royd Hosp Wakef 91-94; Chapl Wakef HA (Mental Health Services) 91-95; Chapl Wakef and Pontefract

Community NHS Trust 95-01; Hd Past/Spiritual Care SW Yorks Mental Health NHS Trust from 02. *2 Weirside, Marsden, Huddersfield HD7 6BU* E-mail michaelgartland4@aol.com

GARTON, Mrs Anne-Marie. b 48. BA MSW CQSW. **d** 02 **p** 03. NSM Caterham *S'wark* from 02. *51 Crescent Road, Caterham CR3 6LH* Tel (01883) 343188
E-mail anne-marie.garton@southwark.anglican.org

GARTON, Capt Jeremy. b 56. Wilson Carlile Coll 78 SEITE 94. **d** 96 **p** 97. C Clapham Team *S'wark* 96-00; P-in-c Caterham Valley 00-03; TV Caterham from 03. *St John's Vicarage, 51 Crescent Road, Caterham CR3 6LH* Tel (01883) 343188 Fax (020) 7863 4120 E-mail jerry@garton.com

✠**GARTON, The Rt Revd John Henry.** b 41. Worc Coll Ox BA67 MA. Cuddesdon Coll 67. **d** 69 **p** 70 **c** 96. CF 69-73; Lect Linc Th Coll 73-78; TR Cov E 78-86; V Cuddesdon and Prin Ripon Coll Cuddesdon 86-96; Hon Can Worc Cathl 87-96; Suff Bp Plymouth *Ex* 96-05; rtd 05; Hon Asst Bp Ox from 05. *c/o P M Garton Esq, 68 Stapleton Road, Headington, Oxford OX3 7LU*

GARTSIDE, Philip Oswin. b 60. Pemb Coll Ox BA82 MA86 Leeds Univ BA92. Coll of Resurr Mirfield 93. **d** 93 **p** 94. C Walton-on-the-Hill *Liv* 93-97; CR from 97. *House of the Resurrection, Stocks Bank Road, Mirfield WF14 0BN* Tel (01924) 483327

GARVIE, Mrs Anna-Lisa Karen. b 48. Luton Univ BA99 Leeds Univ MA05. St Alb Minl Tr Scheme 89. **d** 96 **p** 97. NSM Caddington *St Alb* 96-99; NSM St Paul's Walden 99-01; Chapl Chelsea and Westmr Healthcare NHS Trust 98-01; Co-ord Chapl Hinchingbrooke Health Care NHS Trust 01-09; Chapl Thorpe Hall Hospice from 09. *Thorpe Hall Hospice, Thorpe Road, Longthorpe, Peterborough PE3 6LW* Tel (01733) 330060 Fax 269078

GARWOOD, Simon Frederick. b 62. Reading Univ BA85 Lon Univ PGCE93 Birm Univ BD99. Qu Coll Birm MA00. **d** 00 **p** 01. C Chelmsf All SS 00-03; TV Witham from 03. *18 Witham Lodge, Witham CM8 1HG* Tel (01376) 519017
E-mail sgarwood@keme.co.uk

GASCOIGNE, Philip. b 27. Oak Hill Th Coll. **d** 62 **p** 63. C Blackpool Ch Ch *Blackb* 62-65; V Bootle St Leon *Liv* 65-71; Staff Evang CPAS 71-74; V St Helens St Mark *Liv* 74-77; V Blackpool Ch Ch *Blackb* 77-81; V Blackpool Ch Ch w All SS 81-97; rtd 98; Perm to Offic *Blackb* from 98. *6 King's Close, Staining, Blackpool FY3 0EJ* Tel (01253) 890045

GASH, Christopher Alan Ronald. b 39. EMMTC 83. **d** 86 **p** 87. C Thurmaston *Leic* 86-89; P-in-c Stoke Golding w Dadlington 89-01; rtd 01; Perm to Offic *Cov* 01-03; *Sarum* 03-04; *Ox* 04-06; *St E* 06-09. *37 Stoneygate Drive, Hinckley LE10 1TB*

GASH, Canon Wilfred John. b 31. St Aid Birkenhead 60. **d** 62 **p** 63. C St Mary Cray and St Paul's Cray *Roch* 62-65; C Bexley St Jo 65-67; R Levenshulme St Pet *Man* 67-72; V Clifton 72-94; AD Eccles 81-87; Hon Can Man Cathl 86-97; P-in-c Pendlebury Ch Ch and St Aug 86-87; TR Bolton St Paul w Em 94-96; C Urmston 96-97; Dioc Adv on Evang 89-97; rtd 98; Perm to Offic *Carl* 98-06 and *Blackb* from 08. *11 East Bank, Barrowford, Nelson BB9 6HD* Tel (01282) 611419

GASKELL, Preb John Bernard. b 28. Jes Coll Ox BA52 MA58. Chich Th Coll 59. **d** 60 **p** 61. C Beckenham St Jas *Roch* 60-64; C St Marylebone All SS *Lon* 64-68; C-in-c Grosvenor Chpl 68-79; Warden Liddon Ho Lon 68-79; V Holborn St Alb w Saffron Hill St Pet *Lon* 79-93; AD S Camden 81-86; Preb St Paul's Cathl 85-93; rtd 93; Perm to Offic *Lon* 93-02 and from 07; Hon C St Marylebone All SS 02-07. *12 Up The Quadrangle, Morden College, 19 St Germans Place, London SE3 0PW* Tel (020) 8858 9589

GASKELL, Marion Ingrid. b 52. Wilson Carlile Coll 74 NOC 96. **d** 99 **p** 00. C Thorpe Edge *Bradf* 99-02; TV Shelf w Buttershaw St Aid 02-04; TR from 04. *8 Redwing Drive, Bradford BD6 3YD* Tel (01274) 817978
E-mail marion.gaskell@bradford.anglican.org

GASKELL, Mary. b 50. Nottm Univ BTh81 Bradf and Ilkley Coll CertEd89. Linc Th Coll 77. **dss** 81 **d** 89 **p** 94. Wakef St Jo 81-83; NSM Cleckheaton St Luke and Whitechapel 89-93; NSM Birkenshaw w Hunsworth 93-95; asst Chapl St Jas Univ Hosp NHS Trust Leeds 95-97; Chapl Rishworth Sch Ripponden 97-99; P-in-c Purlwell *Wakef* 00-01; Chapl Dewsbury Health Care NHS Trust 01-02; Chapl Mid Yorks Hosps NHS Trust from 02. *21 Stoney Lane, Chapelthorpe, Wakefield WF4 3JN* Tel (01924) 315110 *or* 816255
E-mail mary.gaskell@midyorks.nhs.uk

GASKELL, Peter John. b 70. Bris Univ MS93 ChB93. Oak Hill Th Coll BA03. **d** 03 **p** 04. NSM Poulton Lancelyn H Trin *Ches* 03-07; NSM Rusholme H Trin *Man* from 09. *47 Linden Park, Manchester M19 2PQ* Tel 07769-682142 (mobile)
E-mail peter@glod.co.uk

GASPER (née COHEN), Mrs Janet Elizabeth. b 47. Birm Univ CertEd70. WMMTC 93. **d** 96 **p** 97. NSM Leominster *Heref* 96-99; C Letton w Staunton, Byford, Mansel Gamage etc 99-01; Hon Chapl RAF 97-01; R Baxterley w Hurley and Wood End and Merevale etc *Birm* from 01; P-in-c Kingsbury from 04. *The Vicarage, Church Lane, Kingsbury, Tamworth B78 2LR* Tel (01827) 874252 E-mail mgasper1@hotmail.com

GASTON, Mrs Lydia Madeleine. b 79. St Andr Univ MA03 Rob Coll Cam BTh09. Ridley Hall Cam 06. **d** 09. C Erdington Ch the K *Birm* from 09. *144 Witton Lodge Road, Perry Common, Birmingham B23 5AP* Tel 07779-006178 (mobile)
E-mail lydgaston@hotmail.co.uk

GASTON, Raymond Gordon. b 62. Leeds Univ BA94. Linc Th Coll MTh94. **d** 96 **p** 97. C Leeds Gipton Epiphany *Ripon* 96-99; V Leeds St Marg and All Hallows 99-07; Tutor Qu Coll Birm from 08. *Flat 12, Queen's Foundation, Somerset Road, Birmingham B15 2QH* Tel 0121-454 1527 Fax 454 8171

GATENBY, Simon John Taylor. b 62. Nottm Univ BA83. St Jo Coll Nottm 84. **d** 87 **p** 88. C Haughton St Mary *Man* 87-90; C Newburn *Newc* 90-93; P-in-c Brunswick *Man* 93-96; R from 96; AD Hulme 99-05. *The Rectory, Hartfield Close, Brunswick, Manchester M13 9YX* Tel 0161-273 2470
E-mail simon@brunswickchurch.freeserve.co.uk

GATES, Alan Raymond. b 46. EAMTC 98. **d** 01 **p** 02. C W w E Mersea and Peldon w Gt and Lt Wigborough *Chelmsf* 01-05; P-in-c Gt Barton *St E* from 05; RD Thingoe from 08. *The Vicarage, Church Road, Great Barton, Bury St Edmunds IP31 2QR* Tel and fax (01284) 787274 Mobile 07974-020379
E-mail alan.gates@virgin.net

GATES, Mrs Frances Margaret. b 44. STETS 01. **d** 04 **p** 05. NSM Portsea St Mary *Portsm* from 04; NSM Portsea St Geo from 04; C NSM Portsea All SS from 04. *114 Kings Road, Southsea PO5 4DW* Tel (023) 9282 0326 Mobile 07951-062226

GATES, John Michael. b 35. Dur Univ BA56. Cranmer Hall Dur 58. **d** 60 **p** 61. C Felixstowe St Jo *St E* 60-67; R Boyton w Capel St Andrew and Hollesley 67-98; P-in-c Shottisham w Sutton 87-92; rtd 98. *9 Foxgrove Lane, Felixstowe IP11 7JS* Tel (01394) 276886

GATES, Richard James. b 46. BA85. Oak Hill Th Coll 82. **d** 85 **p** 86. C Heald Green St Cath *Ches* 85-89; V Norton 89-98; V Bunbury and Tilstone Fearnall from 98. *The Vicarage, Vicarage Lane, Bunbury, Tarporley CW6 9PE* Tel (01829) 260991 Mobile 07715-178750 E-mail rick@prayer.fsnet.co.uk

GATES, Simon Philip. b 60. St Andr Univ MA82 St Jo Coll Dur BA86. Cranmer Hall Dur 84. **d** 87 **p** 88. C Southall Green St Jo *Lon* 87-91; Assoc Min St Andr Ch Hong Kong 91-95; V Clapham Park St Steph *S'wark* 96-06; P-in-c Telford Park St Thos 05-06; V Telford Park from 06; AD Lambeth S from 06. *The Vicarage, 2 Thornton Road, London SW12 0JU* Tel (020) 8671 8276 E-mail sgates2207@aol.com

GATFORD, The Ven Ian. b 40. AKC65. **d** 67 **p** 68. C Clifton w Glapton *S'well* 67-71; TV Clifton 71-75; V Sherwood 75-84; Can Res Derby Cathl 84-99; Adn Derby and Hon Can Derby Cathl 93-05; rtd 05; Perm to Offic *Derby* from 05. *9 Poplar Nook, Allestree, Derby DE22 2DW* Tel (01332) 557567

GATHERCOLE, The Ven John Robert. b 37. Fitzw Ho Cam BA59 MA63. Ridley Hall Cam 59. **d** 62 **p** 63. C Dur St Nic 62-66; C Croxdale 66-69; Bp's Soc and Ind Adv 66-69; Ind Chapl *Worc* 69-87; RD Bromsgrove 77-85; Sen Chapl Worcs Ind Miss 85-01; Hon Can Worc Cathl 80-01; Adn Dudley 87-01; rtd 01; Perm to Offic *Worc* from 01. *Wisteria Cottage, Main Road, Ombersley, Droitwich WR9 0EL* Tel (01905) 620263

GATISS, Lee. b 72. New Coll Ox BA96 MA01. Oak Hill Th Coll BA00. **d** 01 **p** 02. C Barton Seagrave w Warkton *Pet* 01-04; C St Helen Bishopsgate w St Andr Undershaft etc *Lon* from 04. *15 Morgan Street, London E3 5AA* Tel (020) 7283 2231
E-mail l.gatiss@st-helens.org.uk

GATLIFFE, David Spenser. b 45. Keble Coll Ox BA67 Fitzw Coll Cam BA69. Westcott Ho Cam 67. **d** 69 **p** 70. C Oxted *S'wark* 69-72; C Roehampton H Trin 72-75; C S Beddington St Mich 76-77; TV Clapham Old Town 78-87; P-in-c Clapham Ch Ch and St Jo 81-87; TV Clapham Team 87-89; V Wimbledon H Trin and St Pet 89-01; R Lee St Marg from 01; Ldr Post Ord Tr Woolwich Area from 04. *The Rectory, Brandram Road, London SE13 5EA* Tel (020) 8297 1181 *or* 8318 9643

GATRILL, Adrian Colin. b 60. Southn Univ BTh82 FRSA99. Linc Th Coll 83. **d** 85 **p** 86. C W Bromwich St Andr *Lich* 85-88; C W Bromwich St Andr w Ch Ch 88-89; Chapl RAF from 89; Dir of Ords from 06; Perm to Offic *St D* 90-95 and *Ripon* from 00. *Chaplaincy Services, Valiant Block, HQ Air Command, RAF High Wycombe HP14 4UE* Tel (01494) 496800 Fax 496343
E-mail adrian.gatrill@tesco.net

GAUGE, Canon Barrie Victor. b 41. St D Coll Lamp BA62 Selw Coll Cam BA64 MA74. Bp Burgess Hall Lamp. **d** 65 **p** 66. C

Newtown w Llanllwchaiarn w Aberhafesp *St As* 65-68; C Prestatyn 68-73; R Bodfari and Dioc RE Adv 73-76; Perm to Offic *Ches* 76-84; V Birkenhead St Jas w St Bede 84-90; Dir of Resources 90-98; Hon Can Ches Cathl 94-98; C Lache cum Saltney 95-98; Par Development Adv *Derby* 98-06; Can Res Derby Cathl 99-06; Dioc Miss Adv 01-04; rtd 06. *40 Saxon Street, Wrexham LL13 7BD* Tel (01978) 353715 E-mail barrie.gauge@talk21.com

GAUNT, Adam. b 79. St Jo Coll Dur BA00 MA02. St Steph Ho Ox 03. **d** 05 **p** 06. C Middlesbrough Ascension *York* 05-09; R Loftus and Carlin How w Skinningrove from 09. *The Rectory, 11 Micklow Lane, Loftus, Saltburn-by-the-Sea TS13 4JE* Tel (01287) 644047 E-mail adamgauntma@hotmail.com

GAUNT (*née* COTTELL), Mrs Avril Jane. b 50. SRN72 SCM74. S Dios Minl Tr Scheme 92. **d** 95 **p** 97. NSM Yatton Moor *B & W* 95-96 and 97-02; NSM Bourne *Guildf* 96-97; Asst Chapl N Bris NHS Trust 02-05; Perm to Offic *B & W* from 05. *Myrtle Cottage, Ham Lane, Kingston Seymour, Clevedon BS21 6XE* Tel (01934) 832995

GAUNT, Eric Emmerson. b 33. Sarum Th Coll 65. **d** 67 **p** 68. C Hatch End St Anselm *Lon* 67-74; V Neasden cum Kingsbury St Cath 74-80; V Neasden St Cath w St Paul from 80. *St Catherine's Vicarage, Tanfield Avenue, London NW2 7RX* Tel (020) 8452 7322 E-mail dianachapman@madasafish.com

GAUNTLETT, Gilbert Bernard. b 36. Oriel Coll Ox BA59 MA62. Wycliffe Hall Ox 59. **d** 61 **p** 62. C Maidenhead St Andr and St Mary *Ox* 61-64; C Ox St Ebbe w St Pet 64-68; R Nottingham St Nic *S'well* 68-72; Asst Master Leys High Sch Redditch 73-79; Asst Master Stourport High Sch 79-85; rtd 97. *The Tower, Brynygwin Isaf, Dolgellau LL40 1YA* Tel (01341) 423481

GAUSDEN, Canon Peter James. b 32. Qu Coll Birm 57. **d** 60 **p** 61. C Battersea St Pet *S'wark* 60-63; C St Peter-in-Thanet *Cant* 63-68; V Sturry 68-74; R Sturry w Fordwich and Westbere w Hersden 74-97; Dioc Ecum Officer 91-97; Hon Can Cant Cathl 96-97; rtd 97; Perm to Offic *Cant* 97-99 and from 04; Hon C St Nicholas at Wade w Sarre and Chislet w Hoath 99-04. *2 The Paddocks, Collards Close, Monkton, Ramsgate CT12 4JZ* Tel (01843) 825374 E-mail peter@pgausden.fsnet.co.uk

GAVED, Kenneth John Drew. b 31. **d** 95 **p** 96. OLM W Wickham St Jo *S'wark* 95-04 and from 07. *42 Queensway, West Wickham BR4 9ER* Tel (020) 8462 4326

GAVIGAN, Canon Josephine Katherine. b 49. Univ Coll Chich BA00. Sarum Th Coll 93. **d** 96. NSM Boxgrove *Chich* 96-00; C 00-03; Dn-in-c Maybridge from 03; RD Worthing from 05; Can and Preb Chich Cathl from 07. *56 The Boulevard, Worthing BN13 1LA* Tel (01903) 249463 Mobile 07760-277262 E-mail ruraldean@worthingdeanery.org.uk

GAVIN, David Guy. b 63. Birm Univ BA85 St Jo Coll Dur BA90. Cranmer Hall Dur 88. **d** 91 **p** 92. C Parr *Liv* 91-95; TV Toxteth St Philemon w St Gabr and St Cleopas 95-02; P-in-c 02-06; TR from 06. *St Cleopas' Vicarage, Beresford Road, Liverpool L8 4SG* Tel 0151-727 0633 E-mail gavins@uwclub.net

GAVIN (*née* GREGORY), Mrs Judith Rosalind. b 61. Open Univ BA97. St Jo Coll Nottm 99. **d** 01 **p** 02. C Moss Side St Jas w St Clem *Man* 01-04; C Whalley Range St Edm 01-04; C Rhyl w St Ann *St As* 04-05. *Glen Maye, 18B Dyserth Road, Rhyl LL18 4DP* Tel (01745) 332224 E-mail judithanddarrell.gavin@btinternet.com

GAWITH, Canon Alan Ruthven. b 24. Lich Th Coll 54. **d** 56 **p** 57. C Appleby and Murton cum Hilton *Carl* 56-59; C Newton Aycliffe *Dur* 59-61; C-in-c Owton Manor CD 61-67; V Kendal St Geo *Carl* 67-74; Soc Resp Officer *Man* 74-89; Hon Can Man Cathl 82-89; Bp's Adv on AIDS 88-92; rtd 90; Perm to Offic *Man* from 90. *7 Redwaters, Leigh WN7 1JD* Tel (01942) 676641

GAWNE-CAIN, John. b 38. G&C Coll Cam BA61 MA66 CEng MICE. Cuddesdon Coll 74. **d** 76 **p** 77. C Cowley St Jas *Ox* 76-80; P-in-c Ox St Giles 80-85; V Ox St Giles and SS Phil and Jas w St Marg 85-92; P-in-c Uffington w Woolstone and Baulking 92-93; P-in-c Shellingford 92-93; R Uffington, Shellingford, Woolstone and Baulking 93-03; rtd 03; Perm to Offic *Ox* 04-08. *61 St Johns Street, Winchester SO23 0HF* Tel (01962) 851366 E-mail j.gawne-cain@ruralnet.org.uk

GAWTHROP-DORAN, Mrs Sheila Mary. b 37. Birm Univ CertEd. Dalton Ho Bris 68. **dss** 79 **d** 87. Halliwell St Paul *Man* 79-82; New Bury 82-89; Par Dn 87-89; Par Dn Tonge w Alkrington 89-94; rtd 94; Perm to Offic *York* from 95. *35 Swarthdale, Haxby, York YO32 3NZ* Tel (01904) 761247

GAY, Adam Garcia Hugh. b 57. STETS 02. **d** 05 **p** 06. C Bitterne *Win* from 05. *4 Aberdour Close, Southampton SO18 5PF* Tel (023) 8047 3436 E-mail adamgay@totalse.org.uk

GAY, Colin James. b 37. Univ of Wales (Lamp) BA63. Chich Th Coll 63. **d** 65 **p** 66. C W Hackney St Barn *Lon* 65-69; C Hitchin H Sav *St Alb* 69-74; P-in-c Apsley End 74-80; V Chambersbury 80-85; V Barnet Vale St Mark 85-03; rtd 03; Perm to Offic *St Alb* from 03. *Colters, 14 Barleyfield Way, Houghton Regis, Dunstable LU5 5ER* Tel (01582) 862309

GAY, John Charles Nankervis. b 58. ERMC 03. **d** 06 **p** 07. C Wilton *B & W* from 06. *31 Essex Drive, Taunton TA1 4JX* Tel (01823) 336158 E-mail jlmd@surfree.co.uk

GAY, John Dennis. b 43. St Pet Coll Ox BA64 MA68 DPhil69 MSc78. Ripon Hall Ox 64. **d** 67 **p** 68. C Paddington St Jas *Lon* 67-71; P-in-c 71-72; Chapl Culham Coll Abingdon 72-79; Lect Ox Univ 78-80; Dir Culham Inst from 80. *Culham Institute, 15 Norham Gardens, Oxford OX2 6PY* Tel (01865) 284885 Fax 284886 E-mail john.gay@culham.ac.uk

GAY, Canon Perran Russell. b 59. St Cath Coll Cam BA81 MA85 Ex Univ PGCE82 FRGS97. Ripon Coll Cuddesdon BA86. **d** 87 **p** 88. C Bodmin w Lanhydrock and Lanivet *Truro* 87-90; Bp's Dom Chapl and Dioc Officer for Unity 90-94; Can Res and Chan Truro Cathl from 94; Prec from 01; Dir of Tr 94-99; Chapl Epiphany Ho from 06. *52 Daniell Road, Truro TR1 2DA* Tel (01872) 276782 *or* 276491 Fax 277788 E-mail perran@perrangay.com *or* perran@trurocathedral.org.uk

GAY, Stuart. b 66. Oak Hill Th Coll BA94. **d** 00 **p** 01. C Sunningdale *Ox* 00-04; V Margate St Phil *Cant* from 04. *St Philip's Vicarage, 82 Crundale Way, Margate CT9 3YH* Tel (01843) 221589 E-mail stuartgay@btinternet.com

GAYFORD, John. b 37. Lon Univ BDS61 MB, BS65 MD78 FDSRCS64 FRCPsych86. St Jo Sem Wonersh 02. **d** 03. NSM E Grinstead St Mary *Chich* from 03. *Third Acre, 217 Smallfield Road, Horley RH6 9LR* Tel (01342) 842752

GAYLER, Canon Roger Kenneth. b 44. Lich Th Coll 68. **d** 70 **p** 71. C Chingford St Anne *Chelmsf* 70-75; P-in-c Marks Gate 75-81; V from 81; RD Barking and Dagenham from 04; Hon Can Chelmsf Cathl from 99. *The Vicarage, 187 Rose Lane, Romford RM6 5NR* Tel (020) 8599 0415 E-mail rev@r-gayler.fsnet.co.uk

GAYNOR, Christopher Thomas. b 68. **d** 08 **p** 09. C Banbury St Fran *Ox* from 08. *26 Meadowsweet Way, Banbury OX16 1WE* Tel (01295) 271403 E-mail pheechris@yahoo.co.uk

GAYNOR, Mrs Mieke Aaltjen Cornelia. b 43. UEA BA79. St Jo Coll Nottm 02. **d** 03 **p** 04. NSM Hambleden Valley *Ox* 03-09; C Wollaton *S'well* from 09. *32 Deddington Lane, Bramcote, Nottingham NG9 3EW* Tel 0115-928 7765 E-mail mieke.gaynor@btopenworld.com

GAZE, Mrs Sally Ann. b 69. SS Coll Cam BA91 MA95 Birm Univ PGCE92 MPhil98. Qu Coll Birm 94. **d** 96 **p** 97. C Martley and Wichenford, Knightwick etc *Worc* 96-00; C Crickhowell w Cwmdu and Tretower *S & B* 00-02; TR Newton Flotman, Swainsthorpe, Tasburgh, etc *Nor* from 02. *The Rectory, Church Road, Newton Flotman, Norwich NR15 1QB* Tel (01508) 470762 E-mail sally@tasvalley.org

GBEBIKAN, Angela Maria Abïke. b 56. Westcott Ho Cam 02. **d** 04 **p** 05. C Norbury St Steph and Thornton Heath *S'wark* 04-07; P-in-c S Beddington and Roundshaw 07-08; V from 08. *St Michael's Vicarage, Milton Road, Wallington SM6 9RP* Tel (020) 8647 1201 Mobile 07801-065472 E-mail gbebikan@cantab.net

GEACH, Canon Michael Bernard. b 26. Qu Coll Cam BA51 MA56. Westcott Ho Cam 51. **d** 53 **p** 54. C Kenwyn *Truro* 53-56; C Bodmin 56-59; C Helland 56-59; R St Dominic 59-65; Chapl Cotehele Ho Chapl Cornwall 60-65; V Linkinhorne 65-84; R Veryan w Ruan Lanihorne 84-96; Hon Can Truro Cathl 92-96; rtd 96; Perm to Offic *Truro* from 96. *17 Paul's Row, Truro TR1 1HH* Tel (01872) 262927

GEACH, Mrs Sarah Jane. b 50. Trin Coll Carmarthen CertEd73. WEMTC 96. **d** 99 **p** 00. C Pill w Easton in Gordano and Portbury *B & W* 99-02; TV Ross *Heref* 02-07; P-in-c Begelly w Ludchurch and Crunwere *St D* from 07. *The Rectory, New Road, Kilgetty SA68 0YG* Tel (01834) 812078 E-mail sgeach@btinternet.com

GEAKE, Peter Henry. b 17. Trin Hall Cam BA39 MA46. Cuddesdon Coll 45. **d** 47 **p** 48. C Portsea St Mary *Portsm* 47-50; C Southbroom *Sarum* 50-52; R Clovelly *Ex* 52-55; Chapl Canford Sch Wimborne 55-62; V Tattenham Corner and Burgh Heath *Guildf* 62-72; R Fulbeck *Linc* 72-82; P-in-c Carlton Scroop w Normanton 72-82; rtd 82; Perm to Offic *Ox* 94-95 and *Sarum* from 98. *Amesbury Abbey Nursing Home, Amesbury, Salisbury SP4 7EX* Tel (01980) 625748

GEAR, John Arthur. b 37. St Aid Birkenhead 62. **d** 64 **p** 66. C Attleborough *Cov* 64-66; C Attercliffe *Sheff* 66-68; C Sheerness H Trin w St Paul *Cant* 68-73; Asst Youth Adv *S'wark* 73-78; Youth Chapl *Lich* 78-88; V Stafford St Jo and Tixall w Ingestre 88-92; Gen Sec NCEC 92-97; rtd 97; Perm to Offic *Lich* 01-02 and from 04; P-in-c Shrewsbury H Cross 02-03. *Greenside, Lime Kiln Bank, Telford TF2 9NU* Tel (01952) 613487 *or* (01743) 232723

✠**GEAR, The Rt Revd Michael Frederick.** b 34. Dur Univ BA59. Cranmer Hall Dur 59. **d** 61 **p** 62 **c** 93. C Bexleyheath Ch Ch *Roch* 61-64; C Ox St Aldate w H Trin 64-67; V Clubmoor *Liv* 67-71; Rhodesia 71-76; Tutor Wycliffe Hall Ox 76-80; V Macclesfield St Mich *Ches* 80-85; RD Macclesfield 84-88; TR Macclesfield Team 85-88; Adn Ches 88-93; Hon Can Ches Cathl 86-88; Suff Bp Doncaster *Sheff* 93-99; rtd 99; Hon Asst Bp Roch from 99; Hon Asst Bp Cant from 00. *10 Acott Fields, Yalding, Maidstone ME18 6DQ* Tel (01622) 817388 E-mail mike.gear@rochester.anglican.org

GEARY, John Martin. b 52. LRSC77. **d** 08 **p** 09. OLM Heywood *Man* from 08. *30 Conway Close, Heywood OL10 4SG* Tel (01706) 622715 Mobile 07753-462460
E-mail john@johngeary.co.uk

GEARY, Mrs Paula June. b 48. NUI BSc69 HDipEd70. CITC 06. **d** 06 **p** 07. NSM Moviddy Union *C, C & R* from 06. *Lehenaghbeg Farm, Lehenaghbeg, Togher, Cork, Republic of Ireland* Tel (00353) (21) 496 1391
E-mail pjgeary650@hotmail.com

GEBAUER, George Gerhart. b 25. Sarum & Wells Th Coll 71. **d** 73 **p** 74. C Portsdown *Portsm* 73-78; V Purbrook 78-91; rtd 91; Perm to Offic *Portsm* from 91. *52 St John's Road, Locks Heath, Southampton SO31 6NF* Tel (01489) 575172

GEDDES, Canon Gordon David. b 38. St Chad's Coll Dur BA59. **d** 61 **p** 62. C Bishopwearmouth St Mary V w St Pet CD *Dur* 61-65; P-in-c Jarrow 65-68; Teacher Crewe Boys' Gr Sch 68-71; Hd of RS 71-78; Hd of RE Ruskin Sch Crewe 78-90; P-in-c Church Minshull w Leighton and Minshull Vernon *Ches* 90-91; V Leighton-cum-Minshull Vernon 91-05; RD Nantwich 01-06; Hon Can Ches Cathl 04-06; Chapl Mid Cheshire Hosps Trust from 91. *6 Richmond Close, Sandbach CW11 3TX* Tel (01270) 753053 E-mail revggeddes@aol.com
or gordon.geddes@mcht.nhs.uk

GEDDES, Peter Henry. b 51. Trin Coll Bris 84. **d** 86 **p** 87. C Blackpool St Mark *Blackb* 86-88; C Barnston *Ches* 88-92; V Haslington w Crewe Green 92-04; V Partington and Carrington from 04. *St Mary's Vicarage, Manchester Road, Partington, Manchester M31 4FB* Tel 0161-775 3542

GEDDES, Roderick Charles. b 47. Man Univ DipEd78 MPhil85. NOC 88. **d** 91 **p** 93. C Alverthorpe *Wakef* 91-92; C S Ossett 92-94; R Andreas, V Jurby and V Andreas St Jude *S & M* 94-03; P-in-c Gargrave *Bradf* 03-09; P-in-c Gargrave w Coniston Cold from 09. *The Vicarage, Mill Hill Lane, Gargrave, Skipton BD23 3NQ* Tel (01756) 748548
E-mail rod.geddes@bradford.anglican.org

GEDGE, Lloyd Victor. b 23. Cuddesdon Coll 54. **d** 57 **p** 58. C Headington *Ox* 57-60; P-in-c Virden Canada 60-63; V Riverton New Zealand 63-66; C All SS Cathl Edmonton Canada 66-68; P-in-c Edmonton St Steph 68-72; I Edgerton 72-76; I Hanna 76-80; P-in-c N Creake *Nor* 82-83; P-in-c S Creake 82-83; R N and S Creake w Waterden 84-86; rtd 86. *PO Box 794, Viking AB T0B 4N0, Canada* Tel (001) (780) 336 0104

GEDGE, Richard John Anthony. b 70. Bath Univ BEng92 CEng96 MIMechE96. St Jo Coll Nottm MTh09. **d** 09. C Much Woolton *Liv* from 09. *48 Babbacombe Road, Liverpool L16 9JW* E-mail rjagedge@googlemail.com

GEE, Anne Alison. b 43. OBE99. Man Univ MB, ChB66. STETS BA01. **d** 01 **p** 02. NSM Canford Magna *Sarum* 01-06; NSM Horton, Chalbury, Hinton Martel and Holt St Jas from 06. *The Rectory, Hinton Martell, Wimborne BH21 7HD* Tel (01258) 840256 E-mail a.gee@doctors.org.uk

GEE, Mrs Dorothy Mary. b 33. St Jo Coll Nottm 88. **d** 89 **p** 94. Chapl Asst Univ Hosp Nottm 89-95; NSM Plumtree *S'well* 95-97; P-in-c 97-01; rtd 01; Perm to Offic *S'well* from 01. *16 The Leys, Normanton-on-the-Wolds, Keyworth, Nottingham NG12 5NU* Tel 0115-937 4927
E-mail mary.gee@microhelpuk.net

GEE, Canon Edward. b 28. St Deiniol's Hawarden 59. **d** 61 **p** 62. C Hanging Heaton *Wakef* 61-65; V Brownhill 65-75; V Alverthorpe 75-84; R Castleford All SS 84-92; Hon Can Wakef Cathl 87-92; rtd 92; Perm to Offic *Bradf* and *Wakef* from 92. *1 Holme Ghyll, Colne Road, Glusburn, Keighley BD20 8RG* Tel (01535) 630060

GEEN, James William. b 50. Chich Th Coll 76. **d** 79 **p** 80. C Brandon *Dur* 79-84; C Sunderland Red Ho 84-86; P-in-c N Hylton St Marg Castletown 86-89; V 89-91; Dep Chapl HM Pris Dur 91-92; Chapl HM YOI Lanc Farms 92-95; Chapl HM Pris Long Lartin 95-01; Chapl HM Pris Blakenhurst 01-06; CMP from 96. *Address temp unknown* E-mail jacobus@fsmail.net

GEERING, Preb Anthony Ernest. b 43. Columbia Pacific Univ BSc. Kelham Th Coll 62. **d** 68 **p** 69. C Cov St Mary 68-71; New Zealand 71-75; P-in-c Brinklow *Cov* 75-77; R 77-81; V Monks Kirby w Pailton and Stretton-under-Fosse 77-81; R Harborough Magna 77-81; V Pilton w Ashford *Ex* 81-86; P-in-c Shirwell w Loxhore 83-86; R Crediton and Shobrooke 86-01; P-in-c Sandford w Upton Hellions 00-01; R Crediton, Shobrooke and Sandford etc 01; RD Cadbury 93-97; R Chagford, Drewsteignton, Hittisleigh etc from 01; RD Okehampton 02-05; Preb Ex Cathl from 02. *The Rectory, Chagford, Newton Abbot TQ13 8BW* Tel (01647) 433014

GEESON, Brian Alfred. b 30. Qu Coll Ox BA51 Trin & All SS Coll Leeds PGCE76. Qu Coll Birm 54. **d** 55 **p** 56. C Newbold w Dunston *Derby* 55-59; PC Calow 59-64; R Broughton *Bradf* 64-71; TV Seacroft *Ripon* 71-77; Hon C Hanging Heaton *Wakef* 77-87; Hon C Purlwell 87-94; rtd 94; Perm to Offic *Wakef* 94. *32 Willerton Close, Dewsbury WF12 7SH* Tel (01924) 465621

GEILINGER, John Edward. b 27. Lon Univ BSc53 BD58 BA76 MPhil79. Tyndale Hall Bris. **d** 59 **p** 60. C Plymouth St Jude *Ex*

59-61; Lect Trin Th Coll Umuahia Nigeria 63-72; Lect Th Coll of N Nigeria 72-77; Perm to Offic *Portsm* from 79; rtd 92. *Emmaus House, Colwell Road, Freshwater PO40 9LY* Tel (01983) 753030

GEISOW, Hilary Patricia. b 46. Salford Univ BSc67 Warwick Univ PhD71 Nottm Univ PGCE94. St Jo Coll Nottm 01. **d** 03 **p** 04. C Linc St Faith and St Martin w St Pet 03-06; P-in-c Colsterworth Gp 06-08; P-in-c Peakirk w Glinton and Northborough *Pet* from 08; P-in-c Etton w Helpston and Maxey from 08. *The Rectory, 11 Lincoln Road, Glinton, Peterborough PE6 7JR* Tel (01733) 252265
E-mail hilary@geisow.freeserve.co.uk

GELDARD, Preb Mark Dundas. b 50. Liv Univ BA71 Bris Univ MA75. Trin Coll Bris 73. **d** 75 **p** 76. C Aughton Ch Ch *Liv* 75-78; Tutor Trin Coll Bris 78-84; V Fairfield *Liv* 84-88; Dioc Dir of Ords *Lich* 88-07; C Lich St Mich w St Mary and Wall 95-07; P-in-c Wigginton from 07; Preb Lich Cathl from 00. *The Vicarage, Main Road, Wigginton, Tamworth B79 9DN* Tel (01827) 690380 E-mail sue.jackson@lichfield.anglican.org

GELL, Anne Elizabeth. b 63. St Hugh's Coll Ox BA85 MA01 R Free Hosp Sch of Medicine MB, BS90 Surrey Univ BA01. STETS 98. **d** 01 **p** 02. C Headley All SS *Guildf* 01-05; V Wrecclesham from 05. *The Vicarage, 2 King's Lane, Wrecclesham, Farnham GU10 4QB* Tel (01252) 716431
E-mail annegell@lineone.net

GELL, Miss Margaret Florence. b 30. **d** 00 **p** 01. NSM Madeley *Lich* 00-04; rtd 04; Perm to Offic *Lich* from 04. *19 Pear Tree Drive, Madeley, Crewe CW3 9EN* Tel (01782) 750669

GELLI, Frank Julian. b 43. Birkbeck Coll Lon BA78 K Coll Lon MTh82. Ripon Coll Cuddesdon 84. **d** 86 **p** 87. C Chiswick St Nic w St Mary *Lon* 86-89; Chapl Ankara *Eur* 89-91; C Kensington St Mary Abbots w St Geo *Lon* 91-99; rtd 03. *58 Boston Gardens, Brentford TW8 9LP* Tel (020) 8847 4533
E-mail numapomp@talk21.com

GELLING, Canon John Drury. b 22. Pemb Coll Ox BA44 MA48. Wycliffe Hall Ox 44. **d** 54 **p** 55. Hd Master Eccles High Sch 50-64; C Irlam *Man* 54-59; V Rushen *S & M* 64-77; RD Castletown 71-77; R Ballaugh 77-92; P-in-c Michael 77-78; V 78-92; Can St German's Cathl 80-92; rtd 92; Perm to Offic *S & M* from 93. *Uplands, Ballavitchell Road, Crosby, Isle of Man IM4 2DN* Tel (01624) 851223

GELSTON, Anthony. b 35. Keble Coll Ox BA57 MA60 DD85. Ridley Hall Cam 59. **d** 60 **p** 61. C Chipping Norton *Ox* 60-62; Lect Th Dur Univ 62-76; Sen Lect 76-88; Dean Div Faculty 77-79; Reader 89-95; Lic to Offic 62-95; rtd 95. *Lesbury, Hetton Road, Houghton le Spring DH5 8JW* Tel 0191-584 2256
E-mail anthony.gelston@durham.ac.uk

GEMMELL, Ian William Young. b 52. ALAM. St Jo Coll Nottm. **d** 77 **p** 78. C Old Hill H Trin *Worc* 77-81; C Selly Park St Steph and St Wulstan *Birm* 81-83; V Leic St Chris 83-93; RD Christianity S 92-93; P-in-c Gt Bowden w Welham, Glooston and Cranoe 93-02; P-in-c Church Langton w Tur Langton, Thorpe Langton etc 93-99; P-in-c Church Langton cum Tur Langton etc 99-02; R Gt Bowden w Welham, Glooston and Cranoe etc 02-06; RD Gartree I 97-06; Hon Can Leic Cathl 03-06; P-in-c Welford w Sibbertoft and Marston Trussell *Pet* from 06. *The Vicarage, 35 The Leys, Welford, Northampton NN6 6HS* Tel (01858) 571101
E-mail bud.gemmell@btopenworld.com

GENDALL, Stephen Mark. b 63. **d** 89 **p** 90. Lundi St Apollos Zimbabwe 89-01; Youth Chapl 93-01; Can Cen Zimbabwe 00-01; V Lingfield and Crowhurst *S'wark* from 02. *The Vicarage, Vicarage Road, Lingfield RH7 6HA* Tel (01342) 832021 Mobile 07752-063150 E-mail steve@thegendalls.freeserve.co.uk

GENDERS, Nigel Mark. b 65. Oak Hill Th Coll BA92. **d** 92 **p** 93. C New Malden and Coombe *S'wark* 92-96; C Enfield Ch Ch Trent Park *Lon* 96-98; P-in-c Eastry and Northbourne w Tilmanstone etc *Cant* 98-03; P-in-c Woodnesborough w Worth and Staple 03-08; AD Sandwich 06-08; Min to Sandwich Secondary Schs 03-08; Dir of Educn *Cant* from 08. *31 Dover Road, Sandwich CT13 0BS* Tel (01304) 611084
E-mail nmg@f2s.com

GENEREUX, Patrick Edward. b 47. William Carey Coll BSc73 Univ of the South (USA) MDiv78. **d** 78 **p** 79. USA 78-81 and from 82; C Spalding *Linc* 81-82. *621 North 5th Street, Burlington IA 52601-0608, USA* Tel (001) (319) 754 6420
E-mail pgenereux@aol.com

GENOE, Simon. CITC. **d** 09. C Lisburn Ch Ch Cathl from 09. *82 Thornleigh Drive, Lisburn BT28 2DS*
E-mail simon.genoe@gmail.com

GENT, David Robert. b 71. Surrey Univ BSc94. Qu Coll Birm BD97. **d** 98 **p** 99. C Wotton-under-Edge w Ozleworth and N Nibley *Glouc* 98-02; Chapl Yeovil Coll and C Yeovil H Trin w Barwick *B & W* 02-08; P-in-c Martock w Ash from 08. *The Vicarage, 10 Water Street, Martock TA12 6JN* Tel (01935) 826113 E-mail revdgent@aol.com

GENT, Mrs Miriam. b 29. Leeds Univ BA51. SW Minl Tr Course 84. **d** 87 **p** 94. NSM Pinhoe and Broadclyst *Ex* 87-02; Dioc Adv in Adult Tr 96-99; Perm to Offic from 02. *Moss Hayne Cottage, West Clyst, Exeter EX1 3TR* Tel (01392) 467288 Fax 462980

GENT, Miss Susan Elizabeth. K Coll Lon LLB78 Brunel Univ BA95. Wycliffe Hall Ox MPhil96. **d** 97 **p** 98. C Notting Hill St Jo and St Pet *Lon* 97-00; Chapl to City law firms from 00; Hon Assoc P St Paul's Cathl from 00; Dioc Visitor from 01; P-in-c St Martin Ludgate from 05. *3B Amen Court, London EC4M 7BU* Tel (020) 7329 2702 Fax 7248 3104
E-mail susan.gent@ukgateway.net

GENTILELLA, Barbara Catherine. b 55. SEITE 05. **d** 08. NSM Shirley St Jo *S'wark* from 08. *42 Devonshire Way, Croydon CR0 8BR* Tel (020) 8777 4462 E-mail bb2ke@sky.com

GENTRY, Michael John. b 66. St Steph Ho Ox BTh95. **d** 98 **p** 99. C Bromley SS Pet and Paul *Roch* 98-02; V Langton Green from 02. *The Vicarage, The Green, Langton Green, Tunbridge Wells TN3 0JB* Tel and fax (01892) 862072 *or* tel 861889
E-mail michael.gentry@diocese-rochester.org

GEOGHEGAN, Prof Luke. b 62. SS Hild & Bede Coll Dur BA83 Bedf Coll Lon MSc87 CQSW87 FRSA93. SAOMC 87. **d** 00 **p** 01. NSM Spitalfields Ch Ch w All SS *Lon* 00-03; NSM Gt Berkhamsted *St Alb* 03-05; NSM Gt Berkhamsted, Gt and Lt Gaddesden etc from 05; Warden Toynbee Hall from 98. *16 Gravel Path, Berkhamsted HP4 2EF*

GEORGE, Alexander Robert. b 46. K Coll Lon BD69 AKC69. St Aug Coll Cant. **d** 70 **p** 71. C Newmarket St Mary w Exning St Agnes *St E* 70-74; C Swindon Ch Ch *Bris* 74-76; C Henbury 76-79; Lic to Offic 79-80; TV Oldland 80-88; C Ipswich St Aug *St E* 89; C Hadleigh w Layham and Shelley 89-90; P-in-c Assington 90-91; R Assington w Newton Green and Lt Cornard 91-00; P-in-c Hundon 00-03; Hon C 03-04; C Stour Valley from 04; Dioc Moderator for Reader Tr 95-03; Asst Liturg Officer (Formation and Educn) 00-03; rtd 03; Nat Moderator for Reader Tr 04-08. *The Vicarage, 5 Armstrong Close, Hundon, Sudbury CO10 8HD* Tel (01440) 786617
E-mail alecrg@genie.co.uk

GEORGE, Charles Roy. b 32. St Edm Hall Ox BA55 MA59. Cuddesdon Coll 55. **d** 57 **p** 58. C Chorley St Laur *Blackb* 57-60; C Norton *Derby* 60-64; V Eltham St Barn *S'wark* 64-74; V Milton *Portsm* 74-90; R Rowner 90-96; rtd 96; Perm to Offic *Portsm* from 96. *46 The Thicket, Fareham PO16 8PZ* Tel (01329) 288185

GEORGE, David. b 64. Wycliffe Hall Ox 01. **d** 03 **p** 04. C Inkberrow w Cookhill and Kington w Dormston *Worc* 03-07; P-in-c Dudley St Jo from 07. *St John's Vicarage, 8A New Rowley Road, Dudley DY2 8AS* Tel (01384) 236626
E-mail revdave.george@virgin.net

GEORGE, David Michael. b 45. Selw Coll Cam BA66 MA70. Chich Th Coll 70. **d** 73 **p** 74. C Chiswick St Nic w St Mary *Lon* 73-76; C Kensington St Mary Abbots w St Geo 76-78; C Northolt Park St Barn 78-81; Argentina from 81; R Martinez St Mich 82-00; R St Jo Cathl Buenos Aires 00-08; Adn River Plate 84-02; rtd 08. *Pje Dr Rodolfo Rivarola 112-4-10, C1015AAB Buenos Aires, Argentina* Tel (0054) (11) 4372 4596
E-mail davidmg@ciudad.com.ar

GEORGE, Mrs Elizabeth Ann. b 33. Westf Coll Lon BA56. S Dios Minl Tr Scheme 84. **d** 87 **p** 94. NSM Basingstoke *Win* 87-05; Perm to Offic from 05. *71 Camrose Way, Basingstoke RG21 3AW* Tel (01256) 464763
E-mail elizabethgeorge@compuserve.com

GEORGE, The Ven Frederick. b 39. St Luke's Coll Ex TCert61. Chich Th Coll 82. **d** 72 **p** 83. Australia 72-75; Brunei 75-80; The Gambia 80-82 and 83-88; Prin Angl Tr Cen Farafeni 85-88; P-in-c Ringsfield w Redisham, Barsham, Shipmeadow etc *St E* 89-92; R Wainford 92-97; V Jamestown St Helena 97-03; Adn St Helena 99-03; rtd 03; Perm to Offic *Chich* from 03; Perm to Offic St Helena from 04. *Hut's Gate Vicarage, Box 80, St Helena, STHL 1ZZ, South Atlantic*

GEORGE, Henderson Rudolph. b 44. Open Univ BA80 Chelsea Coll Lon MEd85. NTMTC BA07. **d** 07 **p** 08. NSM Clapton St Jas *Lon* from 07. *12 Cowland Avenue, Enfield EN3 7DX* Tel (020) 8804 9224

GEORGE, Nicholas Paul. b 58. St Steph Ho Ox 86. **d** 89 **p** 90. C Leeds St Aid *Ripon* 89-92; C Leeds Richmond Hill 92-96; Chapl Agnes Stewart C of E High Sch Leeds 93-96; V Leeds Halton St Wilfrid *Ripon* 96-02; V Camberwell St Giles w St Matt *S'wark* from 02. *St Giles's Vicarage, 200 Benhill Road, London SE5 7LL* Tel and fax (020) 7703 4504 Mobile 07771-603217
E-mail nick.george@care4free.net

GEORGE (*formerly* COMPTON), **Penelope.** b 55. Bulmershe Coll of HE BEd87. NTMTC 98. **d** 01 **p** 02. C Northolt Park St Barn *Lon* 01-04; TV Hucknall Torkard *S'well* 04-08. *24 Northern Woods, Flackwell Heath, High Wycombe HP10 9JL*

GEORGE, The Rt Revd Randolph Oswald. b 24. Codrington Coll Barbados 46. **d** 50 **p** 51 **c** 76. Barbados 50-53, C Leigh *Lich* 53-55; C Ardwick St Benedict *Man* 55-57; C Bedford Park *Lon* 57-58; C Lavender Hill Ascension *S'wark* 58-60; Trinidad and Tobago 60-71; Hon Can Trinidad 68-71; Guyana from 71; Dean Georgetown 71-76; Suff Bp Stabroek 76-80; Bp Guyana from 80.

Austin House, Kingston, Georgetown 1, Guyana Tel (00592) (2) 63862 Fax 64183

GEORGE, Robert Henry. b 45. FCCA73. WEMTC 99. **d** 01 **p** 02. OLM S Cerney w Cerney Wick and Down Ampney *Glouc* 01-05; NSM Brimpsfield w Birdlip, Syde, Daglingworth etc from 05. *Jedems, Berkeley Close, South Cerney, Cirencester GL7 5UN* Tel (01285) 860973 E-mail member@jedems.wanadoo.co.uk

GEORGE, Roy. *See* GEORGE, Charles Roy

GEORGE-JONES, Canon Gwilym Ifor. b 26. K Coll (NS) 56. **d** 57 **p** 57. R Seaforth St Jas Canada 57-61; V Kirton in Lindsey *Linc* 61-71; R Grayingham 61-71; R Manton 61-71; V Alford w Rigsby 71-92; R Maltby 71-92; R Well 71-92; V Bilsby w Farlesthorpe 71-92; R Hannah cum Hagnaby w Markby 71-92; R Saleby w Beesby 71-92; RD Calcewaithe and Candleshoe 77-85 and 87-89; Can and Preb Linc Cathl 81-01; rtd 92. *42 Kelstern Road, Lincoln LN6 3NJ* Tel (01522) 691896

GEORGE-ROGERS, Gillian Jean Richeldis. b 47. St Mich Coll Llan. **d** 99 **p** 02. C Llanishen 99-05; P-in-c Rhondda Fach Uchaf 05; rtd 06. *Faith House, 82 King's Fee, Monmouth NP25 5BQ* Tel (01600) 716696 E-mail gillian@richeldis.fslife.co.uk

GERARD, Patrick Hoare. b 64. Man Univ BSc86 MSc88. Qu Coll Birm 04. **d** 06 **p** 07. C Solihull *Birm* from 06. *17 Church Hill Close, Solihull B91 3JB* Tel 0121-704 0897 Mobile 07905-967930 E-mail patrick@gerard.net *or* office@solihullparish.org.uk

GERARDO, Brother. *See* ROMO-GARCIA, Brother Gerardo

GERD, Sister. *See* SWENSSON, Sister Gerd Inger

GERMANY AND NORTHERN EUROPE, Archdeacon of. *See* LLOYD, Jonathan Wilford

GERRANS, Daniel. b 58. Em Coll Cam LLB80 MA83 Barrister-at-Law (Middle Temple) 81. SEITE 02. **d** 05 **p** 06. NSM De Beauvoir Town St Pet *Lon* from 05; Chapl to Bp Stepney from 07. *19 College Cross, London N1 1PT*
E-mail daniel.gerrans@xxiv.co.uk

GERRARD, The Ven David Keith Robin. b 39. St Edm Hall Ox BA61. Linc Th Coll 61. **d** 63 **p** 64. C Stoke Newington St Olave *Lon* 63-66; C Primrose Hill St Mary w Avenue Road St Paul 66-69; V Newington St Paul *S'wark* 69-79; V Surbiton St Andr and St Mark 79-89; RD Kingston 84-88; Hon Can S'wark Cathl 85-89; Adn Wandsworth 89-04; rtd 05. *15 Woodbourne Drive, Claygate, Esher KT10 0DR* Tel (01372) 467295
E-mail david.gerrard@gawab.com

GERRARD, Paul Christian Francis. b 58. St Steph Ho Ox 92. **d** 94 **p** 01. C Longton *Lich* 94-95; NSM New Radnor and Llanfihangel Nantmelan etc *S & B* 01-04; NSM Knighton, Norton, Whitton, Pilleth and Cascob 04-07; Perm to Offic from 07. *The Old Vicarage, Norton, Presteigne LD8 2EN* Tel (01544) 260038

GERRISH, David Victor. b 38. St Jo Coll Dur BSc61 MA65. Oak Hill Th Coll 61. **d** 64 **p** 65. C Fareham St Jo *Portsm* 64-66; Asst Chapl K Sch Roch 67-71; Asst Chapl Bryanston Sch 71-73; Chapl 73-77; Chapl Mon Sch 77-86; Chapl Warminster Sch 86-89; R Portland All SS w St Pet *Sarum* 89-96; Chapl Aquitaine *Eur* 96-00; rtd 00; Perm to Offic *Sarum* from 01. *Flat 8, 6 Ricketts Close, Weymouth DT4 7UP* Tel (01305) 789319

GERRY, Brian John Rowland. b 38. Oak Hill Th Coll 69. **d** 71 **p** 72. C Hawkwell *Chelmsf* 71-74; C Battersea Park St Sav *S'wark* 74-77; C Battersea St Geo w St Andr 77-84; V Axmouth w Musbury *Ex* 77-86; R Upton 86-04; rtd 04. *49 Peasland Road, Torquay TQ2 8PA* Tel (01803) 322788

GERRY, Ulric James. b 67. Bris Univ BEng89. Wycliffe Hall Ox BA96. **d** 97 **p** 98. C Hemel Hempstead *St Alb* 97-00; Perm to Offic 01-02; Crosslinks Tanzania from 02. *c/o FCO (Abuja), King Charles Street, London SW1A 2AH*
E-mail ulric_gerry@yahoo.com

GHEST, Richard William Iliffe. b 31. Em Coll Cam BA53 MA57 Lon Univ BA66. Wells Th Coll 53. **d** 55 **p** 56. C Weston-super-Mare St Jo *B & W* 55-57; India 58-63; C Holborn St Geo w H Trin and St Bart *Lon* 63-67; Ceylon 67-68; C Combe Down *B & W* 68-73; C Combe Down w Monkton Combe 73-74; R Tickenham 74-96; rtd 96. *120 Cottrell Road, Roath, Cardiff CF24 3EX* Tel (029) 2048 1597

GHINN, Edward. b 45. Oak Hill Th Coll 71. **d** 74 **p** 75. C Purley Ch Ch *S'wark* 74-77; Chile 77-82; V Sevenoaks Weald *Roch* 82-86; Chapl HM Pris Hull 86-89; Chapl HM Pris Pentonville 89-91; Chapl HM Pris Maidstone 91-96; Brazil 96-98; Min Parkwood CD *Cant* 98-01; Chapl HM Pris Grendon and Spring Hill 01-03; Chapl HM Pris Stocken from 03. *HM Prison Stocken, Stocken Hall Road, Stretton, Oakham LE15 7RD* Tel (01780) 485281 Fax 410681 E-mail g.ghinn@virgin.net

GHOSH, Dipen. b 43. St Jo Coll Nottm 71. **d** 74 **p** 75. C Bushbury *Lich* 74-77; Hon C 86-89; C Wednesfield Heath 89-91; TV Wolverhampton 91-98; TV Bushbury 98-02; Chapl Compton Hospice 98-02; V Wolverhampton St Matt *Lich* from 02. *St Matthew's Vicarage, 14 Sydenham Road, Wolverhampton WV1 2NY* Tel (01902) 453056

GIBB, David Richard Albert. b 68. Lon Bible Coll BA90 Cov Univ MPhil95. **d** 95 **p** 96. C Ox St Ebbe w H Trin and St Pet 95-01; V

Leyland St Andr *Blackb* from 01. *St Andrew's Vicarage, 1 Crocus Field, Leyland PR25 3DY* Tel (01772) 621645
E-mail david.gibb7@ntlworld.com

GIBBARD, Roger. b 48. Southn Univ BA73. Cuddesdon Coll 73. **d** 75 **p** 76. C Portsea St Mary *Portsm* 75-79; P-in-c New Addington *Cant* 79-81; C Ditton St Mich *Liv* 81-82; TV 82-88; Asst Chapl HM Pris Liv 88-89; Chapl HM YOI Hindley 89-92; Chapl HM Pris Risley 92-00; V Wigan St Mich *Liv* 01-04. *97 Barnsley Street, Wigan WN6 7HB* Tel (01942) 233465
E-mail thegibbards@blueyonder.co.uk

GIBBINS, John Grenville. b 53. Aston Tr Scheme 89 Linc Th Coll 89. **d** 91 **p** 92. C Market Harborough *Leic* 91-95; P-in-c Blaby from 95. *The Rectory, Wigston Road, Blaby, Leicester LE8 4FU* Tel 0116-277 2588 E-mail ggibbins@leicester.anglican.org

GIBBON, Matthew. b 79. Trin Coll Carmarthen BA00. St Steph Ho Ox BTh03. **d** 03 **p** 04. C Caerau w Ely *Llan* 03-05; C Aberavon 05-08; P-in-c Treharris, Trelewis and Bedlinog from 08. *The Vicarage, 13 The Oaks, Quakers Yard, Treharris CF46 5HQ* Tel (01443) 410280
E-mail frmatthewgibbon@btinternet.com

GIBBONS, David Austen. b 63. York Univ BSc84. Ch Div Sch of Pacific 93 Ripon Coll Cuddesdon BA94. **d** 94 **p** 95. C Ryde H Trin *Portsm* 94-97; C Swanmore St Mich 94-97; C Gosport Ch Ch 97-01; R Havant 01-08; R Barrington Hills USA from 08. *337 Ridge Road, Barrington IL 60010-2331, USA* Tel (001) (847) 381 0596 E-mail d_gibbons@talk21.com

GIBBONS, David Robin Christian. b 36. Chich Th Coll 82. **d** 84 **p** 85. C Seaford w Sutton *Chich* 84-87; R Harting 87-93; R Harting w Elsted and Treyford cum Didling 93-04; rtd 04. *Richmond Villas, 102 East Street, Selsey, Chichester PO20 0BX* Tel (01243) 602978

GIBBONS, Eric. b 47. Sarum & Wells Th Coll 69. **d** 72 **p** 73. C New Haw *Guildf* 72-76; C Hawley H Trin 76-79; P-in-c Blackheath and Chilworth 79-90; V 90-98; C Shere, Albury and Chilworth 98-99; P-in-c Tongham 99-04; rtd 04. *38 Ambleside Close, Farnborough GU14 0LA* Tel (01252) 540586

GIBBONS, Harvey Lloyd. b 62. Ripon Coll Cuddesdon 97. **d** 99 **p** 00. C Verwood *Sarum* 99-00; C Gillingham 00-02; Dioc Voc Adv and P-in-c Upavon w Rushall and Charlton 02-07; R Warminster St Denys and Upton Scudamore from 07. *The Rectory, 5 Church Street, Warminster BA12 8PG* Tel (01985) 213456 E-mail revdharvey@btinternet.com

GIBBONS, The Ven Kenneth Harry. b 31. Man Univ BSc52. Cuddesdon Coll 54. **d** 56 **p** 57. C Fleetwood St Pet *Blackb* 56-60; NE Sch Sec SCM 60-62; Hon C Leeds St Pet *Ripon* 60-62; C St Martin-in-the-Fields *Lon* 62-65; V New Addington *Cant* 65-70; V Portsea St Mary *Portsm* 70-81; RD Portsm 73-79; Hon Can Portsm Cathl 76-81; Dir Post-Ord Tr *Blackb* 81-83; Acting Chapl HM Forces Weeton 81-85; Dir of Ords 82-90; Adn Lancaster 81-97; P-in-c Weeton 81-85; V St Michaels-on-Wyre 85-97; rtd 97; P-in-c St Magnus the Martyr w St Marg New Fish Street *Lon* 97-03; P-in-c St Clem Eastcheap w St Martin Orgar from 99. *112 Valley Road, Kenley CR8 5BU* Tel (020) 8660 7502 E-mail margaret@gibbons440.fsnet.co.uk

GIBBONS, Mrs Lissa Melanie. b 58. Birm Univ BA79 PGCE80. SAOMC 98. **d** 01 **p** 02. C Risborough *Ox* 01-06; Chapl Bucks Hosps NHS Trust 05-07; TV Monkwearmouth *Dur* from 07. *St Peter's Vicarage, St Peter's Way, Sunderland SR6 0DY* Tel 0191-567 3726 E-mail lissaandtom@btinternet.com

GIBBONS, Paul James. b 37. JP. Chich Th Coll 63. **d** 65 **p** 66. C Croydon St Mich *Cant* 65-72; V Maidstone St Martin from 72. *The Vicarage, 109 Tonbridge Road, Maidstone ME16 8JS* Tel (01622) 752710

GIBBONS, Mrs Susan Janet. b 51. St Mary's Coll Dur BA73 Birm Univ PGCE74. WMMTC 89. **d** 92 **p** 94. NSM Fladbury w Wyre Piddle and Moor etc *Worc* 92-00; Perm to Offic from 00. *The Old School, Bricklehampton, Pershore WR10 3HJ* Tel (01386) 710475

GIBBONS, Thomas Patrick. b 59. St Jo Coll Dur BA82. St Steph Ho Ox 88. **d** 90 **p** 91. C Whorlton *Newc* 90-94; C Gosforth St Nic 94-96; R Radley and Sunningwell *Ox* 96-04; P-in-c Lenborough 04-07; TV Monkwearmouth *Dur* from 07; Chapl Co Durham and Darlington NHS Foundn Trust from 07. *St Peter's Vicarage, St Peter's Way, Sunderland SR6 0DY* Tel 0191-567 3726 E-mail lissaandtom@tesco.net

GIBBONS, Mrs Valerie Mary Lydele. b 49. St Aid Coll Dur BA72 Solicitor 75. Wycliffe Hall Ox 98. **d** 03 **p** 04. OLM Cholsey and Moulsford *Ox* from 03. *Kilifi, Caps Lane, Cholsey, Wallingford OX10 9HF* Tel and fax (01491) 651377 E-mail val.gibbons@btinternet.com

GIBBONS, William Simpson. b 32. TCD BA60 MA64. **d** 61 **p** 62. C Londonderry Ch Ch *D & R* 61-65; I Drumholm and Rossnowlagh 65-70; C Dublin St Ann w St Steph *D & G* 70-72; I Kill 72-95; Can Ch Ch Cathl Dublin 91-95; rtd 95. *Muthaiga, 3 Glenageary Terrace, Dun Laoghaire, Co Dublin, Republic of Ireland* Tel and fax (00353) (1) 214 8699 Mobile 87-218 7771 E-mail wsgibbons@eircom.net

GIBBS, Colin Hugh. b 35. St Mich Coll Llan 82. **d** 84 **p** 85. C

Bistre *St As* 84-87; V Penycae 87-92; rtd 92. *Asaph, 26 Cil y Coed, Ruabon, Wrexham LL14 6TA* Tel (01978) 823550

GIBBS, Colin Wilfred. b 39. Man Univ BA62 Birm Univ CertEd63. St Jo Coll Nottm 71. **d** 73 **p** 74. C Crowborough *Chich* 73-76; C Rodbourne Cheney *Bris* 76-77; C Bickenhill w Elmdon *Birm* 77-80; CF 80-96; Dir Ichthus Ho Homestay 96-06; Chapl Grenville Coll Bideford 99-02; P-in-c Cowden w Hammerwood *Chich* from 06. *The Rectory, Church Street, Cowden, Edenbridge TN8 7JE* Tel (01342) 850221
E-mail ichthushouse@tiscali.co.uk

GIBBS, Edmund. b 38. Fuller Th Sem California DMin81. Oak Hill Th Coll BD62. **d** 63 **p** 64. C Wandsworth All SS *S'wark* 63-66; SAMS Chile 66-70; Educn Sec SAMS 70-77; Ch Progr Manager Bible Soc 77-84; USA from 84; Assoc Prof Evang and Ch Renewal Fuller Th Sem 84-93; Prof Ch Growth from 96; Assoc K Beverly Hills All SS 93-96. *1136 Crowne Drive, Pasadena CA 91107-5911, USA* Tel (001) (626) 794 6393
E-mail edgibbs@fuller.edu

GIBBS (née DE ROBECK), Mrs Fiona Caroline. b 74. St Martin's Coll Lanc BA96. St Jo Coll Nottm MA(TS)99. **d** 00 **p** 01. C Bitterne *Win* 00-05; C Chandler's Ford from 05. *45 Pantheon Road, Chandler's Ford, Eastleigh SO53 2PD* Tel (023) 8026 8433

GIBBS, Mrs Fiorenza Silvia Elisabetta. b 49. SRN71. St Alb Minl Tr Scheme 90. **d** 93 **p** 99. NSM Hitchin *St Alb* 93-96; NSM Pirton 97-99; Asst Chapl N Herts NHS Trust 99-00; Asst Chapl E and N Herts NHS Trust 00-02. Perm to Offic from 02. *12 Bunyon Close, Pirton, Hitchin SG5 3RE* Tel (01462) 711846 or (01438) 781518

GIBBS, Ian Edmund. b 47. Lon Univ BEd69. St Steph Ho Ox 72. **d** 75 **p** 76. C Stony Stratford *Ox* 75-79; V Forest Town *S'well* 79-83; R Diddlebury w Munslow, Holdgate and Tugford *Heref* from 83; R Abdon from 83. *The Rectory, Munslow, Craven Arms SY7 9ET* Tel (01584) 841688

GIBBS, James Millard. b 28. Univ of Michigan BSE51 Nottm Univ PhD68. Seabury-Western Th Sem BD57. **d** 57 **p** 57. USA 57-60; Lic to Offic *S'well* 61-62 and 65-66; C Brandon *Dur* 62-64; Vice-Prin Lich Th Coll 66-71; Lic to Offic *Lich* 66-71; India 72-77; Tutor Qu Coll Birm 78-84; V Stechford *Birm* 84-93; rtd 93; Perm to Offic *Birm* from 93. *13 Lingfield Court, 60 High Street, Harbourne, Birmingham B17 9NE* Tel 0121-426 2108 E-mail jmanddagibbs@aol.com

GIBBS, Jane Anne. b 46. W Midl Coll of Educn CertEd67. EMMTC 03. **d** 06 **p** 07. NSM Hinckley St Mary *Leic* from 06. *4 Kirfield Drive, Hinckley LE10 1SX* Tel (01455) 635934

GIBBS, Jonathan Robert. b 61. Jes Coll Ox MA89 Jes Coll Cam PhD90. Ridley Hall Cam 84. **d** 89 **p** 90. C Stalybridge H Trin and Ch Ch *Ches* 89-92; Chapl Basle w Freiburg-im-Breisgau *Eur* 92-98; R Heswall *Ches* from 98. *The Rectory, Village Road, Heswall, Wirral CH60 0DZ* Tel 0151-342 3471 Fax 342 2275 E-mail jgibbs@heswallparish.co.uk

GIBBS, Michael Robin. b 42. Th Ext Educn Coll 74. **d** 83 **p** 84. NSM Malawi 83-04; Can Upper Shire from 03; Chapl Essex Chs Coun for Ind and Commerce *Chelmsf* from 05. *120 St John's Road, London E17 4JQ* Tel and fax (020) 8523 1375 E-mail micgibbs@talktalk.net

GIBBS, Mrs Patricia Louise. b 39. S'wark Ord Course 91. **d** 94 **p** 95. NSM Croydon H Sav *S'wark* 94-07; Chapl Asst Mayday Healthcare NHS Trust Thornton Heath 94-05; rtd 07. *41 Sandringham Road, Thornton Heath CR7 7AX* Tel (020) 8684 9720

GIBBS, Peter Winston. b 50. Ex Univ BA72 CQSW75. St Jo Coll Nottm. **d** 90 **p** 91. C Hampreston *Sarum* 90-94; P-in-c Ipswich St Matt *St E* 94-99; Assoc P Attenborough *S'well* 99-01; V Toton 01-08; TV N Poole Ecum Team *Sarum* from 08. *St Paul's Vicarage, 16 Rowbarrow Close, Poole BH17 9EA* Tel (01202) 565187 E-mail ladybird1@ntlworld.com

GIBBS, Canon Philip Roscoe. b 33. Codrington Coll Barbados 57. **d** 60 **p** 61. C St Jo Cathl Belize 61-63; P-in-c S Distr Miss 63-70; V Pomona St Matt 70-71; R Corozal 71-74; Hon Can Belize from 71; V Stoke Newington Common St Mich *Lon* 74-87; V Johnsonville New Zealand 87-96; rtd 96. *10 Gardener Street, Levin 5510, New Zealand* Tel (0064) (6) 367 9884 E-mail philip.g@actrix.co.nz

GIBBS, Raymond George. b 55. NTMTC 94. **d** 97 **p** 98. NSM Becontree S *Chelmsf* 97-99; C Dedham 99-04; C Colchester St Mich Myland 04-08; P-in-c from 08; Area Youth Officer 04-08. *352 Mill Road, Mile End, Colchester CO4 5JF* Tel (01206) 843926 E-mail raymond359gibbs@btinternet.com

GIBBS, Richard James. b 68. St Paul's Cheltenham BSc90. St Jo Coll Nottm MTh01. **d** 01 **p** 02. C Southport Ch Ch *Liv* 01-05; Min Banks St Steph CD from 05. *33 Abington Drive, Banks, Southport PR9 8FL* Tel (01704) 546294

GIBBS, Stewart Henry. b 77. CCC Cam BA98 MA PGCE99 Anglia Poly Univ BTh05. Ridley Hall Cam 02. **d** 05 **p** 06. C Grays Thurrock *Chelmsf* from 05. *11 Conrad Gardens, Grays RM16 2TN* Tel (01375) 390370 Mobile 07899-753559

GIBBS, Canon William Gilbert. b 31. Bps' Coll Cheshunt 55. **d** 58

p 59. C Wellington w W Buckland *B & W* 58-61; C Kensington St Mary Abbots w St Geo *Lon* 61-68; V Guilsborough *Pet* 68; V Guilsborough w Hollowell 68-74; V Guilsborough w Hollowell and Cold Ashby 74-98; Jt P-in-c Cottesbrooke w Gt Creaton and Thornby 83-98; Jt P-in-c Maidwell w Draughton, Lamport w Faxton 88-98; Can Pet Cathl 88-98; rtd 98; Perm to Offic *Pet* 98-01 and from 03; P-in-c W Haddon w Winwick and Ravensthorpe 01-03. *Paines Close, Maidwell, Northampton NN6 9JB* Tel (01604) 686424

GIBBS, William John Morris. b 71. Birm Univ BSc94. Ripon Coll Cuddesdon BTh00. **d** 00 **p** 01. C Staines St Mary and St Pet *Lon* 00-03; C Kensington St Mary Abbots w St Geo 03-06; V Redbourn *St Alb* from 06. *The Vicarage, 49 Church End, Redbourn, St Albans AL3 7DU* Tel (01582) 791669

GIBLIN, Brendan Anthony. b 64. K Coll Lon BD86 AKC93 Leeds Univ MA95. Wycliffe Hall Ox 90. **d** 92 **p** 93. C Tadcaster w Newton Kyme *York* 92-96; R Stockton-on-the-Forest w Holtby and Warthill 96-02; P-in-c Middleham w Coverdale and E Witton etc *Ripon* 02-03; R from 03. *The Rectory, Wensley, Leyburn DL8 4HS* Tel (01969) 623736
E-mail bgiblin@toucansurf.com

GIBLING, Derek Vivian. b 31. Wadh Coll Ox BA56 MA63. Wycliffe Hall Ox 70. **d** 72 **p** 73. C Fisherton Anger *Sarum* 72-74; C Yatton Keynell *Bris* 74-77; C Castle Combe 74-77; C Biddestone w Slaughterford 74-77; P-in-c Youlgreave *Derby* 77-82; P-in-c Stanton-in-Peak 77-82; V Youlgreave, Middleton, Stanton-in-Peak etc 82-88; P-in-c Hartington and Biggin 88-90; V Hartington, Biggin and Earl Sterndale 90-96; rtd 96; Perm to Offic *Linc* 96-02; RD Bolingbroke 00-02. *15 Howards Meadow, Glossop SK13 6PZ* Tel (01457) 851423

GIBRALTAR IN EUROPE, Bishop of. See ROWELL, The Rt Revd Douglas Geoffrey

GIBRALTAR, Archdeacon of. See SUTCH, The Ven Christopher David

GIBRALTAR, Dean of. See PADDOCK, The Very Revd John Allan Barnes

GIBSON, Alan. b 35. Birm Univ BSc56 Man Univ MSc72. NW Ord Course 71. **d** 74 **p** 75. C Sale St Anne *Ches* 74-77; V Runcorn St Mich 77-82; Educn Adv *Carl* 82-88; P-in-c Hugill 82-88; V Grange-over-Sands 88-97; rtd 97; Perm to Offic *Derby* from 01. *11 Ecclesbourne Drive, Buxton SK17 9BX* Tel (01298) 22621

GIBSON, Anthony Richard. b 43. Ridley Hall Cam 83. **d** 85 **p** 86. C Rushmere *St E* 85-88; R N Tawton, Bondleigh, Sampford Courtenay etc *Ex* 88-93; RD Okehampton 92-93; P-in-c Tiverton St Pet and Chevithorne w Cove 93-03; rtd 03. *Le Bourg, 82210 Fajolles, France* Tel (0033) (5) 63 94 14 83

GIBSON, Brenda. b 55. St Mary's Coll Dur BSc77 PhD80 Hughes Hall Cam PGCE81 Surrey Univ BA04. STETS 01. **d** 04 **p** 05. NSM Wimborne Minster *Sarum* from 04. *12 Meadow Court, Leigh Road, Wimborne BH21 2BG* Tel (01202) 881472
E-mail brenda@p-b-gibson.demon.co.uk

GIBSON, Catherine Snyder. b 39. Parson's Sch of Design (NY) 57. Ab Dioc Tr Course 82 Edin Th Coll 92. **d** 86 **p** 94. Colombia 86-87; NSM Aberdeen St Marg 87-88; Dioc Hosp Chapl 89-92; C Aberdeen St Mary 93-94; Bp's Chapl for Tr and Educn 93-94; P-in-c Ballater 95-96; R 96-98. P-in-c Aboyne 95-96; R 96-98; P-in-c Braemar 95-97; Assoc P Fort Lauderdale USA 98-04; I Fermoy Union *C, C & R* 04-06; rtd 06; P-in-c Lugano *Eur* 06-07. *Address temp unknown* E-mail kategib@btinternet.com

GIBSON, Charles Daniel. b 48. **d** 03 **p** 04. OLM Wisley w Pyrford *Guildf* from 03. *The Corner Cottage, Send Marsh Road, Ripley, Woking GU23 6JN* Tel (01483) 225317 Fax 223681
E-mail charles@chasdi.freeserve.co.uk

GIBSON, Colin Taylor. b 54. Trin Coll Cam BA77. Oak Hill Th Coll 86. **d** 88 **p** 89. C Thrybergh w Hooton Roberts *Sheff* 88-91; P-in-c Tinsley 91-96; TV Attercliffe, Darnall and Tinsley 96-02; TR Walsall *Lich* from 02; Hon C Walsall St Paul from 05; Hon C Walsall Pleck and Bescot from 05. *St Matthew's Rectory, 48 Jesson Road, Walsall WS1 3AX* Tel (01922) 624012
E-mail c.t.gibson@btinternet.com

GIBSON, David Francis. b 36. Magd Coll Cam BA57 BChir60 MB61. SW Minl Tr Course 84. **d** 90 **p** 91. NSM Newport, Bishops Tawton and Tawstock *Ex* 90-95; Chapl N Devon Healthcare NHS Trust 95-96; Perm to Offic *Ex* from 96. *Little Beara, Marwood, Barnstaple EX31 4EH* Tel (01271) 814876

GIBSON, David Innes. b 31. Oak Hill Th Coll 56. **d** 59 **p** 60. C S Croydon Em *Cant* 59-62; C Washfield *Ex* 62-63; Asst Master and Chapl Blundells Sch Tiverton 63-64; Chapl Sutton Valence Sch Maidstone 64-68; Chapl Dean Close Sch Cheltenham 68-75; Asst Chapl and Ho Master 75-85; Asst Master Brightlands Sch Newnham-on-Severn 85-90; C Cheltenham St Mary, St Matt, St Paul and H Trin *Glouc* 91-96; rtd 96; Perm to Offic *Glouc* 96 97; and from 01. *2 Withyholt Park, Charlton Kings, Cheltenham GL53 9BP* Tel (01242) 511612

GIBSON, Douglas Harold. b 20. Portsm Dioc Tr Course. **d** 87. NSM Portsea St Luke *Portsm* 87-92; Perm to Offic from 92. *83 Middle Street, Southsea PO5 4BW* Tel (023) 9282 9769

GIBSON, Garry Stuart. b 36. Univ Coll Lon BA62 PhD75

Birkbeck Coll Lon BA79. Oak Hill Th Coll 62. **d** 64 **p** 65. C Watford St Mary *St Alb* 64-67; Lect Cambs Coll of Arts and Tech 67-69; Government of Israel Scholar Hebrew Univ 69-70; Asst Master Angl Sch Jerusalem 69-70; Sen Lect Middx Univ 70-97; Hon C Sidmouth, Woolbrook, Salcombe Regis, Sidbury etc *Ex* 96-99; C Stockland, Dalwood, Kilmington and Shute 99-03; C Kilmington, Stockland, Dalwood, Yarcombe etc 03-04. *14 Argus Close, Honiton EX14 1UT* Tel (01404) 44083
E-mail garrygib@yahoo.co.uk

GIBSON, The Ven George Granville. b 36. Cuddesdon Coll 69. **d** 71 **p** 72. C Tynemouth Cullercoats St Paul *Newc* 71-73; TV Cramlington 73-77; V Newton Aycliffe *Dur* 77-85; R Bishopwearmouth St Mich w St Hilda 85-90; TR Sunderland 90-93; RD Wearmouth 85-93; Hon Can Dur Cathl 88-01; Adn Auckland 93-01; rtd 01. *12 West Crescent, Darlington DL3 7PR* Tel (01325) 462526
E-mail granville.gibson@durham.anglican.org

GIBSON, Canon Ian. b 48. Open Univ BA85 MSc FCIPD MCMI. S Dios Minl Tr Scheme 82. **d** 85 **p** 86. NSM Uckfield *Chich* 85-88; NSM Lt Horsted 85-88; NSM Isfield 85-88; V Fairwarp 88-93; P-in-c 94-00; NSM 00-04; V High Hurstwood 88-93; P-in-c 94-00; RD Uckfield 03-04; Bp's Dom Chapl and Research Asst 04-09; Episc V for Min and Bp's Sen Chapl from 09; Can Res and Treas Chich Cathl from 09. *Caigers Cottage, Westergate Street, Woodgate, Chichester PO20 3SQ* Tel (01243) 544534 or 782161 Fax 531332 E-mail ian.gibson@diochi.org.uk

GIBSON, John Murray Hope. b 35. Dur Univ BA58. Cranmer Hall Dur 58. **d** 60 **p** 61. C Chester le Street *Dur* 60-63; C Stockton 63-68; V Denton and Ingleton 68-75; V Swalwell 75-00; Chapl Dunston Hill Hosp Gateshead 80-99; rtd 00; Perm to Offic *Dur* and *Newc* from 01. *50 Church Road, Gosforth, Newcastle upon Tyne NE3 1BJ* Tel 0191-285 2942

GIBSON, Canon John Noel Keith. b 22. MBE89. Ch Coll Cam MA48 Lon Univ BD59. Coll of Resurr Mirfield 45. **d** 47 **p** 48. C S Elmsall *Wakef* 47-51; Antigua 51-56; Virgin Is from 56; Can All SS Cathl 89-92; rtd 92. *PO Box 65, Valley, Virgin Gorda, British Virgin Islands* Tel (001284) 495 5587

GIBSON, Kenneth George Goudie. b 54. Glas Univ MA83 Edin Univ BD87 Strathclyde Univ PGCE95. Edin Th Coll 83. **d** 88 **p** 89. C Glas St Marg 88-90; R E Kilbride 90-98; R Carnoustie *Bre* 98-07. *39 Durham Street, Monifieth, Dundee DD5 4PF* E-mail kenneth.gibson@homecall.co.uk

GIBSON, Laura Mary. See WILFORD, Laura Mary

GIBSON, Mark. b 48. **d** 84. OSB from 67; Abbot of Alton 82-90; Perm to Offic *Win* 84-95; NSM Paddington St Sav *Lon* from 90; NSM Paddington St Mary from 95; Acting Bp's Chapl 90-91; NSM Paddington St Mary Magd 98-03. *6 Park Place Villas, London W2 1SP* Tel (020) 7724 7444 or 7262 3787
E-mail abbotsfancy@aol.com

GIBSON, Nigel Stephen David. b 53. St Barn Coll Adelaide 84. **d** 87 **p** 87. C N Adelaide Ch Ch Australia 87-89; Lect Boston *Linc* 90-91; P-in-c Stamford St Mary and St Mich 91-92; P-in-c Stamford Baron 91-92; R Stamford St Mary and St Martin 92-98; Perm to Offic 98-00; V Kempston Transfiguration *St Alb* 00-04; Chapl Milan w Genoa and Varese *Eur* from 04. *All Saints, via Solferino 17, 20121 Milan, Italy* Tel and fax (0039) (02) 655 2258 E-mail frnigel@boxingkangaroo.org.uk

GIBSON, Mrs Patricia Elizabeth. b 57. Nottm Univ MA02. EMMTC 99. **d** 02 **p** 03. C Wigston Magna *Leic* 02-06; TV Gt Berkhamsted, Gt and Lt Gaddesden etc *St Alb* from 06; Bp's Adv for Women in Min from 07. *The Vicarage, Pipers Hill, Great Gaddesden, Hemel Hempstead HP1 3BY* Tel (01442) 252672
E-mail revteg1@btinternet.com

GIBSON, Paul Saison. b 32. BA LTh Huron Coll Ontario Hon DD90. Coll of Em and St Chad Hon DD88 Vancouver Sch of Th Hon DD95 Montreal Dioc Th Coll Hon DD98 Trin Coll Toronto Hon DD99. **d** 56 **p** 57. C Bloomsbury St Geo w St Jo *Lon* 56-59; R Homer St Geo Canada 59-60; Chapl McGill Univ Montreal 60-66; Prin Hong Kong Union Th Coll 66-72; Consultant Angl Ch of Canada 72-82; Liturg Officer 82-98. *588 Millwood Road, Toronto ON M4S 1K8, Canada* Tel (001) (416) 487 2008

GIBSON, Philip Nigel Scott. b 53. St Jo Coll Dur BA78. Cranmer Hall Dur 79. **d** 79 **p** 80. C Yardley St Edburgha *Birm* 79-82; C Stratford-on-Avon w Bishopton *Cov* 82-84; Chapl SW Hosp Lon 84-91; Chapl St Thos Hosp Lon 84-91; Assoc P Newington St Paul *S'wark* 91-92; Chapl Charing Cross Hosp Lon 92-93; Chapl R Lon Hosp (Whitechapel) 93-94; Chapl Bedford Hosp NHS Trust 95-08. *Sillwood, 1 Wood Lane, Aspley Guise, Milton Keynes MK17 8EJ*

GIBSON, S. Raymond. b 23. Ely Th Coll 60. **d** 62 **p** 63. C Leic St Jas 62-67; Succ Leic Cathl 67-68; Chapl Leic R Infirmary 67-68; Chapl Nottm City Hosp 68-84; V Barlings *Linc* 84-88; rtd 88. *11 Cornell Drive, Nottingham NG3 8RH*

GIBSON, Raymond Frank. b 34. Toronto Bible Coll BTh61 Tyndale Hall Bris 62. **d** 64 **p** 65. C Gt Horton *Bradf* 64-67; C Otley 67-72; V Fairlight *Chich* 72-83; V Hallwood *Ches* 83-85; R Freethorpe, Wickhampton, Halvergate w Tunstall *Nor* 85-99;

P-in-c Reedham w Cantley w Limpenhoe and Southwood 94-99; rtd 99; Perm to Offic *Nor* 99-09. *23 Ramsay Hall, 9-13 Byron Road, Worthing BN11 3HN* Tel (01903) 239957

GIBSON, Canon Robert Swinton. b 26. Wadh Coll Ox BA50 MA55. Wells Th Coll 50. **d** 53 **p** 54. C Greenwich St Alfege w St Pet *S'wark* 53-61; Ind Missr 55-62; Hon Chapl to Bp S'wark 56-67; Sen Chapl S Lon Ind Miss 62-67; Nigeria 67-69; R Guisborough *York* 69-83; RD Guisborough 73-83; TR Halifax *Wakef* 83-94; Hon Can Wakef Cathl 85-94; RD Halifax 86-92; rtd 94; Perm to Offic *Wakef* and *York* from 94. *The Cottage, Main Street, Hutton Buscel, Scarborough YO13 9LL* Tel (01723) 862133

GIBSON, The Ven Terence Allen. b 37. Jes Coll Cam BA61 MA65. Cuddesdon Coll 61. **d** 63 **p** 64. C Kirkby *Liv* 63-66; TV 72-75; TR 75-84; Warden Cen 63 66-75; Youth Chapl 66-72; RD Walton 79-84; Adn Suffolk *St E* 84-87; Adn Ipswich 87-05; rtd 05; Perm to Offic *St E* from 05. *5 Berry Close, Purdis Farm, Ipswich IP3 8SP* Tel (01473) 714756

GIBSON, Thomas Thomson. b 23. Sarum Th Coll 62. **d** 63 **p** 64. C E w W Harnham *Sarum* 63-66; V Rowde 66-74; R Poulshot 67-74; V Badminton w Acton Turville *Glouc* 74-84; P-in-c Hawkesbury 81-84; V Badminton w Lt Badminton, Acton Turville etc 84-93; rtd 93; Perm to Offic *Glouc* 93-96 and from 01; *B & W* and *Sarum* from 95; *Eur* from 99. *9 Lansdown Place West, Bath BA1 5EZ* Tel (01225) 337903 Fax 483676

GIDDENS, Leslie Vernon. b 29. Bps' Coll Cheshunt 54. **d** 56 **p** 57. C Harrow St Pet *Lon* 56-58; C Walthamstow St Benet Fink 58-63; C-in-c Hayes St Nic CD 63-94; rtd 94; Perm to Offic *Lon* from 94. *6 Ashdown Road, Uxbridge UB10 0HY* Tel (01895) 232406

GIDDINGS, Mrs Jaqueline Mary. b 44. St Aid Coll Dur BA67. SW Minl Tr Course 91. **d** 94 **p** 95. C Plympton St Mary *Ex* 94-02; rtd 02. *Grange End, Harrowbeer Lane, Yelverton PL20 6EA* Tel (01822) 854825

GIFFORD, Ms Elizabeth Ann. b 47. St Kath Coll Liv CertEd72 Open Univ BSc96. STETS 99. **d** 02 **p** 03. NSM Trowbridge H Trin *Sarum* 02-09; NSM Studley from 09. *14 Innox Mill Close, Trowbridge BA14 9BA* Tel (01225) 752756 Mobile 07903-269587 E-mail revgif@aol.com

GIFFORD-COLE, David Henry. b 30. San Francisco Th Sem DMin87 ALCD56. **d** 56 **p** 57. C Ashtead *Guildf* 56-59; C Farnham 59-60; Canada from 60. *225 Hoylake Road West, Qualicum Beach BC V9K 1K5, Canada*

✠**GILBERT, The Rt Revd Bruce Carlyle.** b 38. Auckland Univ BSc59. St Jo Coll Auckland STh74. **d** 62 **p** 64 c 85. C Devonport New Zealand 62-64; C Ponsony and Grey Lynn 65; P Asst Panmure 66-68; V Avondale 68-71; Ind Chapl and C Eaglescliffe *Dur* 71-73; Dir Ind Miss Wellington New Zealand 73-79; Dir Th Educn by Ext 80-85; Bp Auckland 85-94; P-in-c Albany Greenhithe 95-00; P-in-c Tamaki St Thos 96-00; Chapl K Sch 97-00; rtd 00. *81 Manaia Road, Tairua 2853, New Zealand* Tel (0064) (7) 864 8727

GILBERT, Anthony John David. b 54. Open Univ BA91 LRSC83. Ripon Coll Cuddesdon 83. **d** 86 **p** 87. C Exning St Martin w Landwade *St E* 86-89; Chapl RAF from 89. *Chaplaincy Services, Valiant Block, HQ Air Command, RAF High Wycombe HP14 4UE* Tel (01494) 496800 Fax 496343 E-mail tngilbert@aol.com

GILBERT, Arthur John. b 57. LTCL76 GBSM79 Reading Univ PGCE80. Coll of Resurr Mirfield 88. **d** 91 **p** 92. C Uppingham w Ayston and Wardley w Belton *Pet* 91-94; C Armley w New Wortley *Ripon* 94-96; V Doncaster St Jude *Sheff* 96-09; AD W Doncaster 00-06; TV Barnstaple *Ex* from 09. *The Vicarage, Sowden Lane, Barnstaple EX32 8BU* Tel (01271) 373837 E-mail frj@gilbert24.plus.com

GILBERT, Canon Barry. b 46. Leeds Univ BA67. Coll of Resurr Mirfield 67. **d** 69 **p** 70. C Malvern Link w Cowleigh *Worc* 69-73; P-in-c Bromsgrove All SS 73-81; V 81-83; P-in-c Lower Mitton 83-88; V 88-92; V Stourport and Wilden 92-06; RD Stourport 93-00 and 02-06; P-in-c Brierley Hill 06-07; TR from 07; Hon Can Worc Cathl from 09. *The Rectory, 2 Church Hill, Brierley Hill DY5 3PX* Tel (01384) 78146 E-mail barry_gilbert@talk21.com

GILBERT, Clive Franklyn. b 55. City of Liv Coll of HE CertEd76 BEd77. SEITE 01. **d** 02 **p** 03. C Paddock Wood *Roch* 02-06; V Dartford St Alb from 06. *St Alban's Vicarage, 51 Watling Street, Dartford DA1 1RW* Tel (01322) 224052 Mobile 07752-676663 E-mail clive.gilbert@diocese-rochester.org

GILBERT, Frederick Joseph. b 29. Lich Th Coll 58. **d** 59 **p** 60. C Westhoughton *Man* 59-62; V Goodshaw 62-68; R Crumpsall St Matt 68-75; RD Cheetham 70-74; RD N Man 74-75; V Rochdale St Aid 75-78; TV Rochdale 78-80; V Westhoughton 80-84; TR 84-87; AD Deane 85-87; R W Bowbrook *Worc* 87-89; R Bowbrook N 89-93; rtd 93; Perm to Offic *Worc* from 93. *Freshways, Main Road, Peopleton, Pershore WR10 2EG* Tel (01905) 841629

GILBERT, Howard Neil. b 73. Southn Univ BA96. Ripon Coll Cuddesdon BTh05. **d** 05 **p** 06. C Dulwich St Barn *S'wark* 05-08. *Address temp unknown* Tel 07887-800478 (mobile) E-mail father.howard@gmail.com

GILBERT, John. *See* GILBERT, Arthur John

GILBERT, John Edwin. b 28. FCA62. Bps' Coll Cheshunt 54. **d** 57 **p** 58. C Luton Ch Ch *St Alb* 57-60; C Gt Berkhamsted 60-64; P-in-c Kemptee India 65-68; Hon Chapl Nagpur Cathl 68-70; Dioc Treas Nagpur 65-70; Perm to Offic *St Alb* 71-77; Lic to Offic 77-86; Hon C Sunnyside w Bourne End 86-89; TV Padgate *Liv* 89-94; rtd 94; Perm to Offic *Heref* from 94. *4 Westgate Drive, Bridgnorth WV16 4QF* Tel (01746) 762611

GILBERT, Mrs Margaret Ann. b 39. CITC 89. **d** 92 **p** 93. NSM Dublin Clontarf *D & G* 92-96; NSM Dublin Santry w Glasnevin and Finglas 96-06; NSM Dublin Drumcondra w N Strand 06-07. *67 Grange Park Road, Raheny, Dublin 5, Republic of Ireland* Tel (00353) (1) 848 1340

GILBERT, Mark. *See* GILBERT, Philip Mark

GILBERT, Ms Mary Rose. b 63. Ridley Hall Cam 94. **d** 97 **p** 97. C Walsall Wood *Lich* 97-00; TV Bilston 00-07; AD Wolverhampton 03-07; V Birm St Paul from 07. *71 Wellington Road, Edgbaston, Birmingham B15 2ET* Tel 0121-440 2337 E-mail mgdartford@aol.com

GILBERT, Michael Victor. b 61. Dur Univ BA84. Trin Coll Bris 92. **d** 94 **p** 95. C Chapeltown *Sheff* 94-97; V Brightside w Wincobank 97-07; Adult Educator Wilson Carlile Coll of Evang from 07. *Wilson Carlile College of Evangelism, 50 Cavendish Street, Sheffield S3 7RZ* Tel 0114-278 7020 E-mail m.gilbert@churcharmy.org.uk

GILBERT, Philip Mark. b 62. Liv Univ BA84. Coll of Resurr Mirfield 84. **d** 87 **p** 88. C Frodsham *Ches* 87-89; C Stockton Heath 89-92; R Tangmere and Oving *Chich* 92-01; Chapl Seaford Coll and P-in-c Graffham w Woolavington 01-09; P-in-c Chich St Wilfrid from 09; Chapl Bp Luffa Sch Chich from 09. *St Wilfrid's House, 7 Durnford Close, Chichester PO19 3AG* Tel (01243) 783853 Mobile 07810-004062 E-mail frmark@mgilbert.clara.co.uk

GILBERT, Raymond. b 34. AKC61. **d** 62 **p** 63. C Newbold w Dunston *Derby* 62-66; PV and Succ S'wark Cathl 66-68; P-in-c Stuntney *Ely* 68-74; Prec and Sacr Ely Cathl 68-74; Min Can Cant Cathl 74-79; Hon Min Can from 79; P-in-c Patrixbourne w Bridge and Bekesbourne 79-81; V 81-00; RD E Bridge 92-98; rtd 00; Perm to Offic *Cant* from 09. *16 Green Acres, Eythorne, Dover CT15 4LX* Tel (01304) 831485

GILBERT, Raymond Frederick. b 44. **d** 93 **p** 94. OLM Stowmarket *St E* from 93. *3 Violet Hill Road, Stowmarket IP14 1NE* Tel (01449) 677700

GILBERT, Roger Charles. b 46. Ex Coll Ox BA69 MA74 Nottm Univ MEd81. St Steph Ho Ox 69. **d** 71 **p** 72. NSM Bridgwater St Mary w Chilton Trinity *B & W* 71-74; NSM Rugeley *Lich* 74-81; NSM Cannock 81-83; NSM Wednesbury St Jas and St Jo from 83; NSM Tividale from 08. *41 Stafford Road, Cannock WS11 4AF* Tel (01543) 570531 E-mail roger.gilbert@talk21.com

GILBERT, Canon Roger Geoffrey. b 37. K Coll Lon BD69 AKC69. **d** 70 **p** 71. C Walton-on-Thames *Guildf* 70-74; R St Mabyn and P-in-c Helland *Truro* 74-81; P-in-c Madron 81-86; R Falmouth K Chas 86-02; Hon Can Truro Cathl 94-02; RD Carnmarth S 94-00; Chapl to The Queen 95-02; rtd 02; Perm to Offic *Eur* from 98. *2 rue de Plouzon, 22690 Pleudihen-sur-Rance, France* Tel (0033) (2) 96 88 28 69

GILBERT, Sidney Horace. b 34. Dur Univ BA58 MA69 Univ of Wales BD62 CertEd83. St Mich Coll Llan 58. **d** 61 **p** 62. C Colwyn Bay *St As* 61-63; C Llanrhos 63-69; R Penley and Bettisfield 69-78; V Brymbo and Bwlchgwyn 78-82; Univ of Wales (Swansea) *S & B* 82-83; R Beeston Regis *Nor* 84-97; Holiday Chapl 84-91; Sen Chapl 91-97; V Llanwddyn and Llanfihangel-yng-Nghwynfa etc *St As* 97-99; rtd 99; Perm to Offic *Ches* 01-04 and from 07; Hon C Odd Rode 04-06. *Mountain View, 23 Holyrood Crescent, Wrexham LL11 2EN* Tel (01978) 358337

GILBERTSON, Canon Michael Robert. b 61. New Coll Ox BA82 MA92 Dur Univ PhD97. St Jo Coll Dur BA91. **d** 97 **p** 98. C Surbiton St Matt *S'wark* 97-00; V Stranton *Dur* from 00; AD Hartlepool from 02; Hon Can Dur Cathl from 08. *The Vicarage, 34 Westbourne Road, Hartlepool TS25 5RE* Tel (01429) 263190 Fax 400118 E-mail michael.gilbertson@durham.anglican.org

GILCHRIST, Alison Roxanne. b 62. Cranmer Hall Dur 02. **d** 04 **p** 05. C Preston St Cuth *Blackb* 04-06; C Fulwood Ch Ch 06-08; TV Marfleet *York* from 08. *St Hilda's House, 256 Annandale Road, Hull HU9 4JY* Tel (01482) 799100

GILCHRIST, David John. b 53. Mert Coll Ox BA75 MA79 Maryvale Inst PGCE08. St Jo Coll Nottm 75. **d** 79 **p** 80. C Gt Ilford St Andr *Chelmsf* 79-81; C Buckhurst Hill 81-84; Chapl Dover Coll 84-95; Chapl Brentwood Sch Essex from 95. *Mitre House, 6 Shenfield Road, Brentwood CM15 8AA* Tel (01277) 224442 E-mail djgilx@btinternet.com

GILCHRIST, Gavin Frank. b 53. AKC74. Coll of Resurr Mirfield 76. **d** 77 **p** 78. C Newbold w Dunston *Derby* 77-80; C Addlestone *Guildf* 80-84; V Blackpool St Mary *Blackb* 84-92; P-in-c Carl St Herbert w St Steph 92-97; V 97-01; V Tynemouth Cullercoats

St Paul *Newc* from 01. *The Vicarage, 53 Grosvenor Drive, Whitley Bay NE26 2JR* Tel and fax 0191-252 4916
E-mail gavingilchrist@btinternet.com

GILCHRIST, Lawrence Edward. b 29. Liv Univ BSc52. NW Ord Course 74. **d** 76 **p** 77. NSM Buxton w Burbage and King Sterndale *Derby* 76-83; V Chinley w Buxworth 83-94; rtd 94; Perm to Offic *St E* 94-03. *9 Santingley Lane, New Crofton, Wakefield WF4 1LG* Tel (01924) 860262

GILCHRIST, Spencer. b 66. QUB BA88. BTh. **d** 91 **p** 92. C Ballynafeigh St Jude *D & D* 91-97; I Connor w Antrim St Patr from 97. *Connor Rectory, Church Road, Kells, Ballymena BT42 3JU* Tel (028) 2589 1254

GILDERSLEVE, Paul. Lon Univ BD. Ridley Hall Cam. **d** 06 **p** 07. NSM Papworth *Ely* from 06. *Manor Farm, 14 Alms Hill, Bourn, Cambridge CB23 2SH* Tel (01954) 718656 *or* 718076
E-mail paulg@miscom.co.uk

GILDING, James Peter. b 33. Leeds Univ BA64. Ely Th Coll 61. **d** 63 **p** 64. C Chorley St Pet *Blackb* 63-66; C Pemberton St Fran Kitt Green *Liv* 66-69; P-in-c Terrington St John *Ely* 69-74; P-in-c Walpole St Andrew 69-74; V Elm 74-81; TR Stanground and Farcet 81-89; V Haslingfield 89-95; R Harlton 89-95; R Haslingfield w Harlton and Gt and Lt Eversden 95-96; rtd 96; Perm to Offic *York* from 98. *14 Main Street, Bishop Wilton, York YO42 1RX* Tel (01759) 368510

GILES, Anthony John. b 50. Aston Univ BSc71 Surrey Univ MSc78 Homerton Coll Cam PGCE86 CEng80 MIET80. SAOMC 01. **d** 04 **p** 05. NSM Stevenage H Trin *St Alb* from 04. *8 Norton Road, Letchworth Garden City SG6 1AB* Tel (01462) 620142 E-mail agiles6203@aol.com

GILES, Anthony Richard. b 68. St Jo Coll Nottm MA00. **d** 01 **p** 02. C Chellaston *Derby* 01-06; P-in-c Epperstone *S'well* from 06; P-in-c Gonalston from 06; P-in-c Oxton from 06; P-in-c Woodborough from 06. *The Vicarage, 12 Lingwood Lane, Woodborough, Nottingham NG14 6DX* Tel 0115-965 3727
E-mail ant.dianne@btopenworld.com

GILES, Brother. *See* SPRENT, Michael Francis

GILES, Edward Alban. b 34. Bps' Coll Cheshunt. **d** 58 **p** 59. C Colne St Bart *Blackb* 58-61; C Warrington St Paul *Liv* 61-63; C Knysna S Africa 63-66; R Eersterus w Silverton 66-70; Chapl HM Pris Camp Hill 70-75; Chapl HM Pris Stafford 75-83; Chapl HM YOI Hollesley Bay Colony 83-94; rtd 94; Sub-Chapl HM Pris Blundeston from 94; Perm to Offic *Nor* 94-00 and *St E* from 94. *The Hollies, Ferry Farm Drive, Sutton Hoo, Woodbridge IP12 3DR* Tel (01394) 387486 E-mail eag1@onetel.net.uk

GILES, Canon Eric Francis. b 34. Sarum Th Coll 61. **d** 63 **p** 64. C Plympton St Mary *Ex* 63-71; R Dumbleton w Wormington *Glouc* 71-77; P-in-c Toddington w Stanley Pontlarge 71-77; R Dumbleton w Wormington and Toddington 77-79; V Churchdown St Jo 79-99; Hon Can Glouc Cathl 95-99; rtd 99; Perm to Offic *Glouc* and *Worc* from 99. *25 Station Road, Pershore WR10 1PN* Tel (01386) 554246

GILES, Gordon John. b 66. Lanc Univ BA88 Magd Coll Cam BA95 MLitt95. Ridley Hall Cam 92. **d** 95 **p** 96. C Chesterton Gd Shep *Ely* 95-98; Min Can and Succ St Paul's Cathl 98-03; V Enfield Chase St Mary from 03; Dir Post-Ord Tr Edmonton Area from 08. *St Mary Magdalene Vicarage, 30 The Ridgeway, Enfield EN2 8QH* Tel (020) 8363 1875
E-mail vicar@saintmarymagdalene.org.uk *or* gjg@ggiles.net

GILES, Graeme John. b 56. Linc Th Coll 82. **d** 85 **p** 86. C Prestbury *Glouc* 85-88; C Paulsgrove *Portsm* 88-96; V Friern Barnet St Pet le Poer *Lon* 96-04. *30A Vine Road, East Molesey KT8 9LF* Tel 07981-708606 (mobile)
E-mail graeme@priest.com

GILES (née WILLIAMS), Mrs Gwenllian. b 34. RSCN55 SRN58 SCM60. WMMTC 88. **d** 92 **p** 94. NSM Bromsgrove St Jo *Worc* 92-00; Perm to Offic 00-03; P-in-c Clifton-on-Teme, Lower Sapey and the Shelsleys 03-04. *Highfield, Bakers Hill, Aveton Gifford, Kingsbridge TQ7 4LA* Tel (01548) 559164

GILES, Canon John Robert. b 36. Em Coll Cam BA60 MA65. Ripon Hall Ox 60. **d** 61 **p** 62. C Lowestoft St Marg *Nor* 61-65; Chapl UEA 65-72; R Kidbrooke St Jas *S'wark* 72-79; Sub-Dean Greenwich 74-79; V Sheff St Mark Broomhall 79-87; Ind Chapl 79-92; Can Res Sheff Cathl 87-92; V Lee Gd Shep w St Pet *S'wark* 92-98; rtd 98; Perm to Offic *St E* from 99. *25 The Terrace, Aldeburgh IP15 5HJ* Tel (01728) 452319

GILES, Kevin Norman. b 40. Lon Univ BD69 Dur Univ MA74. ACT ThL67 MTh78 ThD90. **d** 68 **p** 69. C Mosman St Clem Australia 68-69; C Wollongong 69; Chapl Wollongong Univ Coll 70-72; TV Chester le Street *Dur* 73-74; Chapl Tubingen Univ W Germany 75; Chapl Armidale Univ Australia 75-80; R Kensington 81-95; I Carlton N from 96. *44 Arnold Street, North Carlton Vic 3054, Australia* Tel (0061) (3) 9387 7214 *or* 9380 6387 Fax 9388 9050 E-mail giles@melbpc.org.au

GILES, Peter Michael Osmaston. b 40. Solicitor 65. S Dios Minl Tr Scheme 85. **d** 88 **p** 89. Hon C Wootton Bassett *Sarum* 88-90; Lic to RD Calne from 91; RD Calne 98-03; Chapl St Mary's Sch Calne from 00. *The Old Vicarage, Honeyhill, Wootton Bassett, Swindon SN4 7DY* Tel (01793) 852643 Fax 853191
E-mail gilesoldvic@talk21.com

GILES, The Very Revd Richard Stephen. b 40. Newc Univ BA63 MLitt88 MRTPI71. Cuddesdon Coll 64. **d** 65 **p** 66. C Higham Ferrers w Chelveston *Pet* 65-68; Perm to Offic *Ox* 69; C Oakengates *Lich* 70; C Stevenage St Geo *St Alb* 71-75; P-in-c Howdon Panns *Newc* 75-76; TV Willington 76-79; Bp's Adv for Planning *Pet* 79-87; V Pet St Jude 79-87; Par Development Officer *Wakef* 87-99; P-in-c Huddersfield St Thos 87-93; V 93-99; Hon Can Wakef Cathl 94-99; Can Th Wakef Cathl 98-99; Dean Philadelphia USA 99-08; rtd 08. *5 Lovaine Row, North Shields NE30 4HF* Tel 0191-258 7621 E-mail tynegiles@talktalk.net

GILES, Sarah Jayne. *See* MORRIS, Ms Sarah Jayne

GILES, Susan Jane. b 58. BSc. **dss** 83 **d** 92 **p** 94. Balsall Heath St Paul *Birm* 83-85; Asst Chapl Southmead Hosp Bris 86-90; Asst Chapl HM Rem Cen Pucklechurch 90-96; Asst Chapl HM Pris Bris 92-98; Chapl HM Pris Shepton Mallet 98-01; P-in-c Stockton H Trin *Dur* from 01; Chapl Ian Ramsey Sch Stockton from 01. *4 Greymouth Close, Stockton-on-Tees TS18 5LF* Tel (01642) 585749

GILES, Canon Timothy David. b 46. FCA69. Oak Hill Th Coll 88. **d** 90 **p** 91. C Ipswich St Marg *St E* 90-94; C Reigate St Mary *S'wark* 94-99; P-in-c W Wickham St Jo 99-03; V from 03; Hon Can Offa Nigeria from 06. *The Rectory, 30 Coney Hill Road, West Wickham BR4 9BX* Tel and fax (020) 8462 4001
E-mail timgiles04@googlemail.com

GILKES, Donald Martin. b 47. St Jo Coll Nottm 78. **d** 80 **p** 81. C Conisbrough *Sheff* 80-84; P-in-c Balne 84-86; P-in-c Hensall 84-86; TV Gt Snaith 86-88; V Whittle-le-Woods *Blackb* 88-02; V Normanton *Wakef* from 02. *The Vicarage, High Street, Normanton WF6 1NR* Tel and fax (01924) 893100
E-mail don.gilkes@allsaintsnormanton.org

GILKS, Peter Martin. b 51. Nottm Univ BMus72 SRN77. Ripon Coll Cuddesdon 82. **d** 84 **p** 85. C Bitterne Park *Win* 84-87; TV Basingstoke 87-93; R Abbotts Ann and Upper and Goodworth Clatford 93-98; V Boyatt Wood 98-06; V Chilworth w N Baddesley from 06; P-in-c Ampfield from 08. *The Vicarage, 33 Crescent Road, North Baddesley, Southampton SO52 9HU* Tel (023) 8073 2393 E-mail peter.gilks@ntlworld.com

GILL, Canon Alan Gordon. b 42. Sarum & Wells Th Coll 73. **d** 75 **p** 76. C Wimborne Minster *Sarum* 75-78; R Winterbourne Stickland and Turnworth etc 78-86; V Verwood 86-00; TR Gillingham 00-04; V Gillingham and Milton-on-Stour 04-08; Can and Preb Sarum Cathl 99-08; rtd 08. *1 Cheshire Close, Salisbury SP2 9JT* Tel (01722) 325239
E-mail erznmine@houseofgill.org

GILL, Mrs Carol Ann. b 42. Lady Mabel Coll TCert71. NOC 96. **d** 99 **p** 00. NSM Hanging Heaton *Wakef* 99-07; P-in-c 02-07; rtd 07. *6 Queen's Crescent, Ossett WF8 8AU* Tel (01924) 276021 Mobile 07946-038562 E-mail rev@cgill2.fsnet.co.uk

GILL, Christopher John Sutherland. b 28. Selw Coll Cam BA52 MA70. Ely Th Coll 52. **d** 54 **p** 55. C Portslade St Nic *Chich* 54-58; C Goring-by-Sea 58-60; Chapl St Edm Sch Cant 60-76; Chapl Bennett Memorial Dioc Sch Tunbridge Wells 76-92; Hon C Tunbridge Wells K Chas *Roch* 77-93; rtd 93; Perm to Offic *Roch* from 93. *Flat 1, Hurstleigh, Hurstwood Lane, Tunbridge Wells TN4 8YA* Tel (01892) 528409

GILL, David Alan. b 64. Coll of Resurr Mirfield 98. **d** 00 **p** 01. C Devizes St Jo w St Mary *Sarum* 00-04; P-in-c Brockworth *Glouc* from 04. *The Vicarage, 42 Court Road, Brockworth, Gloucester GL3 4ET* Tel (01452) 862114 E-mail frdavid@houseofgill.org

GILL, David Brian Michael. b 55. Southn Univ BTh88. Sarum & Wells Th Coll 83. **d** 86 **p** 87. C Honiton, Gittisham, Combe Raleigh, Monkton etc *Ex* 86-89; C Teignmouth, Ideford w Luton, Ashcombe etc 89-91; TV Ex St Thos and Em 91-05; RD Christianity 03-05; P-in-c Tamerton Foliot from 05; C Southway from 06; RD Plymouth Moorside from 09. *The Vicarage, 53 Whitson Cross Lane, Tamerton Foliot, Plymouth PL5 4NT* Tel (01752) 771033 E-mail david@dbmg.freeserve.co.uk

GILL, Mrs Gabrielle Mary (Gay). b 40. **d** 90 **p** 94. NSM Timperley *Ches* 90-96; rtd 96; Perm to Offic *Ches* from 97. *The Croft, 3 Harrop Road, Hale, Altrincham WA15 9BU* Tel 0161-928 1800

GILL, Gary George. b 44. Culham Coll Ox CertEd70. Cant Sch of Min 85. **d** 87 **p** 88. C Addlestone *Guildf* 87-90; C Buckland in Dover w Buckland Valley *Cant* 90-98; Chapl Buckland Hosp Dover 90-94; Chapl S Kent Hosps NHS Trust 94-98, C Birchington w Acol and Minnis Bay *Cant* 98-99; rtd 04. *9 Tooting Bec Road, London SW17 8BS* Tel (020) 8672 2179

GILL, Miss Helen Barbara. b 61. K Alfred's Coll Win BEd87. Cranmer Hall Dur. **d** 99 **p** 00. C Newc St Gabr 99-04; P-in-c Tynemouth St Jo from 04. *St John's Vicarage, St John's Terrace, Percy Main, North Shields NE29 6HS* Tel 0191-257 1819
E-mail helen@gill1999.freeserve.co.uk

✠**GILL, The Rt Revd Kenneth Edward.** b 32. Lambeth MA04 Serampore Univ Hon DD06. Hartley Victoria Coll. **d** 58 **p** 60 **c** 72. In Ch of S India 58-80; Bp Karnataka Cen 72-80; Asst Bp Newc 80-98; rtd 99; Hon Asst Bp Newc from 99. *Kingfisher Lodge, 41 Long Cram, Haddington EH41 4NS* Tel (01620) 822113 E-mail k.gill@newcastle.anglican.org

GILL, Michael John. b 59. K Coll Lon BA81 AKC81 Univ of Wales (Cardiff) BD85. St Mich Coll Llan 82. **d** 85 **p** 86. Min Can

St Woolos Cathl 85-90; Chapl St Woolos Hosp Newport 87-90; Succ Heref Cathl and C Heref St Jo 90-93; TV Ebbw Vale *Mon* 93-96; V Tonypandy w Clydach Vale *Llan* 96-09; R Cranford *Lon* from 09. *The Rectory, 34 High Street, Cranford, Hounslow TW5 9RG* Tel (020) 8897 8836

GILL, Paul Joseph. b 45. Ridley Coll Melbourne 73. **d** 74 **p** 74. C Perth St Dav Australia 74-76; C Birm St Martin 77-79; V Pype Hayes 79-89; Perm to Offic *Perth* 89-93; R Perth St Paul 93-00; Sen Chapl HM Min of Justice from 00. *118 Waddell Road, Bicton WA 6157, Australia* Tel (0061) (8) 9317 3912 or 9411 5476 Fax 9411 5542 Mobile 416-021945 E-mail gill@global.com.au

GILL, Peter Stephen. b 48. FCA79. **d** 09. NSM Exning St Martin w Landwade *St E* from 09. *11 Isinglass Close, Newmarket CB8 8HX* Tel (01638) 660335
E-mail petergill861@btinternet.com

GILL, Prof Robin Morton. b 44. K Coll Lon BD66 AKC66 Lon Univ PhD69 Birm Univ MSocSc72. **d** 68 **p** 69. C Rugby St Andr *Cov* 68-71; Papua New Guinea 71-72; Lect Th Edin Univ 72-86; Sen Lect 86-88; Assoc Dean Faculty of Div 85-88; P-in-c Edin SS Phil and Jas 73-75; P-in-c Ford *Newc* 75-87; P-in-c Coldstream *Edin* 87-92; Wm Leech Prof Applied Th Newc Univ 88-92; Mich Ramsey Prof Modern Th Kent Univ from 92; Hon Prov Can Cant Cathl from 92; AD N Downs 02-09; P-in-c Hollingbourne and Hucking w Leeds and Broomfield from 03. *Hucking Court Barn, Church Road, Hucking, Maidstone ME17 1QT* Tel (01622) 884120 E-mail r.gill@kent.ac.uk

GILL, Mrs Ruth Montcrieff. b 48. CITC 01. **d** 04 **p** 05. NSM Cloughjordan w Borrisokane etc *L & K* 04-06; NSM Birr w Lorrha, Dorrha and Lockeen from 06. *Kilgolan House, Kilcormac, Birr, Co Offaly, Republic of Ireland* Tel (00353) (57) 913 5341 Mobile 87-948 4402 E-mail ruth_gill40@hotmail.com

GILL, Miss Sandra Julie. b 67. N Riding Coll of Educn BEd90 Rolle Coll MEd01. SWMTC 03. **d** 06 **p** 07. NSM Kingsteignton and Teigngrace *Ex* from 06. *58 Furze Cap, Kingsteignton, Newton Abbot TQ12 3TF* Tel (01626) 355287
E-mail sandra.gill@btopenworld.com

GILL, Simon David. b 66. Southn Univ BSc87 PhD91. St Jo Coll Nottm BTh00. **d** 01 **p** 02. C Frinton *Chelmsf* 01-05; P-in-c Sudbury w Ballingdon and Brundon *St E* from 05. *5 Clermont Avenue, Sudbury CO10 1ZJ* Tel (01787) 375334
E-mail sallie.simon@tinyworld.co.uk

GILL, Stanley. b 34. Sarum Th Coll 66. **d** 68 **p** 69. C Ipswich St Mary at Stoke w St Pet etc *St E* 68-73 and 78-80; TV 80-82; V Bury St Edmunds St Geo 73-78; P-in-c Childe Okeford, Manston, Hammoon and Hanford *Sarum* 82-89; R The Lulworths, Winfrith Newburgh and Chaldon 89-94; R Hazelbury Bryan and the Hillside Par 94-99; rtd 99; Perm to Offic *Ex* 99-02 and *Sarum* 00-02. *8 Dulverton Hall, Esplanade, Scarborough YO11 2AR* Tel (01723) 340108

GILL, Thomas. b 21. St Aid Birkenhead 62. **d** 63 **p** 64. C Newland St Aug *York* 63-67; V Burstwick w Thorngumbald 67-78; RD S Holderness 74-78; R Brandesburton 78-80; RD N Holderness 80-86; rtd 87; Perm to Offic *York* from 87. *Bellfield, Arnold Lane East, Long Riston, Hull HU11 5HY* Tel (01964) 562282

GILL, Timothy Charles. b 66. Newc Univ BA88 Jes Coll Cam MPhil93 Leeds Univ PhD08. Westcott Ho Cam 89. **d** 92 **p** 93. C N Hull St Mich *York* 92-96; P-in-c Sculcoates St Paul w Ch Ch and St Silas 96-98; P-in-c Hull St Mary Sculcoates 96-98; V York St Luke 98-02; R Adel *Ripon* 02-08; V Roby *Liv* from 08. *The Vicarage, 11 Church Road, Liverpool L36 9TL* Tel 0151-489 1438 E-mail ttimgill@aol.com

GILL, Wilson Ernest. b 55. SAOMC. **d** 05 **p** 06. C Walton H Trin *Ox* 05-09; V Southall Em *Lon* from 09. *37 Dormers Wells Lane, Southall UB1 3HX* Tel (020) 8843 9556
E-mail wilson-gill@tiscali.co.uk

GILLARD, David John. b 66. Ridley Hall Cam 96. **d** 98 **p** 99. C Seaford w Sutton *Chich* 98-02; P-in-c Eastbourne St Elisabeth 02-06; V from 06. *The Vicarage, 11 Baldwin Avenue, Eastbourne BN21 1UJ* Tel (01323) 649728 E-mail djgillard@tiscali.co.uk

GILLARD-FAULKNER, Mrs Sarah Kate. b 80. Coll of Ripon & York St Jo BA01 Glos Univ PGCE02. St Mich Coll Llan BTh06. **d** 09. C Abertillery w Cwmtillery *Mon* from 09. *St Paul's Vicarage, Church Lane, Cwmtillery, Abertillery NP13 1LS* Tel (01495) 212364 Mobile 07900-393358
E-mail sarah_gillard@hotmail.com

GILLESPIE, David Ivan. b 68. TCD BTh01. CITC 98. **d** 01 **p** 02. C Agherton *Conn* 01-04; I Moy w Charlemont *Arm* 04-09; I Dublin St Ann and St Steph *D & G* from 09. *88 Mount Anville Wood, Lower Kilmacud Road, Dublin 14, Republic of Ireland* Tel (00353) (1) 288 0663 or 676 6814 Mobile 86-026 7528
E-mail digillespie15@aol.com

GILLESPIE, Michael David. b 41. EMMTC 86. **d** 89 **p** 90. NSM Countesthorpe w Foston *Leic* from 89. *3 Penfold Drive, Countesthorpe, Leicester LE8 3TP* Tel 0116-278 1130
E-mail mick.gillespie@btinternet.com

GILLESPIE, Canon Nancy Gillian. b 41. TCD MA68. **d** 97 **p** 98. Lib Ossory Cath and C Kilkenny w Aghour and Kilmanagh *C & O* 97-00; I Stradbally w Ballintubbert, Coraclone etc 00-09; P-in-c Maryborough w Dysart Enos and Ballyfin 02-03; Can

Ossory Cathl 06-09; rtd 09. *Address temp unknown* Tel (00353) 87-232 2574 (mobile) E-mail ngilles@iol.ie

GILLETT, Brian Alan Michael. b 42. MRICS73. Chich Th Coll. **d** 82 **p** 83. C Tupsley *Heref* 82-86; R Kingstone w Clehonger, Eaton Bishop etc 86-97; V Baltonsborough w Butleigh, W Bradley etc *B & W* 97-09; Sub-Warden of Readers Wells Adnry 00-02; rtd 09. *1 Barn Close, Somerton TA11 6PH* Tel (01458) 272738

✠**GILLETT, The Rt Revd David Keith.** b 45. Leeds Univ BA65 MPhil68. Oak Hill Th Coll 66. **d** 68 **p** 69 **c** 99. C Watford St Luke *St Alb* 68-71; Sec Pathfinders and CYFA N Area 71-74; Lect St Jo Coll Nottm 74-79; Ch of Ireland Renewal Cen 80-82; V Luton Lewsey St Hugh *St Alb* 82-88; Prin Trin Coll Bris 88-99; Hon Can Bris Cathl 91-99; Suff Bp Bolton *Man* 99-08; rtd 08; Hon Asst Bp Nor from 08. *10 Burton Close, Diss IP22 4YJ* Tel (01379) 640309 E-mail dkgillett@btinternet.com

GILLETT, Victor Henry John. b 31. Open Univ BA83 BTh87 MTh94 ThD06. Clifton Th Coll 59. **d** 62 **p** 63. C Walton Breck *Liv* 62-65; C Wednesfield Heath *Lich* 65-68; V Tipton St Paul 68-76; V Moulton *Pet* 76-92; TV Worthing Ch the King and Chapl Ramsay Hall 92-98; rtd 98; Perm to Offic *Leic* from 98. *Manoah, 50 Stoneygate Drive, Hinckley LE10 1TD* Tel (01455) 239082 E-mail vgillett@manoah.freeserve.co.uk

GILLETT, Vincent. b 30. Lon Univ BSc55 UEA MSc72 Open Univ BA01 FCollP81. Chich Th Coll 59. **d** 61 **p** 62. C Blackpool St Mich *Blackb* 61-63; Chapl Adisadel Coll Ghana 63-66; Chapl Kumasi Univ 66-72; Asst Master St Marg C of E High Sch Aigburth Liv 72-75; Asst Master Halewood Comp Sch 75-79; Hd Master St Wilfrid's Sch Ex 79-84; R Atherington and High Bickington *Ex* 84-94; V Burrington 84-94; rtd 95. *Birchy Barton Lodge, 2 Honiton Road, Exeter EX1 3EA* Tel (01392) 436393
E-mail vincent.gillett@btinternet.com

GILLEY, Margaret Mary. b 54. St Andr Univ MTheol76 Dur Univ PhD97. NEOC 97. **d** 00 **p** 01. C Birtley *Dur* 00-03; P-in-c Stockton St Mark 03; V 03-09; V Elton 03-09; Assoc P Lanchester Deanery from 09. *Moorfield Collierley Vicarage, Bourne Terrace, Stanley DH9 8QS* Tel (01207) 236974
E-mail meg.gilley@durham.anglican.org

GILLHAM, Catherine Anne. b 73. Southn Univ BN95. Trin Coll Bris BA09. **d** 09. C Kempshott *Win* from 09. *1 Lark Close, Basingstoke RG22 5PX* Tel (01256) 361747 Mobile 07873-525602 E-mail catgillham@hotmail.com

GILLHAM, Martin John. b 45. Wilson Carlile Coll IDC66 Qu Coll Birm 72. **d** 75 **p** 76. C Whitley Ch Ch *Ox* 75-78; TV Crowmarsh Gifford w Newnham Murren 78-79; TV Wallingford w Crowmarsh Gifford etc 79-83; V Kintbury w Avington 83-94; Dioc Lay Mın Adv and Warden of Readers 89-97; P-in-c W Wycombe w Bledlow Ridge, Bradenham and Radnage 94-00; R 00; Prov Chapl Third Order SSF 95-99; P-in-c Norham and Duddo *Newc* 00-04; V 04-09; P-in-c Cornhill w Carham 00-09; P-in-c Branxton 00-09; AD Norham 05-09; rtd 09. *Rose Cottage, 25 Rock Village, Rock, Alnwick NE66 3SD*
E-mail m.gillham@virgin.net

GILLHAM, Mrs Patricia Anne. b 40. Wilson Carlile Coll IDC66 Ox Min Course 90. **d** 93 **p** 94. Par Dn Kintbury w Avington *Ox* 93-94; C 94-95; C W Wycombe w Bledlow Ridge, Bradenham and Radnage 95-00; rtd 00; Perm to Offic *Newc* from 00. *Rose Cottage, 25 Rock Village, Rock, Alnwick NE66 3SD*

GILLHESPEY, Canon Clive. b 28. Lon Univ BD73. Cranmer Hall Dur 63. **d** 65 **p** 66. C Barrow St Geo w St Luke *Carl* 65-69; V Flookburgh 69-74; R Barrow St Geo w St Luke 74-81; TR 81-92; Hon Can Carl Cathl 84-92; rtd 92; Perm to Offic *Carl* from 92. *Canon's Court, 43 Holyoake Avenue, Barrow-in-Furness LA13 9LH* Tel (01229) 839041

GILLIAN, Canon Ronald Trevor. b 57. Ulster Univ MTD78 QUB BEd89 TCD BTh93. CITC 90. **d** 93 **p** 94. C Belfast St Donard *D & D* 93-96; I Aghalurcher w Tattykeeran, Cooneen etc *Clogh* from 96; Dir of Ords from 04; Preb Donaghmore St Patr Cathl Dublin from 05. *St Ronan's Rectory, Owenskerry Lane, Killarbran, Fivemiletown BT75 0SR* Tel and fax (028) 8953 1822 Mobile 07977-157637
E-mail colebrooke_clogher@hotmail.com

GILLIBRAND, John Nigel. b 60. Ox Univ BA82 MA86 Lon Univ PGCE83. St Steph Ho Ox BTh87. **d** 88 **p** 89. C Dolgellau w Llanfachreth and Brithdir etc *Ban* 88-90; C Llanbeblig w Caernarfon and Betws Garmon etc 90-91; R Ffestiniog w Blaenau Ffestiniog 91-97; V Llandegfan w Llandysilio 97-02; Nat Co-ord (Wales) Nat Autistic Soc from 02; Lic to Offic *Llan* 02-04; P-in-c Llangeler w Pen-Boyr *St D* from 04. *The Vicarage, Llangeler, Llandysul SA44 5EX* Tel (01559) 371170

GILLIBRAND, Margaret Ann Jane. b 43. **d** 01 **p** 02. OLM Deal St Leon and St Rich and Sholden *Cant* 01-04; Perm to Offic *Eur* 04-07; Asst Chapl Poitou-Charentes 07-09. *La Maison de l'Évêque, Les Picardies, 16420 Lesterts, France* Tel (0033) (5) 45 85 55 94 E-mail gillibrand@onetel.com

✠**GILLIES, The Rt Revd Robert Arthur.** b 51. Edin Univ BD77 St Andr Univ PhD91. Edin Th Coll 73. **d** 77 **p** 78 **c** 07. C Falkirk *Edin* 77-80; C Edin Ch Ch 80-84; Chapl Napier Coll 80-84; Chapl Dundee Univ 84-90; R St Andrews St Andr *St And* 91-07;

Dioc Dir of Ords 96-07; Can St Ninian's Cathl Perth 97-07; Dean St Andr 07; Bp Ab from 07. *Diocesan Office, 39 King's Crescent, Aberdeen AB24 3HP* Tel (01224) 636653 *or* 208142 Fax 636186 *or* 312141 E-mail bishop@aberdeen.anglican.org

GILLIES, Miss Sheila Jennifer. St Martin's Coll Lanc TCert71. **d** 06 **p** 07. OLM Childwall All SS *Liv* from 06. *190 Thomas Drive, Liverpool L14 3LE* Tel 0151-228 4304

GILLING, John Reginald. b 25. Trin Hall Cam BA49 MA51 Down Coll Cam MLitt55. Cuddesdon Coll 53. **d** 55 **p** 56. C Romford St Alb *Chelmsf* 55-58; C Cambridge St Mary Less *Ely* 58-62; Chapl Ch Ch Ox 62-71; V Pimlico St Mary Graham-street *Lon* 71-90; AD Westmr St Marg 79-85; rtd 90; Perm to Offic *Chich* 90-08. *St Mary's Convent, Burlington Lane, London W4 2QE* Tel (020) 8994 4641

GILLINGHAM, John Bruce. b 48. Ch Ch Ox BA69 MA74. St Jo Coll Nottm BA73. **d** 73 **p** 74. C Plymouth St Andr w St Paul and St Geo *Ex* 73-77; C Ox St Aldate w H Trin 78; Chapl Jes Coll Ox 78-88; Chapl Ox Pastorate 79-88; Dioc Missr *Birm* 88-92; R Ox St Clem from 92; AD Cowley from 07. *St Clement's Rectory, 58 Rectory Road, Oxford OX4 1BW* Tel (01865) 248735

GILLINGHAM, Michael John. b 46. Hull Univ MA90. Chich Th Coll 68. **d** 71 **p** 72. C Llanharan w Peterston-super-Montem 71-73; C Skewen 73-76; Neath Deanery Youth Chapl 74-76; Perm to Offic 79-80; TV Kirkby *Liv* 76-77; Youth Chapl Woodchurch *Ches* 77-79; Sen Youth Worker (Bedfordshire) *St Alb* 80-83; Perm to Offic 80-83; TV Sheff Manor 83-88; R Frecheville from 88; Chapl Sheff Sea Cadets from 87; Chapl RNR 90-92; Chapl S Yorks Police *Sheff* from 93. *Frecheville Rectory, Brackenfield Grove, Sheffield S12 4XS* Tel 0114-239 9555 Mobile 0774-606456 E-mail mgillingham@talktalk.net

GILLINGHAM, Mrs Stephanie Ruth. b 60. W Lon Inst of HE CertEd82 Open Univ BA86 Man Univ MEd06. NTMTC BA09. **d** 09. C Galleywood Common *Chelmsf* from 09. *39 Craiston Way, Chelmsford CM2 8ED* Tel (01245) 477818 E-mail stephanie@stmichaelsgalleywood.co.uk

GILLINGS, The Ven Richard John. b 45. St Chad's Coll Dur BA67. Linc Th Coll 68. **d** 70 **p** 71. C Altrincham St Geo *Ches* 70-75; P-in-c Stockport St Thos 75-77; R 77-83; P-in-c Stockport St Pet 78-83; TR Birkenhead Priory 83-93; V Bramhall 93-05; RD Birkenhead 85-93; Hon Can Ches Cathl 92-94; Adn Macclesfield from 94. *5 Robin's Lane, Bramhall, Stockport SK7 2PE* Tel 0161-439 2254 Fax 439 0878 E-mail richard.gillings@chester.anglican.org

GILLION, Alan Robert. b 51. LRAM. Sarum & Wells Th Coll 81. **d** 83 **p** 84. C E Dereham *Nor* 83-86; C Richmond St Mary w St Matthias and St Jo *S'wark* 86-90; P-in-c Discovery Bay Ch Hong Kong 90-98; Chapl Shek Pik Pris 90-98; Bp Kensington's Officer for Evang *Lon* 98-01; P-in-c Upper Chelsea 01-02; V 02-08; R Upper Chelsea H Trin from 08; AD Chelsea from 04. *Upper Chelsea Rectory, 97A Cadogan Lane, London SW1X 9DU* Tel (020) 7730 7270 E-mail rob.gillion@london.anglican.org

GILLIONS, Michael George. b 37. Ch Ch Ox MA65 Keele Univ PGCE74. WEMTC 93. **d** 96 **p** 97. NSM Dorrington w Leebotwood, Longnor, Stapleton etc *Heref* 96-00; NSM Condover w Frodesley, Acton Burnell etc from 00. *The Maltsters, Dorrington, Shrewsbury SY5 7JD* Tel (01743) 718550

GILLMOR, Canon Samuel Frederick. b 29. St Aid Birkenhead. **d** 62 **p** 63. C Carlow Union *C & O* 62-64; I Fenagh Union 64-68; I Maryborough w Dysart Enos 68-79; Can Ossory Cathl 78-79; Can Leighlin Cathl 78-79; I Clane w Donadea *M & K* 79-84; I Mullingar, Portnashangan, Moyliscar, Kilbixy etc 84-93; Can Meath 92-93; Can Achonry w Tubbercurry and Killoran *T, K & A* 93-03; Can Achonry Cathl 93-03; rtd 04. *Back Acre, Carrowdubh, Strandhill, Co Sligo, Republic of Ireland* Tel (00353) (71) 916 8571

GILLON, Patrick. b 51. WMMTC 05. **d** 08 **p** 09. NSM Kingstanding St Mark *Birm* from 08. *161 Beacon Road, Great Barr, Birmingham B43 7DA* Tel 0121-605 2890 Mobile 07792-635831 E-mail patrick_gillon2000@yahoo.co.uk

GILLUM, Thomas Alan. b 55. Ex Univ BSc. Cranmer Hall Dur 87. **d** 89 **p** 90. C Brompton H Trin w Onslow Square St Paul *Lon* 89-94; P-in-c Paddington St Steph w St Luke 94-04; P-in-c S Kensington St Jude 04-06; Warden Community of St Jude from 06. *St Jude's Vicarage, 18 Collingham Road, London SW5 0LX* Tel (020) 7370 1360 E-mail tom.gillum@stjudeschurch.com

GILMAN, Michael. b 35. Man Univ BA57 Sheff Univ PhD99. Ripon Hall Ox 59. **d** 61 **p** 62. C Old Trafford St Jo *Man* 61-64; C Englefield Green *Guildf* 64-69; Historic Buildings Division Gtr Lon Coun 66-86; English Heritage 86-89; rtd 00. *6 Osborne Road, Egham TW20 9RN* Tel (01784) 437106

GILMORE, David Samuel. b 70. Univ of Ulster BSc92 QUB MSSc95 Anglia Poly Univ MA05 CQSW92. EAMTC 01. **d** 03 **p** 04. C Basildon St Martin *Chelmsf* 03-04; C Danbury 04-08; R Soho St Anne w St Thos and St Pet *Lon* from 08. *St Anne's Rectory, 55 Dean Street, London W1D 6AF* Tel (020) 7437 5006 *or* tel and fax 7437 8039 E-mail davidgilmore@btinternet.com

GILMORE, Canon Henry. b 51. Man Univ BA72 TCD BD82. CITC 75. **d** 75 **p** 76. C Arm St Mark w Aghavilly 75-78; C Dublin St Patr Cathl Gp 78-81; I Stranorlar w Meenglas and

Kilteevogue *D & R* 81-84; I Achill w Dugort, Castlebar and Turlough *T, K & A* 84-91; I Moville w Greencastle, Donagh, Cloncha etc *D & R* from 91; Can Raphoe Cathl from 01. *The Rectory, Moville, Co Donegal, Republic of Ireland* Tel (00353) (74) 938 2572 E-mail hgilmore@eircom.net

GILMOUR, Ian Hedley. b 57. Ex Univ LLB Lon Univ BD. Wycliffe Hall Ox 80. **d** 83 **p** 84. C Harold Wood *Chelmsf* 83-86; C Thame w Towersey *Ox* 86-91; V Streatham Vale H Redeemer *S'wark* from 91. *The Vicarage, Churchmore Road, London SW16 5UZ* Tel (020) 8764 5808

GILPIN, Jeremy David. b 59. Pemb Coll Ox BA80 CertEd82. Trin Coll Bris BA88. **d** 88 **p** 89. C Southsea St Jude *Portsm* 88-92; R Itchingfield w Slinfold *Chich* 92-96; Chapl St Hugh's Coll Ox 97-07. *Address temp unknown*

GILPIN, Canon Richard John. b 45. Lon Univ BSc66. Wells Th Coll 67. **d** 70 **p** 71. C Davyhulme Ch Ch *Man* 70-74; Pastor Gustav Adolf Berlin EKD 74-77; R Heaton Norris Ch w All SS 77-83; R Chorlton-cum-Hardy St Clem 83-99; AD Hulme 95-99; V Norley, Crowton and Kingsley *Ches* 99-07; RD Frodsham 03-06; Hon Can Ches Cathl 04-06; rtd 07. *4 Smithy Close, Shocklach, Malpas SY14 7BX* Tel (01829) 250413 E-mail dick@gilpins.org

GILPIN, The Ven Richard Thomas. b 39. Lich Th Coll 60. **d** 63 **p** 64. C Whipton *Ex* 63-66; C Tavistock and Gulworthy 66-69; V 73-91; V Swimbridge 69-73; Preb Ex Cathl from 82; RD Tavistock 87-90; Dioc Dir of Ords 90-91; Adv for Voc and Dioc Dir of Ords 91-96; Sub Dean Ex Cathl 92-96; Adn Totnes 96-05; rtd 05. *7 The Strand, Shaldon, Teignmouth TQ14 0DL* Tel (01626) 873443 E-mail richard.gilpin2@btinternet.com

GIMSON, Francis Herbert. b 54. Reading Univ BSc79. St Jo Coll Nottm 83. **d** 86 **p** 87. C Menston w Woodhead *Bradf* 86-89; C Barnoldswick w Bracewell 89-91; V Langleybury St Paul *St Alb* 91-02; P-in-c Downton *Sarum* 02-06; P-in-c Redlynch and Morgan's Vale 04-06; TR Forest and Avon from 06. *The Vicarage, Barford Lane, Downton, Salisbury SP5 3QA* Tel (01725) 510326 E-mail fgimson@nildram.co.uk

GINEVER, Paul Michael John. b 49. AKC71. **d** 72 **p** 73. C Davyhulme Ch Ch *Man* 72-75; Australia 76-77; C Tettenhall Wood *Lich* 77-80; C Halesowen *Worc* 80; TV 80-86; P-in-c Gt Malvern Ch Ch 86-98; V S Hayling *Portsm* from 98. *The Vicarage, 34 Church Road, Hayling Island PO11 0NT* Tel (023) 9246 2914 *or* 9263 7649 E-mail parishoffice@haylinganglicans.freeserve.co.uk

GINGELL, John Lawrence. b 27. Lon Univ BD55. ALCD55. **d** 55 **p** 56. C Normanton *Derby* 55-58; C Ilkeston St Bart CD 58-61; Toc H Staff Padre 61-70; Asst Chapl S Lon Ind Miss 61-64; Lic to Offic *S'wark* 61-66; Lic to Offic *Lon* 67-70; V Somercotes *Derby* 70-72; Bp's Ind Adv 72-80; rtd 92. *18 Bournville Road, London SE6 4RN* Tel (020) 8690 0148

GINGRICH, Dale Robert. b 64. Midland Lutheran Coll (USA) BSc86 Lutheran Th Sem Gettysburg MDiv93. EAMTC 03. **d** 04 **p** 05. NSM Shingay Gp *Ely* 04-08; TV Gaywood *Nor* from 08; Dioc Ecum Officer from 09. *Church Bungalow, Gayton Road, Gaywood, King's Lynn PE30 4DZ* Tel (01553) 765167 Mobile 07766-706773 E-mail dale.gingrich@norwich.anglican.org

GINN, Daniel Vivian. b 33. Univ of Wales (Cardiff) BSc55 DipEd56. Llan Dioc Tr Scheme 79. **d** 82 **p** 83. NSM Llantwit Major and St Donat's 82-83; NSM Llantwit Major 83-02; TV 88-02; RD Llantwit Major and Cowbridge 94-02; Perm to Offic from 02. *Chenet, 24 Voss Park Drive, Llantwit Major CF61 1YE* Tel (01446) 792774

GINN, Canon Richard John. b 51. Lon Univ BD77 Dur Univ MLitt05 ACIB73 Lambeth STh85. Oak Hill Th Coll 75 Cranmer Hall Dur 77. **d** 79 **p** 80. C Hornsey Ch Ch *Lon* 79-82; C Highgate St Mich 82-85; V Westleton w Dunwich *St E* 85-08; V Darsham 85-08; P-in-c Yoxford, Peasenhall and Sibton 01-08; P-in-c Middleton cum Fordley and Theberton w Eastbridge 01-08; V Yoxmere from 08; Hon Can St E Cathl from 01. *The Vicarage, Darsham Road, Westleton, Saxmundham IP17 3AQ* Tel (01728) 648271 E-mail r.ginn@btinternet.com

GINNO, Albert Charles. b 31. CA Tr Coll 51 Lon Coll of Div 66. **d** 68 **p** 69. C Kemp Town St Mark and St Matt *Chich* 68-72; P-in-c E Hoathly 72-83; V Westham 83-96; rtd 96; Perm to Offic *Chich* from 96. *106 Sorrel Drive, Eastbourne BN23 8BJ* Tel (01323) 761479 Fax 768920

GIRARD, Canon William Nicholas Charles. b 35. Coll of Resurr Mirfield 65. **d** 67 **p** 68. C Yate *Glouc* 67-70; C Westbury-on-Trym St Alb *Bris* 70-73; Chapl K Sch Ely 73-76; V Fenstanton and Hilton *Ely* 76-85; R Balsham and P-in-c W Wickham 85-99; P-in-c Horseheath 85-96; RD Linton 93-94 and 96-99; Hon Can Ely Cathl 97-03; C Alconbury cum Weston 99-00; Hon C 00-03; C Buckworth 99-00; Hon C 00-03; C Gt w Lt Stukeley 99-00; Hon C 00-03; rtd 00; P-in-c Hamerton *Ely* 00-04; RD Leightonstone 00-02; Perm to Offic *Ely* and *Pet* from 05. *Ferrar House, Little Gidding, Huntingdon PE28 5RJ* Tel (01832) 293383

GIRLING, Andrew Martin. b 40. Em Coll Cam BA63 MA67. Wycliffe Hall Ox 63. **d** 65 **p** 66. C Luton w E Hyde *St Alb* 65-69; Chapl Hull Univ 69-75; V Dringhouses 75-00; Can and Preb York Minster 97-00; P-in-c Thurlstone w S Milton *Ex* 00-02; R

Thurlestone, S Milton, W Alvington etc 02-08; rtd 08. *2 Mead Drive, Thurlestone, Kingsbridge TQ7 3TA* E-mail sueand@talktalk.net

GIRLING, David Frederick Charles. b 33. Kelham Th Coll 49 Edin Th Coll 58. **d** 61 **p** 62. C Caister *Nor* 61-65; C Leigh St Clem *Chelmsf* 65-66; CF 66-83; V Prittlewell St Luke *Chelmsf* 83-98; rtd 98; Perm to Offic *Nor* from 98. *37 Dell Road East, Lowestoft NR33 9LA* Tel (01502) 567426

GIRLING, Francis Richard (Vincent). b 28. Worc Coll Ox BA52 MA56 Lon Univ BD65. Coll of Resurr Mirfield 55. **d** 57 **p** 59. CR from 57; rtd 98; Lic to Offic *Wakef* from 98. *House of the Resurrection, Stocks Bank Road, Mirfield WF14 0BN* Tel (01924) 494318

GIRLING, Ian John. b 53. Oak Hill Th Coll 03. **d** 05 **p** 06. C Hubberston *St D* 05-08; TV Aberystwyth from 08. *Holy Trinity Vicarage, Buarth Road, Aberystwyth SY23 1NB* Tel (01970) 617015 E-mail iangirling@yahoo.co.uk

GIRLING, Stephen Paul. b 61. Southn Univ BSc83. Trin Coll Bris BA91. **d** 91 **p** 92. C Ogley Hay *Lich* 91-95; TV S Molton w Nymet St George, High Bray etc *Ex* 95-01; RD S Molton 97-01; V Crofton *Portsm* from 01; RD Fareham from 08. *The Vicarage, 40 Vicarage Lane, Stubbington, Fareham PO14 2JX* Tel and fax (01329) 662007 E-mail girlingsp@aol.com

GIRLING, Canon Timothy Havelock. b 43. Oak Hill Th Coll 63. **d** 67 **p** 68. C Wickford *Chelmsf* 67-70; C Luton w E Hyde *St Alb* 70-74; C Luton All SS w St Pet 74-80; Chapl Luton and Dunstable Hosp 74-80; R Northill w Moggerhanger *St Alb* 80-89; Chapl Glenfield Hosp NHS Trust 89-90; Chapl Glenfrith Hosp 89-93; Chapl Univ Hosps Leic NHS Trust 00-04; Hon Can Leic Cathl 97-04; rtd 04; Chapl Leics Partnership NHS Trust from 04; Perm to Offic *Pet* 04-08 and *Leic* from 04. *36 Winton Avenue, Leicester LE3 1DH* Tel 0116-291 3795 Mobile 07879-418721 E-mail tgirling@ntlworld.com

GIRLING, Vincent. See GIRLING, Francis Richard

GIRTCHEN, John Christopher. b 54. Linc Th Coll 94. **d** 96 **p** 97. C Bourne *Linc* 96-00; V Barrow and Goxhill from 00. *The Vicarage, Thornton Street, Barrow-upon-Humber DN19 7DG* Tel (01469) 530357 E-mail jcgirtchen@lineone.net

GISBOURNE, Michael Andrew. b 65. Leeds Univ BA87 St Martin's Coll Lanc MA09. St Jo Coll Nottm BTh91. **d** 92 **p** 93. C Gateacre *Liv* 92-95; C Marton *Blackb* 95-98; V Freckleton 98-03; V Garstang St Thos from 03. *St Thomas's Vicarage, Church Street, Garstang, Preston PR3 1PA* Tel and fax (01995) 602162 E-mail michael.gisbourne@phonecoop.coop

GISBY, Vivien Barbara. b 56. **d** 08 **p** 09. NSM Sutton St Jas *Ches* from 08. *1 Fearndown Way, Macclesfield SK10 2UF* Tel (01625) 501449 E-mail vivien.gisby@btinternet.com

✠**GITARI, The Most Revd David Mukuba.** b 37. K Coll Lon BA64 BD71 Ashland Univ (USA) Hon DD83 Kent Univ Hon DD98. Trinidad Hall Bris 68. **d** 71 **p** 72 **c** 75. Gen Sec Bible Soc Kenya 71-75; Bp Mt Kenya E 75-90; Bp Kirinyaga 90-97; Dean of Angl Ch of Kenya 94-97; Abp Kenya 96-02; rtd 02. *PO Box 607, 60100 Embu, Kenya* Tel (00254) (161) 30832 Fax 30824 E-mail davidgitari@insightkenya.com

GITTINGS, Graham. b 46. Qu Coll Birm 75. **d** 78 **p** 79. C Caverswall *Lich* 78-81; C Wolverhampton St Matt 81-82; C Walthamstow St Mary w St Steph *Chelmsf* 82-83; C Dagenham 83-89; V Earl Shilton w Elmesthorpe *Leic* from 89. *The Vicarage, Maughan Street, Earl Shilton, Leicester LE9 7BA* Tel (01455) 843961 E-mail ggvicar@aol.com

GITTOES, Julie Anne. b 76. Trevelyan Coll Dur BA98 Graduate Soc Dur MA99 Selw Coll Cam PhD04. Westcott Ho Cam 99. **d** 03 **p** 04. C Hampton Hill *Lon* 03-06; V Hampton All SS from 06. *All Saints' Vicarage, 40 The Avenue, Hampton TW12 3RS* Tel (020) 8941 4424 Mobile 07941-871570 E-mail juliegittoes@googlemail.com

GIVEN, Harold Richard. b 54. Oak Hill Th Coll 75. **d** 78 **p** 79. C Belfast St Clem *D & D* 78-80; C Belfast St Donard 80-83; I Tamlaght O'Crilly Upper w Lower *D & R* 83-92; I Tamlaghtfinlagan w Myroe from 92. *Finlagan Rectory, 77 Ballykelly Road, Limavady BT49 9DS* Tel (028) 7176 2743

GLADSTONE, Robert Michael. b 60. Ch Ch Ox BA82 MA86. Wycliffe Hall Ox 92. **d** 94 **p** 95. C Trentham *Lich* 94-97; C Heigham H Trin *Nor* 97-01; V Rothley *Leic* from 01; RD Goscote from 06. *The Vicarage, 128 Hallfields Lane, Rothley, Leicester LE7 7NG* Tel 0116-230 2241 E-mail rob@rgladstone.wanadoo.co.uk

✠**GLADWIN, The Rt Revd John Warren.** b 42. Chu Coll Cam BA65 MA68. Cranmer Hall Dur. **d** 67 **p** 68 **c** 94. C Kirkheaton *Wakef* 67-71; Tutor St Jo Coll Dur 71-77; Dir Shaftesbury Project 77-82; Sec Gen Syn Bd for Soc Resp 82-88; Preb St Paul's Cathl 84-88; Provost Sheff 88-94; Angl Adv Yorkshire TV 88-94; Bp Guildf 94-03; Bp Chelmsf 03-09; rtd 09. *131A Marford Road, Wheathampstead AL4 8NH* Tel (01582) 834223

GLADWIN, Thomas William. b 35. St Alb Minl Tr Scheme 78. **d** 81 **p** 82. NSM Hertford St Andr *St Alb* 81-82; NSM Digswell and Panshanger 82-86; C 86-96; rtd 96; Perm to Offic *St Alb* from 96. *99 Warren Way, Welwyn AL6 0DL* Tel (01438) 714700

GLAISTER, James Richard. b 30. Oak Hill Th Coll 81. **d** 83 **p** 84. NSM Shrub End *Chelmsf* 83-85; NSM Lawshall w Shimplingthorne and Alpheton *St E* 85-87; NSM Lavenham 87-88; C Felixstowe St Jo 88-95; rtd 95; Perm to Offic *St E* 95-01; Carl 00-02; *Blackb* 02-05. *Les Planchettes, 61350 Saint-Roche-sur-Egrenne, France*

GLAISYER, Canon Hugh. b 30. Oriel Coll Ox BA51 MA55. St Steph Ho Ox 51. **d** 56 **p** 56. C Tonge Moor *Man* 56-62; C Sidcup St Jo *Roch* 62-64; V Milton next Gravesend Ch Ch 64-81; RD Gravesend 74-81; V Hove All SS *Chich* 81-91; Can and Preb Chich Cathl 82-91; RD Hove 82-91; P-in-c Hove St Jo 87-91; Adn Lewes and Hastings 91-97; rtd 97; Perm to Offic *Chich* 97-03; Lic to Offic from 03. *Florence Villa, Hangleton Lane, Ferring, Worthing BN12 6PP* Tel and fax (01903) 244688 Mobile 07712-317118 E-mail h.glaisyer@virgin.net

GLANVILLE-SMITH, Canon Michael Raymond. b 38. Leeds Univ MA95 AKC61. **d** 62 **p** 63. C St Marylebone St Mark w St Luke *Lon* 62-64; C Penzance St Mary *Truro* 64-68; R Worc St Andr and All SS w St Helen 68-74; Dioc Youth Chapl 68-74; V Catshill 74-80; P-in-c Worc St Martin w St Pet 80-81; TR Worc St Martin w St Pet, St Mark etc 81-86; TR Worc SE 86-90; Hon Can Worc Cathl 83-90; Can Res Ripon Cathl 90-07; RD Ripon 96-97; rtd 07. *13 Ure Bank Terrace, Ripon HG4 1JG* Tel (01765) 609428 Mobile 07792-014055 E-mail mglansmith@hotmail.com

GLARE, Michael Francis. b 28. Southn Univ BA54. St Steph Ho Ox 56. **d** 57 **p** 58. C Withycombe Raleigh *Ex* 57-62; C-in-c Goodrington CD 62-65; C Tamerton Foliot 65-70; R Weare Giffard w Landcross 70-76; RD Hartland 74-76; P-in-c Babbacombe 76-80; V 80-87; V Ilsington 87-93; rtd 93; Perm to Offic *Ex* from 94. *Poplar Lodge, 23 Albion Street, Shaldon, Teignmouth TQ14 0DF* Tel (01626) 872679

GLASBY, Alan Langland. b 46. St Jo Coll Nottm 74. **d** 77 **p** 78. C Erith St Paul *Roch* 77-80; C Moor Allerton *Ripon* 80-81; TV 81-87; V Middleton St Mary 87-92; V Bilton 92-00; V Barton and Manfield and Cleasby w Stapleton 00-04; TR E Richmond from 04. *The Vicarage, Silver Garth, Barton, Richmond DL10 6NG* Tel (01325) 377274 Mobile 07970-712484 E-mail alanglasby@btinternet.com

GLASGOW AND GALLOWAY, Bishop of. *Vacant*

GLASGOW AND GALLOWAY, Dean of. See DUNCAN, The Very Revd Gregor Duthie

GLASGOW, Provost of. See HOLDSWORTH, The Very Revd Kelvin

GLASS, Caroline Mary. b 57. Southn Univ BSc79 Open Univ MA(Fd)01 Trin Coll Bris BA06. **d** 06 **p** 07. C Redhill H Trin S'wark from 06. *3 Ringwood Avenue, Redhill RH1 2DY* Tel (01737) 766604 Mobile 07910-066837

GLASS, Kenneth William. b 23. FRSA68. **d** 57 **p** 58. C Ipswich St Matt *St E* 57-59; R Glemsford and P-in-c Somerton 59-63; V Ipswich St Nic 63-73; P-in-c Ipswich St Helen 73; R Sproughton w Burstall 74-76; Perm to Offic 76-04; rtd 83. *31 Finborough Court, Pilgrims Way, Great Finborough, Stowmarket IP14 3AY* Tel (01449) 777004

GLASS, Mrs Yvonne Elizabeth. b 58. EMMTC 94. **d** 97 **p** 98. NSM Bingham *S'well* 97-00; Asst Chapl Nottm City Hosp NHS Trust from 00. *25 Valley Road, West Bridgford, Nottingham NG2 6HG* Tel 0115-846 2125

GLASSPOOL, John Martin. b 59. Kent Univ BA83 Heythrop Coll Lon MTh95 Leeds Univ MA05 RGN87. Westcott Ho Cam 88. **d** 90 **p** 91. C Forest Gate Em w Upton Cross *Chelmsf* 90-93; P-in-c Theydon Garnon 93-95; Chapl St Marg Hosp Epping 93-99; TV Epping Distr *Chelmsf* 95-99; Asst Chapl R Free Hampstead NHS Trust 99-02; Chapl Surrey and Sussex Healthcare NHS Trust from 02. *Chaplaincy Department, East Surrey Hospital, Canada Avenue, Redhill RH1 5RH* Tel (01737) 768511 ext 6120 E-mail john.glasspool@sash.nhs.uk

GLAZEBROOK, William Leng. b 29. Edin Th Coll 76. **d** 76 **p** 77. C Dollar *St And* 76-82; Dioc Supernumerary 83; Chapl Trin Coll Glenalmond 84; P-in-c Glencarse *Bre* 84-87; Dioc Sec 84-87; Chapl HM Pris Perth 85-87; V Broughton Poggs w Filkins, Broadwell etc *Ox* 87-94; Perm to Offic *Bre* 94-08 and *St And* from 98. *10 Rose Terrace, Perth PH1 5HA* Tel (01738) 624913

GLEADALL, John Frederick. b 39. Ripon Hall Ox 66 Sarum Th Coll 69. **d** 70 **p** 71. C S Ashford Ch Ch *Cant* 70-76; P-in-c Hothfield 76-83; P-in-c Westwell 81-83; P-in-c Eastwell w Boughton Aluph 81-83; V Westwell, Hothfield, Eastwell and Boughton Aluph 84-03; rtd 03; Hon C Old Leake w Wrangle *Linc* 03-07; Chapl HM Pris N Sea Camp 07-07. *2 Pinewood Gardens, North Cove, Beccles NR34 7PG* Tel (01502) 476483

GLEAVES, John. b 39. Alsager Coll of Educn CertEd60 Westmr Coll Ox BTh03. NOC 99. **d** 00 **p** 01. NSM Alsager St Mary *Ches* 00-03; P-in-c Alvanley 03-08; rtd 08. *46 Linley Grove, Alsager, Stoke-on-Trent ST7 2PS* Tel (01270) 878169 E-mail j.gleaves@btinternet.com

GLEDHILL, Alan. b 43. Lon Univ BSc(Econ)73. NOC 81. **d** 84 **p** 85. C Knaresborough *Ripon* 84-87; P-in-c Easby 87-88; P-in-c Bolton on Swale 87-88; V Easby w Brompton on Swale and

Bolton on Swale 88-96; Teacher St Fran Xavier Sch Richmond 96-08; Perm to Offic *Ripon* 96-08; rtd 08; P-in-c Gilling and Kirkby Ravensworth *Ripon* from 08. *The Vicarage, High Street, Gilling West, Richmond DL10 5JG* Tel (01748) 824466 Mobile 07906-195390 E-mail gledhill356@btinternet.com

GLEDHILL, Canon James William. b 27. Dur Univ BA52. Westcott Ho Cam 52. **d** 56 **p** 57. C Mexborough *Sheff* 56-59; CF 59-61; C Bywell *Newc* 61-65; V Warden w Newbrough 65-98; RD Hexham 78-88; Hon Can Newc Cathl 88-98; rtd 98; Perm to Offic *Newc* from 98. *Castleview, Castlegate, Jedburgh TD8 6BD* Tel (01835) 862834

✠**GLEDHILL, The Rt Revd Jonathan Michael.** b 49. Keele Univ BA72 Hon DUniv07 Bris Univ MA75. Trin Coll Bris 72. **d** 75 **p** 76 **c** 96. C Marple All SS *Ches* 75-78; C Folkestone H Trin w Ch Ch *Cant* 78-83; V Cant St Mary Bredin 83-96; Tutor Cant Sch of Min 83-96; RD Cant 88-94; Hon Can Cant Cathl 92-96; Suff Bp Southampton *Win* 96-03; Bp Lich from 03. *Bishop's House, 22 The Close, Lichfield WS13 7LG* Tel (01543) 306000 Fax 306009 E-mail bishop.lichfield@lichfield.anglican.org

GLEESON, Robert Godfrey. b 49. Man Univ CQSW74. Qu Coll Birm 83. **d** 85 **p** 86. C Hall Green St Pet *Birm* 85-88; Asst Chapl Mental Health & Elderly Care Services Birm HA 88-90; Chapl 90-94; Chapl Moseley Hall Hosp Birm 90-94; Chapl S Birm Mental Health NHS Trust 94-03; Perm to Offic *Birm* from 03. *180 Pineapple Road, Birmingham B30 2TY* Tel 0121-444 2793 *or* 678 2002 Mobile 07966-188006

GLEN, Mrs Dawn Andrea. b 64. Liv Univ BA86. Westcott Ho Cam 07. **d** 09. C Derby Cathl from 09. *54 Park Grove, Derby DE22 1HF*

GLENDALOUGH, Archdeacon of. *See* ROUNTREE, The Ven Richard Benjamin

GLENFIELD, Samuel Ferran. b 54. QUB BA76 TCD MLitt90 MA94 Ox Univ MTh99. Wycliffe Hall Ox 88. **d** 91 **p** 92. C Douglas Union w Frankfield *C, C & R* 91-94; I Rathcooney Union 94-96; I Kill *D & G* from 96. *The Rectory, Kill o' the Grange, Blackrock, Co Dublin, Republic of Ireland* Tel (00353) (1) 280 1721 *or* tel and fax 289 6442 E-mail office@kotg.ie

GLENNON, James Joseph. b 37. St Mary's Coll Strawberry Hill TCert69 BA70. Franciscan Ho of Studies. **d** 62 **p** 63. C S Woodford *Chelmsf* 64-65; NSM Hadleigh w Layham and Shelley *St E* 88-95; C Hadleigh 95-02; rtd 02; Perm to Offic *St E* from 02. *21 Carlford Court, 112 Parliament Road, Ipswich IP4 5EL* Tel (01473) 721072

GLOUCESTER, Archdeacon of. *See* SIDAWAY, The Ven Geoffrey Harold

GLOUCESTER, Bishop of. *See* PERHAM, The Rt Revd Michael Francis

GLOUCESTER, Dean of. *See* BURY, The Very Revd Nicholas Ayles Stillingfleet

GLOVER, Alan. b 47. SWMTC 96. **d** 99 **p** 00. NSM Bideford, Northam, Westward Ho!, Appledore etc *Ex* from 99. *West Fordlands, Heywood Road, Northam, Bideford EX39 3QA* Tel (01237) 479542

GLOVER, David Charles. b 66. St Jo Coll Dur BA87 St Jo Coll Cam MPhil91. Ridley Hall Cam 87. **d** 90 **p** 91. C Wath-upon-Dearne w Adwick-upon-Dearne *Sheff* 90-92; Chapl Hatf Coll Dur 92-00; P-in-c Dur St Marg 95-00; R Dur St Marg and Neville's Cross St Jo 00-05; P-in-c Washington 05-08; R from 08; AD Chester-le-Street from 08. *27 Wroxton, Washington NE38 7NU* Tel 0191-418 7911 Mobile 07932-683745 E-mail david.glover17@btinternet.com

GLOVER, Mrs Diana Mary. b 50. Kent Univ BA73 MA75. SAOMC. **d** 01 **p** 02. C Aylesbury w Bierton and Hulcott *Ox* 01-05; P-in-c Amersham on the Hill 05-08; V from 08. *The Vicarage, 70 Sycamore Road, Amersham HP6 5DR* Tel (01494) 727553 E-mail diana.glover@btinternet.com

GLOVER, Elisabeth Ann. b 53. Univ Coll Ches BTh99. **d** 98 **p** 99. NSM Thurstaston *Ches* 98-99; C Stockton Heath 00-04; V Eastham from 04. *The Vicarage, 29 Ferry Road, Eastham, Wirral CH62 0AJ* Tel 0151-327 2182 E-mail beth.glover@tesco.net

GLOVER, Janet Mary. b 58. Natal Univ BSc79 UED80. EAMTC 98. **d** 01 **p** 02. NSM Cambridge St Phil *Ely* 01-04; NSM Histon from 04; NSM Impington from 04; Hon Asst Dir of Ords from 07. *139 Waterbeach Road, Landbeach, Cambridge CB25 9FA* Tel (01223) 864931 E-mail janet.glover@ntlworld.com

GLOVER, Canon John. b 48. Kelham Th Coll 67. **d** 71 **p** 72. C Foley Park *Worc* 71-75; TV Sutton *Liv* 75-79; P-in-c Churchill w Blakedown *Worc* 79-84; R 84-87; R Belbroughton w Fairfield and Clent 87-91; Chapl Children's Family Trust from 91; NSM Flint *St As* 92-93; R Halkyn w Caerfallwch w Rhesycae 93-97; V Rhyl w St Ann from 97; Can Cursal St As Cathl 02-09; Sacr from 08. *The Vicarage, 31 Bath Street, Rhyl LL18 3LU* Tel (01745) 353732 Fax 350075 E-mail gloverjohn@supanet.com

GLOVER, Mrs Judith Rosalind. b 53. NEOC 93. **d** 95 **p** 96. C Glendale Gp *Newc* 95-99; P-in-c Alwinton w Holystone and Alnham 99-04; R Upper Coquetdale 04-09; R Alston Moor from 09. *The Parsonage House, Brampton Road, Alston CA9 3AA* Tel (01434) 382558 E-mail judy@alwinton.net

GLOVER, Michael John Myers. b 28. Lon Univ BSc48 CEng MICE MSAICE. Cuddesdon Coll 54. **d** 56 **p** 57. C Leic St Pet 56-60; S Africa 60-73 and from 86; TR Northampton Em *Pet* 74-86; Bp's Chapl E Area Northn 73-74; rtd 93. *PO Box 447, Nongoma, 3950 South Africa* Tel (0027) (358) 310044 Fax 310457

GLOVER, Richard John. b 47. Nottm Univ BTh77. Linc Th Coll 73. **d** 77 **p** 78. C Barrow St Geo w St Luke *Carl* 77-79; C Netherton 79-80; P-in-c Addingham 80-83; P-in-c Edenhall w Langwathby and Culgaith 80-83; V Addingham, Edenhall, Langwathby and Culgaith 83-84; V Bishops Hull *B & W* 84-89; V Shilbottle *Newc* 89-96; V Whittingham and Edlingham w Bolton Chapel 96-00; P-in-c Barton, Pooley Bridge and Martindale *Carl* 00-04; Dioc Adv for Spiritual Direction and Healing 00-04; R Lower Swale *Ripon* from 04. *The Rectory, Manor Lane, Ainderby Steeple, Northallerton DL7 9PY* Tel (01609) 773346 E-mail richard@richardglover.wanadoo.co.uk

GLYN, Aneirin. b 75. St Hugh's Coll Ox MMath98 DPhil02. Oak Hill Th Coll MTh09. **d** 09. C St Helen Bishopsgate w St Andr Undershaft etc *Lon* from 09. *15 Morgan Street, London E3 5AA* Tel 07905-288078 (mobile) E-mail aneirin@gmail.com

GLYN-JONES, Alun. b 38. JP. CCC Cam BA59 MA63. Bps' Coll Cheshunt 60. **d** 61 **p** 62. C Portsea St Mary *Portsm* 61-65; Chapl Hampton Sch Middx 65-76; Hd Master Abp Tenison Gr Sch Croydon 76-88; V Twickenham St Mary *Lon* 88-01; rtd 01; Perm to Offic *B & W; Bris; Sarum* and *Eur* from 01. *23 Bainton Close, Bradford-on-Avon BA15 1SE* Tel (01225) 866874 E-mail acglynj@aol.com

GLYNN, Simon Adrian. b 59. Van Mildert Coll Dur BSc80 Univ Coll Ches BTh99. NOC 96. **d** 99 **p** 00. NSM Carr Mill *Liv* 99-04; C Burscough Bridge 04-09; P-in-c Douglas *Blackb* from 09; C Appley Bridge from 09. *The Vicarage, 5 Tan House Lane, Parbold, Wigan WN8 7HG* Tel (01257) 462350 E-mail simon@simonglynn.plus.com

GOALBY, George Christian. b 55. Leeds Univ BA77. St Jo Coll Nottm 79. **d** 81 **p** 82. C Wakef St Andr and St Mary 81-84; Asst Chapl HM Pris Wakef 84-85; Chapl HM Youth Cust Cen Deerbolt 85-87; Chapl HM Pris Frankland 87-89; V Swinderby *Linc* from 89; CF (ACF) from 04. *All Saints' Vicarage, 27 Station Road, Swinderby, Lincoln LN6 9LY* Tel and fax (01522) 868430

GOATCHER, Mrs Sara Jacoba Helena. b 46. Oak Hill NSM Course 86. **d** 89 **p** 94. NSM S Croydon Em *S'wark* 89-95; C 95-96; R Sutton St Nic 96-06; rtd 06; Perm to Offic *S'wark* 06-07; Hon C Croydon St Jo from 07. *8 Hornchurch Hill, Whyteleafe CR3 0DA* Tel (020) 8660 6198 E-mail sara@goatcher.demon.co.uk

GOATER, Michael Robert. b 46. York Univ BA MA. NOC 89. **d** 92 **p** 93. C Norton *Sheff* 92-94; V Endcliffe 94-99; Chapl Sheff Ind Miss 94-95; Assoc Chapl Sheff Hallam Univ 95-99; Asst Post-Ord Tr Officer 95-99; Dioc Voc Officer 96-99, C Stratford-upon-Avon, Luddington etc *Cov* 99-02; P-in-c Gt Shelford *Ely* from 02; RD Shelford 04-09; RD Granta from 09. *The Vicarage, 12 Church Street, Great Shelford, Cambridge CB22 5EL* Tel (01223) 843654 E-mail michael@mickthevic.org.uk

GOATLY, Ms Ruth Christine. b 50. Leic Univ LLB72 Herts Univ MA98 CQSW74. Westcott Ho Cam 08. **d** 09. NSM Boxmoor St Jo *St Alb* from 09. *23 Beechfield Road, Hemel Hempstead HP1 1PP* Tel (01442) 253102 Mobile 07961-980158 E-mail ruth@goatly.fsnet.co.uk

GOBBETT, Michael George Timothy. b 64. St Chad's Coll Dur BSc86. St Steph Ho Ox BA89 MA98. **d** 90 **p** 91. CMP from 91; C Hartlepool St Aid *Dur* 90-94; P-in-c Norton St Mich 94-95; V 95-05; TR Upper Skerne from 05. *The Rectory, 2 Durham Road, Sedgefield, Stockton-on-Tees TS21 3DW* Tel (01740) 620274 E-mail michael@mgobbett.freeserve.co.uk

GOBEY, Ian Clifford. b 48. WEMTC 94. **d** 96 **p** 97. NSM Whiteshill and Randwick *Glouc* 96-00; NSM Painswick, Sheepscombe, Cranham, The Edge etc 00-07; P-in-c Westbury-on-Severn w Flaxley, Blaisdon etc from 07. *The Vicarage, Adsett, Westbury-on-Severn GL14 1PH* Tel (01452) 760592 E-mail ian@gobey7818.fsnet.co.uk

GOBLE, Christopher. b 75. Univ of Wales (Lamp) BA96. Trin Coll Bris 96. **d** 98 **p** 99. C St Jo in Bedwardine *Worc* 98-01; P-in-c Worc St Clem 01-02; R Brington w Whilton and Norton etc *Pet* 02-08; P-in-c Ilmington w Stretton-on-Fosse etc *Cov* from 08; P-in-c Tredington and Darlingscott from 08. *The Rectory, Valenders Lane, Ilmington, Shipston-on-Stour CV36 4LB* Tel (01608) 682282 E-mail ilmingtonrectory@btinternet.com

GOBLE, Clifford David. b 41. Oak Hill Th Coll 69. **d** 72 **p** 73. C Erith St Paul *Roch* 72-76; C Tunbridge Wells St Jas 76-79; R Southfleet 79-05; RD Gravesend 94-05; Hon Can Roch Cathl 99-05; rtd 05; Perm to Offic *Cant* from 06. *15 Martindown Road, Whitstable CT5 4PX* Tel (01227) 263333

GOBLE (née DUNN), Mrs Sharon Louise. b 71. Univ of Wales (Swansea) BA93 Fitzw Coll Cam BA97. Ridley Hall Cam 95. **d** 98 **p** 99. C Malpas *Mon* 98-01; C Cyncoed 01-02; R Heyford w Stowe Nine Churches and Flore etc *Pet* 02-04; Perm to Offic 04-08; Chapl Shakespeare Hospice from 08. *The Rectory,*

Valenders Lane, Ilmington, Shipston-on-Stour CV36 4LB Tel (01608) 682282 *or* (01789) 266852
E-mail sharon.goble@btinternet.com

GODBER, Canon Francis Giles. b 48. Open Univ BA88. Ridley Hall Cam 72. **d** 75 **p** 76. C Blackheath *Birm* 75-78; C Wolverhampton St Matt *Lich* 78-80; TV Washfield, Stoodleigh, Withleigh etc *Ex* 80-85; R Shenley and Loughton *Ox* 85-88; TR Watling Valley 88-96; Chapl Heatherwood and Wexham Park Hosp NHS Trust 96-00; P-in-c Geddington w Weekley *Pet* from 00; Dioc Ecum Officer from 00; Can Pet Cathl from 03. *The Vicarage, 25 West Street, Geddington, Kettering NN14 1BD* Tel (01536) 742200 E-mail gilbar@telco4u.net

GODDARD, Andrew John. b 67. St Jo Coll Ox BA88 MA93 DPhil96. Cranmer Hall Dur 94. **d** 96 **p** 97. C Cogges and S Leigh *Ox* 96-99; Tutor Wycliffe Hall Ox 99-08; Tutor Trin Coll Bris from 08. *47 Upper Cranbrook Road, Bristol BS6 7UR* Tel 0117-968 0222 E-mail andrew.goddard@trinity-bris.ac.uk

GODDARD, Canon Charles Douglas James. b 47. CITC 67. **d** 70 **p** 71. C Orangefield *D & D* 70-73; C Stormont 73-75; Miss to Seafarers from 75; Sen Chapl and Sec N Ireland from 77; Can Belf Cathl from 05. *7 Abercorn Drive, Carnreagh Road, Hillsborough BT26 6LB* Tel (028) 9268 3592 *or* 9075 1131 E-mail flying@angel.dnet.co.uk

GODDARD, Christopher. b 45. Sarum & Wells Th Coll 79. **d** 81 **p** 82. C Whitehaven *Carl* 81-83; C Barrow St Geo w St Luke 83-85; P-in-c Hayton St Mary 85-90; V Brigham 90-98; V Mosser 90-98; Perm to Offic 00-03; Hon C Cockermouth w Embleton and Wythop 03-05; TV Cockermouth Area from 05. *The Vicarage, 14 Harrot Hill, Cockermouth CA13 0BL* Tel (01900) 824383
E-mail chris.goddard@parishofcockermouth.org.uk

GODDARD, Derek George. b 38. St Martin's Coll Lanc BA97 CEng FIMechE FIMarEST FCMI. Cranmer Hall Dur 94 CBDTI 95. **d** 97 **p** 98. NSM Windermere St Mary and Troutbeck *Carl* 97-01; P-in-c Leven Valley 01-06; rtd 06; P-in-c Palermo w Taormina *Eur* 06-09. *Address temp unknown*
E-mail d.d.goddard@talk21.com

GODDARD, Mrs Doris. b 48. St Mary's Coll Twickenham CertEd70 Open Univ BA80. S'wark Ord Course 93. **d** 96 **p** 97. Chapl John Nightingale Sch W Molesley 96-00; NSM Addlestone *Guildf* 96-98; NSM Botleys and Lyne 98-04; NSM Long Cross 98-04; NSM Chertsey, Lyne and Longcross 04-05; NSM Blackdown *B & W* 05-09; P-in-c Puriton and Pawlett from 09. *The Vicarage, 1 The Rye, Puriton, Bridgwater TA7 8BZ* Tel (01823) 683500 E-mail rev.doris.goddard@btinternet.com

GODDARD, Douglas. *See* GODDARD, Canon Charles Douglas James

GODDARD, Mrs Elaine Clare. b 53. K Alfred's Coll Win CertEd78. WEMTC 96. **d** 99 **p** 00. C Leominster *Heref* 99-04; P-in-c St Weonards 04-07; R from 07; RD Ross and Archenfield from 07. *The Vicarage, Mount Way, St Weonards, Hereford HR2 8NN* Tel (01981) 580307 E-mail email@ecgoddard.co.uk

GODDARD, Elisabeth Ann. b 64. St Hugh's Coll Ox BA89 MA99. Cranmer Hall Dur 94. **d** 96 **p** 97. C Cogges and S Leigh *Ox* 96-99; Chapl Jes Coll Ox 99-04; Tutor Wycliffe Hall Ox 04-08; Hon C Ox St Andr 04-08. *47 Upper Cranbrook Road, Bristol BS6 7UR* Tel 0117-923 2631
E-mail goddardea@gmail.com

GODDARD, Canon Giles William. b 62. Clare Coll Cam MA84. S'wark Ord Course 92. **d** 95 **p** 96. C N Dulwich St Faith *S'wark* 95-98; TR Walworth St Pet 98-09; AD S'wark and Newington 02-07; P-in-c Waterloo St Jo w St Andr from 09; Hon Can S'wark Cathl from 07. *St John's Vicarage, 1 Secker Street, London SE1 8UF* Tel (020) 7633 9819
E-mail gileswgoddard@googlemail.com

GODDARD, Canon Harold Frederick. b 42. Keble Coll Ox BA63 MA69. Cuddesdon Coll 64. **d** 66 **p** 67. C Birm St Pet 66-70; Chapl Dudley Road Hosp Birm 66-70; Chapl HM Pris Birm 68-70; C Alverstoke *Portsm* 70-72; Chapl Gosport Cottage Hosp Portsm 70-72; Chapl HM Det Cen Haslar 70-72; P-in-c Portsea St Geo CD *Portsm* 72-76; Chapl Portsm Cathl 73-76; P-in-c Stoke Prior *Worc* 76-78; P-in-c Wychbold and Upton Warren 77-78; R Stoke Prior, Wychbold and Upton Warren 78-80; Chapl Forelands Orthopaedic Hosp *Worc* 77-80; Chapl R Marsden Hosp Lon and Surrey 80-83; R Martley and Wichenford *Worc* 83-88; P-in-c Knightwick w Doddenham, Broadwas and Cotheridge 85-88; R Martley and Wichenford, Knightwick etc 89-90; Bp's Adv on Min of Healing 84-99; Chapl St Rich Hospice *Worc* 87-94; RD Martley and Worc W 88-90; Chapl Kidderminster Gen Hosp 90-92; P-in-c Hallow *Worc* 91-92; P-in-c Sedgeberrow w Hinton-on-the-Green 92-00; Chapl Evesham Community Hosp *Worc* 93-00; Chapl Worcs Community Healthcare NHS Trust 97-00; Co-ord W Midl Healing Advisers 94-99; RD Evesham *Worc* 97-00; TR Kidderminster St Jo and H Innocents 00-08; Hon Can Worc Cathl 03-08; rtd 08; Perm to Offic *Worc* from 08. *1 Springfield House, Como Road, Malvern WR14 2HS* Tel (01684) 563350 Mobile 07768-106287 E-mail hgoddard@hotmail.com

GODDARD, John David. b 42. Guy's Hosp Medical Sch MB, BS64 MRCP73. **d** 03 **p** 04. OLM Morden *S'wark* from 03. *58 Queen Mary Avenue, Morden SM4 4JR* Tel (020) 8540 5082 E-mail jdg13@blueyonder.co.uk

✠**GODDARD, The Rt Revd John William.** b 47. St Chad's Coll Dur BA69. **d** 70 **p** 71 **c** 00. C S Bank *York* 70-74; C Cayton w Eastfield 74-75; V Middlesbrough Ascension 75-82; RD Middlesbrough 81-87; V Middlesbrough All SS 82-88; Can and Preb York Minster 87-88; Vice-Prin Edin Th Coll 88-92; TR Ribbleton *Blackb* 92-00; Suff Bp Burnley from 00; Bp's Adv on Hosp Chapls from 01; Co-ord for Interfaith Work from 07. *All Saints House, Padiham Road, Burnley BB12 6PA* Tel (01282) 470360 Fax 470361 E-mail bishop.burnley@ntlworld.com

GODDARD, Mrs Margaret. **d** 01 **p** 02. NSM Cockermouth Area *Carl* from 01. *The Vicarage, 14 Harrot Hill, Cockermouth CA13 0BL* Tel (01900) 824383 *or* 826151
E-mail margaret@cateam.org.uk

GODDARD, Ms Marion. b 54. Sarum & Wells Th Coll 87. **d** 89 **p** 94. Par Dn Lewisham St Swithun *S'wark* 89-94; C 94-95; TV Thamesmead 96-04; rtd 04. *1 Hollows Close, Salisbury SP2 8JU* Tel (01722) 338562

GODDARD, Matthew Francis. b 45. Kelham Th Coll 65. **d** 69 **p** 70. C Mansfield St Mark *S'well* 69-72; C Northolt Park St Barn *Lon* 72-78; P-in-c Acton Green St Pet 78-87; R Norwood St Mary 87-96. *27 Hounslow Avenue, Hounslow TW3 2DZ* Tel (020) 8230 6591

GODDARD, Mrs Pamela Gay. b 53. LSE BSc(Econ)74 CQSW77. SAOMC 95 EAMTC 97. **d** 98 **p** 99. C New Catton St Luke w St Aug *Nor* 98-03; Perm to Offic 03-05; NSM Hamworthy *Sarum* 05-07; C Throop *Win* 07-08; C Hamworthy *Sarum* from 08. *The Rectory, 1 St Michael's Close, Poole BH15 4QT* Tel (01202) 674878 E-mail pam.goddard@googlemail.com

GODDARD, Mrs Rosemary Joy. b 48. Philippa Fawcett Coll CertEd69. EAMTC 00. **d** 03 **p** 04. C Linc St Nic w St Jo Newport 03-05; P-in-c Bicker 05-08; P-in-c Donington 08; P-in-c Fleet w Gedney from 08; P-in-c Holbeach Marsh from 08. *The Rectory, Church End, Fleet, Spalding PE12 8NQ* Tel 07740-203149 (mobile) E-mail rosemaryjg@aol.com

GODDARD, Stuart David. b 53. Cen Sch of Art Lon BA76 Middx Poly PGCE82. Trin Coll Bris 91. **d** 93 **p** 94. C Watling Valley *Ox* 93-97; P-in-c Bowthorpe *Nor* 97-00; TV 00-05; P-in-c Hamworthy *Sarum* from 05. *The Rectory, 1 St Michael's Close, Poole BH15 4QT* Tel (01202) 674878
E-mail stuart@goddard7.fsbusiness.co.uk

GODDARD, Canon Sydney Thomas. b 16. St Aid Birkenhead 46. **d** 49 **p** 50. C Ravenhead *Liv* 49-52; C St Helens St Helen 52-55; V Widnes St Ambrose 55-59; Warden World Friendship Ho 59-83; Chapl Liv Maternity Hosp 59-81; V Liv St Sav 59-71; Hon Can Liv Cathl 69-83; rtd 83; Perm to Offic *Ban* from 84. *Ynys Thomas, Bronaber, Trawsfynydd, Blaenau Ffestiniog LL41 4UR* Tel (01766) 540413

GODDARD, Trevor Paul. b 63. NTMTC 03. **d** 06 **p** 07. NSM Kensal Rise St Mark and St Martin *Lon* from 06. *17 Odessa Road, London NW10 5YJ* Tel (020) 8357 2731 Mobile 07957-482926 E-mail trevorgoddard@mac.com

GODDEN, Peter David. b 47. Leeds Univ BA69 MA04 ARCO70. Linc Th Coll 85. **d** 87 **p** 88. C Bearsted w Thurnham *Cant* 87-90; C Hykeham *Linc* 90-91; TV 91-95; P-in-c Linc St Faith-at-Gowts and St Andr 95-99; Hon PV Linc Cathl 90-99; R Armthorpe *Sheff* 99-00; R Owmby Gp *Linc* from 00; RD Lawres 05-06 and from 09; P-in-c Spring Line Gp from 08. *The Vicarage, Main Street, Hackthorn, Lincoln LN2 3PF* Tel (01673) 860856 E-mail peter@owmbygroup.co.uk

GODDEN, Timothy Richard James. b 62. Univ Coll Lon BA84. St Jo Coll Nottm 89. **d** 89 **p** 90. C Tulse Hill H Trin and St Matthias *S'wark* 89-93; TV Horsham *Chich* 93-01; TR Bishopsworth and Bedminster Down *Bris* from 01. *St Peter's Vicarage, 61 Fernsteed Road, Bristol BS13 8HE* Tel and fax 0117-964 2734 E-mail tim@cgodden.fsnet.co.uk

GODECK, John William George. b 30. Chich Th Coll 57. **d** 60 **p** 61. C Wadhurst *Chich* 60-62; C Tidebrook 60-62; C Eastbourne 62-63; R Bondleigh *Ex* 63-78; R Zeal Monachorum 63-78; P-in-c Broadwoodkelly 65-67; R 68-78; R Dunchideock and Shillingford St George w Ide 78-96; RD Kenn 83-89; rtd 96; Perm to Offic *Ex* from 96. *Boxgrove, 6 Barley Lane, Exeter EX4 1TE* Tel (01392) 424224

GODFREY, Ann Veronica. *See* MacKEITH, Mrs Ann Veronica

GODFREY, Canon Brian Ernest Searles. b 37. Lon Univ BSc60 MSc63 PhD72. S'wark Ord Course 78. **d** 81 **p** 82. NSM Hayes *Roch* 81-86; C 86-88; R Kingsdown 88-93; R Sundridge w Ide Hill 93-02; RD Sevenoaks 95-00; Hon Can Roch Cathl 99-03; rtd 02; Perm to Offic *Sarum* from 03. *Rowans, Kingcombe Road, Toller Porcorum, Dorchester DT2 0DG* Tel (01300) 320833 E-mail godfrey@centrenet.co.uk

GODFREY, David Samuel George. b 35. CITC 64. **d** 66 **p** 67. C Londonderry Ch Ch *D & R* 66-68; I Tomregan w Drumlane *K, E & A* 68-72; I Cloonclare 72-79; I Templebreedy *C, C & R* 79-85; I Bray *D & G* 85-97; Can Ch Ch Cathl Dublin 95-97; Dean Kilmore *K, E & A* 97-04; I Kilmore w Ballintemple 97-04;

Preb Mulhuddart St Patr Cathl Dublin 01-04; rtd 04. *37 Earlsfort Meadows, Earlsfort, Lucan, Co Dublin, Republic of Ireland* Tel (00353) (1) 624 1906   Mobile 86-238 9686
E-mail dgodfrey@iol.ie

GODFREY, Edward Colin. b 30. Wells Th Coll 63. **d** 65 **p** 66. C Lyndhurst and Emery Down *Win* 65-69; C Paignton Ch Ch *Ex* 69-73; V Stockland w Dalwood 73-77; Chapl HM Pris Man 77-78; Chapl HM Pris Cant 78-83; Chapl HM Pris Highpoint 83-85 and 90-95; Chapl HM YOI Glen Parva 85-90; rtd 95; Perm to Offic *St E* from 95. *11 De Burgh Place, Clare, Sudbury CO10 8QL*   Tel (01787) 277690

✠**GODFREY, The Rt Revd Harold William.** b 48. AKC71. St Aug Coll Cant 71. **d** 72 **p** 73 **c** 87. C Warsop *S'well* 72-75; TV Hucknall Torkard 75-86; Dioc Ecum Officer 81-82; USPG from 86; R and Adn Montevideo and Can Buenos Aires 86-88; Asst Bp Argentina and Uruguay 87-88; Bp Uruguay 88-98; Bp Peru from 98. *Calle Alcal 336, Urb la Castellana, Santiago de Surco, Lima 33, Peru*   Tel and fax (0051) (1) 422 9160 *or* 448 4855   E-mail wgodfrey@amauta.rcp.net.pe

GODFREY, Ian. b 56. **d** 01 **p** 02. NSM Mill Hill Jo Keble Ch *Lon* from 01. *Sirocco, 40 Hillside Grove, London NW7 2LR* Tel (020) 8959 5123 Fax 8959 1434 E-mail igodfrey@ukonline.co.uk

GODFREY, Jennifer Olwen. **d** 02 **p** 03. C Lasswade *Edin* 02-03; NSM from 03; C Dalkeith 02-03; NSM from 03. *131 Newbattle Abbey Crescent, Dalkeith EH22 3LP* Tel 0131-660 6145 Mobile 07812-923159 E-mail jenniegodfrey@fsmail.net

GODFREY, John Frederick. b 31. Lon Univ LLB53 AKC54 Solicitor 57. Cuddesdon Coll 59. **d** 61 **p** 62. C Battersea St Luke *S'wark* 61-65; Min Reigate St Phil CD 65-72; Public Preacher *St Alb* 73-03; Perm to Offic from 03. *3 Davidge Place, Knotty Green, Beaconsfield HP9 2SR* Tel (01494) 689925 Fax 672930

GODFREY, Kesari Feneka. b 73. Nesamony Memorial Chr Coll Marthandam BSc93 United Th Coll Bangalore BD99. Princeton Th Sem ThM01. **p** 05. Perm to Offic *Birm* 05-07; C Bridlington Priory *York* from 07. *20 The Lawns, Bridlington YO16 6FL* Tel (01262) 675919   Mobile 07709-947056
E-mail revdgodfrey@yahoo.co.uk

GODFREY, Matthew Fenton. b 69. Univ Coll Dur BA91 K Coll Lon MA94. Ripon Coll Cuddesdon MTh04. **d** 04 **p** 05. C Bodmin w Lanhydrock and Lanivet *Truro* 04-09. *Address temp unknown* E-mail nitrogen_narcosis@hotmail.com

GODFREY, Michael. b 49. K Coll Lon BD70 Wolv Univ PGCE97. St Aug Coll Cant AKC72. **d** 72 **p** 73. C Birtley *Dur* 72-75; Ind Chapl 76-79; TV Bilston *Lich* 79-86; TV Wolverhampton 86-93; Chapl Black Country Urban Ind Miss 79-86; Team Ldr 86-93; Preb Lich Cathl 87-93; Dioc Rural Officer *Worc* 04-08 and *Cov* 05-08; R Newport Pagnell w Lathbury and Moulsoe *Ox* from 08. *The Rectory, 81 High Street, Newport Pagnell MK16 8AB* Tel (01908) 611145
E-mail rector_08@btinternet.com

GODFREY, Michael James. b 50. Sheff Univ BEd77. St Jo Coll Nottm 79. **d** 82 **p** 83. C Walton H Trin *Ox* 82-86; C Chadderton Ch Ch *Man* 86-91; V Woodlands *Sheff* 91-03; V Wythall *Birm* from 03. *15 Hawthorne Drive, Hollywood, Birmingham B47 5QT* Tel 0121-430 2775 E-mail mikegodfrey@btinternet.com

GODFREY, Myles. *See* GODFREY, Rumley Myles.

GODFREY, Nigel Philip. b 51. Ripon Coll Cuddesdon BA78 MA84 Lon Guildhall Univ MBA00 MRTPI76. Ripon Coll Cuddesdon 77. **d** 79 **p** 80. C Kennington St Jo w St Jas *S'wark* 79-89; Community of Th Servant 84-93; V Brixton Road Ch Ch *S'wark* 89-01; Prin OLM Scheme 01-07; Chapl S'wark Cathl 02-07; V German *S & M* from 07; Sub-Dean St German's Cathl from 07. *14 The Net, Mariners Wharf, Peel, Isle of Man IM5 1AR* Tel (01624) 851325

GODFREY, Mrs Patricia Ann. b 54. SEITE 01. **d** 04 **p** 05. NSM Dover St Mary *Cant* from 04. *8 Longfield Road, Dover CT17 9QU* Tel (01304) 206019
E-mail trish@godfrey88.screaming.net

GODFREY (née ROGERS), Mrs Pauline Ann. b 58. LMH Ox BA79 MA83 Ox Univ Inst of Educn PGCE80. S Dios Minl Tr Scheme 89. **d** 92 **p** 94. NSM Headley All SS *Guildf* 92-96; C 96-99; Past Tutor Local Min Progr from 96; P-in-c Wyke 99-01; V from 01. *Wyke Vicarage, Guildford Road, Normandy, Guildford GU3 2DA* Tel (01483) 811332
E-mail pag@yerfdog1.screaming.net *or* p.a.g@talktalk.net

GODFREY, Rumley Myles. b 48. S'wark Ord Course. **d** 83 **p** 84. NSM Dorchester *Ox* from 83. *The Old Malthouse, Warborough OX10 7DY* Tel (01865) 858627
E-mail myles@warborough.fsnet.co.uk

GODFREY, Mrs Sarah Joy. b 64. Southn Univ BSc85 Bath Univ PGCE86. STETS 02. **d** 05 **p** 06. NSM Puddletown, Tolpuddle and Milborne w Dewlish *Sarum* from 05. *Bankfield House, Pound Lane, Dewlish, Dorchester DT2 7LZ* Tel (01258) 839067 E-mail sarah.godfrey@tiscali.co.uk

GODFREY, Canon Simon Henry Martin. b 55. TD00. K Coll Lon BD80 AKC80. St Steph Ho Ox 80. **d** 81 **p** 82. C Kettering SS Pet and Paul 81-84; R Crick and Yelvertoft w Clay Coton and Lilbourne 84-89; V Northampton All SS w St Kath 89-98; R Northampton All SS w St Kath and St Pet 98-09; Sen Chapl

Malta and Gozo *Eur* from 09; Can and Chan St Paul's Pro-Cathl Valetta from 09. *St Paul's Anglican Pro-Cathedral, Independence Square, Valetta VLT12, Malta GC* Tel (00356) 2122 5714 Fax 2122 5867 E-mail simonhmgodfrey@googlemail.com

GODFREY, Stanley William. b 24. CEng MIET67. Qu Coll Birm 71. **d** 74 **p** 74. C Sutton Coldfield St Chad *Birm* 74-78; Hon C Handsworth St Andr 78-86; Hon C Worc City St Paul and Old St Martin etc 86-89; Hon C Droitwich Spa 89-96; Perm to Offic from 96. *2 The Pippins, Eckington, Pershore WR10 3PY* Tel (01386) 751184

GODIN, Mrs Mary Louise. b 42. SRN64 QN66. Oak Hill NSM Course 89. **d** 92 **p** 94. NSM Surbiton Hill Ch Ch *S'wark* 92-97; Chapl Kingston and Distr Community NHS Trust 97-01; Team Chapl SW Lon and St George's Mental Health NHS Trust 01-03; Chapl Taunton and Somerset NHS Trust from 03. *Taunton and Somerset NHS Trust, Musgrove Park Hospital, Taunton TA1 5DA* Tel (01823) 333444 ext 2515
E-mail mary.godin@tst.nhs.uk

GODSALL, Canon Andrew Paul. b 59. Birm Univ BA81. Ripon Coll Cuddesdon 86. **d** 88 **p** 89. C Gt Stanmore *Lon* 88-91; C Ealing All SS 91-94; V Hillingdon All SS 94-01; Dir of Ords Willesden Area 99-01; Bp's Chapl and Asst *Ex* 01-06; Dioc Dir of Min from 06; PV Ex Cathl 04-06; Can Res and Chan Ex Cathl from 06. *12 The Close, Exeter EX1 1EZ* Tel (01392) 275756
E-mail andrew.godsall@exeter.anglican.org

GODSALL, Canon Ralph Charles. b 48. Qu Coll Cam BA71 MA75. Cuddesdon Coll 73. **d** 75 **p** 76. C Sprowston *Nor* 75-78; Chapl Trin Coll Cam 78-84; V Hebden Bridge *Wakef* 84-93; V Westmr St Steph w St Jo *Lon* 93-01; Can Res Roch Cathl 01-08; rtd 08; PV Westmr Abbey from 08. *39 Vincent Square, London SW1P 2NP* Tel (020) 7976 5899   Mobile 07786-959540
E-mail canonralph@hotmail.co.uk

GODSELL, David Brian. b 40. Lon Univ BA62. Coll of Resurr Mirfield 65. **d** 67 **p** 68. C Middlesbrough All SS *York* 67-73; CMP from 69; C Stainton-in-Cleveland *York* 73-75; V Byker St Ant *Newc* 75-90; P-in-c Brandon *Dur* 90-94; V 94-04; V Brandon and Ushaw Moor 04-05; rtd 05; Hon C Brandon and Ushaw Moor *Dur* from 05; Chapl St Cuthb Soc Dur from 05. *The Clergy House, Sawmill Lane, Brandon, Durham DH7 8NS* Tel 0191-378 0845

GODSELL, Kenneth James Rowland. b 22. Birm Coll of Educn Dip Teaching50. Qu Coll Birm 75. **d** 76 **p** 77. Sen Lect Westhill Coll of HE Birm 74-85; Hon C Selly Hill St Steph *Birm* 76-81; Hon C Selly Park St Steph and St Wulstan 81-90; rtd 90; Lic to Offic *Birm* 90-96; Perm to Offic *Worc* from 96. *The Quest, Dock Lane, Tewkesbury GL20 7LN* Tel (01684) 772469

GODSON, Alan. b 31. Chi Coll Cam BA61 MA65. Clifton Th Coll 61. **d** 63 **p** 64. C Preston All SS *Blackb* 63-66; Lic to Offic *Man* 66-69; Asst Chapl Emb Ch Paris 69; Dioc Ev *Liv* 69-01; P in c Edge Hill St Mary 72-78; V 78-01; rtd 01; Perm to Offic *Liv* from 01. *28 Handley Court, Aigburth, Liverpool L19 3QS* Tel 0151-427 0255

GODSON, Mark Rowland. b 61. K Coll Lon BD83 AKC83 CertEd84. Linc Th Coll 84. **d** 86 **p** 87. C Hurst Green *S'wark* 86-88; C Fawley *Win* 88-90; TV Wimborne Minster and Holt *Sarum* 90-95; Chapl Forest Healthcare NHS Trust Lon 96-00; P-in-c Bicton, Montford w Shrawardine and Fitz *Lich* 00-06; Chapl Shropshire Co Primary Care Trust 01-06; TR Fordingbridge and Breamore and Hale etc *Win* from 06. *The Rectory, 71 Church Street, Fordingbridge SP6 1BB* Tel (01425) 650855 E-mail team.rector@gmail.com

GODWIN, Canon David Harold. b 45. Kelham Th Coll 67. **d** 71 **p** 72. C Camberwell St Phil and St Mark *S'wark* 71-75; Asst Chapl The Lon Hosp (Whitechapel) 75-79; Chapl R E Sussex Hosp Hastings 79-86; Chapl Over Hosp Glouc 86-92; Chapl Glos R Hosp 86-94; Chapl Glos R Hosp NHS Trust 94-02; Chapl Glos Hosps NHS Foundn Trust 02-05; Hon Can Glouc Cathl 03-05; rtd 05; Perm to Offic *Glouc* from 05. *Mews Two, Wallsworth Hall, Sandhurst Lane, Sandhurst, Gloucester GL2 9PA* Tel (01452) 730435
E-mail davidhgodwin@hotmail.co.uk

GODWIN, Canon Michael Francis Harold. b 35. Nottm Univ BSc57. Ely Th Coll 59. **d** 61 **p** 62. C Farnborough *Guildf* 61-65; V Epsom St Barn 66-85; V Bramley and Grafham 85-98; Hon Can Guildf Cathl 89-98; rtd 00. *14 Lemmington Way, Horsham RH12 5JG* Tel (01403) 273411

GOFF, Philip Francis Michael. b 52. K Coll Lon BD73 AKC73 FBS00 FSA08. St Aug Coll Cant 74. **d** 75 **p** 76. C Ruislip St Martin *Lon* 75-79; Chapl Aldenham Sch Herts 79-82; V Tokyngton St Mich *Lon* 82-89; In RC Ch 89-91; Primary Care Cllr NHS 91-98; Perm to Offic *Lon* 99-00; Chapl to Bp Edmonton 00-04; P-in-c Highgate St Aug from 04; Asst Dir Post-Ord Tr Edmonton Area 03-06. *St Augustine's Vicarage, Langdon Park Road, London N6 5QG* Tel (020) 8374 6985 Mobile 07768-920506 E-mail phildress@blueyonder.co.uk

GOFTON, Canon William Alder. b 31. Dur Univ BA54. Coll of Resurr Mirfield 59. **d** 61 **p** 62. C Benwell St Aid *Newc* 61-64; C N Gosforth 64-69; V Seaton Hirst 69-77; V Newc H Cross 77-89;

RD Newc W 85-89; Hon Can Newc Cathl 88-96; R Bolam w Whalton and Hartburn w Meldon 89-96; P-in-c Nether Witton 89-95; V 95-96; Chapl Kirkley Hall Coll 90-96; rtd 96; Perm to Offic *Newc* from 96. *4 Crossfell, Ponteland, Newcastle upon Tyne NE20 9EA* Tel (01661) 820344 E-mail aggofton@yahoo.co.uk

GOGGIN, Philip Frederick de Jean. b 46. Rhodes Univ BA66 Lon Univ MA73 Keele Univ PhD89 Leeds Univ MA05. NOC 03. **d** 05 **p** 06. NSM Sandbach Heath w Wheelock *Ches* 05-07; P-in-c Leighton-cum-Minshull Vernon from 07. *The Vicarage, Middlewich Road, Minshull Vernon, Crewe CW1 4RD* Tel (01270) 522213 E-mail gail.philip@virgin.net

GOLBOURNE, Winston George. b 30. Univ of W Indies BA53. Virginia Th Sem STM69 Sarum & Wells Th Coll 71. **d** 73 **p** 74. C Bitterne Park *Win* 73-76; Jamaica 76-79; C Handsworth St Andr *Birm* 79-83; V Perry Hill St Geo *S'wark* 83-00; rtd 00; Perm to Offic *Roch* and *S'wark* from 00. *17 Bromley College, London Road, Bromley BR1 1PE*

GOLD, Guy Alastair Whitmore. b 16. TD50. Trin Coll Cam BA38 MA48. Qu Coll Birm 55. **d** 55 **p** 56. C Prittlewell St Pet *Chelmsf* 55-57; Bp's Dom Chapl 58-61; R Wickham Bishops 62-69; R Hasketon *St E* 69-76; rtd 76; Perm to Offic *St E* 76-89. *Grove Court, Beech Way, Woodbridge IP12 4BW* Tel (01394) 383277

GOLDEN, Stephen Gerard. b 61. Lon Univ BA84. St Steph Ho Ox 84. **d** 86 **p** 87. C Reading St Luke w St Bart *Ox* 86-90; CF 90-94; Perm to Offic *Lon* from 07. *35 Lonsdale Road, London SW13 9JP* Tel (020) 8748 5306 E-mail sggolden@btinternet.com

GOLDENBERG, Ralph Maurice. b 45. City Univ FBCO67 FBOA67. Trin Coll Bris 88. **d** 90 **p** 91. C Kinson *Sarum* 90-93; C Edgware *Lon* 93-97; TV Roxeth 97-01; V Bayston Hill *Lich* from 01. *The Vicarage, 42 Eric Lock Road West, Bayston Hill, Shrewsbury SY3 0QA* Tel (01743) 872164 E-mail rgoldenberg@btopenworld.com

GOLDER, Rebecca Marie. *See* ROGERS, Mrs Rebecca Marie

GOLDIE, Prof James Stuart. b 46. Lon Univ BTh73 Edin Univ BEd73 Hon MEd81. Lon Coll of Div BDQ66 ALCD69. **d** 69 **p** 70. C Blackpool St Paul *Blackb* 69-70; C-in-c Penketh CD *Liv* 70-73; Asst Chapl Greystone Heath Sch 70-73; Chapl Kilmarnock Academy 73-75; V Flixton St Jo *Man* 75-78; Chapl Friars Sch Man 75-78; V Skelmersdale St Paul *Liv* 78-80; Chapl Trin Sch Liv 78-80; Lect Man Bible Coll and Dir Man City Miss 80-83; Hon Prof from 81; Chapl Westbrook Hay Sch Hemel Hempstead 83-89; V Pennington w Lindal and Marton *Carl* 89-90; Chapl Bp Wand Sch *Lon* 90-95; Chapl Queenswood Sch Herts 96-97; Hd Master Westcliff Prep Sch 97-03; V Red Sea Area Egypt from 04; Prin El Gouna Internat Sch from 04; rtd 06. *23 Ffordd Naddyn, Glan Conway, Colwyn Bay LL28 4NH* Tel (01492) 593996

GOLDIE, Katrina Ruth. *See* SCOTT, Katrina Ruth

GOLDING, Neil Christopher. b 47. Warwick Univ BA69. S'wark Ord Course 92. **d** 95 **p** 96. C Mitcham Ascension *S'wark* 95-00; P-in-c Croydon Woodside 00-05; V from 05. *St Luke's Vicarage, Portland Road, London SE25 4RB* Tel and fax (020) 8654 9841 E-mail rev_neil@btopenworld.com

GOLDING, Piers Edwin Hugh. b 26. RD76. St Aug Coll Cant 48 Edin Th Coll 50. **d** 53 **p** 54. C Guildf Ch Ch 53-55; C Enfield St Andr *Lon* 55-58; Chapl RN 58-62; Chapl RNR 62-93; V S Bermondsey St Aug *S'wark* 62-93; rtd 93; Perm to Offic *St E* and *S'wark* from 93. *6 White Lion House, Broad Street, Eye IP23 7AF* Tel (01379) 871253

GOLDING, The Ven Simon Jefferies. b 46. CBE02. Brasted Place Coll 70. Linc Th Coll 72. **d** 74 **p** 75. C Wilton *York* 74-77; Chapl RN 77-97; Chapl of the Fleet 97-98 and 00-02; Adn for the RN 97-02; Dir Gen Naval Chapl Service 00-02; QHC from 97; Hon Can Gib Cathl 98-02; rtd 02; Perm to Offic *Ripon* from 02; Dioc Adv for NSM from 08. *Arlanza, Hornby Road, Appleton Wiske, Northallerton DL6 2AF* Tel (01609) 881185 E-mail perce.2000@virgin.net

GOLDING, Stephen. b 57. Keele Univ BA79 CertEd79 Lon Bible Coll BA86. Cant Sch of Min 93. **d** 95 **p** 96. NSM Ramsgate St Luke *Cant* 95-98; Chapl St Lawr Coll Ramsgate 95-98; Chapl Berkhamsted Colleg Sch Herts from 98. *Adelbert House, Mill Street, Berkhamsted HP4 2BA* Tel (01442) 878190 *or* 358201

GOLDING, Trevor. b 58. Ridley Hall Cam 07. **d** 09. C Highbury Ch Ch w St Jo and St Sav *Lon* from 09. *Flat 1, 81B Ball's Pond Road, London N1 4BW* Tel (020) 7354 0741 Mobile 07511-870694 E-mail trevor.golding@googlemail.com

GOLDINGAY, Prof John Edgar. b 42. Keble Coll Ox BA64 Nottm Univ PhD83 Lambeth DD97. Clifton Th Coll 64. **d** 66 **p** 67. C Finchley Ch Ch *Lon* 66-69; Lect St Jo Coll Nottm 70-75; Dir Studies 76-79; Registrar 79-85; Vice-Prin 85-88; Prin 88-97; Prof OT Fuller Th Sem Pasadena from 97. *111 South Orange Grove Apt 108, Pasadena CA 91105-1756, USA* Tel (001) (626) 405 0626 E-mail johngold@fuller.edu

GOLDSMITH, Brian Derek. b 36. Leeds Univ BA64. Coll of Resurr Mirfield 64. **d** 66 **p** 67. C Littlehampton St Mary *Chich* 66-69; C Guildf St Nic 69-73; V Aldershot St Aug 73-81; C-in-c Leigh Park St Clare CD *Portsm* 82-85; C Rowner 85-96; rtd 97;

C Catherington and Clanfield *Portsm* 97-01; Perm to Offic *Win* from 98. *27 White Dirt Lane, Catherington, Waterlooville PO8 0NB* Tel (023) 9259 9462

GOLDSMITH, Christopher David. b 54. York Univ BA76 DPhil79. NTMTC 97. **d** 00 **p** 01. NSM Pitsea w Nevendon *Chelmsf* 00-04; V Warley Ch Ch and Gt Warley St Mary from 04. *The Vicarage, 79 Mount Crescent, Warley, Brentwood CM14 5DD* Tel (01277) 220428 Mobile 07981-912576 E-mail c.goldsmith@btinternet.com

GOLDSMITH, Mrs Ellen Elizabeth. b 48. York Univ BA77 Middx Univ BA06. NTMTC 03. **d** 06 **p** 07. NSM Bentley Common, Kelvedon Hatch and Navestock *Chelmsf* from 06. *The Vicarage, 79 Mount Crescent, Warley, Brentwood CM14 5DD* Tel (01277) 220428 Mobile 07906-979321 E-mail ellen.goldsmith@btinternet.com

GOLDSMITH, John Oliver. b 46. K Coll Lon BD69 AKC69. St Aug Coll Cant 69. **d** 70 **p** 71. C Dronfield *Derby* 70-73; C Ellesmere Port *Ches* 73-74; TV Ellesmere Port 74-81; P-in-c Pleasley *Derby* 81-87; P-in-c Pleasley Hill *S'well* 83-87; V Matlock Bank *Derby* 87-97; RD Wirksworth 92-97; P-in-c Kirk Hallam 97-01; V 01-02; P-in-c Taddington, Chelmorton and Flagg, and Monyash from 02; P-in-c Hartington, Biggin and Earl Sterndale from 02; RD Buxton from 02. *The Vicarage, Church Street, Monyash, Bakewell DE45 1JH* Tel (01629) 812234

GOLDSMITH, Lesley Anne. NTMTC 02. **d** 05 **p** 06. C E Ham w Upton Park St Alb *Chelmsf* 05-08; V Chingford St Edm from 08. *St Edmund's Vicarage, Larkswood Road, London E4 9DS* Tel (020) 8529 5226 E-mail lesley.goldsmith@btinternet.com

GOLDSMITH, Malcolm Clive. b 39. Birm Univ BSocSc60 Aston Univ MSc01. Ripon Hall Ox 60. **d** 62 **p** 63. C Balsall Heath St Paul *Birm* 62-64; Chapl Aston Univ 64-72; Bp's Adv on Ind Soc *S'well* 72-79; R Nottingham St Pet and St Jas 79-85; Gen Sec IVS 85-88; Bp's Personal Exec Asst *Bradf* 88-91; Research Fell Stirling Univ 91-94; R Edin St Cuth 94-02; Dioc Dir of Ords 95-01; rtd 02. *82 Woodfield Park, Colinton, Edinburgh EH13 0RB* Tel 0131-441 9881 Mobile 07795-122622 E-mail mcg@malcy.net

GOLDSMITH, Canon Mary Louie. b 48. K Coll Lon BA70 AKC70. Qu Coll Birm 91. **d** 93 **p** 94. NSM Matlock Bank *Derby* 93-97; NSM Kirk Hallam 97-02; NSM Taddington, Chelmorton and Flagg, and Monyash from 00; Hon Can Derby Cathl from 05. *The Vicarage, Church Street, Monyash, Bakewell DE45 1JH* Tel (01629) 812234

GOLDSMITH, Mrs Pauline Anne. b 40. Linc Th Coll 82. **dss** 84 **d** 87 **p** 94. Waddington *Linc* 86-88; Par Dn 87 88; Par Dn Gt and Lt Coates w Bradley 88-94; TV 94-96; TV Kidderminster St Mary and All SS w Trimpley etc *Worc* 96-01; rtd 01; Perm to Offic *Derby* and *Sheff* from 01. *143 Ravencar Road, Eckington, Sheffield S21 4JR* Tel (01246) 430083

GOLDSMITH, Stephen. b 32. Edin Th Coll. **d** 76 **p** 77. SPCK Staff 53-97; Bookshops Regional Manager SPCK 87-97; NSM Penicuik *Edin* 76-81; NSM Linc St Nic w St Jo Newport 81-90; NSM Gt and Lt Coates w Bradley 90-96; NSM Kidderminster St Mary and All SS w Trimpley etc *Worc* 96-01; Perm to Offic *Derby* and *Sheff* from 01. *143 Ravencar Road, Eckington, Sheffield S21 4JR* Tel (01246) 430083

GOLDSPINK, David. b 35. Open Univ BA81. Lon Coll of Div 62. **d** 65 **p** 66. C Mile Cross *Nor* 65-68; C St Austell *Truro* 68-70; TV Bramerton w Surlingham *Nor* 70-73; Min Gunton St Pet 73-75; R Mutford w Rushmere w Gisleham w N Cove w Barnby 75-81; Asst Chapl HM Pris Man 81-82; Chapl HM Youth Cust Cen Hollesley Bay Colony 82-84; Chapl HM Pris Blundeston 84-88; Perm to Offic *St E* 87-01; rtd 88; Perm to Offic *Nor* from 88. *14 Deepdale, Carlton Colville, Lowestoft NR33 8TU* Tel (01502) 537769

GOLDSTONE-CREASEY, Graham. b 51. Trent Poly BA73. Cranmer Hall Dur 80. **d** 83 **p** 84. C Birstall and Wanlip *Leic* 83-87; C-in-c Wheatley Park St Paul CD *Sheff* 87-92; V Wheatley Park 92-95; P-in-c Gleadless Valley 95-98. *281 Fleetwood Road North, Thornton Cleveleys FY5 4LE* Tel (01253) 862668 E-mail goldstonecreasey1@btinternet.com

GOLDTHORPE, Ms Shirley. b 42. Linc Th Coll 70. **dss** 76 **d** 87 **p** 94. Thornhill Lees *Wakef* 76-78; Birkenshaw w Hunsworth 78-80; Batley St Thos 80-85; Batley All SS 80-85; Purlwell 80-92; Par Dn 87-88; Dn-in-c 88-92; Dn-in-c Horbury Junction 92-94; P-in-c 94-01; rtd 02; Perm to Offic *Wakef* from 02. *10 Orchid View, Alverthorpe, Wakefield WF2 0FG* Tel (01924) 383181 Mobile 07885-462837

GOLLEDGE, Christopher John. b 66. St Mich Coll Llan 89. **d** 92 **p** 93. C Newton Nottage *Llan* 92-95; Perm to Offic *Chich* 95-00. *Address temp unknown*

GOLLEDGE, Miss Patricia Anne. b 55. Trin Coll Bris BA00. **d** 00 **p** 01. C Pontypool *Mon* 00-03; TV 03-09; V Griffithstown from 09. *St Hilda's Vicarage, 2 Sunnybank Road, Griffithstown, Pontypool NP4 5LT* Tel (01495) 763641 E-mail anne.golledge@virgin.net

GOLLOP, Michael John. b 58. Keble Coll Ox BA81 MA85. St Mich Coll Llan BD85. **d** 85 **p** 86. C Newport St Mark *Mon*

85-87; C Bassaleg 87-91; V St Hilary Greenway 91-93; V St Arvans w Penterry, Itton, Devauden etc from 93. *The Vicarage, St Arvans, Chepstow NP16 6EU* Tel (01291) 622064

GOLTON, Alan Victor. b 29. St Jo Coll Ox BA51 MA54 DPhil54. **d** 85 **p** 86. P-in-c Barston *Birm* 87-95; Perm to Offic 95-96; Hon C Grenoble *Eur* 97-00. *Chant du Matin, Les Michallons, 38250 St Nizier du Moucherotte, France* Tel (0033) (4) 76 53 43 77 E-mail avgolton@hotmail.com

GOMERSALL, Ian Douglass. b 56. Birm Univ BSc77 Fitzw Coll Cam BA80 MA85 Dur Univ MA94. Westcott Ho Cam 78. **d** 81 **p** 82. C Darlington St Mark w St Paul *Dur* 81-84; C Barnard Castle w Whorlton 84-86; Chapl HM YOI Deerbolt 85-90; P-in-c Cockfield *Dur* 86-88; R 88-90; Dep Chapl HM Pris Wakef 90-91; Chapl HM Pris Full Sutton 91-97; P-in-c Kexby w Wilberfoss *York* 93-97; TV Man Whitworth 97-03; P-in-c Man Victoria Park from 98; Chapl Man Metrop Univ 97-03; Hon Chapl from 03; AD Ardwick from 08. *St Chrysostom's Rectory, 38 Park Range, Manchester M14 5HQ* Tel 0161-224 6971 Mobile 07711-607625 E-mail fatherian@priest.com

GOMERSALL, Richard. b 45. FCA68. NOC 90. **d** 93 **p** 94. NSM Thurcroft *Sheff* 93-96; NSM Sheff St Matt 96-03; Ind Chapl 98-03; C-in-c Southey Green St Bernard CD from 03. *Dale View House, 14 Wignall Avenue, Wickersley, Rotherham S66 2AX* Tel (01709) 546441 Fax 701900 E-mail fr.gomersall@btinternet.com

GOMES, Jules Francis Paulinus. b 66. Bombay Univ BA86 United Th Coll Serampore MTh97 Selw Coll Cam PhD04. Union Bibl Sem Serampore BD94. **d** 98 **p** 98. India 98-04; Co-ord Chapl Greenwich Univ 04-08; Lect Lon Sch of Th from 08; NSM Harefield *Lon* 08-09; Perm to Offic from 09. *15A Priory Close, Ruislip HA4 8HP* Tel (01895) 672065 *or* (01923) 456403 Mobile 07981-570384 E-mail jules.gomes@lst.ac.uk

✠**GOMEZ, The Most Revd Drexel Wellington.** b 37. Dur Univ BA59. Codrington Coll Barbados 55. **d** 59 **c** 72. Tutor Codrington Coll Barbados 64-68; Bp Barbados 72-93; Bp Coadjutor Nassau and Bahamas 95-96; Dioc Bp 96-01; Bp Bahamas and Turks and Caicos Is 01-08; Abp W Indies 98-08, rtd 09. *Address temp unknown*

GOMM, Timothy Frank. b 64. St Jo Coll Nottm 00. **d** 02 **p** 03. C Kinson *Sarum* 02-04; C Heatherlands St Jo from 04; Community Chapl Rossmore Community Coll from 04. *72 Alexandra Road, Poole BH14 9EW* E-mail tim.gomm@ntlworld.com

GOMPERTZ, Helen Morey. b 40. **d** 06 **p** 07. NSM Kettering St Andr *Pet* from 06. *The Rectory, Church Street, Woodford, Kettering NN14 4EX* Tel (01832) 732477

GOMPERTZ, Canon Peter Alan Martin. b 40. ALCD63 **d** 64 **p** 65. C Eccleston St Luke *Liv* 64-69; Scripture Union 69-73; C Yeovil *B & W* 73-75; V Northampton St Giles *Pet* 75-96; R Aynho and Croughton w Evenley etc 96-06; P-in-c Gt w Lt Addington and Woodford from 06; Can Pet Cathl from 88. *The Rectory, Church Street, Woodford, Kettering NN14 4EX* Tel (01832) 732477 Mobile 07771-615364 E-mail p.gompertz@btinternet.com

GONIN, Christopher Willett. b 33. Man Univ DACE87 MBA92. AKC59. **d** 60 **p** 61. C Camberwell St Geo *S'wark* 60-64; C Stevenage H Trin *St Alb* 64-69; C Bletchley *Ox* 70-73; R Newington St Mary *S'wark* 73-76; Perm to Offic *Bris* 76-77; Hon C Horfield H Trin 77-89; Hon C City of Bris 89-91; V Milton Ernest *St Alb* 92-97; V Thurleigh 92-97; rtd 97; Perm to Offic *St E* from 97. *15 The Gables, Leiston IP16 4UZ* Tel (01728) 635549 E-mail christopher@gonin.wanadoo.co.uk

GOOCH, John Ellerton. b 46. Natal Univ BEcon70. Trin Coll Bris 73. **d** 75 **p** 76. C Pinetown Ch Ch S Africa 75-77; P-in-c Escombe 77-79; P-in-c E London St Sav 80-81; R E London St Mich 81-82; TV Beacon Bay 82-83; P-in-c Casablanca *Eur* 98-07; Perm to Offic from 07. *109 rue Mozart/Kouttoubia, Amerchich 40000, Marrakech, Morocco* Tel (00212) (24) 311600 Mobile 63-203174 E-mail johnpen@swissmail.net

GOOCH, Michael Anthony. b 44. Nottm Coll of Educn TCert66. Cant Sch of Min 90. **d** 93 **p** 94. NSM New Romney w Old Romney and Midley *Cant* 93-97; P-in-c Teynham w Lynsted and Kingsdown 97-08; Bp's Officer for NSM 98-03; rtd 08; Perm to Offic *Cant* from 08. *Little Owls, Tookey Road, New Romney TN28 8ET* Tel (01797) 367858 E-mail mgooch@connectfree.co.uk

GOOD, Alan Raymond. b 39. Bris Sch of Min 83. **d** 85 **p** 86. NSM Horfield St Greg *Bris* 85-97; Chapl Asst Southmead Health Services NHS Trust 97-99; Chapl Asst N Bris NHS Trust from 99. *Southmead Hospital, Westbury-on-Trym, Bristol BS10 5NB* Tel 0117-959 5447, 950 5050 *or* (01454) 415778

GOOD, Andrew Ronald. b 60. Bris Univ BA82. Linc Th Coll 83. **d** 85 **p** 86. C Tupsley St Jo *Chelmsf* 85-88; C Cheshunt *St Alb* 88-91; R Spixworth w Crostwick and Frettenham *Nor* 91-04; Perm to Offic from 04. *20 Ebbisham Drive, Norwich NR4 6HN* Tel (01603) 458501

GOOD, Anthony Ernest. b 28. ARIBA51 Heriot-Watt Univ MSc73. Wells Th Coll 54. **d** 56 **p** 57. C Maidstone All SS *Cant* 56-60; C Reading St Mary V *Ox* 60-62; R Sandhurst 62-70; Perm

to Offic *Ex* 71-82; TR Wallingford w Crowmarsh Gifford etc *Ox* 82-92; RD Wallingford 85-91; rtd 92; Perm to Offic *Ex* from 92. *Cotts Weir Quay, Bere Alston, Yelverton PL20 7BX* Tel (01822) 840524

GOOD, David Howard. b 42. Glouc Sch of Min 84. **d** 87 **p** 88. NSM Bromyard *Heref* 87-92; C Pontesbury I and II 92-95; P-in-c Ditton Priors w Neenton, Burwarton etc 95-98; R Ditton Priors w Neenton, Burwarton etc 98-02; rtd 02; Perm to Offic *Heref* from 02. *26 Farjeon Close, Ledbury HR8 2FU* Tel (01531) 636474

GOOD, Geoffrey. b 27. St Aid Birkenhead. **d** 61 **p** 62. C Roby *Liv* 61-65; V Staincliffe *Wakef* 65-79; V Thornes St Jas w Ch Ch 79-93; rtd 93; Perm to Offic *Wakef* from 93. *147 Thornes Road, Wakefield WF2 8QN* Tel (01924) 378273

GOOD, George Fitzgerald. b 19. TCD BA41. CITC 42. **d** 42 **p** 43. C Drumglass *Arm* 42-45; Clerical V Ch Ch Cathl Dublin 45-49; I Inniskeel w Lettermacaward *D & R* 49-60; I Raphoe w Raymochy 60-67; Can Raphoe Cathl 60-62; Dean Raphoe 62-67; Dean Derry 67-84; I Templemore 67-84; rtd 84. *Cliff Cottage, Portnoo, Co Donegal, Republic of Ireland*

GOOD, Preb John Hobart. b 43. Bps' Coll Cheshunt 66 Coll of Resurr Mirfield 68. **d** 69 **p** 70. C Ex St Jas 69-73; C Cockington 73-75; C Wolborough w Newton Abbot 75-78; P-in-c Exminster 78-80; P-in-c Kenn 78-80; R Exminster and Kenn 80-95; RD Kenn 89-95; TR Axminster, Chardstock, All Saints etc 95-09; Preb Ex Cathl 02-09; Chapl All Hallows Sch Rousdon 98-09; rtd 09; Hon C The Winterbournes and Compton Valence *Sarum* from 09; Hon C Dorchester from 09. *The Rectory, Martinstown, Dorchester DT2 9JZ* Tel (01305) 889466 E-mail jhgood_minster@hotmail.com

✠**GOOD, The Rt Revd Kenneth Raymond.** b 52. TCD BA74 Nottm Univ BA76 NUI HDipEd81 MEd84. St Jo Coll Nottm 75. **d** 77 **p** 78 **c** 02. C Willowfield *D & D* 77-79; Chapl Ashton Sch Cork 79-84; I Dunganstown w Redcross and Conary *D & G* 84-90; I Lurgan Ch the Redeemer *D & D* 90-02; Adn Dromore 97-02; Bp D & R from 02. *The See House, 112 Culmore Road, Londonderry BT48 8JF* Tel (028) 7135 1206 *or* 7126 2440 Fax 7135 2554 E-mail bishop@derry.anglican.org

GOOD, The Ven Kenneth Roy. b 41. K Coll Lon BD66 AKC66. **d** 67 **p** 68. C Stockton St Pet *Dur* 67-70; Chapl Antwerp Miss to Seamen *Eur* 70-74; Japan 74-79; Hon Can Kobe from 74; Asst Gen Sec Miss to Seamen 79-85; Asst Chapl St Mich Paternoster Royal *Lon* 79-85; V Nunthorpe *York* 85-93; RD Stokesley 90-93; Adn Richmond *Ripon* 93-06; rtd 06; Perm to Offic *York* from 07. *18 Fox Howe, Coulby Newham, Middlesbrough TS8 0RU* Tel (01642) 594158 E-mail joken.good@virgin.net

GOOD, Robert Stanley. b 24. TCD BA45 BD47 Kent Univ MA82. TCD Div Sch Div Test 46. **d** 47 **p** 48. C Lurgan Ch the Redeemer *D & D* 47-49; Kenya CMS 50-60; Perm to Offic *Cant* from 61; Sen Div Master Maidstone Gr Sch 62-64; Sen Lect Ch Ch Coll Cant 64-78; Fiji 83-87; Par Educn Officer Herne Bay Ch Ch *Cant* 88-94; rtd 94. *Njiani, 44 Ivanhoe Road, Herne Bay CT6 6EG* Tel (01227) 363561

GOOD, Stuart Eric Clifford. b 37. Wycliffe Hall Ox 63. **d** 64 **p** 65. C Walton H Trin *Ox* 64-67; Australia from 66; Dir Chapl Services Angl Homes Inc 85-05; rtd 05. *6 Enright Circuit, Stanford Gardens, Beeliar WA 6164, Australia* Tel (0061) 418-943337 (mobile) E-mail sbargood@bigpond.net.au

GOODACRE, Canon David Leighton. b 36. AKC59. **d** 60 **p** 61. C Stockton St Chad *Dur* 60-63; C Birtley 63-68; Chapl Sunderland Gen Hosp 69-74; P-in-c Ryhope *Dur* 75-81; V Ovingham *Newc* 81-01; Hon Can Newc Cathl 92-01; rtd 01; Perm to Offic *Newc* from 01. *9 Wilmington Close, Newcastle upon Tyne NE3 2SF* Tel 0191-271 4382

GOODAIR, Janet. *See* CHEESEMAN, Ms Janet

GOODALL, George. b 24. LCP. **d** 86 **p** 87. NSM Bretby w Newton Solney *Derby* 86-94; Perm to Offic from 94. *6 Brizlincote Lane, Burton-on-Trent DE15 0PR* Tel (01283) 562467

GOODALL, James Richard. b 51. Reading Univ BA73 Ox Univ DPhil79 York St Jo Univ MA09. Coll of Resurr Mirfield 08. **d** 09. NSM Hurst Green and Mitton *Bradf* from 09. *Smithy Cottage, Walker Fold, Chaigley, Clitheroe BB7 3LU* Tel (01254) 826746 Mobile 07989-949743 E-mail jamesrgoodall@btinternet.com

GOODALL, Canon John William. b 45. Hull Univ BA69. Ripon Hall Ox 69. **d** 71 **p** 72. C Loughborough Em *Leic* 71-74; C Dorchester *Ox* 74-75; TV 75-80; Tutor Sarum & Wells Th Coll 80-88; Vice Prin S Dios Minl Tr Scheme 80-88; P-in-c Gt Wishford *Sarum* 80-83; P-in-c Colehill 88-96; V from 96; Dioc Dir of Readers 88-95; Can and Preb Sarum Cathl from 07. *The Vicarage, Smugglers Lane, Colehill, Wimborne BH21 2RY* Tel (01202) 883721

GOODALL, Canon Jonathan Michael. b 61. R Holloway Coll Lon BMus83. Wycliffe Hall Ox 86. **d** 89 **p** 90. C Bicester w Bucknell, Caversfield and Launton *Ox* 89-92; Asst Chapl HM Pris Bullingdon 90-92; Min Can, Chapl, and Sacr Westmr Abbey 92-98; Bp's Chapl and Research Asst *Eur* 98-05; Can Gib Cathl from 05; Abp's Chapl and Ecum Officer *Cant* 05-09; Abp's Personal Chapl and Ecum Sec from 09; Hon C Westmr St Matt

Lon 99-03; PV Westmr Abbey from 04. *Lambeth Palace, London SE1 7JU* Tel (020) 7898 1200
E-mail jonathan.goodall@c-of-e.org.uk

GOODALL, Malcolm. b 39. Newc Univ MA93. Carl Dioc Tr Inst 80. **d** 85 **p** 86. NSM Allonby and Cross Canonby *Carl* 85-88; C Auckland St Andr and St Anne *Dur* 88-90; V Grindon and Stillington 90-98; P-in-c Wolsingham and Thornley 98-03; R 03-08; rtd 08. *West Wing, Eden Place, Kirkby Stephen CA17 4AP* Tel (017683) 72320 E-mail mg@malcolmgoodall.co.uk

GOODBODY, Ruth Vivien. b 68. Surrey Univ BA02. Wycliffe Hall Ox 96 STETS 00. **d** 02 **p** 03. C Bourne Valley *Sarum* 02-06; C Stebbing and Lindsell w Gt and Lt Saling *Chelmsf* from 06. *The Vicarage, 7 Ruffels Place, Stebbing, Dunmow CM6 3TJ* Tel (01371) 856080 E-mail the.goodbodies@virgin.net

GOODBODY, Steven John. b 70. Univ of Wales (Cardiff) BD92. Wycliffe Hall Ox 00. **d** 02 **p** 03. C Tunbridge Wells St Jo *Roch* 02-05; C Ex St Leon w H Trin from 05. *27 Barnardo Road, Exeter EX2 4ND* Tel (01392) 277540 Mobile 07768-645172 E-mail sjgoodbody@csi.com

GOODBODY, Timothy Edward. b 66. York Univ BA89. Wycliffe Hall Ox BTh98. **d** 98 **p** 99. C Blandford Forum and Langton Long *Sarum* 98-02; NSM Bourne Valley 02-06; P-in-c Stebbing and Lindsell w Gt and Lt Saling *Chelmsf* from 06. *The Vicarage, 7 Ruffels Place, Stebbing, Dunmow CM6 3TJ* Tel (01371) 856080 E-mail the.goodbodies@virgin.net

GOODBURN, David Henry. b 41. S'wark Ord Course 73. **d** 76 **p** 77. NSM Enfield SS Pet and Paul *Lon* 76-82; Perm to Offic 83-85; NSM Potters Bar *St Alb* 85-88; Chapl RN 88-96; V Luton St Sav *St Alb* from 96. *St Saviour's Vicarage, St Saviour's Crescent, Luton LU1 5HG* Tel (01582) 730445

GOODCHILD, Andrew Philip. b 55. CertEd80. Oak Hill Th Coll BA85. **d** 85 **p** 86. C Barnston *Ches* 85-88; C Hollington St Leon *Chich* 88-89; P-in-c Millbrook *Ches* 89-94; Chapl and Hd RE Kimbolton Sch 94-03. *Sand Pit Lodge, 72 Lynn Road, Dersingham, King's Lynn PE31 6LB* Tel (01485) 543743 Mobile 07748-815479 E-mail mel-andy@tiscali.co.uk

GOODCHILD, Canon John McKillip. b 42. Clare Coll Cam BA64 MA68 Oriel Coll Ox CertEd69. Wycliffe Hall Ox 67. **d** 69 **p** 70. C Clubmoor *Liv* 69-72; CMS Nigeria 72-83; Hon Can Aba from 74; V Ainsdale *Liv* 83-89; TR Maghull 89-98; Prin Dioc Minl Course and Dir OLM *Tr Nor* 98-06; rtd 06. *39 St Michael's Road, Aigburth, Liverpool L17 7AN*

GOODDEN, John Maurice Phelips. b 34. Sarum & Wells Th Coll 70. **d** 72 **p** 75. C Weymouth H Trin *Sarum* 72-74; C Harlow New Town w Lt Parndon *Chelmsf* 74-78; Ind Chapl and Chapl Princess Alexandra Hosp Harlow 78-82, V Moulsham St Jo *Chelmsf* 86-90; R Chipstead and Adv Rural Min *S'wark* 90-04; rtd 04; Perm to Offic *B & W* from 05. *Easter Cottage, 64 Kingston Deverill, Warminster BA12 7HG* Tel (01985) 845318 E-mail goodden@msn.com

GOODE, Anthony Thomas Ryall. b 42. Ex Coll Ox BA64 MA71. Cuddesdon Coll 65. **d** 67 **p** 68. C Wolvercote *Ox* 67-71; P-in-c Edith Weston w Normanton *Pet* 72-74; Chapl RAF 71-91; Asst Chapl-in-Chief 91-97; Chapl to The Queen 95-97; Chapl Abu Dhabi St Andr UAE 97-00; V Hurstbourne Tarrant, Faccombe, Vernham Dean etc *Win* 00-07; rtd 07. *9 rue de la Gargoille, 79600 Marnes, France* Tel (0033) (5) 49 66 79 14 E-mail spetroshbt@aol.com

GOODE, Claire Elizabeth. b 60. Nottm Univ BSc82. EMMTC 04. **d** 08 **p** 09. C St Cluster S'well Deanery from 08. *10 Lantern Lane, East Leake, Loughborough LE12 6QN* E-mail goodepc@ntlworld.com

GOODE, John Laurence. b 48. W Cheshire Coll of Tech TEng70 Federal Univ Minas Gerais Brazil Dip Teaching78. Chich Th Coll 81. **d** 83 **p** 84. C Crewe St Andr *Ches* 83-86; USPG 87-94; Brazil 91-94; TV Ches 94-00; V Latchford Ch Ch from 00. *Christ Church Vicarage, Wash Lane, Warrington WA4 1HT* Tel (01925) 630846

GOODE, Jonathan. b 67. St Martin's Coll Lanc BA89. Qu Coll Birm. **d** 00 **p** 01. C Middleton St Mary *Ripon* 00-04; P-in-c Hartlepool St Hilda *Dur* 04-08; Chapl St Hilda's Sch 04-08; V Denton *Newc* from 08. *The Vicarage, Dunblane Crescent, Newcastle upon Tyne NE5 2BE* E-mail revjgoode@yahoo.com

GOODE, Michael Arthur John. b 40. K Coll Lon BD AKC63. **d** 64 **p** 65. C Sunderland Springwell w Thorney Close *Dur* 64-68; C Solihull *Birm* 68-70; R Fladbury, Wyre Piddle and Moor *Worc* 70-75; P-in-c Foley Park 75-81; V 81-83; RD Kidderminster 81-83; TR Crawley *Chich* 83-93; TR Abingdon and V Shippon *Ox* 93-05; rtd 05. *13 Britannia Square, Worcester WR1 3DG* Tel (01235) 532722 E-mail jenny.goode@btinternet.com

GOODE, Canon Peter William Herbert. b 23. Oak Hill Th Coll 60. **d** 62 **p** 63. C Woodford Wells *Chelmsf* 62-65; V Harold Hill St Paul 65-76; V Gt Warley Ch Ch 76-93; RD Brentwood 89-93; Hon Can Chelmsf Cathl 90-93; rtd 93; Perm to Offic *St Alb* from 93. *52 Slimmons Drive, St Albans AL4 9AP* Tel (01727) 852166

GOODE, Thomas. *See* GOODE, Anthony Thomas Ryall

GOODE, Timothy. b 69. Huddersfield Poly BA90 Roehampton Inst PGCE91. Ripon Coll Cuddesdon 07. **d** 09. C Croydon St Jo

S'wark from 09. *37 Alton Road, Croydon CR0 4LZ* Tel (020) 8643 0192 E-mail musicgoode@hotmail.com

GOODER, Canon Martin Lee. b 37. Sheff Univ BSc58. Oak Hill Th Coll 58. **d** 60 **p** 61. C Barrow St Mark *Carl* 60-63; C Halliwell St Pet *Man* 63-66; R Chorlton on Medlock St Sav 66-71; R Brunswick 71-92; P-in-c Bacup Ch Ch 92-02; Hon Can Man Cathl 98-02; rtd 02; Perm to Offic *Man* from 02. *12 Walton Close, Bacup OL13 9RE* Tel (01706) 872418 E-mail gooder@btopenworld.com

GOODERHAM, Daniel Charles. b 24. St Fran Coll Brisbane 49. **d** 52 **p** 53. Australia 52-60; C Staveley *Derby* 60-61; C Ipswich St Thos *St E* 61-64; V Ipswich St Bart 64-71; R Drinkstone 71-78; R Rattlesden 71-78; RD Lavenham 75-78; V Beckenham St Mich w St Aug *Roch* 78-87; P-in-c Whiteparish *Sarum* 87-89; rtd 89; Perm to Offic *St E* from 89. *58 Millfield, Eye IP23 7DE* Tel (01379) 871589

GOODEY, Philip Julian Frank. b 61. Aston Tr Scheme 87 Trin Coll Bris 89. **d** 92 **p** 93. C Iver *Ox* 92-94; C Hornchurch St Andr *Chelmsf* 94-99; V Wickham Market w Pettistree *St E* 99-01; TR Parkham, Alwington, Buckland Brewer etc *Ex* 01-06; P-in-c Lundy 01-06; R Botley *Portsm* from 06; V Curdridge from 06; R Durley from 06. *The Rectory, 46 High Street, Botley, Southampton SO30 2EA* Tel (01489) 781534 E-mail phil.goodey@me.com

GOODFELLOW, Ian. b 37. St Cath Coll Cam BA61 MA65 Lon Univ PGCE76 Dur Univ PhD83. Wells Th Coll 61. **d** 63 **p** 64. C Dunstable *St Alb* 63-67; Chapl Haileybury Coll 67-71; Asst Chapl St Bede Coll Dur 71-74; Lect and Tutor 71-75; Sen Lect and Tutor SS Hild and Bede Coll Dur 75-78; Sen Cllr Open Univ (SW Region) 78-97; Perm to Offic *Ex* from 89; rtd 02. *Crosslea, 206 Whitchurch Road, Tavistock PL19 9DQ* Tel (01822) 612069 E-mail goodfellow1@lineone.net

GOODFIELD, Dudley Francis. b 40. AKC65. **d** 66 **p** 67. C Bath Twerton-on-Avon *B & W* 66-69; C Lache cum Saltney *Ches* 69-71; C Portishead *B & W* 71-76; V Weston-super-Mare St Andr Bournville 76-82; V Ruishton w Thornfalcon 82-05; rtd 05; Perm to Offic *B & W* from 05. *4 Gillards Close, Rockwell Green, Wellington TA21 9DX* Tel (01823) 660533

GOODGER, Kenneth Andrew. b 67. Univ of Qld BA96. St Fran Coll Brisbane BTh97. **d** 93 **p** 96. C Milton Australia 93-96; C Caloundra 96-99; C Pimlico St Pet w Westmr Ch Ch *Lon* 99-02; R Moorooka and Salisbury Australia 02-06; R Caloundra from 06. *PO Box 52, Caloundra Qld 4551, Australia* Tel (0061) (7) 5491 1866 E-mail m.sanglican@uqconnect.net

GOODHAND, Richard. b 51. Sarum & Wells Th Coll 88. **d** 90 **p** 91. C Wollaton *S'well* 90-93; P-in-c Clarborough w Hayton 93-98; Sub-Chapl HM Pris Ranby 93-96; Asst Chapl 96-98; P-in-c Blidworth *S'well* 98-02; P-in-c Rainworth 98-02; V Blidworth w Rainworth 02-08; P-in-c Ollerton w Boughton from 08. *St Paulinus Vicarage, 65 Larch Road, New Ollerton, Newark NG22 9SX* Tel (01623) 836081 E-mail revrichard@goodhand.org.uk

GOODHEW, David John. b 65. Collingwood Coll Dur BA86 CCC Ox DPhil92 St Jo Coll Dur BA92. Cranmer Hall Dur 90. **d** 93 **p** 94. C Bedminster *Bris* 93-96; Chapl and Fell St Cath Coll Cam 96-01; V Fulford *York* 01-08; P-in-c York St Denys 01-04; Dir Minl Practice Cranmer Hall Dur from 08. *St John's College, 3 South Bailey, Durham DH1 3RJ* Tel 0191-334 3863 Fax 334 3501 E-mail d.j.goodhew@durham.ac.uk

GOODHEW, Mrs Lindsey Jane Ellin. b 66. UEA BA87 St Jo Coll Dur BA92. Cranmer Hall Dur 90. **d** 93 **p** 94. C Bishopsworth *Bris* 93-96; Perm to Offic *Ely* 96-97; Hon C Cambridge St Mark 97-01; Perm to Offic *York* 01-07; Hon C Fulford 07-08. *Address temp unknown*

GOODHEW, Roy William. b 41. Reading Univ BA Univ of Wales (Cardiff) PGCE. S Dios Minl Tr Scheme. **d** 89 **p** 90. C Southampton Maybush St Pet *Win* 89-94; V Hound 94-05; rtd 05; Perm to Offic *Lon* from 06. *121 Edgecot Grove, London N15 5HH* Tel (020) 8802 5101

GOODING, Canon Ian Eric. b 42. Leeds Univ BSc63 BCom65 CEng69 MIProdE68. St Jo Coll Nottm 70. **d** 73 **p** 74. C Wandsworth All SS *S'wark* 73-77; Bp's Ind Adv *Derby* from 77; P-in-c Stanton-by-Dale w Dale Abbey 77-87; R 87-00; P-in-c Risley 94-00; R Stanton-by-Dale w Dale Abbey and Risley from 00; RD Erewash from 98; Hon Can Derby Cathl from 02. *The Rectory, Stanhope Street, Stanton-by-Dale, Ilkeston DE7 4QA* Tel and fax 0115-932 4585 Mobile 07768-917385

GOODING, Ian Peter Slade. b 56. Imp Coll Lon BScEng77 MBCS88. Qu Coll Birm 90. **d** 92 **p** 93. C Swindon Dorcan *Bris* 92-96; TV Langley Marish *Ox* 96-02; Internet Manager Scripture Union from 02; Hon C Woughton *Ox* from 09. *5 Pipston Green, Kents Hill, Milton Keynes MK7 6HT* Tel (01908) 673651 E-mail goodingip@clara.co.uk

GOODING, John Henry. b 47. St Jo Coll Nottm. **d** 84 **p** 85. C Charles w Plymouth St Matthias *Ex* 84-88; C Leeds St Geo *Ripon* 88-93; TV Liskeard, St Keyne, St Pinnock, Morval etc *Truro* 93-94; Lon and SE Consultant CPAS 94-00; Hon C Egham *Guildf* 96-00; Dioc Par Resource Officer 00-03; Dioc Dir Miss, Evang and Par Development from 03. *Diocesan House,*

Quarry Street, Guildford GU1 3XG Tel (01483) 571826 ext 206 *or* (01932) 560407 E-mail john.gooding@cofeguildford.org.uk

GOODING, Paul David Buchanan. b 76. Pemb Coll Ox MA98 Green Coll Ox PGCE01. Ox Min Course 06. d 08. NSM Grove *Ox* from 08. *c/o Crockford, Church House, Great Smith Street, London SW1P 3AZ* E-mail pdbgooding@hotmail.com

GOODLAD, Canon Martin Randall. b 39. Sheff City Coll of Educn TDip60. Linc Th Coll 63. d 66 p 67. C Bramley *Ripon* 66-69; TV Daventry *Pet* 69-71; Asst Dioc Youth Officer 69-71; Asst Dir of Educn *Wakef* 71-74; Youth Work Officer Gen Syn Bd of Educn 74-83; P-in-c Cheam Common St Phil *S'wark* 83-85; V 85-97; RD Sutton 90-97; Hon Chapl St Raphael's Hospice 87-97; V Coulsdon St Andr *S'wark* 97-05; Hon Can S'wark Cathl 96-05; rtd 05; Perm to Offic *S'wark* from 06. *3 Cromer Mansions, Cheam Road, Sutton SM1 2SR* Tel (020) 8915 0555 E-mail hornes27@aol.com

GOODLAND, Michael Eric. b 53. WEMTC 97. d 97 p 98. NSM Ilminster and Distr *B & W* 97-02; NSM Crewkerne w Wayford 02-07; Perm to Offic *Truro* from 07. *Wesley House, Bay Tree Hill, Liskeard PL14 4BG*

GOODLEY, Christopher Ronald. b 47. K Coll Lon BD72 AKC72. d 73 p 74. C Shenfield *Chelmsf* 73-77; C Hanley H Ev *Lich* 77-78; TV 78-83; Chapl Whittington Hosp Lon 83-86; Chapl St Crispin's Hosp Northampton 88-94; Chapl Northampton Community Healthcare NHS Trust 94-01; Chapl Northants Healthcare NHS Trust from 01. *Princess Marina Hospital, Duston, Northampton NN5 6UH* Tel (01604) 595087 *or* 752323 Fax 583795 E-mail christopher.goodley@nht.northants.nhs.uk

GOODMAN, Ms Alice Abigail. b 58. Harvard Univ BA80 Girton Coll Cam BA82 MA86 Boston Univ MDiv97. Ripon Coll Cuddesdon 00. d 01 p 03. C Redditch, The Ridge *Worc* 01-02; C Kidderminster St Mary and All SS w Trimpley etc 02-06; Chapl Trin Coll Cam from 06. *Trinity College, Cambridge CB2 1TQ* Tel (01223) 338400 E-mail aag31@cam.ac.uk

GOODMAN, Andrew Francis Malby. b 56. Lon Univ BA79 Birm Univ MSocSc88 CQSW88. Qu Coll Birm 01. d 03 p 04. C Hamstead St Paul *Birm* 03-07; Co-ord Chapl Bedfordshire Univ from 07. *33 Felix Avenue, Luton LU2 7AE* Tel (01582) 432019 E-mail goodmanco@yahoo.co.uk

GOODMAN, Canon Derek George. b 34. Keble Coll Ox BA57 MA60. Ridley Hall Cam 59. d 61 p 62. C Attenborough *S'well* 61-65; R Eastwood 65-84; Dioc Insp of Schs 65-89; V Woodthorpe 84-89; Dioc Dir of Educn *Leic* 89-96; Hon Can Leic Cathl 90-96; rtd 96; Perm to Offic *Leic* from 96. *1 Brown Avenue, Quorn, Loughborough LE12 8RH* Tel (01509) 415692

GOODMAN, John. b 20. Selw Coll Cam BA42 MA46. Linc Th Coll 47. d 49 p 50. C Kidderminster St Jo *Worc* 49-53; C Marlborough *Sarum* 53-56; V Wootton Bassett 56-65; C Broad Town 56-65; C Salisbury St Mark 65-68; V 68-83; R Wool and E Stoke 83-88; rtd 88; Perm to Offic *Sarum* from 88. *141 Avon Road, Devizes SN10 1PY* Tel (01380) 721267

GOODMAN, John Dennis Julian. b 35. Sarum & Wells Th Coll 74. d 76 p 77. C Cotmanhay Derby 76-79; TV Old Brampton and Loundsley Green 79-86; R Finningley w Auckley *S'well* 86-96; rtd 96; Perm to Offic *Pet* from 96. *6 Mason Close, Thrapston, Kettering NN14 4UQ* Tel (01832) 731194

GOODMAN, Brother Kevin Charles. b 54. Surrey Univ BA06. STETS 03. d 06 p 07. NSM Buckland Newton, Cerne Abbas, Godmanstone etc *Sarum* from 06. *The Friary, Hilfield, Dorchester DT2 7BE* Tel (01300) 341345 E-mail kevinssf@franciscans.org.uk

GOODMAN, Mrs Mairion Kim (Mars). b 73. Leeds Univ BA95. Trin Coll Bris BA03. d 05 p 06. NSM Redland *Bris* from 05. *6 Willoughby Road, Horfield, Bristol BS7 8QX* Tel 0117-989 2597 E-mail mars@redland.org.uk

GOODMAN, Mark Alexander Scott. b 61. Lanc Univ BA84 Nottm Univ BTh90 New Coll Edin MTh97. Linc Th Coll 87. d 90 p 91. C Denton St Lawr *Man* 90-93; R Dalkeith and Lasswade *Edin* 93-06; Dioc Communications Officer 96-06; Can St Mary's Cathl and Syn Clerk 02-06; Chapl Stamford Sch from 06. *Saddlers Cottage, 9A St Peter's Street, Stamford PE9 2PQ* Tel (01780) 763691 Mobile 07947-032739

GOODMAN, Peter William (Bill). b 60. St Cath Coll Cam BA82 Sheff Univ MPhil98. St Jo Coll Nottm 85. d 89 p 90. C Stapenhill w Cauldwell *Derby* 89-92; C Ovenden *Wakef* 92-94; V Halifax St Aug 94-98; Crosslinks Ethiopia 98-05; C Leic H Trin w St Jo 05-08. *1 Reservoir View, Main Street, Saddington, Leicester LE8 0QH* E-mail goodmans@cooptel.net

GOODMAN, Canon Sidney William. b 10. Kelham Th Coll 27. d 33 p 34. C Wigan St Mich *Liv* 33-36; C Gt Grimsby St Mary and St Jas *Linc* 36-39; V Fulstow 39-44; V Habrough 44-55; V Immingham 44-55; V Habrough Gp 55-71; RD Grimsby N 57-64; RD Haverstoe 64-76; Can and Preb Linc Cathl 69-79; P-in-c Wold Newton w Hawerby 71-78; rtd 78; Perm to Offic *Linc* from 78. *c/o Mrs C M Willey, 47 Pilgrim Avenue, Immingham DN40 1DL* Tel (01469) 573495

GOODMAN, Veronica Mary. b 57. Newman Coll Birm BEd80. Qu Coll Birm 06. d 08 p 09. C Dunstable *St Alb* from 08. *33 Felix Avenue, Luton LU2 7LE* Tel (01582) 432019 E-mail ronigoodman@yahoo.co.uk

GOODMAN, Victor Terence. b 46. Liv Univ BSc67 CEng92 MBCS74. EMMTC 82. d 85 p 86. NSM Barwell w Potters Marston and Stapleton *Leic* 85-89; NSM Croft and Stoney Stanton 89-94; P-in-c Whetstone 94-03; TV Hugglescote w Donington, Ellistown and Snibston 03-07; C Coalville and Bardon Hill from 07; C Ravenstone and Swannington from 07. *7 Millers Walk, Ravenstone, Coalville LE67 2BZ* Tel (01530) 832679 E-mail victor.goodman@btinternet.com

GOODMAN, Mrs Victoria Elizabeth Stuart. b 51. RGN74. Trin Coll Bris. d 98 p 99. C Ilminster and Distr *B & W* 98-02; R Blagdon w Compton Martin and Ubley from 02; Dioc Chapl MU from 01. *The Rectory, High Street, Blagdon, Bristol BS40 7TA* Tel (01761) 462495

GOODMAN, William. *See* GOODMAN, Peter William

GOODRICH, Derek Hugh. b 27. Selw Coll Cam BA48 MA54. St Steph Ho Ox 50. d 52 p 53. C Willesden St Andr *Lon* 52-57; V Lodge St Sidwell Guyana 57-67; V Port Mourant 67-71; R New Amsterdam All SS 71-84; Adn Berlice 81-84; V Gen Dio Guyana 82-94; Dean Georgetown 84-93; P-in-c St Aloysius 93-00; rtd 00; Perm to Offic *S'wark* from 03. *The Rectory of St Barnabas, Blackberry Lane, Lingfield RH7 6NJ* Tel (01342) 872873

GOODRICH, Mrs Nancy Elisabeth. b 66. St Hilda's Coll Ox BA88 MA09 ACA93. WMMTC 06. d 09. C St Annes St Thos *Blackb* from 09. *4 The Boulevard, Lytham St Annes FY8 1EH* Tel (01253) 781119 Mobile 07974-250466 E-mail nancy@goodrich.myzen.co.uk

GOODRICH, Canon Peter. b 36. Dur Univ BA58. Cuddesdon Coll 60. d 62 p 63. C Walton St Jo *Liv* 62-66; C Prescot 66-68; V Anfield St Marg 68-72; V Gt Crosby St Faith 72-83; P-in-c Seaforth 76-80; RD Bootle 78-83; TR Upholland 83-94; R Halsall 94-02; Dir Dioc OLM Scheme 94-02; Hon Can Liv Cathl 89-02; rtd 03; Perm to Offic *Liv* from 03. *Dunelm, 16 Hillside Avenue, Ormskirk L39 4TD* Tel (01695) 573285

GOODRIDGE, Elizabeth Jane. b 57. SEITE 06. d 09. NSM S Beddington and Roundshaw *S'wark* from 09. *32 Waterer Rise, Wallington SM6 9DN* Tel (020) 8669 9371 Mobile 07788-755752 E-mail elizabeth.goodridge1@btinternet.com

GOODRIDGE, John Francis James. b 49. Open Univ BA86. WEMTC 04. d 07 p 08. NSM Bristol St Aid w St Geo from 07; NSM E Bris St Ambrose and St Leon from 07; NSM Fishponds All SS from 07; NSM Fishponds St Jo from 07; NSM Fishponds St Mary from 07; NSM Two Mile Hill St Mich from 07. *153 Whittucks Road, Bristol BS15 3PY* Tel 0117-940 1508

GOODRIDGE, Paul Charles. b 54. Leic Univ MSc98 MCIPD84. d 04 p 05. OLM Cheam *S'wark* 04-08; C Beddington from 08. *32 Waterer Rise, Wallington SM6 9DN* Tel (020) 8669 8227 E-mail paul.goodridge1@btinternet.com

GOODRIDGE, Peter Warren. b 66. Liv Univ BA87. Wycliffe Hall Ox 07. d 09. C Tonbridge SS Pet and Paul *Roch* from 09. *14 Salisbury Road, Tonbridge TN10 4PB* Tel (01732) 355200 E-mail pwg@inbox.com

GOODRUM, Mrs Alice. b 30. Lightfoot Ho Dur 58. dss 80 d 87 p 94. Fenham St Jas and St Basil *Newc* 80-91; C 87-91; rtd 91; Perm to Offic *Dur* and *Newc* from 91. *58 West Avenue, South Shields NE34 6BD* Tel 0191-425 3629

GOODSELL, Patrick. b 32. BA88. Linc Th Coll 62. d 64 p 65. C Thornton Heath St Jude *Cant* 64-65; C Croydon St Jo *S'wark* 65-70; V Tenterden St Mich *Cant* 70-78; P-in-c Sellindge w Monks Horton and Stowting 78-84; P-in-c Lympne w W Hythe 82-84; V Sellindge w Monks Horton and Stowting etc 84-92; V Nonington w Wymynswold and Goodnestone etc 92-98; rtd 98; Perm to Offic *Cant* from 98. *3 James Close, Lyminge, Folkestone CT18 8NL* Tel (01303) 863976 E-mail pat_goodsell@sky.com

GOODWIN, Barry Frederick John. b 48. Birm Univ BSc69 PhD77. St Jo Coll Nottm 86. d 88 p 89. C Ware Ch Ch *St Alb* 88-91; P-in-c Stanstead Abbots 91-96; P-in-c Gt Amwell w St Marg 95-96; V Gt Amwell w St Margaret's and Stanstead Abbots 96-99; RD Hertford and Ware 96-99; V Clapham Park All SS *S'wark* 99-05; RD Clapham 02-05; Soc Resp (Par Development) Adv Croydon Adnry from 05. *48 Northampton Road, Croydon CR0 7HT* Tel (020) 8256 9637 E-mail barry.goodwin@southwark.anglican.org

GOODWIN, Bruce William. b 64. Univ of W Aus BA84 DipEd85. Trin Coll Bris 07. d 09. C Thornbury and Oldbury-on-Severn w Shepperdine *Glouc* from 09. *10 Meadowside, Thornbury, Bristol BS35 2EN* Tel 07720-772190 (mobile) E-mail goodwins07@gmail.com

GOODWIN, Daphne Mary. b 35. Lon Univ MB, BS60. STETS 94. d 97 p 98. NSM Ifield *Chich* from 97. *150 Buckswood Drive, Gossops Green, Crawley RH11 8JF* Tel (01293) 612906 E-mail dapheter.goodwin@ukgateway.net

GOODWIN, David Wayne. b 71. Univ of Wales BD95. Cranmer Hall Dur 95. d 97 p 98. C Ches H Trin 97-00; Dep Chapl HM Pris Dur 00-01; Chapl HM YOI Thorn Cross 01-04; Chapl HM Pris Liv 04-07; Chapl HM Pris Kennet from 07. *HM Prison*

317

Kennet, Parkbourn, Liverpool L31 1HX Tel 0151-213 3000 Fax 213 3103

GOODWIN, Mrs Gillian Sheila. b 54. NOC MTh99. **d** 99 **p** 00. C Penkridge *Lich* 99-02; TV Wrockwardine Deanery from 02. *The Vicarage, Church Road, High Ercall, Telford TF6 6BE* Tel (01952) 770206

GOODWIN, Canon John Fletcher Beckles. b 20. Jes Coll Cam BA43 MA46. Ridley Hall Cam 42. **d** 45 **p** 46. C Southall H Trin *Lon* 45-48; C Drypool *York* 48-49; Niger 50-57; Vice-Prin Ripon Hall Ox 57-62; V Merton *Ox* 62-70; V Heanor *Derby* 70-74; V Hazlewood 74-85; V Turnditch 74-85; Adv for In-Service Tr and Chapl to Bp 74-88; Hon Can Derby Cathl 81-85; rtd 85; Perm to Offic *Derby* 85-99. *1 Kirby Place, Oxford OX4 2RX* Tel (01865) 712356

GOODWIN, Ronald Victor. b 33. S'wark Ord Course. **d** 86 **p** 87. NSM Wickford and Runwell *Chelmsf* 86-98; Perm to Offic 98-01; NSM W Hanningfield 01-03; P-in-c 03-06; rtd 06; Perm to Offic *Chelmsf* from 06. *164 Southend Road, Wickford SS11 8EH* Tel (01268) 734447

GOODWIN, Stephen. b 58. Sheff Univ BA80. Cranmer Hall Dur 82. **d** 85 **p** 86. C Lytham St Cuth *Blackb* 85-87; C W Burnley All SS 88-90; TV Headley All SS *Guildf* 90-98; NSM Leek and Meerbrook *Lich* 98-03; Chapl Univ Hosp of N Staffs NHS Trust 03-08; Chapl Douglas Macmillan Hospice Blurton from 08. *2 Lordshire Mews, Armshead Road, Werrington, Stoke-on-Trent ST9 0HJ* Tel (01782) 302418 *or* 344300
E-mail revsgoodwin2@talktalk.net

GOODWIN, Mrs Susan Elizabeth. b 51. Leeds Poly BSc74 Leeds Univ MSc76. St Jo Coll Dur 82. **dss** 84 **d** 87 **p** 94. Norton Woodseats St Chad *Sheff* 84-87; Par Dn 87; Chapl Scargill Ho 87-89; NSM W Burnley All SS *Blackb* 89-90; NSM Headley All SS *Guildf* 90-98; Past Asst Acorn Chr Healing Trust 91-93; P-in-c Wetley Rocks *Lich* 98-09; P-in-c Werrington 08-09; V Werrington and Wetley Rocks from 09. *2 Lordshire Mews, Armshead Road, Werrington, Stoke-on-Trent ST9 0HJ* Tel (01782) 302418 E-mail revsgoodwinx2@talktalk.net

GOODWIN HUDSON, Brainerd Peter de Wirtz. b 34. K Coll Lon BD57 AKC57. Westcott Ho Cam 57. **d** 59 **p** 60. C Morden *S'wark* 59-60; Australia 61-65; Asst Sec CCCS 65-68; Chapl St Lawr Coll Ramsgate 68-74; Chapl Repton Sch Derby 74-94; Chapl Santiago Chile 94-01; rtd 99; Hon C Broadwell, Evenlode, Oddington, Adlestrop etc *Glouc* 02-06. *Brea Heights, Trebetherick, Wadebridge PL27 6SE*
E-mail brainerd@freeuk.com

GOODWINS, Christopher William Hedley. b 36. St Jo Coll Cam BA58 MA62. Linc Th Coll 62. **d** 64 **p** 65. C Lowestoft Ch Ch *Nor* 64-69; V Tamerton Foliot *Ex* 69-98; P-in-c Southway 78-82; rtd 98; P-in-c Isleham *Ely* 99-04; Perm to Offic from 05. *102 The Causeway, Isleham, Ely CB7 5ST* Tel (01638) 780284
E-mail christopher@isleham.freeserve.co.uk

GOODYEAR, Benjamin. b 76. LSE BSc98. Ridley Hall Cam 03. **d** 06 **p** 07. C Balham Hill Ascension *S'wark* 06-09; P-in-c Brixton St Paul w St Sav from 09. *73 Baytree Road, London SW2 5RR* Tel 07866-774354 (mobile)
E-mail thegoodyears@gmail.com

GOODYEAR, Canon Edward Arthur. b 42. Witwatersrand Univ BA63 SS Coll Cam BA67 MA70 Rhodes Univ MTh91. St Paul's Coll Grahamstown 68. **d** 68 **p** 69. S Africa 69-92; Can Cape Town 80-84; R Alverstoke *Portsm* from 92; P-in-c Gosport Ch Ch 97-01; Hon Can Wusasa Nigeria from 99. *The Rectory, Little Anglesey Road, Alverstoke, Gosport PO12 2JA* Tel and fax (023) 9258 1979 *or* 9258 0551 Mobile 07976-921089
E-mail ego.lizg@virgin.net

GOOLD, Peter John. b 44. Lon Univ BD74. St Steph Ho Ox 67. **d** 70 **p** 71. C Chiswick St Nic w St Mary *Lon* 70-73; Chapl Asst R Masonic Hosp Lon 73-74; Chapl Asst Basingstoke Distr Hosp 74-77; Chapl R Marsden Hosp Lon and Surrey 77-80; Chapl N Hants Hosp 80-94; Chapl N Hants Hosps NHS Trust 94-00; Chapl N Hants Loddon Community NHS Trust 94-00; Perm to Offic *Guildf* 94-00; rtd 09. *Aepelford Acre, The Sands, Woodborough, Pewsey SN9 5PR* Tel (01672) 851942

GORDON, Alan Williamson. b 53. Strathclyde Univ BA75 MCIBS79. Wycliffe Hall Ox 98. **d** 98 **p** 99. C Win Ch Ch 98-02; R King's Worthy from 02; R Headbourne Worthy from 02; RD Win from 07. *The Rectory, 4 Campion Way, King's Worthy, Winchester SO23 7QP* Tel (01962) 882166
E-mail alan.gordon98@ntlworld.com

GORDON, The Very Revd Alexander Ronald. b 49. Nottm Univ BPharm71. Coll of Resurr Mirfield 74. **d** 77 **p** 78. C Headingley *Ripon* 77-80; C Fareham SS Pet and Paul *Portsm* 80-83; V Cudworth *Wakef* 83-85; P-in-c Tain *Mor* 85-87; P-in-c Lairg Miss 87-01; P-in-c Brora and Dornoch 88-01; Dioc Dir of Ords 89-01; Can St Andr Cathl Inverness 95-01; Hon Can 02-05; Chapl Strasbourg *Eur* 02-05; Provost St Andr Cathl Inverness from 05. *St Andrew's Lodge, 15 Ardross Street, Inverness IV3 5NS* Tel (01463) 233535 Mobile 07917-668918
E-mail canonalexgordon@btconnect.com

GORDON, Anne. *See* LE BAS, Mrs Jennifer Anne

✠**GORDON, The Rt Revd Archibald Ronald McDonald.** b 27. Ball Coll Ox BA50 MA52. Cuddesdon Coll 50. **d** 52 **p** 53 **c** 75. C Stepney St Dunstan and All SS *Lon* 52-55; Chapl Cuddesdon Coll 55-59; Lic to Offic *Ox* 57-59; V Birm St Pet 59-68; Lect Qu Coll Birm 60-62; Can Res Birm Cathl 67-71; V Ox St Mary V w St Cross and St Pet 71-75; Bp Portsm 75-84; Bp at Lambeth (Hd of Staff) *Cant* 84-91; Asst Bp S'wark 84-91; Bp HM Forces 85-90; Can Res and Sub-Dean Ch Ch *Ox* 91-96; rtd 96; Hon Asst Bp Ox from 91. *Garden Flat B, St Katharine's House, Ormond Road, Wantage OX12 8EA* Tel (01235) 760766
E-mail ronaldgordon.ab@btinternet.com

GORDON, Mrs Avis Patricia. b 52. Man Univ BA73. **d** 08 **p** 09. OLM Clifton *Man* from 08. *47 Agecroft Road West, Prestwich, Manchester M25 9RF* Tel 0161-798 8018

GORDON, Bruce Harold Clark. b 40. Edin Univ MTh96. Cranmer Hall Dur 65. **d** 68 **p** 69. C Edin St Jas 68-71; C Blackheath St Jo *S'wark* 71-74; R Duns *Edin* 74-90; R Lanark and Douglas *Glas* 90-05; rtd 05. *52 Foxknowe Place, Livingston EH54 6TX* Tel (01506) 418466
E-mail brucehc.gordon@virgin.net

GORDON, Donald Ian. b 30. Nottm Univ BA52 PhD64. Westcott Ho Cam 71. **d** 71 **p** 72. NSM Newport *Chelmsf* 71-75; NSM Creeksea w Althorne, Latchingdon and N Fambridge 76-00; rtd 00; Perm to Offic *Chelmsf* from 01. *Holden House, Steeple Road, Latchingdon, Chelmsford CM3 6JX* Tel (01621) 740296 E-mail barbaragordon@tiscali.co.uk

GORDON, Edward John. b 32. Univ of Wales BA52. St Mich Coll Llan 52. **d** 55 **p** 56. C Baglan *Llan* 55-61; C Newcastle w Laleston and Tythegston 61-65; V Ynyshir 65-69; C Bramhall *Ches* 69-72; V Cheadle Hulme All SS 72-79; V Tranmere St Paul w St Luke 79-88; V Sandbach Heath 88-97; Chapl Arclid Hosp 90-93; RD Congleton *Ches* 92-97; P-in-c Wheelock 95-97; rtd 97; Perm to Offic *B & W* from 97. *55 Greenslade Gardens, Nailsea, Bristol BS48 2BJ* Tel (01275) 853404

GORDON, John Michael. b 30. CITC. **d** 83 **p** 84. NSM Dublin St Geo *D & G* 83-85; NSM Dublin Irishtown w Donnybrook from 85. *Ferndale House, Rathmichael, Shankill, Co Dublin, Republic of Ireland* Tel (00353) (1) 282 2421 Fax 282 2954

GORDON, Jonathan Andrew. b 61. Keele Univ BA83 MPhil98 Southn Univ BTh88 Southn Inst MPhil04. Sarum & Wells Th Coll 84. **d** 87 **p** 88. C Wallingford w Crowmarsh Gifford etc *Ox* 87-91; C Tilehurst St Mich 91-93; TV Stoke-upon-Trent *Lich* 93-97; Chapl Southn Solent Univ 98-05; R Northchurch and Wigginton *St Alb* from 05. *St Mary's Rectory, 80 High Street, Northchurch, Berkhamsted HP4 3QW* Tel (01442) 871547
E-mail ebenezer@jonathangordon.wanadoo.co.uk

GORDON, Keith Adrian. b 49. Surrey Univ BSc71 Birm Univ MA02. Open Th Coll 95. **d** 98 **p** 99. Venezuela 98-03; C Caracas St Mary 98-99; Bp's Chapl Dioc Chpl 99-03; P-in-c Tenerife Sur *Eur* from 03. *Residencial Sonia #17, Calle El Mojon, Callao Salvaje, Adeje, 38678 Tenerife* Tel and fax (0034) 922 742 045 Mobile 679 660 277 E-mail kagordon40@hotmail.com

GORDON, Canon Kenneth Davidson. b 35. Edin Univ MA57 Univ of Wales MTh08. Tyndale Hall Bris 58. **d** 60 **p** 61. C St Helens St Helen *Liv* 60-66; V Daubhill *Man* 66-71; R Bieldside *Ab* 71-01; Can St Andr Cathl 81-01; Syn Clerk 96-01; rtd 01; Perm to Offic *Blackb* and *Liv* 01-07; Bp's Warrant *Ab* from 07. *16 Reidford Gardens, Drumoak, Banchory AB31 5AW* Tel (01330) 810260 Mobile 07715-169548
E-mail canonken@btinternet.com

GORDON, Kristy. *See* PATTIMORE, Mrs Kristy

GORDON, Mrs Pamela Anne. b 48. Brighton Coll of Educn CertEd69 BEd70. SAOMC 99. **d** 02 **p** 03. NSM Wargrave w Knowl Hill *Ox* from 02. *Rebeny, 2A Hawthorn Road, Caversham, Reading RG4 6LY* Tel 0118-947 8676 Fax 954 3076
E-mail pam.gordon@ntlworld.com

GORDON, Sister Patricia Ann. b 44. SAOMC. **d** 00 **p** 01. CSMV from 80; NSM Didcot St Pet *Ox* 00-07; NSM Wantage Downs from 07. *St Mary's Convent, Challow Road, Wantage OX12 9DJ* Tel (01235) 774084 Mobile 07884-196004
E-mail sisterpatriciaann@hotmail.co.uk

GORDON, Robert Andrew. b 42. Llan Dioc Tr Scheme 82. **d** 84 **p** 85. C Bargoed and Deri w Brithdir *Llan* 84-87; V Aberpergwm and Blaengwrach 87-94; R Johnston w Steynton *St D* 94-97; R Coshreston w Nash and Upton 97-04; TV Carew 04-07; rtd 07. *6 Oakridge Acres, Tenby SA70 8DB* Tel (01834) 844735

GORDON, Robert John. b 56. Edin Univ MA81. Wycliffe Hall Ox 87. **d** 89 **p** 90. C Wilnecote *Lich* 89-91; C Bideford *Ex* 91-95; P-in-c Feniton, Buckerell and Escot 95-05; P-in-c Tiverton St Pet and Chevithorne w Cove from 05. *St Peter's Vicarage, 29 Moorlands, Tiverton EX16 6UF* Tel (01884) 254079
E-mail robert.j.gordon@btopenworld.com

GORDON, Ronald. *See* GORDON, The Rt Revd Archibald Ronald McDonald

GORDON, Thomas William. b 57. QUB BEd80 Univ of Ulster MA86 TCD BTh89. CITC 85. **d** 89 **p** 90. C Ballymacash *Conn* 89-91; Min Can Belf Cathl 91-95; Chapl and Tutor CITC 91-96; Dir Extra-Mural Studies from 96; Lect Past Th and Liturgy from 01; Consultant Dir Past Formation and NSM 06-09; PV Ch Ch

Cathl Dublin from 96; Co-ord Relig Progr RTE from 99. *CITC, Braemor Park, Dublin 14, Republic of Ireland* Tel (00353) (1) 492 3506 *or* 492 3695 Fax 492 3082
E-mail tomgordon.consultancy@gmail.com

GORDON CLARK, John Vincent Michael. b 29. FCA. S'wark Ord Course 73. **d** 76 **p** 77. NSM Guildf H Trin w St Mary 76-81; NSM Albury w St Martha 81-91; Dioc Chapl to MU 92-95; Lic to Offic 95-99; Hon C Guildf Cathl 91-99; Perm to Offic from 99. *Hillfield, 8 Little Warren Close, Guildford GU4 8PW* Tel (01483) 569027

GORDON-CUMMING, Henry Ian. b 28. Barrister-at-Law (Gray's Inn) 56. Oak Hill Th Coll 54. **d** 57 **p** 58. C Southsea St Jude *Portsm* 57-60; Chapl to Bp Ankole-Kigezi Uganda 61-65; Chapl Ntari Sch 65-67; V Virginia Water *Guildf* 68-78; R Busbridge 78-87; R Lynch w Iping Marsh and Milland *Chich* 87-94; rtd 94; Perm to Offic *Chich* from 94. *Bay Cottage, Brookside, Runcton, Chichester PO20 1PX* Tel (01243) 783395

GORDON-KERR, Canon Francis Alexander. b 39. Dur Univ BA64 MA67 Hull Univ PhD81 DipEd. Wycliffe Hall Ox 65. **d** 67 **p** 68. C Heworth St Mary *Dur* 67-70; Chapl Newc Poly 70-75; Chapl Hull Univ 75-82; V Welton w Melton 82-92; Clergy Tr Officer E Riding 82-92; AD W Hull 87-96; RD Hull 89-96; Can and Preb York Minster 89-98; V Anlaby St Pet 92-98; R Crowland *Linc* 98-04; rtd 04. *Alberic Cottage, Low Road, Barrowby, Grantham NG32 1DD* Tel (01476) 574961

GORDON-TAYLOR, Benjamin Nicholas. b 69. St Jo Coll Dur BA90 MA92 Leeds Univ BA94 Dur Univ PhD08 FRSA99. Coll of Resurr Mirfield 92. **d** 95 **p** 96. C Launceston *Truro* 95-97; C Northampton St Matt *Pet* 97-99; Fell and Chapl Univ Coll Dur 99-04; Lect and Tutor Coll of Resurr Mirfield from 05; Visiting Lect Leeds Univ from 05; Dir Mirfield Liturg Inst from 08. *College of the Resurrection, Stocks Bank Road, Mirfield WF14 0BW* Tel (01924) 490441
E-mail bgordon-taylor@mirfield.org.uk

GORDON-WALKER, Caroline. b 37. LMH Ox BA59. Cranmer Hall Dur 01. **d** 02 **p** 03. NSM Poitou-Charentes *Eur* 02-05; C Aquitaine 05-07; Asst Chapl from 07. *La Vieille Ferme, 24170 St Germain-de-Belvès, France* Tel (0033) (5) 53 29 36 03
E-mail carolinegw@wanadoo.fr

GORE, Canon John Charles. b 29. Leeds Univ BA52. Coll of Resurr Mirfield 52. **d** 54 **p** 55. C Middlesbrough St Jo the Ev *York* 54-59; N Rhodesia 59-64; Zambia 64-75; Can Lusaka 70-75; R Elland *Wakef* 75-84; TR 84-86; RD Brighouse and Elland 77-86; V Wembley Park Aug *Lon* 86-95; P-in-c Tokyngton St Mich 89-90; AD Brent 90-95; rtd 95; P-in-c Heptonstall *Wakef* 95-99; Perm to Offic *Bradf* from 99. *3 Navigation Square, Skipton BD23 1XB* Tel (01756) 792297

GORE, Canon John Harrington. b 24. Em Coll Cam BA49 MA52. Westcott Ho Cam 49. **d** 51 **p** 52. C Deane *Man* 51-54; C Whitstable All SS w St Pet *Cant* 54-59; CF 59-62; V Womenswold *Cant* 62-67; C-in-c Aylesham CD 62-67; R Deal St Leon 67-75; RD Sandwich 70-78; P-in-c Sholden 74-75; R Deal St Leon w Sholden 75-80; R Southchurch H Trin *Chelmsf* 80-90; RD Southend-on-Sea 84-89; Hon Can Chelmsf Cathl 86-90; rtd 90; Perm to Offic *St E* and *Chelmsf* from 90. *8 De Burgh Place, Clare, Sudbury CO10 8QL* Tel (01787) 278558

GORE, Mrs Margaret Lesley. b 44. Westf Coll Lon BA66. ERMC 05. **d** 07 **p** 08. NSM Cherry Hinton St Jo *Ely* 07-09; NSM Linton from 09. *38 Symonds Lane, Linton, Cambridge CB21 4HY* Tel (01223) 891970

GORHAM, Canon Andrew Arthur. b 51. Bris Univ BA73 Birm Univ MA87. Qu Coll Birm 77. **d** 79 **p** 80. C Plaistow St Mary *Roch* 79-82; Chapl Lanchester Poly *Cov* 82-87; TV Warwick 87-95; Chapl Birm Univ 95-00; Bp's Dom Chapl from 00; Hon Can Birm Cathl from 06. *Bishop's Croft, Old Church Road, Harborne, Birmingham B17 0BE* Tel 0121-427 2295 *or* 427 1163 Fax 426 1322
E-mail bishopschaplain@birmingham.anglican.org

GORHAM, The Ven Karen Marisa. b 64. Trin Coll Bris BA95. **d** 95 **p** 96. C Northallerton w Kirby Sigston *York* 95-99; P-in-c Maidstone St Paul *Cant* 99-07; Asst Dir of Ords 02-07; AD Maidstone 03-07; Hon Can Cant Cathl 06-07; Adn Buckingham *Ox* from 07. *The Rectory, Stone, Aylesbury HP17 8RZ* Tel (01865) 208264 Fax (01296) 747424
E-mail archdbuc@oxford.anglican.org

GORICK, Charles. b 32. Reading Univ BA55 Nottm Univ DipEd72. EMMTC 81. **d** 84 **p** 85. NSM W Bridgford *S'well* 84-89; C Gotham 89-97; C Kingston and Ratcliffe-on-Soar 89-97; C Barton in Fabis 89-97; C Thrumpton 89-97; P-in-c Gotham 97-99; rtd 99; Perm to Offic *S'well* from 03. *11 Brookfields Way, East Leake, Loughborough LE12 6HD* Tel (01509) 856960

GORICK, Janet Margaret. b 30. Reading Univ BA54. EMMTC 84. **dss** 86 **d** 87 **p** 94. Hon Par Dn W Bridgford *S'well* 87-95; NSM Gotham 95-99; NSM Barton in Fabis 95-99; NSM Kingston and Ratcliffe-on-Soar 95-99; NSM Thrumpton 95-99; rtd 99; Perm to Offic *S'well* from 03. *11 Brookfields Way, East Leake, Loughborough LE12 6HD* Tel (01509) 856960

GORICK, Martin Charles William. b 62. Selw Coll Cam BA84 MA88. Ripon Coll Cuddesdon 85. **d** 87 **p** 88. C Birtley *Dur* 87-91; Bp's Dom Chapl *Ox* 91-94; V Smethwick *Birm* 94-01; AD Warley 97-01; R Stratford-upon-Avon, Luddington etc *Cov* from 01. *The Vicarage, 7 Old Town, Stratford-upon-Avon CV37 6BG* Tel (01789) 266022 *or* 266316
E-mail office@stratford-upon-avon.org

GORING, Charles Robert. b 60. Nottm Univ BA91. Linc Th Coll 91. **d** 93 **p** 94. C Thornbury *Glouc* 93-96; Perm to Offic *Chich* 97-98; C Mayfield 98-00; V The Hydneye 00-07; C Eastbourne Ch Ch and St Phil from 07; Asst Chapl E Sussex Hosps NHS Trust from 01. *St Philip's House, 10 St Philip's Place, Eastbourne BN22 8LW* Tel (01323) 749653
E-mail jc.goring@googlemail.com

GORRIE, Richard Bingham. b 27. Univ Coll Ox BA49 MA51. Ridley Hall Cam 49. **d** 51 **p** 52. C Ox St Clem 51-54; C Morden S'wark 54-56; Scripture Union Rep (Scotland) 56-92; Chapl Fettes Coll Edin 60-74; Dir Inter-Sch Chr Fellowship (Scotland) 74-80; rtd 92; Perm to Offic *Glas* from 92. *20 Auchlochan Courtyard, New Trows Road, Lesmahagow, Lanark ML11 0GS* Tel (01555) 895076 E-mail gorries@silas57.freeserve.co.uk

GORRINGE, Edward George Alexander. b 63. TD. QUB BA85 Strathclyde Univ MBA00 FCMA06. CITC 04. **d** 07 **p** 08. NSM Aghalee *D & D* 07-09; CF from 09. *c/o MOD Chaplains (Army)* Tel (01980) 615804 Fax 615800 E-mail egag.public@virgin.net

GORRINGE, Prof Timothy Jervis. b 46. St Edm Hall Ox BA69 MPhil75. Sarum Th Coll 69. **d** 72 **p** 73. C Chapel Allerton *Ripon* 72-75; C Ox St Mary V w St Cross and St Pet 76-78; India 79-86; Chapl St Jo Coll Ox 86-96; Reader St Andr Univ from 96; Prof Th Ex Univ from 99. *Department of Theology, Exeter University, Queen's Building, The Queen's Drive, Exeter EX4 4QH* Tel (01392) 264242 E-mail t.j.gorringe@exeter.ac.uk

GORST, Angela Deborah. *See* WYNNE, Mrs Angela Deborah

GORTON, Anthony David Trevor. b 39. Lon Univ BSc65. Oak Hill Th Coll 78. **d** 81 **p** 82. NSM Colney Heath St Mark *St Alb* 81-00; NSM Watford St Pet from 00. *Waterdell, Lane End, Hatfield AL10 9AG* Tel (01707) 263605
E-mail tonygorton@hotmail.com

GORTON, Ian Charles Johnson. b 62. Bp Otter Coll BA84. Sarum & Wells Th Coll 86. **d** 89 **p** 90. C Wythenshawe Wm Temple Ch *Man* 89-92; C Man Apostles w Miles Platting 92-95; P-in-c Abbey Hey 95-03; P-in-c Moston St Chad from 03; P-in-c Moston St Jo from 05. *St Chad's Rectory, 30 Hawthorn Road, Manchester M40 3RH* Tel 0161-681 3203

GORTON (née CARTER), Sarah Helen Buchanan. b 44. St Andr Univ BSc65 DipEd66. TISEC 93. **d** 96 **p** 98. NSM Lenzie *Glas* 96-01; P-in-c Alexandria from 01; Chapl Argyll and Clyde NHS from 01. *The Rectory, Queen Street, Alexandria G83 0AS* Tel (01389) 752633 E-mail shbgorton@btinternet.com

GOSDEN, Timothy John. b 50. Open Univ BA86. Chich Th Coll 74. **d** 77 **p** 78. C Cant All SS 77-81; Asst Chapl Loughb Univ 81-85; Lic to Offic *Cant* 85-87; Chapl Ch Ch Coll of HE Cant 85-87; Sen Chapl Hull Univ 87-94; V Taunton Lyngford *B & W* 94-98; V Harrow St Mary *Lon* from 98. *St Mary's Vicarage, Church Hill, Harrow HA1 3HL* Tel (020) 8422 2652
E-mail timgosden@tiscali.co.uk *or* stmaryharrow@aol.com

GOSHAI, Miss Veja Helena. b 32. SRN57 SCM59 City Univ BSc99. Trin Coll Bris 75. **d** 87 **p** 94. Asst Chapl St Bart Hosp Lon 87-97; rtd 92; Perm to Offic *S'wark* 99-03. *Grace, 26 Bilston Road, Crawford, Cape Town, 7780 South Africa*

GOSLING, David. b 27. SAOMC 95. **d** 98 **p** 99. OLM High Wycombe *Ox* 98-03; Perm to Offic from 02. *72 Hatters Lane, High Wycombe HP13 7NJ* Tel (01494) 443947
E-mail dgosling027@btopenworld.com

GOSLING, David Lagourie. b 39. Man Univ MSc63 Fitzw Coll Cam MA69 Lanc Univ PhD74 MInstP69 CPhys84. Ridley Hall Cam 63. **d** 73 **p** 74. Hon C Lancaster St Mary *Blackb* 73-74; Hon C Kingston upon Hull St Matt w St Barn *York* 74-77; Hon C Cottingham 78-83; Asst Chapl Geneva *Eur* 84-89; C Cambridge Gt St Mary w St Mich *Ely* 89-90; C Dry Drayton 90-94; USPG India 95-99; Perm to Offic *York* from 95 and *Ely* from 01; Fell Clare Hall Cam from 01; Prin Edwardes Coll Peshawar Pakistan from 06. *Clare Hall, Herschel Road, Cambridge CB3 9AL* Tel (01223) 352450 Fax 332333 E-mail dlg26@cam.ac.uk

GOSLING, James Albert. b 41. Oak Hill Th Coll 81. **d** 84 **p** 85. NSM Victoria Docks St Luke *Chelmsf* 84-96; V C Gt Mongeham w Ripple and Sutton by Dover *Cant* 96-01; Hon C Eastry and Northbourne w Tilmanstone etc 96-01; C Kenton, Mamhead, Powderham, Cofton and Starcross *Ex* 01-02. *2 Wordsworth Close, Exmouth EX8 5SQ* Tel (01395) 225278
E-mail jimandjan@jimandjan.fsnet.co.uk

GOSLING, John William Fraser. b 34. St Jo Coll Dur BA58 MA71 Ex Univ PhD78. Cranmer Hall Dur 58. **d** 60 **p** 61. C Plympton St Mary *Ex* 60-68; V Newport 68-78; Org Sec CECS *St Alb* and *Ox* 78-82; C Stratford sub Castle *Sarum* 83-86; Adv on CME 83-86; Perm to Offic 86-91 and from 95; C Swindon Ch Ch *Bris* 91-95; rtd 95. *1 Wiley Terrace, Wilton, Salisbury SP2 0HN* Tel (01722) 742788 E-mail jgosling@givemail.co.uk

GOSNEY, Jeanette Margaret. b 58. Bath Univ BA81 Univ Coll Ches MA05 Nottm Univ PGCE82. St Jo Coll Nottm BTh93 MPhil95. **d** 95 **p** 96. C Ipswich St Marg *St E* 95-98; Chapl Loughb Univ 98; Sen Chapl 98-01; Tutor Trin Coll Bris 01-04; Chapl Repton Sch Derby 04-05; TV Albury, Braughing, Furneux Pelham, Lt Hadham etc *St Alb* from 06. *The Rectory, 7A Green End, Braughing, Ware SG11 2PG* Tel (01920) 822619 E-mail vicar@braughing.org.uk

GOSS, David James. b 52. Nottm Univ BCombStuds. Linc Th Coll. **d** 83 **p** 84. C Wood Green St Mich w Bounds Green St Gabr etc *Lon* 83-86; TV Gleadless Valley *Sheff* 86-89; TR 89-95; V Wheatley Hills from 95. *The Vicarage, 18 Central Boulevard, Doncaster DN2 5PE* Tel (01302) 342047 E-mail geese@talk21.com

GOSS, Kevin Ian. b 56. LRAM75 LTCL76 GRSM77 LGSM80 Hughes Hall Cam PGCE78 Heythrop Coll Lon MA08. S Dios Minl Tr Scheme 89. **d** 92 **p** 93. NSM Ardingly *Chich* 92-98; Asst Chapl Ardingly Coll 92-98; Min Can, Prec and Sacr Cant Cathl 98-03; P-in-c Hockerill *St Alb* from 04; Chapl Herts and Essex Community NHS Trust from 04. *Hockerill Vicarage, 4A All Saints Close, Bishop's Stortford CM23 2EA* Tel (01279) 506542 E-mail allsaintshockerill@btinternet.com

GOSS, Michael John. b 37. Chich Th Coll 62. **d** 65 **p** 66. C Angell Town St Jo *S'wark* 65-68; C Catford St Laur 68-71; P-in-c Lewisham St Swithun 71-81; V Redhill St Jo 81-88; V Studley St Thos and St Luke *Worc* 88-98; C Small Heath *Birm* 98-02; rtd 02; Perm to Offic *Birm* from 02. *8 Mayland Road, Birmingham B16 0NG* Tel 0121-429 6022 E-mail michael.goss@tinyworld.co.uk

GOSSWINN, Nicholas Simon. b 50. Birm Poly FGA80. St D Coll Lamp. **d** 73 **p** 77. C Abergavenny St Mary *Mon* 73-74; C-in-c Bassaleg 74-80; TV Barrow St Geo w St Luke *Carl* 81-87; C Usworth *Dur* 89-90; TV 90-96; P-in-c Sunderland Red Ho 96-02; P-in-c Stockport St Matt *Ches* 02-03. *Alnwick, Queens Park, Millom LA18 5DY*

GOSTELOW (née THOMPSON), Mrs Ruth Jean. b 47. St Alb Minl Tr Scheme 85. **d** 90 **p** 94. Par Dn Stonebridge St Mich *Lon* 90-94; C Ealing St Paul 94-96; TV W Slough *Ox* 96-03; V New Haw *Guildf* from 03. *The Vicarage, 149 Woodham Lane, New Haw, Addlestone KT15 3NJ* Tel and fax (01932) 343187 E-mail rev.ruth@btinternet.com

GOSWELL, Geoffrey. b 34. SS Paul & Mary Coll Cheltenham CertEd68. Glouc Th Course 70. **d** 71 **p** 72. C Cheltenham Em *Glouc* 71-73; C Lydney w Aylburton 73-76; P-in-c Falfield w Rockhampton 76-79; Chapl HM Det Cen Eastwood Park 76-79; Area Sec CMS *Ely* 79-81; *Linc* and *Pet* 79-86; Dep Regional Sec (UK) CMS 86-97; P-in-c Orton Waterville *Ely* 90-96; TV The Ortons, Alwalton and Chesterton 96-97; rtd 97; Perm to Offic *Pet* from 01. *8 Lapwing Close, Northampton NN4 0RT* Tel (01604) 701572 E-mail g.goswell@hotmail.co.uk

GOTHARD, Mrs Anne Marie. b 51. STETS. **d** 00. NSM E Meon and Langrish *Portsm* 00-04; NSM Catherington and Clanfield from 04. *27 Green Lane, Clanfield, Waterlooville PO8 0JU* Tel (023) 9259 6315 Mobile 07939-472796 E-mail rev_gothard@hotmail.com

GOTT, Stephen. b 61. St Jo Coll Nottm 92. **d** 94 **p** 95. C Mount Pellon *Wakef* 94-97; V Greetland and W Vale 97-06; TR Em TM from 06. *The Rectory, 12 Moor Close, Huddersfield HD4 7BP* Tel (01484) 652543 E-mail stephen.gott@btinternet.com

GOUGH, Andrew Stephen. b 60. Sarum & Wells Th Coll 83. **d** 86 **p** 87. C St Leonards Ch Ch and St Mary *Chich* 86-88; C Broseley w Benthall *Heref* 88-90; V Ketley and Oakengates *Lich* 90-93; TV Bickleigh (Plymouth) *Ex* 93; TV Bickleigh and Shaugh Prior 94; P-in-c St Day *Truro* 94-96; V Chacewater w St Day and Carharrack from 96. *The Vicarage, Pink Moors, St Day, Redruth TR16 5NN* Tel (01209) 820275 Mobile 07590-695515 E-mail goughfr@hotmail.com

GOUGH, Andrew Walter. b 55. Bris Univ BA78. Trin Coll Bris 90. **d** 92 **p** 93. C Mossley Hill St Matt and St Jas *Liv* 92-94; C Wavertree H Trin 94-96; Chapl Warw Sch from 96. *9 Griffin Road, Warwick CV34 6QX* Tel (01926) 400533 *or* 776416 E-mail awg@warwickschool.org

GOUGH, Anthony Walter. b 31. Leic Univ MA76 Chicago Th Sem DMin81. Oak Hill Th Coll 57. **d** 60 **p** 61. C Southsea St Simon *Portsm* 60-64; R Peldon *Chelmsf* 64-71; V Rothley *Leic* 71-80; USA 80-81; Chapl St Jo Hosp Aylesbury 81-82; Perm to Offic *Leic* 82-96; rtd 96. *410 Hinckley Road, Leicester LE3 0WA* Tel 0116-285 4284 E-mail tg1@ntlworld.com

GOUGH, Canon Colin Richard. b 47. St Chad's Coll Dur BA69. Cuddesdon Coll 73. **d** 75 **p** 76. C Lich St Chad 75-78; C Codsall 78-84; V Wednesbury St Paul Wood Green 84-92; TR Tettenhall Wood 92-99; TR Tettenhall Wood and Perton 99-01; P-in-c Stannington *Newc* from 01; Dioc Adv for CME from 01; Hon Can Newc Cathl from 06; AD Morpeth from 08. *The Vicarage, Beechlea, Stannington, Morpeth NE61 6HL* Tel (01670) 789122 *or* 0191-270 4153 Fax 0191-270 4101 E-mail colingough@onetel.com *or* c.gough@newcastle.anglican.org

GOUGH, David Kenneth. b 44. St Mark & St Jo Coll Lon TCert66 Open Univ BA93. **d** 07 **p** 08. OLM Kinnerley w Melverley and Knockin w Maesbrook *Lich* from 07. *Ainsdale House, Maesbrook, Oswestry SY10 8QP*

GOUGH, David Norman. b 42. Oak Hill Th Coll 70. **d** 70 **p** 71. C Penn Fields *Lich* 70-73; C Stapenhill w Cauldwell *Derby* 73-77; V Heath 77-86; P-in-c Derby St Chad 86-95; TV Walbrook Epiphany 95-03; P-in-c Codnor and Loscoe 03-07; rtd 07. *7 Mullberry Close, Belper DE56 1RQ* Tel (01773) 599013 E-mail thevic@dsl.pipex.com

GOUGH, David Richard. b 71. St Jo Coll Nottm 06. **d** 08 **p** 09. C Sheff St Jo from 08. *338 Harborough Avenue, Sheffield S2 1UU* Tel 07913-083656 (mobile) E-mail david_gough11@hotmail.com

GOUGH, Derek William. b 31. Pemb Coll Cam BA55 MA59. St Steph Ho Ox 55. **d** 57 **p** 58. C E Finchley All SS *Lon* 57-60; C Roxbourne St Andr 60-66; V Edmonton St Mary w St Jo 66-98; rtd 98; Perm to Offic *Chelmsf* 98-07 and *St Alb* 00-07. *43A Church Street, Market Deeping, Peterborough PE6 8AN* Tel (01778) 341421

GOUGH, Elizabeth. b 54. CBDTI 97. **d** 00 **p** 01. OLM Eden, Gelt and Irthing *Carl* 00-06; TV from 06. *Brackenside Barn, Brampton CA8 2QX* Tel (01697) 746252 E-mail elizabeth.gough3@btinternet.com

GOUGH, Canon Ernest Hubert. b 31. TCD BA53 MA57. TCD Div Sch Div Test 54. **d** 54 **p** 55. C Glenavy *Conn* 54-57; C Lisburn Ch Ch 57-61; P-in-c Belfast St Ninian 61-62; I 62-71; I Belfast St Bart 71-85; I Templepatrick w Donegore 85-97; Can Conn Cathl from 91; rtd 97. *The Caim, 15 Swilly Road, Portstewart BT55 7DJ* Tel (028) 7083 3253 E-mail ehg@thecaim.fsnet.co.uk

GOUGH, Frank Peter. b 32. Lon Coll of Div 66. **d** 68 **p** 69. C Weymouth St Mary *Sarum* 68-70; C Attenborough w Chilwell *S'well* 70-73; R Barrow *Ches* 73-77; P-in-c Summerstown *S'wark* 77-88; RD Tooting 80-88; Dioc Past Sec 88-93; Tutor and Chapl Whittington Coll Felbridge 93-98; rtd 98; Perm to Offic *Roch* 03-07. *7 Burden Way, Guildford GU2 9RB* Tel 07970-199135 (mobile) E-mail frank_gough@msn.com

GOUGH, Canon Jonathan Robin Blanning. b 62. Univ of Wales (Lamp) BA83 Westmr Coll Ox MTh96 FRSA03. St Steph Ho Ox 83. **d** 85 **p** 86. C Braunton *Ex* 85-86; C Matson *Glouc* 86-89; CF 89-01 and 05-08; Abp's Officer for Ecum *Cant* 01-05; Can Gib Cathl 02-05; Public Preacher *Win* from 02; Hon Can Nicosia from 06. *22 Hayes Court, Camberwell New Road, London SE5 0TQ* Tel (020) 7654 7218

GOUGH, Miss Lynda Elizabeth. b 54. SS Hild & Bede Coll Dur BA94 RGN83. Wycliffe Hall Ox 97. **d** 99 **p** 00. C Stranton *Dur* 99-03; V Spennymoor and Whitworth from 03. *The Vicarage, 30 Jubilee Close, Spennymoor DL16 6GA* Tel (01388) 815471

GOUGH, Martyn John. b 66. Univ of Wales (Cardiff) BTh87 Univ of Wales (Lamp) MA05 FRSA04. St Steph Ho Ox 88. **d** 90 **p** 91. C Port Talbot St Theodore *Llan* 90-92; C Roath 92-94; Asst Chapl Milan w Genoa and Varese *Eur* 95-98; Chapl RN from 98; Asst Dir of Ords RN and Voc Adv 07-09; Dir from 09. *Royal Naval Chaplaincy Service, Mail Point 1-2, Leach Building, Whale Island, Portsmouth PO2 8BY* Tel (023) 9262 5055 Fax 9262 5134

GOUGH, Stephen William Cyprian. b 50. Alberta Univ BSc71. Cuddesdon Coll BA80 MA. **d** 79 **p** 80. C Walton St Mary *Liv* 79-83; V New Springs 83-87; V Childwall St Dav 87-06; V Stoneycroft All SS 04-06; Co-ord Chapl HM Pris Risley 06-08; P-in-c Rainford *Liv* from 08. *6 West View, Ormskirk Road, Rainford, St Helens WA11 8BS* Tel (01744) 882200 Mobile 07965-554471 E-mail gough_stephen@btopenworld.com

GOULD, Alan Charles. b 26. **d** 62 **p** 63. C Bromborough *Ches* 62-67; V Audlem and Burleydam 67-80; V Knowbury and P-in-c Coreley and Doddington *Heref* 80-83; P-in-c Cound and Berrington w Betton Strange 83-91; rtd 91; Perm to Offic *Heref* and *Lich* from 91. *32 Mytton Oak Road, Shrewsbury SY3 8UD* Tel (01743) 244820

GOULD, David Robert. b 59. Cov Poly BA81. Cranmer Hall Dur 87. **d** 90 **p** 91. C Rugby *Cov* 90-93; CF 93-94; Perm to Offic *Cov* 01-05; TV Kings Norton *Birm* 05-08; V Smethwick Resurr from 08. *The Vicarage, 69 South Road, Smethwick, Warley B67 7BP* Tel 0121-558 0373 Mobile 07787-199998 E-mail davidgould1@btinternet.com

GOULD, Canon Douglas Walter. b 35. St Jo Coll Cam BA59 MA63. Ridley Hall Cam 59. **d** 61 **p** 62. C Clifton *York* 61-64; C Bridgnorth w Tasley *Heref* 64-67; C Astley Abbotts w Linley 64-67; R Acton Burnell w Pitchford 67-73; P-in-c Cound and Asst Dioc Youth Officer 68-73; P-in-c Frodesley 69-73; V Bromyard and P-in-c Stanford Bishop 73-00; P-in-c Ullingswick and Ocle Pychard 75-98; P-in-c Stoke Lacy, Moreton Jeffries w Much Cowarne etc 76-83; RD Bromyard 73-99; Chapl Bromyard Community Hosp 73-92; Chapl Herefordshire Community Health NHS Trust 92-00; Preb Heref Cathl 83-00; rtd 00; Perm to Offic *Heref* from 00; Hon Can Dar es Salaam from 06. *Highwood Croft, Marden, Hereford HR1 3EW* Tel and fax (01432) 880084 E-mail waltergould@waitrose.com

GOULD, Ms Janet. b 63. LTCL85. Westcott Ho Cam 92. **d** 95 **p** 96. C Pet St Mary Boongate 95-98; C Fleet *Guildf* 98-04; C St Mellons *Mon* 04-05; P-in-c Glan Ely *Llan* from 06. *St Michael's College, 54 Cardiff Road, Llandaff, Cardiff CF5 2YJ* Tel (029) 2056 3116 E-mail jan.gould2@btinternet.com

GOULD, Jonathan George Lillico. b 58. Bris Univ LLB79. Wycliffe Hall Ox 86. **d** 89 **p** 91. Australia 89-93; Schs Worker Scripture Union Independent Schs 93-95; Perm to Offic *S'wark* 93-95; Min Hampstead St Jo Downshire Hill Prop Chpl *Lon* from 95. *The Parsonage, 64 Pilgrim's Lane, London NW3 1SN* Tel (020) 7794 8946 *or* tel and fax 7435 8404 E-mail jonathan@sjdh.org

GOULD, Mrs Pamela Rosemarie. b 41. **d** 01 **p** 02. NSM New Bilton *Cov* 01-03; Asst Chapl HM YOI Onley 01-03; NSM Clifton upon Dunsmore and Newton *Cov* 03-05; P-in-c 05-06; Perm to Offic from 07. *19 Church Road, Church Lawford, Rugby CV23 9EG* Tel (024) 7654 5745 E-mail revpamgould@aol.com

GOULD, Peter Richard. b 34. Univ of Wales BA57. Qu Coll Birm. **d** 62 **p** 63. C Rothwell *Ripon* 62-68; V Allerton Bywater 68-73; Lic to Offic *S'well* 73-76; Chapl Lic Victuallers' Sch Ascot 76-93; V Aberavon H Trin *Llan* 93-99; rtd 99. *Amber Cottage, 1 Load Lane, Weston Zoyland, Bridgwater TA7 0EQ* Tel (01278) 691029

GOULD, Robert Ozburn. b 38. Williams Coll Mass BA59 St Andr Univ PhD63. **d** 78 **p** 83. NSM Edin St Columba 78-80; TV from 83; Hon Dioc Supernumerary 80-83; Hon Chapl Edin Univ 00-04. *33 Charterhall Road, Edinburgh EH9 3HS* Tel 0131-667 7230 E-mail gould@ed.ac.uk

GOULD, Susan Judith. *See* MURRAY, Mrs Susan Judith

GOULD, Walter. *See* GOULD, Canon Douglas Walter

GOULDER, Canon Catherine Helen. b 44. Hull Univ BA65 MA67 Ox Univ DipEd68. NEOC 96. **d** 98 **p** 99. NSM Sutton St Mich *York* 98-02; P-in-c Hotham and N Cave w Cliffe 02-08; Perm to Offic from 08; Can and Preb York Minster from 05. *5 Bishops Croft, Beverley HU17 8JY* Tel (01482) 880553

GOULDING, Amanda. b 53. STETS. **d** 07 **p** 08. NSM Upper Dever *Win* 07-08; NSM Win St Bart from 08. *Long Valley, Deane Down Drove, Littleton, Winchester SO22 6PP* Tel (01962) 884585 E-mail agoulding@btinternet.com

GOULDING, John Gilbert. b 29. Univ Coll Dur BA54 MA59. **d** 88 **p** 89. NSM Kemsing w Woodlands *Roch* 88-91; Hon Nat Moderator for Reader Tr ACCM 90-91; ABM 91-94; NSM Sevenoaks St Luke CD 91-96; Perm to Offic from 97. *Springwood, 50 Copperfields, Kemsing, Sevenoaks TN15 6QG* Tel (01732) 762558

GOULDING, Nicolas John. b 56. Southn Univ BSc78 PhD82. NTMTC 94. **d** 97 **p** 98. NSM St Bart Less *Lon* from 97; Chapl St Bart's and RLSMD Qu Mary and Westf Coll from 97; Perm to Offic *St Alb* from 99. *5 Greatfield Close, Harpenden AL5 3HP* Tel (01582) 461293 *or* (020) 7882 6128 Fax (020) 7982 6076 E-mail n.j.goulding@qmul.ac.uk

GOULDTHORPE, Rachel Carolyn. b 72. Bp Otter Coll 00. **d** 03. NSM Hove *Chich* 03-05; C Moulsecoomb from 05. *The Vicarage, Selham Drive, Brighton BN1 9EL* Tel (01273) 601854 Mobile 07859-066557 E-mail rachelgouldthorpe@netbreeze.co.uk

GOULSTON, Jeremy Hugh. b 68. St Aid Coll Dur BA90. Ripon Coll Cuddesdon 01. **d** 03 **p** 04. C Henfield w Shermanbury and Woodmancote *Chich* 03-07; TV Wallingford *Ox* from 07. *The Vicarage, 34 Thames Mead, Crowmarsh Gifford, Wallingford OX10 8EY* Tel (01491) 837626 E-mail jgoulston@btinternet.com

GOULSTONE, Thomas Richard Kerry. b 36. Univ of Wales (Lamp) BA57. St Mich Coll Llan 57. **d** 59 **p** 60. C Llanbadarn Fawr *St D* 59-61; C Carmarthen St Pet 61-64; V 84-93; V Whitchurch w Solva and St Elvis 64-67; V Gors-las 67-76; V Burry Port and Pwll 76-84; Chapl W Wales Gen Hosp Carmarthen 84-93; Can St D Cathl 86-93; Hon Can St D Cathl from 93; RD Carmarthen 88-92; Adn Carmarthen 91-93; Dean and Lib St As Cathl 93-01; rtd 01. *25 Parc Tyisha, Burry Port SA16 0RR* Tel (01554) 832390

GOUNDREY-SMITH, Stephen John. b 67. Brighton Poly BSc88 MRPharmS89 City Univ MSc94. Aston Tr Scheme 96 Wycliffe Hall Ox BTh01. **d** 99 **p** 00. C Happisburgh, Walcott, Hempstead w Eccles etc *Nor* 99-01; Perm to Offic *Pet* 02-03; NSM Chenderit 03-08; Perm to Offic from 09. *1 The Walnuts, Main Street, Charlton, Banbury OX17 3DR* Tel (01295) 816887 Mobile 07771-741009 E-mail stephen.goundrey-smith@torex.com

GOUNDRY, Canon Ralph Walter. b 31. St Chad's Coll Dur BA56. **d** 58 **p** 59. C Harton Colliery *Dur* 58-62; Prec Newc Cathl 62-65; V Sighill 65-72; V Long Benton 72-96; Hon Can Newc Cathl 94-96; rtd 96; Perm to Offic *York* 96-08. *16 Old Manor Way, Chislehurst BR7 5XS* Tel (020) 8249 9992

GOUPILLON, Mrs Jane Elizabeth. b 50. Univ of Wales (Lamp) BA92 Trin Coll Carmarthen PGCE94. St Mich Coll Llan. **d** 03 **p** 04. C Carmarthen St Dav *St D* 03-05; R Llangwm w Freystrop and Johnston from 05. *The Rectory, Four Winds, 30 The Kilns, Llangwm, Haverfordwest SA62 4NG* Tel (01437) 891317

GOURDIE, Mrs Janice Elizabeth. b 65. Univ of Wales (Ban) BTh04. **d** 04 **p** 05. C Botwnnog w Bryncroes w Llangwnnadl w Penllech *Ban* 04-05; C Llyn and Eifionydd 05-07; P-in-c Denio w Abererch 07-09; V from 09. *Y Ficerdy, Yr Ala, Pwllheli LL53 5BL* Tel (01758) 612305 Mobile 07969-655497 E-mail janicegourdie@hotmail.com

GOURLEY, Malcolm Samuel. b 37. MRPharmS58. NEOC 94. **d** 98 **p** 98. NSM Gt Smeaton w Appleton Wiske and Birkby etc *Ripon* 98-00; NSM Ainderby Steeple w Yafforth and Kirby Wiske etc 00-02; NSM Herrington, Penshaw and Shiney Row *Dur* from 02. *10 Weymouth Drive, Houghton le Spring DH4 7TQ* Tel 0191-385 4076

GOURLEY, William Robert Joseph. b 48. K Coll Lon BD74. CITC 68. **d** 75 **p** 76. C Newtownards *D & D* 75-78; I Currin w Drum and Newbliss *Clogh* 78-81; I Dublin St Geo and St Thos, Finglas and Free Ch *D & G* 81-88; I Dublin Zion Ch from 88. *The Rectory, 18 Bushy Park Road, Rathgar, Dublin 6, Republic of Ireland* Tel (00353) (1) 492 2365 *or* 406 4730 E-mail wilbertgourley@ireland.com

GOVAN, Kesh Rico. b 66. St Jo Coll Dur BA96. Cranmer Hall Dur 93. **d** 96 **p** 97. C Astley Bridge *Man* 96-00; TV Walkden and Lt Hulton 00-04; I Blessington w Kilbride, Ballymore Eustace etc *D & G* 04-07; C Rocester and Croxden w Hollington *Lich* from 07; C Uttoxeter Area from 07. *The Vicarage, Church Lane, Rocester, Uttoxeter ST14 5JZ* Tel (01889) 590424 Mobile 07982-930384 E-mail revkesh@sky.com

GOVENDER, The Very Revd Rogers Morgan. b 60. Natal Univ BTh97. St Paul's Coll Grahamstown 83. **d** 85 **p** 86. C Overport Ch Ch S Africa 85-87; R Greyville St Mary 88-92; R Hayfields St Matt 93-98; Adn Pietermaritzburg 97-98; R Berea St Thos 99-00; P-in-c Didsbury Ch Ch *Man* 01-06; P-in-c Withington St Chris 03-06; AD Withington 04-06; Dean Man from 06. *1 Booth Clibborn Court, Salford M7 4PJ* Tel 0161-792 2801 *or* 833 2220 Fax 839 6218 E-mail dean@manchestercathedral.com

GOW, Iain Douglas. b 60. Denver Univ USA BA83 MIM85. Trin Coll Bris MA94. **d** 94 **p** 95. C Kenilworth St Jo *Cov* 94-97; C Birm St Martin w Bordesley St Andr 97-05; AD Birm City Cen 02-04; New Zealand from 05. *2/82 Knights Road, Rothesay Bay, North Shore, Auckland 1311, New Zealand* Tel (0064) (9) 478 4894

GOW, Peter Draffin. b 52. Bede Coll Dur BEd76. St Jo Coll Nottm 83. **d** 85. C Kingston Hill St Paul *S'wark* 85-86; rtd 86. *Chatsworth Wing, Royal Hospital for Neuro-disability, London SW15 3SW* Tel (020) 8788 5158 E-mail petergow@waacis.edex.co.uk

GOWDEY, Michael Cragg. b 32. Oriel Coll Ox BA56 MA58 Keele Univ CertEd73. Qu Coll Birm. **d** 58 **p** 59. C Ashbourne w Mapleton and Clifton *Derby* 58-63; V Chellaston 63-69; Asst Chapl Ellesmere Coll 69-74; Chapl Trent Coll Nottm 74-81; Educn Chapl *Worc* 81 97; Chapl K Edw Sixth Form Coll Worc 81-97; rtd 97; P-in-c Beeley and Edensor *Derby* 97-02; Perm to Offic from 02. *18 Moorhall Estate, Bakewell DE45 1FP* Tel (01629) 814121

GOWEN, John Frank. b 30. **d** 87 **p** 89. Aux Min Lecale Gp and Cregagh *D & D* 87-91; Lic to Offic 89-99; Aux Min Stormont 99-01; Aux Min Knock 01-05; rtd 05. *36 Downshire Road, Belfast BT6 9JL* Tel (028) 9070 1640 Mobile 07815-301818 E-mail jgowen212@btinternet.com

GOWER, Canon Christopher Raymond. b 45. Nottm Univ BA73 Heythrop Coll Lon MA96 Univ of Wales MTh02 FRSA84. St Jo Coll Nottm 70. **d** 73 **p** 74. C Hounslow H Trin *Lon* 73-76; Hon C N Greenford All Hallows 76-77; P-in-c Willesden Green St Gabr 77-83; P-in-c Brondesbury St Anne w Kilburn H Trin 81-82; Perm to Offic 82-84; P-in-c Yiewsley 84-96; R St Marylebone w H Trin from 97; P-in-c St Marylebone St Cypr 99-02; Hon Can Ilesa from 04; Preb St Paul's Cathl from 07. *21 Beaumont Street, London W1G 6DQ* Tel (020) 7935 8965 *or* 7935 7315 Fax 7486 5493 E-mail office@stmarylebone.org

GOWER, Denys Victor. b 33. Can Sch of Min 85. **d** 87 **p** 88. NSM Gillingham H Trin *Roch* 87-91; NSM Gillingham St Aug 89-91; C Perry Street 91-93; P-in-c Wateringbury w Teston and W Farleigh 93-96; P-in-c 96-00; rtd 00; Ind Chapl *Roch* from 00; Perm to Offic *Roch* from 00 and *Cant* 03-09; Hon Chapl Medway NHS Foundn Trust from 05; PV Roch Cathl from 07. *4 Locarno Avenue, Gillingham ME8 6ET* Tel (01634) 375765 Mobile 07985-781161

GOWER, Nigel Plested. b 37. SS Coll Cam BA62 MA65 Lon Univ PGCE68. Ridley Hall Cam 61. **d** 63 **p** 64. C Walthamstow St Jo *Chelmsf* 63-66; CMS Nigeria 67-78; P-in-c Loscoe *Derby* 78-79; V 79-88; RD Heanor 84-88; R Bamford 88-98; Dioc World Development Officer 90-96; P-in-c Bradwell 96-98; Assoc P Alfreton Deanery 98-02; rtd 02; Perm to Offic *Heref* from 02. *New Cottage, Llanbister Road, Llandrindod Wells LD1 5UW* Tel (01547) 550318

GOWER, Miss Patricia Ann. b 44. Wilson Carlile Coll IDC79 Sarum & Wells Th Coll 88. **d** 88 **p** 94. Chapl Bris Univ 88-91; Hon Par Dn Clifton St Paul 88-91; Par Dn Spondon *Derby* 91-94; C 94-95; P-in-c Hatton 95-98; Asst Chapl HM Pris Sudbury 95-98; Chapl 98-04; rtd 04; Perm to Offic *Derby* from

04. *19 Heronswood Drive, Spondon, Derby DE21 7AX* Tel (01332) 671031

GOWER, Miss Paulette Rose-Mary de Garis. b 70. Plymouth Univ BEd93. Cranmer Hall Dur 01. **d** 03 **p** 04. C Shrewsbury St Geo w Greenfields *Lich* 03-07; TV Hawarden *St As* from 07. *32 Well House Drive, Penymynydd, Chester CH4 0LB* Tel (01244) 540177 E-mail paulettegower@tiscali.co.uk

GOWER, Mrs Sarah Catherine. b 63. Ex Univ BA84 Cam Univ BTh09. Westcott Ho Cam 07. **d** 09. C St Neots *Ely* from 09. *56 Stone Hill, St Neots PE19 6AA* E-mail sarahcgower@btinternet.com

GOWER, Archdeacon of. *See* WILLIAMS, The Ven Robert John

GOWERS, Nicholas Stephen. b 78. Jes Coll Cam MEng02 MA05. Oak Hill Th Coll MTh08. **d** 08. C Ex St Leon w H Trin from 08. *63 Cedars Road, Exeter EX2 4NB* Tel (01392) 286998 E-mail nick@stleonardsexeter.org.uk

GOWING, Wilfred Herbert. b 50. QUB BSc72. NEOC 03. **d** 06 **p** 07. NSM Ripon H Trin from 06. *Littlemead, 20 Springfield Rise, Great Ouseburn, York YO26 9SE* Tel (01423) 331177 Fax 331178 E-mail wilfgowing@btinternet.com

GOWING-CUMBER, Alexander John. b 72. Fitzw Coll Cam MA00 Moorlands Th Coll BA94. Ridley Hall Cam 98. **d** 00 **p** 03. C Vange *Chelmsf* 00-02; C Rayleigh 02-05; TV Grays Thurrock from 05. *The Vicarage, Clockhouse Lane, Grays RM16 6YW* Tel (01375) 482252 E-mail fralexgc@aol.com

GOYMOUR, Mrs Joanna Leigh. b 58. Reading Univ BA79. Dioc OLM tr scheme 99. **d** 02 **p** 03. OLM Bures w Assington and Lt Cornard *St E* from 02. *Dorking Tye House, Dorking Tye, Bures CO8 5JY* Tel (01787) 227494 E-mail jo@acgoymour.freeserve.co.uk

GOYMOUR, Michael Edwyn. b 29. Selw Coll Cam BA51 McGill Univ Montreal BD53. Montreal Dioc Th Coll 51 Wells Th Coll 53. **d** 53 **p** 54. C Bury St Edmunds St Jo *St E* 53-56; C Ipswich St Bart 56-60; R Gamlingay *Ely* 60-68; rtd 92; Perm to Offic *Ely* and *Pet* from 92. *56 Church Drive, Orton Waterville, Peterborough PE2 5HE* Tel (01733) 231535

GRACE, Capt David Leonard. b 55. Wilson Carlile Coll 89 Ripon Coll Cuddesdon 98. **d** 99 **p** 00. CA from 92; C St Leonards and St Ives *Win* 99-04; V 04-09; Chapl Basingstoke and N Hants NHS Foundation Trust from 09; Chapl Hants Partnership NHS Trust from 09. *The North Hampshire Hospital, Aldermaston Road, Basingstoke RG24 9NA* Tel (01256) 473202

GRACE, Mrs Irene. b 36. Nottm Univ BSc58. Guildf Dioc Min Course 96. **d** 98 **p** 99. OLM Stoneleigh *Guildf* 98-06; Perm to Offic from 06. *33 Woodstone Avenue, Stoneleigh, Epsom KT17 2JS* Tel (020) 8393 7280

GRACE, Kenneth. b 24. Leeds Univ BA49. Wycliffe Hall Ox 62. **d** 63 **p** 64. C Tonge w Alkrington *Man* 63-66; R Thwing and V Wold Newton *York* 66-70; Chapl St Andr Sch Worthing 70-76; R Berwick w Selmeston and Alciston *Chich* 76-81; P-in-c Kingston Buci 81-85; R Westbourne 85-90; rtd 90; Perm to Offic *Chich* from 90. *5 Ramsay Hall, 11-13 Byron Road, Worthing BN11 3HN* Tel (01903) 230611

GRACE, Ms Louise Sarah. b 68. Girton Coll Cam BA89. Ripon Coll Cuddesdon BA97 Ch Div Sch of Pacific 97. **d** 98 **p** 99. C Wordsley *Worc* 98-02; R Teme Valley N from 02; RD Stourport from 08. *The Rectory, Lindridge, Tenbury Wells WR15 8JQ* Tel (01584) 881331 E-mail louisegrace@fsmail.net

GRACE, Richard Maurice. b 29. St Chad's Coll Dur BA53. Chich Th Coll. **d** 55 **p** 56. C Toxteth Park St Agnes *Liv* 55-58; C Wolverhampton St Pet *Lich* 58-62; V W Bromwich St Fran 62-78; P-in-c Salt 78-84; P-in-c Sandon w Burston 82-84; V Salt and Sandon w Burston 84-93; rtd 94. *Little Owls, 1 Trinity Close, Crewe CW2 8FD* Tel (01270) 662221

GRACE, Wilfrid Windsor. b 15. ACA39 FCA60. Westcott Ho Cam 52. **d** 53 **p** 54. C Chippenham St Andr w Tytherton Lucas *Bris* 53-57; V Minety w Oaksey 57-71; V Oldland 71-76; V Abbots Leigh w Leigh Woods 76-80; Chapl Ham Green Hosp 79-87; rtd 80; Perm to Offic *B & W* from 81; Hon Chapl Cheshire Home Axbridge from 81. *clo J Grace Esq, 6 Kingston Road, Nailsea, Bristol BS48 4RD*

GRACIE, Anthony Johnstone. b 25. Ch Coll Cam BA48 MA51. Linc Th Coll 57. **d** 59 **p** 60. C Edgbaston St Geo *Birm* 59-62; R Lyndon w Manton and Martinsthorpe *Pet* 62-76; R N Luffenham 66-76; V Odiham w S Warnborough and Long Sutton *Win* 76-85; Perm to Offic *Bris* 85-88; rtd 88. *Colt Corner, Horn Lane, East Hendred, Wantage OX12 8LD* Tel (01235) 821509 E-mail a.gracie@btconnect.com

GRACIE, Canon Bryan John. b 45. MBE06. Open Univ BA81. AKC67. **d** 68 **p** 69. C Whipton *Ex* 68-72; Chapl St Jo Sch Tiffield 72-73; Chapl HM Borstal Stoke Heath 74-78; Asst Chapl HM Pris Liv 74; Chapl HM Youth Cust Cen Feltham 78-85; Chapl HM Pris Birm from 85; Hon Can Birm Cathl from 05. *Chaplain's Office, HM Prison, Winson Green Road, Birmingham B18 4AS* Tel 0121-345 2500 ext 2598 Fax 345 2501

GRAEBE, Canon Denys Redford. b 26. Qu Coll Cam BA48 MA51. Westcott Ho Cam 50. **d** 51 **p** 52. C Hitchin St Mary *St Alb* 51-57; R Gt Parndon *Chelmsf* 57-72; V Norton *St Alb* 72-83; R Kimpton w Ayot St Lawrence 83-92; RD

Wheathampstead 87-92; Hon Can St Alb Abbey 90-92; rtd 92; Perm to Offic *St E* from 92. *5 Sancroft Way, Fressingfield, Eye IP21 5QN* Tel (01379) 588178

GRAESSER, Adrian Stewart. b 42. Tyndale Hall Bris 63. **d** 67 **p** 68. C Nottingham St Jude *S'well* 67-69; C Slaithwaite w E Scammonden *Wakef* 69-72; CF 72-75; V Earl's Heaton *Wakef* 75-81; R Norton Fitzwarren *B & W* 81-86; R Bickenhill w Elmdon *Birm* 86-90; R Elmdon St Nic 90-00; P-in-c Dolton *Ex* 00-05; P-in-c Iddesleigh w Dowland 00-05; P-in-c Monkokehampton 00-05; RD Torrington 02-05; rtd 05; Perm to Offic *Worc* from 09. *7 Mortlake Drive, Martley, Worcester WR6 6QU* Tel (01886) 888628 E-mail adrian.graesser@sky.com

GRAHAM, Alan Robert. b 44. St Edm Hall Ox BA67 MA71. St Steph Ho Ox 67. **d** 70 **p** 71. C Clifton All SS *Bris* 70-74; C Tadley St Pet *Win* 74-77; P-in-c Upper Clatford w Goodworth Clatford 77-79; R Abbotts Ann and Upper and Goodworth Clatford 79-84; V Lyndhurst and Emery Down 84-92; P-in-c Over Wallop w Nether Wallop 92-02; rtd 02. *44 New Forest Drive, Brockenhurst SO42 7QW* Tel (01590) 622324

GRAHAM, Alexander. *See* GRAHAM, The Rt Revd Andrew Alexander Kenny

GRAHAM, Alfred. b 34. Bris Univ BA57. Tyndale Hall Bris. **d** 58 **p** 59. C Chaddesden St Mary *Derby* 58-61; C Bickenhill w Elmdon *Birm* 61-64; V Kirkdale St Lawr *Liv* 64-70; V Stapleford *S'well* 70-83; V Burton Joyce w Bulcote 83-95; V Burton Joyce w Bulcote and Stoke Bardolph 95-97; rtd 97; Perm to Offic *S'well* from 03. *2 Hobsons Acre, Gunthorpe, Nottingham NG14 7FF* Tel 0115-966 3912

GRAHAM, Alistair. *See* GRAHAM, Michael Alistair

✠**GRAHAM, The Rt Revd Andrew Alexander Kenny (Alec).** b 29. St Jo Coll Ox BA52 MA57 Lambeth DD95. Ely Th Coll 53. **d** 55 **p** 56 **c** 77. C Hove All SS *Chich* 55-58; Chapl, Lect Th, and Tutor Worc Coll Ox 58-70; Warden Linc Th Coll 70-77; Can and Preb Linc Cathl 70-77; Suff Bp Bedford *St Alb* 77-81; Bp Newc 81-97; Chmn ACCM 84-87; Chmn Doctrine Commn 87-95; rtd 97; Hon Asst Bp Carl from 97. *Fell End, Butterwick, Penrith CA10 2QQ* Tel (01931) 713147

GRAHAM, Canon Anthony Nigel. b 40. Univ of Wales (Abth) BA62 CertEd70. Ripon Hall Ox 62. **d** 64 **p** 65. C Heref H Trin 64-67; C Birm St Martin 67-69; C Selly Oak St Mary 71-75; V Edgbaston SS Mary and Ambrose 75-83; CMS Miss Partner Nigeria 84-88; Hon Can Jos from 88; V Highworth w Sevenhampton and Inglesham etc *Bris* 88-95; RD Highworth 93-95; P-in-c Coalpit Heath 95-99; V 99-00; rtd 00. *19 Dormer Road, Cheltenham GL51 0AX*

GRAHAM, Anthony Stanley David. b 34. SS Coll Cam BA56 MA60. Cuddesdon Coll 58. **d** 60 **p** 61. C Welwyn Garden City *St Alb* 60-64; Asst Chapl Ipswich Sch 64-65; C Margate St Jo *Cant* 65-68; Chr Aid Area Sec *Chich* 68-99; rtd 99; Perm to Offic *Chich* from 05. *48 Springfield Road, Crawley RH11 8AH* Tel (01293) 526279 E-mail tonygraham@dsl.pipex.com

GRAHAM, Bruce. *See* GRAHAM, William Bruce

GRAHAM, Christopher John. b 55. EMMTC. **d** 03 **p** 04. NSM Ripley *Derby* 03-08; NSM Ilkeston St Jo from 08. *41 Lathkill Drive, Ripley DE5 8HW* Tel (01773) 747223 E-mail chris@graham-family.freeserve.co.uk

GRAHAM, Clifton Gordon. b 53. ARCM72 GRSM74 FRCO75 Coll of Ripon & York St Jo PGCE76. St Steph Ho Ox 90. **d** 92 **p** 93. C Northfield *Birm* 92-93; C Perry Beeches 93-97; P-in-c S Yardley St Mich 97-00; V 00-06; Chapl Birm City Univ from 06. *35 Westhill Close, Birmingham B29 6QQ* Tel 0121-471 1958 *or* 331 5345 E-mail clifton.graham@bcu.ac.uk *or* c.g.g@blueyonder.co.uk

GRAHAM, David. *See* GRAHAM, George David

GRAHAM, Canon Frederick Lawrence. b 35. TCD BA65. CITC 66. **d** 66 **p** 67. C Belfast St Matt *Conn* 66-69; TV Chelmsley Wood *Birm* 69-73; Chief of Ireland Youth Officer 73-78; Bp's C Stoneyford *Conn* 78-88; Bp's C Fahan Lower and Upper *D & R* 88-91; Can Raphoe Cathl 90-01; I Donagheady 91-01; Can Derry Cathl 95-01; rtd 01. *Thuma Mina, 80 Altnahinch Road, Loughguile, Ballymena BT44 9JS* Tel (028) 2764 1016 E-mail fredkade@btinternet.com

GRAHAM, Frederick Louis Roth. b 20. Selw Coll Cam BA47 MA49. Ridley Hall Cam 48. **d** 50 **p** 51. C Shirley *Win* 50-53; R Old Trafford St Jo *Man* 53-61; R Wombwell *Sheff* 61-71; V Thorne 71-77; P-in-c Chilton-super-Polden w Edington *B & W* 77-82; P-in-c Catcott 77-82; V W Poldens 82-86; RD Glastonbury 82-86; rtd 86; Perm to Offic *Win* 86-08. *Flat 11, Manormead, Tilford Road, Hindhead GU26 6RA* Tel (01428) 602500

GRAHAM, George David. b 42. Jes Coll Cam BA64 MA68. St Jo Coll Nottm LTh Lon Coll of Div 66. **d** 71 **p** 72. C Corby St Columba *Pet* 71-74; C Deptford St Jo *S'wark* 74-77; P-in-c Deptford St Pet 77-82; C-in-c Wheatley Park St Paul CD *Sheff* 82-87; TV Dunstable *St Alb* 87-92; V Bromley Common St Luke *Roch* 92-02; R Hayes from 02. *The Rectory, Hayes Street, Bromley BR2 7LH* Tel (020) 8462 1373

GRAHAM, Canon George Edgar. b 55. QUB BA91. Sarum & Wells Th Coll 74 CITC 77. **d** 78 **p** 79. C Lisburn Ch Ch *Conn* 78-81; C Mossley 81-83; I Broomhedge 83-91; I Derriaghy w Colin 91-96; I Ballywillan 96-05; I Dunluce from 05; Can Conn Cathl from 05. *Dunluce Rectory, 17 Priestland Road, Bushmills BT57 8QP* Tel (028) 2073 1221 *or* 2073 0537 E-mail rectordunluce@btconnect.com *or* admindunluce@btconnect.com

GRAHAM, George Gordon. b 17. OBE96. St Chad's Coll Dur BA48 MSc71. **d** 50 **p** 51. C Luton Ch Ch *St Alb* 50-53; C Bakewell *Derby* 53-56; P-in-c Wheatley Hill *Dur* 56-69; V Hunwick 69-88; Chapl Homelands Hosp Dur 80-94; Chapl Bishop Auckland Hospitals NHS Trust 94-98; Chapl S Durham Healthcare NHS Trust 98-02; rtd 88. *3 The Willows, Bishop Auckland DL14 7HH* Tel (01388) 602758

GRAHAM, George Gordon. b 34. Harvard Univ BA55 MDiv JD71. **d** 96 **p** 97. Aux Min Seapatrick *D & D* 97-99; Aux Min Lecale Gp 99-03; P-in-c Castlewellan w Kilcoo from 03. *10 Castlebridge Court, Newcastle BT33 0RF* Tel (028) 4062 2612 *or* 4372 6175 E-mail gorbargrah@aol.com

GRAHAM, Gordon. *See* GRAHAM, Prof Lawrence Gordon

GRAHAM, Gordon Cecil. b 31. JP. Ch Coll Cam BA53 MA57. Ripon Hall Ox 53. **d** 55 **p** 56. C Didsbury St Jas and Em *Man* 55-58; C Rochdale 58-60; R Heaton Mersey 60-67; Chapl Hulme Gr Sch Oldham 67-74; Lic to Offic *Ches* 72-92; rtd 92. *21 The Crescent, Davenport, Stockport SK3 8SL* Tel 0161-483 6011

GRAHAM, Harry John. b 52. Magd Coll Cam BA75 MA86. Trin Coll Bris BA94. **d** 96 **p** 97. C Walkden and Lt Hulton *Man* 96-99; Chapl Salford Coll of Tech 96-99; P-in-c Edgeside *Man* 99-00; TV Rossendale Middle Valley 00-02; Gen Sec Miss without Borders (UK) Ltd from 02. *69 Eyre Court, Finchley Road, London NW8 9TX* Tel (020) 7586 8336 *or* 7940 1370 Fax 7403 7348 E-mail info_uk@mwbi.org

GRAHAM, Ian Maxwell. b 50. CertEd76. Chich Th Coll 86. **d** 88 **p** 89. C Middlesbrough St Thos *York* 88-90; C Stainton-in-Cleveland 90-93; V Hemlington 93-00; V Grangetown from 00. *The Vicarage, Clynes Road, Grangetown, Middlesbrough TS6 7LY* Tel (01642) 453704 E-mail casahild@lineone.net

GRAHAM, James Hamilton. b 54. Trin Hall Cam BA76 MA80 Solicitor 78. Ripon Coll Cuddesdon BA83 MA87. **d** 84 **p** 85. C Harlescott *Lich* 84-88; C Adderley 88-93; C Drayton in Hales 88-93; C Moreton Say 88-93; R Hodnet w Weston under Redcastle 93-00; RD Hodnet 97-00; V Eccleshall from 00. *The Vicarage, Church Street, Eccleshall, Stafford ST21 6BY* Tel (01785) 850351

GRAHAM, John Galbraith. b 21. MBE05. K Coll Cam BA43 MA46. Ely Th Coll 46. **d** 48 **p** 49. C E Dulwich St Jo *S'wark* 48-49; Chapl St Chad's Coll *Dur* 49-52; C Aldershot St Mich *Guildf* 52-55; C-in-c Beaconsfield St Mich CD *Ox* 55-62; Chapl Reading Univ 62-72; C Pimlico St Pet w Westmr Ch Ch *Lon* 72-74; R Houghton w Wyton *Ely* 74-78; rtd 86; Lic to Offic *St E* from 86; Perm to Offic *Ely* from 93. *31 Rectory Lane, Somersham, Huntingdon PE28 3EL* Tel (01487) 842737

GRAHAM, Kevin. *See* GRAHAM, Terence Kevin Declan

GRAHAM, Prof Lawrence Gordon. b 49. OBE96. St Andr Univ MA Dur Univ MA PhD75 FRSE99. St Steph Ho Ox 90. **d** 05. Regius Prof Moral Philosophy Aber Univ 96-05; C Aberdeen St Mary 05-06; Prof Philosophy and Arts Princeton Th Sem USA from 06. *Princeton Theological Seminary, PO Box 821, Princeton NJ 08542, USA* Tel (001) (609) 497 7849

GRAHAM, Mrs Marion McKenzie. b 39. St As Minl Tr Course. **d** 89 **p** 97. NSM Bagillt *St As* 89-93; NSM Flint 93-99 and 00-08; C 99-00; rtd 08. *Sharondale, Bryntirion Road, Bagillt CH6 6BZ* Tel (01352) 734139

GRAHAM, Michael. b 51. CITC BTh95. **d** 95 **p** 96. C Cork St Fin Barre's Union *C, C & R* 95-98; Min Can Cork Cathl 97-98; I Drogheda w Ardee, Collon and Termonfeckin *Arm* from 98; Ch of Ireland Internet Co-ord 99-05; I Kilsaran w Drumcar, Dunleer and Dunany from 07. *St Peter's Rectory, Drogheda, Co Louth, Republic of Ireland* Tel (00353) (41) 987 0073 *or* 983 8791 E-mail office.drogheda@armagh.anglican.org

GRAHAM, Michael Alistair. b 47. CITC 67. **d** 70 **p** 71. C Dublin Clontarf *D & G* 71-75; C Ox St Mich w St Martin and All SS 76-78; P-in-c Dublin Sandymount *D & G* 80-86; I Stillorgan w Blackrock 86-00; Soc Worker E Health Bd Dub 00-09; I Mullingar, Portnashangan, Moyliscar, Kilbixy etc *M & K* from 09. *15 Rock Lodge, Killiney, Co Dublin, Republic of Ireland*

GRAHAM, Nigel. *See* GRAHAM, Canon Anthony Nigel

GRAHAM, Ms Olivia Josephine. b 56. UEA BA84. SAOMC 94. **d** 97 **p** 98. NSM Wheatley *Ox* 97-98; C Risborough 98-01; TV Burnham w Dropmore, Hitcham and Taplow 01-07; Par Development Adv from 07. *Downs View, High Street, Long Wittenham, Abingdon OX14 4QD* Tel (01865) 407062 E-mail graham.glenny@virgin.net

GRAHAM, Peter. b 32. CEng MIMechE. **d** 86 **p** 87. NSM Minchinhampton *Glouc* 86-96; Perm to Offic 96-97; NSM Alderminster and Halford *Cov* 98-02; NSM Butlers Marston and the Pillertons w Ettington 98-02; rtd 02; Perm to Offic *Cov* 02-07. *21 Brick Meadow, Bishops Castle SY9 5DH* Tel (01588) 638176

GRAHAM, Peter Bartlemy. b 23. K Coll Cam BA47 MA52. Ely Th Coll 50. **d** 52 **p** 53. C St Alb Abbey *St Alb* 52-55; V Eaton Bray 55-64; R Harpenden St Nic 64-73; V Aylesbury *Ox* 73-82; Hon Can Ch Ch 79-82; R Elford *Lich* 82-88; Dioc Adv Past Care and Counselling 82-88; rtd 88; Perm to Offic *Sarum* from 88. *Carriers Cottage, Buckland Newton, Dorchester DT2 7DW* Tel (01300) 345287

GRAHAM, Richard William. b 63. Poly of Wales BA86 ACA91. Trin Coll Bris 03. **d** 05 **p** 06. C Savernake *Sarum* 05-09; TV Hemel Hempstead *St Alb* from 09. *St Barnabas Vicarage, Everest Way, Hemel Hempstead HP2 4HY* Tel (01442) 253681 E-mail randmgraham@hotmail.com

GRAHAM, Robert John. b 70. Wycliffe Hall Ox BTh99. **d** 99 **p** 00. C Nailsea H Trin *B & W* 99-04. *Address temp unknown* E-mail revrgraham@btinternet.com

GRAHAM, Ronald Fleming. b 33. Edin Th Coll 67. **d** 69 **p** 69. Chapl St Andr Cathl 69-73; R Glas Gd Shep 73-75; R Glas Gd Shep and Ascension 75-76; CF (TA) 74-76; R Peterhead *Ab* 76-80; Chapl RAF 76-80; Bp's Dom Chapl *Arg* 80-84; Itinerant Priest 80-84; R Lanark *Glas* 84-89; R Douglas 84-89; rtd 89; Hon C Glas St Ninian 90-98. *77 Merryvale Avenue, Giffnock, Glasgow G46 6DE* Tel 0141-569 5090

GRAHAM, Ronald Gaven. b 27. **d** 90 **p** 91. NSM Adare w Kilpeacon and Croom *L & K* 90-92; Dioc Info Officer (Limerick) 91-95; NSM Rathkeale w Askeaton and Kilcornan 92-96; NSM Wexford w Ardcolm and Killurin *C & O* 97-03; rtd 03. *8 Chestnut Grove, Fernyhill, Killinick, Co Wexford, Republic of Ireland* Tel (00353) (53) 915 8369 E-mail rvgraham@eircom.net

GRAHAM, Roy Richard Arthur. b 39. Lon Univ BD63 Open Univ BA78. ALCD62. **d** 63 **p** 64. C Southsea St Jude *Portsm* 63-66; C Morden *S'wark* 66-70; V Tittensor *Lich* 70-79; R Hurworth and Dinsdale w Sockburn *Dur* 79-02; rtd 02. *The School House, Eaglesfield, Lockerbie DG11 3PA* Tel (01461) 500499 E-mail rragraham@onenet.co.uk

GRAHAM, Stig. *See* GRAHAM, William Stig

GRAHAM, Mrs Susan Lochrie. b 46. Sheff Univ PhD01. Yale Div Sch MDiv90. **d** 90 **p** 91. Cow Head Par Canada 90-92; P-in-c Kingsway All SS, St Hilary, Bolton etc 92-96; NSM Ilminster and Distr *B & W* 96-97; Perm to Offic 97-03; NSM Glastonbury w Meare 03-08; NSM Combe Martin, Berrynarbor, Lynton, Brendon etc *Ex* from 08. *The Rectory, Lee Road, Lynton EX35 6BP* Tel (01598) 753251 E-mail s.l.graham@exeter.ac.uk

GRAHAM, Terence Kevin Declan. b 67. NUI BSc89 TCD BTh02. CITC 99. **d** 02 **p** 03. C Knock *D & D* 02-05; I Carrowdore w Millisle from 05. *Carrowdore Rectory, 40 Woburn Road, Millisle, Newtownards BT22 2HY* Tel (028) 9186 2219 Mobile 07973 257193 E-mail carrowdore@down.anglican.org

GRAHAM, Mrs Wendy. b 41. **d** 01 **p** 02. OLM Chalfont St Peter *Ox* from 01. *The Box, Hillfield Road, Chalfont St Peter, Gerrards Cross SL9 0DU* Tel (01753) 885066

GRAHAM, William Bruce. b 37. Univ of New Mexico BA60 Yale Univ MDiv90. **d** 90 **p** 91. Canada 90-97; P-in-c W Poldens *B & W* 97-08; P-in-c Greinton 05-08; RD Glastonbury 03-08. *Address temp unknown*

GRAHAM, William Stig. b 53. Newc Univ BSc75. NEOC. **d** 99 **p** 00. C W Acklam *York* 99-02; Chapl Myton Hamlet Hospice from 02. *2 Winyates Road, Lighthorne Heath, Leamington Spa CV33 9TU* Tel (01926) 640811 *or* 492518 E-mail stiggraham@netscape.net *or* stig.graham@mytonhospice.org

GRAHAM-BROWN, John George Francis. b 34. CA60. Wycliffe Hall Ox 60. **d** 63 **p** 64. C Darlington St Cuth *Dur* 63-67; C Rufforth w Moor Monkton and Hessay *York* 67-73; Sec York Dioc Redundant Chs Uses Cttee 69-89; Asst Sec DBF 73-84; Dioc Past Cttee 73-89; Hon C York St Barn 73-85; P-in-c 85-92; TV Marfleet 92-99; rtd 99; Perm to Offic *St Alb* from 00. *40 Hunters Oak, Hemel Hempstead HP2 7SW* Tel (01482) 402226 E-mail f.graham-brown@tinyonline.co.uk

GRAHAM-ORLEBAR, Ian Henry Gaunt. b 26. New Coll Ox BA49 MA56. Cuddesdon Coll 60. **d** 62 **p** 63. C Hemel Hempstead *St Alb* 62-70; R Barton-le-Cley w Higham Gobion 70-80; R Barton-le-Cley w Higham Gobion and Hexton 80-92; rtd 92; Perm to Offic *Ex* from 94. *Hole Farm, Bickington, Newton Abbot TQ12 6PE* Tel (01626) 821298

GRAINGER, Canon Bruce. b 37. Nottm Univ BA62 Hull Univ MA83. Cuddesdon Coll 62. **d** 64 **p** 65. C Bingley All SS *Bradf* 64-67; Chapl K Sch Cant 67-72; Hon Min Can Cant Cathl 69-72; V Baildon *Bradf* 72-88; V Oxenhope 88-04; Hon Can Bradf Cathl 84-04; Dir of Ords 88-96; Dioc Ecum Officer 96-04; Tutor Bradf Univ 99-03; RD S Craven 02-03; rtd 04; Perm to Offic *Bradf* from 04. *Aspen Lodge, Low Shann Farm, High Spring Gardens Lane, Keighley BD20 6LN* Tel (01535) 611989 E-mail bruce@graspen.gotadsl.co.uk

GRAINGER, Horace. b 34. Carl Dioc Tr Course 82. **d** 85 **p** 86. NSM Barrow St Matt *Carl* 85-89; C Carl St Herbert w St Steph 89-91; TV Penrith w Newton Reigny and Plumpton Wall 91-96;

P-in-c Holme Cultram St Mary 96-00; P-in-c Holme Cultram St Cuth 96-00; rtd 00; NSM Barrow St Aid *Carl* 01-03; NSM S Barrow from 03. *15 Maylands Avenue, Barrow-in-Furness LA13 0AL* Tel (01229) 828603

GRAINGER, Ian. b 66. Cranmer Hall Dur 89. **d** 92 **p** 93. C Whitehaven *Carl* 92-94; C Walney Is 94-97; P-in-c Barrow St Aid 97-02; V Camerton, Seaton and W Seaton from 02. *The Vicarage, Ling Beck Park, Seaton, Workington CA14 1JQ* Tel (01900) 602162 E-mail revd.ian@grainger89.fsnet.co.uk

GRAINGER, Michael Noel Howard. b 40. Trin Coll Carmarthen. **d** 91 **p** 92. NSM Haverfordwest St Martin w Lambston *St D* 91-95; V Maenclochog and New Moat etc 95-05; rtd 05. *1 impasse Edith Piaf, Kerbregent, Plumeliau 56930, France* Tel (0033) (2) 97 51 91 28 Mobile (8) 79 39 24 61

GRAINGER, Prof Roger Beckett. b 34. Birm Univ MA70 Leeds Univ PhD79 Lon Univ BA80 DD90 Huddersfield Poly MPhil88 Bris Univ PhD92 Leeds Metrop Univ BSc98 PhD(Educ)01 Lambeth STh83 FRSA85 FRAI85 CPsychol96 AFBPsS99. Lich Th Coll 64. **d** 66 **p** 69. C W Bromwich All SS *Lich* 66-68; C Walsall 69-73; Chapl Stanley Royd Hosp Wakef 73-90; rtd 91; Hon C Wakef St Jo from 93; Dioc Drama Adv from 98; Prof Extraordinary Potchefstroom Univ S Africa from 01; Hon Chapl Wakef Cathl from 02. *7 Park Grove, Horbury, Wakefield WF4 6EE* Tel (01924) 272742

GRAINGER-SMITH, James Edward. b 71. Nottm Univ BA92. St Jo Coll Nottm MA02. **d** 02 **p** 03. C Hordle *Win* 02-07; R Beeford w Frodingham and Foston *York* from 07. *The Rectory, 11 Glebe Gardens, Beeford, Driffield YO25 8BF* Tel (01262) 488042 E-mail j.j.grainger-smith@lineone.net

GRANDEY, Frederick Michael. b 56. St Jo Coll Ox MA83 BM, BCh84 Newc Univ MSc98 MRCGP90 FFPH04. St Jo Coll Nottm 06. **d** 09. C Haxby and Wigginton *York* from 09. *5 Back Lane, Wigginton, York YO32 2ZH* Tel (01904) 765144 E-mail m.grandey@talk21.com

GRANGE (née FEATHERSTON), Mrs Alice Margery. b 55. Teesside Univ BA97. NEOC. **d** 99 **p** 00. C Pickering w Lockton and Levisham *York* 99-02; TV Crosslacon *Carl* 02-07; P-in-c Middlesbrough St Agnes *York* from 07; Chapl S Tees Hosps NHS Trust from 07. *St Agnes' Vicarage, 1 Broughton Avenue, Middlesbrough TS4 3PX* Tel (01642) 321770 E-mail margery-grange@tiscali.co.uk

GRANNER, Mrs Linda. b 52. Westmr Coll Ox BTh00. WMMTC 01. **d** 03 **p** 04. NSM Bearwood *Birm* 03-06; C Edgbaston St Bart 06-08; C Edgbaston St Geo 06-08; P-in-c Hobs Moat from 08. *St Mary's House, 30 Hobs Meadow, Solihull B92 8PN* Tel 0121-743 4955 E-mail l.granner@sky.com

GRANT, Alistair Sims. b 25. SS Coll Cam BA49 MA53. Sarum Th Coll 49. **d** 51 **p** 52. C Northampton St Jas *Pet* 51-54; C Conisbrough *Sheff* 54-57; Org Sec (E Anglia) CECS 57-58; V Haddenham *Ely* 58-65; rtd 90; Perm to Offic *Ely* 90-00. *56 The Causeway, Burwell, Cambridge CB25 0DU* Tel (01638) 741670

GRANT, Canon Andrew Richard. b 40. Univ of Wales BA2. Chich Th Coll 63. **d** 65 **p** 66. C Kennington St Jo *S'wark* 65-68; Hon C 70-72; Hon C Stockwell Green St Andr 68-70; V Nunhead St Antony 72-79; TR N Lambeth 79-92; USPG Ghana 92-99; Hon Can Kumasi from 02; C Paddington St Jo w St Mich *Lon* 99-01; P-in-c Stockwell St Mich *S'wark* 01-03; P-in-c Stockwell St Andr and St Mich 03-04; V 04-09; rtd 09. *36B Champion Hill, London SE5 8AP* Tel (020) 7738 3167

GRANT, Antony Richard Charles. b 34. Ch Ch Ox BA59 MA64. Coll of Resurr Mirfield 72. **d** 74 **p** 75. C St John's Wood *Lon* 74-77; Novice CR 77-79; CR from 79; Lic to Offic *Wakef* from 80; tt'd 99. *House of the Resurrection, Stocks Bank Road, Mirfield WF14 0BN* Tel (01924) 483332 Fax 490489 E-mail agrant@mirfield.org.uk

GRANT, Arthur Glyndŵr Webber. b 28. St Luke's Coll Ex CertEd49. Wells Th Coll 52. **d** 54 **p** 55. C Cannock *Lich* 54-57; C Penhalonga St Aug Miss R Rhodesia 57-63; C Paignton St Jo *Ex* 63-68; C Bridgton Gd Shep Preston *Chich* 68-76; C Moulsecoomb 76-80; Chapl HM Pris Northeye 80-83; P-in-c Wartling *Chich* 80-83; C Seaford w Sutton 83-87; Sub-Chapl HM Pris Lewes 86-92; rtd 92; Perm to Offic *Ex* 93-95 and 98-06. *The College of St Barnabas, Blackberry Lane, Lingfield RH7 6NJ* Tel (01342) 872832

GRANT, Eric. *See* GRANT, William Frederick

GRANT, Canon Geoffrey. b 27. Lich Th Coll 55. **d** 58 **p** 59. C Swindon New Town *Bris* 58-62; V Eastville St Thos 62-67; V Sherston Magna w Easton Grey 67-75; P-in-c Luckington w Alderton 71-75; P-in-c Woolcott Park 75-78; V Cotham St Mary 76-78; V Cotham St Sav w St Mary 78-81; TR Yate New Town 81-88; Hon Can Bris Cathl 82-92; Dir St Jo Home Bris 89-92; rtd 92; Perm to Offic *Bris* 92-97; Chapl Beaulieu-sur-Mer *Eur* 97-00. *1266 chemin des Espinets, 06570 Saint-Paul-de-Vence, France* Tel (0033) (4) 93 58 78 49

GRANT, Canon Geoffrey Leslie. b 33. Trin Coll Cam BA57 MA61. Ridley Hall Cam 57. **d** 59 **p** 60. C Chelsea St Luke *Lon* 59-64; Chapl Orwell Park Sch Nacton from 64; R Nacton w Levington *St E* 64-78; P-in-c Bucklesham w Brightwell and Foxhall 75-76; R Nacton and Levington w Bucklesham and

Foxhall 78-06; P-in-c Kirton w Falkenham 96-06; R Nacton and Levington w Bucklesham etc from 06; RD Colneys from 86; Hon Can St E Cathl from 94. *The Rectory, Nacton, Ipswich IP10 0HY* Tel (01473) 659232 E-mail canon@nildram.co.uk

GRANT, Glyn. *See* GRANT, Arthur Glyndwr Webber

GRANT, James Neil. b 57. Toorak Coll of Educn BEd80. Trin Coll Melbourne BTh84. **d** 85 **p** 86. C E Frankston Australia 85-87; C Feltham *Lon* 87-89; Chapl Peninsula Sch Mt Eliza Melbourne 89-03; Assoc P Mt Eliza 99-03; Assoc P Richmond St Steph from 04. *21 Bent Street, East Malvern Vic 3145, Australia* Tel (0061) (3) 5976 1773 Mobile 425-721962 E-mail frjames.ststephens@keypoint.com.au

GRANT, John Brian Frederick. b 47. Bris Univ BSc68 MB, ChB71 MD76 FRCS76. Coll of Resurr Mirfield 91. **d** 93 **p** 94. C Doncaster Ch Ch *Sheff* 93-95; C Doncaster H Trin 95-96; Chapl Asst Salford R Hosps NHS Trust 96-07; Hon C Man Victoria Park from 08. *179 Manley Road, Manchester M21 0GY* Tel 0161-860 7488

GRANT, Ms Kerry Jean (Kes). b 65. SEITE 00. **d** 03 **p** 04. NSM Eltham St Sav *S'wark* 03-09; C Bermondsey St Hugh CD from 09; Chapl Lewisham Hosp NHS Trust 05-09; Chapl St Sav and St Olave's Sch Newington *S'wark* from 09. *54 Balin House, Long Lane, London SE1 1YH* Tel 07866-690527 (mobile) E-mail kgrant@ssso.southwark.sch.uk

GRANT, Canon Malcolm Etheridge. b 44. Edin Univ BSc66 BD69. Edin Th Coll 66. **d** 69 **p** 70. C St Mary's Cathl 69-72; C Grantham w Manthorpe *Linc* 72; TV Grantham 72-78; P-in-c Invergordon St Ninian *Mor* 78-81; Provost St Andr Cathl 81-91; R Glas St Mary 81-91; Provost St Andr Cathl Inverness 91-02; R Inverness St Andr 91-02; P-in-c Culloden St Mary-in-the-Fields 91-97; R Strathnairn St Paul 91-97; Hon Can St Andr Cathl Inverness from 02; V Eaton Bray w Edlesborough *St Alb* 02-09; RD Dunstable 04-09; rtd 09; Perm to Offic *St Alb* from 09. *13 Rock Lane, Leighton Buzzard LU7 2QQ* Tel (01525) 372771

GRANT, Murray William. b 36. Chich Th Coll 64. **d** 66 **p** 67. C Stanley *Liv* 66-70; C Munster Square St Mary Magd *Lon* 70-74; C Westmr St Sav and St Jas Less 74-82; P-in-c Albany Street Ch Ch 82; P-in-c Hammersmith H Innocents 83-94; V 94-99; Chapl Naples w Sorrento, Capri and Bari *Eur* 99-03; rtd 04. *12 Ashdown Crescent, London NW5 4QB* Tel (020) 7319 2519

GRANT, Patrick Iain Douglas. b 67. Keble's Coll Win BA88. Cuddesdon Coll BTh93. **d** 96 **p** 97. C Croydon Woodside *S'wark* 96-99; V S Beddington and Roundshaw 99-07; R Perth St Jo *St And* from 07. *23 Comely Bank, Perth PH2 7HU* Tel (01738) 634999 or 625394 E-mail rector@episcopal-perth.org.uk

GRANT, Canon Rodney Arthur. b 26. AKC52. K Coll Lon St Boniface Warminster. **d** 53 **p** 54. C Edin St Jas 53-56; C Musselburgh 56-59; P-in-c Prestonpans 59-60; P-in-c Edin St Aid Miss Niddrie Mains 60-72; R Edin St Jas 72-80; R Edin Ch 72-80; R Edin Ch Ch-St Jas 80-86; R Edin SS Phil and Jas 86-92; Chapl St Columba's Hospice Edin 86-92; Hon Can St Mary's Cathl from 91; rtd 92; P-in-c Edin St Vin from 98. *1F1, 29 Bruntsfield Gardens, Edinburgh EH10 4DY* Tel 0131-229 1857

GRANT, William Frederick (Eric). b 23. Fitzw Ho Cam BA48 MA50 Cam Univ CertEd50. Wycliffe Hall Ox 51. **d** 53 **p** 54. C Islington St Paul Ball's Pond *Lon* 53-57; V Islington All SS 57-60; Hd RE Therfield Sch Leatherhead 60-84; Perm to Offic *Guildf* from 66 and *S'wark* from 89; rtd 88. *Kingfishers, 24 The Avenue, Brockham, Betchworth RH3 7EN* Tel (01737) 842551

GRANTHAM, David George. b 70. Humberside Univ BA94. St Jo Coll Nottm. **d** 07 **p** 08. C Bury St Edmunds Ch St E from 07. *7 Brayfield Close, Bury St Edmunds IP32 7EN* Tel 07877-505965 (mobile) E-mail godistheguy@hotmail.com

GRANTHAM, Michael Paul. b 47. Linc Th Coll. **d** 84 **p** 85. C Gainsborough All SS *Linc* 84-87; R S Kelsey Gp 87-94; R Dunster, Carhampton and Withycombe w Rodhuish *B & W* 94-06; RD Exmoor 03-05; P-in-c Peakirk w Glinton and Northborough *Pet* 06-07; P-in-c Etton w Helpston and Maxey 06-07; rtd 07. *Brook Cottage, 2 Main Street, Breedon-on-the-Hill, Derby DE73 8AN* Tel (01332) 865077

GRANTHAM, Suffragan Bishop of. *See* ELLIS, The Rt Revd Timothy William

GRASBY, Derek. b 56. Bris Univ BA80 MA82. Wesley Coll Bris 77 EAMTC 95. **d** 95 **p** 96. C Harlescott *Lich* 95-96; C W Bromwich St Andr w Ch Ch 96-98; R Newton Heath *Man* 98-02; Chapl UWE *Bris* 02-03; R Farnley *Ripon* from 03. *The Rectory, 16 Cross Lane, Leeds LS12 5AA* Tel 0113-263 8064 Mobile 07834-276382 E-mail grasby@f2s.com

GRATTON, Patricia Margaret. *See* MAGUIRE, Canon Patricia Margaret

GRATY, Canon John Thomas. b 33. Univ Coll Ox BA58 MA60. Coll of Resurr Mirfield 58. **d** 60 **p** 61. C Cov St Mark 60-63; C Hitchin St Mary *St Alb* 63-67; R Cov St Alb 67-75; P-in-c Radway w Ratley 75-77; P-in-c Warmington w Shotteswell 75-77; RD Dassett Magna 76-79; R Warmington w Shotteswell and Radway w Ratley 77-84; Hon Can Cov Cathl 80-96; P-in-c Nuneaton St Mary 84-89; V 89-96; rtd 96; Perm to Offic *Cov* from 96. *10 Kendall Avenue, Stratford-upon-Avon CV37 6SG* Tel (01789) 298856

GRAVELL, Canon John Hilary. b 45. Univ of Wales (Abth) BA65 DipEd66. Bp Burgess Hall Lamp 66. **d** 68 **p** 69. C Aberystwyth *St D* 68-72; R Llangeitho w Blaenpennal 72-81; V Betws Leuci 73-81; V Llan-non 81-95; Can St D Cathl 92-09; V Llandybie 95-09; AD Dyffryn Aman 01-07; rtd 09. *16 Stewart Drive, Ammanford SA18 3BH* Tel (01269) 5943

GRAVES, Jonathan Mark. b 57. BEd. St Steph Ho Ox. **d** 84 **p** 85. C St Leonards Ch Ch and St Mary *Chich* 84-88; C-in-c N Langley CD 88-95; V Stone Cross St Luke w N Langney 95-02; Chapl St Wilfrid's Hospice Eastbourne 94-02; Chapl Grenville Coll Bideford 02-04; Perm to Offic *Chich* from 05. *6 Jervis Avenue, Eastbourne BN23 6DU* Tel (01323) 728601
E-mail fr.jonathan@jgraves.fslife.co.uk

GRAVES, Peter. b 33. EMMTC 78. **d** 81 **p** 82. NSM Roughey *Chich* 81-89; NSM Itchingfield w Slinfold 89-98; Perm to Offic *S'well* from 98. *5 Fletcher Court, The Woodlands, Farnsfield, Newark NG22 8LY* Tel (01623) 882987
E-mail gravesp1@btinternet.com

GRAY, Alan Eric. b 18. Lich Th Coll 38. **d** 41 **p** 42. C Sampford Peverell *Ex* 41-44; CR 44-52; Miss P Penhalonga S Rhodesia 47-51; R St Mark's S Africa 52-56; R Shabani S Rhodesia 56-61; V Lower Beeding *Chich* 61-70; rtd 83. *14 Frederick Road, Malvern WR14 1RS* Tel (01684) 572453
E-mail rjgray@waitrose.com

GRAY, Canon Angela Margery. b 46. St D Coll Lamp. **dss** 73 **d** 80 **p** 97. Aberystwyth *St D* 73-80; C Dafen and Llwynhendy 80-90; C-in-c 90-97; V Llwynhendy from 97; Hon Can St D Cathl from 01. *Clergy House, 10 Bryn Isaf, Llwynhendy, Llanelli SA14 9EX* Tel (01554) 774213

GRAY, Brett Christopher. b 71. Lon Bible Coll BA95 Selw Coll Cam MPhil04. Ridley Hall Cam 02. **d** 04 **p** 05. C Sunnyside w Bourne End *St Alb* 04-07; V St Alb St Mich from 07. *St Michael's Vicarage, St Michaels Street, St Albans AL3 4SL* Tel (01727) 835037 E-mail bcgray@gmail.com

GRAY, Charles Malcolm. b 38. Lich Th Coll 67. **d** 69 **p** 70. C St Geo-in-the-East St Mary *Lon* 69-72; C Bush Hill Park St Mark 72-75; V Winchmore Hill H Trin 75-07; rtd 07; Perm to Offic *Lon* from 07. *16 Alpine Walk, Stanmore HA7 3HU* Tel (020) 8950 7860 E-mail frcmg.stanmore@btinternet.com

GRAY, Ms Christine Angela (Kit). b 46. Nottm Univ BA67 CertEd68. Cranmer Hall Dur 71. **dss** 80 **d** 87 **p** 94. Rawthorpe *Wakef* 74-81; Chapl Nottm Univ 81-88; C Rushmere *St E* 88-94; P-in-c Ringshall w Battisford, Barking w Darmsden etc 94-00; P-in-c Nayland w Wiston from 00. *The Vicarage, Bear Street, Nayland, Colchester CO6 4LA* Tel (01206) 262316

GRAY, Dale Armitage. b 42. Edin Th Coll 62. **d** 92 **p** 93. Dioc Missr *Arg* 92-98; Chapl St Jo Cathl Oban 92-95; P-in-c Cumbrae (or Millport) 95-98, rtd 98; Perm to Offic *Edin* from 05. *The Dovecote, Duke Street, Coldstream TD12 4BN* Tel (01890) 883247

GRAY, David. b 55. Oak Hill Th Coll. **d** 00 **p** 01. C Bestwood Em w St Mark *S'well* 00-04; P-in-c Bulwell St Jo 04-06; V from 06. *St John's Vicarage, Snape Wood Road, Bulwell, Nottingham NG6 7GH* Tel 0115-927 8025
E-mail davidgray72@hotmail.com

GRAY, David Bryan. b 28. RD77. Roch Th Coll 59. **d** 61 **p** 62. C Linc St Giles 61-65; V Thurlby 65-67; P-in-c Ropsley 67-75; P-in-c Sapperton w Braceby 67-75; P-in-c Somerby w Humby 67-75; R Trimley *St E* 75-82; R Orford w Sudbourne, Chillesford, Butley and Iken 82-94; rtd 94; Perm to Offic *St E* from 94. *6 Stowlangtoft Hall Nursing Home, Stowlangtoft, Bury St Edmunds IP31 3JY* Tel (01359) 233511

GRAY, David Cedric. b 53. RMN77. **d** 97 **p** 98. OLM Gorton Em w St Jas *Man* 97-06; OLM Gorton and Abbey Hey from 06. *39 Jessop Street, Gorton, Manchester M18 8TZ* Tel 0161-355 6605 Pager 017623-725682

GRAY, David Michael. b 57. ACIBS80 St Jo Coll Dur BA99. CA Tr Coll 90 Cranmer Hall Dur 97. **d** 99 **p** 00. C Newc H Cross 99-02; V Long Benton St Mary from 02. *St Mary's Vicarage, Blackfriars Way, Newcastle-upon-Tyne NE12 8ST* Tel 0191-266 2326 E-mail revdavegray@aol.com

GRAY, Canon Donald Cecil. b 24. Linc Th Coll 49. **d** 50 **p** 51. C Abington *Pet* 50-53; C Bedford St Paul *St Alb* 53-56; Chapl Bedf Gen Hosp 53-56; C Wilton Place St Paul *Lon* 56-59; V N Holmwood *Guildf* 59-67; RD Dorking 63-67; R Farnham and Chapl Cobgates and Farnham Hosps 67-89; RD Farnham 69-74; Hon Can Guildf Cathl 71-89; rtd 89; Perm to Offic *Win* from 89. *13 Mallard Close, Alresford SO24 9BX* Tel (01962) 734371

GRAY, Canon Donald Clifford. b 30. CBE98 TD70. Liv Univ MPhil81 Man Univ PhD85 FRHistS88 FSA07. AKC55. **d** 56 **p** 57. C Leigh St Mary *Man* 56-60; CF (TA) 58-67; V Westleigh St Pet *Man* 60-67; V Elton All SS 67-74; CF (TAVR) 67-77; QHC 74-77; R Liv Our Lady and St Nic w St Anne 74-87; RD Liv 75-81; Hon Can Liv Cathl 82-87; Chapl to The Queen 82-00; Can Westmr Abbey 87-98; R Westmr St Marg 87-98; Chapl to Speaker of Ho of Commons 87-98; rtd 98; Perm to Offic *Linc*

GRAY, Evan William. b 43. Oak Hill Th Coll 86. **d** 88 **p** 89. C Street w Walton *B & W* 88-92; V Blackpool St Mark *Blackb* 92-03; V Ellel w Shireshead 03-08; rtd 08; Perm to Offic *Blackb* from 08. *39 Boyes Avenue, Catterall, Preston PR3 0HB* E-mail evan.gray@virgin.net

GRAY, James William. SAOMC. **d** 05 **p** 06. NSM Crich and S Wingfield *Derby* from 05. *Holmleigh, Market Place, Crich, Matlock DE4 5DD* Tel (01773) 857921

GRAY (née ROBERTS), Mrs Jennifer. b 55. R Holloway Coll Lon BA76 Somerville Coll Ox PGCE77. SAOMC 00. **d** 03 **p** 04. C Welwyn Garden City *St Alb* from 03. *42 Attimore Road, Welwyn Garden City AL8 6LP* Tel (01707) 321177
E-mail jennygraywgc@aol.com

GRAY, Joan. See BURKITT-GRAY, Mrs Joan Katherine

GRAY, John David Norman. b 38. Oak Hill Th Coll 84. **d** 86 **p** 87. C Portsdown *Portsm* 86-88; C Worthing St Geo *Chich* 88-91; TV Swanborough *Sarum* 91-98; rtd 98; Perm to Offic *Ex* 00-03 and *Portsm* from 03. *15 Charminster Court, 46 Craneswater Park, Southsea PO4 0NU* Tel (023) 9285 1299

GRAY, John Howard. b 39. St Aid Birkenhead 61. **d** 65 **p** 66. C Old Trafford St Cuth *Man* 65-68; C Urmston 68-74; V Oldham Moorside 74-08; rtd 08; Hon C Dulverton and Brushford *B & W* from 08; Hon C Brompton Regis w Upton and Skilgate from 08. *The Vicarage, Brompton Regis, Dulverton TA22 9NL* Tel (01398) 371438

GRAY, Mrs Joy Dora. b 24. SRN46 SCM48. Gilmore Ho 79. **dss** 81 **d** 87 **p** 95. Newick *Chich* 81-94; Hon Par Dn 87-94; NSM Fletching 94-98; Perm to Offic from 98. *10 High Hurst Close, Newick, Lewes BN8 4NJ* Tel (01825) 722965

GRAY, Julian Francis. b 64. Univ of Wales (Lamp) BA86 MA09. Coll of Resurr Mirfield 86. **d** 88 **p** 89. Min Can St Woolos Cathl 88-91; C Bassaleg 91-93; V Overmonnow w Wonastow and Michel Troy 93-98; V King's Sutton and Newbottle and Charlton *Pet* 98-00; V Usk and Monkswood w Glascoed Chpl and Gwehelog 00-03; V Usk and Gwehelog w Llantrisant w Llanllowell from 03. *The Vicarage, Castle Parade, Usk NP15 1AA* Tel (01291) 671441
E-mail usk.vicarage@btinternet.com

GRAY, Lindsay Doreen. b 50. Open Univ BA83 Leic Univ PhD87. Coll of Resurr Mirfield 05. **d** 06 **p** 07. NSM Firbank, Howgill and Killington *Bradf* 06-09; NSM Sedbergh, Cautley and Garsdale 06-09; Ind Chapl and TV Egremont and Haile *Carl* from 09. *1 Bridge End Park, Egremont CA22 2RH* Tel (01946) 822051 E-mail lgray782@btinternet.com

GRAY, Malcolm. See GRAY, Charles Malcolm

GRAY, The Ven Martin Clifford. b 44. Westcott Ho Cam 78. **d** 80 **p** 81. C Gaywood, Bawsey and Mintlyn *Nor* 80-84; V Sheringham 84-94; TR Lowestoft St Marg 94-97; Chapl Lothingland Hosp 95-99; RD Lothingland *Nor* 97-99; Adn Lynn 99-09; rtd 09; Perm to Offic *Nor* from 09. *11 Canns Lane, Hethersett, Norwich NR9 3JE* Tel (01603) 812610
E-mail mandpgray@btinternet.com

GRAY, Melvyn Dixon. b 38. Lon Univ BD86 Dur Univ MA89 PhD07. NEOC 84. **d** 87 **p** 88. C Richmond w Hudswell *Ripon* 87-90; P-in-c Downholme and Marske 88-90; P-in-c Forcett and Aldbrough and Melsonby 90-91; R 91-00; R Mobberley *Ches* 00-04; rtd 04. *19 Windgroves, Chilton, Ferryhill DL17 0RS* Tel (01388) 721870 E-mail windgroves2004@talktalk.net

GRAY, Neil Kenneth. b 48. Kelham Th Coll 67. **d** 71 **p** 72. C Chorley St Laur *Blackb* 71-74; C S Shore H Trin 74-78; P-in-c Preston St Oswald 78-83; C Blackpool St Steph 83-87; Chapl Bolton HA from 87; Chapl Bolton Hosps NHS Trust from 90; Co-ord Spiritual and Cultural Care 90-03; Hd of Chapl from 04; Bp's Adv on Healthcare Chapl *Man* from 08. *The Chaplains' Office, Royal Bolton Hospital, Minerva Road, Farnworth, Bolton BL4 0JR* Tel (01204) 390770 *or* 390390
E-mail neil.gray@rbh.nhs.uk

GRAY, Neil Ralph. b 53. MA. St Steph Ho Ox. **d** 82 **p** 83. C Kennington St Jo w St Jas *S'wark* 82-85; C Somers Town *Lon* 85-88. *3 Parsonage Close, High Wycombe HP13 6DT* Tel (01494) 531875

GRAY, Mrs Patricia Linda. b 51. Univ of Wales (Swansea) BA73 Ches Coll of HE BTh02. NOC 99. **d** 02 **p** 03. NSM Glazebury w Hollinfare *Liv* 02-04; C from 04; Perm to Offic *Man* from 06. *10 Hesnall Close, Glazebury, Warrington WA3 5PB* Tel (01942) 603161 Mobile 07747-772345 E-mail pat.gray@virgin.net

GRAY, Patrick. See GRAY, Sidney Patrick

GRAY, Penelope Jane. See GRAYSMITH, Mrs Penelope Jane

GRAY, Percy. b 28. OBE94 TD71. Lon Univ BA53 St Cath Soc Ox BA55 MA59. Oak Hill Th Coll 50. **d** 55 **p** 56. C Sutton *Liv* 55-58; C Chelsea Ch Ch *Lon* 58-59; V Bermondsey St Crispin w Ch Ch *S'wark* 59-99; CF (TA) 59-67; CF (TAVR) from 67; CF (ACF) from 76; rtd 99; Perm to Offic *S'wark* from 04; OCF from 04. *12 King Edward III Mews, Paradise Street, London SE16 4QH* Tel (020) 7394 7127 E-mail percyvic@aol.com

GRAY, Canon Philip Charles. b 67. Nottm Univ BA91. St Steph Ho Ox 91. **d** 93 **p** 94. C Scarborough St Martin *York* 93-97; TV

Leek and Meerbrook *Lich* 97-01; Bp's Dom Chapl *Blackb* 02-07; P-in-c Ilkley St Marg *Bradf* from 07; Fresh Expressions Min Otley Deanery from 07; Hon Can Ho Ghana from 04. *St Margaret's Vicarage, Wells Road, Ilkley LS29 9JH* Tel (01943) 607015

GRAY, Philip Thomas. b 41. Lon Univ BA65. Chich Th Coll 66. **d** 68 **p** 69. C Leigh St Clem *Chelmsf* 68-74; P-in-c Wickham Skeith *St E* 86-97; V Mendlesham from 74. *The Vicarage, Old Station Road, Mendlesham, Stowmarket IP14 5RS* Tel (01449) 766359

GRAY, Canon Robert James. b 70. TCD BA92 HDipEd93 MA95 Irish Sch of Ecum MPhil97. CITC 94. **d** 96 **p** 97. C Clooney w Strathfoyle *D & R* 96-99; I Ardamine w Kiltennel, Glascarrig etc *C & O* from 99; Treas Ferns Cathl from 04. *Ardamine Rectory, Courtown Harbour, Gorey, Co Wexford, Republic of Ireland* Tel and fax (00353) (53) 942 5423 Mobile 86-684 7621 E-mail ardamine@ferns.anglican.org

GRAY, Sidney Patrick. b 19. Worc Ord Coll. **d** 63 **p** 63. C Skegness *Linc* 63-65; V Dunholme 65-71; R Cliffe at Hoo w Cooling *Roch* 72-78; V Gillingham St Aug 78-84; rtd 84; Perm to Offic *Cant* and *Roch* 84-08. *7 St Stephens Road, Retford DN22 7EZ*

GRAY, Stephen James Norman. b 66. Lon Univ BA89 Hughes Hall Cam PGCE91. Ridley Hall Cam MA00. **d** 00 **p** 01. C Cheltenham Ch Ch *Glouc* 00-03; Chapl RN 03-04; Chapl Sherborne Sch from 04. *Rosslyn House, Acreman Street, Sherborne DT9 3NU* Tel (01935) 813846

GRAY, Mrs Susan Hazel. b 49. Kingston Univ BA06. **d** 09. OLM Hersham *Guildf* from 09. *39 Misty's Field, Walton-on-Thames KT12 2BG* Tel (01932) 242838 E-mail suehgray@btinternet.com

GRAY, Mrs Trudy Ann Jennifer. b 48. Univ of Wales (Abth) BSc69 Aston Univ MSc72. **d** 05 **p** 06. NSM Gt Finborough w Onehouse, Harleston, Buxhall etc *St E* from 05. *The Old Police House, High Road, Great Finborough, Stowmarket IP14 3AA* Tel (01449) 674819 E-mail tajgrayfin@aol.com

GRAY, Mrs Ursula Mary. b 33. K Coll Lon BD56 AKC91 Univ of Wales (Lamp) MA02. **d** 04 **p** 05. NSM Shaston *Sarum* 04-08; Perm to Offic 09. *Rowans, Chavenage Lane, Tetbury GL8 8JW* Tel (01666) 504548 E-mail umg@shaston.plus.com

GRAY-STACK, Martha Mary Stewart. b 35. QUB BA57. **d** 90 **p** 91. NSM Limerick City *L & K* 90-93; Warden of Readers 90-93; NSM Clara w Liss, Moate and Clonmacnoise *M & K* 93-00; Chapl Kingston Coll Co Cork from 00. *16 Kingston College, Mitchelstown, Co Cork, Republic of Ireland* Tel and fax (00353) (25) 258 5975

GRAYSHON, Matthew Richard. b 47. St Jo Coll Nottm BTh81. **d** 81 **p** 82. C Beverley Minster *York* 81-85; V Hallwood *Ches* 85-93; R Hanwell St Mary w St Chris *Lon* from 93. *The Rectory, 91 Church Road, London W7 3BJ* Tel (020) 8567 6185 Fax 8579 8755 E-mail matthewgrayshon@tesco.net

GRAYSHON, Paul Nicholas Walton. b 50. St Jo Coll Dur 81. **d** 83 **p** 84. C Walkden Moor *Man* 83-87; V Radcliffe St Andr 87-07; P-in-c Matlock Bath and Cromford *Derby* from 07. *Holy Trinity Vicarage, 8 Derby Road, Matlock DE4 3PU* Tel (01629) 583924 E-mail nickgrayshon@btopenworld.com

GRAYSMITH (née GRAY), Mrs Penelope Jane. b 63. SS Hild & Bede Coll Dur BA85 Em Coll Cam MPhil88. Westcott Ho Cam 86. **d** 89 **p** 94. Par Dn Evington *Leic* 89-92; Par Dn Cannock *Lich* 92-94; C 94-96; Chapl Asst Mid Staffs Gen Hosps NHS Trust 96-07; Hd Chapl Services Mid Staffs NHS Foundn Trust from 07; Chapl Kath Ho Hospice Stafford from 96. *The Vicarage, 97 Baswich Lane, Stafford ST17 0BN* Tel (01785) 251057 *or* 230930 E-mail penny.graysmith@midstaffs.nhs.uk

GRAYSMITH, Peter Alexander. b 62. UEA BSc83. Westcott Ho Cam 85. **d** 88 **p** 89. C Tettenhall Regis *Lich* 88-89; C Cannock 89-92; TV 92-99; V Rocester and Croxden w Hollington 99-01; V Baswich from 01. *The Vicarage, 97 Baswich Lane, Stafford ST17 0BN* Tel (01785) 251057 E-mail petergraysmith@talktalk.net

GRAYSON, Jane Elizabeth. b 71. **d** 07 **p** 08. OLM Moston St Mary *Man* from 07. *296 St Mary's Road, Manchester M40 0BD* Tel 0161-688 7073 E-mail janegrayson@aol.com

GRAYSON, Robin John. b 53. Mert Coll Ox BA74 DPhil78. Wycliffe Hall Ox 00. **d** 02 **p** 03. C Beaconsfield *Ox* 02-06; P-in-c Langley Marish 06-08; TR from 08. *The Vicarage, 3 St Mary's Road, Slough SL3 7EN* Tel (01753) 542068 Mobile 07801-280475 E-mail r.j.grayson@btinternet.com

GREADY, Andrew John. b 63. Univ Coll Lon BSc84 Newc Univ MA93 Surrey Univ BSc05. St Jo Coll Nottm 86. **d** 89 **p** 90. C Monkwearmouth St Andr *Dur* 89-92; C Bramley St Cath S Africa 92-96; R Sunninghill St Steph 96-99; Chapl St Pet Prep Sch 99; V Shottermill *Guildf* 00-06; Chapl Amesbury Sch 01-06; P-in-c Wynberg St Jo S Africa from 06. *Barnabas House, St John's Terrace, Wynberg 7800, South Africa* Tel (0027) (21) 797 8968 Fax 762 5970 E-mail andrew@greadyfamily.fsnet.co.uk

GREANY, Canon Richard Andrew Hugh. b 44. Qu Coll Ox BA67 MA83. Coll of Resurr Mirfield 67. **d** 69 **p** 70. C Hartlepool St Oswald *Dur* 69-72; C Clifton All SS *Bris* 72-75; Tutor Coll of

Resurr Mirfield 75-78; V Whitworth w Spennymoor *Dur* 78-83; P-in-c Byers Green 78-79; Asst Prin St Alb Minl Tr Scheme 83-88; V Flamstead *St Alb* 83-88; V Hessle *York* 88-94; V Cambridge St Mary Less *Ely* from 94; Dioc Spirituality Officer from 99; Hon Can Ely Cathl from 05; RD Cambridge S from 06. *1B Summerfield, Cambridge CB3 9HE* Tel (01223) 350733 *or* 366202 E-mail greany@lsm.org.uk

GREANY, Mrs Virginia Clare. b 52. Bris Univ BA74 PGCE75 Hull Univ MSc94. Westcott Ho Cam 96 EAMTC 97. **d** 98. Bp's Dn to Local Government *Ely* 98-99; Asst to Dean Trin Hall Cam 98-00. *Trinity Hall, Cambridge CB2 1TJ* Tel (01223) 332500

GREAR, Hugh Massey. b 60. Bris Univ LLB82. SEITE. **d** 00 **p** 01. C Warlingham w Chelsham and Farleigh *S'wark* 00-04; V Upper Tooting H Trin w St Aug from 04. *Holy Trinity Vicarage, 14 Upper Tooting Park, London SW17 7SW* Tel (020) 8672 4790 E-mail hugh.grear@tesco.net

GREASLEY, James Kenneth. b 39. K Coll Lon BD66 AKC66. **d** 67 **p** 68. C Stoke upon Trent *Lich* 67-70; P-in-c Lusaka St Pet Zambia 70-76; V Gt Staughton *Ely* 76-81; Chapl HM Borstal Gaynes Hall 76-81; V Melbourn and Meldreth *Ely* 81-96; RD Shingay 82-96; R Chalfont St Peter *Ox* 96-04; rtd 04; Perm to Offic *Heref* from 05. *Bank Cottage, Norton, Presteigne LD8 2EN* Tel (01544) 267567 E-mail jk.greasley@btinternet.com

GREATBATCH, John Charles. b 56. N Staffs Poly BA80. Coll of Resurr Mirfield 80. **d** 83 **p** 84. C Wednesbury St Paul Wood Green *Lich* 83-88; C Codsall 88-94; V Tipton St Jo 94-97; V Charlestown *Truro* from 97; Chapl Cornwall Healthcare NHS Trust 98-02; Chapl Cen Cornwall Primary Care Trust 02-07. *The Vicarage, Church Road, Charlestown, St Austell PL25 3NS* Tel (01726) 75688 Mobile 07799-078164 E-mail john@obadiah19.fsnet.co.uk

GREATOREX, Mrs Susan Kathleen. b 58. St Hilda's Coll Ox BA79 MA04 Univ of Wales (Cardiff) PGCE80. WEMTC 01. **d** 04 **p** 05. C Keynsham *B & W* 04-08; R Radstock w Writhlington from 08; R Kilmersdon w Babington from 08. *28 Wells Road, Radstock BA3 3RL* Tel (01761) 433917 E-mail susangreatorex@blueyonder.co.uk

GREATREX, Richard Quintin. b 65. K Coll Lon BD86 Surrey Univ BA02. STETS 99. **d** 02 **p** 03. NSM Westbury-on-Trym St Alb *Bris* 02-06; NSM Flax Bourton and Barrow Gurney *B & W* 06-09; NSM Long Ashton w Barrow Gurney and Flax Bourton from 09. *The Rectory, Main Road, Flax Bourton, Bristol BS48 3QJ* Tel (01275) 461179 E-mail rqg1@fsmail.net

GREAVES, Canon John Neville. b 29. Newc Univ MA96 Dur Univ MLitt03. St Aid Birkenhead 58. **d** 61 **p** 62. C Pendleton St Ambrose *Man* 61-62; P-in-c 62-63; C Benchill 63-65; C-in-c Wythenshawe St Rich CD 65-71; V Wythenshawe St Rich 71-73; R Sadberge *Dur* 73-78; V Dur St Cuth 78-94; Chapl New Coll Dur 78-92; Lect NEOC 79-84; Chapl Dur Co Fire Brigade 85-94; RD Durham 91-93; Hon Can Dur Cathl 91-94; rtd 94; Perm to Offic *Ches* 94-97; P-in-c Salt and Sandon w Burston *Lich* 97-00; Past Aux Eccleshall Deanery 00-01; Perm to Offic *Lich* 01-02 and *Heref* from 03. *3 Sitwell Close, Bucknell SY7 0DD* Tel (01547) 530152

GREED, Frederick John. b 44. Trin Coll Bris 79. **d** 81 **p** 82. C Yateley *Win* 81-85; R Ore St Helen and St Barn *Chich* 85-95; R Street w Walton *B & W* from 95; RD Glastonbury from 08. *The Rectory, Vestry Close, Street BA16 0HZ* Tel (01458) 442671 E-mail john.greed@tesco.net

GREEDY, Tegryd Joseph. b 31. St D Coll Lamp 59. **d** 61 **p** 62. C Newbridge *Mon* 61-64; C Bassaleg 64-66; V Newport St Teilo 66-74; Hon C Newport St Mark 80-83; V Goldcliffe and Whitson and Nash 83-90; Ind Chapl 83-90; V Marshfield and Peterstone Wentloog etc 90-96; rtd 96. *42 Churchward Drive, Newport NP19 4SB* Tel (01633) 282159

GREEN, Adrian Paul. b 66. Trin Coll Bris 06. **d** 08 **p** 09. NSM Willowfield *D & D* from 08. *122 Mount Merrion Avenue, Belfast BT6 0FS* Tel (028) 9029 4676 *or* 9045 7654 Mobile 07914-290193 E-mail adrian.familygreen@tiscali.co.uk

GREEN, Alan John Enrique. b 56. Worc Coll Ox BA79 MA83. Linc Th Coll 83. **d** 85 **p** 86. C Kirkby *Liv* 85-88; TV 88-94; Chapl Knowsley Community Coll 87-90; Chapl Worc Coll and C Ox St Giles and SS Phil and Jas w St Marg 94-98; TR St Jo on Bethnal Green *Lon* from 98; AD Tower Hamlets from 06. *St John's Rectory, 30 Victoria Park Square, London E2 9PB* Tel and fax (020) 8980 1742 E-mail alan.green@virgin.net

GREEN, Alison Mary. b 51. Boro Road Teacher Tr Coll BEd74 Wesley Coll Bris MA03 Roehampton Univ PhD07. STETS 02. **d** 04 **p** 05. NSM Bath St Barn w Englishcombe *B & W* 04-06; NSM Monmouth w Overmonnow etc from 06. *Great Manson Hall, Manson Lane, Manson, Monmouth NP25 5RD* Tel (01600) 715538 E-mail alig9@btinternet.com

GREEN, Anthony Brian. b 39. Sussex Univ MA88 Birm Univ CertEd60 ACP66. Bps' Coll Cheshunt 62. **d** 64 **p** 65. C Batheaston w St Cath *B & W* 64-67; Chapl Aiglon Coll and Villars *Eur* 67-71; Hd Master Battisborough Sch Holbeton 71-81; Chapl R Gr Sch Worc 81-83; Hd Master Frewen Coll Rye 83-96; P-in-c New Groombridge *Chich* from 97. *The Vicarage,*

Corsley Road, Groombridge, Tunbridge Wells TN3 9SE Tel and fax (01892) 864265
E-mail fidgreen@groombridge65.fsnet.co.uk

GREEN, Arthur Edward. b 27. Chich Th Coll 58. **d** 59 **p** 60. C Malden St Jas *S'wark* 59-62; C Caterham 62-67; R Burgh Parva w Briston *Nor* 67-75; V Middleton 75-76; V Middleton w E Winch 76-84; R Neatishead w Irstead 84-90; V Barton Turf 84-90; R Neatishead, Barton Turf and Irstead 90-92; rtd 92; Perm to Offic *Portsm* from 92. *10 James Butcher Court, 16 Eastern Villas Road, Southsea PO4 0TD* Tel (023) 9275 0701

GREEN, Barrie. b 51. SS Coll Cam BA72 MA76. Wycliffe Hall Ox 75. **d** 78 **p** 79. C Castle Vale *Birm* 78-81; V W Heath 81-96; RD Kings Norton 87-95; TR Dronfield w Holmesfield *Derby* from 96. *The Rectory, Church Street, Dronfield S18 1QB* Tel (01246) 411531 *or* 412328 Fax 08707-065540
E-mail barrie.green@dwhparish.org.uk

GREEN, Benjamin Charles. b 83. Magd Coll Cam BA04 MA08. Wycliffe Hall Ox MTh08. **d** 08. C Stockton and Preston-on-Tees and Longnewton *Dur* 08-09. *8 High Church Wynd, Yarm TS15 9BQ* Tel (01642) 780950 E-mail revbcg@gmail.com

GREEN, Brian Robert. b 31. Bris Univ BA55. Tyndale Hall Bris 52. **d** 56 **p** 57. C Toxteth Park St Philemon *Liv* 56-58; V Toxteth Park St Philemon w St Silas 58-69; P-in-c Toxteth Park St Gabr 64-69; P-in-c Toxteth Park St Jo and St Thos 64-69; P-in-c Toxteth Park St Jas and St Matt 68-69; V Elsenham *Chelmsf* 69-85; V Henham 69-85; P-in-c Ugley 84-85; V Henham and Elsenham w Ugley 85-89; RD Newport and Stansted 87-89; Perm to Offic *Ex* 90-91; V Tidenham w Beachley and Lancaut *Glouc* 91-97; RD Forest S 95-97; rtd 97; Perm to Offic *Ex* from 97. *1 The Square, Offwell, Honiton EX14 9SA* Tel (01404) 831795

GREEN, Brutus Zachary. b 78. Westcott Ho Cam 07. **d** 09. C Paddington St Jo w St Mich *Lon* from 09. *23 Archery Close, London W2 2BE* Tel 07734-887903 (mobile)
E-mail bru_zac@hotmail.com

GREEN, Catherine Isabel. *See* HITCHENS, Mrs Catherine Isabel

GREEN, Christopher Frederick. b 46. Nottm Univ BTh75 Birm Univ DipEd85 Univ of Wales (Abth) MEd94. Bp Otter Coll CertEd69 Linc Th Coll 71. **d** 75 **p** 76. C Hodge Hill *Birm* 75-77; C S Lafford *Linc* 77-79; P-in-c Worc St Mich 79-82; Hd RS and Lib RNIB New Coll Worc 82-96; V Clipstone *S'well* 96-02; rtd 02; Perm to Offic *Linc* from 03. *Cobwebs, Middlefield Lane, Glenthorn, Market Rasen LN8 2ET* Tel (01673) 878633

GREEN, Christopher Martyn. b 58. New Coll Edin BD80. Cranmer Hall Dur 82. **d** 83 **p** 84. C Virginia Water *Guildf* 83-87; C Bromley Ch Ch *Roch* 87-91; Study Asst the Proclamation Trust 91-92; C Surbiton Hill Ch Ch *S'wark* 92-00; Vice Prin Oak Hill Th Coll from 00; Perm to Offic *Lon* from 02. *Oak Hill Theological College, Chase Side, London N14 4PS* Tel (020) 8449 0467 *or* 8441 0315

GREEN, Mrs Clare Noreen. b 30. SWMTC 84. **d** 88. NSM Bideford *Ex* 88-90; Perm to Offic from 90. *30 Rosebarn Lane, Exeter EX4 5DX* Tel (01392) 272505

GREEN, Daphne Mary. b 55. K Coll Cam BA77 Bradf Univ MBA91 Leeds Univ PhD01 Lon Inst of Educn PGCE79. NOC 95. **d** 98 **p** 99. C Headingley *Ripon* 98-02; Chapl Leeds Metrop Univ 00-02; R Stanningley St Thos 02-08; Abp's Chapl and Researcher *York* from 08. *Bishopthorpe, York YO23 2GE* Tel (01904) 707021 Fax 709204 Mobile 07796-084264

GREEN, David Allen. b 61. Sheff City Poly BA90. Cranmer Hall Dur 00. **d** 02 **p** 03. C Huyton St Geo *Liv* 02-06; TV Walkden and Lt Hulton *Man* from 06. *Peel Rectory, 122 Peel Lane, Little Hulton, Manchester M38 0FD* Tel 0161-799 6300
E-mail peel.rectory@btinternet.com

GREEN, Canon David John. b 54. SWMTC 82. **d** 85 **p** 86. C St Marychurch *Ex* 85-89; C Laira 89-90; V Maughold *S & M* from 90; RD Ramsey 98-08; Dioc Dir of Ords 05-08; Can St German's Cathl from 05. *The Vicarage, Maughold, Isle of Man IM7 1AS* Tel (01624) 812070 E-mail dgreen@mcb.net

GREEN, David Norman. b 37. Magd Coll Cam BA60. Clifton Th Coll 60. **d** 62 **p** 63. C Islington St Mary *Lon* 62-65; C Burley *Ripon* 65-68; Kenya 69-80; P-in-c Brimscombe *Glouc* 81-90; R Woodchester and Brimscombe 90-96; P-in-c Coberley w Cowley 96-97; P-in-c Colesborne 96-97; P-in-c Coberley, Cowley, Colesbourne and Elkstone 97-04; Dioc Rural Adv 96-04; rtd 04; Tanzania from 04. *Diocese of Tabora, PO Box 1408, Tabora, Tanzania*

GREEN, David Robert John. b 73. Sheff Univ BA96. Ridley Hall Cam 06. **d** 08 **p** 09. C Chatham St Phil and St Jas *Roch* from 08. *3A Kit Hill Avenue, Chatham ME5 9ET* Tel (01634) 682991
E-mail mail@revdgreen.org.uk

GREEN, David William. b 53. CertEd75 Nottm Univ BCombStuds84. Linc Th Coll 81. **d** 84 **p** 85. C S Merstham *S'wark* 84-88; C Walton-on-Thames *Guildf* 88-91; V Gillingham H Trin and Chapl Lennox Wood Elderly People's Home *Roch* 91-99; V Strood St Nic w St Mary from 99. *The Vicarage, 3 Central Road, Strood, Rochester ME2 3HF* Tel (01634) 719052
E-mail david.green@diocese-rochester.org

GREEN, Miss Denise Penelope. b 57. Bedf Coll of Educn BEd80 MPhil89. EMMTC 03. **d** 06 **p** 07. C Skirbeck H Trin *Linc* from 06. *15 Sandringham Gardens, Fishtoft, Boston PE21 9QA* Tel (01205) 356722 Mobile 07812-006295

GREEN, Canon Derek George Wilson. b 27. Bris Univ BA53 MA58. Tyndale Hall Bris 48. **d** 53 **p** 54. C Weymouth St Mary *Sarum* 53-55; Chapl RAF 55-58; R N Pickenham w Houghton on the Hill *Nor* 58-89; R S Pickenham 58-89; R N Pickenham w S Pickenham etc 89-93; Hon Can Nor Cathl 78-93; E Region Co-ord Scripture Union 80-92; rtd 93; Perm to Offic *Sarum* 93-07; P-in-c Worlingworth, Southolt, Tannington, Bedfield etc *St E* from 07. *The Rectory, Church Street, Worlingworth, Woodbridge IP13 7NT* Tel (01728) 627975

GREEN, Donald Henry. b 31. Selw Coll Cam BA54 Lon Inst of Educn PGCE55. Qu Coll Birm 81. **d** 83 **p** 84. C Dudley St Aug Holly Hall *Worc* 83-85; V Dudley St Barn 85-90; rtd 90. *The Cuckoo's Nest, 12 Mill Green, Knighton LD7 1EE* Tel (01547) 528289

GREEN, Donald Pentney (Brother Donald). b 25. Leeds Univ BA50. Coll of Resurr Mirfield 50. **d** 52 **p** 53. C Ardwick St Benedict *Man* 52-55; SSF from 55; Sec for Miss SSF 78-96; Lic to Offic *Chelmsf* 58-60 and 69-72; Papua New Guinea 60-63; Chapl HM Pris Kingston (Portsm) 72-76; Lic to Offic *Edin* 76-77; Org Sec Catholic Renewal 77; Lic to Offic *Lich* from 78; rtd 95. *85 Crofton Road, London E13 8QT* Tel (020) 7474 5863
E-mail donaldssf@aol.com

GREEN, Dorothy Mary. b 36. Westf Coll Lon BA58. Selly Oak Coll 60. **dss** 83 **d** 87 **p** 94. Ryde All SS *Portsm* 83-91; C 87-91; Hon C Hempnall *Nor* 91-96; rtd 96; Perm to Offic *B & W* 97-07. *2 Bramwell Lodge, Brighton Road, Woodmancote, Henfield BN5 9SX* Tel (01273) 495501
E-mail revdern17@yahoo.co.uk

GREEN, Douglas Edward. b 17. Sarum Th Coll 47. **d** 50 **p** 51. C Glouc St Paul 50-53; C Malvern Link St Matthias *Worc* 53-56; R Tolladine 56-58; V Bosbury *Heref* 58-78; R Coddington 59-79; V Wellington Heath 59-79; Hon C Minsterley 78-80; rtd 82; Perm to Offic *Worc* from 83. *21 The Quadrangle, Newland, Malvern WR13 5AX* Tel (01684) 568335

GREEN, Canon Duncan Jamie. b 52. Sarum & Wells Th Coll 82. **d** 84 **p** 85. C Uckfield *Chich* 84-87; Dioc Youth Officer *Chelmsf* 87-96; Warden and Chapl St Mark's Coll Res Cen 93-96; TR Saffron Walden w Wendens Ambo, Littlebury etc 96-07; RD Saffron Walden 05-07; C of E Olympic and Paralympic Co-ord from 07; Hon Can Chelmsf Cathl from 03. *86 Princes Road, Buckhurst Hill IG9 5DZ*
E-mail cofeolympiccoordinator@greendj.co.uk

GREEN, Edward Bryan. b 75. Westcott Ho Cam 02. **d** 05 **p** 06. C Soham and Wicken *Ely* 05-09; TV Cherwell Valley *Ox* from 09. *The Rectory, Station Road, Lower Heyford, Bicester OX25 5PD* Tel (01869) 340562 Mobile 07974-107524
E-mail edward.green@cherwellvalleybenefice.org

GREEN, Edward John. b 35. Lich Th Coll. **d** 59 **p** 60. C Longford *Cov* 59-61; C Wigston Magna *Leic* 61-65; V 73-00; V Glenfield 65-73; rtd 00; Perm to Offic *Leic* 00-03 and from 05. *Holly Mount, 27 Greendale Road, Glen Parva, Leicester LE2 9HD* Tel 0116-277 2479

GREEN, Edward Marcus. b 66. Mert Coll Ox BA88 MA92. Wycliffe Hall Ox 90. **d** 94 **p** 95. C Glyncorrwg w Afan Vale and Cymmer Afan *Llan* 94-96; C Aberystwyth *St D* 96-99; P-in-c Pontypridd St Cath w St Matt *Llan* 00-01; V Pontypridd St Cath from 01. *St Catherine's Vicarage, Gelliwastad Grove, Pontypridd CF37 2BS* Tel (01443) 402021
E-mail marcusgreen@manutd.com

GREEN, Canon Edward Michael Bankes. b 30. Ex Coll Ox BA53 MA56 Qu Coll Cam BA57 MA61 BD66 Toronto Univ DD92 Lambeth DD96. Ridley Hall Cam 55. **d** 57 **p** 58. C Eastbourne H Trin *Chich* 57-60; Lect Lon Coll of Div 60-69; Prin St Jo Coll Nottm 69-75; Can Th Cov Cathl 70-76; R Ox St Aldate w H Trin 75-82; R Ox St Aldate w St Matt 82-86; Prof Evang Regent Coll Canada 87-92; Abps' Adv Springboard for Decade of Evang 92-96; rtd 96; Six Preacher Cant Cathl 93-99; Sen Research Fell Wycliffe Hall Ox from 97; Perm to Offic *Ox* from 99. *7 Little Acreage, Marston, Oxford OX3 0PS* Tel (01865) 248387 Fax 792083 E-mail michael.green@wycliffe.ox.ac.uk

GREEN, Mrs Elizabeth Pauline Anne. b 29. Gilmore Ho 69. **dss** 76 **d** 87 **p** 94. Chorleywood Ch Ch *St Alb* 76-87; Par Dn 87-90; C Chipping Sodbury and Old Sodbury *Glouc* 90-95; Asst Dioc Missr 90-95; rtd 95; NSM Chipping Sodbury and Old Sodbury *Glouc* 95-99; Perm to Offic *Glouc*; *Bris* from 99. *The Old House, The Common, Chipping Sodbury, Bristol BS37 6PX* Tel (01454) 311936 E-mail p.green@care4free.net

GREEN, Eric Kenneth. b 18. Tyndale Hall Bris 40. **d** 45 **p** 47. C Heatherlands St Jo *Sarum* 45-48; C Radipole 48-49; C Bucknall and Bagnall *Lich* 49-50; V Halwell w Moreleigh *Ex* 50-53; V Wakef St Mary 53-55; R Peldon *Chelmsf* 55-57; P-in-c Leaden Roding 57-58; R 58-63; V Aythorpe Roding and High Roding 60-63; R All Cannings w Etchilhampton *Sarum* 63-75; V Over Kellet *Blackb* 75-83; rtd 83; Perm to Offic *Bradf* 91-98. *Penlee*

Residential Care Home, 56 Morrab Road, Penzance TR18 4EB Tel (01736) 364102

GREEN, Ernest James. b 31. Pemb Coll Cam BA55 MA62. Linc Th Coll 55. **d** 57 **p** 58. C Rawmarsh *Sheff* 57-60; Sec Th Colls Dept SCM 60-62; Prec and Sacr Bris Cathl 62-65; Min Can 62-65; V Churchill *B & W* 65-78; RD Locking 72-78; V Burrington and Churchill 78-82; Preb Wells Cathl 81-82; V Ryde All SS *Portsm* 82-91; P-in-c Ryde H Trin 82-86; RD E Wight 83-88; TR Hempnall *Nor* 91-96; rtd 96; Perm to Offic *B & W* 97-07. *2 Bramwell Lodge, Brighton Road, Woodmancote, Henfield BN5 9SX* Tel (01273) 495501
E-mail revdern17@yahoo.co.uk

GREEN, Ms Fiona Jenifer. b 67. Rob Coll Cam BA89 MA93. Ridley Hall Cam 02. **d** 05 **p** 06. C Highbury Ch Ch w St Jo and St Sav *Lon* 05-08; C St Jo on Bethnal Green from 08; Co-ord Reader Tr Stepney Area from 08. *The Rectory Flat, Hereford Street, London E2 6EX* Tel 07786-541559 (mobile)
E-mail fionajgreen@yahoo.co.uk

GREEN, Fleur Estelle. b 72. Univ of Wales (Ban) BD94. Ripon Coll Cuddesdon 95. **d** 97 **p** 98. C Blackpool St Jo *Blackb* 97-00; C Lancaster St Mary w St John and St Anne 00-03; P-in-c Blackb St Luke w St Phil 03-04; P-in-c Witton 03-04; V Blackb Christ the King from 04; Asst Dir of Ords from 06. *St Mark's Vicarage, Buncer Lane, Blackburn BB2 6SY* Tel (01254) 676615

GREEN, Frank Gilbert. b 23. Kelham Th Coll 46. **d** 50 **p** 51. C Sheff St Cecilia Parson Cross 50-56; SSM from 52; C Nottingham St Geo w St Jo *S'well* 58-60; Basutoland 59-62; S Africa 62-69 and 84-88; Lesotho 69-84; Lic to Offic *Ox* from 88; rtd 93. *Society of the Sacred Mission, 1 Linford Lane, Willen, Milton Keynes MK15 9DL* Tel (01908) 663749

GREEN, Gary Henry. b 64. Univ of Wales (Cardiff) BD87. St Mich Coll Llan 93. **d** 95 **p** 96. C Baglan *Llan* 95-97; C Neath w Llantwit 97-01; TV Neath 01-02; V Llangiwg *S & B* from 02. *The Vicarage, 10 Uplands Road, Pontardawe, Swansea SA8 4AH* Tel (01792) 862003

GREEN, George James. b 26. Cuddesdon Coll 69. **d** 69 **p** 70. C Handsworth St Mary *Birm* 69-76; R Croughton w Evenley *Pet* 76-88; R Aynho and Croughton w Evenley 88-95; rtd 95; Perm to Offic *Cov* from 95. *Dibbinsdale, Langley Road, Claverdon, Warwick CV35 8PU*

GREEN, Gillian. b 41. Balls Park Coll Hertford TCert61 Open Univ BA83. EAMTC 03. **d** 05 **p** 06. NSM Stour Valley *St E* from 05. *Lady's Green Cottage, Lady's Green, Ousden, Newmarket CB8 8TU* Tel (01284) 850605
E-mail gill@g-green.fsnet.co.uk

GREEN, Mrs Gloria. b 49. STETS 00. **d** 03 **p** 04. NSM Jersey St Brelade *Win* from 03; Asst Chapl Jersey Gp of Hosps 03-04 and from 05. *1 Hibernia Vale, Le Mont les Vaux, St Brelade, Jersey JE3 8AF* Tel (01534) 744804 Fax 08700-941104
E-mail glo@glogreen.com

GREEN, Gordon Sydney. b 33. Ridley Hall Cam 77. **d** 79 **p** 80. C Ipswich St Mary *St E* 79-83; TV Barton Mills, Beck Row w Kenny Hill etc 83-85; TV Mildenhall 85-86; rtd 86; Perm to Offic *St E* from 97. *28 Upton Close, Ipswich IP4 2QQ* Tel (01473) 252188

GREEN, Graham Reginald. b 48. Sarum & Wells Th Coll 71. **d** 74 **p** 75. C Chorley St Laur *Blackb* 74-76; C Padiham 76-79; V Osmondthorpe St Phil *Ripon* 79-94. *3 Northwood Gardens, Colton, Leeds LS15 9HH* Tel 0113-264 3558

GREEN, Imogen Elizabeth. See VIBERT, Imogen Elizabeth

GREEN, Mrs Janice Anne. b 48. NTMTC BA07. **d** 07 **p** 08. NSM Gt Hallingbury and Lt Hallingbury *Chelmsf* from 07; P-in-c from 09. *The Rectory, Wrights Green Lane, Little Hallingbury, Bishop's Stortford CM22 7RE*
E-mail rev.janicegreen@btinternet.com

GREEN, Jeffrey. b 43. Chich Th Coll 76. **d** 78 **p** 79. C Crewkerne w Wayford *B & W* 78-81; C Cockington *Ex* 81-83; R Ripple, Earls Croome w Hill Croome and Strensham *Worc* 83-87; Perm to Offic *Glouc* 02-03; Hon C Boxwell, Leighterton, Didmarton, Oldbury etc 03-06; Hon C Nailsworth w Shortwood, Horsley etc 03-06; rtd 06. *7 Cherry Tree Close, Nailsworth, Stroud GL6 0DX* Tel (01453) 836910

GREEN, Miss Jennifer Mary. b 55. SEN78 SRN81 RM84. Trin Coll Bris 87. **d** 90 **p** 95. C Tong *Bradf* 90-93; Chapl Bradf Cathl 93; CMS from 94; Uganda from 94. *Muhabura Diocese, PO Box 22, Kisoro, Uganda*

GREEN, Jeremy Nigel. b 52. St Andr Univ MA. St Jo Coll Nottm 80. **d** 83 **p** 84. C Dorridge *Birm* 83-86; V Scrooby *S'well* 86-94; V Bawtry w Austerfield and Misson 94-06; AD Bawtry 01-06; P-in-c Haxey *Linc* from 06; P-in-c Owston from 06. *The Vicarage, Church Street, Haxey, Doncaster DN9 2HY* Tel (01427) 752351 E-mail jngreen@lineone.net

GREEN, John. See GREEN, Edward John

GREEN, The Ven John. b 53. Nottm Univ BCombStuds83. Linc Th Coll 80. **d** 83 **p** 84. C Watford St Mich *St Alb* 83-86; C St Alb St Steph 86-91; Chapl RN 91-06; Chapl of the Fleet and Adn for the RN from 06; Hon Can Portsm Cathl from 06. *Royal Naval Chaplaincy Service, Mail Point 1-2, Leach Building, Whale Island, Portsmouth PO2 8BY* Tel (023) 9262 5055 Fax 9262 5134

GREEN, John David. b 29. Lon Univ BD66. Roch Th Coll 63. **d** 66 **p** 66. C Roch St Pet w St Marg 66-72; V Oxshott *Guildf* 72-85; R Weybridge 85-94; rtd 94; Perm to Offic *Guildf* from 94. *103 Bitterne Drive, Woking GU21 3JX* Tel (01483) 727936

GREEN, John Francis Humphrey. b 44. Ex Univ BA65 Heythrop Coll Lon MA96. Westcott Ho Cam 91. **d** 93 **p** 94. C Tadworth *S'wark* 93-96; Chapl St Geo Sch Harpenden 96-01; P-in-c Flamstead *St Alb* from 01; P-in-c Markyate Street from 01; RD Wheathampstead from 09. *The Vicarage, 50 Trowley Hill Road, Flamstead, St Albans AL3 8EE* Tel (01582) 842040
E-mail johnhumphreygreen@hotmail.com

GREEN, Canon John Henry. b 44. K Coll Lon BD72 AKC. **d** 73 **p** 74. C Tupsley *Heref* 73-77; Asst Chapl Newc Univ 77-79; V Stevenage St Hugh Chells *St Alb* 79-85; V St Jo in Bedwardine *Worc* 85-92; Dir of Ords 92-08; P-in-c Guarlford and Madresfield w Newland 92-99; C Fladbury w Wyre Piddle and Moor etc 99-08; P-in-c Bowbrook N from 08; P-in-c Bowbrook S from 08; Hon Can Worc Cathl from 94. *The Parsonage, Church Lane, Tibberton, Droitwich WR9 7NW* Tel (01905) 345242
E-mail jgreen@cofe-worcester.org.uk

GREEN, John Herbert Gardner-Waterman. b 21. Trin Hall Cam BA48 MA58. Wells Th Coll 58. **d** 59 **p** 60. C New Romney w Hope *Cant* 59-63; V Hartlip 63-68; R Sandhurst w Newenden 68-90; RD W Charing 74-81; rtd 90; Perm to Offic *Cant* 90-09 and *Chich* from 98. *Littlefield House, Maytham Road, Rolvenden Layne, Cranbrook TN17 4NS* Tel (01580) 241579

GREEN, Joseph Hudson. b 28. TD76. Dur Univ TCert73. Kelham Th Coll 48. **d** 53 **p** 54. C Norton St Mich *Dur* 53-56; C Heworth St Mary 56-62; V Harton Colliery 62-69; Chapl S Shields Gen Hosp 62-69; CF (TA) 63-67; CF (TAVR) 67-77; V Leadgate *Dur* 69-78; V Dudleston *Lich* 78-85; V Criftins 78-85; R Hodnet w Weston under Redcastle 85-93; RD Hodnet 86-93; rtd 93; Perm to Offic *Lich* from 93. *3 The Paddocks, Market Drayton TF9 3UE* Tel (01630) 658887

GREEN, Julia Ann. See CARTWRIGHT, Julia Ann

GREEN, Canon Karina Beverley. b 61. Ripon Coll Cuddesdon 87. **d** 90 **p** 94. C Lee-on-the-Solent *Portsm* 90-93; Dioc Youth Officer *Guildf* 94-99; Youth and Children's Work Adv *Portsm* 99-03; P-in-c Portsea St Geo 03-05; V from 05; CME Officer from 03; Hon Can Portsm Cathl from 06. *The Vicarage, 8 Queen Street, Portsmouth PO1 3HL* Tel (023) 9283 8713
E-mail karina@stgeorgeschurch.freeserve.co.uk

GREEN, Miss Katharine Marisa. b 81. Bris Univ BA02 St Jo Coll Dur MA08. Cranmer Hall Dur 05. **d** 08 **p** 09. C Kidderminster St Mary and All SS w Trimpley etc *Worc* from 08. *201B Birmingham Road, Kidderminster DY10 2DB* Tel (01562) 825582
E-mail katharine_green@hotmail.com

✠**GREEN, The Rt Revd Laurence Alexander.** b 45. K Coll Lon BD68 AKC68. DMin82 NY Th Sem STM69 St Aug Coll Cant 70. **d** 70 **p** 71 **c** 93. C Kingstanding St Mark *Birm* 70-73; V Erdington St Chad 73-83; Prin Aston Tr Scheme 83-89; Hon C Birchfield *Birm* 84-89; TR Poplar *Lon* 89-93; Area Bp Bradwell *Chelmsf* from 93. *The Bishop's House, Orsett Road, Horndon-on-the-Hill, Stanford-le-Hope SS17 8NS* Tel (01375) 673806 Fax 674222 E-mail b.bradwell@chelmsford.anglican.org

GREEN, Mrs Linda Anne. b 60. Westcott Ho Cam 84. **dss** 86 **d** 87 **p** 94. Borehamwood *St Alb* 86-89; Par Dn 87-89; Par Dn Sheff St Cuth 89-90; Chapl Asst N Gen Hosp Sheff 89-91; Chapl 91-95; Chapl Qu Mary's NHS Trust 96-05; P-in-c Crockenhill All So *Roch* from 06. *The Vicarage, Eynsford Road, Swanley BR8 8JS* Tel (01322) 662157
E-mail revlindagreen@aol.com

GREEN, Mrs Linda Jeanne. b 50. R Holloway Coll Lon BSc72 RGN74 RCNT79. SAOMC 01. **d** 04 **p** 05. C Headington Quarry *Ox* 04-09; P-in-c Banbury from 09. *The Vicarage, 89 Oxford Road, Banbury OX16 9AJ* Tel (01295) 262370 Mobile 07973-802863 E-mail linda@revgreen.wanadoo.co.uk

GREEN, Marcus. See GREEN, Edward Marcus

GREEN, Mrs Margaret Elizabeth. b 34. St Mich Ho Ox 60. **dss** 84 **d** 87 **p** 94. Ecclesall *Sheff* 84-87; Par Dn 87-90; C Doncaster St Jas 90-94; rtd 95; Perm to Offic *Sheff* from 95. *91 Littemoor Lane, Doncaster DN4 0LQ* Tel (01302) 365884

✠**GREEN, The Rt Revd Mark.** b 17. MC45. Linc Coll Ox BA40 MA44 Aston Univ Hon DSc80. Cuddesdon Coll 40. **d** 40 **p** 41 **c** 72. C Glouc St Cath 40-42; CF (EC) 43-46; V Newland St Jo *York* 48-53; CF 53-56; V S Bank *York* 56-58; R Cottingham 58-64; V Bishopthorpe and Acaster Malbis 64-72; Hon Chapl to Abp York 64-72; Can and Preb York Minster 63-72; RD Ainsty 64-68; Suff Bp Aston *Birm* 72-82; Dioc Dir of Ords 80-82; rtd 82; Hon Asst Bp Chich 82-06. *The College of St Barnabas, Blackberry Lane, Lingfield RH7 6NJ* Tel (01342) 872824

GREEN, Martin Charles. b 59. Bris Univ BA81 MPhil86. Wycliffe Hall Ox 82. **d** 84 **p** 85. C Margate H Trin *Cant* 84-88; V Kingston upon Hull St Aid Southcoates *York* 88-94; P-in-c Bishop's Itchington *Cov* from 94; Dioc Children's Officer 94-05; P-in-c Radford Semele from 05. *The Vicarage, 1 Manor Road, Bishop's Itchington, Southam CV47 2QJ* Tel (01926) 613466
E-mail revmcg@aol.com

GREEN, Martyn. b 41. FCA. Ridley Hall Cam 78. **d** 80 **p** 81. C Wetherby *Ripon* 80-83; V Leeds St Cypr Harehills 83-90; V Ossett cum Gawthorpe *Wakef* 90-99; TR Haxby w Wigginton *York* 99-07; rtd 07. *29 Park Row, Knaresborough HG5 0BJ* Tel (01423) 797560

GREEN, Mrs Maureen. b 49. Avery Hill Coll CertEd70 Lon Univ BEd71. EAMTC 95. **d** 98 **p** 02. NSM Ipswich St Jo *St E* from 98; Asst Chapl Ipswich Hosp NHS Trust 98-05; Asst Chapl Local Health Partnerships NHS Trust 98-02; Asst Chapl Cen Suffolk Primary Care Trust 02-05. *Rose Cottage, 41 Cowper Street, Ipswich IP4 5JB* Tel (01473) 434330 E-mail maureengreen@talk21.com

GREEN, Canon Maurice Paul. b 34. MCIMA60. Wells Th Coll 68. **d** 70 **p** 71. C Eaton *Nor* 70-74; R N w S Wootton 74-90; RD Lynn 83-89; Hon Can Nor Cathl 88-96; V Swaffham 90-96; rtd 96; Perm to Offic *St E* from 96. *6 Wimborne Avenue, Ipswich IP3 8QW* Tel (01473) 711061 E-mail m.green25@ntl.com

GREEN, Michael. *See* GREEN, Canon Edward Michael Bankes

GREEN, Muriel Hilda. b 38. SEITE 94. **d** 96 **p** 97. NSM Ealing St Barn 96-98; C 98-00; Hon C Elmstead *Chelmsf* 00-04; P-in-c rtd 06; Perm to Offic *Chelmsf* from 06. *3 Laurence Close, Elmstead Market, Colchester CO7 7EJ* Tel (01206) 820561 E-mail murielgreen@onetel.com

GREEN, Neil Howard. b 57. New Coll Ox BA80 PGCE81. Wycliffe Hall Ox 87. **d** 90 **p** 91. C Finchley St Paul and St Luke *Lon* 90-94; C Muswell Hill St Jas w St Matt 94-98; V Eastbourne All So *Chich* from 98. *All Souls Vicarage, 53 Susans Road, Eastbourne BN21 3TH* Tel (01323) 731366

GREEN, Nicholas. b 67. Cranmer Hall Dur 07. **d** 08 **p** 09. C Marton-in-Cleveland *York* from 08. *31 Grange Wood, Coulby Newham, Middlesbrough TS8 0RT* Tel (01642) 284172 Mobile 07970-164175 E-mail nickygreen@ntlworld.com

GREEN, Paul. b 25. RD. Sarum & Wells Th Coll 72. **d** 74 **p** 75. C Pinhoe *Ex* 74-77; P-in-c 77-79; V 79-85; P-in-c Bishopsteignton 85-88; P-in-c Ideford, Luton and Ashcombe 85-88; rtd 88; Perm to Offic *Ex* from 88. *58 Maudlin Drive, Teignmouth TQ14 8SB* Tel (01626) 777312

GREEN, Paul John. b 48. Sarum & Wells Th Coll 72. **d** 73 **p** 74. C Tuffley *Glouc* 73-76; C Prestbury 76-82; P-in-c Highnam w Lassington and Rudford 82-83; P-in-c Tibberton w Taynton 82-83; R Highnam, Lassington, Rudford, Tibberton etc 84-92; Hon Min Can Glouc Cathl 85-96; V Fairford 92-96; RD Fairford 93-96; rtd 96; Perm to Offic *Glouc* from 98. *19 Prices Road, Abbeymead, Gloucester GL4 4PD* Tel (01452) 614259

GREEN, Pauline. *See* GREEN, Mrs Elizabeth Pauline Anne

GREEN, Penny. *See* GREEN, Miss Denise Penelope

GREEN, Peter. b 38. Ex Univ BSc59. Sarum Th Coll 59. **d** 61 **p** 62. C Romford St Edw *Chelmsf* 61-66; Chapl Trin Coll Kandy Ceylon 66-70; V Darnall *Sheff* 71-80; TV Stantonbury *Ox* 80-87; TV Stantonbury and Willen 87-91; Dcp Chapl HM Pris Belmarsh 91-92; Chapl HM Pris Woodhill 92-03; rtd 03; Perm to Offic *Ox* from 04. *34 North Twelfth Street, Milton Keynes MK9 3BT* Tel (01908) 240634 Fax 240635 Mobile 07808-556213 E-mail peter@pg34.eclipse.co.uk

GREEN, Canon Peter Edwin. b 33. Lich Th Coll. **d** 62 **p** 63. C Sprowston *Nor* 62-65; C-in-c Heartsease St Fran CD 65-73; V Loddon w Sisland 73-91; Hon Can Nor Cathl 86-92; rtd 92; Perm to Offic *Nor* 92-96 and *St E* from 96. *Ambleside, Lowestoft Road, Beccles NR34 7DG* Tel (01502) 717740

GREEN, Peter Geoffrey. b 59. St Andr Univ MA83 Open Univ MA01. Coll of Resurr Mirfield 85. **d** 88 **p** 89. C Pershore w Pinvin, Wick and Birlingham *Worc* 88-91; V Dudley St Barn 91-99; V W Bromwich St Fran *Lich* 99-02; RD W Bromwich 02-04; Chapl Abbots Bromley Sch from 04; P-in-c Hoar Cross w Newchurch *Lich* from 07. *Duttons House, High Street, Abbots Bromley, Rugeley WS15 3BN* Tel (01283) 840528 E-mail chaplain@abbotsbromley.staffs.sch.uk

GREEN, Peter Jamie. b 63. Aston Tr Scheme 87 Oak Hill Th Coll BA93. **d** 93 **p** 94. C Brigg *Linc* 93-97; C Brigg, Wrawby and Cadney cum Howsham 97; P-in-c Billinghay 97-01; V Carr Dyke Gp 01-02; R Kelsey Gp 02-09; Bermuda from 09. *Address temp unknown*

GREEN, Philip Charles. b 53. NOC 91. **d** 94 **p** 95. C Southport Em *Liv* 94-98; P-in-c Crossens 98-03; TV N Meols 03-05; TR from 05. *St John's Vicarage, Rufford Road, Southport PR9 8JH* Tel (01704) 227662 E-mail revphilgreen@crossens1.freeserve.co.uk

GREEN, Canon Philip Harry. b 19. ALCD50. **d** 50 **p** 51. C Keighley *Bradf* 50-53; V Everton St Sav *Liv* 53-57; V Barnoldswick w Bracewell *Bradf* 57-64; V Shipley St Paul 64-77; Hon Can Bradf Cathl 77-82; V Gargrave 77-82; rtd 82; Perm to Offic *Bradf* 82-94 and *Carl* from 82. *102 Kentsford Road, Grange-over-Sands LA11 7BB* Tel (01539) 534395

GREEN, Richard Alistair. b 76. Ex Univ BA97. St Steph Ho Ox BA01. **d** 01 **p** 02. C Cockerton *Dur* 01-05; TV Ludlow *Heref* from 05; Chapl Shropshire Co Primary Care Trust from 05. *St Mary's Vicarage, Donkey Lane, Ashford Carbonel, Ludlow SY8 4DA* Tel (01584) 831113 E-mail richardgreen@ashfordcarbonell.co.uk

GREEN, Richard Charles. b 49. K Coll Lon 68 St Aug Coll Cant 73. **d** 74 **p** 75. C Broseley w Benthall *Heref* 74-79; TV Heref St Martin w St Fran 80-95; C Heref S Wye 95-99; rtd 99; Hon Chapl Heref S Wye 99-02; Chapl from 02. *5 Bardolph Close, Hereford HR2 7QA* Tel (01432) 354588 *or* 353717 Mobile 07976-910881 E-mail rghswtm@aol.com

GREEN, Robert Henry. b 57. K Coll Lon BD79. Wycliffe Hall Ox 81. **d** 83 **p** 84. C Norbury *Ches* 83-86 and from 91; C Knutsford St Jo and Toft 86-88; rtd 88. *122 Cavendish Road, Hazel Grove, Stockport SK7 6JH* Tel (01625) 858680 E-mail rob.green122@ntlworld.com

GREEN, Robert Leonard. b 44. Sarum & Wells Th Coll. **d** 84 **p** 85. C Battersea St Luke *S'wark* 84-89; CF 89-04; P-in-c Southwick w Boarhunt *Portsm* from 05. *The White House, High Street, Southwick, Fareham PO17 6EB* Tel (023) 9237 7568 E-mail revdbobgreen@talktalk.net

GREEN, Robert Stanley. b 42. Dur Univ BA65. Wells Th Coll 65. **d** 67 **p** 68. C Ashford *Cant* 67-73; R Otham 73-80; V Bethersden w High Halden 80-87; R Winterbourne Stickland and Turnworth etc *Sarum* 87-99; R Monkton Farleigh, S Wraxall and Winsley 99-05; rtd 05. *The Bungalow, Wootton Grove, Sherborne DT9 4DL* Tel (01935) 817066 E-mail albertgoat@aol.com

GREEN, Robin. b 47. St As Minl Tr Course. **d** 06 **p** 07. NSM Llangystennin *St As* from 06. *140 Queens Road, Llandudno LL30 1UE* Tel (01492) 876451 E-mail rev.robin@tiscali.co.uk

GREEN, Robin Christopher William. b 43. Leeds Univ BA64 Fitzw Ho Cam BA67. Ridley Hall Cam 65. **d** 68 **p** 69. C S'wark H Trin 68-71; C Englefield Green *Guildf* 71-73; Chapl Whitelands Coll of HE *S'wark* 73-78; Team Ldr Dioc Lay Tr Team 78-84; V W Brompton St Mary w St Pet *Lon* 84-87; USPG 87-90; Perm to Offic *S'wark* 88-90; rtd 03. *The Catch, 53 Sandown Road, Deal CT14 6PE* Tel (01304) 389050

GREEN, Roderick. b 74. Reading Univ BA95 Brunel Univ MA99. Wycliffe Hall Ox MTh07. **d** 07 **p** 08. C Spitalfields Ch Ch w All SS *Lon* from 07. *35 Buxton Street, London E1 5EH* Tel (020) 3216 0045 Mobile 07957-247239 E-mail rodeagreen@googlemail.com

GREEN, Rodney William. b 52. **d** 93 **p** 94. OLM Flixton St Jo *Man* from 93. *85 Arundel Avenue, Flixton, Manchester M41 6MG* Tel 0161-748 7238

GREEN, Roger Thomas. b 43. Oak Hill Th Coll. **d** 79 **p** 80. C Paddock Wood *Roch* 79-83; R High Halstow w All Hallows and Hoo St Mary 83-89; Chapl HM Pris Brixton 89-90; Standford Hill 90-94; Swaleside 94-99; Rochester 99-03; Blantyre Ho 03; Brixton 03-06; rtd 06. *4 Burnt House Close, Wainscott, Rochester ME3 8AU* Tel (01634) 730773 E-mail rogert.green@btinternet.com

GREEN, Preb Ronald Henry. b 27. Lambeth MA86 Bps' Coll Cheshunt 53. **d** 55 **p** 56. C St Marylebone Ch Ch w St Barn *Lon* 55-58; R 58-62; Dioc Youth Tr Officer 62-64; C St Andr Holborn 62-64; RE Adv 63-73; V Hampstead St Steph 64-73; RD N Camden 67-73; V Heston 73-80; Preb St Paul's Cathl 75-83; Jt Dir Lon and S'wark Bd of Educn 79-83; Dir of Educn *Sarum* 83-86; R Chiddingfold *Guildf* 86-91; rtd 91; Perm to Offic *Nor* 91-92; Master St Nic Hosp Salisbury 92-97; Perm to Offic *Sarum* from 98. *20 Ayleswade Road, Salisbury SP2 8DR* Tel (01722) 327660

GREEN (née JARMAN), Mrs Rosemary Susan. b 44. SAOMC 99. **d** 01 **p** 02. OLM Bradfield and Stanford Dingley *Ox* from 01. *1 Buscot Copse, Bradfield, Reading RG7 6JB* Tel 0118-974 4640 Fax 974 4910 E-mail rosemary.s.green@tesco.net

GREEN, Ruth Valerie. *See* JAGGER, Mrs Ruth Valerie

GREEN, Ryan Albert. b 77. Nottm Univ BA99. St Steph Ho Ox MTh05. **d** 05 **p** 06. C The Cookhams *Ox* 05-09; R Swanbourne w Mt Claremont Australia from 09. *The Rectory, Shenton Road, Swanbourne, Perth WA 6010, Australia* E-mail rev_green@hotmail.co.uk

GREEN, Sidney Leonard. b 44. K Coll Lon MTh86 Montessori DipEd84. Oak Hill Th Coll BD72. **d** 72 **p** 73. C Skelmersdale St Paul *Liv* 72-74; C Denton Holme *Carl* 74-76; In Bapt Min 76-85; Chapl Qu Eliz Gr Sch Blackb 85-91; Chapl Epsom Coll 91-01; P-in-c Sway *Win* 01-03; V 03-04; rtd 04; Australia from 04; Asst Min Adelaide H Trin 05; R Adelaide St Luke 06; Chapl Kensington St Matt from 07. *Bethany, 31 Maesbury Circuit, Sturt, Adelaide SA 5047, Australia* Tel (0061) (8) 8358 1406 E-mail sandjgreen@adam.com.au

GREEN, Ms Stella Louise. b 61. Kent Univ BA84. St Mich Coll Llan 01. **d** 03 **p** 04. C Stamford Hill St Thos *Lon* 03-06; R Horsford, Felthorpe and Hevingham *Nor* from 06. *The Rectory, 1B Gordon Godfrey Way, Horsford, Norwich NR10 3SG* Tel (01603) 891754 Mobile 07815-089704 E-mail stellalgreen@hotmail.com

GREEN, Preb Stephen Keith. b 48. Ex Coll Ox BA69 Mass Inst of Tech MSc75. NOC 84. **d** 87 **p** 88. Hong Kong 87-93; Perm to Offic *Lon* 93-00; NSM Kensington St Barn from 01; Preb St Paul's Cathl from 07. *8 Canada Square, London E14 5HQ* Tel (020) 7992 3600 Fax 7991 4344

GREEN, Steven Douglas. b 57. Univ of Wales BA97. Sarum & Wells Th Coll 81. **d** 82 **p** 83. C Hawarden *St As* 82-86; V Mostyn 86-93; V Ffynnongroew 86-93; V Mostyn w Ffynnongroyw 93-99; R Trefnant w Tremeirchion 99-01; R Cefn w Trefnant w Tremeirchion 01-07; V Shotton from 07. *The Vicarage, Chester Road East, Shotton, Deeside CH5 1QD* Tel (01244) 836991 E-mail clwydian1@btopenworld.com

GREEN, Ms Susan Denise. b 66. TCD BA89 HDipEd90. **d** 92 **p** 93. C Antrim All SS *Conn* 92-95; Dioc Youth Officer (Cashel) *C & O* 95-00; Chapl Adelaide and Meath Hosp Dublin 00-09. *The Rectory, Tullow, Co Carlow, Republic of Ireland* Tel and fax (00353) (59) 915 1481 E-mail greens@iolfree.ie

GREEN, Mrs Susan Margaret. b 54. Univ of Wales (Abth) BSc75. SW Minl Tr Course 92. **d** 95 **p** 96. NSM Wiveliscombe w Chipstable, Huish Champflower etc *B & W* 95-05; R Blackdown from 05; C Trull w Angersleigh from 05. *The Vicarage, Pitminster, Taunton TA3 7AZ* Tel (01823) 421232 E-mail suegreen@summit.me.uk

GREEN, Mrs Susannah Ruth. b 83. Jes Coll Cam BA05. Wycliffe Hall Ox MTh08. **d** 08 **p** 09. C Preston-on-Tees and Longnewton *Dur* from 08; C Stockton from 08. *61 Bishopton Road, Stockton-on-Tees TS18 4PD* Tel (01642) 617420

GREEN, Canon Trevor Geoffrey Nash. b 45. BA. Oak Hill Th Coll 81. **d** 84 **p** 85. C Stalybridge H Trin and Ch Ch *Ches* 84-89; V 89-96; V Lache cum Saltney from 96; Hon Can Ches Cathl from 08. *St Mark's Vicarage, 5 Cliveden Road, Chester CH4 8DR* Tel (01244) 671702 *or* 675372 Fax 677818 E-mail trevoratmarks@aol.com

GREEN, Trevor Howard. b 37. Sarum & Wells Th Coll 72. **d** 74 **p** 75. C Bloxwich *Lich* 74-77; C Willenhall St Steph 77-79; P-in-c 79-80; V 80-82; V Essington 82-90; V Bishopswood and Brewood 90-02; P-in-c Coven 00-02; RD Penkridge 94-01; rtd 02; Perm to Offic *Lich* from 02. *113 Stafford Street, Cannock WS12 2EN* Tel (01543) 271159

GREEN, William. b 44. Newc Univ BA66 DipEd67 MA77. NOC 87. **d** 90 **p** 91. NSM Utley *Bradf* 90-97; P-in-c Scarborough St Jas w H Trin *York* 97-00; V Thornton St Jas *Bradf* 00-06; rtd 07; Perm to Offic *Bradf* from 07. *105 Shann Lane, Keighley BD20 6DY* Tel (01535) 669360 E-mail billandagnes@tiscali.co.uk

GREENACRE, Canon Roger Tagent. b 30. Ordre national du Mérite 98. Clare Coll Cam BA52 MA56 Lambeth DD01. Coll of Resurr Mirfield 52. **d** 54 **p** 55. C Hanworth All SS *Lon* 54-59; Chapl Ely Th Coll 59-60; Chapl Summer Fields Sch Ox 60-61; C N Audley Street St Mark *Lon* 62-63; Chapl Liddon Ho Lon 63-65; Chapl Paris St Geo *Eur* 65-75; RD France 70-75; Dioc Ecum Officer *Chich* 75-88; Lect Chich Th Coll 75-89; Can Res Chich Cathl 75-00; Chan 75-97; Prec 97-00; Select Preacher Ox Univ 95; rtd 00; P-in-c Beaulieu-sur-Mer *Eur* from 00. *Le Saint Michel, 9 rue Paul-Doumer, 06310 Beaulieu-sur-Mer, France* Tel and fax (0033) (4) 93 01 45 61

GREENALL, Canon Ronald Gilbert. b 41. St Aid Birkenhead 61. **d** 64 **p** 65. C Adlington *Blackb* 64-67; C Ribbleton 67-69; R Coppull St Jo 69-84; V Garstang St Thos 84-99; RD Garstang 89-96; Hon Can Blackb Cathl 95-99; rtd 99; Perm to Offic *Blackb* from 99. *40 Duckworth Drive, Catterall, Preston PR3 1YS* Tel (01995) 606135

GREENE, Prof Colin John David. b 50. QUB BA73 Fitzw Coll Cam MA75 Nottm Univ PhD. St Jo Coll Nottm 78. **d** 80 **p** 81. NSM Sandiacre *Derby* 80-81; C Loughborough Em *Leic* 81-84; V Thorpe Acre w Dishley 84-89; Evang Tr Consultant Bible Soc 89-91; Tutor Trin Coll Bris 91-95; Th Consultant Bible Soc and Springdale Coll 95-96; Hd Th and Public Policy Bible Soc 96-03; Dean Th and Prof Seattle Pacific Univ USA 03-05. *Address temp unknown* E-mail cgreene@mhgs.edu

GREENE, John Howe. b 22. K Coll Lon AKC48 BD49. **d** 49 **p** 50. C Drayton in Hales *Lich* 49-52; C Stoke upon Trent 52-56; V Wilnecote 56-62; V Lodsworth and R Selham *Chich* 62-69; R Burwash 69-75; R Petworth 75-88; P-in-c Egdean 76-80; R 80-88; RD Petworth 76-88; rtd 88; Perm to Offic *Chich* from 88. *37 Wilderness Road, Hurstpierpoint, Hassocks BN6 9XD* Tel (01273) 833651

GREENE, Paul David O'Dwyer. b 53. Brunel Univ BSc78 Southn Univ DASS81 CQSW81. Oak Hill NSM Course 90. **d** 93 **p** 94. NSM Northwood Em *Lon* from 93. *50 The Drive, Northwood HA6 1HP* Tel (01923) 829605 Fax 828867 Mobile 07870-237104 E-mail paul@pgreene.demon.co.uk

GREENE, Ms Rachel Elizabeth. b 78. Virginia Univ BA01 Peterho Cam MPhil04. Westcott Ho Cam 05 Yale Div Sch 06. **d** 08 **p** 09. C Sturminster Newton, Hinton St Mary and Lydlinch *Sarum* from 08. *The Round House, 23 Drovers, Sturminster Newton DT10 1QZ* E-mail rachelegreene@gmail.com

GREENE, Richard Francis. b 47. TCD BAI70 BA70 MA86 AMIMechE. CITC 03. **d** 06 **p** 07. NSM Waterford w Killea, Drumcannon and Dunhill *C & O* from 06. *Shallon, 2 Pleasant Avenue, Mount Pleasant, Waterford, Republic of Ireland* Tel (00353) (51) 878477 Mobile 87-825 0418 E-mail richard@daralinn.ie

GREENER, The Very Revd Jonathan Desmond Francis. b 61. Trin Coll Cam BA83 MA87. Coll of Resurr Mirfield 89. **d** 91 **p** 92. C S'wark H Trin w St Matt 91-94; Bp's Dom Chapl *Truro* 94-96; V Brighton Gd Shep Preston *Chich* 96-03; Adn Pontefract *Wakef* 03-07; Dean Wakef from 07. *The Deanery, 1 Cathedral Close, Wakefield WF1 2DP* Tel (01924) 239308 *or* 373923 Fax 215054 E-mail jonathan.greener@wakefield-cathedral.org.uk

GREENFIELD, Canon Martin Richard. b 54. Em Coll Cam MA75. Wycliffe Hall Ox MA78. **d** 79 **p** 80. C Enfield Ch Ch Trent Park *Lon* 79-83; CMS from 84; Nigeria 85-94; Hon Can Aba from 89; C Langdon Hills *Chelmsf* 94-95; R Brampton *Ely* from 95; RD Huntingdon 99-04. *The Rectory, 15 Church Road, Brampton, Huntingdon PE28 4PF* Tel (01480) 453341 E-mail m.greenfield@ntlworld.com

GREENFIELD, Norman John Charles. b 27. Leeds Univ BA51. Chich Th Coll 51. **d** 53 **p** 54. C Portsea St Cuth *Portsm* 53-56; C Whitley Ch Ch *Ox* 56-60; V Moorends *Sheff* 60-65; Asst Stewardship Adv *Ox* 65-70; V Littleworth 65-71; V New Marston 71-79; Dioc Stewardship Adv *Chich* 79-88; P-in-c Amberley w N Stoke 79-83; R Guestling and Pett 88-94; rtd 94; Perm to Offic *Chich* from 94. *5 Marlborough Close, Eastbourne BN23 8AN* Tel (01323) 769494

GREENHALGH, Eric. b 20. Tyndale Hall Bris. **d** 63 **p** 64. C Preston St Mary *Blackb* 63-66; P-in-c 66-68; V 68-72; V Partington and Carrington *Ches* 72-81; V Inskip *Blackb* 81-85; rtd 85; Perm to Offic *Blackb* and *Carl* from 85. *Maranatha, 4 Rydal Close, Millom LA18 4QR* Tel (01229) 770995

GREENHALGH, Ian Frank. b 49. Wycliffe Hall Ox 74. **d** 77 **p** 78. C Parr *Liv* 77-80; V Wigan St Barn Marsh Green 80-84; Chapl RAF 84-04; V Clapham-with-Keasden and Austwick *Bradf* from 04; RD Ewecross from 05. *The Vicarage, Clapham Road, Austwick, Lancaster LA2 8BE* Tel (01524) 251313 E-mail ian.greenhalgh@bradford.anglican.org

GREENHALGH, Philip Adrian. b 52. Dur Univ MA05. Ian Ramsey Coll 75 Wycliffe Hall Ox 76. **d** 79 **p** 80. C Gt Clacton *Chelmsf* 79-82; P-in-c Stalmine *Blackb* 82-86; Rep Leprosy Miss E Anglia 86-87; Area Org CECS 88-90; NSM Alston Team *Newc* 90-92; NSM Chulmleigh *Ex* 92-93; NSM Chawleigh w Cheldon 92-93; NSM Wembworthy w Eggesford 92-93; P-in-c Gilsland w Nether Denton *Carl* 93-95; V Millom 95-00; P-in-c Heatherycleugh *Dur* 00-04; P-in-c Westgate 00-04; P-in-c St John in Weardale 00-04; P-in-c Stanhope w Frosterley 02-04; P-in-c Eastgate w Rookhope 02-04; R Upper Weardale 04-07; AD Stanhope 00-07; R Bewcastle, Stapleton and Kirklinton etc *Carl* from 07. *Stapleton Rectory, Roweltown, Carlisle CA6 6LD* Tel (01697) 748660 E-mail philipgreenhalgh@hotmail.com

GREENHALGH, Stephen. b 53. Man Univ MA99. Lon Bible Coll BA81. **d** 81 **p** 82. C Horwich H Trin *Man* 81-84; C Horwich 84-85; Chapl RAF 85-89; Perm to Offic *Blackb* 96-01; *Carl* 01-07; *Man* from 07. *2 Old Chapel Lane, Levens, Kendal LA8 8PX* Tel (01539) 737856

GREENHAM (née MORTIMER), Mrs Helen Teän. b 69. Leeds Univ BA91 Univ of Wales (Swansea) PGCE92. Ripon Coll Cuddesdon 06. **d** 08. C Bridgnorth, Tasley, Astley Abbotts, etc *Heref* from 08. *32 Goodwood Avenue, Bridgnorth WV15 5BD* Tel (01746) 763885 Mobile 07720-543885 E-mail helen.greenham@gmail.com

GREENHILL, Anthony David. b 39. Bris Univ BSc59. Tyndale Hall Bris 61. **d** 63 **p** 64. C Southsea St Jude *Portsm* 63-65; India 65-78; C Kinson *Sarum* 78-81; V Girlington *Bradf* 81-97; C Platt Bridge *Liv* 97-00; rtd 00; Perm to Offic *Bradf* from 01 and *Man* from 05. *65 Lymbridge Drive, Blackrod, Bolton BL6 5TH* Tel (01204) 696509 E-mail admp@greenhill.me.uk

GREENHOUGH, Alan Kenneth. b 40. St D Coll Lamp. **d** 66 **p** 67. C Allestree *Derby* 66-70; C Ilkeston St Mary 70-73; V Bradwell 73-85; R Twyford w Guist w Bintry w Themelthorpe etc *Nor* 85-95; P-in-c Stibbard 94-95; R Twyford, Guist, Bintree, Themelthorpe etc 95-05; rtd 05. *10 Newton Close, Metheringham, Lincoln LN4 3EQ* Tel (01526) 328642

GREENHOUGH, Andrew Quentin. b 68. E Lon Poly BSc89. Wycliffe Hall Ox BTh94. **d** 94 **p** 95. C Partington and Carrington *Ches* 94-98; C Davenham 98-05; P-in-c Moulton 01-05; V New Ferry from 05. *St Mark's Vicarage, New Chester Road, Wirral CH62 1DG* Tel 0151-645 2638 E-mail andy@macvicar.org.uk

GREENHOUGH, Arthur George. b 30. Fitzw Ho Cam BA52 MA56. Tyndale Hall Bris 55. **d** 57 **p** 58. C Wakef St Andr 57-63; R Birkin w Haddlesey *York* 63-85; RD Selby 77-84; P-in-c Hambleton 84-85; R Haddlesey w Hambleton and Birkin 85-00; rtd 01; Perm to Offic *York* from 01. *4 Sandway Drive, Camblesforth, Selby YO8 8JX* Tel (01757) 617347

GREENHOUGH, Geoffrey Herman. b 36. Sheff Univ BA57 Lon Univ BD71. St Jo Coll Nottm 74. **d** 75 **p** 76. C Cheadle Hulme St Andr *Ches* 75-78; R Tilston and Shocklach 78-82; V Hyde St Geo 82-87; V Pott Shrigley 87-00; rtd 00; Perm to Offic *Ches* from 01. *9 Pasey Close, Winsford CW7 3BP* Tel (01606) 556275 E-mail geoffrey@ggreenhough.freeserve.co.uk

GREENISH, Brian Vivian Isitt. b 20. LRCP MRCS Lon Univ MB BS. **d** 89 **p** 89. NSM Bedford St Pet w St Cuth *St Alb* 89-91;

Perm to Offic from 91. *69 Chaucer Road, Bedford MK40 2AL* Tel (01234) 352498

GREENLAND, Martin. b 65. Warwick Univ BSc87. Westcott Ho Cam 94. **d** 97 **p** 98. C Scarborough St Martin *York* 97-00; TV Bramley and Ravenfield w Hooton Roberts etc *Sheff* 00-04; V Ravenfield, Hooton Roberts and Braithwell 04-08; R Acle w Fishley, N Burlingham, Beighton w Moulton *Nor* from 08. *The Rectory, Norwich Road, Acle, Norwich NR13 3BU* Tel (01493) 750393 E-mail martin@s-lidster.fsnet.co.uk

GREENLAND, Paul Howard. b 59. Bath Univ BA80 ACA85. Trin Coll Bris 98. **d** 00 **p** 01. C Caverswall and Weston Coyney w Dilhorne *Lich* 00-03; P-in-c Chelmsf St Andr 03-05; V from 05. *The Vicarage, 88 Chignal Road, Chelmsford CM1 2JB* Tel and fax (01245) 496722 Mobile 07811-539328 E-mail paulhgreenland@care4free.net

GREENLAND, Roy Wilfrid. b 37. St Steph Ho Ox 71. **d** 73 **p** 74. C Wanstead St Mary *Chelmsf* 73-76; V Harlow St Mary Magd 76-83; P-in-c Huntingdon All SS w St Jo *Ely* 83-84; P-in-c Huntingdon St Barn 83-84; P-in-c Huntingdon St Mary w St Benedict 83-84; Bermuda 84-89; V Northampton St Alb *Pet* 89-92; R Waldron *Chich* 92-02; rtd 02; Perm to Offic *Pet* 05-07. *7 Margetts Close, Kenilworth CV8 1EN* Tel (01926) 852560

GREENMAN, David John. b 35. Lon Univ BA59. Oak Hill Th Coll 57. **d** 61 **p** 62. C Wandsworth St Steph *S'wark* 61-63; C Bishopwearmouth St Gabr *Dur* 63-66; C-in-c Bedgrove CD *Ox* 66-74; P-in-c Macclesfield Ch Ch *Ches* 74-77; V 77-81; P-in-c Glouc All SS 81-85; V Glouc St Jas 81-85; V Bare *Blackb* 85-91; V Market Lavington and Easterton *Sarum* 91-99; rtd 99; Perm to Offic *Sarum* and *Win* from 00. *3 Bure Lane, Christchurch BH23 4DJ* Tel (01425) 241034

GREENMAN (née CHESTER), Mrs Irene Mary. b 51. Dioc OLM tr scheme 97. **d** 99 **p** 00. OLM Cornholme *Wakef* 99-00; OLM Cornholme and Walsden from 00. *8 Glenview Street, Cornholme, Todmorden OL14 8LT* Tel and fax (01706) 817296 E-mail irene@stmicks99.freeserve.co.uk

GREENSLADE, Canon Gillian Carol. b 43. Leic Univ BA64 Essex Univ MA78 Nottm Univ PGCE65. EAMTC 93. **d** 96 **p** 97. NSM Dovercourt and Parkeston w Harwich *Chelmsf* 96-00; NSM Colchester, New Town and The Hythe 00-02; R Broxted w Chickney and Tilty etc 02-08; Hon Can Chelmsf Cathl 07-08; rtd 08; Adv for Women's Min (Colchester Area) 05-08; Perm to Offic *Chelmsf* from 08. *24 Quayside Court, The Quay, Harwich CO12 3HH* Tel (01255) 552055

GREENSLADE, Timothy Julian. b 63. St Jo Coll Ox BA86. Oak Hill Th Coll BA95. **d** 95 **p** 96. C Broadwater *Chich* 95-99; TV Radipole and Melcombe Regis *Sarum* from 99. *The Vicarage, 106 Spa Road, Weymouth DT3 5ER* Tel (01305) 771938

GREENSTREET, Mark George. b 68. St Jo Coll Dur BA97. Cranmer Hall Dur 94. **d** 97 **p** 98. C St Alb St Pet *St Alb* 97-99; C Stevenage St Hugh and St Jo 99-01; C Dorridge *Birm* 01-04; V Halton *Ches* 04-09; I Seapatrick *D & D* from 09. *26 Larchwood Avenue, Banbridge BT32 3XH* Tel (028) 4066 9086 E-mail mark-greenstreet@lineone.net

GREENWAY, John. b 32. Bps' Coll Cheshunt 68 Qu Coll Birm 69. **d** 69 **p** 70. C Luton Ch Ch *St Alb* 69-74; C Pulloxhill w Flitton 75-76; P-in-c Marston Morteyne 76-79; P-in-c Lidlington 77-79; P-in-c Marston Morteyne w Lidlington 80-81; R 81-97; rtd 97; Perm to Offic *Portsm* from 98. *73 Northmore Road, Locks Heath, Southampton SO31 6ZW* Tel (01489) 886791

GREENWAY, John Michael. b 34. **d** 96 **p** 97. OLM Gt Yarmouth *Nor* 96-04; Perm to Offic from 04. *17 Hamilton Road, Great Yarmouth NR30 4ND* Tel (01493) 853558

GREENWAY, Margaret Hester. b 26. **d** 87. Downend *Bris* 75-79; Oldland 79-82; Stratton St Margaret w S Marston etc 82-86; rtd 86; Perm to Offic *B & W* 87-95. *5 Weston Lodge, Lower Bristol Road, Weston-super-Mare BS23 2PJ* Tel (01934) 623561

GREENWELL, Christopher. b 49. Linc Th Coll 79. **d** 81 **p** 82. C Scarborough St Martin *York* 81-84; V S Bank 84-89; R Bolton by Bowland w Grindleton *Bradf* 89-92; V Nether Hoyland St Andr *Sheff* 92-96; V Kirkleatham *York* 96-07; rtd 07. *79 Hillshaw Park Way, Ripon HG4 1JU* Tel (01765) 600467 E-mail chris@greenwell49.wanadoo.co.uk

GREENWELL, Canon Paul. b 60. Magd Coll Ox BA81 MA85. St Steph Ho Ox 82. **d** 85 **p** 86. C Hendon and Sunderland *Dur* 85-88; Min Can and Prec Ripon Cathl 88-93; Chapl Univ Coll of Ripon and York St Jo 88-93; V Hunslet St Mary *Ripon* 93-02; Chapl Harrogate and Distr NHS Foundn Trust 02-08; Chapl St Mich Hospice Harrogate 02-08; Convenor Dioc Adv Gp for Chr Healing *Ripon* 03-08; Can Res Ripon Cathl from 08. *St Wilfrid's House, Minster Close, Ripon HG4 1QP* Tel (01765) 600211 E-mail canonpaul@riponcathedral.org.uk

GREENWOOD, Claire. *See* GREENWOOD, Helen Claire

GREENWOOD, David. *See* GREENWOOD, Canon Norman David

GREENWOOD, Elizabeth. *See* GREENWOOD, Mrs Margaret Elizabeth

GREENWOOD, Canon Gerald. b 33. Leeds Univ BA57 Sheff Poly MSc81 Surrey Univ Hon MA93. Linc Th Coll 57. **d** 59 **p** 60. C Rotherham *Sheff* 59-62; V Elsecar 62-70; V Wales 70-77;

P-in-c Thorpe Salvin 74-77; Dioc Sch Officer 77-84; P-in-c Bramley and Ravenfield 77-78; P-in-c Hooton Roberts 77-78; R 78-84; Hon Can Sheff Cathl 80-84; Dioc Dir of Educn 81-84; Hon Can S'wark Cathl 84-97; Dir of Educn 84-97; rtd 97; Perm to Offic *Cant* from 97. *Home Farm Cottage, Westmarsh, Canterbury CT3 2LW* Tel (01304) 812160

GREENWOOD, Canon Gordon Edwin. b 44. Trin Coll Bris 78. **d** 80 **p** 81. C Bootle St Matt *Liv* 80-83; V Hunts Cross 83-93; V Skelmersdale St Paul from 93; P-in-c Skelmersdale Ch at Cen from 02; AD Ormskirk from 06; Hon Can Liv Cathl from 06. *The Vicarage, Church Road, Skelmersdale WN8 8ND* Tel (01695) 722087 E-mail gordongreenwood@stpaulskem.freeserve.co.uk

GREENWOOD, Helen Claire. b 54. Cranmer Hall Dur 05. **d** 06 **p** 07. C Willington *Newc* from 06. *St Mary's Vicarage, 77 Holywell Avenue, Whitley Bay NE26 3AG* Tel 0191-252 2484

GREENWOOD, Ian Richard. b 74. Liv Hope BEd96. St Jo Coll Nottm MTh09. **d** 09. C Burscough Bridge *Liv* from 09. *3 Thistle Court, Burscough, Ormskirk L40 4AW* Tel 07840-829956 (mobile) E-mail iang.nicg@btinternet.com

GREENWOOD, James Peter. b 61. Univ Coll Lon BSc83 St Jo Coll Dur BA90 RIBA87. Cranmer Hall Dur 88. **d** 91 **p** 92. C Belper *Derby* 91-94; CMS Pakistan 95-01; V Islamabad St Thos 95-00; V Silsden *Bradf* from 01; Dioc Spirituality Adv from 05; RD S Craven from 07. *The Vicarage, Briggate, Silsden, Keighley BD20 9JS* Tel (01535) 652204 E-mail peter.greenwood@bradford.anglican.org

GREENWOOD, John Newton. b 44. St Chad's Coll Dur BA69. **d** 70 **p** 71. C Hartlepool H Trin *Dur* 70-72; Lic to Offic from 72; Hd Master Archibald Primary Sch Cleveland 84-97; Asst Chapl HM Pris Holme Ho from 99. *1 Brae Head, Eaglescliffe, Stockton-on-Tees TS16 9HP* Tel (01642) 783200

GREENWOOD, Leslie. b 37. Dur Univ BA59. St Jo Coll Dur. **d** 61 **p** 62. C Birstall *Wakef* 61-63; C Illingworth 64-70; Chapl H Trin Sch Halifax 64-89; V Charlestown 70-91; TV Upper Holme Valley 91-97; Perm to Offic from 97; rtd 00. *2 Trenance Gardens, Greetland, Halifax HX4 8NN* Tel (01422) 373926 E-mail kyandles@aol.com

GREENWOOD, Mrs Margaret Elizabeth. b 34. St Mary's Coll Chelt TCert65 Surrey Univ MA93. St Mich Ho Ox 60. **d** 00. NSM Shepperton *Lon* 00-01; NSM Whitton SS Phil and Jas 01-04; Perm to Offic from 04. *Bundoran Cottage, Vicarage Lane, Staines TW18 1UE* Tel (01784) 458115 E-mail elizabethgreenwood@btinternet.com

GREENWOOD, Canon Michael Eric. b 44. Oak Hill Th Coll 78. **d** 80 **p** 81. C Clubmoor *Liv* 80-83; V Pemberton St Mark Newtown 83-94; V Grassendale 94-00, V Ashton in Makerfield St Thos from 00; Hon Can Liv Cathl from 08. *The Vicarage, 18 Warrington Road, Ashton-in-Makerfield, Wigan WN4 9PL* Tel (01942) 727275 E-mail mikeg@tinyonline.co.uk

GREENWOOD, Canon Norman David. b 52. Edin Univ BMus74 Lon Univ BD78 Nottm Univ MPhil90. Oak Hill Th Coll 76. **d** 78 **p** 79. C Gorleston St Andr *Nor* 78-81; SAMS 81-83; C Cromer *Nor* 83-84; R Appleby Magna and Swepstone w Snarestone *Leic* 84-94; P-in-c Chesterfield H Trin *Derby* 94-95; P-in-c Chesterfield Ch 94-95; R Chesterfield H Trin and Ch Ch 95-99; V S Ramsey St Paul *S & M* from 99; Dir of Ords from 01; RD Ramsey from 08; Chapl HM Pris Is of Man from 05; Hon Can St German's Cathl from 09. *St Paul's Vicarage, Walpole Drive, Ramsey, Isle of Man IM8 1NA* Tel (01624) 812275

GREENWOOD, Peter. *See* GREENWOOD, James Peter

GREENWOOD, Canon Robin Patrick. b 47. St Chad's Coll Dur BA68 MA71 Birm Univ PhD92. **d** 70 **p** 71. C Adel *Ripon* 70-73; Min Can and Succ Ripon Cathl 73-78; V Leeds Halton St Wilfrid 78-86; Dioc Can Res Ripon Cathl 86-95; Dioc Missr and Dir Lay and Post-Ord Tr 86-95; Dir of Min and Hon Can Chelmsf Cathl 95-00; Prov Officer for Min Ch in Wales 01-05; Hon C Canton St Jo *Llan* 02-05; V Monkseaton St Mary *Newc* from 05. *St Mary's Vicarage, 77 Holywell Avenue, Whitley Bay NE26 3AG* Tel 0191-252 2484

GREENWOOD, Roy Douglas. b 27. Tyndale Hall Bris 58. **d** 60 **p** 61. C Ox St Matt 60-62; V Ulpha *Carl* 62-63; V Seathwaite w Ulpha 63-72; P-in-c Haverthwaite 72-74, C Ulverston St Mary w H Trin 74-78; V Egton w Newland 78-86; Assoc Chapl Palma de Mallorca and Balearic Is *Eur* 86-93; Assoc Chapl Palma de Mallorca 93-95; rtd 95. *La Finquita, Apartado 78, 07460 Pollenca (Illes Balears), Spain* Tel (0034) 971 530 966

GREENWOOD, Sharon. **d** 07 **p** 08. NSM Welling *S'wark* from 07. *44 Honiton Road, Welling DA16 3LE* Tel (020) 8854 3541 E-mail sharon.greenwood44@tiscali.co.uk

GREER, Eric Gordon. b 52. Pepperdine Univ BA74. Princeton Th Sem MDiv80. **d** 93 **p** 94. C Southgate St Andr *Lon* 93-96; C Camden Square St Paul 96-00; V Grange Park St Pet from 00. *The Vicarage, Langham Gardens, London N21 1DN* Tel (020) 8360 2294 E-mail egreer@talk21.com

GREETHAM, Canon William Frederick. b 40. Bede Coll Dur CertEd. Cranmer Hall Dur 63. **d** 66 **p** 67. C Heyhouses on Sea *Blackb* 66-69; C Ashton-on-Ribble St Andr 69-71; Chapl

Aysgarth Sch 71-82; C Bedale *Ripon* 72-75; V Crakehall, Hornby and Patrick Brompton and Hunton 75-82; V Kirkby Stephen *Carl* 82-90; R Kirkby Stephen w Mallerstang etc 90-96; RD Appleby 86-91; P-in-c Crosthwaite Kendal 96-05; P-in-c Cartmel Fell 96-05; P-in-c Winster 96-05; P-in-c Witherslack 96-05; Hon Can Carl Cathl 89-05; rtd 05; Perm to Offic *Blackb* and *Carl* from 05. *2 Crosslands, Whittington, Carnforth LA6 2NX* Tel (015242) 71521 E-mail canonbillg@hotmail.co.uk

GREEVES, Roger Derrick. b 43. TCD BA66 MA70 Fitzw Coll Cam BA68 MA73. Westcott Ho Cam 98. **d** 98 **p** 99. In Methodist Ch 68-98; NSM Cam St Edw *Ely* 98-00; Chapl Oakington Immigration Reception Cen 00-01; Chapl Peterho Cam 00-01; Dean Clare Coll Cam 01-08; rtd 08; Perm to Offic *Ely* from 08. *28 Bateman Street, Cambridge CB2 1NB* Tel (01223) 571699 Mobile 07817-032301 E-mail rdg20@cam.ac.uk

GREGG, David William Austin. b 37. Lon Univ BD66 Bris Univ MA69. Tyndale Hall Bris 63. **d** 68 **p** 69. C Barrow St Mark *Carl* 68-71; P-in-c Lindal w Marton 71-75; Communications Sec Gen Syn Bd for Miss and Unity 76-81; Prin Romsey Ho Coll Cam 81-88; V Haddenham w Cuddington, Kingsey etc *Ox* 88-96; P-in-c Newton Longville w Stoke Hammond and Whaddon 96-02; rtd 03; Perm to Offic *Carl* from 03. *Lowick Farm House, Lowick Green, Ulverston LA12 8DX* Tel (01229) 885258

GREGORY, Alan Paul Roy. b 55. K Coll Lon BD77 MTh78 Emory Univ Atlanta PhD94 AKC77. Ripon Coll Cuddesdon 78. **d** 79 **p** 80. C Walton-on-Thames *Guildf* 79-82; Lect Sarum & Wells Th Coll 82-88; Dir Studies 85-88; Assoc R Atlanta St Patr USA 88-94; R Athens Em 94-95; Assoc Prof Ch Hist Episc Th Sem of the SW 95-04; Academic Dean and Prof Ch Hist from 04. *800 West 5th Street #702, Austin TX 78703, USA* Tel (001) (512) 364 3888 Fax 472 3098 E-mail agregory@ssw.edu

GREGORY, Andrew Forsythe. b 71. St Jo Coll Dur BA92. Wycliffe Hall Ox BA96 MA00 DPhil01. **d** 97 **p** 98. C E Acton St Dunstan w St Thos *Lon* 97-99; Asst Chapl Keble Coll Ox 97-99; Chapl Linc Coll Ox 99-03; Research Fell Keble Coll Ox 03-05; Chapl and Fell Univ Coll Ox from 05. *University College, High Street, Oxford OX1 4BH* Tel (01865) 276663 E-mail andrew.gregory@theology.ox.ac.uk

GREGORY, Brian. b 43. Trin Coll Bris. **d** 82 **p** 83. C Burscough Bridge *Liv* 82-85; V Platt Bridge 85-92; V Ben Rhydding *Bradf* 92-06; rtd 06. *9 Strawberry Street, Silsden, Keighley BD20 0AT* Tel (01535) 653056 E-mail brian@bgregory.freeserve.co.uk

✠**GREGORY, The Rt Revd Clive Malcolm.** b 61. Lanc Univ BA84 Qu Coll Cam BA87 MA89 Warwick Univ Hon MA99. Westcott Ho Cam 85. **d** 88 **p** 89 **c** 07. C Margate St Jo *Cant* 88-92; Chapl Warw Univ 92-98; TR Cov E 98-07; Area Bp Wolverhampton *Lich* from 07. *61 Richmond Road, Wolverhampton WV3 9JH* Tel (01902) 824503 Fax 824504 E-mail bishop.wolverhampton@lichfield.anglican.org

GREGORY, Father. *See* DUDDING, Edward Leslie

GREGORY, Graham. b 36. Open Univ BA78. Tyndale Hall Bris 63. **d** 66 **p** 67. C Wandsworth St Mich *S'wark* 68-71; C Hastings Em and St Mary in the Castle *Chich* 71-75; V Douglas St Ninian *S & M* 75-91; Dioc Youth Officer 78-88; Chapl HM Pris Douglas 82-86; RD Douglas *S & M* 86-91; V Wollaton Park *S'well* 91-95; V Lenton Abbey 91-95; rtd 95; Perm to Offic *York* from 98. *15 Keble Drive, Bishopthorpe, York YO23 2TA* Tel (01904) 701679

GREGORY, Ian Peter. b 45. Open Univ BA82 Plymouth Univ PGCE92. Bernard Gilpin Soc Dur 66 Chich Th Coll 67. **d** 70 **p** 71. C Tettenhall Regis *Lich* 70-73; C Shrewsbury H Cross 73-76; P-in-c Walsall St Mary and All SS Palfrey 76-80; R Petrockstowe, Petersmarland, Merton, Meeth etc *Ex* 80-87; TV Ex St Thos and Em 87-91; Hon C S Wimbledon All SS *S'wark* 94-00. *142 Monkleigh Road, Morden SM4 4ER* Tel (020) 8401 6148

GREGORY, John Frederick. b 33. Glouc Sch of Min 75. **d** 78 **p** 78. NSM S Cerney w Cerney Wick *Glouc* 78-81; NSM Coates, Rodmarton and Sapperton etc 81-88; P-in-c Kempsford w Welford 88-98; rtd 98; Perm to Offic *B & W* from 99. *22 Jury Road, Dulverton TA22 9DU* Tel (01398) 323587

GREGORY, Judith Rosalind. *See* GAVIN, Mrs Judith Rosalind

GREGORY, Mary Emma. b 70. Birm Univ BA92 St Jo Coll Dur BA04 MA06. Cranmer Hall Dur 02. **d** 05 **p** 06. C Hatfield *Sheff* 05-08; R Kirk Sandall and Edenthorpe from 08. *The Rectory, 31 Doncaster Road, Kirk Sandall, Doncaster DN3 1HP* Tel (01302) 882861 Mobile 07734-052524 E-mail maryegregory@tiscali.co.uk

GREGORY, Peter. b 35. Cranmer Hall Dur 59. **d** 62 **p** 63. C Pennington *Man* 62-65; C N Ferriby *York* 65-68; V Tonge Fold *Man* 68-72; V Hollym w Welwick and Holmpton *York* 72-77; P-in-c Foston w Flaxton 77-80; P-in-c Crambe w Whitwell and Huttons Ambo 77-80; R Whitwell w Crambe, Flaxton, Foston etc 81-94; rtd 94. *6 High Terrace, Northallerton DL6 1BG* Tel (01609) 776956

GREGORY, Richard Branson. b 33. Fitzw Ho Cam BA58 MA62. Sarum Th Coll 58 Ridley Hall Cam 59. **d** 60 **p** 61. C Sheff

St Cuth 60-62; Asst Chapl Leeds Univ 62-64; V Yeadon St Jo *Bradf* 64-71; R Keighley 71-74; TR Keighley St Andr 74-82; Hon Can Bradf Cathl 71-82; RD S Craven 71-73 and 78-82; P-in-c Broadmayne, W Knighton, Owermoigne etc *Sarum* 82-85; R 85-98; rtd 98; Perm to Offic *Sarum* from 98. *2 Huish Cottages, Sydling, Dorchester DT2 9NS* Tel (01300) 341835

GREGORY, Canon Stephen Simpson. b 40. Nottm Univ BA62 CertEd63. St Steph Ho Ox. **d** 68 **p** 69. C Aldershot St Mich *Guildf* 68-71; Chapl St Mary's Sch Wantage 71-74; R Edgefield *Nor* 74-88; R Holt 74-94; R Holt w High Kelling 94-95; RD Holt 79-84 and 93-95; Hon Can Nor Cathl 94-95; V Prestbury *Glouc* 95-03; P-in-c Pittville All SS 99-03; TR Prestbury and All SS 03-06; RD Cheltenham 00-05; Hon Can Glouc Cathl 04-06; rtd 06; Perm to Offic *Nor* from 08. *Mulberry Cottage, Balfour Road, West Runton, Cromer NR27 9QJ* Tel (01263) 838049

GREGORY, Timothy Stephen. b 48. Sheff City Coll of Educn CertEd70. NOC 96. **d** 99 **p** 00. NSM Deepcar *Sheff* 99-06; NSM Ecclesfield Deanery from 06. *33 St Margaret Avenue, Deepcar, Sheffield S36 2TE* Tel 0114-288 4198 E-mail t.gregory@tiscali.co.uk

GREGORY-SMITH, Hew Quentin. b 69. Univ of Wales (Abth) BSc93. St Mich Coll Llan 98. **d** 01 **p** 02. C Pembroke Gp *St D* 01-04; C Henfynyw w Aberaeron and Llanddewi Aberarth etc 04-07; P-in-c Llanllwchaearn and Llanina from 07. *The Rectory, LLandysul Road, New Quay SA45 9RE* Tel (01545) 571579

GREGSON, Gillian Amy. b 33. Westmr Coll Ox BTh02 CQSW78. **d** 98 **p** 99. OLM Coulsdon St Jo *S'wark* 98-05; Perm to Offic from 05. *3 Coulsdon Road, Coulsdon CR5 2LG* Tel (020) 8660 0304 E-mail gillgregson@waitrose.com

GREGSON, Peter John. b 36. Univ Coll Dur BSc61. Ripon Hall Ox 61. **d** 63 **p** 64. C Radcliffe St Thos *Man* 63-65; C Baguley 65-67; Chapl RN 68-91; V Ashburton w Buckland in the Moor and Bickington *Ex* 91-01; RD Moreton 95-98; rtd 01; Perm to Offic *Sarum* from 01. *Beech Tree Cottage, 18 Rectory Road, Broadmayne, Dorchester DT2 8EG* Tel (01305) 852478

GREIFF, Andrew John. b 64. Huddersfield Univ BA98 Leeds Univ PGCE99 St Jo Coll Dur BA05. Cranmer Hall Dur 03. **d** 05 **p** 06. C Pudsey St Lawr and St Paul *Bradf* 05-08; P-in-c Thornton St Jas from 08; P-in-c Fairweather Green from 08. *The Vicarage, 300 Thornton Road, Thornton, Bradford BD13 3AB* Tel (01274) 833200 E-mail thegoof@hotmail.com

GREIG, George Malcolm. b 28. CA53 St Andr Univ BD95. LNSM course 75. **d** 81 **p** 82. NSM Dundee St Mary Magd *Bre* 81-84; NSM Dundee St Jo 82-84; P-in-c Dundee St Ninian 84-85; Chapl St Paul's Cathl Dundee 85-98; rtd 98; Hon C Dundee St Salvador *Bre* from 98. *61 Charleston Drive, Dundee DD2 2HE* Tel (01382) 566709 E-mail gmg28@btinternet.com

GREIG, John Kenneth. b 38. Natal Univ BA57. **d** 61 **p** 62. C Durban St Thos S Africa 61-65; C Sheldon 65-66; C Friern Barnet St Jas *Lon* 66-69; C Kenton 69-71; Asst Chapl Dioc Coll Rondebosch S Africa 71-76; Chapl 76-78; Chapl Whitelands Coll of HE *S'wark* 78-84; V Purley St Swithun 84-04; Area Ecum Officer (Croydon) 84-04; rtd 04; Perm to Offic *S'wark* from 05. *29 Clive Road, London SW19 2JA* Tel (020) 8715 2784 E-mail jkgreig@hotmail.com

GREIG, Martin David Sandford. b 45. Bris Univ BSc67. St Jo Coll Nottm 72. **d** 75 **p** 76. C Keresley and Coundon *Cov* 75-79; C Rugby 79-83; TV 83-86; V Cov St Geo 86-93; TV Southgate *Chich* 93-01; R Maresfield 01-06; P-in-c Nutley 01-06; rtd 06. *Bodawen, Llangrannog, Llandysul SA44 6SH* Tel (01239) 654257 E-mail mg@bodawen.org.uk

GREIG, Michael Lawrie Dickson. b 48. All Nations Chr Coll 78 St Jo Coll Nottm 94. **d** 96 **p** 97. C Hunningham *Cov* 96-00; C Wappenbury w Weston under Wetherley 96-00; C Offchurch 96-00; C Long Itchington and Marton 96-00; P-in-c Napton-on-the-Hill, Lower Shuckburgh etc from 00; P-in-c Priors Hardwick, Priors Marston and Wormleighton from 09. *The Vicarage, Butt Hill, Napton, Rugby CV47 8NE* Tel (01926) 812383 E-mail mg@biggles99.freeserve.co.uk

GRENFELL, James Christopher. b 69. Qu Coll Ox BA93 MA96 MPhil95 Ox Univ DPhil00. Westcott Ho Cam 98. **d** 00 **p** 01. C Kirkby *Liv* 00-03; P-in-c Sheff Manor 03-06; TR 06-09; P-in-c Ranmoor from 09. *The Vicarage, 389A Fulwood Road, Sheffield S10 3GA* Tel 0114-230 1671 *or* 230 1199 E-mail james.grenfell@sheffield.anglican.org

GRENFELL, Canon Joanne Woolway. b 72. Oriel Coll Ox BA93 DPhil97 Univ of BC MA94. Westcott Ho Cam 98. **d** 00 **p** 01. C Kirkby *Liv* 00-03; Jt P-in-c Sheff Manor 03-06; Can Res Sheff Cathl from 06; Dioc Dir of Ords from 06; Dean of Women's Min from 08. *Sheffield Cathedral, Church Street, Sheffield S1 1HA* Tel 0114-263 6064 Mobile 07775-868259 E-mail joanne.grenfell@sheffield-cathedral.org.uk

GRENHAM-TOZE, Mrs Sharon Carmel. b 66. Reading Univ LLB87 Solicitor 92. Trin Coll Bris 94 SAOMC 96. **d** 98 **p** 00. C Buckingham *Ox* 98-00; C Milton Keynes 00-02; Miss Adv USPG *Lon*, *Ox* and *St Alb* 02-03; NSM Wilshamstead and Houghton Conquest *St Alb* 03-04; Chapl Oakhill Secure Tr Cen 04-05; Perm to Offic *St Alb* from 04; Asst Chapl HM Pris

Woodhill from 08. *HM Prison Woodhill, Tattenhoe Street, Milton Keynes MK4 4DA* Tel (01908) 722000
E-mail sgtoze@btopenworld.com

GRESHAM, Karen Louise. *See* SMEETON, Mrs Karen Louise

GRETTON, Tony Butler. b 29. St Jo Coll Dur BA53. **d** 54 **p** 55. C W Teignmouth *Ex* 54-57; R Norton Fitzwarren *B & W* 57-68; rtd 68; Chapl Glouc Docks Mariners' Ch 73-92; P-in-c Brookthorpe w Whaddon 79-82; Hon C The Edge, Pitchcombe, Harescombe and Brookthorpe 82-89; Perm to Offic from 89. *18 Clover Drive, Hardwicke, Gloucester GL2 4TG* Tel (01452) 721505

GREW, Nicholas David. b 52. Surrey Univ BSc74 MSc75. Wycliffe Hall Ox 93. **d** 95 **p** 96. C Biddulph *Lich* 95-99; P-in-c Knaphill *Guildf* 99-00; V Knaphill w Brookwood from 00. *Trinity House, Trinity Road, Knaphill, Woking GU21 2SY* Tel (01483) 473489
E-mail nickthevic@talktalk.com

GREW, Richard Lewis. b 32. Clare Coll Cam BA54 MA58. Wycliffe Hall Ox 67. **d** 68 **p** 70. C Repton *Derby* 68-73; Asst Chapl Repton Sch Derby 74-93; Lic to Offic *Derby* 73-93; rtd 93; Perm to Offic *Sarum* 94-07. *5 Priory Gardens, Spetisbury, Blandford Forum DT11 9DS* Tel (01258) 857613

GREW, Timothy Richard. b 65. SS Coll Cam MA88. WEMTC 03. **d** 06 **p** 07. NSM Cheltenham H Trin and St Paul *Glouc* from 06. *7 Clarence Square, Cheltenham GL50 4JN* Tel (01242) 519709
E-mail tim.grew@trinity.org

GREY, Andrew James. b 76. St Chad's Coll Dur BA99 MA00. Oak Hill Th Coll 03. **d** 08 **p** 09. C Harold Wood *Chelmsf* from 08. *48 Harold Court Road, Romford RM3 0YX* Tel (01708) 331684
E-mail andrew@stpetersharoldwood.org

GREY, Richard Thomas. b 50. QVRM06 TD94. St D Coll Lamp BA73 Ripon Hall Ox 73. **d** 75 **p** 76. C Blaenavon w Capel Newydd *Mon* 75-77; Ind Chapl 77-02; C Newport St Paul 77-80; CF (TA) from 78; Chapl Aberbargoed Hosp 80-88; V Bedwellty *Mon* 80-88; R Llanwenarth Ultra 88-92; R Govilon w Llanfoist w Llanelen 92-02; RD Abergavenny 98-02; V Brynmawr *S & B* from 02. *The Vicarage, Dumfries Place, Brynmawr, Ebbw Vale NP23 4RA* Tel (01495) 310405

GREY, Canon Roger Derrick Masson. b 38. AKC61. **d** 62 **p** 63. C Darlington H Trin *Dur* 62-63; C Bishopwearmouth St Mich 63-67; V Mabe *Truro* 67-70; Dioc Youth Chapl 67-70; Youth Chapl *Glouc* 70-77; V Stroud H Trin 77-82; Dioc Can Res Glouc Cathl 82-03; Dir of Educn 82-94; Bp's Chapl 94-03; rtd 03; Clergy Widows' Officer (Glouc Adnry) from 03; Perm to Offic from 04. *12 Buckingham Close, Walton Cardiff, Tewkesbury GL20 7QB* Tel (01684) 275742

GREY, Stephen Bernard. b 56. Linc Th Coll 86. **d** 88 **p** 89. C Worsley *Man* 88-93; V Bamford 93-04; P-in-c Rochdale St Geo w St Alb 99-04; P-in-c Preesall *Blackb* 04-05; P-in-c Hambleton w Out Rawcliffe 04-05; V Waterside Par from 05. *St Oswald's Vicarage, Lancaster Road, Knott End-on-Sea, Poulton-le-Fylde FY6 0DU* Tel (01253) 810297

GREY-SMITH, Donald Edward. b 31. ACT ThL64. **d** 64 **p** 65. Australia 64-68 and from 71; W Germany 68-69; C Weeke *Win* 69-71; rtd 96. *6/317 Military Road, Semaphore Park SA 5019, Australia* Tel (0061) (8) 8449 4420

GRIBBEN, John Gibson. b 44. K Coll Lon BD75 QUB MTh81. CITC 73. **d** 75 **p** 76. C Dunmurry *Conn* 75-78; CR from 79; Lic to Offic *Wakef* from 83; rtd 09. *House of the Resurrection, Stocks Bank Road, Mirfield WF14 0BN* Tel (01924) 483339
E-mail jgribben@mirfield.org.uk

GRIBBIN, Canon Bernard Byron. b 35. Bradf Univ MPhil84. St Aid Birkenhead 58. **d** 60 **p** 61. C Maghull *Liv* 60-63; C Prescot 63-65; V Denholme Gate *Bradf* 65-71; V Bankfoot 71-79; Dioc Stewardship Adv 79-86; Prec and Chapl Choral Ches Cathl 86-91; V Ringway 91-96; Dioc Tourism Officer 91-96; Hon Can Ches Cathl 91-96; rtd 96; Perm to Offic *Bradf* from 96. *5 Heather Court, Ilkley LS29 9TZ* Tel (01943) 816253

GRIBBLE, Howard Frank. b 27. Magd Coll Cam BA50 MA56. Ely Th Coll 50. **d** 52 **p** 53. C Leytonstone St Marg w St Columba *Chelmsf* 52-56; N Rhodesia 56-59; Metrop Area Sec UMCA 59-62; V Harlow St Mary Magd *Chelmsf* 62-70; R Lawhitton *Truro* 70-81; R Lezant 70-81; RD Trigg Major 75-79; P-in-c S Petherwin w Trewen 77-79; Chapl R Cornwall Hosps Trust 81-84; rtd 84; Perm to Offic *Truro* from 84. *Westerlies, Marine Drive, Widemouth Bay, Bude EX23 0AQ* Tel (01288) 361528

GRIDDLE, Malcolm George. b 44. Chu Coll Cam BA67 MA71. Linc Th Coll 79. **d** 81 **p** 82. C Farnborough *Roch* 81-84; V Bostall Heath 84-90; V Bexleyheath Ch Ch 90-02; P-in-c Hever, Four Elms and Mark Beech 02-06; R from 06. *The Rectory, Rectory Lane, Hever, Edenbridge TN8 7LH* Tel (01732) 862249
E-mail mg@gribule.net

GRICE, Charles. b 24. MBE83. **d** 58 **p** 59. C Stocksbridge *Sheff* 58-61; R Armthorpe 61-66; Ind Missr 66-69; Ind Chapl 69-73; V Tinsley 69-73; V Oughtibridge 73-76; Gen Sec Ch Lads' and Ch Girls' Brigade 77-91; R Braithwell w Bramley *Sheff* 88-91; rtd 89; Perm to Offic *Sheff* from 89. *57 Deepdale Road, Rotherham S61 2NR* Tel (01709) 557551

GRICE, Canon David Richard. b 32. Keble Coll Ox BA55 MA59. St Steph Ho Ox 55. **d** 57 **p** 58. C Leeds St Aid *Ripon* 57-61; C

Middleton St Mary 61-62; V Woodlesford 62-69; V Leeds St Wilfrid 69-78; TR Seacroft 78-93; Hon Can Ripon Cathl 92-99; P-in-c Thorner 93-95; V 95-99; rtd 99; Perm to Offic *Ripon* from 00. *15 Mead Road, Leeds LS15 9JR* Tel 0113-260 4371
E-mail david@grice12.freeserve.co.uk

GRIDLEY, Miss Susan Mary. b 49. EAMTC 94. **d** 97 **p** 98. NSM Doddinghurst and Mountnessing *Chelmsf* 97-03; Perm to Offic *Bradf* 03-04 and *Chelmsf* from 06. *7 Thracian Close, Colchester CO2 9RN* Tel (01206) 548766

GRIER, James Emerson. b 74. St Pet Coll Ox BA95 MA01. Wycliffe Hall Ox 96. **d** 98 **p** 99. C Ox St Andr 98-02; C Harborne Heath *Birm* 02-07; TV Pinhoe and Broadclyst *Ex* from 07; Dioc Youth Adv from 07. *The Vicarage, Rockbeare, Exeter EX5 2EG* Tel (01404) 822883 E-mail james.grier@exeter.anglican.org

GRIERSON, Peter Stanley. b 42. Lon Univ BD68 Leeds Univ MPhil74. Linc Th Coll 68. **d** 69 **p** 70. C Clitheroe St Mary *Blackb* 69-71; C Aston cum Aughton *Sheff* 71-74; V Preston St Jude w St Paul *Blackb* 74-81; V Blackb St Luke w St Phil 89-97; RD Blackb 91-97; V Burnley St Matt w H Trin 97-02; Perm to Offic *Bradf* from 03. *2 Spindle Mill, Skipton BD23 1NY* Tel (01756) 797175

GRIEVE, David Campbell. b 51. St Jo Coll Dur BA74. Wycliffe Hall Ox 74. **d** 76 **p** 77. C Upton (Overchurch) *Ches* 76-80; C Selston *S'well* 80-82; V Pelton *Dur* 82-89; rtd 89. *The Rectory, 107 Front Street, Cockfield, Bishop Auckland DL13 5AA* Tel (01388) 718447 E-mail davidgrieve@cix.co.uk

GRIEVE (née PIERSSENÉ), Frances Jane. b 55. St Jo Coll Dur BA76. Cranmer Hall Dur 99. **d** 01 **p** 02. C Barnard Castle w Whorlton *Dur* 01-05; P-in-c Cockfield from 05; P-in-c Lynesack from 05. *The Rectory, 107 Front Street, Cockfield, Bishop Auckland DL13 5AA* Tel (01388) 718447
E-mail jane.grieve@durham.anglican.org

GRIEVE, Mrs Judith Margaret. b 52. Goldsmiths' Coll Lon CertEd73. NEOC 91. **d** 94 **p** 96. NSM Choppington *Newc* 94-99; P-in-c Woodhorn w Newbiggin 99-06; V from 06. *The Vicarage, 34A Front Street, Newbiggin-by-the-Sea NE64 6PS* Tel (01670) 817220

GRIEVES, Anthony Michael. b 47. St Alb Minl Tr Scheme 81. **d** 84 **p** 85. NSM Stevenage St Mary Shephall *St Alb* 84-86; NSM Stevenage St Mary Shephall w Aston 86-95; Perm to Offic from 95. *27 Falcon Close, Stevenage SG2 9PG* Tel (01438) 727204

GRIEVES, Ian Leslie. b 56. Bede Coll Dur CertEd77 BEd78. Chich Th Coll 82. **d** 84 **p** 85. C Darlington St Mark w St Paul *Dur* 84-87; C Whickham 87-89; V Darlington St Jas from 89. *St James's Vicarage, Vicarage Road, Darlington DL1 1JW* Tel (01325) 465980 E-mail father_grieves@lineone.net

GRIFFIN, Alan Howard Foster. b 44. TCD BA66 MA69 Peterho Cam PhD71. Sarum & Wells Th Coll 75. **d** 78 **p** 79. Lect Ex Univ 78-01; Asst to Lazenby Chapl 78-92; Sub-Warden Duryard Halls 78-81; Warden 81-84; Sen Warden 84-98; Perm to Offic *Ex* 92-98; C Heavitree w Ex St Paul 98-01; Ex Campus Chapl Plymouth Univ 98-01; R St Andr-by-the-Wardrobe w St Ann, Blackfriars *Lon* from 01; R St Jas Garlickhythe w St Mich Queenhithe etc from 01; CME Officer Two Cities Area 01-08. *St Andrew's House, 35 St Andrew's Hill, London EC4V 5DE* Tel (020) 7248 7546 E-mail rector@standrewbythewardrobe.co.uk

GRIFFIN, Christopher Donald. b 59. Reading Univ BA80 CertEd81. Wycliffe Hall Ox 82. **d** 85 **p** 86. C Gerrards Cross *Ox* 85-88; Chapl Felsted Sch 88-98; Chapl Sedbergh Sch 98-06; Ho Master from 00. *Sedbergh School, Sedbergh LA10 5HG* Tel (01539) 620535

GRIFFIN, Gerald Albert Francis. b 31. Qu Coll Birm 74. **d** 77 **p** 78. NSM Bushbury *Lich* 77-83; Ind Chapl *Dur* 83-88; Chapl HM Pris Man 88-89; Chapl HM Pris Featherstone 89-93; Chapl Toxteth St Philemon w St Gabr and St Cleopas *Liv* 93-96; rtd 96; NSM W Bromwich Deanery *Lich* from 00. *7 Chartwell Drive, Bushbury, Wolverhampton WV10 8JL* Tel (01902) 836414
E-mail revgerrygriffinhome@msn.com

GRIFFIN, Harold Rodan Bristow. b 12. Jes Coll Cam BA33 LLB34 MA43. Ridley Hall Cam 43. **d** 45 **p** 46. C Kirby Moorside w Gillamoor *York* 45-49; C Linthorpe 49-52; C Boylestone *Derby* 52; R Hulland, Atlow and Bradley 52-61; V Framsden *St E* 61-71; R Helmingham 61-71; rtd 77; Perm to Offic *Ely* 91-99. *Highlands, Fitzgerald Road, Woodbridge IP12 1EN* Tel (01394) 383090

GRIFFIN, Joan Angela. b 35. Qu Coll Birm 82. dss 85 **d** 92 **p** 94. Moseley St Mary *Birm* 85-05; NSM 92-05; Chapl Univ Hosp Birm NHS Trust 95-02; Chapl Priory Hosp Birm from 02. *389 Wake Green Road, Birmingham B13 0BH* Tel 0121-777 8772

GRIFFIN, Canon Joseph William. b 48. St Mich Coll Llan 70. **d** 74 **p** 75. C Killay *S & B* 74-78; C Swansea St Thos and Kilvey 78-81; V Troedrhiwgarth *Llan* 81-91; V Llanrhidian w Llanmadoc and Cheriton *S & B* 91-99; RD Gower 94-99; V Swansea St Nic 99-04; RD Swansea 02-04; P-in-c SW Gower 04-06; V from 06; Hon Can Brecon Cathl from 98. *The Rectory, Port Eynon, Swansea SA3 1NL* Tel (01792) 390456
E-mail joe.griffin@virgin.net

GRIFFIN, Keith. b 66. Nottm Trent Univ BA88. Cranmer Hall Dur BA94. **d** 95 **p** 96. C Gedling *S'well* 95-98; V Barkingside

GRIFFIN

St Geo *Chelmsf* 99-02; TV Upper Holme Valley *Wakef* from 02. *The Vicarage, 3 Vicarage Meadows, Holmfirth HD9 1DZ* Tel (01484) 682644 E-mail revdkg@tiscali.co.uk

GRIFFIN, Kenneth Francis. b 21. Lon Univ BSc64. St Jo Coll Nottm 72. **d** 73 **p** 74. C Bexleyheath Ch Ch *Roch* 73-77; R Kingsdown 77-82; rtd 86. *Woodlands, Palmers Cross Hill, Rough Common, Canterbury CT2 9BL* Tel (01227) 457314

GRIFFIN, Mark Richard. b 68. Trin Coll Bris BA93. Westcott Ho Cam 94. **d** 96 **p** 97. C Walmer *Cant* 96-00; V Wingham w Elmstone and Preston w Stourmouth 00-07; V Sevenoaks St Luke *Roch* from 07. *St Luke's House, 30 Eardley Road, Sevenoaks TN13 1XT* Tel (01732) 452462
E-mail revd.mark.griffin@talk21.com

GRIFFIN, Michael. b 59. **d** 01 **p** 01. C Kirkdale St Lawr *Liv* 01-02, P-in-c 02-05; V from 05. *81 Rawcliffe Road, Liverpool L9 1AN* Tel 0151-523 6968 E-mail mike.j.griffin@amserve.net

GRIFFIN, Niall Paul. b 37. TCD BA61 Div Test61. **d** 61 **p** 62. C Newtownards *D & D* 61-63; C Arm St Mark 63-64; C Cross Roads Jamaica 64-66; C Lurgan Ch the Redeemer *D & D* 66-69; Chapl RAF 69-84; Missr Chr Renewal Cen *D & D* 84-89; Nat Dir (Ireland) SOMA UK 89-07; rtd 07. *7 Cloughmore Park, Rostrevor, Newry BT34 3AX* Tel and fax (028) 4173 8959
E-mail n&g@griffin.go-plus.net

GRIFFIN, Nigel Robert. b 50. Univ of Wales (Lamp) BA71. Ripon Hall Ox 71. **d** 73 **p** 74. C Burry Port and Pwll *St D* 73-77; C Carmarthen St Pet 77-79; Youth Chapl 79-86; V Whitland and Kiffig 80-89; Warden of Ords 86-91; V Llangunnor w Cwmffrwd 89-92; RD Carmarthen 91-92; R Aberporth w Tremain and Blaenporth 92-95; R Aberporth w Tremain w Blaenporth and Betws Ifan 95-96; Chapl Morriston Hosp/Ysbyty Treforys NHS Trust 96-99; Chapl Swansea NHS Trust from 99. *Morriston Hospital, Heol Maes Eglwys, Cwmrhydyceirw, Swansea SA6 8EL* Tel (01792) 702222

GRIFFIN, Canon Rutland Basil. b 16. ALCD41. **d** 41 **p** 42. C Aylesbury *Ox* 41-45; C Bp's Hatfield *St Alb* 45-50; V Biggleswade 50-61; V Dartford H Trin *Roch* 61-84; RD Dartford 64-84; Hon Can Roch Cathl 70-84; rtd 84; Perm to Offic *Roch* and *Cant* 84-95; Cov from 97. *c/o Mrs C Kent, 39 Paddockhall Road, Haywards Heath RH16 1HN* Tel (01444) 440642 Fax 08701-334347

GRIFFIN, The Very Revd Victor Gilbert Benjamin. b 24. MRIA TCD BA46 MA57 Hon DD92. CITC 47. **d** 47 **p** 48. C Londonderry St Aug *D & R* 47-51; C Londonderry Ch Ch 51-57; I 57-68; Preb Howth St Patr Cathl Dublin 62-68; Dean St Patr Cathl Dublin 68-91; rtd 91. *7 Tyler Road, Limavady BT49 0DW* Tel (028) 7176 2093

GRIFFISS, Helen Mary. b 48. Univ of Wales (Ban) CertEd69 K Alfred's Coll Win MA98. STETS 97. **d** 00 **p** 01. Miss Adv USPG *Bris, Sarum* and *Win* 00-03; NSM Bransgore *Win* 00-03; C Milton 04-06; P-in-c Mudeford from 06. *All Saints' Vicarage, 22 Kestrel Drive, Christchurch BH23 4DE* Tel (01425) 276267
E-mail revhelen@4afairworld.co.uk

GRIFFITH, Benedict Lloyd. b 64. Trin Coll Carmarthen BA86. Ripon Coll Cuddesdon 04. **d** 06 **p** 07. C Kempston Transfiguration *St Alb* 06-09; V Upper Wye *S & B* from 09. *The Vicarage, 2 Highbury Fields, Llanyre, Llandrindod Wells LD1 6NF* Tel (01597) 822472 Mobile 07960-947137

GRIFFITH, Brian Vann. b 34. Univ Sch Th Abth & Lamp BTh91 MTh94 St D Dioc Tr Course 81. **d** 82 **p** 83. NSM C Aberystwyth *St D* 82-87; NSM Llanfihangel w Llanafan and Llanwnnws etc 87-88; NSM C Llanbadarn Fawr w Capel Bangor and Goginan 88-93; Public Preacher 93-96; NSM Machynlleth w Llanwrin and Penegoes *Ban* 97-99; rtd 99; Perm to Offic *St D* from 00. *14 Ystwyth Close, Penparcau, Aberystwyth SY23 3RU*

GRIFFITH, The Ven David Vaughan. b 36. St D Coll Lamp BA60. Lich Th Coll 60. **d** 62 **p** 63. C Llanfairfechan *Ban* 62-66; C Dolgellau 66-70; R Llanfair Talhaiarn *St As* 70-82; R Llanfairtalhaiarn and Llannefydd 82-85; P-in-c Llangernyw, Gwytherin and Llanddewi 77-85; V Colwyn 85-98; Warden of Readers 91-99; Can Cursal St As Cathl 95-98; P-in-c Berriew and Manafon 98-99; V 99-02; Preb St As Cathl and Adn Montgomery 98-02; rtd 02. *1 Bishop's Walk, St Asaph LL17 0SU* Tel (01745) 582903

GRIFFITH, Donald Bennet. b 17. Dur Univ LTh40. St Aid Birkenhead 36. **d** 40 **p** 41. C Collyhurst St Oswald *Man* 40-43; C Pendlebury St Jo 43-45; P-in-c Pendleton 45-47; V Everton St Cuth *Liv* 47-52; V Lathom 52-58; R Freuma w Thorrington *Chelmsf* 58-66; R Lawford 66-73; R Theydon Garnon 73-77; P-in-c Bradfield 77-82; rtd 82; Perm to Offic *Chelmsf* from 82. *Don Thomson House, Low Road, Harwich CO12 3TS* Tel (01255) 503235

GRIFFITH, Frank Michael. b 24. Bris Univ BSc50. St Aid Birkenhead 58. **d** 60 **p** 61. C Leamington Priors H Trin *Cov* 60-63; C Stratford-on-Avon w Bishopton 63-67; V Rounds Green *Birm* 67-70; R Barford *Cov* 70-78; V Wasperton 70-78; RD Stratford-on-Avon 77-79; R Barford w Wasperton and Sherbourne 78-89; RD Fosse 79-87; rtd 90; Perm to Offic *Cov*

from 90. *Wusi, Armscote Road, Tredington, Shipston-on-Stour CV36 4NP* Tel (01608) 661621
E-mail michaelgriffith1@btinternet.com

GRIFFITH, Glyn Keble Gethin. b 37. St D Coll Lamp BA59. Ridley Hall Cam 67. **d** 69 **p** 70. C Derby St Aug 69-72; C Coity w Nolton *Llan* 72-75; P-in-c Heage *Derby* 75-81; V Allestree St Nic 81-92; R Wilne and Draycott w Breaston 92-01; rtd 01; Perm to Offic *Mon* from 02; *Heref* 02-08; *Glouc* from 04. *3 Cornford Close, Osbaston, Monmouth NP25 3NT* Tel (01600) 719740

GRIFFITH, Canon Hugh Emrys. b 24. St D Coll Lamp BA53. **d** 54 **p** 55. C Welshpool *St As* 54-56; C Abergele 56-58; R Llanfair Talhaiarn 58-61; R Llangeinwen w Llangaffo and Llanfair-yn-y-Cwmwd *Ban* 61-75; R Llanllyfni 75-81; R Amlwch 81-94; RD Twrcelyn 82-94; Can Ban Cathl from 89; rtd 94; Perm to Offic *Ban* from 94. *Llys Caerwynt, Rhos-y-bol, Amlwch LL68 9PR* Tel (01407) 831917

GRIFFITH, Canon John Vaughan. b 33. St D Coll Lamp 53. **d** 58 **p** 59. C Holyhead w Rhoscolyn *Ban* 58-63; R Maentwrog w Trawsfynydd 63-68; Chapl RAF 68-72; V Winnington *Ches* 72-76; V Northwich St Luke and H Trin 76-81; V Sandiway 81-98; Dioc Communications Officer 84-86; Ed Ches Dioc News 84-92; Hon Can Ches Cathl 89-98; rtd 98; Perm to Offic *Ches* from 99. *41 Moss Lane, Cuddington, Northwich CW8 2PT*

GRIFFITH, Justin David. b 48. Imp Coll Lon BScEng74 Cranfield Inst of Tech MSc89. NEOC 03. **d** 06 **p** 07. NSM N Ferriby *York* from 06. *8 North Drive, Swanland, North Ferriby HU14 3QU* Tel (01482) 633581 Mobile 07973-937162
E-mail j@swanland.co.uk

GRIFFITH, Michael. See GRIFFITH, Frank Michael

GRIFFITH, Canon Peter Malcolm. b 43. FRICS71. EAMTC 94. **d** 97 **p** 98. NSM Stilton w Denton and Caldecote etc *Ely* 97-99; R Sawtry and Glatton from 00; RD Yaxley from 07; Hon Can Ely Cathl from 08. *The Rectory, Church Causeway, Sawtry, Huntingdon PE28 5TD* Tel (01487) 830215
E-mail rev.griffith@tiscali.co.uk

GRIFFITH, Sandra. b 44. Open Univ BA94. EAMTC 01. **d** 04 **p** 05. NSM The Ortons, Alwalton and Chesterton *Ely* 04-06; NSM Sawtry and Glatton from 06; Asst Chapl Hinchingbrooke Health Care NHS Trust from 05. *The Rectory, Church Causeway, Sawtry, Huntingdon PE28 5TD* Tel (01487) 830215
E-mail sandra@revgriffith.com

GRIFFITH, Stephen. See GRIFFITH, William Stephen

GRIFFITH, Steven Ellsworth. b 63. Univ of Wales BTh91. St Steph Ho Ox. **d** 87 **p** 88. C Holyhead w Rhoscolyn w Llanfair-yn-Neubwll *Ban* 87-90; CF 90-08; Sen CF from 08. *c/o MOD Chaplains (Army)* Tel (01980) 615804 Fax 615800

GRIFFITH, Mrs Wendy Margaret. b 41. **d** 01 **p** 02. NSM Sixpenny Handley w Gussage St Andrew etc *Sarum* 01-08; NSM Somerton w Compton Dundon, the Charltons etc *B & W* from 08. *The Parsonage, George Street, Charlton Adam, Somerton TA11 7AS* Tel (01458) 224087 Mobile 07720-942996

GRIFFITH, William Stephen. b 52. Univ of Wales (Ban) BA71 FRAS92. Westcott Ho Cam 71. **d** 73 **p** 74. C Llandudno *Ban* 73-76; C Calne and Blackland *Sarum* 76-78; P-in-c Broadwindsor w Burstock and Seaborough 78-79; TV Beaminster Area 79-81; Perm to Offic 81-83; Chapl St Pet Sch York 83-87; C Leeds St Pet *Ripon* 87; Chapl Bearwood Coll Wokingham 87-92; CMS Jordan 92-95; Sen Chapl Univ of Wales (Cardiff) *Llan* 95-96; Chapl Damascus 96-02; P-in-c Yerevan, Baku and Tbilisi *Eur* 03; V Benton *Newc* 04-08; TV Mortlake w E Sheen *S'wark* from 09. *17 Sheen Gate Gardens, London SW14 7PD* Tel (020) 8876 5002 Mobile 07729-278294
E-mail haywalks@hotmail.com

GRIFFITH-JONES, Robin Guthrie. b 56. New Coll Ox BA78 Ch Coll Cam BA88. Westcott Ho Cam 86. **d** 89 **p** 90. C Cantril Farm *Liv* 89-92; Chapl Linc Coll Ox 92-99; Master of The Temple from 99. *The Master's House, Temple, London EC4Y 7BB* Tel (020) 7353 8559
E-mail master@templechurch.com

GRIFFITHS, Ainsley. See GRIFFITHS, John Mark Ainsley

GRIFFITHS, Alan Charles. b 46. Dur Univ BA67. Cranmer Hall Dur 66. **d** 69 **p** 70. C Leic H Apostles 69-72; Lic to Offic *York* 73-77; V Lea Hall *Birm* 77-87; Asst Dir of Educn *Sheff* 87-92; V W Bessacarr 92-02; V Conisbrough from 02. *The Vicarage, 8 Castle Avenue, Conisbrough, Doncaster DN12 3BT* Tel (01709) 864695 E-mail alan.c.griffiths@virgin.net

GRIFFITHS, Alec. b 42. St Chad's Coll Dur BA63. **d** 65 **p** 66. C Glas St Ninian 65-68; C Greenock 68-72; R Glas H Cross 72-79; V Birchencliffe *Wakef* 79-83; Chapl Kingston Hosp Surrey 83-99; rtd 99; Perm to Offic *S'wark* 99-00; Hon C W Acton St Martin *Lon* from 00; Hon C Ealing All SS from 00. *St Martin's Cottage, Hale Gardens, London W3 9SQ* Tel and fax (020) 8896 9009 E-mail alec.griffiths@btopenworld.com

GRIFFITHS, Andrew Taylor. b 68. Jes Coll Ox BA92 MA96. Cranmer Hall Dur 98. **d** 00 **p** 01. C Paris St Mich *Eur* 00-04; C Galleywood Common *Chelmsf* 04-05; V from 05; RD Chelmsf S from 07. *Galleywood Vicarage, 450 Beehive Lane, Chelmsford CM2 8RN* Tel (01245) 353922 Mobile 07969-605059
E-mail andygr.iffiths@yahoo.co.uk

334

GRIFFITHS, Arthur Evan. b 27. ACP66. St Deiniol's Hawarden. **d** 69 **p** 70. Hon C Cleobury Mortimer w Hopton Wafers *Heref* 69-83; C 84-86; P-in-c Knowbury and Coreley and Doddington 86-88; rtd 89; Perm to Offic *Heref* 93-08. *clo S M Griffiths Esq, 14 Serin Close, Kidderminster DY10 4TY*

GRIFFITHS, Beatrice Mary. b 29. Chelsea Coll Lon CertEd60. Westcott Ho Cam 85. **dss** 86 **d** 87 **p** 94. W Bridgford *S'well* 86-87; NSM Wilford Hill 87-99; rtd 99; Perm to Offic *S'well* from 99. *7 Stella Avenue, Tollerton, Nottingham NG12 4EX* Tel 0115-937 4155

GRIFFITHS, Brian John. b 45. Brunel Univ PhD82. **d** 05 **p** 06. OLM Iver *Ox* from 05. *44 Somerset Way, Iver SL0 9AF* Tel (01753) 654768 E-mail brian.griffiths@iverparish.co.uk

GRIFFITHS, Caroline. *See* PRINCE, Caroline Heidi Ann

GRIFFITHS (née MITCHELL), Mrs Clare Elizabeth. b 68. **d** 01 **p** 02. C Caerleon w Llanhennock *Mon* 01-03; Chapl Malvern Girls' Coll 03-06; C Gt Malvern Ch Ch *Worc* from 06. *St Mary's House, 137 Madresfield Road, Malvern WR14 2HD* Tel (01684) 564494

GRIFFITHS, Colin Lindsay. b 50. ACT 75. **d** 79 **p** 80. C Adelaide St Jo Australia 79-81; C Masite Lesotho 82-83; P-in-c Maseru St Jo 84; Chapl St Mich Priory Melbourne 85-87; Prior 87-90; P-in-c Port Augusta 90-95; P-in-c Point Pearce Min Distr 95-96; Assoc P Thornbury 97-98; R Alice Springs and Can Ch Ch Cathl Darwin 99-05; Dioc Admin N Territory 00-05; Perm to Offic *Ox* from 06. *The Well, Newport Road, Willen, Milton Keynes MK15 9AA* Tel (01908) 231986 E-mail colin.griffiths@hotmail.com

GRIFFITHS, Canon David. b 38. St Mich Coll Llan. **d** 67 **p** 68. C Llangollen *St As* 67-71; C Rhyl 71-74; V Kerry 74-77; V Kerry and Llanmerewig 77-82; R Caerwys and Bodfari 82-87; V Gresford 87-97; V Gresford w Holt 97-03; RD Wrexham 97-01; RD Gresford 01-03; Can St As Cathl 90-03; rtd 03. *16 Heol-y-Wal, Bradley, Wrexham LL11 4BY* Tel (01978) 751416

GRIFFITHS, David Bruce. b 44. Sussex Univ BA69 Hull Univ MA83. Linc Th Coll. **d** 82 **p** 83. C Springfield All SS *Chelmsf* 82-84; TV Horwich *Man* 84-92; V Heaton Ch Ch 92-03; P-in-c Ainsworth 03-09; rtd 09. *Woodford, Mill Lane, Horwich, Bolton BL6 6AQ* Tel (01204) 469621 E-mail dandbgriffiths@googlemail.com

GRIFFITHS, David John. b 53. St Jo Coll Nottm BTh93. **d** 94 **p** 95. C Retford St Sav *S'well* 94-96; NSM Thwaites Brow *Bradf* 96-98; P-in-c Oakenshaw cum Woodlands 98-03; V Buttershaw St Paul from 03; Asst Chapl Airedale NHS Trust from 96. *St Paul's Vicarage, 42A Wibsey Park Avenue, Bradford BD6 3QA* Tel (01274) 676359 E-mail david.griffiths@bradford.anglican.org

GRIFFITHS, David Mark. b 41. Univ of Wales (Cardiff) BA67 CertEd71 St Mich Coll Llan 92. **d** 94 **p** 95. C Llwynderw *S & B* 94-96; R Llanbadarn Fawr, Llandegley and Llanfihangel etc 96-02; P-in-c Slebech and Uzmaston w Boulston *St D* 02-06; rtd 06. *17 Catherine's Gate, Merlins Bridge, Haverfordwest SA61 1NB* Tel (01437) 783950 Mobile 07811-647910 E-mail markgriffiths16@btopenworld.com

GRIFFITHS, David Mark. b 59. Kent Univ BA80. Chich Th Coll 81. **d** 83 **p** 84. C Clydach *S & B* 83-84; C Llwynderw 84-88; V Swansea St Nic 88-98; Chapl Swansea Inst of HE 88-98; V Swansea St Gabr from 98; Chapl Swansea NHS Trust from 98. *St Gabriel's Vicarage, Bryn Road, Brynmill, Swansea SA2 0AP* Tel (01792) 464011

GRIFFITHS, The Ven David Nigel. b 27. RD77. Worc Coll Ox BA52 MA56 Reading Univ PhD91 FSA. Linc Th Coll 56. **d** 58 **p** 59. C Northampton St Matt *Pet* 58-61; SPCK HQ Staff 61-67; Chapl RNR 63-77; Hon C Bromley St Andr *Roch* 65-67; V Linc St Mich 67-73; R Linc St Mary Magd w St Paul 67-73; Vice Chan and Lib Linc Cathl 67-73; TR New Windsor *Ox* 73-87; RD Maidenhead 77-82 and 84-87; Chapl to The Queen 77-97; Hon Can Ch Ch *Ox* 83-87; Adn Berks 87-92; rtd 92; Chapl St Anne's Bede Houses Linc 93-00; Perm to Offic *Linc* from 00. *2 Middleton's Field, Lincoln LN2 1QP* Tel (01522) 525753 E-mail bibliophile@britishlibrary.net

GRIFFITHS, David Percy Douglas. b 25. St Mich Coll Llan. **d** 78 **p** 79. C Betws w Ammanford *St D* 78-80; V Llanarth w Mydroilyn, Capel Cynon, Talgarreg etc 80-84; V Llanarth and Capel Cynon w Talgarreg etc 84-86; V Newcastle Emlyn w Llandyfriog and Troed-yr-aur 86-95; rtd 95. *The Poplars, Ebenezer Street, Newcastle Emlyn SA38 9BS* Tel (01239) 711448

GRIFFITHS, David Rowson Hopkin. b 38. Oak Hill Th Coll 59. **d** 62 **p** 63. C Barrow St Mark *Carl* 62-65; OMF Internat from 66; Japan 66-88; Philippines from 88; rtd 03. *clo Miss M Clee, 15 Richmond Mews, Uplands, Swansea SA2 0QU*

GRIFFITHS, David Wynne. b 47. Univ of Wales (Cardiff) BD73 PGCE77 MA85 MEd93 PhD07. St Mich Coll Llan 69. **d** 73 **p** 74. C Gabalfa *Llan* 73-76; Lic to Offic 77-79; Hon C Tonypandy w Clydach Vale 79-80; Hon C Pontypridd St Cath 80-87; Perm to Offic from 87. *13 Heol Tyn-y-Cae, Rhiwbina, Cardiff CF14 6DH*

GRIFFITHS, Ms Elizabeth Leigh. b 61. St Hugh's Coll Ox BA83 MA87 Warwick Univ PGCE84. Ripon Coll Cuddesdon 96. **d** 98

p 99. C Bettws *Mon* 98-99; C Maindee Newport 99-01; TV Cen Swansea and Dioc Chapl Tertiary Educn *S & B* 01-03; C St Martin-in-the-Fields *Lon* 03-09; Dir Past Studies ERMC and Nor Dioc Min Course from 09. *Emmaus House, 64 The Close, Norwich NR1 4DH* Tel (01603) 729814 E-mail liz.griffiths@norwich.anglican.org

GRIFFITHS, Eric. b 33. **d** 02 **p** 04. NSM St Andr-by-the-Wardrobe w St Ann, Blackfriars *Lon* 02-08; NSM St Jas Garlickhythe w St Mich Queenhithe etc 02-08; rtd 08. *The Charterhouse, Charterhouse Square, London EC1M 6AN* Tel (020) 7490 1025 E-mail egcharterhouse@yahoo.co.uk

GRIFFITHS, Garrie Charles. b 53. St Jo Coll Nottm. **d** 77 **p** 78. Canada 77-78; C Stalybridge H Trin and Ch Ch *Ches* 78-81; C Moreton 81-84; V Godley cum Newton Green 84-89; V Bayston Hill *Lich* 89-01; TR Mildenhall *St E* 01-04; V Hadfield *Derby* from 04; RD Glossop from 06. *St Andrew's Vicarage, 122 Hadfield Road, Hadfield, Glossop SK13 2DR* Tel (01457) 852431 E-mail ggriffiths787@btinternet.com

GRIFFITHS, Gerald Brian. b 41. Open Univ BA88. SEITE 97. **d** 00 **p** 01. NSM Cliftonville *Cant* 00-03; TV St Laur in Thanet from 04. *St Christopher's House, Kimberley Road, Ramsgate CT12 6HH* Tel (01843) 594160 E-mail geebeegee@tiscali.co.uk

GRIFFITHS, Gerald Lewis. b 38. Westmr Coll Ox MTh97. Qu Coll Birm. **d** 88 **p** 89. C Wrexham *St As* 88-91; TV 91-95; R Hope 95-00; rtd 00. *10 Ryder Close, Wrexham LL13 9GS* Tel (01978) 355244

GRIFFITHS, Gordon John. b 31. Univ of Wales (Cardiff) BA53. S'wark Ord Course 72. **d** 75 **p** 76. NSM Sutton St Nic *S'wark* 75-78; Asst Chapl Eastbourne Coll 78-81; Perm to Offic *Chich* from 81. *15 Buckhurst Close, Willingdon, Eastbourne BN20 9EF* Tel (01323) 505547

GRIFFITHS, Griff. *See* GRIFFITHS, Stephen David

GRIFFITHS, Harvey Stephen. b 35. Linc Coll Ox BA58 MA62. Linc Th Coll 62. **d** 62 **p** 63. C Frodingham *Linc* 62-65; C Darlington St Cuth *Dur* 65-70; Chapl RN 70-92; P-in-c Southwick w Boarhunt *Portsm* 92-05; rtd 05; Perm to Offic *Portsm* from 05. *27 Burnham Wood, Fareham PO16 7UD* Tel (01329) 232915 Mobile 07747-093365 E-mail harvey@hsgriffiths.fsnet.co.uk

GRIFFITHS, Hugh. b 44. Nottm Univ BEd78. Clifton Th Coll 69. **d** 71 **p** 72. C Mansfield SS Pet and Paul *S'well* 71-77; NSM Stockport St Geo *Ches* from 08. *1 Heath Crescent, Stockport SK2 6JN* Tel 0161-285 9772 E-mail hughgriffiths@hotmail.co.uk

GRIFFITHS, Mrs Jean Rose. b 36. Avery Hill Coll TCert56. S'wark Ord Course 93. **d** 95 **p** 96. NSM Charlton *S'wark* 95-03; Asst Chapl HM Pris Brixton 95-03; Chapl 03-04; rtd 04; Perm to Offic *S'wark* from 04. *32 Weyman Road, London SE3 8RY* Tel (020) 8319 8676 *or* 8588 6051

GRIFFITHS, John Alan. b 48. CPsychol AFBPsS Univ of Wales BSc72 Cape Town Univ MEd76. St Mich Coll Llan 87. **d** 89 **p** 90. C Neath w Llantwit 89-93; V Roath St German 93-95. *All Pine Grange, Bath Road, Bournemouth BH1 2PF* Tel (01202) 314120

GRIFFITHS, John Gareth. b 44. Lich Th Coll 68. **d** 71 **p** 72. C Shotton *St As* 71-73; C Rhyl w St Ann 73-76; V Llanasa 76-95; RD Holywell 89-95; V Rhuddlan from 95. *The Vicarage, Tirionfa, Rhuddlan, Rhyl LL18 6LT* Tel (01745) 591568

GRIFFITHS, John Mark Ainsley. b 68. Man Univ BSc90 MSc91 PGCE92. Ripon Coll Cuddesdon BA97. **d** 98 **p** 99. Min Can Bangor 98-01; P-in-c Denio w Abererch 01-02; V 02-05; Chapl Trin Coll Carmarthen from 05. *Trinity College, College Road, Carmarthen SA31 3EP* Tel (01267) 676767 E-mail ainsley.griffiths@trinity-cm.ac.uk

GRIFFITHS, Mrs Linda Betty. b 48. Trin Coll Carmarthen CertEd69 Gwent Coll of HE BEd96 Open Univ MA97. Mon Dioc Tr Scheme 05. **d** 06. NSM Newbridge *Mon* from 06. *19 Cromwell Road, Risca, Newport NP11 7AF* Tel (01495) 270455 E-mail griff.l@btinternet.com

GRIFFITHS, Malcolm. b 47. St Alb Minl Tr Scheme. **d** 82 **p** 83. NSM Hemel Hempstead *St Alb* 82-86; C 86-87; TV Liskeard, St Keyne, St Pinnock, Morval etc *Truro* 87-96; V Landrake w St Erney and Botus Fleming from 96. *The Vicarage, School Road, Landrake, Saltash PL12 5EA* Tel (01752) 851801

GRIFFITHS, Margaret. *See* MacLACHLAN, Mrs Margaret

GRIFFITHS, Mrs Margarett. b 29. ATCL47 LRAM48. CA Tr Coll 50. **dss** 81 **d** 87. Hackington *Cant* 81-83; Ashford 84-89; Par Dn 87-89; rtd 89. *39 Newington Way, Craven Arms SY7 9PS* Tel (01588) 673848

GRIFFITHS, Mark. *See* GRIFFITHS, David Mark

GRIFFITHS, Mark. b 68. Nottm Univ PhD09. St Jo Coll Nottm 04. **d** 07 **p** 08. C Stoke Poges *Ox* from 07. *21 Freeman's Close, Stoke Poges, Slough SL2 4ER* Tel (01753) 663031 E-mail revmarkgriff@sky.com

GRIFFITHS, Canon Martyn Robert. b 51. Nottm Univ BTh74 St Martin's Coll Lanc PGCE75. Kelham Th Coll 70. **d** 74 **p** 75. C Kings Heath *Birm* 74-77; C-in-c Elmdon Heath CD 77-79; TV Solihull 79-81; Asst Admin Shrine of Our Lady of Walsingham 81-85; V Oldham St Steph and All Martyrs *Man* 85-89; TR Swinton and Pendlebury 89-98; Hon Can Man Cathl 96-98; R

Preston St Jo and St Geo *Blackb* 98-05; Hon Can Blackb Cathl 00-05; R Henley w Remenham *Ox* from 05. *St Mary's Rectory, Hart Street, Henley-on-Thames RG9 2AU* Tel and fax (01491) 577340 E-mail rector.hwr@lineone.net

GRIFFITHS, Meirion. b 38. Clifton Th Coll 63. **d** 66 **p** 67. C Upper Holloway St Pet *Lon* 66-68; C Taunton St Jas *B & W* 68-70; C Radipole *Sarum* 70-74; R Chich St Pancras and St Jo 74-82; R Corwen and Llangar *St As* 82-88; RD Edeyrnion 82-88; C Albany Australia 88; R Collie 89-93; P-in-c Maddington 97-00; rtd 00. *27 Coachwood Way, Maddington WA 6109, Australia* Tel (0061) (8) 9459 2920 Fax 9452 2720 E-mail meirion4@aol.com

GRIFFITHS, Mervyn Harrington. b 15. Ripon Hall Ox 53. **d** 54 **p** 55. C Aigburth *Liv* 54-56; C Grassendale 56-58; C Findon *Chich* 58-59; R Bighton *Win* 59-78; V Bishop's Sutton 59-78; rtd 80; Perm to Offic *Ex* from 80. *7 Barnards Farm, Beer, Seaton EX12 3NF* Tel (01297) 22382

GRIFFITHS, Neville. b 39. Univ of Wales BA63. St D Coll Lamp LTh66. **d** 66 **p** 67. C Newport St Mark *Mon* 66-68; C Cardiff St Jo *Llan* 68-70; Chapl Greystoke Coll Carl 70-76; C Greystoke w Matterdale *Carl* 70-75; TV Greystoke, Matterdale and Mungrisdale 75-76; Chapl Grey Coll Dur 76-81; C Croxdale *Dur* 76-81; R Didsbury Ch Ch *Man* 81-83; P-in-c Lowther and Askham *Carl* 83-84; R 84-88; V Guernsey St Matt *Win* 88-93; R Guernsey St Pierre du Bois 93-02; R Guernsey St Philippe de Torteval 93-02; Vice-Dean Guernsey 99-02; rtd 03. *6 Howlcroft Villas, Neville's Cross, Durham DH1 4DU* Tel 0191-386 4778

GRIFFITHS, Mrs Pamela Verley. **d** 07. NSM Ebbw Vale *Mon* from 07. *3 Ivy Close, Rassau, Ebbw Vale NP23 5SJ* Tel (01495) 303926 Fax 210433

GRIFFITHS, Paul Edward. b 48. St Jo Coll Nottm 86. **d** 88 **p** 89. C Ipswich St Andr *St E* 88-92; P-in-c Tollerton *S'well* 92-00; P-in-c Plumtree 95-97; Ind Chapl and Dioc Adv on Ind Soc 97-00; V Hellesdon *Nor* from 00. *The Vicarage, Broom Avenue, Hellesdon, Norwich NR6 6LG* Tel (01603) 426902

GRIFFITHS, Ms Paula Whitmore Llewellyn. b 49. LMH Ox BA71 MA75 Anglia Ruskin Univ BA09. Westcott Ho Cam 08. **d** 09. NSM Saffron Walden w Wendens Ambo, Littlebury etc *Chelmsf* from 09. *Greatford Cottage, Stocking Green, Radwinter, Saffron Walden CB10 2SS* E-mail paula.greatford@btinternet.com

GRIFFITHS, Percy. *See* GRIFFITHS, David Percy Douglas

GRIFFITHS, Richard Barre Maw. b 43. CCC Ox BA65 MA69 St Jo Coll Dur BA71. Cranmer Hall Dur. **d** 71 **p** 72. C Fulwood *Sheff* 71-74; Hon C Sheff St Jo 74-76; Fell Dept of Bibl Studies Sheff Univ 74-76; C Fulham St Matt *Lon* 76-78; P-in-c 78-83; R Chich St Pancras and St Jo from 83. *St Pancras's Rectory, 9 St John Street, Chichester PO19 1UR* Tel (01243) 536390 *or* 536387 E-mail stpancraschichester@hotmail.com

GRIFFITHS, Prof Richard Mathias. b 35. K Coll Cam BA57 MA61 PhD62 BNC Ox MA66 FIL91 FKC95. Ox Min Course 89 SAOMC 96. **d** 97 **p** 98. Prof French K Coll Lon 90-00; NSM W Woodhay w Enborne, Hampstead Marshall etc *Ox* 97-00; NSM Llantrisant 01-02; NSM Penarth and Llandough from 03. *Waltham House, Bradford Place, Penarth CF64 1AG* Tel (029) 2070 7828 Fax 2070 9699

GRIFFITHS, Canon Robert Herbert. b 53. Chich Th Coll 75. **d** 76 **p** 77. C Holywell *St As* 76-80; CF (TA) 79-87; P-in-c Gyffylliog *St As* 80-84; V Llanfair Dyffryn Clwyd 80-84; V Llanfair DC, Derwen, Llanelidan and Efenechtyd 84-88; Asst Dioc Youth Chapl 81-86; Dioc Youth Chapl 86-91; PV St As and Tremeirchion w Cefn 88-97; Chapl H M Stanley Hosp 88-97; Bp's Visitor and Dioc RE Adv *St As* 88-93; Chapl Glan Clwyd Distr Gen Hosp 93-97; V Llanrhos *St As* from 97; Can St As Cathl from 98; AD Llanrwst from 01; Chapl NW Wales NHS Trust from 97. *Llanrhos Vicarage, 2 Vicarage Road, Llandudno LL30 1PT* Tel (01492) 876152

GRIFFITHS, Robert James. b 52. Nottm Univ BTh82. St Jo Coll Nottm 79. **d** 82 **p** 83. C Kettering St Andr *Pet* 82-85; C Collier Row St Jas and Havering-atte-Bower *Chelmsf* 86-89; R High Ongar w Norton Mandeville 89-97; R Ilmington w Stretton-on-Fosse etc *Cov* 97-99; V Newport *Chelmsf* 99-03; V Newport and Widdington 03-06. *Address temp unknown* E-mail robert.griffiths@btinternet.com

GRIFFITHS, Roger. b 46. Trin Coll Bris 70. **d** 74 **p** 75. C Normanton *Derby* 74-77; C Bucknall and Bagnall *Lich* 77-80; TV 80-83; TV Aberystwyth *St D* 83-86; R Letterston w Llanfair Nant-y-Gof etc from 86; AD Dewisland and Fishguard from 01. *New Letterston Rectory, Nant y Ffynnon, Letterston, Haverfordwest SA62 5SX* Tel (01348) 840336

GRIFFITHS, Roger Michael. b 47. Wycliffe Hall Ox 83. **d** 86 **p** 87. Min Can St D Cathl 86-88; V Pen-boyr 88-94; V Fishguard w Llanychar and Pontfaen w Morfil etc 94-03. *Trebover Farmhouse, Llanychaer, Fishguard SA65 9SA* Tel (01348) 873963 E-mail roger@rogriff.freeserve.co.uk

GRIFFITHS, Russell Howard. b 22. Glouc Th Course 75. **d** 77 **p** 78. NSM Fownhope w Fawley *Heref* 77-80; NSM Brockhampton 77-80; P-in-c Bridstow w Peterstow 80-81; TV Ross w Brampton Abbotts, Bridstow and Peterstow 81-87; rtd

87; Perm to Offic *Heref* from 91. *2 White House Way, Hereford HR1 1PX* Tel (01432) 278562

GRIFFITHS, Sarah. *See* BICK, Mrs Sarah

GRIFFITHS, Shane Owen. b 63. Ripon Coll Cuddesdon 01. **d** 04 **p** 04. C Icknield *Ox* 04-07; P-in-c Mullion *Truro* from 07; P-in-c Cury and Gunnwalloe from 07. *The Vicarage, Nansmellyon Road, Mullion, Helston TR12 7DH* Tel (01326) 240325 E-mail shaneowengriffiths@yahoo.co.uk

GRIFFITHS, Shirley Thelma. b 48. Univ of Wales (Ban) CertEd69 Open Univ BA83 Coll of Ripon & York St Jo MA01. St Deiniol's Hawarden 79. **d** 82 **p** 95. NSM Dyserth and Trelawnyd and Cwm *St As* 82-91; RE Officer 89-95; Min Can St As Cathl 91-95; P-in-c The Cowtons *Ripon* 95-02; RE Adv 95-02; V Abergele *St As* 02-08; V Abergele and St George from 08. *The Vicarage, 28 Lon Dirion, Abergele LL22 8PX* Tel and fax (01745) 833132

GRIFFITHS, Simon Mark. b 62. Ch Ch Coll Cant BA84 Kent Univ MA95. Chich Th Coll. **d** 87 **p** 88. C Cardiff St Jo *Llan* 87-91; Sub-Chapl HM Pris Cardiff 87-91; Chapl and Succ Roch Cath 91-96; Chapl Univ Coll Chich 96-01; V Sheff St Matt from 01. *St Matthew's Vicarage, 29 Winchester Road, Sheffield S10 4EE* Tel 0114-230 5641

GRIFFITHS, Canon Stanley Arthur. b 17. Lon Univ BSc38. Cuddesdon Coll 46. **d** 47 **p** 48. C Southsea St Matt *Portsm* 47-48; C Southsea H Spirit 48-51; C Cowley St Jas *Ox* 51-55; V Northbourne 55-65; V St Neots *Ely* 65-77; RD St Neots 76-82; Hon Can Ely Cathl 76-82; V Buckden 77-82; rtd 82; Perm to Offic *Ely* 82-96 and *York* 82-09. *9 Parkway, St Neots PE19 1EB*

GRIFFITHS, Stephen David (Griff). b 70. Oak Hill Th Coll BA96 Trin Coll Bris. **d** 00 **p** 01. C Cranleigh *Guildf* 00-04; TV Thetford *Nor* from 04. *24 Foxglove Road, Thetford IP24 2XF* Tel (01842) 764601 Mobile 07708-414952 E-mail revgriff@tesco.net

GRIFFITHS, Stephen Mark. b 67. Nottm Univ BTh93 PhD00. St Jo Coll Nottm 90. **d** 93 **p** 94. C Glascote and Stonydelph *Lich* 93-96; P-in-c Stratford New Town St Paul *Chelmsf* 96-02; P-in-c Steeple Bumpstead and Helions Bumpstead 02-05; Tutor Ridley Hall Cam 01-09; TR Linton *Ely* from 09. *4 Broad Green, Steeple Bumpstead, Haverhill CB9 7BW* Tel 07905-861234 (mobile) E-mail smg48@cam.ac.uk

GRIFFITHS, Stephen Robert. b 78. Oak Hill Th Coll BA00 Anglia Poly Univ MA05. Ridley Hall Cam 02. **d** 04 **p** 05. C Normanton *Derby* 04-08; P-in-c Moresby *Carl* from 08. *The Rectory, Low Moresby, Whitehaven CA28 6RR* Tel (01946) 693970 E-mail steph78griff@hotmail.com

GRIFFITHS, Mrs Susan Angela. b 61. St Jo Coll Nottm BTh94. **d** 94 **p** 95. C Ingrow cum Hainworth *Bradf* 94-98; V Wyke 98-03; C Buttershaw St Paul from 03. *St Paul's Vicarage, 42A Wibsey Park Avenue, Bradford BD6 3QA* Tel (01274) 676359 E-mail susan.griffiths@bradford.anglican.org

GRIFFITHS, Canon Sylvia Joy. b 50. Gipsy Hill Coll of Educn CertEd71. St Jo Coll Nottm 85. **dss** 86 **d** 87 **p** 94. Woodthorpe *S'well* 86-90; Par Dn 87-90; Min Bestwood/Rise Park LEP 90-94; TD Bestwood 90-94; TR 94-99; P-in-c Sherwood 99-01; V from 01; Hon Can S'well Minster from 04. *St Martin's Vicarage, Trevose Gardens, Sherwood, Nottingham NG5 3FU* Tel 0115-960 7547 E-mail sylvia.griffiths@homecall.co.uk

GRIFFITHS, Thomas. b 31. AKC57. **d** 58 **p** 59. C Cheadle Hulme All SS *Ches* 58-61; C Oxton 61-63; V Micklehurst 63-72; V Ringway 73-91; V Liscard St Mary w St Columba 91-96; rtd 96; Perm to Offic *Ches* from 96 and *Lich* from 01. *14A High Street, Ellesmere SY12 0EP* Tel (01691) 623589

GRIFFITHS, Canon Tudor Francis Lloyd. b 54. Jes Coll Ox BA76 MA81 Leeds Univ PhD99. Wycliffe Hall Ox 76. **d** 79 **p** 80. C Brecon w Battle *S & B* 79-81; Min Can Brecon Cathl 79-81; C Swansea St Mary w H Trin 81-83; R Llangattock and Llangynidr 83-88; CMS Uganda 89-95; C Newton St Pet *S & B* 96; Dioc Missr *Mon* from 96; V Goldcliffe and Whitson and Nash 96-98; TV Magor 98-03; TR Hawarden *St As* from 03; Can Cursal St As Cathl 07-08; Chan from 08. *The Rectory, 2 Birch Rise, Hawarden CH5 3DD* Tel (01244) 520091

GRIFFITHS, Vyrnach Morgan. b 24. Univ of Wales (Lamp) BA50. St Mich Coll Llan 52. **d** 54 **p** 55. C Llantrisant 54-56; C Ystradyfodwg 56-60; C Cwmavon 60-61; V Clydach Vale 61-63; R Llanfair Talhaiarn *St As* 63-70; V Dinas w Penygraig *Llan* 70-74; R Llanddulas *St As* 74-80; R Llanddulas and Llysfaen 80-89; rtd 89. *10 Cilfan, Pensarn, Abergele LL22 7RD*

GRIFFITHS, Canon William David Aled. b 52. Univ of Wales (Abth) BA74 Man Univ AHA77. St Mich Coll Llan. **d** 83 **p** 84. C Carmarthen St Pet *St D* 83-87; Asst Warden of Ords 84-91; Warden of Ords 91-07; V Llansadwrn w Llanwrda and Manordeilo 87-92; V Llangunnor w Cwmffrwd from 92; Can St D Cathl from 01. *The Vicarage, Llangunnor Road, Carmarthen SA31 2HY* Tel (01267) 236435

GRIFFITHS, William David Maldwyn. b 23. St D Coll Lamp BA47. **d** 50 **p** 51. C Cardigan *St D* 50-54; C Henfynyw w Aberaeron 54-57; P-in-c Llechryd 57-59; V Mathri, St Edrens and Llanrheithan 59-67; V Llanfihangel Genau'r Glyn 67-89; RD Llanbadarn Fawr 87-89; rtd 89. *Bro Enlli, Lower Regent Street, Aberaeron SA46 0HZ* Tel (01545) 570176

GRIFFITHS, William Thomas Gordon. b 48. York Univ BA70 Fitzw Coll Cam BA79. Ridley Hall Cam 78. **d** 80 **p** 81. C Dulwich St Barn *S'wark* 80-83; C Egglescliffe *Dur* 83-85; Ind Chapl 85-90; V Stockton St Jas 90-98; NSM Leamington Hastings and Birdingbury *Cov* 98-03; NSM Grandborough w Willoughby and Flecknoe 98-03; NSM Leam Valley 03-06; Perm to Offic from 06. *24 Park Road, Rugby CV21 2QH* Tel (01788) 547815

GRIGG, Robin Harold. b 44. **d** 07 **p** 08. NSM St Mewan w Mevagissey and St Ewe *Truro* from 07; Chapl R Cornwall Hosps Trust from 07. *Higher Polstreath, School Hill, Mevagissey, St Austell PL26 6TH* Tel (01726) 843708

GRIGG, Simon James. b 61. Warwick Univ BA82 MA83 Southn Univ BTh90. Chich Th Coll 87. **d** 90 **p** 91. C Cowley St Jas *Ox* 90-94; C W Hampstead St Jas *Lon* 94-95; V Munster Square Ch Ch and St Mary Magd 95-06; R Covent Garden St Paul from 06. *Flat 3, 35 Craven Street, London WC2N 5NF* Tel (020) 7836 5221 Mobile 07958-472568
E-mail simon.grigg@btopenworld.com

GRIGG, Canon Terence George. b 34. Kelham Th Coll 54. **d** 59 **p** 60. C Brookfield St Anne, Highgate Rise *Lon* 59-62; Chapl Lee Abbey 63-66; Chapl and Lect St Luke's Coll Ex 66-70; V Stainton-in-Cleveland *York* 70-83; R Cottingham 83-04; Can and Preb York Minster 90-04; rtd 04; Hon Can Koforidua from 84; Hon Can Ho from 06. *The Canon's House, 14 Grove Street, Norton, Malton YO17 9BG* Tel (01653) 691157

GRIGG, William John Frank. b 27. Ripon Hall Ox. **d** 66 **p** 67. C Wigan All SS *Liv* 66-67; C Leek St Luke *Lich* 67-69; C Fenton 69-74; C St Stephen by Saltash *Truro* 74-76; TV Redruth 76-79; TV Laneast w St Clether and Tresmere 79-81; P-in-c Wendron 81-85; TV Helston and Wendron 85-91; rtd 91. *St Germoe, 23 Dunheved Fields, Launceston PL15 7HS* Tel (01566) 772878

GRIGGS, Canon Alan Sheward. b 33. Trin Hall Cam BA56 MA60. Westcott Ho Cam 58. **d** 60 **p** 61. C Arnold *S'well* 60-63; Succ S'wark Cathl 63-66; Ind Chapl 66-71; C Leeds H Trin *Ripon* 71-81; V 81-91; Soc and Ind Adv 71-81; Hon Can Ripon Cathl 84-98; Soc Resp Officer 91-98; rtd 98; Perm to Offic *Ripon* from 98. *32 St Chad's Avenue, Leeds LS6 3QF* Tel 0113-275 8100
E-mail alan@griggs32.freeserve.co.uk

GRIGGS, Mrs Anthea Mary. b 37. Homerton Coll Cam TCert57 New Coll Edin BA86. SAOMC. **d** 00 **p** 01. NSM Sunningdale *Ox* 00-05; Lic to Offic *Edin* from 06. *8/1 Rattray Drive, Edinburgh EH10 5TH* Tel 0131-447 2448
E-mail amgriggs@freenetname.co.uk

GRIGGS, Frederick John. b 20. Peterho Cam BA48 MA53. Linc Th Coll. **d** 50 **p** 51. C Stand *Man* 50-53; C Writtle *Chelmsf* 53-55; P-in-c The Chignals w Mashbury 55-58; V Chelmsf St Andr 58-62; R Colne Engaine 62-80; P-in-c Frating w Thorrington 80-03; rtd 05. *6 Church Vean, Halton, Halesworth IP19 8PR* Tel (01986) 875298

✠**GRIGGS, The Rt Revd Ian Macdonald.** b 28. Trin Hall Cam BA52 MA56 Westcott Ho Cam. **d** 54 **p** 55 **c** 87. C Portsea St Cuth *Portsm* 54-59; Dioc Youth Chapl *Sheff* 59-64; Bp's Dom Chapl 59-64; V Sheff St Cuth 64-71; V Kidderminster St Mary *Worc* 71-82; Hon Can Worc Cathl 77-84; TR Kidderminster St Mary and All SS, Trimpley etc 82-84; Preb Heref Cathl 84-94; Adn Ludlow 84-87; P-in-c Tenbury St Mich 84-87; Suff Bp Ludlow 87-94; rtd 94; Hon Asst Bp Carl from 94. *Rookings, Patterdale, Penrith CA11 0NP* Tel (01768) 482064
E-mail ian.griggs@virgin.net

GRIGOR, Miss Alice Moira (Tirsh). b 49. Ripon Coll Cuddesdon 94. **d** 96 **p** 97. C Curry Rivel w Fivehead and Swell *B & W* 96-98; C Nailsea Ch Ch w Tickenham 98-00; TV Ross *Heref* 00-06; P-in-c Quinton and Welford w Weston *Glouc* from 06. *The Rectory, Church Lane, Welford on Avon, Stratford-upon-Avon CV37 8EL* Tel (01789) 751576
E-mail tirshgrigor@hotmail.co.uk

GRIGOR, David Alexander. b 29. St Aid Birkenhead 51. **d** 54 **p** 55. C Hengrove *Bris* 54-57; C Marshfield w Cold Ashton 57-60; V Newport *Ex* 60-67; V Paignton St Paul Preston 67-73; R Rio de Janeiro Ch Ch Brazil 73-74; Hon C Heavitree *Ex* 74-77; Chapl Ex Sch 74-77; Chapl Brighton Coll 77-89; Chapl Warminster Sch 89-93; rtd 93; Perm to Offic *Win* 02-06 and *Portsm* 03-06. *42 Russell Crescent, Wollaton, Nottingham NG8 2BQ* Tel 0115-928 9036

GRIGSBY, Peter Edward. b 31. Magd Coll Cam MA56 CertEd56. NEOC 85. **d** 88 **p** 89. NSM Haxby w Wigginton *York* 88-90; C Brayton 90-92; TV 92-97; rtd 97; Perm to Offic *Chich* 98-01 and from 04. *4 The Hop Garden, South Harting, Petersfield GU31 5QL* Tel (01730) 825295

GRIGSON, Richard John Stephen. b 60. Man Univ BA83. Qu Coll Birm 86. **d** 88 **p** 89. C W Bromwich St Fran *Lich* 88-92; V Smallthorne from 92; P-in-c Brown Edge from 05. *St Saviour's Vicarage, Ford Green Road, Stoke-on-Trent ST6 1NX* Tel (01782) 835941 Fax (07092) 214726
E-mail richard.grigson@lichfield.anglican.org

GRIMASON, The Very Revd Alistair John. b 57. CITC 76. **d** 79 **p** 80. C Belfast H Trin *Conn* 79-82; C Dublin Drumcondra w N Strand *D & G* 82-84; I Navan w Kentstown, Tara, Slane, Painestown etc *M & K* 84-91; Dioc Youth Officer (Meath) 90-94; Dioc Info Officer (Meath) 90-96; I Tullamore w Durrow, Newtownfertullagh, Rahan etc 91-00; Preb Tipper St Patr Cathl Dublin 92-00; Can Meath *M & K* 92-00; Chan Kildare Cathl 98-00; Dean Tuam *T, K & A* from 00; I Tuam w Cong and Aasleagh from 00. *Deanery Place, Cong, Claremorris, Co Mayo, Republic of Ireland* Tel and fax (00353) (94) 954 6017
E-mail deantuam@hotmail.com

GRIME, Arthur Michael. b 28. Kelham Th Coll 48. **d** 52 **p** 53. Basutoland 52-55; C Ealing St Barn *Lon* 55-57; C Pimlico St Gabr 57-59; C Greenford H Cross 59-62; V Fulham St Pet 62-66; V Chiswick St Paul Grove Park 66-88; rtd 89; Perm to Offic *Chich* 89-01. *29 Eton Close, Datchet, Slough SL3 9BE* Tel (01753) 545802

GRIME, William John Peter. b 38. St Jo Coll Ox BA60 MA66. Cuddesdon Coll 69. **d** 70 **p** 71. C Blackb St Jas 70-74; Chapl St Martin's Coll of Educn 74-77; V Seascale *Carl* 77-78; P-in-c Irton w Drigg 77-78; V Seascale and Drigg 78-05; rtd 05; Perm to Offic *York* from 05. *Bridge House, Snape, Bedale DL8 2SZ* Tel (01677) 470077 E-mail wjpgrime@gmail.com

GRIMLEY, The Very Revd Robert William. b 43. Ch Coll Cam BA66 MA70 Wadh Coll Ox BA68 MA76 UWE Hon DLitt04. Ripon Hall Ox 66. **d** 68 **p** 69. C Radlett *St Alb* 68-72; Chapl K Edw Sch Birm 72-84; Hon C Moseley St Mary *Birm* 72-84; V Edgbaston St Geo 84-97; Dean Bris from 97. *The Deanery, 20 Charlotte Street, Bristol BS1 5PZ* Tel 0117-926 2443 *or* 926 4879 Fax 925 3678 E-mail dean@bristol.anglican.org

GRIMSBY, Suffragan Bishop of. *See* ROSSDALE, The Rt Revd David Douglas James

GRIMSDALE, Mrs Margaret. b 24. SRN48. Gilmore Course 80. dss 82 **d** 87. Stoke Poges *Ox* 82-88; Hon Par Dn 87-88; Hon Par Dn Burrington and Churchill *B & W* 88-90; rtd 90; Perm to Offic *B & W* 90-94. *Widecombe House, Barrington Road, Torquay TQ1 2QJ* Tel (01803) 298692

GRIMSHAW, Eric Fenton Hall. b 34. Bris Univ BA57. Tyndale Hall Bris 54. **d** 58 **p** 59. C Moss Side St Jas *Man* 58-61; C Leyland St Andr *Blackb* 61-64; V Preston St Mark 64-72; V Mirehouse *Carl* 72-91; Hon Can Carl Cathl 86-91; V Knowsley *Liv* 91-99; rtd 99; Perm to Offic *Liv* from 99. *22 Lynwood Avenue, Aughton, Ormskirk L39 5BB* Tel (01695) 424864

GRIMSTER, Barry John. b 49. Ex Univ BA70. Trin Coll Bris 72. **d** 74 **p** 75. C S Lambeth St Steph *S'wark* 74-77; C New Malden and Coombe 77-82; P-in-c Deptford St Jo 82-84; V Deptford St Jo w H Trin 84-89; V Woking St Pet *Guildf* 89-01; TR from 02. *The Rectory, 28 High Street, Old Woking, Woking GU22 9ER* Tel (01483) 762707 E-mail bjay1@onetel.com

GRIMWADE, Canon John Girling. b 20. Keble Coll Ox BA48 MA52. Cuddesdon Coll 48. **d** 50 **p** 51. C Kingston All SS *S'wark* 50-55; C Ox St Mary V 55-56; PC Londonderry *Birm* 56-62; R Caversham *Ox* 62-81; Hon Can Ch Ch 73-90; Chapl to The Queen 80-90; R Caversham St Pet and Mapledurham etc *Ox* 81-83; P-in-c Stonesfield 83-89; rtd 89; Perm to Offic *Glouc* and *Ox* from 89. *88 Alexander Drive, Cirencester GL7 1UJ* Tel (01285) 885767

GRIMWOOD, Andrew Stuart. b 68. Ex Univ BA89. St Mich Coll Llan BD97. **d** 98 **p** 99. C Llangynwyd w Maesteg 98-01; P-in-c Rhyl w St Ann *St As* 01-04; R Llanllwchaiarn and Newtown w Aberhafesp from 04; AD Cedewain from 08. *The Rectory, 3 Old Barn Lane, Newtown SY16 2PT* Tel (01686) 622260
E-mail andy18b@tiscali.co.uk

GRIMWOOD, Canon David Walter. b 48. Lon Univ BA70 K Coll Lon BD73 AKC73. **d** 74 **p** 75. C Newc St Geo 74-78; C Wholrton 78-80; TV Totton *Win* 80-93; Adv to Coun for Soc Resp *Roch* and *Cant* 93-02; Chief Exec Ch in Soc *Roch* and *Cant* 02-09; Hon Can Roch Cathl 97-09; Perm to Offic *Cant* from 09. *56 Postley Road, Maidstone ME15 6TR* Tel (01622) 764625 Mobile 07960-369681 E-mail d.grimwood@zedakah.co.uk

GRINDELL, James Mark. b 43. Nottm Univ BA66 Bris Univ MA69. Wells Th Coll 66. **d** 68 **p** 69. C Bushey Heath *St Alb* 68-72; C Ex St Dav 72-74; Chapl St Audries Sch W Quantoxhead 74-83; Chapl Berkhamsted Colleg Sch Herts 83-86; Chapl Denstone Coll Uttoxeter 86-91; Chapl Portsm Gr Sch 91-03; rtd 03; Hon Chapl Portsm Cathl from 91. *6A Victoria Place, Ryde PO33 2PX* Tel (01983) 613463

GRINHAM, Garth Clews. b 36. Oak Hill Th Coll 61. **d** 64 **p** 65. C Beckenham Ch Ch *Roch* 64-68; C Wallington *S wark* 68-71; V Erith St Paul *Roch* 71-76; Asst Sec CPAS 76-81; Hon C Knockholt *Roch* 76-81; V Southport Ch Ch *Liv* 81-94; V Douglas St Ninian *S & M* 94-01; rtd 01; Perm to Offic *Liv* from 01. *8 Ottery Close, Southport PR9 9GE* Tel (01704) 213468

GRINHAM, Julian Clive. b 39. Birkbeck Coll Lon BA65. Oak Hill Th Coll 79. **d** 81 **p** 82. C Blackb Ch Ch w St Matt 81-83; Nat Sec Pathfinders CPAS 83-89; Dir CYPECS 89-94; V Normanton *Derby* 94-00; rtd 00; Perm to Offic *Nor* from 01. *85 Gwyn Crescent, Fakenham NR21 8NE* Tel (01328) 853068

GRINSELL, Robert Paul. b 62. Ch Ch Coll Cant BA86 PGCE89. Trin Coll Bris MA03. **d** 03 **p** 04. C Foord St Jo *Cant* 03-07; P-in-c Hawkinge w Acrise and Swingfield from 07. *The Rectory, 78*

Canterbury Road, Hawkinge, Folkestone CT18 7BP Tel (01303) 893215 E-mail robgrinsell@tiscali.co.uk

GRINSTED, Richard Anthony. b 43. Leic Univ BSc65. Oak Hill Th Coll 67. **d** 70 **p** 71. C Egham *Guildf* 70-73; C Woodford Wells *Chelmsf* 73-76; P-in-c Havering-atte-Bower 76-84; R Ditton *Roch* 84-94; R Chulmleigh *Ex* 94-96; R Chawleigh w Cheldon 94-96; R Wembworthy w Eggesford 94-96; R Chulmleigh, Chawleigh w Cheldon, Wembworthy etc 96-00; rtd 00. *Stonehouse, Christow, Exeter EX6 7NE* Tel (01647) 252653

GRISCOME, David. b 47. Oak Hill Th Coll BA88 TCD Div Sch 89. **d** 89 **p** 90. C Glendermott *D & R* 89-91; I Clondehorkey w Cashel 91-95; I Mevagh w Glenalla 91-95; Bp's C Calry *K, E & A* 95-97; I 97-00; Dean Elphin and Ardagh 99-04; I Sligo w Knocknarea and Rosses Pt 99-04; Perm to Offic *Cant* 04-06; I Convoy w Monellan and Donaghmore *D & R* from 06; Bp's Dom Chapl from 07. *The Rectory, Convoy, Co Donegal, Republic of Ireland* Tel (00353) (74) 910 1898 E-mail david@keida.wanadoo.co.uk

✠**GRISWOLD, The Most Revd Frank Tracy.** b 37. Harvard Univ AB59 Oriel Coll Ox BA62 MA66. Gen Th Sem NY 59 Hon DD85 Seabury-Western Th Sem Hon DD85. **d** 62 **p** 63 **c** 85. C Bryn Mawr Redeemer 63-67; R Yardley St Andr 67-74; R Philadelphia St Martin-in-the-Fields 74-85; Bp Coadjutor Chicago 85-87; Bp Chicago 87-97; Presiding Bp 98-06; rtd 06. *Episcopal Church Center, 815 Second Avenue, New York, NY 10017, USA* Tel (001) (212) 716 6276 *or* 867 8400 Fax 490 3298 E-mail pboffice@episcopalchurch.org

GROARKE, Ms Nicola Jane. b 62. Lanc Univ BA84. Ridley Hall Cam. **d** 00 **p** 01. C Balham Hill Ascension *S'wark* 00-08; V Canonbury St Steph *Lon* from 08. *St Stephen's Vicarage, 9 River Place, London N1 2DE* Tel (020) 7359 4164 *or* tel and fax 7226 7526 E-mail nikki@stsc.org.uk

GROEPE, Canon Thomas Matthew Karl. b 51. St Pet Coll Natal 76. **d** 78 **p** 79. S Africa 78-83 and from 88; Hon C Waterloo St Jo w St Andr *S'wark* 83-88. *PO Box 1932, Cape Town, 8000 South Africa* Tel and fax (0027) (21) 465 4946 *or* tel 461 9566 E-mail karlgroepe@mweb.co.za

GROOCOCK, Christopher John. b 59. St Jo Coll Nottm 89. **d** 92 **p** 93. C Shawbury *Lich* 92-95; V Hengoed w Gobowen 95-00; CF from 00. *c/o MOD Chaplains (Army)* Tel (01980) 615804 Fax 615800

GROOCOCK, Craig Ronald. WMMTC 03. **d** 05 **p** 06. C Kenilworth St Nic *Cov* 05-08; P-in-c Harbury and Ladbroke from 08. *The Rectory, 2 Vicarage Lane, Harbury, Leamington Spa CV33 9HA* Tel (01926) 612377 Mobile 07811-395169 E-mail craiggroocock@aol.com

GROOM, Mrs Susan Anne. b 63. Univ of Wales BA85 Hughes Hall Cam MPhil86 Lon Bible Coll MA94 Open Univ MPhil00. St Jo Coll Nottm 94. **d** 96 **p** 97. C Harefield *Lon* 96-99; C Eastcote St Lawr 99-01; P-in-c Yiewsley 01-03; V 03-07; Dir Lic Min Kensington Area from 07. *St Augustine's Vicarage, 117 Queens Gate, London SW7 5LP* Tel (020) 7225 2168 E-mail sue.groom@london.anglican.org

GROSSCURTH, Stephen. b 55. Sarum & Wells Th Coll 81. **d** 84 **p** 85. C Southport H Trin *Liv* 84-87; C Amblecote *Worc* 87-89; V Walton St Jo *Liv* 89-95; Chapl S Man Univ Hosps NHS Trust from 95. *Wythenshawe Hospital, Southmoor Road, Manchester M23 9LT* Tel 0161-291 2298 *or* (01925) 821124 Fax 0161-946 2603

GROSSE, Anthony Charles Bain. b 30. Oak Hill Th Coll 58. **d** 61 **p** 62. C Chislehurst Ch Ch *Roch* 61-65; C Washfield *Ex* 65-71; TV Washfield, Stoodleigh, Withleigh etc 71-73; R Hemyock 73-86; P-in-c Clayhidon 76-86; R Hemyock w Culm Davy and Clayhidon 87-93; R Hemyock w Culm Davy, Clayhidon and Culmstock 93-96; rtd 96; Perm to Offic *Ex* from 96. *17 Frog Street, Bampton, Tiverton EX16 9NT* Tel (01398) 331981 E-mail acgrosse@btinternet.com

GROSSE, Peter George. b 43. St Steph Ho Ox 02. **d** 03 **p** 04. NSM Reading St Matt *Ox* 03-06; NSM Tilehurst St Mary from 06; NSM Tilehurst St Geo from 06. *18 Rangewood Avenue, Reading RG30 3NN* Tel 0118-959 4573 E-mail petergrosse@supanet.com

GROSSE, Richard William. b 52. Solicitor 77 Mid Essex Tech Coll LLB73. Ridley Hall Cam 86. **d** 88 **p** 89. C Soham *Ely* 88-91; C Bedale *Ripon* 91-93; C-in-c Thornton Watlass w Thornton Steward 91-93; V Barton and Manfield w Cleasby 93-95; V Barton and Manfield and Cleasby w Stapleton 95-99; R Keelby Gp *Linc* 99-04; R Callander *St And* from 04; R Aberfoyle from 04. *St Mary's Rectory, Main Street, Aberfoyle, Stirling FK8 3UJ* Tel and fax (01877) 382887 E-mail richard_grosse@hotmail.com

GROSU, Iosif. b 60. Iasi Univ BTh92. RC Inst Iasi. **d** 89 **p** 89. In RC Ch 89-93; C Darlington St Cuth *Dur* 96-99; C Stockton St Jo and Stockton St Jas 99-02; TV Ch the K 02-08; P-in-c Purston cum S Featherstone *Wakef* 08-09; P-in-c Featherstone 08-09; V from 09. *The Vicarage, Victoria Street, Featherstone, Pontefract WF7 5EZ* Tel (01977) 792288 E-mail iosif@grosu.freeserve.co.uk

GROSVENOR, Royston Johannes Martin. b 47. K Coll Lon BD70 AKC. **d** 71 **p** 72. C Pontesbury I and II *Heref* 71-75; C Bishopston *Bris* 75-79; P-in-c Croydon St Pet S End *Cant* 79-81; V Croydon St Pet 81-84; V Croydon St Pet *S'wark* 85-87; R Merstham and Gatton 87-97; V Tidenham w Beachley and Lancaut *Glouc* from 97; P-in-c St Briavels w Hewelsfield from 05; AD Forest S 04-09. *Tidenham Vicarage, Gloucester Road, Tutshill, Chepstow NP16 7DH* Tel (01291) 622442 E-mail roystongrosvenor@tidenham42.freeserve.co.uk

GROUNDSELL, Ms Melanie Anne. b 65. Colchester Inst of Educn BA87 Brooklands Coll PGCE99 Glos Univ BA03 LTCL89 FLCM90. STETS MA07. **d** 07 **p** 08. NSM Camberley St Mich Yorktown *Guildf* from 07. *2 Longmeadow, Frimley, Camberley GU16 8RR* Tel (01276) 501027 Mobile 07722-518052 E-mail m.groundsell@clarinetandpianoinfrimley.co.uk

GROVE, Lynn. b 43. Lon Univ MB, BS67. Cranmer Hall Dur 03. **d** 04 **p** 05. NSM Pickering w Lockton and Levisham *York* from 04. *37 Eastgate, Pickering YO18 7DU* Tel (01751) 477574 E-mail lynngrove43@hotmail.com

GROVER, Wilfrid John. b 29. Lich Th Coll 55. **d** 58 **p** 59. C Northampton St Alb *Pet* 58-61; C Boyne Hill *Ox* 61-65; V Cookham 65-85; RD Maidenhead 82-85; Warden Christchurch Retreat Ho *Glouc* 85-93; rtd 89; Perm to C Jedburgh *Edin* from 93. *5 The Stables, Buccleuch Chase, St Boswells, Melrose TD6 0HE* Tel (01835) 824435

GROVES, Caroline Anne. b 41. **d** 05 **p** 06. OLM Norbiton *S'wark* from 05. *16 Beaufort Road, Kingston upon Thames KT1 2TQ* Tel (020) 8549 1585 E-mail sicaro@blueyonder.co.uk

GROVES, Elizabeth Ann. Bp Otter Coll 94. **d** 97. NSM Soberton w Newtown *Portsm* 97-01; NSM Botley, Durley and Curdridge 01-06; NSM Wickham 06; NSM Shedfield and Wickham from 07. *The Rectory, Southwick Road, Wickham, Fareham PO17 6HR* Tel (01329) 832134 E-mail akeagroves@aol.com

GROVES, James Alan. b 32. CCC Cam BA58 MA62. Wells Th Coll 58. **d** 60 **p** 61. C Milton next Gravesend Ch Ch *Roch* 60-64; C Beckenham St Jas 64-66; V Orpington St Andr 66-98; rtd 98; Perm to Offic *Chich* from 98. *9 Wykeham Road, Hastings TN34 1UA* Tel (01424) 200839

GROVES, Preb Jill. b 61. Univ Coll Lon BSc82. St Jo Coll Nottm MA93. **d** 93 **p** 94. C Tenbury *Heref* 93-98; P-in-c Hope Bowdler w Eaton-under-Heywood from 98; P-in-c Cardington from 98; P-in-c Rushbury from 98; Preb Heref Cathl from 09. *The Rectory, Hope Bowdler, Church Stretton SY6 7DD* Tel (01694) 722918 E-mail jill@grovesfamily.org.uk

GROVES, Justin Simon John. b 69. Lon Bible Coll BA93. Ridley Hall Cam 00. **d** 02 **p** 03. C Glouc St Cath 02-05; C Newport St Paul *Mon* 05-07; P-in-c from 07. *52 Oakfield Road, Newport NP20 4LX* Tel (01633) 419775

GROVES, Margaret Ann. b 49. Nottm Univ BEd71 BPhil88. EMMTC 95. **d** 98 **p** 99. NSM Farnsfield *S'well* from 98; NSM Bilsthorpe from 98. *Churchill House, Church Hill, Bilsthorpe, Newark NG22 8RU* Tel (01623) 870679

GROVES, Peter John. b 70. New Coll Ox BA92 MA96 DPhil96. Westcott Ho Cam 95. **d** 97 **p** 98. C Leigh-on-Sea St Marg *Chelmsf* 97-99; Lib Pusey Ho 99-01; Asst Chapl and Tutor Keble Coll Ox 01-02; Chapl and Fell BNC Ox 02-06; Hon C Ox St Mary Magd 01-04; P-in-c from 05. *15 Beaumont Street, Oxford OX1 2NA* Tel (01865) 247836 E-mail peter.groves@theology.ox.ac.uk

GROVES, Canon Philip Neil. b 62. Man Univ BA84. St Jo Coll Nottm 86. **d** 88 **p** 89. C Holbeck *Ripon* 88-91; CMS 91-99; Lect St Phil Th Coll Kongwa Tanzania 91-98; Hon Can Mpwampwa from 98; TV Melton Mowbray *Leic* 99-05; Listening Process Facilitator on Human Sexuality Angl Communion from 06. *Anglican Communion Office, 16 Tavistock Crescent, London W11 1AP* Tel (020) 7313 3907 E-mail phil.groves@anglicancommunion.org *or* rev.phil@ntlworld.com

GROVES, Robert John. b 42. Trin Coll Bris 74. **d** 76 **p** 77. C Norwood St Luke *S'wark* 76-79; P-in-c Clapham Park All SS 79-86; V Anerley *Roch* 86-95; TV Canford Magna *Sarum* 95-98; TR Tollington *Lon* 98-02; rtd 02; Perm to Offic *Cant* and *Roch* from 02. *12 Oatfield Close, Cranbrook TN17 3NH* Tel (01580) 715756 E-mail bob_groves@lineone.net

GROWNS, John Huntley. b 28. Chich Th Coll 57. **d** 60 **p** 61. C Hayes St Mary *Lon* 60-64; C Addlestone *Guildf* 64-67; C-in-c Kempston Transfiguration CD *St Alb* 67-74; R Stevenage St Geo 74-82; R Felpham w Middleton *Chich* 82-88; P-in-c Westmill w Gt Munden *St Alb* 88-89; P-in-c Westmill 89-93; Dioc Stewardship Adv 88-93; rtd 93; Perm to Offic *Chich* 93-04 and *St Alb* 93-00. *5 Little London Gardens, Ely CB6 1BF* Tel (01353) 772794

GRUBB, Greville Alexander (Alex). b 36. Saltley Tr Coll Birm CertEd60. St Jo Coll Nottm 72. **d** 74 **p** 75. C Rushden w Newton Bromswold *Pet* 74-77; Chapl St D Coll Llandudno 77-89; Chapl Casterton Sch Lancs 90-96; rtd 96; Perm to Offic *Blackb* from 96 and *Bradf* from 02. *Beckstones, 21 Littledale Road, Brookhouse, Lancaster LA2 9PH* Tel (01524) 770512

GRUNDY, Anthony Brian. b 36. Pemb Coll Cam BA62 MA87. Ridley Hall Cam 61. **d** 63 **p** 64. C Hatcham St Jas *S'wark* 63-66; C Margate H Trin *Cant* 66-68; C Brixton Hill St Sav *S'wark* 68-70; V Assington *St E* 70-76; TV Much Wenlock w Bourton *Heref* 76-81; TV Wenlock 81-82; TR 82-88; RD Condover 86-88; R Burghfield *Ox* 88-02; rtd 02; Perm to Offic *Chich* from 03. *29 Gerald Road, Worthing BN11 5QQ* Tel (01903) 507213

GRUNDY, Christopher John. b 49. ACA72. Trin Coll Bris 74. **d** 77 **p** 78. C Maidstone St Luke *Cant* 77-81; Argentina 81-82; Chile 82-84; Perm to Offic *Guildf* 84-96; NSM Guildf Ch Ch w St Martha-on-the-Hill 96-99; C Shere, Albury and Chilworth 99-06; TV Drypool *York* from 06. *St John's Vicarage, 383 Southcoates Lane, Hull HU9 3UN* Tel (01482) 781090 E-mail chris@grundy.org.uk

GRUNDY, David. *See* GRUNDY, Julian David

GRUNDY, Jocelyn Pratchitt. b 22. Trin Coll Cam MA. Westcott Ho Cam 64. **d** 66 **p** 67. C Guildf H Trin w St Mary 66-68; R Shere 68-73; V Fleet 73-83; C Aldershot St Mich 83-87; rtd 87; Perm to Offic *Guildf* from 87. *Richmond Cottage, School Hill, Seale, Farnham GU10 1HY* Tel (01252) 782238

GRUNDY, Judith Michal Towers Mynors. b 54. Lady Spencer Chu Coll of Educn CertEd76 Ox Univ BEd77. Trin Coll Bris 85. **d** 93 **p** 94. NSM Kensal Rise St Mark and St Martin *Lon* 93-95; NSM Snettisham w Ingoldisthorpe and Fring *Nor* 95-04; R Denver and Ryston w Roxham and W Dereham etc *Ely* from 04. *The Rectory, Ryston Road, Denver, Downham Market PE38 0DP* Tel (01366) 383226 E-mail judith.grundy@ely.anglican.org

GRUNDY, Julian David. b 60. St Andr Univ MA83. Trin Coll Bris BA88. **d** 89 **p** 90. C Lancaster St Thos *Blackb* 89-92; C Kensal Rise St Mark and St Martin *Lon* 92-95; R Snettisham w Ingoldisthorpe and Fring *Nor* 95-03; Perm to Offic *Ely* from 08. *The Rectory, Ryston Road, Denver, Downham Market PE38 0DP* Tel (01366) 387727 E-mail david@grundyd.fslife.co.uk

GRUNDY, Canon Malcolm Leslie. b 44. Open Univ BA76. St Boniface Warminster AKC68. **d** 69 **p** 70. C Doncaster St Geo *Sheff* 69-72; Ind Chapl 72-80; Dir of Educn *Lon* 80-86; TR Huntingdon *Ely* 86-91; Hon Can Ely Cathl 88-94; Dir Avec 91-94; Adn Craven *Bradf* 94-05; Dir Foundn for Ch Leadership 05-09; rtd 09; Perm to Offic *York* from 09. *4 Portal Road, York YO26 6BQ* Tel (01904) 787387 Mobile 07950-816641 E-mail malcolm.grundy@live-wires.org

GRUNDY, Paul. b 55. BD77 AKC. Linc Th Coll 79. **d** 80 **p** 81. C Ryhope *Dur* 80-82; C Ferryhill 82-85; TV Cramlington *Newc* 85-87; TV Swinton and Pendlebury *Man* 87-90; V Wingate Grange *Dur* 90-95; R Willington and Sunnybrow 95-07; P-in-c Usworth from 07. *Usworth Vicarage, 14 Prestwick Close, Washington NE37 2LP* Tel 0191-416 7604

GRÜNEBERG, Keith Nigel. *See* BEECH-GRÜNEBERG, Keith Nigel

GRUNEWALD, Gottfried Johannes. b 38. Loyola Univ Chicago MPS92. Th Faculty Frankfurt 66. **d** 69 **p** 69. Denmark 70-95; C Dunbar *Edin* 95-97; R Dollar *St And* 98-05; rtd 05. *Teglparken 8, 8860 Ulstrup, Denmark* Tel (0045) 864 6341 E-mail grunewald@email.dk

GRYLLS, Ms Catherine Anne. b 70. **d** 00 **p** 01. C Hall Green St Pet *Birm* 00-04; P-in-c Balsall Heath St Paul 04-07; P-in-c Edgbaston SS Mary and Ambrose 04-07; P-in-c Balsall Heath and Edgbaston SS Mary and Ambrose 07-08; V from 08. *St Ambrose Vicarage, 15 Raglan Road, Birmingham B5 7RA* Tel 0121-440 2196

GRYLLS, Canon Michael John. b 38. Qu Coll Cam BA62 MA66. Linc Th Coll 62. **d** 64 **p** 65. C Sheff Gillcar St Silas 64-67; C-in-c Dunscroft CD 67-70; V Herringthorpe 70-78; V Amport, Grateley, Monxton and Quarley *Win* 78-89; RD Andover 85-89; V Whitchurch w Tufton and Litchfield 89-03; Hon Can Win Cathl 01-03; rtd 03; Perm to Offic *Worc* from 04. *41 Church Street, Evesham WR11 1DY* Tel (01386) 442086

GUBBINS, Andrew Martin. b 65. York Univ BA86 Keele Univ 93. St Jo Coll Nottm LTh93. **d** 96 **p** 97. C Harrogate St Mark *Ripon* 96-00; P-in-c Osmondthorpe St Phil 00-03; V Leeds All SS w Osmondthorpe from 03. *St Philip's Vicarage, 68 Osmondthorpe Lane, Leeds LS9 9EF* Tel 0113-249 7371

GUBBINS (née O'BRIEN), Mrs Mary. b 68. Leeds Univ BSc90. St Jo Coll Nottm BTh93. **d** 94 **p** 95. C Middleton St Mary *Ripon* 94-96; C Bilton 96-99; Perm to Offic from 99. *St Philip's Vicarage, 68 Osmondthorpe Lane, Leeds LS9 9EF* Tel 0113-249 7371

GUDGEON, Canon Michael John. b 40. Qu Coll Cam BA63 MA67. Chich Th Coll 65. **d** 66 **p** 67. C Kings Heath *Birm* 66-72; Asst Chapl K Edw Sch Birm 69-72; Chapl and Tutor Cuddesdon Coll 72-75; V Hawley H Trin *Guildf* 75-80; V Minley 75-80; Adult Educn Adv *Chich* 80-87; Can Res Portsm Cathl 87-90; Dioc Dir of Educn 87-90; V Hove St Thos *Chich* 90-93; TV Hove 93-94; Bp's Chapl *Eur* 94-98; Dir of Ords 94-97; Can Gib Cathl 96-06; P-in-c Worthing St Andr *Chich* 98-05; rtd 05. *11 Gloucester Road, Littlehampton BN17 7BT* Tel (01903) 739682 E-mail michaelgudgeon@aol.com

GUERNSEY, Dean of. *See* MELLOR, The Very Revd Kenneth Paul

✠**GUERRERO, The Rt Revd Orlando.** b 45. Episc Sem of Ecuador. **p** 80 **c** 95. P Puerto la Cruz H Trin 80-93; Interim P Caracas St Mary 80-84; Bp Venezuela from 95. *Apartado 49-143, Avenida Caron 100, Colinas de Bello Monte, Caracas 1042-A, Venezuela* Tel (0058) (2) 753 0723 Fax 751 3180

GUEST, David. b 41. Dur Univ BA62. Coll of Resurr Mirfield 70. **d** 72 **p** 73. C Horsforth *Ripon* 72-75; C Richmond 75-76; C Richmond w Hudswell 76-78; R Middleham 78-81; R Middleham and Coverham w Horsehouse 81-86; V W Rainton and E Rainton *Dur* 86-03; RD Houghton 92-94 and 96-97; rtd 03; Perm to Offic *Ripon* from 03. *Lindisfarne, 3 New Croft, Horsforth, Leeds LS18 4TD* Tel 0113-258 0521

GUEST, David Andrew. b 61. Chich Th Coll BTh92. **d** 92 **p** 93. C Prenton *Ches* 92-94; C Ches H Trin 94-97; Assoc P Douglas All SS and St Thos *S & M* 97-00; Dioc Communications Officer 97-00; Relig Adv Manx Radio 97-00; Bp's Dom Chapl 98-00; Dioc Communications Officer *Chich* from 00; C Hove 00-03; C Southwick from 03. *St Peter's House, 107A Gardner Road, Portslade, Brighton BN41 1PN* Tel (01273) 592125 *or* 425791 Fax 421041 E-mail david.guest@diochi.org.uk

GUEST, Derek William. b 55. NOC 90. **d** 93 **p** 94. C Cheadle Hulme St Andr *Ches* 93-99; V from 99. *2 Orrishmere Road, Cheadle Hulme, Cheadle SK8 5HP* Tel 0161-486 9306 E-mail revdguest@yahoo.co.uk

GUEST, Ernest Anthony. b 64. NTMTC 99. **d** 02 **p** 03. C Gt Ilford St Jo *Chelmsf* 02-05; V Barkingside St Laur from 05. *St Laurence's Vicarage, Donington Avenue, Ilford IG6 1AJ* Tel (020) 8518 3113 Mobile 07810-516356 E-mail ernie@eguest.fsnet.co.uk

GUEST, Mrs Helen. b 54. Totley Thornbridge Coll CertEd75 Nottm Univ MA02. EMMTC 99. **d** 02 **p** 03. NSM Brimington *Derby* 02-05; C Hatton 05-07; P-in-c Killamarsh from 07; C Barlborough and Renishaw from 07. *The Rectory, Sheepcote Road, Killamarsh, Sheffield S21 1DU* Tel 0114-248 2769 E-mail revsguest@btinternet.com

GUEST, John. b 36. Trin Coll Bris 59. **d** 61 **p** 62. C Barton Hill St Luke w Ch Ch *Bris* 61-64; C Liv St Sav 65-66; USA from 66; rtd 01. *30 Myrtle Hill Road, Sewickley PA 15143-8700, USA*

GUEST, John Andrew Kenneth. b 55. Univ of Wales (Lamp) BA78. Wycliffe Hall Ox 78. **d** 80 **p** 81. C Eastwood *S'well* 80-84; TV Toxteth St Philemon w St Gabr and St Cleopas *Liv* 84-89; C Cranham Park *Chelmsf* 89-93; P-in-c Stanford-le-Hope w Mucking 93-03; R from 03. *The Rectory, The Green, Stanford-le-Hope SS17 0EP* Tel (01375) 672271 E-mail gof4god@aol.com

GUEST, Michael. b 52. EMMTC. **d** 99 **p** 00. NSM Heath *Derby* 99-07; NSM Killamarsh from 07; NSM Barlborough and Renishaw from 07. *The Rectory, Sheepcote Road, Killamarsh, Sheffield S21 1DU* Tel 0114-248 2769 E-mail revsguest@btinternet.com

GUEST, Simon Llewelyn. b 56. Univ of Wales (Lamp) BA78 CertEd79. St Mich Coll Llan 83. **d** 85 **p** 86. C Bassaleg *Mon* 85-88; C Cwmbran 88-89; TV 89-91; V Raglan w Llandenny and Bryngwyn 91-95; V Rockfield and Dingestow Gp from 05; AD Raglan-Usk 01-05; AD Monmouth from 06. *The Vicarage, Dingestow, Monmouth NP25 4DY* Tel (01600) 740206

GUEST-BLOFELD, Thomas. b 35. St D Coll Lamp BA59. Cranmer Hall Dur 59. **d** 62 **p** 63. C Maltby *Sheff* 62-63; C Goole 63-66; C Pocklington w Yapham-cum-Meltonby, Owsthorpe etc *York* 67-68; C Ely 68-70; C Pemberton St Jo *Liv* 70-72; V Walton St Jo 72-74; V Barkisland w W Scammonden *Wakef* 74-80; V Smallbridge *Man* 80-82; C Irlam 83-86; rtd 87. *43 Banborhaew, M005, Tamboon Maesai, Amper Muang, Amper Changwat Phayao, 5600, Thailand* Tel (0066) (8) 7184 3624

GUILDFORD, Bishop of. *See* HILL, The Rt Revd Christopher John

GUILDFORD, Dean of. *See* STOCK, The Very Revd Victor Andrew

GUILFORD, John Edward. b 50. S & M Dioc Tr Inst 94. **d** 99 **p** 00. OLM Lonan *S & M* from 99; OLM Laxey from 99. *Tremissary House, Strathallan Road, Douglas, Isle of Man IM2 4PN* Tel and fax (01624) 672001 Mobile 07624-494274 E-mail revjohnnyg@manx.net

GUILLAN, Miss Barbara Doris. b 19. S'wark Ord Course 45. **d** 87. NSM St Stythians w Perranarworthal and Gwennap *Truro* 87-89; rtd 89; Perm to Offic *Truro* 89-94. *St Cecilia's Nursing Home, 1 Hitchen Lane, Shepton Mallet BA4 5TZ* Tel (01749) 342809

GUILLE, The Very Revd John Arthur. b 49. Southn Univ BTh79. Sarum & Wells Th Coll 73. **d** 76 **p** 77. C Chandler's Ford *Win* 76-80; P-in-c Bournemouth St Jo 80-84; P-in-c Bournemouth St Mich 83-84; V Bournemouth St Jo w St Mich 84-89; R Guernsey St Andr 89-99; Adn Win 99-07; Can Res Win Cathl 99-07; Dean S'well from 07. *The Residence, Southwell NG25 0HP* Tel (01636) 812593 *or* 812649

GUILLEBAUD, Mrs Jette Margaret. b 48. Ex Univ BA70 UWE Hon MA98 FRSA62. Ripon Coll Cuddesdon 03. **d** 05 **p** 06. NSM Sarum Cathl from 05. *The Dovecot, Mount Sorrel, Broad Chalke, Salisbury SP5 5HQ* Tel (01722) 781281 Mobile 07985-576739 E-mail maggieguillebaud@salcath.co.uk

GUILLEBAUD, Miss Margaret Jean. b 43. MBE03. Edin Univ BSc66. Cranmer Hall Dur 79. **dss** 80 **d** 87 **p** 94. New Malden and Coombe *S'wark* 80-84; Carlton Colville w Mutford and Rushmere *Nor* 84-91; Par Dn 87-91; Par Dn Rodbourne Cheney *Bris* 91-94; C 94-95; CMS Rwanda 95-08; rtd 08; Perm to Offic *Birm* from 08. *7 Poplar Road, Dorridge, Solihull B93 8DD* Tel (01564) 770113 E-mail mguillebaud@rwanda1.com

GUILLEMIN, Thierry Jean-Louis. b 62. Coll of Resurr Mirfield 08. **d** 01 **p** 01. In RC Ch 01-07; Perm to Offic *Wakef* 08-09; C Heckmondwike from 09; C Liversedge w Hightown from 09. *The Vicarage, 14 Knowler Hill, Liversedge WF15 6LJ* Tel (01924) 403837 Mobile 07778-577008
E-mail t.guillemin@btinternet.com

GUINNESS, Alexander. *See* GUINNESS, Graham Alexander

GUINNESS, Christopher Paul. b 43. Lon Coll of Div 64. **d** 67 **p** 68. C Farnborough *Guildf* 67-70; C Tulse Hill H Trin *S'wark* 70-74; C Worting *Win* 74-78; P-in-c S Lambeth St Steph *S'wark* 78-89; V 89-91; RD Lambeth 86-90; C Ches Square St Mich w St Phil *Lon* 91-97; Living Waters Trust 98-00; Chapl Ealing Hosp NHS Trust 00-01; Chapl Hammersmith Hosps NHS Trust 01-08; Chapl Imp Coll Healthcare NHS Trust from 08. *14 Goldsboro Road, London SW8 4RR* Tel (020) 7720 2301 *or* 8846 1056 E-mail lisaguinness@hotmail.com

GUINNESS, Canon Garry Grattan. b 40. Em Coll Cam BA64 MA68. Ridley Hall Cam 64. **d** 66 **p** 67. C Wallington *S'wark* 66-69; C St Marylebone All So w SS Pet and Jo *Lon* 69-72; P-in-c Clifton H Trin, St Andr and St Pet *Bris* 72-79; V Watford St Luke *St Alb* 79-90; Hon Can Kigeme from 02; rtd 05. *37 Stowell Crescent, Wareham BH20 4PT* Tel (01929) 550215

GUINNESS, Graham Alexander. b 60. Edin Th Coll 82. **d** 85 **p** 86. Dioc Youth Chapl *Mor* 85-88; C Elgin w Lossiemouth 85-88; Asst P Glas St Ninian 88-90; R Tighnabruaich *Arg* 90-91 and 94-99; R Dunoon 90-99; Miss to Seamen 90-99; R Fort William *Arg* from 99. *St Andrew's Rectory, Parade Road, Fort William PH33 6BA* Tel and fax (01397) 702979
E-mail ftwilliam@argyll.anglican.org

GUINNESS, Canon Peter Grattan. b 49. Man Univ BSc71 CertEd73. St Jo Coll Nottm 80. **d** 82 **p** 83. C Normanton *Wakef* 82-87; V Fletchamstead *Cov* 87-91; V Lancaster St Thos *Blackb* from 91; Hon Can Blackb Cathl from 04. *St Thomas's Vicarage, 33 Belle Vue Terrace, Lancaster LA1 4TY* Tel (01524) 590410 E-mail peter@st.tees.org.uk

GUINNESS, Canon Robin Gordon. b 38. St Jo Coll Cam MA61. Ridley Hall Cam 63. **d** 63 **p** 64. C Bedworth *Cov* 63-66; CMS 66-68; Canada from 68. *1243-109 Front Street East, Toronto ON M5A 4P7, Canada* E-mail rguinnness@primus.ca

GUISE, John Christopher. b 29. Cheltenham & Glouc Coll of HE MA94 MRPharmS51. WMMTC 90. **d** 83 **p** 84. NSM Alfrick, Lulsley, Suckley, Leigh and Bransford *Worc* 83-94; NSM Martley and Wichenford, Knightwick etc 94-00; Perm to Offic from 00. *Marsh Cottage, Leigh, Worcester WR6 5LE* Tel (01886) 832336

GUISE, Stephen. b 48. Win Sch of Art BA75. Chich Th Coll 85. **d** 87 **p** 88. C Bexhill St Pet *Chich* 87-90; TV Haywards Heath St Wilfrid 90-94; V Kirdford 94-97; Chapl Community of Servants of the Cross 97-01; P-in-c Amberley w N Stoke and Parham, Wiggonholt etc *Chich* 99-03; TV Bridport *Sarum* 03-07; rtd 07; Perm to Offic *Chich* 07-09; P-in-c Sidlesham from 09. *The Vicarage, Church Farm Lane, Sidlesham, Chichester PO20 7RE* Tel (01243) 641237

GUITE, Ayodeji Malcolm. b 57. Pemb Coll Cam BA80 MA84 Newc Poly PGCE82 Dur Univ PhD93. Ridley Hall Cam 88. **d** 90 **p** 91. C Ely 90-93; TV Huntingdon 93-98; Chapl Anglia Poly Univ 98-03; Chapl Girton Coll Cam from 03. *Girton College, Cambridge CB3 0JG* Tel (01223) 338999
E-mail mg320@cam.ac.uk

GUITE, Mrs Frances Clare. b 56. Leeds Univ BA08. Coll of Resurr Mirfield 06. **d** 08 **p** 09. C Westleigh St Pet *Man* from 08; C Westleigh St Paul from 09. *12 Garden Vale, Leigh WN7 5SY* Tel 07791-328624 (mobile) E-mail francesguite@yahoo.co.uk

GUITE, Canon Margaret Ann. b 53. Girton Coll Cam BA74 MA78 St Jo Coll Dur PhD81. Cranmer Hall Dur 75. **dss** 79 **d** 87 **p** 94. Warlingham w Chelsham and Farleigh *S'wark* 79-82; Cherry Hinton St Jo *Ely* 82-86; Tutor Westcott Ho Cam 82-90; Tutor Wesley Ho Cam 87-90; NSM Ely 90-93; NSM Chettisham 90-93; NSM Prickwillow 90-93; NSM Huntingdon 93-99; V Fenstanton 99-06; V Hilton 99-06; RD Huntingdon 05-06; P-in-c Cambridge St Mark from 06; Hon Can Ely Cathl from 04. *St Mark's Vicarage, 13 Barton Road, Cambridge CB3 9JZ* Tel (01223) 327621 E-mail margaret.guite@ntlworld.com

GUIVER, Paul Alfred (George). b 45. St Chad's Coll Dur BA68. Cuddesdon Coll 71. **d** 73 **p** 74. C Mill End and Heronsgate w W Hyde *St Alb* 73-76; P-in-c Bishop's Frome *Heref* 76-82; P-in-c Castle Frome 76-82; P-in-c Acton Beauchamp and Evesbatch 76-82; CR from 85; Superior from 02; Lic to Offic *Wakef* from 85. *House of the Resurrection, Stocks Bank Road, Mirfield WF14 0BN* Tel (01924) 483301
E-mail gguiver@mirfield.org.uk

GUIVER, Roger William Antony. b 53. Edin Univ MA75 St Chad's Coll Dur BA78. Coll of Resurr Mirfield. **d** 82 **p** 83. C Rekendyke *Dur* 82-85; Chapl Middlesbrough Gen Hosp 85-93; P-in-c Middlesbrough St Columba w St Paul *York* 85-94; V Acomb Moor 94-97; V Middlesbrough St Thos 97-00. *Swang Farm, Glaisdale, Whitby YO21 2QZ* Tel (01947) 897210

GULL, William John. b 42. Ripon Hall Ox 63. **d** 65 **p** 66. C Worksop Priory *S'well* 65-69; C Newark St Mary 69-71; P-in-c Mansfield St Lawr 71-77; V 77-78; Chapl HM YOI Lowdham Grange 78-90; R Lambley *S'well* 78-91; V Sneinton St Cypr 91-99; rtd 99; Perm to Offic *S'well* from 03. *37 Hazel Grove, Mapperley, Nottingham NG3 6DQ* Tel 0115-920 8071
E-mail wjgull@btopenworld.com

GULLAND, John Robertson. b 46. Open Univ BA76 Chelsea Coll Lon MA82 Avery Hill Coll CertEd70 ACIB. Oak Hill Th Coll 88. **d** 90 **p** 91. NSM Woodside Park St Barn *Lon* 90-92; Lic to Offic *S & M* 91-09; NSM Castletown 92-09; Chapl K Wm Coll 92-09; P-in-c Corfu *Eur* from 09. *21 L Mavili Street, Kerkyra, Corfu 491 00, Greece* Tel and fax (0030) (2661) 031467
E-mail holytrin@otenet.gr

GULLIDGE, Philip Michael Nowell. b 60. Univ of Wales (Swansea) BSc82 Univ of Wales (Cardiff) BD93. St Mich Coll Llan 90. **d** 93 **p** 94. C Neath w Llantwit 93-97; V Treharris w Bedlinog 97-03; V Treharris, Trelewis and Bedlinog 04-08; V Llantwit Fardre from 08. *The Vicarage, Church Village, Pontypridd CF38 1EP* Tel (01443) 202538
E-mail philipgullidge@aol.com

GULLIFORD, Mrs Susan Diane. b 49. W Midl Coll of Educn BEd86. WMMTC 97. **d** 00 **p** 01. NSM Tettenhall Regis *Lich* 00-02; C Wednesfield 02-04; Perm to Offic from 04. *2 James Street, Willenhall WV13 1SS*
E-mail sue.gulliford@btinternet.com

GULLIFORD, William Douglas FitzGerald. b 69. Selw Coll Cam BA91 MA95. Westcott Ho Cam. **d** 94 **p** 95. C Banstead *Guildf* 94-97; C Wilton Place St Paul *Lon* 97-00; Chapl Guildhall Sch of Music and Drama 97-01; P-in-c St Dunstan in the West 00-08; V from 08; Gen Sec Angl and E Churches Assn from 00; Bp's Chapl *Lon* 00-02; R St Mary le Strand w St Clem Danes 02-08; Dioc Bp's Chapl for E Orthodox Affairs from 02; Dir of Ords *Eur* from 03. *184A Fleet Street, London EC4A 2HD* Tel and fax (020) 7405 1929 E-mail william.gulliford@london.anglican.org

GULLY, Mrs Carol Glenys. b 57. Coll of Ripon & York St Jo BEd79. NOC 02. **d** 05 **p** 06. NSM Castleton Moor *Man* 05-09; NSM Kirkholt from 09. *Oakenrod and Bamford Vicarage, 389 Bury and Rochdale Old Road, Heywood OL10 4AT* Tel (01706) 369610 E-mail revdcggully@aol.com

GULLY, Paul David. b 59. Shoreditch Coll Lon BEd81. Trin Coll Bris BA95. **d** 95 **p** 96. C Radcliffe *Man* 95-99; TV New Bury 99-05; V Oakenrod and Bamford from 05. *Oakenrod and Bamford Vicarage, 389 Bury and Rochdale Old Road, Heywood OL10 4AT* Tel (01706) 369610 E-mail revdpaulgully@aol.com

GULVIN, Philip Christopher. b 53. BSc76. St Jo Coll Nottm 82. **d** 85 **p** 86. C Northwood H Trin *Lon* 85-89; TV Sanderstead All SS *S'wark* 89-96; V Croydon St Matt 96-99; C W Wickham St Fran 99-02; C W Wickham St Fran and St Mary 02-04; rtd 04. *2 Ellis Close, Five Oak Green, Tonbridge TN12 6PQ*
E-mail gulvins@tiscali.co.uk

GUMBEL, Jonathan Philip. b 82. **d** 09. C Brighton St Pet *Chich* from 09. *Address temp unknown* E-mail brighton@htb.org.uk

GUMBEL, Nicholas Glyn Paul. b 55. Trin Coll Cam MA76. Wycliffe Hall Ox MA86. **d** 86 **p** 87. C Brompton H Trin w Onslow Square St Paul *Lon* 86-05; V from 05. *Holy Trinity Vicarage, 73 Princes Gate Mews, London SW7 2PP* Tel (020) 7052 0263 *or* 7052 0264 Fax 7589 3390
E-mail roslyn.dehaan@htb.org.uk

GUMMER, Dudley Harrison. b 28. Roch Th Coll 61. **d** 63 **p** 64. C Deptford St Paul *S'wark* 63-65; C Melton Mowbray w Thorpe Arnold *Leic* 65-68; C-in-c E Goscote CD 68-75; V E Goscote 75-78; V Luton St Anne *St Alb* 78-88; R Albury w St Martha *Guildf* 88-95; rtd 95; Perm to Offic *Chich* from 95 and *Portsm* from 03. *Wyndham House, The Gardens, West Ashling, Chichester PO18 8DX* Tel (01243) 573002

GUNASEKERA, Nilanka Keith (Kit). b 72. Ridley Hall Cam 04. **d** 06 **p** 07. C Brentford *Lon* from 06. *34 Brook Road South, Brentford TW8 0NN* Tel 07968-591695 (mobile)
E-mail kit_gunasekera@yahoo.com

GUNN, Jeffrey Thomas. b 47. St Chad's Coll Dur BA77 Kent Univ MA95. Coll of Resurr Mirfield 77. **d** 79 **p** 80. C Prestbury *Glouc* 79-82; P-in-c Coldham, Elm and Friday Bridge *Ely* 82-87; V Larkfield *Roch* 87-94; P-in-c Leybourne 87-94; V Petts Wood 94-99; Dean Ballarat Australia 99-04; V Eastbourne St Sav and St Pet *Chich* from 05. *St Saviour's Vicarage, Spencer Road, Eastbourne BN21 4PA* Tel (01323) 722317

GUNN, Robert. b 35. Oak Hill Th Coll 59. **d** 62 **p** 63. C Upper Holloway St Jo *Lon* 62-66; C Woking St Jo *Guildf* 66-69; Scripture Union 69-71; R Necton w Holme Hale *Nor* 71-77; V Tottenham St Jo *Lon* 77-81; V Gt Cambridge Road St Jo and St Jas 82-85; V Luton St Fran *St Alb* 85-90; Chapl Luton

Airport 90-95; rtd 95; Perm to Offic *St Alb* from 95. *95 Edgewood Drive, Luton LU2 8ER* Tel (01582) 416151

GUNN-JOHNSON, The Ven David Allan. b 49. Lambeth STh85 MA95. St Steph Ho Ox 79. **d** 81 **p** 82. C Oxhey St Matt *St Alb* 81-84; C Cheshunt 84-88; TR Colyton, Southleigh, Offwell, Widworthy etc *Ex* 88-03; RD Honiton 90-96; Preb Ex Cathl 99-03; Adn Barnstaple from 03; Dioc Warden of Readers from 04. *Stage Cross, Sanders Lane, Bishops Tawton, Barnstaple EX32 0BE* Tel (01271) 375475 Fax 377934
E-mail archdeacon.of.barnstaple@exeter.anglican.org

GUNNER, Canon Laurence François Pascal. b 36. Keble Coll Ox BA59 MA63. Wells Th Coll 59. **d** 61 **p** 62. C Charlton Kings St Mary *Glouc* 61-65; C Hemel Hempstead *St Alb* 65-69; Hd RE Adeyfield Secondary Modern Sch 67-69; Chapl Bloxham Sch 69-86; Chapl Tudor Hall Sch 70-84; Sen Chapl Marlborough Coll 86-96; Can Windsor 96-06; Can Steward 97-06; rtd 06. *Contin Mains, Contin, Strathpeffer IV14 9ES* Tel and fax (01997) 421996 Mobile 07836-369729
E-mail laurence@gunner.co.uk

GUNNER, Mrs Susanna Mary. b 58. St Jo Coll Dur BA80 SS Coll Cam PGCE81. ERMC 05. **d** 08 **p** 09. C N Walsham and Edingthorpe *Nor* from 08; Dioc Lay Development Co-ord from 07. *36 Vicarage Street, North Walsham NR28 9DQ* Tel (01692) 405501 E-mail susanna.ainsworth@ukonline.co.uk

GUNSTONE, Canon John Thomas Arthur. b 27. St Chad's Coll Dur BA48 MA55. Coll of Resurr Mirfield 50. **d** 52 **p** 53. C Walthamstow St Jas *Gt Chelmsf* 52-53; C Forest Gate St Edm 53-58; C-in-c Rush Green St Aug CD 58-71; Chapl Barn Fellowship Winterborne Whitechurch 71-75; Tutor Sarum & Wells Th Coll 71-75; Sec Gtr Man Co Ecum Coun 75-80; Lic to Offic *Man* 75-80; Hon Can Man Cathl 80-92; rtd 92; Perm to Offic *Man* 03. *12 Deneford Road, Didsbury, Manchester M20 2TD* Tel 0161-434 8351

GUNTER, Timothy Wilson. b 37. Leeds Univ BA59 St Jo Coll Cam BA62 MA66. Ridley Hall Cam 59. **d** 62 **p** 63. C Beverley Minster *York* 62-65; C Hornsea and Goxhill 65-70; V Silsden *Bradf* 70-80; V Sunninghill *Ox* 80-03; rtd 03; Perm to Offic *Worc* from 04. *2 Hillstone Court, Victoria Road, Malvern WR14 2TE* Tel (01684) 899377 E-mail gunters@gmail.com

GURD, Brian Charles (Simon). b 44. Sarum & Wells Th Coll 72. **d** 74 **p** 75. OSP from 67; Lic to Offic *Win* 74-82; Prior Alton Abbey 79-82; C Shepherd's Bush St Steph w St Thos *Lon* 82-84; NSM Willesborough *Cant* 85-87; V Bethersden w High Halden 87-95; R Etchingham and V Hurst Green 95-97; V Langney 97-01; R Yarm *York* from 01. *The Rectory, 6 Westgate, Yarm TS15 9QT* Tel (01642) 781115

GURDON, Mrs June Mary. b 38. Sarum Th Coll 83. **dss** 85 **d** 87 **p** 94. Jersey St Sav *Win* 85-86; Jersey St Mary 86-88; Par Dn 87-88; Par Dn Jersey St Brelade 88-94; C 94-00; rtd 00; Perm to Offic *Win* from 00. *Dower House Alfriston, La Route d'Ebenezer, Trinity, Jersey JE3 3EH* Tel (01534) 863245 Mobile 07797 736280

GURNER (formerly RAVEN), Mrs Margaret Ann. b 54. Westmr Univ BSc76 City Univ MSc87. Ridley Hall Cam 03. **d** 05 **p** 06. C Woodhall Spa Gp *Linc* 05-08; P-in-c Cheveley 05-08; P-in-c Wood Ditton w Saxon Street from 08; P-in-c Kirtling from 08; P-in-c Ashley w Silverley from 08. *The Rectory, 132 High Street, Cheveley, Newmarket CB8 9DG* Tel (01638) 730770
E-mail ann.raven@btopenworld.com

GURNEY, Miss Ann. b 27. Lambeth STh92. Gilmore Ho 45. **dss** 54 **d** 87 **p** 94. Lewisham St Jo Southend *S'wark* 54-56; Warden Berridge Ho Coll of Educn 56-59; Prin Gilmore Ho 59-70; Bp's Adv for Lay Min *Lon* 70-87; rtd 87; Hon C Eltham H Trin *S'wark* 94-98; Perm to Offic from 98. *3 Brecon Court, Greenacres, London SE9 5BG* Tel (020) 8850 4083

GURNEY, Canon Dennis Albert John. b 31. OBE02. Lon Coll of Div. **d** 67 **p** 68. C Boscombe St Jo *Win* 67-69; V Hurstbourne Tarrant and Faccombe 70-77; R Jersey St Ouen w St Geo 77-84; Hon Chapl Miss to Seafarers from 84; Chapl ICS UAE 84-01; Can Bahrain from 98; rtd 01; Perm to Offic *Ex* and *B & W* from 02. *3 Stevens Cross Close, Sidford, Sidmouth EX10 9QJ* Tel (01395) 515362 Mobile 07789-111226
E-mail dennis.gurney@.virgin.net

GURR, Mrs Mary Sandra. b 42. SAOMC 95. **d** 98 **p** 99. C Easthampstead *Ox* 98-02; TV High Wycombe from 02. *The Vicarage, 245 Micklefield Road, High Wycombe HP13 7HU* Tel (01494) 520323
E-mail marygurr@stmichaelshouse.freeserve.co.uk

GURR, Stephen John. b 72. Kent Univ BA94. Trin Coll Bris MLitt97. **d** 97 **p** 98. C Ore St Helen and St Barn *Chich* 97-00; C Goring-by-Sea 00-03; V Findon w Clapham and Patching 03-06; Chapl St Barn Ho Worthing from 07; Chapl Chestnut Tree Ho Arundel from 07. *St Barnabas House, Columbia Drive, Worthing BN13 2QF* Tel (01903) 534030

GUSH, Laurence Langley. b 23. Lon Univ BSc44. NW Ord Course 73. **d** 76 **p** 77. NSM Sheff St Matt 76-82; NSM Aston cum Aughton 82-84; NSM Aston cum Aughton and Ulley 84-89; rtd 89. *3 New Court, Eyam, Hope Valley S32 5RL* Tel (01433) 631818

GUSSMAN, Canon Robert William Spencer Lockhart. b 50. Ch Ch Ox BA72 MA76. Coll of Resurr Mirfield BA74. **d** 75 **p** 76. C Pinner *Lon* 75-79; C Northolt St Jos 79-81; P-in-c Sutton *Ely* 81-82; V 82-89; P-in-c Witcham w Mepal 81-82; R 82-89; RD Ely 86-89; V Alton St Lawr *Win* 89-02; Hon Can Win Cathl 99-02; rtd 02; Perm to Offic *Win* from 02. *6A Patrick's Close, Liss GU33 7ER* Tel (01730) 893545

GUTHRIE, Adrian Malcolm. b 57. Goldsmiths' Coll Lon BEd80. Wycliffe Hall Ox 01. **d** 03 **p** 04. C Ickenham *Lon* 03-05; R from 05. *St Giles's Rectory, 38 Swakeley's Road, Ickenham, Uxbridge UB10 8BE* Tel (01895) 622970 E-mail am.guthrie@virgin.net

GUTHRIE, Nigel. b 60. Bris Univ BA82 LRAM78 ARCO80 ARCM81. Ripon Coll Cuddesdon BA87 MA91. **d** 88 **p** 89. C Cov St Jo 88-91; Chapl Cov Cathl 91-94; V Chellaston *Derby* 94-02; RD Melbourne 99-02; R Crediton, Shobrooke and Sandford etc *Ex* from 02. *The Rectory, Church Street, Crediton EX17 2AQ* Tel (01363) 772669 or 773226
E-mail rev.guthrie@btinternet.com

GUTSELL, Canon David Leonard Nicholas. b 35. Sheff Univ BA59. ALCD61. **d** 61 **p** 62. C Clapham Common St Barn *S'wark* 61-65; V Upper Tulse Hill St Matthias 65-76; RD Clapham and Brixton 74-75; V Patcham *Chich* 76-93; Can and Preb Chich Cathl 89-00; V Polegate 93-00; rtd 00; C Peacehaven and Telscombe Cliffs *Chich* 01-05; C Southease 01-05; C Piddinghoe 01-05; Perm to Offic from 05. *6 Solway Avenue, Brighton BN1 8UJ* Tel (01273) 554434
E-mail davidgutsell@googlemail.com

GUTSELL, Eric Leslie. b 44. Goldsmiths' Coll Lon TCert65. Ox NSM Course 79. **d** 82 **p** 83. NSM Gt Faringdon w Lt Coxwell *Ox* 82-88; NSM Shrivenham w Watchfield and Bourton 82-99; Asst Chapl HM Pris Wormwood Scrubs 99-00; Chapl HM Pris Coldingley 00-03; Chapl HM Pris Erlestoke 03-04; rtd 04; Perm to Offic *Ox* from 05. *54 Folly View Road, Faringdon SN7 7DH* Tel (01367) 240886 E-mail ericgutsell@virgin.net

GUTTERIDGE, David Frank. b 39. Man Univ BSc61 Lon Inst of Educn PGCE62 DipEd67 Birkbeck Coll Lon MSc73. WMMTC 82. **d** 85 **p** 87. NSM Droitwich *Worc* 85-87; NSM Droitwich Spa 87-93; C Shrawley, Witley, Astley and Abberley 93-98; Chapl Abberley Hall Sch Worc 93-97; Dioc Tertiary Educn Officer *Worc* 97-99; NSM Ombersley w Doverdale 98-99; TV Malvern Link w Cowleigh 99-02; rtd 02. *79 Tan House Lane, Malvern WR14 1LQ* Tel (01886) 833578
E-mail dgutteridge@cofe-worcester.org.uk

GUTTERIDGE, John. b 34. Oak Hill Th Coll 60. **d** 63 **p** 64. C Deptford St Luke *S'wark* 63-66; C Southgate *Chich* 66-70; P-in-c Brixton Road Ch Ch *S'wark* 70-73; P-in-c Manuden w Berden *Chelmsf* 73-76; Distr Sec (N Lon, Herts and Essex) BFBS 76-82; Hon C Walthamstow St Gabr 79-82; V 82-95; Chapl Thorpe Coombe Psycho-Geriatric Hosp 83-95; rtd 95; Perm to Offic *Chelmsf* from 95. *52 Hatch Road, Pilgrims Hatch, Brentwood CM15 9PX* Tel (01277) 375401
E-mail john_gutteridge@hotmail.com

GUTTERIDGE, John Philip. b 52. QUB BA74. Chich Th Coll 75. **d** 78 **p** 79. C Leeds St Aid *Ripon* 78-82; C Manston 82-85; P-in-c Beeston Hill H Spirit 85-00; Perm to Offic from 03. *4 Amberton Garth, Leeds LS8 3JW*

GUTTRIDGE (née EVANS), Mrs Frances Margaret Bethan. b 54. Reading Univ BSc75 Univ of Wales (Cardiff) PGCE76. STETS. **d** 00 **p** 01. C Weston-super-Mare St Andr Bournville *B & W* 00-04; V 04-09; C St Decumans from 09; C Williton from 09. *47 Brendon Road, Watchet TA23 0HU* Tel (01984) 631103 Mobile 07778-137454 E-mail bethanguttridge@hotmail.com

GUTTRIDGE, John Arthur. b 26. Trin Hall Cam BA51 MA55. Westcott Ho Cam 51. **d** 53 **p** 54. C Rugby St Andr *Cov* 53-59; Lect Wells Th Coll 59-61; Chapl 61-63; Vice-Prin 63-66; Bp's Dom Chapl *Wakef* 66-68; Dir Post-Ord Tr 66-68; Dir of Further Tr *Dur* 68-74; Dir Studies Sarum & Wells Th Coll 74-78; C Bilston St Leon *Lich* 78-79; TV Bilston 80-84; V Wall 84-90; V Stonnall 84-90; rtd 91. *The Charterhouse, Charterhouse Square, London EC1M 6AN* Tel (020) 7251 6357

GUY, Mrs Alison. b 43. CQSW69. WMMTC 95. **d** 98 **p** 99. NSM Minchinhampton *Glouc* 98-04; C Bisley, Chalford, France Lynch, and Oakridge 04-08. *7 Tooke Road, Minchinhampton, Stroud GL6 9DA* Tel (01453) 883906
E-mail alisonguy@metronet.co.uk

GUY, Ian Towers. b 47. Newc Univ MB, BS70 MSc89 MRCGP. NEOC. **d** 83 **p** 84. NSM Saltburn-by-the-Sea *York* 83-88; NSM Skelton w Upleatham 88-92; Perm to Offic from 92. *14 North Terrace, Skelton-in-Cleveland, Saltburn-by-the-Sea TS12 2ES* Tel (01287) 650309 Mobile 07092-298033
E-mail ian.guy@gp-a81630.nhs.uk

GUY, John Richard. *See* MORGAN-GUY, John Richard

GUY, Kate Anne. b 26. **d** 88 **p** 94. OLM Welton *Linc* 88-92; OLM Welton and Dunholme w Scothern 92-96; Perm to Offic 96-02. *2 Eastfield Close, Welton, Lincoln LN2 3NB* Tel (01673) 860285

GUY, Peter-John. b 71. Bournemouth Univ BA93. Oak Hill Th Coll BA03. **d** 03 **p** 04. C Eastbourne All So *Chich* 03-07; C

Lindfield from 07. *46 Noahs Ark Lane, Lindfield, Haywards Heath RH16 2LT* Tel (01444) 487866
E-mail pjgerdaguy@hotmail.com

GUY, Simon Edward Walrond. b 39. St Andr Univ MA61. St D Coll Lamp LTh67. **d** 67 **p** 68. C Bris St Mary Redcliffe w Temple etc 67-68; C Knowle St Martin 68-71; C Bishopston 71-75; V Westwood *Sarum* 75-81; TV Melksham 81-82; TV Wednesfield *Lich* 82-90; R Heaton Moor *Man* 90-02; P-in-c Heaton Norris Ch w All SS 99-01; TV Heatons 02-04; rtd 04. *1 Holley Close, Exminster, Exeter EX6 8SS* Tel (01392) 823084
E-mail sewguy@supanet.com

GUYANA, Bishop of. See GEORGE, The Rt Revd Randolph Oswald

GUYMER, Canon Raymond John. b 41. AKC64. St Boniface Warminster. **d** 65 **p** 66. C W Bromwich All SS *Lich* 65-70; Chapl HM Pris Wormwood Scrubs 70-71 and 84-93; Chapl HM Borstal Portland 71-78; Chapl HM Youth Cust Cen Hollesley Bay Colony 78-84; Chapl HM Pris Win 93-01; Hon C Upper Itchen *Win* 02-06; Hon Can Win Cathl 99-06; rtd 06. *16 St Mary's Gardens, Hilperton Marsh, Trowbridge BA14 7PG* Tel (01225) 751063

GUZEK, Mrs Bridget Louise. b 47. York Univ BA70 Keswick Hall Coll PGCE79. STETS 05. **d** 08 **p** 09. NSM E Clevedon w Clapton in Gordano etc *B & W* from 08. *16 Woodlands Road, Clevedon BS21 7QD* E-mail bridgetguzek@blueyonder.co.uk

GWILLIAM, Christopher. b 44. St Chad's Coll Dur BA65. **d** 67 **p** 68. C Chepstow *Mon* 67-70; C Risca 70-72; V Cwmtillery 72-75; V Hartlepool St Oswald *Dur* 75-82; Relig Progr Producer Radio Tees 82-87; C Stockton w St Jo 82-83; R Longnewton w Elton 83-87; Relig Progr Producer Radio Nottm *S'well* 87-93; Relig Progr Producer BBC Network Radio 93-95; rtd 04. *Les Perreaux, 71140 Maltat, France* Tel (0033) (3) 85 84 87 57
E-mail christopher.gwilliam@googlemail.com

GWILLIAMS, Canon Dianna Lynn. b 57. California Univ BA78 K Coll Lon MA01. S'wark Ord Course 89. **d** 92 **p** 94. NSM Peckham St Sav *S'wark* 92-97; C Dulwich St Barn 97-99; V from 99; P-in-c Peckham St Sav from 07; AD Dulwich from 05; Hon Can S'wark Cathl from 06; Dean of Women's Min from 09; Chapl Alleyn's Foundn Dulwich from 99. *St Barnabas's Vicarage, 38 Calton Avenue, London SE21 7DG* Tel (020) 8693 1524 *or* 8693 2936 Fax 8693 0203
E-mail dianna.gwilliams@stbarnabasdulwich.org

GWILLIM, Allan John. b 51. Coll of Resurr Mirfield 87. **d** 89 **p** 90. C Skerton St Luke *Blackb* 89-94; P-in-c Ellel 94-98; V Fleetwood St Pet 98-06; V Leyland St Jas 06-08; V Ocker Hill *Lich* from 08. *St Mark's Vicarage, Ocker Hill Road, Tipton DY4 0UT* Tel 0121-556 0678
E-mail allan.gwillim@btinternet.com

GWILT, Stephen Gary. b 59. **d** 88 **p** 89. S Africa 88-94; Chapl Glouc Docks Mariners' Ch 95-00; C Moreton *Ches* 00-03; R High Halstow w All Hallows and Hoo St Mary *Roch* from 03. *The Rectory, 2 Cooling Road, High Halstow, Rochester ME3 8SA* Tel (01634) 250637

GWINN, Brian Harvey. b 35. MIQA75. St Alb Minl Tr Scheme 83. **d** 86 **p** 87. NSM Wheathampstead *St Alb* 86-88; Ind Chapl 88-95; RD Hatfield 93-95; P-in-c Watton at Stone 95-99; P-in-c Bramfield w Stapleford and Waterford 96-99; R Bramfield, Stapleford, Waterford etc 99-01; rtd 01; Perm to Offic *St Alb* from 01. *32 Wick Avenue, Wheathampstead, St Albans AL4 8QB* Tel (01582) 629903 Mobile 07966-469754
E-mail gwinns@ntlworld.com

GWYNN, Phillip John. b 57. Univ of Wales BA87. St Mich Coll Llan 87. **d** 89 **p** 90. C Clydach *S & B* 89-93; V Swansea St Thos and Kilvey 93-00; Hon Chapl Miss to Seafarers 93-00; V Tycoch *S & B* from 00; Chapl Swansea NHS Trust from 00. *The Vicarage, 26 Hendrefoilan Road, Swansea SA2 9LS* Tel and fax (01792) 204476 Mobile 07946-351787
E-mail rev.gwynn@virgin.net

GWYNNE, Robert Durham. b 44. Qu Coll Birm 67. **d** 70 **p** 72. C N Hammersmith St Kath *Lon* 70-75; C Ramsey *Ely* 76-78; TV Old Brumby *Linc* 78-81; P-in-c Goxhill and Thornton Curtis 81-83; C Edmonton All SS w St Mich *Lon* 83-84; rtd 86. *127 Eastfield Road, Louth LN11 7AS* Tel (01507) 600966

GWYTHER, Canon Geoffrey David. b 51. St D Coll Lamp. **d** 74 **p** 75. C Pembroke Dock *St D* 74-77; C Milford Haven 77-81; V Llawhaden w Bletherston and Llanycefn 81-88; R Prendergast w Rudbaxton from 88; AD Daugleddau from 01; Can St D Cathl from 01. *Prendergast Rectory, 5 Cherry Grove, Haverfordwest SA61 2NT* Tel (01437) 762625

GWYTHER, Ronald Lloyd. b 23. Lon Univ BA85 Southn Univ MA97. St Fran Coll Brisbane ThL47. **d** 47 **p** 48. Australia 48-50; Perm to Offic *Ox* 50-51; Australia 51-56; C Broadstairs *Cant* 56-60; R Pinxton *Derby* 60-73; CF (TA) 71-88; V Swanley St Mary *Roch* 73-89; rtd 89; Perm to Offic *Portsm* from 89. *St Helen's, 20 Maylings Farm Road, Fareham PO16 7QU* Tel (01329) 230990

GYLE, Alan Gordon. b 65. Aber Univ MA87 Ox Univ BA91 Univ of E Lon MA09 FRSA99. St Steph Ho Ox. **d** 92 **p** 93. C Acton Green *Lon* 92-94; Min Can, Succ and Dean's V Windsor 94-99;

Chapl Imp Coll and R Coll of Art 99-04; P-in-c Wilton Place St Paul *Lon* 01-03; V from 03; PV Westmr Abbey from 07; Dir Development Two Cities Area *Lon* from 08. *St Paul's Vicarage, 32 Wilton Place, London SW1X 8SH* Tel and fax (020) 7201 9990 *or* tel 7201 9999 E-mail alan@stpaulsknightsbridge.org

GYLES, Ms Sonia. b 76. TCD BTh01. CITC 98. **d** 01 **p** 02. C Taney *D & G* 01-04; I Dublin Sandford w Milltown from 04. *The Rectory, Sandford Close, Ranelagh, Dublin 6, Republic of Ireland* Tel (00353) (1) 497 2983 Fax 496 4789
E-mail sandford@dublin.anglican.org

H

HAARHOFF, Robert Russell. b 46. St Paul's Coll Grahamstown 89 Th Ext Educn Coll 91. **d** 90 **p** 91. Zimbabwe 91-02; Harare Cathl 91-94; I Makonde 94-02; P-in-c Astley, Clive, Grinshill and Hadnall *Lich* from 02; RD Wem and Whitchurch from 08. *The Vicarage, Shrewsbury Road, Hadnall, Shrewsbury SY4 4AG* Tel (01939) 210241 E-mail robhaarhoff@tiscali.co.uk

HABERMEHL, Canon Kenneth Charles. b 22. Em Coll Cam BA46 MA48. Chich Th Coll 47. **d** 49 **p** 50. C Luton St Chris Round Green CD *St Alb* 49-53; C Luton Ch Ch 53-56; V Caddington 56-65; V Kempston All SS 65-87; Hon Can St Alb 81-87; rtd 87; Perm to Offic *St Alb* 87-93 and from 00. *34 Bedford Road, Aspley Guise, Milton Keynes MK17 8DH* Tel (01908) 584710

HABERSHON, Kenneth Willoughby. b 35. MBE01. New Coll Ox BA57 MA60. Wycliffe Hall Ox 57. **d** 59 **p** 60. C Finchley Ch Ch *Lon* 59-66; Sec CYFA 66-74; CPAS Staff 74-90; Hon C Slaugham *Chich* from 84; Ldr Mayfield CYFA 90-00; Sec Ch Patr Trust 90-07; Sec Peache Trustees from 90; rtd 00. *Truckers Ghyll, Horsham Road, Handcross, Haywards Heath RH17 6DT* Tel (01444) 400274 E-mail kandmhab@btopenworld.com

✠**HABGOOD, The Rt Revd and Rt Hon Lord (John Stapylton).** b 27. PC83. K Coll Cam BA48 MA51 PhD52 Dur Univ Hon DD75 Cam Univ Hon DD84 Aber Univ Hon DD88 Huron Coll Hon DD90. Cuddesdon Coll 53. **d** 54 **p** 55 **c** 73. C Kensington St Mary Abbots w St Geo *Lon* 54-56; Vice-Prin Westcott Ho Cam 56-62; R Jedburgh *Edin* 62-67; Prin Qu Coll Birm 67-73; Hon Can Birm Cathl 71-73; Bp Dur 73-83; Abp York 83-95; rtd 95. *18 The Mount, Malton YO17 7ND*

HABGOOD, Simon. See LAWRENCE, Simon Peter

HABGOOD, Stephen Roy. b 52. Open Univ MBA95 Fitzw Coll Cam MSt01. St Mich Coll Llan 75. **d** 77 **p** 78. C Whitchurch *Llan* 77-80; Perm to Offic *Worc* 85-91. *Yew Tree Cottage, Wharf Road, Gnosall, Stafford ST20 0DA* Tel (01785) 824244

HABIBY, Canon Samir Jamil. b 33. Phillips Univ BA55 MA56. Ch Div Sch of Pacific MDiv58 Episc Th Sem Kentucky DD. **d** 58 **p** 59. R Hinesville St Phil USA 58-98 and from 04; P-in-c Lausanne *Eur* 98-04; rtd 04. *24 Sawyers Crossing Road, Swanzey NH 03446, USA* Tel and fax (001) (603) 357 8778

HACK, Arthur John. b 52. Bris Univ BEd75 St Paul's Cheltenham CertEd74. **d** 08 **p** 09. NSM Alstonfield, Butterton, Ilam etc *Lich* from 08; Warden Dovedale Ho from 89. *Dovedale House, Ilam, Ashbourne DE6 2AZ* Tel (01335) 350365 Mobile 07749-294386
E-mail warden@dovedalehouse.org.uk

HACK, Canon Rex Hereward. b 28. ACA56 FCA67 Pemb Coll Cam BA50 MA56. Ripon Hall Ox 58. **d** 59 **p** 60. C Ashton-upon-Mersey St Mary Magd *Ches* 59-62; C Ellesmere Port 62-65; V Norton Cuckney *S'well* 65-69; V Bramhall *Ches* 69-93; RD Cheadle 87-92; Hon Can Ches Cathl 90-93; rtd 93; Perm to Offic *Ches* from 93. *Marshmead, 8A Pownall Avenue, Bramhall, Stockport SK7 2HE* Tel 0161-439 0300

✠**HACKER, The Rt Revd George Lanyon.** b 28. Ex Coll Ox BA52 MA56. Cuddesdon Coll 52. **d** 54 **p** 55 **c** 79. C Bris St Mary Redcliffe w Temple 54-59; Chapl St Boniface Coll Warminster 59-64; V Bishopwearmouth Gd Shep *Dur* 64-71; R Tilehurst St Mich *Ox* 71-79; Suff Bp Penrith *Carl* 79-94; Hon Can Carl Cathl 79-94; Episc Adv for the Angl Young People's Assn 87-94; rtd 94; Hon Asst Bp Carl from 94. *Keld House, Milburn, Penrith CA10 1TW* Tel (01768) 361506
E-mail bishhack@btopenworld.com

HACKER HUGHES, Katherine Lucy. b 60. York Univ BA81. Westcott Ho Cam 90. **d** 92 **p** 94. Par Dn S Woodham Ferrers *Chelmsf* 92-94; C 94-95; NSM Maldon All SS w St Pet 95-98; Chapl Chelmsf Cathl 98-01; P-in-c Gt Waltham w Ford End 01-05; Adv relationship and family issues (Bradwell Area) 01-03; Perm to Offic *Chelmsf* from 06; Chapl Mid-Essex Hosp Services NHS Trust 06-07; Chapl Farleigh Hospice from 07. *1 Swiss Avenue, Chelmsford CM1 2AD* Tel (01245) 600969 *or* 457300
E-mail katyhh@lineone.net

HACKETT, Bryan Malcolm. b 66. Magd Coll Ox BA88 MA93 Cam Univ BA92 MA03. Westcott Ho Cam 90. **d** 93 **p** 94. C Willington *Newc* 93-97; TV Radcliffe *Man* 97-03; P-in-c Prestwich St Mary from 03. *The Rectory, Church Lane, Prestwich, Manchester M25 1AN* Tel 0161-773 2912
E-mail bryan.hackett@btinternet.com

HACKETT, Canon Frank James. b 33. Birm Univ MA77 AMIMechE68 MBIM72 MIIM79. Bps' Coll Cheshunt 62. **d** 64 **p** 65. C Feltham *Lon* 64-69; Ind Chapl *Lich* 69-73; Ind Chapl Port of Lon *Chelmsf* 73-98; P-in-c N Ockendon 79-93; Hon Can Chelmsf Cathl 93-98; Ind Chapl *Chelmsf* 93-98; rtd 98; Perm to Offic *Lon* 98-02 and from 05; *Chelmsf* from 99. *11 Fairfield Avenue, Upminster RM14 3AZ* Tel (01708) 221461

HACKETT, Glyndwr. See HACKETT, The Ven Ronald Glyndwr

HACKETT, John Nigel. b 32. Trin Hall Cam BA55 MA59. Ely Th Coll. **d** 59 **p** 60. C Handsworth St Mary *Birm* 59-66; V Handsworth St Jas 66-82; P-in-c Balsall Common 82-83; V 83-95; Perm to Offic *B & W* from 96; rtd 97. *Honeymead, Duck Lane, Kenn, Clevedon BS21 6TP* Tel (01275) 876591

HACKETT, Peter Edward. b 25. Magd Coll Ox BA48 MA51 ALCD60. **d** 60 **p** 61. C Lenton *S'well* 60-62; C Attenborough w Bramcote 62-63; V Lenton Abbey 63-67; R Acton Beauchamp and Evesbatch w Stanford Bishop *Heref* 67-71; V Choral Heref Cathl 72-76; P-in-c St Weonards w Orcop 76-79; P-in-c Tretire w Michaelchurch and Pencoyd 76-79; P-in-c Garway 76-79; P-in-c Welsh Newton w Llanrothal 77-79; V Rounds Green *Birm* 79-87; C Sutton Coldfield H Trin 87-90; rtd 90; NSM Shipton Moyne w Westonbirt and Lasborough *Glouc* 91-94; Perm to Offic *Birm* and *Worc* 94-99; *Heref* from 00. *96 The Pastures, Lower Bullingham, Hereford HR2 6EX* Tel (01432) 272462

HACKETT, The Ven Ronald Glyndwr. b 47. Hatf Coll Dur BA70. Cuddesdon Coll 70. **d** 72 **p** 73. C Pembroke St Mary w St Mich *St D* 72-75; C Bassaleg *Mon* 75-78; V Blaenavon w Capel Newydd 78-84; Chapl R Gwent Hosp 84-90; V Newport St Paul *Mon* 84-90; V Newport Ch Ch 90-01; Adn Mon 01-08; R Mamhilad and Llanfihangel Pontymoile 01-03; R Mamhilad w Monkswood and Glascoed Chapel 03-08; Adn Newport from 08. *The Archdeaconry, 93 Stow Hill, Newport NP20 4EA* Tel (01633) 215012
E-mail archdeacon.newport@churchinwales.org.uk

HACKETT, Victoria Anne. b 52. St Gabr Coll Lon CertEd73 Open Univ BA91. SEITE 97. **d** 00 **p** 01. NSM Earlsfield St Andr *S'wark* from 00. *40 Freshford Street, London SW18 3TF* Tel (020) 8947 3755 E-mail v.ah@btopenworld.com

HACKING, Philip Henry. b 31. St Pet Hall Ox BA53 MA57. Oak Hill Th Coll 53. **d** 55 **p** 56. C St Helens St Helen *Liv* 55-58; C-in-c Edin St Thos 59-68; V Fulwood *Sheff* 68-97; rtd 97; Perm to Offic *Sheff* from 98. *61 Sefton Court, Sefton Road, Sheffield S10 3TT* Tel 0114 230 1321

HACKING, Rodney Douglas. b 53. K Coll Lon BD74 AKC74 Man Univ MA83. St Aug Coll Cant 75. **d** 76 **p** 78. C Byker St Mich *Newc* 76-77; C Eltham St Jo *S'wark* 77-79; Ind Chapl *Ripon* 80-85; R Upwell St Pet and Outwell *Ely* 85-88; Vice Prin S Dios Minl Tr Scheme 89-93; V Bolton-le-Sands *Blackb* 93-97; R The Wainfleet Gp *Linc* 03-06; rtd 06. *16 Eskrigge Court, Lancaster LA1 2LA* Tel (01524) 32884
E-mail rdnyhacking@aol.com

HACKING, Stuart Peter. b 60. St Pet Coll Ox BA82 MA. Oak Hill Th Coll 83. **d** 85 **p** 86. C Shipley St Pet *Bradf* 85-88; C Darfield *Sheff* 88-91; V Thornton St Jas *Bradf* 91-00; P-in-c Frizinghall St Marg from 00. *7 Redbeck Vale, Shipley BD18 3BN* Tel (01274) 580166 Fax (07020) 972854
E-mail stuart.hacking@bradford.anglican.org

HACKL, Aileen Patricia. b 41. Wycliffe Hall Ox 00. **d** 01 **p** 02. C Vienna *Eur* 01-09; NSM from 09. *Hardtmuthgasse 28/3/20, A-1100 Vienna, Austria* Tel and fax (0043) (1) 600 3083
E-mail aileen_hackl@hotmail.com

HACKNEY, Archdeacon of. See DENNEN, The Ven Lyle

HACKSHALL, Brian Leonard. b 33. K Coll Lon BD53 AKC53. **d** 57 **p** 58. C Portsea St Mary *Portsm* 57-62; C Westbury-on-Trym St Alb *Bris* 62-64; V Avonmouth St Andr 64-71; Miss to Seamen 71-79; C Crawley *Chich* 79; TV 79-98; Ind Chapl 89-98; rtd 98. *5 St Michael Street, Brecon LD3 9AB* Tel (01874) 611319

HACKWOOD, The Ven Paul Colin. b 61. Huddersfield Poly BSc84 Bradf Univ MBA05. Qu Coll Birm 86. **d** 89 **p** 90. C Horton *Bradf* 89-93; Soc Resp Adv *St Alb* 93-97; V Thornbury *Bradf* 97-05; Adn Loughborough *Leic* from 05; Can Res Leic Cathl from 07. *The Archdeaconry, 21 Church Road, Glenfield, Leicester LE3 8DP* Tel 0116-231 1632 Fax 253 2889
E-mail paul.hackwood@leccofe.org

HADDEN, Timothy. b 48. Brighton Poly BSc72 Surrey Univ MSc75. **d** 05 **p** 06. OLM Watling Valley *Ox* from 05. *13 Willets Rise, Shenley Church End, Milton Keynes MK5 6JW* Tel (01908) 507794 Mobile 07889-614386
E-mail tim@willets13.freeserve.co.uk

HADDLETON, Peter Gordon. b 53. UEA BA74 Southn Univ BTh80. Sarum & Wells Th Coll 76. **d** 79 **p** 80. C Thamesmead *S'wark* 79-83; TV Bridgnorth, Tasley, Astley Abbotts, etc *Heref* 83-91; TV Heref S Wye 91-98; TR 98-07; TR Worc St Barn w Ch

Ch from 07. *St Barnabas' Vicarage, Church Road, Worcester WR3 8NX* Tel (01905) 23785 Fax 352142
E-mail peter.haddleton@talk21.com

HADDOCK, Malcolm George. b 27. Univ of Wales (Cardiff) BA56 CertEd73. St Deiniol's Hawarden 87. **d** 80 **p** 81. NSM Newport Ch Ch *Mon* 80-85; NSM Risca 85-87; C 87-89; C Caerleon 89-96; rtd 96; Lic to Offic *Mon* from 96. *48 Cambria Close, Caerleon, Newport NP18 1LF* Tel (01633) 422960

HADDON-REECE (*née* **STREETER**)**, Mrs Christine Mary.** b 50. St Jo Coll Nottm BTh81 LTh81. dss 83 **d** 87 **p** 94. Monkwearmouth St Andr *Dur* 83-85; Stranton 85-87; Par Dn 87-90; Par Dn Lastingham w Appleton-le-Moors, Rosedale etc *York* 90-94; C 94-97; V Topcliffe, Baldersby w Dishforth, Dalton etc 97-08; V Middle Esk Moor from 08. *St Hilda's Vicarage, Egton, Whitby YO21 1UT*

HADFIELD, Prof Brigid. b 50. Edin Univ LLB72 QUB LLM77 Essex Univ PhD03. EAMTC 02. **d** 03 **p** 04. NSM Wivenhoe *Chelmsf* 03-06; NSM Shrub End from 06. *12 Thornton Drive, Colchester CO4 5WB* Tel (01206) 843426
E-mail bhadf@essex.ac.uk

HADFIELD, Christopher John Andrew Chad. b 39. Jes Coll Cam BA61. Wells Th Coll 63. **d** 65 **p** 66. C Wigton w Waverton *Carl* 65-68; Teacher Newlands Sch Seaford 70-06; Lic to Offic *Mor* from 92; Perm to Offic *Chich* from 96. *15 The Fridays, East Dean, Eastbourne BN20 0DH* Tel (01323) 422050

HADFIELD, Derek. b 34. **d** 01 **p** 02. OLM Folkestone H Trin w Ch Ch *Cant* 01-04; OLM Sandgate St Paul w Folkestone St Geo 01-04; rtd 04; Perm to Offic *Cant* from 04. *135 Capel Court, Capel-le-Ferne, Folkestone CT18 7AZ* Tel (01303) 244862
E-mail dhaddy49@tiscali.co.uk

HADFIELD, Douglas. b 22. K Coll Cam BA44 MA49. St Jo Coll Nottm 84. **d** 88 **p** 89. NSM Lenzie *Glas* 88-92; rtd 92; Perm to Offic *Glas* from 92 and *Pet* from 94. *8 Church Street, Helmdon, Brackley NN13 5QJ* Tel (01295) 760679
E-mail douglas.hadfield@firelight.co.uk

HADFIELD, Graham Francis. b 48. Bris Univ BSc69. Cranmer Hall Dur 69. **d** 73 **p** 74. C Blackpool St Thos *Blackb* 73-76; CF 76-99; Asst Chapl Gen 99-04; QHC 02-04; P-in-c Nottingham St Jude *S'well* from 04. *St Jude's Vicarage, Woodborough Road, Nottingham NG3 5HE* Tel 0115-960 4102
E-mail graham@hadf48.fsnet.co.uk

HADFIELD, Jonathan Benedict Philip John. b 43. Lon Univ BA64 Jes Coll Cam BA67 MA72. Edin Th Coll 66. **d** 68 **p** 69. C Fort William *Arg* 68-70; Chapl K Sch Glouc from 70; Hon Min Can Glouc Cathl from 70. *Dulverton House, King's School, Pitt Street, Gloucester GL1 2BG* Tel (01452) 521251

HADFIELD, Norman. b 39. Doncaster Coll of Educn TEng78. St Mich Coll Llan 89 Llan Dioc Tr Scheme 83. **d** 86 **p** 87. NSM Ferndale w Maerdy *Llan* 86-90; C Llanblethian w Cowbridge and Llandough etc 90-92; V Resolven w Tonna 92-04; RD Neath 01-03; rtd 04. *42 Lakeside, Cwmdare, Aberdare CF44 8AX* Tel (01685) 872764

HADJIOANNOU, John. b 56. Ch Coll Cam BA78 MA81. SAOMC 95. **d** 97 **p** 98. C Linslade *Ox* 97-00; V Kinsley w Wragby *Wakef* from 00; P-in-c Felkirk from 05. *Kinsley Vicarage, Wakefield Road, Fitzwilliam, Pontefract WF9 5BX* Tel (01977) 610497 E-mail john@minster.co.uk

HADLEY, Ann. See HADLEY, Preb Elizabeth Ann

HADLEY, Charles Adrian. b 50. Trin Coll Cam BA71 MA75. Cuddesdon Coll 73. **d** 75 **p** 76. C Hadleigh w Layham and Shelley *St E* 75-78; C Bracknell *Ox* 78-82; R Blagdon w Compton Martin and Ubley *B & W* 82-92; RD Chew Magna 88-92; R Somerton w Compton Dundon, the Charltons etc 92-04; Chapl Ex Univ from 04. *2 Velwell Road, Exeter EX4 4LE* Tel (01392) 435384

HADLEY, David Charles. b 42. **d** 02 **p** 03. NSM Kenley *S'wark* from 02; NSM Purley St Barn from 08. *21 Park Road, Kenley CR8 5AQ* Tel (020) 8763 6206

HADLEY, Preb Elizabeth Ann. b 33. St Jo Coll Nottm 80. dss 81 **d** 87 **p** 94. Aspley *S'well* 81-85; Stone St Mich w Aston St Sav *Lich* 85-92; Par Dn 87-92; P-in-c Myddle 92-97; R 97-99; P-in-c Broughton 92-97; V 97-99; Dioc Voc Officer 92-99; Preb Lich Cathl 97-99; rtd 99; P-in-c Harvington *Worc* 99-00; Perm to Offic from 00. *6 Peninsular Road, Norton, Worcester WR5 2SE* Tel (01905) 353710

HADLEY, John Spencer Fairfax. b 47. Ch Ch Ox BA70 MA73. Coll of Resurr Mirfield BA72. **d** 73 **p** 74. C Stoke Newington St Mary *Lon* 73-77; C High Wycombe *Ox* 77-81; TV 82-87; P-in-c Clifton St Paul *Bris* 87-91; Sen Chapl Bris Univ 87-91; Chapl Hengrave Hall Ecum Cen 91-94; Ecum Assoc Min Chelsea Methodist Ch 94-97; Hon C Chelsea St Luke and Ch Ch *Lon* 94-97; Chapl Westcott Ho Cam 97-02; P-in-c Horfield H Trin *Bris* from 02. *Horfield Rectory, Wellington Hill, Bristol BS7 8ST* Tel 0117-924 6185 E-mail john-hadley@tiscali.co.uk

HADLEY, Stuart James. b 55. K Coll Lon BD76 AKC76. St Steph Ho Ox 77. **d** 78 **p** 79. C Mansfield St Mark *S'well* 78-82; V Cowbit *Linc* 82-86; Perm to Offic 86-88; NSM W w E Allington and Sedgebrook 88-95; NSM Saxonwell 95-96; NSM Woolsthorpe 88-95; NSM Harlaxton Gp 95-96; Perm to Offic

97-99; NSM Barkston and Hough Gp from 99. *35 Wensleydale Close, Grantham NG31 8FH* Tel (01476) 575854
E-mail hadleystuart@hotmail.com

HADLOW, Mrs Jennifer Lesley. b 48. **d** 01 **p** 02. OLM Herne *Cant* from 01; OLM Reculver and Herne Bay St Bart from 04. *2 Hicks Forstal Cottages, Hicks Forstal Road, Hoath, Canterbury CT3 4NA* Tel (01227) 711516
E-mail jennyhadlow@hotmail.com

HAGAN, Canon Kenneth Raymond. b 40. Fairfax Univ Australia BA97. St Jo Coll Morpeth 62. **d** 64 **p** 65. C Charlestown Australia 64-69; C Cessnock 69-70; R E Pilbara 70-75; C Portsea St Mary *Portsm* 75-78; P-in-c Wolvey, Burton Hastings and Stretton Baskerville *Cov* 78-81; P-in-c Withybrook w Copston Magna 78-81; P-in-c Shilton w Ansty 78-81; OCF 78-81; Dir St Mungo Community 82-88; R Hamilton Australia 89-98; R Portland 98-05; Can Ballarat from 99; rtd 05; P-in-c Heveningham *St E* 04-07. *35B Narrunga Avenue, Buff Point NSW 2262, Australia* Tel (0061) (2) 4399 3523

HAGAN, Matthew Henry. b 59. TCD MPhil09. CITC. **d** 06 **p** 07. NSM Derryloran *Arm* from 06. *10 Kingarve Road, Dungannon BT71 6LQ* Tel (028) 8772 4356 Mobile 07778-038454
E-mail mhhagan@hotmail.com

HAGENBUCH, Mrs Andrea. b 63. STETS 05. **d** 08 **p** 09. C Corfe Castle, Church Knowle, Kimmeridge etc *Sarum* from 08. *5 Townsend Road, Corfe Castle, Wareham BH20 5ET* Tel (01292) 481105 E-mail stephenhagenbuch@hotmail.com

HAGGAN, David Anthony. b 25. QUB LLB49 Barrister-at-Law 70. S'wark Ord Course 87. **d** 89 **p** 90. NSM Reigate St Mary *S'wark* 89-05; Perm to Offic from 05. *2 Fairford Close, Reigate RH2 0EY* Tel (01737) 246197

HAGGAR, Keith Ivan. b 38. MRPharmS61. Cant Sch of Min 87. **d** 90 **p** 91. NSM Woodnesborough w Worth and Staple *Cant* 90-98; Perm to Offic from 98; Chapl St Bart Hosp Sandwich 00-03. *Burtree Cottage, The Street, Worth, Deal CT14 0DE* Tel (01304) 613599

HAGGER, Jonathan Paul. b 59. St Jo Coll Nottm BTh95. **d** 95 **p** 96. C Newsham *Newc* 95-97; C Newc St Gabr 97-00; P-in-c Cresswell and Lynemouth 00-02; C Newc St Fran from 02. *18 Cotswold Gardens, Newcastle upon Tyne NE7 7AE* Tel 0191-281 2059

HAGGIS, Richard. b 66. Ch Ch Ox BA88 MA95 Nottm Univ MA95. Linc Th Coll. **d** 95 **p** 96. C Romford St Edw *Chelmsf* 95-98; Chapl Trin Coll Cam 98-00; C St Giles-in-the-Fields *Lon* 00-03; C Upper Chelsea H Trin 04-06. *26 Bampton Close, Littlemore, Oxford OX4 6NN* Tel (01865) 749520 Mobile 07788-704044 E-mail rh.giles@btopenworld.com

HAGGIS, Timothy Robin. b 52. New Coll Ox BA75 MA79. St Jo Coll Nottm. **d** 82 **p** 83. C Chilwell *S'well* 82-86; TV Hucknall Torkard 86-94; Chapl Trent Coll Nottm from 94. *Trent College, Long Eaton, Nottingham NG10 4AD* Tel 0115-849 4980
E-mail tim.haggis@trentcollege.net

HAGON, Roger Charles. b 58. Nottm Univ BA80. St Steph Ho Ox 82. **d** 85 **p** 86. C Charlton St Luke w H Trin *S'wark* 85-88; C St Helier 88-95; V Kenley from 95; P-in-c Purley St Barn from 01. *The Vicarage, 3 Valley Road, Kenley CR8 5DJ* Tel (020) 8660 3263 E-mail hagons@kenley82.freeserve.co.uk

HAGUE, David Hallett. b 59. Univ Coll Lon BScEng81 MSc82. Ridley Hall Cam 91. **d** 93 **p** 94. C Luton St Mary *St Alb* 93-96; V Stevenage St Pet Broadwater 96-09; P-in-c Romford Gd Shep *Chelmsf* from 09. *Good Shepherd Vicarage, 97 Collier Row Lane, Romford RM5 3BA* Tel (01708) 726423

HAHNEMAN, Geoffrey Mark. b 54. Baylor Univ (USA) BA77 Virginia Th Sem MDiv80 Ox Univ DPhil87. **d** 80 **p** 80. C Boston Advent USA 80-84; Hon C Ox St Mary Magd 85-87; Asst Chapl Brussels *Eur* 87-90; Can Minneapolis Cathl USA 90-94; R Portsmouth Trin Ch 95-00; R Bridgeport St Jo from 05. *154 Jackman Avenue, Fairfield CT 06825-1724, USA* Tel (001) (203) 362 0890 *or* 335 2528
E-mail rector@saintjohnbridgeport.org

HAIG, Alistair Matthew. b 39. K Coll Lon BD63 AKC63. **d** 64 **p** 65. C Forest Gate St Edm *Chelmsf* 64-67; C Laindon w Basildon 67-71; V S Woodham Ferrers 71-78; P-in-c Bath H Trin *B & W* 78-83; R 83-89; R Bocking St Mary *Chelmsf* 89-95; Dean Bocking 89-95; rtd 00. *17 Maidenburgh Street, Colchester CO1 1UB* Tel (01206) 795275

HAIG, Canon Andrew Livingstone. b 45. Keble Coll Ox BA67. Coll of Resurr Mirfield 67. **d** 69 **p** 70. C Elton All SS *Man* 69-75; R Brantham *St E* 75-76; R Brantham w Stutton 76-82; RD Samford 81-82; P-in-c Haverhill 82; TR Haverhill w Withersfield, the Wrattings etc 82-90; RD Clare 84-87; Chapl Qu Eliz Hosp King's Lynn 90-94; Chapl King's Lynn and Wisbech Hosps NHS Trust from 94; Hon Can Nor Cathl from 07. *The Chaplain's Office, Queen Elizabeth Hospital, Gayton Road, King's Lynn PE30 4ET* Tel (01553) 613613 ext 2642

HAIG, Canon Murray Nigel Francis. b 39. Univ of Wales (Lamp) BA62. Kelham Th Coll. **d** 66 **p** 67. C Felixstowe St Jo *St E* 66-72; C Morpeth *Newc* 72-74; V Byker St Mich 74-79; V Byker St Mich w St Lawr 79-81; I Benwell St Jas 81-85; TR Benwell 85-91; TR Cramlington 91-97; Hon Can Newc Cathl 95-05;

P-in-c Alnwick 97-98; V 98-05; rtd 05. *4 Farm Well Place, Prudhoe NE42 5FB* Tel (07801) 495616
E-mail d.haig@abbeyfield.com

HAIGH, Alan Bernard. b 42. NEOC 87. **d** 90 **p** 91. NSM Thorner *Ripon* from 90. *4 The Paddock, Thorner, Leeds LS14 3JB* Tel 0113-289 2870

HAIGH, Nicholas James. b 71. Sheff Univ BA00 St Jo Coll Dur MA04. Cranmer Hall Dur 02. **d** 04 **p** 05. C Bredbury St Mark *Ches* 04-06; P Missr Huddersfield *Wakef* from 06. *50 Longcroft, Huddersfield HD5 8XW* Tel (01484) 315511 Mobile 07876-782888 E-mail nickhaigh@breathemail.net

HAIGH, Nicolas Peter. b 57. Teesside Poly BEd84. Ripon Coll Cuddesdon 07. **d** 09. C Eastbourne St Mary *Chich* from 09. *6 Bay Pond Road, Eastbourne BN21 1HX* Tel (01323) 641536 or 07966-187349 E-mail nickhaigh95@hotmail.com

HAIGH, Richard Michael Fisher. b 30. Dur Univ BA57. Cranmer Hall Dur 57. **d** 59 **p** 60. C Stanwix *Carl* 59-62; CMS India 63-67 and 68-70; R Salford St Clem w St Cypr Ordsall *Man* 71-75; R Holcombe 75-85; V Unsworth 85-93; R Brough w Stainmore, Musgrave and Warcop *Carl* 93-97; rtd 97; Perm to Offic *Carl* from 98. *21 Templand Park, Allithwaite, Grange-over-Sands LA11 7QS* Tel (01539) 532312

HAILES, Derek Arthur. b 38. Coll of Resurr Mirfield. **d** 82 **p** 83. C Sneinton St Cypr *S'well* 82-84; V Kneesall w Laxton 84-85; P-in-c Wellow 84-85; V Kneesall w Laxton and Wellow 85-88; V Sneinton St Steph w St Alb 88-95; P-in-c Bury H Trin *Man* 95-03; rtd 03; Perm to Offic *S'well* from 05. *14 Manor Road, Carlton, Nottingham NG4 3AY* Tel 0115-987 3314

HAILS, Canon Brian. b 33. JP71. ACMA62 FCMA76. NEOC 77. **d** 81 **p** 82. NSM Harton Dur 81-87; Ind Chapl 87-99; Hon Can Dur Cathl 93-99; TR Sunderland 96-99; rtd 99. *The Coach House, Church Lane, Whitburn, Sunderland SR6 7JL* Tel 0191-529 5297 E-mail canon-hails@ukonline.co.uk

HAINES, Andrew Philip. b 47. LSE BSc68. Oak Hill Th Coll 84. **d** 87 **p** 88. C Enfield Ch Ch Trent Park *Lon* 87-91; V Hillmorton *Cov* from 91. *The Vicarage, Hoskyn Close, Rugby CV21 4LA* Tel (01788) 576279 E-mail andrew@cahaines.fsnet.co.uk

HAINES, Daniel Hugo. b 43. TD89. Lon Univ BDS68 MRCS73. **d** 79 **p** 84. Hon C Bhunya Swaziland 79-80; Hon C Falkland Is 80-82; Hon C Hatcham St Cath *S'wark* 84-99; Perm to Offic from 99. *56 Vesta Road, London SE4 2NH* Tel (020) 7635 0305 E-mail 113270.506@compuserve.com

HAINES, Canon Robert Melvin. b 31. Coll of Resurr Mirfield 71. **d** 73 **p** 74. C Derringham Bank *York* 73-76; P-in-c Newport St Steph 76-79; TV Howden 80-82; R Turriff *Ab* 82-97; R Cuminestown 82-97; R Banff 82-97; P-in-c Portsoy 94-97; P-in-c Buckie 94-97; rtd 97; NSM Turriff *Ab* from 97; Hon Can St Andr Cathl from 01. *Ceol-na-Mara, 11 Scotstown, Banff AB45 1LA* Tel (01261) 818258

HAINES, Stephen Decatur. b 42. Freiburg Univ MA68 Fitzw Coll Cam BA70 MA74. **d** 71 **p** 72. C Fulham St Dionis Parson's Green *Lon* 71-76; C Finchley St Mary 76-78; Hon C Clapham Old Town *S'wark* 83-87; Hon C Clapham Team 87-88; Hon C Camberwell St Giles w St Matt 88-94; Hon Chapl S'wark Cathl from 92. *3 Lyndhurst Square, London SE15 5AR* Tel (020) 7703 4239

HAINSWORTH, Richard John. b 79. Jes Coll Cam BA01 MA03. St Mich Coll Llan 04. **d** 06 **p** 07. C Newtown w Llanllwchaiarn w Aberhafesp *St As* 06-07; C Llanllwchaiarn and Newtown w Aberhafesp 07-08; C Wrexham from 08. *The Vicarage, 37 Acton Gate, Wrexham LL11 2PW* Tel (01978) 266685 Mobile 07886-117922 E-mail rich_hainsworth@yahoo.co.uk

HAIR, James Eric. b 48. Lon Univ BA69 MPhil92. St Steph Ho Ox 69. **d** 72 **p** 73. C Fishponds St Jo *Bris* 72-75; C Bushey *St Alb* 75-79; P-in-c Lake *Portsm* 79-81; V 81-88; P-in-c Shanklin St Sav 79-81; V 81-88; TV Totton *Win* 88-95; C Portchester *Portsm* 96-97; Community Mental Health Chapl Portsm Health Care NHS Trust 97-02; Community Mental Health Chapl Hants Partnership NHS Trust from 02; Chapl Team Ldr E Hants Primary Care Trust from 99; Asst to RD Fareham *Portsm* 97-98 and 99. *219 West Street, Fareham PO16 0ET* Tel (01329) 825231

HAITH, James Rodney. b 69. Ex Univ BA. Ridley Hall Cam 02. **d** 04 **p** 05. C Brompton H Trin w Onslow Square St Paul *Lon* from 04. *23 Pooles Lane, London SW10 0RH* Tel 08456-447533 Mobile 07833-705271 E-mail jamie.haith@htb.org.uk

HAKE (née JACKSON), Mrs Ruth Victoria. b 78. Univ Coll Dur BA99 Fitzw Coll Cam BA01 MA05. Ridley Hall Cam 99. **d** 02 **p** 03. C York St Mich-le-Belfrey 02-05; CF(V) 04-05; Chapl RAF from 05. *Chaplaincy Services, HQ Personnel and Training Command, RAF High Wycombe HP14 4UE* Tel (01494) 496800 Fax 496343

HALAHAN, Maxwell Crosby. b 30. Lon Univ BSc52 Southn Univ CertEd78. Westcott Ho Cam 54. **d** 56 **p** 57. C Forton *Portsm* 56-60; C Liv Our Lady and St Nic 60-62; Dom Chapl to Bp Nassau and the Bahamas 62-64; C Widley w Wymering *Portsm* 64-66; C-in-c Cowes St Faith CD 66-70; V Cowes St Faith 70-77; Hon C Portsea St Sav 77-84; rtd 84; Perm to Offic *Portsm* 84-94. *4 Coach House Mews, Old Canal, Southsea PO4 8HD*

HALBERT, Mrs Elizabeth Mary. b 58. Liv Hope BA97 PGCE98. **d** 06 **p** 07. OLM Sefton and Thornton *Liv* from 06. *15 Third Avenue, Crosby, Liverpool L23 5SA* Tel 0151-281 1390 E-mail lizhalbert1000@msn.com

HALE, Antony Jolyon (Jon). b 56. Newc Univ BA79 MRTPI89. Sarum & Wells Th Coll 86. **d** 88 **p** 89. C Monkseaton St Mary *Newc* 88-92; P-in-c Tandridge *S'wark* 92-97; C Oxted 92-97; C Oxted and Tandridge 97-98; V Crawley Down All SS *Chich* from 98. *The Vicarage, Vicarage Road, Crawley Down, Crawley RH10 4JJ* Tel (01342) 714922 E-mail aj@jkcahale.plus.com

HALE, David Nigel James. b 43. SEITE 00. **d** 03 **p** 04. NSM Aylesham w Adisham *Cant* from 03; NSM Nonington w Wymynswold and Goodnestone etc from 03. *Chilton House, 43 The Street, Ash, Canterbury CT3 2EN* Tel (01304) 813161 *or* (01843) 862991 E-mail halenigelval@hotmail.com

HALE, John Frederick. b 29. Fitzw Ho Cam BA54 MA58. Tyndale Hall Bris. **d** 55 **p** 56. C Heigham H Trin *Nor* 55-58; C Paddington St Jas *Lon* 58-61; V St Leonards St Ethelburga *Chich* 61-79; C Prestonville St Luke 79-90; R Rotherfield w Mark Cross 90-92; rtd 92; Perm to Offic *Chich* from 92. *51 Brangwyn Drive, Brighton BN1 8XB* Tel (01273) 554944

HALE, Jon. *See* HALE, Antony Jolyon

HALE, Keith John Edward. b 53. Sheff Poly BSc75. St Jo Coll Nottm MA94. **d** 91 **p** 92. C Greasbrough *Sheff* 91-94; P-in-c Tankersley 94-95; R Tankersley, Thurgoland and Wortley from 95; Ind Chapl 96-01; Bp's Rural Adv from 01; AD Tankersley from 07. *The Rectory, 9 Chapel Road, Tankersley, Barnsley S75 3AR* Tel (01226) 744140 E-mail revkeith.hale@virgin.net

HALE (née McKAY), Mrs Margaret McLeish (Greta). b 37. RN76. WEMTC 92. **d** 95 **p** 96. OLM Bream *Glouc* 95-01; NSM 01-04; NSM Newland and Redbrook w Clearwell 04-06; NSM Coleford, Staunton, Newland, Redbrook etc from 06. *1 The Bungalow, High Street, Clearwell, Coleford GL16 8JS* Tel (01594) 832400 E-mail gretahale@hotmail.com

HALE, Nigel. *See* HALE, David Nigel James

HALE, Roger Anthony. b 41. MCIH85. Brasted Th Coll 68 Oak Hill Th Coll 70. **d** 72 **p** 73. C Blackb Sav 72-75; C Burnley St Pet 75-77; Chapl Burnley Gen Hosp 75-77; V Fence in Pendle *Blackb* 77-82; Chapl Lancs Ind Miss 77-82; NSM Tottenham St Mary *Lon* 88-91; R Cheddington w Mentmore and Marsworth *Ox* 91-06; rtd 06; Perm to Offic *Ox* from 06. *Chiltern House, 12 High Street, Cheddington, Leighton Buzzard LU7 0RQ* Tel (01296) 668114 E-mail rogertherector@yahoo.co.uk

HALES, Peter John. b 45. Open Univ BSc02. ERMC 08. **d** 08. Chapl Coutances *Eur* from 08. *4 rue le Mascaret, 50220 Précey, France* Tel (0033) (2) 33 58 86 76 Fax (6) 87 53 20 13 E-mail halesphx2@aol.com

HALES, Sandra Louise. Lon Univ BSc94 Univ Coll Lon MSc96 TCD BTh02 RGN. CITC. **d** 02 **p** 02. C Lucan w Leixlip *D & G* 02-06; I Celbridge w Straffan and Newcastle-Lyons from 06. *The Rectory, Maynooth Road, Celbridge, Co Kildare, Republic of Ireland* Tel (00353) (1) 628 8231 E-mail slhales@eircom.net

HALEY, Thomas Arthur. b 52. NTMTC 98. **d** 98 **p** 99. NSM Old Ford St Paul and St Mark *Lon* 98-02; NSM Hackney Marsh from 02; TV from 07. *All Souls' Vicarage, 44 Overbury Street, London E5 0AJ* Tel (020) 8525 2863 E-mail tomarcic@aol.com

HALFORD, David John. b 47. JP84. Didsbury Coll Man CertEd69 Open Univ BA75 DipEd86 Man Univ MEd79 ACP72. **d** 96 **p** 97. OLM Royton St Anne *Man* from 96. *33 Broadway, Royton, Oldham OL2 5DD* Tel and fax 0161-633 4650

HALFPENNY, Brian Norman. b 36. CB90. St Jo Coll Ox BA60 MA64. Wells Th Coll 60. **d** 62 **p** 63. C Melksham *Sarum* 62-65; Chapl RAF 65-83; Sen Chapl RAF Coll Cranwell 82-83; Asst Chapl-in-Chief RAF 83-88; Chapl-in-Chief RAF 88-91; QHC 85-91; Can and Preb Linc Cathl 89-91; TR Redditch, The Ridge *Worc* 91-01; rtd 01; Perm to Offic *Glouc* from 02. *80 Roman Way, Bourton-on-the-Water, Cheltenham GL54 2EW* Tel (01451) 821589

HALIFAX, Archdeacon of. *See* FREEMAN, The Ven Robert John

HALKES, Canon John Stanley. b 39. SWMTC 87. **d** 90 **p** 91. NSM St Buryan, St Levan and Sennen *Truro* 90-92; P-in-c Lanteglos by Fowey 92-04; P-in-c Lansallos 03-04; Hon Can Truro Cathl 03-08; rtd 04. *Reading Room Cottage, Mixton Farm, Lerryn, Lostwithiel PL22 0QE*

HALL, Alan Maurice Frank. b 28. FCCA. Sarum & Wells Th Coll 86. **d** 89 **p** 90. NSM Winterbourne Stickland and Turnworth etc *Sarum* 89-97; Perm to Offic *Sarum* 97-00 and *St Alb* from 00. *2 Barnes Road, Wooton, Bedford MK43 9FA* Tel (01234) 764676

✠**HALL, The Rt Revd Albert Peter.** b 30. St Jo Coll Cam BA53 MA56. Ridley Hall Cam 53. **d** 55 **p** 56 **c** 84. C Birm St Martin 55-60; S Rhodesia 60-65; Rhodesia 65-70; R Birm St Martin 70-84; Hon Can Birm Cathl 75-84; Suff Bp Woolwich *S'wark* 84-91; Area Bp Woolwich 91-96; Chmn ACUPA 90-96; rtd 96; Asst Bp Birm from 96. *27 Jacey Road, Birmingham B16 0LL* Tel 0121-455 9240

HALL, Canon Alfred Christopher. b 35. Trin Coll Ox BA58 MA61. Westcott Ho Cam 58. **d** 61 **p** 62. C Frecheville *Derby*

61-64; C Dronfield 64-67; V Smethwick St Matt *Birm* 67-70; V Smethwick St Matt w St Chad 70-75; Can Res Man Cathl 75-83; Hon Can 83-90; Dioc Adult Educn Officer 75-83; Dioc World Development Officer 76-88; V Bolton St Pet 83-90; Co-ord Chr Concern for One World 90-00; rtd 96; Hon Can Ch Ch *Ox* 00-01; Perm to Offic from 03. *The Knowle, Philcote Street, Deddington, Banbury OX15 0TB* Tel (01869) 338225 Fax 337766 E-mail achall@globalnet.co.uk

HALL, Mrs Ann Addington. b 34. Ex Univ CertEd71. SW Minl Tr Course 82. **d**ss 85 **d** 87 **p** 94. Ex St Mark 85-90; Hon Par Dn 87-90; Perm to Offic 90-92; NSM Cen Ex from 92. *5 Harringcourt Road, Exeter EX4 8PQ* Tel (01392) 278717

HALL, Arthur John. b 23. Bris Univ BSc48. Sarum & Wells Th Coll 74. **d** 76 **p** 77. NSM Portishead *B & W* 76-88; Perm to Offic from 88; Chapl St Brandon's Sch Clevedon 86-91. *34 Beechwood Road, Portishead, Bristol BS20 8EP* Tel (01275) 842603

HALL, Barry George. b 38. Solicitor 62. Oak Hill Th Coll 78. **d** 81 **p** 82. NSM Stock Harvard *Chelmsf* 81-90; NSM W Hanningfield 90-02; P-in-c 93-02; Perm to Offic from 02. *Harvard Cottage, Swan Lane, Stock, Ingatestone CM4 9BQ* Tel (01277) 840387

HALL, Brian. b 59. Aston Tr Scheme 90 Oak Hill Th Coll 92. **d** 94 **p** 95. C Mansfield St Jo *S'well* 94-96; C Skegby 96-99; P-in-c Sutton in Ashfield St Mich 99-04; R Carlton-in-the-Willows from 04. *St Paul's Rectory, Church Street, Nottingham NG4 1BJ* Tel 0115-961 1644 E-mail revbhall@aol.com

HALL, Canon Brian Arthur. b 48. Ex Univ BEd70. Cuddesdon Coll 73. **d** 75 **p** 76. C Hobs Moat *Birm* 75-79; V Smethwick 79-93; R Handsworth St Mary from 93; AD Handsworth 99-05 and 06-08; Hon Can Birm Cathl from 05. *Handsworth Rectory, 288 Hamstead Road, Birmingham B20 2RB* Tel 0121-554 3407 E-mail brian.a.hall@btinternet.com

HALL, Mrs Carolyn Ruth. **d** 08 **p** 09. NSM Builth and Llanddewi'r Cwm w Llangynog etc *S & B* from 08. *The Vicarage, 1 North Road, Builth Wells LD2 3BT* Tel (01982) 552355 E-mail nigeldhall@hotmail.com

HALL, Charles John. b 40. JP. ALCD68. **d** 68 **p** 69. C Upton (Overchurch) *Ches* 68-72; C Morden *S'wark* 72-76; V Hyson Green *S'well* 76-84; V Stapleford 84-97; RD Beeston 90-97; TR Thetford *Nor* 97-05; RD Thetford and Rockland 99-03; rtd 05; Perm to Offic *Nor* from 05. *24 Mill Road, Reepham, Norwich NR10 4JU* Tel (01603) 879194 E-mail hallthetrec@tesco.net

HALL, Ms Christine Beryl. b 52. Southn Univ BSc73 Leeds Univ MA06. NTMTC BA08. **d** 08 **p** 09. NSM Stepney St Dunstan and All SS *Lon* from 08; Chapl Guy's and St Thos' NHS Foundn Trust from 08; Chapl Lon Fire Brigade from 08. *6 Arbour Square, London E1 0SH* Tel (020) 7790 9961 E-mail christine.b.hall@btinternet.com

HALL, Christine Mary. b 45. K Coll Lon BD67 MPhil86. **d** 87. NSM Bickley *Roch* 87-92; Vice-Prin Chich Th Coll 92-95; Lic to Offic *Chich* 95-03. *The Old School, East Marden, Chichester PO18 9JE* Tel (01243) 535244

HALL, Christopher. *See* HALL, Canon Alfred Christopher

HALL, Darryl Christopher. b 69. Cranmer Hall Dur 07. **d** 09. C Knaresborough *Ripon* from 09. *9 Castle Yard, Knaresborough HG5 8AS* Tel (01423) 869845 Mobile 07930-177337 E-mail horlix@aol.com

HALL, David Anthony. b 43. Reading Univ BA66. Qu Coll Birm 79. **d** 81 **p** 82. C Norton *St Alb* 81-85; TV Hitchin 85-93; P-in-c Bidford-on-Avon *Cov* 93; V 93-08; RD Alcester 05-08; rtd 08. *Holyoake Farm Cottage, Little Alne, Wooton Wawen, Henley-in-Arden B95 6HW* E-mail davidahall@onetel.com

HALL, David Martin. b 66. Avery Hill Coll BA89. Oak Hill Th Coll BA00. **d** 00 **p** 01. C Bebington *Ches* 00-03; P-in-c Danehill *Chich* 03-05; V from 05. *The Vicarage, Lewes Road, Danehill, Haywards Heath RH17 7ER* Tel (01825) 790269

HALL, Denis. b 43. Lon Coll of Div 65. **d** 69 **p** 70. C Netherton *Liv* 69-71; C Roby 72-75; V Wigan St Steph 75-90; V Newton-le-Willows from 90. *The Vicarage, 243 Crow Lane East, Newton-le-Willows WA12 9UB* Tel (01925) 290545 E-mail allsaints@3tc4u.net

HALL, Derek. *See* HALL, Canon John Derek

HALL, Derek Guy. b 26. Tyndale Hall Bris 50. **d** 51 **p** 52. C Preston All SS *Blackb* 51-54; C Halliwell St Pet *Man* 54-56; C-in-c Buxton Trin Prop Chpl *Derby* 56-58; V Blackb St Jude 58-67; R Fazakerley Em *Liv* 67-74; TR 74-81; V Langdale *Carl* 81-86; rtd 86; Perm to Offic *Carl* from 86. *14 Gale Park, Ambleside LA22 0BN* Tel (01539) 433144

HALL, Elaine Chegwin. b 59. Liv Univ MTh01 RGN82. NOC 94. **d** 97 **p** 98. C Frankby w Greasby *Ches* 97-01; V Stretton and Appleton Thorn from 01; RD Gt Budworth from 03. *The Vicarage, Stretton Road, Stretton, Warrington WA4 4NT* Tel (01925) 730276 E-mail petera.hall@care4free.net

HALL, Fiona Myfanwy Gordon. b 63. Regents Th Coll BA95 Roehampton Inst PGCE96 Anglia Ruskin Univ MA04. Ridley Hall Cam 02. **d** 04 **p** 05. C Southampton Maybush St Pet *Win* 04-06; C Maybush and Southampton St Jude 06-07; Asst Chapl R Berks NHS Foundn Trust from 08. *St John's Convent, Linden Hill Lane, Kiln Green, Reading RG10 9XP* Tel 0118-940 4311

HALL, Frances. *See* SHOESMITH, Mrs Judith Frances

HALL, Geoffrey Hedley. b 33. Bris Univ BA55. St Steph Ho Ox 63. **d** 65 **p** 66. C Taunton H Trin *B & W* 65-67; CF 67-80; Sen CF 80-86; P-in-c Ambrosden w Arncot and Blackthorn *Ox* 72-75; V Barnsley St Edw *Wakef* 86-98; rtd 98; Perm to Offic *St And* from 98 and *Bre* from 99. *Montana Villa, 39 Haston Crescent, Perth PH2 7XD* Tel (01738) 636802 Mobile 07803-578499 E-mail geoffreyhall@blueyonder.co.uk

HALL, George Richard Wyndham. b 49. Ex Univ LLB71. Wycliffe Hall Ox BA74 MA78. **d** 75 **p** 76. C Walton H Trin *Ox* 75-79; C Farnborough *Guildf* 79-84; Bp's Chapl *Nor* 84-87; R Saltford w Corston and Newton St Loe *B & W* from 87; Chapl Bath Coll of HE 88-90; RD Chew Magna *B & W* 97-03. *The Rectory, 12 Beech Road, Saltford, Bristol BS31 3BE* Tel and fax (01225) 872275 E-mail richardhall@blueyonder.co.uk

HALL, Canon George Rumney. b 37. LVO99 CVO03. Westcott Ho Cam 60. **d** 62 **p** 63. C Camberwell St Phil *S'wark* 62-65; C Waltham Cross *St Alb* 65-67; R Buckenham w Hassingham and Strumpshaw *Nor* 67-74; Chapl St Andr Hosp Thorpe 67-72; Chapl HM Pris Nor 72-74; V Wymondham *Nor* 74-87; RD Humbleyard 86-87; R Sandringham w W Newton 87-94; P-in-c Flitcham 87-94; P-in-c Wolferton w Babingley 87-94; R Sandringham w W Newton and Appleton etc 95-03; P-in-c Castle Rising 87-03; P-in-c Hillington 87-03; Hon Can Nor Cathl 87-03; RD Heacham and Rising 89-01; Dom Chapl to The Queen 87-03; Chapl to The Queen 89-07; rtd 03; Perm to Offic *Nor* from 03. *Town Farm Cottage, Lynn Road, Bircham, King's Lynn PE31 6RJ* Tel (01485) 576134

HALL, Mrs Gillian Louise. b 45. Univ of Wales (Ban) MPhil06. NOC 87. **d** 90 **p** 94. NSM Earby *Bradf* 90-96; NSM Gisburn 96-01; NSM Hellifield 96-01; Perm to Offic 01-02; Chapl Airedale NHS Trust 02-04; Hon C Sutton w Cowling and Lothersdale *Bradf* from 05. *Mitton House, Lothersdale, Keighley BD20 8HR* Tel (01535) 636144 E-mail gill@hessledodge.freeserve.co.uk

HALL, Harold Henry Stanley Lawson. b 23. Qu Coll Birm 56. **d** 58 **p** 59. C Bishopwearmouth Ch Ch *Dur* 58-61; C Winlaton 61-65; V Consett 65-69; V Newton Aycliffe 69-76; R Whitburn 76-89; rtd 89. *9 Balmoral Terrace, East Herrington, Sunderland SR3 3PR* Tel 0191-528 0108

HALL, Harry. b 41. Open Univ BA93. Chich Th Coll 91. **d** 91 **p** 92. C Boston *Linc* 91-92; C Bourne 92-94; P-in-c Sutterton w Fosdyke and Algarkirk 94-97; R Sutterton, Fosdyke, Algarkirk and Wigtoft 97-99; V Barnsley St Edw *Wakef* 99-05; Chapl ATC 99-05; I Ardstraw w Baronscourt, Badoney Lower etc *D & R* from 05. *The Rectory, 2 Bunderg Road, Newtownstewart BT78 4NQ* Tel (028) 8166 1342 E-mail slk248@hotmail.com

HALL, Miss Helen Constance Patricia Mary. b 77. Peterho Cam BA99 MA03 St Jo Coll Dur BA05 Solicitor 02. Cranmer Hall Dur 03. **d** 06 **p** 07. C Maindee Newport *Mon* from 06. *16 Kensington Place, Newport NP19 8GL* Tel (01633) 281053 Mobile 07919-538077 E-mail bititt@yahoo.co.uk

HALL, Canon Hubert William Peter. b 35. Ely Th Coll 58. **d** 60 **p** 61. C Louth w Welton-le-Wold *Linc* 60-62; C Gt Grimsby St Jas 62-69; C Gt Grimsby St Mary and St Jas 69-71; Hon Chapl Miss to Seafarers 71-01; V Immingham *Linc* 71-01; RD Haverstoe 86-01; Can and Preb Linc Cathl 89-01; rtd 01; Perm to Offic *Linc* from 01. *6 Abbey Rise, Barrow-upon-Humber DN19 7TF* Tel (01469) 531504 E-mail hwphall@talktalk.net

HALL, Ian Alfred. b 60. NOC 99. **d** 03. In RC Ch 86-98; C Whitkirk *Ripon* 99-02; TV Swinton and Pendlebury *Man* 02-09; P-in-c Winton from 09. *St Augustine's Vicarage, 23 Hospital Road, Pendlebury, Swinton, Manchester M27 4EY* Tel 0161-794 4298 E-mail carolian86@yahoo.co.uk

HALL, Ian Michael. b 48. Mansf Coll Ox MA70 Leeds Univ CertEd71. Carl Dioc Tr Course 85. **d** 88 **p** 89. NSM Eskdale, Irton, Muncaster and Waberthwaite *Carl* 88-05. *Address temp unknown*

HALL, James. b 28. Wollongong Univ BA78. CITC 53. **d** 56 **p** 57. C Belfast St Mich *Conn* 56-59; I Cleenish *Clogh* 59-62; R Openshaw *Man* 63-68; C-in-c Figtree Australia 68-71; R 72-79; Lic to Offic Dio Sydney 81-89 and 93-03; R Morley w Deopham, Hackford, Wicklewood etc *Nor* 89-92; R High Oak 92-93; rtd 93. *319/2 Huntley Road, St Luke's Retirement Village, Dapto NSW 2530, Australia* Tel (0061) (2) 4262 7881 E-mail jmhall@ihug.com.au

HALL, Canon James Robert. b 24. TCD BA48 MA54. **d** 49 **p** 50. C Seagoe *D & D* 49-51; C Lisburn Ch Ch *Conn* 51-59; I Belfast St Mich 59-66; I Finaghy 66-89; Can Belf Cathl 82-89; rtd 89. *3 Coachman's Way, Hillsborough BT26 6HQ* Tel (028) 9268 9678

HALL, Mrs Jane Daphne. b 60. Trent Poly BA92 Solicitor 93. **d** 09. NSM Clopton w Otley, Swilland and Ashbocking *St E* from 09. *Countryside, Gibraltar Road, Otley, Ipswich IP6 9LL* Tel (01473) 785251 E-mail allthealls@tiscali.co.uk

HALL, Jeffrey Ernest. b 42. Linc Th Coll 73. **d** 75 **p** 76. C Brampton St Thos *Derby* 75-78; C Whittington and New Whittington 78-81; TV Riverside *Ox* 81-90; Ind Chapl Slough

Deanery 81-89; R Anstey *Leic* 90-97; TR Hugglescote w Donington, Ellistown and Snibston 97-08; rtd 08. *6 Hardy Court, Marlott Road, Gillingham SP8 4FR* Tel (01747) 826936 Mobile 07876-540343

HALL, The Ven John Barrie. b 41. Sarum & Wells Th Coll 82. **d** 84 **p** 85. Chapl St Edward's Hosp Cheddleton 84-88; C Cheddleton *Lich* 84-88; V Rocester 88-94; V Rocester and Croxden w Hollington 94-98; RD Uttoxeter 91-98; Adn Salop from 98; V Tong from 98; P-in-c Donington 98-00. *Tong Vicarage, Shifnal TF11 8PW* Tel (01902) 372622 Fax 374021 E-mail archdeacon.salop@lichfield.anglican.org

HALL, John Bruce. b 33. Covenant Th Sem St Louis MTh80 DMin85. ALCD60. **d** 60 **p** 61. C Kingston upon Hull H Trin *York* 60 67; C Beverley Minster 67-68; V Clapham Park St Steph *S'wark* 68-76; R Tooting Graveney St Nic 76-03; rtd 03; Perm to Offic *S'wark* from 03. *44 Mayford Road, London SW12 8SD* Tel (020) 8673 6869 E-mail jbewhall@macunlimited.net

HALL, John Charles. b 46. Hull Univ BA71 Spurgeon's Coll MTh05. Ridley Hall Cam 71. **d** 73 **p** 74. C Bromley Common St Aug *Roch* 73-77; C Westbury-on-Trym St Alb *Bris* 78-80; C-in-c Bishop Auckland Woodhouse Close CD *Dur* 82-90; P-in-c Gt and Lt Glemham, Blaxhall etc *St E* 90-91; P-in-c Rodney Stoke w Draycott *B & W* 91-01; Dioc Ecum Officer 91-01; V Southmead *Bris* from 01. *St Stephen's Vicarage, Wigton Crescent, Bristol BS10 6DR* Tel 0117-950 7164 Mobile 07811-316249 E-mail sarasgarden@blueyonder.co.uk

HALL, John Curtis. b 39. CEng73 MIMechE73. Coll of Resurr Mirfield 80. **d** 82 **p** 83. C Pet Ch Carpenter 82-86; TV Heavitree w Ex St Paul 86-93; R Bow w Broad Nymet 93-04; V Colebrooke 93-04; R Zeal Monachorum 93-04; RD Cadbury 97-02; rtd 04. *37 Lawn Drive, Chudleigh, Newton Abbot TQ13 0LS* Tel (01626) 853245

HALL, Canon John Derek. b 25. St Cuth Soc Dur BA50. Linc Th Coll 50. **d** 52 **p** 53. C Redcar *York* 52-54; C Newland St Jo 54-57; V Boosbeck w Moorsholm 57-61; V Middlesbrough St Oswald 61-68; Chapl St Luke's Hosp Middlesbrough 61-67; V York St Chad 68-90; Chapl Bootham Park Hosp 68-85; Can and Preb York Minster 85-90; rtd 90; Chapl Castle Howard 90-02; Perm to Offic *York* from 98. *25 Fairfields Drive, Skelton, York YO30 1YP* Tel (01904) 470978

HALL, John Edmund. b 49. Open Univ BA84 Birm Univ MPhil05 Warwick Univ PhD06 CQSW76. Trin Coll Bris BA89. **d** 89 **p** 90. C Winchmore Hill St Paul *Lon* 89-92; V Edmonton St Aldhelm 92-01; Dir Soc Resp *Cov* from 01. *The Rectory, Spring Hill, Bubbenhall, Coventry CV8 3BD* Tel (024) 7630 2345 or 7671 0500 Fax 7671 0550 E-mail john.hall@covcofe.org

HALL, Canon John Kenneth. b 32. Qu Coll Birm 61. **d** 63 **p** 64. C Ilminster w Whitelackington *B & W* 63-66; P-in-c Mackworth St Fran *Derby* 66-69; V Blackford *B & W* 69-76; R Chapel Allerton 69-76; New Zealand from 77; Can St Pet Cathl Waikato 85-91; rtd 93. *24 Pohutukawa Drive, RD 1, Katikati 3177, New Zealand* Tel and fax (0064) (7) 863 4465 E-mail gee.jay@paradise.net.nz

HALL, John MacNicol. b 44. Glas Univ BSc65 MB, ChB69 St Jo Coll Cam BA73 MA76 Nottm Univ MTh88 MSc93 MRCGP75. Westcott Ho Cam 71. **d** 86 **p** 86. NSM Clarendon Park St Jo w Knighton St Mich *Leic* 86-89; Perm to Offic *Ely* 89-91; *St Alb* 90-92; *Birm* from 91. *85 Galton Road, Smethwick B67 5JX* Tel 0121-434 3957

HALL, John Michael. b 47. BD. Oak Hill Th Coll 68. **d** 73 **p** 74. C Walthamstow St Mary w St Steph *Chelmsf* 73-76; C Rainham 76-79; P-in-c Woodham Mortimer w Hazeleigh 79-93; P-in-c Woodham Walter 79-93; Ind Chapl 79-93; R Fairstead w Terling and White Notley etc from 93; RD Witham 01-07. *The Rectory, New Road, Terling, Chelmsford CM3 2PN* Tel (01245) 233256 E-mail rev.john.hall@tinyworld.co.uk

HALL, Canon John Michael. b 62. Leeds Univ BA. Coll of Resurr Mirfield 83. **d** 86 **p** 87. C Ribbleton *Blackb* 86-89; C Carnforth 89-92; V Lt Marsden 92-98; V Lt Marsden w Nelson St Mary 98; V Warton St Oswald w Yealand Conyers 98-08; AD Tunstall 05-08; P-in-c Fleetwood St Dav from 08; P-in-c Fleetwood St Pet from 08; Hon Can Bloemfontein Cathl from 01; Hon Can Blackb Cathl from 09. *The Vicarage, 49 Mount Road, Fleetwood FY7 6QZ* E-mail johnbloem@aol.com

HALL, The Very Revd John Robert. b 49. St Chad's Coll Dur BA71. Cuddesdon Coll 73. **d** 75 **p** 76. C Kennington St Jo *S'wark* 75-78; P-in-c S Wimbledon All SS 78-84; V Streatham St Pet 84-92; Dioc Dir of Educn *Blackb* 92-98; Hon Can Blackb Cathl 92-94 and 2001-06; Can Res 94-98; Gen Sec Nat Soc 98-06; Gen Sec C of E Bd of Educn 98-02; Chief Educn Officer and Hd Educn Division Abps' Coun 03-06; Hon C S Norwood St Alb *S'wark* 03-06; Dean Westmr from 06. *The Deanery, Dean's Yard, London SW1P 3PA* Tel (020) 7654 4801 Fax 7654 4883 E-mail john.hall@westminster-abbey.org

HALL, John Terence Peter. b 67. St Jo Coll Dur BA98. Cranmer Hall Dur. **d** 98 **p** 99. C Towcester w Easton Neston *Pet* 98-01; P-in-c Blakesley w Adstone and Maidford etc 01-07; C Greens Norton w Bradden and Lichborough 06-07; R Lambfold from

07; RD Towcester from 09. *The Vicarage, Collswell Lane, Blakesley, Towcester NN12 8RB* Tel and fax (01327) 860507 E-mail fr-john@lambfold.org.uk

HALL, Jonathan. b 62. Ch Ch Coll Cant BA83 MCIPD94. STETS BTh99. **d** 99 **p** 00. C Weymouth H Trin *Sarum* 99-03; R Whippingham w E Cowes *Portsm* from 03; RD W Wight from 07. *The Rectory, 69 Victoria Grove, East Cowes PO32 6DL* Tel (01983) 200107

HALL, Kenneth Robert James. b 59. St Jo Coll Nottm 95. **d** 98 **p** 99. NSM Derryloran *Arm* 98-02; C Drumglass w Moygashel 02-03; C Brackaville w Donaghendry and Ballyclog 03-04; I from 04. *Holy Trinity Rectory, 82 Dungannon Road, Coalisland, Dungannon BT71 4HT* Tel (028) 8774 0243 E-mail krjhall@btinternet.com

HALL, Keven Neil. b 47. Auckland Univ BSc PhD74. K Coll Lon BD AKC79. **d** 79 **p** 80. New Zealand 79-87; NSM Shepherd's Bush St Steph w St Thos *Lon* 91-95 and 98-00; NSM W Acton St Martin 96-98; Asst Chapl NW Lon Hosp NHS Trust 00-07; Chapl Nat Soc for Epilepsy 91-03. *Flat B, Rutland House, 30 Greencroft Gardens, London NW6 3LT* Tel 07930-353717 (mobile) E-mail kevenhall@hotmail.com

HALL, Leslie. b 37. Man Univ BSc59. EMMTC 83. **d** 86 **p** 87. NSM Freiston w Butterwick and Benington *Linc* 86-02; Perm to Offic 02-05; Dioc NSM Officer 94-97. *29 Brand End Road, Butterwick, Boston PE22 0ET* Tel (01205) 760375

HALL, Mrs Lilian Evelyn Mary. b 42. SWMTC 02. **d** 05 **p** 06. NSM Ludgvan, Marazion, St Hilary and Perranuthnoe *Truro* from 05. *Pillar House, Ludgvan, Penzance TR20 8EY* Tel (01736) 740824 E-mail johnandlily.hall@btinternet.com

HALL, Mrs Linda Charlotte. b 50. Cam Inst of Educn CertEd72. St Alb Minl Tr Scheme 85 Oak Hill Th Coll 91. **d** 92 **p** 94. NSM St Alb St Steph *St Alb* 92-98; NSM Sandridge 98-99; C Ipswich All Hallows *St E* 99-00; Perm to Offic 01; TV Cwmbran Mon 01-08; P-in-c Maesglas and Duffryn from 08. *The Vicarage, Old Cardiff Road, Newport NP20 3AT*

HALL, Mrs Marigold Josephine. b 29. Linc Th Coll 81. **dss** 83 **d** 87. Chapl Asst Hellesdon Hosp Nor 83-94; Nor St Pet Parmentergate w St Jo 83-87; C 87-94; rtd 90; Perm to Offic *Nor* from 94. *36 Cavendish House, Recorder Road, Norwich NR1 1BW* Tel (01603) 625933

HALL, Ms Melanie Jane. b 55. Ex Univ BA78. Ripon Coll Cuddesdon 01. **d** 03 **p** 04. C Stepney St Dunstan and All SS *Lon* 03-06; rtd 06. *28 St Gabriel's Manor, 25 Cormont Road, London SE5 9RH* Tel (020) 7587 1766 E-mail melanie.jh@btopenworld.com

HALL, Michael Alan. b 76. Univ of Wales (Lamp) BA98. Ripon Coll Cuddesdon 99. **d** 01 **p** 02. C Wellington Ch Ch *Lich* 01-05; V Chelmsf All SS from 05. *All Saints' Vicarage, 76A Kings Road, Chelmsford CM1 4HP* Tel (01245) 281706 E-mail revd.michael@btinternet.com

HALL, Canon Michael Anthony. b 41. St Paul's Coll Grahamstown LTh64. **d** 64 **p** 65. S Africa 64-01; C E London St Alb 65-67; C Queenstown St Mich 67-69; R Port Elizabeth All SS 70-78; R E London All SS 78-81; R Queenstown St Mich w Tarkastad St Mary 81-91; Adn Aliwal N 81-01; R Barkly E St Steph and P-in-c Dordrecht St Aug 91-01; Hon Can Grahamstown from 01; P-in-c Lapford, Nymet Rowland and Coldridge *Ex* 01-03; TV N Creedy from 03. *The Rectory, Bow, Crediton EX17 6HS* Tel (01363) 82566 Mobile 07751-798670 E-mail micksandhall@btopenworld.com

HALL, Michael Edward. b 32. Fitzw Ho Cam BA57 MA61. Ridley Hall Cam 68. **d** 69 **p** 70. C Aspley *S'well* 69-73; P-in-c Bulwell St Jo 73-75; V 75-81; P-in-c Tyler's Green *Ox* 81-90; V 90-00; rtd 00. *5 Hawkings Meadow, Marlborough SN8 1UR* Tel (01672) 511713

HALL, Murray. b 34. K Coll Lon. **d** 61 **p** 62. C Eaton *Nor* 61-64; C Shalford *Guildf* 64-67; V Oxshott 67-72; P-in-c Runham *Nor* 72-80; R Filby w Thrigby w Mautby 72-80; P-in-c Stokesby w Herringby 72-80; R Filby w Thrigby, Mautby, Stokesby, Herringby etc 80-94; rtd 94; Perm to Offic *Nor* 94-07. *64 Nursery Close, Acle, Norwich NR13 3EH* Tel (01493) 751287

HALL, Nicholas Charles. b 56. **d** 86 **p** 87. C Hyde St Geo *Ches* 86-89; C Cheadle 89-91; NSM from 91. *58 Warren Avenue, Cheadle SK8 1ND* Tel 0161-491 6758 Fax 491 0285 E-mail nick@domini.org

HALL, Canon Nigel David. b 46. Univ of Wales (Cardiff) BA67 BD76 Lon Univ CertEd68. St Mich Coll Llan 73. **d** 76 **p** 77. C Cardiff St Jo *Llan* 76-81; R Llanbadarn Fawr, Llandegley and Llanfihangel etc *S & B* 81-95; RD Maelienydd 89-95; V Builth and Llandewi'r Cwm w Llangynog etc from 95; Can Brecon Cathl from 99; Prec 99-00; Treas 00-04; Chan from 04; AD Builth from 04. *The Vicarage, 1 North Road, Builth Wells LD2 3BT* Tel (01982) 552355

HALL (née WANSTALL), Canon Noelle Margaret. b 53. Wolfs Coll Cam BEd76. Sarum & Wells Th Coll 84. **dss** 86 **d** 87 **p** 94. Hythe *Cant* 86-89; Par Dn 87-89; Par Dn Reculver and Herne Bay St Bart 89-94; C 94-95; Dioc Adv in Women's Min 92-99; Asst Dir Post-Ord Tr 94-97; P-in-c Sittingbourne St Mary 95-00; P-in-c Cant St Martin and St Paul 00-02; R from 02; P-in-c

Blean 07-09; Hon Can Cant Cathl from 96; AD Cant from 05. *The Rectory, 13 Ersham Road, Canterbury CT1 3AR* Tel (01227) 462686 *or* tel and fax 768072 E-mail noelle@thinker117.freeserve.co.uk

HALL, Peter. See HALL, Canon Hubert William Peter

HALL, Peter. See HALL, The Rt Revd Albert Peter

HALL, Peter Douglas. b 60. Oak Hill Th Coll BA92. **d** 92 **p** 93. C Bromyard *Heref* 92-96; C Dorridge *Birm* 96-01; V Fareham St Jo *Portsm* from 01. *St John's Vicarage, 3A Upper St Michael's Grove, Fareham PO14 1DN* Tel (01329) 284203 *or* 280762 E-mail revpdhall@btinternet.com

HALL, Philip Edward Robin. b 36. Oak Hill Th Coll 64. **d** 67 **p** 68. C Ware Ch Ch *St Alb* 67-70; C Rayleigh *Chelmsf* 70-73; R Lewin w Catwick *York* 73-85; P-in-c Mayfield *Lich* 85-95; P-in-c Ilam w Blore Ray and Okeover 89-95; Res Min Canwell, Hints and Drayton Bassett 95-01; rtd 01; Perm to Offic *Sheff* from 01 and *Derby* from 02. *45 St Alban's Road, Sheffield S10 4DN* Tel 0114-229 5032

HALL, Richard. See HALL, George Richard Wyndham

HALL, Richard Alexander Bullock. b 71. Ex Univ BA93 Edin Univ MTh95 BD98. TISEC 95. **d** 98 **p** 99. C Boxmoor St Jo *St Alb* 98-01; CF 01-09; Hon Min Can Ripon Cathl 06-09; P-in-c Kirkby Stephen w Mallerstang etc *Carl* from 09. *The Vicarage, Vicarage Lane, Kirkby Stephen CA17 4QX* Tel (017683) 71204 E-mail richard.moonhall@btinternet.com

HALL, Robert Arthur. b 35. Lon Univ BSc66. NW Ord Course 74. **d** 77 **p** 78. C York St Paul 77-79; R Elvington w Sutton on Derwent and E Cottingwith 79-82; Chapl Tiffield Sch Northants 82-84; V Bessingby and Carnaby *York* 84-88; V Fulford 88-00; P-in-c York St Denys 97-00; rtd 00; Perm to Offic *York* from 00. *11 Almond Grove, Filey YO14 9EH* Tel (01723) 518355 E-mail robertandjune@cwctv.net

HALL, Robert Stainburn. b 72. Qu Coll Cam BA93. St Steph Ho Ox 96. **d** 98 **p** 99. C Worc SE 98-01; TV Halas from 01. *St Margaret's Vicarage, 55 Quarry Lane, Halesowen B63 4PD* Tel 0121-550 8744

HALL, Roger John. b 53. MBE97. Linc Th Coll. **d** 84 **p** 85. C Shrewsbury St Giles w Sutton and Atcham *Lich* 84-87; CF 87-07; Warden Amport Ho 98-01; Chapl Guards Chpl Lon 01-03; Asst Chapl Gen 03-07; Dir Ords 98-02 and Warden of Readers 98-07; QHC 06-07; Dep P in O from 07; Chapl St Pet-ad-Vincula at HM Tower of Lon from 07; Chapl Bacon's Coll from 07. *The Chaplain's Residence, HM Tower of London, London EC3N 4AB* Tel (020) 3166 6796 E-mail roger.hall@hrp.org.uk

HALL, Ronald Cecil. b 20. St Aid Birkenhead 63. **d** 65 **p** 66. C Tamworth *Lich* 65-69; R Talke 69-74; V Birstwith *Ripon* 74-90; P-in-c Thornthwaite w Thruscross and Darley 76-77; rtd 90. *Wickham House, Kingsmead, Farm Road, Bracklesham Bay, Chichester PO20 8JU* Tel (01243) 671190

HALL, Mrs Rosalyn. b 58. NEOC 04. **d** 07 **p** 08. C Washington *Dur* from 07. *38 Brancepeth Road, Washington NE38 0LA* Tel 07790-209472 (mobile) E-mail rosalyn44@hotmail.com

HALL, Sonia Winifred. See RUDD, Mrs Sonia Winifred

HALL, Stephen Clarence. b 23. Kelham Th Coll 46. **d** 51 **p** 52. C Killingworth *Newc* 51-53; C Newc H Cross 53-56; Rhodesia 56-77; S Africa from 77; R Makoni 56-69; P-in-c Bonda 59-62; R Mabelreign 62-68; Chapl Univ Coll of Rhodesia 68-77; Chapl Michaelhouse Sch 77-86; R Richard's Bay St Andr 86-97; rtd 97. *PO Box 102124, Meer-en-See, Zululand, 3901 South Africa* Tel (0027) (351) 32293

HALL, Stephen Philip. b 56. Ripon Coll Cuddesdon. **d** 84 **p** 85. C Camberwell St Giles *S'wark* 84-88; Chapl Brighton Poly *Chich* 88-92; TV Bicester w Bucknell, Caversfield and Launton *Ox* 92-02; Sub Chapl HM Pris Bullingdon 92-02; TV Southampton (City Cen) *Win* from 02. *The Deanery, 100 Chapel Road, Southampton SO14 5GL* Tel (023) 8063 3134

HALL, Prof Stuart George. b 28. New Coll Ox BA52 MA55 BD72. Ripon Hall Ox 53. **d** 54 **p** 55. C Newark w Coddington *S'well* 54-58; Tutor Qu Coll Birm 58-62; Lect Th Nottm Univ 62-73; Sen Lect 73-78; Prof Ecclesiastical Hist K Coll Lon 78-90; Perm to Offic *St Alb* 80-86 and *S'wark* 86-90; R Pittenweem *St And* 90-98; R Elie and Earlsferry 90-98; rtd 93. *Hopedene, 15 High Street, Elie, Leven KY9 1BY* Tel and fax (01333) 330145 E-mail sgh1@st-andrews.ac.uk

HALL, Thomas Bartholomew Berners. b 39. St Fran Coll Brisbane 63 ThL65. **d** 65 **p** 66. Australia 65-75 and from 82; C Townsville Cathl 65-66; C Rockhampton Cathl 66-69; P-in-c Emerald 69-70; R 70-75; P-in-c Whitehawk *Chich* 75-82; V Inglewood and Texas 82-89; V Pine Rivers S 85-89; R Strathpine from 89. *2 Lindale Court, Cashmere Qld 4500, Australia* Tel (0061) (7) 3882 0880 *or* 3881 2090 Mobile 428-711719 E-mail tombbhall@ozemail.com.au

HALL, Timothy Patrick. b 65. Bucks Coll of Educn BSc87 Oak Hill Th Coll BA93. Trin Coll Bris 99. **d** 01 **p** 02. C Kingsnorth and Shadoxhurst *Cant* 01-04; P-in-c Crowfield w Stonham Aspal and Mickfield *St E* from 04; P-in-c Coddenham w Gosbeck and Hemingstone w Henley from 04; RD Bosmere 07-08. *The*

Rectory, The Street, Stonham Aspal, Stowmarket IP14 6AQ Tel (01449) 711409 E-mail tph@tesco.net

HALL, Timothy Robert. b 52. Dur Univ BA74. St Jo Coll Nottm LTh87. **d** 87 **p** 88. C Hawarden *St As* 87-89; Chapl St D Coll Llandudno from 90. *Woodpecker Cottage, St David's College, Llandudno LL30 1RD* Tel (01492) 581224

HALL, William. b 34. Hull Univ BSc(Econ)56. NEOC 89. **d** 92 **p** 93. NSM Bishopwearmouth St Nic *Dur* 92-01; rtd 01. *31 Nursery Road, Silksworth Lane, Sunderland SR3 1NT* Tel 0191-528 4843

HALL, Canon William Cameron. b 40. K Coll Lon 60. **d** 65 **p** 66. C Thornaby on Tees St Paul *York* 65-68; Chapl to Arts and Recreation *Dur* 68-05; V Grindon 71-80; Hon Can Dur Cathl from 89; Sen Chapl Actors' Ch Union 89-04; Perm to Offic *York* from 89; Hon Sen Research Fell Sunderland Univ from 98. *41 Ellerby Mews, Thornley, Durham DH6 3FB* Tel (01429) 820869 E-mail billhalluk@yahoo.co.uk

HALL-MATTHEWS, Preb John Cuthbert Berners. b 33. Univ of Qld BA55 K Coll Lon PGCE65. Coll of Resurr Mirfield 58. **d** 60 **p** 61. C Woodley St Jo the Ev *Ox* 60-63; C Is of Dogs Ch Ch and St Jo w St Luke *Lon* 63-65; Asst Chapl Ch Hosp Horsham 65-72; Chapl R Hosp Sch Holbrook 72-75; V Tupsley *Heref* 75-90; P-in-c Hampton Bishop and Mordiford w Dormington 77-90; RD Heref City 84-90; Preb Heref Cathl 85-90; TR Wolverhampton *Lich* 90-98; TR Cen Wolverhampton 98-02; Preb Lich Cathl 01-02; rtd 02. *Hillcrest, Corvedale Road, Halford, Craven Arms SY7 9BT* Tel (01588) 672706 E-mail jotricia@hall-matthews.freeserve.co.uk

HALL-THOMPSON, Colin Lloyd. b 51. JP. TCD. **d** 84 **p** 85. C Dublin Rathfarnham *D & G* 84-86; Bp's C Clonmel Union *C, C & R* 86-91; Chapl Fort Mitchel Pris 86-91; Chapl Port of Cork 86-91; I Kilbride *Conn* 91-03; I Ballymacarrett *D & D* from 03; Hon Chapl Miss to Seafarers from 91. *32 Ascot Park, Belfast BT5 6LW* Tel (028) 9065 7180 *or* 9073 8396 E-mail colin.hall-thompson@ntlworld.com

HALLAM, Mrs Janet Kay. b 59. EN(G)79 RGN01. STETS 05. **d** 08. NSM Newport St Jo *Portsm* from 08; NSM Newport St Thos from 08. *Maranatha, 10 Broadwood Lane, Newport PO30 5NE* Tel (01983) 529973 Mobile 07955-381319 E-mail jezjanet@btinternet.com

HALLAM, Lawrence Gordon. b 31. Lich Th Coll 61. **d** 63 **p** 64. C Brighton St Martin *Chich* 63-68; R Cocking w Bepton 68-71; V Eastbourne Ch Ch 71-84; V Bexhill St Barn 84-87; rtd 87; Perm to Offic *Chich* 87-92. *18 Eaton Court, Eaton Gardens, Hove BN3 3PL* Tel (01273) 772328

HALLAM, Mrs Marilyn. **d** 03 **p** 04. NSM Hayes *Roch* from 03. *83 Pickhurst Rise, West Wickham, Bromley BR4 0AE* Tel (020) 8777 2246 E-mail lyn.hallam@diocese-rochester.org

HALLAM, Nicholas Francis. b 48. Univ Coll Ox BA71 MA81 Glas Univ PhD76 MB, ChB81 MRCPath91. Ox NSM Course 84. **d** 87 **p** 88. NSM Ox St Clem 87-93; NSM Balerno *Edin* 93-05; NSM Hawkshead and Low Wray w Sawrey and Rusland etc *Carl* from 06; NSM Ambleside w Brathay from 06; Perm to Offic *Edin* from 06. *Wetherlam, Hawkshead, Ambleside LA22 0NR* Tel (01539) 436069 E-mail nick.hallam@uwclub.net

HALLAM, Canon Peter Hubert. b 33. Trin Hall Cam BA56 MA60. Westcott Ho Cam 56. **d** 58 **p** 59. C Heyhouses on Sea *Blackb* 58-62; Asst Chapl and Tutor St Bede Coll Dur 62-67; V Briercliffe *Blackb* 67-98; Hon Can Blackb Cathl 92-98; rtd 98; Perm to Offic *Blackb* from 02. *57 Grassington Drive, Burnley BB10 2SP* Tel (01282) 441070

HALLAM, Stuart Peter. b 66. St Martin's Coll Lanc BA92 Wolfs Coll Cam BTh99. Westcott Ho Cam 96. **d** 99 **p** 00. C Battersea St Mary *S'wark* 99-02; Chapl RN from 02. *Royal Naval Chaplaincy Service, Mail Point 1-2, Leach Building, Whale Island, Portsmouth PO2 8BY* Tel (023) 9262 5055 Fax 9262 5134 E-mail revhallam@aol.com

✠**HALLATT, The Rt Revd David Marrison.** b 37. Southn Univ BA59 St Cath Coll Ox BA62 MA66. Wycliffe Hall Ox 59. **d** 63 **p** 64 **c** 94. C Maghull *Liv* 63-67; PC Totley *Derby* 67-75; R Didsbury St Jas *Man* 75-80; R Barlow Moor 76-80; TR Didsbury St Jas and Em 80-89; Adn Halifax *Wakef* 89-94; Area Bp Shrewsbury *Lich* 94-01; Asst Bp Sheff from 01; rtd 02. *1 Merbeck Grove, High Green, Sheffield S35 4HE* Tel 0114-284 4440 E-mail david.hallatt@btopenworld.com

HALLATT, John Leighton. b 34. St Pet Coll Ox BA58 MA62. Wycliffe Hall Ox 58. **d** 60 **p** 61. C Ipswich St Jo *St E* 60-63; C Warrington St Paul *Liv* 63-66; V Wadsley *Sheff* 66-72; V Hindley St Pet *Liv* 72-75; Area Sec (Scotland and Dios Newc and Dur) CMS 75-83; N Sec CMS 78-83; TR Cramlington *Newc* 83-90; V Monkseaton St Mary 90-99; rtd 99; Perm to Offic *Newc* from 99. *16 Eastfield Avenue, Whitley Bay NE25 8LT* Tel 0191-252 9518

HALLETT, Miss Caroline Morwenna. b 51. Nottm Univ BSc72 PGCE74 Univ of Wales (Ban) BTh05. EAMTC 03. **d** 05 **p** 06. C Sole Bay *St E* from 05. *31 The Flies, Reydon, Southwold IP18 6YS* Tel (01502) 722663 E-mail challett@myself.com

HALLETT, Howard Adrian. b 43. Man Univ MPhil90. Oak Hill Th Coll BA81. **d** 81 **p** 82. C Walshaw Ch Ch *Man* 81-84; V Stoke sub Hamdon *B & W* 84-99; RD Ivelchester 91-95; V Kea *Truro*

99-05; rtd 05; Perm to Offic *Truro* from 05. *Tremanda, La Vague, Feock, Truro TR3 6RQ* Tel (01872) 862564

HALLETT, Miss Jacqueline Victoria (Lyn). b 54. Ex Univ BA75 PGCE76. Linc Th Coll 94. **d** 94 **p** 95. C Crook and Stanley *Dur* 94-99; P-in-c Crook 99-01; R 01-04; P-in-c Castleside 04-05; rtd 05. *39 St Mary's Avenue, Crook DL15 9HY* Tel (01388) 766665

HALLETT, Keith Philip. b 37. Tyndale Hall Bris 61. **d** 64 **p** 65. C Higher Openshaw *Man* 64-68; C Bushbury *Lich* 68-71; P-in-c Drayton Bassett 71-72; R 72-90; V Fazeley 71-90; P-in-c Hints 78-83; V 83-90; C-in-c Canwell CD 78-83; V Canwell 83-90; RD Tamworth 81-90; P-in-c Buckhurst Hill *Chelmsf* 90-93; TR 93-02; rtd 02; Perm to Offic *B & W* from 03. *46 Balmoral Way, Worle, Weston-super-Mare BS22 9AL* Tel (01934) 413711 E-mail kph@webtribe.net

HALLETT, Peter. b 49. Bath Univ BSc72. Oak Hill Th Coll. **d** 76 **p** 77. C Brinsworth w Catcliffe *Sheff* 76-79; P-in-c Doncaster St Jas 80-81; V 81-86; R Henstridge and Charlton Horethorne w Stowell *B & W* 86-07; P-in-c Abbas and Templecombe w Horsington 06-07; R Abbas and Templecombe, Henstridge and Horsington from 07. *The Vicarage, Church Street, Henstridge, Templecombe BA8 0QE* Tel and fax (01963) 362266 E-mail halatvic@aol.com

HALLETT, Peter Duncan. b 43. CCC Cam BA66 MA68. Westcott Ho Cam 69. **d** 71 **p** 72. C Sawston *Ely* 71-73; C Lyndhurst and Emery Down *Win* 73-78; C Skegness and Winthorpe *Linc* 78-80; P-in-c Samlesbury *Blackb* 80-91; Asst Dir RE 80-00; C Leyland St Ambrose 91-94; V Lostock Hall 00-09; P-in-c Farington Moss 03-09; V Lostock Hall and Farington Moss 09; rtd 09; Perm to Offic *Blackb* from 09. *Fosbrooke House, 8 Clifton Drive, Lytham St Annes FY8 5RQ* Tel (01253) 667052

HALLETT, Raymond. b 44. EMMTC 85. **d** 88 **p** 89. NSM Hucknall Torkard *S'well* 88-01; NSM Basford St Leodegarius 01-03. *26 Nursery Close, Hucknall, Nottingham NG15 6DQ* Tel 0115-953 7677

HALLIDAY, Christopher Norton Robert. b 48. Bradf Univ PhD99. NOC 82. **d** 85 **p** 86. C Davyhulme St Mary *Man* 85-87; Lect Bolton St Pet 87-90; I Rathdrum w Glenealy, Derralossary and Laragh *D & G* 90-00; R Valley Lee St Geo SU00-05; Perm to Offic *Man* 07-08; TR Saddleworth from 08. *Lydgate Vicarage, Stockport Road, Lydgate, Oldham OL4 4JJ* Tel (01457) 872117 E-mail christopher@olg.com

HALLIDAY, Mrs Diana Patricia. b 40. ALA66. NOC 89. **d** 92 **p** 94. NSM Burley in Wharfedale *Bradf* 92-95; NSM Harden and Wilsden 95-97; P-in-c Cullingworth 97-05; Chapl Airedale NHS Trust 04-05; rtd 06. *7 Kirkstall Gardens, Keighley BD21 5PN* Tel (01535) 606048 Mobile 07774-235844 E-mail revdi@halliday2000.fsnet.co.uk

HALLIDAY, Edwin James. b 35. NW Ord Course 70. **d** 73 **p** 74. C New Bury *Man* 73-76; V Bolton St Phil 76-82; Dioc Communications Officer 82-88; V Radcliffe St Thos and St Jo 82-90; R Gt Lever 90-02; rtd 02; Perm to Offic *Man* from 02. *8 Oxford Close, Farnworth, Bolton BL4 0NF* Tel (01204) 792347

HALLIDAY, Geoffrey Lewis. b 40. Lon Coll of Div LTh66. **d** 66 **p** 67. C W Bridgford *S'well* 66-72; V Woodborough 72-78; P-in-c St Dav Bermuda 78-80; V Rampton *S'well* 80-81; P-in-c Laneham 80-81; P-in-c Treswell and Cottam 80-81; V Rampton w Laneham, Treswell and Cottam 81-85; V Attenborough 85-88; Perm to Offic *Derby* 91-92; NSM Ilkeston St Mary 92-03; rtd 03; Perm to Offic *Derby* from 03. *Frog Hollow, 323 Heanor Road, Ilkeston DE7 8TN* Tel 0115-930 8607 Mobile 07799-111093 E-mail fayandgeoff@froghollow.f9.co.uk

HALLIDAY, Jean Douglas. b 47. NTMTC 99. **d** 01 **p** 02. NSM Forest Gate Em w Upton Cross *Chelmsf* 01-02; NSM E Ham w Upton Park St Alb 02-05; NSM Becontree S from 05; Dioc Child Protection Adv from 05. *St John's Flat, 522A Goresbrook Road, Dagenham RM9 4XB* Tel and fax (020) 8593 0616 E-mail jhalliday@chelmsford.anglican.org

HALLIDAY, Louisa. b 42. Open Univ BA77 BA94. STETS. **d** 00 **p** 01. NSM Wylye and Till Valley *Sarum* from 00. *Station House, Great Wishford, Salisbury SP2 0PA* Tel (01722) 790618 E-mail greatwishford@yahoo.co.uk

HALLIDAY, Paula Patricia. *See* ROBINSON, Paula Patricia

✠**HALLIDAY, The Rt Revd Robert Taylor.** b 32. Glas Univ MA54 BD57. Edin Th Coll 55. **d** 57 **p** 58 **c** 90. C St Andrews St Andr *St And* 57-60; C Glas St Marg 60-63; Lect NT Edin Th Coll 63-74; R Edin H Cross 63-83; Tutor Edin Univ 69-71; Can St Mary's Cathl 73-83; R St Andrews St Andr *St And* 83-90; Tutor St Andr Univ 84-90; Bp Bre 90-96; rtd 96; Lic to Offic *Edin* from 97. *28 Forbes Road, Edinburgh EH10 4ED* Tel 0131-221 1490

HALLING, William Laurence. b 43. Linc Coll Ox BA64 MA68 Lon Univ BD68. Tyndale Hall Bris 66. **d** 68 **p** 69. C Beckenham St Jo *Roch* 68-72; C Walton H Trin *Ox* 72-78; V Barrow St Mark *Carl* 78-86; R Kirkheaton *Wakef* 86-04; Chapl Mill Hill Hosp Huddersfield 86-95; rtd 04; Perm to Offic *Wakef* from 04; Dioc Adv on Environmental Issues from 08. *56 Westborough Drive, Halifax HX2 7QL* Tel (01422) 320829 E-mail halling@uwclub.net

HALLIWELL, Christopher Eigil. b 57. Newc Univ BA78. Trin Coll Bris 89. **d** 91 **p** 92. C Mildenhall *St E* 91-94; R Wrentham w Benacre, Covehithe, Frostenden etc 94-97; TV Sileby, Cossington and Seagrave *Leic* 97-01; V Preston St Cuth *Blackb* from 01. *St Cuthbert's Vicarage, 20 Black Bull Lane, Fulwood, Preston PR2 3PX* Tel (01772) 717346

HALLIWELL, Ivor George. b 33. St Cath Coll Cam BA57 MA60. Wells Th Coll 58. **d** 60 **p** 60. C Hanworth St Geo *Lon* 60-62; C Willenhall *Cov* 62-65; C-in-c Whitley St Jas CD 65-68; V Whitley 68-72; V Corton *Nor* 72-77; P-in-c Hopton 72-74; V 74-77; Asst Chapl HM Pris Pentonville 77; Chapl HM Pris Ex 77-83; Chapl HM Pris Jersey 75-80; Vice-Dean Jersey *Win* 85-99; Tutor S Dios Minl Tr Scheme 92-96; rtd 96; Hon C Jersey Grouville *Win* 96-99; Hon Can Win Cathl 98-99; Perm to Offic from 99. *1 Alliance Cottages, Awbridge Hill, Romsey SO51 0HF* Tel (01794) 830395 E-mail halliwells@jerseymail.co.uk

HALLOWS, John Martin. b 50. Birm Univ BA78 Lon Univ PGCE82 E Lon Univ MSc93. Oak Hill Th Coll 92. **d** 94 **p** 95. C Boxmoor St Jo *St Alb* 94-98; TV Bracknell *Ox* 98-01; V Barrowford and Newchurch-in-Pendle *Blackb* from 01. *St Thomas's Vicarage, Wheatley Lane Road, Barrowford, Nelson BB9 6QS* Tel and fax (01282) 613206 E-mail jhallows@compuserve.com

HALLS, Canon Peter Ernest. b 38. Bris Univ BA62. Tyndale Hall Bris 59. **d** 64 **p** 65. C Blackb St Barn 64-67; C Bromley Ch Ch *Roch* 67-70; V Halvergate w Tunstall *Nor* 70-79; V Freethorpe w Wickhampton 71-79; P-in-c Beighton and Moulton 77-79; V Tuckswood 79-90; RD Nor S 86-90; R Brooke, Kirstead, Mundham w Seething and Thwaite 90-03; RD Depwade 91-97 and 01-03; Hon Can Nor Cathl 99-03; rtd 03; Perm to Offic *Nor* from 03. *1 Church Farm Close, Weston Longville, Norwich NR9 5JY* Tel (01603) 880835

HALLS, Susan Mary. *See* HEMSLEY HALLS, Susan Mary

HALMSHAW, Mrs Stella Mary. b 36. Brighton Coll of Educn TCert57. St Alb Minl Tr Scheme 81. **dss** 84 **d** 87 **p** 96. Radlett *St Alb* 84-01; Par Dn 87-93; Hon C 93-01; Chapl Herts Univ 93-96; rtd 96; P-in-c Wittersham w Stone-in-Oxney and Ebony *Cant* from 01. *The Rectory, The Street, Wittersham, Tenterden TN30 7EA* Tel (01797) 270142

HALSALL, Graham. b 61. Sheff Univ BA82 Westmr Coll Ox PGCE84. St Steph Ho Ox MTh00. **d** 00 **p** 01. C Preston St Jo and St Geo *Blackb* 00-02; C Torrisholme 02-04; P-in-c Bamber Bridge St Sav from 04. *St Saviour's Vicarage, Church Road, Bamber Bridge, Preston PR5 6AJ* Tel (01772) 335374 E-mail graham@halsall4461.reeserve.co.uk

HALSALL, Mrs Isobel Joan. b 47. Liv Univ CertEd71. Local Minl Tr Course 91. **d** 94 **p** 95. OLM Walshaw Ch Ch *Man* 94-05; NSM Cockermouth Area *Carl* from 05. *The Vicarage, Bridekirk, Cockermouth CA13 0PE* Tel (01900) 826557 E-mail stbridgets@tiscali.co.uk

HALSEY, Anthony Michael James. b 35. K Coll Cam BA56 MA62 Solicitor 64. St Jo Coll Nottm 73. **d** 75 **p** 76. C Derby St Werburgh 75-77; Chapl Canford Sch Wimborne 78-87; TV Sanderstead All SS *S'wark* 87-89; Perm to Offic *Portsm* from 89; rtd 00. *Woodlands, South Road, Liphook GU30 7HS* Tel (01428) 724459 E-mail halseys@southroad.fsbusiness.co.uk

HALSEY, Brother John Walter Brooke. b 33. Cam Univ BA57. Westcott Ho Cam 61. **d** 61 **p** 62. C Stocksbridge *Sheff* 61-65; Community of the Transfiguration Midlothian from 65; Ind Chapl Edin 65-69. *Hermitage of the Transfiguration, 23 Manse Road, Roslin EH25 9LF*

HALSON, Bryan Richard. b 32. Jes Coll Cam BA56 MA60 Liv Univ MA72 Geneva Univ 59. Ridley Hall Cam 57. **d** 59 **p** 60. C Coulsdon St Andr *S'wark* 59-62; Lic to Offic *Ches* 63-68; Tutor St Aid Birkenhead 63-65; Sen Tutor 65-68; Vice-Prin 68-69; Lect Alsager Coll of Educn 69-72; Prin Lect Crewe and Alsager Coll of HE 72-90; Perm to Offic *Ches* from 97. *1 Victoria Mill Drive, Willaston, Nantwich CW5 6RR*

HALSTEAD, James. b 74. Nottm Univ BA97. Oak Hill Th Coll MTh09. **d** 09. C Gee Cross *Ches* from 09. *121 Dowson Road, Hyde SK14 5HJ* Tel 0161-366 5083 E-mail jameshalstead@mac.com

HALSTEAD, Stuart. NTMTC 02. **d** 05 **p** 06. C Houghton Regis *St Alb* 05-08; C Kilburn St Aug w St Jo *Lon* from 08. *122 Dibdin House, Maida Vale, London W9 1QG* Tel (020) 7328 9301 E-mail stuart.halstead@btopenworld.com

HALTON, Tony James. b 66. Dundee Univ BSc88 City Univ MSc01 RGN94. NTMTC BA06. **d** 06 **p** 07. NSM W Hendon St Jo *Lon* from 06. *29 Pageant Road, St Albans AL1 1NB* Tel (01727) 893229 E-mail tonyjhalton@hotmail.com

✠**HAMBIDGE, The Most Revd Douglas Walter.** b 27. Lon Univ BD58. ALCD53 Angl Th Coll (BC) DD70. **d** 53 **p** 54 **c** 69. C Dalston St Mark w St Bart *Lon* 53-56; Canada 56-93 and from 95; R Cassiar 56-58; R Smithers 58-64; R Fort St John 64-69; Can Caledonia 65-69; Bp Caledonia 69-80; Bp New Westmr 80; Abp New Westmr and Metrop BC 81-93; Prin St Mark's Th Coll Dar es Salaam 93-95; Asst Bp Dar es Salaam 93-95; Chan Vancouver Sch of Th from 95. *1621 Golf Club Drive, Delta BC V4M 4E6, Canada* Tel (001) (604) 948 1931 E-mail hambidge@vst.edu

HAMBIDGE, John Robert. b 29. Birm Univ MA02. Sarum Th Coll. **d** 55 **p** 56. C Tynemouth H Trin W Town *Newc* 55-57; C Middlesbrough St Ju the Ev *York* 58-63; C Clerkenwell H Redeemer w St Phil *Lon* 63-64; C Richmond St Mary *S'wark* 64-66; V Richmond St Jo 66-76; R Swanscombe *Roch* 76-84; V Aberedw w Llandeilo Graban and Llanbadarn etc *S & B* 84-91; P-in-c Sibson w Sheepy and Ratcliffe Culey *Leic* 91-94; P-in-c Orton-on-the-Hill w Twycross etc 92-94; R The Sheepy Gp 95-97; rtd 97; Perm to Offic *Lich* from 99. *99 Elizabeth Drive, Tamworth B79 8DE* Tel (01827) 61526 E-mail john@hambidge.com

HAMBLEN, John William Frederick. b 24. Sarum Th Coll 64. **d** 65 **p** 66. C Weymouth H Trin *Sarum* 66-68; C Marlborough 68-70; V Chardstock 70-77; P-in-c Lytchett Matravers 77-83; P-in-c Burpham *Chich* 83-89; Dioc Stewardship Adv 83-89; rtd 89; Perm to Offic *Ex* from 89. *2 Woodridge Mead, Bishops Lydeard, Taunton TA4 3PQ*

HAMBLIN, Derek Gordon Hawthorn. b 35. SWMTC 94. **d** 96 **p** 97. NSM S Brent and Rattery *Ex* 96-01; Chapl Larnaca Cyprus 01-02; Asst Chapl Dubai UAE 03-04; Perm to Offic *Ex* and Cyprus and the Gulf from 04. *2 Brookwood Close, South Brent TQ10 9DH* Tel (01364) 72388 *or* (00357) (24) 620455 E-mail derekthecleric1@aol.com

HAMBLIN, John Talbot. b 38. St Steph Ho Ox 64. **d** 66 **p** 67. C Newc St Jo 66-70; C Covent Garden St Paul *Lon* 70-71; C St Marylebone Ch Ch w St Barn 71-72; C St Marylebone Ch Ch w St Paul 72-73; C Hendon St Mary 73-76; V Tottenham Ch Ch W Green 76-77; P-in-c Hornsey St Pet 76-77; V W Green Ch Ch w St Pet 77-96; rtd 98. *42 Evelyn Lancaster House, St Marks Lane, Horsham RH12 5PU* Tel (01403) 252095

HAMBLIN, Mrs Karen Elizabeth. b 59. St Mary's Coll Dur BA80 Homerton Coll Cam PGCE82. St Jo Coll Nottm 05. **d** 07 **p** 08. C Long Eaton St Jo *Derby* from 07. *5 Mendip Close, Long Eaton, Nottingham NG10 4NY* Tel 0115-973 2646 Mobile 07711-664649

HAMBLIN, Canon Roger Noel. b 42. Ripon Hall Ox 67. **d** 70 **p** 71. C Scotforth *Blackb* 70-73; C Altham w Clayton le Moors 73-76; V Cockerham w Winmarleigh 76-87; V Cockerham w Winmarleigh and Glasson 87-00; P-in-c Wray w Tatham and Tatham Fells 00-03; V E Lonsdale from 03; Hon Can Blackb Cathl from 04. *The Vicarage, Main Street, Wray, Lancaster LA2 8QF* Tel (01524) 221030

HAMBLING, Paul Gary. b 73. St Steph Ho Ox 05. **d** 07 **p** 08. C Woodbridge St Mary *St E* from 07. *40 Old Barrack Road, Woodbridge IP12 4ET* Tel (01394) 446051 E-mail curate@stmaryswoodbridge.org

HAMBORG, Graham Richard. b 52. Bris Univ BSc73 Nottm Univ BA76 MTh77. St Jo Coll Nottm 74. **d** 77 **p** 78. C Tile Cross *Birm* 77-80; C Upton cum Chalvey *Ox* 80-82; TV 82-86; V Ruscombe and Twyford 86-04; AD Sonning 03-04; CME Adv *Chelmsf* from 04; C Gt Baddow from 04; C Lt Baddow from 05. *The Rectory, Colam Lane, Little Baddow, Chelmsford CM3 4SY* Tel (01245) 222454 E-mail revghamborg@hotmail.com

HAMBROOK, Peter John. b 37. **d** 01 **p** 02. OLM Gt Mongeham w Ripple and Sutton by Dover *Cant* 01-04; OLM Deal St Leon w St Rich and Sholden etc from 04; OLM Ringwould w Kingsdown and Ripple etc from 05. *4 Brewery Cottages, Northbourne Road, Great Mongeham, Deal CT14 0HA* Tel (01304) 364457 E-mail peter@4brewerycotts.fsnet.co.uk

HAMEL COOKE, Ian Kirk. b 17. Birm Univ BA39. Chich Th Coll 39. **d** 41 **p** 42. C Bedminster St Fran *Bris* 41-43; C Alton All SS *Win* 43-48; V N Baddesley 48-55; R Hartest w Boxted *St E* 55-63; V Addlestone *Guildf* 63-75; R Tittleshall w Godwick and Wellingham *Nor* 75-76; R Tittleshall w Godwick, Wellingham and Weasenham 76-82; rtd 82; Perm to Offic *Nor* 82-09. *Millfield, Norton Road, Great Ashfield, Bury St Edmunds IP31 3HJ* Tel (01359) 244453

HAMER, David Handel. b 41. Cape Town Univ BA61 Trin Coll Ox BA66. Coll of Resurr Mirfield 62. **d** 66 **p** 67. S Africa 66-73; C Claremont 66-70; Chapl St Paul's Coll Grahamstown 70-73; Chapl Blundell's Sch Tiverton 73-01; rtd 01. *Jaspers Green, Uplowman, Tiverton EX16 7DP* Tel (01884) 829130

HAMER, Irving David. b 59. **d** 84 **p** 85. C Newton Nottage *Llan* 84-88; C Roath 88-90; V Llansawel, Briton Ferry 90-00; V Roath St Martin from 00; Miss to Seafarers from 90. *St Martin's*

Vicarage, Strathnairn Street, Roath, Cardiff CF24 3JL Tel (029) 2048 2295 E-mail fr.irving.hamer@ntlworld.com

HAMER, Mrs Penelope Ann. MA FIBMS. **d** 00 **p** 01. NSM Hartpury w Corse and Staunton *Glouc* from 00. *Catsbury Cottage, Corsend Road, Hartpury GL19 3BP* Tel (01425) 700314 E-mail revpennyahamer@aol.com

HAMER, Canon Val. b 52. Leeds Univ BA74. S'wark Ord Course 83. **dss** 86 **d** 87 **p** 94. Warlingham w Chelsham and Farleigh *S'wark* 86-88; Par Dn 87-88; Par Dn Caterham 88-94; C 94-96; RD Caterham 95-96; Sub Chapl HM Pris Wandsworth 88-95; V Addiscombe St Mildred *S'wark* 96-02; Ldr Post Ord Tr Croydon Area 94-99; Can Res and Chan Heref Cathl 02-08; Dioc Missr and P-in-c Coychurch, Llangan and St Mary Hill from 08. *The Rectory, 9 Heol Cae Tyla, Coychurch, Bridgend CF35 5HR.* Tel (01656) 656313 E-mail valhamer@churchinwales.org.uk

HAMEY, Geoffrey Allan. b 25. Lon Univ BSc47. S'wark Ord Course 75. **d** 78 **p** 79. NSM Pinner *Lon* 78-83; P-in-c Fincham *Ely* 83-84; P-in-c Marham 83-84; P-in-c Shouldham 83-84; P-in-c Shouldham Thorpe 83-84; V 84-88; rtd 88; Hon C Winkleigh *Ex* 88-96; Perm to Offic *Ex* 96-02; *Lich* from 02. *15 Victoria Gardens, Lichfield WS13 8BG* Tel (01543) 416079

✠**HAMID, The Rt Revd David.** b 55. McMaster Univ Ontario BSc78. Trin Coll Toronto MDiv81 Hon DD05. **d** 81 **p** 82 **c** 02. C Burlington St Chris Canada 81-83; R Burlington St Jo 83-87; Miss Co-ord Gen Syn of Angl Ch of Canada 87-96; Hon Can Santo Domingo 93-02; Dir Ecum Affairs ACC 96-02; Suff Bp Eur from 02; Hon Asst Bp Roch from 03; Hon C Orpington St Andr from 03. *14 Tufton Street, London SW1P 3QZ* Tel (020) 7898 1160 Fax 7898 1166 E-mail david.hamid@europe.c-of-e.org.uk

HAMIL, Sheila. b 49. Northd Coll of Educn TCert71. NEOC 92. **d** 95 **p** 98. NSM Wallsend St Luke *Newc* 95-97; NSM Long Benton St Mary 97-02; NSM Willington 02-06; rtd 06; Perm to Offic *Newc* from 06. *5 Kings Road, Wallsend NE28 7QT* Tel 0191-287 3449 E-mail sheila@sheilahamil.co.uk

HAMILL-STEWART, Simon Francis. b 32. Pemb Coll Cam BA56. NOC 77. **d** 80 **p** 81. NSM Neston *Ches* 80-83; C 83-86; V Over St Jo 86-00; Dioc Ecum Officer 92-00; rtd 00; Perm to Offic *Ches* 00-01 and from 04; C Middlewich w Byley 01-03. *87 Warmingham Lane, Middlewich CW10 0DJ* Tel (01606) 737329

HAMILTON, Gerald Murray Percival. b 14. Ch Coll Cam BA37 MA41. Ridley Hall Cam 37. **d** 39 **p** 40. C Shirley *Win* 39-40; Bp's Dom Chapl 40-41; C Odiham w S Warnborough and Long Sutton 41-44; C Leeds St Pet *Ripon* 44-46; V Ashton-upon-Mersey St Mary Magd *Ches* 46-51; Relig Broadcasting Org BBC N Region 52-65; Lic to Offic *Ches* 51-65; Can Res Newc Cathl 65-67; Bp's Ind and Community Adv 65-67; Prin Lect Coll of Ripon & York St Jo 67-78; R Crayke w Brandsby and Yearsley *York* 78-82; rtd 82; Perm to Offic *York* from 82. *The Rectory, Duck Street, Steeple Langford, Salisbury SP3 4NH* Tel (01722) 790192 E-mail peter@standrewgate.demon.co.uk

HAMILTON, Graham. See HAMILTON, William Graham

HAMILTON, James Davy. b 20. Hatf Coll Dur 38. Edin Th Coll 40. **d** 43 **p** 45. C Kirkcaldy *St And* 43-46; C Wokingham St Paul *Ox* 46-49; Chapl RAF 49-55; C St Athan *Llan* 49-50; C Boscombe Down 50-52; C Amersham *Ox* 55-62; R Sandford w Upton Hellions *Ex* 62-79; P-in-c Ashprington 79-81; P-in-c Cornworthy 79-81; R Ashprington, Cornworthy and Dittisham 81-83; C Weymouth St Paul *Sarum* 83-85; rtd 85; Perm to Offic *Ex* from 85. *21 Langaton Lane, Exeter EX1 3SP* Tel (01392) 466747

HAMILTON, John Frederick. b 57. Leeds Univ BA78. Edin Th Coll 78. **d** 80 **p** 81. C Whitkirk *Ripon* 80-83; C Leeds Belle Is St Jo w St Barn 83-86; V Oulton w Woodlesford 86-94; V Cookridge H Trin from 94. *Cookridge Vicarage, 53 Green Lane, Cookridge, Leeds LS16 7LW* Tel 0113-267 4921 Fax 261 2102 Mobile 07780-677341 E-mail sulaco57@btopenworld.com

HAMILTON, John Hans Patrick. b 44. K Coll Lon BD66 AKC67 Lon Univ DipAdEd76 FCMI96. St Boniface Warminster 66. **d** 67 **p** 68. C Cleobury Mortimer w Hopton Wafers *Heref* 67-69; C Sanderstead All SS *S'wark* 69-73; V Battersea St Mary-le-Park 73-75; Perm to Offic *Ely* 75-90; Dir of Educn *Derby* 90-95; P-in-c Cliddesden and Ellisfield w Farleigh Wallop etc *Win* 95-00; Perm to Offic 00-03; P-in-c Dungeon Hill and The Caundles w Folke and Holwell *Sarum* 03-07; TR Wylye and Till Valley from 07. *The Rectory, Duck Street, Steeple Langford, Salisbury SP3 4NH* Tel (01722) 790198 E-mail john@montoid2.fsnet.co.uk

HAMILTON, John Nicholas. b 49. Trin Coll Cam BA71 MA75. Ridley Hall Cam 72. **d** 75 **p** 76. C Ealing Dean St Jo *Lon* 75-79; C Stoughton *Guildf* 79-83; R Denton St Lawr *Man* 83-88; R The Sherbornes w Pamber *Win* from 88. *The Rectory, Vyne Road, Sherborne St John, Basingstoke RG24 9HX* Tel (01256) 850434 E-mail jnh@btinternet.com

HAMILTON, Nigel John. See TABER-HAMILTON, Nigel John

HAMILTON, Canon Noble Ridgeway. b 23. TD66. TCD BA45 MA49. **d** 47 **p** 48. C Dundela St Mark *D & D* 47-51; C Holywood 51-55; I Belfast St Clem 55-61; I Seapatrick 61-89;

Can Dromore Cathl 66-89; Prec 75-84; Chan 84-89; rtd 89; Lic to Offic *D & D* from 90. *67 Meadowvale, Waringstown, Craigavon BT66 7RL* Tel (028) 3888 2064

HAMILTON, Paul Stuart. b 69. Univ of Wales (Ban) BTh02. EAMTC. **d** 02 **p** 03. C Hawkwell *Chelmsf* 02-06; V Ingrave St Nic and St Steph from 06. *The Vicarage, Thorndon Gate, Ingrave, Brentwood CM13 3RG* Tel (01277) 812190 E-mail pshamilton@btinternet.com

HAMILTON, Richard Alexander. b 46. Pemb Coll Cam BA67 MA87 Brunel Univ PGCE97. S Dios Minl Tr Scheme 82. **d** 85 **p** 86. NSM Guernsey St Sampson *Win* 85-89; C Highgate St Mich *Lon* 89-91; P-in-c Tottenham H Trin 91-96; Master Denbigh High Sch Luton 96-98; TV The Ortons, Alwalton and Chesterton *Ely* from 98. *The Rectory, 67 Church Drive, Orton Waterville, Peterborough PE2 5HE* Tel (01733) 238877 Mobile 07958-317512 E-mail hamvic@aol.com

HAMILTON, William Graham. b 63. New Coll Ox BA86. Wycliffe Hall Ox BA95. **d** 95 **p** 96. C Ivybridge w Harford *Ex* 95-99; V Bovey Tracey SS Pet, Paul and Thos w Hennock from 99. *The Vicarage, Coombe Cross, Bovey Tracey, Newton Abbot TQ13 9EP* Tel (01626) 833813 E-mail revgraham.hamilton@btopenworld.com

HAMILTON, William Joseph Taylor. b 40. Univ Coll Ches MTh00. **d** 97 **p** 98. NSM Ches 97-02; C Thurlstone, S Milton, W Alvington etc *Ex* 02-07; rtd 07; Perm to Offic *Ches* from 07. *39 Vincent Drive, Chester CH4 7RQ* Tel (01244) 677843 E-mail bill@hamiltonb.freeserve.co.uk

HAMILTON-BROWN, James John. b 35. Lon Univ BSc59. Ridley Hall Cam 59. **d** 61 **p** 62. C Attenborough w Bramcote *S'well* 61-67; V Bramcote 67-76; R and D Officer Abps' Coun on Evang 76-79; Lic to Offic *Sarum* 76-81 and 91-95; TR Dorchester 81-91; Sec Par and People 91-95; P-in-c Tarrant Valley 95-99; C Tollard Royal w Farnham, Gussage St Michael etc 99-00; rtd 00; Perm to Offic *Sarum* from 00. *The Old Mill, Spetisbury, Blandford Forum DT11 9DF* Tel (01258) 453939 E-mail jumperhb@aol.com

HAMILTON-MANON, Phillipp Robert Christian. b 49. BA88. St Steph Ho Ox 89. **d** 90 **p** 91. C Norton St Mary *Dur* 90-94; P-in-c Cleadon Park 94-95; V 95-97; TV Lewes All SS, St Anne, St Mich and St Thos *Chich* 97-00; R Lewes St Anne from 00. *St Anne's Rectory, 57 St Anne's Crescent, Lewes BN7 1SD* Tel (01273) 472545 E-mail hamilton-manon@aol.com

HAMLET, Paul Manning. b 42. Open Univ BA81 Ex Univ MEd96 Univ of Wales (Lamp) MTh04 Lambeth STh84 FCollP96. Kelham Th Coll 61. **d** 66 **p** 67. C Rumboldswyke *Chich* 66-69; C Ely 69-73; Hon C Ipswich St Bart *St E* 73-84; Chapl Wellington Sch Somerset 84-94; Chapl Ipswich Sch 94-02; CF (TAVR) 88-99; CF (ACF) from 99; rtd 02; Perm to Offic *St E* from 02. *5 Wineanton Close, Ipswich IP4 3EE* Tel (01473) 724413 E-mail paul.hamlet@btopenworld.com

HAMMERSLEY, Peter. b 41. Lon Univ BD78 Birm Univ MEd87 PhD97. Kelham Th Coll 60. **d** 65 **p** 66. C Oadby *Leic* 65-69; R Linstead Jamaica 70-73; Chapl and Hd RE DeCarteret Coll Mandeville 73-77; Chapl K Sch and Min Can Worc Cathl 77-84; V Foley Park 84-90; TV Kidderminster St Jo and H Innocents 90-91; Dioc Warden of Readers 91; Vice-Prin Aston Tr Scheme 91-97; Adult RE Researcher St Pet Saltley Trust 98-99; Chapl HM Pris Hewell Grange from 98; Chapl HM Pris Brockhill from 06. *52 Hanbury Road, Droitwich WR9 8PR* Tel (01905) 798590 Fax 776197 Mobile 07754-545482 E-mail hammersley@tiscali.co.uk

HAMMERSLEY, Peter Angus Ragsdale. b 35. Linc Th Coll 74. **d** 76 **p** 77. C Stafford *Lich* 76-79; P-in-c W Bromwich St Andr 79-83; V 83-88; P-in-c W Bromwich Ch Ch 85-88; V Streetly 88-98; RD Walsall 90-98; C Ledbury *Heref* 98-00; Team Chapl W Heref 98-00; rtd 01; Assoc TV Ledbury *Heref* 01-04; Perm to Offic from 04. *15 Pound Close, Tarrington, Hereford HR1 4AZ* Tel (01432) 890609

HAMMERSLEY, Susan. b 67. Nottm Univ BA90. Ripon Coll Cuddesdon BA07. **d** 07 **p** 08. C Ecclesfield *Sheff* from 07. *15 Nursery Drive, Ecclesfield, Sheffield S35 9XU* Tel 0114-245 7661 E-mail suehammersley@tiscali.co.uk

HAMMETT, The Ven Barry Keith. b 47. CB06. Magd Coll Ox BA71 MA74. St Steph Ho Ox 71. **d** 74 **p** 75. C Plymouth St Pet *Ex* 74-77; Chapl RN 77-02; Chapl of the Fleet and Adn for the RN 02-06; Dir Gen Naval Chapl Service 02-06; QHC from 99; Hon Can Portsm Cathl from 02; Can Gib Cathl from 03; rtd 06; Perm to Offic *Portsm* from 07. *1 de Port Heights, Corhampton, Southampton SO32 3DA*

HAMMILL, Anthony Lawrence. b 71. Linc Coll Ox BA92 MA97 Univ Coll Lon MSc95 Anglia Ruskin Univ MA08 Fitzw Coll Cam MPhil08. Ridley Hall Cam 05. **d** 08 **p** 09. C Chalk *Roch* from 08. *6 Dene Holm Road, Northfleet, Gravesend DA11 8LE* E-mail anthony.hammill@diocese-rochester.org

HAMMON, David Edward. b 48. St Mich Coll Llan 99. **d** 01 **p** 02. C Pembroke Dock *St D* 01-04; Perm to Offic 04-08. *2 Dunmore Apartments, Warren Street, Tenby SA70 7JT* Tel (01834) 842785 Mobile 07779-711239 E-mail davidhammon@lineone.net

HAMMOND, Andrew Charles Raphael. b 63. Clare Coll Cam BA86 K Coll Cam MPhil07 LRAM91. Westcott Ho Cam 05. **d** 07 **p** 08. C St John's Wood *Lon* from 07. *3 Cochrane Street, London NW8 7PA* Tel 07884-185207 (mobile) E-mail andrewchoo7@hotmail.com

HAMMOND, Mrs Barbara Watson. b 33. Lanc Univ MA79 Bp Otter Coll TCert53 ACP70. S'wark Ord Course 89. **d** 92 **p** 94. NSM Upper Norwood St Jo *S'wark* 92-94; Hon C Spring Park All SS 94-97; Perm to Offic *S'wark* 97-02 and *Portsm* from 98. *27 Maisemore Gardens, Emsworth PO10 7JU* Tel (01243) 370531 E-mail barbara@br2811.demon.co.uk

HAMMOND, Canon Brian Leonard. b 31. Bris Univ BSc54. Wells Th Coll 56. **d** 58 **p** 59. C Clapham H Trin *S'wark* 58-62; V Walworth All SS and St Steph 62-72; V S Merstham 72-87; RD Reigate 80-86; Hon Can S'wark Cathl 83-97; V Spring Park All SS 87-97; rtd 97; Perm to Offic *S'wark* 97-02 and *Portsm* from 98; *Chich* from 05. *27 Maisemore Gardens, Emsworth PO10 7JU* Tel (01243) 370531 Mobile 07802-482974 E-mail brian@br2811.demon.co.uk

HAMMOND, Carolyn John-Baptist. b 64. St Jo Coll Ox MA90 Univ Coll Ox DPhil93 CCC Cam BA97 MA02. Westcott Ho Cam 95. **d** 98 **p** 99. C Gamlingay w Hatley St George and E Hatley *Ely* 98-99; C Gamlingay and Everton 99-01; R 01-05; Dean G&C Coll Cam from 05. *Gonville and Caius College, Trinity Street, Cambridge CB2 1TA* Tel (01223) 332400 Fax 332456 E-mail cjbh2@cam.ac.uk

HAMMOND, David Geoffrey. b 80. Glos Univ BA02. Cranmer Hall Dur 02. **d** 04 **p** 05. NSM Preston-on-Tees and Longnewton *Dur* 04-06; C 06-08; Pioneer Missr and P-in-c Nottingham St Sav *S'well* from 08. *St Saviour's Vicarage, Arkwright Walk, Nottingham NG2 2JU* Tel 0115-952 4860 Mobile 07939-464095 E-mail dave@saviours.org.uk

HAMMOND, Diana Mary. b 46. **d** 99 **p** 00. OLM Bishopstrow and Boreham *Sarum* 99-04; OLM Upper Wylye Valley from 04. *41 Bishopstrow, Warminster BA12 9HN* Tel (01985) 214495 E-mail rhlignum@blueyonder.co.uk

HAMMOND, Kathryn Mary. b 49. JP. LCTP 07. **d** 08 **p** 09. NSM Linton in Craven *Bradf* from 08; NSM Burnsall w Rylstone from 08. *15 Brooklyn, Threshfield, Skipton BD23 5ER* Tel (01756) 751871 E-mail ckham@tiscali.co.uk

HAMMOND, Canon Lindsay John. b 57. Southn Univ BA83. Sarum & Wells Th Coll 84. **d** 86 **p** 87. C Ashford *Cant* 86-90; V Appledore w Brookland, Fairfield, Brenzett etc 90-03; P-in-c Stone-in-Oxney 95-03; RD S Lympne 95-01; P-in-c Westwell and Hothfield from 03; P-in-c Charing w Charing Heath and Lt Chart from 06; Hon Min Can Cant Cathl 93-08; Hon Can from 08. *The Vicarage, Eastwell Lane, Westwell, Ashford TN25 4LQ* Tel (01233) 712576 E-mail applevic@clara.co.uk

HAMMOND, Martin James. b 62. St Jo Coll Nottm 03. **d** 05 **p** 06. C Walmley *Birm* 05-08; C Erdington 08-09; TV Bedworth *Cov* from 09. *2 Bryony Close, Bedworth CV12 0GG* Tel (024) 7664 4693 E-mail revmartinh@blueyonder.co.uk

HAMMOND, Peter Clark. b 27. Linc Coll Ox BA49 MA53. Wells Th Coll 51. **d** 52 **p** 53. C Willesborough *Cant* 52-55; C Croydon St Jo 55-59; R Barham 60-66; V Walmer 66-85; V Rolvenden 85-89; rtd 89; Perm to Offic *Ely* from 89. *19 Hardwick Street, Cambridge CB3 9JA* Tel (01223) 467425

HAMNETT, Herbert Arnold. b 22. K Coll Lon BSc49. Qu Coll Birm 49. **d** 51 **p** 52. C Greenhill St Jo *Lon* 51-54; C Horsham *Chich* 55-60; R Yapton w Ford 60-87; rtd 87; Perm to Offic *St E* 87-97. *Clarence House, Stradbrooke Road, Fressingfield, Eye IP21 5PP* Tel (01379) 588082

HAMPEL, Canon Michael Hans Joachim. b 67. Univ Coll Dur BA89 St Chad's Coll Dur MA02 FRSA02. Westcott Ho Cam 90. **d** 93 **p** 94. C Whitworth w Spennymoor *Dur* 93-97; Min Can, Prec and Sacr Dur Cathl 97-02; Sen Tutor St Chad's Coll Dur 02-04; Can Res St E Cathl from 04; Sub Dean from 08. *1 Abbey Precincts, Bury St Edmunds IP33 1RS* Tel (01284) 761982 Fax 768655 Mobile 07947-070210 E-mail michael.hampel@dunelm.org.uk

HAMPSON, Claude Eric. b 25. Rhodes Univ BA49. St Paul's Coll Grahamstown LTh50. **d** 50 **p** 51. C Pietermaritzburg Cathl S Africa 50-54; C Greenford H Cross *Lon* 54-58; Sec Fellowship of SS Alb and Sergius 58-60; Brotherhood of St Barn Australia 60-66, R Mt Isa and Adn of the W 67-74; P-in-c Mekong Vietnam 74-75; V Kilburn St Aug w St Jo *Lon* 75-77; R Branxton Australia 77-82; rtd 85. *17/250 Jersey Road, Woollahra NSW 2025, Australia* Tel (0061) (2) 9327 8215

HAMPSON, David. b 46. Chich Th Coll 69. **d** 72 **p** 73. C Penrith *Carl* 72-78; V Crosscrake 78-95; V Crosscrake and Preston Patrick 95; P-in-c Arnside 95-97; rtd 97. *81 Rectory Road, North Ashton, Wigan WN4 0QD* Tel (01942) 728760

HAMPSON, Miss Judith Elizabeth. b 50. I M Marsh Coll of Physical Educn Liv BEd72 Open Univ BA89. Ripon Coll Cuddesdon 90. **d** 92 **p** 94. C Alnwick *Newc* 92-96; R Allendale w Whitfield 96-05; V Haydon Bridge and Beltingham w Henshaw from 05. *The Vicarage, Haydon Bridge, Hexham NE47 6LL* Tel (01434) 684307 E-mail rev.jude@dsl.pipex.com

HAMPSON, Michael John. b 67. Jes Coll Ox BA88. Ripon Coll Cuddesdon 88. **d** 91 **p** 92. C W Burnley All SS *Blackb* 91-93; C Harlow St Mary Magd *Chelmsf* 93-00; V Church Langley 00-04. *Station House, Arkholme, Carnforth LA6 1AZ* Tel 07712-477003 (mobile) E-mail michael@michaelhampson.freeserve.co.uk

HAMPSON, Robert Edward. b 58. LSE BSc80 Heythrop Coll Lon BA91 MTh93. Ridley Hall Cam. **d** 97 **p** 98. C Chingford SS Pet and Paul *Chelmsf* 97-01; V Wanstead H Trin Hermon Hill from 01. *Holy Trinity Vicarage, 185 Hermon Hill, London E18 1QQ* Tel (020) 8530 3029 E-mail roberthampson@btopenworld.com

HAMPSTEAD, Archdeacon of. *See* LAWSON, The Ven Michael Charles

HAMPTON, Alison Jean. b 61. St Mary's Coll Twickenham BA98. SEITE 98. **d** 01 **p** 02. C Notting Dale St Clem w St Mark and St Jas *Lon* 01-04; P-in-c Burrough Hill Pars *Leic* 04-06; Chapl Brooksby Melton Coll 04-06; P-in-c Husbands Bosworth w Mowsley and Knaptoft etc *Leic* 06-09; P-in-c Arnesby w Shearsby and Bruntingthorpe 06-09; R Hexagon from 09. *The Rectory, Honeypot Lane, Husbands Bosworth, Lutterworth LE17 6LY* Tel (01858) 880351 E-mail gladthatilive@hotmail.com

HAMPTON, Canon Carla Irene. b 47. ARCM67 GRSM68. NTMTC 96. **d** 99 **p** 00. Asst Chapl Mid-Essex Hosp Services NHS Trust 98-02; Chapl Team Ldr 02-04; NSM Chelmsf St Andr 99-04; NSM Gt and Lt Leighs and Lt Waltham 04-06; P-in-c Gt Waltham w Ford End from 06; RD Chelmsf N from 07; Hon Can Chelmsf Cathl from 08. *1 Glebe Meadow, Great Waltham, Chelmsford CM3 1EX* Tel (01245) 364081 E-mail carla@hamptonc.freeserve.co.uk

HAMPTON, Canon John Waller. b 28. Linc Coll Ox BA51 MA58. Westcott Ho Cam 51. **d** 53 **p** 54. C Rugby St Andr *Cov* 53-56; Chapl St Paul's Sch Hammersmith 56-65; Chapl St Paul's Girls' Sch Hammersmith 60-65; V Gaydon w Chadshunt *Cov* 65-69; Asst Dir RE 65-70; C-in-c Warwick St Nic 69-75; Fell Qu Coll Birm 75-76; P-in-c Wetton *Lich* 76-82; P-in-c Alstonfield 76-82; P-in-c Sheen 76-80; RD Alstonfield 80-82; P-in-c Butterton 80-82; P-in-c Warslow and Elkstones 80-82; P-in-c Broadway *Worc* 82-91; V 91-93; RD Evesham 87-93; Hon Can Worc Cathl 88-93; rtd 93; Perm to Offic *Ab* from 93. *41 Craigton Terrace, Aberdeen AB15 7RN* Tel (01224) 310074

HAMPTON, Stephen William Peter. b 72. Magd Coll Cam BA93 MA97 Ex Coll Ox MSt99 DPhil02. Wycliffe Hall Ox BA95 MA98. **d** 96 **p** 97. C St Neots *Ely* 96-98; Chapl and Fell Ex Coll Ox 98-03; Sen Tutor St Jo Coll Dur 04-07; Hon Min Can Dur Cathl 05-07; Fell and Dean Peterho Cam from 07. *Peterhouse, Cambridge CB2 1RD* Tel (01223) 338217 Fax 337578 E-mail swph2@cam.ac.uk

HAMPTON DAVIES, David Arthur Guy. *See* DAVIES, David Arthur Guy Hampton

HANAWAY, Peter Louis. b 47. Open Univ BA85 Middx Univ BA02. NTMTC 99. **d** 02 **p** 03. NSM Westmr St Matt *Lon* from 02. *711 Duncan House, Dolphin Square, London SW1V 3PP* Tel (020) 7798 8478 Mobile 07947-722219 E-mail peter.hanaway@cwctv.com

HANCE, Mrs Joy. b 47. Cam Inst of Educn. SAOMC 99. **d** 02 **p** 03. NSM Cherbury w Gainfield *Ox* from 02. *The Vicarage, Buckland, Faringdon SN7 8QN* Tel (01367) 870618 Mobile 07752-187014 E-mail joysmail@talk21.com

HANCE, Mrs Marion. b 49. **d** 01 **p** 02. OLM Cheddington w Mentmore and Marsworth *Ox* 01-08; NSM Quantock Coast *B & W* from 08. *Shardloes, Staple Lane, West Quantoxhead, Taunton TA4 4DE* E-mail marion2212.hance@virgin.net

HANCE, Stephen John. b 66. Portsm Poly BSc89 Nottm Univ BTh92 MA93. St Jo Coll Nottm 90. **d** 93 **p** 94. C Southsea St Jude *Portsm* 93-96; TV Tollington *Lon* 96-99; V Balham Hill Ascension *S'wark* from 99. *Ascension Vicarage, 22 Malwood Road, London SW12 8EN* Tel (020) 8673 7666 or 8675 8626 Fax 8516 9429 *or* 8673 3796 E-mail stephen.hance@virgin.net

HANCOCK, Mrs Barbara. b 40. TCert60. EMMTC 93. **d** 96 **p** 04. NSM Caythorpe *Linc* 96-08; Perm to Offic from 08. *Fulbeck Cottage, Sudthorpe Hill, Fulbeck, Grantham NG32 3LE* Tel (01400) 272644 E-mail bchancock@lineone.net

HANCOCK, Christopher David. b 54. Qu Coll Ox BA75 MA80 St Jo Coll Dur BA78 PhD84. Cranmer Hall Dur. **d** 82 **p** 83. C Leic H Trin w St Jo 82-85; Chapl Magd Coll Cam 85-88, USA 88-94; V Cambridge H Trin *Ely* 94-02; Dean Bradf 02-04. *3 College Farm Cottages, Garford, Abingdon OX13 5PF* Tel (01865) 392804 E-mail chancock@btinternet.com

HANCOCK, Mrs Eleanor Mary Catherine. b 55. Huddersfield Univ CertEd91. CBDTI. **d** 05 **p** 06. C Carl H Trin and St Barn 05-08; P-in-c from 08. *104 Housesteads Road, Carlisle CA2 7XG* Tel and fax (01228) 527106 Mobile 07763-482542 E-mail emhancock@hartington.fsworld.co.uk

HANCOCK, Miss Gillian. b 59. St Jo Coll Nottm 05. **d** 07 **p** 08. C Iffley *Ox* from 07. *Church House, The Oval, Oxford OX4 4SE* Tel (01865) 747857 Mobile 07919-064612 E-mail gillhancock@btinternet.com

HANCOCK, Mrs Helen Margaret. b 62. Rob Coll Cam MA85. SEITE 06. **d** 09. NSM New Malden and Coombe *S'wark* from 09. *29 Rosebery Avenue, New Malden KT3 4JR* Tel (020) 8942 6987 E-mail hhancock29@gmail.com

HANCOCK, Ivor Michael. b 31. Lon Univ BD60. Linc Th Coll 65. **d** 66 **p** 67. C Havant *Portsm* 66-69; V Gosport Ch 69-76; P-in-c Southend St Alb *Chelmsf* 76-80; V Hawley H Trin *Guildf* 80-96; V Minley 80-96; RD Aldershot 83-88; rtd 96; Perm to Offic *Ox* from 98. *Assisi, 15 Whaley Road, Wokingham RG40 1QA* Tel 0118-962 9976

HANCOCK, Canon John Clayton. b 36. Dur Univ BA58. Cranmer Hall Dur. **d** 60 **p** 61. C Newbarns w Hawcoat *Carl* 60-65; V Church Coniston 65-76; R Torver 66-76; P-in-c Heversham 76-77; V 77-93; V Heversham and Milnthorpe 93-05; rtd 05; Hon Can Carl Cathl from 98; Hon C Levens from 05. *Fairfield, Sandside, Milnthorpe LA7 7HW* Tel (01539) 563659

HANCOCK, John Martin. b 55. Ealing Coll of Educn BA78. Wycliffe Hall Ox 97. **d** 99 **p** 00. C Bedford St Jo and St Leon *St Alb* 99-04; V Old Hill H Trin *Worc* from 04. *The Vicarage, 58 Wrights Lane, Cradley Heath B64 6RD* Tel (01384) 412987

HANCOCK, Canon John Mervyn. b 38. St Jo Coll Dur BA61 MA70 Hertf Coll Ox BA63 MA66. Cranmer Hall Dur 63. **d** 64 **p** 65. C Bishopwearmouth St Gabr *Dur* 64-67; V Hebburn St Jo 67-87; RD Jarrow 83-92; V S Westoe 87-03; C Jarrow w Simonside St Aid w St Steph 92-95; Hon Can Dur Cathl 88-03; rtd 03; C Chilton Moor *Dur* 07-08. *9 Railway Cottages, Dubmire, Houghton le Spring DH4 6LE* Tel 0191-385 7491 E-mail kda77@dial.pipex.com

HANCOCK, Malcolm James. b 50. Leeds Univ MA02 AGSM73. Sarum & Wells Th Coll 85. **d** 87 **p** 88. C Sandhurst *Ox* 87-90; P-in-c Bradbourne and Brassington *Derby* 90-92; TV Wirksworth 92-95; V Tunbridge Wells K Chas *Roch* 95-02; R Beckenham St Geo from 02. *The Rectory, 14 The Knoll, Beckenham BR3 5JW* Tel (020) 8650 0983 *or* 8663 6996 Fax 8658 4914 E-mail malcolm.hancock@diocese-rochester.org

HANCOCK, Martin. *See* HANCOCK, John Martin

HANCOCK, Mrs Mary. b 52. Imp Coll Lon BSc73 ARCS73. Ridley Hall Cam 04. **d** 07 **p** 08. C Fen Orchards *Ely* from 07. *The Vicarage, Main Road, Friday Bridge, Wisbech PE14 0HJ* Tel (01945) 860382

HANCOCK, Ms Mary Joy. b 40. Auckland Univ BA61 Auckland Teachers' Coll PGCE62 Man Univ CQSW69. S'wark Ord Course 91. **d** 94 **p** 95. NSM Merton St Mary *S'wark* 94-01; NSM Colliers Wood Ch 01-06; NSM Upper Tooting H Trin w St Aug from 06. *55 Huntspill Street, London SW17 0AA* Tel (020) 8946 8984

HANCOCK, Nigel John. b 35. K Coll Cam BA63 MA67. EAMTC 86. **d** 89 **p** 91. NSM Cambridge St Mary Less *Ely* 89-00; PV St Jo Coll Cam 95-99; Perm to Offic *Ely* from 00. *5 Atherton Close, Cambridge CB4 2BE* Tel (01223) 355828

HANCOCK, Preb Paul. b 43. AKC66. **d** 67 **p** 68. C Wednesbury St Paul Wood Green *Lich* 67-70; C Rugeley 70-73; V Rickerscote 73-75; R Blisland w St Breward *Truro* 75-78; V Mansfield St Lawr *S'well* 78-82; P-in-c Charleton *Ex* 82-83; P-in-c E Portlemouth, S Pool and Chivelstone 82-83; R Charleton w Buckland Tout Saints etc 83-95; RD Woodleigh 86-95; P-in-c Plymouth Crownhill Ascension 95-99; V 99-09; Preb Ex Cathl 03-09; rtd 09. *27 Paddock Drive, Ivybridge PL21 0UB* Tel (01752) 690655 E-mail hazelnut33@aol.com

HANCOCK, The Ven Peter. b 55. Selw Coll Cam BA76 MA79. Oak Hill Th Coll BA80. **d** 80 **p** 81. C Portsdown *Portsm* 80-83; C Radipole and Melcombe Regis *Sarum* 83-87; V Cowplain *Portsm* 87-99; RD Havant 93-98; Hon Can Portsm Cathl from 97; Adn The Meon from 99; Dioc Dir Miss 03-06. *Victoria Lodge, 36 Osborn Road, Fareham PO16 7DS* Tel (01329) 828100 *or* 280101 Fax 281603 Mobile 07974 000134 E-mail admeon@portsmouth.anglican.org

HANCOCK, Peter Ernest. b 33. Man Univ BA54. Qu Coll Birm 54. **d** 56 **p** 57. C Wigston Magna *Leic* 56-59; C Hucknall Torkard *S'well* 59-61; V Sutton in Ashfield St Mich 61-65; Dioc Youth Officer *Portsm* 65-73; R Broughton Astley *Leic* 73-86; Dioc Adv for Min of Health and Healing *B & W* 86-93; rtd 94; Perm to Offic *B & W* from 98. *24 Mulberry Road, Congresbury, Bristol BS49 5HD* Tel (01934) 838920

HANCOCK, Peter Thompson. b 31. G&C Coll Cam BA54 MA58. Ridley Hall Cam 54. **d** 56 **p** 57. C Beckenham Ch Ch *Roch* 56-59; Chapl St Lawr Coll Ramsgate 59-62; Chapl Stowe Sch 62-67; Asst Chapl and Lect Br Embassy Ch Paris *Eur* 67-70; V Walton H Trin *Ox* 70-80; Canada 80-84; V Northwood H Trin *Lon* 84-94; rtd 94; Perm to Offic *Ox* 99-07. *High Lawns, Woodhouse Lane, Holmbury St Mary, Dorking RH5 6NN* Tel (01483) 205430

HANCOCK, Reginald Legassicke (Rex). b 28. Trin Coll Cam BA51 MA57. Clifton Th Coll 60. **d** 61 **p** 62. C Finchley Ch Ch *Lon* 61-63; CF 63-82; R Quantoxhead *B & W* 82-93; rtd 93; Perm to Offic *B & W* from 94. *Stowleys, Bossington Lane, Porlock, Minehead TA24 8HD* Tel (01643) 862327

HANCOCK, Richard Manuel Ashley. b 69. LRPS02. Linc Th Coll 94 Westcott Ho Cam 95. **d** 97 **p** 98. C Didcot St Pet *Ox*

97-00; P-in-c Shrivenham w Watchfield and Bourton 00-03; V Shrivenham and Ashbury from 03; AD Vale of White Horse from 05. *St Andrew's Vicarage, Shrivenham, Swindon SN6 8AN* Tel (01793) 780183 E-mail vicar@standrews-shrivenham.fsnet.co.uk

HANCOCK, Mrs Vittoria Ruth. b 74. Univ of Wales (Ban) BSc95 BD99. Cranmer Hall Dur 91. **d** 01 **p** 02. C Llanberis w Llanrug *Ban* 01-04; C Dolgellau w Llanfachreth and Brithdir etc 04-05; Chapl St As Cathl and Dioc Evang Officer from 06. *Woodcroft, Upper Denbigh Road, St Asaph LL17 0BG* Tel (01745) 730176

HANCOCKS, Graeme. b 58. Univ of Wales (Ban) BD79 Oslo Univ 87. Linc Th Coll 79. **d** 81 **p** 82. C Denbigh and Nantglyn *St As* 81-84; Asst Chapl Oslo St Edm *Eur* 84-88; Chapl Stockholm 88-89; Chapl Marseille w St Raphaël, Aix-en-Provence etc 89; Chapl Gothenburg w Halmstad, Jönköping etc 90-93; Chapl Southn Univ Hosps NHS Trust 93-98; Chapl Trafford Healthcare NHS Trust 98-02; Chapl Leeds Teaching Hosps NHS Trust from 02. *St James University Hospital, Beckett Street, Leeds LS9 7TF* Tel 0113-206 5935 E-mail graeme.hancocks@leedsth.nhs.uk

HAND, Michael. *See* HAND, Peter Michael

HAND, Michael Anthony (Tony). b 63. SROT York Univ BA84 DipCOT88. St Jo Coll Nottm MA95. **d** 95 **p** 96. C Lutterworth w Cotesbach *Leic* 95-98; C Lutterworth w Cotesbach and Bitteswell 99-01; V Acomb H Redeemer *York* from 01; Chapl Manor Sch from 01. *The Vicarage, 108 Boroughbridge Road, York YO26 6AB* Tel (01904) 798593 E-mail holyredeemer01@hotmail.com

HAND, Canon Nigel Arthur. b 54. St Jo Coll Nottm. **d** 84 **p** 85. C Birm St Luke 84-88; C Walton H Trin *Ox* 88-89; TV 89-97; C Selly Park St Steph and St Wulstan *Birm* 97-04; P-in-c Selly Park Ch Ch 04-08; AD Moseley 04-07; Can Res Birm Cathl from 08. *12 Nursery Drive, Handsworth, Birmingham B20 2SW* E-mail n.hand1@btinternet.com

HAND, Peter Michael. b 42. Univ Coll Ox BA63 Lon Univ BSc75. Sarum & Wells Th Coll 77. **d** 80 **p** 81. NSM Shaston *Sarum* 80-81; C Tisbury 81-83; C Glastonbury St Jo w Godney *B & W* 83-84; C Glastonbury w Meare, W Pennard and Godney 84-87; V High Littleton 87-99; RD Midsomer Norton 92-98; R Winford w Felton Common Hill 99-07; Warden of Readers Bath Adnry 98-06; rtd 07. *27 Stancombe View, Winchcombe, Cheltenham GL54 5LE*

HAND, Philip Ronald. b 53. Spurgeon's Coll BA78. **d** 03 **p** 04. NSM Southampton (City Cen) *Win* from 03. *52 Cranbury Avenue, Southampton SO14 0LT* Tel (023) 8049 4490

✠**HANDFORD, The Rt Revd George Clive.** b 37. CMG07. Hatf Coll Dur BA61. Qu Coll Birm 61. **d** 63 **p** 64 **c** 90. C Mansfield SS Pet and Paul *S'well* 63-67; Lebanon 67-74; Dean Jerusalem 74-78; UAE 78-83; Adn Gulf 78-83; V Kneesall w Laxton *S'well* 83-84; P-in-c Wellow 83-84; RD Tuxford and Norwell 83-84; Adn Nottingham 84-90; Suff Bp Warw *Cov* 90-96; Bp Cyprus and the Gulf 96-07; Pres Bp Episc Ch Jerusalem and Middle E 02-07; rtd 07; Hon Asst Bp Ripon and Leeds from 07. *Wayside, 1 The Terrace, Kirby Hill, Boroughbridge, York YO51 9DQ* Tel (01423) 325406 E-mail gchandford@aol.com

HANDFORD, John Richard. b 32. Sydney Univ BSc52 Univ Coll Lon MSc58 Surrey Univ MA84 Heythrop Coll Lon MTh96 Lon Univ PhD04. Lon Coll of Div 68. **d** 69 **p** 70. Asst Chapl Wellington Coll Berks 69-87; Hon C Windlesham *Guildf* 87-92; Perm to Offic 92-02. *Desiderata, 33 Chertsey Road, Windlesham GU20 6EW* Tel (01276) 472397

HANDFORD, Maurice. b 25. Oak Hill Th Coll 48. **d** 52 **p** 53. C Dublin Miss Ch *D & G* 52-55; Org & Deputation Sec ICM (N & Midl) 55-58; C-in-c Buxton Trin Prop Chpl *Derby* 58-87; I Clondevaddock w Portsalon and Leatbeg *D & R* 87-90; Bp's Dom Chapl 88-90; rtd 90; Perm to Offic *Ches* from 90 and *Derby* from 92. *11 Woburn Court, Towers Road, Poynton, Stockport SK12 1DF* Tel (01625) 850509

HANDFORTH, Canon Richard Brereton. b 31. St Pet Coll Ox BA55 MA60. Westcott Ho Cam 63. **d** 64 **p** 65. C Hornchurch St Andr *Chelmsf* 64-65; Warden St Steph Coll Hong Kong 65-73; Chapl CMS Fellowship Ho Chislehurst 73-75; Hon C Chislehurst St Nic *Roch* 73-75; Home Educn Sec CMS 75-83; V Biggin Hill *Roch* 83-88; Inter-change Adv CMS 88-96; Hon C Plaistow St Mary *Roch* 95-04; Hon Can Lagos from 95; rtd 96; Perm to Offic *Roch* from 01. *40 Sheppard's College, London Road, Bromley BR1 1PF* Tel (020) 8460 0238 E-mail richardhandforth@virgin.net

HANDLEY, The Ven Anthony Michael. b 36. Selw Coll Cam BA60 MA64. Chich Th Coll 60. **d** 62 **p** 63. C Thorpe St Andr *Nor* 62-66; C Gaywood, Bawsey and Mintlyn 66-72; V Hellesdon 72-81; RD Nor N 80-81; Adn Nor 81-93; Adn Norfolk 93-02; rtd 02; Perm to Offic *Nor* from 02. *25 New Street, Sheringham NR26 8EE* Tel (01263) 820928

HANDLEY, Dennis Francis. b 57. MIE79 TEng(CEI)80. Coll of Resurr Mirfield 82. **d** 85 **p** 86. C Headingley *Ripon* 85-88; C Rothwell 88-92; V Liversedge *Wakef* 92-97; V Ripponden and Barkisland w W Scammonden 97-06; TR Almondbury w Farnley Tyas from 06; Dioc Rural Officer from 04. *The Rectory,*

2 Westgate, Almondbury, Huddersfield HD5 8XE Tel (01484) 309469 E-mail dennishandley01@aol.com

HANDLEY, John. b 38. Oak Hill Th Coll. d 83 p 84. C Witton w Brundall and Braydeston *Nor* 83-86; R Reedham w Cantley w Limpenhoe and Southwood 86-93; P-in-c E w W Harling and Bridgham w Roudham 93-95; R E w W Harling, Bridgham w Roudham, Larling etc 95-05; P-in-c Garboldisham w Blo' Norton, Riddlesworth etc 94-96; RD Thetford and Rockland 95-98; rtd 05; Perm to Offic *Nor* from 05. *6 Barton Close, Swaffham PE37 7SB* Tel (01760) 336328

HANDLEY, Michael. *See* HANDLEY, The Ven Anthony Michael

HANDLEY, Neil. b 40. St Aid Birkenhead 64. d 67 p 68. C Ashton Ch Ch *Man* 67-70; C Stretford All SS 70-73; C Tonge 73; C-in-c Bolton St Jo Breightmet CD 74-79; V Bolton St Jo 79-80; R Broughton St Jo 80-87; Perm to Offic *Eur* from 90. *La Taire du Grel, 24250 Domme, France* Tel (0033) (5) 53 28 23 42

HANDLEY, Timothy John. b 63. St Steph Ho Ox 94. d 96 p 97. C St Marychurch *Ex* 96-98; Perm to Offic *Cant* from 06. *All Saints' House, Churchview Road, Twickenham TW2 5BX* Tel (020) 8894 3580

HANDLEY MACMATH, Terence. b 59. Goldsmiths' Coll Lon BA80 K Coll Cam MA98. Westcott Ho Cam 91. d 94 p 95. NSM Southwold *St E* 94-95; Perm to Offic *St Alb* 96-99; C St Alb St Pet 99-05; V Harrow Weald All SS *Lon* 05-07; Chapl R Free Hampstead NHS Trust from 07. *The Chaplain's Office, Royal Free Hospital, Pond Street, London NW3 2QG* Tel (020) 7830 2742

HANDY, Thomas. b 79. Ex Univ BA02 Bris Univ PGCE05. Trin Coll Bris MA09. d 09. C Shepton Mallet w Doulting *B & W* from 09. *24 Walnut Grove, Shepton Mallet BA4 4HX* E-mail thomashandy100@hotmail.com

HANFORD, Canon William Richard. b 38. Keble Coll Ox BA60 MA64 Lon Univ BD66 Univ of Wales LLM95. St Steph Ho Ox 60. d 63 p 64. C Roath St Martin *Llan* 63-67; C Llantwit Major 67-68; PV Llan Cathl 68-72; Chapl RN 72-76; Hon Chapl Gibraltar Cathl 74-76; Hon C Eastbourne St Sav and St Pet *Chich* 76-77; C Brighton St Pet 77-78; Can Res and Prec Guildf Cathl 78-83; Hon Can 03-09; V Ewell 83-09; Tutor and Lect Chich Th Coll 79-86; rtd 09; Perm to Offic *Guildf* and *Llan* from 09. *15 Austin Avenue, Laleston, Bridgend CF32 0LG* Tel (01656) 656892 *or* (020) 8786 0552 E-mail wrhanford@btinternet.com

HANKE, Canon Hilary Claire. b 53. Qu Coll Birm BTheol93. d 93 p 94. C Kempsey and Severn Stoke w Croome d'Abitot *Worc* 93-97; TV Wordsley 97-99; Convenor for Women's Min 98-05; P-in-c Reddal Hill St Luke 01-08; V from 08; Hon Can Worc Cathl from 98; RD Dudley from 04. *St Luke's Vicarage, Upper High Street, Cradley Heath B64 5HX* Tel and fax (01384) 569940 E-mail hchanke@btinternet.com

HANKEY, Miss Dorothy Mary. b 38. CertEd65. Trin Coll Bris 75. dss 78 d 87 p 94. Wigan St Jas w St Thos *Liv* 78-84; Middleton *Man* 84-85; Litherland Ch Ch *Liv* 85-89; Par Dn 87-89; Par Dn Blackpool St Mark *Blackb* 89-94; C 94-95; C Blackpool St Paul 95-98; rtd 98; Perm to Offic *Blackb* from 98. *89 Rutland Avenue, Poulton-le-Flyde FY6 7RX* Tel (01253) 890645

HANKEY, Rupert Christopher Alers. b 60. Sheff Univ LLB82. Wilson Carlile Coll 86 St Jo Coll Nottm MTh06. d 07 p 08. C Bedford St Jo and St Leon *St Alb* from 07. *53 Hillesden Avenue, Elstow, Bedford MK42 9AJ* Tel (01234) 358307 Mobile 07891-472077 E-mail rupert3@tesco.net

HANKINS, Clifford James. b 24. Chich Th Coll 70. d 72 p 73. C Henfield *Chich* 72-76; V Fernhurst 76-84; V Mithian w Mount Hawke *Truro* 84-89; rtd 89; Hon C W Wittering and Birdham w Itchenor *Chich* from 90. *2 Kestrel Close, East Wittering, Chichester PO20 8PQ* Tel (01243) 672164

HANLEY, Mirt Joseph. b 74. Univ Coll Ches BA95. CITC BTh03. d 03 p 04. Aux Min Tralee w Kilmoyley, Ballymacelligott etc *L & K* from 03. *The New Rectory, Kilgobbin, Camp, Dingle, Co Kerry, Republic of Ireland* Tel (00353) (66) 713 0230 Mobile 87-619 4733 E-mail mairtjhanley@hotmail.com

HANLON, Michael James. b 50. St Jo Coll Nottm 96. d 98 p 99. C Tamworth *Lich* 98-00; C Melbourne St Jo Australia from 00. *25 The Eyrie, Lilydale Vic 3140, Australia* Tel (0061) (3) 9739 5235 *or* 9739 3541 E-mail mikeruth@alphalink.com.au

HANLON, Thomas Kyle. b 72. QUB BA94 TCD BTh97. d 97 p 98. C Bangor St Comgall *D & D* 97-00; I Dromore *Clogh* 00-06; I Fivemiletown from 06; Chapl to Bp Clogh from 03. *Fivemiletown Rectory, 160 Ballagh Road, Fivemiletown BT75 0QP* Tel (028) 8952 1030 *or* 8952 2422 E-mail tkhanlon@btinternet.com

HANMER, Sister Phoebe Margaret. b 31. Edin Univ MA54. d 96 p 97. NSM Brakpan S Africa 96-00; NSM Actonville 00-03; Perm to Offic *Ox* 99-00 and *Birm* from 04. *366 High Street, Smethwick B66 3PD* Tel and fax 0121-558 0094

HANMER, Canon Richard John. b 38. Peterho Cam BA61 MA65. Linc Th Coll 62. d 64 p 65. C Sheff St Swithun 64-69; Bp's Chapl *Nor* 69-73; V Cinderhill *S'well* 73-81; V Eaton *Nor* 81-94; Dioc Chapl MU 91-94; Hon Can Nor Cathl 93-94; Can Res Nor Cathl 94-04; P-in-c Nor St Mary in the Marsh 94-04;

rtd 04; Perm to Offic *Nor* from 04. *18 Quebec Road, Dereham NR19 2DR* Tel (01362) 655092

HANNA, Miss Elizabeth. b 50. QUB BA73 Lon Bible Coll BA79 Milltown Inst Dub MA01. CITC 99. d 01 p 02. C Bangor Abbey *D & D* 01-04; I Magherally w Annaclone 04-08; I Belfast St Nic *Conn* from 08. *St Nicolas' Rectory, 15 Harberton Park, Belfast BT9 6TW* Tel (028) 9066 7753 Mobile 07801-946909 E-mail hannamanor@compuserve.com

HANNA, Isaac James. b 70. York St Jo Coll MA03. CITC 07. d 08 p 09. Bp's C Dungiven w Bovevagh *D & R* from 08. *The Rectory, 14 Main Street, Dungiven, Londonderry BT47 4LB* Tel and fax (028) 7774 1226 E-mail issac17@btinternet.com

HANNA, John. b 44. Lon Bible Coll BA83. Westcott Ho Cam 86. d 87 p 88. C Denton Ch Ch *Man* 87-91; V Higher Walton *Blackb* 91-98; C Marple All SS *Ches* 98-02; TV Burrington, Chawleigh, Cheldon, Chulmleigh etc *Ex* from 02; RD S Molton 03-09. *The Vicarage, The Square, Witheridge, Tiverton EX16 8AE* Tel (01884) 860764

HANNA, Patricia Elizabeth. TCD BA HDipEd QUB BD NUU MA. d 99 p 00. Aux Min Nenagh *L & K* from 99; Aux Min Drumcliffe w Kilnasoolagh from 00. *St Columba's Rectory, Bindon Street, Ennis, Co Clare, Republic of Ireland* Tel (00353) (65) 682 0109 Mobile 87-660 6003 E-mail patricia.hanna@ul.ie

HANNA, Peter Thomas. b 45. ACII66 GIFireE75. CITC 85. d 88 p 89. NSM Cork St Fin Barre's Union *C, C & R* 88-95; Min Can Cork Cathl from 92; Dioc Info Officer 94-95; Aux Min Cork St Luke Union 95-00; Aux Min Kinsale Union 00-04; Aux Min Douglas Union w Frankfield from 04. *Mount Windsor, Farnahoe, Inishannon, Co Cork, Republic of Ireland* Tel and fax (00353) (21) 477 5470 E-mail hanna7@gofree.indigo.ie

HANNA, Canon Robert Charles. b 49. Oak Hill Th Coll 75. d 77 p 78. C Coleraine *Conn* 77-82; I Convoy w Monellan and Donaghmore *D & R* 82-94; Can Raphoe Cathl 88-94; I Drumcliffe w Kilnasoolagh *L & K* from 94; Can Limerick, Killaloe and Clonfert Cathls from 00; Chan from 04. *St Columba's Rectory, Bindon Street, Ennis, Co Clare, Republic of Ireland* Tel (00353) (65) 682 0109 Mobile 86-356 0864 E-mail bobhanna@eircom.net

HANNA, Steven John. b 70. Oak Hill Th Coll BA02. d 02 p 03. C Dagenham *Chelmsf* 02-07; V Becontree St Elisabeth from 07. *St Elisabeth's Vicarage, Hewett Road, Dagenham RM8 2XT* Tel (020) 8517 0355 E-mail stevenhanna@yahoo.com

HANNAFORD, Prof Robert. b 53. Ex Univ BEd76 MA78 PhD87. St Steph Ho Ox 78. d 80 p 81. C Ex St Jas 80-83; Chapl Ex Univ 83-88; Tutor St Steph Ho Ox 89-92; Sen Lect Ch Ch Coll Cant 92-99; Prof Chr Th Univ Coll Chich 99-01; Hon C Bury w Houghton and Coldwaltham and Hardham *Chich* 99-01; Th Consultant Bp Horsham 99-01; Can and Preb Chich Cathl from 00; Prof Th St Martin's Coll Lanc 02-05; Dean of Faculty 05-07; Dean of Faculty Cumbria Univ from 07; Hon C Tunstall w Melling and Leck *Blackb* 02-03; Hon C E Lonsdale from 03. *The Vicarage, Church Lane, Tunstall, Carnforth LA6 2RQ* Tel (01524) 274376 E-mail rhannaford@ktdbroadband.com

HANNAH, Darrell Dale. b 62. Grand Canyon Univ BA85 S Bapt Th Sem MDiv89 Regent Coll Vancouver ThM92 Magd Coll Cam PhD96. WMMTC 00. d 03 p 03. NSM Edgbaston St Geo *Birm* 03-04; NSM Iffley *Ox* 04-07; NSM Earley St Pet 07-08; R Ascot Heath from 08. *All Saints' Rectory, London Road, Ascot SL5 8DQ* Tel (01344) 621200 E-mail drddhannah@yahoo.co.uk

HANNAH, Kimberley Victoria. *See* WILLIAMS, Mrs Kimberley Victoria

HANNAM, Robert Stephen. b 46. CertEd69. d 05 p 06. NSM Rastrick St Matt *Wakef* 05-08; NSM Rastrick from 08. *33 Lyndhurst Road, Brighouse HD6 3RX* Tel (01484) 716053 E-mail stephenr.hannam@btinternet.com

HANNEN, Robert John. *See* DAVIES-HANNEN, Robert John

✠**HANNON, The Rt Revd Brian Desmond Anthony.** b 36. TCD BA59 MA62. TCD Div Sch Div Test61. d 61 p 62 c 86. C Clooney *D & R* 61-64; I Desertmartin 64-69; I Londonderry Ch Ch 69-82; I Enniskillen *Clogh* 82-86; Preb Clogh Cathl 82-84; Dean Clogh 85-86; Bp Clogh 86-01; rtd 01. *Drumconnis Top, 202 Mullaghmeen Road, Ballinamallard, Enniskillen BT94 2DZ* Tel (028) 6638 8557 Fax 6638 8086 E-mail bdah@btinternet.com

HANNY, Mrs Annette Elizabeth. b 49. Keele Univ MA95. WMMTC 02. d 05 p 06. NSM Oldbury, Langley and Londonderry *Birm* from 05. *93 St Mary's Road, Smethwick B67 5DG* Tel 0121-420 2858 Mobile 07970-841662 E-mail annette.hanny@hobtpct.nhs.uk

HANOVA, Petra. *See* ELSMORE, Ms Petra

HANSELL, Peter Michael. b 76. Selw Coll Cam BA97 MA01 MPhil99 PhD02. Qu Coll Birm 03. d 05 p 06. C Moseley St Mary *Birm* 05-07; C Moseley St Mary and St Anne 07-09; Reader Initial Tr Adv *Cov* from 09. *56 Wyken Croft, Coventry CV2 3AD* E-mail petermhansell@hotmail.com

HANSEN, Mrs Moira Jacqueline. b 55. K Coll Lon BSc76. Oak Hill Th Coll BA88. d 88 p 96. Par Dn Finchley Ch Ch *Lon* 88-91; Par Dn Broadwater *Chich* 91-94; Chapl Oak Hill Th Coll 94-00; P-in-c Stanton *St E* 00-04; P-in-c Hopton, Market Weston,

Barningham etc 00-04; R Stanton, Hopton, Market Weston, Barningham etc 04-06; rtd 06. *49 Turnstone Drive, Bury St Edmunds IP32 7GT* Tel (01284) 717191
E-mail moira@hansenj.fsnet.co.uk

HANSFORD, Gordon John. b 40. Southn Univ BSc61. Trin Coll Bris 77. **d** 79 **p** 80. C Ex St Leon w H Trin 79-82; C Shirley *Win* 82-87; R Landcross, Littleham, Monkleigh etc *Ex* 87-96; TV Bideford, Northam, Westward Ho!, Appledore etc 96-99; P-in-c Monkleigh 96-99; RD Hartland 96-99; V Paul *Truro* 99-07; rtd 07. *14 Chilpark, Fremington, Barnstaple EX31 3BY*
E-mail hansford@tinyworld.co.uk

HANSFORD, Ruth Patricia. b 68. K Coll Lon BSc90 Surrey Univ MSc96 Sch of Pharmacy Lon PhD00. Trin Coll Bris BA02. **d** 03 **p** 04. C Parkham, Alwington, Buckland Brewer etc *Ex* 03-07; P-in-c Hatherleigh, Meeth, Exbourne and Jacobstowe from 07. *The Rectory, Hatherleigh, Okehampton EX20 3JY* Tel (01837) 810314 Mobile 07718-765936
E-mail maggiethecat@waitrose.com

HANSON, Christopher. b 48. Ox Univ BTh02. Wycliffe Hall Ox 87. **d** 89 **p** 90. C Heref St Pet w St Owen and St Jas 89-91; C Plymouth St Andr w St Paul and St Geo *Ex* 91-93; C Devonport St Mich 93-94; TV Shebbear, Buckland Filleigh, Sheepwash etc 94-97; TV Langley Marish *Ox* 97-08; V Victoria Docks Ascension *Chelmsf* from 08. *The Vicarage, 5 Broadgate Road, London E16 3TL* Tel (020) 7476 5999
E-mail revhansonctwcc@aol.com

HANSON, Dale Robert. b 57. Fitzw Coll Cam BA78 MA81 Univ of BC MA80. Ridley Hall Cam 81. **d** 84 **p** 85. C Much Woolton *Liv* 84-87; Assoc Min Kowloon St Andr Hong Kong 87-91; TV Billingham St Aid *Dur* 91-95; C Dur St Nic 95-98; V 98-07; C Kowloon St Andr Hong Kong from 07. *Shatin Anglican Church, PO Box 1627, Shatin Central PO, Shatin, NT, Hong Kong, China* Tel (00852) 2694 9928 Fax 2695 0580
E-mail standrew@pacific.net.hk

HANSON, Edward William. b 51. Salem State Coll (USA) BA73 Tufts Univ MA78 Boston Coll PhD92 Episc Div Sch MDiv00. Ripon Coll Cuddesdon 00. **d** 01 **p** 02. C Linc St Botolph and Linc St Pet-at-Gowts and St Andr 01-04; P-in-c Orsett and Bulphan and Horndon on the Hill *Chelmsf* 04-06; R from 06; RD Thurrock from 08. *The Rectory, School Lane, Orsett, Grays RM16 3JS* Tel (01375) 891254 E-mail rector@hobnob.org.uk

HANSON, Canon John Westland. b 19. OBE74. St Jo Coll Dur BA41 MA44. **d** 43 **p** 44. C Louth w Welton-le-Wold *Linc* 43-50; Chapl and Lect RAF Flying Coll Manby 50-76; R Grimoldby w Manby 50-76; RD E Louthesk 60-68; Chief Examiner Relig Studies Cam Univ 66-82; Can and Preb Linc Cathl 67-02; RD Louthesk 68-77; V Woodhall Spa and Kirkstead 76-88; P-in-c Langton w Woodhall 76-88; rtd 88. *Brookfield, 28 Tor-o-Moor Road, Woodhall Spa LN10 6TD* Tel (01526) 352554

HANSON, Keith. b 59. Cranmer Hall Dur 99. **d** 01 **p** 02. C Armley w New Wortley *Ripon* 01-04; C Whitkirk 04-06; P-in-c Illingworth *Wakef* 06-09; Chapl H Trin Sch Halifax 06-09; P-in-c Harlaxton Gp *Linc* from 09. *The Rectory, 6 Rectory Lane, Harlaxton, Grantham NG32 1HD* Tel (01476) 594608
E-mail revkeef@hotmail.com

HANSON, Mrs Margaret Patricia. b 45. Ripon Coll Cuddesdon 04. **d** 05 **p** 06. NSM Ifield *Chich* from 05. *Birch Cottage, 7 Barnwood, Crawley RH10 7TH* Tel (01293) 535569
E-mail margaret.hanson1@tesco.net

HANSON, Michael Beaumont. b 49. Univ Coll Ox MA70 PGCE71. NOC 81. **d** 84 **p** 85. Chapl Leeds Gr Sch and NSM Leeds St Geo *Ripon* 84-99; rtd 99; Perm to Offic *Carl* from 99. *5 The Crofts, Crosby, Maryport CA15 6SP* Tel (01900) 816630
E-mail mikeandchristinehanson@sky.com

HANSON, Peter Richard. b 45. ARCM. Chich Th Coll 72. **d** 75 **p** 76. C Forest Gate St Edm *Chelmsf* 75-79; C Chingford SS Pet and Paul 79-81; V Leytonstone H Trin Harrow Green 81-86; Dep Chapl HM Pris Wandsworth 86-88; Chapl HM Pris Lewes 88-91; rtd 91; Perm to Offic *Chich* from 91. *Flat 2, 39 St Anne's Crescent, Lewes BN7 1SB* Tel (01273) 471714

HANSON, Robert Arthur. b 35. Keele Univ BA57. St Steph Ho Ox 57 St Mich Coll Llan 59. **d** 60 **p** 61. C Longton St Mary and St Chad *Lich* 60-65; Chapl St Mary's Cathl *Edin* 65-69; R Glas St Matt 69-79; R Paisley H Trin 79-87; V Walsall St Andr *Lich* 87-93; Perm to Offic *Worc* 94-97; C Kentish Town *Lon* 97-01; Hon C 02-06; rtd 02; Perm to Offic *Lon* from 06. *7B Fraser Regnart Court, Mackenzie Road, London NW5 4HU* Tel (020) 7284 3634 Mobile 07951-154384
E-mail bob.hanson@tiscali.co.uk

HANSON, Timothy David. b 68. Oak Hill Th Coll BA95. **d** 95 **p** 96. C Boscombe St Jo *Win* 95-00; V Wharton *Ches* from 00. *The Vicarage, 165 Crook Lane, Winsford CW7 3DR* Tel (01606) 593215 *or* 861860 E-mail tiohanson@aol.com

HANWELL, David John. b 46. Leic Univ CertEd74 UEA BEd94. **d** 98 **p** 99. OLM Mundford w Lynford, Cranwich and Ickburgh w Langford *Nor* 98-04; OLM Cockley Cley w Gooderstone 99-04; P-in-c from 04; OLM Gt and Lt Cressingham w Threxton 99-04; C from 04; OLM Hilborough w Bodney 99-04; C from 04; OLM Oxborough w Foulden and Caldecote 99-04; C from 04.

The Rectory, Elm Place, Gooderstone, King's Lynn PE33 9BX Tel (01366) 328856 E-mail david.hanwell@btopenworld.com

HAOKIP (*formerly YAM*), **Canon David Tongkhoyam.** b 60. Serampore Univ BTh89 Madras Univ MDiv92. H Cross Coll Rangoon. **d** 84 **p** 85. Missnr Jla 83-93; Hon Can Sittwe from 09; India 93-95; Korea 96-97; Perm to Offic *S'wark* 99; TV Southampton (City Cen) *Win* 00-05; V E Ham St Geo *Chelmsf* from 05. *The Vicarage, Buxton Road, London E6 3NB* Tel (020) 8472 2111 Mobile 07817-702358
E-mail dthaokip1@yahoo.co.uk

HAPGOOD-STRICKLAND, Canon Peter Russell. b 57. St Steph Ho Ox BA83. **d** 83 **p** 84. C Ashford *Cant* 83-86; C Sheerness H Trin w St Paul 86-90; V Blackb St Thos w St Jude 90-97; P-in-c Burnley St Andr w St Marg 97; V Burnley St Andr w St Marg and St Jas from 98; Hon Can Blackb Cathl from 05. *St Andrew's Vicarage, 230 Barden Lane, Burnley BB10 1JD* Tel (01282) 423185 E-mail standrews@marsdens.net

HARARE, Bishop of. *See* GANDIYA, The Rt Revd Chad Nicholas

HARBIDGE, The Ven Adrian Guy. b 48. St Jo Coll Dur BA70. Cuddesdon Coll 73. **d** 75 **p** 76. C Romsey *Win* 75-80; V Bournemouth St Andr 80-86; V Chandler's Ford 86-99; RD Eastleigh 93-99; Adn Bournemouth from 99. *Glebe House, 22 Bellflower Way, Chandler's Ford, Eastleigh SO53 4HN* Tel and fax (023) 8026 0955 E-mail adrian.harbidge@dial.pipex.com

HARBORD, Canon Paul Geoffrey. b 56. JP99. Keble Coll Ox BA78 MA86. Chich Th Coll 81. **d** 83 **p** 84. C Rawmarsh w Parkgate *Sheff* 83-86; C Doncaster St Geo 86-90; C-in-c St Edm Anchorage Lane CD 90-95; V Masbrough 95-03; Bp's Chapl from 03; Hon Can Sheff Cathl from 07. *4 Clarke Drive, Sheffield S10 2NS* Tel 0114-266 1932 *or* 230 2170 Mobile 07898-485428
E-mail geoffrey.harbord@sheffield.anglican.org

HARBORD, Philip James. b 56. St Cath Coll Ox BA77. Cranmer Hall Dur 78. **d** 80 **p** 81. C Enfield St Andr *Lon* 80-83; CMS Pakistan 84-88; C Clay Hill St Jo and St Luke *Lon* 88-91; Chapl Wexham Park Hosp Slough 91-92; Chapl Upton Hosp Slough 91-92; Chapl Heatherwood and Wexham Park Hosp NHS Trust 92-95; Chapl Leic Gen Hosp NHS Trust 95-98; Chapl Fosse Health NHS Trust 98-99; Chapl Leics and Rutland Healthcare NHS Trust 99-01; P-in-c Cosby *Leic* 01-07; P-in-c Whetstone 03-07; rtd 07. *47 Maple Avenue, Blaby, Leicester LE8 4AT* Tel 0116-277 6522 E-mail philipjharbord@btinternet.com

HARBOTTLE, Anthony Hall Harrison. b 25. LVO79. Ch Coll Cam BA50 MA53. Wycliffe Hall Ox 50. **d** 52 **p** 53. C Boxley *Cant* 52-54; C St Peter-in-Thanet 54-60; R Sandhurst w Newenden 60-68; Chapl in Windsor Gt Park 68-81; Chapl to The Queen 64-95; R E Dean w Friston and Jevington *Chich* 81-95; P-in-c 95-96; rtd 96; Perm to Offic *Chich* from 97. *44 Summerdown Road, Eastbourne BN20 8DQ* Tel (01323) 730881

HARBRIDGE, Philip Charles Anthony. b 65. K Coll Lon LLB88 AKC88 Ch Coll Cam BA98 MA02. Westcott Ho Cam. **d** 99 **p** 00. C Hampton All SS *Lon* 99-02; Chapl Ch Coll Cam 02-07; Chapl Millfield Sch Somerset from 07. *Millfield School, Street BA16 0YD* Tel (01458) 442291
E-mail pch@millfieldschool.com

HARCOURT, Canon Giles. b 36. Westcott Ho Cam 68. **d** 71 **p** 72. C Bishopwearmouth St Mich w St Hilda *Dur* 71-73; C Fishponds St Mary *Bris* 73-75; Bp's Dom Chapl *S'wark* 75-78; Lic to Offic 78-79; V S Wimbledon H Trin and St Pet 79-88; V Greenwich St Alfege 88-04; Hon Chapl RN Coll Greenwich 89-99; RD Greenwich Thameside *S'wark* 94-98; Boro Dean Greenwich 94-98; Hon Can S'wark Cathl 96-04; rtd 05; Perm to Offic *Chich* from 05. *1A Trinity Trees, Eastbourne BN21 3LA* Tel (01323) 638790

HARCOURT, Paul George. b 67. Em Coll Cam BA88 MA92. Wycliffe Hall Ox BA91. **d** 92 **p** 93. C Moreton *Ches* 92-95; C Woodford Wells *Chelmsf* 95-00; V from 00. *All Saints' Vicarage, 4 Inmans Row, Woodford Green IG8 0NH* Tel (020) 8504 0266 Fax 8504 9640 E-mail pharcourt@btconnect.com

HARCOURT-NORTON, Michael Clive. *See* NORTON, Michael Clive Harcourt

HARDACRE (*née* **BROOKFIELD**), **Mrs Patricia Anne.** b 50. St Mary's Coll Dur BA72 St Jo Coll Dur MA74. Cranmer Hall Dur. **dss** 84 **d** 87 **p** 94. Kingston upon Hull St Nic *York* 84-86; Acomb St Steph 86-96; Par Dn 87-94; C 94-96; TV Preston Risen Lord *Blackb* 96-07; rtd 07; Perm to Offic *Blackb* from 07. *17 Fairfield Drive, Clitheroe BB7 2PE* Tel (01200) 429341
E-mail anne@anneporage.fsnet.co.uk

HARDAKER, Canon Ian Alexander. b 32. K Coll Lon BD59 AKC59. **d** 60 **p** 61. C Beckenham St Geo *Roch* 60-65; R Eynsford w Lullingstone 65-70; V Chatham St Steph 70-85; RD Roch 78-85; Hon Can Roch Cathl 83-98; Clergy Appts Adv 86-98; Chapl to The Queen 94-02; rtd 99; Perm to Offic *B & W* from 00. *The Old Post Office, Huish Champflower, Taunton TA4 2EY* Tel (01984) 623409

HARDCASTLE, Ian Kenneth Dalton. b 56. Auckland Univ BE78 ME80. St Jo Coll Nottm MTh04. **d** 04 **p** 05. C Denton Holme

Carl 04-09; V Whangaparaoa Peninsula New Zealand from 09. *3/39 Wade River Road, Whangaparaoa 0932, New Zealand* Tel (0064) (9) 424 0939 E-mail vicar@ststephenswgp.org.nz

HARDCASTLE, Nigel John. b 47. Reading Univ BSc68. Qu Coll Birm. **d** 72 **p** 73. C Weoley Castle *Birm* 72-75; C Handsworth St Andr 75-78; V Garretts Green 78-86; Exec Sec Ch Computer Project BCC 86-89; R Emmer Green *Ox* 89-99; V Reading St Luke w St Bart from 99. *St Luke's Vicarage, 14 Erleigh Road, Reading RG1 5LH* Tel and fax 0118-926 2372
E-mail nigel@hardcastle33.fsnet.co.uk

HARDCASTLE, Roger Clive. b 52. Southn Univ BSc73. Qu Coll Birm. **d** 78 **p** 79. C Walton St Mary *Liv* 78-82; V Pemberton St Fran Kitt Green 82-94; TV Padgate 94-96; V Birchwood 96-06; rtd 06. *15 Ullswater Avenue, Orrell, Wigan WN5 8PF* Tel (01942) 513568 E-mail rhardcastle@btopenworld.com

HARDIE, John Blair. b 16. MBE46. LDS FDS MRCS38 MRCSE66. Edin Th Coll 73. **d** 76 **p** 76. Chapl St Paul's Cathl Dundee 76-86; rtd 86; Hon C Carnoustie *Bre* from 86. *4 Lammerton Terrace, Dundee DD4 7BW* Tel (01382) 860836

HARDIE, Canon Stephen. b 41. AKC67. **d** 68 **p** 69. C Roxbourne St Andr *Lon* 68-73; C Colchester St Mary V *Chelmsf* 73-76; R Wivenhoe 76-92; TR Dovercourt and Parkeston 92-96; P-in-c Harwich 92-96; R Dovercourt and Parkeston w Harwich 96-04; TR Harwich Peninsula 04-05; P-in-c Ramsden Crays w Ramsden Bellhouse 02-05; RD Harwich 97-04; Hon Can Chelmsf Cathl 02-05; rtd 05; Perm to Offic *St E* from 06 and *Nor* from 09. *The Croft, 2 Lowestoft Road, Worlingham, Beccles NR34 7EH* Tel (01502) 711625

HARDING, Alan. b 45. St Jo Coll Ox BA67 MA73 Pemb Coll Ox DPhil92. Oak Hill NSM Course 89. **d** 93 **p** 94. NSM Lt Heath *St Alb* 93-99; P-in-c S Mymms and Ridge 99-05; Perm to Offic *St E* 05-08 and *St Alb* from 05; NSM S Hartismere *St E* from 08. *The Old Guildhall, Mill Street, Gislingham, Eye IP23 8JT* Tel (01379) 783361

HARDING, Alec James. b 61. St Andr Univ MA83 DTh. Cranmer Hall Dur 86. **d** 89 **p** 90. C Thirsk *York* 89-93; TV Heref St Martin w St Fran 93-95; TV Heref S Wye 95-00; V Barnard Castle w Whorlton *Dur* from 00; AD Barnard Castle from 03. *The Vicarage, Parson's Lonnen, Barnard Castle DL12 8ST* Tel (01833) 637018 E-mail aleckim@barney16.fsnet.co.uk

HARDING, Andrew Barry. b 66. Westcott Ho Cam 97. **d** 99 **p** 00. C Rainham *Roch* 99-03; V Hoo St Werburgh from 03. *The Vicarage, Vicarage Lane, Hoo, Rochester ME3 9BB* Tel (01634) 250291 E-mail andy.harding@diocese-rochester.org

HARDING, Benjamin Lee. b 75. Bris Univ BA97. Trin Coll Bris BA07. **d** 07. C Cullompton, Willand, Uffculme, Kentisbeare etc *Ex* from 07. *16 Gravel Walk, Cullompton EX15 1DA* Tel (01884) 34585 E-mail benharding@boardermail.com

HARDING, Canon Brenda Kathleen. b 39. Bedf Coll Lon BA60 K Coll Lon BD62 Lon Inst of Educn PGCE65. St Deiniol's Hawarden 91. **d** 92 **p** 94. NSM Lancaster Ch Ch *Blackb* from 92; Acting Vice-Prin CBDTI 04-05; Hon Can Blackb Cathl from 05. *14 Ascot Close, Lancaster LA1 4LT* Tel (01524) 660/1

HARDING, Canon Brian Edward. b 38. ALCD65. **d** 65 **p** 66. C Chislehurst Ch Ch *Roch* 65-68; P-in-c Baxenden *Blackb* 68-70; V 70-88; V Douglas 88-07; Hon Can Blackb Cathl 96-07; rtd 07. *8 Lon Eirlys, Prestatyn LL19 9JZ* Tel (01745) 851615 E-mail beharding@tiscali.co.uk

HARDING, Clifford Maurice. b 22. Leeds Univ BA47. Coll of Resurr Mirfield 46. **d** 48 **p** 49. C Tonge Moor *Man* 48-54; Nyasaland 54-56; CF 56-59; V Oldham St Jo *Man* 59-65; Lic to Offic *Blackb* 65-87; rtd 87; Perm to Offic *Blackb* from 87. *31 Riley Avenue, Lytham St Annes FY8 1HZ* Tel (01253) 725138

HARDING, Colin Ronald Stansby. b 32. RGN71 FVCM92. Bp Otter Coll 94. **d** 97. NSM Aldingbourne, Barnham and Eastergate *Chich* from 97. *Spindle Trees, 67 Elm Grove, Barnham, Bognor Regis PO22 0HJ* Tel (01243) 552579

HARDING, James Owen Glyn. b 42. Sussex Univ BA65. NEOC 04. **d** 06 **p** 07. NSM Nether w Upper Poppleton *York* from 06. *63 Station Road, Upper Poppleton, York YO26 6PZ* Tel (01904) 784495

HARDING, John Stuart Michael. b 45. St Jo Coll Nottm 79. **d** 81 **p** 82. C Clifton *S'well* 81-87; V Broxtowe 87-98; Perm to Offic *Chelmsf* 98-01 and *M & K* 01-02; rtd 07. *Greystone Farm, 9 Liscable Road, Newtownstewart BT78 4EF*

HARDING, John William Christopher. b 31. St Jo Coll Dur BA55. **d** 58 **p** 59. C Wigan St Cath *Liv* 58-60; C Much Woolton 60-63; V Whiston 63-73; V Birkdale St Jo 73-97; rtd 97; Perm to Offic *Liv* from 98. *17 Baytree Close, Southport PR9 8RE* Tel (01704) 507654

HARDING, Ms Lesley Anne. b 58. Westcott Ho Cam 98 SEITE 99. **d** 01 **p** 02. C Walmer *Cant* 01-03; C Broadstairs 03-04; Perm to Offic 05-07; NSM Barkston and Hough Gp *Linc* from 07. *The Rectory, Barkston Road, Marston, Grantham NG32 2HN* Tel (01400) 251590 E-mail revlesleyanne@tesco.net

HARDING, Mrs Marion. b 33. Gilmore Course 75. **dss** 85 **d** 87 **p** 94. Hertford St Andr *St Alb* 85-87; Par Dn 87-93; rtd 93; NSM Lt Amwell *St Alb* 93-97; Perm to Offic from 97. *41 Calton Avenue, Hertford SG14 2ER*

HARDING, Mrs Mary Elizabeth. b 46. SRN67. STETS 97. **d** 00 **p** 01. NSM Shaston *Sarum* from 00; Chapl Westmr Memorial Hosp Shaftesbury from 02. *21 Brionne Way, Shaftesbury SP7 8SL* Tel (01747) 850464 E-mail mary.harding3@virgin.net

HARDING, Michael Anthony John. b 37. Brasted Th Coll 67 Sarum Th Coll 68. **d** 71 **p** 72. C Forest Hill Ch Ch *S'wark* 71-72; C Catford St Laur 72-74; C Leominster *Heref* 74-77; R Neenton and V Ditton Priors 77-86; P-in-c Aston Botterell w Wheathill and Loughton 77-86; P-in-c Burwarton w N Cleobury 77-86; R Ditton Priors w Neenton, Burwarton etc 86-94; V E Budleigh w Bicton and Otterton *Ex* 94-03; rtd 03; Perm to Offic *Sarum* from 03. *The Beaches, 22 Middlehill Road, Colehill, Wimborne BH21 2SD* Tel (01202) 884775
E-mail michaelharding@talktalk.net

HARDING, Preb Michael David. b 38. Man Univ BA61. Lich Th Coll 61. **d** 63 **p** 64. C Hednesford *Lich* 63-67; C Blurton 67-70; V Newcastle St Paul 70-99; RD Newcastle 87-97; Preb Lich Cathl 89-99; rtd 99; Perm to Offic *Lich* from 00. *7 Staines Court, Stone ST15 8XF* Tel (01785) 811737
E-mail mdharding@argonet.co.uk

HARDING, Peter Gordon. b 45. Lon Univ BA70 Open Univ BA88 MA90. Cranmer Hall Dur. **d** 79 **p** 80. C Kirkheaton *Wakef* 79-82; NSM New Sleaford *Linc* 90-00. *67 The Drove, Sleaford NG34 7AS* Tel (01529) 307231
E-mail peter@harding6.orangehome.co.uk

HARDING, Mrs Ren Elaine Lois. b 56. Glos Univ BA05. Trin Coll Bris MA07. **d** 07 **p** 08. C Rainham *Roch* from 07. *60 Childscroft Road, Rainham, Gillingham ME8 7SN* Tel (01634) 231538 Mobile 07836-644782
E-mail renharding@hotmail.co.uk

HARDING, Richard Michael. b 42. St Alb Minl Tr Scheme 80. **d** 83 **p** 84. C Pershore w Pinvin, Wick and Birlingham *Worc* 83-86; V Longdon, Castlemorton, Bushley, Queenhill etc 86-95; P-in-c Catshill and Dodford 95-97; V 97-02; P-in-c Stokenham w Sherford and Beesands, and Slapton *Ex* 02-05; R 05-09; R Stokenham, Slapton, Charleton w Buckland etc from 09. *The Vicarage, Stokenham, Kingsbridge TQ7 2ST* Tel (01548) 580385

HARDING, Richard Warrington. b 60. Trin Coll Bris 05. **d** 07 **p** 08. C Broadway w Wickhamford *Worc* 07-09; C Old Hill H Trin from 09. *15 Highland Road, Cradley Heath B64 5NB*

HARDING, Rolf John. b 22. Oak Hill Th Coll 41 Lon Coll of Div 46. **d** 49 **p** 50. C Sydenham H Trin *S'wark* 49-52; C Harold Wood *Chelmsf* 52-53; Min Harold Hill St Paul CD 53-61; V Coopersale 61-91; Chapl St Marg Hosp Epping 73-91; Chapl W Essex HA 86-91; rtd 91; Perm to Offic *B & W* 91-05; Asst Chapl R United Hosp Bath NHS Trust 92-94. *11 Westbrook Park, Weston, Bath BA1 4DP* Tel (01225) 484968

HARDING, Miss Sylvia. b 23. St Mich Ho Ox 55. **dss** 64 **d** 87. Rodbourne Cheney *Bris* 57-66; Midl Area Sec CPAS 66-71; Patchway 71-78; Sec Coun of Women's Min Bris 77-84; rtd 84; Westbury-on-Trym St Alb *Bris* 86-92; Hon Par Dn 87-92; Perm to Offic *Bris* and *B & W* from 92. *53 Brampton Way, Portishead, Bristol BS20 6YW* Tel (01275) 847046 or 848634

HARDINGHAM, Paul David. b 52. Lon Univ BSc74 Fitzw Coll Cam BA77. Ridley Hall Cam 75. **d** 78 **p** 79. C Cambridge St Martin *Ely* 78-81; C Jesmond Clayton Memorial *Newc* 81-88; C Harborne Heath *Birm* 88-91; R Ipswich St Matt *St E* 91-04; V Halliwell St Pet *Man* from 04. *St Peter's Vicarage, 1 Sefton Road, Bolton BL1 6HT* Tel (01204) 848567
E-mail paul@hardingham60.freeserve.co.uk

HARDINGHAM, Paul Ernest. b 57. **d** 06 **p** 07. OLM Gosberton, Gosberton Clough and Quadring *Linc* from 06; OLM Glen Gp from 07. *The Red House, 97 High Street, Gosberton, Spalding PE11 4NA* Tel (01775) 840803

HARDMAN, Bryan Edwin. b 29. Lon Univ BD60 Selw Coll Cam PhD64 K Coll Lon MTh75. Moore Th Coll Sydney. **d** 55 **p** 55. C Hurstville Australia 55-60; Perm to Offic *Ely* 60-65; V Cambridge St Andr Less 65-68; Prin Bible Coll of S Australia 68-83; Prin Karachi Dioc Sem Pakistan 83-86; Prin Discipleship Tr Cen Singapore 87-94; Nat Dir Interserve Korea 94-97; Visiting Prof Tyndale Univ Canada 99-00; rtd 01; Lic to Offic Adelaide from 06. *197 Kappler Court, 1215 Grand Junction Rd, Hope Valley, SA 5090, Australia* Tel (0061) (8) 8265 6494
E-mail hardmanbryan@gmail.com

HARDMAN, The Ven Christine Elizabeth. b 51. Lon Univ BSc(Econ)73. St Alb Minl Tr Scheme 81 **dss** 84 **d** 87 **p** 94. Markyate Street *St Alb* 84-88; Par Dn 87-88; Tutor St Alb Minl Tr Scheme 88-91; Course Dir 91-96; C Markyate Street 94-96; V Stevenage H Trin 96-01; RD Stevenage 99-01; Adn Lewisham *S'wark* 01-08; Adn Lewisham and Greenwich from 08. *129A Honor Oak Park, London SE23 3LD* Tel (020) 8699 8207 or 7939 9408 Fax 8699 9259 or 7939 9465
E-mail christine.hardman@southwark.anglican.org

HARDMAN, Geoffrey James. b 41. Birm Univ BA63. NOC 77. **d** 80 **p** 81. NSM Latchford St Jas *Ches* 80-93; NSM Haydock St Jas *Liv* from 94. *48 Denbury Avenue, Stockton Heath, Warrington WA4 2BW* Tel (01925) 264064
E-mail geoff@ghardman.freeserve.co.uk

HARDMAN, Mrs Pamela. b 39. **d** 01 **p** 02. NSM Bramhall *Ches* 01-07; NSM Prestbury from 07. *38 Deva Close, Poynton, Stockport SK12 1HH* Tel (01625) 877936
E-mail pamela.prestbury@yahoo.co.uk

HARDMAN, Canon Peter George. b 35. Man Univ BSc56. Ridley Hall Cam 58. **d** 60 **p** 61. C Oldham St Paul *Man* 60-63; NW England Area Sec SCM 63-64; NW England Area Sec CEM 64-67; Asst Chapl Marlborough Coll 67-72; Chapl 72-79; P-in-c Wareham *Sarum* 79-80; TR 80-00; Chapl Wareham Hosp 80-92; Chapl Dorset Health Care NHS Trust 92-00; Can and Preb Sarum Cathl 87-00; RD Purbeck 89-99; rtd 00; Perm to Offic *Sarum* from 00 and *B & W* from 02. *55 Palairet Close, Bradford-on-Avon BA15 1US* Tel (01225) 867198
E-mail peterhardman@onetel.com

HARDS, Mrs Valerie Joy. STETS. **d** 08 **p** 09. NSM Whippingham w E Cowes *Portsm* from 08. *Dallimores, Barton Estate, East Cowes PO32 6NR* Tel (01983) 883943

HARDWICK, The Very Revd Christopher George. b 57. Open Univ BA94 Birm Univ MA96 PhD00 ACIB79. Ripon Coll Cuddesdon 90. **d** 92 **p** 93. C Worc SE 92-95; R Ripple, Earls Croome w Hill Croome and Strensham 95-00; R Upton-on-Severn, Ripple, Earls Croome etc 00-05; RD Upton 97-05; Hon Can Worc Cathl 03-05; Dean Truro from 05; R Truro St Mary from 05. *The Deanery, The Avenue, Truro TR1 1HR* Tel (01872) 272661 *or* 276782 Fax 277788
E-mail dean@trurocathedral.org.uk

HARDWICK, Dennis Egerton. b 27. St Deiniol's Hawarden. **d** 82 **p** 83. NSM Lache cum Saltney *Ches* 82-85; P-in-c Backford 85-88; P-in-c Capenhurst 87-88; R Backford and Capenhurst 88-93; rtd 93; Perm to Offic *Chich* from 93. *11 Prime Close, Walberton, Arundel BN18 0PL* Tel (01243) 551379

HARDWICK, Canon Graham John. b 42. Qu Coll Birm 68. **d** 70 **p** 71. C Watford St Mich *St Alb* 70-73; C N Mymms 73-75; Youth Officer Cov Cathl 75-81; Chapl Lanchester Poly 76-81; V Nuneaton St Nic 81-95; Ind Chapl and P-in-c New Bilton 95-07; Hon Can Cov Cathl 04-07; rtd 08. *150 Pytchley Road, Rugby CV22 5NG* Tel (01788) 544011 Fax 333256
E-mail revgjh@btinternet.com

HARDWICK, John Audley. b 28. Em Coll Cam BA51 MA55. Westcott Ho Cam 51. **d** 53 **p** 54. C Selby Abbey *York* 53-56; Chapl St Edm Sch Hindhead 56-60; Chapl Aysgarth Sch 60-62; Chapl St Edm Sch Hindhead 62-86; Asst Hd Master 73-90; rtd 93; Perm to Offic *Ches* 95-09. *26 Gracey Court, Woodland Road, Broadclyst, Exeter EX5 3GA*

HARDWICK, The Ven Robert. b 56. St Jo Coll Nottm 91. **d** 93 **p** 94. C Beeston *S'well* 93-97; V Scawby, Redbourne and Hibaldstow *Linc* 97-01; RD Yarborough 00-01; R Swift Current Canada from 01; Adn Swift Current from 02. *731 North Hill Drive, Swift Current SK S9H 1X4, Canada* Tel (001) (306) 773 8871 E-mail rob.hardwick@shaw.ca

HARDWICK, Canon Susan Frances. b 44. Warwick Univ BA81. Qu Coll Birm 82. **dss** 85 **d** 87 **p** 94. Chilvers Coton w Astley *Cov* 85-91; C 87-91; Dioc Disabilities Officer 91-96; Chapl Hereward Coll 91-96; Chapl FE Colls 94-09; Hon C New Bilton 96-98; FE Field Officer Team Co-ord (W Midl) 97-09; Chapl Rainsbrook Secure Tr Cen 99-09; Hon Can Cov Cathl 04-09; rtd 09. *150 Pytchley Road, Rugby CV22 5NG* Tel (01788) 544011 Fax 333256 E-mail revgjh@btinternet.com

HARDWICKE, Stephen Michael. b 57. Herts Coll BA85 Lon Bible Coll MA87 K Coll Lon MTh92. Westcott Ho Cam 93. **d** 95 **p** 96. C Leagrave *St Alb* 95-01; P-in-c Cowley *Lon* 01-03; R from 03. *St Laurence Rectory, Church Road, Cowley, Uxbridge UB8 3NB* Tel and fax (01895) 232728
E-mail stevehardwicke660@hotmail.com

HARDY, Ms Alison Jane. b 61. St Anne's Coll Ox BA82 MA96. NOC 92. **d** 95 **p** 96. C Flixton St Mich *Man* 95-98; Lect Bolton St Pet 98-00; P-in-c Irlam 00-05; R Stand from 05. *Stand Rectory, 32 Church Lane, Whitefield, Manchester M45 7NF* Tel 0161-766 2619 E-mail alisonhardy@fsmail.net

HARDY, Anthony. b 36. **d** 86 **p** 87. NSM Malden St Jas *S'wark* 86-06; Perm to Offic from 06. *48 Blake's Lane, New Malden KT3 6NR* Tel (020) 8949 0703 E-mail aehardy@waitrose.com

HARDY, Canon Anthony William. b 56. Open Univ BEd79 MEd86 Open Univ BSc00. St Jo Coll Nottm LTh88. **d** 88 **p** 89. C Pennington *Man* 88-91; V Eccleston St Luke *Liv* 91-00; Min Consultant CPAS 00-09; Dioc Evang (iv Man 00-02; Can Ev Man Cathl from 09. *30 Rathen Road, Manchester M20 4GH* Tel 0161-438 2834
E-mail canon.evangelist@manchestercathedral.org

HARDY, Canon Brian Albert. b 31. St Jo Coll Ox BA54 MA58. Westcott Ho Cam 55. **d** 57 **p** 58. C Rugeley *Lich* 57-62; Chapl Down Coll Cam 62-66; C-in-c Livingston Miss *Edin* 66-74; Preb Heref Cathl 74-78; Ch Planning Officer Telford 74-78; RD Telford Severn Gorge 75-78; Chapl Edin Th Coll 78-82; Chapl Edin R Infirmary 82-86; R Edin St Columba 82-91; Dean Edin 86-91; Hon Can St Mary's Cathl from 91; R St Andrews All SS *St And* 91-96; rtd 96. *3/3 Starbank Road, Edinburgh EH5 3BN* Tel 0131-551 6783

HARDY, Christopher Richard. b 52. R Holloway Coll Lon BMus77 Southn Univ BTh90. Chich Th Coll 87. **d** 90 **p** 91. C Kenton *Lon* 90-95; V E Finchley All SS from 95. *All Saints' Vicarage, Twyford Avenue, London N2 9NH* Tel and fax (020) 8883 9315 Mobile 07785-728272
E-mail christopherhardy@btinternet.com

HARDY, Miss Janet Frances. b 59. Newc Univ BA81 CertEd82. Trin Coll Bris 87. **d** 89 **p** 94. Par Dn Sheff St Paul 89-92; TD Gt Snaith 92-94; TV 94-96; V Pitsmoor Ch Ch 96-01; V Thorpe Hesley from 01. *The Vicarage, 30 Barnsley Road, Thorpe Hesley, Rotherham S61 2RR* Tel 0114-246 3487

HARDY, John Christopher. b 61. St Jo Coll Dur BA83 Dur Univ MA95 New Coll Edin BD92 Ox Univ MLitt00. Aston Tr Scheme 87 Coates Hall Edin 89. **d** 92 **p** 93. C Walker *Newc* 92-95; Fell Chapl Magd Coll Ox 95-98; TV Benwell *Newc* 98-03; R Alston Moor 03-08; R Newmarket St Mary w Exning St Agnes *St E* from 08. *The Rectory, 21 Hamilton Road, Newmarket CB8 0NY* Tel (01638) 660729

HARDY, Canon John Lewis Daniel. b 26. St Chad's Coll Dur BA51. **d** 52 **p** 53. C Hucknall Torkard *S'well* 52-58; V Harworth 58-65; V Sutton in Ashfield St Mary 65-85; R Keyworth 85-93; P-in-c Stanton-on-the-Wolds 85-93; RD S Bingham 91-93; Hon Can S'well Minster 92-93; rtd 93; Perm to Offic *S'well* from 93. *10 Redhill Lodge Drive, Nottingham NG5 8JH* Tel 0115-926 7370

HARDY, Joseph. b 42. RMN64. CA Tr Coll 68. **d** 05 **p** 05. C Tralee w Kilmoyley, Ballymacelligott etc *L & K* from 05. *18 Woodlee, Monavally, Tralee, Co Kerry, Republic of Ireland* Tel (00353) (66) 712 6733

HARDY, Mrs Lesley Anne. b 53. Nottm Univ BA75 St Luke's Coll Ex PGCE76. **d** 05 **p** 06. OLM Lydd *Cant* 05-09; Perm to Offic from 09. *The Rectory, The Street, Barham, Canterbury CT4 6PA* Tel (01227) 831340

HARDY, Michael Frederick Bryan. b 36. Selw Coll Cam BA60 MA64. Linc Th Coll 60. **d** 62 **p** 63. C Pontefract St Giles *Wakef* 62-66; C Lightcliffe 66-69; V Hightown 69-78; V Birkby 78-85; C Boultham *Linc* 88-89; V Misterton and W Stockwith *S'well* 89-01; rtd 01; Perm to Offic *S'well* from 01. *23 Anderson Way, Lea, Gainsborough DN21 5EF* Tel (01427) 614468

HARDY, Michael Henry. b 33. Qu Coll Birm 85. **d** 86 **p** 87. C Leic St Jas 86-88; R Arnesby w Shearsby and Bruntingthorpe 88-94; RD Guthlaxton I 91-94; TV Bradgate Team 94-99; rtd 99; Perm to Offic *Leic* and *Pet* from 99. *14 Dean's Street, Oakham LE15 6AF* Tel (01572) 722591

HARDY, Michael John. b 35. Keble Coll Ox BA58 MA66. Cuddesdon Coll 59. **d** 61 **p** 62. C Dalton-in-Furness *Carl* 61-64; C Harborne St Pet *Birm* 64-68; Min Can Ripon Cathl 68-73; Appt and Tr Sec USPG 73-80; R Stretford St Pet *Man* 80-91; P-in-c Newton Hall *Dur* 91-96; TR Keighley St Andr *Bradf* 96-00; rtd 00; Perm to Offic *Wakef* from 01. *5 Dean Avenue, Netherthong, Holmfirth HD9 3UJ* Tel (01484) 687987

HARDY, Mrs Norma Patricia. b 59. SS Hild & Bede Coll Dur BEd81 St Chad's Coll Dur CertEd08. **d** 08. OLM Hillside *Dur* from 08. *15 Mount Pleasant, Dipton, Stanley DH9 9BL* Tel (01207) 570558 E-mail pat@ianhardy.net

HARDY, Canon Paul Richard. b 30. K Coll Cam BA52 MA56. St Steph Ho Ox 57. **d** 59 **p** 60. C Corringham *Chelmsf* 59-61; C Prittlewell All SS 61-64; USPG Tanzania 64-95; Can Dar-es-Salaam 74-88; Can Zanzibar and Tanga 88-95; Hon Can from 95; rtd 95; Perm to Offic *Roch* from 95. *22 Bromley College, London Road, Bromley BR1 1PE* Tel (020) 8290 1289
E-mail paul@prhardy.co.uk

HARDY, Miss Pauline. b 41. CertEd. Linc Th Coll 85. **d** 87 **p** 94. Par Dn Walsall Wood *Lich* 87-89; Par Dn Buckingham *Ox* 89-93; C Buckingham w Radclive cum Chackmore 93-97; C Nash w Thornton, Beachampton and Thornborough 96-97; C Buckingham 97-03; C Watling Valley 03-06; rtd 06. *32 Campbell Road, Plymouth PL9 8UE* E-mail pauline@revhardy.plus.com

✠**HARDY, The Rt Revd Robert Maynard.** b 36. CBE01. Clare Coll Cam BA60 MA64 Hull Univ Hon DD92. Cuddesdon Coll 60. **d** 62 **p** 63 **c** 80. C Langley St Aid CD *Man* 62-64; C Langley All SS and Martyrs 64-65; Chapl and Lect Th Selw Coll Cam 65-72; V Boreham Wood All SS *St Alb* 72-75; Dir St Alb Minl Tr Scheme 75-80; P-in-c Aspley Guise *St Alb* 75-79; P-in-c Husborne Crawley w Ridgmont 76-79; R Aspley Guise w Husborne Crawley and Ridgmont 80-87; Bp Linc 87-01; Bp HM Pris 85-01; rtd 01; Hon Asst Bp Carl from 01. *Carleton House, Back Lane, Langwathby, Penrith CA10 1NB* Tel (01768) 881210

HARDY, Sam Richard Ian. b 71. Wall Hall Coll Aldenham BEd95 Open Univ MA00. Wycliffe Hall Ox BTh04. **d** 04. C Parr *Liv* 04-05. *Knarside, Woodhead Road, Tintwistle, Glossop SK13 1JX* E-mail sam.hardy@tiscali.co.uk

HARDY, Stephen John Arundell. b 49. SEITE 95. **d** 97 **p** 98. NSM Marden *Cant* 97-00; P-in-c Lydd 00-09; AD Romney 03-08; P-in-c Barham w Bishopsbourne and Kingston from 09. *The Rectory, The Street, Barham, Canterbury CT4 6PA* Tel (01227) 831340 E-mail stephenhardy1@mac.com

HARE, Christopher Sumner. b 49. Solicitor 73. WEMTC 92. **d** 95 **p** 96. NSM Saltford w Corston and Newton St Loe *B & W* 95-01; P-in-c Timsbury and Priston from 01; RD Midsomer Norton from 07; Bp's Officer for Ord NSM (Bath Adnry) 07-08. *The Rectory, South Road, Timsbury, Bath BA2 0EJ* Tel (01761) 479660 E-mail chrishare@stmarystimsbury.org

HARE, David. b 46. Qu Coll Birm 81. **d** 83 **p** 83. SSF 67-94; Bp's Dom Chapl *Birm* 83-87; V Handsworth St Mich 87-97; R Newton Regis w Seckington and Shuttington 97-03; rtd 03; Perm to Offic *Birm* from 03. *118 Southam Road, Birmingham B28 0AD* Tel 0121-777 3493 E-mail dandjhare@hallgreen118.fsnet.co.uk

HARE, Douglas Stewart. b 27. Bris Univ BA51 Lon Inst of Educn PGCE52. Wycliffe Hall Ox 82. **d** 96 **p** 97. NSM Margate H Trin *Cant* 96-99; rtd 99; Perm to Offic *Sarum* from 00. *8 Lady Down View, Tisbury, Salisbury SP3 6LL* Tel (01747) 871544

HARE, Frank Richard Knight. b 22. Trin Hall Cam BA46 MA48. Cuddesdon Coll 46. **d** 48 **p** 49. C Dennington *St E* 48-51; C Eastbourne St Mary *Chich* 51-54; R Rotherfield 54-62; V Steyning 62-70; R Ashurst 62-70; TV Raveningham *Nor* 70-71; TR Barnham Broom 71-79; V Buxton w Oxnead 79-86; R Lammas w Lt Hautbois 79-86; rtd 86; Perm to Offic *St E* from 86. *14 Lee Road, Aldeburgh IP15 5HG* Tel (01728) 453372

HARE, Michael John. b 41. Lon Univ MD71 Cam Univ MA77. EAMTC 00. **d** 02 **p** 03. NSM E Leightonstone *Ely* 02-06; NSM Buckworth and Alconbury cum Weston 04-06; Perm to Offic *St E* 06-09; NSM Woodbridge St Mary from 09. *The Q Tower, 14 South Hill, Felixstowe IP11 2AA* Tel (01394) 670264 E-mail hare@waitrose.com

HARE, Richard William. b 66. Bris Univ BSc88 PhD94. Cranmer Hall Dur BA95. **d** 95 **p** 96. C Coulsdon St Jo *S'wark* 95-98; C Coventry Caludon 98-99; TV 99-07; AD Cov E 01-07; TR Bedworth from 07. *The Rectory, 1 Linden Lea, Bedworth CV12 8UD* Tel (024) 7631 0219 E-mail thehares@ic24.net

✠**HARE, The Rt Revd Thomas Richard.** b 22. Trin Coll Ox BA48 MA53. Westcott Ho Cam 48. **d** 50 **p** 51. C Haltwhistle *Newc* 50-52; Bp's Dom Chapl *Man* 52-59; Can Res Carl Cathl 59-65; R Barrow St Geo w St Luke 65-69; Adn Westmorland and Furness 65-71; Hon Can Carl Cathl 65-71; V Winster 69-71; Suff Bp Pontefract *Wakef* 71-92; rtd 92. *Wood Cottage, Mirehouse, Underskiddaw, Keswick CA12 4QE* Tel (01768) 772996

✠**HARE DUKE, The Rt Revd Michael Geoffrey.** b 25. Trin Coll Ox BA49 MA51 St Andr Univ Hon DD94. Westcott Ho Cam 50. **d** 52 **p** 53 **c** 69. C St John's Wood *Lon* 52-56; V Bury St Mark *Man* 56-62; Past Dir Clinical Th Assn Nottm 62-64; Past Consultant 64-69; V Daybrook *S'well* 64-69; Bp St And 69-94; rtd 94. *2 Balhousie Avenue, Perth PH1 5HN* Tel (01738) 622642 E-mail bishmick@blueyonder.co.uk

HARES, David Ronald Walter. b 40. Qu Coll Cam BA63 MA67 CertEd. Westcott Ho Cam 64. **d** 66 **p** 67. C Cannock *Lich* 66-69; Chapl Peterho Cam 69-72; Asst Master Chesterton Sch Cam 72-74; V Kesgrave *St E* 74-98; R Lt Barningham, Blickling, Edgefield etc *Nor* 98-05; rtd 05; Perm to Offic *Nor* from 05. *17 Trory Street, Norwich NR2 2RH* Tel (01603) 626392 E-mail dh@davidhares.freeserve.co.uk

HAREWOOD, John Rupert. b 24. Man Univ BA48. Sarum & Wells Th Coll 76. **d** 79 **p** 80. NSM Taunton St Jas *B & W* 79-82; TV Camelot Par 82-89; rtd 89; Perm to Offic *Ex* from 92. *19 Swains Road, Budleigh Salterton EX9 6HU* Tel (01395) 445802

HARFORD, Julian Gray. b 29. Univ Coll Ox BA52 MA59 Lon Univ PGCE58. Qu Coll Birm. **d** 64 **p** 65. C W End *Win* 64-67; C Chearsley w Nether Winchendon *Ox* 67-77; C Chilton All SS 72-77; R Westbury w Turweston, Shalstone and Biddlesden 77-86; C Chenies and Lt Chalfont 86-87; C Chenies and Lt Chalfont, Latimer and Flaunden 87-95; rtd 95; Perm to Offic *Sarum* from 95. *14 Dial Close, Seend, Melksham SN12 6NP* Tel (01380) 828306

HARFORD, The Ven Michael Rivers Dundas. b 26. Trin Coll Cam BA49 MA51. Westcott Ho Cam 50. **d** 52 **p** 53. C Ashton-on-Ribble St Andr *Blackb* 52-55; Perm to Offic *Edin* 55-56; C Singapore Cathl and Chapl Univ of Malaya 56-60; C Kuala Lumpur St Mary 60-62; V Childwall St Dav *Liv* 66-71; R Katanning Australia 71-76; Adn Albany 76-79; R Bicton and Attadale 79-86; R Guildford 86-91; Adn Swan 86-89; Adn Mitchell 90-91; rtd 91. *Unit 12, 18 Bridges Road, Melville WA 6156, Australia* Tel (0061) (8) 9319 1538 Mobile 410-566896 E-mail venmike@optusnet.com.au

HARFORD, Timothy William. b 58. Nottm Univ BTh89. Linc Th Coll 86. **d** 89 **p** 90. C Minehead *B & W* 89-93; R Knebworth *St Alb* 93-03; Children's Soc from 03. *The Children's Society, Edward Rudolf House, Margery Street, London WC1X 0JL* Tel (020) 7841 4400 E-mail twh@childsoc.org.uk

HARGER, Robin Charles Nicholas. b 49. BTh. Sarum & Wells Th Coll 78. **d** 81 **p** 82. C Charlton Kings St Mary *Glouc* 81-85; C Folkestone St Mary and St Eanswythe *Cant* 85-89; TV Langley and Parkfield *Man* 89-95; TV Bournemouth Town Cen *Win* from 95. *The Vicarage, 2A St Anthony's Road, Bournemouth BH2 6PD* Tel (01202) 554355 E-mail robin.harger2@btopenworld.com

HARGRAVE, Canon Alan Lewis. b 50. Birm Univ BSc73 PhD77. Ridley Hall Cam 87. **d** 89 **p** 90. C Cambridge H Trin w St Andr Gt *Ely* 89-92; C Cambridge H Trin 92-93; C-in-c Fen Ditton 93-94; V Cambridge H Cross 94-04; Can Res Ely Cathl from 04. *Powchers Hall, The College, Ely CB7 4DL* Tel (01353) 660304 *or* 667735 Fax 665658 E-mail alan.hargrave@cathedral.ely.anglican.org

HARGRAVES, Mrs Christobel Mary Kathleen. b 58. Man Poly BSc79 Open Univ MBA RGN83. SAOMC 03. **d** 06 **p** 07. C Goring w S Stoke *Ox* 06-07; C Goring and Streatley w S Stoke 07-09; R Shelswell from 09. *The Rectory, Water Stratford Road, Finmere, Buckingham MK18 4AT* Tel (01280) 847184 E-mail chris.hargraves@psaconnect.com

HARGREAVE, James David. b 44. K Coll Lon BA66 Lon Univ PGCE68 ALCM89 LTCL90. Coll of Resurr Mirfield 70. **d** 73 **p** 74. C Houghton le Spring *Dur* 73-77; C Gateshead St Cuth w St Paul 77-79; V Trimdon 79-87; C-in-c Stockton Green Vale H Trin CD 87-94; V Hedon w Paull *York* 94-02; rtd 02. *1 The Avenue, Crescent Street, Cottingham HU16 5QT* Tel (01482) 844297

HARGREAVES, Andrew David. b 74. Homerton Coll Cam BEd97. Trin Coll Bris BA08. **d** 08 **p** 09. C Shirley *Win* from 08. *16 Radway Road, Southampton SO15 7PW* Tel (023) 8077 0474 Mobile 07801-062986 E-mail adhargreaves@btinternet.com

HARGREAVES, Arthur Walsh. b 34. Man Univ MB, ChB FRCSE MRCS FRCSGlas. St Deiniol's Hawarden 89. **d** 90 **p** 91. NSM Baguley *Man* 90-04; rtd 04; Perm to Offic *Man* from 04. *33 Chelford Road, Knutsford WA16 8NN* Tel (01565) 654343

HARGREAVES, John. b 43. St Jo Coll Nottm 86. **d** 88 **p** 89. C Werneth *Man* 88-91; TV Rochdale 91-96; C Man Gd Shep 96-97; Perm to Offic *Liv* 96-97; C Manchester Gd Shep and St Barn 97-98; rtd 98; Perm to Offic *Man* 06-09. *Penola, Wyebank, Bakewell DE45 1BH*

HARGREAVES, John Rodney. b 36. Open Univ BA74. Didsbury Methodist Coll 59 St Deiniol's Hawarden 74. **d** 75 **p** 75. In Methodist Ch 63-74; C Pontypool *Mon* 75-77; C Llanedeyrn 77-79; Chapl HM Pris Aylesbury 79-83; Sen Chapl HM Pris Stafford 83-88; Asst Chapl Gen of Pris (N) 88-90; Asst Chapl Gen of Pris 90-96; R Stone St Mich and St Wulfad w Aston St Sav *Lich* 96-01; rtd 01; Master St Jo Hosp Lich 01-04; Perm to Offic from 04. *217 Newcastle Road, Stone ST15 8LF* Tel (01785) 814765 E-mail jrhargreaves@easynet.co.uk

HARGREAVES, John Wilson. b 46. Aber Univ BScFor67. Westcott Ho Cam 84. **d** 86 **p** 87. C Rugby *Cov* 86-90; TV Daventry, Ashby St Ledgers, Braunston etc *Pet* 90-97; Chapl Daventry Tertiary Coll 94-97; P-in-c Pinxton *Derby* 97-01; R 01-02; TR E Scarsdale from 02. *The Rectory, Rectory Road, Upper Langwith, Mansfield NG20 9RE* Tel (01623) 748505

HARGREAVES, Mrs Julia Gay. b 61. EMMTC 04. **d** 07 **p** 08. NSM Glenfield *Leic* 07-08; NSM Upper Soar from 08. *66 Underwood Drive, Stoney Stanton, Leicester LE9 4TD* Tel (01455) 272827 E-mail simonw.hargreaves@btinternet.com

HARGREAVES, Ms Marise. b 60. Leeds Univ BA81. Cranmer Hall Dur 82. **dss** 85 **d** 94 **p** 95. Yeadon St Jo *Bradf* 85-87; NSM Bradf St Clem 94-96; NSM Buttershaw St Paul 96-00; C Eccleshill 00-03; Perm to Offic 03-09; Chapl Derby Hosps NHS Foundation Trust from 09. *Chaplaincy, Royal Derby Hospital, Uttoxeter Road, Derby DE22 3NE* Tel (01332) 340131

HARGREAVES, Mark Kingston. b 63. Oriel Coll Ox BA85 MA89 Rob Coll Cam PhD91 W Lon Inst of HE PGCE86. Ridley Hall Cam 87. **d** 91 **p** 92. C Highbury Ch Ch w St Jo and St Sav *Lon* 91-94; C Ealing St Steph Castle Hill 94-97; C Notting Hill St Jo and St Pet 97-02; V Notting Hill St Pet from 03; AD Kensington from 06. *48 Ladbroke Road, London W11 3NW* Tel (020) 7221 9841 E-mail mark@nottinghillchurch.org.uk

HARGREAVES-STEAD, Terence Desmond. b 32. Edin Th Coll 60. **d** 63 **p** 64. C Walney Is *Carl* 63-66; Chapl Withington Hosp Man 66-72; V Westleigh St Paul *Man* 72-06; Chapl Wigan and Leigh Health Services NHS Trust 96-01; Chapl Wrightington Wigan and Leigh NHS Trust 01-06; rtd 07. *4 Hartford Green, Westhoughton, Bolton BL5 2GL* Tel (01942) 859929

HARINGTON, Roger John Urquhart. b 48. Trin Hall Cam BA70 MA71. Coll of Resurr Mirfield 72. **d** 75 **p** 76. C Liv Our Lady and St Nic w St Anne 75-78; Asst Chapl Leeds Univ and Poly 78-81; TV Moor Allerton 81-86; Dioc Drama Adv (Jabbok Theatre Co) 86-95; V Leeds Gipton Epiphany 95-02. *21 Spencer Place, Leeds LS7 4DQ* Tel 0113-240 0769 E-mail jabbok@gn.apc.org

HARKER, Harold Aidan. b 35. **d** 82 **p** 83. OSB from 53; C Reading St Giles *Ox* 82-83; Lic to Offic 83-87; C Halstead St Andr w H Trin and Greenstead Green *Chelmsf* 87-89; P-in-c Belchamp St Paul 89-97; R Belchamp Otten w Belchamp Walter and Bulmer etc 97-00; rtd 00; Lic to Offic *Chelmsf* from 00. *38 Sheppard's College, London Road, Bromley BR1 1PE* Tel (020) 8464 1206

HARKER, Ian. b 39. Dur Univ BA61. Lich Th Coll Moray Ho Edin 66. **d** 63 **p** 64. C Knottingley *Wakef* 63-66; Perm to Offic 66-70; C Notting Hill *Lon* 70-75; Chapl Newc Univ 75-83; Master Newc St Thos Prop Chpl 75-83; Perm to Offic *Chelmsf*

99-01; C Plaistow and N Canning Town 01; C Loughton St Jo 01-02; V Leytonstone H Trin Harrow Green from 02. *The Vicarage, 4 Holloway Road, London E11 4LD* Tel and fax (020) 8539 7760 E-mail harkatvic@aol.com

HARKER, John Hadlett. b 37. Dur Univ BSc59 Newc Univ PhD67 CEng MIChemE64 MInstE64 CChem MRSC65 FIChemE80. NEOC 81. **d** 84 **p** 85. C Earsdon *Newc* 84-87; P-in-c Long Horsley 87-91; V Bassenthwaite, Isel and Setmurthy *Carl* 91-94; TR Howden *York* 94-96; P-in-c Willerby w Ganton and Folkton 96-98; rtd 98; Perm to Offic *Newc* 98-01 and from 04; Hon C Newc St Andr and St Luke 01-04. *30 Station Road, Kenton Bank Foot, Newcastle upon Tyne NE13 8AG* Tel 0191-286 3206 E-mail harker@thestell.freeserve.co.uk

HARKER, Stephan John. b 47. Em Coll Cam BA68 MA72. Westcott Ho Cam 70. **d** 72 **p** 73. C Marton *Blackb* 72-76; C Preston St Matt 76-79; C Fleetwood St Pet 79-80; Sen Chapl Charterhouse Sch Godalming 81-07; Chapl from 07. *Firview, 63 Peperharow Road, Godalming GU7 2PL* Tel (01483) 422155 E-mail sjh@charterhouse.org.uk

HARKIN, Canon John Patrick. b 53. Open Univ BA92. Oak Hill Th Coll 87. **d** 89 **p** 90. C Wisley w Pyrford *Guildf* 89-93; P-in-c Mickleham 93-98; Chapl Box Hill Sch Surrey 93-98; R Jersey St Ouen w St Geo *Win* from 98; Vice-Dean Jersey from 01; Hon Can Win Cathl from 09. *The Rectory, La Route au Marais, St Ouen, Jersey JE3 2GG* Tel (01534) 481800 Fax 484202 E-mail harkin@jerseymail.co.uk

HARKIN, Terence James. b 46. Lon Bible Coll BA82 New Coll Edin MTh94. **d** 95 **p** 96. In Bapt Min 86-95; C Edin H Cross 95-96; C S Queensferry 95-96; P-in-c from 96. *6 Wellhead Close, South Queensferry EH30 9WA* Tel 0131-319 1099 *or* 331 1958 E-mail tjharkin@priorychurch.com

HARKINS, James Robert. b 27. Minnesota Univ BA49. Seabury-Western Th Sem MTh53. **d** 52 **p** 52. USA 52-60, 72-79 and 91-93; Colombia 60-72; Dominica 79-85; Venezuela 85-91; Chapl Venice w Trieste *Eur* 94-99; P-in-c Menton 99-01; rtd 01. *Soleil du Menton, 2 Sent Pigautier, 06500 Menton, France* Tel (0033) (4) 9357 2025

HARKNETT, David Philip. b 74. St Pet Coll Ox BA97. Oak Hill Th Coll BA03. **d** 03 **p** 04. C Radipole and Melcombe Regis *Sarum* 03-07; TV Melbury from 07. *The Vicarage, Corscombe, Dorchester DT2 0NU* Tel (01935) 891247 E-mail davidharknett@hotmail.com

HARKNETT, Linda. b 48. Open Univ BA81 Croydon Coll CertEd92. SEITE 97. **d** 00 **p** 01. NSM Sutton St Nic *S'wark* 00-03; Chapl Epsom and St Helier NHS Trust 00-03; Chapl Whitelands Coll Surrey Univ Roehampton 03-07; Dioc FE and HE Chapl Officer 03-07; P-in-c Headley w Box Hill *Guildf* from 07. *The Rectory, Church Lane, Headley, Epsom KT18 6LE* Tel (01372) 377327 Mobile 07799 903167

HARLAND, Brenda. **d** 08. NSM Thatcham *Ox* from 08. *St Mary's Church Office, Church Gate, Thatcham RG19 3PN* Tel (01635) 862277 E-mail brenda.harland@ntlworld.com

HARLAND, Canon Harold William James. b 35. Hertf Coll Ox BA59 MA63. Clifton Th Coll 59. **d** 60 **p** 61 **p** 62. C Reigate St Mary *S'wark* 61-64; C Farnborough *Guildf* 64-68; V Walmley *Birm* 68-74; V Bromley Ch Ch *Roch* 74-86; V Foord St Jo *Cant* 86-00; Dir Post-Ord Tr 93-97; Hon Can Cant Cathl 94-00; rtd 00; Perm to Offic *Cant* from 00. *121 Station Road West, Canterbury CT2 8DE* Tel (01227) 764699 E-mail harlandh992@aol.com

HARLEY, Brother Martin Mortimer. b 25. K Coll Lon 48. **d** 53 **p** 54. C Bris St Agnes w St Simon 53-56; Lic to Offic *Sarum* 56-62; SSF from 56; Chapl St Fran Sch Hooke 58-61; Papua New Guinea 61-79; Australia from 87; Hon Gen SSF from 91; rtd 95. *The Hermitage of St Bernadine, PO Box 46, Stroud NSW 2425, Australia* Tel (0061) (2) 4994 5372 Fax 4994 5527

HARLEY, Canon Brian Nigel. b 30. Clare Coll Cam BA53 MA57. Cuddesdon Coll 53. **d** 55 **p** 56. C Basingstoke *Win* 55-60; TV 71-73; TR 73-80; C W End 60-61; C-in-c Southn St Chris Thornhill CD 61-71; V Eastleigh 80-93; RD Eastleigh 85-93; rtd 93; Perm to Offic *Win* from 93; Bp's Dom Chapl 94-96. *18 Phillimore Road, Southampton SO16 2NR* Tel (023) 8055 1049

HARLEY, Mrs Carol Anne. b 46. **d** 00 **p** 01. OLM Tettenhall Wood and Perton *Lich* from 00. *2 Tyrley Close, Compton, Wolverhampton WV6 8AP* Tel (01902) 755316 E-mail allynharley@lineone.net

HARLEY, Christopher David. b 41. Selw Coll Cam BA63 MA69 Bris Univ PGCE64 Columbia Bible Sem DMin92 Utrecht Univ PhD02. Clifton Th Coll 64. **d** 66 **p** 67. C Finchley Ch Ch *Lon* 66-69; Hon C 75-78; Ethiopia 70-75; Hd of UK Miss CMJ 75-78; Lect All Nations Chr Coll Ware 78-85; Prin 85-93; Chmn Lon Inst of Contemporary Christianity 88-89; Chmn CMJ 89-90; Crosslinks 93-06; Gen Dir OMF Internat 93-05; NSM Bromley Ch Ch *Roch* 93-96; NSM Singapore 96-06; rtd 06. *6 Michigan Way, Exeter EX4 5EU* Tel (01392) 207190 E-mail harleydavid@omf.net

HARLEY, David Bertram. b 22. Down Coll Cam BA50 MA55. Westcott Ho Cam 55. **d** 56 **p** 58. Asst Master Bedford Sch 50-58; C Biddenham *St Alb* 56-58; Chapl Stamford Sch 58-87; rtd 87;

Confrater Browne's Hosp Stamford from 87; Lic to Offic *Linc* 59-94; Perm to Offic from 94. *Beggars' Roost, Priory Road, Stamford PE9 2ES* Tel (01780) 763403

HARLEY, The Ven Michael. b 50. AKC73 Ch Ch Coll Cant CertEd74 Lambeth STh92 Kent Univ MPhil95. St Aug Coll Cant 74. **d** 75 **p** 76. C Chatham St Wm *Roch* 75-78; C-in-c Weeke *Win* 78-81; V Southampton St Mary Extra 81-86; V Hurstbourne Tarrant, Faccombe, Vernham Dean etc 86-99; ACORA Link Officer 91-94; Dioc Rural Officer 95-97; RD Andover 95-99; V Chandler's Ford 99-09; Tutor STETS 03-06; Hon Can Win Cathl 06-09; Adn Win from 09; P-in-c Win St Cross w St Faith from 09; Master St Cross Hosp from 09. *22 St John Street, Winchester SO23 8HF* Tel (01962) 869442 E-mail michael.harley@winchester.anglican.org

HARLEY, Nigel. *See* HARLEY, Canon Brian Nigel

HARLEY, Peter David. b 59. Sheff Univ BSc82 Warwick Univ MBA86. **d** 09. OLM Horwich and Rivington *Man* from 09. *6 Barford Grove, Lostock, Bolton BL6 4NQ* Tel (01204) 694611 E-mail peter.harley@talktalk.net

HARLEY, Canon Robert Patterson. b 53. St Andr Univ MA75 Cam Univ CertEd76 Glas Univ PhD89 Edin Univ BD97. **d** 97 **p** 98. C Edin St Thos 97-00; Chapl Lothian Univ Hosps NHS Trust 98-00; P-in-c Kirriemuir *St And* from 00; Can St Ninian's Cathl Perth from 08. *128 Glengate, Kirriemuir DD8 4JG* Tel (01575) 575515 E-mail robert.harley@virgin.net

HARLEY, Roger Newcomb. b 38. Ely Th Coll 61. **d** 64 **p** 65. C Plymouth St Pet *Ex* 64-66; C Heston *Lon* 66-69; C Maidstone All SS w St Phil and H Trin *Cant* 69-73; R Temple Ewell w Lydden 73-79; P-in-c Shirley St Geo 79-81; V 81-85; V Croydon H Sav *S'wark* 85-95; V Forest Row *Chich* 95-03; rtd 03; Perm to Offic *Cant* from 03. *7 Roman Way, St Margarets-at-Cliffe, Dover CT15 6AH* Tel (01304) 851720 E-mail rnharley@tesco.net

HARLING, Timothy Charles. b 80. Fitzw Coll Cam BA04. Westcott Ho Cam 02. **d** 05 **p** 06. C Romsey *Win* 05-09; Chapl HM Pris Peterborough from 09. *HM Prison Peterborough, Saville Road, Peterborough PE3 7PD* Tel (01733) 217500

HARLOW, Antony Francis. b 24. Pemb Coll Cam BA50 MA55. Oak Hill Th Coll 84. **d** 85 **p** 86. NSM Watford St Luke *St Alb* 85-86; CMS 86-91; Uganda 86-91; NSM Watford St Pet *St Alb* 92-96; Perm to Offic *St Alb* 90-98 and *B & W* from 98. *1 Jubilee Homes, Langford Road, Langford, Bristol BS40 5HU* Tel (01934) 862605

HARLOW, Canon Derrick Peter. b 30. St Jo Coll Cam BA53 MA57. Ridley Hall Cam 53. **d** 55 **p** 56. C Barking St Marg *Chelmsf* 55-58; V Leyton Em 58-63; V Goodmayes All SS 63-75; R Thundersley 76-83; TR Saffron Walden w Wendens Ambo and Littlebury 83-95; Hon Can Chelmsf Cathl 94-95; rtd 95; Perm to Offic *Ely* from 95 and *Chelmsf* from 98. *26 Kintbury, Duxford, Cambridge CB22 4RR* Tel (01223) 721405

HARLOW, Mrs Elizabeth Gilchrist. b 27. MSc50. Oak Hill Th Coll 85. **d** 91 **p** 94. NSM St Alb St Luke *St Alb* 91-94; NSM Watford St Luke 94-96; Perm to Offic *St Alb* 90-98 and *B & W* from 98. *1 Jubilee Homes, Langford Road, Langford, Bristol BS40 5HU* Tel (01934) 862605

HARLOW, Kathryn. b 78. Southn Univ BSc99. Wycliffe Hall Ox BTh07. **d** 07 **p** 08. C Foord St Jo *Cant* from 07. *2 Chalk Close, Folkestone CT19 5TD* Tel (01303) 256356 E-mail rev_kathryn@hotmail.co.uk

HARLOW-TRIGG, Richard John St Clair. b 63. Cam Univ BA85 MA88. Cranmer Hall Dur 87. **d** 89 **p** 90. C Hyson Green *S'well* 89-91; C Basford w Hyson Green 91-94; C Mansfield SS Pet and Paul 94-97; TV Newark 97-01; Chapl Mid Sussex NHS Trust 01-02; Chapl Brighton and Sussex Univ Hosps NHS Trust from 02; Chapl St Pet and St Jas Hospice N Chailey 02-05. *The Princess Royal Hospital, Lewes Road, Haywards Heath RH16 4EX* Tel (01444) 441881 ext 4232 E-mail richard.harlow-trigg@bsuh.nhs.uk

HARLOW, Archdeacon of. *See* WEBSTER, The Ven Martin Duncan

HARMAN, Kathleen Joyce. b 49. **d** 03 **p** 04. C Llangynwyd w Maesteg 03-08; R Dowlais and Penydarren from 08. *The Rectory, Gwernllwyn Road, Dowlais, Merthyr Tydfil CF48 3NA* Tel (01685) 722118

HARMAN, Leslie Davies. b 46. Nottm Univ BTh76. St Jo Coll Nottm LTh75. **d** 76 **p** 77. C Wandsworth All SS *S'wark* 76-78; C Godstone 78-82; V Thorncombe w Winsham and Cricket St Thomas *B & W* 82-87; TV Hitchin *St Alb* 87-95; V Royston from 95; RD Buntingford 96-01. *The Vicarage, 20 Palace Gardens, Royston SG8 5AD* Tel (01763) 243145 *or* 788933

HARMAN, Michael John. b 48. Chich Th Coll 71. **d** 74 **p** 75. C Blackpool St Steph *Blackb* 74-79; Chapl RN 79-06; rtd 06; Perm to Offic *Ex* and *Truro* from 06; P-in-c Wembury *Ex* from 08. *18 Furzeacre Close, Plymouth PL7 5DZ* Tel (01752) 338910 Mobile 07836-377820 E-mail revmikeharman@blueyonder.co.uk

HARMAN, Theodore Allan. b 27. Linc Coll Ox BA52 MA56 Hatf Coll Dur MA90. Wells Th Coll 52. **d** 54 **p** 55. C Hawkshead and Low Wray *Carl* 54-55; C Kirkby Stephen w Mallerstang 55-57; Asst Chapl Sedbergh Sch 57-84; Sen Chapl 84-87; Tutor

Hatf Coll Dur from 88; Admissions Tutor 89-90; Lib and Coll Officer 91-02; Acting Chapl 99-00; Fell from 00; Perm to Offic *Dur* from 88. *Flat D1, Hatfield College, North Bailey, Durham DH1 3RQ* Tel 0191-334 2626 Fax 334 3101
E-mail t.a.harman@durham.ac.uk

HARMER, Timothy James. b 47. Birm Univ CertEd68. St Jo Coll Nottm BA95. **d** 95 **p** 96. C Studley *Cov* 95-98; V Tanworth *Birm* 98-05; P-in-c Helsington *Carl* from 05; P-in-c Underbarrow from 05; RD Kendal from 08. *Sunnybank, Underbarrow, Kendal LA8 8HG* Tel (01539) 568865
E-mail revtim.harmer@virgin.net

HARMSWORTH, Canon Roger James. b 46. Univ of W Ontario BA87. Huron Coll Ontario MDiv90. **d** 90 **p** 90. Canada 90-96; I Maryborough w Dysart Enos and Ballyfin *C & O* 96-01; I Killanne w Killegney, Rossdroit and Templeshanbo from 01; Treas Ferns Cathl 03-04; Chan from 04. *The Rectory, Clonroche, Enniscorthy, Co Wexford, Republic of Ireland* Tel and fax (00353) (53) 924 4180 E-mail therev@iol.ie

HARNDEN, Peter John. b 63. Coll of Resurr Mirfield 96. **d** 98 **p** 99. C Staplehurst *Cant* 98-02; V Tokyngton St Mich *Lon* from 02. *The Vicarage, St Michael's Avenue, Wembley HA9 6SL* Tel (020) 8902 3290 E-mail harny@cwcom.net
or harny@boltblue.net

HARNEY, Janice. b 56. **d** 02 **p** 03. OLM Pennington *Man* 02-06; Perm to Offic from 06. *29 Green Lane, Leigh WN7 2TL* Tel and fax (01942) 671481 Mobile 07811-764355
E-mail jan.harney@btinternet.com

HARNISH, Robert George. b 64. Univ of Ottawa BSc87 Worc Coll Ox DPhil90 MA92. Wycliffe Hall Ox 90. **d** 93 **p** 94. C Chinnor w Emmington and Sydenham etc *Ox* 93-95; Chapl and Dean of Div New Coll Ox 96-01; Chapl Eliz Coll Guernsey from 01. *11 Saumarez Street, St Peter Port, Guernsey GY1 2PT* Tel (01481) 713298 *or* 726544

HARONSKI, Boleslaw. b 46. Pemb Coll Ox BA68 MA72 DPhil73. St Mich Coll Llan 80 Westcott Ho Cam 82. **d** 82 **p** 83. C Maindee Newport *Mon* 82-85; V Llanishen w Trellech Grange and Llanfihangel etc 85-89; V Blackwood 89-92. *45 St Julian's Road, Newport NP9 7GN*

✠**HARPER, The Most Revd Alan Edwin Thomas.** b 44. OBE96. Leeds Univ BA65. CITC 75. **d** 78 **p** 79 **c** 02. C Ballywillan *Conn* 78-80; I Moville w Greencastle, Upper Moville etc *D & R* 80-82; I Londonderry Ch Ch 82-86; I Belfast Malone St Jo *Conn* 86-02; Preb St Audoen St Patr Cathl Dublin 90-01; Adn Conn 96-02; Prec Belf Cathl 96-02; Bp Conn 02-07; Abp Arm from 07. *Diocesan Office, Church House, 46 Abbey Street, Armagh BT61 7DZ* Tel (028) 3752 2858
E-mail archbishop@armagh.anglican.org

HARPER, Alan Peter. b 50. Man Univ BA73 FCA83. Ripon Coll Cuddesdon 86. **d** 88 **p** 89. C Newport w Longford and Chetwynd *Lich* 88-91; P-in-c Wilnecote 91-94; V Codsall 98-07; Preb Lich Cathl 02-07, RD Penkridge 06-07; Bp's Dom Chapl *Derby* from 07. *2 Mayfair Court, Milford Road, Duffield, Belper DE56 4EL* Tel (01332) 843169
E-mail chaplain@bishopofderby.org

HARPER, Barry. See HARPER, Canon Malcolm Barry

HARPER, Brian John. b 61. Liv Univ BA82. CITC. **d** 85 **p** 86. C Portadown St Columba *Arm* 85-88; C Drumglass 88-89; I Errigle Keerogue w Ballygawley and Killeshil 89-93; I Mullavilly from 93. *89 Mullavilly Road, Tandragee, Craigavon BT62 2LX* Tel (028) 3884 0221 *or* 3884 1918
E-mail mullavilly@btinternet.com

HARPER, Clive Stewart. b 35. FCIS71. Ridley Hall Cam 80. **d** 82 **p** 83. C Bromyard *Heref* 82-85; P-in-c Bredenbury and Wacton w Grendon Bishop 85-89; P-in-c Edwyn Ralph and Collington w Thornbury 85-89; P-in-c Pencombe w Marston Stannett and Lt Cowarne 85-89; R Bredenbury w Grendon Bishop and Wacton etc 89-92; R Bilton *Cov* 92-02; rtd 02; Hon C Churchover w Willey *Cov* 02-05; Perm to Offic from 05. *Kairos, 18 Whimbrel Close, Rugby CV23 0WG* Tel (01788) 541041
E-mail harper@clival.freeserve.co.uk

HARPER, David Laurence. b 51. Qu Coll Cam BA73 MA77 PhD78. Wycliffe Hall Ox BA80. **d** 80 **p** 81. C Mansfield SS Pet and Paul *S'well* 80-84; C Wollaton 84-87; V Brinsley w Underwood 87-94; R Bingham from 94; AD Bingham 00-03; AD E Bingham 03-07. *The Rectory, Bingham, Nottingham NG13 8DR* Tel (01949) 837335
E-mail dl.harper@btopenworld.com

HARPER, Geoffrey. b 32. Hertf Coll Ox BA55 MA59. Coll of Resurr Mirfield. **d** 57 **p** 58. C Cov St Pet 57-60; C Handsworth St Mich *Birm* 60-62; C-in-c Kingstanding St Mark CD 62-71; V Kingstanding St Mark 71-73; R Sheviock *Truro* 73-80; R Antony w Sheviock 80-82; V Paul 82-98; Dioc Development Rep 86-98; rtd 98; Perm to Offic *Truro* 99-04. *9 Galloway Close, Fleet GU51 2TJ* Tel (01252) 501509
E-mail juan.geoff@ntlworld.com

HARPER, Canon Geoffrey Roger. b 57. Jes Coll Cam BA79 MA83. St Jo Coll Nottm 81. **d** 84 **p** 85. C Belper *Derby* 84-87; C Birstall and Wanlip *Leic* 87-90; TV Tettenhall Regis *Lich* 90-97; C Aldridge 97-02; Chapl Douglas MacMillan Hospice Stoke-on-

Trent 04-07; Perm to Offic *Lich* 02-07; C W Bromwich Gd Shep w St Jo 07-09; C Bilston from 09; Hon Can W Ankole from 05. *34 Somerset Road, Walsall WS4 2DP* Tel (01922) 611484 Mobile 07954-409635 E-mail roger.harper@blueyonder.co.uk

HARPER, Gordon. b 32. Oak Hill Th Coll 64. **d** 66 **p** 67. C Halliwell St Pet *Man* 66-71 and 84-99; P-in-c Brinsworth *Sheff* 71-75; V Brinsworth w Catcliffe 76-84; rtd 99. *15 New Church Road, Bolton BL1 5QP* Tel (01204) 849413

HARPER, Gordon William Robert. b 48. Wellington Univ (NZ) BA70 St Chad's Coll Dur BA74 Nottm Univ PhD89. Coll of Resurr Mirfield 74. **d** 75 **p** 76. C Battyeford *Wakef* 75-76; New Zealand 76-80; P-in-c Byers Green *Dur* 80-83; V Evenwood 83-89; R Wolviston 89-00; V Billingham St Mary 97-01; P-in-c Winlaton from 01. *The Rectory, Winlaton, Blaydon-on-Tyne NE21 6PL* Tel and fax 0191-414 3165
E-mail drgwr&jharper@westbill.freeserve.co.uk

HARPER, Ian. b 54. AKC78. Oak Hill Th Coll 79. **d** 80 **p** 81. C Sidcup St Jo *Roch* 80-83; C Bushey *St Alb* 83-87; TV Thamesmead *S'wark* 87-92; TR N Lambeth 92-00; V Homerton St Luke *Lon* from 00; AD Hackney 04-09. *St Luke's Vicarage, 23 Cassland Road, London E9 7AL* Tel (020) 8525 0950 *or* 8985 2263 E-mail sluke.hackney@london.anglican.org

HARPER, James. b 35. St Luke's Coll Ex TDip57. SWMTC. **d** 90 **p** 91. NSM Pendeen w Morvah *Truro* 90-97. *1 Millstream Mews, 50 Beaconsfield Road, Christchurch BH23 1QT* Tel (01202) 477138

HARPER, John Anthony. b 46. AKC69. **d** 70 **p** 71. C Pet St Mary Boongate 70-73; C Abington 73-75; V Grendon w Castle Ashby 75-82; Asst Dioc Youth Chapl 75-82; R Castor w Sutton and Upton 82-94; TV Riverside *Ox* 94-04; V Meppershall and Shefford *St Alb* from 04; RD Shefford from 08. *The Rectory, Church Road, Meppershall, Shefford SG17 5NA* Tel (01462) 813334 E-mail j.harper@ukgateway.net

HARPER, John Hugh. b 34. ALAM62 Hertf Coll Ox BA57 MA61. Wells Th Coll 57. **d** 59 **p** 60. C Twerton *B & W* 59-62; R Chapel Allerton 62-69; V Blackford 62-69; V Halsetown *Truro* 69-91; RD Penwith 84-88; P-in-c S Brent *Ex* 91; V S Brent and Rattery 91-99; rtd 99; Perm to Offic *Chelmsf* 00-04. *19 Winston Rise, Four Marks, Alton GU34 5HP* Tel (01420) 563227

HARPER, Joseph Frank. b 38. Hull Univ BA60 MA86 MPhil98. Linc Th Coll 80. **d** 81 **p** 82. C Preston St Cuth *Blackb* 81-83; C Lancaster St Mary 83-87; V Bamber Bridge St Aid 87-92; V Kinsley w Wragby *Wakef* 92-99; R Newhaven *Chich* 99-04; rtd 04. *30 Greenways, Consett DH8 7DE* Tel (01207) 590962

HARPER, Canon Malcolm Barry. b 37. Dur Univ BSc59. Wycliffe Hall Ox 59. **d** 61 **p** 62. C Harold Wood *Chelmsf* 61-65; C Madeley *Heref* 65-68; V Slaithwaite w E Scammonden *Wakef* 68-75; V Walmley *Birm* 75-03; Hon Can Birm Cathl 96-03; rtd 03; Perm to Offic *Birm* from 03. *1 Welcombe Drive, Sutton Coldfield B76 1ND* Tel 0121-351 3990
E-mail canonbarryharper@tiscali.co.uk

HARPER, Mrs Margaret. b 51. Nottm Coll of Educn TCert73 Nottm Univ BEd74. SAOMC 98. **d** 01 **p** 02. C Slough *Ox* 01-05; P-in-c Leeds St Cypr Harehills *Ripon* 05-09; P-in-c Burmantofts St Steph and St Agnes 05-09; TV Ely from 09. *20 Barton Road, Ely CB7 4DE* Tel (01353) 666064
E-mail margaretharper@waitrose.com

HARPER, Martin Nigel. b 48. FRICS88 Cant Ch Ch Univ Coll PGCE95. S Dios Minl Tr Scheme 82. **d** 85 **p** 86. NSM St Leonards Ch Ch and St Mary *Chich* 85-93; NSM Rye 94-95; R Brede w Udimore from 08. *31 Manor Road, Bexhill-on-Sea TN40 1SP* Tel (01424) 210838 Mobile 07760-197954
E-mail martin.harper@tiscali.co.uk

HARPER, Canon Maurice. b 20. St Steph Ho Ox 60. **d** 62 **p** 63. C Upminster *Chelmsf* 62-67; V Gt Ilford St Mary 67-71; R Upminster 71-85; RD Havering 80-85; Hon Can Chelmsf Cathl 84-85; rtd 85; Perm to Offic *Chelmsf* and *Nor* from 85; *Chich* from 05. *30 Cookham Dene, Buckhurst Road, Bexhill-on-Sea TN40 1RU* Tel (01424) 222189
E-mail canonmauriceharper@o2.co.uk

HARPER, Michael Sydney. b 36. Portsm Dioc Tr Course 86. **d** 87. NSM Leigh Park St Clare CD *Portsm* 87-88; NSM Warren Park 88-05; NSM Leigh Park 96-05; rtd 05; Perm to Offic *Portsm* from 07. *17 Hampage Green, Warren Park, Havant PO9 4HJ* Tel (023) 9245 4275 E-mail michael_harper06@tiscali.co.uk

HARPER, Richard Michael. b 53. Univ of Wales PhD78. St Steph Ho Ox BA80 MA87. **d** 81 **p** 82. C Holt *Nor* 81-84; C-in-c Grahame Park St Aug CD *Lon* 84-88; Sub-Warden and Dir Studies St Mich Coll Llan 88-93; Lect Th Hist Univ of Wales (Cardiff) 88-93; R St Leonards Ch Ch and St Mary *Chich* 94-03; RD Hastings 02-03; V Weymouth St Paul *Sarum* from 03. *St Paul's Vicarage, 58 Abbotsbury Road, Weymouth DT4 0BJ* Tel (01305) 778821

HARPER, Roger. See HARPER, Canon Geoffrey Roger

HARPER, Roger. b 43. Man Univ BSc64 FCA80. Local Minl Tr Course 84. **d** 87 **p** 88. NSM Onchan *S & M* 87-97; NSM Douglas St Geo from 97. *The Barns, Strawberry Fields, Croit-e-Caley, Colby, Isle of Man IM9 4BZ* Tel (01624) 842466

HARPER, Rosemary Elizabeth. b 55. Birm Univ BA76 ARCM75 LRAM78. NTMTC 96. **d** 99 **p** 00. C Amersham *Ox* 99-03; P-in-c Gt Missenden w Ballinger and Lt Hampden 03-07; V from 07; Chapl to Bp Buckingham from 06. *The Rectory, Church Street, Amersham HP7 0BD* Tel (01494) 728988
E-mail rosie51619@aol.com

HARPER, Thomas Reginald. b 31. Dur Univ BA57 MA67. **d** 58 **p** 59. C Corbridge w Halton *Newc* 58-60; C Byker St Mich 60-62; V Ushaw Moor *Dur* 62-67; Asst Chapl HM Pris Dur 62-67; N Sec CMS 67-74; V Thornthwaite *Carl* 74-75; V Thornthwaite cum Braithwaite and Newlands 76-90; TV Bellingham/Otterburn Gp *Newc* 90-91; TV N Tyne and Redesdale 91-92; TR 92-98; RD Bellingham 93-98; rtd 98; Perm to Offic *Carl* from 98. *Dunelm, Old Lake Road, Ambleside LA22 0DH* Tel (01539) 433556

HARPER, Timothy James Lincoln. b 54. Lon Univ BMus76 MA96 CertEd LRAM. Wycliffe Hall Ox 84. **d** 86 **p** 87. C Morden *S'wark* 86-90; V Deptford St Pet 90-97; R Amersham *Ox* from 97. *The Rectory, Church Street, Amersham HP7 0DB* Tel (01494) 724426 *or* 729380 Fax 08701-639596
E-mail tjlharper@aol.com

HARPHAM, Mrs Diana Joan. b 44. MCSP66. St Alb Minl Tr Scheme 94. **d** 98 **p** 99. NSM Harrold and Carlton w Chellington *St Alb* 98-01; NSM Bromham w Oakley and Stagsden from 01. *The Old Police House, 40 Stagsden Road, Bromham, Bedford MK43 8PT* Tel (01234) 823222 Fax 825577
E-mail di@harpham.com

HARRATT, Philip David. b 56. Magd Coll Ox BA79 MA83. Ripon Coll Cuddesdon 82. **d** 85 **p** 86. C Ewyas Harold w Dulas, Kenderchurch etc *Heref* 85-88; V Chirbury 88-09; V Marton 88-09; V Trelystan 88-09; P-in-c Middleton 02-09; RD Pontesbury 01-08; Preb Heref Cathl 03-09; V Embleton w Rennington and Rock *Newc* from 09. *The Vicarage, Embleton, Alnwick NE66 3UW* Tel (01661) 576660

HARREX, David Brian. b 54. Trin Coll Bris 87. **d** 89 **p** 90. C Bedminster St Mich *Bris* 89-93; V Pilning w Compton Greenfield 93-00; RD Westbury and Severnside 97-99; AD Bris W 99-00; TR Yate New Town from 00; C Frampton Cotterell and Iron Acton from 07. *The Rectory, 97 Canterbury Close, Yate, Bristol BS37 5TU* Tel (01454) 311483
E-mail davidharrex@hotmail.com

HARRIES, Henry Rayner Mackintosh. b 30. MBE67. Chich Th Coll 53. **d** 55 **p** 56. C Hastings H Trin *Chich* 55-58; Chapl RAF 58-79; Asst Chapl-in-Chief RAF 79-84; QHC 83-84; P-in-c Gt Brickhill w Bow Brickhill and Lt Brickhill *Ox* 84-86; R 86-94; RD Mursley 91-94; rtd 95; Perm to Offic *Chelmsf* from 94. *2 Fyfield Road, Ongar CM5 0AH* Tel (01277) 363741

HARRIES, John Edward. b 60. Bris Univ BSc81 PhD84. Wycliffe Hall Ox 94. **d** 96 **p** 97. C Hyde St Geo *Ches* 96-00; P-in-c Walton from 00; C Latchford St Jas from 00; Chapl Sir Thos Boteler High Sch from 03. *13 Hillfoot Crescent, Stockton Heath, Warrington WA4 6SB* Tel (01925) 262939
E-mail stjohnswalton@btinternet.com

HARRIES, Mrs Judith Janice. b 43. SRN67 Trin Coll Bris BA93 Bris Univ PGCE94. WEMTC 99. **d** 01 **p** 02. NSM Bath St Sav w Swainswick and Woolley B & W 01-03; Hon C Farmborough, Marksbury and Stanton Prior 03-08. *19 Victoria Buildings, Bath BA2 3EH* Tel (01225) 332418
E-mail judithharries@hotmail.com

HARRIES, Malcolm David. b 44. BA99. Oak Hill Th Coll 94. **d** 96 **p** 97. C Rock Ferry *Ches* 96-00; P-in-c Godley cum Newton Green from 00. *The Vicarage, 43 Sheffield Road, Hyde SK14 2PR* Tel 0161-368 2159 E-mail liberteharries@aol.com

HARRIES, Rayner. *See* HARRIES, Henry Rayner Mackintosh

✠**HARRIES OF PENTREGARTH, The Rt Revd Lord (Richard Douglas).** b 36. Selw Coll Cam BA61 MA65 Lon Univ Hon DD94 FKC83 FRSL96. Cuddesdon Coll 61. **d** 63 **p** 64 **c** 87. C Hampstead St Jo *Lon* 63-69; Chapl Westf Coll Lon 67-69; Tutor Wells Th Coll 69-71; Warden Sarum & Wells Th Coll 71-72; V Fulham All SS *Lon* 72-81; Dean K Coll Lon 81-87; Consultant to Abps Cant and York on Inter-Faith Relns 86-06; Bp Ox 87-06; rtd 06; Asst Bp S'wark from 06; Hon Prof Th K Coll Lon from 06. *House of Lords, London SW1A 0PW*
E-mail harriesr@parliament.uk

HARRINGTON, Christopher Robert. b 57. Wilson Carlile Coll 99 ERMC 06. **d** 08 **p** 09. C Middle Rasen Gp *Linc* from 08. *5 The Orchards, Middle Rasen, Market Rasen LN8 3TL* Tel (01673) 844657 E-mail c.r.harrington@btinternet.com

HARRINGTON, John Christopher Thomas. b 43. Qu Coll Birm 71. **d** 74 **p** 75. C Northampton St Mich *Pet* 74-76; C Paston 76-79; R Doddington *Ely* 79-82; R Benwick St Mary 79-82; R Doddington w Benwick 82-83; CF (TA) 75-85; Chapl Doddington Co Hosp 79-83; V Eastbourne St Mich *Chich* 83-02; R Selsey from 02; Chapl RNLI from 03. *The Rectory, 75 St Peter's Crescent, Selsey, Chichester PO20 0NA* Tel (01243) 601984 E-mail jctharrington@tiscali.co.uk

HARRINGTON, William Harry. b 33. AKC57. **d** 58 **p** 59. C Childwall All SS *Liv* 58-60; C Sutton 60-64; V Ditton St Mich 64-76; V Mossley Hill St Barn 76-83; V Highfield 83-01; rtd 01; Perm to Offic *Liv* from 03. *4 Crowther Drive, Winstanley, Wigan WN3 6LY* Tel (01942) 225021

HARRIS, Mrs Alison Ann. b 54. Univ of Wales (Abth) BA75 Westmr Coll Ox PGCE76 Ches Univ MTh07. Qu Coll Birm 07. **d** 08 **p** 09. C Neston *Ches* from 08. *The Vicarage, Church Road, Saughall, Chester CH1 6EN* Tel (01244) 880213 Mobile 07969-005978 E-mail alisonannharris@hotmail.co.uk

HARRIS, Arthur Emlyn Dawson. b 27. Ex Univ BSc47. S'wark Ord Course 83. **d** 86 **p** 87. NSM Frant w Eridge *Chich* 86-87; P-in-c Withyham St Mich 87-95; rtd 95; Perm to Offic *Sarum* 96-07. *53A The Close, Salisbury SP1 2EL* Tel (01722) 339886
E-mail closecelts@aol.com

HARRIS, Bernard Malcolm. b 29. Leeds Univ BA54. Coll of Resurr Mirfield 54. **d** 56 **p** 57. C Shrewsbury St Chad *Lich* 56-60; C Porthill 60-61; V Birches Head 61-66; V W Bromwich St Jas 66-78; V Sedgley All SS 78-93; rtd 93; Perm to Offic *Worc* from 93 and *Lich* from 09. *6 Beacon Lane, Sedgley, Dudley DY3 1NB* Tel (01902) 663134 E-mail bernard.harris@care4free.co.uk

HARRIS, Brian. *See* HARRIS, The Ven Reginald Brian

HARRIS, Brian. b 33. Man Univ BSc. Qu Coll Birm 79. **d** 80 **p** 81. C Lich St Chad 80-81; Perm to Offic *Ches* 82-87; NSM Warburton 87-88; P-in-c 88-92; R Gt and Lt Casterton w Pickworth and Tickencote *Pet* 92-98; RD Barnack 94-98; rtd 98; Perm to Offic *Pet* 99-07 and *St Alb* 06-07. *16 Westminster Green, Chester CH4 7LE* Tel (01244) 675824
E-mail meadowbrook@waitrose.com

HARRIS, Brian William. b 38. K Coll Lon BD61 AKC61. St Boniface Warminster 61. **d** 62 **p** 63. C Liversedge *Wakef* 62-65; C Kirkby *Liv* 65-70; V Dalton 70-79; V Aberford w Saxton *York* 79-91; V Hemingbrough 91-95; rtd 95; Perm to Offic *York* from 95; Dom Chapl to Bp Selby 95-03; Rtd Clergy and Widows Officer (York Adnry) from 99. *2 Furness Drive, Rawcliffe, York YO30 5TD* Tel (01904) 638214
E-mail harrischap@ntlworld.com

HARRIS, Catherine Elizabeth. *See* EDMONDS, Mrs Catherine Elizabeth

HARRIS, Charles Edward. b 20. Roch Th Coll 63. **d** 65 **p** 66. C Hertford St Andr *St Alb* 65-71; R Sywell w Overstone *Pet* 71-90; rtd 90; Perm to Offic *Chich* from 92. *The College of St Barnabas, Blackberry Lane, Lingfield RH7 6NJ* Tel (01342) 870607

HARRIS, Cyril Evans. b 30. Linc Th Coll 61. **d** 63 **p** 64. C Beaconsfield *Ox* 63-68; V Stoke Poges 68-98; rtd 98; Perm to Offic *Ox* 99-07 and *St Alb* from 98. *The Gables, 8 De Parys Avenue, Bedford MK40 2TW* Tel (01234) 344927

HARRIS, David Rowland. b 46. Ch Ch Ox BA69 MA72. Wycliffe Hall Ox 70. **d** 73 **p** 74. C Virginia Water *Guildf* 73-76; C Clifton Ch Ch w Em *Bris* 76-79; Scripture Union 79-85; V Bedford Ch Ch *St Alb* 85-99; R Ex St Leon w H Trin from 99. *St Leonard's Rectory, 27 St Leonard's Road, Exeter EX2 4LA* Tel (01392) 255681 *or* 255449 E-mail dandsharris@hotmail.com

HARRIS, Derrick William. b 21. **d** 63 **p** 64. C Birkdale St Jo *Liv* 63-67; V Billinge 67-81; V Walton *Ches* 81-87; rtd 88; Perm to Offic *Ches* and *Liv* from 88. *3 Melrose Avenue, Southport PR9 9UY* Tel (01704) 213828

HARRIS, Duncan Roy. b 46. **d** 89 **p** 90. Chapl Miss to Seamen 89-98; UAE 89-92; Cyprus 92-97; P-in-c Patrington w Hollym, Welwick and Winestead *York* 98-05; R from 05. *The Rectory, Northside, Patrington, Hull HU12 0PA* Tel (01964) 630327 Fax 630366 E-mail fr.duncan@tiscali.co.uk

HARRIS, Mrs Elaine Sarah. b 43. SWMTC 02. **d** 03 **p** 04. NSM Dyffryn *Llan* 03-06; P-in-c Penyfai from 06. *The Vicarage, Pen-y-fai, Bridgend CF31 4LS* Tel (01656) 651719
E-mail fforestgoch@hotmail.com

HARRIS, Canon Ernest John. b 46. QUB BD75. **d** 75 **p** 76. C Lisburn Ch Ch *Conn* 75-78; C Coleraine 78-83; I Belfast St Kath 83-90; I Ballinderry from 90; Preb Conn Cathl from 06. *The Rectory, 124 Ballinderry Road, Ballinderry Upper, Lisburn BT28 2NL* Tel (028) 9265 1310

HARRIS, Geoffrey Daryl. b 39. Open Univ BA83. St Aid Birkenhead 63. **d** 66 **p** 67. C Eston *York* 66-70; C Iffley *Ox* 70-75; V Bubwith *York* 75-78; V Bubwith w Ellerton and Aughton 78-79; P-in-c Stillingfleet w Naburn 79-80; R Escrick and Stillingfleet w Naburn 80-95; Chapl Qu Marg Sch York 83-94; Hon C Okehampton w Inwardleigh, Bratton Clovelly etc *Ex* 96-99; P-in-c Ashwater, Halwill, Beaworthy, Clawton etc 99-01; R 01-03; rtd 03; C Okehampton w Inwardleigh, Bratton Clovelly etc *Ex* from 07. *St Bridget's House, Bridestowe, Okehampton EX20 4ER* Tel (01837) 861644
E-mail the.harrisclan1@tinyonline.co.uk

HARRIS, George. b 36. Sarum Th Coll 66. **d** 68 **p** 69. C Shildon *Dur* 68-70; CF 70-74; P-in-c Doddington *Ely* 74-75; R 75-78; R Benwick St Mary 74-78; V Shotton *Dur* 78-86; V Stockton St Mark 86-87; V Chilton Moor 87-94; P-in-c Lyons 96, R 96-99; rtd 99. *49 Dunelm Drive, Houghton le Spring DH4 5QQ* Tel 0191-584 8608

HARRIS, Harriet Anne. b 68. Oriel Coll Ox BA90 New Coll Ox DPhil94. St Steph Ho Ox. **d** 00 **p** 01. C Ox St Mary V w St Cross

and St Pet 00-06; Chapl Wadham Coll from 00. *33 Minster Road, Oxford OX4 1LY* Tel (01865) 202835 *or* 277905
E-mail harriet.harris@wadh.ox.ac.uk

HARRIS, James. b 54. CITC 99. **d** 02 **p** 03. Aux Min Ballybeen *D & D* 02-05; C Belfast St Brendan from 05. *8 Grangewood Avenue, Dundonald, Belfast BT16 1GA* Tel (028) 9050 6074 Mobile 07761-066421 E-mail harrisj639@aol.com

HARRIS, Canon James Nigel Kingsley. b 37. St D Coll Lamp BA60. Sarum Th Coll. **d** 62 **p** 63. C Painswick *Glouc* 62-65; C Glouc St Paul 65-67; V Slad 67-77; V Cam 77-78; P-in-c Stinchcombe 77-78; V Cam w Stinchcombe 78-82; V Stonehouse 82-02; Chapl Glos R Hosp NHS Trust 92-02; rtd 02; Hon Can Antsiranana Madagascar from 00; Perm to Offic *Glouc* from 03. *14 Shalford Close, Cirencester GL7 1WG* Tel (01285) 885641

HARRIS, James Philip. b 59. Westf Coll Lon BA82 Univ of Wales PGCE97. St Mich Coll Llan BD86. **d** 86 **p** 87. C Newport St Paul *Mon* 86-89; C Bedwellty 89-91; V Newport St Matt 91-96; Chapl Univ of Wales Inst Cardiff *Llan* 97-99; Chapl Glam Univ 99-03; V Gwernaffield and Llanferres *St As* 03-09; V Bwlchgwyn and Minera from 09. *The Vicarage, Church Road, Minera, Wrexham LL11 3DA* Tel (01978) 753133
E-mail jharris3@glam.ac.uk

HARRIS, Jeremy David. b 63. Leeds Metrop Univ MA00 Univ of Wales (Lamp) BA04 Cardiff Univ MPhil07 FCCA92. St Mich Coll Llan 05. **d** 07 **p** 08. C Monmouth w Overmonnow etc from 07. *St Thomas's Vicarage, St Thomas's Square, Monmouth NP25 5ES* Tel 07710-410950 (mobile)
E-mail jeremyharris@hotmail.com

HARRIS, Jeremy Michael. b 64. St Steph Ho Ox BTh93. **d** 93 **p** 94. C Newport St Julian *Mon* 93-95; C Ebbw Vale 95-97; TV 97-98; Dioc Youth Chapl 96-98; TV Bracknell *Ox* 98-05; V Boyne Hill from 05. *The Vicarage, Westmorland Road, Maidenhead SL6 4HB* Tel (01628) 626921
E-mail jeremy_m_harris@compuserve.com

HARRIS, The Very Revd John. b 32. Univ of Wales (Lamp) BA55. Sarum Th Coll 55. **d** 57 **p** 58. V Pontnewynydd *Mon* 57-60; C Bassaleg 60-63; V Penmaen 63-69; V Newport St Paul 69-84; RD Newport 77-93; V Maindee Newport 84-93; Can St Woolos Cathl 84-93; Dean Brecon *S & B* 93-98; V Brecon St Mary and Battle w Llanddew 93-98; rtd 98; Lic to Offic *Mon* from 98. *40 Mounton Drive, Chepstow NP16 5EH* Tel (01291) 621233

HARRIS, Canon John. b 45. St Steph Ho Ox 72. **d** 75 **p** 76. C Wanstead St Mary *Chelmsf* 75-84; V Penponds *Truro* 84-91; V St Gluvias from 91; RD Carnmarth S from 00; Hon Can Truro Cathl from 01. *The Vicarage, St Gluvias, Penryn TR10 9LQ* Tel (01326) 373356

HARRIS, John. b 54. Leeds Univ BSc75. St Jo Coll Nottm LTh86. **d** 86 **p** 87. C S Ossett *Wakef* 86-90; V Moldgreen 90-97; P-in-c S Ossett 97-04; V from 04. *36 Manor Road, Ossett, Wakefield WF5 0AU* Tel (01924) 263311 *or* 281732
E-mail johnharris@ccso.fsnet.co.uk

HARRIS, John Brian. b 53. Hertf Coll Ox BA76. Ripon Coll Cuddesdon 87. **d** 89 **p** 90. C Witton *Ches* 89-93; R Thurstaston 93-99; V Stockton Heath 99-04; P-in-c Gt Saughall from 04. *The Vicarage, Church Road, Saughall, Chester CH1 6EN* Tel (01244) 880213 E-mail brian@jbharris.fsnet.co.uk

HARRIS, Canon John Peter. b 33. St D Coll Lamp BA57. **d** 58 **p** 59. Chapl St Woolos Hosp Newport 58-63; C Newport St Woolos *Mon* 58-60; Chapl St Woolos Cathl 60-63; CF (TA) 59-63; CF 63-82; V Chepstow *Mon* 82-98; RD Chepstow 85-97; Can St Woolos Cathl 93-98; rtd 98; Lic to Offic *Mon* from 98. *7 Victoria Way, Undy, Caldicot NP26 3NW* Tel (01633) 882423

HARRIS, John Stuart. b 29. Hertf Coll Ox BA52 MA56. Wells Th Coll 52. **d** 54 **p** 55. C Epsom St Martin *Guildf* 54-58; C Guildf H Trin w St Mary 58-63; R Bentley 63-72; V Milford 72-87; R Walton-on-the-Hill 87-98; Dioc Ecum Officer 87-92; rtd 98; Perm to Offic *Roch* from 00. *6 Pearse Place, Lamberhurst, Tunbridge Wells TN3 8EJ* Tel (01892) 890582

HARRIS, Mrs Judith Helen. b 53. Chelsea Coll Lon TCert64 Westmr Coll Ox MTh03. St Alb Minl Tr Scheme 83. **dss** 86 **d** 87 **p** 94. Leagrave *St Alb* 86-87; Hon Par Dn 87-91; TD Dunstable 91-94; TV 94-03; rtd 03; Perm to Offic *Truro* from 03. *Belmont, Fore Street, Porthleven, Helston TR13 9HN* Tel (01326) 563090
E-mail revdjhharris@ntlworld.com

HARRIS, Canon Kenneth. b 28. NW Ord Course 70. **d** 72 **p** 73. NSM Upton Ascension *Ches* 72-77; NSM Eccleston and Pulford 77-80; P-in-c Hargrave 80-81; V 81-94; Exec Officer Dioc Bd for Soc Resp 84-94; Hon Can Ches Cathl 91-94; rtd 94; Perm to Offic *Ches* 94-96 and from 00; P-in-c Ashton Hayes 96-98; P-in-c Alvanley 98-99. *Delsa, Willington Road, Willington, Tarporley CW6 0ND* Tel (01829) 751880

HARRIS, Lawrence Rex Rowland. b 35. St Cath Coll Cam BA59 MA63. Ely Th Coll. **d** 61 **p** 62. C Carrington *S'well* 61-63; Chapl Rampton Hosp Retford 63-66; V Sturton w Littleborough *S'well* 66-71; V Bole w Saundby 66-71; R Clowne *Derby* 71-04; RD Bolsover and Staveley 81-86; rtd 04; Perm to Offic *Derby* from 04. *131 North Road, Clowne, Chesterfield S43 4PQ*

HARRIS, Leslie Gerald Conley Eyre. b 44. Culham Coll of Educn CertEd66 St Jo Coll Nottm LTh00 FRGS83. Wycliffe Hall Ox 71. **d** 75 **p** 76. Kenya 75-99; Chapl Banda Sch Nairobi 75-99; NSM Karen St Fran 75-99; NSM Kiambu St Paul 84-99; NSM Limuru All SS 90-99; C Sawley *Derby* 00-03; R Pinxton from 03. *The Rectory, 49 Town Street, Pinxton, Nottingham NG16 6HH* Tel (01773) 580024

HARRIS, Linda Margaret. b 55. Man Univ BSc76 UMIST MSc78 Birkbeck Coll Lon MSc98. Wycliffe Hall Ox 03. **d** 05 **p** 06. C Cannock *Lich* 05-08; P-in-c Hatch Warren and Beggarwood *Win* from 08. *Immanuel House, 29 Lapin Lane, Basingstoke RG22 4XH* Tel (01256) 472632
E-mail revlinda@btinternet.com

HARRIS, Margaret Claire (Sister Margaret Joy). b 53. RGN85 Homerton Coll Cam BEd78. Ridley Hall Cam 90. **d** 92. Par Dn Stevenage All SS Pin Green *St Alb* 92-93; C 93-95; CSMV 95-99; OSB from 99. *St Mary's Abbey, 52 Swan Street, West Malling ME19 6JX* Tel (01732) 843309

HARRIS, Mark Jonathan. b 66. St Cath Coll Cam BA88 MA92 PhD92. Ripon Coll Cuddesdon BA01. **d** 02 **p** 03. C Cowley St Jas *Ox* 02-04; Chapl Oriel Coll Ox from 04. *Oriel College, Oxford OX1 4EW* Tel (01865) 276580
E-mail chaplain@oriel.ox.ac.uk

HARRIS, Martin John. b 54. Trin Coll Cam BA76 MA. Wycliffe Hall Ox 82. **d** 85 **p** 86. C Lindfield *Chich* 85-88; C Galleywood Common *Chelmsf* 88-91; V Southchurch Ch Ch 91-08; RD Southend-on-Sea 00-05; TR Harlow Town Cen w Lt Parndon from 08. *The Rectory, 43 Upper Park, Harlow CM20 1TW* Tel (01279) 411100 *or* 434243
E-mail martinharris@martinharris.messages.co.uk

HARRIS, Michael. b 34. St Mark & St Jo Coll Lon CertEd56 ACP65 MIL76. Qu Coll Birm. **d** 83 **p** 84. NSM Bournville *Birm* 83-90; NSM Stirchley 90-96; Chapl Univ of Cen England in Birm 92-99; Dean NSMs 96-99; rtd 00; Perm to Offic *Birm* and *Cov* from 00. *33 Bosley Close, Shipston-on-Stour CV36 4QA* Tel and fax (01608) 661672 Mobile 07811-489713
E-mail revmichael@harrisann.fsnet.co.uk

HARRIS, Michael Andrew. b 53. Ian Ramsey Coll 74 Trin Coll Bris 75. **d** 78 **p** 79. C St Paul's Cray St Barn *Roch* 78-82; C Church Stretton *Heref* 82-87; Res Min Penkridge w Stretton *Lich* 87-90; Res Min Penkridge Team 90-92; V Amington *Birm* from 92; AD Polesworth from 07. *The Vicarage, 224 Tamworth Road, Amington, Tamworth B77 3DE* Tel (01827) 62573
E-mail mike.harris26@ntlworld.com

HARRIS, Nicholas Bryan. b 60. Down Coll Cam BA81 MA85. Ridley Hall Cam 82. **d** 85 **p** 86. C Walney Is *Carl* 85-88; C S'wark Ch Ch 88-92; Perm to Offic *Chich* 92-08. *Wheelwrights, High Street, Fairwarp, Uckfield TN22 3BP*
E-mail box534@yahoo.co.uk

HARRIS, Owen. b 50. Univ of Wales (Swansea) BSc(Econ)71 PGCE72. St Mich Coll Llan. **d** 94 **p** 95. C Bassaleg *Mon* 94-98; TV Cwmbran 98-01; V Maindee Newport 01-02; rtd 02. *2 Marine Cottages, Ferryside SA17 5SB* Tel (01267) 267095

✠**HARRIS, The Rt Revd Patrick Burnet.** b 34. Keble Coll Ox BA58 MA63. Clifton Th Coll 58. **d** 60 **p** 61 **c** 73. C Ox St Ebbe w St Pet 60-63; SAMS 63-81; Adn N Argentina 70-73; Bp 73-80; R Kirkheaton *Wakef* 81-85; Asst Bp Wakef 81-85; Sec C of E Partnership for World Miss 86-88; Asst Bp Ox 86-88; Bp S'well 88-99; rtd 99; Asst Bp Linc 99-05 and Eur from 99; Hon Asst Bp Glouc from 05. *Apartment B, Ireton House, Pavilion Gardens, Cheltenham GL50 2SR* Tel (01242) 231376
E-mail pandvharris@blueyonder.co.uk

HARRIS, Canon Paul. b 55. St Paul's Cheltenham BEd79. Oak Hill Th Coll 82. **d** 84 **p** 85. C Billericay and Lt Burstead *Chelmsf* 84-87; TV Cheltenham St Mary, St Matt, St Paul and H Trin *Glouc* 87-93; V Bitterne *Win* 93-97; UK Evang Co-ord Evang Alliance 97-02; C Portswood Ch Ch 04; TR Cheltenham St Mark *Glouc* from 04; Hon Can Glouc Cathl from 09. *St Mark's Rectory, Fairmount Road, Cheltenham GL51 7AQ* Tel (01242) 690007 E-mail harrisrevpaul@aol.com

HARRIS, Paul Ian. b 45. MSc. Qu Coll Birm. **d** 82 **p** 83. C The Quinton *Birm* 82-86; V Atherstone *Cov* from 86. *40 Holte Road, Atherstone CV9 1HN* Tel (01827) 713200
E-mail paulih@ntlworld.com

HARRIS, Paul Michael. b 58. Chelsea Coll Lon BSc79 Oak Hill Th Coll BA89 Bath Coll of HE CertEd82 Open Univ BA04. **d** 89. C Finchley Ch Ch *Lon* 89-90; Asst Master St Luke's Sch W Norwood 90-91; Master and Asst Chapl Brent Internat Sch Manila 91-92; Volunteer Miss Movement Sunningdale 93-94; Past Asst St Joseph's RC Ch Dorking 94-95; Form Master Merton Court Prep Sch Sidcup 95-97; Asst Master Clewborough Ho Prep Sch Camberley 98-01; Teacher St Nic Sch for Girls Church Crookham 01-02; Teacher Culford Prep Sch Bury St Edmunds 02-04; Teacher St Marg Prep Sch Calne 05-07. *Maes-yr-Haf, 4 Penllain, Penparc, Cardigan SA43 1RJ* Tel (01239) 613797 E-mail paul.harris.007@hotmail.co.uk

HARRIS, Peter Frank. b 43. WMMTC 89. **d** 92 **p** 93. NSM Lich Ch Ch 92-96; NSM Ogley Hay 96-00; NSM Rushall 00-03; Perm to Offic from 03. *94 Ogley Hay Road, Burntwood WS7 2HU* Tel (01543) 319163

HARRIS, Peter Malcolm. b 52. Em Coll Cam BA74 MA79. Trin Coll Bris. **d** 80 **p** 81. C Upton (Overchurch) *Ches* 80-83; Crosslinks from 83; Portugal 93-97; France from 97. *rue de Meunier 4, Ribet, 13990 Fontvieille, France* Tel (0033) (8) 77 35 61 53 (mobile) E-mail harris@crosslinks.org

HARRIS, Peter Samuel. b 68. Dundee Univ BA98 St Jo Coll Dur BA04. Cranmer Hall Dur 02. **d** 04 **p** 05. C Walton and Trimley *St E* 04-07; R Dalkeith *Edin* from 07; R Lasswade from 07. *The Rectory, 7 Ancrum Bank, Dalkeith EH22 3AY* Tel 0131-663 7000 E-mail revpharris@googlemail.com

HARRIS, Raymond. b 36. Nottm Univ BA58. Lich Th Coll 58. **d** 60 **p** 61. C Clifton St Fran *S'well* 60-63; C Davyhulme St Mary *Man* 63-66; V Bacup Ch Ch 66-82; R Dunsby w Dowsby *Linc* 82-87; R Rippingale 82-87; R Rippingale Gp 87-94; rtd 94. *2 The Bungalow, High Street, Swaton, Sleaford NG34 0JU* Tel (01529) 421343

HARRIS, Canon Raymond John. b 29. Leeds Univ BA51. Coll of Resurr Mirfield 51. **d** 53 **p** 54. C Workington St Mich *Carl* 53-59; V New Swindon St Barn Gorse Hill *Bris* 59-94; Hon Can Bris Cathl 80-94; RD Cricklade 82-88; rtd 94. Perm to Offic *Glouc* from 94. *46 Courtbrook, Fairford GL7 4BE* Tel (01285) 713965

HARRIS, Rebecca Jane. *See* SWYER, Mrs Rebecca Jane

HARRIS (née LEE), Mrs Rebecca Susan. b 62. Man Univ BA85. Trin Coll Bris 93. **d** 95 **p** 96. C Cirencester *Glouc* 95-99; TV Gt Chesham *Ox* from 99. *Christ Church Vicarage, 95 Latimer Road, Chesham HP5 1QQ* Tel and fax (01494) 773318

HARRIS, The Ven Reginald Brian. b 34. Ch Coll Cam BA58 MA61. Ridley Hall Cam. **d** 59 **p** 60. C Wednesbury St Bart *Lich* 59-61; C Uttoxeter w Bramshall 61-64; V Bury St Pet *Man* 64-70; V Walmsley 70-80; RD Walmsley 70-80; Adn Man 80-98; Can Res Man Cathl 80-98; rtd 98. Perm to Offic *Derby* from 98. *9 Cote Lane, Hayfield, Stockport SK22 2HL* Tel (01663) 746321

HARRIS, Robert. *See* WYNFORD-HARRIS, Robert William

HARRIS, Robert Douglas. b 57. BEd. Chich Th Coll 80. **d** 82 **p** 83. C Portsea St Mary *Portsm* 82-87; V Clevedon St Jo *B & W* 87-92; R Felpham w Middleton *Chich* 92-99; R Felpham 99-04; RD Arundel and Bognor 99-04; P-in-c Southwick 04-06; R from 06. *The Rectory, 22 Church Lane, Southwick, Brighton BN42 4GB* Tel (01273) 592389 E-mail robertharris@staroftheseea.freeserve.co.uk

HARRIS, Robert James. b 45. Nottm Univ MA02 ALCD73. St Jo Coll Nottm 69. **d** 72 **p** 73. C Sheff St Jo 72-76; C Goole 76-78; V Bramley and Ravenfield 78-91; P-in-c Boulton *Derby* 91-99; RD Melbourne 96-99; P-in-c Hazlewood 99-02; P-in-c Hazlewood and Milford 02-05; V Hazelwood, Holbrook and Milford from 05. *The Vicarage, Hob Hill, Hazelwood, Belper DE56 4AL* Tel (01332) 840161 E-mail robert@kneetinnit.fsnet.co.uk

HARRIS, Mrs Ruth. b 60. Hull Univ BA82 Liv Univ MArAd84. NOC 01. **d** 04 **p** 05. C Kinsley w Wragby *Wakef* 04-07; C Felkirk 05-07; P-in-c Wrenthorpe from 07. *The Vicarage, 121 Wrenthorpe Road, Wrenthorpe, Wakefield WF2 0JS* Tel (01924) 373758 E-mail ruth.harris11@btinternet.com

HARRIS, Sian Elizabeth. b 54. Kingston Poly BSocSc75. WEMTC 03. **d** 06 **p** 07. NSM Leominster *Heref* 06-09; C Llanbadarn Fawr, Llandegley and Llanfihangel etc *S & B* from 09; C Llanbister w Llanbadarn Fynydd w Llananno etc from 09. *The Vicarage, Llanbister, Llandrindod Wells LD1 6TN* E-mail sianharris@f2s.com

HARRIS, Suzanne Sarah. CITC. **d** 09. NSM Dublin Booterstown *D & G* from 09. *Caneel, 3 Belmont Green, Blackrock, Co Dublin, Republic of Ireland* Tel (00353) 87-935 4869 (mobile) E-mail curate.booterstown@dublin.anglican.org

HARRIS, Thomas William. b 54. Univ of Wales (Lamp) MA04 AKC76. Linc Th Coll 77. **d** 78 **p** 79. C Norton Woodseats St Chad *Sheff* 78-81; V Barnby Dun 81-91; P-in-c Kirk Bramwith and Fenwick 81-85; Chapl RN 91-94; R Draycot *Bris* 94-02; P-in-c Cawston w Booton and Brandiston etc *Nor* from 02; Chapl Norfolk and Nor Univ Hosp NHS Trust 02-07; Chapl Cawston Park Hosp from 07. *The Rectory, Ames Court, Cawston, Norwich NR10 4AN* Tel (01603) 871282 E-mail tomwharris@tiscali.co.uk

HARRIS, William Edric Mackenzie. b 46. Sarum & Wells Th Coll 72. **d** 75 **p** 76. C Langney *Chich* 75-79; C Moulsecoomb 80-81; TV 81-85; R W Grinstead from 85. *The Rectory, Steyning Road, West Grinstead, Horsham RH13 8LR* Tel (01403) 710339 E-mail williamem.harris@virgin.net

HARRIS, William Fergus. b 36. CCC Cam BA59 MA63 Edin Univ DipEd70. Yale Div Sch 59 Westcott Ho Cam 60. **d** 62 **p** 63. C St Andrews St Andr *St And* 62-64; Chapl Edin Univ 64-71; R Edin St Pet 71-83; R Perth St Jo *St And* 83-90; Hon C 90-08; rtd 90; Prov Archivist 91-02; Lic to Offic *St And* from 08. *35 St Mary's Drive, Perth PH2 7BY* Tel (01738) 621379

HARRIS-DOUGLAS, John Douglas. b 34. Ripon Hall Ox 65. **d** 66 **p** 67. C Ringwood *Win* 66-67; C Baswich *Lich* 67-71; R St Tudy *Truro* 71-74; R St Tudy w Michaelstow 74-76; Adv in Children's Work and Asst Dir Educn 71-76; R Fiskerton *Linc*

76-79; Dir of Educn and Adv RE 76-79; P-in-c Thormanby *York* 79-84; V Brafferton w Pilmoor and Myton-on-Swale 79-84; V Brafferton w Pilmoor, Myton-on-Swale etc 84-97; rtd 97. Perm to Offic *York* from 97. *Tanglewood Cottage, Newton-upon-Ouse, York YO30 2BN* Tel (01347) 848219

HARRIS-EVANS, William Giles. b 46. AKC68. Bangalore Th Coll. **d** 70 **p** 71. C Clapham H Trin *S'wark* 70-74; Sri Lanka 75-78; V Benhilton *S'wark* 78-86; TR Cov E 86-93; TR Brighouse and Clifton *Wakef* 93-99; V Petersfield *Portsm* from 99; R Buriton from 99. *The Vicarage, Shackleford House, 12 Dragon Street, Petersfield GU31 4AB* Tel and fax (01730) 264138 *or* 260213 E-mail petersfield@stpeters.fsbusiness.co.uk

HARRIS-WHITE, John Emlyn. b 34. St Aid Birkenhead 59. **d** 62 **p** 63. C Cricklade w Latton *Bris* 62-63; C Kingswood 63-66; C Ashton-on-Ribble St Andr *Blackb* 66-69; V Heyhouses 69-71; Chapl Roundway Hosp Devizes 71-77; Chapl R Variety Children's Hosp 77-89; Chapl K Coll and Belgrave Hosps Lon 77-89; Regional Community Relns Co-ord 89-93; rtd 94; Hon C Folkestone St Pet *Cant* 97-01. *40 Tippet Knowes Road, Winchburgh, Broxburn EH52 6UL*

HARRISON, Alastair Lee. b 22. ALCD51. **d** 51 **p** 52. C Stoke Damerel *Ex* 51-54; Chapl RAF 54-67; Chapl Miss to Seamen 67-77; Lic to Offic *D & G* 77-83; Lic to Offic *M & K* 77-83; C Dublin St Ann w St Mark and St Steph *D & G* 83-92; rtd 92. *8 Grosvenor Place, Rathgar, Dublin 6, Republic of Ireland* Tel (00353) (1) 497 6053

HARRISON, Alison Edwina. *See* HART, Mrs Alison Edwina

HARRISON, Mrs Barbara Ann. b 41. Man Univ BA63 Leic Univ CertEd64. EMMTC 85. **d** 88 **p** 94. C Immingham *Linc* 88-94; P-in-c Habrough Gp 94-99; V 99-01; rtd 02; Perm to Offic *Linc* from 02. *3 Windsor Mews, Louth LN11 9AY* Tel (01507) 610015

HARRISON, Canon Barbara Anne. b 34. Westf Coll Lon BA56 CertEd57 Hull Univ MA85. Linc Th Coll 76. **dss** 79 **d** 87 **p** 94. Lakenham St Jo *Nor* 79-80; Chapl York Univ 80-88; TD Sheff Manor 88-93; Par Dn Holts CD *Man* 93-94; C-in-c 94-98; Dioc UPA Officer 93-98; Chapl Rochdale Healthcare NHS Trust 98-04; C Bury Ch King *Man* 98-01; C Bury St Paul 98-04; P-in-c Kirkholt 01-04; Hon Can Man Cathl 02-04; rtd 04; Perm to Offic *Man* from 04. *66 Gainsborough Drive, Rochdale OL11 2QT* Tel (01706) 639872

HARRISON, Bernard Charles. b 37. St Mich Coll Llan 61. **d** 64 **p** 65. C Toxteth Park St Marg *Liv* 64-69; C Hindley All SS 69-71; V Wigan St Geo 71-02; rtd 02. *66 Brookhouse Street, Wigan WN1 3EY* Tel (01942) 244500

HARRISON, Brian John. b 35. FCP. Glouc Sch of Min 83. **d** 86 **p** 89. NSM Broseley w Benthall *Heref* 86-93; Perm to Offic 94-97. *17 Hafren Road, Little Dawley, Telford TF4 3HJ* Tel (01952) 591891

HARRISON, Bruce. b 49. Linc Th Coll 86. **d** 88 **p** 89. C Syston *Leic* 88-90; C Whitby *York* 90-93; V Glaisdale 93-99; R Brotton Parva 99-04; V Coatham and Dormanstown 04-08; Chapl Tees and NE Yorks NHS Trust 04-07; rtd 08; Perm to Offic *York* from 08. *The Vicarage, 10 Allendale Road, New Marske, Redcar TS11 8HN* Tel (01642) 484833 E-mail br218@hotmail.com

HARRISON, Bruce Mountford. b 49. AKC71. **d** 72 **p** 73. C Hebburn St Cuth *Dur* 72-75; C Bethnal Green St Jo w St Simon *Lon* 75-77; P-in-c Bethnal Green St Bart 77-78; TV Bethnal Green St Jo w St Bart 78-80; C-in-c Pennywell St Thos and Grindon St Oswald CD *Dur* 80-85; V Sunderland Pennywell St Thos 85-90; V Gateshead St Helen from 90. *The Vicarage, 7 Carlton Terrace, Gateshead NE9 6DE* Tel 0191-487 6510

HARRISON, Christine Amelia. b 49. STETS 94. **d** 98 **p** 99. NSM Goldsworth Park *Guildf* from 98. *2 Abercorn Way, Woking GU21 3NY* Tel (01483) 750645 E-mail revchrissie@btinternet.com

HARRISON, Christopher Dennis. b 57. Clare Coll Cam BA79 BA86. Westcott Ho Cam 84. **d** 87 **p** 88. C Camberwell St Geo *S'wark* 87-92; V Forest Hill 92-96; P-in-c Fenny Bentley, Kniveton, Thorpe and Tissington *Derby* 96-98; P-in-c Parwich w Alsop-en-le-Dale 96-98; R Fenny Bentley, Thorpe, Tissington, Parwich etc 98-09; RD Ashbourne 98-09; P-in-c Nottingham All SS, St Mary and St Pet *S'well* from 09. *2 Tennis View, Tattershall Drive, Nottingham NG7 1AD* Tel 0115-941 8927 E-mail christopher.d.harrison@btinternet.com

HARRISON, Christopher Joseph. b 38. AKC61 Hull Univ CertEd68 Bris Univ BEd75. **d** 62 **p** 63. C Bottesford *Linc* 62-67; C Elloughton *York* 67-68; Asst Master Bishop's Cleeve Primary Sch 68-74; Sen Master 74-78; Dep Hd 78-96; P-in-c Farmington *Glouc* 69-73; C Tredington w Stoke Orchard and Hardwicke 74-86; rtd 96; Perm to Offic *Glouc* from 87. *Appledore, 93 Stoke Road, Bishops Cleeve, Cheltenham GL52 8RP* Tel (01242) 673452

HARRISON, Crispin. *See* HARRISON, Michael Burt

HARRISON, Sister Cécile. b 29. Bp Lonsdale Coll TCert51. St Steph Ho Ox 97. **d** 97 **p** 97. CGA from 66; Lic to Offic *Eur* from 97. *Prasada, Quartier Subrane, Montauroux, 83440 Fayence, France* Tel and fax (0033) (4) 94 47 74 26 E-mail cga.prasada@wanadoo.fr

HARRISON, David Daniel. b 62. St Paul's Cheltenham BA84 Leeds Univ MA85 Westmr Coll Ox PGCE88. Westcott Ho Cam 03. **d** 05 **p** 06. C Beckenham St Geo *Roch* 05-09; P-in-c Woodnesborough w Worth and Staple *Cant* from 09. *The Vicarage, The Street, Woodnesborough, Sandwich CT13 0NQ* Tel (01304) 613056

HARRISON, David Henry. b 40. Tyndale Hall Bris 65. **d** 68 **p** 69. C Bolton St Paul *Man* 68-72; V Bircle 72-83; V Southport SS Simon and Jude *Liv* 83-91; TR Fazakerley Em 91-99; V Toxteth Park Ch Ch and St Mich w St Andr 99-05; rtd 05; Perm to Offic *Blackb* from 06. *55 The Oval, Shevington, Wigan WN6 8EN* Tel (01257) 400084 E-mail getrevdave@hotmail.com

HARRISON, David Samuel. b 44. Univ of Wales (Ban) BSc67. St Mich Coll Llan 67. **d** 70 **p** 71. C Canton St Jo *Llan* 70-74; C Witton *Ches* 74-78; V Sutton St Geo 78-96; P-in-c Henbury 96-01; V 01-06; rtd 06. *50 Cherryfields Road, Macclesfield SK11 8RF* Tel (01625) 268460

HARRISON, Miss Doreen. b 32. Leeds Univ BA53 PGCE54 Lanc Univ MLitt78 MA(Ed)79. **d** 92 **p** 94. C Ambleside w Brathay *Carl* 92-96; Asst P Colton 96-01; P-in-c 01-02; Asst P Rusland 96-01; P-in-c 01-02; Asst P Satterthwaite 96-01; P-in-c 01-02; rtd 02; Perm to Offic *Carl* 02-07. *Fox How, Ambleside LA22 9LL* Tel (01539) 433021

HARRISON, Francis Russell. b 20. EAMTC. **d** 82 **p** 83. NSM Felixstowe St Jo *St E* 82-85; Asst Chapl Ipswich Hosp 85-87; rtd 87; Perm to Offic *St E* 87-03. *The Strands, London Road, Copdock, Ipswich IP8 3JF* Tel (01473) 730292

HARRISON, Fred Graham. b 41. Lon Univ BSc62. Ridley Hall Cam 80. **d** 82 **p** 83. C Lenton *S'well* 82-85; V Ruddington 85-04; rtd 04; Perm to Offic *Ches* from 05. *18 Holly Bank, Hollingworth, Hyde SK14 8QL* Tel (01457) 765955 E-mail fg.harrison@virgin.net

HARRISON, Guy Patrick. b 58. Ox Univ MTh99. Sarum & Wells Th Coll 92. **d** 94 **p** 95. C Wimborne Minster and Holt *Sarum* 94-96; C Wimborne Minster 96-97; Chapl Dorothy House Hospice Winsley 97-01; Chapl Stoke Mandeville Hosp NHS Trust 01-07; Chapl Team Ldr W Lon Mental Health NHS Trust from 07. *The Chaplaincy Department, West London Mental Health NHS Trust, Uxbridge Road, Southall UB1 3EU* Tel (020) 8354 8354 E-mail guy.harrison@wlmht.nhs.uk

HARRISON, Herbert Gerald. b 29. Oak Hill Th Coll 53. **d** 56 **p** 57. C Chesterfield H Trin *Derby* 56-59; C Cambridge St Andr Less *Ely* 59-64; Miss to Seamen 64-74; Kenya 64-68; Port Chapl Ipswich 68-74; V Ipswich All SS *St E* 74-81; P-in-c Elmsett w Aldham 81-88; P-in-c Kersey w Lindsey 81-88; R Horringer cum Ickworth 88-94; rtd 94; Perm to Offic *St E* from 94. *15 Lynwood Avenue, Felixstowe IP11 9HS* Tel (01394) 283764

HARRISON, Ian David. b 45. Imp Coll Lon BSc66. Oak Hill Th Coll 93. **d** 96 **p** 97. NSM Tunbridge Wells St Jo *Roch* 96-99; P-in-c Chiddingstone w Chiddingstone Causeway from 99. *The Rectory, Chiddingstone, Edenbridge TN8 7AH* Tel and fax (01892) 870478 E-mail ian@therectory.fsbusiness.co.uk

HARRISON (née HOLLINRAKE), Mrs Jean Margaret. b 28. Bolton Teacher Tr Coll TCert64. Wakef Dioc Reader Tr 82. **d** 93 **p** 96. NSM Perth St Ninian *St And* 93-96; NSM Stanley 96-98; Bp's Chapl 95-99. *Address temp unknown*

HARRISON, Joanne Elizabeth. SAOMC. **d** 05 **p** 06. NSM Wokingham St Paul *Ox* from 05. *25 Harvard Road, Owlsmoor, Sandhurst GU47 0XB* Tel (01276) 34409

HARRISON, John. *See* HARRISON, Steven John

HARRISON, John. b 49. Fitzw Coll Cam BA71 MA74. Westcott Ho Cam 74. **d** 77 **p** 78. C Nunthorpe *York* 77-81; C Acomb St Steph 81-83; C-in-c St Aid 81-83; V Heptonstall *Wakef* 83-91; R Stamford Bridge Gp *York* 91-02; V Easingwold w Raskelf from 02; RD Easingwold from 05. *The Vicarage, Church Hill, Easingwold, York YO61 3JT* Tel (01347) 821394

HARRISON, John Northcott. b 31. St Jo Coll Cam BA54. Westcott Ho Cam 54. **d** 56 **p** 57. C Moor Allerton *Ripon* 56-59; C Bedale 59-61; V Hudswell w Downholme 61-64; Youth Chapl *Dur* 64-68; V Auckland St Andr and St Anne 68-76; Community Chapl Stockton-on-Tees 76-83; TR Southampton (City Cen) *Win* 83-88; V Bris Ch the Servant Stockwood 88-96; RD Brislington 89-95; Chapl St Brendan's Sixth Form Coll 90-96; rtd 96; Perm to Offic *B & W* and *Bris* from 96. *8 Moorham Road, Winscombe BS25 1HS* Tel (01934) 844403

HARRISON, Josephine Mary. b 42. **d** 97 **p** 98. NSM Yatton Keynell *Bris* 97-99; NSM By Brook 99-01; Perm to Offic *B & W* 01-02 and from 07; NSM Wellington and Distr 02-07. *Pippins, 18 Cox Road, Wellington TA21 9RD* Tel and fax (01823) 669525

HARRISON, Keith. *See* HARRISON, Peter Keith

HARRISON, Lyndon. b 57. St Mich Coll Llan 91. **d** 93 **p** 94. C Ebbw Vale *Mon* 93-96; TV 96-01; TV Caldicot 01-05; TR from 05. *St Mary's Rectory, 39 Church Road, Caldicot NP26 4HN* Tel (01291) 420221

HARRISON, Mrs Marion Jeanne. b 56. SAOMC 04. **d** 07 **p** 08. C Watercombe *Sarum* from 07. *9 High Trees, Broadmayne, Dorchester DT2 8ER* Tel (01305) 853027 Mobile 07932-521776

HARRISON, Martin. b 58. Bris Univ BA89. Trin Coll Bris 86. **d** 89 **p** 90. C Heworth H Trin *York* 89-94; Chapl York Distr Hosp

HARRISON, Matthew Henry. b 64. Univ Coll Dur BA85 Union Th Sem (NY) STM93. St Steph Ho Ox BA88 MA92. **d** 89 **p** 90. C Whickham *Dur* 89-92; C Owton Manor 93-95; USA 92-93; Asst Chapl Paris St Geo *Eur* 95-02; Perm to Offic 02-04; C Paddington St Jas *Lon* 04-07; Chapl Paris St Geo *Eur* from 07. *St George, 7 rue Auguste-Vacquerie, 75116 Paris, France* Tel (0033) (1) 47 20 22 51 E-mail office@stgeorgesparis.com

HARRISON, Maureen. **d** 08. OLM Sutton *Liv* from 08. *89 Farndon Avenue, Sutton Manor, St Helens WA9 4DN* E-mail maureen.harrison@talktalk.net

HARRISON, Michael Anthony. b 48. Westhill Coll Birm CertCYW72 Huddersfield Poly CertEd88 Leeds Poly BA91 Leeds Univ MA98. NOC 94. **d** 97 **p** 98. NSM Thornhill and Whitley Lower *Wakef* 97-99; TV Wrexham *St As* 99-03; V Ruabon from 03. *The Vicarage, Park Street, Ruabon, Wrexham LL14 6LF* Tel (01978) 810176 E-mail whernside@aol.com

HARRISON, Michael Burt (Crispin). b 36. Leeds Univ BA59 Trin Coll Ox BA62 MA66. Coll of Resurr Mirfield 59. **d** 63 **p** 64. C W Hartlepool St Aid *Dur* 63-64; C Middlesbrough All SS *York* 64-66; Lic to Offic *Wakef* 67-69 and 78-87; CR from 68; S Africa 69-77 and 87-97; Registrar Coll of the Resurr Mirfield 78-84; Vice-Prin 84-87; Superior CR 97-02. *St Peter's Priory, PO Box 991, Southdale, 2135 South Africa* Tel (0027) (11) 434 2504 Fax 434 4556 E-mail crpriory@acenet.co.za

HARRISON, Canon Michael Robert. b 63. Selw Coll Cam BA84 K Coll Lon PhD97 Bradf Univ MA03. Ripon Coll Cuddesdon BA89 Union Th Sem (NY) STM90. **d** 90 **p** 91. C S Lambeth St Anne and All SS *S'wark* 90-94; Bp's Chapl to Students *Bradf* 94-98; Chapl Bradf Univ 94-98; Chapl Bradf and Ilkley Community Coll 94-98; V Eltham H Trin *S'wark* 98-06; RD Eltham and Mottingham 05-06; Dir Min and Miss *Leic* from 06; Hon Can Leic Cathl from 06. *11 Paterson Drive, Woodhouse Eaves, Loughborough LE12 8RL* Tel (01509) 891670 E-mail mikeharrison7@hotmail.com

HARRISON, Canon Noel Milburn. b 27. Leeds Univ MPhil75 PhD80. St Aid Birkenhead 54. **d** 57 **p** 58. C Doncaster St Jas *Sheff* 57-60; Chapl Yorkshire Res Sch for Deaf Doncaster 60-68; C Woodlands *Sheff* 60-62; Chapl to the Deaf 60-68; Hd Master Elmete Hall Sch Leeds 68-84; Hon C Whitgift w Adlingfleet and Eastoft 83-84; Hon C Abbeydale St Jo 84-86; Dioc Dir of Educn 84-94; R Tankersley 86-94; Hon Can Sheff Cathl 88-94; rtd 94; Perm to Offic *Sheff* from 94 and *Linc* 95-99. *Aidan House, 118 High Street, Crowle, Scunthorpe DN17 4DR*

HARRISON, Mrs Nona Margaret. b 50. Open Univ BA80. S Dios Minl Tr Scheme 92. **d** 95 **p** 96. NSM E w W Wellow and Sherfield English *Win* 95-99; NSM Barton Stacey and Bullington etc 99; NSM Hurstbourne Priors, Longparish etc 00-08. *5 Chichester Close, East Wellow, Romsey SO51 6EY* Tel (01 /94) 323154

HARRISON, Oliver. b 71. SS Paul & Mary Coll Cheltenham BA93. St Jo Coll Nottm MA95. **d** 97 **p** 98. Asst Chapl The Hague *Eur* 97-00; C Walmley *Birm* 00-04; C-in-c Grove Green LEP *Cant* 04-08; V Wilnecote *Lich* from 08. *The Vicarage, 64 Glascote Lane, Wilnecote, Tamworth B77 2PH* Tel (01827) 260560 E-mail oliver.harrison@tiscali.co.uk

HARRISON, Miss Patricia Mary. b 35. St Kath Coll Lon CertEd65 Open Univ BA74. St Mich Ho Ox IDC59. **dss** 85 **d** 87 **p** 94. NSM Nunthorpe *York* 85-98; rtd 98; Perm to Offic *York* from 98. *22 Lamonby Close, Nunthorpe, Middlesbrough TS7 0QG* Tel (01642) 313524

HARRISON, Paul Graham. b 53. Sarum & Wells Th Coll 76. **d** 79 **p** 80. C Brixham w Churston Ferrers *Ex* 79-82; C Portsea N End St Mark *Portsm* 82-87; V Tiverton St Andr *Ex* 87-94; Chapl Tiverton and Distr Hosp 90-94; P-in-c Astwood Bank *Worc* 94-05; TV Redditch Ch the K 05-08; P-in-c Churchill-in-Halfshire w Blakedown and Broome from 08; Chapl to the Deaf from 94; Perm to Offic *Cov* from 94. *The Rectory, 5 Mill Lane, Blakedown, Kidderminster DY10 3ND* Tel (01562) 700144 E-mail p.g.harrison@btinternet.com *or* dda@cofe-worcester.org.uk

HARRISON, Paul Thomas. b 57. Nor Sch of Art BA80 Leic Poly PGCE88 Coll of Ripon & York St Jo MA99. Qu Coll Birm 95. **d** 97 **p** 98. C Northallerton w Kirby Sigston *York* 97-01; TV Usworth *Dur* 01-05; V Dalton le Dale and New Seaham from 05. *The Vicarage, 269 Station Road, Seaham SR7 0BH* Tel 0191-581 3270

HARRISON, Mrs Penelope Ann. b 58. St Andr Univ MA79. Qu Coll Birm MA09. **d** 09. C Hamstead St Paul *Birm* from 09. *119 Lechlade Road, Birmingham B43 5NE* Tel 0121-357 1428 Mobile 07722-446222 E-mail penny_h123@hotmail.com

HARRISON, Peter. *See* HARRISON, Robert Peter

HARRISON, Peter Keith. b 44. Open Univ BA85. St Aid Birkenhead. **d** 68 **p** 69. C Higher Bebington *Ches* 68-71; C Walmsley *Man* 71-74; V Lumb in Rossendale 74-79; V Heywood St Marg 79-87; V Hey 87-95; AD Saddleworth 93-95; Chapl

Athens w Kifissia *Eur* 95-98; V Aston Cantlow and Wilmcote w Billesley *Cov* 98-02; V W Burnley All SS *Blackb* 02-09; rtd 09; Perm to Offic *Blackb* from 09. *57 West Cliffe, Lytham St Annes FY8 5DR* E-mail harrison.ssc@virgin.net

HARRISON, The Ven Peter Reginald Wallace. b 39. Selw Coll Cam BA62. Ridley Hall Cam 62. **d** 64 **p** 65. C Barton Hill St Luke w Ch Ch *Bris* 64-69; Chapl Greenhouse Trust 69-77; Dir Northorpe Hall Trust 77-84; TR Drypool *York* 84-98; AD E Hull 88-98; Adn E Riding 98-06; Can and Preb York Minster 94-06; rtd 06; Perm to Offic *York* from 06. *10 Priestgate, Sutton-on-Hull, Hull HU7 4QR* Tel (01482) 797110 E-mail peter@harrisons.karoo.co.uk

HARRISON, Canon Philip Hubert. b 37. Sarum & Wells Th Coll 77. **d** 79 **p** 80. C Wymondham *Nor* 79-83; V Watton w Carbrooke and Ovington 83-92; R Drayton w Felthorpe 92-02; Hon Can Nor Cathl 99-02; rtd 02; Perm to Offic *Nor* from 02. *The Fairstead, 1 Back Street, Horsham St Faith, Norwich NR10 3JP* Tel (01603) 893087

HARRISON, Mrs Rachel Elizabeth. b 53. NEOC 98. **d** 01 **p** 02. C Skelton w Upleatham *York* 01-04; P-in-c New Marske 04-06; V from 06; P-in-c Wilton 04-06; V from 06; Ind Chapl from 04. *The Vicarage, 10 Allendale Tee, New Marske, Redcar TS11 8HN* Tel (01642) 484833 E-mail rachelhere@hotmail.com

HARRISON, Richard Kingswood. b 61. Linc Coll Ox BA83 MA88 Leeds Univ BA90. Coll of Resurr Mirfield 88. **d** 91 **p** 92. C Reading St Giles *Ox* 91-93; Asst Chapl Merchant Taylors' Sch Northwood 93-96; Chapl Ardingly Coll 96-02; R Shill Valley and Broadshire *Ox* 02-04; Chapl Uppingham Sch 04-09; Chapl Lancing Coll from 09. *Ladywell House, Lancing College, Lancing BN15 0RW* Tel (01273) 465931

HARRISON, Robert Peter. b 28. Chich Th Coll. **d** 60 **p** 61. C Ealing Ch the Sav *Lon* 60-64; C Hammersmith SS Mich and Geo White City Estate CD 64-66; P-in-c Fulham St Pet 66-73; V 73-94; rtd 94; Perm to Offic *Chich* from 94. *8 Broadwater Way, Worthing BN14 9LP* Tel (01903) 217073

HARRISON, Robert William. b 62. Mansf Coll Ox BA84. Qu Coll Birm 87. **d** 89 **p** 90. C Sholing *Win* 89-93; Communications Adv to Bp Willesden *Lon* 93-97; C Cricklewood St Gabr and St Mich 93-97; V Hillingdon St Jo from 97. *St John's Vicarage, Royal Lane, Uxbridge UB8 3QR* Tel (01895) 461945 E-mail rob.harrison@london.anglican.org

HARRISON, Rodney Lovel Neal. b 46. MBE87. Dur Univ BA67. Ripon Coll Cuddesdon 93. **d** 95 **p** 96. C N w S Wootton *Nor* 95-98; P-in-c Gt and Lt Bedwyn and Savernake Forest *Sarum* 98-02; TV Savernake from 02. *The Vicarage, Church Street, Great Bedwyn, Marlborough SN8 3PF* Tel (01672) 870779 E-mail rodney@rlnh-ejhh.demon.co.uk

HARRISON, Rosemary Jane. b 53. Bradf Coll of Educn CertEd76. Trin Coll Bris 83. **d** 87 **p** 94. NSM Southway *Ex* 87-89; NSM Kinson *Sarum* 89-96. *28 First Avenue, Havant PO9 2QN* Tel (023) 9245 5226

HARRISON, Roy. *See* HARRISON, Canon William Roy

HARRISON, Russell. *See* HARRISON, Francis Russell

HARRISON, Miss Ruth Margaret. b 33. BEM85. FRSA94. Ripon Coll Cuddesdon 02. **d** 02 **p** 03. NSM Baddiley and Wrenbury w Burleydam *Ches* from 02. *2 Heywood Cottages, Heywood Lane, Audlem, Crewe CW3 0EX* Tel (01270) 812010

HARRISON, Shirley Ann. b 56. Leic Univ BA76. NOC 02. **d** 05 **p** 06. C Saddleworth *Man* 05-08; P-in-c Denton Ch Ch from 08. *Christ Church Rectory, 1 Windmill Lane, Denton, Manchester M34 3RN* Tel 0161-336 4456 Mobile 07956-080121 E-mail revdsah@yahoo.co.uk

HARRISON, Steven John. b 47. Univ of Wales (Abth) BSc68 PhD74 FRMetS74. St And Dioc Tr Course 87. **d** 90 **p** 91. NSM Alloa *St And* 90-94; NSM Bridge of Allan 94-02; NSM Spittal *Newc* from 02; NSM Scremerston from 02; P-in-c from 06. *St John's Vicarage, 129 Main Street, Spittal, Berwick-upon-Tweed TD15 1RP* Tel (01289) 307342 E-mail johnandaveril@aol.com

HARRISON, Canon William Roy. b 34. Dur Univ BA58. Cranmer Hall Dur 57. **d** 59 **p** 60. C Kingswood *Bris* 59-62; Kenya 62-65; P-in-c Gt Somerford *Bris* 66; V Soundwell 66-99; Hon Can Bris Cathl 92-99; rtd 99; Perm to Offic *Bris* from 99. *20 Pool Road, Bristol BS15 1XL* Tel 0117-967 9802

HARRISON-SMITH, Ms Fiona Jane. b 74. Huddersfield Univ BMus96 Ox Brookes Univ BA03 Leeds Univ MA07. Coll of Resurr Mirfield 05. **d** 07 **p** 08. C Redcar *York* from 07. *34 Ings Road, Redcar TS10 2DL* Tel (01642) 498241 Mobile 07709-914786 E-mail fharrisonsmith@aol.com

HARRISON-WATSON, Carole. *See* FORD, Mrs Carole

HARRISSON, John Anthony Lomax. b 47. Ex Univ BA72. Qu Coll Birm 72. **d** 74 **p** 75. C Loughton St Jo *Chelmsf* 74-81; V Chingford St Anne 81-98; TV Aldrington *Chich* 98-04; TV Golden Cap Team *Sarum* from 04. *The Vicarage, West Hill Road, Lyme Regis DT7 3LW* Tel (01297) 443134

HARROLD, Canon Jeremy Robin. b 31. Hertf Coll Ox BA54 BSc56 MA58. Wycliffe Hall Ox. **d** 59 **p** 60. C Rushden *Pet* 59-61; Bp's Chapl *Lon* 61-64; Australia 64-67; V Harlesden St Mark *Lon* 67-72; V Hendon St Paul Mill Hill 72-84; V Stowmarket *St E* 84-96; RD Stowmarket 90-96; Hon Can St E Cathl 94-96;

rtd 96; Perm to Offic *St E* from 96. *18 Wilkinson Way, Woodbridge IP12 1SS* Tel (01394) 380127

HARRON, Gareth Andrew. b 71. QUB BA92. CITC BTh95. **d** 95 **p** 96. C Willowfield *D & D* 95-98; C Dromore Cathl 98-02; I Magheralin w Dollingstown from 02. *The Rectory, 12 New Forge Road, Magheralin, Craigavon BT67 0QJ* Tel (028) 9261 1273 E-mail gareth@gharron.freeserve.co.uk

HARRON, James Alexander. b 37. GIMechE61. St Aid Birkenhead 63. **d** 65 **p** 66. C Willowfield *D & D* 65-69; I Desertmartin *D & R* 69-80; Dep Sec BCMS (Ireland) 80-84; I Aghalee *D & D* 84-03; Preb Dromore Cathl 02-03; Chapl HM Pris Maghaberry 86-03; rtd 03. *8 Churchill Avenue, Lurgan, Craigavon BT66 7BW* Tel and fax (028) 3834 6543

HARROP, Stephen Douglas. b 48. St Jo Coll York CertEd74 Man Univ DipAdEd90. Edin Th Coll 77. **d** 79 **p** 82. C Middlesbrough St Martin *York* 79-80; C Cayton w Eastfield 80-82; C Oldham *Man* 82-84; V Oldham St Barn 84-89; P-in-c Em Ch Hong Kong 89-93; Ind Chapl and TV Kidderminster St Mary and All SS w Trimpley etc *Worc* 93-95; Chapl Kidderminster Coll 93-95; Sandwell Chs Link Officer *Birm* 95-96; Dep Chapl HM Pris Brixton 96-97; Chapl Taichung St Jas Taiwan 97-98; R Lower Merion St Jo USA 98-99; R Essington St Jo 99-03; Perm to Offic *Man* 03-04; C Elton St Steph 04-05; P-in-c 05-08; Chapl HM Pris Forest Bank from 08. *HM Prison Forest Bank, Agecroft Road, Pendlebury, Manchester M27 8FB* Tel 0161-925 7037 E-mail esharrop@aol.com

HARRY, Bruce David. b 40. JP77. Culham Coll Ox CertEd60. NOC 83. **d** 86 **p** 87. NSM Liscard St Thos *Ches* 86-91; NSM Eastham 91-94; C New Brighton St Jas 94-96; C New Brighton Em 94-96; C New Brighton St Jas w Em 96-98; NSM 98-02; NSM New Brighton All SS 98-02; P-in-c 02-03; Perm to Offic from 03. *21 Sandymount Drive, Wallasey CH45 0LJ* Tel 0151-639 7232

HART (formerly HARRISON), Mrs Alison Edwina. b 53. Newc Univ BEd75. Linc Th Coll 84. **dss** 86 **d** 87 **p** 94. Loughborough Em *Leic* 86-89; Par Dn 87-89; C Stockton *Dur* 89-92; P-in-c Lynesack and Cockfield 92-95; P-in-c Ebchester 95-96; R 96-97; V Medomsley 96-97; V Newc H Cross 97-01; P-in-c Ulgham and Widdrington 01-06; P-in-c Beckermet St Jo and St Bridget w Ponsonby *Carl* from 06. *St John's Vicarage, 11 Lowrey Close, Beckermet CA21 2YX* Tel (01946) 841327 E-mail alison.harrison3@btopenworld.com

HART, Allen Sydney George. b 38. Chich Th Coll 64. **d** 67 **p** 68. C N Wembley St Cuth *Lon* 67-71; C W Bromwich All SS *Lich* 71-74; TV Hucknall Torkard *S'well* 74-80; V Annesley Our Lady and All SS 80-86; V Bilborough St Jo 86-99; RD Nottingham W 94-99; P-in-c Clarborough w Hayton 99-03; Asst Chapl HM Pris Ranby 99-03; rtd 03; Perm to Offic *S'well* from 03. *3 Castleton Close, Hucknall, Nottingham NG15 6TD* Tel 0115-955 2067 E-mail a.hart557@ntlworld.com

HART, André Hendrik. b 62. Cape Town Univ BA86. St Steph Ho Ox 89. **d** 91 **p** 92. C Newbold w Dunston *Derby* 91-95; P-in-c Clifton and Norbury w Snelston 95-02; Chapl S Derbyshire Community Health Services NHS Trust 95-02; V Westbury-on-Trym H Trin *Bris* from 02. *Holy Trinity Vicarage, 44 Eastfield Road, Westbury-on-Trym, Bristol BS9 4AG* Tel 0117-962 1536 *or* 950 8644

HART, Anthony. b 35. St Mich Coll Llan 77. **d** 79 **p** 80. NSM Jersey St Helier *Win* 79-81; C Heref All SS 81-82; C Kingstone 82-84; C Eaton Bishop 82-84; C Clehonger 82-84; R Sutton St Nicholas w Sutton St Michael 84-88; R Withington w Westhide 84-88; R Jersey St Mary *Win* 88-01; rtd 01; Perm to Offic *Win* from 02. *Villa Rapallo, Mont de la Trinite, St Helier, Jersey JE2 4NJ* Tel (01534) 739146 Mobile 07797-750435 E-mail hart@localdial.com

HART, Colin Edwin. b 45. Leeds Univ BA66 PGCE67 MPhil89 Fitzw Coll Cam BA73 MA77 K Coll Lon MTh76 Man Univ PhD98. Trin Coll Bris 74. **d** 74 **p** 75. C Ware Ch Ch *St Alb* 74-78; TV Sheff Manor 78-80; V Wombridge *Lich* 80-87; Lect St Jo Coll Nottm 87-01; Public Preacher *S'well* 87-01; Hon C Chilwell 87-91; Hon C Trowell 91-01; Perm to Offic *Ches* from 09. *47 Deveraux Drive, Wallasey CH44 4DG* Tel 0151-630 0749 E-mail hart206@btinternet.com

HART, Dagogo. b 50. Birm Bible Inst 77. **d** 82 **p** 83. C Niger Delta St Cypr 82-88; V 93-96; Chapl to Bp Niger Delta 83-88; Res Min Niger Delta Ch 89-92; Can Res St Steph Cathl Niger Delta 97-00; C W Bromwich St Jas w St Paul *Lich* 01-06; V from 06. *3 Tiverton Drive, West Bromwich B71 1DA* Tel 0121-553 0601

HART, David. b 48. Edge Hill Coll of HE BEd80 Liv Univ MEd87 Ches Coll of HE BPhil94. NOC 91. **d** 94 **p** 95. NSM Ashton-in-Makerfield St Thos *Liv* 94-02; NSM Wigan W Deanery 02-05. *12 Ratcliffe Road, Aspull, Wigan WN2 1YE* Tel (01942) 832918

HART, David Alan. b 54. Rhodes Univ BTh86 MTh89 PhD92 Bournemouth Univ DEd08. **d** 81 **p** 82. R Auckland Park St Pet S Africa 82-86; Sub Dean Kimberley Cathl 86-90; Chapl Cape Town Univ 90-94; NSM Cape Town Cathl 94-98; Chapl Bournemouth and Poole Coll of FE *Sarum* 99-06; Co-ord of IME from 07; Vice Prin Sarum OLM Scheme from 07; Asst Dioc

Dir of Ords from 07. *61 Felton Road, Poole BH14 0QR* Tel (01722) 411944 E-mail david.hart@salisbury.anglican.org

HART, David Leonard. b 42. Ripon Hall Ox 68. **d** 71 **p** 72. C Castle Vale *Birm* 71-73; Chapl All SS Hosp Birm 73-94; Chapl Services Manager N Birm Mental Health Trust 94-03; Manager Past Care Birm and Solihull Mental Health Trust 03-05; rtd 06; Lic to Offic *Arg* from 06. *15 Kirk Brae, Morvern, Oban PA34 5XW* Tel (01967) 421201 E-mail dhart29819@aol.com

HART, David Maurice. b 35. Univ Coll Dur BSc57. Clifton Th Coll 59. **d** 61 **p** 62. C Bolton St Paul *Man* 61-64; C Hamworthy *Sarum* 64-70; R W Dean w E Grimstead 70-81; R Farley w Pitton and W Dean w E Grimstead 81-90; V Steeple Ashton w Semington and Keevil 90-03; rtd 03. *9 Field Close, Westbury BA13 3AG* Tel (01373) 827912

HART, Canon Dennis Daniel. b 22. Linc Th Coll 45. **d** 48 **p** 49. C Abbots Langley *St Alb* 48-49; C Bedford St Paul 49-53; CF 53-55; V St Alb St Sav *St Alb* 55-92; Hon Can St Alb 74-92; RD St Alb 84-90; rtd 92. *7 Bassett Close, Redbourn AL3 7JY* Tel (01582) 794464

HART, Dennis William. b 30. JP. Open Univ BA. Oak Hill Th Coll 75. **d** 78 **p** 79. NSM Clacton St Paul *Chelmsf* 78-04; Perm to Offic 04-07. *Maranatha, 15 Albert Gardens, Clacton-on-Sea CO15 6QN* Tel (01255) 431794

HART, Edwin Joseph. b 21. Oak Hill Th Coll 56. **d** 58 **p** 59. C Harlow New Town w Lt Parndon *Chelmsf* 58-60; C Leyton 60-61; C-in-c Cranham Park St Luke CD 61-69; V Cranham Park 69-71; R Markfield *Leic* 71-89; rtd 89; Perm to Offic *Leic* from 89. *c/o Ms G Gordon, 1 Meadow Lane, Markfield LE67 9WT*

HART, Geoffrey Robert. b 49. TISEC 93. **d** 95 **p** 96. P-in-c Edin St Salvador 96-98; C Edin St Cuth 96-98; Lic to Offic 98-00; TV Edin St Marg 00-04; NSM Edin St Dav 04-09; P-in-c Edin St Marg from 09. *27 Links View, Port Seton, Prestonpans EH32 0EZ* Tel (01875) 811147 Mobile 07963-463551 E-mail geoff@lovehart.demon.co.uk

HART, Mrs Gillian Mary. b 57. Sheff City Poly BA79. Carl Dioc Tr Inst 92. **d** 95 **p** 96. C Burgh-by-Sands and Kirkbampton w Kirkandrews etc *Carl* 95-99; C Aikton 95-99; C Orton St Giles 95-99; Dioc Youth Officer 99-03; Chapl St Martin's Coll Carl 99-03; R Barony of Burgh *Carl* from 03; Adv for Women in Min from 08. *The Rectory, Burgh-by-Sands, Carlisle CA5 6AW* Tel (01228) 576324 E-mail hart.gill@btopenworld.com

HART, Graham Cooper. b 36. S Dios Minl Tr Scheme 88. **d** 91 **p** 92. NSM Filton *Bris* 91-93; NSM Downend 93-01. *11 West Hill, Portishead, Bristol BS20 6LQ* Tel (01275) 840363

HART, Canon Graham Merril (Merry). b 23. Ridley Coll Melbourne 65. **d** 77 **p** 77. Tanzania 69-84; CMS 72-83; Can Musoma from 85; Chapl Ostend w Knokke and Bruges *Eur* 84-93; Miss to Seamen 84-93; rtd 93; Perm to Offic *S'wark* from 93. *8 Alexander Court, 57 Kidbrooke Grove, London SE3 0LH* Tel (020) 8858 3731

HART, James. b 53. Dur Univ BA75 DipEd76 Lon Univ BD96 MIL84. Oak Hill Th Coll 86. **d** 88 **p** 89. C Starbeck *Ripon* 88-90; SAMS Argentina 90-96; R Buenos Aires St Sav 91-95; Chapl Bishop's Stortford Coll 96-00; Chapl Felsted Sch 00-06; Dioc FE Officer *Chelmsf* from 00; P-in-c Steeple Bumpstead and Helions Bumpstead from 06. *The Vicarage, 3 Church Street, Steeple Bumpstead, Haverhill CB9 7DG* Tel (01440) 730914 E-mail james@harthome.org

HART, John Peter. b 39. Bris Sch of Min 80. **d** 84 **p** 85. NSM Malmesbury w Westport and Brokenborough *Bris* 84-88; C Yatton Moor *B & W* 89-90; V Bridgwater H Trin 90-96; Chapl HM Pris The Mount 96-01; P-in-c Sarratt *St Alb* 96-04; P-in-c Chipperfield St Paul 01-04; rtd 04; Perm to Offic *Pet* from 05. *4 Waverley Gardens, Stamford PE9 1BH* Tel (01780) 754756

HART, Julia Lesley. b 43. **d** 08 **p** 09. NSM Nettleham *Linc* from 08. *Shrewsbury Cottage, Nettleham Lane, Scothern, Lincoln LN2 2TY* Tel (01673) 862426 E-mail jldf.hart@btinternet.com

HART, Mark. b 61. Chu Coll Cam BA82 Cam Univ MA86 PhD86. Trin Coll Bris BA98. **d** 98 **p** 99. C Bromborough *Ches* 98-02; V Plemstall w Guilden Sutton from 02; RD Ches from 09. *The Vicarage, Wicker Lane, Guilden Sutton, Chester CH3 7EL* Tel (01244) 300306 E-mail markhart61@googlemail.com

HART, Merril. See HART, Canon Graham Merril

HART, Canon Michael Anthony. b 50. AKC71. St Aug Coll Cant 72. **d** 73 **p** 74. C Southwick St Columba *Dur* 73-76; C Hendon St Alphage *Lon* 76-78; P-in-c Eltham Park St Luke *S'wark* 78-83, V 83-85; R Newington St Mary 85-96; P-in-c Camberwell St Mich w All So w Em 85-96; RD S'wark and Newington 93-96; P-in-c Chaldon 96-97; P-in-c Caterham 96-97; TR 98-05; RD Caterham 98-05; Hon Can S'wark Cathl 01-05; Can Missr from 05. *483A Southwark Park Road, London SE16 2JP* Tel (020) 7237 0563 or 7939 9411 Fax 7939 9467 E-mail michael.hart@southwark.anglican.org

HART, Preb Michael Stuart. b 39. Univ of Wales (Lamp) BA61 Lanc Univ MA72. Wycliffe Hall Ox 61. **d** 63 **p** 64. C W Bromwich St Jas *Lich* 63-66; C Tarrington w Stoke Edith *Heref* 66-67; C Putney St Mary *S'wark* 67-70; V Accrington St Mary *Blackb* 70-82; RD Accrington 76-82; Hon Can Blackb Cathl

81-91; V Walton-le-Dale 82-91; TR Heavitree w Ex St Paul 91-02; P-in-c Ex St Mary Steps 01-02; TR Heavitree and St Mary Steps 02-07; P-in-c Exwick 05-07; Preb Ex Cathl 02-07; rtd 07; Hon C Bath H Trin *B & W* from 09. *20 The Grove, Hallatrow, Bristol BS39 6ES* Tel (01225) 423718 Mobile 07786-516076 E-mail m.hart254@btinternet.com

HART, Peter. See HART, John Peter

HART, Peter Osborne. b 57. St Jo Coll Nottm. **d** 92 **p** 93. C Shipley St Pet *Bradf* 92-97; TV Walsall *Lich* 97-03; TV Cannock from 03. *St Luke's Vicarage, 18 Queen Street, Cannock WS11 1AE* Tel (01543) 579660

HART, Peter William. b 60. Liv Univ BA82 Université de Haute Normandie MèsL84 Univ of Wales (Swansea) MPhil92. Sarum & Wells Th Coll 86. **d** 88 **p** 89. C Llansamlet *S & B* 88-89; C Sketty 89-92; P-in-c Warndon St Nic *Worc* 92-97; R Berkhamsted St Mary *St Alb* 97-04; V Kew St Phil and All SS w St Luke *S'wark* from 04; Ecum Adv Kingston Area from 05. *St Philip's Vicarage, 70 Marksbury Avenue, Richmond TW9 4JF* Tel (020) 8392 1425 or 8332 1324 E-mail pwhart1@aol.com

HART, Robert William. b 76. R Holloway & Bedf New Coll Lon BSc97 Leeds Univ BA01 MA04. Coll of Resurr Mirfield 99. **d** 02 **p** 03. C Haydock St Jas *Liv* 02-06; R Hemsworth *Wakef* from 06. *The Rectory, 3 Church Close, Hemsworth, Pontefract WF9 4SJ* Tel (01977) 610507 Mobile 07970-229469 E-mail frrobert@parishofhemsworth.org.uk

HART, Ronald George. b 46. BSc CQSW77. Sarum & Wells Th Coll. **d** 85 **p** 86. C Sittingbourne St Mich *Cant* 85-88; C Walton H Trin *Ox* 88-89; TV 89-96; R Broughton Gifford, Gt Chalfield and Holt *Sarum* 96-05; Chapl UWE *Bris* 05-07; C Mangotsfield 06-07; R Vale of White Hart *Sarum* from 07. *The Rectory, Holwell, Sherborne DT9 5LF* Tel (01963) 23035 E-mail ronhart1@yahoo.co.uk

HART, Mrs Sheila Elizabeth. b 49. ERMC. **d** 08 **p** 09. NSM Whinlands *St E* from 08. *3 Keats Close, Saxmundham IP17 1WJ* Tel (01728) 602456 E-mail sheila.hart@tesco.net

HART, Tony. b 36. CCC Cam BA59 MA63. Cuddesdon Coll 59. **d** 61 **p** 62. C Middlesbrough All SS *York* 61-64; Bp's Dom Chapl *Dur* 64-67; Hon Chapl 67-72; C Owton Manor CD 67-70; V Harton Colliery 70-71; TR S Shields All SS 71-83; RD Jarrow 77-83; Can Res Dur Cathl 83-92; V Easingwold w Raskelfe *York* 92-97; V 97-01; RD Easingwold 97-00; rtd 01; Perm to Offic *Newc* from 02. *13 Stobhill Villas, Morpeth NE61 2SH* Tel (01670) 519017

HART, Prof Trevor Andrew. b 61. St Jo Coll Dur BA82 Aber Univ PhD89. **d** 88 **p** 88. NSM Bieldside *Ab* 88-95; NSM St Andrews St Andr *St And* from 95; Prof Div St Mary's Coll St Andr Univ from 95; Prin St Mary's Coll from 95. *St Mary's College, South Street, St Andrews KY16 9JU* Tel (01334) 462864 E-mail tah@st-andrews.ac.uk

HART, Mrs Valerie Mary. b 44. Sheff Univ MEd89 Wolv Univ MSc95 Nottm Univ MA08 RSCN. EMMTC 06. **d** 08 **p** 09. NSM Derby St Andr w St Osmund from 08. *4 Kingswood Avenue, Belper DE56 1TU* Tel (01773) 821417

HARTE, Frederick George. b 25. AKC53. **d** 54 **p** 55. C Lewisham St Jo Southend *S'wark* 54-57; C Eltham H Trin 57-60; V Bellingham St Dunstan 60-73; V Plumstead St Nic 73-84; V Sutton Bridge *Linc* 84-90; rtd 90; Master St Jo Hosp Bath and P-in-c of Chpl 90-00; Perm to Offic *Guildf* from 00. *Heartsease, 5 Vale Road, Claygate, Esher KT10 0NJ* Tel and fax (01372) 802548 E-mail f.harte@gmx.net

HARTE, The Ven Matthew Scott. b 46. TCD BA70 MA74. CITC 71. **d** 71 **p** 72. C Bangor Abbey *D & D* 71-74; C Ballynafeigh St Jude 74-76; I Ardara w Glencolumbkille, Inniskeel etc *D & R* 76-98; I Dunfanaghy, Raymunterdoney and Tullaghbegley from 98; Adn Raphoe from 83; Preb Howth St Patr Cathl Dublin from 07. *The Rectory, Horn Head Road, Dunfanaghy, Letterkenny, Co Donegal, Republic of Ireland* Tel (00353) (74) 913 6187 Fax 913 6051 E-mail archdeacon@raphoe.anglican.org

HARTERINK, Mrs Joy Frances. b 49. Essex Univ BA71 Hughes Hall Cam CertEd72 Lon Univ MSc87. Oak Hill NSM Course 89. **d** 92 **p** 94. NSM Richmond H Trin and Ch Ch *S'wark* 92-05; Chapl Richmond Coll 97-01; Perm to Offic *Guildf* from 05. *9 Eastmead, Woking GU21 3BP* Tel (01483) 751179 E-mail joyharterink@yahoo.com

HARTLAND, David Robson. b 33. Qu Coll Birm 64. **d** 66 **p** 67. C Brierley Hill *Lich* 66-71; V Hartshill 71-76; V Moxley 76-85; V Willenhall St Steph 85-99; rtd 99; Perm to Offic *Lich* and *Worc* from 00. *80 Clifton Street, Bilston WV14 9HB* Tel (01902) 563262

HARTLAND, Ian Charles. b 49. K Coll Lon BD72 AKC72 PGCE73 MTh76. Sarum & Wells Th Coll 83. **d** 84 **p** 85. C Orpington All SS *Roch* 84-87; Sen Lect Ch Ch Coll Cant 87-95; Adv RE Kent Coun 96-04; HMI of Schs from 04. *Ivy Lodge, 4 The Terrace, Canterbury CT2 7AJ* Tel (01227) 472836 E-mail ian.hartland@ofsted.gov.uk

HARTLAND, Michael. **d** 08. NSM Sutton *S'wark* from 08. *63 Park Lane, Carshalton SM5 3EE* Tel (020) 8401 6706 E-mail mandjhartland@blueyonder.co.uk

HARTLESS, Mrs Berengaria Isabella de la Tour. b 52. Univ of Wales (Cardiff) BSc74 Goldsmiths' Coll Lon PGCE76 Liv Univ MA03. Ox Min Course 90. **d** 93 **p** 94. Par Dn High Wycombe *Ox* 93-94; C 94-97; P-in-c Seer Green and Jordans 97-00; OLM Tr Officer (Bucks) 97-00; Dioc Prin of OLM from 00. *St Michael's Vicarage, Faringdon Road, Abingdon OX14 1BG*
E-mail beren.hartless@oxford.anglican.org

HARTLEY, Mrs Anne Theresa. b 52. St Cuth Soc Dur BSc74 Worc Coll of Educn PGCE75. **d** 03 **p** 04. OLM Shipton-under-Wychwood w Milton, Fifield etc *Ox* from 03. *The Old House, Upper Milton, Milton-under-Wychwood, Chipping Norton OX7 6EX* Tel (01993) 830160 Mobile 07976-025101
E-mail annethartley@hotmail.com

HARTLEY, Brian. b 41. NOC 82. **d** 85 **p** 86. NSM Royton St Paul *Man* 85-91; NSM Oldham St Steph and All Martyrs 91-94; TV E Farnworth and Kearsley 94-97; TR New Bury 97-06; P-in-c Gt Lever 03-06; AD Farnworth 98-05; rtd 06; Perm to Offic *Man* from 06. *21 Penryn Avenue, Royton, Oldham OL2 6JR* Tel (01706) 849132 E-mail brian_hartley@tiscali.co.uk

HARTLEY, Colin Redfearn. b 60. Cant Ch Ch Univ Coll BA98. Ridley Hall Cam 02. **d** 04 **p** 05. C Herne Bay Ch Ch *Cant* 04-08; TV Langley Marish *Ox* from 08. *Christ the Worker Vicarage, Parlaunt Road, Slough SL3 8BB* Tel (01753) 596722
E-mail rev.hartley@btinternet.com

HARTLEY, Daniel George. b 73. Leeds Univ BA95. Coll of Resurr Mirfield 96. **d** 99 **p** 00. C Richmond w Hudswell *Ripon* 99-03; Chapl HM YOI Deerbolt from 03. *HM YOI Deerbolt, Bowes Road, Barnard Castle DL12 9BG* Tel (01833) 633325
E-mail daniel.hartley@hmps.gsi.gov.uk

HARTLEY, Denis. b 54. NTMTC BA07. **d** 07. NSM Wood Green St Mich w Bounds Green St Gabr etc *Lon* from 07. *33 Stanmore Road, London N15 3PR* Tel (020) 8374 0915 Mobile 07957-227764 E-mail dhart74802@blueyonder.co.uk

HARTLEY, Dianna Lynn. *See* GWILLIAMS, Canon Dianna Lynn

HARTLEY, Graeme William. b 68. Ripon Coll Cuddesdon 05. **d** 07 **p** 08. C Sherborne w Castleton, Lillington and Longburton *Sarum* from 07. *32 Abbots Way, Sherborne DT9 6DT* Tel (01935) 389910 E-mail revd.graeme@btinternet.com

HARTLEY, Graham William Harrington. b 21. Ripon Hall Ox 61. **d** 62 **p** 63. C N Meols *Liv* 62-65; V Kano St Geo Nigeria 65-66; V Knowsley *Liv* 66-72; V Langdale *Carl* 72-81; TV Egremont and Haile 81-85; TV Whitehaven 85-88; rtd 88; Perm to Offic *Carl* from 88. *6 Meadowside, Chapel Stile, Ambleside LA22 9JE* Tel (01539) 437322

HARTLEY, Helen-Ann Macleod. b 73. St Andr Univ MTheol95 Princeton Th Sem ThM96 Worc Coll Ox MPhil00 DPhil05. SAOMC 03. **d** 05 **p** 06. C Wheatley *Ox* 05-07; C Littlemore from 07; Lect Ripon Coll Cuddesdon from 05; Tutor from 09. *43 Fairfax Gate, Holton, Oxford OX33 1QE* Tel (01865) 874466 Mobile 07981-914832
E-mail helen-ann.hartley@ripon-cuddesdon.ac.uk

HARTLEY, Herbert. b 28. AKC52. **d** 53 **p** 54. C Blackpool H Cross *Blackb* 53-55; C Reading St Giles *Ox* 55-58; V Ruscombe and Twyford 58-66; Chapl RN 66-73; C Langley Marish *Ox* 73-77; R Hedsor and Bourne End 77-93; rtd 93. *The College of St Barnabas, Blackberry Lane, Lingfield RH7 6NJ* Tel (01342) 872858

HARTLEY, John Peter. b 56. Cam Univ BA78 Leeds Univ PhD82 Dur Univ BA84. Cranmer Hall Dur 82. **d** 85 **p** 86. C Spring Grove St Mary *Lon* 85-88; C Bexleyheath St Pet *Roch* 88-91; P-in-c Hanford *Lich* 91-00; Faith in the City Officer (Potteries) 91-00; V Eccleshill *Bradf* from 00. *The Vicarage, 2 Fagley Lane, Bradford BD2 3NS* Tel (01274) 636403 Mobile 07811-915320 E-mail john.hartley@bradford.anglican.org

HARTLEY, Canon John William. b 47. St Jo Coll Dur BA69. Linc Th Coll 70. **d** 72 **p** 73. C Poulton-le-Fylde *Blackb* 72-76; C Lancaster St Mary 76-79; V Barrowford 79-87; V Salesbury from 87; AD Whalley from 01; Hon Can Blackb Cathl from 09. *St Peter's Vicarage, 49A Ribchester Road, Blackburn BB1 9HU* Tel (01254) 248072 E-mail john@salesbury49a.freeserve.co.uk

HARTLEY, Julian John. b 57. Oak Hill Th Coll BA85. **d** 85 **p** 86. C Eccleston Ch Ch *Liv* 85-89; V Goose Green 89-00; P-in-c Mosley Common *Man* 00-06; TV Astley, Tyldesley and Mosley Common from 06. *St John's Vicarage, Mosley Common Road, Worsley, Manchester M28 4AN* Tel 0161-790 2957 Fax 799 0314 E-mail rev.hartley@hartley.me.uk

HARTLEY, Michael Leslie. b 56. Leeds Univ BSc77. Ripon Coll Cuddesdon 87. **d** 89 **p** 90. C Standish *Blackb* 89-93; V Bamber Bridge St Aid 93-98; TR Colne and Villages 98-08; P-in-c Warton St Paul from 08; Dioc Ecum Officer from 08. *The Vicarage, Church Road, Warton, Preston PR4 1BD* Tel (01772) 632227 E-mail blackburndeo@googlemail.com

HARTLEY, Nigel John. b 48. Portsm Poly BA. St Jo Coll Nottm. **d** 83 **p** 84. C Ipswich St Marg *St E* 83-86; P-in-c Hintlesham w Chattisham 86-95; Dioc Radio Officer 86-95; P-in-c Gt Finborough w Onehouse, Harleston, Buxhall etc 95-04; RD Stowmarket 96-99; V Aldeburgh w Hazlewood from 04; RD

Saxmundham from 05. *The Vicarage, Church Walk, Aldeburgh IP15 5DU* Tel (01728) 452223
E-mail nigel.hartley@stedmundsbury.anglican.org

HARTLEY, Paul. b 51. Nottm Univ BTh88. Linc Th Coll 85. **d** 88 **p** 89. C Clitheroe St Mary *Blackb* 88-91; TV Guiseley w Esholt *Bradf* 91-97; R Ackworth *Wakef* from 97. *The Rectory, Cross Hill, Ackworth, Pontefract WF7 7EJ* Tel (01977) 602751
E-mail rev.paulhartley@btinternet.com

HARTLEY, Canon Peter. b 44. St Cath Coll Cam BA66 MA69 Avery Hill Coll PGCE67. Sarum & Wells Th Coll 77. **d** 78 **p** 79. Hon C Freemantle *Win* 78-79; Chr Educn Officer *Pet* 79-81; Dir of Educn 81-90; Dir Coun of Educn and Tr *Chelmsf* from 90; Hon Can Chelmsf Cathl from 92; Perm to Offic *Nor* from 04. *St Clare, Links Drive, Chelmsford CM2 9AW* Tel (01245) 251461
E-mail hartleyp@chelmsford.anglican.org

HARTLEY, Peter Mellodew. b 41. Qu Coll Cam BA63 MA66 Lon Univ MSc71 FICE. S'wark Ord Course 80. **d** 83 **p** 84. NSM Salfords *S'wark* 83-97; Chapl Surrey and Sussex Healthcare NHS Trust 97-02; rtd 02; Perm to Offic *Chich* from 00 and *S'wark* from 02. *Old Timbers, North Lane, West Hoathly RH19 4QF* Tel (01342) 811238
E-mail petefionahartley@ukonline.co.uk

HARTLEY (née ARCHER), Sarah Elizabeth. b 66. Charing Cross Hosp Medical Sch MB, BS89 Heythrop Coll Lon MA03 MRCGP95. Ripon Coll Cuddesdon BA99 MA07. **d** 00 **p** 01. C Dulwich St Barn *S'wark* 00-03; C Shepherd's Bush St Steph w St Thos *Lon* 03-07; PV Westmr Abbey 07-08; Perm to Offic *Lon* 07-08 and *B & W* from 08. *Flat 3, 17 Edward Street, Bath BA2 4DU* Tel (01225) 480650 Mobile 07717-718569
E-mail searcher@doctors.org.uk

HARTLEY, Stephen William Mark. b 50. St Chad's Coll Dur BA71. Westcott Ho Cam 72. **d** 74 **p** 75. C Holbrooks *Cov* 74-76; C Styvechale 76-79; P-in-c Snitterfield w Bearley 79-81; V 81-83; V Exhall 83-88; V Tilehurst St Cath *Ox* 88-95; TR Cowley St Jas 95-06; TR Hermitage 06-08; TR Cov E from 08. *St Peter's Rectory, Charles Street, Coventry CV1 5NP* Tel (024) 7622 8383
E-mail stephen.hartley@btinternet.com

HARTLEY, Stewart John Ridley. b 47. St Jo Coll Nottm 78. **d** 80 **p** 81. C Altham w Clayton le Moors *Blackb* 80-84; P-in-c Nelson St Phil 84-91; V 91-98; V Gt Marsden w Nelson St Phil 99-03; Hon Can Blackb Cathl 99-03; V Bermondsey St Anne and St Aug *S'wark* from 03; V Bermondsey St Jas w Ch Ch and St Crispin from 03. *St Anne's Vicarage, 10 Thorburn Square, London SE1 5QH* Tel (020) 7237 3950
E-mail stewarthartley@btinternet.com

HARTLEY, Susan Mary. b 49. Newc Univ MB, BS73 MRCGP77. SEITE 99. **d** 02 **p** 03. NSM Spitalfields Ch Ch w All SS *Lon* 02-07; NSM Hainault *Chelmsf* from 07; Asst Chapl St Joseph's Hospice Hackney from 06. *272 New North Road, Ilford IG6 3BT* Tel (020) 8500 4592
E-mail suemhartley@btinternet.com

HARTLEY, Canon Bruce John. b 42. Ex Univ BA64 Linacre Coll Ox BA66 MA. Ripon Hall Ox 64. **d** 66 **p** 67. C S Stoneham *Win* 66-69; Chapl and Tutor Ripon Hall Ox 69-74; V Knowl Hill w Littlewick *Ox* 74-78; Chapl Southn Univ 78-83; V Sholing 83-07; AD Southampton 93-01; Hon Can Win Cathl 93-07; rtd 07. *9 Ash Close, Southampton SO19 5SD* Tel (023) 8090 5420
E-mail bruce.hartnell@ukgateway.net

HARTNELL, Graham Philip. b 50. **d** 08 **p** 08. NSM Flackwell Heath *Ox* from 08. *36 Minniacy Road, Loudwater, High Wycombe HP10 9RL* Tel (01494) 521783
E-mail g.hartnell@talktalk.net

HARTOPP, Mrs Penelope Faye. b 55. Ripon Coll Cuddesdon. **d** 03 **p** 04. C Studley *Cov* 03-04; C Cov E 04-07; TV Godalming *Guildf* from 07. *The Vicarage, 29 Franklyn Road, Godalming GU7 2LD* Tel (01483) 424710 Mobile 07884-314752
E-mail penniehartopp@googlemail.com

HARTREE, Steven John. b 45. FFA78. WEMTC 96. **d** 99 **p** 00. NSM Highbridge *B & W* 99-03; P-in-c Tintinhull w Chilthorne Domer, Yeovil Marsh etc from 03. *The Rectory, Vicarage Street, Tintinhull, Yeovil BA22 8PY* Tel (01935) 822655

HARTROPP, Andrew James. b 59. Southn Univ BSc80 PhD85 K Coll Lon PhD03. Oak Hill Th Coll BA95. **d** 98 **p** 99. C Watford *St Alb* 98-01; C Watford Ch Ch 01-08; Teacher Henrietta Barnett Sch 01-06; NSM White Waltham w Shottesbrooke *Ox* from 08; NSM Waltham St Lawrence from 08. *The Parsonage, School Road, Waltham St Lawrence, Reading RG10 0NU* Tel 0118-934 4841 E-mail a.hartropp@btinternet.com

HARTWELL, Mrs Jeanette May. b 65. Aston Univ BSc88. Qu Coll Birm BA07. **d** 08 **p** 08. C Brereton and Rugeley *Lich* from 07. *4 Cardigan Avenue, Rugeley WS15 1LG* Tel (01889) 582355

HARVEY, Alan Douglas. b 25. FRSH82. Melbourne Coll of Div 78. **d** 79 **p** 81. Australia 79-86; Perm to Offic *Ely* 86-87; V Wiggenhall St Germans and Islington 88-95; V Wiggenhall St Mary Magd 88-95; rtd 95; Perm to Offic *Cant* from 95. *17 Bay View Road, Broadstairs CT10 2EA* Tel (01843) 862794

HARVEY, Alison Christine Vera. b 57. Open Univ BA97 Nottm Univ MA03. EMMTC 01. **d** 03 **p** 04. C Horncastle Gp *Linc* 03-07; P-in-c Mablethorpe w Trusthorpe from 07. *The Rectory,*

88 Wellington Road, Mablethorpe LN12 1HT Tel (01507) 473159 Mobile 07789-835039
E-mail harvey524@btinternet.com

HARVEY, Canon Anthony Ernest. b 30. Worc Coll Ox BA53 MA56 DD83. Westcott Ho Cam 56. **d** 58 **p** 59. C Chelsea Ch Ch *Lon* 58-62; Ch Ch Ox 62-69; Warden St Aug Coll Cant 69-75; Lect Th Ox Univ 76-82; Chapl Qu Coll Ox 77-82; Can and Lib Westmr Abbey 82-99; Sub-Dean and Adn Westmr 87-99; rtd 99; Perm to Offic *Glouc* from 00. *Mendelssohn Cottage, Broadway Road, Willersey, Broadway WR12 7BH* Tel (01386) 859260

HARVEY, Anthony Peter. b 42. Birm Univ BSc63 MSc64. Wycliffe Hall Ox 79. **d** 81 **p** 82. C Stoke Damerel *Ex* 81-84; Canada 84-90; Chapl HM YOI Deerbolt 91-92; Chapl HM Pris Wakef 92-95; Chapl HM Pris Kirkham 95-01; rtd 07; Canada from 07. *259 White Road, Harrington QC J8G 2T3, Canada* Tel (001) (514) 626 2665

HARVEY, Brian. b 51. Hatf Poly BA74. St As Minl Tr Course 02. **d** 05 **p** 06. NSM Cilcain and Nannerch and Rhydymwyn *St As* 05-09; P-in-c 06-09; R Flint from 09. *The Rectory, Allt Goch, Flint CH6 5NF* Tel (01352) 733274
E-mail brianharvey@mac.com

HARVEY, Carol Roberta. b 47. NUU BA89. CITC 03. **d** 06 **p** 07. NSM Carnmoney *Conn* from 06. *26 Larne Road, Carrickfergus BT38 7DX* Tel (028) 9335 1654
E-mail carolrharvey@hotmail.com

HARVEY, Christopher John Alfred. b 41. S'wark Ord Course 66. **d** 69 **p** 70. C Grays Thurrock *Chelmsf* 69-73; C Gt Baddow 73-75; V Berechurch St Marg w St Mich 75-94; R Tendring and Lt Bentley w Beaumont cum Moze 94-00; P-in-c Alresford 00-08; rtd 08; Perm to Offic *Chelmsf* from 08. *Bethel, 9 Laburnum Crescent, Kirby Cross, Frinton-on-Sea CO13 0QQ* Tel (01255) 678649 E-mail chris.anne@tiscali.co.uk

HARVEY, The Ven Cyril John. b 30. Univ of Wales (Lamp) BA51. Coll of Resurr Mirfield 51. **d** 53 **p** 54. C Caerau w Ely *Llan* 53-57; C Milford Haven *St D* 57-61; V Castlemartin and Warren 61-65; R Begelly w Kilgetty 65-73; V Haverfordwest St Martin w Lambston 73-88; Can St D Cathl from 85; R Tenby 88-96; Adn St D 91-96; rtd 96. *10 Oakwood Grove, Slade Lane, Haverfordwest SA61 2HF* Tel (01437) 768036

HARVEY, Canon Debra Eileen. b 54. SWMTC. **d** 94 **p** 95. NSM Camborne *Truro* from 94; Chapl w Deaf People from 94; Hon Can Truro Cathl from 03. *Ankorva Salow, Tehidy Road, Camborne TR14 0NA* Tel (01209) 716282 Mobile 07774-975268 Fax and minicom as telephone
E-mail hippo@ankorva.freeserve.co.uk

HARVEY, Desmond Victor Ross. b 37. QUB BA59. Princeton Th Sem ThM63 Fuller Th Sem California DMin93 St Mich Coll Llan 93. **d** 95 **p** 96. Presbyterian Min 65-95; C Cwmbran *Mon* 95-97; TV 97; Perm to Offic from 97; Offg Chapl RAF from 98. *Mallory, Llanmaes, Llantwit Major CF61 2XR* Tel and fax (01446) 792753

HARVEY, Ian Malcolm. b 51. **d** 03 **p** 04. NSM Burnie Australia 03-07; NSM Filwood Park *Bris* 07-09; C S Barrow *Carl* from 09. *98A Roose Road, Barrow-in-Furness LA13 9RL*
E-mail ian_harvey@blueyonder.co.uk

HARVEY, John. b 30. S'wark Ord Course. **d** 65 **p** 66. C Lewisham St Jo Southend *S'wark* 65-73; V Bellingham St Dunstan 73-78; TV Bourne Valley *Sarum* 78-81; TR 81-87; R Kilkhampton w Morwenstow *Truro* 87-90; rtd 90; Perm to Offic *Roch* 90-99. *18 Ramsay Hall, 11-13 Byron Road, Worthing BN11 3HN*

HARVEY, John Christopher. b 65. Univ of Wales (Lamp) BA86 Nottm Univ BTh89. Linc Th Coll 86. **d** 89 **p** 90. C Dwygyfylchi *Ban* 89-93; V Llangrannog w Llandysiliogogo w Penbryn *St D* 93-02; RD Glyn Aeron 99-02; P-in-c Llangystennin *St As* 02-04; R 04-09; Dioc Voc Adv 08-09; V Meliden and Gwaenysgor from 09. *The Vicarage, Ffordd Penrhwylfa, Prestatyn LL19 8HN* Tel (01745) 856220

HARVEY, John Mark. b 64. QUB BEd87 TCD BTh93. CITC 90. **d** 93 **p** 94. C Portadown St Columba *Arm* 93-96; I Monaghan w Tydavnet and Kilmore *Clogh* 96-01; Dioc Communications Officer 97-00; Miss Officer (Ireland) CMS 01-05; I Ballybeen *D & D* from 05. *1 Grahamsbridge Road, Dundonald, Belfast BT16 2DB* Tel (028) 9048 0834 Mobile 07966-332310
E-mail rector@stmarysballybeen.com

HARVEY, Lt Col John William Arthur. b 43. Guildf Dioc Min Course 98. **d** 01 **p** 02. OLM Aldershot St Aug *Guildf* from 01. *59 Knoll Road, Fleet GU51 4PT* Tel (01252) 622793
E-mail father.john@talktalk.net

HARVEY, Lance Sydney Crockford. b 25. Ridley Hall Cam 67. **d** 69 **p** 70. C Mortlake w E Sheen *S'wark* 69-74; P-in-c Woolwich St Thos 75-86; V Lee Gd Shep w St Pet 86-92; RD E Lewisham 87-91; rtd 92; Perm to Offic *Truro* 92-06. *17 Lariggan Road, Penzance TR18 4NJ*

HARVEY, Lincoln. b 69. Univ of Wales (Swansea) BA92 K Coll Lon MA01 PhD08. SEITE. **d** 09. NSM St John-at-Hackney *Lon* from 09. *1 Dr Spurstowe House, 36 Navarino Road, London E8 1AF* Tel 07855-866823 (mobile)
E-mail lincoln.harvey@gmail.com

HARVEY, Margaret Claire. b 41. Univ of Wales (Abth) BA62 DipEd63 Lon Univ BD68. Dalton Ho Bris 66. **dss** 68 **d** 80 **p** 97. Flint *St As* 68-74; Lect Trin Coll Bris 74-80; Connah's Quay *St As* 79-80; C 80-86; Bp's Adv for Continuing Clerical Educn 86-98; Hon C Corwen and Llangar 86-87; Dn-in-c Bryneglwys 87-97; P-in-c 97-02; rtd 02. *Coleg y Groes, The College, Corwen LL21 0AU* Tel (01490) 412169 E-mail colegygroes@talk21.com

HARVEY, Mark. *See* HARVEY, John Mark

HARVEY, Murray Alexander. b 63. Univ of Qld BA85 Deakin Univ Australia DHSc03 MAPsS87. St Fran Coll Brisbane BTh91. **d** 91 **p** 92. Australia 91-02; C Milton 92-93; C Stafford 94-95; P-in-c Tamborine Mt St Geo 95-02; V Glen Gp *Linc* from 02. *The Vicarage, 19 Spalding Road, Pinchbeck, Spalding PE11 3UD* Tel and fax (01775) 725698
E-mail murray.harvey@spaldingchurches.org

HARVEY, Canon Norman Roy. b 43. Nottm Univ DipAE86. Wycliffe Hall Ox 66. **d** 69 **p** 70. C Clay Cross *Derby* 69-72; C Dronfield 72-76; TV 76-79; P-in-c Rowsley 79-89; Dioc Youth Officer 79-83; Dioc Adv in Adult and Youth Educn 83-89; TR Eckington w Handley and Ridgeway 89-01; R Eckington and Ridgeway 01-08; RD Bolsover and Staveley 00-05; Hon Can Derby Cathl 00-08; rtd 08. *62 Parklands View, Aston, Sheffield S26 2GW* Tel 0114-287 2243
E-mail norman.harvey2@btopenworld.com

HARVEY, Oliver Paul. b 33. Magd Coll Ox BA55 MA59. Cuddesdon Coll 57. **d** 59 **p** 60. C S Norwood St Mark *Cant* 59-61; C Hythe 61-64; Zambia 64-71; Chapl Cant Coll of Tech 71-77; Hon C Cant St Martin and St Paul 73-77; Chapl K Sch Roch 77-88; C Roch 88-90; V Gillingham St Mary 90-00; RD Gillingham 98-00; rtd 00; Perm to Offic *Roch* 00-03 and *B & W* from 05. *11 Henley Road, Taunton TA1 5BN* Tel (01823) 272825

HARVEY, Miss Pamela Betty. b 33. Dalton Ho Bris IDC59. **dss** 68 **d** 87 **p** 95. Nottingham St Ann *S'well* 68-72; Bestwood St Matt 72-76; CPAS Staff 76-93; Dir Consultants Division CPAS 93-99; rtd 99; Hon C Glenfield *Leic* 95-04; Perm to Offic from 04. *72 Chestnut Road, Glenfield, Leicester LE3 8DB* Tel 0116-232 2959 E-mail pam.harvey@ukgateway.net

HARVEY, Mrs Patricia Ann. b 45. Qu Coll Birm. **dss** 82 **d** 87 **p** 94. Gospel Lane St Mich *Birm* 82-85; Exhall *Cov* 85-89; C 87-89; TD Droitwich Spa *Worc* 89-94; TV 94-97; P-in-c Finstall 97-00; V 00-02; rtd 02; Perm to Offic *Heref* from 02 and *Worc* from 04. *15 Mount Orchard, Tenbury Wells WR15 8DW* Tel (01584) 819444 E-mail patricia.harvey3@virgin.net

HARVEY, Canon Patrick Arnold. b 58. TCD BA MA. CITC 82. **d** 85 **p** 86. C Bandon Union *C, C & R* 85-88; Dean's V Limerick St Mich *L & K* 88-91; Dioc Info Officer 88-91; I Abbeyleix w Ballyroan etc *C & O* from 91; Can Ossory Cathl from 97. *The Rectory, Abbeyleix, Portlaoise, Co Laois, Republic of Ireland* Tel and fax (00353) (57) 873 1243
E-mail abbeyleix@leighlin.anglican.org

HARVEY, Paul. *See* HARVEY, Oliver Paul

HARVEY, Robert Martin. b 30. S'wark Ord Course 69. **d** 70 **p** 71. C Sutton New Town *S'wark* 70-75; C Leatherhead *Guildf* 76-78; V Wadworth w Loversall *Sheff* 78-96; RD Doncaster 94-97; rtd 96; Perm to Offic *Sheff* from 96. *44 Castlegate, Tickhill, Doncaster DN11 9QU* Tel (01302) 746532

HARVEY, Robin Grant. b 43. Clare Coll Cam BA64 MA68 Univ of NSW PhD74. Linc Th Coll 85. **d** 87 **p** 88. C Keynsham *B & W* 87-91; R E w W Harptree and Hinton Blewett 91-97; Chapl Surrey Univ 98-02; P-in-c Cuddington 02-07; V 07-08; rtd 08. *21 St Cadoc House, Temple Street, Keynsham, Bristol BS31 1HD* Tel 0117-986 2295
E-mail rgharvey.194@btinternet.com

HARVEY, Roland. b 68. St Jo Coll Nottm 99. **d** 01 **p** 02. C Skelmersdale St Paul *Liv* 01-05; P-in-c Pemberton St Fran Kitt Green from 05. *The Vicarage, 42 Sherborne Road, Orrell, Wigan WN5 0JA* Tel (01942) 213227 Mobile 07817-901455

HARVEY, Simon John. b 63. Trin Coll Bris BA00. **d** 00 **p** 01. C Walsall St Paul *Lich* 00-03; TV Oadby *Leic* from 03; Warden of Readers from 05. *St Paul's House, Hamble Road, Oadby, Leicester LE2 4NX* Tel 0116-271 0519
E-mail simon@sjharvey.org.uk

HARVEY, Steven Charles. b 58. Reading Univ BA79 Cam Univ PGCE80 Ox Univ BA83 MA88. Ripon Coll Cuddesdon 81. **d** 84 **p** 85. C Oldham *Man* 84-87; Chapl and Hd RS St Pet Sch York 87-96; Sen Dep Hd Kingswood Sch Bath 96-03; Sen Provost and Educn Officer Woodard Corp 03-06; Hd Master Bury Gr Sch from 06; Perm to Offic *Blackb* and *Man* from 06. *41 Bury New Road, Ramsbottom, Bury BL0 0AR* Tel (01706) 822690

HARVEY, Trevor John. b 43. Sheff Univ BA64 K Coll Lon MA94. Coll of Resurr Mirfield 64. **d** 66 **p** 67. C Kingswinford St Mary *Lich* 66-72; V Upper Gornal 72-77; V Meir 77-86; Chapl St Geo Sch Windsor 86-99; Min Can Windsor 86-99; Chapl Ellesmere Coll 99-03; rtd 03; C Meir Heath and Normacot *Lich* 03-07; Perm to Offic from 07. *1 Rolt Close, Stone ST15 8YX* Tel (01785) 813266
E-mail revdtjharvey@yahoo.co.uk

HARVEY, Mrs Verity Margaret. b 48. Bris Univ BA69 Saltley Tr Coll Birm DipEd70. SAOMC 99. **d** 02 **p** 03. NSM Radlett *St Alb* 02-05; NSM Bushey from 05. *28 Field Road, Watford WD19 4DR* Tel (01923) 492863

HARVEY, Wendy Marion. b 46. SEITE 06. **d** 09. NSM Hurst Green *S'wark* from 09. *Surrey Beeches West, Westerham Road, Westerham TN16 2EX* Tel (01959) 562340 Mobile 07973-428683 E-mail wendyharvey@talktalk.net

HARVEY-NEILL, Nicola Lisa Jane. b 69. QUB BD91 TCD MPhil95. CITC BTh94. **d** 95 **p** 96. Dioc C *T, K & A* 95-96; C Galway w Kilcummin 96-97; Dioc Youth Adv (Limerick) *L & K* 97-01; Chapl Villier's Sch Limerick 98-01; Chapl Limerick Univ 98-01; Perm to Offic from 01. *Modreeny Rectory, Cloughjordan, Co Tipperary, Republic of Ireland* Tel and fax (00353) (505) 42183 Mobile 87-250 0570 F-mail nickihn@eircom.net *or* snnneill@iol.ie

HARVIE, Robert. b 53. **d** 04 **p** 05. OLM Godalming *Guildf* from 04. *7 Ockford Ridge, Godalming GU7 2NP* Tel (01483) 415931 E-mail rhl.swift@ukonline.co.uk *or* robbie.harvie@godalming.org.uk

HARWOOD, Ms Ann Jane. b 73. SEITE. **d** 08. C Winslow w Gt Horwood and Addington *Ox* from 08. *39 Vicarage Road, Winslow, Buckingham MK18 3BJ* Tel 07903-652927 (mobile) E-mail annharwood73@googlemail.com

HARWOOD (formerly SOUTH), Mrs Gillian. b 51. NEOC 87. **d** 90 **p** 94. C Rothbury *Newc* 90-93; C Morpeth 93-97; V Amble 97-06; Chapl Northumbria Healthcare NHS Trust from 06. *Wansbeck General Hospital, Woodhorn Lane, Ashington NE63 9JJ* Tel (01670) 521212 E-mail gillysouth@btopenworld.com

HARWOOD, Canon John Rossiter. b 26. Selw Coll Cam BA51 MA55. Wycliffe Hall Ox 51. **d** 53 **p** 54. C Handsworth St Mary *Birm* 53-55; Tutor Trin Coll Umuahia Nigeria 57-64; Warden Minl Tr Cen Freetown Sierra Leone and Bp's Dom Chapl 64-67; Home Educn Sec CMS 67-75; V Cheltenham Ch Ch *Glouc* 75-91; RD Cheltenham 84-89; Hon Can Glouc Cathl 85-91; rtd 91; Perm to Offic *Ex* 91-99; *Chich* and *Portsm* from 00. *8 Kingsey Avenue, Emsworth PO10 7HP* Tel (01243) 372215

HARWOOD, Mary Ann. b 46. Cam Inst of Educn CertEd68. Ox Min Course 04. **d** 07 **p** 08. NSM Burghfield *Ox* from 07. *5 Bainbridge Road, Calcot, Reading RG31 7BE* Tel and fax 0118-967 8145 Mobile 07721-437316 E-mail maryh@globalnet.co.uk

HARWOOD, Peter James. b 64. Birm Univ MB88 ChB88. Wycliffe Hall Ox BA93. **d** 94 **p** 95. C Cov H Trin 94-97; C Kensington St Barn *Lon* 97-02; V Woking Ch Ch *Guildf* from 02; Chapl Woking Hospice from 06. *Christ Church Vicarage, 10 Russetts Close, Woking GU21 4BH* Tel (01483) 762100 E-mail peter.harwood@christchurchwoking.org

HASELHURST (née STERLING), Mrs Anne. b 51. Macalester Coll (USA) BA73. EAMTC 89. **d** 92 **p** 94. Par Dn Bury St Edmunds St Jo *St E* 92-94; C 94-95; V Fordham St Pet *Ely* 95-06; P-in-c Kennett 95-06; P-in-c Isleham 05-06; R Cupar *St And* from 06; R Ladybank from 06. *13 Robertson Road, Cupar KY15 5YR* Tel (01334) 652982 E-mail annehaselhurst@talktalk.net

HASELOCK, Canon Jeremy Matthew. b 51. York Univ BA73 BPhil74. St Steph Ho Ox BA82 MA86. **d** 83 **p** 84. C Pimlico St Gabr *Lon* 83-86; C Paddington St Jas 86-88; Bp's Dom Chapl *Chich* 88-91; P-in-c Boxgrove 91-94; V 94-98; Dioc Adv on Liturgy 91-98; Can and Preb Chich Cathl 94-98; Can Res and Prec Nor Cathl from 98. *34 The Close, Norwich NR1 4DZ* Tel (01603) 619169 Fax 766032

HASKETT, Mrs Fiona Ann. b 55. SEITE 01. **d** 04 **p** 05. NSM Leigh *Roch* 04-09; V Hints *Lich* from 09; V Whittington w Weeford from 09. *5 Bramley Way, Lichfield WS14 9SB* Tel (01543) 432233 E-mail fiona.haskett@btopenworld.com

HASKEY, Alyn Rex. b 51. EMMTC 02. **d** 04 **p** 05. NSM Sneinton St Chris w St Phil *S'well* from 04; NSM Nottingham St Sav from 04; NSM Nottingham St Nic from 04; Dioc Ev from 09. *Flat 1, 6 Vickers Street, Nottingham NG3 4LD* Tel 0115-960 5489 E-mail alynhaskey@freedomministries.freeserve.co.uk

HASKINS, Thomas. b 41. TCD BA72. CITC 71. **d** 73 **p** 74. C Larne and Inver *Conn* 73-78; C Antrim All SS 78-83; I Belfast St Mark 83-90; I Dublin Clontarf *D & G* 90-02; I Dublin St Ann and St Steph 02-08; Can Ch Ch Cathl Dublin 99-08; rtd 08. *7 Gorse Haven, Coolboy, Tinahely, Co Wicklow, Republic of Ireland* Tel (00353) (402) 34997

HASLAM, Andrew James. b 57. Univ Coll Dur BSc78 Coll of Ripon & York St Jo PGCE79 Lambeth STh84. Trin Coll Bris 80. **d** 83 **p** 84. C Leyland St Andr *Blackb* 83-86; C Hartford *Ches* 86-88; V Grimsargh *Blackb* 88-98; V St Helens St Mark *Liv* 98-05; V Birkenhead Ch Ch *Ches* from 05. *Christ Church Vicarage, 7 Palm Grove, Prenton CH43 1TE* Tel 0151-652 5647 E-mail vicar@christchurch.birkenhead

HASLAM, Canon Frank. b 26. Bris Univ BA50. Tyndale Hall Bris 49. **d** 51 **p** 52. C Halliwell St Paul *Man* 51-55; Uganda 56-60; C Wednesfield Heath *Lich* 60-61; V Wolverhampton St Matt 61-65; V Blackpool Ch Ch *Blackb* 65-70; V Macclesfield St Mich *Ches* 71-80; Dir of Resources 80-91; Hon Can Ches Cathl 81-91; rtd 91; Perm to Offic *Ches* from 91; P-in-c Bistre *St As* 99-00. *Brackendale, Chester Road, Buckley CH7 3AH* Tel (01244) 549291

HASLAM, James Robert. b 31. Open Univ BA74. Bps' Coll Cheshunt 55. **d** 57 **p** 58. C Penwortham St Mary *Blackb* 57-63; V Cockerham 63-74; V Cockerham w Winmarleigh 74-76; V Gt Harwood St Bart 76-88; V Fairhaven 88-95; rtd 95; Perm to Offic *Blackb* from 95. *5 Willow Trees Drive, Blackburn BB1 8LB* Tel (01254) 697092

HASLAM, Mrs Jane. b 70. Leeds Poly BA92. Trin Coll Bris BA97. **d** 97 **p** 98. C Minehead *B & W* 97-00; Perm to Offic *Newc* 00-03; C Balkwell 03-04; P-in-c Purton *Bris* from 04. *The Vicarage, 2 Kingsacre, Hyde Lane, Purton, Swindon SN5 4DU* Tel (01793) 770210 E-mail jane.haslam@virgin.net

HASLAM, John Gordon. b 32. Birm Univ LLB53. Qu Coll Birm 75. **d** 77 **p** 77. Hon C Bartley Green *Birm* 77-79; Hon C Moseley St Mary 79-96; Chapl to The Queen 89-02; Perm to Offic *Heref* from 97. *16 Mill Street, Ludlow SY8 1BE* Tel and fax (01584) 876663

HASLAM, Michael Henry. b 72. Buckingham Univ BA93. Trin Coll Bris BA94 MA94. **d** 97 **p** 98. C Minehead *B & W* 97-00; Chapl Newc Univ 00-04; C Purton and Dioc Ecum Officer *Bris* 04-06; P-in-c N Swindon St Andr from 06. *The Vicarage, 2 Kingsacre, Hyde Lane, Purton, Swindon SN5 4DU* Tel (01793) 770210 Mobile 07817-703929 E-mail mike.haslam@bristoldiocese.org

HASLAM, Robert John Alexander. b 34. CCC Cam BA58. Coll of Resurr Mirfield 58. **d** 60 **p** 61. C Rawmarsh w Parkgate *Sheff* 60-66; Perm to Offic *Edin* 66-73 and *Carl* 73-77; P-in-c Peebles *Edin* 77-81; V Darnall *Sheff* 81-85; Hon C Bermondsey St Hugh CD *S'wark* 86-88; R Clydebank *Glas* 88-98; Chapl Mlaga *Eur* 98-03. *Flat 1/1, 134 Fergus Drive, Glasgow G20 6AT* Tel 0141-945 4132

HASLER, Canon John Joseph. b 45. Univ of Wales (Cardiff) MPhil99. Qu Coll Birm 89. **d** 90 **p** 91. C Horfield H Trin *Bris* 90-93; V Bris St Andr Hartcliffe 93-01; V Bris Lockleaze St Mary Magd w St Fran from 01; AD City 03-06; Hon Can Bris Cathl from 08. *The Vicarage, Copley Gardens, Bristol BS7 9YE* Tel 0117-951 2516

HASLER, Kevin John. b 56. RGN80 RMN80. St Mich Coll Llan 03. **d** 06 **p** 07. NSM Raglan w Llandenny and Bryngwyn *Mon* 06-08; NSM Llangwm Uchaf and Llangwm Isaf w Gwernesney etc from 08. *The Steps, Old Abergavenny Road, Brynglyn, Raglan, Usk NP15 2AA* Tel (01291) 690163 Mobile 07592-822022 E-mail kevin@hasler.org.uk *or* kevin@llangwm-parishes.org.uk

HASSALL, Mrs Elizabeth Claire. b 80. R Holloway Coll Lon BSc01. Trin Coll Bris BA08. **d** 09. C Bempton w Flamborough, Reighton w Speeton *York* from 09. *Briel Cottage, Bridlington Road, Flamborough, Bridlington YO15 1PW* Tel (01262) 851385

HASSALL, William Edwin. b 41. St Jo Coll Nottm 75. **d** 77 **p** 78. C Wellington w Eyton *Lich* 77-80; C Farewell 80-82; V 82-93; C Gentleshaw 80-82; V 82-93; P-in-c Cheddleton 93-94; Asst Chapl Birm Heartlands and Solihull NHS Trust 98-01; Chapl Team Ldr 01-06; rtd 06; Perm to Offic *Lich* from 97 and *Birm* from 06. *17 Bradwell Lane, Rugeley WS15 4RW* Tel (01543) 670739

HASSAN, Brian Joseph. b 67. CITC 05. **d** 08 **p** 09. NSM Clooney w Strathfoyle *D & R* 08-09; NSM Faughanvale from 09. *96 Castle Park, Limavady BT49 0SB* Tel (028) 7776 6281 Mobile 07828-668342 E-mail brian.hassan2@btinternet.com

HASSELL, David Edwin. b 38. WMMTC 87. **d** 90 **p** 91. NSM Worc SE 90-93; C Abberton, Naunton Beauchamp and Bishampton etc 93-94; P-in-c Abberton, The Flyfords, Naunton Beauchamp etc 94-04; rtd 04; Perm to Offic *Worc* from 04. *14 Napleton Lane, Kempsey, Worcester WR5 3PT* Tel (01905) 828096

HASSELL, John Charles. b 44. FCA. Sarum & Wells Th Coll 81. **d** 83 **p** 84. C Tottenham St Paul *Lon* 83-86; C Fingringhoe w E Donyland *Chelmsf* 86-90; V Moulsham St Jo 90-00; TR Grays Thurrock 00-05; RD Thurrock 01-03; rtd 06; Perm to Offic *Chelmsf* from 06. *17A Second Avenue, Westcliff-on-Sea SS0 8HX* Tel (01702) 333267 E-mail john@hassall2000.fsnet.co.uk

HASTE, James Victor William. b 36. St Mich Th Coll Crafers 64. **d** 68 **p** 70. C Ormond Australia 68-69; C Roehampton H Trin *S'wark* 70-72; P-in-c Boroko Papua New Guinea 72-76; Sec ABM Vic Australia 76-81; I Armadale w Hawksburn 81-86; I Vermont S 86-89; Inter-Ch Trade and Ind Chapl 89-94; rtd 01; Lic to Offic The Murray 99-05; Perm to Offic Melbourne from 05. *17 Park View Drive, Aspendale Vic 3195, Australia* Tel (0061) (3) 9588 2805 Mobile 407-044086 E-mail baha@picknowl.com.au

HASTED, Marcus Arthur David. b 35. Qu Coll Birm 63. **d** 66 **p** 67. C Woodchurch *Ches* 66-69; C W Kirby St Bridget 69-72; V Farndon 72-76; V Farndon and Coddington 76-79; Perm to Offic 98-00 and from 02; NSM Liscard St Mary w St Columba 00-02. *62 South Road, West Kirby, Wirral CH48 3HQ* Tel 0151-625 0428

HASTEY, Erle. b 44. St Mich Coll Llan 66. **d** 68 **p** 69. C Pontefract St Giles *Wakef* 68-71; C Almondbury 71-74; V

Purlwell 74-79; P-in-c Batley Carr 76-79; V Ynyshir *Llan* 79-86; V Tylorstown w Ynyshir 86-87; V Tonyrefail w Gilfach Goch 87-97; P-in-c Llandyfodwg 87-97; V Tonyrefail w Gilfach Goch and Llandyfodwg 97-99; V Pyle w Kenfig 99-04; rtd 04. *2 Cambray Close, Porthcawl CF36 3PY* Tel (01656) 783935

HASTIE-SMITH, Timothy Maybury. b 62. Magd Coll Cam MA84. Wycliffe Hall Ox 85. d 88 p 89. C Ox St Ebbe w H Trin and St Pet 88-91; Chapl Stowe Sch 91-98; Hd Master Dean Close Sch Cheltenham 98-08; TV Fairford Deanery *Glouc* from 08. *The Parsonage, High Street, Kempsford, Fairford GL7 4ET* Tel (01285) 810773 E-mail tim.hastie-smith@hotmail.com

HASTINGS, David Kerr. b 40. St Luke's Coll Ex CertEd63. Ox NSM Course 84. d 87 p 88. Hd Master St Edburg's Sch Bicester 82-89; Asst Chapl HM Pris Grendon and Spring Hill 87-89; NSM Bicester w Bucknell, Caversfield and Launton *Ox* 87-89; Chapl HM Pris Reading 90-92; P-in-c Gt Wishford *Sarum* 92; P-in-c S Newton 92; P-in-c Stapleford w Berwick St James 92; P-in-c Winterbourne Stoke 92; R Lower Wylye and Till Valley 92-95; Chapl HM Pris Ex 96-01; Perm to Offic *Ex* from 01; rtd 01. *26 Hoopern Street, Exeter EX4 4LY* Tel (01392) 498233

HASTINGS, The Ven Gary Lea. b 56. NUU BA82 MA87 TCD BTh93. CITC 90. d 93 p 94. C Galway w Kilcummin *T, K & A* 93-95; I Aughaval w Achill, Knappagh, Dugort etc 95-09; I Galway w Kilcummin from 09; Dom Chapl to Bp Tuam from 94; Can Tuam Cathl from 00; Adn Tuam from 06. *The Rectory, Taylor's Hill, Galway, Republic of Ireland* Tel (00353) (91) 521914 E-mail gryhastings@iol.ie

HASTROP, Paul. b 39. Wells Th Coll 70. d 72 p 73. C Parkstone St Osmund *Sarum* 72-76; C Penzance St Mary w St Paul *Truro* 76-79; V St Blazey 79-87; TV Bournemouth St Pet w St Swithun, H Trin etc *Win* 87-94; TV Thornaby on Tees *York* 94-96; P-in-c Portsea St Sav *Portsm* 96-03; rtd 03. Perm to Offic *Portsm* from 08. *23 Chawton Close, Winchester SO22 6HY* Tel (01962) 883061

HASTWELL, James Sydney. b 37. Roch Th Coll 67. d 69 p 70. C Croydon St Aug *Cant* 69-73; C Hurstpierpoint *Chich* 73-75; P-in-c Twineham 76; P-in-c Sayers Common 76; P-in-c Albourne 76; R Albourne w Sayers Common and Twineham 76-88; V Forest Row 88-94; rtd 97; Perm to Offic *Chich* from 97. *54 Ridgewood Gardens, Bexhill-on-Sea TN40 1TS* Tel (01424) 220510

HASWELL, Jeremy William Drake. b 60. Ridley Hall Cam. d 08. C St Alb St Paul *St Alb* from 08. *46 Brampton Road, St Albans AL1 4PT* Tel (01727) 847236 Mobile 07717-762539 E-mail jeremy@haswells.fsnet.co.uk

HATCH, Canon George Andrew. b 29. Leeds Univ BA. Coll of Resurr Mirfield 51. d 53 p 54. C S Farnborough *Guildf* 53-55; Windward Is 55-63; Barbados from 63; R St Mary Barbados 63 73; Asst Dir Chr Action Development in Caribbean 73-83; R St Jas Barbados 83-94; rtd 94. *St James, Barbados* Tel (001809) 432 0700

HATCH, Richard Francis. b 36. Qu Coll Cam BA60 MA64. Cuddesdon Coll 60. d 62 p 63. C Leigh St Mary *Man* 62 66; PC Peel Green 66-71; V Barton w Peel Green 71-75; Dioc Broadcasting Officer 73-85; R Birch St Jas and Fallowfield 75-78; Lic Preacher 78-08; rtd 01. *c/o Mr P A Macniven, 15 Faircross Way, St Albans AL1 4RT*

HATCHETT, Michael John. b 49. Enfield Coll BSc72 K Coll Lon BD77 AKC77. Linc Th Coll 77. d 78 p 79. C Halstead St Andr *Chelmsf* 78-79; C Halstead St Andr w H Trin and Greenstead Green 79-81; C Greenstead 81-85; V Gt Totham 85-01; R Gt Totham and Lt Totham w Goldhanger 01-06; RD Witham 96-01; Dioc Chapl MU 04-06; R Melton and Ufford *St E* from 06. *The Rectory, 1 Station Road, Melton, Woodbridge IP12 1PX* Tel and fax (01394) 380279 E-mail mikehatchett2004@yahoo.co.uk

HATCHETT, Mrs Ruth Merrick. b 54. K Coll Lon BD77 AKC77 Open Univ BA92. EAMTC 03. d 05 p 06. NSM Tolleshunt Knights w Tiptree and Gt Braxted *Chelmsf* 05-06; NSM Melton and Ufford *St E* from 06. *The Rectory, 1 Station Road, Melton, Woodbridge IP12 1PX* Tel and fax (01394) 380279 E-mail rmhatchett@yahoo.com

HATCHLEY, Canon Walter John. b 24. Lon Univ BA65. Coll of Resurr Mirfield 64. d 66 p 67. C Monkseaton St Pet *Newc* 66-69; C Gosforth All SS 69-72; C Cullercoats St Geo 72; TV 72-78; V Newc St Fran 78 93; RD Newc E 83-92; Hon Can Newc Cathl 90-93; rtd 93; Perm to Offic *Newc* from 93. *4 Woodthorne Road, Jesmond, Newcastle upon Tyne NE2 3PB*

HATCHMAN, Ms Elizabeth Mary. b 63. St Andr Univ MA85. Selly Oak Coll Qu Coll Birm BD92. d 93 p 94. C Aston SS Pet and Paul *Birm* 93-96; C Rowley Regis 96-00; Chapl St Geo Hosp 16 Cen 00-04; Perm to Offic from 05. *21 Westfield Road, Birmingham B14 7SX* Tel 0121-441 2711

HATCHMAN, Hugh Alleyne. b 28. Qu Coll Cam BA52 MA56. Ridley Hall Cam 52. d 54 p 55. C E Twickenham St Steph *Lon* 54-56; C Morden *S'wark* 56-59; E Midl Area Sec CPAS 59-63; V New Catton St Luke *Nor* 63-79; Chapl Bexley Hosp Kent 79-93; rtd 93. *Braemar, North Lyminge, Lyminge, Folkestone CT18 8EF* Tel (01303) 862369

HATFIELD, Rebecca Alison. *See* LUMLEY, Rebecca Alison

HATHAWAY, Canon David Alfred Gerald. b 48. St Mich Coll Llan. d 72 p 73. C Newport St Julian *Mon* 72-74; P-in-c Oakham w Hambleton and Egleton *Pet* 74-77; V Newport St Matt *Mon* 77-83; CF (TA) from 78; V Abertillery *Mon* 83-88; V Rumney from 88; Hon Can St Woolos Cathl 91-05; Can from 05. *The Vicarage, 702 Newport Road, Runney, Cardiff CF3 4DF* Tel (029) 2079 7882

HATHAWAY, John Albert. b 24. Sarum Th Coll 59. d 60 p 61. C Fleet *Guildf* 60-64; C Cowley St Jas *Ox* 64-66; V Holmwood *Guildf* 66-71; V Westborough 71-74; V Newmarket All SS *St E* 74-82; V Acton w Gt Waldingfield 82-85; R W Downland *Sarum* 85-90; rtd 90; Perm to Offic *Sarum* from 94. *12 St Edwards Court, Shaftesbury SP7 8LZ* Tel (01747) 851950

HATHAWAY, Martin Charles. b 48. St Jo Coll Nottm 93. d 95 p 96. C Weddington and Caldecote *Cov* 95-99; V Potters Green 99-04; C The Heyfords w Rousham and Somerton *Ox* 04-05; C Fritwell w Souldern and Ardley w Fewcott 04-05; TV Dunstable *St Alb* from 05. *20 Friars Walk, Dunstable LU6 3JA* Tel (01582) 668996 E-mail revd.martinhathaway@tiscali.co.uk

HATHAWAY, Vivienne Ann. b 57. Bucks Chilterns Univ Coll BSc96. Westcott Ho Cam 00. d 02 p 03. C Bp's Hatfield *St Alb* 02-05; C Bp's Hatfield, Lemsford and N Mymms 05-07; P-in-c Stevenage St Mary Shephall w Aston from 07. *St Mary's Vicarage, 148 Hydean Way, Shephall, Stevenage SG2 9YA* Tel (01438) 351963 E-mail vivienne@vhathaway.freeserve.co.uk

HATHERLEY, Peter Graham. b 46. Univ of Wales (Cardiff) BSc67 PhD70. St Mich Coll Llan 70. d 72 p 73. C Ystrad Mynach *Llan* 72-75; Hon C Tonyrefail 75-88; Perm to Offic from 88. *Treetops, The Derwen, Bridgend CF35 6HD* Tel (01656) 662196

HATHERLEY, Victor Charles. b 17. St Aug Coll Cant 63. d 64 p 64. C Crewkerne *B & W* 64-68; R E Harptree 68-73; R E w W Harptree 73-76; R E w W Harptree and Hinton Blewett 76-82; rtd 82; Perm to Offic *B & W* 83-91 and *Sarum* from 91. *10 Fairview Road, Broadstone BH18 9AX* Tel (01202) 692855

HATHORNE (née MARSH), Mrs Carol Ann. b 44. W Midl Coll of Educn BA83. WMMTC 88. d 91 p 94. Par Dn Wednesbury St Paul Wood Green *Lich* 91-93; NSM Pensnett *Worc* 93-97; TV Cannock *Lich* 97-01; NSM Willenhall H Trin from 05. *Holy Trinity Vicarage, 20 Church Road, Willenhall WV12 5PT* Tel (01922) 476416 E-mail hathorne@btinternet.com

HATHORNE, Mark Stephen. b 51. Boston Univ MDiv76. d 00 p 00. C Willenhall H Trin *Lich* 00-01; TV 01-06; TR from 06; P-in-c Bentley 06-09. *Holy Trinity Vicarage, 20 Church Road, Willenhall WV12 5PT* Tel (01922) 476416 E-mail m.s.hathorne@virgin.net

HATHWAY, Ross Arthur. b 56. Moore Th Coll Sydney BTh86. d 86 p 87. C Tamworth St Pet Australia 87-88; C Corby St Columba *Pet* 89-92; R Null w Angclulgh *B & W* 92-02. R Kellyville St Steph Australia from 03. *45 President Road, Kellyville NSW 2155, Australia* Tel (0061) (2) 9629 6255 E-mail kellyvilleanglican@bigpond.com

HATREY, David Nigel. b 57. SS Mark & Jo Univ Coll Plymouth CertEd79 BEd90 Ex Univ MA01. SWMTC 90. d 93 p 94. NSM S Hill w Callington *Truro* 93-01; Hon C Street w Walton *B & W* from 01. *Pilgrims Way, Chilton Polden Hill, Edington, Bridgwater TA7 9AL* Tel (01278) 723616 E-mail hatreys@micehouse.fsnet.co.uk

HATTAN, Jeffrey William Rowland. b 49. Cranmer Hall Dur 83. d 85 p 86. C Eston w Normanby *York* 85-89; TV 89-95; V Hunmanby w Muston from 95. *The Vicarage, 6 Northgate, Hunmanby, Filey YO14 0NT* Tel (01723) 890294 E-mail jeff@all-saints.freeserve.co.uk

HATTON, Jane Elizabeth. b 53. SAOMC 95. d 98 p 99. NSM Stevenage St Pet Broadwater *St Alb* 98-04; Asst Chapl E and N Herts NHS Trust from 04. *2 Dancote, Park Lane, Knebworth SG3 6PB* Tel (01438) 811039 E-mail janehatton@dial.pipex.com

HATTON, Jeffrey Charles. b 49. K Coll Lon BD70 Bris Univ MA72. Westcott Ho Cam 72 Episc Th Sch Cam Mass 73. d 74 p 75. C Nor St Pet Mancroft 74-78; C Earlham St Anne 78-79; Relig Broadcasting Asst IBA 79-82; Hon C Kensington St Barn *Lon* 79-84; Hon C Fulham All SS 85-89; R Win All SS w Chilcomb and Chesil 89-94; Dioc Communications Officer 89 94; P in-c Salisbury St Thos and St Edm *Sarum* 94-99; R 99-05; rtd 05; Hon C Chalke Valley *Sarum* from 06. *4 Longhill Drive, Salisbury SP2 8TD* Tel (01722) 501409 E-mail charles.hatton51@ntlworld.com

HATTON, Michael Samuel. b 44. St Jo Coll Dur BA72. Cranmer Hall Dur. d 74 p 75. C Dudley St Jas *Worc* 74-75; C N Lynn w St Marg and St Nic *Nor* 75-77; C Walsall Wood *Lich* 78-79; Min Shelfield St Mark CD 79-89; V Middleton St Cross *Ripon* 89-97; V Ingol *Blackb* from 97. *St Margaret's Vicarage, 1A St Margaret's Close, Ingol, Preston PR2 3ZU* Tel (01772) 727208 E-mail spike.ingol@virgin.net

HATTON, Trevor. b 55. Oak Hill Th Coll BA86. d 86 p 87. C Chilwell *S'well* 86-90; R Trowell 90-95; Chapl Nottm Trent Univ

95-99; P-in-c Nottingham St Nic 99-02; R 02-07; rtd 07. *53 Ashchurch Drive, Nottingham NG8 2RB* E-mail trev_ali@tiscali.co.uk

HATTON, Mrs Vivienne Gloria. b 57. Birm Univ BA03. St Jo Coll Nottm MA06. **d** 06 **p** 07. C Wednesfield Heath *Lich* from 06. *2A Victoria Road, Wednesfield, Wolverhampton WV11 1RZ* Tel (01902) 738096 E-mail viviennehatton@blueyonder.co.uk

HATWELL, Timothy Rex. b 53. Oak Hill Th Coll BA85. **d** 85 **p** 86. C Tonbridge St Steph *Roch* 85-90; V Cudham and Downe 90-07; V Falconwood from 07. *The Vicarage, The Green, Welling DA16 2PD* Tel (020) 8298 0065 Mobile 07799-601546 E-mail tim.hatwell@diocese-rochester.org

HAUGHTON, Peter Steele. b 57. K Coll Lon BD84 MA90. Westcott Ho Cam 84. **d** 86 **p** 87. C Cheam Common St Phil *S'wark* 86-90; Chapl Lon Univ Medical Schs 90-94; Educn Adv Lon Univ Medical Schs 94-95; P-in-c Kingston Vale St Jo 95-03; Adv in Ethics and Law K Coll Lon from 03. *95 Bullar Road, Southampton SO18 1GT* Tel 07815-803920 (mobile) E-mail peter.haughton@btinternet.com

HAVARD, Alan Ernest. b 27. Qu Coll Birm 79. **d** 81 **p** 82. NSM Rugby St Matt *Cov* 81-84; C Portishead *B & W* 84-96; V Mickleover All SS *Derby* 86-96; rtd 96; Perm to Offic *Derby* from 96. *7 Headingley Court, Littleover, Derby DE3 6XS*

HAVARD, David William. b 56. Man Univ BA84. Qu Coll Birm 84. **d** 85. C Man Clayton St Cross w St Paul 85-88; Canada 88-02; Perm to Offic *Sheff* from 03. *33 Hallcar Street, Sheffield S4 7JY* Tel 0114-272 9695 E-mail deacondave@onetel.com

HAVELL, Edward Michael. b 38. Dur Univ BA65. Ridley Hall Cam 66. **d** 68 **p** 69. C Ecclesall *Sheff* 68-71; C Roch St Justus 71-74; P-in-c Holbeach Hurn *Linc* 74-75; C Hollington St Jo *Chich* 75-85; TV Rye 85-92; C E Dereham and Scarning *Nor* 92; rtd 93; Perm to Offic *Chich* from 99. *4 Gammons Way, Sedlescombe, Battle TN33 0RQ* Tel (01424) 870864

HAVENS, Mrs Anita Sue. b 44. Univ of Mass BSEd67 Clark Univ (USA) MA72 Hughes Hall Cam BA79. Cranmer Hall Dur MA83. **dss** 84 **d** 87 **p** 94. Gateshead Hosps 84-87; Par Dn Cen Telford *Lich* 87-90; Ind Chapl 87-90; Ind Chapl *Liv* 90-96; TV Man Whitworth 96-99; Chapl Man Univ 96-99; R Birch St Agnes w Longsight St Jo w St Cypr 99-01; rtd 01; Perm to Offic *Carl* from 03. *Stone Cottage, Kirkby Thore, Penrith CA10 1UE* Tel (01768) 362682 E-mail sue.havens@lineone.net

HAVEY, Kenneth Richard. b 61. St Steph Ho Ox 95. **d** 97 **p** 98. C Corringham *Chelmsf* 97-98; C Leigh St Clem 98-02; R from 02. *St Clement's Rectory, 80 Leigh Hill, Leigh-on-Sea SS9 1AR* Tel (01702) 475967 E-mail frkenneth@leighhill.plus.com

HAVILAND, Andrew Mark James. b 65. Leeds Univ BEd87. STETS 02. **d** 05 **p** 06. NSM N Holmwood *Guildf* 05-08; Chapl Bryanston Sch from 08. *Bryanston School, Blandford DT11 0PX* Tel (01258) 452411 Mobile 07855-823255 E-mail amjh@talktalk.net

HAVILAND, Edmund Selwyn. b 24. K Coll Cam BA49 MA51. Wells Th Coll 49. **d** 51 **p** 52. C St Helier *S'wark* 51-55; C-in-c Bermondsey St Hugh CD 55-58; V Ockbrook *Derby* 58-68; V E Peckham *Roch* 68-78; R E Peckham and Nettlestead 78-84; S Africa 84-85; Dep Chapl HM Pris Brixton 85-89; rtd 89; Perm to Offic *Guildf* from 89. *Hill Farm, Thursley, Godalming GU8 6QQ* Tel (01252) 702115

HAWES, Andrew Thomas. b 54. Sheff Univ BA77 Em Coll Cam MA79. Westcott Ho Cam 77. **d** 80 **p** 81. C Gt Grimsby St Mary and St Jas *Linc* 80-84; P-in-c Gedney Drove End 84-86; P-in-c Sutton St Nicholas 84-86; V Lutton w Gedney Drove End, Dawsmere 86-89; V Edenham w Witham on the Hill 89-00; V Edenham w Witham on the Hill and Swinstead from 00; RD Beltisloe from 97. *The Vicarage, Church Lane, Edenham, Bourne PE10 0LS* Tel and fax (01778) 591358

HAWES, The Ven Arthur John. b 43. UEA BA86. Chich Th Coll 65. **d** 68 **p** 69. C Kidderminster St Jo *Worc* 68-72; P-in-c Droitwich 72-76; R Alderford w Attlebridge and Swannington *Nor* 76-92; Chapl Hellesdon and David Rice Hosps and Yare Clinic 76-92; RD Sparham *Nor* 81-91; Mental Health Act Commr 86-94; Hon Can Nor Cathl 88-95; TR Gaywood 92-95; Adn Linc and Can and Preb Linc Cathl 95-08; rtd 08. *49 Thamespoint, Fairways, Teddington TW11 9PP* Tel (020) 8274 2635 Mobile 07808-249834 E-mail arthur.hawes@yahoo.co.uk

HAWES, Joseph Patricius. b 65. St Chad's Coll Dur BA87. St Steph Ho Ox 88. **d** 91 **p** 92. C Clapham Team *S'wark* 91-96; P-in-c Barnes St Mich 96-97; TV Barnes 97-03; V Fulham All SS *Lon* from 03. *All Saints' Vicarage, 70 Fulham High Street, London SW6 3LG* Tel (020) 7371 5202 *or* 7736 6301 E-mail vicarasfulham@aol.com

HAWES, Mary Elizabeth. b 56. SEITE 94. **d** 00 **p** 01. Dioc Children's Adv *Lon* 98-06; Nat Children's Adv Abps' Coun from 06; NSM Streatham St Leon *S'wark* from 00. *9 Roman Rise, London SE19 1JG* Tel (020) 8761 0231 E-mail mary.hawes@c-of-e.org.uk

HAWES, Michael Rowell. b 31. AKC61. **d** 62 **p** 63. C Epsom St Martin *Guildf* 62-65; Chapl RAF 65-86; R Newnham w Nately Scures w Mapledurwell etc *Win* 86-97; rtd 97; Perm to

Offic *Win* from 97. *7 Holly Lane, Ashley, New Milton BH25 5RF* Tel (01425) 620698

HAWES, Ms Rachel. b 54. St Hugh's Coll Ox BA76 MA80. STETS 05. **d** 07 **p** 08. NSM Kensington St Mary Abbots w Ch Ch and St Phil *Lon* from 07. *26 Talbot Road, London W2 5LJ* Tel (020) 7792 3909 Mobile 07768-875590 E-mail rachel.hawes@lawcol.co.uk

HAWKEN, Canon Andrew Robert. b 58. K Coll Lon BD81 AKC81. St Steph Ho Ox 83. **d** 85 **p** 86. C Ex St Dav 85-88; TV Witney *Ox* 88-93; V Benson from 93; AD Aston and Cuddesdon 02-07; Hon Can Ch Ch from 09. *The Vicarage, Church Road, Benson, Wallingford OX10 6SF* Tel and fax (01491) 201668 Mobile 07711-664877 E-mail andrew.hawken@ntlworld.com

HAWKEN, Rosalind Mary. b 56. York Univ BA77 Univ of Wales (Cardiff) BTh02. St Mich Coll Llan 99. **d** 02 **p** 03. C Swansea St Thos and Kilvey *S & B* 02-03; C Gorseinon 03-07. *Society of the Sacred Cross, Tymawr Convent, Lydart, Monmouth NP25 4RN* Tel (01600) 860244

HAWKER, The Ven Alan Fort. b 44. Hull Univ BA65. Clifton Th Coll 65. **d** 68 **p** 69. C Bootle St Leon *Liv* 68-71; C Fazakerley Em 71-73; V Goose Green 73-81; TR Southgate *Chich* 81-98; Can and Preb Chich Cathl 91-98; RD E Grinstead 94-98; Hon Can Bris Cathl from 98; Adn Swindon 98-99; Adn Malmesbury from 99. *Church Paddock, Church Lane, Kington Langley, Chippenham SN15 5NR* Tel (01249) 750085 Fax 750086 E-mail alan.hawker@bristol5.gotadsl.co.uk

HAWKER, Brian Henry. b 34. AKC61 St Boniface Warminster 61. **d** 62 **p** 63. C Hemel Hempstead *St Alb* 62-66; R Stone w Hartwell w Bishopstone *Ox* 66-69; Chapl St Jo Hosp Stone 66-69; V W Wycombe 69-72; Past Consultant Clinical Th Assn 72-83; Past Consultant 83-94; Public Preacher *S'well* 72-76; rtd 94; Perm to Offic *B & W* 76-83; *Truro* 83-90; and *Leic* from 99. *12 Burfield Avenue, Loughborough LE11 3AZ* Tel (01509) 261439

HAWKER, Canon Peter John. b 37. OBE96. Ex Univ BA59. Wycliffe Hall Ox 69. **d** 70 **p** 71. Asst Chapl Berne *Eur* 70-76; Chapl Berne w Neuchâtel 76-89; Adn Switzerland 86-04; Chapl Zürich w St Gallen, Baden and Zug 90-00; Can Brussels Cathl 86-04; rtd 04. *Schulgasse 10, 3280 Murten, Switzerland* Tel (0041) (26) 670 6221 Fax 670 6219 E-mail phawker@anglican.ch

HAWKES, Mrs Cecilia Mary (Cilla). b 48. Reading Univ BSc69 Canley Coll of Educn DipEd71. EAMTC 99. **d** 02 **p** 03. NSM Takeley w Lt Canfield *Chelmsf* from 02; Voc Officer Colchester Area from 08. *Greenfields, Felsted, Dunmow CM6 3LF* Tel and fax (01371) 856480 E-mail cilla@hawkesfarming.co.uk

HAWKES, Mrs Elisabeth Anne. b 56. GRNCM78 PGCE80 Kent Univ MA97. Linc Th Coll 86. **d** 88 **p** 97. Hon Par Dn Finham *Cov* 88-90; Hon Par Dn Bexhill St Pet *Chich* 90-97; Asst to RD Oundle *Pet* 97-98; NSM Oundle 98-01; NSM Benefield and Southwick w Glapthorn 99-00; Perm to Offic *Cant* 00-04; Hon Min Can Cant Cathl from 03; NSM Reculver and Herne Bay St Bart from 04; NSM Hoath H Cross from 04; Dioc Adv in Liturgy from 04. *The Vicarage, 25 Dence Park, Herne Bay CT6 6BQ* Tel and fax (01227) 360948 E-mail liz@hawkes48.freeserve.co.uk

HAWKES, Mrs Helen Vanda. b 50. Surrey Univ BA01. STETS 98. **d** 01 **p** 02. NSM N Hayling St Pet and Hayling Is St Andr *Portsm* 01-05; NSM Bedhampton from 05. *67 East Lodge Park, Farlington, Portsmouth PO16 1BZ* Tel (023) 9221 9005 Mobile 07719-828113 E-mail vanda.hawkes@btinternet.com

HAWKES, Keith Andrew. b 28. Oak Hill Th Coll 72. **d** 74 **p** 75. C Gt Yarmouth *Nor* 74-77; C-in-c Bowthorpe CD 77-83; Chapl Düsseldorf *Eur* 77-83; TV Quidenham *Nor* 83-88; TR 88-90; RD Thetford and Rockland 86-90; R Wickmere w Lt Barningham, Itteringham etc 90-96; Dioc Rural Officer 90-94; P-in-c Saxthorpe w Corpusty, Blickling, Oulton etc 94-96; R Lt Barningham, Blickling, Edgefield etc 96-98; Bp's Chapl 98; rtd 98; Perm to Offic *Nor* 98-00 and from 04; P-in-c Guiltcross 00-02; Chapl Norwich Primary Care Trust 00-02; Chapl Riddlesworth Hall Sch Nor from 04. *Peel Cottage, West Church Street, Kenninghall, Norwich NR16 2EN* Tel and fax (01953) 888533 E-mail revkahawkes@aol.com

HAWKES, Martyn John. b 71. Nottm Univ BA94 St Jo Coll Dur BA01. Cranmer Hall Dur 99. **d** 02 **p** 03. C Is of Dogs Ch Ch and St Jo w St Luke *Lon* 02-05; C Brownswood Park from 05; C Stoke Newington St Mary from 05. *St John's Vicarage, 2A Gloucester Drive, London N4 2LW* Tel (020) 8211 0729 E-mail mj_hawkes@yahoo.co.uk

HAWKES, Nigel Anthony Robert. b 59. UEA BSc80 Edin Univ MSc82. Ripon Coll Cuddesdon 00. **d** 02 **p** 03. C Chase *Ox* 02-04; C Chipping Norton 04-05; TV Dorchester from 05. *The Vicarage, 49 The Green North, Warborough, Wallingford OX10 7DW* Tel (01865) 858381

HAWKES, Ronald Linton. b 54. St Jo Coll York CertEd75 Leeds Univ BEd76 Kent Univ MA96. Linc Th Coll 85. **d** 87 **p** 88. C Finham *Cov* 87-90; TV Bexhill St Pet *Chich* 90-97; V Oundle *Pet* 97-00; P-in-c Benefield and Southwick w Glapthorn 99-00; Dir Post-Ord Tr 98-00; Chapl St Edm Sch Cant 00-03; V Reculver and Herne Bay St Bart *Cant* from 03; P-in-c Hoath H Cross from 04; Hon Min Can Cant Cathl from 01; AD Reculver from 06. *The Vicarage, 25 Dence Park, Herne Bay CT6 6BQ* Tel and fax (01227) 360948 E-mail revronald@hotmail.com

HAWKES, Vanda. *See* HAWKES, Mrs Helen Vanda

HAWKETT, Graham Kenneth. b 20. Bps' Coll Cheshunt 61. **d** 63 **p** 64. C Farncombe *Guildf* 63-67; V Wyke 67-85; rtd 85; Perm to Offic *Guildf* from 85. *Bede House, Beech Road, Haslemere GU27 2BX* Tel (01428) 656430

HAWKEY, James Douglas Thomas. b 79. Girton Coll Cam BA01 MA05 Selw Coll Cam MPhil02 PhD08. Westcott Ho Cam 03 St Thos Aquinas Pontifical Univ Rome 06. **d** 07 **p** 08. C Portsea St Mary *Portsm* from 07. *166 Shearer Road, Portsmouth PO1 5LS* Tel 07919-342457 (mobile) E-mail jamiehawkey@googlemail.com *or* curate@portseaparish.co.uk

HAWKINGS, Timothy Denison. b 55. Ex Univ BA78. St Jo Coll Nottm BA80. **d** 81 **p** 82. C Penn *Lich* 81-85; TV Stafford 85-94; TR Stratton St Margaret w S Marston etc *Bris* 94-05; P-in-c Axbridge w Shipham and Rowberrow *B & W* from 05; P-in-c Mark w Allerton from 08; RD Axbridge from 08. *The Rectory, Cheddar Road, Axbridge BS26 2DL* Tel (01934) 732261

HAWKINS, The Very Revd Alun John. b 44. K Coll Lon BA66 AKC66 Univ of Wales (Ban) BD81. St Deiniol's Hawarden 78. **d** 81 **p** 82. C Dwygyfylchi *Ban* 81-84; R Llanberis 84-89; Tutor Ban Dioc NSM Course 85-90; Dir of Ords *Ban* 86-90; V Knighton and Norton *S & B* 89-93; Chapl Knighton Hosp 89-93; TR Bangor 93-06; Adult Educn Officer from 93; Sec Dioc Bd of Miss from 93; Can Res and Can Missr Ban Cathl 93-00; Adn Ban 00-04; Dean Ban from 04. *The Deanery, Cathedral Close, Glanrafon, Bangor LL57 1LH* Tel (01248) 362840 Fax 353882

HAWKINS, Andrew Robert. b 40. St Andr Univ BSc64. St Chad's Coll Dur BA68. **d** 69 **p** 70. C Sutton St Nic *S'wark* 69-73; C Wimbledon 73-77; TV Cramlington *Newc* 77-81; R Clutton w Cameley *B & W* 81-89; Chapl City of Bath Coll of FE from 89; Perm to Offic *B & W* from 90. *18 Wally Court Road, Chew Stoke, Bristol BS40 8XN* Tel (01275) 332422 E-mail andrewr.hawkins@virgin.net

HAWKINS (née BRAZIER), Mrs Annette Michaela. b 59. Brighton Univ BEd95 Homerton Coll Cam BTh. Ridley Hall Cam 07. **d** 09. C Ore St Helen and St Barn *Chich* from 09. *37 Filsham Road, St Leonards-on-Sea TN38 0PA* Tel (01424) 423859 Mobile 07900-332791 E-mail annette@jhbd.co.uk

HAWKINS, Canon Bruce Alexander. b 44. Qu Coll Ox BA66 MA71. Sarum Th Coll 66. **d** 68 **p** 69. C Epsom St Martin *Guildf* 68-71; Dioc Youth Chapl *Cant* 72-81; Hon Min Can Cant Cathl 73-99; Dep Dir of Educn 81-86; V Walmer 86-05; RD Sandwich 94-00; Hon Can Cant Cathl 99-05; rtd 05; Perm to Offic *Cant* from 05. *88 The Gateway, Dover CT16 1LQ* Tel (01304) 240820

HAWKINS, Canon Clive Ladbrook. b 53. St Pet Coll Ox BA76 MA79. Trin Coll Bris 80. **d** 82 **p** 83. C Win Ch Ch 82-86; R Eastrop from 86; AD Basingstoke 00-08; Hon Can Win Cathl from 05. *Eastrop Rectory, 2A Wallis Road, Basingstoke RG21 3DW* Tel (01256) 355507 *or* 464249 E-mail clive.hawkins@stmarys-basingstoke.org.uk

✠**HAWKINS, The Rt Revd David John Leader.** b 49. Nottm Univ BTh73. St Jo Coll Nottm 69 ALCD73. **d** 73 **p** 74 **c** 02. C Bebington *Ches* 73-76; Nigeria 76-82; C Ox St Aldate w St Matt 83-86; V Leeds St Geo *Ripon* 86-99; TR 99-02; Area Bp Barking *Chelmsf* from 02. *Barking Lodge, 35A Verulam Avenue, London E17 8ES* Tel (020) 8509 7377 Fax 8521 4097 E-mail b.barking@chelmsford.anglican.org

HAWKINS, David Kenneth Beaumont. b 36. Em Coll Saskatoon LTh63. **d** 63 **p** 64. C Northminster Canada 63-69; C Belleville Ch Ch 69-71; I Wellington 71-79; I Barriefield w Pittsburgh 80-85; C St Alb St Paul *St Alb* 85-87; C Hednesford *Lich* 87-92; R Buildwas and Leighton w Eaton Constantine etc 92-95; TV Wrockwardine Deanery 95-01; rtd 01. *PO Box 454, 131 Westward Crescent, Wellington ON K0K 3L0, Canada* Tel (001) (613) 399 5666 E-mail rowenadavid@sympatico.ca

HAWKINS, Donald John. b 39. K Coll Lon BD62 AKC62. St Boniface Warminster 62. **d** 63 **p** 64. C Winlaton *Dur* 63-66; C Gateshead St Mary 66-69; C Ryhope 69-71; R Cockfield 71-79; Chapl N Staffs R Infirmary Stoke-on-Trent 79-89; Chapl Stoke-on-Trent City Gen Hosp 89-93; Chapl Staffs Hosp NHS Trust 93-99; Chapl Co-ord 94-99; rtd 99; Perm to Offic *Lich* from 99. *12 The Avenue, Hartshill, Stoke-on-Trent ST4 6BJ* Tel and fax (01782) 620691 E-mail hawkins@12ave.freeserve.co.uk

HAWKINS, Canon Francis John. b 36. Ex Coll Ox BA61 MA63. Chich Th Coll 59. **d** 61 **p** 62. C Tavistock and Gulworthy *Ex* 61-64; Lect Chich Th Coll 64-73; Vice-Prin 73-75; V E Grinstead St Mary *Chich* 75-81; Can Res and Treas Chich Cathl 81-01; V Sidlesham 81-89; Dir of Ords 89-01; rtd 01; Perm to Offic *Chich* from 01. *6 Priory Road, Chichester PO19 1NS* Tel (01243) 771921

HAWKINS, Ian Clinton. b 27. Roch Th Coll 63. **d** 65 **p** 66. C Boulton *Derby* 65-68; V Cotmanhay 68-77; V Ospringe *Cant* 77-85; P-in-c Eastling 77-85; P-in-c Goodnestone H Cross w

Chillenden and Knowlton 85; P-in-c Womenswold 85; V Nonington w Wymynswold and Goodnestone etc 85-92; rtd 92; Perm to Offic *Derby* from 92. *7 Main Road, Bradwell, Hope Valley S33 9JG* Tel (01433) 621360 E-mail ian.hawkins4@virgin.net

HAWKINS, James Reginald. b 39. Ex Univ BA61 Hull Univ MA00. Westcott Ho Cam 61. **d** 63 **p** 64. C Cannock *Lich* 63-66; C Wem 66-67; C Cheddleton 67-69; R Yoxall 69-77; R The Quinton *Birm* 77-84; V Bosbury w Wellington Heath etc *Heref* 84-96; P-in-c Ancaster Wilsford Gp *Linc* 96-99; R 99-04; RD Loveden 97-03; rtd 04. *14 Pound Pill, Corsham SN13 9JA* Tel (01249) 715353 E-mail james.hawkins39@btopenworld.com

HAWKINS, John Arthur. b 45. Kelham Th Coll 64. **d** 69 **p** 70. C Cov St Alb 70-73; C Fletchamstead 73-77; V Whitley 77-81; TV Northampton Em *Pet* 81-90; TV Gt Chesham *Ox* 90-98; C Thorpe St Andr *Nor* from 98. *8 Hampden Drive, Thorpe St Andrew, Norwich NR7 0UT* Tel (01603) 431868

HAWKINS, John Charles Lacey. b 18. Linc Th Coll 40. **d** 42 **p** 43. C Dalton-in-Furness *Carl* 42-44; C Workington St Mich 44-48; V Allonby w W Newton 48-53; V Thornton w Allerthorpe *York* 53-60; R Stockton-on-the-Forest w Holtby and Warthill 60-77; R Sigglesthorne and Rise w Nunkeeling and Bewholme 77-83; rtd 83; Perm to Offic *York* 83-96. *4 Bromley College, London Road, Bromley BR1 1PE* Tel (020) 8460 1469

HAWKINS, John Colin. b 50. SEITE 97. **d** 00 **p** 01. NSM W Wickham St Jo *S'wark* 00-04; P-in-c Burwash Weald *Chich* from 04. *The Vicarage, Burwash Common, Etchingham TN19 7NA* Tel (01435) 883287 E-mail john.c.hawkins@btinternet.com

HAWKINS, John Edward Inskipp. b 63. K Coll Lon BD85. Qu Coll Birm 86. **d** 88 **p** 89. C Birchfield *Birm* 88-92; C Poplar *Lon* 92-93; TV 93-99; V W Hendon St Jo from 99; P-in-c Colindale St Matthias from 07; AD W Barnet from 04. *St John's Vicarage, Vicarage Road, London NW4 3PX* Tel and fax (020) 8202 8606 E-mail jeih.stj@aladdinscave.org

HAWKINS, Jonathan Desmond. b 53. FRICS93. Ox Min Course 04. **d** 07 **p** 08. NSM Walton H Trin *Ox* from 07. *22 Limes Avenue, Aylesbury HP21 7HA* Tel (01296) 428631 Fax 339239 Mobile 07976-281699 E-mail jon@jdhawkins.co.uk

HAWKINS, Nicholas Milner. b 45. Univ of Wales (Swansea) BA MSc. **d** 01. Par Dn Dingestow and Llangovan w Penyclawdd etc *Mon* 01-02; Perm to Offic *Ban* 02-03; NSM Nefyn w Tudweiliog w Llandudwen w Edern 03-08; P-in-c Botwnnog w Bryncroes w Llangwnnadl w Penllech from 08. *Bryn Mor, Llangwnadl, Pwllheli LL53 8NS* Tel (01758) 770582 Fax 770228 Mobile 07870-264385 E-mail nick.hawkins@btinternet.com

HAWKINS, Noel. b 46. St Jo Coll Nottm 82. **d** 84 **p** 85. C Worksop St Jo *S'well* 84-86; C Wollaton Park 86-89; TV Billericay and Lt Burstead *Chelmsf* 89-95; TV Keynsham *B & W* 95-00; V Brislington St Chris and St Cuth 00-08; V Brislington St Chris from 09; P-in-c Hengrove from 06. *The Vicarage, 35 Wick Crescent, Bristol BS4 4HG* Tel 0117-977 6351 E-mail noel-lynda@hawkins99.freeserve.co.uk

HAWKINS, Miss Patricia Sally. b 59. LMH Ox BA80 MA84 Ex Univ BPhil85 Ox Univ BTh04 CQSW85. St Steph Ho Ox 99. **d** 01 **p** 02. C Stafford *Lich* 01-04; V Oxley from 04; AD Wolverhampton from 08. *The Vicarage, Lymer Road, Oxley, Wolverhampton WV10 6AA* Tel (01902) 783342 E-mail pathawkins@btinternet.com

HAWKINS, Paul Henry Whishaw. b 46. Ex Coll Ox BA68 MA74 SS Coll Cam MA84. St Steph Ho Ox 70. **d** 72 **p** 73. C Fawley *Win* 72-75; C Ealing St Steph Castle Hill *Lon* 75-77; P-in-c Dorney *Ox* 77-78; TV Riverside 78-81; Chapl SS Coll Cam 82-87; V Plymstock *Ex* 87-97; RD Plymouth Sutton 91-96; TR Plymstock and Hooe 97-00; Preb Ex Cathl 98-00; P-in-c St Pancras w St Jas and Ch Ch *Lon* 00-02; V from 02. *St Pancras Vicarage, 6 Sandwich Street, London WC1H 9PL* Tel (020) 7388 1630 *or* tel and fax 7388 1461 E-mail st.pancras@lineone.net

HAWKINS, Peter Edward. b 35. Leeds Univ BA60. Coll of Resurr Mirfield 60. **d** 62 **p** 63. C Forest Gate St Edm *Chelmsf* 62-65; C Sevenoaks St Jo *Roch* 65-68; Chapl Metrop Police Cadet Corps Tr Sch 68-73; P-in-c Knowle H Nativity *Bris* 73; TV Knowle 73-79; V Westbury-on-Trym H Trin 79-87; TR Solihull *Birm* 87-96; Hon Can Birm Cathl 92-96; rtd 00. *Back Street Cottage, 15 St Andrew's Road, Stogursey, Bridgwater TA5 1TE* Tel and fax (01278) 733635 E-mail peh.stogursey@tiscali.uk

HAWKINS, Peter Michael. b 38. Kelham Th Coll 58. **d** 63 **p** 64. India 63-69; Asn Miss to Calcutta 64-66; C Calcutta Cathl 64-66; C-in-c Kidderpore 66-68; V Asansol w Burnpur 68-69; C Manningham St Paul and St Jude *Bradf* 70-72; C Bradf Cathl 72-75; V Allerton 75-90; V Pet H Spirit Bretton 90-07; P-in-c Marholm 90-95; rtd 07. *Belle Vue Nord, Mane Guelo, 56690 Landaul, France* Tel (0033) (2) 97 59 90 83 E-mail peter.hawkins@orange.fr

HAWKINS, Richard Randal. b 39. **d** 65 **p** 66. C Bushbury *Lich* 65-68; V Woodford St Mary *Chelmsf* 68-71; S Africa from 71; rtd 04. *7 Chapter Close, 6 Taunton Road, Pietermaritzburg, 3201 South Africa*

✠**HAWKINS, The Rt Revd Richard Stephen.** b 39. Ex Coll Ox BA61 MA65 Ex Univ BPhil76. St Steph Ho Ox 61. **d** 63 **p** 64

c 88. C Ex St Thos 63-66; C Clyst St Mary 66-75; TV Clyst St George, Aylesbeare, Clyst Honiton etc 75-78; TV Cen Ex 78-81; Bp's Officer for Min and Jt Dir Ex and Truro NSM Scheme 78-81; Dioc Dir of Ords 79-81; Adn Totnes 81-88; P-in-c Oldridge and Whitestone 81-87; Suff Bp Plymouth 88-96; Suff Bp Crediton 96-04; rtd 04; Hon Asst Bp Ex from 05. *3 Westbrook Close, Exeter EX4 8BS* Tel (01392) 462622

HAWKINS, Richard Whishaw. b 51. Coll of Resurr Mirfield 93. **d** 95 **p** 96. C Weymouth H Trin *Sarum* 95-99; P-in-c Hey *Man* 99-06; TR Medlock Head from 06; AD Rochdale 03-09. *St John's Vicarage, 1 Owen Fold, Oldham OL4 3DT* Tel 0161-626 3630 E-mail richard.hawkins107@ntlworld.com

HAWKINS, Roger David William. b 33. K Coll Lon BD58 AKC58. **d** 59 **p** 60. C Twickenham St Mary *Lon* 59-61; C Heston 61-64; C Dorking w Ranmore *Guildf* 64-65; V Mitcham St Mark *S'wark* 65-74; V Redhill St Matt 74-91; P-in-c Warlingham w Chelsham and Farleigh 91-97; TR 97-98; rtd 98. *2 Grove Court, Falkland Grove, Dorking RH4 3DL* Tel (01306) 885817

HAWKINS, Roger Julian. b 32. Ripon Hall Ox 59. **d** 61 **p** 62. C-in-c Newall Green CD *Man* 61-63; Chapl RAF 63-67; R Mawgan in Pyder *Truro* 67-75; R Lanteglos by Camelford w Advent 75-78; R Newmarket St Mary w Exning St Agnes *St E* 78-85; P-in-c Coltishall w Gt Hautbois *Nor* 85-87; R Coltishall w Gt Hautbois and Horstead 87-90; Chapl Whiteley Village *Guildf* 90-94; rtd 97; Perm to Offic *Win* 01-02 and *Sarum* 02-08. *3 Norman Cockaday Court, Holt NR25 6JA* Tel (01263) 710004

HAWKINS, Steven Andrew. b 51. Nottm Univ BEd75 Open Univ BSc91 Bris Poly ADEd90. STETS 95. **d** 98 **p** 99. C Horfield H Trin *Bris* 98-02; V Brislington St Anne 02-08; P-in-c Knowle St Martin from 08. *St Martin's Vicarage, 46 St Martin's Road, Bristol BS4 2NG* Tel 0117-977 6275 Mobile 07929-485006 E-mail fr.stevenhawkins@googlemail.com

HAWKINS, Susan. b 47. Doncaster Coll of Educn CertEd69 Ches Coll of HE BTh99. NOC 95. **d** 99 **p** 00. NSM Prestbury *Ches* 99-02; P-in-c Marthall and Chapl David Lewis Cen for Epilepsy 02-09; rtd 09; Perm to Offic *Ches* from 09. *3 Thorne Close, Prestbury, Macclesfield SK10 4DE* Tel (01625) 829833 E-mail dvs.hawkins@btinternet.com

HAWKINS, Timothy St John. b 59. CCC Ox BA82. Trin Coll Bris BA87. **d** 87 **p** 88. C Cheltenham St Mary, St Matt, St Paul and H Trin *Glouc* 87-90; C Cowplain *Portsm* 90-94; V Pennycross *Ex* 94-96; P-in-c St Keverne *Truro* 96-05; P-in-c Gulval and Madron from 05. *The Vicarage, Church Road, Madron, Penzance TR20 8SW* Tel (01736) 360992 E-mail revtimhawkins@hotmail.co.uk

HAWKINS, William Arthur. b 18. Clifton Th Coll 50. **d** 53 **p** 54. C Ellacombe *Ex* 53-54; C Totnes 54-58; R Ashill w Broadway *B & W* 58-74; R Herstmonceux *Chich* 74-83; rtd 83; Perm to Offic *Chich* from 84. *Three Gables, 17 Heighton Road, Newhaven BN9 0RB* Tel (01273) 513694

HAWKSWORTH, Maldwyn Harry. b 45. Aston Univ CertEd74. St Jo Coll Nottm 87. **d** 89 **p** 90. C Penn *Lich* 89-94; TV Bloxwich 94-09; P-in-c Yoxall from 09; Local Min Adv (Wolverhampton) from 09. *The Rectory, Savey Lane, Yoxall, Burton-on-Trent DE13 8PD* Tel (01543) 473202

HAWKSWORTH, Peter John Dallas. b 54. St Jo Coll Ox BA75 MA79 Solicitor 79. Sarum & Wells Th Coll 89. **d** 91 **p** 92. C Warminster St Denys, Upton Scudamore etc *Sarum* 91-95; P-in-c Salisbury St Mark 95-99; V 99-05; RD Salisbury 03-05; Perm to Offic from 07. *Little Acre, Tollard Road, Winterslow, Salisbury SP5 1PY* E-mail onehundredkilos@btinternet.com

HAWLEY, Canon Anthony Broughton. b 41. St Pet Coll Ox BA67 MA71. Westcott Ho Cam 67. **d** 69 **p** 70. C Wolverhampton St Pet *Lich* 69-72; C-in-c Bermondsey St Hugh CD *S'wark* 73-84; Hon PV S'wark Cathl 83-84; TR Kirkby *Liv* 84-02; AD Walton 93-02; Hon Can Liv Cathl 96-02; Can Res Liv Cathl from 02. *2 Cathedral Close, Liverpool L1 7BR* Tel 0151-708 0932 or 709 6271 E-mail canon.hawley@liverpoolcathedral.org.uk

HAWLEY, Georgina. b 45. **d** 01 **p** 02. Australia 01-02 and from 07; NSM Chippenham St Pet *Bris* 02-03; Perm to Offic 03-07. *32A Wishart Street, Gwelup WA 6018, Australia* Tel (0061) (8) 9446 4021 E-mail georginahawley@hotmail.co.uk

HAWLEY, The Ven John Andrew. b 50. K Coll Lon BD71 AKC71. Wycliffe Hall Ox 72. **d** 74 **p** 75. C Kingston upon Hull H Trin *York* 74-77; C Bradf Cathl Par 77-80; V Woodlands *Sheff* 80-91; TR Dewsbury *Wakef* 91-02; Hon Can Wakef Cathl 98-02; Adn Blackb from 02. *19 Clarence Park, Blackburn BB2 7FA* Tel (01254) 262571 Pager 07623-110608 Fax (01254) 263394 E-mail archdeacon.blackburn@milestonenet.co.uk

HAWLEY, William David Llewellyn. b 41. Univ of W Aus BCom77 Murdoch Univ Aus BD94. **d** 92 **p** 95. Hon C Bullcreek w Bateman Australia 92-94; Hon C Kwinana 94-95; Dioc Registrar and Assoc P Spearwood w Hilton 95-98; R Hilton 98-00; TV By Brook *Bris* 01-07; C Colerne w N Wraxall 06-07; rtd 07. *32A Wishart Street, Gwelup WA 6018, Australia* Tel (0061) (8) 9446 4021

HAWNT, John Charles Frederick. b 30. Westwood Cen Zimbabwe 72. **d** 75 **p** 76. Zimbabwe 75-81; C Rugby *Cov* 81-85; R Lydeard St Lawrence w Brompton Ralph etc *B & W* 85-00; rtd

00. *39 St Andrew Road, Houghton, Johannesburg, 2198 South Africa* Tel (0027) (11) 487 3259

HAWORTH (née ARMSTRONG), Fiona Heather. b 65. Reading Univ BSc86 Nottm Univ PhD90. St Jo Coll Nottm BTh94. **d** 97 **p** 98. C Sutton in Ashfield St Mary *S'well* 97-02; TV Kidderminster St Mary and All SS w Trimpley etc *Worc* 02-09; Chapl Worc Univ from 09. *Address temp unknown*

HAWORTH, Julie. b 59. St Mich Coll Llan. **d** 09. C Wigan All SS and St Geo *Liv* from 09. *63 Kendal Street, Wigan WN6 7DJ*

HAWORTH, Mark Newby. b 50. Aber Univ BSc73 MICFor81. Westcott Ho Cam 88. **d** 90 **p** 91. C Cherry Hinton St Andr *Ely* 90-93; C Teversham 90-93; P-in-c Swaffham Bulbeck and Swaffham Prior w Reach 93-94; V 94-02; Sub Warden of Readers 95-02; RD Fordham 96-02; Chapl Framlingham Coll 03; Chapl to Bp Pet 03-05; TR Pendleton *Man* 05-09; P-in-c Lower Kersal 06-09; TR Salford All SS from 09. *The Rectory, 92 Fitzwarren Street, Salford M6 5RS* Tel 0161-745 7608 Mobile 07932-160009 E-mail father.mark@virgin.net

HAWORTH, Paul. b 47. G&C Coll Cam BA68 MA72. Westcott Ho Cam 75. **d** 78 **p** 79. C Hornchurch St Andr *Chelmsf* 78-81; C Loughton St Mary and St Mich 81-88; TV Waltham H Cross 88-92; TR Becontree S 92-00; P-in-c S Woodham Ferrers from 00. *The Vicarage, 18 Victoria Road, South Woodham Ferrers, Chelmsford CM3 5LR* Tel (01245) 322134 E-mail preacherman@pewend.org

HAWORTH, Stanley Robert. b 48. St Jo Coll Dur BA69. Sarum & Wells Th Coll 71. **d** 73 **p** 74. C Skipton H Trin *Bradf* 73-76; C Bradf Cathl 76-78; C Grantham *Linc* 78; TV 78-82; V Deeping St James 82-96; V Middlewich w Byley *Ches* 96-01; P-in-c Forcett and Aldbrough and Melsonby *Ripon* from 01; Adn Richmond from 08. *The Vicarage, 1 Appleby Close, Aldbrough St John, Richmond DL11 7TT* Tel (01325) 374634 E-mail stantherevman@hotmail.com

HAWORTH, Stuart. b 43. **d** 94 **p** 95. OLM Bradshaw *Man* 94-01; OLM Turton Moorland Min 01-08; rtd 08. *178 Turton Road, Bolton BL2 3EE* Tel (01204) 594506

HAWRISH, Mary-Beth Louise Ladine. **d** 09. OLM Oxshott *Guildf* from 09. *Cedar House, Sandy Lane, Cobham KT11 2EP* Tel (01932) 864695 E-mail mhawrish@yahoo.co.uk

HAWTHORN, The Ven Christopher John. b 36. Qu Coll Cam BA60 MA64. Ripon Hall Ox 60. **d** 62 **p** 63. C Sutton St Jas *York* 62-66; V Kingston upon Hull St Nic 66-72; V E Coatham 72-79; V Scarborough St Martin 79-91; RD Scarborough 82-91; Can and Preb York Minster 87-01; Adn Cleveland 91-01; rtd 01; Perm to Offic *York* from 01. *43 Barley Rise, Strensall, York YO32 5AB* Tel (01904) 492060

HAWTHORN, David. b 63. Chich Th Coll 87. **d** 90 **p** 91. C Hartlepool H Trin *Dur* 90-94; C Middlesbrough All SS *York* 94-95; P-in-c Thornaby on Tees 95-96; V S Thornaby 96-02; P-in-c Brighton Annunciation *Chich* 02-04; V Hollinwood and Limeside *Man* from 04. *St Margaret's Vicarage, 61 Chapel Road, Oldham OL8 4QQ* Tel and fax 0161-681 4541 E-mail hawthorn@supanet.com

HAWTHORN, Philip Alan. b 58. Essex Univ BSc79. Ripon Coll Cuddesdon 05. **d** 07 **p** 08. C Hardington Vale *B & W* from 07. *38 Church Lane, Rode, Frome BA11 6PN* Tel (01373) 831234 Mobile 07973-350560 E-mail philiphawthorn@btinternet.com

HAWTHORN, Thomas Russell. b 18. MBE90. Imp Coll Lon BSc48. **d** 82 **p** 82. Mexico 82-84; Perm to Offic *Nor* from 84; Sub Chapl HM Pris Blundeston 86-94. *82 Wollaston Road, Lowestoft NR32 2PF* Tel (01502) 518741

HAWTHORNE, Canon Andrew. b 68. Jes Coll Ox BA89 MA93 K Coll Lon PhD04. Chich Th Coll BTh93. **d** 93 **p** 94. C Christchurch *Win* 93-97; TV Dorchester *Sarum* 97-00; rtd 00; Hon Can Kinkizi from 04; C Christchurch *Win* from 05. *68 Arnewood Road, Southbourne, Bournemouth BH6 5DN* Tel (01202) 569163 E-mail andrewahawthorne@aol.com

HAWTHORNE, John William. b 32. St Aug Coll Cant 74. **d** 77 **p** 78. C Boxley *Cant* 77-80; P-in-c Otham 80-82; P-in-c Langley 80-82; R Otham w Langley 82-83; TR Preston w Sutton Poyntz and Osmington w Poxwell *Sarum* 83-87; R Tetbury w Beverston *Glouc* 87-01; rtd 01; Perm to Offic *Ex* from 02. *19 Long Street, Devizes SN10 1NN* Tel (01380) 728056 E-mail honitonhawthorne@aol.com

HAWTHORNE, Canon William James (Jim). b 46. MBE01. TCD 66 Ch of Ireland Tr Coll 66. **d** 69 **p** 70. C Gilnahirk *D & D* 69-72; Asst Chapl Miss to Seamen 72-76; C Boultham *Linc* 76-78; C Bracebridge Heath 78-90; Dioc Adv for Relig Broadcasting 80-90; Chapl Palma de Mallorca and Balearic Is *Eur* 90-93; Chapl Palma de Mallorca 93-01; P-in-c Menorca 97-98; Can Gib Cathl 97-01; rtd 01. *16-08 Victoria Centre, Milton Street, Nottingham NG1 3PL* Tel 0115-840 7913 E-mail williamjameshawthorne@hotmail.com

✠**HAWTIN, The Rt Revd David Christopher.** b 43. Keble Coll Ox BA65 MA70. Wm Temple Coll Rugby 65 Cuddesdon Coll 66. **d** 67 **p** 68 **c** 99. C Pennywell St Thos and Grindon St Oswald CD *Dur* 67-71; C Stockton St Pet 71-74; C-in-c Leam Lane CD 74-79; R Washington 79-88; Dioc Ecum Officer 88-91; Adn Newark *S'well* 92-99; Suff Bp Repton *Derby* 99-06; rtd 06; Hon

Asst Bp Sheff from 07. *162 Greenhill Avenue, Sheffield S8 7TF*
Tel 0114-274 0006

HAY, David Frederick. b 38. MA67. Qu Coll Birm 82. **d** 84 **p** 85. C
Prenton *Ches* 84-88; V Stockport St Sav 88-96; P-in-c Gt
Saughall 96-03; rtd 03; Perm to Offic *Ches* from 04; Hon Min
Can Ches Cathl from 04. *2 Moel View Road, Buckley CH7 2BT*
Tel (01244) 541342

HAY, Ian Gordon. b 52. Dundee Univ MA73 Edin Univ BD76
CertEd84. Edin Th Coll 73. **d** 76 **p** 77. C Dumfries *Glas* 76-79;
Dioc Chapl *Bre* 79-81; R Brechin 81-85; Asst Chapl H Trin Sch
Halifax 85-88; Dioc Youth Officer *Carl* 89-98; Sen Development
Worker Youth Link Scotland from 98. *The Ross House,
Pittendreich, Kinross KY13 9HD* Tel (01592) 840820
E-mail youthlink-scot@sol.co.uk

HAY, Jack Barr. b 31. Bps' Coll Cheshunt 57. **d** 60 **p** 61. C Byker
St Ant *Newc* 60-63; C Killingworth 63-68; V Cowgate 68-77; V
Woodhorn w Newbiggin 77-96; rtd 96; Perm to Offic *Newc* from
96. *7 Glebelands, Corbridge NE45 5DS* Tel (01434) 632979

HAY, Joanna Jane Louise. *See* DOBSON, Mrs Joanna Jane
Louise

HAY, John. b 43. St D Coll Lamp 63. **d** 67 **p** 68. C Ynyshir *Llan*
67-70; C Cardiff St Mary and St Steph w St Dyfrig etc 70-74; V
Llanwynno 74-78; P-in-c Weston-super-Mare All SS *B & W*
78-80; TV Weston-super-Mare Cen Par 80-85; P-in-c
Handsworth St Mich *Birm* 85-86; NSM Eastbourne St Sav and
St Pet *Chich* 88-91; V Buckley *St As* 91-96; P-in-c Ardwick
St Benedict *Man* 96-99; C Hollinwood and Oldham St Chad
Limeside 99-01; rtd 01. *1 Rothesay House, 21 Clyde Road,
St Leonards-on-Sea TN38 0QE*

HAY, The Very Revd John. b 45. CITC 77. **d** 79 **p** 80. C
Newtownards *D & D* 79-81; I Galloon w Drummully *Clogh*
81-89; I Donacavey w Barr 89-03; Can Clogh Cathl 91-03; Dean
Raphoe *D & R* from 03; I Raphoe w Raymochy and Clonleigh
from 03. *Maranatha, The Deanery, Raphoe, Lifford, Co Donegal,
Republic of Ireland* Tel (00353) (74) 914 5226 *or* (028) 8284 0377
E-mail dean@raphoe.anglican.org
or johnhayraphoe@eircom.net

HAY, Miss Lesley Jean Hamilton. b 48. St Andr Univ MA71.
Westcott Ho Cam 04 Yale Div Sch 05. **d** 06 **p** 07. C Shrivenham
and Ashbury *Ox* 06-08; C Bethany USA 08; Asst R Hamden
from 08. *Address temp unknown*
E-mail lesley.hay@ukonline.co.uk

HAY, Margaret Ann. b 47. Brunel Univ BTech71 W Sussex Inst of
HE PGCE95. STETS 02. **d** 05 **p** 06. NSM Elson *Portsm* from 05.
Bodinnick, 12 Longwater Drive, Gosport PO12 2UP Tel (023)
9234 3303

HAY, Canon Nicholas John. b 56. Sheff Poly BSc85. St Jo Coll
Nottm 85. **d** 88 **p** 89. C Blackb Redeemer 88-91; C Hellesdon
Nor 91-95; R Wistford *Chelmsf* 95-01; Sen Chapl HM Pris
Ashfield from 01; Hon Can Bris Cathl from 09. *HMP Prison and
YOI Ashfield, Shortwood Road, Pucklechurch, Bristol BS16 9QJ*
Tel 0117-303 8128 *or* 303 8000
E-mail chaplaincy@premiercustodial.com

HAY, Richard. b 42. CMG92. Ball Coll Ox BA63. Cranmer Hall
Dur 94. **d** 96 **p** 97. C Hastings St Clem and All SS *Chich* 96-99; V
Addlestone *Guildf* 99-07; RD Runnymede 02-07; rtd 07; Perm to
Offic *Guildf* from 07. *15 Fox Close, Woking GU22 8LP* Tel
(01932) 343585 E-mail richard.hay3@btinternet.com

HAYCOCK, Edward. d 09. OLM Gnosall and Moreton *Lich* from
09. *390 New Inn Lane, Stoke-on-Trent ST4 8BW* Tel (01782)
641867

HAYCRAFT, Roger Brian Norman. b 43. Oak Hill Th Coll 69.
d 73 **p** 74. C Belsize Park *Lon* 73-76; C Yardley St Edburgha
Birm 76-79; V Hornchurch H Cross *Chelmsf* 79-03; rtd 03; Perm
to Offic *Chelmsf* from 04. *12 Hannards Way, Hainault IG6 3TB*
Tel (020) 8501 1718

HAYDAY, Canon Alan Geoffrey David. b 46. Kelham Th Coll 65.
d 69 **p** 70. C Evington *Leic* 69-72; C Spalding *Linc* 72-78; V
Cherry Willingham w Greetwell 78-86; RD Lawres 84-86; TR
Brumby 86-02; RD Manlake 93-99; Can and Preb Linc Cathl
00-02; Dean St Chris Cathl Bahrain 02-09; rtd 09. *22 Kestral
Drive, Louth LN11 0GE* E-mail windhover22@live.co.uk

HAYDEN, Carol Toni. b 64. NOC. **d** 05 **p** 06. NSM Ainsworth
Man 05-09; NSM Bury St Pet from 09. *38 Launceston Road,
Radcliffe, Manchester M26 3UN* Tel 0161-724 0514
E-mail revchayden@aol.com

HAYDEN, The Ven David Frank. b 47. Lon Univ BD71. Tyndale
Hall Bris 67. **d** 71 **p** 72. C Silverhill St Matt *Chich* 71-75; C
Galleywood Common *Chelmsf* 75-79; R Redgrave cum
Botesdale w Rickinghall *St E* 79-84; RD Hartismere 81-84; V
Cromer *Nor* 84-02; P-in-c Gresham 84-98; Chapl Cromer and
Distr Hosp Norfolk 84-94; Chapl Norfolk and Nor Health Care
NHS Trust 94-00; Chapl Fletcher Hosp Norfolk 85-00; RD
Repps *Nor* 95-02; Hon Can Nor Cathl from 96; Adn Norfolk
from 02. *8 Boulton Road, Thorpe St Andrew, Norwich NR7 0DF*
Tel and fax (01603) 702477
E-mail archdeacon.norfolk@4frontmedia.co.uk

HAYDEN, Eric Henry Ashmore. b 26. ACII65. Sarum & Wells Th
Coll 71. **d** 73 **p** 74. C Horsham *Chich* 73-78; V Cuckfield 78-92;

rtd 92; P-in-c Tilshead, Orcheston and Chitterne *Sarum* 92-97;
Perm to Offic *Sarum* and *Ox* 98-08. *3 Heather Bank, Haywards
Heath RH16 1HY* Tel (01444) 412169

✠**HAYDEN, The Rt Revd John Donald.** b 40. Lon Univ BD62.
Tyndale Hall Bris 63. **d** 65 **p** 66 **c** 04. C Macclesfield Ch Ch *Ches*
65-68; C H Spirit Cathl Dodoma Tanzania 68-69; V Moshi
70-77; Home Sec USCL 77-83; TV Ipswich St Mary at Stoke w
St Pet *St E* 83-94; P-in-c Bury St Edmunds St Mary 94-99; V
99-04; Asst Bp Mt Kilimanjaro from 04; Hon Asst Bp Ches from
08. *45 Birkenhead Road, Meols, Wirral CH47 5AF* Tel 0151-632
0448 E-mail johnhayden@dsl.pipex.com

HAYDEN, Canon Mark Joseph James. b 68. St Thos Aquinas
Pontifical Univ Rome BD93. H Cross Coll Clonliffe 88. **d** 92
p 93. In RC Ch 92-99; C Monkstown *D & G* 99-01; I Gorey w
Kilnahue, Leskinfere and Ballycanew *C & O* from 01; Can Treas
Ferns Cathl from 07. *The Rectory, The Avenue, Gorey, Co
Wexford, Republic of Ireland* Tel and fax (00353) (53) 942 1383
E-mail gorey@ferns.anglican.org

HAYDOCK, Canon Alan. b 41. Kelham Th Coll 60. **d** 65 **p** 66. C
Rainworth *S'well* 65-68; C Hucknall Torkard 68-71; TV 71-74; V
Bilborough St Jo 74-80; R E Bridgford 80-82; R E Bridgford and
Kneeton 82-06; RD Bingham 84-94; Hon Can S'well Minster
86-06; rtd 06. *29 The Teasels, Bingham, Nottingham NG13 8TY*
Tel (01949) 875805 Mobile 07944-569661

HAYDON, Keith Frank. b 46. Cuddesdon Coll 73. **d** 75 **p** 76. C De
Beauvoir Town St Pet *Lon* 75-77; C Wells St Thos w Horrington
B & W 77-80; TV Weston-super-Mare Cen Par 80-84; TV
Cowley St Jas *Ox* 84-87; TR 87-95; V Walsingham, Houghton
and Barsham *Nor* 95-96; P-in-c 96-99; rtd 01; Hon C Sutton on
Plym *Ex* from 09; Hon C Plymouth St Simon and St Mary from
09; C Sutton on Plym from 09; C Plymouth St Simon and
St Mary from 09. *Address withheld by request*

HAYE, Alfred Kirby. b 40. Lon Univ BA67 Saltley Tr Coll Birm
TCert65. **d** 05 **p** 06. OLM Delaval *Newc* 05-09; C Salcombe and
Malborough w S Huish *Ex* from 09. *The Vicarage, Marlborough,
Kingsbridge TQ7 3RR* E-mail kirby@haye1.fsnet.co.uk

HAYES, Brian Richard Walker. b 33. Qu Coll Birm 81. **d** 83 **p** 84.
C Cheadle Hulme All SS *Ches* 83-87; C Sheff St Cecilia Parson
Cross 87-88; C Sheff St Leon Norwood 88-91; V Gazeley w
Dalham, Moulton and Kentford *St E* 91-02; P-in-c Higham
Green 98-02; rtd 02; Hon C W Felton *Lich* 02-07; Perm to Offic
from 07. *8 Lutton Close, Oswestry SY11 2GZ*
E-mail brianhayes@cwcom.net

HAYES, Bruce John. b 75. UCD BA97 TCD BTh01. CITC 98.
d 01 **p** 02. C Cregagh *D & D* 01-04; I Abbeystrewry Union
C, C & R from 04; Warden of Readers from 08. *The Rectory,
Coronea Drive, Skibbereen, Co Cork, Republic of Ireland* Tel
(00353) (28) 21234 E-mail abbeystrewryunion@eircom.net

HAYES, Carmen Miranda. b 61. TCD BTh08. **d** 08 **p** 09. C
Portadown St Mark *Arm* from 08. *Killynoomain Drive,
Portadown, Craigavon BT63 5JJ* Tel (028) 3833 5813 Mobile
07907-579913 E-mail carmenmirandahayes@hotmail.com

HAYES, Christopher John. b 64. Univ of Wales IN Leeds Univ
MA RGN. Cranmer Hall Dur. **d** 96 **p** 97. C Burton Fleming w
Fordon, Grindale etc *York* 96-99; R Buckrose Carrs 99-06;
P-in-c Weaverthorpe w Helperthorpe, Luttons Ambo etc 03-06;
C Heworth Ch Ch 06-07. *Address temp unknown*
E-mail chris@buckrose.org.uk

HAYES, David Malcolm Hollingworth. b 42. K Coll Lon BD68
AKC68 MPhil97. **d** 69 **p** 70. C Upper Teddington SS Pet and
Paul 69-70; C Ruislip St Martin 70-75; P-in-c Ludford *Heref*
75-80; P-in-c Ashford Carbonell w Ashford Bowdler 75-80; V
Eastcote St Lawr *Lon* 80-90; R Cant St Pet w St Alphege and
St Marg etc 90-07; P-in-c Blean 03-07; Master Eastbridge Hosp
90-07; Guardian of the Greyfriars 97-07; rtd 07. *Forge Cottage,
3 North Row, Warminster BA12 9AD* Tel (01985) 212929
E-mail dmhforge@btinternet.com

HAYES, David Roland Payton. b 37. Hertf Coll Ox BA62 MA66.
Coll of Resurr Mirfield 62. **d** 64 **p** 65. C Woodley St Jo the Ev *Ox*
64-67; C Emscote *Cov* 67-69; C Farnham Royal *Ox* 69-75; P-in-c
75-78; P-in-c Lathbury 78-79; P-in-c Newport Pagnell 78-79; R
Newport Pagnell w Lathbury 79-85; RD Newport 80-85; Chapl
Renny Lodge Hosp 85-87; R Newport Pagnell w Lathbury and
Moulsoe *Ox* 85-86; P-in-c 86-87; P-in-c Bucknell w Buckton,
Llanfair Waterdine and Stowe *Heref* 87-91; V Bucknell w Chapel
Lawn, Llanfair Waterdine etc 91-94; RD Clun Forest 91-94;
P-in-c Presteigne w Discoed, Kinsham and Lingen 94-00; P-in-c
Knill 97-00; R Presteigne w Discoed, Kinsham, Lingen and
Knill 00-01; rtd 01; Perm to Offic *Heref* from 01. *3 Redcar
Avenue, Hereford HR4 9TJ* Tel (01432) 261466

HAYES, David Thomas. b 70. Yorks Min Course. **d** 09. NSM
Leeds Belle Is St Jo and St Barn *Ripon* from 09. *15 Windsor
Mount, Leeds LS15 7DD* Tel 0113-232 6588 Mobile
07739-364755 E-mail dandh.whitkirk.uk@lineone.net

HAYES, Denise Angela. b 62. NOC 02. **d** 05 **p** 06. C Ashton-in-
Makerfield St Thos *Liv* from 05. *79 Greenfields Crescent, Ashton-
in-Makerfield, Wigan WN4 8QY* Tel (01942) 272681 Mobile
07736-523168 E-mail denisehayes4@aol.com

HAYES, Canon John Henry Andrew. b 52. BSc. Wycliffe Hall Ox 82. **d** 84 **p** 85. C Moreton *Ches* 84-87; R Barrow 87-94; Bp's Chapl 87-94; P-in-c Runcorn St Mich 94-04; P-in-c Runcorn All SS 94-05; P-in-c Runcorn H Trin 04-05; V Runcorn All SS w H Trin from 05; Hon Can Ches Cathl from 08. *The Vicarage, 1 Highlands Road, Runcorn WA7 4PS* Tel (01928) 572417
E-mail revjohnhayes@ntlworld.com

HAYES, Mrs Marion Anne. b 51. Leeds Univ BA05 Liv Inst of Educn CertEd72. NOC 02. **d** 05 **p** 06. NSM Runcorn All SS w H Trin *Ches* from 05. *The Vicarage, 1 Highlands Road, Runcorn WA7 4PS* Tel (01928) 572417
E-mail marion.hayes@ntlworld.com

HAYES, Michael Gordon William. b 48. St Cath Coll Cam BA69 MA73 PhD73. Ridley Hall Cam 73. **d** 75 **p** 76. C Combe Down w Monkton Combe *B & W* 75-78; C Cambridge H Trin *Ely* 78-81; V Bathampton *B & W* 81-88; V Clevedon St Andr and Ch Ch 88-95; C Belper *Derby* 95-00; P-in-c Drayton in Hales *Lich* 00-07; RD Hodnet 01-06; P-in-c Chilton Cantelo, Ashington, Mudford, Rimpton etc *B & W* from 07. *The New Rectory, Camel Street, Marston Magna, Yeovil BA22 8DD* Tel (01935) 850536
E-mail mhhayes@freeuk.com

HAYES, Michael John. b 52. Lanc Univ BA73. Coll of Resurr Mirfield 75. **d** 78 **p** 79. C Notting Hill *Lon* 78-81; C-in-c Hammersmith SS Mich and Geo White City Estate CD 81-88; Perm to Offic 98-00; NSM Norwood St Mary 00-03; Chapl Heart of Kent Hospice from 05. *22 Ridley Road, Rochester ME1 1UL* Tel (01622) 792200
E-mail mike.hayes@diocese-rochester.org

HAYES, Mrs Miranda Jane. b 57. STETS BA06. **d** 06 **p** 07. C Dorking w Ranmore *Guildf* from 06. *79 Ashcombe Road, Dorking RH4 1LX* Tel (01306) 822065
E-mail mail@mirandahayes.org

HAYES, Richard. b 39. K Coll Lon BD68 AKC68. **d** 69 **p** 70. C Dartford H Trin *Roch* 69-72; C S Kensington St Steph *Lon* 72-76; V Ruislip Manor St Paul 76-82; V Ealing St Pet Mt Park 82-91; R St Edm the King and St Mary Woolnoth etc 91-99; rtd 99; Perm to Offic *Lich* 99-04 and *Heref* from 00; Hon C Shrewsbury St Alkmund *Lich* 04-07; Hon C Shrewsbury St Chad, St Mary and St Alkmund from 07; OCF from 09. *26 St John's Hill, Shrewsbury SY1 1JJ* Tel (01743) 244668
E-mail l.r.hayes@btinternet.com

HAYES, Richard Henry. b 65. St Jo Coll Nottm 89. **d** 92 **p** 93. C Southborough St Pet w Ch Ch and St Matt *Roch* 92-95; C Downend *Bris* 95-97; V Gravesend St Mary *Roch* 97-02; R Clymping and Yapton w Ford *Chich* from 02. *The Rectory, St Mary's Meadow, Yapton, Arundel BN18 0EE* Tel (01243) 552962 Mobile 07944-804933 E-mail hayesrev@supanet.com

HAYES, Mrs Rosemarie Eveline. b 51. Brighton Coll of Educn CertEd72. NOC 88. **d** 91 **p** 94. Par Dn Manston *Ripon* 91-94; C 94-95; C Beeston 95-00; V Horsforth from 00; P-in-c Kirkstall from 06. *St Margaret's Vicarage, Church Lane, Horsforth, Leeds LS18 5LA* Tel 0113-258 2481
E-mail rosemarie@hayes2482.fsnet.co.uk

HAYES, Mrs Sarah Caroline. b 61. Qu Coll Birm. **d** 09. NSM Hall Green St Pet *Birm* from 09. *25 Valentine Road, Birmingham B14 7AN* Tel 0121-441 1264
E-mail shayes@sarahhayessolicitors.co.uk

HAYES, Stephen Anthony. b 57. St Jo Coll Dur BA80 S Bank Univ PGCE96. SAOMC 97. **d** 99 **p** 00. NSM Kingham w Churchill, Daylesford and Sarsden *Ox* 99-01; NSM Chipping Norton 01-06; Chapl Kingham Hill Sch Oxon 99-06; Teacher Arnold Lodge Sch Leamington Spa from 06. *9 Hastings Hill, Churchill, Chipping Norton OX7 6NA* Tel (01608) 658267
E-mail hayesfamily@freeuk.com

HAYES, Timothy James. b 62. **d** 89 **p** 90. C Lache cum Saltney *Ches* 89-94; P-in-c Dukinfield St Jo 94-99; V from 99. *37 Harold Avenue, Dukinfield SK16 5NH* Tel 0161-308 4708

HAYHOE, Geoffrey John Stephen. b 57. Portsm Univ BSc00. Qu Coll Birm 01. **d** 03 **p** 04. C Felixstowe St Jo *St E* 03-06; V Geraldine New Zealand from 06. *The Parish Office, 77 Talbot Street, Geraldine 7930, New Zealand* Tel (0064) (3) 693 9691
E-mail john@hayhoe.net

HAYLER, Peter John. b 65. R Holloway Coll Lon BSc87 Univ of Wales MPhil02. Wilson Carlile Coll 89 St Mich Coll Llan 99. **d** 00 **p** 04. Ind Chapl *Mon* 95-03; C Pontnewydd 00-03; C Magor 03-06; TV Magor 06-09; C Cambridge St Edw w St Mich *Ely* from 09; Chapl Univ Staff Cam from 09. *Great St Mary's, St Mary' Passage, Cambridge CB2 3PQ* Tel (01223) 741718
E-mail haylers@dialstart.net

HAYLES, Graham David. b 39. Clifton Th Coll 64. **d** 67 **p** 68. C Gipsy Hill Ch Ch *S'wark* 67-70; C Heatherlands St Jo *Sarum* 70-74; V W Streatham St Jas *S'wark* 74-90; TR Hinckley H Trin *Leic* 90-03; rtd 03; Perm to Offic *S'wark* from 04. *19 Park Road, Redhill RH1 1BT* Tel (01737) 761732

HAYLETT, David William. b 44. **d** 05 **p** 06. OLM Dorchester *Ox* from 05. *8 Westfield Road, Long Wittenham, Abingdon OX14 4RF* Tel (01865) 407382
E-mail familyhaylett@yahoo.com

HAYMAN, Mrs Audrey Doris. b 41. St Mary's Coll Chelt 61 Bris Univ CertEd61 Cov Coll of Educn 65. Glouc Sch of Min 88. **d** 91 **p** 94. NSM Matson *Glouc* 91-98; P-in-c Falfield w Rockhampton 98-02; P-in-c Oldbury-on-Severn 98-02; Perm to Offic 02-04; NSM Barnwood from 04. *32 Corncroft Lane, Matson, Gloucester GL4 6XU* Tel (01452) 411786
E-mail adhayman@yahoo.co.uk

HAYMAN, Canon Robert Fleming. b 31. Princeton Univ BA53. Gen Th Sem (NY) MDiv56. **d** 56 **p** 56. USA 56-88; I Drumcliffe w Lissadell and Munninane *K, E & A* 88-92; Preb Elphin Cathl 88-92; rtd 92. *1102 East Boston Street, Seattle WA 98102-4128, USA* Tel (001) (206) 860 7565

HAYNES, Anthony. *See* HAYNES, Michael Anthony Richard

HAYNES, Miss Catherine Mary. b 68. Man Univ BA90. St Mich Coll Llan BD95. **d** 96 **p** 97. C Llantwit Major 96-99; C Coity w Nolton 99-01; P-in-c Llangammarch w Llanganten and Llanlleonfel etc *S & B* 01-03; P-in-c Irfon Valley 03-06; R from 06; V Blaenau Irfon from 06. *The Rectory, Maes Glas, Llangammarch Wells LD4 4EE* Tel (01591) 620482
E-mail cmhaynes@compuserve.com

HAYNES, Clifford. b 33. Cam Univ MA60. Linc Th Coll 80. **d** 82 **p** 83. C Lightcliffe *Wakef* 82-85; V Bradshaw 85-98; rtd 98; Perm to Offic *Carl* from 98. *East Lyn, Lazonby, Penrith CA10 1BX* Tel (01768) 897018

HAYNES (née RYDER), Mrs Jennifer Ann. b 40. Bath Spa Univ Coll BSc99. **d** 04 **p** 06. OLM Potterne w Worton and Marston *Sarum* 04-06; OLM Southbroom from 06. *15 Mill Road, Worton, Devizes SN10 5SF* Tel (01380) 723911

HAYNES, Canon John Richard. b 35. Ely Th Coll 60. **d** 63 **p** 64. C Bollington St Jo *Ches* 63-67; C Ches St Jo 67-68; C Davenham 68-70; Rhodesia 70-80; Zimbabwe 80-90; Sub-Dean Bulawayo Cathl 78-83; Hon Can Matabeleland from 90; V Bishop's Stortford *St Alb* 90-00; rtd 00; Perm to Offic *B & W* from 01. *53 Stag Way, Glastonbury BA6 9PR* Tel (01458) 830686

HAYNES, John Stanley. b 30. WMMTC. **d** 82 **p** 83. NSM Westwood *Cov* 82-84; C Radford Semele and Ufton 84-85; V 85-95; rtd 95; Perm to Offic *Cov* from 95. *64 Rugby Road, Cubbington, Leamington Spa CV32 7JF* Tel (01926) 330016

HAYNES, Leonard Thomas. b 17. **d** 69 **p** 70. C Lutterworth w Cotesbach *Leic* 69-73; C-in-c Swinford w Catthorpe, Shawell and Stanford 73-74; V 74-83; rtd 83; Perm to Offic *Leic* 83-02 and from 05; *Birm* 95-97. *c/o E J Haynes Esq, 33 Belcher Close, Heather, Coalville LE67 2RN*

HAYNES, Michael Anthony Richard (Tony). b 47. Heythrop Coll Lon MA95 Univ of Wales (Cardiff) LLM03. NTMTC 98. **d** 00 **p** 01. NSM Tottenham St Paul *Lon* 00-05; Hon C W Green Ch Ch w St Pet from 05. *Christ Church Vicarage, Waldeck Road, London N15 3EP* Tel (020) 8889 9677

HAYNES, Canon Michael Thomas Avery. b 32. AKC61. St Boniface Warminster 61. **d** 62 **p** 63. C Hebden Bridge *Wakef* 62-64; C Elland 64-68; V Thornhill Lees 68-82; V Lindley 82-97; Hon Can Wakef Cathl 82-97; rtd 97; Perm to Offic from 97. *Longwood Edge Cottage, 86 Lamb Hall Road, Huddersfield HD3 3TJ*

HAYNES, The Very Revd Peter. b 25. Selw Coll Cam BA49 MA54. Cuddesdon Coll 50. **d** 52 **p** 53. C Stokesley *York* 52-54; C Hessle 54-58; V Drypool St Jo 58-63; Asst Dir RE *B & W* 63-70; Youth Chapl 63-70; V Glastonbury St Jo 70-72; V Glastonbury St Jo w Godney 72-74; Adn Wells, Can Res and Preb Wells Cathl 74-82; Dean Heref and V Heref St Jo 82-92; rtd 92; Perm to Offic *B & W* 92-04 and *Heref* 05-09. *Flat 2, 1A Salterns Way, Poole BH14 8JR* Tel (01202) 707862

HAYNES, Peter Nigel Stafford. b 39. Hertf Coll Ox BA62 MA66. Cuddesdon Coll 62. **d** 64 **p** 65. C Norwood All SS *Cant* 64-68; C Portsea N End St Mark *Portsm* 68-72; Asst Chapl Brussels *Eur* 72-76; TV Banbury *Ox* 76-80; Asst Sec (Internat Affairs) Gen Syn Bd Soc Resp 80-85; P-in-c E Peckham and Nettlestead *Roch* 85-92; R Bredgar w Bicknor and Frinsted w Wormshill etc *Cant* 92-99; rtd 99. *1 Vesper Cottage, Cage Lane, Smarden, Ashford TN27 8QD* Tel (01233) 770367

HAYNES, Valerie Elizabeth Mary-Benedict. b 53. Cant Ch Ch Univ BA09. St Steph Ho Ox 03. **d** 05 **p** 06. C Sheerness H Trin w St Paul *Cant* 05-09; Perm to Offic from 09. *The Vicarage, North Road, Queenborough ME11 5HA* Tel (01795) 662648 Mobile 07803-798475 E-mail revhaynes@btinternet.com

HAYSMORE, Geoffrey Frederick. b 39. Bps' Coll Cheshunt 63. **d** 66 **p** 67. C St Marylebone St Mark w St Luke *Lon* 66-69; C Stockton St Chad *Dur* 69-72; C-in-c Town End Farm CD 72-77; Perm to Offic *York* from 95; rtd 01. *139 Lambton Road, Middlesbrough TS4 2ST* Tel (01642) 275259

HAYTER, Mary Elizabeth. *See* BARR, Mary Elizabeth

HAYTER, Raymond William. b 48. Oak Hill Th Coll 74. **d** 77 **p** 78. C Bermondsey St Jas w Ch Ch *S'wark* 77-80; C Sydenham H Trin 81-83; Asst Chapl HM Pris Brixton 83-84; Chapl HM Youth Cust Cen Stoke Heath 84-88; Chapl HM Pris Maidstone 88-91; CF 91-08; Chapl HM Pris Standford Hill from 08. *HM Prison Standford Hill, Church Road, Eastchurch, Sheerness ME12 4AA* Tel (01795) 884559

HAYTER, Sandra. *See* RAILTON, Sandra

HAYTON, John Anthony. b 45. TD81. Heythrop Coll Lon MA00 ACII70. Oak Hill Th Coll 93. **d** 96 **p** 97. NSM St Alb St Mich *St Alb* from 96; OCF 02-08. *89 Harpenden Road, St Albans AL3 6BY* Tel (01727) 761719 *or* 835037 Fax 765832 *or* 811744 E-mail john.hayton@ntlworld.com

HAYTON, Mark William. b 59. St Steph Ho Ox 85. **d** 88 **p** 89. C Sittingbourne St Mich *Cant* 88-91; C Kennington 91-94; R Broadstairs 94-07; RD Thanet 96-01; P-in-c Folkestone Trin from 07. *Holy Trinity Vicarage, 21 Manor Road, Folkestone CT20 2SA* Tel (01303) 253831 E-mail markhayton@supanet.com

HAYTON, Norman Joseph Patrick. b 32. MRICS57. Sarum Th Coll 69. **d** 71 **p** 72. C Lytham St Cuth *Blackb* 71-74; V Wesham 74-79; V Chorley St Geo 79-80; NSM Kells *Carl* 84-85; P-in-c Flimby 85-90; V Barrow St Jas 90-94; TV Egremont and Haile 94-97; P-in-c Distington 97-00; rtd 00; P-in-c Charnock Richard *Blackb* 01-05; Perm to Offic *Ches* from 05. *6 Chinley Close, Sale M33 3LT* Tel 0161-962 2000 E-mail normanhayton@hotmail.com

HAYWARD, Canon Alan Richard. b 25. Open Univ BA72. Wycliffe Hall Ox 54. **d** 56 **p** 57. C Dudley St Fran *Worc* 56-59; C-in-c Wollescote CD 59-65; V Wollescote 65-85; Hon Can Worc Cathl 85-91; R Alvechurch 85-91; rtd 91; Perm to Offic *Worc* 91-01. *2 St Kenelm's Court, St Kenelm's Road, Romsley, Halesowen B62 0NF* Tel (01562) 710749

HAYWARD, Canon Christopher Joseph. b 38. TCD BA63 MA67. Ridley Hall Cam 63. **d** 65 **p** 66. C Hatcham St Jas *S'wark* 65-69; Warden Lee Abbey Internat Students' Club Kensington 69-74; Chapl Chelmsf Cathl 74-77; P-in-c Darlaston All SS *Lich* 77-83; Ind Chapl 77-83; Can Res Bradf Cathl 83-92; R Linton in Craven 92-03; P-in-c Burnsall w Rylstone 97-03; RD Skipton 93-98; Hon Can Bradf Cathl 92-03; rtd 03; Perm to Offic *Bradf* from 04. *12 Ron Lawton Crescent, Burley in Wharfedale, Ilkley LS29 7ST* Tel (01943) 865261 E-mail chris.hayward@bradford.anglican.org

HAYWARD, Derek. *See* HAYWARD, The Ven John Derek Risdon

HAYWARD, Jane. *See* HAYWARD, Ms Pamela Jane

HAYWARD, Jeffrey Kenneth. b 47. St Jo Coll Nottm BTh74. **d** 74 **p** 75. C Stambermill *Worc* 74-77; C Woking St Jo *Guildf* 77-83; V Springfield H Trin *Chelmsf* 83-88; Chapl HM Pris Chelmsf 86-00; Area RD Chelmsf 86-88; RD Chelmsf 88-93; RD Chelmsf N 93-95; Hon Can Chelmsf Cathl 93-98; Chapl HM Pris Wakef 00-05; Chapl HM Pris Long Lartin from 05. *HM Prison Long Lartin, South Littleton, Evesham WR11 8TZ* Tel (01386) 835100 Fax 835101

HAYWARD, Mrs Jennifer Dawn. b 38. WMMTC 85. **d** 88 **p** 94. NSM Gt Malvern St Mary *Worc* 88-90; NSM Gt Malvern Ch Ch 88-90; Par Dn 90-94; C 94-96; TV Warndon *Derby* 96-04; rtd 04; Perm to Offic *Worc* from 04. *26 Barley Crescent, Long Meadow, Worcester WR4 0HW* Tel (01905) 29545

HAYWARD, John Andrew. b 63. Nottm Univ BTh89 MHCIMA83. Linc Th Coll 86. **d** 89 **p** 90. C Seaford w Sutton *Chich* 89-92; C St Pancras H Cross w St Jude and St Pet *Lon* 92-95; V Kentish Town St Martin w St Andr 95-08; AD S Camden 05-08; V Merton St Mary *S'wark* from 08. *The Vicarage, 3 Church Path, London SW19 3HJ* Tel (020) 8543 6192 E-mail vicar@stmarysmerton.org.uk

HAYWARD, The Ven John Derek Risdon. b 23. OBE00. Trin Coll Cam BA56 MA64. Westcott Ho Cam 56. **d** 57 **p** 58. C Sheff St Mary w St Simon w St Matthias 57-59; V Sheff Gillcar St Silas 59-63; V Isleworth All SS *Lon* 64-94; Adn Middx 74-75; Gen Sec Lon Dio 75-93; rtd 94; Perm to Offic *B & W* 94-04. *29A Great Pulteney Street, Bath BA2 4BU* Tel (01225) 336305 Fax 421862

HAYWARD, Preb John Talbot. b 28. Selw Coll Cam BA52 MA56. Wells Th Coll 52. **d** 54 **p** 55. C S Lyncombe *B & W* 54-58; R Lamyatt 58-71; V Bruton w Wyke Champflower and Redlynch 58-71; RD Bruton 62-71; R Weston-super-Mare St Jo 71-75; Preb Wells Cathl from 73; TR Weston-super-Mare Cen Par 75-92; rtd 92; Perm to Offic *B & W* from 92. *5 Chelswood Avenue, Weston-super-Mare BS22 8QP* Tel (01934) 628431

HAYWARD, Martin. b 45. WMMTC 07. **d** 07 **p** 08. Dir Internat Min *Cov* from 07; NSM Cov St Fran N Radford from 07. *47 Benedictine Road, Coventry CV3 6GW* Tel (024) 7652 1205 Mobile 07917-182579 E-mail martin.hayward@coventrycathedral.org.uk

HAYWARD, Ms Pamela Jane. b 52. RGN82. Westcott Ho Cam 84. **d** 87 **p** 94. Par Dn Northampton St Mary *Pet* 87-90; Par Dn Bris St Mary Redcliffe w Temple etc 90-94; C 94-96; V Eastville St Anne w St Mark and St Thos from 96. *266 Glenfrome Road, Bristol BS5 6TS* Tel and fax 0117-952 0202

HAYWARD, Peter Noel. b 26. Leeds Univ BA48 BD78. Coll of Resurr Mirfield 48. **d** 50 **p** 51. C S Elmsall *Wakef* 50-56; C Sheldon *Birm* 56-60; C-in-c Garretts Green CD 60-69; V Garretts Green 69-70; V N Cave w Cliffe *York* 70-00; R Hotham 70-00; RD Howden 78-86; P-in-c Newbald 97-00; rtd 00; Perm to Offic *Carl* from 00; Hon C Solway Plain from 02. *The Old Chapel, Allonby, Maryport CA15 6QH* Tel (01900) 881466

HAYWARD, Mrs Sarah. b 77. St Mary's Coll Strawberry Hill BA99. St Jo Coll Nottm MTh06. **d** 08 **p** 09. C Dibden *Win* from 08. *Church House, 2 Corsair Drive, Dibden, Southampton SO45 5UF* Tel 07828-046193 (mobile) E-mail curate@dibdenchurches.org

HAYWARD, Timothy David Mark. b 78. St Andr Univ MTheol00. Westcott Ho Cam 07. **d** 09. C Buckden w the Offords Ely from 09. *19 Church Street, Buckden, St Neots PE19 5SJ* Tel (01480) 819665 Mobile 07988-994481 E-mail timhayward@hotmail.co.uk

HAYWARD, William Richmond. b 42. JP98. NY Th Sem BA90 NY Th Sem MPS91. Chich Th Coll 88. **d** 88 **p** 90. Bermuda from 88; Miss to Seafarers from 91. *8 Seabright Avenue, Paget DV 04, Bermuda* Tel and fax (001441) 236 3221

HAYWARD-WRIGHT, Mrs Diane. b 51. WEMTC 06. **d** 09. NSM Inkberrow w Cookhill and Kington w Dormston *Worc* from 09. *1 Church Drive, Cookhill, Alcester B49 5JH* Tel (01527) 892727 Mobile 07815-520107 E-mail diane@shopwright.co.uk

HAYWOOD, James William. b 36. Chich Th Coll 69. **d** 73 **p** 74. C Leeds Halton St Wilfrid *Ripon* 73-76; C Workington St Jo *Carl* 76-78; V Clifton 78-84; P-in-c Barrow St Jas 84-85; V 85-89; V Crosby Ravensworth 89-94; R Asby 89-94; V Bolton 89-94; rtd 98. *19 Bramham Road, Whitwood, Castleford WF10 5PA*

HAYWOOD, Preb Keith Roderick. b 48. Oak Hill Th Coll 84. **d** 86 **p** 87. C Fazeley *Lich* 86-90; TV Leek and Meerbrook 90-01; Acting TR Hanley H Ev 01-03; TR from 03; Preb Lich Cathl from 07. *Rectory, 35 Harding Road, Hanley, Stoke-on-Trent ST1 3BQ* Tel (01782) 266066 E-mail krhaywood@xalt.co.uk

HAZEL, Sister. *See* SMITH, Sister Hazel Ferguson Waide

HAZELL, The Ven Frederick Roy. b 30. Fitzw Ho Cam BA53 MA59. Cuddesdon Coll 54. **d** 56 **p** 57. C Ilkeston St Mary *Derby* 56-59; C Heanor 59-62; V Marlpool 62-63; Chapl Univ of W Indies 63-66; C St Martin-in-the-Fields *Lon* 66-68; V Croydon H Sav *Cant* 68-84; RD Croydon 72-78; Hon Can Cant Cathl 73-84; P-in-c Croydon H Trin 77-80; Adn Croydon *S'wark* 84-93; rtd 93; P-in-c Chard, Furnham w Chaffcombe, Knowle St Giles etc *B & W* 95-99; P-in-c Tardebigge *Worc* 00-03; Perm to Offic *Birm* from 00 and *Worc* from 04. *1 Chapelside, Clapton Row, Bourton-on-the-Water, Cheltenham GL54 2DN* Tel (01451) 821140

HAZELL, Thomas Jeremy. b 35. Bris Univ LLB56 PhD01. St D Coll Lamp 56. **d** 58 **p** 59. C Newport St Paul *Mon* 58-61; C Derby St Jo 61-64; V Arksey *Sheff* 64-69; Sen Student Cllr Univ of Wales (Cardiff) Llan 69-89; rtd 95. *Castlewood Barn, Ponde, Llandefalle, Brecon LD3 0NR* Tel (01874) 754030

HAZELTON, John. b 35. St Cath Coll Cam BA56 MA60 Bris Univ MLitt74 Newc Univ BPhil80. Wells Th Coll 59. **d** 61 **p** 62. C Twerton *B & W* 61-65; V Pitcombe w Shepton Montague 65-72; Lect SS Hild and Bede Dur 72-79; Asst Master Dame Allan's Schs Newc 79-88; Chapl 88-95; rtd 95; Perm to Offic *Dur* from 97. *36 Orchard Drive, Durham DH1 1LA* Tel 0191-384 6606

HAZELTON, Michael John. b 53. UEA BA76 Bedf Coll Lon PhD81 Heythrop Coll Lon BD89. **d** 90 **p** 91. Asst Chapl Helsinki *Eur* 94-95; Asst Chapl Zürich w Winterthur 95-98; R Mablethorpe w Trusthorpe *Linc* 98-02; R Saxonwell 02-05; V Danby w Castleton and Commondale *York* from 05; V Westerdale from 05; V Moorsholm from 09. *The Vicarage, Yall Flats Lane, Danby, Whitby YO21 2NQ* Tel (01287) 660388 E-mail mjh_uk@hotmail.com

HAZELTON, Robert Henry Peter. b 22. Wells Th Coll 65. **d** 67 **p** 68. C Eastover *B & W* 67-69; C Milton 69-76; V Peasedown St John 76-80; V Peasedown St John w Wellow 80-89; rtd 90; Perm to Offic *B & W* 90-06. *37 High Meadows, Midsomer Norton, Bath BA3 2RY* Tel (01761) 419675

HAZELWOOD, Ms Jillian. b 32. Bp Otter Coll CertEd52 St Alb Minl Tr Scheme 82. **d** 87 **p** 94. NSM Wheathampstead *St Alb* 87-02; Perm to Offic from 02. *14 Butterfield Road, Wheathampstead, St Albans AL4 8PU* Tel and fax (01582) 833146

HAZLEDINE, Basil William. b 18. St Pet Hall Ox BA42 MA45. Wycliffe Hall Ox 42. **d** 43 **p** 44. C Highfield *Ox* 43-46; C Gerrards Cross 46-51; V Barking St Patr *Chelmsf* 51-55; R Twineham and V Sayers Common *Chich* 55-60; V Stoughton *Guildf* 60-70; V Westlands St Andr *Lich* 70-77; P-in-c Whatfield w Semer *St E* 77-78; R 78-81; P-in-c Nedging w Naughton 77-81; R Whatfield w Semer, Nedging and Naughton 81-84; rtd 84. *1 David Gresham House, 226 Pollards Oak Road, Oxted RH8 0JP* Tel (01883) 717763

HAZLEHURST, Anthony Robin. b 43. Man Univ BSc64. Tyndale Hall Bris 65. **d** 68 **p** 69. C Macclesfield Ch Ch *Ches* 68-71; C Bushbury *Lich* 71-75; P-in-c New Clee *Linc* 75-85; TV Deane *Man* 85-96; V Harwood 96-07; rtd 07; Perm to Offic *Man* from 07. *1 Maybury Close, Ramsbottom, Bury BL0 9WG* Tel (01706) 281661 E-mail robinhaz@btinternet.com

HAZLEHURST, David. b 32. Liv Univ BSc54. St Steph Ho Ox 55. **d** 57 **p** 58. C Sheff Arbourthorne 57-59; C Doncaster Ch Ch 59-61; C W Wycombe *Ox* 61-63; P-in-c Collyhurst St Jas *Man* 66-67; V Blackrod 67-79; V Halliwell St Marg 79-84; R Sutton

St Nic *S'wark* 84-94; rtd 94; Perm to Offic *S'wark* from 95; Perm to Offic *Guildf* 95-99. *3 Up The Quadrangle, Morden College, 19 St Germans Place, London SE3 0PW* Tel (020) 8853 1180

HAZLEHURST, David John Benedict (Benny). b 63. Trin Coll Bris 88. **d** 91 **p** 92. C Plumstead St Jo w St Jas and St Paul *S'wark* 91-98; Estates Outreach Worker (S'wark Adnry) 98-02; V Brixton Road Ch Ch 02-05; R Puddletown, Tolpuddle and Milborne w Dewlish *Sarum* from 05. *The Vicarage, The Square, Puddletown, Dorchester DT2 8SL* Tel (01305) 848216 Mobile 07973-498590 E-mail bennyandmel@lineone.net

HAZLEHURST, Robin. *See* HAZLEHURST, Anthony Robin

HAZLETT, Stephen David. b 56. TCD BTh88. CITC. **d** 88 **p** 89. C Ballywillan *Conn* 88-90; I Rathcoole 90-95; I Dunluce 95-00; Ind Chapl *Dur* from 00; TV Sunderland 00-07; Chapl Sunderland Minster from 07. *14 The Oaks West, Sunderland SR2 8HZ* Tel 0191-565 4121
E-mail stephen.hazlett@lineone.net

HAZLEWOOD, Andrew Lord. b 54. BSc. Wycliffe Hall Ox. **d** 82 **p** 83. C Leckhampton SS Phil and Jas w Cheltenham St Jas *Glouc* 82-85; C Waltham H Cross *Chelmsf* 85-89; R Pedmore *Worc* from 89; P-in-c Wollaston from 09; RD Stourbridge from 07. *The Rectory, Pedmore Lane, Stourbridge DY9 0SW* Tel (01562) 884856 *or* 887287
E-mail andrewhazlewood@hotmail.com
or stpeterspedmore@hotmail.com

HAZLEWOOD, David Paul. b 47. Sheff Univ MB, ChB70 Campion Hall Ox BA72 MA77. Wycliffe Hall Ox 70. **d** 73 **p** 74. C Chapeltown *Sheff* 73-75; Singapore 76; Indonesia 76-88; R Ipswich St Helen *St E* 88-97; V Shirley *Win* from 97. *The Vicarage, 2B Wordsworth Road, Southampton SO15 5LX* Tel (023) 8077 4329 E-mail david.hazlewood@ukgateway.net

HAZLEWOOD, William Peter Guy. b 71. De Montfort Univ BA97. St Steph Ho Ox BTh01. **d** 01 **p** 02. C Knowle H Nativity and Easton All Hallows *Bris* 01-04; P-in-c Iver Heath *Ox* 04-08; R from 08. *The Rectory, 2 Pinewood Close, Iver SL0 0QS* Tel (01753) 654470 E-mail frwill@hazlewoodhq.co.uk

HEAD, David Nicholas. b 55. Pemb Coll Cam BA77 MA81 Westmr Coll of Educn MTh01. Westcott Ho Cam 78. **d** 81 **p** 82. C Surbiton St Andr and St Mark *S'wark* 81-84; C St Marylebone w H Trin *Lon* 84-89; TV Clapham Team *S'wark* 89-96; Chapl Trin Hospice Lon 89-96; Chapl Princess Alice Hospice Esher 96-03; R Lyng, Sparham, Elsing, Bylaugh, Bawdeswell etc *Nor* from 03. *The Rectory, Rectory Road, Lyng, Norwich NR9 5RA* Tel and fax (01603) 872381
E-mail david@davidhead.plus.com

HEAD, Canon Derek Leonard Hamilton. b 34. ALCD58. **d** 58 **p** 59. C Bexleyheath Ch Ch *Roch* 58-61; C Wisley w Pyrford *Guildf* 61-66; C-in-c Ewell St Paul Howell Hill CD 66-73; R Headley All SS 73-81; TR 81-82; RD Farnham 80-82; V Chertsey 82-99; Hon Can Guildf Cathl 83-99; RD Runnymede 88-93; Dir Post-Ord Tr 90-94; rtd 99; Perm to Offic *Win* from 00. *9 Tangmere Close, Mudeford, Christchurch BH23 4LZ* Tel (01425) 276545 E-mail headd@onetel.com

HEAD, Canon Ivan Francis. b 53. Univ of W Aus BA75 Glas Univ PhD85. Melbourne Coll of Div BD78. **d** 79 **p** 79. Australia 79-81 and from 85; C Uddingston *Glas* 81-85; C Cambuslang 81-85; Dir Angl Inst Theol Perth 85-91; Warden Ch Coll Tasmania Univ 91-94; Warden St Paul's Coll Sydney Univ from 95. *St Paul's College, University of Sydney NSW 2006, Australia* Tel (0061) (2) 9550 7444 *or* 9557 1447 Fax 9519 7246
E-mail ihead@mail.usyd.edu.au

HEAD, Peter Ernest. b 38. Lon Univ BSc59. Ridley Hall Cam 61. **d** 63 **p** 64. C Fulwood *Sheff* 63-66; C Belper *Derby* 66-68; Hd RE Shoeburyness Sch Southend-on-Sea 69-74; Hd RE Bilborough Coll 74-79; Public Preacher *S'well* 74-79; NSM Bramcote 74-79; Vice-Prin Totton Coll Southn 79-93; Hon C Hordle *Win* 94-02; rtd 03; Perm to Offic *Win* from 02. *44 Lentune Way, Lymington SO41 3PF* Tel and fax (01590) 678097
E-mail peter_head@bigfoot.com

HEADING, Margaret Anne. b 66. Leeds Univ BSc88 Man Univ PhD91 Aston Univ PGCE99. Wycliffe Hall Ox BA01. **d** 02 **p** 03. C Fletchamstead *Cov* 02-05; V Ingleby Greenhow, Bilsdale Priory etc *York* from 05. *3 Holmemead, Great Broughton, Middlesbrough TS9 7HQ* Tel (01642) 710045
E-mail anne.heading@tesco.net

HEADING, Canon Richard Vaughan. b 43. Lon Univ BSc65 ARCS65. Coll of Resurr Mirfield 66. **d** 68 **p** 69. C Heref St Martin 68-75; P-in-c Birches Head and Northwood *Lich* 75-77; TV Hanley H Ev 77-82; V Heref H Trin 82-92; TR Bedminster *Bris* 92-08; AD Bris S 01-06; Hon Can Bris Cathl 01-08; rtd 08. *18 Timberdine Avenue, Worcester WR5 2BD* Tel (01905) 360998 E-mail richard.heading@gmx.co.uk

HEADLAND, James Frederick. b 20. Clifton Th Coll 51. **d** 53 **p** 54. C Barnsbury St Andr *Lon* 53-55; C Spitalfields Ch Ch w All SS 55-57; V Upper Tulse Hill St Matthias *S'wark* 57-65; R Church Pulverbatch *Heref* 65-81; P-in-c Smethcott w Woolstaston 65-81; R Reedham w Cantley w Limpenhoe and Southwood *Nor* 81-86; rtd 86; Perm to Offic *Heref* from 86 and

Lich 88-00. *3 Ashford Avenue, Pontesbury, Shrewsbury SY5 0QN* Tel (01743) 790565

HEADLEY, Miss Carolyn Jane. b 50. K Coll Lon MA94 MCSP71. Oak Hill Th Coll BA83. **dss** 83 **d** 87 **p** 94. Kensal Rise St Mark and St Martin *Lon* 83-87; Par Dn Uxbridge 87-90; TD 90-92; Warden of Readers (Willesden Area) 88-92; Tutor Wycliffe Hall Ox 94-05; P-in-c W Meon and Warnford *Portsm* 05-07; Chapl Portsm Hosps NHS Trust from 07. *31 Canal Wharf, Chichester PO19 8EY* Tel (01243) 774558 Mobile 07777-617516 E-mail carolynheadley@btinternet.com

HEADS, John. b 27. Bps' Coll Cheshunt 60. **d** 62 **p** 63. C Beamish *Dur* 61-64; C Monkwearmouth St Andr 64-65; C Stockton St Chad 65-70; rtd 94. *18 Green Crescent, Golcar, Huddersfield HD7 4RF* Tel (01484) 651232

HEAGERTY, Alistair John. b 42. MBE86. Oriel Coll Ox BA63 MA67. Lon Coll of Div BD68. **d** 68 **p** 69. C Margate H Trin *Cant* 68-72; CF 72-97; Chapl R Memorial Chpl Sandhurst 92-97; TV Kingswood *Bris* 97-08; rtd 08. *44 Ferney Road, East Barnet, Barnet EN4 8LF* Tel (020) 3234 1003
E-mail alistair@heagerty.freeserve.co.uk

HEAK, Philip George. b 70. QUB BA92. CITC BTh95. **d** 95 **p** 96. C Ballymacash *Conn* 95-98; C Galway w Kilcummin *T, K & A* 98-00; Dioc Youth Officer (Cashel) *C & O* 00-06; I Naas w Kill and Rathmore *M & K* from 06. *15 Spring Gardens, Naas, Co Kildare, Republic of Ireland* Tel (00353) (45) 897206 Mobile 86-817 2356 E-mail pheak@eircom.net

HEAL, David Walter. b 37. Ox Univ MA63. Trin Coll Carmarthen. **d** 90 **p** 91. NSM Henfynyw w Aberaeron and Llanddewi Aberarth *St D* 90-96; Hon Asst Chapl Algarve *Eur* 96-98; Chapl Madeira 98-03; rtd 03; Perm to Offic *St D* from 04. *Cae Gwair Bach, Llanon SY23 5LZ* Tel (01974) 202596

HEAL, Miss Felicity Joan. b 42. Portsm Dioc Tr Course 89. **d** 92. NSM Bramshott and Liphook *Portsm* 92-95; NSM Blendworth w Chalton w Idsworth 95-97; Perm to Offic from 97. *40 Rushes Road, Petersfield GU32 3BW* Tel (01730) 260410 Mobile 07712-249608 E-mail fj.heal@ntlworld.com

HEALD, William Roland. b 40. St Jo Coll Auckland 72. **d** 74 **p** 75. C Howick New Zealand 74; C Kaitaia 75; C Auckland St Paul Symonds Street 76-78; C Bournville *Birm* 78-79; V Henderson New Zealand 79-82; V Auckland St Paul Symonds Street 84-93; V S Kensington St Luke *Lon* 93-07; rtd 07; V Kaitaia New Zealand from 07. *47 Church Street, Kaitaia 0441, New Zealand* Tel (0064) (9) 408 0524 E-mail bill.heald@virgin.net

HEALE, Nicholas James. b 67. St Cath Coll Ox BA89 DPhil95 Leeds Univ BA94. Coll of Resurr Mirfield 95. **d** 95 **p** 96. C Syston *Leic* 95-99; V Blackpool St Mich *Blackb* from 99. *St Michael's Vicarage, Calvert Place, Blackpool FY3 7RU* Tel (01253) 397755

HEALE, Walter James Grenville. b 40. Wycliffe Hall Ox 77. **d** 79 **p** 80. C Walsall *Lich* 79-82; TV Marfleet *York* 82-89; TR 89-94; R Easington w Skeffling, Kilnsea and Holmpton 94-05; P-in-c Owthorne and Rimswell w Withernsea 00-05; rtd 05; P-in-c Easington w Skeffling, Kilnsea and Holmpton *York* 05-06; Perm to Offic from 06. *18 Sloe Lane, Beverley HU17 8ND*

HEALES, John. b 48. K Coll Lon BD71 AKC71 PGCE72. St Mich Coll Llan 75. **d** 76 **p** 77. C Cwmbran *Mon* 76-78; Chapl Rendcomb Coll Cirencester 78-82; Chapl Mon Sch 84-88; V Penhow, St Brides Netherwent w Llandavenny etc *Mon* from 88. *The New Rectory, Llanvaches, Newport NP26 3AY* Tel (01633) 400901

HEALEY, James Christopher. b 44. Linc Th Coll 84. **d** 86 **p** 87. C Boultham *Linc* 86-90; TV Gt Grimsby St Mary and St Jas 90-91; I Narraghmore and Timolin w Castledermot etc *D & G* 91-93; I New Ross *C & O* 93-97; Dean Lismore 97-99; I Lismore w Cappoquin, Kilwatermoy, Dungarvan etc 97-99; Chan Cashel Cathl 97-99; Prec Waterford Cathl 97-99; Can Ossory Cathl 97-99; I Arvagh w Carrigallen, Gowna and Columbkille *K, E & A* 99-02; P-in-c Winthorpe and Langford w Holme *S'well* 02-03; R Coddington and Winthorpe and Langford w Holme 03-05; rtd 05. *12 Ridgeway, Nettleham, Lincoln LN2 2TL* Tel (01522) 753622

HEALEY, Michael Harry Edmund. b 74. Mansf Coll Ox MA01 Leeds Univ BA03. Coll of Resurr Mirfield 01. **d** 04 **p** 05. C Norton *Sheff* 04-07; P-in-c Beighton from 07. *The Vicarage, 27 Tynker Avenue, Beighton, Sheffield S20 1DX* Tel 0114-248 7635
E-mail mheheyaley@hotmail.com

HEALY (née THOROLD), Mrs Alison Susan Joy. b 59. St Jo Coll Dur BA80. Ripon Coll Cuddesdon 97 SEITE 03. **d** 06 **p** 07. NSM Shooters Hill Ch Ch *S'wark* from 06. *68 Charlton Lane, London SE7 8LA* Tel (020) 8858 1736 Mobile 07962-318728 E-mail vicardancer@supanet.com

HEANEY, Canon James Roland. b 59. **d** 85 **p** 86. C Ballynafeigh St Jude *D & D* 85-88; C Lisburn Ch Ch Cathl 88-90; I Dunganstown w Redcross and Conary *D & G* from 90; Can Ch Ch Cathl Dublin from 05. *The Rectory, Redcross, Co Wicklow, Republic of Ireland* Tel and fax (00353) (404) 41637
E-mail heaneyr@indigo.ie

HEANEY, Michael Roger. b 43. TCD BA66 HDipEd67 MA69. CITC 74. **d** 76 **p** 77. Chapl St Columba's Coll Dub 76-09; rtd 09.

Montana, Scholarstown Road, Dublin 16, Republic of Ireland Tel (00353) (1) 493 1167 *or* 493 2219 E-mail mheaney@iol.ie

HEANEY, Robert Stewart. d 01 **p** 02. C Dunboyne Union *M & K* 01-04; Perm to Offic *Ox* from 05. *Regent's Park College, Pusey Street, Oxford OX1 2LB* Tel (01865) 280000 ext 28357 E-mail robert.heaney@theology.ox.ac.uk

HEANEY, Samuel Stewart. b 44. Open Univ BA79 Ulster Univ BEd83 Lon Univ BD93 QUB MPhil99. St Deiniol's Hawarden 92. **d** 92 **p** 93. In Presbyterian Ch 85-92; C Knockbreda *D & D* 92-96; I Belfast H Trin and St Silas *Conn* 96-02; I Ballyrashane w Kildollagh 02-09; rtd 09. *3 Edgewood Court, Antrim BT41 4PG* Tel (028) 9446 1076

HEANEY, Timothy Daniel. b 59. Trin Coll Bris BA04. **d** 04 **p** 05. C Dursley *Glouc* 04-08; P-in-c Paul *Truro* from 08. *The Vicarage, 1 St Pol-de-Leon View, Paul, Penzance TR19 6US* Tel (01736) 731261 E-mail tim@heaney.org.uk *or* timheaney@paulchurch.co.uk

HEANEY, Wendy Anne. b 42. St Alb Minl Tr Scheme 90. **d** 95 **p** 96. NSM Clifton and Southill *St Alb* 95-99; Asst Chapl HM Pris Bedf 95-99; Chapl 99-02; Lic to Offic *St Alb* 99-02; rtd 02; Perm to Offic *St Alb* from 03. *34 Meadow Way, Letchworth Garden City SG6 3JB* Tel (01462) 641303

HEANS, Simon John. b 56. Peterho Cam BA77 MA81. St Steph Ho Ox 92. **d** 94 **p** 95. Asst Chapl Lancing Coll 94-99; NSM Lancing St Mich *Chich* 94-99; Chapl R Gr Sch Worc 99-00; C Brighton Resurr *Chich* 00-04; V Beckenham St Barn *Roch* from 04. *St Barnabas' Vicarage, Oakhill Road, Beckenham BR3 6NG* Tel (020) 8650 3332 Fax 8658 2429 E-mail simon.heans@diocese-rochester.org

HEAP, David Leonard. b 58. Man Univ BA79. Cranmer Hall Dur 82. **d** 85 **p** 86. C Clitheroe St Jas *Blackb* 85-88; C Blackb St Gabr 88-92; V Bare from 92. *St Christopher's Vicarage, 12 Elm Grove, Morecambe LA4 6AT* Tel (01524) 411363 E-mail davidheap@readingroom.freeserve.co.uk

HEAPS, Richard Peter. b 35. Bernard Gilpin Soc Dur 58 Qu Coll Birm 58. **d** 61 **p** 62. C Castle Bromwich SS Mary and Marg *Birm* 61-65; C-in-c Erdington St Chad CD 65-70; V Nechells 70-81; RD Aston 75-81; V Marston Green 81-86; P-in-c Shrawley and Witley w Astley *Worc* 86-92; R Shrawley, Witley, Astley and Abberley 92-01; rtd 01; Perm to Offic *Worc* from 01. *9 Timberdyne Close, Rock, Kidderminster DY14 9RT* Tel (01299) 832376

HEARD, Charles. b 19. S'wark Ord Course 62. **d** 65 **p** 66. C Plumstead St Nic *S'wark* 65-71; C Blackheath All SS 71-72; V Barnes H Trin 72-84; rtd 84; Hon C E Wickham *S'wark* 04 07; Perm to Offic from 07. *5 Elmfield Court, Wickham Street, Welling DA16 3DF* Tel (020) 8855 9809

HEARD, James Barrie. b 66. Brunel Univ BA98 K Coll Lon MA01. Ridley Hall Cam 03. **d** 06 **p** 07. C Fulham All SS *Lon* from 06. *70A Fulham High Street, London SW6 3LG* Tel 07867-508919 (mobile)

HEARD, Richard Adrian. b 72. Univ of Wales (Swansea) BSc94 Hull Univ PGCE96. St Jo Coll Nottm 06. **d** 08 **p** 09. C Hackenthorpe *Sheff* from 08. *5 Grassington Drive, Sheffield S12 4NE* Tel 07818-850347 (mobile) E-mail rev.richardheard@yahoo.co.uk

HEARD, Stephen Edward. b 53. NTMTC 02. **d** 04. NSM Bush Hill Park St Mark *Lon* from 04. *43 Speed House, Barbican, London EC2Y 8AT* Tel (020) 7638 9501 Mobile 07939-263657 E-mail stephen.heard3@btinternet.com

HEARL, Maria Christina. b 47. New Hall Cam BA69 Ex Univ MA98 PhD07 PGCE70. SWMTC 03. **d** 07 **p** 08. NSM Ex St Dav from 07. *16 Twyford Place, Tiverton EX16 6AP* Tel (01884) 256380 E-mail mariahearl@btinternet.com

HEARN, John Henry. b 49. Trin Coll Bris. **d** 82 **p** 83. C Epsom Common Ch Ch *Guildf* 82-85; C Ringwood *Win* 85-88; Chapl Basingstoke Distr Hosp 88-91; Chapl Luton and Dunstable Hosp 91-96; C Ampthill w Millbrook and Steppingley *St Alb* 96-99; P-in-c Wymington w Podington 99-03; V W Acklam *York* from 03. *St Mary's Vicarage, 50 Church Lane, Middlesbrough TS5 7EB* Tel (01642) 814701 E-mail john.hearn@tesco.net

HEARN, Jonathan. b 58. Leeds Univ BA81 GradIPM85. Westcott Ho Cam 89. **d** 91 **p** 92. C Tuffley *Glouc* 91-94; C Milton *Win* 94-02; P-in-c Warwick St Paul *Cov* 02-03; TV Warwick from 03. *St Paul's Vicarage, 33 Stratford Road, Warwick CV34 6AS* Tel (01926) 419814

HEARN, Canon Peter Brian. b 31. St Jo Coll Dur 52. **d** 55 **p** 56. C Frodingham *Linc* 55-59; R Belton SS Pet and Paul 59-64; PC Manthorpe w Londonthorpe 59-64; V Billingborough 64-73; V Sempringham w Pointon and Birthorpe 64-73; V Flixborough w Burton upon Stather 73-96; RD Manlake 87-93; Can and Preb Linc Cathl 92-01; rtd 96; Perm to Offic *Linc* from 01. *7 St Andrews Drive, Burton-upon-Stather, Scunthorpe DN15 9BY* Tel (01724) 720510

HEARN, Stephen Isaac Raphael. b 79. Linc Coll Ox BA04 MA08. St Steph Ho Ox 06 Ven English Coll Rome 08. **d** 09. C Market Deeping *Linc* from 09. *16 Church Street, Deeping St James, Peterborough PE6 8HD* Tel (01778) 344516 E-mail stephen.hearn@lincoln.oxon.org

HEARN, Thomas Peter. b 18. Selw Coll Cam BA40 MA45. Linc Th Coll 40. **d** 42 **p** 43. C Oxhey St Matt *St Alb* 42-45; C Cirencester *Glouc* 45-52; V Childswyckham 52-62; R Aston Somerville 52-62; RD Winchcombe 60-62; R Stratton w Baunton 62-75; V France Lynch 75-83; rtd 84; Perm to Offic *Glouc* from 84. *9 Cotswold Close, Cirencester GL7 1XP* Tel (01285) 655627 E-mail hearn.petvon@amserve.net

HEARN, Trevor. b 36. Sarum Th Coll 61. **d** 64 **p** 65. C Hounslow St Steph *Lon* 64-67; Miss to Seafarers 67-01; UAE 92-01; rtd 01; Perm to Offic *Bris* from 01. *37 Elberton Road, Bristol BS9 2PZ* Tel 0117-983 6526 E-mail tandv@hearn3136.fsnet.co.uk

HEARTFIELD, Canon Peter Reginald. b 27. Chich Th Coll 61. **d** 63 **p** 64. C Hurstpierpoint *Chich* 63-67; V Brighton St Alb Preston 67-73; Chapl Kent and Cant Hosp 73-92; Chapl Nunnery Fields Hosp Cant 73-92; Six Preacher Cant Cathl 79-84; Hon Can Cant Cathl 84-92; rtd 92; Perm to Offic *Cant* from 00. *13 Lanfranc Gardens, Harbledown, Canterbury CT2 8NJ* Tel and fax (01227) 451621

HEASLIP, William John (Jack). b 44. TCD BA66. CITC 79. **d** 80 **p** 81. Chapl Mt Temple Sch Dub 80-86; Bp's C Aughaval w Burrishoole, Knappagh and Louisburgh *T, K & A* 86-88; I Aughaval w Achill, Knappagh, Dugort etc 88-95; Radio Officer (Tuam) 90-95; I Cork St Luke Union *C, C & R* 95-98; Colann Renewal Min *T, K & A* from 98. *Cloghadockan, Turlough, Castlebar, Co Mayo, Republic of Ireland* Tel (00353) (94) 902 5282 E-mail jackheaslip@eircom.net

HEATH, Mrs Cynthia Grace. b 46. St Mark & St Jo Coll Lon TCert68 Open Univ BA85 ARCM66 GRSM68. WMMTC 94. **d** 97 **p** 98. NSM Penkridge *Lich* 97-00; TV 00-07. *2 Hall Farm Road, Brewood, Stafford ST19 9EZ* Tel (01902) 850175

HEATH, Henry. b 40. FCII77. Oak Hill Th Coll 77. **d** 80 **p** 81. NSM Lexden *Chelmsf* 80-86; C Colne Engaine 86; NSM Halstead St Andr w H Trin and Greenstead Green 86-90; NSM W w E Mersea 90-95; R Stanway 95-02; rtd 02; Perm to Offic *Chelmsf* 02-05; P-in-c Wormingford, Mt Bures and Lt Horkesley from 05. *The Vicarage, Church Road, Wormingford, Colchester CO6 3AZ* Tel and fax (01787) 227398 E-mail heathatquayside@aol.com

HEATH, Mrs Janet. b 45. EMMTC 89. **d** 91 **p** 94. Par Dn Rainworth *S'well* 91-94; C 94-96; C Mansfield Woodhouse 96-99; rtd 00; Perm to Offic *S'well* from 00. *17 The Hollies, Sherwood Park, Rainworth, Mansfield NG21 0FZ* Tel (01623) 490422 E-mail janheath@supanet.com

HEATH, John Henry. b 41. Chich Th Coll 69. **d** 71 **p** 72. C Crediton *Ex* 71-74; C Tavistock and Gulworthy 74-76; C Brixham 76-77; C Brixham w Churston Ferrers 77-79; R Bere Ferrers 79-85; P-in-c Moretonhampstead, N Bovey and Manaton 85-88; R 88-93; P in c Lifton 93-99; P-in-c Kelly w Bradstone 93-99; P-in-c Broadwoodwidger 93-99; R Lifton, Broadwoodwidger, Coryton, Stowford etc 99-01; V Lifton, Broadwoodwidger, Stowford etc 01-03; rtd 03; Perm to Offic *Heref* from 04. *30 Wye Way, Victoria Bridge, Hereford HR1 2NP*

HEATH, Julie Ann. b 62. EMMTC. **d** 06 **p** 07. NSM Kegworth, Hathern, Long Whatton, Diseworth etc *Leic* 06-08. *Fairmount House, 87 Leicester Road, Ashby-de-la-Zouch LE65 1DD* E-mail jaheath@globalnet.co.uk

HEATH, Martin Jonathan. b 68. St Jo Coll Nottm 07. **d** 09. C Gt Wyrley *Lich* from 09. *6 Clover Ridge, Cheslyn Hay, Walsall WS6 7DP* Tel 07847-370572 (mobile) E-mail martinjheath@talktalk.net

HEATH, Mrs Wendy Hillary. b 47. WMMTC 95. **d** 98 **p** 99. NSM Rugeley *Lich* 98-99; C 00-01; P-in-c Brereton 01-06; TV Brereton and Rugeley from 06. *The Vicarage, 72 Main Road, Brereton, Rugeley WS15 1DU* Tel (01889) 582466 E-mail wen_heath@hotmail.com

HEATH-WHYTE, David Robert. b 68. Fitzw Coll Cam BA89. Wycliffe Hall Ox BTh98. **d** 98 **p** 99. C Gt Chesham *Ox* 98-02; V Frogmore *St Alb* from 02. *Holy Trinity Vicarage, 39 Frogmore, St Albans AL2 2JU* Tel (01727) 872172 E-mail david@hotfrog.info

HEATHCOTE, Warwick Geoffrey. b 46. Th Ext Educn Coll 97. **d** 00 **p** 01. C Grahamstown Cathl S Africa 00-03; C Cirencester *Glouc* 03-09; P-in-c Stratton, N Cerney, Baunton and Bagendon from 09. *The Rectory, 94 Gloucester Road, Cirencester GL7 2LJ* Tel (01285) 653359 E-mail warwick.heathcote@sky.com

HEATHER, James Eric. b 34. **d** 98 **p** 99. OLM Hook *S'wark* from 98. *276 Hook Road, Chessington KT9 1PF* Tel (020) 8397 0063

HEATHER, Mark Duncan Grainger. b 62. Leic Poly LLB83 Leeds Univ BA99. Coll of Resurr Mirfield 97. **d** 99 **p** 00. C Leeds St Aid *Ripon* 99-03; V Leeds Halton St Wilfrid from 03. *St Wilfrid's Vicarage, Selby Road, Leeds LS15 7NP* Tel 0113-264 7000 E-mail mark.heather@bigfoot.com

HEATHER, Mrs Sally Patricia. b 51. Avery Hill Coll BEd73. STETS 99. **d** 02 **p** 03. NSM Michelmersh and Awbridge and Braishfield etc *Win* 02-06; TV Basingstoke from 06. *75 Cumberland Avenue, Basingstoke RG22 4BQ* Tel (01256) 422665 E-mail spheather@gmail.com

HEATHFIELD, Simon David. b 67. Birm Univ BMus88 Fitzw Coll Cam BTh99. Ridley Hall Cam 96. **d** 99 **p** 00. C Heswall *Ches* 99-02; Voc and Min Adv CPAS 02-05; TR Walthamstow *Chelmsf* from 06. *St Mary's Rectory, 117 Church Hill, London E17 3BD* Tel (020) 8520 4281 *or* 8520 1430
E-mail simonh@walthamstowchurch.org.uk

HEATLEY, Cecil. *See* HEATLEY, Canon William Cecil

HEATLEY, David Henry. b 50. Kent Univ BA72. Qu Coll Birm 86. **d** 88 **p** 89. C Liss *Portsm* 88-91; V Newchurch and Arreton 91-99; R Greatham w Empshott and Hawkley w Prior's Dean from 99; Dioc Rural Officer from 98. *The Vicarage, Hawkley, Liss GU33 6NF* Tel (01730) 827459 E-mail dhheatley@aol.com

HEATLEY, Canon William Cecil. b 39. QUB BA61. Ridley Hall Cam 62. **d** 64 **p** 65. C Ballymacarrett St Patr *D & D* 64-69; C Herne Hill St Paul *S'wark* 69-74; TV Sanderstead All SS 75-82; P-in-c Peckham St Sav 82-87; V 87-07; RD Dulwich 97-02; Hon Can S'wark Cathl 01-07; rtd 07; Perm to Offic *S'wark* from 07. *37 Bromley College, London Road, Bromley BR1 1PE* Tel (020) 8460 9505 E-mail cecilheatley@yahoo.com

HEATON, Alan. b 36. K Coll Lon BD64 AKC64 Nottm Univ MTh76. **d** 65 **p** 66. C Stockton St Chad *Dur* 65-68; C Englefield Green *Guildf* 68-70; C Winlaton *Dur* 70-74; Chapl Derby Lonsdale Coll 74-79; V Alfreton 79-87; RD Alfreton 81-86; TR Clifton *S'well* 87-93; P-in-c Rolleston w Fiskerton, Morton and Upton 93-96; rtd 97; Perm to Offic *Liv* from 97. *29 The Parchments, Newton-le-Willows WA12 0DX* Tel (01925) 292209

HEATON, Sister Elizabeth Ann. b 65. Bath Coll of HE BSc87. Ripon Coll Cuddesdon. **d** 00 **p** 01. C Lostwithiel, St Winnow w St Nectan's Chpl etc *Truro* 00-03; CSF from 03. *The Community of St Francis, Compton Durville, South Petherton TA13 5ES* Tel (01460) 240473 E-mail liz.hn@btopenworld.com

HEATON, Joseph Anthony Turnley. b 70. Univ of Wales (Abth) BSc91 PhD95 St Jo Coll Dur BA08. Cranmer Hall Dur 06. **d** 08 **p** 09. C Ribbesford w Bewdley and Dowles *Worc* from 08. *18 Brook Vale, Bewdley DY12 1BQ* Tel (01299) 401455

HEATON, Julian Roger. b 62. LSE BSc(Econ)83. St Steph Ho Ox BA86 MA92. **d** 87 **p** 88. C Stockport St Thos w St Pet *Ches* 87-90; Chapl Asst Qu Medical Cen and Univ Hosp Nottm 90-92; V Knutsford St Cross 92-01; P-in-c Altrincham St Jo 01-05; Voc Officer (Macclesfield Adnry) 01-05; V Sale St Anne from 05. *St Anne's Vicarage, Church Road West, Sale M33 3GD* Tel 0161-973 4145 E-mail julian.heaton@talktalk.net

HEATON, Nicholas Mark. b 70. Leeds Metrop Univ BEd92 Ches Coll of HE BTh04. NOC 01. **d** 04 **p** 05. C Linthorpe *York* 04-08; TV Morley *Wakef* from 08. *The Vicarage, Rooms Lane, Morley, Leeds LS27 9PA* Tel 0113-252 6836
E-mail rev.nick@ntlworld.com

HEATON, Timothy. b 59. STETS 08. **d** 08. NSM Upper Stour *Sarum* from 08. *Grange Cottage, Chaffeymoor, Bourton, Gillingham SP8 5BY* Tel (01747) 841076

HEAVER, Derek Cyril. b 47. St Jo Coll Nottm BTh69. **d** 73 **p** 74. C Win Ch Ch 73-77; CF 77-02; rtd 02. *Orchard Cottage, 2 Myrtle Close, Puncknowle, Dorchester DT2 9EH* Tel and fax (01308) 898466 E-mail delsaun@eurobell.co.uk

HEAVISIDES, Canon Neil Cameron. b 50. Selw Coll Cam BA72 MA76 Ox Univ BA74 MA85. Ripon Hall Ox 72. **d** 75 **p** 76. C Stockton St Pet *Dur* 75-78; Succ S'wark Cathl 78-81; V Seaham w Seaham Harbour *Dur* 81-88; P-in-c Edington and Imber, Erlestoke and E Coulston *Sarum* 88-89; R 89-93; Can Res Glouc Cathl from 93. *7 College Green, Gloucester GL1 2LX* Tel (01452) 523987 E-mail nheavisides@gloucestercathedral.org.uk

HEAWOOD, Canon Alan Richard. b 32. G&C Coll Cam BA54 MA58. Union Th Sem (NY) BD56 Ripon Hall Ox 56. **d** 57 **p** 58. C Horwich H Trin *Man* 57-59; C Weaste 59-60; C Beverley Minster *York* 60-62; Chapl and Lect St Pet Coll Saltley 62-65; R Hockwold w Wilton *Ely* 65-72; R Weeting 65-72; V Melbourn 72-80; V Meldreth 72-80; P-in-c Teversham 80-90; Adult Educn Sec 80-89; Dir of Educn 80-98; Hon Can Ely Cathl 80-98; rtd 98; Perm to Offic *Ely* from 98. *10 Westberry Court, Grange Road, Cambridge CB3 9BG* Tel (01223) 460088

HEAZELL, Pamela Fletcher. b 50. NTMTC 96. **d** 99 **p** 00. NSM Hayes St Nic CD *Lon* 99-01; NSM N Greenford All Hallows 01-04; P-in-c 04-08; V from 08. *72 Horsenden Lane North, Greenford UB6 0PD* Tel (020) 8933 7700
E-mail pfheazell@aol.com

HEBBERN, Geoffrey Alan. b 43. MBE98. **d** 05 **p** 06. OLM Bridport *Sarum* from 05. *11 Hawthorn Close, Weymouth DT4 9UG* Tel and fax (01305) 772205
E-mail ghebbern@hotmail.com

HEBBLETHWAITE, Anne Brian Leslie. b 39. Magd Coll Ox BA61 MA67 Magd Coll Cam BA63 MA68 BD84. Westcott Ho Cam 62. **d** 65 **p** 66. C Elton All SS *Man* 65-68; Chapl Qu Coll Cam 68; Dean of Chpl and Fell 69-94; Asst Lect Div Cam Univ 73-77; Lect 77-99; Can Th Leic Cathl 82-00; rtd 99; Perm to Offic *Ely* from 02. *The Old Barn, 32 High Street, Stretham, Ely CB6 3JQ* Tel (01353) 648279 Mobile 07740-307568
E-mail blh1000@cam.ac.uk

HEBBLEWHITE, David Ernest. b 52. Hull Univ BA81 Nottm Univ MA82 CQSW82. St Jo Coll Nottm MA95. **d** 97 **p** 98. C

Melton Mowbray *Leic* 97-00; TV Cannock *Lich* 00-07; P-in-c Countesthorpe w Foston *Leic* from 07. *The Vicarage, 102 Station Road, Countesthorpe, Leicester LE8 5TB* Tel 0116-278 4442 *or* 277 8643

HEBBORN, Roy Valentine Charles. S Dios Minl Tr Scheme 83. **d** 86 **p** 87. NSM Lewes All SS, St Anne, St Mich and St Thos *Chich* 86-00; NSM Lewes St Anne 00-01; rtd 01; Perm to Offic *Chich* from 03. *27 Greater Paddock, Ringmer, Lewes BN8 5LH* Tel (01273) 812005 E-mail roy.hebborn@connectfree.co.uk

HEBDEN, Mrs Cynthia Margaret. b 47. Univ of Wales (Ban) BTh94. **d** 94 **p** 97. NSM Llanfairpwll w Penmynydd *Ban* 94-95; C Twrcelyn Deanery 95-96; C Knighton St Mary Magd *Leic* 96-99; P-in-c Higham-on-the-Hill w Fenny Drayton and Witherley 99-02; P-in-c Stoke Golding w Dadlington 01-02; R Fenn Lanes Gp 02-03; V Shepshed and Oaks in Charnwood from 03; RD Akeley E from 06. *1 Charles Hall Close, Shepshed, Loughborough LE12 9UP* Tel (01509) 508550
E-mail cynthia.hebden@talktalk.net

HEBDEN, John Percy. b 18. Sheff Univ 46 Lon Univ 67. St Aid Birkenhead 58. **d** 60 **p** 60. C Skipton H Trin *Bradf* 60-62; R Kirby Misperton *York* 63-67; V Laxey *S & M* 70-83; V Lonan 80-83; rtd 84; Hon C Douglas St Geo and St Barn *S & M* 84-95. *Begra, Clayhead Road, Baldrine, Isle of Man IM4 6DN* Tel (01624) 861296

HEBDEN, Keith Oliver. b 76. Univ of Wales (Ban) BD98 MTh00 Warwick Univ PGCE01 Birm Univ PhD08. Qu Coll Birm 07. **d** 09. C Matson *Glouc* from 09. *58 Haycroft Drive, Matson, Gloucester GL4 6XX* Tel (01452) 311041

HEBDEN, Peter. b 43. Wigan Coll of Tech MICE67. St As Minl Tr Course 92. **d** 95 **p** 96. NSM Twrcelyn Deanery *Ban* 95-96; NSM Glen Magna cum Stretton Magna etc *Leic* 96-98; Chapl to Asst Bp Leic 98-99; NSM Barwell w Potters Marston and Stapleton 00-02; Perm to Offic from 02. *1 Charles Hall Close, Shepshed, Loughborough LE12 9UP* Tel (01509) 508550
E-mail hebdens@leicester.anglican.org

HEBER, Andrew John. b 63. Nottm Univ BA86 MA89 CQSW89. Trin Coll Bris BA99. **d** 99 **p** 00. C Parr *Liv* 99-03; TV Kirkby from 03. *St Andrew's Vicarage, 63 Roughwood Way, Liverpool L33 4DU* Tel 0151-548 7969 E-mail gill.heber@bigfoot.com

HEBER PERCY, Canon Christopher John. b 41. St Jo Coll Cam BA64 MA68. Wells Th Coll 66. **d** 68 **p** 69. C Leigh St Mary *Man* 68-71; Asst Ind Chapl 71-80; P-in-c Oldham St Andr 75-78; TV Oldham 78-80; Ind Chapl *Win* 80-90; N Humberside Ind Chapl *York* 90-06; AD E Hull 98-06; Can and Preb York Minster 05-06; rtd 06. *59 Swarcliffe Road, Harrogate HG1 4QZ* Tel (01423) 884076 E-mail percy@lindisandchris.karoo.co.uk

HECTOR, Noel Antony. b 61. Sheff Univ LLB83 Barrister-at-Law 84. Oak Hill Th Coll BA91. **d** 91 **p** 92. C Rodbourne Cheney *Bris* 91-92; C Bris St Mary Redcliffe w Temple etc 92-95; R Wrington w Butcombe *B & W* 95-03; R E Clevedon w Clapton in Gordano etc from 03; Chapl N Bris NHS Trust from 03. *The Rectory, All Saints' Lane, Clevedon BS21 6AU* Tel and fax (01275) 873257 E-mail eastcleveub@blueyonder.co.uk

HEDDERLY, Katherine. b 63. St Hugh's Coll Ox BA85 MA94. NTMTC BA06. **d** 06 **p** 07. C Bedford Park *Lon* 06-09; C St Martin-in-the-Fields from 09. *Flat 2, 6 St Martin's Place, London WC2N 4JH*

HEDDLE, Duncan. b 34. Wadh Coll Ox BA57 MA61 DPhil64. **d** 86 **p** 86. Chapl Aber Univ from 86; P-in-c Bucksburn from 90. *2 Douglas Place, High Street, Aberdeen AB24 3EA* Tel (01224) 485975 *or* 272888 E-mail d.heddle@abdn.ac.uk

HEDGE, Peter Andrew. b 62. New Coll Ox MA90. Coll of Resurr Mirfield 90. **d** 93 **p** 94. C Thornbury *Bradf* 93-97; V Queensbury from 97. *7 Russell Hall Lane, Queensbury, Bradford BD13 2AJ* Tel (01274) 815516

HEDGECOCK, Jonathan James. b 64. Imp Coll Lon BScEng86 CEng MIET89. **d** 07 **p** 08. OLM Guildf H Trin w St Mary from 07. *8 Foxglove Gardens, Guildford GU4 7ES* Tel (01483) 502199 Mobile 07785-766631
E-mail jonathan.hedgecock@powerplanning.com

HEDGER, Canon Graham. b 57. Lon Bible Coll BA79. Ridley Hall Cam 81. **d** 83 **p** 84. C Walton *St E* 83-86; TV Mildenhall 86-91; R Swainsthorpe w Newton Flotman *Nor* 91-94; Dioc Evang Officer 91-94; Perm to Offic *St E* 95-99; Bp's Chapl and Liaison Officer 99-07; Bp's Policy and Liaison Officer from 07; P-in-c Clopton w Otley, Swilland and Ashbocking from 09; Hon Can St E Cathl from 04. *14 St Peter's Close, Charsfield, Woodbridge IP13 7RG* Tel (01473) 277042
E-mail graham@stedmundsbury.anglican.org

HEDGES, Mrs Anne Violet. b 53. Ripon Coll Cuddesdon 87. **d** 89 **p** 94. C Thetford *Nor* 89-94; P-in-c Garboldisham w Blo' Norton, Riddlesworth etc 94-97; R Guiltcross 97-00; Chapl Riddlesworth Hall Sch Nor 93-00; Dep Chapl HM Pris Leeds 00-01; Chapl HM Pris Leic 01-05; Chapl HM Pris Highpoint 05-09; Chapl HM Pris Coltishall from 09. *HM Prison at RAF Coltishall, Coltishall, Norwich NR10 5AJ* Tel (01603) 266800 E-mail anne.hedges@hmps.gsi.gov.uk

HEDGES, Canon Dennis Walter. b 29. Sarum Th Coll. **d** 62 **p** 63. C Walton-on-Thames *Guildf* 62-66; C Westborough 66-69; V

Blackheath and Chilworth 69-79; R Farncombe 79-94; RD Godalming 84-89; Hon Can Guildf Cathl 92-94; rtd 94; Perm to Offic *Guildf* and *Win* from 94; *Portsm* from 99. *21 Lincoln Green, Alton GU34 1SX* Tel and fax (01420) 542624 Mobile 07989-110454 E-mail dennisw.hedges@lineone.net

HEDGES, Ian Charles. b 55. Sarum & Wells Th Coll 79. **d** 82 **p** 83. C Chessington *Guildf* 82-85; C Fleet 85-90; Dioc Adv on Homelessness from 87; V S Farnborough from 90; Tr Officer for Past Assts 91-00. *The Vicarage, 1 St Mark's Close, Farnborough GU14 6PP* Tel (01252) 544711
E-mail smarksfbro@btinternet.com

HEDGES, Canon Jane Barbara. b 55. St Jo Coll Dur BA78. Cranmer Hall Dur 78. **dss** 80 **d** 87 **p** 94. Fareham H Trin *Portsm* 80-83; Southampton (City Cen) *Win* 83-87; Par Dn 87-88; Dioc Stewardship Adv *Portsm* 88-93; Can Res Portsm Cathl 93-01; P-in-c Honiton, Gittisham, Combe Raleigh, Monkton etc *Ex* 01-03; TR 03-06; RD Honiton 03-06; Can Steward Westmr Abbey from 06. *2 Little Cloister, London SW1P 3PL* Tel (020) 7654 4867 *or* 7654 4815 Fax 7654 4811
E-mail jane.hedges@westminster-abbey.org

HEDGES, Mrs Jane Rosemary. b 44. RGN65. S Dios Minl Tr Scheme 86. **d** 89 **p** 94. NSM Gillingham *Sarum* 89-04; NSM Gillingham and Milton-on-Stour 04-08; Lic to RD Blackmore Vale from 08. *Dene Hollow, Wyke Road, Gillingham SP8 4NG* Tel (01747) 822812 E-mail denehollow@msn.com

HEDGES, John Michael Peter. b 34. Leeds Univ BA60. Ripon Hall Ox 60. **d** 61 **p** 62. C Weaste *Man* 61-65; V Ashton St Pet 65-74; C Easthampstead *Ox* 74-85; V Tilehurst St Geo 85-91; C Thatcham 91-94; TV 94-99; rtd 99; Perm to Offic *Ox* from 99. *39 Mallard Way, Grove, Wantage OX12 0QG* Tel (01235) 766834

HEDGES, Leslie Norman. b 26. Bris Univ BA51 Lon Univ BD56. Clifton Th Coll 48. **d** 53 **p** 54. C Summerstown *S'wark* 53-55; C Wolverhampton St Luke *Lich* 55-56; C Reigate St Mary *S'wark* 56-59; V Clapham Park All SS 59-70; V Findern *Derby* 70-82; V Willington 70-82; V Trowbridge St Thos and W Ashton *Sarum* 82-91; rtd 91; Perm to Offic *Truro* from 91. *16 Penwerris Road, Truro TR1 3QS* Tel (01872) 279858

HEDLEY, Charles John Wykeham. b 47. R Holloway Coll Lon BSc69 PhD73 Fitzw Coll Cam BA75 MA79. Westcott Ho Cam 73. **d** 76 **p** 77. C Chingford St Anne *Chelmsf* 76-79; C St Martin-in-the-Fields Lon 79-84 and 85-86; P-in-c 84-85; Chapl Ch Coll Cam 86-90; TR Gleadless *Sheff* 90-99; R Westmr St Jas *Lon* from 99. *St James's Rectory, 197 Piccadilly, London W1J 9LL* Tel (020) 7734 4511 Fax 7734 7449
E-mail ch@chsplace.freeserve.co.uk

HEDLEY, Mrs Julia Margaret. b 56. Goldsmiths' Coll Lon BA78 Bedf Coll Lon MSc85 Liv Univ MTh03 SRN80. NOC 97. **d** 00 **p** 01. C Altrincham St Geo *Ches* 00-04; PV Ches Cathl 04-07; Bps' Dom Chapl *B & W* from 07. *The Palace, Wells BA5 2PD* Tel (01749) 672341 Fax 679355
E-mail julia.hedley@bathwells.anglican.org

HEDLEY, William Clifford. b 35. Tyndale Hall Bris 65. **d** 67 **p** 68. C Hensingham *Carl* 67-69; C Rainhill *Liv* 69-71; C St Helens St Helen 71-73; V Low Elswick *Newc* 73-81; V Kingston upon Hull St Aid Southcoates *York* 81-87; TV Heworth H Trin 87-94; V Norton juxta Malton 94-97; C Newburn *Newc* 97-01; rtd 01. *21 Laburnum Grove, Sunniside, Newcastle upon Tyne NE16 5LY* Tel 0191-488 2908

HEDWORTH, Paul Simon James. b 56. Worc Coll of Educn BEd78. Qu Coll Birm BA(Theol)84. **d** 04 **p** 05. NSM Bacup and Stacksteads *Man* 04-06; Chapl Qu Eliz Gr Sch Blackb 98-06; Chapl Bromsgrove Sch from 06. *Bromsgrove School, Worcester Road, Bromsgrove B61 7DU* Tel (01527) 579679 Mobile 07966-503194 E-mail hedworthfamily@yahoo.co.uk

HEELEY, Mrs Janet. b 45. **d** 00 **p** 01. OLM Lich St Chad from 00. *43 High Grange, Lichfield WS13 7DU* Tel (01543) 251600
E-mail janet.heeley@talktalk.net

HEELEY, Robert Francis. b 54. NOC 06. **d** 08 **p** 09. NSM Hadfield *Derby* from 08. *3 Chesham Close, Hadfield, Glossop SK13 1QX* Tel (01457) 855541 E-mail rob.heeley@uwclub.net

HEELEY, Mrs Ruth Mary. b 41. Qu Coll Birm 04. **d** 06 **p** 07. NSM Halas *Worc* from 06. *4 Cherry Tree Lane, Halesowen B63 1DU* Tel 0121-550 7622 E-mail ruthmh@hotmail.co.uk

HEENAN, Vivienne Mary. b 48. Univ of Wales (Abth) BA70 SS Paul & Mary Coll Cheltenham PGCE90. STETS 03. **d** 06 **p** 07. NSM Niton *Portsm* from 06; NSM Whitwell from 06. *Dolphins House, Boxers Lane, Niton, Ventnor PO38 2BH* Tel and fax (01983) 730352 Mobile 07740-780767
E-mail vivienne.heenan@tiscali.co.uk

HEFFER, Thomas Patrick Peter. b 69. K Coll Lon BD90 AKC90 Univ of Wales (Cardiff) LLM03. Ripon Coll Cuddesdon 94. **d** 96 **p** 97. C Sprowston w Beeston *Nor* 96-98; Bp's Chapl and Press Officer 98-01; Min Sec Miss to Seafarers 01-05; Dir Chapl 05-09; Sec Gen from 09; Lic to Offic *Lon* and Perm to Offic *St Alb* from 01. *The Mission to Seafarers, St Michael Paternoster Royal, College Hill, London EC4R 2RL* Tel (020) 7248 5202 Fax 7248 4761 E-mail secgen@missiontoseafarers.org

HEFFER, William John Gambrell. b 30. AKC55. **d** 56 **p** 57. C Biggleswade *St Alb* 56-59; C Clacton St Jas *Chelmsf* 59-61; V

Langford *St Alb* 61-67; V Luton All SS 67-73; P-in-c Eaton Socon 73-75; V 75-77; Lic to Offic 78-81; R Wingrave w Rowsham, Aston Abbotts and Cublington *Ox* 81-88; R Wilden w Colmworth and Ravensden *St Alb* 88-91; C Leighton Buzzard w Eggington, Hockliffe etc 91-94; rtd 94; Perm to Offic *St Alb* 94-00 and from 01; *Ox* 97-01; P-in-c Empingham and Exton w Horn w Whitwell *Pet* 00-01. *Domus, 35 Pebblemoor, Edlesborough, Dunstable LU6 2HZ* Tel (01525) 220618

HEFFERNAN, Anna Elizabeth. *See* LINDSEY, Anna Elizabeth

HEFFERNAN, Ms May Olive. b 52. Maria Grey Coll Lon CertEd74 Lon Univ BD93. Aston Tr Scheme 88 Westcott Ho Cam 93. **d** 93 **p** 94. C Duddeston w Nechells *Birm* 93-97; P-in-c Ward End 97-03; rtd 03. *22 Ladysmith Close, Christchurch BH23 3DR*

HEGARTY, Gerald. b 52. QUB BA74 BD81. Union Th Coll Belf 78. **d** 86 **p** 87. NSM Leic H Trin w St Jo 86-87; P-in-c Sibson w Sheepy and Ratcliffe Culey 87-90; Tutor Wycliffe Hall Ox 90-95; Chapl St Edm Hall Ox 90-96 and from 04; Tutor SAOMC *Ox* 96-99; Vice Prin 00-05; Vice Prin Ox Min Course from 05. *39 Lakeside, Oxford OX2 8JF* Tel (01865) 557847

HEIDT, John Harrison. b 32. Yale Univ BA54 Ox Univ BLitt67 DPhil75. Nashotah Ho BD57 MDiv69. **d** 56 **p** 57. USA 57-75; C Ox St Mary Magd 75-80; V Up Hatherley *Glouc* 80-96; P-in-c Cheltenham St Steph 89-95; USA from 96; rtd 97. *204 North Rosemont Avenue, Dallas TX 75208-5413, USA* Tel (001) (214) 948 3442 Fax 941 0339

HEIGHT (*formerly* WATKINS), Susan Jane. b 58. Qu Coll Birm. **d** 01 **p** 02. C Edgbaston St Germain *Birm* 01-05; TV Salter Street and Shirley from 05. *18 Widney Lane, Solihull B91 3LS* Tel 0121-705 6586 E-mail sue-watkins@blueyonder.co.uk

HEIGHTON, Miss Janet Elizabeth. b 67. Leeds Poly BSc92. Ripon Coll Cuddesdon. **d** 00 **p** 01. C Leeds Gipton Epiphany *Ripon* 00-04; P-in-c 04-07; TV Upholland *Liv* from 07. *158 Back Lane, Birleywood, Skelmersdale WN8 9BX* Tel (01695) 728091 E-mail janet@christtheservantchurch.org.uk

HEIL, Janet. b 53. Liv Univ BEd75 St Jo Coll Dur BA84. Cranmer Hall Dur. **dss** 85 **d** 87 **p** 94. Ashton Ch Ch *Man* 85-91; Par Dn 87-91; Par Dn Scotforth *Blackb* 91-94; C 94-95; V Gt Harwood St Bart 95-06; P-in-c Gt Harwood St Jo 02-06; Hon Can Blackb Cathl 04-06; Chapl Oslo w Bergen, Trondheim and Stavanger *Eur* from 06. *Harald Hårfagres Gate 2 (L512), 0363 Oslo, Norway* Tel (0047) 2269 2214 Fax 2269 2163

HEINZE, Canon Rudolph William. b 31. Concordia Coll (USA) BSc56 CertEd56 De Paul Univ (USA) MA59 Univ of Iowa PhD65. **d** 86 **p** 87. NSM London Colney St Pet *St Alb* 86-98; Lect Oak Hill Th Coll 86-98; Sen Tutor 88-94; Vice-Prin 94-97; Visiting Scholar from 99; Hon Can Port Sudan from 94; Hon Prof Middx Univ from 98. *1714D Lakecliffe Drive, Wheaton IL 60181-8368, USA* Tel (001) (630) 588 8954
E-mail revrudi@aol.com

HELEN, Sister. *See* LODER, Sister Helen

HELEY, John. b 28. Lon Univ BA72. Bps' Coll Cheshunt 54. **d** 56 **p** 57. C Claremont St Sav S Africa 57-61; C Wimborne Minster *Sarum* 61-62; V Narborough w Narford *Nor* 62-67; R Pentney St Mary Magd w W Bilney 62-67; V Catton 67-69; Lic to Offic *Ox* 69-72; R E w W Rudham *Nor* 72-75; P-in-c Houghton 72-74; V 74-75; V Hunstanton St Edm 75-82; V Hunstanton St Edm w Ringstead 82-83; rtd 88. *24 Kestrel Close, Burnham Market, King's Lynn PE31 8EF* Tel (01328) 730036

HELFT, Gunter. b 23. Lon Univ BA48. Ely Th Coll 46. **d** 48 **p** 49. Chapl Essex Home Sch Chelmsf 48-52; C Chelmsf Ascension 48-49; C Billesley Common *Birm* 52-53; Miss to Seamen 53-62; Japan 53-57; Sudan 57; Sec HQ 57-62; Bp's Youth Officer *Ox* 62-65; Tr Officer C of E Youth Coun 65-67; Hd Master Abp Temple's Sch Lambeth 67-71; Hd Master Don Valley High Sch S Yorkshire 71; rtd 80; Perm to Offic *Worc* from 87. *19 Kenwood Avenue, Worcester WR4 9BD* Tel (01905) 29797
E-mail ghelft@btinternet.com

HELLARD, Dawn Yvonne Lorraine. b 47. St Mich Coll Llan 89. **d** 91 **p** 97. C Llantwit Major 91-95; TV Cowbridge 95-05; rtd 05. *10 Maes Lloi, Aberthin, Cowbridge CF71 7HA* Tel (01446) 772460

HELLEWELL, John. b 63. Bris Univ BSc86 BTh93 Nottm Univ MA94. St Jo Coll Nottm 93. **d** 94 **p** 95. C Greasbrough *Sheff* 94-98; P-in-c High Hoyland, Scissett and Clayton W *Wakef* 98-04; V Mount Pellon 04-09; V Halifax St Aug and Mount Pellon from 09; Warden of Readers from 04. *The Vicarage, Church Lane, Halifax HX2 0EF* Tel (01422) 365027
E-mail revjhell@blueyonder.co.uk

HELLICAR, Hugh Christopher. b 37. Qu Coll Birm 69. **d** 70 **p** 71. C Bromyard *Heref* 70-73; C Bishop's Castle w Mainstone 73-75; Perm to Offic *S'wark* 77-85 and Chich 83-93; NSM Hove *Chich* 93-98; rtd 02. *74 Marina, St Leonards-on-Sea TN38 0BJ* Tel (01424) 444072

HELLIER, Jeremy Peter. b 53. K Coll Lon BD75 AKC75 QTS01. St Aug Coll Cant 75. **d** 76 **p** 77. C Walton *St E* 76-79; C Ipswich St Fran 79-80; C Wolborough w Newton Abbot *Ex* 80-82; CF 82-84; R Pendine w Llanmiloe and Eglwys Gymyn w Marros *St D* 84-89; TR Widecombe-in-the-Moor, Leusdon, Princetown etc *Ex* 89-94; CF (TAVR) 90-03; RD Moreton *Ex* 91-94; Chapl and Hd RE Wellington Sch Somerset from 94; Hon Chapl Miss to Seafarers from 02. *Wellington School, Wellington TA21 8NT* Tel (01823) 668827 *or* 668837 Fax 668844 Mobile 07971-588184 E-mail jeremyhellier@hotmail.com

HELLINGS, Mrs Tara Charmian Lashmar. b 68. Ch Ch Ox MA90. STETS 06. **d** 09. NSM Alton St Lawr *Win* from 09. *Serendib, 1 Poacher's Field, South Warnborough, Hook RG29 1RB* Tel (01256) 862810 Mobile 07932-184873 E-mail tartzhellings@yahoo.co.uk

HELLIWELL (*née* SWALLOW), **Mrs Judith Hazel.** b 46. Dioc OLM tr scheme 99. **d** 01 **p** 02. OLM Meltham *Wakef* from 01. *3 Upper Wilshaw, Meltham, Holmfirth HD9 4EA* Tel (01484) 851158

HELLMUTH, Miss Lynn. b 61. Lon Bible Coll BA82 Birm Univ PGCE83. Wycliffe Hall Ox 00. **d** 02 **p** 03. C Twickenham Common H Trin *Lon* 02-05; TV Crawley *Chich* 05-08; V Stoneleigh *Guildf* from 08. *The Vicarage, 59 Stoneleigh Park Road, Epsom KT19 0QU* Tel (020) 8393 3738 E-mail lynnhellmuth@yahoo.co.uk

HELLYER, Ian Anthony. b 66. Lanc Univ BSc91 Nottm Univ BTh95. Linc Th Coll 92. **d** 95 **p** 96. C Poulton-le-Fylde *Blackb* 95-01; R Moretonhampstead, Manaton, N Bovey and Lustleigh *Ex* from 01. *The Rectory, 3 Grays Meadow, Moretonhampstead, Newton Abbot TQ13 8NB* Tel (01647) 441098 E-mail hellyer@surfaid.org

HELLYER, Stephen John. b 56. St Cath Coll Cam BA77 MA81. Wycliffe Hall Ox 82. **d** 84 **p** 85. C Plymouth St Andr w St Paul and St Geo *Ex* 84-88; Chapl Lee Abbey 88-89; Lon and SE Consultant CPAS 90-94; C Nottingham St Nic *S'well* 94-98; P-in-c Ox St Matt from 98. *St Matthew's Vicarage, Marlborough Road, Oxford OX1 4LW* Tel (01865) 243434 E-mail steve@hellyers.fsworld.co.uk

HELM, Alistair Thomas. b 53. Aston Univ BSc75. EAMTC 88. **d** 91 **p** 92. NSM Leic St Jas 91-95; NSM Humberstone 95-03; NSM Ascension TM 03-04; NSM Emmaus Par Team 04-09; NSM Giggleswick and Rathmell w Wigglesworth *Bradf* from 09. *The Vicarage, Bankwell Road, Giggleswick, Settle BD24 0AP* E-mail alistair.helm@btinternet.com

HELM, Catherine Mary. b 64. St Martin's Coll Lanc BEd86. St Jo Coll Nottm 03. **d** 05 **p** 06. C Heswall *Ches* 05-09; V Burton and Shotwick from 09. *The Vicarage, Vicarage Lane, Burton, Neston CH64 5TJ* Tel 0151-336 4070

HELM, Nicholas. b 57. Surrey Univ BSc81. St Jo Coll Nottm 85. **d** 88 **p** 89. C Old Ford St Paul w St Steph and St Mark *Lon* 88-92; TV Nethertorpe *Sheff* 92-93; V Sheff St Bart 93-98; Bp's Chapl 99-03; Bp's Adv in Spirituality from 99; Chapl Whirlow Grange Conf Cen Sheff from 99. *23 Hill Turrets Close, Sheffield S11 9RE* Tel 0114-235 0191 Fax 235 2275 E-mail nick@bishopscroft.idps.co.uk

HELMS, David Clarke. b 50. Boston Univ BA72. Yale Div Sch MDiv77. **d** 77 **p** 77. USA 77-88; Ind Chapl *Worc* 88-97; Ind Chapl Teesside *York* 97-02; Dir Workplace Min for Ch in Soc *Roch* from 05. *3 Royal Oak Terrace, Gravesend DA12 1JU* Tel (01474) 321593 Mobile 07957-193816 E-mail davidh@churchinsociety.org

HELYER, Patrick Joseph Peter. b 15. ALCD39 FRGS83. Wycliffe Hall Ox 38. **d** 38 **p** 39. C Maidstone St Paul *Cant* 38-41; Asst Chapl Miss to Seamen 41-42; Chapl RNVR 42-46; V St Nicholas at Wade w Sarre *Cant* 46-50; Chapl RAN Australia 51-61; V Rolvenden *Cant* 62-66; R Frome St Quintin w Evershot and Melbury Bubb *Sarum* 66-71; R Ch Ch Cathl Falkland Is 71-75; Hon Can Port Stanley 72-75; R Streat w Westmeston *Chich* 75-78; P-in-c Tristan da Cunha 78-81; rtd 81; Perm to Offic *Heref* 84-00; *Glouc* from 84. *c/o J A Helyer Esq, 1 Mews Gardens, Northford Road, Dartmouth TQ6 9ET* Tel (01803) 833392

HEMINGRAY, Raymond. b 47. Leeds Univ LLB68 Solicitor 71. ERMC 04. **d** 07 **p** 08. Dioc Registrar *Pet* from 74; NSM Castor w Sutton and Upton w Marholm from 07. *4 Holywell Way, Peterborough PE3 6SS* Tel (01733) 262523 Fax 330280 Mobile 07860-227354 E-mail rh@raymondhemingray.co.uk

HEMINGWAY, Peter. b 32. S'wark Ord Course 72. **d** 75 **p** 76. NSM Belmont *S'wark* 75-79; C Herne Hill St Paul 79-81; V Headstone St Geo *Lon* 81-92; V N Harrow St Alb 87-02; rtd 02. *Chelmerton, 138 Winthrope Road, Bury St Edmunds IP33 3XW* Tel (01284) 705070

HEMMING, Terry Edward. b 47. Calvin Coll Michigan MA84. S Dios Minl Tr Scheme 88. **d** 90 **p** 91. NSM E Win 90-09; Chapl St Swithun's Sch Win 95-07; NSM Hurstbourne Priors, Longparish etc *Win* from 09. *St Nicholas House, Longparish, Andover SP11 6PG* Tel (01264) 720215 E-mail revhemm@yahoo.co.uk

HEMMING-CLARK, Stanley Charles. b 29. Peterho Cam BA52 MA56. Ridley Hall Cam 52. **d** 54 **p** 55. C Redhill H Trin *S'wark* 54-56; C Woking St Jo *Guildf* 56-59; V Crockenhill All So *Roch* 59-97; rtd 97; Perm to Offic *Guildf* from 97. *St Anthony's, 22 Ashcroft, Shalford, Guildford GU4 8JT* Tel (01483) 568197

HEMMINGS, Ms Jane Marie. b 68. Lon Univ BD91 AKC91 Heythrop Coll Lon MTh95 Southn Univ PGCE08. NTMTC 01.

d 03 **p** 04. C Bishop's Waltham and Upham *Portsm* 03-08; NSM 07-08; NSM Akeman *Ox* from 08. *The Rectory, Troy Lane, Kirtlington, Kidlington OX5 3HA* Tel (01869) 350224 E-mail dauphin.jg@btinternet.com

HEMMINGS, Keith. b 43. **d** 97. Par Dn Bedwellty *Mon* 97-05; Par Dn Bedwellty w New Tredegar 05-06; Perm to Offic from 06. *Penydarren, Park Drive, Bargoed CF81 8PJ* Tel (01443) 830662

HEMMINGS, Roy Anthony. b 48. Univ of Wales (Cardiff) BD85 MTh00. St Mich Coll Llan 82. **d** 86 **p** 87. C Rhyl w St Ann *St As* 86-90; CF 90-08; V Maybush and Southampton St Jude *Win* from 08. *Maybush Vicarage, Sedbergh Road, Southampton SO16 9HJ* Tel (023) 8070 3443 Mobile 07710-774431 E-mail padreroy48@aol.com

HEMPHILL, John James. b 44. TCD BA68 MA72. Oak Hill Th Coll 71. **d** 73 **p** 74. C Dundonald *D & D* 73-78; I Balteagh w Carrick *D & R* 78-02; I Ballyhalbert w Ardkeen *D & D* from 02. *Ballyeasboro Rectory, 187 Main Road, Portavogie, Newtownards BT22 1DA* Tel (028) 4277 1234 Mobile 07890-012843

HEMSLEY, David Ridgway. b 36. AKC61. **d** 61 **p** 62. C Penhill *Bris* 61-64; C Highworth w Sevenhampton and Inglesham etc 64-66; C Surbiton St Andr *S'wark* 66-70; P-in-c Tingewick w Water Stratford *Ox* 70-75; P-in-c Radclive 72-75; PM N Marston w Granborough etc 75-81; P-in-c Quainton 75-81; TV Schorne 81-90; P-in-c Lt Missenden 90-93; V 93-01; rtd 01; Perm to Offic *Ox* from 03; AD Buckingham from 09. *27 Overn Avenue, Buckingham MK18 1LG* Tel (01280) 814636

HEMSLEY HALLS, Susan Mary. b 59. Cranmer Hall Dur 93. **d** 95 **p** 96. C Wilnecote *Lich* 95-00; P-in-c Attenborough *S'well* from 00; Dioc Chapl amongst Deaf People from 00. *Vale Cottage, 19 Church Lane, Attenborough, Beeston NG9 6AS* Tel 0115-925 9602 E-mail mail@smca.fsworld.co.uk

HEMSTOCK, Julian. b 51. Trent Poly BSc74 CEng MIProdE. Sarum & Wells Th Coll 89. **d** 91 **p** 92. C Carrington *S'well* 91-94; C Basford St Aid 94-97; Asst Chapl Qu Medical Cen Nottm Univ Hosp NHS Trust 97-03; Chapl from 03. *Queen's Medical Centre University Hospital, Derby Road, Nottingham NG7 2UH* Tel 0115-924 9924 ext 43799 E-mail julian.hemstock@qmc.nhs.uk

HEMSTOCK, Mrs Pat. b 51. Sarum & Wells Th Coll 89. **d** 91 **p** 95. Par Dn Carrington *S'well* 91-94; Par Dn Basford St Aid 94-95; C 95-97; P-in-c 97-05; V Calverton from 05. *The Vicarage, Crookdole Lane, Calverton, Nottingham NG14 6GF* Tel 0115-965 2552 E-mail pat.hemstock@btinternet.com

HEMSWORTH, John Alan. b 45. FGA67. Man OLM Scheme 99. **d** 02 **p** 03. OLM Droylsden St Andr *Man* from 02. *13 Keston Avenue, Droylsden, Manchester M43 6BL* Tel 0161-292 7356

HENCHER, John Bredon. b 31. Lich Th Coll 58. **d** 60 **p** 61. C Pershore w Wick *Worc* 60-62; Bp's Dom Chapl 63-64; V Amblecote 64-70; Perm to Offic *Glouc* 72-74; Dioc RE Adv *Heref* 74-80; Lic to Offic 80-87; Perm to Offic *Mon* 87-00; Asst Chapl Mon Sch 87-00; Chapl from 00. *The Tank House, Weston, Pembridge, Leominster HR6 9JE* Tel (01544) 388540

HENDERSON, Canon Alastair Roy. b 27. BNC Ox BA51 MA54. Ridley Hall Cam 52. **d** 54 **p** 55. C Ex St Leon w H Trin 54-57; Travelling Sec IVF 57-60; C St Mary le Bow w St Pancras Soper Lane etc *Lon* 58-60; V Barton Hill St Luke w Ch Ch *Bris* 60-68; P-in-c Bris St Phil and St Jacob w Em 67-68; V Stoke Bishop 68-92; Lect Clifton Th Coll 69-71; Lect Trin Coll Bris 71-73; RD Westbury and Severnside *Bris* 73-79; Hon Can Bris Cathl 80-92; rtd 92; Perm to Offic *Ex* from 92. *3 Garden Court, Cricketfield Lane, Budleigh Salterton EX9 6PN* Tel (01395) 446147

HENDERSON, Andrew Douglas. b 36. Trin Coll Cam BA60 MA64 Liv Univ DASS65 MBASW. Cuddesdon Coll 60. **d** 62 **p** 63. C Newington St Paul *S'wark* 62-64; Hon C Camberwell St Luke 65-80; Perm to Offic *Lon* 85-06 and *Chich* from 06. *4 Western Terrace, Brighton BN1 2LD* Tel (01273) 327829

HENDERSON, Ashley. *See* HENDERSON, Peter Ashley

HENDERSON, Colin. *See* HENDERSON, Francis Colin

HENDERSON, David. *See* HENDERSON, Robert David Druitt

HENDERSON, David. b 35. Oak Hill NSM Course. **d** 83 **p** 84. NSM Rush Green *Chelmsf* 83-00; Perm to Offic from 00. *Le Strange Cottages, 2-8 Hunstanton Road, Heacham, King's Lynn PE31 7HH* Tel (01485) 572150

HENDERSON, Mrs Elizabeth. b 42. CITC 96. **d** 99 **p** 00. C Ballymacash *Conn* 99-00; C Finaghy from 00; Asst Chapl Belfast City Hosp Health and Soc Services Trust 99-05; Asst Chapl Down Lisburn Health and Soc Services Trust from 05. *39 Garvey Court, Lisburn BT27 4DG* Tel (028) 9260 7146 E-mail hclerics@tesco.net

HENDERSON, Francis Colin. b 35. St Cath Coll Cam BA59 MA63. Cuddesdon Coll 60. **d** 62 **p** 63. C Croydon St Jo *Cant* 62-67; V Westwood *Cov* 67-75; V Chilvers Coton w Astley 75-80; P-in-c Wolston 80; P-in-c Church Lawford w Newnham Regis 80; V Wolston and Church Lawford 80-85; USA from 85; rtd 00. *1364 Katella Street, Laguna Beach CA 92651-3437, USA* Tel (001) (949) 497 2239 E-mail echenderson@earthlink.net

HENDERSON, The Ven Janet. b 57. St Jo Coll Dur BA88 RGN82. Cranmer Hall Dur 85. **d** 88 **p** 94. Par Dn Wisbech SS Pet and Paul *Ely* 88-90; Par Dn Bestwood *S'well* 90-93; Tutor

St Jo Coll Nottm 92-97; Lect Worship 93-97; NSM Bramcote *S'well* 94-97; Lect Worship and Tutor Ridley Hall Cam 97-01; Dir Studies 00-01; P-in-c Nuthall *S'well* 01-07; Dean of Women's Min 01-07; AD Beeston 06-07; Hon Can S'well Minster 03-07; Adn Richmond *Ripon* from 07. *Hoppus House, Hutton Conyers, Ripon HG4 5DX* Tel and fax (01765) 601316
E-mail janeth@riponleeds-diocese.org.uk

HENDERSON, Mrs Janet Elizabeth. b 53. N Lon Poly BSc75. Ripon Coll Cuddesdon 05. **d** 06 **p** 07. NSM Ellesborough, The Kimbles and Stoke Mandeville *Ox* from 06. *Brook Farm, Marsh Road, Little Kimble, Aylesbury HP22 5XS* Tel (01296) 613241
E-mail brook-farm@supanet.com

HENDERSON, Judith Ann. b 37. **d** 89 **p** 94. NSM Sheringham *Nor* 89-92; NSM Brampton St Thos *Derby* 92-00; Perm to Offic *Sarum* from 00. *Blackmore House, Stone Lane, Wimborne BH21 1HD* Tel (01202) 881422

HENDERSON, The Ven Julian Tudor. b 54. Keble Coll Ox BA76 MA81. Ridley Hall Cam 77. **d** 79 **p** 80. C Islington St Mary *Lon* 79-83; V Hastings Em and St Mary in the Castle *Chich* 83-92; V Claygate *Guildf* 92-05; RD Emly 96-01; Adn Dorking from 05; Hon Can Guildf Cathl from 02. *The Old Cricketers, Portsmouth Road, Ripley, Woking GU23 6ER* Tel (01483) 479300
E-mail julian.henderson@cofeguildford.org.uk

HENDERSON, Nicholas Paul. b 48. Selw Coll Cam BA73 MA77. Ripon Hall Ox 73. **d** 75 **p** 76. C St Alb St Steph *St Alb* 75-78; Warden J F Kennedy Ho Cov Cathl 78-79; C Bow w Bromley St Leon *Lon* 79-85; P-in-c W Acton St Martin 85-96; V from 96; P-in-c Ealing All SS 89-95; V from 96. *The Parishes Office, 25 Birch Grove, London W3 9SP* Tel (020) 8992 2333 *or* 8248 0608 Fax 8993 5812
E-mail nicholashenderson@btinternet.com

HENDERSON, Olive Elizabeth. b 48. St Jo Coll Nottm. **d** 97 **p** 98. Aux Min Tallaght *D & G* 97-99; P-in-c Moviddy Union *C, C & R* 99-01; P-in-c Rathdrum w Glenealy, Derralossary and Laragh *D & G* 01-04; C 04-07; I 07-08; I Killeshin w Cloydagh and Killabban *C & O* from 08. *The Rectory, Ballickmoyler, Co Carlow, Republic of Ireland* Tel (00353) (59) 862 5321 Mobile 87-218 1891

HENDERSON, Patrick James. b 57. R Holloway Coll Lon BA78 Surrey Univ PGCE01. St Steph Ho Ox 83. **d** 86 **p** 87. C Hornsey St Mary w St Geo *Lon* 86-90; V Whetstone St Jo 90-95; In RC Ch 95-01; Perm to Offic 01-02; C Hornsey H Innocents 02-07; C Stroud Green H Trin 02-04; P-in-c 04-07; V from 07; C Hornsey H Innocents from 07; Chapl Greig City Academy from 02. *Holy Trinity Vicarage, Granville Road, London N4 4EL* Tel (020) 8340 2051 Mobile 07947-714893
E-mail pjhenderson2001@yahoo.co.uk

HENDERSON, Peter Ashley. b 59. St Martin's Coll Lanc PGCE00. CBDTI 02. **d** 05 **p** 06. NSM Arnside *Carl* 05-08; NSM Kendal H Trin from 08. *2 Lowther Park, Kendal LA9 6RS* Tel (01539) 736079 E-mail janash@btinternet.com

HENDERSON, Richard. b 69. St Jo Coll Nottm 04. **d** 06 **p** 07. C Beccles St Mich and St Luke *St E* 06-09; TV Sole Bay from 09. *The Rectory, 45 Wangford Road, Reydon, Southwold IP18 6PZ*
E-mail richhenderson@btinternet.com

✠**HENDERSON, The Rt Revd Richard Crosbie Aitken.** b 57. Magd Coll Ox MA84 DPhil84. St Jo Coll Nottm 83. **d** 86 **p** 87 **c** 98. C Chinnor w Emmington and Sydenham etc *Ox* 86-89; I Abbeystrewry Union *C, C & R* 89-95; I Ross Union 95-98; Dean Ross 95-98; Chan Cork Cathl 95-98; Bp T, K & A from 98. *Bishop's House, Knockglass, Crossmolina, Ballina, Co Mayo, Republic of Ireland* Tel (00353) (96) 31317 Fax 31775
E-mail bptuam@iol.ie

HENDERSON, Robert. b 43. TCD 66 Lambeth STh94. **d** 69 **p** 70. C Drumglass *Arm* 69-72; Chapl Miss to Seamen 72-77; Sen Chapl Mombasa Kenya 77-78; I Mostrim w Granard, Clonbroney, Killoe etc *K, E & A* 78-82; I Belfast St Matt *Conn* 82-92; I Kilroot and Templecorran 92-98; rtd 98. *39 Garvey Court, Lisburn BT27 4DG* Tel (028) 9260 7146
E-mail hclerics@tesco.net

HENDERSON, Robert David Druitt. b 41. St Edm Hall Ox MA64 Brunel Univ MA77 K Alfred's Coll Win PGCE88. **d** 03 **p** 04. OLM Wylye and Till Valley *Sarum* from 03. *Orchard House, Salisbury Road, Steeple Langford, Salisbury SP3 4NQ* Tel (01722) 790388 E-mail henderson.family@virgin.net

HENDERSON, Mrs Shirley Claire. b 49. Surrey Univ BA02. Bp Otter Coll 94. **d** 96 **p** 02. NSM Gatcombe, Chale and Shorwell w Kingston *Portsm* 96-00; NSM Whitwell, Niton and St Lawrence 00-03; P-in-c Shedfield 03-06; R Shedfield and Wickham 07; TV Parkham, Alwington, Buckland Brewer etc *Ex* from 07; RD Hartland from 09. *The Vicarage, Hartland, Bideford EX39 6BP* Tel (01237) 440229 E-mail rev_shirley@hotmail.com

HENDERSON, Terry James. b 45. St Deiniol's Hawarden 76. **d** 77 **p** 77. C Wrexham *St As* 77-79; Wilson Carlile Coll of Evang 79-81; TV Langtree *Ox* 81-87; P-in-c Aston Cantlow and Wilmcote w Billesley *Cov* 87-90; V 90-97; V St Peter-in-Thanet *Cant* 97-02; R Elmley Castle w Bricklehampton and Combertons *Worc* from 02. *The Rectory, 22 Parkwood, Elmley Castle, Pershore WR10 3HT* Tel (01386) 710394
E-mail terryhenderson@onetel.com

HENDERSON, William Ernest. b 53. CEng81 MICE81 Southn Univ BSc75. St Jo Coll Nottm 87. **d** 89 **p** 90. C Win Ch Ch 89-93; V Stanley *Wakef* from 93. *The Vicarage, 379 Aberford Road, Stanley, Wakefield WF3 4HE* Tel (01924) 822143 *or* 835746
E-mail billh@stpeters-stanley.org.uk

HENDERSON, William Ralph. b 32. Oak Hill Th Coll 65. **d** 67 **p** 68. C Littleover *Derby* 67-68; C Nottingham St Sav *S'well* 68-74; V Alne *York* 75-92; Chapl York Distr Hosp 86-92; rtd 92; Perm to Offic *York* from 92. *15 Drakes Close, Huntington, York YO32 9QN* Tel (01904) 761741

HENDRICKSE, Canon Clarence David. b 41. Nottm Univ PGCE73 CEng MIMechE71. St Jo Coll Nottm 71. **d** 74 **p** 75. C St Helens St Helen *Liv* 74-76; C Netherley Ch Ch CD 76-77; TV 78-87; V Liv Ch Ch Norris Green 87-93; V Eccleston Ch Ch 93-06; Hon Can Liv Cathl 96-06; rtd 06. *Highfield, 17 Meadow Road, Windermere LA23 2EU* Tel (015394) 43058
E-mail revdhendrickse@onetel.com

HENDRY, Mrs Helen Clare. b 58. Lanc Univ BA79 Cam Univ PGCE80. Reformed Th Sem Mississippi MA85 Oak Hill Th Coll 94. **d** 95. Lect Oak Hill Th Coll from 86; NSM Muswell Hill St Jas w St Matt *Lon* from 95. *44 The Grove, London N3 5JR* Tel (020) 8882 2186 *or* 8883 6277 E-mail clareh@oakhill.ac.uk

HENDRY, Leonard John. b 34. St D Coll Lamp 65. **d** 68 **p** 69. C Minchinhampton *Glouc* 68-71; C Bishop's Cleeve 71-74; V Cheltenham St Mich 74-78; V Horsley and Newington Bagpath w Kingscote 78-82; Chapl Salonika *Eur* 82-91; rtd 94. *Stratigi 34, Pilea, 543 52 Salonika, Greece* Tel (00353) (31) 281193

HENDY, Canon Graham Alfred. b 45. St Jo Coll Dur BA67 MA75 Fitzw Coll Cam CertEd Univ of Wales (Lamp) MTh03 MPhil07. Sarum Th Coll 67. **d** 70 **p** 71. C High Wycombe *Ox* 70-75; TV 75-78; R Upton cum Chalvey 78-83; TR 83-90; R S Walsham and Upton *Nor* 90-97; Dioc Lay Tr Officer 90-97; Can Res S'well Minster 97-02; R Upper Itchen *Win* 02-08; rtd 08. *74 Bath Road, Wells BA5 3LJ* Tel (01749) 677003

HENEY, William Butler. b 22. Potchefstroom Univ BA99. CITC. **d** 60 **p** 61. C Seagoe *D & D* 60-63; I Carrickmacross *Clogh* 64-73; I Newbridge w Carnalway and Kilcullen *M & K* 73-95; Treas Kildare Cathl 81-86; Can Kildare Cathl 81-95; Adn Kildare 86-94; rtd 95; Chapl Mageough Home *D & G* from 96. *14 Trees Road, Mount Merrion, Blackrock, Co Dublin, Republic of Ireland* Tel (00353) (1) 288 9773

HENGIST, Barry. b 59. N Lon Poly BA88. Ripon Coll Cuddesdon 07. **d** 09. C Weybridge *Guildf* from 09. *87 Greenlands Road, Weybridge KT13 8PS* Tel (01932) 821196 Mobile 07917 068209 E-mail barryhengist@f2s.com

HENLEY, Claud Michael. b 31. Keble Coll Ox BA55 MA59. Chich Th Coll 55. **d** 57 **p** 58. C Cowley St Jas *Ox* 57-60; C Wetherby *Ripon* 60-63; C Brighton St Pet *Chich* 63-69; V Brighton St Jo 69-75; V New Groombridge 75-96; rtd 96; Perm to Offic *Chich* from 97. *12 Barn Stables, De Montfort Road, Lewes BN7 1ST* Tel (01273) 472467

HENLEY, David Edward. b 44. Sarum & Wells Th Coll 69. **d** 72 **p** 73. C Fareham H Trin *Portsm* 72-76; C-in-c Leigh Park St Clare CD 76-78; R Freshwater 78-87; RD W Wight 83-87; R Meonstoke w Corhampton cum Exton 87-02; R Droxford 87-02; RD Bishop's Waltham 93-98; Hon Can Portsm Cathl 96-02; TR Chalke Valley *Sarum* from 02; RD Chalke from 07. *The Vicarage, Newtown, Broad Chalke, Salisbury SP5 5DS* Tel (01722) 780262 E-mail david.henley257@btinternet.com

HENLEY, Dean. b 64. St Chad's Coll Dur BA93. Westcott Ho Cam 95. **d** 95 **p** 96. C Farncombe *Guildf* 95-99; TV Hale w Badshot Lea 99-06; R Campton, Clophill and Haynes *St Alb* from 06. *The Rectory, 4A North Lane, Haynes, Bedford MK45 3PW* Tel (01234) 381235
E-mail deanhenley@waitrose.com

HENLEY, John Francis Hugh. b 48. SS Mark & Jo Coll Chelsea CertEd69. St Mich Coll Llan. **d** 82 **p** 83. C Griffithstown *Mon* 82-85; V St Hilary Greenway 85-90; P-in-c Fulham St Etheldreda w St Clem *Lon* from 90. *St Etheldreda's Vicarage, Doneraile Street, London SW6 6EL* Tel (020) 7736 3809

HENLEY, Michael. *See* HENLEY, Claud Michael

✠**HENLEY, The Rt Revd Michael Harry George.** b 38. CB91. Lon Coll of Div. **d** 61 **p** 62 **c** 95. C St Marylebone w H Trin *Lon* 61-64; Chapl RN 64-68 and 74-89; Chapl of the Fleet and Adn for the RN 89-93; Dir Gen Naval Chapl Services 92-93; Chapl St Andr Univ 68-72; Chapl R Hosp Sch Holbrook 72-74; QHC 89-93; Hon Can Gib Cathl 89-93; P-in-c Pitlochry *St And* 94-95; Bp St And 95-04; rtd 04. *West Chattan, Mavis Haugh, 108 Hepburn Gardens, St Andrews KY16 9LT* Tel (01334) 473167

HENLY, Francis Michael. b 25. Sarum Th Coll. **d** 67 **p** 68. C E w W Harnham *Sarum* 67-70; P-in-c Stour Provost w Todbere 70-75; P-in-c Rowde 75-79; V 79-83; R Poulshot 79-83; V Bishop's Cannings, All Cannings etc 83-92; rtd 92; Perm to Offic *Sarum* from 92. *Oldbury View, Middle Lane, Cherhill, Calne SN11 8XX* Tel (01249) 815191

HENNING, Mrs Judy. b 49. Portsm Univ MSc99. S Dios Minl Tr Scheme 85. **d** 88 **p** 97. C Catherington and Clanfield *Portsm* 88-91; C Leigh Park 91-92; Perm to Offic 94-96; Min in Whiteley and Asst to RD Fareham 96-99; C-in-c Whiteley CD 99-04;

P-in-c Old Cleeve, Leighland and Treborough *B & W* 04-06; R from 06. *The Rectory, Old Cleeve, Minehead TA24 6HN* Tel (01984) 640576 E-mail judy.henning@btinternet.com

HENNINGS, John Richard (Brother John). b 58. Sheff Univ BA80. Spurgeon's Coll BA87. **d** 07 **p** 08. SSF from 05; Perm to Offic *Ripon* from 09. *25 Karnac Road, Leeds LS8 5BL* Tel 0113-226 0647 E-mail johnssf@franciscans.org.uk

HENRY, Cornelius Augustus. b 70. K Coll NY BA92 Heythrop Coll Lon MA06. NTMTC 07. **d** 09. C Hornchurch St Andr *Chelmsf* from 09. *49 Burnway, Hornchurch RM11 3SN* Tel (01708) 442868 E-mail cahenry70@yahoo.com

HENRY, Miss Jacqueline Margaret. b 40. Open Univ BA82. Trin Coll Bris 77. **dss** 83 **d** 87 **p** 94. Deptford St Jo *S'wark* 79-82; Catshill and Dodford *Worc* 83-86; The Lye and Stambermill 86-87; Par Dn 87-89; Educn Chapl 89-93; C Tolleshunt Knights w Tiptree and Gt Braxted *Chelmsf* 94-97; Chapl amongst Deaf People 94-97; TV Stantonbury and Willen *Ox* 97-02; rtd 02; Perm to Offic *Cant* from 02. *114 Maidstone Road, Rochester ME1 3DT* Tel (01634) 829183

HENRY, Peter. b 49. BTh. St Jo Coll Nottm. **d** 84 **p** 85. C Sinfin Moor and Blagreaves St Andr CD *Derby* 84-89; V Guernsey St Jo *Win* 89-97; P-in-c Sawley *Derby* 97-01; R 01-06; rtd 06. *5 Les Casquets, Amherst Road, St Peter Port, Guernsey GY1 2DH* Tel (01481) 715699

HENRY, Canon Stephen Kenelm Malim. b 37. Brasted Th Coll 58 Bps' Coll Cheshunt 60. **d** 62 **p** 63. C Leic St Phil 62-67; CF 67-70; V Woodhouse *Wakef* 70-01; Hon Can Wakef Cathl 00-01; rtd 01; Perm to Offic *Wakef* from 01. *1 Yorkstone, Crosland Moor, Huddersfield HD4 5NQ* Tel (01484) 644807 E-mail mandsmalim64@btinternet.com

HENSHALL, Keith. See HENSHALL, Ronald Keith

✠HENSHALL, The Rt Revd Michael. b 28. St Chad's Coll Dur BA54. **d** 56 **p** 57 **c** 76. C Sewerby w Marton *York* 56-59; C Bridlington Quay H Trin 56-59; C-in-c Micklehurst CD *Ches* 59-62; V Micklehurst 62-63; V Altrincham St Geo 63-76; Hon Can Ches Cathl 72-76; Suff Bp Warrington *Liv* 76-96; rtd 96; Perm to Offic *Liv* 96-03 and *York* 96-99; Hon Asst Bp York from 99. *28 Hermitage Way, Sleights, Whitby YO22 5HG* Tel (01947) 811233

HENSHALL, Nicholas James. b 62. Wadh Coll Ox BA84 MA88. Ripon Coll Cuddesdon 85. **d** 88 **p** 89. C Blyth St Mary *Newc* 88-92; V Scotswood 92-02; Can Res Derby Cathl 02-08; V High Harrogate Ch Ch *Ripon* from 08. *Christ Church Vicarage, 11 St Hilda's Road, Harrogate HG2 8JX* Tel (01423) 883390

HENSHALL, Ronald Keith. b 54. Loughb Coll of Educn CertEd76. Chich Th Coll 87. **d** 89 **p** 90. C Ribbleton *Blackb* 89-92; TV 95-98; P-in-c Charlestown and Lowlands Nevis 92-95; V Ellel w Shireshead 98-02; Cyprus 02-05; Chapl R Alexandra and Albert Sch Reigate 05-06; P-in-c Lerwick *Ab* from 06; P-in-c Burravoe from 06. *St Magnus's Rectory, 14 Greenfield Place, Lerwick ZE1 0AQ* Tel (01595) 693862 E-mail keithhenshall@btinternet.com

HENSHAW, Nicholas Newell. b 49. Rhodes Univ BA72. Cuddesdon Coll 73. **d** 75 **p** 76. C Beaconsfield *Ox* 75-78; Chapl Wellington Coll Berks 78-80; C Pimlico St Pet w Westmr Ch Ch *Lon* 80-82; Chapl Sevenoaks Sch from 82; Hon C Sevenoaks St Nic *Roch* from 82; Perm to Offic *St E* from 08. *Sevenoaks School, High Street, Sevenoaks TN13 1HU* Tel (01732) 455133

HENSON, Carolyn. b 44. Bedf Coll Lon BA65 Nottm Univ MTh88 PhD97 Solicitor 75. EMMTC 82. **dss** 85 **d** 87 **p** 94. Braunstone *Leic* 85-89; Par Dn 87-89; Adult Educn and Tr Officer *Ely* 89-91; NSM Sutton and Witcham w Mepal 89-95; Chapl Gt Ormond Street Hosp for Children NHS Trust 95-96; NSM Cainscross w Selsley *Glouc* 96-97; Vice Prin EMMTC *S'well* 97-01; R Morley w Smalley and Horsley Woodhouse *Derby* 02-05; rtd 05; Chapl St Mich Hospice Harrogate from 09. *6 Parkfield, Stillington, York YO61 1JW* E-mail carolyn.henson@virgin.net

HENSON, Joanna. **d** 06 **p** 07. NSM Egton-cum-Newland and Lowick and Colton *Carl* from 06. *Woodside Cottage, Colton, Ulverston LA12 8HE* Tel (01229) 861800 E-mail joannahenson@aol.com

HENSON, John David. b 49. EMMTC. **d** 00 **p** 01. NSM Beckingham w Walkeringham *S'well* 00-02; NSM Gringley-on-the-Hill 00-02; NSM Misterton and W Stockwith 02-05; C 06-07; C Beckingham w Walkeringham and Gringley 06-07; P-in-c Beckingham and Walkeringham and Misterton etc from 07; Asst Chapl HM Pris Whatton 00-05; Sen Police Chapl *S'well* from 03. *The Vicarage, 4 Church Lane, Misterton, Doncaster DN10 4AL* Tel (01427) 890270 E-mail jd.henson@btinternet.com

HENSON, Canon John Richard. b 40. Selw Coll Cam BA62 MA66. Ridley Hall Cam 62. **d** 65 **p** 66. C Ollerton *S'well* 65-68; Univs Sec CMS 68-73; Chapl Scargill Ho 73-78; V Shipley St Paul *Bradf* 78-83; TR Shipley St Paul and Frizinghall 83-91; V Ilkeston St Mary *Derby* 91-99; V Mackleover St Jo 99-05; Dioc Ecum Officer 96-05; Hon Can Derby Cathl 00-05; rtd 05; Perm to Offic *Derby* from 05. *6 Ganton Close, Nottingham NG3 3ET* E-mail john.henson3@ntlworld.com

HENSON, Shaun Christopher. b 64. E Nazarene Coll (USA) BA94 Duke Univ (USA) MDiv98 Regent's Park Coll Ox DPhil07. Wycliffe Hall Ox 03. **d** 04 **p** 05. C Blenheim *Ox* from 04; Chapl St Hugh's Coll Ox from 07. *St Hugh's College, St Margarets Road, Oxford OX2 6LE,* or *19 Park Close, Bladon, Woodstock OX20 1RN* Tel (01993) 813603 Mobile 07795-547555 E-mail shaun.henson@st-hughs.ox.ac.uk

HENSTRIDGE, Edward John. b 31. Ex Coll Ox BA55 MA59 FCIPD77. Wells Th Coll 55. **d** 57 **p** 58. C Milton *Portsm* 57-62; V Soberton w Newtown 62-69; Lic to Offic *Derby* 69-71; Perm to Offic *Guildf* 72-84 and from 02; Lic to Offic 84-02; Bp's Officer for NSMs 97-01. *Hunters Moon, Lower Ham Lane, Elstead, Godalming GU8 6HQ* Tel (01252) 702272 E-mail johnhn@globalnet.co.uk

HENTHORNE, Thomas Roger. b 30. EAMTC. **d** 79 **p** 80. Hd Master St Mary's Sch St Neots 67-93; NSM St Neots *Ely* 79-04; Perm to Offic from 04. *Stapeley, 45 Berkley Street, Eynesbury, St Neots PE19 2NE* Tel (01480) 472548 E-mail roger.henthorne@tesco.net

HENTON, John Martin. b 48. AKC71 St Luke's Coll Ex DipEd72. St Aug Coll Cant 74. **d** 74 **p** 75. C Woolwich St Mary w H Trin *S'wark* 74-77; C Cotham St Mary *Bris* 77-78; C Cotham St Sav w St Mary 78-80; R Filton 80-87; Chapl Ex Sch and St Marg Sch 87-91; V Ex St Dav *Win* 91-09; rtd 09. *Upexe Cottage, Upexe, Exeter EX5 5ND* Tel (01392) 860038 E-mail j.henton@tesco.net

HENWOOD, Mrs Gillian Kathleen. b 56. ABIPP81 Lanc Univ MA97. CBDTI 94. **d** 97 **p** 98. NSM Whitechapel w Admarsh-in-Bleasdale *Blackb* 97-01; Rural Chapl 00-03; Bp's Adv for Leisure and Tourism 01-03; C Westmr St Jas *Lon* 03-04; V Nunthorpe *York* 04-09; P-in-c Riding Mill *Newc* from 09; Chapl Shepherd's Dene Retreat Ho from 09; Adv for Spirituality and Spiritual Direction from 09. *The Vicarage, Riding Mill NE44 6AT* E-mail gillhenwood@hotmail.com

HENWOOD, Martin John. b 58. DL05. Glas Univ BD81. Ripon Coll Cuddesdon. **d** 85 **p** 86. C Dartford H Trin *Roch* 85-88; C St Martin-in-the-Fields *Lon* 88-93; V Dartford H Trin *Roch* from 93. *The Vicarage, High Street, Dartford DA1 1RX* Tel (01322) 222782

HENWOOD, Canon Peter Richard. b 32. St Edm Hall Ox BA55 MA69. Cuddesdon Coll 56. **d** 57 **p** 58. C Rugby St Andr *Cov* 57-62; C-in-c Gleadless Valley CD *Sheff* 62-71; V Plaistow St Mary *Roch* 71-97; RD Bromley 79-96; Hon Can Roch Cathl 88-97; rtd 97. *Wayside, 1 Highfield Close, Sandling Road, Saltwood, Hythe CT21 4QP* Tel (01303) 230039

HENWOOD (née OAKLEY), Mrs Susan Mary. b 55. Salford Univ BSc76. St Jo Coll Nottm 84. **d** 87 **p** 88. Par Dn Armthorpe *Sheff* 87-91; C Howell Hill *Guildf* 91-96; Perm to Offic *Cov* 02-04; NSM Bidford-on-Avon from 04. *24 High Street, Bidford-on-Avon, Alcester B50 4BU* Tel (01789) 490630

HEPPER, Christopher Michael Alan. b 55. St Jo Coll Nottm 90. **d** 92 **p** 93. C High Harrogate Ch Ch *Ripon* 92-95; P-in-c Dom Chapl 95-99; Chapl Poitou-Charentes *Eur* from 99. *Les Vallées d'Epinoux, 86400 Savigne, France* Tel (0033) (5) 49 97 04 21 Fax 49 97 04 37 Mobile (6) 85 05 34 62 E-mail chaplain.goodshepherd@wanadoo.fr

HEPPER, William Raymond. b 62. Kingston Poly BA83. Trin Coll Bris BA98. **d** 98 **p** 99. C Spring Grove St Mary *Lon* 98-01; CMS Egypt 01-04; NSM Greenford H Cross *Lon* 05-08; Perm to Offic from 08. *Address temp unknown* E-mail heppers@dataxprs.com.eg

HEPPLE, Gordon. b 32. Edin Th Coll. **d** 63 **p** 68. C Billingham St Cuth *Dur* 63-64; C Ryhope 64; Perm to Offic 66-68; C Wingate Grange 68-69; C Heworth St Mary 69; C Gateshead St Mary 69-71; P-in-c Low Team 71-72; R Lyons 72-79; V Basford St Aid *S'well* 79-84; V Blackhill *Dur* 84-95; rtd 97; Perm to Offic *Win* from 97. *66B Ringwood Road, Christchurch BH23 5RE* Tel (01425) 279068

HEPTINSTALL, Mrs Lillian. b 49. EMMTC 99. **d** 02 **p** 03. NSM Chilwell *S'well* from 02. *8 Cranston Road, Bramcote, Nottingham NG9 3GU* Tel 0115-916 4588 E-mail heptinstall@ntlworld.com

HEPWORTH, Canon Ernest John Peter. b 51. K Coll Lon BD65 AKC65 Hull Univ MA87. **d** 66 **p** 67. C Headingley *Ripon* 66-69; Asst Chapl St Geo Hosp Lon 69-71; C Gt Grimsby St Mary and St Jas *Linc* 71-72; TV 72-74; V Crosby 74-80; V Barton upon Humber 80-04; RD Yarborough 86-92; Can and Preb Linc Cathl 94-04; rtd 04. *63 Ferriby Road, Barton-upon-Humber DN18 5LQ* Tel (01652) 661363 E-mail ehep01@aol.com

HEPWORTH, Michael David Albert. b 37. Em Coll Cam BA59 MA63 Lon Inst of Educn PGCE60. Ridley Hall Cam 65. **d** 67 **p** 68. C Eastbourne All SS *Chich* 67-69; Teacher Eastbourne Coll 67-69; Asst Chapl Bedford Sch 69-72; Chapl 72-83; Hd Master Birkdale Sch 83-98; Perm to Offic *Derby* and *Sheff* from 83. *29 Stumperlowe Park Road, Sheffield S10 3QP* Tel 0114-230 6016 E-mail hepworthmj@tiscali.co.uk

HEPWORTH, Michael Edward. b 29. Leeds Univ BA51. NW Ord Course 74. **d** 77 **p** 78. NSM Timperley *Ches* 77-98; Perm to Offic from 00. *56 Ridgeway Road, Timperley, Altrincham WA15 7HD* Tel 0161-980 5104

HERAPATH, Jonathan James. b 67. Westmr Coll Ox Brookes Univ PGCE02. St Steph Ho Ox MTh06. d 05 p 06. C Cowley St Jo *Ox* 05-07; Chapl SS Helen and Kath Sch Abingdon from 07. *2 Moberly Close, Oxford OX4 1HX* Tel 07745-405150 (mobile) E-mail jonathanherapath@02.co.uk

HERBERT, Christopher John. b 37. Dur Univ BA60. Cranmer Hall Dur 60. d 62 p 63. C Huyton Quarry *Liv* 62-65; C Rainford 65-68; V Impington *Ely* 68-78; RD N Stowe 76-78; V Gt Shelford 78-97; RD Shelford 80-85; rtd 97. *North Place, Crown Street, Great Bardfield, Braintree CM7 4ST* Tel (01371) 810516

✠HERBERT, The Rt Revd Christopher William. b 44. Univ of Wales (Lamp) BA65 Bris Univ PGCE65 Leic Univ MPhil02 PhD08 Herts Univ Hon DLitt03. Wells Th Coll 65. d 67 p 68 c 95. C Tupsley *Heref* 67-71; Dioc RE Adv 71-76; Dioc Dir RE 76-81; Preb Heref Cathl 76-81; V Bourne *Guildf* 81-90; Hon Can Guildf Cathl 85-95; Adn Dorking 90-95; Bp St Alb 95-09; rtd 09. Hon Asst Bp Guildf from 09. *1 Beacon Close, Wrecclesham, Farnham GU10 4PA* Tel (01252) 795600 E-mail cherbert@threeabbeys.org.uk

HERBERT, Clair Geoffrey Thomas. b 36. Tyndale Hall Bris 61. d 64 p 65. C Nottingham St Sav *S'well* 64-67; C Harwell *Ox* 67-70; C Chilton All SS 67-70; V Bucklebury w Marlston 70-80; Chapl Brighton Coll Jun Sch 80-83; Hon C Upton (Overchurch) *Ches* 85-86; C 86-88; V Collier Row St Jas and Havering-atte-Bower *Chelmsf* 88-01; rtd 01; Perm to Offic *Ripon* from 01. *24 Birstwith Grange, Birstwith, Harrogate HG3 3AH* Tel (01423) 771315 E-mail geoffnval@vwclub.net

HERBERT, Clare Marguerite. b 54. St Hild Coll Dur BA76 New Coll Edin MTh78. Linc Th Coll 79. dss 81 d 87 p 94. Clifton St Paul *Bris* and Asst Chapl Bris Univ 81-84; Hon Par Dn Bris St Mary Redcliffe w Temple etc 87-90; Dioc Past Care Adv *Lon* 92-95; Hon C Clapham Team *S'wark* 94-96; C St Martin-in-the-Fields *Lon* 96-98; R Soho St Anne w St Thos and St Pet 98-07; Dean of Women's Min Two Cities Area 01-07; Nat Co-ord Inclusive Ch from 07. *37 Sydenham Hill, London SE26 6SH* Tel 07504-577210 (mobile) E-mail herbert.clare@googlemail.com

HERBERT, Canon David Alexander Sellars. b 39. Bris Univ BA60. St Steph Ho Ox 65. d 67 p 68. C St Leonards Ch Ch *Chich* 67-81; V Bickley *Roch* 81-09. Hon Can Roch Cathl 92-09; rtd 09. *47 Holmdale Road, Chislehurst BR7 6BY* Tel 07748-997586 (mobile) E-mail david.herbert@intcone.net

HERBERT, Canon David Roy. b 54. K Coll Lon BD73 AKC73. d 74 p 75. C Sheff St Aid w St Luke 74-76; C Sheff Manor 76-78; TV Gleadless Valley 78-83; TV Ellesmere Port *Ches* 83-93; V Tarvin 93-09; Continuing Minl Tr Officer 03-09; Clergy Development Officer from 09; Hon Can *Ches* Cathl from 08. *25 Blackstairs Road, Ellesmere Port CH66 1TX* Tel 0151-356 4554 E-mail david.herbert@chester.anglican.org

HERBERT, Mrs Denise Bridget Helen. b 42. SRN72 SCM74. Ripon Coll Cuddesdon. d 95 p 96. C Ocean View S Africa 95-97; C Grahamstown Cathl 97-99; Sub-Dean 99-00; R Jedburgh *Edin* 00-08; rtd 08. *8 Everest Road, Earlston TD4 6HB*

HERBERT, Geoffrey. See HERBERT, Clair Geoffrey Thomas

HERBERT, Geoffrey William. b 38. Ox Univ MA62 Birm Univ PhD72. Qu Coll Birm 80. d 82 p 83. C Hall Green Ascension *Birm* 82-85; R Sheldon 85-95; rtd 95; Perm to Offic *Birm* from 95; Co-ord for Spiritual Direction 00-05. *28 Lulworth Road, Birmingham B28 8NS* Tel 0121-777 2684 E-mail gandjherbert@tesco.net

HERBERT, Graham Victor. b 61. St Jo Coll Nottm BA02. d 02 p 03. C Strood St Nic w St Mary *Roch* 02-06; P-in-c Grain w Stoke from 06. *1 Parsonage Cottages, The Street, Upper Stoke, Rochester ME3 9RT* Tel (01634) 272564 E-mail graham.herbert@diocese.rochester.org

HERBERT, Jonathan Patrick. b 62. Bris Univ BA86. Linc Th Coll 86. d 88 p 89. C Kirkby *Liv* 88-91; TV Blakenall Heath *Lich* 91-96; Pilsdon Community from 96. *Pilsdon Manor, Pilsdon, Bridport DT6 5NZ* Tel (01308) 868308 Fax 868161

HERBERT, Malcolm Francis. b 53. K Coll Lon BD74 AKC74 St Mary's Coll Chelt CertEd75. Trin Coll Bris 76. d 77 p 78. C Wotton-under-Edge w Ozleworth and N Nibley *Glouc* 77-79; C Milton B & W 79-80; C Worle 80-85; V Woking Ch Ch *Guildf* 86-02; RD Woking 94-99; Dioc Dir of Ords *Bris* 02-07; C Kington St Michael and Chippenham St Paul w Hardenhuish etc 02-05; C Chippenham St Paul *Lon* from 07. *14 Lampton Park Road, Hounslow TW3 4HB* Tel (020) 8570 3066

HERBERT, Michael. b 35. Nottm Univ BA57. St D Coll Lamp 59. d 61 p 62. C Paston *Pet* 61-65; C Northampton All SS w St Kath 65-67; R Sutton w Upton 67-72; Asst Youth Chapl 67-72; Ind Chapl 72-84; P-in-c Pitsford 79-84; Ind Chapl *Worc* 84-01; TV Redditch, The Ridge 84-01; Chapl NE Worcs Coll 86-01; rtd 01; Perm to Offic *Worc* from 01. *33 Abbey Road, Redditch B97 4BL* Tel and Fax (01527) 69997

HERBERT, Canon Ronald. b 53. Worc Coll Ox BA75 MA80 Lon Univ BD78 W Kentucky Univ MA79. Oak Hill Th Coll 75. d 79 p 80. C Welling *Roch* 79-82; Hon Can Falconwood 89-90; V Becontree S w Chelmsf 90-00. Can Chelmsf Cathl 02-07; V

Stonebridge St Mich *Lon* from 07. *St Michael's Vicarage, Hillside, London NW10 8LB* Tel (020) 8965 7443 E-mail ronald.herbert@virgin.net

HERBERT, Mrs Rosemary. b 44. Westf Coll Lon BSc65. Qu Coll Birm 81. dss 85 d 87. Malvern Link w Cowleigh *Worc* 85-91; Hon Par Dn 87-91; NSM Malvern H Trin and St Jas from 91. *4 Cedar Avenue, Malvern WR14 2SG* Tel (01684) 572497

HERBERT, Stephen Edward. b 54. Hastings Coll Nebraska BA76 Bemidji State Univ MA81. Seabury-Western Th Sem MDiv87. d 87 p 87. V Lake City Grace Ch USA 87-90; Asst P Vancouver St Jas Canada 90-00; TV Wythenshawe *Man* 00-06; TR 06-09; P-in-c Byker St Martin *Newc* from 09; P-in-c Byker St Mich w St Lawr from 09. *St Martin's Vicarage, 152 Roman Avenue, Newcastle upon Tyne NE6 2RJ* E-mail stephenherbert@supanet.com

HERBERT, Canon Timothy David. b 57. Man Univ BA78 MPhil88 PhD04. Ridley Hall Cam 79. d 81 p 82. C Macclesfield St Mich *Ches* 81-85; V Wharton 85-93; Asst CME Officer 90-93; P-in-c Thanington *Cant* 93-98; Dir of Ords 93-98; Dir Dioc Tr Inst *Carl* from 99; C Cotehill and Cumwhinton 99-00; Hon Can Carl Cathl 99; C Scotby and Cotehill w Cumwhinton from 00. *The Vicarage, Cotehill, Carlisle CA4 0DY* Tel (01228) 561745 Fax 562366 E-mail therbert@globalnet.co.uk

✠HERD, The Rt Revd William Brian. b 31. Clifton Th Coll 55. d 58 p 59 c 76. C Wolverhampton St Luke *Lich* 58-61; Uganda 61-77; Adn Karamoja 70-75; Bp Karamoja 76-77; Deputation Sec (Ireland) BCMS 77-89; C Harrow Trin St Mich *Lon* 89-93; V Gresley *Derby* 93-98; rtd 98; Perm to Offic *Sarum* from 98. *Karibu, 13 Ambleside, Weymouth DT3 5HH* Tel (01305) 770257

HEREFORD, Archdeacon of. See COLMER, The Ven Malcolm John

HEREFORD, Bishop of. See PRIDDIS, The Rt Revd Anthony Martin

HEREFORD, Dean of. See TAVINOR, The Very Revd Michael Edward

HEREWARD, John Owen. b 53. FRCSE82 Lon Univ MB, BS77. Ridley Hall Cam 89. d 91 p 92. C W Ealing St Jo w St Jas *Lon* 91-95; P-in-c Hanwell St Mellitus w St Mark from 95; Dir Post-Ord Tr from 97; AD Ealing 98-03. *St Mellitus Vicarage, 1 Church Road, London W7 3BA* Tel (020) 8567 6535 E-mail john@jhereward.fsnet.co.uk

HEREWARD-ROTHWELL, Canon Michael John. b 46. MA Tulane Univ (USA) DPhil03. Chich Th Coll 74. d 78 p 79. C Chelmsf All SS 78-82; C Clacton St Jas 82-85; V Thorpe *Guildf* from 85; Hon Can Guildf Cathl from 99. *The Vicarage, Church Approach, Egham TW20 8TQ* Tel and fax (01932) 565986

HERITAGE, Barry. b 35. Clifton Th Coll 59. d 61 p 62. C Wolverhampton St Jude *Lich* 61-65; C Chaddesden St Mary *Derby* 65-67; V Kidsgrove *Lich* 67-76, NE Area Sec CPAS 76-89; V Elloughton and Brough w Brantingham *York* 89-93; C York St Paul 93-00; rtd 00; Perm to Offic *York* from 00. *32 St Swithins Walk, York YO26 4UF* Tel (01904) 786077

HERKES, Richard Andrew. b 54. Kent Univ BA75. STETS 99. d 02 p 03. NSM Polegate *Chich* from 02. *31 Wannock Lane, Eastbourne BN20 9SB* Tel (01323) 488328 E-mail rherkes@hotmail.com

HERKLOTS, Canon John Radu. b 31. Trin Hall Cam BA53 MA61. Westcott Ho Cam 54. d 55 p 56. C Attercliffe w Carbrook *Sheff* 55-60; C Stoke Damerel *Ex* 60-65; V Devonport St Bart 65-72; V Denmead *Portsm* 72-97; RD Havant 82-87; Hon Can Portsm Cathl 86-97; rtd 97; Perm to Offic *Heref* 97-02 and *Portsm* from 03. *14 Derwent Road, Lee-on-the-Solent PO13 8JG* Tel (023) 9255 2652

HERON, David George. b 49. AKC72. d 73 p 74. C Stockton St Chad *Dur* 73-77; C Beamish 77-81; R Willington and Sunnybrow 81-95; V Dipton and Leadgate from 95. *The Vicarage, St Ives Road, Leadgate, Consett DH8 7SN* Tel (01207) 503918 E-mail frdavidheron@aol.com

HERON, George Dobson. b 34. TD. Cranmer Hall Dur 58. d 61 p 62. C Benfieldside *Dur* 61-65; C Winlaton 65-68; V Dunston St Nic 68-77; P-in-c Dunston Ch Ch 74-77; V Dunston 77-82; V Gateshead St Helen 82-89, rtd 94; Perm to Offic *Dur* 94-96 and *Newc* from 94. *36 Woodlands Road, Shotley Bridge, Consett DH8 0DE* Tel (01207) 507733

HERON, Nicholas Peter. b 60. Man Univ BA81 Southn Univ BTh86. Sarum & Wells Th Coll 84. d 84 p 85. C Brinnington w Portwood *Ches* 84-87; Chapl RAF from 87. *Chaplaincy Services, Valiant Block, HQ Air Command, RAF High Wycombe HP14 4UE* Tel (01494) 496800 Fax 496343

HERON, Simon Alexander. b 68. Ridley Hall Cam 05. d 07 p 08. C Frindsbury w Upnor and Chattenden *Roch* from 07. *18 Honeypot Close, Rochester ME2 3DU* Tel (01634) 717847 Mobile 07768-525512 E-mail siheron@yahoo.com

HERRICK, Andrew Frederick. b 58. Univ of Wales (Lamp) BA80. Wycliffe Hall Ox 80. d 82 p 83. C Aberystwyth *St D* 82-85; P-in-c Llangeitho and Blaenpennal w Betws Leucu etc 85-86; R 86-88; Youth Chapl 86-88; R Aberporth w Tremain and Blaenporth 88-91; Succ St D Cathl 91-94; V Betws w

Ammanford 94-00; TV Aberystwyth from 00. *Fenton, Queens Square, Aberystwyth SY23 2HL* Tel (01970) 624537

HERRICK, David William. b 52. Middx Poly BSc73. St Jo Coll Nottm 79. **d** 82 **p** 83. C Ipswich St Matt *St E* 82-85; C Nor St Pet Mancroft w St Jo Maddermarket 85-88; V Bury St Edmunds St Geo *St E* 88-96; P-in-c Gt Barton 96-99; Dir Studies Dioc Min Course from 99; Vice Prin from 04. *24 Cromwell Road, Ely CB6 1AS* Tel (01353) 662909 Fax 662056

HERRICK (*formerly* COWLEY), Mrs Jean Louie Cameron. b 39. Sarum Dioc Tr Coll CertEd59. SAOMC 94. **d** 96 **p** 97. NSM Chorleywood Ch Ch *St Alb* 96-02; NSM Hermitage *Ox* 02-05; Perm to Offic *Glouc* from 05. *52 Cambrian Road, Walton Cardiff, Tewkesbury GL20 7RP* Tel (01684) 295598
E-mail jean.herrick@tesco.net

HERRICK (*née* RENAUT), Canon Vanessa Anne. b 58. York Univ BA80 Fitzw Coll Cam MA96 LTCL75. St Jo Coll Nottm 80 Ridley Hall Cam 94. **d** 96 **p** 97. C St E Cathl Distr 96-99; Chapl Fitzw Coll Cam 99-02; Fell 01-02; Tutor Ridley Hall Cam 99-02; Dir Min and Vocation *Ely* from 03; Hon Can Ely Cathl from 03. *24 Cromwell Road, Ely CB6 1AS* Tel (01353) 662909 Fax 662056 Mobile 07778-496340
E-mail vanessa.herrick@ely.anglican.org

HERROD, Mrs Kathryn. b 59. Warwick Univ BSc80 Matlock Coll of Educn PGCE81. St Jo Coll Nottm MA97. **d** 97 **p** 98. C Wollaton *S'well* 97-01; R Warsop from 01. *The Rectory, Church Road, Warsop, Mansfield NG20 0SL* Tel (01623) 843290
E-mail revkathryn@aol.com

HERRON, Robert Gordon John. b 36. MCIPD75. Wycliffe Hall Ox 65. **d** 77 **p** 78. C Ditton St Mich *Liv* 77-80; C W Kirby St Bridget *Ches* 80-82; R Gorton Our Lady and St Thos *Man* 82-00; rtd 00. *The Gables, 13 West Road, Bowden, Altrincham WA14 2LD*

HERSCHEL, Richard James. b 27. Villanova Univ USA MA72. **d** 57 **p** 57. USA 57-81 and 84-97; TV Cannock *Lich* 82-84; rtd 92. *80B King Street, Norwich NR1 1PG* Tel (01603) 614873

HERTFORD, Archdeacon of. *See* JONES, The Ven Trevor Pryce

HERTFORD, Suffragan Bishop of. *See* FOSTER, The Rt Revd Christopher Richard James

HERTH, Daniel Edwin. b 36. Xavier Univ Cincinnati BS58. Ch Div Sch of Pacific MDiv83. **d** 83 **p** 84. C Oakland St Paul USA 83-86; R Alameda Ch Ch 86-97; NSM Gt and Lt Ouseburn w Marton cum Grafton etc *Ripon* 98-01; Chapl HM YOI Wetherby from 99. *The Garden House, 32 Mallorie Park Drive, Ripon HG4 2QF* Tel and fax (01765) 602558 Mobile 07779-379420 E-mail danieleherthsr@hotmail.com

HERVÉ, Canon John Anthony. b 49. TD94. Open Univ BA81 Wolv Univ PGCE95. Lich Th Coll 70. **d** 73 **p** 74. C Middlesbrough All SS *York* 73-76; CF 76-81; P-in-c Handsworth St Andr *Birm* 81-86; Hon C Cowley St Jo *Ox* 86-90; Tutor St Steph Ho Ox 86-90; V Sparkbrook St Agatha w Balsall Heath St Barn *Birm* from 90; P-in-c Highgate from 05; Hon Can Birm Cathl from 05. *The Clergy House, 120 Stanhope Street, Birmingham B12 0XB* Tel 0121-440 4605
E-mail fr.john@saintagathas.org.uk

HERVEY, Mrs Mary Diana. b 41. St Hugh's Coll Ox BA63. St And Dioc Tr Course 83 TISEC 96. **d** 92 **p** 94. Par Dn Cupar *St And* 92-94; Asst Chapl St Andr Univ 94-97; Asst P Cen Fife Team 94-97; C Ulverston St Mary w H Trin *Carl* 97-00; P-in-c Barrow St Jo 00-06; rtd 06. *Rigg Cottage, Bardsea, Ulverston LA12 9QU* E-mail revdih@aol.com

HESELTINE, Mrs Barbara Joan. b 42. Keele Univ BA65. S'wark Ord Course 85. **d** 88 **p** 94. NSM Addington *S'wark* 88-98; Perm to Offic *Truro* from 98; NSM Feock from 02. *The Lodge, Penpol, Devoran, Truro TR3 6NA* Tel and fax (01872) 870039 Mobile 07767-264060 E-mail barbara.heseltine@tiscali.co.uk

HESELWOOD, Eric Harold. b 43. Oak Hill Th Coll 84. **d** 86 **p** 87. C Farnborough *Roch* 86-88; V Biggin Hill 88-96; V Orpington All SS 96-98; V Bromley Common St Aug 98-05; rtd 05; Perm to Offic *Roch* 06-08; P-in-c Cudham and Downe from 08. *34 Victoria Gardens, Biggin Hill, Westerham TN16 3DJ* Tel and fax (01959) 509131 E-mail eric.heselwood@ntlworld.com

HESELWOOD, Mrs Hilda. b 39. CA Tr Coll 61. **dss** 85 **d** 87 **p** 94. CA from 63; Bromley Common St Luke *Roch* 85-00; Par Dn 87-94; C 94-00; rtd 00; Perm to Offic *Roch* from 00. *34 Victoria Gardens, Biggin Hill, Westerham TN16 3DJ* Tel and fax (01959) 509131

HESFORD-LOCKE, Richard Nigel. b 61. Coll of Resurr Mirfield 92. **d** 94 **p** 95. C Middlesbrough Ascension *York* 94-97; C Paignton St Jo *Ex* 97-98; rtd 98. *2 Windyhill Drive, Bolton BL3 4TH*

HESKETH, Canon Philip John. b 64. K Coll Lon BD86 AKC86 PhD94. Ripon Coll Cuddesdon 92. **d** 94 **p** 95. C Bearsted w Thurnham *Cant* 94-98; V Chatham St Steph *Roch* 98-05; Can Res Roch Cathl from 05. *East Canonry, Kings Orchard, Rochester ME1 1TG* Tel (01634) 841491 *or* 843366

HESKETH, The Ven Ronald David. b 47. CB04. Bede Coll Dur BA68 FRGS02. Ridley Hall Cam 69 St Mich Coll Llan 71. **d** 71 **p** 72. C Southport H Trin *Liv* 71-74; Asst Chapl Miss to Seamen 74-75; Chapl RAF 75-98; Command Chapl RAF 98-01; Chapl-

in-Chief RAF 01-06; Can and Preb Linc Cathl 01-06; Voc Officer *Worc* from 06; QHC from 01. *The Old Police Station, Bredon Road, Tewkesbury GL20 5BZ* Tel (01684) 299773
E-mail vera&ron.hesketh@dunelm.org.uk

HESKINS, Georgiana Mary. b 48. K Coll Lon BD81 AKC81 MTh93. Westcott Ho Cam 81. **dss** 83 **d** 87 **p** 94. Cobbold Road St Sav w St Mary *Lon* 83-85; St Botolph Aldgate w H Trin Minories 85-87; Par Dn 87; Perm to Offic *S'wark* 88-93; Par Dn Kidbrooke St Jas 93-95; Tutor S'wark Ord Course 93-94; Tutor SEITE 94-98; Teacher Eltham Coll 98-02; Asst Chapl Qu Eliz Hosp NHS Trust from 03; Hon Chapl S'wark Cathl from 95. *Queen Elizabeth Hospital NHS Trust, Stadium Road, London SE18 4QH* Tel (020) 8836 6831 Mobile 07776-122350
E-mail georgiana@lineone.net

HESKINS, Jeffrey George. b 55. Heythrop Coll Lon MA94 Princeton Th Sem DMin00 AKC78. Chich Th Coll 80. **d** 81 **p** 82. C Primrose Hill St Mary w Avenue Road St Paul *Lon* 81-85; Enfield Deanery Youth Officer 85-88; C Enfield Chase St Mary 85-88; TV Kidbrooke St Jas *S'wark* 88-95; R Charlton St Luke w H Trin 95-02; P-in-c Old Charlton St Thos 02; R Charlton 02-07; Dioc Dir of Ords *Linc* from 07; Min Can and PV Linc Cathl from 08. *Church House, The Old Palace, Lincoln LN2 1PU* Tel (01522) 504029 Fax 504051
E-mail jeffrey.heskins@lincoln.anglican.org

HESLAM, Peter Somers. b 63. Hull Univ BA89 Keble Coll Ox DPhil94 Trin Coll Cam BA96 MA01. Ridley Hall Cam 93. **d** 96 **p** 97. C Huntingdon *Ely* 96-99; Min Stukeley Meadows LEP 99; Dir Studies EAMTC 99-00; Tutor Ridley Hall Cam from 99; Dir Capitalism Project Lon Inst of Contemporary Chr 00-04; Hon C Cherry Hinton St Jo *Ely* from 00; Fell Faculty of Div Cam Univ from 05. *Glebe House, 64A Glebe Road, Cambridge CB1 7SZ* Tel (01223) 722822 E-mail psh20@cam.ac.uk

HESLOP, Alan. *See* HESLOP, James Alan

HESLOP, Andrew James. b 66. Man Univ BA87 PGCE88. **d** 03 **p** 04. OLM Turton Moorland Min *Man* from 03; Chapl Wrightington Wigan and Leigh NHS Trust from 07; Perm to Offic *Blackb* from 07. *The Chaplaincy, Royal Albert Edward Infirmary, Wigan Lane, Wigan WN1 2NN* Tel (01942) 244000

HESLOP, David Anthony. b 45. BSc DipEd MTh Birm Univ MLitt97. St Jo Coll Nottm 81. **d** 83 **p** 84. C Willenhall H Trin *Lich* 83-86; V Gresley *Derby* 86-92; V Marston on Dove w Scropton 92-95; Chapl Derby Univ 95-99; V Castle Donington and Lockington cum Hemington *Leic* 99-03; Chapl E Midl Airport 99-03; Prin OLM and Integrated Tr *Sarum* 03-07; Co-ord for Learning and Discipleship from 07. *25 Lime Kiln Way, Salisbury SP2 8RN* Tel (01722) 417616 *or* 411944 Fax 08701-301824 E-mail david.heslop@salisbury.anglican.org *or* revdave@heslops.co.uk

HESLOP, Harold William. b 40. Leeds Univ BA62 Open Univ BA72. Ox NSM Course 75. **d** 78 **p** 79. NSM Stoke Mandeville *Ox* 78-91; NSM Wendover 82-00; NSM Ellesborough, The Kimbles and Stoke Mandeville 91-94. *Farmside House, 42 Beechburn Park, Crook DL15 8NA* Tel (01388) 765903

HESLOP, James Alan. b 37. Codrington Coll Barbados 61. **d** 64 **p** 65. C Bartica Guyana 64-68; P-in-c Long Is Nassau 68-71; C Ch Ch Cathl 71-72; C Haxby w Wigginton *York* 72-74; TV 74-76; V York St Olave w St Giles 76-87; V Northampton All SS w St Kath *Pet* 87-88; R Felpham w Middleton *Chich* 88-92; TR Howden *York* 92-94; Warden Coll of St Barn Lingfield 94-95; Warden Morley Retreat and Conf Ho *Derby* 95-98; R Kirkbride and V Lezayre St Olave Ramsey *S & M* 98-99; P-in-c Woburn w Eversholt, Milton Bryan, Battlesden etc *St Alb* 99-03; rtd 03; Chapl Soc of St Marg 04-05; P-in-c Pau *Eur* 05-06. *1 Coniston Close, Bognor Regis PO22 8ND* Tel (01243) 869499

HESLOP, Michael Andrew. b 47. Trin Coll Bris 73. **d** 76 **p** 77. C Burmantofts St Steph and St Agnes *Ripon* 76-80; V Thorpe Edge *Bradf* 80-87; TV Penrith w Newton Reigny and Plumpton Wall *Carl* 87-91; V Silloth 91-01; V Kettlewell w Conistone, Hubberholme etc *Bradf* 01-07; Perm to Offic *Carl* from 07. *8 Lowscales Drive, Cockermouth CA13 9DR* Tel (01900) 829542

HESS, Paul Austin. b 67. Cape Town Univ BA89. St Bede's Coll Umtata. **d** 93 **p** 93. C Matroosfontein S Africa 92-94; NSM Eythorne and Elvington w Waldershare etc *Cant* 95-96; C Storrington *Chich* 96-99; Chapl Hurstpierpoint Coll 99-05; Chapl Eton Coll from 05. *Eton College, Windsor SL4 6DW* Tel (01753) 671161 E-mail pahess@tiscali.co.uk

HETHERINGTON, Andrew. b 50. Sheff Univ BSc71. Wycliffe Hall Ox 71. **d** 74 **p** 75. C Leic H Trin w St Jo 74-78; C Leic H Apostles 78-82; V Bootle St Mary w St Paul *Liv* 82-93; TR W Swindon and the Lydiards *Bris* 93-01; P-in-c Chedgrave, Ellenhall and Seighford-with-Creswell *Lich* 01-06; V Chebsey, Creswell, Ellenhall, Ranton etc from 06. *The Vicarage, The Green, Seighford, Stafford ST18 9PQ* Tel (01785) 282829

HETHERINGTON, Mrs Charlotte Elizabeth. b 51. Girton Coll Cam BA74 Maria Grey Coll Lon PGCE75 Heythrop Coll Lon MA02. SAOMC 95. **d** 98 **p** 99. NSM Stratfield Mortimer and Mortimer W End etc *Ox* 98-04; C Portsea St Mary *Portsm* from 04. *Flat 10, 1 Bill Sargent Crescent, Portsmouth PO1 1UP* Tel (023) 9282 6892 E-mail charlottehetherington@hotmail.com

HETHERINGTON, Mrs Glynis Catherine. b 48. EMMTC 93. d 93 p 94. NSM E and W Leake, Stanford-on-Soar, Rempstone etc *S'well* 93-99; R from 99. *The Rectory, 3 Bateman Road, East Leake, Loughborough LE12 6LN* Tel (01509) 852228

HETHERINGTON, John Carl. b 52. Hull Univ BTh93. Linc Th Coll 82. d 84 p 85. C Crosby *Linc* 84-88; TV Cleethorpes 88-93; Chapl RAF 93-07; R Monk Fryston and S Milford *York* from 07. *The Rectory, Main Street, Hillam, Leeds LS25 5HH* Tel and fax (01977) 682357 Mobile 07903-450228
E-mail hetherington556@btinternet.com

HETHERINGTON, Mrs Rachel Marie. b 65. ERMC 05. d 08. NSM Northampton St Mich w St Edm *Pet* from 08; NSM Northampton H Sepulchre w St Andr and St Lawr from 08. *13 Woodrush Way, Moulton, Northampton NN3 7HU* Tel (01604) 459864 E-mail rh10@ntlworld.com

HETLING, William Maurice. b 37. AKC61. d 62 p 63. C Eltham St Barn *S'wark* 62-66; C Horley 66-71; C Kingston Jamaica 71-72; R Highgate 72-73; P-in-c Porus 74-75; C-in-c Farnham Royal S CD *Ox* 75-78; TV W Slough 78-80 and 88-91; TR 80-88; TV Parkstone St Pet w Branksea and St Osmund *Sarum* 91-96; P-in-c Reading St Barn *Ox* 96-99; rtd 99; Perm to Offic *Chich* 99-06. *12 Manor Close, Storrington, Pulborough RH20 4LF*

HEWES, John. b 29. Nottm Univ BA50. Chich Th Coll 79. d 81 p 82. C Buckland in Dover w Buckland Valley *Cant* 81-84; P-in-c Elmsted w Hastingleigh 84-89; P-in-c Crundale w Godmersham 84-89; RD W Bridge 88-89; R Lydd 89-95; RD S Lympne 89-95; rtd 95; Perm to Offic *Cant* from 95. *Brambledown, Tamley Lane, Hastingleigh, Ashford TN25 5HW* Tel (01233) 750214

HEWES, Timothy William. b 50. Sheff Univ BDS74. SAOMC 98. d 01. NSM Abingdon *Ox* from 01. *55 Lower Radley, Abingdon OX14 3AY* Tel (01235) 523963 Mobile 07771-880117
E-mail tim@rdlf.uninet.co.uk

HEWETSON, The Ven Christopher. b 37. Trin Coll Ox BA60 MA64. Chich Th Coll 67. d 69 p 70. C Leckhampton St Pet *Glouc* 69-71; C Wokingham All SS *Ox* 71-73; V Didcot St Pet 73-82; R Ascot Heath 82-90; RD Bracknell 86-90; P-in-c Headington Quarry 90-94; Hon Can Ch Ch 92-94; RD Cowley 94; Adn Ches 94-02; rtd 02; Bp's Adv for Spirituality *Ex* 03-07; Perm to Offic *Ches* from 05. *The Old Estate House, The Square, North Molton, South Molton EX36 3HP* Tel (01598) 740573
E-mail cahewetson@tiscali.co.uk

HEWETSON, David Geoffrey. b 31. S'wark Ord Course 71. d 74 p 75. NSM Brighton St Mich *Chich* 74-06; rtd 06; Perm to Offic *Chich* from 07. *Flat 1, 166 Dyke Road, Brighton BN1 5PU* Tel (01273) 275776

HEWETSON, Canon Robin Jervis. b 39. AKC63 K Coll Lon MA93. d 64 p 65. C Thorpe St Andr *Nor* 64-67; C E Dereham w Hoe 67-69; TV Mattishall w Mattishall Burgh 69-72; R Ingham w Sutton 72-78; R Catfield 75-78; R Taverham w Ringland 78-89; P-in-c Marsham 89-92; P-in-c Burgh 89-92; Dioc Ecum Officer 89-04; Exec Officer Norfolk Ecum Coun 89-04; R Marsham w Burgh-next-Aylsham 92-04; Hon Can Nor Cathl 01-04; rtd 04; Perm to Offic *Nor* from 04. *83 Soame Close, Aylsham, Norwich NR11 6JF* Tel (01263) 734325

HEWETSON, Canon Valerie Patricia. b 44. St Mary's Coll Dur BSc66 MSc70 Leeds Univ MA75. Linc Th Coll 89. d 91 p 94. C Kingston upon Hull St Nic *York* 91-94; V Barmby Moor w Allerthorpe, Fangfoss and Yapham 94-98; V Barmby Moor Gp from 98; Can and Preb York Minster from 01; RD S Wold 01-07. *The Vicarage, St Helen's Square, Barmby Moor, York YO42 4HF* Tel (01759) 305971

HEWETT, Andrew David. b 63. Univ of Wales (Lamp) BA. Chich Th Coll 84. d 86 p 87. C Caldicot *Mon* 86-90; Chapl RAF from 90. *Chaplaincy Services, Valiant Block, HQ Air Command, RAF High Wycombe HP14 4UE* Tel (01494) 496800 Fax 496343

HEWETT, Maurice Gordon. b 28. Lon Univ BA53. Oak Hill Th Coll 49. d 54 p 55. C Gipsy Hill Ch Ch *S'wark* 54-57; C Maidstone St Faith *Cant* 57-60; R Chevening *Roch* 60-95; rtd 95; Perm to Offic *Roch* and *Cant* from 95; Hon Wing Chapl ATC 96-04. *Rosings, 12 The Thicketts, Sevenoaks TN13 3SZ* Tel and fax (01732) 464734

HEWETT, Canon Roger Leroy. b 45. St Mich Coll Llan 93. d 95 p 96. C Whitchurch *Llan* 95-98; R Blaina and Nantyglo *Mon* from 98; AD Blaenau Gwent from 05; Can St Woolos Cathl from 08. *The Rectory, Station Road, Blaina NP13 3BW* Tel (01495) 290130

HEWISON, Alan Stuart. b 30. SS Mark & Jo Univ Coll Plymouth BEd82. K Coll Lon. d 57 p 58. C S Mymms K Chas *Lon* 57-60; C Bourne *Guildf* 60-63; Chapl RN 63-79; Perm to Offic *Ex* from 79; rtd 95. *8 Hazelwood Crescent, Plymouth PL9 8BL*

HEWITSON, John Kenneth. b 48. Curtin Univ Aus BA Flinders Univ Aus MA96. Adelaide Coll of Div ThL70 ACT ThSchol83. d 71 p 72. C Swindon Ch Ch *Bris* 71-74; Australia from 74; C Spearwood 74-76; R Balga 76-77; Chapl Royal Perth Hosp 79-83; R Lockridge 83-86; R Eliz 92-97; Chapl Trin Coll 93-98; Chapl Kormilda Coll Darwin from 99; R Freds Pass from 00. *PO Box 346, Humpty Doo NT 0836, Australia* Tel (0061) (8) 8983 3947 Fax 8983 3951 E-mail jah@octa4.net.au

HEWITT, Christopher James Chichele (Chich). b 45. Witwatersrand Univ BSc68 UNISA BA78 MTh92 LTCL69. St Paul's Coll Grahamstown. d 78 p 79. S Africa 78-99; Chapl St Paul's Coll Grahamstown 84-86; Warden 86-92; Can Grahamstown Cathl 88-93; Chan 92; Sub-Dean 93; Dean and Adn Grahamstown 93-98; USA 99; TR Radcliffe *Man* 00-09; AD Radcliffe and Prestwich 02-09; P-in-c Swinton H Rood from 09. *Holy Rood Vicarage, 33 Moorside Road, Swinton, Manchester M27 3EL* Tel 0161-794 2464 E-mail chich@rink-hewitt.co.uk

HEWITT, Colin Edward. b 52. Man Poly BA80 Em Coll Cam BA82 MA86. Westcott Ho Cam 80. d 83 p 84. C Radcliffe St Thos and St Jo *Man* 83-84; C Langley and Parkfield 84-86; R Byfield w Boddington *Pet* 86-89; R Byfield w Boddington and Aston le Walls 89-91; Chapl RAF 91-09; V Brentwood St Thos *Chelmsf* from 09. *St Thomas's Vicarage, 91 Queens Road, Brentwood CM14 4EY* Tel (01277) 225700
E-mail fathercolin@live.co.uk

HEWITT, David Warner. b 33. Selw Coll Cam BA56 MA60. Wells Th Coll 57. d 59 p 60. C Longbridge *Birm* 59-61; C Sheldon 61-64; V Smethwick Old Ch 64-70; V Smethwick 70-78; P-in-c Littlehampton St Jas *Chich* 78-85; P-in-c Wick 78-85; V Littlehampton St Mary 78-85; TR Littlehampton and Wick 86-89; Perm to Offic *Eur* from 95; rtd 98; Hon Asst Chapl Gtr Athens *Eur* 00-03; Perm to Offic *Chelmsf* from 07. *18 Orchard Close, Weaverhead Lane, Thaxted, Dunmow CM6 2JX* Tel (01371) 830591 E-mail tangulls@the.forthnet.gr

HEWITT, Canon Francis John Adam. b 42. St Chad's Coll Dur BA64. d 66 p 67. C Dewsbury Moor *Wakef* 66-69; C Huddersfield St Jo 69-73; V King Cross 73-81; V Lastingham w Appleton-le-Moors, Rosedale etc *York* 81-94; RD Helmsley 85-94; V Pickering 94-95; V Pickering w Lockton and Levisham 95-07; RD Pickering 94-06; Can and Preb York Minster 97-07; rtd 07; Perm to Offic *York* from 07. *Michaelmas Cottage, 3 Lime Chase, Kirkbymoorside, York YO62 6BX* Tel (01751) 430322
E-mail fandb.michaelmas1@btinternet.com

HEWITT, Canon Garth Bruce. b 46. St Jo Coll Dur BA68. Lon Coll of Div LTh70. d 70 p 71. C Maidstone St Luke *Cant* 70-73; Staff Evang CPAS 73-79; Hon C W Ealing St Jo w St Jas *Lon* 73-81; Dir Amos Trust 88-96; World Affairs Adv *Guildf* 94-96; Regional Co-ord (Lon and SE) Chr Aid from 96; Perm to Offic *S'wark* 96-04; P-in-c All Hallows Lon Wall 97-99; V from 99; Hon Can Jerusalem from 06. *Christian Aid, All Hallows on the Wall, 83 London Wall, London EC2M 5ND* Tel (020) 7496 1680 or 7588 2638 Fax 7496 1684 E-mail ghewitt@christian-aid.org

HEWITT, Geoffrey Williams. b 48. Leeds Univ BA69. Wells Th Coll 70. d 72 p 73. C Heywood St Luke *Man* 72-74; Ind Chapl 74-77; P-in-c Hulme St Geo 74-77; R Mamhilad and Llanfihangel Pontymoile *Mon* 77-80; Ind Chapl 77-80; V Arthog w Fairbourne *Ban* 80-89; R Llangelynnin w Rhoslefain 87-89; TV Bangor 89-94; Dioc Soc Resp Officer 89-02; P in c Pentir 94-02; Hon Can Ban Cathl 99-02; RD Ogwen 00-02; P-in-c Draycot *Bris* from 02. *Draycot Rectory, Seagry Road, Sutton Benger, Chippenham SN15 4RY* Tel and fax (01249) 720070 Mobile 07950-497580
E-mail geoffrey@revhewitt.freeserve.co.uk

HEWITT, Guy Arlington Kenneth. b 67. Univ of W Indies BSc92 MSc94. SEITE 00. d 04 p 05. C Ch Ch Barbados 04-06 and 07-08; P-in-c Ruby H Trin 06-07. *33 Tino Terrace, Warners, Christ Church BB15104, Barbados* Tel (001) (246) 437 6569 Mobile 435 6052 E-mail guyhewitt@gmail.com

HEWITT, John Kaffrell. b 34. St Aid Birkenhead 60. d 63 p 64. C Woking Ch Ch *Guildf* 63-66; P-in-c Sudbury w Ballingdon and Brundon *St E* 66-70; V 70-80; V Portsdown *Portsm* 80-96; Perm to Offic *Win* from 97. *45 Knowland Drive, Milford-on-Sea, Lymington SO41 0RH* Tel (01590) 644473

HEWITT, Kenneth Victor. b 30. Lon Univ BSc49 CertEd51 MSc53. Cuddesdon Coll 60. d 62 p 63. C Maidstone St Martin *Cant* 62-64; C Croydon St Mich 64-67; P-in-c S Kensington St Aug *Lon* 67-73; V 73-95; Asst Chapl Lon Univ 67-73; rtd 95; Perm to Offic *Roch* from 95. *41 Bromley College, London Road, Bromley BR1 1PE* Tel (020) 8464 0014

HEWITT, Michael David. b 49. K Coll Lon BD79 AKC79 CertEd. Qu Coll Birm 79. d 80 p 81. C Bexleyheath Ch Ch *Roch* 80-84; C Buckland in Dover w Buckland Valley *Cant* 84-89; R Ridgewell w Ashen, Birdbrook and Sturmer *Chelmsf* from 89. *The Rectory, Church Lane, Ridgewell, Halstead CO9 4SA* Tel (01440) 785355

HEWITT, Patrick. See HEWITT, Canon William Patrick

HEWITT, Paul Stephen Patrick. b 59. TCD BA82 MA87. CITC 83. d 86 p 87. C Ballymacash *Conn* 86-89; C Ballymena w Ballyclug 89-91; I Glencraig *D & D* from 91. *The Parish Office, 6 Seahill Road, Craigavad, Holywood BT18 0DA* Tel (028) 9042 3903 or 9042 1847 E-mail glencraigoffice@btconnect.com

HEWITT, Peter. See HEWITT, Thomas Peter James

HEWITT, Robert Samuel. b 51. QUB BSc73. CITC 77. d 80 p 81. C Dundela St Mark *D & D* 80-84; R Donaghadee 84-92. *3 The Trees, New Road, Donaghadee BT21 0EJ* Tel (028) 9188 2594

HEWITT, Stephen Wilkes. b 49. Fitzw Coll Cam MA71. St Jo Coll Nottm 88. d 90 p 91. C Eaton *Nor* 90-93; V Warwick

St Paul *Cov* 93-01; Perm to Offic *Newc* 01-02; P-in-c High Spen and Rowlands Gill *Dur* 02-05; V 05-09; TR Cramlington *Newc* from 09. *33 Twyford Close, Cramlington NE23 1PH*
E-mail sandshewitt@hotmail.com

HEWITT, Thomas Peter James. b 24. St Andr Univ MA50. St Steph Ho Ox 50. **d** 52 **p** 53. C Ellesmere Port *Ches* 52-56; C Leytonstone St Marg w St Columba *Chelmsf* 56-60; V Barlby *York* 60-65; V Godshill *Portsm* 65-93; rtd 93. *c/o C L Wiggins Esq, Jerome and Co Solicitors, 98 High Street, Newport PO30 1BD*

HEWITT, Timothy James. b 67. St D Coll Lamp BD88. Ripon Coll Cuddesdon 89. **d** 91 **p** 92. C Milford Haven *St D* 91-94; C Llanelli 94-96; P-in-c Llan-non 96-97; V Clydach *S & B* 98-07; V Ystalyfera from 07; Dioc Voc Adv from 07. *The Vicarage, Glan yr Afon Road, Ystalyfera, Swansea SA9 2EP* Tel (01639) 842257

HEWITT, Canon William Patrick. b 48. Nottm Univ BTh79. Linc Th Coll 75. **d** 79 **p** 80. C Workington St Jo *Carl* 79-83; V Flookburgh 83-87; V Barrow St Matt 87-90; V Lowick and Kyloe w Ancroft *Newc* 90-96; R Ford and Etal 96-96; RD Norham 91-96; I Fanlobbus Union *C, C & R* 96-07; I Bandon Union from 07; Can Cork Cathl from 00; Can Cloyne Cathl from 00. *The Rectory, Castle Road, Bandon, Co Cork, Republic of Ireland* Tel (00353) (23) 41259 *or* tel and fax 29818
E-mail bandon@cork.anglican.org

HEWLETT, Mrs Caroline Joan. b 68. Coll of Ripon & York St Jo BEd92 St Jo Coll Dur BA01. Cranmer Hall Dur 99. **d** 01 **p** 02. C Leeds St Geo *Ripon* 01-04; C Aldborough w Boroughbridge and Roecliffe 04-06; Chapl Leeds Combined Court Cen 03-06; V Swaledale from 06. *The Vicarage, Reeth, Richmond DL11 6TR* Tel (01748) 886429 Mobile 07866-750211
E-mail carolinehewlett@hotmail.com

HEWLETT, David Bryan. b 49. Bris Univ BEd72. Qu Coll Birm 77. **d** 79 **p** 80. C Ludlow *Heref* 79-81; TV 81-84; V Marden w Amberley and Wisteston 84-92; Lect Glouc Sch for Min 84-92; Field Officer for Lay Min *Heref* 84-91; CME Officer 86-92; Dir Post-Ord Tr 91-92; Hd Master St Fran Sch Pewsey 92-94; Co-ord Chapl Frenchay Healthcare NHS Trust Bris 94-00; Dir Past Studies OLM Scheme and CME Adv *Linc* 00-04; Par Development Adv (South) 00-04; R Pontesbury I and II *Heref* 04-08; V Corbridge w Halton and Newton Hall *Newc* from 08; AD Corbridge from 09. *The Vicarage, Greencroft Avenue, Corbridge NE45 5DW* Tel (01434) 632128
E-mail david.hewlett3@btopenworld.com

HEWLETT, David Jonathon Peter. b 57. Dur Univ BA79 PhD83. Ridley Hall Cam 82. **d** 83 **p** 84. C New Barnet St Jas *St Alb* 83-86; Lect CITC 86-90; P-in-c Feock *Truro* 91-95; Jt Dir SWMTC 91-95; Prin 95-03; Adv Local Ord Min 91-95; Hon Can Truro Cathl 01-03; Prin Qu Coll Birm from 03. *71 Farquhar Road, Edgbaston, Birmingham B15 2QP* Tel 0121-452 2612 *or* 452 2603 Fax 454 8171 E-mail d.hewlett@queens.ac.uk

HEWLETT, Guy Edward. b 59. Thames Poly CertEd89 Open Univ BA90. Oak Hill Th Coll 96. **d** 96 **p** 97. NSM Sudbury St Andr *Lon* 96-99; C Harrow Trin St Mich 99-05; V Harrow Weald St Mich from 05. *74 Bishop Ken Road, Harrow HA3 7HR* Tel (020) 8861 1710 E-mail guyhewlett@lineone.net

HEWLETT-SMITH, Peter Brian. b 40. OBE87. Ripon Coll Cuddesdon 06. **d** 06. NSM Heckfield w Mattingley and Rotherwick *Win* 06-07; NSM Whitewater from 07. *10 Winchfield Court, Pale Lane, Winchfield, Hook RG27 8SP* Tel (01252) 842163 Mobile 07799-404206
E-mail peter.hewlettsmith@gmail.com

HEWLINS, Pauline Elizabeth. *See* SEAMAN, Mrs Pauline Elizabeth

HEWSON, Mrs Rose Raylene. b 47. SAOMC 96. **d** 99 **p** 00. NSM High Wycombe *Ox* 99-02; NSM Burnham w Dropmore, Hitcham and Taplow 02-08; NSM Hitcham from 08. *Hitcham Vicarage, 1 The Precincts, Burnham, Slough SL1 7HU* Tel (01628) 602881 E-mail rosie@hewsons.net

HEWSON, Thomas Robert. b 45. Man Univ BA66. S'wark Ord Course 85. **d** 89 **p** 90. C Chinnor w Emmington and Sydenham etc *Ox* 89-92; TV Burnham w Dropmore, Hitcham and Taplow 92-08; V Hitcham from 08. *Hitcham Vicarage, 1 The Precincts, Burnham, Slough SL1 7HU* Tel and fax (01628) 602881
E-mail trh@hewsons.net

HEYCOCKS, Christian John. b 71. Univ of Wales (Ban) BA93 MA96. Westcott Ho Cam 94 CITC 97. **d** 97 **p** 98. C Rhyl w St Ann *St As* 97-00; Chapl RN 00-06; Chapl Univ Staff Cam and C Cambridge Gt St Mary w St Mich *Ely* 06-09; V Sheringham *Nor* from 09. *The Vicarage, 10 North Street, Sheringham NR26 8LW* Tel (01263) 822089
E-mail rev.heycocks15@btinternet.com

HEYES, Andrew Robin. b 61. Man Univ BA93. St Steph Ho Ox 93. **d** 95 **p** 96. C Tonge Moor *Man* 95-00; V Glodwick 00-06; R Tampa St Clem USA from 06. *3817 Beneraid Street, Land o' Lakes FL 34638, USA* Tel (001) (813) 995 5364
E-mail aheyes@tampabay.rr.com

HEYES, Robert John. b 46. STETS 00. **d** 03 **p** 04. NSM Bramley and Grafham *Guildf* 03-08; NSM Shamley Green from 08.

Juniper Cottage, 22 Eastwood Road, Bramley, Guildford GU5 0DS Tel (01483) 893706 Fax 894001
E-mail bobheyes@onetel.com

HEYGATE, Stephen Beaumont. b 48. Loughb Univ BSc71 CQSW73 PhD89. St Jo Coll Nottm 86. **d** 88 **p** 89. C Aylestone St Andr w St Jas *Leic* 88-90; V Cosby 90-00; V Evington from 00; P-in-c Leic St Phil 00-04; Bp's Adv for Healing and Deliverance from 04. *Evington Vicarage, Stoughton Lane, Stoughton, Leicester LE2 2FH* Tel 0116-271 2032
E-mail stephenheygate@btinternet.com

HEYHOE, Canon Jonathan Peter. b 53. Man Univ BA75. Trin Coll Bris 77. **d** 80 **p** 81. C Woking St Pet *Guildf* 80-83; C Heatherlands St Jo *Sarum* 83-91; Chr Renewal Cen Rostrevor 91-95; Perm to Offic *D & D* 91-97; I Ballybay w Mucknoe and Clontibret *Clogh* from 98; Preb Clogh Cathl from 06. *The Rectory, Knocknamaddy, Ballybay, Co Monaghan, Republic of Ireland* Tel (00353) (42) 974 1102 Mobile 87-418 1427
E-mail ballybay@clogher.anglican.org *or* jheyhoe@esatclear.ie

HEYWOOD, Mrs Anne Christine. b 44. Sarum Th Coll. **d** 97 **p** 98. C Talbot Village *Sarum* 97-01; TV Shaston from 01. *St James's Vicarage, 34 Tanyard Lane, Shaftesbury SP7 8HW* Tel (01747) 852193

HEYWOOD, Anthony. *See* HEYWOOD, Richard Anthony

HEYWOOD, David Stephen. b 55. Selw Coll Cam BA76 MA80 SS Hild & Bede Coll Dur PhD89. St Jo Coll Dur 80. **d** 86 **p** 87. C Cheltenham St Luke and St Jo *Glouc* 86-90; TV Sanderstead All SS *S'wark* 90-98; V Edensor *Lich* 98-03; Deanery and Min Development Officer 03-06; Lect Past Th Ripon Coll Cuddesdon from 06. *3 College Field, Cuddesdon, Oxford OX44 9HL* Tel (01865) 874974 *or* 877444
E-mail david.heywood@ripon-cuddesdon.ac.uk

HEYWOOD, Deiniol John Owen. *See* KEARLEY-HEYWOOD, Deiniol John Owen

HEYWOOD, Geoffrey Thomas. b 26. St Mich Coll Llan 60. **d** 62 **p** 63. C Porthmadog *Ban* 62-64; C Llandudno 64-67; V Caerhun w Llangelynin 67-74; Asst Chapl HM Pris Liv 74-75; Chapl HM Pris Ex 75-77; Chapl HM Pris Wakef 77-79; Chapl HM YOI Eastwood Park 79-90; Chapl HM Pris Leyhill 79-90; rtd 90; Perm to Offic *Glouc* 94-05. *5 Meadow Road, Leyhill, Wotton-under-Edge GL12 8HW*

HEYWOOD, Mrs Margaret Anne (Meg). b 52. Luton Coll of HE BSc81. EMMTC 04. **d** 07 **p** 07. Chapl Ox Min Course from 06; NSM Ox St Clem 07-08. *3 College Field, Cuddesdon, Oxford OX44 9HL* Tel (01865) 874974
E-mail meg_heywood@hotmail.com

HEYWOOD, Michael Herbert. b 41. Liv Univ BSc63. Clifton Th Coll 63. **d** 65 **p** 66. C Low Elswick *Newc* 65-68; C St Helens St Mark *Liv* 68-75; Leprosy Miss Area Org NE and Cumbria 75-85; S Lon, Surrey and Berks 85-91; Internat Publicity and Promotional Co-ord 91-01; Hon C New Malden and Coombe *S'wark* 01-06; rtd 06. *9 Dryburn Road, Durham DH1 5AJ* Tel 0191-386 0087 E-mail biddyandmike@lineone.net

HEYWOOD, Peter. b 46. Cranmer Hall Dur 72. **d** 75 **p** 76. C Blackley St Andr *Man* 75-78; C Denton Ch Ch 78-80; V Constable Lee 80-01; rtd 01; Perm to Offic *Man* from 01. *12 Heys Close, Cloughfold, Rossendale BB4 7LW* Tel (01706) 222169

HEYWOOD, Richard Anthony. b 77. St Jo Coll Dur BA99. Oak Hill Th Coll 04. **d** 07 **p** 08. C Lt Shelford *Ely* from 07. *5 Garden Fields, Little Shelford, Cambridge CB22 5HH* Tel 07804-671405 (mobile) E-mail tony.heywood@talk21.com

HEZEL, Adrian. b 43. Chelsea Coll Lon BSc64 PhD67. NOC 78. **d** 81 **p** 82. NSM Mirfield *Wakef* 81-89; C 89-99; V Shelley and Shepley 90-99; V Hoylake *Ches* 99-08; rtd 08. *14 John Yeoman Close, Little Neston, Neston CH64 4BF* Tel 0151-336 3773
E-mail ahezel@btinternet.com

HIBBARD, John. b 42. **d** 03 **p** 04. NSM Stewkley w Soulbury and Drayton Parslow *Ox* 03-06; Perm to Offic 06-08; NSM Fenny Stratford from 08. *Chapel Side, 6 Nearton End, Swanbourne, Milton Keynes MK17 0SL* Tel (01296) 720449

HIBBERD, Brian Jeffery. b 35. Fitzw Coll Cam MA62 Southn Univ MA84. Ridley Hall Cam 58. **d** 60 **p** 61. C Cambridge H Trin *Ely* 60-63; C Doncaster St Mary *Sheff* 63-66; Asst Master Price's Sch Fareham 66-69; Warblington Sch Havant 69-71; Hd Soc and RS Carisbrooke High Sch 71-84; Distr Health Promotion Officer Is of Wight 84-88; SW Herts 88-90; Hd RS Goffs Sch Cheshunt 90-95; rtd 95; Teacher Qu Sch Bushey 95-97; Teacher R Masonic Sch for Girls Rickmansworth 97-00; Hon C Abbots Langley *St Alb* 00-01; Perm to Offic from 01. *50 Rosehill Gardens, Abbots Langley WD5 0HF* Tel (01923) 267391

HIBBERD, Carol Anne. b 59. Kent Univ BA80. S'wark Ord Course 89. **d** 92 **p** 94. NSM Gospel Lane St Mich *Birm* 92-94; C 94-98; C Coleshill 98-02; Chapl Marie Curie Cen Warren Pearl 02-06. *Address temp unknown*

HIBBERD, John. b 60. Wadh Coll Ox MA82. Trin Coll Bris BA89. **d** 89 **p** 90. C Northolt St Mary *Lon* 89-92; C-in-c Southall Em CD 92-94; Min of Miss Through Faith Miss *Ely* from 95. *Celandine, 1 School Lane, Swavesey, Cambridge CB24 4RL* Tel (01954) 200285 E-mail john.hibberd3@ntlworld.com

HIBBERD, John Charles. b 38. Bernard Gilpin Soc Dur 62 Chich Th Coll 63. **d** 66 **p** 67. C W Drayton 66-70; C Noel Park St Mark 70-72; C Ealing St Steph Castle Hill 72-75; V Gunnersbury St Jas 75-84; V Whitton SS Phil and Jas 84-86; Finance and Trust Sec Lon Dioc Fund 87-98; Perm to Offic 87-98; rtd 98. *18 Pursley Close, Sandown PO36 9QP* Tel (01983) 401036

HIBBERT, Miss Anne Mary Elizabeth. Southn Univ BA81. Trin Coll Bris 81. **dss** 83 **d** 87 **p** 94. Muswell Hill St Jas w St Matt *Lon* 83-86; Leic H Trin w St Jo 86-87; Par Dn 87-90; Perm to Offic *Cov* from 90; Evang Co-ord and Adv CPAS 90-98; Churches Millennium Exec 98-99; Miss & Spirituality Adv BRF 99-03; Dir Well Chr Healing Cen from 03. *The Well Christian Healing Centre, PO Box 3407, Leamington Spa CV32 6ZH* Tel (01926) 888003 Mobile 07973-563667 E-mail anne@wellhealing.org

HIBBERT, Charles Dennis. b 24. Linc Th Coll 69. **d** 70 **p** 71. C Radcliffe-on-Trent *S'well* 70-73; P-in-c Ladybrook 73-77; V 77-79; V Boughton 79-85; V Ollerton 79-85; R Nuthall 85-89; rtd 89; Perm to Offic *S'well* from 89. *27 Nottingham Road, Kimberley, Nottingham NG16 2NB* Tel 0115-938 6302

HIBBERT, Peter John. b 43. Hull Univ BA71 Lon Univ CertEd72 MA79. Sarum & Wells Th Coll 85. **d** 88 **p** 89. C Newsome and Armitage Bridge *Wakef* 88-92; P-in-c Newton Flowery Field *Ches* 92-00; P-in-c Hyde St Thos 97-00; V Handsworth St Jas *Birm* 00-08; rtd 08; P-in-c Altarnon w Bolventor, Laneast and St Clether *Truro* from 08. *The Rectory, Altarnun, Launceston PL15 7SJ* Tel (01566) 880134 E-mail hibbert631@btinternet.com

HIBBERT, Prof Peter Rodney. b 53. Man Univ LLB74 Nottm Univ MA99 Solicitor 77. EMMTC 96. **d** 99 **p** 00. C Knighton St Mary Magd *Leic* 99-01; Perm to Offic *Leic* from 01 and *Birm* from 03. *Grange Cottage, 37 Rushes Lane, Lubenham, Market Harborough LE16 9TN* Tel (01858) 433174

HIBBERT, Richard Charles. b 62. Trin Coll Bris BA93. **d** 96 **p** 97. C Luton St Mary *St Alb* 96-00; V Bedford Ch Ch from 00. *Christ Church Vicarage, 115 Denmark Street, Bedford MK40 3TJ* Tel and fax (01234) 359342 E-mail vicar@christchurchbedford.org.uk

HIBBINS, Neil Lance. b 60. St Anne's Coll Ox BA82 MA87. St Mich Coll Llan 83. **d** 85 **p** 86. C Griffithstown *Mon* 85-87; C Pontypool 87-88; TV Pontypool 88-92; Walsall Hosps NHS Trust 92-96; Asst Chapl Manor Hosp Walsall 92-96; R Norton Canes *Lich* from 96. *The Rectory, 81 Church Road, Norton Canes, Cannock WS11 9PQ* Tel (01543) 278969 E-mail neil_hibbins@lycos.com

HIBBS, Peter Wilfred. b 56. NOC 05. **d** 08 **p** 09. NSM Gt Snaith *Sheff* from 08. *Peveril, High Street, Snaith, Goole DN14 9HJ* Tel (01405) 862517 Mobile 07885-348498

HICHENS, Anthony. b 29. AKC59. **d** 60 **p** 61. C Ashford St Hilda *Lon* 60-64; C Leeds St Wilfrid *Ripon* 64-66; V Waramuri Guyana 67-75; P-in-c Stratton Audley w Godington *Ox* 76-83; P-in-c Finmere w Mixbury 76-78; P-in-c Fringford w Hethe and Newton Purcell 78-83; R Stratton Audley and Godington, Fringford etc 83-95; rtd 95; Perm to Offic *Pet* 95-07. *3 Brookside Mews, 666 Town Bush Road, Oak Park, Pietermaritzburg, 3201 South Africa* Tel (0027) (33) 347 3762

HICKES, Roy Edward. b 31. St Aid Birkenhead 56. **d** 59 **p** 60. C New Bury *Man* 59-63; C Winford *Ripon* 63-65; R Oldham St Andr *Man* 65-69; V Smallbridge 69-79; R Winford *B & W* 79-81; R Winford w Felton Common Hill 81-88; RD Chew Magna 85-88; Chapl Costa Blanca *Eur* 88-92; rtd 92; Perm to Offic *B & W* and *Bris* from 92; Hon C Wrington w Butcombe *B & W* 97-98. *17 Haycombe, Bristol BS14 0AJ* Tel (01275) 544750 E-mail royhickes@blueyonder.co.uk *or* randwhickes@blueyonder.co.uk

HICKFORD, Canon Michael Francis. b 53. Edin Th Coll 84. **d** 86 **p** 87. Chapl St Jo Cathl Oban 86-89; R Alexandria *Glas* 89-95; P-in-c Dingwall and Strathpeffer *Mor* 95-03; Dean *Mor* 98-03; R Inverness St Andr and Provost St Andr Cathl *Inverness* 03-04; Chapl NHS Highland from 04; Hon Can St Andr Cathl Inverness from 07. *New Craigs Hospital, 8 Leachkin Road, Inverness IV3 8NP* Tel (01463) 704000 ext 2426 Mobile 07795-238928 E-mail michael.hickford@nhs.net

HICKLING, John. b 34. Handsworth Coll *Birm* 56. Launde Abbey 69. **d** 69 **p** 70. In Methodist Ch 59-69; C Melton Mowbray w Thorpe Arnold *Leic* 69-71; TV 71-75; R Waltham on the Wolds w Stonesby and Saltby 75-84; R Aylestone St Andr w St Jas 84-93; R Husbands Bosworth w Mowsley and Knaptoft etc 93-96; rtd 96; Perm to Offic *Leic* from 99. *28 Oxford Drive, Melton Mowbray LE13 0AL* Tel (01664) 560770

HICKMAN, John William. b 38. Barrister-at-Law (Middle Temple) 69 Qu Coll Cam LLM81. Oak Hill Th Coll 92. **d** 95 **p** 96. NSM Sevenoaks St Nic *Roch* 95-98; P-in-c Stedham w Iping *Chich* 98-04; rtd 04; Perm to Offic *Chich* from 05. *Bywood, Selham Road, West Lavington, Midhurst GU29 0EG* Tel (01730) 810821

HICKS, Miss Barbara. b 42. Cranmer Hall Dur BA71. **dss** 85 **d** 87 P. Norton Woodseats St Paul *Sheff* 85-87; Par Dn Sheff St Jo ... Chapl Shrewsbury Hosp 96-02; rtd 02; Perm to

Offic *Sheff* from 06. *87 Underwood Road, Sheffield S8 8TG* Tel 0114-255 8087

HICKS, Ms Eunice. b 41. Trin Coll Bris BA00. WEMTC 01. **d** 01 **p** 02. NSM Chew Magna w Dundry and Norton Malreward *B & W* 01-06; NSM Rowledge and Frensham *Guildf* from 06. *The Vicarage, The Street, Frensham, Farnham GU10 3DT* Tel (01252) 792137 E-mail priest@frenshamchurches.org.uk

HICKS, Francis Fuller. b 28. Sarum & Wells Th Coll 71. **d** 74 **p** 75. C Broadstone *Sarum* 74-78; P-in-c Kington Magna and Buckhorn Weston 78-79; TV Gillingham 79-86; P-in-c Portland St Jo 86-89; V 89-93; rtd 93; Perm to Offic *B & W* and *Sarum* from 93. *Windyridge, 21 Castle Road, Sherborne DT9 3RW* Tel (01935) 814837

HICKS, Hazel Rebecca. b 54. Open Univ BA92. CITC 05. **d** 08 **p** 09. NSM Annagh w Drumaloor, Cloverhill and Drumlane *K, E & A* from 08. *Garvary Lodge, 49 Teemore Road, Derrylin, Enniskillen BT92 9QB* Tel (028) 6774 8422 Mobile 07770-852362 E-mail hazel6004@yahoo.co.uk

HICKS, Miss Joan Rosemary. b 60. Homerton Coll Cam BEd83. Westcott Ho Cam 87. **d** 90 **p** 94. C Wendover *Ox* 90-95; C Earley St Pet 95-98; P-in-c Beech Hill, Grazeley and Spencers Wood 98-05; P-in-c Cox Green from 05. *The Vicarage, 9 Warwick Close, Maidenhead SL6 3AL* Tel (01628) 622139 E-mail joanhicks@compuserve.com

HICKS, John Michael. b 67. Crewe & Alsager Coll BA89 K Coll Lon MA01 K Alfred's Coll Win PGCE90. NTMTC 02. **d** 05 **p** 06. NSM Grosvenor Chpl *Lon* 05-09; NSM Westmr St Steph w St Jo from 09. *167 John Ruskin Street, London SE5 0PQ* Tel (020) 7641 5930 Mobile 07971-670092 E-mail jnhx@hotmail.com

HICKS (née HODGSON), Julia Ruth. b 66. Somerville Coll Ox BA88 UEA PGCE89. Westcott Ho Cam 06. **d** 08 **p** 09. C Bridgwater St Mary and Chilton Trinity *B & W* from 08. *11 Alexandra Road, Bridgwater TA6 3HE* Tel 07812-179381 (mobile) E-mail juliahicks@tiscali.co.uk

HICKS, Richard Barry. b 32. Dur Univ BA55. Sarum Th Coll 59. **d** 61 **p** 62. C Wallsend St Luke *Newc* 61-64; C Tynemouth Ch Ch 64-69; V Tynemouth St Jo 69-75; V Prudhoe 75-82; TV Swanborough *Sarum* 82-86; R Hilperton w Whaddon and Staverton etc 86-97; rtd 97; Perm to Offic *Newc* from 97 and *Carl* from 98. *Lane House, Sawmill Lane, Brampton CA8 1DA* Tel (01697) 72156

HICKS, Robert Buxton. b 66. Ex Univ BSc90. Westcott Ho Cam 06. **d** 08 **p** 09. C Bridgwater St Fran *B & W* from 08. *11 Alexandra Road, Bridgwater TA6 3HE* Tel 07968-153988 (mobile) E-mail tbhicks@tiscali.co.uk

HICKS, Stuart Knox. b 34. Univ of W Ontario BA56 Huron Coll LTh59 Ox Univ DipEd67. **d** 58 **p** 60. Canada 58-65; C Allerton Liv 65-66; Hon C Rye Park St Cuth *St Alb* 68-72; Lic to Offic *B & W* 72-87 and 88-95; Chapl Magdalen Chpl Bath 80-86; Chapl Partis Coll Bath 88-90; rtd 99. *Folly Orchard, The Folly, Saltford, Bristol BS31 3JW* Tel (01225) 873391

HICKS, Mrs Valerie Joy. b 47. SRN69. Cant Sch of Min 82. **dss** 85 **d** 87 **p** 94. Roch 85-89; Hon Par Dn 87-89; Par Dn Thatcham *Ox* 89-93; TD Aylesbury w Bierton and Hulcott 93-94; TV 94-00; P-in-c Dordon *Birm* 00-09; V from 09; Dioc Chapl MU from 01. *St Leonard's Vicarage, Watling Street, Dordon, Tamworth B78 1TE* Tel (01827) 892294 E-mail val.hicks@tesco.net

HICKS, Canon William Trevor. b 47. Hull Univ BA68 Fitzw Coll Cam BA70 MA74. Westcott Ho Cam 68. **d** 70 **p** 71. C Cottingham *York* 70-73; C Elland *Wakef* 73-76; V Walsden 76-81; V Knottingley 81-92; R Castleford All SS 92-96; P-in-c Womersley and Kirk Smeaton 96-00; RD Pontefract 94-99; V Bolsover *Derby* from 00; RD Bolsover and Staveley from 05; Hon Can Derby Cathl from 07. *The Vicarage, Church Street, Bolsover, Chesterfield S44 6HB* Tel (01246) 824888 E-mail trevorhicks1@aol.com

HICKSON, Gordon Crawford Fitzgerald. b 51. CCC Cam MA76. **d** 06 **p** 07. NSM Ox St Aldate from 06. *40 Pembroke Street, Oxford OX1 1BP* Tel (01865) 242000 Mobile 07713-688079 E-mail gordon.hickson@staldates.org.uk

HIDE, Timothy John. b 71. Roehampton Inst BA95. St Steph Ho Ox 97. **d** 99 **p** 00. C Woodford St Mary w St Phil and St Jas *Chelmsf* 99-01; C Upminster 01-05; Asst P Forest Gate Em w Upton Cross 05-06; Perm to Offic 06-08, TV Canvey Is from 08. *St Anne's House, 51 St Anne's Road, Canvey Island SS8 7LS* Tel (01268) 514412 Fax 08707-622402 E-mail frtimhide@btinternet.com

HIDER, David Arthur. b 46. Lon Univ BSc67. Sarum & Wells Th Coll 86. **d** 89 **p** 90. NSM Southbourne w W Thorney *Chich* 89-91; C Goring-by-Sea 91-94; P-in-c Peacehaven and Telscombe Cliffs 94-99; V from 99; P-in-c Telscombe w Piddinghoe and Southease 94-99; V Telscombe Village from 99; V Piddinghoe 99; V Southease from 99. *The Vicarage, 41 Bramber Avenue, Peacehaven BN10 8HR* Tel and fax (01273) 583149 E-mail revd_d_hider@msn.com

HIDER, Mrs Melanie Anne. b 53. UEA BA91 Homerton Coll Cam PGCE92. **d** 06 **p** 07. OLM Nor Lakenham St Alb and

St Mark from 06. *10 Brian Avenue, Norwich NR1 2PH* Tel (01603) 622373 E-mail melaniehider@beemerz.co.uk

HIGGINBOTTOM, Richard. b 48. Lon Univ BD74. Oak Hill Th Coll. d 74 p 75. C Kenilworth St Jo *Cov* 74-77; C Finham 77-79; P-in-c Attleborough 79-81; V 81-84; Asst Chapl HM Pris Brixton 84-85; Chapl HM Pris Roch 85-92; Camp Hill 92-00; HM YOI Dover 00-03; rtd 03; Perm to Offic *Cant* 03-07. *c/o Crockford, Church House, Great Smith Street, London SW1P 3AZ* Tel 07779-775081 (mobile)

HIGGINBOTTOM, Richard William. b 51. Man Univ BA73 MA75. Edin Th Coll 83. d 85 p 86. C Knighton St Mary Magd *Leic* 85-87; C Northleach w Hampnett and Farmington *Glouc* 87-89; V Hayfield *Derby* 89-93; CPAS Min Adv for Scotland from 93. *2 Highfield Place, Bankfoot, Perth PH1 4AX* Tel (01738) 440877 *or* 787429 Mobile 07963-625835 E-mail rhigginbottom@cpas.org.uk

HIGGINS, Anthony Charles. b 46. d 97 p 98. OLM Swanage and Studland *Sarum* from 97. *The Old School House, School Lane, Studland, Swanage BH19 3AJ* Tel (01929) 450691 E-mail revtonyhiggins@btinternet.com

HIGGINS, Bernard. b 42. Leic Poly BPharm63 PhD66 MRPharmS68. St Jo Coll Nottm 89. d 91 p 92. C Stockport St Geo *Ches* 91-94; C Stockport SW 94-95; P-in-c Dunham Massey St Marg and St Mark 95-98; V 98-00; rtd 00; Perm to Offic *Blackb* and *Carl* from 01. *16 Inglemere Close, Arnside, Carnforth LA5 0AP* Tel (01524) 761000

HIGGINS, Frank Roylance. b 34. Open Univ BA74 MEd83. Bps' Coll Cheshunt 59. d 62 p 63. C Sunderland *Dur* 62-64; C S Westoe 64-66; P-in-c Smethwick St Mich *Birm* 66-67; V 67-70; V Garretts Green 70-75; Lic to Offic *Worc* 76-84; Perm to Offic *Birm* 81-87; Hon C Feckenham w Bradley *Worc* 84-87; R Ripple, Earls Croome w Hill Croome and Strensham 87-95; RD Upton 92-95; rtd 95; P-in-c Church Lench w Rous Lench and Abbots Morton *Worc* 95-00; Perm to Offic from 00. *Verona, Abberton Road, Bishampton, Pershore WR10 2LU* Tel and fax (01386) 462694

HIGGINS, Geoffrey Minta. b 27. New Coll Ox BA52 MA56. Cuddesdon Coll 52. d 54 p 55. C Pet St Mary Boongate 54-56; CF 56-77; Hong Kong from 77. *12-C Far East Consortium Building, 29 On Lok Road, Yuen Long, New Territories, Hong Kong* Tel (00852) 479 9374

HIGGINS, Canon Godfrey. b 39. St Chad's Coll Dur BA61 DipEd63. d 63 p 64. C Brighouse *Wakef* 63-66; C Huddersfield St Jo 66-68; R High Hoyland w Clayton W 68-75; V Marsden 75-83; V Pontefract St Giles 83-04; Hon Can Wakef Cathl 93-04; rtd 04. *2 Holme View, Ilkley LS29 9EL* Tel (01943) 603861

HIGGINS, John. b 44. Lon Bible Coll MTh98. Trin Coll Bris 71. d 73 p 74. C Clapham St Jas *S'wark* 73-74; C Ruskin Park St Sav and St Matt 74-77; C Hamworthy *Sarum* 77-80; V Bordesley St Andr *Birm* 80-83; V Bishop Sutton and Stanton Drew and Stowey *B & W* 83-09; rtd 09; Perm to Offic *Nor* from 09. *129 St Martins Way, Thetford IP24 3QB* Tel (01842) 752655 E-mail rev.johnhiggins@btopenworld.com

HIGGINS, John Leslie. b 43. Open Univ BA79 Birm Univ MEd89 Univ of Cen England in Birm CQSW75. Lich Th Coll 64. d 66 p 67. C Sale St Anne *Ches* 66-69; C Bredbury St Mark 69-72; V Wharton 72-74; Hon C Annan and Lockerbie *Glas* 75-79; V Coseley Ch Ch *Lich* 79-89; R Arthuret *Carl* 89-96; Soc Resp Officer and Child Protection Co-ord 90-00; C Brampton and Farlam and Castle Carrock w Cumrew 96-00; Hon Can Carl Cathl 96-00; rtd 00; Hon C Annan *Glas* from 00; Perm to Offic *Carl* from 01. *Green Croft Cottage, The Haggs, Ecclefechan, Lockerbie DG11 3ED* Tel (01576) 300796 Fax 300790 Mobile 07867-505644 E-mail john_l_higgins@lineone.net

HIGGINS, Canon Kenneth. b 56. TCD BTh93. CITC 90. d 93 p 94. C Cregagh *D & D* 93-96; Bp's C Movilla 96-00; I 01-09; I Belfast St Donard from 09; Can Down Cathl from 06. *St Donard's Rectory, 421 Beersbridge Road, Belfast BT5 5DU* Tel (028) 9065 2321 Mobile 07986-866690 E-mail revkenhiggins@hotmail.com

HIGGINS, The Very Revd Michael John. b 35. Birm Univ LLB57 G&C Coll Cam LLB59 PhD62. Ridley Hall Cam 63. d 65 p 65. C Ormskirk *Liv* 65-67; Selection Sec ACCM 67-74; Hon C St Marylebone St Mark w St Luke *Lon* 69-74; P-in-c Woodlands *B & W* 74-80; V Frome St Jo 74-80; TR Preston St Jo *Blackb* 80-91; Dean Ely 91-03; rtd 03; Perm to Offic *Ely* from 05. *Twin Cottage, North Street, Great Dunham, King's Lynn PE32 2LR* Tel (01328) 701058

HIGGINS, Richard Ellis. b 63. Univ of Wales BA84. St Mich Coll Llan 86. d 89 p 90. C Bargoed and Deri w Brithdir *Llan* 89-92; Zimbabwe 92-94; V Penmaen and Crumlin *Mon* 94-99; Chapl Glan Hafren NHS Trust 94-99; V Rhymney *Mon* 99-02; Chapl Pet Hosps NHS Trust from 03. *Chaplaincy Services, Peterborough Hospital NHS Trust, Thorpe Road, Peterborough PE3 6DA* Tel (01733) 874345 E-mail richard.higgins@pbh-tr.nhs.uk

HIGGINS, Rupert Anthony. b 59. Man Univ BA80. Wycliffe Hall Ox 82. d 85 p 86. C Plymouth St Andr w St Paul and St Geo *Ex* 85-90; C-in-c St Paul 88-90; Assoc V Clifton Ch Ch w Em *Bris*

90-95; V S Croydon Em *S'wark* 95-02; C Langham Place All So *Lon* 02-05; P-in-c Clifton Ch Ch w Em *Bris* from 05. *Christ Church Vicarage, 16 Mortimer Road, Clifton, Bristol BS8 4EY* Tel 0117-974 3404 E-mail rupert@christchurchclifton.org.uk

HIGGINS, Canon Timothy John. b 45. Bris Univ BEd70 Lanc Univ MA74. Cranmer Hall Dur. d 79 p 80. C Northampton All SS w St Kath *Pet* 79-82; V Whitton St Aug *Lon* 82-90; AD Hampton 86-90; TR Aylesbury w Bierton and Hulcott *Ox* 90-06; RD Aylesbury 94-04; Hon Can Ch Ch 00-06; Can Res Bris Cathl from 06; P-in-c City of Bris 06-08; P-in-c Bris St Steph w St Jas and St Jo w St Mich etc from 08. *City Rectory, Apartment 8, 10 Unity Street, Bristol BS1 5HH* Tel 0117-929 4984 E-mail city.canon@bristol-cathedral.co.uk

HIGGINSON, Andrew John. b 62. Bradf Univ BTech85. Trin Coll Bris 02. d 04 p 05. C Quarrington w Old Sleaford *Linc* 04-08; C Silk Willoughby 04-08; P-in-c Freiston, Butterwick w Bennington, and Leverton from 08. *The Rectory, Butterwick Road, Freiston, Boston PE22 0LF* Tel (01205) 760480 E-mail andrewj.higginson@btopenworld.com

HIGGINSON, Richard Andrew. b 53. St Jo Coll Cam BA74 Man Univ PhD82. EAMTC 02. d 04 p 05. NSM Cambridge St Phil *Ely* from 04; Dir of Studies Ridley Hall Cam from 05. *15 Guest Road, Cambridge CB1 2AL* Tel (01223) 315667 *or* 741074 E-mail rah41@cam.ac.uk

HIGGINSON, Stanley. d 08. NSM Wigan St Mich *Liv* from 08. *12 Clifton Crescent, Wigan WN1 2LB* E-mail stanley.higginson33@yahoo.co.uk

HIGGON, David. Univ of Wales (Swansea) BA75 Birm Univ MBA96 Nottm Univ MA99. EMMTC 96. d 00 p 01. NSM Crich and S Wingfield *Derby* 00-04; Chapl HM Pris Dovegate 04-05; Perm to Offic *Derby* 05-07; Chapl HM Pris Ranby from 07. *HM Prison, Ranby, Retford DN22 8EU* Tel (01777) 862000 E-mail dhiggon@btopenworld.com

HIGGOTT, Bryn Graham. b 54. Birm Poly BA76 Solicitor 79. NEOC 03. d 06 p 07. NSM Thirsk *York* 06-08. *The Barton, Westcombe Hill, Colebrooke, Crediton EX17 5DL* Tel (01363) 82859 E-mail bghiggott@googlemail.com

HIGGS, Andrew Richard Bowen. b 53. Man Univ BSc75. St Jo Coll Nottm 81. d 85 p 86. C Droylsden St Mary *Man* 85-88; C Harlow Town Cen w Lt Parndon *Chelmsf* 88-95; TV 95-02; Chapl Princess Alexandra Hosp NHS Trust 96-02; R Stifford *Chelmsf* from 02. *The Rectory, High Road, North Stifford, Grays RM16 5UE* Tel (01375) 372733 E-mail andy@higgs4a.fsnet.co.uk

HIGGS, Michael John. b 53. Sarum & Wells Th Coll 76. d 80 p 81. C Cant St Martin and St Paul 80-84; C Maidstone St Martin 84-88; R Egerton w Pluckley 88-03; rtd 03. *8 Robinsons Mill, Mellis, Eye IP23 8DW* Tel (01379) 783926

HIGGS, Owen Christopher Goodwin. b 63. St Anne's Coll Ox BA84 MA88. St Steph Ho Ox 90. d 93 p 94. C Teddington St Mark and Hampton Wick *Lon* 93-96; C Lon Docks St Pet w Wapping St Jo 96-00; V Petts Wood *Roch* from 00. *The Vicarage, Willett Way, Orpington BR5 1QE* Tel (01689) 829971

HIGHAM, Gerald Norman. b 40. St Aid Birkenhead 64. d 68 p 69. C Garston *Liv* 68-71; C Blundellsands St Nic 71-73; V Bolton All So w St Jas *Man* 73-78; V Tonge w Alkrington 78-84; P-in-c Edenfield 84-86; P-in-c Stubbins 84-86; V Edenfield and Stubbins 86-03; rtd 03; Perm to Offic *Blackb* from 03. *71 Cherry Tree Way, Rossendale BB4 4JZ* Tel (01706) 210143 E-mail revg.higham@rotary1280.org

HIGHAM, Canon Jack. b 33. Linc Coll Ox BA56 MA60 Union Th Sem (NY) STM61. Qu Coll Birm 58. d 60 p 61. C Handsworth *Sheff* 60-64; V Handsworth Woodhouse 64-70; USA 70-78; R Stoke Bruerne w Grafton Regis and Alderton *Pet* 78-83; RD Towcester 82-83; Can Res, Chan and Lib Pet Cathl 83-03; rtd 03; Perm to Offic *S'well* from 04. *44 Alma Hill, Kimberley, Nottingham NG16 2JF* Tel 0115-938 6063

HIGHAM, John Leonard. b 39. Wycliffe Hall Ox 62. d 65 p 66. C Prescot *Liv* 65-71; V Hollinfare 71-74; Adult and Youth Service Adv Knowsley 74-76; TV Padgate 76-84; V Farnworth 84-89; TR Sutton 89-02; rtd 02; Perm to Offic *Liv* from 03. *86 Ormskirk Road, Rainford, St Helens WA11 8DB*

HIGHAM (née ANNS), Canon Pauline Mary. b 49. Bris Univ BEd71. EMMTC 87. d 90 p 94. Par Dn Wirksworth w Alderwasley, Carsington etc *Derby* 90-92; Par Dn Lt Berkhamsted and Bayford, Essendon etc *St Alb* 92-94; C 94-96; P-in-c 96-05; R from 05; Jt RD Hertford and Ware from 05; Hon Can St Alb from 06. *1 Little Berkhamsted Lane, Little Berkhamsted, Hertford SG13 8LU* Tel (01707) 875940 Fax 875289

HIGHTON, Philip William. b 70. Liv Univ BSc91 Nottm Univ MSc92. Oak Hill Th Coll BA05. d 05 p 06. C Knutsford St Jo and Toft *Ches* 05-09; V Cheadle All Hallows from 09. *All Hallows' Vicarage, 222 Councillor Lane, Cheadle SK8 2JG* Tel 0161-428 9071 *or* 428 2804 E-mail phil_highton@tiscali.co.uk

HIGHTON, William James. b 31. St Deiniol's Hawarden. d 83 p 83. NSM Thornton Hough *Ches* 82-84; C Cheadle 84-89; Walton 88-99; rtd 99; Perm to Offic *Carl* from 01. *... Drive, Burton-in-Kendal, Carnforth LA6 1NF ...*

HIGMAN, John Charles. b 62. Plymouth Poly BSc84 MRSC01. SWMTC 03. **d** 06 **p** 07. NSM Peter Tavy, Mary Tavy, Lydford and Brent Tor *Ex* from 06. *Balwynd, Bal Lane, Mary Tavy, Tavistock PL19 9PE* Tel (01822) 810431

HIGTON, Anthony Raymond. b 42. Lon Sch of Th BD65. Oak Hill Th Coll 65. **d** 67 **p** 68. C Newark Ch Ch *S'well* 67-69; C Cheltenham St Mark *Glouc* 70-75; R Hawkwell *Chelmsf* 75-99; Gen Dir CMJ 99-05; R Jerusalem Ch Ch 03-05; R N w S Wootton *Nor* 06-09; rtd 09; rtd 09. *17 Church View, Marham, King's Lynn PE33 9HW* Tel (01760) 338342 Mobile 07815-891582 E-mail tony@higton.info

HILARY, Sister. *See* JORDINSON, Vera

HILBORN, David Henry Kyte. b 64. Nottm Univ BA85 PhD94 Mansf Coll Ox MA88. **d** 02 **p** 02. C Acton St Mary *Lon* 02-06; Dir Studies NTMTC from 06. *North Thames Ministerial Training Course, The Crypt, St George-in-the-East, 16 Cannon Street Road, London E1 0BH* Tel (020) 7481 9477 Fax 7481 8907 E-mail studies@ntmtc.org.uk *or* dhilborn@btinternet.com

HILBORN, Mrs Mia Alison Kyte. b 63. City Univ BSc84 Mansf Coll Ox MA87. **d** 02 **p** 02. Chapl Team Ldr Guy's and St Thos' NHS Foundn Trust from 01; NSM N Lambeth *S'wark* from 02. *Guy's and St Thomas' NHS Foundation Trust, St Thomas Street, London SE1 9RT* Tel (020) 7188 5588 Mobile 07740-779585 E-mail mia.hilborn@gstt.sthames.nhs.uk

HILDITCH, Canon Janet. b 59. St Andr Univ MTheol81 PhD87. NOC 92. **d** 94 **p** 95. C Kirkholt *Man* 94-98; Chapl Rochdale Healthcare NHS Trust 97-98; Chapl N Man Health Care NHS Trust 98-00; Chapl Tameside and Glossop Acute Services NHS Trust from 00; Hon Can Man Cathl from 04. *Tameside General Hospital, Fountain Street, Ashton-under-Lyne OL6 9EW* Tel 0161-331 6000

HILDRED, David. b 61. Bath Univ BSc83 CertEd83. Wycliffe Hall Ox 86. **d** 89 **p** 90. C Westcliff St Mich *Chelmsf* 89-92; C Rayleigh 92-96; V Sidcup St Andr *Roch* from 96; AD Sidcup 03-08. *The Vicarage, St Andrew's Road, Sidcup DA14 4SA* Tel (020) 8300 4172 E-mail david.hildred@diocese-rochester.org

HILDRETH, Sarah Frances. b 72. St Mich Coll Llan BTh05. **d** 05 **p** 06. C Hawarden *St As* 05-08; V Bagillt from 08; P-in-c Mostyn from 08. *The Vicarage, Bryntirion Road, Bagillt CH6 6BZ* Tel (01352) 732732 Mobile 07752-261931 E-mail revsarah3005@btinternet.com

HILES, Janet Rita. b 39. SAOMC 96. **d** 98 **p** 99. OLM Dorchester *Ox* 98-03; rtd 03; Perm to Offic *Portsm* from 04. *Malabar, The Broadway, Totland Bay PO39 0AN* Tel (01983) 752765 E-mail chrishiles@4thenet.co.uk

HILES, John Michael. b 32. Qu Coll Cam BA57 MA61. Ripon Th Coll 57. **d** 59 **p** 60. C Clifton St Jas *Sheff* 59-62; V Bramley St Fran 62-69; Hon C Holmfirth *Wakef* 69-89; Hon C Upper Holme Valley 89-91; Lic to Offic 91-97; Perm to Offic *Wakef* 97-03 and *Sarum* from 03. *22 Oldfield Road, Bishopdown, Salisbury SP1 3GQ* Tel (01722) 349951

HILL, Mrs Anne Doreen. b 40. **d** 88 **p** 94. Par Dn Bexleyheath St Pet *Roch* 88-90; Sub Chapl HM Pris Belmarsh 91-96; Dep Chapl 96-99; Hon C Lee St Mildred *S'wark* 93-04; rtd 04; Perm to Offic *Sarum* 05-08. *64 St Mary's Road, Poole BH15 2LL* Tel (01202) 666076 E-mail adhill40@hotmail.com

HILL, Barry Leon. b 79. Wycliffe Hall Ox BTh05. **d** 05 **p** 06. C Loughborough Em and St Mary in Charnwood *Leic* 05-09; Dioc Miss Enabler from 09. *1 Old Vicarage Mews, Sileby, Loughborough LE12 7FZ* E-mail barry@hill-home.co.uk

HILL, Canon Charles Bernard. b 50. Sheff Univ BA71 Qu Coll Ox DPhil76. Cant Sch of Min 91. **d** 94 **p** 95. NSM Sandgate St Paul w Folkestone St Geo *Cant* 94-98; NSM Folkestone H Trin w Ch 98-04; Eur Sec Coun for Chr Unity 99-08; Can Gib Cathl 03-08; P-in-c Benenden *Cant* from 08; P-in-c Sandhurst w Newenden from 08. *The Vicarage, The Green, Benenden, Cranbrook TN17 4DL* Tel (01580) 240658 E-mail cbh.mail@ntlworld.com

HILL, Charles Merrick. b 52. Strathclyde Univ BA74. Qu Coll Birm. **d** 80 **p** 81. C Silksworth *Dur* 80-83; C Stockton St Pet 83-85; TV Southampton (City Cen) *Win* 85-87; V Portsea St Geo *Portsm* 87-94; P-in-c Bodenham w Hope-under-Dinmore, Felton etc *Heref* 94-04; P-in-c Hellingly and Upper Dicker *Chich* 04-05; V from 05. *The Vicarage, 14 Orchard Grange, Lower Dicker, Hailsham BN27 3PA* Tel (01323) 440246

HILL, Charles Winston. b 78. Lanc Univ BA99. St Steph Ho Ox 00. **d** 03 **p** 04. C Lt Marsden w Nelson St Mary *Blackb* 03-04; C Blackb St Thos w St Jude 04-07; C Blackb St Mich w St Jo and H Trin 04-07; Chapl HM Pris Preston 07-08; Chapl HM Pris Hindley 08-09; P-in-c Burnley St Mark *Blackb* from 09; P-in-c W Burnley All SS from 09. *St Mark's Vicarage, 9 Rossendale Road, Burnley BB11 5DQ* Tel (01282) 428178

✠**HILL, The Rt Revd Christopher John.** b 45. K Coll Lon BD67 AKC67 MTh68. **d** 69 **p** 70 **c** 96. C Tividale *Lich* 69-73; C Codsall 73-74; Abp's Asst Chapl on Foreign Relns *Cant* 74-81; ARCIC from 74; Sec 74-90; Abp's Sec for Ecum Affairs *Cant* 82-89; Hon Can Cant Cathl 82-89; Chapl to The Queen 87-96; Can Res and Prec St Paul's Cathl 89-96; Select Preacher Ox Univ 90; Area Bp Stafford *Lich* 96-04; Bp Guildf from 04; Clerk of the Closet from 05. *Willow Grange, Woking Road, Guildford GU4 7QS* Tel (01483) 590500 Fax 590501 E-mail bishop.christopher@cofeguildford.org.uk

HILL, Christopher Murray. b 57. Lanchester Poly Cov BA78. Ox Min Course 05. **d** 07 **p** 08. NSM Warfield *Ox* from 07. *7 Shorland Oaks, Bracknell RG42 2JZ* Tel (01344) 867687 Mobile 07792-205124 E-mail chrismurrayhill@btopenworld.com

HILL, The Ven Colin. b 42. Leic Univ BSc64 Open Univ PhD88. Ripon Hall Ox 64. **d** 66 **p** 67. C Leic Martyrs 66-69; C Braunstone 69-71; Lect Ecum Inst Thornaby Teesside 71-72; V Worsbrough St Thos and St Jas *Sheff* 72-78; Telford Planning Officer *Lich* 78-96; RD Telford and Telford Severn Gorge *Heref* 80-96; Preb Heref Cathl 83-96; Can Res Carl Cathl 96-04; Dioc Sec 96-04; Adn Carl Cathl 96-04; Adn Carlisle and Furness 04-08; rtd 08. *1A Briery Bank, Arnside, Carnforth LA5 0HW* Tel (01524) 762629

HILL, Canon Colin Arnold Clifford. b 29. OBE96. Bris Univ 52 Univ of Wales (Ban) MPhil03. Ripon Hall Ox 55. **d** 57 **p** 58. C Rotherham *Sheff* 57-61; V Brightside St Thos 61-64; R Easthampstead *Ox* 64-73; Chapl RAF Coll Bracknell 68-73; V Croydon St Jo *Cant* 73-84; V Croydon St Jo *S'wark* 85-94; Chapl Abp Whitgift Foundn 73-94; Hon Can Cant Cathl 75-84; Hon Can S'wark Cathl 85-94; Chapl to The Queen 90-99; rtd 94. *Silver Birches, 70 Preston Crowmarsh, Wallingford OX10 6SL* Tel and fax (01491) 836102 E-mail colin.sb@btopenworld.com

HILL, David Rowland. b 34. Lon Univ BSc55. Qu Coll Birm. **d** 59 **p** 60. C Upper Tooting H Trin *S'wark* 59-61; C Cheam 61-63; C Richmond St Mary 63-68; V Sutton St Nicholas *Linc* 68-82; V Pinchbeck 82-99; rtd 99; Perm to Offic *Linc* 99-02 and from 05; *Pet* from 04. *24 London Road, Spalding PE11 2TA* Tel (01775) 768912 E-mail revdandj.hill@virgin.net

HILL, David Royston. b 68. Westmr Coll Ox BTh96. ERMC 04. **d** 06 **p** 07. C Dereham and Distr *Nor* 06-09; R Quidenham Gp from 09. *The Rectory, Church Hill, Banham, Norwich NR16 2HN* Tel (01953) 887562 Mobile 07906-227109 E-mail revdrhill@dsl.pipex.com

HILL, Derek Stanley. b 28. AKC53. **d** 53 **p** 54. C Rushmere *St E* 53-55; S Africa 55-57; C Boreham Wood All SS *St Alb* 57-59; V Crowfield *St E* 59-67; P-in-c Stonham Aspal 59-61; R 61-67; V Bury St Edmunds St Geo 67-73; P-in-c Ampton w Lt Livermere and Ingham 68-73; V Gazeley w Dalham 73-75; P-in-c Lidgate w Ousden 73-74; P-in-c Gt Bradley 74-78; V Gazeley w Dalham and Moulton 75-78; V Gt Barton 78-86; V Bury St Edmunds All SS 86-93; rtd 93; Perm to Offic *St E* from 93. *Whinwillow, 38 Maltings Garth, Thurston, Bury St Edmunds IP31 3PP* Tel (01359) 230770

HILL, Elizabeth Jayne Louise. *See* DAVENPORT, Elizabeth Jayne Louise

HILL, Ernest. *See* HILL, George Ernest

HILL, Eugene Mark. b 48. Univ of Wales (Lamp) BA71. Sarum Th Coll 71. **d** 73 **p** 74. C Sutton St Nic *S'wark* 73-77; Hon C 77-80; Asst Chapl Em Sch Wandsworth 77-87; Chapl 87-04; Hon C St Helier *S'wark* 83-84; Hon C Caterham 84-98; Dir Chr Studies Course 85-04; Perm to Offic 98-07; P-in-c Croydon St Jo from 07. *22 Bramley Hill, South Croydon CR2 6LT* Tel (020) 8688 1387

HILL, Geoffrey Lionel. b 45. WEMTC 96. **d** 03 **p** 04. OLM Thornbury and Oldbury-on-Severn w Shepperdine *Glouc* 03-06; Perm to Offic Cyprus and the Gulf from 07. *4 Kalamionas Villas, Vasilikon Anavargos, 8025 Paphos, Cyprus* Tel (00357) (26) 910123 E-mail gl.hill@cytanet.com

HILL, George Ernest. b 25. St Jo Coll Nottm. **d** 85 **p** 87. OLM Selston *S'well* 85-95; Perm to Offic from 95. *105 Main Road, Jacksdale, Nottingham NG16 5HR* Tel (01773) 603446

HILL, Giles. *See* HILL, The Rt Revd Michael John Giles

HILL, Canon Gillian Beryl. b 53. Open Univ BA86 Portsm Univ PhD06. S Dios Minl Tr Scheme 87. **d** 90 **p** 94. NSM Southsea St Jude *Portsm* 90-95; C Southsea St Pet 95-01; V Catherington and Clanfield from 01; Hon Can Portsm Cathl from 03. *The Vicarage, 330 Catherington Lane, Catherington, Waterlooville PO8 0TD* Tel (023) 9259 3228 *or* 9259 3139 E-mail gillhill@inglisrd.freeserve.co.uk

HILL, Ian Maxwell. b 60. Loughb Univ BSc81 MCIT85. EMMTC 92. **d** 95 **p** 96. NSM Thurnby Lodge *Leic* 95-00; NSM Thurmaston 00-08; NSM Syston from 08. *Shady Ash, 4 Sturrock Close, Thurnby, Leicester LE7 9QP* Tel 0116-243 1609

HILL, Ian Richard. b 69. Wycliffe Hall Ox 04. **d** 06 **p** 07. C Fareham St Jo *Portsm* from 06. *7A Upper St Michaels Grove, Fareham PO14 1DN* Tel (01329) 317395

HILL, James. *See* HILL, Kenneth James

HILL, James Alexander Hart. b 82. K Coll Lon BA05. St Steph Ho Ox 05. **d** 07 **p** 08. C Tottenham St Paul *Lon* from 07. *The Curate's Flat, St Paul's Vicarage, 60 Park Lane, London N17 0JR* Tel (020) 8885 1395 E-mail frjameshill@hotmail.co.uk

HILL, James Arthur. b 47. Ulster Univ BEd85. CITC 69. **d** 72 **p** 73. C Ballymena w Ballyclug *Conn* 72-74; C Arm St Mark w Aghavilly 74-78; C Derg w Termonamongan *D & R* 78-79; I Inver w Mountcharles, Killaghtee and Killybegs 79-87. *53 Dufferin Avenue, Bangor BT20 3AB* Tel (028) 9146 9090

HILL, James Stuart. b 75. Ridley Hall Cam 06. **d** 09. NSM Cov H Trin from 09. *85 Stoney Road, Coventry CV3 6HH* Tel (024) 7626 9053 E-mail james.anglican@gmail.com

HILL, Mrs Janice. Sheff Univ BEd79. St Jo Coll Nottm 05. **d** 07 **p** 08. C Formby H Trin *Liv* from 07. *19 Hampton Road, Liverpool L37 6EJ* Tel (01704) 870796 E-mail janicehill.htc@talktalk.net

HILL, Mrs Jennifer Clare. b 50. City Univ BSc71 FBCO72. EAMTC 94. **d** 97 **p** 98. NSM Bottesford and Muston *Leic* 97-98; C Glen Parva and S Wigston 98-01; C Walsall Wood *Lich* 01-08; V Shelfield and High Heath from 08; AD Walsall from 05. *Church House, 25 Green Lane, Shelfield, Walsall WS4 1RN* Tel (01922) 692550

HILL, Mrs Jennifer Susan. b 50. Ex Univ BTh06 ALCM71 LLCM72 Gipsy Hill Coll of Educn CertEd75. SWMTC 03. **d** 06 **p** 07. C St Mewan w Mevagissey and St Ewe *Truro* from 06. *14 Socotra Drive, Trewoon, St Austell PL25 5SQ* Tel (01726) 63387 E-mail jenny@primrosemusic.fslife.co.uk

HILL, John. b 56. S'wark Ord Course. **d** 89 **p** 90. NSM Upper Norwood St Jo *S'wark* 89-94; Chapl RN from 94; Dir of Ords RN and Voc Adv 04-09. *Royal Naval Chaplaincy Service, Mail Point 1-2, Leach Building, Whale Island, Portsmouth PO2 8BY* Tel (023) 9262 5055 Fax 9262 5134

HILL, John Michael. b 34. FCA. Oak Hill NSM Course 81. **d** 85 **p** 86. NSM Rayleigh *Chelmsf* 85-96; Perm to Offic *Lon* 85-92; Chapl Rochford Gen Hosp 93-95; Chapl Southend Health Care NHS Trust 95-99; NSM Rochford *Chelmsf* 96-04; Perm to Offic from 04. *25D Belchamps Way, Hockley SS5 4NT* Tel (01702) 203287 E-mail michaelhill25@yahoo.co.uk

HILL, Mrs Judith Anne. b 47. RGN68. STETS 99. **d** 02 **p** 03. OLM Wool and E Stoke *Sarum* from 02. *9 High Street Close, Wool, Wareham BH20 6BW* Tel (01929) 462888 E-mail reverendjudy@tiscali.co.uk

HILL, Kenneth James. b 43. Leic Univ BA64 Lon Univ BD68. Oak Hill Th Coll 65. **d** 69 **p** 70. C Southall Green St Jo *Lon* 69-72; C Blackheath Park St Mich *S'wark* 72-75; C Bath Abbey w St Jas *B & W* 75-83; P-in-c Bath St Mich w St Paul 75-82; R 82-83; R Huntspill 83-91; Omega Order 91-98; Perm to Offic *B & W* and *Bris* 91-98; C Somerton w Compton Dundon, the Charltons etc *B & W* 98-07; rtd 07. *14 White Horse Road, Winsey, Bradford-on-Avon BA15 2JZ* Tel (01225) 864119 E-mail kjhill@tiscali.co.uk

HILL, Laurence Bruce. b 43. AKC67. **d** 69 **p** 70. C Feltham *Lon* 69-72; C-in-c Hampstead St Steph 72-77; V Finchley H Trin from 77. *Holy Trinity Vicarage, 91 Church Lane, London N2 0TH* Tel and fax (020) 8883 8720 E-mail frlaurencehill@yahoo.co.uk

HILL, Mrs Leonora Anne. b 59. Bath Univ BSc81 Westmr Coll Ox PGCE93. Ox Min Course 05. **d** 08 **p** 09. C Charlton Kings St Mary *Glouc* from 08. *20 Glynrosa Road, Charlton Kings, Cheltenham GL53 8QS* Tel (01242) 248858 Mobile 07773-137653 E-mail plcdhill@btinternet.com

HILL, Malcolm Crawford. b 43. Oak Hill Th Coll 68. **d** 71 **p** 72. C Maidstone St Luke *Cant* 71-74; C Longfleet *Sarum* 74-79; V Bexleyheath St Pet *Roch* 79-90; V Lee St Mildred *S'wark* 90-04; rtd 04; Perm to Offic *Sarum* from 05. *64 St Mary's Road, Poole BH15 2LL* Tel (01202) 666076 E-mail adhill40@hotmail.com

HILL, Mrs Marjorie Ann. b 38. MCSP60. St Jo Coll Nottm 92. **d** 94 **p** 95. C Hull St Martin w Transfiguration *York* 94-99; P-in-c Willerby w Ganton and Folkton 99-03; rtd 03; Perm to Offic *York* 03-06; P-in-c Sigglesthorne w Nunkeeling and Bewholme 06-09; RD N Holderness 07-08. *New Rectory, Main Street, Sigglesthorne, Hull HU11 5QA* Tel (01964) 533033

HILL, Mark. *See* HILL, Eugene Mark

HILL, Martyn William. b 43. Man Univ BSc64 Univ of Wales (Ban) PhD70 MInstP68 CPhys85. Westcott Ho Cam 90. **d** 92 **p** 93. C Horninglow *Lich* 92-95; TV Hawarden *St As* 95-00; V Bistre 00-05; rtd 05; Perm to Offic *St As* from 05. *Llys Penmaen, Penmaenpool, Dolgellau LL40 1YD* Tel (01391) 423305 Mobile 07835-238522 E-mail machillpenmaen@aol.com

HILL, Matthew Anthony Robert. b 71. Leeds Univ BA93 Univ of Wales (Cardiff) BD96. St Mich Coll Llan 94. **d** 97 **p** 98. C Cardiff St Jo *Llan* 97-00; Min Can Llan Cathl 00-04; P-in-c Dowlais and Penydarren 04-05; R 05-07; Chapl Univ of Wales (Lamp) *St D* from 07. *Fairfield, North Road, Lampeter SA48 7HZ* Tel (01570) 422238 E-mail m.hill@lamp.ac.uk

HILL, Michael. *See* HILL, John Michael

HILL, Michael. b 32. TD77. AKC55. **d** 56 **p** 57. C Tynemouth Cullercoats St Paul *Newc* 56-59; C Drayton in Hales *Lich* 59-61; V Milton 61-64; V Preston Gubbals 64-73; V Leaton 64-76; CF (TA) 65-67; CF (TAVR) 67-87; V Oswestry St Oswald *Lich* 76-87; P-in-c Trefonen 80-83; V Sunningdale *Ox* 87-97; rtd 97; Perm to Offic *Lich* from 97. *20 Winterton Way, Bicton Heath, Shrewsbury SY3 5PA* Tel (01743) 341076

✠HILL, The Rt Revd Michael Arthur. b 49. Ridley Hall Cam 74. **d** 77 **p** 78 **c** 98. C Addiscombe St Mary *Cant* 77-81; C Slough *Ox* 81-83; P-in-c Chesham Bois 83-90; R 90-92; RD Amersham 89-92; Adn Berks 92-98; Area Bp Buckm 98-03; Bp Bris from 03.

Bishop's Office, 58A High Street, Winterbourne, Bristol BS36 1JQ Tel (01454) 777728 E-mail bishop@bristoldiocese.org

HILL, The Rt Revd Michael John Giles. b 43. S Dios Minl Tr Scheme 82. **d** 84 **p** 86. Community of Our Lady and St John from 67; Abbot from 90; Perm to Offic *Win* 84-92; Public Preacher from 92; Perm to Offic *Portsm* from 04. *Alton Abbey, Abbey Road, Beech, Alton GU34 4AP* Tel (01420) 562145 *or* 563575 Fax 561691

HILL, Miss Naomi Jean. b 75. Coll of Ripon & York St Jo BA96. Wycliffe Hall Ox BTh06. **d** 06 **p** 07. C Northampton St Giles *Pet* from 06. *18 The Avenue, Cliftonville, Northampton NN1 5BT* Tel (01604) 632489 Mobile 07855-060410 E-mail naomi_hill@hotmail.com

HILL, Nora. b 47. Univ of Wales BA95 PGCE97. St Mich Coll Llan 00. **d** 03 **p** 04. NSM Llandogo w Whitebrook Chpl and Tintern Parva *Mon* from 03. *3 Warwick Close, Chepstow NP16 5BU* Tel (01291) 626784

HILL, Patricia Frances. b 49. RGN90. SEITE 96. **d** 99 **p** 00. NSM Hythe *Cant* 99-01; Asst Chapl E Kent Hosps NHS Trust 99-00; Team Ldr Chapl from 01. *Springville, Sandling Road, Saltwood, Hythe CT21 4QJ* Tel (01303) 266649 *or* (01233) 633331 ext 88381 E-mail patricia.hill@ekht.nhs.uk

HILL, Peppie. *See* HILL, Stephanie Jane

HILL, Canon Peter. b 36. AKC60. St Boniface Warminster 60. **d** 61 **p** 62. C Gt Berkhamsted *St Alb* 61-67; R Bedford St Mary 67-69; P-in-c 69-70; V Goldington 69-79; V Biggleswade 79-90; RD Biggleswade 80-85; Hon Can St Alb 85-90; V Holbeach *Linc* 90-01; RD Elloe E 94-99; P-in-c The Suttons w Tydd 99-01; rtd 01; Perm to Offic *Nor* from 01 and *Ely* from 06. *Rayner Cottage, Low Street, Sloley, Norwich NR12 8HD* Tel (01692) 538744

HILL, The Ven Peter. b 50. Man Univ BSc71 Nottm Univ MTh90. Wycliffe Hall Ox 81. **d** 83 **p** 84. C Porchester *S'well* 83-86; V Huthwaite 86-95; P-in-c Calverton 95-04; RD S'well 97-01; Dioc Chief Exec 04-07; Adn Nottingham from 07; Hon Can S'well Minster 01-07. *4 Victoria Crescent, Sherwood, Nottingham NG5 4DA* Tel 0115-985 8641 E-mail archdeacon-nottm@southwell.anglican.org

HILL, Canon Richard Brian. b 47. Dur Univ BA68. Cranmer Hall Dur 68 Westcott Ho Cam 70. **d** 71 **p** 72. C Cockermouth All SS w Ch Ch *Carl* 71-74; C Barrow St Geo w St Luke 74-76; V Walney Is 76-83; Dir of Clergy Tr 83-90; P-in-c Westward, Rosley-w-Woodside and Welton 83-90; V Gosforth All SS *Newc* 90-05; rtd 05; Hon Can Newc Cathl from 05; Chapl St Mary Magd and H Jes Trust from 06; Asst Dioc Ecum Officer *Newc* from 08. *56 St Mary Magdalene Hospital, Claremont Road, Newcastle upon Tyne NE2 4NN* Tel 0191-261 2648 E-mail r.b.hill@lineone.net

HILL, Richard Hugh Oldham. b 52. CCC Ox BA74 BA77 MA78. Wycliffe Hall Ox 75. **d** 78 **p** 79. C Harold Wood *Chelmsf* 78-81; C Hampreston *Sarum* 81-86; TV N Ferriby *York* 86-97; V Swanland 97-08; R Church Stretton *Heref* from 08. *The Rectory, Ashbrook Meadow, Carding Mill Valley, Church Stretton SY6 6JF* Tel (01694) 722585

HILL, Robert Arthur. b 59. Trent Poly BSc83 Open Univ BA93. ACT 96. **d** 01 **p** 02. Sen Chapl Miss to Seafarers Australia 95-03; C Kettering SS Pet and Paul 03-08; Soc Resp Adv from 08. *19 Greenhill Road, Kettering NN15 7LW* Tel and fax (01536) 523603 E-mail robert@peterandpaul.org.uk

HILL, Robert Joseph. b 45. Oak Hill Th Coll BA81. **d** 81 **p** 82. C W Derby St Luke *Liv* 81-84; P-in-c Devonport St Mich *Ex* 84-97; Chapl Morden Coll Blackheath 97-99; TV Manningham *Bradf* 99-04; P-in-c Davyhulme Ch Ch *Man* from 04. *Christ Church Vicarage, 14 Welbeck Avenue, Urmston, Manchester M41 0GJ* Tel 0161-748 2018 E-mail rjh@credo-ergo-sum.fsnet.co.uk

HILL, Robin. b 35. Cranmer Hall Dur 59. **d** 62 **p** 63. C Aspley *S'well* 62-65; V Mansfield St Aug 65-71; R Hulland, Atlow and Bradley *Derby* 71-76; R Nollamara Australia 76-82; R Armadale 82-86; P-in-c Alkmonton, Cubley, Marston Montgomery etc *Derby* 86-93; P-in-c Ticknall, Smisby and Stanton-by-Bridge 93-99; P-in-c Barrow-on-Trent w Twyford and Swarkestone 94-99; rtd 99; Assoc P Fremantle Australia 99-05. *55B Yeovil Crescent, Bicton WA 6157, Australia* Tel (0061) (8) 9319 3447

HILL, Rodney Maurice. b 44. Leeds Univ BA67 FCIPD. Ripon Coll Cuddesdon 04. **d** 05 **p** 06. NSM N Hinksey and Wytham *Ox* from 05. *13 Hobson Road, Oxford OX2 7JX* Tel (01865) 426804 E-mail rodneymauricehill@hotmail.com

HILL, Canon Roger Anthony John. b 45. Liv Univ BA67 Lincacre Coll Ox BA69 MA. Ripon Hall Ox 67. **d** 70 **p** 71. C St Helier *S'wark* 70-74; C Dawley Parva *Lich* 74-75; C Cen Telford 76-77; TV 77-81; TR 81-88; TR Newark *S'well* 88-02; RD Newark 90-95; Hon Can S'well Minster 98-02; R Man St Ann 02-07; AD Hulme 05-07; Bp's Missr from 07; Hon Can Man Cathl from 02; Chapl to The Queen from 01. *The Rectory, 296 Wilbraham Road, Chorlton-cum-Hardy, Manchester M21 0UU* Tel 0161-881 1229 E-mail missioner@bishopscourt.manchester.anglican.org

HILL, Simon George. b 53. Reading Univ BSc75 MSc78. S'wark Ord Course 80. **d** 83 **p** 84. NSM Croydon St Aug *Cant* 83-84;

HILLS

Swaziland 84-86; Fiji 86-88; NSM Croydon St Aug *S'wark* 88-90; Tanzania 90-94; Uganda 94-96; Swaziland 96-98; Perm to Offic *Chich* and *S'wark* 99-02; P-in-c Cockfield w Bradfield St Clare, Felsham etc *St E* 02-04; R Bradfield St Clare, Bradfield St George etc from 04; RD Lavenham from 09. *The Rectory, Howe Lane, Cockfield, Bury St Edmunds IP30 0HA* Tel (01284) 828385 Mobile 07747-022903
E-mail revsimon@dial.pipex.com

HILL, Simon James. b 64. Sheff Univ BA85 Ex Univ PGCE88. Ripon Coll Cuddesdon BA84. **d** 95 **p** 96. C Manston *Ripon* 95-98; TV Dorchester *Ox* 98-03; Dir Berinsfield Progr Ripon Coll Cuddesdon 98-03; R Backwell w Chelvey and Brockley *B & W* from 03. *The Rectory, 72 Church Lane, Backwell, Bristol BS48 3JJ* Tel (01275) 462391

HILL, Stephanie Jane (**Peppie**). b 67. K Coll Lon LLB88. Wycliffe Hall Ox BTh05. **d** 05. C Loughborough Em and St Mary in Charnwood *Leic* 05-06. *1 Old Vicarage Mews, Sileby, Loughborough LE12 7FZ* E-mail pep@hill-home.co.uk

HILL, Stuart Graeme. b 64. Ripon Coll Cuddesdon BTh97. **d** 97 **p** 98. C Usworth *Dur* 97-99; C Monkwearmouth 99-01; TV 01-06; V Upper Derwent *York* from 06. *The Vicarage, 4 Cayley Lane, Brompton-by-Sawdon, Scarborough YO13 9DL* Tel (01723) 859694

HILL, Trevor Walton. b 30. Leeds Univ BA57. Coll of Resurr Mirfield. **d** 59 **p** 60. C Bollington St Jo *Ches* 59-62; C Woodchurch 62-64; V Addingham *Carl* 64-67; V Carl H Trin 67-71; R Wetheral w Warwick 71-80; P-in-c Doddington w Wychling *Cant* 80-82; P-in-c Newnham 80-82; rtd 95. *59 Medina Avenue, Newport PO30 1HG*

HILL, Walter Henry. **d** 06 **p** 07. Aux Min Cloyne Union *C, C & R* from 06. *Quetta, Glenatore, Conna, Co Cork, Republic of Ireland* Tel and fax (00353) (58) 56147 E-mail whill45@eircom.net

HILL, William. b 44. Man Univ BSc66 CEng73 MICE73. SEITE 95. **d** 98 **p** 99. NSM Farnham *Guildf* 98-01; P-in-c Smallburgh w Dilham w Honing and Crostwight *Nor* 01-05; rtd 05; Perm to Offic *Nor* from 05; RD St Benet from 09. *Grange Farm House, Yarmouth Road, Worstead, North Walsham NR28 9LX* Tel (01692) 404917 E-mail revd.william.hill@btinternet.com

HILL-BROWN, Rachel Judith. b 65. Westmr Coll Ox BEd88. St Jo Coll Nottm MTh07. **d** 07. C Knowle *Birm* from 07. *54 Glendon Way, Dorridge, Solihull B93 8SY* Tel (01564) 772472 E-mail rhillbrown@ukonline.co.uk

HILL-BROWN, Timothy Duncan. b 65. Westmr Coll Ox BA87. Wycliffe Hall Ox 91. **d** 93 **p** 94. C Sparkhill w Greet and Sparkbrook *Birm* 93-97; C Sutton Coldfield H Trin 97-99; P-in-c Short Heath 99-00; V 00-06; V Dorridge from 06. *54 Glendon Way, Dorridge, Solihull B93 8SY* Tel (01564) 772472 E-mail duncan@ukonline.co.uk

HILLARY, Leslie Tyrone James. b 59. Cranmer Hall Dur 84. **d** 87 **p** 88. C Monkseaton All SS *York* 87-89; C Stainton-in-Cleveland 89-91; CF from 91. *c/o MOD Chaplains (Army)* Tel (01980) 615804 Fax 615800

HILLAS, Ms Patricia Dorothy. b 66. E Lon Univ BA91 Middx Univ BA02. NTMTC 98. **d** 02 **p** 03. C Kensal Rise St Mark and St Martin *Lon* 02-05; V Northolt Park St Barn from 05. *The Vicarage, Raglan Way, Northolt UB5 4SX* Tel and fax (020) 8422 3775 E-mail mountainskies@btinternet.com

HILLEBRAND, Frank David. b 46. AKC68. St Boniface Warminster 68. **d** 69 **p** 70. C Wood Green St Mich *Lon* 69-72; C Evesham *Worc* 72-75; V Worc H Trin 75-80; V Kidderminster St Jo 80-90; TR Kidderminster St Jo and H Innocents 90-91; TV High Wycombe *Ox* 91-95; TR 95-00; Team Chapl Portsm Hosps NHS Trust 00-06; rtd 06. *40 Woodfield Park Road, Emsworth PO10 8BG* Tel (01243) 378846
E-mail frankandsue68@btinternet.com

HILLEL, Laurence Christopher Francis. b 54. Bris Univ BA76 Sheff Univ PGCE78 SOAS Lon MA84. Cuddesdon Coll 98. **d** 98 **p** 99. C Pinner *Lon* 98-00; NSM Eastcote St Lawr 01-04; Chapl Bp Ramsey Sch 01-04; NSM Brondesbury St Anne w Kilburn H Trin *Lon* from 04. *49 Keslake Road, London NW6 6DH* Tel (020) 8968 3898 E-mail revhillel@aol.com

HILLER, Ms Frances. b 53. Greenwich Univ BA93. NTMTC 07. **d** 09. Chapl to Suff Bp Eur from 09; Perm to Offic *S'wark* from 09. *14 Tufton Street, London SW1P 3QZ* Tel (020) 7898 1161 E-mail frances.hiller@c-of-e.org.uk

HILLIAM, Mrs Cheryl. b 49. EMMTC. **d** 94 **p** 95. C Linc St Faith and St Martin w St Pet 94-98; P-in-c S Ormsby Gp from 98. *The Rectory, South Ormsby, Louth LN11 8QT* Tel (01507) 480236

HILLIARD, David. b 57. TCD BTh91. CITC 88. **d** 91 **p** 92. C Holywood *D & D* 91-94; C Seagoe 94-96; I Tartaraghan w Diamond *Arm* from 96. *The Rectory, 5 Tarthlogue Road, Portadown BT62 1RB* Tel and fax (028) 3885 1289
E-mail tartaraghan@armagh.anglican.org

HILLIARD, Canon George Percival St John. b 45. TCD BA67. **d** 69 **p** 70. C Seapatrick *D & D* 69-73; C Carrickfergus *Conn* 73-76; I Fanlobbus Union *C, C & R* 76-85; Dean Cloyne 85-02; Prec Cork Cathl 85-02; I Cloyne Union 85-02; Chapl Univ Coll Cork from 02; Can Cork and Cloyne Cathls from 02. *The*

Chaplaincy, Iona, College Road, Cork, Republic of Ireland Tel (00353) (21) 490 2444 E-mail gchilliard@hotmail.com *or* gphilliard@ucc.ie

HILLIARD, Ms Lorelli Alison. b 60. St Mary's Coll Dur BSc82 Dur Univ MA07. Cranmer Hall Dur 04. **d** 06 **p** 07. C Drypool *York* from 06. *2 Harcourt Drive, Hull HU9 2AR* Tel (01482) 323840 E-mail lorelli@dunelm.org.uk

HILLIARD, Martin. b 45. TCD BA69 BTh08. CITC 05. **d** 08 **p** 09. C Larne and Inver *Conn* from 08; C Glynn w Raloo from 08. *23 Glenburn Avenue, Glynn, Larne BT40 3DJ* Tel (028) 2827 6129 Mobile (00353) 86-108 7432

HILLIARD, Robert Godfrey. b 52. Portsm Univ BA(Ed)97 MA02. St Mich Coll Llan 72. **d** 75 **p** 76. C Whitchurch *Llan* 75-80; Chapl RNR 77-80; Chapl RN 80-06; Hon Chapl Portsm Cathl 03-06; Chapl Bradfield Coll Berks from 06. *Bradfield College, Bradfield, Reading RG7 6AU* Tel 0118-964 4763
E-mail ghilliard@bradfieldcollege.org.uk

HILLIARD, Russell Boston. b 57. Univ of N Carolina BA82 Zürich Univ Lic89 Vanderbilt Univ (USA) PhD95. St Jo Coll Nottm 01. **d** 03 **p** 04. C Zürich *Eur* 03-06; Perm to Offic 06-09; Asst Chapl Basle from 09. *Rebweg 12, 8309 Nürensdorf, Switzerland* Tel and fax (0041) (44) 836 9245 Mobile 79-501 4904 E-mail r.hilliard@anglicanbasel.ch

HILLIER, Andrew. b 68. RGN92. SWMTC 99. **d** 02 **p** 03. C Castle Cary w Ansford *B & W* 02-05; Chapl RN from 05. *Royal Naval Chaplaincy Service, Mail Point 1-2, Leach Building, Whale Island, Portsmouth PO2 8BY* Tel (023) 9262 5055 Fax 9262 5134 E-mail andrewhillier@bigfoot.com

HILLIER, Derek John. b 30. Sarum Th Coll 61. **d** 63 **p** 64. C Salisbury St Mark *Sarum* 63-65; C Weymouth H Trin 65-66; R Caundle Bishop w Caundle Marsh and Holwell 66-75; R The Caundles and Holwell 75-81; R The Caundles w Folke and Holwell 81-02; P-in-c Pulham 70-78; rtd 02; Perm to Offic *Sarum* and *B & W* from 02. *Sarum House, Bishop's Caundle, Sherborne DT9 5ND* Tel and fax (01963) 23243

HILLIER, John Frederick. b 43. ARIBA67. **d** 01 **p** 02. OLM Merton St Mary *S'wark* 01-06; Perm to Offic *St Alb* 07; NSM Sandridge from 07. *21 Gonnerston, Mount Pleasant, St Albans AL3 4SY* Tel (01727) 812821 Mobile 07802-646374

HILLIER (*née* CHAPMAN), Mrs Linda Rosa. b 54. Middx Univ BA04. NTMTC 01. **d** 04 **p** 05. C W Drayton *Lon* 04-07; Faith and Work Development Officer Slough *Ox* from 07. *79 Torbay Road, Harrow HA2 9QG* Tel (020) 8864 5728
E-mail lindarosahillier@msn.com

HILLIER, Mrs Marilyn Jean. b 51. Ches Coll of HE CertEd73. NTMTC BA08. **d** 08 **p** 09. NSM Gt Parndon *Chelmsf* from 08. *23 Chapel Hill, Stansted CM24 8AD* Tel (01279) 813833 E mail lynhillier@btinternet.com

HILLIER, The Ven Michael Bruce. b 49. St Barn Coll Adelaide ThD73. **d** 74 **p** 75. C Plympton Australia 74-76; Assoc P Walkerville 76-80; C Tewkesbury w Walton Cardiff *Glouc* 81-86; P-in-c Whyalla Australia from 94; Adn Eyre Peninsula from 01. *37 Wood Terrace, PO Box 244, Whyalla SA 5600, Australia* Tel (0061) (8) 8644 0391 Fax 8644 0657
E-mail mjhillier@ozemail.com.au

HILLIER, Timothy John. b 55. Westmr Coll Ox CertEd77. Oak Hill Th Coll 94. **d** 96 **p** 97. C Chertsey *Guildf* 96-00; V 00-04; V Chertsey, Lyne and Longcross from 04; RD Runnymede from 07. *The Vicarage, London Street, Chertsey KT16 8AA* Tel and fax (01932) 563141 E-mail hillier@timp33.freeserve.co.uk

HILLMAN, Clive Ralph. b 71. York Univ BSc92. St Steph Ho Ox BA93. **d** 96 **p** 97. C Kingston upon Hull St Alb *York* 96-00; TV Ifield *Chich* 00-02; Chapl St Jo Coll Cam 02-06; V Betws-y-Coed and Capel Curig w Penmachno etc *Ban* from 06. *The Vicarage, Betws-y-Coed LL24 0AD* Tel (01690) 710313
E-mail crh41@cam.ac.uk

HILLMAN, John Anthony. b 32. St Chad's Coll Dur BA53. St Mich Coll Llan 54. **d** 55 **p** 56. C Llangollen *St As* 56-60; C Silvertown S Africa 60-64; P-in-c Matroosfontein 64-72; R Noorder Paarl 72-75; R Durbanville 75-80; R Somerset W 80-86; TV Wolstanton *Lich* 86-91; P-in-c E Goscote w Ratcliffe and Rearsby *Leic* 91-93; TV Syston 93-98; rtd 98. *7 Hafod Road West, Penrhyn Bay, Llandudno LL30 3PN* Tel (01492) 541374

HILLMAN, Jonathan. b 68. Man Univ BEng90. Ridley Hall Cam. **d** 00 **p** 01. C N Wingfield, Clay Cross and Pilsley *Derby* 00-03; TV Cove St Jo *Guildf* from 03. *Firecroft, 21 St John's Road, Farnborough GU14 9RL* Tel (01252) 543502
E-mail st.johns@parishofcove.org.uk

HILLMAN, Peter. b 69. Spurgeon's Coll Lon BD. NTMTC. **d** 07 **p** 08. C Rayleigh *Chelmsf* from 07. *20 Lambeth Road, Benfleet SS7 4BN* Tel (01268) 461753 E-mail pete@legacyweb.org

HILLMAN, Sarah Catherine. b 68. Selw Coll Cam BA90 MA94. St Jo Coll Nottm MA05. **d** 03 **p** 04. C Sandy *St Alb* 03-06; P-in-c Barkway, Reed and Buckland w Barley from 06. *The Rectory, 135 High Street, Barkway, Royston SG8 8ED* Tel (01763) 848077 E-mail sarah.c.hillman@tesco.net

HILLS, Alan Arthur. b 49. Sussex Univ BA73 Ches Coll of HE MEd94. **d** 09. OLM Ashton Ch Ch *Man* from 09. *41 Bollington*

391

Road, Stockport SK4 5ER Tel 0161-432 2964 Fax 477 7459 Mobile 07752-162333 E-mail alan.hills@stockport.gov.uk

HILLS, Mrs Christine Ann. b 54. NTMTC BA05. **d** 05 **p** 06. C Romford Gd Shep *Chelmsf* 05-08; C Blackmore and Stondon Massey from 08. *323 Pettits Lane North, Romford RM1 4PH* Tel (01708) 787464 E-mail chris-hills@ntlworld.com

HILLS, Elaine. b 45. RN67. Mon Dioc Tr Scheme 02. **d** 04 **p** 08. NSM Caerleon w Llanhennock *Mon* from 04. *6 Anthony Drive, Caerleon, Newport NP18 3DS* Tel (01633) 421248 Mobile 07967-349096 E-mail elainehills@tiscali.co.uk

HILLS, Kenneth Hugh. b 30. Univ of NZ BCom54. Ripon Hall Ox 55. **d** 57 **p** 58. C Handsworth St Mary *Birm* 57-59; V Wanganui Paroch Distr New Zealand 59-61; V Porirua 61-67; Ind Chapl *Birm* 67-74; Chapl Aston Univ 74-82; rtd 91; Community Member Cluny Hill Coll 93-00. *2 O'Neills Place, Church Road, Holywood BT18 9BU* Tel (028) 9042 1545 E-mail ken.hills@findhorn.org *or* k_h@onetel.com

HILLS, Lee Anthony. b 74. St Jo Coll Nottm 04. **d** 06. Deanery Missr *Birm* 06-08. *23 Jubilee Gardens, Birmingham B23 5HS* Tel 0121-382 6887 Mobile 07796-137423 E-mail lee@djvicar.co.uk

HILLS, Michael John. b 58. MBE09. BA82. Westcott Ho Cam 87. **d** 88 **p** 89. C Workington St Jo *Carl* 88-91; Perm to Offic *Newc* 91-93; TV Seaton Hirst 93-98; Chapl RN from 98. *Royal Naval Chaplaincy Service, Mail Point 1-2, Leach Building, Whale Island, Portsmouth PO2 8BY* Tel (023) 9262 5055 Fax 9262 5134 E-mail revmikehills@hotmail.com

HILLS, Michael Rae Buchanan. b 52. Univ of Wales (Lamp) BA81 Ex Univ BPhil83. St Steph Ho Ox 92. **d** 94 **p** 95. C Kingston upon Hull St Nic *York* 94-97; V Newington w Dairycoates 97-03; P-in-c 03-06; P-in-c Kingston upon Hull St Nic 05-06; N Humberside Ind Chapl 03-06; Sen Chapl from 07; Hon C Newington w Dairycoates 07-08; P-in-c Kingston upon Hull St Mary from 08. *St John's Vicarage, 203 St George's Road, Hull HU3 3SP* Tel (01482) 214551 E-mail vicar@kanga.karoo.co.uk

HILLS, Michael William John. b 54. Univ of Wales (Lamp) BA84. Westcott Ho Cam 85. **d** 87 **p** 88. C Reddish *Man* 87-91; V Bolton St Phil 91-00; V Northampton St Mich w St Edm *Pet* from 00; P-in-c Northampton H Sepulchre w St Andr and St Lawr 04-07; V from 07. *The Vicarage, 94 St Georges Avenue, Northampton NN2 6JF* Tel (01604) 230316 *or* 408111 Fax 635673 E-mail mickkhills@btconnect.com

HILLS, Richard Leslie. b 36. Qu Coll Cam BA60 MA63 UMIST PhD68 FMA83. St Deiniol's Hawarden 85. **d** 87 **p** 88. C Urmston *Man* 87-89; C Gt Yarmouth *Nor* 89-90; NSM Mottram in Longdendale *Ches* 90-01; Perm to Offic from 01. *Stamford Cottage, 47 Old Road, Mottram, Hyde SK14 6LW* Tel (01457) 763104

HILLS, Roger Malcolm. b 42. Oak Hill Th Coll 83. **d** 86 **p** 87. NSM Mill Hill Jo Keble Ch *Lon* 86-98; NSM Mill Hill St Mich 86-98; Perm to Offic 98-00; V Queensbury All SS 00-07; rtd 07; Perm to Offic *Lon* from 08. *22 Sefton Avenue, London NW7 3QD* Tel (020) 8959 1931 E-mail roger.hills2@btinternet.com

HILLS, Sarah Ann St Leger. b 65. Sheff Univ MB, ChB89 Leeds Univ MA07. NOC 04. **d** 07 **p** 08. C Millhouses H Trin *Sheff* from 07. *102 Ashdell Road, Sheffield S10 3DB* Tel 0114-267 0982 E-mail sarahandrichard91@talktalk.net

HILLS, Stephen Alan. b 59. Sheff Univ BA81. Ridley Hall Cam 97. **d** 99 **p** 00. C Southborough St Pet w Ch Ch and St Matt etc *Roch* 99-02; TV from 02. *The Rectory, Rectory Drive, Bidborough, Tunbridge Wells TN3 0UL* Tel (01892) 528081 E-mail stephen.hills@diocese-rochester.org

HILLYER, Charles Norman. b 21. Lon Univ BD48 Lambeth STh67. ALCD48. **d** 48 **p** 49. C Finchley Ch Ch *Lon* 48-51; C New Malden and Coombe *S'wark* 51-54; V Hanley Road St Sav w St Paul *Lon* 54-59; Chapl City of Lon Maternity Hosp 54-59; V Ponsbourne St Alb 59-70; Chapl Tolmers Park Hosp 59-70; Lib Tyndale Ho Cam 70-73; Org Ed UCCF 73-79; Sec Tyndale Fellowship Bibl Research Cam 73-75; P-in-c Hatherleigh *Ex* 79-81; V 81-86; rtd 86; Perm to Offic *Sarum* 89-03 and *Leic* from 03. *10 Smyth Close, Market Harborough LE16 7NS* Tel (01858) 432179 E-mail norman.hillyer@btinternet.com

HILTON, Clive. b 30. K Coll Lon 54. **d** 58 **p** 59. C Wythenshawe Wm Temple Ch CD *Man* 58-61; C Newton Heath All SS 61-62; C-in-c Oldham St Chad Limeside CD 62-65; V Oldham St Chad Limeside 65-70; P-in-c Gravesend H Family *Roch* 70-71; R Killamarsh *Derby* 71-88; R Broughton w Loddington and Cransley etc *Pet* 88-91; rtd 92; Perm to Offic *Pet* and *Linc* from 98; *Ely* 05-08. *73A Tattershall Drive, Market Deeping, Peterborough PE6 8BZ* Tel (01778) 346217

HILTON, Ian Anthony. b 57. St Jo Coll Nottm 83. **d** 86 **p** 87. C Nottingham St Sav *S'well* 86-90; C Aspley 90-97; P-in-c Colchester, New Town and The Hythe *Chelmsf* 97-02; R from 02; RD Colchester from 04. *The Rectory, 24 New Town Road, Colchester CO1 2EF* Tel (01206) 530320 E-mail ian.hilton@ntlworld.com

HILTON, John. b 49. Ex Univ BA70. Cuddesdon Coll 71. **d** 73 **p** 74. C W Derby St Jo *Liv* 73-79; V Orford St Andr 79-96; V

Leeds St Wilfrid *Ripon* from 96. *St Wilfrid's Vicarage, Chatsworth Road, Leeds LS8 3RS* Tel 0113-249 7724 E-mail john@the-oak-403.demon.co.uk

HILTON-TURVEY, Geoffrey Michael. b 34. Oak Hill Th Coll 80. **d** 81 **p** 82. C Bispham *Blackb* 81-85; V Inskip 85-99; rtd 99; Perm to Offic *Heref* from 00. *20 Cralves Mead, Tenbury Wells WR15 8EX* Tel (01584) 811153 E-mail gmh-t@gmh-t.freeserve.co.uk

HILTON-TURVEY, Keith Geoffrey Michael. b 59. Oak Hill Th Coll BA03. **d** 03 **p** 04. C S Mimms Ch Ch *Lon* from 03. *8 Wentworth Road, Barnet EN5 4NT* Tel (020) 8441 0645 E-mail kht@fideste.freeserve.co.uk

HINA, Christine Magdeleine. b 66. SAOMC. **d** 01 **p** 02. C Stevenage St Hugh and St Jo *St Alb* 01-06; C Stevenage St Nic and Graveley from 06. *1 Vallansgate, Stevenage SG2 8PY* Tel (01438) 236536 E-mail christine@anih.freeserve.co.uk

HINCHCLIFFE, Garry Anthony Frank. b 68. New Coll Edin BD94. Edin Th Coll 90. **d** 94 **p** 95. C Dumfries *Glas* 94-97; P-in-c Motherwell and Wishaw 97-00; V Hampsthwaite and Killinghall *Ripon* 00-04; V Hampsthwaite and Killinghall and Birstwith from 04. *The Vicarage, Church Lane, Hampsthwaite, Harrogate HG3 2HB* Tel (01423) 770337 E-mail garry.hinchcliffe@btinternet.com

HINCHEY, Peter John. b 30. LTCL53. Chich Th Coll 55. **d** 58 **p** 59. C Malden St Jo *S'wark* 58-61; V Rosherville *Roch* 61-67; V Gillingham St Aug 67-72; V Bromley St Andr 72-74; Hon Chapl to Bp 74-78; Hon C Lamorbey H Redeemer 76-78; R Foots Cray 78-81; Perm to Offic *Chich* 92-94; rtd 94; Hon C Rotherhithe St Mary w All SS *S'wark* 94-98; Perm to Offic *Chelmsf* 95-03; *St E* from 97; *Chich* 03-09. *Ash Lodge, Southolt Road, Bedfield, Woodbridge IP13 7HH* Tel (01728) 627134 E-mail hincheypj@hotmail.com

HINCKLEY, Paul Frederick. b 61. Cranfield Inst of Tech MSc85. Ridley Hall Cam 92. **d** 94 **p** 95. C Ovenden *Wakef* 94-99; TV Billericay and Lt Burstead *Chelmsf* 99-06; R Yateley *Win* from 06. *The Vicarage, 99 Reading Road, Yateley GU46 7LR* Tel (01252) 873133

✠**HIND, The Rt Revd John William.** b 45. Leeds Univ BA66. Cuddesdon Coll 70. **d** 72 **p** 73 **c** 91. C Catford (Southend) and Downham *S'wark* 72-76; V Forest Hill Ch Ch 76-82; P-in-c Forest Hill St Paul 81-82; Prin Chich Th Coll 82-91; Wiccamical Preb Chich Cathl 82-91; Area Bp Horsham 91-93; Bp Eur 93-01; Asst Bp Chich 93-01; Bp Chich from 01. *The Palace, Chichester PO19 1PY* Tel (01243) 782161 Fax 531332 E-mail bishop.chichester@diochi.org.uk

HIND, Mrs Ruth Elizabeth. b 71. Cen Lancs Univ BA93. St Jo Coll Nottm MTh01. **d** 02 **p** 03. C Caldbeck, Castle Sowerby and Sebergham *Carl* 02-06; V Hutton Cranswick w Skerne, Watton and Beswick *York* from 06. *The Vicarage, 5 Howl Lane, Hutton, Driffield YO25 9QA* Tel (01377) 270402 E-mail ruthhind@tiscali.co.uk

HINDER, Doreen Patterson. b 38. Open Univ BA95. Selly Oak Coll 60 Bris Bapt Coll 68. **d** 97 **p** 98. NSM Stanwix *Carl* 97-99; P-in-c Glenurquhart *Mor* 99-03; rtd 03. *Hardies Byre, Kirkhill, Inverness IV5 7PP* Tel (01463) 831729

HINDER, Richard Alan. b 46. Birm Univ BSc67 CCC Cam PhD71 FRAS70 CEng82 FIEE80. S'wark Ord Course 04. **d** 07 **p** 08. NSM Croydon St Matt *S'wark* from 07. *18 Mapledale Avenue, Croydon CR0 5TB* Tel (020) 8123 5256 E-mail richard@richardhinder.com

HINDLE (formerly PARKER), Anne Margaret. b 57. Leeds Univ BSc78. EAMTC 96. **d** 99 **p** 00. C Greenstead w Colchester St Anne *Chelmsf* 99-04; TV 04-08; P-in-c Kingsley and Foxt-w-Whiston *Lich* from 08. *The Rectory, Holt Lane, Kingsley, Stoke-on-Trent ST10 2BA* Tel (01538) 754754 Mobile 07703-571879 E-mail anne.hindle@hotmail.co.uk

HINDLE, Miss Penelope Jane Bowyn. b 45. Trin Coll Bris 76. dss 84 **d** 87 **p** 94. Stoneycroft All SS *Liv* 84-89; Par Dn 87-89; Asst Chapl Broadgreen Hosp Liv 87-89; Asst Chapl R Free Hosp Lon 89-93; Chapl N Herts NHS Trust 93-02; rtd 02; Perm to Offic *B & W* from 07. *Cleeve House, Level Lane, Charlton Horethorne, Sherborne DT9 4NN* Tel (01963) 220055

HINDLEY, Canon Andrew David. b 59. Univ of Wales (Lamp) BA. Sarum & Wells Th Coll. **d** 82 **p** 83. C Huddersfield St Pet *Wakef* 82-84; C Huddersfield St Pet and All SS 84-86; P-in-c Holmfield 86-91; R Ribchester w Stidd *Blackb* 91-96; Bp's Adv for Leisure and Tourism 91-96; Chapl Ribchester Hosp from 91; Can Res Blackb Cathl from 96. *22 Billinge Avenue, Blackburn BB2 6SD* Tel (01254) 261152 *or* 51491 Fax 689666 E-mail andrew.hindle@blackburn.anglican.org

HINDLEY, Canon Anthony Talbot. b 41. Bernard Gilpin Soc Dur 61 Oak Hill Th Coll 62. **d** 66 **p** 67. C Stoke next Guildf St Jo 66-69; C Eldoret Kenya 70-72; V Menengai 72-78; C Redhill H Trin *S'wark* 78-79; P-in-c Eastbourne All So *Chich* 79-83; V 83-86; V S Malling 86-98; R Wainford *St E* 98-06; RD Beccles and S Elmham 00-03; Hon Can St E Cathl 05-06; Perm to Offic *St E* and *Nor* from 07. *Amani @ Mile End, Church Road, Earsham, Bungay NR35 2TL* Tel (01986) 894749 Mobile 07766-546601 E-mail anthony.hindley@ireverend.com

HINDLEY, John Philip Talbot. b 76. Ex Univ BA96 Oak Hill Th Coll BA01. **d** 01 **p** 02. C Astley Bridge *Man* 01-04; Assoc Miss Partner Crosslinks from 04. *5 Haydn Avenue, Manchester M14 4DJ* Tel 0161-226 6860 Mobile 07790-007390 E-mail john@theplant.net

HINDLEY, Michael Alexander. b 72. Man Metrop Univ BA94. Wycliffe Hall Ox BTh05. **d** 05 **p** 06. C Clubmoor *Liv* 05-09; TV Fazakerley Em from 09. *Emmanuel Rectory, Higher Lane, Liverpool L9 9DJ* Tel 0151-525 5229 Mobile 07980-912768 E-mail revd.mike@btinternet.com

HINDLEY, Roger Dennis. b 48. Birm Univ BA70 Ox Univ BA77 MA83. Ripon Coll Cuddesdon 75 Qu Coll Birm 77. **d** 78 **p** 79. C Rubery *Birm* 78-81; C Henbury *Bris* 81-83; V Erdington St Chad *Birm* 83-89; V Hill 89-05; AD Sutton Coldfield 96-02; Hon Can Birm Cathl 00-05; TR Willington *Newc* from 05. *St Mary's Vicarage, 67 Churchill Street, Wallsend NE28 7TE* Tel 0191-262 8208 E-mail rdhindley@yahoo.co.uk

HINDLEY, Thomas Richard. b 31. ARIBA54 Sheff Univ BA53 Lon Univ BD66. Clifton Th Coll 61. **d** 63 **p** 64. C Kenilworth St Jo *Cov* 63-67; C Cheadle *Ches* 67-70; R Harpurhey Ch Ch *Man* 70-95; R Harpurhey St Steph 72-95; rtd 96; Perm to Offic *Man* from 96. *15 Twyford Close, Didsbury, Manchester M20 2YR* Tel 0161-438 0387

HINDS, Francis. b 73. Bath Univ BSc96 Edge Hill Coll of HE PGCE98. Wycliffe Hall Ox 96. **d** 08. C Haydock St Mark *Liv* from 08; Dir Pioneer Min from 08. *1 Brookside Close, Haydock, St Helens WA11 0UQ* Tel 07736-176826 (mobile)

HINDS, Kenneth Arthur Lancelot. b 30. K Coll Lon BA00 Birkbeck Coll Lon MA04. Bps' Coll Cheshunt. **d** 64 **p** 65. C Sawbridgeworth *St Alb* 64-67; C Gt Berkhamsted 67-71; V Boreham Wood St Mich 71-75; Trinidad and Tobago 75-79; P-in-c Gt Ilford St Luke *Chelmsf* 79-81; V 81-95; rtd 95; Perm to Offic *Chelmsf* from 95. *214 Aldborough Road South, Ilford IG3 8HF* Tel (020) 8598 2963 E-mail frkalhinds@ntlworld.com

HINE, John Victor. b 36. Open Univ BA82. Carl Dioc Tr Course 85. **d** 88 **p** 89. NSM Dean *Carl* 88-92; NSM Clifton 88-92; C Millom 92-94; P-in-c Gt Broughton and Broughton Moor 94-02; P-in-c Brigham 99-02; rtd 02; Perm to Offic *Carl* from 02. *4 The Paddocks, Thursby, Carlisle CA5 6PB* Tel (01228) 712704 E-mail hine.hine@virgin.net

HINE, Keith Ernest. b 50. Bradf Univ BA Leeds Univ CertEd. NOC 89. **d** 89 **p** 90. C Wilmslow *Ches* 89-94; V Bowdon 94-08; R Tarporley from 08. *The Rectory, High Street, Tarporley CW6 0AG* Tel (01829) 732491 E-mail hine@line24.freeserve.co.uk

HINE, Patrick Lewis. b 45. **d** 06 **p** 07. OLM Horfield H Trin *Bris* from 06. *16 Red House Lane, Bristol BS9 3RZ* Tel 0117-962 3861 E-mail patrick.hine@horfieldparishchurch.org.uk

HINES, Richard Arthur. b 49. Imp Coll Lon MSc73 PhD76 K Coll Lon MTh89. Oak Hill Th Coll 82. **d** 84 **p** 85. C Mile Cross *Nor* 84-87; Lect Oak Hill Th Coll 87-97; Vice-Prin NTMTC 94-97; R Happisburgh, Walcott, Hempstead w Eccles etc *Nor* 97-07; C Bacton w Edingthorpe w Witton and Ridlington 04-07; R Bacton, Happisburgh, Hempstead w Eccles etc 07; R Falkland Is from 07. *PO Box 160, The Deanery, 17 Ross Road, Stanley, Falkland Islands FIQQ 1ZZ* Tel (00500) 21100 E-mail christchurch@horizon.co.fk

HINEY, Thomas Bernard Felix. b 35. MC61. Open Univ BA07. Ridley Hall Cam 67. **d** 69 **p** 70. C Edgbaston St Aug *Birm* 69-71; CF 71-91; Chapl R Hosp Chelsea 91-01; Chapl Mercers' Coll Holborn 99-01; rtd 01. *7B Dagmar Road, Exmouth EX8 2AN* Tel (01395) 270688 E-mail thiney@onetel.net

HINGE, Canon David Gerald Francis. b 30. FRSA57. Wells Th Coll 64. **d** 66 **p** 67. C Brookfield St Anne, Highgate Rise *Lon* 66-69; C N Greenford All Hallows 69-71; V Winton *Man* 71-78; R Etherley *Dur* 78-96; Hon Can Dur Cathl 90-00; rtd 96. *9 Hillside, Ingleton, Darlington DL2 3JH* Tel (01325) 732002

HINGE, Derek Colin. b 36. Imp Coll Lon BSc58 CChem60 MRSC60. St Alb Minl Tr Scheme 84. **d** 88 **p** 89. NSM Bishop's Stortford St Mich *St Alb* from 88. *12 Avenue Road, Bishop's Stortford CM23 5NU* Tel (01279) 652173 E-mail derek.hinge@btinternet.com

HINGLEY, Christopher James Howard. b 48. Trin Coll Ox BA69 MA71. Wycliffe Hall Ox 81. **d** 80 **p** 81. C St Jo Cathl Bulawayo Zimbabwe 80-81; C Hillside Ascension 82-84; Tutor Wycliffe Hall Ox 84-88; Chapl Whitestone Sch Bulawayo 89-04; Headmaster Petra High Sch Bulawayo 04-06; R Petra Schs Bulawayo from 06. *Whitestone School, Private Bag 4, Bulawayo, Zimbabwe* E-mail hingley@yoafrica.com

HINGLEY (née EDWARDS), Mrs Helen. b 55. Natal Univ BSW75. St Steph Ho Ox 94. **d** 96 **p** 97. C Gravelly Hill *Birm* 96-01; TV Cen Wolverhampton *Lich* 01-05; P-in-c Hamstead St Bernard *Birm* from 05; AD Handsworth from 08. *The Vicarage, 147 Churchill Street, Great Barr, Birmingham B43 5BB* Tel 0121-358 1286 E-mail h.hingley@btinternet.com

HINGLEY, Robert Charles. b 46. Ball Coll Ox BA69 MA74 Birm Univ CertEd73. Qu Coll Birm. **d** 73 **p** 74. C Charlton St Luke w H Trin *S'wark* 73-76; Asst Warden Iona Abbey 76-77; TV

Langley Marish *Ox* 77-83; V Balsall Heath St Paul *Birm* 83-90; Perm to Offic 90-91; V Birm St Luke 91-96; Lic to Offic 96-05; Hon C Hamstead St Bernard from 05; Perm to Offic *Lich* from 01. *The Vicarage, 147 Hamstead Road, Great Barr, Birmingham B43 5BB* Tel 0121-357 4534

HINGLEY, Roderick Stanley Plant. b 51. St Chad's Coll Dur BA72. St Steph Ho Ox 74. **d** 75 **p** 76. C Lower Gornal *Lich* 75-79; C Tividale 79-82; C Broseley w Benthall *Heref* 82-84; C Wanstead St Mary *Chelmsf* 84-92; V Romford St Alb from 92. *St Alban's Vicarage, 3 Francombe Gardens, Romford RM1 2TH* Tel (01708) 473580

HINGSTON, Barry David. b 63. LSE BSc(Econ)84. NTMTC BA08. **d** 08 **p** 09. C Ealing St Paul *Lon* from 08. *20 Brookbank Avenue, London W7 3DW* Tel (020) 8578 2910 Mobile 07710-359483 E-mail barryhingston@btinternet.com

HINKLEY, Maureen. b 41. **d** 04. NSM Hollington St Jo *Chich* from 04. *8 Wadhurst Close, St Leonards-on-Sea TN37 7AZ* Tel (01424) 754872 E-mail hinkley@wadhurstclose.fsnet.co.uk

HINKS, David John. b 63. STETS 04. **d** 07 **p** 08. C Cowes H Trin and St Mary *Portsm* from 07. *St Faith's House, 2 St Faith's Road, Cowes PO31 7HH* Tel (01983) 280197 Mobile 07766-355196 E-mail julie@hinks42.freeserve.co.uk

HINKS (née CHAMBERS), Mrs Marion Patricia. b 48. Univ of Wales BDS72. SWMTC 97. **d** 97 **p** 98. NSM Plymstock and Hooe *Ex* from 97. *52 Southland Park Road, Wembury, Plymouth PL9 0HQ* Tel (01752) 862439 Mobile 07889-291228 E-mail marion@southlandpark.freeserve.co.uk

HINKSMAN, Adrian James Terence. b 43. Open Univ BA76. SAOMC 96. **d** 99 **p** 00. NSM Hemel Hempstead *St Alb* 99-02; Dioc CME Officer and NSM St Alb St Mary Marshalswick 02-07; rtd 07; NSM King's Walden and Offley w Lilley *St Alb* from 07. *33 Sycamore Close, St Ippolyts, Hitchin SG4 7SN* Tel (01462) 458260 E-mail adrian_hinksman@hotmail.com

HINKSMAN, Barrie Lawrence James. b 41. K Coll Lon BD64 AKC64 Birm Univ PhD02. St Boniface Warminster 64. **d** 65 **p** 66. C Crosby *Linc* 65-67; Locum Development Officer Scunthorpe Coun of Chs 67-69; C Chelmsley Wood *Birm* 69-72; TV 72-75; P-in-c Offchurch *Cov* 75-79; Bp's Adv for Lay Tr 75-79; Perm to Offic 89-90; Hon Chapl Cov Cathl 90-01; Perm to Offic *Birm* from 01; Hon Sen Fell Warw Univ from 02. *c/o Crockford, Church House, Great Smith Street, London SW1P 3AZ*

HINSLEY, Robert Charles. b 77. Univ of Wales (Abth) BTh98. Cranmer Hall Dur 03. **d** 05 **p** 06. C Carlton-in-Lindrick and Langold w Oldcotes *S'well* 05-08; P-in-c Felixstowe St Jo *St E* from 08. *The New Vicarage, 54 Princes Road, Felixstowe IP11 7PL* Tel (01394) 286552 E-mail roberthinsley@tiscali.co.uk

HINTON, Mrs Frances Mary. b 43. EN(G)85. EMMTC 89. **d** 92 **p** 94. Dn Hornsey Rise Whitehall Park Team *Lon* 92-94; C 94-97; C Upper Holloway 97; TV Barking St Marg w St Patr *Chelmsf* 97-04; rtd 04. *5 Little Thorpe Lane, Thorpe-on-the-Hill, Lincoln LN6 9BL* Tel (01522) 688886

HINTON, Geoffrey. b 34. Bede Coll Dur BA56 Em Coll Cam MA67 Sussex Univ PGCE72. Ridley Hall Cam 58. **d** 60 **p** 61. C Cheltenham St Mary *Glouc* 60-61; C Beverley Minster *York* 61-65; C Newark St Mary *S'well* 70-71; rtd 99. *1 Northmoor Place, Oxford OX2 6XB* Tel (01865) 510267

HINTON, James William. b 63. Cov Poly BSc84 Leeds Univ PGCE86. St Jo Coll Nottm 00. **d** 02 **p** 03. C Thornbury *Bradf* 02-05; P-in-c Bowling St Steph from 05; C Lt Horton from 05. *St Stephen's Vicarage, 48 Newton Street, Bradford BD5 7BH* Tel (01274) 720784 or 391537 E-mail jimmy.hinton@bradford.anglican.org

HINTON, Michael Ernest. b 33. K Coll Lon 53 St Boniface Warminster 56. **d** 57 **p** 58. C Babbacombe *Ex* 57-60; S Africa 60-66; P-in-c Limehouse St Pet *Lon* 66-68; R Felmingham *Nor* 68-72; R Suffield 68-72; P-in-c Colby w Banningham and Tuttington 68-72; Bahamas 72-76; P-in-c Mylor w Flushing *Truro* 76-77; V 77-80; R The Deverills *Sarum* 82-87; Bermuda 87-89; Virgin Is 89-91; Chapl Sequoian Retreat and Conf Progr from 91; rtd 89; Perm to Offic *St E* 00-01; *Ex* from 02. *Le Petit Pain, St Ann's Chapel, Kingsbridge TQ7 4IIQ* Tel (01548) 810124 E-mail lacton.int@virgin.net

HINTON, Michael George. b 27. Mert Coll Ox BA48 MA51 Reading Univ PhD59. S Dios Minl Tr Scheme 81. **d** 83 **p** 84. NSM Weston-super-Mare St Paul *B & W* 83-85; NSM Sibertswold w Coldred *Cant* 85-87; NSM Eythorne and Elvington w Waldershare etc 87-95; Perm to Offic from 95. *212 The Gateway, Dover CT16 1LL* Tel and fax (01304) 204198 E-mail michael@hintonm.demon.co.uk

HINTON, Nigel Keith. b 49. Univ Coll Lon BSc70 Worc Coll of Educn PGCE73 Lon Univ MA87. Oak Hill NSM Course 89. **d** 92 **p** 93. NSM Cudham and Downe *Roch* 92-07; Perm to Offic *Lon* from 03. *Address temp unknown*

HINTON, Paul Robin George. b 64. St Jo Coll Dur BA86. Qu Coll Birm BA05. **d** 05 **p** 06. C Rowley Regis *Birm* 05-09; V Warley Woods from 09. *St Hilda's Vicarage, Abbey Road,*

Smethwick, Warley B67 5NQ   Tel 0121-429 1384 Fax 420 2386
Mobile 07777-603188 E-mail revpaulhinton@btinternet.com
HINTON, Robert Matthew. b 69. Lanc Univ BA91. Cranmer Hall
Dur BA97. d 97 p 98. C Lache cum Saltney Ches 97-99; C
Cheadle Hulme St Andr 99-02; V Hale Barns w Ringway from
02. Ringway Vicarage, Wicker Lane, Hale Barns, Altrincham
WA15 0HQ Tel 0161-980 3955 or 980 3234
E-mail revrobhinton@hotmail.com
HIPKINS, Leslie Michael. b 35. Univ Coll Dur BA57 ACIS60.
Oak Hill Th Coll 78 Westcott Ho Cam 89. d 81 p 82. NSM
Halstead St Andr w H Trin and Greenstead Green Chelmsf
81-87; C Tolleshunt Knights w Tiptree and Gt Braxted 87-89;
P-in-c Cratfield w Heveningham and Ubbeston etc St E 89-00;
rtd 00; Perm to Offic St E from 01. Laundry Farm, Thorington,
Halesworth IP19 9JF Tel (01502) 478675
HIPPISLEY-COX, Stephen David. b 63. Sheff Univ BSc85
PhD92 Peterho Cam BA98. Westcott Ho Cam 96. d 99 p 00. C
Ollerton w Boughton S'well 99-02; NSM Wilford Hill 02-07;
P-in-c Willoughby-on-the-Wolds w Wysall and Widmerpool
from 07. The Rectory, Keyworth Road, Wysall, Nottingham
NG12 5QQ Tel 0115-945 2714
E-mail s.d.hippisley-cox@ntlworld.com
HIRD, Matthew. b 83. Jes Coll Ox BA04. St Jo Coll Nottm MA09.
d 09. C Penn Lich from 09. Penhelig, Wynne Crescent,
Wolverhampton WV4 4SW
E-mail matthew_hird@hotmail.com
HIRONS, Malcolm Percy. b 36. Oriel Coll Ox BA59 MA62.
Wycliffe Hall Ox 59. d 61 p 62. C Edgbaston St Aug Birm 61-64;
Chapl Warw Sch 64-65; C Beverley Minster York 65-69; V
Barnby upon Don Sheff 69-80; P-in-c Kirk Bramwith 75-80;
P-in-c Fenwick 75-80; V Norton Woodseats St Paul 80-98; rtd
98; Perm to Offic Nor from 98. Broome Lodge, 8 Lincoln Square,
Hunstanton PE36 6DL Tel (01485) 532385
HIRST, Alan. b 44. CQSW74. Linc Th Coll 79. d 81 p 82. C
Newton Heath All SS Man 81-84; Chapl to the Deaf 84-88; V
Oldham St Chad Limeside 88-91; Dep Chapl HM Pris Liv
91-92; Chapl HM Pris Ranby 92-96 and 00-07; Chapl HM Pris
Wakef 96-99; NSM Retford S'well from 07. 8 Maple Drive,
Elkesley, Retford DN22 8AX
HIRST, Anthony Melville (Anthony Mary). b 50. Cuddesdon Coll
74. d 77 p 78. C S Gillingham Roch 77-80; C Coity w Nolton
Llan 80-83; OSB from 81; R Hallaton w Horninghold, Allexton,
Tugby etc Leic 83-90; R Arthog w Fairbourne w Llangelynnin w
Rhoslefain Ban 90-97; R Montgomery and Forden and
Llandyssil St As 97-04; V Bedford Leigh Man 04-09; P-in-c S
Ashford St Fran Cant from 09; P-in-c S Ashford Ch Ch from 09.
Christ Church Vicarage, Beaver Road, Ashford TN23 7SR Tel
(01233) 620600 E-mail ahirst@avnet.co.uk
HIRST, Mrs Carol Anne. b 46. Yorks Min Course 06. d 09. NSM
Ripponden Wakef from 09; NSM Barkisland w W Scammonden
from 09. 86 Crow Wood Park, Halifax HX2 7NR Tel (01422)
363095 Mobile 07797-210297
E-mail carolhirst1@btinternet.com
HIRST, David William. b 37. Man Univ BA78. Brasted Th Coll
59 St Aid Birkenhead 61. d 63 p 64. C Clayton Man 63-64; C
Bury St Jo 64-66; C Wythenshawe Wm Temple Ch 67-70; V
Oldham St Chad Limeside 70-79; V Friezland 79-91; R Ashton
St Mich 91-95; Chapl HM Pris Buckley Hall 95-00; Chapl
HM Pris Wolds 00-02; rtd 02; Perm to Offic Blackb from 09.
8 Priory Mews, Lytham St Annes FY8 4FT Tel 07833-353837
(mobile)
HIRST, Canon Godfrey Ian. b 41. Univ of Wales (Lamp) BA63
MBIM. Chich Th Coll 63. d 65 p 66. C Brierfield Blackb 65-68;
Ind Chapl Liv 68-71; TV Kirkby 71-75; Ind Chapl Blackb 75-94;
P-in-c Treales 75-87; Hon Can Blackb Cathl 83-87 and 94-06;
Can Res 87-94; V Lytham St Cuth 94-06; AD Kirkham 98-06;
rtd 06; Perm to Offic Blackb from 06. 11 Arundel Road, Lytham
St Annes FY8 1AF Tel (01253) 732474 Mobile 07885-118331
E-mail ghirst1@compuserve.com
HIRST, John Adrian. b 49. St Jo Coll Nottm BTh78. d 78 p 79. C
Cheltenham St Mark Glouc 78-84; TV 84-85; TV Swan Ox
85-89; R Denham from 89. The Rectory, Ashmead Lane,
Denham, Uxbridge UB9 5BB Tel (01895) 832771
HIRST, Mrs Judith. b 54. St Mary's Coll Dur BA76 LMH Ox
PGCE77 Hull Univ MA86 St Jo Coll Dur BA94. Cranmer Hall
Dur 91. d 94 p 95. Bp's Adv in Past Care and Counselling Dur
94-00; C Dur St Oswald 94-00; Dir Min Formation Cranmer
Hall Dur 00-07; Local Min Development Officer Dur and Newc
from 07. Easdale, St Hild's Lane, Durham DH1 1QL Tel
0191-334 8540 E-mail judy.hirst@durham.ac.uk
HIRST, Malcolm. b 62. Ilkley Coll BA84. Moorlands Bible Coll
86 Trin Coll Bris BA00. d 00 p 01. C Bromley Common St Aug
Roch 00-03; C Farnborough 03-08. Address temp unknown
E-mail malcolm@port-vale.freeserve.co.uk
HIRST, Mrs Rachel Ann. b 58. Portsm Poly BA79 Hull Univ
PGCE81 ACII85. NEOC 99. d 02 p 03. NSM Clifton York
02-04; C 04-06; Par Development and Tr Officer (York Adnry)
from 06. The Rectory, Sandy Lane, Stockton on the Forest, York
YO32 9UR Tel (01904) 400811

HISCOCK, Donald Henry. b 26. St Mich Th Coll Crafers 50 ACT
ThL56. d 53 p 54. Australia 53 and from 65; SSM 54-82; C
Averham w Kelham S'well 56-58; Lic to Offic 58-59; S Africa
59-60; Basutoland 60-61; rtd 92. 12 Charsley Street, Willagee
WA 6156, Australia Tel (0061) (8) 9314 5192
HISCOCK, Gary Edward. b 43. Oak Hill Th Coll BA90. d 90
p 91. C Cheltenham St Luke and St Jo Glouc 90-94;
C Hardwicke, Quedgeley and Elmore w Longney 95-96; rtd
96. 25 Bournside Road, Cheltenham GL51 3AL Tel (01242)
513002
HISCOCK, Peter George Harold. b 31. Wadh Coll Ox BA54
MA66. Ely Th Coll 54. d 58 p 59. C Edgehill St Dunstan Liv
58-61; C Kirkby 61-64; C Southport St Luke 64-66; Asst Dean
of Residence TCD 66-68; Dean of Res TCD 68-73; Min Can St
Patr Cathl Dublin 67-70; Chapl St Steph Coll Delhi 73-76; TV
Jarrow Dur 77-82; Chapl Univ Coll Dur 82-87; P-in-c
Dinnington Newc 87-88; TV Ch the King 88-94; RD Newc Cen
87-94; rtd 94; Perm to Offic Lon from 95. 8 Banbury Road,
London E9 7DU Tel (020) 8986 2252
HISCOCK, Phillip George. b 47. Southn Univ CertEd68
MPhil90 MCIPD83. STETS 95. d 98 p 99. NSM Portchester
and Chapl Portsm Docks 98-02; Chapl Dunkirk Miss to
Seafarers Eur 02-08; C Alverstoke Portsm from 08. 36 Gomer
Lane, Gosport PO12 2SA Tel and fax (023) 9234 6881 Mobile
07830-362149 E-mail phillip.hiscock@ntlworld.com
HISCOCKS, Nicholas Robin Thomas. b 75. Keble Coll Ox BA96
MA01 Anglia Poly Univ MA01. Ridley Hall Cam 99. d 01 p 02.
C Bromley Ch Ch Roch from 01. 34 Wickham Chase, West
Wickham BR4 0BL Tel (020) 8777 4292
E-mail nicholas.hiscocks@diocese-rochester.org
HISCOX, Miss Denise. b 47. Lon Univ TCert68 Lanchester Poly
Cov BSc78. WMMTC 98. d 01 p 02. NSM Cov St Mary 01-05;
NSM Leamington Priors All SS 05-07; NSM Leamington Spa H
Trin and Old Milverton 05-07; Perm to Offic 07-08; NSM
Willenhall from 08. 48 Wainbody Avenue North, Coventry
CV3 6DB Tel (024) 7641 1034 E-mail denise@dhiscox.co.uk
HISCOX, Jonathan Ronald James. b 64. Qu Coll Birm 87. d 89
p 90. C Wiveliscombe B & W 89-93; P-in-c Donyatt w Horton,
Broadway and Ashill 93-94; TV Ilminster and Distr 94-02; R
Rowde and Bromham Sarum from 02. The Rectory, High Street,
Bromham, Chippenham SN15 2HA Tel (01380) 859750
HISLOP, Martin Gregory. b 55. Jas Cook Univ Townsville BA78
Univ of S Aus MEd88. d 92 p 93. C N Mackay St Ambrose
Australia 92-93; Dir Studies St Barn Coll of Min 93-94; Chapl
Ballarat Univ 95-98; Asst Chapl St Mich Gr Sch and Assoc P E
St Kilda 98; C Kingston St Luke S'wark 00-01; P-in-c 01-05; V
from 05. St Luke's Vicarage, 4 Burton Road, Kingston upon
Thames KT2 5TE Tel (020) 8546 4064
E-mail mhislop@btinternet.com
HISLOP, Mrs Patricia Elizabeth. b 42. Heythrop Coll Lon
MA03. d 08 p 09. OLM Ewhurst Guildf from 08. 2 Napper Place,
Cranleigh GU6 8DG Tel (01483) 274359
E-mail patricia.hislop@dsl.pipex.com
HITCH, Canon Kim William. b 54. Leic Univ BSc75 K Coll Lon
MA94 Birm Univ MPhil08. Trin Coll Bris 76. d 78 p 79. C
Beccontree St Mary Chelmsf 78-80; C Hurton Quarry Liv 80-83;
V Hatcham St Jas S'wark 83-91; TR Kidbrooke 91-02; R
Kidbrooke St Jas from 02; Lewisham Adnry Ecum Officer
03-06; Dir Ords (Woolwich Area) from 05; AD Charlton from
06; Hon Can S'wark Cathl from 08. St James's Rectory, 62
Kidbrooke Park Road, London SE3 0DU Tel (020) 8856 3438
E-mail kim.hitch@tiscali.co.uk
HITCHCOCK, David. b 37. MCIEH. S'wark Ord Course 70. d 73
p 74. NSM Milton next Gravesend Ch Ch Roch 73-94; NSM
Chalk 96-98; CF (ACF) from 79; Perm to Offic Lon 93-02; NSM
St Andr-by-the-Wardrobe w St Ann, Blackfriars 02-09; NSM
St Jas Garlickhythe w St Mich Queenhithe etc 02-09. 148 Old
Road East, Gravesend DA12 1PF Tel (01474) 361091
E-mail hitch5@btinternet.com
HITCHEN, Miss Lisa Jan. b 73. Linc Univ NZ BPR&TM95
Graduate Sch of Educn Dip Teaching01. Trin Coll Bris BA09.
d 09. C Brinnington w Portwood Ches from 09. 10 Jura Close,
Dukinfield SK16 4DE Tel 0161-339 9850 Mobile 07769-800915
E-mail lisahitchen.angel@gmail.com
HITCHENS (née GREEN), Mrs Catherine Isabel. b 48. Cant Sch
of Min 89. d 92 p 94. C Willesborough Cant 92-96; Sen Asst P E
Dereham and Scarning Nor 96-97; Asst Chapl HM Pris Wayland
96-97; Chapl HM Pris Leic 97-00; Chapl HM YOI Castington
00-02; Chapl HM Pris Cant from 02. The Chaplain's Office, HM
Prison, 46 Longport, Canterbury CT1 1PJ Tel (01227) 862984
HITCHINER, Mrs Elizabeth Ann. b 59. Birm Univ BSc80.
WEMTC 03. d 06 p 07. NSM Kingstone w Clehonger, Eaton
Bishop etc Heref from 06. Dunan House, Clehonger, Hereford
HR2 9SF Tel (01432) 355980
HITCHINER, Sally Ann. b 80. Wycliffe Hall Ox. d 09. C W
Ealing St Jo w St Jas Lon from 09. 41 Leighton Road, London
W13 9EL Tel (020) 8567 0241 Mobile 07761-661529
E-mail sallyhitchiner@hotmail.co.uk

HITCHING, His Honour Judge Alan Norman. b 41. Ch Ch Ox BA62 MA66 BCL63 Barrister-at-Law (Middle Temple) 64. **d** 01 **p** 02. NSM High Ongar w Norton Mandeville *Chelmsf* 01-06; Perm to Offic from 06. *9 Monkhams Drive, Woodford Green IG8 0LG* Tel (020) 8504 4260
E-mail anhitching@btinternet.com

HITCHINS, Graham Edward David. b 54. S Dios Minl Tr Scheme 91. **d** 94 **p** 95. C Bishop's Waltham *Portsm* 94-97; C Upham 94-97; C Honiton, Gittisham, Combe Raleigh, Monkton etc *Ex* 97-98; TV 98-03; Chapl RN from 03. *Royal Naval Chaplaincy Service, Mail Point 1-2, Leach Building, Whale Island, Portsmouth PO2 8BY* Tel (023) 9262 5055 Fax 9262 5134

HITCHMAN, Keith John. b 62. Middx Univ BSc90. Trin Coll Bris BA95. **d** 95 **p** 96. C Bestwood *S'well* 95-99; Chapl Glos Univ 99-04; C Cheltenham St Mary, St Matt, St Paul and H Trin *Glouc* 04-07; TV Cheltenham H Trin and St Paul from 07. *60 All Saints Road, Cheltenham GL52 2AH*
E-mail keith.hitchman@trinityuk.org

HITCHMOUGH, William. b 30. NOC. **d** 81 **p** 82. NSM Penketh *Liv* 81-83; Chapl Warrington Distr Gen Hosp 83-99; Perm to Offic *Liv* 83-03 and *Guildf* from 00. *4 Rex Court, Haslemere GU27 1LJ* Tel (01428) 661504

HIZA, Douglas William. b 38. Richmond Univ Virginia BA60 MDiv63 Mankato State Univ MS70. Virginia Th Sem 60. **d** 63 **p** 64. C Calvary Cathl Sioux Falls USA 63-65; V Sioux Falls Gd Shep 65-66; V Vermillion St Paul 66-69; V New Ulm St Pet 71-80; Chapl Mankato State Univ 74-80; Chapl Hackney Hosp Gp Lon 80-95; Chapl Homerton Hosp Lon 80-95; Perm to Offic *S'wark* from 96. *10 Meynal Crescent, London E9 7AS* Tel (020) 8985 7832 *or* 7253 3107 E-mail general@joanhudson.co.uk

HJORTH, Rolf Gunnar Leer. b 25. St Jo Coll Ox BA46 MA50 AMICE. Wycliffe Hall Ox 61. **d** 62 **p** 63. C Cumnor *Ox* 62-65; V Bramfield and Walpole *St E* 65-69; V Oulton *Lich* 69-78; Chapl Ostend w Knokke and Bruges *Eur* 78-84; Chapl Düsseldorf 85-90; rtd 90; Perm to Offic *Lich* from 99. *6 Darwin Close, Lichfield WS13 7ET* Tel (01543) 253774
E-mail rolf.hjorth@carefree.net

HOAD, Anne Elizabeth. b 42. Bris Univ BA63. **dss** 69 **d** 94 **p** 95. Asst Chapl Imp Coll *Lon* 69-74; S'wark Lay Tr Scheme 74-77; Brixton St Matt *S'wark* 77-80; Charlton St Luke w H Trin 80-94; Project Worker Community of Women and Men 88-91; Voc Adv Lewisham from 91; Asst Chapl Lewisham Hosp 92-03; from 03. *14 Silk Close, London SE12 8DL* Tel (020) 8297 8761

HOAD, Miss Rosemary Claire. b 60. Cranmer Hall Dur 92. **d** 94 **p** 95. C Epsom St Martin *Guildf* 94-97; TV Brentford *Lon* 97-05; V Spring Grove St Mary from 05. *St Mary's Vicarage, Osterley Road, Isleworth TW7 4PW* Tel (020) 8560 3555
E-mail rosemary.hoad@btinternet.com

HOARE, Carol. b 46. Lon Univ BA68 Birm Univ CertEd69. Qu Coll Birm 86 WMMTC 86. **d** 91 **p** 94. NSM Curdworth *Birm* 91-00; Perm to Offic from 00. *14 Elms Road, Sutton Coldfield B72 1JF* Tel 0121-354 1117 E-mail c.hoare@btinternet.com

HOARE, David Albert Sylvester. b 47. **d** 95. C Gibraltar Cathl 95-00. *3 Governor's Lane, Gibraltar*

HOARE, Canon David Marlyn. b 33. Bps' Coll Cheshunt 60. **d** 63 **p** 64. C Ampthill w Millbrook and Steppingley *St Alb* 63-67; C Bushey 67-70; V Harlington 70-79; V Oxhey All SS 76-81; V Hellesdon *Nor* 81-98; Hon Can Nor Cathl 95-98; rtd 98; Perm to Offic *Nor* from 98. *42 Starling Close, Aylsham, Norwich NR11 6XG* Tel (01263) 734565

HOARE, Diana Charlotte. Kent Univ BA78. WEMTC 02. **d** 05 **p** 06. C Bishop's Castle w Mainstone, Lydbury N etc *Heref* from 05. *The Vicarage, Lydbury North SY7 8AU* Tel (01588) 680609 Mobile 07989-432280 E-mail diana@stonescribe.com *or* curate@ridgewaychurches.org

HOARE (née CULLING), Elizabeth Ann. b 58. St Mary's Coll Dur BA76 St Jo Coll Dur PhD87 Rob Coll Cam BA88 PGCE80. Ridley Hall Cam 86. **d** 89 **p** 94. Par Dn S Cave and Ellerker w Broomfleet *York* 89-92; Tutor Cranmer Hall Dur 93-95; P-in-c Cherry Burton *York* 95-00; Abp's Sen Adv on Rural Affairs 95-98; Abp's Adv for Spiritual Direction 98 00; Chapl Bp Burton Coll York 95-00; Perm to Offic *York* 01-02; NSM Cowesby 02-07; NSM Felixkirk w Boltby 02-07; NSM Kirby Knowle 02-07; NSM Leake w Over and Nether Silton and Kepwick 02-07; Tutor and Lect Cranmer Hall Dur 02-07; Tutor Wycliffe Hall Ox from 07. *Wycliffe Hall, 54 Banbury Road, Oxford OX2 6PW* Tel (01865) 274200 *or* 873412
E-mail liz.wildgoose@bigfoot.com

HOARE, Janet Francis Mary. See MILES, Ms Janet Francis Mary

HOARE, Patrick Gerard. See GERARD, Patrick Hoare

HOARE, Patrick Reginald Andrew Reid (Toddy). b 47. TD80 and Bar 88. Hull Univ MA90. Wycliffe Hall Ox 77. **d** 80 **p** 81. C Guisborough *York* 80-83; P-in-c Felixkirk w Boltby 83-07; P-in-c Kirby Knowle 83-07; P-in-c Leake w Over and Nether Silton and Kepwick 83-07; P-in-c Cowesby 83-07; Chapl Yorks Agric Soc

92-09; CF (TA) 82-99; rtd 07; Perm to Offic *Ox* from 07. *Pond Farm House, Holton, Oxford OX33 1PY* Tel (01865) 873412
E-mail toddy100@btinternet.com

HOARE, Roger John. b 38. Tyndale Hall Bris 63. **d** 66 **p** 67. C Stoughton *Guildf* 66-70; C Chesham St Mary *Ox* 70-73; V Bath St Bart *B & W* 73-83; V Gt Faringdon w Lt Coxwell *Ox* 83-89; Deputation Appeals Org (NE Lon) Children's Soc 89-93; P-in-c Lambourne w Abridge and Stapleford Abbotts *Chelmsf* 93-03; Ind Chapl 93-03; rtd 03; Perm to Offic *Chelmsf* from 04. *44 Anchor Road, Tiptree, Colchester CO5 0AP* Tel (01621) 817236 E-mail rogerhoare@aol.com

✠**HOARE, The Rt Revd Rupert William Noel.** b 40. Trin Coll Ox BA61 MA66 Fitzw Ho Cam BA64 MA84 Birm Univ PhD73. Kirchliche Hochschule Berlin 61 Westcott Ho Cam 62. **d** 64 **p** 65 **c** 93. C Oldham St Mary w St Pet *Man* 64-67; Lect Qu Coll Birm 68-72; Can Th Cov Cathl 70-76; R Man Resurr 72-78; Can Res Birm Cathl 78-81; Prin Westcott Ho Cam 81-93; Area Bp Dudley and Hon Can Worc Cathl 93-00; Dean Liv 00-07; rtd 07; Hon Asst Bp Man from 08. *14 Shaw Hall Bank Road, Greenfield, Oldham OL3 7LD* Tel (01457) 820375

HOARE, Canon Simon Gerard. b 37. AKC61. **d** 62 **p** 63. C Headingley *Ripon* 62-65; C Adel 65-68; R Spofforth 68-71; R Spofforth w Kirk Deighton 71-77; V Rawdon *Bradf* 77-85; Hon Can Bradf Cathl 85-02; R Carleton and Lothersdale 85-02; Dioc Ecum Officer 85-94; rtd 02; Perm to Offic *Ripon* from 02. *Skell Villa, 20 Wellington Street, Ripon HG4 1PH* Tel (01765) 692187
E-mail sghoare@freenetname.co.uk

HOARE, Toddy. See HOARE, Patrick Reginald Andrew Reid

HOARE, Mrs Valerie Mary. b 54. Ex Univ BTh07. SWMTC 04. **d** 07 **p** 08. NSM Chard St Mary *B & W* from 07. *Cherrybrook, Underway, Combe St Nicholas, Chard TA20 3NS* Tel (01460) 68799 E-mail cherrybrook@hotmail.com

HOBBINS, Mrs Susan. b 47. Birm Univ CertEd68. STETS 04. **d** 07 **p** 08. NSM Hatherden w Tangley, Weyhill and Penton Mewsey *Win* 07-09; NSM Pastrow from 09. *Whistlers Farm, Tangley, Andover SP11 0SB* Tel and fax (01264) 735533
E-mail suehobbins@yahoo.com

HOBBS, Antony Ewan Talbot. b 25. Ripon Hall Ox 58. **d** 60 **p** 61. C Cuckfield *Chich* 62-64; V Staplefield Common 64-89; rtd 89; Perm to Offic *Chich* from 89. *Chippers, Chalvington, Hailsham BN27 3TE* Tel (01321) 811243

HOBBS (*formerly* **DUFFUS), Mrs Barbara Rose.** b 51. EMMTC 95. **d** 98 **p** 99. C Linc St Faith and St Martin w St Pet 98-00; C Grantham 00-02; P-in-c Brothertoft Gp 02-04; Mental Health Chapl SE Lincs 02-04; P-in-c Hastings St Clem and All SS *Chich* 04-08; rtd 08. *Courtyard Cottage, Main Road Westfield, Hastings TN35 4QE* Tel (01424) 756479 Mobile 07962-892156
E-mail barbara.r.hobbs@googlemail.com

HOBBS, Basil Ernest William. b 22. St Chad's Coll Dur BA49. **d** 51 **p** 52. C Mitcham St Mark *S'wark* 51-54; CF 54-68, IIon C Paddington H Trin w St Paul *Lon* 70-72; Asst Chapl St Mary's Hosp Praed Street Lon 69-72; Novice CR 72-74; Past Consultant Clinical Th 74-84; Lic to Offic *S'well* 74-83; Chapl HM Pris Nottm 81-84; Hon C Nottingham St Andr *S'well* 83-84; C 84-86; TV Clifton 86-87; rtd 87; Perm to Offic *S'well* 87-00 and *Leic* from 99. *17 Stuart Court, High Street, Kibworth, Leicester LE8 0LR* Tel 0116-279 6367

HOBBS, Christopher Bedo. b 61. Jes Coll Cam BA83 BTh90. Ridley Hall Cam 88. **d** 91 **p** 92. C Langham Place All So *Lon* 91-95; C Hull St Jo Newland *York* 95-00; V Selly Park St Steph and St Wulstan *Birm* from 00. *18 Selly Wick Road, Selly Park, Birmingham B29 7JA* Tel 0121-472 0050 *or* 472 8253

HOBBS, Christopher John Pearson. b 60. Sydney Univ BA82 K Coll Lon BD89 AKC89. Wycliffe Hall Ox 89. **d** 91 **p** 92. C S Mimms Ch Ch *Lon* 91-94; C Jesmond Clayton Memorial *Newc* 94-97; V Oakwood St Thos *Lon* from 97. *St Thomas's Vicarage, 2 Sheringham Avenue, London N14 4UE* Tel (020) 8360 1749 *or* tel and fax 8245 9152
E-mail christopher.hobbs@blueyonder.co.uk

HOBBS, Edward Quincey. b 74. Bris Univ BSc95. Wycliffe Hall Ox BA99. **d** 00 **p** 01. C Stapenhill w Cauldwell *Derby* 00-03; C Newbury *Ox* 03-08; C Brompton H Trin w Onslow Square St Paul *Lon* from 08. *Holy Trinity Church, Brompton Road, London SW7 1JA* Tel 08456-447533
E-mail eqhobbs@gmail.com

HOBBS, Ian. See HOBBS, Kenneth Ian

HOBBS, James. b 42. K Alfred's Coll Win CertEd64 Open Univ BA89 Hull Univ MA94. Linc Th Coll 66. **d** 68 **p** 69. C Moseley St Mary *Birm* 68-73; V Kingstanding St Mark 73-77; R Rushbrooke *St E* 77-78; R Bradfield St Geo 77-80; P-in-c Bradfield St Clare 77-80; P-in-c Felsham w Gedding 77-80; R Bradfield St George w Bradfield St Clare etc 80-84; P-in-c Gt and Lt Whelnetham 84-85; R Gt and Lt Whelnetham w Bradfield St George 85-90; Ecum Chapl for F&HE Grimsby *Linc* 90-97; Chapl Humberside Univ (Grimsby Campus) 90-97; Gen Preacher 92-97; V Ingham w Cammeringham w Fillingham 97-01; R Aisthorpe w Scampton w Thorpe le Fallows etc 97-01; P-in-c Burton by Linc 97-01; rtd 01; Perm to Offic *Linc* 01-04.

Courtyard Cottage, Main Road, Westfield, Hastings TN35 4QE Tel (01424) 756479 Mobile 07726-302341 E-mail hobbs.jim1@googlemail.com

HOBBS, Mrs Joan Rosemary. b 39. Chelsea Coll Lon TDip61. WEMTC 97. **d** 00 **p** 01. NSM Cheltenham St Mary, St Matt, St Paul and H Trin *Glouc* 00-02; Perm to Offic 02-04; NSM Brimpsfield w Birdlip, Syde, Daglingworth etc from 04. *Manor Farmhouse, Woodmancote, Cirencester GL7 7EF* Tel and fax (01285) 831244 E-mail joan@hobbsjr.fsnet.co.uk

HOBBS, John Antony. b 36. S Dios Minl Tr Scheme. **d** 87 **p** 88. NSM Crowborough *Chich* from 87. *May Cottage, Alice Bright Lane, Crowborough TN6 3SQ* Tel (01892) 653909

HOBBS, Jonathan Noel Alan. b 70. Oak Hill Th Coll BA03. **d** 03 **p** 04. C Lindfield *Chich* 03-07; R Maresfield from 07; V Nutley from 07. *16 The Paddock, Maresfield, Uckfield TN22 2HQ* Tel (01825) 764536 E-mail jon@hobbs99.freeserve.co.uk

HOBBS, Kenneth Brian. b 47. Sussex Univ BA68 Lon Inst of Educn PGCE70. NTMTC 98. **d** 98 **p** 99. NSM Howell Hill *Guildf* 98-01; NSM Shere, Albury and Chilworth from 01. *Yeoman's Acre, Farley Green, Albury, Guildford GU5 9DN* Tel (01483) 202165 E-mail hobbs@farleygreen.net

HOBBS, Kenneth Ian. b 50. Oak Hill Th Coll 74. **d** 77 **p** 78. C Southborough St Pet w Ch Ch and St Matt *Roch* 77-80; C Hoole *Ches* 80-84; V Barnston 84-95; P-in-c Bedworth *Cov* 95; TR 95-01; RD Nuneaton 00-01; TR Radipole and Melcombe Regis *Sarum* from 01; RD Weymouth and Portland from 08. *39 Icen Road, Weymouth DT3 5JL* Tel (01305) 785553 E-mail teamrector@radipoleparish.f2s.com

HOBBS, Leslie Robert. b 42. Sussex Univ BA64 Lon Bible Coll BD67. EAMTC. **d** 02 **p** 03. NSM Somerleyton, Ashby, Fritton, Herringfleet etc *Nor* 02-09; R from 09. *Nother End Cottage, Blacksmiths Loke, Lound, Lowestoft NR32 5LS* Tel (01502) 732536 Mobile 07833-753704

HOBBS, Ms Maureen Patricia. b 54. Surrey Univ BSc76 Warwick Univ 92. Westcott Ho Cam 95. **d** 97 **p** 98. C Shrewsbury St Chad w St Mary *Lich* 97-01; R Baschurch and Weston Lullingfield w Hordley 01-09; P-in-c Pattingham w Patshull from 04; RD Trysull from 09; Dioc Adv for Women in Min from 04. *The Vicarage, 20 Dartmouth Avenue, Pattingham, Wolverhampton WV6 7DP* Tel (01902) 700257 E-mail hobbsmaureen@yahoo.co.uk

HOBBS, Michael Bedo. b 30. Fitzw Ho Cam BA58 MA62. Clifton Th Coll 58. **d** 60 **p** 61. C Southsea St Jude *Portsm* 60-63; Paraguay 63-65; Argentina 65-67; V Potters Green *Cov* 68-75; Distr Sec BFBS 75-82; R Plaxtol *Roch* 82-96; Dioc Missn Audits Consultant 90-96; rtd 96; Perm to Offic *Sarum* from 96. *Falcons, Barkers Hill, Semley, Shaftesbury SP7 9BH* Tel (01747) 828920

HOBBS, Ms Sarah Kathleen. b 72. Liv Univ BA94 UMIST BSc98 PGCE95. Wycliffe Hall Ox BA05. **d** 05 **p** 06. C W Ealing St Jo w St Jas *Lon* 05-08; V Blockhouse Bay New Zealand from 08. *429A Blockhouse Bay Road, Blockhouse Bay, Auckland 0600, New Zealand* Tel (0064) (9) 627 8779 E-mail sarah@churchofthesaviour.org.nz

HOBBS, Sarah Louise. b 47. WEMTC 01. **d** 04 **p** 05. NSM Westbury-on-Severn w Flaxley, Blaisdon etc *Glouc* from 05. *Folly Cottage, Adsett Lane, Adsett, Westbury-on-Severn GL14 1PQ* Tel (01452) 760337 E-mail sarah@qhobbs.wanadoo.co.uk

HOBBS, Simon John. b 59. St Steph Ho Ox BA82 MA. **d** 83 **p** 84. C Middlesbrough Ascension *York* 83-85; C Stainton-in-Cleveland 85-88; C St Marylebone All SS *Lon* 88-90; P-in-c Paddington St Pet 90-94; C-in-c Grosvenor Chpl 94-08; C Hanover Square St Geo 94-08; Chapl Bonn w Cologne *Eur* from 08. *Kaiser-Friedrich-Strasse 19, 53113 Bonn, Germany* Tel and fax (0049) (2246) 302565 Mobile 170-693 5538 E-mail bkchaplain@mac.com

HOBDAY, Hannah Elizabeth. b 80. Jes Coll Ox BA03 Cam Univ BA06. Ridley Hall Cam 04. **d** 07 **p** 08. C Cliftonville *Cant* 07-09; C Margate H Trin 07-09. *Address temp unknown* Tel 07792-923575 (mobile) E-mail hannah.sutcliffe1@alumni.jesus.ox.ac.uk

HOBDAY, Peter Hugh Francis. b 34. IEng90. Oak Hill NSM Course 99. **d** 00 **p** 01. NSM Perivale *Lon* 00-05; Perm to Offic *Lon* 05-07 and *Pet* from 07. *18 Juniper Close, Towcester NN12 6XP* Tel (01327) 359045 Mobile 07778-007370 E-mail petehobday@aol.com

HOBDAY, Philip Peter. b 81. Ex Coll Ox BA02 MA09 Fitzw Coll Cam BA05 MA09. Ridley Hall Cam 03. **d** 06 **p** 07. C St Peter-in-Thanet *Cant* 06-09; Chapl Cant Ch Ch Univ 06-09; Chapl and Fell Magd Coll Cam from 09. *Magdalene College, Cambridge CB3 0AG* Tel (01223) 332129 Mobile 07717-056951 E-mail pph21@cam.ac.uk

HOBDEN, Canon Brian Charles. b 38. Oak Hill Th Coll 63. **d** 66 **p** 67. C S Lambeth St Steph *S'wark* 66-70; C Cheadle *Ches* 70-76; R Brandon USA 76-87; R Prescott St Jo 87-98; R Mesilla Park St Jas from 98; rtd 03. *3160 Executive Hills Road, Las Cruces NM 88011-4724, USA* Tel (001) (505) 521 9435 Fax 526 4821 E-mail stjames@lascruces.com

HOBDEN, Christopher Martin. b 49. Lon Univ BSc71. Oak Hill

Th Coll 80. **d** 87 **p** 88. NSM St Marylebone All So w SS Pet and Jo *Lon* 87-88; NSM Langham Place All So 88-95. *10 Kent Terrace, London NW1 4RP*

HOBDEN, David Nicholas. b 54. K Coll Lon BD76 AKC76 Cam Univ PGCE. Ripon Coll Cuddesdon 77. **d** 78 **p** 79. C Marlborough *Sarum* 78-80; C Salisbury St Thos and St Edm 81-85; V Shalford *Guildf* 85-99; Asst Chapl R Surrey Co Hosp NHS Trust 99-00; Sen Chapl from 00. *Department of Pastoral Care, Royal Surrey County Hospital, Egerton Road, Guildford GU2 5XX* Tel (01483) 406835 *or* 571122 E-mail cmhobden@aol.com *or* dhobden@royalsurrey.nhs.uk

HOBDEN, Geoffrey William. b 46. Trin Coll Bris 80. **d** 82 **p** 83. C Ex St Leon w H Trin 82-86; V Weston-super-Mare Ch Ch *B & W* 86-06; V Weston super Mare Ch Ch and Em from 06; RD Locking 93-99. *Christ Church Vicarage, 18 Montpelier, Weston-super-Mare BS23 2RH* Tel (01934) 624376 Fax 641016 E-mail geoff@ccwsm.org.uk

HOBLEY, Ms Susan Elizabeth. b 51. Newc Univ BA74 Dur Univ PGCE75. NEOC 98. **d** 01 **p** 02. NSM Millfield St Mark and Pallion St Luke *Dur* 01-05; C Sheff St Mark Broomhill from 05. *9 Betjeman Gardens, Sheffield S10 3FW* Tel 0114-266 4343 E-mail sue@stmarkssheffield.co.uk

HOBROUGH, Mrs Margaret Edith. b 40. OBE97. Man Univ BA63 Newc Univ MEd75 K Coll Lon MTh80 FRSA94. STETS 01. **d** 03 **p** 04. NSM Godalming *Guildf* 03-05; NSM Warkworth and Acklington *Newc* from 05. *3 St Lawrence Terrace, Warkworth, Morpeth NE65 0XE* Tel (01665) 711203 E-mail margarethobrough@v21.me.uk

HOBSON, Alexander. See HOBSON, John Alexander

HOBSON, Anthony Peter. b 53. St Jo Coll Cam BA74. St Jo Coll Nottm 75. **d** 77 **p** 78. C Brunswick *Man* 77-82; R Stretford St Bride 82-92; TR Hackney Marsh *Lon* 92-00; V Leic Martyrs 00-08; Dir Cathl Square Project from 09. *4 Church Road, Aylestone, Leicester LE2 8LB* Tel 0116-283 3251 E-mail petehobson@me.com

HOBSON, Barry Rodney. b 57. Open Univ BA98. Wilson Carlile Coll 82 EAMTC 97. **d** 98 **p** 99. CA from 85; C Warboys w Broughton and Bury w Wistow *Ely* 98-01; P-in-c Roxwell *Chelmsf* 01-07; RD Chelmsf N 06-07; V Hornchurch St Andr from 07. *The Vicarage, 222 High Street, Hornchurch RM12 6QP* Tel (01708) 454594 *or* 441571 E-mail b.hobson@btinternet.com

HOBSON, Jeremy Graeme. b 71. Lon Univ BMedSci95 MB, BS96. Oak Hill Th Coll BA03. **d** 03 **p** 04. C Eastbourne H Trin *Chich* 03-07; C Clerkenwell St Jas and St Jo w St Pet *Lon* 07-08; Lic to AD Islington from 08. *47 Grange Grove, London N1 2NP* Tel (020) 7251 1190 E-mail thehobsons@onetel.com

HOBSON, John Alexander (Alex). b 70. LMH Ox BA91 MA02 York Univ MA94. Wycliffe Hall Ox BA01. **d** 02 **p** 03. C Aynho and Croughton w Evenley etc *Pet* 02-05; Chapl RAF from 05. *Chaplaincy Services, Valiant Block, HQ Air Command, RAF High Wycombe HP14 4UE* Tel (01494) 496800 Fax 496343 E-mail hobson@oxfree.com

HOBSON, Canon Patrick John Bogan. b 33. MC53. Magd Coll Cam BA56 MA60 Ox Brookes Univ BA08. S'wark Ord Course 75 Qu Coll Birm 77. **d** 79 **p** 80. C St Jo in Bedwardine *Worc* 79-81; R Clifton-on-Teme, Lower Sapey and the Shelsleys 81-88; TR Waltham H Cross *Chelmsf* 88-98; Hon Can Chelmsf Cathl 95-98; rtd 98. *24 Cunliffe Close, Oxford OX2 7BL* Tel and fax (01865) 556206 E-mail patrick.hobson@btinternet.com

HOBSON, Peter. See HOBSON, Anthony Peter

HOBSON, Mrs Yvonne Mary. b 45. Ex Univ BTh03. SWMTC 00. **d** 03 **p** 04. C St Illogan *Truro* 03-06; C Paul from 06. *8 Donnington Road, Penzance TR18 4PQ* Tel (01736) 364354 E-mail yvonnehobson@btinternet.com

HOCKEN, Glen Rundle. b 59. Kent Univ BA80 Southlands Coll Lon PGCE90 ACA84. Wycliffe Hall Ox 90. **d** 92 **p** 93. C Cogges *Ox* 92-94; C Cogges and S Leigh 94-96; C Boldmere *Birm* 96-99; TV Southgate *Chich* 99-06; Chapl HM Pris Lewes from 06; Chapl St Pet and St Jas Hospice N Chailey from 05. *The Chaplain's Office, HM Prison, Brighton Road, Lewes BN7 1EA* Tel (01273) 785100 Fax 785101

HOCKEY, Ms Christine Helen. St Mich Coll Llan. **d** 09. NSM Maindee Newport *Mon* from 09. *134 Christchurch Road, Newport NP19 7SB* Tel (01633) 768900

HOCKEY (née LOOMES), Gaenor Mary. b 65. Hull Univ BA92 RGN86. St Jo Coll Nottm MPhil93. **d** 96 **p** 97. C Charles w Plymouth St Matthias *Ex* 96-00; C Devonport St Aubyn 00-05; Perm to Offic 05-06; P-in-c Seer Green and Jordans *Ox* from 06. *43 Long Grove, Seer Green, Beaconsfield HP9 2YN* Tel (01494) 675013

HOCKEY, Paul Henry. b 49. Oak Hill Th Coll BA86. **d** 86 **p** 87. C Dalton-in-Furness *Carl* 86-89; R Clifton, Brougham and Cliburn 89-94; V Fremington *Ex* from 94; Chapl Children's Hospice SW 97-07; RD Barnstaple from 07. *The Vicarage, Fremington, Barnstaple EX31 2NX* Tel (01271) 373879

HOCKING, Canon Hugh Michael Warwick. b 12. VRD54. Ch Coll Cam BA34 MA38. Westcott Ho Cam 34. **d** 36 **p** 37. C Hackney St Jo *Lon* 36-37; C Stoke Damerel *Ex* 37-39; Chapl

RNVR 39-46; V Madron w Morvah *Truro* 46-54; Chapl Poltair Hosp 50-54; V Bris St Ambrose Whitehall 54-62; R Guildf H Trin w St Mary 62-77; Chapl St Luke's Hosp Guildf 63-77; Hon Can Guildf Cathl 68-77; rtd 77; Chapl W Cornwall Hosp Penzance 78-97; Perm to Offic *Ex* from 97. *23 Gracey Court, Woodland Road, Broadclyst, Exeter EX5 3GA* Tel (01392) 465170

HOCKING, Paul Frederick. b 43. Chich Th Coll 84. **d** 86 **p** 87. C Whitton and Thurleston w Akenham *St E* 86-89; V Ipswich All Hallows 89-91; P-in-c Gt Cornard 91-98; V Nsettleton w Swallow w Drinkstone 98-03; R 03-05; rtd 05; Perm to Offic *St E* from 05. *32 Spriteshall Lane, Trimley St Mary, Felixstowe IP11 9QY* Tel (01394) 277600 E-mail mhock33733@aol.com

HOCKLEY, Paul William. b 47. Chu Coll Cam BA68 MA72 Nottm Univ BA73. St Jo Coll Nottm 71. **d** 74 **p** 75. C Chatham St Phil and St Jas *Roch* 74-78; C Tunbridge Wells St Jo 78-81; V Penketh *Liv* from 81. *St Paul's Vicarage, 6 Poplar Avenue, Penketh, Warrington WA5 2EH* Tel (01925) 723492 Fax 486945 E-mail paul-hockley@lineone.net

HOCKLEY, Canon Raymond Alan. b 29. LRAM53 Em Coll Cam MA71. Westcott Ho Cam 56. **d** 58 **p** 59. C Endcliffe *Sheff* 58-61; P-in-c Wicker w Neepsend 61-63; Chapl Westcott Ho Cam 63-68; Chapl Em Coll Cam 68-76; Can Res and Prec York Minster 76-95; rtd 95; Perm to Offic *York* from 95. *26 Buckingham Mews, Sutton Coldfield B73 5PR* Tel 0121-354 7083

HOCKNULL, Mark Dennis. b 63. Surrey Univ BSc85 Univ Coll Lon PhD89 St Jo Coll Dur BA93. Cranmer Hall Dur 91. **d** 94 **p** 95. C Prenton *Ches* 94-96; C Runcorn All SS and Runcorn St Mich 96-99; V Gt Meols 99-05; CME Officer *Linc* from 05; Lic Preacher from 05. *105 Nettleham Road, Lincoln LN2 1RU* Tel (01522) 560521 *or* 504050 E-mail mark.hocknull@lincoln.anglican.org

HOCKRIDGE, Joan. b 25. Girton Coll Cam BA47 MA50. St Steph Ho Ox 82. **dss** 83 **d** 87 **p** 94. Ealing Ascension Hanger Hill *Lon* 83-88; Hon C 87-88; Hon C Hanger Hill Ascension and W Twyford St Mary 88-92; Hon C Hillingdon St Jo 92-95; Perm to Offic 95-00. *17 Mead Way, Ruislip HA4 7QW* Tel (01895) 622643

HODDER, Christopher John. b 75. Huddersfield Univ BA96. St Jo Coll Nottm BTh00. **d** 01 **p** 02. C Loughborough Em and St Mary in Charnwood *Leic* 01-05; Chapl Derby Univ from 05; Chapl Derby Cathl from 05. *1 Peet Street, Derby DE22 3RF* Tel (01332) 594172 *or* 591878 E-mail c.hodder@derby.ac.uk

HODDER, John Kenneth. b 45. Edin Univ MA68. Cuddesdon Coll 71. **d** 73 **p** 74. C Kibworth Beauchamp *Leic* 73-76; C Whittlesey *Ely* 76-80; R Downham 80-87; P-in-c Coveney 80-81; R 81-87; R Nunney and Witham Friary, Marston Bigot etc *B & W* from 87. *The Rectory, High Street, Nunney, Frome BA11 4LZ* Tel (01373) 836732

HODDER, Trevor Valentine. b 31. Bps' Coll Cheshunt 65. **d** 67 **p** 68. C Oxhey All SS *St Alb* 67-70; C Digswell 70-73; V Colchester St Anne *Chelmsf* 74-96; rtd 96; Perm to Offic *Chelmsf* from 00. *30 Drury Road, Colchester CO2 7UX* Tel (01206) 766480

HODGE, Albert. b 40. NOC 84. **d** 87 **p** 88. C Huyton St Geo *Liv* 87-89; P-in-c Widnes St Paul 89-97; Chapl Halton Coll of FE 89-97; C Linton in Craven and Burnsall w Rylstone *Bradf* 97-05; rtd 05; Perm to Offic *Man* from 06. *Sunnyhurst, 50 Sandfield Road, Bacup OL13 9PD* Tel (01706) 873285 E-mail sergeant1832@aol.com

HODGE, Anthony Charles. b 43. AKC66. **d** 67 **p** 68. C Carrington *S'well* 67-69; C Bawtry w Austerfield 69-72; C Misson 69-72; Grenada 72-74; Trinidad and Tobago 74-76; V Tuckingmill *Truro* 76-78; V Worksop St Paul *S'well* 78-81; P-in-c Patrington w Hollym, Welwick and Winestead *York* 81-86; R 86-88; V York St Olave w St Giles 88-08; V York St Helen w St Martin 97-08; Chapl York Coll for Girls 88-96; rtd 08; P-in-c Duloe, Herodsfoot, Morval and St Pinnock *Truro* from 08. *The Rectory, Duloe, Liskeard PL14 4PW* Tel (01503) 264229 Mobile 07717-877430 E-mail anthonyhodge401@msn.com

HODGE, Colin. b 39. Sarum & Wells Th Coll. **d** 83 **p** 84. NSM Wareham *Sarum* 84-87; C Parkstone St Pet w Branksea and St Osmund 87-89; V Lilliput 89-00; rtd 00; Perm to Offic *Sarum* from 01. *35 Stowell Crescent, Wareham BH20 4PT* Tel (01929) 553222

HODGE, Canon Michael Robert. b 34. Pemb Coll Cam BA57 MA61. Ridley Hall Cam 57. **d** 59 **p** 60. C Harpurhey Ch Ch *Man* 59; C Blackpool St Mark *Blackb* 59-62; V Stalybridge Old St Geo *Man* 62-67; R Cobham w Luddesdowne and Dode *Roch* 67-81; Hon Can Roch Cathl 81-99; R Bidborough 81-99; rtd 99; Hon C Chale *Portsm* 99-06; Hon C Gatcombe 99-06; Hon C Shorwell w Kingston 99-06; Asst to RD W Wight 99-06; Perm to Offic from 06. *Braxton Cottage, Halletts Shute, Norton, Yarmouth PO41 0RH* Tel and fax (01983) 761121 Mobile 07941-232983 E-mail michael.hodge.1954@pem.cam.ac.uk

HODGE, Nigel John. b 61. BTh83 Open Univ BSc97 MIBiol98. St Mich Coll Llan 83. **d** 85 **p** 86. C Mynyddislwyn *Mon* 85-87; C Machen 87-89; TV Ebbw Vale 89-91; V Abercarn 91-98; Lic to

Offic from 99. *6 Maple Terrace, Abercarn, Newport NP11 5JF* Tel (01495) 249014

HODGES, Ian. Ridley Hall Cam. **d** 05 **p** 06. C Llantrisant from 05. *36 Danygraig Heights, Talbot Green, Pontyclun CF72 8FD* Tel (01443) 226508 E-mail ianhodges@parishofllantrisant.org.uk

HODGES, Mrs Jane Anne Christine. b 62. SEITE. **d** 09. C Poplar *Lon* from 09. *164 St Leonard's Road, London E14 6PW* E-mail sussexjane@hotmail.com

HODGES, Jasper Tor. b 62. Leeds Univ BSc84 Sheff Univ MEng85 Lon Univ PGCE87. Trin Coll Bris BA94. **d** 94 **p** 95. C Holbeck *Ripon* 94-97; C Ealing St Steph Castle Hill *Lon* 97-04; V Arbourthorne and Norfolk Park *Sheff* from 04. *St Paul's and St Leonard's Vicarage, 458B East Bank Road, Sheffield S2 2AD* Tel 0114-239 8533 Fax 08701-687299 E-mail jasper@live.freeserve.co.uk

HODGES, Keith Michael. b 53. Southn Univ BTh82 Heythrop Coll Lon MA04. Chich Th Coll 77. **d** 80 **p** 81. C Sydenham St Phil *S'wark* 80-84; Perm to Offic 85; C Leatherhead *Guildf* 86-89; V Aldershot St Aug from 89. *St Augustine's Vicarage, Holly Road, Aldershot GU12 4SE* Tel (01252) 320840 E-mail father.keith@ntlworld.com

HODGES, Mrs Laura. b 53. SAOMC 01. **d** 04 **p** 05. NSM Abingdon *Ox* from 04; Chapl SW Oxon Primary Care Trust from 07. *38 Baker Road, Abingdon OX14 5LW* Tel (01235) 527654 E-mail laura.hodges@btinternet.com

HODGES, Miss Stefanie Margaret. b 54. Trin Coll Bris 93. **d** 97 **p** 98. C Croydon Ch Ch *S'wark* 97-99; C Sutton St Nic 99-02; TV Mildenhall *St E* 02-08; TR Westborough *Guildf* from 08. *St Francis's Vicarage, Beckingham Road, Guildford GU2 8BU* Tel (01483) 546412 E-mail stefanie@mhodges.co.uk

HODGES, Mrs Valerie Irene. b 44. **d** 06. NSM Newbridge *Mon* from 06. *Ty-Pwll House, The Pant, Newbridge, Newport NP11 5GF* Tel (01495) 244676 E-mail val.hodges@btinternet.com

HODGETT, Ms Tina Elizabeth. b 64. Leic Univ MBA05 Sheff Univ PGCE90 St Mary's Coll Dur BA88. Ridley Hall Cam 06. **d** 08 **p** 09. C Bestwood Em w St Mark *S'well* from 08. *5 Hatton Close, Arnold, Nottingham NG5 9QG* Tel 0115-952 4715 Mobile 07759-909106

HODGETTS, Alan Paul. b 54. Birm Poly BSc78 Heythrop Coll Lon MA96. St Steph Ho Ox 79. **d** 82 **p** 83. C Perry Barr *Birm* 82-85; C Broseley w Benthall *Heref* 85-87; V Effingham w Lt Bookham *Guildf* 87-96; R Merrow 96-06; Chapl HM Pris Woodhill from 06. *The Chaplaincy Department, HM Prison Woodhill, Tattenhoe Street, Milton Keynes MK4 4DA* Tel (01908) 722000 ext 2097 E-mail alan.hodgetts@hmps.gsi.gov.uk

HODGETTS, Colin William John. b 40. St D Coll Lamp BA61 Ripon Hall Ox 61. **d** 63 **p** 64. C Hackney St Jo *Lon* 63-68; Hon C St Martin-in-the-Fields 70-76; C Creeksea w Althorne *Chelmsf* 76-79; Perm to Offic *Ex* 84-03; C Parkham, Alwington, Buckland Brewer etc 03-06; Hon C from 06; rtd 06. *Quincott, Cheristow, Hartland, Bideford EX39 6DA* Tel (01237) 441426 E-mail julia@hartland.swinternet.co.uk

HODGETTS, Harry Samuel. b 30. Chich Th Coll 63. **d** 65 **p** 66. C Harton Colliery *Dur* 65-68; C Penzance St Mary *Truro* 68-70; V Penwerris 70-79; V Kettering St Mary *Pet* 79-94; rtd 95; Perm to Offic *Win* 03-09. *The Flat, Etal Manor, Etal, Cornhill-on-Tweed TD12 4TL* Tel (01890) 820378

HODGINS, Miss Kylie Anne. b 68. SEITE 98 Ridley Hall Cam 00. **d** 02 **p** 03. C Histon and Impington *Ely* 02-07; Chapl Sherborne Sch for Girls 07-08; P-in-c Cottenham *Ely* from 08; P-in-c Rampton from 09. *The Rectory, 6 High Street, Cottenham, Cambridge CB24 8SA* Tel (01954) 250454 E-mail kylie@gumnut.me.uk

HODGINS, Philip Arthur. b 57. Lanc Univ BA78 Bradf Univ MBA90 MCIPD94. Linc Th Coll 82. **d** 85 **p** 86. C Norton *Ches* 85-88; V Whitkirk *Ripon* 88-89; Perm to Offic *Bradf* 89-90 and *Chich* 91-02; Hon C Chiddingly w E Hoathly *Chich* 02-04; P-in-c 04-09; R from 09; RD Uckfield from 06. *The Rectory, Rectory Close, East Hoathly, Lewes BN8 6EG* Tel (01825) 840270 E-mail philhodgins@btinternet.com

HODGKINSON, Canon John. b 27. Trin Hall Cam BA51 MA55. Linc Th Coll 51. **d** 53 **p** 54. C Penrith St Andr *Carl* 53-56; C Linc St Nic w St Jo Newport 56-58; C-in-c Lin St Jo Bapt CD 58-63; V Linc St Jo 63-66; R Old Brumby 66-71; V Kendal H Trin *Carl* 71-90; Hon Can Carl Cathl 84-90; rtd 90; Perm to Offic *Carl* from 90. *Boxtree Barn, Levens, Kendal LA8 8NZ* Tel (01539) 560806 E-mail boxtreebarn@hotmail.com

HODGKINSON, John David. b 57. Birm Univ BA78 Edin Univ BD89. Edin Th Coll 86. **d** 89 **p** 90. C Briercliffe *Blackb* 89-92; C Darwen St Cuth w Tockholes St Steph 92-94; R Harrington *Carl* 94-00; V Walney Is from 00. *The Vicarage, Promenade, Walney, Barrow in Furness LA14 3QU* Tel (01229) 471268

HODGSON, Ms Amanda Jane. b 66. Westmr Coll Ox BA88 Heythrop Coll Lon MA99. Westcott Ho Cam 94. **d** 96 **p** 97. C Epping Distr *Chelmsf* 96-01; TV Wythenshawe *Man* 01-07; R

Streatham St Leon *S'wark* from 07. *The Rectory, 1 Becmead Avenue, London SW16 1UH* Tel (020) 8769 4366
E-mail rectorstleonards@btinternet.com

HODGSON, Anthony Owen Langlois. b 35. Ripon Hall Ox 60. **d** 62 **p** 63. C Stiffkey w Morston and Blakeney w Lt Langham *Nor* 62-65; C Paddington Ch Ch *Lon* 66-70; Area Sec (Beds & Cambs) Chr Aid 70-74; (Herts & Hunts) 70-73; (Rutland & Northants) 73-74; V Gt w Lt Gidding and Steeple Gidding *Ely* 77-81; Warden Dovedale Ho 81-89; P-in-c Ilam w Blore Ray and Okeover *Lich* 81-89; Dir Chr Rural Cen 89-91; C Checkley and Stramshall 91-97; TV Uttoxeter Area 97-00; rtd 00. *9 Trent House, Station Road, Oundle, Peterborough PE8 4DE* Tel (01832) 275343 E-mail hodgsons@phonecoop.coop

HODGSON, Antony Robert. b 66. Dundee Univ MA88 Jes Coll Cam BA92 MA96 Lanc Univ MA04. Westcott Ho Cam 90 Ven English Coll Rome 92. **d** 93 **p** 94. C Chorley St Geo *Blackb* 93-96; C Lytham St Cuth 96-99; V St Annes St Marg from 99. *St Margaret's Vicarage, 24 Chatsworth Road, Lytham St Annes FY8 2JN* Tel (01253) 722648

HODGSON, Barbara Elizabeth. b 46. N Riding Coll of Educn BEd85. NEOC 06. **d** 08 **p** 09. NSM Bridlington Em *York* from 08. *79 St James Road, Bridlington YO15 3PQ* Tel (01262) 675014 Mobile 07907-593234 E-mail vidara1972@talktalk.net

HODGSON, Christopher. b 24. Oriel Coll Ox BA49 MA54. Qu Coll Birm 50. **d** 52 **p** 53. C Cheltenham Ch Ch *Glouc* 52-55; C Liv Our Lady and St Nic 55-57; V Anfield St Columba 57-64; V Pembury *Roch* 64-82; Chapl Pembury Hosp Tunbridge Wells 66-82; R Aynho w Newbottle and Charlton *Pet* 82-85; Chapl Burrswood Chr Cen 85-94; C Castle Bromwich St Clem *Birm* 86-94; rtd 94. *Appledore, 29 Bramber Road, Seaford BN25 1AG* Tel (01323) 890735

HODGSON, Canon David George. b 54. Coll of Resurr Mirfield. **d** 82 **p** 83. C Stainton-in-Cleveland *York* 82-87; R Loftus 87; P-in-c Carlin How w Skinningrove 87; R Loftus and Carlin How w Skinningrove 87-93; V Middlesbrough Ascension from 93; P-in-c S Bank 03-07; RD Middlesbrough 98-05; Can and Preb York Minster from 01. *The Ascension Vicarage, Penrith Road, Middlesbrough TS3 7JR* Tel (01642) 244857

HODGSON, Canon David Peter. b 56. Fitzw Coll Cam BA77 MA81 Nottm Univ BA82 MTh85. St Jo Coll Nottm 80. **d** 83 **p** 84. C Guiseley w Esholt *Bradf* 83-86; Asst Chapl Loughb Univ 86-89; P-in-c Hatfield Broad Oak *Chelmsf* 89-90; P-in-c Bush End 89-90; P-in-c Hatfield Broad Oak and Bush End 90-97; Ind Chapl Harlow 89-97; R Wokingham All SS *Ox* from 97; AD Sonning from 04; Hon Can Ch Ch from 09. *The Rectory, 2A Norreys Avenue, Wokingham RG40 1TU* Tel 0118-979 2999 E-mail david@allsaints.prestel.co.uk

HODGSON, Gary Stuart. b 65. Ridley Hall Cam 95. **d** 98 **p** 99. C S Ossett *Wakef* 98-01; V Kirkburton 01-07; Chapl Huddersfield Univ and Hon C Fixby and Cowcliffe from 07. *The Rectory, 10 The Dell, Huddersfield HD2 2FD* Tel (01484) 545079 E-mail g.hodgson@hud.ac.uk

HODGSON, George. b 36. Qu Coll Birm 75. **d** 78 **p** 79. NSM Wordsley *Lich* 78-93; NSM Wordsley *Worc* from 93; Perm to Offic 84-93. *1 Newfield Drive, Kingswinford DY6 8HY* Tel (01384) 292543 Mobile 07811-753160
E-mail george@hodgson25.freeserve.co.uk

HODGSON, Mrs Helen Mary. b 66. NOC 01. **d** 04 **p** 05. C Emley and Flockton cum Denby Grange *Wakef* 04-05; NSM Kirkburton 05-07; Asst to RD Huddersfield from 07. *The Rectory, 10 The Dell, Huddersfield HD2 2FD* Tel (01484) 545079 E-mail hm.hodgson@ntlworld.com

HODGSON, John. b 35. St Jo Coll Cam MA62 Lon Univ BD61. St Deiniol's Hawarden 80. **d** 81 **p** 82. Hon C Padiham *Blackb* 81-84; C W Burnley All SS 85-87; V 87-95; rtd 95; Perm to Offic *Worc* 95-02 and *Glouc* 98-02. *8 Rivergreen, Amble, Morpeth NE65 0GZ* Tel (01665) 713203

HODGSON, Kenneth Jonah. b 36. Open Univ BA79 CQSW89. Oak Hill Th Coll. **d** 69 **p** 70. C Rainford *Liv* 69-72; C Fazakerley Em 72-74; TV 74-78; Soc Worker 78-96; CF 79-82; rtd 96; Wallasey St Hilary *Ches* 01-03; Perm to Offic from 03. *134 Rake Lane, Wallasey, Merseyside CH45 1JW* Tel and fax 0151-639 2980

HODGSON, Roger Vaughan. b 27. Magd Coll Cam BA49 MA54. Cuddesdon Coll 55. **d** 56 **p** 57. C Westmr St Matt *Lon* 56-59; C Pimlico St Pet w Westmr Ch Ch 59-65; R Lt Hadham *St Alb* 65-78; Chapl Oporto *Eur* 78-80; Chapl and Lect St Deiniol's Lib Hawarden 81-82; V Coldwaltham *Chich* 82-92; rtd 92; Asst Chapl Costa Blanca *Eur* 92-94; Perm to Offic *Chich* from 94. *2 Bakers Arms Hill, Arundel BN18 9DA* Tel (01903) 884708

HODGSON, The Ven Thomas Richard Burnham. b 26. FRMetS88. Lon Coll of Div BD52 ALCD52. **d** 52 **p** 53. C Crosthwaite Kendal *Carl* 52-55; C Stanwix 55-59; V Whitehaven St Nic 59-65; R Aikton 65-67; Bp's Dom Chapl and V Raughton Head w Gatesgill 67-73; Dir of Ords 70-74; Hon Can Carl Cathl 72-91; V Grange-over-Sands 73-79; RD Windermere 76-79; Adn W Cumberland 79-91; V Mosser 79-83; rtd 91; Perm to Offic

Carl from 91. *58 Greenacres, Wetheral, Carlisle CA4 8LD* Tel (01228) 561159

HODGSON, Vernon Charles. b 34. MRPharmS58 Lon Univ BPharm58. Llan Dioc Tr Scheme 83. **d** 86 **p** 87. NSM Roath *Llan* 86-91; C Caerphilly 91-93; V Llanbister w Llanbadarn Fynydd w Llananno *S & B* 93-97; V Llanddewi Ystradenni 94-97; V Llanbister w Llanbadarn Fynydd w Llananno etc 97-01; rtd 01. *114 Carisbrooke Way, Cyncoed, Cardiff CF23 9HX* Tel (029) 2045 3403

HODKINSON, George Leslie. b 48. Qu Coll Birm 86. **d** 88 **p** 89. C Hall Green St Pet *Birm* 88-91; TV Solihull 91-96; P-in-c Billesley Common 96-00; V 00-05; AD Moseley 01-02; rtd 05; Chapl Countess of Chester Hosp NHS Foundn Trust from 05; Chapl Cheshire and Wirral Partnerships NHS Trust from 05. *2 Birch Close, Four Crosses, Llanymynech SY22 6NH* Tel (01691) 839946 *or* (01244) 364543

HODSON, Gordon George. b 35. St Chad's Coll Dur BA59. **d** 60 **p** 61. C Tettenhall Regis *Lich* 60-64; C Rugeley 64-68; V Shrewsbury St Mich 68-74; V Kinnerley w Melverley 74-87; P-in-c Knockin w Maesbrook 75-87; P-in-c Chebsey 87-91; P-in-c Seighford, Derrington and Cresswell 87-91; V Chebsey, Ellenhall and Seighford-with-Creswell 91-00; rtd 00; Perm to Offic *Lich* from 01. *27 Oak Drive, Oswestry SY11 2RU* Tel (01691) 662849

HODSON, Keith. b 53. Hatf Coll Dur BA74. Wycliffe Hall Ox 77. **d** 80 **p** 81. C Ashton-upon-Mersey St Mary Magd *Ches* 80-84; C Polegate *Chich* 84-92; V Baddesley Ensor w Grendon *Birm* 92-08; R Beckbury, Badger, Kemberton, Ryton, Stockton etc *Lich* from 08. *The Rectory, Beckbury, Shifnal TF11 9DG* Tel (01952) 750474 E-mail keithhodson@talk21.com

HODSON, Miss Margaret Christina. b 39. Linc Th Coll 88. **d** 90 **p** 94. Par Dn Old Trafford St Jo *Man* 90-94; C 94-95; P-in-c Calderbrook and Shore 95-01; rtd 01. *53 Lon Thelwal, Benllech, Tyn-y-Gongl LL74 8QH* Tel (01248) 852990

HODSON, Mrs Margot Rosemary. b 60. Bris Univ BSc82 PGCE83 Ox Brookes Univ BA06. All Nations Chr Coll 87 SAOMC 99. **d** 01 **p** 02. C Grove *Ox* 01-04; Chapl Jes Coll Ox 04-09; P-in-c Haddenham w Cuddington, Kingsey etc *Ox* from 09. *The Vicarage, 27A The Gables, Haddenham, Aylesbury HP17 8AD* Tel (01844) 291244
E-mail vicar@haddenhamstmarys.org

HODSON, Canon Raymond Leslie. b 42. St Chad's Coll Dur BSc64. **d** 66 **p** 67. C Adlington *Blackb* 66-68; C Cleveleys 68-72; V Ewood 72-77; V Nazeing *Chelmsf* 77-84; R Ampthill w Millbrook and Steppingley *St Alb* 84-95; Chapl Madrid *Eur* 95-04; Can Gib Cathl 02-04; rtd 04. *Mataro 1, 1 dcha, 28034 Madrid, Spain*

HODSON, Trevor. b 57. Sheff Univ BA78 Padgate Coll of Educn PGCE79 Leeds Univ MA06. NOC 04. **d** 06 **p** 07. NSM Broadheath *Ches* from 06. *40 Riversdale, Woolston, Warrington WA1 4PZ* Tel (01925) 811952
E-mail t.hodson@lathom.lancs.sch.uk

HODSON, William. b 42. Man Univ BA. Cranmer Hall Dur 81. **d** 82 **p** 83. C Ashton St Mich *Man* 82-86; V Tintwistle *Ches* 86-93; P-in-c Weston 93-99; rtd 99. *10 St Anne's Road, Horwich, Bolton BL6 7EJ* Tel (01204) 696172
E-mail bill.hodson@btopenworld.com

HOEY, David Paul. b 57. QUB BD79. CITC 79. **d** 81 **p** 82. C Belfast Whiterock *Conn* 81-83; C Portadown St Mark *Arm* 83-84; I Cleenish w Mullaghdun *Clogh* 84-90; I Magheracross 90-03; Dir of Ords 91-03; Can Clogh Cathl 95-03; Min Consultant for Ireland CPAS from 03. *44 Laragh, Ballycassidy, Enniskillen BT4 2JT* Tel (028) 6632 9655 Mobile 07712-873322
E-mail dphoey@btinternet.com *or* phoey@cpas.org.uk

HOEY, The Ven Raymond George. b 46. TCD BA70 MA. **d** 72 **p** 73. C Portadown St Mark *Arm* 72-78; I Camlough w Mullaglass from 78; Dom Chapl to Abp *Arm* from 86; Adn *Arm* from 92. *2 Maytown Road, Bessbrook, Newry BT35 7LY* Tel and fax (028) 3083 0301 E-mail archdeacon@armagh.anglican.org *or* rghoey@btinternet.com

HOEY, William Thomas. b 32. CITC 64. **d** 66 **p** 67. C Belfast St Mary *Conn* 66-68; C Lisburn Ch Ch 69-72; I Ballinderry 72-78; I Belfast St Simon w St Phil 78-02; rtd 02. *11 Carnshill Court, Belfast BT8 6TX* Tel (028) 9079 0595

HOFBAUER, Canon Andrea Martina. b 71. Johannes Gutenberg Univ Mainz Ox Univ MTh04. St Steph Ho Ox 00. **d** 02 **p** 03. C Teignmouth, Ideford w Luton, Ashcombe etc *Ex* 02-05; Chapl Ex Univ 05-09; Tutor SWMTC 05-09; PV Ex Cathl 06-09; Prec Wakef Cathl from 09. *4 Cathedral Close, Wakefield WF1 2DP* Tel (01924) 200191
E-mail andi.hofbauer@wakefield-cathedral.org.uk

HOFFMANN, Jonathan Mark. b 60. Cranmer Hall Dur 95. **d** 97 **p** 99. C Eaton *Nor* 97-98; C Horsell *Guildf* 98-02; TV Aston cum Aughton w Swallownest and Ulley *Sheff* 02-06; P-in-c Freshford, Limpley Stoke and Hinton Charterhouse *B & W* from 06. *The Rectory, Crowe Lane, Freshford, Bath BA2 7WB* Tel (01225) 723135

HOGAN, Edward James Martin. b 46. Trin Coll Bris. **d** 85 **p** 86. C St Austell *Truro* 85-88; V Gt Broughton and Broughton Moor

Carl 88-94; V St Stythians w Perranarworthal and Gwennap *Truro* from 94; RD Carnmarth N 03-08. *The Vicarage, Old Vicarage Close, Stithians, Truro TR3 7DZ* Tel (01209) 860123
E-mail vicar@stythian.org

HOGAN, Miss Jennie. b 75. Goldsmiths' Coll Lon BA99 Fitzw Coll Cam BA03. Westcott Ho Cam 01. **d** 04 **p** 05. C Westmr St Steph w St Jo *Lon* 04-07; C All Hallows by the Tower etc from 07; Chapl Chelsea Coll from 07. *159 Wapping High Street, London E1W 3NQ* Tel (020) 7481 0901 *or* 7488 4772 Fax 7488 3333 E-mail jenniehogan@mac.com
or jennie@allhallowsbythetower.org.uk

HOGAN, John James. b 24. St Edm Hall Ox BA51 MA56. Wells Th Coll 51. **d** 53 **p** 54. C Cannock *Lich* 53-55; C Drayton in Hales 55-58; V Woore 58-84; P-in-c Norton in Hales 82-84; V Woore and Norton in Hales 84-89; rtd 89; Perm to Offic *Lich* 89-00. *Wrekin Prospect, Audlem Road, Woore, Crewe CW3 9RJ* Tel (01630) 647677

HOGAN, William Riddell. b 22. Qu Coll Birm 48. **d** 51 **p** 52. C Brighouse *Wakef* 51-54; Singapore 55-58; V Greetland *Wakef* 59-73; V Greetland and W Vale 73-80; V Kellington w Whitley 80-87; rtd 89. *15 The Pastures, Carlton, Goole DN14 9QF* Tel (01405) 862233

HOGARTH, Alan Francis. b 58. Oak Hill Th Coll BA89. **d** 89 **p** 90. C Felixstowe SS Pet and Paul *St E* 89-93; R Beckington w Standerwick, Berkley, Rodden etc *B & W* 93-04; P-in-c Basildon w Aldworth and Ashampstead *Ox* 04-08; P-in-c Heapey and Withnell *Blackb* from 08. *34 Kittiwake Road, Heapey, Chorley PR6 9BA* Tel (01257) 231868
E-mail alan.hogarth@gmail._com

HOGARTH, Joseph. b 32. Edin Th Coll 65. **d** 67 **p** 67. C Walney Is *Carl* 67-71; V Whitehaven St Jas 71-76; V Millom H Trin w Thwaites 76-82; V Maryport 82-91; V Consett *Dur* 91-97; rtd 97; Perm to Offic *Roch* from 99. *56A Bexley Lane, Dartford DA1 4DD* Tel (01322) 526733

HOGARTH, Peter Robert. b 61. Bath Univ MSc97. Trin Coll Bris BA01. **d** 01 **p** 02. C Martock w Ash *B & W* 01-04; Asst Chapl Oslo w Bergen, Trondheim and Stavanger *Eur* from 04. *dragabergveien 11, 4085 Hundvåg, Stavanger, Norway* Tel (0047) 5155 5488 E-mail revpastorpete@yahoo.co.uk

HOGBEN, The Ven Peter Graham. b 25. Bps' Coll Cheshunt 60. **d** 61 **p** 62. C Hale *Guildf* 61-64; V Westborough 64-71; V Ewell 71-82; Hon Can Guildf Cathl 79-90; RD Epsom 80-82; Adn Dorking 82-90; rtd 90; Perm to Offic *Guildf* from 90. *3 School Road, Rowledge, Farnham GU10 4EJ* Tel (01252) 793533

HOGG, Mrs Ann Grant. b 46. St Andr Univ MA68 Hughes Hall Cam PGCE70. NOC 99. **d** 02 **p** 03. NSM Bromborough *Ches* 02-04; Perm to Offic *St Alb* 04-05; NSM Watford Ch Ch 05-06; NSM Aldenham, Radlett and Shenley from 06. *The Vicarage, Church Fields, Christchurch Crescent, Radlett WD7 8EE* Tel (01923) 856606 E-mail wijoho@aol.com

HOGG, Anthony. b 42. Univ of Wales (Lamp) BA63. Linc Th Coll 64 Chich Th Coll 78. **d** 78 **p** 79. NSM Ridgeway *Ox* 78-86; C 90-91; NSM W w E Hanney 86-88; Hd Master New Coll Sch Ox 88-89; P-in-c Hanney, Denchworth and E Challow *Ox* 91-92; V from 92. *The Vicarage, Winter Lane, West Hanney, Wantage OX12 0LF* Tel (01235) 868863 E-mail victory@ukgateway.net

HOGG, Matthew. b 79. **d** 08 **p** 09. C Brompton H Trin w Onslow Square St Paul *Lon* from 08. *Flat 3, 145 Saltram Crescent, London W9 3JT* Tel (020) 8968 4101
E-mail matt.hogg@htb.org.uk

HOGG, Neil Richard. b 46. BSc69. Ridley Hall Cam 82. **d** 84 **p** 85. C Bingham *S'well* 84-87; TV Bushbury *Lich* 87-00; V Worksop St Jo *S'well* from 00. *St John's Vicarage, 1B Shepherds Avenue, Worksop S81 0JD* Tel (01909) 489868 Mobile 07585-816697 E-mail shepherd1b@njhogg.fsnet.co.uk

HOGG, William John. b 49. New Coll Ox MA71 Lon Univ CertEd72 Crewe & Alsager Coll MSc88. Edin Th Coll 86. **d** 88 **p** 89. C Oxton *Ches* 88-93; R Bromborough 93-04; P-in-c Radlett *St Alb* 04-05; TR Aldenham, Radlett and Shenley from 05. *The Vicarage, Church Fields, Christchurch Crescent, Radlett WD7 8EE* Tel (01923) 856606 E-mail wijoho@aol.lcom

HOGG, William Ritson. b 47. Leeds Univ BSc69. Qu Coll Birm. **d** 72 **p** 73. C Bordesley St Oswald *Birm* 72-76; TV Seacroft *Ripon* 76-82; V Hunslet St Mary 82-88; V Catterick 88-97; rtd 07. *c/o Crockford, Church House, Great Smith Street, London SW1P 3AZ* E-mail bill.denise@yahoo.co.uk

HOGGARD, Mrs Jean Margaret. b 36. NW Ord Course 76. **dss** 79 **d** 87 **p** 94. Northowram *Wakef* 79-94; Par Dn 87-94; C Ovenden 94-00; rtd 00; Perm to Offic *Wakef* from 01. *13 Joseph Avenue, Northowram, Halifax HX3 7HJ* Tel (01422) 201475

HOGGER, Clive Duncan. b 70. Sheff Univ MA92. Ridley Hall Cam 06. **d** 08 **p** 09. C Fletchamstead *Cov* from 08. *5 The Oaklands, Coventry CV4 9SY* E-mail rev2b@tiscali.co.uk

HOGWOOD, Brian Roy. b 38. Bps' Coll Cheshunt. **d** 65 **p** 92. NSM Thetford *Nor* 91-93; Hon C from 93; Chapl Addenbrooke's NHS Trust 98-99. *31 Byron Walk, Thetford IP24 1JX* Tel (01842) 753915

HOLBEN, Bruce Frederick. b 45. STETS 99. **d** 02 **p** 03. NSM W Wittering and Birdham w Itchenor *Chich* from 02. *3 Elmstead*

Gardens, West Wittering, Chichester PO20 8NG Tel (01243) 514129 Mobile 07940-759060

HOLBROOK, Ms Barbara Mary. b 58. Nottm Trent Univ BA94 Nottm Univ MA04. EMMTC 02. **d** 04 **p** 05. C Chesterfield H Trin and Ch Ch *Derby* 04-08; P-in-c Kimberley *S'well* from 08; P-in-c Nuthall from 08. *The Rectory, 1 Eastwood Road, Kimberley, Nottingham NG16 2HX* Tel 0115-938 3565 Mobile 07766-732514

HOLBROOK, Colin Eric Basford. *See* BASFORD HOLBROOK, Colin Eric

HOLBROOK, Canon John Edward. b 62. St Pet Coll Ox BA83 MA87. Ridley Hall Cam 82. **d** 86 **p** 87. C Barnes St Mary *S'wark* 86-89; C Bletchley *Ox* 89-93; C N Bletchley CD 89-93; V Adderbury w Milton 93-02; RD Deddington 00-02; R Wimborne Minster *Sarum* from 02; P-in-c Witchampton, Stanbridge and Long Crichel etc from 02; P-in-c Horton, Chalbury, Hinton Martel and Holt St Jas from 06; RD Wimborne from 04; Chapl S and E Dorset Primary Care Trust from 02; Can and Preb Sarum Cathl from 06. *The Rectory, 17 King Street, Wimborne BH21 1DZ* Tel (01202) 882340
E-mail john.holbrook@ukonline.co.uk

HOLBROOKE-JONES, Canon Stanley Charles. b 27. Dur Univ BA58 MA77. Cranmer Hall Dur 58. **d** 60 **p** 61. C Gravesend St Jas *Roch* 60-63; C Streatham Immanuel w St Anselm *S'wark* 63-66; V W Bromwich H Trin *Lich* 66-79; V W Exe 79-88; R Poole *Sarum* 88-97; Miss to Seafarers from 88; Can and Preb Sarum Cathl 96-97; rtd 97; Perm to Offic *Sarum* from 97. *27 Clarendon Road, Broadstone BH18 9HT* Tel (01202) 460433

HOLCOMBE, Canon Graham William Arthur. b 50. Open Univ BA99. St Mich Coll Llan. **d** 80 **p** 81. C Neath w Llantwit 80-84; Asst Youth Chapl 81-84; PV Llan Cathl 84-86; V Pentyrch 86-00; V Pentyrch w Capel Llanilltterne 00-02; Can Llan Cathl from 02. *1 White House, Cathedral Green, Llandaff, Cardiff CF5 2EB* Tel (029) 2056 9521

HOLDAWAY, Mark Daniel James. b 78. Selw Coll Cam MA02. Oak Hill Th Coll BA07. **d** 07 **p** 08. C Bury St Edmunds St Mary *St E* from 07. *18 Vinery Road, Bury St Edmunds IP33 2JR*

HOLDAWAY, Simon Douglas. b 47. Lanc Univ BA73 Sheff Univ PhD81. NOC 78. **d** 81 **p** 82. NSM Gleadless *Sheff* from 81; Sen Lect Sheff Univ from 81. *Address temp unknown*

HOLDAWAY, Canon Stephen Douglas. b 45. Hull Univ BA67. Ridley Hall Cam 67. **d** 70 **p** 71. C Southampton Thornhill St Chris *Win* 70-73; C Tardebigge *Worc* 73-78; Ind Chapl 73-78; Ind Chapl *Linc* 78-93; Co-ord City Cen Group Min 81-93; TR Louth from 93; RD Louthesk from 95; Can and Preb Linc Cathl from 00. *The Rectory, 49 Westgate, Louth LN11 9YE* Tel (01507) 603213 *or* 610247 Fax 602991
E-mail stephen.holdaway@btinternet.com

HOLDEN, Canon Arthur Stuart James. b 23. ALCD51. **d** 51 **p** 52. C Barking St Marg *Chelmsf* 51-54; P-in-c Berechurch 54-55; V 55-61; V Earls Colne 61-82; P-in-c White Colne 66-67; V 68-82; V Earls Colne and White Colne 82-88; Hon Can Chelmsf Cathl 80-88; rtd 88; Perm to Offic *Chelmsf* from 88. *10 Wroxham Close, Colchester CO3 3RQ* Tel (01206) 560845

HOLDEN, Christopher Graham. b 78. Lanc Univ BA06. Westcott Ho Cam 07. **d** 09. C Carnforth *Blackb* from 09. *10 Croasdale Close, Carnforth LA5 9UN* Tel 07790-202429 (mobile) E-mail wilfridcgh@hotmail.com

HOLDEN, Geoffrey. b 26. FCII54. Oak Hill Th Coll 57. **d** 59 **p** 60. C Crookes St Thos *Sheff* 59-61; C Belper *Derby* 61-63; C Woking St Jo *Guildf* 63-66; R Bath St Mich w St Paul *B & W* 66-73; Chapl Bath Gp Hosps 73-91; rtd 91; Perm to Offic *B & W* from 91. *32 Crescent Gardens, Bath BA1 2NB* Tel (01225) 427933

HOLDEN, Geoffrey Ralph. b 25. Ripon Hall Ox 64. **d** 65 **p** 66. C Sparkhill St Jo *Birm* 65-68; C Walsall *Lich* 68-71; R Longton St Jas 71-75; rtd 90. *Aberscethin, Talybont LL43 2AR* Tel (01341) 247538

HOLDEN, Jack Crawford (Simon). b 30. Leeds Univ BA59. Coll of Resurr Mirfield 59. **d** 61 **p** 61. C Middlesbrough All SS *York* 61-64; Lic to Offic *Wakef* 65-69 and from 98; CR from 67; Asst Chapl Univ Coll *Lon* 69-74; rtd 98. *House of the Resurrection, Stocks Bank Road, Mirfield WF14 0BN* Tel (01924) 494318

HOLDEN, Canon John. b 33. MBE76. Sheff Univ MA02 ACMA62. Ridley Hall Cam 65 Selly Oak Coll 71. **d** 67 **p** 68. C Flixton St Jo CD *Man* 67-71; Uganda 71-75; V Aston SS Pet and Paul *Birm* 75-87; RD Aston 86-87; Hon Can Birm Cathl 86-87; R Ulverston St Mary w H Trin *Carl* 87-98; RD Furness 90-94; Hon Can Carl Cathl 91-94; rtd 98; Perm to Offic *Carl* from 98 and *Heref* from 99. *3 Alison Road, Church Stretton SY6 7AT* Tel (01694) 724167

HOLDEN, John Norman. b 35. Heythrop Coll Lon MA97. Oak Hill Th Coll 91. **d** 95 **p** 96. NSM Codicote *St Alb* 95-96; Perm to Offic *St Alb* from 96 and *Ely* from 00. *4 Chapel Row, Shay Lane, Upper Dean, Huntingdon PE28 0LU* Tel (01234) 708928

HOLDEN, John Worrall. b 44. K Coll Lon AKC67. **d** 70 **p** 71. C Derby St Bart 70-72; Lic to Offic 72-74; Hon C St Helier *S'wark* 74-77; Hon C St Marylebone All SS *Lon* 80-83; Hon C St Botolph Aldgate w H Trin Minories 84-95. *4 Foster Lane, London EC2V 6HH*

HOLDEN, Mark Noel. b 61. Collingwood Coll Dur BA82 Edin Univ CQSW85 Warwick Univ TCert93 Birm Univ MA95. Qu Coll Birm 93. **d** 95 **p** 96. C Brumby *Linc* 95-99; P-in-c Wragby 99-00; R Wragby Gp from 00. *The Vicarage, Church Street, Wragby, Lincoln LN8 5RA* Tel (01673) 857825
HOLDEN, Norman. *See* HOLDEN, John Norman
HOLDEN, Paul Edward. b 53. BSc75 CEng79 MIM MIBF. Trin Coll Bris 82. **d** 86 **p** 87. C Harpurhey Ch Ch *Man* 86-88; C Harpurhey St Steph 88-93; Sen Min Harpurhey LEP 88-93. *2 Baywood Street, Harpurhey, Manchester M9 5XJ* Tel 0161-205 2938
HOLDEN, Richard Gary. **d** 04 **p** 05. C Louth *Linc* 04-07; P-in-c Clee from 07; P-in-c Cleethorpes St Aid from 07. *Old Clee Vicarage, 202 Clee Road, Grimsby DN32 8NG* Tel (01472) 581570 E-mail revrichard.holden@btinternet.com
HOLDEN, Mrs Rita. b 45. SAOMC 98. **d** 01 **p** 03. OLM Burghfield *Ox* 01-02; NSM Droitwich Spa *Worc* from 02. *40 Nightingale Close, Droitwich WR9 7HB* Tel (01905) 772787 Mobile 07814-621389 E-mail rita@openv.clara.co.uk
HOLDEN, Simon. *See* HOLDEN, Jack Crawford
HOLDEN, Stuart. *See* HOLDEN, Canon Arthur Stuart James
HOLDER, Adèle Claire. *See* REES, Ms Adèle Claire
HOLDER, Canon John William. b 41. Chester Coll CertEd61 Open Univ BA73 Bath Univ MEd85. Trin Coll Bris MA94. **d** 87 **p** 88. C Brockworth *Glouc* 87-91; P-in-c Avening w Cherington 91-95; V Cinderford St Jo 95-05; P-in-c Lydbrook 99-03; P-in-c Coberley, Cowley, Colesbourne and Elkstone from 05; Hon Can Glouc Cathl from 03. *The Rectory, Cowley, Cheltenham GL53 9NJ* Tel (01242) 870183
E-mail canon.john@holder-net.co.uk
HOLDER, Kenneth William. b 29. Sarum Th Coll 60. **d** 61 **p** 62. C Crawley *Chich* 61-65; C-in-c Wick CD 65-73; V Hangleton 73-79; R Rotherfield 79-81; R Rotherfield w Mark Cross 81-83; Chapl Eastbourne Coll 83-84; C Farnborough *Roch* 85; TV Mildenhall *St E* 87-92; R Redgrave cum Botesdale w Rickinghall 92-99; rtd 99; Perm to Offic *Chich* from 01. *Flat 3, 13 Granville Road, Eastbourne BN20 7HE* Tel (01323) 410868
HOLDER, Rodney Dennis. b 50. Trin Coll Cam BA71 MA75 Ch Ch Ox MA75 DPhil78 FRAS75 CPhys91 MInstP91 CMath95 FIMA95. Wycliffe Hall Ox BA96. **d** 97 **p** 98. C Long Compton, Whichford and Barton-on-the-Heath *Cov* 97-01; C Wolford w Burmington 97-01; C Cherington w Stourton 97-01; C Barcheston 97-01; Perm to Offic 01-02; P-in-c The Claydons *Ox* 02-05; Course Dir Faraday Inst for Science and Relig from 06. *The Faraday Institute, St Edmund's College, Cambridge CB3 0BN* Tel (01223) 741224 or 364577
E-mail rodney.holder@virgin.net
HOLDING, Kenneth George Frank. b 27. Sarum & Wells Th Coll 75. **d** 77 **p** 78. C Bexley St Mary *Roch* 77-80; Min Joydens Wood St Barn CD 80-85; R Mereworth w W Peckham 85-92; rtd 92; Perm to Offic *York* 92-04; P-in-c Willerby w Ganton and Folkton from 04. *Willerby Vicarage, Wains Lane, Staxton, Scarborough YO12 4SF* Tel (01944) 710364
HOLDRIDGE, The Ven Bernard Lee. b 35. Lich Th Coll 64. **d** 67 **p** 68. C Swinton *Sheff* 67-71; V Doncaster St Jude 71-81; R Rawmarsh w Parkgate 81-88; RD Rotherham 86-88; V Worksop Priory *S'well* 88-94; Adn Doncaster *Sheff* 94-01; rtd 01; Perm to Offic *Sheff* 01-06 and *Guildf* from 06. *35 Denehyrst Court, York Road, Guildford GU1 4EA* Tel (01483) 570791
HOLDSTOCK, Adrian Charles. b 51. Peterho Cam BA MA75 Nottm Univ MA03 CEng MIMechE MCMI. EMMTC 00. **d** 03 **p** 04. NSM Bosworth and Sheepy Gp *Leic* from 03; NSM Nailstone and Carlton w Shackerstone from 07. *34 Herald Way, Burbage, Hinckley LE10 2NX* Tel (01455) 251066 Mobile 07792-452669 E-mail adriancholdstock@yahoo.co.uk
HOLDSWORTH, Ian Scott. b 52. Sheff Poly BA75. Oak Hill Th Coll BA81. **d** 81 **p** 82. C Denham *Ox* 81-84; P-in-c S Leigh 84-89; P-in-c Cogges 84-88; V 88-89; Perm to Offic *Pet* 95; NSM Brackley St Pet w St Jas 96-99; P-in-c Northampton St Mary 99-04; V from 04. *St Mary's Vicarage, Towcester Road, Northampton NN4 9EZ* Tel (01604) 761104 Mobile 07930-391511 E-mail ianholdworth@aol.com
HOLDSWORTH, The Ven John Ivor. b 49. Univ of Wales (Abth) BA70 Univ of Wales (Cardiff) BD73 MTh75. St Mich Coll Llan 70. **d** 73 **p** 74. C Newport St Paul *Mon* 73-77; CF (TAVR) 75-90; V Abercraf and Callwen *S & B* 77-86; Bp's Chapl for Th Educn 80-97; V Gorseinon 86-97; Hon Lect Th Univ of Wales (Swansea) 88-96; Prin and Warden St Mich Coll Llan 97-03; Lect Th Univ of Wales (Cardiff) 97-03; Adn St D from 03; V Steynton from 03. *The New Vicarage, Steynton, Milford Haven SA73 1AW* Tel (01646) 692867
E-mail archdeacon.stdavids@churchinwales.org.uk
HOLDSWORTH, The Very Revd Kelvin. b 66. Man Poly BSc89 St Andr Univ BD92 Edin Univ MTh96. TISEC 95. **d** 97 **p** 98. Prec St Ninian's Cathl Perth 97-00; R Bridge of Allan 00-06; Chapl Stirling Univ 00-06; Provost St Mary's Cathl from 06; R Glas St Mary from 06. *300 Great Western Road, Glasgow G4 9JB* Tel 0141-530 8643 E-mail kelvin@thurible.net *or* provost@thecathedral.org.uk

HOLDSWORTH, Michael Andrew. b 65. Univ Coll Dur BA88. Ripon Coll Cuddesdon BA92 MA96. **d** 93 **p** 94. C Cannock *Lich* 93-97; TV Sheff Manor 97-99; Tutor Ripon Coll Cuddesdon 97-99. *Address temp unknown*
HOLE, The Very Revd Derek Norman. b 33. De Montfort Univ Hon DLitt99 Leic Univ Hon LLD05. Linc Th Coll 57. **d** 60 **p** 61. C Knighton St Mary Magd *Leic* 60-62; S Africa 62-64; C Kenilworth St Nic *Cov* 64-67; R Burton Latimer *Pet* 67-73; V Leic St Jas 73-92; Hon Can Leic Cathl 83-92; RD Christianity S 83-92; Provost Leic 92-99; Chapl to The Queen 85-93; rtd 99; Perm to Offic *Leic* from 00. *25 Southernhay Close, Leicester LE2 3TW* Tel 0116-270 9988
E-mail dnhole@leicester.anglican.org
HOLE, Toby Kenton. b 72. Dur Univ BA94 MA95 Cam Univ BTh06. Ridley Hall Cam 03. **d** 06 **p** 07. C Islington St Mary *Lon* from 06. *14 Cross Street, London N1 2BG* Tel (020) 7354 3185 *or* 7226 3400 E-mail holes@freeuk.com
HOLFORD, Andrew Peter. b 62. Nottm Univ BSc84. Cranmer Hall Dur 87. **d** 90 **p** 91. C Waltham Cross *St Alb* 90-93; C Northampton St Benedict *Pet* 93-95; V Pet Ch Carpenter 95-04; TR Baldock w Bygrave and Weston *St Alb* from 04. *The Rectory, 9 Pond Lane, Baldock SG7 5AS* Tel (01462) 894398
E-mail andrewholford@ukonline.co.uk
HOLFORD, Canon John Alexander. b 40. Chich Th Coll 65. **d** 67 **p** 68. C Cottingley *Bradf* 67-71; C Baildon 71-73; P-in-c Bingley H Trin 73-74; V 74-86; V Woodhall 86-93; C Shelf 93-94; TV Shelf w Buttershaw St Aid 94-99; rtd 99; P-in-c Embsay w Eastby *Bradf* 99-04; Hon Can Bradf Cathl 03-04; Perm to Offic from 04. *3 Wheelwrights Court, Hellifield, Skipton BD23 4LX* Tel (01729) 851740 E-mail john.holford@bradford.anglican.org
HOLFORD, Margaret Sophia. b 39. SAOMC 95. **d** 98 **p** 99. NSM Stevenage St Andr and St Geo *St Alb* 98-03; NSM Ickleford w Holwell 03-05; NSM Holwell, Ickleford and Pirton from 05. *Icknield House, Westmill Lane, Ickleford, Hitchin SG5 3RN* Tel (01462) 432794 Fax 436618
HOLGATE, David Andrew. b 54. Cape Town Univ BA77 Port Eliz Univ BA89 Rhodes Univ MTh90 PhD94. All Nations Chr Coll 80. **d** 82 **p** 84. S Africa 82-93; C Uitenhage St Kath 82-84; Asst P Port Elizabeth St Hugh 84-87; P-in-c Somerset E All SS 88-89; St Paul's Coll Grahamstown 90-93; CME Officer *Chelmsf* 93-96; P-in-c Felsted 93-96; V Felsted and Lt Dunmow 96-97; Dean of Studies STETS from 97; Vice-Prin from 01. *19 The Close, Salisbury SP1 2EE* Tel (01722) 424820 Fax 424811
E-mail daholgate@stets.ac.uk
✠**HOLLAND, The Rt Revd Alfred Charles.** b 27. St Chad's Coll Dur BA50. **d** 52 **p** 53 **c** 70. C W Hackney St Barn *Lon* 52-54; Australia 55-78 and from 94; R Scarborough 55-70; Asst Bp Perth 70-77; Bp Newcastle 78-92; rtd 92; Chapl St Geo Coll Jerusalem 93-94. *21 Sullivan Crescent, Wanniassa ACT 2903, Australia* Tel (0061) (2) 6231 8368
E-mail acjmholland@bigpond.com
✠**HOLLAND, The Rt Revd Edward.** b 36. AKC64. **d** 65 **p** 66 **c** 86. C Dartford H Trin *Roch* 65-69; C Mill Hill Jo Keble Ch *Lon* 69-72; Prec Gib Cathl 72-74; Chapl Naples Ch Ch 74-79; Chapl Bromley Hosp 79-86; V Bromley St Mark *Roch* 79-86; Suff Bp Eur 86-95; Dean Brussels 86-95; Area Bp Colchester *Chelmsf* 95-01; rtd 01; Hon Asst Bp Lon from 02; Hon Asst Bp Eur from 02. *37 Parfrey Street, London W6 9EW* Tel (020) 8746 3636
E-mail ed.holland@btopenworld.com
HOLLAND, Geoffrey. *See* HOLLAND, William Geoffrey Bretton
HOLLAND, Mrs Gillaine. b 67. Kent Inst of Art & Design BA89. STETS 05. **d** 08 **p** 09. C Epsom St Martin *Guildf* 08-09; C Woking St Mary from 09. *11 Upper Edgeborough Road, Guildford GU1 2BJ* Tel 07969-067116 (mobile)
E-mail gillaineholland@sky.com
HOLLAND, Glyn. b 59. Hull Univ BA Bris Univ CertEd. Coll of Resurr Mirfield 83. **d** 85 **p** 86. C Brighouse St Martin *Wakef* 85-89; V Ferrybridge 89-96; Chapl Pontefract Gen Infirmary 89-96; V Middlesbrough All SS *York* from 96. *All Saints' Vicarage, 14 The Crescent, Middlesbrough TS5 6SQ* Tel (01642) 820304
HOLLAND, Jesse Marvin Sean. b 66. Westmr Coll Ox MTh03. Oak Hill Th Coll BA97. **d** 98 **p** 99. C Thundersley *Chelmsf* 98-02; P-in-c Tedburn St Mary, Whitestone, Oldridge etc *Ex* 02-06; V Buller New Zealand 06-08; P-in-c Lyneham w Bradenstoke *Sarum* from 08. *The Vicarage, The Green, Lyneham, Chippenham SN15 4PD* Tel (01249) 892475
E-mail revdjmsholland@aol.com
HOLLAND, John Stuart. b 52. Sarum & Wells Th Coll 77. **d** 80 **p** 81. C Wylde Green *Birm* 80-83; C Swanage and Studland *Sarum* 83-85; P-in-c Handley w Pentridge 85-88; TV Preston w Sutton Poyntz and Osmington w Poxwell 88-95; P-in-c Failsworth St Jo *Man* 95-01; V Ashton Ch Ch 01-07; P-in-c Carbis Bay w Lelant *Truro* 07; P-in-c Towednack from 08; P-in-c Zennor from 08. *The Vicarage, Porthrepta Road, Carbis Bay, St Ives TR26 2LD* Tel (01736) 796206 Mobile 07718-483817 E-mail vicar-cbl@fsmail.net
HOLLAND, Lesley Anne. *See* LEON, Mrs Lesley Anne

HOLLAND, Mrs Linda. b 48. Sarum & Wells Th Coll 91. **d** 93 **p** 94. Par Dn Queensbury All SS *Lon* 93-94; C 94-96; C Enfield St Jas 96-01; V Coney Hill *Glouc* from 01. *St Oswald's Vicarage, Coney Hill, Gloucester GL4 7LX* Tel (01452) 523618
E-mail revlynne@batzion.fsnet.co.uk

HOLLAND, Matthew Francis. b 52. Lon Univ BA73. Qu Coll Birm. **d** 79 **p** 80. C Ecclesall *Sheff* 79-83; TV Gleadless Valley 83-86; TR 86-88; V Sheff Gillcar St Silas 88-92; V Sheff St Silas Broomhall 92-98; V Southsea St Simon *Portsm* from 98. *St Simon's Vicarage, 6 Festing Road, Southsea PO4 0NG* Tel (023) 9273 3068

HOLLAND, Paul William. b 55. Coll of Resurr Mirfield 78. **d** 80 **p** 81. C Parkstone St Pet w Branksea and St Osmund *Sarum* 80-83; CR 85-93; Asst Chapl Musgrove Park Hosp 93; Asst Chapl St Helier Hosp Carshalton 93-96; C Croydon St Jo *S'wark* 96-04; TV Barnes from 04. *39 Elm Bank Gardens, London SW13 0NX* Tel (020) 8876 5230 E-mail pauholl@mac.com

HOLLAND, Peter Christie. b 36. St Andr Univ BSc60. Cranmer Hall Dur 60. **d** 62 **p** 63. C Darlington St Jo *Dur* 62-64; C Bishopwearmouth Ch Ch 64-69; V Tudhoe 69-77; V New Seaham 77-89; V Totternhoe, Stanbridge and Tilsworth *St Alb* 89-01; rtd 02; Perm to Offic *Dur* from 02. *Bracken Ridge, Woodland, Bishop Auckland DL13 5RH* Tel (01388) 718881
E-mail hollandpeter90@supanet.com

HOLLAND, Simon Geoffrey. b 63. MHCIMA83. Trin Coll Bris BA. **d** 91 **p** 92. C Reigate St Mary *S'wark* 91-95; Chapl Lee Abbey 95-99; C Guildf St Sav 99-07; P-in-c Bath Walcot *B & W* from 07. *The Rectory, 6 Rivers Street, Bath BA1 2PZ* Tel (01225) 334748 E-mail simonholland150@hotmail.com

HOLLAND, Simon Paul. b 56. Westcott Ho Cam 79. **d** 81 **p** 82. C Uckfield *Chich* 81-84; TV Lewes All SS, St Anne, St Mich and St Thos 84-88; TR 88-91; R Glas St Matt 91-95; P-in-c Glas *Chich* from 96. *The Rectory, 97 Barnham Road, Barnham, Bognor Regis PO22 0EQ* Tel (01243) 554077
E-mail simonholland578@btinternet.com

HOLLAND, Mrs Tessa Christine. b 59. Hull Univ BA81. STETS 00. **d** 03 **p** 04. NSM Storrington *Chich* 03-05; NSM Pulborough 05-07; Lic to Offic from 07. *Wild Fortune, Sandgate Lane, Storrington, Pulborough RH20 3HJ* Tel (01903) 740487
E-mail wildfortune@btinternet.com

HOLLAND, William Geoffrey Bretton. b 36. Magd Coll Cam BA59 MA63. Westcott Ho Cam 61. **d** 63 **p** 64. C Cannock *Lich* 63-66; C Paddington Ch Ch *Lon* 66-69; Chapl Magd Coll Cam 69-73; V Twyford *Win* 74-78; V Twyford and Owslebury and Morestead 78-84; Chapl Twyford Sch *Win* 84-90; rtd 01. *68A Warwick Way, London SW1V 1RZ* Tel (020) 7630 8334

HOLLANDS, Derek Gordon. b 45. Brasted Th Coll Chich Th Coll 72. **d** 74 **p** 75. C Banstead *Guildf* 74-77; C Cranleigh 77-79; C Haywards Heath St Wilfrid *Chich* 79-80; TV 80-82; Chapl Hillingdon Area HA 82-86; Chapl W Suffolk Hosp Bury St Edm 86-95; Pres Coll Health Care Chapls 92-94; Sen Chapl R Cornwall Hosps Trust 95-98; rtd 99. *Oaklands Lodge, Lawshall Road, Hawstead, Bury St Edmunds IP29 5NR* Tel (01284) 386196 E-mail derek.hollands@tesco.net

HOLLANDS, Percival Edwin Macaulay. b 36. Edin Th Coll 57. **d** 60 **p** 61. C Greenock *Glas* 60-64; C Aberdeen St Mary 64-65; P-in-c Aberdeen St Clem 65-68; R Cruden Bay 68-70; CF 70-82; C Ribbleton *Blackb* 82-83; TV 83-88; C Penwortham St Mary 88-92; V Farington 92-98; rtd 98; Perm to Offic *Nor* from 00. *30 Teasel Road, Attleborough NR17 1XX* Tel (01953) 457372

HOLLANDS, Ray Leonard. b 42. MRICS02 MASI MRSH MCIOB. S'wark Ord Course 68. **d** 71 **p** 72. NSM Hanworth All SS *Lon* 71-77, 85-91, 95-98 and 02-03; NSM Hanworth St Geo 77-85; NSM Marshwood Vale *Sarum* 81-91; NSM Upper Sunbury St Sav *Lon* 91-10; rtd 03. *Yew Tree Cottage, Marshwood, Bridport DT6 5QF* Tel (01297) 678566
E-mail rlh.ltd@virgin.net

HOLLETT, Catherine Elaine. *See* DAKIN, Mrs Catherine Elaine

HOLLEY, Paul Robert. b 65. St Jo Coll Dur 91. **d** 94 **p** 95. C Tonge w Alkrington *Man* 94-98; P-in-c Salford St Phil w St Steph 98-00; P-in-c Salford Sacred Trin 99-00; R Salford Sacred Trin and St Phil 00-03; P-in-c La Côte *Eur* from 03. *7 chemin du Couchant, 1260 Nyon, Switzerland* Tel (0041) (22) 364 0030 E-mail paul.holley@lineone.net

HOLLIDAY, Andrew. b 62. St Steph Ho Ox 89. **d** 92 **p** 93. C Marton *Blackb* 92-95; C Poulton-le-Fylde 95-97; V Leyland St Jas 97-04; AD Leyland 02-04; P-in-c Darwen St Pet w Hoddlesden from 04. *The Rectory, St Peter's Close, Darwen BB3 2EA* Tel (01254) 702411

HOLLIDAY, Arthur. b 22. St Jo Coll Dur 80. **d** 81 **p** 82. Hon C Allerton *Bradf* 81-84; Hon C Thornton St Jas 84-91; Perm to Offic 91-01. *Address temp unknown*

HOLLIDAY, Peter Leslie. b 48. FCA79 Birm Univ BCom70 MA92. Qu Coll Birm 81. **d** 83 **p** 84. C Burton *Lich* 83-87; P-in-c Longdon 87-93; PV and Subchanter Lich Cath 87-93; R Stratford-on-Avon w Bishopton *Cov* 93-00; Dir St Giles Hospice

Lich from 00; Chan's V Lich Cathl from 02. *St Giles Hospice, Fisherwick Road, Lichfield WS14 9LH* Tel (01543) 432031
E-mail plh@clara.net

HOLLIDAY, William. b 33. Qu Coll Cam BA56 MA60 McGill Univ Montreal BD58 LTh58. Montreal Dioc Th Coll 56 Linc Th Coll 58. **d** 58 **p** 59. C Stanningley St Thos *Ripon* 58-63; C Romaldkirk 63-64; India 64-77; V Thwaites Brow *Bradf* 77-86; RD S Craven 82-86; P-in-c Horton 86-98; P-in-c Bradf St Oswald Chapel Green 91-98; RD Bowling and Horton 95-98; rtd 98; Perm to Offic *Bradf* from 99. *61 Woodside Crescent, Bingley BD16 1RE* Tel (01274) 568413

HOLLIDAY, William John. b 49. Middleton St Geo Coll of Educn TCert72. CBDTI 05. **d** 07 **p** 08. NSM Kendal St Thos *Carl* from 07. *2 Michaelson Road, Kendal LA9 5JQ* Tel (01539) 730701 E-mail billholliday@googlemail.com

HOLLIMAN, The Ven John James. b 44. St D Coll Lamp BA66. **d** 67 **p** 68. C Tideswell *Derby* 67-71; CF 71-99; QHC 94-99; Dep Chapl Gen 96-99; Adn for the Army 96-99; V Funtington and Sennicotts *Chich* 99-09; R W Stoke 99-09; RD Westbourne 04-09; rtd 09. *3 Littledown, Shaftesbury SP7 9HD* Tel (01747) 853637

HOLLIN, Ian. b 40. Open Univ BA76 DCC91. Sarum Th Coll 67. **d** 70 **p** 71. C Lancaster Ch Ch *Blackb* 70-72; C S Shore H Trin 72-75; C Marton Moss 72-75; V Morecambe St Lawr 75-78; V Blackpool St Mary 78-83; PV and Succ Ex Cathl 83-87; Counsellor Coun for Chr Care and Tr 87-91; Admin Boniface Cen Ex 91-93; TV Maltby *Sheff* 93-96; R Handsworth 96-08; rtd 08; Perm to Offic *Blackb* from 08. *30 Sumpter Croft, Penwortham, Preston PR1 9UJ* Tel (01772) 749806

HOLLINGDALE, Derek Leslie. b 32. Ex & Truro NSM Scheme. **d** 83 **p** 84. NSM Tuckingmill *Truro* 83-85; NSM Illogan 85-92; NSM Treslothan 92-95; NSM Mithian w Mount Hawke 95-98; Perm to Offic from 05. *53 Tregrea, Beacon, Camborne TR14 7ST* Tel (01209) 612938

HOLLINGHURST, Canon Anne Elizabeth. b 64. Trin Coll Bris BA96. **d** 96 **p** 97. C Nottingham St Sav *S'well* 96-99; Chapl Derby Univ and Derby Cathl 99-05; Bp's Dom Chapl *Man* from 05; Can Res Man Cathl from 05. *Bishopscourt, Bury New Road, Salford M7 4LE* Tel 0161-792 2096 *or* 788 8461 Fax 792 6826 E-mail chaplain@bishopscourt.manchester.anglican.org

HOLLINGHURST, Preb Stephen. b 59. St Jo Coll Nottm 81. **d** 83 **p** 84. C Hyde St Geo *Ches* 83-86; C Cropwell Bishop w Colston Bassett, Granby etc *S'well* 86-90; R Pembridge w Moor Court, Shobdon, Staunton etc *Heref* 90-02; R Presteigne w Discoed, Kinsham, Lingen and Knill from 02; RD Kington and Weobley 95-02 and from 07; Preb Heref Cathl from 08. *The Rectory, St David's Street, Presteigne LD8 2BP* Tel (01544) 267777 E-mail steve.hollinghurst@lineone.net

HOLLINGHURST, Stephen Patrick. b 63. Hull Univ BA84. Trin Coll Bris BA93 MA93. **d** 96 **p** 97. C Nottingham St Sav *S'well* 96-99; Chapl Nottm Trent Univ 99-03; Researcher CA from 03; Perm to Offic *Derby* 00-04; Chapl Derby Cathl 04-05. *197A Lancaster Road, Salford M6 8NB* Tel 0161-788 8461

HOLLINGS, Ms Daphne. b 46. WMMTC 02. **d** 05 **p** 06. NSM Adbaston, High Offley, Knightley, Norbury etc *Lich* from 05. *247 Stone Road, Stafford ST16 1LA* Tel (01785) 211329 E-mail daphne.hollings@tiscali.co.uk

HOLLINGS, Miss Patricia Mary. b 39. CertEd59. S'wark Ord Course 84. **d** 87. Par Dn Wyke *Bradf* 87-94; C 94-96; rtd 96; Perm to Offic *Bradf* from 96. *1 Greenacre Way, Wyke, Bradford BD12 9DJ* Tel (01274) 677439

HOLLINGS, Robert George. b 48. St Jo Coll Nottm. **d** 94 **p** 95. C Cotmanhay *Derby* 94-97; TV Godrevy *Truro* 97-02; V Newhall *Derby* from 02. *St John's Vicarage, Church Street, Newhall, Swadlincote DE11 0HY* Tel (01283) 214685
E-mail bobandjacqui@btinternet.com

HOLLINGSHURST, Christopher Paul. b 63. St Chad's Coll Dur BA85 Westmr Coll Ox PGCE86 Anglia Poly Univ MA04. Ridley Hall Cam 96. **d** 99 **p** 00. C Bourn and Kingston w Caxton and Longstowe *Ely* 99-00; C Papworth 00-03; V Hook *S'wark* from 03. *The Vicarage, 278 Hook Road, Chessington KT9 1PF* Tel (020) 8397 3521
E-mail chris.hollingshurst1@btopenworld.com

HOLLINGSHURST, Robert Peter. b 38. Ridley Hall Cam 64. **d** 67 **p** 68. C Roxeth Ch Ch *Lon* 67-70; C Attenborough w Chilwell *S'well* 70-73; C Ramsgate St Luke *Cant* 74-75; Chapl to the Deaf 78-80; TV Louth *Linc* 80-84; Chapl to the Deaf *Sarum* 84-87; P-in-c Odstock w Nunton and Bodenham 84-96; P-in-c Britford and Charlton All Saints 89-96; R Gt and Lt Gaddesden *St Alb* 96-04; rtd 04; Perm to Offic *Chich* from 04. *Tudor Croft, 3 Tudor Close, Seaford BN25 2LU* Tel (01323) 892186
E-mail rpholl38@aol.com

HOLLINGSWORTH, Geoffrey. b 53. MCIPD85 Leeds Poly 74. NOC 86. **d** 86 **p** 87. C Thorne *Sheff* 86-89; V Rawcliffe 89-96; V Airmyn, Hook and Rawcliffe from 96. *The Vicarage, 12 Church Lane, Hook, Goole DN14 5PN* Tel (01405) 763654

HOLLINGSWORTH, James William. b 69. Southn Univ BA91 SS Coll Cam BA96. Aston Tr Scheme 92 Ridley Hall Cam 94. **d** 97 **p** 98. C Mildenhall *St E* 97-01; R Barcombe *Chich* from 01.

The Rectory, 1 The Grange, Barcombe, Lewes BN8 5AT Tel (01273) 400260 E-mail james@barcombe.net

HOLLINGSWORTH, Miss Paula Marion. b 62. Van Mildert Coll Dur BSc83 Univ of Wales (Lamp) MA08. Trin Coll Bris BA91. d 91 p 94. C Keynsham *B & W* 91-95; C Balsall Heath St Paul *Birm* 95-98; Tutor Crowther Hall CMS Tr Coll Selly Oak 95-01; P-in-c Houghton-on-the-Hill, Keyham and Hungarton *Leic* from 01; Bp's Adv for CME 01-04. *The Rectory, 16 Main Street, Houghton-on-the-Hill, Leicester LE7 9GD* Tel 0116-241 2226 E-mail pmhollingsworth@btinternet.com

HOLLINGTON, David Mark. b 61. MCIEH83. Trin Coll Bris BA94. d 94. C Wednesbury St Paul Wood Green *Lich* 94-95; C Cannock 95-96. *Address temp unknown*

HOLLINRAKE, Jean Margaret. *See* HARRISON, Mrs Jean Margaret

HOLLINS, Mrs Beverley Jayne. b 68. Univ of Wales (Abth) BLib90. SAOMC 00. d 03 p 04. C Milton Keynes *Ox* 03-06; Lic to Offic 06-07; Newport Deanery Development Facilitator from 07. *3 Castle Meadow Close, Newport Pagnell MK16 9EJ* Tel (01908) 614943 E-mail newportddf@talktalk.net

HOLLINS, John Edgar. b 35. St Jo Coll Cam BA58 MA62. Oak Hill Th Coll 58. d 60 p 61. C Whalley Range St Edm *Man* 60-63; C Highbury Ch Ch *Lon* 63-66; C St Alb St Paul *St Alb* 66-71; Hon C Halliwell St Paul *Man* 71-72; C Ravenhill St Jo 72-73; Perm to Offic *Birm* 79-81; V Millbrook *Ches* 81-89; rtd 89; Perm to Offic *Truro* from 89. *1 Russell House, Station Road, Liskeard PL14 4BS* Tel (01579) 349697

HOLLINS (formerly SHIPP), Patricia Susan. b 54. Univ of Wales BA76. St Paul's Coll Grahamstown 77 Linc Th Coll 81. d 83 p 94. C Cyncoed *Mon* 83-87; Par Dn Lawrence Weston *Bris* 89-91; Par Dn Henbury 91-94; V Longwell Green 94-99; Hon Can Bris Cathl 97-99; Chapl Mt Vernon and Watford Hosps NHS Trust 99-00; Sen Co-ord Chapl W Herts Hosps NHS Trust 00-04; Lead Chapl (E) *Caring for the Spirit* NHS Project 04-09; P-in-c Boxley w Detling *Cant* from 09. *The Vicarage, The Street, Boxley, Maidstone ME14 3DX* Tel (01622) 758606 E-mail s.hollins540@btinternet.com

HOLLIS, Anthony Wolcott Linsley. b 40. McGill Univ Montreal BA61 Long Is Univ MA76. Gen Th Sem NY MDiv64. d 64 p 65. USA 64-92 and from 02; V Lonaconing St Pet 66-67; Chapl US Army 67-79; R Sherwood Ch Cockeysville 79-92; R St George St Pet Bermuda 92-02; rtd 02. *712 Murdock Road, Baltimore MD 21212, USA*

HOLLIS, The Ven Arnold Thaddeus. b 33. JP87. Stockton State Coll New Jersey BA74 NY Th Sem MDiv74 STM76 DMin78. Codrington Coll Barbados 56. d 59 p 60. C Wakef St Jo 60-62; Br Guiana 62-64; P-in-c Horbury Bridge *Wakef* 64-66; C Loughton St Jo *Chelmsf* 66-69; USA 69-77; Bermuda from 77; Hon Chapl RN from 77; Chapl HM Pris from 77; Chapl Miss to Seafarers from 90; Hon Can Bermuda Cathl from 87; Adn Bermuda 96-03; rtd 03. *3 Middle Road, Sandys 5B 0Z, Bermuda* Tel (001441) 234 0834 *or* 234 2025 Fax 234 2723 E-mail athol@logic.bm

HOLLIS, Christopher Barnsley. b 28. Clare Coll Cam BA52 MA59. Wells Th Coll 60. d 62 p 63. C Baildon *Bradf* 62-64; V Esholt 64-66; V Heaton St Barn 66-85; RD Airedale 73-82; Hon Can Bradf Cathl 77-85; Chapl HM YOI Medomsley 85-90; V Medomsley *Dur* 85-90; P-in-c Denholme Gate *Bradf* 90-95; rtd 95; Perm to Offic *Bradf* from 95. *52 Wilmer Drive, Bradford BD9 4AS* Tel (01274) 546722

HOLLIS, Derek. b 60. Loughb Univ BA82. Cranmer Hall Dur 83. d 86 p 87. C Evington *Leic* 86-89; C Arnold *S'well* 89-93; V Beckingham w Walkeringham 93-03; P-in-c Gringley-on-the-Hill 95-03; V Beckingham w Walkeringham and Gringley 03-05; Hon Chapl Miss to Seafarers 03-04; Bp's Adv on Rural Affairs *S'well* from 04; P-in-c Elston w Elston Chapelry from 05; P-in-c E Stoke w Syerston from 05; P-in-c Shelton from 05; P-in-c Sibthorpe from 05; P-in-c Staunton w Flawborough from 05; P-in-c Kilvington from 05. *The Rectory, Top Street, Elston, Newark NG23 5NP* Tel (01636) 525383 E-mail rural.adviser@southwell.anglican.org

HOLLIS, Douglas John. b 32. S Dios Minl Tr Scheme. d 84 p 85. NSM Haywards Heath St Wilfrid *Chich* 84-98; Perm to Offic from 98. *Windrush, 1A High Point, Haywards Heath RH16 3RU* Tel (01444) 453688 E-mail douglas@cornerhouse.fslife.co.uk

HOLLIS, Mrs Lorna Mary. b 60. Cranmer Hall Dur 05. d 06 p 07. NSM Scarborough St Jas w H Trin *York* from 06; Asst Chapl Scarborough and NE Yorks Healthcare NHS Trust from 06. *30 Hartford Court, Filey Road, Scarborough YO11 2TP* Tel (01723) 351395 E-mail gmholl@supanet.com

HOLLIS, Rebecca Catherine. *See* MATHEW, Rebecca Catherine

HOLLIS, Timothy Knowles. b 28. RN Coll Dartmouth 45. St Steph Ho Ox 54. d 58 p 59. C Oatlands *Guildf* 58-60; C Crawley *Chich* 60-63; C Sotterley w Willingham *St E* 63-69; R Sotterley, Willingham, Shadingfield, Ellough etc 69-76; Gen Sec L'Arche UK 77-93; rtd 93; Perm to Offic *Chich* 93-02 and *Glouc* from 03. *9 Abbots Court Drive, Twyning, Tewkesbury GL20 6JJ* Tel (01684) 274903

HOLLIS, Mrs Valerie Elizabeth. b 40. Maria Grey Coll Lon CertEd61. St Alb Minl Tr Scheme 89. d 92 p 94. NSM Kempston Transfiguration *St Alb* 92-06; NSM Officer Bedford Adnry from 06. *33 Silverdale Street, Kempston, Bedford MK42 8BE* Tel (01234) 853397 E-mail nsmobeds@stalbans.anglican.org

HOLLOWAY, Canon David Dennis. b 43. Lich Th Coll 65. d 68 p 69. C Cricklade w Latton *Bris* 68-71; C Bris St Agnes and St Simon w St Werburgh 71-74; V Bitton 74-78; TV E Bris 78-80; P-in-c Tormarton w W Littleton 80-83; Dioc Ecum Officer 83-93; Hon C Bris St Mich 89-93; V Horfield St Greg 93-00; RD Horfield 97-99; Chapl St Monica Home Westbury-on-Trym 00-07; Hon Can Bris Cathl 92-07; rtd 07. *76 Marsworth Road, Pitstone, Leighton Buzzard LU7 9AS* Tel (01296) 662765 Mobile 07974-648556

HOLLOWAY, David Ronald James. b 39. Univ Coll Ox BA62 MA66. Ridley Hall Cam 65. d 67 p 68. C Leeds St Geo *Ripon* 67-71; Tutor Wycliffe Hall Ox 71-72; V Jesmond Clayton Memorial *Newc* from 73. *The Vicarage, 7 Otterburn Terrace, Jesmond, Newcastle upon Tyne NE2 3AP* Tel 0191-281 2001 *or* 281 2139

HOLLOWAY, Graham Edward. b 45. Chich Th Coll 69. d 72 p 73. C W Drayton *Lon* 72-75; P-in-c Hawton *S'well* 75-80; V Ladybrook 80-85; P-in-c Babworth 85-87; R Babworth w Sutton-cum-Lound 87-97; RD Retford 88-93; C Mansfield Woodhouse 97-04; P-in-c Mansfield St Aug from 04; P-in-c Pleasley Hill from 04. *St Augustine's Vicarage, 46 Abbott Road, Mansfield NG19 6DD* Tel (01623) 621247 E-mail padreg@btinternet.com

HOLLOWAY, Keith Graham. b 45. Linc Coll Ox BA67. Cranmer Hall Dur. d 73 p 74. C Gt Ilford St Andr *Chelmsf* 73-78; Hon C Squirrels Heath 78-80; Min Chelmer Village CD 80-87; V E Springfield 87-89; P-in-c Gt Dunmow 89-96; R Gt Dunmow and Barnston 96-02; R Upper Colne from 02. *The Rectory, Church Road, Great Yeldham, Halstead CO9 4PT* Tel and fax (01787) 236055 E-mail kanddway@aol.com

HOLLOWAY, Michael Sinclair. b 50. UEA BSc74 Southn Univ PGCE75. STETS 99. d 02 p 03. NSM Catherington and Clanfield *Portsm* 02-07; C Bishop's Cleeve *Glouc* 07-08; TV Bishop's Cleeve and Woolstone w Gotherington etc from 08. *The Rectory, 67 Malleson Road, Gotherington, Cheltenham GL52 9EX* Tel (01242) 675559 E-mail revmike.holloway@btinternet.com

✠**HOLLOWAY, The Rt Revd Prof Richard Frederick.** b 33. Lon Univ BD63 NY Th Sem STM68 Strathclyde Univ DUniv94 Aber Univ Hon DD95 Napier Univ Edin DLitt00 Glas Univ DD01 FRSE95. Edin Th Coll 58. d 59 p 60 c 86. C Glas St Ninian 59-63; P-in-c Glas St Marg 63-68; R Edin Old St Paul 68-80; R Boston The Advent MA USA 80-84; V Ox St Mary Magd 84-86; Bp Edin 86-00; Primus 92-00; rtd 00; Gresham Prof of Div 97-01. *6 Blantyre Terrace, Edinburgh EH10 5AE* Tel 0131-446 0696 Mobile 07710-254500 E-mail holloway.doc@googlemail.com

HOLLOWAY, Roger Graham. b 33. OBE97. Selw Coll Cam BA58 MA61. S'wark Ord Course 75. d 78 p 80. Hong Kong 78-80 and 85-88; Japan 80-84; PV Westmr Abbey from 88; Nat Dir ICF 91-96; Lic to Offic *Lon* from 94; Preacher Gray's Inn from 97; Lic Preacher *Lon* from 97. *Flat 6, 2 Porchester Gardens, London W2 6JL* Tel (020) 7402 4937 Fax 7402 4683

HOLLOWAY, Simon Anthony. b 50. Sussex Univ BSc72. Trin Coll Bris 76. d 79 p 81. C Bushbury *Lich* 79-81; C Castle Church 81-84; P-in-c Sparkbrook Ch Ch *Birm* 84-91; V 91-02; AD Bordesley 92-02; TV Horley *S'wark* from 02. *St Wilfrid's Vicarage, Horley Row, Horley RH6 8DF* Tel (01293) 771869 Mobile 07986-274393 E-mail holloway.horley@virgin.net

HOLLOWOOD, Christopher George. b 54. K Alfred's Coll Win BEd76 Open Univ MA97. Ripon Coll Cuddesdon 83. d 86 p 87. C Tupsley *Heref* 86-89; R Much Birch w Lt Birch, Much Dewchurch etc 89-92; Hd RS Haywood High Sch Heref 92-97; Sen Teacher St Aug Upper Sch Ox 97-00; Dep Hd N Bromsgrove High Sch 00-02; Headmaster Bp Llan Ch in Wales High Sch Cardiff from 02. *170 Kings Road, Cardiff CF11 9DG* Tel (029) 2056 2485 E-mail c.hollowood@ntlworld.com

HOLLOWOOD, Graham. b 56. Anglia Ruskin Univ MA07. St Steph Ho Ox 97. d 99 p 00. C Newport St Julian *Mon* 99-02; V Newport All SS 02-08; V Glodwick *Man* from 08. *St Mark's Vicarage, 1 Skipton Street, Oldham OL8 2JF* Tel and fax 0161-624 4964 Mobile 07748-106718 E-mail graham.hollowood@virgin.net

HOLLYWELL, Julian Francis. b 70. Liv Univ BSc91 Leeds Univ MA05. NOC 03. d 05 p 06. C W Didsbury and Withington St Chris *Man* 05-08; V Spondon *Derby* from 08. *St Werburgh's Vicarage, Gascoigne Drive, Spondon, Derby DE21 7GL* Tel (01332) 673573 Mobile 07963-420564

HOLMAN, Francis Noel. b 37. Sarum Th Coll 62. d 65 p 66. C Weston Favell *Pet* 65-68; C Eckington *Derby* 68-71; Asst Chapl St Thos Hosp Lon 72-77; Chapl Hope Hosp Salford 77-02; Chapl Salford R Hosp 77-93; Chapl Ladywell Hosp 77-99; Chapl Man and Salford Skin Hosp 88-94; rtd 02; Perm to Offic

Man from 03. *90 Rocky Lane, Eccles, Manchester M30 9LY* Tel 0161-707 1180

HOLMAN, Geoffrey Gladstone. b 32. AKC56. **d** 57 **p** 58. C Eltham St Barn *S'wark* 57-60; CF 60-73; Dep Asst Chapl Gen 73-80; Asst Chapl Gen 80-84; QHC 82-84; V Wetwang and Garton-on-the-Wolds w Kirkburn *York* 84-92; RD Harthill 87-92; rtd 92; P-in-c Askham Bryan *York* 93-01; Perm to Offic from 01. *3 Westholme Drive, York YO30 5TH* Tel (01904) 624419 E-mail samegus@btopenworld.com.uk

HOLMDEN, Miss Maria Irene. b 50. Trent Poly TCert72 BEd73. Oak Hill Th Coll 90. **d** 92 **p** 94. Par Dn Stratford St Jo and Ch Ch w Forest Gate St Jas *Chelmsf* 92-94; C 94-96; P-in-c Leyton All SS 96-01; V from 01. *All Saints' Vicarage, 47 Melbourne Road, London E10 7HF* Tel (020) 8558 8139 E-mail mholmden@tiscali.co.uk

HOLME, Thomas Edmund. b 49. Selw Coll Cam BA71 MA75. Coll of Resurr Mirfield 71. **d** 73 **p** 74. C Wyther *Ripon* 73-76; C Wimbledon *S'wark* 76-78; TV 78-79; Hermondsey St Anne 79-81; V Stamford Baron *Pet* 83-89; P-in-c Tinwell 83-89; Hon Min Can Pet Cathl 84-89; Prec Worc Cathl 89-95; P-in-c Penshurst and Fordcombe *Roch* 95-05; R from 05. *The Rectory, High Street, Penshurst, Tonbridge TN11 8BN* Tel (01892) 870316

HOLMES, Alan Stewart. b 57. St Andr Univ BSc80 MInstPkg88. Ox NSM Course 85. **d** 88 **p** 89. NSM Shinfield *Ox* 88-95; NSM Beech Hill, Grazeley and Spencers Wood 95-98. *Address temp unknown*

HOLMES, Andrew Keith. b 69. Univ of Wales BEng93. St Mich Coll Llan BTh96. **d** 96 **p** 97. C Clydach *S & B* 96-98; C Swansea St Thos and Kilvey 98-00; P-in-c New Radnor and Llanfihangel Nantmelan etc 00-03; V Penrhiwceiber, Matthewstown and Ynysboeth *Llan* from 03. *The Vicarage, Penrhiwceiber, Mountain Ash CF45 3YF* Tel (01443) 473716 E-mail frandrew@penrhiwceiber.plus.com

HOLMES (née PLATT), Mrs Anne Cecilia. b 46. Birm Univ BA67 Ox Univ DipEd68 MInstGA96. SAOMC 99. **d** 02 **p** 03. NSM Marston w Elsfield *Ox* from 02; Chapl Headington Sch 02-04; Asst Chapl Oxon & Bucks Mental Health Partnership NHS Trust 04-09. *59 Oxford Road, Old Marston, Oxford OX3 0PH* Tel (01865) 794916 Mobile 07831-254727 E-mail anne@acholmes.demon.co.uk

HOLMES, Anthony David Robert. b 38. Oak Hill Th Coll 75. **d** 77 **p** 78. C Iver *Ox* 77-81 and 00-05; V Bucklebury w Marlston 81-00; rtd 05. *16 Lawrence Close, Aylesbury HP20 1DY* Tel (01296) 398945

HOLMES, Brian. b 41. NEOC 92. **d** 95 **p** 96. NSM Darlington St Matt and St Luke *Dur* 95-98; V 98-08; rtd 08. *2 Christchurch Close, Darlington DL1 2YL* Tel (01325) 482255 E-mail revbholmes@tiscali.co.uk

HOLMES (née KENYON), Caroline Elizabeth. b 40. SRN62. NOC 04. **d** 05 **p** 06. NSM Hale and Ashley *Ches* from 05. *1 Broomfield House, 134 Hale Road, Hale, Altrincham WA15 9HJ* Tel 0161-233 0761 E-mail caroline.holmes@btinternet.com

HOLMES, Clive Horace. b 31. Ox NSM Course. **d** 83 **p** 84. NSM Cumnor *Ox* 83-98; Perm to Offic from 98. *108 New Road, East Hagbourne, Didcot OX11 9JZ* Tel (01235) 811996

HOLMES, Craig Walter. b 72. Southn Univ BSc95 R Holloway & Bedf New Coll Lon PhD01 Fitzw Coll Cam BA03 MA07 CCC Cam MPhil04. Ridley Hall Cam 01. **d** 07 **p** 08. C Egham *Guildf* from 07. *33 Grange Road, Egham TW20 9QP* Tel (01784) 479695

HOLMES, David Roy. b 34. FCIPD75. Ox NSM Course 81. **d** 84 **p** 85. NSM Ox SS Phil and Jas w St Marg 84-85; NSM Ox St Giles and SS Phil and Jas w St Marg 85-99; Lic to Offic 99-00; Perm to Offic *St Alb* 00-06. *Address temp unknown*

HOLMES, Frank. b 22. NW Ord Course 75. **d** 78 **p** 79. NSM Hyde St Geo *Ches* 78-81; C Poynton 81-87; rtd 87; Perm to Offic *Ches* from 87. *277 Stockport Road, Marple, Stockport SK6 6ES* Tel 0161-449 9289

HOLMES, Geoffrey. *See* HOLMES, Robert John Geoffrey

HOLMES, Geoffrey Robert. b 67. Nottm Univ BSc89. Ridley Hall Cam BA92. **d** 93 **p** 94. C Clifton St Jas *Sheff* 93-98; V Worsbrough St Thos and St Jas 98-05. *16 Vernon Road, Worsbrough, Barnsley S70 5BD* E-mail geoffrey.r.holmes@tesco.net

HOLMES, Grant Wenlock. b 54. St Steph Ho Ox BA78 MA83. **d** 79 **p** 80. C Bendinck *S'wark* 79-82; C-in-c S Kenton Annunciation CD *Lon* 82-86; Tutor Chich Th Coll 86-87; Bp's Dom Chapl *Chich* 86-88; V Mayfield 88-99; P-in-c Mark Cross 97-99; Asst Chapl Lewisham Hosp NHS Trust 99-01; Lead Chapl Kingston Hosp NHS Trust Surrey from 01; Hon C Barnes *S'wark* 01-06. *Kingston Hospitals NHS Trust, Galsworthy Road, Kingston upon Thames KT2 7QB* Tel (020) 8546 7711 ext 2292 E-mail grant.holmes@kingstonhospital.nhs.uk

HOLMES, Jane Margaret. b 52. Ridley Hall Cam 05. **d** 07 **p** 08. C Stamford Ch w Ch *Linc* from 07. *17 Turnpole Close, Stamford PE9 1DT*

HOLMES, Mrs Janet Ellen. b 61. Wolv Univ BSc95 RCN MSc99 RGN83. Qu Coll Birm MA09. **d** 09. C Hadley and Wellington

Ch Ch *Lich* from 09. *Sutton Bank Farm, Sutton, Newport TF10 8DD* Tel (01952) 813658 E-mail janeteholmes@btinternet.com

HOLMES, Canon John Robin. b 42. Leeds Univ BA64. Linc Th Coll 64. **d** 66 **p** 67. C Wyther *Ripon* 66-69; C Adel 69-73; V Beeston Hill St Luke 73-76; V Holbeck 76-86; RD Armley 82-86; V Manston 86-93; Hon Can Ripon Cathl 89-98; Dioc Missr 93-98; Can Missr *Wakef* 98-07; rtd 07. *31 Detroit Avenue, Leeds LS15 8NU* Tel 07712-044364 (mobile) E-mail john@kingfisher5.force9.co.uk

HOLMES, Jonathan Michael. b 49. Qu Coll Cam BA70 MA74 VetMB73 PhD78 MRCVS73. Ridley Hall Cam 87. **d** 88 **p** 89. Chapl Qu Coll Cam from 88; Dean of Chpl from 94. *Queens' College, Cambridge CB3 9ET* Tel (01223) 335545 Fax 335522 E-mail jmh38@cam.ac.uk

HOLMES, Nigel Peter. b 48. Nottm Univ BTh72 Lanc Univ CertEd72 Lon Univ BD76 Sheff Univ MEd84. Kelham Th Coll. **d** 72 **p** 73. C Barrow St Matt *Carl* 72-75; C Derby St Bart 75-78; P-in-c Gt Barlow 78-84; V Carl St Herbert w St Steph 84-91; V Keswick St Jo 91-94; V Mexborough *Sheff* 94-97; P-in-c Nether Hoyland St Pet 97-98; P-in-c Nether Hoyland St Andr 97-98; V Hoyland 98-07; AD Tankersley 04-07; V Monk Bretton *Wakef* 07-09; rtd 09. *172 Wath Road, Elsecar, Barnsley S74 8JG* Tel (01226) 745993 E-mail paxlives@btinternet.com

HOLMES, Mrs Patricia Ann. b 52. Bris Univ BA89 MA90. NOC 96. **d** 97 **p** 98. C Almondbury w Farnley Tyas *Wakef* 97-00; V Northowram from 00. *The Vicarage, Church Walk, Northowram, Halifax HX3 7HF* Tel (01422) 202551

HOLMES, Peter Anthony. b 55. Univ of Wales (Ban) BA77 Brighton Poly CertEd78. Trin Coll Bris. **d** 88 **p** 89. C Croydon Ch Ch *S'wark* 88-93; V Norbiton from 93; RD Kingston 97-00. *The Vicarage, 21 Wolsey Close, Kingston upon Thames KT2 7ER* Tel (020) 8942 8330 or 8546 3212 E-mail revrock@yahoo.co.uk

HOLMES, Prof Peter Geoffrey. b 32. Bris Univ BSc59 MSc69 Leic Univ PhD74 CEng FIEE. St Deiniol's Hawarden 74. **d** 76 **p** 77. NSM Glen Parva and S Wigston *Leic* 76-02; Prof Nottm Poly 85-92; Prof Nottm Trent Univ 92-96; rtd 02; Perm to Offic *Leic* from 02. *19 Windsor Avenue, Glen Parva, Leicester LE2 9TQ* Tel 0116-277 4534 E-mail peterholmes@iee.org

HOLMES, Peter John. b 41. Reading Univ TCert63 Open Univ BA76 K Coll Lon BA96 AKC96 MA97 Glas Univ PhD02. St Steph Ho Ox 03. **d** 04 **p** 05. NSM Beaconsfield *Ox* 04-08; Perm to Offic from 08. *10 Park Lawn, Farnham Royal, Slough SL2 3AP* Tel (01753) 646673 E-mail peter.holmes@dial.pipex.com

HOLMES, Robert John Geoffrey. b 28. TCD BA53 MA57. Ely Th Coll 56. **d** 57 **p** 58. C Whitton St Aug CD *Lon* 57-59; C St Pancras w St Jas and Ch Ch 59-63; C Stepney St Dunstan and All SS 63-66; C Stepney St Aug w St Phil 66-68; Chapl The Lon Hosp (Whitechapel) 63-68; R Middelburg, Steynsburg and Colesburg S Africa 68-74; Perm to Offic *Ely* 74 and *Chich* 74-76; R Telscombe w Piddinghoe and Southease *Chich* 76-93; P-in-c Barlavington, Burton w Coates, Sutton and Bignor 93-96; rtd 95; Perm to Offic *Chich* 95-01. *7 Buckhurst Road, Telscombe Cliffs, Peacehaven BN10 7AH*

HOLMES, Roger Cockburn. b 46. Jes Coll Ox BA70 MA84 Edin Univ BD76. Edin Th Coll 73. **d** 84 **p** 85. Canada 84-88; R Ditchingham w Pirnough *Nor* 88-90; R Hedenham 88-90; R Broome 88-90; R Ditchingham, Hedenham and Broome 90-93; V Helmsley *York* 93-97; Perm to Offic *Wakef* 07. *16 Heslington Road, York YO10 5AT* Tel (01904) 629640 E-mail fatherholmes@hotmail.com

HOLMES, Roy Grant. b 37. Ox NSM Course 83. **d** 86 **p** 87. NSM Wokingham St Paul *Ox* from 86. *58 Copse Drive, Wokingham RG41 1LX* Tel 0118-978 4141

HOLMES, Stephen. b 54. St Andr Univ MTheol84. Chich Th Coll 84. **d** 86 **p** 87. C Croydon St Jo *S'wark* 86-89; C Tewkesbury w Walton Cardiff *Glouc* 89-92; P-in-c Bournemouth St Luke *Win* 92-94; V from 94. *St Luke's Vicarage, 31 Lonsdale Road, Bournemouth BH3 7LY* Tel (01202) 516653

HOLMES, Stephen John. b 50. CertEd72. Trin Coll Bris 81 Sarum & Wells Th Coll 88. **d** 89 **p** 90. C Skegness and Winthorpe *Linc* 89-93; P-in-c Mablethorpe w Trusthorpe 93-97; V Hadleigh St Barn *Chelmsf* 97-07; R Gt and Lt Leighs and Lt Waltham from 07. *141 Main Road, Great Leighs, Chelmsford CM3 1NP* Tel (01245) 361955 E-mail familyholmes@hotmail.co.uk

HOLMES, Susan. **d** 06 **p** 07. NSM Scotby and Cotehill w Cumwhinton *Carl* from 06. *Woodside, Great Corby, Carlisle CA4 8LL* Tel (01228) 560617 E-mail susan@gtcorby.plus.com

HOLMES, Theodore John. b 47. EMMTC 02. **d** 06 **p** 07. NSM Somercotes *Derby* from 06. *18 Leabrooks Road, Somercotes, Alfreton DE55 4HB* Tel (01773) 540186 Mobile 07837-574881 E-mail theodore.holmes@btopenworld.com

HOLMES, William John. b 49. **d** 97 **p** 98. Aux Min Billy w Derrykeighan *Conn* 97-02; Aux Min Ballymoney w Finvoy and Rasharkin from 02. *14 Glenlough Park, Coleraine BT52 1TY* Tel (028) 7035 5993

HOLMYARD, Deborah. *See* FRAZER, Deborah

HOLNESS, Edwin Geoffrey Nicholas. b 39. RGN. Sarum Th Coll 68. **d** 71 **p** 72. C Upper Beeding and Bramber w Botolphs *Chich* 71-74; C Munster Square St Mary Magd *Lon* 74-75; Perm to Offic *Chich* 75-76 and 77-99; C Brighton Annunciation 76-77; Chapl Brighton Hosp Gp 77-94; Chapl R Sussex Co Hosp Brighton 77-94; P-in-c Southwick St Pet *Chich* 99-02; rtd 02. *41 Wivelsfield Road, Saltdean, Brighton BN2 8FP* Tel (01273) 307025

HOLROYD, John Richard. b 54. Liv Univ BA75 PGCE77. Wycliffe Hall Ox 78. **d** 81 **p** 82. C Gt Stanmore *Lon* 81-84; Min Can, V Choral and Prec St E Cathl 84-89; TV Wolverton *Ox* 89-96; P-in-c Maidenhead St Luke from 96. *St Luke's Vicarage, 26 Norfolk Road, Maidenhead SL6 7AX* Tel (01628) 783033 E-mail rholroyd@dircon.co.uk

HOLROYD, Stephen Charles. b 56. UEA BA79. St Jo Coll Nottm 84. **d** 87 **p** 88. C Barton Seagrave w Warkton *Pet* 87-91; V Eye 91-97; V Silsoe, Pulloxhill and Flitton *St Alb* from 97. *The Vicarage, Firtree Road, Silsoe, Bedford MK45 4DU* Tel (01525) 862380 E-mail silsoe.vicarage@tesco.net

HOLT, Mrs Claire Frances. b 66. Bris Univ BSc88 Kingston Poly PGCE89. STETS 02. **d** 05 **p** 06. C N Farnborough *Guildf* from 05; Chapl HM Pris Coldingley from 05. *27 Church Road East, Farnborough GU14 6QJ* Tel (01252) 655010 Mobile 07900-583403 E-mail clairefholt@hotmail.com

HOLT, Canon David. b 44. St Jo Coll Dur BSc67. **d** 70 **p** 71. C Blackley St Pet *Man* 70-73; C Radcliffe St Thos 73-74; C Radcliffe St Thos and St Jo 74-75; V Ashton St Pet 75-79; Dioc Youth Officer *Guildf* 80-85; V Bagshot 85-97; RD Surrey Heath 92-97; V Fleet 97-03; RD Aldershot 98-03; Hon Can Guildf Cathl 99-03; rtd 03; Perm to Offic *Guildf* from 03. *62 Lynwood Drive, Mytchett, Camberley GU16 6BY* Tel (01276) 507538 Mobile 07974-354411 E-mail david.holt@ntlworld.com

HOLT, Canon Douglas Robert. b 49. MA. Ridley Hall Cam. **d** 82 **p** 83. C Cambridge St Barn *Ely* 82-84; P-in-c 84-86; V 86-91; V Ealing St Mary *Lon* 91-98; Can Res Bris Cathl from 98; Dir Par Development Team from 98. *9 Leigh Road, Clifton, Bristol BS8 2DA* Tel 0117-973 7427

HOLT, Francis Thomas. b 38. Edin Th Coll 79. **d** 81 **p** 82. C Cullercoats St Geo *Newc* 81-83; C Ponteland 83-86; Chapl Worc Coll of HE 86-89; R Worc St Clem 86-93; V Finstall 93-96; Chapl Menorca *Eur* 96-97; Perm to Offic *Worc* from 97; rtd 98. *10 Ash Close, Malvern WR14 2WF* Tel (01684) 575507

HOLT, Jack Derek. b 38. Trin Coll Bris 71. **d** 73 **p** 74. C Daubhill *Man* 73-76; P-in-c Thornham w Gravel Hole 76-79; V 79-83; R Talke *Lich* 83-93; V Cotmanhay *Derby* 93-03; Chapl Derbyshire Mental Health Services NHS Trust 93-03; rtd 03; Perm to Offic *Lich* from 03. *31 Hatherton Close, Newcastle ST5 7SN* Tel (01782) 560845

HOLT, James Edward. b 49. St Martin's Coll Lanc BA94 PGCE95. NOC 99. **d** 02 **p** 04. NSM Holme-in-Cliviger w Worsthorne *Blackb* 02-03; NSM Whalley from 03. *5 Graham Street, Padiham, Burnley BB12 8RW* Tel (01282) 778319

HOLT, Keith. b 37. CPFA62. S'wark Ord Course. **d** 82 **p** 83. NSM Selsdon St Jo w St Fran *Cant* 82-84; NSM Selsdon St Jo w St Fran *S'wark* 85-07; Perm to Offic from 07. *12 Ridge Langley, South Croydon CR2 0AR* Tel (020) 8651 1815

HOLT, Mrs Lucinda Jane. b 65. Open Univ BSc00. Wycliffe Hall Ox 01. **d** 03 **p** 04. C Newton Longville and Mursley w Swanbourne etc *Ox* 03-06; TV Riverside 06-08; V Eton w Eton Wick, Boveney and Dorney from 08. *The Vicarage, 69A Eton Wick Road, Eton Wick, Windsor SL4 6NE* Tel (01753) 852268 E-mail andrew-lucy@tinyworld.co.uk

HOLT, Michael. b 38. Univ of Wales (Lamp) BA61. St D Coll Lamp. **d** 63 **p** 64. C Stand *Man* 63-69; V Bacup St Jo 69-03; AD Rossendale 98-00; rtd 03. *22 Windermere Road, Bacup OL13 9DN* Tel (01706) 877976

HOLT, Shirley Ann. b 48. **d** 98 **p** 99. OLM High Oak, Hingham and Scoulton w Wood Rising *Nor* from 98. *Westfield, 59 Church Lane, Wicklewood, Wymondham NR18 9QH* Tel (01953) 603668 E-mail saholt@talk21.com

HOLT, Stuart Henry. b 57. Bath Coll of HE BEd78. Ridley Hall Cam 84. **d** 87 **p** 88. C Locks Heath *Portsm* 87-90; Chapl RAF 90-91; C Worthing St Geo *Chich* 91-93; C Portchester *Portsm* 93-95; Perm to Offic 02-03; P-in-c Soberton w Newtown 03-09; P-in-c Droxford from 09; P-in-c Meonstoke w Corhampton cum Exton from 09; AD Bishop's Waltham from 09. *The Rectory, Rectory Lane, Meonstoke, Southampton SO32 3NF* Tel (01489) 878222 E-mail stuart.holt2@btopenworld.com

HOLT, Susan Mary. b 45. Coll of Ripon & York St Jo MA98. NOC 97. **d** 97 **p** 98. NSM Longwood *Wakef* 97-00; NSM Liversedge w Hightown from 00. *229/231 Stainland Road, Holywell Green, Halifax HX4 9AJ* Tel (01422) 376481 E-mail susan@micromundi.net

HOLTAM, Nicholas Roderick. b 54. Collingwood Coll Dur BA75 K Coll Lon BD78 AKC78 FKC05 Dur Univ MA89 Hon DCL05. Westcott Ho Cam 78. **d** 79 **p** 80. C Stepney St Dunstan and All SS *Lon* 79-83; Tutor Linc Th Coll 83-88; V Is of Dogs Ch Ch and St Jo w St Luke *Lon* 88-95; V St Martin-in-the-Fields

from 95. *Flat 3, 6 St Martin's Place, London WC2N 4JJ* Tel (020) 7766 1100 Fax 7839 5163 E-mail clergy@smitf.org

HOLTH, Oystein Johan. b 31. Open Univ BA75. AKC54. **d** 54 **p** 55. C Greenford H Cross *Lon* 54-56; Br N Borneo and Sarawak 56-63; E Malaysia 63-67; Chapl OHP 67-75; Chapl St Hilda's Sch Whitby 67-75; P-in-c Pimlico St Barn *Lon* 75-97; Ind Chapl 75-97; rtd 97; Perm to Offic *Lon* from 97. *13 Dollis Park, London N3 1HJ* Tel (020) 8346 8131

HOLY, Ravi. b 69. K Coll Lon MA09. Trin Coll Bris BA05. **d** 05 **p** 06. C Battersea St Luke *S'wark* from 05. *30 Canford Road, London SW11 6NZ* Tel (020) 8772 0463 Mobile 07930-401963 E-mail raviholy@aol.com

HOLYER, Vincent Alfred Douglas. b 28. Ex Univ BA54. Oak Hill Th Coll 54. **d** 56 **p** 57. C Bethnal Green St Jas Less *Lon* 56-58; C Braintree *Chelmsf* 58-61; V Islington All SS *Lon* 61-65; R St Ruan w St Grade *Truro* 65-85; V Constantine 85-91; rtd 91; Perm to Offic *Truro* from 91. *32 Valley Gardens, Illogan, Redruth TR16 4EE* Tel (01209) 211509

HOLZAPFEL, Mrs Christine Anne. b 53. Ex Univ BA74 PGCE75. WMMTC 04. **d** 07 **p** 08. C Worc SE from 07. *The Rectory, 3 Oakfield Drive, Kempsey, Worcester WR5 3PP* Tel (01905) 821719 Mobile 07749-898698 E-mail cherrytree@tesco.net

HOLZAPFEL, Peter Rudolph. b 51. St Jo Coll Nottm 84. **d** 86 **p** 87. C St Jo in Bedwardine *Worc* 86-89; R Kempsey and Severn Stoke w Croome d'Abitot from 99. *The Rectory, 3 Oakfield Drive, Kempsey, Worcester WR5 3PP* Tel (01905) 820202

HOMDEN, Peter David. b 56. Moorlands Coll BA06. STETS 07. **d** 09. C Heatherlands St Jo *Sarum* from 09. *42 Milborne Crescent, Poole BH12 4ET* Tel (01202) 241437 Mobile 07841-699094 E-mail homdenhome@btinternet.com

HOMER, Alan Fellows. b 30. Ridley Hall Cam 61. **d** 63 **p** 64. C Heref St Jas 63-66; V Brixton Hill St Sav *S'wark* 66-73; Dep Chapl HM Pris Brixton 66-70; CF (TA) 70-73; CF 73-76; V Heeley *Sheff* 75-87; R Cheveley *Ely* 87-95; R Ashley w Silverley 87-95; V Wood Ditton w Saxon Street 87-95; V Kirtling 87-95; RD Linton 94-95; rtd 95; Perm to Offic *Bris* from 95 and *Ox* 95-01. *62 The Willows, Highworth, Swindon SN6 7PH* Tel and fax (01793) 764023

HOMER, Antony James. b 72. La Sainte Union Coll BTh95 Leeds Univ MA02 Southn Univ PGCE96. Coll of Resurr Mirfield 00. **d** 02 **p** 03. C St Leonards Ch Ch and St Mary *Chich* 02-06; C Hornsey St Mary w St Geo *Lon* 06-07; V Winchmore Hill H Trin from 07; Chapl Bp Stopford's Sch Enfield from 06; CMP from 04. *Holy Trinity Vicarage, King's Avenue, London N21 3NA* Tel (020) 8364 2724 E-mail franton yh@hotmail.com

HOMEWOOD, Michael John. b 33. Wells Th Coll 69. **d** 71 **p** 72. C Ilfracombe H Trin *Ex* 71-72; C Ilfracombe, Lee and W Down 72-75; P-in-c Woolacombe 76-78; TV Ilfracombe, Lee, W Down, Woolacombe and Bittadon 78-82; TR S Molton w Nymet St George, High Bray etc 82-97; RD S Molton 93-95; rtd 97; Perm to Offic *Sarum* from 97. *5 Avon Drive, Wareham BH20 4EL* Tel (01929) 556216

HOMEWOOD, Peter Laurence de Silvie. b 58. Oriel Coll Ox BA80 MA84. St Steph Ho Ox 90. **d** 92 **p** 93. C Ruislip St Martin *Lon* 92-96; R Hayes St Mary from 96; P-in-c Hayes St Anselm 03-07. *The Rectory, 170 Church Road, Hayes UB3 2LR* Tel (020) 8573 2470 E-mail peter@hayes-rectory.demon.co.uk

HOMFRAY, John Bax Tayler. b 29. Keble Coll Ox BA52 MA. Ridley Hall Cam 52. **d** 54 **p** 55. C Kingswood *Bris* 54-57; C Leckhampton St Pet *Glouc* 57-64; V Staverton w Boddington 64-86; V Staverton w Boddington and Tredington etc 87-95; rtd 95; Perm to Offic *Glouc* from 95. *Ellerslie Nursing Home, 108 Albert Road, Cheltenham GL52 3JB* Tel (01242) 514384

HOMFRAY, Kenyon Lee James. b 55. TCD BTh99 MA03 Univ of Wales (Cardiff) LLM02. CITC 96. **d** 99 **p** 00. C Convoy w Monellan and Donaghmore *D & R* 99-02; I 02-05; I Buncloody w Kildavin, Clonegal and Kilrush *C & O* from 05. *The Rectory, Bunclody, Enniscorthy, Co Wexford, Republic of Ireland* Tel (00353) (53) 937 7652

HONE, Canon Frank Leslie. b 11. Kelham Th Coll 32. **d** 38 **p** 39. C Sheff Arbourthorne 38-40; CF (EC) 40-45; C Sheff St Anne and St Phil 45-46; C Rotherham 46-49; V Brightside St Thos 49-53; R Attercliffe w Carbrook 53-60; P-in-c Sheff St Swithun 60-66; V Frodingham *Linc* 66-78; RD Manlake 69-76; Can and Preb Linc Cathl 72-78; rtd 78; Perm to Offic *Linc* from 78. *Morcote, 13 Roselea Avenue, Welton, Lincoln LN2 3RT* Tel (01673) 861548

HONES, Simon Anthony. b 54. Sussex Univ BSc75. Qu Coll Birm. **d** 79 **p** 80. C Win Ch Ch 79-82; C Basing 82-88; Min Chineham CD 88-90; V Surbiton St Matt *S'wark* 90-08; TR from 08. *St Matthew's Vicarage, 20 Kingsdowne Road, Surbiton KT6 6JZ* Tel (020) 8399 4853 E-mail simon.hones@blueyonder.co.uk

HONEY, Mrs Elizabeth Katherine. b 81. Keble Coll Ox MA07. Wycliffe Hall Ox 06. **d** 09. C Furze Platt *Ox* from 09. *46 Bridle Road, Maidenhead SL6 7RP* Tel (01628) 674654 Mobile 07918-171770 E-mail beth.honey@hotmail.co.uk

HONEY, Canon Frederick Bernard. b 22. Selw Coll Cam BA48 MA72. Wells Th Coll 48. **d** 50 **p** 51. C S'wark St Geo 50-52; C

Claines St Jo *Worc* 52-55; V Wollaston 55-87; RD Stourbridge 72-83; Hon Can Worc Cathl 75-87; rtd 87. *38 Park Farm, Bourton-on-the-Water, Cheltenham GL54 2HF* Tel (01451) 822218

HONEY, Canon Thomas David. b 56. Lon Univ BA78. Ripon Coll Cuddesdon 80. **d** 83 **p** 84. C Mill End and Heronsgate w W Hyde *St Alb* 83-86; C Stepney St Dunstan and All SS *Lon* 86-89; TV High Wycombe *Ox* 89-95; P-in-c Headington Quarry 95-07; Can Res and Treas Ex Cathl from 07. *9 Cathedral Close, Exeter EX1 1EZ* Tel (01392) 279367
E-mail tom.honey@ukonline.co.uk

HONEYMAN, Jennifer Mary. b 73. Univ Coll Ches BA08. NOC 05. **d** 08 **p** 09. C Crosland Moor and Linthwaite *Wakef* from 08. *The Vicarage, Church Lane, Linthwaite, Huddersfield HD7 5TA* Tel 07710-034457 (mobile) E-mail jandchoneyman@aol.com

HONG KONG ISLAND, Bishop of. *See* KWONG KONG KIT, The Most Revd Peter

HONG KONG SHENG KUNG HUI, Archbishop of. *See* KWONG KONG KIT, The Most Revd Peter

HONNER, Canon Robert Ralph. b 15. St Chad's Coll Dur BA37 MA40. **d** 38 **p** 39. C Gt Crosby St Faith *Liv* 38-41; P-in-c Wigan St Andr 41-44; C Rugby St Andr *Cov* 44-49; V Derby St Barn 49-53; V Melbourne 54-72; RD Melbourne 54-67; Hon Can Derby Cathl 58-80; V Beeley and Edensor 72-80; RD Bakewell and Eyam 73-78; rtd 80; Perm to Offic *Derby* from 80. *clo Mrs K M Pollard, 8 Alma Hill, Kimberley, Nottingham NG16 2JF* Tel (01159) 459072

HONNOR, Jonathan Michael **Bellamy.** b 62. Leeds Univ BA84 Cant Ch Ch Univ Coll PGCE89. Stavanger Sch of Miss and Th 98. **p** 00. Norway 00-03; C Leigh Park and Warren Park *Portsm* 03-08; P-in-c Aylesham w Adisham *Cant* from 08. *The Rectory, Dorman Avenue North, Aylesham, Canterbury CT3 3BL* Tel (01304) 840266

HONNOR, Mrs Marjorie Rochefort. b 27. Birm Univ BA48. Cranmer Hall Dur 79. dss 81 **d** 87 **p** 94. Church Oakley and Wootton St Lawrence *Win* 81-87; Par Dn 87-89; rtd 89; Perm to Offic *Win* from 98. *33C Surrey Road, Bournemouth BH4 9HR* Tel (01202) 761021

HONOR MARGARET, Sister. *See* McILROY, Sister Honor Margaret

HONOUR, Colin Reginald. b 44. Lanc Univ CertEd69 Man Univ AdDipEd75 Newc Univ MEd80. NOC 88. **d** 91 **p** 92. NSM Walmsley *Man* 91; C Middleton 92-94; R Holcombe 94-01; P-in-c Hawkshaw Lane 99-01; P-in-c Aldingham, Dendron, Rampside and Urswick *Carl* 01-03; R from 03. *The Vicarage, Church Road, Great Urswick, Ulverston LA12 0TA* Tel (01229) 581383 E-mail cnchonour@btinternet.com

HONOUR, Derek Gordon. b 59. Bath Univ BSc84. St Jo Coll Nottm. **d** 89 **p** 90. C High Wycombe *Ox* 89-91; C Brightside w Wincobank *Sheff* 91-94; P-in-c Dawley St Jerome *Lon* 94-01; C Derby St Alkmund and St Werburgh 01-05; V Stoke Hill *Guildf* from 05. *St Peter's House, 37 Hazel Avenue, Guildford GU1 1NP* Tel (01483) 572078 E-mail derekhonour@compuserve.com

HONOUR, Mrs Joanna Clare. b 61. Westmr Coll Ox BEd83. St Jo Coll Nottm 86. **d** 89 **p** 94. Par Dn High Wycombe *Ox* 89-91; Par Dn Brightside w Wincobank *Sheff* 91-94; C 94; Dep Chapl HM Pris Wandsworth 95-97; Chapl HM Pris The Mount 97; NSM Dawley St Jerome *Lon* 96-01; Chapl HM Pris Foston Hall 01-05; Chapl HM Pris Coldingley 06-09; Chapl HM Pris Whatton from 09. *HM Prison Whatton, New Lane, Whatton, Nottingham NG13 9FQ* Tel (01949) 803200 Fax 803201
E-mail jo.honour@hmps.gsi.gov.uk

HONOUR, Jonathan Paul. b 68. Ox Brookes Univ BSc90 Greenwich Univ PGCE91. St Jo Coll Nottm MA98. **d** 99 **p** 00. C Tonbridge St Steph *Roch* 99-03; TV Woodley *Ox* 03-08; V Guernsey H Trin *Win* from 08. *Holy Trinity Vicarage, Brock Road, St Peter Port, Guernsey GY1 1RS* Tel (01481) 724382 Mobile 07752-241255 E-mail jonathanhonour@googlemail.com

HOOD, Mrs Doreen. b 38. Open Univ BA90 SRN59 RFN61. NEOC 90. **d** 93 **p** 94. NSM Cullercoats St Geo *Newc* 93-99; NSM Monkseaton St Pet 99-00; P-in-c Newc St Hilda 00-03; rtd 03. *24 Keswick Drive, North Shields NE30 3EW* Tel 0191-253 1762

HOOD, Mrs Elizabeth Mary. b 57. Ex Univ BA79. ERMC 05. **d** 08. C Boxmoor St Jo *St Alb* from 08. *136A Abbots Road, Abbots Langley WD5 0BL* Tel (01923) 263924
E-mail lizziehood@aol.com

HOOD, Leslie. b 23. NEOC. **d** 85 **p** 85. NSM Seaham w Seaham Harbour *Dur* 85-90; NSM Dalton le Dale 90-93; NSM Hawthorn 90-93; rtd 93; Perm to Offic *Dur* from 93. *3 Queen Street, Seaham SR7 7SR* Tel 0191-581 2658
E-mail leslie@hood71.freeserve.co.uk

HOOD, Mrs Linda. b 47. Leeds Univ BA68. St Jo Coll Nottm 07. **d** 09. NSM Chase Terrace *Lich* from 09. *13 Mossbank Avenue, Burntwood WS7 4UN* Tel (01543) 301728 Mobile 07786-987114
E-mail linda.hood@stjohnscommunitychurch.org.uk

HOOD, Peter Michael. b 47. Sheff Univ BSc68. Wycliffe Hall Ox 70. **d** 73 **p** 74. C Soundwell *Bris* 73-76; P-in-c Walcot St Andr CD

76-77; TV Swindon St Jo and St Andr 77-80; V Esh and Hamsteels *Dur* 80-88; V Stockton St Paul 88-00; P-in-c Herrington 00-05; P-in-c Penshaw 00-05; P-in-c Shiney Row 00-05; R Herrington, Penshaw and Shiney Row 05-07; Lic to Adn Sunderland and Houghton Deanery from 07. *1 Victory Street East, Hetton le Hole, Houghton le Spring DH5 9DN* Tel 0191-526 9187
E-mail peter.hood@rohlfing-hood.freeserve.co.uk

HOOD, Canon Thomas Henry Havelock. b 24. Chich Th Coll 51. **d** 54 **p** 55. C Stella *Dur* 54-57; Australia from 57; Hon Can Brisbane from 88; rtd 93. *18 Moonyean Street, Bellbird Park Qld 4300, Australia* Tel (0061) (7) 3288 5106
E-mail havelock@gil.com.au

HOOGERWERF, John Constant. b 50. Bris Poly BA85 MCIH86. Oscott Coll (RC) 68. **d** 73 **p** 74. In RC Ch 73-84; NSM Davyhulme Ch Ch *Man* 84-93; Perm to Offic *Heref* 93-04; NSM Mold *St As* 04; Lic to Offic from 04. *2 Llys y Foel, Mold CH7 1EX* Tel (01352) 750701

HOOK, Ian Kevin. b 57. Trin Coll Bris 93. **d** 95 **p** 96. C Dalton-in-Furness *Carl* 95-98; C Newbarns w Hawcoat 98-01; V Barrow St Mark from 01; RD Barrow from 06. *St Mark's Vicarage, Rawlinson Street, Barrow-in-Furness LA14 1BX* Tel (01229) 820405 E-mail ian@hooki.freeserve.co.uk

HOOK, Neil. b 73. Univ of Wales (Swansea) BA94 Univ of Wales (Cardiff) BD96. St Mich Coll Llan 94. **d** 97 **p** 98. C Brecon St Mary and Battle w Llanddew *S & B* 97-99; Min Can Brecon Cathl 97-99; P-in-c Llanllyr-yn-Rhos w Llanfihangel Helygen 99-00; V Upper Wye 00-05; P-in-c Trallwng w Bettws Penpont w Aberyskir etc from 05; P-in-c Cynog Honddu from 08. *2 The Gardens, Cradoc, Brecon LD3 9LR* Tel (01874) 621533

HOOKER, Richard Malcolm Neil. b 38. Lon Univ BDS63 LDS63. Guildf Dioc Min Course. **d** 98 **p** 99. OLM Ashtead *Guildf* from 98. *Lanacre Cottage, 4 Farm Close, Fetcham KT22 9BJ* Tel (01372) 372446 Mobile 07802-961686
E-mail rmnhooker@fsmail.net

HOOKWAY, John Leonard Walter. b 73. St Jo Coll Dur BSc95. St Jo Coll Nottm MTh04. **d** 04 **p** 05. C St Alb St Paul *St Alb* 04-07; C Howell Hill w Burgh Heath *Guildf* from 07. *18 Nonsuch Walk, Sutton SM2 7NG* Tel (020) 8873 1961
E-mail johnh@saintpauls.co.uk

HOOLE, Charles. b 33. St Aid Birkenhead 61. **d** 63 **p** 64. C Skerton St Luke *Blackb* 63-65; P-in-c Preston St Jas 65-69; V Lostock Hall 69-73; Chapl HM Pris Eastchurch 74-75; V St Annes St Marg *Blackb* 75-81; V S Shore St Pet 81-92; C Laneside 92-94; rtd 95; Perm to Offic *Blackb* from 95. *32 Hanover Crescent, Blackpool FY2 9DL* Tel (01253) 353564

HOOPER, Preb Derek Royston. b 33. St Edm Hall Ox BA57 MA65. Cuddesdon Coll 57. **d** 59 **p** 60. C Gt Walsingham *Nor* 59-62; C Townstall w Dartmouth *Ex* 62-65; V Lynton and Brendon 65-69; C Littleham w Exmouth 70-72; TV 72-79; R Wrington w Butcombe *B & W* 79-94; Preb Wells Cathl 93-94; rtd 94; Perm to Offic *Ex* 95; B & W 95-00. *23 Dagmar Road, Exmouth EX8 2AN* Tel (01395) 272831

HOOPER, Geoffrey Michael. b 39. MBE00. Univ of Wales (Ban) MA07. K Coll Lon 61. **d** 66 **p** 67. C Chesterfield St Mary and All SS *Derby* 66-69; Chapl RAF 69-74; P-in-c Hook Norton w Swerford and Wigginton *Ox* 74-80; P-in-c Gt Rollright 75-80; R Hook Norton w Gt Rollright, Swerford etc 80-82; Warden Mansf Ho Univ Settlement Plaistow 82-00; Dir 86-00; rtd 03. *Ty'n Twll, Penbodlas, Llaniestyn, Pwllheli LL53 8SD* Tel (01758) 730526 E-mail geoffreyhooper@penbodlas.wanadoo.co.uk

HOOPER, Ian. b 44. St Jo Coll York CertEd67. Trin Coll Bris. **d** 88 **p** 89. C Martlesham w Brightwell *St E* 88-92; R Pakenham w Norton and Tostock 92-09; RD Ixworth 03-09; rtd 09; Perm to Offic *St E* from 09. *26 Drake Close, Stowmarket IP14 1UP*

✠**HOOPER, The Rt Revd Michael Wrenford.** b 41. Univ of Wales (Lamp) BA63. St Steph Ho Ox 63. **d** 65 **p** 66 **c** 02. C Bridgnorth St Mary *Heref* 65-70; P-in-c Habberley 70-81; R 78-81; V Minsterley 70-81; RD Pontesbury 75-80; Preb Heref Cathl 81-02; V Leominster 81-85; TR Leominster 85-97; P-in-c Eyton 81-85; RD Leominster 81-97; P-in-c Eye, Croft w Yarpole and Lucton 91-97; Adn Heref 97-02; Suff Bp Ludlow 02-09; Adn Ludlow 02-09; rtd 09. *6 Avon Drive, Eckington, Pershore WR10 3BU* Tel (01386) 751589
E-mail bishopmichael@btinternet.com

HOOPER, Canon Paul Denis Gregory. b 52. Man Univ BA75 Ox Univ BA80 MA87. Wycliffe Hall Ox 78. **d** 81 **p** 82. C Leeds St Geo *Ripon* 81-84; Dioc Youth Officer 84-87; Bp's Dom Chapl 87-95; Dioc Communications Officer 87-97; V Harrogate St Mark from 95; AD Harrogate 05-09; Dir Clergy Development from 09; Hon Can Ripon Cathl from 08. *9 Fulwith Gate, Harrogate HG2 8HS*

HOOPER, Peter George. b 62. BSc PhD. EMMTC. **d** 06 **p** 07. C Melton Mowbray *Leic* from 06. *1 Palmerston Road, Melton Mowbray LE13 0SS* Tel (01664) 561499

HOOPER, Sydney Paul. b 46. QUB BA68 Lanc Univ CertEd69. **d** 85 **p** 87. NSM Killaney w Carryduff *D & D* 85-91; Lic to Offic from 91; NSM Belfast St Chris 01-03; NSM Ballymacarrett from

03. *26 Manse Park, Carryduff, Belfast BT8 8RX* Tel (028) 9081 5607 *or* 9056 6289

HOOPER, William Gilbert. b 38. Ex Univ BA60. St Mich Coll Llan. **d** 82 **p** 83. C Hubberston w Herbrandston and Hasguard etc *St D* 82-85; R Llangwm and Freystrop 85-97; R Llangwm w Freystrop and Johnston 97-04; rtd 04. *5 Pen-y-Ffordd, St Clears, Carmarthen SA33 4DX* Tel (01994) 230069

HOOTON, David James. b 50. St Kath Coll Liv CertEd73. NOC 83. **d** 86 **p** 87. NSM Pemberton St Mark Newtown *Liv* 86-89; C Ashton-in-Makerfield St Thos 89-92; V Bryn from 92. *The Vicarage, 12 Bryn Road, Ashton-in-Makerfield, Wigan WN4 0AA* Tel (01942) 727114

HOPCRAFT, Jonathan Richard. b 34. Oriel Coll Ox BA55 DipEd66 MA66. Westcott Ho Cam 57. **d** 59 **p** 60. C Cannock *Lich* 59-63; N Rhodesia 63-64; S Rhodesia 64-65; Hon C Olton *Birm* 66-68; Antigua 68-72; C Gt Grimsby St Mary and St Jas *Linc* 72; TV 72-76; P-in-c E Stockwith 76-84; V Blyton w Pilham 76-84; P-in-c Laughton w Wildsworth 76-84; TV Bilston *Lich* 84-90; P-in-c Wolverhampton St Jo 90-98; C Wolverhampton 97-98; TV Cen Wolverhampton 98-00; rtd 00; Perm to Offic *Chelmsf* from 01. *13 Nabbott Road, Chelmsford CM1 2SW* Tel (01245) 263983 E-mail jonhopcraft@supanet.com

HOPE, Charles Henry. b 64. Regent's Park Coll Ox BA87 MA90. St Jo Coll Dur BA90. **d** 90 **p** 91. C Tynemouth St Jo *Newc* 90-94; V 94-03; P-in-c Prudhoe 03-07; V from 07. *The Vicarage, 5 Kepwell Court, Prudhoe NE42 5PE* Tel (01661) 836059 Mobile 07884-070619 E-mail charleshope@btopenworld.com

HOPE, Colin Frederick. b 49. St Mich Coll Llan 73. **d** 76 **p** 77. C Warrington St Elphin *Liv* 76-80; V Newton-le-Willows 80-84; CSWG from 84; Lic to Offic *Chich* from 88. *The Monastery, Crawley Down, Crawley RH10 4LH* Tel (01342) 712074

HOPE, Edith. b 43. Lanc Univ MA86 SRN64 SCM66. Wycliffe Hall Ox 89. **d** 91 **p** 94. Par Dn Droylsden St Mary *Man* 91-94; Par Dn Ecclesall *Sheff* 94; C 94-01; V Crosspool 01-08; rtd 08. *46 Gisborne Road, Sheffield S11 7HB* Tel 0114-263 1230 E-mail edithhope@btinternet.com

HOPE, Robert. b 36. Dur Univ BSc61. Clifton Th Coll 61. **d** 63 **p** 64. C Woking St Mary *Guildf* 63-66; C Surbiton Hill Ch Ch *S'wark* 66-68; Th Students' Sec IVF 68-71; Hon C Wallington *S'wark* 69-71; C Ox St Ebbe w St Pet 71-74; V Walshaw Ch Ch *Man* 74-87; TR Radipole and Melcombe Regis *Sarum* 87-93; rtd 93; Perm to Offic *St D* from 93. *1A Swiss Valley, Felinfael, Llanelli SA14 8BS* Tel (01554) 759199

HOPE, Susan. b 49. St Jo Coll Dur BA83 Sheff Univ MA04. Cranmer Hall Dur 80. **dss** 83 **d** 87 **p** 94. Boston Spa *York* 83-86; Brightside w Wincobank *Sheff* 86-97; Par Dn 87-89; Dn-in-c 89-94; V 94-97; V Chapeltown 97-02; Dioc Missr 02-07; RD Tankersley 00-02; Hon Can Sheff Cathl 00-09; Dir Tr Wilson Carlile Coll of Evang 07-08; P-in-c Shipley St Paul *Bradf* from 09; Dioc Adv in Evang from 09; Six Preacher Cant Cathl from 99. *The Vicarage, Oak Avenue, Bingley BD16 1ES* Tel (01274) 561949 Mobile 07736-774937

✠**HOPE OF THORNES, The Rt Revd and Rt Hon Lord (David Michael).** b 40. KCVO95 PC91. Nottm Univ BA62 Linacre Ho Ox DPhil65 Hon FGCM94. St Steph Ho Ox 62. **d** 65 **p** 66 **c** 85. C W Derby St Jo *Liv* 65-67 and 68-70; Chapl Bucharest *Eur* 67-68; V Orford St Andr *Liv* 70-74; Prin St Steph Ho Ox 74-82; V St Marylebone All SS *Lon* 82-85; Master of Guardians Shrine of Our Lady of Walsingham 82-93; Bp Wakef 85-91; Bp Lon 91-95; Dean of HM Chpls Royal and Prelate of OBE 91-95; Abp York 95-05; rtd 05; P-in-c Ilkley St Marg *Bradf* 05-06; Hon Asst Bp Bradf from 05; Hon Asst Bp Eur from 07; Hon Asst Bp Blackb from 08. *2 Aspinall Rise, Hellifield, Skipton BD23 4JT*

HOPEWELL, Jeffery Stewart. b 52. Leic Univ BA75 ACA79. EMMTC 82. **d** 85 **p** 86. NSM Houghton on the Hill w Keyham *Leic* 85-88; NSM Houghton-on-the-Hill, Keyham and Hungarton 88-91; C Syston 91-93; TV Syston 93-97; Bp's Ecum Adv 91-97; P-in-c Wymeswold and Prestwold w Hoton 97-04; V Old Dalby, Nether Broughton, Saxelbye etc from 04; Dioc Ecum Officer from 03. *The Vicarage, Church Lane, Old Dalby, Melton Mowbray LE14 3LB* Tel (01664) 820064 E-mail jshopewell@btinternet.com

HOPKIN, David James. b 67. Birm Univ BTh92 CertEd91. Ripon Coll Cuddesdon 98. **d** 99 **p** 00. C Wickford and Runwell *Chelmsf* 99-02; TV Penistone and Thurlstone *Wakef* 02-06; TR from 06. *The Vicarage, Shrewsbury Road, Penistone, Sheffield S36 6DY* Tel (01226) 370954 E-mail david.hopkin@hotmail.com *or* stjohns.pen@hotmail.com

HOPKIN, Mrs Angela Joan. b 42. Bp Otter Coll Chich CertEd64. S Dios Minl Tr Scheme 92. **d** 95 **p** 96. NSM Kingsbury H Innocents *Lon* from 95. *3 Regal Way, Harrow HA3 0RZ* Tel (020) 8907 1045 E-mail hopkinsangl@aol.com

HOPKINS, Miss Barbara Agnes. b 28. Lon Univ BSc60 Imp Coll Lon MPhil67. St Alb Minl Tr Scheme 82. **dss** 85 **d** 87. Bedford All SS *St Alb* 85-86; Chapl Asst Bedf Gen Hosp 86-88; Bedford St Mich *St Alb* 86-88; Hon Par Dn 87-88; Chapl Asst N Lincs Mental Health Unit 89-91; rtd 91; Perm to Offic *Linc* 93-95. *6 Olsen Court, Olsen Rise, Lincoln LN2 4UZ* Tel (01522) 513359

HOPKINS, Brenda Alison. b 63. St Martin's Coll Lanc BA95 Anglia Poly Univ MA97. Westcott Ho Cam 95. **d** 97 **p** 98. C Camberwell St Geo *S'wark* 97-00; Chapl Nor City Coll of F&HE 00-03. *Rose Tree Cottage, The Green, Stokesby, Great Yarmouth NR29 3EX* E-mail bhopkins@ccn.ac.uk

HOPKINS, Christopher Freeman. b 41. Dur Univ BA63. Wells Th Coll 63. **d** 65 **p** 66. C Spring Park *Cant* 65-69; C Mafeking S Africa 69-70; R Potchefstroom 70-78; Lic to Offic Botswana 78-81; R Beckley and Peasmarsh *Chich* from 81. *The Rectory, School Lane, Peasmarsh, Rye TN31 6UW* Tel and fax (01797) 230255 E-mail fr-christopher_hopkins@bigfoot.com

HOPKINS, Gillian Frances. b 55. Bedf Coll Lon BA76 SS Mark & Jo Univ Coll Plymouth PGCE77 Cam Inst of Educn MA91. NTMTC BA07. **d** 07 **p** 08. C Wickford and Runwell *Chelmsf* from 07. *8 Honington Close, Wickford SS11 8XB* Tel (01268) 560286 E-mail gill_hopkins@yahoo.co.uk

HOPKINS, Henry Charles. b 46. RD87. Edin Th Coll 65. **d** 71 **p** 72. C Dundee St Salvador *Bre* 71-74; C Dundee St Martin 71-74; Chapl RNVR 72-81; R Monifieth *Bre* 74-78; Chapl Miss to Seamen Kenya 78-85; Singapore 85-92; Offg Chapl NZ Defence Force 89-92; Chapl Miss to Seamen Teesside 92-94; V Middlesbrough St Thos *York* 94-97; V N Thornaby from 97. *St Paul's Vicarage, 60 Lanehouse Road, Thornaby, Stockton-on-Tees TS17 8EA* Tel and fax (01642) 868086 E-mail harry.hopkins@ntlworld.com

HOPKINS, Hugh. b 33. TCD BA. **d** 62 **p** 63. C Ballymena *Conn* 62-64; C Belfast Ch Ch 64-67; I Ballintoy 67-72; I Belfast St Ninian 72-81; I Mossley 81-86; I Ballywillan 86-96; Can Belf Cathl 94-96; rtd 96. *2 Bush Gardens, Ballyness, Bushmills BT57 8AE* Tel (028) 2073 2981

HOPKINS, Ian Richard. b 70. Dur Univ BA92 Ox Univ BTh00. **d** 00 **p** 01. C Edin St Thos 00-04; R from 04. *16 Belgrave Road, Edinburgh EH12 6NF* Tel 0131-334 4434 *or* 316 4292 E-mail rector@saintthomas.org.uk

HOPKINS, John Dawson. b 39. Chich Th Coll 85. **d** 87 **p** 88. C Walker *Newc* 87-89; C Newc St Fran 89-92; V Horton 92-00; rtd 00; Perm to Offic *Newc* from 01. *Amen Cottage, 31 High Fair, Wooler NE71 6PA* Tel (07790) 915763

HOPKINS, Kenneth Victor John. b 45. Univ Coll Lon BA66 Lon Univ BD69 Hull Univ PhD84. Tyndale Hall Bris 66. **d** 69 **p** 70. C S Mimms Ch Ch *Lon* 69-72; C Branksome St Clem *Sarum* 72-75; P-in-c Trowbridge St Thos 75-76; V 76-81; R Wingfield w Rowley 76-81; Chapl and Lect NE Surrey Coll of Tech 81-84; Hd Student Services Essex Inst of HE 84-88; Kingston Poly 88-92; Kingston Univ 92-98; Dean of Students 98-03; Pro Vice-Chan 04-06; rtd 06. *Quarry Cottage, Duke Street, Withington, Hereford HR1 3QD* Tel (01432) 850933

HOPKINS, Lionel. b 48. Open Univ BA82. St D Coll Lamp. **d** 71 **p** 72. C Llandeilo Tal-y-bont *S & B* 71-74; C Morriston 74-78; P-in-c Waunarllwydd 78-80; V 80-86; Youth Chapl 84-86; V Llangyfelach 86-96; P-in-c Swansea Ch Ch 96-00; Chapl HM Pris Swansea from 96. *HM Prison, 200 Oystermouth Road, Swansea SA1 3SR* Tel (01792) 464030

HOPKINS, Miss Patricia Mary. b 46. Kingston Poly BEd78. Trin Coll Bris 83. **dss** 85 **d** 87 **p** 94. Gorleston St Andr *Nor* 85-88; C 87-88; C Woking St Jo *Guildf* 88-90; TD Barnham Broom *Nor* 90-94; TV 94-97; V Otford *Roch* 97-07; rtd 07; Perm to Offic *Nor* from 08. *Hill Cottage, Broomhill, East Runton, Cromer NR27 9PF* Tel (01263) 512338

HOPKINS, Peter. b 54. Nottm Univ BSc75 Imp Coll Lon MSc79. Oak Hill Th Coll BA86. **d** 86 **p** 87. C Gee Cross *Ches* 86-90; R Gt Gonerby *Linc* 90-95; R Barrowby and Gt Gonerby from 95; RD Grantham 01-09. *The Rectory, 7 Long Street, Great Gonerby, Grantham NG31 8LN* Tel and fax (01476) 565737 E-mail peterhoppy@worldonline.co.uk

HOPKINS, Richard Clive John. b 74. Nottm Univ BA95 Ex Univ PGCE97. Wycliffe Hall Ox BTh02. **d** 02 **p** 03. C Duffield *Derby* 02-05; C Duffield and Lt Eaton 05-06; P-in-c Sileby, Cossington and Seagrave *Leic* 06-09; R from 09. *The Rectory, 11 Mountsorrel Lane, Sileby, Loughborough LE12 7NF* Tel (01509) 812493 E-mail hopkins@richardcj.fsnet.co.uk

HOPKINS, Robert James Gardner. b 42. Bris Univ BSc64 ACA76 FCA81. St Alb Minl Tr Scheme. **d** 79 **p** 80. NSM Chorleywood Ch Ch *St Alb* 79-83; NSM Parr Mt *Liv* 83-97; NSM Crookes St Thos *Sheff* 97-09; NSM Philadelphia St Thos from 09; Dir Angl Ch Planting Initiatives from 92. *70 St Thomas Road, Sheffield S10 1UX* Tel and fax 0114-267 8266 *or* 278 9378 E-mail admin@acpi.org.uk

HOPKINS, Victor John. b 44. UEA LLB82. CBDTI 06. **d** 07 **p** 08. NSM Sedbergh, Cautley and Garsdale *Bradf* from 07. *Brantrigg, Winfield Road, Sedbergh LA10 5AZ* Tel (015396) 21455 E-mail brantrigg@btinternet.com

HOPKINSON, The Ven Barnabas John. b 39. Trin Coll Cam BA63 MA67. Linc Th Coll 63. **d** 65 **p** 66. C Langley All SS and Martyrs *Man* 65-67; C Cambridge Gt St Mary w St Mich *Ely* 67-71; Asst Chapl Charterhouse Sch Godalming 71-75; P-in-c Preshute *Sarum* 75-76; TV Marlborough 76-81; RD Marlborough 77-81; TR Wimborne Minster and Holt 81-86; Can and Preb Sarum Cathl 83-04; RD Wimborne 85-86; Adn

Sarum 86-98; P-in-c Stratford sub Castle 87-98; Adn Wilts 98-04; rtd 04. *Tanners Cottage, 22 Frog Street, Bampton, Tiverton EX16 9NT* Tel (01398) 331611

HOPKINSON, Benjamin Alaric. b 36. Trin Coll Ox BA59. Chich Th Coll 59. **d** 61 **p** 62. C Pallion *Dur* 61-66; Rhodesia 66-67; Botswana 67-74; Hon C Sherwood *S'well* 74-77; Hon C Carrington 74-77; V Lowdham 77-85; R Whitby *York* 85-95; Miss to Seafarers from 85; V Stainton w Hilton *York* 95-01; Chapl Cleveland Constabulary 95-01; rtd 01; Perm to Offic *Newc* from 01. *11 Watershaugh Road, Warkworth, Morpeth NE65 0TT* Tel and fax (01665) 714213 E-mail dumela@dial.pipex.com

HOPKINSON, Colin Edward. b 57. BA LLB. Ridley Hall Cam. **d** 84 **p** 85. C Chadwell *Chelmsf* 84-87; C Canvey Is 87-90; P-in-c E Springfield 90-98; RD Chelmsf N 95-99; R Langdon Hills from 98. *The Rectory, 105A Berry Lane, Basildon SS16 6AP* Tel (01268) 542156 E-mail cchopkinson@aol.com

HOPKINSON, David John. b 47. Ox NSM Course. **d** 79 **p** 80. NSM Wardington *Ox* 79-80; Hon C Didcot St Pet 80-83; C Headingley *Ripon* 83-87; P-in-c Leeds All So 87-91; R Middleton Tyas w Croft and Eryholme 91-95; V Leeds Belle Is St Jo and St Barn 95-98; rtd 98; Perm to Offic *Ripon* 98-06. *11 Old Well Head, Halifax HX1 2BN* Tel (01422) 361226

HOPKINSON, William Humphrey. b 48. Lon Univ BSc69 Dur Univ MA78 Nottm Univ MPhil84 Man Poly MSc90 California State Univ MEd00 ARIC73. Cranmer Hall Dur. **d** 77 **p** 78. C Normanton *Derby* 77-80; C Sawley 80-82; V Birtles *Ches* 82-87; Dir Past Studies NOC 82-94; Dir Course Development 90-94; CME Officer *Ches* 87-94; P-in-c Tenterden St Mich *Cant* 94-96; Dir Min and Tr 94-02; Hon Can Cant Cathl 01-02; Perm to Offic 03-06; World Faith Manager Harmondsworth Immigration Removal Cen 04-05; Registrar Lon Academy of HE from 05. *London Academy of Higher Education, Boardman House, 64 Broadway, London E15 1NT* Tel (020) 8432 0388 Mobile 07734-202750 E-mail whhopkinson@f2s.com

HOPLEY, David. b 37. Wells Th Coll 62. **d** 65 **p** 66. C Frome St Jo *B & W* 65-68; R Staunton-on-Arrow w Byton and Kinsham *Heref* 68-81; P-in-c Lingen 68-81; P-in-c Aymestrey and Leinthall Earles 72-81; R Buckland Newton, Long Burton etc *Sarum* 81-02; rtd 02; Perm to Offic *B & W* from 07. *Sunnyside, Clatworthy, Taunton TA4 2EH* Tel (01984) 623842

HOPLEY, Gilbert. b 40. Univ of Wales (Ban) BA62. St D Coll Lamp LTh65. **d** 65 **p** 66. C St As and Tremeirchion *St As* 65-73; Warden Ch Hostel Ban 73-76; Chapl Univ of Wales (Ban) 73-76; V Meifod and Llangynyw *St As* 76-79; Chapl St Marg Sch Bushey 79-87; Hd Master St Paul's Cathl Choir Sch 87-97. *Plas Afon, Pentrefelin, Criccieth LL52 0PT* Tel (01766) 523588

HOPPER, Peter Edward. b 60. **d** 99 **p** 00. OLM Bermondsey St Mary w St Olave, St Jo etc *S'wark* 99-05. *56 Reverdy Road, London SE1 5QD* Tel (020) 7237 1543 or 7525 1831 E-mail phopper@phopper.screaming.net

HOPPER, Peter John. b 37. Univ Coll Dur BSc59 Lon Univ PGCE60. NOC 89. **d** 91 **p** 91. C Aston cum Aughton and Ulley *Sheff* 91-93; C Aston cum Aughton w Swallownest, Todwick etc 93-94; P-in-c Braithwell w Bramley 94-95; TV Bramley and Ravenfield w Hooton Roberts etc 95-00; rtd 00; Perm to Offic *Worc* from 00. *21 Hornsby Avenue, Worcester WR4 0PN* Tel (01905) 731618 E-mail peterjhopper@supanet.com

HOPPER, Robert Keith. b 45. St Jo Coll Dur 74. **d** 77 **p** 78. C Oxclose *Dur* 77-80; C Hebburn St Jo 80-82; V Lobley Hill 82-04; P-in-c Marley Hill 02-04; V Hillside from 04. *All Saints' Vicarage, Rowanwood Gardens, Gateshead NE11 0DP* Tel and fax 0191-460 4409 Mobile 07960-754744 E-mail bob.hopper@durham.anglican.org

HOPPERTON, Thomas. b 33. Chich Th Coll 71. **d** 73 **p** 74. C Cheam *S'wark* 73-89; P-in-c St Alb Ch 76-89; P-in-c Rotherhithe St Kath w St Barn 89-92; P-in-c S Bermondsey St Bart 91-92; V Bermondsey St Kath w St Bart 92-01; rtd 01; Perm to Offic *York* from 03. *8 Croft Heads, Sowerby, Thirsk YO7 1ND* Tel (01845) 524210 E-mail fathertom21@aol.com

HOPTHROW, Mrs Elizabeth Rosemary Gladys. b 45. **d** 01 **p** 02. NSM Aylesham w Adisham *Cant* 01-04; NSM Nonington w Wymynswold and Goodnestone etc 01-04; NSM Barham w Bishopsbourne and Kingston from 04; Chapl Pilgrims Hospice Cant from 01. *146 The Street, Kingston, Canterbury CT4 6JQ* Tel (01227) 830070 or 812610 Mobile 07977-754920 E-mail lizziehopthrow@quista.net

HOPWOOD, Adrian Patrick. b 37. N Lon Poly BSc61 CBiol MIBiol MCIWEM. Ox Min Course 87. **d** 90 **p** 91. NSM Chesham Bois *Ox* 90-93; NSM Amersham 93-95; NSM Ridgeway 95-05; rtd 05; Perm to Offic *B & W* from 06. *15 Waverley, Somerton TA11 6SH* Tel (01458) 274527

HOPWOOD OWEN, Mrs Karen. b 58. Padgate Coll of Educn CertEd79 St Martin's Coll Lanc DASE90. **d** 95 **p** 96. OLM Peel Man 95-99; OLM Walkden and Lt Hulton from 99. *168 Manchester Road, Tyldesley, Manchester M29 8WY* Tel (01942) 894850

HORAN, Joan Anne. b 53. BA74 DipEd75. **d** 05 **p** 06. Australia 05-09; P-in-c Feltwell and Methwold *Ely* from 09; P-in-c Hockwold w Wilton from 09; P-in-c Weeting from 09; C

Northwold and Wretton w Stoke Ferry etc from 09. *The Rectory, 7 Oak Street, Feltwell, Thetford IP26 4DD* Tel (01842) 828034 E-mail jahoran@yahoo.co.uk

HORAN, John Champain. b 52. WMMTC 95. **d** 98 **p** 99. NSM Leckhampton SS Phil and Jas w Cheltenham St Jas *Glouc* 98-08; Dioc Communications Officer 01-02. *38 Leckhampton Road, Cheltenham GL53 0BB* Tel (01242) 235370 E-mail horan.jc@btinternet.com

HORBURY, Prof William. b 42. Oriel Coll Ox BA64 MA67 Clare Coll Cam BA66 PhD71 DD00 FBA97. Westcott Ho Cam 64. **d** 69 **p** 70. Fell Clare Coll Cam 68-72; CCC Cam from 78; R Gt w Lt Gransden *Ely* 72-78; Lect Div Cam Univ 84-98; Prof Jewish and Early Chr Studies from 98; P-in-c Cambridge St Botolph *Ely* from 90. *5 Grange Road, Cambridge CB3 9AS* Tel (01223) 363529 Fax 462751

HORDER, Mrs Catharine Joy. b 51. Battersea Coll of Educn CertEd72 UWE BA98. S Dios Minl Tr Scheme 92. **d** 95 **p** 96. C Burrington and Churchill *B & W* 95-00; TV Yatton Moor from 00. *1 Miller Road, Cleeve, Bristol BS49 4NL* Tel (01934) 833152 E-mail cathy.horder@btinternet.com

HORDER, Peter Alan Trahair. b 43. **d** 97 **p** 98. OLM Madron *Truro* 97-01; OLM Gulval 99-01; OLM Gulval and Madron from 01. *Kourion, 38 Boscathnoe Way, Heamoor, Penzance TR18 3JS* Tel (01736) 360813

HORDERN, Peter John Calveley. b 35. Jes Coll Cam BA59 MA64 McMaster Univ Ontario PhD72. Linc Th Coll 59. **d** 61 **p** 62. C Billingham St Aid *Dur* 61-65; Canada from 65; rtd 00. *346 Aberdeen Avenue, Brandon MB R7A 1N4, Canada* Tel (001) (204) 727 3324

HORE, Leslie Nicholas Peter. b 40. SWMTC 99. **d** 02 **p** 03. OLM Treverbyn *Truro* from 02. *Tremore, Hallaze Road, Penwithick, St Austell PL26 8YW* Tel (01726) 851750 E-mail peterhore@hotmail.co.uk

HORE, Michael John. b 50. Man Univ BSc71. Linc Th Coll 75. **d** 78 **p** 79. C Maidstone St Martin *Cant* 78-81; C St Peter-in-Thanet 81-83; R Storrington *Chich* 83-93; RD Storrington 90-93; V Goring-by-Sea 93-02; R Cottenham *Ely* 02-07; R Upminster *Chelmsf* from 07. *The Rectory, 4 Gridiron Place, Upminster RM14 2BE* Tel (01708) 220174 E-mail mrthore@yahoo.co.uk

HORLESTON, Kenneth William. b 50. Oak Hill Th Coll BA86. **d** 86 **p** 87. C Wednesfield Heath *Lich* 86-89; V Blagreaves *Derby* 89-00; P-in-c Horsley 00-02; P-in-c Denby 00-02; V Horsley and Denby from 02; C Morley w Smalley and Horsley Woodhouse 06-07. *The Vicarage, Church Street, Horsley, Derby DE21 5BR* Tel (01332) 880284 E-mail kenhorleston@tiscali.co.uk

HORLOCK, Andrew John. b 51. Bath Univ BSc74 Open Univ MPhil89 Nottm Univ PhD99. Ridley Hall Cam 03. **d** 05 **p** 06. C Crich and S Wingfield *Derby* 05-08; P-in-c Lugano *Eur* from 08. *St Edward the Confessor, via Maraini 6, 6900 Lugano, Switzerland* Tel (0041) (91) 968 1149 E-mail andrewhorlock@hotmail.com

HORLOCK, The Very Revd Brian William. b 31. OBE78. Univ of Wales (Lamp) BA55. Chich Th Coll 55. **d** 57 **p** 58. C Chiswick St Nic w St Mary *Lon* 57-61; C Witney *Ox* 61-62; V N Acton St Gabr *Lon* 62-68; Chapl Oslo w Bergen, Trondheim and Stavanger *Eur* 68-89; RD Scandinavia 75-79; Adn 80-89; Hon Can Brussels Cathl 80-89; Dean Gib 89-98; Chapl Gib 89-98; rtd 98; Perm to Offic *Eur* from 98; Hon C Wootton Bassett *Sarum* from 98. *1 Richard's Close, Wootton Bassett, Swindon SN4 7LE* Tel (01793) 848344 Fax 848378

HORLOCK, Peter Richard. b 76. UWE BA97. Oak Hill Th Coll BA04. **d** 04 **p** 05. C Rusholme H Trin *Man* from 04. *26 Croasdale Avenue, Manchester M14 6GU* Tel 0161-249 3957 Mobile 07890-860022 E-mail peter@plattchurch.org

HORLOCK, Timothy Edward. b 72. Anglia Poly Univ BSc94 Bath Univ PGCE96. Ridley Hall Cam 05. **d** 07 **p** 08. C Bedford Ch Ch *St Alb* from 07. *161 Dudley Street, Bedford MK40 3SY* Tel 07787-968843 (mobile) E-mail alextim_horlock@hotmail.com

HORN, Colin Clive. b 39. CEng MIMechE. Cant Sch of Min. **d** 83 **p** 84. NSM Yalding w Collier Street *Roch* 83-91; V Kemsing w Woodlands 91-98; RD Shoreham 94-98; rtd 99; Perm to Offic *B & W* 00-07. *Saw Mill Cottage, Leigh Street, Leigh upon Mendip, Radstock BA3 5QQ* Tel and fax (01373) 812736 Mobile 07885-523190 E-mail colinhorn@hotmail.com

HORNBY (née CHRISTIAN), Mrs Helen. b 47. K Coll Lon BA68 AKC68 Lon Inst of Educn PGCE69. Cranmer Hall Dur 00. **d** 02 **p** 03. C Briercliffe *Blackb* 02-07; C Blackpool St Jo from 07. *2 Arnside Avenue, Lytham St Annes FY8 3SA* Tel (01253) 711215

HORNE, Brian Edward. b 37. CEng68 MRAeS68 MIET68 EurIng92 Lon Univ BSc62 PhD78. WEMTC 92. **d** 95 **p** 96. OLM Cheltenham St Mark *Glouc* from 95. *87A Rowanfield Road, Cheltenham GL51 8AF* Tel (01242) 236786 E-mail lynbrihorne@btinternet.com

HORNE, Jack Kenneth. b 20. Linc Th Coll 68. **d** 70 **p** 71. C Danbury *Chelmsf* 70-75; V Frampton *Linc* 75-85; rtd 85; Perm to Offic *Linc* from 01. *154 Kenilworth Road, Grantham NG31 9UH* Tel (01476) 578867

HORNE, Mona Lyn Denison. b 38. Gipsy Hill Coll of Educn TCert58. WEMTC 98. **d** 99 **p** 00. OLM Cheltenham St Mark *Glouc* from 99. *87A Rowanfield Road, Cheltenham GL51 8AF* Tel (01242) 236786 Fax 691869
E-mail lynbrihorne@btinternet.com

HORNE, Simon Timothy. b 62. Ball Coll Ox BA86 MA90 Birm Univ PhD99 RN(MH)89. Qu Coll Birm BD94. **d** 95 **p** 96. C Basingstoke *Win* 95-99; C Fordingbridge 99-01; TV Fordingbridge and Breamore and Hale etc from 01. *29 Shaftesbury Street, Fordingbridge SP6 1JF* Tel 07502-146758 (mobile) E-mail simon.horne31@googlemail.com

HORNER, Eric. b 43. EMMTC 87. **d** 90 **p** 91. C Boultham *Linc* 90-93; P-in-c Frampton w Kirton in Holland 93-97; V Kirton in Holland 97-04; rtd 05. *24 Hurn Close, Ruskington, Sleaford NG34 9FE* Tel (01526) 834043 E-mail erichorner04@aol.com

HORNER, Graham. b 57. Grey Coll Dur BSc78 ACA81. St Jo Coll Nottm 93. **d** 93 **p** 94. C Longdon-upon-Tern, Rodington, Uppington etc *Lich* 93-95; C Wrockwardine Deanery 95-96; TV 96-02; TR 02-07; RD Wrockwardine 02-07; V Gt Wyrley from 07. *The Vicarage, 1 Cleves Crescent, Cheslyn Hay, Walsall WS6 7LR* Tel (01922) 414309
E-mail horner314@btinternet.com

HORNER, John Henry. b 40. Leeds Univ BA62 Middx Poly MA87. Oak Hill Th Coll 76. **d** 79 **p** 80. NSM Datchworth w Tewin *St Alb* 79-85; NSM Ware St Mary 85-91; C S Ashford Ch Ch *Cant* 91-94; C Bp's Hatfield *St Alb* 94-99; V Sandridge 99-02; rtd 02; P-in-c Broxbourne w Wormley *St Alb* 03-04. *41 St Leonard's Road, Hertford SG14 3JW* Tel (01992) 423725
E-mail john.horner1@ntlworld.com

HORNER, Richard Murray. b 61. Dur Univ BSc83. NTMTC 93. **d** 96 **p** 97. C Sherborne w Castleton and Lillington *Sarum* 96-99; Chapl Rugby Sch from 99. *11 Horton Crescent, Rugby CV22 5DJ* Tel (01788) 544939

HORNER, Sally. b 68. City Univ BSc94. Westcott Ho Cam 06. **d** 08 **p** 09. C Peckham St Jo w St Andr *S'wark* from 08. *10 Buller Close, London SE15 6UJ* Tel (020) 7639 0084
E-mail sally@sallyhorner.co.uk

HORNSBY, Edgar. b 23. AKC50. **d** 51 **p** 52. C Portsea St Mary *Portsm* 51-55; Chapl RAF 55-69; St Mary's Hall and Brighton Coll 69-74; Chapl St Swithun's Sch Win 74-88; rtd 88; Perm to Offic *B & W* 88-04 and *Sarum* 01-06. *4 Stirling Road, Chichester PO19 7DJ* Tel (01243) 536711

HORNSBY, William John. b 49. RIBA79. SEITE 98. **d** 01 **p** 02. C Faversham *Cant* 01-04; C Preston next Faversham, Goodnestone and Graveney 02-04; P-in-c Newington w Hartlip and Stockbury 04-07; P-in-c Iwade and Upchurch w Lower Halstow 05-07; Perm to Offic 07-08; V Goudhurst w Kilndown from 08. *The Vicarage, Back Lane, Goudhurst, Cranbrook TN17 1AN* Tel (01580) 211332

HOROBIN, Timothy John. b 60. St Jo Coll Nottm 92. **d** 94 **p** 95. C Nelson St Phil *Blackb* 94-98; P-in-c Blackpool St Paul 98-00; Perm to Offic 05-06; Lic to Offic from 06. *75 Main Street, Warton, Carnforth LA5 9PJ* Tel (01524) 733037 Mobile 07811-074063

HORREX, Mrs Gay Lesley. b 42. **d** 96 **p** 97. OLM Walton-on-Thames *Guildf* 96-07; rtd 07; Perm to Offic *Guildf* from 07 and *Portsm* from 08. *25 Pine Walk, Liss GU33 7AT* Tel (01730) 893827 E-mail glhorrex@homecall.co.uk

HORROCKS, Judith Anne. b 53. Univ of Calgary BSc76 Keele Univ MA99. St Jo Coll Nottm. **dss** 82 **d** 87 **p** 94. Denton Ch Ch *Man* 82-85; Whalley Range St Edm 85-97; Par Dn 87-97; C 94-97; Chapl Man R Infirmary 88-90; Chapl Christie Hosp NHS Trust Man 95-03; Chapl S Man Univ Hosps NHS Trust 98-03; Lic Preacher *Man* 97-03; Hon Can Man Cathl 02-03; Multifaith Chapl Co-ord Sheff Hallam Univ 03-05; Chapl St Ann's Hospice Manchester from 05. *Five Saints Rectory, 130A Highfield Road, Farnworth, Bolton BL4 0AJ* Tel (01204) 572334 Fax 08709-138446

HORROCKS, Oliver John. b 30. Clare Coll Cam BA53 MA57. Westcott Ho Cam 53. **d** 55 **p** 56. C Moss Side Ch Ch *Man* 55-58; C Arnold *S'well* 58-60; R Ancoats *Man* 62-67; R Barthomley *Ches* 67-96; rtd 96; Perm to Offic *Ches* from 98. *36 Station Road, Alsager, Stoke-on-Trent ST7 2PD* Tel (01270) 877284

HORROCKS, Robert James. b 56. Grey Coll Dur BSc78. St Jo Coll Nottm. **d** 82 **p** 83. C Denton Ch Ch *Man* 82-85; R Whalley Range St Edm 85-97; P-in-c Bolton St Paul w Em 97-06; P-in-c Daubhill 05-06; TR New Bury w St Paul from 06. *Five Saints Rectory, 130A Highfield Road, Farnworth, Bolton BL4 0AJ* Tel (01204) 572334 Fax 08709-138446
E-mail revbobhorrocks@yahoo.co.uk

HORSEMAN, Christopher Michael. b 54. Bris Sch of Min 84 Trin Coll Bris 87. **d** 88 **p** 89. C Weston-super-Mare Cen Par *B & W* 88-92; TV Yatton Moor 92-02; NSM 02-08. *6 Westaway Park, Yatton, Bristol BS49 4JU* Tel (01934) 834537
E-mail cfhors@globalnet.co.uk

HORSEMAN, Colin. b 46. Lon Coll of Div ALCD69 BD70 STh75. **d** 70 **p** 71. C Higher Openshaw *Man* 70-74; C Darfield *Sheff* 75-78; V Stainforth 78-88; V Heeley 88-95; P-in-c Ducklington *Ox* 95-99; P-in-c Gt Horkesley *Chelmsf* 99-02;

P-in-c W Bergholt 00-02; R W Bergholt and Gt Horkesley from 02; RD Dedham and Tey 03-08. *The Rectory, Ivy Lodge Road, Great Horkesley, Colchester CO6 4EN* Tel (01206) 271242
E-mail revcolin@tiscali.co.uk

HORSEY, Maurice Alfred. b 30. ACIB. S'wark Ord Course 61. **d** 64 **p** 65. C Oxhey All SS *St Alb* 64-67; C Coulsdon St Jo *S'wark* 67-71; P-in-c Champion Hill St Sav 71-76; Hon C Lewisham St Swithun 84-86; P-in-c Woolwich St Thos 86-90; R 90-94; rtd 94; Chapl Costa del Sol W *Eur* 94-98; Perm to Offic from 99. *6/47 Marina de Casares, 29690 Casares (Malaga), Spain* Tel (0034) 952 892 166 E-mail dorothy@tiscali.es

HORSEY, Stanley Desmond. b 20. Ely Th Coll 46. **d** 49 **p** 50. C S Clevedon *B & W* 49-51; C Leigh-on-Sea St Marg *Chelmsf* 51-53; C Barbourne *Worc* 53-55; V Edgbaston St Jas *Birm* 55-60; V Brighton St Martin *Chich* 60-67; V Hove St Barn 67-77; V Hove St Barn and St Agnes 77-85; rtd 85; Perm to Offic *Chich* from 85. *27A Amesbury Crescent, Hove BN3 5RD* Tel (01273) 732081

HORSFALL, Andrew Stuart. b 64. Qu Coll Birm 93. **d** 06 **p** 06. Methodist Min 95-06; Chapl E Lancs Hosps NHS Trust 05-09; Chapl Co-ord from 09; NSM Feniscowles *Blackb* from 06. *Royal Blackburn Hospital, Haslingden Road, Blackburn BB2 3HH* Tel (01254) 736849 E-mail revhors@aol.com

HORSFALL, David John. b 55. Bris Poly BA77. St Jo Coll Nottm 87. **d** 89 **p** 90. C Chaddesden St Mary *Derby* 89-92; V Swadlincote from 92; RD Repton 99-09. *The Vicarage, Church Street, Swadlincote DE11 8LF* Tel (01283) 217756
E-mail djhorsfall@hotmail.com

HORSFALL, Keith. b 39. Tyndale Hall Bris 62. **d** 65 **p** 66. C Walton Breck *Liv* 65-68; C Fazakerley Em 68-70; C Mile Cross *Nor* 70-73; V Gayton 73-80; TR Parr *Liv* 80-90; V Leyland St Andr *Blackb* 90-00; P-in-c Willand *Ex* 00-01; TV Cullompton, Willand, Uffculme, Kentisbeare etc 01-05; rtd 05. *6 rue du Coq, 79110 Tillou, France* Tel (0033) (5) 49 29 73 14
E-mail ritaandkeith@hotmail.com

HORSHAM, Archdeacon of. See COMBES, The Ven Roger Matthew

HORSHAM, Area Bishop of. See SOWERBY, The Rt Revd Mark Crispin Rake

HORSINGTON, Timothy Frederick. b 44. Dur Univ BA66. Wycliffe Hall Ox 67. **d** 69 **p** 70. C Halewood *Liv* 69-72; C Farnworth 72-75; C-in-c Widnes St Jo 72-75; P-in-c Llangarron w Llangrove *Heref* 75-82; P-in-c Whitchurch w Ganarew 77-82; R Llangarron w Llangrove, Whitchurch and Ganarew 83-84; R Highclere and Ashmansworth w Crux Easton *Win* 84-09; rtd 09. *27 Arlington Close, Yeovil BA21 3TB* Tel (01935) 410731

HORSLEY, Canon Alan Avery. b 36. St Chad's Coll Dur BA58 Pacific States Univ MA84 PhD85. Qu Coll Birm 58. **d** 60 **p** 61. C Daventry *Pet* 60-63; C Reading St Giles *Ox* 63-64; C Wokingham St Paul 64-66; V Yeadon St Andr *Bradf* 66-71; R Heyford w Stowe Nine Churches *Pet* 71-78; RD Daventry 76-78; V Oakham w Hambleton and Egleton 78-81; V Oakham, Hambleton, Egleton, Braunston and Brooke 81-86; Can Pet Cathl 79-86; V Lanteglos by Fowey *Truro* 86-88; Provost St Andr Cathl Inverness 88-91; R Inverness St Andr 88-91; P-in-c Culloden St Mary-in-the-Fields 88-91; P-in-c Strathnairn St Paul 88-91; V Mill End and Heronsgate w W Hyde *St Alb* 91-01; RD Rickmansworth 00-01; rtd 01; Perm to Offic *Pet* from 03. *3 Leicester Terrace, Northampton NN2 6AJ* Tel (01604) 628868 E-mail alanahorsley@hotmail.co.uk

HORSLEY, Amelia Mary Elizabeth. b 69. K Alfred's Coll Win BEd91. St Jo Coll Nottm MA97. **d** 98 **p** 99. C Southampton Maybush St Pet *Win* 98-01; Teacher Mansel Infant Sch Southampton 01; Teacher Highfields Primary Sch Leic from 01; Dep Hd from 05. *9 Aylestone Drive, Leicester LE2 8SB* Tel 0116-283 7710 E-mail amehorsley@aol.com

HORSLEY, Peter Alec. b 56. Leeds Metrop Univ CertEd98. Cranmer Hall Dur 99. **d** 01 **p** 02. C Acomb St Steph *York* 01-05; P-in-c Wheldrake w Thorganby 05-08; R Derwent Ings from 08. *The Rectory, Church Lane, Wheldrake, York YO19 6AW* Tel (01904) 448230

HORSMAN, Andrew Alan. b 49. Otago Univ BA70 Man Univ MA72 PhD75. St Steph Ho Ox BA80 MA87. **d** 81 **p** 82. C Hillingdon All SS *Lon* 81-84; C Lt Stanmore St Lawr 84-87; TV Haxby w Wigginton *York* 87-98; V Acomb Moor from 98; P-in-c York All SS N Street from 03. *The Vicarage, 2 Sherringham Drive, York YO24 2SE* Tel (01904) 706047
E-mail andrew@jasdn.freeserve.co.uk

HORSWELL, Kevin George. b 55. Jes Coll Cam BA77 MA81 Nottm Univ BA81. St Jo Coll Nottm 79. **d** 82 **p** 83. C Bootle Ch Ch *Liv* 82-86; Chapl LMH Ox 86-91; C Ox St Giles and SS Phil and Jas w St Marg 86-91; R Dodleston *Ches* 91-00; R Llanaber w Caerdeon *Ban* from 00. *The Rectory, Mynach Road, Barmouth LL42 1RL* Tel (01341) 280516

HORTA, Nelson Pinto. b 40. Lisbon Univ Lic80 Catholic Univ of Portugal LicTh92. **d** 65 **p** 69. Portugal from 65; V Setbal H Spirit 69-71; V Lisbon St Paul 71-96; Asst Chapl Gtr Lisbon *Eur* 97-00. *Quinta da Cerieira, rua C, Lote 261, Vale de Figueira-Sobreda, 2800 Almada, Portugal* Tel (00351) (1) 295 7943

HORTON, Alan Michael. b 47. Univ of Wales BScTech71. Linc Th Coll 92. **d** 92 **p** 93. C Bexleyheath Ch Ch *Roch* 92-95; P-in-c Slade Green 95-99; V 99-03; P-in-c Southborough St Thos 03-08; rtd 08. *3 Bracken Row, Thurston, Bury St Edmunds IP31 3PT* Tel (01359) 231976 E-mail alan@horton28.plus.com

HORTON, Andrew Charles. b 50. Ex Univ BA71. Sarum Th Coll 71. **d** 73 **p** 74. C Westbury-on-Trym St Alb *Bris* 73-76; R Westfield St Pet USA 76-79; R Hamburg Trin Ch 79-87; R Chardon 88; P-in-c Battersea St Mich *S'wark* 90-92; V 92-98; Local Min Officer Kingston Area 94-98; TR Selsdon St Jo w St Fran 98-03. *Address temp unknown*

HORTON, Anne. *See* HORTON, Canon Roberta Anne

HORTON, Cathy Lynne Bosworth. b 62. BA JD. SEITE. **d** 99 **p** 00. NSM Warlingham w Chelsham and Farleigh *S'wark* 99-03; Assoc P Shaker Heights USA 03-07. *Address temp unknown*

HORTON, Canon Christopher Peter. b 26. Leeds Univ BA49. Coll of Resurr Mirfield 49. **d** 51 **p** 52. C Blyth St Mary *Newc* 51-55; C Delaval 55-59; V Grangetown *York* 59-91; Can and Preb York Minster 85-91; rtd 91; Perm to Offic *Newc* from 91. *51 Well Ridge Close, Seaton Grange, Whitley Bay NE25 9PN* Tel 0191-251 0742

HORTON, David Harold. b 49. St Jo Coll Dur BA72. NEOC 82. **d** 86 **p** 87. C Enfield St Jas *Lon* 86-90; Min Joydens Wood St Barn CD *Roch* 90-93; V Joydens Wood St Barn 93-99; P-in-c Rosherville 99-04; rtd 04. *5B Hawes Road, Bromley BR1 3JS* Tel (020) 8466 9211 E-mail davidhhorton@yahoo.com

HORTON, Canon Jeremy Nicholas Orkney. b 44. Cranmer Hall Dur 64. **d** 68 **p** 69. C Dalton-in-Furness *Carl* 68-70; C Penrith 70-73; V Hudswell w Downholme and Marske *Ripon* 73-75; R Middleton Tyas and Melsonby 75-81; P-in-c Croft 78-81; P-in-c Eryholme 78-81; V Wortley de Leeds 81-93; V Middleton St Mary 93-98; RD Armley 96-98; V Kirby-on-the-Moor, Cundall w Norton-le-Clay etc from 98; Jt AD Ripon 01-04; Hon Can Ripon Cathl from 01; rtd 09. *Address temp unknown* Tel 07927-209028 (mobile) E-mail nickhorton199@btinternet.com

HORTON, John. b 49. STETS 05. **d** 07 **p** 08. NSM Exhall w Wixford *Cov* from 07. *St Giles's House, 222 Coventry Road, Exhall, Coventry CV7 9BH* Tel (024) 7631 1582 E-mail john@horton6677.freeserve.co.uk

HORTON, John Ward. b 27. Leeds Univ BA50. Coll of Resurr Mirfield 50. **d** 52 **p** 53. C Balkwell CD *Newc* 52-55; C E Coatham *York* 55-58; C-in-c Acomb Moor CD 58-71; V Acomb Moor 71-93; rtd 93; Perm to Offic *Newc* from 93. *39 Billy Mill Lane, North Shields NE29 8BZ* Tel 0191-296 4082

HORTON, Mrs Joy. b 52. CertEd73 Kent Univ MA98. SEITE 94. **d** 97 **p** 98. C Dartford St Edm *Roch* 97-01; Chapl Bromley Hosps NHS Trust 01-02; C Erith St Jo *Roch* 02-03; Perm to Offic 03-04; Chapl Burrswood Chr Cen 04-08; Perm to Offic *St E* from 09. *3 Bracken Row, Thurston, Bury St Edmunds IP31 3PT* Tel (01359) 231976

HORTON, Melanie Jane. b 64. Birm Poly LLB85 Solicitor 86. Ripon Coll Cuddesdon BA95. **d** 96 **p** 97. C Lich St Chad 96-00; Chapl R Masonic Sch for Girls Rickmansworth 00-03; Chapl St Edm Sch Cant 03-08; R Colwall w Upper Colwall and Coddington *Heref* from 08. *The Rectory, Walwyn Road, Colwall, Malvern WR13 6EG* Tel (01684) 540330 Mobile 07748-842825 E-mail colwallrector@tiscali.co.uk

HORTON, Michael John. b 56. St Jo Coll Cam BA80 MA83 Univ of Wales (Swansea) PGCE83. Wycliffe Hall Ox BA88 MA92. **d** 89 **p** 90. C Northallerton w Kirby Sigston *York* 89-92; C Ulverston St Mary w H Trin *Carl* 92-94; V Lightwater *Guildf* 94-04; Chapl Wrekin Coll Telford from 04. *Five Gables, Prospect Road, Wellington, Telford TF1 3BE* Tel (01952) 415059 E-mail michael@hortonfamily.co.uk *or* mjhorton@wrekincollege.ac.uk

HORTON, Nicholas. *See* HORTON, Canon Jeremy Nicholas Orkney

HORTON, Ralph Edward. b 41. S'wark Ord Course 75. **d** 78 **p** 79. C Streatham St Leon *S'wark* 78-81; TV Catford (Southend) and Downham 81-88; V Ashford St Matt *Lon* from 88. *The Vicarage, 99 Church Road, Ashford TW15 2NY* Tel (01784) 252459

HORTON, Canon Roberta Anne. b 44. Leic Univ BSc66 CertEd67 Nottm Univ BCombStuds82. Linc Th Coll 79. **dss** 82 **d** 87 **p** 94. Cambridge St Jas *Ely* 82-86; Beaumont Leys *Leic* 86-91; Par Dn 87-91; Dioc Dir of Tr 91-00; P-in-c Swithland 94-99; R Woodhouse, Woodhouse Eaves and Swithland from 00; Hon Can Leic Cathl from 94. *The Rectory, 157 Main Street, Swithland, Loughborough LE12 8TQ* Tel and fax (01509) 891163 E-mail rahorton@leicester.anglican.org

HORTON, Mrs Wilma Alton. b 46. **d** 06 **p** 07. OLM Alford w Rigsby *Linc* from 06. *6 Wilyman Close, Sandilands, Mablethorpe LN12 2UG* Tel (01507) 443383 E-mail malc.horton@tiscali.co.uk

HORWELL, Elizabeth. b 54. Southn Univ BSc76 Essex Univ MA77 Birm Univ PhD84 Wolv Univ PGCE94. ERMC 04. **d** 07 **p** 08. C Wanstead St Mary w Ch Ch *Chelmsf* from 07. *13 Wanstead Place, London E11 2SW* Tel (020) 8530 4970 Mobile 07835-450837 E-mail ehorwell@hotmail.com

HORWOOD, Graham Frederick. b 34. Univ of Wales (Cardiff) BA55. Coll of Resurr Mirfield 55. **d** 57 **p** 58. C Llantrisant 57-61; C Roath St Sav 61-62; C Roath 62-66; V Clydach Vale 66-77; V Canton St Luke 77-99; rtd 99. *26 Heol-yr-Onnen, Llanharry, Pontyclun CF72 9NJ* Tel (01443) 225777 E-mail ghorwood@freeuk.com

HOSKIN, Brian. *See* HOSKIN, Henry Brian

HOSKIN, Canon David William. b 49. Hatf Coll Dur BSc71. Wycliffe Hall Ox 72. **d** 75 **p** 76. C Bridlington Priory *York* 75-78; C Rodbourne Cheney *Bris* 78-79; C Bebington *Ches* 79-82; R Lockington and Lund and Scorborough w Leconfield *York* 82-88; V Beverley St Mary from 88; RD Beverley 97-07; Can and Preb York Minster from 05. *St Mary's Vicarage, 15 Molescroft Road, Beverley HU17 7DX* Tel and fax (01482) 881437 E-mail office@stmarysbeverley.org.uk

HOSKIN, Canon Eric James. b 28. St Chad's Coll Dur BA50. **d** 52 **p** 53. C Coney Hill *Glouc* 52-54; C Stroud 54-57; R Ruardean 57-63; P-in-c Lydbrook 61-63; V Cheltenham Em 63-70; R Dursley 70-86; RD Dursley 77-85; Hon Can Glouc Cathl 81-86; R Easington w Liverton *York* 86-96; rtd 96; Perm to Offic *York* from 96. *37A Algarth Rise, Pocklington, York YO42 2HX* Tel (01759) 305798

HOSKIN, Henry Brian. b 32. NW Ord Course 72. **d** 75 **p** 76. NSM Chesterfield St Aug *Derby* 75-79; NSM Bolsover 79-83; NSM Old Brampton and Loundsley Green 83-88; P-in-c Gt Barlow 88-94; rtd 97; Perm to Offic *Derby* from 97. *25 Barn Close, Chesterfield S41 8BD* Tel (01246) 201550

HOSKING, Canon Harold Ernest. b 19. Lich Th Coll 51. **d** 53 **p** 54. C Penwerris *Truro* 53-56; R Mawgan in Pyder 56-61; V Newlyn St Pet 61-69; V Newquay 69-74; TR Redruth 74-80; R Redruth w Lanner 80-84; Hon Can Truro Cathl 78-84; rtd 84; Perm to Offic *Ex* and *Truro* 84-03; *Ely* from 03. *11 Greenfield Close, Stapleford, Cambridge CB22 5BT* Tel (01223) 840468

HOSKINS, Hugh George. b 46. S Dios Minl Tr Scheme. **d** 84 **p** 85. NSM Hilperton w Whaddon and Staverton etc *Sarum* 84-87; C Calne and Blackland 87-90; R W Lavington and the Cheverells 90-97; TR Upper Wylye Valley 97-04; RD Heytesbury 00-03; TR Pewsey and Swanborough from 04; P-in-c Upavon w Rushall and Charlton from 07. *The Rectory, Church Street, Pewsey SN9 5DL* Tel (01672) 564357 Fax 563203 E-mail hahoskins@aol.com

HOSKINS, John Paul. b 74. Univ Coll Dur BA95 MA96 MLitt07 Trin Coll Cam BA99 MA04. Westcott Ho Cam 97 Ripon Coll Cuddesdon 05. **d** 07 **p** 08. C Bakewell *Derby* from 07. *The Vicarage, Curbar Lane, Curbar, Calver, Hope Valley S32 3YF* Tel (01433) 630979 E-mail hoskjp@tiscali.co.uk

HOSKINS, Mrs Rosemary Anne. b 56. Surrey Univ BA03. Wesley Coll Bris 99 STETS 01. **d** 02 **p** 03. NSM Camelot Par *B & W* 02-06; NSM Cam Vale from 06; Warden of Readers Wells Adnry from 05. *Springfields, Weston Bampfylde, Yeovil BA22 7HZ* Tel (01963) 440026 E-mail revrose@weston-bampfylde.freeserve.co.uk

HOTCHEN, Stephen Jeffrie. b 50. Bradf Coll of Educn. Linc Th Coll 85. **d** 87 **p** 88. C Morpeth *Newc* 87-90; TV High Wycombe *Ox* 90-91; R Dingwall and Strathpeffer *Mor* 91-94; V Rickerscote *Lich* 94-04; R Aylmerton, Runton, Beeston Regis and Gresham *Nor* 04-07; P-in-c Altofts *Wakef* from 07. *The Vicarage, 72A Church Road, Normanton WF6 2QG* Tel (01924) 892299 Mobile 07976-387199 E-mail sjhotchen@aol.com

HOTCHIN, Mrs Hilary Moya. b 52. Birm Univ CertEd73. WMMTC 88. **d** 88 **p** 94. NSM Redditch St Steph *Worc* 88-91; Par Dn Handsworth *Sheff* 91-94; C 94-96; TV Maltby 96-98; NSM Marfleet *York* 06-08; NSM Sutton St Mich from 08. *8 Whisperwood Way, Bransholme, Hull HU7 4JT* Tel (01482) 828015

HOUGH, Adrian Michael. b 59. Hertf Coll Ox BA80 MA84 DPhil84 MRSC CChem. Ripon Coll Cuddesdon BA91. **d** 92 **p** 93. C Martley and Wichenford, Knightwick etc *Worc* 92-96; Asst P Evesham Deanery 96-97; V Badsey w Aldington and Offenham and Bretforton 97-04; Perm to Offic *Worc* 05-06; Bp's Chapl and Asst *Ex* from 06. *2 West Avenue, Exeter EX4 4SD* Tel (01392) 214867 *or* 272362 E-mail adrian.amhough@btinternet.com

HOUGH, Miss Carole Elizabeth. b 59. Lon Hosp SRN81. St Jo Coll Nottm 87. **d** 91 **p** 94. C Beoley *Worc* 91-95; Asst Chapl Addenbrooke's NHS Trust 95-98; Chapl Milton Keynes Hosp NHS Foundn Trust from 98; Chapl Milton Keynes Primary Care Trust from 98. *Milton Keynes General Hospital, Standing Way, Milton Keynes MK6 5LD* Tel (01908) 660033 ext 2215

HOUGH, Michael Jeremy. b 61. Wilson Carlile Coll Oak Hill Th Coll 00. **d** 02 **p** 03. C Redhill H Trin *S'wark* 02-06; P-in-c Woodmansterne from 06. *The Rectory, Woodmansterne Street, Banstead SM7 3NL* Tel (01737) 352849 Mobile 07939-088867 E mail micklmough@hotmail.com

HOUGH, Peter George. b 40. Dur Univ BA62. Wells Th Coll 62. **d** 64 **p** 65. C Stocking Farm CD *Leic* 64-68; V Leic St Aid 68-76; V Knutton *Lich* 76-05; P-in-c Silverdale and Alsagers Bank 93-94; V Alsagers Bank 01-05; rtd 05. *2 Station Road, Keele, Newcastle ST5 5AH* Tel (01782) 624282

HOUGH, Sharron Lesley. b 54. **d** 01 **p** 02. OLM Willenhall H Trin *Lich* 01-05; C Bentley 05-09; P-in-c from 09. *10 Pineneedle Croft, Willenhall WV12 4BY* Tel (01902) 410458

HOUGH, Wendy Lorraine. b 63. Trin Coll Bris BA94 LLAM81. Cranmer Hall Dur 98. **d** 00 **p** 01. C The Hague *Eur* 00-03; Asst Chapl Berne w Neuchâtel 05-07; C Bris St Mary Redcliffe w Temple etc from 07; Chapl St Mary Redcliffe and Temple Sch from 07. *2 Colston Parade, Bristol BS1 6RA* Tel 0117-929 1519 E-mail wendy@stmaryredcliffe.co.uk

HOUGHTON, Christopher Guy. b 64. W Surrey Coll of Art & Design BA86. Oak Hill Th Coll BA89. **d** 89 **p** 90. C Mossley Hill St Matt and St Jas *Liv* 89-92; C Ashton-in-Makerfield St Thos 92-95; C Southport St Phil and St Paul 95-96; Chapl Chorley and S Ribble NHS Trust 96-01; rtd 01; Perm to Offic *Blackb* from 03. *35 Deerfold, Chorley PR7 1UD*

HOUGHTON, David John. b 47. Edin Univ BSc(Econ)68. Cuddesdon Coll 69. **d** 71 **p** 72. C Prestbury *Glouc* 71-74; Prec Gib Cathl 74-76; Chapl Madrid 76-78; C Croydon St Jo *Cant* 78-80; Chapl Warw Sch 80-85; P-in-c Isleworth St Fran *Lon* 85-90; USA 90-91; TV Clapham Team *S'wark* 91-01; RD Clapham 93-01; V Clapham H Spirit 02; Chapl Paris St Geo *Eur* 02-07; P-in-c Surbiton St Andr and St Mark *S'wark* from 07. *14 The Ridge, Surbiton KT5 8HX* Tel (020) 8399 6053 E-mail davidhoughton@wanadoo.fr

HOUGHTON, Mrs Evelyn Mabel. b 44. Stockwell Coll of Educn TCert65. Oak Hill NSM Course 92. **d** 94 **p** 95. NSM Bedford St Jo and St Leon *St Alb* 94-98; C Reading St Agnes w St Paul *Ox* from 98. *St Paul's House, 3 Whitley Wood Lane, Reading RG2 8PN* Tel 0118-986 2513

HOUGHTON, Geoffrey John. b 59. Ridley Hall Cam 87. **d** 90 **p** 91. C Sholing *Win* 90-94; P-in-c Jersey All SS 94-99; V 99-09; P-in-c Jersey St Simon 94-99; V 99-09; P-in-c Jersey H Trin 05-06; R from 06; Vice-Dean Jersey from 99; Hon Chapl Jersey Hospice from 96. *Holy Trinity Rectory, La Rue du Presbytere, Trinity, Jersey JE3 5JB* Tel and fax (01534) 861110 E-mail geoffhoughton@jerseymail.co.uk *or* gjh@super.net.uk

HOUGHTON, Graham. *See* HOUGHTON, Peter Graham

HOUGHTON, Hugh Alexander Gervase. b 76. St Jo Coll Cam BA97 MPhil98 MA01 Leeds Univ BA02 Birm Univ PhD06. Coll of Resurr Mirfield 00. **d** 03 **p** 04. NSM Weoley Castle *Birm* 03-06; NSM Headington Quarry *Ox* 06-09; Perm to Offic *Birm* from 09; Research Fell Birm Univ from 06. *68 Camp Lane, Handsworth, Birmingham B21 8JR* Tel 0121-682 1150 E-mail h.a.g.houghton@bham.ac.uk

HOUGHTON, Ian David. b 50. Lanc Univ BA71 Newc Univ CertEd74. Sarum & Wells Th Coll 80. **d** 82 **p** 83. C Newc St Geo 82-85; Chapl Newc Poly 85-92; Chapl Univ of Northumbria at Newc 92-95; Master Newc St Thos Prop Chpl 90-95; Black Country Urban Ind Miss *Lich* 95-04; Res Min Bilston 95-04; Chapl Pet City Cen 04-08; C Pet St Jo 04-08; P-in-c Osmotherley w Harlsey and Ingleby Arncliffe *York* 08-09; V from 09; P-in-c Leake w Over and Nether Silton and Kepwick 08-09; V from 09; P-in-c Felixkirk w Boltby 08-09; V from 09; P-in-c Kirby Knowle 08-09; V from 09; P-in-c Cowesby 08-09; R from 09. *Leake Vicarage, Knayton, Thirsk YO7 4AZ* Tel (01485) 537277 E-mail ian.houghton@ukonline.co.uk

HOUGHTON, James Robert. b 44. AKC67 St Luke's Coll Ex CertEd73. **d** 68 **p** 69. C Herrington *Dur* 68-70; Asst Dioc Youth Chapl *Bris* 70-72; Perm to Offic *Ex* 73-74; C Heavitree 74-78; Perm to Offic *Lon* 78-80 and 83-88; Hon C W Drayton 80-83; Chapl Greycoat Hosp Sch 83-88; Chapl Stonar Sch Melksham 88-95; Chapl St Mary and St Anne's Sch Abbots Bromley 95-99; R Buxted and Hadlow Down *Chich* 99-02; V Eastbourne St Mich 02-08; rtd 09; Perm to Offic *Cant* from 09. *12A Marlborough Court, Earls Avenue, Folkstone CT20 2PN* Tel 07955-242324 (mobile) E-mail jamiehoughton@live.com

HOUGHTON, Canon John Caswell. b 16. Dur Univ BA38 LTh38. St Boniface Warminster 34. **d** 39 **p** 40. C Wolverton St Geo *Ox* 39-42; Zambia 42-74; Warden Dioc Th Sem N Rhodesia 47-52; Can N Rhodesia 60-62; Adn N Rhodesia 62-64; Adn S Zambia 64-70; Can Lusaka 71-74; Promotions Sec Feed the Minds 74-81; rtd 81; Perm to Offic *Ox* 82-07. *42 Caton House, Epsom Grove, Bletchley, Milton Keynes MK3 5NR*

HOUGHTON, Josephine Elizabeth. b 80. Birm Univ BA01 PhD07. St Steph Ho Ox BA09. **d** 09. C Handsworth St Andr *Birm* from 09. *68 Camp Lane, Handsworth, Birmingham B21 8JR* Tel 0121-682 1150 E-mail josephine@houghtons.org.uk

HOUGHTON, Peter Graham. b 51. St Jo Coll Nottm 85. **d** 87 **p** 88. C Toxteth Park St Clem *Liv* 87-91; Chapl Winwick Hosp Warrington 91-94; Chapl Warrington Community Health Care NHS Trust 94-98; Chapl HM Pris Styal 98-01; Chapl St Helens and Knowsley Hosps NHS Trust 04-05. *40 Grange Drive, Penketh, Warrington WA5 2JN*

HOUGHTON, Prof Peter John. b 47. Chelsea Coll Lon BPharm68 PhD73 FRPharmS93 FRSC94. Dioc OLM tr scheme 05. **d** 08. NSM Balham Hill Ascension *S'wark* from 08. *7 Culverden Road, London SW12 9LR* Tel (020) 8673 7884 Mobile 07734-747688 E-mail peter.houghton@kcl.ac.uk

HOUGHTON, Mrs Rosemary Margaret Anne. b 46. **d** 00 **p** 01. OLM Earlham *Nor* from 00. *74 St Mildred's Road, West Earlham, Norwich NR5 8RS* Tel (01603) 502752 Mobile 07808-774811 E-mail rosemary.houghton@ntlworld.com

HOUGHTON, Mrs Susan Jeanette. b 39. Qu Mary Coll Lon BSc61 Nottm Univ PGCE62. WMMTC 98. **d** 99 **p** 00. OLM Dursley *Glouc* 99-02; rtd 02; NSM Offwell, Northleigh, Farway, Cotleigh etc *Ex* 02-09. *2 Combewater Cottages, Wilmington, Honiton EX14 9SQ* Tel (01404) 831887 E-mail susanhoughton@lineone.net *or* davidjohnhoughton@lineone.net

HOUGHTON, Thomas. b 17. NW Ord Course 71. **d** 74 **p** 75. NSM Newcastle w Butterton *Lich* 74-82; Perm to Offic from 82. *Madeley Manor Nursing Home, Heighley Castle Way, Madeley, Crewe CW3 9HF* Tel (01782) 750610

HOUGHTON, Timothy John. b 56. Kingston Poly BSc88. Oak Hill Th Coll BA93. **d** 97 **p** 98. C Normanton *Derby* 97-03. *Address temp unknown*

HOULDEN, Prof James Leslie. b 29. Qu Coll Ox BA52 MA56. Cuddesdon Coll 53. **d** 55 **p** 56. C Hunslet St Mary and Stourton *Ripon* 55-58; Tutor Chich Th Coll 58-59; Chapl 59-60; Chapl Trin Coll Ox 60-70; Prin Cuddesdon Coll 70-75; Prin Ripon Coll Cuddesdon 75-77; V Cuddesdon *Ox* 70-77; Hon Can Ch Ch 76-77; Sen Lect NT Studies K Coll Lon 77-87; Prof Th 87-94; rtd 94; Perm to Offic *S'wark* 94-99 and *Birm* from 99. *5 The Court, Fen End Road West, Knowle, Solihull B93 0AN* Tel (01564) 777138 E-mail leslie.houlden@btopenworld.com

HOULDING, Preb David Nigel Christopher. b 53. AKC76. **d** 77 **p** 78. C Hillingdon All SS *Lon* 77-81; C Holborn St Alb w Saffron Hill St Pet 81-85; V Hampstead St Steph w All Hallows from 85; AD N Camden 01-02; Preb St Paul's Cathl from 04. *All Hallows' House, 52 Courthope Road, London NW3 2LD* Tel (020) 7267 7833 *or* 7267 6317 Fax 7267 6317 Mobile 07710-403294 E-mail fr.houlding@lineone.net

HOULDSWORTH, Raymond Clifford. b 30. Bps' Coll Cheshunt 64. **d** 66 **p** 67. C Egham Hythe *Guildf* 66-70; C Cranbrook *Cant* 70-76; V Hernhill 76-82; V Minster w Monkton 82-95; rtd 95; Perm to Offic *Mon* from 95. *St Illtyd's, 11 Craig Road, Six Bells, Abertillery NP13 2LR* Tel (01495) 321934

HOULT, Roy Anthony. b 35. AKC58. **d** 59 **p** 60. C Walton St Mary *Liv* 59-63; Canada from 63; Hon Can Koot 75-79. *381 Huron Street, Toronto ON M5S 2G5, Canada*

HOULTON, David Andrew. b 58. Bradf Univ BEng80 MPhil86 CEng90 EurIng90 FIChemE98. Wycliffe Hall Ox 07. **d** 09. C Old Trafford St Bride *Man* from 09. *78 Northumberland Road, Manchester M16 9PP* E-mail david.houlton@wycliffe.ox.ac.uk

HOULTON, Neil James. b 54. STETS 04. **d** 07 **p** 08. NSM Pokesdown St Jas *Win* from 07. *27 Rebbeck Road, Bournemouth BH7 6LW* Tel (01202) 462476 E-mail neil.houlton@ntlworld.com

HOUNSELL, Mrs Susan Mary. b 49. STETS 04. **d** 07 **p** 08. NSM W Monkton *B & W* from 07. *33 Home Orchard, Hatch Beauchamp, Taunton TA3 6TG* Tel (01823) 480545 E-mail susanhounsell@tiscali.co.uk

HOUSE, Graham Ivor. b 44. Oak Hill Th Coll BA80. **d** 80 **p** 81. C Ipswich St Jo *St E* 80-84; V Ipswich St Andr 84-00; R Monks Eleigh w Chelsworth and Brent Eleigh etc 00-03; rtd 03; Perm to Offic *St E* from 03. *6 Through Duncans, Woodbridge IP12 4EA* Tel (01394) 386066 Mobile 07966-169372

HOUSE, Jack Francis. b 35. Bris Univ BEd70 Lon Univ MA80 Univ of Wales MTh94. Bris & Glouc Tr Course 79. **d** 80 **p** 81. NSM Bedminster *Bris* 80-92; Perm to Offic 92-94; NSM Knowle H Nativity 94-03; NSM Easton All Hallows 98-03; NSM Brislington St Anne 03-05; rtd 05; Perm to Offic *Bris* from 05. *48 Hendre Road, Bristol BS3 2LR* Tel 0117-966 1144 E-mail rhouse3766@aol.com

HOUSE, Mrs Janet. b 45. UEA BA67 Keswick Hall Coll PGCE68 Sussex Univ MA80. Ripon Coll Cuddesdon 93. **d** 95 **p** 96. C Swindon Ch Ch *Bris* 95-99; TV Worc SE 99-06; rtd 06; Perm to Offic *Nor* from 06. *11 Caernarvon Road, Norwich NR2 3HZ* Tel (01603) 762259 E-mail jhouse@waitrose.com

HOUSE, Miss Maureen Ruth (Mo). b 33. St Mich Ho Ox 56 LNSM course 95. **d** 98 **p** 99. NSM Charlton *S'wark* from 98. *88 Speedwell Street, London SE8 4AT* Tel (020) 8691 1637 *or* 8316 7695 E-mail plumbhouse@88speedwell.freeserve.co.uk

HOUSE, Simon Hutchinson. b 30. Peterho Cam BA65 MA67. Cuddesdon Coll 61. **d** 64 **p** 65. C Sutton St Jas *York* 64-67; C Acomb St Steph 67-69; V Allestree St Nic *Derby* 69-81; RD Duffield 74-81; V Bitterne Park *Win* 81-91; rtd 91; Perm to Offic *Win* from 91. *22 Stanley Street, Southsea PO5 2DS* Tel (023) 9283 8592

HOUSE, Vickery Willis. b 45. Kelham Th Coll. **d** 69 **p** 70. C Crediton *Ex* 69-76; TV Sampford Peverell, Uplowman, Holcombe Rogus etc 76-81; R Berwick w Selmeston and Alciston *Chich* 81-90; Chapl Ardingly Coll 90-94; V Brighton St Bart *Chich* from 94. *16 Richmond Terrace, Brighton BN2 9SA* Tel (01273) 685142 *or* 620491 Fax 572215 E-mail stbarts@fastnet.co.uk

HOUSEMAN, Patricia Adele. *See* CAMPION, Mrs Patricia Adele

HOUSLEY, Andrew Arthur. b 67. Wilson Carlile Coll 91 Ridley Hall Cam 00. **d** 02 **p** 03. C Ormskirk *Liv* 02-06; V Litherland St Phil 06-09; R Aughton St Mich and Bickerstaffe from 09. *The Rectory, 10 Church Lane, Aughton, Ormskirk L39 6SB* Tel (01695) 423204 E-mail andrewjohousley@ukonline.co.uk

HOUSMAN, Arthur Martin Rowand. b 53. MA CertEd. Trin Coll Bris 81. **d** 83 **p** 84. C Croydon Ch Ch Broad Green *Cant* 83-84; C Croydon Ch Ch *S'wark* 85-87; TV Stratton St Margaret w S Marston etc *Bris* 87-93; Chapl Peterhouse Sch Zimbabwe 93-98; Chapl Nor Sch 98-07; Hon PV Nor Cathl 98-07; Hon C Raveningham Gp from 08. *Orchards, Beccles Road, Raveningham, Norwich NR14 6NW* Tel (01508) 548322 Mobile 07790-944860 E-mail orchardsone@uwclub.net

HOUSTON, Canon Arthur James. b 54. Trin Coll Bris BA87. **d** 87 **p** 88. C Chatham St Phil and St Jas *Roch* 87-91; I Carrigaline Union *C, C & R* 91-99; Can Cork Cathl 95-99; Can Ross Cathl 95-99; Dir of Ords 96-99; V Margate H Trin *Cant* 99-08; P-in-c Maidstone St Paul from 08; AD Thanet 02-08; AD Maidstone from 08; Hon Can Cant Cathl from 03. *4 Church Square, Lenham, Maidstone ME17 2PJ* Tel (01622) 858202 E-mail arthurjhouston@googlemail.com

HOUSTON, David William James. b 52. Th Ext Educn Coll. **d** 93 **p** 95. C Lyttelton S Africa 93-96; R Sabie w Lydenburg 96-00; P-in-c Elmsted w Hastingleigh *Cant* 00-06; P-in-c Petham and Waltham w Lower Hardres etc 00-06; V Stone Street Gp 06; R Southfleet *Roch* from 06. *The Rectory, Hook Green Road, Southfleet, Gravesend DA13 9NQ* Tel (01474) 833252 E-mail david@houstonclan.net

HOUSTON, Edward Davison. b 31. TCD BA56. **d** 57 **p** 58. C Conwall Union *D & R* 57-59; India 59-88; V Whittlebury w Paulerspury *Pet* 89-01; P-in-c Wicken 89-01; rtd 01; Perm to Offic *Pet* from 01. *38 Meadow Street, Market Harborough LE16 7JZ* Tel (01858) 433309

HOUSTON, Helen Sarah. b 70. Bris Univ BA91. St Jo Coll Nottm MA95. **d** 95 **p** 96. C Bourne *Guildf* 95-98; Perm to Offic *Bris* 98-99; Hon C Chippenham St Pet 99-00; C Ballyholme *D & D* 02-04; C Stretton and Appleton Thorn *Ches* 04-05; Asst to RD Gt Budworth 05; Chapl St Rocco's Hospice from 05; Hon C Stockton Heath *Ches* from 08. *St Rocco's Hospice, Lockton Lane, Bewsey, Warrington WA5 5BW* Tel (01925) 575780 *or* 211466 Fax 419777 E-mail helen@davehouston.fsnet.co.uk

HOUSTON, Kenneth. *See* HOUSTON, Prof Samuel Kenneth

HOUSTON, Maurice Iain. b 48. TISEC 99. **d** 02 **p** 03. C Edin Old St Paul 02-05; R Melrose from 05. *The Rectory, 20 High Cross Avenue, Melrose TD6 9SU* Tel (01896) 822626 Mobile 07866-074568 E-mail morrishouston@btinternet.com

HOUSTON, Michael Alexander. b 46. Lanc Univ MA92. Linc Th Coll 86. **d** 88 **p** 89. C Longton *Blackb* 88-91; C Woughton *Ox* 91-92; TV 92-98; TR 98-99; TR Gd Shep TM *Carl* 99-07; rtd 07. *East Wing, Eden Place, Kirkby Stephen CA17 4AP* Tel (01768) 371356 E-mail mike.greystoke@tiscali.co.uk

HOUSTON, Michael James. b 41. Dub Bible Coll St Jo Coll Nottm. **d** 95 **p** 97. Aux Min *D & D* 95-99; P-in-c Ballyphilip w Ardquin 99-07; Chapl Kyrenia St Andr Cyprus from 07. *PO Box 171, Girne, Mersin 10, Turkey* Tel (0090) (392) 815 4329 E-mail standrews@gawab.com

HOUSTON, Prof Samuel Kenneth. b 43. QUB BSc64 PhD67 FIMA73 MILT. CITC 81. **d** 85 **p** 86. NSM Belfast St Jas w St Silas *Conn* 85-91; NSM Belfast St Andr from 91; Prof Mathematical Studies Ulster Univ from 96. *29 North Circular Road, Belfast BT15 5HB* Tel (028) 9077 1830 *or* 9036 6953 Fax 9036 6859 Mobile 07929-725319 E-mail sk.houston@north-circular.demon.co.uk

HOUSTON, William Paul. b 54. QUB BSSc76 TCD BTh78. CITC 78. **d** 81 **p** 82. C Carrickfergus *Conn* 81-83; C Bangor St Comgall *D & D* 83-86; I Gilford 86-90; I Carnalea 90-99; I Clondalkin w Rathcoole *D & G* from 99; Min Can St Patr Cathl Dublin from 00. *The Rectory, 5 Monastery Road, Clondalkin, Dublin 22, Republic of Ireland* Tel (00353) (1) 459 2160

HOVENDEN, Gerald Eric. b 53. York Univ BA75 Ox Univ MA85. Wycliffe Hall Ox 78. **d** 81 **p** 82. C Pitsmoor w Ellesmere *Sheff* 81-85; Chapl Lyon w Grenoble and St Etienne *Eur* 85-90; TV S Gillingham *Roch* 90-97; TR Southborough St Pet w Ch Ch and St Matt etc from 98. *The Vicarage, 86 Prospect Road, Southborough, Tunbridge Wells TN4 0EG* Tel (01892) 528534 *or* tel and fax 513680 E-mail gerald.hovenden@diocese-rochester.org

HOVEY, Richard Michael. b 58. Imp Coll Lon BScEng79 Cranfield Inst of Tech MBA84 CEng83 MIET83 EurIng92. Cranmer Hall Dur 93. **d** 95 **p** 96. C Cheddar *B & W* 95-99; TV Gtr Corsham *Bris* 99-01; TV Gtr Corsham and Lacock 01-05; S Team Ldr CMS from 05. *80 High Street, Corsham SN13 0HF* Tel (01249) 715407 E-mail crockford@richardhovey.co.uk

HOVIL, Jeremy Richard Guy. b 65. K Coll Lon BSc86 Spurgeon's Coll Lon MTh99 Stellenbosch Univ ThD05. Wycliffe Hall Ox BTh95. **d** 95 **p** 96. C Kensington St Barn *Lon* 95-99; Crosslinks

Uganda 00-07; Field Dir Trust in Chr S Africa from 07. *11 Upper Towers Road, Muizenberg, Cape Town, 7945 South Africa* Tel (0027) (21) 788 3313 Mobile 76-120 5888 E-mail jem@trustinchrist.org

HOVIL, Richard Guy. b 29. Ex Coll Ox BA51 MA57. Ridley Hall Cam. **d** 55 **p** 56. C Finchley Ch Ch *Lon* 55-58; Staff Worker Scripture Union 58-71; Chapl Monkton Combe Sch Bath 71-83; V Fremington *Ex* 83-94; rtd 94; Perm to Offic *Sarum* from 94. *22 The Downlands, Warminster BA12 9PN* Tel (01985) 214337 E-mail ricjanhovil@blueyonder.co.uk

HOW, Gillian Carol. *See* BUNCE, Gillian Carol

HOW, Canon John Maxloe. b 15. Magd Coll Cam BA37 MA49. Westcott Ho Cam 39. **d** 39 **p** 40. C Norton St Mary *Dur* 39-44; P-in-c W Pelton 44-45; P-in-c Stella 46-47; V Thornley 47-51; V Monkwearmouth St Andr 51-59; V Barton w Pooley Bridge *Carl* 59-73; RD Penrith 61-73; Hon Can Carl Cathl 72-81; V Kirkby Lonsdale w Mansergh 73-76; TR Kirkby Lonsdale 76-81; rtd 81; Perm to Offic *Carl* from 81. *The Laurels, 3 Belle Isle Terrace, Grange-over-Sands LA11 6EA* Tel (01539) 534117

HOWARD, Alan James. b 45. Bris Univ BA69. Clifton Th Coll. **d** 71 **p** 72. C Welling *Roch* 71-74; C Cromer *Nor* 74-78; V Sidcup St Andr *Roch* 78-86; V Leyton St Cath *Chelmsf* 86-93; V Leyton St Cath and St Paul 93-00; rtd 05. *4 Bower Close, Romford RM5 3SR* Tel (01708) 760905

HOWARD, Andrew. b 63. Man Univ BA95 Leeds Univ MA97. Coll of Resurr Mirfield 95. **d** 97 **p** 98. C Worksop Priory *S'well* 97-01; V Hemlington *York* 01-05; Chapl Teesside Univ from 05; C Middlesbrough St Jo the Ev from 05; C Middlesbrough St Columba w St Paul from 05. *St John's Vicarage, 45 Lothian Road, Middlesbrough TS4 2HS* Tel (01642) 242926

HOWARD, Arthur Calvin. b 60. Leeds Univ LLB82 Barrister 83. Wycliffe Hall Ox 00. **d** 03 **p** 04. C Heswall *Ches* 03-04; C Weston 04-07. *14 St Michael's Close, Blackburn BB2 5DG* E-mail calvin.howard@btinternet.com

HOWARD, Charles William Wykeham. b 52. Southn Univ BTh81. Sarum & Wells Th Coll 76. **d** 79 **p** 80. C St Mary-at-Latton *Chelmsf* 79-82; Chapl RN 82-06; Chapl Midi-Pyrénées and Aude *Eur* 06-09. *18 Vincent Way, Martock TA12 6DG* E-mail charles.howard@orange.fr

HOWARD, Clive Eric. b 65. Oak Hill Th Coll BA99. **d** 99 **p** 00. C Chipping Sodbury and Old Sodbury *Glouc* 99-03; V Tipton St Matt *Lich* from 03. *St Matthew's Vicarage, Dudley Road, Tipton DY4 8DJ* Tel 0121-557 1929 E-mail clive-howard@rev65.fsnet.co.uk

HOWARD, Daniel James. b 71. Nottm Univ BA94. Oak Hill Th Coll 04. **d** 06 **p** 07. C Deane *Man* from 06. *10 Salterton Drive, Bolton BL3 3RG* Tel (01204) 855112 Mobile 07891-937278

HOWARD, David John. b 47. Brasted Th Coll 68 Ripon Hall Ox 70. **d** 72 **p** 73. C Benchill *Man* 72-75; C Sedgley All SS *Lich* 75-77; C-in-c Lostock CD *Man* 77-85; V Lt Hulton 85-88; Perm to Offic 90-91; C E Leake *S'well* 91-92; C Costock 91-92; C Rempstone 91-92; C Stanford on Soar 91-92; C W Leake w Kingston-on-Soar and Ratcliffe-on-Soar 91-92; C E and W Leake, Stanford-on-Soar, Rempstone etc 92-94; P-in-c Bilborough w Strelley 94-98; Chapl HM YOI Werrington Ho 98-03; Chapl HM Pris Drake Hall from 03. *HM Prison and YOI Drake Hall, Eccleshall, Stafford ST21 6LQ* Tel (01785) 774144 E-mail david.howard3@hmps.gsi.gov.uk

HOWARD, David John. b 51. Lon Univ BSc73. Oak Hill Th Coll 74. **d** 77 **p** 78. C Radipole and Melcombe Regis *Sarum* 77-83; R Tredington and Darlingscott w Newbold on Stour *Cov* 83-90; P-in-c Binley 90-94; V 94-04; RD Cov E 95-99; V Potterne w Worton and Marston *Sarum* from 04. *The Vicarage, 4 Rookes Lane, Potterne, Devizes SN10 5NF* Tel (01380) 723189 E-mail howard@binleyvicarage.fsnet.co.uk

HOWARD, Mrs Erika Kathryn. b 49. SRN70 SCM72. S Dios Minl Tr Scheme 88. **d** 91 **p** 94. NSM New Shoreham and Old Shoreham *Chich* 91-94; C Kingston Buci 94-03; V Sompting from 03. *The Vicarage, West Street, Sompting, Lancing BN15 0AP* Tel (01903) 234511 E-mail rev.erikahoward@ntlworld.com

HOWARD, Canon Francis Curzon. b 27. St Aid Birkenhead 54. **d** 57 **p** 58. C Claughton cum Grange *Ches* 57-60; C Cheltenham St Paul *Glouc* 60-62; V Sheff St Barn 62-65; R Sandys Bermuda 65-71; Asst P Westfield Atonement USA 71-76; R Tariffville 76-98; rtd 98; Can Kaduna from 95. *PO Box 423, 116 Terry's Plain Road, Simsbury CT 06070-1829, USA* Tel (001) (860) 658 1897

HOWARD, Frank Thomas. b 36. Lon Univ BSc57. Bps' Coll Cheshunt 59. **d** 61 **p** 62. C Macclesfield St Mich *Ches* 61-64; C Claughton cum Grange 64-66; V Lache cum Saltney 66-76; R Stanton *St E* 76-97; RD Ixworth 79-85; P-in-c Hempnall *Nor* 97-01; rtd 01; Perm to Offic *Nor* from 01. *55 Heywood Avenue, Diss IP22 4DN* Tel (01379) 640819

HOWARD, Geoffrey. b 30. Barrister-at-Law 83 Lon Univ LLB77. EMMTC. **d** 85 **p** 86. NSM Barton *Ely* 85-87; NSM Coton 85-87; C W Walton 87-92; TV Daventry, Ashby St Ledgers, Braunston etc *Pet* 92-97; rtd 97; Perm to Offic *Ely* 97-00 and from 07.

11 Porson Court, Porson Road, Cambridge CB2 8ER Tel (01223) 300738

HOWARD, Geoffrey. b 45. St Jo Coll Dur BA68. Cranmer Hall Dur 67. **d** 71 **p** 72. C Cheetham Hill *Man* 71-74; C Denton Ch Ch 75-77; V Pendleton St Ambrose 77-91; AD Salford 86-94; TR Pendleton St Thos w Charlestown 91-94; Perm to Offic from 05. *20 May Road, Swinton, Manchester M27 5FR*

HOWARD, George Granville. b 47. Trin Coll Bris. **d** 88 **p** 89. C Downend *Bris* 88-92; V Clifton H Trin, St Andr and St Pet 92-99; Bp's Officer for Miss and Evang 92-99; V W Streatham St Jas *S'wark* from 99; AD Tooting 02-07. *St James's Vicarage, 236 Mitcham Lane, London SW16 6NT* Tel (020) 8664 6059 *or* 8677 3947 E-mail ghoward@ukonline.co.uk

HOWARD, George Victor Richard. b 69. Northn Univ MBA06. Ripon Coll Cuddesdon 07. **d** 09. C Iver *Ox* from 09. *18 Somerset Way, Iver SL0 9AF* E-mail georgehoward01@btinternet.com

HOWARD, John. *See* HOWARD, Nicolas John

HOWARD, John Alexander. b 27. Wesley Coll Leeds 48 Coll of Resurr Mirfield 66. **d** 67 **p** 68. C Almondbury *Wakef* 67-71; V Skelmanthorpe 71-81; R Fortrose *Mor* 81-94; R Cromarty 81-94; R Arpafeelie 81-94; rtd 94; Perm to Offic *Glouc* from 94. *2 Webbs Cottages, Stratford Road, Mickleton, Chipping Campden GL55 6SW*

HOWARD, Canon John Robert. b 60. NUI BA HDipEd. **d** 84 **p** 85. C Donaghcloney w Waringstown *D & D* 84-88; I Belfast St Ninian *Conn* 88-94; Bp's Dom Chapl 88-94; Chapl Ulster Univ 88-94; I Annahilt w Magherahamlet *D & D* from 94; Can Dromore Cathl from 06; Chapl HM Pris Maghaberry from 96. *Annahilt Rectory, 15 Ballykeel Road, Hillsborough BT26 6NW* Tel (028) 9263 8218 E-mail jrobert.howard@btinternet.com

HOWARD, Mrs Judith Marion. b 46. WEMTC 98. **d** 01 **p** 02. NSM Glouc St Jas and All SS from 01. *Paulmead, Wells Road, Bisley, Stroud GL6 7AG* Tel (01452) 770776 E-mail judy.howard@homecall.co.uk

HOWARD, Keith. b 55. St Jo Coll Nottm 81. **d** 84 **p** 85. C Llanidloes w Llangurig *Ban* 84-87; R Llansantffraid Glan Conwy and Eglwysbach *St As* 87-00; V Heapey and Withnell *Blackb* 00-07; V Hooton Ches from 07. *Hooton Vicarage, Chester Road, Childer Thornton, Ellesmere Port CH66 1QF* Tel 0151-339 1655

HOWARD, Martin John Aidan. b 68. Lon Univ BA90 Open Univ MA96. St Jo Coll Nottm MA97. **d** 97 **p** 98. C Billericay and Lt Burstead *Chelmsf* 97-01; TV Kinson *Sarum* 01-06; TV Hampreston 06-08; TR from 08. *The Vicarage, 3 Dudsbury Road, West Parley, Ferndown BH22 8RA* Tel (01202) 876552 E-mail office@stmarys-ferndown.org.uk

HOWARD, Canon Michael Charles. b 35. Selw Coll Cam BA58 MA63 CQSW72. Wycliffe Hall Ox 58. **d** 60 **p** 61. C Stowmarket *St E* 60-64; CMS Nigeria 64-71; Hon Can Ondo 70-71; Hon C Southborough St Pet w Ch Ch and St Matt *Roch* 72-73; Perm to Offic *Ox* from 73; rtd 00. *17 Milton Road, Bloxham, Banbury OX15 4HD* Tel (01295) 720470

HOWARD, Natalie Delia. b 51. St Mich Coll Llan 99. **d** 02 **p** 03. NSM Magor *Mon* from 02. *8 The Meadows, Magor, Caldicot NP26 3LA* Tel (01633) 881714

HOWARD, Nicolas John. b 61. Nottm Univ BTh90. Aston Tr Scheme 85 Linc Th Coll 87. **d** 90 **p** 91. C Bracknell *Ox* 90-94; P-in-c Oldham St Chad Limeside *Man* 94-96; Perm to Offic *Birm* 96-99. *11 Chesterfield Court, Middleton Hall Road, Birmingham B30 1AF* Tel 0121-459 4975

HOWARD, Norman. b 26. AKC57. St Boniface Warminster 57. **d** 58 **p** 59. C Friern Barnet St Jas *Lon* 58-62; Jamaica 62-69; USA from 69; rtd 91. *766 Lake Forest Road, Clearwater FL 33765-2231, USA* Tel (001) (813) 799 3929

HOWARD, Paul David. b 47. Lancaster Poly Cov BA69. St Jo Coll Nottm 74. **d** 77 **p** 78. C Bedworth *Cov* 77-83; V Newchapel *Lich* 83-93; V Stretton w Claymills 93-04; P-in-c Talke from 04; Chapl Newcastle-under-Lyme Primary Care Trust from 07. *The Rectory, 26 Crown Bank, Talke, Stoke-on-Trent ST7 1PU* Tel (01782) 782348 E-mail paul@howard510.freeserve.co.uk

HOWARD, Peter Leslie. b 48. Nottm Univ BTh77 Birm Univ MA80 Leeds Univ MEd91. St Jo Coll Nottm LTh77. **d** 77 **p** 78. C Gospel Lane St Mich *Birm* 77-81; P-in-c Nechells 81-85; V Stanley *Wakef* 85-92; P-in-c Nor Heartsease St Fran from 92; Dioc UPA/CUF Link Officer from 02; RD Nor E from 06. *St Francis's Vicarage, 100 Rider Haggard Road, Norwich NR7 9UQ* Tel (01603) 702799 E-mail plhoward@btinternet.com

HOWARD, Robert. *See* HOWARD, Canon John Robert

HOWARD, Canon Robert Weston (Robin). b 28. Pemb Coll Cam BA49 MA53. Westcott Ho Cam 51. **d** 53 **p** 54. C Bishopwearmouth St Mich *Dur* 53-56; C Cambridge Gt St Mary w St Mich *Ely* 56-60; Hong Kong 60-66; V Prenton *Ches* 66-75; RD Frodsham 74-82; P-in-c Dunham-on-the-Hill 75-77; V Helsby and Dun 75-77; V Helsby and Dunham-on-the-Hill 77-82; Hon Can Ches Cathl 78-82; V Moseley St Mary *Birm* 82-88; V Chalke Valley W *Sarum* 88-93; rtd 93; Perm to Offic *St D* and *Heref* 93-08; *Ox* from 08. *4 Hitchmans Drive, Chipping Norton OX7 5BG* Tel (01608) 641248

HOWARD, Ronald. b 40. AMIBF65 AMICME01. Cranmer Hall Dur 86. **d** 88 **p** 89. C Baildon *Bradf* 88-92; P-in-c Sutton 92-96; P-in-c St Tudy w St Mabyn and Michaelstow *Truro* 96-00; P-in-c Keyingham w Ottringham, Halsham and Sunk Is *York* 00-03; R 03-08; RD S Holderness 04-06; rtd 08; Perm to Offic *York* from 08. *Silver Gates, Withernsea Road, Hollym, Withernsea HU19 2QH* Tel (01964) 611270 E-mail fatherronald@btinternet.com

HOWARD, Simon Charles. b 60. Birm Univ BA81. Ridley Hall Cam 90. **d** 92 **p** 93. C Cambridge St Martin *Ely* 92-96; Chapl St Bede's Sch Cam 92-96; P-in-c Earley Trin *Ox* 96-05; P-in-c Ruscombe and Twyford from 05. *The Vicarage, Ruscombe, Reading RG10 9UD* Tel 0118-934 1092 *or* 934 1685 E-mail revsimon@lineone.net

HOWARD, Ms Susan. b 65. Lanc Univ BA86. Ripon Coll Cuddesdon 88. **d** 91 **p** 94. C Ditton St Mich *Liv* 91-94; C Kirkby 94-97; Adv for Youth and Young Adults *Man* 97-00; Governor HM Pris Styal from 01. *HM Prison, Styal, Wilmslow SK9 4HR* Tel (01625) 532141

HOWARD, Thomas Norman. b 40. St Aid Birkenhead 64. **d** 67 **p** 68. C Farnworth and Kearsley *Man* 67-70; C Prestwich St Marg 70-73; V Heyside 73-85; Warden Lamplugh Ho Angl Conf Cen 85-90; Hon C Langtoft w Foxholes, Butterwick, Cottam etc *York* 85-87; C 87-90; V Fence and Newchurch-in-Pendle *Blackb* 90-00; Dioc Ecum Officer 90-95; rtd 00; Hon C Stalybridge H Trin and Ch Ch *Ches* 01-03; Perm to Offic from 03. *36 Bridgeside, Carnforth LA5 9LF* Tel (01524) 736552

HOWARD, William Alfred. b 47. St Jo Coll Dur BA69. Wycliffe Hall Ox 74. **d** 77 **p** 79. C Norbiton *S'wark* 77-80; C Mile Cross *Nor* 80-84; R Grimston, Congham and Roydon from 84; Chapl Norfolk Constabulary from 00. *The Rectory, Watery Lane, Grimston, King's Lynn PE32 1BQ* Tel (01485) 600335 E-mail william.howard@dunelm.org.uk

HOWARD-COWLEY, Joseph Charles. b 27. Trin Coll Cam BA53 MA56. Wells Th Coll 53. **d** 55 **p** 56. C Newmarket All SS *St E* 55-58; Chapl Aycliffe Approved Sch Co Dur 58-61; V Aldringham *St E* 61-86; rtd 86; Perm to Offic *St E* 86-93 and *Truro* 93-03. *36 Bath Road, Wootton Bassett, Swindon SN4 7DF*

HOWARD JONES, Preb Raymond Vernon. b 31. AKC54. **d** 55 **p** 56. C Hutton *Chelmsf* 55-58; CF 58-62; V Walpole St Andrew *Ely* 62-64; Chapl St Crispin's Hosp Northampton 64-70; V Brockhampton w Fawley *Heref* 64-66; V Fownhope 70-86; RD Heref Rural 77-81; Preb Heref Cathl 81-97; Communications Adv and Bp's Staff Officer 86-97; rtd 97; Perm to Offic *Heref* from 97. *Kingfishers, Breinton, Hereford HR4 7PP* Tel (01432) 279371

HOWARTH, Christopher. b 47. Ch Ch Coll Cant CertEd69 Open Univ BA76. S Dios Minl Tr Scheme. **d** 83 **p** 84. NSM Uckfield *Chich* from 83; NSM Lt Horsted from 83; NSM Isfield from 83. *137 Rocks Park Road, Uckfield TN22 2BD* Tel (01825) 765352

HOWARTH, Mrs Henriette. b 66. Utrecht Univ MTh94. Wycliffe Hall Ox 91. **d** 04 **p** 05. C Sparkbrook Ch Ch *Birm* 04-05; C Springfield 05-09; Perm to Offic from 09. *172 Woodlands Road, Sparkhill, Birmingham B11 4ET* Tel 0121-777 1989 E-mail hentob@tiscali.co.uk

HOWARTH, Miles. b 58. **d** 08 **p** 09. OLM Failsworth St Jo *Man* from 08. *15 Grimshaw Street, Failsworth, Manchester M35 0DF* Tel 0161-688 7710 Mobile 07718-326321 E-mail miles@howarth8023.freeserve.co.uk

HOWARTH, Robert Francis Harvey. b 31. S'wark Ord Course 71. **d** 72 **p** 73. C St Marylebone All So w SS Pet and Jo *Lon* 72-73; C St Helen Bishopsgate w St Martin Outwich 73-78; V Harlow St Mary and St Hugh w St Jo the Bapt *Chelmsf* 78-88; P-in-c Victoria Docks Ascension 88-96; rtd 96. *Lochhill, Palnackie, Castle Douglas DG7 1PW* Tel (01556) 600363

HOWARTH, Canon Ronald. b 26. TCD BA51 MA54. Linc Th Coll 50. **d** 52 **p** 53. C Gannow *Blackb* 52-55; Nigeria 55-89; rtd 91. *4 Kingston Court, Walton Street, Oxford OX2 6ES* Tel (01865) 553046

HOWARTH, Toby Matthew. b 62. Yale Univ BA86 Birm Univ MA91 Free Univ of Amsterdam PhD01. Wycliffe Hall Ox 89. **d** 92 **p** 93. C Derby St Aug 92-95; Crosslinks India 95-00; The Netherlands 00-02; Vice Prin and Tutor Crowther Hall CMS Tr Coll Selly Oak 02-04; P-in-c Springfield *Birm* from 04; Bp's Adv on Inter-Faith Relns from 05. *172 Woodlands Road, Sparkhill, Birmingham B11 4ET* Tel 0121-777 1989 E-mail hentob@aya.yale.edu

HOWAT, Jeremy Noel Thomas. b 35. Em Coll Cam BA59 MA62. Ridley Hall Cam 59. **d** 63 **p** 64. C Sutton *Liv* 63-65; C Kirk Ella *York* 65-66; C Bridlington Quay Ch Ch 66-69; R Wheldrake 69-78; Dioc Youth Officer 69-74; SAMS Argentina 78-81 and 90-97; P-in-c Newton upon Ouse *York* 81-82; V Shipton w Overton 81-82; P-in-c Skelton by York 81-82; R Skelton w Shipton and Newton on Ouse 82-89; C Elloughton and Brough w Brantingham 97-99; rtd 99; Perm to Offic *York* from 00. *18 Petersway, York YO30 6AR* Tel (01904) 628946 E-mail jnth@ntlworld.com

HOWDEN, Canon John Travis. b 40. RIBA62. Sarum Th Coll 66. **d** 69 **p** 70. C S Gillingham *Roch* 69-72; C Banbury *Ox* 72-73; Lic to Offic *York* 73-74; Hon C Hull St Jo Newland 74-81; Hon C Stock Harvard *Chelmsf* 82-86; R Doddinghurst and Mountnessing 86-91; P-in-c Pleshey and Warden Pleshey Retreat Ho 91-00; R Wickham Bishops w Lt Braxted 00-05; Hon Can Chelmsf Cathl 97-05; rtd 05; Perm to Offic *Chelmsf* from 05. *12A Back Road, Writtle, Chelmsford CM1 3PD* Tel (01245) 422023 E-mail johnhowden@realemail.co.uk

HOWDLE, Glyn. b 50. Bp Lonsdale Coll BEd72. St Alb Minl Tr Scheme 90. **d** 01 **p** 02. NSM Aspenden, Buntingford and Westmill *St Alb* from 01. *58 Ermine Street, Thundridge, Ware SG12 0SY* Tel and fax (01920) 469632 Mobile 07909-920437 E-mail glynjosealicia@howdle.fslife.co.uk

HOWE, Alan Raymond. b 52. Nottm Univ BTh79. St Jo Coll Nottm 76. **d** 80 **p** 81. C Southsea St Simon *Portsm* 80-83; C Bexleyheath St Pet *Roch* 83-86; TV Camberley St Paul *Guildf* 86-93; P-in-c Mansfield St Jo *S'well* 93-96; P-in-c Wollaton Park 96-02; V 02-05; AD Nottingham W 99-05; V Chilwell from 05. *Christ Church Vicarage, 8 College Road, Beeston, Nottingham NG9 4AS* Tel 0115-925 7419 E-mail ar.howe1@ntlworld.com

HOWE, Anthony Graham. b 72. Qu Coll Ox BA93 MA99. St Steph Ho Ox BA00. **d** 01 **p** 02. C Newbury *Ox* 01-04; Dioc Communications Officer *Wakef* 04-05; C Athersley and Monk Bretton 05-06; V Staincliffe and Carlinghow from 06. *The Vicarage, Staincliffe Hall Road, Batley WF17 7QX* Tel (01924) 473343 Mobile 07795-095157 E-mail fatherhowe@tiscali.co.uk

HOWE, Charles. b 30. Lon Univ BD65 Univ BA79. Tyndale Hall Bris 55. **d** 58 **p** 59. C Willowfield *D & D* 58-60; C Derryloran *Arm* 60-64; C Belfast St Bart *Conn* 64-65; I Tullyaughnish w Kilmacrennan and Killygarvan *D & R* 65-72; I Londonderry St Aug 73-95; Can Derry Cathl 85-95; Dioc Org and Tutor for Aux Min 93-95; rtd 95. *43 Ashburn Avenue, Londonderry BT47 5QE* Tel (028) 7131 2305 E-mail charleshowe1@hotmail.com

HOWE, Canon David Randall. b 24. St Jo Coll Cam BA51 MA55. Wells Th Coll 51. **d** 53 **p** 54. C Basingstoke *Win* 53-59; V Rotherwick, Hook and Greywell 59-70; R Bossington w Broughton 70-81; R Broughton w Bossington and Mottisfont 81-86; R Broughton, Bossington, Houghton and Mottisfont 86-89; Hon Can Win Cathl 87-89; rtd 89; Perm to Offic *Sarum* and *Win* 89-05; *Ox* from 06. *Easter Cottage, 36 Britwell Road, Burnham, Slough SL1 8AG* Tel (01628) 603046

HOWE, Miss Frances Ruth. b 28. ACIB67. Cranmer Hall Dur IDC80. **dss** 80 **d** 87 **p** 94. Newc St Andr 80-82; Chapl Asst R Victoria Infirmary Newc 80-87; Chapl Wylam and Fleming Ch Hosp 82-87; Chapl St Oswald's Hospice Newc 86-92; C Newc Epiphany 87-90; rtd 92; Hon C Delaval *Newc* 92-98; Perm to Offic from 98. *18 Mason Avenue, Whitley Bay NE26 1AQ* Tel 0191-252 5163

HOWE, The Ven George Alexander. b 52. St Jo Coll Dur BA73. Westcott Ho Cam 73. **d** 75 **p** 76. C Peterlee *Dur* 75-79; C Norton St Mary 79-81; V Hart w Elwick Hall 81-85; R Sedgefield 85-91; RD Sedgefield 89-91; V Kendal H Trin *Carl* 91-00; RD Kendal 94-00; Hon Can Carl Cathl from 94; Adn Westmorland and Furness from 00; Bp's Adv for Ecum Affairs from 01. *The Vicarage, Windermere Road, Lindale, Grange-over-Sands LA11 6LB* Tel (01539) 534717 Fax 535090 E-mail archdeacon.south@carlislediocese.org.uk

HOWE, Canon John. b 36. Ex Coll Ox BA58 MA63. St Steph Ho Ox 58. **d** 61 **p** 62. C Horninglow *Lich* 61-64; C Sedgley All SS 64-66; V Ocker Hill 66-73; V Gnosall 73 79; P in c Hoar Cross 79-82; Preb Lich Cathl 83-88; V Hoar Cross w Newchurch 83-88; Can Res Lich Cathl 88-96; Master St Jo Hosp Lich 96-00; rtd 00; Perm to Offic *Lich* from 01. *9 Cherry Street, The Leys, Tamworth B79 7ED* Tel (01827) 57817

HOWE, Canon Nicholas Simon. b 60. Man Univ BA81 K Coll Lon MTh85. Ridley Hall Cam 86. **d** 88 **p** 89. C Lich St Chad 88-92; TV Leeds City *Ripon* 92-01; Dioc Dir of Ords and Post-Ord Tr *Sheff* 01-06; Chapl Sheff Cathl 01-06; Can Res Sheff Cathl 03-06; Chapl Stockholm w Gävle and Västerås *Eur* from 06. *The English Church of Stockholm, Styrmansgatan 1, SE-114 54, Stockholm, Sweden* Tel (0046) (8) 663 8248 Fax 663 8911 E-mail anglican.church@chello.se

HOWE, Canon Rex Alan. b 29. Ch Coll Cam BA53 MA57. Coll of Resurr Mirfield 53. **d** 55 **p** 56. C Barnsley St Pet *Wakef* 55-57; C Helmsley *York* 57-60; V Middlesbrough St Martin 60-67; V Redcar 67-73; V Kirkleatham 67-73; RD Guisborough 67-73; Dean Hong Kong 73-76; Adn 75-76; TR Grantham *Linc* 77-85; RD Grantham 78-85; Can and Preb Linc Cathl 81-85; V Canford Cliffs and Sandbanks *Sarum* 85-94; RD Poole 92-94; rtd 94; Perm to Offic *Sarum* from 94. *18 St Nicholas Hospital, 5 St Nicholas Gate, Salisbury SP1 2SW* Tel (01722) 326677

HOWE, Roy William. b 38. ALCD67. **d** 66 **p** 67. C Bradf Cathl 66-70; C Barnoldswick w Bracewell 70-72; V Yeadon St Jo 72-79; P-in-c Bainton *York* 79-86; P-in-c Middleton-on-the-Wolds 79-86; P-in-c N Dalton 79-86; RD Harthill 81-87; C Watton w Beswick and Kilnwick 82-86; R Bainton w N Dalton, Middleton-on-the-Wolds etc 86-87; TV Penrith w Newton Reigny and Plumpton Wall *Carl* 87-92; Dioc Chapl to Agric and Rural Life 87-92; V Cornhill w Carham *Newc* 92-98; V Branxton

92-98; P-in-c Coddenham w Gosbeck and Hemingstone w Henley *St E* 98-03; rtd 03; Perm to Offic *St E* from 04. *Ballaclague, 2 Halvasso Vean, Longdowns, Penryn TR10 9DN* Tel (01209) 860552

HOWE, Ruth. *See* HOWE, Miss Frances Ruth

HOWE, William Ernest. b 25. MRICS51. Westcott Ho Cam 68. **d** 70 **p** 71. C Anston *Sheff* 70-73; V 84-92; C Woodsetts 70-73; V Greasbrough 73-84; rtd 92; Perm to Offic *Sheff* from 92 and *S'well* from 97. *21 Broad Bridge Close, Kiveton Park, Sheffield S26 6SL* Tel (01909) 779779

HOWELL, Andrew John. b 44. Clifton Th Coll 68. **d** 71 **p** 72. C Halliwell St Pet *Man* 71-77; V Facit 77-95; P-in-c Smallbridge and Wardle from 95. *The Vicarage, 151 Wardle Road, Rochdale OL12 9JA* Tel (01706) 713529

HOWELL, David. b 29. Clifton Th Coll 56. **d** 59 **p** 60. C Tipton St Martin *Lich* 59-62; V W Bromwich St Paul 62-71; V Deptford St Jo *S'wark* 71-81; Dir and Chapl Home of Divine Healing Crowhurst 81-89; rtd 90; Dir Ch Coun for Health and Healing 91-93; Hon Dioc Adv on Health and Healing *B & W* 93-00; Perm to Offic from 01. *60 Andrew Allan Road, Rockwell Green, Wellington TA21 9DY* Tel (01823) 664529 E-mail revshowell@waitrose.com

HOWELL (*formerly* WILLIAMS), **David Paul.** b 61. Coll of Resurr Mirfield 91. **d** 93 **p** 94. C Leic St Aid 93-97; P-in-c Edvin Loach w Tedstone Delamere etc *Heref* from 97. *The Rectory, Whitbourne, Worcester WR6 5RP* Tel (01886) 821285

HOWELL, Geoffrey Peter. b 52. Selw Coll Cam BA75 MA78 Leeds Univ MA01 K Alfred's Coll Win PGCE77 LTCL82. Cranmer Hall Dur 85. **d** 87 **p** 88. C Hartlepool St Luke *Dur* 87-90; TV Burford I *Heref* 90-94; TV Burford II w Greete and Hope Bagot 90-94; TV Burford III w Lt Heref 90-94; TV Tenbury 90-94; P-in-c Cradley w Mathon and Storridge 94-97; Succ Heref Cathl 97-99; Chapl Heref Cathl Jun Sch 97-99; Perm to Offic *Heref* from 99; Min Can St Woolos Cathl from 02. *1 Hereford Road, Weobley HR4 8SW* Tel (01544) 319284 E-mail geoffrey.howell@tesco.net

HOWELL, Mrs Heather Ellen. b 40. Bp Otter Coll Chich TCert60 Sussex Univ BA83. Ripon Coll Cuddesdon 00. **d** 01 **p** 02. NSM Newhaven *Chich* 01-06; P-in-c Fletching from 06. *The Vicarage, Mill Lane, Fletching, Uckfield TN22 3SR* Tel (01825) 723880 E-mail heather.howell@tiscali.co.uk

HOWELL, Martin John Hope. b 38. Bris Univ BA62. Tyndale Hall Bris 59. **d** 64 **p** 65. C Bolton St Paul *Man* 64-67; C Bishopsworth *Bris* 67-70; V Swindon St Aug 70-81; TR Stratton St Margaret w S Marston etc 81-93; RD Cricklade 88; RD Highworth 88-93; Chapl Lee Abbey 93-98; Chapl St Pet Via del Mar Chile 99-03; rtd 03; Hon C Salcombe and Malborough w S Huish *Ex* 03-08. *7 Glen Walk, Exeter EX4 5EA* Tel (01548) 562402

HOWELL, Roger Brian. b 43. ALCD67. **d** 67 **p** 68. C Battersea Park St Sav *S'wark* 67-71; C Southgate *Chich* 71-76; V Pendeen and P-in-c Sancreed *Truro* 76-81; V Bedgrove *Ox* 81-91; R Purley 91-08; RD Bradfield 94-04; rtd 08; Perm to Offic *Ox* from 08. *246 Burwell Meadow, Witney OX28 5JJ* Tel (01993) 706893 E-mail rbh@bradean.fsnet.co.uk

HOWELL, Ronald William Fullerton. b 51. Man Univ BA72 CertEd Ox Univ BA78 MA. Ripon Coll Cuddesdon 76. **d** 79 **p** 80. C Newc St Fran 79-81; C Warmsworth *Sheff* 81-82; Dioc Educn Officer 82-85; V Millhouses H Trin 85-93; R Thornhill and Whitley Lower *Wakef* 93-96. *11 Hartington Road, Aldeburgh IP15 5HD* Tel (01728) 453000

HOWELL, Simon Gordon. b 63. Sheff Univ BMus84 Bath Coll of HE PGCE85 ACII90. Ridley Hall Cam 00. **d** 03 **p** 04. C Northwood Em *Lon* 03-06; TV Keynsham *B & W* from 06. *9 Chelmer Grove, Keynsham, Bristol BS31 1QA* Tel 0117-377 9798 E-mail revsimonhowell@blueyonder.co.uk

HOWELL, Preb Walter Ernest. b 17. St D Coll Lamp BA49. **d** 50 **p** 51. C Bromley St Mich *Lon* 50-56; V Somers Town 56-68; V Kentish Town St Benet and All SS 68-79; Preb St Paul's Cathl 78-84; V Alexandra Park St Sav 79-84; rtd 84; Perm to Offic *York* from 90. *6 Wattlers Close, Copmanthorpe, York YO23 3XR* Tel (01904) 702615

HOWELL-JONES, Canon Peter. b 62. Huddersfield Poly BMus84 Bretton Hall Coll PGCE85. St Jo Coll Nottm 90 MA96. **d** 93 **p** 94. C Walsall *Lich* 93-98; V Boldmere *Birm* 98-05; Can Res Birm Cathl from 05; Bp's Adv for Miss from 05; Asst Dean from 07. *Birmingham Cathedral, Colmore Row, Birmingham B3 2QB* Tel 0121-262 1840 Fax 262 1860 E-mail actingdean@birminghamcathedral.com

HOWELLS, Chan Arthur Glyn. b 32. Univ of Wales (Lamp) BA54. St Mich Coll Llan 54. **d** 56 **p** 57. C Oystermouth *S & B* 56-58; C Llangyfelach and Morriston 58-64; R Llandefalle and Llyswen w Boughrood etc 64-69; Youth Chapl 67-71; V Landore 70-80; Dioc Missr 80-89; Can Brecon Cathl 80-89; Can Treas 89-94; Dir St Mary's Coll Swansea 82-89; V Swansea St Jas *S & B* 89-98; Chan Brecon Cathl 94-98; RD Swansea 96-98; rtd 98. *2 Lilliput Lane, West Cross, Swansea SA3 5AQ* Tel (01792) 402123

HOWELLS, David. b 55. Grey Coll Dur BA78. Ripon Coll Cuddesdon 79. **d** 81 **p** 82. C Birtley *Dur* 81-84; Canada from 84. *5551 West Saanich Road, Victoria BC V9E 2G1, Canada* E-mail smaaac@telus.net

HOWELLS, David Morgan. b 24. Qu Coll Birm 72. **d** 75 **p** 76. NSM Radford *Cov* 75-87; rtd 87; Perm to Offic *Cov* 87-03 and *Roch* 98-03. *14 St Werburgh's Court, Pottery Road, Rochester ME3 9AP* Tel (01634) 251544

HOWELLS (formerly SMITHAM), Mrs Elizabeth Ann. b 62. St D Coll Lamp BA90 Univ of Wales (Lamp) MA04. St Mich Coll Llan. **d** 92 **p** 97. C Llangiwg *S & B* 92-94; C Morriston 94-98; P-in-c Llanfair-is-gaer and Llanddeiniolen *Ban* 98-00; V 00-03; V Llanddeiniolen w Llanfair-is-gaer etc 03-04; V Clydau w Egremont and Llanglydwen etc *St D* 04-06; P-in-c Llanpumsaint w Llanllawddog 06-08; V Llanilar w Rhostie and Llangwyryfon etc from 09. *The Vicarage, Llanafan, Aberystwyth SY23 4AZ* Tel (01974) 261185

HOWELLS, Euryl. b 60. Univ of Wales (Cardiff) BD93. St Mich Coll Llan 90. **d** 93 **p** 94. C Deanery of Emlyn *St D* 93-97; V Llangeler w Pen-Boyr 97-03; P-in-c Tre-lech a'r Betws w Abernant and Llanwinio 03-06; Chapl Carmarthenshire NHS Trust 06-08; Chapl R Devon and Ex NHS Foundn Trust 08-09; V Grwp Bro Ystwyth a Mynach *St D* from 09. *The Vicarage, Llanafan, Aberystwyth SY23 4AZ* Tel (01974) 261185

HOWELLS, Garfield Edwin. b 18. K Coll Lon 53 St Boniface Warminster 53. **d** 54 **p** 55. C Sanderstead All SS *S'wark* 54-57; CF 57-60; R Kingsdown *Roch* 60-64; Australia from 64; rtd 83. *301/17 Hefron Street, Rockingham WA 6168, Australia* Tel (0061) (8) 9592 8337

HOWELLS, Gordon. b 39. Univ of Wales (Cardiff) BSc61 DipEd62. Ripon Coll Cuddesdon 86. **d** 88 **p** 89. C Atherstone *Cov* 88-89; C Lillington 89-92; R Clymping and Yapton w Ford *Chich* 92-97; P-in-c Rackheath and Salhouse *Nor* 97-04; Chapl among Deaf People 97-04; rtd 04. *53 Abbey Road, Rhos on Sea, Colwyn Bay LL28 4NR* Tel (01492) 525899 E-mail g.howells.norwich@virgin.net

HOWELLS, Richard Grant. b 62. Univ of Wales (Lamp) BA83. Westcott Ho Cam 83 and 92. **d** 93 **p** 94. NSM Harston w Hauxton and Newton *Ely* from 93. *The Old School House, 8 High Street, Harston, Cambridge CB22 7PX* Tel (01223) 871902

HOWELLS, Mrs Sandra Jane. b 52. FBDO77. Mon Dioc Tr Scheme 90. **d** 93 **p** 97. NSM Caerwent w Dinham and Llanfair Discoed etc *Mon* 93-97; C Griffithstown 97-00; V Penallt and Trellech 00-07; V Trellech and Penallt from 07. *The Vicarage, Penallt, Monmouth NP25 4SE* Tel (01600) 716622

HOWES, Alan. b 49. Chich Th Coll 76. **d** 79 **p** 80. C Bilborough St Jo *S'well* 79-82; TV Newark w Hawton, Cotham and Shelton 82-89; TV Newark 89-94; P-in-c Coseley St Chad *Worc* 94-96; V from 96. *St Chad's Vicarage, 3 Oak Street, Coseley, Bilston WV14 9TA* Tel (01902) 882285 Mobile 07941-284048 E-mail alan@heavensdoor.co.uk

HOWES, David. b 30. Open Univ BA75. Roch Th Coll 62. **d** 64 **p** 65. C Highweek *Ex* 64-67; C Clyst St George 67-71; P-in-c Woolfardisworthy w Kennerleigh 71-72; P-in-c Washford Pyne w Puddington 71-72; TR N Creedy 72-73; Perm to Offic 74-77; C Walworth *S'wark* 77-78; P-in-c Roundshaw LEP 78-83; R S'wark St Geo 83-90; P-in-c S'wark St Jude 84-90; P-in-c Risley *Derby* 90-93; Bp's Ind Adv 90-93; rtd 93; Perm to Offic *Derby* 93-00; S'well 95-00; Win from 01. *1 St George's Close, Lower Street, Salisbury SP2 8HA* Tel (01722) 323484

HOWES, Miss Judith Elizabeth. b 44. SRN RSCN. Ripon Coll Cuddesdon 83. **d** 89 **p** 94. Par Dn Ex St Sidwell and St Matt 89-92; Par Dn Brixham w Churston Ferrers and Kingswear 92-94; C 94-95; TV E Darlington *Dur* 95-97; TR 97-02; P-in-c Washington 02-04; P-in-c S Shields St Simon 04-08; C Hedworth 04-08; rtd 08. *37 Middleton Close, Seaton, Seaham SR7 0PQ* Tel 0191-581 1729

HOWES, Mrs Kathleen Valerie. b 44. Surrey Univ BA05. STETS 03. **d** 05 **p** 06. NSM Droxford and Meonstoke w Corhampton cum Exton *Portsm* 05-08; NSM Cosham 08-09. *1 St George's Close, Lower Street, Salisbury SP2 8HA* Tel (01722) 323484 E-mail valerie.howes@btinternet.com

HOWES, Michael John Norton. b 43. Hull Univ BA66. Linc Th Coll 66. **d** 68 **p** 69. C Gt Berkhamsted *St Alb* 68-71; C Ampthill w Millbrook and Steppingley 71-72; Chapl RAF 72-88; V Thurlby w Carlby *Linc* 88-95; V Ness Gp 95-97; R Bassingham 97-00; V Aubourn w Haddington 97-00; V Carlton-le-Moorland w Stapleford 97-00; R Thurlby w Norton Disney 97-00; P-in-c Ashill w Saham Toney *Nor* 01-03; rtd 03. *182 Rookery Lane, Lincoln LN6 7PH* Tel (01522) 801514 E-mail mike.howes50@ntlworld.com

HOWES, Canon Norman Vincent. b 36. AKC61. **d** 62 **p** 63. C Radford *Cov* 62-66; V Napton on the Hill 66-72; V Exhall 72-83; R Walton d'Eiville and V Wellesbourne 83-03; RD Fosse 87-93; Hon Can Cov Cathl 89-03; rtd 03; Perm to Offic *Cov* from 03. *6 Brookside Avenue, Wellesbourne, Warwick CV35 9RZ* Tel (01789) 470902 E-mail norman@nhowes.freeserve.co.uk

HOWES, Valerie. *See* HOWES, Mrs Kathleen Valerie

HOWES, William John Lawrence. b 46. EAMTC. **d** 00 **p** 01. NSM Lexden *Chelmsf* 00-04; NSM Coggeshall w Markshall from 04. *26 Westfield Drive, Coggeshall, Colchester CO6 1PU* Tel and fax (01376) 561826 Mobile 07718-048574 E-mail frbill_105@fsmail.net

HOWITT, Mrs Barbara Gillian. b 39. K Coll Lon BD60 PGCE61 MA95. EAMTC 99. **d** 00 **p** 01. NSM Longthorpe *Pet* 00-09; rtd 09; Perm to Offic *Pet* from 09. *8 Wakerley Drive, Orton Longueville, Peterborough PE2 7WF* Tel (01733) 391092

HOWITT, Ivan Richard. b 56. Kent Univ BA81. Sarum & Wells Th Coll 83. **d** 85 **p** 86. C Herne Bay Ch Ch *Cant* 85-87; C St Laur in Thanet 87-90; R Owmby and Normanby w Glentham *Linc* 90-91; P-in-c Spridlington w Saxby and Firsby 90-91; R Owmby Gp 91-99; RD Lawres 96-99; Chapl Hull Miss to Seafarers 99-03; V Hedon w Paull *York* 03-09; P-in-c Sand Hutton from 09; P-in-c Whitwell w Crambe and Foston from 09. *The Vicarage, Sand Hutton, York YO41 1LB* Tel (01904) 468443 Mobile 07739-316019 E-mail ivanhowitt@ivanhowitt.karoo.co.uk

HOWITT, John Leslie. b 28. Lon Coll of Div 60. **d** 62 **p** 63. C Attenborough w Bramcote *S'well* 62-66; Chapl Rampton Hosp Retford 66-71; P-in-c Treswell and Cottam *S'well* 68-71; Chapl HM Pris Cardiff 71-75; Chapl HM Youth Cust Cen Dover 75-79; Chapl HM Pris Dartmoor 79-83; Chapl HM Pris Cant 83-87; Chapl HM Det Cen Aldington 83-87; Perm to Offic *Cant* 87-88; V Shobnall *Lich* 88-94; rtd 94; Perm to Offic *Chich* from 94. *7 Wish Court, Ingram Crescent West, Hove BN3 5NY* Tel (01273) 414535

HOWITZ (formerly TEDD), Christopher Jonathan Richard. b 74. Ch Ch Ox MEng96. Oak Hill Th Coll BA00. **d** 00 **p** 01. C Harpurhey Ch Ch *Man* 00-04; P-in-c Higher Openshaw from 05. *St Clement's Rectory, Ashton Old Road, Manchester M11 1HF* Tel 0161-370 1538

HOWLES, Kenneth. b 56. Oak Hill Th Coll 91. **d** 93 **p** 94. C Leyland St Andr *Blackb* 93-96; C Livesey 96-97; C Ewood 96-97; P-in-c 97-99; V 99-03; P-in-c Blackb Sav 01-03; V Chorley St Jas from 03. *St James's Vicarage, St James's Place, Chorley PR6 0NA* Tel (01257) 263153 E-mail kenhowles@btinternet.com

HOWLETT, Mrs Elizabeth Mary. b 58. Southn Univ BA80. WMMTC 99. **d** 01 **p** 02. C Salter Street and Shirley *Birm* 01-04; Bp's Adv for Lay Adult Educn and Tr from 04. *6 Greenside, Shirley, Solihull B90 4HH* Tel (01564) 702233 E-mail liz@birmingham.anglican.org

HOWLETT, Richard Laurence. b 56. Kent Univ BA79. Trin Coll Bris. **d** 94 **p** 95. C Louth *Linc* 94-98; R Marston Morteyne w Lidlington *St Alb* 98-05; V Goldington from 05. *St Mary's Vicarage, Church Lane, Goldington, Bedford MK41 0AP* Tel (01234) 355024 E-mail richard@revhowlett.fslife.co.uk

HOWLETT, Victor John. b 43. S Dios Minl Tr Scheme 90. **d** 93 **p** 94. NSM Bris St Andr w St Bart 93-95; NSM Bishopston and Bris St Matt and St Nath 95-96; C Gtr Corsham 95-99; V Wick w Doynton and Dyrham 99-05; AD Kingswood and S Glos 02-05; P-in-c Stratton St Margaret w S Marston etc from 05. *The Rectory, Kenwin Close, Swindon SN3 4NY* Tel (01793) 822793 E-mail victorhowlett@charis.co.uk

HOWMAN, Anne Louise. b 43. Ex Univ BA97. SWMTC 97. **d** 99 **p** 00. NSM Ex St Dav 99-02; C Salcombe and Malborough w S Huish 02-07; rtd 08. *28 Sentrys Orchard, Exminster, Exeter EX6 8UD* E-mail alhow@btinternet.com

HOWORTH, Sister Rosemary. b 44. Newnham Coll Cam MA. Westcott Ho Cam. **d** 98 **p** 99. NSM Derby St Andr w St Osmund from 98. *The Convent of the Holy Name, Morley Road, Oakwood, Derby DE21 6HP* Tel (01332) 671716

HOWSE, Elizabeth Ann. *See* SMITH, Mrs Elizabeth Ann

HOWSE, Martin David. b 58. Steph Ho Ox 97. **d** 99 **p** 00. C Colchester St Jas and St Paul w All SS etc *Chelmsf* 99-03; V Rush Green from 03. *St Augustine's Vicarage, 78 Birkbeck Road, Romford RM7 0QP* Tel (01708) 741460 Fax 732093 Mobile 07770-928167 E-mail martin.howse@virgin.net

HOWSON, Christopher Stewart. b 69. Bradf Univ BA94 St Jo Coll Dur BA02 CQSW94. Cranmer Hall Dur 99. **d** 02 **p** 03. C Tong *Bradf* 02-05; Miss P Bradf Adnry from 05. *Desmond Tutu House, 2 Ashgrove, Great Horton Road, Bradford BD7 1BN* Tel (01274) 727034 E-mail chrishowson@yahoo.com

HOWSON, James Edward. b 62. Ridley Hall Cam 97 EAMTC 98. **d** 00 **p** 01. C Cogges and S Leigh *Ox* 00-05; Perm to Offic *Ox* and *Eur* 05-06; P-in-c Kiev *Eur* 06-08; R Alfriston w Lullington, Litlington and W Dean *Chich* from 09. *The Rectory, Sloe Lane, Alfriston, Polegate BN26 5UP* Tel (01323) 870376 E-mail jameshowson@rocketmail.com

HOY, Michael John. b 30. Reading Univ BSc52. Oak Hill Th Coll 57. **d** 59 **p** 60. C Worthing St Geo *Chich* 59-62; C Tulse Hill H Trin *S'wark* 62-66; R Danby Wiske w Yafforth and Hutton Bonville *Ripon* 66-76; V Camelsdale *Chich* 76-87; V St Marsden *Blackb* 87-96; rtd 96. *35 Hardwick Park, Banbury OX16 1YF* Tel (01295) 268744

HOY, Stephen Anthony. b 55. Leeds Poly BA76. Linc Th Coll 92. **d** 94 **p** 95. C Glen Parva and S Wigston *Leic* 94-98; V Linc St Jo

from 98. *St John's Vicarage, 102 Sudbrooke Drive, Lincoln LN2 2EF* Tel (01522) 525621
E-mail stephen@hoy997.freeserve.co.uk

HOYAL, Richard Dunstan. b 47. Ch Ch Ox BA67 MA71 BA78. Ripon Coll Cuddesdon 76. **d** 79 **p** 80. C Stevenage St Geo *St Alb* 79-83; V Monk Bretton *Wakef* 83-89; V Ilkley St Marg *Bradf* 89-04; Dir of Ords 96-04; Hon Can Bradf Cathl 03-04; P-in-c Clifton All SS w St Jo *Bris* from 04; P-in-c Easton All Hallows from 04. *All Saints' Vicarage, 68 Pembroke Road, Bristol BS8 3ED* Tel 0117-974 1355
E-mail richard@rdhoyal.fsnet.co.uk

HOYLAND, John Gregory. b 50. Sussex Univ BEd73. Wycliffe Hall Ox 75. **d** 78 **p** 79. C Pudsey St Lawr *Bradf* 78-81; P-in-c Long Preston 81-84; V Long Preston w Tosside 84; CPAS Staff 85-87; Chapl York St Jo Coll 87-01; Lect York St Jo Univ from 01; Perm to Offic *York* from 01. *18 Caxton Avenue, York YO26 5SN* Tel (01904) 784140 *or* 716533

HOYLE, David Fredric. b 46. Lon Bible Coll. **d** 02 **p** 03. NSM Northwood Em *Lon* 02-05. *23 Cranleigh Gardens, Bournemouth BH6 5LE* Tel (01202) 386305 E-mail david.f.hoyle@lineone.net

HOYLE, Canon David Michael. b 57. CCC Cam BA80 MA83 PhD91. Ripon Coll Cuddesdon 84. **d** 86 **p** 87. C Chesterton Gd Shep *Ely* 86-88; Chapl and Fell Magd Coll Cam 88-91; Dean and Fell 91-95; V Southgate Ch Ch *Lon* 95-02; Dir Post-Ord Tr Edmonton Area 00-02; Dioc Officer for Min *Glouc* from 02; Dioc Can Res Glouc Cathl from 02. *4 College Green, Gloucester GL1 2LR* Tel (01452) 410022 ext 231
E-mail dhoyle@glosdioc.org.uk

HOYLE, Pamela Margaret. *See* CLOCKSIN, Mrs Pamela Margaret

HOYLE, Stephen Jonathan. b 64. Leeds Univ BA87. Ripon Coll Cuddesdon 88. **d** 90 **p** 91. C Lt Stanmore St Lawr *Lon* 90-93; C Lon Docks St Pet w Wapping St Jo 93-96; Perm to Offic 01-02; TV Withycombe Raleigh *Ex* from 02. *St John's Vicarage, 3 Diane Close, Exmouth EX8 5QG* Tel (01395) 270094

HRYZIUK, Petro. b 57. Lanc Univ BEd80 Open Univ MA95. St Jo Coll Nottm 89. **d** 90 **p** 91. C Huyton St Geo *Liv* 90-93; C Goose Green 93-96; C Wavertree H Trin 96-98; TV Maghull 98-05; Chapl Shrewsbury and Telford NHS Trust from 05. *Chaplaincy Department, Royal Shrewsbury Hospital, Mytton Oak Road, Shrewsbury SY3 8XQ* Tel (01743) 261000
E-mail petroh@hotmail.com

HUARD, The Ven Geoffrey Robert. b 43. N Bapt Th Sem Illinois DMin95. Clifton Th Coll 65. **d** 70 **p** 71. C Barking St Marg *Chelmsf* 70-73; C Everton St Ambrose w St Tim *Liv* 73-74; C Everton St Pet 74-76; R Redfern and Waterloo Australia 76-78; R S Sydney St Sav 78-89; Adn Sydney and Cumberland 89-93; Adn Liverpool 93-08; C-in-c Cabramatta 97-99; R Chester Hill w Sefton 01-03; R Bankstown from 03. *34 Wigram Road, Austinmer NSW 2515, Australia* Tel (0061) (2) 4268 4243 Mobile 43-995 1571 E-mail gchuard@smartchat.net.au

HUBAND, Richard William. b 39. Trin Coll Cam BA62 MA66. Qu Coll Birm 76. **d** 78 **p** 79. C Norton *St Alb* 78-81; R Aspley Guise w Husborne Crawley and Ridgmont 81-91; V Elstow 91-03; rtd 03. *5 Shooters Paddock, Layton Lane, Shaftesbury SP7 8AB* Tel (01747) 854741

HUBBARD, David Harris. b 33. St Pet Coll Ox BA57 MA61 K Coll Lon MTh88. Ridley Hall Cam 59. **d** 60 **p** 61. C Dalston St Mark w St Bart *Lon* 60-63; C Stoke Newington St Olave 63-67; Hon C 67-68; Asst Master Dalston Sch 67-75; Hon C Hornsey Ch Ch 69-70; V 70-82; AD W Haringey 78-85; V Highgate All SS 82-02; rtd 02; Hon C W Hampstead St Cuth *Lon* 02-04; Perm to Offic from 04. *35 Sheppards College, London Road, Bromley BR1 1PF* Tel (020) 8695 7477

HUBBARD, Mrs Elisabeth Ann. b 41. EAMTC 82. **dss** 85 **d** 87 **p** 94. Cambridge H Trin w St Andr *Ely* 85-86; Cherry Hinton St Jo 86-92; Par Dn 87-92; Par Dn Milton 92-94; C 94-95; R Willingham and Rampton 95-00; rtd 00; NSM Ely 01-06; Perm to Offic from 06. *3 Lodge Gardens, Haddenham, Ely CB6 3TR* Tel (01353) 741472

HUBBARD, Mrs Gillian. b 63. RGN84. WEMTC 05. **d** 08 **p** 09. NSM Glouc St Paul from 08. *9 Pipers Grove, Highnam, Gloucester GL2 8NJ* Tel (01452) 413063 Mobile 07985-080680 E-mail gillyhubbard@hotmail.co.uk

HUBBARD, Haynes Quinton. b 68. Dalhousie Univ BA89. Wycliffe Coll Toronto MDiv95. **d** 96 **p** 96. C Elora Canada 96-99; R Dunville 99-07; Sen Chapl Algarve *Eur* from 07. *St Vincent, Casa do Jarim, Parque da Praia, Vila da Luz, 8600 Lagos, Portugal* Tel (00351) (282) 789660

HUBBARD, Ian Maxwell. b 43. TheolP83 ACP83 Surrey Univ BEd84 Goldsmiths' Coll Lon MA86. Sarum & Wells Th Coll 69. **d** 73 **p** 74. Hon C S'wark H Trin w St Matt 73-78; Hon C Camberwell St Mich w All So w Em 78-87; Hon C Dulwich St Barn 87-90; C Battersea St Mary 90-92; V Winscombe *B & W* 92-98; TR Yatton Moor from 98; RD Portishead from 02. *The Rectory, 1 Well Lane, Yatton, Bristol BS49 4HT* Tel (01934) 835859 E-mail ian@hubbardi.freeserve.co.uk

HUBBARD, Ms Judith Frances. b 49. St Alb Minl Tr Scheme 79. **dss** 82 **d** 87 **p** 94. Hemel Hempstead *St Alb* 82-86; Longden and

Annscroft w Pulverbatch *Heref* 86-87; Hon C 87-91; Vice Prin WEMTC 91-97; Acting Prin 94-95; Hon C Leominster *Heref* 94-97; Cathl Chapl and Visitors' Officer *Glouc* 97-02; I Kinneigh Union *C, C & R* 02-09; Warden of Readers 05-08; P-in-c Frampton on Severn, Arlingham, Saul etc *Glouc* from 09. *1 The Passage, High Street, Arlingham, Gloucester GL2 7JN* Tel (01452) 741609 E-mail judithfrances@gmail.com

HUBBARD, The Ven Julian Richard Hawes. b 55. Em Coll Cam BA76 MA81. Wycliffe Hall Ox BA80 MA85. **d** 81 **p** 82. C Fulham St Dionis Parson's Green *Lon* 81-84; Chapl Jes Coll and Tutor Wycliffe Hall Ox 84-89; Selection Sec ACCM 89-91; Sen Selection Sec ABM 91-93; V Bourne *Guildf* 93-99; P-in-c Tilford 97-99; RD Farnham 96-99; Can Res Guildf Cathl and Dir Minl Tr 99-05; Adn Ox and Can Res Ch Ch from 05. *Archdeacon's Lodging, Christ Church, Oxford OX1 1DP* Tel and fax (01865) 276185 E-mail archdoxf@oxford.anglican.org

HUBBARD, Laurence Arthur. b 36. Qu Coll Cam BA60 MA64. Wycliffe Hall Ox 60 CMS Tr Coll Chislehurst 65 CMS Tr Coll Selly Oak 93. **d** 62 **p** 63. C Widcombe *B & W* 62-65; CMS Kenya 66-73; V Pype Hayes *Birm* 73-79; P-in-c Norwich-over-the-Water Colegate St Geo 79-85; P-in-c Nor St Aug w St Mary 79-85; CMS 85-97; Area Sec *Cant* and *Roch* 85-93; Chapl Damascus, Syria 93-97; Miss to Seamen Aqaba, Jordan 97-00; rtd 00; Perm to Offic *Glouc* from 01. *31 Saddlers Road, Quedgeley, Gloucester GL2 4SY* Tel (01452) 728061

HUBBARD, Peter James. b 72. York Univ BA93 Nottm Univ PGCE97. Trin Coll Bris BA03. **d** 04 **p** 05. C Hinckley H Trin *Leic* 04-08; R Karrinyup Australia from 08. *53 Burroughs Road, Karrinyup, Perth WA 6018, Australia* Tel (0061) (8) 9341 5572 E-mail peterhubbardkac@bigpond.com

HUBBARD, Roy Oswald. b 32. Lich Th Coll 62. **d** 64 **p** 65. C Baswick *Lich* 64-68; P-in-c Ash 68-70; V Stevenage St Pet Broadwater *St Alb* 71-78; V Flitwick 78-90; RD Ampthill 87-90; R Sharnbrook and Knotting w Souldrop 90-96; rtd 96; Perm to Offic *St Alb* and *Pet* from 96. *11 Cowslip Close, Rushden NN10 0UD* Tel (01933) 419210

HUBBLE, Canon Raymond Carr. b 30. Wm Temple Coll Rugby 60. **d** 61 **p** 62. C Newbold w Dunston *Derby* 61-64; Chapl RAF 64-80; Asst Chapl-in-Chief RAF 80-85; QHC 84-85; P-in-c Odiham w S Warnborough and Long Sutton *Win* 85; P-in-c Odiham 85-86; V 86-95; RD Odiham 88-95; Hon Can Win Cathl 94-95; rtd 95; Perm to Offic *Win* from 95. *Dormers, Centre Lane, Everton, Lymington SO41 0JP*

HUBBLE, Canon Trevor Ernest. b 46. Bernard Gilpin Soc Dur 69 Chich Th Coll 70. **d** 76 **p** 77. C Eltham St Barn *S'wark* 76-79; C St Agnes Mission Teyateyameng Lesotho 80-81; R Quthing H Trin 81-85; Adn S Lesotho 84-87; Warden Angl Tr Cen and Dir Chr Educn 85-87; Co-ord of Tr for Lay Min S Africa 87-89; R Matatiele St Steph 89-00; Adn Matatiele 91-00; V Gen Umzimvubu 95-00; Shared Min Tr Officer *Dur* 00-07; C Esh, Hamsteels, Langley Park and Waterhouses 00-07; Warden Lee Abbey Internat Students' Club Kensington from 07. *Lee Abbey International Students' Club, 57-67 Lexham Gardens, London W8 6JJ* Tel (020) 7244 2709 Fax 7244 8702
E-mail warden@leeabbeylondon.com

HUCKETT, Andrew William. b 50. AKC72. St Aug Coll Cant 72. **d** 73 **p** 74. C Chipping Sodbury and Old Sodbury *Glouc* 73-76; Miss to Seafarers from 76; Chapl Flushing 76-79; Chapl Teesside 79-82; Chapl Lagos Nigeria 82-85; Chapl Mombasa Kenya 85-86; Chapl Milford Haven 86-92; Chapl Medway Ports 92-03; Staff Chapl and Chapl Thames/Medway 03-05; Chapl Southampton from 05. *Southampton Seafarers' Centre, 12/14 Queens Terrace, Southampton SO14 3BP* Tel (023) 8033 3106 *or* 8071 4083 Mobile 07836-261324
E-mail southampton@mtsmail.org

HUCKLE, John Walford (Wally). b 39. EMMTC. **d** 89 **p** 90. C Nottingham St Pet and St Jas *S'well* 89-00; Commercial Chapl Nottingham City Cen 89-00; Dioc Adv on Ind Soc 96-97; rtd 00; Perm to Offic *S'well* from 00. *6 Lime Close, Radcliffe-on-Trent, Nottingham NG12 2DF* Tel 0115-933 2278
E-mail wally.huckle@ntlworld.com

HUCKLE, Peter. b 46. Ox Univ Inst of Educn CertEd69 Auckland Univ DipEd71. Educn for Min (NZ). **d** 90 **p** 91. New Zealand 90-91; Hon C N Walsham w Antingham *Nor* 91-92; C Gt Yarmouth 92-94; TV 94-96; Min Can and Chapl St Paul's Cathl 96-97; Asst Chapl Athens and Perm to Offic *Eur* 97; SSJE from 97; Superior from 02. *St Edward's House, 22 Great College Street, London SW1P 3QA* Tel (020) 7222 9234 Fax 7799 2641 E-mail superior@ssje.org.uk

HUCKLE, Stephen Leslie. b 48. Ch Ch Ox BA70 BA72 MA74. Coll of Resurr Mirfield 73. **d** 75 **p** 76. C Wednesbury St Paul Wood Green *Lich* 75-78; C Aylesbury *Ox* 78-85; C Farnham Royal w Hedgerley 85-88; V Fenny Stratford 88-98; V Stirchley *Birm* 98-05; P-in-c Kempston All SS *St Alb* from 05; P-in-c Biddenham from 05. *The Vicarage, Church End, Kempston, Bedford MK43 8RH* Tel (01234) 852241

HUCKLE, Walford. *See* HUCKLE, John Walford

HUDD, Philip Simon. b 68. Westmr Coll Ox BA90 Lanc Univ MA06. Westcott Ho Cam 91. **d** 93 **p** 94. C Kirkby *Liv* 93-97; TV

97-99; V Lancaster Ch Ch *Blackb* from 99; AD Lancaster from 04. *Christ Church Vicarage, 1 East Road, Lancaster LA1 3EE* Tel (01524) 34430 E-mail p.hudd@uwclub.net

HUDDLESON, Robert Roulston. b 32. QUB BA55 TCD Div Test57. **d** 57 **p** 58. C Ballymena *Conn* 57-59; C Belfast St Jas 59-63; Ethiopia 65-69; Exec Asst WCC Geneva 69-75; Dep Sec Gen Syn Bd for Miss and Unity 75-81; Admin Sec *Dur* 81-86; Dioc Sec *Ex* 86-97; rtd 97; Perm to Offic *Ex* from 97. *6 Newton Court, Bampton, Tiverton EX16 9LG* Tel (01398) 331412

HUDDLESTON, Geoffrey Roger. b 36. TCD BA63 MA67. Ridley Hall Cam 63. **d** 65 **p** 66. C Tonbridge SS Pet and Paul *Roch* 65-69; Chapl RAF 69-85; V Lyonsdown H Trin *St Alb* 85-00; RD Barnet 94-99; rtd 00; Perm to Offic *Lich* from 01. *The Granary, Bellamour Lodge Farm, Colton Road, Colton, Rugeley WS15 3NZ* Tel (01889) 574052

HUDDLESTON, Mark Geoffrey. b 68. Bath Univ BSc90. Wycliffe Hall Ox 06. **d** 08 **p** 09. C Heigham H Trin *Nor* from 08. *14 Trinity Street, Norwich NR2 2BQ* Tel (01603) 443785 E-mail mhuddleston@onetel.com

HUDGHTON, John Francis. b 56. BA. Cranmer Hall Dur 81. **d** 83 **p** 84. C Stockport St Geo *Ches* 83-85; C Witton 85-87; C Stockport St Alb Hall Street 87-90; V Thornton-le-Moors w Ince and Elton 90-95; Chapl RAF 95-01; P-in-c Burnby *York* 01-03; P-in-c Londesborough 01-03; P-in-c Nunburnholme and Warter and Huggate 01-03; P-in-c Shiptonthorpe and Hayton 01-03; TR Buxton w Burbage and King Sterndale *Derby* from 03. *The Rectory, 7 Lismore Park, Buxton SK17 9AU* Tel (01298) 22151 E-mail rectorofbuxton@hotmail.com

HUDSON, Andrew Julian. b 57. Cranmer Hall Dur 93. **d** 93 **p** 94. C Moldgreen *Wakef* 93-97; P-in-c Lundwood 97-01; V Dodworth 01-04; Ind Chapl *Chelmsf* from 04; C Aveley and Purfleet from 04. *St Stephen's Vicarage, London Road, Purfleet RM19 1QD* Tel (01708) 891242 Mobile 07989-988496 E-mail hudsona6@aol.com

HUDSON, Anthony George. b 39. NOC. **d** 84 **p** 85. C Harrogate St Mark *Ripon* 84-87; P-in-c Hampsthwaite 87-96; P-in-c Killinghall 87-94; V Hampsthwaite and Killinghall 96-99; rtd 99; Perm to Offic *Ripon* from 00. *26 Beckwith Crescent, Harrogate HG2 0BQ* Tel (01423) 858740

HUDSON, Brainerd Peter de Wirtz Goodwin. *See* GOODWIN HUDSON, Brainerd Peter de Wirtz

HUDSON, Charles Edward Cameron. b 73. Univ Coll Ox BA94 MA08. Wycliffe Hall Ox BA07. **d** 08 **p** 09. C St Margaret's-on-Thames *Lon* from 08. *All Souls' Church, Northcote Road, Twickenham TW1 1PB* Tel (020) 8891 6820 E-mail charleshudson@allsoulschurch.org.uk

HUDSON, Christopher John. b 45. Bedf Coll Lon BSc68 MCIH73. Cranmer Hall Dur. **d** 77 **p** 78. C Bath Weston St Jo *B & W* 77-80; Youth Chapl 77-80; P-in-c Baltonsborough w Butleigh and W Bradley 80-84; V 84-87; P-in-c Shirwell w Loxhore *Ex* 87-89; P-in-c Kentisbury, Trentishoe, E Down and Arlington 88-89; TR Shirwell, Loxhore, Kentisbury, Arlington, etc 90-91; P-in-c Trentishoe 90-91; RD Shirwell 88-91; R Huntspill *B & W* 91-94; rtd 01; Perm to Offic *B & W* from 98 and *Ex* from 06. *Achray, 5 Conigar Close, Hemyock, Cullompton EX15 3RE* Tel (01823) 680170 E-mail revchris@mhbruton.eclipse.co.uk

HUDSON, Clive. b 42. Nor City Coll CertEd66. **d** 03 **p** 04. OLM Redenhall, Harleston, Wortwell and Needham *Nor* from 03; Perm to Offic *St E* from 08. *9 Shotford Road, Harleston IP20 9JH* Tel (01379) 853284 E-mail clive.hudson@talktalk.net

HUDSON, Canon Gerald Ernest. b 20. Ex Coll Ox BA42 MA46. Westcott Ho Cam 42. **d** 43 **p** 44. C Deptford St Paul *S'wark* 43-47; C Raynes Park St Sav 47-51; V Catford St Laur 51-60; V Roehampton H Trin 60-71; Hon Can S'wark Cathl 68-80; Prin S'wark Ord Course 71-80; R St Mary le Bow w St Pancras Soper Lane etc *Lon* 80-85; rtd 85; Perm to Offic *Cant* 85-99; Dir Post-Ord Tr 86-88. *10 Medina Avenue, Whitstable CT5 4EN* Tel (01227) 276548

HUDSON, John. b 47. FRSA CertSS. Linc Th Coll. **d** 83 **p** 84. C Merton St Mary *S'wark* 83-86; C Kirk Ella *York* 86-88; P-in-c Lenborough *Ox* 88-93; V Lenborough 93-03; P-in-c Tingewick w Water Stratford, Radclive etc 89-93; P-in-c Water Stratford 93-00; P-in-c Reading St Matt from 03. *St Matthew's Vicarage, 205 Southcote Lane, Reading RG30 3AX* Tel 0118-957 3755

HUDSON, John. b 51. Oak Hill Th Coll 84. **d** 86 **p** 87. C Leyland St Andr *Blackb* 86-89; V Coppull from 89. *The Vicarage, Chapel Lane, Coppull, Chorley PR7 4NA* Tel (01257) 791218

HUDSON, Canon John Cecil. b 22. Selw Coll Cam BA46 MA48. Qu Coll Birm BD51. **d** 48 **p** 49. C Darlington St Cuth *Dur* 48-53; CF (TA) 50-57; TR Usworth *Dur* 53-57; V Padiham *Blackb* 57-68; RD Burnley 65-68; RD Whalley 68-83; V Clitheroe St Mary 68-85; Hon Can Blackb Cathl 79-85; rtd 85; Perm to Offic *Blackb* and *Bradf* from 85. *29 Eastfield Drive, West Bradford, Clitheroe BB7 4TQ* Tel (01200) 423531

HUDSON, Canon John Leonard. b 44. AKC66. **d** 67 **p** 68. C Dodworth *Wakef* 67-70; Prec Wakef Cathl 70-73; V Ravensthorpe 73-80; V Royston 80-09; P-in-c Carlton 90-09; RD

Barnsley 93-04; Hon Can Wakef Cathl 98-09; rtd 09; Perm to Offic *Wakef* from 09. *Millbank Cottage, Thorpe Bassett, Malton YO17 8LU* Tel (01944) 718518 E-mail john.hudson@uku.co.uk

HUDSON, John Peter. b 42. AKC64. St Boniface Warminster 64. **d** 65 **p** 66. C S Shields St Hilda w St Thos *Dur* 65-68; Chapl RN 68-84; V Mellor *Blackb* 84-07; rtd 07; Perm to Offic *Blackb* from 07. *Hazel Mount, Bailrigg Lane, Bailrigg, Lancaster LA1 4XP* Tel (01524) 848693

HUDSON, Prof John Richard Keith. b 35. St Pet Coll Ox BA60 MA64 State Univ NY PhD83. Linc Th Coll 60. **d** 62 **p** 63. C Tettenhall Wood *Lich* 62-65; Chapl and Lect Bp Grosseteste Coll Linc 65-71; Staff Officer Gen Syn Bd of Educn 72-73; Australia 73-79; Lect Riverina Coll of Advanced Educn Wagga 73-74; Lect Mt Gravatt Coll of Advanced Educn Brisbane 74-79; Master and Chapl Yardley Court Sch Tonbridge 79-82; Teaching Asst State Univ NY USA 82-83; Asst Prof Louisiana State Univ Alexandria 83-85; Asst R Alexandria St Jas 84-85; R Camden St Paul Delaware 85-05; Prof Wesley Coll Dover 85-92; Chapl Delaware Hospice 92-96; rtd 01. *1300 Morris Avenue, Villanova PA 19085-2131, USA* Tel (001) (610) 525 3131 E-mail jrkh65@msn.com

HUDSON, John Stephen Anthony. b 49. S Dios Minl Tr Scheme 85 Chich Th Coll 86. **d** 88 **p** 89. C Horsham *Chich* 88-91; TV Littlehampton and Wick from 91. *The Vicarage, 40 Beaconsfield Road, Wick, Littlehampton BN17 6LN* Tel (01903) 724990

HUDSON, Peter John. b 66. **d** 03 **p** 04. OLM Deptford St Paul *S'wark* 03-07; NSM Lewisham St Steph and St Mark from 07. *7A Blackheath Rise, London SE13 7PN* Tel (020) 8318 0483 Mobile 07908-640369 E-mail frpeter@sky.com

HUDSON, Philip Howard. b 50. St Steph Ho Ox 89. **d** 91 **p** 92. C Poulton-le-Fylde *Blackb* 91-95; V Blackpool St Wilfrid from 95. *St Wilfrid's Vicarage, 8 Langdale Road, Blackpool FY4 4RT* Tel (01253) 761532

HUDSON, Stephen. *See* HUDSON, John Stephen Anthony

HUDSON, Trevor. b 32. Dur Univ BA56. Cranmer Hall Dur. **d** 58 **p** 59. C Doncaster St Mary *Sheff* 58-62; C Attercliffe 62-64; V Stannington 64-79; V Abbeydale St Jo 79-88; V Worsbrough St Mary 88-95; rtd 95; Perm to Offic *Sheff* from 95. *Spring Villa Garden, 136A Langsett Road South, Oughtibridge, Sheffield S35 0HA* Tel 0114-286 3559

HUDSON, Walter Gerald. b 29. **d** 95 **p** 96. Hon C Eccleston Park *Liv* 95-99; Perm to Offic from 99. *31 Springfield Lane, Eccleston, St Helens WA10 5EW* Tel (01744) 24919

HUDSON, Wilfred. b 23. St Jo Coll Dur BA49. **d** 51 **p** 52. C Doncaster St Mary *Sheff* 51-56; V Brampton Bierlow 56-64; V Anston 64-74; V Woodsetts 64-74; V Sharrow St Andr 74-88; rtd 88; Perm to Offic *Sheff* from 88. *128 Totley Brook Road, Sheffield S17 3QU* Tel 0114-236 5558

HUDSON-WILKIN, Mrs Rose Josephine. b 61. WMMTC 89. **d** 91 **p** 94. Par Dn Wolverhampton St Matt *Lich* 91-94; C 94-95; C W Bromwich Gd Shep w St Jo 95-98; Black Anglican Concern 95-98; V Dalston H Trin w St Phil and Haggerston All SS *Lon* from 98; Chapl to The Queen from 08. *The Vicarage, Livermere Road, London E8 4EZ* Tel (020) 7254 5062 E-mail revdrose@aol.com

HUDSPETH, Ralph. b 46. **d** 06 **p** 07. NSM Ripley w Burnt Yates *Ripon* from 06. *10 Winksley Grove, Harrogate HG3 2SZ* Tel (01423) 561918 Mobile 07867-772986 E-mail ralphhudspeth@hotmail.com

HUDSPITH, Colin John. b 46. Nottm Univ BA67. SW Minl Tr Course 93. **d** 96 **p** 97. C Pilton w Ashford *Ex* 96-97; C Barnstaple 97-99; C Shirwell, Loxhore, Kentisbury, Arlington, etc 99-00; TV from 00. *The Rectory, Shirwell, Barnstaple EX31 4JU* Tel (01271) 850436

HUDSPITH, Ernest. b 26. Open Univ BA73. Qu Coll Birm 61. **d** 64 **p** 65. PV S'well Minster 64-67; Prec Gib Cathl 67-68; NSM Twickenham St Mary *Lon* 69-74; rtd 94; Perm to Offic *Chich* from 01. *12 Homegate House, The Avenue, Eastbourne BN21 3YE* Tel (01323) 439488

HUDSPITH, Mrs Susan Mary. b 49. St Alb Minl Tr Scheme 79. **dss** 82 **d** 87 **p** 94. Luton St Chris Round Green *St Alb* 82-92; Par Dn 87-88; NSM 88-92; Perm to Offic 92-94 and 00-05; NSM Luton St Mary 94-00; NSM Stevenage St Pet Broadwater 05-08; Perm to Offic from 08. *15 Waverley Close, Stevenage SG2 8RU* Tel (01438) 725030 E-mail geoff-sue.hudspith@virgin.net

HUGGETT, Christopher Roy. b 49. Hull Univ BA72 CertEd73. Linc Th Coll 79. **d** 93 **p** 94. C Accrington St Jo w Huncoat *Blackb* 93-95; C Cleveleys 95-97; P-in-c Scorton 97-99; V Scorton and Barnacre and Calder Vale 99-02; P-in-c Leyburn w Bellerby *Ripon* from 02. *The Vicarage, I'Anson Close, Leyburn DL8 5LF* Tel (01969) 622251 E-mail c.huggett@freenet.co.uk

HUGGETT, David John. b 34. Lon Univ BSc56 Southn Univ PhD59. Clifton Th Coll 64. **d** 67 **p** 68. C Heatherlands St James *Sarum* 67-70; C Cambridge St Sepulchre *Ely* 70-73; R Nottingham St Nic *S'well* 73-92; Cyprus 93-99; rtd 99. *101 Admirals Walk, West Cliff Road, Bournemouth BH2 5HF* Tel (01202) 558199

HUGGETT, John Victor James. b 39. Dur Univ BA64. Tyndale Hall Bris 64. **d** 66 **p** 67. C Hailsham *Chich* 66-69; C Worthing St Geo 69-71; C Woking St Pet *Guildf* 71-73; C Buckhurst Hill *Chelmsf* 73-76; V Meltham Mills *Wakef* 76-78; V Wilshaw 76-78; rtd 79; Jt Ldr Breath Fellowship from 79; Perm to Offic *Wakef* 79-84 and *Roch* from 84. *Breath Ministries Healing Centre, Weald House, 10A High Street, Tunbridge Wells TN1 1UX* Tel (01892) 512520 E-mail cjphuggett@yahoo.co.uk

HUGGETT, Kevin John. b 62. St Jo Coll Dur BA83. Trin Coll Bris 88. **d** 91 **p** 92. C Gt Ilford St Andr *Chelmsf* 91-94; Regional Manager for Uganda and Sudan CMS 94-01; Hon C Tonbridge SS Pet and Paul *Roch* 98-01; Chapl Lanc Univ from 01. *11 Alderman Road, Lancaster LA1 5FW* Tel (01524) 843091 *or* 594082/71 E-mail k.huggett@lancaster.ac.uk

HUGGETT, Michael George. b 38. Bris Univ BA60 Birm Univ CertEd61. EMMTC 85. **d** 88 **p** 89. C Sawley *Derby* 88-92; C Chaddesden St Phil 92-93; P-in-c Alkmonton, Cubley, Marston Montgomery etc 93-99; R 99-04; rtd 04. *12 Murray Road, Mickleover, Derby DE3 9LE*

HUGGINS, Stephen David. b 53. Sussex Univ BEd75 K Coll Lon MA80 Leic Univ DipEd79. STETS. **d** 01 **p** 02. NSM Bexhill St Aug *Chich* 01-02; NSM Sedlescombe w Whatlington 02-07; P-in-c Turners Hill 07-09; Angl Chapl Worth Sch 07-09; TV Bexhill St Pet *Chich* from 09. *20 Glassenbury Drive, Bexhill-on-Sea TN40 2NY* E-mail frshuggins@aol.com

HUGHES, Canon Adrian John. b 57. Newc Univ BA78 St Jo Coll Dur BA82. Cranmer Hall Dur 80. **d** 83 **p** 84. C Shard End *Birm* 83-86; TV Solihull 86-90; TV Glendale Gp *Newc* 90-94; P-in-c Belford 94-95; V Belford and Lucker 95-96; V Ellingham 95-02; AD Bamburgh and Glendale 97-06; Asst Dioc Dir of Ords 98-06; V Cullercoats St Geo from 06; AD Tynemouth from 09; Hon Can Newc Cathl from 05. *St George's Vicarage, 1 Beverley Gardens, North Shields NE30 4NS* Tel 0191-252 1817 E-mail revajh@btinternet.com

HUGHES, Canon Alan. b 46. TD. Edin Th Coll 71. **d** 74 **p** 75. C Edin St Cuth 74-76; P-in-c Edin St Luke 76-78; C Marske in Cleveland *York* 78-81; V New Marske 81-84; V Kirkbymoorside w Gillamoor, Farndale etc 84-94; CF 84-94; V Berwick H Trin and St Mary *Newc* from 94; Hon Can Newc Cathl from 08. *The Vicarage, Parade, Berwick-upon-Tweed TD15 1DF* Tel and fax (01289) 306136 Mobile 07941-757412 E-mail berwick.church@bigwig.net *or* skypilot@bigwig.net

HUGHES, Albert William. b 48. S Dios Minl Tr Scheme 90. **d** 92 **p** 93. Community of Our Lady and St John from 70; Prior from 90; Perm to Offic *Win* from 96. *Alton Abbey, Abbey Road, Beech, Alton GU34 4AP* Tel (01420) 562145 *or* 563575 Fax 561691

HUGHES, Alexander James. b 75. Greyfriars Ox BA97 MA03 St Edm Coll Cam MPhil99. Westcott Ho Cam 98. **d** 00 **p** 01. C Headington Quarry *Ox* 00-03; Bp's Dom Chapl *Portsm* 03-08; P-in-c Southsea St Pet from 08; P-in-c Portsea St Luke from 08. *St Peter's House, Playfair Road, Southsea PO5 1EQ* Tel (023) 9281 1999 E-mail alex.hughes@portsmouth.anglican.org

HUGHES, Allan Paul. b 45. Glam Coll of Educn CertEd69 Open Univ BA91. Abp's Sch of Min 01. **d** 02 **p** 03. Chapl St Olave's Sch York 02-05; NSM Skelton w Shipton and Newton on Ouse *York* 02-03; Asst to RD Easingwold 03-04; NSM York All SS Pavement w St Crux and St Mich from 04; NSM York St Denys from 04. *All Saints' Rectory, 52 St Andrewgate, York YO1 7BZ* Tel (01904) 643813 E-mail revd_al@hotmail.co.uk

HUGHES, Andrew Karl William. b 58. St Steph Ho Ox 07 WEMTC 08. **d** 08 **p** 09. NSM N Cheltenham *Glouc* 08-09; C W Bromwich St Fran *Lich* from 09. *210 Friar Park Road, Wednesbury WS10 0GA* Tel 0121-505 4466 E-mail andrewhughes303@btinternet.com

HUGHES, Andrew Terrell. b 29. Bris Univ BA56 DipEd. Coll of Resurr Mirfield 64. **d** 66 **p** 67. C Weston-super-Mare St Sav *B & W* 66-70; C Yeovil St Jo w Preston Plucknett 70-73; TV Yeovil 73-83; R Wincanton 83-88; rtd 89; Perm to Offic *Sarum* from 89. *2 Cove Street, Weymouth DT4 8TS* Tel (01305) 778639

HUGHES, Miss Angela Mary. b 52. Avery Hill Coll CertEd75. St Steph Ho Ox 90. **d** 92 **p** 94. Par On Kidderminster St Mary and All SS w Trimpley etc *Worc* 92-94; C 94-96; P-in-c Gilmorton w Peatling Parva and Kimcote etc *Leic* 96-01; RD Guthlaxton II 99-01; R Wyberton *Linc* 01-09; V Frampton 01-09; RD Holland W 04-09; R Carnoustie *Bre* from 09; R Monifieth from 09. *Holy Rood Rectory, 58 Maule Street, Carnoustie DD7 6AB* Tel (01241) 852202

HUGHES, Arthur John. b 41. MCIOB71 MRICS78. WEMTC 03. **d** 05 **p** 06. NSM Church Stretton *Heref* from 05. *Jacey, 2 Lawley Close, Church Stretton SY6 6EP* Tel (01694) 722582 E-mail jhnhughes6@aol.com

HUGHES, Arthur Lewis. b 36. St Deiniol's Hawarden 65. **d** 68 **p** 69. C Holywell *St As* 68-71; Lect Watford St Mary *St Alb* 71-75; V Thornton in Lonsdale w Burton in Lonsdale *Bradf* 75-84; V Daubhill *Man* 84-89; V Castle Town *Lich* 89-00; Chapl Staffs Univ 91-00; rtd 00; Perm to Offic *Ches* 00-04 and *Pet* from 05. *31 Hunt Close, Towcester NN12 7AD* Tel (01327) 358257

HUGHES, Benjamin John. b 65. Golds Coll Lon BEd91 Lon Metrop Univ MA08. Cranmer Hall Dur BTh97. **d** 99 **p** 00. NSM

Fulham St Matt *Lon* 99-03; Chapl RN 03; Perm to Offic *Lon* from 04 and *S'wark* from 08. *101 Herne Hill Road, London SE24 0AD* E-mail benbassforty@yahoo.co.uk

HUGHES, Bernard Patrick. b 35. Oak Hill Th Coll. **d** 65 **p** 66. C Fulham St Matt *Lon* 65-69; Chapl St Steph Hosp Lon 69-89; Chapl St Mary Abbots Hosp Lon 69-97; Chapl Westmr Hosp Lon 89-94; Chapl Westmr Children's Hosp Lon 89-94; Sen Chapl Chelsea and Westmr Healthcare NHS Trust 94-97; rtd 97; Perm to Offic *Bris* and *Sarum* from 97. *Charis, 6 Priory Park, Bradford-on-Avon BA15 1QU* Tel (01225) 868679

HUGHES, Bertram Arthur Edwin. b 23. Clifton Th Coll 64. **d** 66 **p** 67. C Taunton St Jas *B & W* 66-68; C Ramsgate St Luke *Cant* 68-70; Australia 70-76; P-in-c Swanton Abbott w Skeyton *Nor* 76-80; P-in-c Scottow 76-80; Australia 80-83; R Reymerston w Cranworth, Letton, Southburgh etc *Nor* 83-84; rtd 84; Perm to Offic *Ex* from 90. *88 Winslade Road, Sidmouth EX10 9EZ* Tel (01395) 512452

HUGHES, Miss Carol Lindsay. b 51. Cam Inst of Educn CertEd72 Nottm Univ BEd86. Trin Coll Bris 91. **d** 93 **p** 94. C Ilkeston St Mary *Derby* 93-97; P-in-c Langley Mill 97-02; V 02-06; P-in-c Oakwood from 06; RD Heanor 99-06. *The Vicarage, 239 Morley Road, Oakwood, Derby DE21 4TB* Tel (01332) 667803 E-mail c.l.hughes@fsmail.net

HUGHES, Christopher Clarke. b 40. MRAC61. ALCD65. **d** 65 **p** 66. C Broadclyst *Ex* 65-68; C Chenies and Lt Chalfont *Ox* 68-70; TV Lydford w Bridestowe and Sourton *Ex* 70-72; TV Lydford, Brent Tor, Bridestowe and Sourton 72-74; V Buckland Monachorum 74-83; R Ashtead *Guildf* 83-98; R Aboyne and Ballater *Ab* 98-03; rtd 03. *Stone Farmhouse, Thorveton, Exeter EX5 5LL* Tel (01884) 855250

HUGHES, Clive. b 54. Univ of Wales BA77 MA82. St Mich Coll Llan BD95. **d** 95 **p** 96. C Carmarthen St Dav *St D* 95-97; TV Aberystwyth 97-04; P-in-c Hanmer, Bronington, Bettisfield, Tallarn Green *St As* from 04. *The Vicarage, Hanmer, Whitchurch SY13 3DE* Tel (01948) 830468 E-mail clive@hughes2003.fsnet.co.uk

HUGHES, David Anthony. b 25. Trin Coll Cam BA48 MA55. Linc Th Coll 74. **d** 76 **p** 77. C Boston *Linc* 76-78; V Graffoe 78-90; rtd 90; Perm to Offic *Linc* from 91. *27 St Clement's Road, Ruskington, Sleaford NG34 9AF* Tel (01526) 832618

HUGHES, David Howard. b 55. Univ of Wales (Ban). St Mich Coll Llan. **d** 79 **p** 80. C Llanrhos *St As* 79-82; C Eckington w Handley and Ridgeway *Derby* 82-83; C Staveley and Barrow Hill 83-85; TV 85-89; V Whitworth St Bart *Man* 89-00. *2 Cromwell Road, Chesterfield S40 4TH* Tel (01246) 277361

HUGHES, Canon David Michael. b 41. Oak Hill Th Coll BD67. **d** 68 **p** 69. C Tunbridge Wells St Jo *Roch* 68-73; C Crookes St Thos *Sheff* 73-81; V Normanton *Wakef* 81-90; TR Didsbury St Jas and Em *Man* 90-09; AD Withington 00-04; Hon Can Man Cathl 06-09; rtd 09. *41 Cross Lane, Marple, Stockport SK6 6DG* Tel 07929-114143 (mobile) E-mail davidmichaelhughes@btinternet.com

HUGHES, Debbie Ann. *See* PEATMAN, Mrs Debbie Ann

HUGHES, Elfed. b 53. St Mich Coll Llan BD75 PhD03. **d** 77 **p** 78. C Skewen *Llan* 77-80; TV Ystradyfodwg w Gelli, Rhigos and Tonpentre 80-81; P-in-c Pentre CD 81-85; V Pentre 85-87; Chapl Wales Poly 87-91; V Llanilltusant 91-97; rtd 97; Perm to Offic *Llan* from 99; *Ban*, *St D* and *Mon* from 02; *Glouc* from 04; *Lon* from 06; USPG Miss Adv for Ch in Wales 02-06 and *Glouc* 04-06; Ch Relns Manager (Dep Dir) 06-08; Dir Britain and Ireland Team from 08. *19 Heol Brynteg, Tonyrefail, Porth CF39 8DL* Tel (020) 7378 5696 E-mail elfedh@uspg.org.uk

HUGHES, Mrs Elizabeth Jane. b 58. K Coll Lon BD81 AKC81. Ripon Coll Cuddesdon 81. **dss** 83 **d** 87 **p** 94. Chipping Barnet w Arkley *St Alb* 83-86; Dunstable 86-87; Hon Par Dn 87-93; NSM Boxmoor St Jo 93-03; Chapl Hospice of St Fran Berkhamsted from 99. *17 Lansdowne Road, Luton LU3 1EE* Tel (01582) 730722 E-mail liz.hughes@stfrancis.org

HUGHES, The Ven Evan Arthur Bertram. b 25. St D Coll Lamp BA48 LTh50. **d** 50 **p** 51. C Abergwili w Llanfihangel-uwch-Gwili *St D* 50-53; C Llanelli 53-58; India 59-69; Adn Bhagalpur 65-66; C Llanstadwel *St D* 70-73; Pakistan 73-74; R Johnston w Steynton *St D* 74-80; Can St D Cathl 80-85; V Newcastle Emlyn 80-81; V Newcastle Emlyn w Llandyfriog and Troed-yr-aur 81-86; Adn Carmarthen 85-91; V Llanegwad w Llanfynydd 86-88; V Cynwil Elfed and Newchurch 88-91; rtd 91. *104 Bronwydd Road, Carmarthen SA31 2AW* Tel (01267) 237155

HUGHES, Canon Evelyn. b 31. Gilmore Ho 73. **dss** 79 **d** 87 **p** 94. Fetcham *Guildf* 79-82; Dioc Adv Lay Min 82-86; Farnborough 83-87; C 87-92; Bp's Adv for Women's Min 87-94; Dn-in-c Badshot Lea CD 92-94; C-in-c 94-96; Hon Can Guildf Cathl 94-96; rtd 96; Perm to Offic *Guildf* from 96. *4 Oaklands, Haslemere GU27 3RD* Tel (01428) 651576

HUGHES, Gareth Francis. b 73. St Jo Coll Dur MSc94 GInstP94. St Mich Coll Llan BD98. **d** 98 **p** 99. C Haughton le Skerne *Dur* 98-02; TV White Horse *Sarum* 02-06. *The Oriental Institute, Pusey Lane, Oxford OX1 2LE* Tel (01865) 278200

HUGHES, The Very Revd Geraint Morgan Hugh. b 34. Keble Coll Ox BA58 MA63. St Mich Coll Llan 58. **d** 59 **p** 60. C Gorseinon *S & B* 59-63; C Oystermouth 63-68; R Llanbadarn Fawr, Llandegley and Llanfihangel etc 68-76; R Llandrindod w Cefnllys 76-87; R Llandrindod w Cefnllys and Disserth 87-98; Can Brecon Cathl 89-98; Prec Brecon Cathl 95-98; RD Maelienydd 95-98; Dean Brecon 98-00; V Brecon St Mary and Battle w Llanddew 98-00; rtd 00. *Hafod, Cefnllys Lane, Penybont, Llandrindod Wells LD1 5SW* Tel (01597) 851830

HUGHES, Canon Gerald Thomas. b 30. Univ Coll BD63 MTh. Qu Coll Birm 72. **d** 72 **p** 73. Lic to Offic *Cov* 72-80; P-in-c Birdingbury 80-81; P-in-c Leamington Hastings 80-81; V Leamington Hastings and Birdingbury 81-82; V Dunchurch 82-89; RD Rugby 85-89; Can Res Cov Cathl 89-94; rtd 94; Perm to Offic *Cov* and *Worc* from 94. *Loafers' Cottage, Lazy Lane, Fladbury, Pershore WR10 2QL* Tel (01386) 860650 E-mail gerald@loafers.plus.net

HUGHES, Canon Gwilym Berw. b 42. St Mich Coll Llan. **d** 68 **p** 69. C Conwy w Gyffin *Ban* 68-71; V Llandinorwig 71-75; TV Llandudno 75-80; V Dwygyfylchi 80-96; RD Arllechwedd 88-96; V Bodelwyddan *St As* from 96; Can Cursal St As Cathl from 08. *The Vicarage, Bodelwyddan, Rhyl LL18 5UR* Tel (01745) 583034

HUGHES, Gwilym Lloyd. b 48. Univ of Wales (Cardiff) BD76 MA79 Univ of Wales (Ban) CertEd84. St Mich Coll Llan 71. **d** 99 **p** 00. NSM Caerwys and Bodfari *St As* from 99; Warden of Readers 99-02. *Adlonfa, Bodfari, Denbigh LL16 4DA* Tel (01745) 710385

HUGHES, Canon Gwyndaf Morris. b 36. Univ of Wales (Lamp) BA57 St Cath Soc Ox 57. St Steph Ho Ox 58 St Mich Coll Llan 59. **d** 59 **p** 60. C Glanogwen *Ban* 59-62; Chapl RN 62-78; R Llanfairpwll w Penmynydd *Ban* 78-90; R Beaumaris 90-03; RD Tindaethwy 88-02; AD 02-03; Can Ban Cathl 95-99; Prec 97-99; Preb 99-03; rtd 03. *Cae Pysgodlyn, Waterloo Port, Caernarfon LL55 1LW* Tel (01286) 677461

HUGHES, Canon Hazel. b 45. St Jo Coll Dur 75. **dss** 78 **d** 87 **p** 94. Lower Mitton *Worc* 78-81; Worc St Martin w St Pet, St Mark etc 82-87; Par Dn Worc SE 87-88; Dn-in-c Wribbenhall 88-94; V 94; P-in-c from 94; Chapl to Mentally Handicapped from 94; Hon Can Worc Cathl from 95. *Wribbenhall Vicarage, Trimpley Lane, Bewdley DY12 1JJ* Tel (01299) 402196 Mobile 07986-251938 E-mail hazel.hughes1@btopenworld.com

HUGHES, Heather Alice. b 48. Open Univ BA91 Kent Univ 97. **d** 99 **p** 00. NSM Pembury *Roch* from 99. *7 Henwoods Crescent, Pembury TN2 4LJ* Tel (01892) 822764 E-mail heather.hughes@diocese-rochester.org

HUGHES, Hugh. b 13. St D Coll Lamp BA35. St Mich Coll Llan 35. **d** 36 **p** 37. C Llanfaethlu w Llanfwrog *Ban* 36-41; C Holyhead 41-45; V Dolwyddelan 45-56; R Llanbeulan w Llanfaelog and Tal-y-Llyn 56-69; R Llaneugrad w Llanallgo and Penrhoslugwy etc 73-82; RD Twrcelyn 80-82; rtd 82; Perm to Offic *Ban* from 86. *Cefnwyffordd, Ffordd Caergybi, Llanfairpwllgwyngyll LL61 5SX*

HUGHES, Ian. b 67. Aston Tr Scheme Trin Coll Bris BA00. **d** 00 **p** 01. C Halton *Ches* 00-04; P-in-c Seacombe from 04; P-in-c Poulton from 06. *Seacombe Vicarage, 5 Brougham Road, Wallasey CH44 6PN* Tel 0151-638 3677 E-mail i_hughes@hotmail.com

HUGHES, Ian Peter. b 55. Fitzw Coll Cam BA76 MA93. Ridley Hall Cam 05. **d** 07 **p** 08. C Wadhurst *Chich* from 07. *The Vicarage, Bardown Road, Stonegate, Wadhurst TN5 7EJ* Tel (01580) 201855 Mobile 07718-909695 E-mail ian@hughes.name

HUGHES, Preb Ivor Gordon. b 45. Culham Coll of Educn CertEd68 Westmr Coll Ox MTh94. Ripon Coll Cuddesdon 75. **d** 77 **p** 78. C Newport w Longford *Lich* 77-79; Children's Work Officer CMS 79-82; V Gt and Lt Bedwyn and Savernake Forest *Sarum* 82-86; P-in-c Urchfont w Stert 86-90; TR Redhorn 90-92; Nat Children's Officer Gen Syn Bd of Educn 92-95; R Yeovil w Kingston Pitney *B & W* 95-06; Preb Wells Cathl 02-06; RD Yeovil 04-06; Chapl St Marg Hospice Yeovil 04-06; P-in-c Klamath Falls and Bonanza USA 06-08; rtd 08. *6 Cole Mead, Bruton BA10 0DL* Tel (01749) 814873

HUGHES, Mrs Jackie Louise. b 50. ACP81 Birm Poly BEd86. WMMTC 89. **d** 92. NSM Edgbaston St Geo *Birm* 92-05; Tutor Qu Coll Birm 96-05; Lic to Offic *Birm* from 05. *267 Stoney Lane, Yardley, Birmingham B25 8YG* Tel 0121-628 4184 *or* 454 8597

HUGHES, James Thomas. b 74. St Anne's Coll Ox BA95 Liv Hope PGCE97. Oak Hill Th Coll BA02. **d** 03 **p** 04. C Virginia Water *Guildf* 03-07; C Hartford *Ches* from 07. *52 Stones Manor Lane, Hartford, Northwich CW8 1NU* Tel (01606) 77740 E-mail james@christchurchgreenbank.org

HUGHES, John. *See* HUGHES, Arthur John

HUGHES, John David. b 58. Leeds Univ BA79 Man Univ PGCE82. Ripon Coll Cuddesdon 97. **d** 99 **p** 00. C Wythenshawe *Man* 99-06; P-in-c Old Trafford St Jo from 06. *St John's Rectory, 1 Lindum Avenue, Manchester M16 9NQ* Tel 0161-872 0500 E-mail john_dhughes@yahoo.co.uk

HUGHES, John Lloyd. b 48. **d** 08 **p** 09. NSM Abergavenny St Mary w Llanwenarth Citra *Mon* from 08. *Emmanuel, 7*

Orchard Close, Gilwern, Abergavenny NP7 0EN Tel (01873) 831580 E-mail john997hughes@btinternet.com

HUGHES, John Malcolm. b 47. Man Univ BSc68. Coll of Resurr Mirfield 68. **d** 71 **p** 72. C Newton Nottage *Llan* 71-78; V Llanwynno 78-92; R Cadoxton-juxta-Barry from 92; AD Penarth and Barry from 08. *The Rectory, 21 Rectory Road, Cadoxton, Barry CF63 3QB* Tel and fax (01446) 406690 E-mail johnmhughes@ntlworld.com

HUGHES, John Mark David. b 78. Jes Coll Cam BA00 MA04 Mert Coll Ox MSt02 Em Coll Cam PhD05. Westcott Ho Cam 01. **d** 05 **p** 06. C Ex St Dav 05-09; Chapl Jes Coll Cam from 09. *Jesus College, Jesus Lane, Cambridge CB5 8BL* Tel (01223) 339339 Mobile 07967-744033 E-mail jmdh3@cantab.net

HUGHES, Canon John Patrick. b 41. Oak Hill Th Coll. **d** 67 **p** 68. C Chorleywood St Andr *St Alb* 67-71; C E Twickenham St Steph *Lon* 71-76; TV High Wycombe *Ox* 77-92; Chapl Wycombe Hosp 77-83; V Harborne Heath *Birm* from 92; Hon Can Birm Cathl from 99. *St John's Vicarage, 99 Wentworth Road, Birmingham B17 9ST* Tel 0121-428 2093 *or* 427 4601 Fax 428 1934 E-mail jphughes@stjohns-church.co.uk

HUGHES, John Tudor. b 59. Nottm Univ BSc81 Univ of Wales (Cardiff) BD84. St Mich Coll Llan 81. **d** 84 **p** 85. C Mold *St As* 84-88; Asst Dioc Youth Chapl 86-90; Dioc Youth Chapl 90-97; Min Can St As Cathl 88-90; Min St As and Tremeirchion 88-90; V Holt 90-96; V Buckley 96-04; RD Mold 00-03; V Gresford from 04. *The Vicarage, Church Green, Gresford, Wrexham LL12 8RG* Tel (01978) 852236

HUGHES, Leonard Mordecai. b 50. St Jo Coll Nottm 95. **d** 97 **p** 98. NSM N Evington *Leic* from 97. *68 Trevino Drive, Leicester LE4 7PH* Tel 0116-266 9979

HUGHES, Lindsay. *See* HUGHES, Miss Carol Lindsay

HUGHES, Martin Conway. b 40. Ex Coll Ox BA61 MA67. Chich Th Coll. **d** 63 **p** 64. C Roehampton H Trin *S'wark* 63-67; C Addlestone *Guildf* 67-71; V Burpham 71-88; V Shamley Green 88-05; RD Cranleigh 90-95; rtd 05; Perm to Offic *Portsm* from 05. *22 Siskin Close, Bishops Waltham, Southampton SO32 1RQ* Tel (01489) 890365 E-mail martin@mchughes.org.uk

HUGHES, Matthew James. b 66. K Coll Lon BD88. Westcott Ho Cam 89. **d** 91 **p** 92. C Heston *Lon* 91-94; C Fulham All SS 94-96; TV St Laur in Thanet *Cant* 96-01; R Farnborough *Roch* from 01. *The Rectory, Farnborough Hill, Orpington BR6 7EQ* Tel (01689) 856931 E-mail jmath@btinternet.com

HUGHES, Michael John Minto. b 50. Liv Univ MB, ChB74 Westmr Coll Ox MTh94. Wycliffe Hall Ox 76. **d** 79 **p** 80. C Stranton *Dur* 79-82; Chapl Intercon Ch Soc Peru 82-86; Perm to Offic *Dur* 86-87 and *Carl* 87-89; TV Thetford *Nor* 89-97; P-in-c Downham *Ely* 97-05; Hon C Ely from 05. *Georgian House, 6A Station Road, Ely CB7 4BS* Tel (01353) 615682 E-mail mikeandsue.hughes@ntlworld.com

HUGHES, Neville Joseph. b 52. NUU BA79 MBIM93. CITC 97. **d** 91 **p** 92. NSM Mullabrack w Markethill and Kilcluney *Arm* 91-98; I from 00; C Portadown St Mark 98-00. *The Rectory, 6 Mullurg Road, Markethill BT60 1QN* Tel (028) 3755 1092

HUGHES, The Ven Paul Vernon. b 53. Ripon Coll Cuddesdon 79. **d** 82 **p** 83. C Chipping Barnet w Arkley *St Alb* 82-86; TV Dunstable 86-93; P-in-c Boxmoor St Jo 93-98; V 98-03; RD Hemel Hempstead 96-03; Adn Bedford from 03. *17 Landsowne Road, Luton LU3 1EE* Tel (01582) 730722 Fax 877354 E-mail archdbedf@stalbans.anglican.org

HUGHES, Mrs Penelope Patricia. b 47. Sheff Univ LLB. WMMTC 95. **d** 98 **p** 99. NSM Whitley *Cov* 98-01; NSM Leamington Spa H Trin and Old Milverton 01-03; P-in-c Berkswell 03-08; rtd 08. *8 Albany Terrace, Leamington Spa CV32 5LP* Tel (01926) 330204 E-mail penhughes@aol.com

HUGHES, Peter. b 79. Nottm Univ BSc02. Westmr Th Cen 06. **d** 08 **p** 09. C Bryanston Square St Mary w St Marylebone St Mark *Lon* from 08. *St Mary's Offices, 245 Old Marylebone Road, London NW1 5QT* Tel (020) 7258 5040 E-mail pete@stmaryslondon.com

HUGHES, Peter John. b 43. Melbourne Univ BA67 Ch Ch Ox BPhil77. Trin Coll Melbourne 64 ACT 69. **d** 70 **p** 70. C Warrnambool Australia 70-72; C Croydon St Jo 72-74; Perm to Offic *Ox* 75-77; Chapl Ripon Coll Cuddesdon 77-79; Chapl Lon Univ 79-84; Australia from 84; rtd 08. *clo P J Miller & Co, PO Box 626, North Sydney NSW 2059, Australia* E-mail pjmillerandco@ozemail.com.au

HUGHES, Peter John. b 59. Wolv Poly BA83 Lon Univ PGCE85. Wycliffe Hall Ox 90. **d** 92 **p** 93. C Ecclesall *Sheff* 92-96; V Kimberworth 96-05; R Wickersley from 05. *The Rectory, 5 Church Lane, Wickersley, Rotherham S66 1ES* Tel (01709) 543111

HUGHES, Peter Knowles. b 61. Sarum & Wells Th Coll 87. **d** 90 **p** 91. C Whitchurch *Bris* 90-93; Perm to Offic *Worc* 93-97 and from 02; Chapl Univ Coll Worc 97-02. *Woodside Farmhouse, Blakes Lane, Guarlford, Malvern WR13 6NZ* Tel (01684) 311308

HUGHES, Philip. b 47. St Jo Coll Nottm 79. **d** 81 **p** 82. C Dolgellau w Llanfachreth and Brithdir etc *Ban* 81-83; Asst Youth Chapl 82-83; R Llaneugrad w Llanallgo and Penrhoslugwy etc 83-95; R Llanberis w Llanrug 95-03; Dioc

Youth Chapl 93-98; RD Arfon 00-02; R Llanfair-pwll and Llanddaniel-fab etc from 03; AD Tindaethwy and Menai from 07. *The Rectory, Ffordd Caergybi, Llanfairpwllgwyngyll LL61 5SX* Tel and fax (01248) 713746
E-mail revphiliphughes@yahoo.co.uk

HUGHES, Philip Geoffrey John. b 60. Nottm Univ BCombStuds82. Qu Coll Birm 86. **d** 89 **p** 90. C Sedgley All SS *Worc* 89-94; V Boscoppa *Truro* 94-96; Chapl Gatwick Airport and Chapl Sussex Police 96-02; P-in-c Harmondsworth *Lon* 02-07; Chapl Heathrow Airport 02-07; Chapl Metrop Police 02-07; V Seghill *Newc* from 07; Chapl Northumbria Police from 07. *Seghill Vicarage, Mares Close, Seghill, Cramlington NE23 7EA* Tel 0191-298 0925
E-mail p.hughes.1@btinternet.com

HUGHES, Philip John. b 70. Trin Coll Bris BA07. **d** 07 **p** 08. C Ashby-de-la-Zouch and Breedon on the Hill *Leic* from 07. *5 Ulleswater Crescent, Ashby-de-la-Zouch LE65 1FH* Tel (01530) 413166 *or* 564208 E-mail phil2overflowing@tesco.net

HUGHES, Philip Stephen. b 34. Dur Univ BA59. Coll of Resurr Mirfield 59. **d** 62 **p** 63. C Horfield St Greg *Bris* 62-66; C Bedminster St Mich 66-69; P-in-c Chippenham St Pet 69-71; V 71-83; TR Bedminster 83-91; V Ashton Keynes, Leigh and Minety 91-00; rtd 00; Perm to Offic *Worc* from 00. *19 Fairways, Pershore WR10 1HA* Tel (01386) 552375

HUGHES, Richard Clifford. b 24. Pemb Coll Cam BA57 MA59. Ely Th Coll 48. **d** 50 **p** 51. C Wandsworth St Anne *S'wark* 50-53; S Rhodesia 53-65; S Africa 65-86; Adn Pinetown 75-80; Australia from 86; rtd 89. *1/184 Springfield Road, Blackburn North Vic 3130, Australia* Tel (0061) (3) 9894 4889
E-mail cherryh@smart.net.au

HUGHES, Richard Jeffrey. b 47. Trin Coll Carmarthen CertEd68. St Mich Coll Llan 74. **d** 76 **p** 77. C Llanbeblig w Caernarfon and Betws Garmon etc *Ban* 76-78; Dioc Youth Chapl 78-82; TV Holyhead w Rhoscolyn w Llanfair-yn-Neubwll 78-83; R Llanfachraeth 83-92; R Llangefni w Tregaean and Llangristiolus etc 92-95; TV Llanbeblig w Caernarfon and Betws Garmon etc 95-06; V Llanddeiniolen w Llanfair-is-gaer etc from 06. *Hafoty, 30 Bryn Rhos, Rhosbodrual, Caernarfon LL55 2BT* Tel (01286) 674181

HUGHES, Richard Millree. b 33. Univ of Wales BA56 MA79. St Mich Coll Llan 56. **d** 58 **p** 59. C Mold *St As* 58-61; V Choral St As Cathl 61-64; V Towyn 64-67; Asst Master Marlborough Sch Woodstock 77-79; R Whitchurch St Mary *Ox* 79-00; rtd 00. *Le Village, Saint-Antoine, 32340 Miradoux, France* Tel (0033) (5) 62 28 69 08 Mobile 07798-790369 E-mail rmillree@aol.com

HUGHES, Robert Elistan-Glodrydd. b 32. Trin Coll Ox BA54 MA58 Birm Univ MLitt85. Westcott Ho Cam 55. **d** 57 **p** 58. C Stoke *Cov* 57-61; Ind Chapl *S'wark* 61-64; Birm Univ 64-87; Chapl 64-69; Lodgings Warden and Student Welfare Adv 69-87; Dir Housing Study Overseas Students Trust 88-91; Perm to Offic *Ban* 88-94; V Harlech and Llanfair-juxta-Harlech etc 94-99; rtd 97. *Clogwyn Melyn, Ynys, Talsarnau LL47 6TP* Tel (01766) 780257 E-mail shebob.clog1@virgin.net

HUGHES, Robert John. b 46. Liv Univ MB, ChB69. St Jo Coll Nottm 05. **d** 07 **p** 08. NSM Davenham *Ches* from 07. *90 Hartford Road, Davenham, Northwich CW9 8JF* Tel (01606) 350132
E-mail john_thia@hotmail.com

HUGHES, Robert Leslie. b 52. Qu Coll Birm 88. **d** 00 **p** 01. C The Quinton *Birm* 00-05; P-in-c Appleby Gp *Leic* 05-08; TV Woodfield Team from 08. *The Rectory, 17 Rectory Lane, Appleby Magna, Swadlincote DE12 7BQ* Tel (01530) 272651
E-mail robert@hazrobhughes.demon.co.uk

HUGHES, Rodney Thomas. b 39. Dur Univ BA60. Wycliffe Hall Ox 60. **d** 62 **p** 63. C Edin St Thos 62-65; C Harlow New Town w Lt Parndon *Chelmsf* 65-67; R Haworth *Bradf* 67-74; R W Knighton w Broadmayne *Sarum* 74-77; R Broadmayne, W Knighton, Owermoigne etc 77-82; V Crosthwaite Keswick *Carl* 82-02; rtd 02; Perm to Offic *Carl* from 02. *2 Bewcastle Close, Carlisle CA3 0PU* Tel (01228) 401680

HUGHES, Roger. *See* HUGHES, Canon William Roger

HUGHES, Mrs Sally Lorraine. b 59. Open Univ BA98. EAMTC 99. **d** 02 **p** 03. NSM Gretton w Rockingham and Cottingham w E Carlton *Pet* 02-05; Asst Chapl Kettering Gen Hosp NHS Trust 02-04; P-in-c Stoke Albany w Wilbarston and Ashley etc *Pet* from 05; Rural Adv Oakham Adnry from 05. *28 Rushton Road, Wilbarston, Market Harborough LE16 8QL* Tel and fax (01536) 770998 E-mail sally@hughes.uk.com

HUGHES, Mrs Sheila. b 52. NOC 92. **d** 95 **p** 96. NSM Birkenhead Priory *Ches* 95-97; C 97-99; P-in-c Northwich St Luke and H Trin 99-01; V 01-07; Bp's Adv for Women in Min 00-07; Chapl Mid Cheshire Hosps Trust 99-07; P-in-c Barrow St Jo *Carl* from 07. *St John's Vicarage, James Watt Terrace, Barrow-in-Furness LA14 2TS* Tel (01229) 821101 *or* 835909
E-mail revsheilahughes@hotmail.co.uk

HUGHES, Sheila Norah. b 40. **d** 06 **p** 07. NSM Ellesmere Port *Ches* from 06. *13 Bridle Way, Great Sutton, Ellesmere Port CH66 2NJ* Tel 0151 339 9777
E-mail sheila.hughes67@ntlworld.com

HUGHES, Steven Philip. b 52. MBE01. St Jo Coll Dur BA80. Ridley Hall Cam 80. **d** 82 **p** 83. C Chilvers Coton w Astley *Cov* 82-86; TV Kings Norton *Birm* 86-91; Perm to Offic *Eur* 92-96; Asst Chapl Bucharest 96-98; P-in-c Bucharest w Sofia 98-01; P-in-c Belgrade 98-00; P-in-c Hoole *Blackb* 02-09; Inter-Faith Development Officer Chs Together from 09. *6 Park Avenue, Much Hoole, Preston PR4 4QL* Tel 07754-177689 (mobile)
E-mail steven.hughes24@btinternet.com

HUGHES, Trystan Owain. b 72. Univ of Wales (Ban) BD94 PhD98. Wycliffe Hall Ox MTh. **d** 05 **p** 07. C Llantwit Major 05-09; C Whitchurch from 09. *16 St John's Crescent, Whitchurch, Cardiff CF14 7AF* Tel (029) 2062 5947
E-mail trystan_hughes@hotmail.com

HUGHES, Ms Valerie Elizabeth. b 53. Birm Univ BA75 CertEd76. Wycliffe Hall Ox 85. **d** 87 **p** 94. C Hallwood *Ches* 87-90; Par Dn Garston *Liv* 90-93; Asst Chapl Liv Univ 93; TD Gateacre 93-94; TV 94-00; C St Helens St Helen 00-09; TV Newton from 09. *Emmanuel Rectory, 333 Wargrave Road, Newton-le-Willows WA12 8RR* Tel (01925) 224920

HUGHES, William. *See* HUGHES, Albert William

HUGHES, William Piers Maximillian. b 76. Ex Univ BA99. Ripon Coll Cuddesdon 99. **d** 01 **p** 02. C Cley Hill Warminster *Sarum* 01-05; V Blackmoor and Whitehill *Portsm* from 05. *The Vicarage, Blackmoor, Liss GU33 6BN* Tel (01420) 473548
E-mail will-hattie@lineone.net

HUGHES, Canon William Roger. b 47. ACCA MCIPD MBIM. Trin Coll Carmarthen. **d** 91 **p** 92. NSM Llan-non *St D* 91-93; Dio Officer for Soc Resp from 93; V Llangathen w Llanfihangel Cilfargen etc from 93; Hon Can St D Cathl 06-09; Can from 09; AD Llangadog and Llandeilo from 06. *The Vicarage, Llangathen, Carmarthen SA32 8QD* Tel (01558) 668455

HUGHMAN, June Alison. b 58. Kingston Poly BSc81 Southn Univ PhD84. Trin Coll Bris 86. **d** 89 **p** 94. Par Dn Penge St Jo *Roch* 89-93; C Woking Ch Ch *Guildf* 93-98; V Croydon Ch Ch *S'wark* 98-00; C Uxbridge *Lon* from 00; Town Cen Min from 00. *84 Harefield Road, Uxbridge UB8 1PN* Tel and fax (01895) 254121 *or* tel 258766 E-mail junehughman@tiscali.co.uk

HUGO, Canon Keith Alan. b 41. Nottm Univ BA62. Chich Th Coll 62. **d** 64 **p** 65. C Pontefract St Giles *Wakef* 64-68; C Chesterfield St Mary and All SS *Derby* 68-71; V Allenton and Shelton Lock 71-77; Dioc Communications Officer *Sarum* 77-89; V Potterne 77-84; V Worton 77-84; V Potterne w Worton and Marston 84-89; R Wyke Regis 89-06; Can and Preb Sarum Cathl 84-06; RD Weymouth 94-04; rtd 06. *15 Steepdene, Poole BH14 8TE* Tel (01202) 734971
E-mail keith.hugo@ntlworld.com

HUISH, Barnaby Thomas. b 71. St Chad's Coll Dur BA94 MA95. Ripon Coll Cuddesdon BA98. **d** 99 **p** 00. C Darlington H Trin *Dur* 99-02; Prec and Min Can St Alb Abbey 02-06; R Dur St Marg and Neville's Cross St Jo from 06. *St Margaret's Rectory, 10 Westhouse Avenue, Durham DH1 4FH*

HUITSON, Christopher Philip. b 45. Keble Coll Ox BA66 MA70. Cuddesdon Coll 67. **d** 69 **p** 70. C Croydon St Sav *Cant* 69-71; Soc Service Unit St Martin-in-the-Fields Lon 71-73; C St Alb St Pet *St Alb* 73-77; V Cople 77-78; P-in-c Willington 77-78; V Cople w Willington 78-89; V Leavesden 89-96; V Totteridge from 96; RD Barnet 99-05. *The Vicarage, 44 Totteridge Village, London N20 8PR* Tel (020) 8445 6787 Fax 8445 8757
E-mail c.huitson@btinternet.com

HULBERT, Hugh Forfar. b 22. Bris Univ BA49. Bible Churchmen's Coll Bris 46. **d** 50 **p** 51. C Summerstown *S'wark* 50-53; C Felixstowe SS Pet and Paul *St E* 53-55; Min Collier Row St Jas CD *Chelmsf* 55-59; SW Area Sec CPAS 59-63; V Portsea St Luke *Portsm* 63-75; V Worthing H Trin *Chich* 75-81; C-in-c Hove H Trin CD 81-85; C Hailsham 86-87; rtd 87; Perm to Offic *Chich* from 87. *8 Ramsay Hall, 11-13 Byron Road, Worthing BN11 3HN* Tel (01903) 209594

HULBERT, John Anthony Lovett. b 40. Trin Coll Cam BA63 MA67. Wells Th Coll 64. **d** 66 **p** 67. C Fareham H Trin *Portsm* 66-70; R Wickham 70-79; RD Bishop's Waltham 74-79; V Bedford St Andr *St Alb* 79-92; RD Bedford 87-92; V Leighton Buzzard w Eggington, Hockliffe etc 92-03; Hon Can St Alb 91-03; C Stansted *Chich* 03-04; P-in-c Lynch w Iping Marsh and Milland from 04. *Lynch Rectory, Fernhurst Road, Milland, Liphook GU30 7LU* Tel and fax (01428) 741285
E-mail anthonic@stlukeschurches.org

HULBERT, Canon Martin Francis Harrington. b 37. Dur Univ BSc58 MA62. Ripon Hall Ox 58. **d** 60 **p** 61. C Buxton *Derby* 60-63; C Eglingham *Newc* 63-67; C-in-c Loundsley Green Ascension CD *Derby* 67-71; P-in-c Frecheville 71-73; R Frecheville and Hackenthorpe *Sheff* 73-77; P-in-c Hathersage *Derby* 77-83; V 83-90; RD Bakewell and Eyam 81-90; R Brailsford w Shirley and Osmaston w Edlaston 90-93; V Tideswell 93-02; RD Buxton 96-99; Hon Can Derby Cathl 89-02; rtd 02; Perm to Offic *Derby* from 02. *16 Lismore Road, Buxton SK17 9AZ* Tel (01298) 79566
E-mail martin.hulbert1@btinternet.com

HULETT, Peter. b 31. CEng MIMechE62 Leeds Univ CertEd74. Wycliffe Hall Ox 75. **d** 77 **p** 78. C Eastwood *S'well* 77-80; C

Granby w Elton 80-83; V Gilling and Kirkby Ravensworth *Ripon* 83-90; P-in-c Bishop Monkton and Burton Leonard 90-96; rtd 96; Perm to Offic *Bradf* from 96. *2 Cardan Drive, Ilkley LS29 8PH* Tel (01943) 604202

HULL, Mrs Bernadette Mary. b 46. E Lon Univ BA92 PGCE93. NTMTC 99. **d** 02 **p** 03. NSM Becontree S *Chelmsf* 02-04; NSM Marks Gate 04-09; P-in-c Romford Ascension Collier Row from 09. *Ascension Vicarage, 68 Collier Row Road, Romford RM5 2BA* Tel (01708) 741658 Mobile 07990-730293 E-mail bernadettehull@btinternet.com

HULL, David John. b 44. Linc Th Coll 88. **d** 90 **p** 91. C Mansfield Woodhouse *S'well* 90-93; P-in-c Mansfield St Lawr 93-00; V Mosbrough *Sheff* 00-03; V Elmton *Derby* from 03; P-in-c Whitwell from 05. *The Vicarage, 1 Elmton Road, Creswell, Worksop S80 4HD* Tel (01909) 721264

HULL, John Hammond. b 36. Brasted Th Coll 58 Sarum Th Coll 60. **d** 61 **p** 62. C Gt Clacton *Chelmsf* 61-66; Area Chapl (E Anglia) Toc H 66-70; (Midl Region) 70-75; Lic to Offic *Chelmsf* 66-75; Chapl Toc H HQ 75-82; Lic to Offic *Ox* from 75. *66 Grenville Avenue, Wendover, Aylesbury HP22 6AL* Tel (01296) 624487

HULL, The Very Revd Thomas Henry. b 55. QUB BD79. NTMTC 94. **d** 97 **p** 98. C Kidbrooke *S'wark* 97-99; TV 99-01; I Lecale Gp *D & D* from 01; Min Can Down Cathl 03-06; Dean Down from 06. *Lecale Rectory, 9 Quoile Road, Downpatrick BT30 6SE* Tel (028) 4461 3101 *or* 4461 4922 Fax 4461 4456 E-mail henryhull@downcathedral.org

HULL, Timothy David. b 60. Lon Bible Coll 87 K Coll Lon PhD97. St Jo Coll Nottm BTh90. **d** 90 **p** 91. C Leyton St Mary w St Edw *Chelmsf* 90-95; Chapl Havering Coll of F&HE 94-98; C Harold Hill St Geo *Chelmsf* 95-98; TV Becontree W 98-05; Co-ord NTMTC 98-01; Registrar 01-05; Tutor St Jo Coll Nottm from 05. *2 Peache Way, Chilwell Lane, Bramcote, Nottingham NG9 3DX* Tel 0115-943 6988 E-mail t.hull@stjohns-nottm.ac.uk

HULL, Suffragan Bishop of. *See* FRITH, The Rt Revd Richard Michael Cokayne

✠**HULLAH, The Rt Revd Peter Fearnley.** b 49. K Coll Lon BD71 AKC71 FRSA93. Cuddesdon Coll 73. **d** 74 **p** 75 **c** 99. Asst Chapl St Edw Sch Ox 74-77; C Summertown *Ox* 74-77; Chapl Sevenoaks Sch 77-82; Hon C Sevenoaks St Nic *Roch* 77-82; Ho Master Internat Cen Sevenoaks Sch 82-87; Hon C Kippington 82-87; Sen Chapl K Sch and Hon Min Can Cant Cathl 87-92; Hd Master Chetham's Sch of Music 92-99; Hon Can Man Cathl 96-99; Area Bp Ramsbury *Sarum* 99-05; Prin Northn Academy from 05. *Northampton Academy, Billing Brook Road, Northampton NN3 8NH* Tel (01604) 402811 Fax 414265 E-mail bishop.peter@northampton-academy.org

HULLETT, Frederick Graham. St Jo Coll York CertEd53 Leeds Univ BA58. Coll of Resurr Mirfield 58. **d** 60 **p** 61. C Acton Green St Pet *Lon* 60-61; C W Hackney St Barn 61-64; C Paddington St Mary 64-67; Hon C 67-69; P-in-c Haggerston St Aug w St Steph 69-73; Lic to Offic 73-84; Perm to Offic *Linc* from 84; rtd 91. *16 James Street, Lincoln LN2 1QE* Tel (01522) 523516

HULLYER, Paul Charles. b 68. Anglia Poly Univ MA98 Lambeth MA04 FRSA04. Aston Tr Scheme 92 Westcott Ho Cam 94. **d** 97 **p** 98. C Stoke Newington St Mary *Lon* 97-00; C Addlestone *Guildf* 00-03; V Hillingdon All SS *Lon* 03-08; V Pinner from 08. *The Vicarage, 2 Church Lane, Pinner HA5 3AA* Tel (020) 8866 3869 E-mail paul.hullyer@tiscali.co.uk

HULME, Alan John. b 60. Birm Univ BSc81. Wycliffe Hall Ox BA90. **d** 91 **p** 92. C Chilwell *S'well* 91-96; TV Roxeth *Lon* 96-02; V S Harrow St Paul 02-08; TR Ely from 08. *St Mary's Vicarage, St Mary's Street, Ely CB7 4HF* Tel (01353) 662308 *or* 659550 E-mail alanjhulme@aol.com

HULME (née ASHLEY), Mrs Jane Isobel. b 59. Birm Univ BSc81. **d** 05 **p** 06. NSM S Harrow St Paul *Lon* 05-08; NSM Ely from 08. *St Mary's Vicarage, St Mary's Street, Ely CB7 4ER* Tel (01353) 662308 E-mail janehulme@aol.com

HULME, Ms Juliette Mary. b 57. Whitelands Coll Lon BEd81. Cranmer Hall Dur 94. **d** 94 **p** 95. C Crayford *Roch* 94-98; C Leatherhead *Guildf* 98-01; CF 02-05; Perm to Offic *Sarum* 05-08; Chapl Wells Cathl Sch from 06. *18 Vicars Close, Wells BA5 2UJ* Tel (01749) 834207 E-mail j.hulme@wells-cathedral-school.com

HULME, Norman. b 31. Kelham Th Coll 50. **d** 54 **p** 55. C Blackb St Pet 54-57; C Blakenall Heath *Lich* 57-59; V Gannow *Blackb* 59-64; V Anwick *Linc* 64-74; V S Kyme 64-74; V Moulton 74-83; V Earl Shilton w Elmesthorpe *Leic* 83-88; Chapl Harperbury Hosp Radlett 88-96; rtd 96. *Moorcroft, 9 Birch Grove, Spalding PE11 2HL* Tel (01775) 710127 E-mail norjoan@yahoo.co.uk

HULME, Susan. d 08 **p** 09. NSM Kinsley w Wragby *Wakef* from 08. *4 Balmoral Drive, Knottingley WF11 8RQ* Tel (01977) 676808

HULME, Suffragan Bishop of. *Vacant*

HULSE, William John. b 42. Dur Univ BA65. Linc Th Coll 65. **d** 67 **p** 68. C S Westoe *Dur* 67-70; Lic to Offic *Newc* 70-72; C Far Headingley St Chad *Ripon* 72-76; R Swillington 76-88; V

Shadwell 88-95; V Oulton w Woodlesford 95-02; P-in-c Spennithorne w Finghall and Hauxwell from 02; Chapl MU from 03. *The Rectory, Spennithorne, Leyburn DL8 5PR* Tel (01969) 623010

HULT, Mrs Anna Eva Hildegard. b 73. Lund Univ Sweden MTh. Lund Inst Past Th 97. **p** 98. C Norrahammar Sweden 98-99; Asst V Ignaberga 99-00; Asst V Genard 00-03; Perm to Offic *Ely* 02-03; P-in-c Witchford w Wentworth 03-08; Spiritual Dir Växjö Sweden from 08. *Address temp unknown*

HUME, Miss Clephane Arrol. b 46. Open Univ BA87 Edin Univ MTh98 DipOT68. Edin Dioc NSM Course 88. **d** 92 **p** 94. NSM Edin St Jo from 92. *30 Findhorn Place, Edinburgh EH9 2JP* Tel 0131-667 2996 Fax 668 3568 E-mail cah@clephaneh.plus.com

HUME, Ernest. b 45. Linc Th Coll 77. **d** 79 **p** 80. C Ilkeston St Mary *Derby* 79-81; C Sheff Manor 81-82; TV 82-88; V Norton Woodseats St Chad 88-99; V Woodhouse St Jas 99-02; rtd 02. *Shadwell, 6 Canal Bridge, Killamarsh, Sheffield S21 1DJ* Tel 0114-248 1769 E-mail ehume@vicarage51.freeserve.co.uk

HUME, Martin. b 54. Coll of Resurr Mirfield 89. **d** 91 **p** 92. C Brentwood St Thos *Chelmsf* 91-94; P-in-c Corringham 94-04; V E Wickham *S'wark* from 04. *St Michael's Vicarage, Upper Wickham Lane, Welling DA16 3AP* Tel (020) 8304 1214 E-mail martinhume@aol.com

HUMMERSTONE, Jeremy David. Mert Coll Ox BA65 MA70. Wells Th Coll 70. **d** 72 **p** 73. C Helmsley *York* 72-75; C Pockley cum E Moors 72-75; P-in-c Manningford Bruce w Manningford Abbots *Sarum* 75; TV Swanborough 75-80; P-in-c Frithelstock *Ex* 80-81; P-in-c Gt Torrington 80-81; P-in-c Lt Torrington 80-81; V Gt and Lt Torrington and Frithelstock from 81. *The Vicarage, Calf Street, Torrington EX38 8EA* Tel (01805) 622166 E-mail jdhummerstone@tiscali.co.uk

HUMPHREY, Mrs Betty. b 37. St Mich Ho Ox 59. **d** 90 **p** 94. C Hardwicke, Quedgeley and Elmore w Longney *Glouc* 90-93; Dn-in-c Swindon w Uckington and Elmstone Hardwicke 93-94; P-in-c 94-96; R 96-98; rtd 98; Perm to Offic *Glouc* from 00. *11 Lower Orchard, Tibberton, Gloucester GL19 3AX* Tel (01452) 790790

HUMPHREY, David Lane. b 57. Maine Univ BA79. St Jo Coll Nottm 84. **d** 88 **p** 89. C Springfield All SS *Chelmsf* 88-91; C Thundersley 91-96; V Standon *St Alb* 96-04; RD Bishop's Stortford 01-04; R Portland St Matt USA from 04. *11229 NE Prescott Street, Portland OR 97220-2457, USA* Tel (001) (503) 252 5720 E-mail humphrey@iinet.com

HUMPHREY, Derek Hollis. b 37. Chich Th Coll 69. **d** 72 **p** 73. C Havant *Portsm* 72-75; C Southsea H Spirit 75-78; V Finsbury Park St Thos *Lon* 78-88; V S Patcham *Chich* 88-03; rtd 03; C Clayton w Keymer *Chich* 03-05; C Bolney 05-07; C Lurgashall, Lodsworth and Selham from 07. *The Rectory, Lodsworth, Petworth GU28 9DE* Tel (01798) 861741

HUMPHREY, Canon George William. b 38. Lon Bible Coll BD61 Lon Univ CertEd74. Oak Hill Th Coll 61. **d** 62 **p** 63. C Heigham H Trin *Nor* 62-64; P-in-c Buckenham w Hassingham and Strumpshaw 64-67; Chapl St Andr Hosp Norwich 64-67; Asst Master Mexborough Gr Sch 67-69; Hd RE Cheadle Gr Sch 69-76; Hon C Cheadle Hulme St Andr *Ches* 70-76; P-in-c Kellington w Whitley *Wakef* 76-80; Teacher Thurnscoe Comp Sch 76-80; RE Insp Glos Co Coun and Dio *Glouc* 80-93; Dioc RE Adv 93-99; Hon Can Glouc Cathl 95-99; rtd 00; Perm to Offic *Glouc* from 00. *11 Lower Orchard, Tibberton, Gloucester GL19 3AX* Tel (01452) 790790

HUMPHREY, Heather Mary. b 46. CertEd68. WMMTC 87. **d** 90 **p** 94. NSM Overbury w Teddington, Alstone etc *Worc* 90-96; NSM Berrow w Pendock, Eldersfield, Hollybush etc 96-98; C Coseley Ch Ch 98-00; V from 00. *The Vicarage, Church Road, Coseley, Bilston WV14 8YB* Tel (01902) 353551

HUMPHREY, Timothy Martin. b 62. Ex Univ BA83. St Jo Coll Nottm 86. **d** 89 **p** 90. C Wallington *S'wark* 89-92; P-in-c 92-97; C Oakley w Wootton St Lawrence *Win* 97-02; Faith Development Field Officer 97-02; V Kensington St Barn *Lon* from 02. *St Barnabas' Vicarage, 23 Addison Road, London W14 8LH* Tel (020) 7471 7019 *or* 7471 7000 Fax 7471 7001 E-mail tim@stbk.org.uk

HUMPHREYS, Mrs Anne-Marie (Anna). b 44. SRN67 K Coll Lon BD92 AKC92 Man Univ MA96. NOC 92. **d** 95 **p** 96. NSM Manchester Gd Shep and St Barn 95-98; NSM Burnage St Nic 98-03; Chapl Cen Man Healthcare NHS Trust 96-01; Chapl Cen Man/Man Children's Univ Hosp NHS Trust 01-06. *Tyn-y-Coed, Henryd Road, Conwy LL32 8YF* Tel (01492) 573396

HUMPHREYS, Brian Leonard. b 29. MChS51 SRCh. Bp Attwell Tr Inst. **d** 87 **p** 88. NSM Maughold *S & M* 87-91; NSM S Ramsey St Paul 91-92; NSM Andreas 92-94; Perm to Offic from 94. *Thie Cassan Yack, Jack's Lane, Port E Vullen, Ramsey, Isle of Man IM7 1AW* Tel (01624) 813694

HUMPHREYS, Daniel Robert. b 74. K Coll Lon BA95 AKC95 Leeds Univ BA99. Coll of Resurr Mirfield 97. **d** 00 **p** 01. C Scarborough St Martin *York* 00-02; C Kilburn St Aug w St Jo *Lon* 02-08; V Willesden St Matt from 08. *St Matthew's Vicarage, 77 St Mary's Road, London NW10 4AU* Tel (020) 8965 3748 E-mail dhumphreys566@btinternet.com

HUMPHREYS, James Graham. b 36. Liv Univ BEng57 PhD60. Trin Coll Bris 61. d 63 p 64. C Denton Holme *Carl* 63-66; C St Helens St Mark *Liv* 66-68; V Houghton *Carl* 68-79; V Bramcote *S'well* 79-93; RD Beeston 85-90; rtd 93; Perm to Offic *S'well* 93-01; Perm to Offic *Carl* from 01. *383 London Road, Carlisle CA1 3HA* Tel (01228) 597108

HUMPHREYS, John Louis. b 51. Jes Coll Cam BA72 MA76 Nottm Univ BA75. St Jo Coll Nottm 73. d 76 p 77. C W Bromwich Gd Shep w St Jo *Lich* 76-79; C Woodford Wells *Chelmsf* 79-83; V Werrington *Lich* 83-08; Chapl HM YOI Werrington Ho 83-98; Perm to Offic *Lich* from 09. *18 Omega Way, Stoke-on-Trent ST4 8TF* Tel and fax (01782) 658575

HUMPHREYS, Canon Kenneth Glyn. b 28. Bps' Coll Cheshunt 64. d 66 p 67. C New Windsor St Jo *Ox* 66-67; C Whitley Ch Ch 67-70; V Compton 70-74; R Compton w E Ilsley 74-75; C Wokingham All SS 75-77; Chapl Lucas Hosp Wokingham (Almshouses) 77-81; V California *Ox* 81-94; RD Sonning 86-88; Hon Can Ch Ch 91-94; rtd 95; Perm to Offic *Ox* from 96. *3 Milton Court, Milton Road, Wokingham RG40 1DQ* Tel 0118-977 2096

HUMPHREYS, Mrs Lydia Ann. b 60. Sarum & Wells Th Coll 91. d 93 p 94. C Gaywood *Nor* 93-95 and 95-97; TV Cov E from 97. *St Margaret's Vicarage, 18 South Avenue, Coventry CV2 4DR* Tel and fax (024) 7645 7344
E-mail lydia@humphreys.clara.co.uk

HUMPHREYS, Canon Philip Noel. b 34. Bps' Coll Cheshunt 62. d 64 p 65. C Plymouth St Andr *Ex* 64-68; Chapl Lee Abbey 68-73; V Porchester *S'well* 73-82; RD W Bingham 82-87; P-in-c W Leake w Kingston-on-Soar and Ratcliffe-on-Soar 82-87; R W Bridgford 82-00; Hon Can S'well Minster 93-00; rtd 00; Perm to Offic *S'well* from 01. *2 Kirkfell Close, West Bridgford, Nottingham NG2 6QT*

HUMPHREYS, Canon Roger John. b 45. CertEd66 Open Univ BA76. Wycliffe Hall Ox 81. d 83 p 84. Chapl Dragon Sch Ox 83-87; C Ox St Andr 83-87; V Carterton 87-94; R Bladon w Woodstock 94-05; TR Blenheim 05-09; AD Woodstock 01-06; Chapl Cokethorpe Sch Witney from 09; Hon Can Ch Ch *Ox* from 05. *Cokethorpe School, Witney OX29 7PU* Tel (01993) 703921 E-mail rev.rog@zen.co.uk

HUMPHREYS, Stephen Robert Beresford. b 52. K Coll Lon BA98. K Coll Lon 74. d 76 p 77. C Northwood Hills St Edm *Lon* 76-79; C Manningham St Mary and Bradf St Mich 79-81; Chapl Bradf R Infirmary 82-86; C Leeds St Pet *Ripon* 87-90; Perm to Offic *B & W* 94-99; C Selworthy, Timberscombe, Wootton Courtenay etc 02-07; C Porlock and Porlock Weir w Stoke Pero etc from 07. *Stowey Farm, Timberscombe, Minehead TA24 7BW* Tel (01643) 841265 Mobile 07973-409536

HUMPHREYS, William Alfred. b 18. Lich Th Coll 54. d 56 p 57. C Stone St Mich *Lich* 56-60; V Fazeley 60-65; V Prees 65-83; P-in-c Fauls 66-70; V 70-83; RD Wem and Whitchurch 80-83; rtd 83; Perm to Offic *Heref* 83-97. *Bryncroft, 4 Seabridge Meadow, Bucknell SY7 0AP* Tel (01547) 530597

HUMPHRIES, Anthony Roy. b 49. Lon Univ BSc73. Wycliffe Hall Ox. d 94 p 95. C Worksop St Jo *S'well* 94-96; C Retford St Sav 96-98; TV Grantham *Linc* 98-00; TV Bestwood *S'well* 00-03; V Branston w Tatenhill *Lich* 03-07. *57 Yeoman Street, Bonsall, Matlock DE4 2AA* Tel (01283) 568926
E-mail revtonyhumphries@hotmail.com

HUMPHRIES, Benjamin Paul. b 56. Man Univ BA77 FRGS85. Qu Coll Birm 82. d 85 p 86. C Hall Green Ascension *Birm* 85-88; P-in-c Belmont *Man* 88-96; Fieldworker USPG *Bluckb, Bradf, Carl* and *Wakef* 96-98; Area Co-ord Chr Aid (Cumbria, Lancs and Isle of Man) 98-07; C Shepherd's Bush St Steph w St Thos *Lon* from 07. *St Michael and St George Vicarage, 1 Commonwealth Avenue, London W12 7QR* Tel (020) 8743 7100 Mobile 07712-460860
E-mail ben.humphries@london.anglican.org

HUMPHRIES, Betty. See HUMPHRIES, Miss Marion Betty

HUMPHRIES, Catherine Elizabeth. See NICHOLLS, Mrs Catherine Elizabeth

HUMPHRIES, Canon Christopher William. b 52. St Jo Coll Cam BA73 MA77 Lon Inst of Educn CertEd74. St Jo Coll Nottm 77. d 79 p 80. C Eccleshill *Bradf* 79-82; Chapl Scargill Ho 82-86; TV Guiseley w Esholt *Bradf* 86-91; V Filey *York* 91-05; RD Scarborough 98-04; Can Ches Cathl from 05. *9 Abbey Street, Chester CH1 2JF* Tel (01244) 313812
E-mail canon.humphries@chestercathedral.com

HUMPHRIES, David. See HUMPHRIES, William David

HUMPHRIES, David Graham. b 48. St Mich Coll Llan 67. d 71 p 72. C Neath w Llantwit 71-72; C Bishop's Cleeve *Glouc* 81-83; C Cirencester 83-87; V Glouc St Steph 87-96; P-in-c Mickleton 96-03; Assoc P Up Hatherley 03-06; rtd 06; Chapl Glouc Charities Trust from 06. *16 St Margaret's, London Road, Gloucester GL1 3PH* Tel (01452) 529582

HUMPHRIES, David John. b 51. BSc CertEd BD. Edin Th Coll. d 84 p 85. C Styvechale *Cov* 84-88; V Greetland and W Vale *Wakef* 88-96; V Shawbury *Lich* from 96; V Stanton on Hine Heath from 96; R Moreton Corbet from 96. *The Vicarage, Church Road, Shawbury, Shrewsbury SY4 4NH* Tel (01939) 250419

HUMPHRIES, Donald. b 43. Bris Univ BA66. Clifton Th Coll 66. d 68 p 69. C Selly Hill St Steph *Birm* 68-74; Chapl Warw Univ 74-79; V Bedford Ch Ch *St Alb* 79-85; V Cambridge H Trin w St Andr Gt *Ely* 85-92; V Cambridge H Trin 92-94; rtd 94; Perm to Offic *Ely* from 94. *25 Park Avenue, Beverley HU17 7AT* Tel (01482) 871471

HUMPHRIES, Miss Dorothy Maud. b 22. Bedf Coll Lon BA44 Lon Univ DipEd45. Gilmore Course 85. dss 79 d 87 p 94. Kidderminster Deanery *Worc* 79-97; NSM 87-97; Perm to Offic from 98. *16 George Law Court, Anchorfields, Kidderminster DY10 1PZ* Tel (01562) 824459

HUMPHRIES, Grahame Leslie. b 44. Lon Coll of Div ALCD70 LTh. d 71 p 72. C Wandsworth St Mich *S'wark* 71-74; C Slough *Ox* 74-77; P-in-c Arley *Cov* 77-82; R 82-84; Norfolk Churches' Radio Officer 84-96; P-in-c Bawdeswell w Foxley 84-96; P-in-c Mayfield *Lich* 96-02; Local Min Adv (Stafford) 96-02; RD Uttoxeter 98-02; P-in-c Blockley w Aston Magna and Bourton on the Hill *Glouc* from 02; Local Min Officer from 02. *The Vicarage, The Square, Blockley, Moreton-in-Marsh GL56 9ES* Tel (01386) 700283

HUMPHRIES, Mrs Janet Susan. b 46. SAOMC 02. d 04 p 05. NSM Potton w Sutton and Cockayne Hatley *St Alb* 04-07; NSM Caldecote, Northill and Old Warden from 07. *7 Shakespeare Drive, Upper Caldecote, Biggleswade SG18 9DD* Tel (01767) 220365 E-mail janet.humphries1@ntlworld.com

HUMPHRIES, John. b 49. St Mich Coll Llan 73. d 76 p 77. C Pontnewynydd *Mon* 76-78; C Ebbw Vale 78-81; V Pet Ch Carpenter 81-86; P-in-c King's Cliffe 86-87; R King's Cliffe w Apethorpe 87-93; R King's Cliffe 93-97; V Finedon 97-09; Chapl Northants Fire and Rescue Service 03-09; TR Mynyddislwyn *Mon* from 09. *The Rectory, Vicarage Lane, Pontllanfraith, Blackwood NP12 2DP* Tel (01495) 224240 Mobile 07976-370434 E-mail frjohn13@aol.com

HUMPHRIES, Mrs Julie Ann. b 64. Birm Univ BA02. Qu Coll Birm 06. d 08 p 09. C Redditch H Trin *Worc* from 08. *4 Marshfield Close, Redditch B98 8RW* Tel (01527) 60670 E-mail julie1hum@tiscali.co.uk

HUMPHRIES, Miss Marion Betty. b 29. Open Univ BA84. Selly Oak Coll 51. dss 80 d 87 p 94. Newmarket St Mary w Exning St Agnes *St E* 80-82; Acomb St Steph *York* 83-86; Scarborough St Martin 86-93; Par Dn 87-93; C Cayton w Eastfield 94; rtd 94; Perm to Offic *Nor* from 95. *27 Wells Road, Walsingham NR22 6DL* Tel (01328) 820489

HUMPHRIES, Richard James Robert. b 44. FRAM95. EAMTC 99. d 01 p 02. NSM Heybridge w Langford *Chelmsf* 01-02; NSM Maldon All SS w St Pet from 02; Asst Chapl Mid-Essex Hosp Services NHS Trust 01-04; Chapl Colchester Hosp Univ NHS Foundn Trust from 04. *1 Prince of Wales Road, Great Totham, Maldon CM9 8PX* Tel (01621) 892922 Mobile 07803-281036 E-mail richard.humphries1@btopenworld.com

HUMPHRIES, Robert William. b 36. Open Univ BA87. SWMTC 96. d 99 p 00. OLM Kenwyn w St Allen *Truro* from 99. *27 Penhalls Way, Playing Place, Truro TR3 6EX* Tel (01872) 862827 E-mail rev.hob@tiscali.co.uk

HUMPHRIES, Mrs Susan Joy. b 45. Open Univ BSc98. Cranmer Hall Dur 05. d 06 p 07. NSM Beverley Minster *York* 06-09; NSM N Cave w Cliffe from 09; NSM Hotham from 09. *The Vicarage, Church Lane, North Cave, Brough HU15 2LW* Tel (01430) 470716
E-mail humphries22@humphries.22.kavoo.co.uk

HUMPHRIES, William David. b 57. QUB BEd LTCL. CITC. d 86 p 87. C Ballyholme *D & D* 86-90; Min Can Belf Cathl from 89; V Choral 90-93; C Belfast St Anne *Conn* 90-93; I Stormont *D & D* from 93. *St Molua's Rectory, 3 Rosepark, Belfast BT5 7RG* Tel (028) 9048 2292 *or* 9041 9171
E-mail stormont@down.anglican.org

HUMPHRIS, Richard. b 44. Sarum & Wells Th Coll 69. d 72 p 73. C Cheltenham St Luke and St Jo *Glouc* 72-77; C Lydney w Aylburton 77-82; Chapl RAF 82-85; TV Kippax w Allerton Bywater *Ripon* 85-92; RSPCA 92-95; rtd 95; Perm to Offic *York* from 98. *33 Field Avenue, Thorpe Willoughby, Selby YO8 9PS* Tel (01757) 291030

HUMPHRISS, Canon Reginald George. b 36. Kelham Th Coll 56. d 61 p 62. C Londonderry *Birm* 61-63; Asst Dir RE *Cant* 63-66; Dioc Youth Chapl 63-66; V Preston next Faversham 66-72; P-in-c Goodnestone St Bart and Graveney 71-72; V Spring Park 72-76; R Cant St Martin and St Paul 76-90; R Saltwood 90-01; RD Cant 82-88; Hon Can Cant Cathl 85-01; RD Elham 93-00; rtd 01; Perm to Offic *Cant* from 01. *Winsole, Faussett, Lower Hardres, Canterbury CT4 7AH* Tel (01227) 765264

HUMPHRY, Toby Peter. b 66. Man Univ BA88. Ripon Coll Cuddesdon BA90 MA96 Qu Coll Birm 92. d 93 p 94. C Westhoughton *Man* 93-96; C Westhoughton and Wingates 97; TV Atherton 97-99; TV Atherton and Hindsford 99-02; TV Atherton and Hindsford w Howe Bridge 02-03; Chapl K Sch Ely from 03. *The King's School, Barton Road, Ely CB7 4DB* Tel (01353) 659653 E-mail chaplain@kings-ely.cambs.sch.uk

HUMPHRYES, Garry James. b 62. Coll of Resurr Mirfield 92. **d** 95 **p** 96. C Lt Marsden *Blackb* 95-98; C Darwen St Cuth w Tockholes St Steph 98-00; V Nelson St Bede 00-03; V Morecambe St Barn 03-08; Dioc Race and Community Relns Officer 98-03; CF from 08. *c/o MOD Chaplains (Army)* Tel (01980) 615804 Fax 615800

HUMPHRYS, Kevin Luke. b 73. Surrey Univ BA97. St Steph Ho Ox. **d** 99 **p** 00. C Moulsecoomb *Chich* 99-03. *2 Adur Court, 463 Brighton Road, Lancing BN15 8LF* Tel (01903) 609260 E-mail kevinhumphrys@hotmail.com

HUMPHRYS, Laura Frances. b 53. Goldsmiths' Coll Lon PGCE77. STETS 00. **d** 03 **p** 04. NSM Gatcombe, Chale and Shorwell w Kingston *Portsm* 03-07; Chapl HM Pris Parkhurst from 07. *HM Prison Parkhurst, Clissold Road, Newport PO30 5NX* Tel (01983) 554000
E-mail laura.humphrys@virgin.net

HUNDLEBY, Alan. b 41. **d** 86 **p** 87. OLM Fotherby *Linc* 86-02; NSM Barnoldby le Beck from 02. *35 Cheapside, Waltham, Grimsby DN37 0HE* Tel (01472) 827159

HUNG, Frank Yu-Chi. b 45. Birm Univ BSc68 BA75 Liv Univ MSc71. Wycliffe Hall Ox 76. **d** 78 **p** 79. C Walton H Trin *Ox* 78-82; C Spring Grove St Mary *Lon* 82-85; TV Wexcombe *Sarum* 85-92; V Hatcham St Jas *S'wark* 92-98; Chapl Goldsmiths' Coll Lon 95-98; Chapl S Bank Univ from 98. *151 Graham Road, London SW19 3SL* Tel (020) 8542 1612 or 7815 6419

HUNGERFORD, Robin Nicholas. b 47. Redland Coll of Educn CertEd74. Trin Coll Bris 86. **d** 88 **p** 89. C Swindon Dorcan *Bris* 88-92; TV Melbury *Sarum* 92-01; P-in-c Winterbourne Stickland and Turnworth etc 01-05; V Winterborne Valley and Milton Abbas from 05. *The Rectory, North Street, Winterborne Stickland, Blandford Forum DT11 0NL* Tel and fax (01258) 880482 E-mail rjnk@rhungerford.freeserve.co.uk

HUNNISETT, John Bernard. b 47. AKC73. **d** 73 **p** 74. C Charlton Kings St Mary *Glouc* 73-77; C Portsea St Mary *Portsm* 77-80; V Badgeworth w Shurdington *Glouc* 80-87; R Dursley 87-99; TR Ross *Heref* 99-07; RD Ross and Archenfield 02-07; Chapl Huggens Coll Northfleet *Roch* from 07. *Chaplain's House, Huggens College, College Road, Northfleet DA11 9DL* Tel (01474) 352428 E-mail chaplain@huggenscollege.org

HUNNYBUN, Martin Wilfrid. b 44. Oak Hill Th Coll 67. **d** 70 **p** 71. C Ware Ch Ch *St Alb* 70-74; C Washfield, Stoodleigh, Withleigh etc *Ex* 74-75; TV 75-80; R Braunston *Pet* 80-85; Asst Chapl HM Pris Onley 80-85; R Berry and Kangaroo Valley Sydney Australia 85-94; Sen Chapl Angl Retirement Villages 94-98; TV Parkham, Alwington, Buckland Brewer etc *Ex* 98-00; Dioc Ecum Adv 98-00; R Glebe Australia 00-03. *43 Geards Road, PO Box 136, Cygnet Tas 7112, Australia* Tel (0061) (3) 6295 0013 or 6295 1767 E-mail mhunnybun@bigpond.com

HUNT, Alan. b 31. GIMechE51 GIPE51. St Mich Coll Llan 65. **d** 67 **p** 68. C Standish *Blackb* 67-72; V Clitheroe St Paul Low Moor 72-76; Lic to Offic 76-85; rtd 85; Perm to Offic *Blackb* from 85. *68 Coniston Drive, Walton-le-Dale, Preston PR5 4RQ* Tel (01772) 339554

HUNT, Andrew Collins. b 54. Reading Univ BA77 Hull Univ PGCE79. St Alb Minl Tr Scheme 82 Sarum & Wells Th Coll 89 WEMTC 99. **d** 00 **p** 01. NSM Cainscross w Selsley *Glouc* 00-02; NSM Wells St Thos w Horrington *B & W* from 07. *67 Wells Road, Glastonbury BA5 9BY* Tel (01458) 830914

HUNT, Ashley Stephen. b 50. St Jo Coll Nottm 81. **d** 83 **p** 84. C Southchurch H Trin *Chelmsf* 83-86; TV Droitwich *Worc* 86-87; USA 88-91; TV Melton Gt Framland *Leic* 92-93; TV Melton Mowbray 93-98; TV Grantham *Linc* 98-00; Chapl Mental Health 98-01; C Stamford All SS w St Jo 00-01; TV Mynyddislwyn *Mon* from 02. *The Vicarage, Commercial Road, Cwmfelinfach, Ynysddu, Newport NP11 7HW* Tel (01495) 200257 E-mail louhunt3@aol.com

HUNT, Beverley Cecilia. b 49. **d** 08 **p** 09. NSM E Molesey *Guildf* from 08. *422 Hurst Road, West Molesey KT8 1QS* Tel (020) 8979 8616

HUNT, Mrs Christina. b 24. Qu Mary Coll Lon BSc45. S Dios Minl Tr Scheme 78. dss 81 **d** 87 **p** 94. Alderbury and W Grimstead *Sarum* 81-87; Hon Par Dn 87-91; Hon Par Dn Alderbury Team 91-94; rtd 94; Perm to Offic *Sarum* 94-08. *The Heather, Southampton Road, Alderbury, Salisbury SP5 3AF* Tel (01722) 710601

HUNT, Christopher Paul Colin. b 38. Ch Coll Cam BA62 MA62. Clifton Th Coll 63. **d** 65 **p** 66. C Widnes St Paul *Liv* 65-68; Singapore 68-70; Malaysia 70-71; Hon C Foord St Jo *Cant* 72-73; Iran 74-80; Overseas Service Adv CMS 81-91; P-in-c Claverdon w Preston Bagot *Cov* 91-02; rtd 02; Perm to Offic *Worc* from 04. *Birchfield House, 18 Oaklands, Malvern WR14 4JE* Tel (01684) 575883

HUNT, David John. b 35. Kelham Th Coll 60. **d** 65 **p** 66. C Bethnal Green St Jo w St Simon *Lon* 65-69; C Mill Hill St Mich 69-73; R Staple Fitzpaine, Orchard Portman, Thurlbear etc *B & W* 73-79; P-in-c E Coker w Sutton Bingham 79-88; V E

Coker w Sutton Bingham and Closworth 88-00; RD Merston 85-94; rtd 00; Perm to Offic *B & W* from 01. *Meadowside, Head Street, Tintinhull, Yeovil BA22 8QH* Tel (01935) 824554

HUNT, Derek Henry. b 38. ALCD61. **d** 62 **p** 63. C Roxeth Ch Ch *Lon* 62-66; C Radipole *Sarum* 66-70; P-in-c Shalbourne w Ham 70-72; V Burbage 72-73; V Burbage and Savernake Ch Ch 73-78; P-in-c Hulcote w Salford *St Alb* 78-88; R Cranfield 78-88; R Cranfield and Hulcote w Salford 88-95; rtd 95; Perm to Offic *St Alb* 95-98. *26 Jowitt Avenue, Kempston, Bedford MK42 8NW*

HUNT, Ernest Gary. b 36. Univ Coll Dur BA57. Carl Dioc Tr Inst 90. **d** 93 **p** 94. NSM Salesbury *Blackb* 93-95; NSM Blackb St Mich w St Jo and H Trin 95-98; NSM Balderstone 98-01; rtd 01; Perm to Offic *Blackb* from 01. *Dunelm, 10 Pleckgate Road, Blackburn BB1 8NN* Tel (01254) 52531

HUNT, Miss Gabrielle Ann. b 59. STETS 05. **d** 08 **p** 09. C Salisbury St Fran and Stratford sub Castle *Sarum* from 08; C Bourne Valley from 09. *20 Thistlebarrow Road, Salisbury SP1 3RT* Tel (01722) 415250 E-mail gale.hunt@btinternet.com

HUNT, Giles Butler. b 28. Trin Hall Cam BA51 MA55. Cuddesdon Coll 51. **d** 53 **p** 54. C N Evington *Leic* 53-56; C Northolt St Mary *Lon* 56-58; Bp's Dom Chapl *Portsm* 58-59; Bp's Chapl *Nor* 59-62; R Holt 62-67; R Kelling w Salthouse 63-67; C Pimlico St Pet w Westmr Ch Ch *Lon* 67-72; V Barkway w Reed and Buckland *St Alb* 72-79; V Preston next Faversham, Goodnestone and Graveney *Cant* 79-92; rtd 92; Perm to Offic *Nor* from 92. *The Cottage, The Fairstead, Cley-next-the-Sea, Holt NR25 7RJ* Tel (01263) 740471

HUNT, Canon Ian Carter. b 34. Chich Th Coll 61. **d** 64 **p** 65. C Plymouth St Pet *Ex* 64-67; C Daventry *Pet* 67-70; V Northampton St Paul 70-91; Can Pet Cathl 81-99; V Wellingborough All Hallows 91-99; rtd 99; Chapl Allnutt's Hosp Goring Heath 99-08. *Old School Cottage, Goring Heath, Reading RG8 7RR* Tel (01491) 680261

HUNT, James Allen. b 49. Linc Th Coll 92. **d** 92 **p** 93. C Huddersfield St Pet and All SS *Wakef* 92-95; V Longwood from 95. *St Mark's Vicarage, 313 Vicarage Road, Huddersfield HD3 4HJ* Tel and fax (01484) 314163
E-mail jandchunt1@ntlworld.com

HUNT, James Castle. b 66. Univ of Ulster BSc90 MRICS92. Wycliffe Hall Ox 02. **d** 04 **p** 05. C N Farnborough *Guildf* 04-08; R Bishop's Waltham *Portsm* from 08; R Upham from 08. *The Rectory, Free Street, Bishops Waltham, Southampton SO32 1EE* Tel (01489) 892618

HUNT, Jeremy Mark Nicholas. b 46. Open Univ BA73 FRGS70. Ridley Hall Cam 83. **d** 85 **p** 86. C Leckhampton SS Phil and Jas w Cheltenham St Jas *Glouc* 85-87; Asst Chapl Vevey w Château d'Oex and Villars *Eur* 87-89; Chapl Berne w Neuchâtel 89-90; Dep Chapl HM Pris Pentonville 94-95; Chapl HM Pris Highpoint 95-05; TV Bury St Edmunds All SS w St Jo and St Geo *St E* 05-06; rtd 06; Perm to Offic *St E* from 06. *44 Queens Road, Bury St Edmunds IP33 3EP* Tel (01284) 723918

HUNT, John Barry. b 46. Lich Th Coll 70 Qu Coll Birm 72. **d** 73 **p** 74. C Auckland St Andr and St Anne *Dur* 73-77; C Consett 77-79; R Lyons 79-89; P-in-c Hebburn St Cuth 89-05; P-in-c Hebburn St Oswald 01-05; V Hebburn St Cuth and St Oswald from 05. *St Cuthbert's Vicarage, Argyle Street, Hebburn NE31 1RD* Tel 0191-422 1145

HUNT, John Edwin. b 38. ARCO Dur Univ BA60 DipEd. EMMTC 78. **d** 81 **p** 82. NSM Newbold w Dunston *Derby* 81-92; NSM Chesterfield St Mary and All SS 92-02. *4 Ardsley Road, Ashgate, Chesterfield S40 4DG* Tel (01246) 275141
E-mail fredwin@cwcom.net

HUNT, John Stewart. b 37. Nor Ord Course 75. **d** 78 **p** 79. NSM Hunstanton St Edm *Nor* 78-81; NSM Hunstanton St Mary w Ringstead Parva, Holme etc 81-86; NSM Sedgeford w Southmere 84-86; C Lowestoft and Kirkley 86-89; R Blundeston w Flixton and Lound 89-93; P-in-c Kessingland w Gisleham 93-99; R Kessingland, Gisleham and Rushmere 99-00; rtd 00; Perm to Offic *Nor* from 00. *10 Peddars Drive, Hunstanton PE36 6HF* Tel (01485) 533424

HUNT, The Ven Judith Mary. b 57. Bris Univ BVSc80 Lon Univ PhD85 Fitzw Coll Cam BA90 MRCVS80. Ridley Hall Cam 88. **d** 91 **p** 94. Par Dn Heswall *Ches* 91-94; C 94-95; P-in-c Tilston and Shocklach 95-03; Bp's Adv for Women in Min 95-00; Can Res Ches Cathl 03-09; Dioc Dir of Min 03-09; Adn Suffolk *St E* from 09. *Glebe House, The Street, Ashfield, Stowmarket IP14 6LX* Tel (01728) 685497 Fax 685969
E-mail archdeacon.judy@stedmundsbury.anglican.org

HUNT, Kevin. b 59. St Jo Coll Dur BA80 Ox Univ BA84 MA88. St Steph Ho Ox 81. **d** 84 **p** 85. C Mansfield St Mark *S'well* 84-85; C Hendon and Sunderland *Dur* 85-88; V Sunderland St Mary and St Pet 88-95; TR Jarrow 95-02; V Walker *Newc* from 02; Asst Dioc Dir of Ords from 03; AD Newc E from 04. *Walker Vicarage, Middle Street, Newcastle upon Tyne NE6 4DB* Tel 0191-262 3666 E-mail kevin@hunt10.plus.com

HUNT, Mark. *See* HUNT, Jeremy Mark Nicholas

HUNT, Miss Nicola Mary. b 54. SRN77 RSCN77 RHV87. Ripon Coll Cuddesdon 93. **d** 95 **p** 96. C Broughton Astley and Croft w Stoney Stanton *Leic* 95-98; C Plymouth Em, St Paul Efford and

St Aug *Ex* 98-01; V Ermington and Ugborough from 01. *The Vicarage, Lutterburn Street, Ugborough, Ivybridge PL21 0NG* Tel (01752) 897360

HUNT, Paul. *See* HUNT, Christopher Paul Colin

HUNT, Paul Edwin. b 47. Ripon Coll Cuddesdon 93. **d** 95 **p** 96. C Cleobury Mortimer w Hopton Wafers etc *Heref* 95-98; P-in-c Fritwell w Souldern and Ardley w Fewcott *Ox* 98-05; TR Cherwell Valley from 05; AD Bicester and Islip 05-08. *The Vicarage, 44 Forge Place, Fritwell, Bicester OX27 7QQ* Tel (01869) 346739 E-mail paul@cherwellvalleybenefice.co.uk

HUNT, Paul Michael. b 57. St Chad's Coll Dur BA79 K Coll Lon PGCE80 MA96 Univ of Wales (Lamp) MTh04. Chich Th Coll 91. **d** 92 **p** 93. Chapl Brighton Coll 92-93; NSM St Leonards SS Pet and Paul *Chich* 92-93; Chapl Mill Hill Sch Lon 93-98; Hon C Hendon St Paul Mill Hill *Lon* 95-98; P in O 96-98; V Southgate St Andr *Lon* 98-05; Warden of Readers Edmonton Area 01-05; Chapl Em Sch Wandsworth from 05. *Emanuel School, Battersea Rise, London SW11 1HS* Tel (020) 8870 4171 E-mail pmh@emanuel.org.uk

HUNT, Canon Peter John. b 35. AKC58. St Boniface Warminster. **d** 59 **p** 60. C Chesterfield St Mary and All SS *Derby* 59-61; C Matlock and Tansley 61-63; Chapl Matlock Hosp 61-63; Lect Matlock Teacher Tr Coll 61-63; V Tottington *Man* 63-69; CF (TA) 65-67 and from 75; V Bollington St Jo *Ches* 69-76; R Wilmslow 76-98; Hon Can Ches Cathl 94-02; P-in-c Brereton w Swettenham 98-02; rtd 02; Perm to Offic *Ches* from 02. *1 Varden Town Cottages, Birtles Lane, Over Alderley, Macclesfield SK10 4RZ* Tel (01265) 829593 E-mail canonhari@aol.com

HUNT, Richard William. b 46. G&C Coll Cam BA67 MA71. Westcott Ho Cam 68. **d** 72 **p** 73. C Bris St Agnes and St Simon w St Werburgh 72-77; Chapl Selw Coll Cam 77-84; V Birchfield *Birm* 84-01; R Chich St Paul and Westhampnett from 01; RD Chich from 06. *The Rectory, Tower Close, Chichester PO19 1QN* Tel (01243) 531624 E-mail richard@hunts.fsnet.co.uk

HUNT, Ms Rosalind Edna Mary. b 55. Man Univ BA76. St Steph Ho Ox 86. **d** 88 **p** 94. Chapl Jes Coll Cam 88-92; Hon Chapl to the Deaf *Ely* 92-04; C Cambridge St Jas 00. *Flat 1, Thorne House, Wilmslow Road, Manchester M14 6DW* Tel 0161-257 0238 E-mail ros.hunt@virgin.net

HUNT, Canon Russell Barrett. b 35. NY Univ Virginia Univ Fitzw Ho Cam. Westcott Ho Cam 73. **d** 75 **p** 76. C Leic St Mary 75-78; V Leic St Gabr 78-82; Chapl Leic Gen Hosp 82-95; Hon Can Leic Cathl 88-95; rtd 95. *33 Braunstone Avenue, Leicester LE3 0JH* Tel 0116-254 9101

HUNT, Simon John. b 60. Pemb Coll Ox BA81 MA85. St Jo Coll Nottm 87. **d** 90 **p** 91. C Stalybridge St Paul *Ches* 90-93; C Heysham *Blackb* 93-99; V Higher Walton from 99. *The Vicarage, Blackburn Road, Higher Walton, Preston PR5 4EA* Tel (01772) 335406 E-mail shunt@aschurchhw.co.uk

HUNT, Stephen. b 38. Man Univ BSc61 MSc62 PhD64 DSc80. Carl Dioc Tr Inst 88. **d** 91 **p** 92. C Broughton *Blackb* 91-95; Chapl Preston Acute Hosps NHS Trust 94-95; V Preston Em *Blackb* 95-03; rtd 03; Perm to Offic *Blackb* from 05. *8 Wallace Lane, Forton, Preston PR3 0BA* Tel (01524) 792563

HUNT, Timothy Collinson. b 65. ASVA91 Univ of Wales (Cardiff) BD95 Ox Univ MTh98. Ripon Coll Cuddesdon 95. **d** 97 **p** 98. C Ex St Dav 97-01; Chapl Blundell's Sch Tiverton from 01. *1B Hillands, 39 Tidcombe Lane, Tiverton EX16 4EA* Tel (01884) 242343 E-mail tc@collhunt.fsnet.co.uk

HUNT, Vera Susan Henrietta. b 33. MBE06. S Dios Minl Tr Scheme 88. **d** 91 **p** 94. Hon Chapl RAD from 91; Perm to Offic *Lon* from 03. *54 Highway Avenue, Maidenhead SL6 5AQ* Tel (01628) 623909 E-mail _vera@sh-hunt.fsnet.co.uk

HUNTE (née FRANKLIN), Ms Roxanne Fay. b 60. Gama Filho Univ Brazil BSc93 Huron Univ MBA94 Leeds Univ BA08. Coll of Resurr Mirfield 07. **d** 09. C Newington St Mary *S'wark* from 09. *89 Ambergate Street, London SE17 3RZ* Tel (020) 7735 1894 Mobile 07747-896779

HUNTER, Allan Davies. b 36. Univ of Wales (Lamp) BA57. Coll of Resurr Mirfield 57. **d** 59 **p** 60. C Cardiff St Jo *Llan* 59-68; V Llansawel 68-76; Youth Chapl 71-77; V Llansawel w Briton Ferry 76-79; V Canton St Cath 79-01; rtd 01. *9 Avonridge, Thornhill, Cardiff CF14 9AU* Tel (029) 2069 3054 E-mail allanhunter@talk21.com

HUNTER, David Hilliard Cowan. b 48. Massey Univ (NZ) BA92. St Jo Coll Auckland LTh74. **d** 73 **p** 74. C Stoke New Zealand 73-75; C Christ Church Cathl 75-78; V Waimea 78-79; Chapl Tongariro Pris Farm 79-85; Chapl Waikune Pris 81-85; Chapl Rangipo Pris 81-85; Chapl Rimutaka Pris and Pris Staff Coll 86-92; P Asst Silverstream 86-92; Chapl NZ Army 88-92; P Asst Marton 92-97; P Asst Cambridge 91-01; Chapl Bruton Sch for Girls 02; P-in-c Stevington *St Alb* 03-06; Chapl Rockhampton Gr Sch Australia from 06. *Rockhampton Grammar School, Archer Street, Rockhampton Qld 4700, Australia* Tel (0061) (7) 4936 0600

HUNTER, Edwin Wallace. b 43. NUI BA83 FCIM. CITC 91. **d** 94 **p** 95. NSM Cork St Fin Barre's Union *C, C & R* from 94; Min Can Cork Cathl from 95; Bp's Dom Chapl from 03. *Cedar Lodge, Church Road, Carrigaline, Co Cork, Republic of Ireland* Tel (00353) (21) 437 2338 E-mail enjhunter@eircom.net

HUNTER, Canon Frank Geoffrey. b 34. Keble Coll Ox BA56 MA60 Fitzw Coll Cam BA58 MA62. Ridley Hall Cam 57. **d** 59 **p** 60. C Bircle *Man* 59-62; C Jarrow Grange *Dur* 62-65; V Kingston upon Hull St Martin *York* 65-72; V Linthorpe 72-76; V Heslington 76-99; RD Derwent 78-98; Can and Preb York Minster 85-99; rtd 99; Perm to Offic *Wakef* from 01. *2 Flexbury Avenue, Morley, Leeds LS27 0RG* Tel 0113-253 9213

HUNTER, Graham. b 78. K Coll Lon BA02. Ridley Hall Cam 05. **d** 07 **p** 08. C Holloway St Mary Magd *Lon* from 07. *1 Sophia Close, London N7 8SR*

HUNTER, Ian Paton. b 20. Em Coll Cam BA46 MA50. Tyndale Hall Bris 40. **d** 43 **p** 47. C Harrington *Pet* 43-47; C Portman Square St Paul *Lon* 47-50; V Furneux Pelham w Stocking Pelham *St Alb* 50-54; V Moulton *Pet* 54-60; V Danehill *Chich* 60-67; R Plumpton w E Chiltington 67-77; V Burwash Weald 77-83; P-in-c Stonegate 83-85; rtd 85; Perm to Offic *Chich* 86-08. *The College of St Barnabas, Blackberry Lane, Lingfield RH7 6NJ* Tel (01342) 872856

HUNTER, James. b 38. Union Th Coll Belf BD90. **d** 92 **p** 92. In Presbyterian Ch of Ireland 82-92; V Werneth *Man* 92-98; V Woking St Paul *Guildf* 98-05; Asst Chapl HM Pris Coldingley 01-05; rtd 06; Perm to Offic *Pet* from 06. *39 Meadow Street, Market Harborough LE16 7JY* E-mail jimo.hunter@virgin.net

HUNTER, John Crichton. b 38. Univ of Wales (Cardiff) BA59 DipEd60 LTCL. St Steph Ho Ox 98. **d** 99 **p** 00. NSM Walham Green St Jo w St Jas *Lon* 99-05; NSM S Kensington St Steph 05-08; Perm to Offic from 08. *57 Manor Court, 23 Bagleys Lane, London SW6 2BN* Tel (020) 7736 7544 E-mail frjohnhunter@hotmail.com

HUNTER, Canon John Gaunt. b 21. St Jo Coll Dur BA49 Leeds Univ MA94 Lanc Univ MPhil08. Ridley Hall Cam 49. **d** 51 **p** 52. C Bradf Cathl 51-54; C Compton Gifford *Ex* 54-56; V Bootle St Matt *Liv* 56-62; Prin Bp Tucker Coll Uganda 62-65; V Altcar *Liv* 65-78; Dioc Missr 65-71; Abp York's Adv in Miss 71-78; Hon Can Liv Cathl 71-78; R Buckhurst Hill *Chelmsf* 78-79; TR 79-89; Dioc Adv in Evang *Bradf* 89-92; rtd 92; Perm to Offic *Bradf* from 92. *Westhouse Lodge, Lower Westhouse, Ingleton, Carnforth LA6 3NZ* Tel (01524) 241305

HUNTER, Mrs Linda Margaret. b 47. STETS 95. **d** 98. NSM Wootton *Portsm* 98-02; NSM Chale, Gatcombe and Shorwell w Kingston 02-05; NSM Ruskington Gp *Linc* from 07. *12 Hillside Estate, Ruskington, Sleaford NG34 9TJ*

HUNTER, Lionel Lawledge Gleave. b 24. ALCD53. **d** 53 **p** 54. C Leic H Trin 53-56; C Northampton St Giles *Pet* 56-58; C Everton St Chrys *Liv* 58-59; P-in-c Liv St Mich 59-61; Chile 61-72; R Diddlebury w Bouldon and Munslow *Heref* 72-75; P-in-c Abdon w Clee St Margaret 73-75; P-in-c Holdgate w Tugford 73-75; Canada 75-85; V N Elmham w Billingford *Nor* 85-89; R N Elmham w Billingford and Worthing 89-90; rtd 90; Perm to Offic *Heref* 93-07. *Flat 3, Manormead, Tilford Road, Hindhead GU26 6RA* Tel (01428) 602500

HUNTER, Malcolm Leggatt. b 61. Middx Univ BA97 MA97. SAOMC 03. **d** 05 **p** 07. NSM Old St Pancras Lon 05-06; C 06-09; Chapl HM Pris Bronzefield from 09. *HM Prison Bronzefield, Woodthorpe Road, Ashford TW15 3JZ* Tel (01784) 425690

HUNTER, Michael John. b 45. CCC Cam BA67 MA71 PhD71 Ox Univ BA75. Wycliffe Hall Ox 73. **d** 76 **p** 77. C Partington and Carrington *Ches* 76-79; CMS 80-90; Uganda 80-89; C Penn Fields *Lich* 90-02; RD Trysull 97-02; V Dore *Sheff* from 02. *The Vicarage, 51 Vicarage Lane, Dore, Sheffield S17 3GY* Tel 0114-236 3335 E-mail dorevicar@aol.com

HUNTER, Canon Michael Oram. b 40. K Coll Lon BD64 AKC64. **d** 65 **p** 66. C Tividale *Lich* 65-68; C Harrogate St Wilfrid *Ripon* 68-70; V Hawksworth Wood 70-78; V Whitkirk 78-86; TR Gt Grimsby St Mary and St Jas *Linc* from 86; Can and Preb Linc Cathl from 89. *29 Park Drive, Grimsby DN32 0EG* Tel (01472) 342933 or 358610 Fax 250751 E-mail mo.hunter@virgin.net

HUNTER, Paul. b 55. Huddersfield Poly BEd82 Cliff Coll MA05. Chich Th Coll 86. **d** 88 **p** 90. C Weymouth H Trin *Sarum* 88-92; P-in-c Hucknall Torkard *S'well* 92; TV 92-96; V Thurcroft *Sheff* 96-06; R Cleethorpes *Linc* from 06. *3 Taylors Avenue, Cleethorpes DN35 0LF* Tel (01472) 291156 E-mail paul@paulhunter03.wanadoo.co.uk

HUNTER, Paul Graham. b 64. Sheff Univ LLB85 Solicitor 86. St Jo Coll Nottm MA96. **d** 04 **p** 05. Prin Morogoro Bible Coll Tanzania 04-06; Perm to Offic *Blackb* from 08. *1 Ferndale Close, Leyland PR25 3BS* Tel (01772) 624492 Mobile 07731-924289 E-mail pp.hunter@sky.com

HUNTER, Peter Wells. b 52. Bris Univ BSc73. Trin Coll Bris BA91. **d** 91 **p** 92. C New Borough and Leigh *Sarum* 91-97; P-in-c Warminster Ch Ch from 97. *The Vicarage, 13 Avon Road, Warminster BA12 9PR* Tel (01985) 212219 E-mail peter.wh@btopenworld.com

HUNTER, Robert. b 36. Man Univ BSc60. Clifton Th Coll. **d** 63 **p** 64. C Chadderton Ch Ch *Man* 63-65; C Balderstone 65-69; C Newburn *Newc* 69-73; TV Sutton St Jas and Wawne *York* 73-81;

V Bilton St Pet 81-82; Hon C N Hull St Mich 82-91; TV Howden 91-97; P-in-c Ashton St Pet *Man* 97-99; TV Ashton 00-01; rtd 01; Perm to Offic *Bradf* from 02. *50 Kendall Avenue, Shipley BD18 4DY* Tel (01274) 584884

HUNTER, Stephen Albert Paul. b 52. JP96. NOC 01. **d** 04 **p** 05. NSM Ecclesall *Sheff* from 04. *Overhill, Townhead Road, Dore, Sheffield S17 3GE* Tel 0114-236 9978 Fax 275 9769 Mobile 07739-949473 E-mail stephen_hunter@btconnect.com

HUNTER SMART, Ian Douglas. b 60. St Jo Coll Dur BA83 MA99. Edin Th Coll 83. **d** 85 **p** 86. C Cockerton *Dur* 85-89; TV Jarrow 89-92; TV Sunderland 92-98; Chapl Sunderland Univ 92-98; Ecum Chapl Newcastle Coll of H&FE 98-00; Perm to Offic *Dur* from 98. *33 Barbary Drive, Sunderland SR6 0RB* Tel 0191-567 1966 E-mail ihs@dunelm.org.uk

HUNTER SMART, William David. b 75. Bris Univ BSc97. Wycliffe Hall Ox BA01. **d** 02 **p** 03. C Watford *St Alb* 02-05; C Muswell Hill St Jas w St Matt *Lon* from 05. *67 St James's Lane, London N10 3QY* Tel (020) 8444 1316
E-mail will.huntersmart@st-james.org.uk

HUNTINGDON AND WISBECH, Archdeacon of. *See* McCURDY, The Ven Hugh Kyle

HUNTINGDON, Suffragan Bishop of. *See* THOMSON, The Rt Revd David

HUNTLEY, David Anthony. b 32. AMInstT56 MRTvS78 MILT98. Lon Bible Coll BA60 Fuller Sch of World Miss MTh81 Trin Coll Singapore 65. **d** 64 **p** 65. OMF Internat from 61; Singapore 61-71; Indonesia 72-73; Philippines 74-75; Hong Kong 77-81; Seychelles 82-87; Thailand 88-97; NSM S Croydon Em 76-77, 81-82, 87-88, 91-92 and 98-04. *42 Farnborough Avenue, South Croydon CR2 8HD* Tel (020) 8657 5673

HUNTLEY, Denis Anthony. b 56. Saltley Tr Coll Birm CertEd77. Qu Coll Birm 77. **d** 80 **p** 81. C Llanblethian w Cowbridge and Llandough etc 80-83; TV Glyncorrwg w Afan Vale and Cymmer Afan 83-86; R 86-89; Chapl Asst Walsgrave Hosp Cov 89-92; Chapl Halifax Gen Hosp 92-94; Chapl Calderdale Healthcare NHS Trust 94-97; C Leeds City *Ripon* 97-02; Chapl to the Deaf 97-02; Chapl amongst Deaf People and Adv for Deaf Min 02-06; Chapl amongst Deaf and Deaf-blind People *Chelmsf* from 06. *17 Oakham Close, Langdon Hills, Basildon SS16 6NX* Tel (01268) 490471 *or* 546026
E-mail denis.huntley@btinternet.com

HUNTLEY, Heidi Anne. b 71. Ripon Coll Cuddesdon 07. **d** 09. C Sydenham St Bart *S'wark* from 09. *1 Ashleigh Court, 81 Lawrie Park Road, London SE26 6EX* Tel (020) 8659 9598
E-mail hahlive@yahoo.co.uk

HUNTLEY, Stuart Michael. b 73. BEng BA. Trin Coll Bris. **d** 08 **p** 09. C Jersey St Lawr *Win* from 08. *35 Nomond Avenue, La Pouquelaye, St Helier, Jersey JE2 3FW* Tel (01534) 758569 Mobile 07949-195026 E-mail stuart.huntley@jerseymail.co.uk

HUNTRESS, Franklin Elias. b 33. Berkeley Div Sch STM62. **d** 62 **p** 63. C Malden St Paul USA 62-65; C Ches St Mary 65-68; C Waltham Abbey *Chelmsf* 68-73; C Manchester Grace Ch USA 73-77; V Leic St Gabr 77-81; R Schuylerville USA 81-85; R New Bedf St Martin 85-91; C Skegness and Winthorpe *Linc* 91-93; P-in-c Long Bennington w Foston 93-94; Asst P Boston All SS USA 95-02; Asst P Boston Advent 98-01. *5C Independence Way, Glover Landing, Marble Head MA 01945-4659, USA* Tel (001) (781) 631 4785

HUNWICKE, John William. b 41. Hertf Coll Ox BA64 MA67. St Steph Ho Ox. **d** 67 **p** 68. C Beaconsfield *Ox* 67-70; C Newington St Paul *S'wark* 70-73; Hd of Th Lancing Coll 73-01; rtd 01; C Lifton, Broadwoodwidger, Stowford etc *Ex* 01-07; Hon C Ox St Thos from 07. *John Coombs House, 28 St Thomas Street, Oxford OX1 1JL* Tel (01865) 246080

HURCOMBE, Thomas William. b 45. BD74 AKC76. **d** 76 **p** 77. C Hampstead All So *Lon* 76-79; C Is of Dogs Ch Ch and St Jo w St Luke 79-83; C Bromley All Hallows 83-89; C E Greenwich Ch Ch w St Andr and St Mich *S'wark* 89-96; Ind Chapl 89-97; Dioc Urban Missr 90-96; Greenwich Waterfront Chapl 96-98; C Charlton St Luke w H Trin 97-98; P-in-c S Norwood St Mark from 98. *St Mark's Vicarage, 101 Albert Road, London SE25 4JE* Tel (020) 8656 6329 E-mail hurcomt@aol.com

HURD, Alun John. b 52. Trin Coll Bris BA86 New Coll Edin MTh97. **d** 86 **p** 87. C Chertsey *Guildf* 86-90; Chapl St Pet Hosp Chertsey 86-90; V W Ewell *Guildf* 90-04; Chapl NE Surrey Coll Ewell 01-05; CF (TA) 99-05; Distr P Lower Yorke Peninsular Australia 05-07; P-in-c Gt Wakering w Foulness *Chelmsf* from 08; P-in-c Barling w Lt Wakering from 08. *The Vicarage, 2 New Road, Great Wakering, Southend-on-Sea SS3 0AH* Tel (01702) 217493 Mobile 07941-417135
E-mail alun.john.hurd@googlemail.com

HURD, Mrs Brenda Edith. b 44. Sittingbourne Coll DipEd75. Cant Sch of Min 87. **d** 92 **p** 94. NSM Birling, Addington, Ryarsh and Trottiscliffe *Roch* 92-02; P-in-c Wrotham from 02; RD Shoreham from 06. *The Rectory, Borough Green Road, Wrotham, Sevenoaks TN15 7RA* Tel (01732) 882211
E-mail brenda.hurd@diocese-rochester.org
or b.hurd@virgin.net

HURD, John Patrick. b 37. CertEd65 Open Univ BA73 Kent Univ MA92. S Dios Minl Tr Scheme 77. **d** 80 **p** 81. NSM Billingshurst *Chich* 80-82 and 89-94; NSM Itchingfield w Slinfold 82-89. *Groomsland Cottage, Parbrook, Billingshurst RH14 9EU* Tel (01403) 782167

HURFORD, Colin Osborne. b 33. Qu Coll Ox BA55 MA59. Wells Th Coll 55. **d** 57 **p** 58. C Barnoldswick w Bracewell *Bradf* 57-61; C Warrington St Elphin *Liv* 61-63; Malaysia 63-70; P-in-c Annscroft *Heref* 71-79; P-in-c Longden 71-79; P-in-c Pontesbury III 71-79; R Longden and Annscroft 79-85; P-in-c Church Pulverbatch 81-85; R Longden and Annscroft w Pulverbatch 85-86; Tanzania 86-87; TR Billingham St Aid *Dur* 87-96; rtd 96; Perm to Offic *Heref* from 96 and *Lich* from 01. *14 Station Road, Pontesbury, Shrewsbury SY5 0QY* Tel (01743) 792605

✠**HURFORD, The Rt Revd Richard Warwick.** b 44. OAM99. Trin Coll Bris BA96 Univ of Wales MTh02 ACertCM71 Hon FGCM96 MACE81. St Jo Coll Morpeth. **d** 69 **p** 70 **c** 01. Prec Grafton Cathl Australia 69-70; P-in-c Tisbury *Sarum* 71-73; R 73-75; R Tisbury and Swallowcliffe w Ansty 75-76; TR Tisbury 76-78; P-in-c Chilmark 76-78; TR Coffs Harbour Australia 78-83; Dean Grafton 83-97; Adn The Clarence and Hastings 85-87; Adn Grafton 87-92; R Sydney St Jas 97-01; Bp Bathurst from 01. *Bishopscourt, 288 William Street, PO Box 23, Bathurst NSW 2795, Australia* Tel (0061) (2) 6331 3550 *or* 6331 1722 Fax 6331 3660 *or* 6332 2772 E-mail bxbishop@ix.net.au

HURLE, Canon Anthony Rowland. b 54. Lon Univ BSc Em Coll Cam PGCE. Wycliffe Hall Ox 80. **d** 83 **p** 84. C Ipswich St Mary at Stoke w St Pet *St E* 83-87; TV Barking St Marg w St Patr *Chelmsf* 87-92; V St Alb St Paul *St Alb* from 92; RD St Alb 95-05; Hon Can St Alb from 05. *St Paul's Vicarage, 7 Brampton Road, St Albans AL1 4PN* Tel and fax (01727) 836810 *or* tel 846281 E-mail tony@stpauls-stalbans.org
or vicar@stpauls-stalbans.org

HURLE (née POWNALL), Mrs Lydia Margaret. b 53. SRN SCM. Wycliffe Hall Ox 78. **dss** 81 **d** 94 **p** 95. Ipswich St Mary at Stoke w St Pet etc *St E* 81-83; NSM St Alb St Paul *St Alb* from 93. *St Paul's Vicarage, 7 Brampton Road, St Albans AL1 4PN* Tel and fax (01727) 836810 E-mail tony.hurle@ntlworld.com

HURLEY, Daniel Timothy. b 37. St Mich Coll Llan 68. **d** 70 **p** 71. C Llanfabon 70-73; CF 73-79; R W Walton *Ely* 79-86; V Cwmdauddwr w St Harmon and Llanwrthwl *S & B* 86-02; rtd 02. *39 Ellesmere Orchard, Emsworth PO10 8TP* Tel (01243) 376923

HURLEY, Mark Tristan. b 57. Trin Coll Bris BA89. Sarum & Wells Th Coll 89. **d** 91 **p** 92. C Gainsborough All SS *Linc* 91-94; TV Grantham 94-00; V Donington and Bicker 00-02; Perm to Offic *Ox* 08-09; Hon C Wolverton from 09. *42 Fegans Court, Stony Stratford, Milton Keynes MK11 1LS* Tel (01908) 568809

HURLEY, Robert. b 64. Univ of Wales (Cardiff) BD86. Ridley Hall Cam 88. **d** 90 **p** 91. C Dagenham *Chelmsf* 90-93; C Egg Buckland *Ex* 93-96; C Devonport St Budeaux 96; P-in-c Camberwell All SS *S'wark* 96-99; V 99-02; R Oldbury *Sarum* 02-04. *9 Forester Road, Bath BA2 6QF*
E-mail janeandbobhurley@aol.com

HURLOCK, Ronald James. b 31. BSc PhD. St Deiniol's Hawarden. **d** 83 **p** 84. C Oxton *Ches* 83-87; Chapl Asst Man R Infirmary 87-91; rtd 91. *78 Garwood Close, Westbrook, Warrington WA5 5TF* Tel (01925) 444583

HURLSTON, Mrs Jean Margaret. b 54. Crewe Coll of Educn CertEd75 Keele Univ BEd76. **d** 06 **p** 07. OLM High Crompton *Man* from 06. *24 Taunton Lawns, Ashton-under-Lyne OL7 9EL* Tel and fax 0161-344 2854 Mobile 078885-406808
E-mail jeanhurlston@btinternet.com

HURN, Mrs June Barbara. b 32. Birm Univ CertEd53. Cant Sch of Min 87. **d** 90 **p** 94. NSM Chislehurst St Nic *Roch* from 90. *Hawkswing, Hawkwood Lane, Chislehurst BR7 5PW* Tel (020) 8467 2320

HURRELL, John William. b 25. Ripon Hall Ox 65. **d** 66 **p** 67. C Painswick *Glouc* 66-68; C Glouc St Geo 68-70; C Thornbury 70-73; V Glouc St Steph 73-86; V Deerhurst, Apperley w Forthampton and Chaceley 86-90; rtd 90; Perm to Offic *B & W* from 90. *1 Church View, Porlock, Minehead TA24 8NA* Tel (01643) 862488

HURREN, Timothy John. b 46. York Univ BA74 ACIB70. NEOC 99. **d** 02 **p** 03. NSM High Harrogate St Pet *Ripon* 02-06; C from 06. *1 South Park Road, Harrogate HG1 5QU* Tel (01423) 541696 E-mail tim.hurren@ntlworld.com

HURRY, Lynn Susan. b 59. Middx Univ BA05. NTMTC 02. **d** 05 **p** 06. C Southchurch H Trin *Chelmsf* 05-08; V St Mary-at-Latton from 08. *St Mary-at-Latton Vicarage, The Gowers, Harlow CM20 2JP* Tel (01279) 424005
E-mail revlynn@btinternet.com

HURST, Alaric Desmond St John. b 24. New Coll Ox BA50 MA70. Wells Th Coll 48. **d** 51 **p** 53. C Huddersfield H Trin *Wakef* 51-52; C Leeds St Geo *Ripon* 52-54; Bp's Chapl for Rehabilitation *Roch* 55-56; C St Steph Walbrook and St Swithun etc *Lon* 57-59; V Pudsey St Paul *Bradf* 59-63; V Writtle *Chelmsf*

63-69; rtd 89. *9 Ganderton Court, Pershore WR10 1AW* Tel (01905) 840939

HURST, Antony. b 38. Trin Coll Cam MA61 LSE MSc(Econ)71 Bris Coll DipEd64. S'wark Ord Course 79. **d** 83 **p** 84. NSM S'wark H Trin w St Matt 83-89; NSM S'wark Ch 89-96; NSM St Martin-in-the-Fields *Lon* from 96. *33 Hugh Street, London SW1V 1QJ* Tel (020) 7828 2844

HURST, Brian Charles. b 58. Nottm Univ BA Sheff Univ MA07. Ripon Coll Cuddesdon 82. **d** 84 **p** 85. C Cullercoats St Geo *Newc* 84-87; C Prudhoe 87-88; TV Willington 88-95; V Denton 95-03; RD Newc W 97-98; TV Glendale Gp 03-09; V Bamburgh from 09; V Ellingham from 09; AD Bamburgh and Glendale from 06. *The Vicarage, 7 The Wynding, Bamburgh NE69 7DB* Tel (01668) 214748 E-mail brian.hurst1@btopenworld.com

HURST, Colin. b 49. Linc Th Coll 88. **d** 90 **p** 91. C Wavertree H Trin *Liv* 90-93; C Croft and Stoney Stanton *Leic* 93-95; TV Broughton Astley and Croft w Stoney Stanton 95-97; V Wigan St Andr *Liv* from 97; AD Wigan W 03-05; AD Wigan 05-08; Hon Can Liv Cathl 03-08. *St Andrew's Vicarage, 3A Mort Street, Wigan WN6 7AU* Tel (01942) 243514 E-mail churst6000@aol.com

HURST, Colin. b 58. Westmr Coll Ox BA90. St Jo Coll Nottm MA95. **d** 95 **p** 96. C Warboys w Broughton and Bury w Wistow *Ely* 95-98; P-in-c Wisbech St Mary 98-04; P-in-c Guyhirn w Ring's End 98-04; V Wisbech St Mary and Guyhirn w Ring's End etc 05-07; P-in-c Eye *Pet* from 07; P-in-c Newborough from 07; P-in-c Thorney Abbey *Ely* from 07. *The Vicarage, Thorney Road, Eye, Peterborough PE6 7UN* Tel (01733) 222334 E-mail cehurst@globalnet.co.uk

HURST, Canon Jeremy Richard. b 40. Trin Coll Cam BA61 MA MPhil FCP. Linc Th Coll 62. **d** 64 **p** 65. C Woolwich St Mary w H Trin *S'wark* 64-69; Perm to Offic *Ex* 69-76 and *Ox* 76-84; TV Langley Marish *Ox* 84-85; TR 85-05; Hon Can Ch Ch 05; Chapl Thames Valley Univ 92-98; rtd 05. *Hortus Lodge, 22A Bolton Avenue, Windsor SL4 3JF* Tel (01753) 863693 E-mail jeremyhurst@lineone.net

HURST, John. b 31. NW Ord Course 76. **d** 79 **p** 80. C Flixton St Jo *Man* 79-82; P-in-c Hindsford 82-86; V 86-88; V Halliwell St Paul 88-93; rtd 93; Perm to Offic *Man* from 99. *26 Cornwall Avenue, Bolton BL5 1DZ* Tel (01204) 659233

HURT, Mrs Grenda Mary. b 36. JP91. LSE BSc(Econ)63. STETS 96. **d** 99 **p** 01. NSM Freshwater *Portsm* from 99; NSM Yarmouth from 99; Asst Chapl Isle of Wight Healthcare NHS Trust 03-05; Chapl Earl Mountbatten Hospice 03-05. *Easterholme, Tennyson Road, Yarmouth PO41 0PR* E-mail grenda.hurt@tiscali.co.uk

✠**HURTADO, The Rt Revd Jorge A Perera.** b 34. **d** 57 **p** 58 **c** 94. Bp Cuba from 94. *Calle 6 No 273, Vedado, Plaza de la Revolución, Havana 4, 10400, Cuba* Tel (0053) (7) 35655, 38003, 321120 *or* 312436 Fax 333293 E-mail episcopal@ip.etecsa.cu

HUSS, David Ian. b 75. Jes Coll Ox MPhys97. Wycliffe Hall Ox BA07. **d** 07 **p** 08. C Banbury St Paul *Ox* from 07. *10 Hardwick Park, Banbury OX16 1YD* Tel 07766-026041 (mobile) E-mail david@huss.org.uk

HUSSEY, Martin John. b 47. STETS 96. **d** 99 **p** 00. NSM Thames Ditton *Guildf* from 99. *94 Wellington Close, Walton-on-Thames KT12 1BE* Tel (01932) 221914 E-mail martinhussey_uk@yahoo.co.uk

HUTCHENS, Tony Blair. b 42. Univ of Michigan BA64 Univ of Chicago MA69. Seabury-Western Th Sem MDiv88. **d** 88 **p** 88. USA 88-05; P-in-c Glenurquhart *Mor* from 05. *St Ninian's Cottage, 32 Milton, Drumnadrochit, Inverness IV63 6UA* Tel (01456) 450158 E-mail hollyhutchens@btinternet.com

HUTCHEON, Mrs Elsie. b 39. RGN63 CertEd UEA MEd98. EAMTC 89. **d** 92 **p** 94. NSM Heigham St Thos *Nor* 92-02; P-in-c Heigham St Barn w St Bart from 02; RD Nor S from 06. *St Barnabas's Vicarage, 1 Russell Street, Norwich NR2 4QT* Tel (01603) 627859 E-mail elsie@rev.demon.co.uk

HUTCHIN, David William. b 37. Man Univ MusB58 CertEd59 DipEd59 LRAM ARCM LTCL. Glouc Sch of Min 85. **d** 88 **p** 89. NSM Northleach w Hampnett and Farmington *Glouc* 88-94; NSM Cold Aston w Notgrove and Turkdean 88-94; NSM Chedworth, Yanworth and Stowell, Coln Rogers etc 94-01; RD Northleach 96-99; Perm to Offic *Leic* 01-06 and *Derby* 02-06; *Ripon* from 06. *Bank Side Garden, Glasshouses, Harrogate HG3 5QY* Tel (01423) 712733

HUTCHINGS, Colin Michael. b 36. Clifton Th Coll 66. **d** 68 **p** 69. C Worksop St Jo *S'well* 68-71; C Hampreston *Sarum* 71-76; TV Tisbury 76-82; R Waddesdon w Over Winchendon and Fleet Marston *Ox* 82-00; rtd 00; Perm to Offic *Pet* from 01. *Nimrod, 4 The Beeches, Pattishall, Towcester NN12 8LT* Tel (01327) 830563

HUTCHINGS, Ian James. b 49. Ches Coll of HE MA03. Clifton Th Coll 69 Trin Coll Bris 72. **d** 73 **p** 74. C Parr *Liv* 73-77; C Timperley *Ches* 77-81; V Partington and Carrington 81-96; V Huntington from 96; Chapl Bp's Blue Coat C of E High Sch from 96. *St Luke's Vicarage, 14 Celandine Close, Huntington, Chester CH3 6DT* Tel and fax (01244) 347345 *or* tel 344705 E-mail ihutchings@aol.com

HUTCHINGS, James Benjamin Balfour. b 62. Ex Univ BA84. STETS 03. **d** 06 **p** 07. C Ex St Jas from 06. *Glenn House, 96 Old Tiverton Road, Exeter EX4 6LD* Tel (01392) 202983 E-mail jhutchings@mail.com

HUTCHINGS, John Denis Arthur. b 29. Keble Coll Ox BA53 MA59 MSc59. Chich Th Coll 58. **d** 60 **p** 61. C St Pancras w St Jas and Ch Ch *Lon* 60-63; Asst Chapl Denstone Coll Uttoxeter 63-67 and 79-83; C Stepney St Dunstan and All SS *Lon* 67-78; V Devonport St Boniface *Ex* 83-86; TR Devonport St Boniface and St Phil 86-93; P-in-c Lydford and Brent Tor 93-95; rtd 96; Perm to Offic *Ex* from 96. *Maisonette, 40 Brook Street, Tavistock PL19 0HE* Tel (01822) 616946

HUTCHINS, Paul. b 79. Coll of Resurr Mirfield 99 NOC 04. **d** 05 **p** 06. C Royton St Paul *Man* from 05. *136 Denbydale Way, Royton, Oldham OL2 5TE* Tel 0161-628 0141 Mobile 07818-022678 E-mail fr.hutchins@btinternet.com

HUTCHINSON, Alison Joyce. b 62. Leeds Univ BA84 RMN90. Aston Tr Scheme 92 Ripon Coll Cuddesdon 94. **d** 97 **p** 98. C Benfieldside *Dur* 97-00; C Bishopwearmouth St Nic 00-02; Perm to Offic *Carl* 02-07; C Penrith w Newton Reigny and Plumpton Wall 07-08; Perm to Offic from 09. *The Rectory, Leven Close, Stokesley, Middlesbrough TS9 5AP* Tel (01642) 710405 E-mail alison.hutchinson@btinternet.com

HUTCHINSON, Canon Andrew Charles. b 63. Univ of Wales (Ban) BA84 MEd96. Aston Tr Scheme 85 Chich Th Coll 87. **d** 89 **p** 90. C Burnley St Cath w St Alb and St Paul *Blackb* 89-92; C Shrewsbury St Chad w St Mary *Lich* 92-94; Chapl Heref Cathl Sch 94-97; Succ Heref Cathl 94-97; Chapl Solihull Sch from 97; Can St Jo Pro-Cathl Katakwa from 00. *2 St Alphege Close, Church Hill Road, Solihull B91 3RQ* Tel 0121-704 3708

HUTCHINSON, Andrew George Pearce. b 78. Glos Univ BA01 PGCE02. Oak Hill Th Coll BA08. **d** 08 **p** 09. C Normanton *Derby* from 08. *18 Lawnlea Close, Sunnyhill, Derby DE23 1XQ* Tel (01332) 769503 Mobile 07877-831506 E-mail andy_hutchinson@hotmail.com

HUTCHINSON, Andrew Paul. b 65. Trin Hall Cam BA87 MA91 Solicitor 90. Aston Tr Scheme 92 Ripon Coll Cuddesdon BTh97. **d** 97 **p** 98. C Stanley *Dur* 97-99; C Sunderland 99-01; TV 01-02; Chapl Sunderland Univ 99-02; TV Penrith w Newton Reigny and Plumpton Wall *Carl* 02-09; Chapl Cumbria Campus Cen Lancs Univ 02-07; Chapl Cumbria Univ 07-09; R Stokesley w Seamer *York* from 09. *The Rectory, Leven Close, Stokesley, Middlesbrough TS9 5AP* Tel (01642) 710405 E-mail paul.hutchinson5@btinternet.com

HUTCHINSON, Mrs Barbara Anne. b 55. **d** 05 **p** 06. OLM Holbeach Fen *Linc* from 05. *3 Sholtsgate, Whaplode, Spalding PE12 6TZ* Tel (01406) 422354

HUTCHINSON, Canon Cyril Peter. b 37. Dur Univ BA61. Wm Temple Coll Rugby 61. **d** 63 **p** 64. C Birm St Paul 63-67; Prin Community Relns Officer 66-69; Dir Bradf SHARE 69-76; Hon C Manningham *Bradf* 75-76; V Clayton 76-83; RD Bowling and Horton 80-83; TR Keighley St Andr 83-94; Hon Can Bradf Cathl 84-03; rtd 94; Hon C Keighley All SS *Bradf* 94-03. *Wellcroft, Laycock Lane, Laycock, Keighley BD22 0PN* Tel (01535) 606145

HUTCHINSON, David. See HUTCHINSON, Canon William David

HUTCHINSON, David Bamford. b 29. QUB BSc53 TCD Div Test55 QUB DipEd57. **d** 55 **p** 56. C Lisburn Ch Ch *Conn* 55-57; Uganda 57-65; I Kilkccl *D & D* 66-75; I Willowfield 75-82; V Longfleet *Sarum* 82-94; rtd 94; Perm to Offic *Sarum* 94-99. *Bethany, 3 Panorama Road, Poole BH13 7RA* Tel (01202) 664964

HUTCHINSON, Hugh Edward. b 27. CEng FICE. Bps' Coll Cheshunt. **d** 61 **p** 62. C Limehouse St Anne *Lon* 61-64; C Townstall w Dartmouth *Ex* 64-67; V Ex St Mark 67-75; P-in-c Foston on the Wolds *York* 75-77; R N Frodingham 75-77; R Beeford w Lissett 75-77; R Beeford w Frodingham and Foston 77-80; RD N Holderness 79-80; P-in-c Appleton Roebuck w Acaster Selby 80-84; P-in-c Etton w Dalton Holme 84-91; rtd 91; Perm to Offic *York* from 91. *33 Limestone Grove, Burniston, Scarborough YO13 0DH* Tel (01723) 871116

HUTCHINSON, Jeremy Olpherts. b 32. Oriel Coll Ox BA55 MA60. St Jo Coll Dur. **d** 57 **p** 58. C Shoreditch St Leon *Lon* 57-60; V Hoxton St Jo w Ch 60-78; Hon C Hackney 78-85; C Highbury Ch Ch w St Jo and St Sav 85-91; P-in-c Hanley Road St Sav w St Paul 91-92; TV Tollington 92-96; rtd 96; Perm to Offic *Lon* from 96. *8 Casimir Road, London E5 9NU* Tel (020) 8806 6492

HUTCHINSON, John Charles. b 44. K Coll Lon 64. **d** 69 **p** 70. C Portsea All SS *Portsm* 69-73; TV Fareham H Trin 73-78; P-in-c Pangbourne *Ox* 78-86; P-in-c Tidmarsh w Sulham 84-86; R Pangbourne w Tidmarsh and Sulham 86-96; Perm to Offic from 07. *90 Fir Tree Avenue, Wallingford OX10 0PL* Tel (01491) 832445 E-mail cavea@btinternet.com

HUTCHINSON, Jonathan Graham. b 62. Bris Univ BA01. Trin Coll Bris 98. **d** 01 **p** 02. C Church Stretton *Heref* 01-04; P-in-c Aspley *S'well* from 04. *St Margaret's Vicarage, 319 Aspley Lane,*

Nottingham NG8 5GA Tel 0115-929 2920 *or* tel and fax 929 8899 E-mail jghutchinson@btinternet.com

HUTCHINSON, Jonathan Mark. b 45. Cant Sch of Min 85. **d** 89 **p** 90. NSM Wickham Market w Pettistree and Easton *St E* 89-93; V Thorington w Wenhaston, Bramfield etc 94-97; TV Ipswich St Mary at Stoke w St Pet and St Fran 97-02; Perm to Offic *B & W* from 02. *27 Milton Lane, Wells BA5 2QS* Tel (01749) 676096

HUTCHINSON, Canon Julie Lorraine. b 55. WMMTC 90. **d** 93 **p** 94. C Northampton St Mary *Pet* 93-95; P-in-c Morcott w Glaston and Bisbrooke 95-97; P-in-c Lyddington w Stoke Dry and Seaton etc 97-02; V 03; Dir of Ords and Voc from 03; Can Pet Cathl from 04. *The Rectory, Raunds Road, Stanwick, Wellingborough NN9 6PP* Tel (01933) 626203

HUTCHINSON, June. *See* HUTCHINSON, Mrs Margaret June

HUTCHINSON, Mrs Karen Elizabeth. b 64. LMH Ox BA85 MA89 Kent Univ MA06 Solicitor 89. Wycliffe Hall Ox. **d** 01 **p** 02. C Alton St Lawr *Win* 01-06; V Crondall and Ewshot *Guildf* from 06. *The Vicarage, Farm Lane, Crondall, Farnham GU10 5QE* Tel (01252) 850379

HUTCHINSON, Mrs Margaret June. b 45. ERMC 03. **d** 06 **p** 07. C Midi-Pyrénées and Aude *Eur* from 06. *Le Cru, 46150 Thedirac, France* Tel and fax (0033) (5) 65 21 68 52 E-mail hutchinsonlecru@compuserve.com

HUTCHINSON, Mark. *See* HUTCHINSON, Jonathan Mark

HUTCHINSON, Moreen Anne. b 46. Ulster Univ BA84. CITC 98. **d** 01 **p** 02. NSM Larne and Inver *Conn* 01-04; P-in-c Ardclinis and Tickmacrevan w Layde and Cushendun from 04; Bp's Dom Chapl from 08. *St Mary's Rectory, 76 Largy Road, Carnlough, Ballymena BT44 0JJ* Tel and fax (028) 2888 5593 E-mail moreen.hutchinson@btinternet.com

HUTCHINSON, Paul. *See* HUTCHINSON, Andrew Paul

HUTCHINSON, Paul Edward. b 33. K Coll Lon. **d** 59 **p** 60. C Bromley St Mich *Lon* 59-63; C Mill Hill St Mich 63-66; C Sandridge *St Alb* 66-73; V St Alb St Mary Marshalswick 73-80; V Tunstall *Lich* 80-91; RD Stoke N 82-91; V Lower Gornal 91-93; V Lower Gornal *Worc* 93-98; rtd 98; Perm to Offic *Lich* from 99. *55 Mill Hayes Road, Burslem, Stoke-on-Trent ST6 4JB* Tel (01782) 813361

HUTCHINSON, Miss Pauline. b 49. St Jo Coll Nottm 88. **d** 90 **p** 94. Par Dn Sherwood *S'well* 90-94; C 94-95; TV Newark 95-09; Chapl Newark Hosp NHS Trust 95-04; rtd 09. *18 Cardinal Hinsley Close, Newark NG24 4NQ* Tel (01636) 681931

HUTCHINSON, Peter. *See* HUTCHINSON, Canon Cyril Peter

HUTCHINSON, Peter Francis. b 52. Sarum & Wells Th Coll 87. **d** 89 **p** 90. C Honiton, Gittisham, Combe Raleigh, Monkton etc *Ex* 89-93; V Valley Park *Win* from 93. *35 Raglan Close, Eastleigh SO53 4NH* Tel (023) 8025 5749 E-mail st.francis@ukgateway.net

HUTCHINSON, Raymond John. b 51. Liv Univ BSc73. Westcott Ho Cam 73. **d** 76 **p** 77. C Peckham St Jo *S'wark* 76-78; C Peckham St Jo w St Andr 78-79; C Prescot *Liv* 79-81; V Edgehill St Dunstan 81-87; P-in-c Litherland Ch 87-89; P-in-c Waterloo Park 87-89; V Waterloo Ch Ch and St Mary 90-97; Chapl Wigan and Leigh Health Services NHS Trust 97-01; P-in-c Wigan All SS *Liv* 04-08; P-in-c Wigan St Geo 05-08; R Wigan All SS and St Geo from 08. *The Rectory, 6 Wrightington Street, Wigan WN1 2BX* Tel (01942) 244459 E-mail hutchinsons@glebehouse.fslife.co.uk

HUTCHINSON, Canon Stephen. b 38. St Chad's Coll Dur BA60. **d** 62 **p** 63. C Tividale *Lich* 62-68; V Walsall St Andr 68-73; R Headless Cross *Worc* 73-81; TR Redditch, The Ridge 81-91; RD Bromsgrove 85-91; V Stourbridge St Thos 91-03; Hon Can Worc Cathl 88-03; rtd 03; Perm to Offic *Worc* from 03. *251 Stourbridge Road, Kidderminster DY10 2XJ* Tel (01562) 631658

HUTCHINSON, Canon William David. b 27. Wycliffe Hall Ox 55. **d** 57 **p** 58. C Ipswich St Jo *St E* 57-60; R Combs 60-65; V Ipswich St Aug 65-76; R Ewhurst *Guildf* 76-81; V Aldeburgh w Hazlewood *St E* 81-92; RD Saxmundham 83-88; Hon Can St E Cathl 87-92; rtd 92. *Hazelwood, 1 Birch Close, Woodbridge IP12 4UA* Tel (01394) 383760

HUTCHINSON CERVANTES, Canon Ian Charles. b 62. Cant Univ (NZ) BSc84 Reading Univ MSc86 Jes Coll Cam BA89 MA92. Westcott Ho Cam 86. **d** 89 **p** 90. C Iffley *Ox* 89-92; USPG 92-04; Locum P Caracas Cathl Venezuela 93; P-in-c El Cayo St Andr Belize 93-97; USPG Staff 97-04; Chapl Madrid *Eur* from 04; Hon Can Madrid Cathl from 01; Hon Can Buenos Aires from 02. *St George's Anglican Church, Nez de Balboa 43, 28001 Madrid, Spain* Tel and fax (0034) 915 765 109 E-mail irhutch@ya.com

✠**HUTCHISON, The Most Revd Andrew Sandford.** b 38. Montreal Dioc Th Coll Hon DD93. Trin Coll Toronto. **d** 69 **p** 70 **c** 70. Canada from 69; Dean Montreal 84-90; Bp Montreal 90-04; Primate of Angl Ch of Canada from 04. *80 Hayden Street, Toronto ON M4Y 3G2, Canada* Tel (001) (416) 924 9119 Fax 924 0211 E-mail primate@national.anglican.ca

HUTCHISON, Geoffrey John. b 52. Trin Hall Cam MA76 Lon Univ CertEd76. Ridley Hall Cam 77. **d** 79 **p** 80. C Harold Wood

Chelmsf 79-83; CF 83-89; Warden Viney Hill Chr Adventure Cen 89-96; P-in-c Viney Hill *Glouc* 89-96; V Wadsley *Sheff* from 96. *The Vicarage, 91 Airedale Road, Sheffield S6 4AW* Tel 0114-234 8481 E-mail rev.hutch@googlemail.com

HUTCHISON, Ross. b 61. Wadh Coll Ox BA83 MA86 DPhil88. SEITE 03. **d** 06 **p** 07. NSM Newington St Mary *S'wark* from 06. *12A Cumberland Mansions, West End Lane, London NW6 1LL* Tel (020) 7794 6087 E-mail ross.hutchison@kpmg.co.uk

HUTT, Colin Villette. b 32. FCA. Glouc Sch of Min 87. **d** 89 **p** 90. NSM Ludlow *Heref* 89-93; C Ludlow, Ludford, Ashford Carbonell etc 93-94; TV Tenbury 94-01; rtd 01; Perm to Offic *Heref* from 01. *Broxwell, Livesey Road, Ludlow SY8 1EX* Tel (01584) 877959 Fax 831659 E-mail broxwell@hotmail.com

HUTT, Canon David Handley. b 38. Lambeth MA05 AKC68. **d** 69 **p** 70. C Bedford Park *Lon* 69-70; C Westmr St Matt 70-73; PV and Succ S'wark Cathl 73-78; Chapl K Coll Taunton 78-82; V Bordesley SS Alb and Patr *Birm* 82-86; V St Marylebone All SS *Lon* 86-95; Can Steward Westmr Abbey 95-05; Sub-Dean and Adn Westmr 99-05; rtd 05; Perm to Offic *Lon* and *Eur* from 06. *3CC Morpeth Terrace, London SW1P 1EW*

HUTTON, Elizabeth. *See* HUTTON, Susan Elizabeth

HUTTON, Griffith Arthur Jeremy. b 31. Trin Hall Cam BA56 MA59. Linc Th Coll 56. **d** 58 **p** 59. C Hexham *Newc* 58-60; C Gosforth All SS 60-65; V Whitegate *Ches* 65-71; V Whitegate w Lt Budworth 71-78; R Dowdeswell and Andoversford w the Shiptons etc *Glouc* 78-91; V Newnham w Awre and Blakeney 91-96; rtd 96; Perm to Offic *Heref* from 99. *Hill House, Stoke Lacy, Bromyard HR7 4RE* Tel (01432) 820423

HUTTON, Joseph Charles. b 21. DFC41. Westcott Ho Cam 63. **d** 65 **p** 66. C St Marychurch *Ex* 65-67; V Warborough *Ox* 67-70; V Earley St Pet 70-75; R Ludgvan *Truro* 75-79; rtd 79. *2 Baines Close, Bourton-on-the-Water, Cheltenham GL54 2PU*

HUTTON, Mrs Serena Quartermaine. b 35. Nottm Univ BA57 Lon Univ BA73 Stranmillis Coll PGCE68 FRSA87. SAOMC 95. **d** 98 **p** 99. OLM Chinnor, Sydenham, Aston Rowant and Crowell *Ox* from 98. *Elma Cottage, The Green, Kingston Blount, Chinnor OX9 4SE* Tel (01844) 354173

HUTTON, Susan Elizabeth. b 70. Univ of Wales (Cardiff) BD91. Ripon Coll Cuddesdon 93. **d** 95 **p** 96. C W Parley *Sarum* 95-99; C Trowbridge H Trin 99-05; P-in-c from 05. *The Rectory, 26 Holbrook Lane, Trowbridge BA14 0PP* Tel (01225) 751275 E-mail rev.beth@virgin.net

HUTTON-BURY, David. b 44. BA. **d** 94 **p** 95. Aux Min Geashill w Killeigh and Ballycommon *M & K* 94-97; Aux Min Clane w Donadea and Coolcarrigan 97-00; Aux Min Mullingar, Portnashangan, Moyliscar, Kilbixy etc 00-05; Aux Min Clane w Donadea and Coolcarrigan from 05. *Chorleyville Farm, Tullamore, Co Offaly, Republic of Ireland* Tel (00353) (57) 932 1813

HUXHAM, Hector Hubert. b 29. Bris Univ BA55. Tyndale Hall Bris 52. **d** 56 **p** 57. C Eccleston St Luke *Liv* 56-58; C Heworth H Trin *York* 59-60; V Burley *Ripon* 61-66; Chapl St Jas Univ Hosp Leeds 67-94; rtd 94; Perm to Offic *Bradf* 94-98 and *Ripon* from 94. *3 Oakwell Oval, Leeds LS8 4AL* Tel 0113-266 8851

HUXHAM, Canon Peter Richard. b 38. Worc Coll Ox BA61 MA74. St Steph Ho Ox 61. **d** 63 **p** 64. C Gillingham *Sarum* 63-67; C Osmondthorpe St Phil *Ripon* 67-70; V Parkstone St Osmund *Sarum* 70-75; TR Parkstone St Pet w Branksea and St Osmund 75-92; RD Poole 85-92; Can and Preb Sarum Cathl 85-92; Chapl Taunton and Somerset NHS Trust 92-03. *3 Salterns House, 34 Brownsea View Avenue, Poole BH14 8LQ* Tel (01202) 707431

HUXLEY, Edward Jonathan. b 74. Bris Univ BEng95. Trin Coll Bris BA04. **d** 05 **p** 06. C Sea Mills *Bris* 05-08. *Address temp unknown*

HUXLEY, Canon Stephen Scott. b 30. Linc Th Coll 53. **d** 56 **p** 57. C Cullercoats St Geo *Newc* 56-59; C Eglingham 59-60; C N Gosforth 60-63; V Nether Witton and Hartburn and Meldon 63-65; V Tynemouth Priory 65-74; V Warkworth and Acklington 74-78; P-in-c Tynemouth St Jo 78-81; V 81-87; Hon Can Newc Cathl 82-92; V Wylam 87-92; rtd 92; Perm to Offic *Newc* from 92. *35 Castle Street, Norham, Berwick-upon-Tweed TD15 2LQ* Tel (01289) 382356

HUXTABLE, Christopher Michael Barclay. b 61. Ex Univ BA83 Qu Coll Cam PGCE84. St Steph Ho Ox 93. **d** 95 **p** 96. C Chich 95-98; C Haywards Heath St Wilfrid 98-99; TV 99-01; Chapl Geelong Gr Sch (Timbertop) Australia 01-04; Chapl St Mary's Sch Wantage 04-05; C Blewbury, Hagbourne and Upton *Ox* 05-06; C S w N Moreton, Aston Tirrold and Aston Upthorpe 05-06; R Mansfield Australia from 06. *The Rectory, PO Box 261, Mansfield Vic 3724, Australia* Tel (0061) (3) 5775 2036 E-mail anglicanmansfield@gmail.com

HUXTABLE, Michael George. b 29. St Jo Coll Cam BA50 MA54. S Dios Minl Tr Scheme 87. **d** 90 **p** 91. NSM Fisherton Anger *Sarum* 90-01; Perm to Offic from 01. *10 Trews Weir Reach, Exeter EX2 4EG* Tel (01392) 277332

HUXTABLE, Peter Alexander. b 68. Southn Univ BEng90. St Jo Coll Nottm MTh01. **d** 01 **p** 02. C Kidderminster St Geo *Worc* 01-05; V Bestwood Em w St Mark *S'well* from 05. *Emmanuel*

Vicarage, 10 Church View Close, Arnold, Nottingham NG5 9QP Tel 0115-920 8879

HUYTON, Stuart. b 37. St D Coll Lamp BA62. **d** 63 **p** 64. C Kingswinford H Trin *Lich* 63-66; C Leek St Edw 66-69; V Wigginton 69-76; V Wombourne 76-89; RD Trysull 79-84; P-in-c Bobbington 85-89; TR Wombourne w Trysull and Bobbington 89-95; V Lt Aston 95-04; rtd 04. *14 Crosbie Close, Chichester PO19 8RZ* Tel (01243) 790119

HUYTON, Canon Susan Mary. b 57. Birm Univ BA79. Qu Coll Birm 83. **d** 86 **p** 97. C Connah's Quay *St As* 86-89; C Wrexham 89-90; Dn-in-c 90-91; TV 91-99; V Gwersyllt from 99; AD Gresford from 05; Can Cursal St As Cathl from 08. *The Vicarage, Old Mold Road, Gwersyllt, Wrexham LL11 4SB* Tel (01978) 756391 E-mail suehyton@aol.com

HUZZEY, Peter George. b 48. Trin Coll Bris 74. **d** 76 **p** 77. C Bishopsworth *Bris* 76-79; V 86-96; C Downend 79-80; TV Kings Norton *Birm* 80-86; TR Bishopsworth and Bedminster Down *Bris* 97-00; RD Bedminster 98-99; TR Kingswood from 00. *Holy Trinity Vicarage, High Street, Kingswood, Bristol BS15 4AD* Tel 0117-967 3627 E-mail peterhuzzey@tiscali.co.uk

HYATT, Robert Keith. b 34. Em Coll Cam BA59 MA63. Ridley Hall Cam 58. **d** 60 **p** 61. C Cheltenham St Mary *Glouc* 60-63; Asst Chapl K Edw Sch Witley 63-65; C Godalming *Guildf* 65-69; Hong Kong 69-78; V Claygate *Guildf* 78-91; TV Whitton *Sarum* 91-96 and 99-00; TR 96-99; rtd 00; Perm to Offic *B & W* 00-04 and *Bris* from 02; May Moore Chapl Malmesbury *Bris* 02-05; Chapl Kennet and N Wilts Primary Care Trust 02-05. *19 Dark Lane, Malmesbury SN16 0BB* Tel (01666) 829026 *or* 826666 E-mail bobnhelen@onetel.com

HYDE, Ann. b 42. **d** 09. NSM Bramhall *Ches* from 09. *Mellor View, 25 St Martin's Road, Marple, Stockport SK6 7BY*

HYDE, Mrs Denise. b 54. WEMTC 05. **d** 08 **p** 09. OLM Fairford and Kempsford w Whelford *Glouc* 08; OLM Fairford Deanery from 09. *14 Park Street, Fairford GL7 4JJ* Tel (01285) 713285 Mobile 07816-500269 E-mail nisehyde@hotmail.co.uk

HYDE, Dennis Hugh. b 23. Leeds Univ BA56. Sarum Th Coll 60. **d** 60 **p** 61. C Farncombe *Guildf* 60-62; C Burgh Heath 62-65; V Shottermill 65-74; Past Consultant Clinical Th Assn 74-80; rtd 88. *c/o Miss M E M Hyde, 18 Lindsay Road, New Haw, Addlestone KT15 3BD* Tel (01932) 354682

HYDE, Edgar Bonsor. b 29. Clifton Th Coll 59. **d** 61 **p** 62. C Weston-super-Mare Ch Ch *B & W* 61-66; C Chipping Campden *Glouc* 66-70; R Longborough w Condicote and Sezincote 70-78; R Longborough, Sezincote, Condicote and the Swells 78-99; rtd 99; Perm to Offic *Glouc* from 99. *1 Turnpike Close, Primrose Court, Moreton-in-Marsh GL56 0JJ* Tel (01608) 652456

HYDE, Mrs Jacqueline. WEMTC. **d** 09. NSM Leckhampton SS Phil and Jas w Cheltenham St Jas *Glouc* from 09. *2 Liddington Road, Cheltenham GL53 0AJ* Tel (01242) 234955

HYDE, Jeremy Richard Granville. b 52. Sch of Pharmacy Lon BPharm75 PhD80. SAOMC 01. **d** 04 **p** 05. NSM Furze Platt *Ox* from 04; AD Maidenhead and Windsor from 08. *2A Belmont Park Road, Maidenhead SL6 6HT* Tel (01628) 621651 E-mail jeremyrhyde@aol.com

HYDE-DUNN, Keith Frederick. b 43. Sarum Th Coll. **d** 69 **p** 70. C Selukwe St Athan Rhodesia 69-72; C Horsham *Chich* 73-77; P-in-c Fittleworth 77-86; P-in-c Graffham w Woolavington 86-00; Perm to Offic from 01; rtd 04. *The Hermitage, Church Place, Pulborough RH20 1AF* Tel (01798) 873892

HYDER-SMITH, Brian John. b 45. FInstAM MCMI MBIM. EAMTC 84. **d** 8/ **p** 88. NSM Huntingdon *Ely* 87-90; P-in-c Abbots Ripton w Wood Walton 90-98; P-in-c Kings Ripton 90-98; C Whittlesey, Pondersbridge and Coates 98-99; TV 99-04; rtd 04. *La Cachette, Le Val Pien, 61470 Le Bosc-Renoult, France* Tel (0033) (2) 33 12 57 51 E-mail cachette66@hotmail.com

HYDON, Ms Veronica Weldon. b 52. N Lon Poly BA73 Maria Grey Coll Lon CertEd74. Aston Tr Scheme 87 Westcott Ho Cam 89. **d** 91 **p** 94. Par Dn Poplar *Lon* 91-94; C 94-95; P-in-c Roxwell *Chelmsf* 95-00; Lay Development Officer 95-00; V Forest Gate Em w Upton Cross 00-03; Assoc V Timperley *Ches* 03-07; V Bollington from 07. *The Vicarage, 35A Shrigley Road, Bollington, Macclesfield SK10 5RD* Tel (01625) 573162 E-mail vhydon@hotmail.com

HYETT, Dawn Barbara. b 53. Cyncoed Coll CertEd74 Open Univ BA79. WEMTC 99. **d** 02 **p** 03. NSM Bromyard *Heref* 02-08; NSM Bromyard and Stoke Lacy from 09. *Roberts Hill, Norton, Bromyard HR7 4PB* Tel (01885) 483747

HYETT, Derek Walter. b 79. Leeds Univ BA05. Coll of Resurr Mirfield 02. **d** 05 **p** 06. C Edmonton St Alphege *Lon* 05-08; C Ponders End St Matt 05-08. *Address temp unknown*

HYLAND, Cecil George. b 38. TCD BA62 MA78. CITC Div Test. **d** 63 **p** 64. C Belfast St Nic *Conn* 63-66; C Monkstown *D & G* 66-68; Ch of Ireland Youth Officer 68-73; Chapl TCD 73-79; I Tullow *D & G* 79-90; I Howth 90-05; Dir of Ords (Dub) 91-98; Can Ch Ch Cathl Dublin 91-05; Cen Dir of Ords 98-05; rtd 05. *34 The Vale, Skerries Road, Skerries, Co Dublin, Republic of Ireland* Tel (00353) (1) 810 6884 Mobile 86-838 5317 E-mail cecilhyland@hotmail.com

HYSLOP, Mrs Catherine Graham Young. b 53. Carl Dioc Tr Inst 90. **d** 92 **p** 94. NSM St Bees *Carl* 92-95; NSM Upperby St Jo 95-98; C 98-03; C S Carl from 03. *St John's Vicarage, Manor Road, Upperby, Carlisle CA2 4LH* Tel (01228) 523380 E-mail jim.hyslop@talk21.com

HYSLOP, Canon Thomas James (Jim). b 54. St Andr Univ BD76. Edin Th Coll 76. **d** 78 **p** 79. C Whitehaven *Carl* 78-81; C Walney Is 81-83; P-in-c Gt Broughton and Broughton Moor 83-85; V 85-88; V Kells 88-95; P-in-c Upperby St Jo 95-97; V 97-03; TR S Carl from 03; Dioc Chapl MU from 02; Hon Can Carl Cathl from 06. *St John's Vicarage, Manor Road, Upperby, Carlisle CA2 4LH* Tel (01228) 523380 E-mail jim.hyslop@talk21.com

HYSON, Peter Raymond. b 51. Open Univ BA80 Bris Univ MSc05. Oak Hill Th Coll BA86. **d** 87 **p** 88. C Billericay and Lt Burstead *Chelmsf* 87-92; TV Whitton *Sarum* 92-99; Perm to Offic *Lon* from 07. *23 Havana Road, London SW19 8EJ* Tel (020) 8715 0093 Mobile 07951-767113 E-mail peter@change-perspectives.com

I

I'ANSON, Frederick Mark. b 43. MRAC68. Carl Dioc Tr Inst 89. **d** 92 **p** 93. NSM Sedbergh, Cautley and Garsdale *Bradf* 92-98; P-in-c Kirkby-in-Malhamdale w Coniston Cold 98-08; rtd 08. *The Bowers, Firbank, Sedbergh LA10 5EG* Tel (015396) 21757 Mobile 07815-552778 E-mail mark@mmia.demon.co.uk

IBADAN SOUTH, Bishop of. See AJETUNMOBI, The Rt Revd Jacob Ademola

IBALL, Charles Martin John. b 40. Lich Th Coll 67. **d** 69 **p** 70. C Dudley St Edm *Worc* 69-73; C W Bromwich St Jas *Lich* 73-76; V Oxley 76-80; Hon C Whittington w Weeford from 86; Hon C Clifton Campville w Edingale and Harlaston 96-06; Hon C Hints from 06; rtd 04. *75 Carlcroft, Stoneydelph, Tamworth B77 4DW* Tel (01827) 896644

IBBETSON, Stephen Andrew. b 59. Portsm Poly BSc82. STETS 04. **d** 07 **p** 08. NSM Southbroom *Sarum* from 07. *12 Moonrakers, London Road, Devizes SN10 2DY* Tel (01380) 721953 E-mail s.ibbetson@btinternet.com

IBBOTSON, Miss Tracy Alexandra. b 63. Cranmer Hall Dur 01. **d** 03 **p** 04. C Todmorden *Wakef* 03-08; V Airedale w Fryston from 08. *Holy Cross Vicarage, The Mount, Castleford WF10 3JN* Tel (01977) 553157 E-mail tracy.ibbotson@tiscali.co.uk

IBIAYO, David Akindayo Oluwarotimi. b 71. Lagos Univ BSc. Ridley Hall Cam. **d** 06 **p** 07. C Barking St Marg w St Patr *Chelmsf* from 06. *48 Sunningdale Avenue, Barking IG11 7GF* Tel (020) 8227 1131 Mobile 07904-846028 E-mail david_ibiayo@hotmail.com

IDDON, Roy Edward. b 40. TCert61 Lanc Univ MA88. NOC 83. **d** 83 **p** 84. Hd Teacher St Andr Primary Sch Blackb from 83; NSM Bolton St Matt w St Barn *Man* 83-88; Lic to AD Walmsley 88-93; NSM Walmsley 93-01; NSM Turton Moorland Min 01-04; NSM Bolton St Phil from 04. *28 New Briggs Fold, Egerton, Bolton BL7 9UL* Tel (01204) 306589

IDLE, Christopher Martin. b 38. St Pet Coll Ox BA62. Clifton Th Coll 62. **d** 65 **p** 66. C Barrow St Mark *Carl* 65-68; C Camberwell Ch Ch *S'wark* 68-71; P-in-c Poplar St Matthias *Lon* 71-76; R Limehouse 76-89; R N Hartismere *St E* 89-95; Perm to Offic *S'wark* 95-03 and *St E* 01-03; rtd 03; Perm to Offic *Roch* from 04. *16 Cottage Avenue, Bromley BR2 8LQ* Tel and fax (020) 8462 1749

IEVINS, Mrs Catherine Ruth. b 54. LMH Ox BA77 MA80 Solicitor 81. EAMTC 98. **d** 01 **p** 02. C Pet Ch Carpenter 01-05; Perm to Offic 05-06; R Polebrook and Lutton w Hemington and Luddington 06-07; C Barnwell w Tichmarsh, Thurning and Clapton 06-07; R Barnwell, Hemington, Luddington in the Brook etc from 07. *The Rectory, Main Street, Polebrook, Peterborough PE8 5LN* Tel (01832) 270162 E-mail cievins@yahoo.co.uk

IEVINS, Peter Valdis. b 54. St Jo Coll Ox BA75 MA81 Solicitor 79. Westcott Ho Cam 86. **d** 88 **p** 89. C Sawston and Babraham *Ely* 88-91; NSM Pet Ch Carpenter 01-06; Lic to Offic from 06. *The Rectory, Main Street, Polebrook, Peterborough PE8 5LN* Tel (01832) 270162 E-mail peter.ievins@dca.gsi.gov.uk

IGENOZA, Andrew Olu. b 50. Ife Univ Nigeria BA75 Man Univ PhD82. Immanuel Coll Ibadan 87. **d** 88 **p** 89. Nigeria 88-99; C Gorton St Phil *Man* 00-01. *17 Northmoor Road, Longsight, Manchester M12 4NF* Tel 0161-248 8758

IGWE, Oliver Chimezie. b 72. St Paul's Univ Coll Awka Nigeria BA90 St Jo Coll Dur MA01. **d** 96 **p** 97. Nigeria 96-02; Perm to Offic *Birm* 03-05; Lic to Offic 05-07. *Address temp unknown*

IJAZ, Luke Anthony. b 76. Univ Coll Lon MSci99 Lon Inst of Educn PGCE01. Wycliffe Hall Ox BA06. **d** 07 **p** 08. C Wallington *S'wark* from 07. *54 Stanley Park Road, Carshalton SM5 3HW* Tel (020) 8647 7605 E-mail luke_ijaz@hotmail.com

IKIN, Gordon Mitchell. b 30. AKC57. **d** 58 **p** 59. C Leigh St Mary *Man* 58-61; V Westleigh St Paul 61-72; V Thornham St Jas 72-95; rtd 95; Perm to Offic *Man* 95-08. *3 Lygon Lodge, Newland, Malvern WR13 5AX*

ILES, Canon Paul Robert. b 37. FRCO65 Fitzw Coll Cam BA59 MA64 St Edm Hall Ox MA80. Sarum Th Coll 59. **d** 61 **p** 62. Chapl Bp Wordsworth Sch Salisbury 61-67; C Salisbury St Mich *Sarum* 61-64; Min Can Sarum Cathl 64-67; C Bournemouth St Pet *Win* 67-72; R Filton *Bris* 72-79; V Ox SS Phil and Jas w St Marg 79-83; Can Res and Prec Heref Cathl 83-03; rtd 03; Hon C Prestbury and All SS *Glouc* 03-08; Hon C N Cheltenham from 08. *24 Willowherb Close, Prestbury, Cheltenham GL52 5LP* Tel (01242) 579456

ILIFFE, Mrs Felicity Mary. b 57. Glam Univ BA79 Normal Coll Ban PGCE82. SEITE 06 WEMTC 07. **d** 09. C Ledbury *Heref* from 09. *21 Biddulph Way, Ledbury HR8 2HP* Tel (01531) 636561 E-mail revfliss@googlemail.com

ILLING, Eric James. b 33. Kelham Th Coll 54 Chich Th Coll 55. **d** 57 **p** 58. C Leeds St Aid *Ripon* 57-60; C Leeds All SS 60-62; C E Grinstead St Swithun *Chich* 62-65; V Middleton St Mary *Ripon* 65-74; R Felpham w Middleton *Chich* 74-81; Chapl R Devon and Ex Hosp (Wonford) 81-91; TR Heavitree w SS St Paul 81-91; R Bradninch and Clyst Hydon 91-94; rtd 94; Perm to Offic *B & W* from 94 and *Eur* from 98. *25 Pikes Crescent, Taunton TA1 4HS* Tel (01823) 289203

ILLINGWORTH, John Patrick Paul. b 34. New Coll Ox BA59 MA63. Chich Th Coll 61. **d** 63 **p** 64. C Brighouse *Wakef* 63-66; C Willesden St Andr *Lon* 66-70; Chapl Gothenburg w Halmstad and Jönköping *Eur* 70-74; Perm to Offic *Chich* 74; V Ryhill *Wakef* 74-82; R Weston Longville w Morton and the Witchinghams *Nor* 82-04; P-in-c Alderford w Attlebridge and Swannington 94-04; RD Sparham 95-00; rtd 04; Perm to Offic *Nor* from 04. *1 The Paddock, Top Common, East Runton, Cromer NR27 9PR* Tel (01263) 515710

ILORI, Emmanuel. b 57. **d** 04 **p** 05. NSM New Addington *S'wark* from 04. *12 Birdhurst Avenue, South Croydon CR2 7DX* Tel 07734-929501 (mobile) E-mail emmanuel@ilori.freeserve.co.uk

ILOTT, Philip Edwin. b 36. Roch Th Coll 66. **d** 68 **p** 69. C Leavesden *St Alb* 68-71; C-in-c Godshill CD *Portsm* 71-77; V Mayfield *Chich* 77-81; V Bexhill St Barn 81-84; rtd 84; Perm to Offic *Chich* 85-97. *Durlock, 15 Shining Cliff, Hastings TN34 2GT*

ILSLEY (née ROGERS), Mrs Anne Frances. b 50. Heythrop Coll Lon BA00 RGN72. Wycliffe Hall Ox 00. **d** 02 **p** 03. NSM Harefield *Lon* 02-06; NSM Dorchester *Ox* from 06. *The Vicarage, High Street, Long Wittenham, Abingdon OX14 4QQ* Tel (01865) 407605 Mobile 07956-374624 E-mail annefi36@aol.com

ILSON, John Robert. b 37. Leeds Univ BSc59 Lon Univ BD64 CertEd65. ALCD63. **d** 64 **p** 65. C Kennington St Mark *S'wark* 64-67; C Sydenham H Trin 67-70; Asst Dir RE *Sheff* 70-77; R Hooton Roberts 70-75; R Hooton Roberts w Ravenfield 75-77; P-in-c Kidderminster St Geo *Worc* 77-81; TR 81-85; P-in-c Powick 85-96; Chapl N Devon Healthcare NHS Trust 97-08; rtd 04. *14 Bromley College, London Road, Bromley BR1 1PE* Tel 020-8460 3927 E-mail jilson1@tiscali.co.uk

ILTON, Mrs Jennifer Jane. b 38. S Dios Minl Tr Scheme 92. **d** 95 **p** 96. NSM Jersey St Sav *Win* from 95. *38 Maison St Louis, St Saviour, Jersey JE2 7LX* Tel (01534) 722327

ILYAS, Marilyn. b 51. Oak Hill Th Coll 92. **d** 95 **p** 96. C Roch 95-98; TV S Chatham H Trin 98-01; TR from 01. *26 Mayford Road, Chatham ME5 8SZ* Tel (01634) 660922 E-mail marilyn.ilyas@diocese-rochester.org

IMPEY, Miss Joan Mary. b 35. Dalton Ho Bris 65. **dss** 74 **d** 87 **p** 94. Kennington St Mark *S'wark* 64-77; Barking St Marg w St Patr *Chelmsf* 75-81; Harwell w Chilton *Ox* 81-87; Par Dn 87-92; Par Dn Didcot All SS 92-94; C 94-97; rtd 98; Perm to Offic *Ox* from 99. *15 Loder Road, Harwell, Didcot OX11 0HR* Tel (01235) 820346

IMPEY, Canon Patricia Irene. b 45. Birm Univ BA67 Lanc Univ MPhil01. Carl Dioc Tr Course 88. **d** 90 **p** 94. Par Dn Blackpool St Paul *Blackb* 90-94; C 94-95; Chapl Asst Victoria Hosp Blackpool 94-95; Asst Chapl Norfolk and Nor Hosp 95-96; Hon C Sprowston w Beeston *Nor* 96; R King's Beck 96-02; V Ecclesfield *Sheff* from 02; Bp's Adv for Women's Min 03-06; Dean of Women's Min 06-08; Hon Can Sheff Cathl from 04. *The Vicarage, 230 The Wheel, Ecclesfield, Sheffield S35 9ZB* Tel 0114-257 0002 E-mail patriciaimpey@btinternet.com

IMPEY, Richard. b 41. Em Coll Cam BA63 MA67 Harvard Univ ThM67. Ridley Hall Cam 67. **d** 68 **p** 69. C Birm St Martin 68-72; Dir of Tr *B & W* 72-79; Dir of Ords 76-79; V Blackpool St Jo *Blackb* 79-95; RD Blackpool 84-90; Hon Can Blackb Cathl 89-95; Dioc Dir of Tr *Nor* 95-00; P-in-c Heigham St Barn w

St Bart 00-02; V Wentworth *Sheff* 02-06; Bp's Adv in Par Development from 04; rtd 06. *The Vicarage, 230 The Wheel, Ecclesfield, Sheffield S35 9ZB* Tel 0114-257 0002

INALL, Mrs Elizabeth Freda. b 47. Univ of Wales (Lamp) MA06. St Alb Minl Tr Scheme 88. **d** 92 **p** 94. NSM Tring *St Alb* 92-01; C Harpenden St Nic from 01. *10 Cross Way, Harpenden AL5 4RA* Tel (01582) 713007 E-mail elizabeth.inall@virgin.net

INCE, Peter Reginald. b 26. Bp's Coll Calcutta 48. **d** 51 **p** 52. India 51-55; C Leek St Luke *Lich* 55-57; C Milton 57-59; C Lewisham St Jo Southend *S'wark* 59-62; R Loddington w Cransley *Pet* 62-75; V Snibston *Leic* 75-79; R Mickleham *Guildf* 79-92; rtd 92; Perm to Offic *Guildf* from 92. *Bickerton, 8 Rockdale, Headley Road, Grayshott, Hindhead GU26 6TU* Tel (01428) 604694

IND, Dominic Mark. b 63. Lanc Univ BA87. Ridley Hall Cam 87. **d** 90 **p** 91. C Birch w Fallowfield *Man* 90-93; SSF 93-95; Perm to Offic *Glas* 95-96; C Byker St Martin *Newc* 96-98; C Walker 96-98; P-in-c Cambuslang and Uddingston *Glas* 98-07; R Bridge of Allan *St And* from 07; Chapl Stirling Univ from 07. *21 Fountain Road, Bridge of Allan FK9 4AT* Tel (01786) 832368 E-mail dom.ind@btinternet.com

IND, Philip William David. b 35. K Coll Lon BD82. Wycliffe Hall Ox 74 Cranmer Hall Dur 59. **d** 65 **p** 66. C Ipswich St Jo *St E* 65-67; C Charlton Kings St Mary *Glouc* 67-71; R Woolstone w Gotherington and Oxenton 71-74; Chapl Alleyn's Sch Dulwich 76-81; C Beckenham St Geo *Roch* 83-85; V Bromley St Jo 85-87; Perm to Offic *Ox* 88-91 and from 95; P-in-c Hurley 91-92; P-in-c Stubbings 91-92; rtd 92. *Stilegate, Tugwood Common, Cookham, Maidenhead SL6 9TT* Tel (01628) 477425 E-mail mtpipind@aol.com

✠**IND, The Rt Revd William.** b 42. Leeds Univ BA64. Coll of Resurr Mirfield 64. **d** 66 **p** 67 **c** 87. C Feltham *Lon* 66-71; C Northolt St Mary 71-73; TV Basingstoke *Win* 73-87; Vice-Prin Aston Tr Scheme 79-82; Dioc Dir of Ords *Win* 82-87; Hon Can Win Cathl 84-87; Suff Bp Grantham *Linc* 87-97; Dean Stamford 87-97; Can and Preb Linc Cathl 87-97; Bp Truro 97-08; rtd 08. *15 Dean Close, Melksham SN12 7EZ*

INDER, Patrick John. b 30. K Coll Lon BD54 AKC54 Huddersfield Univ MA98. St Boniface Warminster. **d** 55 **p** 56. C St Margaret's-on-Thames *Lon* 55-57; C Golders Green 57-61; V Hanwell St Mellitus 61-77; R Rawmarsh w Parkgate *Sheff* 77-80; rtd 80; Hon C Sheff St Matt 82-88; Perm to Offic *Wakef* from 98 and *Win* from 02. *Roucoulement, rue de la Brigade, St Andrews, Guernsey GY6 8RQ* Tel (01481) 234343 E-mail roucoulement@cwgsy.net

INDIAN OCEAN, Archbishop of the Province of the. See ERNEST, The Most Revd Gerald James Ian

INESON, David Antony. b 36. ALCD62. **d** 62 **p** 63. C Sandal St Helen *Wakef* 62-65; C Birm St Geo 66-71; V Horton *Bradf* 71-80; RD Bowling and Horton 78-80; V Sedbergh, Cautley and Garsdale 80-86; C Firbank, Howgill and Killington 81-86; TV Langley and Parkfield *Man* 86-88; TR Banbury *Ox* 92-98; R 98-01; rtd 01; Perm to Offic *Ripon* from 01. *11 Church Close, Redmire, Leyburn DL8 4HF* Tel (01969) 624631 E-mail d.ineson@tiscali.co.uk

INESON, Emma Gwynneth. b 69. Birm Univ BA92 MPhil93 PhD98. Trin Coll Bris BA99. **d** 00 **p** 01. C Dore *Sheff* 00-03; Chapl Lee Abbey 03-06; Partnership P Inner Ring Partnership *Bris* from 06; NSM Bris St Matt and St Nath from 06; Tutor Trin Coll Bris from 07. *St Matthew's Vicarage, 11 Glentworth Road, Bristol BS6 7EG* Tel 0117-942 4186 E-mail emmaineson@blueyonder.co.uk

INESON, Mathew David. b 69. Birm Univ BEng91. Trin Coll Bris BA99 MA00. **d** 00 **p** 01. NSM Dore *Sheff* 00-03; Chapl Lee Abbey 03-06; P-in-c Bris St Matt and St Nath from 06; Min Inner Ring Partnership from 06. *St Matthew's Vicarage, 11 Glentworth Road, Bristol BS6 7EG* Tel 0117-942 4186 Mobile 07896-997604 E-mail mat.ineson@bristol.anglican.org

INESON, Matthew. b 68. Leeds Univ BA00. Coll of Resurr Mirfield 97. **d** 00 **p** 01. C Owton Manor *Dur* 00-03; V Dalton *Sheff* from 03. *The Vicarage, 2 Vicarage Close, Dalton, Rotherham S65 3QL* Tel (01709) 850377 Mobile 07780-686310 E-mail frmatt_@excite.com

INGALL, David Lenox. b 81. Jes Coll Cam MA08. Wycliffe Hall Ox BA08. **d** 09. C Holborn St Geo w H Trin and St Bart *Lon* from 09. *Flat 3, 58 Lamb's Conduit Street, London WC1N 3LW* Tel 07968-119017 (mobile) E-mail davidingall@gmail.com

INGAMELLS, Ronald Sidney. b 32. FCIPD92. AKC56. **d** 57 **p** 58. C Leeds Gipton Epiphany *Ripon* 57-59; C Gt Yarmouth *Nor* 59-64; Dioc Youth Officer 64-79; Hon C Nor St Pet Mancroft 64-79; P-in-c Lemsford *St Alb* 79-02; Sec Tr Development and Chr Educn Nat Coun YMCAs 79-92; Consultant to Romania Euro Alliance YMCAs 93-97; rtd 02; Perm to Offic *Ely* from 03. *2 Aragon Close, Buckden, St Neots PE19 5TY* Tel (01480) 811608

✠**INGE, The Rt Revd John Geoffrey.** b 55. St Chad's Coll Dur BSc77 MA94 PhD02 Keble Coll Ox PGCE79. Coll of Resurr Mirfield. **d** 84 **p** 85 **c** 03. Asst Chapl Lancing Coll 84-86; Jun Chapl Harrow Sch 86-89; Sen Chapl 89-90; V Wallsend St Luke *Newc* 90-96; Can Res Ely Cathl 96-03; Vice-Dean 99-03; Suff Bp

Huntingdon 03-07; Bp Worc from 07. *The Bishop's Office, The Old Palace, Deansway, Worcester WR1 2JE* Tel (01905) 731599 Fax 739382 E-mail bishop.worcester@cofe-worcester.org.uk

INGHAM, Anthony William. b 55. Ven English Coll Rome PhB75 STB78 NOC 98. **d** 78 **p** 79. In RC Ch 78-98; NSM Tottington *Man* 99-01; CF from 01. *c/o MOD Chaplains (Army)* Tel (01980) 615804 Fax 615800

INGHAM, Miss Dawn. b 48. **d** 04 **p** 05. C Brownhill *Wakef* 04-07; P-in-c Wakef St Andr and St Mary from 07. *St Andrew's Vicarage, Johnston Street, Wakefield WF1 4DZ* E-mail dawn124@fsmail.net

INGHAM, John Edmund. b 34. Reading Univ BA56. Clifton Th Coll 58. **d** 60 **p** 61. C Rodbourne Cheney *Bris* 60-63; C Tunbridge Wells St Jo *Roch* 63-67; V Sevenoaks Weald 67-82; V Farrington Gurney *B & W* 82-92; V Paulton 82-92; RD Midsomer Norton 88-91; R Aspley Guise w Husborne Crawley and Ridgmont *St Alb* 92-99; rtd 99; Perm to Offic *B & W* from 00. *10 Milton Lane, Wookey Hole, Wells BA5 1DG* Tel (01749) 677529

INGHAM, Malcolm John. b 68. Wycliffe Hall Ox BTh99. **d** 99 **p** 00. C Moreton-in-Marsh w Batsford, Todenham etc *Glouc* 99-03; C Leckhampton SS Phil and Jas w Cheltenham St Jas 03-04; TV The Ortons, Alwalton and Chesterton *Ely* from 04; P-in-c Elton w Stibbington and Water Newton from 06. *St Andrew's Rectory, 4 Alwalton Hall, Alwalton, Peterborough PE7 3UN* Tel (01733) 239289 Mobile 07974-394984 E-mail mail@malcolm-ingham.fsnet.co.uk

INGHAM, Mrs Carol Helen. *See* PHARAOH, Carol Helen

INGHAM, Mrs Pamela. b 47. MBE96. NEOC 93. **d** 96 **p** 97. C Newc Epiphany 96-99; C Fawdon 99-00; P-in-c 00-06; Dioc Development Officer for Partners in Community Action from 06. *St Luke's Vicarage, 15 Claremont Street, Newcastle upon Tyne NE2 4AH* Tel 0191-221 1009 E-mail pimbe@aol.com

INGLE-GILLIS, William Clarke. b 68. Baylor Univ (USA) BA90 MA95 K Coll Lon PhD04. Westcott Ho Cam 02. **d** 04 **p** 05. C Caldicot *Mon* 04-08; Dioc Soc Resp Officer 06-08; P-in-c Caerwent w Dinham and Llanfair Discoed etc from 08; Tutor St Mich Coll Llan from 07. *1 Vicarage Gardens, Caerwent, Caldicot NP26 5BH* Tel and fax (01291) 424484 E-mail w.c.ingle-gillis@cantab.net

INGLEBY, Canon Anthony Richard. b 48. Keele Univ BA72. Trin Coll Bris. **d** 83 **p** 84. C Plymouth St Jude *Ex* 83-88; R Lanreath *Truro* 88-97; V Pelynt 88-97; RD W Wivelshire 96-97; P-in-c Stoke Climsland 97-05; P-in-c Linkinhorne 03-05; P-in-c Liskeard and St Keyne from 05; Chapl Cornwall and Is of Scilly Primary Care Trust 05-09; Hon Can Truro Cathl from 04; RD W Wivelshire from 08. *The Rectory, Church Street, Liskeard PL14 3AQ* Tel (01579) 342178 E-mail tony@ingleby100.freeserve.co.uk

INGLEDEW, Peter David Gordon. b 48. AKC77 Jo Dalton Coll Man CertEd73 Croydon Coll DASS92 CQSW92 Univ Coll Chich BA03. St Steph Ho Ox 77. **d** 78 **p** 79. C Whorlton *Newc* 78-81; C Poplar *Lon* 81-83; TV 83-85; V Tottenham H Trin 85-90; Perm to Offic *Chich* from 90. *11 St Luke's Terrace, Brighton BN2 2ZE* Tel (01273) 689765 Fax 389115 E-mail david.ingledew2@ntlworld.com

INGLESBY, Eric Vredenburg (Paul). b 15. Qu Coll Ox BA46 MA63. Wycliffe Hall Ox 63. **d** 64 **p** 64. C Plymouth Crownhill Ascension *Ex* 64-66; R Caythorpe *Linc* 66-70; C Scilly Is *Truro* 70-73; C Plymouth St Andr w St Paul and St Geo *Ex* 73-76; rtd 76. *43 Palmers Road, Glastonbury BA6 9PB* Tel (01458) 833591

INGLESBY, Richard Eric. b 47. Birm Univ BSc69 Bris Univ CertEd74. Wycliffe Hall Ox 85. **d** 87 **p** 88. C Cheltenham Ch Ch *Glouc* 87-92; P-in-c Paulton *B & W* 92-94; V 94-01; P-in-c Farrington Gurney 92-94; V 94-01; P-in-c Moxley *Lich* 01-09; V from 09; C Darlaston All SS from 01; C Darlaston St Lawr from 01; Ecum Adv (Wolverhampton Area) 04-08; RD Wednesbury from 05. *The Vicarage, 5 Sutton Road, Moxley, Wednesbury WS10 8SG* Tel and fax (01902) 653084

INGLIS, Kelvin John. b 62. Ripon Coll Cuddesdon MTh00. **d** 00 **p** 01. C Southampton Maybush St Pet *Win* 00-04; V Whitchurch w Tufton and Litchfield from 04. *The Vicarage, Church Street, Whitchurch RG28 7AS* Tel (01256) 892535

INGLIS-JONES, Valentine Walter. b 72. UEA BA94 Univ of N Lon PGCE95 Cam Univ BTh07. Ridley Hall Cam 04. **d** 07 **p** 08. C Combe Down w Monkton Combe and S Stoke *B & W* from 07. *13A Fox Hill, Bath BA2 5QL* Tel (01225) 840305 Mobile 07888-679079 E-mail vwi20@cam.ac.uk

INGRAM, Canon Bernard Richard. b 40. Lon Coll of Div 66. **d** 66 **p** 67. C Bromley Common St Aug *Roch* 66-70; C Gravesend St Geo 70-74; Chapl Joyce Green Hosp Dartford 75-83; V Dartford St Edm *Roch* 75-83; V Strood St Fran 83-04; RD Strood 91-97; Hon Can Roch Cathl 00-04; rtd 04; Perm to Offic *Heref* from 05. *1 Hillview Cottage, Upper Colwall, Malvern WR13 6DII* Tel and fax (01684) 544175

INGRAM, Gary Simon. b 58. K Coll Lon BD AKC. Ripon Coll Cuddesdon. **d** 83 **p** 84. Chapl Nelson and Colne Coll 92-98; C Spalding *Linc* 83-87; C Heaton Ch Ch *Man* 87-89; V Colne H Trin *Blackb* 89-98; RD Pendle 96-98; R Poulton-le-Sands w

Morecambe St Laur 98-09; AD Lancaster 98-04; P-in-c Ferring *Chich* from 09. *The Vicarage, 19 Grange Park, Ferring, Worthing BN12 5LS* Tel (01903) 241645 E-mail garyingram@care4free.net

INGRAM (née BURDEN), Mrs Joanna Mary. b 50. EMMTC 04. **d** 07 **p** 08. NSM Aston on Trent, Elvaston, Weston on Trent etc *Derby* from 07. *25 The Woodlands, Melbourne, Derby DE73 8DP* Tel (01332) 862548 E-mail joanna.ingram@rdplus.net

INGRAM, Canon Peter Anthony. b 53. NOC 83. **d** 86 **p** 87. C Maltby *Sheff* 86-89; TV Gt Snaith 89-92; R Adwick-le-Street w Skelbrooke 92-05; AD Adwick 01-05; V Millhouses H Trin from 05; AD Ecclesall from 07; Hon Can Sheff Cathl from 05. *The Vicarage, 80 Millhouses Lane, Sheffield S7 2HB* Tel 0114-236 2838 E-mail revingram@hotmail.co.uk

INGRAMS, Peter Douglas. b 56. Wheaton Coll Illinois BA77 Ox Univ BA80. Wycliffe Hall Ox 78. **d** 83 **p** 84. C Rowner *Portsm* 83-86; C Petersfield w Sheet 86-90; V Sheet 90-96; V Locks Heath 96-07; Local Min Officer *Cant* from 07. *12 Guildford Road, Canterbury CT1 3QD*

INKPIN, David Leonard. b 32. Liv Univ BSc54 CChem MRSC55. EMMTC 83. **d** 86 **p** 87. NSM Legsby, Linwood and Market Rasen *Linc* 86-04; Perm to Offic from 04. *Weelsby House, Legsby Road, Market Rasen LN8 3DY* Tel (01673) 843360 E-mail inkpens@yahoo.co.uk

INKPIN, Jonathan David Francis. b 60. Mert Coll Ox MA81 Dur Univ PhD96. Ripon Coll Cuddesdon BA85. **d** 86 **p** 87. C Hackney *Lon* 86-88; Tutor Ripon Coll Cuddesdon 88-90; C Cuddesdon *Ox* 88-90; TV Gateshead *Dur* 90-95; C Stanhope w Frosterley 95-01; C Eastgate w Rookhope 95-01; Dioc Rural Development Officer 95-01; Australia from 01. *78 Henry Parry Drive, PO Box 4255, Gosford East NSW 2250, Australia* Tel (0061) (2) 4324 2630

INMAN, Malcolm Gordon. b 33. Edin Th Coll 58. **d** 60 **p** 61. C Lundwood *Wakef* 60-63; C Heckmondwike 63-70; V Wrenthorpe 70-75; Chapl Cardigan Hosp 70-73; Asst Chapl Pinderfields Gen Hosp Wakef 72-73; V Cleckheaton St Jo *Wakef* 75-98; rtd 98; Perm to Offic *Wakef* 00-07; Hon C Staincliffe and Carlinghow from 07. *14 Briestfield Road, Thornhill Edge, Dewsbury WF12 0PW* Tel (01924) 437171

INMAN, Mark Henry. b 31. Lon Univ BSc53. EAMTC 80. **d** 83 **p** 84. Hon C Orford w Sudbourne, Chillesford, Butley and Iken *St E* 83-85; Chapl HM YOI Hollesley Bay Colony 85-91; Hon C Alderton w Ramsholt and Bawdsey *St E* 85-92; P-in-c 92-00; P-in-c Shottisham w Sutton 92-00; TV Wilford Peninsula 00-01; rtd 01; Perm to Offic *Nor* from 01. *Mill Farm House, Newton Road, Sporle, King's Lynn PE32 2DB* Tel (01760) 722544

INMAN, Martin. b 50. K Coll Lon BD72 AKC73. St Aug Coll Cant 72. **d** 73 **p** 74. C Bridgnorth St Mary *Heref* 73-77; C Parkstone St Pet w Branksea and St Osmund *Sarum* 77-79; V Willenhall St Anne *Lich* 79-85; Chapl Yeovil Distr Gen Hosp 85-91; TV Yeovil *B & W* 85-88; R Barwick 88-91; Chapl Jersey Gen Hosp 91-99; Chapl Whittington Hosp NHS Trust 99-03; TV Smestow Vale *Lich* 03-09; RD Trysull 06-09; rtd 09. *28 Market Lane, Wolverhampton WV4 4UJ* Tel 07980-920462 (mobile) E-mail martininman@hotmail.co.uk

INMAN, Canon Thomas Jeremy. b 45. Rhodes Univ BA67. St Steph Ho Ox 67. **d** 69 **p** 70. C Deptford St Paul *S'wark* 69-72; C Bellville S Africa 72-73; R Malmesbury 73-76; P-in-c Donnington *Chich* 76-80; V Hangleton 80-86; V Bosham from 86; RD Westbourne 91-99; Can and Preb Chich Cathl from 00. *The Vicarage, Bosham Lane, Bosham, Chichester PO18 8HX* Tel (01243) 573228 Mobile 07941-834914 E-mail tjinman45@aol.com

INNES, Donald John. b 32. St Jo Coll Ox BA54 MA. Westcott Ho Cam 56. **d** 56 **p** 57. C St Marylebone St Mark Hamilton Terrace *Lon* 56-58; C Walton-on-Thames *Guildf* 58-67; Chapl Moor Park Coll Farnham 67-76; P-in-c Tilford *Guildf* 76-97; rtd 97; Perm to Offic *Guildf* from 97. *Watchetts, 67A Upper Hale Road, Farnham GU9 0PA* Tel (01252) 734597

INNES, Donald Keith. b 33. St Jo Coll Ox BA56 MA60 Lon Univ BD58 Bris Univ MPhil01. Clifton Th Coll 56. **d** 58 **p** 59. C Harold Hill St Paul *Chelmsf* 58-61; C Ealing Dean St Jo *Lon* 61-65; V Westacre and R Gayton Thorpe w E Walton *Nor* 65-70; V Woking St Paul *Guildf* 70-78; R Alfold and Loxwood 78-88; V Doddington w Wychling *Cant* 88-90; V Newnham 88-90; V Doddington, Newnham and Wychling 90-97; rtd 97; Perm to Offic *Chich* from 98. *High Elms, Lewes Road, Ringmer, Lewes BN8 5NE* Tel (01273) 814995

INNES, James Michael. b 32. Lon Univ BA56 BD59. Clifton Th Coll 58. **d** 59 **p** 60. C Blackpool St Thos *Blackb* 59-62; Tutor Clifton Th Coll 62-65; V Burton All SS *Lich* 65-73; V Ashton-upon-Mersey St Mary Magd *Ches* 73-90; P-in-c Brereton w Swettenham 90-91; R 91-97; Dioc Clergy Widows and Retirement Officer 93-97; rtd 97; Perm to Offic *Derby* from 97. *22 Sandown Avenue, Mickleover, Derby DE3 0QQ* Tel (01332) 516691 E-mail jminnes.9@tiscali.co.uk

INNES, Canon Robert Neil. b 59. K Coll Cam BA82 MA85 St Jo Coll Dur BA91 Dur Univ PhD95. Cranmer Hall Dur 89. **d** 95 **p** 96. C Dur St Cuth 95-97; C Shadforth and Sherburn w

Pittington 97-99; Lect St Jo Coll Dur 95-99; P-in-c Belmont *Dur* 99-00; V 00-05; Sen Chapl and Chan Brussels Cathl from 05. *Avenue Princesse Paola 15, 1410 Waterloo, Belgium* Tel (0032) (2) 511 7183 E-mail chaplain@htbrussels.com

INNES, Ms Ruth. b 56. New Coll Edin BD00. TISEC 97. **d** 00 **p** 01. Prec St Ninian's Cathl Perth 00-02; P-in-c Linlithgow and Bathgate *Edin* 02-06; P-in-c Edin St Mark from 06. *St Mark's Rectory, 32 Durham Avenue, Edinburgh EH15 1PA* Tel 0131-258 2456 E-mail ruth@ruthinnes.me.uk

INSLEY, Canon Michael George Pitron. b 47. Trin Coll Ox BA69 MA70 Nottm Univ MPhil85. Wycliffe Hall Ox 69. **d** 72 **p** 73. C Beckenham Ch Ch *Roch* 72-76; P-in-c Cowden 76-79; Lect St Jo Coll Nottm 79-85; V Tidebrook and Wadhurst *Chich* 85-98; P-in-c Stonegate 95-98; Can and Preb Chich Cathl 94-98; P-in-c Horsmonden and Dioc Rural Officer *Roch* 98-03; V Bromley Common St Luke from 03; Hon Can Th Roch Cathl from 06. *St Luke's Vicarage, 20 Bromley Common, Bromley BR2 9PD* Tel (020) 8464 2076 E-mail michael.insley@diocese-rochester.org

INSTON, Brian John. b 47. SAOMC 95. **d** 98 **p** 99. C Bentley *Sheff* 98-01; V Balby from 01; AD W Doncaster from 07. *St John's Vicarage, 6 Greenfield Lane, Doncaster DN4 0PT* Tel and fax (01302) 853278 Mobile 07990-513120

INVERNESS, Provost of. *See* GORDON, The Very Revd Alexander Ronald

✠**INWOOD, The Rt Revd Richard Neil.** b 46. Univ Coll Ox BSc70 MA73 Nottm Univ BA73. St Jo Coll Nottm 71. **d** 74 **p** 75 **c** 03. C Fulwood *Sheff* 74-78; C St Marylebone All So w SS Pet and Jo *Lon* 78-81; V Bath St Luke *B & W* 81-89; R Yeovil w Kingston Pitney 89-95; Preb Wells Cathl 90-95; Adn Halifax *Wakef* 95-03; Suff Bp Bedford *St Alb* from 03; Cen Chapl MU from 05. *Bishop's Lodge, Bedford Road, Cardington, Bedford MK44 3SS* Tel (01234) 831432 Fax 831484 E-mail bishopbedford@stalbans.anglican.org

IPGRAVE, The Ven Michael Geoffrey. b 58. Oriel Coll Ox BA78 MA94 St Chad's Coll Dur PhD00 SOAS Lon MA04. Ripon Coll Cuddesdon BA81. **d** 82 **p** 83. C Oakham, Hambleton, Egleton, Braunston and Brooke *Pet* 82-85; Asst P Chiba Resurr Japan 85-87; TV Leic Ascension 87-90; TV Leic H Spirit 91-95; TR 95-99; P-in-c Leic St Mary 93-94; Bp's Adv on Relns w People of Other Faiths 91-99; Bp's Dom Chapl 92-99; Hon Can Leic Cathl 94-04; Adv Inter-Faith Relns Abp's Coun 99-04; Sec Ch's Commission Inter Faith Relns 99-04; Hon C Leic Presentation 02-04; Adn S'wark from 04; P-in-c S'wark St Geo w St Alphege and St Jude 06-07. *49 Colombo Street, London SE1 8DP* Tel (020) 7939 9409 *or* 7771 2858 Fax 7939 9467 E-mail michael.ipgrave@southwark.anglican.org

IPSWICH, Archdeacon of. *Vacant*

IQBAL, Javaid. b 71. St Jo Coll Nottm BA97. **d** 97 **p** 99. C Lahore St Thos Pakistan 97-99; P-in-c Lahore Ch Ch 99-00; Dir Miss and Evang Raiwind 98-99; Perm to Offic *Leic* 00-05; C Evington 05-07; P-in-c Thurmaston 07-08; TV Syston from 08. *The Vicarage, 828 Melton Road, Thurmaston, Leicester LE4 8BE* Tel 0116-269 2555 Mobile 07782-169987 E-mail javaidiqbal7@aol.com

IREDALE, Simon Peter. b 56. Cam Univ BA78 MPhil80. Wycliffe Hall Ox 83. **d** 86 **p** 87. C Thirsk *York* 86-89; Asst Chapl Norfolk and Nor Hosp 89-90; P-in-c Kexby w Wilberfoss *York* 90-93; Sub-Chapl HM Pris Full Sutton 90-93; Chapl RAF 93-06. *5 Grange Road, Albrighton, Wolverhampton WV7 3LD*

IRELAND, David Arthur. b 45. Mert Coll Ox BA67 MA71 MICFM87. Cuddesdon Coll 67. **d** 69 **p** 70. C Chapel Allerton *Ripon* 69-72; C Harpenden St Nic *St Alb* 72-76; R Clifton 76-84; Perm to Offic *Guildf* 91-00; NSM Leatherhead and Mickleham from 01; Chapl Box Hill Sch from 05. *The Rectory, Old London Road, Mickleham, Dorking RH5 6EB* Tel (01372) 378335 E-mail rev.ireland43@btinternet.com

IRELAND, Leslie Sydney. b 55. York Univ BA76. St Jo Coll Nottm 83. **d** 86 **p** 87. C Harwood *Man* 86-89; C Davyhulme St Mary 89-90; V Bardsley 90-99; R Levenshulme St Andr and St Pet 99-06; P-in-c Levenshulme St Mark 05-06; R Levenshulme from 06; AD Heaton from 04. *The Rectory, 27 Errwood Road, Levenshulme, Manchester M19 2PN* Tel 0161-224 5877 E-mail lesireland@compuserve.com

IRELAND, Mrs Lucy Annabel. b 53. Univ of Zimbabwe BSc74. St Jo Coll Nottm. **dss** 85 **d** 87 **p** 95. Mansfield St Jo *S'well* 85-87; Hon Par Dn Harwood *Man* 87-89; NSM Bardsley 90-99; C Levenshulme St Andr and St Pet 99-06; C Levenshulme from 06. *The Rectory, 27 Errwood Road, Levenshulme, Manchester M19 2PN* Tel 0161-224 5877 E-mail lesireland@compuserve.com

IRELAND, Mark Campbell. b 60. St Andr Univ MTheol81 Sheff Univ MA01. Wycliffe Hall Ox 82. **d** 84 **p** 85. C Blackb St Gabr 84-87; C Lancaster St Mary 87-89; Sub-Chapl HM Pris Lanc 87-89; V Baxenden *Blackb* 89-97; Dioc Missr *Lich* 98-07; TV Walsall 98-07; V Wellington All SS w Eyton from 07. *All Saints' Vicarage, 35 Crescent Road, Wellington, Telford TF1 3DW* Tel (01952) 641251 Fax 625924 E-mail mark.ireland@lichfield.anglican.org

IRELAND, Mrs Mary Janet. b 52. EMMTC 96. **d** 99 **p** 00. NSM

Kibworth and Smeeton Westerby and Saddington *Leic* 99-02; C Lutterworth w Cotesbach and Bitteswell 02-05; P-in-c Glen Magna cum Stretton Magna etc from 05. *St Cuthbert's Vicarage, Church Road, Great Glen, Leicester LE8 9FE* Tel 0116-259 2238 E-mail mary_ireland@btinternet.com

IRELAND, Mrs Sharran. b 49. SEITE 95. **d** 98 **p** 99. C Appledore w Brookland, Fairfield, Brenzett etc *Cant* 98-01; TV St Laur in Thanet 01-03; TR from 03. *The Rectory, 2 Newington Road, Ramsgate CT11 0QT* Tel (01843) 592478

IRESON, David Christopher. b 45. Man Univ TCert67 Birm Univ BEd80. St Steph Ho Ox. **d** 93 **p** 94. C Minehead *B & W* 93-97; V St Decumans 97-08; rtd 08. *50 Camperdown Terrace, Exmouth EX8 1EQ* Tel (01395) 263307 E-mail decuman@hotmail.co.uk

IRESON, Ms Gillian Dorothy. b 39. Gilmore Ho 67. **dss** 72 **d** 87 **p** 94. Stepney St Dunstan and All SS *Lon* 72-99; Par Dn 87-94; C 94-99; rtd 99; Perm to Offic *Nor* from 00. *67 Glebe Road, Norwich NR2 3JH* Tel (01603) 451969

IRESON, Philip. b 52. Newc Univ BSc73. St Jo Coll Nottm. **d** 84 **p** 85. C Owlerton *Sheff* 84-87; V The Marshland 87-94; Perm to Offic *Linc* 90-93; Chapl HM YOI Hatfield 91-92; Bp's Rural Adv *Sheff* 91-00; R Firbeck w Letwell 94-01; V Woodsetts 94-01; Chapl HM Pris and YOI Doncaster from 01. *HM Prison Doncaster, Marshgate, Doncaster DN5 8UX* Tel (01302) 760870 Fax 760851 E-mail philip@ireson.freeserve.co.uk

IRESON, Richard Henry. b 46. Linc Th Coll 69. **d** 71 **p** 72. C Spilsby w Hundleby *Linc* 71-74; TV Grantham w Manthorpe 74-76; R Claypole 76-79; P-in-c Westborough w Dry Doddington and Stubton 76-77; R 77-79; R Bratoft w Irby-in-the-Marsh 79-86; V Burgh le Marsh 79-86; V Orby 79-86; R Welton-le-Marsh w Gunby 79-86; R Wyberton 86-01; RD Holland W 95-97; V Frampton 97-01; V Alford w Rigsby 01-06; R Well 01-06; R Saleby w Beesby and Maltby 01-06; V Bilsby w Farlesthorpe 01-06; R Hannah cum Hagnaby w Markby 01-06; R N Beltisloe Gp from 06. *12 School Lane, Ropsley, Grantham NG33 4BT* Tel (01476) 585237 E-mail r.ireson@uwclub.net

IRETON, Paul. b 65. Cranmer Hall Dur 99. **d** 01 **p** 02. C Southway *Ex* 01-06; P-in-c Torquay St Jo and Ellacombe from 06. *Silver Hill Lodge, Meadfoot Road, Torquay TQ1 2JP* Tel (01803) 392813 E-mail revpireton@eurobell.co.uk

IRETON, Robert John. b 56. Bris Univ BEd. Oak Hill Th Coll BA. **d** 84 **p** 85. C Bromley Ch Ch *Roch* 84-87; TV Greystoke, Matterdale, Mungrisdale etc *Carl* 87-90; V Falconwood *Roch* 90-97; V Stanwix *Carl* 97-04; P-in-c Erith St Jo *Roch* from 04; Chapl Trin Sch Belvedere from 04. *St John's Church House, 100 Park Crescent, Erith DA8 3DZ* Tel (01322) 332555

IRONS, Nigel Richard. b 55. Aston Univ BSc77. St Jo Coll Nottm MA95. **d** 97 **p** 98. C Newchapel *Lich* 97-00; V Burton All SS w Ch Ch from 00. *All Saints' Vicarage, 242 Blackpool Street, Burton-on-Trent DE14 3AU* Tel (01283) 565134 E-mail mail@nigelirons.co.uk

IRONSIDE, John Edmund. b 31. Peterho Cam BA55 MA59. Qu Coll Birm 55. **d** 57 **p** 58. C Spring Park *Cant* 57-60; C Guernsey St Sampson *Win* 60-63; Thailand 63-66; V Guernsey St Jo *Win* 66-72; V Sholing 72-82; R Guernsey St Sampson 82-98; Miss to Seamen 82-98; rtd 98; Perm to Offic *Win* 98-07; P-in-c Guernsey St Andr from 07. *The Rectory, Route de St Andre, St Andrew, Guernsey GY6 8XN* Tel and fax (01481) 239636 *or* tel 238568 E-mail ironside@cwgsy.net

IRVINE, Mrs Andrea Mary. b 49. Sussex Univ BA70 Ox Univ PGCE71. NTMTC 99. **d** 02. NSM Cov H Trin 02-05; Perm to Offic 05-06; NSM Cov Cathl from 06. *The Deanery, 11 Priory Row, Coventry CV1 5EX* Tel (024) 7663 1448 *or* 7652 1200 E-mail amirvine@lineone.net

IRVINE, Barry. *See* IRVINE, William Barry

IRVINE (*formerly* SADLER), **Ann Penrith.** b 50. STETS 98. **d** 01 **p** 02. C Len Valley *Cant* 01-04; P-in-c Aylesham w Adisham 04-08; C Nonington w Wymynswold and Goodnestone etc 04-08; Perm to Offic from 08. *The Rectory, 69 Swalecliffe Court, Whitstable CT5 2NF* Tel (01227) 792826 E-mail revann@uwclub.net

IRVINE, Mrs Catherine Frances. b 70. K Coll Lon BA97. Ripon Coll Cuddesdon 99. **d** 01 **p** 02. C Romsey *Win* 01-05; TV Richmond St Mary w St Matthias and St Jo S'wark from 05. *St Matthias's House, 22 Cambrian Road, Richmond TW10 6JQ* Tel and fax (020) 8948 7217

IRVINE, Canon Christopher Paul. b 51. Nottm Univ BTh75 Lanc Univ MA76 St Martin's Coll Lanc PGCE77. Kelham Th Coll 73. **d** 76 **p** 76. Chapl Lanc Univ 76-77; C Stoke Newington St Mary *Lon* 77-80; Chapl Sheff Univ 80-85; Chapl St Edm Hall Ox 85-90; Tutor St Steph Ho Ox 85-90; Vice-Prin 91-94; V Cowley St Jo Ox 94-98; Prin Coll of Resurr Mirfield 98-07; Can Res and Lib Cant Cathl from 07. *19 The Precincts, Canterbury CT1 2EP* Tel (01227) 762862 E-mail irvinec@canterbury-cathedral.org

IRVINE, Clyde. *See* IRVINE, James Clyde

IRVINE, David John. b 50. Trin Coll Cam BA72 MA75. NOC 91. **d** 94 **p** 95. C Hexham *Newc* 94-99; P-in-c Blanchland w Hunstanworth and Edmundbyers etc from 99; P-in-c Slaley from

99; P-in-c Healey from 03; P-in-c Whittonstall from 03. *The Vicarage, Slaley, Hexham NE47 0AA* Tel (01434) 673609

IRVINE, Donald Andrew. b 45. Trin Coll Bris 94. **d** 96 **p** 97. C Allington and Maidstone St Pet *Cant* 96-99; P-in-c Harrietsham w Ulcombe 99-02; P-in-c Lenham w Boughton Malherbe 00-02; R Len Valley 02-07; Hon C Whitstable from 07. *The Rectory, 69 Swalecliffe Court Drive, Whitstable CT5 2NF* Tel (01227) 792826 E-mail revirvine@aol.com

IRVINE, Gerard Philip. b 30. QUB BA52. Edin Th Coll 56. **d** 56 **p** 57. Chapl St Andr Cathl 56-58; Prec St Andr Cathl 58-59; C Belfast Malone St Jo *Conn* 61-66; Chapl Community of St Jo Ev Dublin 67-77; C Dublin Sandymount *D & G* 77-97; rtd 97. *12A Carraig na Greine House, Coliemore Road, Dalkey, Co Dublin, Republic of Ireland* Tel (00353) (1) 230 1430

IRVINE, James Clyde. b 35. QUB BA57 NUU BPhil(Ed)83. CITC 59. **d** 59 **p** 60. C Belfast St Luke *Conn* 59-62; C Lisburn Ch Ch Cathl 62-65; R Duneane w Ballyscullion 65-69; I Kilbride 69-74; Hd of RE Ballyclare High Sch 73-98; Bp's C Killead w Gartree 98-05; rtd 05. *1A Rathmena Avenue, Ballyclare BT39 9HX* Tel (028) 9332 2933 E-mail irvine@killead61.fsnet.co.uk

IRVINE, The Very Revd John Dudley. b 49. Sussex Univ BA70. Wycliffe Hall Ox BA80. **d** 81 **p** 82. C Brompton H Trin w Onslow Square St Paul *Lon* 81-85; P-in-c Kensington St Barn 85-94; V 94-01; Dean Cov from 01; P-in-c Cov St Fran N Radford from 06. *The Deanery, 11 Priory Row, Coventry CV1 5EX* Tel and fax (024) 7663 1448 *or* tel 7652 1200 E-mail john.irvine@coventrycathedral.org.uk

IRVINE, Preb John Graham Gerard Charles. b 20. Mert Coll Ox BA42 MA46. St Steph Ho Ox 42. **d** 45 **p** 46. C Knowle H Nativity *Bris* 45-48; C Longton St Mary and St Chad *Lich* 48-51; C Soho St Anne w St Thos and St Pet *Lon* 51-53; Lon Dioc Home Missr Cranford 53-61; V Earl's Court St Cuth w St Matthias 61-69; V Westmr St Matt 69-86; Preb St Paul's Cathl 82-86; rtd 86; Perm to Offic *Chich* from 86. *42 Montpelier Road, Brighton BN1 3BA* Tel (01273) 730039

IRVINE, Simon Timothy. b 74. CITC 00. **d** 03 **p** 04. C Dublin Ch Ch Cathl Gp 03-06; Chapl Dublin Sandymount from 06; Chapl Rathdown Sch from 06. *St Mary's Lodge, 28A Clyde Lane, Ballsbridge, Dublin 4, Republic of Ireland* Tel (00353) 87-944 4113 (mobile)

IRVINE, Stanley. b 35. TCD. **d** 83 **p** 84. C Arm St Mark w Aghavilly 83-85; I Kilmoremoy w Castleconnor, Easkey, Kilglass etc *T, K & A* 85-94; Dom Chapl to Bp Tuam 88-94; I Stranorlar w Meenglas and Kilteevogue *D & R* 94-05; Bp's Dom Chapl 01-05; Can Raphoe Cathl 02-05; rtd 05. *3 Inisfayle Crescent, Bangor BT19 1DT* Tel (028) 9146 2012

IRVINE, Mrs Suzanne. b 74. Huddersfield Univ BA96. St Jo Coll Nottm 99. **d** 03 **p** 04. C Wrose *Bradf* 03-06; Chapl Ripley St Thos C of E High Sch Lanc *Blackb* from 06. *Ripley St Thomas School, Ashton Road, Lancaster LA1 4RS* Tel (01524) 64496 Fax 847069 E-mail chocsxxx@hotmail.com

IRVINE, William Barry. b 48. QUB BD75. St Jo Coll Nottm 75. **d** 76 **p** 77. C Belfast St Mich *Conn* 76-80; C Mansfield SS Pet and Paul *S'well* 80-84; V Chapel-en-le-Frith *Derby* 84-90; Chapl Cheltenham Gen and Delancey Hosps 90-94; Chapl E Glos NHS Trust 94-02; Chapl Glos Hosps NHS Foundn Trust from 02. *Cheltenham General Hospital, Sandford Road, Cheltenham GL53 7AN* Tel (01242) 222222 ext 4286 *or* 274286

IRVINE-CAPEL, Luke Thomas. b 75. Greyfriars Ox BA97 MA01 Leeds Univ MA99. Coll of Resurr Mirfield 97. **d** 99 **p** 00. C Abertillery w Cwmtillery w Six Bells *Mon* 99-01; Chapl Gwent Tertiary Coll 99-01; Min Can St Woolos Cathl 01-03; Sub-Chapl HM Pris Cardiff 02-03; R Cranford *Lon* 03-08; V Pimlico St Gabr from 08. *St Gabriel's Vicarage, 30 Warwick Square, London SW1V 2AD* Tel (020) 7834 7520

IRVING, Canon Andrew. b 27. St Deiniol's Hawarden 62. **d** 65 **p** 66. C Benwell St Jas *Newc* 65-69; C Langley Marish *Ox* 69-73; V Moulsford 73-81; Canada from 81; rtd 92. *204-4630 Ponderosa Drive, Peachland BC V0H 1X5, Canada* Tel (001) (604) 767 9582

IRVING, Canon Michael John Derek. b 43. LVO07. BEd80. Qu Coll Birm 80. **d** 81 **p** 82. C Coleford w Staunton *Glouc* 81-84; V Dean Forest H Trin 84-91; RD Forest S 88-91; P-in-c Hempsted and Dir of Ords 91-96; R Minchinhampton 96-08; Hon Can Glouc Cathl 94-08; rtd 08. *9 Canton Acre, Painswick, Stroud GL6 6QX* E-mail irvings@vale-view.co.uk

IRWIN, Albert Samuel. b 14. TCD BA38 MA44. CITC 38. **d** 38 **p** 39. C Bury St Pet *Man* 38-42; C Bolton St Pet 42-45; Lect 45-47; Chapl RNVR 47-48; C Gillingham *Sarum* 48-49; C Buenos Aires St Jo Argentina 49-52; Chapl St Geo Coll Quilmes 52-54; V Apethorpe w Woodnewton *Pet* 54-59; R Clyst St Mary and Clyst St George *Ex* 59-61; V Stamford Baron *Pet* 61-81; P-in-c Tinwell 77-81; rtd 81; Lic to Offic *Pet* 81-85; Perm to Offic from 85; *Linc* 91-00. *19 Water Street, Stamford PE9 2NJ* Tel (01780) 763495

IRWIN, John Nesbitt Cottier. b 27. Mert Coll Ox BA50 MA53 SEN79. SW Minl Tr Course 86. **d** 87 **p** 88. NSM Buckfastleigh w Dean Prior *Ex* from 87. *56 Plymouth Road, Buckfastleigh TQ11 0DH* Tel (01364) 643044

IRWIN, Mrs Patricia Jane. b 49. CBDTI 02. **d** 05 **p** 06. NSM S Carl from 05. *31 Blackwell Road, Carlisle CA2 4AB* Tel (01228) 526885

IRWIN, Patrick Alexander. b 55. BNC Ox BA77 MA81 Edin Univ BD81. Edin Th Coll 77 Liturgisches Inst Trier 79. **d** 81 **p** 82. Hon C Cambridge St Botolph *Ely* 81-84; Chapl BNC Ox 84-92; Lect Th 86-92; CF 92-99; Sen CF from 99; Chapl Guards Chpl Lon 05-07; Dir of Ords 05-07; Chapl Udruga Hrvata Sv Dominik Gorazde 94-95; Perm to Offic *D & G* from 87; *Arm* from 96; *Eur* from 08; Hon V Choral Arm Cathl 02-07. *c/o MOD Chaplains (Army)* Tel (01980) 615804 Fax 615800 E-mail patalexirwin@yahoo.co.uk

IRWIN, Stewart. b 53. Sarum & Wells Th Coll 80. **d** 83 **p** 84. C Brighouse *Wakef* 83-87; V Stockton St Jo *Dur* 87-95; V Howden-le-Wear and Hunwick from 95. *The Vicarage, Hunwick, Crook DL15 0JU* Tel (01388) 604456

IRWIN, Miss Susan Elizabeth. b 47. Cranmer Hall Dur 77. **dss** 79 **d** 87 **p** 94. Harborne St Faith and St Laur *Birm* 79-82; Caterham *S'wark* 82-88; Par Dn 87-88; Par Dn Kidlington w Hampton Poyle *Ox* 88-94; C 94-95; TV Gt Marlow w Marlow Bottom, Lt Marlow and Bisham 95-06; R Powick and Guarlford and Madresfield w Newland *Worc* from 06. *The Vicarage, 31 The Greenway, Powick, Worcester WR2 4RZ* Tel (01905) 830270 Mobile 07703-350301 E-mail vicarage@powickparish.org.uk

IRWIN, Canon William George. b 53. QUB BSc77. CITC 80. **d** 80 **p** 81. C Lisburn St Paul *Conn* 80-83; C Seagoe *D & D* 83-85; C Newtownards w Movilla Abbey 85-88; I Ballymacash *Conn* from 88; Preb Conn Cathl from 04. *St Mark's Rectory, 97 Antrim Road, Lisburn BT28 3EA* Tel (028) 9266 2393 E-mail wgirwin@btopenworld.com

IRWIN-CLARK, Peter Elliot. b 49. Univ Coll Lon LLB71 Barrister 72. Cranmer Hall Dur BA80. **d** 81 **p** 82. C Kirkheaton *Wakef* 81-86; V Shirley *Win* 86-96; Perm to Office *Chich* 96-97 and *S'wark* 97; V Prestonville St Luke *Chich* 97-03; Missr Warham Trust and Faith Development Officer (Basingstoke Adnry) *Win* 03-08; TR Broadwater *Chich* from 08. *The Rectory, 8 Sompting Avenue, Worthing BN14 8HN* Tel (01903) 823996 E-mail panddic@surfaid.org

ISAAC, Canon David Thomas. b 43. Univ of Wales BA65. Cuddesdon Coll 65. **d** 67 **p** 68. C Llandaff w Capel Llanilltern 67-71; P-in-c Swansea St Jas *S & B* 71-73; Chapl Ch in Wales Youth Coun 73-77; V Llangiwg *S & B* 77-79; Dioc Youth Officer *Ripon* 79-83; Nat Officer for Youth Work Gen Syn Bd of Educn 83-90; Can Res Portsm Cathl from 90; Dioc Dir of Educn 90-06; Hd Miss and Discipleship from 06. *1 Pembroke Close, Portsmouth PO1 2NX* Tel (023) 9281 8107 *or* 9282 2053 Fax 9229 5081 Mobile 07768-997220 E-mail david.isaac@portsmouth.anglican.org

ISAAC, Edward Henry. b 20. Qu Coll Cam BA42 MA46. Ridley Hall Cam 45. **d** 47 **p** 48. C Wednesbury St Bart *Lich* 47-51; V Liv St Phil 51-56; V Knowsley 56-61; V Garston 61-66; V Millom St Geo *Carl* 66-85; rtd 85; Perm to Offic *Carl* from 86. *31 Lowther Road, Millom LA18 4PE* Tel (01229) 772332

ISAACS, John Kenneth. b 36. Cam Univ MA. EAMTC. **d** 82 **p** 83. NSM Ely 82-85; Chapl K Sch Ely 85-94; Lic to Offic *Ely* 85-94; P-in-c Denver 94-02; P-in-c Ryston w Roxham 94-02; P-in-c W Dereham 94-02; R Denver and Ryston w Roxham and W Dereham etc 02-03; rtd 03; Perm to Offic *Ely* from 03. *18 Barton Road, Ely CB7 4DE* Tel (01366) 666936

ISAACSON, Alan Timothy. b 55. York Univ BA77 Sheff Univ PGCE84 Leeds Univ MA97. NOC 94. **d** 96 **p** 97. C Kimberworth *Sheff* 96-99; TV Brinsworth w Catcliffe and Treeton 99-03; TV Rivers Team 03-07; R Bradfield from 07; Dioc Discipleship Development Officer from 07. *The Rectory, High Bradfield, Bradfield, Sheffield S6 6LG* Tel 0114-285 1225 E-mail alan.isaacson@sheffield.anglican.org

ISAACSON, Hilda Ruth. b 57. NOC 07. **d** 09. C Deepcar *Sheff* from 09. *The Rectory, High Bradfield, Bradfield, Sheffield S6 6LG* Tel 0114-285 1225 Mobile 07762-075687 E-mail hilda.isaacson@sheffield.anglican.org

ISABEL, Sister. See KEEGAN, Frances Ann

ISAM, Miss Margaret Myra Elizabeth (Wendy). b 35. Nottm Univ BEd73. EMMTC 78. **dss** 81 **d** 87 **p** 94. Humberston *Linc* 81-84; Gt Grimsby St Andr and St Luke 85-93; Dn-in-c 87-93; P-in-c Gt Grimsby St Andr w St Luke and All SS 94-97; V 97-00; rtd 00; Perm to Offic *Linc* from 00. *18 Grainsby Avenue, Cleethorpes DN35 9PA* Tel (01472) 699821 Mobile 07950-464542

ISBISTER, Charles. b 27. Chich Th Coll 58. **d** 60 **p** 61. C Tynemouth Ch Ch *Newc* 60-64; C Boyne Hill *Ox* 64-67; V Cookridge H Trin *Ripon* 67-93; rtd 93; Perm to Offic *Ripon* from 01. *2 Church Mount, Horsforth, Leeds LS18 5LE* Tel 0113-239 0813 Mobile 07714-356059

ISHERWOOD, Canon David Owen. b 46. BA68 Lon Univ MA95 MPhil87. Ridley Hall Cam 76. **d** 78 **p** 79. C Sanderstead All SS *S'wark* 78-82; C Horley 82-84; TV 84-88; P-in-c Streatham Immanuel and St Andr 88-89; V 89-95; TR Clapham Team 95-01; V Clapham H Trin and St Pet from 02; Hon Can S'wark Cathl from 06. *25 The Chase, London SW4 0NP* Tel (020) 7498

6879 *or* 7627 0941 Fax 7978 1327 *or* 7627 5065
E-mail rector@holytrinityclapham.org
or david.htc@lineone.net

ISHERWOOD, Robin James. b 56. Hull Univ BA78 Uppsala Univ MDiv92. Ripon Coll Cuddesdon 92. **d** 94 **p** 95. C Bramhall *Ches* 94-98; V Alsager St Mary from 98; Hon Chapl ATC from 99. *St Mary's Vicarage, 37 Eaton Road, Alsager, Stoke-on-Trent ST7 2BQ* Tel (01270) 875748 E-mail vicar@pit6.fsnet.co.uk

ISHERWOOD, Samuel Peter. b 34. Lon Coll of Div ALCD62 LTh74. **d** 62 **p** 63. C Bacup St Sav *Man* 62-65; C Man Albert Memorial Ch 65-67; V Livesey *Blackb* 67-79; V Handforth *Ches* 79-99; RD Cheadle 92-99; rtd 99; Perm to Offic *York* from 00. *1 Andrew Drive, Huntington, York YO32 9YF* Tel (01904) 438116

✠**ISINGOMA, The Most Revd Henri Kahwa.** Bp Katanga 01-07; Bp Boga 07-09; Abp Congo from 09. *Address temp unknown*

ISIORHO, David John Phillip. b 58. Liv Poly BA80 Warwick Univ MA93 Bradf Univ PhD98. Westcott Ho Cam 87. **d** 90 **p** 91. C Nuneaton St Mary *Cov* 90-93; P-in-c Bradf St Oswald Chapel Green 93-96; P-in-c Brereton *Lich* 96-00; P-in-c Arthingworth, Harrington w Oxendon and E Farndon *Pet* 00-05; P-in-c Maidwell w Draughton, Lamport w Faxton 01-05; V Kempston Transfiguration *St Alb* 05-09; V Handsworth St Jas *Birm* from 09. *St James's Vicarage, 21 Austin Road, Birmingham B21 8NJ* Tel 0121-554 4151
E-mail davidisiorho@catholic.org

ISIORHO (née NORTHALL), Mrs Linda Barbara. b 50. Birm Univ BA72 Worc Coll of Educn PGCE75. Qu Coll Birm 88. **d** 90 **p** 94. C Wood End *Cov* 90-91; Perm to Offic *Cov* 91-93 and *Bradf* 93-94; NSM Low Moor St Mark *Bradf* 94-96; Perm to Offic *Lich* 96-97; NSM Alrewas 97-00; Perm to Offic *Pet* 01-05. *St James's Vicarage, 21 Austin Road, Birmingham B21 8NJ* Tel 0121-554 4151

ISITT, Canon David Edgar Reid. b 28. K Coll Cam BA49 MA53. Wells Th Coll 51. **d** 53 **p** 54. C Westbury-on-Trym H Trin *Bris* 53-56; Chapl K Coll Cam 56-60; V Haslingfield *Ely* 60-68; R Harlton 60-68; Chapl St Edw K and Martyr Cam 68-77; Asst Chapl Trin Hall Cam 68-77; Can Res Bris Cathl 77-86; Dir Dioc Sch of Min 77-86; P-in-c Bris Ch Ch w St Ewen and All SS 80-82; Dioc Dir of Ords 81-86; Lic to Offic *Ely* 87-93; Acting Dean Trin Hall Cam 89; Tutor Westcott Ho 90; Chapl Fitzw Coll Cam 90-93; rtd 93; Perm to Offic *Ely* from 99. *41 Fulbrooke Road, Cambridge CB3 9EE* Tel (01223) 571763

ISITT, Norman. b 34. St Jo Coll Dur BA56. Cranmer Hall Dur. **d** 59 **p** 60. C Loughton St Mary *Chelmsf* 59-62; C Moulsham St Jo 62-64; Billericay Co Sch 64-90; Squirrels Heath Sch Romford 64-90; Althorpe and Keadby Co Sch 66-95; rtd 95. *21 Cambridge Avenue, Bottesford, Scunthorpe DN16 3LT* Tel (01724) 851489

ISKANDER, Mrs Susan Mary Mackay. Ox Univ BA85 MBA93. NTMTC 05. **d** 08 **p** 09. NSM Writtle w Highwood *Chelmsf* from 08. *44 Maltese Road, Chelmsford CM1 2PA*
E-mail revsusaniskander@gmail.com

ISLE OF WIGHT, Archdeacon of. *See* BASTON, The Ven Caroline

ISON, Andrew Phillip. b 60. Imp Coll Lon BEng82 Penn Univ MSE83 Univ Coll Lon PhD87 Bris Univ BA01 CEng92 MIChemE92. Trin Coll Bris 99. **d** 01 **p** 02. C Cleethorpes *Linc* 01-05; V Bestwood Park w Rise Park *S'well* 05-07; Chapl Voorschoten *Eur* from 07. *Chopinlaan 17, 2253 BS Voorschoten, The Netherlands* Tel (0031) (71) 561 3020
E-mail minister@stjames.nl

ISON, The Very Revd David John. b 54. Leic Univ BA76 Nottm Univ BA78 K Coll Lon PhD85. St Jo Coll Nottm 76. **d** 79 **p** 80. C Deptford St Nic and St Luke *S'wark* 79-85; Lect CA Tr Coll Blackheath 85-88; V Potters Green *Cov* 88-93; Jt Dir SW Minl Tr Course *Ex* 93-95; Dioc Officer for CME 93-05; Bp's Officer for NSMs 97-05; Can Res Ex Cathl 95-05; Chan 97-05; Dean Bradf from 05. *The Deanery, 1 Cathedral Close, Bradford BD1 4EG* Tel (01274) 777722 Fax 777730
E-mail dean@bradford.anglican.org

ISON, Mrs Hilary Margaret. b 55. Leic Univ BA76 E Lon Univ MA02. Gilmore Course 77. **d** 87 **p** 94. NSM Deptford St Nic and St Luke *S'wark* 87-88; NSM Potters Green *Cov* 88-90; C Rugby 90-93; Chapl Ex Hospiscare 93-00; C Ex St Mark, St Sidwell and St Matt 99-02; Bp's Adv for Women in Min 02-05; Area Tutor SWMTC 03-05; PV Ex Cathl 04-05; Tutor Coll of Resurr Mirfield 05-08; Selection Sec Min Division from 08; Hon C Calverley Deanery *Bradf* from 06. *The Deanery, 1 Cathedral Close, Bradford BD1 4EG* Tel (01274) 777727
E-mail hilary.ison@c-of-e.org.uk

ISSBERNER, Norman Gunther Erich. b 34. Fitzw Ho Cam BA58 MA61. Clifton Th Coll 57. **d** 59 **p** 60. C Croydon Ch Ch Broad Green *Cant* 59-61; C Surbiton Hill Ch Ch *S'wark* 61-66; V Egham *Guildf* 66-75; V Wallington *S'wark* 75-86; UK Chmn Africa Inland Miss from 77; Adv on Miss and Evang *Chelmsf* 86-91; P-in-c Castle Hedingham 91-93; V Clacton St Paul 93-99; RD St Osyth 94-99; rtd 99; Perm to Offic *Chelmsf* from 99. *14 Darcy Close, Frinton-on-Sea CO13 0RR* Tel (01255) 673548

ITALY AND MALTA, Archdeacon of. *See* BOARDMAN, The Ven Jonathan

ITUMU, John Murithi. b 65. Lon Bible Coll 01. **d** 02 **p** 03. C Cricklewood St Gabr and St Mich *Lon* 02-07; C Herne Hill *S'wark* from 07. *8 Ruskin Walk, London SE24 9LZ* Tel (020) 7274 3663 Mobile 07946-000364 E-mail joitumu@hotmail.com

IVE, Jeremy George Augustus. b 57. Rhodes Univ BA81 Ch Coll Cam PhD86 K Coll Lon MPhil95. Wycliffe Hall Ox 89. **d** 91 **p** 92. NSM Ivybridge w Harford *Ex* 91-95; P-in-c Abbotskerswell 95-99; P-in-c Tudeley cum Capel w Five Oak Green *Roch* from 99. *The Vicarage, Sychem Lane, Five Oak Green, Tonbridge TN12 6TL* Tel and fax (01892) 836653 Mobile 07720-841169
E-mail jeremy.ive@diocese-rochester.org *or* jeremy@tudeley.org

IVE (née KNOTT), Mrs Pamela Frances. b 58. Bedf Coll of Educn BEd79. Wycliffe Hall Ox 88. **d** 90. NSM Ivybridge w Harford *Ex* 90-95; Par Dn Abbotskerswell 95-99; Par Dn Tudeley cum Capel w Five Oak Green *Roch* from 99. *The Vicarage, Sychem Lane, Five Oak Green, Tonbridge TN12 6TL* Tel and fax (01892) 836653 *or* tel 835548
E-mail pamela.ive@diocese-rochester.org
or pamela@tudeley.org

IVELL, Robert William. b 45. Lon Univ BSc71 Liv Univ CertEd. Ridley Hall Cam 83. **d** 85 **p** 86. C Wadsley *Sheff* 85-88; V Laughton w Throapham 88-96; V Wadworth w Loversall 96-06; rtd 06. *1 Wellbank, 20 Burrell Street, Crieff PH7 4DT* Tel (01764) 652057

IVES, Raymond Charles. b 27. St Mark & St Jo Coll Lon CertEd50. **d** 95 **p** 96. OLM Croydon St Pet *S'wark* 95-04; Perm to Offic from 04. *60 Windermere Road, West Wickham BR4 9AW* Tel (020) 8777 4956 E-mail revrayives@aol.com

IVES, Mrs Susan Ethel. b 48. EAMTC 98. **d** 01 **p** 02. NSM Moulsham St Luke *Chelmsf* 01-08; NSM Chelmsf St Andr from 08; Educn and Par Links Adv Chelmsf Deaneries from 07. *47 Long Brandocks, Writtle, Chelmsford CM1 3JL* Tel (01245) 420325 Mobile 07964-538485
E-mail sives@chelmsford.anglican.org

IVESON, Mrs Patricia Jill. b 35. Cam Univ CertEd55 K Coll Lon BD76 AKC76. **dss** 81 **d** 87 **p** 94. Wilmington *Roch* 81-87; Hon Par Dn 87-94; Hon C from 94; Chapl Dartford and Gravesham NHS Trust 87-04. *The Birches, 15 Wallis Close, Wilmington, Dartford DA2 7BE* Tel (01322) 279100 Mobile 07811-286219 E-mail pat.iveson@diocese-rochester.org

IVESON, Robert George. b 70. Oak Hill Th Coll BA01. **d** 01 **p** 02. C Cheadle All Hallows *Ches* 01-04; C-in-c Cheadle Hulme Em CD from 04. *198 Bruntwood Lane, Cheadle Hulme, Cheadle SK8 6BE* Tel 0161-485 1154 E-mail rob.iveson@btinternet.com

IVESON, Ronald Edward. b 68. Ches Coll of HE RMN92. Aston Tr Scheme 95 Oak Hill Th Coll BA00. **d** 00 **p** 01. C Lache cum Saltney *Ches* 00-03; V Bidston from 03. *The Vicarage, 6 Statham Road, Prenton CH43 7XS* Tel 0151-652 4852 *or* 653 4584
E-mail roniveson@hotmail.com

IVIN, Miss Maureen. b 34. Gilmore Ho 60. **dss** 85 **d** 87 **p** 94. Grays Thurrock *Chelmsf* 85-99; Par Dn 87-94; TV 94-99; rtd 99; Perm to Offic *Chelmsf* from 00. *40 Cleveland Drive, Westcliff-on-Sea SS0 0SU* Tel (01702) 346660

IVISON, Norman William. b 54. Hull Univ BA75 DipEd76. Trin Coll Bris. **d** 82 **p** 83. C Barrow St Mark *Carl* 82-85; Ecum Liaison Officer BBC Radio Furness 82-85; Chapl Barrow Sixth Form Coll 83-85; Dioc Broadcasting Officer *Lich* 85-91; Relig Progr Producer BBC Radio Stoke 85-91; Hon C Bucknall and Bagnall *Lich* 85-91; Asst Producer Relig Progr BBC TV Man 91-93; Producer Relig Progr BBC TV Man 93-05; Dir Tr and Events Fresh Expressions from 05; Perm to Offic *Blackb* from 98. *44 Peel Park Avenue, Clitheroe BB7 1JR* Tel and fax (01200) 442004 Mobile 07885-866317
E-mail norman.ivison@freshexpressions.org.uk

IVORSON, David. b 51. Mansf Coll Ox MA73 York Univ BPhil75 ACA80. SEITE 05. **d** 08 **p** 09. NSM E Grinstead St Swithun *Chich* from 08. *Woodhurst, Portland Road, East Grinstead RH19 4DZ* Tel (01342) 316451 Mobile 07787-155154
E-mail david@ivorson.com

IVORY, Canon Christopher James. b 54. Reading Univ BSc76. Qu Coll Birm. **d** 81 **p** 82. C Waltham Cross *St Alb* 81-84; C Is of Dogs Ch Ch and St Jo w St Luke *Lon* 84-88; V Streatham Ch Ch *S'wark* 88-03; Lambeth Adnry Ecum Officer 90-95; RD Streatham 00-03; R King's Lynn St Marg w St Nic *Nor* from 03; RD Lynn from 08; Hon Can Nor Cathl from 08. *St Margaret's Vicarage, St Margaret's Place, King's Lynn PE30 5DL* Tel (01553) 767090 E-mail vicar@stmargaretskingslynn.org.uk

IWANUSCHAK, Victor. b 51. Coll of Ripon & York St Jo MA00. NOC 97. **d** 00 **p** 01. C Pontefract All SS *Wakef* 00-03; P-in-c from 03. *All Saints' Vicarage, Grenton, South Baileygate, Pontefract WF8 2JL* Tel (01977) 695590 Mobile 07734-710254
E-mail iwanuschak@triom.net

IZOD, Mrs Wendy Janet. b 47. Sheff Univ BSc(Econ)68. SEITE 98. **d** 01 **p** 02. NSM Hever, Four Elms and Mark Beech *Roch* from 01; Chapl ATC from 01. *West Lodge, Stick Hill, Edenbridge*

TN8 5NJ Tel (01342) 850738 Fax 850077 Mobile 07703-107496
E-mail izod.calligraphy@btinternet.com
IZZARD, David Antony. b 55. Trin Coll Bris 92. **d** 94 **p** 95. C E
Bris 94-98; V Sea Mills from 98. *St Edyth's Vicarage, Avonleaze,
Bristol BS9 2HU* Tel 0117-968 1912 *or* 968 6965
E-mail clan.izzard@ukgateway.net
IZZARD, Ms Susannah Amanda. b 59. Hatf Poly BA82 Birm
Univ MEd93 Wolv Univ PGCE92. Trin Coll Bris BA86. **dss** 86
d 87 **p** 01. Birm St Martin w Bordesley St Andr 86-89; Par Dn
87-89; C Handsworth St Jas 89-91; Asst Chapl Qu Eliz Hosp
Birm 90-91; Lect Birm Univ 93-02; NSM Selly Oak St Mary
from 01; Bp's Adv for Pastoral Care from 07. *2 Hemyock Road,
Birmingham B29 4DG* Tel and fax 0121-243 3745
E-mail susannah.izzard@blueyonder.co.uk

J

JABLONSKI, Andrew Philip. Ridley Hall Cam. **d** 09. NSM
Grantham, Harrowby w Londonthorpe *Linc* from 09.
12 Lincoln Close, Grantham NG31 8RQ
JABLONSKI, Mrs Anne Judith. b 54. Girton Coll Cam BA76.
Ridley Hall Cam 07. **d** 09. C Grantham *Linc* from 09. *12 Lincoln
Close, Grantham NG31 8RQ* Tel 07759-661836 (mobile)
E-mail annejab@ntlworld.com
JACK, Alexander Richard. b 30. Leeds Univ BSc55 MSc66. Oak
Hill Th Coll 69. **d** 71 **p** 72. C Penn Fields *Lich* 71-78; P-in-c
78-83; R Barnston and Lt Dunmow *Chelmsf* 83-95; RD
Dunmow 88-95; rtd 95; Perm to Offic *Lich* from 95.
30 Bellencroft Gardens, Wolverhampton WV3 8DT Tel (01902)
763481
JACK, Canon Henry Graham. b 21. K Coll Lon AKC48 BD49.
d 49 **p** 50. C Hornsey Ch Ch *Lon* 49-50; C Steyning *Chich* 52-56;
R Warbleton 56-61; V Alfriston and Lullington 61-65; RD
Seaford 64-65; Sub-Dean St Andr Cathl Chile 65-74; Hon Can
Chile 66-74; R Trowbridge St Jas *Sarum* 74-87; Can and Preb
Sarum Cathl 83-87; rtd 87; Perm to Offic *Sarum* from 87. *285A
The Common, Holt, Trowbridge BA14 6QJ* Tel (01225) 782776
JACK, Judith Ann. b 54. Wycliffe Hall Ox 03. **d** 05 **p** 06. C Tetbury,
Beverston and Long Newnton *Glouc* from 05. *The Rectory,
Shipton Moyne, Tetbury GL8 8PW* Tel (01666) 880132
E-mail jackpot@waitrose.com
JACK, Paul. b 65. QUB BSc92 Univ Coll Galway MSc94 TCD
BTh99. CITC 96. **d** 99 **p** 00. C Jordanstown *Conn* 99-01; C
Seagoe *D & D* 01-07; I Belfast St Simon w St Phil *Conn* from 07;
Bp's Dom Chapl from 08. *106 Upper Lisburn Road, Belfast
BT10 0BB* Tel (028) 9061 7562
E-mail paul@jack11.wanadoo.co.uk
JACK, Philip Andrew. b 76. Nottm Univ BA98. Oak Hill Th Coll
BA08. **d** 08 **p** 09. C Ox St Ebbe w H Trin and St Pet from 08.
81 Marlborough Road, Oxford OX1 4LX Tel 07972-078148
(mobile) E-mail phil.a.jack@gmail.com
JACKLIN, John Frederick. b 30. Oak Hill Th Coll 72. **d** 72 **p** 72.
Chile 72-75; C Roxeth Ch Ch *Lon* 75-78; V Selston *S'well* 78-95;
rtd 95; Perm to Offic *Derby* from 95. *5 Rose Avenue, Borrowash,
Derby DE7 3GA* Tel (01332) 669670
JACKS, David. b 59. Nottm Univ BTh87 Birm Univ MA95
PhD08. Linc Th Coll 84. **d** 87 **p** 88. C Oakham, Hambleton,
Egleton, Braunston and Brooke *Pet* 87-90; V Weedon Bec w
Everdon 90-98; P-in-c Dodford 96-98; V Weedon Bec w Everdon
and Dodford 98-01; V Llandrillo-yn-Rhos *St As* from 01.
Llandrillo Vicarage, 36 Llandudno Road, Colwyn Bay LL28 4UD
Tel (01492) 548878 Mobile 07850-597891
E-mail david@llandrillo.fsbusiness.co.uk
JACKSON, Alan. b 44. Newc Univ BA67 DipEd68 MEd79.
NEOC 79. **d** 81 **p** 82. NSM Jesmond H Trin *Newc* 81-82; Chapl
Bp Wand Sch Sunbury-on-Thames 82-89; V Hanworth St Rich
Lon from 89. *St Richard's Vicarage, 35 Forge Lane, Feltham
TW13 6UN* Tel (020) 8898 0241
E-mail alan.jackson@london.anglican.org
JACKSON, Canon Arthur Malcolm. b 31. TCD BA54 MA60.
TCD Div Sch Div Test 54. **d** 54 **p** 55. C Templecorran Union
Conn 54-57; C Dublin Santry Union *D & G* 57-58; Bp's V and
Registrar *C & O* 58-61; I Monasterevan *M & K* 61-68; I
Narraghmore w Fontstown and Timolin *D & G* 68-88; I
Narraghmore and Timolin w Castledermot etc 88-91; I Killanne
w Killegney, Rossdroit and Templeshanbo *C & O* 91-00; Preb
Ferns Cathl 93-96; Bp's Dom Chapl *C & O* 96-98; Chan Ferns Cathl
96-98; Prec Ferns Cathl 98-00; rtd 00. *2 Church Road, Bunclody,
Enniscorthy, Co Wexford, Republic of Ireland* Tel (00353) (53)
937 5066

JACKSON, Barry. b 30. St Jo Coll Cam BA53 DipEd54 MA57.
Westcott Ho Cam 63. **d** 65 **p** 66. C Stockport St Geo 65-68;
C Bridgwater St Mary, Chilton Trinity and Durleigh *B & W*
68-70; P-in-c Thurloxton 70-75; Chapl Wycliffe Coll Glos 75-88;
V Heathfield *Chich* 88-97; rtd 97; Perm to Offic *Chich* from 98.
11 Gleneigh Walk, Robertsbridge TN32 5DQ Tel (01580)
880067
JACKSON, Barry James. b 65. Sheff Univ BEng87. St Jo Coll
Nottm 05. **d** 07 **p** 08. C Leamington Priors St Mary *Cov* from 07.
*The Vicarage, 7 Church End, Radford Semele, Leamington Spa
CV31 1TA* Tel (01926) 470459
E-mail barry.jackson@talktalk.net
JACKSON, The Very Revd Brandon Donald. b 34. Liv Univ
LLB56 Bradf Univ Hon DLitt90. Wycliffe Hall Ox. **d** 58 **p** 59. C
New Malden and Coombe *S'wark* 58-61; C Leeds St Geo *Ripon*
61-65; V Shipley St Pet *Bradf* 65-77; Relig Adv Yorkshire TV
69-79; Provost Bradf 77-89; Dean Linc 89-97; rtd 97; Perm to
Offic *Ripon* from 98. *1 Kingston Way, Market Harborough
LE16 7XB* Tel (01858) 462425 E-mail brandon.j@talktalk.net
JACKSON, Christopher John Wilson. b 45. St Pet Coll Ox BA67
MA87. Ridley Hall Cam 69. **d** 72 **p** 73. C Putney St Marg *S'wark*
72-76; C Battersea St Pet and St Paul 76-79; TV Preston St Jo
Blackb 79-87; P-in-c Sandal St Cath *Wakef* 87-90; V Shenley
Green *Birm* 90-01; AD Kings Norton 95-99; P-in-c Chesterfield
H Trin and Ch Ch *Derby* from 01. *31 Newbold Road, Chesterfield
S41 7PG* Tel (01246) 273508 E-mail jacks31@btinternet.com
JACKSON, Miss Cynthia. b 42. S'wark Ord Course 93. **d** 96 **p** 97.
NSM Wimbledon *S'wark* from 96. *39 Panmuir Road, London
SW20 0PZ* Tel (020) 8947 5940 *or* 7361 2396
JACKSON, Canon David. b 33. Leeds Univ BA60. Coll of Resurr
Mirfield 60. **d** 62 **p** 63. C Lewisham St Steph *S'wark* 62-65; P-in-c
New Charlton H Trin 65-69; C Charlton St Luke w St Paul
69-72; Sen Tutor Coll of the Resurr Mirfield 72-75; R Clapham
H Trin 75-78; P-in-c Clapham St Pet 76-78; TR Clapham Old
Town 78-84; Hon Can S'wark Cathl 80-96; V Battersea St Mary-
le-Park 84-89; V Surbiton St Andr and St Mark 89-96; rtd 96;
Chapl St Mich Convent Ham 96-03. *18 Tower Lane, Bearsted,
Maidstone ME14 4JJ* Tel (01622) 730041
JACKSON, David. b 48. Open Univ BA85. St Deiniol's Hawarden
91. **d** 91 **p** 92. C Scotforth *Blackb* 91-95; C Banbury *Ox* 95-96;
TV 96-98; V Banbury St Hugh 98-07; V Banbury St Fran from
07; Chapl Ox Radcliffe Hosps NHS Trust 95-00. *St Francis'
House, Highlands, Banbury OX16 7FA* Tel (01295) 275449
E-mail vicardavyjax@tiscali.co.uk
JACKSON, David Hilton. b 62. Stanford Univ BA84 Princeton
Th Sem MDiv90 Ox Univ MSt94. Wycliffe Hall Ox 94. **d** 95
p 96. C Ox St Andr 95-98; TV Thame 98-00; USA from 00;
Assoc R and Chapl Upland St Mark 01-03; Sen Assoc for Par
Life Pasadena All SS from 03. *614 Occidental Drive, Claremont
CA 91711, USA* E-mail david.jackson@cgu.edu
JACKSON, David Reginald Estcourt. b 25. OBE. Qu Coll Cam
BA45 MA49. St Jo Coll Dur 80. **d** 81 **p** 82. Hon C Douglas
Blackb 81-82; C 82-87; rtd 90. *64 The Common, Parbold, Wigan
WN8 7EA* Tel (01257) 462671
JACKSON, David Robert. b 51. Lon Univ BDS. Linc Th Coll 81.
d 83 **p** 84. C Hatcham St Cath *S'wark* 83-87; V Sydenham St
Bart 87-93; Perm to Offic *Lon* 03-05; Hon C St Martin-in-the-
Fields from 05. *168 Manor Park, London SE13 5RH* Tel (020)
8297 9132 E-mail djsaab@aol.com
JACKSON, David William. b 53. Goldsmiths' Coll Lon BA75
PGCE76. Cranmer Hall Dur 90. **d** 92 **p** 93. C Desborough *Pet*
92-95; C Eastham *Ches* 95-98; P-in-c Taverham w Ringland *Nor*
98-05; R Taverham 05-06; R Redenhall, Harleston, Wortwell and
Needham from 06. *The Rectory, 10 Swan Lane, Harleston
IP20 9AN* Tel (01379) 852068 E-mail redrec@tiscali.co.uk
JACKSON, Canon Derek. b 26. Ex Coll Ox BA51 MA55.
Westcott Ho Cam 51. **d** 53 **p** 54. C Radcliffe-on-Trent *S'well*
53-56; C Frome St Jo *B & W* 56-57; V Eaton Socon *St Alb* 57-63;
V Boxmoor St Jo 63-74; V Bishop's Stortford St Mich 74-85;
Hon Can St Alb 82-85; Bermuda 85-89; P-in-c Cerne Abbas w
Godmanstone and Minterne Magna *Sarum* 89-95; rtd 95; Chapl
Menorca *Eur* 95-96; Perm to Offic *St Alb* from 96 and *Chelmsf*
from 97. *88 Stansted Road, Bishop's Stortford CM23 2DZ* Tel
(01279) 652664
JACKSON, Canon Derek Reginald. b 49. K Coll Lon BD72
AKC72. **d** 73 **p** 74. C Westhoughton *Man* 73-75; C Kendal H
Trin *Carl* 75-78; V Pennington w Lindal and Marton 78-83;
Warden of Readers 82-92; V Kendal St Geo 83-94; Hon Can
Carl Cathl 89-00; V Applethwaite 94-96; P-in-c Troutbeck 94-96;
V Windermere St Mary and Troutbeck 96-00; RD Windermere
98-00; Can Res Bradf Cathl 00-03; P-in-c Bingley All SS from 03;
RD Airedale from 05. *Woodlands, 26 Falcon Road, Bingley
BD16 4DW* Tel (01274) 563113
E-mail derekjackson2901@hotmail.com
JACKSON, Doreen May. b 35. SRN. S Dios Minl Tr Scheme. **d** 88
p 94. NSM Fareham H Trin *Portsm* 88-05; rtd 05. *134 Oak Road,
Fareham PO15 5HR* Tel (01329) 841429
JACKSON, Mrs Elizabeth Mary. b 41. Man Univ BA67 Leeds
Univ MA01. Ox Min Course 90. **d** 92 **p** 94. Chapl Asst Reading

Hosps 86-95; NSM Reading St Mary w St Laur *Ox* 92-94; Chapl R Berks and Battle Hosps NHS Trust 95-02; NSM Reading Deanery *Ox* 02-07. *The Hayloft, 2 Hall Court, Tallentire, Cockermouth CA13 0PU* Tel (01900) 825799
E-mail mjack2bl@aol.com

JACKSON, The Ven Frances Anne (Peggy). b 51. Somerville Coll Ox BA72 MA76 ACA76 FCA81. Ripon Coll Cuddesdon 85. **d** 87 **p** 94. C Ilkeston St Mary *Derby* 87-90; TM Hemel Hempstead *St Alb* 90-94; TV 94-98; TR Mortlake w E Sheen *S'wark* 98-09; RD Richmond and Barnes 00-05; Hon Can S'wark Cathl 03-09; Dean of Women's Min 04-09; Adn Llan from 09; P-in-c Penmark w Llancarfan w Llantrithyd from 09. *The Rectory, Llancarfan, Barry CF62 3AJ* Tel (01446) 750053 Fax 08701-323319
E-mail archdeacon.llandaff@churchinwales.org.uk

JACKSON, Miss Freda. b 41. Bp Otter Coll TCert61. **d** 92 **p** 94. OLM Middleton *Man* 92-94; OLM Middleton w Thornham from 94. *783 Manchester Old Road, Middleton, Manchester M24 4RE* Tel 0161-653 5876

JACKSON, Ms Gillian Rosemary. b 52. Newc Univ BA75 PGCE76 Aber Univ MLitt80 Nottm Univ MA04 AFBPsS. EMMTC 01. **d** 04 **p** 05. NSM Bosworth and Sheepy Gp *Leic* from 04. *Keeper's Cottage, Help out Mill, Shackerstone, Nuneaton CV13 0BT* Tel (01530) 264122 *or* 0116-248 7424
E-mail gill.jackson@leccofe.org

JACKSON, Harry Francis. b 30. K Coll Lon BD61 AKC61 Ex Univ BTh05 FBCO80. Sarum Th Coll 61. **d** 62 **p** 62. Bermuda 62-65; C Cobham *Guildf* 65-69; R Ash 69-96; Chapl RAF Farnborough 80-96; rtd 96; P-in-c Mawnan *Truro* 96-01; Perm to Offic from 02. *Rosnython, Treliever Road, Mabe Burnthouse, Penryn TR10 9EX* Tel (01326) 372532
E-mail harry.jackson4@btinternet.com

JACKSON, Hilary Walton. b 17. St Chad's Coll Dur BA40 MA48. **d** 46 **p** 47. C Selby Abbey *York* 46-49; C Middlesbrough All SS 49-51; V Thornley *Dur* 51-56; V Beamish 56-66; V Heighington 66-82; rtd 82. *127 Bates Avenue, Darlington DL3 0UE* Tel (01325) 243794
E-mail hilary.jackson@durham.anglican.org

JACKSON, Ian. b 53. Jes Coll Ox BA75. Linc Th Coll 76. **d** 78 **p** 79. C Holbeach *Linc* 78-82; V Newsome *Wakef* 82-85; V Newsome and Armitage Bridge 85-03; TR Em TM 03-04; P-in-c Corfe Castle, Church Knowle, Kimmeridge etc *Sarum* from 04. *The Rectory, East Street, Corfe Castle, Wareham BH20 5EE* Tel (01929) 480257

JACKSON, Mrs Isobel Margaret. b 69. Uganda Chr Univ BD04. **d** 04. CMS Uganda 04-05; C Lismore w Cappoquin, Kilwatermoy, Dungarvan etc *C & O* from 05. *The Rectory, Church Lane, Stradbally, Co Waterford, Republic of Ireland* Tel (00353) (51) 293129 Mobile 86-743 5424
E-mail isobel@nijackson.com *or* curate@lismore.anglican.org

JACKSON, Mrs Janet Lesley. b 45. CQSW78. NEOC 93. **d** 96 **p** 97. NSM Whorlton *Newc* 96-98; Chapl St Oswald's Hospice Newc 98-07. *1 St Andrews Road, Hexham NE46 2EY* Tel (01434) 602929

JACKSON, Mrs Joan. b 44. Bolton Coll of Educn CertEd71 Lanc Univ MA98. CBDTI 95. **d** 98 **p** 99. NSM Staveley, Ings and Kentmere *Carl* 98-00; Chapl Furness Hosps NHS Trust 98-00; Asst Chapl Bradf Hosps NHS Trust 00-04; NSM Bingley H Trin *Bradf* 03-07; Perm to Offic from 07. *Woodlands, 26 Falcon Road, Bingley BD16 4DW* Tel (01274) 563113

JACKSON, John Edward. b 29. K Coll Lon BD57 AKC57. St Boniface Warminster 57. **d** 58 **p** 59. C Crofton Park St Hilda w St Cypr *S'wark* 58-61; V Bremhill w Foxham *Sarum* 61-69; V Netheravon w Fittleton 69-73; V Netheravon w Fittleton and Enford 73-85; OCF 69-85; V Salisbury St Mark *Sarum* 85-92; P-in-c Bryngwyn and Newchurch and Llanbedr etc *S & B* 92-96; rtd 96. *Llwyndyrys Care Home, Llechryd, Cardigan SA43 2QP* Tel (01239) 682263

JACKSON, Miss Kathryn Dianne. b 64. Leeds Univ BA87 MA01. St Steph Ho Ox 87. **d** 90 **p** 94. Par Dn Headingley *Ripon* 90-94; C Hawksworth Wood 94-00; P-in-c Scarborough St Columba *York* from 00; Chapl St Cath Hospice Scarborough from 00. *160 Dean Road, Scarborough YO12 7JH* Tel (01723) 375070 E-mail kathryn.jackson@st-catherineshospice.org.uk

JACKSON, Kenneth William. b 58. NEOC 01. **d** 04 **p** 05. C Guisborough *York* 04-08; V Kirkleatham from 08. *The Vicarage, 130 Mersey Road, Redcar TS10 4DF* Tel (01642) 758018
E-mail mal_jacko@hotmail.com

JACKSON, Miss Lisa Helen. b 79. Reading Univ BA(Ed)01 Cam Univ BA06. Ridley Hall Cam 04. **d** 07 **p** 08. C Patcham *Chich* from 07. *78A Mackie Avenue, Brighton BN1 8RB* Tel (01273) 502866 Mobile 07989-761575 E-mail lisa@joyful.co.uk

JACKSON, Malcolm. b 58. NEOC 01. **d** 04 **p** 05. C Guisborough *York* 04-08; V Kirkleatham from 08. *The Vicarage, 130 Mersey Road, Redcar TS10 4DF* Tel (01642) 758018
E-mail mal_jacko@hotmail.com

JACKSON, Mrs Margaret Elizabeth. b 47. Lon Univ BSc68 MSc95 Univ of Wales (Lamp) MTh05 FCIPD91. S'wark Ord Course 80. **dss** 83 **d** 92 **p** 94. Surbiton Hill Ch Ch *S'wark* 83-84;

Saffron Walden w Wendens Ambo and Littlebury *Chelmsf* 84-85; Dulwich St Barn *S'wark* 86-97; Hon C 92-97; Personal Asst to Bp S'wark 92-94; Selection Sec Min Division 96-00 and from 03; NSM Churt *Guildf* 98-00; NSM The Bourne and Tilford from 00; Convenor STETS 00-02; Dioc Dir of Ords S'wark 05-06. *67 Parkhurst Fields, Churt, Farnham GU10 2PQ* Tel (01428) 714411 Fax 714426
E-mail revjackson@btinternet.com

JACKSON, Mrs Margaret Elizabeth. b 47. Mon Dioc Tr Scheme. **d** 87 **p** 94. C Chepstow *Mon* 87-90; C Exhall *Cov* 90-92; C Leamington Priors All SS 92-96; R Hulme Ascension *Man* 96-99; V Alstonfield, Butterton, Ilam etc *Lich* 99-08; RD Alstonfield 00-03; R Stonehaven *Bre* from 08; Dioc Interfaith from 08. *3 Ramsay Road, Stonehaven AB39 2HJ* Tel (01569) 764264 E-mail maggie.jackson@virgin.net

JACKSON, Margaret Jane. b 50. RGN72. S'wark Ord Course 89. **d** 92 **p** 94. Par Dn Hatcham St Cath *S'wark* 92-94; C 94-98; V Mottingham St Edw from 98. *St Edward's Vicarage, St Keverne Road, London SE9 4AQ* Tel (020) 8857 6278
E-mail margaretjjackson@compuserve.com

JACKSON, Ms Marie Ann. b 45. Nottm Univ BSc66. SAOMC 98. **d** 98 **p** 99. OLM High Wycombe *Ox* from 98. *19 New Road, Sands, High Wycombe HP12 4LH* Tel (01494) 530728

JACKSON, Mark Harding. b 51. Open Univ BA87. Sarum & Wells Th Coll 76. **d** 79 **p** 80. C Hobs Moat *Birm* 79-83; Chapl RN from 83. *Royal Naval Chaplaincy Service, Mail Point 1-2, Leach Building, Whale Island, Portsmouth PO2 8BY* Tel (023) 9262 5055 Fax 9262 5134

JACKSON, Martin. b 56. Clare Coll Cam BA77 MA81 St Jo Coll Dur BA80 MA97. Cranmer Hall Dur. **d** 81 **p** 82. C Houghton le Spring *Dur* 81-84; C Bishopwearmouth St Mich w St Hilda 84-86; TV Winlaton 86; V High Spen and Rowlands Gill 86-94; P-in-c Benfieldside 94-97; V from 97; AD Lanchester 00-06. *St Cuthbert's Vicarage, Church Bank, Consett DH8 0NW* Tel (01207) 503019 E-mail martin.jackson@durham.anglican.org

JACKSON, Matthew Christopher. b 75. Univ of Wales (Abth) BD96 MTh98. Ripon Coll Cuddesdon. **d** 01 **p** 02. C King's Lynn St Marg w St Nic *Nor* 01-05; V Pembury *Roch* from 05. *The Vicarage, 4 Hastings Road, Pembury, Tunbridge Wells TN2 4PD* Tel and fax (01892) 824761
E-mail matthew@pemburychurch.net

JACKSON, Mrs Melanie Jane Susann. b 60. UWE BA83 Leic Univ MA94. SWMTC 97. **d** 00 **p** 01. C Ottery St Mary, Alfington, W Hill, Tipton etc *Ex* 00-04; Perm to Offic 04-08; NSM Linc St Jo from 08. *22 Kennington Close, Dunholme, Lincoln LN2 3QN* Tel (01673) 866129
E-mail melaniejackson.amia@btinternet.com

✠**JACKSON, The Rt Revd Michael Geoffrey St Aubyn.** b 56. TCD BA79 MA82 St Jo Coll Cam BA81 MA85 PhD86 Ch Ch Ox MA89 DPhil89. CITC 86. **d** 86 **p** 87 **c** 02. C Dublin Zion Ch *D & G* 86-89; Chapl Ch Ch Ox 89-97; Student 93-97; Dean Cork C, C & R 97-02; I Cork St Fin Barre's Union 97-02; Chapl and Asst Lect Univ Coll Cork 98-02; Chapl Cork Inst of Tech 98-02; Bp Clogh from 02. *The See House, Ballagh Road, Fivemiletown BT75 0QP* Tel and fax (028) 8952 2475
E-mail bishop@clogher.anglican.org

JACKSON, Michael Ian. b 51. Southn Univ BA73. STETS 00. **d** 03 **p** 04. Dir St Jo Win Charity from 87; NSM Twyford and Owslebury and Morestead etc *Win* from 03. *Hill Farm Lodge, Morestead, Winchester SO21 1LZ* Tel (01962) 777277 *or* 854226
E-mail mijackson@ukgateway.net

JACKSON, Canon Michael James. b 44. Liv Univ BEng65 Newc Univ PhD84 CEng69 MICE69. NEOC 82. **d** 84 **p** 85. C Houghton le Spring *Dur* 84-87; V Millfield St Mark 87-95; V Ponteland *Newc* 95-07; AD Newc W 03-07; Hon Can Newc Cathl 06-07; rtd 07. *1 St Andrews Road, Hexham NE46 2EY* Tel (01434) 602929

JACKSON, Michael Richard. b 31. Selw Coll Cam BA54 MA58. Westcott Ho Cam 54. **d** 56 **p** 57. C Gosforth All SS *Newc* 56-62; R Dinnington *Sheff* 62-76; V Swinton 76-97; rtd 97; Perm to Offic *Sheff* from 97. *10 Elmhirst Drive, Rotherham S65 3ED* Tel (01709) 531065

JACKSON, Nicholas David. b 64. Wadh Coll Ox MA75 Bris Univ PGCE76. Wycliffe Hall Ox 06. **d** 08 **p** 09. C Branksome Park All SS *Sarum* from 08. *30 Canford Cliffs Road, Poole BH13 7AA* Tel (01202) 722967 Mobile 07816 553927
E-mail nick@thejacksons.freeserve.co.uk

JACKSON, Norman. b 20. CEng MIMechE53. S'wark Ord Course 74. **d** 77 **p** 78. NSM Erith Ch Ch *Roch* 77-82; NSM Bishopstoke *Win* 82-95; rtd 95; Perm to Offic *Win* 95-04. *7 Otter Close, Eastleigh SO50 8NF* Tel (023) 8069 5045

JACKSON, Paul Andrew. b 65. NEOC 05. **d** 08 **p** 09. NSM Haxby and Wigginton *York* from 08. *44 Windmill Way, Haxby, York YO32 3NJ* Tel (01904) 763921 E-mail pjacko99@aol.com

JACKSON, Peggy. *See* JACKSON, The Ven Frances Anne

JACKSON, Peter. *See* JACKSON, Thomas Peter

JACKSON, Peter Charles. b 71. Univ of Northumbria at Newc BA95. Oak Hill Th Coll BA01. **d** 02 **p** 03. C Lowestoft Ch Ch

Nor 02-07; P-in-c Kendray *Sheff* from 07. *St Andrew's Vicarage, 84 Hunningley Lane, Barnsley S70 3DT* Tel (01226) 205826 E-mail jacko.pete@googlemail.com

JACKSON, Peter Jonathan Edward. b 53. St Pet Coll Ox BA74 MA78 PGCE78. St Steph Ho Ox 79. **d** 79 **p** 80. Lect Westmr Coll Ox 79-80; Hon C Ox St Mich w St Martin and All SS 79-80; C Malvern Link w Cowleigh *Worc* 79-82; Chapl Aldenham Sch Herts 82-89; Chapl and Hd RE Harrow Sch 89-01; Lect K Coll Lon 92-99; Dir Chr Educn and Assoc R Washington St Patr USA 01-03; V Southgate Ch Ch *Lon* from 03. *The Vicarage, 1 The Green, London N14 7EG* Tel (020) 8882 0917 *or* 8886 0384 E mail pcter.jackson@london.anglican.org

JACKSON, Peter Lewis. b 34. Bps' Coll Cheshunt 63. **d** 66 **p** 67. C Stockingford *Cov* 66-67; C Kenilworth St Nic 67-72; P-in-c Napton on the Hill 72-75; V 75-89; V Lower Shuckburgh 75-89; R Napton-on-the-Hill, Lower Shuckburgh etc 89-99; rtd 99; Perm to Offic *Cov* from 99. *66 Arthur Street, Kenilworth CV8 2HE* Tel (01926) 864234

JACKSON, Philip Michael. b 74. Chelt & Glouc Coll of HE BA95 Brunel Univ PGCE97. Trin Coll Bris BA05. **d** 06 **p** 07. C W Kilburn St Luke w St Simon and St Jude *Lon* 06-09; C Reigate St Mary *S'wark* from 09. *63 Chart Lane, Reigate RH2 7EA* Tel 07545-054022 (mobile) E-mail phil.jackson74@googlemail.com

JACKSON (née PRICE), Mrs Rachel Anne. b 57. **d** 03 **p** 04. OLM Barnham Broom and Upper Yare *Nor* from 03. *Red Hall, Red Hall Lane, Southburgh, Thetford IP25 7TG* Tel (01362) 821032 Fax 820145 E-mail revrachel@edwardjacksonltd.com

JACKSON, Richard Charles. b 61. Ch Ch Ox BA83 Cranfield Inst of Tech MSc85. Trin Coll Bris 92. **d** 94 **p** 95. C Lindfield *Chich* 94-98; V Rudgwick from 98; RD Horsham from 05. *The Vicarage, Cox Green Close, Rudgwick, Horsham RH12 3DD* Tel (01403) 822127 E-mail rjac187233@aol.com

JACKSON, Richard Hugh. b 44. St Jo Coll York CertEd66 UEA MA84. **d** 98 **p** 99. OLM Stalham and E Ruston w Brunstead *Nor* 98-00; OLM Stalham, E Ruston, Brunstead, Sutton and Ingham from 00. *5 Rivermead, Stalham, Norwich NR12 9PH* Tel (01692) 581389 E-mail richard.jackson@intamail.com

JACKSON, Robert. b 69. Nottm Univ BA01. St Jo Coll Nottm 98. **d** 01 **p** 02. C Altham w Clayton le Moors *Blackb* 01-03; C Blackb St Gabr 03-05; TV Westhoughton and Wingates *Man* from 05. *The Vicarage, 91 Chorley Road, Westhoughton, Bolton BL5 3PG* Tel (01942) 812119 Mobile 07703-824849 E-mail jacksonsrt@aol.com

JACKSON, Robert Brandon. b 61. Lanchester Poly Cov BA86 Ox Univ BA88 MA95. Wycliffe Hall Ox 86. **d** 89 **p** 90. C Bromley Common St Aug *Roch* 89-92; P-in-c Stowe *Ox* 92-97; Asst Chapl Stowe Sch 92-97; Chapl Ld Wandsworth Coll Basingstoke 97-02; Chapl Stowe Sch from 02. *Stowe School, Buckingham MK18 5EH* Tel (01280) 818000 *or* 818144 E-mail rjackson@stowe.co.uk

JACKSON, Robert Fielden. b 35. St D Coll Lamp BA57. Sarum Th Coll 57. **d** 59 **p** 60. C Altham w Clayton le Moors *Blackb* 59-62; C Lytham St Cuth 62-64; V Skerton St Chad 64-69; V Preesall 69-90; RD Garstang 85-89; V Wray w Tatham and Tatham Fells 90-00; rtd 00; Perm to Offic *Blackb* from 01. *8 Squirrel's Chase, Lostock Hall, Preston PR5 5NE* Tel (01772) 338756

JACKSON, The Ven Robert William. b 49. K Coll Cam MA73 Man Univ MA. St Jo Coll Nottm 78. **d** 81 **p** 82. C Fulwood *Sheff* 81-84; V Grenoside and Chapl Grenoside Hosp 84 92; V Scarborough St Mary w Ch Ch and H Apostles *York* 92-01; Springboard Missr 01-04; Adn Walsall *Lich* from 04. *9 Glebe Park, Eyam, Sheffield S32 5RH* Tel (01433) 631212 E-mail archbob@gmail.com

JACKSON, Roger. b 57. Chich Th Coll 85. **d** 88 **p** 89. C Hale *Guildf* 88-92; V Barton w Peel Green *Man* 92-95; P-in-c Long Crendon w Chearsley and Nether Winchendon *Ox* 95-00; V 00-08; V Clevedon St Jo *B & W* from 08. *St John's Vicarage, 1 St John's Road, Clevedon BS21 7TG* Tel (01275) 341830

JACKSON, Canon Roger Brumby. b 31. Dur Univ BSc53 DipEd54. Ridley Hall Cam 57. **d** 59 **p** 60. C Rowner *Portsm* 59-61; C Drypool St Columba w St Andr and St Pet *York* 61-64; Asst Chapl HM Pris Hull 61-64; V Plumstead St Jas w St Jo *S'wark* 65-68; P-in-c Plumstead St Paul 65-68; V Plumstead St Jo w St Jas and St Paul 68-74; Sub-Dean Woolwich 71-74; Chapl Hulton Hosp Bolton 74-94; Chapl Bolton Hosp NHS Trust 94-01; V Deane *Man* 74-80; TR 80-01; AD Deane 80-85; Hon Can Man Cathl 90-01; rtd 01; Perm to Offic *Man* from 01. *17 Bentworth Close, Westhoughton, Bolton BL5 2GN* Tel (01942) 813209

JACKSON, Preb Roland Francis. b 20. Univ of Wales (Lamp) BA42. St Mich Coll Llan 42. **d** 44 **p** 45. C Risca *Mon* 44-49; C Chepstow St Arvan's w Penterry 49-54; R Haughton *Lich* 54-61; V Stafford St Paul Forebridge 61-72, RD Eccleshall 72-82; Chapl HM Pris Drake Hall 75-85; V Eccleshall *Lich* 72-85; Preb Lich Cathl 82-85; rtd 85; Perm to Offic *Lich* from 85. *Treginnis, 29 Meadow Drive, Haughton, Stafford ST18 9HQ* Tel (01785) 780571

JACKSON, Canon Ronald William. b 37. Lon Univ MA71 ALCD. **d** 69 **p** 70. C Crofton *Portsm* 69-74; V Wolverhampton St Matt *Lich* 74-85; V Bloxwich 85-89; C Tamworth 89-92; Bp's Officer for Par Miss and Development *Bradf* 92-98; Hon Can Bradf Cathl 94-98; rtd 98; Perm to Offic *Bradf* from 98. *94 Primrose Lane, Bingley BD16 4QP* Tel and fax (01274) 510642 E-mail rw.jackson@btinternet.com

JACKSON, Ruth Ellen. b 69. Dub City Univ BBS91. CITC BTh02. **d** 02 **p** 03. C Portadown St Mark *Arm* 02-05; C Carrigrohane Union *C, C & R* from 05. *24 Ard Dara View, Station Road, Blarney, Co Cork, Republic of Ireland* Tel (00353) (21) 438 3103 E-mail rjblarney@eircom.net

JACKSON, Ruth Victoria. *See* HAKE, Mrs Ruth Victoria

JACKSON (née STAFF), Mrs Susan. b 59. Leeds Univ BA82. Ridley Hall Cam 88. **d** 90 **p** 94. Par Dn Mickleover All SS *Derby* 90-93; Par Dn Chatham St Wm *Roch* 93-94; C 94-97; TV Walton Milton Keynes *Ox* from 97. *The Rectory, London Road, Broughton, Milton Keynes MK10 9AA* Tel (01908) 667846

JACKSON, Thomas Peter. b 27. Univ of Wales (Lamp) BA50. St Mich Coll Llan 50. **d** 52 **p** 53. C Swansea St Mary and H Trin *S & B* 52-58; Area Sec (S Midl and S Wales) UMCA 58-60; V Glouc St Steph 60-73; R Upton St Leonards 73-92; RD Glouc N 82-91; rtd 92; Perm to Offic *Glouc* from 92. *44 Grebe Close, Gloucester GL4 9XL* Tel (01452) 533769

JACKSON, Wendy Pamela. b 45. Th Ext Educn Coll 99. **d** 00 **p** 02. Community P Woodlands S Africa 02-03; C Crediton, Shobrooke and Sandford etc *Ex* 03-05; P-in-c Southway from 05; C Tamerton Foliot from 06. *The Vicarage, 70 Inchkeith Road, Plymouth PL6 6EJ* Tel (01752) 782256 E-mail wendy@davwen.freeserve.co.uk

JACKSON, William Stafford. b 48. Sunderland Poly DCYW83 Sunderland Univ CertEd96. Linc Th Coll 86. **d** 89 **p** 90. C Heworth St Mary *Dur* 89-91; C Tudhoe Grange 91-92; Churches' Regional Commn in the NE 97-01; NSM Dipton and Leadgate 03-08; V Burnham *Ox* from 08. *The Rectory, The Precincts, Burnham, Slough SL1 7HU* Tel (01628) 559992 Mobile 07793-750652 E-mail jackson.bill39@yahoo.co.uk

JACKSON, Canon William Stanley Peter. b 39. St Mich Coll Llan 63. **d** 66 **p** 67. C Llandrindod w Cefnllys *S & B* 66-69; C Gowerton w Waunarlwydd 69-73; V Cricadarn w Gwenddwr and Alltmawr 73-79; R Llanfeugan w Llanthetty etc 79-04; Dioc GFS Chapl 84-92; Can Res Brecon Cathl 90-04; Prec 98-99; Treas 99-00; Chan 00-04; Dioc Communications Officer 92-94; RD Crickhowell 98-02; rtd 04. *9 St Peter's Avenue, Fforestfach, Swansea SA5 5BX* Tel (01792) 541229 E-mail canonjacko@aol.com

JACKSON-STEVENS, Preb Nigel. b 42. St Steph Ho Ox. **d** 68 **p** 69. C Babbacombe *Ex* 68-73; V Swimbridge 73-75; P-in-c Buckland 73-75; V Swimbridge and W Buckland 75-84; P-in-c Mortehoe 84-85; P-in-c Ilfracombe, Lee, Woolacombe, Bittadon and Bittadon 84-85; TR Ilfracombe, Lee, Woolacombe, Bittadon etc 85-08; RD Barnstaple 93-97; Preb Ex Cathl 95-08; rtd 08. *Rose Cottage, Eastacombe, Barnstaple EX31 3NT* Tel (01271) 325283

JACOB, Mrs Amelia Stanley. b 52. Punjab Univ BA73. Oak Hill Th Coll. **d** 90 **p** 94. NSM Asian Chr Congregation All SS Tufnell Park *Lon* 90-92; NSM Alperton from 92. *62 Clifford Road, Wembley HA0 1AE* Tel (020) 8429 8633 *or* 8902 4592 E-mail stjames2000@breathemail.net

JACOB, John Lionel Andrew. b 26. Selw Coll Cam BA50 MA54 Westcott Ho Cam 50. **d** 52 **p** 53. C Brightside St Thos *Sheff* 52-55; C Maltby 55-58; V Doncaster Intake 58-67; V Sheff St Aid w St Luke 67-75; TR Sheff Manor 75-82; R Waddington *Linc* 82-91; rtd 91; Perm to Offic *Linc* 91-00. *Flat 21, Manormead, Tilford Road, Hindhead GU26 6RA* Tel (01428) 602559

JACOB, Canon Joseph. b 38. CITC 65. **d** 68 **p** 69. C Belfast St Aid *Conn* 68-70; Bp's Dom Chapl 70-71; I Kilscoran *C & O* 71-80; I Geashill *M & K* 80-83; Asst Warden Ch's Min of Healing 83-86; Gen Sec (Ireland) CMJ 87-91; I Ardamine, Kilnamanagh w Monamolin *C & O* 91-98; Preb Ferns Cathl 96-98; rtd 98. *Crannaulin, Clonmullen, Bunclody, Co Wexford, Republic of Ireland* Tel (00353) (53) 937 7532

JACOB, Neville Peter. b 60. Kent Univ BA82 Leeds Metrop Univ PGCE86. Ripon Coll Cuddesdon 94. **d** 96 **p** 97. C Market Harborough *Leic* 96-97; C Market Harborough Transfiguration 96-97; C Market Harborough and The Transfiguration etc 97-99; Chapl Miss to Seafarers 99-03; P-in-c Copythorne *Win* from 03; Chapl Ibex from 03. *The Vicarage, Pine Ridge, Romsey Road, Cadnam, Southampton SO40 2NN* Tel and fax (023) 8081 4769 E-mail raveknave@tinyworld.co.uk

JACOB, The Ven William Mungo. b 44. Hull Univ LLB66 Linacre Coll Ox BA69 MA73 Ex Univ PhD. St Steph Ho Ox 70. **d** 70 **p** 71. C Wymondham *Nor* 70-73; Asst Chapl Ex Univ 73-75; Dir Past Studies Sarum & Wells Th Coll 75-80; Vice-Prin 77-80; Selection Sec and Sec Cttee for Th Educn ACCM 80-86; Warden Linc Th Coll 85-96; Can and Preb Linc Cathl 86-96; Hon C Linc Minster Gp 88-96; Adn Charing Cross *Lon* from 96; Bp's Sen Chapl 96-00; R St Giles-in-the-Fields from 00. *15A Gower Street,*

London WC1E 6HW Tel (020) 7636 4646 *or* 7323 1992 Fax 7937 2560 *or* 7323 4102
E-mail archdeacon.charingcross@london.anglican.org

JACOBS, Mrs Brenda Mary. b 61. Birm Univ BA85 Glos Univ PGCE04. WEMTC 06. **d** 09. C Holmer w Huntington *Heref* from 09. *155 Godiva Road, Leominster HR6 8TB* Tel (01568) 610167 E-mail mail@jacobs4.fsnet.co.uk

JACOBS, Prof Michael David. b 41. Ex Coll Ox BA63 MA67. Chich Th Coll 63. **d** 65 **p** 66. C Walthamstow St Pet *Chelmsf* 65-68; Chapl Sussex Univ 68-72; Student Cllr Leic Univ 72-84; Lect 84-97; Sen Lect 97-00; Dir Past Care *Derby, Linc* and *S'well* 84-94; Visiting Prof Bournemouth Univ from 03. *12 Atlantic Road, Swanage BH19 2EG* Tel and fax (01929) 423068

JACOBS, Neville Robertson Eynesford. b 32. Lon Coll of Div ALCD59. **d** 59 **p** 60. C Chesham St Mary *Ox* 59-62; CMS 62-67; C Keynsham *B & W* 67 71; R Croscombe and Dinder 72-80; R Pilton w Croscombe, N Wootton and Dinder 80-83; V Biddenham *St Alb* 83-89; V Chipping Sodbury and Old Sodbury *Glouc* 89-97; RD Hawkesbury 91-96; rtd 97; Perm to Offic *S'wark* from 98. *22 Comforts Farm Avenue, Hurst Green, Oxted RH8 9DH* Tel (01883) 714127

JACOBS, Peter John. b 33. JP. MICFM. SEITE 96. **d** 96 **p** 97. NSM Boughton under Blean w Dunkirk and Hernhill *Cant* 96-99; NSM Murston w Bapchild and Tonge 99-02; rtd 02; Perm to Offic *Cant* from 02. *13 Crown Gardens, Canterbury CT2 8LQ* Tel (01227) 455733 E-mail peter@pjacobs72.freeserve.co.uk

JACOBSON, Ian Andrew. b 61. FRGS94. STETS 02. **d** 05 **p** 06. NSM Ewell St Fran *Guildf* 05-08; NSM Headley w Box Hill from 08; CF (TA) from 07. *34 Woodlands Road, Epsom KT18 7HW* Tel (01372) 742281
E-mail andrew.jacobson@waitrose.com

JACQUES, Barry John. b 52. Open Univ BSc95. Wycliffe Hall Ox 00. **d** 02 **p** 03. NSM Attleborough *Cov* 02-03; C Weddington and Caldecote 03-07; Perm to Offic from 07. *6 Easedale Close, Nuneaton CV11 6EX* Tel (024) 7635 3400
E-mail barry@bjjacques.screaming.net

JACQUES, Mrs Margaret Irene. b 53. St Jo Coll Nottm BA03. **d** 03 **p** 04. C W Hallam and Mapperley w Stanley *Derby* 03-07; P-in-c Morton and Stonebroom w Shirland from 07. *The Rectory, Main Road, Shirland, Alfreton DE55 6BB* Tel (01773) 836003 E-mail margaret@ajacques.plus.com

JACQUES, Martin. b 62. Ch Ch Coll Cant BA05. Coll of Resurr Mirfield 00. **d** 02 **p** 03. C Margate St Jo *Cant* 02-06; P-in-c Bucharest w Sofia *Eur* 06-09; P-in-c Gainford *Dur* from 09; P-in-c Winston from 09. *The Vicarage, Low Green, Gainford, Darlington DL2 3DS* Tel (01325) 733268 Mobile 07706-875741
E-mail martinjacques@gmail.com

JACQUET, Linda. b 44. Hatf Poly BA84. ERMC 06. **d** 08 **p** 09. NSM Bungay H Trin w St Mary *St E* from 08. *The Old Red House, Barley Green, Stradbroke, Eye IP21 5LY* Tel (01379) 388846 Mobile 07890-216889 E-mail l.jacquet@tiscali.co.uk

JACQUET, Trevor Graham. b 56. Man Univ BSc77. Oak Hill Th Coll BA88. **d** 88 **p** 89. C Deptford St Nic and St Luke *S'wark* 88-92; Chapl HM Pris Brixton 92-95; Chapl HM Pris Elmley 95-08; Chapl HM Pris Belmarsh from 08. *HM Prison Belmarsh, Western Way, London SE28 0EB* Tel (020) 8331 4400 Fax 8331 4401 E-mail trevor@jacquet2.freeserve.co.uk

JACSON, Edward Shallcross Owen. b 38. St Steph Ho Ox 61. **d** 64 **p** 65. C Yate *Glouc* 64-67; C Churchdown 67-70; P-in-c Sandhurst 70-75; V Sherborne w Windrush and the Barringtons 75-76; V Sherborne, Windrush, the Barringtons etc 76-80; TV Shaston *Sarum* 80-87; Lic to Offic 87-03; Perm to Offic from 03. *Grove Farm House, Melbury Abbas, Shaftesbury SP7 0DE* Tel (01747) 853688

JAGE-BOWLER, Christopher William. b 61. Nottm Univ BA83 Ch Ch Ox PGCE84 Down Coll Cam BA89 MA95. Ridley Hall Cam 87. **d** 90 **p** 91. C Downend *Bris* 90-94; Chapl Bris Univ 94-96; C Bris St Mich and St Paul 94-96; Asst Chapl Berlin *Eur* 96-97; Chapl from 97. *Goethestrasse 31, 13158 Berlin, Germany* Tel and fax (0049) (30) 917 2248 E-mail office@stgeorges.de

JAGGER, The Ven Ian. b 55. K Coll Cam BA77 MA81 St Jo Coll Dur BA80 MA75. Cranmer Hall Dur 78. **d** 82 **p** 83. C Twickenham St Mary *Lon* 82-85; P-in-c Willen *Ox* 85-87; TV Stantonbury and Willen 87-94; TR Fareham H Trin *Portsm* 94-98; Dioc Ecum Officer 94-96; RD Fareham 96-98; Can Missr 98-01; Adn Auckland *Dur* 01-06; Dioc Rural Development Officer 01-06; Adn Dur and Can Res Dur Cathl from 06. *15 The College, Durham DH1 3EQ* Tel 0191-384 7534 *or* 386 6915
E-mail archdeacon.of.durham@durham.anglican.org

JAGGER, Peter John. b 38. Lambeth MA71 Leeds Univ MPhil76 PhD87 FR.HistS78. Wesley Coll Leeds 62 Coll of Resurr Mirfield 67. **d** 68 **p** 69. C Leeds All SS *Ripon* 68-71; V Bolton w Redmire 71-77; Warden and Chief Lib St Deiniol's Lib Hawarden 77-97; Dir of Self Supporting Min 77-97; Lic to Offic *St As* 77-02; rtd 97; Perm to Offic *St E* from 03. *Redmire, 12 Eastlands, Stradbroke, Eye IP21 5JA* Tel (01379) 384292

JAGGER (née GREEN), Mrs Ruth Valerie. b 56. Ex Univ CertEd77. Ox NSM Course 87. **d** 90 **p** 94. NSM Stantonbury and Willen *Ox* 90-94; NSM Fareham H Trin *Portsm* 94-98; NSM

Portsm Deanery 98-01; Perm to Offic *Dur* from 02. *15 The College, Durham DH1 3EQ* Tel 0191-384 7534 *or* 386 6915

JAGO, Christine May. b 52. SRN73. **d** 94 **p** 95. OLM St Buryan, St Levan and Sennen *Truro* from 94. *Boscarne House, St Buryan, Penzance TR19 6HR* Tel (01736) 810374 Fax 810070
E-mail wandcmjago@btinternet.com

JAGO, David. b 48. Shoreditch Coll Lon CertEd69 Birm Univ BPhil77. St Steph Ho Ox 95. **d** 97 **p** 98. C S Bank *York* 97-00; V Middlesbrough St Martin w St Cuth 00-05; V Kingston upon Hull St Alb from 05. *St Alban's Vicarage, 62 Hall Road, Hull HU6 8SA* Tel (01482) 446639

JAKEMAN, Francis David. b 47. Leeds Univ BSc69. Cuddesdon Coll 71. **d** 74 **p** 75. C Gt Grimsby St Mary and St Jas *Linc* 74-77; Ind Chapl *Lon* 77-88; V Harrow Weald All SS 88-03; V Bexleyheath Ch Ch *Roch* from 03; AD Erith from 04. *57 Townley Road, Bexleyheath DA6 7HY* Tel (020) 8301 5086 Mobile 07734-436879 E-mail francis.jakeman@diocese rochester.org

JALLAND, Hilary Gervase Alexander. b 50. Ex Univ BA72. Coll of Resurr Mirfield 74. **d** 76 **p** 77. C Ex St Thos 76-80; C Portsea St Mary *Portsm* 80-86; V Hempton and Pudding Norton 86-90; TV Hawarden *St As* 90-93; R Llandysilio and Penrhos and Llandrinio etc 93-03; V Towyn and St George 03-06; rtd 06. *2 Church Cottages, Green Square, High Street, Llanfyllin SY22 5AB* Tel (01691) 649119 Mobile 07814-132259
E-mail hgaj@jalland1504.freeserve.co.uk

JAMES, Andrew Nicholas. b 54. BSc76. Trin Coll Bris 77. **d** 80 **p** 81. C Prescot *Liv* 80-83; C Upholland 83-85; V Hindley Green 85-91; V Dean Forest H Trin *Glouc* 91-06; RD Forest S 97-03; P-in-c Hardwicke and Elmore w Longney 06-09; V from 09. *Church House, Cornfield Drive, Hardwicke, Gloucester GL2 4QJ* Tel (01452) 720015 E-mail vicarage@inbox.com

JAMES, Andrew Peter. b 69. Glam Univ BSc96 Univ of Wales (Cardiff) BTh99. St Mich Coll Llan 96. **d** 99 **p** 00. C Roath *Llan* 99-01; C Radyr 01-06; TV Whitchurch from 06. *3 Lon Ganol, Cardiff CF14 6EB* Tel (029) 2065 4406
E-mail frjames@totalise.co.uk

JAMES, Anne Loraine. b 45. St Jo Coll Nottm. **d** 90 **p** 94. NSM Ellon and Cruden Bay *Ab* 90-99; NSM Alford 99-02; P-in-c from 02. *St Andrew's House, 53 Main Street, Alford AB33 8PX* Tel (01975) 564006 E-mail revanne.alford@virgin.net

JAMES, Barry Paul. b 49. BSc. Sarum & Wells Th Coll. **d** 82 **p** 83. C Bitterne Park *Win* 82-86; V Southampton St Mary Extra 86-00; R Fawley from 00. *The Rectory, 1 Sheringham Close, Southampton SO45 1SQ* Tel (023) 8089 3552
E-mail bpjames@email.com

JAMES, Brian. *See* JAMES, The Ven David Brian

JAMES, Brother. *See* PICKEN, James Hugh

JAMES, Brunel Hugh Grayburn. b 70. Selw Coll Cam BA93 MA97 Leeds Univ MA02. Wycliffe Hall Ox BA97. **d** 98 **p** 99. C Thornbury *Bradf* 98-02; R Barwick in Elmet *Ripon* 02-08; Abp's Dom Chapl *York* from 08. *Palace Gardens Cottage, Bishopthorpe Road, York YO23 2QD* Tel (01904) 772381 Mobile 07969-492793 E-mail brunel.james@archbishopofyork.org

JAMES, Miss Carolyn Anne. b 65. Coll of Ripon & York St Jo BA87 Nottm Univ BTh91 Leeds Univ MA03. Linc Th Coll 88. **d** 91 **p** 94. Par Dn Middleton St Mary *Ripon* 91-94; C Wetherby 94-97; V Kirkstall 97-05; Chapl and Sen Warden Bp Grosseteste Coll Linc from 05. *Bishop Grosseteste College, Newport, Lincoln LN1 3DY* Tel (01522) 583607 E-mail carolyn.james@bgc.ac.uk

JAMES, Christyan Elliot. b 68. Westcott Ho Cam. **d** 09. C Maidstone St Martin *Cant* from 09. *85 Loose Road, Maidstone ME15 7DA* Tel (01622) 679432 E-mail christyanj@yahoo.co.uk

✠**JAMES, The Rt Revd Colin Clement Walter.** b 26. K Coll Cam BA49 MA51. Cuddesdon Coll 50. **d** 52 **p** 53 **c** 73. C Stepney St Dunstan and All SS *Lon* 52-55; Asst Chapl Stowe Sch 55-56; Chapl 56-59; Asst in Relig Broadcasting BBC 59-60; Relig Broadcasting Org W Region BBC 60-67; V Bournemouth St Pet *Win* 67-73; P-in-c Bournemouth St Steph 70-73; Dir of Tr 72-77; Can Res Win Cathl 73-77; Suff Bp Basingstoke 73-77; Bp Wakef 77-85; Bp Win 85-95; rtd 95; Hon Asst Bp B & W 95-01; Hon Asst Bp Win from 03. *Long Meadow, 3 Back Street, Winchester SO23 9SB* Tel and fax (01962) 868874

JAMES, Colin Robert. b 39. Magd Coll Ox BA61 MA65 DipEd62. SAOMC 03. **d** 96 **p** 97. NSM Wokingham All SS *Ox* from 96. *7 Sewell Avenue, Wokingham RG41 1NT* Tel 0118-978 1515

JAMES, David. *See* JAMES, Richard David

JAMES, The Ven David Brian. b 30. FCA52 Univ of Wales (Swansea) BA63. St Mich Coll Llan 55. **d** 57 **p** 58. C Llandeilo Tal-y-bont *S & B* 57-59; C Swansea Ch Ch 59-63; V Bryngwyn and Newchurch and Llanbedr etc 63-70; R Llanfeugan w Llanthetty and Glyncollwng etc 70-79; V Ilston w Pennard 79-94; Hon Can Brecon Cathl 87-89; RD Gower 89-94; Can Brecon Cathl 89-94; Chan Brecon Cathl 93-94; Adn Brecon 94-99; P-in-c Llanllyr-yn-Rhos w Llanfihangel Helygen 94-99; Adn Gower 99-00; rtd 00. *1 Llys Ger-y-Llan, Pontarddulais, Swansea SA4 8HJ* Tel and fax (01792) 881323

✠**JAMES, The Rt Revd David Charles.** b 45. Ex Univ BSc66 PhD71. St Jo Coll Nottm BA73. **d** 73 **p** 74 **c** 98. C Portswood Ch

Ch *Win* 73-76; C Goring-by-Sea *Chich* 76-78; Chapl UEA *Nor* 78-82; V Ecclesfield *Sheff* 82-90; RD Ecclesfield 87-90; V Portswood Ch Ch *Win* 90-98; Hon Can Win Cathl 98; Suff Bp Pontefract *Wakef* 98-02; Bp Bradf from 02. *Bishopscroft, Ashwell Road, Heaton, Bradford BD9 4AU* Tel (01274) 545414 Fax 544831 E-mail bishop@bradford.anglican.org

JAMES, David Clive. b 40. Bris Univ BA61 K Coll Lon DipEd87. Lich Th Coll 62 St Steph Ho Ox 64. **d** 65 **p** 66. C Portslade St Nic *Chich* 65-68; C Haywards Heath St Wilfrid 68-71; Chapl Brighton Poly 71-75; Perm to Offic from 75. *22 Bradford Road, Lewes BN1 1RB* Tel (01273) 471851 E-mail davidcjames@talktalk.net

JAMES, David Henry. b 45. Univ of Wales MB, BCh68 Univ of Wales (Swansea) MA92 MRCPsych75. SWMTC 95. **d** 98. NSM Truro Cathl 98-00; rtd 00; Perm to Offic *Truro* 00-03 and *Sarum* 03-05; Lic to Offic *Arg* from 06. *Glencruitten House, Glencruitten, Oban PA34 4QB* Tel (01631) 562431 E-mail david.james.855@btinternet.com

JAMES, Preb David Howard. b 47. Ex Univ BA70 MA73 Pemb Coll Cam CertEd72. Linc Th Coll 81. **d** 83 **p** 84. C Tavistock and Gulworthy *Ex* 83-86; C E Teignmouth 86-88; C W Teignmouth 86-88; P-in-c Bishopsteignton 88-89; P-in-c Ideford, Luton and Ashcombe 88-89; TV Teignmouth, Ideford w Luton, Ashcombe etc 90-95; P-in-c Sidmouth, Woolbrook, Salcombe Regis, Sidbury etc 95-97; TR from 97; Preb Ex Cathl from 99; RD Ottery from 03. *The Rectory, Glen Road, Sidmouth EX10 8RW* Tel (01395) 514223 E-mail rev.davidjames@btinternet.com

JAMES, David William. b 55. Birm Univ BA99. Coll of Resurr Mirfield 86. **d** 88 **p** 88. C New Rossington *Sheff* 88-90; V Yardley Wood *Birm* 90-95; P-in-c Allens Cross 95-96; V 96-06; P-in-c Rubery from 05. *160A New Road, Rubery, Rednal, Birmingham B45 9JA* Tel 0121-460 1278 Mobile 07511-918806 E-mail david.james5@btinternet.com

JAMES, Derek George. b 27. Sarum & Wells Th Coll 72. **d** 74 **p** 75. C Petersfield w Sheet *Portsm* 74-77; P-in-c Gosport Ch Ch 77-81; V 81-96; RD Gosport 90-96; rtd 96; Perm to Offic *Portsm* from 96. *2 Pyrford Close, Alverstoke, Gosport PO12 2RP* Tel (023) 9258 4753

JAMES, Canon Eric Arthur. b 25. K Coll Lon AKC50 BD51 FKC78 Trin Coll Cam MA55 Lambeth DD93 FRSA92. **d** 51 **p** 52. C Westmr St Steph w St Jo *Lon* 51-55; Chapl Trin Coll Cam 55-59; Warden Trin Coll Miss Camberwell 59-64; V Camberwell St Geo *S'wark* 59-64; Dir Par and People 64-69; Can Res and Prec S'wark Cathl 66-73; Dioc Missr *St Alb* 73-83; Can Res St Alb 73-83; Hon Can 83-90; Preacher Gray's Inn 78-97; Dir Chr Action 79-90; Hon Dir from 90; Chapl to The Queen 84-95; Extra Chapl to The Queen from 95; rtd 90; Perm to Offic *S'wark* 90-02. *Charterhouse Sutton's Hospital, The Charterhouse, Charterhouse Square, London EC1M 6AN*

JAMES, Gerwyn. *See* JAMES, Joshua John Gerwyn

JAMES, Gillian Mary. b 49. **d** 99. OLM Bassaleg *Mon* 99-05. *69 Hollybush Road, Cyncoed, Cardiff CF2 4SZ* Tel (029) 2073 2673

JAMES, Glyn. *See* JAMES, Henry Glyn

JAMES, Canon Godfrey Walter. b 36. Univ of Wales (Lamp) BA58 Univ of Wales (Cardiff) MA60 St Pet Coll Ox DipEd61 BA63 MA67. St Mich Coll Llan 63. **d** 64 **p** 65. C Canton St Jo *Llan* 64-71; V Williamstown 71-85; V Kenfig Hill 85-01; Hon Can Llan Cathl 96-01; rtd 01. *23 Crossfield Avenue, Porthcawl CF36 3LA*

✠**JAMES, The Rt Revd Graham Richard.** b 51. Lanc Univ BA72 Hon FGCM92. Cuddesdon Coll 72. **d** 75 **p** 76 **c** 93. C Pet Ch Carpenter 75-79; C Digswell *St Alb* 79-82; TV Digswell and Panshanger 82-83; Sen Selection Sec and Sec Cand Cttee ACCM 83-87; Abp's Chapl *Cant* 87-93; Hon Can Dallas from 87; Suff Bp St Germans *Truro* 93-99; Bp Nor from 99. *The Bishop's House, Norwich NR3 1SB* Tel (01603) 629001 Fax 761613 E-mail bishop@bishopofnorwich.org

JAMES, Henley George. b 31. Sarum & Wells Th Coll 79. **d** 81 **p** 82. C Tottenham H Trin *Lon* 81-85; C Cricklewood St Pet 85-88; P-in-c 88-89; V Bearwood *Birm* 89-97; rtd 97. *11 Brosil Avenue, Birmingham B20 1LB* Tel 0121-523 4243

JAMES, Henry Glyn. b 26. Keble Coll Ox BA50 MA58 Toronto Univ MEd74. Wycliffe Hall Ox 50. **d** 52 **p** 53. C Edgbaston St Aug *Birm* 52-54; C Surbiton St Matt *S'wark* 54-57; Housemaster Kingham Hill Sch Oxon 57-62; Chapl St Lawr Coll Ramsgate 62-68; Canada 68-73; Hon C Kidmore End *Ox* 74-77; K Jas Coll of Henley 74-87; Hon C Remenham *Ox* 77-88; Chapl The Henley Coll 87-88; Chapl Toulouse *Eur* 88-91; rtd 91; Perm to Offic *Win* from 93. *13 Harbour Road, Bournemouth BH6 4DD* Tel (01202) 427697 E-mail glyn.james1@ntlworld.com

JAMES, Herbert Royston Joseph. b 22. Sarum Th Coll 65. **d** 67 **p** 68. C Whipton *Ex* 67-75; V Shaugh Prior 75-83; V Ipplepen w Torbryan 83-87; rtd 87; Perm to Offic *Ex* from 90. *188 Hamlin Lane, Exeter EX1 2SH*

JAMES, Prof Ian Nigel. b 48. Leeds Univ BSc69 Man Univ PhD74. SAOMC 99. **d** 02 **p** 03. NSM Bracknell *Ox* 02-04; NSM

Winkfield and Cranbourne from 04. *2 Kyle Close, Bracknell RG12 7DF* Tel (01344) 451155 Mobile 07808-207422 E-mail dr.i.n.james@btinternet.com

JAMES, Jeffrey Aneurin. b 53. Univ of Wales (Cardiff) BScEcon80 Bris Univ MSc85 MHSM83. WEMTC 98. **d** 01 **p** 02. NSM Minchinhampton *Glouc* 01-07; NSM Painswick, Sheepscombe, Cranham, The Edge etc from 07. *Jays Cottage, Keble Road, France Lynch, Stroud GL6 8LW* Tel (01453) 882481 E-mail jayscott@dsl.pipex.com

JAMES, Jeremy Richard. b 52. Jes Coll Cam BA73 MA77 York Univ CertEd77. Cranmer Hall Dur 86. **d** 88 **p** 89. C Broxbourne w Wormley *St Alb* 88-91; C Hailsham *Chich* 91-99; V Wadhurst from 99; V Tidebrook from 99; P-in-c Stonegate from 99; RD Rotherfield from 03. *The Vicarage, High Street, Wadhurst TN5 6AA* Tel (01892) 782083 E-mail jeremy@jrjames.freeserve.co.uk

JAMES, Mrs Joanna Elizabeth. b 72. SAOMC. **d** 06 **p** 07. C Northwood Em *Lon* from 06. *64 Chester Road, Northwood HA6 1BH* Tel (01923) 825019 E-mail jo.james@ecn.org.uk

JAMES, John Charles. b 35. Keble Coll Ox BA59. Linc Th Coll 68. **d** 70 **p** 71. C S Shields St Hilda w St Thos *Dur* 70-77; P-in-c Jarrow Docks 77-78; Adn Seychelles 78-92; V Mylor w Flushing *Truro* 92-05; rtd 06. *172 Westoe Road, South Shields NE33 3PH*

JAMES, John David. b 23. CCC Cam MA. Wells Th Coll. **d** 50 **p** 51. C Romford St Edw *Chelmsf* 50-54; C Cannock *Lich* 54-56; R Wickham Bishops *Chelmsf* 56-61; V Stansted Mountfitchet 61-71; V Clacton St Jas 71-84; R Poulshot *Sarum* 84-87; V Rowde 84; R Rowde and Poulshot 84-88; rtd 88; Perm to Offic *Heref* from 92. *15 Beaconsfield Park, Ludlow SY8 4LY* Tel (01584) 873754

JAMES, John Hugh Alexander. b 56. St Jo Coll Dur BA78. St Mich Coll Llan. **d** 81 **p** 82. C Newton Nottage *Llan* 81-84; Prov Youth and Children's Officer Ch in Wales 84-92; V Llanfihangel-ar-arth *St D* 92-97; V Llanfihangel-ar-arth w Capel Dewi 97-04; RD Emlyn 01-04; V Cydweli and Llandyfaelog from 04; AD Cydweli 05-07. *The Vicarage, Vicarage Lane, Kidwelly SA17 4SY* Tel (01554) 890295 E-mail ficerdy@tiscali.co.uk

JAMES, John Morgan. b 21. Lon Univ BD43 MTh45. ALCD43. **d** 44 **p** 45. C Leyton St Mary w St Edw *Chelmsf* 44-47; C Southend St Sav Westcliff 47-50; Prec Chelmsf Cathl 50-53; V Kemp Town St Mark *Chich* 53-65; R Balcombe 65-67; V Sunbury *Lon* 67-77; RD Kemp Town *Chich* 55-65; Dir Coll of Preachers 77-85; Lic to Offic *Guildf* 77-86; rtd 85. *Fair Winds, 126 Pagham Road, Pagham, Bognor Regis PO21 4NN* Tel (01243) 264250

JAMES, John Paul. b 30. Sarum Th Coll 58. **d** 60 **p** 61. C Milton *Portsm* 60-65; C Stanmer w Falmer and Moulsecoomb *Chich* 65-69; PC Brighton H Trin 69-71; Canada from 71; R Saguenay St Jean 71; Dean Quebec 77-87; R Westmount St Matthias 87-96; rtd 96. *301-97 Huron Street, Stratford ON N5A 5S7, Canada* Fax (001) (519) 273 9226 E-mail helenandpaul@rogers.com

JAMES, Joshua John Gerwyn. b 31. St D Coll Lamp BA52. **d** 54 **p** 55. C Haverfordwest St Mary w St Thos *St D* 54-56; C Llanaber w Caerdeon *Ban* 56-57; CF 57-76; V Tidenham w Beachley and Lancaut *Glouc* 76-80; R Aberdovey *Ban* 80-82; V Quinton w Marston Sicca *Glouc* 82-90; RD Campden 88-90; P-in-c Upper Chelsea St Simon *Lon* 90-96; rtd 96; Perm to Offic *S'wark* from 97. *25 The Watergardens, Warren Road, Kingston upon Thames KT2 7LF* Tel (020) 8974 6889

JAMES, Mrs Julie Margaret. b 55. Shenstone Coll of Educn BEd77. Qu Coll Birm 01. **d** 04 **p** 05. NSM Salwarpe and Hindlip w Martin Hussingtree *Worc* 04-06; NSM St Jo in Bedwardine from 06. *Wyche Cottage, Plough Road, Tibberton, Droitwich WR9 7NQ* Tel (01905) 345688 Mobile 07751-465241 E-mail julie.m.james@btinternet.com

JAMES, Keith Edwin Arthur. b 38. Sarum & Wells Th Coll 85. **d** 87 **p** 88. C Hempnall *Nor* 87-91; R Roughton and Felbrigg, Metton, Sustead etc 91-98; V Ascension Is 98-01; rtd 02; Chapl Laslett's *Worc* 02-04; Perm to Offic *Nor* from 05. *30 Woodland Rise, Tasburgh, Norwich NR15 1NF* Tel (01508) 470032

JAMES, Keith Nicholas. b 69. Leeds Univ BA91. St Jo Coll Nottm MA93. **d** 93 **p** 94. C Crosby *Linc* 93-96; P-in-c Cherry Willingham w Greetwell 96-00; R S Lawres Gp 00-03; RD Lawres 01-03; R Ribbesford w Bewdley and Dowles *Worc* from 03; RD Kidderminster from 07. *The Rectory, 57 Park Lane, Bewdley DY12 2HA* Tel (01299) 402275 or 404773 E-mail kn.james@btinternet.com

JAMES, Malcolm. b 37. CEng MICE MIStructE. NOC 80. **d** 83 **p** 84. NSM Ripponden *Wakef* from 83. *Lower Stones, Bar Lane, Rishworth, Sowerby Bridge HX6 4EY* Tel (01422) 822483 Fax 825992 E-mail malcolm@mjconsultancy.demon.co.uk

JAMES, Mark Nicholas. b 55. Jes Coll Ox BA77 MA80 PGCE79. Ridley Hall Cam 03. **d** 05 **p** 06. C Gt Dunmow and Barnston *Chelmsf* 05-09; R Bentley Common, Kelvedon Hatch and Navestock from 09. *The Rectory, 2 Church Road, Kelvedon Hatch, Brentwood CM14 5TJ* Tel (01277) 373486 Mobile 07884-185835 E-mail revmarkjames@btinternet.com

JAMES, Martin. b 40. ACII. **d** 94 **p** 95. OLM N Farnborough *Guildf* 94-08; OLM Camberley St Martin Old Dean 08-09; NSM from 09. *43 Ashley Road, Farnborough GU14 7HB* Tel (01252) 544698 E-mail martinjean.james@ntlworld.com

JAMES, Michael Howard. b 55. Bris Univ LLB73 Solicitor 92. WEMTC 04. **d** 06 **p** 07. NSM Clifton H Trin, St Andr and St Pet *Bris* 06-08; NSM Westbury Park LEP from 08. *10 Hill Drive, Failand, Bristol BS8 3UX* Tel (01275) 393729 E-mail jamfam@jamfam4.wanadoo.co.uk *or* cranmer1662@hotmail.co.uk

JAMES, Michael John. b 29. ALA53 Heriot-Watt Univ CQSW81. Ho of Resurr Mirfield 57. **d** 59 **p** 60. C Applethwaite *Carl* 59-61; C Carl H Trin 61-63; C-in-c Carl St Luke Morton CD 63-67; R Lambley w Knaresdale *Newc* 67-72; Rossie Sch Montrose 75-83; Prin Redding Ho Falkirk 83-86; rtd 93. *28 Windsor Street, Edinburgh EH7 5JR* Tel 0131-556 4935

JAMES, Paul Maynard. b 31. Univ of Wales (Ban) BA52 Fitzw Ho Cam BA54 MA58. Ridley Hall Cam 56. **d** 57 **p** 58. C Newhaven *Chich* 57-60; Kenya 60-65; SW Area Sec CCCS 65-68; V Shrewsbury St Julian *Lich* 68-76; V Shrewsbury H Trin w St Julian 76-90; P-in-c Woore and Norton in Hales 90-98; Adn Salop's Adv on Evang 90-98; RD Hodnet 93-97; rtd 98; Perm to Offic *Heref* and *Lich* from 00. *Nettledene, Elms Lane, Little Stretton, Church Stretton SY6 6RD* Tel (01694) 722559

JAMES, Canon Peter David. b 42. Keble Coll Ox BA63 Lon Univ BD67. Tyndale Hall Bris 64. **d** 67 **p** 68. C Haydock St Mark *Liv* 67-69; C Ashton-in-Makerfield St Thos 69-74; V Whiston 74-80; V Harlech and Llanfair-juxta-Harlech etc *Ban* 80-94; R Botwnnog w Bryncroes 94-07; Hon Can Ban Cathl 02-07; rtd 07. *Tabor, Llithfaen, Pwllheli LL53 6NL* Tel (01758) 750202 E-mail peterjames@botwnnog.fsnet.co.uk

JAMES, Raymond John. b 36. Linc Th Coll 85. **d** 87 **p** 88. C Cov E 87-91; V Wolvey w Burton Hastings, Copston Magna etc 91-01; rtd 01. *46 Conmore, Pershore WR10 1HX* Tel (01336) 556537

JAMES, Richard Andrew. b 44. Mert Coll Ox BA67 MA70. Tyndale Hall Bris. **d** 70 **p** 71. C Bebington *Ches* 70-73; C Histon *Ely* 73-77; Chapl Guildf Coll of Tech 77-80; C Guildf St Sav w Stoke-next-Guildford 77-80; Ecum Chapl Bedf Coll of HE *St Alb* 81-83; TV Ipsley *Worc* 84-89; R Mulbarton w Kenningham *Nor* 89-92; rtd 93. *5 Kirkby Close, Ripon HG4 2DS* Tel (01765) 604511

JAMES, Richard David. b 45. Cheltenham & Glouc Coll of HE MA97. Lon Coll of Div 66. **d** 70 **p** 71. C Boultham *Linc* 70-74; C New Waltham 74-77; TV Cleethorpes 77-87; TR E Bris 87-99; V E Bris St Ambrose and St Leon from 99. *St Ambrose Vicarage, 487 Whitehall Road, Bristol BS5 7DA* Tel 0117-951 2270 Mobile 07749-243407

JAMES, Richard David. b 65. Clare Coll Cam MA88 Lon Hosp MB, BChir90. Ridley Hall Cam 92. **d** 95 **p** 96. C Clifton Ch Ch w Em *Bris* 95-98; C Enfield Ch Ch Trent Park *Lon* 98-00; V from 00. *The Vicarage, 2A Chalk Lane, Cockfosters, Barnet EN4 9JQ* Tel (020) 8441 1230 *or* tel and fax 8449 0556 E-mail richard@ccc1.fsnet.co.uk

JAMES, Richard Lindsay. b 39. Kelham Th Coll 61. **d** 66 **p** 67. C Seacroft *Ripon* 66-74; rtd 04. *3 Cavendish Mews, Hove BN3 1AZ* Tel (01273) 324672

JAMES, Richard William. b 47. St D Coll Lamp. **d** 75 **p** 76. C Hubberston *St D* 75-78; R Pendine w Llanmiloe and Eglwys Gymyn w Marros 78-83; V Caerwent w Dinham and Llanfair Discoed etc *Mon* 83-84; Chapl Gothenburg w Halmstad, Jönköping etc *Eur* 84-89; P-in-c Shooters Hill Ch Ch *S'wark* 89-97; V Plumstead St Mark and St Marg 97-07; rtd 07. *Gärdesvägen 9H, 87162 Härnösand, Sweden* Tel (0046) (611) 435557 E-mail eva.jame@comhem.se

JAMES, Robert William. b 79. Kent Univ BA01 SOAS Lon MA02 CCC Cam MPhil03. Westcott Ho Cam 02. **d** 05 **p** 06. C St Edm Way and Bradfield St Clare, Bradfield St George etc *St E* 05-07. *Address temp unknown* E-mail robdogcollar@yahoo.co.uk

JAMES, Roger Michael. b 44. K Coll Lon BD66 AKC66. **d** 69 **p** 70. C Frindsbury w Upnor *Roch* 69-72; Lic to Offic *St Alb* 73-78; C Digswell 78-81; R Knebworth 81-92; P-in-c Upper Tean and Local Min Adv (Stafford) *Lich* 92-99; Dir Cottesloe Chr Tr Progr *Ox* 99-03; R Cusop w Blakemere, Bredwardine w Brobury etc *Heref* 03-09; RD Abbeydore 06-09; rtd 09. *Ty Siloh, Llandeilo'r Fan, Brecon LD3 8UD* Tel (01874) 636126 E-mail tysiloh@googlemail.com

JAMES, Roy. *See* JAMES, Herbert Royston Joseph
JAMES, Sandra Kay. *See* GARDNER, Mrs Sandra Kay
JAMES, Sarah Alison Livingston. b 38. FCA73. **d** 06 **p** 06. NSM Churchdown *Glouc* from 06. *Canton House, New Street, Painswick, Stroud GL6 6XH* Tel (01452) 812809 E-mail saljames@zetnet.co.uk

JAMES, Ms Sheridan Angharad. b 71. Univ of Wales (Abth) BA93 PGCE94 MPhil00. SEITE 04. **d** 07 **p** 08. C Catford (Southend) and Downham *S'wark* from 07. *59 Southend Lane, London SE6 3AB* Tel (020) 8697 6538 *or* 8461 1479 Mobile 07703-291594

JAMES, Stephen Lynn. b 53. Oak Hill Th Coll BA86. **d** 86 **p** 87. C Heigham H Trin *Nor* 86-89; C Vancouver St Jo Canada 89-93; R Bebington *Ches* 93-06; R Rusholme H Trin *Man* from 06. *Holy Trinity Rectory, Platt Lane, Manchester M14 5NF* Tel 0161-224 1123 Fax 224 1144 E-mail office@plattchurch.org

JAMES, Stephen Nicholas. b 51. Reading Univ MA87 Bris Univ EdD95 ARCM72 LTCL72 FTCL73 FRSA00. SAOMC 01. **d** 04 **p** 05. NSM Hanney, Denchworth and E Challow *Ox* 04-07; P-in-c Goetre w Llanover *Mon* from 07. *The Rectory, Nantyderry, Abergavenny NP7 9DW* Tel (01873) 880378 E-mail sueandstephen@btinternet.com

JAMES, Mrs Susan Margaret. b 58. SRN81 RSCN81 St Jo Coll Dur BA04. Cranmer Hall Dur 00. **d** 04 **p** 05. NSM Derby St Paul 04-07. *267 Victoria Avenue, Ockbrook, Derby DE72 3RL* Tel (01332) 673551 E-mail suzejames@hotmail.com

JAMES, Mrs Veronica Norma. b 59. STETS 99. **d** 02 **p** 03. NSM Ashton Keynes, Leigh and Minety *Bris* 02-05; R Merriott w Hinton, Dinnington and Lopen *B & W* from 05. *The Rectory, Church Street, Merriott TA16 5PS* Tel (01460) 73226 E-mail flojoefred@hotmail.com

JAMES, William Glynne George. b 39. Trin Coll Carmarthen 82. **d** 85 **p** 86. NSM Gorseinon *S & B* from 85. *23 Cecil Road, Gowerton, Swansea SA4 3DF* Tel (01792) 872363

JAMESON, David Kingsbury. b 28. Mert Coll Ox BA50 MA55. Qu Coll Birm 50. **d** 53 **p** 54. C Leominster *Heref* 53-56; C Portsm Cathl 56-60; Dioc Youth Officer 58-61; V Gosport Ch Ch 60-65; V Portsea St Cuth 65-70; V Enfield Jes Chpl *Lon* 70-74; RD Nuneaton *Cov* 74-79; V Nuneaton St Nic 74-80; Org Sec (Leics and Northants) CECS 80-82; P-in-c Forty Hill Jes Ch *Lon* 82-87; V 87-91; rtd 91; Hon C Okehampton w Inwardleigh, Bratton Clovelly etc *Ex* 94-96; Hon C St Giles-in-the-Fields *Lon* 96-99; Perm to Offic *Chelmsf* 99-00 and *Cov* from 01. *20 Grasmere Crescent, Nuneaton CV11 6ED* Tel (024) 7674 6957

JAMESON, Canon Dermot Christopher Ledgard. b 27. TCD BA49 MA54. CITC 49. **d** 50 **p** 51. C Seagoe *D & D* 50-53; C Holywood 53-57; I Kilkeel 57-62; I Donaghcloney w Waringstown 62-79; Can Dromore Cathl 77-93; I Kilbroney 79-93; Treas Dromore Cathl 81-83; Prec Dromore Cathl 83-90; Chan Dromore Cathl 90-93; rtd 93. *Concord, 10B Kilbroney Road, Rostrevor, Newry BT34 3BH* Tel (028) 4173 9728

JAMESON, Geoffrey Vaughan. b 27. Culham Coll Ox CertEd51. Wycliffe Hall Ox 68. **d** 70 **p** 71. C Buckingham *Ox* 70-73; R Exton w Whitwell *Pet* 73-86; V Marystowe, Coryton, Stowford, Lewtrenchard etc *Ex* 86-90; rtd 90; Perm to Offic *Portsm* from 91 and *Win* from 93. *18 Eglantine Walk, Cowplain, Waterlooville PO8 9BG* Tel (023) 9257 1112

JAMESON, Howard Kingsley. b 63. Warwick Univ BSc84. Trin Coll Bris 99. **d** 02 **p** 03. C Wareham *Sarum* 02-05; P-in-c Monkton Farleigh, S Wraxall and Winsley from 05. *The Rectory, 6 Millbourn Close, Winsley, Bradford-on-Avon BA15 2NN* Tel (01225) 722230 E-mail howard.jameson@virgin.net

JAMESON, Peter. b 31. Trin Coll Cam BA54 MA60. Linc Th Coll. **d** 62 **p** 63. C Earl's Court St Cuth w St Matthias *Lon* 62-68; C Notting Hill St Clem 68-72; C Notting Hill St Clem and St Mark 72-74; TV Notting Hill 74-77; V Stoke Newington St Olave 77-95; rtd 95; Perm to Offic *Chich* from 95. *Colemans, Warren Lane, Cross in Hand, Heathfield TN21 0TB* Tel (01435) 863414

JAMIESON, Douglas. *See* JAMIESON, William Douglas
JAMIESON, Guy Stuart. b 66. Leeds Univ BA98. Ripon Coll Cuddesdon. **d** 00 **p** 01. C Woodhall *Bradf* 00-03; V Southowram and Claremount *Wakef* from 03. *St Anne's Vicarage, Church Lane, Southowram, Halifax HX3 9TD* Tel (01422) 365229 E-mail guy.jamieson@virgin.net

JAMIESON, Kenneth Euan Oram. b 24. Roch Th Coll 60. **d** 62 **p** 63. C Bromley SS Pet and Paul *Roch* 62-66; R Colchester St Mary Magd *Chelmsf* 66-71; V Bexleyheath St Pet *Roch* 71-78; P-in-c Maidstone St Faith 78-83; P-in-c Maidstone St Paul 78-83; Ind Chapl *St Alb* 83-89; rtd 89; Perm to Offic *B & W* from 89. *4 Ashley Road, Taunton TA1 5BP* Tel (01823) 289367

JAMIESON, Canon Marilyn. b 52. Cranmer Hall Dur IDC80. **d** 91 **p** 94. Par Dn Bensham *Dur* 91-93; Par Dn Ryton w Hedgefield 93-94; Chapl Metro Cen Gateshead 94-02 and from 06; Bp's Sen Chapl 02-05; Hon C Ryton 05-06; Hon Can Dur Cathl from 97. *Barmoor House, 64 Main Road, Ryton NE40 3AJ* Tel 0191-413 4592

JAMIESON, Mrs Moira Elizabeth. b 50. **d** 08. C Lenzie *Glas* from 08. *5 Pinewood Place, Kirkintilloch, Glasgow G66 4JN* Tel 0141-775 1161 Mobile 07977-096446 E-mail moira.jamieson@ntlworld.com

JAMIESON, Peter Grant. b 64. Liv Univ BA87. Coll of Resurr Mirfield 93. **d** 93 **p** 94. C Charlton Kings St Mary *Glouc* 93-96. *3 Belmont Mews, Upper High Street, Thame OX9 3EJ* Tel (01844) 212895

JAMIESON, Miss Rosalind Heather. b 49. CertEd71. St Jo Coll Dur 79. **dss** 81 **d** 87 **p** 94. Queensbury All SS *Lon* 81-85; Richmond H Trin and Ch Ch *S'wark* 85-87; Par Dn 87-91; Par Dn Burmantofts St Steph and St Agnes *Ripon* 91-94; C 94-99;

TV Seacroft from 99. *St Richard's Vicarage, Ramshead Hill, Leeds LS14 1BX* Tel 0113-273 2527
E-mail jamheat2002@tiscali.co.uk

JAMIESON, Mrs Susan Jennifer. b 49. Liv Univ SRN71. Dioc OLM tr scheme 97. **d** 00 **p** 01. OLM Clubmoor *Liv* from 00. *15 Winsford Road, Liverpool L13 0BJ* Tel 0151-475 7562 Mobile 07879-425277 E-mail susiejam@blueyonder.co.uk

JAMIESON, Thomas Lindsay. b 53. N Lon Poly BSc74. Cranmer Hall Dur. **d** 77 **p** 78. C Gateshead Fell *Dur* 77-80; C Gateshead 80-84; TV 84-90; P-in-c Gateshead St Cuth w St Paul 90-91; TV Bensham 91-93; P-in-c Ryton w Hedgefield 93-95; R 95-05; R Ryton from 05; AD Gateshead W 94-98. *Barmoor House, 64 Main Road, Ryton NE40 3AJ* Tel 0191-413 4592
E-mail atl.jamieson@talk21.com

JAMIESON, William Douglas. b 38. Oak Hill Th Coll 63. **d** 66 **p** 67. C Shrewsbury St Julian *Lich* 66-68; C Bucknall and Bagnall 68-70; C Otley *Bradf* 70-74; TV Keighley 74-81; V Utley 81-00; rtd 00; Perm to Offic *Ches* from 00. *11 The Quay, Frodsham, Warrington WA6 7JG* Tel (01928) 731085 Mobile 07974-947838 E-mail douglasjamieson@lineone.net

JAMISON, William Mervyn Noel. b 66. CITC 03. **d** 07 **p** 08. NSM Ballybeen *D & D* from 07. *Millview House, 1 Old Ballygowan Road, Comber, Newtownards BT23 5NP* Tel (028) 9187 1962 E-mail rev.merv@btinternet.com

JANES, Austin Steven. b 75. York Univ BA97. Ripon Coll Cuddesdon 06. **d** 08 **p** 09. C Crewe St Andr w St Jo *Ches* from 08. *26 Laura Street, Crewe CW2 6HA* Tel (01270) 215866
E-mail austinjanes@btinternet.com

JANES, David Edward. b 40. Lon Univ BSc67. Glouc Sch of Min 86. **d** 89 **p** 90. NSM Church Stretton *Heref* 89-00; rtd 00; Perm to Offic *Heref* from 00. *Bourton Westwood Farm, 3 Bourton Westwood, Much Wenlock TF13 6QB* Tel (01952) 727393

JANICKER, Laurence Norman. b 47. SS Mark & Jo Coll Chelsea DipEd69. St Jo Coll Nottm 83. **d** 85 **p** 86. C Beverley Minster *York* 85-89; R Lockington and Lund and Scorborough w Leconfield 89-94; V Cov St Geo 94-08; rtd 08; Perm to Offic *Nor* from 09. *136 Manor Road, Newton St Faith, Norwich NR10 3LG* Tel (01603) 898614 E-mail laurencejanicker@btinternet.com

JANSMA, Henry Peter. b 57. NE Bible Coll (USA) BA79 Westmr Th Sem (USA) MA85 St Jo Coll Dur PhD91. Linc Th Coll 89. **d** 91 **p** 92. C Spalding *Linc* 91-96; P-in-c Cleethorpes St Aid 96-97; V 97-01; R Haddon Heights St Mary USA from 01. *501 Green Street, Haddon Heights NJ 08035-1903, USA* Tel (001) (856) 547 0565 *or* 547 3240 Fax 310 0565
E-mail stmaryshh@juno.com

JANSSON, Maria Patricia. b 55. Milltown Inst Dub MRelSc92. CITC 00. **d** 01 **p** 02. C Galway w Kilcummin *T, K & A* 01-02; C Wexford w Ardcolm and Killurin *C & O* 02-04; I from 04; C Kilscoran w Killinick and Mulrankin 02-04; P-in-c from 04. *The Rectory, Park, Wexford, Republic of Ireland* Tel (00353) (53) 914 0652 *or* 912 2377 Mobile 87-225 5793
E-mail miajansson@eircom.net

JANVIER, Philip Harold. b 57. Trin Coll Bris BA87. **d** 87 **p** 88. C Much Woolton *Liv* 87-90; TV Toxteth St Philemon w St Gabr and St Cleopas 90-97; TR Gateacre from 97. *St Stephen's Rectory, Belle Vale Road, Liverpool L25 2PQ* Tel and fax 0151-487 9338

JAONA, Ramahalefitra Hyacinthe Arsène. b 70. St Paul's Th Coll Ambatoharanana Madagascar 89. **d** 94 **p** 96. Madagascar 94-97 and from 98; C Caldicot *Mon* 97-98. *Mission Angelican, BP 126, 206 Antalaha, Antsiranana, Madagascar*

JAQUES, Geoffrey Sanderson. b 48. Man Univ BSc. NEOC 94. **d** 97 **p** 98. NSM Gt Ayton w Easby and Newton under Roseberry *York* from 97. *132 Roseberry Crescent, Great Ayton, Middlesbrough TS9 6EW* Tel (01642) 722979

JAQUISS, Mrs Gabrielle Clair. b 56. Clare Coll Cam BA79 MA83 LRAM76. NOC 06. **d** 08 **p** 09. NSM Bowdon *Ches* from 08. *Ingersley, Belgrave Road, Bowdon, Altrincham WA14 2NZ* Tel 0161-928 0717 Mobile 07843-375494
E-mail clairjq@aol.com

JARAM, Peter Ellis. b 45. Lon Univ BSc70 CEng77 MIET77 MBIM88. Linc Th Coll 94. **d** 94 **p** 95. C Bridlington Priory *York* 94-96; C Rufforth w Moor Monkton and Hessay 96-97; C Healaugh w Wighill, Bilbrough and Askham Richard 96-97; P-in-c 97-01; Chapl Askham Bryan Coll 97-01; V Brompton by Sawdon w Hutton Buscel, Snainton etc *York* 01-05; Perm to Offic *York* from 05. *74 Eastgate, Pickering YO18 7DY* Tel (01751) 477831 E-mail pwj74@btinternet.com

JARDIN, Kenneth. b 35. TCD 67. **d** 69 **p** 70. Chapl R Sch Arm 69-72; C Arm St Mark 69-72; Chapl RAF 72-78; V Barlings *Linc* 78-83; P-in-c Stainton-by-Langworth 78; P-in-c Scothern w Sudbrooke 78; Chapl Monte Carlo *Eur* 83-87; P-in-c Sudbury and Somersal Herbert *Derby* 87-92; Dep Chapl HM Open Pris Foston Hall and Sudbury 87-92; P in c Kirk Langley 92-03; P-in-c Mackworth All SS 92-03; P-in-c Mugginton and Kedleston 92-03; rtd 03. *10C Coolmoyne House, Dunmurry, Belfast BT17 9EW* Tel (028) 9062 7442

JARDINE, Canon Anthony. b 38. Qu Coll Birm 64. **d** 67 **p** 68. C

Baldock w Bygrave and Clothall *St Alb* 67-71; C N Stoneham *Win* 71-73; P-in-c Ecchinswell cum Sydmonton 73-79; P-in-c Burghclere w Newtown 78-79; R Burghclere w Newtown and Ecchinswell w Sydmonton 79-87; R Wonston and Stoke Charity w Hunton 87-97; P-in-c Chawton and Farringdon 97-04; Dioc Rural Officer 97-04; Hon Can Win Cathl 99-04; rtd 04; Hon C Knight's Enham and Smannell w Enham Alamein *Win* 04-08; Perm to Offic *Heref* from 09. *Longdendale, 4 Victoria Road, Kington HR5 3BX* E-mail rev_jardine@hotmail.com

JARDINE, David Eric Cranswick. b 30. CCC Ox BA53 MA57. Wycliffe Hall Ox 53. **d** 55 **p** 56. C Wavertree St Mary *Liv* 55-58; C Liv All So Springwood 58-62; C Horley *S'wark* 62-65; V Mitcham Ch Ch 65-72; V Iford *Win* 72-89; R Smannell w Enham Alamein 89-96; rtd 96; Perm to Offic *Sheff* from 96. *387 Redmires Road, Sheffield S10 4LE* Tel 0114-230 8721
E-mail ema98dej@sheffield.ac.uk

JARDINE, Canon David John (Brother David). b 42. QUB BA65. CITC 67. **d** 67 **p** 68. C Ballymacarrett St Patr *D & D* 67-70; Asst Chapl QUB 70-73; SSF from 73; Asst Chapl HM Pris Belfast 75-79; Chapl 79-85; USA 85-88; Sen Asst Warden Ch of Ireland Min of Healing 88-92; Dir Divine Healing Min 92-08; Can Belf Cathl from 07. *3 Richmond Park, Stranmillis, Belfast BT9 5EF* Tel (028) 9066 6200 *or* 9031 1532

JARDINE, Canon Norman. b 47. QUB BSc72. Trin Coll Bris 74. **d** 76 **p** 77. C Magheralin *D & D* 76-78; C Dundonald 78-80; Bp's C Ballybeen 80-88; I Willowfield 88-00; Dir Think Again 00-04; I Ballynafeigh St Jude from 04; Can Belf Cathl from 03. *10 Mornington, Belfast BT7 3JS* Tel (028) 9050 4976
E-mail norman.jardine2@ntlworld.com

JARDINE, Thomas Parker. b 44. Oak Hill Th Coll BA87. **d** 87 **p** 88. C Crowborough *Chich* 87-91; R Dersingham w Anmer and Shernborne *Nor* 91-00; P-in-c Southport SS Simon and Jude *Liv* 00-03; V Southport SS Simon and Jude w All So from 03; C Southport All SS from 03. *The Vicarage, 128 Roe Lane, Southport PR9 7PJ* Tel (01704) 227095

JARMAN, Christopher (Kit). b 38. QUB BA63. Wells Th Coll 69. **d** 71 **p** 72. C Leckhampton SS Phil and Jas *Glouc* 71-73; Chapl RN 73-93; Chapl Rossall Sch Fleetwood 94; R Stirling *St And* 94-03; Chapl ATC 97-03; rtd 03; Warrant from 04. *Ground Floor Flat 2, 4 Branksome Park, Longsdale Road, Oban PA34 5JZ* Tel and fax (01631) 563535

JARMAN, John Geoffrey. b 31. IEng. S'wark Ord Course 75. **d** 78 **p** 79. NSM Chigwell *Chelmsf* 78-81; NSM Leytonstone St Marg w St Columba 81-87; C Walthamstow St Sav 87-89; V Gt Bentley and P-in-c Frating w Thorrington 89-92; C Wanstead St Mary w Ch Ch 92-95; rtd 95; Perm to Offic *Chelmsf* from 95. *18 Hillside Crescent, Holland-on-Sea, Clacton-on-Sea CO15 6PB* Tel (01255) 812746

JARMAN, Michael Robert. **d** 09. NSM Caerleon w Llanhennock *Mon* from 09. *4 Hafod Mews, Caerleon Road, Ponthir, Newport NP18 1PY* Tel (01633) 423619
E-mail michael@ahlan48.fsnet.co.uk

JARMAN, Robert Joseph. b 59. Van Mildert Coll Dur BA90. **d** 92 **p** 93. C Llanishen and Lisvane 92-93; C Whitchurch 93-94. *47 Penydre, Rhiwbina, Cardiff CF14 6EJ*

JARRATT, Canon Robert Michael. b 39. K Coll Lon BD62 AKC62 NY Th Sem DMin85. **d** 63 **p** 64. C Corby St Columba *Pet* 63-67; Lay Tr Officer *Sheff* 67-71; Ind Chapl *S'wark* 72-80; P-in-c Betchworth 76-80; V Ranmoor *Sheff* 80-01; P-in-c Worsbrough and Dir Post-Ord Tr 01-05; RD Hallam 87-94; Hon Can Sheff Cathl 95-05; rtd 05. *42 Storthwood Court, Storth Lane, Sheffield S10 3HP* Tel 0114-230 7036
E-mail michaeljarratt42@yahoo.co.uk

JARRATT, Stephen. b 51. Edin Univ BD76 St Kath Coll Liv CertEd77. **d** 78 **p** 79. C Horsforth *Ripon* 78-81; C Stanningley St Thos 81-84; P-in-c Fishponds St Jo *Bris* 84-85; V 85-92; V Chapel Allerton *Ripon* 92-04; AD Allerton 97-04; TR Clifton *S'well* 04-08; AD W Bingham 07-08; P-in-c Haxby and Wigginton *York* from 08. *The Rectory, 3 Westfield Close, Wigginton, York YO32 2JG* Tel (01904) 760455
E-mail steveandnicky@thejarratts.freeserve.co.uk

✠**JARRETT, The Rt Revd Martyn William.** b 44. K Coll Lon BD67 AKC67 Hull Univ MPhil91. **d** 68 **p** 69 **c** 94. C Bris St Geo 68-70; C Swindon New Town 70-74; C Northolt St Mary *Lon* 74-76; V Northolt St Jos 76-81; V Hillingdon St Andr 81-83; P-in-c Uxbridge Moor 82-83; V Uxbridge St Andr w St Jo 83-85; Selection Sec ACCM 85-88; Sen Selection Sec 89-91; V Chesterfield St Mary and All SS *Derby* 91-94; Suff Bp Burnley *Blackb* 94-00; Hon Can Blackb Cathl 94-00; Suff Bp Beverley (PEV) *York* from 00; Hon Can Bp Dur, Ripon and Sheff from 00; Hon Asst Bp Man, S'well and Wakef from 01; Hon Asst Bp Bradf from 02; Hon Asst Bp Liv from 03; Hon Can Wakef Cathl from 01. *3 North Lane, Roundhay, Leeds LS8 2QJ* Tel 0113-265 4280 Fax 265 4281
E-mail bishop-of-beverley@3-north-lane.fsnet.co.uk

JARRETT, René Isaac Taiwo. b 49. Milton Margai Teachers' Coll Sierra Leone TCert79 Lon Inst of Educn BEd94. Sierra Leone Th Hall 80. **d** 83 **p** 85. Dn Freetown St Luke Sierra Leone 83-85;

C Freetown Bp Elwin Memorial Ch 85-89; Hon C St Pancras w St Jas and Ch Ch *Lon* 89-95; C Bloomsbury St Geo w Woburn Square Ch Ch from 95. *2 Woburn Mansions, Torrington Place, London WC1E 7HL* Tel (020) 7580 5165 Mobile 07853-348143 E-mail jarrorene@yahoo.co.uk

JARROW, Suffragan Bishop of. *See* BRYANT, The Rt Revd Mark Watts

JARVIS, Ian Frederick Rodger. b 38. Bris Univ BA60. Tyndale Hall Bris 61. **d** 63 **p** 64. C Penge St Jo Ch w H Trin *Roch* 63-67; C Bilston St Leon *Lich* 67-71; V Lozells St Silas *Birm* 71-76; V Chaddesden St Mary *Derby* 76-95; V Newhall 95-02; rtd 02; Perm to Offic *Derby* from 02. *29 Springfield Road, Midway, Swadlincote DE11 0BZ* Tel (01283) 551589

JARVIS, Mrs Lynda Claire. b 46. Southn Univ CQSW87. STETS 95. **d** 98 **p** 99. C Chandler's Ford *Win* 98-01; rtd 01. *Largo Santana 3, Tavira, 8800-701 Algarve, Portugal* Tel (00351) (281) 323553 Mobile 961-166240

JARVIS, Miss Mary. b 35. Leeds Univ BA57 Lon Univ CertEd59. Cranmer Hall Dur 78. **dss** 80 **d** 87 **p** 94. Low Harrogate St Mary *Ripon* 80-84; Wortley de Leeds 84-87; C 87-88; C Upper Armley 88-94; C Holbeck 94-95; rtd 95; Perm to Offic *Ripon* from 01. *71 Burnsall Croft, Leeds LS12 3LH* Tel 0113-279 7832 E-mail mjarvis@amserve.com

JARVIS, Nathan John. b 73. Ox Brookes Univ BA97 Leeds Univ MA04. St Steph Ho Ox BTh06. **d** 06 **p** 07. C Hartlepool H Trin *Dur* from 06. *43 Alderwood Close, Hartlepool TS27 3QR* Tel (01429) 894013 E-mail fr.nathan@yahoo.com

JARVIS, Mrs Pamela Ann. b 51. Sussex Univ BEd74. SWMTC 97. **d** 00 **p** 01. C Braunton *Ex* 00-03; C Combe Martin, Berrynarbor, Lynton, Brendon etc 03-04; TV from 04. *The Rectory, Lee Road, Lynton EX35 6BP* Tel (01598) 753251 Mobile 07773-900523 E-mail pajarvis@ntlworld.com

JARVIS, Peter Timothy. b 64. St Jo Coll Nottm 02. **d** 04 **p** 05. C Thatcham *Ox* 04-06; TV from 06. *The Vicarage, 1 Cowslip Crescent, Thatcham RG18 4DE* Tel (01635) 867336 Mobile 07775-440507 E-mail revdpj@btinternet.com

JARVIS, Rupert Charles Melbourn. b 69. St Andr Univ MA92 Univ of Wales (Swansea) MPhil96. Cuddesdon Coll 96. **d** 98 **p** 99. C Swansea St Mary w H Trin *S & B* 98-99; Min Can Brecon Cathl 99-01; CF 01-08; Asst Chapl Shiplake Coll Henley 08-09; Chapl Denstone Coll Uttoxeter from 09. *Denstone College, Uttoxeter ST14 5HN* Tel (01889) 590484

JARVIS, Stephen John. b 55. WEMTC 04. **d** 07 **p** 08. NSM Bisley, Chalford, France Lynch, and Oakridge *Glouc* from 07. *8 Ollney Road, Minchinhampton, Stroud GL6 9BX* Tel (01453) 884545 Mobile 07921-548467 E-mail stephen@sjarvis.freeserve.co.uk

JARVIS, Steven. WEMTC. **d** 07 **p** 08. NSM Ludlow *Heref* from 07. *3 Townsend Close, Ludlow SY8 1UN* Tel (01584) 874284

JARY, Ms Helen Lesley. b 69. Lanc Univ BA91. St Jo Coll Nottm 05. **d** 07 **p** 08. C Oulton Broad *Nor* from 07. *3 Windward Way, Lowestoft NR33 9HF* Tel (01502) 502166 Mobile 07990-501683 E-mail helen.jary@ukf.net

JASON, Mark Andrew. b 73. Madras Univ BA94 S Asia Inst for Advanced Chr Studies MA96. Gurukul Lutheran Th Coll & Research Inst BD00. **p** 01. India 01-03; Perm to Offic *Ab* from 03. *31 Gladstone Place, Aberdeen AB10 6UX* Tel (01224) 321714 E-mail m.a.jason@abdn.ac.uk

JASPER, Prof David. b 51. Jes Coll Cam BA72 MA76 Keble Coll Ox BD80 Dur Univ PhD83 Ox Univ DD02 Uppsala Univ Hon ThD07 FRSE06. **d** 76 **p** 77. C Buckingham *Ox* 76-79; C Sherborne St Oswald 80; Chapl Hatf Coll Dur 81-88; Dir Cen Study of Lit and Th Dur 88-91; Prin St Chad's Coll Dur 88-91; Reader and Dir Cen Study of Lit and Th Glas Univ from 91; Vice-Dean of Div 95-98; Dean of Div 98-02; Lic to Offic *Glas* 91-08; NSM Hamilton from 08. *Netherwood, 124 Old Manse Road, Wishaw ML2 0EP* Tel and fax (01698) 373286 E-mail d.jasper@arts.gla.ac.uk

JASPER, David Julian McLean. b 44. Dur Univ BA66. Linc Th Coll 66. **d** 68 **p** 69. C Redruth *Truro* 68-72; TV 72-75; V St Just in Penwith 75-86; P-in-c Sancreed 82-86; C Reading St Matt *Ox* 96-00; P-in-c 00-02; R S Petherton w the Seavingtons *B & W* from 02. *The Rectory, Hele Lane, South Petherton TA13 5DY* Tel (01460) 240377 Mobile 07767-814533 E-mail david.jasper@virgin.net

JASPER, James Roland. b 32. CA Tr Coll 56 NEOC 82. **d** 84 **p** 84. C Newburn *Newc* 84-86; V Ansley *Cov* 86-97; rtd 97; Perm to Offic *Leic* from 97 and *Cov* from 03. *69 Edward Road, Newbold Verdon, Leicester LE9 9LG* Tel (01455) 822567

JASPER, Jonathan Ernest Farley. b 50. AKC72. St Aug Coll Cant 73. **d** 73 **p** 74. C Cheshunt *St Alb* 73-75; C Bedford St Paul 75-77; C Bedford St Pet w St Cuth 75-77; Chapl Southn Univ 77-80; Chapl Lon Univ Medical Students 80-86; PV Chich Cathl 86-89; P-in-c Earls Colne and White Colne *Chelmsf* 89-94; P-in-c Colne Engaine 89-94; R Earls Colne w White Colne and Colne Engaine 95-02; C Christchurch *Win* 02-08; Perm to Offic from 08. *7 Tyndale Close, Bournemouth BH9 3SF* Tel (01202) 534037 E-mail jefjasper@btinternet.com

JAUNDRILL, John Warwick. b 47. MCIM81. Qu Coll Birm 86. **d** 88 **p** 89. C Bistre *St As* 88-91; P-in-c Towyn and St George

91-92; V 92-02; C Llanrhos from 06. *5 Traeth Penrhyn, Penrhyn Bay, Llandudno LL30 3RN* Tel (01492) 544845

JAY, Colin. b 62. Keble Coll Ox BA85 St Jo Coll Dur BA89. Cranmer Hall Dur 87. **d** 90 **p** 91. C Bishopwearmouth St Gabr *Dur* 90-94; C Newton Aycliffe 94; TV 94-96; TV Gt Aycliffe 96-03; AD Sedgefield 99-03; Chapl Co Dur & Darlington Priority Services NHS Trust from 03. *Earls House Hospital, Lanchester Road, Durham DH1 5RD* Tel 0191-333 6262 E-mail colsar@netscapeonline.co.uk

JAY, Ms Nicola Mary. b 37. SRN58. NEOC 88. **d** 91 **p** 94. Par Dn Whitburn *Dur* 91-94; C 94-95; P-in-c Sacriston and Kimblesworth 95-00; rtd 00. *29 Church Street, Sacriston, Durham DH7 6JL* Tel 0191-371 0152

JAY, Richard Hylton Michael. b 31. Bris Univ BEd75. Sarum & Wells Th Coll 77. **d** 79 **p** 80. NSM Bath St Barn w Englishcombe *B & W* 79-81; NSM Saltford w Corston and Newton St Loe 81-88; R Hatch Beauchamp w Beercrocombe, Curry Mallet etc 89-97; rtd 97; Perm to Offic *B & W* from 97. *Stableside, 5 Princess Road, Taunton TA1 4SY* Tel (01823) 335531

JAYNE, Martin Philip. b 49. Man Univ BA71 MRTPI73. Carl Dioc Tr Course 87. **d** 90 **p** 91. NSM Natland *Carl* from 90; Dioc Officer for NSM 04-08. *12 Longmeadow Lane, Natland, Kendal LA9 7QZ* Tel (01539) 560942 E-mail martjay@btinternet.com

JEANES, Gordon Paul. b 55. Ox Univ BCL79 MA80 BD90 Univ of Wales (Lamp) PhD99. St Steph Ho Ox 80. **d** 82 **p** 83. C S Wimbledon H Trin and St Pet *S'wark* 82-85; C Surbiton St Andr and St Mark 85-90; Chapl St Chad's Coll Dur 90-93; Sub-Warden St Mich Coll Llan 94-98; Lect Th Univ of Wales (Cardiff) 94-98; V Wandsworth St Anne *S'wark* 98-08; P-in-c Wandsworth St Faith 05-08; V Wandsworth St Anne w St Faith from 08; Dioc Voc Adv from 99. *St Anne's Vicarage, 182 St Ann's Hill, London SW18 2RS* Tel (020) 8874 2809 E-mail gordon.jeanes@virgin.net

JEANS, The Ven Alan Paul. b 58. MIAAS84 MIBCO84 Southn Univ BTh89 Univ of Wales (Lamp) MA03. Sarum & Wells Th Coll 86. **d** 89 **p** 90. C Parkstone St Pet w Branksea and St Osmund *Sarum* 89-93; P-in-c Bishop's Cannings, All Cannings etc 93-98; Par Development Adv from 98; Can and Preb Sarum Cathl from 02; Adn Sarum from 03; RD Alderbury 05-07; Dioc Dir of Ords from 07. *Herbert House, 118 Lower Road, Salisbury SP2 9NW* Tel (01722) 336290 *or* (01380) 840373 Fax (01722) 411990 *or* (01380) 848247 E-mail adsarum@salisbury.anglican.org

JEANS, David Bockley. b 48. Mert Coll Ox BA71 MA80 PGCE73 Man Univ MPhil98. Trin Coll Bris 83. **d** 85 **p** 86. C Clevedon St Andr and Ch Ch *B & W* 85-88; V Wadsley *Sheff* 88-96; Dir Studies Wilson Carlile Coll of Evang 96; Prin 97-06; Dean Coll of S Cross New Zealand 06-08; P-in-c Deepcar *Sheff* from 08. *St John's Vicarage, 27 Carr Road, Deepcar, Sheffield S36 2PQ* Tel 0114-288 5138

JEAPES (*née* **PORTER**), **Mrs Barbara Judith.** b 47. Cam Inst of Educn TCert68. Carl Dioc Tr Inst 91. **d** 94 **p** 95. NSM Egremont and Haile *Carl* from 94. *15 Millfields, Beckermet CA21 2YY* Tel (01946) 841489 E-mail barbara.jeapes@btinternet.com

JEAVONS, Mrs Margaret Anne. b 51. Liv Poly BA72 Bris Univ BA01 St Kath Coll Liv PGCE74. Trin Coll Bris 99. **d** 01 **p** 02. C Totnes w Bridgetown, Berry Pomeroy etc *Ex* 01-05; V Sutton St Mich *York* from 05. *St Michael's Vicarage, 751 Marfleet Lane, Hull HU9 4TJ* Tel (01482) 374509 E-mail mjeavons@btopenworld.com

JEAVONS, Maurice. b 32. Ely Th Coll 60. **d** 62 **p** 63. C Longton St Jo *Lich* 62-68; V Wednesfield St Greg 68-81; V Lower Gornal 81-90; NSM Willenhall St Anne 92-93; C Tunstall 93-99; rtd 99; Hon C Wolverhampton St Steph *Lich* 99-09; Perm to Offic from 09. *17 Colaton Close, Wolverhampton WV10 9BB* Tel (01902) 351118

JEE, Jonathan Noel. b 63. BNC Ox BA84 MA88. Wycliffe Hall Ox 85. **d** 88 **p** 89. C Brampton St Thos *Derby* 88-92; TV Hinckley H Trin *Leic* 92-00; V Leamington Priors St Paul *Cov* from 00. *The Vicarage, 15 Lillington Road, Leamington Spa CV32 5YS* Tel (01926) 772132 *or* 427149 E-mail jonathan.jee@ntlworld.com

JEFF, Canon Gordon Henry. b 32. St Edm Hall Ox BA56 MA60. Wells Th Coll 59. **d** 61 **p** 62. C Sydenham St Bart *S'wark* 61-64; C Kidbrooke St Jas 64-66; V Clapham St Paul 66-72; V Raynes Park St Sav 73-79; RD Merton 77-79; V Carshalton Beeches 79-86; P-in-c Petersham 86-90; Chapl St Mich Convent 90-96; Hon Can S'wark Cathl 93-96; rtd 96; Perm to Offic *B & W* from 07. *9 Barnetts Well, Draycott, Cheddar BS27 3TF* Tel (01934) 744943

JEFFCOAT, Rupert Edward Elessing. b 70. St Cath Coll Cam BA92 MA96 FRCO91. WMMTC 02. **d** 05. NSM Brisbane Cathl Australia from 05. *GPO Box 421, Brisbane Qld 4001, Australia* Tel (0061) (7) 3835 2231 E-mail rjeffcoat@freenetname.co.uk

JEFFERIES, Michael Lewis. b 45. St Jo Coll Nottm. **d** 87 **p** 88. C Pudsey St Lawr and St Paul *Bradf* 87-93; V Beckenham St Jo *Roch* 93-00; TV Modbury, Bigbury, Ringmore w Kingston etc

Ex from 00. *The Vicarage, 3 Little Gate, Loddiswell, Kingsbridge TQ7 4RB* Tel (01548) 550841

JEFFERIES, Preb Phillip John. b 42. St Chad's Coll Dur BA65 MA91. **d** 67 **p** 68. C Tunstall Ch Ch *Lich* 67-71; C Wolverhampton St Pet 71-74; P-in-c Oakengates 74-80; V 80-82; P-in-c Ketley 78-82; V Horninglow 82-00; RD Tutbury 97-00; TR Stafford 00-07; Bp's Adv on Hosp Chapl 82-06; Preb Lich Cathl 99-07; rtd 07; Perm to Offic *Lich* from 07. *16 Morley's Hill, Burton-on-Trent DE13 0TA* Tel (01283) 544013

JEFFERS, Cliff Peter. b 69. CITC BTh98. **d** 98 **p** 99. C Limerick City *L & K* 98-01; I Clonenagh w Offerlane, Borris-in-Ossory etc *C & O* 01-04; I Athy w Kilberry, Fontstown and Kilkea *D & G* from 04. *The Rectory, Church Road, Athy, Co Kildare, Republic of Ireland* Tel (00353) (59) 863 1446 Fax 863 1490
E-mail athy@glendalough.anglican.org

JEFFERS, Neil Gareth Thompson. b 78. St Jo Coll Ox BA99 MA05. Oak Hill Th Coll MTh07. **d** 07 **p** 08. C Lowestoft Ch Ch *Nor* from 07. *10 Station Road, Lowestoft NR32 4QF* Tel (01502) 508695 Mobile 07769-586260
E-mail neiljeffers2003@yahoo.co.uk

JEFFERSON, Charles Dudley. b 55. St Pet Coll Ox BA78 MA81. Ridley Hall Cam 79. **d** 81 **p** 82. C Chadkirk *Ches* 81-84; C Macclesfield St Pet 84-85; C Macclesfield Team 85-89; R Elworth and Warmingham 89-99; Chapl Framlingham Coll 99-01; Chapl Rendcomb Coll Cirencester 01-09; P-in-c Rendcomb *Glouc* 01-09; R Thrapston, Denford and Islip *Pet* from 09. *The Rectory, 48 Oundle Road, Thrapston, Kettering NN14 4PD* Tel (01832) 732393
E-mail revjefferson@tiscali.co.uk

JEFFERSON, David Charles. b 33. Leeds Univ BA57. Coll of Resurr Mirfield 57. **d** 59 **p** 60. C Kennington Cross St Anselm *S'wark* 59-62; C Richmond St Mary 62-64; Chapl Wilson's Gr Sch Camberwell 64-93; Chapl Wilson's Sch Wallington 75-99; Public Preacher *S'wark* 64-74; Hon C Carshalton Beeches 74-04; rtd 93; Perm to Offic *S'wark* from 04. *15 Sandown Drive, Carshalton SM5 4LN* Tel (020) 8669 0640 *or* 8773 2931

JEFFERSON, Michael William. b 41. K Coll Lon AKC64. WMMTC 96. **d** 98 **p** 99. C Four Oaks *Birm* 98-02; P-in-c Longdon *Lich* 02-08; Local Min Adv (Wolverhampton) 02-08; rtd 08; Perm to Offic *Lich* and *Portsm* from 09. *9 Soma House, 380 Springfield Road, Sutton Coldfield B75 7JH* Tel 0121-329 2214

✠**JEFFERTS SCHORI, The Most Revd Katharine.** b 54. Stanford Univ BS74 Oregon State Univ MS77 PhD83. Ch Div Sch of Pacific MDiv94 Hon DD01. **d** 94 **p** 94 **c** 01. C Corvallis Gd Samaritan USA 94-01; Chapl Benton Hospice Service 95-00; Instructor Oregon State Univ 96-99; Bp Nevada 01-06; Presiding Bp from 06. *Episcopal Church Center, 815 Second Avenue, New York NY 10017, USA* Tel (001) (212) 716 6271 Fax 490 3298
E-mail pboffice@episcopalchurch.org

JEFFERY, Graham. b 35. Qu Coll Cam BA58. Wells Th Coll 58. **d** 60 **p** 61. C Southampton Maybush St Pet *Win* 60-63; Australia 63-66; C E Grinstead St Swithun *Chich* 66-68; C-in-c The Hydneye CD 68-74; V Wick 74-76; C Hove 76-78; P-in-c Newtimber w Pyecombe 78-82; R Poynings w Edburton, Newtimber and Pyecombe 82-92; P-in-c Sullington and Thakeham w Warminghurst 92-95; rtd 96; P-in-c Poynings w Edburton, Newtimber and Pyecombe *Chich* 97-99; Perm to Offic from 00. *Eton Cottage, Compton, Chichester PO18 9HD* Tel (023) 9263 1220

JEFFERY (*née* **CAW**), **Mrs Hannah Mary.** b 69. Birm Univ BMus91. St Jo Coll Nottm MA95. **d** 95 **p** 96. C Northampton St Giles *Pet* 95-99; Hon C Hanger Hill Ascension and W Twyford St Mary *Lon* 99-04; TV Northampton Em *Pet* from 04. *9 Botmead Road, Northampton NN3 5JF* Tel (01604) 787954
E-mail jeffery@xalt.co.uk

JEFFERY, Mrs Jennifer Ann. b 45. Philippa Fawcett Coll CertEd66. STETS. **d** 02 **p** 03. NSM Wilton *B & W* from 02; Chapl Bp Henderson Sch from 07. *4 Southwell, Trull, Taunton TA3 7HU* Tel (01823) 286589
E-mail jenny@jajeffery.freeserve.co.uk

JEFFERY, Jonathan George Piers. b 63. Man Univ LLB84. Ripon Coll Cuddesdon 95. **d** 97 **p** 98. C Lee-on-the-Solent *Portsm* 97-01; V Leigh Park from 01; V Warren Park from 01. *The Vicarage, Riders Lane, Havant PO9 4QT* Tel (023) 9247 5276

JEFFERY, Kenneth Charles. b 40. Univ of Wales BA64 Linacre Coll Ox BA67 MA70. St Steph Ho Ox 64. **d** 67 **p** 68. C Swindon New Town *Bris* 67-68; C Summertown *Ox* 68-71; C Brighton St Pet *Chich* 71-77; V Ditchling 77-00; rtd 05. *62 Fruitlands, Malvern WR14 4XA* Tel (01684) 567042
E-mail kenneth@jeffery333.fslife.co.uk

JEFFERY, Michael Frank. b 48. Linc Th Coll 74. **d** 76 **p** 77. C Caterham Valley *S'wark* 76-79; C Tupsley *Heref* 79-82; P-in-c Stretton Sugwas 82-84; P-in-c Bishopstone 83-84; P-in-c Kenchester and Bridge Sollers 83-84; V Whiteshill *Glouc* 84-92; P-in-c Randwick 92; V Whiteshill and Randwick 93-02; TV Bedminster *Bris* from 02. *St Paul's Vicarage, 2 Southville Road, Bristol BS3 1DG* Tel 0117-908 6996

JEFFERY, Peter James. b 41. Leeds Univ BSc63. Oak Hill Th Coll 64. **d** 66 **p** 67. C Streatham Park St Alb *S'wark* 66-70; C Northampton St Giles *Pet* 70-73; C Rushden St Pet 73-76; C Rushden w Newton Bromswold 77-78; V Siddal *Wakef* 78-85; V Sowerby Bridge w Norland 85-98; P-in-c Cornholme 98-00; P-in-c Walsden 98-00; V Cornholme and Walsden 00-05; rtd 05. *12 Highcroft Road, Todmorden OL14 5LZ* Tel (01706) 839781
E-mail jeffrey@cornden.freeserve.co.uk

JEFFERY, Peter Noel. b 37. Pemb Coll Ox BA60 MA64. Linc Th Coll 60. **d** 62 **p** 63. C W Smethwick *Birm* 62-64; P-in-c Bordesley St Andr 64-69; R Turvey *St Alb* 69-98; P-in-c Stevington 79-98; rtd 98. *Franconia Cottage, The Gardens, Adstock, Buckingham MK18 2JF* Tel (01296) 715770

JEFFERY, Richard William Christopher. b 43. Ex Univ BA65. Coll of Resurr Mirfield 66. **d** 68 **p** 69. C Widley w Wymering *Portsm* 68-71; C Salisbury St Mich *Sarum* 71-74; TV Ridgeway 74-80; V Stanford in the Vale w Goosey and Hatford *Ox* 80-89; V Topsham *Ex* from 89; RD Aylesbeare 01-07. *The Vicarage, Globefields, Topsham, Exeter EX3 0EZ* Tel (01392) 876120
E-mail knocksink@eurobell.co.uk

JEFFERY, The Very Revd Robert Martin Colquhoun. b 35. K Coll Lon BD58 AKC58 Birm Univ Hon DD99 FRSA91. **d** 59 **p** 60. C Grangetown *Dur* 59-61; C Barnes St Mary *S'wark* 61-63; Asst Sec Miss and Ecum Coun Ch Assembly 64-68; Sec Dept Miss and Unity BCC 68-71; V Headington *Ox* 71-78; RD Cowley 73-78; P-in-c Tong *Lich* 78-83; V 83-87; Dioc Missr 78-80; Adn Salop 80-87; Dean Worc 87-96; Can Res and Sub-Dean Ch Ch *Ox* 96-02; Select Preacher Ox Univ 91, 97, 98 and 02; rtd 02. *47 The Manor House, Bennett Crescent, Cowley, Oxford OX4 2UG* Tel (01865) 749706
E-mail rmcj@btopenworld.com

JEFFERYES, June Ann. b 37. Dur Univ BA58. WMMTC 87. **d** 90 **p** 94. NSM Caverswall *Lich* 90-92; NSM Caverswall and Weston Coyney w Dilhorne 92-02; rtd 02; Perm to Offic *Lich* from 02. *24 Glen Drive, Alton, Stoke-on-Trent ST10 4DJ* Tel (01538) 702150

JEFFERYES, Preb Neil. b 37. St Andr Univ BSc60 Lon Univ BD62. Tyndale Hall Bris 60. **d** 63 **p** 64. C St Helens St Helen *Liv* 63-68; V Barrow St Mark *Carl* 68-77; RD Furness 74-77; P-in-c Tetsworth *Ox* 77-81; P-in-c Adwell w S Weston 77-81; P-in-c Stoke Talmage w Wheatfield 77-81; RD Aston 81-85; R Tetsworth, Adwell w S Weston, Lewknor etc 81-86; V Caverswall *Lich* 86-92; P-in-c Dilhorne 86-92; RD Cheadle 91-98; V Caverswall and Weston Coyney w Dilhorne 92-02; Preb Lich Cathl 97-02; rtd 02; Perm to Offic *Lich* from 02. *24 Glen Drive, Alton, Stoke-on-Trent ST10 4DJ* Tel (01538) 702150
E-mail neil@jefferyes.freeserve.co.uk

JEFFORD, Mrs Margaret June. b 50. Univ of Wales RGN81. St Mich Coll Llan 94. **d** 96 **p** 97. C Risca *Mon* 96-98; C Pontypool 98-00; TV 00-02; V Newbridge w Crumlin 02-04; V Newbridge from 04. *St Paul's Vicarage, High Street, Newbridge, Newport NP11 4FW* Tel (01495) 243975

JEFFORD, Peter Ernest. b 29. AKC53. **d** 54 **p** 55. C Berkeley *Glouc* 54-57; C Petersfield w Sheet *Portsm* 57-61; Chapl Churcher's Coll 57-61; R Rollesby w Burgh w Billockby *Nor* 62-71; V Watton 71-81; V Watton w Carbrooke and Ovington 81-82; Offg Chapl RAF 71-82; P-in-c Brampford Speke *Ex* 82-83; P-in-c Cadbury 82-83; P-in-c Thorverton 82-83; P-in-c Upton Pyne 82-83; TR Thorverton, Cadbury, Upton Pyne etc 83-92; rtd 92; Perm to Offic *Ox* 92-96 and from 03; Hon C Ox St Mary V w St Cross and St Pet 96-99; P-in-c Whitchurch St Mary 00-03; Chapl Plater Coll 96-05. *27 Ashlong Road, Headington, Oxford OX3 0NH* Tel (01865) 760593

JEFFORD, Ronald. b 46. St Mich Coll Llan. **d** 91 **p** 92. C Ebbw Vale *Mon* 91-94; TV 94-95; R Bedwas and Rudry 95-98; V Abersychan and Garndiffaith 98-03; TV Mynyddislwyn 03-05; rtd 05. *St Paul's Vicarage, High Street, Newbridge, Newport NP11 4FW* Tel (01495) 243975

JEFFREE, Robin. b 29. AKC54. **d** 55 **p** 56. C N Harrow St Alb *Lon* 55-59; C Hendon St Mary 59-62; V Manea *Ely* 62-67; V Hartford 67-83; R Denver 83-94; V Ryston w Roxham 83-94; V W Dereham 83-94; rtd 94; Perm to Offic *Nor* from 94. *3 Church Lane, Hindolveston, Dereham NR20 5BT* Tel (01263) 861857

JEFFREY, Katrina. *See* METZNER, Mrs Katrina

JEFFREYS, David John. b 45. S Dios Minl Tr Scheme 89. **d** 92 **p** 93. NSM Bexhill St Barn *Chich* 92-95; Chapl Hastings and Rother NHS Trust 95-02; Chapl E Sussex Hosps NHS Trust 02-05; Chapl Team Ldr 05-07; Chapl Eastbourne Hosps NHS Trust from 07. *Eastbourne District General Hospital, King's Drive, Eastbourne BN21 2UD* Tel (01323) 417400 ext 4145

JEFFREYS (*née* **DESHPANDE**), **Mrs Lakshmi Anant.** b 64. Liv Univ BSc86 Ex Univ PGCE87. Wycliffe Hall Ox BTh94. **d** 94 **p** 95. C Long Eaton St Jo *Derby* 94-97; Chapl Nottm Trent Univ 98-03; Perm to Offic *Derby* 03-04; Dioc Miss Adv from 04. *43 White Street, Derby DE22 1HB* Tel (01332) 224432
E-mail lakshmi.jeffreys@derby.anglican.org

JEFFREYS, Timothy John. b 58. Man Univ BSc79. Cranmer Hall Dur 83. **d** 86 **p** 87. C Goodmayes All SS *Chelmsf* 86-88; Perm to Offic *S'wark* 92-93; Hon C S Lambeth St Anne and All

SS 93-96; C Croydon St Jo 96-06; V Brixton Road Ch Ch from 06. *The Vicarage, 96 Brixton Road, London SW9 6BE* Tel (020) 7793 0621 E-mail tim.jeffreys@btopenworld.com

JEFFRIES, Frances Alyx. b 59. Bris Poly BA82 Solicitor 83. **d** 04 **p** 05. OLM Gainsborough and Morton *Linc* from 04. *33 Balfour Street, Gainsborough DN21 2LF* Tel (01427) 678569 E-mail frances@33gains.fsnet.co.uk

JEFFRIES, Keith. b 48. St Steph Ho Ox 91. **d** 93 **p** 94. C St Marychurch *Ex* 93-96; TV Wood Green St Mich w Bounds Green St Gabr etc *Lon* 96-98; V The Hydneye *Chich* 98-00; Chapl Univ of Greenwich *Roch* 00-02; Chapl Kent Inst of Art and Design 00-02; Chapl Tenerife Sur *Eur* 02-03; Perm to Offic *Roch* 03-04; Bp's Adv on Chr/Muslim Relns *Birm* 04-07; Chapl Oakington Immigration Reception Cen 07-09; rtd 09. *Edificio las Tejas, Bloque 3, Vivenda 12, Lugar Pasitos 38, Pueblo de Mogan, 35140 Las Palmas, Spain* E-mail fatherkeithjeffries@hotmail.com

JELF, Miss Pauline Margaret. b 55. Chich Th Coll 88. **d** 90 **p** 94. Par Dn Clayton *Lich* 90-94; C Knutton 94-98; P-in-c Silverdale and Alsagers Bank 94-98; Perm to Offic 98-02; C Clayton 02; C Betley and Madeley 02-04; C Trent Vale 03-06. *11 Stafford Avenue, Newcastle ST5 3BN* Tel (01785) 639545

JELLEY, Ian. b 54. Newc Univ MA94. NEOC 89. **d** 91 **p** 92. C Jarrow *Dur* 91-95; P-in-c Leam Lane 95-96; Chapl HM Pris Holme Ho 96-01; R Grindon, Stillington and Wolviston *Dur* 01-03; rtd 03. *Address temp unknown*

JELLEY, James Dudley. b 46. Linc Th Coll 78. **d** 80 **p** 81. C Stockwell Green St Andr *S'wark* 80-85; V Camberwell St Phil and St Mark 85-93; Perm to Offic 93-96; V Camberwell St Luke from 96; RD Camberwell 00-06. *St Luke's Vicarage, 30 Commercial Way, London SE15 5JQ* Tel and fax (020) 7703 5587

JELLEY (née CAPITANCHIK), Mrs Sophie Rebecca. b 72. Leeds Univ BA93. Wycliffe Hall Ox MPhil97. **d** 97 **p** 98. C Shipley St Pet *Bradf* 97-00; CMS Uganda 00-03; C Churt and Hindhead *Guildf* from 03. *St John's Vicarage, Old Kiln Lane, Churt, Farnham GU10 2HX* Tel (01428) 713368 E-mail sophie@jelley.f9.co.uk

JENKIN, The Revd Canon the Hon Charles Alexander Graham. b 54. BScEng. Westcott Ho Cam 81. **d** 84 **p** 85. C Binley *Cov* 84-88; TV Canvey Is *Chelmsf* 88-94; TR Melton Mowbray *Leic* 94-08; RD Framland 98-02; Hon Can Leic Cathl 06-08; V Ipswich St Mary-le-Tower *St E* from 08; Bp's Interfaith Adv from 09. *The Vicarage, 18 Kingsfield Avenue, Ipswich IP1 3TA* Tel and fax (01473) 289001 E-mail charles@jenkin.uk.net

JENKIN, Christopher Cameron. b 36. BNC Ox BA61 MA64. Clifton Th Coll 61. **d** 63 **p** 64. C Walthamstow St Mary *Chelmsf* 63-68; C Surbiton Hill Ch Ch *S'wark* 68-78; V Newport St Jo *Portsm* 78-88; TR Newbarns w Hawcoat *Carl* 88-01; rtd 01; Perm to Offic *Carl* from 01. *Beckside, Orton, Penrith CA10 3RX* Tel (01539) 624410

JENKINS, Alan David. b 60. Bris Poly BA83 Spurgeon's Coll MTh02. Wycliffe Hall Ox 93. **d** 95 **p** 96. C Tunbridge Wells St Jas w St Phil *Roch* 95-01; TV S Gillingham 01-07; R Gt Bookham *Guildf* from 07. *The Rectory, 2A Fife Way, Bookham, Leatherhead KT23 3PH* Tel (01372) 452405 E-mail alan.jenkins@stnicolasbookham.org.uk

JENKINS, Allan Kenneth. b 40. Lon Univ BD63 AKC63 MTh69 PhD85. St Mich Coll Llan 63. **d** 64 **p** 65. C Llanblethian w Cowbridge 64-70; Lect Serampore Coll India 70-76; V Llanarth w Clytha, Llansantffraed and Bryngwyn *Mon* 76-78; Dir of Studies Chich Th Coll 78-83; P-in-c Fowlmere and Thriplow *Ely* 83-87; Sen Tutor EAMTC 84-87; Sen Chapl Cardiff Colls 87-95; Dioc Dir Post-Ord Tr *Llan* 88-95; P-in-c Sidlesham *Chich* 95-08; Tutor Chich Univ 95-09. *6 Clive Mews, Loftus Street, Cardiff CF5 1HY* Tel (029) 2035 9076 Mobile 07788-427159 E-mail allankjenkins@tiscali.co.uk

JENKINS, Miss Anne Christina. b 47. Birm Univ BA70 Hull Univ CertEd71 St Jo Coll Dur BA77. Cranmer Hall Dur 75. **dss** 78 **d** 87 **p** 94. E Coatham *York* 78-81; OHP 81-87; Perm to Offic *York* 81-87; Ghana 87-88; Par Dn Beeston *Ripon* 88-93; Par Dn Leeds Gipton Epiphany 93-94; V Leeds St Marg and All Hallows 94-99; rtd 99; Perm to Offic *York* from 00. *28 Hill Cottages, Rosedale East, Pickering YO18 8RG* Tel (01751) 417130

JENKINS, Audrey Joan. b 36. TCert61. St D Coll Lamp. **d** 01. Par Dn Marshfield and Peterstone Wentloog etc *Mon* 01-06; NSM Llanrumney from 06. *10 Cwrt Pencraig, 8 Caerau Crescent, Newport NP20 4HG* Tel (01633) 263470 E-mail glyn.jenkins@homecall.co.uk

JENKINS, Catherine. b 34. SWMTC 04. **d** 05 **p** 06. NSM Silverton, Butterleigh, Bickleigh and Cadeleigh *Ex* from 05. *Butterleigh House, Butterleigh, Cullompton EX15 1PH* Tel (01884) 855379

JENKINS, Clifford Thomas. b 38. Westmr Coll Ox MTh02 IEng MIEIecIE. Sarum & Wells Th Coll 74. **d** 77 **p** 78. Chapl Yeovil Coll 77-86; Hon C Yeovil w Kingston Pitney *B & W* 77-80; P-in-c 80-86; Chs FE Liaison Officer *B & W, Bris* and *Glouc* 87-90; Perm to Offic *B & W* from 87; FE Adv Gen Syn Bd of

Educn and Meth Ch 90-98; rtd 98. *Bethany, 10 Grove Avenue, Yeovil BA20 2BB* Tel (01935) 475043 E-mail clifford.jenkins@virgin.net

JENKINS, Clive Ronald. b 57. Chich Univ BA08. Ripon Coll Cuddesdon 81. **d** 84 **p** 85. C E Grinstead St Swithun *Chich* 84-87; C Horsham 87-88; TV 88-90; Dioc Youth Chapl 90-96; P-in-c Amberley w N Stoke and Parham, Wiggonholt etc 93-96; V Southbourne w W Thorney from 96. *The Vicarage, 271 Main Road, Southbourne, Emsworth PO10 8JE* Tel (01243) 372436

JENKINS, David. *See* JENKINS, Canon William David

JENKINS, David. *See* JENKINS, Preb Richard David

✠**JENKINS, The Rt Revd David Edward.** b 25. Qu Coll Ox BA51 MA54 Dur Univ DD87. Linc Th Coll 52. **d** 53 **p** 54 **c** 84. C Birm Cathl 53-54; Lect Qu Coll Birm 53-54; Chapl Qu Coll Ox 54-69; Lect Th Ox Univ 55-69; Can Th Leic Cathl 66-82; Dir WCC Humanum Studies 69-73; Dir Wm Temple Foundn Man 73-78; Jt Dir 79-94; Prof Th and RS Leeds Univ 79-84; Bp Dur 84-94; rtd 94; Hon Asst Bp Ripon and Leeds from 94. *Ashburne, Cotherstone, Barnard Castle DL12 9PR* Tel (01833) 650804 Fax 650714

JENKINS, Canon David Harold. b 61. SS Coll Cam BA84 MA87 Ox Univ BA88 MA94 FSAScot01. Ripon Coll Cuddesdon 86. **d** 89 **p** 90. C Chesterton Gd Shep *Ely* 89-91; C Earley St Pet *Ox* 91-94; V Blackpool St Mich *Blackb* 94-99; V Broughton 99-04; AD Preston 04; Can Res Carl Cathl 04-07; Dir of Educn from 04. *1 The Abbey, Carlisle CA3 8TZ* Tel (01228) 597614 *or* 538086 Fax 815409 E-mail director.education@carlislediocese.org.uk

JENKINS, David Noble. b 25. CCC Cam BA47 MA50. Cuddesdon Coll 48. **d** 50 **p** 51. C Northampton St Matt *Pet* 50-54; Chapl Hurstpierpoint Coll 54-59; USPG 60-65; Chapl Eastbourne Coll 66-74; V Jarvis Brook *Chich* 75-90; rtd 90; Perm to Offic *Chich* from 92. *25 Ramsay Hall, 9-13 Byron Road, Worthing BN11 3HN* Tel (01903) 207524 E-mail dnjlittleb@waitrose.com

JENKINS, David Roland. b 32. Kelham Th Coll 55. **d** 59 **p** 60. C Middlesbrough St Jo the Ev *York* 59-60; C Kingston upon Hull St Alb 60-64; C Roehampton H Trin *S'wark* 64-68; V Dawley St Jerome *Lon* 68-73; R Harlington 73-98; rtd 98; Perm to Offic *Lon* from 99. *21F Cleveland Road, Cowley, Uxbridge UB8 2DR* Tel (01895) 253761

JENKINS, David Thomas. b 43. Ox Univ MA94 RIBA70. S'wark Ord Course 76. **d** 79 **p** 80. NSM Merthyr Tydfil and Cyfarthfa *Llan* 79-86; NSM Brecon St David w Llanspyddid and Llanilltyd *S & B* 86-91; P-in-c Llangiwg 91-92; V 92-01; Chapl Puerto de la Cruz Tenerife *Eur* 02-09; rtd 09. *Apartado 68, Parque Taoro, Puerto de la Cruz, 38400 Tenerife, Canary Islands* Tel (0034) 922 384 038 Fax 922 388 285 E-mail djenkins@tinyonline.co.uk

JENKINS, The Ven David Thomas Ivor. b 29. K Coll Lon BD52 AKC52 Birm Univ MA63. **d** 53 **p** 54. C Bilton *Cov* 53-56; V Wolston 56-61; Asst Dir RE *Carl* 61-63; V Carl St Barn 63-72; V Carl St Cuth 72-76; P-in-c Carl St Mary w St Paul 72-76; V Carl St Cuth w St Mary 76-91; Dioc Sec 84-95; Hon Can Carl Cathl 76-91; Can Res 91-95; Adn Westmorland and Furness 95-99; rtd 99; Perm to Offic *Carl* from 00. *Irvings House, Sleagill, Penrith CA10 3HD* Tel (01931) 714400

JENKINS, Eric Robert. b 52. Poly Cen Lon BSc74. STETS 97. **d** 00 **p** 01. C Weybridge *Guildf* 00-04; R Cobham and Stoke D'Abernon from 04; RD Leatherhead from 08. *The Vicarage, St Andrew's Walk, Cobham KT11 3EQ* Tel (01932) 862109 Mobile 07747-844689 E-mail er.jenkins@btinternet.com

JENKINS, Mrs Fiona. b 59. Dur Univ BSc80 York St Jo Coll MA04. St Jo Coll Nottm 04. **d** 06 **p** 07. C Settle *Bradf* 06-08; C Linton in Craven from 08; C Kettlewell w Conistone, Hubberholme etc from 08; C Burnsall w Rylstone from 08. *The Rectory, Church Lane, Burnsall, Skipton BD23 6BP* Tel (01756) 720331 E-mail fiona.jenkins@bradford.anglican.org

JENKINS, The Very Revd Frank Graham. b 23. St D Coll Lamp BA47 Jes Coll Ox BA49 MA53. St Mich Coll Llan 49. **d** 50 **p** 51. C Llangeinor 50-53; Chapl Llan Cathl 53-60; CF (TA) 56-61; V Abertillery *Mon* 60-64; V Risca 64-75; Can St Woolos Cathl 67-76; V Caerleon 75-76; Dean Mon 76-90; rtd 90; Lic to Offic *Mon* from 90. *Rivendell, 209 Christchurch Road, Newport NP19 7QL* Tel (01633) 255278

JENKINS, Garry Frederick. b 48. Southn Univ BTh79. Chich Th Coll 75. **d** 79 **p** 80. C Kingsbury St Andr *Lon* 79-84; C Leigh St Clem *Chelmsf* 84-88; P-in-c Brentwood St Geo 88-94; V from 94; Chapl NE Lon Mental Health Tr from 02. *The Vicarage, 28 Robin Hood Road, Brentwood CM15 9EN* Tel (01277) 213618 E-mail g.f.jenkins@amserve.com

JENKINS, Canon Gary John. b 59. York Univ BA80 CertEd81. Oak Hill Th Coll BA89. **d** 89 **p** 90. C Norwood St Luke *S'wark* 89-94; P-in-c St Helier 94-95; V 95-01; V Redhill H Trin from 01; Hon Can *S'wark* Cathl from 06. *4 Carlton Road, Redhill RH1 2BX* Tel (01737) 779917 E-mail gary@htredhill.com

JENKINS, Canon Jeanette. b 42. St Jo Coll Nottm 83. **dss** 84 **d** 86 **p** 94. NSM Kilmarnock *Glas* 84-94; NSM Irvine St Andr LEP 84-94; NSM Ardrossan 84-94; Asst Chapl Crosshouse Hosp

86-94; Chapl Ayrshire Hospice 90-02; Can St Mary's Cathl from 99. *4 Gleneagles Avenue, Kilwinning KA13 6RD*   Tel (01294) 553383   Mobile 07775-595901
E-mail revj.jenkins@btinternet.com

JENKINS, John Francis. b 46. Ripon Hall Ox 77 Ripon Coll Cuddesdon 75. **d** 77 **p** 78. C Filton *Bris* 77-79; C Bris St Andr Hartcliffe 79-84; P-in-c Bris H Cross Inns Court 84-85; V 85-95; R Odcombe, Brympton, Lufton and Montacute *B & W* from 95. *The Rectory, Street Lane, Higher Odcombe, Yeovil BA22 8UP*   Tel (01935) 863034

JENKINS, John Howard David. b 51. Birm Univ BA72. St Steph Ho Ox 72. **d** 74 **p** 75. C Milford Haven *St D* 74-77; PV Llan Cathl 77-81; Chapl Lowther Coll and V Choral St As Cathl 81-84; C Neath w Llantwit 84-86; Chapl Colston's Sch Bris 86-91; Chapl Blue Coat Sch Birm 91-04; Chapl R Masonic Sch for Girls Rickmansworth from 04. *Royal Masonic School, Rickmansworth Park, Rickmansworth WD3 4HF*   Tel (01923) 725338 *or* 773593

JENKINS, John Morgan. b 33. Open Univ BA96. Mon Dioc Tr Scheme 82. **d** 85 **p** 86. NSM Cwmbran *Mon* 85-02; rtd 02. *5 Ridgeway Avenue, Newport NP20 5AJ*   Tel (01633) 662231

JENKINS, John Raymond. b 26. K Coll Lon 52. **d** 53 **p** 54. C Wrexham *St As* 53-56; Hon C 77-82; C Welshpool 56-57; V Mochdre 57-65; V Llandysul *St D* 65-67; V Llanfair Caereinion w Llanllugan *St As* 67-70; V Llanychaearn w Llanddeiniol *St D* 82-91; rtd 91; Chapl Lanzarote *Eur* 95-97. *Hafan, Main Street, Llanon SY23 5HH*   Tel (01974) 202212

JENKINS, John Richard. b 68. Dundee Univ LLB90 Leeds Univ MA98. St Steph Ho Ox BA94. **d** 94 **p** 95. C Brighouse and Clifton *Wakef* 94-97; C Barnsley St Mary 97-99; Dir Affirming Catholicism from 05. *St Matthew's House, 20 Great Peter Street, London SW1P 2BU*   Tel (020) 7233 0235
E-mail director@affirmingcatholicism.org.uk

JENKINS, Julian James. b 56. St Mich Coll Llan 97. **d** 99 **p** 00. C Whitchurch *Llan* 99-01; TV Aberavon 01-05; TV Cowbridge from 05. *The Vicarage, 2 Court Close, Aberthin, Cowbridge CF71 7EH*   Tel (01446) 773889

JENKINS, Canon Lawrence Clifford. b 45. AKC70 Open Univ BA77. St Aug Coll Cant. **d** 71 **p** 72. C Osmondthorpe St Phil *Ripon* 71-74; C Monkseaton St Mary *Newc* 74-78; V Shiremoor 78-84; V Wheatley Hills *Sheff* 84-95; RD Doncaster 92-95; V Greenhill from 95; Hon Can Sheff Cathl from 08. *St Peter's Vicarage, Reney Avenue, Sheffield S8 7FN*   Tel and fax 0114-237 7422   E-mail lawrie.jenkins@ukgateway.net

JENKINS, Canon Paul Morgan. b 44. Sussex Univ BEd68 Fitzw Coll Cam BA73 MA76. Westcott Ho Cam 71. **d** 74 **p** 75. C Forest Gate St Edm *Chelmsf* 74-77; Chapl Bryanston Sch 77-85; P-in-c Stourpaine, Durweston and Bryanston *Sarum* 77-83; Asst Chapl and Housemaster Repton Sch Derby 84-89; Dean of Chpl 89-91; R Singleton *Chich* 91-97; V E Dean 91-97; V W Dean 91-97; Dir St Columba's Retreat and Conf Cen 97-07; Chapl Community of St Pet Woking 03-07; P-in-c Dunsfold and Hascombe *Guildf* from 07; Hon Can Guildf Cathl from 05. *The Rectory, Church Green, Dunsfold, Godalming GU8 4LT*   Tel (01483) 200207   Mobile 07973-848941
E-mail pjenkins44@aol.com

JENKINS (née RICHARDSON), Pauline Kate. b 41. RGN62 Nottm Univ CertEd80 RNT83. St Jo Coll Nottm 91. **d** 94 **p** 98. Uganda 94-96; Perm to Offic *S'well* 96-98; NSM Selston 98-01; NSM Annesley w Newstead 01-03; rtd 03; Perm to Offic *S'well* from 03. *The Cottage, 5 Main Street, Stathern, Melton Mowbray LE14 4HW*   Tel (01949) 869474

JENKINS, Richard. *See* JENKINS, John Richard

JENKINS, Preb Richard David. b 33. Magd Coll Cam BA58 MA. Westcott Ho Cam 59. **d** 61 **p** 62. C Staveley *Derby* 61-64; C Billingham St Aid *Dur* 64-68; V Walsall Pleck and Bescot *Lich* 68-73; R Whitchurch 73-97; RD Wem and Whitchurch 85-95; P-in-c Tilstock and Whixall 92-95; Preb Lich Cathl 93-97; rtd 97; Perm to Offic *Lich* from 99. *The Council House, Council House Court, Castle Street, Shrewsbury SY1 2AU*   Tel (01743) 270051

JENKINS, Richard Morvan. b 44. St Mich Coll Llan 65. **d** 69 **p** 70. C Tenby *St D* 69-73; V Llanrhian w Llanhywel and Carnhedryn etc 73-80; R Johnston w Steynton 80-93; V St Ishmael's w Llan-saint and Ferryside 93-09; rtd 09. *Geirionydd, 7 Dwynant, Furnace Road, Burry Port SA16 0YQ*

JENKINS, Robert. *See* JENKINS, Eric Robert

JENKINS, Canon Robert Francis. b 33. BNC Ox BA57 MA59. Wycliffe Hall Ox 57. **d** 59 **p** 60. C Hall Green Ascension *Birm* 59-63; V Dosthill and Wood End 63-71; V Brandwood 71-85; V Sutton Coldfield St Columba 85-97; Hon Can S Malawi from 87; rtd 97; Perm to Offic *Birm* from 97 and *Lich* from 00. *4 The Pines, Lichfield WS14 9XA*   Tel (01543) 252176

JENKINS, Canon Timothy David. b 52. Pemb Coll Ox BA73 MLitt77 MA82 St Edm Ho Cam BA84. Ridley Hall Cam 82. **d** 85 **p** 86. C Kingswood *Bris* 85-87; Sen Chapl Nottm Univ 88-92; Dean Jes Coll Cam from 92; Can Th Leic Cathl from 04. *50 Stanley Road, Cambridge CB5 8BL*   Tel (01223) 363185 *or* 339303   E-mail tdj22@jesus.cam.ac.uk

JENKINS, Canon William David. b 42. Birm Univ BA63. St D Coll Lamp LTh65. **d** 65 **p** 66. C Gorseinon *S & B* 65-67; C Llanelli *St D* 67-72; V Clydach *S & B* 72-82; Chapl Gwynedd Hosp NHS Trust 82-97; V Llanrhos *St As* 82-97; RD Llanrwst 84-96; Can Cursal St As Cathl 93-97; TR Tenby *St D* 97-07; rtd 07. *Kildare, 96 Conway Road, Llandudno LL30 1PP*   Tel 07791-738018 (mobile)

JENKINSON, Margaret. b 40. MCSP62. Carl Dioc Tr Inst 89. **d** 92 **p** 94. NSM Preesall *Blackb* 92-96; NSM Lanercost, Walton, Gilsland and Nether Denton *Carl* 96-04; P-in-c Lorton and Loweswater w Buttermere from 04. *The Vicarage, Loweswater, Cockermouth CA13 0RU*   Tel (01900) 85237
E-mail mgtandhenry@aol.com

JENKINSON, Rachel Elisabeth. b 66. Somerville Coll Ox BA87 Cranfield Univ MBA99. Ridley Hall Cam 05. **d** 07 **p** 08. C Chorleywood Ch Ch *St Alb* from 07. *4 Berry Way, Rickmansworth WD3 7EY*   Tel (01923) 447185

JENKYNS, Preb Henry Derrik George. b 30. Sarum Th Coll 57. **d** 60 **p** 61. C Kettering SS Pet and Paul 60-64; V Shrewsbury St Geo *Lich* 64-71; V Wednesbury St Paul Wood Green 71-76; V Stokesay *Heref* 76-86; P-in-c Acton Scott 76-86; RD Condover 80-86; Preb Heref Cathl 83-96; R Kington w Huntington, Old Radnor, Kinnerton etc 86-96; rtd 96; Perm to Offic *Heref* from 96. *Llantroft, Newcastle, Craven Arms SY7 8PD*   Tel (01588) 640314

JENKYNS, John Thomas William Basil. b 30. Univ of Wales (Lamp) BA54 St Cath Coll Ox BA57 MA62. Wycliffe Hall Ox 54. **d** 57 **p** 58. C Neasden cum Kingsbury St Cath *Lon* 57-60; C S Lyncombe *B & W* 60-64; V Gt Harwood St Bart *Blackb* 64-66; R Colne St Bart 66-69; V Chard St Mary *B & W* 69-87; Preb Wells Cathl 87; V Swaffham *Nor* 87-89; V Overbury w Teddington, Alstone etc *Worc* 89-95; rtd 95. *2 Clos y Fran, Glais, Swansea SA7 9TH*   Tel (01792) 842765

JENKYNS, Stephen. b 60. Univ of Wales (Cardiff) BTh02. St Mich Coll Llan 99. **d** 02 **p** 03. C Penarth w Lavernock *Llan* 02-04; C Penarth and Llandough 04-06; TV Cyncoed *Mon* from 06. *40 Felbrigg Crescent, Pontprennau, Cardiff CF23 8SE*   Tel (029) 2054 0955

JENNER, Miss Brenda Ann. b 54. Culham Coll Ox BEd80. St Jo Coll Nottm 86. **d** 88. Par Dn Leigh St Mary *Man* 88-92; Par Dn Leic Ch Sav 92-94. *18 Chatsworth Avenue, Wigston, Leicester LE18 4LF*

JENNER, Michael Albert. b 37. Oak Hill Th Coll 75. **d** 77 **p** 78. C Mile Cross *Nor* 77-80; P-in-c Easton *Ely* 80-86; P-in-c Ellington 80-86; P-in-c Grafham 80-86; P-in-c Spaldwick w Barham and Woolley 80-86; Perm to Offic *Roch* from 01; rtd 02. *Heathgate Cottage, Langton Road, Langton Green, Tunbridge Wells TN3 0BA*   Tel (01892) 535136 Fax 535146   Mobile 07831-826954

JENNER, Peter John. b 56. Chu Coll Cam BA77 PhD80 MA81. St Jo Coll Nottm 82. **d** 85 **p** 86. C Upperby St Jo *Carl* 85-88; Chapl Reading Univ 88-96; P-in-c Mellor *Derby* 96-99; V 99-06; V Mellor *Ches* from 06; RD Chadkirk from 08. *The Vicarage, Church Road, Mellor, Stockport SK6 5LX*   Tel 0161-427 1203
E-mail jennerfamily@btinternet.com

JENNER, William George. b 37. Nottm Univ BSc59 K Coll Lon PGCE60. **d** 97 **p** 98. OLM Gillingham w Geldeston, Stockton, Ellingham etc *Nor* 97-05; Perm to Offic from 05. *3 Woodland Drive, Kirby Cane, Bungay NR35 2PT*   Tel (01508) 518229

JENNETT, The Ven Maurice Arthur. b 34. St Jo Coll Dur BA60. Cranmer Hall Dur 60. **d** 62 **p** 63. C Marple All SS *Ches* 62-67; V Withnell *Blackb* 67-75; V Stranton *Dur* 75-91; Crosslinks Zimbabwe 92-99; Asst P Nyanga St Mary Magd 92-93; R 93-99; Can and Adn Manicaland N 97; rtd 99; Perm to Offic *Ripon* from 01. *2 Southfield Avenue, Ripon HG4 2NR*   Tel (01765) 607842   E-mail maurice@mjennett.fsnet.co.uk

JENNINGS, Anne. *See* SMITH, Mrs Anne

JENNINGS, Prof Barry Randall. b 39. Southn Univ BSc61 PhD64 DSc76 DEng01 FInstP70 FRSC95. SWMTC 96. **d** 98 **p** 99. Prof Physics Reading Univ from 84; NSM St Germans *Truro* 98-00; NSM S Hill w Callington 00-08; rtd 08; Perm to Offic *Truro* from 08. *Pitt Meadow, St Dominic, Saltash PL12 6SX*   Tel and fax (01579) 350940

JENNINGS, Clive John. b 57. Trin Coll Bris. **d** 00 **p** 01. C Milton *B & W* 00-02; V Clevedon St Andr and Ch Ch from 02. *12 Princes Road, Clevedon BS21 7SZ*   Tel (01275) 872134
E-mail clive.jennings@blueyonder.co.uk

✠**JENNINGS, The Rt Revd David Willfred Michael.** b 44. AKC66. **d** 67 **p** 68 **c** 00. C Walton St Mary *Liv* 67-69; C Christchurch *Win* 69-73; V Hythe 73-80; V Romford St Edw *Chelmsf* 80-92; RD Havering 85-92; Hon Can Chelmsf Cathl 87-92; Adn Southend 92-00; Suff Bp Warrington *Liv* 00-09; rtd 09. *Laurel Cottage, High Street, Northleach, Cheltenham GL54 3ET*   Tel (01451) 860743

JENNINGS, Duncan William. b 54. UWE MA. STETS 05. **d** 08 **p** 09. C Southampton Thornhill St Chris *Win* from 08. *22 Lydgate Green, Southampton SO19 6LP*   Tel (023) 8040 5313

JENNINGS, Canon Frederick David. b 48. K Coll Lon BD73 AKC73 Loughb Univ MPhil98. St Aug Coll Cant 73. **d** 74 **p** 75.

C Halesowen *Worc* 74-77; Perm to Offic *Birm* 78-80; Perm to Offic *Leic* 78-80 and 85-87; P-in-c Snibston 80-85; Community Relns Officer 81-84; P-in-c Burbage w Aston Flamville 87-91; R from 91; Hon Can Leic Cathl from 03. *The Rectory, New Road, Burbage, Hinckley LE10 2AW* Tel (01455) 230512 Fax 250833 E-mail revdavidjennings@btinternet.com

JENNINGS, Harold Andrew. b 15. ATCL35 LTCL36 FTCL37 MRST39 LRAM39. St Deiniol's Hawarden 63. **d** 63 **p** 64. C Swansea St Gabr *S & B* 63-67; R Aberedw w Llandeilo Graban etc 67-79; V Knighton and Norton 79-85; Hon C Llanbister and Llanbadarn Fynydd w Llananno 85-87; rtd 87. *Finsbury, Beaufort Road, Llandrindod Wells LD1 5EL* Tel (01597) 824892

JENNINGS, Ian. b 47. Leeds Univ MA98. NOC 95. **d** 97 **p** 97. NSM Hackenthorpe *Sheff* 97-01; Asst Chapl HM Pris Doncaster 97-98; Chapl HM Pris and YOI Doncaster 98-01; V Sheff St Cuth 01-06; TR Aston cum Aughton w Swallownest and Ulley from 06. *The Rectory, 91 Worksop Road, Aston, Sheffield S26 2EB* Tel 0114-287 2272

JENNINGS, Ian Richard. b 65. Liv Univ BA88 Wolv Poly PGCE91. Trin Coll Bris 07. **d** 09. C Pedmore *Worc* from 09. *25 Sandhurst Avenue, Pedmore, Stourbridge DY9 0XQ* Tel 07722-019096 (mobile) E-mail ianandsuejennings@googlemail.com

JENNINGS, Janet. b 38. SCM71 SRN74. Oak Hill Th Coll BA87. **d** 88 **p** 97. Par Dn Stevenage St Pet Broadwater *St Alb* 88-90; Perm to Offic *St As* from 92. *Pound House, Forden, Welshpool SY21 8NU* Tel (01938) 580400

JENNINGS, Jonathan Peter. b 61. K Coll Lon BD83. Westcott Ho Cam 84. **d** 86 **p** 87. C Peterlee *Dur* 86-89; C Darlington St Cuth 89-92; Dioc Communications Officer *Man* 92-95; Broadcasting Officer Gen Syn 95-01; Perm to Offic *S'wark* 95-98; Hon C Banstead *Guildf* 98-04; Abp Cant's Press Sec 01-08; Perm to Offic *Cant* and *Roch* 05-08; P-in-c Gillingham St Aug *Roch* from 08. *St Augustine's Vicarage, Rock Avenue, Gillingham ME7 5PW* Tel (01634) 850288 E-mail revjpj@aol.com

JENNINGS, Mervyn. b 39. Sarum & Wells Th Coll 83. **d** 85 **p** 86. C Knowle *Bris* 85-89; P-in-c Cressing and Rural Youth Development Officer *Chelmsf* 89-93; V Barkingside St Fran 93-08; rtd 08; Perm to Offic *Chelmsf* from 08. *36 Harris Close, Romford RM3 8PQ* Tel (01708) 341043 E-mail father.mervyn.jennings@o2.co.uk

JENNINGS, Mrs Pamela. b 49. SRN71. NEOC 05. **d** 08 **p** 09. NSM Scarborough St Mary w Ch Ch and H Apostles *York* from 08. *26 Ling Hill, Scarborough YO12 5HS* Tel (01723) 365528 E-mail kenandpamjennings@gmail.com

JENNINGS, Peter James. b 28. Univ of Wales (Lamp) BA56. St D Coll Lamp LTh57. **d** 57 **p** 58. C Dudley St Jo *Worc* 57-60; C Dudley St Thos 61-64; Chapl HM Borstal Portland 64-66; Chapl HM Pris Wakef 66-70; Chapl HM Pris Liv 70-76; RD Walton *Liv* 75-76; Chapl HM Pris Styal 76-77 and 88-92; N Regional Chapl 76-82; Asst Chapl Gen (N) 82-88; Perm to Offic *Man* 77-89 and from 00; *Ches* from 79; and fra 93. *6 St Ann's Road South, Cheadle SK8 3DZ* Tel 0161-437 8828

JENNINGS, Robert Henry. b 46. St Jo Coll Dur BA69 MA79. Qu Coll Birm. **d** 72 **p** 73. C Dursley *Glouc* 72-74; C Coleford w Staunton 75-78; TV Bottesford w Ashby *Linc* 78-83; TV Witney *Ox* 83-89; V Lane End w Cadmore End from 89. *The Vicarage, 7 Lammas Way, Lane End, High Wycombe HP14 3EX* Tel (01494) 881913

JENNINGS, Thomas Robert. b 24. TCD BA47 MA51. **d** 48 **p** 49. C Drumragh *D & R* 48-51; CF 51-67; I Killeshandra *K, E & A* 67-70; I Newcastle w Newtownmountkennedy and Calary *D & G* 70-92; Can Ch Ch Cathl Dublin 88-92; rtd 92. *66 Seacourt, Newcastle, Greystones, Co Wicklow, Republic of Ireland* Tel (00353) (1) 281 0777 Mobile 87-763 3418 E-mail bojen@yahoo.co.uk

JENNINGS, Walter James. b 37. Birm Univ BMus60 MA90. Qu Coll Birm 77. **d** 80 **p** 81. Hon C Hampton in Arden *Birm* 80-84; Chapl St Alb Aided Sch Highgate Birm 84-86; C Wotton-under-Edge w Ozleworth and N Nibley *Glouc* 86-89; V Pittville All SS 89-98; rtd 98; Chapl Beauchamp Community 98-00; Perm to Offic *Worc* from 98. *Flat 7, Leamington Court, Wells Road, Malvern WR14 4HF* Tel (01684) 561513 E-mail walter.linda@virgin.net

JENNO, Charles Henry. b 25. Wells Th Coll 65. **d** 66 **p** 67. C Shirehampton *Bris* 66-69; C Fishponds St Mary 69-73; V Thornes St Jas w Ch Ch *Wakef* 73-78; V Carleton 78-82; V E Hardwick 78-82; rtd 82; Perm to Offic *Wakef* from 82. *32 Tower Avenue, Upton, Pontefract WF9 1EE* Tel (01977) 640925

JENSEN, Alexander Sönderup. b 68. Tübingen Univ 94 St Jo Coll Dur PhD01 Ox Univ MTh01. St Steph Ho Ox 97. **d** 99 **p** 00. C Norton St Mich *Dur* 99-02; Lect CITC 02-05; Lect Murdoch Univ Australia from 05. *School of Social Sciences and Humanities, Murdoch University, South Street, Murdoch, W Australia 6150* Tel (0061) (8) 9360 6625 Fax 9360 6480 E-mail a.jensen@murdoch.edu.au

JENSEN, Erik Henning. b 33. Copenhagen Univ BPhil51 Harvard Univ STM54 Worc Coll Ox BLitt58 DPhil69. Ripon Hall Ox 56. **d** 58 **p** 59. C Highwood *Chelmsf* 58-59; C

Simanggang Sarawak 59-61; Borneo 61-62; Malaysia 63-03; rtd 02. *The Rock House, Maugersbury, Stow-on-the-Wold GL54 1HP* Tel (01451) 830171

✠**JENSEN, The Most Revd Peter Frederick.** b 43. Lon Univ BD70 Sydney Univ MA76 Ox Univ DPhil80. Moore Th Coll Sydney. **d** 69 **p** 70 **c** 01. C Broadway Australia 69-76; Perm to Offic *Ox* 76-79; Lect Moore Th Coll 73-76 and 80-84; Prin 85-01; Can Sydney 89-01; Abp Sydney from 01. *PO Box Q190, QVB PO NSW 1230, Australia* Tel (0061) (2) 9265 1521 Fax 9265 1504

JENSON, Philip Peter. b 56. Ex Coll Ox BA78 MA82 Down Coll Cam BA80 MA86 PhD88. Ridley Hall Cam 80. **d** 87 **p** 88. C Gt Warley Ch Ch *Chelmsf* 87-89; Lect Trin Coll Bris 89-05; Lect Ridley Hall Cam from 05. *Ridley Hall, Cambridge CB3 9HG* Tel (01223) 741080 Fax 741081 E-mail ppj22@cam.ac.uk

JEPP, Malcolm Leonard. b 44. SWMTC 06. **d** 09. NSM Meneage Truro from 09. *Polpidnick Cottage, Porthallow, St Keverne, Helston TR12 6PL* Tel and fax (01326) 281031 Mobile 07797-505539 E-mail lenjepp@jeppassociates.co.uk

JEPP (née NUGENT), Mrs Mary Patricia. b 55. Mt St Vincent Univ Canada BA79 Univ of New Brunswick BEd80 Open Univ MA03. ERMC 05. **d** 08 **p** 09. C Godmanchester *Ely* from 08. *59 London Road, Godmanchester, Huntingdon PE29 2HZ* Tel (01480) 411734 E-mail m.jepp@btinternet.com

JEPPS, Philip Anthony. b 34. BNC Ox BA58 MA68. Wycliffe Hall Ox 58. **d** 60 **p** 73. C Elton All SS *Man* 60; Perm to Offic *Pet* 70-73; R Church w Chapel Brampton 74-80; P-in-c Harlestone 79-80; V Kettering St Andr 80-94; V Conisbrough *Sheff* 94-01; rtd 01; Perm to Offic *Heref* from 01. *2 Eagle Cottages, Church Lane, Orleton, Ludlow SY8 4HT* Tel (01568) 780517

JEPSON, Joanna Elizabeth. b 76. Trin Coll Bris BA99 Cam Univ MA03. Ridley Hall Cam 01. **d** 03 **p** 04. C Plas Newton *Ches* 03-06; Chapl Lon Coll of Fashion from 06; P-in-c Fulham St Pet from 06. *St Peter's Vicarage, 2 St Peter's Terrace, London SW6 7JS* Tel (020) 3080 0904 E-mail joeyjep@yahoo.com

JERMAN, Edward David. b 40. Trin Coll Carmarthen CertEd61. **d** 87 **p** 88. NSM Llandrygarn w Bodwrog and Heneglwys etc *Ban* from 87. *Tryfan, Trefor, Holyhead LL65 3YT* Tel (01407) 720856

JERMY, Jack. b 22. ACP65. Ripon Hall Ox 64. **d** 65 **p** 66. Hd Master SS Simon and Jude Primary Sch Bolton 62-80; C Bolton SS Simon and Jude *Man* 65-74; P-in-c Rivington 74-93; NSM Horwich and Rivington 93-95; rtd 95; Perm to Offic from 95. *179 Preston Road, Whittle-le-Woods, Chorley PR6 7PR* Tel (01257) 480466

JERMY, Stuart John. b 66. Middx Univ BEd90. Wycliffe Hall Ox 01. **d** 03 **p** 04. C New Thundersley *Chelmsf* 03-07; V St Martins and Weston Rhyn *Lich* from 07. *The Vicarage, Church Lane, St Martins, Oswestry SY11 3AP* Tel (01691) 778468 Mobile 07801-071443 E-mail sjermy@toucansurf.com

JERSEY, Dean of. *See* KEY, The Very Revd Robert Frederick

JERVIS, Christopher. b 53. Loughb Univ BEd75. Wycliffe Hall Ox 80. **d** 82 **p** 83. C Woodford Wells *Chelmsf* 82-85; Chapl Felsted Sch 85-87; Chapl Canford Sch Wimborne from 87. *Merryvale, Canford Magna, Wimborne BH21 3AF* Tel (01202) 887722 E-mail cj@canford.com

JERVIS, William Edward. b 47. MRICS74. Linc Th Coll 74. **d** 77 **p** 78. C W Bromwich All SS *Lich* 77-80; C Horsham *Chich* 80-86; R W Tarring from 86. *West Tarring Rectory, Glebe Road, Worthing BN14 7PF* Tel (01903) 235043 Fax 218877

JESSETT, David Charles. b 55. K Coll Lon BD77 AKC77 MTh. Westcott Ho Cam 78. **d** 79 **p** 80. C Aveley *Chelmsf* 79-82; C Walthamstow St Pet 82-85; P-in-c Hunningham *Cov* 85-91; P-in-c Wappenbury w Weston under Wetherley 85-91; Progr Dir Exploring Chr Min Scheme 85-91; Dir CME 87-90; Perm to Offic 90-97; P-in-c Barford w Wasperton and Sherbourne from 97; P-in-c Hampton Lucy w Charlecote and Loxley from 07. *The Rectory, Church Lane, Barford, Warwick CV35 8ES* Tel (01926) 624238 E-mail david@jessetts.freeserve.co.uk

JESSIMAN, Elaine Rae. b 59. Wall Hall Coll Aldenham BEd95. STETS 05. **d** 08 **p** 09. C Leigh Park *Portsm* from 08. *The Vicarage, 61 Hart Plain Avenue, Waterlooville PO8 8RG* Tel (023) 9226 4551 E-mail elaine.jessiman@ntlworld.com

JESSIMAN, Timothy Edward. b 59. Portsm Univ MA06. Oak Hill Th Coll 88. **d** 91 **p** 92. C Baldock w Bygrave *St Alb* 91-95; C Bideford *Ex* 95-96; TV Bideford, Northam, Westward Ho!, Appledore etc 96-00; Chapl Grenville Coll Bideford 95-00; Chapl N Devon Healthcare NHS Trust 98-00; P-in-c Hartplain *Portsm* 00-06; V from 06. *The Vicarage, 61 Hart Plain Avenue, Waterlooville PO8 8RG* Tel (023) 9226 4551 E-mail tim.jessiman@ntlworld.com

JESSON, Alan Francis. b 47. TD89. Ealing Coll of Educn 70 Loughb Univ MLS77 Selw Coll Cam MA87 ALA70 FLA91 MBIM82. EAMTC 88. **d** 91 **p** 92. NSM Swavesey *Ely* 91-95; NSM Fen Drayton w Conington and Lolworth etc 95-00; CF (ACF) 92-96; Sen Chapl ACF from 96; R Outwell *Ely* from 00; R Upwell St Pet from 00; Perm to Offic *Nor* from 01. *The Rectory, 5 New Road, Upwell, Wisbech PE14 9AB* Tel (01945) 772213 Fax 07075-055234 E-mail alan.jesson@ely.anglican.org

JESSON, George Albert Oswald (Ossie). b 54. Trin Coll Bris 90. **d** 92 **p** 93. C Thorpe Acre w Dishley *Leic* 92-01; C Chilwell *S'well* 01-08. *The Rectory, Lincoln Road, East Markham, Newark NG22 0SH* Tel (01777) 870965
E-mail revo.jesson@ntlworld.com

JESSON, Julia Margaret. b 54. St Matthias Coll Bris CertEd75 Nottm Univ MA04. EMMTC 01. **d** 04 **p** 05. NSM Stapleford *S'well* 04-07; C Kimberley 07-08; P-in-c E Markham w Askham, Headon w Upton and Grove from 08; P-in-c Dunham w Darlton, Ragnall, Fledborough etc from 08. *The Rectory, Lincoln Road, East Markham, Newark NG22 0SH* Tel (01777) 870965 E-mail julia.jesson@ntlworld.com

JESSOP, Mrs Gillian Mary. b 48. Hatf Poly BSc71 Nottm Univ MEd85 Homerton Coll Cam PGCE80. EAMTC 91. **d** 94 **p** 95. C Gt Yarmouth *Nor* 94-97; R Gt w Lt Addington and Woodford *Pet* 97-02; R Paston from 02; Asst Dir Tr for Readers 00-02; Dir from 02. *The Rectory, 236 Fulbridge Road, Peterborough PE4 6SN* Tel (01733) 578228 E-mail rev.gill@tesco.net

JESSOP, John Edward. b 46. RMCS BSc71 CEng78 MIET78. S Dios Minl Tr Scheme 87 Ridley Coll Melbourne 89. **d** 90 **p** 90. Australia 90-02; C Mooroolbark 90-91; P-in-c S Yarra 92-93; I Blackburn St Jo 93-98; I Kew H Trin 98-02; P-in-c Brimpsfield w Birdlip, Syde, Daglingworth etc *Glouc* 02-04; R from 04; AD Cirencester from 08. *The Rectory, Church Road, Daglingworth, Cirencester GL7 7AG* Tel and fax (01285) 640782

JESSUP, William Roy. b 27. Lon Univ BSc48 CertEd. Ridley Hall Cam 59. **d** 61 **p** 62. C Walton *St E* 61-64; R Tuddenham St Mary w Cavenham 64-83; P-in-c Eriswell 75-78; Assoc Min Ipswich All SS 83-85; R Toppesfield and Stambourne *Chelmsf* 85-92; rtd 92; Perm to Offic *Chelmsf* and *St E* from 92. *71 Brain Valley Avenue, Black Notley, Braintree CM77 8LT* Tel (01376) 322554

JESTY, Mrs Helen Margaret. b 51. York Univ BA72. Cranmer Hall Dur BA81. **dss** 82 **d** 87. S Lambeth St Steph *S'wark* 82-86; Norbiton 86-93; Par Dn 87-90; Hon Par Dn 91-93. *Fairfield, 1 Downside Road, Winchester SO22 5LT* Tel (01962) 849190

JESUDASON, Leslie Peter Prakash. b 58. Wycliffe Hall Ox 05. **d** 07 **p** 08. C Throop *Win* from 07. *51 Langford Way, Bournemouth BH8 0NY* Tel (01202) 526731 *or* 525525
E-mail l.jesudason@hotmail.co.uk

JEVONS, Alan Neil. b 56. Ex Univ BA77 Selw Coll Cam BA80 MA84. Ridley Hall Cam. **d** 81 **p** 82. C Halesowen *Worc* 81-84; C Heywood St Luke w All So *Man* 84-87; TV Heref St Martin w St Fran 87-93; P-in-c Much Birch w Lt Birch, Much Dewchurch etc 93-02; RD Ross and Archenfield 98-02; TR Tenbury 02-07; Preb Heref Cathl 02-07; RD Ludlow 05-07; V Llyn Safaddan *S & B* from 07; Dioc Tourism Officer from 07. *The Vicarage, Llangorse, Brecon LD3 7UG* Tel (01874) 658298
E-mail alanjevons@mac.com

JEVONS, Harry Clifford. b 46. Bp Otter Coll 01. **d** 04 **p** 05. C Ifield *Chich* 04-07; C Milton *Win* from 07. *St Peter's House, 25 Ashley Common Road, New Milton BH25 5AJ* Tel (01425) 612644 Mobile 07881-527050
E-mail harryjevons@supanet.com

JEWELL, Alan David John. b 59. St Cath Coll Ox MA86. Wycliffe Hall Ox 83. **d** 86 **p** 87. C Walton H Trin *Ox* 86-91; TV Sutton *Liv* 91-97; TV Halewood 97-01; TR from 01. *The Rectory, 3 Rectory Drive, Halewood, Liverpool L26 6LJ* Tel 0151-487 5610 E-mail alandjjewell@btopenworld.com

JEWELL, Charles John. b 15. Bps' Coll Cheshunt 46. **d** 49 **p** 50. C Swindon St Aug *Bris* 49-52; CF 52-58; C-in-c Patchway CD *Bris* 58-61; Chapl Tristan da Cunha 61 and 71-74; Area Sec (N Ireland) USPG 62-69; Area Sec USPG *Ex* and *Truro* 69-71; R Durban St Raphael 74-78; R Sydenham 78-87; rtd 87; Perm to Offic *Ex* 87-08. *3 Rectory Road, Sutton SM1 1QW* Tel (020) 8641 7721

JEWELL, Mrs Maureen Ann. b 34. Reading Univ CertEd72. Chich Th Coll 90. **d** 91 **p** 95. NSM Parklands St Wilfrid CD *Chich* 91-94; NSM Storrington 94-97; Perm to Offic 97-09. *Address temp unknown*

JEWELL, Raymond Frederick. b 27. CA Tr Coll 56. **d** 05 **p** 05. NSM Tuffley *Glouc* from 05. *1 Bybrook Gardens, Tuffley, Gloucester GL4 0HQ*

JEWITT, Martin Paul Noel. b 44. AKC69. St Aug Coll Cant. **d** 70 **p** 71. C Usworth *Dur* 70-74; TV 77-78; Papua New Guinea 74-77; V Balham Hill Ascension *S'wark* 78-93; R N Reddish *Man* 93-99; V Thornton Heath St Paul *S'wark* from 99. *The Vicarage, 1 Norbury Avenue, Thornton Heath CR7 8AH* Tel (020) 8653 2762 Mobile 07949-938307
E-mail scarpaul@btinternet.com

JEWSBURY, Jonathan Mark. b 64. St Jo Coll Dur BA86. NEOC 04. **d** 06 **p** 07. NSM E Rainton *Dur* from 06; NSM W Rainton from 06. *62 Grange Road, Durham DH1 1AL*
E-mail j.jewsbury100@durhamlea.org.uk

JEYNES, Anthony James. b 44. AKC68. **d** 69 **p** 70. C Ellesmere Port *Ches* 69-73; C Birkenhead St Pet w St Matt 73-75; R Oughtrington 75-80; C Timperley 80-85; C Eastham 85-89; V New Brighton St Jas 89-96; P-in-c New Brighton Em 94-96; R Tarleton *Blackb* 96-04; P-in-c Kyrenia St Andr and Chapl N

Cyprus 04-07; Chapl Paphos from 07. *PO Box 61083, 8130 Kato Paphos, Cyprus* Tel (00357) (26) 953337
E-mail chap.house@cytanet.com.cy

JOACHIM, Margaret Jane. b 49. FGS91 St Hugh's Coll Ox BA70 MA74 W Midl Coll of Educn PGCE71 Birm Univ PhD77. S Dios Minl Tr Scheme 91. **d** 94 **p** 95. NSM Ealing St Barn *Lon* 94-97; NSM Ealing St Pet Mt Park from 97. *8 Newburgh Road, London W3 6DQ* Tel (020) 8723 4514 *or* 8754 4547 E-mail margaret.joachim@london.anglican.org

JOB, Canon Evan Roger Gould. b 36. Magd Coll Ox BA60 MA64 ARCM55. Cuddesdon Coll 60. **d** 62 **p** 63. C Liv Our Lady and St Nic 62-65; V New Springs 65-70; Min Can and Prec Man Cathl 70-74; Prec and Sacr Westmr Abbey 74-79; Can Res, Prec and Sacr Win Cathl 79-94; Vice-Dean Win 91-94; Select Preacher Ox Univ 74 and 91; rtd 01; Perm to Offic *Win* from 94 and *Portsm* from 04. *Kitwood Farmhouse, Kitwood Lane, Ropley, Alresford SO24 0DB* Tel (01962) 772303

JOBBER, Barry William. b 38. N Staffs Poly BA84. Cuddesdon Coll 73. **d** 75 **p** 76. C Fenton *Lich* 76-79; V Goldenhill 79-80; Perm to Offic *Ches* 90-02; NSM Middlewich w Byley 02-08; NSM Witton from 08. *16 Angus Grove, Middlewich CW10 9GR* Tel (01606) 737386 Mobile 07974-380234
E-mail barry.jobber@uwclub.net

JOBLING, Jeremy Charles. b 72. Natal Univ BSc95. Wycliffe Hall Ox 03. **d** 05 **p** 06. C Watford *St Alb* 05-08; C Kenilworth S Africa from 08. *16 Summerley Road, Kenilworth, 7708 South Africa* Tel (0027) (21) 797 6332
E-mail jeremy.jobling@googlemail.com

JOBSON, Clifford Hedley. b 31. St Jo Coll Dur BA54 MA81. **d** 56 **p** 57. C Hall Green Ascension *Birm* 56-59; C Ambleside w Rydal *Carl* 59-60; R Arthuret 60-62; CF 62-73; Dep Asst Chapl Gen 73-78; Asst Chapl Gen 78-84; QHC from 80; V Fleet *Guildf* 84-96; rtd 96; Perm to Offic *B & W* 96-06. *Vine Cottage, 25 Silver Street, South Petherton TA13 5AL* Tel (01460) 241783

JOEL, Mrs Mary Tertia. b 35. **d** 99 **p** 00. OLM Blyth Valley *St E* 99-05; rtd 05; Perm to Offic *St E* from 05. *38 Saxmundham Road, Aldeburgh IP15 5JE* Tel (01728) 454886 Mobile 07790-910554
E-mail maryt@joel12.freeserve.co.uk

JOHN, Alexander Dominic. b 26. Madras Univ BA47. Episc Sem Austin Texas MDiv63. **d** 63 **p** 64. C Millhouses H Trin *Sheff* 63-65; Switzerland 65-68; India 68-78; Australia from 78; rtd 85. *12 Bentwood Avenue, Woodlands WA 6018, Australia* Tel (0061) (8) 9445 3530 E-mail remo@space.net.au

✠**JOHN, The Rt Revd Andrew Thomas Griffith.** b 64. Univ of Wales LLB. St Jo Coll Nottm BA. **d** 89 **p** 90 **c** 08. C Cardigan w Mwnt and Y Ferwig *St D* 89-91; C Aberystwyth 91-92; TV 92-99; V Henfynyw w Aberaeron and Llanddewi Aberarth etc 99-06; V Pencarreg and Llanycrwys 06-08; Adn Cardigan 06-08; Bp Ban from 08. *Ty'r Esgob, Upper Garth Road, Bangor LL57 2SS* Tel (01248) 362895
E-mail bishop.bangor@churchinwales.org.uk

JOHN, Canon Arun Andrew. b 54. **d** 77 **p** 78. India 77-96; S Africa 97-04; TV Manningham *Bradf* from 04. *St Paul's Rectory, 63 St Paul's Road, Manningham, Bradford BD8 7LS* Tel (01274) 490550 E-mail stpauls@legend.co.uk

JOHN, Barbara. b 34. Gilmore Ho. **dss** 67 **d** 80 **p** 97. Merthyr Tydfil *Llan* 67-71; Loughton St Jo *Chelmsf* 71-73; Newport St Woolos *Mon* 73-78; Asst Chapl Univ Hosp of Wales Cardiff 78-85; C Radyr *Llan* 85-00; rtd 00. *14 Pace Close, Cardiff CF5 2QZ* Tel (029) 2055 2989

JOHN, Canon Beverley Hayes. b 49. Qu Coll Birm 83. **d** 85 **p** 86. C Oystermouth *S & B* 85-87; C Morriston 87-88; V Cefn Coed w Vaynor from 88; AD Brecon from 99; Can Res Brecon Cathl from 04. *Ty Cefn Coed, 6 Lamb Road, Penderyn, Aberdare CF44 9JU* Tel (01685) 811810

JOHN, Brother. *See* HENNINGS, John Richard

JOHN, Caroline Victoria. b 64. Cam Univ BA86 MA90. St Jo Coll Nottm. **d** 90. NSM Cardigan w Mwnt and Y Ferwig *St D* 90-91; NSM Aberystwyth 91-96. *Ty'r Esgob, Upper Garth Road, Bangor LL57 2SS* Tel (01248) 362895

JOHN, Canon David Michael. b 36. Univ of Wales (Lamp) BA57. St Mich Coll Llan 57. **d** 59 **p** 60. C Pontypool *Mon* 59-61; C Roath *Llan* 61-66; Asst Chapl HM Pris Liv 66-67; Chapl HM Pris Ex 67-68; V Ystrad Rhondda *Llan* 68-76; V Pontyclun w Talygarn 76-84; R Newton Nottage 84-91; Can Llan Cathl 85-91; rtd 91; Perm to Offic *Llan* and *Mon* from 91. *1 Hornbeam Close, St Mellons, Cardiff CF3 0JA* Tel (029) 2079 7496

JOHN, David Wyndham. b 61. Lon Bible Coll. NTMTC. **d** 01 **p** 02. NSM Hampstead Em W End *Lon* 01-04; NSM W Hampstead St Cuth from 04; P-in-c from 06. *13 Kingscroft Road, London NW2 3QE* Tel (020) 8452 1913 Mobile 07719-333389

JOHN, The Ven Elwyn Crebey. b 36. Univ of Wales (Lamp) BA57. St Mich Coll Llan 57. **d** 59 **p** 60. C Llangiwg *S & B* 59-62; C Llandrindod w Cefnllys 62-66; V Beguildy and Heyope 66-79; Youth Chapl 72-79; Chapl Agric and Rural Soc 77-03; V Builth and Llanddewi'r Cwm w Llangynog etc 79-95; Can Brecon Cathl 88-95; Can Res Brecon Cathl 95-03; Prec 94-95; Treas 95-98; Chan 98-03; V Brecon St Mary w Llanddew 95-01; Adn Brecon

99-03; rtd 03. *17 Cae Castell, Builth Wells LD2 3BE* Tel (01982) 551553

JOHN, Canon James Richard. b 21. Ch Coll Cam BA47 MA49. Cuddesdon Coll 47. **d** 49 **p** 50. C Sidcup Ch Ch *Roch* 49-52; V Gillingham St Mary 52-66; RD Gillingham 60-66; V Bolton St Jas w St Chrys *Bradf* 66-78; R Guiseley 78-83; RD Otley 80-86; P-in-c Esholt 82-83; TR Guiseley w Esholt 83-87; Hon Can Bradf Cathl 83-87; rtd 87; Perm to Offic *Bradf* from 87. *37 Croft House Drive, Otley LS21 2ER* Tel (01943) 461998

JOHN, The Very Revd Jeffrey Philip Hywel. b 53. Hertf Coll Ox BA75 Magd Coll Ox DPhil84. St Steph Ho Ox BA77 MA78. **d** 78 **p** 79. C Penarth w Lavernock *Llan* 78-80; Asst Chapl Magd Coll Ox 80-82; Fell and Dean of Div 84-91; Chapl and Lect BNC Ox 82-84; V Eltham H Trin *S'wark* 91-97; Chan and Can Th S'wark Cathl 97-04; Bp's Adv for Min 97-04; Dean St Alb from 04. *The Deanery, Sumpter Yard, St Albans AL1 1BY* Tel (01727) 890203 Fax 890227 E-mail dean@stalbanscathedral.org.uk

JOHN, Mrs Marie. b 48. **d** 04 **p** 05. OLM Camberwell St Geo *S'wark* from 04. *8 Caroline Gardens, Asylum Road, London SE15 2SQ* Tel (020) 7635 5534

JOHN, Mark Christopher. b 61. SS Mark & Jo Univ Coll Plymouth BA83. St Steph Ho Ox 84. **d** 87 **p** 88. C Treboeth *S & B* 87-90; V Swansea St Mark and St Jo 90-94; Chapl HM Pris Swansea 91-94; Chapl HM Pris Usk and Prescoed 94-97; Chapl HM Pris Cardiff from 97; Lic to Offic *Mon* from 99. *HM Prison Cardiff, Knox Road, Cardiff CF24 0UG* Tel (029) 2043 3100 ext 3233 Fax 2043 3318

JOHN, Meurig Hywel. b 46. St D Coll Lamp 67. **d** 71 **p** 72. C Llanelli Ch Ch *St D* 71-74; V Penrhyncoch and Elerch 74-79; V Llanfihangel Aberbythych 79-81; R Cilgerran w Bridell and Llantwyd 81-83; V Gwaun-cae-Gurwen 83-89; V Llanfihangel Genau'r-glyn and Llangorwen 89-95; V Newcastle Emlyn w Llandyfriog etc 95-01; Assoc V Lampeter and Llanddewibrefi Gp 01-03; rtd 03. *Arosfa, Llanybri, Carmarthen SA33 5HQ* Tel (01267) 241096

JOHN, Napoleon. b 55. Punjab Univ BA76. Lahetysteologisen Inst Ryttyla Finland 84 Oak Hill Th Coll BA93. **d** 93 **p** 94. C Leyton St Mary w St Edw *Chelmsf* 93-96; C Leyton St Mary w St Edw and St Luke 96-97; P-in-c Becontree St Elisabeth 97-04; V 04-07; TR Walton and Trimley *St E* from 07. *1 Parsonage Close, Felixstowe IP11 2QR* Tel (01394) 284803 E-mail napojohn@hotmail.com

JOHN, Nigel. b 59. Univ of Wales (Cardiff) BA87 Selw Coll Cam MPhil90. Westcott Ho Cam 88. **d** 91 **p** 92. C Carmarthen St Pet *St D* 91-94; Chapl Roehampton Inst *S'wark* 94-96; V Gors-las *St D* 96-98; V Llanelli Ch Ch 98-02; Chapl Univ of Wales (Swansea) *S & B* from 02. *23 Mayals Avenue, Blackpill, Swansea SA3 5DE* Tel (01792) 401703

JOHN, Richard. *See* JOHN, Canon James Richard

JOHN, Robert Michael. b 46. Edin Univ BSc67 Man Univ MSc68 PhD70 Otago Univ BD78. St Jo Coll Auckland 76. **d** 78 **p** 79. New Zealand 78-87 and from 88; C Swansea St Jas *S & B* 87-88. *38 Cowan Street, Ponsonby, Auckland 1011, New Zealand* Tel (0064) (9) 376 8303 *or* 307 4949

JOHN, Stephen Michael. b 63. Univ of Wales (Lamp) BA85. Coll of Resurr Mirfield 87. **d** 89 **p** 90. C Coity w Nolton *Llan* 89-91; C Merthyr Dyfan 91-94; V Tredegar St Geo *Mon* 94-99; Chapl HM Pris Gartree 99-04; TV Tenby *St D* from 04. *9 Lamack Vale, Tenby SA70 8DN* Tel (01834) 844330

JOHN-FRANCIS, Brother. *See* FRIENDSHIP, Roger Geoffrey

JOHNES, Philip Sydney. b 45. St Mich Coll Llan 90. **d** 92 **p** 93. C Cardigan w Mwnt and Y Ferwig *St D* 92-95; V Llanegwad w Llanfynydd from 95. *Llanegwad Vicarage, Heol Alltyferin, Nantgaredig, Carmarthen SA32 7NE* Tel and fax (01267) 290142 E-mail pjohnes@aol.com

JOHNES, Adam Aubrey. b 34. TCD BA57 MA76 NUU BA75. CITC Div Test 58. **d** 58 **p** 59. C Aghalee *D & D* 58-61; C Derriaghy *Conn* 61-63; I Billy 63-77; I Billy w Derrykeighan 77-03; Can Conn Cathl 98-03; rtd 03. *26 Chatham Road, Armoy, Ballymoney BT53 8TT* Tel (028) 2075 1978

JOHNS, Canon Bernard Thomas. b 36. Birm Univ BSc58. St Mich Coll Llan 61. **d** 63 **p** 64. C Aberavon *Llan* 63-65; C St Andrews Major w Michaelston-le-Pit 65-70; V Cardiff St Andr and St Teilo 70-76; Asst Dioc Dir of Educn 72-91; V Roath 76-88; R Wenvoe and St Lythans 88-02; Dioc Dir Community Educn 91-02; Can Llan Cathl 96-02; rtd 02. *Bay Tree Cottage, 13 Badgers Meadow, Pwllmeyric, Chepstow NP16 6UE* Tel (01291) 623254

JOHNS, Mrs Patricia Holly. b 33. Girton Coll Cam BA56 MA60 Hughes Hall Cam PGCE57. Ox NSM Course 87. **d** 90 **p** 94. NSM Wantage *Ox* 90-94; NSM Marlborough *Sarum* 94-95; rtd 95; Perm to Offic *Sarum* 95-08. *1 Priory Lodge, 93 Brown Street, Salisbury SP1 2BX* Tel (01722) 328007

JOHNS, Canon Ronald Charles. b 37. TD. Dur Univ BA59. Wells Th Coll 59. **d** 61 **p** 62. C Wigan All SS *Liv* 61-66; TV Kirkby 66-75; Ho Master Ruffwood Sch Kirkby 70-75; TV Maghull 75-79; Dep Hd Master Maghull Old Hall High Sch 75-79; P-in-c Borrowdale *Carl* 79-84; V 84-89; RD Derwent 81-89; Hon Can Carl Cathl 87-89; Can Res 89-94; R Caldbeck, Castle Sowerby

and Sebergham 94-00; rtd 01; Perm to Offic *Nor* from 01. *3 Kings Road, Coltishall, Norwich NR12 7DX*

JOHNS, Thomas Morton. b 43. Oak Hill Th Coll 67. **d** 70 **p** 71. C N Meols *Liv* 70-73; C Farnborough *Guildf* 73-76; P-in-c Badshot Lea CD 76-83; Dep Chapl HM Pris Man 83; Chapl HM Youth Cust Cen Wellingborough 83-88; Chapl HM YOI Swinfen Hall 88-90; Chapl Tr Officer 88-95; Chapl HM Pris Service Coll 90-95; Asst Chapl Gen of Pris (HQ) 95-01; Acting Chapl Gen 00-01; P-in-c Colbury *Win* 02-08; Chapl Hants Constabulary 02-08; rtd 08. *74 Coronation Road, Aldershot GU11 3QA* Tel (01252) 322876 Mobile 07974-025478 E-mail tom@mortonjohns.fsnet.co.uk

JOHNS, Trevor Charles. b 33. St D Coll Lamp BA58. **d** 58 **p** 59. C Pembroke St Mary w St Mich *St D* 58-61; R Walwyn's Castle w Robeston W 61-67; CF 67-75; V Spittal and Treffgarne *St D* 75-79; C Tring *St Alb* 79-80; TV Tring 80-85; V Knighton and Norton *S & B* 85-86; V Merthyr Cynog and Dyffryn Honddu etc 86-98; rtd 98. *109 Hoel-y-Banc, Bancffosfelen, Llanelli SA15 5DF*

JOHNS, William Price. b 28. Keble Coll Ox BA51 MA56. St Mich Coll Llan 52. **d** 53 **p** 54. C Whitchurch *Llan* 53-56; C Pontypridd St Cath 56-59; Min Can Brecon Cathl 59-62; V Wellington *Heref* 62-78; R Wellington w Pipe-cum-Lyde and Moreton-on-Lugg 78-93; P-in-c Ford 63-69; rtd 93; Perm to Offic *Llan* from 93. *12 Deepdale Close, Cardiff CF23 5LR* Tel (029) 2048 3762

JOHNSEN, Edward Andrew. b 67. Birm Univ BTheol89. Qu Coll Birm 95. **d** 97 **p** 98. C Birm St Luke 97-01; C Handsworth St Mary 01-04; Perm to Offic 05-06; TV Eden, Gelt and Irthing *Carl* from 06. *The Vicarage, Hayton, Brampton CA8 9HR* Tel (01228) 670248 E-mail mail@johnsen3671.fsworld.co.uk

JOHNSON, Amanda Saffery. b 58. K Alfred's Coll Win BEd83. Wycliffe Hall Ox. **d** 97 **p** 98. C Oxhey All SS *St Alb* 97-00; C Bricket Wood 00-02; Teacher Bp Wand Sch Sunbury-on-Thames 02-04; C Dorking St Paul *Guildf* 05-09; C Bisley and W End from 09. *6 Falkland Road, Dorking RH4 3AB* Tel 07905-893394 (mobile) E-mail amandola@tesco.net

JOHNSON, Andrew Paul. b 56. W Surrey Coll of Art & Design BA79 Kent Coll for Careers CertEd82 TCD BTh96. CITC 93. **d** 96 **p** 97. C Penarth w Lavernock *Llan* 96-99; R Walton W w Talbenny and Haroldston W *St D* from 99. *The Rectory, Walton West, Little Haven, Haverfordwest SA62 3UB* Tel (01437) 781279

JOHNSON, Andrew Peter. b 67. Westf Coll Lon BA89 St Jo Coll Nottm MA98 LTh99. Aston Tr Scheme 94. **d** 99 **p** 00. C Hitchin *St Alb* 99-03; V Batley All SS and Purlwell *Wakef* from 03. *The Vicarage, Churchfield Street, Batley WF17 5DL* Tel and fax (01924) 473049 E-mail johnsons@care4free.net

JOHNSON, Andrew Robert. b 68. Jes Coll Ox MA96 Univ of Wales (Abth) MLib93 PhD96. Cranmer Hall Dur 03. **d** 05 **p** 06. C Carmarthen St Pet *St D* 05-08; P-in-c Llanfihangel Ystrad and Cilcennin w Trefilan etc from 08. *Ystrad Vicarage, Felinfach, Lampeter SA48 8AE* E-mail andrewj@evemail.net

JOHNSON, Mrs Angela Carolyn Louise. b 52. RGN76. STETS 00. **d** 03 **p** 04. NSM Catherington and Clanfield *Portsm* 03-07; NSM Denmead from 07. *90 Downhouse Road, Waterlooville PO8 0TY* Tel (023) 9264 4595 E-mail angela.johnson52@ntlworld.com

JOHNSON, Anthony. *See* JOHNSON, Edward Anthony

JOHNSON, Anthony Arthur Derry. b 15. Kelham Th Coll 31. **d** 39 **p** 40. C Pinner *Lon* 39-42; C Willesden St Andr 42-44; C Winchmore Hill H Trin 44-49; V Brookfield St Anne, Highgate Rise 49-60; V Mill Hill St Mich 60-73; R Chalfont St Giles *Ox* 73-80; rtd 80; Perm to Offic *Sarum* from 80. *Garden Close, Long Street, Sherborne DT9 3DD* Tel (01935) 813469

JOHNSON, Anthony Peter. b 45. K Coll Lon BD76 AKC76 MTh79. Wells Th Coll 67. **d** 70 **p** 71. C Goldington *St Alb* 70-73; C Hainault *Chelmsf* 73-76; TV Loughton St Mary 76-81; V Scunthorpe All SS *Linc* 81-85; V Alkborough 85-87; Chapl Man Univ and TV Man Whitworth 87-96; P-in-c Chorlton-cum-Hardy St Werburgh 96-00; R 00-05; P-in-c Yardley St Cypr Hay Mill *Birm* 05-08; V from 08. *St Barnabas' Vicarage, 51 Over Green Drive, Kingshurst, Birmingham B37 6EY* Tel 0121-770 3972 E-mail a.johnson05@tiscali.co.uk

JOHNSON, Canon Anthony Trevor. b 27. CCC Ox BA51 MA55. Cuddesdon Coll 51. **d** 53 **p** 54. C Wareham w Arne *Sarum* 53-57; C Melksham 57-60; R Tarrant Gunville, Tarrant Hinton etc 60-67; R Upton Scudamore 67-85; V Warminster St Denys 67-85; RD Heytesbury 71-76; Can and Preb Sarum Cathl 75-92; P-in-c Horningsham 76-85; P-in-c Semley and Sedgehill 85-86; R E Knoyle, Semley and Sedgehill 86-92; rtd 92; Perm to Offic *Sarum* from 92. *Coombe Warren, Hindon Lane, Tisbury, Salisbury SP3 6QQ* Tel (01747) 870130

JOHNSON, Anthony Warrington. b 40. Goldsmiths' Coll Lon CertEd60. St Jo Coll Nottm 86. **d** 88 **p** 89. C Lutterworth w Cotesbach *Leic* 88-92; V Countesthorpe w Foston 92-06; P-in-c Arnesby w Shearsby and Bruntingthorpe 94-01; rtd 06; Hon C Lutterworth w Cotesbach and Bitteswell *Leic* from 06. *The*

Vicarage, Lutterworth Road, Bitteswell, Lutterworth LE17 4RX Tel (01455) 557562

JOHNSON, Miss Barbara. b 45. St Jo Coll Nottm 04. **d** 07 **p** 08. NSM Royston *St Alb* 07-08; NSM Goldington from 08; Chapl Beds and Luton Fire and Rescue Service from 07. *4 Hicks Lane, Girton, Cambridge CB3 0JS* Tel (01223) 276282 Mobile 07768-560646 E-mail barbara.johnson@bedsfire.com

JOHNSON, Barry Charles Richard. b 48. EAMTC 96. **d** 99 **p** 00. NSM Billericay and Lt Burstead *Chelmsf* 99-01; C Gt Burstead 01-02; C Bowers Gifford w N Benfleet 02-04; P-in-c Woodham Mortimer w Hazeleigh 04-06; R Vange from 06; P-in-c Bowers Gifford w N Benfleet from 07. *Vange Rectory, 782 Clay Hill Road, Basildon SS16 4NG* Tel (01268) 581574 E-mail johnson@buers.freeserve.co.uk

JOHNSON, Beverley Charles. b 35. Bp Gray Coll Cape Town 59. **d** 61 **p** 62. S Africa 61-67 and from 91; C Woodstock St Mary 61-64; C Clanwilliam St Jo 64-65; C Plumstead St Mark 65-67; C Southsea St Pet *Portsm* 68-69; C Southwick St Cuth CD *Dur* 70-71; P-in-c Waterhouses 71-80; R Burnmoor 80-85; V Brandon 85-89; Australia 89-91; Asst P Sea Point St Jas 91-01; rtd 01. *43 Oxford Street, Goodwood, 7460 South Africa* Tel and fax (0027) (21) 592 1180 Mobile 82-202 5260

JOHNSON, Mrs Brenda Margaret. b 47. TISEC 93. **d** 00. NSM Edin St Salvador 00-03; NSM Wester Hailes St Luke 00-03; NSM Edin Gd Shep from 03. *58 Ratho Park Road, Ratho, Newbridge EH28 8PQ* Tel 0131-333 1742 Mobile 07713-154744 E-mail brenmj@btinternet.com

JOHNSON, Brian. b 42. S'wark Ord Course 84. **d** 87 **p** 88. NSM Dulwich St Barn *S'wark* 87-92; NSM Herne Hill 92-94; Perm to Offic 94-96; Chapl HM Pris Man 96-01; P-in-c Rotterdam *Eur* 01-02; Operations Manager ICS 03; Perm to Offic *Ches* from 04. *11A Lynton Park Road, Cheadle Hulme, Cheadle SK8 6JA* Tel 0161-485 3787 E-mail revbfg@ntlworld.com

JOHNSON, Christopher Dudley. b 26. Worc Coll Ox BA44 MA51. Cuddesdon Coll 53. **d** 56 **p** 57. C Basingstoke *Win* 56-61; V Bethnal Green St Barn *Lon* 61-67; V Eton w Eton Wick and Boveney *Ox* 67-88; rtd 91; Perm to Offic *Sarum* from 96. *Lavinces Cottage, Netherbury, Bridport DT6 5LL*

JOHNSON, Christopher Frederick. b 43. MRICS67. Ripon Hall Ox 71. **d** 74 **p** 75. C Chatham St Steph *Roch* 74-78; V Slade Green 78-85; V Wilmington 85-95; R Chevening 95-09; rtd 09. *7 Kennedy Gardens, Sevenoaks TN13 3UG* Tel (01732) 456626 E-mail c.f.johnson@waitrose.com

JOHNSON, Christopher Paul. b 47. St Jo Coll Nottm BTh74. **d** 74 **p** 75. C Normanton *Wakef* 74-78; P-in-c Dewsbury St Mark 78-82; V Harden and Wilsden *Bradf* 82-88; P-in-c Holbeck *Ripon* 88-94; V 94-97; Asst Chapl Leeds Teaching Hosps NHS Trust 97-01; Chapl Bradf Hosps NHS Trust from 01. *Bradford Royal Infirmary, Duckworth Lane, Bradford BD9 6RJ* Tel (01274) 542200 E-mail chris.johnson@bradfordhospitals.nhs.uk

JOHNSON, Christopher Robert. b 43. Lon Coll of Div 66. **d** 70 **p** 71. C Everton St Geo *Liv* 70-71; C Childwall All SS 71-75; TV Gateacre 75-76; TV Bushbury *Lich* 76-87; R Burslem from 87. *The Rectory, 16 Heyburn Crescent, Burslem, Stoke-on-Trent ST6 4DL* Tel (01782) 838932

JOHNSON, Canon Colin Gawman. b 32. Leeds Univ BA59. Coll of Resurr Mirfield 59. **d** 61 **p** 62. C Barrow St Matt *Carl* 61-67; V 90-96; V Addingham 67-71; V Carl H Trin 71-80; V Wigton 80-90; Hon Can Carl Cathl 85-96; rtd 96; Perm to Offic *Carl* from 97. *Hemp Garth, Ireby, Wigton CA7 1EA* Tel (01697) 371578

JOHNSON, Colin Leslie. b 41. Trin Coll Cam MA65. Cheshunt Coll Cam 62. **d** 93 **p** 94. Publications Dir Chr Educn Movement from 89; NSM Brailsford w Shirley and Osmaston w Edlaston *Derby* 93-04; Perm to Offic from 04. *33 The Plain, Brailsford, Ashbourne DE6 3BZ* Tel (01335) 360591 E-mail cj@acjohnson.plus.com

JOHNSON, Colin Stewart. b 46. SEITE 99. **d** 02 **p** 03. NSM Borden *Cant* 02-05; C Charlton-in-Dover 05-06. P-in-c from 06. *Holywell House, 3 Monastery Avenue, Dover CT16 1AB* Tel and fax (01304) 201143 Mobile 07740-775277 E-mail frcj@dsl.pipex.com

JOHNSON, Cyril Francis. b 22. St Cath Coll Cam BA49 MA54. Ely Th Coll 50. **d** 52 **p** 53. C Twickenham All Hallows *Lon* 52-56; C Kingsthorpe *Pet* 56-61; R Harpole 61-87; rtd 87; Perm to Offic *Chich* from 01. *16 Blake's Way, Eastbourne BN23 6EW* Tel (01323) 723491

JOHNSON, David. *See* JOHNSON, John David

JOHNSON, David Alan. b 43. Lon Univ BSc63 PhD67. Trin Coll Bris 78. **d** 80 **p** 81. C Watford *St Alb* 80-85; V Idle *Bradf* 85-08; P-in-c Greengates 08; rtd 08. *15 Blackburn Close, Bearpark, Durham DH7 7TQ* Tel 0191-373 7953 E-mail david@fss.me.uk

JOHNSON, David Bryan Alfred. b 36. Hartsham Th Coll 56. **d** 61 **p** 62. C Streatham St Paul *S'wark* 61-63; Malaysia 63-71; V Worc St Mich 71-74; Warden Lee Abbey Internat Students' Club Kensington 74-77; V Plumstead St Mark and St Marg *S'wark* 77-86; Chapl W Park Hosp Epsom 86-96; Chapl Laslett's *Worc* 96-01; rtd 96. *3 St Birinus Cottages, Wessex Way, Bicester OX26 6DX* Tel (01869) 320839

JOHNSON, David Clark. b 15. Tyndale Hall Bris 61. **d** 62 **p** 63. C Chippenham St Paul *Bris* 62-64; C Chippenham St Paul w Langley Burrell 64-65; V Bishopsworth 65-74; V Stratton St Margaret 75-78; TR Stratton St Margaret w S Marston etc 78-80; rtd 80; Perm to Offic *Bris* from 80. *St Joseph's Home, 66 Cotham Hill, Bristol BS6 6JX* Tel 0117-973 3815

JOHNSON, David Francis. b 32. Univ Coll Ox BA55 MA59. Westcott Ho Cam 55. **d** 57 **p** 58. C Earlsdon *Cov* 57-59; C Willenhall 59-61; C Attenborough w Bramcote *S'well* 61-62; V Ravenstone w Weston Underwood *Ox* 62-66; V Crewe Ch Ch *Ches* 66-70; P-in-c Crewe St Pet 67-70; V Thornton w Allerthorpe *York* 70-79; V N Hull St Mich 79-81; V Leyburn w Bellerby *Ripon* 81-88; V Coxwold and Husthwaite *York* 88-97; rtd 97; Perm to Offic *York* 98-03 and *Heref* from 05. *Nursery Cottage, The Park, Wormelow, Hereford HR2 8EQ* Tel (01981) 540967

JOHNSON, David John. b 49. Lanc Univ BA72. Linc Th Coll 78. **d** 81 **p** 82. C Stockport St Thos *Ches* 81-84; OGS from 83; C Stockton Heath *Ches* 84-88; V Tranmere St Paul w St Luke 88-99; P-in-c Antrobus 99-02; P-in-c Aston by Sutton 99-02; P-in-c Lt Leigh and Lower Whitley 99-02; V Antrobus, Aston by Sutton, Lt Leigh etc 02-07; C Coppenhall from 07. *St Raphael, 149 Broad Street, Crewe CW1 3UD* Tel (01270) 250256

JOHNSON, David Richard. b 67. Birm Univ BSc88. Ripon Coll Cuddesdon BA92 MA97. **d** 94 **p** 95. C Horfield H Trin *Bris* 94-97; V Two Mile Hill St Mich 97-01; Asst Chapl Haileybury Coll 01-02; Chapl Dauntsey's Sch Devizes from 02. *20 High Street, West Lavington, Devizes SN10 4HQ* Tel (01380) 814573 E-mail johnsoda@dauntseys.wilts.sch.uk

JOHNSON, David William. b 40. Oak Hill Th Coll BD64. **d** 65 **p** 66. C Tunbridge Wells St Jas *Roch* 65-68; C Kirby Muxloe *Leic* 68-72; V Burton Joyce w Bulcote *S'well* 72-83; V Mitford and Chapl Northgate Mental Handicap Unit Morpeth 83-87; Asst Chapl R Victoria Infirmary Newc 87-89; Chapl R Shrewsbury Hosps NHS Trust 89-04; rtd 04. *42 Hartlands, Bedlington NE22 6JG* Tel (01670) 828693

JOHNSON, David William. b 53. Selw Coll Cam BA76. Ripon Coll Cuddesdon 76. **d** 78 **p** 79. C Fulham St Etheldreda w St Clem *Lon* 78-82; Communications Sec Gen Syn Bd for Miss and Unity 82-87; PV Westmr Abbey 85-87; R Gilmorton w Peatling Parva and Kimcote etc *Leic* 87-91; R Cogenhoe *Pet* 91-95; R Whiston 93-95; rtd 95; Perm to Offic *Ox* from 00. *Seaview Cottage, 115 Hurst Street, Oxford OX4 1HE* Tel (01865) 793393

JOHNSON, Preb Derek John. b 36. St Aid Birkenhead 65. **d** 68 **p** 69. C Eccleshall *Lich* 68-73; C Stafford St Mary 73-75; Chapl New Cross Hosp Wolv 75-96; Preb Lich Cathl 83-96; rtd 96; Perm to Offic *St E* from 96. *6 St Paul's Close, Aldeburgh IP15 5BQ* Tel (01728) 452474

JOHNSON, Canon Diana Margaret. b 46. MCSP68 SRP68. Cranmer Hall Dur 92. **d** 94 **p** 95. C Birtley *Dur* 94-99; TV Gateshead 99-06; AD Gateshead 03-06; P-in-c Belmont 06-07; V Belmont and Pittington from 07; Hon Can Dur Cathl from 06. *Belmont Vicarage, Broomside Lane, Durham DH1 2QW* Tel 0191-386 1545

JOHNSON, Mrs Diane Pearl. b 47. Leeds Univ BA68 Cam Univ PGCE69. EAMTC 95. **d** 98 **p** 99. NSM Gt Bowden w Welham, Glooston and Cranoe *Leic* 98-01; C Evington and Leic St Phil 01-04; P-in-c Leic St Phil 04-07; rtd 07. *16 Oaklands Park, Market Harborough LE16 8EU* Tel (01858) 434118 E-mail grahamanddiane@ntlworld.com

JOHNSON, Canon Donald Arnold. b 28. Linc Coll Ox BA51 MA59. Cuddesdon 51. **d** 53 **p** 54. C Henfield *Chich* 53-55; C Horsham 55-59; V Oving w Merston 59-68; Bp's Dom Chapl 59-68; V Hellingly 68-78; V Upper Dicker 68-78; R W Stoke 78-98; V Funtington and Sennicotts 78-98; Can and Preb Chich Cathl 96-98; rtd 98; Perm to Offic *Chich* from 99. *Vectis, Commonside, Westbourne, Emsworth PO10 8TA* Tel (01243) 371433

JOHNSON, Mrs Dorothy. Leic Univ BSc89 Ox Univ MTh95 RGN FRSH91. Qu Coll Birm 77. dss 80 **d** 87 **p** 94. Coventry Caludon 80-81; Wolston and Church Lawford 81-86; NSM Stoneleigh w Ashow 87-08; Bp's Asst Officer for Soc Resp 87-96. *The Firs, Stoneleigh Road, Bubbenhall, Coventry CV8 3BS* Tel and fax (024) 7630 3712 E-mail firsjohn@supanet.com

JOHNSON, Douglas Leonard. b 45. Trin Coll Bris 70 Lon Bible Coll MA95. **d** 73 **p** 74. C New Malden and Coombe *S'wark* 73-76; P-in-c Upper Tulse Hill St Matthias 76-82; CPAS Staff 82-88; Lect and Tutor CA Coll 88-91; Dir Crossways Chr Educn Trust 92-08; Hon C Wimbledon Em Ridgway Prop Chpl *S'wark* 83-08; Lect Cornhill Tr Course 95-08; Kenya from 08. *Address temp unknown*

JOHNSON, Edward Anthony (Tony). b 32. Univ of Wales (Swansea) BSc54. St Steph Ho Ox 79. **d** 81 **p** 82. C Wolvercote w Summertown *Ox* 81-84; P-in-c Ramsden 84-87; P-in-c Finstock and Fawler 84-87; P-in-c Wilcote 84-87; V Ramsden, Finstock and Fawler, Leafield etc 87-92; rtd 92; Hon C Kennington *Ox* 92-98; Perm to Offic from 98. *15 Cranbrook Drive, Kennington, Oxford OX1 5RR* Tel (01865) 739751

JOHNSON, Mrs Elizabeth Jane. b 47. St Hilda's Coll Ox MA69. Wycliffe Hall Ox 84. **dss** 86 **d** 87 **p** 94. NSM Ox St Aldate w St Matt 86-91; NSM Marston 91-94; NSM Ox St Clem 94-95; NSM Islip w Charlton on Otmoor, Oddington, Noke etc 95-99; OLM Officer (Dorchester) 99-00; Asst Chapl Oxon Mental Healthcare NHS Trust 00-04; NSM Bladon w Woodstock *Ox* 99-04; NSM Shill Valley and Broadshire 04-09. *11 Oakey Close, Alvescot, Bampton OX18 2PX* Tel (01993) 846169
E-mail lizjohn@crecy.fsnet.co.uk

JOHNSON, Miss Emma Louise. b 82. St Mary's Coll Dur BA05 MA06. Ridley Hall Cam 07. **d** 09. C Cockfield *Dur* from 09; C Lynesack from 09. *The Vicarage, Brookside, Evenwood, Bishop Auckland DL14 9RA*
E-mail emmajohnson139@googlemail.com

JOHNSON, Eric. b 38. Nottm Univ BSc60 Open Univ BA92 SS Paul & Mary Coll Cheltenham MA94. Qu Coll Birm 74. **d** 77 **p** 78. Sen Lect Cov Tech Coll 66-91; NSM Earlsdon *Cov* 77-81; NSM Wolston and Church Lawford 81-86; NSM Stoneleigh w Ashow and Baginton 90-98; FE Liaison Officer *B & W, Bris* and *Glouc* 91-93; Dioc Dir of Educn *Worc* 93-98; rtd 98; Assoc Dir of Discipleship Development *Cov* from 98. *The Firs, Stoneleigh Road, Bubbenhall, Coventry CV8 3BS* Tel and fax (024) 7630 3712 Mobile 07773-748967 E-mail firsjohn@supanet.com

JOHNSON, Frances Josephine. b 53. Leeds Univ CertEd74 Open Univ BA90. NOC 02. **d** 05 **p** 06. C Hall Green St Pet *Birm* 05-08; V Kingshurst from 08. *St Barnabas' Vicarage, 51 Overgreen Drive, Birmingham B37 6EY* Tel 0121-770 3972
E-mail j.johnson2@tiscali.co.uk

JOHNSON, Geoffrey Kemble. b 22. RD71. Roch Th Coll 62. **d** 64 **p** 65. C Hayes *Roch* 64-68; R Worlingham *St E* 68-84; rtd 84; Perm to Offic *Nor* 84-00 and *St E* from 84. *53 St Walstans Road, Taverham, Norwich NR8 6NG* Tel (01603) 860626

JOHNSON, Geoffrey Stuart. b 39. ALCD65 Wolv Poly DipEd Sussex Univ DPhil01. **d** 65 **p** 66. C Worksop St Jo *S'well* 65-68; Taiwan 68-71; C St Andr Cathl Singapore 71-76; Aber Univ 76-78; Perm to Offic *Heref* 78-82; P-in-c Hoarwithy, Hentland and Sellack 82-84; Chapl Horton Hosp Epsom 84-90; Distr Chapl Brighton HA 90-94; Managing Chapl Brighton Healthcare NHS Trust 94-99; rtd 99; Chapl S Downs Health NHS Trust 00-06; Chapl Sussex Partnership NHS Trust from 06; Perm to Offic *Chich* from 01. *5 Garden Mews, 15 Beachy Head Road, Eastbourne BN20 7QP* Tel (01323) 644083

JOHNSON, Gillian Margaret. b 55. Bretton Hall Coll CertEd76 Coll of Ripon & York St Jo MA03. NOC 00. **d** 03 **p** 04. C Thornhill and Whitley Lower *Wakef* 03-07; C Mirfield from 07; Curriculum Development Officer Dioc Bd Educn from 07. *5 Wood Mount, Overton, Wakefield WF4 4SB* Tel (01924) 262181 Mobile 07880-901201
E-mail gilljohnson99@hotmail.com

JOHNSON, Gordon Edward. b 27. Oak Hill Th Coll 76. **d** 77 **p** 78. C Scarborough St Mary w Ch Ch and H Apostles *York* 77-82; V Hutton Cranswick w Skerne 82-86; P-in-c Watton w Beswick and Kilnwick 82-86; V Hutton Cranswick w Skerne, Watton and Beswick 86-88; V Bubwith w Skipwith 88-93; rtd 93; Perm to Offic *York* and *Ripon* from 93. *Greenacres, Lovesome Hill, Northallerton DL6 2PB* Tel (01609) 881512

JOHNSON, Graham. b 37. Westcott Ho Cam 66. **d** 68 **p** 69. C Stafford St Mary *Lich* 68-71; C Wombourne 71-74; Youth Chapl 74-77; P-in-c Tong 76-77; Res Min Wednesfield St Thos 77-78; TV 79-82; P-in-c Milwich and Weston upon Trent 82-88; P-in-c Gayton w Fradswell 84-88; V Fradswell, Gayton, Milwich and Weston 88-90; TV Wolstanton 90-96; V Oxley 96-02; rtd 03. *Ty Pab, 4 Church Street, Tremadog, Porthmadog LL49 9RA* Tel (01766) 513744 E-mail graham@typab.freeserve.co.uk

JOHNSON, Graham James. b 43. Southn Hall Ba67. Coll of Resurr Mirfield. **d** 70 **p** 71. C Heckmondwike *Wakef* 70-73; C Pet St Jude 73-76; V Gt w Lt Harrowden and Orlingbury 76-83; R Daventry 83-92; TR Daventry, Ashby St Ledgers, Braunston etc 92; RD Daventry 88-92; Chapl Danetre Hosp 83-93; P-in-c Loddington *Leic* 93-99; Warden Launde Abbey 93-99; RD Framland 94-96; Bp's Chapl and Interfaith Adv 00-02; P-in-c Humberstone 02-03; P-in-c Thurnby Lodge 02-03; TR Ascension TM 03-06; rtd 06. *16 Oaklands Park, Market Harborough LE16 8EU* Tel (01858) 434118
E-mail grahamanddiane@ntlworld.com

JOHNSON, Canon Hilary Ann. b 51. RGN72 RHV74. S'wark Ord Course 82. **dss** 85 **d** 87 **p** 94. Hon Par Dn Salfords *S'wark* 85-90; Chapl St Geo Hosp Lon 90-94; Chapl St Geo Healthcare NHS Trust Lon from 94; Assoc P Wimbledon *S'wark* from 95; Hon Can S'wark Cathl from 07. *St George's Hospital, Blackshaw Road, London SW17 0QT* Tel (020) 8725 3070, 8725 3071 or 8397 0952 Fax 8725 1621
E-mail hilary.johnson@stgeorges.nhs.uk

JOHNSON, Ian Lawrence. b 44. Wells Th Coll 68. **d** 71 **p** 72. C Benhilton *S'wark* 71-73; C Weymouth H Trin *Sarum* 73-76; R Pewsey 76-81; R Maiden Newton and Valleys 81-83; Youth Officer (Sherborne Area) 81-83; Dioc Youth Officer 83-88; TR Langley and Parkfield *Man* 88-95; P-in-c Haughton St Anne

95-99; Dioc Adv on Evang 95-99; TR Southampton (City Cen) *Win* 99-08; rtd 08. *Farthing Cottage, 71 St Andrew Street, Tiverton EX16 6PL* Tel (01884) 251974

JOHNSON, Ian Leslie. b 51. Bede Coll Dur TCert73. Wycliffe Hall Ox 91. **d** 93 **p** 94. C Evington *Leic* 93-96; Sub Chapl HM Pris Gartree 96-97; C Foxton w Gumley and Laughton and Lubenham *Leic* 96-97; C Foxton w Gumley and Laughton 97-00; P-in-c from 00; Sub Chapl HM Pris Gartree from 97. *The Vicarage, Vicarage Drive, Foxton, Market Harborough LE16 7RJ* Tel (01858) 545245 E-mail ijoh270951@aol.com

JOHNSON (*née* SILINS), Ms Jacqueline. b 62. Coll of Ripon & York St Jo BA85. Ripon Coll Cuddesdon 01. **d** 03 **p** 04. C Torpoint *Truro* 03-08; P-in-c Harworth *S'well* from 08. *The Vicarage, Tickhill Road, Harworth, Doncaster DN11 8PD* Tel (01302) 744157 Mobile 07905-354723
E-mail jackie@benedict.f9.co.uk

✠**JOHNSON, The Rt Revd James Nathaniel.** b 32. Wells Th Coll 63. **d** 64 **p** 65 **c** 85. C Lawrence Weston *Bris* 64-66; P-in-c St Paul's Cathl St Helena 66-69; V 69-71; Hon Can from 75; Area Sec USPG *Ex* and *Truro* 72-74; R Combe Martin *Ex* 74-80; V Thorpe Bay *Chelmsf* 80-85; Bp St Helena 85-91; R Byfield w Boddington and Aston le Walls *Pet* 91-92; Asst Bp Pet 91-92; V Hockley *Chelmsf* 92-97; Asst Bp Chelmsf 92-97; Can Chelmsf Cathl 94-97; rtd 97; Hon Asst Bp Chelmsf 97-04; Hon Asst Bp Ox from 04; Perm to Offic *Cov* from 05. *St Helena, 28 Molyneux Drive, Bodicote, Banbury OX15 4AP* Tel (01295) 255357 E-mail bpjnj@onetel.com

JOHNSON, Canon John Anthony. b 18. Selw Coll Cam BA48 MA53 St Jo Coll Dur. **d** 51 **p** 52. C Battersea St Mary *S'wark* 51-54; C Merton St Mary 54-56; V Balderton *S'well* 56-60; V Mansfield Woodhouse 60-70; V Beeston 70-85; RD Beeston 81-85; Hon Can S'well Minster 82-85; rtd 86; Perm to Offic *Blackb* 90-02. *Driftwood, Ireleth Road, Askam-in-Furness LA16 7JD* Tel (01229) 462291

JOHNSON, John Cecil. b 23. Peterho Cam BA48. Ely Th Coll 57. **d** 59 **p** 60. C Whitton SS Phil and Jas *Lon* 59-70; P-in-c Fulham St Andr Fulham Fields 70-73; V 73-88; rtd 88; Perm to Offic *Lich* from 88 and *Heref* from 90. *13 Selkirk Drive, Sutton Hill, Telford TF7 4JE* Tel (01952) 588407

JOHNSON, John David. b 38. Handsworth Coll Birm 60 Claremont Sch of Th 65 St Deiniol's Hawarden 71. **d** 71 **p** 72. C Heref St Martin 71-73; P-in-c Ewyas Harold w Dulas 73-79; P-in-c Kilpeck 73-79; P-in-c St Devereux w Wormbridge 73-79; P-in-c Kenderchurch 73-79; P-in-c Bacton 78-79; TR Ewyas Harold w Dulas, Kenderchurch etc 79-81; R Kentchurch w Llangua, Rowlestone, Llancillo etc 79-81; Chapl Napsbury Hosp St Alb 81-96; Chapl Horizon NHS Trust Herts 96-00; Chapl Barnet Healthcare NHS Trust 96-00; Chapl Barnet and Chase Farm Hosps NHS Trust 00-05; Chapl Herts Partnerships NHS Trust 02-03; rtd 03. *25 Church Lane, Eaton Bray, Dunstable LU6 2DJ* Tel (01525) 222319

JOHNSON, Josephine. *See* JOHNSON, Frances Josephine

JOHNSON, Mrs Julie Margaret. b 47. **d** 98 **p** 99. OLM Welton and Dunholme w Scothern *Linc* 98-07; NSM Edgeley and Cheadle Heath *Ches* from 07. *10 Delaford Close, Stockport SK3 8XA* Tel 0161-456 6463 E-mail johnson-julie2@sky.com

JOHNSON, Kathryn Ann. **d** 03 **p** 04. C Wrexham *St As* 03-04; C Prestatyn from 04. *The Vicarage, First Avenue, 109 High Street, Prestatyn LL19 9AR* Tel (01745) 853780

JOHNSON, Keith Henry. b 64. Keele Univ BA91 CQSW91 Leeds Univ BA97. Coll of Resurr Mirfield 95. **d** 97 **p** 98. C W Bromwich St Fran *Lich* 97-00; P-in-c Willenhall St Giles 00-05; V 05-06; Perm to Offic *Lon* 06-08 and *Lich* from 07; P-in-c Handsworth *Sheff* from 08. *St Mary's Rectory, Handsworth Road, Handsworth, Sheffield S13 9BZ* Tel 0114-269 2403 Mobile 07988-405572 E-mail keithhjohnson@hotmail.com

JOHNSON, Keith Martyn. b 68. St Jo Coll Nottm 04. **d** 06 **p** 07. C Ipsley *Worc* from 06. *77 Edgmond Close, Redditch B98 0JQ* Tel (01527) 526703 E-mail keithandrachel.johnson@tesco.net

JOHNSON, The Very Revd Keith Winton Thomas William. b 37. K Coll Lon BD63 Open Univ MA06 AKC63. **d** 64 **p** 65. C Dartford H Trin *Roch* 64-69; Chapl Kuwait 69-73; V Erith St Jo *Roch* 73-80; V Bexley St Jo 80-91; V Royston *St Alb* 91-94; R Sandon, Wallington and Rushden w Clothall 94-97; Dean St Chris Cathl Bahrain 97-02; rtd 02; Hon C Balsham, Weston Colville, W Wickham etc *Ely* from 04; RD Linton 07-09. *The Vicarage, The Causeway, West Wratting, Cambridge CB21 5NA* Tel (01223) 291265 E-mail keith1412@hotmail.com

JOHNSON, Kenneth William George. b 53. Hull Univ BA76 PGCE77. EMMTC 92. **d** 95 **p** 96. NSM Ilkeston H Trin *Derby* 95-99; NSM Sandiacre from 99; Chapl Bluecoat Sch Nottm from 02. *18 Park Avenue, Awsworth, Nottingham NG16 2RA* Tel 0115-930 7830 E-mail kjohnson@bluecoat.nottingham.sch.uk

JOHNSON, Miss Lesley Denise. b 47. WMMTC 95. **d** 98 **p** 99. NSM Stockingford *Cov* 98-01; TV Cov E from 01. *St Alban's Vicarage, Mercer Avenue, Coventry CV2 4PQ* Tel and fax (024) 7645 2493

JOHNSON, Malcolm Arthur. b 36. Univ Coll Dur BA60 MA64 Lon Metrop Univ Hon MA02 Lambeth MA06 FSA04.

Cuddesdon Coll 60. **d** 62 **p** 63. C Portsea N End St Mark *Portsm* 62-67; Chapl Qu Mary Coll *Lon* 67-74; V St Botolph Aldgate w H Trin Minories 74-92; P-in-c St Ethelburga Bishopgate 85-89; AD The City 85-90; Master R Foundn of St Kath in Ratcliffe 93-97; Bp's Adv for Past Care and Counselling *Lon* 97-01; rtd 02; Perm to Offic *Lon* from 07 and *Guildf* from 09. *1 Foxgrove Drive, Woking GU21 4DZ* Tel (01483) 720684
E-mail malcolm.johnson4@btinternet.com

JOHNSON, Canon Malcolm Stuart. b 35. AKC60. **d** 61 **p** 62. C Catford St Laur *S'wark* 61-64; Hon C Hatcham St Cath 66-76; P-in-c Kingstanding St Luke *Birm* 76-77; V 77-82; P-in-c Peckham St Jo w St Andr *S'wark* 82-92; V 92-03; Hon Can Sabongidda-Ora from 98; rtd 04. *34 Sheppard's College, London Road, Bromley BR1 1PF* Tel (020) 8466 5276

JOHNSON, Canon Margaret Anne Hope. b 52. Fitzw Coll Cam BA95. Ridley Hall Cam 93. **d** 95 **p** 96. C Northampton Em *Pet* 95-97; P-in-c 97-98; TR from 98; Adv in Women's Min 03-06; Can Pet Cathl from 04. *13 Booth Lane North, Northampton NN3 6JG* Tel (01604) 648974 E-mail revmahj@aol.com

JOHNSON, Margaret Joan (Meg). b 41. S'wark Ord Course 92. **d** 95 **p** 96. NSM Sanderstead St Mary *S'wark* 95-04. *73 St Peter's Street, South Croydon CR2 7DG* Tel (020) 8686 1711 E-mail meg.johnson@southwark.anglican.org

JOHNSON, Mark. b 62. Leic Poly BSc84 Loughb Univ PhD88. Ripon Coll Cuddesdon 88. **d** 94 **p** 95. C Bishop's Cleeve *Glouc* 94-98; TV Heref S Wye from 98. *The Vicarage, 1 Holme Lacy Road, Hereford HR2 6DD* Tel (01432) 353275 or 353717 Fax 352412 E-mail s.wye.team.ministry@talk21.com

JOHNSON, Michael. b 42. Birm Univ BSc63. S'wark Ord Course 68. **d** 71 **p** 72. C Kidbrooke St Jas *S'wark* 71-74; NSM Eynsford w Farningham and Lullingstone *Roch* 74-89; NSM Selling w Throwley, Sheldwich w Badlesmere etc *Cant* from 89. *1 Halke Cottages, North Street, Sheldwich, Faversham ME13 0LR* Tel (01795) 536583 Mobile 07860-635728 E-mail onehalke@aol.com

JOHNSON, Canon Michael Anthony. b 51. Ex Univ BA76. Ripon Coll Cuddesdon 76 Ch Div Sch of the Pacific (USA) 77. **d** 78 **p** 79. C Primrose Hill St Mary w Avenue Road St Paul *Lon* 78-81; C Hampstead St Jo 81-85; TV Mortlake w E Sheen *S'wark* 85-93; V Wroughton *Bris* from 93; RD Wroughton 97-99; AD Swindon 99-06; Hon Can Bris Cathl from 99. *The Vicarage, Church Hill, Wroughton, Swindon SN4 9JS* Tel (01793) 812301 Fax 814582 E-mail canonmike@hotmail.com

JOHNSON, Michael Colin. b 37. S'wark Ord Course 77. **d** 80 **p** 81. NSM New Eltham All SS *S'wark* 80-84; NSM Woldingham 84-98; rtd 98; Perm to Offic *Chich* 99-07. *The College of St Barnabas, Blackberry Lane, Lingfield RH7 6NJ* Tel (01342) 872832 E-mail tandem@collegeofstbarnabas.com

JOHNSON, Michael Gordon. b 45. Kelham Th Coll 64. **d** 68 **p** 69. C Holbrooks *Cov* 68-72; C Cannock *Lich* 72-75; V Coseley Ch Ch 75-79; P-in-c Sneyd 79-82; R Longton 82-88; Chapl Pilgrim Hosp Boston 88-96; TV Jarrow *Dur* 96-98; Chapl Monkton and Primrose Hill Hosp 96-98; R Burghwallis and Campsall *Sheff* from 98. *The Vicarage, High Street, Campsall, Doncaster DN6 9AF* Tel (01302) 700286

JOHNSON, Michael Robert. b 68. Aston Business Sch BSc90. Ridley Hall Cam 94. **d** 97 **p** 98. C E Greenwich *S'wark* 97-00; C Perry Hill St Geo 00-03; Chapl W Lon YMCA 03-05; C Wokingham All SS *Ox* from 05. *2A Ashridge Road, Wokingham RG40 1PQ* 1el 0118-979 0098 E-mail thebluegnu@yahoo.co.uk

JOHNSON, Mrs Nancy May. b 46. TCert67 Sheff Poly MA86. NOC 00. **d** 02 **p** 03. NSM Sheff Cathl 02-04; Asst Chapl Sheff Teaching Hosps NHS Foundn Trust from 04. *121 Rustlings Road, Sheffield S11 7AB* Tel 0114-266 6456 E-mail nancy@121rustlings.freeserve.co.uk

JOHNSON, Nigel Edwin. b 41. AKC64 St Boniface Warminster 64. **d** 65 **p** 66. C Poulton-le-Sands *Blackb* 65-68; Chapl RN 68-93; Perm to Offic *Cant* 93-00 and *Carl* from 00; rtd 99. *Mell View, 9 Thirlmere Park, Penrith CA11 8QS* Tel (01768) 899865

JOHNSON, Canon Nigel Victor. b 48. ARCM68 LTCL75 Cam Univ DipEd69. Linc Th Coll 80. **d** 82 **p** 83. C Lindley *Wakef* 82-85; P-in-c Upperthong 85-87; Perm to Offic *Derby* 88-89; NSM Calow and Sutton cum Duckmanton 89-90; R 90-00; RD Bolsover and Staveley 98-00; V Newbold w Dunston from 00; RD Chesterfield from 02; Hon Can Derby Cathl from 05. *Newbold Rectory, St John's Road, Chesterfield S41 8QN* Tel (01246) 450374 E-mail nvjohnson@tiscali.co.uk

JOHNSON, Paul James. b 56. Teesside Coll of Educn BEd80 Dur Sch of Educn MA95. NEOC 06. **d** 09. NSM Whorlton w Carlton and Faceby *York* from 09. *18 Priorwood Gardens, Ingleby Barwick, Stockton-on-Tees TS17 0XH* Tel (01642) 761941 E-mail paul.johnson53@ntlworld.com

JOHNSON, Peter Colin. b 64. SS Mark & Jo Univ Coll Plymouth BEd87 Univ of Wales (Lamp) PhD00. SWMTC 97. **d** 00 **p** 01. NSM Godrevy *Truro* from 00. *Seascape, Trewelloe Road, Praa Sands, Penzance TR20 9SU* Tel (01736) 763407 E-mail peterjohnson9@btconnect.com

JOHNSON, Canon Peter Frederick. b 41. Melbourne Univ BA63 Ch Ch Ox BA68 MA72. St Steph Ho Ox 68. **d** 69 **p** 70. C

Banbury *Ox* 69-71; Tutor St Steph Ho Ox 71-74; Chapl St Chad's Coll Dur 74-80; Vice-Prin 78-80; Chapl K Sch Cant 80-90; Perm to Offic *Cant* 80-81; Hon Min Can Cant Cathl 81-90; Can Res Bris Cathl 90-08; rtd 08; Perm to Offic *Ox* from 08. *4 St John's Road, Windsor SL4 3QN* Tel (01753) 865914 E-mail pfjohnson@virgin.net

JOHNSON, Prof Peter Stewart. b 44. Nottm Univ BA65 PhD70. Cranmer Hall Dur 01. **d** 03 **p** 04. NSM Dur St Nic from 03. *126 Devonshire Road, Durham DH1 2BH* Tel 0191-386 6334 Mobile 07949-680467

JOHNSON, Philip Anthony. b 69. All Nations Chr Coll BA97 MA98 FIBMS94. Ridley Hall Cam 00. **d** 02 **p** 03. C Witham *Chelmsf* 02-06; P-in-c Holland-on-Sea from 06. *The Vicarage, 297 Frinton Road, Holland-on-Sea, Clacton-on-Sea CO15 5SP* Tel (01255) 812420 E-mail revdphilip@aol.com

JOHNSON, Phillip Thomas. b 75. City Univ BA03. Ripon Coll Cuddesdon 06. **d** 08 **p** 09. C Cheam *S'wark* from 08. *4 Tudor Close, Sutton SM3 8QS* Tel (020) 8395 1443 Mobile 07815-018846 E-mail curate@cheamparish.org.uk

JOHNSON (née DAVIES), Rhiannon Mary Morgan. b 69. St Anne's Coll Ox BA90 MA96 Univ of Wales (Cardiff) PhD94 BD96. St Mich Coll Llan 94. **d** 97 **p** 98. C Whitchurch *Llan* 97-99; NSM Walton W w Talbenny and Haroldston W *St D* 99-00; Chapl Trin Coll Carmarthen 00; NSM Walton W w Talbenny and Haroldston W *St D* 00-08; P-in-c Walwyn's Castle w Robeston W from 08. *The Rectory, Walton West, Little Haven, Haverfordwest SA62 3UB* Tel (01437) 781279

JOHNSON, Richard Miles. b 59. Bris Univ BSc82. St Jo Coll Nottm 87. **d** 90 **p** 91. C Bromley SS Pet and Paul *Roch* 90-94; USPG/CMS Philippines 94-97; Ind Chapl *Roch* 97-06; C Bexleyheath Ch Ch 97-06; Ind Chapl *Worc* from 06; TV Redditch H Trin from 06. *120 Carthorse Lane, Redditch B97 6SZ* Tel (01527) 61936 E-mail dickim@globalnet.co.uk

JOHNSON, Canon Robert Kenneth. b 48. NOC 83. **d** 86 **p** 87. C Hattersley *Ches* 86-88; C Brinnington w Portwood 88-90; V Gospel Lane St Mich *Birm* 90-97; P-in-c Birm St Geo 97-07; R 07; Hon Can Birm Cathl 05-07; rtd 07. *9 Briants Piece, Hermitage, Thatcham RG18 9SX* Tel (01635) 203419 E-mail robkj@btopenworld.com

JOHNSON, Canon Robin Edward Hobbs. b 39. Fitzw Ho Cam BA61 MA65. Ripon Hall Ox 61. **d** 63 **p** 64. C Tyldesley w Shakerley *Man* 63-66; Lic to Offic *Leic* 66-71; V Castleton Moor *Man* 71-77; Dir of Ords 76-81; V Prestwich St Gabr 77-81; V Heaton Ch Ch 81-91; Hon Can Man Cathl 86-91; TR Dorchester *Sarum* 91-00; RD Dorchester 99-00; rtd 00; Chapl Torrevieja *Eur* 00-03. *10 The Knowles, 2 Blundellsands Road West, Crosby, Liverpool L23 6AB*

JOHNSON, Ronald George. b 33. Chich Th Coll 75. **d** 76 **p** 77. NSM Shipley *Chich* 76-79; C Brighton St Matthias 79-82; R Barlavington, Burton w Coates, Sutton and Bignor 82-93; rtd 93; Perm to Offic *Chich* from 93. *1 Highdown Drive, Littlehampton BN17 6HJ* Tel (01903) 732210

JOHNSON, The Very Revd Samuel Hugh Akinsope. b 30. K Coll Lon BD61. Lich Th Coll 52. **d** 55 **p** 56. C Whitechapel St Paul w St Mark *Lon* 55-58; C Sunbury 58-59; C Lisson Grove w St Marylebone St Matt w Em 59-60; C St Martin-in-the-Fields 60-62; Nigeria from 63; Provost Lagos Cathl 70-95; rtd 95. *1 Oba Nle Aro Crescent, Ilupeju, PO Box 10021, Marina, Lagos, Nigeria*

JOHNSON (née ROWE), Mrs Shiela. b 43. CITC 93. **d** 96 **p** 97. Aux Min Urncy w Denn and Derryheen *K, E & A* 96-97; Aux Min Boyle and Elphin w Aghanagh, Kilbryan etc 97-01; Aux Min Roscommon w Donamon, Rathcline, Kilkeevin etc 97-01; P-in-c Clondevaddock w Portsalon and Leatbeg *D & R* 02-08; rtd 08. *Rainbow's End, Carrickmacafferty, Derrybeg, Co Donegal, Republic of Ireland*

JOHNSON, Stanley. b 42. QUB BSc63 TCD BTh89. CITC 86. **d** 89 **p** 90. C Kilmore w Ballintemple, Kildallan etc *K, E & A* 89-97; Adn Elphin and Ardagh 97-01; Can Elphin Cathl 97-01; I Templemichael w Clongish, Clooncumber etc 97-01; I Clondehorkey w Cashel *D & R* 01-09; Can Raphoe Cathl 08-09; rtd 09. *Rainbow's End, Carrickmacafferty, Derrybeg, Co Donegal, Republic of Ireland* E-mail johnsons@esatclear.ie

JOHNSON, Stephen. b 57. Cranmer Hall Dur. **d** 00 **p** 01. C Longton *Blackb* 00-02; C Longridge 03-04; V Preston Em from 04; Chapl Cen Lancs Univ from 08. *Emmanuel Vicarage, 2 Cornthwaite Road, Fulwood, Preston PR2 3DA* Tel (01772) 717136 Mobile 07790-917504

JOHNSON, Stephen Ashley. b 79. York Univ BA01 MA02. Wycliffe Hall Ox BTh06. **d** 06 **p** 07. C Sunningdale *Ox* 06-09; V Sunninghill and S Ascot from 09. *Sunninghill Vicarage, Church Lane, Ascot SL5 7DD* Tel (01344) 873202 Mobile 07799-834250 E-mail steve79@tiscali.co.uk

JOHNSON, Stephen William. b 63. Trent Poly BEd86 Keele Univ MA94 Univ Coll Ches BA05 ALCM85. NOC 02. **d** 05 **p** 06. NSM Betley *Lich* 05-08; NSM Keele 05-08; NSM Madeley 05-08; NSM Silverdale 05-08. *86 Dunnocksfold Road, Alsager, Stoke-on-Trent ST7 2TW* Tel (01270) 874066 Mobile 07766-411090 E-mail sjohnsonone@talktalk.net

JOHNSON, Stuart. *See* JOHNSON, Geoffrey Stuart

JOHNSON, Mrs Susan Constance. b 46. EAMTC 01. **d** 03 **p** 04. NSM Heald Green St Cath *Ches* 03-07. *11A Lynton Park Road, Cheadle Hulme, Cheadle SK8 6JA* Tel 0161-485 3787 E-mail revsusan@ntlworld.com

JOHNSON, Miss Susan Elaine. b 44. R Holloway Coll Lon BA66. EAMTC 99. **d** 03 **p** 03. C Münich Ascension and V Ingolstadt H Trin 03-06; NSM Cwmbran *Mon* 06-09; TV Papworth *Ely* from 09. *The Rectory, 2 Short Street, Bourn, Cambridge CB23 2SG* Tel (01954) 717422 Mobile 07919-232211 E-mail revsusan44@btinternet.com *or* susan.johnson@ely.anglican.org

JOHNSON, Terence John. b 44. Cov Poly BA89. ALCD70. **d** 69 **p** 70. C Woodside *Ripon* 69-72; C Leeds St Geo 72-76; C Heworth H Trin *York* 76-81; V Budbrooke *Cov* 81-97; Chapl Wroxall Abbey Sch 83-93; V Stone Ch Ch and Oulton *Lich* 97-02; P-in-c Collingtree w Courteenhall and Milton Malsor *Pet* 02-08; rtd 08. *18 Northgate, Towcester NN12 6HT* Tel (01327) 351408 E-mail terencejohnson194@btinternet.com

JOHNSON, Thomas Bernard. b 44. BA CertEd. Oak Hill Th Coll. **d** 84 **p** 85. C Birkenhead St Jas w St Bede *Ches* 84-88; R Ashover and Brackenfield *Derby* 88 01; P-in-c Wessington 99-01; R Ashover and Brackenfield w Wessington 01-03; Hon Chapl Derbyshire St Jo Ambulance from 91; RD Chesterfield 97-02; V Swanwick and Pentrich from 03. *The Vicarage, 4 Broom Avenue, Swanwick, Alfreton DE55 1DQ* Tel (01773) 602684 E-mail t.b.johnson@virgin.net

JOHNSON, Victor Edward. b 45. Linc Th Coll 83. **d** 85 **p** 86. C Garforth *Ripon* 85-90; Dioc Video Officer 90-92; V Wyther 92-00; V Shelley and Shepley *Wakef* 00-01; rtd 01; Perm to Offic *Bradf* 02-04. *Low Farm, Marsh Lane Gardens, Kellington, Goole DN14 0PG* Tel (01977) 661629 E-mail vej@onetel.com

JOHNSON, Victoria Louise. b 75. Leic Univ BSc96 PhD00 SS Coll Cam BA06. Westcott Ho Cam 04 Yale Div Sch 06. **d** 07 **p** 08. C Baguley *Man* from 07. *39 Dalebrook Road, Sale M33 3LD* Tel 0161-973 3046 Mobile 07761-030755 E-mail vickyjohnson@cantab.net

JOHNSTON, Alexander Irvine. b 47. Keele Univ BA70 LRAM. St Alb Minl Tr Scheme 77. **d** 80 **p** 81. NSM Hockerill *St Alb* 80-95; NSM High Wych and Gilston w Eastwick 95-96; TV Bottesford w Ashby *Linc* 96-01; P-in-c St Germans *Truro* from 01. *The Vicarage, Quay Road, St Germans, Saltash PL12 5LY* Tel (01503) 230690 E-mail alecjohnston@btinternet.com

JOHNSTON, Allen Niall. b 61. Sussex Univ BTh92 Kent Univ MA97 AMBIM87 MISM87 MInstD00. Sarum & Wells Th Coll 89. **d** 92 **p** 93. C Roehampton H Trin *S'wark* 92-95; Dir Past Services Richmond, Twickenham and Roehampton NHS Trust 95-98; Tutor SEITE 95-97; Perm to Offic *Eur* 01-02; Sierra Leone 02-03; Asst P St Jo Cathl Freetown 03; Perm to Offic *Ely* from 03 and *D & R* from 04. *50 Vestry Court, 5 Monck Street, London SW1P 2BW* E-mail niall@nialljohnston.org

JOHNSTON, Austin. b 50. Huddersfield Poly CertEd76 BEd90. Chich Th Coll 92. **d** 94 **p** 95. C Peterlee *Dur* 94-97; C Stockton St Pet 97-00; TR Stanley and Tanfield 00-01; TR Ch the K from 01. *The Rectory, Church Bank, Stanley DH9 0DU* Tel (01207) 233936

JOHNSTON, Brian. *See* JOHNSTON, Wilfred Brian

JOHNSTON, Mrs Carole Ann. b 58. Worc Coll of Educn BA84. St Jo Coll Nottm 04. **d** 06 **p** 07. C Ilkley All SS *Bradf* from 06. *7 Rose Bank, Burley in Wharfedale, Ilkley LS29 7PQ* Tel (01943) 865077 E-mail carole.johnston@virgin.net

JOHNSTON, Charles Walter Barr. b 38. Lon Univ BSc61. Oak Hill Th Coll 62. **d** 64 **p** 65. C Holloway St Mark w Em *Lon* 64-68; Argentina from 68; SAMS 70-03; rtd 03. *c/o A Johnston Esq, 27 Cloister Crofts, Leamington Spa CV32 6QG* Tel (01926) 336136

JOHNSTON, David. *See* JOHNSTON, Thomas David

JOHNSTON, David George Scott. b 66. Avery Hill Coll BA88. SEITE 00. **d** 03 **p** 04. C Frindsbury w Upnor and Chattenden *Roch* 03-06; R Longfield from 06. *The Rectory, 67 Main Road, Longfield DA3 7PQ* Tel (01474) 702201 E-mail cathryn.johnston@ntlworld.com

JOHNSTON, Canon Donald Walter. b 28. Trin Coll Melbourne BA51 Lon Univ PGCE52 Em Coll Cam BA63 MA67. Ridley Hall Cam 64. **d** 64 **p** 65. C Cottingham *York* 64-66; Australia from 66; Min Nunawading Melbourne 67-69; Chapl Brighton Gr Sch Melbourne 70-73; Chapl Melbourne C of E Gr Sch 74-84; Angl Bd of Miss 85-90; Chapl H Name Sch Dogura 85; Hd Martyrs' Memorial Sch Popondetta 86-89; Hon Commissary from 91; Can Papua New Guinea from 90; rtd 90. *22 Albert Street, PO Box 114, Point Lonsdale Vic 3225, Australia* Tel (0061) (3) 5258 2139 *or* 9690 0549 Fax 5258 3994 E-mail dncjohnston@al.com.au

JOHNSTON, Duncan Howard. b 63. Hull Univ BA85 Nottm Univ MA93. St Jo Coll Nottm 91. **d** 93 **p** 94. C Werrington *Pet* 93-96; V Gt Doddington and Wilby 96-01; Dioc Adv in Local Miss *Dur* 02-03; R Fremont St Jo USA from 03. *515 East Pine Street, Fremont MI 49412-1739, USA* Tel (001) (231) 924 7120 E-mail djepisc@joimail.com

JOHNSTON, Edith Violet Nicholl. b 28. **d** 87. Par Dn Bentley *Sheff* 87-88; rtd 88; Perm to Offic *Sheff* 88-08. *30 Sharman Road, Belfast BT9 5FW* Tel (028) 9066 6776

JOHNSTON, Elizabeth Margaret. b 37. QUB BA58 DipEd69 Serampore Univ BD87. Dalton Ho Bris. **d** 81 **p** 94. BCMS India 62-92; C Belfast St Chris *D & D* 93-94; Bp's C 94-03; Can Down Cathl 01-03; rtd 03. *103 Ballydorn Road, Killinchy, Newtownards BT23 6QB* Tel (028) 9754 2518 Mobile 07980-123181 E-mail elizabeth_johnston@amserve.com

JOHNSTON, Frank. *See* JOHNSTON, William Francis

JOHNSTON, Geoffrey Stanley. b 44. Aston Univ MBA81 Birm Univ CertEd78. Kelham Th Coll 64. **d** 68 **p** 69. C Blakenall Heath *Lich* 68-72 and 73-75; C St Buryan, St Levan and Sennen *Truro* 72-73; P-in-c Willenhall St Steph *Lich* 75-76; C W Bromwich All SS 76-77; Lect W Bromwich Coll of Commerce and Tech 78-82; Ind Chapl *Worc* 82-94; P-in-c H Halesowen 82-94; NSM Dudley St Fran 94-99; P-in-c 99-08; P-in-c Dudley St Edm 04-08; rtd 08; P-in-c Nerja and Almuécar *Eur* from 08. *Church House, Calle Jilguero, Urbanizacion Almijara 2 Sur, Nerja, 29780 (Mlaga), Spain* Tel (0034) 952 521 339 E-mail anglicansnerja@yahoo.com

JOHNSTON, Mrs Helen Kay. b 48. SRN70. SAOMC 95. **d** 98 **p** 99. OLM Banbury St Paul *Ox* 98-01; P-in-c Flimby *Carl* 01-03; C Netherton 01-03; Perm to Offic *Derby* from 04. *2 Clough Mill, Slack Lane, Little Hayfield, High Peak SK22 2NJ* Tel (01663) 741900 E-mail kaybees@supanet.com

JOHNSTON, Miss Henrietta Elizabeth Ann. b 59. St Jo Coll Dur BA03. Cranmer Hall Dur 01. **d** 03 **p** 04. C Cov H Trin 03-07; C Dorridge *Birm* from 07. *2 Hurst Green, Bentley Heath, Solihull B93 8AE* Tel (01564) 775494 Mobile 07796-948904 E-mail hennie.johnston@tiscali.co.uk

JOHNSTON, Kay. *See* JOHNSTON, Mrs Helen Kay

JOHNSTON, Malcolm. *See* JOHNSTON, William Malcolm

JOHNSTON, Michael David Haigh. b 44. S Dios Minl Tr Scheme 88. **d** 91 **p** 92. NSM Wootton *Portsm* 91-95; NSM Ryde H Trin 95-99; NSM Swanmore St Mich 95-99; P-in-c Cowes St Faith 99-03; Asst Chapl Isle of Wight NHS Primary Care Trust from 03; Chapl HM Pris Kingston (Portsm) 03-05; The Chaplaincy, St Mary's Hospital, Newport PO30 5TG Tel (01983) 524081 E-mail rvdmikej@fastmail.fm

JOHNSTON, Michael Edward. b 68. TCD BA97 MA04. CITC BTh00. **d** 00 **p** 01. Bp's V Kilkenny Cathl 00-03; C Kilkenny w Aghour and Kilmanagh 00-03; V Waterford w Killea, Drumcannon and Dunhill 03-09; I Shinrone w Aghancon etc *L & K* from 09. *St Mary's Rectory, Shinrone, Birr, Co Offaly, Republic of Ireland* Tel (00353) (505) 47164 E-mail shinrone@killaloe.anglican.org

JOHNSTON, Niall. *See* JOHNSTON, Allen Niall

JOHNSTON, Mrs Patricia Anne. b 42. Ou Coll Birm 05. **d** 06 **p** 07. NSM Rubery *Birm* from 06. *St Chad's Parish Office, 160A New Road, Rednal, Birmingham B45 9JA* Tel 0121-460 1278

JOHNSTON, Canon Robert John. b 31. Oak Hill Th Coll 62. **d** 64 **p** 65. C Bebington *Ches* 64-68; I Lack *Clogh* 68-99; Can Clogh Cathl 89-99; rtd 99. *2 Beechcroft, Semicock Road, Ballymoney BT53 6NF* Tel (028) 2766 9317

JOHNSTON, Thomas Cosbey. b 15. Em Coll Cam BA40 MA44. Ridley Hall Cam 40. **d** 42 **p** 43. C Handsworth St Mary *Birm* 42-48; New Zealand from 48. *254 Main Road, Mancks Bay, Christchurch 8081, New Zealand* Tel (0064) (3) 384 1224

JOHNSTON, Thomas David. b 52. Salford Univ BSc78 TCD MPhil03. NOC 98. **d** 98 **p** 99. Dioc Communications Officer *Man* 96-00; NSM Bolton St Paul w Em 98-00; I Sixmilecross w Termonmaguirke *Arm* 00-03; Dir Communications *Liv* 03-05; P-in-c Daubhill *Man* 05-06. *Address temp unknown* Tel 07967-105999 (mobile)

JOHNSTON, Trevor Samuel. b 72. Ulster Univ BMus96 TCD BTh01. CITC 98. **d** 01 **p** 02. C Carrickfergus *Conn* 01-04; C Jordanstown from 04; Chapl Jordanstown and Belf Campuses Ulster Univ from 04. *105 Jordanstown Road, Newtownabbey BT37 0NT* Tel (028) 9050 6444 *or* 9036 6404 Mobile 07776-178248 E-mail trev@tjohnston.net *or* t.johnston@ulst.ac.uk

JOHNSTON, Wilfred Brian. b 44. TCD BA67 MA70. Div Test 68. **d** 68 **p** 70. C Seagoe *D & D* 68-73; I Inniskeel *D & R* 73-82; I Castlerock w Dunboe and Fermoyle 82-02; Bp's C Gweedore, Carrickfin and Templecrone 02-08; Dioc Registrar 89-06; Can Derry Cathl 92-02; Preb 99-02; Can Raphoe Cathl 05-08; rtd 08. *2 The Apple Yard, Coleraine BT51 3PP* Tel (028) 7032 6406 E-mail b.johnston@talk21.com

JOHNSTON, William Derek. b 40. CITC 68. **d** 68 **p** 69. V Choral Derry Cathl 68-70; I Swanlinbar w Templeport *K, E & A* 70-73; I Billis Union 73-84; Glebes Sec (Kilmore) 77-03; I Annagh w Drumaloor and Cloverhill 84-87; Preb Kilmore Cathl 85-89; I Annagh w Drumgoon, Ashfield etc 87-99; Adn Kilmore 89-03; I Lurgan w Billis, Killinkere and Munterconnaught 99-03; rtd 03. *Ballaghanea, Mullagh Road, Virginia, Co Cavan, Republic of Ireland* Tel (00353) (49) 854 9960 Mobile 86-832 9911

JOHNSTON, William Francis (Frank). b 30. CB83. TCD BA55 MA69. **d** 55 **p** 56. C Orangefield *D & D* 55-59; CF 59-77; Asst

Chapl Gen 77-80; Chapl Gen 80-87; P-in-c Winslow *Ox* 87-91; RD Claydon 89-94; R Winslow w Gt Horwood and Addington 91-95; rtd 95; Perm to Offic *Ex* from 95. *Lower Axehill, Chard Road, Axminster EX13 5ED* Tel (01297) 33259

JOHNSTON, Canon William John. b 35. Lon Univ BA85 MA90 PhD. CITC 67. **d** 70 **p** 71. C Belfast St Donard *D & D* 70-72; C Derg *D & R* 72-78; I Drumclamph w Lower and Upper Langfield 78-91; I Kilskeery w Trillick *Clogh* from 91; Preb Clogh Cathl from 04; Prec from 09. *The Rectory, 130 Kilskeery Road, Trillick, Omagh BT78 3RJ* Tel (028) 8956 1228

JOHNSTON, William Malcolm. b 48. SAOMC 92. **d** 95 **p** 96. NSM Banbury *Ox* 95-01; P-in-c Netherton *Carl* 01-03; C Flimby 01-03; Perm to Offic *Derby* from 04. *2 Clough Mill, Slack Lane, Little Hayfield, High Peak SK22 2NJ* Tel (01663) 741900 E-mail kaybees@supanet.com

JOHNSTON, William McConnell. b 33. TCD BA57. **d** 58 **p** 59. C Ballymena w Ballyclug Conn 58-61; C Belfast St Thos 61-63; C Finaghy 63-66; R Kambula S Africa 66-74; Dean Eshowe 74-86; R Mtubatuba 86-99; rtd 00; Perm to Offic *Chich* from 04. *Honeysuckle Cottage, Redford, Midhurst GU29 0QG* Tel (01428) 741131

JOHNSTON-HUBBOLD, Clifford Johnston. b 19. Lon Univ BA76 BD80. St Aid Birkenhead 49. **d** 52 **p** 53. C Stanwix *Carl* 52-55; V Gt Broughton 55-59; R Sedgeberrow *Worc* 59-73; P-in-c Hinton-on-the-Green 72-73; R Sedgeberrow w Hinton-on-the-Green 73-92; rtd 92; Perm to Offic *Worc* from 92. *2 Mills Close, Broadway WR12 7RB* Tel (01386) 852199

JOHNSTONE, William Henry Green. b 26. **d** 92 **p** 94. Belize 92-98; Hon C Tollard Royal w Farnham, Gussage St Michael etc *Sarum* 98-01; Hon C Chase from 01; OCF 94-98 and from 01. *Church Cottage, Chettle, Blandford Forum DT11 8DB* Tel (01258) 830396 E-mail padrewmchettle@aol.com

JOINT, Canon Michael John. b 39. Sarum & Wells Th Coll 79. **d** 79 **p** 79. CA from 61; Hon C Chandler's Ford *Win* 79-83; Youth Chapl 79-83; V Lymington 83-95; Co-ord Chapl R Bournemouth and Christchurch Hosps NHS Trust 96-03; Hon Can Win Cathl 00-03; rtd 03; Perm to Offic *Win* 03-04. *20 Wavendon Avenue, Barton on Sea, New Milton BH25 7LS* Tel (01425) 628952 E-mail michjoin@aol.com

JOLLEY, Andrew John. b 61. Nottm Univ BSc83 PhD06 Warwick Univ MBA88 CEng88 MIMechE88. St Jo Coll Nottm BTh97. **d** 98 **p** 99. C Sparkhill w Greet and Sparkbrook *Birm* 98-02; V Aston SS Pet and Paul 02-08; P-in-c Aston St Jas 05-08; P-in-c Nechells 05-08; V Aston and Nechells from 08; AD Aston from 05. *The Vicarage, Sycamore Road, Aston, Birmingham B6 5UH* Tel 0121-327 5856 E-mail andy@astonnechellscofe.com

JOLLY, Leslie Alfred Walter. b 16. AKC40. **d** 40 **p** 41. C Bow w Bromley St Leon *Lon* 40-42; C Cheam Common St Phil *S'wark* 42-50; C Mottingham St Andr 50-52; V Newington St Matt 52-57; R Chaldon 57-85; rtd 85; Perm to Offic *S'wark* 85-94 and *York* 85-04. *12 Roseneath Court, Greenwood Gardens, Caterham CR3 6RX* Tel (01883) 332463

JONAS, Alan Charles. b 56. Leeds Univ BA79 Univ of Wales (Abth) PGCE80 Wycliffe Hall Ox 92. **d** 94 **p** 95. C Hersham *Guildf* 94-98; P-in-c Westcott from 98; Chapl Priory Sch 01-07. *The Vicarage, Guildford Road, Westcott, Dorking RH4 3QB* Tel (01306) 885309 E-mail alchasjonas@aol.com

JONAS, Ian Robert. b 54. St Jo Coll Nottm BTh80. **d** 80 **p** 81. C Portadown St Mark *Arm* 80-82; C Cregagh *D & D* 82-85; BCMS Sec *D & G* 85-90; V Langley Mill *Derby* 90-97; I Kilgariffe Union *C, C & R* 97-09; I Carrigrohane Union from 09. *The Rectory, Church Hill, Carrigrohane, Co Cork, Republic of Ireland* Tel (00353) (21) 487 1106 E-mail revianjonas@yahoo.co.uk

JONES, Alan David. b 32. ALCD58. **d** 58 **p** 59. C Ipswich All SS *St E* 58-60; C Southend St Jo *Chelmsf* 60-64; V Leyton St Cath 64-70; V Hatfield Broad Oak and P-in-c Bush End 70-77; V Theydon Bois 77-88; P-in-c Finchingfield and Cornish Hall End 88-93; rtd 94; Perm to Offic *Chelmsf* and *St E* from 94. *3 Grammar School Place, Sudbury CO10 2GE* Tel (01787) 370864

JONES, Alan John. b 47. Nottm Univ BA71. Coll of Resurr Mirfield 71. **d** 73 **p** 74. C Sedgley St Mary *Lich* 73-76; C Cov St Jo 76-78; V Bromwich St Fran *Lich* 78-94; V Ettingshall from 94; AD Wolverhampton from 03. *The Vicarage, Farrington Road, Wolverhampton WV4 6QH* Tel (01902) 884616

JONES, Alan Pierce. See PIERCE-JONES, Alan

JONES, Albert. b 13. K Coll Lon 37. **d** 41 **p** 42. C Farnworth and Kearsley *Man* 41-46; P-in-c 45-46; C Felixstowe St Jo *E* 46-47; C Headstone St Geo *Lon* 47-49; R Stretford All SS *Man* 49-52; Trinidad and Tobago 52-56; V Farnworth St Pet *Man* 56-58; Area Sec USPG *York* 58-63; V Tillingham *Chelmsf* 63-66; R Dengie w Asheldham 63-66; R Stifford 66-72; P-in-c Stondon Massey 72-79; R Doddinghurst 72-79; rtd 79; Perm to Offic *Chelmsf* from 79. *29 Seaview Road, Brightlingsea, Colchester CO7 0PP* Tel (01206) 303994

JONES, Alison. See JONES, Ms Helen Alison

JONES, Alison. See WAGSTAFF, Ms Alison

JONES, Alun. b 52. Leeds Univ BA96. Cuddesdon Coll 94. **d** 96 **p** 97. C Newc St Geo 96-98; C Cowgate 98-99; C Fenham St Jas and St Basil 99-04; P-in-c Carl St Herbert w St Steph 04-07; V from 07. *St Herbert's Vicarage, Blackwell Road, Carlisle CA2 4RA* Tel (01228) 523375 E-mail alun52@btinternet.com

JONES, Alwyn Humphrey Griffith. b 30. Leeds Univ BSc51. Coll of Resurr Mirfield 53. **d** 55 **p** 56. C W Hackney St Barn *Lon* 55-58; C-in-c Dacca St Thos E Pakistan 58-64; Ox Miss to Calcutta India 65-68; Chapl R Bombay Seamen's Soc 68-73; P-in-c Bedminster St Fran *Bris* 73-75; TR Bedminster 75-83; TV Langport Area *B & W* 83-85; Dep Chapl HM Pris Nor 85; Chapl HM Pris Preston 85-89; Chapl HM Pris Ashwell 89-91; C Acton Green *Lon* 91-93; rtd 93; NSM Langport Area *B & W* 93-98; Perm to Offic *B & W* and *Bris* from 98. *4 All Saints' House, 1 Upper York Street, Bristol BS2 8NT* Tel 0117-923 2331 E-mail alwyn_j@btinternet.com

JONES, Alyson Elizabeth. See DAVIE, Mrs Alyson Elizabeth

JONES, Mrs Andrea Margaret. b 46. Qu Coll Birm 88. **d** 90 **p** 94. Par Dn Kidderminster St Geo *Worc* 90-94; TV 94-95; C Penn Fields *Lich* 95-00; C Gt Wyrley 00-06; rtd 06. *57 Woodward Road, Kidderminster DY11 6NY* Tel (01562) 823555 E-mail aam@jones46.fsbusiness.co.uk

JONES, Andrew. See JONES, Ian Andrew

JONES, Canon Andrew. b 61. Univ of Wales (Ban) BD82 PGCE82 TCD BTh85 MA91 Univ of Wales MPhil93. CITC 82 St Geo Coll Jerusalem 84. **d** 85 **p** 86. Min Can Ban Cathl 85-88; R Dolgellau 88-92; Warden of Readers 91-92; Dir Past Studies St Mich Coll Llan 92-96; Lect Th Univ of Wales (Cardiff) 92-96; Visiting Prof St Geo Coll Jerusalem from 94; Research Fell from 96; R Llanbedrog w Llannor w Llanfihangel etc *Ban* 96-01; R Llanbedrog w Llannor and Llangian from 01; Dioc CME and NSM Officer 96-00; AD Llyn and Eifionydd from 99; Hon Can Ban Cathl 04-05; Can from 05; Dioc Dir of Ords from 06. *Ty'n Llan Rectory, Llanbedrog, Pwllheli LL53 7TU* Tel and fax (01758) 740919 E-mail andrewjon@supanet.com

JONES, Andrew. b 64. York Univ BA85. Westmr Th Sem (USA) MDiv91 St Jo Coll Nottm 92. **d** 94 **p** 95. C Win Ch Ch 94-98; C St Helen Bishopsgate w St Andr Undershaft etc *Lon* from 98. *89 Forest Road, London E8 3BL* Tel (020) 7254 5942 E-mail a.jones@st-helens.org.uk

JONES, Andrew Christopher. b 47. Southn Univ BA69 PhD75. Ridley Hall Cam 78. **d** 80 **p** 81. C Wareham *Sarum* 80-83; P-in-c Symondsbury 83; P-in-c Chideock 83; R Symondsbury and Chideock 84-91; V Shottermill *Guildf* 91-99; P-in-c Bishopsnympton, Rose Ash, Mariansleigh etc *Ex* from 99. *The Rectory, Bishops Nympton, South Molton EX36 4NY* Tel (01769) 550427 E-mail a.c.jones@bnrec.f9.co.uk

JONES, Andrew Collins. b 62. Univ Coll Dur BA83 MA84 MLitt92. St Steph Ho Ox 88. **d** 90 **p** 91. C Llangefni w Tregaean and Llangristiolus etc *Ban* 90-94; C Hartlepool St Aid *Dur* 94-98; Chapl Hartlepool Gen Hosp 94-98; R Hendon *Dur* from 98; CMP from 99. *St Ignatius' Rectory, Bramwell Road, Sunderland SR2 8BY* Tel 0191-567 5575

JONES, Anne. See FURNESS, Christine Anne

JONES, Anthony. b 43. WEMTC 99. **d** 01 **p** 02. OLM Lydney *Glouc* 01-07; NSM Woolaston w Alvington and Aylburton from 07. *The Rectory, Main Road, Alvington, Lydney GL15 5AT* Tel (01594) 529387 Mobile 07860-331755 E-mail jones_rev@yahoo.co.uk

JONES, Canon Anthony Spacie. b 34. AKC58. **d** 59 **p** 60. C Bedford St Martin *St Alb* 59-63; Br Guiana 63-66; Guyana 66-71; V Ipswich All Hallows *St E* 72-80; RD Ipswich 78-86; Bp's Dom Chapl 80-82; V Rushmere 82-91; Hon Can St E Cathl 83-99; R Brantham w Stutton 91-99; P-in-c Bentley w Tattingstone 95-99; rtd 99; Perm to Offic *St E* from 99. *6 Frittilary Close, Pinewood, Ipswich IP8 3QT* Tel (01473) 601848 E-mail tonyjones.pinewood@btinternet.com

JONES, Barbara Christine. b 48. St Hugh's Coll Ox BA71 MA74 Lady Spencer Chu Coll of Educn PGCE74. CBDTI 97. **d** 00 **p** 01. NSM Bolton-le-Sands *Blackb* from 00. *11 Sandown Road, Lancaster LA1 4LN* Tel (01524) 65598 E-mail jones@barbara.bbfree.co.uk

JONES, Barry Mervyn. b 46. St Chad's Coll Dur BA68. **d** 70 **p** 71. C Bloxwich *Lich* 70-72; C Norwood All SS *Cant* 72-76; C New Addington 76-78; Chapl Mayday Univ Hosp Thornton Heath 78-86; Chapl Qu and St Mary's Hosps Croydon 78-86; Chapl Bromsgrove and Redditch DHA 86-94; Chapl Alexandra Hosp Redditch 86-94; Chapl Alexandra Healthcare NHS Trust Redditch 94-00; Chapl Worcs Acute Hosps NHS Trust 00-05; Perm to Offic *Worc* from 05. *46 Barlich Way, Lodge Park, Redditch B98 7JP* Tel (01527) 520659

JONES, Canon Basil Henry. b 26. Bps' Coll Cheshunt 63. **d** 64 **p** 65. C Gt Berkhamsted *St Alb* 64-67; V Leagrave 68-74; RD Luton 71-74; P-in-c Bedford St Paul 74-75; V Wigginton 75-93; Hon Can St Alb 82-93; rtd 93; Perm to Offic *St Alb* from 00. *17 Lochnell Road, Northchurch, Berkhamsted HP4 3QD* Tel (01442) 864485 E-mail bazilhjones@aol.com

JONES, Benjamin Jenkin Hywel. b 39. Univ of Wales BA61. St Mich Coll Llan 61. **d** 64 **p** 65. C Carmarthen St Pet *St D*

64-70; V Cynwyl Gaeo w Llansawel and Talley 70-79; R Llanbadarn Fawr 79-82; V Llanbadarn Fawr w Capel Bangor and Goginan 82-92; V Llanychaearn w Llanddeiniol 92-05; Warden of Readers from 82; Can St D Cathl 86-90; RD Llanbadarn Fawr 89-90; Adn Cardigan 90-06; rtd 06. *Dowerdd, Waun Fawr, Aberystwyth SY23 3QF* Tel (01970) 617100

JONES, Benjamin Tecwyn. b 17. Univ of Wales BA38. K Coll Lon 38. d 40 p 41. C Hawarden *St As* 40-45; C Pleasley *Derby* 45-46; C Ormskirk *Liv* 46-49; R Rufford *Blackb* 49-55; V S Shore St Pet 55-65; C Oldham St Mary w St Pet *Man* 65-69; Hd Master and Chapl St Mary's Sch Bexhill-on-Sea 69-71; V Blackb St Luke 71-72; P-in-c Griffin 71-72; V Blackb St Luke w St Phil 72-83; rtd 83; Perm to Offic *Blackb* from 83. *21 Fosbrooke House, 8 Clifton Drive, Lytham St Annes FY8 5RQ*

JONES, Bernard Lewis. b 48. Llan Dioc Tr Scheme 89. d 93 p 94. NSM Aberaman and Abercwmboi w Cwmaman *Llan* 93-99; V Hirwaun from 99; AD Cynon Valley from 08. *The New Vicarage, 6 Redhill Close, Hirwaun, Aberdare CF44 9NZ* Tel (01685) 811316

JONES, Brenda. *See* CAMPBELL, Mrs Brenda

JONES, Brenda. b 50. Cranmer Hall Dur 02. d 04 p 05. C Jarrow *Dur* 04-07; C-in-c Bishop Auckland Woodhouse Close CD from 07. *18 Watling Road, Bishop Auckland DL14 6RP* Tel (01388) 604807

JONES, Brian. BSc. d 94 p 96. Lic to Offic *D & D* from 94. *16 Massey Avenue, Belfast BT4 2JS*

JONES, Canon Brian Howell. b 35. Univ of Wales MPhil96. St Mich Coll Llan. d 61 p 62. C Llangiwg *S & B* 61-63; C Swansea St Mary and H Trin 63-70; R New Radnor w Llanfihangel Nantmelan etc 70-75; V Llansamlet 75-89; Dioc Dir of Stewardship 82-89; P-in-c Capel Coelbren 89-95; Dioc Missr 89-95; Can Res Brecon Cathl 89-00; Can Treas 98-00; Chan 99-00; RD Cwmtawe 89-93; V Killay 95-00; rtd 00. *12 Harlech Crescent, Sketty, Swansea SA2 9LP* Tel (01792) 421115

JONES, Canon Brian Michael. b 34. Trin Coll Bris 79 Oak Hill Th Coll BA82. d 84 p 84. CMS 82-93; Sierra Leone 84-93; Can Bo from 91; C Frimley *Guildf* 93-99; rtd 99; Perm to Offic *Newc* 00-01; Hon C N Tyne and Redesdale from 01-08. *20 Campfield Road, Ulverston LA12 9PB* E-mail bmj.retired@btopenworld.com

JONES, Canon Brian Noel. b 32. Edin Th Coll 59. d 62 p 63. C Monkseaton St Mary *Newc* 62-65; C Saffron Walden *Chelmsf* 65-69; P-in-c Swaffham Bulbeck *Ely* 69-75; Dioc Youth Officer 69-75; RD St Ives 75-83 and 87-89; V Ramsey 75-89; V Upwood w Gt and Lt Raveley 75-89; P-in-c Ramsey St Mary's 82-89; Hon Can Ely Cathl 85-97; V Cherry Hinton St Jo 89-97; RD Cambridge 94-97; rtd 97; Perm to Offic *Nor* from 97. *11 Winns Close, Holt NR25 6NQ* Tel (01263) 713645

JONES, Brian Robert. b 53. Surrey Univ BSc76. SAOMC 02. d 05 p 06. NSM Greenham *Ox* from 05. *27 Three Acre Road, Newbury RG14 7AW* Tel (01635) 34875

JONES, Canon Bryan Maldwyn. b 32. St Mich Coll Llan. d 62 p 63. C Swansea St Barn *S & B* 62-69; V Trallwng and Betws Penpont 69-75; V Trallwng, Bettws Penpont w Aberyskir etc 75-00; RD Brecon II 80-91; RD Brecon 91-99; Hon Can Brecon Cathl 92-00; rtd 00. *Plas Newydd, 8 Camden Crescent, Brecon LD3 7BY* Tel (01874) 625063

JONES, Bryan William. b 30. Selw Coll Cam BA53 MA57. Linc Th Coll 53. d 55 p 56. C Bedminster Down *Bris* 55-58; C Filton 58-62; P-in-c Bedminster St Mich 62-65; V 65-72; P-in-c Moorfields 72-75; TV E Bris 75-95; rtd 95; Perm to Offic *Bris* from 95. *89 Canterbury Close, Yate, Bristol BS37 5TU* Tel (01454) 316795

JONES, Bryn Parry. b 49. Univ of Wales BSc98 MCIH98 FCIH03. St As Minl Tr Course 04. d 06. NSM Connah's Quay *St As* from 06. *7 Fron Las, Pen y Maes, Holywell CH8 7HX* Tel (01352) 714781

JONES, Bryon. b 34. Open Univ BA84. St D Coll Lamp 61. d 64 p 65. C Port Talbot St Theodore *Llan* 64-67; C Aberdare 68-69; C Up Hatherley *Glouc* 69-71; C Oysterrmouth *S & B* 71-74; V Camrose *St D* 74-77; V Camrose and St Lawrence w Ford and Haycastle 77-04; rtd 04. *31 New Road, Haverfordwest SA61 1TU* Tel (01437) 760596

JONES, Mrs Carol. b 45. d 04 p 05. OLM Shirley St Geo *S'wark* from 04. *50 Belgrave Court, Sloane Walk, Croydon CR0 7NW* Tel (020) 8777 6247 E-mail caroljonesolm@yahoo.co.uk

JONES, Miss Celia Lynn. b 54. Trin Coll Bris. d 01 p 08. C Bris St Paul's 01-08; C Barton Hill St Luke w Ch Ch and Moorfields from 08. *15 St Werburghs Park, Bristol BS2 9YT* Tel 0117-955 6258 E-mail celialynn@supanet.com

JONES, Charles Derek. b 37. K Coll Lon BD60 AKC60. d 61 p 62. C Stockton St Chad *Dur* 61-64; C Becontree St Elisabeth *Chelmsf* 64-66; C S Beddington St Mich *S'wark* 66-73; Lic to Offic *Ex* 73-77; Perm to Offic *Liv* 77-99; rtd 02. *4 Bryn Glas, Graigfechan, Ruthin LL15 2EX* Tel (01824) 705015

JONES, Christopher Howell. b 50. BA FCCA. Oak Hill Th Coll 80. d 83 p 84. C Leyton St Mary w St Edw *Chelmsf* 83-86; C Becontree St Mary 86-90; P-in-c Bootle St Matt *Liv* 90-93; V 93-99; AD Bootle 97-99; V Ormskirk from 99; Chapl W

Lancashire NHS Trust from 99. *The Vicarage, Park Road, Ormskirk L39 3AJ* Tel (01695) 572143

JONES, Christopher John Stark. b 39. Lon Univ BA60 AKC60. Wells Th Coll 63. d 65 p 66. C Stanmore *Win* 65-67; C Bournemouth St Pet 67-71; C W Wycombe *Ox* 71-75; TV High Wycombe 75-77; V Wokingham St Sebastian 77-84; R Didsbury Ch Ch *Man* 84-00; rtd 00; Perm to Offic *Ches* from 01. *5 Trueman Close, Prenton CH43 7YR* Tel 0151-513 3436

JONES, Christopher Mark. b 54. St Pet Coll Ox BA75 MA79 Selw Coll Cam MPhil80. Ridley Hall Cam 77. d 80 p 81. C Putney St Marg *S'wark* 80-83; C Ham St Andr 83-86; Chapl HM Rem Cen Latchmere Ho 83-86; Chapl St Jo Coll Dur 87-93; Tutor Cranmer Hall Dur 87-93; Chapl and Fell St Pet Coll Ox 93-04; Home Affairs Policy Adv Abps' Coun Bd for Soc Resp from 04. *Archbishops' Council, Church House, Great Smith Street, London SW1P 3AZ* Tel (020) 7898 1531 Fax 7898 1536 E-mail christopher.jones@c-of-e.org.uk

JONES, Christopher Mark. b 56. St Jo Coll Cam BA78 MA82 Wycliffe Hall Ox BA81 MA85. d 82 p 83. C Walsall *Lich* 82-84; Chapl St Jo Coll Cam 84-89; Chapl Eton Coll from 89; Ho Master from 97. *The Hopgarden, Eton College, Windsor SL4 6EQ* Tel (01753) 671065 Fax 671067 E-mail c.m.jones@etoncollege.org.uk

JONES, Christopher Yeates. b 51. STETS 97. d 00 p 01. NSM Yeovil St Mich *B & W* from 00. *20 Bedford Road, Yeovil BA21 5UQ* Tel (01935) 420886 Mobile 07803-371617 E-mail cyjones@care4free.net

JONES, Clifford Albert. b 20. Edin Th Coll 54. d 56 p 57. C Dundee St Salvador *Bre* 56-58; C Linc St Swithin 58-59; C Grantham St Wulfram 59-60; R Dundee St Salvador *Bre* 60-69; V Bradford *B & W* 69-74; V Bridgwater St Jo 74-78; RD Bridgwater 76-80; R Bridgwater St Jo w Chedzoy 78-80; P-in-c Timsbury 80-85; R Timsbury and Priston 85; rtd 85; P-in-c Nor St Geo Tombland 85-90; Hon C St Marylebone All SS *Lon* 90-94; Perm to Offic *Nor* 94-99 and *Lon* from 97. *c/o The Revd Canon M Sanders, The Rectory, Woodbridge Road, Grundisburgh, Woodbridge IP13 6UF* Tel (01473) 735182

JONES, Clive. b 51. BA82. Oak Hill Th Coll 79. d 82 p 83. C Brunswick *Man* 82-85; V Pendlebury St Jo 85-96; V Attleborough *Cov* from 96. *Attleborough Vicarage, 5 Fifield Close, Nuneaton CV11 4TS* Tel (024) 7635 4114 E-mail clivej@hta1.freeserve.co.uk

JONES, Clive Morlais Peter. b 40. Univ of Wales (Cardiff) BA63 CertEd64 LTCL71. Chich Th Coll 64. d 66 p 67. C Llanfabon 66-70; PV Llan Cathl 70-75; R Gelligaer 75-85; Prec and Can Llan Cathl 84-85; R Tilehurst St Mich *Ox* 85-94; Chapl Costa Blanca *Eur* 94-97; V Newton St Pet *S & B* 97-06; P-in-c Haarlem *Eur* from 07. *Diakenhuisweg 77, 2033 AP Haarlem, The Netherlands* Tel (0031) (23) 547 3760 E-mail cdjones@planet.nl

JONES, Clive Wesley. b 68. St Steph Ho Ox 95. d 98 p 99. C Swanley St Mary *Roch* 98-02; P-in-c Belvedere St Aug 02-07; V from 07; Chapl Trin Sch Belvedere 02-04. *The Vicarage, St Augustine's Road, Belvedere DA17 5HH* Tel (020) 8311 6307 E-mail clive.jones@diocese-rochester.org *or* frclive@tiscali.co.uk

JONES, Colin Stuart. b 56. Southn Univ LLB77. Coll of Resurr Mirfield 81. d 84 p 85. C Mountain Ash *Llan* 84-86; C Castle Bromwich SS Mary and Marg *Birm* 86-89; V Kingshurst 89-94; V Perry Barr 94-05; P-in-c Wordsley *Worc* 05-07; TR from 07. *The Rectory, 13 Dunsley Drive, 13 Dunsley Drive, Stourbridge DY8 5RA* Tel (01384) 400709

JONES, Cyril Ernest. b 29. St D Coll Lamp BA54. d 56 p 57. C Llanedy *St D* 56-60; C Llanelli 60-63; V Mydroilyn w Dihewyd 63-66; V Llanybydder 66-73; V Llanybydder and Llanwenog w Llanwnnen 73-78; V Betws w Ammanford 78-81; V Cynwyl Gaeo w Llansawel and Talley 81-94; rtd 94. *21 Pentardulais Road, Tycroes, Ammanford SA18 3QD* Tel (01269) 596421

JONES, Daniel. b 78. St Andr Univ MTheol01 PGCE02. Qu Coll Birm 06. d 08 p 09. NSM Barbourne *Worc* from 08. *48 Lavender Road, Worcester WR3 7AE* Tel (01905) 28715 E-mail daniel_a_jones@btopenworld.com

JONES, David. *See* JONES, Preb Wilfred David

JONES, David. *See* JONES, Canon William David

JONES, David. b 55. CA Tr Coll 74 St Steph Ho Ox 83. d 85 p 86. C Fleur-de-Lis *Mon* 85-87; V Ynysddu 87-93; V Blackwood 93-08; AD Bedwellty 06-08; V Landore *S & B* from 08; V Treboeth from 08. *St Alban's Vicarage, Heol Fach, Treboeth, Swansea SA5 9DE* Tel (01792) 310586

JONES, David Arthur. b 44. Liv Univ BA66 Sussex Univ MA68. St D Coll Lamp LTh74. d 74 p 75. C Tenby *St D* 74-76; C Chepstow *Mon* 76-78; P-in-c Teversal *S'well* 78-81; R 81-91; Chapl Sutton Cen 78-89; V Radford All So w Ch Ch and St Mich 91-04; Adv to Urban Priority Par 96-01; Officer for Urban Life and Miss from 04. *37 Devonshire Road, Nottingham NG5 2EW* Tel 0115-962 2115 E-mail urban.officer@southwell.anglican.org

JONES, Chan David Frederick Donald. b 19. Univ of Wales (Abth) BA41. Westcott Ho Cam 41. d 43 p 44. C Henfynyw w Aberaeron *St D* 43-46; C Carmarthen St Pet 46-53; V Pencarreg

53-64; Lect Bp Burgess Th Hall Lamp 59-72; V Betws w Ammanford 64-78; RD Dyffryn Aman 72-78; Can St D Cathl 75-88; Chan St D Cathl 83-88; V Felin-foel 78-88; rtd 88. *clo Jane Howarth, Lingan House, 3 Clos y Ddraenen, Llanelli SA14 8ED*

JONES, David Gornal. b 47. d 74 p 75. In RC Ch 75-80; Asst P Durban St Paul 87-88; R Durban St Aid 89-91; Justice and Reconciliation Officer Natal 92-94; Port Chapl Miss to Seafarers Walvis Bay 95-00; Vlissingen (Flushing) *Eur* 00-02; R Ayr, Girvan and Maybole *Glas* 02-06; V Sunderland St Thos and St Oswald *Dur* from 06. *St Thomas's Vicarage, Parkhurst Road, Sunderland SR4 9DB* Tel 0191-534 2100
E-mail dgjones@clara.co.uk

JONES, David Hugh. b 34. St D Coll Lamp BA56. St Mich Coll Llan 58. d 58 p 59. C Swansea St Mary and H Trin *S & B* 58-61; Inter-Colleg Sec SCM (Liv) 61-63; Hon Chapl Liv Univ 61-63; C Swansea St Pet *S & B* 63-69; V Llanddewi Ystradenni and Abbey Cwmhir 69-75; R Port Eynon w Rhosili and Llanddewi and Knelston 75-83; V Swansea St Barn 83-92; rtd 92. *16 Lon Ger-y-Coed, Cockett, Swansea SA2 0YH*

✠JONES, The Rt Revd David Huw. b 34. Univ of Wales (Ban) BA55 Univ Coll Ox BA58 MA62. St Mich Coll Llan 58. d 59 p 60 c 93. C Aberdare *Llan* 59-61; C Neath w Llantwit 61-65; V Crynant 65-69; V Cwmavon 69-74; Lect Th Univ of Wales (Cardiff) 74-78; Sub-Warden St Mich Coll Llan 74-78; V Prestatyn *St As* 78-82; Dioc Ecum Officer 78-82; Dean Brecon *S & B* 82-93; V Brecon w Battle 82-83; V Brecon St Mary and Battle w Llanddew 83-93; Asst Bp St As 93-96; Bp St D 96-01; rtd 02. *31 The Cathedral Green, Llandaff, Cardiff CF5 2EB*

JONES, Prof David Huw. b 49. Univ of Wales MB, BCh72 Chelsea Coll Lon MSc78 Univ of Wales MD79 FRCR83 FRCP96. EAMTC 95. d 98 p 99. NSM Trumpington *Ely* 98-02; Perm to Offic from 02. *17 Barrow Road, Cambridge CB2 8AP* Tel and fax (01223) 358458 E-mail drhuw@btopenworld.com

JONES, David Ian Stewart. b 34. Selw Coll Cam BA57 MA61. Westcott Ho Cam 57. d 59 p 60. C Oldham *Man* 59-63; V Elton All SS 63-66; Chapl Eton Coll 66-70; Sen Chapl 70-74; Hd Master Bryanston Sch 74-82; P-in-c Bris Ch Ch w St Ewen and All SS 82-84; P-in-c Bris St Steph w St Nic and St Leon 82-84; Soc Resp Adv 84-85; Dir Lambeth Endowed Charities 85-94; Hon PV S'wark Cathl 85-94; rtd 94; Perm to Offic *Ox* from 08. *3 Brackenwood, Naphill, High Wycombe HP14 4TD* Tel (01494) 564040

JONES, David James Hammond. b 45. Kelham Th Coll 65. d 70 p 70. C Cheadle *Lich* 70-73; Hon C W Bromwich All SS 78-83; Hon C Primrose Hill St Mary w Avenue Road St Paul *Lon* 91-03; Hon C Regent's Park St Mark 03-08; Perm to Offic from 08. *11 Ridgebourne Road, Shrewsbury SY3 9AA*
E-mail david@colourwash.co.uk

JONES, David Mark. b 73. St Mich Coll Llan 03. d 06 p 07. C Llansamlet *S & B* 06-08; Min Can Brecon Cathl from 08. *The Clergy House, Cathedral Close, Brecon LD3 9DP* Tel (01874) 623886

JONES, David Michael. b 48. Chich Th Coll 75. d 78 p 79. C Yeovil *B & W* 78-84; C Barwick 81-84; V Cleeve w Chelvey and Brockley 84-92; V Heigham St Barn w St Bart *Nor* 92-00; V Writtle w Highwood *Chelmsf* from 00. *The Vicarage, 19 Lodge Road, Writtle, Chelmsford CM1 3HY* Tel (01245) 421282
E-mail revmjoneswrittle@aol.com

JONES, David Ormond. b 46. Llan Dioc Tr Scheme 90. d 94 p 95. NSM Resolven w Tonna *Llan* 94-01; C Skewen 01-07; N Neath from 07. *30 Henfaes Road, Tonna, Neath SA11 3EX* Tel (01639) 770930 E-mail ormond.jones@ntlworld.com

JONES, David Raymond. b 34. Univ of Wales (Lamp) BA54 St Cath Coll Ox BA57 MA61. Wycliffe Hall Ox 58. d 58 p 59. C Ex St Dav 58-60; C Bideford 60-63; Chapl Grenville Coll Bideford 63-66; Chapl RN 66-89; QHC 84-89; Dir and Warden Divine Healing Miss Crowhurst 89-97; rtd 97; Perm to Offic *Chich* from 97. *Mill View, North Fields Lane, Westergate, Chichester PO20 3UH* Tel (01243) 543179

JONES, David Robert. b 37. Dur Univ BA59 QUB MA83 MBIM83. Cranmer Hall Dur. d 69 p 70. C Middleton *Man* 69-72; CF 72-92; V Staindrop *Dur* 92-04; rtd 04. *8 Heugh Wynd, Craster, Alnwick NE66 3TL* Tel (01665) 576313

JONES, David Robert Deverell. b 50. Sarum & Wells Th Coll 72. d 75 p 78. C Altrincham St Geo *Ches* 75-76; C Clayton *Lich* 77-80; Carriacou 80-81; P-in-c Baschurch *Lich* 81-83; R Baschurch and Weston Lullingfield w Hordley 83-96; RD Ellesmere 85-95; P-in-c Criftins 94-96; P-in-c Dudleston 94-96; P-in-c Jersey St Luke *Win* 96-99; V from 99; P-in-c Jersey St Jas 96-99; V from 99; R Jersey St Mary 02-07. *The Vicarage, Longueville Farm, Longueville Road, St Saviour, Jersey JE2 7WG* Tel (01534) 851445 Mobile 07797-757765

JONES, David Roy. b 47. Hull Univ BA74 CQSW76 Man Univ DipAdEd76 Bradf Univ MA85. NOC 77. d 80 p 81. C New Bury *Man* 80-83; NSM Ringley w Prestolee 92-97; NSM Belmont 97-01; TV Turton Moorland Min from 01. *The Vicarage, High Street, Bemont, Bolton BL7 8AP* Tel (01204) 811221

JONES, David Sebastian. b 43. St Cath Coll Cam BA67 MA73. Linc Th Coll 66. d 68 p 69. C Baguley *Man* 68-71; C Bray and Braywood *Ox* 71-73; V S Ascot 73-07; AD Bracknell 96-04; Chapl Heatherwood Hosp E Berks 81-94; Chapl Heatherwood and Wexham Park Hosp NHS Trust 94-07; rtd 07. *Fairhaven, 1 St Clement's Terrace, Mousehole, Penzance TR19 6SJ* Tel (01736) 732938 E-mail sebastianjones@talk21.com

JONES, David Victor. b 37. St Jo Coll Dur BA59. Cranmer Hall Dur Bossey Ecum Inst Geneva 61. d 62 p 63. C Farnworth *Liv* 62-65; CF 65-68; Asst Master Hutton Gr Sch Preston 68-97; rtd 02. *10 Houghton Close, Penwortham, Preston PR1 9HT* Tel (01772) 745306 E-mail d.v.jones@btinternet.com

JONES, David William. b 42. St Mark & St Jo Coll Lon CertEd64 Open Univ BA79. SEITE 97. d 00 p 01. NSM Coxheath, E Farleigh, Hunton, Linton etc *Roch* from 00; Perm to Offic *Cant* from 04. *13 Woodlands, Coxheath, Maidstone ME17 4EE* Tel (01622) 741474 E-mail david.jones@diocese-rochester.org

JONES, Denise Gloria. b 56. Cov Univ BA93 Leeds Univ MA06. WMMTC 95. d 98 p 99. C Hobs Moat *Birm* 98-02; C Olton and Chapl S Birm Mental Health NHS Trust 02-06; Chapl Manager Birm Women's Healthcare NHS Trust 06-08; TV Bridgnorth, Tasley, Astley Abbotts, etc *Heref* from 08. *41 Innage Lane, Bridgnorth WV16 4HS* Tel (01746) 763637 Mobile 07747-385006 E-mail revddee@aol.com

JONES, Miss Diana. b 46. Qu Coll Birm 89. d 91 p 94. Par Dn Harnham *Sarum* 91-94; C 94-95; C Tidworth, Ludgershall and Faberstown 95-00; P-in-c Hazelbury Bryan and the Hillside Par 00-06; rtd 06. *47 Gloucester Road, Trowbridge BA14 0AB* Tel (01225) 755826

JONES, Canon Dick Heath Remi. b 32. Jes Coll Cam BA56. Linc Th Coll 56. d 58 p 59. C Ipswich St Thos *St E* 58-61; C Putney St Mary *S'wark* 61-65; P-in-c Dawley Parva *Lich* 65-75; P-in-c Lawley 65-75; RD Wrockwardine 70-72; P-in-c Malins Lee 72-75; RD Telford 72-80; P-in-c Stirchley 74-75; TR Cen Telford 75-80; Preb Lich Cathl 76-80; TR Bournemouth St Pet w St Swithun, H Trin etc *Win* 80-96; RD Bournemouth 90-95; Hon Can Win Cathl 91-96; rtd 96; Perm to Offic *Sarum* from 96. *Maltings, Church Street, Fontmell Magna, Shaftesbury SP7 0NY* Tel (01747) 812071 E-mail dick.jones@talk21.com

JONES, Donald. b 50. BA BSc. St Jo Coll Nottm 79. d 82 p 83. C Hutton *Chelmsf* 82-86; C E Ham w Upton Park St Alb 86-88; TV 88-96; V Nuneaton St Nic *Cov* from 96; RD Nuneaton 01-06. *61 Ambleside Way, Nuneaton CV11 6AU* Tel (024) 7634 6900

JONES, Edward. b 36. Dur Univ BA60. Ely Th Coll 60. d 62 p 63. C S Shields St Hilda w St Thos *Dur* 62-65; C Cleadon Park 65-68; V Hebburn St Cuth 68-79; R Winlaton 79-00; rtd 00; Perm to Offic *Dur* from 00 and *Newc* from 01. *10 Melkridge Gardens, Benton, Newcastle upon Tyne NE7 7GQ* Tel 0191-266 4388

JONES, Miss Elaine Edith. b 58. St Jo Coll Nottm BA99. d 99 p 00. C Gainsborough and Morton *Linc* 99-02; C Netherton *Carl* 02-04; TV Maryport, Netherton and Flimby 04-05; Lay Tr Officer 02-05; V Binley *Cov* from 05. *The Vicarage, 68 Brandon Road, Binley, Coventry CV3 2JF* Tel (024) 7663 6334
E-mail elaine.jones@stbarts-binley.org.uk

JONES, Canon Elaine Joan. b 50. Oak Hill Th Coll. d 87 p 94. Par Dn Tottenham H Trin *Lon* 87-92; Par Dn Clay Hill St Jo and St Luke 92-94; C St Botolph Aldgate w H Trin Minories 94-96; V Hackney Wick St Mary of Eton w St Aug 96-04; AD Hackney 99-04; Can Res Derby Cathl from 04. *22 Kedleston Road, Derby DE22 1GU* Tel (01332) 208995
E-mail canon.pastor@derbycathedral.org
or canon.pastor@ukonline.co.uk

JONES, Mrs Elizabeth Mary. b 48. QUB BA69. NOC 88. d 91 p 94. Par Dn Kippax w Allerton Bywater *Ripon* 91-94; C 94-95; R Swillington 95-00; TV Wordsley *Worc* 00-02; rtd 02. *33 Pill Way, Clevedon BS21 7UW* Tel (01275) 876297

JONES, Mrs Elizabeth Somerset. b 49. St Jo Coll Nottm. d 88 p 94. NSM Duns *Edin* 88-99; NSM Selkirk 89-90; Dioc Dir of Ords 95-05; NSM Dalkeith from 02; NSM Lasswade from 02. *255 Carnethie Street, Rosewell EH24 9DR* Tel 0131-653 6767 Fax 653 3646 E-mail esomersetjones@btinternet.com

JONES, Emile Conrad Modupe Kojo. b 50. Univ of Sierra Leone BA74 MA BD. Trin Coll Bris 74. d 77 p 78. C Kissy St Patr Sierra Leone 77-78; C Freetown H Trin 78-81; Asst Chapl and Lect OT Studies Fourah Bay Coll 81-85; Chapl Heidelberg *Eur* 86-97; Miss Partner CMS 97-03; C Holloway St Mary Magd *Lon* 97-04; Asst Chapl Whittington Hosp NHS Trust from 04; Hon C Walthamstow St Pet *Chelmsf* from 05; Hon C Tollington *Lon* from 05. *1 Beech Court, 28 Bisterne Avenue, London E17 3QX* Tel (020) 8521 1213 E-mail mynaekj@yahoo.co.uk

JONES, Canon Eric Vernon. b 26. Ely Th Coll 57. d 59 p 60. C S Shore H Trin *Blackb* 59-63; V Preston St Matt 64-77; R Chorley St Laur 77-91; Hon Can Blackb Cathl 81-91; rtd 91; Perm to Offic *Blackb* from 91. *23 Rivington Avenue, Adlington, Chorley PR6 9PX* Tel (01257) 480482

JONES, Ernest Edward Stephen. b 39. Lon Univ BD76. St D Coll Lamp. d 66 p 67. C N Meols *Liv* 66-69; C Kirkby 69-71; V

Farnworth All SS *Man* 71-75; P-in-c Bempton *York* 75-78; R Rufford *Blackb* 78-84; V Cropredy w Gt Bourton and Wardington *Ox* 84-90; R York St Clem w St Mary Bishophill Senior 90-98; P-in-c York All SS N Street 90-98; V Northampton St Benedict *Pet* 98-05; rtd 05; P-in-c Wootton w Glympton and Kiddington *Ox* from 05. *The Rectory, 22 Castle Road, Wootton, Woodstock OX20 1EG* Tel (01993) 812543
E-mail stephen@samarnic.wanadoo.co.uk

JONES, Evan Hopkins. b 38. St Mich Coll Llan 65. **d** 67 **p** 68. C Churston Ferrers w Goodrington *Ex* 67-70; C Tavistock and Gulworthy 70-73; R Ashprington and V Cornworthy 73-78; R S Hackney St Jo w Ch Ch *Lon* 78-92; AD Hackney 84-89; V Islington St Jas w St Pet 92-08; rtd 08; Perm to Offic *Lon* from 08. *5 St James's Close, Bishop Street, London N1 8PH* Tel (020) 7226 0104 E-mail fr.evan@virgin.net

JONES, Evan Trefor. b 32. Univ of Wales (Ban) BA54. Coll of Resurr Mirfield 54. **d** 56 **p** 57. C Ban St Mary 56-62; V Llandinorwig 62-71; TV Llanbeblig w Caernarfon and Betws Garmon etc 71-84; Ed dioc magazine *The Link* 79-89; R Llanfairfechan w Aber 84-97; Can Ban Cathl 95-97; rtd 97. *19 Marlborough Place, Vaughan Street, Llandudno LL30 1AE* Tel (01492) 878411

JONES, Frederick Morgan. b 19. Univ of Wales (Lamp) BA40 BD49. St Mich Coll Llan 42. **d** 42 **p** 43. C Llanelli St Paul *St D* 42-50; Org Sec (Wales) Ind Chr Fellowship 50-53; C-in-c Llwynhendy CD *St D* 52-56; C Llanelli 56-57; V Penrhyncoch and Elerch 57-61; R Llanbedrog and Penrhos *Ban* 61-74; R Llanbedrog w Llannor w Llanfihangel etc 74-84; C Llangefni w Tregaean and Llangristiolus etc 84-85; rtd 85; Perm to Offic *Ban* from 85. *15 Ponc-y-Fron, Llangefni LL77 7NY* Tel (01248) 722850

JONES, Gareth. b 35. St Aid Birkenhead 58. **d** 61 **p** 62. C Doncaster Ch Ch *Sheff* 61-65; Min Can Ripon Cathl 65-68; Chapl RAF 68-85; St Jo Cathl Hong Kong 85-89; R Spofforth w Kirk Deighton *Ripon* 89-00; rtd 00; Perm to Offic *Ripon* from 00 and *Dur* from 02. *36 Whitcliffe Lane, Ripon HG4 2JL* Tel (01765) 601745 E-mail garjones1549@yahoo.co.uk

JONES, Gareth Edward John Paul. b 79. Leeds Univ BA06. Coll of Resurr Mirfield 03. **d** 06 **p** 07. C Brighton St Mich *Chich* from 06. *59 Avalon, West Street, Brighton BN1 2RP* Tel (01273) 729888 E-mail fathergarethjones@gmail.com

JONES, Gareth Lewis. b 42. K Coll Lon BD64 AKC64. **d** 65 **p** 66. C Risca *Mon* 65-70; Perm to Offic *Win* 70-74; *Newc* 74-75; *Sarum* 75; C Pontesbury I and II *Heref* 75-77; P-in-c Presteigne w Discoed 77-79; TV Hemel Hempstead *St Alb* 79-86; R Longden and Annscroft w Pulverbatch *Heref* 86-93; TV Leominster 93-07; rtd 07; Perm to Offic *Heref* from 08. *33 Danesfield Drive, Leominster HR6 8HP* Tel (01568) 620453

JONES, Prof Gareth Lloyd. b 38. Univ of Wales BA61 Selw Coll Cam BA63 MA67 Yale Univ STM69 TCD BD70 Lon Univ PhD75. Episc Sem Austin Texas Hon DD90 Westcott Ho Cam 62. **d** 65 **p** 66. C Holyhead w Rhoscolyn *Ban* 65-68; USA 68-70; P-in-c Merton *Ox* 70-72; Tutor Ripon Hall Ox 72; Sen Tutor 73-75; Lect Ex Coll Ox 73-77; Tutor and Lib Ripon Coll Cuddesdon 75-77; Lect Th Univ of Wales (Ban) 77-89; Sen Lect 89-95; Reader and Hd of Sch from 95; Prof from 98; Sub-Dean Faculty of Th 80-89; Dean 89-92; Chan Ban Cathl from 90; Select Preacher Ox Univ 89. *22 Bron-y-Felin, Llandegfan, Menai Bridge LL59 5UY* Tel (01248) 712786

JONES, Glyn Evan. b 44. Lon Coll of Div ALCD67 LTh. **d** 67 **p** 68. C Gt Horton *Bradf* 67-70; SAMS Argentina 71-78; V Idle *Bradf* 78-84; V Hyson Green *S'well* 84-87; V Nottingham St Steph 84-87; V Hyson Green St Paul w St Steph 87-89; V Hyson Green 89-91; V Basford w Hyson Green 91-92; V Worksop St Jo 92-99; RD Worksop 93-99; V Nottingham St Sav 99-08; rtd 08. *65 Conifer Crescent, Nottingham NG11 9EP* Tel 0115-846 9947 Mobile 07885-816697 E-mail chezjones@ntlworld.com

JONES, Canon Glyndwr. b 35. St Mich Coll Llan. **d** 62 **p** 63. C Clydach *S & B* 62-64; C Llangyfelach 64-67; C Sketty 67-70; V Bryngwyn and Newchurch and Llanbedr etc 70-72; Miss to Seafarers 72-00; Swansea 72-76; Port of Lon 76-81; Aux Min Sec 81-85; Asst Gen Sec 85-90; Sec Gen 90-00; V St Mich Paternoster Royal *Lon* 91-00; rtd 01; Hon Can Kobe Japan from 88; Chapl to The Queen 90-05; Perm to Offic *Chelmsf* from 91. *5 The Close, Grays RM16 2XU* Tel (01375) 375053
E-mail glynita.tomdavey@blueyonder.co.uk

JONES, Glynn. b 56. NEOC 91. **d** 94 **p** 95. NSM Glendale Gp *Newc* 94-97; Sen Chapl HM Pris Leeds 97-99; Chapl HM Pris Dur 99-00; Chapl HM YOI Wetherby 00-05; Chapl HM Pris Wymott 06-07; Co-ord Chapl HM Pris Haverigg from 07. *HM Prison, North Lane, Haverigg, Millom LA18 4NA* Tel (01229) 713152 *or* 713025 E-mail glynn.jones@hmps.gsi.gov.uk

JONES, Godfrey Caine. b 36. Dur Univ BA59 Lon Univ CertEd60 Birm Univ MEd71. St Deiniol's Hawarden 76. **d** 78 **p** 79. Hd Humanities Denbigh High Sch 75-81; NSM Ruthin w Llanrhydd *St As* 78-81; C 83-84; Sen Lect Matlock Coll 81-83; P-in-c Llanfwrog and Clocaenog and Gyffylliog 84-85; R 85-93; V Ruabon 93-02; RD Llangollen 93-02; rtd 02; Min Pradoe *Lich*

02-08; Perm to Offic from 08. *Idoma, Penylan, Ruabon, Wrexham LL14 6HP* Tel (01978) 812102
E-mail dorothy.e.jones@btopenworld.com

JONES, Gordon Howlett. b 26. G&C Coll Cam BA47 MA51. Westcott Ho Cam 49. **d** 51 **p** 52. C Milton *Win* 51-54; Study Sec SCM and C St Helen Bishopsgate w St Martin Outwich *Lon* 54-58; V Claremont H Angels *Man* 58-63; R Northenden 63-79; P-in-c Hilmarton and Highway *Sarum* 79-83; V Bremhill w Foxham and Hilmarton 83-92; RD Calne 84-88; rtd 92; Perm to Offic *Sarum* from 92. *63 New Park Street, Devizes SN11 8SB* Tel (01380) 720950

JONES, Canon Gordon Michael Campbell. b 33. St D Coll Lamp BA56. St Jo Coll Dur 56. **d** 58 **p** 59. C Maindee Newport *Mon* 58-60; C Penhow, St Brides Netherwent w Llandavenny etc 60-63; V Magor w Redwick 63-68; V Southern Cross Australia 68-71; R Kirkby Thore w Temple Sowerby *Carl* 72-73; R Kirkby Thore w Temple Sowerby and Newbiggin 73-79; P-in-c Accrington St Jas *Blackb* 79-81; P-in-c Accrington St Andr 81-83; Chapl Ahmadi Kuwait 83-91; R Swardeston w E Carleton, Intwood, Keswick etc *Nor* 91-96; Chapl Limassol St Barn and Miss to Seafarers 96-03; Can Nicosia 01-03; rtd 03; Perm to Offic *Blackb* 03-08 and *Cov* from 08. *2 Margetts Close, Kenilworth CV8 1EN* Tel and fax (01926) 856759

JONES, Graham Frederick. b 37. Leeds Univ BA60 GradIPM63. ALCD66. **d** 66 **p** 67. C Chesterfield H Trin *Derby* 66-70; C Leeds St Geo *Ripon* 70-73; P-in-c Newcastle St Geo *Lich* 73-83; New Zealand 83-87; P-in-c Westcote w Icomb and Bledington *Glouc* 89-94; rtd 94. *7 Keynsham Bank, Cheltenham GL52 6ER* Tel (01242) 238680

JONES, Griffith Trevor. b 56. BSc MPS Univ of Wales BD. **d** 87 **p** 88. C Llandrygarn w Bodwrog and Heneglwys etc *Ban* 87-89; R Llangefni w Tregaean and Llangristiolus etc 89-91; TV Bangor 91-94; Chapl Ysbyty Gwynedd 91-94; Lic to Offic 94-00. *8 Carreg-y-Gad, Llanfairpwllgwyngyll LL61 5QF* Tel (01248) 713094

JONES, Preb Griffith Walter Hywyn. b 24. St Mich Coll Llan 47. **d** 50 **p** 51. C Llanaber *Ban* 50-52; Chapl RAF 52-67; V Betws y Coed *Ban* 67-69; V Betws y Coed and Capel Curig 70-78; R Holyhead w Rhoscolyn w Llanfair-yn-Neubwll 78-87; Can and Preb Ban Cathl 78-90; RD Llifon and Talybolion 80-85; Spiritual Dir Cursillo Cymru 81-90; V Ynyscynhaearn w Penmorfa and Porthmadog *Ban* 87-90; rtd 90; Lic to Offic *St As* from 90 and *Ban* 90-96. *Cysgod y Coed, 12 Church View, Ruabon, Wrexham LL14 6TD* Tel (01978) 822206

JONES, Canon Griffith William. b 31. St D Coll Lamp BA53 LTh55. **d** 55 **p** 56. C Llanycil w Bala and Frongoch *St As* 55-58; V Llandrillo 58-66; V Llandrillo and Llandderfel 66-96; RD Penllyn 83-96; Can Cursal St As Cathl from 87; rtd 96. *45 Yr Hafan, Bala LL23 7AU* Tel (01678) 520217

JONES, Gwynfryn Lloyd. b 35. Univ of Wales (Lamp) BA59. St Mich Coll Llan 59. **d** 61 **p** 62. C Rhyl w St Ann *St As* 61-64; C Prestatyn 64-67; V Whitford 67-75; V Llay 75-83; V Northop 83-98; rtd 98. *Tryfan, 41 Snowdon Avenue, Bryn-y-Baal, Mold CH7 6SZ* Tel (01352) 751036

JONES, Gwynn Rees. b 32. St D Coll Lamp BA55. **d** 57 **p** 58. C Llangystennin *St As* 57-59; C Llanrhos 59-64; R Cefn 64-68; R Llanfyllin 68-80; V Bistre 80-89; R Flint 89-97. *3 Lon Derw, Abergele LL22 7EA* Tel (01745) 825188

JONES, Canon Harold Desmond. b 22. Sarum Th Coll 52. **d** 55 **p** 56. C Bushey Heath *St Alb* 55-58; C Stevenage 58-64; V Milton Ernest and Thurleigh 64-80; RD Sharnbrook 70-81; Hon Can St Alb 78-90; V Sharnbrook 80-82; P-in-c Knotting w Souldrop 80-82; R Sharnbrook and Knotting w Souldrop 82-90; P-in-c Felmersham 82-87; RD Sharnbrook 86-90; rtd 90; Perm to Offic *St Alb* 00-04. *8 Capel Court, The Burgage, Prestbury, Cheltenham GL52 3EL* Tel (01242) 576510

JONES, Harold Philip. b 49. Leeds Univ BA72 St Jo Coll Dur BA84. Cranmer Hall Dur 82. **d** 85 **p** 86. C Scartho *Linc* 85-88; V Dodworth *Wakef* 88-91; C Penistone and Thurlstone 91-95; C Scunthorpe All SS *Linc* 95-96; TV Brumby 96-02; Chapl Derby Hosps NHS Foundation Trust from 02. *Derbyshire Royal Infirmary, London Road, Derby DE1 2QY* Tel (01332) 347141 Fax 290559 E-mail harold.jones@derbyhospitals.nhs.uk

JONES, Haydn Llewellyn. b 42. Edin Th Coll 63. **d** 65 **p** 66. C Towcester w Easton Neston *Pet* 65-68; C Northampton St Matt 68-72; CF 72-97; Perm to Offic *Roch* 97-98; Ex from 98; rtd 99. *11 Lady Park Road, Livermead, Torquay TQ2 6UA* Tel (01803) 690483

JONES (née JAMES), Ms Helen Alison. b 59. St Andr Univ BSc81. EMMTC 93. **d** 96 **p** 97. C Brocklesby Park *Linc* 96-98; Perm to Offic 06-08; C Bassingham Gp from 08. *8 Doe Close, Witham St Hughs, Lincoln LN6 9UW* Tel (01522) 869417 Mobile 07814-789817 E-mail alison@hajones.freeserve.co.uk

JONES, Hester. See JONES, Susannah Hester Everett

JONES, Hilary Christine. b 55. Ch Ch Coll Cant CertEd76 Lon Univ BEd77. SEITE. **d** 99 **p** 00. C Kennington *Cant* 99-02; R Cheriton St Martin from 02; P-in-c Cheriton All So w Newington from 06; Bp's Adv for Women's Min from 04; AD

Elham from 08. *St Martin's Rectory, Horn Street, Folkestone CT20 3JJ* Tel (01303) 238509 E-mail hilarycjones@lycos.co.uk
JONES, Howard. *See* JONES, John Howard
JONES, Hugh Vaughan. b 44. **d** 07 **p** 08. C Holyhead *Ban* from 07. *Ty Sant Elbod, 3 Harbour View, Holyhead LL65 2HL* Tel (01407) 761320 Mobile 07795-578932
E-mail hughvaughan.santelbod@btinternet.com
JONES, Hughie. *See* JONES, The Ven Thomas Hughie
JONES, Huw. *See* JONES, Prof David Huw
JONES, Hywyn. *See* JONES, Preb Griffith Walter Hywyn
JONES, Ian. b 63. Trin Coll Carmarthen BEd88. St Mich Coll Llan 95. **d** 97 **p** 98. NSM Tycoch *S & B* 97-01; NSM Swansea St Nic 01-04; Chapl Wymondham Coll from 04. *Staff House 8, Wymondham College, Golf Links Road, Wymondham NR18 9SX* Tel (01953) 607120 E-mail ianjones99@yahoo.com
JONES, Ian Andrew. b 65. Lanc Univ BA87. St Mich Coll Llan. **d** 90 **p** 91. C Caerphilly *Llan* 90-96; Chapl RAF from 96. *Chaplaincy Services, Valiant Block, HQ Air Command, RAF High Wycombe HP14 4UE* Tel (01494) 496800 Fax 496343
JONES, Idris. b 31. **d** 88 **p** 94. NSM Llanfihangel Ysgeifiog and Llanffinan etc *Ban* 88-97; NSM Llangefni w Tregaean and Llangristiolus etc 98-01; NSM Llanfihangel Ysgeifiog w Llangristiolus etc 01-02. *8 Swn yr Engan, Gaerwen LL60 6LS* Tel (01248) 421777
✠**JONES, The Rt Revd Idris.** b 43. St D Coll Lamp BA64 NY Th Sem DMin86. Edin Th Coll 64. **d** 67 **p** 68 **c** 98. C Stafford St Mary *Lich* 67-70; Prec St Paul's Cathl Dundee 70-73; P-in-c Gosforth All SS *Newc* 73-80; R Montrose and Inverbervie *Bre* 80-89; Can St Paul's Cathl Dundee 84-92; Chapl Angl Students Dundee Univ 89-92; P-in-c Invergowrie 89-92; TR S Ayrshire TM 92-98; Bp Glas 98-09; Primus 06-09; rtd 09; Hon Fell Univ of Wales (Lamp) from 07. *27 Donald Wynd, Largs KA30 8TH* E-mail idrisjones43@hotmail.co.uk
JONES, Ivor Wyn. b 56. Trin Coll Bris 92. **d** 94 **p** 95. C Gabalfa *Llan* 94-97; TV Daventry, Ashby St Ledgers, Braunston etc *Pet* 97-01; P-in-c Dawley St Jerome *Lon* 01-08; C-in-c Harlington Ch Ch CD 03-08; V W Hayes from 08. *St Jerome's Lodge, 42 Corwell Lane, Uxbridge UB8 3DE* Tel (020) 8561 7393 *or* 8573 1895 E-mail wynjones@blueyonder.co.uk
JONES, James Richard. b 65. SS Hild & Bede Coll Dur BA87 Open Univ MBA95. Wycliffe Hall Ox 02. **d** 04 **p** 05. C Ashtead *Guildf* 04-08; P-in-c Burscough Bridge *Liv* from 08. *St John's Vicarage, 253 Liverpool Road South, Ormskirk L40 7TD* E-mail jrj37@aol.com
✠**JONES, The Rt Revd James Stuart.** b 48. Ex Univ BA70 PGCE71 Hull Univ Hon DD99 Lincs & Humberside Univ Hon DLitt01. Wycliffe Hall Ox 81. **d** 82 **p** 83 **c** 94. C Clifton Ch Ch w Em *Bris* 82-90; V S Croydon Em *S'wark* 90-94; Suff Bp Hull *York* 94-98; Bp Liv from 98; Bp HM Pris from 07. *Bishop's Lodge, Woolton Park, Liverpool L25 6DT* Tel 0151-421 0831 Fax 428 3055 E-mail bishopslodge@liverpool.anglican.org
JONES, Canon Jaqueline Dorian. b 58. K Coll Lon BD80 AKC80 MTh81. Westcott Ho Cam 84. **dss** 86 **d** 87 **p** 94. Epsom St Martin *Guildf* 86-91; C 87-91; Chapl Chelmsf Cathl 91-97; V Bridgemary *Portsm* 97-03; Can Res S'well Minster from 03. *2 Vicars Court, Southwell NG25 0HP* Tel (01636) 813188
JONES, Jeffrey Lloyd. b 66. Univ of Wales (Abth) BD87 PGCE90. Wycliffe Hall Ox 95. **d** 97 **p** 98. C Lampeter Pont Steffan w Silian *St D* 97; C Carmarthen St Dav 97-00; TV Llantwit Major 00-08; V Llanddeiniolen w Llanfair-is-gaer etc *Ban* from 08. *The Vicarage, Y Felinheli LL56 4SQ* Tel (01248) 670212
JONES, Jennifer Margaret. b 49. Lon Univ CertEd. Cranmer Hall Dur 87. **d** 89 **p** 94. C Musselburgh *Edin* 89-93; Dn-in-c 93-94; P-in-c 94-95; R 95-02; C Prestonpans 89-93; Dn-in-c 93-94; P-in-c 94-95; R 95-02; Lic to Offic *Mor* from 02. *2 Stables, Balvatin Cottages, Perth Road, Newtonmore PH20 1BB* Tel (01540) 673042
JONES, John Bernard. b 49. Qu Coll Birm 86. **d** 88 **p** 89. C Mold *St As* 88-91; P-in-c Treuddyn and Nercwys and Eryrys 91-92; V Treuddyn w Nercwys from 92; RD Mold 95-00. *The Vicarage, Ffordd y Llan, Treuddyn, Mold CH7 4LN* Tel (01352) 770919 E-mail revjbj@hotmail.com
JONES, John Brian. St Mich Coll Llan. **d** 05 **p** 06. NSM Gors-las *St D* from 05. *Penpentre, 79 Carmarthen Road, Cross Hands, Lanelli SA14 6SU* Tel (01269) 842236
JONES, John David Emrys. b 36. Trin Coll Carmarthen. **d** 96 **p** 97. NSM Llanfihangel Ystrad and Cilcennin w Trefilan etc *St D* 96-97; P-in-c Llangeitho and Blaenpennal w Betws Leucu etc 97-06; Lic to Offic from 06. *Dolfor, Ciliau Aeron, Lampeter SA48 8DE* Tel (01570) 470569
JONES, Canon John Francis Williams. b 26. St D Coll Lamp 48. **d** 52 **p** 53. C Glanadda *Ban* 52-55; C Porthmadog 55-57; V Llandrygarn w Bodwrog and Heneglwys etc 57-96; RD Menai and Malltraeth 75-97; Hon Can Ban Cathl 81-83; Can from 83; Preb from 90; rtd 96; AD Malltraeth *Ban* 03-06. *Llandrygarn Vicarage, Tynlon, Holyhead LL65 3AZ* Tel (01407) 720234
✠**JONES, John Hellyer.** b 20. Birm Univ LDS43. Westcott Ho Cam 65. **d** 67 **p** 68. C Haddenham *Ely* 67-70; P-in-c Lolworth 70-79

and 81-85; P-in-c Conington 75-79 and 81-85; R Houghton w Wyton 79; rtd 85; Perm to Offic *Ely* 85-02. *13 High Street, Haddenham, Ely CB6 3XA* Tel (01353) 740530
E-mail jonhadnam@ntlworld.com
JONES, John Howard. b 48. New Coll Ox BA69 MA73 K Coll Cam CertEd70. Sarum & Wells Th Coll 76. **d** 77 **p** 78. C Salisbury St Mark *Sarum* 77-78; C Morriston *S & B* 78-80; Dir of Ords 80-83; V Gowerton 80-83; V Swansea St Jas 85-89; Chapl Alleyn's Sch Dulwich 89-08; Hon C Dulwich St Barn *S'wark* 90-08; rtd 08. *53 Gilkes Crescent, London SE21 7BP* Tel (020) 8299 4826
JONES, John Trevor. b 14. St D Coll Lamp BA42. **d** 43 **p** 44. C Rhosddu *St As* 43-52; C Timperley *Ches* 52-53; V Barnton 53-60; V Poulton 60-81; rtd 81; Perm to Offic *Ches* from 82. *21 Sandy Lane, Wallasey CH45 3JY* Tel 0151-639 4794
JONES, Joyce Rosemary. b 54. Newnham Coll Cam BA76 MA82 Coll of Ripon & York St Jo MA97 Solicitor 79. NOC 94. **d** 97 **p** 98. C Pontefract All SS *Wakef* 97-00; NSM Cumberworth, Denby and Denby Dale 00-01; Dioc Voc Adv 00-01; Asst Chapl Kirkwood Hospice Huddersfield 00-01; P-in-c Shelley and Shepley *Wakef* from 01. *Oakfield, 206 Barnsley Road, Denby Dale, Huddersfield HD8 8TS* Tel and fax (01484) 862350
E-mail joycerjones@aol.com
JONES, Mrs Julie Denise. b 63. CBDTI 03. **d** 06 **p** 07. C Darwen St Pet w Hoddlesden *Blackb* from 06. *44 Minster Crescent, Darwen BB3 3PY* Tel (01254) 703796 Mobile 07814-500855
E-mail julie.jones.bpl@btinternet.com
JONES, Mrs Karen Elizabeth. b 64. Univ of Ulster BA87. Wycliffe Hall Ox 04. **d** 06 **p** 07. C Northolt Park St Barn *Lon* 06-07; NSM Longwell Green *Bris* from 08. *119 North Road, Stoke Gifford, Bristol BS34 8PE* Tel 0117-979 1656 Mobile 07876-752745 E-mail admin@karenjones.org.uk
JONES, Kathryn Mary. *See* BUCK, Kathryn Mary
JONES (née SANDELLS-REES), Ms Kathy Louise. b 68. Univ of Wales (Ban) BTh96. Qu Coll Birm 90. **d** 92 **p** 97. C Holyhead w Rhoscolyn w Llanfair-yn-Neubwll *Ban* 92-94; C Bangor 94-95; Chapl Gwynedd Hosp Ban 94-99; P-in-c Bangor 95-99; P-in-c Betws-y-Coed and Capel Curig w Penmachno etc 99-06; Chapl Newcastle upon Tyne Hosps NHS Foundn Trust from 06. *Freeman Hospital, Freeman Road, High Heaton, Newcastle upon Tyne NE7 7DN* Tel 0191-233 6161
JONES, Mrs Katie Ann. b 74. **d** 99 **p** 00. NSM Sutton Courtenay w Appleford *Ox* 99-04; Perm to Offic *Cant* from 04. *The Headmaster's House, Dover College, Effingham Crescent, Dover CT17 9RH* Tel (01304) 205969
JONES, The Very Revd Keith Brynmor. b 44. Selw Coll Cam BA65 MA69. Cuddesdon Coll 67. **d** 69 **p** 70. C Limpsfield and Titsey *S'wark* 69-72; Dean's V St Alb Abbey 72-76; P-in-c Boreham Wood St Mich 76-79; TV Borehamwood 79-82; V Ipswich St Mary-le-Tower *St E* 82-96; RD Ipswich 92-96; Hon Can St E Cathl 93-96; Dean Ex 96-04; Dean York from 04. *The Deanery, York YO1 7JQ* Tel (01904) 557202 *or* 623618 Fax 557204 E-mail dean@yorkminster.org
JONES, Keith Bythell. b 35. BA CertEd ACP. Trin Coll Bris. **d** 83 **p** 84. C Bris St Mary Redcliffe w Temple etc 83-86; C Filton 86-88; TV Yate New Town 88-95; rtd 95; Perm to Offic *Mon* from 95. *3 Woodlands Close, St Arvans, Chepstow NP16 6EF* Tel (01291) 622377
JONES, Keith Ellison. b 47. Wycliffe Hall Ox 72. **d** 75 **p** 76. C Everton St Chrys *Liv* 75-79; C Buckhurst Hill *Chelmsf* 79-81, TV 81-88; TR Leek and Meerbrook *Lich* 88-99; V Formby H Trin *Liv* from 99; AD Sefton 05-08; Hon Can Liv Cathl 05-08. *Holy Trinity Vicarage, 2A Brows Lane, Liverpool L37 3HZ* Tel and fax (01704) 386464 E-mail keith.hfvicarage@blueyonder.co.uk
JONES, Kingsley Charles. b 45. Birm Univ BSc66 Open Univ BA75. Sarum Th Coll 66. **d** 69 **p** 70. C Penwortham St Mary *Blackb* 69-72; C Broughton 72-74; P-in-c Gt Wollaston *Heref* 74-77; Chapl RAF 77-83; V Colwich w Gt Haywood *Lich* 83-94; V Winshill *Derby* 94-01; P-in-c Glouc St Aldate from 01. *St Aldate's Vicarage, Finlay Road, Gloucester GL4 6TN* Tel (01452) 523906
JONES, Lesley Anne. b 46. Luton Coll of HE CertEd77. SAOMC 01. **d** 04 **p** 06. NSM Gravenhurst, Shillington and Stondon *St Alb* 04-06; NSM Leagrave from 06. *91 Manton Drive, Luton LU2 7DL* Tel (01582) 616888
E-mail lesleyjones31647@aol.com
JONES, Leslie Joseph. b 23. Linc Th Coll. **d** 57 **p** 58. C Penhill *Bris* 57-60; C-in-c Lockleaze St Mary CD 60-62; V Bris Lockleaze St Mary Magd w St Fran 62-69; V Bedminster St Aldhelm 69-75; TV Bedminster 75-80; V Abbots Leigh w Leigh Woods 80-88; rtd 88; Perm to Offic *Bris* from 88. *4 Summerleaze, Bristol BS16 4ER* Tel 0117-965 3597
JONES, Lloyd. *See* JONES, Jeffrey Lloyd
JONES, Lloyd. *See* JONES, Prof Gareth Lloyd
JONES, Miss Mair. b 41. Cartrefle Coll of Educn TCert61. St Mich Coll Llan 91. **d** 93 **p** 97. C Llangollen w Trevor and Llantysilio *St As* 93-97; V Llandrillo and Llandderfel 97-00; R Llanelian w Betws-yn-Rhos w Trofarth 00-03; R Llanelian

03-08; P-in-c Brynmaen 04-08; rtd 08. *5 Ffordd Bugail, Colwyn Bay LL29 8TN* Tel (01492) 517866
E-mail mair@jones6527.fsnet.co.uk

JONES, Malcolm. *See* JONES, Philip Malcolm

JONES, Malcolm Francis. b 44. Open Univ BA88 Hull Univ MA96 Univ of Wales (Cardiff) LLM05. Chich Th Coll 67. **d** 70 **p** 71. C Prestbury *Ches* 70-73; Chapl RAF 73-81; R Heaton Reddish *Man* 81-84; CF (ACF) 82-84 and from 98; CF (TA) 83-84; CF 84-93; CF (R of O) 93-99; TV Cleethorpes *Linc* 93-97; V Ryde H Trin *Portsm* from 97; V Swanmore St Mich from 97. *The Vicarage, 11 Wray Street, Swanmore, Ryde PO33 3ED* Tel (01983) 562984 Mobile 07710-543155
E-mail frmalcolmjones@hotmail.com

JONES, Malcolm Stuart. b 41. Sheff Univ BA62. Linc Th Coll 64. **d** 66 **p** 67. C Monkseaton St Mary *Newc* 66-69; C Ponteland 69 72; Chapl Lake Maracaibo Venezuela 73-75; C Hexham *Newc* 75-77; P-in-c Killingworth 77-92; V Delaval 92-01; TV Ch the King 01-07; rtd 07. *13 Valeside, Newcastle upon Tyne NE15 9LA*

JONES, Maldwyn Lloyd. b 17. St D Coll Lamp BA39. **d** 40 **p** 41. C Gorseinon *S & B* 40-43; Lic to Offic *Ox* 43-46; Chapl Nichteroy All SS Brazil 46-48; Hd Master St Paul's Sch Sao Paulo 48-50; Chapl Ch Ch Cathl Falkland Is 50-51; Chapl RN 52-68; Chapl Shattuck Sch Faribault USA 68-70; Chapl Lon Nautical Sch 71-72; Lic to Offic *Ban* 72-82; rtd 82; Perm to Offic *Ban* from 82. *12 Springfield Street, Dolgellau LL40 1LY* Tel (01341) 421715

JONES, Ms Margaret. b 28. TCD BA53 Man Univ PGCE54 Lon Univ BD66. **d** 87 **p** 94. NSM Stanstead Abbots *St Alb* 87-88; NSM Grappenhall *Ches* 89-98; Perm to Offic *Ches* from 98. *19 Hill Top Road, Grappenhall, Warrington WA4 2ED* Tel (01925) 261992

JONES, Mrs Margaret Angela. b 53. Wolv Univ CertEd91. Qu Coll Birm BA99. **d** 99 **p** 00. C Pershore w Pinvin, Wick and Birlingham *Worc* 99-03; TV Solihull *Birm* from 03. *St Helen's House, 6 St Helen's Road, Solihull B91 2DA* Tel 0121-704 2878
E-mail magz@sthelens@cpadsl.co.uk

JONES, Mrs Margaret Anne. b 47. Lon Univ TCert68 Ches Coll of HE BTh04. NOC 01. **d** 04 **p** 05. NSM Altrincham St Geo *Ches* 04-07; C from 07; C Altrincham St Jo from 07; Chapl Trin C of E High Sch Man 05-07. *12 Moorland Avenue, Sale M33 3FH* Tel 0161-973 8020 Mobile 07748-645596
E-mail margaret_jones@talk21.com

JONES, Margaret Mary. b 47. Oak Hill Th Coll 92. **d** 95 **p** 96. C Sydenham H Trin *S'wark* 95-98; V Anerley St Paul *Roch* 98-09; TV Anerley from 09. *St Paul's Vicarage, Hamlet Road, London SE19 2AW* Tel (020) 8653 0978

JONES, Mark. *See* JONES, Christopher Mark

JONES, Mark. b 70. Warwick Univ BSc92 Univ of Wales PGCE93. Ripon Coll Cuddesdon 06. **d** 08 **p** 09. C Old Basing and Lychpit *Win* from 08. *6 Copse View Close, Chineham, Basingstoke RG24 8EZ* Tel (01256) 323794
E-mail mark.kennington@btinternet.com

JONES, Mark Andrew. b 60. Southn Univ BSc82 Sussex Univ PGCE83. Oak Hill Th Coll BA91. **d** 91 **p** 92. C Wolverhampton St Luke *Lich* 91-96; I Inishmacsaint *Clogh* 96-01; V Padiham w Hapton and Padiham Green *Blackb* from 01. *The Vicarage, 1 Arbory Drive, Padiham, Burnley BB12 8JS* Tel (01282) 772442
E-mail jones.rectory@care4free.net

JONES, Mark Vincent. b 60. Liv Univ BA81. **d** 84 **p** 85. C Whitchurch *Llan* 84-89; V Pwllgwaun w Llanddewi Rhondda 89-90; CF from 90. *c/o MOD Chaplains (Army)* Tel (01980) 615804 Fax 615800

JONES, Martin. b 58. Leeds Univ BA07. NOC 04. **d** 07 **p** 08. NSM Winwick *Liv* from 07; Chapl St Helens and Knowsley Hosps NHS Trust from 08. *7 Longwood Close, Rainford, St Helens WA11 7QJ* Tel (01744) 889938
E-mail martinjones9558@aol.com

JONES, Martin Patrick. b 62. K Coll Lon BDS85. Dioc OLM tr scheme 02. **d** 05 **p** 06. NSM Kingsnorth and Shadoxhurst *Cant* 05-09; Perm to Offic from 09. *3 Hewitts Place, Willesborough, Ashford TN24 0AH* Tel (01233) 613271
E-mail martin.jones62@ntlworld.com

JONES, Mrs Mary Catherine Theresa Bridget. b 41. Westhill Coll Birm CertEd77 Birm Univ BA80. Qu Coll Birm 04. **d** 05 **p** 06. NSM Bromsgrove St Jo *Worc* from 05. *15 Greyfriars Drive, Bromsgrove B61 7LF* Tel (01527) 837018
E-mail theresa@supalife.com

JONES, Canon Mary Nerissa Anna. b 41. MBE02. Qu Mary Coll Lon BA86 FRSA91. Ripon Coll Cuddesdon 86. **d** 88 **p** 94. Par Dn St Botolph Aldgate w H Trin Minories *Lon* 88-93; P-in-c Wood End *Cov* 93-95; V 95-01; Hon Can Cov Cathl 01; rtd 01; P-in-c Askerswell, Loders and Powerstock *Sarum* from 01; P-in-c Symondsbury from 07. *The Vicarage, Loders, Bridport DT6 3SA* Tel (01308) 425419 E-mail nerissa@eurobell.co.uk

JONES, Canon Mary Valerie. b 37. Univ of Wales (Ban) BD84. St Deiniol's Hawarden 84. **d** 85 **p** 97. C Holyhead w Rhoscolyn w Llanfair-yn-Neubwll *Ban* 85-87; C Ynyscynhaearn w Penmorfa and Porthmadog 87-90; Dn-in-c Llansantffraid Glyn Ceirog and

Llanarmon etc *St As* 90-97; V 97-98; R Overton and Erbistock and Penley 98-04; RD Bangor Isycoed 98-04; Can Cursal St As Cathl 01-04; rtd 04. *Cysgod y Coed, 12 Church View, Ruabon, Wrexham LL14 6TD* Tel (01978) 822206
E-mail valerie@hywyn.freeserve.co.uk

JONES, Matthew Christopher Howell. b 74. Leeds Univ BSc95 Cam Univ BTh01. Westcott Ho Cam 98. **d** 01 **p** 02. C Cheshunt *St Alb* 01-05; V Southgate St Andr *Lon* from 05. *St Andrew's Vicarage, 184 Chase Side, London N14 5HN* Tel (020) 8886 7523
E-mail mchjones@lineone.net

JONES, Maurice Maxwell Hughes. b 32. Clifton Th Coll 56. **d** 60 **p** 61. C Islington St Andr w St Thos and St Matthias *Lon* 60-63; Argentina 63-71; C Whitchurch *Llan* 72-73; Area Sec (NW England) SAMS 73-77; V Haydock St Mark *Liv* 78-87; V Paddington Em Harrow Road *Lon* 87-97; rtd 98. *Glyn Orig, Cemmaes, Machynlleth SY20 9PR* Tel and fax (01650) 511632

JONES, Canon Melville Kenneth. b 40. Open Univ BA82. St D Coll Lamp. **d** 66 **p** 67. C Aberdare *Llan* 66-71; C Caerau w Ely 71-72; Chapl Pontypridd Hosps 72-89; V Graig *Llan* 72-89; P-in-c Cilfynydd 86-89; V Llantwit Fardre 89-07; Chapl E Glam Hosp 89-99; RD Pontypridd 99-05; Hon Can Llan Cathl 04-07; Chapl Pontypridd and Rhondda NHS Trust 99-01; rtd 07. *Nanteos, 7 Meadow Hill, Church Village, Pontypridd CF38 1RX* Tel (01443) 217213 E-mail melville_k.jones@virgin.net

JONES, Michael. *See* JONES, David Michael

JONES, Michael. *See* JONES, Canon Gordon Michael Campbell

JONES, Michael. b 49. Leeds Univ BA71 Man Univ MA73. Qu Coll Birm 83. **d** 85 **p** 86. C Leigh St Mary *Man* 85-88; C-in-c Holts CD 88-93; V Hamer 93-05; Perm to Offic 06-08. *Ty Coch Cottage, Llangynhafal, Ruthin LL15 1RT*
E-mail mike@ashborn.force9.co.uk

JONES, Michael Adrian. b 62. Reading Univ BSc83 PGCE84. Trin Coll Bris 07. **d** 09. C Bath Weston All SS w N Stoke and Langridge *B & W* from 09. *23 Lucklands Road, Bath BA1 4AX*
E-mail adrianjones.bath@tiscali.co.uk

JONES, Michael Barry. b 48. MCIEH88 MIOSH88. ERMC 04. **d** 07 **p** 08. NSM Whittlesey, Pondersbridge and Coates *Ely* from 07. *20 White Horse Gardens, March PE15 8AG* Tel (01354) 653456

JONES, Michael Christopher. b 67. Southn Univ BSc88. St Jo Coll Nottm MTh03 MA04. **d** 04 **p** 05. C Aldridge *Lich* 04-07; V Lilleshall and Muxton from 07. *The Vicarage, 25 Church Road, Lilleshall, Newport TF10 9HE* Tel (01952) 604281

JONES, Michael Denis Dyson. b 39. CCC Cam BA62 MA66 Lon Univ MSc73. Wycliffe Hall Ox. **d** 76 **p** 77. C Plymouth St Andr w St Paul and St Geo *Ex* 76-81; V Devonport St Budeaux 81-00; RD Plymouth Devonport 93-95; TV Barnstaple 00-07; RD Barnstaple 03-07; rtd 07. *The Spinney, 40 West Drive, Harrow HA3 6TS* Tel (020) 8954 1530 E-mail mddjamj@onetel.com

JONES, Michael Emlyn. b 47. Aber Univ MB, ChB72 MRCP75 FRCP95. **d** 79 **p** 79. Asst P Moshi St Marg Tanzania 79-82; NSM Duns *Edin* 83-99; NSM Dalkeith from 02; NSM Lasswade from 02. *255 Carnethie Street, Rosewell EH24 9DR* Tel 0131-440 2602 or 653 6767 Fax 653 3646 Mobile 07710-276208
E-mail michaelejones@doctors.org.uk

JONES, Michael Gerald. b 46. Ban Ord Course 05. **d** 07 **p** 08. NSM Ystumaner *Ban* from 07. *Bryn-Hyfryd, 1 St Mary's Terrace, Arthog LL39 1BQ* Tel (01341) 250406

JONES, Michael Kevin. b 57. Llan Ord Course 94. **d** 98 **p** 99. NSM Caerau w Ely *Llan* 98-00; NSM Cen Cardiff 01; P-in-c Tremorfa St Phil CD 02-05; Area Fundraising Manager Children's Soc *Llan* and *Mon* 98-00; Ch Strategy Manager Wales 01-02; Lic to Offic *Llan* 05-09; V Mountain Ash and Miskin from 09. *5 Lon-y-Felin, Cefn Pennar, Mountain Ash CF45 4ES* Tel (01443) 473700

JONES, Morgan. *See* JONES, Frederick Morgan

JONES, Canon Neil Crawford. b 42. Univ of Wales BA63 K Coll Lon BD66 AKC66. **d** 67 **p** 68. C Holywell *St As* 67-69; C Rhyl w St Ann 69-73; C Christchurch *Win* 73-77; V Stanmore 77-84; RD Win 82-84; V Romsey 84-07; RD Romsey 89-94; Hon Can Win Cathl 93-07; rtd 07. *1 The Brambles, Rosemary Lane, Leintwardine, Craven Arms SY7 0LR* Tel (01547) 540333

JONES, Nerissa. *See* JONES, Canon Mary Nerissa Anna

JONES, Canon Neville George. b 36. Univ of Wales (Ban) BA59. St Mich Coll Llan 59. **d** 61 **p** 62. C Broughton *St As* 61-65; C Newcastle *Llan* 65-68; V Laleston w Tythegston 68-84; V Llanishen and Lisvane 84-93; V Llanishen 93-02; Hon Can Llan Cathl 96-02; rtd 02. *21 Cwm Gwynlais, Tongwynlais, Cardiff CF15 7HU* Tel (029) 2081 1150

JONES, Nicholas Godwin. b 58. St Jo Coll Cam BA81 MA84 Hughes Hall Cam PGCE90. Ridley Hall Cam 91. **d** 93 **p** 94. C Cambridge H Trin *Ely* 93-97; Chapl St Bede's Sch 94-97; C Fulbourn w Gt and Lt Wilbraham 97-00; V Harston w Hauxton and Newton 00-03; V Gt Horton *Bradf* from 03. *The Vicarage, 30 Bartle Close, Bradford BD7 4QH* Tel (01274) 521456 *or* 572002 Mobile 07957-387698
E-mail nick.jones@bradford.anglican.org
or vicarofstjohns@aol.com

JONES, Nicholas Peter. b 55. St Mich Coll Llan. **d** 82 **p** 83. C St Andrews Major w Michaelston-le-Pit *Llan* 82-84; C Aberdare 84-88; Youth Chapl 85-89; V Abercynon 88-96; R Llanilid w Pencoed from 96. *The Rectory, 60 Coychurch Road, Pencoed, Bridgend CF35 5NA* Tel (01656) 860337

JONES, Nigel David. b 69. Qu Coll Cam MA95. Westcott Ho Cam 97. **d** 00 **p** 01. C Abbots Langley *St Alb* 00-03; TV Dunstable 03-08; V Caversham St Andr *Ox* from 08. *St Andrew's Vicarage, Harrogate Road, Reading RG4 7PW* Tel 0118-947 2788

JONES, Nigel Ivor. b 54. Sheff Univ MMin04. WMMTC 91. **d** 94 **p** 95. C Shirley *Birm* 94-99; TV Salter Street and Shirley 99-01; V Olton 01-08; rtd 08. *41 Innage Lane, Bridgnorth WV16 4HS* Tel (01746) 763637 Mobile 07857-828300
E-mail revnigel@aol.com

JONES, Norman. b 50. Oak Hill Th Coll BA83. **d** 83 **p** 84. C Ulverston St Mary w H Trin *Carl* 83-87; Hong Kong 88-92; TR Eccles *Man* 92-01; AD Eccles 95-00; R Haslemere and Grayswood *Guildf* from 01; RD Godalming 02-07; Chapl Wispers Sch Haslemere from 01. *The Rectory, 7 Derby Road, Haslemere GU27 1BS* Tel (01428) 658107 *or* tel and fax 644578 E-mail revnjones@aol.com

✠**JONES, The Rt Revd Noël Debroy.** b 32. CB86. Univ of Wales (Lamp) BA53. Wells Th Coll 53. **d** 55 **p** 56 **c** 89. C Tredegar St Jas *Mon* 55-57; C Newport St Mark 57-60; V Kano Nigeria 60-62; Chapl RN 62-84; Chapl of the Fleet and Adn for the RN 84-89; QHC from 83; Hon Can Gib Cathl from 86; Bp S & M 89-03; rtd 03; Hon Asst Bp York from 03. *The Sudreys, Pickering Road, Thornton Dale, Pickering YO18 7LH*
E-mail holy.noellee@sagainternet.co.uk

JONES, Ormond. *See* JONES, David Ormond

JONES, Mrs Patricia Ann. b 43. **d** 97 **p** 98. OLM Bincombe w Broadwey, Upwey and Buckland Ripers *Sarum* 97-05. *23 Camedown Close, Weymouth DT3 5RB* Tel (01305) 813056

JONES, Mrs Patricia Anne. b 55. CSS81. Oak Hill Th Coll 92. **d** 95. NSM Mill Hill Jo Keble Ch *Lon* 95-01; NSM Queensbury All SS 01-08; Perm to Offic from 08. *The Flat, St Paul's School, The Ridgeway, London NW7 1QU* Tel (020) 8201 1583

JONES, Canon Patrick Geoffrey Dickson. b 28. Ch Ch Ox BA51 MA55 Aber Univ MLitt98. St Deiniol's Hawarden 79. **d** 82 **p** 83. NSM Sandbach *Ches* 82-84; R Aboyne 84-96; R Ballater 84-96; P-in-c Braemar 84-96; rtd 96; Hon Can St Andr Cathl from 01. *Byebush of Fedderate, New Deer, Turriff AB53 6UL* Tel (01771) 644110 E-mail pg.dj@tiscali.co.uk

JONES, Patrick George. b 42. Cant Ch Ch Univ Coll MA99. Lich Th Coll 69. **d** 72 **p** 73. C Chesterton St Geo *Ely* 72-75; P-in-c Waterbeach 75-78; P-in-c Landbeach 76-78; R Charlton-in-Dover *Cant* 78-90; Chapl Cautley Ho 90-06; rtd 06. *28 North Salts, Rye TN31 7NU* Tel (01797) 222958

JONES, Paul Anthony. b 72. Cov Univ BSc95. Ripon Coll Cuddesdon BTh99. **d** 99 **p** 00. C Dolgellau w Llanfachreth and Brithdir etc *Ban* 99-02; P-in-c Ffestiniog w Blaenau Ffestiniog 02-04; Perm to Offic *Newc* 06-07; Hon C Long Benton St Mary from 07. *10 Manor Grove, Benton, Newcastle upon Tyne NE7 7XQ* Tel 0191-270 1429 E-mail monty@classicfm.net

JONES, Paul Evan. b 62. York Univ BA84 CPFA89. SEITE 02. **d** 05 **p** 06. C Kingstanding St Luke *Birm* 05-09; P-in-c Babbacombe *Ex* from 09. *Babbacombe Vicarage, 4 Cary Park, Torquay TQ1 3NH* Tel (01803) 323002
E-mail liberty.hall@tiscali.co.uk

JONES, Paul Terence. b 35. Dur Univ BA60. Qu Coll Birm 60. **d** 62 **p** 63. C Rainford *Liv* 62-65; C Skelmersdale St Paul 65-68; V Huyton Quarry 68-78; V Widnes St Ambrose 78-00; rtd 00; Perm to Offic *Liv* from 00. *9 Hunter Court, Prescot L34 2UH* Tel 0151-430 6057

JONES, Penelope Howson. b 58. Girton Coll Cam BA80 MA83 LGSM79. Ripon Coll Cuddesdon BA85 MA88. **dss** 86 **d** 87 **p** 94. Hackney *Lon* 86-87; Par Dn 87-88; Tutor Ripon Coll Cuddesdon 88-90; Par Dn Cuddesdon *Ox* 88-90; Perm to Offic *Dur* 92-95; Dir Practical Th NEOC *Newc* 93-97; Hon C Eastgate w Rookhope *Dur* 93-97; Hon C Stanhope w Frosterley 93-97; Perm to Offic *York* 93-97; P-in-c Stanhope w Frosterley *Dur* 97-01; P-in-c Eastgate w Rookhope 97-01; Woman Adv in Min 97-01; Hon Can Dur Cathl 98-01; Sen Assoc P Gosford Australia from 01. *78 Henry Parry Drive, PO Box 4255, Gosford East NSW 2250, Australia* Tel (0061) (2) 4324 2630
E-mail redimp@bigpong.com

JONES, Canon Peter Anthony Watson. b 53. AKC75. Sarum & Wells Th Coll 76. **d** 77 **p** 78. C Hessle *York* 77-81; C Stainton-in-Cleveland 81-82; P-in-c Weston Mill *Ex* 82-84; Chapl Plymouth Poly 82-90; V Gt Ayton w Easby and Newton-in-Cleveland *York* 90-92; C Devonport St Aubyn *Ex* 92-98; P-in-c Yealmpton and Brixton 98-01; Team Chapl Portsm Hosps NHS Trust 01-05; Chapl Portsm Univ 05-09; Can Res Portsm Cathl 05-09; R Havant from 09; Dioc Interfaith Adv from 06. *St Faith's Rectory, 5 Meadowlands, Havant PO9 2RP* Tel (023) 9248 3485
E-mail canon@stfaith.com

JONES, Peter Charles. b 57. Univ of Wales BA81 MA82 PGCE97. St Mich Coll Llan 80. **d** 83 **p** 84. C Pontnewynydd *Mon* 83-85; C Bassaleg 85-87; TV Cwmbran 87-94; V Blaenavon w Capel Newydd 94-01; Chapl CME 00-01; Chapl and Fell Trin Coll Carmarthen 01-05; V Llangennech and Hendy *St D* from 05; AD Cydweli from 08. *The Vicarage, 2A Mwrwg Road, Llangennech, Llanelli SA14 8UA* Tel (01554) 820324

JONES, Peter David. b 48. S'wark Ord Course 89. **d** 92 **p** 93. NSM Coulsdon St Andr *S'wark* 92-04; Perm to Offic from 04. *79 Beverley Road, Whyteleafe CR3 0DU* Tel (020) 8668 6398

JONES, Peter Gordon Lewis. b 31. Llan Dioc Tr Scheme. **d** 82 **p** 83. NSM Llangynwyd w Maesteg 82-84; Deputation Appeals Org (S & M Glam) CECS 84-87; Appeals Manager (Wales and Glouc) Children's Soc 87-97; NSM Pyle w Kenfig *Llan* 89-97; rtd 97. *18 Fulmar Road, Porthcawl CF36 3UL* Tel (01656) 785455 Mobile 07785-755399

JONES, Peter Henry. b 50. Qu Coll Cam MA72 Ex Univ CertEd73 Bradf Univ MSc81 Nottm Univ MA05. EMMTC 02. **d** 05 **p** 06. NSM Annesley w Newstead *S'well* from 05. *3 Roland Avenue, Nuthall, Nottingham NG16 1BB* Tel 0115-975 1868
E-mail maryandpeterjones@btinternet.com

JONES, Peter Owen. b 64. Hull Univ BSc86. Oak Hill Th Coll BA08. **d** 08 **p** 09. C Hubberston *St D* from 08. *95 Waterloo Road, Hakin, Milford Haven SA73 3PE* Tel (01646) 697649
E-mail peter@ojones.plus.com

JONES, Peter Robin. b 42. Open Univ BA75 Bp Otter Coll Chich CertEd68. EMMTC 79. **d** 82 **p** 83. NSM Doveridge *Derby* 82-97; NSM Doveridge, Scropton, Sudbury etc from 98; Bp's Inspector of Th Colls and Courses from 98; Perm to Offic *Lich* from 93. *4 Cross Road, Uttoxeter ST14 7BN* Tel (01889) 565123
E-mail rev.jon@talktalk.net

JONES, Canon Peter Russell. b 48. St Jo Coll Cam BA71 MA75 Univ of Wales MTh86. Wycliffe Hall Ox. **d** 75 **p** 76. C Northampton All SS w St Kath *Pet* 75-79; C Ban Cathl 79-81; Min Can Ban Cathl 79-81; R Pentraeth and Llanddyfnan 81-85; V Conwy w Gyffin from 85; Lect Univ of Wales (Ban) 89-95; AD Arllechwedd *Ban* from 96; Can and Treas Ban Cathl from 99. *The Vicarage, Rose Hill Street, Conwy LL32 8LD* Tel (01492) 593402

JONES, The Ven Philip Hugh. b 51. Solicitor. Chich Th Coll 92. **d** 94 **p** 95. C Horsham *Chich* 94-97; V Southwater 97-05; RD Horsham 02-04; Adn Lewes and Hastings from 05. *27 The Avenue, Lewes BN7 1QT* Tel (01273) 479530
E-mail archlandh@diochi.org.uk

JONES, Philip Malcolm. b 43. Qu Coll Birm. **d** 04 **p** 05. NSM Birm St Paul 04-08; P-in-c Heathfield St Rich *Chich* from 08. *St Richard's Vicarage, Hailsham Road, Heathfield TN21 8AF* Tel (01435) 862744 E-mail malcolm@peri.co.uk

JONES, Philip Smith. b 53. St Mich Coll Llan 75. **d** 79 **p** 80. C Milford Haven *St D* 79-82; Asst Chapl Miss to Seamen 82-84; C Orford St Andr *Liv* 84-85; C Walton St Luke 85-87; C Gt Crosby St Faith 87; C Blundellsands St Nic 87-88; Perm to Offic *St D* 05-07; Hon C Cwm Gwendraeth 07-08; P-in-c Llansteffan and Llan-y-bri etc from 08. *The Vicarage, Church Road, Llansteffan, Carmarthen SA33 5JT* Tel (01267) 241280
E-mail meryljones@lothlorien22.freeserve.co.uk

JONES, Philip Thomas Henry. b 34. Qu Coll Birm 58. **d** 60 **p** 61. C Castle Bromwich SS Mary and Marg *Birm* 60-67; C Reading St Mary V *Ox* 67-72; C-in-c Reading All SS CD 72-75; V Reading All SS 75-93; Perm to Offic *Portsm* from 97; Hon Chapl Portsm Cathl from 97. *13 Oyster Street, Portsmouth PO1 2HZ* Tel (023) 9275 6676

JONES, Canon Phillip Bryan. b 34. St Mich Coll Llan. **d** 61 **p** 62. C Hope *St As* 61-64; C Llanrhos 64-67; V Kerry 67-74; R Newtown w Llanllwchaiarn w Aberhafesp 74-97; RD Cedewain 76-97; Sec Ch in Wales Prov Evang Cttee 80-83; Hon Can St As Cathl 86-93; Can 93-97; rtd 97. *7 Dalton Drive, Shrewsbury SY3 8DA* Tel (01743) 351426

JONES, Phillip Edmund. b 56. Man Poly BA78 Fitzw Coll Cam BA84 MA88 GradCIPD79. Westcott Ho Cam 82. **d** 85 **p** 86. C Stafford St Jo and Tixall w Ingestre *Lich* 85-89; TV Redditch, The Ridge *Worc* 89-95; TV Worc SE 95-08; Ind Chapl 89-08; Team Ldr Worcs Ind Miss 01-08; Team Ldr and Chapl Faith at Work in Worcs from 08; C Worc St Barn w Ch Ch from 08. *7 Egremont Gardens, Worcester WR4 0QH* Tel (01905) 755037
E-mail phillipjones@faithatwork.co.uk

JONES, Phyllis Gwendoline Charlotte. b 44. **d** 05 **p** 06. OLM Talbot Village *Sarum* from 05. *Bluebell Cottage, 112 Wallisdown Road, Bournemouth BH10 4HY* Tel (01202) 528956
E-mail revphyllisjones@fsmail.net

JONES, Ray. *See* JONES, David Raymond

JONES, Raymond. b 43. NOC 99. **d** 02 **p** 03. NSM Ashton-in-Makerfield St Thos *Liv* 02-03; C Widnes St Mary w St Paul 03-05; V 05-08; rtd 08. *4 Norlands Park, Widnes WA8 5BH*

JONES, Raymond Alban. b 34. RGN55 RMN63. Chich Th Coll 64. **d** 67 **p** 68. C Ocker Hill *Lich* 67-70; C Truro St Paul 70-71; Chapl Selly Oak Hosp Birm 71-76; USPG Bahamas 76-79; Chapl Hospice of Our Lady and St Jo Willen 80-83; Chapl St Jas Hosp Balham 83-87; NSM Leamington Spa H Trin and Old Milverton *Cov* 87-92; TV Probus, Ladock and Grampound w Creed and St Erme *Truro* 92-94; rtd 94; Perm to Offic *Sarum* from 09. *2 St Catherine's Terrace, Rodden Row, Abbotsbury, Weymouth DT3 4JL* Tel (01305) 871836

JONES, Raymond Blake. b 29. K Coll Lon BD54 AKC54. **d** 55 **p** 56. C Fenny Stratford *Ox* 55-58; C Lt Brickhill 55-58; C Wooburn 58-60; C Southbourne St Kath *Win* 60-66; R Braiseworth *St E* 66-76; V Eye 66-76; P-in-c Yaxley 74-77; RD Hartismere 76-77; V Eye w Braiseworth and Yaxley 77; R Ufford 77-82; Chapl St Audry's Hosp Melton 77-82; V Southbourne St Kath *Win* 82-95; rtd 95; Perm to Offic *Win* from 95. *4 Russell Drive, Riverslea, Christchurch BH23 3PA* Tel (01202) 473205

JONES, Raymond Sydney. b 35. MSERT71. Glouc Th Course 85. **d** 87 **p** 88. NSM Madley *Heref* 87-89; NSM Preston-on-Wye w Blakemere 87-89; NSM Madley w Tyberton, Preston-on-Wye and Blakemere 89; Chapl St Mich Hospice Hereford 90-00; Perm to Offic *Heref* 00-06. *The Old Cedars, Much Birch, Hereford HR2 8HR* Tel (01981) 540851

JONES, Canon Raymond Trevor. b 35. Linc Th Coll. **d** 82 **p** 83. C Rushmere *St E* 82-85; Bp's Dom Chapl 85-86; CF 86-91; TV Ridgeway *Sarum* 91-97; Relig Programmes Producer BBC Wiltshire Sound 91-97; Chapl Fuengirola St Andr *Eur* 97-00; P-in-c Ypres from 00; P-in-c Ostend 06-08; Can Gib Cathl from 04. *MLK Haiglaan 12, B 8900, Ypres, Belgium* Tel (0032) (5) 721 5685 Fax 721 5927 E-mail raymondstg@hotmail.com

JONES, Ms Rhiannon Elizabeth. b 72. Ex Univ BA93 Brunel Univ MA95 Anglia Poly Univ MA05. Ridley Hall Cam 98. **d** 00 **p** 01. C Huntingdon *Ely* 00-04; R Fulbourn from 04; V Gt Wilbraham from 04; R Lt Wilbraham from 04. *The Rectory, 2 Apthorpe Street, Fulbourn, Cambridge CB21 5EY* Tel (01223) 880337 E-mail rhiannon.jones@ely.anglican.org

JONES, Richard. *See* JONES, James Richard

JONES, Richard. b 23. BEM. St Deiniol's Hawarden 74. **d** 76 **p** 77. NSM Welshpool w Castle Caereinion *St As* 76-94; rtd 94. *Sherwood, Rhos Common, Llandrinio, Llanymynech SY22 6RN* Tel (01691) 830534

JONES, Canon Richard. b 28. St D Coll Lamp 54. **d** 56 **p** 57. C Llanaber w Caerdeon *Ban* 56-61; R Aberffraw w Llangwyfan 61-74; CF (TA) 61-71; V Llanfairisgaer *Ban* 74-79; Bp's Private Chapl 78-82; V Llanfair-is-gaer and Llanddeiniolen 79-89; RD Arfon 82-89; Can Ban Cathl from 86; V Llandegfan w Llandysilio 89-96; Chapl ATC from 90; rtd 96; Perm to Offic *Ban* from 96. *Bryniau, Rhostrehwfa, Llangefni LL77 7YS* Tel (01248) 724609

JONES, Richard Christopher Bentley. b 53. Pemb Coll Ox BA77 MA79. SEITE 03. **d** 06 **p** 07. NSM Clapham H Trin and St Pet *S'wark* from 06. *68 Mysore Road, London SW11 5SB* Tel (020) 7228 8965 E-mail rcb.jones@tiscali.co.uk

JONES, Richard Eifion. b 23. St D Dioc Tr Course 80 St Mich Coll Llan 84. **d** 82 **p** 83. NSM Llangennech and Hendy *St D* 82-84; C Llanbadarn Fawr w Capel Bangor and Goginan 84-86; V Llangadog and Gwynfe w Llanddeusant 86-91; rtd 91. *Gercoed, 186 St Teilo Street, Pontarddulais, Swansea SA4 8LH* Tel (01792) 882234

JONES, Richard Keith. b 40. Jes Coll Ox BA63. Wycliffe Hall Ox 61. **d** 63 **p** 64. C Blaenavon w Capel Newydd *Mon* 63-67; C Mynyddislwyn 67-71; C Pontypool 71; V Abercarn 71-81; V Penhow, St Brides Netherwent w Llandavenny etc 81-88. *32 Quantock Court, South Esplanade, Burnham-on-Sea TA8 1DL* Tel (01278) 458123

JONES, Robert. b 26. Lon Univ BA52 K Coll Lon BD65 Hull Univ MA82. St Deiniol's Hawarden 79. **d** 80 **p** 81. NSM Doncaster St Mary *Sheff* 80-81; C Halifax St Jo Bapt *Wakef* 81-83; P-in-c Dewsbury St Mark 83-84; TV Dewsbury 84-92; rtd 92; P-in-c Halifax St Jo *Wakef* 92-95; Perm to Offic 95-04 and from 06. *46 College Avenue, Huddersfield HD3 3LQ* Tel (01484) 531982

JONES, Robert. b 40. **d** 80 **p** 81. C St Laur in Thanet *Cant* 80-83. *Erbacher Strasse 72, 64287 Darmstadt, Germany* Tel (0049) (6151) 422913

JONES, Robert. b 45. Culham Coll Ox CertEd67. St Steph Ho Ox. **d** 85 **p** 86. C High Wycombe *Ox* 85-89; V Beckenham St Barn *Roch* 89-90; C Swanley St Mary 90-91; C Edenbridge from 91; C Crockham Hill H Trin from 91. *The Vicarage, Oakdale Lane, Crockham Hill, Edenbridge TN8 6RL* Tel (01732) 866515 Fax 864352 E-mail bob.jones@diocese-rochester.org

JONES, Robert Cecil. b 32. Univ of Wales (Abth) BA54 DipEd55. Qu Coll Birm 84. **d** 86 **p** 87. C Llanbadarn Fawr w Capel Bangor and Goginan *St D* 86-88; R Llanllwchaearn and Llanina 88-91; R Newport w Cilgwyn and Dinas w Llanllawer 91-98; rtd 98; Perm to Offic *Derby* from 05. *Old Craigstead Works, High Street, Stoney Middleton, Hope Valley S32 4TL* Tel (01433) 631857

JONES, Robert David. b 73. UCD BSc97 TCD BTh07. CITC 04. **d** 07 **p** 08. C Dublin St Patr Cathl Gp from 07. *25 Knockwaree Avenue, Dublin 12, Republic of Ireland* Tel (00353) 86-285 4098 (mobile)

JONES, Canon Robert George. b 42. St Mich Coll Llan 93. **d** 95 **p** 96. NSM Treboeth *S & B* 95-02; P-in-c Treboeth 02-07; P-in-c Landore 03-07; Can Res Brecon Cathl 06-07; rtd 07. *Green*

Gables, 42 Heol Fach, Treboeth, Swansea SA5 9DE Tel (01792) 540530

JONES, Canon Robert George. b 55. Hatf Coll Dur BA77 Ox Univ BA79 MA87. Ripon Coll Cuddesdon 77. **d** 80 **p** 81. C Foley Park *Worc* 80-84; V Dudley St Fran 84-92; TR Worc St Barn w Ch Ch 92-06; Dir Development from 06; RD Worc E 99-05; Hon Can Worc Cathl from 03. *4 Silverdale Avenue, Worcester WR5 1PY* Tel (01905) 769590 E-mail rjones@cofe-worcester.org.uk

JONES, Robert Ivan. b 33. Bede Coll Dur CertEd57. Westcott Ho Cam 85. **d** 85 **p** 86. NSM Wymondham *Nor* 85-86; C Epsom St Martin *Guildf* 87-89; V Hutton Cranswick w Skerne, Watton and Beswick *York* 89-94; RD Harthill 92-97; V Wetwang and Garton-on-the-Wolds w Kirkburn 94-98; V Waggoners 98-00; rtd 00; P-in-c Newbald *York* 00-04; Perm to Offic from 04. *North Wing, Saxby Hall, 72 Main Street, Saxby-All-Saints, Brigg DN20 0QB* Tel (01652) 618036 E-mail beemajo@onetel.com

JONES, The Very Revd Robert William. b 55. Open Univ BA85 MA88. Ian Ramsey Coll 75 Chich Th Coll 76 TCD Div Sch 77. **d** 79 **p** 80. C Seapatrick *D & D* 79; C Bangor Abbey 81-83; I Drumgath w Drumgooland and Clonduff 83-89; I Finaghy *Conn* 89-93; I Kilwaughter w Cairncastle and Craigy Hill 94-98; I Athlone w Benown, Kiltoom and Forgney *M & K* 98-02; Dean Clonmacnoise from 02; I Trim and Athboy Gp from 02. *St Patrick's Deanery, Loman Street, Trim, Co Meath, Republic of Ireland* Tel (00353) (46) 943 6698 Mobile 87-290 8344 E-mail trimdeanery@iolfree.ie

JONES, Robert William Aplin. b 32. Univ of Wales (Cardiff) BSc52 MSc65 FRSC71 CChem72. St Deiniol's Hawarden 72. **d** 73 **p** 74. C Bassaleg *Mon* 73-77; V Nantyglo 77-82; Perm to Offic 82-86; R Colwinston w Llandow and Llysworney 86-95; rtd 95; Perm to Offic *St D* from 99. *Golwg-y-Lan, Heol Castell Ganol, Newport SA42 0RR* Tel (01239) 820297 Mobile 07968-173759

JONES, Robin Dominic Edwin. b 78. St Chad's Coll Dur BA00 K Coll Lon MA01. St Steph Ho Ox MTh07. **d** 04 **p** 05. C Ealing Ch the Sav *Lon* 04-08; V Hammersmith St Luke from 08. *St Luke's Vicarage, 450 Uxbridge Road, London W12 0NS* Tel (020) 8749 7523 Mobile 07779-299924 E-mail fr.robin@stlukesw12.com

JONES, Roderick. b 48. Leeds Univ BA70 PGCE72. Westmr Th Sem (USA) 73 Oak Hill Th Coll 74. **d** 76 **p** 77. C Beckenham Ch Ch *Roch* 76-80; C Uphill *B & W* 80-84; R Springfield All SS *Chelmsf* 84-90; Selection Sec ABM 91-96; V Horsell *Guildf* from 96. *The Vicarage, Wilson Way, Horsell, Woking GU21 4QJ* Tel (01483) 772134 E-mail rjones2558@aol.com

JONES, Canon Roger. b 49. St Mich Coll Llan 84. **d** 86 **p** 87. C Llangynwyd w Maesteg 86-90; V Wiston w Walton E and Clarbeston *St D* 90-01; V Pembroke Gp 01-04; TV Monkton from 04; Can St D Cathl from 09. *The Vicarage, Lower Lamphey Road, Pembroke SA71 4AF* Tel and fax (01646) 682710 Mobile 07971-528933 E-mail roger@revjones.fsnet.co.uk

JONES, Russell Frederick. b 59. Man Univ BA77 Edin Univ BD84. Edin Th Coll 81. **d** 84 **p** 85. C Croxteth *Liv* 84-87; V Edgehill St Dunstan 87-98; R Glas St Bride 98-08; Hon Chapl Glas Univ 00-06. *14B Hatfield Drive, Glasgow G12 0YA* Tel 0141-339 7989 E-mail howisonandjones@btinternet.com

JONES, Mrs Sally. b 41. **d** 09. NSM Teme Valley N *Worc* from 09. *2 Old School House, Eastham, Tenbury Wells WR15 8PB* Tel (01584) 781526

JONES, Samuel. b 44. CITC. **d** 86 **p** 87. C Agherton *Conn* 86-88; I Connor w Antrim St Patr 88-97; I Whitehead and Islandmagee 97-01; Bp's C Kilbroney *D & D* from 01. *The Vicarage, 15 Kilbroney Road, Rostrevor, Newry BT34 3BH* Tel (028) 4173 8293

JONES, Sarah Charlotte. b 57. SRN79. SAOMC 01. **d** 04 **p** 05. NSM Forest Edge *Ox* from 04. *4 Tower Hill, Witney OX28 5ER* Tel (01993) 200483 E-mail sarahtandem@hotmail.com

JONES, Ms Sarah Jane. b 61. St Hugh's Coll Ox BA95 MA03 Northumbria Univ MSc02. Westcott Ho Cam 02. **d** 04 **p** 05. C Ross *Heref* 04-07; P-in-c 07-08; V Ross w Walford from 08. *The Rectory, Church Street, Ross-on-Wye HR9 5HN* Tel (01989) 562175 E-mail sarah@revsarah.demon.co.uk

JONES, Sebastian. *See* JONES, David Sebastian

JONES, Sharon. b 74. Liv Univ MA00 PhD05. Westcott Ho Cam 05. **d** 07 **p** 08. C Warwick *Cov* from 07. *1 All Saints Road, Warwick CV34 5NL* E-mail rev.sharonjones@googlemail.com

JONES, Mrs Sharon Ann. b 46. St Kath Coll Liv BA82. Cranmer Hall Dur 83. **dss** 85 **d** 87 **p** 94. Rubery *Birm* 85-89; Par Dn 87-89; C-in-c Chelmsley Wood St Aug CD 89-92; Perm to Offic *Newc* 92-93; Chapl HM Pris Acklington 93-97; Chapl HM YOI Castington 97-00; Chapl HM Pris Forest Bank 00-06; P-in-c Dearnley *Man* from 06; AD Salford 03-06; AD Rochdale 06-09. *St Andrew's Vicarage, Arm Road, Littleborough OL15 8NJ* Tel (01706) 378466 Mobile 07738-966271 E-mail vicar@dearnleyvicarage.plusnet.com

JONES, Mrs Shelagh Deirdre. b 46. St Mary's Coll Dur BA68. NEOC 01. **d** 04 **p** 05. NSM Burnby *York* from 04; NSM Londesborough from 04; NSM Nunburnholme and Warter and Huggate from 04; NSM Shiptonthorpe and Hayton from 04;

Chapl HM YOI Wetherby from 04. *HM Young Offender Institution, York Road, Wetherby LS22 5ED* Tel (01937) 544325 Fax 544201 Mobile 07971-054674
E-mail revd-shelagh@amserve.com

JONES, Canon Sian Eira. b 63. Univ of Wales (Lamp) BA84 Southn Univ BTh88. Sarum & Wells Th Coll 85. **d** 88 **p** 97. C Llan-llwch w Llangain and Llangynog *St D* 88-93; Dn-in-c Llansteffan and Llan-y-bri etc 93-97; V 97-06; AD Carmarthen 00-06; TR Llanelli from 06; Can St D Cathl from 09. *The Vicarage, 1 Cysgod y Llan, Llanelli SA15 3HD* Tel (01554) 772072

JONES, Sian Hilary. *See* WIGHT, Mrs Sian Hilary

JONES, Simon. b 63. Trin Coll Bris BA89. **d** 89 **p** 90. C Hildenborough *Roch* 89-93; C Crofton *Portsm* 93-96; C Northwood Em *Lon* 96-01; Min in charge Ignite 01-07; TR Stoke Gifford *Bris* from 07. *119 North Road, Stoke Gifford, Bristol BS34 8PE* Tel 0117-979 1656 *or* 969 2486 Fax 959 9264
E-mail simon@st-michaels-church.org.uk

JONES, Simon Matthew. b 72. SS Hild & Bede Coll Dur BA93 MA94 Selw Coll Cam PhD00 Ox Univ MA02 DPhil03. Westcott Ho Cam 95. **d** 99 **p** 00. C Tewkesbury w Walton Cardiff and Twyning *Glouc* 99-02; Chapl and Fell Mert Coll Ox from 02. *Merton College, Oxford OX1 4JD* Tel (01865) 276365 *or* 281793 Fax 276361 E-mail simon.jones@merton.ox.ac.uk

JONES, Stella Frances. TCD BTh02. CITC. **d** 02 **p** 03. C Bandon Union *C, C & R* 02-05; I Clonenagh w Offerlane, Borris-in-Ossory etc *C & O* from 05. *Clonenagh Rectory, Portlaoise Road, Mountrath, Co Laois, Republic of Ireland* Tel (00353) (57) 873 2146 E-mail clonenagh@ossory.anglican.org

JONES, Stephen. *See* JONES, Ernest Edward Stephen

JONES, Stephen Frederick. b 53. Magd Coll Ox BA75 MA79 Lon Univ BD89 Leeds Univ MA96. Linc Th Coll BCombStuds84. **d** 84 **p** 85. C Kingswinford St Mary *Lich* 84-87; Min Can, Succ and Dean's V Windsor 87-94; C Howden *York* 94-96; Chapl St Elphin's Sch Matlock 96-01; C Worksop Priory *S'well* 01-03; R Longton *Lich* from 03. *The Rectory, Rutland Road, Stoke-on-Trent ST3 1EH* Tel (01782) 595098

JONES, Stephen Leslie. b 59. Hull Univ BA80 Lanc Univ MA06. Sarum & Wells Th Coll 82. **d** 85 **p** 86. C Perry Barr *Birm* 85-88; C Blackpool St Steph *Blackb* 88-90; V Greenlands 90-95; V Carnforth from 95. *The Vicarage, North Road, Carnforth LA5 9LJ* Tel (01524) 732948
E-mail stephenjones17@hotmail.com

JONES, Stephen Richard. b 49. Heythrop Coll Lon MA01. Oak Hill Th Coll 72. **d** 75 **p** 76. C Welling *Roch* 75-79; C Cheltenham St Mark *Glouc* 79-82; V Shiregreen St Jas and St Chris *Sheff* 82-86; P-in-c Harold Hill St Geo *Chelmsf* 86-88; V 88-97; P-in-c Harold Hill St Paul 94-95; V Kippington *Roch* 97-08; RD Sevenoaks 00-05; R Ightham from 08. *The Rectory, Bates Hill, Ightham, Sevenoaks TN15 9BG* Tel (01732) 884176
E-mail srjones49@hotmail.com
or stephen.jones@diocese-rochester.org

JONES, Stephen William. b 46. K Coll Lon BD70 AKC70. **d** 71 **p** 72. C Streatham St Pet *S'wark* 71-76; C Leeds St Pet *Ripon* 76-79; C Leeds Richmond Hill 79-85; R Gourock *Glas* 85-88; V Porthleven w Sithney *Truro* 88-94; Miss to Seamen 88-94; P-in-c Portsea Ascension *Portsm* 96-00; V Grimsby St Aug *Linc* from 00. *St Augustine's Vicarage, 145 Legsby Avenue, Grimsby DN32 0LA* Tel (01472) 877109

JONES, Stewart William. b 57. Heriot-Watt Univ BA79 Bris Univ BA88. Trin Coll Bris 86. **d** 88 **p** 89. C Stoke Bishop *Bris* 88-92; P-in-c Brislington St Luke 92-97; Abp's Chapl and Dioc Missr *Cant* 97-03; P-in-c Cant All SS 01-05; AD Cant and Hon Prov Can Cant Cathl 02-05; R Birm St Martin w Bordesley St Andr from 05. *St Martin's Rectory, 37 Barlows Road, Birmingham B15 2PN* Tel 0121-604 0850 Mobile 07793-724949
E-mail stewart@bullring.org

JONES, Mrs Susan. b 55. Liv Hope BA03 St Jo Coll Dur MA05. Cranmer Hall Dur 03. **d** 05 **p** 06. C Skelmersdale St Paul *Liv* 05-09; TV Maghull and Melling from 09. *23 Green Link, Maghull L31 8DW* Tel 0151-526 6626
E-mail rev_sue@talktalk.net

JONES, Susan Helen. b 60. Trin Coll Carmarthen BEd2 MPhil94 Univ of Wales (Ban) PhD. Ripon Coll Cuddesdon 93. **d** 95 **p** 97. Chapl Univ of Wales (Swansea) *S & B* 95-98; Hon C Sketty 95-98; Dir Past Studies St Mich Coll Llan 98-00; TV Bangor from 00; AD Ogwen from 07. *Deiniol, 31 Trefonwys, Bangor LL57 2HU* Tel (01248) 355530
E-mail suejone@netscapeonline.co.uk

JONES, Susan Jean. b 47. Bp Grosseteste Coll CertEd68 Heythrop Coll Lon MA01. SAOMC 93. **d** 96 **p** 97. C S Ascot *Ox* 96-07; NSM 01-07; rtd 07. *Fairhaven, 1 St Clement's Terrace, Mousehole, Penzance TR19 6SJ* Tel (01736) 732938
E-mail sebastian143@btinternet.com

JONES, Susannah Hester Everett. **d** 07 **p** 08. NSM Bris St Mary Redcliffe w Temple etc from 07. *18 Fairfield Road, Montpellier, Bristol BS6 5JP* E-mail hester.jones@stmaryredcliffe.co.uk

JONES, Tegid Owen. b 27. Univ of Wales (Abth) LLB47. St Deiniol's Hawarden. **d** 68 **p** 69. C Rhosddu *St As* 68-71; C

Wrexham 71-75; R Marchwiel 75-83; R Marchwiel and Isycoed 83-92; RD Bangor Isycoed 86-92; rtd 92. *Teglys, 2 Bungalow, Pentre, Chirk, Wrexham LL14 5AW*

JONES, Theresa. *See* JONES, Mrs Mary Catherine Theresa Bridget

JONES, Thomas Glyndwr. b 41. Clifton Th Coll 65. **d** 65 **p** 66. C Islington St Mary *Lon* 65-69; USA from 69. *4425 Colchester Court, Columbus GA 31907-1682, USA* Tel (001) (706) 569 0314
E-mail welshwiz@knology.net

JONES, Canon Thomas Graham. b 33. St D Coll Lamp BA57. **d** 59 **p** 60. C Llanelli *St D* 59-64; V Ysbyty Cynfyn 64-69; V Ysbyty Cynfyn w Llantrisant 69-72; V Llanelli Ch Ch 72-94; RD Cydweli 89-93; V Carmarthen St Dav 94-00; Hon Can St D Cathl 93-99; Can from 99; RD Carmarthen 98-00; rtd 00. *32 Pen y Morfa, Llangunnor, Carmarthen SA31 2NP* Tel (01267) 231846

JONES, The Ven Thomas Hughie. b 27. Univ of Wales BA49 LLM94 Lon Univ BD53 Leic Univ MA72 FRSA. St Deiniol's Hawarden. **d** 66 **p** 67. Hon C Evington *Leic* 66-76; Hon C Kirby Muxloe 76-81; Dioc Adult Educn Officer 81-85; R Church Langton w Thorpe Langton and Tur Langton 81-85; Hon Can Leic Cathl 83-86; R Church Langton w Tur Langton, Thorpe Langton etc 85-86; Adn Loughborough 86-92; rtd 92; Perm to Offic *Leic* from 92. *Four Trees, 68 Main Street, Thorpe Satchville, Melton Mowbray LE14 2DQ* Tel (01664) 840262
E-mail thj@connectfree.co.uk

JONES, Thomas Percy Norman Devonshire. b 34. St Jo Coll Ox BA58 MA61 Lambeth MLitt02. Cuddesdon Coll 58. **d** 60 **p** 61. C Portsea St Cuth *Portsm* 60-61; C Portsea N End St Mark 61-67; Asst Chapl Portsm Tech Coll 67-70; Chapl Portsm Poly 70-73; Chapl Trin Coll Hartford USA 73-74; V Folkestone St Sav *Cant* 75-81; V Regent's Park St Mark *Lon* 81-00; rtd 00; Perm to Offic *Lon* from 00; Dir Art and Chr Enquiry Trust 94-06. *107 Crundale Avenue, London NW9 9PS* Tel and fax (020) 8204 7970 E-mail tomdevonshirejones@tiscali.co.uk

JONES, Canon Thomas Peter. b 20. Ex Coll Ox BA43 MA46. St Mich Coll Llan 43. **d** 45 **p** 46. C Wrexham *St As* 45-48; C Llandrillo-yn-Rhos 48-57; R Erbistock and Overton 57-78; Can St As Cathl 78-84; Preb and Prec St As Cathl 84-86; RD Bangor Isycoed 80-86; R Overton and Erbistock and Penley 83-86; rtd 86; Perm to Offic *Cov* 86-98; *St As* from 98. *18 All Hallows Close, Retford DN22 7UP* Tel (01777) 700481

JONES, Timothy Llewellyn. b 67. York Univ BA90. Ripon Coll Cuddesdon BA94. **d** 94 **p** 95. C Middlesbrough St Martin *York* 94-96; P-in-c Rounton w Welbury 96-02; Chapl HM YOI Northallerton 96-99; Adv for Young Adults and Voc (Cleveland) 99-02; R Corinth St Paul USA 02-07; P-in-c York St Hilda from 07; P-in-c York St Lawr w St Nic from 07. *St Hilda's Vicarage, 155 Tang Hall Lane, York YO10 3SD* Tel (01904) 412196 Mobile 07525-776406 E-mail tim.jones@yorklandh.org

JONES, Timothy Richard Nigel. b 54. Collingwood Coll Dur BSc75 Birm Univ MSc76 FGS. Trin Coll Bris 84. **d** 86 **p** 87. C Hailsham *Chich* 86-91; V Madley w Tyberton, Preston-on-Wye and Blakemere *Heref* 91-00; R Madley w Tyberton, Peterchurch, Vowchurch etc 00-06; V Taunton St Jas *B & W* from 06. *69 Richmond Road, Taunton TA1 1EN* Tel (01823) 333194
E-mail timjones@tesco.net

JONES, Trevor Blandon. b 43. Oak Hill Th Coll 77. **d** 80 **p** 81. NSM Homerton St Barn w St Paul *Lon* 80-83; NSM Harlow New Town w Lt Parndon *Chelmsf* 83-90; C 90-92; V Leyton Em 92-01; rtd 02; Perm to Offic *Chelmsf* from 03. *5 Wheatley Close, Sawbridgeworth CM21 0HS* Tel (01279) 600248
E-mail rev.trev@lineone.net

JONES, Trevor Edwin. b 49. Heythrop Coll Lon MA05. Ripon Coll Cuddesdon 74. **d** 76 **p** 77. C Cannock *Lich* 76-79; C Middlesbrough Ascension *York* 79-81; V Oldham St Steph and All Martyrs *Man* 81-84; V Perry Beeches *Birm* 84-90; P-in-c Saltley 90-93; P-in-c Shaw Hill 90-93; V Saltley and Shaw Hill 93-97; R Lon Docks St Pet w Wapping St Jo from 97. *St Peter's Clergy House, Wapping Lane, London E1W 2RW* Tel (020) 7481 2985 Fax 7265 1100
E-mail fatherjones@stpeterslondondocks.org.uk
or frtejones@aol.com

JONES, The Ven Trevor Pryce. b 48. Southn Univ BEd76 BTh79 Univ of Wales (Cardiff) LLM04. Sarum & Wells Th Coll 73. **d** 76 **p** 77. C Glouc St Geo 76-79; Warden Bp Mascall Cen *Heref* 79-84; Dioc Communications Officer 81-86; TR Heref S Wye 84-97; Preb Heref Cathl 93-97; OCF 85-97; Adn Hertford and Hon Can St Alb from 97. *Glebe House, St Mary's Lane, Hertingfordbury, Hertford SG14 2LE* Tel (01992) 581629 Fax 535349 E-mail archdhert@stalbans.anglican.org.uk

JONES, Canon Tudor Howell. b 39. Univ of Wales (Cardiff) BD91. St Mich Coll Llan. **d** 68 **p** 69. C Clydach *S & B* 68-72; C Swansea St Pet 72-75; V Ystradfellte 75-79; V Llangiwg 79-91; V Manselton 91-05; RD Penderi 98-05; Can Res Brecon Cathl 00-05; rtd 05. *15 Glasfryn Close, Cockett, Swansea SA2 0FP*

JONES, Victor Harvey. b 25. St D Coll Lamp BA53. Coll of Resurr Mirfield. **d** 55 **p** 56. C Canton St Luke *Llan* 55-57; C Caerau w Ely 57-61; Chapl RN 62-76; Perm to Offic *Truro* 77-80;

C Portishead *B & W* 80-83; rtd 83; Perm to Offic *Ex* 92-98 and *Chich* from 04. *17 Beech Road, Findon, Worthing BN14 0UR* Tel (01903) 873461

JONES, Preb Wilfred David. b 22. Keble Coll Ox BA47 MA48. St Mich Coll Llan 47. **d** 48 **p** 49. C Aberaman *Llan* 48-50; C Cardiff St Jo 50-55; Chapl Kelly Coll Tavistock 55-62; V St Decumans *B & W* 62-76; V Ilminster w Whitelackington 76-92; RD Ilminster 78-87; Preb Wells Cathl from 81; rtd 92; Perm to Offic *B & W* 92-06. *Dragons, Lambrook Road, Shepton Beauchamp, Ilminster TA19 0NA* Tel (01460) 240967

JONES, Wilfred Lovell. b 39. Lon Univ BD71 Cam Univ CertEd. St D Coll Lamp. **d** 63 **p** 64. C Llanllyfni *Ban* 63-65; C Llanbeblig w Caernarfon 65-68; V Llanwnog w Penstrowed 68-73; V Llanwnnog and Caersws w Carno 73-75; Asst Chapl Dover Coll 77-90; Chapl Wrekin Coll Telford 91-94; V Llangollen w Trevor and Llantysilio *St As* 94-04; AD Llangollen 03-04; rtd 04. *7 Beech Hollows, Lavister, Rossett LL12 0DA* Tel (01244) 579225

JONES, Canon William. b 30. BTh92. St Mich Coll Llan 54. **d** 55 **p** 56. C Denio w Abererch *Ban* 55-60; V Aberdaron and Bodferin 60-66; R Llandwrog 66-71; R Llanstumdwy, Llangybi w Llanarmon 71-74; R Dolbenmaen w Llanystymdwy w Llangybi etc 74-99; RD Eifionydd 75-99; Can *Ban* Cathl 84-93; Can and Treas Ban Cathl 93-99; rtd 99; Perm to Offic *Ban* from 99. *Y Fachwen, Rhoshirwaun, Pwllheli LL53 8LB* Tel (01758) 760262

JONES, Canon William David. b 28. St D Coll Lamp BA48 Lon Univ BD57 Leeds Univ MA73. St Mich Coll Llan 48. **d** 51 **p** 52. C Risca *Mon* 51-54; C Chepstow St Arvan's w Penterry 54-55; C St Geo-in-the-East w Ch Ch w St Jo *Lon* 55-59; C Farnham Royal *Ox* 59-64; Lect Div Culham Coll 65-67; Hd RS Doncaster Coll of Educn 67-74; Vice-Prin St Bede Coll Dur 74; Vice-Prin SS Hild and Bede Coll Dur 75-89; Lect Th Dur Univ 75-89; Dir of Miss Ch in Wales 89-93; Metropolitical and Hon Can St D Cathl 90-93; rtd 93; Perm to Offic *Glouc* 93-08. *Triscombe Lodge, 55 Llantrisant Road, Cardiff CF5 2PU* Tel (029) 2019 3914 E-mail wdavidjones@ntlworld.com

JONES, William Douglas. b 28. St Fran Coll Brisbane ThL56. **d** 56 **p** 58. Australia 56-58; Papua New Guinea 58-72; C Manston *Ripon* 72-75; V Middleton St Mary 75-87; V Ireland Wood 87-94; rtd 94; Perm to Offic *Ripon* from 94. *6 Willow Court, Pool in Wharfedale, Otley LS21 1RX* Tel 0113-284 2028

JONES, William Edward Benjamin. b 19. TCD BA43 MA53. TCD Div Sch Div Test44. **d** 44 **p** 45. C Belfast St Thos *Conn* 44-47; C Sudbury St Andr *Lon* 47-50; CF 50-54; V Edmonton St Pet w St Martin *Lon* 54-59; V N Wembley St Cuth 59-81; V Ripley *Guildf* 81-87; Chapl HM Pris Send 81-87; rtd 87; Perm to Offic *Nor* from 87. *37 Bircham Road, Reepham, Norwich NR10 4NG* Tel (01603) 870738

JONES, William John. b 59. St Mich Coll Llan 91. **d** 93 **p** 94. C Pembroke Dock w Cosheston w Nash and Upton *St D* 93-96; C Tenby 96; TV 96-99; V Llanrhian w Llanhywel and Carnhedryn etc 99-00; rtd 00. *13 George Street, Milford Haven SA73 2AY* Tel (01646) 697094

JONES, William Lincoln. b 19. St D Coll Lamp BA41 St Mich Coll Llan 41. **d** 43 **p** 44. C Roath *Llan* 43-47; C Wooburn *Ox* 47-50; C Bridgwater w Chilton *B & W* 50-55; V Langford Budville w Runnington 55-60; V Winscombe 60-71; V Bishops Lydeard 71-73; V Bishops Lydeard w Cothelstone 73-80; P-in-c Bagborough 78-80; R Bishops Lydeard w Bagborough and Cothelstone 80-84; rtd 84; Perm to Offic *Ex* from 86. *Holme Lea, Well Mead, Kilmington, Axminster EX13 7SQ* Tel (01297) 32744

JONES, Mrs Wyn. **d** 01 **p** 02. OLM Linslade *Ox* 01-08; OLM Ouzel Valley *St Alb* from 08. *2 Woodside Way, Linslade, Leighton Buzzard LU7 7PN* Tel (01525) 373638

JONES, Wyn. *See* JONES, Ivor Wyn

JONES-BLACKETT, Enid Olive. b 40. Reading Univ BA61. **d** 97 **p** 98. OLM Hellesdon *Nor* from 97. *8 Fastolf Close, Hellesdon, Norwich NR6 5RE* Tel (01603) 414895 E-mail enidjonesblackett@btinternet.com

JONES-CRABTREE, Stephen. b 56. Nottm Univ BTh80. Linc Th Coll 76. **d** 80 **p** 81. C Chorley St Pet *Blackb* 80-83; C Blackpool St Steph 83-84; C Penwortham St Mary 84-88; R Mareham-le-Fen and Revesby *Linc* 88-02; R Hameringham w Scrafield and Winceby 98-02; V Mareham on the Hill 98-02; R Washingborough w Heighington and Canwick from 02. *The Rectory, Church Hill, Washingborough, Lincoln LN4 1EJ* Tel (01522) 800240 E-mail stephen.jones-crabtree@ukonline.co.uk

JONGMAN, Kären Anngel Irene. b 43. EMMTC 97. **d** 01 **p** 02. NSM Northampton St Mary *Pet* 01-03; NSM Guilsborough w Hollowell and Cold Ashby 03-04; P-in-c Walgrave w Hannington and Wold and Scaldwell from 04; Chapl Northants Fire and Rescue Service from 03. *The Rectory, Lower Green, Walgrave, Northampton NN6 9QF* Tel and fax (01604) 781974 Mobile 07980-881252 E-mail jongman@ncounterus.co.uk

JORDAN, Anne. b 42. RGN66. **d** 02 **p** 03. OLM Crofton *Wakef* from 02. *95 Ashdene Avenue, Crofton, Wakefield WF4 1LY* Tel (01924) 865527 Mobile 07450-475184

JORDAN, Anthony John. b 50. Birm Univ BEd73. LNSM course. **d** 83 **p** 84. Asst Chapl Uppingham Sch 83-86; NSM Uppingham w Ayston and Wardley w Belton *Pet* 83-86; Asst Chapl Sherborne Sch 86-87; NSM Bournemouth St Fran *Win* 88-03; Perm to Offic *Leic* 04-06; NSM Leic St Aid 06-08; V Eyres Monsell from 08. *St Hugh's Vicarage, 51 Pasley Road, Leicester LE2 9BU* Tel 0116-278 0940 Mobile 07798-860106 E-mail fathertonyjordan@ntlworld.com

JORDAN, Darryl Mark. b 62. Univ of Texas at Dallas BSc85 S Methodist Univ Dallas MDiv05. Perkins Sch of Th (USA) 01. **d** 04 **p** 04. C Dallas Ch USA 04-05; C Bishop's Stortford St Mich *St Alb* from 05. *Cowell House, 24 Apton Road, Bishop's Stortford CM23 3SN* Tel (01279) 654414 E-mail revdarryl@saintmichaelweb.org.uk

JORDAN, Mrs Elizabeth Ann. b 58. New Hall Cam MA82. St Jo Coll Nottm 82. **d** 87 **p** 94. Par Dn Blackpool St Jo *Blackb* 87-90; Par Dn Ewood 90-94; C 94-95; Asst Dir of Ords 90-95; Min Shelfield St Mark CD *Lich* 95-00; Local Min Adv (Wolverhampton) 95-05; OLM Course Ldr and Team Ldr Min Division 03-05; Dir Local Min Development from 06. *17 Blackberry Lane, Walsall Wood, Walsall WS9 9RQ* Tel (01543) 820352 E-mail elizabeth.jordan@lichfield.anglican.org

JORDAN, John Charles. b 37. CQSW81. NOC 84. **d** 87 **p** 88. C Southport Em *Liv* 87-90; V Abram and Bickershaw 90-95; V Bempton w Flamborough, Reighton w Speeton *York* 95-00; rtd 01; Perm to Offic *York* from 05. *35 Hollycroft, Barnston, Driffield YO25 8PP* Tel (01262) 468925 E-mail john@jordan55.freeserve.co.uk

JORDAN, Lindy. **d** 09. C Costa del Sol E *Eur* from 09. *Address temp unknown*

JORDAN, Miss Pamela Mary. b 43. Univ of Wales (Cardiff) BSc64 Ox Univ DipEd65. WEMTC 02. **d** 05 **p** 06. NSM Coalbrookdale, Iron-Bridge and Lt Wenlock *Heref* from 05; Perm to Offic *Lich* from 05. *2 Madeley Wood View, Madeley, Telford TF7 5TF* Tel (01952) 583254

JORDAN, Patrick Glen. b 69. SEITE 01. **d** 04 **p** 05. C Charlton S'wark 04-07; C Catford (Southend) and Downham 07-08; TV from 08. *233 Bellingham Road, London SE6 1EH* Tel (020) 8697 3220 E-mail patrickorpaula@hotmail.com

JORDAN, Peter Harry. b 42. Leeds Univ BA64 Leeds Coll of Educn PGCE65. Cranmer Hall Dur 70. **d** 73 **p** 74. C Nottingham St Ann w Em *S'well* 73-77; C Edgware *Lon* 77-82; V Everton St Chrys *Liv* 82-94; Dioc Ev and V Bootle St Mary w St Paul 94-02; Chapl Barcelona *Eur* 02-08; rtd 08; Perm to Offic *Eur* from 08. *11 Stanford Avenue, Wallasey CH45 5AP* Tel 0151-639 7860 E-mail peterybarbara@gmail.com

JORDAN, Richard William. b 56. Lanchester Poly Cov BSc78. St Jo Coll Nottm 83. **d** 87 **p** 88. C Blackpool St Jo *Blackb* 87-90; V Ewood 90-95; Perm to Offic *Lich* 95-97 and from 06; Co-ord Walsall Town Cen Min 97-00; Ch Links Projects Officer 00-06; Asst Min Walsall St Paul 97-06; Dioc Ch and Soc Officer *Derby* from 06. *17 Blackberry Lane, Walsall Wood, Walsall WS9 9RQ* Tel (01543) 820638 *or* (01332) 388668 E-mail richard.jordan@derby.anglican.org

JORDAN, Robert Brian. b 43. Qu Coll Birm 68. **d** 69 **p** 70. C Norton St Mich *Dur* 69-73; C Hastings St Clem and All SS *Chich* 73-74; C Carshalton *S'wark* 74-81; V Catford St Andr 81-08; rtd 08. *5 St Patrick's Road, Deal CT14 6AN* Tel (01304) 368607

JORDAN, Ronald Henry. b 30. K Coll Lon. **d** 57 **p** 58. C Clerkenwell H Redeemer w St Phil *Lon* 57-58; C Southgate Ch Ch 58-59; C Edmonton St Mary w St Jo 62-69; Hon C 86-94; V Wood Green St Mich 69-73; Hon C Finchley H Trin 80-86; Perm to Offic from 94; rtd 95. *120 Church Lane, London N2 0TB* Tel (020) 8883 7828

JORDAN, Thomas. b 36. NW Ord Course 76. **d** 79 **p** 80. NSM Prenton *Ches* 79-84; NSM Egremont St Jo 84-91; C 91-96; Ind Chapl 91-96; TV Birkenhead Priory 96-01; rtd 01; Perm to Offic *Ches* from 02. *31 Willowbank Road, Birkenhead CH42 7JU* Tel 0151-652 4212 E-mail jordan@farndene.freeserve.co.uk

JORDAN, Trevor. b 44. Lon Hosp MB, BS67 LRCP68 MRCS68 Nottm Univ MA99. EMMTC 96. **d** 03 **p** 04. NSM Seamer *York* 03-07; Perm to Offic from 07. *8 Alderson Crescent, Scarborough YO12 4JT* Tel 07887-537244 (mobile) E-mail trevor@trevorsweb.net

JORDINSON, Vera (Sister Hilary). b 37. Liv Univ BA60 CertEd61. Westcott Ho Cam 88. **d** 89 **p** 94. CSF from 74; Prov Sec 90-01; Gen Sec 96-02; Sec for Miss SSF 96-99; Gift Aid Sec from 01; Lic to Offic *Heref* 89-92; Perm to Offic *Lich* 90-92; *Birm* 92-94 and 97-06; *B & W* from 06; NSM Birchfield *Birm* 94-96. *St Francis Convent, Compton Durville, South Petherton TA13 5ES* Tel (01460) 240473 Fax 242360 E-mail hilarycsf@franciscans.org.uk

JORYSZ, Ian Herbert. b 62. Van Mildert Coll Dur BSc84 MA95 Liv Univ PhD87. Ripon Coll Cuddesdon BA89 MA95. **d** 90 **p** 91. C Houghton le Spring *Dur* 90-93; C Ferryhill 93-95; Research Officer to Bp of Bradwell from 95; P-in-c S Weald *Chelmsf* 95-00; V from 00; RD Brentwood from 08. *The*

Vicarage, Wigley Bush Lane, South Weald, Brentwood *CM14 5QP* Tel (01277) 212054 Fax 262388 E-mail ian@jorysz.com

JOSS, Martin James Torquil. b 60. Univ of Wales (Lamp) BA79. EAMTC 03. **d** 03 **p** 04. C Harlow Town Cen w Lt Parndon *Chelmsf* 03-07; P-in-c Coalville and Bardon Hill *Leic* from 07; C Ravenstone and Swannington from 07. *Christ Church Vicarage, 28 London Road, Coalville LE67 3JA* Tel (01530) 838287 Mobile 07875-494588 E-mail martin@thejosses.co.uk

JOUSTRA, The Very Revd Jan Tjeerd. b 57. Univ of Tasmania BA83 La Trobe Univ Vic MA97. Melbourne Coll of Div BTh91. **d** 89 **p** 91. Australia 89-97; C Melbourne E 90-91; C Wangaratta Cathl 91-93; R Rutherglen w Chiltern 93-97; P-in-c St Steph Chpl Hong Kong 97-03; Sen Chapl St Jo Cathl 00-03; Chapl Monte Carlo *Eur* 04-07; Dean Hamilton New Zealand from 07. *PO Box 338, Hamilton, New Zealand*

JOWETT, Ms Hilary Anne. b 54. Hull Univ BA75. Cranmer Hall Dur IDC80. **dss** 82 **d** 87 **p** 94. Sheff St Jo 80-83; Brampton Bierlow 83-87; Par Dn 87-89; Hon Par Dn Sharrow St Andr 89-95; Chapl Nether Edge Hosp Sheff 89-95; C Sheff St Mark Broomhill 95-97; C Mosbrough 97-00; TR Gleadless from 00. *The Rectory, 243 Hollinsend Road, Sheffield S12 2EE* Tel 0114-239 0757 E-mail hilary.jowett@izrmail.com

JOWETT, Canon Nicholas Peter Alfred. b 44. St Cath Coll Cam BA66 MA Bris Univ CertEd67. Qu Coll Birm 72. **d** 75 **p** 76. C Wales *Sheff* 75-78; TV Sheff Manor 78-83; V Brampton Bierlow 83-89; V Psalter Lane St Andr from 89; Dioc Ecum Adv from 01; Hon Can Sheff Cathl from 06. *Shirley House, 31 Psalter Lane, Sheffield S11 8YL* Tel 0114 258 6550 E-mail njowett@standrewspsalterlane.org.uk

JOWITT, Andrew Robert Benson. b 56. Down Coll Cam BA78 PGCE79 MA81. Wycliffe Hall Ox 88. **d** 90 **p** 91. C Northampton Em *Pet* 90-94; C Barking St Marg w St Patr *Chelmsf* 94-98; TV 98-00; TV Stantonbury and Willen *Ox* from 00; Bp's Officer for Evang from 00. *Church House, 1A Atterbrook, Bradwell, Milton Keynes MK13 9EY* Tel (01908) 320850

JOWITT, David Arthur Benson. b 25. St Jo Coll Ox BA49 MA53. Sarum Th Coll 49. **d** 51 **p** 52. C Heckmondwike *Wakef* 51-56; C Harrogate St Wilfrid *Ripon* 56-59; V Kirkby Fleetham 60-69; R Langton on Swale 60-69; OGS from 65; Superior 75-81; P-in-c Edin St Ninian 69-77; Dioc Supernumerary 77-80; Chapl Edin R Infirmary 77-80; Syn Clerk *Edin* 77-90; Can St Mary's Cathl 77-90; Vice-Provost 81-86; P-in-c S Queensferry 86-90; rtd 90; Hon C Edin Old St Paul 91-99; Perm to Offic *S'wark* from 01. *16 The Quadrangle, Morden College, 19 St German's Place, London SE3 0PW* Tel (020) 8305 0811

JOWITT, John Frederick Benson. b 23. Oak Hill Th Coll 57. **d** 59 **p** 59. Uganda 59-63; CF 63-73; R Thrandeston, Stuston and Brome w Oakley *St E* 73-82; V Docking *Nor* 82-83; P-in-c Gt Bircham 82-83; R Docking w the Birchams 83-88; P-in-c Stanhoe w Barwick 85-88; R Docking w The Birchams and Stanhoe w Barwick 88; rtd 88; Perm to Offic *Nor* 88-06 and *St E* from 90. *White Lodge, The Street, North Cove, Beccles NR34 7PN* Tel (01502) 476404

JOY, Bernard David. b 50. Sarum & Wells Th Coll 90. **d** 92 **p** 93. C Shortlands *Roch* 92-94; C Henbury *Bris* 94-96; V Bristol St Aid w St Geo 96-03; P-in-c Bridgwater St Fran *B & W* 03-07; V from 07. *The Vicarage, Saxon Green, Bridgwater TA6 4HZ* Tel (01278) 422744 Mobile 07796-678478 E-mail rev.obejoyful@htopenworld.com

JOY, Canon Matthew Osmund Clifton. b 40. St Edm Hall Ox BA62 MA66. St Steph Ho Ox 62. **d** 64 **p** 65. C Brinksway *Ches* 64-66; C Southwick St Columba *Dur* 66-69; V Hartlepool H Trin 69-85; V Rotherham St Paul, St Mich and St Jo Ferham Park *Sheff* 85-88; V Masbrough 88-95; RD Rotherham 88-93; P-in-c Bordesley St Benedict *Birm* 95-01; V 01-05; Bp's Adv on Chr/Muslim Relns 95-05; rtd 05; Perm to Offic *Wakef* from 05 and *Sheff* from 06. *Lindisfarne, Eddyfield Road, Oxspring, Sheffield S36 8YH* Tel (01226) 762276

JOYCE, Canon Alison Jane. b 59. Univ of Wales (Swansea) BA81 Bris Univ MLitt87 Birm Univ PhD00 SS Coll Cam PGCE84. Ripon Coll Cuddesdon BA87 MA94. **d** 88 **p** 94. Par Dn Chalgrove w Berrick Salome *Ox* 88-90; Tutor WMMTC 90-95; Tutor Qu Coll Birm 95-96; NSM Moseley St Anne *Birm* 96-04; Dean NSMs 00-03; NSM Birm Cathl 04-05; P-in-c Edgbaston St Bart from 05; Chapl Birm Univ from 05; Chapl Elmhurst Sch for Dance from 05; Hon Can Birm Cathl from 06. *The Vicarage, 1B Arthur Road, Edgbaston, Birmingham B15 2UW* Tel 0121-454 0070 E-mail ajjoyce@grinners.demon.co.uk

JOYCE, Anthony Owen. b 35. Selw Coll Cam BA60 MA64. Wycliffe Hall Ox 60. **d** 62 **p** 63. C Birm St Martin 62-67; Rhodesia 67-70; V Birm St Luke 70-79; V Downend *Bris* 79-01; RD Stapleton 83-89; rtd 01; Perm to Offic *Bris* from 01. *116 Jellicoe Avenue, Stapleton, Bristol BS16 1WJ* Tel 0117-956 2510 E-mail tony@joycet.freeserve.co.uk

JOYCE, Gordon Franklin. b 51. Birm Univ BA72. St Jo Coll Nottm 86. **d** 88 **p** 89. C Didsbury St Jas and Em *Man* 88-92; V

Tonge w Alkrington 92-06; C Bury St Mary from 06. *1A Pimhole Road, Bury BL9 7EY* Tel 0161-764 1157

JOYCE, Graham Leslie. b 49. Lon Univ CertEd71. Trin Coll Bris 87. **d** 89 **p** 90. C Heald Green St Cath *Ches* 89-93; R Church Lawton from 93. *The Rectory, 1 Liverpool Road West, Church Lawton, Stoke-on-Trent ST7 3DE* Tel and fax (01270) 882103 E-mail grahamljoyce@btinternet.com

JOYCE, John Barnabas Altham. b 47. St Chad's Coll Dur BA69 Lon Univ DipEd86. St Steph Ho Ox 72. **d** 74 **p** 75. C Reading St Giles *Ox* 74-77; C Cowley St Jo 77-80; Dioc Youth and Community Officer 80-87; V Hangleton *Chich* 87-94; Dioc Adv for Schs and Dir Educn 94-99; R Hurstpierpoint from 99. *The Rectory, 21 Cuckfield Road, Hurstpierpoint, Hassocks BN6 9RP* Tel (01273) 832203 E-mail rector@hurstrectory.co.uk

JOYCE, Kingsley Reginald. b 49. MBE00 TD91. Man Univ BSc70. Cuddesdon Coll 70. **d** 73 **p** 74. C High Wycombe *Ox* 73-76; C Fingest 76-79; C Hambleden 76-79; C Medmenham 76-79; C Fawley (Bucks) 76-79; C Turville 76-79; P-in-c Hambleden Valley 79-80; R 80-87; R Friern Barnet St Jas *Lon* 87-91; CF 91-08; Chapl Naples w Sorrento, Capri and Bari *Eur* from 08. *Christ Church, Afsouth (Naples), BFPO 8, London* Tel (0039) (081) 411842 Fax 409789 E-mail vicar@christchurchnaples.org

JOYCE, Margaret. b 47. Oak Hill NSM Course 86. **d** 89 **p** 94. NSM Chadwell Heath *Chelmsf* 89-92; NSM Bath Odd Down w Combe Hay *B & W* from 92; Chapl Bath and West Community NHS Trust from 95. *69 Bloomfield Rise, Bath BA2 2BN* Tel (01225) 840864 E-mail margaretjoyce@stphilipstjames.org

JOYCE, Paul David. b 70. Qu Coll Birm 00. **d** 02 **p** 03. C Perry Beeches *Birm* 02-05; V Eastwood St Dav *Chelmsf* from 05. *St David's Vicarage, 400 Rayleigh Road, Leigh-on-Sea SS9 5PT* Tel (01702) 523126 E-mail joycefamily400@btinternet.com

JOYCE, Miss Penelope Anne. b 53. St Mary's Coll Chelt CertEd74. Wycliffe Hall Ox. **d** 00 **p** 01. C Ox St Clem 00-03; C Cogges and S Leigh 03-09. *Address temp unknown* Tel 07808-181885 (mobile) E-mail pennyre.joyce@virgin.net

JOYCE, Philip Rupert. b 38. Selw Coll Cam BA68 MA72. Cranmer Hall Dur 68. **d** 70 **p** 71. C Newland St Jo *York* 70-73; C Woolwich St Mary w H Trin *S'wark* 73-77; Chapl Thames Poly 73-77; Chapl S Bank Poly 77-79; rtd 03. *37 Fulcher Avenue, Cromer NR27 9SG* Tel (01263) 519405 E-mail philipjoyce@ntlworld.com

JOYCE, Raymond. b 37. Keele Univ BA60 MA67 Linc Coll Ox BA62 MA68 Leic Univ MA97. St Steph Ho Ox 78. **d** 80 **p** 81. NSM Normanton *Derby* 80-83; NSM Derby St Alkmund and St Werburgh 83-87; Lic to Offic 87-97; NSM Mickleover All SS 97-00; Perm to Offic from 01. *23 Hindscarth Crescent, Mickleover, Derby DE3 9NN* Tel (01332) 519001

JOYCE, Canon Terence Alan. b 57. St Jo Coll Nottm BTh84. **d** 84 **p** 85. C Mansfield SS Pet and Paul *S'well* 84-88; V Greasley 88-00; Dioc Dir of Ords from 99; Dir Post-Ord Support and Tr from 01; Hon Can S'well Minster from 02. *86 Main Road, Ravenshead, Nottingham NG15 9GW* Tel (01623) 489819 E-mail tjoyce@southwell.anglican.org

JOYNER, Mrs Susan Diane. b 58. Nene Coll Northn BA79 Open Univ MA99 Leic Univ PGCE84. NEOC 05. **d** 08 **p** 09. NSM Upper Coquetdale *Newc* from 08. *The Old Church, Harbottle, Morpeth NE65 7DQ* Tel (01669) 650385 E-mail suejoyner2@aol.com

JUBA, Bishop of. See MARONA, The Most Revd Joseph Biringi Hassan

JUCKES, Jonathan Sydney. b 61. St Andr Univ MA83. Ridley Hall Cam BA87. **d** 88 **p** 89. C Sevenoaks St Nic *Roch* 88-92; Proclamation Trust 92-95; C St Helen Bishopsgate w St Andr Undershaft etc *Lon* 95-98; TR Kirk Ella and Willerby *York* from 98. *The Rectory, 2 School Lane, Kirk Ella, Hull HU10 7NR* Tel (01482) 653040 E-mail juckes@juckes.karoo.co.uk

JUDD, Adrian Timothy. b 67. Lanc Univ BA88 St Jo Coll Dur BA92. Cranmer Hall Dur 90 Trin Coll Singapore 92. **d** 93 **p** 94. C Dudley St Aug Holly Hall *Worc* 93-97; V Stockbridge Village *Liv* 97-99; V Went Valley *Wakef* from 00. *The Vicarage, Marlpit Lane, Darrington, Pontefract WF8 3AB* Tel (01977) 704744

JUDD, Colin Ivor. b 35. Dur Univ BA61. Ridley Hall Cam 61. **d** 63 **p** 64. C Stratford St Jo w Ch Ch *Chelmsf* 63-66; C Kimberworth *Sheff* 66-68; Area Sec CMS *Bradf* and *Wakef* 68-80; V Bradf St Columba w St Andr 80-00; rtd 00; Perm to Offic *Bradf* from 01. *57 Grosvenor Road, Shipley BD18 4RB* Tel (01274) 584775

JUDD, Mrs Nicola Jane. b 51. Birm Coll of Educn CertEd72. S Dios Minl Tr Scheme 87. **d** 90 **p** 94. NSM Abbotts Ann and Upper and Goodworth Clatford *Win* from 90; Adv for NSM from 01. *13 Belmont Close, Andover SP10 2DE* Tel (01264) 363364 E-mail nicola.judd@ukonline.co.uk

JUDD, The Very Revd Peter Somerset Margesson. b 49. Trin Hall Cam BA71. Cuddesdon Coll 71. **d** 74 **p** 75. C Salford St Phil w St Steph *Man* 74-76; Chapl Clare Coll Cam 76-81; C Burnham *Ox* 81-82; TV Burnham w Dropmore, Hitcham and Taplow

82-88; V Iffley 88-97; RD Cowley 94-97; Provost Chelmsf 97-00; Dean Chelmsf from 00. *The Deanery, 3 Harlings Grove, Chelmsford CM1 1YQ* Tel (01245) 354318 *or* 294480
E-mail dean@chelmsfordcathedral.org.uk

JUDD, Susan Elizabeth. b 48. Bris Univ BSc74 Univ of Wales MA04 ACA80. STETS 05. **d** 08 **p** 09. NSM Portsm Cathl from 08. *16 Bepton Down, Petersfield GU31 4PR* Tel (01730) 266819
E-mail susan.judd@ntlworld.com

JUDGE, Andrew Duncan. b 50. Cape Town Univ BCom72 Keble Coll Ox MA81. Pietermaritzburg Th Sem 82. **d** 83 **p** 84. S Africa 83-01; C Westville 84-87; R Prestbury 88-94; R Westville 94-01; TV Keynsham *B & W* from 01. *St Francis's Vicarage, Warwick Road, Keynsham, Bristol BS31 2PW* Tel 0117-373 7478
E-mail revjudge@blueyonder.co.uk

JUDGE, Mark Rollo. b 60. Chich Th Coll BTh92. **d** 92 **p** 93. C Forest Gate St Edm *Chelmsf* 92-96; V Gt Ilford St Luke 96-01; Asst Chapl Barking Havering and Redbridge Hosps NHS Trust from 01. *Harold Wood Hospital, Gubbins Lane, Harold Wood, Romford RM3 0BE* Tel (01708) 345533 *or* 746090 ext 2633 Fax 708465 E-mail markjudge_new.uk@excite.co.uk

JUDSON, Miss Christine Alison. b 64. Surrey Univ BSc86 Birm Univ PGCE88. Ripon Coll Cuddesdon 05. **d** 07 **p** 08. C Highbridge *B & W* from 07. *3 Brunels Way, Highbridge TA9 3LF* Tel (01278) 795732

JUDSON, Mrs Mary Ruth. b 47. Bretton Hall Coll DipEd68. NEOC 89. **d** 92 **p** 94. Par Dn Chester le Street *Dur* 92-94; C 94-96; V Millfield St Mark and Pallion St Luke 96-04; V Hartlepool St Luke from 04. *St Luke's Vicarage, 5 Tunstall Avenue, Hartlepool TS26 8NF* Tel (01429) 272893
E-mail mary.judson@durham.anglican.org

JUDSON, Paul Wesley. b 46. Leic Poly ATD71. Cranmer Hall Dur 87. **d** 89 **p** 90. C Lobley Hill *Dur* 89-92; C Chester le Street 92-96; Ed Dioc Publications and Sec Dioc Bd of Soc Resp 96-98; C Millfield St Mark and Pallion St Luke 96-04; C Hartlepool St Luke from 04; Dioc Publications Officer from 98; Dioc Dir of Communications from 02. *St Luke's Vicarage, 5 Tunstall Avenue, Hartlepool TS26 8NF* Tel (01429) 272893
E-mail director.of.communications@durham.anglican.org

JUDSON, Peter. b 39. Lon Univ BSc61 Plymouth Univ PGCE87. SWMTC 99. **d** 02 **p** 03. OLM Bude Haven and Marhamchurch *Truro* 02-09; rtd 09. *Meadowcroft, Bagbury Road, Bude EX23 8QJ* Tel and fax (01288) 356597 Mobile 07970-115538

JUKES, The Very Revd Keith Michael. b 54. Leeds Univ BA76. Linc Th Coll 77. **d** 78 **p** 79. C Wordsley *Lich* 78-81; C Wolverhampton 81-83; C-in-c Stoneydelph St Martin CD 83-90; TR Glascote and Stonydelph 90-91; RD Tamworth 90-91; TR Cannock and V Hatherton 91-97; Preb Lich Cathl 96-97; P-in-c Selby Abbey *York* 97-99; V 99-07; Dean Ripon from 07. *The Minster House, Bedern Bank, Ripon HG4 1PE* Tel (01765) 602609 *or* 603462 E-mail deankeith@riponcathedral.org.uk

JUKES (*née* **WEATHERHOGG**)**, Mrs Susanne.** b 56. Leeds Univ BA77 Coll of Ripon & York St Jo PGCE78. NEOC 98. **d** 01 **p** 02. C Monk Fryston and S Milford *York* 01-05; P-in-c 05-07; Assoc Min Aldborough w Boroughbridge and Roecliffe *Ripon* 07-09; Asst Dir of Ords from 07; Chapl HM Pris Full Sutton from 09. *The Chaplaincy, HM Prison Full Sutton, York YO41 1PS* Tel (01759) 475100 Fax 371206

JUMP, Elizabeth Anne. b 63. Liv Inst of Educn BA95. NOC 97. **d** 00 **p** 01. C Walkden and Lt Hulton *Man* 00-03; P-in-c Elton St Steph 03-05; C Ashton ch Ch 05-06; Perm to Offic 06-07; TV Blackbourne *St E* from 07. *The Rectory, Church Road, Honington, Bury St Edmunds IP31 1RG* Tel (01359) 269265
E-mail revlizj@btinternet.com

JUMP, Paul Gordon. b 77. St Andr Univ BSc99. Oak Hill Th Coll 04. **d** 07 **p** 08. C Rusholme H Trin *Man* from 07. *2 The Grange, Manchester M14 5NY* Tel 0161-256 6547

JUNG, Mrs Jennifer Margaret. b 61. STETS 95. **d** 98 **p** 99. NSM Fareham H Trin *Portsm* 98-02. *42 Clifton Road, Winchester SO22 5BU*

JUPE, Canon Derek Robert. b 26. TCD BA53 Div Test54 MA67. **d** 54 **p** 55. C Lurgan Ch the Redeemer *D & D* 54-57; C Dublin Harold's Cross *D & G* 57-60; I Easkey w Kilglass *T, K & A* 60-65; Deputation Sec (Ireland) BCMS 65-72; R Man St Jerome w Ardwick St Silas 72-78; V Ardsley *Sheff* 78-83; I Tempo and Clabby *Clogh* 83-92; Can Clogh Cathl 89-92; rtd 92; Perm to Offic *Cov* 92-05 and *Edin* from 05. *4 Leithen Mills, Innerleithen EH44 6JJ* Tel (01896) 831701

✠**JUPP, The Rt Revd Roger Alan.** b 56. St Edm Hall Ox BA78 MA82 Surrey Univ PGCE96. Chich Th Coll 79. **d** 80 **p** 81 **c** 03. C Newbold w Dunston *Derby* 80-83; C Cowley St Jo *Ox* 83-85; C Islington St Jas w St Phil *Lon* 85-86; V Lower Beeding *Chich* 86-90; Dom Chapl to Bp Horsham 86-91; V Burgess Hill St Jo 90-93; TR Burgess Hill St Jo w St Edw 93-94; Perm to Offic 97-98; C Aldwick 98-00; Prin Newton Th Coll Papua New Guinea 00-03; Bp Popondota 03-05; Hon Asst Bp Chich from 05; P-in-c St Leonards Ch Ch and St Mary 05-06; R from 06. *Christ Church Rectory, 3 Silchester Road, St Leonards-on-Sea TN38 0JB* Tel (01424) 444052
E-mail rajupp1@hotmail.com

JUPP, Vincent John. b 64. St Jo Coll Nottm BA(ThM)06. **d** 00 **p** 01. C Evington *Leic* 00-03; TV Ascension TM 03-07; TR from 07. *Christ Church Vicarage, 73 Nursery Road, Leicester LE5 2HQ* Tel 0116-241 3848
E-mail vince@nursery73.plus.com

JUSTICE, Keith Leonard. b 42. Wolv Univ BSc68 CEng83 MIMechE83. Wycliffe Hall Ox 91. **d** 93 **p** 94. C Penwortham St Mary *Blackb* 93-96; C Dovercourt and Parkeston w Harwich *Chelmsf* 96-98; V Wentworth *Sheff* 98-01; Chapl Rotherham Gen Hosps NHS Trust 98-01; Chapl Rotherham Priority Health Services NHS Trust 98-01; R Melrose *Edin* 01-04; P-in-c Royton St Anne *Man* 04-08; P-in-c Lawton Moor from 08. *The Vicarage, Orton Road, Manchester M23 0LH* Tel 0161-998 2461
E-mail keith.justice@ntlworld.com

JUSTICE, Simon Charles. b 66. Univ of Wales (Lamp) BD88 Edin Univ MTh90. Cranmer Hall Dur 90. **d** 92 **p** 93. C Tilehurst St Mich *Ox* 92-95; R Troy St Paul USA 95-01; R Tigard St Jas 01-04; Can All SS Cathl Albany 98-04; R Edin Ch Ch 04-06; R Corvallis Gd Samaritan USA from 06. *445 NW Elizabeth Drive, Corvallis OR 97330, USA*
E-mail simon.justice@googlemail.com

JUTE, Danald Anak. b 66. Edin Univ BD92. Edin Th Coll 89. **d** 92 **p** 93. Tutor Epiphany Ho Th Coll Kuching Malaysia 92-98; C St Thos Cathl Kuching 98-02; C Bearsden w Milngavie *Glas* 04-08; P-in-c Glas St Oswald from 08. *3 Golf Road, Rutherglen, Glasgow G73 4JW* Tel 0141-634 5555 Mobile 07918-110503
E-mail djuteepiscopal@yahoo.co.uk

JUTSUM, Linda Mary. *See* ELLIOTT, Mrs Linda Mary

K

KABOLEH, David Reardon. b 64. Westmr Coll Ox MTh00. Trin Coll Nairobi 88. **d** 90 **p** 91. C-in-c Nairobi St Phil 90-92; TV Nairobi St Luke and Immanuel 93-95; NSM Hoddesdon *St Alb* 95-97; NSM Ox St Matt 97-99; NSM Blackbird Leys 99-02; NSM Ox St Aldate 03-04; NSM Akeman 04-07; P-in-c Worminghall w Ickford, Oakley and Shabbington from 07. *The Rectory, 32A The Avenue, Worminghall, Aylesbury HP18 9LE* Tel (01844) 338839 E-mail kaboleh@aol.com

KACHIWANDA, Evans Esau. b 62. Univ of Malawi BA97. Bp Patteson Th Coll (Solomon Is) 87 Virginia Th Sem MTh04. **d** 89 **p** 91. Chapl to Bp S Malawi 91-92; Sch and Coll Chapl 92-93; Angl Progr Dir 97-98; Chapl and Teacher Malosa Sch 99-04; Headmaster 01-02; Prov Sec Cen Africa 04-05; Lect and Dean of Studies Leonard Kamungu Th Coll 05-06; Perm to Offic *Blackb* from 07. *4 Cumberland Court, West Road, Lancaster LA1 5QE* Tel 07942-048252 (mobile) E-mail ekachiwanda@hotmail.com

✠**KAFITY, The Rt Revd Samir.** b 33. Beirut Univ BA57. Near E Sch of Th 57. **d** 57 **p** 58 **c** 86. Israel 57-64 and 77-98; Lebanon 64-77; Adn Jerusalem 77-82; Bp Jerusalem 84-98; Pres Bp Episc Ch Jerusalem and Middle E 86-96; rtd 98. *11964 Callado Road, San Diego CA 92128, USA*

KAGGWA, Nelson Sonny. b 58. E Lon Univ BA91. Bp Tucker Coll Mukono 77. **d** 80 **p** 80. Kenya 80-83; USA 83; Hon C Ox SS Phil and Jas w St Marg 84-85; C W Ham *Chelmsf* 86-87; TV Walthamstow St Mary w St Steph 87-92; Perm to Offic *Sheff* 92-95; V Sheff St Paul 96-97; rtd 98. *Al-Salam, 36 Standish Gardens, Sheffield S5 8YD* Tel 0114-273 1428 Fax 273 1348 Mobile 07989-261278 E-mail kaggwanelsonibrahim@msn.com

KAJUMBA, The Ven Daniel Steven Kimbugwe. b 52. S'wark Ord Course. **d** 85 **p** 86. C Goldington *St Alb* 85-87; Uganda 87-99; TV Horley *S'wark* 99-01; Adn Reigate from 01. *84 Higher Drive, Purley CR8 2HJ* Tel (020) 8660 9276 *or* 8681 5496 Fax 8686 2074 Mobile 07949-594460
E-mail daniel.kajumba@southwark.anglican.org

KAKURU (*née* **ASHBRIDGE**)**, Mrs Clare Patricia Esther.** b 80. QUB BTh03 MTh07. **d** 07 **p** 08. C Donaghcloney w Waringstown *D & D* from 07. *3 Banbridge Road, Waringstown, Craigavon BT66 7QA* Tel (028) 3882 0109

KALENIUK, Nicholas George. b 69. WEMTC. **d** 09. C Claines St Jo *Worc* from 09. *41 Drovers Way, Worcester WR3 8QD*

KALSI, Mrs Gina Louise. b 68. Leeds Univ BA09. NOC 06. **d** 09. C Netherthorpe St Steph *Sheff* from 09. *73 Burgoyne Road, Sheffield S6 3QB* Tel 0114-233 1455 Mobile 07808-578721
E-mail ginalkalsi@hotmail.co.uk

KALUS, Rupert. b 57. St Jo Coll Dur BA85 MA93 BA01 M Sussex Inst of HE PGCE87. Cranmer Hall Dur 99. **d** 02 **p** 03. C Dur N 02-06; P-in-c Shildon 06-07; V from 08. *St John's Vicarage, 1A Burnie Gardens, Shildon DL4 1ND* Tel (01388) 774494

KAMBLE-HANSELL, Anupama. b 76. Pune Univ India BSc97 Serampore Univ BD03 Birm Univ MA06. **d** 02 **p** 04. Perm to Offic *Nor* 03; C Birm St Martin w Bordesley St Andr 04-08; Chapl Aston Univ 05-08; TV Coventry Caludon from 08. *56 Wyken Croft, Coventry CV2 3AD* Tel (024) 7662 2007 E-mail anupamakamble@hotmail.com

KAMEGERI, Stephen. *See* NSHIMYE, Stephen Kamegeri

KAMPALA, Bishop of. *See* OROMBI, The Most Revd Henry Luke

KAMUYU, Elpiety Wanjiku. b 53. St Jo Coll Nottm 06. **d** 93 **p** 09. Kenya 93-01; NSM Edgware *Lon* 01-03; NSM Bilborough w Strelley *S'well* 04-06; C Lenton from 08. *99 Allington Avenue, Lenton, Nottingham NG7 1JY* Tel 0115-845 3922 Mobile 07985-424139 E-mail pietykamuyu@yahoo.co.uk

KANE, Peter David Colin. b 72. K Coll Lon BMus92 Fitzw Coll Cam BA05 MA09 ARCO91 ARCM94. Wycliffe Hall Ox BA08. **d** 09. C Chich St Paul and Westhampnett from 09. *37 Somerstown, Chichester PO19 6AL* Tel (01243) 539849 E-mail p.kane.03@cantab.net

KANERIA, Rajni. b 57. Bath Univ BPharm82. Wycliffe Hall Ox 83. **d** 86 **p** 87. C Hyson Green *S'well* 86-87; C Hyson Green St Paul w St Steph 87-89; C Harold Hill St Geo *Chelmsf* 89-91; TV Oadby *Leic* 91-97. *32 Rendall Road, Leicester LE4 6LE* Tel 0116-266 6613

KAOMA, John Kafwanka. b 66. Trin Coll Melbourne BTh97 Ridley Coll Melbourne MA00. St Jo Sem Lusaka 90. **d** 93 **p** 94. C Chingola St Barn Zambia 93-94; Perm to Offic Melbourne Australia 94-00; Lect St Jo Coll Lusaka Zambia 00-03; Prin 01-03; Regional Manager (S Africa) CMS 03-06; Research Officer Miss Dept Angl Communion Office 06-09; Dir for Miss from 09; Perm to Offic *Lon* from 06. *11 Silverhall Street, Isleworth TW7 6RF* Tel (020) 7313 3940 Fax 7313 3999 Mobile 07901-987239
E-mail john.kafwanka@anglicancommunion.org

KARAMURA, Grace Patrick. b 62. Nat Teachers' Coll Uganda DipEd89 Rob Coll Cam MPhil95 Leeds Univ PhD98. Bp Tucker Coll Mukono BD92. **d** 92 **p** 93. C All SS Cathl Kampala Uganda 92-93; C Ebbw Vale *Mon* 98-01; TV 01-03; V Pontyclun w Talygarn *Llan* from 03. *The Vicarage, Heol Miskin, Pontyclun CF72 9AJ* Tel and fax (01443) 225477
E-mail gracekaramu@hotmail.com

KARRACH, Herbert Adolf. b 24. TCD BA46 MB, BCh48 BAO48. EAMTC 85. **d** 88 **p** 89. NSM Snettisham w Ingoldisthorpe and Fring *Nor* 88-95; Perm to Offic from 95. *Narnia, 5 Docking Road, Fring, King's Lynn PE31 6SQ* Tel (01485) 518346

KASHOURIS, Peter Zacharias. b 66. Peterho Cam BA89 MA93. St Steph Ho Ox 92. **d** 94 **p** 95. C Hampstead St Jo *Lon* 94-97; R Hartlepool St Hilda *Dur* 97-03; P-in-c Dur St Oswald 03-06; P-in-c Dur St Oswald and Shincliffe from 06; Dioc Ecum Officer from 03. *St Oswald's Vicarage, Church Street, Durham DH1 3DG* Tel 0191-374 1681 E-mail p.j.kashouris@durham.anglican.org

KASIBANTE, Amos Sebadduka. b 54. Trin Coll Cam BA83 MA87 Yale Univ STM89. Bp Tucker Coll Mukono 76 Berkeley Div Sch 88. **d** 79 **p** 80. C Lyantonde Uganda 79-80; Tutor Bp Tucker Coll Mukono 83-92; Tutor Coll of Ascension Selly Oak 93-95; Prin Simon of Cyrene Th Inst 95-97; Vice Prin St Mich Coll Llan 97-02; Chapl Leic Univ 02-09. *Address temp unknown* E-mail amos.kasibante@virgin.net

KASOZI, Jackson Nsamba. b 50. Bp Tucker Coll Mukono BD91 Birm Univ MPhil94 All Nations Chr Coll MA00. **d** 83 **p** 84. Uganda 84-92 and 96-99; V St Andr Cathl Mityana 84-88; Adn 86-88; Chapl to Bp W Buganda 91-92; Perm to Offic *Cov* 93-94; Adn W Buganda 95-98; Acting Dean St Paul's Cathl 98-99; NSM Limehouse *Lon* 00-02; NSM Old Ford St Paul and St Mark 02-03; C Harold Hill St Geo *Chelmsf* 04-08; rtd 08. *c/o Christian Vision Uganda, PO Box 37269, Kampala, Uganda* E-mail christian.vision.uganda@live.com

KASSELL, Colin George Henry. b 42. Wycliffe Hall Ox 66. **d** 68 **p** 69. In RC Ch 69-75; Perm to Offic *Ox* 76-77; C Denham 77-80; V Brotherton *Wakef* 80-84; Chapl and Past Ldr St Cath Hospice Crawley 84-91; R Rogate w Terwick and Trotton w Chithurst *Chich* 91-94; C Heene 94-06; Chapl Worthing Hosp 94-07; rtd 07; P-in-c Worthing St Andr *Chich* from 06. *Park House, 3 Madeira Avenue, Worthing BN11 2AT* Tel (01903) 526571 Mobile 07802-259310
E-mail colin.kassell@ntlworld.com

KATE, Sister. *See* BURGESS, Kate Lamorna

KAUNHOVEN, Anthony Peter. b 55. Leeds Univ BA78 Coll of Ripon & York St Jo PGCE79. Edin Th Coll 79. **d** 81 **p** 82. C Leeds St Aid *Ripon* 81-84; C Hawksworth Wood 84-89; V Upper Nidderdale 89-91; Hon C Rawdon *Bradf* 96-99; P-in-c Old Brampton *Derby* 99-07; P-in-c Barlow 04-07; P-in-c Bakewell from 07; C Ashford w Sheldon and Longstone from 07; P-in-c Rowsley from 07; Dioc Ecum Officer from 01. *The Vicarage, South Church Street, Bakewell DE45 1FD* Tel (01629) 812256 E-mail jazzyrector@aol.com

KAVANAGH, John Paul. b 63. St Fran Coll Brisbane BTh94. **d** 94 **p** 96. C Indooroopilly Australia 94-95; C Centenary Suburbs

96-98; R Forest Lake 98; P-in-c Texas w Inglewood 99-00; Chapl Wolston Park Hosp and Asst Chapl R Brisbane Hosp 00-02; Chapl Matthew Flinders Angl Coll 02-08; I Kells Gp *C & O* from 08. *The Priory, Kells, Co Kilkenny, Republic of Ireland* Tel (00353) (56) 772 8367 Mobile 85-840 2404
E-mail jpandmary@gmail.com

KAVANAGH, Canon Michael Lowther. b 58. York Univ BA80 Newc Univ MSc82 Leeds Univ BA86 MBPsS90. Coll of Resurr Mirfield 84. **d** 87 **p** 88. C Boston Spa *York* 87-91; V Beverley St Nic 91-97; RD Beverley 95-97; Abp's Dom Chapl and Dioc Dir of Ords 97-05; Chapl HM Pris Full Sutton 06-08; Angl Adv HM Pris Service from 08; Can Th Liv Cathl from 09. *Chaplaincy HQ, HM Prison Service, Room 410, Abell House, John Islip Street, London SW1P 4LH* Tel (020) 7217 8678

KAY, Mrs Audrey Elizabeth. b 60. NOC 04. **d** 07 **p** 08. NSM Ramsbottom and Edenfield *Man* from 07. *61 Greenbank Road, Radcliffe, Manchester M26 4FR* Tel 0161-725 8093 Mobile 07752-526140 E-mail kaynacg@aol.com

KAY, Dennis. b 57. St As Minl Tr Course 96. **d** 99 **p** 00. NSM Llangystennin *St As* 99-01; NSM Colwyn Bay w Brynymaen 01-03; NSM Petryal 03-07. *41 Ffordd Ffynnon, Rhuddlan, Rhyl LL18 2SP* Tel 07748-312067 (mobile)

KAY, George Ronald. b 24. Sarum & Wells Th Coll 74. **d** 77 **p** 78. NSM Bemerton *Sarum* 77-87; rtd 87; Perm to Offic *Sarum* 89-00. *The Lodge, 157 Wilton Road, Salisbury SP2 7JH* Tel (01722) 338326

KAY, Ian Geoffrey. NOC. **d** 89 **p** 90. NSM Rochdale *Man* 89-91 and from 95; NSM Heywood St Luke w All So 91-95. *161 Norden Road, Rochdale OL11 5PT* Tel (01706) 639497

KAY, Marjory Marianne Kate. b 61. **d** 97. NSM Godshill *Portsm* 97-05. *76A East Street, Bridport DT6 3LL* Tel (01308) 422453

KAYE, Alistair Geoffrey. b 62. Reading Univ BSc85. St Jo Coll Nottm 87. **d** 90 **p** 91. C Gt Horton *Bradf* 90-94; C Rushden w Newton Bromswold *Pet* 94-98; V Upper Armley *Ripon* 98-08; Armley Deanery Missr from 08; AD Armley 05-08. *27 Hough End Lane, Leeds LS13 4EY* Tel 0113-257 3702 Mobile 07881-804104 E-mail alistair@armley.freeserve.co.uk

KAYE, Bruce Norman. b 39. Lon Univ BD64 Sydney Univ BA66 Basel Univ DrTheol75. Moore Th Coll Sydney ThL64. **d** 64 **p** 65. Australia 64-66 and from 83; Perm to Offic *Dur* 67-69; Tutor St Jo Coll Dur 68-75; Sen Tutor 75-83; Vice Prin 79-83; rtd 04. *217 Hopetown Avenue, Watsons Bay NSW 2030, Australia* Tel (0061) (2) 9337 6795

KAYE, Canon Gerald Trevor. b 32. Man Univ BSc54. Oak Hill Th Coll. **d** 56 **p** 57. C Widnes St Ambrose *Liv* 56-58; C St Helens St Mark 58-62; V Brixton Hill St Sav *S'wark* 62-65; Canada 65-85; Hon Can Keewatin 70-75; Adn Patricia 75-78; V Slough *Ox* 85-97; rtd 97; Lic to Offic *Arg* from 08. *Craiguanach, Torlundy, Fort William PH33 6SW* Tel (01397) 705395
E-mail eleanorado@aol.com

KAYE, Peter Alan. b 47. K Coll Lon BD71 AKC71 Leic Univ MA82 CQSW82. St Aug Coll Cant 71. **d** 72 **p** 73. C Fulham All SS *Lon* 72-74; Chapl Rubery Hill, Jo Conolly and Jos Sheldon Hosps Birm 74-80; Hon C Northfield *Birm* 80-83; Perm to Offic 99-06; P-in-c Stirchley from 06. *Stirchley Vicarage, 18 Pineapple Grove, Birmingham B30 2TJ* Tel 0121-443 1371 Mobile 07790-268754 E-mail peterakaye@googlemail.com

KAYE, Mrs Sharon Vernie. b 72. Bradf Coll of Educn BEd97 Trin Coll Bris 06. **d** 08 **p** 09. C Yeadon *Bradf* from 08. *37 Millbank, Yeadon, Leeds LS19 7AY* Tel 07871-768774 (mobile) E-mail verniekaye@hotmail.com

KAYE, Stephen Michael. b 72. Trin Coll Bris 06. **d** 08 **p** 09. C Calverley *Bradf* from 08. *37 Millbank, Yeadon, Leeds LS19 7AY* Tel 07756-274011 (mobile) E-mail mr.kaye.is@gmail.com

KAYE, Timothy Henry. b 52. Linc Th Coll 77. **d** 80 **p** 81. C Warsop *S'well* 80-83; C Far Headingley St Chad *Ripon* 83-86; P-in-c Birkby *Wakef* 86; TV N Huddersfield 86-91; R Stone St Mich w Aston St Sav *Lich* 91-95; V S Kirkby *Wakef* from 95. *The Vicarage, Bull Lane, South Kirkby, Pontefract WF9 3QD* Tel and fax (01977) 642795 E-mail mail@kaye5.fsworld.co.uk

KAYE-BESLEY, Mrs Lesley Kathleen. b 47. Cam Inst of Educn CertEd69 Kingston Univ MA94 FRSA85. **d** 04 **p** 05. OLM Walton-on-Thames *Guildf* from 04. *Minggay, 1 Park Road, Esher KT10 8NP* Tel (01372) 465185
E-mail lesley@waltonparish.org.uk

KAZIRO, Godfrey Sam. b 48. BDSc Lon Univ MSc FDSRCPSGlas FFDRCSI. **d** 02 **p** 03. OLM Waterloo St Jo w St Andr *S'wark* from 02. *19 Hampshire Road, Hornchurch RM11 3EU* Tel (01708) 441609

KEAL, Barry Clifford. b 57. Leeds Univ BA06. NOC 03. **d** 06 **p** 07. NSM Halsall, Lydiate and Downholland *Liv* from 06. *46 Eastway, Liverpool L31 6BS* Tel 0151-526 4508
E-mail barry@keal.me.uk

KEANE, Christian John. b 74. Rob Coll Cam BA95 MA99. Wycliffe Hall Ox BA06 MA06. **d** 06 **p** 07. C Eastrop *Win* from 06. *15 Camwood Close, Basingstoke RG21 3BL* Tel (01256) 330712 E-mail chris.keane@stmarys-basingstoke.org.uk

KEANE, Damien. d 08 **p** 09. C Bandon Union *C, C & R* from 08. *3 The Pines, Kilbrittain Road, Bandon, Co Cork, Republic of Ireland* Tel (00353) (23) 43009
E-mail damiengkeane@gmail.com
or bandoncurate@gmail.com

KEARLEY-HEYWOOD, Deiniol John Owen. b 73. K Coll Lon BA95 Peterho Cam MPhil03. Westcott Ho Cam 02. **d** 04 **p** 05. C Paddington St Jo w St Mich *Lon* 04-08; R Prestwood and Gt Hampden *Ox* from 08. *The Rectory, 140 Wycombe Road, Prestwood, Great Missenden HP16 0HJ* Tel (01494) 866530
E-mail rector@htprestwood.org.uk

KEARNEY, Mrs Sandra. b 55. Bolton Inst of HE BSc89 Univ Coll Ches BTh04. NOC 01. **d** 04 **p** 05. C Blackpool Ch Ch w All SS *Blackb* 04-08; P-in-c Ordsall and Salford Quays *Man* from 08. *The Rectory, Parsonage Close, Salford M5 3GS* Tel 0161-872 0800 E-mail revsandra@btinternet.com

KEARNS, Andrew Philip. b 76. Wycliffe Hall Ox. **d** 09. C Maidenhead St Andr and St Mary *Ox* from 09. *1 Hemsdale, Maidenhead SL6 6SL* Tel 07990-574431 (mobile)
E-mail andrewpkearns@gmail.com

KEARNS, Mrs Mary Leah. b 38. **d** 87 **p** 94. Par Dn Morden *S'wark* 87-88; Asst Chapl HM Pris Holloway 88-98; rtd 99; Perm to Offic *Guildf* from 01. *48 The Orchard, North Holmwood, Dorking RH5 4JT* Tel (01306) 886858

KEARNS, Philip Gillin. b 59. Ripon Coll Cuddesdon 90. **d** 92 **p** 93. C Winchmore Hill St Paul *Lon* 92-97; V N Shoebury *Chelmsf* 97-02; TR Wickford and Runwell from 02; RD Basildon from 09. *The Rectory, 120 Southend Road, Wickford SS11 8EB* Tel (01268) 733147 Mobile 07747-826066
E-mail philip@pkearns.fsnet.co.uk

KEARON, Canon Kenneth Arthur. b 53. TCD BA76 MA79 MPhil91. CITC 78. **d** 81 **p** 82. C Raheny w Coolock *D & G* 81-84; Lect TCD 82-90; Dean of Res TCD 84-90; I Tullow *D & G* 91-99; Can Ch Ch Cathl Dublin from 95; Dir Irish Sch Ecum 99-05; Sec Gen ACC from 05; Hon Prov Can Cant Cathl from 06. *Anglican Communion Office, 16 Tavistock Crescent, London W11 1AX* Tel (020) 7313 3900 Fax 7313 3999
E-mail kkearon@tcd.ie

KEARTON, Janet Elizabeth. b 54. Univ Coll Lon BSc78 Birkbeck Coll Lon MSc81. NEOC 01. **d** 04 **p** 05. C Richmond w Hudswell and Downholme and Marske *Ripon* 04-08; V Hipswell from 08. *The Vicarage, 7 Forest Drive, Colburn, Catterick Garrison DL9 4PN* Tel (01748) 833320 Mobile 07816-278267
E-mail revjan@btinternet.com

KEAST, William. b 43. Univ Coll Ox BA65 DipEd66. **d** 88 **p** 89. OLM Scotton w Northorpe *Linc* from 88. *4 Crapple Lane, Scotton, Gainsborough DN21 3QT* Tel (01724) 763190
E-mail wkeast@hotmail.com

KEATING, Mrs Ann Barbara. b 53. Open Univ BA85. STETS 06. **d** 09. NSM Fisherton Anger *Sarum* from 09. *1 The Old Orchard, High Street, Netheravon, Salisbury SP4 9QW* Tel (01980) 671010 Mobile 07510-588007
E-mail ann.keating@winchester.ac.uk

KEATING, Christopher Robin. b 39. K Coll Lon BD AKC84. Sarum Th Coll 62. **d** 65 **p** 66. C Baildon *Bradf* 65-67; CF 67-72; V Thornton Heath St Paul *Cant* 72-79; C Harold Hill St Geo *Chelmsf* 85-89; V Goodmayes All SS 89-07; rtd 07; Perm to Offic *York* from 09. *Ghyll View, Goathland, Whitby YO22 5AP* Tel (01947) 896406

KEATING, Geoffrey John. b 52. Open Univ BA94. St Steph Ho Ox 81. **d** 84 **p** 85. C Lancaster Ch Ch w St Jo and St Anne *Blackb* 84-85; C Rotherham *Sheff* 85-87; V Bentley 87-91; V Penponds *Truro* 91-96; V Pet St Jude from 96. *St Jude's Vicarage, 49 Atherstone Avenue, Peterborough PE3 9TZ* Tel and fax (01733) 264169 *or* 268816 E-mail geoffkeatg@aol.com

KEAY, Alfred David. b 26. Aston Univ MSc72. Qu Coll Birm 76. **d** 79 **p** 80. Hon C Penkridge w Stretton *Lich* 79-82; C Rugeley 82-85; V Cheswardine 85-95; V Hales 85-95; rtd 95; Perm to Offic *Lich* from 98. *2 The Coppice, Farcroft Gardens, Market Drayton TF9 3UA* Tel (01630) 657924

KEAY, Charles Edward. b 70. Glos Univ BA94. St Steph Ho Ox 01. **d** 03 **p** 04. C Havant *Portsm* 03-07; P-in-c Alford w Rigsby *Linc* from 07. *The Vicarage, 15 Bilsby Road, Alford LN13 9EW* Tel (01507) 466768

KEDDIE, Canon Tony. b 37. Qu Coll Birm 63. **d** 66 **p** 67. C Barnoldswick w Bracewell *Bradf* 66-69; C New Bentley *Sheff* 69-71; TV Seacroft *Ripon* 71-79; V Kippax 79-85; TR Kippax w Allerton Bywater 85-92; R Fountains Gp 92-02; Hon Can Ripon Cathl 94-02; rtd 02; Perm to Offic *Ripon* from 02. *2 Westcroft, Station Road, Otley LS21 3HX* Tel (01943) 464146

KEEBLE, Leslie Bruce. b 32. Spurgeon's Coll Lon BD59. Bapt Th Sem Ruschlikon Zürich ThM63. **d** 08 **p** 08. NSM Harwell w Chilton *Ox* from 08. *13 Limetrees, Chilton, Didcot OX11 0HW* Tel (01235) 852203 E-mail bk@brucekeeble.org.uk

KEEBLE, Stephen Robert. b 56. K Coll Lon BD84 AKC84 MA98. Westcott Ho Cam 85. **d** 87 **p** 88. C Lt Stanmore St Lawr *Lon* 87-90; C Headstone St Geo 90-93; P-in-c 93-98; V from 98. *St George's Vicarage, 96 Pinner View, Harrow HA1 4RJ* Tel and fax (020) 8427 1253 E-mail megpointer@supanet.com

KEECH, Canon April Irene. b 52. Penn State Univ BA76. Trin Coll Bris BA89. **d** 89 **p** 92. C Walthamstow St Luke *Chelmsf* 89-92; USA 92-95; V Deptford St Jo w H Trin *S'wark* 95-02; Asst Dioc Dir of Ords 96-00; Hon Can S'wark Cathl from 99; V Hoxton St Jo w Ch Ch *Lon* from 02. *St John's Vicarage, Crondall Street, London N1 6PT* Tel (020) 7739 9823 *or* 7739 9302

KEEGAN, Donald Leslie. b 37. ACII. CITC 65. **d** 68 **p** 69. C Drumragh w Mountfield *D & R* 68-72; I Birr w Lorrha, Dorrha and Lockeen *L & K* 72-02; Can Killaloe Cathl 80-82; Treas Killaloe Cathl 82-87; Prec Limerick and Killaloe Cathls 87-89; Adn Killaloe, Kilfenora, Clonfert etc 89-02; rtd 02. *279 Redford Park, Greystones, Co Wicklow, Republic of Ireland* Tel (00353) (1) 201 7259 E-mail donkee@eircom.net

KEEGAN, Frances Ann (Sister Isabel). b 44. SEN74. Franciscan Study Cen 87. **d** 99 **p** 00. NSM Sherborne w Castleton and Lillington *Sarum* 99-01; NSM Golden Cap Team 01-08; NSM Crosslacon *Carl* from 08. *The Vicarage, Arlecdon, Frizington CA26 3UB* Tel (01946) 861353
E-mail annmarie.isabel@zen.co.uk

KEEGAN, Graham Brownell. b 40. Nottm Univ CertEd68. NOC 81. **d** 84 **p** 85. C Highfield *Liv* 84-87; V Ince St Mary 87-95; V Newton in Makerfield St Pet 95-05; rtd 05. *5 Scott Road, Lowton, Warrington WA3 2HD* Tel (01942) 713809

KEELER, Alan. b 58. City Univ BSc81. St Jo Coll Nottm MA01. **d** 90 **p** 91. C Paddock Wood *Roch* 90-94; V Blendon 94-06; V Plaistow St Mary from 06. *St Mary's Vicarage, 74 London Lane, Bromley BR1 4HE* Tel (020) 8460 1827
E-mail alan.keeler@diocese-rochester.org

KEELEY, John Robin. b 38. G&C Coll Cam BA62. Clifton Th Coll 62. **d** 64 **p** 65. C Onslow Square St Paul *Lon* 64-66; C Hove Bp Hannington Memorial Ch *Chich* 66-69; C Harborne Heath *Birm* 69-72; V Leic H Trin 72-74; V Leic H Trin w St Jo 74-80; Perm to Offic *St Alb* 81-86; NSM Carterton *Ox* 89-95; Tutor EAMTC *Ely* 95-99; TV Bishopsnympton, Rose Ash, Mariansleigh etc *Ex* 99-03; RD S Molton 01-03; rtd 03. *74 Pacific Parade, Mount Tamborine Qld 4272, Australia* Tel (0061) (7) 5545 0966 E-mail robandpaulkeeley@bigpond.com

KEELING, Peter Frank. b 34. Kelham Th Coll. **d** 58 **p** 59. C S Elmsall *Wakef* 58-63; C Barnsley St Mary 63-67; V Ravensthorpe 67-73; V Cudworth 73-83; R Downham Market w Bexwell *Ely* 83-00; RD Fincham 83-94; V Crimplesham w Stradsett 85-00; rtd 00; P-in-c Hempton and Pudding Norton 00-04; Perm to Offic from 04. *23 Cleaves Drive, Walsingham NR22 6EQ* Tel (01328) 820310

KEEN, David Mark. b 69. Oriel Coll Ox BA91. St Jo Coll Nottm BTh96 MPhil98. **d** 98 **p** 99. C Yeovil w Kingston Pitney *B & W* 98-02; C Haughton le Skerne *Dur* 02-06; C Preston Plucknett *B & W* from 06. *3 Poplar Drive, Yeovil BA21 3UL* Tel (01935) 422286 E-mail david.keen@ukonline.co.uk

KEEN, Michael Spencer. b 41. St Pet Coll Ox BA68 MA72 GRSM62 ARCM Reading Univ CertEd. Westcott Ho Cam 68. **d** 73 **p** 74. NSM W Derby St Jo *Liv* 73-74; NSM Stanley 74-77; Chs Youth and Community Officer Telford *Lich* 77-82; Dioc Unemployment Officer *Sheff* 82-89; NSM Brixton Road Ch Ch *S'wark* 89-92; Employment Development Officer 89-92; Perm to Offic 92-99; NSM Camberwell St Giles w St Matt 99-01. *B54 Du Cane Court, Balham High Road, London SW17 7JE* Tel (020) 8772 0186

KEEN, Miriam Frances. b 65. Ex Univ BSc87 Westmr Coll of Educn PGCE89. Wycliffe Hall Ox 03. **d** 05 **p** 06. C Cogges and S Leigh *Ox* from 05; C N Leigh from 08. *The Vicarage, New Yatt Road, North Leigh, Witney OX29 6TT* Tel (01933) 773844
E-mail miri@coggesparish.com

KEENAN, Leslie Herbert (Bertie). b 32. Cranmer Hall Dur. **d** 66 **p** 67. C Anston *Sheff* 66-70; C Woodsetts 66-70; Chapl HM Borstal Pollington 70-78; V Balne *Sheff* 70-78; V Poughill *Truro* 78-99; rtd 99; Perm to Offic *Chich* from 01. *Rosedene, Southdown Road, Seaford BN25 4JS* Tel (01323) 899507

KEENE, Canon David Peter. b 35. Westcott Ho Cam. **d** 58 **p** 59. C Radcliffe-on-Trent *S'well* 58-61; C Mansfield SS Pet and Paul 61-64; V Nottingham St Cath 64-71; R Bingham 71-81; Dioc Dir of Ords 81-90; Can Res S'well Minster 81-97; rtd 97; Perm to Offic *S'well* from 02. *Averham Cottage, Church Lane, Averham, Newark NG23 5RB* Tel (01636) 708601 E-mail keene@averham.fsnet.co.uk

KEENE, Mrs Muriel Ada. b 35. dss 83 **d** 87 **p** 94. Dioc Lay Min Adv *S'well* 87-88; Asst Dir of Ords 88-90; Dn-in-c Saxton 90-93; Dn-in-c Epperstone 90-94; Dn-in-c Gonalston 90-94; NSM Lowdham w Caythorpe, and Gunthorpe 94-00; rtd 95; Perm to Offic *S'well* from 05. *Averham Cottage, Church Lane, Averham, Newark NG23 5RB* Tel (01636) 708601
E-mail keene@averham.fsnet.co.uk

KEEP, Andrew James. b 55. Collingwood Coll Dur BA77 Yale Univ STM84. Sarum & Wells Th Coll 78. **d** 80 **p** 81. C Banstead *Guildf* 80-83; Chapl Qu Eliz Hosp Banstead 80-83; USA 83-84; Chapl Cranleigh Sch Surrey 84-98; Chapl Wells Cathl Sch 98-01; PV Wells Cathl 01-06; Chapl Mill Hill Sch Lon from 07. *Mill Hill School, The Ridgeway, London NW7 1QS* Tel (020) 8959 1176 Mobile 07740-647813 E-mail andrew.keep@lineone.net

KEEP, Hugh Charles John Martin. b 45. Qu Coll Birm 90. **d** 92 **p** 93. C Aston Cantlow and Wilmcote w Billesley *Cov* 92-95; P-in-c Hampton Lucy w Charlecote and Loxley 95-02; Chapl Rainsbrook Secure Tr Cen 02-05; Perm to Offic *Cov* from 05. *4 Old Town, Stratford-upon-Avon CV37 6BG* Tel (01789) 414142 E-mail hrkeepnet@aol.com

KEETON, Barry. b 40. Dur Univ BA61 MA69 MLitt78 K Coll Lon BD63 AKC63. **d** 64 **p** 65. C S Bank *York* 64-67; C Middlesbrough St Cuth 67-69; C Kingston upon Hull St Alb 70-71; V Appleton-le-Street w Amotherby 71-74; Dioc Ecum Adv 74-81; R Ampleforth w Oswaldkirk 74-78; V Howden 78-79; P-in-c Barmby on the Marsh 78-79; P-in-c Laxton w Blacktoft 78-79; P-in-c Wressell 78-79; TR Howden 80-91; Can and Preb York Minster 85-91; RD Howden 86-91; TR Lewes All SS, St Anne, St Mich and St Thos *Chich* 91-96; R Cov St Jo 96-01; RD Cov N 97-01; rtd 01; Perm to Offic *Sheff* from 01 and *York* from 05. *19 Shardlow Gardens, Bessacarr, Doncaster DN4 6UB* Tel (01302) 532045 E-mail barry.k3@ukonline.co.uk

KEFFORD, Canon Peter Charles. b 44. Nottm Univ BTh74. Linc Th Coll 70. **d** 74 **p** 75. C W Wimbledon Ch Ch *S'wark* 74-77; C All Hallows by the Tower etc *Lon* 77-81; C-in-c Pound Hill CD *Chich* 81; TV Worth 82-83; TR 83-92; V Henfield w Shermanbury and Woodmancote 92-01; Can Res and Treas Chich Cathl from 01; Adv for Ord Min and Dioc Dir of Ords 01-06; Dioc Adv for Min from 07. *12 St Martin's Square, Chichester PO19 1NR* Tel (01243) 783509 Fax 812499 E-mail peter.kefford@diochi.org.uk

KEGG, Barry. b 47. Oak Hill Th Coll BA99. EAMTC 02. **d** 05 **p** 06. NSM Mattishall and the Tudd Valley *Nor* from 05. *The Vicarage, Back Lane, Mattishall, Dereham NR20 3PU* Tel (01362) 850243 E-mail gordonkegg@waitrose.com

KEGG, Gordon Rutherford. b 45. Reading Univ BSc66 Imp Coll Lon PhD71 Lon Univ CertEd74. Oak Hill Th Coll 88. **d** 90 **p** 91. C Luton Lewsey St Hugh *St Alb* 90-94; TV Hemel Hempstead 94-01; P-in-c Mattishall w Mattishall Burgh, Welborne etc *Nor* 01-08; P-in-c Hockering, Honingham, E and N Tuddenham 04-08; R Mattishall and the Tudd Valley from 08. *The Vicarage, Back Lane, Mattishall, Dereham NR20 3PU* Tel (01362) 850243 E-mail gordonkegg@waitrose.com

KEIGHLEY, Mrs Amanda Jane. b 56. Garnett Coll Lon CertEd85 Leeds Univ MA98. Cranmer Hall Dur 04. **d** 07 **p** 08. NSM Is of Dogs Ch Ch and St Jo w St Luke *Lon* from 07. *86 Saunders Ness Road, London E14 3EA* Tel (020) 7517 9628 Mobile 07889-486354 E-mail 42xfv@dsl.pipex.com

KEIGHLEY, Andrew Kenneth. b 62. Nottm Univ LLB84 Solicitor 85. Wycliffe Hall Ox 94. **d** 97 **p** 98. C Westminster St Jas the Less *Lon* 97-00; NSM 00-04; C Brompton H Trin w Onslow Square St Paul 04-06; P-in-c W Hampstead Trin from 06. *Holy Trinity Vicarage, 1A Akenside Road, London NW3 5BS* Tel (020) 7794 2975 Mobile 07747-611577

KEIGHLEY, David John. b 48. Open Univ BA88 CertEd. Sarum & Wells Th Coll 82. **d** 83 **p** 84. C Sawbridgeworth *St Alb* 83-86; TV Saltash *Truro* 86-89; V Lanlivery w Luxulyan 89-00; P-in-c The Candover Valley *Win* 00-08; P-in-c Wield 03-08; P-in-c Hurstbourne Tarrant, Faccombe, Vernham Dean etc from 08. *The Vicarage, The Dene, Hurstbourne Tarrant, Andover SP11 0AH* Tel (01264) 736222 Mobile 07736-799262 E-mail davidkeighley@hotmail.com

KEIGHLEY, Martin Philip. b 61. Edin Univ MA83. Westcott Ho Cam 86. **d** 88 **p** 89. C Lytham St Cuth *Blackb* 88-91; C Lancaster St Mary 91-93; R Halton w Aughton 93-00; V Poulton-le-Fylde 00-04; V Poulton Carleton and Singleton from 04; AD Poulton from 08. *The Vicarage, 7 Vicarage Road, Poulton-le-Fylde FY6 7BE* Tel (01253) 883086 E-mail martinkeighley@btconnect.com

KEIGHLEY, Thomas Christopher. b 51. Open Univ BA85. NEOC 00. **d** 03 **p** 04. NSM Upper Nidderdale *Ripon* 03-06; NSM Dacre w Hartwith and Darley w Thornthwaite 06-07; NSM Is of Dogs Ch Ch and St Jo w St Luke *Lon* from 07; Chapl St Joseph's Hospice Hackney from 09. *86 Saunders Ness Road, London E14 3EA* Tel (020) 7517 9628 Mobile 07740-721032 E-mail nurprc@nursing.u-net.com

KEIGHTLEY, Canon Peter Edward. b 17. Leeds Univ BA41. Coll of Resurr Mirfield 41. **d** 43 **p** 44. C Wellingborough All Hallows *Pet* 43-45; C Solihull *Birm* 45-49; C Cirencester *Glouc* 50-53; V Glouc St Paul 53-59; V Widley w Wymering *Portsm* 59-67; V Southsea H Spirit 67-76; Chapl St Mary's Hosp Portsm 76-82; Hon Can Portsm Cathl 81-82; rtd 82; Perm to Offic *Portsm* 83-08. *The College of St Barnabas, Blackberry Lane, Lingfield RH7 6NJ* Tel (01342) 870260

KEIGHTLEY, Canon Thomas. b 44. CITC 79. **d** 79 **p** 80. C Seagoe *D & D* 79-83; I Belvoir from 83; Can Down Cathl from 95; Treas from 01; Prec from 01. *The Rectory, 86B Beechill Road, Belfast BT8 7QN* Tel (028) 9064 3777 Mobile 07919-366660 E-mail tmgkkly@googlemail.com

KEIGHTLEY, Trevor Charles. b 54. St Jo Coll Nottm. **d** 03 **p** 04. C Wombwell *Sheff* 03-07; V Worsbrough Common w

Worsbrough St Thos from 07. *St Thomas's Vicarage, 80 Kingwell Road, Worsbrough, Barnsley S70 4HG* Tel (01226) 286505 E-mail trevorkeightley@aol.com

KEILLER, Canon Jane Elizabeth. b 52. Westmr Coll Ox BEd74. Cranmer Hall Dur 76. **dss** 80 **d** 87 **p** 94. Cambridge H Trin w St Andr Gt *Ely* 80-86; NSM Cambridge St Barn 86-88 and 90-94; NSM Cambridge H Cross 95-02; Chapl and Tutor Ridley Hall Cam from 96; Hon Can Ely Cathl from 05. *68 Pierce Lane, Cambridge CB21 5DL* Tel (01223) 575776 *or* tel and fax 741076 E-mail jk271@cam.ac.uk

KEIR, Mrs Gillian Irene. b 44. Westf Coll Lon BA66 Somerville Coll Ox BLitt70 Lon Univ MA95. SAOMC 95. **d** 98 **p** 99. NSM St Alb St Steph *St Alb* from 98; NSM Officer St Alb Adnry from 06. *17 Battlefield Road, St Albans AL1 4DA* Tel (01727) 839392

KEIRLE, Michael Robert. b 62. Trin Coll Bris BA89. **d** 89 **p** 90. C Orpington Ch Ch *Roch* 89-92; Zimbabwe 92-95; R Keston *Roch* 95-03; R Guernsey St Martin *Win* from 03. *St Martin's Rectory, La Grande Rue, St Martin, Guernsey GY4 6RR* Tel (01481) 238303 Fax 237710 E-mail mrkeirle@cwgsy.net

KEITH, Andrew James Buchanan. b 47. Qu Coll Cam BA69 MA73. Wycliffe Hall Ox 71. **d** 74 **p** 75. C Warrington St Elphin *Liv* 74-77; C Southgate *Chich* 77-80; C-in-c Broadfield CD 80-82; P-in-c Walberton w Binsted 82-85; P-in-c Aldingbourne 83-85; Chapl Oswestry Sch 85-95; Chapl HM Pris Liv 95-96; Chapl HM Pris Preston 96-01; Chapl HM Pris Garth 01-06; NSM Chipping Norton *Ox* from 07. *Juxon House, Little Compton, Moreton-in-Marsh GL56 0SE* Tel (01608) 674856 E-mail keith@janda.go-plus.net

KEITH, Gary Mark Wayne. b 71. Ripon Coll Cuddesdon 01. **d** 03 **p** 04. C Botley, Curdridge and Durley *Portsm* 03-06; Chapl RNR 05-06; Chapl RN 06-08; C N Hants Downs *Win* from 08. *The Vicarage, The Bury, Odiham, Hook RG29 1ND* Tel (01256) 704154 Mobile 07971-448049 E-mail thebishmeister@btinternet.com

KEITH, John. b 25. LRAM50 LGSM50 AGSM51. Cuddesdon Coll 60. **d** 62 **p** 63. C Lee-on-the-Solent *Portsm* 62-65; C Raynes Park St Sav *S'wark* 65-68; rtd 90. *7 Torr An Eas, Glenfinnan PH37 4LS* Tel (01397) 722314

KELHAM, Adèle. b 46. St Andr Univ BSc69. Cranmer Hall Dur. **d** 98 **p** 99. Asst Chapl Zürich *Eur* 98-01; P-in-c Bishop Middleham *Dur* 01-05; AD Sedgefield 03-05; P-in-c Lausanne *Eur* from 05; Dioc Adv for Women's Min from 05. *Avenue Floréal 3, 1006 Lausanne, Switzerland* Tel (0041) (21) 312 6563 E-mail info@christchurch-lausanne.ch

KELK, Michael Anthony. b 48. Sarum & Wells Th Coll. **d** 83 **p** 84. C Ross w Brampton Abbotts, Bridstow and Peterstow *Heref* 83-86; P-in-c Burghill 86-97; P-in-c Stretton Sugwas 86-97; P-in-c Walford and St John w Bishopswood, Goodrich etc 97-02; P-in-c Llangarron w Llangrove, Whitchurch and Ganarew 02-08. *Address temp unknown*

KELLAGHER, Christopher John Bannerman. b 55. Aber Univ MA79 UMIST MSc88. STETS MA09. **d** 09. NSM Aldershot H Trin *Guildf* from 09. *8 Elsenwood Crescent, Camberley GU15 2BA* Tel (01276) 508193 E-mail jkellagher@ntlworld.com

KELLAND, Kenneth William Jerome. b 16. S'wark Ord Course 65. **d** 66 **p** 67. C Addlestone *Guildf* 66-69; C Sholing *Win* 69-74; V Weston 74-82; rtd 82; Hon C Odiham w S Warnborough and Long Sutton *Win* 82-85; Hon C Herriard w Winslade and Long Sutton etc 85-86. *50 Wooteys Way, Alton GU34 2JZ* Tel (01420) 85325

KELLEHER, Mrs Cheryl. b 56. Sheff Univ BA97. NOC 98. **d** 01 **p** 02. NSM Worsbrough St Mary *Sheff* 01-03; Perm to Offic from 04. *10 Fieldsend, Oxspring, Sheffield S36 8WH* Tel (01226) 763236 E-mail cheryl@kelnet.co.uk

KELLEN, David. b 52. St Mich Coll Llan 70. **d** 75 **p** 76. C Mynyddislwyn *Mon* 75-77; C Risca 77-78; C Malpas 78-81; V Newport All SS 81-88; V St Mellons from 88; R Michaelston-y-Fedw 89-96. *The Vicarage, Ty'r Winch Road, St Mellons, Cardiff CF3 5UP* Tel (029) 2079 6560

KELLETT, Garth. See KELLETT, Ronald Garth

KELLETT, Neil. b 41. Bps' Coll Cheshunt 64. **d** 66 **p** 67. C Ex St Thos 66-72; C Win H Trin 72-74; P-in-c Redditch St Geo *Worc* 74-77; Canada from 77. *39 Fox Avenue, St John's NL A1B 2H8, Canada* Tel (001) (709) 726 2883

KELLETT, Richard. b 64. Leeds Univ BSc85 PhD89. St Jo Coll Nottm BTh95 MA96. **d** 96 **p** 97. C Nottingham St Jude *S'well* 96-00; P-in-c Skegby 00-02; P-in-c Teversal 00-02; R Skegby w Teversal from 02; AD Newstead from 06. *The Vicarage, Mansfield Road, Skegby, Sutton-in-Ashfield NG17 3ED* Tel and fax (01623) 558800 E-mail richard@kellett.com

KELLETT, Ronald Garth. b 41. NOC 04. **d** 05 **p** 06. NSM Ilkley St Marg *Bradf* from 05. *8 Kingsway Drive, Ilkley LS29 9AG* Tel (01943) 601906 E-mail 01943601906@talktalk.net

KELLEY, Neil George. b 64. ARCM85. Westcott Ho Cam 88. **d** 91 **p** 92. C E Bedfont *Lon* 91-93; C Chiswick St Nic w St Mary 93-97; C Kirkby *Liv* 97-99; V Gt Crosby St Faith and Waterloo Park St Mary from 99; Dioc Adv on Worship and Liturgy from

06. *The Vicarage, Milton Road, Waterloo, Liverpool L22 4RE* Tel and fax 0151-928 3342 Mobile 07980-872203
E-mail frneilkelley@tiscali.co.uk

KELLY, Canon Albert Norman. b 21. TCD BA43 MA63. **d** 44 **p** 45. C Donaghcloney *D & D* 44-46; C Belfast Malone St Jo *Conn* 46-55; I Billy 55-63; C Dorking w Ranmore *Guildf* 63-66; C-in-c New Haw CD 66-72; V New Haw 72-78; RD Chertsey 73-75; RD Runnymede 75-78; V Egham Hythe 78-86; Hon Can Guildf Cathl 80-86; rtd 86; USPG Area Sec 88-93. *21 Rosetta Road, Belfast BT6 0LQ* Tel (028) 9069 3921

KELLY, Mrs Ann Clarke Thomson. b 60. WMMTC 04. **d** 07 **p** 08. C Stafford St Jo and Tixall w Ingestre *Lich* from 07. *31 The Oval, Stafford ST17 4LQ* Tel (01785) 251683
E-mail scottyann@blueyonder.co.uk

KELLY, Brian Eugene. b 56. Otago Univ BA77 Dunedin Coll PGCE79 Bris Univ PhD93. Trin Coll Bris BA89. **d** 90 **p** 91. NSM Redland *Bris* 90-93; C Scarborough St Mary w Ch Ch and H Apostles *York* 93-96; Dean Chpl Cant Ch Ch Univ Coll 96-03; Perm to Offic *Cant* from 06. *2 Riverside Close, Bridge, Canterbury CT4 5BN* Tel (01227) 831380
E-mail brian@kelly1915.fsnet.co.uk

KELLY, Canon Brian Horace. b 34. St Jo Coll Dur BA57 MA69. **d** 58 **p** 59. C Douglas St Geo and St Barn *S & M* 58-61; V Foxdale 61-64; V Bolton All So w St Jas *Man* 64-73; V Maughold *S & M* 73-77; Dir of Ords 76-93; V German 77-06; Can and Prec St German's Cathl 80-06; RD Castletown and Peel 97-04; rtd 06. *16 Slieau Whallian Park, St Johns, Isle of Man IM4 3JH* Tel (01624) 801479

KELLY, Canon Charles. b 31. Liv Univ BA52. Lich Th Coll 54. **d** 56 **p** 57. C Tranmere St Paul *Ches* 56-59; C-in-c Grange St Andr CD 59-63; P-in-c Grange St Andr 63-65; V 65-67; R Coppenhall 67-82; V W Kirby St Andr 82-01; Hon Can Ches Cathl 86-01; rtd 01; Perm to Offic *Ches* from 01. *26 Lyndhurst Road, Hoylake, Wirral CH47 7BP* Tel 0151-632 0335

KELLY, Desmond Norman. b 42. Oak Hill Th Coll 89. **d** 90 **p** 91. C Braintree *Chelmsf* 90-94; P-in-c Sible Hedingham 94-95; P-in-c Castle Hedingham 94-95; R Sible Hedingham w Castle Hedingham 95-08; rtd 08. *Wykhams, Mill Common, Westhall, Halesworth IP19 8RQ* Tel (01502) 575493
E-mail rev.des@btinternet.com

KELLY, Canon Edward William Moncrieff. b 28. AKC57. **d** 57 **p** 58. C Petersfield w Sheet *Portsm* 57-60; Papua New Guinea 60-65; Dioc Sec Samarai and Hon Chapl Miss to Seamen 61; V Gosport Ch Ch *Portsm* 65-69; Hon C Eltham St Jo *S'wark* 69-87; Org Sec New Guinea Miss 69-77; Org Sec Papua New Guinea Ch Partnership 77-87; Hon Can Papua New Guinea from 78; TR Trowbridge H Trin *Sarum* 87-94; Chapl St Jo Hosp Trowbridge 87-94; Acting RD Bradford 91-92; rtd 94; Perm to Offic *Portsm* from 94. *133 Borough Road, Petersfield GU32 3LP* Tel (01730) 260399

KELLY, John Adrian. b 49. Qu Coll Birm 70. **d** 73 **p** 74. C Formby St Pet *Liv* 73-77; Org Sec CECS *Liv, Blackb* and *S & M* 77-92; Deputation Appeals Org (Lancs and Is of Man) 88-92; Perm to Offic *Liv* 77-05; *Bradf* 77-00; Man 88-97. *39 Cornwall Way, Southport PR8 3SG*

KELLY, Canon John Dickinson. b 42. Nottm Univ BA63. Ripon Hall Ox 63. **d** 65 **p** 66. C Egremont *Carl* 65-67; C Upperby St Jo 67-70; V Arlecdon 70-73; V Barrow St Aid 73-79; V Milnthorpe 79-83; V Beetham and Milnthorpe 83-85; V Camerton St Pet 85-88; P-in-c Camerton H Trin W Seaton 86-88; V Camerton, Seaton and W Seaton 88-01; P-in-c Kells 01-05; Hon Can Carl Cathl from 00; Chapl N Cumbria Acute Hosps NHS Trust 03-05; rtd 05; P-in-c Kirkland, Lamplugh w Ennerdale *Carl* 05-07; Hon C Whitehaven from 07. *The Vicarage, Oakfield Court, Hillcrest, Whitehaven CA28 7UY* Tel (01946) 861310

KELLY, John Graham. b 60. Lanc Univ LLB82 Sheff Univ PhD95 Solicitor 84. St Jo Coll Nottm BTh91. **d** 94 **p** 95. C Normanton *Derby* 94-97; P-in-c Ockbrook 97-01; Lect St Jo Coll Nottm 01-07; rtd 07. *34 Hopping Hill, Milford, Belper DE56 0RJ* Tel (01773) 599066
E-mail jgkelly34@btinternet.com

KELLY, Malcolm Bernard. b 46. St Mich Coll Llan 72. **d** 74 **p** 75. C Tranmere St Paul w St Luke *Ches* 74-77; Chapl Bebington Hosp from 76; C Barnston *Ches* 77-80; R Thurstaston 80-92; R Grappenhall from 92. *The Rectory, 17 Hill Top Road, Stockton Heath, Warrington WA4 2ED* Tel (01925) 261546

KELLY, Martin Herbert. b 55. Selw Coll Cam MA90. Aston Tr Scheme 78 Ripon Coll Cuddesdon 80. **d** 83 **p** 84. C Clapham Old Town *S'wark* 83-87; Chapl and Fell Selw Coll Cam 87-92; Chapl Newnham Coll Cam 87-92; Chapl St Piers Hosp Sch Lingfield *S'wark* 95-01; C Limpsfield and Titsey 95-01; Chapl Basildon and Thurrock Gen Hosps NHS Trust 03-04; Chapl Dartford and Gravesham NHS Trust from 04. *Darent Valley Hospital, Darenth Wood Road, Dartford DA2 8DA* Tel (01322) 428100 ext 4640
E-mail martin.kelly@dvh.nhs.uk

KELLY, Nigel James (Ned). b 60. N Staffs Poly BSc83. Ripon Coll Cuddesdon 83. **d** 86 **p** 87. C Cen Telford *Lich* 86-90; TV 90-92; Chapl RN from 92. *Royal Naval Chaplaincy Service, Mail*

Point 1-2, Leach Building, Whale Island, Portsmouth PO2 8BY* Tel (023) 9262 5055 Fax 9262 5134

KELLY, Paul. b 60. Qu Coll Birm 02. **d** 04 **p** 05. C Ogley Hay *Lich* 04-07; V Stafford St Paul Forebridge from 07. *St Paul's Vicarage, 31 The Oval, Stafford ST17 4LQ* Tel (01785) 224634 Mobile 07815-452616

KELLY, Canon Peter Hugh. b 46. Sarum & Wells Th Coll 81. **d** 84 **p** 85. C Fareham H Trin *Portsm* 84-87; Chapl and Prec Portsm Cathl 87-90; V Eastney 90-97; P-in-c Swanmore St Barn 97-06; V from 07; RD Bishop's Waltham 03-09; Hon Can Portsm Cathl from 07. *The Vicarage, Church Road, Swanmore, Southampton SO32 2PA* Tel (01489) 892105
E-mail peterkelly@swanmore.net

KELLY, Stephen Alexander. b 61. Man Univ BSc84. Ridley Hall Cam 03. **d** 05 **p** 06. C Meole Brace *Lich* 05-08; C Cen Telford from 08. *28 Bartholomew Road, Lawley Village, Telford TF4 2PW* Tel (01952) 501305 E-mail steve.kelly7@virgin.net

KELLY, Canon Stephen Paul. b 55. Keble Coll Ox BA77 MA07 Leeds Univ MA06. Linc Th Coll 77. **d** 79 **p** 80. C Illingworth *Wakef* 79-82; C Knottingley 82-84; V Alverthorpe 84-93; Dioc Ecum Officer 88-93; TR Bingley All SS *Bradf* 93-03; P-in-c Woolley *Wakef* from 03; Dioc CME Officer from 03; Hon Can Wakef Cathl from 08. *The Vicarage, Church Street, Woolley, Wakefield WF4 2JU* Tel (01226) 382550
E-mail stephen.kelly@wakefield.anglican.org

KELLY, Canon William. b 35. Dur Univ BA58. Lambeth STh75 Wycliffe Hall Ox 58. **d** 60 **p** 61. C Walney St Mary *Carl* 60-66; R Distington 66-71; V Barrow St Matt 71-81; RD Furness 77-81; Hon Can Carl Cathl 79-00; Dir of Ords 81-97; V Dalston 81-92; RD Carl 83-88; P-in-c Raughton Head w Gatesgill 86-92; P-in-c Maryport 92-97; P-in-c Flimby 93-96; P-in-c Arthuret and Nicholforest and Kirkandrews on Esk 97-00; rtd 00; Perm to Offic *Carl* from 00. *73 Upperby Road, Carlisle CA2 4JE* Tel (01228) 511535

KELLY, William Norman. b 21. St Aid Birkenhead. **d** 64 **p** 65. Miss to Seamen 64-66; C Douglas St Geo and St Barn *S & M* 66-69; V Wingates *Man* 69-75; Perm to Offic 76-84; Chapl HM Pris Liv 77-78; Chapl HM Borstal Stoke Heath 78-84; V Castletown *S & M* 84-92; rtd 92; Perm to Offic *S & M* from 92. *9 Millhope Close, Hope Street, Castletown, Isle of Man IM9 1DJ* Tel (01624) 824768

KELSEY, George Robert. b 61. Imp Coll Lon BSc83 Newc Univ MSc84 PhD92. Cranmer Hall Dur 95. **d** 97 **p** 98. C Denton *Newc* 97-01; TV Glendale Gp from 01. *Eglingham Vicarage, The Village, Eglingham, Alnwick NE66 2TX* Tel (01665) 578250
E-mail robert@josephkelsey.fsnet.co.uk

KELSEY, Michael Ray. b 22. FEPA57. Wycliffe Hall Ox 60. **d** 62 **p** 63. C Lower Broughton St Clem *Man* 62-64; V Ingleby Greenhow *York* 64-68; V Scarborough St Jas 68-71; Asst to the Gen Sec USCL 71-74; V Blackheath St Jo *S'wark* 74-87; rtd 87; Perm to Offic *St E* 88-05. *20 Sweet Briar, Marcham, Abingdon OX13 6PD* Tel (01865) 391835

✠**KELSHAW, The Rt Revd Terence.** b 36. Pittsburgh Th Sem DMin86. Oak Hill Th Coll. **d** 67 **p** 68 **c** 89. C Clifton Ch Ch w Em *Bris* 67-71; C Woking St Jo *Guildf* 71-73; V Bris H Trin 73-75; P-in-c Easton St Gabr w St Laur 73-75; V Easton H Trin w St Gabr and St Lawr 75-80; P-in-c Barton Hill St Luke w Ch Ch 76-80; USA from 80; Bp Rio Grande 89-05; rtd 05. *12321 Key West Drive NE, Albuquerque NM 87111-2734, USA* Tel (001) (505) 299 0475 E-mail tkelshaw@aol.com

KELSO, Andrew John. b 47. Lon Univ BA70 LRAM73. St Jo Coll Nottm 83. **d** 85 **p** 86. C Gorleston St Mary *Nor* 85-87; C Hellesdon 87-90; TV Ipsley *Worc* from 90; rtd 09. *2 The Close, Throckmorton, Pershore WR10 2JU* Tel (01386) 462087 Mobile 07795-431382 E-mail andykelso@blueyonder.co.uk

KEMM, William St John. b 39. Birm Univ BA62 MA65. Ridley Hall Cam 62. **d** 64 **p** 65. C Kingswinford H Trin *Lich* 64-68; C Hednesford 68-71; V Hanbury 71-76; R Berrow and Breane *B & W* 76-92; V Hertford All SS *St Alb* 92-06; rtd 06. *Holtye, Nether Lane, Nutley, Uckfield TN22 3LE* Tel (01825) 713704
E-mail billkemm@waitrose.com

KEMP, Canon Allan. b 43. Bps' Coll Cheshunt 65 Oak Hill Th Coll 67. **d** 68 **p** 69. C Tunbridge Wells St Jas *Roch* 68-76; V Becontree St Mary *Chelmsf* 76-90; RD Barking and Dagenham 81-86; V Gt w Lt Chesterford 90-07; Hon Can Chelmsf Cathl 99-07; rtd 07. *6 Freemans Orchard, Newent GL18 1TX* Tel (01531) 822041 E-mail canonkemp@waitrose.com

KEMP, Prof Anthony Eric. b 34. St Mark & St Jo Coll Lon CertEd57 LTCL63 FTCL63 Lon Inst of Educn DipEd70 Sussex Univ MA71 DPhil79 Hon FASE77. PSA97 Sydney Univ FBPsS97 Helsinki Univ Hon MusDoc03. SAOMC 96. **d** 98 **p** 99. NSM Wokingham All SS *Ox* 98-05; NSM Wokingham St Paul from 05. *18 Blagrove Lane, Wokingham RG41 4BA* Tel and fax 0118-978 2586 E-mail a.e.kemp@btinternet.com

KEMP, Ms Audrey. b 26. MSR49. Gilmore Ho 62. **dss** 69 **d** 87 **p** 94. Cranford *Lon* 67-70; S Ockendon Hosp 70-71; N Greenford All Hallows *Lon* 71-72; Feltham 72-80; Brentford St Faith 80-83; Hanworth All SS 83-85; Hanworth St Geo 85-87; Par Dn 87-88; rtd 88; Perm to Offic *B & W* 88-89 and 99-07; Hon

Par Dn Ditcheat w E Pennard and Pylle 89-94; P-in-c 94-95; Perm to Offic *Win* 95-98. *Flat 5, Manormead, Tilford Road, Hindhead GU26 6RA* Tel (01428) 602500

KEMP, Christopher Michael. b 48. K Coll Lon BD71 AKC71. St Aug Coll Cant 75. **d** 76 **p** 77. C Weaverham *Ches* 76-79; C Latchford St Jas 79-82; P-in-c Sandbach Heath 82-88; V Macclesfield St Paul 88-89; C Cheadle Hulme All SS 89-93; C Oxton 93-98; P-in-c Seacombe 98-02; P-in-c Brereton w Swettenham 02-05; P-in-c Brereton w Eaton and Hulme Walfield from 05. *The Rectory, Brereton Park, Brereton, Sandbach CW11 1RY* Tel (01477) 533263

✠**KEMP, The Rt Revd Eric Waldram.** b 15. Ex Coll Ox BA36 MA40 BD44 DD61 Sussex Univ Hon DLitt FRHistS51 DLitt01. St Steph Ho Ox 36. **d** 39 **p** 40 **c** 74. C Newtown St Luke *Win* 39-41; Lib Pusey Ho 41-46; Chapl Ch Ch Ox 43-46; Tutor and Chapl Ex Coll Ox 46-69; Can and Preb Linc Cathl 52-01; Chapl to The Queen 67-69; Dean Worc 69-74; Bp Chich 74-01; rtd 01. *5 Alexandra Road, Chichester PO19 7LX* Tel (01243) 780647

KEMP, Geoffrey Bernard. b 20. Lon Univ BD43. ALCD42. **d** 43 **p** 44. C Leyton All SS *Chelmsf* 43-46; C Woodford St Mary 46-49; V Barkingside St Laur 49-60; V Hadleigh St Barn 60-79; R Kelvedon Hatch 79-86; V Navestock 79-86; rtd 86; Perm to Offic *Chelmsf* and *St E* from 86. *24 Roman Way, Felixstowe IP11 9NJ* Tel (01394) 276691

KEMP, John Graham Edwin. b 29. Bris Univ BA51 PGCE52 Lon Univ BD65. Wells Th Coll 63. **d** 65 **p** 66. C Maidenhead St Luke *Ox* 65-70; R Rotherfield Greys 70-78; V Highmore 70-78; Dep Dir Tr Scheme for NSM 78-84; P-in-c Taplow 78-82; TV Burnham w Dropmore, Hitcham and Taplow 82-84; Prin EAMTC 84-92; rtd 92; Chapl Kyrenia Cyprus 92-95; Perm to Offic *St E* from 95. *Lea Cottage, The Street, Middleton, Saxmundham IP17 3NJ* Tel (01728) 648324
E-mail revdjgk@waitrose.com

KEMP, John Robert Deverall. b 42. City Univ BSc65 BD69. Oak Hill Th Coll 66. **d** 70 **p** 71. C Fulham Ch Ch *Lon* 70-73; C Widford *Chelmsf* 73-79; P-in-c New Thundersley 79-84; V 84-98; Chapl HM Pris Bullwood Hall 79-98; R S Shoebury *Chelmsf* 98-09; rtd 09; Perm to Offic *Chelmsf* from 09. *36 Macmurdo Road, Leigh-on-Sea SS9 5AQ*

KEMP, Mrs Pamela Ann. b 52. Coll of St Matthias Bris CertEd73 RMN98. Ripon Coll Cuddesdon BTh07. **d** 02 **p** 03. C Portland All SS w St Pet *Sarum* 02-04; C Verwood 04-06; R Highnam, Lassington, Rudford, Tibberton etc *Glouc* from 06. *The Rectory, 25 Maidenhall, Highnam, Gloucester GL2 8DL* Tel (01452) 525567 Mobile 07989-604543
E-mail pamelakemp@btinternet.com

KEMP, Ralph John. b 71. Wye Coll Lon BSc93 Trin Hall Cam BTh04. Ridley Hall Cam 01. **d** 04 **p** 05. C Astbury and Smallwood *Ches* 04-07; V Burton and Shotwick 07-08; NSM Plas Newton w Ches Ch Ch from 09. *87 High Street, Tarvin, Chester CH3 8JA* Tel 07762-847211 (mobile)
E-mail rjk30@cam.ac.uk

KEMP, Trevor George. b 62. Trin Coll Bris 98. **d** 00 **p** 01. C Old Catton *Nor* 00-03; V S Nutfield w Outwood *S'wark* from 03. *The Vicarage, 136 Mid Street, South Nutfield, Redhill RH1 5RP* Tel (01737) 822211 E-mail rev-trev@cc-nutfield.org.uk
or sixkemps@tinonli.co.uk

KEMP, William. b 67. St Anne's Coll Ox BA91 Brunel Univ PGCE92 Wolfs Coll Cam BTh99. Ridley Hall Cam 96. **d** 99 **p** 00. C Kensington St Barn *Lon* 99-04; P-in-c Mid-Sussex Network Ch *Chich* from 04; C Hurstpierpoint from 04. *12 Western Road, Hurstpierpoint BN6 9TA* Tel (01273) 835829

KEMPSTER, Miss Helen Edith. b 49. **d** 00 **p** 01. OLM Weybridge *Guildf* 00-06; OLM Esher from 06. *28 Dorchester Road, Weybridge KT13 8PE* Tel (01932) 845861
E-mail helen.kempster@btinternet.com

KEMPSTER, Robert Alec. b 29. Selw Coll Cam MA53. Coll of Resurr Mirfield 53. **d** 55 **p** 56. C W Hackney St Barn *Lon* 55-57; C-in-c S'wark All Hallows CD 57-70; PV S'wark Cathl 57-60; Chapl Evelina Children's Hosp 57-70; Chapl Guy's Hosp Lon 70-81; Chapl Nat Hosp for Nervous Diseases Lon 81-89; Chapl Convent Companions Jes Gd Shep W Ogwell 89; rtd 90; Perm to Offic *Ex* from 90. *15A Seymour Road, Newton Abbot TQ12 2PT*

KEMPTHORNE, Renatus. b 39. Wadh Coll Ox MA64. Wycliffe Hall Ox 60. **d** 62 **p** 63. C Stoke *Cov* 62-65; Lect St Jo Coll Auckland New Zealand 65-68; R Wytham *Ox* 68-75; Chapl Bp Grosseteste Coll Linc 75-83; V Waimea New Zealand 83-90; Th Consultant 90-96; Researcher and Educator from 97; rtd 04. *140 Nile Street, Nelson 7010, New Zealand* Tel (0064) (3) 546 7447 E-mail kempthorne@xtra.co.nz

KENCHINGTON, Canon Jane Elizabeth Ballantyne. b 58. Hull Univ BSc79 Trin Coll Bris MA05 Hughes Hall Cam PGCE83. Westcott Ho Cam 88. **d** 90 **p** 94. C Winchcombe, Gretton, Sudeley Manor etc *Glouc* 90-96; Perm to Offic 96-99; NSM Dursley 99-02; Dir Reader Tr and Tutor WEMTC 01-06; Dean of Women Clergy from 06; Hon Can Glouc Cathl from 06. *7 Warren Croft, North Nibley, Dursley GL11 6EN* Tel (01453) 546509 E-mail jane@kenchington.plus.com

KENCHINGTON, Paul Henry. b 54. Worc Coll Ox MA76. St Jo Coll Nottm BA81. **d** 82 **p** 83. C Scarborough St Mary w Ch Ch and H Apostles *York* 82-85; C Caversham St Pet and Mapledurham etc *Ox* 85-89; V Hucclecote *Glouc* 89-00; V Kowloon St Andr Hong Kong 00-05; Chapl Versailles w Chevry *Eur* from 05. *31 rue du pont Colbert, 78000 Versailles, France* Tel (0033) (1) 39 02 79 45 E-mail office@stmarksversailles.org

KENDAL, Gordon McGregor. b 46. Dundee Univ MA70 Mansf Coll Ox BA72 MA76 Lon Univ BA73 PhD79 MA98 St Andr Univ PhD08 Jordanhill Coll Glas PGCE88. Edin Th Coll 72. **d** 74 **p** 75. C Bracknell *Ox* 74-77; C Wokingham All SS 77-79; Chapl and Fell Linc Coll Ox 79-83; R Edin St Pet 83-87; Man Gr Sch 88-92; Gen Sec Fellowship of St Alb and St Sergius 92-96; V S Lambeth St Anne and all SS *S'wark* 96-00. *10 Bamff Road, Alyth, Blairgowrie PH11 8DT* Tel (01828) 633400

KENDAL, Henry David. b 59. ASVA83. Lon Bible Coll 90 Oak Hill NSM Course 92. **d** 94 **p** 95. C Roxeth *Lon* 94-99; C Woodside Park St Barn 99-06; V from 06. *78 Woodside Avenue, London N12 8TB* Tel (020) 8343 7776 or 8343 5775 Mobile 07977-521656 Fax (020) 8446 7492 or 8343 5771
E-mail henrykendal@compuserve.com
or henrykendal@stbarnabas.co.uk

KENDAL, Canon Stephen. b 35. Leeds Univ BA59. Coll of Resurr Mirfield 59. **d** 61 **p** 62. C Seaton Hirst *Newc* 61-63; C Newc St Geo 63-66; C Gosforth All SS 66-70; Ind Chapl *Llan* 70-78; Ind Chapl *Dur* 78-91; Hon C Houghton le Spring 78-90; Ind Chapl *Worc* 91-00; Hon Can Worc Cathl 98-00; rtd 00; Perm to Offic *Heref* from 00. *15 Coneybury View, Broseley TF12 5AX* Tel (01952) 882447 E-mail wimkiddy@aol.com

KENDALL, Edward Oliver Vaughan. b 33. Dur Univ BA59. Ridley Hall Cam 59. **d** 61 **p** 62. C Corsham *Bris* 61-64; C Portsea St Mary *Portsm* 64-67; Asst Chapl HM Pris Pentonville 67-68; Chapl HM Borstal Portland 68-71; Lic to Offic *Bradf* 71-94; rtd 94. *10 Halsteads Cottages, Settle BD24 9QJ* Tel and fax (01729) 822207

KENDALL, Frank. b 40. CCC Cam BA62 MA68 FRSA90. S'wark Ord Course 74. **d** 74 **p** 75. NSM Lingfield *S'wark* 74-75 and 78-82; NSM Sketty *S & B* 75-78; NSM Limpsfield and Titsey *S'wark* 82-84; Lic to Offic *Man* 84-89 and *Liv* 89-96; NSM Adnry St Helens *Liv* 96-00; Perm to Offic from 01; NSM Farington Moss and Lostock Hall *Blackb* 03-06; Perm to Offic from 06. *52 Kingsway, Penwortham, Preston PR1 0ED* Tel (01772) 748021

KENDALL, Giles. b 57. Lon Univ BA80 Univ Coll Lon BSc86 Lon Univ PhD90. STETS BTh98. **d** 98 **p** 99. C Wareham *Sarum* 98-01; V Sawston *Ely* 01-08; P-in-c Babraham 01-08; P-in-c Kingswinford St Mary *Worc* from 08. *The Rectory, 17 Penzer Street, Kingswinford DY6 7AA* Tel (01384) 273716
E-mail revg.kingswinford@btinternet.com

KENDALL, Gordon Sydney. b 41. **d** 72 **p** 74. NSM Old Ford St Paul w St Steph and St Mark *Lon* 72-82; NSM Homerton St Luke 89-92; Asst Chapl Hackney and Homerton Hosp Lon 87-92; Chapl S Devon Healthcare NHS Trust 92-06; rtd 06. *Shiloh, Beech Trees Lane, Ipplepen, Newton Abbot TQ12 5TW* Tel (01803) 814054

KENDRA, Neil Stuart. b 46. JP96. Leeds Univ BA67 Bradf Univ MSc80 PhD84. Linc Th Coll 67. **d** 69 **p** 70. C Allerton *Liv* 69-72; Ldr Leeds City Cen Detached Youth Work Project 73-75; Dioc Youth Officer *Ripon* 75-77; Lect Ilkley Coll 77-78; Sen Lect Bradf and Ilkley Community Coll 78-88; Hd Community and Youth Studies St Martn's Coll 88-94; Hd Applied Soc Sciences 94-06; Hd Sch Soc Sciences and Business Studies 01-06; P-in-c Settle *Bradf* from 06; P-in-c Giggleswick and Rathmell w Wigglesworth from 08. *Cravendale, Belle Hill, Giggleswick, Settle BD24 0BA* Tel (01729) 825307
E-mail neil.kendra@totalise.co.uk

KENDREW, Geoffrey David. b 42. K Coll Lon BD66 AKC66. **d** 67 **p** 68. C Bourne *Guildf* 67-70; C Haslemere 70-76; V Derby St Barn 76-95; R Deal St Leon w St Rich and Sholden etc *Cant* 95-07; Chapl E Kent NHS and Soc Care Partnership Trust 00-06; Chapl Kent & Medway NHS and Soc Care Partnership Trust 06-07; rtd 07. *2 Mill Lane, Butterwick, Boston PE22 0JE* Tel (01205) 760977 E-mail david-kendrew@supanet.com

KENDRICK, Dale Evans. b 62. Ch Ch Coll Cant BA86 Nottm Univ MA87 Leeds Univ MA95. Coll of Resurr Mirfield 94. **d** 95 **p** 96. C Tividale *Lich* 95-96; C Blakenall Heath 96-97; C Stafford 97-98; Dep Chapl HM Pris Birm 98-01; Chapl HM Pris Drake Hall 01-03; Dep Chapl RAF 03-04; Chapl HM YOI Werrington Ho from 04. *HM Youth Custody Centre, Werrington, Stoke-on-Trent ST9 0DX* Tel (01782) 463300 Fax 463301

KENDRICK, Canon Desmond Max. b 22. Leeds Univ BA47. Wycliffe Hall Ox 50. **d** 52 **p** 53. C Glodwick St Mark *Man* 52-54; Chapl Leeds Road Hosp Bradf 54-77; V Bradf St Clem 54-77; RD Bradf 63-73; Hon Can Bradf Cathl 64-89; V Otley 77-89; Chapl Wharfdale Gen Hosp 77-90; rtd 89; Perm to Offic *Bradf* from 89. *26 Ashtofts Mount, Guiseley LS20 9DB* Tel (01943) 870430

KENDRICK, Mrs Helen Grace. b 66. Bris Univ BA88. SAOMC 96. **d** 99 **p** 00. C Icknield *Ox* 99-03; P-in-c Sutton Courtenay w

Appleford from 03. *The Vicarage, 3 Tullis Close, Sutton Courtenay, Abingdon OX14 4BD* Tel (01235) 848297 E-mail helen@kendricks.fsnet.co.uk

KENNAR, Thomas Philip. b 66. Surrey Univ BA08. STETS 02. **d** 05 **p** 06. C Warblington w Emsworth *Portsm* 05-08; Chapl Portsm Coll 06-08; TR Portsea N End St Mark *Portsm* from 08. *The Rectory, 3A Wadham Road, Portsmouth PO2 9ED* Tel (023) 9234 2661 E-mail tomkennar@googlemail.com

KENNARD, Mark Philip Donald. b 60. Man Univ BSc82. Cranmer Hall Dur 85. **d** 88 **p** 89. C Newark w Hawton, Cotham and Shelton *S'well* 88-89; C Newark 89-91; C Cropwell Bishop w Colston Bassett, Granby etc 91-93; P-in-c Shireoaks 93-99; Chapl Bassetlaw Hosp and Community Services NHS Trust 93-96; Chapl RAF from 99. *Chaplaincy Services, Valiant Block, HQ Air Command, RAF High Wycombe HP14 4UE* Tel (01494) 496800 Fax 496343

KENNEDY, Alan. b 52. Liv Univ BSc95. NOC 01. **d** 03 **p** 04. C Westbrook St Phil *Liv* 03-07; TV Mossley Hill from 07. *The Vicarage, Rose Lane, Liverpool L18 8DB* Tel 0151-724 1915

KENNEDY, Ms Alison Mary. b 66. K Coll Lon BMus87 Heythrop Coll Lon MA95 LTCL90. NTMTC 96. **d** 99 **p** 00. C De Beauvoir Town St Pet *Lon* 99-02; TV Walthamstow *Chelmsf* 02-07; TV N Lambeth *S'wark* from 07. *10 Wincott Street, London SE11 4NT* Tel (020) 7820 9445 E-mail alison_m_kennedy@hotmail.com

KENNEDY, Anthony Reeves. b 32. Roch Th Coll 64. **d** 67 **p** 68. C Ross *Heref* 67-69; C Marfleet *York* 69-71; TV 72-76; V Lightwater *Guildf* 76-83; V W Ham *Chelmsf* 83-89; V Lutton w Gedney Drove End, Dawsmere *Linc* 89-94; Perm to Offic *Chich* from 94 and *Win* from 01; rtd 97. *40 Haydock Close, Alton GU34 2TL* Tel (01420) 549860 E-mail anthreev.kennedy@virgin.net

KENNEDY, Miss Carolyn Ruth. b 59. Univ of Wales (Ban) BA81 GradCertEd(FE)85. Ripon Coll Cuddesdon BA90. **d** 91 **p** 94. C Frodingham *Linc* 91-95; Chapl Cov Univ 95-00; R Uffington Gp *Linc* from 00. *The Rectory, 67 Main Road, Uffington, Stamford PE9 4SN* Tel (01780) 481786 E-mail rector@uffingtongroup.org.uk

KENNEDY, David George. b 46. Hull Univ BEd71 MA76. Linc Th Coll 77. **d** 79 **p** 80. C Linc St Faith and St Martin w St Pet 79-82; V Bilton St Pet *York* 82-90; V New Seaham *Dur* 90-92; Chapl Lincs and Humberside Univ 92-97; P-in-c Barrow St Matt *Carl* 97-99; TR 99-03; Chapl Furness Coll 97-03; P-in-c Blackb St Aid 03-04; V Blackb St Fran and St Aid 04-06; Chapl Nord Pas de Calais *Eur* 06-08; P-in-c Bierley *Bradf* from 08. *St John's Vicarage, Bierley Lane, Bradford BD4 6AA* Tel (01274) 681397 E-mail therevdavid@hotmail.com

KENNEDY, Canon David John. b 57. St Jo Coll Dur BA78 Nottm Univ MTh81 Birm Univ PhD96. St Jo Coll Nottm 79. **d** 81 **p** 82. C Tudhoe Grange *Dur* 81-87; C Merrington 84-87; Tutor Qu Coll Birm 88-96; R Haughton le Skerne *Dur* 96-01; Can Res Dur Cathl from 01; Vice-Dean from 09. *7 The College, Durham DH1 3EQ* Tel 0191-375 0242 Fax 386 4267 E-mail canon.precentor@durhamcathedral.co.uk

KENNEDY, Gary. b 63. Qu Coll Birm BA02. **d** 03 **p** 04. C New Bury *Man* 03-06; C New Bury w Gt Lever 06; P-in-c Bolton SS Simon and Jude from 06. *The Vicarage, 15 Lowick Avenue, Bolton BL3 2DS* Tel (01204) 365063 E-mail therev@talktalk.net

KENNEDY, Ian Duncan. b 53. **d** 04 **p** 05. OLM Whitnash *Cov* 04-07; NSM Leek Wootton 07-08; P-in-c Fillongley and Corley from 08. *The Vicarage, Holbeche Crescent, Fillongley, Coventry CV7 8ES* Tel (01676) 540320 E-mail reviankennedy@aol.com

KENNEDY, James Ernest. b 20. TCD BA46 MA51. CITC 46. **d** 46 **p** 47. C Kilnamanagh w Kilcormack, Castle Ellis etc *C & O* 46-48; C Ahoghill *Conn* 48; P-in-c Portglenone 48-51; I 51-60; I Agherton 60-67; I Errigal w Desertoghill *D & R* 67-81; rtd 81. *38 Prospect Road, Portstewart BT55 7LQ* Tel (028) 7083 2052

KENNEDY, Mrs Jane Rowston. b 47. Dudley Coll of Educn CertEd70 Leic Univ DipEd93. EMMTC 04. **d** 07 **p** 08. NSM Gilmorton, Peatling Parva, Kimcote etc *Leic* from 07. *17 Cromwell Close, Walcote, Lutterworth LE17 4JJ* Tel (01455) 554065 E-mail jane@kennedyjane.wanadoo.co.uk

KENNEDY, Jason Grant. b 68. Oak Hill Th Coll BA95. **d** 98 **p** 99. C Beccles St Mich *St E* 98-01; R Hollington St Leon *Chich* 01-05; C Tonbridge St Steph *Roch* from 05. *20 Woodfield Road, Tonbridge TN9 2LQ*

KENNEDY, John Frederick. b 42. Birm Univ BSc64 PhD67 DSc73. Qu Coll Birm 05. **d** 06 **p** 07. NSM Edgbaston St Geo *Birm* from 06. *St George's Church Office, 1 Westbourne Crescent, Edgbaston, Birmingham B15 3DQ* Tel 0121-454 2303 E-mail office@stgeorgesedgbaston.org.uk

KENNEDY, Joseph. b 69. Edin Univ BSc91 BD94 Moray Ho Coll of Educn PGCE97 St Hugh's Coll Ox MSt00 Keble Coll Ox DPhil06. St Steph Ho Ox 98. **d** 02 **p** 03. C Stratfield Mortimer and Mortimer W End etc *Ox* 02-03; C Abingdon 03-05; Dean of Chpl, Chapl and Fell Selw Coll Cam 05-08; Chapl Newnham Coll Cam 05-08; Prin Coll of Resurr Mirfield from 08. *College of the Resurrection, Stocks Bank Road, Mirfield WF14 0BW* Tel (01924) 490441 Fax 492738 E-mail jkennedy@mirfield.org.uk

KENNEDY, Canon Michael Charles. b 39. TCD BA63 MA79 BD79 Open Univ PhD87. TCD Div Sch 61. **d** 63 **p** 64. C Drumglass *Arm* 63-66; I Lisnadill w Kildarton from 66; Warden Dioc Guild of Lay Readers from 74; Hon V Choral Arm Cathl from 75; Tutor for Aux Min (Arm) from 82; Preb Yagoe St Patr Cathl Dublin from 92. *Lisnadill Rectory, 60 Newtownhamilton Road, Armagh BT60 2PW* Tel (028) 3752 3630 E-mail michaelkennedy2@btinternet.com

KENNEDY, Paul Alan. b 67. ACA92. St Steph Ho Ox BA95. **d** 95 **p** 96. C Romford St Andr *Chelmsf* 95-98; C Cheam *S'wark* 98-01; V Steep and Froxfield w Privett *Portsm* 01-08; R E Win from 08; Bp's Adv on Healing *Portsm* from 04. *The Rectory, 19 Petersfield Road, Winchester SO23 0JD* Tel (01962) 853777 Mobile 07877-211303 E-mail rectoreastwinchester@googlemail.com

KENNEDY, Paul Joseph Alan. b 57. Newc Univ MA93. Sarum & Wells Th Coll 81. **d** 84 **p** 85. C Shildon w Eldon *Dur* 84-86; C Shotton *St As* 86-88; V Waterhouses *Dur* 88-93; V Denton *Newc* 93-95; CF 95-98; P-in-c Leam Lane *Dur* 98-99; V 99-05; P-in-c S Westoe from 05. *St Michael's Vicarage, Westoe Road, South Shields NE33 3PD* Tel 0191-422 1299

KENNEDY, Brother Philip Bartholomew. b 47. STETS 95. **d** 98 **p** 99. SSF from 77; Hon C Plaistow and N Canning Town *Chelmsf* from 08. *St Matthias' Vicarage, 45 Mafeking Road, London E16 4NS* Tel (020) 7511 7848 E-mail philipbartholomewssf@googlemail.com

KENNEDY, Ross Kenneth. b 40. Edin Th Coll 83. **d** 85 **p** 86. C Hexham *Newc* 85-89; TV Glendale Gp 89-93; TR Ch the King 93-05; rtd 05; Hon C Dunfermline *St And* from 05. *12 Calaisburn Place, Dunfermline KY11 4RD* Tel (01383) 625887 E-mail rk.kennedy@btinternet.com

KENNEDY, Samuel (Uell). b 51. Heriot-Watt Univ BSc72. CBDTI 06. **d** 07 **p** 08. NSM Baildon *Bradf* from 07; Development Officer Min and Miss from 02. *The Moorings, Hunsingore, Wetherby LS22 5HY* Tel (01535) 650531 E-mail uell@kadugli.org.uk

KENNEDY, Wendy Patricia. b 58. STETS 00. **d** 03 **p** 04. NSM Warren Park and Leigh Park *Portsm* 03-07; Dioc Sec from 07; Perm to Offic from 07. *13 Ashcroft Lane, Waterlooville PO8 0AX* Tel (023) 9241 3190 E-mail wendy.kennedy@portsmouth.anglican.org

KENNEDY, William Edmund. b 20. QUB BA43 TCD BA45 MA48. **d** 45 **p** 46. C Seagoe *D & D* 45-48; C Ballynafeigh St Jude 48-57; I Ballyculter w Kilclief 57-85; rtd 85. *Redburn Nursing Home, 89 Belfast Road, Ballynahinch BT24 8EB* Tel (028) 9756 3554

KENNERLEY, Katherine Virginia (Ginnie). Somerville Coll Ox BA58 MA65 TCD BA86 Princeton TS Sem DMin98. CITC 86. **d** 88 **p** 90. Lect Applied Th CITC 88-93; NSM Bray *D & G* 88-93; I Narraghmore and Timolin w Castledermot etc 93-05; Can Ch Ch Cathl Dublin 96-05; rtd 05. *4 Seafield Terrace, Dalkey, Co Dublin, Republic of Ireland* Tel (00353) (1) 275 0737 Mobile 87-647 5092 E-mail kennerley@eircom.net

KENNETT-ORPWOOD, Jason Robert. b 59. St Mich Coll Llan. **d** 78 **p** 79. Chapl St Woolos Cathl 78-82; Chapl St Woolos Hosp Newport 79-82; Dioc Youth Chapl *Mon* 82-85; V Cwmcarn 82-85; TV Wrexham *St As* 85-89; Dioc Ecum Officer 94-99; Chapl Wrexham Maelor Hosp 86-89; V Bistre 89-99. *94 Erddig Road, Wrexham LL13 7DR*

KENNEY, Canon Peter. b 50. Edin Univ BD75. Edin Th Coll 73. **d** 76 **p** 77. C Cullercoats St Geo *Newc* 76-81; TV Whorlton 81-88; TR Ch the King 88-93; P-in-c Newc St Jo 93-02; P-in-c Gosforth St Hugh 02-09; P-in-c Chapel House from 09; Dioc Adv in Past Care and Counselling from 02; Hon Can Newc Cathl from 04. *The Vicarage, 44 Queensbury Drive, North Walbottle, Newcastle upon Tyne NE15 9XF* Tel 0191-229 0136 E-mail kenney@globalnet.co.uk

KENNING, Canon Michael Stephen. b 47. St Chad's Coll Dur BA68. Westcott Ho Cam 69. **d** 71 **p** 72. C Hythe *Cant* 71-75; TV Bow w Bromley St Leon *Lon* 75-77; C-in-c W Leigh CD *Portsm* 77-81; V Lee-on-the-Solent 81-92; R N Waltham and Steventon, Ashe and Deane *Win* from 92; RD Whitchurch 03-08; Hon Can Win Cathl from 09. *The Rectory, North Waltham, Basingstoke RG25 2BQ* Tel and fax (01256) 397256 E-mail michael.kenning@ukgateway.net

KENNINGTON, John Paul. b 61. Collingwood Coll Dur BA85. St Steph Ho Ox BA87 MA92. **d** 88 **p** 89. C Headington *Ox* 88-91; C Dulwich St Clem w St Pet *S'wark* 91-94; TV Mortlake w E Sheen 94-01; V Battersea St Mary from 01. *St Mary's Vicarage, 32 Vicarage Crescent, London SW11 3LD* Tel (020) 7585 3986 *or* tel and fax 7228 9648 E-mail pkennington@clara.net

KENNY, Charles John. b 39. QUB BA61 MEd78 LGSM74. CITC 69. **d** 69 **p** 70. C Belfast St Paul *Conn* 69-71; Hd of RE Grosvenor High Sch 71-94; V Choral Belf Cathl 94-00; Can Treas 95-00; rtd 00; Lic to Offic *Conn* from 84. *45 Deramore*

Drive, Belfast BT9 5JS Tel (028) 9066 9632 *or* 9032 8332 Fax 9023 8855 E-mail c.kenny142@btinternet.com

KENNY, Frederick William Bouvier. b 28. TCD BA53 DipEd54 MA56. **d** 56 **p** 57. C Ballymacarrett St Patr *D & D* 56-58; C Blackpool St Jo *Blackb* 58-61; V Preston St Paul 61-66; Chapl Preston R Infirmary 61-66; Youth Adv CMS (Lon) 66-70; Youth Sec (Ireland) CMS 70-75; I Belfast St Clem *D & D* 75-80; V Preston St Cuth *Blackb* 80-86; TV Bushbury *Lich* 86-90; P-in-c Stambridge *Chelmsf* 90-97; Chapl Southend Community Care Services NHS Trust 90-97; rtd 97; Perm to Offic *Pet* 97-99 and *Chelmsf* from 99. *89 Cavendish Gardens, Westcliff-on-Sea SS0 9XP* Tel (01702) 344791 E-mail c-jkenny@dial.pipex.com

KENNY, Mark Anthony. b 74. Leeds Univ BA97 PGCE98. NTMTC 02. **d** 04 **p** 05. NSM Covent Garden St Paul *Lon* 04-08; NSM Aldersbrook *Chelmsf* from 08. *110 Perth Road, Ilford IG2 6AS* Tel (020) 8554 2492 Mobile 07974-572074 E-mail mark.kenny@btinternet.com

KENRICK, Kenneth David Norman. b 44. Liv Univ RMN. Ripon Hall Ox 70 NW Ord Course 77. **d** 77 **p** 78. C Stockport St Geo *Ches* 77-83; R Stockport St Thos 83-85; R Stockport St Thos w St Pet from 86; Chapl St Thos and Cheadle Royal Hospitals from 88. *St Thomas's Rectory, 25 Heath Road, Stockport SK2 6JJ* Tel 0161-483 2483 E-mail truefaith_@hotmail.com

KENSINGTON, Area Bishop of. *See* WILLIAMS, The Rt Revd Paul Gavin

KENT, Barry James. b 41. **d** 02 **p** 03. OLM Kinson *Sarum* 02-07; NSM Hordle *Win* from 07. *Church Cottage, Sway Road, Tiptoe, Lymington SO41 6FR* Tel (01425) 616670 E-mail kenthome@tiscali.co.uk

KENT, Christopher Alfred. b 48. Birm Univ BSc69 PhD72 CEng77 MIChemE77. St Jo Coll Nottm 82. **d** 84 **p** 85. C Bucknall and Bagnall *Lich* 84-86; Hon C Halesowen *Worc* 86-96; NSM Reddal Hill St Luke 96-01; NSM The Lye and Stambermill from 01. *40 County Park Avenue, Halesowen B62 8SP* Tel 0121-550 3132 E-mail c.a.kent@bham.ac.uk

KENT, Miss Cindy. b 45. SEITE 05. **d** 07 **p** 08. NSM Whetstone St Jo *Lon* from 07. *24 Queens Avenue, London N20 0JE* Tel (020) 8445 3682 Mobile 07879-642100 E-mail cindykent58@hotmail.com

KENT, David. b 44. CEng MIMechE. NOC. **d** 83 **p** 84. NSM Huddersfield St Pet and All SS *Wakef* 83-98; NSM Newsome and Armitage Bridge 98-03; NSM Em TM from 03. *2 Hillside Crescent, Huddersfield HD4 6LY* Tel (01484) 324049 Mobile 07949-762186 E-mail david.kent3@ntlworld.com

KENT, Frank. b 44. Open Univ BA82 ARCM76. Ridley Hall Cam. **d** 86 **p** 87. C Faversham *Cant* 86-89; R Lyminge w Paddlesworth, Stanford w Postling etc 89-99; P-in-c Sittingbourne St Mich 99-00; V Sittingbourne St Mary and St Mich 01-04; R Eastry and Northbourne w Tilmanstone etc 04-07; rtd 07. *3 Balfour Road, Walmer, Deal CT14 7HU* Tel (01304) 375080 *or* 619366 E-mail revkent@francikent.freeserve.co.uk

KENT, Hugh. *See* KENT, Richard Hugh

KENT, Keith Meredith. b 32. St Aid Birkenhead 55. **d** 58 **p** 59. C Fulwood Ch Ch *Blackb* 58-60; C Everton St Chrys *Liv* 60-62; C Litherland St Phil 64-68; P-in-c Everton St Polycarp 68-74; V Liv All So Springwood 74-78; V Carr Mill 78-86; V Beddgelert *Ban* 86-91; rtd 91; Perm to Offic *Blackb* from 91. *14 Crow Hills Road, Penwortham, Preston PR1 0JE* Tel (01772) 746831

KENT, Mrs Mary. b 51. Birm Univ BA72. St Steph Ho Ox 06. **d** 08 **p** 09. NSM Alvcston *Cov* from 08. *Elmhurst, Little Alne, Wootton Wawen, Henley-in-Arden B95 6HW* Tel (01789) 488150

KENT, Canon Michael Patrick. b 31. St Edm Hall Ox BA50 MA52. Cuddesdon Coll 50. **d** 52 **p** 53. C W Hartlepool St Aid *Dur* 52-57; C-in-c Pennywell St Thos and Grindon St Oswald CD 57-70; V Cockerton 70-93; RD Darlington 79-84; Hon Can Dur Cathl 83-98; rtd 93; Chapl St Chad's Coll *Dur* 94-95. *Beddall House, Sherburn Hospital, Durham DH1 2SE* Tel 0191-372 0269

KENT, Richard Hugh. b 38. Worc Coll Ox BA61 MA63. Chich Th Coll 61. **d** 63 **p** 64. C Emscote *Cov* 63-66; C Finham 66-70; V Parkend *Glouc* 70-75; V Glouc St Aldate 75-86; Chapl and Warden Harnhill Healing Cen 86-96; R N Buckingham *Ox* 96-04; AD Buckingham 00-04; rtd 04; Perm to Offic *Pet* from 05. *10 Booth Close, Pattishall, Towcester NN12 8JP* Tel (01327) 836231 E-mail hugh.k@talk21.com

KENT, Ms Susan Elizabeth. b 52. St Aid Coll Dur BA74 St Mary's Coll Newc PGCE77. Ripon Coll Cuddesdon 98. **d** 00 **p** 01. C Westgate Common *Wakef* 00-03; P-in-c Oxclose *Dur* 03-08; R Upper Weardale from 08. *The Rectory, 48 Front Street, Stanhope, Bishop Auckland DL13 2UE* Tel (01388) 528722 Mobile 07884-024202 E-mail revsusan@arken.freeserve.co.uk

KENT-WINSLEY, Cindy. *See* KENT, Miss Cindy

KENTIGERN-FOX, Canon William Poyntere Kentigern. b 38. AKC63. **d** 64 **p** 65. C S Mimms St Mary and Potters Bar *Lon* 64-67; C S Tottenham 67-70; R Barrowden and Wakerley *Pet* 70-76; P-in-c Duddington w Tixover 70-76; P-in-c Morcott w S Luffenham 75-77; R Barrowden and Wakerley w S Luffenham 77-79; R Byfield w Boddington 79-86; V Northampton St Mich w St Edm 86-95; V Raunds 95-03; Can Pet Cathl 94-03; RD

Higham 97-02; rtd 03. *41 Parkfield Road, Ruskington, Sleaford NG34 9HT* Tel (01526) 830944

KENWARD, Roger Nelson. b 34. Selw Coll Cam BA58 MA62. Ripon Hall Ox 58. **d** 60 **p** 61. C Paddington St Jas *Lon* 60-63; Chapl RAF 64-82; Asst Chapl-in-Chief RAF 82-89; P-in-c Lyneham w Bradenstoke *Sarum* 72-76; QHC 85-89; R Laughton w Ripe and Chalvington *Chich* 90-95; Chapl Laughton Lodge Hosp 90-95; rtd 95; NSM Chiddingly w E Hoathly *Chich* 96; Perm to Offic from 96. *The Coach House, School Hill, Old Heathfield, Heathfield TN21 9AE* Tel (01435) 862618

KENWAY, Ian Michael. b 52. Leeds Univ BA74 Bris Univ PhD86. Coll of Resurr Mirfield 74. **d** 76 **p** 77. C Cov E 76-79; C Southmead *Bris* 79-81; P-in-c Shaw Hill *Birm* 82-88; Asst Sec Gen Syn Bd for Soc Resp 88-93; Chapl Essex Univ 93-99; Dir Studies Cen for Study of Th 93-99; Perm to Offic *S & B* from 01. *The Beast House, Cwmdu, Crickhowell NP8 1RT* Tel (01874) 730143 Mobile 07748-223090 Fax 07092-315825 E-mail iank@cischr.org

KENWAY, Robert Andrew. b 56. Bris Univ BA78. Westcott Ho Cam 80. **d** 82 **p** 83. C Birchfield *Birm* 82-85; C Queensbury All SS *Lon* 87-89; R Birm St Geo 89-97; V Calne and Blackland *Sarum* from 97. *The Vicarage, Vicarage Close, Calne SN11 8DD* Tel (01249) 812340 E-mail bobandsadie.kenway@btopenworld.com

KENYA, Archbishop of. *See* WABUKALA, The Most Revd Eliud

KENYON, Lee Stuart. b 78. Lanc Univ BA01 Leeds Univ BA04 MA05. Coll of Resurr Mirfield 02. **d** 05 **p** 06. C Darwen St Cuth w Tockholes St Steph *Blackb* 05-09; P-in-c Calgary St Jo Canada from 09. *St John's Rectory, 1421 8th Avenue SE, Calgary AB T2G 0N1, Canada* E-mail leekenyon@fsmail.net

KEOGH, Anthony. b 35. St Mich Coll Llan 63. **d** 66 **p** 67. C Aberaman and Abercwmboi *Llan* 66-70; Hon C Penarth All SS 70-76; R Jersey H Trin *Win* 76-05; rtd 05. *9 La Ville des Chenes, St John, Jersey JE3 4BG* Tel (01534) 869655 E-mail jill.keogh@virgin.net

KEOGH, Henry James. b 39. TCD BA61 NUI BMus65. **d** 62 **p** 63. C Cork St Fin Barre's Cathl 62-65; C Belfast St Luke *Conn* 65-66; C Dromore Cathl 66-68; I Castlecomer *C & O* 68-85; I Kilscoran w Killinick and Mulrankin 85-02; Hon Chapl Miss to Seafarers 85-02; Preb Ferns Cathl 96-02; rtd 02. *5 Ard na Gréine, Dark Road, Midleton, Co Cork, Republic of Ireland* Tel (00353) (21) 463 0841

KEOGH, Paul Anthony. b 37. Order of Friars Minor 55. **d** 62 **p** 63. In RC Ch 62-66; Hon C Eltham Park St Luke *S'wark* 00-07; Perm to Offic from 07. *78 Greenvale Road, London SE9 1PD* Tel (020) 8850 9958 *or* 8303 4786

KEOGH, Robert Gordon. b 56. CITC. **d** 84 **p** 85. C Mossley *Conn* 84-87; I Taunagh w Kilmactranny, Ballysumaghan etc *K, E & A* 87-90; I Swanlinbar w Tomregan, Kinawley, Drumlane etc 90-02; Preb Kilmore Cathl 98-02; I Drumclamph w Lower and Upper Langfield *D & R* from 02. *Drumclamph Rectory, 70 Greenville Road, Castlederg BT81 7NU* Tel (028) 8167 1433 E-mail rkeogh@utvinternet.com

KEOWN, Paul. b 53. Univ of Wales (Swansea) BA95 PGCE97 LGSM76. Ripon Coll Cuddesdon 00 St Steph Ho Ox BTh06. **d** 02 **p** 03. C Llansamlet *S & B* 02-04; P-in-c Swansea St Nic 04-07; R Haddington *Edin* 07-08; V Salfords *S'wark* from 08. *The Vicarage, Honeycrock Lane, Redhill RH1 5DF* Tel (01737) 764712 E-mail frpaulkeown@mac.com

KER, Desmond Agar-Ellis. b 15. Wells Th Coll 58. **d** 58 **p** 60. C Wyken *Cov* 58-59; C Dawlish *Ex* 60-61; C Cockington 61-69; V Bovey Tracey St Jo 69-80; rtd 80; Perm to Offic *S'wark* 84-92; Perm to Offic *Chich* 92-97. *Flat 36, St Clements Court, Wear Bay Crescent, Folkestone CT19 5AU*

KER, Robert Andrew. **d** 05 **p** 06. Aux Min Larne and Inver *Conn* from 05. *24 Ravensdale, Newtownabbey BT36 6FA* Tel (028) 9083 6901 E-mail a.ker@btinternet.com

KERLEY, Brian Edwin. b 36. St Jo Coll Cam BA57 MA61. Linc Th Coll 59. **d** 61 **p** 62. C Sheerness H Trin w St Paul *Cant* 61-64; C St Laur in Thanet 64-69; C Coulsdon St Andr *S'wark* 69-76; P-in-c Fulbourn *Ely* 76-77; R 77-03; P-in-c Gt and Lt Wilbraham 86-03; RD Quy 83-93 and 97-00; rtd 03; Perm to Offic *Ely* from 03. *11 Dalton Way, Ely CB6 1DS* Tel (01353) 665641 E-mail brian.kerley@ely.anglican.org

KERLEY, Patrick Thomas Stewart. b 42. Linc Th Coll. **d** 85 **p** 86. Hon C Thorpe St Andr *Nor* 85-90; C Wymondham 90-94; C Gt Yarmouth 94-95; TV 95-00; TV Wilford Peninsula *St E* 00-07; rtd 07; Perm to Offic *Nor* from 08. *3 St Leonard's Close, Wymondham NR18 0JF* Tel (01953) 606618 Mobile 07940-739769

KERNER, Vivienne Jane. b 49. Liv Univ CertEd71 BEd72. WEMTC 91. **d** 94 **p** 95. NSM Glouc St Jas and All SS 94-01; NSM Glouc St Mark and St Mary de Crypt w St Jo etc 01-02; Perm to Offic 02-04; NSM Hardwicke and Elmore w Longney 04-07; Hon Chapl Leckhampton Court Hospice 03-07, NSM Charfield and Kingswood *Glouc* from 07. *The Rectory, 36 Wotton Road, Charfield, Wotton-under-Edge GL12 8TG* Tel (01454) 261751 E-mail vivienne.kerner@btinternet.com

KERNEY, Barbara. *See* SHERLOCK, Mrs Barbara Lee Kerney

KERR, Mrs Alison. b 76. Ripon Coll Cuddesdon 06. **d** 09. C Lytchett Minster *Sarum* from 09. *Corfe View, Jenny's Lane, Lytchett Matravers, Poole BH16 6BP* Tel 07833-450780 (mobile) E-mail rev.allie@hotmail.com

KERR, Andrew Harry Mayne. b 41. TCD BA63. Melbourne Coll of Div MMin98. **d** 65 **p** 66. C Belfast St Luke *Conn* 65-68; SCM Sec (Ireland) 68-72; C Clooney *D & R* 72-74; Australia from 74; C Swinburne 74-80; I Dallas 80-88; I Mont Albert 88-94; P-in-c W Geelong from 96. *101 Katrina Street, Blackburn North Vic 3130, Australia* Tel (0061) (3) 5221 6694 *or* 9893 4946 Fax 9893 4946 E-mail ahmkerr@hotmail.com

KERR, Mrs Anita Dawn Christina. b 63. SRN81 SCM86 PGCE04. CITC 04. **d** 07 **p** 08. Aux Min Sligo w Knocknarea and Rosses Pt *K, E & A* from 07. *Rosa Cottage, Drumnacool, Boyle, Co Sligo, Republic of Ireland* Tel (00353) (71) 916 5467 E-mail st_kerr@btopenworld.com

KERR, Anthony. b 43. Sheff Univ BA64 Man Univ CertEd65. NOC. **d** 85 **p** 86. NSM Greenfield *Man* 85-87; NSM Leesfield 87-97; P-in-c Oldham St Steph and All Martyrs 97-02; NSM Lydgate w Friezland 02-03; NSM Saddleworth from 03. *16 Netherlees, Spring Lane, Oldham OL4 5BA* Tel 0161-620 6512

KERR, Arthur Henry. LRAM47 TCD BA48. **d** 49 **p** 50. C Templemore *D & R* 49-50; C Dublin Harold's Cross *D & G* 50-57; ICM 57-60; Chapl Rotunda Hosp 60-75; Lic to Offic *Conn* 88-94; P-in-c Clondevaddock w Portsalon and Leatbeg *D & R* 94-01; rtd 01. *Halothane, 172 Mountsandel Road, Coleraine BT52 1JE* Tel (028) 7034 4940

KERR, Bryan Thomas. b 70. QUB BD91 TCD MPhil96. CITC 94. **d** 96 **p** 97. C Enniskillen *Clogh* 96-99; I Garrison w Slavin and Belleek 99-05; I Lisbellaw from 05; Dioc Communications Officer from 00. *The Rectory, Faughard, Lisbellaw, Enniskillen BT94 5ES* Tel (028) 6638 7219 E-mail rector@lisbellaw.net *or* dco@clogher.anglican.org

KERR, Charles. *See* KERR, Ewan Charles

KERR, Charles Alexander Gray. b 33. Open Univ BA75 Birm Univ MA83 MA88. Edin Th Coll 63. **d** 67 **p** 68. C Hawick *Edin* 67-70; C Edgbaston St Geo *Birm* 70-72; Chapl Birm Skin Hosp 70-75; P-in-c Quinton Road W St Boniface *Birm* 72-79; V 79-84; R Musselburgh *Edin* 84-86; P-in-c Prestonpans 84-86; NSM Reighton w Speeton *York* 89-91; P-in-c Burton Pidsea and Humbleton w Elsternwick 91-95; V Anlaby Common St Mark 95; rtd 96; Perm to Offic *York* 96-02. *8 Lyster Road, Fordingbridge SP6 1QY*

KERR, David James. b 36. TCD BA58 MA61 BD61 HDipEd66. TCD Div Sch Div Test 59. **d** 60 **p** 61. C Belfast Trin Coll Miss *Conn* 60-63; Dean's V St Patr Cathl Dublin 63-66; Chapl Beechwood Park Sch St Alb 66-01; Hon C Flamstead *St Alb* 74-00; Perm to Offic from 00; rtd 01. *Trumpton Cottage, 12A Pickford Road, Markyate, St Albans AL3 8RU* Tel (01582) 841191 E-mail kerr_david@hotmail.com

KERR, Derek Preston. b 64. TCD BTh90. Oak Hill Th Coll 85. **d** 90 **p** 91. C Belfast St Donard *D & D* 90-93; C Carrickfergus *Conn* 93-96; I Devenish w Boho *Clogh* 96-07; I Drummaul w Duneane and Ballyscullion *Conn* from 07. *The Vicarage, 1A Glenkeen, Randalstown, Antrim BT41 3JX* Tel (028) 9447 2561

KERR, Miss Dora Elizabeth. b 41. QUB BA65 Southn Univ DipEd66. St Jo Coll Nottm 82. **dss** 84 **d** 87 **p** 94. Becontree St Mary *Chelmsf* 84-88; Par Dn 87-88; Par Dn Rushden w Newton Bromswold *Pet* 88-93; C Finham and Chapl Walsgrave Hosps NHS Trust 94-00; C Belper *Derby* 00-07; rtd 07. *23 Worcester Close, Allesley, Coventry CV5 9FZ* Tel (024) 7640 2413 E-mail elizabeth@ekerr.freeserve.co.uk

KERR, Ewan Charles. b 74. Fitzw Coll Cam BA96 MA00. Ripon Coll Cuddesdon MTh01. **d** 01 **p** 02. C Nor St Pet Mancroft w St Jo Maddermarket 01-04; Chapl Glenalmond Coll *St And* 04-07; Chapl St Edw Sch Ox from 07. *281 Woodstock Road, Oxford OX2 7NY* Tel (01865) 510210

KERR, Frank George. b 52. **d** 05 **p** 06. OLM Levenshulme *Man* from 05. *4 Limefield Terrace, Levenshulme, Manchester M19 2EP* Tel 0161-225 4200 E-mail frankkerr@btinternet.com

KERR, George Cecil. b 36. TCD BA60 MA65. CITC 60. **d** 60 **p** 61. C Coleraine *Conn* 60-63; Div Master Annandale Gr Sch Belf 63-65; Dean of Res QUB 65-74; Lic to Offic *D & D* 75-00; rtd 00. *12 Berkeley Grove, Warrenpoint BT34 3TS*

KERR, Canon Jean. b 46. Man Univ MA93 SS Hild & Bede Coll Dur CertEd69. NOC 84. **d** 87 **p** 94. NSM Peel *Man* 87-93; Par Dn Dixon Green 88-89; Par Dn New Bury 89-93; Par Dn Gillingham St Mark *Roch* 93-94; C 94-98; Chapl Medway Secure Tr Cen 98-01; Warden of Cn 98-05; NSM Roch St Justus 01-05; Hon Can Roch Cathl 03-05; Can Missr from 05; Tr Officer for Lay Min Educn 03-05; Bp's Officer for Miss and Unity from 05. *Prebendal House, Kings Orchard, Rochester ME1 1TG* Tel and fax (01634) 844508 E-mail jean.kerr@rochester.anglican.org

KERR, John Maxwell. b 43. Toronto Univ BASc66 Leeds Univ MSc70 MSOSc88. Linc Th Coll 75. **d** 77 **p** 78. C New Windsor *Ox* 77-80; Asst Chapl Cheltenham Coll 80-81; Chapl 81-82; NSM Win St Lawr and St Maurice w St Swithun 82-94; Chapl Win Coll 82-97; Hd RS 86-97; Visiting Lect Dept of Continuing

Educn Ox Univ 92-04; rtd 02; Perm to Offic *Portsm* 03-04; USA from 05. *111 Rolfe Road, Williamsburg VA 23185-3920, USA* E-mail jmk@kerr.newnet.co.uk

KERR, Canon Nicholas Ian. b 46. Em Coll Cam BA68 MA72. Westcott Ho Cam 74. **d** 77 **p** 78. C Merton St Mary *S'wark* 77-80; C Rainham *Roch* 80-84; Chapl Joyce Green Hosp Dartford 84-90; V Dartford St Edm *Roch* 84-90; V Lamorbey H Redeemer from 90; RD Sidcup 98-03; Hon Can Roch Cathl from 02. *The Vicarage, 64 Day's Lane, Sidcup DA15 8JR* Tel (020) 8300 1508 Mobile 07885-619595 E-mail nicholas.kerr@diocese-rochester.org *or* nicholasian@mac.com

KERR, Paul Turner. b 47. Man Univ MA92. Cranmer Hall Dur 68. **d** 71 **p** 72. C Kingston upon Hull St Martin *York* 71-72; C Linthorpe 72-76; C Cherry Hinton St Jo *Ely* 76-78; Chapl Addenbrooke's Hosp Cam 76-78; TV Rochdale *Man* 78-84; Chapl Birch Hill Hosp Rochdale 78-84; V New Bury 84-87; TR 87-93; C Gillingham St Mark *Roch* 93-98; RD Gillingham 96-98; V Roch St Justus from 98; RD Roch from 02. *St Justus's Vicarage, 1 Binnacle Road, Rochester ME1 2XR* Tel (01634) 841183 *or* tel and fax 818353 E-mail paul.kerr@diocese-rochester.org *or* kerrevan@global.net

KERR, Canon Stephen Peter. b 46. TCD BA68 Edin Univ BD71 MPhil80. **d** 71 **p** 72. C Belfast H Trin *Conn* 72-76; C Ballywillan 76-78; Lect Linc Th Coll 78-87; Dioc Officer for Adult Educn and Minl Tr *Worc* 87-99; P-in-c Ombersley w Doverdale from 87; Bp's Th Adv 99-07; P-in-c Hartlebury from 98; Hon Can Worc Cathl from 93; RD Droitwich from 07. *The Rectory, Main Road, Ombersley, Droitwich WR9 0EW* Tel (01905) 620950 E-mail peter.kerr@cofe-worcester.org

KERR, Terence Philip. b 54. QUB BD97. CITC 97. **d** 99 **p** 00. C Antrim All SS *Conn* 99-01; I Drummaul w Duneane and Ballyscullion 01-07; I Belfast St Aid from 07. *12 Royal Lodge Mews, Belfast BT8 7YT* Tel (028) 9079 0977 Mobile 07727-877830 E-mail terryrevkerr@talktalk.net

KERRIDGE, Donald George. b 32. Bede Coll Dur CertEd72 Hull Univ BA84. Wesley Coll Leeds 57 Bps' Coll Cheshunt 61. **d** 62 **p** 63. C Manston *Ripon* 62-66; C Hawksworth Wood 66-71; Asst Chapl Brentwood Sch Essex 72-74; Lic to Offic *Linc* 81-89; R Tetney, Marshchapel and N Coates 89-91; P-in-c Linc St Swithin 91-95; P-in-c Linc St Swithin w All SS 95-99; Asst Chapl Linc Co Hosp 91-94; rtd 99; Perm to Offic *S'wark* from 03. *28 Caverleigh Way, Worcester Park KT4 8DG* Tel (020) 8337 3886

KERRIN, Albert Eric. b 26. Aber Univ MA51. Edin Th Coll 51. **d** 53 **p** 54. C Dumfries *Glas* 53-55; P-in-c Cambuslang w Newton Cathl Miss 55-57; R Alford *Ab* 57-69; P-in-c Portpatrick *Glas* 69-98; P-in-c Stranraer 69-98; rtd 91; Perm to Offic *Glas* from 98. *15 London Road, Stranraer DG9 8AF* Tel (01776) 702822

KERRISON, Mrs Anne Edmonstone. b 23. Cranmer Hall Dur 69. **dss** 77 **d** 87 **p** 94. Hellesdon *Nor* 76-78; Ind Miss 78-79; Lic to Offic 79-88; Perm to Offic 88-94; NSM Hevingham w Hainford and Stratton Strawless 94-96; Perm to Offic 96-08. *Sloley Lodge, Sloley, Norwich NR12 8HE* Tel (01692) 538253

KERRY, Martin John. b 55. Ox Univ MA78. St Jo Coll Nottm BA81 MTh83. **d** 82 **p** 83. C Everton St Geo *Liv* 82-85; Lic to Offic *S'well* 85-04; Chapl Asst Nottm City Hosp 85-89; Chapl 89-94; Hd Chapl Nottm City Hosp NHS Trust 94-04; Lead Chapl (NE) *Caring for the Spirit* NHS Project 04-07; Chapl Manager Sheff Teaching Hosps NHS Foundn Trust from 07. *Chaplaincy Services, Royal Hallamshire Hospital, Glossop Road, Sheffield S10 2JF* Tel 0114-271 2718 E-mail martin.kerry@sth.nhs.uk

KERSHAW, John Harvey. b 51. Coll of Resurr Mirfield 84. **d** 86 **p** 87. C Hollinwood *Man* 86-89; V Audenshaw St Hilda from 89; Chapl Tameside Gen Hosp 90-94; Chapl Tameside and Glossop NHS Trust 94-95. *St Hilda's Vicarage, Denton Road, Audenshaw, Manchester M34 5BL* Tel 0161-336 2310

KERSHAW, Savile. b 37. Bernard Gilpin Soc Dur 60 Chich Th Coll 61. **d** 64 **p** 65. C Staincliffe *Wakef* 64-66; C Saltley *Birm* 66-68; C Birm St Aid Small Heath 68-72; Perm to Offic 88-02; rtd 02. *74 Longmore Road, Shirley, Solihull B90 3EE* Tel 0121-744 3470

KERSLAKE, Mrs Mary. b 39. Mary MacMillan Tr Coll Bradf QTS60. **d** 05 **p** 06. OLM Hethersett w Canteloff w Lt and Gt Melton *Nor* from 05. *Melton Vista, Green Lane, Little Melton, Norwich NR9 3LE* Tel (01603) 811228 E-mail hjbk@btinternet.com

KERSLEY, Stuart Casburn. b 40. CEng MIET. Trin Coll Bris. **d** 82 **p** 83. C Lancing w Coombes *Chich* 82-87; TV Littlehampton and Wick 87-90; R Kingston Buci 90-98; V Kirdford 98-06; rtd 06; Hon C Appleshaw, Kimpton, Thruxton, Fyfield etc *Win* from 06. *St Peter's Vicarage, High Street, Shipton Bellinger, Tidworth SP9 7UF* Tel (01980) 842244

KERSWILL, Canon Anthony John. b 39. Lambeth STh85. Linc Th Coll 72. **d** 73 **p** 73. C Boultham *Linc* 73-76; P-in-c N Kelsey and Cadney 76-83; V Gainsborough St Geo 83-91; V Bracebridge 91-00; P-in-c Linc St Swithin 00-01; V Linc All SS 01-05; RD Christianity 96-02; Can and Preb Linc Cathl 02-05;

rtd 05; Chapl Trin Hosp Retford from 05. *The Rectory Farm, Rectory Road, Retford DN22 7AY* Tel (01777) 862533
E-mail kerswill@btinternet.com

KERTON-JOHNSON, Peter. b 41. St Paul's Coll Grahamstown. **d** 81 **p** 82. S Africa 81-99; Perm to Offic *Sarum* 99-00; P-in-c Stoke sub Hamdon *B & W* from 00; Chapl St Marg Hospice Yeovil from 07. *The Vicarage, 1 Castle Street, Stoke-sub-Hamdon TA14 6RE* Tel (01935) 822529 Fax 818289
E-mail kertonjohnson@btopenworld.com

KESLAKE, Peter Ralegh. b 33. Sarum & Wells Th Coll. **d** 83 **p** 84. C Glouc St Geo w Whaddon 83-86; P-in-c France Lynch 86-91; V Chalford and France Lynch 91-03; rtd 03; Perm to Offic *Glouc* from 04. *4 Farmcote Close, Eastcombe, Stroud GL6 7EG*

KESTER, Jonathan George Frederick. b 66. Ex Univ BA90. Coll of Resurr Mirfield 91. **d** 93 **p** 94. C Cheshunt *St Alb* 93-96; Chapl to Bp Edmonton *Lon* 96-00; Hon C Munster Square Ch Ch and St Mary Magd 96-00; V Gt Ilford St Mary *Chelmsf* 00-08; P-in-c Hampstead Em W End *Lon* from 08; Asst Dir of Ords from 09; CMP from 00. *Emmanuel Vicarage, Lyncroft Gardens, London NW6 1JU* Tel (020) 7435 1911 E-mail frjonathan@mac.com

KESTEVEN, Elizabeth Anne. b 79. Newc Univ LLB01. St Steph Ho Ox 05. **d** 08 **p** 09. C Bris St Steph w St Jas and St Jo w St Mich etc from 08. *78 Leighton Road, Southville, Bristol BS3 1NU* Tel 07973-917720 (mobile)
E-mail simon@kesteven.orangehome.co.uk

KESTON, Marion. b 44. Glas Univ MB, ChB68 Edin Univ MTh95. St And Dioc Tr Course 87 Edin Th Coll 92. **d** 90 **p** 94. NSM W Fife Team Min *St And* 90-93; C Dunfermline 93-96; Priest Livingston LEP *Edin* 96-04; P-in-c Kinross *St And* from 04. *Hattonburn Lodge, Milnathort, Kinross KY13 0SA* Tel (01577) 866834 E-mail marion.keston@btinternet.com

KETLEY, Christopher Glen. b 62. Aston Tr Scheme 91 Coll of Resurr Mirfield 93. **d** 95 **p** 96. C Gt Crosby St Faith *Liv* 95-98; C Swinton and Pendlebury *Man* 98-00; V Belfield 00-08. *8 Gordon Street, Elgin IV30 1JQ* E-mail cgketley@waitrose.com

KETLEY, Michael James. b 39. Oak Hill Th Coll 79. **d** 81 **p** 82. C Bedhampton *Portsm* 81-85; R St Ive w Quethiock *Truro* 85-86; NSM Basildon St Andr w H Cross *Chelmsf* 89-90; C Barkingside St Cedd 90-92; P-in-c 92-95; R Hadleigh St Jas 95-08; rtd 08; Perm to Offic *Chelmsf* from 08. *40 Commonhall Lane, Hadleigh, Benfleet SS7 2RN* Tel (01702) 556318
E-mail mikeketley@aol.com

KETTLE, Alan Marshall. b 51. Leeds Univ BA72. Wycliffe Hall Ox MA78. **d** 78 **p** 79. C Llantwit Fardre 78-81; Prov RF Adv Ch in Wales 81-84; Chapl Llandovery Coll 84-92; P-in-c Cil-y-Cwm and Ystrad-ffin w Rhandir-mwyn etc *St D* 85-92; Chapl W Buckland Sch Barnstaple from 92; Lic to Offic *Ex* from 92. *2 West Close, West Buckland, Barnstaple EX32 0ST* Tel (01598) 760542

KETTLE, David John. b 47. Bris Univ BSc69 MLitt86 Fitzw Coll Cam BA75 MA79. Westcott Ho Cam 73. **d** 76 **p** 77. C Bris St Andr Hartcliffe 76-79; C Fishponds All SS 79-80; P-in-c 81-83; Perm to Offic *St E* 83-91; New Zealand 91-97; NSM Anglesey Gp *Ely* from 99. *11 Redgate Road, Girton, Cambridge CB3 0PP* Tel (01223) 277505 E-mail kettled@fastmail.co.uk

KETTLE, Martin Drew. b 52. New Coll Ox BA74 Selw Coll Cam BA76 Cam Univ MA85. Ridley Hall Cam 74. **d** 77 **p** 78. C Enfield St Andr *Lon* 77-80; Chapl Ridley Hall Cam 80-84; V Hendon St Paul Mill Hill *Lon* 85-98; AD W Barnet 90-95; Perm to Offic *Ely* 03-04; Hon C Huntingdon 04-06; Hon C E Leightonstone from 06. *The Vicarage, Church Way, Alconbury, Huntingdon PE28 4DX* Tel 07770-273923 (mobile)
E-mail mdkettle@msn.com

KETTLE, Mrs Patricia Mary Carole. b 41. Worc Coll of Educn CertEd61. Dalton Ho Bris 66. **d** 87 **p** 94. C Wonersh *Guildf* 87-98; C Wonersh w Blackheath 98-01; rtd 01; Perm to Offic *Guildf* from 02. *Wakehurst Cottage, Links Road, Bramley GU5 0AL* Tel (01483) 898856

KETTLE, Peter. b 51. K Coll Lon BD74 AKC74. St Aug Coll Cant 74. **d** 75 **p** 76. C Angell Town St Jo *S'wark* 75-78; C Putney St Mary 78-80; V Raynes Park St Sav 80-85; Perm to Offic *S'wark* from 85 and Lon from 03. *46 Allenswood, Albert Drive, London SW19 6JX* Tel (020) 8785 3797
E-mail peter.kettle@btinternet.com

KEULEMANS, Andrew Francis Charles. b 68. Univ of Wales (Abth) BSc90. St Jo Coll Nottm BTh93. **d** 94 **p** 95. C Mold *St As* 94-97; TV Wrexham 97-02; Chapl Loretto Sch Musselburgh from 02. *Pinkie House, Loretto School, Linkfield Road, Musselburgh EH21 7AF* Tel 0131-653 4429
E-mail keulemaa@loretto.com

KEVILL-DAVIES, Christopher Charles. b 44. AKC69. St Aug Coll Cant 70. **d** 70 **p** 71. C Folkestone St Sav *Cant* 70-75; V Yaxley *Ely* 75-78; R Chevington w Hargrave and Whepstead w Brockley *St E* 78-86; Perm to Offic *St Alb* 86-89; NSM Stansted Mountfitchet *Chelmsf* 87-89; R Barkway, Reed and Buckland w Barley *St Alb* 89-97; R Chelsea St Luke and Ch Ch *Lon* 97-05; rtd 06; Perm to Offic *S'wark* from 06. *York House, 35 Clapham Common South Side, London SW4 9BS* Tel (020) 7622 9647
E-mail christopherkd@hotmail.com

KEVIN, Brother. *See* GOODMAN, Brother Kevin Charles

KEVIS, Lionel William Graham. b 55. York Univ BA. Wycliffe Hall Ox 83. **d** 86 **p** 87. C Plaistow St Mary *Roch* 86-90; R Ash and Ridley 90-00; P-in-c Bidborough 00-02; P-in-c Leigh from 00; RD Tonbridge from 03. *The Vicarage, The Green, Leigh, Tonbridge TN11 8QJ* Tel (01732) 833022

KEW, William Richard. b 45. Lon Univ BD69. ALCD68. **d** 69 **p** 70. C Finchley St Paul Long Lane 69-72; C Stoke Bishop *Bris* 72-76; USA 76-07; C Hamilton and Wenham 76-79; R Rochester All SS 79-85; Exec Dir SPCK 85-95; Co-ord Russian Min Network 95-00; Convenor US Angl Congregation 00-02; V Franklin Apostles 02-06; R Franklin Resurr 06-07; Development Dir Ridley Hall Cam from 07. *Ridley Hall, Ridley Hall Road, Cambridge CB3 9HG* Tel (01223) 741080 Fax 741081
E-mail richardkew@aol.com

KEY, Christopher Halstead. b 56. St Jo Coll Dur BA77 K Coll Lon MTh78. Ridley Hall Cam 79. **d** 81 **p** 82. C Balderstone *Man* 81-84; C Wandsworth All SS *S'wark* 84-88; C-in-c W Dulwich Em CD 88-93; V W Dulwich Em 93-95; R Ore St Helen and St Barn *Chich* from 95; RD Hastings from 03. *St Helen's Rectory, 266 Elphinstone Road, Hastings TN34 2AG* Tel (01424) 425172
E-mail chriskey5@talktalk.net

KEY, The Very Revd Robert Frederick. b 52. Bris Univ BA73. Oak Hill Th Coll 74. **d** 76 **p** 77. C Ox St Ebbe w St Pet 76-80; C Wallington *S'wark* 80-85; V Eynsham and Cassington *Ox* 85-91; V Ox St Andr 91-01; Gen Dir CPAS 01-05; Dean Jersey *Win* from 05; P-in-c Jersey St Helier from 05. *The Deanery, David Place, St Helier, Jersey JE2 4TE* Tel (01534) 720001
E-mail deanofjersey@gov.je *or* robert_f_key@yahoo.com

KEY, Roderick Charles Halstead. b 57. MTh. **d** 84 **p** 85. C Up Hatherley *Glouc* 84-87; V Glouc St Paul 87-04; TR Trunch *Nor* from 04. *The Rectory, Knapton Road, Trunch, North Walsham NR28 0QE* Tel (01263) 722725 *or* 834603

KEY, Roger Astley. b 49. Coll of Resurr Mirfield 72. **d** 74 **p** 75. Perm to Offic *Wakef* 74-75; P-in-c Khomasdal Grace Ch Namibia 75-77; R Luderitz 77-81; Adn The South 77-80; R Walvis Bay 81-85; Personal Asst to Bp Windhoek 85-86; Dean Windhoek 86-00; V Hopton w Corton *Nor* from 00. *The Vicarage, 51 The Street, Corton, Lowestoft NR32 5HT* Tel (01502) 730977 Mobile 07733-028048
E-mail thekeybunch@aol.com *or* rogerkey30@hotmail.com

KEYES, Graham George. b 44. St Cath Coll Cam BA65 MA68 Lanc Univ MA74 Nottm Univ MTh85 MPhil92. EMMTC 82. **d** 84 **p** 85. C Evington *Leic* 84-86; Vice-Prin NEOC 86-89; C Monkseaton St Mary *Newc* 86-89; P-in-c Newc St Hilda 89-94; TV Ch the King 94-99; rtd 99. *1 East Avenue, Newcastle upon Tyne NE12 9PH* Tel 0191-259 9024
E-mail simeon.and.anna@talk21.com

KEYMER, Philip John. b 72. Bris Univ BSc93. Oak Hill Th Coll 96. **d** 99 **p** 00. C Partington and Carrington *Ches* 99-02; C Cheadle 02-04; Perm to Offic *Man* from 05. *10 Central Avenue, Levenshulme, Manchester M19 2EN* Tel 0161-224 2384
E-mail phil.keymer@ntlworld.com

KEYS, Christopher David. b 56. Southn Univ BTh95. Trin Coll Bris. **d** 02 **p** 03. C Fressingfield, Mendham etc *St E* 02-04; C Ipswich St Helen, H Trin, St Luke 04-05; P-in-c Swineshead and Brothertoft Gp *Linc* 05-07; P-in-c Weston Zoyland w Chedzoy *B & W* from 07. *The Vicarage, Church Lane, Weston Zoyland, Bridgwater TA7 0EP* Tel (01278) 691098
E-mail revchriskeys@btconnect.com

KEYT, Fitzroy John. b 34. Linc Th Coll. **d** 67 **p** 68. C Highters Heath *Birm* 67-70; Hon C Sheldon 70-73; Australia from 73; V Miles 73-76; R Rayton 76-86; R Coolangatta 86-98; P-in-c Clayfield 98-01. *58 Thompson Street, Zillmere Qld 4034, Australia* Tel (0061) (7) 3314 3011
E-mail dskeyt@optusnet.com.au

KEYTE, Douglas Joseph Henry. b 18. St Jo Coll Cam BA40 MA46. Wycliffe Hall Ox 46. **d** 48 **p** 49. C Kersal Moor *Man* 48-51; C Newall Green St Fran 51-54; Chapl K Wm's Coll Is of Man 55-57; Ghana 57-61; Asst Master Co Gr Sch for Girls Sale 61-75; Hon C Charlestown *Man* 75-89; rtd 83; Hon C Pendleton St Thos w Charlestown *Man* 89-95; Hon C Pendleton 95-09; Hon C Salford All SS from 09. *26 Heathfield Close, Sale M33 2PQ* Tel 0161-973 2844

KHAKHRIA, Rohitkumar Prabhulal (Roy). b 60. Sheff Univ BSc82 PGCE83. Oak Hill Th Coll 94. **d** 96 **p** 97. C Muswell Hill St Jas w St Matt *Lon* 96-01; C Stoughton *Guildf* 01-04; V Boscombe St Jo *Win* from 04. *St John's Vicarage, 17 Browning Avenue, Bournemouth BH5 1NR* Tel (01202) 396667 *or* tel and fax 301916 E-mail roy.khakhria@lycosmax.co.uk

KHAMBATTA, Neville Holbery. b 48. St Chad's Coll Dur BA74. S'wark Ord Course 81. **d** 84 **p** 85. Asst Chapl Em Sch Wandsworth 84-87; Hon C Thornton Heath St Jude w St Aid *S'wark* 84-87; Asst Warden Horstead Cen 87-01; Hon C Coltishall w Gt Hautbois and Horstead *Nor* 87-01; V Ludham, Potter Heigham, Hickling and Catfield from 01. *The Vicarage, Norwich Road, Ludham, Great Yarmouth NR29 5QA* Tel (01692) 678282 E-mail khambatta@lineone.net

KHARITONOVA, Natalia. *See* CRITCHLOW, Natalia

KHOO, Boon-Hor. b 31. FBCO. Llan Dioc Tr Scheme. **d** 87 **p** 88. NSM Llandaff w Capel Llanilltern 87-96; Perm to Offic from 96. *38 The Cathedral Green, Llandaff, Cardiff CF5 2EB* Tel (029) 2056 1478

KICHENSIDE, Mark Gregory. b 53. Nottm Univ BTh83. St Jo Coll Nottm 80. **d** 83 **p** 84. C Orpington Ch Ch *Roch* 83-86; C Bexley St Jo 86-90; V Blendon 90-93; V Welling 93-00; R Flegg Coastal Benefice *Nor* 00-05; RD Gt Yarmouth 02-05; TV High Oak, Hingham and Scoulton w Wood Rising from 05. *The Rectory, Attleborough Road, Hingham, Norwich NR9 4HP* Tel (01953) 850211 E-mail mark@kiche.enterprise-plc.com

KIDD, Anthony John Eric. b 38. Solicitor. Oak Hill NSM Course. **d** 89 **p** 90. NSM Rawdon *Bradf* 89-91; C Ilkley All SS 91-93; Perm to Offic *Bradf* 93-95 and *York* 95-96; Hon C Gt and Lt Driffield *York* 96-98; Perm to Offic 98-04; P-in-c The Beacon 04-08; Perm to Offic *Chich* and *York* from 08. *7 Victoria Grove, Ilkley LS29 9BN* Tel 07795-109090 (mobile)

KIDD, Canon Carol Ivy. b 47. Trent Park Coll of Educn CertEd69. Oak Hill Th Coll 92. **d** 95 **p** 96. C Bootle St Mary w St Paul *Liv* 95-99; TV Speke St Aid 99-05; TR from 05; Hon Can Liv Cathl from 03. *All Saints' Vicarage, Speke Church Road, Liverpool L24 3TA* Tel 0151-486 0292

KIDD, John Alan. b 32. Pemb Coll Cam BA58 MA61. Ridley Hall Cam 57. **d** 61 **p** 62. C Onslow Square St Paul *Lon* 61-65; R Bloemhof S Africa 65-67; Chapl Jinja Uganda 67-69; P-in-c Mayfair Ch Ch *Lon* 69-75; V 75-79; V Virginia Water *Guildf* 79-88; Lic to Offic 88-94; rtd 94. *1 Blayds Lane, Spring Street, Easingwold, York YO61 3BL* Tel (01347) 823201

KIDD, Kerry. **d** 08. NSM Alverthorpe *Wakef* from 08. *49 Wrenthorpe Lane, Wrenthorpe, Wakefield WF2 0PX* Tel (01924) 368811 E-mail kskrpe@hotmail.com

KIDD, Maurice Edward. b 26. **d** 55 **p** 56. C Wembley St Jo *Lon* 55-58; C Middleton *Man* 58-61; Chapl Pastures Hosp Derby 61-69; Chapl Guild of Health Lon 69-72; R Hanworth St Geo *Lon* 72-82; R Chartham *Cant* 82-91; rtd 91; Perm to Offic *Cant* from 91 and *Lon* 96-97. *4 Cornwallis Circle, Whitstable CT5 1DU* Tel (01227) 282658

KIDD, Timothy. b 24. St Chad's Coll Dur BA48 MA53 Nottm Univ MA57 MPhil71 MEd80 Lambeth STh74. **d** 50 **p** 51. C Mexborough *Sheff* 50-52; Lect Boston *Linc* 52-56; PC Grantham St Anne 56-65; Offg Chapl RAF 56-65; Asst Dioc Youth Chapl 59-65; Prin Lect Kesteven Coll of Educn 65-79; Hon C Harlaxton, Lt Ponton and Stroxton 66-72; Gen Preacher *Linc* 73-90; Visiting Lect Univ Evansville (USA) 79-86; Teacher K Sch Grantham 80-90; rtd 90; Perm to Offic *Leic* 89-03. *14 Woodlands Drive, Grantham NG31 9DJ* Tel (01476) 563273

KIDDLE, Canon John. b 58. Qu Coll Cam BA80 MA83 Heythrop Coll Lon MTh02. Ridley Hall Cam 79. **d** 82 **p** 83. C Ormskirk *Liv* 82-86; V Huyton Quarry 86-91; V Watford St Luke *St Alb* 91-08; RD Watford 99-04; Officer for Miss and Development from 08; Hon Can St Alb from 05. *19 Stanbury Avenue, Watford WD17 3HW* Tel (01923) 460083 *or* (01727) 851748 E-mail john.kiddle@stalbans.anglican.org

KIDDLE, Mark Brydges. b 34. ACP61. Wycliffe Hall Ox. **d** 63 **p** 64. C Scarborough St Luke *York* 63-66; C Walthamstow St Sav *Chelmsf* 66-71; V Nelson St Bede *Blackb* 71-76; V Perry Common *Birm* 76-79; R Grayingham *Linc* 79-84; V Kirton in Lindsey 79-84; R Manton 79-84; Hon C St Botolph Aldgate w H Trin Minories *Lon* 85-91; Hon C St Clem Eastcheap w St Martin Orgar 91-08. *12 Tudor Rose Court, 35 Fann Street, London EC2Y 8DY* E-mail mk@fpsi.org

KIDDLE, Martin John. b 42. Open Univ BA80. St Jo Coll Nottm 74. **d** 76 **p** 77. C Gt Parndon *Chelmsf* 76-80; Asst Chapl HM Pris Wakef 80-81; Asst Chapl HM Youth Cust Cen Portland 81-88; Chapl HM Pris Cardiff 88-97; Chapl HM Pris Channings Wood 97-02; rtd 02; Perm to Offic *Ex* from 02. *2 Cricketfield Close, Chudleigh, Newton Abbot TQ13 0GA* Tel (01626) 853980 E-mail mkiddle@talktalk.net

KIDDLE, Miss Susan Elizabeth. b 44. Birm Univ BSc66 Nottm Univ CertEd67. **d** 89 **p** 95. OLM Waddington *Linc* 89-97; OLM Bracebridge 98-06; Perm to Offic from 06. *16 Sycamore Drive, Waddington, Lincoln LN5 9DR* Tel (01522) 722010

KIGALI, Bishop of. *See* KOLINI, The Most Revd Emmanuel Musaba

KIGGELL, Mrs Anne. b 36. Liv Univ BA57. SAOMC 99. **d** 02 **p** 03. OLM Basildon w Aldworth and Ashampstead *Ox* from 02. *Straight Ash, Ashampstead Common, Reading RG8 8QT* Tel (01635) 201385 E-mail anne.kiggell@virgin.net

KIGHTLEY, Canon David John. b 39. AKC67. **d** 68 **p** 69. C Plymouth St Andr *Ex* 68-70; C Ex St Dav 70-73; Chapl Greenwich Distr Hosp & Brook Gen Hosp Lon 73-76; P-in-c Chippenham *Ely* 76-96; P-in-c Snailwell 76-96; P-in-c Isleham 76-96; RD Fordham 95-96; P-in-c Feltwell 96-98; P-in-c Methwold 96-98; R Feltwell and Methwold 98-05; RD Feltwell 96-04; RD Fincham 98-04; RD Fincham and Feltwell 04-05; Hon Can Ely Cathl 00-05; rtd 05; Perm to Offic *Nor* from 06 and *Ely* from 07. *53 Churchill Road, Thetford IP24 2JZ* Tel (01842) 753079 E-mail davidkightley@aol.com

KILBEY, Mrs Sarah. b 39. MBE98. Edin Univ MA75 Man Poly CETD82. Bp Otter Coll TDip59 Edin Dioc NSM Course 84. **d** 93 **p** 97. NSM Edin St Columba 93-96; NSM Edin St Martin from 96. *77 Morningside Park, Edinburgh EH10 5EZ* Tel 0131-447 2378

KILBOURN-MACKIE, Canon Mary Elizabeth. b 26. Toronto Univ BA48 Harvard Univ MA49. Trin Coll Toronto MDiv78 Hon DD02. **d** 77 **p** 78. Canada 77-00; C Norway St Jo and Chapl Toronto Gen Hosp 78-80; Dir Chapl Toronto 80-89; Hon Can Toronto from 95; Perm to Offic *Sarum* and *B & W* from 01. *17 Chatham Court, Station Road, Warminster BA12 9LS* Tel (01985) 216167 E-mail meskm1807@hotmail.co.uk

KILCOOLEY, Christine. *See* ROBINSON, Mrs Christine

KILDARE, Archdeacon of. *See* STEVENSON, The Ven Leslie Thomas Clayton

KILDARE, Dean of. *See* MARSDEN, The Very Revd John Joseph

KILFORD, John Douglas. b 38. Oak Hill Th Coll 73. **d** 75 **p** 76. C Beckenham St Jo *Roch* 75-80; P-in-c Sinfin Moor *Derby* 80-83; V Penge St Jo *Roch* 83-92; Staff Member Ellel Min 92-03; rtd 03; Perm to Offic *Truro* 03-07. *33 London Road, Godmanchester, Huntingdon PE29 2HZ*

KILFORD, William Roy. b 38. Bris Univ BA60. Sarum & Wells Th Coll 82. **d** 84 **p** 85. C Herne *Cant* 84-87; Chapl Wm Harvey Hosp Ashford 87-93; R Mersham w Hinxhill *Cant* 87-93; P-in-c Sevington 87-93; V Reculver and Herne Bay St Bart 93-95; Chapl Paphos Cyprus 95-98; P-in-c Doddington, Newnham and Wychling *Cant* 98-02; P-in-c Lynsted w Kingsdown 98-02; P-in-c Norton 98-02; AD Ospringe 01-02; rtd 02; Chapl Nord Pas de Calais *Eur* 02-04; Hon C Burton Fleming w Fordon, Grindale etc *York* 04-08; Chapl St Jo Hosp Cant from 08. *1 St John's House, 40 Northgate, Canterbury CT1 1BE* Tel (01227) 764935

KILGOUR, The Very Revd Richard Eifl. b 57. Edin Univ BD85. Edin Th Coll 81. **d** 85 **p** 86. C Wrexham *St As* 85-88; V Whitford 88-97; Ind Chapl 89-97; R Newtown w Llanllwchaiarn w Aberhafesp 97-03; RD Cedewain 01-03; Provost St Andr Cathl from 03; R Aberdeen St Andr from 03; P-in-c Aberdeen St Ninian from 03. *St Andrew's Cathedral, King Street, Aberdeen AB24 5AX* Tel (01224) 640119 E-mail provost@aberdeen.anglican.org *or* newrect@hotmail.com

KILLALA AND ACHONRY, Archdeacon of. *Vacant*

KILLALA, Dean of. *See* PATTERSON, The Very Revd Susan Margaret

KILLALOE, KILFENORA AND CLONFERT, Dean of. *See* WHITE, The Very Revd Stephen Ross

KILLALOE, KILFENORA, CLONFERT AND KILMACDUAGH, Archdeacon of. *See* CARNEY, The Ven Richard Wayne

KILLE, Vivian Edwy. b 30. Tyndale Hall Bris 60. **d** 62 **p** 63. C Dublin Miss Ch *D & G* 62-66; I Emlaghfad *T, K & A* 66-74; I Aghadrumsee w Clogh and Drumsnatt 74-05; Can Clogh Cathl 93-05; rtd 05. *16 Greer House, 115 Castlereagh Road, Belfast BT5 5FF* Tel (028) 9073 1135 E-mail vek@hallelujah.demon.co.uk

KILLOCK, Alfred Kenneth. b 26. Cranmer Hall Dur 72. **d** 74 **p** 75. C Moor Allerton *Ripon* 74-79; Hon C Bolton St Jas w St Chrys *Bradf* 79-83; P-in-c Oakenshaw cum Woodlands 84-90; P-in-c Allerton 90-91; rtd 91; Perm to Offic *Bradf* from 91. *15 Warwick Road, Bradford BD4 7RA* Tel (01274) 394462

KILLWICK, Canon Simon David Andrew. b 56. K Coll Lon BD80 AKC80. St Steph Ho Ox 80. **d** 81 **p** 82. C Worsley *Man* 81-84; TV 84-97; P-in-c Moss Side Ch Ch 97-06; R from 06; Hon Can Man Cathl from 04; AD Hulme from 07. *Christ Church Rectory, Monton Street, Manchester M14 4LT* Tel and fax 0161-226 2476 E-mail frskillwick@tiscali.co.uk

KILMISTER, David John. b 46. Open Univ BA88. **d** 06 **p** 07. OLM Chippenham St Paul w Hardenhuish etc *Bris* from 06; OLM Kington St Michael from 06. *22 The Common, Langley Burrell, Chippenham SN15 4LQ* Tel and fax (01249) 650926 Mobile 07747-331971 E-mail dave@kilmister.eclipse.co.uk

KILMORE, Archdeacon of. *Vacant*

KILMORE, Dean of. *See* FERGUSON, The Very Revd Wallace Raymond

KILMORE, ELPHIN AND ARDAGH, Bishop of. *See* CLARKE, The Rt Revd Kenneth Herbert

KILNER, Canon Frederick James. b 43. Qu Coll Cam BA65 MA69. Ridley Hall Cam 67. **d** 70 **p** 71. C Harlow New Town w Lt Parndon *Chelmsf* 70-74; C Cambridge St Andr Less *Ely* 74-79; P-in-c Milton 79-88; R 88-94; P-in-c Ely 94-96; P-in-c Chettisham 94-96; P-in-c Prickwillow 94-96; P-in-c Stretham w Thetford 94-96; P-in-c Stuntney 95-96; TR Ely 96-08; Hon Can Ely Cathl 88-08; Hon C Woodhurst and Somersham w Pidley and Oldhurst from 08. *125 High Street, Somersham, Huntingdon PE28 3EN* Tel (01487) 842864 E-mail kilner@btinternet.com

KILNER, James Martin. b 51. Solicitor 77. St Jo Coll Nottm BA03. **d** 07 **p** 07. P-in-c Sheff St Bart 07-08; V Grenoside from

08. *St Mark's Vicarage, 19 Graven Close, Grenoside, Sheffield S35 8QT* Tel 0114-246 7513 Mobile 07931-582547
E-mail martin.kilner@sheffield.anglican.org

KILNER, Mrs Valerie June. b 42. Univ of Wales (Abth) BSc64 Hughes Hall Cam PGCE65 MICFM91. EAMTC 98. **d** 98 **p** 99. NSM Ely 98-08; Perm to Offic from 08. *125 High Street, Somersham, Huntingdon PE28 3EN* Tel (01487) 842864
E-mail kilner@btinternet.com

KILPATRICK, Alan William. b 64. Oak Hill Th Coll BA96. **d** 96 **p** 97. C Ealing St Paul *Lon* 96-01; Assoc R Mt Pleasant USA 01-04; P-in-c Prestonville St Luke *Chich* from 04. *St Luke's Vicarage, 64A Old Shoreham Road, Brighton BN1 5DD* Tel (01273) 552267

KILSBY, Miss Joyce (Jocelyn). b 40. Univ Coll Lon BSc62 Ox Univ DipEd63. NOC 98. **d** 01 **p** 02. NSM Stanley *Wakef* from 01. *18 Hazelwood Court, Outwood, Wakefield WF1 3HP* Tel (01924) 824396 E-mail hilkil.hazco@virgin.net

KIMARU, Benson Mbure. b 54. St Andr Coll Kabare 81. **d** 83 **p** 84. V Mitunguu Kenya 85; Dioc Radio Producer 86-88; Asst to Provost Nairobi 88; V Kangaru 89-90; V Kayole 91-94; V Nyari 95-98; V Maringo 99-02; V Githurai 03-05; Perm to Offic *Sheff* 06-07; NSM Brightside w Wincobank from 07. *The Vicarage, Manchester Road, Thurlstone, Sheffield S36 9QS* Tel (01226) 764225 Mobile 07919-988131
E-mail bensonkimaru@yahoo.com

KIMBALL, Melodie Irene. b 49. **d** 99 **p** 06. USA 99-01; Chapl Asst S Man Univ Hosps NHS Trust 01-02; Asst Chapl Qu Medical Cen Nottm Univ Hosp NHS Trust 02-03; Chapl Leeds Mental Health Teaching NHS Trust from 03; Hon C Far Headingley St Chad *Ripon* from 06. *The Becklin Centre, Alma Street, Leeds LS9 7BE* Tel 0113-305 6639
E-mail melodie.kimball@leedsmh.nhs.uk

KIMBER, Geoffrey Francis. b 46. Univ Coll Lon BA67 Birm Univ MPhil01. St Jo Coll Nottm 86. **d** 88 **p** 89. C Buckhurst Hill *Chelmsf* 88-92; R Arley *Cov* 92-02; P-in-c Ansley 97-02; CMS Romania 02-07; R Birm Bp Latimer w All SS from 07. *Winson Green Vicarage, 28 Handsworth New Road, Birmingham B18 4PT* Tel 0121-598 9093 E-mail geoff.kimber@gmail.com

KIMBER, Mrs Gillian Margaret. b 48. Bedf Coll Lon BA70. Oak Hill Th Coll 89. **d** 91. NSM Buckhurst Hill *Chelmsf* 91-92; C Arley *Cov* 92-97; C Ansley 97-02; CMS Romania 02-07; Perm to Offic *Birm* from 08. *Winson Green Vicarage, 28 Handsworth New Road, Birmingham B18 4PT* Tel 0121-554 2221
E-mail gill.kimber@btinternet.com

KIMBER, Mrs Hazel Olive. b 33. Lon Univ CertEd73. **d** 95 **p** 96. OLM W Dulwich Em *S'wark* from 95. *18 Michaelson House, Kingswood Estate, London SE21 8PX* Tel (020) 8670 5298

KIMBER, John Keith. b 45. Bris Univ BSc66. St Mich Coll Llan. **d** 69 **p** 70. C Caerphilly *Llan* 69-72; Chapl Birm Univ 72-75; TR Bris St Agnes and St Simon w St Werburgh 75-82; P-in-c Bris St Paul w St Barn 80-82; Hon C Westbury-on-Trym H Trin 82-83; Area Sec (Wales) USPG 83-89; TR Halesowen *Worc* 89-92; Chapl Geneva *Eur* 92-01; Chapl Monte Carlo 01-02; TR Cen Cardiff *Llan* 02-06; V City Par St Jo from 07. *The Vicarage, 16 Queen Anne Square, Cardiff CF10 3ED* Tel (029) 2022 0375
E-mail jkk@ntlworld.com

KIMBER, Jonathan Richard. b 69. K Coll Cam BA91 MA95 St Jo Coll Dur MA02. Cranmer Hall Dur 99. **d** 02 **p** 03. C Weston Favell *Pet* 02-05; P-in-c Northampton St Benedict from 05. *St Benedict's Vicarage, 16 Sentinel Road, Northampton NN4 9UF* Tel (01604) 768624 E-mail jrkimber@yahoo.co.uk

KIMBER, Stuart Francis. b 53. Qu Eliz Coll Lon BSc74 Fitzw Coll Cam BA MA83. Ridley Hall Cam 77. **d** 80 **p** 81. C Edgware *Lon* 80-83; C Cheltenham St Mark *Glouc* 83-84; TV 84-92; C Hawkwell *Chelmsf* 92-01; V Westcliff St Andr from 01. *St Andrew's Vicarage, 65 Electric Avenue, Westcliff-on-Sea SS0 9NN* Tel (01702) 302255
E-mail revskimber@blueyonder.co.uk

KIMBERLEY, Countess of (Carol Lylie Wodehouse). b 51. St Hugh's Coll Ox BA73 CertEd74 MA77. Ripon Coll Cuddesdon 87. **d** 89 **p** 94. NSM Hambleden Valley *Ox* 89-02; P-in-c Hormead, Wyddial, Anstey, Brent Pelham etc *St Alb* from 02; RD Buntingford from 06. *The Vicarage, Great Hormead, Buntingford SG9 0NT* Tel (01763) 289258

KIMBERLEY, John Harry. b 49. Brasted Th Coll 72 St Steph Ho Ox 74. **d** 76 **p** 77. C W Tarring *Chich* 76-79; C Portslade St Nic 79-82; C-in-c Findon Valley CD 82-89; V Findon Valley 89-90; V E Preston w Kingston 90-95; Chapl Eastbourne Hosps NHS Trust 95-06. *Address temp unknown*

KIMBERLEY, The Ven Owen Charles Lawrence. b 27. Univ of NZ BCom53. Tyndale Hall Bris 57. **d** 59 **p** 60. C Higher Openshaw *Man* 59-62; New Zealand 62-94; C Nelson All SS 62-64; V Motupiko 64-69; V Kaikoura 69-76; V Tahunanui 76-85 76-85; Can Nelson Cathl 77-78; Adn Waimea 78-92; V Richmond 85-92; Egypt 94-98; Chapl Port Said 94-98; Adn Egypt 96-98. *11B Gilbert Street, Richmond, Nelson 7020, New Zealand* Tel (0064) (3) 544 2115 E-mail okimberley@xtra.co.nz

KIME, Thomas Frederick. b 28. Linc Coll Ox BA50 MA53. Cuddesdon Coll 54. **d** 56 **p** 57. C Forest Gate St Edm *Chelmsf*

56-58; S Africa 58-74; R Ellisfield w Farleigh Wallop and Dummer *Win* 74-83; P-in-c Cliddesden 82-83; R Cliddesden and Ellisfield w Farleigh Wallop etc 83-94; rtd 94; Perm to Offic *Win* from 94. *6 Morley College, Market Street, Winchester SO23 9LF* Tel (01962) 870240

KINAHAN, Canon Timothy Charles. b 53. Jes Coll Cam BA75. CITC 77. **d** 78 **p** 79. C Carrickfergus *Conn* 78-81; Papua New Guinea 81-84; I Belfast Whiterock *Conn* 84-90; I Gilnahirk *D & D* 90-06; I Helen's Bay from 06; Can Belf Cathl from 04. *The Rectory, 2 Woodland Avenue, Helen's Bay, Bangor BT19 1TX* Tel (028) 9185 3601

KINCH, Christopher David. b 81. K Alfred's Coll Win BTh02. St Steph Ho Ox 03. **d** 05 **p** 06. C Long Eaton St Laur *Derby* 05-09; TV Swindon New Town *Bris* from 09. *3 Briar Fields, Swindon SN1 2QN* Tel (01793) 536679
E-mail christopherkinch@btinternet.com

KINCHIN-SMITH, John Michael. b 52. Fitzw Coll Cam MA. Ridley Hall Cam 79. **d** 82 **p** 83. C Sanderstead All SS *S'wark* 82-87; TV Halesworth w Linstead, Chediston, Holton etc *St E* 87-92; R Mursley w Swanbourne and Lt Horwood *Ox* 92-02; R Newton Longville and Mursley w Swanbourne etc 03-06; R Chinnor, Sydenham, Aston Rowant and Crowell from 06. *The Rectory, High Street, Chinnor OX39 4DH* Tel (01844) 351309
E-mail johnks1881@aol.com

KINDER, David James. b 55. EAMTC 01. **d** 04 **p** 05. NSM Warboys w Broughton and Bury w Wistow *Ely* 04-08; Chapl HM Pris Littlehey from 08. *Chaplain, HM Prison Littlehey, Perry, Huntingdon PE28 0SR* Tel (01480) 333252
E-mail david.kinder@hmps.gsi.gov.uk

KINDER, Mark Russell. b 66. Univ of Wales (Swansea) BA(Econ)88. St Jo Coll Nottm 91. **d** 94 **p** 95. C Pheasey *Lich* 94-98; TV Tettenhall Regis 98-07; P-in-c Walsall St Paul from 07; C Walsall from 07. *St Paul's Vicarage, 57 Mellish Road, Walsall WS4 2DG* Tel (01922) 624963

KINDER, Mrs Sylvia Patricia. b 61. Ridley Hall Cam 03. **d** 05 **p** 06. C Warboys w Broughton and Bury w Wistow *Ely* 05-09; C Werrington *Pet* from 09. *6 Davids Close, Peterborough PE4 5AN* Tel 07876-204624 (mobile) E-mail sylviakinder@tesco.net

KING, Mrs Angela Margaret. b 45. Bedf Coll Lon BA67 Lon Inst of Educn PGCE68. SEITE 00. **d** 03 **p** 04. NSM Bromley St Andr *Roch* from 03. *4 Avondale Road, Bromley BR1 4EP* Tel and fax (020) 8402 0847 E-mail angelaking45@hotmail.com

KING, Anthony Richard. b 34. Trin Hall Cam BA58. Ely Th Coll 58 Linc Th Coll 61. **d** 62 **p** 63. C Benwell St Jas *Newc* 62-64; C Thirsk w S Kilvington *York* 64-67; V Halifax St Aug *Wakef* 67-74; R Upton on Severn *Worc* 74-99; RD Upton 86-92; rtd 99; Perm to Offic *Ex* from 99. *4 The Elms, Colyford, Colyton EX24 6QU* Tel (01297) 552666

KING, Benjamin John. b 74. Down Coll Cam BA96 MA00 Harvard Univ MTh03. Westcott Ho Cam 97. **d** 00 **p** 00. C Boston the Advent USA 00-06; Chapl Harvard Univ from 06. *2 Garden Street, Cambridge MA 02138, USA* Tel (001) (617) 495 4340 E-mail episcopal_chaplaincy@harvard.edu

KING, Benjamin William. b 76. Dijon Univ BA97 Man Univ BA98 Univ Coll Lon MA Cam Univ BA05. Ridley Hall Cam 03. **d** 06 **p** 07. C Stanwix *Carl* from 06. *54 Eden Street, Carlisle CA3 9LH* Tel (01228) 526721 Mobile 07752-708207
E-mail kingbw2001@yahoo.com

KING, Brian Henry. b 39. Chich Th Coll 63. **d** 65 **p** 66. C Castle Bromwich SS Mary and Marg *Birm* 65-67; C Southwick St Mich *Chich* 68-70; V Southwater 70-73; C Brighton St Alb Preston 73-74; TV Brighton Resurr 74-75; V Eastbourne St Elisabeth 75-96; rtd 96; Perm to Offic *Chich* from 96. *7 Bracken Road, Eastbourne BN20 8SH* Tel (01323) 431118

KING, Caroline Naomi. b 62. New Coll Edin BD94. Ripon Coll Cuddesdon 94. **d** 97 **p** 98. C Wheatley *Ox* from 97. *The Vicarage, Holton, Oxford OX33 1PR* Tel (01865) 873451
E-mail caroline.king1@ntlworld.com

KING, Christopher John. b 56. Chelsea Coll Lon BSc78 CertEd79. St Jo Coll Nottm LTh87. **d** 88 **p** 89. C Wandsworth All SS *S'wark* 88-92; Canada from 92; R Geraldton w Jellicoe, Longlac, Collins etc 92-97; R Toronto Lt Trin Ch from 97. *425 King Street East, Toronto ON M5A 1L3, Canada* Tel (001) (416) 367 2074 Fax 367 2074 E-mail chrisking@sympatico.ca

KING, Clare Maria. b 68. St Andr Univ BD91 K Coll Lon MPhil98. Westcott Ho Cam 91. **d** 94. Hon C Norbury St Phil *S'wark* 94-96; Chapl Croydon Coll 95-96; Asst Chapl Cen Sheff Univ Hosps NHS Trust 96-01; C Leic Presentation 02-08; C Leic St Chad from 08. *The Vicarage, 12 Saddington Road, Fleckney, Leicester LE8 8AW* Tel 0116-240 2215

KING, Mrs Daphne Eileen. b 37. EMMTC 78. **dss** 81 **d** 87 **p** 94. Theddlethorpe *Linc* 84-89; Dn-in-c 87-89; Saltfleetby 84-89; Dn-in-c 87-89; Dn-in-c Healing and Stallingborough 89-94; P-in-c 94-97; rtd 97; Perm to Offic *Linc* 99-02. *28 Charles Street, Louth LN11 0LE* Tel (01507) 606062
E-mail daphneking@lud28.freeserve.co.uk

KING, David Charles. b 52. K Coll Lon 73 Coll of Resurr Mirfield 77. **d** 78 **p** 79. C Saltburn-by-the-Sea *York* 78-81; Youth Officer 81-85; P-in-c Crathorne 81-85; Par Educn Adv *Wakef* 85-91;

Min Coulby Newham LEP *York* 91-94; P-in-c Egton w Grosmont 94-00; P-in-c Goathland and Glaisdale 99-00; V Middle Esk Moor 00-07. *Address temp unknown*

KING, David Frederick. b 32. Sarum Th Coll 59. **d** 61 **p** 72. C Hanworth All SS *Lon* 61-62; Hon C Andover St Mich *Win* 71-83; P-in-c 83-88; V 88-90; Chapl R S Hants Hosp 90-92; Chapl Countess Mountbatten Hospice 90-92; Chapl Andover District Community Health Care NHS Trust from 92; Perm to Offic *Win* 92-97; rtd 97; P-in-c Smannell w Enham Alamein *Win* 97-04. *158 Weyhill Road, Andover SP10 3BG* Tel (01264) 365694

KING, David John. b 67. W Sussex Inst of HE BEd91. St Steph Ho Ox 98. **d** 00 **p** 01. C Bexhill St Pet *Chich* 00-03; TV 03-08; V Eastbourne St Andr from 08. *St Andrew's Vicarage, 425 Seaside, Eastbourne BN22 7RT* Tel (01323) 723739

KING, David Michael. b 73. St Jo Coll Dur BA95 PGCE96 Cam Univ BA02. Ridley Hall Cam 00. **d** 03 **p** 04. C Claygate *Guildf* 03-07; C Redhill H Trin *S'wark* from 07. *29 St John's Meadow, Blindley Heath, Lingfield RH7 6JU* Tel 07901-700958 (mobile) E-mail rev.d.king@btinternet.com

KING, Canon David Russell. b 42. Univ of Wales (Lamp) BA67. St D Coll Lamp. **d** 68 **p** 69. C Barrow St Geo w St Luke *Carl* 68-72; P-in-c Kirkland 72-74; V Edenhall w Langwathby 72-73; P-in-c Culgaith 72-73; V Edenhall w Langwathby and Culgaith 73-74; V Flookburgh 75-79; V Barrow St Jas 79-82; P-in-c Bolton w Ireby and Uldale 82-83; R 83-90; R Burgh-by-Sands and Kirkbampton w Kirkandrews etc 90-00; P-in-c Aikton and Orton St Giles 95-00; R Barony of Burgh 00-02; P-in-c Gt Broughton and Broughton Moor 02-05; V Brigham, Gt Broughton and Broughton Moor 05-07; Hon Can Carl Cathl 01-07; rtd 07. *27 King Street, Aspatria, Wigton CA7 3AF* Tel (01697) 323580 E-mail candrking@dsl.pipex.com

KING, David William Anthony. b 42. Ch Ch Ox BA63 MA68. Westcott Ho Cam 63. **d** 65 **p** 66. C Cayton w Eastfield *York* 65-68; C Southbroom *Sarum* 68-71; V Holt St Jas 71-72; R Hinton Parva 71-72; V Holt St Jas and Hinton Parva 72-75; P-in-c Horton and Chalbury 73-75; R Holt St Jas, Hinton Parva, Horton and Chalbury 75-79; TV Melton Mowbray w Thorpe Arnold *Leic* 79-83; V Foxton w Gumley and Laughton and Lubenham 83-90; P-in-c Boreham *Chelmsf* 90-00; R Tendring and Lt Bentley w Beaumont cum Moze 00-06; rtd 06; Perm to Offic *Ely* from 06. *14 The Hythe, Reach, Cambridge CB25 0JQ* Tel (01638) 742924

KING, Dennis. b 31. ACA53 FCA64. EMMTC 73. **d** 76 **p** 77. NSM Chesterfield St Mary and All SS *Derby* 76-00; Perm to Offic from 00. *Hillcrest, Stubben Edge, Ashover, Chesterfield S45 0EU* Tel (01246) 590279

KING, Dennis Keppel. b 33. Lich Th Coll 63. **d** 65 **p** 66. C Eccleston St Thos *Liv* 65-68; C W Derby St Mary 68-71; V Aintree St Giles 71-96; rtd 96; Perm to Offic *York* from 96 and *Liv* 00-05. *8 Whiteoak Avenue, Easingwold, York YO61 3GB* Tel (01347) 822625 E-mail dennis.k.king@btinternet.com

KING, Derek Edwin Noel. b 31. Qu Mary Coll Lon BSc54 Birkbeck Coll Lon PhD60. **d** 93 **p** 94. OLM Nacton and Levington w Bucklesham etc *St E* from 93. *Vindelis, 1 Eastcliff, Felixstowe IP11 9TA* Tel and fax (01394) 270815

KING, Donald. b 32. ISM82. Chich Th Coll. **d** 86. NSM Forton *Portsm* 86-98; Perm to Offic from 98. *8 Burnett Road, Gosport PO12 3AH* Tel (023) 9252 3440

KING, Canon Fergus John. b 62. St Andr Univ MA Edin Univ BD89. Edin Th Coll 86. **d** 89 **p** 90. Chapl St Jo Cathl Oban 89-92; C Oban St Jo 89-92; Tanzania 92-98; Hon Can and Can Th Tanga from 01; Perm to Offic *S'wark* 99-03; Hon C Thamesmead 03-05; R Kotara South Gd Shep Australia from 05. *The Rectory, 10 Melissa Avenue, Adamstown Heights NSW 2289, Australia* Tel (0061) (2) 4943 0103 E-mail revfking@bigpond.net.au

KING, George Henry. b 24. St Alb Minl Tr Scheme. **d** 79 **p** 80. Hon C Flamstead *St Alb* 79-98; Dioc Agric Chapl 90-98; Perm to Offic from 98. *Chad Lane Farm, Chad Lane, Flamstead, St Albans AL3 8HW* Tel (01582) 841648

KING, Mrs Gillian Daphne. b 38. EMMTC 79. **dss** 83 **d** 87 **p** 94. Knighton St Jo *Leic* 83-85; Clarendon Park St Jo w Knighton St Mich 86-89; Par Dn 87-89; Chapl Kingston and Esher Mental Health Services 89-93; Chapl Kingston and Esher Community Health Unit 93-97; Chapl Long Grove Hosp Epsom 90-92; Chapl Tolworth Hosp Surbiton 91-97; Chapl Kingston and Distr Community NHS Trust 94-99; TV Hale w Badshot Lea *Guildf* 97-99; V Egham Hythe 99-05; rtd 05. *2 Fieldhurst Close, Addlestone KT15 1NN* Tel (01932) 846348 Mobile 07775-724090 E-mail revdgking@tiscali.co.uk

KING, James Anthony. b 46. CBE76. K Coll Lon BA69 AKC69 Lon Inst of Educn DipEd77. SAOMC 99. **d** 01 **p** 02. NSM Gerrards Cross and Fulmer *Ox* 01-03; NSM S Tottenham St Ann *Lon* 03-08; NSM Chalfont St Peter *Ox* from 08. *7 Meadowcroft, Chalfont St Peter, Gerrards Cross SL9 9DH* Tel (01753) 887386 E-mail jim@jimking.co.uk

KING, Canon Jeffrey Douglas Wallace. b 43. AKC67. **d** 68 **p** 69. C S Harrow St Paul *Lon* 68-71; C Garforth *Ripon* 71-74; V Potternewton 74-83; TR Moor Allerton 83-99; RD Allerton

85-89; P-in-c Thorner and Dioc Ecum Officer 99-08; Hon Can Ripon Cathl 90-08; rtd 08; Perm to Offic *Ripon* from 09. *27 Badger Wood Glade, Wetherby LS22 7XR* Tel (01937) 588177

KING, Jennifer. b 48. **d** 08 **p** 09. OLM Chorlton-cum-Hardy St Clem *Man* from 08. *8 St Clements Road, Manchester M21 9HU* Tel 0161-861 0898 Mobile 07918-702572 E-mail jennifer.king60@btinternet.com

KING, Jennifer Mary. b 41. Lon Univ BDS65 MSc75 PhD. Ripon Coll Cuddesdon 86. **d** 88 **p** 94. NSM S Hackney St Mich w Haggerston St Paul *Lon* 88-99; Chapl St Bart's and RLSMD Qu Mary and Westf Coll from 98; NSM St John-at-Hackney from 99. *83 Victoria Park Road, London E9 7NA* Tel (020) 7377 7000 ext 3069 or 7377 7167 E-mail jenny.king@qmul.ac.uk

KING, Jeremy Norman. See CLARK-KING, Jeremy Norman

KING, John. b 05 **p** 06. NSM Buckingham *Ox* from 05. *Wood End Farm, 2 Wood End, Nash, Milton Keynes MK17 0EL* Tel (01908) 501860 E-mail john@kingsfold100.freeserve.co.uk

KING, John. b 38. S'wark Ord Course 77. **d** 80 **p** 81. C Gillingham *Roch* 80-85; Min Joydens Wood St Barn CD 85-90; V Borstal 90-98; Chapl HM Pris Cookham Wood 90-98; Chapl The Foord Almshouses 90-98; rtd 98; Perm to Offic *Cant* from 99. *14 Lamberhurst Way, Cliftonville, Margate CT9 3HH* Tel (01843) 229405 Mobile 07889-277195

KING, John Andrew. b 50. Qu Coll Birm 72. **d** 75 **p** 76. C Halesowen *Worc* 75-77; C Belper Ch Ch and Milford *Derby* 78-81; Perm to Offic from 87. *11 Well Lane, Milford, Belper DE56 0QQ* Tel (01332) 841810

KING, John Charles. b 27. St Pet Hall Ox BA51 MA55. Oak Hill Th Coll 51. **d** 53 **p** 54. C Slough *Ox* 53-57; V Ware Ch Ch *St Alb* 57-60; Ed *C of E Newspaper* 64-68; Lic to Offic *St Alb* 60-70; Teacher St Fran Bacon Sch St Alb 68-71; Boston Gr Sch 71-88; Lic to Offic *Linc* 74-92; rtd 92. *6 Somersby Way, Boston PE21 9PQ* Tel (01205) 363061

KING, John Colin. b 39. Cuddesdon Coll 69. **d** 71 **p** 72. C Cookham *Ox* 71-75; Youth Chapl *B & W* 75-80; P-in-c Merriott 76-80; P-in-c Hinton w Dinnington 79-80; R Merriott w Hinton, Dinnington and Lopen 80-04; rtd 04. *Les Chênes, Les Arquies, St Henri, 46000 Cahors, France* Tel (0033) (5) 65 31 14 46

KING, Joseph Stephen. b 39. St Chad's Coll Dur BA62 MPhil83. **d** 64 **p** 65. C Lewisham St Mary *S'wark* 64-69; Hon C Milton next Gravesend Ch Ch *Roch* 70-85; V 85-07; rtd 07. *40 Thistledown, Gravesend DA12 5EU* Tel (01474) 748121 E-mail patandjoe48@blueyonder.co.uk

KING, Mrs Katharine Mary. b 63. St Hugh's Coll Ox BA85 MA89 SS Coll Cam BA88. Ridley Hall Cam 86. **d** 89 **p** 94. C Ipswich St Aug *St E* 89-91; NSM Bures 92-02; NSM Bures w Assington and Lt Cornard from 02. *The Vicarage, Church Square, Bures CO8 5AA* Tel (01787) 227315 Mobile 07885-863687 E-mail katharine@kmking.fsnet.co.uk

KING, Malcolm Charles. b 37. Chich Th Coll 67. **d** 70 **p** 71. C Mill End *St Alb* 70-72; Chapl RAF 72-76; R W Lynn *Nor* 76-81; V Croxley Green All SS *St Alb* 81-90; V Grimsby St Aug *Linc* 90-99; Asst Local Min Officer 90-95; V Bury w Houghton and Coldwaltham and Hardham *Chich* 99-02; rtd 02; OGS from 90; Perm to Offic *Chich* from 02; Warden Community of St Pet Woking 02-03. *25 Riverside Court, Station Road, Pulborough RH20 1RG* Tel (01798) 875213

KING, Malcolm Stewart. b 56. Sarum & Wells Th Coll 77. **d** 80 **p** 81. C Farnham *Guildf* 80-83; C Chertsey and Chapl St Pet Hosp Chertsey 83-86; V Egham Hythe *Guildf* 86-91; TR Cove St Jo 91-98; RD Aldershot 93-98; V Dorking w Ranmore 98-04; Hon Can Guildf Cathl 99-04; RD Dorking 01-04; P-in-c Portsea N End St Mark *Portsm* 04-06; TR 06-07; Warden Iona Community *Arg* from 07; Lic to Offic from 08. *The Abbey, Isle of Iona PA76 6SN* Tel (01681) 700404 Fax 700460 E-mail malcolmsking@gmail.com or warden@iona.org.uk

KING (née COWIE), Mrs Margaret Harriet. b 53. Glas Univ BSc76 AMA85 FMA97. TISEC 95. **d** 98 **p** 99. NSM Montrose and Inverbervie *Bre* 98-05; Dioc Dir of Ord 00-05; TV N Hinckford *Chelmsf* from 05. *The Vicarage, Great Henny, Sudbury CO10 7NW* Tel (01787) 269385 Mobile 07855-558056 E-mail mandgking39@hotmail.com

KING, Marie. b 40. CertEd74. **d** 03 **p** 04. OLM Addiscombe St Mildred *S'wark* from 03. *8 Annandale Road, Croydon CR0 7HP* Tel (020) 8654 2651 E-mail marieking@8annan.fsnet.co.uk

KING, Martin Harry. b 42. St Jo Coll Cam MA68 MBCS85. SAOMC 03. **d** 05 **p** 06. NSM Wheathampstead *St Alb* from 05; Dioc Environment Officer from 08. *29 Parkfields, Welwyn Garden City AL8 6EE* Tel (01707) 328905 E-mail martin@king-priestley.freeserve.co.uk

KING, Martin Peter James. b 73. Bris Univ BEng95. Oak Hill Th Coll BA05. **d** 05 **p** 06. C Leamington Priors St Paul *Cov* from 05. *49 Wathen Road, Leamington Spa CV32 5UY* Tel (01926) 451439 E-mail mssking@hotmail.com

KING, Martin Quartermain. b 39. Reading Univ BA61. Cuddesdon Coll 62. **d** 64 **p** 65. C S Shields St Hilda w St Thos *Dur* 64-66; C Newton Aycliffe 66-71; V Chilton Moor 71-78; R Middleton St George 78-91; R Sedgefield 91-04; RD Sedgefield

474

91-96; Chapl Co Dur & Darlington Priority Services NHS Trust 91-04; rtd 04. *3 White House Drive, Sedgefield, Stockton on Tees TS21 3BX* Tel (01740) 620424
E-mail martin.king@durham.anglican.org

KING, Michael Charles. Worc Coll Ox BA56 MA60. Coll of Resurr Mirfield. **d** 62 **p** 63. Hon C Hampstead All So *Lon* 62-65; Ed Asst SCM Press 62-65; C Thorpe St Andr *Nor* 66-69; Ed Sec BRF 69-90; Hon C Queensbury All SS *Lon* 69-79; Hon C Lt Stanmore St Lawr 80-90; R Cawston w Haveringland, Booton and Brandiston *Nor* 91-96; P-in-c Heydon 94-96; R Cawston w Booton and Brandiston etc 96-01; rtd 01; Perm to Offic *Leic* from 01. *84 Beacon Road, Loughborough LE11 2BH* Tel (01509) 563103

KING, Nathan Richard. b 68. Whitelands Coll Lon BA89 Univ of Wales (Cardiff) BTh94 Man Univ MA00. St Mich Coll Llan 91. **d** 94 **p** 95. C Hawarden *St As* 94-99; P-in-c 99-00; P-in-c Coreley and Doddington *Heref* 00-02; P-in-c Knowbury w Clee Hill 00-02; TV Ellesmere Port *Ches* 02-07. *Thornycroft, Aston Hill, Ewloe CH5 3AL* E-mail nathanking@onetel.com

KING, Nicholas Bernard Paul. b 46. Wycliffe Hall Ox 72. **d** 75 **p** 76. C Pitsmoor w Wicker *Sheff* 75-78; C Erdington St Barn *Birm* 78-80; C Sutton Coldfield H Trin 80-84; V Lynesack *Dur* 84-92; rtd 93. *16 Chatsworth Avenue, Bishop Auckland DL14 6AX* Tel (01388) 605614

KING, Peter Duncan. b 48. TD. K Coll Lon LLB70 AKC70 Fitzw Coll Cam BA72 MA77. Westcott Ho Cam 70. **d** 80 **p** 81. Hon C Notting Hill 68-84; Hon C Mortlake w E Sheen *S'wark* from 84; Dean MSE from 99. *49 Leinster Avenue, London SW14 7JW* Tel (020) 8876 8997 Fax 8287 9329
E-mail kingpd@hotmail.com

KING, Peter John Ryland. b 49. **d** 09. NSM Northampton Em *Pet* from 09. *7 Manor Road, Pitsford, Northampton NN6 9AR* Tel (01604) 880522

KING, Peter William Stephen. b 65. St Steph Ho Ox BTh01. **d** 01 **p** 02. C Abertillery w Cwmtillery w Six Bells *Mon* 01-06; C Abertillery w Cwmtillery 06; CF from 06. *c/o MOD Chaplains (Army)* Tel (01980) 615804 Fax 615800

KING, Miss Philipa Ann. b 65. Westcott Ho Cam 91. **d** 95 **p** 96. C Cambridge Ascension *Ely* 95-00; TV 00-02; TR from 02. *2 Stretten Avenue, Cambridge CB4 3EP* Tel (01223) 462414 Mobile 07816-833363 E-mail pipking@btinternet.com

KING, Richard Andrew. b 51. Linc Th Coll. **d** 84 **p** 85. C Bramhall *Ches* 84-87; V Heald Green St Cath 87-92; P-in-c Ashprington, Cornworthy and Dittisham *Ex* 92-99; RD Totnes 97-99; P-in-c Torquay St Jo and Ellacombe 99-02; P-in-c Stoneleigh and Dioc Spirituality Adv *Guildf* 02-07; P-in-c S Framland *Leic* from 08. *The Rectory, 7 Sycamore Lane, Wymondham, Melton Mowbray LE14 2AZ* Tel (01572) 787238 E-mail rking11@hotmail.com

KING, Richard David. b 63. Oak Hill Th Coll 87. **d** 90 **p** 91. C Foord St Jo *Cant* 90-94; P-in-c Orlestone w Snave and Ruckinge w Warehorne 94-02; Dioc Ecum Officer 97-02; CA Field Officer *Cant, Lon, Roch* and *S'wark* 02-06; C Charing w Charing Heath and Lt Chart *Cant* from 06; Dioc Missr from 06. *The Vicarage, Pett Lane, Charing, Ashford TN27 0DL* Tel (01233) 712598
E-mail richard.d.king@tesco.net

KING, Robert Dan. b 57. Sarum & Wells Th Coll 92. **d** 94 **p** 95. C Heref H Trin 94-97; TV W Heref 97-00; V Weobley w Barnesfield and Norton Canon from 00; P-in-c Letton w Staunton, Byford, Mansel Gamage etc 00-04; R from 04. *The Vicarage, Church Road, Weobley, Hereford HR4 8SD* Tel (01544) 318415 E-mail bobking@wbsnct.co.uk

KING, Canon Robin Lucas Colin. b 59. Dundee Univ MA81. Ridley Hall Cam 87. **d** 89 **p** 90. C Ipswich St Aug *St E* 89-92; V Bures 92-02; C Assington w Newton Green and Lt Cornard 00-02; V Bures w Assington and Lt Cornard from 02; RD Sudbury from 06; Hon Can St E Cathl from 08. *The Vicarage, Church Square, Bures CO8 5AA* Tel (01787) 227315 Mobile 07050-222719 E-mail robin@rlcking.freeserve.co.uk

KING, Tony Christopher. b 62. Lanc Univ BA83. Coll of Resurr Mirfield 83. **d** 86 **p** 87. C Stansted Mountfitchet *Chelmsf* 86-89; USPG 89-92; Botswana 90-92; C Chingford SS Pet and Paul *Chelmsf* 92-93. *252 Brettenham Road, London E17 5AY*

KING, Canon Walter Raleigh. b 45. New Coll Ox BA67 MA74. Cuddesdon Coll 71. **d** 74 **p** 75. C Wisbech SS Pet and Paul *Ely* 74-77; C Barrow St Geo w St Luke *Carl* 77-79; P-in-c Clifford *Heref* 79-83; P-in-c Cusop 79-83; P-in-c Hardwick 79-83; P-in-c Whitney w Winforton 81-84; R Cusop w Clifford, Hardwicke, Bredwardine etc 83-86; R Heref St Nic 86-92; Dir of Ords 86-92; Preb Heref Cathl 86-92; TR Huntingdon *Ely* 92-01; RD Huntingdon 94-99; Hon Can Ely Cathl 99-01; Vice Dean and Can Res Chelmsf Cathl from 01. *83 Ridgewell Avenue, Chelmsford CM1 2GF* Tel (01245) 267773 *or* 294493
E-mail vicedean@chelmsfordcathedral.org.uk

KING, Zoë Elizabeth. St Mich Coll Llan. **d** 06 **p** 07. C Neath *Llan* from 06. *18 Woodland Road, Neath SA11 3AL* Tel (01639) 635738

KING-SMITH, Giles Anthony Beaumont. b 53. Univ Coll Ox BA75. Trin Coll Bris 86. **d** 88 **p** 89. C Gtr Corsham *Bris* 88-92; V Two Mile Hill St Mich 92-96; TV Ilfracombe, Lee, Woolacombe,

Bittadon etc *Ex* from 96. *The Vicarage, Springfield Road, Woolacombe EX34 7BX* Tel (01271) 870467

KING-SMITH, Philip Hugh (Brother Robert Hugh). b 28. CCC Cam BA52 MA56. Cuddesdon Coll 52. **d** 54 **p** 55. C Stockton St Pet *Dur* 54-59; V Bishopwearmouth Gd Shep 59-64; SSF from 64; USA from 66; rtd 98. *San Damiano, 573 Dolores Street, San Francisco CA 94110-1164, USA* Tel (001) (415) 861 1372 Fax 861 7952

KINGCOME, John Parken. b 18. CEng50 MIMechE50. Sarum Th Coll 65. **d** 67 **p** 68. C Melksham *Sarum* 67-70; P-in-c Woodborough w Manningford Bohun etc 70-72; R Swanborough 72-75; TR Swanborough 75-79; RD Pewsey 75-84; Custos St Jo Hosp Heytesbury 79-84; rtd 84; Perm to Offic *B & W* from 85-95 and *Bris* from 92. *Stonecrop, The Butts, Biddestone, Chippenham SN14 7DY* Tel (01249) 713412

KINGDON, Mrs Margaret Victoria. b 44. SAOMC 95. **d** 98 **p** 99. OLM Wokingham St Sebastian *Ox* 98-03. *60 Pinewood Avenue, Crowthorne RG45 6RP* Tel (01344) 774625

KINGHAM, Derek Henry. b 29. Oak Hill Th Coll 56. **d** 58 **p** 59. C Deptford St Jo *S'wark* 58-60; C Normanton *Derby* 60-63; R Gaulby w Kings Norton and Stretton Parva *Leic* 63-73; V Bacup St Sav *Man* 73-95; rtd 95; Perm to Offic *Carl* from 95. *12 Castle Green Close, Kendal LA9 6AT* Tel (01539) 727008

KINGHAM, Mair Josephine. *See* TALBOT, Canon Mair Josephine

KINGMAN, Paul Henry Charles. b 64. Reading Univ BSc86. Wycliffe Hall Ox BTh95. **d** 95 **p** 96. C Whitton *Sarum* 95-99; C Harold Wood *Chelmsf* 99-03; V Stone Ch Ch and Oulton *Lich* from 03. *Christ Church Vicarage, Bromfield Court, Stone ST15 8ED* Tel (01785) 812669

KINGS, Mrs Frances Bridget (Biddi). b 48. City Univ BSc70 Birm Univ MSc77. WEMTC 00. **d** 03 **p** 04. NSM Eckington and Defford w Besford *Worc* 03-06; NSM Powick and Guarlford and Madresfield w Newland 06-08; Perm to Offic from 08. *Merebrook Farm, Hanley Swan, Worcester WR8 0DX* Tel (01684) 310950 E-mail biddi@merebrook.clara.co.uk

✠**KINGS, The Rt Revd Graham Ralph.** b 53. Hertf Coll Ox BA77 MA80 Utrecht Univ PhD02. Ridley Hall Cam 78. **d** 80 **p** 81 **c** 09. C Harlesden St Mark *Lon* 80-84; CMS Kenya 85-91; Dir Studies St Andr Inst Kabare 85-88; Vice Prin 89-91; Lect Miss Studies Cam Th Federation 92-00; Overseas Adv Henry Martyn Trust 92-95; Dir Henry Martyn Cen Westmr Coll Cam 95-00; Hon C Cambridge H Trin *Ely* 92-96; Hon C Chesterton St Andr 96-00; V Islington St Mary *Lon* 00-09; Area Bp Sherborne *Sarum* from 09. *Sherborne House, Tower Hill, Iwerne Minster, Blandford Forum DT11 8NH* Tel (01298) 857659 *or* tel and fax 857961

KINGS, Mrs Jean Alison. *See* THORN, Mrs Jean Alison

KINGSBURY, Canon Richard John. b 41. Lon Univ BA63. Linc Th Coll 65. **d** 67 **p** 68. C Wallsend St Luke *Newc* 67-69; C Monkseaton St Mary 69-70; Chapl K Coll Lon 70-75; V Hungerford and Denford *Ox* 75-83; R Caversham St Pet and Mapledurham 83-07; Hon Can Ch Ch 92-07; rtd 07. *14 Emgate, Bedale DL8 1AL* Tel and fax (01677) 424530
E-mail rj.kingsbury@tinyworld.co.uk

KINGSLEY, Brian St Clair. b 26. St Steph Ho Ox 56. **d** 59 **p** 60. C Tilehurst St Mich *Ox* 59-63; CSWG from 63; Prior from 85. *The Monastery of the Holy Trinity, Cuttinglye Lane, Crawley Down, Crawley RH10 4LH* Tel (01342) 712074

KINGSLEY, Miss Mary Phyllis Lillian. b 48. ERMC. **d** 09. NSM Croxley Green All SS *St Alb* from 09. *19 The Cloisters, Rickmansworth WD3 1HL* Tel (01923) 771172

KINGSLEY-SMITH, John Sydney. b 45. ARCM. Ridley Hall Cam 78. **d** 80 **p** 81. C Nailsea H Trin *B & W* 80-84; TV Whitton *Sarum* 84-91; V Chorleywood Ch Ch *St Alb* 91-01; RD Rickmansworth 98-01; rtd 01; Perm to Offic *St Alb* from 01. *29 Lewes Way, Croxley Green, Rickmansworth WD3 3SW* Tel (01923) 249949

KINGSMILL-LUNN, Brooke. *See* LUNN, Preb Brooke Kingsmill

KINGSTON, Canon Albert William. b 47. Bernard Gilpin Soc Dur 68 Oak Hill Th Coll 69. **d** 72 **p** 73. C Walton Breck *Liv* 72-74; C Templemore *D & R* 74-76; I Kildallon w Newtowngore and Corrawallen *K, E & A* 76-82; Bp's C Ardagh w Tashinny, Shrule and Kilcommick from 82; Can and Preb Elphin Cathl from 95. *Oakhill Lodge, Rathmore, Ballymahon, Co Longford, Republic of Ireland* Tel (00353) (90) 643 8945 Mobile 87-919 5473

KINGSTON, Mrs Avril Dawson. b 34. Local Minl Tr Course 91. **d** 94 **p** 95. Aux Min Douglas Union w Frankfield *C, C & R* 94-02; rtd 02. *Ballymartin House, Glencairn, Co Waterford, Republic of Ireland* Tel (00353) (58) 56227
E-mail akingston@esatclear.ie

KINGSTON (née LUCAS), Mrs Barbara Margaret. b 44. Lon Univ CertEd70. **d** 06 **p** 07. NSM Lee Gd Shep w St Pet *S'wark* from 06. *375 Westmount Road, London SE9 1NS* Tel (020) 8856 6468 E-mail barbarakingston44@yahoo.co.uk

KINGSTON, Desmond. *See* KINGSTON, John Desmond George

KINGSTON, Canon Eric. b 24. **d** 69 **p** 70. C Ballymacarrett St Patr *D & D* 69-72; C Knock 72-76; I Annahilt w Magherahamlet 76-93; rtd 93; Can and Prec Dromore Cathl 93. *38 Kinedale Park, Ballynahinch BT24 8YS* Tel (028) 9756 5715

KINGSTON, George Mervyn. b 47. CITC 70. **d** 73 **p** 74. C Comber *D & D* 73-77; C Belfast St Donard 77-80; Min Can Down Cathl 80-84; Bp's C Lecale Gp 82-84; Bp's C Belfast St Andr *Conn* 84-90; I Ballymascanlan w Creggan and Rathcor *Arm* 90-03; V Choral Arm Cathl 03-07; rtd 07. *The Cloisters, 36 Seahill Road, Holywood BT18 0DJ* Tel and fax (028) 9042 5016 Mobile 07816-462107 E-mail creggan@iolfree.ie

KINGSTON, John Desmond George. b 40. TCD BA63 MA66. CITC 64. **d** 64 **p** 65. C Arm St Mark 64-70; Hon V Choral Arm Cathl 69-70; Chapl Portora R Sch Enniskillen 70-01; Lic to Offic *Clogh* 70-01; Can Clogh Cathl 96-01; rtd 01. *Ambleside, 45 Old Rossory Road, Enniskillen BT74 7LF* Tel (028) 6632 4493

KINGSTON, Canon Kenneth Robert. b 42. TCD BA65 MA69. **d** 66 **p** 67. C Enniscorthy *C & O* 66-69; C Ballymena *Conn* 70-72; C Drumragh w Mountfield *D & R* 72-78; I Badoney Lower w Greenan and Badoney Upper 78-84; I Desertmartin w Termoneeny from 84; Can Derry Cathl from 97. *25 Dromore Road, Desertmartin, Magherafelt BT45 5JZ* Tel (028) 7963 2455

KINGSTON, Malcolm Trevor. b 75. QUB BSc97 MSc98 TCD BTh04. CITC 01. **d** 04 **p** 05. C Portadown St Mark *Arm* 04-07; I Kilmore St Aid w St Sav from 07. *38 Vicarage Road, Portadown, Craigavon BT62 4HF* Tel (028) 3833 2664 E-mail malcolm.kingston@btinternet.com

KINGSTON, Michael Joseph. b 51. K Coll Lon BD73 AKC73. St Aug Coll Cant 73. **d** 74 **p** 75. C Reading H Trin *Ox* 74-77; C New Eltham All SS *S'wark* 77-83; V Plumstead Ascension 83-94; Sub-Dean Greenwich N 92-94; V Sydenham St Bart from 94; RD W Lewisham from 04. *St Bartholomew's Vicarage, 4 Westwood Hill, London SE26 6QR* Tel (020) 8778 5290 E-mail thekingstons@btopenworld.com

KINGSTON, Michael Marshall. b 54. St Jo Coll Nottm MA94. **d** 96 **p** 97. C Drayton w Felthorpe *Nor* 96-99; R Gt and Lt Plumstead w Thorpe End and Witton 99-09; RD Blofield 06-08; Chapl Norfolk Community Health and Care 01-09; TR Hempnall *Nor* from 09. *The Rectory, The Street, Hempnall, Norwich NR15 2AD* Tel (01508) 498157

KINGSTON, Robert George. b 46. TCD BA68 Div Test69. **d** 69 **p** 72. C Belfast St Thos *Conn* 69-72; C Kilkenny St Canice Cathl 72-75; I Ballinasloe w Taughmaconnell *L & K* 77-79; I Maryborough w Dysart Enos and Ballyfin *C & O* 79-85; I Lurgan w Billis, Killinkere and Munterconnaught *K, E & A* 85-88; Registrar Kilmore 87-92; I Lurgan etc w Ballymachugh, Kildrumferton etc 88-92; I Tallaght *D & G* 92-98; Warden of Readers 93-98; I Mallow Union *C, C & R* 98-07; I Carrickmacross w Magheracloone *Clogh* from 07. *The Rectory, Drumconrath Road, Carrickmacross, Co Monaghan, Republic of Ireland* Tel (00353) (42) 966 1931 E-mail rgk@eircom.net

KINGSTON, Roy William Henry. b 31. Chich Th Coll 60. **d** 62 **p** 63. C Leeds St Aid *Ripon* 62-66; S Africa 66-73; V Bramley *Ripon* 74-81; TR Hemel Hempstead *St Alb* 81-85; TR Fareham H Trin *Portsm* 85-93; RD Alverstoke 89-90; RD Fareham 90-93; P-in-c Hambledon 93-97; rtd 97; Perm to Offic *Guildf*, *Portsm* and *Win* from 97. *8 Pengilly Road, Farnham GU9 7XQ* Tel (01252) 711371 Mobile 07855-457670 E-mail roy@roykingston.plus.com

KINGSTON-UPON-THAMES, Area Bishop of. *See* CHEETHAM, The Rt Revd Richard Ian

KINGTON, Canon David Bruce. b 45. Trin Coll Bris 72. **d** 72 **p** 73. C Wellington w Eyton *Lich* 72-77; C Boscombe St Jo *Win* 77-81; R Michelmersh, Timsbury, Farley Chamberlayne etc 81-98; R Michelmersh and Awbridge and Braishfield etc from 98; RD Romsey 95-05; Hon Can Win Cathl from 02. *The Rectory, Braishfield Road, Braishfield, Romsey SO51 0PR* Tel (01794) 368335 E-mail dbkington@dbkington.worldonline.co.uk

KINNA, Preb Michael Andrew. b 46. Chich Th Coll 84. **d** 86 **p** 87. C Leominster *Heref* 86-90; TV Wenlock 90-93; R Broseley w Benthall, Jackfield, Linley etc from 94; P-in-c Coalbrookdale, Iron-Bridge and Lt Wenlock from 07; RD Telford Severn Gorge from 03; Preb Heref Cathl from 07. *The Rectory, Church Street, Broseley TF12 5DA* Tel and fax (01952) 882647 E-mail mak@ridewise.fsnet.co.uk

KINNAIRD, Jennifer. b 41. Hull Univ BA62 Ex Univ PGCE63. NEOC 94. **d** 97 **p** 98. NSM Corbridge w Halton and Newton Hall *Newc* from 97. *17 Glebelands, Corbridge NE45 5DS* Tel (01434) 632695 E-mail j.kinnaird@btopenworld.com

KINNAIRD, Keith. b 42. Chich Th Coll 72. **d** 75 **p** 76. C Didcot St Pet *Ox* 75-78; C Abingdon w Shippon 78-82; P-in-c Sunningwell 82-90; P-in-c Radley 88-90; R Radley and Sunningwell 90-95; Chapl Abingdon Hosp 79-92; V Old Shoreham *Chich* 95-00; V New Shoreham 95-00; V Caversham St Andr *Ox* 00-07; Voc Adv and Adv for Min of Healing 00-07; rtd 07; Perm to Offic *Ox* from 07. *2 Weaver Row, Garston Lane, Wantage OX12 7DZ* Tel and fax (01235) 760867 E-mail keithkinnaird@btinternet.com

KINSELLA, Nigel Paul. b 66. Wolv Univ LLB95. Westcott Ho Cam 00. **d** 02 **p** 03. C Attleborough w Besthorpe *Nor* 02-03; C Quidenham Gp 03-05; R E w W Harling, Bridgham w Roudham, Larling etc from 05. *The Rectory, Church Road, East Harling, Norwich NR16 2NB* Tel (01953) 717235 E-mail nigelkinsella@btinternet.com

KINSEY, Bruce Richard Lawrence. b 59. K Coll Lon BD81 AKC81 MTh86 MA94. Wycliffe Hall Ox. **d** 84 **p** 85. C Gt Stanmore *Lon* 84-88; C Shepherd's Bush St Steph w St Thos 88-91; Chapl and Fell Down Coll Cam 91-01; Hd Philosophy and RS Perse Sch Cam from 01; Perm to Offic *Ely* from 07. *The Perse School, Hills Road, Cambridge CB2 8QF* Tel (01223) 3568266 E-mail brkinsey@perse.co.uk

KINSEY, Paul. b 56. Nottm Univ BTh89. Linc Th Coll 86. **d** 89 **p** 90. C Connah's Quay St As 89-91; Min Can St As 91-94; Asst Chapl Univ Coll Lon Hosps NHS Trust 94-00; R S Lynn *Nor* from 00; Ind Chapl from 00. *All Saints' Rectory, 33 Goodwins Road, King's Lynn PE30 5QX* Tel (01553) 771779 E-mail fatherpaul@allsaintskingslynn.org.uk

KINSEY, Russell Frederick David. b 34. Sarum Th Coll 59. **d** 62 **p** 63. C Twerton *B & W* 62-66; C N Cadbury 66-76; C Yarlington 66-76; P-in-c Compton Pauncefoot w Blackford 66-76; P-in-c Maperton 66-76; P-in-c N Cheriton 66-76; TV Camelot Par 76-79; V Pill 79-82; P-in-c Easton-in-Gordano w Portbury and Clapton 80-82; V Pill w Easton in Gordano and Portbury 82-92; rtd 92. *25 Newbourne Road, Weston-super-Mare BS22 8NF*

KINSMEN, Barry William. b 40. Chan Sch Truro. **d** 74 **p** 75. NSM Padstow *Truro* 74-78; Dioc Adv in RE 79-95; P-in-c St Issey 80-81; P-in-c Lt Petherick 80-81; R St Issey w St Petroc Minor 81-95; rtd 95; Perm to Offic *Truro* from 95. *14 Old School Court, School Hill, Padstow PL28 8ED* Tel (01841) 532507

KIPLING, Miss Susan Jane. b 49. Girton Coll Cam BA70 MA73. Westcott Ho Cam 04. **d** 06 **p** 08. C Old Basing and Lychpit *Win* 06-07; C N Hants Downs from 07. *Bartons, Weston Patrick, Basingstoke RG25 2NX* Tel (01256) 862208 E-mail suekipling@yahoo.co.uk

KIPPAX, Canon Michael John. b 48. Open Univ BA82. SWMTC 89. **d** 92 **p** 93. C Camborne *Truro* 92-95; C Woughton *Ox* 95-96; TV 96-98; R St Illogan *Truro* from 98; Hon Can Truro Cathl from 08. *The Rectory, Robartes Terrace, Illogan, Redruth TR16 4RX* Tel (01209) 842233 E-mail mike@saint-illogan.org.uk

KIRBY, Barbara Anne June (Sister Barbara June). b 34. St Andr Univ MA55. SAOMC 95. **d** 96 **p** 97. NSM Cowley St Jo *Ox* 96-05; rtd 06; Perm to Offic *Ox* from 06. *Convent of the Incarnation, Fairacres, Oxford OX4 1TB* Tel (01865) 721301

KIRBY, Bernard William Alexander (Alex). b 39. Keble Coll Ox BA62. Coll of Resurr Mirfield 62. **d** 65 **p** 72. C Is of Dogs Ch Ch and St Jo w St Luke *Lon* 65-66; Hon C Battersea St Phil *S'wark* 72; Hon C Battersea St Phil w St Bart 73-76; Perm to Offic 76-78 and 83-95. *28 Prince Edward Road, Lewes BN7 1BE* Tel (01273) 474935 Fax 486685

KIRBY, David Anthony. b 42. Dur Univ BA64 PhD68 Huddersfield Univ Hon DLitt98. NOC 84. **d** 87 **p** 88. NSM Crosland Moor *Wakef* 87-00; Asst Chapl Algarve Eur 00-05; Perm to Offic *Ripon* from 05. *4 North Mead, Bramhope, Leeds LS16 9DT* Tel 0113-267 8695 E-mail revdakirby@hotmail.com

KIRBY, David Graham. b 58. Univ of Wales (Cardiff) BA80. Wycliffe Hall Ox BA85 MA92. **d** 86 **p** 87. C Northallerton w Kirby Sigston *York* 86-89; C Southport Ch Ch *Liv* 89-92; R Bishop Burton w Walkington *York* 92-07; R Weston Favell *Pet* from 07. *The Rectory, Churchway, Weston Favell, Northampton NN3 3BX* Tel (01604) 784679

KIRBY, Mrs Joan Florence. b 32. St Hugh's Coll Ox MA57 Lon Univ BA66. St Alb Minl Tr Scheme 79. **d** 87 **p** 94. NSM Hemel Hempstead *St Alb* 87-90; C Blisland w St Breward *Truro* 90-94; NSM Cardynham 94-96; rtd 96; Perm to Offic *Truro* 96-04. *25 East Street, Martock TA12 6NG* Tel (01935) 825959

KIRBY, Miss Kathryn Margaret. b 52. Girton Coll Cam BA74 MA78 Hughes Hall Cam PGCE75 Leeds Univ MA08 MCLIP82. Coll of Resurr Mirfield 06. **d** 07 **p** 08. NSM Sale St Paul *Ches* 07-09; NSM Gatley from 09. *18 Pulford Road, Sale M33 3LP* Tel 0161-962 8049 Mobile 07745-434266 E-mail k.m.kirby@btinternet.com *or* kathy.kirby@mbs.ac.uk

KIRBY, Maurice William Herbert. b 31. K Coll Lon CertEd AKC. **d** 55 **p** 56. C Eltham Park St Luke *S'wark* 55-56; C Horley 56-59; C Westbury *Sarum* 59-62; R Poulshot w Worton 62-66; P-in-c Gt Cheverell 65; P-in-c Burcombe 66-68; V 68-70; V Salisbury St Mich 70-73; Chapl SS Helen and Kath Sch Abingdon 73-79; Chapl and Hd RS Wrekin Coll Telford 79-84; V Frensham *Guildf* 84-93; Dir of Reader Tr 84-93; rtd 93; Perm to Offic *Ex* 93-94; *Chich* 94-97; *York* 01-03 and from 04. *12 Rosthwaite Drive, Skelton-in-Cleveland, Saltburn-by-the-Sea TS12 2WJ*

KIRBY, Meg. b 50. STETS 03. **d** 06 **p** 07. NSM Portsea St Cuth *Portsm* 06-09; NSM Calne and Blackland *Sarum* from 09. *7 Richmond Road, Calne SN11 9UW* Tel (01249) 815964 Mobile 07757-646807 E-mail meg@kirby.myzen.co.uk *or* calnepcc@gotadsl.co.uk

KIRBY, Paul Michael. b 51. Wycliffe Hall Ox 74 Seabury-Western Th Sem DMin99. **d** 76 **p** 77. C Gateacre *Liv* 76-79; C Barton Seagrave w Warkton *Pet* 79-83; V Bidston *Ches* 83-93; V Ormskirk *Liv* 93-99; Team Ldr Chapl E Kent Hosps NHS Trust 99-00; Sen Team Ldr Chapl from 00; Chapl Manager E and Coastal Kent Primary Care Trust from 08; Bp's Adv for Hosp Chapl *Cant* from 02. *William Harvey Hospital, Kennington Road, Willesborough, Ashford TN24 0LZ* Tel (01233) 633331 Mobile 07811-134383 E-mail paul.kirby@ekht.nhs.uk

KIRBY, Richard Arthur. b 48. Lon Univ BSc69. **d** 05 **p** 06. OLM Wellington All SS w Eyton *Lich* 05-07; Perm to Offic from 07. *4 Donnerville Gardens, Admaston, Telford TF5 0DE* Tel (01952) 411358 E-mail richard.kirby@lichfield.anglican.org

KIRBY, Simon Thomas. b 67. Lon Bible Coll BA92. NTMTC 00. **d** 03 **p** 04. C Woodside Park St Barn *Lon* 03-06; Lic Preacher from 06; Chapl Wren Academy from 08. *48 Bawtry Road, London N20 0ST* Tel (020) 8361 1545 Mobile 07967-838272

KIRBY, Stennett Roger. b 54. St Pet Coll Ox BA75 MA79. Sarum & Wells Th Coll 75. **d** 77 **p** 78. C Belsize Park *Lon* 77-79; NSM Plumstead St Nic *S'wark* 88; C Leic Ch Sav 90-91; TV Hanley H Ev *Lich* 91-95; P-in-c Walsall St Pet 95-01; V 01-07; V W Ham *Chelmsf* from 07. *The Vicarage, 94 Devenay Road, London E15 4AZ* Tel (020) 8519 0955 E-mail skcse15@virgin.net

KIRK, Alastair James. b 71. St Jo Coll Dur BSc93 PhD98 Fitzw Coll Cam BA06. Ridley Hall Cam 04. **d** 07 **p** 08. C Tong *Bradf* from 07. *207 Broadstone Way, Bradford BD4 9BT* Tel (01274) 685256 Mobile 07725-991073
E-mail alastair_kirk@yahoo.co.uk

KIRK, Andrew. *See* KIRK, John Andrew

KIRK, Clive John Charles. b 37. TD81. FIBMS66. Guildf Dioc Min Course 95. **d** 98 **p** 99. OLM E Molesey St Paul *Guildf* 98-04; NSM E Horsley and Ockham w Hatchford and Downside from 04. *The Rectory, Ockham Lane, Ockham, Woking GU23 6NP* Tel (01483) 210167 E-mail candakirk@lineone.net

KIRK, Miss Erika Cottam. b 55. Nottm Univ LLB76 Solicitor 81. St Jo Coll Nottm MA98. **d** 98 **p** 99. NSM Epperstone, Gonalston, Oxton etc *S'well* 98-03; NSM Burton Joyce w Bulcote and Stoke Bardolph *S'well* 03-08; NSM Edingley w Halam from 08. *24 St Helen's Crescent, Burton Joyce, Nottingham NG14 5DW* Tel 0115-931 4125
E-mail erika.kirk@ntu.ac.uk

KIRK, Canon Gavin John. b 61. Southn Univ BTh Heythrop Coll Lon MA. Chich Th Coll 83. **d** 86 **p** 87. C Seaford w Sutton *Chich* 86-89; Chapl and Succ Roch Cath 89-91; Min Can 89-91; Hon PV 91-98; Asst Chapl K Sch Roch 91-98; Can Res Portsm Cathl 98-03; Can Res and Prec Linc Cathl from 03. *The Precentory, 16 Minster Yard, Lincoln LN2 1PX* Tel (01522) 523644
E-mail precentor@lincolncathedral.com

KIRK, Geoffrey. b 45. Keble Coll Ox BA67. Coll of Resurr Mirfield 71. **d** 72 **p** 73. C Leeds St Aid *Ripon* 72-74; C St Marylebone St Mark w St Luke *Lon* 74-76; C Kennington St Jo *S'wark* 77-79; C Kennington St Jo w St Jas 79-81; P-in-c Lewisham St Steph and St Mark 81-87; V from 87. *St Stephen's Vicarage, Cressingham Road, London SE13 5AG* Tel (020) 8318 1295 Fax 8318 1446

KIRK, George. b 14. Kelham Th Coll 32. **d** 38 **p** 39. C Norbury St Oswald *Cant* 38-41; C Sheff St Cuth 41-43; Chapl City Gen Hosp 41-43; P-in-c Brightside St Thos 43-44; V 44-48; V Bentley 48-56; R Aston cum Aughton 56-80; P-in-c Ulley 57-65; V 65-80; RD Laughton 72-79; rtd 80; Chapl to Rtd Clergy and Clergy Widows Officer *Sheff* 80-86; Lic to Offic 86-93; Perm to Offic from 93. *Hanbury House, Main Street, Ulley, Sheffield S26 3YD* Tel 0114-287 3314

KIRK, Miss Geraldine Mercedes. b 49. Hull Univ MA89. **d** 87 **p** 94. Ind Chapl *Linc* 87-99; P-in-c Bridgwater St Jo *B & W* from 99; Chapl Somerset Primary Care Trust from 99. *St John's Vicarage, Blake Place, Bridgwater TA6 5AU* Tel (01278) 422540 E-mail geraldine@geraldinekirk.wanadoo.co.uk

KIRK, Henry Logan. b 52. Adelaide Univ BA74 New Coll Edin BD77 K Coll Lon MA96. **d** 80 **p** 81. Chapl Dioc Coll Cape Prov S Africa 80-85; Asst Master Haileybury Coll 86; Asst Chapl Rugby Sch 86-93; Dep Hd Dulwich Coll Prep Sch 93-94; NSM S Dulwich St Steph *S'wark* 93-94; C Linslade *Ox* 94-96; Chapl Birkenhead Sch Merseyside 96-03; Chapl Abingdon Sch from 04. *Abingdon School, Park Road, Abingdon OX14 1DA* Tel (01235) 849112 *or* 534674 E-mail henry.kirk@abingdon.org.uk

KIRK, John Andrew. b 37. Lon Univ BD61 AKC61 MPhil75 Fitzw Ho Cam BA63. Ridley Hall Cam 61. **d** 63 **p** 64. C Finchley Ch Ch *Lon* 63-66; Argentina 66-79; SAMS 79-81; CMS 82-90; Dean of Miss Selly Oak Coll Birm 90-99; Dept of Th Birm Univ 99-02; Perm to Offic *Glouc* from 99; rtd 02. *The Old Stable, Market Square, Lechlade GL7 3AB* Tel (01367) 253254

KIRK, Natalie Roberta. *See* GARRETT, Natalie Roberta

KIRK, Peter Fenwick. b 30. Leeds Univ 50. **d** 83 **p** 84. NSM Bathgate *Edin* 83-91; NSM Linlithgow 83-91; NSM Bathgate from 92. *18 Inch Crescent, Bathgate EH48 1EU* Tel (01506) 655369

KIRK, Canon Steven Paul. b 59. Ex Univ LLB80 Univ of Wales (Cardiff) BD87 LLM94. St Mich Coll Llan 84. **d** 87 **p** 88. C

Ebbw Vale *Mon* 87-89; PV Llan Cathl 89-91; PV and Succ 91-94; V Port Talbot St Agnes w Oakwood 94-01; TR Aberavon 01-07; AD Margam 06-07; V Ystrad Mynach w Llanbradach from 07; Can Llan Cathl from 07. *The Vicarage, Nelson Road, Ystrad Mynach, Hengoed CF82 7EG* Tel (01443) 813246

KIRKBRIDE, Martin Lea. b 51. Oak Hill Th Coll BA94. **d** 97 **p** 98. C Lancaster St Thos *Blackb* 97-00; TV Hampreston *Sarum* 00-05; V Lenton *S'well* from 05. *The Vicarage, 35A Church Street, Nottingham NG7 2FF* Tel 0115-970 1059
E-mail martinkirkbride@aol.com

KIRKBY, Canon John Victor Michael. b 39. Lon Univ BScEng62 BD73. Ridley Hall Cam 65. **d** 67 **p** 68. C Muswell Hill St Jas *Lon* 67-70; Chapl Hatf Poly *St Alb* 71-75; V Wootton 75-86; RD Elstow 82-86; R Byfleet *Guildf* 86-92; P-in-c Potten End w Nettleden *St Alb* 92-97; V 97-05; TV Gt Berkhamsted, Gt and Lt Gaddesden etc 05-08; Chapl Ashridge Management Coll 92-08; rtd 08; Perm to Offic *St Alb* from 08; Can Masindi Uganda from 09. *3 Hillside Gardens, Berkhamsted HP4 2LE* Tel (01442) 872725 E-mail jvmkirkby@aol.com

KIRKE, Miss Annie Noreen. b 74. Univ of Wales (Cardiff) BA96 Reading Univ MA04. Westmr Th Cen 06. **d** 08 **p** 09. C Bryanston Square St Mary w St Marylebone St Mark *Lon* from 08. *10A Cavendish Parade, Clapham Common South Side, London SW4 9DP* Tel (020) 7258 5040 Mobile 07971-128498
E-mail annie@stmaryslondon.com

KIRKE, Clive Henry. b 51. Ridley Hall Cam. **d** 83 **p** 84. C Ainsdale *Liv* 83-86; Gen Asst Bootle Deanery 86-89; P-in-c Litherland St Andr 89-98; V Ingrow cum Hainworth *Bradf* from 98. *St John's Vicarage, Oakfield Road, Keighley BD21 1BT* Tel (01555) 604069 E-mail clive.kirke@bradford.anglican.org *or* thekirks@fsmail.net

KIRKER, Richard Ennis. b 51. Sarum & Wells Th Coll 72. **d** 77. C Hitchin *St Alb* 77-78; Chief Exec LGCM 79-08. *10 Coopers Close, London E1 4BB* Tel (020) 7791 1802 Mobile 07798-805428 E-mail richard@richardkirker.com

KIRKHAM, Alan. b 46. **d** 01 **p** 02. OLM Parr *Liv* from 01. *21 Avondale Road, Haydock, St Helens WA11 0HJ* Tel (01744) 28046

KIRKHAM, Clifford Gerald Frank. b 34. Open Univ BA91. Sarum & Wells Th Coll 72. **d** 74 **p** 75. C Worle *B & W* 74-76; C E Preston w Kingston *Chich* 76-78; C Goring-by-Sea 78-80; C-in-c Maybridge CD 80-82; V Maybridge 82-88; R N Chapel w Ebernoe 88-99; Chapl for Rural Affairs 89-99; rtd 99; Perm to Offic *Nor* from 99. *5 Meadow Way, Rollesby, Great Yarmouth NR29 5HA* Tel (01493) 749036

✠**KIRKHAM, The Rt Revd John Dudley Galtrey.** b 35. Trin Coll Cam BA59 MA63. Westcott Ho Cam 60. **d** 62 **p** 63 **c** 76. C Ipswich St Mary le Tower *St E* 62-65; Bp's Chapl *Nor* 65-69; P-in-c Rockland St Mary w Hellington 67-69; Papua New Guinea 69-70; C St Martin-in-the-Fields *Lon* 70-72; C Westmr St Marg 70-72; Abp's Dom Chapl *Cant* 72-76; Suff Bp Sherborne *Sarum* 76-81; Area Bp Sherborne 81-01; Can and Preb Sarum Cathl 77-01; Abp's Adv to the Headmasters' Conf from 90; Bp HM Forces 92-01; rtd 01; Hon Asst Bp Sarum from 01; Can and Preb Sarum Cathl from 02. *Flamstone House, Flamstone Street, Bishopstone, Salisbury SP5 4BZ* Tel (01722) 780221 E-mail jdkirkborne@salisbury.anglican.org

KIRKHAM, June Margaret. b 54. EMMTC 99. **d** 02 **p** 03. C Nottingham St Jude *S'well* 02-06; P-in-c Broxtowe from 06. *St Martha's Vicarage, 135 Frinton Road, Nottingham NG8 6GR* Tel 0115-927 8837 E-mail june@kirkham7260.fsnet.co.uk

KIRKHAM, Stephen Gawin. b 51. MC74. Ridley Hall Cam 96. **d** 98 **p** 99. C Histon and Impington *Ely* 98-02; P-in-c N Leigh *Ox* 02-07; rtd 07. *2 College Row, Crawley, Witney OX29 9TP* Tel (01993) 706405 E-mail sg.kirkham@btinternet.com

KIRKLAND, Richard John. b 53. Leic Univ BA75. St Jo Coll Dur 76. **d** 79 **p** 80. C Knutsford St Jo and Toft *Ches* 79-82; C Bebington 82-89; V Poulton Lancelyn H Trin 89-95; V Hoole from 95. *All Saints' Vicarage, 2 Vicarage Road, Chester CH2 3HZ* Tel (01244) 322056
E-mail j.kirkland@hender.org.uk

KIRKMAN, Richard Marsden. b 55. Cranmer Hall Dur. **d** 87 **p** 88. C Bridlington Priory *York* 87-90; TV Thirsk 90-96; R Escrick and Stillingfleet w Naburn from 96; RD Derwent from 01. *The Rectory, York Road, Escrick, York YO19 6EY* Tel (01904) 728406 E-mail rmkquanta@telco4u.net

KIRKMAN, Trevor Harwood. b 51. Trin Hall Cam BA73 MA77. EMMTC 94. **d** 96 **p** 97. NSM Hickling w Kinoulton and Broughton Sulney *S'well* 96-01; NSM Keyworth and Stanton-on-the-Wolds and Bunny etc from 01; Dioc Registrar and Bp's Legal Adv *Leic* from 02. *The Old Vicarage, 43 Church Lane, Long Clawson, Melton Mowbray LE14 4ND* Tel (01664) 822270 Fax (01509) 238833 E-mail trevorkirkman@btinternet.com

KIRKPATRICK, The Very Revd Jonathan Richard. b 58. CA81 Goldsmiths' Coll Lon BA85 Otago Univ MBA02. Wilson Carlile Coll 78 S'wark Ord Course 83. **d** 85 **p** 85. C Lewisham St Mary *S'wark* 85-87; Chapl Lewisham Hosp 85-87; Selection Sec ACCM 88-91; Sec Aston Tr Scheme 89-91; Hon C Noel Park St Mark *Lon* 88-91; V Christchurch St Mich New Zealand

91-96; Dean Dunedin 96-01; V Gen 97-01; Lic to Offic Auckland from 02. *33 Haycock Avenue, Mount Roskill, Auckland 1041, New Zealand* Tel (0064) (9) 627 7225 E-mail jonrk@xtra.co.nz

KIRKPATRICK, Nigel David Joseph. b 68. CITC BTh96. d 96 p 97. C Portadown St Columba *Arm* 96-99; C Lecale Gp *D & D* 99-01; I Killinchy w Kilmood and Tullynakill 01-07; I Gilnahirk from 07. *The Rectory, 237 Lower Braniel Road, Belfast BT5 7NQ* Tel (028) 9079 1748 E-mail gilnahirk@down.anglican.org

KIRKPATRICK, Reginald. b 48. d 07 p 08. OLM Ditchingham, Hedenham, Broome, Earsham etc *Nor* from 07. *18 Clark Road, Ditchingham, Bungay NR35 2QQ* Tel (01986) 893645 E-mail regkirkpatrick@aol.com

KIRKPATRICK, Roger James (Brother Damian). b 41. FCA. d 86 p 87. SSF from 66; Guardian Belf Friary 80-88; Birm 89-93; Prov Min 91-02; NSM Belfast St Pet *Conn* 86-88; Chapl R Victoria Hosp Belf 86-88; Lic to Offic *Linc* 94-96; *Lon* 97-01; *Sarum* 01-03; V Holy Is *Newc* from 03. *The Vicarage, Holy Island, Berwick-upon-Tweed TD15 2RX* Tel (01289) 389216 E-mail damianssf@franciscans.org.uk

KIRKPATRICK, William John Ashley. b 27. SEN SRN RMN. Sarum Th Coll 63. d 68 p 70. NSM St Mary le Bow w St Pancras Soper Lane etc *Lon* 68-70; NSM Soho St Anne w St Thos and St Pet 70-75; SSF 76-79; NSM S Kensington St Aug *Lon* 79-80; NSM Earl's Court St Cuth w St Matthias 80-98; rtd 98; Perm to Offic *Lon* from 98. *c/o Ms V R F Tschudin, 26 Cathcart Road, London SW10 9NN*

KIRKUP, Nigel Norman. b 54. K Coll Lon BD79 AKC79. d 80 p 80. Hon C Catford (Southend) and Downham *S'wark* 80-83; Hon C Surbiton St Andr and St Mark 83-85; Hon C Shirley St Geo 85-93; Perm to Offic *Lon* 96-09. *10 Norfolk Buildings, Brighton BN1 2DZ* Tel 07817-458076 (mobile) E-mail nigelkirkup@hotmail.com

KIRKWOOD, Canon David Christopher. b 40. Pemb Coll Ox BA63. Clifton Th Coll 63. d 65 p 66. C Wilmington *Roch* 65-68; C Green Street Green 68-72; Youth and Area Sec BCMS 72-73; Educn and Youth Sec 73-80; Hon C Sidcup Ch Ch *Roch* 74-80; V Rothley *Leic* 80-92; RD Goscote II 84-88; RD Goscote 88-90; P-in-c Toxteth St Philemon w St Gabr and St Cleopas *Liv* 92-95; TR 95-01; TR Harlow Town Cen w Lt Parndon *Chelmsf* 01-07; AD Toxteth and Wavertree *Liv* 96-01; AD Harlow *Chelmsf* 04-07; Hon Can Chelmsf Cathl 07; rtd 07. *7 Dunoon Close, Sinfin, Derby DE24 9NF* E-mail davidk@minternet.org

KIRKWOOD, Jack. b 21. Worc Ord Coll 62. d 63 p 64. C Penwerris *Truro* 63-66; V Torpoint 66-73; V Turton *Man* 73-81; P-in-c Castleton All So 81-82; Hon C Heywood St Luke 82-84; rtd 86; Perm to Offic *Blackb* from 86 and *York* 89-94. *5 Duddle Lane, Walton-le-Dale, Preston PR5 4UP*

KIRLEW, John Richard Francis. b 52. STETS 92. d 05 p 06. NSM Castle Cary w Ansford *B & W* 05-08; P-in-c Colwyn *S & B* from 08; Dioc Rural Life Adv from 09. *The Rectory, Llanelwedd, Builth Wells LD2 3TY* Tel (01982) 551288 E-mail richard.kirlew@btinternet.com

KIRTLEY, Georgina. b 44. St Jo Coll Dur BA94. Cranmer Hall Dur. d 95 p 96. NSM Barnard Castle w Whorlton *Dur* 95-00; Chapl HM YOI Deerbolt from 00; Bp's Asst Adv Self-Supporting Min from 00. *Ryelands, Stainton, Barnard Castle DL12 8RB* Tel (01833) 630871

KIRTON, Canon Richard Arthur. b 43. Dur Univ BA67 MA73. Wycliffe Hall Ox 68. d 69 p 70. C Warsop *S'well* 69-72; C Newark St Mary 72-75; Lect Kolej Theoloji Malaysia 76-79; Dean of Studies Th Sem Kuala Lumpur 79-82; P-in-c Kuala Lumpur St Gabr 79-81; Hon Can Kuala Lumpur from 88; P-in-c Bleasby w Halloughton *S'well* 83-89; V Thurgarton w Hoveringham 83-89; V Thurgarton w Hoveringham and Bleasby etc 89-91; Bp's Adv on Overseas Relns 85-91; Tutor Wilson Carlile Coll of Evang 91-98; P-in-c Ollerton w Boughton *S'well* 98-08; rtd 08. *Hill Top, Mosscar Close, Warsop, Mansfield NG20 0BW* Tel (01623) 842915 Mobile 07803-627574 E-mail richardkirton1@btinternet.com

KISH, Paul Alexander. b 68. K Coll Lon BD92 AKC92 Leeds Univ MA96. St Steph Ho Ox 96. d 98 p 99. C Prestbury *Glouc* 98-01; Chapl Sutton Valence Sch Kent from 01. *1 Holdgate House, South Lane, Sutton Valence, Maidstone ME17 3BG* Tel (01622) 842814 or 842289 Fax 844208 Mobile 07760-355434 E-mail chaplain@svs.org.uk

KISSELL, Barrington John. b 38. Lon Coll of Div 64. d 67 p 68. C Camborne *Truro* 67-71; C Chorleywood St Andr *St Alb* 71-00; C Bryanston Square St Mary w St Marylebone St Mark *Lon* from 00; Dir Faith Sharing Min from 74. *Garden Flat, 19 Lena Gardens, London W6 7PY* Tel (020) 7258 5040 E-mail bkissell@aol.com

KISSELL, Jonathan Mark Barrington. b 66. Trin Coll Bris 99. d 01 p 02. C Stevenage St Pet Broadwater *St Alb* 01-05; C Dublin St Patr Cathl Gp from 05. *76 North Circular Road, Dublin 7, Republic of Ireland* Tel (00353) (1) 473 5100 E-mail jonathankissell@hotmail.com

KITCHEN, Ian Brian. b 60. Worc Coll Ox BA81 Southn Univ PGCE82. Wycliffe Hall Ox 98. d 00 p 01. C Brandesburton and Leven w Catwick *York* 00-03; P-in-c Coxwold and Husthwaite

from 03; P-in-c Crayke w Brandsby and Yearsley from 03. *The Rectory, Church Hill, Crayke, York YO61 4TA* Tel (01347) 821876

KITCHEN, Martin. b 47. N Lon Poly BA71 K Coll Lon BD76 AKC77 Man Univ PhD88. S'wark Ord Course 77. d 79 p 80. Lect CA Tr Coll Blackheath 79-83; Hon C Kidbrooke St Jas *S'wark* 79-83; Chapl Man Poly 83-88; TV Man Whitworth 83-86; TR 86-88; Adv In-Service Tr *S'wark* 88-95; Dioc Co-ord of Tr 95-97; Can Res S'wark Cathl 88-97; Can Res Dur Cathl 97-05; Sub-Dean 99-05; Dean Derby 05-07; P-in-c S Rodings *Chelmsf* from 08. *The Rectory, Stortford Road, Leaden Roding, Dunmow CM6 1GY* Tel (01279) 876147 E-mail martinx.kitchen@btinternet.com

KITCHENER, Christopher William. b 46. Open Univ BA. Sarum & Wells Th Coll 82. d 84 p 85. C Bexleyheath Ch Ch *Roch* 84-88; V Gravesend St Mary 88-97; V Biggin Hill 97-07; V St Mary Cray and St Paul's Cray from 07. *The Vicarage, Main Road, Orpington BR5 3EN* Tel (01689) 827697 E-mail chris.kitchener@diocese-rochester.org

KITCHENER, Mrs Evarina Carol. b 51. Stockwell Coll of Educn CertEd70 Heythrop Coll Lon MA00. Cant Sch of Min 89. d 92 p 94. NSM Gravesend St Mary *Roch* 92-97; NSM Biggin Hill 97-07; Asst Chapl Bromley Hosps NHS Trust 98-99; Distr Evang Miss Enabler S Prov URC 99-01; Par Development Officer *Roch* 01-07; C Chislehurst St Nic from 07. *The Vicarage, Main Road, Orpington BR5 3EN* Tel (01689) 827697 E-mail carol.kitchener@diocese-rochester.org

KITCHENER, Canon Michael Anthony. b 45. Trin Coll Cam BA67 MA70 PhD71. Cuddesdon Coll 70. d 71 p 72. C Aldwick *Chich* 71-74; C Caversham *Ox* 74-77; Tutor Coll of Resurr Mirfield 77-83; Prin NEOC *Dur* 83-90; Hon Can Newc Cathl 84-90; Can Res and Chan Blackb Cathl 90-95; P-in-c Rydal and Warden Rydal Hall *Carl* 95-96; Ldr Rydal Hall Community 95-99; Can Res Nor Cathl 99-05; Dioc Dir of Ords 99-04; Bp's Officer for Ord and Initial Tr 04-05; rtd 05; Perm to Offic *Edin* from 06. *Ivy Hatch, St Boswells, Melrose TD6 0AD* Tel (01835) 822035 E-mail kitcheners@yahoo.co.uk

KITCHIN, Kenneth. b 46. Trin Coll Bris. d 89 p 90. C Barrow St Mark *Carl* 89-93; C Dalton-in-Furness 93-95; P-in-c Dearham 95-01; P-in-c Clifton 01-07; P-in-c Dean 01-07; P-in-c Mosser 01-07; R Clifton, Dean and Mosser from 07. *The Vicarage, 1 Clifton Gardens, Great Clifton, Workington CA14 1TT* Tel (01900) 603886 E-mail kenkitchin@uk2k.com

KITCHING, Daphne. b 48. Yorks Min Course. d 09. NSM Swanland from 09. *21 Old Pond Place, North Ferriby HU14 3JE* Tel (01482) 635159

KITCHING, David Monro. b 26. New Coll Ox BA49. Ridley Hall Cam 80. d 82 p 83. C Hornchurch St Andr *Chelmsf* 82-86; P-in-c Graveley w Papworth St Agnes w Yelling etc *Ely* 86-90; rtd 91; Perm to Offic *Ely* from 91. *20 Victoria Park, Cambridge CB4 3EL* Tel (01223) 365687

KITCHING, Miss Elizabeth. b 49. Trent Park Coll of Educn CertEd74. St Jo Coll Nottm. d 01 p 02. C Northallerton w Kirby Sigston *York* 01-05; P-in-c Cloughton and Burniston w Ravenscar etc from 05. *The Vicarage, Mill Lane, Cloughton, Scarborough YO13 0AB* Tel (01723) 870270 Mobile 07889-425025

KITCHING, Paul. b 53. GTCL LTCL. Coll of Resurr Mirfield 80. d 83 p 84. C Hessle *York* 83-86; P-in-c Crathorne 86-98; Youth Officer 86-98; rtd 98; P-in-c Crathorne *York* from 98. *The Rectory, Crathorne, Yarm TS15 0BB* Tel (01642) 701158 Fax 700806 E-mail paulkitching@btinternet.com

KITELEY, Robert John. b 51. Hull Univ BSc73 Univ of Wales (Abth) MSc75 Lon Univ PhD82. Trin Coll Bris. d 83 p 84. C Bebington *Ches* 83-88; C Hoole 88-91; V Plas Newton 91-99; R Ashtead *Guildf* from 99. *The Rectory, Ashdene, Dene Road, Ashtead KT21 1EE* Tel and fax (01372) 805182 E-mail bobkiteley@ntlworld.com

KITLEY, Canon David Buchan. b 53. St Jo Coll Dur BA. Trin Coll Bris 78. d 81 p 82. C Tonbridge St Steph *Roch* 81-84; C-in-c Southall Em CD *Lon* 84-91; V Dartford Ch Ch *Roch* 91-09; RD Dartford 98-07; V Kippington from 09; Bp's Adv for Overseas Links from 09; Hon Can Roch Cathl from 05; Hon Can Mpwampwa from 05. *The Vicarage, 59 Kippington Road, Sevenoaks TN13 2LL* Tel (01732) 452112 E-mail kitley@clara.net

KITTERINGHAM, Canon Ian. b 35. CCC Cam BA59 MA63. Westcott Ho Cam 59. d 61 p 62. C Rotherham *Sheff* 61-64; C Eltham H Trin *S'wark* 64-66; V Battersea St Mary-le-Park 66-73; V Reigate St Mark 73-80; V Caterham Valley 80-85; RD Caterham 84-85; V Wandsworth Common St Mary 85-00; RD Tooting 88-93; Hon Can S'wark Cathl 95-00; rtd 00; Perm to Offic *Cov* 02-07. *33 Central Place, Station Road, Wilmslow SK9 1BU* Tel (01625) 530512

KITTS, Joseph. b 27. Tyndale Hall Bris 59. d 60 p 61. C Parr *Liv* 60-63; C Bootle St Leon 63-66; V Southport SS Simon and Jude 66-74; USA 74-94; rtd 92. *Windyridge, Cottage Lane, St Martin's, Oswestry SY11 3BL* Tel (01691) 777090

KIVETT, Michael Stephen. b 50. Bethany Coll W Virginia BA72. Chr Th Sem Indiana MDiv76 Sarum & Wells Th Coll 76. **d** 77 **p** 78. C Harnham *Sarum* 77-80; C E Dereham *Nor* 80-83; R S Walsham and V Upton 83-88; Chapl Lt Plumstead Hosp 84-88; V Chard St Mary *B & W* 88-99; TR Chard and Ilminster 99-04; RD Crewkerne and Ilminster 93-98; R Staplegrove w Norton Fitzwarren from 04. *The Rectory, Rectory Drive, Staplegrove, Taunton TA2 6AP* Tel (01823) 272787
E-mail kivett@btinternet.com

KLIMAS, Miss Lynda. b 58. Jes Coll Cam BA89 MA93. Cranmer Hall Dur 89. **d** 90 **p** 94. Par Dn Sandy *St Alb* 90-93; Par Dn Bishop's Stortford St Mich 93-94; C 94-98; P-in-c Weston and C Baldock w Bygrave 98-03; TV Baldock w Bygrave and Weston 03-04; V Cople, Moggerhanger and Willington from 04. *The Vicarage, 3 Grange Lane, Cople, Bedford MK44 3TT* Tel (01234) 838431

KNAPP, Antony Blair. b 48. Imp Coll Lon BSc68. NOC 86. **d** 89 **p** 90. C Bolton St Jas w St Chrys *Bradf* 89-92; V Kettlewell w Conistone, Hubberholme etc 92-00; TR Swindon Dorcan *Bris* from 00. *23 Sedgebrook, Swindon SN3 6EY* Tel (01793) 525130
E-mail tonybknapp@aol.com

KNAPP, Bryan Thomas. b 61. Trin Coll Bris BA91. **d** 91 **p** 92. C S Gillingham *Roch* 91-95; V Chatham St Paul w All SS 95-09; V Paddock Wood from 09. *The Vicarage, 169 Maidstone Road, Paddock Wood, Tonbridge TN12 6DZ* Tel (01892) 833917
E-mail bryan.knapp@diocese-rochester.org

KNAPP, Jeremy Michael. b 67. Westhill Coll Birm BEd91. Ripon Coll Cuddesdon BTh99. **d** 99 **p** 00. C Hill *Birm* 99-02; TV Salter Street and Shirley 02-09; V Olton from 09. *St Margaret's Vicarage, 5 Old Warwick Road, Solihull B92 7JU* Tel 0121-706 2318 E-mail jeremy.knapp@btinternet.com

KNAPP (*née* STOCKER), **Mrs Rachael Ann.** b 64. Bris Univ BA86. Trin Coll Bris BA91. **d** 91 **p** 94. C Ditton *Roch* 91-95; C Chatham St Paul w All SS 95-08; Chapl Bennett Memorial Dioc Sch Tunbridge Wells from 08. *The Vicarage, 169 Maidstone Road, Paddock Wood, Tonbridge TN12 6DZ* Tel (01892) 833917 *or* 521595 E-mail knapp@bennett.kent.sch.uk

KNAPPER, Peter Charles. b 39. Lon Univ BA61. St Steph Ho Ox 61. **d** 63 **p** 64. C Carl H Trin 63-68; V Westfield St Mary 68-76; V Bridekirk 76-83; P-in-c Blackheath Ascension *S'wark* 83-96; P-in-c Holmwood *Guildf* 96-03; TV Surrey Weald 03-04; rtd 04; Perm to Offic *S'wark* from 09. *20 Boyne Road, London SE13 5AW* Tel (020) 8473 1501
E-mail peter@pknapper.fsnet.co.uk

KNARESBOROUGH, Suffragan Bishop of. See BELL, The Rt Revd James Harold

KNEE, Geoffrey. b 31. Whitelands Coll Lon CertEd71 Anglia Poly Univ MA05. CA Tr Coll 56 Glouc Sch of Min 91. **d** 92 **p** 93. NSM Hampton *Worc* 92-97; Chapl St Richard's Hospice Worc 95-97; NSM Badsey w Aldington and Offenham and Bretforton *Worc* 97; rtd 97; Perm to Offic *Worc* from 98. *8 Mayfair, Fairfield, Evesham WR11 1JJ* Tel (01386) 443574
E-mail geoff@kneehome.freeserve.co.uk

KNEE, Jacob Samuel. b 66. LSE BSc(Econ)87 MSc(Econ)88. Ripon Coll Cuddesdon BA92. **d** 93 **p** 94. C Ashby-de-la-Zouch St Helen w Coleorton *Leic* 93-96; C Boston *Linc* 96-00; Chapl Boston Coll of FE 96-00; V Cam w Stinchcombe *Glouc* 00-07; R Billings St Steph USA from 07. *1241 Crawford Drive, Billings MT 59102, USA* Tel (001) (406) 259 5017 Fax 259 1150
E-mail jknee@globalnet.co.uk

KNEE-ROBINSON, Keith Frederick. b 40. Thames Poly BSc75 MICE76. SAOMC 99. **d** 01 **p** 02. OLM Caversham St Pet and Mapledurham w Chazey *Ox* from 01. *8 Hewett Close, Reading RG4 7ER* Tel 0118-947 7868 E-mail kkrmill@globalnet.co.uk

KNEEN, Michael John. b 55. Univ Coll Lon BSc76 MSc77 St Jo Coll Dur BA85. Cranmer Hall Dur 83. **d** 86 **p** 87. C Bishop's Castle w Mainstone *Heref* 86-90; TV Bridgnorth, Tasley, Astley Abbotts, etc 90-08; TV Leominster from 08. *The Rectory, Church Street, Leominster HR6 8NH* Tel (01568) 615709
E-mail michael@kneenmichael.orangehome.co.uk

KNELL, John George. b 35. Cant Sch of Min 79. **d** 82 **p** 83. Hd Master St Geo C of E Middle Sch Sheerness 80-87; NSM Sheerness H Trin w St Paul *Cant* 82-87; NSM Minster-in-Sheppey 87-06; rtd 06; Perm to Offic *Cant* from 06-08. *The Annex, Old Mill House, Old Mill Drive, Pulham St Mary, Diss IP21 4NB*

KNELL, Canon Raymond John. b 27. Qu Coll Cam BA48 MA52. Ridley Hall Cam 50. **d** 52 **p** 53. C Bishopwearmouth St Gabr *Dur* 52-57; C S Shields St Hilda 57-58; P-in-c Hebburn St Oswald 58-67; V Castleside 67-76; V Heworth St Mary 76-93; RD Gateshead 83-87; Hon Can Dur Cathl 87-93; rtd 93. *40 St Andrew's Drive, Low Fell, Gateshead NE9 6JU* Tel 0191-442 1069

KNIBBS, Peter John. b 55. Birm Univ BDS78 DDS93. SWMTC 04. **d** 07 **p** 08. NSM St Illogan *Truro* from 07. *Hillywych, Sunnyvale Road, Portreath, Redruth TR16 4NE* Tel (01209) 842005 E-mail peter.knibbs@lineone.net

KNICKERBOCKER, Driss Richard. b 39. Univ of Michigan BA63 MDiv68 Ox Univ DPhil81. **d** 68 **p** 69. USA 68-76; C St Marylebone w H Trin *Lon* 78-81; C Chelsea St Luke 81-83;

P-in-c Isleworth St Fran 83-85; USA from 85; rtd 04. *985 Pierpont Street, Rahway NJ 07065-3114, USA*

KNIFTON, Gladys Elizabeth. b 52. Kingston Univ BSc95 SRN73 SCM75 TCert84. NTMTC 95. **d** 98 **p** 99. NSM Churt *Guildf* 98-01; Asst Chapl Surrey Hants Borders NHS Trust 01-05; Chapl Acorn Chr Foundn from 05; Hon C Grayshott *Guildf* from 07. *Bryanston, Boundary Road, Grayshott, Hindhead GU26 6TX* Tel and fax (01428) 604977
E-mail elizabeth@knifton.com *or* eknifton@acornchristian.org

KNIGHT, The Very Revd Alexander Francis (Alec). b 39. OBE06. St Cath Coll Cam BA61 MA65. Wells Th Coll. **d** 63 **p** 64. C Hemel Hempstead *St Alb* 63-68; Chapl Taunton Sch 68-75; Dir Bloxham Project 75-81; Dir of Studies Aston Tr Scheme 81-83; P-in-c Easton and Martyr Worthy *Win* 83-91; Adn Basingstoke 90-98; Can Res Win Cathl 91-98; Dean Linc 98-06; rtd 06. *Shalom, Clay Street, Whiteparish, Salisbury SP5 2ST* Tel (01794) 884402 E-mail sheelagh_knight@hotmail.com

KNIGHT, Andrew. b 67. **d** 06 **p** 07. C Wolstanton *Lich* from 06. *St Barnabas' Vicarage, Oldcastle Avenue, Newcastle ST5 8QG* Tel (01782) 636161 E-mail andykn@aol.com

KNIGHT, Canon Andrew James. b 50. Grey Coll Dur BA72 Ox Univ BA74 MA81. Wycliffe Hall Ox 72. **d** 75 **p** 76. Min Can Brecon Cathl 75-78; C Brecon w Battle 75-78; C Morriston 78-82; V 89-00; V Llanwrtyd w Llanddulas in Tir Abad etc 82-89; RD Cwmtawe 97-00; V Sketty from 00; Can Res Brecon Cathl 98-04; Treas from 04. *The Vicarage, De La Beche Road, Sketty, Swansea SA2 9AR* Tel (01792) 202767
E-mail andrewknight@phonecoop.coop

KNIGHT, Mrs Ann. b 54. Lanc Univ CertEd75. Trin Coll Bris. **dss** 84 **d** 87 **p** 94. Wigan St Jas w St Thos *Liv* 84-87; Par Dn 87-90; C Costessey *Nor* 90-96; R Gt and Lt Ellingham, Rockland and Shropham etc 96-03; Chapl Norwich Primary Care Trust 96-02; P-in-c Worthen *Heref* 03-07; P-in-c Hope w Shelve 03-07; TV Ross 07-08; V Brampton from 08. *The Rectory, Brampton Abbotts, Ross-on-Wye HR9 7JD* Tel (01989) 562010

KNIGHT, Arthur Clifford Edwin. b 42. Univ of Wales BSc64. Wells Th Coll 64. **d** 66 **p** 67. C Llangyfelach and Morriston *S & B* 66-68; C Oystermouth 68-73; Chapl RAF 73-95; Perm to Offic *Heref* 95-97; P-in-c Brant Broughton and Beckingham *Linc* 97-99; P-in-c Credenhill w Brinsop and Wormsley etc *Heref* from 99; RD Heref Rural 05-07. *26 Meadow Drive, Credenhill, Hereford HR4 7EE* Tel (01432) 760530

KNIGHT, Mrs Barbara. b 46. St Alb Minl Tr Scheme 86. **d** 90 **p** 94. NSM Weston and Ardeley *St Alb* 90-95; C Norton 95-97; R Barkway, Reed and Buckland w Barley 97-05; rtd 05. *Grace House, 5 Ditchburn Road, South Charlton, Alnwick NE66 2JU* Tel (01665) 579455

KNIGHT, Mrs Barbara Mary. b 43. SRN64 SCM70. EMMTC 94. **d** 97 **p** 98. NSM Market Harborough and The Transfiguration etc *Leic* 97-99; C Church Langton cum Tur Langton etc 99-02; P-in-c Billesdon and Skeffington 02; R Church Langton cum Tur Langton etc 02-07; rtd 07; Perm to Offic *Blackb* from 07. *1 Whittlewood Drive, Accrington BB5 5DJ* Tel (01254) 395549 E-mail revbarbarak@btopenworld.com

KNIGHT, Brenda Evelyn. b 27. SAOMC 96. **d** 98 **p** 99. OLM Wheatley *Ox* 98-09; Perm to Offic from 09. *22 Middle Road, Stanton St John, Oxford OX33 1HD* Tel (01865) 351227

KNIGHT, Christopher. b 61. Wycliffe Hall Ox 94. **d** 96 **p** 97. C Banbury *Ox* 96-98; C Banbury St Paul 98-01; Chapl HM Pris Lowdham Grange from 01. *HM Prison Lowdham Grange, Nottingham NG14 7DQ* Tel 0115-966 9308
E-mail 2cv@clara.net

KNIGHT, Christopher Colson. b 52. Ex Univ BSc73 Man Univ PhD77 SS Coll Cam MA90. Sarum & Wells Th Coll BTh83. **d** 81 **p** 82. Chapl St Mary's Cathl 81-84; V Chesterton *Cov* 84-87; R Lighthorne 84-87; V Newbold Pacey w Moreton Morrell 84-87; Chapl and Fell SS Coll Cam 87-92; Sen Research Assoc St Edm Coll Cam from 92. *Hope Cottage, Hindringham Road, Walsingham NR22 6DR* Tel (01328) 820108

KNIGHT, Clifford. See KNIGHT, Arthur Clifford Edwin

KNIGHT, David Alan. b 59. Lanc Univ BA81. Ripon Coll Cuddesdon 82. **d** 85 **p** 86. C Stretford All SS *Man* 85-88; C Charlestown 88-89; TV Pendleton St Thos w Charlestown 89-94; V Tysoe w Oxhill and Whatcote *Cov* 94-05; RD Shipston 04-05; Chapl Marie Curie Hospice Solihull from 06; Chapl St Richard's Hospice Worc from 06. *Marie Curie Hospice, 911-913 Warwick Road, Solihull B91 3ER* Tel 0121-254 7800
E-mail david.knight@mariecurie.org.uk

KNIGHT, David Charles. b 32. Clare Coll Cam BA55 MA59. Tyndale Hall Bris 55. **d** 57 **p** 58. C Cambridge St Paul *Ely* 57-58; C St Alb Ch Ch *St Alb* 58-61; C-in-c Wimbledon Em Ridgway Prop Chpl *S'wark* 61-67; Publications Sec BCMS 67-68; Ed Asst *The Christian* 68-69; V Lanmarth *Truro* 69-75; RD Carnmarth N 72-75; V Fremington *Ex* 75-83; C Edmonton All SS w St Mich *Lon* 83; Chapl N Middx Hosp 83; rtd 94; Perm to Offic *Chelmsf* from 94. *Tudor Court, High Street, Hatfield Broad Oak, Bishop's Stortford CM22 7HF* Tel (01279) 718650
E-mail david-knight@amserve.com

KNIGHT, Canon David Charles. b 45. Lon Univ BA66 St Edm Hall Ox BA68 MA73 ATCL63. St Steph Ho Ox 68. **d** 70 **p** 71. C Northwood H Trin *Lon* 70-73; C Stevenage All SS Pin Green *St Alb* 73-77; C Cippenham CD *Ox* 77-78; TV W Slough 78-83; Dep Min Can Windsor from 81; Ecum Officer to Bp Willesden 83-91; R Lt Stanmore St Lawr *Lon* 83-91; Prec and Can Res Chelmsf Cathl 91-01; V Ranmoor *Sheff* 01-08; rtd 08; Perm to Offic *Ox* from 09. *12 Bankside, Headington, Oxford OX3 8LT* Tel (01865) 761476

KNIGHT, Canon David Lansley. b 33. Em Coll Cam BA58 MA61 PGCE76. Ridley Hall Cam 57. **d** 59 **p** 60. C Chatham St Steph *Roch* 59-63; C Plymouth St Andr *Ex* 63-65; V Gravesend St Aid *Roch* 65-71; V Bexley St Mary 71-98; RD Sidcup 93-97; Hon Can Roch Cathl 97; rtd 98; Perm to Offic *Chich* from 98. *1 Newlands Avenue, Bexhill-on-Sea TN39 4HA* Tel (01424) 212120

KNIGHT (née SMITH), Frances Mary. b 48. St Jo Coll York CertEd69. EMMTC 98. **d** 03 **p** 04. NSM Braunstone *Leic* 03-07; NSM The Abbey Leic from 07. *32 Aster Way, Burbage, Hinckley LE10 2UQ* Tel (01455) 618218
E-mail frances@knight-t.freeserve.co.uk

KNIGHT, Gavin Rees. b 65. St Andr Univ MTheol94. Ripon Coll Cuddesdon MTh96. **d** 98 **p** 99. C Solihull *Birm* 98-02; P-in-c Fulham St Andr Fulham Fields *Lon* 02-05; P-in-c Fulham St Alb w St Aug 04-05; Chapl Mon Sch from 05. *Monmouth School, Almshouse Street, Monmouth NP25 3XP* Tel (01600) 713143 Fax 772701 E-mail chaplain@monmouthschool.org.uk

KNIGHT, Henry Christian. b 34. Fitzw Ho Cam BA62 MA66. Ridley Hall Cam 62. **d** 63 **p** 64. Succ Bradf Cathl 63-64; Chapl 64-66; Chapl Tel Aviv Israel 67-79; CMJ 79-86; V Allithwaite *Carl* 86-93; rtd 93; Perm to Offic *Leic* from 93. *20 Saxon Way, Ashby-de-la-Zouch LE65 2JR* Tel (01530) 460709

KNIGHT, Canon John Bernard. b 34. Fuller Th Sem California DMin91 ACIS60. Oak Hill Th Coll 61. **d** 65 **p** 66. C Morden *S'wark* 65-69; USA 69-71; V Summerfield *Birm* 71-07; Hon Can Birm Cathl 01-07; rtd 07. *102 High Haden Road, Cradley Heath B64 7PN* Tel 0121-559 0108

KNIGHT, Canon John Francis Alan Macdonald. b 36. Coll of Resurr Mirfield 59. **d** 61 **p** 62. C Gwelo S Rhodesia 61-66; R Melfort 66-68; C Highlands and P-in-c Chikwata 68-70; Lic to Offic Mashonaland 70-75; R Umtali 76-81; Dean Mutare 81-87; TR Northampton Em *Pet* 87-97; RD Northn 88-92; P-in-c Greens Norton w Bradden and Lichborough 97-05; Bp's Adv for Min of Healing 99-05; Can Pet Cathl 01-05; rtd 05; Perm to Offic *Pet* from 06. *16 Glebe Drive, Brackley NN13 7BX* Tel (01280) 706258 E-mail jfam@knight40.freeserve.co.uk

KNIGHT, Jonathan Morshead. b 59. Fitzw Coll Cam BA81 MA85 Jes Coll Cam PhD91 Jes Coll Ox MA87 Worc Coll Ox DPhil02 W Lon Inst of HE PGCE82 Sheff Univ PGCE00. Wycliffe Hall Ox 86. **d** 88 **p** 89. C Hillingdon St Jo *Lon* 88-91; NSM Baslow *Derby* 91-92; NSM Curbar and Stoney Middleton 91-92; Lect Bibl Studies Sheff Univ 91-92; Research Fell 92-94; NSM Sheff St Paul 92-94; Bp's Research Asst *Ely* 94-98; Min Whittlesford LEP 95-96; Bp's Dom Chapl 96; Sec Doctrine Commn 96-98; P-in-c Holywell w Needingworth *Ely* 98-01; Tutor Westcott Ho Cam 98-99; OCF from 99; CF (TAVR) 00-03; Hon Lect Th Kent Univ from 00; Asst Master Man Gr Sch 02; Chapl Worc Coll Ox 02-03; Visiting Fell York St Jo Univ from 07; Hon Research Fell Man Univ from 09. *154 Woodrow Avenue, Hayes UB4 8QP* Tel (020) 8574 4322
E-mail jonathanknight5@hotmail.com

KNIGHT, Mrs June. b 28. Glouc Sch of Min 85. **d** 87 **p** 94. NSM Leckhampton SS Phil and Jas w Cheltenham St Jas *Glouc* 87-96; rtd 96; Perm to Offic *Glouc* from 96. *31 St Michael's Road, Woodlands, Cheltenham GL51 5RP* Tel (01242) 517911

KNIGHT, Mrs June Elizabeth. b 42. St Alb Minl Tr Scheme 90. **d** 93 **p** 94. NSM Stanstead Abbots *St Alb* 93-96; NSM Gt Amwell w St Margaret's and Stanstead Abbots 96-97; NSM Lt Hadham w Albury 97-98; NSM Bishop's Stortford St Mich from 98. *The White Cottage, Albury Hall Park, Albury, Ware SG11 2HX* Tel (01279) 771756
E-mail june.k.knight@btopenworld.com

KNIGHT, Keith Kenneth. b 36. Southn Univ BSc58. Wycliffe Hall Ox 59. **d** 62 **p** 63. C Lower Darwen St Jas *Blackb* 62-64; C Leyland St Andr 64-68; P-in-c Blackb All SS 68-71; Dioc Youth Chapl 71-88; Hon C Burnley St Pet 71-74; Warden Scargill Ho 88-01; rtd 01; Perm to Offic *Bradf* from 01. *4 The Hawthorns, Sutton-in-Craven, Keighley BD20 8BP* Tel (01535) 632920

KNIGHT, Mrs Margaret Owen. b 34. Oak Hill Th Coll 78. **dss** 80 **d** 87 **p** 94. Chorleywood St Andr *St Alb* 80-04; Par Dn 87-94; C 94-04; rtd 94; Perm to Offic *St Alb* from 04. *15A Blacketts Wood Drive, Chorleywood, Rickmansworth WD3 5PY* Tel (01923) 283832 E-mail moknight@waitrose.com

KNIGHT, Canon Michael Richard. b 47. St Jo Coll Dur BA69 MA79 Fitzw Coll Cam BA73 MA78 St Cross Coll Ox MA92. Westcott Ho Cam 71. **d** 74 **p** 75. C Bishop's Stortford St Mich *St Alb* 74-75; C Bedford St Andr 75-79; Chapl Angl Students Glas 79-86; V Riddings and Ironville *Derby* 86-91; Lib Pusey Ho 91-94; Fell St Cross Coll Ox 92-94; V Chesterfield St Mary and

All SS *Derby* from 94; P-in-c Chesterfield St Aug 05-09; Hon Can Derby Cathl from 06. *28 Cromwell Road, Chesterfield S40 4TH* Tel (01246) 232937 *or* 206506
E-mail vicar.chesterfield@virgin.net

KNIGHT, Paul James Joseph. b 50. Oak Hill Th Coll. **d** 84 **p** 85. C Broadwater St Mary *Chich* 84-87; R Itchingfield w Slinfold 87-92; Chapl Highgate Sch Lon from 92. *15A Bishopswood Road, London N6 4PB* Tel (020) 8348 9211 *or* 8340 1524
E-mail paul.knight@highgateschool.org.uk

KNIGHT, Paul Jeremy. b 53. **d** 94 **p** 95. CA 77-04; C Moreton Say *Lich* 94-97; V Birstall *Wakef* from 97. *St Peter's Vicarage, King's Drive, Birstall, Batley WF17 9JJ* Tel and fax (01924) 473715
E-mail rev.paul@ntlworld.com *or* vicar@stpetersbirstall.org.uk

KNIGHT, Peter John. b 51. AKC73 Ch Ch Coll Cant CertEd77. Sarum & Wells Th Coll 79. **d** 80 **p** 81. C Greenford H Cross *Lon* 80-83; C Langley Marish *Ox* 83; NSM W Acton St Martin *Lon* 88-90; C E Acton St Dunstan w St Thos 90-92; V Malden St Jo *S'wark* 92-02; Co-ord Chapl HM Pris Long Lartin 02-05; TR Malvern Link w Cowleigh *Worc* from 05. *St Matthias' Rectory, 12 Lambourne Avenue, Malvern WR14 1NL* Tel (01684) 566054
E-mail revpeterknight@hotmail.com

KNIGHT, Peter Malcolm. b 55. Cam Univ BA76 Lon Hosp MB, BS76 MRCGP85. Trin Coll Bris BA94. **d** 94 **p** 95. C Quidenham *Nor* 94-97; R Thurton from 97; RD Loddon 99-05. *The Rectory, 29 Ashby Road, Thurton, Norwich NR14 6AX* Tel (01508) 480738

KNIGHT, Peter Michael. b 47. St Luke's Coll Ex BEd71. Trin Coll Bris 90. **d** 92 **p** 93. C Bris Ch the Servant Stockwood 92-95; Chapl St Brendan's Sixth Form Coll 92-94; C W Swindon and the Lydiards *Bris* 95-96; TV 96-07; P-in-c The Claydons *Ox* 07-09; TV The Claydons and Swan from 09. *The Rectory, Queen Catherine Road, Steeple Claydon, Buckingham MK18 2PY* Tel (01296) 738055 E-mail peterknight15@tiscali.co.uk

KNIGHT, Philip Stephen. b 46. Ian Ramsey Coll 74. **d** 77 **p** 78. C Pennycross *Ex* 77-80; C Epsom St Martin *Guildf* 80-83; V Clay Hill St Jo *Lon* 83-86; TV Washfield, Stoodleigh, Withleigh etc *Ex* 86-90; Chapl ATC from 86; Chapl S Warks Hosps 90-94; Chapl S Warks Health Care NHS Trust 94-05; Perm to Offic *Cov* from 05. *37 Lodge Crescent, Warwick CV34 6BB* Tel (01926) 403053
E-mail psk54@hotmail.co.uk

KNIGHT, Canon Roger George. b 41. Culham Coll Ox CertEd63. Linc Th Coll 65. **d** 67 **p** 68. C Bris St Andr Hartcliffe 67-69; Hd Master Twywell Sch Kettering 69-74; V Naseby *Pet* 74-79; P-in-c Haselbeech 74-79; R Clipston w Naseby and Haselbech 79-82; P-in-c Kelmarsh 79-82; TR Corby SS Pet and Andr w Gt and Lt Oakley 82-88; R Irthlingborough 88-99; RD Higham 89-94; R Burton Latimer 99-03; Can Pet Cathl 92-03; rtd 03; Perm to Offic *Pet* from 03. *9 Hollow Wood Road, Burton Latimer, Kettering NN15 5RB* Tel (01536) 721726
E-mail rogerknight01@yahoo.co.uk

KNIGHT, Roger Ivan. b 54. K Coll Lon BD79 AKC79. Ripon Coll Cuddesdon 79. **d** 80 **p** 81. C Orpington All SS *Roch* 80-84; C St Laur in Thanet *Cant* 84-87; R Cuxton and Halling *Roch* from 87. *The Rectory, 6 Rochester Road, Cuxton, Rochester ME2 1AF* Tel (01634) 717134 E-mail roger.knight@diocese-rochester.org *or* rogerknight@aol.com

KNIGHT, Stephen. *See* KNIGHT, Philip Stephen

KNIGHT, Ms Sue Elizabeth. b 47. Southlands Coll Lon CertEd68. SEITE 01. **d** 03 **p** 04. NSM Lee St Mildred *S'wark* from 03. *101 Lyme Farm Road, London SE12 8JH* Tel (020) 8852 1781

KNIGHT, Mrs Susan Jane. b 57. Open Univ BSc99. NTMTC BA09. **d** 09. C Harlow Town Cen w Lt Parndon *Chelmsf* from 09. *92 Ram Gorse, Harlow CM20 1PZ* Tel 07801-701084 (mobile) E-mail sue@kerryknight.co.uk

KNIGHT, Mrs Susan Margaret. **d** 02 **p** 03. C Clydach *S & B* 02-03; C Cen Swansea 04-05; TV from 05. *The Vicarage, 27 Bowen Street, Swansea SA1 2NA* Tel (01792) 473047

KNIGHT, Suzanne. b 55. **d** 00 **p** 01. NSM Reading St Jo *Ox* from 00. *9 Victoria Way, Reading RG1 3HD* Tel 0118-967 5645
E-mail suz-knight@yahoo.co.uk

KNIGHT, William Lawrence. b 39. Univ Coll Lon BSc61 PhD65. Coll of Resurr Mirfield 75. **d** 77 **p** 78. C Bp's Hatfield *St Alb* 77-81; Asst Chapl Brussels Cathl 81-84; V Pet H Spirit Bretton 84-89; P-in-c Marholm 84-89; TR Riverside *Ox* 89-04; rtd 04. *90 Norfolk Gardens, Littlehampton BN17 5PF* Tel (01903) 716750 E-mail knightsmvd@dial.pipex.com

KNIGHTS, Christopher Hammond. b 61. St Jo Coll Dur BA83 PhD88. Linc Th Coll 87. **d** 89 **p** 90. C Stockton St Pet *Dur* 89-92; C Chich St Paul and St Pet 92-94; Tutor Chich Th Coll 92-94; V Ashington *Newc* 94-00; V Monkseaton St Mary 00-04; Dioc Moderator Reader Tr from 03; P-in-c Scotswood from 04. *St Margaret's Vicarage, 14 Heighley Street, Newcastle upon Tyne NE15 6AR* Tel 0191-274 6322
E-mail knights@time4you.plus.com

KNIGHTS, James William. b 34. AKC66. **d** 67 **p** 68. C Kettering St Andr *Pet* 67-71; V Braunston w Brooke 71-81; V Dudley St Jo *Worc* 81-97; rtd 97; Perm to Offic *Worc* from 98. *192 Brook Farm Road, Malvern WR14 3SL* Tel (01684) 561358

KNIGHTS JOHNSON, Nigel Anthony. b 52. Ealing Tech Coll BA74 Westmr Coll Ox MTh99. Wycliffe Hall Ox 78. **d** 80 **p** 81. C Beckenham Ch Ch *Roch* 80-84; CF 84-07; P-in-c Ockley, Okewood and Forest Green *Guildf* from 07. *The Rectory, Stane Street, Ockley, Dorking RH5 5SY* Tel (01306) 711550
E-mail nknightsj@hotmail.com

KNILL-JONES, Jonathan Waring (Jack). b 58. Univ Coll Lon BSc79. St Jo Coll Nottm 88. **d** 90 **p** 91. C Northolt St Jos *Lon* 90-94; C Hayes St Nic CD 94-99; V Airedale w Fryston *Wakef* 99-07; V Teddington SS Pet and Paul and Fulwell *Lon* from 07; Chapl Richmond and Twickenham Primary Care Trust from 08. *The Vicarage, 1 Bychurch End, Teddington TW11 8PS* Tel (020) 8977 0054 E-mail jackknill@aol.com

KNOPP, Alexander Edward Robert. b 09. St Jo Coll Cam BA33 MA37. Ridley Hall Cam 32. **d** 34 **p** 35. C Loughton St Mary *Chelmsf* 34-38; C Prittlewell St Mary 38-40; R Nevendon 40; R N Benfleet w Nevendon 41-48; V Walthamstow St Jo 48-50; V Pampisford *Ely* 50-59; V Babraham 50-59; R Quendon w Rickling *Chelmsf* 59-68; R Gt Yeldham 68-73; R Gt w Lt Snoring *Nor* 73-76; rtd 76; Perm to Offic *Ely* 77-00. *6 Rose Lane, Melbourn, Royston SG8 6AD* Tel (01763) 262143

KNOTT, Graham Keith. b 53. Oak Hill Th Coll BA80. **d** 80 **p** 81. C Normanton *Derby* 80-83; C Ripley 83-87; TV Newark w Hawton, Cotham and Shelton *S'well* 87-89; TV Newark 89-97; P-in-c Mansfield St Jo 97-06; AD Mansfield 03-06; P-in-c Croajingolong Australia 06-09; P-in-c Watford *St Alb* from 09. *St Mary's Vicarage, 14 Cassiobury Drive, Watford WD17 3AB* Tel (01923) 254005 E-mail graham.knott@stmaryswatford.org

KNOTT, Preb Janet Patricia. b 50. Avery Hill Coll CertEd71. S Dios Minl Tr Scheme MTS91. **d** 92 **p** 94. NSM Clutton w Cameley *B & W* 92-99; Chapl R Sch Bath 94-98; Chapl R High Sch Bath 98-99; R Farmborough, Marksbury and Stanton Prior *B & W* from 99; Chapl Bath Spa Univ from 99; RD Chew Magna *B & W* from 04; Preb Wells Cathl from 07. *The Rectory, Church Lane, Farmborough, Bath BA3 1AN* Tel (01761) 479311 E-mail rayjanknott@btinternet.com

KNOTT, Pamela Frances. *See* IVE, Mrs Pamela Frances

KNOTT, Miss Wendy Gillian. b 47. Adelaide Univ BA78. Melbourne Coll of Div BD95. **d** 94 **p** 96. NSM Sandy Bay Australia 94-98; NSM New Town St Jas 98-01; NSM Franklin w Esperance 01-05; Hon Chapl Ch Coll Tasmania 97-06; R Wick *Mor* from 06; P-in-c Thurso from 06. *5 Naver Place, Thurso KW14 7PZ* Tel (01847) 893393
E-mail rev.wendy@btinternet.com

KNOWD, George Alexander. b 31. St Deiniol's Hawarden. **d** 88 **p** 89. NSM Aghalurcher w Tattykeeran, Cooneen etc *Clogh* 88-91; Dioc Communications Officer 89-90 and 92-97; NSM Ballybay w Mucknoe and Clontibret 91-92; C 92-94; I 94-97; I Clonmel w Innislounagh, Tullaghmelan etc *C & O* 97-06; Can Ossory Cathl 05-06; rtd 06. *Sunhaven, Knockally Road, Fethard, Co Tipperary, Republic of Ireland* Tel and fax (00353) (52) 30821 Mobile 87-284 2350 E-mail gknowd@eircom.net

KNOWERS, Stephen John. b 49. K Coll Lon BD72 AKC72. **d** 73 **p** 74. C Bp's Hatfield *St Alb* 73-77; C Cheshunt 77-81; P-in-c Barnet Vale St Mark 81-83; V 83-85; Chapl S Bank Poly *S'wark* 85-92; Chapl S Bank Univ 92-94; V Croydon St Pet 94-06; P-in-c Croydon St Aug 04-06; V S Croydon St Pet and St Aug 06-07; V Shirley St Jo from 07. *The Vicarage, 49 Shirley Church Road, Croydon CR0 5EF* Tel (020) 8654 1013
E-mail frstiiv@hotmail.com

KNOWLES, Andrew John. b 66. Wimbledon Sch of Art BA88. St Jo Coll Nottm 05. **d** 07 **p** 08. C Long Buckby w Watford *Pet* from 07; C W Haddon w Winwick and Ravensthorpe from 07. *The Vicarage, 4 West End, West Haddon, Northampton NN6 7AY* Tel (01788) 510535

KNOWLES, Canon Andrew William Allen. b 46. St Cath Coll Cam BA68 MA72. St Jo Coll Nottm 69. **d** 71 **p** 72. C Leic H Trin 71-74; C Cambridge H Trin *Ely* 74-77; C Woking St Jo *Guildf* 77-81; V Goldsworth Park 81-93; V Wyke 93-98; Dioc Officer Educn and Development of Lay People 93-98; Can Res Chelmsf Cathl from 98. *2 Harlings Grove, Chelmsford CM1 1YQ* Tel (01245) 355041 or 294484
E-mail andrew.knowles@btinternet.com

KNOWLES, Charles Howard. b 43. Sheff Univ BSc65 Fitzw Coll Cam BA69 MA73. Westcott Ho Cam 67. **d** 69 **p** 70. C Bilborough St Jo *S'well* 69-72; V Choral S'well Minster 72-82; V Cinderhill 82-94; AD Nottingham W 91-94; V Cov St Mary 94-06; AD Cov S 96-02; C Burnsall w Rylstone *Bradf* 06-08; C Linton in Craven 06-08; C Kettlewell w Conistone, Hubberholme etc 06-08; rtd 08. *Ivy Cottage, Linton, Skipton BD23 5HH* E-mail charles.h.knowles@dial.pipex.com

KNOWLES, Clay. *See* KNOWLES, Melvin Clay

KNOWLES, Clifford. b 35. Open Univ BA82. NW Ord Course 74. **d** 77 **p** 78. C Urmston *Man* 77-80; V Chadderton St Luke 80-87; V Heywood St Luke w All So 87-95; AD Heywood and Middleton 92-95; Perm to Offic *Linc* 95-98; rtd 00; Perm to Offic *Linc* from 02. *12B Far Lane, Coleby, Lincoln LN5 0AH* Tel (01522) 810720

KNOWLES, Canon Eric Gordon. b 44. WMMTC 79. **d** 82 **p** 83. NSM Gt Malvern St Mary *Worc* 82-83; NSM Malvern H Trin and St Jas 83-90; NSM Lt Malvern, Malvern Wells and Wyche 90-99; NSM Lt Malvern 99-00; P-in-c from 00; Hon Can Worc Cathl from 05. *45 Wykewane, Malvern WR14 2XD* Tel (01684) 567439

KNOWLES, George. b 37. **d** 95 **p** 96. NSM Hucknall Torkard *S'well* 95-02; rtd 02; Perm to Offic *S'well* from 02. *8 North Hill Avenue, Hucknall, Nottingham NG15 7FE* Tel 0115-955 9822
E-mail g.knowles3@ntlworld.com

✠**KNOWLES, The Rt Revd Graeme Paul.** b 51. AKC73. St Aug Coll Cant 73. **d** 74 **p** 75 **c** 03. C St Peter-in-Thanet *Cant* 74-79; C Leeds St Pet *Ripon* 79-81; Chapl and Prec Portsm Cathl 81-87; Chapter Clerk 85-87; V Leigh Park 87-93; RD Havant 90-93; Adn Portsm 93-99; Dean Carl 99-03; Bp S & M 03-07; Dean St Paul's *Lon* from 07. *The Deanery, 9 Amen Court, London EC4M 7BU* Tel (020) 7236 2827 Fax 7332 0298
E-mail thedean@stpaulscathedral.org.uk

KNOWLES, Irene. *See* KNOWLES, Margaret Irene

KNOWLES, Mrs Jane Frances. b 44. GGSM66 Lon Inst of Educn TCert67. Ox Min Course 90. **d** 93 **p** 94. NSM Sandhurst *Ox* 93-97; C Wargrave 97-99; P-in-c Ramsden, Finstock and Fawler, Leafield etc 99-01; V Forest Edge from 01; rtd 09. *41 Martin's Road, Keevil, Trowbridge BA14 6NA* Tel (01380) 870325 E-mail janeknowles@tiscali.co.uk

KNOWLES, John Geoffrey. b 48. Man Univ BSc69 Ox Univ PGCE70 Lon Univ MSc75 FRSA. WMMTC 95. **d** 98 **p** 99. NSM The Lickey *Birm* 98-99; R Hutcheson's Gr Sch 99-04; P-in-c Woodford *Ches* from 05; Dioc Warden of Readers from 05. *The Vicarage, 531 Chester Road, Woodford, Stockport SK7 1PR* Tel 0161-439 2286 E-mail john.knowles2@virgin.net

KNOWLES, Margaret Irene. b 48. EAMTC 96. **d** 99 **p** 00. C Gt Yarmouth *Nor* 99-03; TV from 03; RD Gt Yarmouth from 05; Chapl Norfolk & Waveney Mental Health NHS Foundn Trust from 00. *18 Royal Avenue, Great Yarmouth NR30 4EB* Tel and fax (01493) 857292 Mobile 07713-30382
E-mail revmik@btinternet.com

KNOWLES, Melvin Clay. b 43. Stetson Univ (USA) BA66 Ex Univ MA73. Ripon Coll Cuddesdon 75. **d** 77 **p** 78. C Minchinhampton *Glouc* 77-80; St Helena 80-82; TV Haywards Heath St Wilfrid *Chich* 82-88; Adult Educn Adv 88-94; TR Burgess Hill St Jo w St Edw 94-00; V Burgess Hill St Jo from 00. *St John's Vicarage, Park Road, Burgess Hill RH15 8HG* Tel (01444) 232582

KNOWLES, Philip Andrew. b 63. Leeds Univ BA07. NOC 04. **d** 07 **p** 08. C Blackb St Mich w St Jo and H Trin from 07; C Blackb St Thos w St Jude from 07. *10 Copse Close, Blackburn BB1 6NJ* Tel (01254) 670853
E-mail philip.knowles1@btinternet.com

KNOWLES, The Very Revd Philip John. b 48. MA PhD BTh LTCL ALCM LLAM. CITC 76. **d** 76 **p** 77. C Lisburn St Paul *Conn* 76-79; I Cloonclare w Killasnett and Lurganboy *K, E & A* 79-87; I Gorey w Kilnahue *C & O* 87-89; I Gorey w Kilnahue, Leskinfere and Ballycanew 89-95; Preb Ferns Cathl 91-95; Dean Cashel from 95; I Cashel w Magorban, Tipperary, Clonbeg etc from 95; Chan Waterford Cathl from 95; Chan Lismore Cathl from 95; Can Ossory and Leighlin Cathls from 96; Can St Patr Cathl Dublin from 08. *The Deanery, Cashel, Co Tipperary, Republic of Ireland* Tel (00353) (62) 61232 or 61944
E-mail knowlesph@iolfree.ie

KNOWLES, Richard John. b 47. EAMTC 00. **d** 01 **p** 02. C Burlingham St Edmund w Lingwood, Strumpshaw etc *Nor* 01-04; TV Gt Yarmouth from 04. *18 Royal Avenue, Great Yarmouth NR30 4EB* Tel (01493) 308711 Mobile 07855-165008
E-mail revrjk@btinternet.com

KNOWLES-BROWN, Canon John Henry. b 30. AKC53. **d** 54 **p** 55. C Hertford St Andr *St Alb* 54-58; C Bushey 58-61; Chapl RAF 61-65; C-in-c Farley Hill St Jo CD *St Alb* 65-69; V Farley Hill St Jo 69-72; V Totteridge 72-95; RD Barnet 79-89; Hon Can St Alb 85-95; rtd 95; Perm to Offic *Ex* from 97. *1 Ascerton Close, Sidmouth EX10 9BS* Tel (01395) 579286

KNOWLING, Richard Charles. b 46. K Coll Lon BSc67 St Edm Hall Ox BA70 MA89. St Steph Ho Ox 69. **d** 71 **p** 72. C Hobs Moat *Birm* 71-75; C Shrewsbury St Mary w All SS and St Mich *Lich* 75-77; V Rough Hills 77-83; Dir Past Th Coll of Resurr Mirfield 83-90; V Palmers Green St Jo *Lon* 90-05; AD Enfield 96-01; V Edmonton St Alphege from 05; P-in-c Ponders End St Matt from 05. *St Alphege's Vicarage, Rossdale Drive, London N9 7LG* Tel (020) 8245 3588
E-mail richard.knowling@london.anglican.org

KNOX, Canon Geoffrey Martin. b 44. Dur Univ BA66 Sheff City Coll of Educn DipEd73. St Chad's Coll Dur 63. **d** 67 **p** 68. C Newark St Mary *S'well* 67-72; Perm to Offic *Derby* 72-74; V Woodville 74-81; RD Repton 79-81; V Long Eaton St Laur 81-00; V Somercotes from 00; RD Alfreton from 04; Hon Can Derby Cathl from 08. *The Vicarage, 114 Nottingham Road, Somercotes, Alfreton DE55 4LY* Tel (01773) 602840

KNOX, Iain John Edward. b 46. TCD BA70 MA74 Hull Univ BPhil76. CITC 71. **d** 71 **p** 72. C Belfast Malone St Jo *Conn* 71-74; Bp's Dom Chapl 72-74; Perm to Offic *D & R* 74-76; I Gweedore Union 76-80; I Clonmel w Innislounagh, Tullaghmelan etc *C & O* 80-96; Bp's Dom Chapl 82-97; Press and Radio Officer (Cashel) 90-95; Dioc Info Officer (Cashel and Waterford) 92-95; Lic to Offic from 96; V Choral Cashel Cathl from 03. *Rossnowlagh, Heywood Road, Clonmel, Co Tipperary, Republic of Ireland* Tel (00353) (52) 27107 Mobile 87-236 8186

KNOX, Canon Ian Stephen. b 44. Leeds Univ LLB64 Solicitor 66 Brunel Univ MPhil03. **d** 05 **p** 05. Perm to Offic *Cov* 05-06 and *Newc* from 06; Exec Dir 40:3 Trust from 05. *16 East Moor, Loughoughton, Alnwick NE66 3JB* Tel (01665) 572939
E-mail office@fortythreetrust.com

KNOX, Matthew Stephen. b 75. Man Univ BSc98 Newc Univ PGCE02 St Jo Coll Dur BA07. Cranmer Hall Dur 04. **d** 07 **p** 08. C Newburn *Newc* from 07. *St Mary's Parsonage, Newburn Road, Newcastle upon Tyne NE15 9AB* Tel 0191-267 4553
E-mail knoxmatthew2@hotmail.com

KNUCKEY, William Thomas. b 47. Qu Coll Birm 02. **d** 05 **p** 06. NSM Amington *Birm* from 05. *6 Davis Road, Tamworth B77 3HP* Tel (01827) 56043 Mobile 07966-512759
E-mail bill.knuckey@btinternet.com

KOHNER, Canon Jeno George. b 31. K Coll Lon BD56 AKC56 Concordia Univ Montreal MA82. Westcott Ho Cam 56. **d** 57 **p** 58. C Eccleston St Thos *Liv* 57-60; Canada from 60; Hon Can Montreal from 75. *H3-850 Lakeshore Drive, Dorval QC H9S 5T9, Canada* Tel (001) (514) 631 0066

KOLAWOLE, Canon Peter Adeleke. b 36. Immanuel Coll Ibadan 91. **d** 85 **p** 86. C Lagos Abp Vining Memorial Ch Nigeria 85-87; P Isolo St Paul 88-96; P Lagos Cathl 97-99; Can Res 99-03; Perm to Offic *Chelmsf* from 04. *58 Shaftesbury Point, High Street, London E13 0AB* Tel (020) 8471 5144

✠**KOLINI, The Most Revd Emmanuel Musaba.** b 44. Balya Bible Coll Uganda 67 Can Werner Coll Burundi 68 Bp Tucker Coll Mukono 75. **d** 69 **c** 80. Uganda 69-79; Kyangwali 69-74; Bulinda 77-79; Zaïre 80-97; Adn Bukavu 80; Asst Bp Bukavu 81-85; Bp Shaba 86-97; Bp Kigali from 97; Abp Rwanda from 98. *PO Box 61, Kigali, Rwanda* Tel (00250) 576340 Fax 573213 *or* 576504
E-mail ek@rwanda1.com

KOLOGARAS, Mrs Linda Audrey. b 48. Humberside Univ BA97. EMMTC 89. **d** 95 **p** 96. NSM Gt and Lt Coates w Bradley *Linc* 95-98; C Immingham 98-02; R Rosewood Australia 03-07. *Address temp unknown*

KOMOR, Michael. b 60. Univ of Wales BSc83. Chich Th Coll 83. **d** 86 **p** 87. C Mountain Ash *Llan* 86-89; C Llantwit Major 89-91; TV 91-00; V Ewenny w St Brides Major 00-05; R Coity, Nolton and Brackla from 05; AD Bridgend from 04. *Nolton Rectory, Merthyr Mawr Road North, Bridgend CF31 3NH* Tel (01656) 652247 E-mail mkomor@talk21.com

KONIG, Peter Montgomery. b 44. Westcott Ho Cam 80. **d** 82 **p** 83. C Oundle *Pet* 82-86; Chapl Westwood Ho Sch Pet 86-92; Chapl Pet High Sch 92-95; Chapl Worksop Coll Notts 95-99; Chapl Glenalmond Coll *St And* 99-04; rtd 04; Perm to Offic *Pet* from 04. *Crossways, Main Street, Yarwell, Peterborough PE8 6PR* Tel (01780) 782873 E-mail pandakonig@talktalk.net

KOPSCH, Hartmut. b 41. Sheff Univ BA63 Univ of BC MA66 Lon Univ PhD70. Trin Coll Bris 78. **d** 80 **p** 81. C Cranham Park *Chelmsf* 80-85; V Springfield *Birm* 85-92; V Dover St Martin *Cant* 92-96; R Bath Walcot *B & W* 96-06; rtd 06; Perm to Offic *Glouc* from 07. *2 Courtfield View, The Reddings, Lydbrook GL17 9ST* Tel (01594) 862685
E-mail harmutandjane@gmail.com

KOREA, Presiding Bishop of. *Vacant*

KORNAHRENS, Wallace Douglas. b 43. The Citadel Charleston BA66 Gen Th Sem (NY) STB69. **d** 69 **p** 70. USA 69-72; C Potters Green *Cov* 73-75; Chapl Community of Celebration Wargrave Oxon 75-76; P-in-c Cumbrae (or Millport) *Arg* 76-78; R Grantown-on-Spey *Mor* 78-83; R Rothiemurchus 78-83; R Edin H Cross from 83. *Holy Cross Rectory, 18 Barnton Gardens, Edinburgh EH4 6AF* Tel 0131-336 2311

KOSLA, Mrs Ann Louise. b 56. Middx Univ BA04. NTMTC 01. **d** 04 **p** 05. NSM Thorley *St Alb* 04-07; NSM Chelmsf S Deanery from 08. *7 Yonge Close, Boreham, Chelmsford CM3 3GY* Tel (01245) 465773 E-mail ann.kosla@sky.com

KOSLA, Charles Antoni. b 58. Ridley Hall Cam 97. **d** 99 **p** 00. C Widford *Chelmsf* 99-03; C Thorley *St Alb* 03-07; Dioc Adv for Miss and Par Development *Chelmsf* from 07; Hon C C E Springfield from 08. *7 Yonge Close, Boreham, Chelmsford CM3 3GY* Tel (01245) 294419 *or* 465773
E-mail ckosla@chelmsford.anglican.org

KOTHARE, Jayant Sunderrao. b 41. Bombay Univ BA Heidelberg Univ MDiv. **d** 86 **p** 87. C Handsworth St Mich *Birm* 86-89; C Southall St Geo *Lon* 89-92; TV Thamesmead *S'wark* 92-97; Dioc Community Relns Officer *Man* 97-00; P-in-c Moston St Chad 97-02; rtd 02. *27 Charlesworth Court, 18 Bingley Close, Manchester M11 3RF*

KOUSSEFF, Mrs Karen Patricia. b 60. Ex Univ BA83. STETS 06. **d** 09. NSM Lower Dever *Win* from 09. *15 Long Barrow Close, South Wonston, Winchester SO21 3ED* Tel (01962) 885114 E-mail kkousseff@tiscali.co.uk

KOVOOR, George Iype. b 57. Delhi Univ BA77 Serampore Univ BD80. Union Bibl Sem Yavatmal 78. **d** 80 **p** 80. Chapl Leprosy Miss Hosp Kothara India 80-81; Assoc Presbyter Shanti Nivas Ch Faridabad 82; Presbyter Santokh Majra 83; Dean St Paul's Cathl Ambala 84-88; Chapl St Steph Hosp Delhi 88-90; C Derby St Aug 90-94; Min Derby Asian Chr Min Project 90-94; Tutor Crowther Hall CMS Tr Coll Selly Oak 94-97; Prin 97-05; Hon Can Worc Cathl 01-05; Prin Trin Coll Bris from 05; Chapl to The Queen from 03. *Trinity College, Stoke Hill, Bristol BS9 1JP* Tel 0117-968 2803 *or* 968 2646 Fax 968 7470
E-mail principal@trinity-bris.ac.uk

KRAFT, (née STEVENS), Mrs Jane. b 45. SRN66 SCM68. NTMTC 01. **d** 03 **p** 04. NSM Finchley St Mary *Lon* 03-07; TV Chipping Barnet *St Alb* from 07. *St Stephen's Vicarage, 1 Spring Close, Barnet EN5 2UR* Tel (020) 8275 0858 Mobile 07803-868482 E-mail revd.janekraft@btinternet.com

KRAMER, Beaman Kristopher (Kris). b 67. Mars Hill Coll (USA) BS88 Duke Univ (USA) MTS95. Wycliffe Hall Ox MTh98. **d** 98 **p** 99. C Hersham *Guildf* 98-99; C Paddington St Jo w St Mich *Lon* 99-00; R Radford Grace USA from 00. *Grace Rectory, 204 Fourth Street, Radford VA 24141-1523, USA* Tel (001) (540) 731 3276 E-mail frkris@i-plus.net

KRAMER, Mrs Caroline Anne. b 70. Wycliffe Hall Ox BTh98. **d** 98. C Oatlands *Guildf* 98-99; USA from 00. *Grace Rectory, 204 Fourth Street, Radford VA 24141-1523, USA* Tel (001) (540) 731 3276 E-mail revkramer@cwcom.net

KROLL, Una Margaret Patricia. b 25. Girton Coll Cam MB51 BChir51. S'wark Ord Course 68. **d** 88 **p** 97. NSM Monmouth 88-97; Lic to Offic 97-04. *6 Hamilton House, 57 Hanson Street, Bury BL9 6LR* Tel 0161-797 7877

KRONBERGS, Paul Mark. b 55. NEOC 02. **d** 05 **p** 06. NSM Middlesbrough St Columba w St Paul *York* from 05. *39 Northumberland Grove, Stockton-on-Tees TS20 1PB* Tel (01642) 890571 E-mail paul.kronbergs@ntlworld.com

KRONENBERG, John Simon. b 59. Greenwich Univ BSc85 Open Univ BA00 MRICS87 MBEng94. Ripon Coll Cuddesdon 02. **d** 02 **p** 03. C Chandler's Ford *Win* 02-06; V Hinchley Wood *Guildf* from 06. *The Vicarage, 98 Manor Road North, Esher KT10 0AD* Tel (020) 8786 6391 Mobile 07956-517065
E-mail j.kronenberg@btinternet.com

KRONENBERG, Selwyn Thomas Denzil. b 32. Univ of Wales (Swansea) BA54 St Cath Soc Ox BA57 MA60 Leic Univ MA72 California Univ MA82. Wycliffe Hall Ox 54. **d** 57 **p** 58. C Surbiton St Matt *S'wark* 57-59; C Luton St Mary *St Alb* 59-61; P-in-c Loscoe *Derby* 61-65; Lect RE Bulmershe Coll 65-67; Whitelands Coll from 67; Perm to Offic *Guildf* from 77; rtd 97. *58 Woodfield Lane, Ashtead KT21 2BS* Tel (01372) 272505

KROUKAMP, Nigel John Charles. b 53. Cen Lancs Univ BSc93 Bolton Inst of HE CertEd86 RNMH75 RGN78. LCTP 05. **d** 08 **p** 09. NSM Colne and Villages *Blackb* from 08. *56 Kelswick Drive, Nelson BB9 0SZ* Tel (01282) 698261 Mobile 07725-858433 E-mail nigelkroukamp@hotmail.com

KRZEMINSKI, Stefan. b 51. Nottm Univ BTh77. Linc Th Coll 74. **d** 77 **p** 78. C Sawley *Derby* 77-79; Asst Chapl Bluecoat Sch Nottm 79-86; Hon C W Hallam and Mapperley *Derby* 84-96; Hd of RE Nottm High Sch from 86; Perm to Offic *Derby* from 96. *12 Newbridge Close, West Hallam, Ilkeston DE7 6LY* Tel 0115-930 5052

KUHRT, The Ven Gordon Wilfred. b 41. Lon Univ BD63 Middx Univ DProf01. Oak Hill Th Coll 65. **d** 67 **p** 68. C Illogan *Truro* 67-70; C Wallington *S'wark* 70-73; V Shenstone *Lich* 73-79; P-in-c S Croydon Em *Cant* 79-81; V S Croydon Em *S'wark* 81-89; RD Croydon Cen *Cant* 81-86; Hon Can S'wark Cathl 87-89; Adn Lewisham 89-96; Chief Sec ABM 96-98; Dir Min Division Abps' Coun 99-06; rtd 06; Hon C Tredington and Darlingscott *Cov* from 06; Hon C Ilmington w Stretton-on-Fosse etc from 06. *The Rectory, Tredington, Shipston-on-Stour CV36 4NG* Tel (01608) 661264
E-mail omkuhrt@tiscali.co.uk

KUHRT, Martin Gordon. b 69. Nottm Univ LLB88. Trin Coll Bris 93. **d** 96 **p** 97. C Morden *S'wark* 96-00; Chapl Lee Abbey 00-02; TV Melksham *Sarum* 02-08; C Atworth w Shaw and Whitley 07-08; C Broughton Gifford, Gt Chalfield and Holt 07-08; P-in-c Bedgrove *Ox* from 08. *The Vicarage, 252 Wendover Road, Aylesbury HP21 9PD* Tel (01296) 435546
E-mail mgkuhrt555@btinternet.com

KUHRT, Stephen John. b 69. Man Univ BA91 Lon Inst of Educn PGCE93. Wycliffe Hall Ox BA03. **d** 03 **p** 04. C New Malden and Coombe *S'wark* 03-07; P-in-c from 07. *12 Roseberry Avenue, New Malden KT3 4JS* Tel (020) 8942 2523

KUIN LAWTON, Theresa. b 69. St Aid Coll Dur BA91 TCD MPhil96. Ox Min Course 05. **d** 07 **p** 08. NSM Bampton w

Clanfield *Ox* from 07; Chapl Magd Coll Sch Ox from 09. *Manor Croft, Church Close, Bampton OX18 2LW* Tel (01993) 850468
E-mail tessa.lawton@onetel.com

KUMAR, Suresh. b 59. Madras Univ MSc81 Leic Univ MA91 Alagappa Univ MA05. Serampore Th Coll BD85. **d** 85 **p** 88. India 85-08; C Braunstone Park *Leic* 08-09; TV Emmaus Par Team from 09. *10 Park Hill Drive, Leicester LE2 8HR* Tel 0116-283 4031 Mobile 07824-813202
E-mail suresh@skumar.plus.com

KURK, Pamela Ann. b 56. Univ of Wales (Ban) BTh06. **d** 04 **p** 05. NSM Wandsworth St Mich w St Steph *S'wark* from 04; Chapl St Cecilia's Wandsworth C of E Sch from 07. *64 Pulborough Road, London SW18 5UJ* Tel (020) 8265 8985 Mobile 07774-437471 E-mail thekurks@aol.com
or akurk@saintcecilias.wandsworth.sch.uk

KURRLE, Canon Stanley Wynton. b 22. OBE82. Melbourne Univ BA47 St Cath Soc Ox BA50 MA54. Wycliffe Hall Ox 49. **d** 52 **p** 53. C Sutton *Liv* 52-54; Australia from 54; Fell St Paul's Coll Univ of Sydney from 69; Can Sydney 81-95; Can Emer 95. *25 Marieba Road, PO Box 53, Kenthurst NSW 2156, Australia* Tel (0061) (2) 9654 1334 Mobile 427-277919 Fax 9654 1368 E-mail mathourastation@bigpond.com

KURTI, Peter Walter. b 60. Qu Mary Coll Lon LLB82 K Coll Lon MTh89. Ch Div Sch of Pacific 82 Ripon Coll Cuddesdon 83. **d** 86 **p** 87. C Prittlewell *Chelmsf* 86-90; Chapl Derby Coll of HE 90-92; Chapl Derby Univ 92-94; Dep Hd Relig Resource and Research Cen 90-94; Australia from 94; Perm to Offic *Perc* 94-97; R Scarborough 97-01; R Sydney St Jas from 01. *Level 1, 169-171 Phillip Street, Sydney NSW 2000, Australia* Tel (0061) (2) 9363 3335 *or* 9232 3022 Mobile 412-049271 Fax 9232 4182 E-mail peter.kurti@bigpond.com

KUSTNER, Ms Jane Lesley. b 54. Lanchester Poly Cov BA76 FCA79. St Steph Ho Ox 03. **d** 05 **p** 06. C Waterloo St Jo w St Andr *S'wark* 05-08; P-in-c Lewisham St Swithun from 08. *St Swithun's Vicarage, 191 Hither Green Lane, London SE13 6QE* Tel 00734-113741 (mobile)
E-mail jane.kustner@btinternet.com

✠**KWONG KONG KIT, The Most Revd Peter.** b 36. Kenyon Coll Ohio BD65 DD86 Hong Kong Univ DD00. Bexley Hall Div Sch Ohio MTh71 DD98. **d** 65 **p** 66 **c** 81. P-in-c Hong Kong Crown of Thorns 65-66; C Hong Kong St Paul 71-72; Bp Hong Kong and Macao 81-98; Bp Hong Kong Is from 98; Abp Hong Kong Sheng Kung Hui from 98. *Bishop's House, 1 Lower Albert Road, Hong Kong, China* Tel (00852) 2526 5355 Fax 2525 2537
E-mail office1@hkskh.org

KYEI-BAFFOUR, Jacob Owusu. b 62. Kwame Nkrumah Univ Ghana BA02 Univ of the Arts Lon MA05. St Nic Th Coll Ghana 90. **d** 93 **p** 94. C Jameso-Nkwatah Ghana 93-94; Perm to Offic *S'wark* 94-95; P-in-c Cape Coast St Monica Ghana 95-98; Asst Chapl Kwame Nkrumah Univ 98-02; Asst P Ch Cathl Cape Coast 02-03; Perm to Offic *Lon* 03-06; Hon C Willesden Green St Andr and St Fran from 06. *150 Ellesmere Road, London NW10 1JT* Tel (020) 8452 7897 Mobile 07906-718708
E-mail kyei_baffourcl@fsmail.net

KYLE, Miss Sharon Patricia Culvinor. b 55. Open Univ BA90 Edin Univ BD94 MTh96. Coates Hall Edin 91. **d** 94 **p** 95. C Edin SS Phil and Jas 94-96; C Neston *Ches* 96-99; TV Kirkby *Liv* 99-01. *22 Oak Tree Close, Kingsbury, Tamworth B78 2JF* Tel (01827) 874445

KYRIACOU, Brian George. b 42. Lon Univ LLB64. Oak Hill Th Coll 79. **d** 81 **p** 82. C Becontree St Mary *Chelmsf* 81-83; C Becontree St Cedd 83-85; C Becontree W 85; TV 85-87; V Shiregreen St Jas and St Chris *Sheff* 87-92; TV Schorne *Ox* 92-98; V Edmonton All SS w St Mich *Lon* 98-07; rtd 07; Perm to Offic *Chelmsf* from 07. *58 Morant Road, Colchester CO1 2JA* Tel (01206) 522069 Mobile 07970-719094
E-mail brian.kyriacou@ntlworld.com

KYRIAKIDES-YELDHAM, Preb Anthony Paul Richard. b 48. Birkbeck Coll Lon BSc82 Warwick Univ MSc90 CQSW83 CPsychol91. K Coll Lon BD73 AKC73. **d** 74 **p** 75. C Dalston H Trin w St Phil *Lon* 74-78; NSM Lon Docks St Pet w Wapping St Jo 79-81; NSM Hackney Wick St Mary of Eton w St Aug 81-85; NSM Wandsworth Common St Mary *S'wark* 85-87; Chapl Wandsworth HA Mental Health Unit 87-93; Chapl Springfield Univ Hosp Lon 87-93; Perm to Offic *Ex* 94-98; Lic to Offic 98-08; Sen Chapl Plymouth Hosps NHS Trust 98-08; P-in-c Kingsbridge and Dodbrooke *Ex* from 08; Preb Ex Cathl from 07. *Dodbrooke Rectory, Church Street, Kingsbridge TQ7 1NW* Tel (01548) 856231 Mobile 07929-775228
E-mail tony.yeldham@talk21.com

KYTE, Eric Anthony. b 62. Leeds Univ BSc84 PGCE85. Trin Coll Bris BA98. **d** 98 **p** 99. C Pudsey St Lawr and St Paul *Bradf* 98-01; P-in-c Gisburn from 01; P-in-c Hellifield from 01. *St Mary's Vicarage, Gisburn, Clitheroe BB7 4HR* Tel (01200) 415935
E-mail eric.kyte@bradford.anglican.org
or reverickyte@onetel.com

KYUMU MOTUKU, Norbert. See CHUMU MUTUKU, Norbert

L

LABDON, David William. b 64. St Jo Coll Nottm 07. **d** 09. C Bebington *Ches* from 09. *125 West Vale, Neston CH64 0TJ* Tel 0151-336 7865 E-mail davidlabdon@btinternet.com

LABDON, John. b 32. Oak Hill Th Coll. **d** 84 **p** 85. C Formby H Trin *Liv* 84-87; P-in-c St Helens St Mark 87-97; rtd 97; Perm to Offic *Ches* from 97. *28 Burton Road, Little Neston, Neston CH64 9RA* Tel 0151-336 7039

LABOUREL, Elaine Odette. b 58. St Jo Coll Nottm 03. **d** 05 **p** 06. C Paris St Mich *Eur* 05-08; P-in-c Rouen All SS 06-08; Asst Chapl Versailles from 08. *4 avenue de Savigny, 91700 Ste Geneviève des Bois, France* Tel (0033) (1) 69 04 09 91 Mobile (6) 60 59 65 98 E-mail elaine.labourel@wanadoo.fr

LABRAN, Stuart. b 79. Leeds Univ BA00 PGCE02 Clare Coll Cam MPhil09. Westcott Ho Cam 07. **d** 09. C Stratford-upon-Avon, Luddington etc *Cov* from 09. *2 St John's Close, Stratford-upon-Avon CV37 9AB* Tel (01789) 268836
E-mail stuartlabran@hotmail.com

LACEY, Allan John. b 48. Sheff Univ MA02. Wycliffe Hall Ox. **d** 82 **p** 83. C Greasbrough *Sheff* 82-85; R Treeton 85-92; V Thorpe Hesley 92-00; R Rossington 00-07; CMS Uganda from 07. *Church Mission Society, Watlington Road, Oxford OX4 6BZ* Tel 08456-201799 E-mail allanlacey@btinternet.com

LACEY, Mrs Carol Ann. b 62. Qu Coll Birm 07. **d** 09. NSM Leic St Anne, St Paul and St Aug from 09. *Willow Cottage, 22A Chapel Street, Blaby, Leicester LE8 4GB* Tel 0116-278 8817 Mobile 07971-519705
E-mail carolannlacey@googlemail.com

LACEY, Eric. b 33. Cranmer Hall Dur 69. **d** 71 **p** 72. C Blackpool St Jo *Blackb* 71-75; V Whittle-le-Woods 75-88; R Heysham 88-98; rtd 98; Perm to Offic *Blackb* from 98. *143 Bredon Avenue, Chorley PR7 6NS* Tel (01257) 273040

LACEY, Nigel Jeremy. b 59. St Jo Coll Nottm BTh94. **d** 94 **p** 95. C Mildenhall *St E* 94-97; C Selly Park St Steph and St Wulstan *Birm* 97-01; P-in-c W Wycombe w Bledlow Ridge, Bradenham and Radnage *Ox* 01-09; R from 09. *The Rectory, Church Lane, West Wycombe, High Wycombe HP14 3AH* Tel (01494) 529988 E-mail nigel.lacey@whsmithnet.co.uk

LACK, Catherine Mary. b 59. Clare Coll Cam BA81 Ox Univ MTh00 ARCM. Qu Coll Birm 90. **d** 92 **p** 94. Par Dn Leiston *St E* 92-94; C 94-95; TV Ipswich St Mary at Stoke w St Pet 95-97; TV Ipswich St Mary at Stoke w St Pet and St Fran 97-98; Chapl Keele Univ 98-07; Cultural and Relig Affairs Manager Yarl's Wood Immigration Removal Cen 07-08; Warden Ferrar House Lt Gidding Community 08-09; Chapl Newc Univ from 09; Master Newc St Thos Prop Chpl from 09. *9 Chester Crescent, Newcastle upon Tyne NE2 1DH*

LACK, Martin Paul. b 57. St Jo Coll Ox MA79 MSc80. Linc Th Coll 83. **d** 86 **p** 87. C E Bowbrook and W Bowbrook *Worc* 86-89; C Bowbrook S and Bowbrook N 89-90; R Teme Valley S 90-01; rtd 01. *Colbridge Cottage, Bottom Lane, Whitbourne, Worcester WR6 5RT* Tel (01886) 821978

LACKEY, Michael Geoffrey Herbert. b 42. Oak Hill Th Coll 73. **d** 75 **p** 76. C Hatcham St Jas *S'wark* 75-81; V New Barnet St Jas *St Alb* 81-91; V Hollington St Jo *Chich* 91-02; Dir Crowhurst Chr Healing Cen 02-05; rtd 05; Hon C St Margaret's and Stanstead Abbots *St Alb* from 05. *30 South Street, Stanstead Abbotts, Ware SG12 8AJ* Tel (01920) 872077 E-mail glackey@toucansurf.com

LACKEY, William Terence Charles. b 32. St Mich Coll Llan 80. **d** 82 **p** 83. C Wrexham *St As* 82-85; V Gwersyllt 85-93; R Trefnant 93-98; rtd 98. *24 Old Farm Road, Rhostyllen, Wrexham LL14 4DX* Tel (01978) 311969

LACY, Melanie June. b 75. TCD BA98 All Hallows Coll Dublin MA00. CITC 98. **d** 00. C Bangor St Comgall *D & D* 00-02; N Ireland Regional Co-ord Crosslinks 02-06; C Knutsford St Jo and Toft *Ches* from 06. *6 Lilac Avenue, Knutsford WA16 0AZ*

LACY, Sarah Frances. b 49. Sarum Th Coll 93. **d** 96 **p** 97. C Weston Zoyland w Chedzoy *B & W* 96-00; C Middlezoy and Othery and Moorlinch 00-01; R Berrow and Breane from 01. *The Rectory, 1 Manor Way, Berrow, Burnham-on-Sea TA8 2RG* Tel (01278) 751057 E-mail sally@lacys.freeserve.co.uk

LACY-SMITH, Mrs Joanna. b 55. STETS 05. **d** 08 **p** 09. OLM Dorchester *Sarum* from 08. *2 Ackerman Road, Dorchester DT1 1NZ* Tel (01305) 266721
E-mail jolacysmith@copperstream.co.uk

LADD, Mrs Anne de Chair. b 56. Nottm Univ BA78 CQSW80. St Jo Coll Nottm. dss 86 **d** 87 **p** 94. Bucknall and Bagnall *Lich* 86-91; Dar Dn 87-91; NSM Bricket Wood *St Alb* 91-01; Chapl Garden Ho Hospice Letchworth 98-06; Befriending Co-ord Mencap from 07; Perm to Offic *Ely* from 01. *57 St Barnabas Road, Cambridge CB1 2BX* Tel (01223) 316228

LADD, John George Morgan. b 36. Univ of Wales (Ban) BA58 MA65. St Mich Coll Llan. **d** 90 **p** 91. NSM Nevern and Y Beifil w Eglwyswrw and Meline etc *St D* 90-92; NSM Llandysilio w

Egremont and Llanglydwen etc 92-93; V Gwaun-cae-Gurwen 93-04; rtd 04. *Penybanc, Rhiw Road, Swansea SA9 2RE*

LADD, Nicholas Mark. b 57. Ex Univ BA78 Selw Coll Cam BA81. Ridley Hall Cam 79. **d** 82 **p** 83. C Aston SS Pet and Paul *Birm* 82-86; TV Bucknall and Bagnall *Lich* 86-91; V Bricket Wood *St Alb* 91-01; V Cambridge St Barn *Ely* 01-09; Dean St Jo Coll Nottm from 09. *St John's College, Chilwell Lane, Bramcote, Beeston, Nottingham NG9 3DS* Tel 0115-925 1114 Fax 943 6438

✠**LADDS, The Rt Revd Robert Sidney.** b 41. Lon Univ BEd71 LRSC72. Cant Sch of Min 79. **d** 80 **p** 81 **c** 99. C Hythe *Cant* 80-83; R Bretherton *Blackb* 83-91; Chapl Bp Rawstorne Sch Preston 83-87; Bp's Chapl for Min and Adv Coun for Min *Blackb* 86-91; P-in-c Preston St Jo 91-96; P Preston St Jo and St Geo 96-97; Hon Can Blackb Cathl 93-97; Adn Lancaster 97-99; Suff Bp Whitby *York* 99-08; rtd 09; Hon C Hendon St Mary and Ch Ch *Lon* from 09. *Christ Church House, 76 Brent Street, London NW4 2ES* Tel (020) 8202 8123

LADIPO, Canon Adeyemi Olalekan. b 37. Trin Coll Bris 63. **d** 66 **p** 76. C Bilston St Leon *Lich* 66-68; Nigeria 68-84; V Canonbury St Steph *Lon* 85-87; Sec for Internat Miss BCMS 87-90; Hon C Bromley SS Pet and Paul *Roch* 89-90; V Herne Hill *S'wark* 90-99; Hon Can Jos from 95; V S Malling *Chich* 99-02; rtd 02; Perm to Offic *Chich* from 03 and *S'wark* from 07. *63 Elm Grove, London SE15 5DB* Tel (020) 7639 8150

LAFFORD, Sylvia June. b 46. Middx Univ BA04. NTMTC 01. **d** 04 **p** 05. NSM Hayes St Edm *Lon* from 04. *17 Audley Court, Pinner HA5 3TQ* Tel (020) 8868 2574
E-mail sylvialafford@aol.com

LAIDLAW, Juliet. See MONTAGUE, Mrs Juliet

LAIN-PRIESTLEY, Ms Rosemary Jane. b 67. Kent Univ BA89 K Coll Lon MA02. Carl Dioc Tr Course 92. **d** 96 **p** 97. C Scotforth *Blackb* 96-98; C St Martin-in-the-Fields *Lon* 98-06; Dean of Women's Min Two Cities Area from 06. *13D Hyde Park Mansions, Cabbell Street, London NW1 5BD* Tel 07941-265316 (mobile) E-mail rosemarylainpriestley@btopenworld.com

LAING, Canon Alexander Burns. b 34. RD90. Edin Th Coll 57. **d** 60 **p** 61. C Falkirk *Edin* 60-62; C Edin Ch Ch 62-70; Chapl RNR 64-91; P-in-c Edin St Fillan 70-74; Chapl Edin R Infirmary 74-77; Dioc Supernumerary *Edin* from 77; R Helensburgh *Glas* 77-03; Can St Mary's Cathl 87-03; rtd 03; Lic to Offic *Glas* from 06. *13 Drumadoon Drive, Helensburgh G84 9SF* Tel (01436) 675705

LAING, William Sydney. b 32. TCD BA54 MA62. **d** 55 **p** 56. C Dublin Crumlin *D & G* 55-59; C Dublin St Ann 59-65; I Carbury *M & K* 65-68; I Dublin Finglas *D & G* 68-80; I Tallaght 80-91; Can Ch Ch Cathl Dublin 90-94; Preb 84-97; I Dublin Crumlin w Chapelizod 91-97; rtd 97. *42 Hazelwood Crescent, Clondalkin, Dublin 22, Republic of Ireland* Tel (00353) (1) 459 3893 Mobile 87-760 1210

LAIRD, Alisdair Mark. b 60. Auckland Univ BA84. Trin Coll Bris BA92. **d** 92 **p** 93. C Linthorpe *York* 92-98; V Hull St Cuth 98-06; P-in-c Alne and Brafferton w Pilmoor, Myton-on-Swale etc 06-07; Lic to Offic 07-08; Perm to Offic from 08; Chapl Hull and E Yorks Hosps NHS Trust from 09. *Hull Royal Infirmary, Anlaby Road, Hull HU3 2JZ* Tel (01482) 875875
E-mail al@lairds.org.uk

LAIRD, Canon John Charles. b 32. Sheff Univ BA53 MA54 St Cath Coll Ox BA58 MA62 Lon Univ DipEd70. Ripon Hall Ox 56. **d** 58 **p** 59. C Cheshunt *St Alb* 58-62; Chapl Bps' Coll Cheshunt 62-64; Vice-Prin 64-67; Prin 67-69; V Keysoe w Bolnhurst and Lt Staughton *St Alb* 69-01; Hon Can St Alb 87-02; Lic to Offic from 01. *The Chaplaincy, Fore Street Lodge, Hatfield Park, Hatfield AL9 5NQ* Tel (01707) 274941

LAIRD, Robert George (Robin). b 42. TCD Div Sch 58 Edin Th Coll 63. **d** 65 **p** 66. C Drumragh *D & R* 65-68; CF 68-93; QHC 91-93; Sen Chapl Sedbergh Sch 93-98; Lic to Offic *Bradf* 93-98; rtd 98; Perm to Offic *Ex* and *Sarum* from 98. *Barrule, Hillside Road, Sidmouth EX10 8JD* Tel (01395) 513948

LAIRD, Stephen Charles Edward. b 66. Oriel Coll Ox BA88 MA92 MSt93 K Coll Lon MTh91 Kent Univ PhD06 FRSA00. Wycliffe Hall Ox MPhil96. **d** 94 **p** 95. C Ilfracombe, Lee, Woolacombe, Bittadon etc *Ex* 94-98; Chapl Kent Univ 98-03; Dean of Chapl from 03; Hon Lect from 98; Hon C Hackington from 03; Chapl Kent Inst of Art and Design 98-02; P-in-c Blean *Cant* from 09. *Landon, Giles Lane, Canterbury CT2 7LR* Tel (01227) 827491 *or* 787476 Mobile 07970-438840
E-mail s.c.e.laird@kent.ac.uk

LAKE, David Michael. b 57. St Mary's Sem Oscott 76. St Jo Coll Nottm BA01. **d** 01 **p** 02. C Lilleshall, Muxton and Sheriffhales *Lich* 01-05; P-in-c Crick and Yelvertoft w Clay Coton and Lilbourne *Pet* from 05. *The Rectory, Main Road, Crick, Northampton NN6 7TU* Tel (01788) 822147
E-mail davidlake@mailserver97.freeserve.co.uk

LAKE, Eileen Veronica. See CREMIN, Mrs Eileen Veronica

LAKE, Kevin William. b 57. St Mich Coll Llan 97. **d** 99 **p** 00. C Penarth w Lavernock *Llan* 99-02; Chapl Marie Curie Cen Holme Tower 02-04; P-in-c Cwm Ogwr *Llan* 04-06; P-in-c Llandyfodwg and Cwm Ogwr 06-08; V Aberdare St Fagan from

08. *5 Redwood Court, Aberdare CF44 8RX* Tel (01685) 881435
E-mail kevin.lake1@btinternet.com

LAKE, Canon Stephen David. b 63. Southn Univ BTh. Chich Th Coll 85. **d** 88 **p** 89. C Sherborne w Castleton and Lillington *Sarum* 88-92; P-in-c Branksome St Aldhelm 92-96; V 96-01; RD Poole 00-01; Can Res and Sub-Dean St Alb from 01. *The Old Rectory, Sumpter Yard, St Albans AL1 1BY* Tel (01727) 890201 Fax 850944 E-mail subdean@stalbanscathedral.org.uk

LAKE, Thomas Wesley Cellan. b 77. Univ Coll Lon MEng01. Oak Hill Th Coll BTh08. **d** 08 **p** 09. C Enfield Ch Ch Trent Park *Lon* from 08. *2 Chalk Lane, Barnet EN4 9JQ*
E-mail curate@cockfosters.org.uk

LAKE, Vivienne Elizabeth. b 48. Westcott Ho Cam 84. **dss** 86 **d** 87 **p** 94. Chesterton Gd Shep *Ely* 86-90; C 87-90; Ecum Min K Hedges Ch Cen 87-90; NSM Bourn Deanery 90-01; NSM Papworth Everard 94-96; Perm to Offic from 01. *15 Storey's House, Mount Pleasant, Cambridge CB3 0BZ* Tel (01223) 369523

LAKE, Wynne Vaughan. b 34. St D Coll Lamp BA55. St Mich Coll Llan 55. **d** 57 **p** 58. C Cadoxton-juxta-Barry *Llan* 57-61; C Roath St Sav 61-64; V Oakwood 64-67; V Oakwood w Bryn 67-72; R Shirenewton and Newchurch *Mon* 72-77; rtd 99. *32 Belvedere Close, Kittle, Swansea SA3 3LA*

LAKER, Clive Sheridan. b 59. Greenwich Univ BSc92 RGN82. Aston Tr Scheme 93 SEITE 95. **d** 98 **p** 99. C Bridlington Quay Ch Ch *York* 98-00; C Bridlington Em 00-01; TV Bucknall *Lich* 01-04; C Surbiton St Mark *S'wark* 04-08; TV from 08. *127 Hamilton Avenue, Surbiton KT6 7QA* Tel (020) 8397 4294
E-mail lakerfamily@ntlworld.com

LAKER, Grace. See SWIFT, Mrs Grace

LAKEY, Elizabeth Flora. b 46. DipOT69 Open Univ BA81. SAOMC 98. **d** 01 **p** 02. OLM Nettlebed w Bix, Highmoor, Pishill etc *Ox* from 01. *Bank Farm, Pishill, Henley-on-Thames RG9 6HJ* Tel and fax (01491) 638601 Mobile 07799-752933
E-mail bankfarm@btinternet.com

LAMB, Mrs Alison. b 60. Ches Coll of HE BTh04. NOC 01. **d** 04 **p** 05. C Rossington *Sheff* 04-08; V Worsbrough w Elsecar from 08. *The Vicarage, Wath Road, Elsecar, Barnsley S74 8HJ* Tel (01226) 351806 E-mail alison.lamb@sheffield.anglican.org

LAMB, Miss Alyson Margaret. b 55. LMH Ox BA77 MA80. Ridley Hall Cam 03. **d** 05 **p** 06. C York St Mich-le-Belfrey from 05. *157 Haxby Road, York YO31 8JL* Tel (01904) 674653
E-mail alyson@st-michael-le-belfrey.org

LAMB, Bruce. b 47. Keble Coll Ox BA69 MA73. Coll of Resurr Mirfield 70. **d** 73 **p** 74. C Romford St Edw *Chelmsf* 73-76; C Canning Town St Cedd 76-79; V New Brompton St Luke *Roch* 79-83; Chapl RN 83-87; C Rugeley *Lich* 87-88; V Trent Vale 88-92; Bereavement Cllr Cruse 94-99; Hon C Chorlton-cum-Hardy St Clem *Man* 98-99; Asst Chapl N Man Health Care NHS Trust 99-02; P-in-c Barton w Peel Green *Man* from 02. *St Michael's Vicarage, 684 Liverpool Road, Eccles, Manchester M30 7LP* Tel 0161-789 3751

LAMB, Bryan John Harry. b 35. Leeds Univ BA60. Coll of Resurr Mirfield 60. **d** 62 **p** 63. C Solihull *Birm* 62-65 and 88-89; Asst Master Malvern Hall Sch Solihull 65-74; Asst Master Arden Sch and Hd of Light Hall Adult Educn Cen 74-88; V Wragby *Linc* 89; Dioc Dir of Readers 89; Perm to Offic *Birm* from 89; rtd 95. *27 Ladbrook Road, Solihull B91 3RN* Tel 0121-705 2489

LAMB, Canon Christopher Avon. b 39. Qu Coll Ox BA61 MA65 Birm Univ MA78 PhD87. Wycliffe Hall Ox BA63. **d** 63 **p** 64. C Enfield St Andr *Lon* 63-69; Pakistan 69-75; Tutor Crowther Hall CMS Tr Coll Selly Oak 75-78; Co-ord BCMS/CMS Other Faiths Th Project 78-87; Dioc Community Relns Officer *Cov* 87-92; Can Th Cov Cathl from 92; Sec Inter Faith Relns Bd of Miss 92-99; R Warmington w Shotteswell and Radway w Ratley *Cov* 99-06; rtd 06; Perm to Offic *Cov* from 06. *8 Brookside Avenue, Wellesbourne, Warwick CV35 9RZ* Tel (01789) 842060
E-mail christophertinalamb@tiscali.co.uk

LAMB, David Andrew. b 60. Liv Inst of HE BA94 Man Univ MA01. NOC 90. **d** 94 **p** 95. C Formby H Trin *Liv* 94-97; C St Helens St Matt Thatto Heath 97-98; C Halewood 98-01; Lect Liv Hope 99-00; V Birkenhead St Jas w St Bede *Ches* 01-08; NSM Wallasey St Nic w All SS from 08. *66 Chapelhill Road, Wirral CH46 9QN*

LAMB, Graeme William. b 68. Open Univ BA. Trin Coll Bris 99. **d** 01 **p** 02. C Heald Green St Cath *Ches* 01-06; P-in-c Whaley Bridge 06-09. *Address temp unknown*
E-mail graeme@graemelamb.com

LAMB, Mrs Jean Evelyn. b 57. Reading Univ BA79 Nottm Univ MA88. St Steph Ho Ox 81. **dss** 84 **d** 87 **p** 94. Leic H Spirit 84-87; Asst Chapl Leic Poly 84-87; Par Dn Beeston *S'well* 89-91; Hon C and Artist in Res Nottingham St Mary and St Cath 92-95; Hon Par Dn Sneinton St Steph w St Alb 97-01; NSM Rolleston w Fiskerton, Morton and Upton 01-02; Perm to Offic 02-04; C Bilborough St Jo from 04; C Bilborough w Strelley from 04. *St Alban's House, 3 Dale Street, Nottingham NG2 4JX* Tel 0115-958 5892 Mobile 07851-792552

LAMB, Nicholas Henry. b 52. St Jo Coll Dur BA74. St Jo Coll Nottm 76. **d** 79 **p** 80. C Luton Lewsey St Hugh *St Alb* 79-84;

Bethany Fellowship 84-86; In Bapt Min 86-94; Perm to Offic *Chich* 97-99; C E Grinstead St Swithun 99-04; V Forest Row from 04. *The Vicarage, Ashdown Road, Forest Row RH18 5BW* Tel (01342) 822595 E-mail revnicklamb@gmail.com

LAMB, Peter Francis Charles. b 15. St Cath Coll Cam BA37 MA41. Wells Th Coll 37. **d** 38 **p** 39. C Wellingborough All Hallows *Pet* 38-42; C Somersham w Pidley and Colne *Ely* 42-48; Chapl RNVR 46-48; C Sherborne w Castleton and Lillington *Sarum* 48-51; The Gambia 51-57; V Winkleigh *Ex* 57-70; RD Chulmleigh 62-63; R Mells w Vobster, Whatley and Chantry *B & W* 70-77; rtd 77; Perm to Offic *B & W* from 77. *6 Parsons Close, Long Sutton, Langport TA10 9LN* Tel (01458) 241481

LAMB, Philip Richard James. b 42. Sarum & Wells Th Coll. **d** 83 **p** 84. C Wotton-under-Edge w Ozleworth and N Nibley *Glouc* 83-86; TV Worc SE 86-91; R Billingsley w Sidbury, Middleton Scriven etc *Heref* 91-96; R St Dominic, Landulph and St Mellion w Pillaton *Truro* from 96. *The Rectory, St Mellion, Saltash PL12 6RN* Tel (01579) 350061 E-mail frlamb@stmellion141.freeserve.co.uk

LAMB, Phillip. b 68. NEOC 00. **d** 03 **p** 04. C Bridlington Priory *York* 03-06; V Hornsea w Atwick from 06. *The Vicarage, 9 Newbegin, Hornsea HU18 1AB* Tel (01964) 532531 Mobile 07803-239611 E-mail phil_lamb2002@yahoo.co.uk

LAMB, Scott Innes. b 64. Edin Univ BSc86 Fitzw Coll Cam BA92. Aston Tr Scheme 88 Ridley Hall Cam 90. **d** 93 **p** 94. C E Ham w Upton Park St Alb *Chelmsf* 93-97; V W Holloway St Luke *Lon* 97-00; P-in-c Hammersmith H Innocents 00-03; Chapl RN 03-09; V Bexley St Jo *Roch* from 09. *St John's Vicarage, 29 Parkhill Road, Bexley DA5 1HX* Tel (01322) 521786 Mobile 07917-534488 E-mail s.i.lamb@blueyonder.co.uk

LAMB, Canon William Robert Stuart. b 70. Ball Coll Ox BA91 MA95 Peterho Cam MPhil94. Westcott Ho Cam 92. **d** 95 **p** 96. C Halifax *Wakef* 95-98; TV Penistone and Thurlstone 98-01; Chapl Sheff Univ from 01; Can Res Sheff Cathl from 05. *119 Ashdell Road, Sheffield S10 3DB* Tel 0114-266 9243 *or* 222 8923 E-mail w.lamb@shef.ac.uk

LAMBERT, Antony. *See* LAMBERT, John Clement Antony

LAMBERT, David Francis. b 40. Oak Hill Th Coll 72. **d** 74 **p** 75. C Paignton St Paul Preston *Ex* 74-77; C Woking Ch Ch *Guildf* 77-84; P-in-c Willesden Green St Gabr *Lon* 84-91; P-in-c Cricklewood St Mich 85-91; V Cricklewood St Gabr and St Mich 92-93; R Chenies and Lt Chalfont, Latimer and Flaunden *Ox* 93-01; Chapl Izmir (Smyrna) w Bornova *Eur* 01-03; TV Brixham w Churston Ferrers and Kingswear *Ex* 03-05; rtd 05. *54 Brunel Road, Broadsands, Paignton TQ4 6HW* Tel (01803) 842076

LAMBERT, David Hardy. b 44. AKC46. **d** 67 **p** 68. C Marske in Cleveland *York* 67-72; V 85-09; V N Ormesby 73-85; RD Guisborough 86-91; rtd 09. *13 Fellbriggs Drive, Marske-by-the-Sea, Redcar TS11 6BU* Tel (01642) 482896 E-mail david@lambert9139.freeserve.co.uk

LAMBERT, David Joseph. b 48. Coll of Resurr Mirfield 99. **d** 01 **p** 02. C Camberwell St Geo *S'wark* 01-04; C Walworth St Jo 04-06; V Stoke Newington St Faith, St Matthias and All SS *Lon* from 06. *St Matthias Vicarage, Wordsworth Road, London N16 8DD* Tel (020) 7254 5063 E-mail frdavidlambert@aol.com

LAMBERT, David Nathaniel. b 34. Headingley Meth Coll 58 Linc Th Coll 66. **d** 66 **p** 67. In Methodist Ch 58-66; C Canwick *Linc* 66-68; C-in-c Bracebridge Heath CD 68-69; R Saltfleetby All SS w St Pet 69-73; R Saltfleetby St Clem 70-73; V Skidbrooke 70-73; V Saltfleetby 73-80; R Theddlethorpe 74-80; RD Louthesk 76-82; R N Ormsby w Wyham 80; R Fotherby 81-94; rtd 94; Perm to Offic *Linc* 94-03; *York* and *Ripon* 03-05; *Dur* from 06. *Sandcroft, Market Place, Houghton-le-Spring DH5 8AJ* Tel 0191-584 1387

LAMBERT, Ian Anderson. b 43. Lon Univ BA72 Nottm Univ MTh87. Ridley Hall Cam 66. **d** 67 **p** 68. C Bermondsey St Mary w St Olave, St Jo etc *S'wark* 67-70; R Lluidas Vale Jamaica 71-75; Chapl RAF 75-98; rtd 98; P-in-c N and S Muskham *S'well* 01-03; P-in-c Averham w Kelham 01-03; Bp's Adv for Past Care and Counselling from 04. *34 Hayside Avenue, Balderton, Newark NG24 3GB* Tel (01636) 659101 Mobile 07788-171958 E-mail revianlambert@mac.com

LAMBERT, John Clement Antony. b 28. St Cath Coll Cam BA48 MA52. Cuddesdon Coll 52. **d** 52 **p** 53. C Hornsea and Goxhill *York* 52-55; C Leeds St Pet *Ripon* 55-59; R Carlton in Lindrick *S'well* 59-93; rtd 93; Perm to Offic *Derby* from 93 and *S'well* 93-00. *139 Longedge Lane, Wingerworth, Chesterfield S42 6PR* Tel (01246) 551774

LAMBERT, John Connolly. b 61. Univ of Wales (Ban) BTh04. EAMTC 01. **d** 04 **p** 05. C Paris St Mich *Eur* 04-08; C Preston-on-Tees and Longnewton *Dur* from 08. *The Vicarage, Quarry Road, Eaglescliffe, Stockton-on-Tees TS16 9BD* Tel (01642) 789814 E-mail johnlambert@allsaints-church.co.uk

LAMBERT, Malcolm Eric. b 58. Leic Univ BSc80 Fitzw Coll Cam BA89 Nottm Univ MPhil02 RMN84. Ridley Hall Cam 87. **d** 90 **p** 91. C Humberstone *Leic* 90-94; R S Croxton Gp 94-99; V Birstall and Wanlip 99-05; TR Leic Resurr 05-07; RD Christianity N 05-07; Warden of Readers 97-05; Dir Angl Th

Inst Belize from 08. *St Ann's Rectory, 37-39 Trinity Boulevard, PO Box 413, Belmopan, Belize* E-mail malcolm.lambert@gmail.com

LAMBERT, Michael Roy. b 25. Univ Coll Dur BSc49. Cuddesdon Coll 52. **d** 52 **p** 53. C Middlesbrough St Oswald *York* 52-56; C Romsey *Win* 56-59; C Cottingham *York* 59-64; Chapl Hull Univ 59-64; V Saltburn-by-the-Sea 64-72; P-in-c Shaftesbury H Trin *Sarum* 72-73; R Shaston 74-78; R Corfe Mullen 78-91; rtd 91; Perm to Offic *Glouc* from 91. *16 Pheasant Way, Cirencester GL7 1BL* Tel (01285) 654657

LAMBERT, Neil James. b 58. Goldsmiths' Coll Lon BA81. Ridley Hall Cam 02. **d** 04 **p** 05. C Wisley w Pyrford *Guildf* 04-08; V Ash Vale from 08. *The Vicarage, 203 Vale Road, Ash Vale, Aldershot GU12 5JE* Tel (01252) 325295 Mobile 07812-385392

LAMBERT, Miss Olivia Jane. b 48. Matlock Coll of Educn BEd70. Trin Coll Bris 84. dss 86 **d** 87 **p** 94. York St Luke 86-90; Par Dn 87-90; Chapl York Distr Hosp 86-90; Par Dn Huntington *York* 90-94; C 94-95; TV 95-00; TV Marfleet 00-07; C Harrogate St Mark *Ripon* 07-08; rtd 08. *58 Almsford Drive, Harrogate HG2 8EE* Tel (01423) 810357 E-mail oliviajlambert@aol.com

LAMBERT, Peter George. b 29. Coll of Resurr Mirfield 86. **d** 87 **p** 88. NSM Rothwell w Orton, Rushton w Glendon and Pipewell *Pet* 87-93; P-in-c Corby Epiphany w St Jo 93-96; rtd 96; Perm to Offic *Pet* from 96. *4 Cogan Crescent, Rothwell, Kettering NN14 6AS* Tel (01536) 710692

LAMBERT, Canon Philip Charles. b 54. St Jo Coll Dur BA75 Fitzw Coll Cam BA77 MA81. Ridley Hall Cam 75. **d** 78 **p** 79. C Upper Tooting H Trin *S'wark* 78-81; C Whorlton *Newc* 81-84; P-in-c Alston cum Garrigill w Nenthead and Kirkhaugh 84-87; TV Alston Team 87-89; R Curry Rivel w Fivehead and Swell *B & W* 89-01; RD Crewkerne and Ilminster 98-01; TR Dorchester *Sarum* 01-06; RD Dorchester 02-06; Can Res Truro Cathl from 06. *Foxhayes, 3 Knights Hill, Truro TR1 3UY* Tel (01872) 272866 E-mail philiplambert@dsl.pipex.com

LAMBERT (née JOHNSON), Mrs Ruth Alice Edna. b 59. Leic Univ BA80 PGCE93 Nottm Univ MA01 RGN85. EMMTC 98. **d** 01 **p** 02. C Mountsorrel Ch Ch and St Pet *Leic* 01-04; Chapl Univ Hosps Leic NHS Trust 04-07; P-in-c Belmopan St Ann Belize from 08. *St Ann's Rectory, 37-39 Trinity Boulevard, PO Box 413, Belmopan, Belize* E-mail ruth.lambert@gmail.com

LAMBETH, Archdeacon of. *See* SKILTON, The Ven Christopher John

LAMBOURN, David Malcolm. b 37. Lanc Univ BEd76 Man Univ MEd78 Warwick Univ PhD01. Linc Th Coll 63. **d** 65 **p** 66. C Camberwell St Geo *S'wark* 65-67; C Mottingham St Andr 67-70; rtd 03. *28 Frederick Road, Birmingham B15 1JN* Tel 0121-242 3953 E-mail david.lambourn@blueyonder.co.uk

LAMBOURNE, John Brian. b 36. Chich Th Coll 62. **d** 65 **p** 66. C Cant St Greg 65-67; C St Mary in the Marsh 67-68; C E Grinstead St Swithun *Chich* 68-70; C Storrington and Sullington 70-76; V Salehurst 76-06; CF (TA) 87-96; Agric Chapl and Bp's Adv on Rural Affairs *Chich* 89-06; rtd 06; Chapl Vinehall Sch Robertsbridge from 06. *2 Walden Terrace, Lower Lake, Battle TN33 0AU* Tel (01580) 880408

LAMDIN, Canon Keith Hamilton. b 47. Bris Univ BA69. Ripon Coll Cuddesdon 86. **d** 86 **p** 87. Adult Educn Officer *Ox* 83-98; Team Ldr Par Resources Dept from 88; Dioc Dir Tr 94-08; Prin Sarum Coll from 08; NSM Cowley St Jo *Ox* 98-06; P-in-c Upper Kennet *Sarum* from 08; Hon Can Ch Ch *Ox* from 97; Hon Can Kimberley S Africa from 08; Can and Preb Sarum Cathl from 09. *2 Forge Close, West Overton, Marlborough SN8 4PG* Tel (01672) 861550 E-mail klamdin@sarum.ac.uk

LAMEY, Richard John. b 77. Keble Coll Ox BA98 MA02 Em Coll Cam BA01 MA05. Westcott Ho Cam 99. **d** 02 **p** 03. C Stockport SW *Ches* 02-05; P-in-c Newton in Mottram from 05; RD Mottram from 08. *St Mary's Vicarage, 39 Bradley Green Road, Hyde SK14 4NA* Tel 0161-368 1489 E-mail richardlamey@btinternet.com

LAMMAS, Miss Diane Beverley. b 47. Trin Coll Bris 76. dss 79 **d** 87 **p** 94. Lenton Abbey *S'well* 79-84; Wollaton Park 79-84; E Regional Co-ord and Sec for Voc and Min CPAS 84-89; Hon C Cambridge St Paul *Ely* 87-90; Voc and Min Adv CPAS 89-92; Sen Voc and Min Adv CPAS 92-95; R Hethersett w Canteloff w Lt and Gt Melton *Nor* from 95; RD Humbleyard 98-03. *The Rectory, 27 Norwich Road, Hethersett, Norwich NR9 3AR* Tel (01603) 810273 E-mail di.lammas@freeuk.com

LAMMENS, Erwin Bernard Eddy. b 62. Catholic Univ Leuven BA86 Gregorian Univ Rome MDiv90. Grootseminarie Gent 84. **d** 87 **p** 88. In RC Ch 87-98; Asst Chapl Antwerp St Boniface *Eur* 98-05; TV Harwich Peninsula *Chelmsf* from 05. *The Vicarage, Church Hill, Ramsey, Harwich CO12 5EU* Tel (01255) 880291 E-mail erwinlammens@btinternet.com

LAMMING, Sarah Rebecca. b 77. Middx Univ BA02. Westcott Ho Cam 03 Yale Div Sch 05. **d** 06 **p** 07. C Handsworth St Jas *Birm* 06-09; USA from 09. *30 South 22nd Street Apt 4, Philadelphia PA 19103, USA* E-mail sarah@sarahlamming.com

LAMOND, Stephen Paul. b 64. Trin Coll Bris BA99. **d** 99 **p** 00. C Weston-super-Mare Ch Ch *B & W* 99-02; C Congresbury w

Puxton and Hewish St Ann 02-03; Chapl RAF from 03. *Chaplaincy Services, Valiant Block, HQ Air Command, RAF High Wycombe HP14 4UE* Tel (01494) 496800 Fax 496343

LAMONT, Canon Euphemia Margaret (Fay). b 53. N Coll of Educn BA98. TISEC 00. **d** 00 **p** 00. C Monifieth and Carnoustie *Bre* 00-07; P-in-c Dundee St Ninian from 07; Can St Paul's Cathl Dundee from 08. *St Ninian's Church House, Kingsway East, Dundee DD4 7RW* Tel (01382) 453818 Mobile 07931-222092 E-mail fay.lamont@sky.com

LAMONT, Roger. b 37. Jes Coll Ox BA60 MA62 MBACP00. St Steph Ho Ox 59. **d** 61 **p** 62. C Northampton St Alb *Pet* 61-66; V Mitcham St Olave *S'wark* 66-73; V N Sheen St Phil and All SS 73-85; P-in-c Richmond St Luke 82-85; Chapl St Lawr Hosp Caterham 85-94; Chapl Lifecare NHS Trust 92-99; Chapl Surrey Oaklands NHS Trust 99-01; rtd 01; Perm to Offic *S'wark* from 01. *8 Montague Drive, Caterham CR3 5BY* Tel (01883) 340803

LAMONT, Ms Veronica Jane (Ronni). b 56. Bp Grosseteste Coll CertEd77 Anglia Poly Univ MA06. St Jo Coll Nottm 90. **d** 92 **p** 94. Par Dn St Alb St Pet *St Alb* 92-94; C 94-96; TV Hemel Hempstead 96-01; V Bexley St Jo *Roch* 01-08; Perm to Offic *Cant* and *Roch* from 08. *86 Ufton Lane, Sittingbourne ME10 1EX* Tel 07802-793910 (mobile) E-mail ronni@lamonts.org.uk

LAMPARD, Ms Ruth Margaret. b 65. St Jo Coll Dur BA87 Jes Coll Cam BA99 MA04 Heythrop Coll Lon MA04. Westcott Ho Cam 97 Berkeley Div Sch 99. **d** 00 **p** 01. C Ealing St Pet Mt Park *Lon* 00-01; C Eastcote St Lawr 01-04; Hon C Norton *St Alb* 05-06; Perm to Offic *S'wark* from 06; Chapl to Bp Kensington *Lon* 07-08; C W Brompton St Mary w St Peter and St Jude from 08. *144 Elsenham Street, London SW18 5NP* Tel (020) 8874 7768 E-mail ruth.lampard@london.anglican.org

LANCASTER, Mrs Jennifer. b 48. NEOC 00. **d** 03 **p** 04. C Walker *Newc* 03-07; TV Jarrow *Dur* from 07. *St Andrew's House, Borough Road, Jarrow NE32 5BL* Tel 0191-423 4109 *or* 489 1925 E-mail jenny.lancaster@gmail.com

LANCASTER, John Rawson. b 47. BSc. NOC. **d** 82 **p** 83. C Bolton St Jas w St Chrys *Bradf* 82-86; V Barnoldswick w Bracewell from 86. *The Vicarage, 131 Gisburn Road, Barnoldswick BB18 5JU* Tel (01282) 812028 Fax 850346 E-mail john.lancaster@bradford.anglican.org

LANCASTER, Norman. b 13. Leeds Univ BA36. Coll of Resurr Mirfield 36. **d** 38 **p** 39. C Skegness *Linc* 38-41; C New Cleethorpes 41-42; C Gt Grimsby St Jas 42-47; V Caistor w Holton le Moor and Clixby 47-52; PC Louth H Trin 52-57; V Keddington 52-57; V Hogsthorpe 57-62; Chapl Butlin's Holiday Camps 59-62; R Panton w Wragby 62-71; V Langton by Wragby 62-71; R Gt Coates 71-77; PC Aylesby 71-77; rtd 77; Perm to Offic *Linc* 77-95. *10 Dulverton Hall, Esplanade, Scarborough YO11 2AR* Tel (01723) 340106

LANCASTER, Ronald. b 31. MBE93. FRSC83 CChem83 St Jo Coll Dur BA53 MA56. Cuddesdon Coll 55. **d** 57 **p** 58. C Morley St Pet w Churwell *Wakef* 57-60; C High Harrogate St Pet *Ripon* 60-63; Lic to Offic *Ely* 63-88; Chapl Kimbolton Sch 63-88; Asst Chapl 88-91; Perm to Offic *Ely* from 88; rtd 96. *7 High Street, Kimbolton, Huntingdon PE28 0HB* Tel (01480) 860498 Fax 861277

LANCASTER, Mrs Susan Louise. b 47. Leic Univ BA79. EMMTC 88. **d** 93 **p** 94. NSM Clarendon Park St Jo w Knighton St Mich *Leic* 93-97; Perm to Offic 97-01; NSM Roundhay St Edm *Ripon* from 01. *38 Talbot Avenue, Leeds LS17 6SB* Tel 0113-228 0145

LANCASTER, Archdeacon of. *See* BALLARD, The Ven Peter James

LANCASTER, Suffragan Bishop of. *See* PEARSON, The Rt Revd Geoffrey Seagrave

LANCHANTIN, Mrs Eveline. b 51. Sorbonne Univ Paris BA79 MA80 MPhil83. Protestant Inst of Th Paris BDiv95 MDiv99. **d** 07 **p** 08. C Ashford *Cant* from 07. *24 Sweet Bay Crescent, Ashford TN23 3QA* Tel (01233) 661664 Mobile 07806-483434 E-mail santiago31@free.fr

LAND, Michael Robert John. b 43. Ripon Hall Ox BA72 MA. **d** 72 **p** 73. C Newbury St Nic *Ox* 72-75; TV Chigwell *Chelmsf* 75-80; V Walthamstow St Andr 80-08; rtd 08; Perm to Offic *Heref* from 08. *20 St Mary's Lane, Burghill, Hereford HR4 7QL* Tel (01432) 760452 E-mail land117@btinternet.com

LANDALL, Capt Allan Roy. b 55. Qu Coll Birm BA98. **d** 98 **p** 99. C Thurnby w Stoughton *Leic* 98-02; R Wisbech *Ely* from 02. *The Vicarage, Church Road, Wisbech PE13 3RA* Tel (01945) 583740 E-mail arlandall@btinternet.com

LANDALL, Richard. b 57. St Jo Coll Dur 85. **d** 88 **p** 89. C Nailsea H Trin *B & W* 88-92; CF 92-99; TV Westborough *Guildf* 99-01; R Armthorpe *Sheff* from 01. *The Rectory, Church Street, Armthorpe, Doncaster DN3 3AD* Tel and fax (01302) 831231 E-mail richard.landall@virgin.net

LANDEN, Edgar Sydney. b 23. ARCM46 FRCO46 St Jo Coll Dur BA54 BMus55. **d** 55 **p** 56. Succ Leeds *Ripon* 55-58; Prec Chelmsf Cathl 58-60; V Bathampton *B & W* 60-65; Perm to Offic *Glouc* 65-69; C Cirencester 69-76; Min Can Ch Ch *Ox* 76-88; V Wytham 76-88; rtd 88; Perm to Offic *B & W* 88-98. *The*

Old Vicarage, Bakers Hill, Tiverton EX16 5NE Tel (01884) 256815

LANDER, Mrs Eileen. b 47. **d** 09. NSM Maidstone St Paul *Cant* from 09. *47 Bargrove Road, Maidstone ME14 5RT* Tel (01622) 685975 E-mail eileenlander@yahoo.co.uk

LANDER, Mrs Elizabeth Anne. b 69. St Andr Univ BSc93 Ox Univ PGCE94. Wycliffe Hall Ox 00. **d** 02 **p** 03. C Glascote and Stonydelph *Lich* 02-07; NSM Beckenham St Jo *Roch* from 08. *2 Repton Court, The Avenue, Beckenham BR3 5EN* Tel (020) 8639 0412 Mobile 07790-212302 E-mail landerliz@yahoo.co.uk

LANDER, John Stanley. b 55. **d** 04 **p** 05. OLM Uttoxeter Area *Lich* from 04. *9 Overcroft, Bramshall, Uttoxeter ST14 5NQ* Tel (01889) 565228 E-mail john_lander@lineone.net

LANDMAN, Denis Cooper. b 21. MBE60 OM(Ger)80. Lon Univ BA41 DipEd52. St Deiniol's Hawarden 79. **d** 82 **p** 83. Hon C Tranmere St Paul w St Luke *Ches* 82-86; Australia from 86; C Southport St Pet 86-88; P-in-c Biggera Waters 88-92; rtd 92. *1/24 Stretton Drive, Helensvale Qld 4212, Australia* Tel (0061) (7) 5573 4660 Mobile 407-758376

LANDMANN, Ulrike Helene Kathryn. b 57. **d** 06 **p** 07. NSM Balsall Heath and Edgbaston SS Mary and Ambrose *Birm* from 06. *57 Lea House Road, Birmingham B30 2DB*

LANDRETH, Mrs Mavis Isabella (Isabel). b 32. SEN81. Gilmore Ho 67. **dss** 74 **d** 87. Walthamstow St Sav *Chelmsf* 70-75; Sanderstead All SS *S'wark* 76-79; Sheff St Cuth 84-85; N Gen Hosp Sheff 84-85; Icklesham *Chich* 86-87; Hon Par Dn 87-89; Perm to Offic from 89. *16 St Bartholomew's Close, Chichester PO19 3EP* Tel (01243) 537832

LANE, Alexander John. b 71. Leeds Univ BA02. Coll of Resurr Mirfield 99. **d** 02 **p** 03. C Eastbourne St Andr *Chich* 02-06; C Littlehampton and Wick 06-08; V Hunslet w Cross Green *Ripon* from 08; CMP from 08. *The Vicarage, Church Street, Hunslet, Leeds LS10 2QY* E-mail fr.alex.lane@googlemail.com

LANE, Andrew Harry John. b 49. MBE92. Lanc Univ BA71. Cuddesdon Coll 71. **d** 73 **p** 74. C Abingdon w Shippon *Ox* 73-78; Chapl Abingdon Sch 75-78; Chapl RAF 78-94; rtd 94; Perm to Offic *Nor* 94-01; Public Preacher from 01; RD Repps 02-05. *Society of St Luke, 32B Beeston Common, Sheringham NR26 8ES* Tel (01263) 825623 Fax 820334 E-mail anthony@ssluke.org.uk

LANE, Anthony James. b 29. Leeds Univ BA53. Coll of Resurr Mirfield 53. **d** 55 **p** 56. C Tilehurst St Mich *Ox* 55-60; Min Can Win Cathl 60-63; R Handley w Pentridge *Sarum* 64-80; V Thurmaston *Leic* 80-85; TV Bournemouth St Pet w St Swithun, H Trin etc *Win* 85-93; rtd 93. *5 Richards Way, Salisbury SP2 8NT* Tel (01722) 332163

LANE, Canon Antony Kenneth. b 58. Ripon Coll Cuddesdon 84. **d** 87 **p** 88. C Crediton and Shobrooke *Ex* 87-90; C Amblecote *Worc* 90-94; C Sedgley All SS 94-95; TV 95-00; R Crayford *Roch* from 00; Hon Can Roch Cathl from 09. *The Rectory, 1 Claremont Crescent, Crayford, Dartford DA1 4RJ* Tel (01322) 522078 Mobile 07931-603470 E-mail antony.lane@diocese-rochester.org

LANE, Bernard Charles. b 59. Cam Coll of Art & Tech BA81 Anglia Poly Univ MA01. Trin Coll Bris BA91 Ridley Hall Cam 99. **d** 01 **p** 02. C Sittingbourne St Mary and St Mich *Cant* 01-05. *Lawrence Weston Vicarage, 335 Long Cross, Bristol BS11 0NN* Tel 0117-982 5863 E-mail lane@train66.fsnet.co.uk

LANE, Christopher George. b 48. Sarum & Wells Th Coll 84. **d** 86 **p** 87. C Petersfield *Portsm* 86-90; P-in-c Barton 90-95; Perm to Offic from 95. *Carisbrooke Priory, 39 Whitcombe Road, Carisbrooke, Newport PO30 1YS* Tel (01983) 523354

LANE, Denis John Victor. b 29. Lon Univ LLB49 BD55. Oak Hill Th Coll 50. **d** 53 **p** 54. C Deptford St Jo *S'wark* 53-56; C Cambridge St Steph CD *Ely* 56-59; OMF S Perak Malaysia 60-66; Promotion Sec OMF Singapore 66-70; Overseas Dir 70-82; Dir Home Min 82-88; Internat Min 88-94; Lic to Offic *Chich* 91-94; rtd 94; Perm to Offic *Chich* from 94. *2 Parry Drive, Rustington, Littlehampton BN16 2QY* Tel and fax (01903) 785430

LANE, Ms Elizabeth Jane Holden. b 66. St Pet Coll Ox BA89 MA93. Cranmer Hall Dur 91. **d** 93 **p** 94. C Blackb St Jas 93-96; Perm to Offic 96-99; Family Life Educn Officer *Ches* 00-02; TV Stockport SW 02-07; Asst Dir of Ords 05-07; V Hale and Ashley from 07. *St Peter's Vicarage, 1 Harrop Road, Hale, Altrincham WA15 9BU* Tel 0161-928 4182 E-mail libby.lane@btinternet.com

LANE, George David Christopher. b 68. St Pet Coll Ox BA89 MA93. Cranmer Hall Dur 91. **d** 93 **p** 94. C Blackb St Jas 93-96; C Beverley Minster *York* 96-99; V Heald Green St Cath *Ches* 99-07; Perm to Offic *Ches* from 07 and *Man* from 08. *St Peter's Vicarage, 1 Harrop Road, Hale, Altrincham WA15 9BU* Tel 0161-928 4182 E-mail george_dcl@yahoo.co.uk

LANE, Canon Gerald. b 29. Bede Coll Dur BA52 MA96. Sarum Th Coll 52. **d** 54 **p** 55. C Camberwell St Giles *S'wark* 54-58; C Gillingham St Aug *Roch* 58-59; V Camberwell St Phil and St Mark *S'wark* 59-67; V Plumstead St Nic 67-73; V Gillingham St Aug *Roch* 73-78; V Hadlow 78-94; Hon Can Roch Cathl

87-94; rtd 94; Perm to Offic *Roch* 94-97; Perm to Offic *St Alb* 97-03. *6 Windsor Drive, Norristhorpe, Liversedge WF15 7RA* Tel (01924) 235254

LANE, Iain Robert. b 61. CCC Ox BA83. Ripon Coll Cuddesdon BA86 MA88. **d** 87 **p** 88. C Rotherhithe St Mary w All SS *S'wark* 87-91; V Bierley *Bradf* 91-00; Can Res St Alb 00-08; Admin St Alb Cen for Chr Studies from 08; Perm to Offic from 08. *Hill House, Wild Hill, Hatfield AL9 6EB* Tel (01707) 660485
E-mail iain.lane@christianstudies.org.uk

LANE, John Ernest. b 39. OBE94. MBIM76 Cranfield Info Tech Inst MSc80. Handsworth Coll Birm 58. **d** 80 **p** 80. In Meth Ch 62-80; Hon C Peckham St Jo w St Andr *S'wark* 80-95; Hon C Greenwich St Alfege 98-99; Dir St Mungo Housing Assn 80-94; Dir Corporate Affairs from 94; Perm to Offic 95-98. *2 Tregony Rise, Lichfield WS14 9SN* Tel (01543) 415078

LANE, Mrs Lilian June. b 37. Stockwell Coll Lon TCert59. **d** 02 **p** 03. OLM E Knoyle, Semley and Sedgehill *Sarum* 02-08; OLM St Bartholomew 08-09; Chapl St Mary's Sch Shaftesbury from 09. *Ashmede, Watery Lane, Donhead St Mary, Shaftesbury SP7 9DP* Tel (01747) 828427

LANE, Mrs Linda Mary. b 41. Lon Univ BD87 ACIB66. Gilmore Ho. **dss** 82 **d** 87 **p** 94. Hadlow *Roch* 82-94; Hon Par Dn 87-94; Perm to Offic 94-96; C Dartford H Trin 96-97; V Kensworth, Studham and Whipsnade *St Alb* 97-03; rtd 03; Perm to Offic *Wakef* from 05. *6 Windsor Drive, Norristhorpe, Liversedge WF15 7RA* Tel (01924) 235254

LANE, Malcolm Clifford George. b 48. JP. ACIB. St D Coll Lamp. **d** 02 **p** 05. Par Dn Abergavenny St Mary w Llanwenarth Citra *Mon* 02-08; P-in-c Michaelston-y-Fedw from 08; Asst Chapl Gwent Healthcare NHS Trust from 02. *The Rectory, Michaelston-y-Fedw, Cardiff CF3 6XS*
E-mail st8711@msn.com

LANE, Martin Guy. b 70. Oak Hill Th Coll BA08. **d** 08 **p** 09. C Herne Bay Ch Ch *Cant* from 08. *66 Linden Avenue, Herne Bay CT6 8TZ* Tel (01227) 371457 Mobile 07765-861939
E-mail martlane@hotmail.com

LANE, Martin John. b 69. Open Univ BSc03 Cardiff Univ LLM08. Coll of Resurr Mirfield 92. **d** 95 **p** 96. C Liss *Portsm* 95-98; C Warren Park and Leigh Park 98-00; TV Littlehampton and Wick *Chich* 00-04; P-in-c Harting w Elsted and Treyford cum Didling from 04. *The Rectory, The Street, South Harting, Petersfield GU31 5QB* Tel (01730) 825234
E-mail martinjlane@btinternet.com

LANE, Mrs Pamela. b 44. **d** 00 **p** 01. OLM Betley *Lich* from 00. *Brandon, Main Road, Betley, Crewe CW3 9BH* Tel (01270) 820258

LANE, Richard Peter. b 60. Linc Th Coll 85. **d** 88 **p** 89. C Towcester w Easton Neston *Pet* 88-91; Asst Chapl Oslo w Bergen, Trondheim, Stavanger etc *Eur* 91-93; V Writtle w Highwood *Chelmsf* 93-99; Chapl Whitelands Coll Roehampton Inst *S'wark* 99-03; P-in-c W Wimbledon Ch Ch 03-04; V from 04. *The Vicarage, 16 Copse Hill, London SW20 0HG* Tel (020) 8946 4491

LANE, Robert David. b 66. St Steph Ho Ox 05. **d** 07 **p** 08. C Corringham *Chelmsf* from 07. *St John's House, Springhouse Road, Corringham, Stanford-le-Hope SS17 7LF* Tel (01375) 641276 Mobile 07907 224748
E-mail robert.lane2@ntlworld.com

LANE, Ms Rosalind Anne. b 69. Trevelyan Coll Dur BA91 Heythrop Coll Lon MPhil93 Man Univ MA01. Westcott Ho Cam. **d** 95 **p** 96. C Huddersfield St Pet and All SS *Wakef* 95-99; Sub Chapl HM Pris and YOI New Hall 97-99; Asst Chapl HM Pris and YOI Doncaster 99-01; Chapl 01; Chapl HM Pris Wymott 01-05; Chapl HM Pris Kirkham 05-08; Perm to Offic *Ely* from 08. *The Precentor's House, 32 High Street, Ely CB7 4JU* Tel (01353) 660335

LANE, Roy Albert. b 42. Bris Sch of Min 82. **d** 85 **p** 86. NSM Bedminster *Bris* 85-97; Perm to Offic 97-02; NSM Bishopsworth and Bedminster Down from 02. *20 Ashton Drive, Bristol BS3 2PW* Tel 0117-983 0747 Mobile 07747-808972
E-mail roypeg@blueyonder.co.uk

LANE, Simon. *See* DOUGLAS LANE, Charles Simon Pellew

LANE, Stuart Alexander Rhys. *See* LANE, Alexander John

LANE, Terry. b 50. STETS 94. **d** 97 **p** 98. NSM Freemantle *Win* 97-99; Chapl HM Pris Kingston (Portsm) 99-01; Chapl HM Pris Parkhurst 01-06; Co-ord Chapl HM Pris Win from 06. *HM Prison Winchester, Romsey Road, Winchester SO22 5DF* Tel (01962) 723000

LANE, Mrs William Henry Howard. b 63. Bris Poly BA85. Trin Coll Bris 00. **d** 02 **p** 03. C Frome H Trin *B & W* 02-06; P-in-c Woolavington w Cossington and Bawdrip 06-08; V from 09; RD Sedgemoor from 09. *The Rectory, 7 Vicarage Road, Woolavington, Bridgwater TA7 8DX* Tel (01278) 683408
E-mail lanc@wkja.wanadoo.co.uk

LANG, Geoffrey Wilfrid Francis. b 33. St Jo Coll Ox BA56 MA61. Cuddesdon Coll 56. **d** 58 **p** 59. C Spalding *Linc* 58-61; Asst Chapl Leeds Univ 61-62; C Chesterton St Luke *Ely* 62-63; C-in-c Chesterton Gd Shep CD 63-69; V Chesterton Gd Shep 69-72; V Willian *St Alb* 72-76; Dioc Dir of Educn 72-76; R N

LANG, The Very Revd John Harley. b 27. LRAM Em Coll Cam MA60 K Coll Lon AKC49 BD60 Keele Univ Hon DLitt88. St Boniface Warminster 49. **d** 52 **p** 53. C Portsea St Mary *Portsm* 52-57; PV and Sacr S'wark Cathl 57-60; Chapl Em Coll Cam 60-64; Asst Hd Relig Broadcasting BBC 64-67; Hd Relig Progr BBC Radio 67-71; Hd Relig Broadcasting BBC 71-80; C Sacombe *St Alb* 73-80; Chapl to The Queen 77-80; Dean Lich 80-93; rtd 93; Perm to Offic *Glouc* 93-96. *1 Abbotsdene, 6 Cudnall Street, Charlton Kings, Cheltenham GL53 8HT* Tel and fax (01242) 577742 E-mail jhlang@email.com

LANG, Nicholas. b 45. SEITE 94. **d** 97 **p** 98. NSM Beckenham St Jo *Roch* 97-98; NSM Penge Lane H Trin 98-01; Chapl St Chris Hospice Lon 00; V Beckenham St Jo *Roch* from 01. *St John's Vicarage, 249 Eden Park Avenue, Beckenham BR3 3JN* Tel and fax (020) 8650 6110 Mobile 07968-985051
E-mail nick.lang@diocese-rochester.org
or niklang@ntlworld.com

LANG, William David. b 51. K Coll Lon BD74 MA94 AKC74. St Aug Coll Cant 74. **d** 75 **p** 76. C Fleet *Guildf* 75-79; C Ewell St Fran 79-82; C W Ewell 79-82; V Holmwood 82-92; R Elstead from 92; V Thursley from 92. *The Rectory, Thursley Road, Elstead, Godalming GU8 6DG* Tel (01252) 703251
E-mail william@lang.net

LANGAN, Mrs Eleanor Susan. b 56. Homerton Coll Cam BEd78. Ripon Coll Cuddesdon 84. **d** 87 **p** 94. Hon Par Dn Grays Thurrock *Chelmsf* 87-89; Lic to Offic 89-94; NSM Creeksea w Althorne, Latchingdon and N Fambridge 94-95; NSM S Woodham Ferrers 95-99; NSM Overstrand, Northrepps, Sidestrand etc 99-03; Chapl Norfolk and Nor Univ Hosp NHS Trust from 00. *The Rectory, 22A Harbord Road, Overstrand, Cromer NR27 0PN* Tel (01263) 579350 *or* (01603) 287470
E-mail eleanor.langan@nnuh.nhs.uk

LANGAN, Michael Leslie. b 54. Cam Univ BA PGCE. Cranmer Hall Dur. **d** 84 **p** 85. C Grays Thurrock *Chelmsf* 84-89; R Creeksea w Althorne, Latchingdon and N Fambridge 89-95; RD Maldon and Dengie 92-95; P-in-c S Woodham Ferrers 95-99; R Overstrand, Northrepps, Sidestrand etc from 99; RD Repps from 05. *The Rectory, 22A Harbord Road, Overstrand, Cromer NR27 0PN* Tel (01263) 579350 E-mail ml@netcom.co.uk

LANGDON, John Bonsall. b 21. Linc Coll Ox BA51 MA55. Ripon Hall Ox 52. **d** 54 **p** 55. C Erith St Jo *Roch* 54-57; C Christchurch *Win* 57-60; Min Can Ripon Cathl 60-63; R Swillington 63-75; P-in-c Wrangthorn 75-76; V Leeds All Hallows w St Simon 75-76; V Leeds All Hallows w Wrangthorn 76-87; P-in-c Woodhouse St Mark 85-87; V Woodhouse and Wrangthorn 87-92; rtd 92; Perm to Offic *Ripon* from 92; Hon Min Can Ripon Cathl from 02. *32 Magdalen's Road, Ripon HG4 1HT* Tel (01765) 606814

LANGDON, Ms Susan Mary. b 48. RN69. Ripon Coll Cuddesdon 01. **d** 03 **p** 04. C Amesbury *Sarum* 03-06; Jt Ldr Pilgrimage Community of St Wite from 06. *St Wite House, Whitchurch Canonicorum, Bridport DT6 6RQ* Tel (01297) 489401 E-mail stwitehouse@btinternet.com

LANGDON-DAVIES, Mrs Stella Mary. b 44. Bris Univ BSc85 Nottm Univ MBA97. St Jo Coll Nottm MTh01. **d** 01 **p** 02. C Stamford All SS w St Jo *Linc* 01-04; V Herne *Cant* 04-06; P-in-c Saxonwell *Linc* 06-08; rtd 08. *5 Manor Paddock, Allington, Grantham NG32 2DL* Tel (01400) 281395 Mobile 07976-380659
E-mail stellalangdondavies@btinternet.com

LANGDOWN, Jennifer May. b 48. STETS 95. **d** 98 **p** 99. C S Petherton w the Seavingtons *B & W* 98-02; R Curry Rivel w Fivehead and Swell from 02. *The Rectory, Curry Rivel, Langport TA10 0HQ* Tel (01458) 251375

LANGE-SMITH, Michael Leslie. b 56. Bris Univ BSc83 Lon Bible Coll MA90. Trin Coll Bris 87. **d** 90 **p** 91. C Greendale Zimbabwe 91-92; R Melfort 93-98; Dir Th Educn by Ext Coll of Zimbabwe 99-02; R Chinnor, Sydenham, Aston Rowant and Crowell *Ox* 03-05; P-in-c Jersey Grouville *Win* 05-06; R from 06. *The Rectory, La Rue à Don, Grouville, Jersey JE3 9GB* Tel (01534) 853073

LANGFORD, Mrs Carol Mary. b 60. Southn Univ BTh93 MTh97 SS Mark & Jo Univ Coll Plymouth PGCE06. STETS 03. **d** 06 **p** 07. C Parkstone St Pet and St Osmund w Branksea *Sarum* 06-09; C Lilliput from 09; Chapl Talbot Heath Sch Bournemouth from 09. *The Vicarage, 55 Lilliput Road, Poole BH14 8JX* Tel (01202) 708567
E-mail carol.langford@tinyworld.co.uk

LANGFORD, David Laurence. b 51. **d** 88 **p** 89. OLM Scotton w Northorpe *Linc* from 88. *1 Westgate, Scotton, Gainsborough DN21 3QX* Tel (01724) 763139

LANGFORD, Prof Michael John. b 31. New Coll Ox BA54 MA58 Cam Univ MA59 Lon Univ PhD66. Westcott Ho Cam 55. **d** 56 **p** 57. C Bris St Nath w St Kath 56-59; Chapl Qu Coll Cam 59-63; C Hampstead St Jo *Lon* 63-67; Philosophy Dept Memorial Univ Newfoundland 67-96; Prof Philosophy 82-96; Prof Medical Ethics 87-96; rtd 96; Perm to Offic *Ely* from 96.

19 High Street, Dry Drayton, Cambridge CB23 8BS Tel (01954) 789593 E-mail ml297@hermes.cam.ac.uk

LANGFORD, Peter Francis. b 54. Sarum & Wells Th Coll 76. **d** 79 **p** 80. C N Ormesby *York* 79-82; Ind Chapl 83-91; V Middlesbrough St Chad 91-96; R Easington w Liverton 96-07; rtd 07. *19 York Road, Brotton, Saltburn-by-the-Sea TS12 2XF* Tel (01287) 678046 E-mail peterlan2@aol.com

LANGFORD, Peter Julian. b 33. Selw Coll Cam BA58. Westcott Ho Cam 59. **d** 60 **p** 61. C E Ham St Mary *Chelmsf* 60-67; Hon C 67-71; Hon C Beccles St Mich *St E* 71-76; Warden Ringsfield Hall Suffolk 71-87; P-in-c Ringsfield w Redisham *St E* 76-80; TV Seacroft *Ripon* 87-98; rtd 98; Perm to Offic *St E* from 99. *22 Alexander Road, Beccles NR34 9UD* Tel (01502) 710034

LANGHAM, Paul Jonathan. b 60. Ex Univ BA81 Fitzw Coll Cam BA86 MA91. Ridley Hall Cam 84. **d** 87 **p** 88. C Bath Weston All SS w N Stoke *B & W* 87-91; Chapl and Fell St Cath Coll Cam 91-96; V Combe Down w Monkton Combe and S Stoke *B & W* from 96; Examining Chapl from 04. *Church Office, Avenue Place, Combe Down, Bath BA2 5EE* Tel (01225) 835835 *or* 833152 E-mail vicar@htcd.co.uk

LANGILLE, Canon Melvin Owen. b 58. St Mary's Univ Halifax NS BA79. Atlantic Sch of Th MDiv82. **d** 82 **p** 83. Dn-in-c Falkland Canada 82; R Lockeport and Barrington 83-86; R French Village 87-90; R Cole Harbour St Andr 90-96; R Yarmouth H Trin 97-03; P-in-c Brora *Mor* from 03; P-in-c Dornoch from 03; Syn Clerk and Can St Andr Cathl Inverness from 07. *An t-Errain Beag, 42 Ross Street, Golspie, Sutherland KW10 6SA* Tel (01408) 633341 Mobile 07780-512990 E-mail mel@langille.freeserve.co.uk

LANGLEY, Ms Emma Louise. b 70. Bris Univ BA93 MA98. STETS 01. **d** 03 **p** 04. C Horfield H Trin *Bris* 03-07; P-in-c Westbury-on-Trym St Alb from 07; Min Westbury Park LEP from 07. *St Alban's Vicarage, 21 Canowie Road, Bristol BS6 7HR* Tel 0117-951 9771 Mobile 07974-658619 E-mail emmalang@aol.com

LANGLEY, Canon Myrtle Sarah. b 39. TCD BA61 HDipEd62 MA67 Bris Univ PhD76 Lon Univ BD66 FRAI. Dalton Ho Bris 64. **d** 88 **p** 94. Dir Chr Development for Miss *Liv* 87-89; Dir Dioc Tr Inst *Carl* 90-98; Dioc Dir of Tr 90-98; Hon Can Carl Cathl 91-98; P-in-c Long Marton w Dufton and w Milburn 98-06; rtd 06. *Grania, 9 St John's Close, Cotehill, Carlisle CA4 0ED* Tel (01228) 562679 E-mail canonmlangley@hotmail.com

LANGLEY, The Ven Robert. b 37. St Cath Soc Ox BA61. St Steph Ho Ox. **d** 63 **p** 64. C Aston cum Aughton *Sheff* 63-68; Midl Area Sec Chr Educn Movement 68-71; HQ Sec Chr Educn Movement 71-74; Prin Ian Ramsey Coll Brasted 74-77; Can Res St Alb and Dir St Alb Minl Tr Scheme 77-85; Can Res Newc Cathl 85-01; Dioc Missr 85-98; Dioc Dir of Min and Tr 98-01; Adn Lindisfarne 01-07; Local Min Development Officer 01-07; rtd 08; Perm to Offic *York* from 08. *Brook House, Middlewood Lane, Fylingthorpe, Whitby YO22 4TT* Tel (01947) 880355 E-mail kca85@dial.pipex.com

LANGMAN, Barry Edward. b 46. Master Mariner 73. Cant Sch of Min 87. **d** 90 **p** 91. NSM St Margarets-at-Cliffe w Westcliffe etc *Cant* 90-92; C Sandgate St Paul w Folkestone St Geo 92-95; P-in-c Headcorn 95-01; V 01-08; rtd 08; Perm to Offic *Cant* from 08. *19 Hazel Heights, Lodge Wood Drive, Ashford TN25 4GF* Tel (01233) 664199

LANGRELL, Gordon John. b 35. Cant Univ (NZ) BA58. Ridley Hall Cam 65. **d** 67 **p** 68. C Tonbridge SS Pet and Paul *Roch* 67-71; New Zealand from 71; rtd 05. *11A Henry Wigram Drive, Hornby, Christchurch 8042, New Zealand* Tel (0064) (3) 348 9554 E-mail gorlang@paradise.net.nz

✠**LANGRISH, The Rt Revd Michael Laurence.** b 46. Birm Univ BSocSc67 Fitzw Coll Cam BA73 MA77. Ridley Hall Cam 71. **d** 73 **p** 74 **c** 93. C Stratford-on-Avon w Bishopton *Cov* 73-76; Chapl Rugby Sch 76-81; P-in-c Offchurch *Cov* 81-87; Dioc Dir of Ords 81-87; P-in-c Rugby 87-91; Hon Can Cov Cathl 90-93; TR Rugby 91-93; Suff Bp Birkenhead *Ches* 93-00; Bp Ex from 00. *The Palace, Exeter EX1 1HY* Tel (01392) 272362 Fax 430923 E-mail bishop.of.exeter@exeter.anglican.org

✠**LANGSTAFF, The Rt Revd James Henry.** b 56. St Cath Coll Ox BA77 MA81 Nottm Univ BA80. St Jo Coll Nottm 78. **d** 81 **p** 82 **c** 04. C Farnborough *Guildf* 81-84 and 85-86; P-in-c 84-85; P-in-c Duddeston w Nechells *Birm* 86; V 87-96; RD Birm City 95-96; Bp's Dom Chapl 96-00; P-in-c Short Heath 98-00; R Sutton Coldfield H Trin 00-04; AD Sutton Coldfield 02-04; Suff Bp Lynn *Nor* from 04. *The Old Vicarage, Castle Acre, King's Lynn PE32 2AA* Tel (01760) 755553 Fax 755085 Mobile 07989-330582 E-mail bishoplynn@norwich.anglican.org

LANGSTON, Clinton Matthew. b 62. Derby Coll of Educn BCombStuds86. Qu Coll Birm 87. **d** 90 **p** 91. C Shirley *Birm* 90-94; CF from 94. *c/o MOD Chaplains (Army)* Tel (01980) 615804 Fax 615800

LANGTON, Robert. b 45. SAOMC 97. **d** 00 **p** 01. C Boyne Hill *Ox* 00-03; Chapl St Mich Hospice 03-08; TV Cwmbran *Mon* from 08. *The Vicarage, 87 Bryn Eglwys, Croesyceiliog, Cwmbran NP44 2LF* Tel (01633) 483945

LANHAM, Geoffrey Peter. b 62. Cam Univ MA84 Ox Univ MPhil86. Wycliffe Hall Ox 86. **d** 89 **p** 90. C Southborough St Pet w Ch Ch and St Matt *Roch* 89-92; C Harborne Heath *Birm* 92-00; C Birm St Paul 00-07; Deanery Missr 00-09; C Birm Cathl 07-09; V Selly Park Ch Ch from 09. *16 Over Mill Drive, Selly Oak, Birmingham B29 7JL* E-mail geoff@b1church.net

LANHAM, Richard Paul White. b 42. Dur Univ BA64. Wycliffe Hall Ox 65. **d** 67 **p** 68. C Gerrards Cross *Ox* 67-69; C Horwich H Trin *Man* 69-72; C Worsley 72-74; V Accrington St Andr *Blackb* 74-80; V Shillington *St Alb* 80-85; V Upper w Lower Gravenhurst 80-85; rtd 85; Perm to Offic *St Alb* from 85. *10 Alexander Close, Clifton, Shefford SG17 5RB* Tel (01462) 813520

LANKESTER, Mrs Jane Elizabeth. b 53. Qu Mary Coll Lon BScEcon74 SS Mark & Jo Univ Coll Plymouth MA04. SWMTC 05. **d** 08. NSM Totnes w Bridgetown, Berry Pomeroy etc *Ex* from 08. *Beeches, 4 Greenfield Drive, South Brent TQ10 9QF* Tel (01364) 72948 Mobile 07812-945622 E-mail jane@lankester.entadsl.com

LANKSHEAR, Jane Frances. *See* MAINWARING, Jane Frances

LANSDALE, Canon Charles Roderick. b 38. Leeds Univ BA59. Coll of Resurr Mirfield 59. **d** 61 **p** 62. C Nunhead St Antony *S'wark* 61-65; Swaziland 65-71; V Benhilton *S'wark* 72-78; TR Catford (Southend) and Downham 78-87; TR Moulsecoomb *Chich* 87-97; V Eastbourne St Mary 97-08; Can and Preb Chich Cathl 98-08; rtd 08; Perm to Offic *Chich* from 08. *102 Channel View Road, Eastbourne BN22 7LJ* Tel (01323) 646655

LANYON-HOGG, Mrs Anne Chester. b 49. St Anne's Coll Ox BA71 MA75 Worc Coll of Educn PGCE92. WEMTC 01. **d** 04 **p** 05. NSM Colwall w Upper Colwall and Coddington *Heref* from 04; NSM Malvern H Trin and St Jas *Worc* from 07. *7 Lockyear Close, Colwall, Malvern WR13 6NR* Tel (01684) 541979 Mobile 07890-995297 E-mail annelh@tiscali.co.uk

LANYON JONES, Keith. b 49. Southn Univ BTh79. Sarum & Wells Th Coll 74. **d** 77 **p** 78. C Charlton Kings St Mary *Glouc* 77-81; Sen Chapl Rugby Sch 81-99; Lic to Offic *Truro* 83-00; P-in-c St Cleer from 00; C St Ive and Pensilva w Quethiock from 02; Chapl Kelly Coll Tavistock from 08. *The Vicarage, St Cleer, Liskeard PL14 5DN* Tel (01579) 343240 E-mail lanyon67@hotmail.com

LAPAGE, Michael Clement. b 23. Selw Coll Cam BA47 MA73. Clifton Th Coll 60. **d** 61 **p** 62. C Weithaga Kenya 61-65; V Nanyuki 65-72; Chapl Bedford Sch 73-75; Chapl Lyon w Grenoble *Eur* 76-79; V Walford w Bishopswood *Heref* 79-88; P-in-c Goodrich w Welsh Bicknor and Marstow 83-88; rtd 88; Perm to Offic *Ex* from 88. *Moorlands, 20 Watts Road, Tavistock PL19 8LG* Tel (01822) 615901

LAPHAM, Canon Fred. b 31. Univ of Wales (Lamp) BA53 PhD00. Vancouver Sch of Th BA58. **d** 55 **p** 55. Canada 55-59; C Wallasey St Hilary *Ches* 59-62; V Over St Jo 62-70; V Upton Ascension 70-82; R Grappenhall 82-91; RD Gt Budworth 85-91; Hon Can Ches Cathl 88-91; rtd 91. *1 Coppice Gate, Lyth Hill, Shrewsbury SY3 0BT* Tel (01743) 872284

LAPWOOD, Robin Rowland John. b 57. Selw Coll Cam MA. Ridley Hall Cam 80. **d** 82 **p** 83. C Bury St Edmunds St Mary *St E* 82-86; P-in-c Bentley w Tattingstone 86-93; P-in-c Copdock w Washbrook and Belstead 86-93; TV High Wycombe *Ox* 93-96; P-in-c Marcham w Garford 96-02; Asst Master Summer Fields Sch Ox from 02. *Summer Fields School, Mayfield Road, Oxford OX2 7EN* Tel (01865) 454433 E-mail robin.lapwood@bigfoot.com

LARCOMBE, Paul Richard. b 57. Portsm Poly BSc79 CEng MIET. Trin Coll Bris 94. **d** 96 **p** 97. C Werrington *Pet* 96-98; C Longthorpe 98-00; V Pet St Paul 00-07; TR Worle *B & W* from 07. *The Vicarage, 93 Church Road, Worle, Weston-super-Mare BS22 9EA* Tel (01934) 510694

LARGE, William Roy. b 40. Dur Univ BA DipEd. Edin Th Coll 82. **d** 84 **p** 85. C Leamington Priors All SS *Cov* 84-88; V Bishop's Tachbrook 88-99; Warden of Readers and Sen Tutor 83-99; TV N Tyne and Redesdale *Newc* 99-01; TR 01-05; rtd 05. *4 Osborne Court, Osborne Avenue, Newcastle upon Tyne NE2 1LE* Tel 0191-281 1894

LARK, William Donald Starling. b 35. Keble Coll Ox BA59 MA63. Wells Th Coll 59. **d** 61 **p** 62. C Wyken *Cov* 61-64; C Christchurch *Win* 64-66; V Yeovil St Mich *B & W* 66-75; V Earley St Pet *Ox* 75-85; V Prittlewell *Chelmsf* 85-88; V Dawlish *Ex* 88-00; rtd 00; P-in-c Lanzarote *Eur* 00-05. *Las Alondras, 6 Cummings Court, Cummings Cross, Liverton, Newton Abbot TQ12 6HJ* Tel (01626) 824966 E-mail lanzalarks2000@yahoo.co.uk

LARKEY, Mrs Deborah Frances. b 63. Univ of Wales (Abth) BA85 Liv Inst of Educn PGCE90. **d** 98 **p** 99. OLM Toxteth St Cypr w Ch Ch *Liv* 98-01; OLM Edge Hill St Cypr w St Mary 01-04; V Toxteth 04-07; TV Pewsey and Swanborough *Sarum* from 07. *The Vicarage, Church Road, Woodborough, Pewsey SN9 5PH* Tel (01672) 851746 E-mail deborah.larkey@pewswan.org.uk

LARKIN, Andrew Brian. b 70. Warwick Univ BEng92 PhD95. Trin Coll Bris BA06. **d** 06 **p** 07. C Littleover *Derby* 06-08; C Brailsford w Shirley, Osmaston w Edlaston etc from 08. *Corner Cottage, Church Lane, Brailsford, Ashbourne DE6 3BX* Tel (01335) 360360 E-mail andy@larkin.me.uk

LARKIN, Mrs Karen Maria. b 74. Qu Coll Birm BA08. **d** 08 **p** 09. C Coleshill *Birm* from 08; C Maxstoke from 08. *52 Oakthorpe Drive, Birmingham B37 6HY* Tel 0121-694 4442 Mobile 07956-923653 E-mail karen_larkin@hotmail.co.uk

LARKIN, Canon Peter John. b 39. BSc62. **d** 62 **p** 63. C Liskeard w St Keyne *Truro* 62-65; C Rugby St Andr *Cov* 65-67; Sec Bp Cov Call to Miss 67-68; V Kea *Truro* 68-78; P-in-c Bromsgrove St Jo *Worc* 78-81; R Torquay St Matthias, St Mark and H Trin *Ex* 81-97; Can Sokoto Nigeria 91-98; Can Kaduna from 98; TR Plymouth Em, St Paul Efford and St Aug *Ex* 97-00; rtd 00; Perm to Offic *Ex* from 00. *Picklecombe, 57 Babbacombe Downs Road, Torquay TQ1 3LP* Tel (01803) 326888 E-mail larkin@petermolly.freeserve.co.uk

LARKIN, Simon George David. b 69. Birm Univ BSocSc90 PGCE91 Reading Univ MA96. Trin Coll Bris BTh09. **d** 09. C Kensington St Barn *Lon* from 09. *17 Devonport Road, London W12 8NZ* Tel 07954-600258 (mobile) E-mail me@sarahsi.com

LARLEE, David Alexander. b 78. Univ of W Ontario MA01. Wycliffe Hall Ox BTh04. **d** 04 **p** 05. NSM Battersea Rise St Mark *S'wark* from 04. *24 Parma Crescent, London SW11 1LT* Tel (020) 7326 9426 *or* 7223 6188 E-mail david_larlee@yahoo.com

LARNER, Gordon Edward Stanley. b 30. Brasted Th Coll 54 Oak Hill Th Coll 55. **d** 59 **p** 60. C Peckham St Mary Magd *S'wark* 59-62; C Luton w E Hyde *St Alb* 62-68; V Lower Sydenham St Mich *S'wark* 68-73; Ind Chapl 73-84; Chapl HM Pris Ranby 84-92; rtd 92. *Glen Rosa, Meshaw, South Molton EX36 4NE*

LARSEN, Clive Erik. b 55. St Jo Coll Nottm 88. **d** 90 **p** 91. C Weaverham *Ches* 90-92; C Alvanley and Helsby and Dunham-on-the-Hill 92-95; P-in-c Cheadle Heath 95-02; P-in-c N Reddish *Man* from 05. *The Rectory, 551 Gorton Road, Stockport SK5 6NX* Tel 0161-223 0692 Mobile 07789-915263 E-mail clive.larsen@ntlworld.com

LASHBROOKE, David. b 60. Ex Univ BA87. Ripon Coll Cuddesdon 90. **d** 92 **p** 93. C Sherborne w Castleton and Lillington *Sarum* 92-95; P-in-c Weymouth St Paul 95-99; V 99-02; V St Marychurch *Ex* from 02. *The Vicarage, Hampton Avenue, Torquay TQ1 3LA* Tel (01803) 329054 *or* 327661 E-mail frdavid@wdi.co.uk

LASKEY, Cyril Edward. b 44. RMN71 RGN74. Llan Dioc Tr Scheme 85. **d** 88 **p** 89. NSM Troedrhiwgarth *Llan* 88-93; NSM Caerau St Cynfelin 94-01; P-in-c Glyncorrwg and Upper Afan Valley from 01. *207 Bridgend Road, Maesteg CF34 0NL* Tel (01656) 734639

LASKEY, Stephen Allan. b 56. Manitoba Univ BA85. St Jo Coll Winnipeg MDiv88. **d** 89 **p** 89. C Labrador W Canada 89; C Battle Harbour 89-91; R 91-96; R Goulds St Paul 96-99; Assoc P Foxtrap All SS 00-01; C Paddington St Jo w St Mich *Lon* 01-02; P-in-c Sydenham H Trin *S'wark* 02-07; P-in-c Forest Hill St Aug 03-07; V Sydenham H Trin and St Aug from 07. *Holy Trinity Vicarage, 1 Sydenham Park Road, London SE26 4DY* Tel (020) 8699 5303 E-mail stephenlaskey@onetel.com

LASLETT, Christopher John. b 42. Leeds Univ BA64 Lon Univ PGCE73. Lich Th Coll 64. **d** 66 **p** 67. C Bradf St Clem 66-69; C Upper Armley *Ripon* 69-70; Perm to Offic *Dur* 71-72; Hon C Stranton 79-81; Perm to Offic *Ripon* 87-88; rtd 07. *1 Locksley Grange, 74 St Marychurch Road, Torquay TQ1 3HX* Tel (01803) 310613 E-mail mfl@ntlworld.com

LAST, Eric Cyril. b 30. Oak Hill Th Coll 77. **d** 79 **p** 80. C Wandsworth All SS *S'wark* 79-83; V Earlsfield St Andr 83-88; V S Merstham 88-96; Asst RD Reigate 92-96; rtd 96; Hon C Upper Tean *Lich* from 96. *29 Vicarage Road, Tean, Stoke-on-Trent ST10 4LE* Tel and fax (01538) 723551 E-mail eric.last1@btopenworld.com

LAST, Harold Wilfred. b 17. ARCM52 ARCO53 CCC Cam BA38 MA42. Linc Th Coll 39. **d** 40 **p** 41. C Bolton St Jas *Bradf* 40-44; C Woodbridge St Mary *St E* 44-45; Lect K Coll Lon 45-53; Dir of Music St Bees, St Olave's & Felstead Schs 53-73; rtd 73. *Flat 1, Knapton House, North Walsham Road, Knapton, North Walsham NR28 0RT* Tel (01263) 720084

LAST, Michael Leonard Eric. b 60. St Jo Coll Nottm 92. **d** 94 **p** 95. C Tettenhall Wood *Lich* 94-98; V Pelsall 98-02; V Alton w Bradley-le-Moors and Oakamoor w Cotton 02-09; P-in-c Mayfield and Denstone w Ellastone and Stanton 06-09; I Saskatchewan Gateway Canada from 09. *St Alban's Church, PO Box 604, Moosomin SK S0G 3N0, Canada* Tel (001) (306) 435 3003 Fax 435 2717 E-mail michael.l.e.last@btinternet.com

LAST, Norman Percy George. b 31. BA CertEd. Sarum & Wells Th Coll 77 Wycliffe Hall Ox 80. **d** 81 **p** 82. C Walton-on-Thames *Guildf* 81-83; C Farnham 83-87; R Monks Eleigh w Chelsworth and Brent Eleigh etc *St E* 87-90; P-in-c Bradworthy *Ex* 91-97; rtd 97; Perm to Offic *Ex* from 98; C Stansted *Chich* 00-02. *9 Wensley Gardens, Emsworth PO10 7RA* Tel (01243) 374174

LATHAM, Christine Elizabeth. b 46. S'wark Ord Course 87. **d** 90 **p** 94. Par Dn Battersea St Pet and St Paul *S'wark* 90-94; Par Dn S'wark Ch Ch 94; C 94-97; C Merstham and Gatton 97-05; Chapl E Surrey Learning Disability NHS Trust 97-05; Chapl R Marsden NHS Foundn Trust from 05. *46 Myrtle Road, Sutton SM1 4BX* Tel (020) 8395 4701

LATHAM, Henry Nicholas Lomax. b 64. Reading Univ BA86. Wycliffe Hall Ox BTh93. **d** 93 **p** 94. C Aberystwyth *St D* 93-99; P-in-c Stoke Poges *Ox* 99-08; V from 08. *The Vicarage, Park Road, Stoke Poges, Slough SL2 4PE* Tel (01753) 642261 E-mail harryandtracy@isaiah61.freeserve.co.uk

LATHAM, John Montgomery. b 37. Univ of NZ BA Cam Univ MA Cant Univ (NZ) MEd. Westcott Ho Cam 60. **d** 62 **p** 63. C Camberwell St Geo *S'wark* 62-65; Chapl Trin Coll Cam 65-70; Chapl Wanganui Colleg Sch New Zealand 71-79; Min Enabler N New Brighton 96-01; V Christchurch St Luke 98-02; rtd 02. *43 Rugby Street, Christchurch 8014, New Zealand* Tel (0064) (3) 355 6654 Fax 355 6658 E-mail latham@xtra.co.nz

LATHAM, John Westwood. b 31. Ely Th Coll 57. **d** 60 **p** 61. C Cleckheaton St Jo *Wakef* 60-63; C Hemel Hempstead *St Alb* 63-65; C Wakef Cathl 65-67; V Outwood 67-72; TV Daventry w Norton *Pet* 72-79; V Flore w Dodford and Brockhall 79-96; rtd 96; Perm to Offic *Leic* from 97. *53 Lubenham Hill, Market Harborough LE16 9DG* Tel (01858) 469023

LATHAM, Robert Norman. b 53. Qu Coll Birm 82. **d** 85 **p** 86. C Tamworth *Lich* 85-89; TV Wordsley 89-96; P-in-c Hallow *Worc* 96-97; R Hallow and Grimley w Holt from 97. *Hallow Vicarage, 26 Baveney Road, Worcester WR2 6DS* Tel (01905) 748711 E-mail robert@hallowvicarage.freeserve.co.uk

LATHAM, Roger Allonby. b 69. Leic Univ BA90 Warwick Univ MA92 Leeds Univ PGCE93 Nottm Univ PhD07. St Jo Coll Nottm BTh98. **d** 99 **p** 00. C Paston *Pet* 99-02; TV Cartmel Peninsula *Carl* from 02; Officer for IME 4-7 from 08; Vice-Prin LCTP from 09. *The Vicarage, Boarbank Lane, Allithwaite, Grange-over-Sands LA11 7QR* Tel (01539) 532437 E-mail lathams@home71.swinternet.co.uk

LATHAM (*née* WEBSTER), Mrs Rosamond Mary. b 54. Coll of Ripon & York St Jo BEd90 MA00. Westcott Ho Cam 00. **d** 02 **p** 03. C Frodingham *Linc* 02-05; TV Dur N 05-07; TV Dorchester *Ox* from 07. *The Vicarage, Cherwell Road, Berinsfield, Wallingford OX10 7PB* Tel (01865) 340460 Mobile 07779-784320 E-mail bbdparishoffice@googlemail.com

LATHAM, Trevor Martin. b 56. BD84. Ripon Coll Cuddesdon 84. **d** 86 **p** 87. C Cantril Farm *Liv* 86-89; TV Croxteth Park 89-98; V 98-99; TR Walton-on-the-Hill from 99. *The Rectory, Walton Village, Liverpool L4 6TJ* Tel and fax 0151-525 3130 E-mail trevor.latham@talktalk.net

LATHE, Canon Anthony Charles Hudson. b 36. Jes Coll Ox BA59 MA64. Lich Th Coll 59. **d** 61 **p** 62. C Selby Abbey *York* 61-63; V Hempnall *Nor* 63-72; R Woodton w Bedingham 63-72; R Fritton w Morningthorpe w Shelton and Hardwick 63-72; R Topcroft 63-72; R Banham 72-76; TR Quidenham 76-83; P-in-c New Buckenham 78-79; V Heigham St Thos 83-94; Hon Can Nor Cathl 87-99; RD Nor S 90-94; P-in-c Sheringham 94-99; rtd 99; Perm to Offic *Nor* 99-06. *15A Kingsdale Road, Berkhamsted HP4 3BS* Tel (01442) 863115

LATIFA, Andrew Murdoch. b 73. Univ of Wales (Abth) BTh96 Univ of Wales (Cardiff) MTh00. St Mich Coll Llan 99. **d** 01 **p** 02. C Betws w Ammanford *St D* 01-03; C Llangynwyd w Maesteg 03-05; CF from 05. *c/o MOD Chaplains (Army)* Tel (01980) 615804 Fax 615800

LATIMER, Clifford James. b 45. City Univ BSc68. **d** 99 **p** 00. OLM Burntwood *Lich* from 99. *24 Dove Close, Burntwood WS7 9JL* Tel (01543) 671471 E-mail cliff.latimer@btinternet.com

LATTEY, Susan. See CUMMING-LATTEY, Mrs Susan Mary Ruth

LATTIMORE, Anthony Leigh. b 35. Dur Univ BA57. Lich Th Coll 60. **d** 62 **p** 63. C Aylestone *Leic* 62-66; C-in-c Eyres Monsell CD 66-69; V Eyres Monsell 69-73; V Somerby, Burrough on the Hill and Pickwell 73-86; RD Goscote I 80-86; R Glenfield 86-95; rtd 95; Perm to Offic *Leic* and *Pet* from 95. *28 Elizabeth Way, Uppingham, Oakham LE15 9PQ* Tel (01572) 823193

LATTY, Howard James. b 54. SRCh71. WEMTC 98. **d** 01 **p** 02. NSM Bath St Mich w St Paul *B & W* 01-08; NSM Chewton Mendip w Ston Easton, Litton etc from 08. *The Rectory, Lower Street, Chewton Mendip, Radstock BA3 4GP* Tel (01761) 241189 E-mail howard.latty@yahoo.co.uk

LAU, Paul Chow Sing. b 49. Nat Chengchi Univ BA74 Chinese Univ of Hong Kong MDiv80. **d** 80 **p** 81. Hong Kong 80-82 and 83-94; C Hong Kong H Trin 80-82; Macao 82-83; V Macao St Mark 82-83; P-in-c Hong Kong Ch of Our Sav 83-94; New Zealand 94-01; V Ang Chinese Miss Ch *Wellington* 94-01; Chapl Chinese Congregation *Lon* from 01. *3 Strutton Court, 54 Great Peter Street, London SW1P 2HH* Tel (020) 7233 4027 *or* 7766 1106 E-mail paul.lau@smitf.org

LAUCKNER, Averil Ann. b 55. Lanc Univ BSc76. Ripon Coll Cuddesdon 03. **d** 04 **p** 05. C Royston *St Alb* 04-07; C Lich St Mich w St Mary and Wall 07-09; C Lich Ch Ch 07-09; P-in-c

from 09. *Christ Church Vicarage, 95 Christ Church Lane, Lichfield WS13 8AL* Tel (01543) 410751
E-mail averil.lauckner@btinternet.com

LAUGHTON, Derek Basil. b 24. Worc Coll Ox BA49 MA52. Westcott Ho Cam 49. **d** 51 **p** 52. C Wareham w Arne *Sarum* 51-53; CF 53-56; C Hemel Hempstead St Mary *St Alb* 56-59; V Stretton cum Wetmoor *Lich* 59-64; Chapl Wellington Sch Somerset 64-73; Chapl Ardingly Coll 73-77; R Plumpton w E Chiltington *Chich* 77-88; Perm to Offic *B & W* from 88; rtd 89. *13 Pyles Thorne Road, Wellington TA21 8DX* Tel (01823) 667386

LAURENCE, Brother. *See* EYERS, Frederick Thomas Laurence

LAURENCE, The Ven John Harvard Christopher. b 29. Trin Hall Cam BA53 MA57. Westcott Ho Cam 53. **d** 55 **p** 56. C Linc St Nic w St Jo Newport 55-59; V Crosby 59-74; Can and Preb Linc Cathl 74-79 and 85-94; Dioc Missr 74-79; Bp's Dir of Clergy Tr *Lon* 80-85; Adn Lindsey *Linc* 85-94; rtd 94; Perm to Offic *Linc* 94-97. *5 Haffenden Road, Lincoln LN2 1RP* Tel (01522) 531444

LAURENCE, Julian Bernard Vere. b 60. Kent Univ BA82. St Steph Ho Ox 86. **d** 88 **p** 89. C Yeovil St Mich *B & W* 88-91; Chapl Yeovil Coll 90-91; Chapl Yeovil Distr Gen Hosp 91; P-in-c Barwick *B & W* 91-94; V Taunton H Trin from 94. *Holy Trinity Vicarage, 18 Holway Avenue, Taunton TA1 3AR* Tel (01823) 337890 E-mail jlaurence@htvicarage.fsnet.co.uk

LAURIE, Canon Donovan Hugh. b 40. Man Univ MSc. Oak Hill NSM Course. **d** 82 **p** 83. NSM Cudham and Downe *Roch* 82-84; C Tunbridge Wells St Jas 84-88; P-in-c Ventnor St Cath *Portsm* 88-99; V 99-04; P-in-c Ventnor H Trin 88-99; V 99-04; P-in-c Bonchurch 00-03; R 03-04; Hon Chapl St Cath Sch Ventnor 88-04; Hon Can Portsm Cathl from 01; rtd 04. *24 Cleveland, Tunbridge Wells TN2 3NF* Tel (01892) 539951
E-mail don@dlaurie.fsbusiness.co.uk

LAUT, Graham Peter. b 37. Chich Th Coll 63. **d** 67 **p** 68. C Corringham *Chelmsf* 67-68; C Leytonstone St Marg w St Columba 68-71; P-in-c Leytonstone St Andr 71-75; V 75-80; V Romford Ascension Collier Row 80-06; rtd 06; Perm to Offic *Chelmsf* from 07. *11 Archers Close, Billericay CM12 9YF* Tel (01277) 630395 E-mail glaut10497@aol.com

LAUTENBACH, Edward Wayne. b 59. Univ Coll Ches BTh04. St Paul's Coll Grahamstown 85. **d** 88 **p** 88. C Weltevredenpark St Mich S Africa 88-89; Asst P Florida St Gabr 89-91; Sen Asst P Bryanston St Mich 91-94; R Bryanston St Pet 94-99; P-in-c Grange St Andr *Ches* 99-04; P-in-c Runcorn H Trin 99-04; V Prenton from 04. *The Vicarage, 1 Vicarage Close, Birkenhead CH42 8QX* Tel 0151-608 1808
E-mail waynelautenbach@sky.com

LAUTENBACH, Mrs Glynnis Valerie. b 59. Leeds Univ BA08. NOC 05. **d** 08 **p** 09. C Oxton *Ches* from 08. *The Vicarage, 1 Vicarage Close, Birkenhead CH42 8QX*
E-mail glynn.laut@sky.com

LAVERACK, John Justin. b 51. Keele Univ BA CertEd Bris Univ BA. Bris Bapt Coll 76 Ex & Truro NSM Scheme 81. **d** 82 **p** 83. In Bapt Ch 79-81; C Braunton *Ex* 82-84; V Ex St Mark 84-92; Perm to Offic 92-98. *Tynewydd, Cwm Rhyd, Blaenwaun, Whitland SA34 0DB* Tel (01994) 419731
E-mail laverack@connect-wales.co.uk

LAVERTY, Canon Walter Joseph Robert. b 49. CITC 70 Glouc Th Course 73. **d** 73 **p** 74. C Belfast St Donard *D & D* 73-77; C Ballymacarrett St Patr 77-82; I Kilwarlin Upper w Kilwarlin Lower 82-86; I Orangefield w Moneyreagh from 86; Warden of Readers from 96; Can Down Cathl 97-00; Preb 97-00; Treas from 01. *The Rectory, 397 Castlereagh Road, Belfast BT5 6AB* Tel and fax (028) 9070 4493

LAVERY, Edward Robinson. Lon Univ BA. St Aid Birkenhead 65. **d** 67 **p** 68. C Belfast Trin Coll Miss *Conn* 67-69; C Belfast St Mary Magd 69-71; CF (TA) 70-95; OCF from 75; I Belfast St Phil *Conn* 71-74; I Craigs w Dunaghy and Killagan 74-83; I Ballymoney w Finvoy and Rasharkin 83-05; Dioc Info Officer 83-05; Can Conn Cathl 96-05; Treas 98-01; Chan 01-05; rtd 05; P-in-c Ballyscullion *D & R* from 09. *11 Drumnamallaght Park, Ballymoney BT53 7QZ* Tel (028) 2766 9147

LAW, Andrew Philip. b 61. BNC Ox BA83 MA93 G&C Coll Cam PGCE86 Leic Univ MBA04. WEMTC 90. **d** 93 **p** 94. C Tupsley w Hampton Bishop *Heref* 93-95; Chapl Heref Sixth Form Coll 94-95; Chapl City of Lon Freemen's Sch 95-97; Lic to Offic *Guildf* 95-97; Chapl and Hd RS Heref Cathl Sch 97-02; Chapl Malvern Coll from 02; Ho Master 05-07; Perm to Offic *Heref* from 02. *The Chaplain's House, College Road, Malvern WR14 3DD* Tel (01684) 581540 Fax 581617
E-mail apl@malcol.org

LAW, David Richard. b 60. **d** 01 **p** 02. NSM Ashton-upon-Mersey St Martin *Ches* from 01. *2 Winston Close, Sale M33 6UG* Tel 0161-962 0297

LAW, Mrs Elizabeth Ann. b 49. Doncaster Coll of Educn CertEd70 Loughb Univ MA01. EAMTC 99. **d** 01 **p** 02. C Wickham Bishops w Lt Braxted *Chelmsf* 01-05; P-in-c Rattlesden w Thorpe Morieux, Brettenham etc *St E* 05-08; R from 08; Asst Dioc Dir of Ords from 08. *The Rectory, High Street, Rattlesden, Bury St Edmunds IP30 0RA* Tel (01449) 737993 E-mail rev.liz@btinternet.com

LAW, Gordon Peter. b 35. Bernard Gilpin Soc Dur 59 Chich Th Coll 60. **d** 64 **p** 65. C Walthamstow St Barn and St Jas Gt *Chelmsf* 64-67; C Southchurch H Trin 67-68; C Plaistow St Andr 68-69; Chapl Aldersbrook Medical Unit 69-83; P-in-c Forest Gate All SS 69-74; V 74-83; V Romford St Jo 83-97; rtd 97; Perm to Offic *Chelmsf* from 97. *40 Molram's Lane, Great Baddow, Chelmsford CM2 7AH* Tel (01245) 477272

LAW, Jeremy Stuart Alan. b 67. RMN93 Man Metrop Univ BSc96. Westcott Ho Cam. **d** 00 **p** 01. C Newton Heath *Man* 00-01; C Wythenshawe 01-04; P-in-c Lawton Moor 04-07; Chapl Cen Man/Man Children's Univ Hosp NHS Trust from 07. *Manchester Royal Infirmary, Cobbett House, Oxford Road, Manchester M13 9WL* Tel 0161-276 1234
E-mail jeremylaw@ntlworld.com

LAW, Jeremy Thomson. b 61. Univ of Wales (Abth) BSc82 Southn Univ BTh89 Ox Univ DPhil00. **d** 87 **p** 88. C Wimborne Minster and Holt *Sarum* 87-90; C Highfield *Ox* 90-94; Chapl Ex Univ 94-03; Dean of Chpl Cant Ch Ch Univ from 03. *Canterbury Christ Church University College, North Holmes Road, Canterbury CT1 1QU* Tel (01227) 767700
E-mail jl89@cant.ac.uk

LAW, John Francis. b 35. Bps' Coll Cheshunt 65. **d** 67 **p** 68. C Styvechale *Cov* 67-71; P-in-c Cov St Anne and All SS 71-73; TV Cov E 73-77; P-in-c Fillongley 77-82; P-in-c Corley 77-82; V Fillongley and Corley 82-00; RD Nuneaton 90-95; rtd 00; Perm to Offic *Cov* from 00. *10 Brodick Way, Nuneaton CV10 7LH* Tel (024) 7632 5582

LAW, Canon John Michael. b 43. Open Univ BA79. Westcott Ho Cam 65. **d** 68 **p** 69. C Chapel Allerton *Ripon* 68-72; C Ryhope *Dur* 72-73; Mental Health Chapl Fulbourn Hosp Cam 74-04; Chapl Ida Darwin Hosp Cam 74-96; Hon Can Ely Cathl 04-05; rtd 04; PV Ely Cathl from 06; Perm to Offic from 08. *2 Suffolk Close, Ely CB6 3EW* Tel (01353) 659084

LAW, Nicholas Charles. b 58. Trin Coll Bris BA89. **d** 89 **p** 90. C Goldington *St Alb* 89-92; C Teignmouth, Ideford w Luton, Ashcombe etc *Ex* 92-97; R Bere Ferrers from 97. *The Rectory, Bere Alston, Yelverton PL20 7HH* Tel (01822) 840229
E-mail nicklaw@breathemail.net

LAW, Peter James. b 46. Ridley Hall Cam 85. **d** 87 **p** 88. C Bournemouth St Jo w St Mich *Win* 87-91; V Chineham 91-96; V Luton Lewsey St Hugh *St Alb* from 96. *St Hugh's Vicarage, 367 Leagrave High Street, Luton LU4 0ND* Tel (01582) 605297 *or* 664433 Fax 472726 E-mail sth367@btinternet.com *or* admin@sthughslewsey.fsnet.co.uk

LAW, Richard Anthony Kelway. b 57. UWIST BEng79. St Jo Coll Nottm MA(TS)01 99. **d** 01 **p** 02. C Brundall w Braydeston and Postwick *Nor* 01-04; V Hollingworth w Tintwistle *Ches* from 04. *The Vicarage, 10 Church Street, Tintwistle, Glossop SK13 1JR* Tel (01457) 852575 E-mail richardaklaw@tiscali.co.uk

LAW, Richard Lindsey. b 34. Univ Coll Ox BA58 MA63 St Pet Coll Birm DipEd70. Cuddesdon Coll 58. **d** 60 **p** 61. C Leighton Buzzard *St Alb* 60-63; Trinidad and Tobago 63-67; V Stottesdon *Heref* 67-72; P-in-c Farlow 67-72; Chapl Framlingham Coll 72-83; V Leigh-on-Sea St Marg *Chelmsf* 83-91; Warden Framlingham Ho of Prayer and Retreat 91-94; rtd 96. *19 Durns Road, Wotton-under-Edge GL12 7JD*

LAW, Canon Robert Frederick. b 43. St Aid Birkenhead 67. **d** 69 **p** 70. C Bengeo *St Alb* 69-72; C Sandy 72-76; P-in-c St Ippolyts 76-81; Chapl Jersey Gp of Hosps 81-84; V Crowan w Godolphin *Truro* 84-92; RD Kerrier 90-91; R St Columb Major w St Wenn 92-02; RD Pydar 95-02; P-in-c St Minver 02-05; Hon Can Truro Cathl 98-05; rtd 05; Perm to Offic *York* from 07. *Iona, 3 Vale Cottages, Stillington, York YO61 1LA* Tel (01347) 810754 Mobile 07842-111525 E-mail robfwa-2@tiscali.co.uk

LAW, Robert James. b 31. Lon Univ MB, BS55. Ridley Hall Cam 62. **d** 64 **p** 65. C Barnehurst *Roch* 64-66; C Edgware *Lon* 66-72; V Halwell w Moreleigh *Ex* 72-94; P-in-c Woodleigh and Loddiswell 76-79; R 79-94; rtd 94. *38 Wheatlands Road, Paignton TQ4 5HU* Tel (01803) 559450

LAW, Simon Anthony. b 55. Middx Univ BA93. NTMTC 94. **d** 96 **p** 97. NSM Forest Gate St Mark *Chelmsf* 96-98; C Becontree W 98-99; TV 99-02; TR 02-07; V Becontree St Cedd from 07. *St Cedd's Vicarage, 185 Lodge Avenue, Dagenham RM8 2HQ* Tel (020) 8592 5900 E-mail simon@revlaw.co.uk

LAW-JONES, Peter Deniston. b 55. Newc Univ BA77 Man Univ PGCE81 Nottm Univ BTh87 Lanc Univ MA03. Linc Th Coll 84. **d** 87 **p** 88. C Chorley St Laur *Blackb* 87-91; V Feniscliffe 91-96; V St Annes St Thos from 96; Chapl Blackpool, Wyre and Fylde Community NHS Trust 97-04. *The Vicarage, St Thomas Road, Lytham St Annes FY8 1JL* Tel (01253) 723750
E-mail peter@law-jones.fsnet.co.uk

LAWAL, Miss Basirat Adebanke Amope (Ade). b 67. Lon Bible Coll BTh02. SAOMC 03. **d** 05 **p** 06. C Blurton *Lich* 05-09; V Wyther *Ripon* from 09. *Wyther Vicarage, Houghley Lane, Leeds LS13 4AU* Tel 0113-279 8014 E-mail rev.chick@hotmail.co.uk

LAWES, David Alan. b 33. Lon Bible Coll BD57 PGCE58 Lon Inst of Educn MA70. Cranmer Hall Dur 90. **d** 91 **p** 92. NSM

Shaston *Sarum* 91-94; Hon C Diptford, N Huish, Harberton and Harbertonford *Ex* 94-98; rtd 98; Perm to Offic *Sarum* 98-07. *47 Grosvenor Road, Shaftesbury SP7 8DP* Tel (01747) 855621

LAWES, Geoffrey Hyland. b 37. St Jo Coll Dur BA58 Hertf Coll Ox BA60 MA64 Newc Univ PGCE76 MEd79. Cranmer Hall Dur 61. **d** 63 **p** 64. C Millfield St Mark *Dur* 63-66; C Jarrow Grange 66-69; Hon C 69-86; Lic to Offic 86-90; V Collierley w Annfield Plain 90-05; rtd 05; Hon C Satley, Stanley and Tow Law *Dur* from 05. *Netherwood, St Mary's Avenue, Crook DL15 9HY* Tel (01388) 766585

LAWES, Stephen George. b 40. Nottm Univ PGCE75. St Jo Coll Nottm BTh74. **d** 82 **p** 83. NSM Hillmorton *Cov* 82-86; NSM Daventry Deanery *Pet* 87-03. *Irrisfree, Barleyfield, Kilbrittain, Co Cork, Republic of Ireland*

LAWES, Timothy Stanley. b 57. Nottm Univ BTh88. Linc Th Coll 85. **d** 88 **p** 89. C Wymondham *Nor* 88-92; R Felmingham, Skeyton, Colby, Banningham etc 92-96; Sweden from 96; Asst V Byske 98-09. *Address temp unknown*

LAWLESS, Mrs Patricia Elizabeth. b 36. Bris Univ BA58 PGCE59. S Dios Minl Tr Scheme 91. **d** 93 **p** 94. NSM Frome Ch Ch *B & W* 93-95; NSM Mells w Buckland Dinham, Elm, Whatley etc 96; NSM Frome St Jo and St Mary 96-00; Chapl Victoria Hosp Frome 96-98; rtd 00; Perm to Offic *B & W* from 00. *22 Braithwaite Way, Frome BA11 2XG* Tel (01373) 466106

LAWLEY, Peter Gerald Fitch. b 52. Chich Th Coll 77. **d** 80 **p** 81. C Pet St Jo 80-83; C Daventry 83-87; P-in-c Syresham w Whitfield 87-90; TV Cen Telford *Lich* 90-98; V Priors Lee and St Georges from 98. *The Vicarage, Ashley Road, Telford TF2 9LF* Tel and fax (01952) 612923 E-mail peterlawley@talktalk.net

LAWLEY, Rosemary Ann. b 47. WMMTC 00. **d** 03 **p** 04. NSM Kinver and Enville *Lich* 03-07; TV Kidderminster St Mary and All SS w Trimpley etc *Worc* from 07; Ind Chapl from 07. *186 Birmingham Road, Kidderminster, Worcester DY10 2SJ* Tel (01562) 748274 E-mail rosemarylawley@tiscali.co.uk

LAWLOR, Colin Robert. b 63. Lanc Univ BA89 MPhil97 St Martin's Coll Lanc PGCE90. Chich Th Coll 90. **d** 93 **p** 94. C Moulsecoomb *Chich* 93-97; TV 97-99; Chapl Brighton Univ from 99. *204 Bevendean Crescent, Brighton BN2 4RD* Tel 07733-225263 (mobile) E-mail c.r.lawlor@bton.ac.uk

LAWLOR, Paul. b 60. Nottm Univ BSc82. St Jo Coll Nottm 06. **d** 08 **p** 09. C Warsop *S'well* from 08. *19 Wood Street, Warsop NG20 0AX* Tel (01623) 844517 Mobile 07807-611090 E-mail paul@pjlawlor.me.uk

LAWRANCE, Hugh Norcliffe. b 49. N Riding Coll of Educn BEd79. Linc Th Coll 83. **d** 85 **p** 86. C Lindley *Wakef* 85-87; C Barkisland w W Scammonden 87-92; C Ripponden 87-92; C Knottingley 92-98; C Thorp Arch w Walton *York* 98-00; C Boston Spa 98-00; C Clifford 98-00; P-in-c Bramham and Clifford 00-08; C Whitby w Ruswarp from 08. *17 Upgang Lane, Whitby YO21 3DT* E-mail frhugh@norcliffe.com

LAWRANCE, Robert William. b 63. Jes Coll Ox BA85 MA89 Man Univ MA93. Ripon Coll Cuddesdon BA87. **d** 88 **p** 89. C Astley *Man* 88-91; Lect Bolton St Pet 91-94; V Bury St Jo w St Mark 94-00; Chapl Bury Healthcare NHS Trust 95-00; Dir of Ords *Dur* 00-08; Chapl Hatf Coll Dur 00-05; Chapl Collingwood Coll Dur 05-08; TR Dur N from 08. *St Cuthbert's Vicarage, 1 Aykley Court, Durham DH1 4NW* Tel 0191-386 0146

LAWRENCE, Charles Anthony Edwin. b 53. AKC75. St Aug Coll Cant 75. **d** 76 **p** 77. C Mitcham St Mark *S'wark* 76-80; C Haslemere *Guildf* 80-82; P-in-c Ashton H Trin *Man* 82-84; V 84-93; AD Ashton-under-Lyne 91-93; V Saddleworth 93-97; V Effingham w Lt Bookham *Guildf* 97-05; Chapl Manor Ho Sch 97-05; R Shere, Albury and Chilworth *Guildf* from 05. *The Rectory, The Spinning Walk, Shere, Guildford GU5 9HN* Tel and fax (01483) 202394 E-mail fathercharles@hotmail.co.uk

LAWRENCE, Christopher David. b 55. Wycliffe Hall Ox 01. **d** 03 **p** 04. C Wadhurst *Chich* 03-07; C Tidebrook 03-07; C Stonegate 03-07; P-in-c Framfield from 07. *The Vicarage, Brookhouse Lane, Framfield, Uckfield TN22 5NH* Tel (01825) 890365 Mobile 07941-557537 E-mail cdsjlawrence@tiscali.co.uk

LAWRENCE, Christopher David. b 73. Liv Jo Moores Univ BEd98. Ridley Hall Cam 03. **d** 05 **p** 06. C Letchworth St Paul w Willian *St Alb* 05-08; Chapl RAF from 08. *Chaplaincy Services, Valiant Block, HQ Air Command, RAF High Wycombe HP14 4UE* Tel (01494) 496800 Fax 496343 E-mail revchrislawrence@yahoo.co.uk

LAWRENCE, Canon David Ian. b 48. Univ Coll Lon BSc74 AIMLS71 MIBiol76. Glouc Sch of Min 84 Sarum & Wells Th Coll 87. **d** 88 **p** 89. C Wotton St Mary *Glouc* 88-91; P-in-c Cheltenham St Mich 91-93; V 93-06; V Coleford, Staunton, Newland, Redbrook etc from 06; Hon Can Glouc Cathl from 06. *The Vicarage, 40 Boxbush Road, Coleford GL16 8DN* Tel (01594) 833379 E-mail dandhlawrence@tiscali.co.uk

LAWRENCE, Miss Helen. b 30. St Mich Ho Ox 62. **dss** 74 **d** 87 **p** 94. Braintree *Chelmsf* 74-87; Par Dn 87-90; rtd 90; Perm to Offic *Chelmsf* 90-08. *28 Storeys House, Mount Pleasant, Cambridge CB3 0BZ*

LAWRENCE, Isaac Sartaj. b 72. Peshawar Univ BSc95 Philippine Chr Univ MBA97. **d** 08 **p** 09. C Ripon H Trin from 08. *14 Filey Avenue, Ripon HG4 2DH* Tel (01765) 603146 Mobile 07837-395770 E-mail isaaclawrence28@yahoo.co.uk

LAWRENCE, James Conrad. b 62. St Jo Coll Dur BA85. Ridley Hall Cam 85. **d** 87 **p** 88. Min Bar Hill LEP *Ely* 87-93; Deanery Adv in Evang 90-93; CPAS Evang 93-98; Perm to Offic *Cov* from 93; Springboard Missr from 97; CPAS Dir Evang Projects from 99. *Cotton Mill Spinney, Cubbington, Leamington Spa CV32 7XH* Tel (01926) 426761 or 334242 Fax 337613 E-mail jlawrence@cpas.org.uk

LAWRENCE, Mrs Janet Maureen. b 43. Hockerill Teacher Tr Coll TCert64. Ox Min Course 89. **d** 92 **p** 94. Hon Par Dn Bletchley *Ox* 92-94; NSM N Bletchley CD 94-05; rtd 05; Perm to Offic *Ox* 05-08; Hon C Gayhurst w Ravenstone, Stoke Goldington etc from 08. *The Rectory, Mount Pleasant, Stoke Goldington, Newport Pagnell MK16 8LL* Tel (01908) 551221 E-mail jmlawrence@talktalk.net

LAWRENCE, John Graham Clive. b 47. ACIB. Trin Coll Bris. **d** 78 **p** 79. C Chatham St Phil and St Jas *Roch* 78-83; V Roch St Justus 83-97; Asst Chapl HM Pris Roch 83-97; UK Dir CMJ 97-00; Internat Co-ord Light to the Nations UK from 00; Chapl Maidstone and Tunbridge Wells NHS Trust 03-04; Chapl W Kent NHS and Soc Care Trust 05-06; Chapl Kent & Medway NHS and Soc Care Partnership Trust 06-08; Chapl Team Ldr Bucks Hosps NHS Trust from 08. *Wycombe General Hospital, Alexander Road, High Wycombe HP11 2TT* Tel (01494) 425072 E-mail john.lawrence@buckshop.nhs.uk

LAWRENCE, Mrs Judith Patricia. b 53. WEMTC 01. **d** 04 **p** 05. C Glastonbury w Meare *B & W* 04-09. *Address temp unknown* Tel 07969-381488 (mobile) E-mail lawrence@wedmore100.fsnet.co.uk

LAWRENCE, Canon Leonard Roy. b 31. Keble Coll Ox BA56 MA59. Westcott Ho Cam 56. **d** 58 **p** 59. C Stockport St Geo *Ches* 58-62; V Thelwall 62-68; V Hyde St Geo 68-75; V Prenton 75-96; Hon Can Ches Cathl 86-96; rtd 96; Perm to Offic *Ches* from 96; Acorn Chr Foundn from 97. *39 Mockbeggar Drive, Wallasey CH45 3NN* Tel 0151-346 9438

LAWRENCE, Leslie. b 44. S'wark Ord Course 86. **d** 88 **p** 89. NSM Stanwell *Lon* 88-92; C Hounslow H Trin w St Paul 92-97; P-in-c Norwood St Mary 97-06; R from 06; rtd 09. *22 Chestnut Road, Ashford TW15 1DG* Tel 07765-551637 (mobile) E-mail leslie.lawrence@tesco.net

LAWRENCE, Martin Kenneth. b 59. Univ Coll Dur BA82. St Steph Ho Ox 94. **d** 96 **p** 97. C Wanstead St Mary w Ch Ch *Chelmsf* 96-00; PV Westmr Abbey 99-00; Chapl Malta and Gozo *Eur* 00-01; C Becontree S *Chelmsf* 02; C Romford St Edw 02-05; P-in-c Cranham 05-08; rtd 08. *4 Hart Road, Dorking RH4 1JS* Tel 07905-290849 (mobile) E-mail martin@lawrence.net

LAWRENCE, Norman. b 45. Lon Univ BEd75. S'wark Ord Course 77. **d** 80 **p** 81. NSM Hounslow H Trin *Lon* 80-88; NSM Hounslow H Trin w St Paul from 88. *89 Bulstrode Avenue, Hounslow TW3 3AE* Tel (020) 8572 6292 E-mail nlawrence@lampton.hounslow.sch.uk

LAWRENCE, Canon Patrick Henry Andrew. b 51. TCD Div Test 79 BA81. **d** 81 **p** 82. C Templemore *D & R* 81-84; C Kilkenny St Canice Cathl 84-85; I Templebreedy w Tracton and Nohoval *C, C & R* 85-92; I Geashill w Killeigh and Ballycommon *M & K* 92-98; Can Kildare Cathl 92-09; Adn Kildare 93-09; Adn Meath 97-09; Warden of Readers 97-09; I Julianstown and Colpe w Drogheda and Duleek 98-09; I Monkstown *D & G* from 09; Preb Monmohenock St Patr Cathl Dublin from 00. *62 Monkstown Road, Monkstown, Co Dublin, Republic of Ireland* Tel (00353) (1) 280 6596 E-mail patricklawrence@eircom.net

LAWRENCE, Canon Peter Anthony. b 36. Lich Th Coll 67. **d** 69 **p** 70. C Oadby *Leic* 69-74; P-in-c Northmarston and Granborough *Ox* 74-81; P-in-c Hardwick St Mary 74-81; P-in-c Quainton 76-81; P-in-c Oving w Pitchcott 76-81; TR Schorne 81-91; RD Claydon 84-88; V Ivinghoe w Pitstone and Slapton 91-97; Hon Can Ch Ch 97; rtd 97; Perm to Offic *Ox* 99-07 and *Worc* from 01. *Hill House, Back Lane, Malvern WR14 2HJ* Tel (01684) 564075

LAWRENCE, Ralph Guy. b 55. Trin Coll Bris 87. **d** 89 **p** 90. C Cotmanhay *Derby* 89-93; P-in-c Tansley, Dethick, Lea and Holloway 93-04; R Ashover and Brackenfield w Wessington from 04; C N Wingfield, Clay Cross and Pilsley from 06. *The Rectory, Narrowleys Lane, Ashover, Chesterfield S45 0AU* Tel (01246) 590246 E-mail ralphlawrence@tiscali.co.uk

LAWRENCE, Roy. See LAWRENCE, Canon Leonard Roy

LAWRENCE (née MASON), Sarah Catherine. b 79. K Coll Lon BA02 PGCE03 Chu Coll Cam MPhil06. Ridley Hall Cam 05. **d** 08. NSM Carr Dyke Gp *Linc* from 08. *21 Thorpe Place, Tattershall, Lincoln LN4 4NT* Tel (01526) 342648 E-mail revsarahlawrence@yahoo.co.uk

LAWRENCE, Simon Peter. b 60. TD. Nottm Univ BTh88 MA97 Indiana State Univ DMin01. St Jo Coll Nottm 88. **d** 89 **p** 90. C Holbeach *Linc* 88-90; C Alford w Rigsby 90-91; R Rattlesden w Thorpe Morieux and Brettenham *St E* 91-93; V Churchdown *Glouc* 93; V Maenclochog w Henry's Moat and Mynachlogddu

etc *St D* 93-94; R Overstrand, Northrepps, Sidestrand etc 95-98; CF (TA) 89-05; CF (ACF) 90-05; Perm to Offic *Nor* 02-06; Public Preacher 06-07; R Stalham, E Ruston, Brunstead, Sutton and Ingham from 07. *The Rectory, Camping Field Lane, Stalham, Norwich NR12 9DT* Tel (01692) 580250
E-mail simon.stalham@btinternet.com

LAWRENCE, Timothy Hervey. b 25. Ripon Hall Ox 58. **d** 60 **p** 61. C Newmarket All SS *St E* 60-62; V Kentford w Higham Green 62-84; P-in-c Herringswell 78-84; rtd 84. *The Dairy, Parsonage Farm, Parsonage Downs, Dunmow CM6 2AT* Tel (01371) 874818

LAWRENCE (née FOREMAN), Mrs Vanessa Jane. b 73. Ch Ch Coll Cant BA95. Westcott Ho Cam. **d** 00 **p** 01. C N Stoneham *Win* 00-04; NSM Swaythling 04-07; NSM Chilworth w N Baddesley from 07; NSM Ampfield from 08. *Roselea, Nutburn Road, North Baddesley, Southampton SO52 9DZ* Tel (023) 8073 6671 E-mail vanessalawrence@waitrose.com

LAWRENCE, Victor John. b 43. ACII. Oak Hill Th Coll. **d** 83 **p** 84. C Paddock Wood *Roch* 83-87; R Milton next Gravesend w Denton 87-09; RD Gravesend 05-09; rtd 09. *7 Sarnia House, 17 Darley Road, Eastbourne BN20 7PE*
E-mail victorjlaw@googlemail.com

LAWRENCE-MARCH, David Lawrence. b 61. Univ of Wales (Lamp) BA83. Coll of Resurr Mirfield 83. **d** 85 **p** 86. C Pet St Jude 85-89; Chapl St Aug Sch Kilburn 89-92; C Kilburn St Aug w St Jo *Lon* 89-90; C Paddington St Mary 90-92; Chapl Bearwood Coll Wokingham 92-96; R Holt w High Kelling *Nor* 96-98; Sen Chapl Bedford Sch 98-09; Chapl Ardingly Coll from 09. *Ardingly College, Haywards Heath RH17 6SQ* Tel (01444) 892656 E-mail father.david@ardingly.com

LAWRENSON, Michael. b 35. Leeds Univ BA60 Liv Univ CertSS65 Newc Univ DASS69. Coll of Resurr Mirfield 60. **d** 74 **p** 74. NSM Glenrothes *St And* 74-90; Dioc Supernumerary 90-95; Chapl HM Pris Perth 91-95; NSM Glenrothes *St And* 95-00; NSM Leven 95-00; NSM Lochgelly 95-00; NSM St Andrews St Andr 95-00; rtd 00. *Hollyburn, West Port, Falkland, Cupar KY15 7BW* Tel (01337) 857311
E-mail lawrenson@hollyburn.plus.com

LAWRENSON, Ronald David. b 41. CITC 68. **d** 71 **p** 72. C Seapatrick *D & D* 71-78; Min Can Down Cathl 78-79; V Choral Belf Cathl 79-86; Bp's C Tynan w Middletown *Arm* 86-93; Hon V Choral Arm Cathl 87-02; Bp's C Tynan w Middletown 92-93; I Donaghmore w Upper Donaghmore 93-98; rtd 02. *Riverbrook Apartments, 9A Brooklands Drive, Whitehead, Carrickfergus BT38 9SL* Tel (028) 9337 3625

LAWRIE (née VENTON), Ms Kathryn Magdelana. b 56. Reading Univ BA78. NEOC 03. **d** 06 **p** 07. C Skelton w Upleatham *York* from 06. *19 Whernside, Skelton-in-Cleveland, Saltburn-by-the-Sea TS12 2FP* Tel (01287) 653364

LAWRIE, Paul Edward. b 12. Freiburg Univ LLD35 St Cath Soc Ox BA48 MA53. Wycliffe Hall Ox 46. **d** 48 **p** 49. C Walkley *Sheff* 48-51; C Thrybergh 51-54; V Drax 54-64; R Todwick 64-78; rtd 78; Chapl Rotherham Distr Gen Hosp 78-85; Hon C Handsworth Woodhouse *Sheff* 85-88; Hon C Aston cum Aughton w Swallownest, Todwick etc 88-92; Perm to Offic from 92. *15 Haddon Way, Aston, Sheffield S26 2EH* Tel 0114-287 4864

LAWRIE, Peter Sinclair. b 39. Clifton Th Coll 62. **d** 65 **p** 66. C Derby St Chad 65-68; C Toxteth Park St Philemon w St Silas *Liv* 68-71; V Ramsey St Mary's w Ponds Bridge *Ely* 71-81; V Whitwick St Jo the Bapt *Leic* 81-96; P-in-c Felixstowe SS Pet and Paul *St E* 96-03; rtd 03. *71 Lincroft, Oakley, Bedford MK43 7SS* Tel (01234) 824055 E-mail p.lawrie@talk21.com

LAWRINSON, Leslie Norman. b 35. IEng MCIPD90 MCMI84. **d** 99 **p** 00. OLM Onchan *S & M* 99-05; NSM Scarisbrick *Liv* 05-08. *8 Hillary Wharf Apartments, South Quay, Douglas, Isle of Man IM1 5BL* Tel (01624) 627664 Mobile 07749-687469
E-mail leslawrinson05@aol.com

LAWRY, Mrs Fianach Alice Moir. b 35. St And Dioc Tr Course 85. **d** 88 **p** 94. NSM Dollar *St And* from 88; Chapl HM Pris Glenochil 91-07. *Sunnybank, Muckhart, Dollar FK14 7JN* Tel (01259) 781426 E-mail f.lawry@virgin.net

LAWRY, Richard Henry. b 57. Bris Univ BA79 Wolfs Coll Cam PGCE81. St Jo Coll Nottm MA01. **d** 99 **p** 00. C Macclesfield Team *Ches* 99-02; P-in-c Stalybridge St Paul 02-06; V 06-09; V Norbury from 09. *Norbury Vicarage, 75 Chester Road, Hazel Grove, Stockport SK7 5PE* Tel 0161-483 8640
E-mail richardlawry@talk21.com

LAWS, Clive Loudon. b 54. UEA BEd76 Leeds Univ CertEd75. Wycliffe Hall Ox 79. **d** 82 **p** 83. C Newcastle w Butterton *Lich* 82-85; C Gabalfa *Llan* 85-88; R Pendine w Llanmiloe and Eglwys Gymyn w Marros *St D* 89-94; CF 89-94; Perm to Offic *B & W* 95-96; C Portishead 96-02; TV 02-08; P-in-c High Laver w Magdalen Laver and Lt Laver etc *Chelmsf* from 08; Chapl St Clare Hospice from 08. *The Lavers Rectory, Magdalen Laver, Ongar CM5 0ES* Tel (01279) 426774
E-mail clive_anne@yahoo.co.uk

LAWSON, Canon Alma Felicity. b 51. St Hugh's Coll Ox BA73 MA78. St Jo Coll Nottm. **d** 98 **p** 99. Dean of Min and Dir of Ords *Wakef* 93-00; Hon C Wakef Cathl 98-00; V Gildersome from 00; Hon Can Wakef Cathl from 01. *St Peter's House, 2A Church Street, Gildersome, Morley, Leeds LS27 7AF* Tel and fax 0113-253 3339 E-mail felicity.lawson@tiscali.co.uk

LAWSON, Anne. *See* LAWSON, Miss Sarah Anne

LAWSON, David McKenzie. b 47. Glas Univ MA69 Edin Univ BD76. Edin Th Coll 73. **d** 76 **p** 77. C Glas St Mary 76-82; V Keighley All SS *Bradf* 82-85; Chapl Asst Univ Coll Hosp Lon 85-91; Hon C St Pancras w St Jas and Ch Ch *Lon* 86-91; R Smithfield St Bart Gt 91-93; Hon C Paddington St Jas 94-00; TV Chambersbury *St Alb* 00-03; TR from 03; RD Hemel Hempstead from 08. *St Mary's Vicarage, 7 Belswains Lane, Hemel Hempstead HP3 9PN* Tel (01442) 261610 Mobile 07939-473717 E-mail davidmlawson@lineone.net

LAWSON, David William. b 50. ACA. Linc Th Coll. **d** 82 **p** 83. C Stafford *Lich* 82-85; TV Redruth w Lanner *Truro* 85-87; P-in-c Whitley *Cov* 87-93; Chapl Whitley Hosp Cov 87-94; Chapl Gulson Road Hosp Cov 87-94; Chapl Cov and Warks Hosp 87-94; V S Leamington St Jo *Cov* from 93. *St John's Vicarage, Tachbrook Street, Leamington Spa CV31 3BN* Tel (01926) 422208

LAWSON, Felicity. *See* LAWSON, Canon Alma Felicity

LAWSON, The Very Revd Frederick Quinney (Rick). b 45. Leic Univ BA. St Steph Ho. **d** 83 **p** 84. Hon C Loughborough Em *Leic* 83-86; NSM Somerby, Burrough on the Hill and Pickwell 86-87; USA from 87; Hon Can Salt Lake City 87-02; Dean from 02. *4294 Adonis Drive, Salt Lake City UT 84124, USA* Tel (001) (801) 595 5380 *or* 322-3400 Fax 278 5903
E-mail rlawson@stmarkscathedral-ut.org

LAWSON, Gary Austin. b 53. Man Univ BA80. Ripon Coll Cuddesdon 80. **d** 82 **p** 83. C Nunhead St Antony *S'wark* 82-86; Hon C Reddish *Man* 86-87; Hon C Longsight St Jo w St Cypr 87-88; V Wythenshawe St Rich 88-98; Chapl Bolton Inst of F&HE 98-03; C Bolton St Pet 98-03; TR Westhoughton and Wingates from 03. *The Rectory, Market Street, Westhoughton, Bolton BL5 3AZ* Tel (01942) 859251

LAWSON, James Barry. b 68. Edin Univ MA91 New Coll Ox DPhil96. Coll of Resurr Mirfield 98. **d** 99 **p** 00. C Poplar *Lon* 99-02; Chapl CCC Cam 02-07; Bp's Sen Chapl *Sarum* 07-08; V Stoke Newington Common St Mich *Lon* from 09. *St Michael's Vicarage, 55 Fountayne Road, London N16 7ED* Tel (020) 8806 4225

LAWSON, Canon John Alexander. b 62. Sheff Univ BA84 Nottm Univ MA97 PhD06. St Jo Coll Nottm 85. **d** 87 **p** 88. C Wellington All SS w Eyton *Lich* 87-92; TV Dewsbury *Wakef* 92-98; P-in-c Birchencliffe 98-05; Dioc Vocations Adv and Asst Dir of Ords 02-05; Can Res Wakef Cathl from 05; Dioc Dir Tr from 05; Warden Wakef Min Scheme from 06. *7 Belgravia Road, Wakefield WF1 3JP* Tel (01924) 380182 *or* 371802
E-mail jal@bh-cc.co.uk

LAWSON, Jonathan Halford. b 68. St Chad's Coll Dur BA90 Heythrop Coll Lon MA04. Westcott Ho Cam 91. **d** 93 **p** 94. C Sedgefield *Dur* 93-96; C Usworth 96-97; TV NE Epping Distr *Chelmsf* 00-04; Chapl St Hild and St Bede Coll *Dur* from 04. *The College of St Hild and St Bede, St Hild's Lane, Durham DH1 1SZ* Tel 0191-334 8522 Fax 334 8501
E-mail j.h.lawson@durham.ac.uk

LAWSON, June Margaret. b 62. Birm Univ BA83 Didsbury Coll of Educn PGCE84 St Jo Coll York MA02. NOC 00. **d** 02 **p** 03. C Huddersfield H Trin *Wakef* 02-05; Dir Adult Chr Educn Mirfield Cen 05-08; Dir Mirfield Cen from 08; Hon C Wakef Cathl from 05; Dean of Women's Min from 09. *The Mirfield Centre, Stocks Bank Road, Mirfield WF14 0BW* Tel (01924) 481911 E-mail jlawson@mirfield.org.uk

LAWSON, Matthew James. b 67. St Andr Univ MTheol91 FRSA02. Ripon Coll Cuddesdon MTh94. **d** 94 **p** 95. C Bedford St Andr *St Alb* 94-97; Chapl and Hd RS St Jo Sch Leatherhead 97-07; Tutor Dioc Min Course *Guildf* 98; Chapl Hurstpierpoint Coll from 07. *Hurstpierpoint College, College Lane, Hurstpierpoint, Hassocks BN6 9JS* Tel (01273) 833636 Fax 835257 Mobile 07768-515950 E-mail frlawson@aol.com

LAWSON, The Ven Michael Charles. b 52. Sussex Univ BA75. Trin Coll Bris 75. **d** 78 **p** 79. C Horsham *Chich* 78-81; C St Marylebone All So w SS Pet and Jo *Lon* 81-87; V Bromley Ch *Roch* 87-99; Adn Hampstead *Lon* from 99. *London Diocesan House, 36 Causton Street, London SW1P 4AU* Tel (020) 7932 1190 Fax 7932 1192
E-mail archdeacon.hampstead@london.anglican.org

LAWSON, Rick. *See* LAWSON, The Very Revd Frederick Quinney

LAWSON, Robert William. b 60. MIBiol89. CITC 05. **d** 08 **p** 09. NSM Galloway w Straffan and Newcastle-Lyons *D & G* from 08. *6 Roselawn Close, Castleknock, Dublin 15, Republic of Ireland* Tel (00353) (1) 820 5129 Mobile 86-394 3151
E-mail lawson.rw@gmail.com

LAWSON, Russell Thomas. b 70. Leeds Univ BA92 Ox Univ BTh98. St Steph Ho Ox 98. **d** 98 **p** 99. C Cheshunt *St Alb* 98-02; C Cheam *S'wark* 02-06; TV 06-07; P-in-c S Norwood St Alb from 07. *The Vicarage, 6 Dagmar Road, London SE25 6HZ* Tel 07703-176001 (mobile) E-mail rtl70@btopenworld.com

LAWSON, Miss Sarah <u>Anne</u>. b 66. Ches Coll of HE BA87. Ridley Hall Cam. **d** 00 **p** 01. C Hollingworth w Tintwistle *Ches* 00-05; V Haslington w Crewe Green from 05. *The Vicarage, 163 Crewe Road, Haslington, Crewe CW1 5RL* Tel (01270) 582388 E-mail revanne@uwclub.net

LAWSON-JONES, Christopher <u>Mark</u>. b 68. Open Univ BA98. St Mich Coll Llan 98. **d** 00 **p** 01. C Risca *Mon* 00-03; Chapl Cross Keys Campus Coleg Gwent 00-03; TV Cyncoed 03-06; P-in-c Magor 06-09; TR Magor from 09. *The Rectory, Redwick Road, Magor, Caldicot NP26 3GU* Tel (01633) 880266 E-mail mark@lawson-jones.freeserve.co.uk

LAWTON, David Andrew. b 62. Man Univ BA83. Cranmer Hall Dur. **d** 00 **p** 01. C Deptford St Jo w H Trin *S'wark* 00-04; TV Walton H Trin *Ox* from 04. *60 Grenville Road, Aylesbury HP21 8EY* Tel (01296) 424175 Mobile 07799-713358 E-mail revdave15@aol.com

LAXON, Canon Colin John. b 44. FRSA. Cant Sch of Min 86. **d** 89 **p** 90. C Folkestone St Mary and St Eanswythe *Cant* 89-94; P-in-c Barrow St Jas *Carl* 94-01; Soc Resp Officer 01-09; C Brampton and Farlam and Castle Carrock w Cumrew 01-02; TV Eden, Gelt and Irthing 02-06; C Carl St Cuth w St Mary 06-09; Hon Can Carl Cathl 06-09; rtd 09. *15 Knowefield Avenue, Carlisle CA3 9BQ* Tel (01228) 544215

LAY, Mrs Alison Margaret. b 57. **d** 07. OLM Needham Market w Badley *St E* 07-08; OLM Combs and Lt Finborough from 08. *Hideaway, Park Road, Needham Market, Ipswich IP6 8BH* Tel (01449) 721115 E-mail ali@divineone.f9.co.uk

LAY, Brian Robert. b 37. Bernard Gilpin Soc Dur 59 Chich Th Coll 60. **d** 63 **p** 64. C Battyeford *Wakef* 63-66; C Belhus Park *Chelmsf* 66-73; P-in-c Sutton on Plym *Ex* 73-80; V 80-07; rtd 07; Perm to Offic *Ex* from 08. *18 Dunstone Drive, Plymouth PL9 8SQ* Tel (01752) 407348

LAY, Geoffrey Arthur. b 54. Leic Poly BA77 Man Univ MA83 Lon Univ BD88. Ridley Hall Cam 90. **d** 92 **p** 93. C St Neots *Ely* 92-95; P-in-c Long Stanton w St Mich 95-01; P-in-c Dry Drayton 95-99; R Chailey *Chich* 01-06; Chapl Chailey Heritage Hosp Lewes 01-06; rtd 06. *77 Firle Road, Peacehaven BN10 7QH* Tel (01273) 588048 E-mail geofflay@btinternet.com

LAYBOURNE, Michael Frederick. b 37. Qu Coll Birm 81. **d** 83 **p** 84. C High Elswick St Phil *Newc* 83-85; C High Elswick St Phil and Newc St Aug 86; C Cramlington 86-87; TV 87-95; C Killingworth 95-02; rtd 02; Perm to Offic *Newc* from 02. *16 Rockcliffe Gardens, Whitley Bay NE26 2NL* Tel 0191-251 0115 E-mail mikelaybourne@waitrose.com

LAYCOCK, Charles. b 37. Open Univ BA88. NOC 80. **d** 83 **p** 84. C Astley Bridge *Man* 83-86; R Crumpsall 86-94; V Ashton Ch Ch 94-00; Perm to Offic *Ches* from 03. *23 The Mere, Ashton-under-Lyne OL6 9NH* Tel 0161-330 2824

LAYCOCK, Lawrence. b 42. St Deiniol's Hawarden 86. **d** 89 **p** 90. C Blackpool St Mich *Blackb* 89-94; Perm to Offic Worsthorne 94-99; P-in-c Holme 96-99; V Holme-in-Cliviger w Worsthorne 99-08; rtd 08; Hon C Burnley St Steph *Blackb* from 08; AD Burnley from 04. *St Stephen's Vicarage, 154 Todmorden Road, Burnley BB11 3ER* Tel (01282) 424733 E-mail revrover@btinternet.com

LAYNESMITH, Mark David. b 74. York Univ BA97 MA99. Ripon Coll Cuddesdon BA01. **d** 02 **p** 03. C Tadcaster w Newton Kyme *York* 02-05; Chapl Reading Univ from 05. *30 Shinfield Road, Reading RG2 7BW* Tel 0118-987 1495

LAYTON, Miss Norene. b 39. Trin Coll Bris 84. **dss** 86 **d** 87 **p** 94. Lindfield *Chich* 86-92; Par Dn 87-92; Par Dn Loughborough Em *Leic* 92-94; C Loughborough Em and St Mary in Charnwood 94-96; V Hengrove *Bris* 96-04; rtd 04. *104 Outwoods Drive, Loughborough LE11 3LU* Tel (01509) 218127

LE BAS, Mrs Jennifer <u>Anne</u>. b 60. Hull Univ BSc81 Univ of Wales (Lamp) MA06. S Dios Minl Tr Scheme 90. **d** 93 **p** 94. C Alverstoke *Portsm* 93-96; C Elson 97-01; P-in-c Gosport Ch Ch and Dioc FE Officer 01-04; Perm to Offic *Roch* 05-06; P-in-c Seal St Pet from 06. *The Vicarage, Church Street, Seal, Sevenoaks TN15 0AR* Tel (01732) 762955 E-mail annelebas@dsl.pipex.com

LE BILLON, Mrs Janet. b 42. STETS 99. **d** 02 **p** 03. NSM Guernsey St Jo *Win* 02-06; NSM Guernsey Ste Marie du Castel from 06; NSM Guernsey St Matt from 06; Chapl States of Guernsey Bd of Health from 02. *Tranquillité, Clos des Quatre Vents, St Martin, Guernsey GY4 6SU* Tel (01481) 234283

LE COUTEUR, Miss Tracy. STETS. **d** 09. NSM Jersey St Clem *Win* from 09. *2 La Cachette, La Cache du Bourg, St Clement, Jersey JE2 6FX* Tel (01534) 857693 E-mail tracylecouteur@hotmail.com

LE DIEU, Miss Heather Muriel. b 41. Birm Univ BA62 MA67. St Jo Coll Dur 77. **dss** 79 **d** 87. Birchfield *Birm* 79-82; Kings Heath 82-84; Walsall Pleck and Bescot *Lich* 84-88; Par Dn 87-88; rtd 88. *159 Swarthmore Road, Selly Oak, Birmingham B29 4NW* Tel 0121-475 1236

LE GRICE, Elizabeth <u>Margaret</u>. b 53. Man Univ BA75 MA(Theol)78. Nor Bapt Coll 75 Westcott Ho Cam 87. **d** 88 **p** 97.

In Bapt Ch 78-82; C Whitchurch *Llan* 88-95; Chapl among the Deaf SE Wales *Mon* from 95; Lic to Offic from 95. *9 Hawarden Road, Newport NP19 8JP*

LE GRYS, Alan Arthur. b 51. K Coll Lon BD73 AKC73 MTh90. St Aug Coll Cant 73. **d** 74 **p** 75. C Harpenden St Jo *St Alb* 74-77; C Hampstead St Jo *Lon* 77-81; Chapl Westf Coll and Bedf Coll 81-84; V Stoneleigh *Guildf* 84-91; Lect Ripon Coll Cuddesdon 91-96; Prin SEITE 96-05; Hon PV Roch Cathl from 96. *265 Dale Street, Chatham ME4 6QR* Tel (01634) 402678 *or* 832299 Fax 819347 Mobile 07958-547053 E-mail alan@alegrys.freeserve.co.uk

LE ROSSIGNOL, Richard Lewis. b 52. Aston Univ BSc75. Oak Hill Th Coll BA79. **d** 79 **p** 80. C E Ham St Paul *Chelmsf* 79-81; C Willesborough w Hinxhill *Cant* 81-85; Perm to Offic 85-94; NSM Brabourne w Smeeth 94-01; NSM Mersham w Hinxhill and Sellindge 01-06; NSM Smeeth w Monks Horton and Stowting and Brabourne 06-07; P-in-c from 07; P-in-c Mersham w Hinxhill and Sellindge from 07. *The Rectory, Church Road, Smeeth, Ashford TN25 6SA* Tel (01303) 812697 E-mail rlerossi@ntlworld.com

LE SÈVE, Mrs Jane <u>Hilary</u>. b 63. SS Hild & Bede Coll Dur BA86. EAMTC 01. **d** 04 **p** 05. NSM Brightlingsea *Chelmsf* 04-08; TV Greenstead w Colchester St Anne from 08. *The Vicarage, 1 Blackwater Avenue, Colchester CO4 3UY* Tel 05602-299409 E-mail revhilary@btinternet.com

LE SUEUR, Paul John. b 38. Lon Univ BSc59. Wycliffe Hall Ox 60. **d** 62 **p** 63. C Mortlake w E Sheen *S'wark* 62-65; C Witney *Ox* 65-69; R Sarsden w Churchill 69-74; P-in-c Clifton Hampden 74-77; P-in-c Rotherfield Greys H Trin 77-82; V 82-90; V Blacklands Hastings Ch Ch and St Andr *Chich* 90-97; V Ticehurst and Flimwell 97-00; rtd 00; Perm to Offic *Chich* from 01. *80 Barnhorn Road, Bexhill-on-Sea TN39 4QA* Tel (01424) 844747 E-mail halomanpaul@talk21.com

LE VASSEUR, Mrs Linda Susan. b 48. Shenstone Coll of Educn CertEd70. S Dios Minl Tr Scheme 92. **d** 95 **p** 96. NSM Guernsey Ste Marie du Castel *Win* 95-01; NSM Guernsey St Matt 95-01; NSM Guernsey St Sav from 01; NSM Guernsey St Marguerite de la Foret from 01. *Coin des Arquets, Les Arquets, St Pierre du Bois, Guernsey GY7 9HE* Tel (01481) 264047

LE VAY, Clare Forbes Agard Bramhall Joanna. b 41. St Anne's Coll Ox BA64 MA66 Univ of Wales (Abth) MSc72 PhD86. Westcott Ho Cam 86. **d** 88 **p** 94. C Stamford Hill St Thos *Lon* 88-89; C Hackney 89-92; Asst Chapl Brook Gen Hosp Lon 92-95; Asst Chapl Greenwich Distr Hosp Lon 92-95; Chapl Greenwich Healthcare NHS Trust 95-01; Perm to Offic *S'wark* 02-06 and *Lon* 04-06. *Winton, Beards Lane, Stroud GL5 4HD* Tel (01453) 751096 Mobile 07816-468112 E-mail clarelevay@yahoo.com

LE-WORTHY, Michael Raymond. b 50. **d** 98 **p** 99. OLM Glascote and Stonydelph *Lich* from 98. *15 Abbey Road, Glascote, Tamworth B77 2QE* Tel (01827) 55762 E-mail michael.leworthy1@btinternet.com

LEA, Carolyn Jane. *See* COOKE, Carolyn Jane

LEA, Canon Montague <u>Brian</u>. b 34. OBE00. St Jo Coll Cam BA55 Lon Univ BD71. St Jo Coll Nottm 68. **d** 71 **p** 72. C Northwood Em *Lon* 71-74; Chapl Barcelona *Eur* 74-79; V Hove Bp Hannington Memorial Ch *Chich* 79-86; AD 14 France *Eur* 86-94; Chapl Paris St Mich 86-94; Hon Can Gib Cathl from 95; R Chiddingly w E Hoathly *Chich* 94-96; Chapl The Hague *Eur* 96-00; rtd 01; Perm to Offic *Chich* from 01. *35 Summerdown Lane, East Dean, Eastbourne BN20 0LE* Tel (01323) 423226 E-mail brian.lea@freedom255.co.uk

LEA, Norman. b 42. JP89. Univ of Wales (Lamp) BA67. Coll of Resurr Mirfield 66. **d** 68 **p** 69. C Newton St Pet *S & B* 68-71; C Oystermouth 71-73; C Brecon w Battle 73-74; TV Cwmbran *Mon* 74-77; V Talgarth and Llanelieu *S & B* 77-84; V Port Talbot St Theodore *Llan* 84-95; Hon Chapl Miss to Seafarers 84-08; V Cadoxton-juxta-Neath *Llan* 95-08; P-in-c Tonna 04-08; rtd 08. *67 Leonard Street, Neath SA11 3HW*

LEA, Canon Richard John Rutland. b 40. Trin Hall Cam BA63 MA67. Westcott Ho Cam 63. **d** 65 **p** 66. C Edenbridge *Roch* 65-68; C Hayes 68-71; V Larkfield 71-86; P-in-c Leybourne 76-86; RD Malling 79-84; V Chatham St Steph 86-88; Can Res and Prec Roch Cathl 88-98; V Iffley *Ox* 98-06; rtd 06. *The Gate House, Malling Abbey, Swan Street, West Malling ME19 6LP* Tel (01732) 522887 E-mail richard.lea@lineone.net

LEA-WILSON, Nicholas <u>Hugh</u>. b 61. Man Poly BA83 Univ Coll Ches BA08 MLI90. NOC 05. **d** 08. C Gateacre *Liv* from 08. *12 Dudlow Gardens, Liverpool L18 2HA* Tel 0151-488 0990 Fax 487 8480 Mobile 07968-290553 E-mail hugh.leawilson@virgin.net

LEACH, Alan Charles Graham. b 46. Univ Coll Ches BTh04 Master Mariner 73 NOC 04. **d** 05 **p** 06. NSM Neston *Ches* 05-08; NSM Heswall from 08. *8 Hill Top Lane, Ness, Neston CH64 4EL* Tel 0151-336 5046 Mobile 07802-624123 E-mail alan.leach5@btinternet.com

LEACH, Alan William Brickett. b 28. MSc CEng FIStructE FASI FICE. S'wark Ord Course. **d** 89 **p** 90. NSM Forest Row *Chich*

89-98; Perm to Offic from 98. *High Beeches, Priory Road, Forest Row RH18 5HP* Tel (01342) 823778
E-mail alanleach@mail.adsl4less.com

LEACH, Miss Bethia Morag. b 62. Sheff Univ BA84 Liv Inst of Educn PGCE85. Ripon Coll Cuddesdon 95. **d** 97 **p** 98. C Stafford *Lich* 97-00; TV Bilston 00-07; V Pensnett *Worc* from 07. *St Mark's Vicarage, Vicarage Lane, Pensnett, Brierley Hill DY5 4JH* Tel (01384) 262666

LEACH, Gerald. b 27. Sarum & Wells Th Coll 85. **d** 73 **p** 74. NSM Cyncoed *Mon* 73-86; C 86-87; V Dingestow and Llangovan w Penyclawdd etc 87-94; rtd 94; Perm to Offic *Heref* from 95; Lic to Offic *Mon* from 98. *19 Grange Park, Whitchurch, Ross-on-Wye HR9 6EA* Tel (01600) 890397

LEACH, James Roger. b 66. Ball Coll Ox BA89 MA99. Wycliffe Hall Ox BA98. **d** 99 **p** 00. C Knowle *Birm* 99-06; C Gerrards Cross and Fulmer *Ox* from 06. *3 The Uplands, Gerrards Cross SL9 7JQ* Tel (01753) 886480
E-mail james@jrleach.freeserve.co.uk

LEACH, John. b 52. K Coll Lon BD79 AKC79 St Jo Coll Dur MA83 Lambeth STh02. **d** 81 **p** 82. C N Walsham w Antingham *Nor* 81-85; C Crookes St Thos *Sheff* 85-89; V Styvechale *Cov* 89-97; Dir Angl Renewal Min 97-02; R Jersey St Lawr *Win* 02-04; Par Development Adv *Mon* 04-09; V Foord St Jo *Cant* from 09. *St John's Vicarage, 4 Cornwallis Avenue, Folkestone CT19 5JA* Tel (01303) 250805
E-mail revjohn.leach@tiscali.co.uk

LEACH, Mrs Rebecca Mary. b 65. St Aid Coll Dur BA87 Bris Univ PGCE90. ERMC 05. **d** 08 **p** 09. C E Barnet *St Alb* from 08. *122 Hazelwood Drive, St Albans AL4 0UZ* Tel (01727) 840182
E-mail p.r.leach@ntlworld.com

LEACH, Robert Neville. b 54. Trin Coll Bris 91. **d** 93 **p** 94. C Towcester w Easton Neston *Pet* 93-96; P-in-c Cowley *Lon* 96-01; P-in-c Brandon and Santon Downham w Elveden *St E* 01-04; P-in-c Lakenheath 02-04; R Brandon and Santon Downham w Elveden etc from 04. *The Rectory, 40 London Road, Brandon IP27 0HY* Tel (01842) 811907

LEACH, Samuel Mark. b 76. Westmr Coll Ox BEd99. Ridley Hall Cam 05. **d** 08 **p** 09. C Walsall St Paul *Lich* from 08. *11 The Cloisters, Walsall WS4 2AJ* Tel 07915-668714 (mobile)
E-mail samuelmw@hotmail.co.uk

LEACH, Stephen Lance. b 42. St Steph Ho Ox 66. **d** 69 **p** 70. C Higham Ferrers w Chelveston *Pet* 69-72; TV Ilfracombe H Trin *Ex* 72-74; V Barnstaple St Mary 74-77; R Goodleigh 74-77; P-in-c Barnstaple St Pet w H Trin 76-77; P-in-c Landkey 77-79; TR Barnstaple and Goodleigh 77-79; TR Barnstaple, Goodleigh and Landkey 79-82; V Paignton St Jo 82-95; Chapl Paignton and Kings Ash Hosps 82-95; Gen Sec ACS 95-08; Public Preacher *Birm* from 95; rtd 07; Perm to Offic *Ex* from 07. *16 Kings Avenue, Paignton TQ3 2AR* Tel (01803) 552335

LEACH, Stephen Windsor. b 47. St Chad's Coll Dur BSc70 Linacre Coll Ox BA72 MA76. Ripon Hall Ox 70. **d** 73 **p** 74. C Swinton St Pet *Man* 73-77; C Oldham St Chad Limeside 77-79; V Shaw 79-87; V St Just in Penwith *Truro* from 87; V Sancreed from 87. *The Vicarage, St Just, Penzance TR19 7UB* Tel (01736) 788672

LEACH, Timothy Edmund. b 41. Dur Univ BA63. Ridley Hall Cam 63. **d** 65 **p** 66. C Ecclesfield *Sheff* 65-68; C Stocksbridge 68-71; C-in-c W Bessacarr CD 71-80; V Goole and Hon Chapl Miss to Seamen 80-95; V Wath-upon-Dearne *Sheff* 95-08; rtd 08; Perm to Offic *Sheff* from 09. *6 Sawn Moor Avenue, Thurcroft, Rotherham S66 9DQ* Tel (01709) 701263
E-mail komedy@btopenworld.com

LEADBEATER, Canon Nicolas James. b 20. Univ of Wales BA43 LLM95. St Steph Ho Ox 45. **d** 45 **p** 46. C Abergavenny H Trin *Mon* 45-47; C Coleford w Staunton *Glouc* 47-55; PC Moreton Valence and V Whitminster 55-67; V Westcote 67-72; P-in-c Icomb 67-72; V Westcote w Icomb 72-79; V Westcote w Icomb and Bledington 79-88; Hon Can Glouc Cathl 83-88; rtd 88; Perm to Offic *Glouc* 88-06. *19 The Cotswold Home, Woodside Drive, Bradwell Grove, Burford OX18 4XA* Tel (01993) 823182

LEADER, Miss Janette Patricia. b 46. EAMTC 94. **d** 97 **p** 98. C Desborough, Brampton Ash, Dingley and Braybrooke *Pet* 97-01; V Wellingborough St Barn from 01. *St Barnabas' Vicarage, St Barnabas Street, Wellingborough NN8 3HB* Tel and fax (01933) 226337 E-mail revjanleader@talktalk.net

LEADER, Stephen. b 64. Ripon Coll Cuddesdon 99. **d** 01 **p** 02. C Battersea St Luke *S'wark* 01-04; V Enfield St Jas *Lon* from 04. *St James's Vicarage, 144 Hertford Road, Enfield EN3 5AY* Tel (020) 7640 9932 E-mail therevstelea@waitrose.com

LEAF, Edward David Hugh. b 65. Oak Hill Th Coll BA97. **d** 98 **p** 99. C Bath St Bart *B & W* 98-01; C Minehead 01-05; V Chadderton Em *Man* from 05. *Emmanuel Vicarage, 15 Chestnut Street, Chadderton, Oldham OL9 8HB* Tel 0161-688 8655 *or* 681 1310 E-mail david.leaf@btinternet.com

LEAH, William Albert. b 34. K Coll Lon BA56 AKC57 K Coll Cam MA63. Ripon Hall Ox 60. **d** 62 **p** 63. C Falmouth K Chas *Truro* 62-63; Chapl K Coll Cam 63-67; Min Can Westmr Abbey 67-74; V Hawkhurst *Cant* 74-83; Hon Min Can Cant Cathl

78-83; V St Ives *Truro* 83-94; rtd 98. *Trerice Cottage, Sancreed Newbridge, Penzance TR20 8QR* Tel (01736) 810987

LEAHY, David Adrian. b 56. Open Univ BA90. Qu Coll Birm. **d** 85 **p** 86. C Tile Cross *Birm* 85-88; C Warley Woods 88-91; V Hobs Moat 91-07; AD Solihull 97-04; V Four Oaks from 07. *The Vicarage, 26 All Saints Drive, Sutton Coldfield B74 4AG* Tel 0121-308 5315 E-mail a.leahy@virgin.net

LEAK, Adrian Scudamore. b 38. Ch Ch Ox BA60 MA65 BD89. Cuddesdon Coll 64. **d** 66 **p** 67. C Cov St Mark 66-69; C Dorchester *Ox* 69-73; V Badsey *Worc* 73-80; V Wickhamford 73-80; P-in-c Monkwearmouth St Pet *Dur* 80-81; V Choral and Archivist York Minster 81-86; Can Res and Prec Guildf Cathl 86-90; Hon C Guildf H Trin w St Mary 96-00; Hon C Worplesdon 00-06; P-in-c Withyham St Mich *Chich* from 06. *The Rectory, Withyham, Hartfield TN7 4BA* Tel (01892) 770241
E-mail adrian.leak@btinternet.com

LEAK, Harry Duncan. b 30. St Cath Coll Cam BA53 MA57. Ely Th Coll 53. **d** 54 **p** 55. S Africa 54-57; Portuguese E Africa 57-61; C Eccleshall *Lich* 62-64; V Normacot 64-66; C Stoke upon Trent 66-68; V Hanley All SS 68-71; R Swynnerton 71-80; Perm to Offic 80-03; rtd 92. *15 Sutherland Road, Tittensor, Stoke-on-Trent ST12 9JQ* Tel (01782) 374341

LEAK, John Michael. b 42. St Jo Coll Nottm. **d** 84 **p** 85. NSM Beeston *Ripon* 84-87; C Far Headingley St Chad 87-88; Hon C 88-90; C Headingley 90-95; TV Bramley 95-98; rtd 98. *23 Arthington Close, Tingley, Wakefield WF3 1BT* Tel 0113-253 3763

✠**LEAKE, The Rt Revd David.** b 35. CBE03. ALCD59. **d** 59 **p** 60 c 69. C Watford *St Alb* 59-61; Lect 61-63; SAMS Argentina 63-69; Asst Bp Paraguay 69-73; Asst Bp N Argentina 69-80; Bp 80-90; Bp Argentina 90-02; rtd 02; Hon Asst Bp Nor from 03; Perm to Offic from 03. *The Anchorage, Lower Common, East Runton, Cromer NR27 9PG* Tel (01263) 513536
E-mail david@leake8.wanadoo.co.uk

LEAKE, Duncan Burton. b 49. Leeds Univ BA71 Leeds and Carnegie Coll PGCE72 Keele Univ MA85. Oak Hill Th Coll 90. **d** 92 **p** 93. C Stanwix *Carl* 92-97; C Chasetown *Lich* 97-00; V Chase Terrace from 00. *The Vicarage, 3 Chapel Street, Burntwood WS7 1NL* Tel (01543) 306649 *or* 304611 Fax 304642 E-mail duncan.leake@ntlworld.com

LEAKEY, Ian Raymond Arundell. b 24. K Coll Cam BA47 MA49. Ridley Hall Cam 48. **d** 50 **p** 51. C Litherland St Jo and St Jas *Liv* 50-53; Rwanda Miss 53-73; Can Burundi 66; V Cudham *Roch* 73-76; P-in-c Downe 76; V Cudham and Downe 76-89; rtd 89; Perm to Offic *Sarum* from 89. *5 Shelley Drive, Salisbury SP1 3JZ* Tel (01722) 329243

LEAKEY, Peter Wippell. b 39. Lon Univ BSc60. Trin Coll Bris 73. **d** 75 **p** 76. C Colne St Bart *Blackb* 75-79; V Copp 79-85; V Pennington *Man* 85-05; AD Leigh 93-00; Hon Can Man Cathl 02-05; rtd 05. *28 Gilda Road, Worsley, Manchester M28 1BP* Tel 0161-703 8076

LEAL, Malcolm Colin. b 33. Chich Th Coll 72. **d** 75 **p** 76. NSM Shoreham St Giles CD *Chich* 75-87; Chapl NE Surrey Coll Ewell 87-95; NSM Arundel w Tortington and S Stoke *Chich* 88-95; Perm to Offic 95-06. *8 West Park Lane, Goring-by-Sea, Worthing BN12 4EK* Tel (01903) 244160

LEALMAN, Helen. b 46. NOC 03. **d** 05 **p** 06. NSM Ben Rhydding *Bradf* 05-06; NSM Bolton St Jas w St Chrys from 06. *8 Parkfield Road, Shipley BD18 4EA* Tel (01274) 584569
E-mail helen.lealman@bradford.anglican.org

LEAMY, Stuart Nigel. b 46. Pemb Coll Ox BA68 MA73 ACA76 FCA81. Sarum Th Coll 68. **d** 70 **p** 71. C Upholland *Liv* 70-78; Lic to Offic *Lon* 78-83 and 94-97; NSM Pimlico St Mary Bourne Street from 97. *92 Gloucester Road, Hampton TW12 2UJ* Tel (020) 8979 9068 E-mail leamy@blueyonder.co.uk

LEAN, The Very Revd David Jonathan Rees. b 52. Coll of Resurr Mirfield 74. **d** 75 **p** 76. C Tenby *St D* 75-81; V Llanrhian w Llanhywel and Carnhedryn etc 81-88; V Haverfordwest St Martin w Lambston 88-00; RD Roose 99-00; Can St D Cathl from 00; TV Dewisland 01-09; TR from 09; Dean St D from 09. *The Deanery, St Davids, Haverfordwest SA62 6RD* Tel (01437) 720456

LEANING, The Very Revd David. b 36. Lambeth MA01 Nottm Trent Univ Hon MA03. Lich Th Coll 58. **d** 60 **p** 61. C Gainsborough All SS *Linc* 60-65; R Warsop *S'well* 65-76; RD Kington and Weobley *Heref* 76-80; R Kington w Huntington 76-80; Adn Newark *S'well* 80-91; Provost S'well 91-00; Dean 00-06; P-in-c Rolleston w Fiskerton, Morton and Upton 91-93; P-in-c Edingley w Halam 02-06; rtd 06; Perm to Offic *S'well* from 06. *52 Greetwell Road, Lincoln LN2 4AX* Tel (01522) 531361 Fax 521903 E-mail davidleaning@btinternet.com

LEAR, Peter Malcolm. b 45. FCMA. SEITE 95. **d** 98 **p** 99. NSM Ham St Andr *S'wark* 98-03; NSM Wandsworth St Anne 03-04; NSM Upper Coquetdale *Newc* from 04. *The Rectory, High Street, Rothbury, Morpeth NE65 7TO* Tel (01669) 620482
E-mail peter@learpm.demon.co.uk

LEARMONT, Oliver James. b 62. UEA BA83 Wolv Univ LLM96 SS Coll Cam BTh07. Westcott Ho Cam 05. **d** 07 **p** 08. C

Hitchin *St Alb* from 07. *67 Whitehill Road, Hitchin SG4 9HP* Tel 07966-459315 (mobile) E-mail oliver@learmont.com

LEARMOUTH, Michael Walter. b 50. FCA. Oak Hill Th Coll 84. **d** 84 **p** 85. C Harlow St Mary and St Hugh w St Jo the Bapt *Chelmsf* 84-89; V Hainault 89-97; TR Harlow Town Cen w Lt Parndon 97-00; TR Barnsbury *Lon* from 00; AD Islington from 08. *The Rectory, 10 Thornhill Square, London N1 1BQ* Tel (020) 7607 9039 *or* 7607 4552
E-mail michael@learmouth.fsworld.co.uk

LEARY, Thomas Glasbrook. b 42. AKC66. **d** 67 **p** 68. C W Bromwich All SS *Lich* 67-70; TV Croydon St Jo *Cant* 70-75; C Limpsfield and Titsey *S'wark* 75-83; V Sutton New Town St Barn 83-92; V Merton St Mary 92-07; RD Merton 98-01; rtd 07. *South Barn, Knighton LD7 1NE* Tel (01547) 529194
E-mail glassbrook@msn.com

LEATHARD, Preb Brian. b 56. Sussex Univ BA Cam Univ MA Loughb Univ PhD91. Westcott Ho Cam 79. **d** 82 **p** 83. C Seaford w Sutton *Chich* 82-85; Chapl Loughb Univ 85-89; V Hampton Hill *Lon* 89-06; R Chelsea St Luke and Ch Ch from 06; Dir of Ords from 99; Preb St Paul's Cathl from 05. *The Rectory, 64A Flood Street, London SW3 5TE* Tel (020) 7352 6331 *or* 7351 7365 E-mail brianleathard@chelseaparish.org

LEATHERBARROW, Ronald. b 35. Chester Coll TCert59. NW Ord Course 71. **d** 75 **p** 76. C Eccleston Ch Ch *Liv* 75-80; C Eccleston St Thos 80-83; R Kirklinton w Hethersgill and Scaleby *Carl* 83-86; R Blackley St Mark White Moss *Man* 86-99; rtd 99. *1 Chapel Street, St Helens WA10 2BG* Tel (01744) 614426

LEATHERS, Brian Stanley Peter. b 61. Nottm Univ BSc83. Oak Hill Th Coll BA89. **d** 89 **p** 90. C Watford *St Alb* 89-92; C Welwyn w Ayot St Peter 92-96; V Heacham *Nor* 96-99; P-in-c Stapenhill Immanuel *Derby* 99-00; V from 00. *Immanuel Vicarage, 150 Hawthorn Crescent, Burton-on-Trent DE15 9QW* Tel (01283) 563959 E-mail briantopsey@googlemail.com

LEATHES, David Burlton de Mussenden. b 49. St Jo Coll Nottm 90. **d** 92 **p** 93. C Kirkby Stephen w Mallerstang etc *Carl* 92-00; C Brough w Stainmore, Musgrave and Warcop 94-00. *Low Beck House, Rookby, Kirkby Stephen CA17 4HX* Tel (01768) 371713

LEATHLEY, Susan Mary. b 57. Bath Univ BPharm78 Trin Coll Bris MA98 MRPharmS. Oak Hill Th Coll 92. **d** 94 **p** 98. C Weston-super-Mare Ch Ch *B & W* 94-95; C Toxteth St Philemon w St Gabr and St Cleopas *Liv* 97-01; TV Maghull 01-08; TV Mildenhall *St E* from 08. *The Rectory, 8 Church Walk, Mildenhall, Bury St Edmunds IP28 7ED* Tel (01638) 711930
E-mail sueleathley@aol.com

LEATHLEY, Terence Michael. b 63. Coll of Resurr Mirfield 99. **d** 01 **p** 02. C Whitby w Aislaby and Ruswarp *York* 01-04; TV 04-07; V S Bank from 07; V Middlesbrough St Thos from 07. *The Vicarage, 259 Normanby Road, Middlesbrough TS6 6TB* Tel 07678-986916 (mobile)

LEATON, Martin John. b 46. Clifton Th Coll 68. **d** 71 **p** 72. C Kenilworth St Jo *Cov* 71-74; C Stratford-on-Avon w Bishopton 74-77; P-in-c Meriden 77-81; R Meriden and Packington 82-84; R Heanton Punchardon w Marwood *Ex* 84-87; Perm to Offic 95-97; P-in-c Rampton w Laneham, Treswell, Cottam and Stokeham *S'well* 97-06, P-in-c N and S Leverton 03-06; rtd 06; Hon C Tysoe w Oxhill and Whatcote *Cov* from 06. *The Vicarage, Peacock Lane, Tysoe, Warwick CV35 0SG* Tel (01295) 680201
E mail martinleaton@yahoo.co.uk

LEAVER, David Noel. b 63. Hatf Coll Dur BA85. Wycliffe Hall Ox 89. **d** 91 **p** 92. C Blackheath Park St Mich *S'wark* 91-95; C Upton (Overchurch) *Ches* 95-98; C Wilmslow 98-99; Perm to Offic from 99. *42 Hill Top Avenue, Cheadle Hulme, Cheadle SK8 7HY* Tel 0161-485 4302
E-mail davidleaver@btconnect.com

LEAVER, Mrs Janice Patricia. b 56. EAMTC 03. **d** 06 **p** 07. C Desborough, Brampton Ash, Dingley and Braybrooke *Pet* 06-09; TV Wilford Peninsula *St E* from 09. *The Vicarage, 11 Walnut Tree Avenue, Rendlesham, Woodbridge IP12 2GG* Tel 07913-977218 (mobile) E-mail revdjleaver@googlemail.com

LEAVER (*née* SMYTH), Mrs Lucinda Elizabeth Jane (Liz). b 67. New Hall Cam BA88 MA92. Wycliffe Hall Ox BTh93. **d** 93 **p** 94. C Cambridge St Barn *Ely* 93-97; Chapl St Kath Hall Liv Inst of HE 97-98; TV Stockport SW *Ches* 99-01; Chapl Stockport Gr Sch from 99. *42 Hill Top Avenue, Cheadle Hulme, Cheadle SK8 7HY* Tel 0161-485 4302 E-mail liz.leaver@boltblue.net

LEAVER, Prof Robin Alan. b 39. Groningen Univ DTh87. Clifton Th Coll 62. **d** 64 **p** 65. C Gipsy Hill Ch Ch *S'wark* 64-67; C Gt Baddow *Chelmsf* 67-71; P-in-c Reading St Mary Castle Street Prop Chpl *Ox* 71-77; P-in-c Cogges 77-84; Chapl Luckley-Oakfield Sch Wokingham 73-75; Lect Wycliffe Hall Ox 84-85; Prof Ch Music Westmr Choir Coll USA 84-08; Visiting Prof Liturgy Drew Univ 88-00; Visiting Prof Juilliard Sch from 04; Visiting Prof Yale Univ from 08; Visiting Prof QUB from 08. *10 Spur Road Extension, Dover NH 03802-9116, USA* Tel (001) (603) 343 4251 E-mail leaver@rider.edu

LEAVES (*née* CRAIG), Julie Elizabeth. b 63. Southn Univ BTh87. Sarum & Wells Th Coll 82. **dss** 86 **d** 87 **p** 92. Thatcham

---

Ox 86-87; Par Dn 87-88; Hong Kong 88-92; Assoc P Fremantle Australia 92-95; Chapl St Mary's Angl Girls' Sch Karrinyup from 96. *Wollaston College, Wollaston Road, Mount Claremont WA 6010, Australia* Tel (0061) (8) 9383 2774 *or* 9341 9102 Fax 9341 9222 E-mail jleaves@stmarys.wa.edu.au

LEAVES, Nigel. b 58. Keble Coll Ox BA80 MA83 K Coll Lon PGCE81 MA86. Sarum & Wells Th Coll 84. **d** 86 **p** 87. C Boyne Hill *Ox* 86-88; Chapl Hong Kong Cathl 88-92; Australia from 92; Abp's Chapl and R W Perth *Perth* 92-98; Tutor and Research Fell Murdoch Univ 98-00; Warden Wollaston Coll & Dir Cen for Belief, Spirituality and Aus Culture from 00. *Wollaston College, Wollaston Road, Mount Claremont WA 6010, Australia* Tel (0061) (8) 9384 5511 *or* tel and fax 9383 2774 Fax 9385 3364
E-mail leaves@iinet.net.au

LEAWORTHY, John Owen. b 40. Univ of Wales (Swansea) BSc62. Oak Hill Th Coll 80. **d** 82 **p** 83. C Compton Gifford *Ex* 82-85; C Plymouth Em w Efford 85-86; P-in-c Marks Tey w Aldham and Lt Tey *Chelmsf* 86-88; R 88-89; Chapl HM Pris Full Sutton 89-91; NSM Portree *Arg* 96-04; rtd 05; Perm to Offic *Chelmsf* from 05. *46 Wilkin Drive, Tiptree, Colchester CO5 0QP* Tel (01621) 810905 E-mail jleaworthy@tesco.net

LECK, Stuart David. b 62. ACIB84. SEITE 03. **d** 06 **p** 07. NSM Brockley Hill St Sav *S'wark* from 06. *55 Algiers Road, London SE13 7JD* Tel (020) 8314 5848
E-mail stuart.leck@btinternet.com

LECKEY, The Very Revd Hamilton. b 29. TCD BA51 MA58. **d** 51 **p** 52. C Ballymacarrett St Martin *D & D* 51-55; C Bangor St Comgall 55-60; I Drumgooland w Kilcoo 60-62; I Comber 62-79; Private Chapl Bp Down 62-73; Dir of Ords 62-87; I Bangor Abbey 79-96; Can Down Cathl 74-87; Dean Down 87-96; rtd 96. *34 Beechfield Drive, Bangor BT19 7ZW* Tel (028) 9146 9370

LECKEY, Paul Robert. b 61. QUB. Ripon Coll Cuddesdon Aston Tr Scheme. **d** 96 **p** 97. C Eastleigh *Win* 96-01; P-in-c Upton St Leonards *Glouc* from 01. *The Rectory, Bond End Road, Upton St Leonards, Gloucester GL4 8AG* Tel (01452) 617443
E-mail paul@pleckey.abel.co.uk

LECLÉZIO, Ms Marie Katryn. b 62. Natal Univ BA83 All Nations Chr Coll MA00. WEMTC 05. **d** 08 **p** 09. C Halas *Worc* from 08. *36 Albrighton Road, Halesowen B63 4JY* Tel and fax 0121-501 1913 E-mail katryn.leclezio@virgin.net

LEDBETTER, Shannon Carroll. b 64. Louisville Univ (USA) BA85 Liv Univ PhD00. Virginia Th Sem MTS96. **d** 03 **p** 04. NSM Knowsley *Liv* 03-08; NSM W Derby St Mary and St Jas from 08. *7 Cathedral Close, Liverpool L1 7BR* Tel 07720-072787 (mobile) E-mail scledbetter2008@yahoo.co.uk

LEDGARD, Canon Frank William Armitage. b 24. Wells Th Coll 49. **d** 52 **p** 53. C Ipswich St Mary le Tower *St E* 52-55; V Tottington *Man* 55-62; V Kirkby Malzeard w Dallow Gill *Ripon* 62-66; R Bedale 66-87; RD Wensley 79-85; Hon Can Ripon Cathl 80-89; Bp's Adv on Chr Healing 87-89; rtd 89; Perm to Offic *Ripon* from 89. *c/o Wrigleys Solicitors, 19 Cookridge Street, Leeds LS2 3AG* Tel 0113-244 6100 Fax 244 6101

LEDGER, James Henry. b 23. Oak Hill Th Coll 68. **d** 70 **p** 71. C Spitalfields Ch Ch w All SS *Lon* 70-75; V Chitts Hill St Cuth 75-91; rtd 91; Perm to Offic *Lon* 91-96; St Alb from 93. *6 Acorn Street, Hunsdon, Ware SG12 8PB* Tel (01279) 842878

LEDGER, Mrs Margaret Phyllis. b 47. **d** 04 **p** 05. OLM Newburn *Newc* from 04. *14 Woodside Avenue, Throckley, Newcastle upon Tyne NE15 9BE* Tel 0191-267 2953
E-mail margaret.p.ledger@btinternet.com

LEDWARD, John Archibald. b 30. Lon Univ BD58 Man Univ MA81 ThD FRSA85. ALCD57. **d** 58 **p** 59. C St Helens St Helen *Liv* 58-62; V Dearham *Carl* 62-66; V Mirehouse 66-71; V Daubhill *Man* 71-77; R Newcastle w Butterton *Lich* 77-88; P-in-c Kirby Bedon w Bixley and Whitlingham 92-94; R Rockland St Mary w Hellington, Bramerton etc 94-95; RD Loddon 92-95; rtd 95; Perm to Offic *Nor* from 95. *41 Lackford Close, Brundall, Norwich NR13 5NL* Tel (01603) 714745

LEE, Agnes Elizabeth. b 31. Open Univ BA87 Whitelands Coll Lon TCert51 ACP76. NOC 97. **d** 98 **p** 99. NSM Dewsbury *Wakef* 98-02; rtd 02; Perm to Offic *Wakef* from 02. *1 Moor Park Court, Dewsbury WF12 7AU* Tel (01924) 467319

LEE, Mrs Anne Louise. b 65. St Jo Coll Nottm BTh90. Wycliffe Hall Ox 94. **d** 95 **p** 96. C Wembley St Jo *Lon* 95-98; NSM S Gillingham *Roch* 98-07; Jt P-in-c Locking *B & W* 07-09; Jt P-in-c Hutton and Locking from 09. *The Vicarage, The Green, Locking, Weston-super-Mare BS24 8DA* Tel (01934) 823556
E-mail revdannelee@yahoo.co.uk

LEE, Anthony Maurice. b 35. Bps' Coll Cheshunt 62. **d** 65 **p** 66. C Pinner *Lon* 65-71; Asst Youth Chapl *Glouc* 71-72; V Childswyckham 72-73; R Aston Somerville 72-73; V Childswyckham w Aston Somerville 73-91; P-in-c Buckland 88-91; P-in-c Stanton w Snowshill 88-91; R Childswyckham w Aston Somerville, Buckland etc 91-94; RD Winchcombe 86-94; rtd 94. *11 Holly Close, Broadclyst, Exeter EX5 3JB*

LEE, Canon Brian. b 37. Linc Th Coll 78. **d** 80 **p** 81. C Duston *Pet* 80-84; P-in-c Spratton 84-89; V 89-06; Jt P-in-c Maidwell w Draughton, Lamport w Faxton 89-01; Jt P-in-c Cottesbrooke w Gt Creaton and Thornby 89-06; RD Brixworth 94-01; Can Pet Cathl 98-06; rtd 06; Perm to Offic *Pet* from 06. *8 Clive Close, Kettering NN15 5BQ* Tel (01536) 519734
E-mail brian.lee18@btopenworld.com

LEE, Canon Brian Ernest. b 32. ACA59 FCA70. Linc Th Coll 60. **d** 62 **p** 63. C Birch St Jas *Man* 62-65; C Withington St Paul 65-66; R Abbey Hey 66-70; Hon C Gatley *Ches* 86-88; V Egremont St Jo 88-97; RD Wallasey 91-96; OGS from 92; Hon Can Ches Cathl 96-97; rtd 97; Perm to Offic *Nor* from 97. *St Fursey House, Convent of All Hallows, Ditchingham, Bungay NR35 2DZ* Tel (01986) 892308 Fax 894215

LEE, Brian John. b 51. K Coll Lon BD78 AKC78. Coll of Resurr Mirfield 78. **d** 79 **p** 80. C Ham St Rich *S'wark* 79-82; C Surbiton St Andr and St Mark 82-85; V Shirley St Geo 85-93; V St Botolph Aldgate w H Trin Minories *Lon* 93-08; rtd 08. *10 Norfolk Buildings, Brighton BN1 2PZ*

LEE, Clifford Samuel (Sam). b 53. **d** 95 **p** 96. NSM S Elmham and Ilketshall *St E* from 95. *Packway Lodge, Flixton, Bungay NR35 1NR* Tel (01986) 782300

LEE, Clive Warwick. b 34. St Pet Coll Ox BA58 MA62 Ox Univ PGCE73. Coll of Resurr Mirfield 58. **d** 60 **p** 61. C W End *Win* 60-64; C Upper Norwood St Jo *Cant* 65-69; Chapl Vinehall Sch Robertsbridge 69-94; rtd 94; Perm to Offic *Cant* from 04. *28 St Radigund's Street, Canterbury CT1 2AA* Tel (01227) 780624

LEE, Colin John Willmot. b 21. Wycliffe Hall Ox 57. **d** 59 **p** 59. C Gravesend St Jas *Roch* 59-62; V Dartford St Edm 62-67; Bp's Ind Adv *Derby* 67-91; C-in-c Ilkeston St Bart CD 67-69; P-in-c Stanton by Dale 69-76; V Ilkeston St Jo 76-91; rtd 91; Perm to Offic *Derby* and *S'well* from 91. *3 Buttermead Close, Trowell, Nottingham NG9 3QT* Tel 0115-949 7608

LEE, The Ven David John. b 46. Bris Univ BSc67 Fitzw Coll Cam BA76 MA79 Birm Univ PhD96. Ridley Hall Cam 74. **d** 77 **p** 78. C Putney St Marg *S'wark* 77-80; Tutor Bp Tucker Th Coll Uganda 80-86; Tutor Crowther Hall CMS Tr Coll Selly Oak 86-91; P-in-c Wishaw and Middleton *Birm* 91-96; Can Res Birm Cathl 96-04; Dir Dioc Bd for Miss 96-04; Adn Bradf from 04. *St Paul's Vicarage, 47 Kirkgate, Shipley BD18 3EH* Tel (01274) 200698 *or* tel and fax 730196 Mobile 07711-671351
E-mail david.lee@bradford.anglican.org

LEE, The Ven David Stanley. b 30. Univ of Wales (Cardiff) BSc51. St Mich Coll Llan 56. **d** 57 **p** 58. C Caerau w Ely *Llan* 57-60; C Port Talbot St Agnes 60-70; Ind Chapl 60-70; R Merthyr Tydfil 70-72; Chapl Merthyr Tydfil Hosp 70-91; R Merthyr Tydfil and Cyfarthfa *Llan* 72-91; RD Merthyr Tydfil 82-91; Can Llan Cathl 84-97; Adn Llan 91-97; R Llanfabon 91-97; rtd 97; Perm to Offic *Llan* from 97; *Mon* from 98. *2 Old Vicarage Close, Llanishen, Cardiff CF14 5UZ* Tel (029) 2075 2431

LEE, David Wight Dunsmore. b 39. Wells Th Coll 61. **d** 63 **p** 64. C Middlesbrough St Oswald *York* 63-67; C Northallerton w Kirby Sigston 67-69; R Limbe w Thyolo and Mulanje Malawi 69-71; R S Highlands 71-75; V Newington Transfiguration 76-81; P-in-c Sheriff Hutton 81-85; P-in-c Sheriff Hutton and Farlington 85-97; V Sheriff Hutton, Farlington, Stillington etc 97-04; rtd 04; Perm to Offic *York* from 04. *Kirkstone Cottage, Main Street, Oswaldkirk, York YO62 5XT* Tel (01439) 788283
E-mail dwdlee@talk21.com

LEE, Derek Alfred. **d** 00. Hon Par Dn Llantilio Pertholey w Bettws Chpl etc *Mon* 00-05; Hon Par Dn Llanfihangel Crucorney w Oldcastle etc from 05. *94 Croesonen Parc, Abergavenny NP7 6PF* Tel (01873) 855042

LEE, Edmund Hugh. b 53. Trin Coll Ox BA75 MA79 Goldsmiths' Coll Lon BMus83 K Coll Lon MA98. Ripon Coll Cuddesdon 93. **d** 95 **p** 96. C Malden St Jas *S'wark* 95-99; TV Mortlake w E Sheen 99-08. *67 North Worple Way, London SW14 8PP* Tel (020) 8876 5270 E-mail edknife@aol.com

LEE, Elizabeth. *See* LEE, Agnes Elizabeth

LEE, Gilbert (Sai Kuen). b 51. Hong Kong Univ BD80 Kent Univ MA98. Chung Chi Coll Hong Kong 77. **d** 80 **p** 81. C Angl Ch Hong Kong 80-81; V 81-88; NSM St Martin-in-the-Fields *Lon* 88-00; Chapl to Chinese in London 88-00; I St Jo Chinese Ch Toronto 00-07; I Markham All SS from 07. *142 Dunbar Crescent, Markham ON L3R 6V8, Canada* Tel (001) (905) 946 1637 Fax 946 9782 E-mail allsts@arex.com

LEE, Henry. b 31. St Chad's Coll Dur BA53 Bede Coll Dur PGCE71. **d** 55 **p** 56. C Hendon St Ignatius *Dur* 55-60; C Dur St Marg 60-65; V Medomsley 65-75; Chapl Darlington Memorial Hosp 75-79; V Darlington H Trin *Dur* 75-82; V Brompton w Deighton *York* 82-90; rtd 90; Perm to Offic *York* from 90. *103 Benfieldside Road, Consett DH8 0RS* Tel (01207) 592170

LEE, Hugh. *See* LEE, John Charles Hugh Mellanby

LEE, Canon Hugh Gordon Cassels. b 41. St Andr Univ BSc64. Edin Th Coll 64. **d** 67 **p** 68. C Dumfries *Glas* 67-70; C Totteridge *St Alb* 70-73; R Glas St Jas 73-80; R Bishopbriggs 80-86; R

St Fillans *St And* 86-89; R Crieff and Comrie 86-01; P-in-c Muthill 86-01; P-in-c Lochearnhead 89-01; R Dunoon *Arg* 01-06; Dioc Dir of Ord from 06; Can St Jo Cathl Oban from 04; Can Cumbrae from 04. *Chapel Hall, Toward, Dunoon PA23 7UA* Tel (01369) 870237 E-mail fish4hill@yahoo.co.uk

LEE, Miss Iris Audrey Olive. b 26. Gilmore Ho. **dss** 76 **d** 87. N Weald Bassett *Chelmsf* 76-87; rtd 87; NSM Clacton St Jas *Chelmsf* 87-00; Chapl Clacton Hosp 90-95; Perm to Offic 00-04. *30 Marine Court, Marine Parade West, Clacton-on-Sea CO15 1ND* Tel (01255) 423719

LEE, Mrs Jayne Christine. b 53. Dundee Univ MA75. **d** 06 **p** 07. OLM Roberttown w Hartshead *Wakef* from 06; OLM Heckmondwike from 06; OLM Liversedge w Hightown from 06. *58 Prospect View, Liversedge WF15 8BD* Tel (01924) 401264 E-mail jayneclee@hotmail.com

LEE, Mrs Jennifer. b 42. Westf Coll Lon BA64 CQSW78. NOC 01. **d** 03 **p** 04. NSM Millhouses H Trin *Sheff* 03-06; NSM Compton w Shackleford and Peper Harow *Guildf* from 07. *The Old Cottage Barn, Peper Harow Park, Peper Harow, Godalming GU8 6BQ* Tel (01483) 424468 E-mail revjenn@btinternet.com

LEE, John. b 47. Univ of Wales (Swansea) BSc70 MSc73 MInstLAM87. Ripon Hall Ox 73. **d** 75 **p** 76. C Swansea St Pet *S & B* 75-78; C St Botolph Aldgate w H Trin Minories *Lon* 79-84; P-in-c Chiddingstone w Chiddingstone Causeway *Roch* 84-89; R 89-98; Clergy Appts Adv from 98. *The Wash House, Lambeth Palace, London SE1 7JU* Tel (020) 7898 1898 Fax 7898 1899 E-mail admin.caa@c-of-e.org.uk

LEE, John Charles Hugh Mellanby. b 44. Trin Hall Cam BA66 MA69 Brunel Univ MTech71. Ox NSM Course 78. **d** 81 **p** 82. NSM Amersham on the Hill *Ox* 81-88; NSM Ox St Aldate w St Matt 88-93; NSM Wheatley 93-95; Dioc Development Officer Miss in Work and Economic Life 95-02; P-in-c Ox St Mich w St Martin and All SS from 02. *12 Walton Street, Oxford OX1 2HG* Tel and fax (01865) 316245
E-mail hugh.lee@btinternet.com

LEE, John Michael Andrew. b 62. Leeds Univ BA84. Trin Coll Bris 88. **d** 90 **p** 91. C Norbiton *S'wark* 90-94; C Leic H Trin w St Jo 94-02; R York St Paul from 02. *St Paul's Rectory, 100 Acomb Road, York YO24 4ER* Tel (01904) 792304
E-mail john_lee@lineone.net

LEE, John Samuel. b 47. Chich Th Coll 74. **d** 77 **p** 78. C Bramley *Ripon* 77-80; C Bideford *Ex* 81-84; TV Littleham w Exmouth 84-90; P-in-c Sidbury 90-91; TV Sidmouth, Woolbrook, Salcombe Regis, Sidbury etc 91-04; rtd 04. *Westward Ho!, Torpark Road, Torquay TQ2 5BQ* Tel (01803) 293086
E-mail johnslee@glensidf.freeserve.co.uk

LEE, Joseph Patrick. b 53. St Jos Coll Upholland 72 Ushaw Coll Dur 75. **d** 78 **p** 79. In RC Ch 78-99; Hon C Charlton *S'wark* 99-09; Hon C E Greenwich from 09. *45 Chestnut Rise, London SE18 1RJ* Tel (020) 8316 4674 Mobile 07956-294429 Fax 8317 7304 E-mail joe_lee@lineone.net

LEE, Mrs Judith Mary. b 44. Doncaster Coll of Educn TCert65. **d** 06 **p** 07. OLM Frenchay and Winterbourne Down *Bris* from 06. *8 Beaufort Road, Frampton Cotterell, Bristol BS36 2AD* Tel (01454) 772381 E-mail jrplee@btinternet.com

LEE, Canon Kenneth Peter. b 45. Em Coll Cam BA67 MA71. Cuddesdon Coll 67. **d** 69 **p** 70. C Stoke Poges *Ox* 69-72; C Witton *Ches* 72-74; V Frankby w Greasby 74-92; R Christleton from 92; Hon Can Ches Cathl from 05. *The Rectory, Birch Heath Lane, Christleton, Chester CH3 7AP* Tel (01244) 335663
E-mail kpeter.lee@btinternet.com

LEE, Luke Gun-Hong. b 37. Univ of Yon Sei BTh62. St Jo Coll Morpeth 64. **d** 67 **p** 68. Lic to Offic Taejon Korea 67-79; C Bloxwich *Lich* 79-83; TV Dunstable *St Alb* 83-90; V Croxley Green All SS 90-07; rtd 07. *101 Larkvale, Aylesbury HP19 0YP* Tel (01296) 423133 E-mail luke.gh.lee@gmail.com

LEE, Miss Lynley Hoe. b 52. St Jo Coll Nottm BTh89 K Coll Lon MA93. **d** 90 **p** 94. Par Dn Pitsea *Chelmsf* 90-95; Singapore 95-98; C Gt Ilford St Andr *Chelmsf* 99-02; TV Grays Thurrock 02-07; Chapl Salford R Hosps NHS Foundn Trust from 07. *Hope Hospital, Stott Lane, Salford M6 8HD* Tel 0161-789 7373
E-mail lynleyhoe@aol.com

LEE, Mrs Margaret. b 48. Coll of Ripon & York St Jo BEd71. NEOC 03. **d** 06 **p** 07. NSM Houghton le Spring *Dur* from 06. *2 Rectory View, Shadforth, Durham DH6 1LF* Tel 0191-372 0595 E-mail margaretlee595@hotmail.com

LEE, Martin Paul. b 66. Aston Tr Scheme 91 Linc Th Coll 93 St Steph Ho Ox 94. **d** 96 **p** 97. C Wells St Thos w Horrington *B & W* 96-00; P-in-c Brent Knoll, E Brent and Lympsham 00-01; R 01-08; RD Axbridge 03-08; V Long Benton *Newc* from 08. *The Vicarage, 3 Station Road, Benton, Newcastle upon Tyne NE12 8AN* Tel 0191-266 1921 E-mail frmlee@aol.com

LEE, Michael. b 45. **d** 07 **p** 08. OLM Chickerell w Fleet *Sarum* from 07. *45 Lower Way, Chickerell, Weymouth DT3 4AR* Tel (01305) 777031 E-mail michaellynda@googlemail.com

LEE, Nicholas Knyvett. b 54. Trin Coll Cam BA76 MA77. Cranmer Hall Dur 82. **d** 85 **p** 86. C Brompton H Trin w Onslow Square St Paul *Lon* from 85; Chapl R Brompton and Harefield

NHS Trust 86-90 and from 94. *St Paul's Church House, Onslow Square, London SW7 3NX* Tel 08456-447533
E-mail nicky.lee@htb.org.uk

LEE, Peter. *See* LEE, Canon Kenneth Peter

LEE, Peter Alexander. b 44. Hull Univ BSc(Econ)65. Ex & Truro NSM Scheme 80. **d** 83 **p** 84. NSM Ex St Sidwell and St Matt 83-89; NSM Ex St Dav 90-98; C Paignton St Jo 98-01; Perm to Offic 01-03; Hon C Ex St Dav from 03. *Windyridge, Beech Avenue, Exeter EX4 6HF* Tel (01392) 254118

✠**LEE, The Rt Revd Peter John.** b 47. St Jo Coll Cam BA69 MA73 CertEd70 Lambeth BD06. Ridley Hall Cam 70 St Jo Coll Nottm 72. **d** 73 **p** 74 **c** 90. C Onslow Square St Paul *Lon* 73-76; S Africa from 76; V-Gen and Bp Ch the K from 90. *PO Box 1653, Rosettenville, 2130 South Africa* Tel (0027) (11) 435 0097 *or* 942 1179 Fax 435 2868 E-mail dckpeter@netactive.co.za

LEE, Peter Kenneth. b 44. Selw Coll Cam BA66 MA69. Cuddesdon Coll 67. **d** 69 **p** 70. C Manston *Ripon* 69-72; C Bingley All SS *Bradf* 72-77; Chapl Bingley Coll of Educn 72-77; V Cross Roads cum Lees *Bradf* 77-90; V Auckland St Pet *Dur* 90-09; Tutor NEOC 91-09; rtd 09; Tutor NEITE from 03; Tutor to Curates *York* from 09. *2 Winston Court, Northallerton DL6 1PY* Tel (01609) 777539

LEE, Canon Raymond John. b 30. St Edm Hall Ox BA53 MA57. Tyndale Hall Bris 54. **d** 56 **p** 57. C Tooting Graveney St Nic *S'wark* 56-59; C Muswell Hill St Jas *Lon* 59-62; V Woking St Mary *Guildf* 62-70; V Gt Crosby St Luke *Liv* 70-82; Dioc Adv NSM 79-95; V Allerton 82-94; P-in-c Altcar 94-98; Hon Can Liv Cathl 89-95; rtd 95; Perm to Offic *Liv* 98-02; Hon C Bootle from 02. *15 Barkfield Lane, Liverpool L37 1LY* Tel (01704) 872670

LEE, Richard. *See* LEE, Thomas Richard

LEE, Richard Alexander. b 63. St Jo Coll Nottm BTh91. **d** 91 **p** 92. C Gt Stanmore *Lon* 91-95; C Edgware 95-98; TV S Gillingham *Roch* 98-07; Jt P-in-c Locking *B & W* 07-09; Jt P-in-c Hutton and Locking from 09. *The Vicarage, The Green, Locking, Weston-super-Mare BS24 8DA* Tel (01934) 823556
E-mail revdannelee@yahoo.co.uk

LEE, Robert David. b 53. QUB BD75. CITC 77. **d** 77 **p** 78. C Comber *D & D* 77-83; I Mt Merrion 83-87; CMS 89-92; Egypt 89-97; R Peebles *Edin* from 97; P-in-c Innerleithen from 97. *The Rectory, 45 Edderston Road, Peebles EH45 9DT* Tel and fax (01721) 720571 E-mail rdlee@dsl.pipex.com

LEE, Robert William. b 31. Keele Univ BA54 St Cath Soc Ox BA58 MA63. Ripon Hall Ox 56. **d** 59 **p** 60. C Dawley St Jerome *Lon* 59-62; C Bromley H Trin *Roch* 62-65; R Clayton *Man* 65-70; P-in-c Man St Paul 65-70; TV Hemel Hempstead *St Alb* 70-72; TV Corby SS Pet and Andr w Gt and Lt Oakley 72-80; V Weedon Lois w Plumpton and Moreton Pinkney etc 80-88; R Thornhams Magna and Parva, Gislingham and Mellis *St E* 88-96; rtd 96; Perm to Offic *Bradf* and *Carl* from 96. *2 Guldrey Fold, Sedbergh LA10 5DY* Tel (01539) 621907

LEE, Roderick James. b 50. Linc Th Coll 88. **d** 90 **p** 91. C Rushden w Newton Bromswold *Pet* 90-93; C Kingsthorpe w Northampton St Dav 93-94; TV 94-99; R Mears Ashby and Hardwick and Sywell etc 99-04; P-in-c Corby St Columba from 04; RD Corby from 07. *St Columba's Vicarage, 157 Studfall Avenue, Corby NN17 1LG* Tel (01536) 204158 *or* 261436
E-mail rlee103400@aol.com

LEE, Sai Kuen. *See* LEE, Gilbert

LEE, Sam. *See* LEE, Clifford Samuel

LEE, Steven Michael. b 56. Van Mildert Coll Dur BA78. Trin Coll Bris 80. **d** 83 **p** 84. C Beckenham St Jo *Roch* 83-86; C Leic Martyrs 86-90; V Coalville and Bardon Hill 90-95; P-in-c Kibworth and Smeeton Westerby and Saddington 95-00; P-in-c Foxton w Gumley and Laughton 96-00; R Kibworth and Smeeton Westerby and Saddington 00-06; Chapl St Lawr Coll Ramsgate 06-08; R Newcastle w Butterton *Lich* from 08. *The Rectory, Seabridge Road, Newcastle ST5 2HS* Tel (01782) 616397 E-mail revslee@btinternet.com

LEE, Stuart Graham. b 73. Roehampton Inst BA94. St Steph Ho Ox BTh00. **d** 00 **p** 01. C Eltham H Trin *S'wark* 00-03; TV Wimbledon from 03. *St Matthew's House, 10 Coombe Gardens, London SW20 0QU* Tel (020) 8944 1010

LEE, Stuart Michael. b 67. SEITE 06. **d** 09. NSM St Jo on Bethnal Green *Lon* from 09. *29 Brierly Gardens, London E2 0TE* Tel (020) 8980 1699 Mobile 07855-703766
E-mail stuartm.lee@virgin.net

LEE, Thomas Richard. b 52. AKC73 FRSA03. St Aug Coll Cant 74. **d** 75 **p** 76. C Leam Lane CD *Dur* 75-80; Chapl RAF 80-09; Prin Armed Forces Chapl Cen Amport Ho 03-06; Hon C St Mary le Strand w St Clem Danes *Lon* 06-09; QHC 06-09; TR Egremont and Haile *Carl* from 09. *The Rectory, Grove Road, Egremont CA22 2LU* Tel and fax (01946) 820268
E-mail lee535877@aol.com

LEE, Veronica. b 47. Redland Coll of Educn CertEd68 Open Univ BA84 Bris Poly MEd89. S1ETS 02. **d** 05 **p** 06. NSM Bishopston and St Andrews *Bris* from 05. *48 Chesterfield Road, Bristol BS6 5DL* Tel 0117-949 8325 E-mail vronlee@hotmail.com

LEE WARNER, Canon Theodore John. b 22. Univ Coll Ox BA49 MA54. Wells Th Coll 50. **d** 51 **p** 52. C S Westoe *Dur* 51-55; P-in-c

Cassop cum Quarrington 55-59; V Peterlee 59-63; V Darlington H Trin 63-74; Chapl Darlington Memorial Hosp 63-74; V Norton St Mary *Dur* 74-80; RD Barnard Castle 80-87; V Gainford 80-87; R Winston 80-87; Hon Can Dur Cathl 83-87; rtd 87. *112 Cleveland Terrace, Darlington DL3 8JA* Tel (01325) 467585

LEECE, Roderick Neil Stephen. b 59. Wadh Coll Ox BA81 MA85 Leeds Univ BA84 ARCM85. Coll of Resurr Mirfield 82. **d** 85 **p** 86. C Portsea St Mary *Portsm* 85-91; V Stamford Hill St Bart *Lon* 91-05; R Hanover Square St Geo from 05. *21A Down Street, London W1J 7AW* Tel (020) 7629 0874
E-mail rleece@lineone.net

LEECH, Kenneth. b 39. Lon Univ BA61 AKC61 Trin Coll Ox BA63 MA71 Lambeth DD98. St Steph Ho Ox 62. **d** 64 **p** 65. C Hoxton H Trin w St Mary *Lon* 64-67; C Soho St Anne w St Thos and St Pet 67-71; Tutor St Aug Coll Cant 71-74; R Bethnal Green St Matt *Lon* 74-79; Field Officer Community & Race Relns Unit BCC 80; Race Relns Officer Gen Syn Bd for Soc Resp 81-87; Hon C Notting Hill St Clem and St Mark *Lon* 82-85; Hon C Notting Dale St Clem w St Mark and St Jas 85-88; Dir Runnymede Trust 87-90; Hon C St Botolph Aldgate w H Trin Minories *Lon* 91-04; rtd 04; Perm to Offic *Ches* from 06. *89 Manchester Road, Mossley, Ashton-under-Lyne OL5 9LZ* Tel (01457) 835119 E-mail kenleech@aol.com

LEEDS, Archdeacon of. *See* BURROWS, The Ven Peter

LEEFIELD, Michael John. b 37. Liv Univ BA60 K Coll Lon BD65 AKC65. St Boniface Warminster 62. **d** 66 **p** 67. C Gt Yarmouth *Nor* 66-70; V Trowse 70-75; V Arminghall 70-75; R Caistor w Markshall 70-75; Chapl Norfolk and Nor Hosp 70-75; V Lydney w Aylburton *Glouc* 75-84; RD Forest S 82-84; Lic to Offic from 85; rtd 01. *Brays Court, Awre, Newnham GL14 1EP* Tel (01594) 510483

LEEKE, Charles Browne. b 39. Stranmillis Coll CertEd62. CITC 80. **d** 83 **p** 84. C Ballymoney w Finvoy and Rasharkin *Conn* 83-86; I Faughanvale *D & R* 86-97; Chapl Port Londonderry Miss to Seamen 92-97; Bp's Dom Chapl *D & R* 92-96; Can Derry Cathl 96-00; I Drumragh w Mountfield 97-00; Reconciliation Development Officer *D & R* from 00; Can Dromore Cathl 05-06; rtd 06; I Dromara w Garvaghy *D & D* from 08. *The Rectory, 58 Banbridge Road, Dromara, Dromore BT25 1NE* Tel (028) 9753 3063 E-mail charlie@reconcile-think.fsnet.co.uk

LEEKE, Canon Stephen Owen. b 50. EAMTC 82 Ridley Hall Cam 83. **d** 84 **p** 85. C Cherry Hinton St Andr *Ely* 84-87; P-in-c Warboys 87-91; P-in-c Bury 87-91; P-in-c Wistow 87-91; R Warboys w Broughton and Bury w Wistow 91-01; RD St Ives 92-01; V Cambridge St Martin from 01; Hon Can Ely Cathl from 05. *St Martin's Vicarage, 127 Suez Road, Cambridge CB1 3QD* Tel (01223) 214203
E-mail stephen.leeke@ely.anglican.org

LEEMAN, John Graham. b 41. NOC 78. **d** 80 **p** 81. NSM Hull St Mary Sculcoates *York* 80-96; Perm to Offic 96-99; Hon C Hull St Mary Sculcoates 99-04; P-in-c from 04; Hon C Hull St Steph Sculcoates 99-04; Hon C Sculcoates St Paul w Ch Ch and St Silas 99-04. *1 Snuff Mill Lane, Cottingham HU16 4RY* Tel (01482) 840355

LEEMING, Jack. b 34. Kelham Th Coll 56. **d** 61 **p** 62. C Sydenham St Phil *S'wark* 61-64; Chapl RAF 64-84; Chapl Salisbury Gen Infirmary 84-89; R Barford St Martin, Dinton, Baverstock etc *Sarum* 89-99; rtd 99; Perm to Offic *Sarum* from 01. *8 Bower Gardens, Salisbury SP1 2RL* Tel (01722) 416800

LEEMING, Mrs Janice Doreen. b 45. EMMTC 97. **d** 00 **p** 01. NSM Lenton *S'well* 00-06; NSM Radford All So w Ch Ch and St Mich from 06; NSM Radford St Pet from 06. *5 Hollinwell Avenue, Wollaton, Nottingham NG8 1JY* Tel 0115-928 2145

LEEMING, John Maurice. b 24. CEng MIMechE MIProdE FIED. NW Ord Course 72. **d** 75 **p** 76. NSM Endcliffe *Sheff* 75-78; C Norton 78-80; V Bolsterstone 80-89; Jt Min Stocksbridge Chr Cen LEP 80-89; Ind Chapl 81-89; rtd 89; Perm to Offic *S'well* from 89; *Sheff* from 93; *Derby* from 98. *Beck House, Toftdyke Lane, Clayworth, Retford DN22 9AH* Tel (01777) 817795 E-mail maurice@leeming02.freeserve.co.uk

LEES, Allan Garside. b 39. **d** 99 **p** 00. OLM Hurst *Man* from 99. *1 Exeter Drive, Ashton-under-Lyne OL6 8BZ* Tel 0161-339 3105

LEES, Brian James. b 52. Lon Univ BA74 Leeds Univ BA08 Univ of Wales (Abth) PGCE75. NOC 05. **d** 08 **p** 09. NSM Hutton Cranswick w Skerne, Watton and Beswick *York* from 08. *The Old Post House, Beswick, Driffield YO25 9AS* Tel (01377) 270806 E-mail brian.lees@tinyworld.co.uk

LEES, Charles Alan. b 38. RGN TCert. WMMTC 78. **d** 81 **p** 82. NSM Yardley St Cypr Hay Mill *Birm* 81-84 and 86-87; Hon C Dorridge 84-86; Chapl E Birm Hosp 85-87; Hon C Leamington Spa H Trin and Old Milverton *Cov* 89-90; Perm to Offic *Birm* 95-01. *8 Fairlawn Close, Leamington Spa CV32 6EN*

LEES, Fitzwilliam (Bill). b 58. Fitzw Coll Cam BA80 Birkbeck Coll Lon MA86 FCIPD. NOC 01. **d** 04 **p** 05. NSM Wilmslow *Ches* from 04; Asst Dir of Ords from 07. *110 Grove Park, Knutsford WA16 8QB* Tel (01565) 631625
E-mail johnlees@dsl.pipex.com

LEES, John Raymond. b 57. Selw Coll Cam BA78 MA82. St Steph Ho Ox 89. **d** 91 **p** 92. C Eastbourne St Mary *Chich* 91-93; Min Can and Succ St Paul's Cathl 93-98; TR Swindon New Town *Bris* 98-01; Asst to AD Swindon and C Highworth w Sevenhampton and Inglesham etc 01-02; Perm to Offic *Lon* 02-05; *Pet* and *Ely* 04-06; Can Res and Prec Wakef Cathl 06-09; rtd 09; Perm to Offic *Lich* from 09. *71 Merridale Road, Wolverhampton WV3 9SE* Tel (01902) 714744 E-mail frjrl@btinternet.com

LEES, Mrs Kathleen Marion. b 30. Birkbeck Coll Lon BA60. S'wark Ord Course 77. **dss** 80 **d** 87 **p** 94. Epping St Jo *Chelmsf* 80-86; Hon C Hunstanton St Mary w Ringstead Parva, Holme etc *Nor* 87-88; Perm to Offic 88-94; Chapl King's Lynn and Wisbech Hosps NHS Trust 94-00; NSM Gaywood *Nor* 94-00; rtd 00; Perm to Offic *Nor* from 00. *20 North Hirne Court, St Anns Street, King's Lynn PE31 1LT* Tel (01553) 661294

LEES, Peter John. b 39. St Jo Coll Nottm 91. **d** 95 **p** 96. NSM Buckie and Turriff *Ab* 95-00; P-in-c Fraserburgh 00-01; R 01-06; rtd 06; Hon C Turriff *Ab* from 06. *7 Whitefield Court, Buckie AB56 1EY* Tel (01542) 835011 Mobile 07929-668027

LEES, Stephen. b 55. St Jo Coll York CertEd77 BEd78 Nottm Univ MA96. St Jo Coll Nottm 88. **d** 90 **p** 91. C Mansfield St Jo *S'well* 90-93; TV Bestwood 93-98; V Baxenden *Blackb* 98-08; P-in-c Halifax All SS *Wakef* from 08. *All Saints' Vicarage, Greenroyd Avenue, Halifax HX3 0LP* E-mail theleeslot@tiscali.net

LEES, Stephen David. b 63. Sheff City Poly BA84 Bradf Coll of Educn PGCE92 St Jo Coll Dur BA09. Cranmer Hall Dur 07. **d** 09. C Frizinghall St Marg *Bradf* from 09. *2B Nab Lane, Shipley BD18 4HB* E-mail stelees2004@yahoo.co.uk

LEES, Stuart Charles Roderick. b 62. Trin Coll Bris BA. **d** 89 **p** 90. C Woodford Wells *Chelmsf* 89-93; C Brompton H Trin w Onslow Square St Paul *Lon* 93-97; Chapl Stewards Trust 93-97; P-in-c Fulham Ch Ch 97-03; V from 03. *Christ Church Vicarage, 40 Clancarty Road, London SW6 3AA* Tel (020) 7736 4261 E-mail stuart@ccfulham.com

LEES-SMITH, Anthony James. b 77. Selw Coll Cam BA99 MA02 St Jo Coll Dur BA08 Westmr Inst of Educn PGCE02. Cranmer Hall Dur 06. **d** 09. C Chesterton Gd Shep *Ely* from 09. *258 Milton Road, Cambridge CB4 1LQ* Tel 07967-353857 (mobile) E-mail singers99@talktalk.net

LEES-SMITH, Christopher John (Brother Edward). b 21. CCC Ox BA49 MA65. Cuddesdon Coll 48. **d** 50 **p** 51. C Pallion *Dur* 50-54; SSF from 54; Lic to Offic *Sarum* 57-62; Perm to Offic *Newc* 62-74; Guardian Alnmouth Friary 65-74; Chapl Third Order SSF 74-91; rtd 91. *The Friary, Alnmouth, Alnwick NE66 6NJ* Tel (01665) 830213

LEESE, Arthur Selwyn Mountford. b 09. K Coll Lon BD31 AKC31 St Cath Soc Ox BA33 MA44. Ripon Hall Ox 31. **d** 33 **p** 34. C Bexleyheath Ch Ch *Roch* 33-37; C Cockington *Ex* 37-39; C Langley Mill *Derby* 39-51; V Hawkhurst *Cant* 51-74; rtd 74; Perm to Offic *Cant* from 74 and *Chich* 75-08. *84 Wickham Avenue, Bexhill-on-Sea TN39 3ER* Tel (01424) 213137

LEESE, Mrs Jane Elizabeth. b 50. Man Univ BA(Econ)72 Avery Hill Coll PGCE73. Sarum Th Coll 93. **d** 96 **p** 97. NSM Kempshott *Win* 96-01; NSM Herriard w Winslade and Long Sutton etc 01-08; NSM N Hants Downs from 08. *The Parsonage, Gaston Lane, South Warnborough, Hook RG29 1RH* Tel (01256) 862843 E-mail jane.leese@ukgateway.net

LEESON, Bernard Alan. b 47. Bris Univ CertEd68 Open Univ BA75 Southn Univ MA78 Sheff Univ PhD97 FCollP92 FRSA92. EMMTC 84. **d** 87 **p** 88. Dep Hd Master Ripley Mill Hill Sch 80-91; NSM Breadsall *Derby* 87-91; Hd St Aid C of E Tech Coll Lancs 91-06; Clergy Support and Development Officer *Blackb* 06-09; Perm to Offic 91-92; Lic to Offic from 92; NSM Officer 92-96; rtd 06. *The Lodge, Daggers Lane, Preesall, Poulton-le-Fylde FY6 0QN* Tel (01253) 811020 E-mail alan.leeson@fsmail.net

LEESON, David Harry Stanley. b 45. Glouc Th Course 82. **d** 85 **p** 86. NSM Stratton w Baunton *Glouc* 85-94; NSM N Cerney w Bagendon 91-94; NSM Stratton, N Cerney, Baunton and Bagendon from 95. *83 Cheltenham Road, Stratton, Cirencester GL7 2JB* Tel (01285) 651186

LEESON, Mrs Sally Elizabeth. b 57. Sussex Univ BA79. Westcott Ho Cam 83. **dss** 85 **d** 87 **p** 94. Battersea St Pet and St Paul *S'wark* 85-90; Par Dn 87-90; Par Dn Limpsfield and Titsey 90-94; Perm to Offic from 94; Chapl Bp Wand Sch Sunbury-on-Thames from 05. *32 Albany Road, New Malden KT3 3NY* Tel (020) 8942 5198

LEFFLER, Christopher. b 33. Em Coll Cam BA57 MA61. Linc Th Coll. **d** 59 **p** 60. C Bermondsey St Mary w St Olave and St Jo *S'wark* 59-60; C Herne Hill St Paul 60-63; C-in-c Canley CD *Cov* 63-67; R Gt and Lt Glemham *St E* 67-72; R Badwell Ash w Gt Ashfield, Stowlangtoft etc 72-82; R Trimley 82-99; rtd 99; Perm to Offic *St E* from 99. *308 High Street, Felixstowe IP11 9QJ* Tel (01394) 672279 E-mail chrisleffler@quista.net

LEFFLER, Jeremy Paul (Jem). b 62. Westmr Coll Ox BEd88. Wycliffe Hall Ox BTh94. **d** 94 **p** 95. C Ormskirk *Liv* 94-97; C Much Woolton 97-00; P-in-c Widnes St Ambrose 00-03; V from 03. *St Ambrose Vicarage, 45 Hargreaves Court, Widnes WA8 0QA* Tel and fax 0151-420 8044 E-mail info@stambrose.fsnet.co.uk

LEFROY, John Perceval. b 40. Trin Coll Cam BA62. Cuddesdon Coll 64. **d** 66 **p** 67. C Maidstone St Martin *Cant* 66-69; C St Peter-in-Thanet 69-74; V Barming Heath 74-82; V Upchurch w Lower Halstow 82-05; P-in-c Iwade 95-05; rtd 05. *23 Heather Avenue, Melksham SN12 6FX* Tel (01225) 704012 E-mail jclefroy@tiscali.co.uk

LEFROY (née CLARK), Kathleen Christine. See ENGLAND, Mrs Kathleen Christine

LEFROY, Matthew William. b 62. Trin Coll Cam BA84 Keele Univ PGCE91. St Jo Coll Nottm MTh02. **d** 02 **p** 03. C Portswood Ch Ch *Win* 02-06; TV Madeley *Heref* from 06. *The Vicarage, Park Lane, Madeley, Telford TF7 5HN* Tel (01952) 588958 E-mail matthew@mjlefroy.freeserve.co.uk

LEFROY-OWEN, Neal. b 62. Bradf Univ BA99. NOC 00. **d** 03 **p** 04. C Sandal St Cath *Wakef* 03-06; Asst Chapl HM Pris Hull 06-08; Chapl HM Pris Lindholme from 08. *HM Prison Lindholme, Bawtry Road, Hatfield Woodhouse, Doncaster DN7 6EE* Tel (01302) 848829 E-mail neal@own21.fslife.co.uk

LEGG, Adrian James. b 52. St Jo Coll Nottm BTh82. **d** 82 **p** 83. C Haughton le Skerne *Dur* 82-85; C Llanishen and Lisvane 85-89; V Llanwddyn and Llanfihangel-yng-Nghwynfa etc *St As* 89-93; V Llansadwrn w Llanwrda and Manordeilo *St D* from 93. *The Vicarage, Llanwrda SA19 8HD* Tel (01550) 777343 E-mail ajlegg@tiscali.co.uk

LEGG, Joanna Susan Penberthy. See PENBERTHY, Canon Joanna Susan

LEGG, Margaret. b 50. SEITE. **d** 07 **p** 08. NSM Paddington St Jo w St Mich *Lon* from 07. *9 Wilton Street, London SW1X 7AF* Tel (020) 7235 4944

LEGG, Peter Ellis. b 51. STETS 02. **d** 05 **p** 06. NSM Radipole and Melcombe Regis *Sarum* from 05. *449 Dorchester Road, Weymouth DT3 5BW* Tel (01305) 815342 Mobile 07779-334520 E-mail pleggwey@aol.com

LEGG, Richard. b 37. Selw Coll Cam BA62 MA66 Brunel Univ MPhil77 NY Th Sem DMin85. Coll of Resurr Mirfield 63. **d** 65 **p** 66. C Ealing St Pet Mt Park *Lon* 65-68; Chapl Brunel Univ 68-78; Wychcroft Ho (Dioc Retreat Cen) *S'wark* 78-81; C Chipping Barnet w Arkley *St Alb* 81-83; TV 83-85; R St Buryan, St Levan and Sennen *Truro* 85-93; Subwarden St Deiniol's Lib Hawarden 93; Perm to Offic *Ches* 93; TV Beaminster Area *Sarum* 93-97; P-in-c Veryan w Ruan Lanihorne *Truro* 97-00; rtd 01; Perm to Offic *Truro* 03-09. *27A Bath Road, Wells BA5 3HR* Tel (01749) 670468 E-mail richardlegg@blue-earth.co.uk

LEGG, Roger Keith. b 35. Lich Th Coll 61. **d** 63 **p** 64. C Petersfield w Sheet *Portsm* 63-66; C Portsea St Mary 66-70; Rhodesia 70-75; V Clayton *Lich* 75-00; rtd 01; Perm to Offic *Lich* from 01. *High Crest, Chapel Lane, Hookgate, Market Drayton TF9 4QP* Tel (01630) 672766 E-mail rogjud@aol.com

LEGG, Miss Ruth Helen Margaret. b 52. Hull Univ BA74 Homerton Coll Cam CertEd75. Trin Coll Bris 86. **d** 88 **p** 94. C Clevedon St Andr and Ch Ch *B & W* 88-92; C Nailsea Ch Ch 92-96; C Nailsea Ch Ch w Tickenham 96-97; V Pill, Portbury and Easton-in-Gordano from 97. *The Rectory, 17 Church Road, Easton-in-Gordano, Bristol BS20 0PQ* Tel (01275) 372804

LEGGATE, Colin Archibald Gunson. b 44. Bris Sch of Min 86. **d** 88 **p** 89. NSM Brislington St Luke 88-97; Asst Chapl Frenchay Healthcare NHS Trust Bris 97-99; Asst Chapl N Bris NHS Trust from 99. *Frenchay Hospital, Frenchay Park Road, Bristol BS16 1LE* Tel 0117-970 1212 *or* 965 1434

LEGGE, Robert James. b 63. BSc92. Ox Min Course. **d** 09. *Address temp unknown* E-mail rjlegge@live.co.uk

LEGGETT, James Henry Aufrere. b 61. Oak Hill Th Coll 91. **d** 93 **p** 94. C Hensingham *Carl* 93-97; C-in-c Ryde St Jas Prop Chpl *Portsm* from 97. *84 Pellhurst Road, Ryde PO33 3BS* Tel (01983) 565621 *or* 566381 E-mail jleggett@onetel.com

LEGGETT, Nicholas William Michael. b 62. St Steph Ho Ox 00. **d** 02 **p** 04. C Clevedon St Jo *B & W* 02-06; P-in-c Bridgwater H Trin and Durleigh 06-07; V from 07; Hon Chapl ATC from 04. *The New Vicarage, Hamp Avenue, Bridgwater TA6 6AN* Tel (01278) 433637 Mobile 07762-156380 E-mail leggett1uwe@yahoo.co.uk

LEGGETT, Vanessa Gisela. See CATO, Ms Vanessa Gisela

LEGH, Mrs Jane Mary. b 52. Southn Univ BSc73. Qu Coll Birm 08. **d** 09. NSM Alkmonton, Cubley and Marston Montgomery *Derby* from 09; NSM Boylestone, Church Broughton, Dalbury, etc from 09; NSM Doveridge, Scropton, Sudbury etc from 09. *Cubley Lodge, Cubley, Ashbourne DE6 2FB* Tel (01335) 330297 E-mail jane.legh@cubleylodge.com

LEGOOD, Giles Leslie. b 67. K Coll Lon BD88 AKC88 Heythrop Coll Lon MTh98 Derby Univ DMin04. Ripon Coll Cuddesdon 90. **d** 92 **p** 93. C N Mymms *St Alb* 92-95; Chapl R Veterinary Coll *Lon* 95-07; Chapl R Free and Univ Coll Medical Sch 95-07; Chapl RAuxAF 04-07; Chapl RAF from 08.

Chaplaincy Services, Valiant Block, HQ Air Command, RAF High Wycombe HP14 4UE Tel (01494) 496800 Fax 496343

LEGRAND, Nigel Stuart. b 51. STETS 96. **d** 99 **p** 00. NSM Boscombe St Jo *Win* 99-03; NSM Pokesdown All SS 03-07; NSM Holdenhurst and Iford from 07; NSM Southbourne St Chris from 03. *50 Meon Road, Bournemouth BH7 6PP* Tel (01202) 428603 Fax 300400 E-mail nlegrandfamily@aol.com

LEHANEY, Frank George. b 44. MCIT75 MILT99 MIAM78. **d** 99 **p** 00. OLM Brockham Green *S'wark* 99-07; NSM from 07; OLM Leigh 99-07; NSM from 07; Chapl Surrey and Sussex Healthcare NHS Trust from 99. *Twelve Trees, Small's Hill Road, Leigh, Reigate RH2 8PE* Tel (01306) 611201

LEICESTER, Archdeacon of. *See* ATKINSON, The Ven Richard William Bryant

LEICESTER, Bishop of. *See* STEVENS, The Rt Revd Timothy John

LEICESTER, Dean of. *See* FAULL, The Very Revd Vivienne Frances

LEIGH, Mrs Alison Margaret. b 40. CertEd63 Goldsmiths' Coll Lon BEd75. Sarum & Wells Th Coll 85. **d** 87 **p** 94. C Chessington *Guildf* 87-90; C Green Street Green *Roch* 90-92; Dn-in-c E Peckham and Nettlestead 92-94; P-in-c 94-95; R 95-01; rtd 01; Perm to Offic *Heref* from 02. *17 Orchard Green, Marden, Hereford HR1 3ED* Tel (01432) 882032 E-mail alison.leigh@which.net

LEIGH, Arnold Robert. b 36. AKC60. **d** 61 **p** 62. C Lewisham St Mary *S'wark* 61-66; C Stockwell Green St Andr 66-69; V 69-72; TV Withycombe Raleigh *Ex* 72-74; TR 74-80; V Devonport St Bart 80-93; P-in-c Moretonhampstead, N Bovey and Manaton 93-96; R Moretonhampstead, Manaton, N Bovey and Lustleigh 96-00; rtd 00; Perm to Offic *Win* from 03. *1 Southwick Road, Bournemouth BH6 5PR* Tel (01202) 420135

LEIGH, Dennis Herbert. b 34. Lon Univ BSc56. Chich Th Coll 58. **d** 60 **p** 61. C Roehampton H Trin *S'wark* 60-62; C E Wickham 62-67; C Plumstead St Mark and St Marg 67-73; C Corby Epiphany w St Jo *Pet* 73-74; C Paston 84-86; C Aylestone St Andr w St Jas *Leic* 86-95; rtd 95; Perm to Offic *Pet* from 95 and *Leic* from 00. *14 Willowbrook Road, Corby NN17 2EB* Tel (01536) 263405

LEIGH, Mary Elizabeth. b 42. K Coll Lon BA64 Univ of Wales (Lamp) MMin06. Westcott Ho Cam 89. **d** 91 **p** 94. NSM Chesterfield St Mary and All SS *Derby* 91-92; C Hall Green Ascension *Birm* 92-94; Asst P Yardley St Edburgha 94-97; Chapl and Tutor NOC 97-08; rtd 08; Perm to Offic *Lich* from 99. *Downing Cottage, Jaggers Lane, Hathersage, Hope Valley S32 1AZ* Tel 07796-980636 (mobile) E-mail maryelizabethleigh@gmail.com

LEIGH, Michael John. b 69. Leeds Univ BA02 LWCMD93. Coll of Resurr Mirfield 00. **d** 02 **p** 03. C N Hull St Mich *York* 02-06; P-in-c Newby from 06. *St Mark's Vicarage, 77 Green Lane, Scarborough YO12 6HT* Tel (01723) 363205

LEIGH, Raymond. b 37. Lon Univ BEd81. Clifton Th Coll 65. **d** 68 **p** 69. C Chadwell *Chelmsf* 68-71; Chapl RAF 71-77; Asst Master Swakeleys Sch Hillingdon 81-88; NSM Hillingdon St Jo *Lon* 87-88; C Rowley Regis *Birm* 88-90; V Londonderry 90-95; R Westbury w Turweston, Shalstone and Biddlesden *Ox* 95-99; CF (ACF) 95-02; rtd 99; Perm to Offic *Chich* 99-07 and *Guildf* from 07. *10 Nursery Close, Epsom KT17 1NH* Tel (020) 8394 2477 Mobile 07745 493014 E-mail rayleigh37@talktalk.net

LEIGH, Richenda Mary Celia. b 71. St Mary's Coll Strawberry Hill BA93. Ripon Coll Cuddesdon BTh98. **d** 99 **p** 00. C Dalston H Trin w St Phil and Haggerston All SS *Lon* 99-02; Asst Chapl R Free Hampstead NHS Trust 02-05; Chapl Lon Metrop Univ from 05. *St Luke's Church House, 21 Roscoe Street, London EC1Y 8PT* Tel (020) 7320 2379 Mobile 07971-659534

LEIGH, Roy Stephen. b 28. Imp Coll Lon BSc49. S'wark Ord Course 87. **d** 90 **p** 92. NSM Green Street Green *Roch* 90-92; NSM E Peckham and Nettlestead 92-00; Perm to Offic *Roch* 01 and *Heref* from 02. *17 Orchard Green, Marden, Hereford HR1 3ED* Tel (01432) 882032 E-mail r.s.leigh@reading.ac.uk

LEIGH-HUNT, Edward Christopher. b 22. Univ Coll Dur BA47. Ely Th Coll 48. **d** 50 **p** 51. C Wandsworth St Anne *S'wark* 50-54; C Bethnal Green St Matt *Lon* 54-56; C Lewisham St Jo Southend *S'wark* 56-57; C Ealing St Barn *Lon* 57-66; C St Bart Less 66-73; Chapl Asst St Bart Hosp Lon 66-73; Chapl Middx Hosp 73-86; rtd 87; Perm to Offic *Lon* 95-02. *The College of St Barnabas, Blackberry Lane, Lingfield RH7 6NJ* Tel (01342) 872823

LEIGH-HUNT, Nicolas Adrian. b 46. MIEx70. Qu Coll Birm 85. **d** 87 **p** 88. C Tilehurst St Geo *Ox* 87-91; TV Wexcombe *Sarum* 91-99; TR 99-02; TR Savernake from 02; RD Pewsey from 97. *The Vicarage, 5 Eastcourt, Burbage, Marlborough SN8 3AG* Tel and fax (01672) 810238 E-mail leighhunt@aol.com

LEIGHLIN, Dean of. *See* WYNNE, The Very Revd Frederick John Gordon

LEIGHTON, Adrian Barry. b 44. LTh. Lon Coll of Div 65. **d** 69 **p** 70. C Erith St Paul *Roch* 69-72; C Ipswich St Marg *St E* 72-75; P-in-c Ipswich St Helen 75-82; R 82-88; P-in-c Holbrook w Freston and Woolverstone 88-97; P-in-c Wherstead 94-97; R

Holbrook, Freston, Woolverstone and Wherstead 97-98; RD Samford 90-93; P-in-c Woore and Norton in Hales *Lich* 98-09; Local Min Adv (Shrewsbury) 99-09; rtd 09. *2 Tollgate Drive, Audlem, Crewe CW3 0EA* Tel (01270) 812209

LEIGHTON, Alan Granville Clyde. b 37. MInstM AMIDHE. S'wark Ord Course 73. **d** 76 **p** 77. C Silverhill St Matt *Chich* 76-79; C Eston *York* 79-82; V 82-84; TR Eston w Normanby 84-02; rtd 02; Perm to Offic *York* from 02. *Priory Lodge, 86B Church Lane, Eston, Middlesbrough TS6 9QR* Tel (01642) 504798 Fax 283016 E-mail aleighton@argonet.co.uk

LEIGHTON, Anthony Robert. b 56. Trin Coll Bris BA88. **d** 88 **p** 89. C Harrow Trin St Mich *Lon* 88-92; TV Ratby cum Groby *Leic* 92-94; TR Bradgate Team 94-00; P-in-c Newtown Linford 95-98; V Thorpe Acre w Dishley 00-08; NSM S Croxton Gp from 08. *The Rectory, 19 Main Street, South Croxton, Leicester LE7 3RJ* Tel (01664) 840245 E-mail tony0leighton@btinternet.com

LEIGHTON, Mrs Susan. b 58. Bretton Hall Coll BEd80. Trin Coll Bris BA89. **d** 89 **p** 94. Par Dn Harrow Weald All SS *Lon* 89-92; NSM Ratby cum Groby *Leic* 92-96; C Bradgate Team 96-00; Asst Warden of Readers 96-00; NSM Thorpe Acre w Dishley 00-08; TV S Croxton Gp from 08. *The Rectory, 19 Main Street, South Croxton, Leicester LE7 3RJ* Tel (01664) 840245 E-mail susan.leighton2@btinternet.com

LEIPER, Nicholas Keith. b 34. SS Coll Cam BA55 MB58 BChir58 MA65. St Jo Coll Nottm LTh82. **d** 84 **p** 85. C Biddston *Ches* 84-87; TV Gateacre *Liv* 87-92; P-in-c Bickerstaffe 92-94; P-in-c Melling 92-94; V Bickerstaffe and Melling 94-00; rtd 00; Perm to Offic *Liv* from 00. *31 Weldale House, Chase Close, Southport PR8 2DX* Tel (01704) 566393

LEITCH, Peter William. b 36. FCA58 ATII59. Coll of Resurr Mirfield 83. **d** 85 **p** 86. C Newsome and Armitage Bridge *Wakef* 85-88; P-in-c Upper Hopton 88-91; P-in-c Mirfield Eastthorpe St Paul 88-91; Chapl Rouen Miss to Seamen *Eur* 92-94; Sen Chapl Rotterdam Miss to Seamen 94-97; Chapl Felixstowe Miss to Seafarers *St E* 97-01; rtd 01; Perm to Offic *St E* from 01. *104 St Andrew's Road, Felixstowe IP11 7ED* Tel (01394) 285320

LEITHEAD, Mrs Lynette. b 54. SEITE. **d** 08 **p** 09. NSM Kippington *Roch* from 08. *45 Chipstead Park, Sevenoaks TN13 2SL* Tel (01732) 742272 Mobile 07958-145959 E-mail lynetteleithead@hotmail.co.uk

LEMMEY, William Henry Michael. b 59. Jes Coll Cam BA81 Jes Coll Ox PGCE82. Westcott Ho Cam 03. **d** 05 **p** 06. C Milton *Win* 05-09; R Porlock and Porlock Weir w Stoke Pero etc *B & W* from 09. *The Rectory, Parsons Street, Porlock, Minehead TA24 8QL* Tel (01643) 863172 E-mail billlemmey@yahoo.co.uk

LENDRUM, William Henry. b 24. TCD BA50 MA62. CITC 50. **d** 50 **p** 51. C Belfast St Mich *Conn* 50-53; C Lisburn Ch Ch Cathl 53-61; P-in-c Belfast Whiterock 61-69; I Belfast St Mary Magd 69-91; Can Conn Cathl 87-91; rtd 91. *38 Lancefield Road, Belfast BT9 6LL* Tel (028) 9028 0635 Mobile 07929-117924

LENG, Bruce Edgar. b 38. St Aid Birkenhead 68. **d** 69 **p** 70. C Sheff St Swithun 69-74; TV Speke St Aid *Liv* 74-78; TV Yate New Town *Bris* 78-82; R Handsworth *Sheff* 82-95; R Thrybergh 95-05; Warden for Past Workers 96-05; rtd 05. *41 Hall Close Avenue, Whiston, Rotherham S60 4AH* Tel (01709) 533819 E-mail bruce@faith.f9.co.uk

LENNARD, Mrs Elizabeth Jemima Mary Patricia (Mary Pat). b 21. Edin Dioc NSM Course 78. **dss** 82 **d** 86 **p** 94. Falkirk *Edin* 82-86; Hon C 86-91; Asst Dioc Supernumerary 91-96; rtd 92; Hon C Grangemouth *Edin* 96-04; Hon C Bo'ness 96-04. *36 Heugh Street, Falkirk FK1 5QR* Tel (01324) 623240

LENNOX, James. b 12. TCD BA36 MA40. Div Test 37. **d** 38 **p** 39. C Houghton le Spring *Dur* 38-43; C Darlington St Cuth 43-47; V Woodhouse *Wakef* 47-63; V Bingley All SS *Bradf* 63-77; rtd 77; Perm to Offic *Bradf* from 77. *30 Hazel Beck, Cottingley Bridge, Bingley BD16 1LZ* Tel (01274) 560189

LENNOX, Joan Baxter. *See* LYON, Joan Baxter

LENNOX, William Ernest Michael. b 28. Selw Coll Cam BA52 MA63 Leeds Univ CertEd55. K Coll Lon 62. **d** 63 **p** 64. C Bramley *Ripon* 63-66; C Margate St Jo *Cant* 66-71; R Kingsnorth 71-73; R Shadoxhurst 71-73; R Kingsnorth w Shadoxhurst 73-93. *6 rue Aux Savons, Le Boisle, 80150 Crécy-en-Ponthieu, France*

LENOX-CONYNGHAM, Andrew George. b 44. Magd Coll Ox BA65 MA73 CCC Cam PhD73. Westcott Ho Cam 72. **d** 74 **p** 75. C Poplar *Lon* 74-77; TV 77-80; Chapl Heidelberg *Eur* 80-82 and 91-96; Chapl Ch Coll Cam 82-86; Chapl and Fell St Cath Coll Cam 86-91; V Birm St Luke from 96; AD Birm City Cen from 04. *St Luke's Vicarage, 29 Bradshaw Close, Birmingham B15 2DD* Tel 0121-666 6089 *or* 622 2435 Fax 622 4532 E-mail lenox@birm.eclipse.co.uk

LENS VAN RIJN, Robert Adriaan. b 47. St Jo Coll Nottm 78. **d** 80 **p** 81. C Gt Baddow *Chelmsf* 80-83; C Edgware *Lon* 83-86; C Derby St Pet and Ch Ch w H Trin 86-90; Chapl Eindhoven *Eur* 91-00; Burrswood Chr Hosp from 04. *Bright's Cottage, Burrswood, Groombridge, Tunbridge Wells TN3 9PU* Tel (01892) 863266

LENTHALL, Mrs Nicola Yvonne. b 73. Southn Univ BA95. Westcott Ho Cam. **d** 99 **p** 00. C Leighton Buzzard w Eggington, Hockliffe etc *St Alb* 99-03; V Kensworth, Studham and Whipsnade from 03. *The Vicarage, Clay Hall Road, Kensworth, Dunstable LU6 3RF* Tel (01582) 872223

LENTON, Colin William. b 23. CertEd. Cuddesdon Coll 80. **d** 81 **p** 81. NSM Cowley St Jo *Ox* 81-82; NSM Oakley 82-85; V Langtoft w Foxholes, Butterwick, Cottam etc *York* 85-89; rtd 89; Perm to Offic *Ripon* and *York* from 89. *Flat 3, 24 South Drive, Harrogate HG2 8AU* Tel (01423) 564751

LENTON, John Robert. b 46. Ex Coll Ox BA69 Harvard Univ MBA74. Oak Hill Th Coll. **d** 00. NSM Muswell Hill St Jas w St Matt *Lon* 00-09; NSM Hampstead St Jo Downshire Hill Prop Chpl from 09. *St James's Vicarage, St James's Lane, London N10 3DB* Tel (020) 8444 2579 Mobile 07714-237235 E-mail johnlenton@iname.com

LENTON, Patricia Margarita. *See* DICKIN, Mrs Patricia Margarita

LEON (*née* HOLLAND), **Mrs Lesley Anne.** b 52. Univ Coll Chich BA04. STETS 04. **d** 07 **p** 08. NSM Northanger *Win* from 07. *11A Tilmore Gardens, Petersfield GU32 2JQ* E-mail lesley.leon@ntlworld.com

LEONARD, Ms Ann Cressey. b 50. Open Univ BA90. S Dios Min l Tr Scheme 90. **d** 94 **p** 95. C Portsea St Cuth *Portsm* 94-96; C Farlington 96-00; Asst to RD Petersfield 00-03; Deanery Co-ord for Educn and Tr 00-03; V Hayling Is St Andr from 03; V N Hayling St Pet from 03; Dioc Ecum Officer from 02. *29 Selsmore Road, Hayling Island PO11 9JZ* E-mail ann.leonard@ukgateway.net

LEONARD, John Francis. b 48. Lich Th Coll 69. **d** 72 **p** 73. C Chorley St Geo *Blackb* 72-75; C S Shore H Trin 75-80; V Marton Moss 81-89; V Kingskerswell w Coffinswell *Ex* from 89; P-in-c Abbotskerswell from 06. *The Vicarage, Pound Lane, Kingskerswell, Newton Abbot TQ12 5DW* Tel (01803) 407217 *or* 873006 E-mail kingskerswell.parish.church@tinyworld.co.uk

LEONARD, Canon John James. b 41. Southn Univ BSc62. Sarum Th Coll 63. **d** 65 **p** 66. C Loughborough Em *Leic* 65-70; V New Humberstone 70-78; C-in-c Rushey Mead CD 78-85; V Leic St Theodore 85-05; Hon Can Leic Cathl 96-05; RD Christianity N 97-05; rtd 05. *1339 Melton Road, Syston, Leicester LE7 2EP* Tel 0116-269 2691

LEONARD, Peter Michael. b 47. Portsm Poly BSc MRTPI. Sarum & Wells Th Coll 82. **d** 84 **p** 85. C Llantwit Major 84-88; V Cymmer and Porth 88-96; R Colwinston, Llandow and Llysworney from 96; AD Vale of Glam 02-08. *The Rectory, Llandow, Cowbridge CF71 7NT* Tel and fax (01656) 890205 E-mail peter@theleonards.org.uk

LEONARD, Peter Philip. b 70. Trin Coll Bris BA94. **d** 97 **p** 98. C Haslemere *Guildf* 97-00; C Haslemere and Grayswood 00-01; C Woodham 01-06. *Address withheld by request* Tel 07817-722219 (mobile) E-mail rev.peterleonard@ntlworld.com

LEONARD, Vaughan Thomas. b 51. Coll of Resurr Mirfield 94. **d** 96 **p** 97. C Broadstone *Sarum* 96-99; C Worth Chich 99-00; TV 00-06; V Leesfield *Man* from 06. *St Thomas Vicarage, 2 Wild Street, Lees, Oldham OL4 5AD* Tel 0161-624 3731 E-mail frvaughan@presbyter.co.uk

LEONARD-JOHNSON, Canon Philip Anthony. b 35. Selw Coll Cam BA58 MA60. Linc Th Coll 63. **d** 65 **p** 66. C Wymondham *Nor* 65-68; Zimbabwe 69-82; V Drayton in Hales *Lich* 82-92; R Adderley 82-92; P-in-c Moreton Say 88-92; S Africa 92-98; rtd 97; Hon Can Grahamstown from 97; Perm to Offic *Lich* from 99. *Hillside, Mount Lane, Market Drayton TF9 1AG* Tel (01630) 655480

LEONARDI, Jeffrey. b 49. Warwick Univ BA71. Carl Dioc Tr Course 85. **d** 88 **p** 89. C Netherton *Carl* 88-91; V Cross Canonby 91-97; V Allonby 91-97; Bp's Adv for Past Care and Counselling *Lich* from 97; Asst Min Colton, Colwich and Gt Haywood from 97. *The New Rectory, Bellamour Way, Colton, Rugeley WS15 3JW* Tel and fax (01889) 570897 E-mail jeff.leonardi@btinternet.com

LEPINE, Canon Jeremy John. b 56. BA. St Jo Coll Nottm 82. **d** 84 **p** 85. C Harrow Trin St Mich *Lon* 84-88; TV Horley *S'wark* 88-95; Evang Adv Croydon Area Miss Team 95-02; Dioc Evang Adv and Hon Chapl S'wark Cathl 97-02; R Wollaton *S'well* from 02; AD Nottingham N from 08; Hon Can S'well Minster from 09. *St Leonard's Rectory, 143 Russell Drive, Nottingham NG8 2BD* Tel 0115-928 1798 E-mail jerry.lepine@btopenworld.com

LEPPINGTON, Dian Marjorie. b 46. Leeds Univ BA85. Cranmer Hall Dur 81. **dss** 83 **d** 87 **p** 94. Potternewton *Ripon* 83-85; Ind Chapl 85-97; Chapl Teesside Univ 97-04; Can and Preb York Minster 03-04; Par Resources Adv *Man* from 05. *3 Booth-Clibborn Court, Salford M7 4PJ* Tel 0161-828 1446 E-mail dleppington@manchester.anglican.org

LERRY, Keith Doyle. b 49. St Mich Coll Llan 69. **d** 72 **p** 73. C Caerau w Ely *Llan* 72-75; C Roath St Martin 75-84; V Glyntaff from 84. *The Vicarage, Glyntaff Road, Pontypridd CF37 4AS* Tel (01443) 402535

LERVY, Hugh Martin. b 68. Univ of Wales (Lamp) BA89. Qu Coll Birm 89. **d** 91 **p** 92. C Brecon St Mary and Battle w Llanddew *S & B* 91-93; C Oystermouth 93-95; V Glantawe 95-00; V Morriston from 00. *The Vicarage, Vicarage Road, Morriston, Swansea SA6 6DR* Tel (01792) 771329 Mobile 07976-725644 E-mail hugh@lervy.freeserve.co.uk

LESITER, The Ven Malcolm Leslie. b 37. Selw Coll Cam BA61 MA65. Cuddesdon Coll 61. **d** 63 **p** 64. C Eastney *Portsm* 63-66; C Hemel Hempstead *St Alb* 66-71; TV 71-73; V Leavesden 73-88; RD Watford 81-88; V Radlett 88-93; Hon Can St Alb Abbey 90-93; Adn Bedford 93-03; rtd 03; Perm to Offic *Ely* from 03 and *Chelmsf* from 04. *349 Ipswich Road, Colchester CO4 0HN* Tel (01206) 841479

LESLIE, Christopher James. b 42. Open Univ BA75. Wycliffe Hall Ox 97. **d** 05 **p** 06. NSM Loddon Reach *Ox* from 05. *Church Farm House, Church Lane, Shinfield, Reading RG2 9BY* Tel 0118-988 8642 E-mail chris_leslie@compuserve.com

LESLIE, David Rodney. b 43. Liv Univ MEd94 Birm Univ PhD01 AKC67. **d** 68 **p** 69. C Belmont *Lon* 68-71; C St Giles Cripplegate w St Bart Moor Lane etc 71-75; TV Kirkby *Liv* 76-84; TR Ditton St Mich 84-98; V Ditton St Mich w St Thos 98-03; V Croxteth Park 03-08; rtd 08. *10 Eversley Close, Frodsham WA6 6AZ* Tel (01928) 723463 E-mail david_leslie@lineone.net

LESLIE, Richard Charles Alan. b 46. ACIB71. St Alb Minl Tr Scheme 76. **d** 79 **p** 91. NSM Redbourn *St Alb* 79-88; NSM Newport Pagnell w Lathbury and Moulsoe *Ox* 88-94; Stewardship Adv St Alb Adnry *St Alb* 94-97; TV Borehamwood 97-05; TV Elstree and Borehamwood from 05. *St Michael's Vicarage, 142 Brook Road, Borehamwood WD6 5EQ* Tel (020) 8953 2362 *or* 8905 1365 E-mail rcaleslie@idreamtime.com

LESTER, David Charles. b 46. BSc. **d** 99 **p** 00. NSM Trowell *S'well* 99-02; NSM Trowell, Awsworth and Cossall 02-06; rtd 06. *25 Ruby Street, Saltburn-by-the-Sea TS12 1EF* E-mail d.lester@ntlworld.com

LESTER, The Very Revd Trevor Rashleigh. b 50. CITC 83 St Deiniol's Hawarden 92. **d** 89 **p** 90. NSM Douglas Union w Frankfield *C, C & R* 89-93; C Kilkenny w Aghour and Kilmanagh *C & O* 93-95; Bp's V Ossory Cathl 93-95; Dioc Registrar (Ossory, Ferns and Leighlin) 93-95; Dioc Lib St Canice's Lib 93-95; I Abbeystrewry Union *C, C & R* 95-03; Dean Waterford *C & O* from 03; I Waterford w Killea, Drumcannon and Dunhill from 03. *The Deanery, 41 Grange Park Road, Waterford, Republic of Ireland* Tel (00353) (51) 874119 E-mail dean@waterford.anglican.org

L'ESTRANGE, Timothy John Nicholas. b 67. Surrey Univ BA90. St Steph Ho Ox BA92 MA96. **d** 93 **p** 94. C Hawkesworth w Linstead, Chediston, Holton etc *St E* 93-96; Dom Chapl to Bp Horsham *Chich* 96-98; R Beeding and Bramber w Botolphs 98-08; R Monken Hadley *Lon* from 08. *The Rectory, Hadley Common, Barnet EN5 5QD* Tel (020) 8449 2414

LETALL, Ronald Richard. b 29. ACII76. Linc Th Coll 82. **d** 84 **p** 85. C Scarborough St Martin *York* 84-86; C Middlesbrough St Thos 86-88; R Kirby Misperton w Normanby, Edston and Salton 88-90; TV Louth *Linc* 90-94; rtd 94; Perm to Offic *Sheff* from 95; *Wakef* 95-97; *Chich* 97-99 and from 01. *20 Greenwood Drive, Angmering, Littlehampton BN16 4ND* Tel (01903) 859469 E-mail ronald@letall.fsnet.co.uk

LETCHER, Canon David John. b 34. K Coll Lon 54. Chich Th Coll 56. **d** 58 **p** 59. C St Austell *Truro* 58-62; C Southbroom *Sarum* 62-64; R Odstock w Nunton and Bodenham 64-72; RD Alderbury 68-73 and 77-82; V Downton 72-85; Can and Preb Sarum Cathl 79-99; TV Dorchester 85-97; RD Dorchester 89-95; rtd 97; Perm to Offic *Sarum* from 97; (ACF) 97-00. *6 Longmoor Street, Poundbury, Dorchester DT1 3GN* Tel (01305) 257764 E-mail letcher@uwclub.net

LETHBRIDGE, Christopher David. b 43. NOC 90. **d** 93 **p** 94. NSM S Elmsall *Wakef* 93-95; C Knottingley 95-97; R Badsworth 97-01; P-in-c Bilham *Sheff* from 01; Chapl HM YOI Hatfield 01-03; Chapl HM Pris Moorland from 03. *Bilham Vicarage, Churchfield Road, Clayton, Doncaster DN5 7DH* Tel (01977) 643756

LETHEREN, William Neils. b 37. St Aid Birkenhead 61. **d** 64 **p** 65. C Liv St Mich 64-67; V 71-75; C Kirkdale St Athanasius 67-69; C Walsall Wood *Lich* 69-71; V W Derby St Jas *Liv* 75-84; R Newton in Makerfield Em 84-88; V Garston 88-04; rtd 04. *24 Pitville Avenue, Liverpool L18 7JG* Tel 0151-724 5543

LETSCHKA, Mrs Alison. b 58. Sussex Univ BA79 Anglia Ruskin Univ BA08. Westcott Ho Cam 06. **d** 08 **p** 09. C Haywards Heath St Wilfrid *Chich* from 08. *The Presentation Vicarage, 1 Marylands, New England Road, Haywards Heath RH16 3JZ* Tel (01444) 454179 Mobile 07950-152229 E-mail acletschka@yahoo.co.uk

LETSOM-CURD, Clifford John. *See* CURD, Clifford John Letsom

LETSON, Barry. b 55. Univ of Wales (Lamp) BA77. St Deiniol's Hawarden 82. **d** 83 **p** 84. C Flint *St As* 83-86; V Llansantffraid Glyn Ceirog and Llanarmon etc 86-89; R Montgomery and Forden and Llandyssil 89-96; RD Pool 92-96; V Mountain Ash *Llan* 96-97; V Mountain Ash and Miskin 97-02; V Crickhowell w Cwmdu and Tretower *S & B* from 02. *The Rectory, Rectory Road, Crickhowell NP8 1DW* Tel (01873) 810017

LETTERS, Mark Ian. b 68. Keble Coll Ox BA89 MA93 Magd Coll Cam PGCE90. SAOMC 03. **d** 05 **p** 06. NSM Ox St Barn and St Paul 05-07; Asst Chapl Campsfield Ho Immigration Removal Cen 05-07; NSM Waterloo All SS Brussels (ECUSA) 07-08; Denmark and Sweden from 09. *Address withheld by request* E-mail culeitreach@msn.com

LETTS, The Ven Kenneth John. b 42. Melbourne Univ BA65 DipEd67. Coll of Resurr Mirfield 68. **d** 71 **p** 72. C Mt Waverley St Steph Australia 71-74; Chapl Melbourne C of E Gr Sch 74-81; P-in-c Albert Park 81-94; Sen Chapl St Mich Sch 82-94; Chapl Nice w Vence *Eur* from 94; Can Gib Cathl from 04; Adn France from 07. *11 rue de la Buffa, 06000 Nice, France* Tel (0033) (4) 93 87 19 83 Fax 93 82 25 09 E-mail anglican@free.fr

LEUNG, Peter. b 36. Trin Coll Singapore BTh60 St Andr Univ PhD73. SE Asia Sch of Th MTh69. **d** 60 **p** 61. Singapore 60-62 and 65-76; Br N Borneo 62-63; Malaysia 63-65; Lect Congr Coll Man 76-77; USPG 77-83; Perm to Offic *Roch* 83-89; BCC 83-90; CTBI from 90; Perm to Offic *S'wark* 88-94; Can C Shortlands *Roch* 90-01; Regional Sec (S and E Asia) CMS 91-99; rtd 99. *35 Tufton Gardens, West Molesey KT8 1TD* Tel (020) 8650 4157

LEVASIER, James Arjen. b 67. Heriot-Watt Univ BSc95. Wycliffe Hall Ox 07. **d** 09. C Ashtead *Guildf* from 09. *17 Loraine Gardens, Ashtead KT21 1PD* Tel 07886-113394 (mobile) E-mail levasier@googlemail.com

LEVASIER, Joanna Mary. b 68. Jes Coll Cam BA89 MA90. Wycliffe Hall Ox 07. **d** 09. C Ashtead *Guildf* from 09. *17 Loraine Gardens, Ashtead KT21 1PD* E-mail j.levasier@ntlworld.com

LEVELL, Peter John. b 40. Bris Univ BA62 CertEd63. STETS 99. **d** 02 **p** 03. NSM Guildf St Sav from 02. *23 Mountside, Guildford GU2 4JD* Tel (01483) 871656 E-mail plevell@ntlworld.com

LEVER, Julian Lawrence Gerrard. b 36. Fitzw Coll Cam BA60 MA64. Sarum Th Coll 60. **d** 62 **p** 63. C Amesbury *Sarum* 62-66; R Corfe Mullen 66-78; RD Wimborne 73-75; P-in-c Wilton w Netherhampton and Fugglestone 78-82; R 82-86; R Salisbury St Martin 86-94; Perm to Offic *Win* from 96; rtd 98. *6 St John's Close, Wimborne BH21 1LY* Tel (01202) 848249

LEVERTON, James. See LEVERTON, Peter James Austin

LEVERTON, Mrs Judith. b 55. Eaton Hall Coll of Educn CertEd76. St Jo Coll Nottm 02. **d** 04 **p** 05. C Doncaster St Jas *Sheff* 04-07; TV Rivers Team from 07; Chapl to Deaf People from 09. *The Rectory, Church Lane, Treeton, Rotherham S60 5PZ* Tel 0114-269 6542 Mobile 07960-573529 E-mail judy.leverton@yahoo.co.uk

LEVERTON, Michael John. b 52. K Coll Lon BD76 AKC76 MTh77. Cant Sch of Min 84. **d** 87 **p** 88. NSM Elham w Denton and Wootton *Cant* 87-92; C Yelverton, Meavy, Sheepstor and Walkhampton *Ex* 92-93; TV 93-98; C Tavistock and Gulworthy 98-00; P-in-c Stevenage All SS Pin Green *St Alb* from 00. *All Saints' Vicarage, 100 Derby Way, Stevenage SG1 5TJ* Tel (01438) 318706 E-mail michael.leverton@btinternet.com

LEVERTON, Peter James Austin. b 33. Nottm Univ BA55. Ripon Coll Cuddesdon 79. **d** 81 **p** 82. C St Jo in Bedwardine *Worc* 81-84; V Worc St Mich 84-88; TR Worc St Barn w Ch Ch 88-92; V Riddings and Ironville *Derby* 92-00; rtd 00; Perm to Offic *Derby* from 00. *2 George Street, Langley Mill, Nottingham NG16 4DJ* Tel (01773) 710243 E-mail jim@rev-levs.freeserve.co.uk

LEVERTON, Peter Robert. b 25. Lich Th Coll 59. **d** 60 **p** 61. C Shepshed *Leic* 60-64; Australia 64-69; V Marshchapel *Linc* 70-73; V Grainthorpe w Conisholme 70-73; R N Coates 70-73; Miss to Seamen 73-77; P-in-c Brislington St Luke 77-84; V Avonmouth St Andr 84-87; Ind Chapl 84-87; P-in-c Ugborough *Ex* 87-91; P-in-c Ermington 88-91; rtd 91; Perm to Offic *Ex* from 91. *4 Drakes Avenue, Sidford, Sidmouth EX10 9QY* Tel (01395) 579835

LEVETT, The Ven Howard. b 44. AKC67. **d** 68 **p** 69. C Rotherhithe St Mary w All SS *S'wark* 68-72; P-in-c Walworth St Jo 72-77; V Walworth St Jo 77-80; P-in-c Walworth Lady Marg w St Mary 78; RD S'wark and Newington 78-80; Adn Egypt 80-94; Miss to Seafarers from 80; JMECA from 80; V Holborn St Alb w Saffron Hill St Pet *Lon* from 94. *St Alban's Clergy House, 18 Brooke Street, London EC1N 7RD* Tel (020) 7405 1831 Fax 7430 2551 Mobile 07815-111429 E-mail secretary@saintalbanthemartyr.org.uk

LEVICK, Brian William. b 30. Solicitor 51. Westcott Ho Cam 63. **d** 64 **p** 65. C Bourne *Linc* 64-69; C Deeping St James 69-70; C Hemel Hempstead *St Alb* 70-71; TV 71-77; Hon C Sedbergh, Cautley and Garsdale *Bradf* 77-83; V Firbank, Howgill and Killington 77-83; V Cononley w Bradley 83-90; Methodist Min 83-90; rtd 90; C Kettlewell w Conistone, Hubberholme etc *Bradf* 90-93; Hon C New Sleaford *Linc* 93-97; Dioc Ecum Officer 93-97; Ecum Officer Chs Together Lincs and S Humberside 93-97; Perm to Offic *Bradf* from 99. *42 Robin Lane, Bentham, Lancaster LA2 7AG* Tel (01524) 261473

LEVISEUR, Nicholas Templer. b 56. Magd Coll Ox MA82 Barrister 79. STETS 97 Ven English Coll Rome 00. **d** 00 **p** 01.

NSM Hartfield w Coleman's Hatch *Chich* from 00. *Tye House East, Edenbridge Road, Hartfield TN7 4JR* Tel (01892) 770451

LEVY, Christopher Charles. b 51. Southn Univ BTh82. Sarum & Wells Th Coll 79. **d** 82 **p** 83. C Rugby *Birm* 82-85; C Stratford-on-Avon w Bishopton *Cov* 85-87; TV Clifton *S'well* 87-95; V Egmanton from 95; R Kirton from 95; V Walesby from 95; P-in-c Kneesall w Laxton and Wellow from 07; Chapl Center Parcs Holiday Village from 01. *St Edmund's Vicarage, Walesby, Newark NG22 9PA* Tel (01623) 860522 E-mail chris@walesbyvic.fsnet.co.uk

LEW, Henry. b 39. **d** 96 **p** 97. Manager Brabazon Trust Sheltered Housing 96-00; NSM Dublin Whitechurch *D & G* 96-99; Lic to Offic from 99; NSM Powerscourt w Kilbride from 00. *Lotts Cottage, Drummin West, The Downs, Delgany, Co Wicklow, Republic of Ireland* Tel (00353) (1) 287 2957 Mobile 87-628 8049 E-mail healew@iol.ie

LEWER ALLEN, Mrs Patricia (Paddy). b 47. UNISA BA79 HDipEd85 Cape Town Univ BA86 SRN70. Th Ext Educn Coll 94. **d** 97 **p** 98. P-in-c Dunbar *Edin* 98-08; R Comrie *St And* from 08; R Crieff from 08; R Lochearnhead from 08. *3B Gavelmore Street, Crieff PH7 4DN* E-mail paddyallen@aol.com

LEWERS, The Very Revd Benjamin Hugh. b 32. Selw Coll Cam BA60 MA64. Linc Th Coll. **d** 62 **p** 63. C Northampton St Mary *Pet* 62-65; C Hounslow Heath St Paul *Lon* 65-68; C-in-c Hounslow Gd Shep Beavers Lane CD 65-68; Chapl Heathrow Airport 68-75; V Newark St Mary *S'well* 75-80; TR Newark w Hawton, Cotham and Shelton 80-81; P-in-c Averham w Kelham 79-81; Provost Derby 81-97; rtd 98; Perm to Offic *Sarum* from 98 and *B & W* from 00. *Thimble Cottage, Marshwood, Bridport DT6 5QF* Tel (01297) 678515

LEWES AND HASTINGS, Archdeacon of. See JONES, The Ven Philip Hugh

LEWES, Area Bishop of. See BENN, The Rt Revd Wallace Parke

LEWIS, Prof Andrew Dominic Edwards. b 49. St Jo Coll Cam LLB71 MA74. SWMTC 04. **d** 07 **p** 08. NSM St Endellion w Port Isaac and St Kew *Truro* from 07; NSM St Minver from 07. *Drakes, 15 Rose Hill, Port Isaac PL29 3RL* Tel (01208) 880947 E-mail a.d.e.lewis@ucl.ac.uk

LEWIS, Ann Theodora Rachel. b 33. Univ of Wales (Ban) BA55. Qu Coll Birm 78. **d** 80 **p** 97. C Swansea St Mary w H Trin *S & B* 80-96; Chapl St Mary's Coll 90-96; rtd 96; Public Preacher *St D* from 96. *Fisherywish, Maes yr Eglwys, Llansaint, Kidwelly SA17 5JE* Tel (01267) 267386

LEWIS, Arthur Jenkin Llewellyn. b 42. Univ of Wales (Cardiff) MPS67 BPharm. Coll of Resurr Mirfield 71. **d** 73 **p** 74. C Cardiff St Jo *Llan* 73-78; C Christchurch *Win* 78-82; R Lightbowne *Man* 82-04; rtd 07. *25 Dene Street Gardens, Dorking RH4 2DN* Tel (01306) 879743

LEWIS, Arthur Roland. b 20. St Edm Hall Ox BA41 MA45. St Steph Ho Ox 41. **d** 43 **p** 44. C Sutton in Ashfield St Mich *S'well* 43-45; C Stirchley *Birm* 45-47; UMCA Miss Msalabani Zanzibar 47-49; Kizara 49-50; P-in-c Msalabani 50-53; P-in-c Kihurio 53-55; C Zanzibar Is 55-57; P-in-c Milo Tanganyika 56-58; P-in-c Rusape S Rhodesia 58-60; P-in-c Mandea 60-69; R Makoni 69-76; Adn Inyanga 66-71; Lic to Offic 77-80; Lic to Offic S Africa 80-87; rtd 87; Perm to Offic *Birm* 88-99. *The College of St Barnabas, Blackberry Lane, Lingfield RH7 6NJ* Tel (01342) 872870 E-mail arthur_r_lewis@compuserve.com

LEWIS, Brian James. b 52. Cant Univ (NZ) BA75. St Jo Coll Auckland 76. **d** 78 **p** 79. C Ashburton New Zealand 78-80; C Shrub End *Chelmsf* 80-82; P-in-c Colchester St Barn 82-84; V 84-88; P-in-c Romford St Andr 88-90; R 90-99; RD Havering 93-97; R Lt Ilford St Mich from 99. *The Rectory, 124 Church Road, London E12 6HA* Tel (020) 8478 2182 E-mail brian@littleilford.fsnet.co.uk

LEWIS, The Very Revd Christopher Andrew. b 44. Bris Univ BA69 CCC Cam PhD74. Westcott Ho Cam 71. **d** 73 **p** 74. C Barnard Castle *Dur* 73-76; Dir Ox Inst for Ch and Soc 76-79; Tutor Ripon Coll Cuddesdon 76-79; Sen Tutor 79-81; Vice-Prin 81-82; P-in-c Aston Rowant w Crowell *Ox* 78-81; V Spalding *Linc* 82-87; Can Res Cant Cathl 87-94; Dir of Minl Tr 89-94; Dean St Alb 94-03; Dean Ch Ch *Ox* from 03. *The Deanery, Christ Church, Oxford OX1 1DP* Tel (01865) 276161 Fax 276238 E-mail jan.bolongaro@christ-church.ox.ac.uk

LEWIS, Canon Christopher Gouldson. b 42. K Coll Cam BA64 MA68. Cuddesdon Coll 65. **d** 67 **p** 68. C Gosforth All SS *Newc* 67-71; Sarawak 71-74; V Luton St Chris Round Green *St Alb* 74-80; RD Reculver *Cant* 80-86 and 92-93; V Whitstable All SS w St Pet 80-84; TR Whitstable 84-93; Dir Post-Ord Tr 88-93; Hon Can Cant Cathl 91-93; Can Res Bradf Cathl 93-01; Bp's Officer for Min and Tr 93-01; P-in-c Riding Mill *Newc* 01-07; Chapl Shepherd's Dene Retreat Ho 01-07; Adv for Spirituality and Spiritual Direction 02-07; Hon Can Newc Cathl from 07; rtd 07. *The Old School, Bingfield, Hexham NE46 4HR* Tel (01434) 672729

LEWIS, David Antony. b 48. Dur Univ BA69 Nottm Univ MTh84. St Jo Coll Nottm 81. **d** 83 **p** 84. C Gateacre *Liv* 83-86; V Toxteth St Cypr w Ch Ch 86-01; V Edge Hill St Cypr w St Mary

01-07; AD Liv N 94-03; Urban Development Adv 07-08; rtd 08. *Address temp unknown*

LEWIS, David Hugh. b 45. Oak Hill Th Coll 88. **d** 90 **p** 91. C Oakham, Hambleton, Egleton, Braunston and Brooke *Pet* 90-94; R Ewhurst *Guildf* 94-99; V Southway *Ex* 99-03; RD Plymouth Moorside 01-03; P-in-c Anglesey Gp *Ely* 03-04; V from 04. *The Vicarage, 86 High Street, Bottisham, Cambridge CB25 9BA* Tel (01223) 812367
E-mail revdavidhlewis@msn.com

LEWIS, David Tudor. b 61. Jes Coll Cam BA83. Trin Coll Bris BA88. **d** 88 **p** 89. C Tile Cross *Birm* 88-91; C Woking St Jo *Guildf* 91-95; TV Carl H Trin and St Barn 95-97; Chapl Carl Hosps NHS Trust 95-97; Asst Chapl Oslo w Bergen, Trondheim and Stavanger *Eur* 97-04; TV E Richmond *Ripon* from 04. *The Rectory, Great Smeaton, Northallerton DL6 2EP* Tel (01609) 881205 E-mail dtlewis@freenet.co.uk

LEWIS, David Tudor Bowes. b 63. Keele Univ BA85 Univ of Wales (Cardiff) BTh90. St Mich Coll Llan 87. **d** 90 **p** 91. C Llangollen w Trevor and Llantysilio *St As* 90-93; C Bistre 93-97; V Berse and Southsea 97-02; V Bwlchgwyn w Berse w Southsea 02-04; R Overton and Erbistock and Penley from 04. *The Rectory, 4 Sundorne, Overton, Wrexham LL13 0EB* Tel (01978) 710229

LEWIS, Canon David Vaughan. b 36. Trin Coll Cam BA60 MA64. Ridley Hall Cam 60. **d** 62 **p** 63. C Rugby St Matt *Cov* 62-65; Asst Chapl K Edw Sch Witley 65-71; Hon C Rainham *Chelmsf* 71-76; V Stoke Hill *Guildf* 76-87; V Wallington *S'wark* 87-03; Hon Can S'wark Cathl 95-03; RD Sutton 97-00; rtd 03; Perm to Offic *Ely* from 03. *11 The Meadows, Haslingfield, Cambridge CB23 1JD* Tel (01223) 874029

LEWIS, Canon David Watkin. b 40. Univ of Wales (Lamp) BA61. Wycliffe Hall Ox 61. **d** 63 **p** 64. C Skewen *Llan* 63-66; Field Tr Officer Prov Youth Coun Ch in Wales 66-68; C Gabalfa 68-71; P-in-c Marcross w Monknash and Wick 71-73; R 73-83; RD Llantwit Major and Cowbridge 81-83; V Baglan from 83; Can Llan Cathl from 00; Treas Llan Cathl from 04. *The Vicarage, 29 Church Road, Port Talbot SA12 8ST* Tel (01639) 812199

LEWIS, Edward John. b 58. JP93. Univ of Wales BEd80 BA82 Surrey Univ MA07 FRSA97 MInstD01. Chich Th Coll 82. **d** 83 **p** 84. C Llangiwg *S & B* 83-85; C Morriston 85-87; Asst Chapl Morriston Hosp 85-87; V Tregaron w Ystrad Meurig and Strata Florida *St D* 87-89; Chapl Tregaron Hosp 87-89; Chapl Manor Hosp Walsall 89-92; Distr Co-ord Chapl Walsall Hosps 90-92; Sen Chapl Walsall Hosps NHS Trust 92-00; Chapl Walsall Community Health Trust 92-00; Chief Exec and Dir Tr Gen Syn Hosp Chapl Coun from 00; Perm to Offic *Lich* from 00 and *St Alb* from 02; Visiting Lect St Mary's Univ Coll Twickenham from 04; PV Westmr Abbey from 07; Chapl to The Queen from 08. *Hospital Chaplaincies Council, Church House, Great Smith Street, London SW1P 3AZ* Tel (020) 7898 1892 Fax 7898 1891 Mobile 07957-529646 E-mail edward.lewis@c-of-e.org.uk

LEWIS, Ella Pauline. b 41. SWMTC 94. **d** 98. NSM Paignton Ch Ch and Preston St Paul *Ex* 98-07; NSM Torquay St Luke from 07. *Roselands, 5 Great Headland Road, Paignton TQ3 2DY* Tel (01803) 555171 E-mail paulinelewis@eclipse.co.uk

LEWIS, Elsie Leonora. b 26. Cranmer Hall Dur 72. **dss** 78 **d** 87 **p** 94. S Westoe *Dur* 78-80; Ryton 80-86; rtd 86. *53 Cushy Cow Lane, Ryton NE40 3NL* Tel 0191-413 5845

LEWIS, Eric. b 36. Sarum & Wells Th Coll 74. **d** 77 **p** 78. NSM Oldbury *Sarum* 77-92; C Weymouth St Paul 92-94; P-in-c Portland St Jo 94-99; Chapl Weymouth Coll 94-97; Asst Chapl Dorset Community NHS Trust 95-99; rtd 99; Chapl Costa Blanca *Eur* 01-07; Perm to Offic *St D* from 07. *St Mary Mead, 2 Aeron Court, Talsarn, Lampeter SA48 8QB* Tel (01570) 471204

LEWIS, Eric. b 47. NEOC 04. **d** 07 **p** 08. NSM Monkseaton St Mary *Newc* from 07. *27 Well Ridge Close, Whitley Bay NE25 9PN* Tel 0191-251 3456
E-mail carolanderic129@aol.com

LEWIS, Frederick Norman. b 23. Leeds Univ BA47. Coll of Resurr Mirfield 47. **d** 49 **p** 50. C Haydock St Jas *Liv* 49-51; C Dresden *Lich* 51-55; C Stafford St Mary 55-56; V Wednesfield St Thos 56-65; V Shrewsbury St Chad 65-69; V Kingswinford St Mary 69-88; rtd 88; Perm to Offic *Lich* from 88. *27 Bramblewood Drive, Wolverhampton WV3 9DB* Tel (01902) 334934

LEWIS, Gary. b 61. Lanc Univ BA85. Ripon Coll Cuddesdon 86. **d** 89 **p** 90. C Blackb St Mich w St Jo and H Trin 89-92; C Altham w Clayton le Moors 92-95; V Lea 95-01; V Skerton St Luke from 01. *St Luke's Vicarage, Slyne Road, Lancaster LA1 2HU* Tel (01524) 63249

LEWIS, Graham Rhys. b 54. Loughb Univ BTech76 Cranfield Inst of Tech MBA89. SEITE 95. **d** 98 **p** 99. NSM S Gillingham *Roch* from 98. *53 Oastview, Gillingham ME8 8JG* Tel (01634) 373036 *or* tel and fax 389224 Mobile 07740-915826 E-mail graham.lewis@diocese-rochester.org

LEWIS, Gwynne. See LEWIS, Hywel Gwynne

LEWIS, Ms Hannah Margaret. b 71. CCC Cam BA93 MA96 Birm Univ PhD03. Qu Coll Birm 95. **d** 97 **p** 98. C Cannock *Lich* 97-00; NSM Cen Telford 00-06; Team Ldr Past Services for Deaf

Community *Liv* from 06. *9 Hougoumont Avenue, Liverpool L22 0LL* Tel 0151-705 2130
E-mail hannah.lewis@liverpool.anglican.org

LEWIS, Hubert Godfrey. b 33. Univ of Wales (Lamp) BA59. **d** 60 **p** 61. C Merthyr Tydfil *Llan* 60-64; C Caerphilly 64-66; Perm to Offic *S'wark* 66-76 and *Cant* 76-82; Hon C Shirley St Jo *S'wark* 82-93; Hon C Whitchurch *Llan* from 94. *2 Heol Wernlas, Cardiff CF14 1RY* Tel (029) 2061 3079

LEWIS, Hywel Gwynne. b 37. FCA75. St D Dioc Tr Course 94. **d** 97 **p** 98. NSM Henfynyw w Aberaeron and Llanddewi Aberarth etc *St D* 97-07; rtd 07; Perm to Offic *St D* from 07. *Danycoed, Lampeter Road, Aberaeron SA46 0ED* Tel (01545) 570577

LEWIS, Ian. b 33. Lon Univ MB, BS57. Oak Hill Th Coll 61. **d** 63 **p** 64. C Heatherlands St Jo *Sarum* 63-66; Ethiopia 66-73; Hon C Bath Walcot *B & W* 75-77; Lic to Offic 78-98; Hon C Bath St Bart 80-04; rtd 98; Perm to Offic *B & W* from 04. *22C Ashley Road, Bathford, Bath BA1 7TT* Tel (01225) 859818
E-mail ian@iclewis.co.uk

LEWIS, Ian Richard. b 54. Sheff Univ BA76 Ox Univ BA83 MA87. Wycliffe Hall Ox 81. **d** 84 **p** 85. C Rusholme H Trin *Man* 84-88; C Sandal St Helen *Wakef* 88-91; V Bath St Bart *B & W* from 91. *St Bartholomew's Vicarage, 5 Oldfield Road, Bath BA2 3ND* Tel and fax (01225) 422070
E-mail ianlewis@stbartsbath.org

LEWIS, James Edward. b 22. St D Coll Lamp BA50. **d** 51 **p** 52. C Gorseinon *S & B* 51-52; C Defynnog 52-56; R Llangynllo w Troed-yr-aur *St D* 56-61; V Brynamman 61-72; R Llangathen w Llanfihangel Cilfargen 72-82; V Llangathen w Llanfihangel Cilfargen etc 82-90; RD Llangadog and Llandeilo 85-89; rtd 90. *The Flat, 3 St Mary's Street, Carmarthen SA31 1TN* Tel (01267) 221660

LEWIS, James Michael. b 51. Trin Coll Carmarthen CertEd73 Open Univ BA86 MA91. St Mich Coll Llan 98. **d** 02 **p** 03. NSM Laleston w Tythegston and Merthyr Mawr *Llan* 02-09; NSM Laleston and Merthyr Mawr from 09. *19 Austin Avenue, Laleston, Bridgend CF32 0LG* Tel (01656) 660648 Mobile 07931-300206 E-mail mike.lewis11@virgin.net

LEWIS, Jean Anwyl. b 34. Surrey Univ BA03. K Coll Lon MA05. **d** 05 **p** 06. OLM Windlesham *Guildf* from 05. *2 Hillside Cottages, Broadway Road, Windlesham GU20 6BY* Tel (01276) 472681
E-mail jean.lewis1@btopenworld.com

LEWIS, Jocelyn Vivien. b 49. Trevelyan Coll Dur BSc70 Sheff Univ PhD75. EMMTC 91. **d** 94 **p** 95. NSM Brimington *Derby* 94-99; P-in-c Whittington 99-09; Dioc Dir Reader Tr 99-09; P-in-c New Whittington 04-09; rtd 09. *13 Gower Crescent, Chesterfield S40 4LX* Tel (01246) 229539

LEWIS, The Ven John Arthur. b 34. Jes Coll Ox BA56 MA60. Cuddesdon Coll 58. **d** 60 **p** 61. C Prestbury *Glouc* 60-63; C Wimborne Minster *Sarum* 63-66; R Eastington and Frocester *Glouc* 66-70; V Nailsworth 70-78; Chapl Memorial and Querns Hosp Cirencester 78-88; V Cirencester *Glouc* 78-88; RD Cirencester 84-88; Hon Can Glouc Cathl 85-98; Adn Cheltenham 88-98; rtd 98; Perm to Offic *Glouc* from 98. *5 Vilverie Mead, Bishop's Cleeve, Cheltenham GL52 7YY* Tel (01242) 678425

LEWIS, John Edward. b 31. SS Mark & Jo Coll Chelsea CertEd53. Qu Coll Birm 83. **d** 85 **p** 86. C Leominster *Heref* 85-87; TV 87-95; rtd 95; Perm to Offic *Heref* from 97. *The Holms, 253 Godiva Road, Leominster HR6 8TB* Tel (01568) 612280

LEWIS, John Goddard. b 52. Houston Bapt Univ (USA) BA74 JD77 Ox Univ 98. Virginia Th Sem MDiv97. **d** 97. USA 97-98 and from 01; Hon C Bladon w Woodstock *Ox* 98-01; Min Cen for Faith in the Workplace San Antonio from 01. *2015 NE Loop 410, San Antonio TX 78217, USA* Tel (001) (210) 599 4224
E-mail john.lewis@theworkshop-sa.org

LEWIS, John Herbert. b 42. Selw Coll Cam BA64 MA68. Westcott Ho Cam 64. **d** 66 **p** 67. C Wyken *Cov* 66-70; C Bedford St Andr *St Alb* 70-73; Lib Pusey Ho and Bp's Chapl for Graduates *Ox* 73-77; TV Woughton 78-82; TV Gt Chesham 82-88; P-in-c Newport Pagnell w Lathbury and Moulsoe 88-91; R 91-07; rtd 07; Perm to Offic *Ox* from 08. *54 Sparrows Way, Oxford OX4 7GE*

LEWIS, John Horatio George. b 47. Southn Univ BEd72 MA85. Ox NSM Course 86. **d** 89 **p** 90. NSM Newbury *Ox* 89-04; Perm to Offic *Win* 94-04; P-in-c Borden *Cant* 05-08; V from 08; AD Sittingbourne from 09. *The Vicarage, School Lane, Borden, Sittingbourne ME9 8JS* Tel (01795) 472986 Mobile 07973-406622 E-mail fr.johnlewis@tiscali.co.uk

✠**LEWIS, The Rt Revd John Hubert Richard.** b 43. AKC66. **d** 67 **p** 68. **c** 92. C Hexham *Newc* 67-70; Ind Chapl 70-77; Communications Officer *Dur* 77-82; Chapl for Agric *Heref* 82-87; Adn Ludlow 87-92; Suff Bp Taunton *B & W* 92-97; Bp St E 97-07; rtd 07. *92 Victoria Road, Diss IP22 4JG* Tel (01379) 650766 E-mail lewis310@btinternet.com

LEWIS, John Malcolm. b 41. Reading Univ BEd. Trin Coll Bris. **d** 82 **p** 83. C Kingswood *Bris* 82-85; TV Weston-super-Mare Cen Par *B & W* 85-91; Dioc Children's Adv *Nor* 91-97; TV Bishopsworth and Bedminster Down *Bris* 97-06; Hon Min Can

Bris Cathl 04-06; rtd 06. *35 Lodge Way, Weymouth DT4 9UU* Tel (01305) 776560 E-mail monandjohn@btinternet.com

LEWIS, John Percival. b 19. TCD BA44. CITC 47. **d** 47 **p** 48. C Galway *T, K & A* 47-51; I Knappagh 51-74; Can Tuam Cathl from 70; I Omey w Ballynakill, Errislannan and Roundstone 73-91; Provost Tuam 73-91; rtd 91. *McBride Home, Westport, Co Mayo, Republic of Ireland*

LEWIS, John Pryce. b 65. Trin Coll Carmarthen BA87. Wycliffe Hall Ox 92. **d** 94 **p** 95. C Carmarthen St Pet *St D* 94-97; V Nevern and Y Beifil w Eglwyswrw and Meline etc 97-07; V Henfynyw w Aberaeron and Llanddewi Aberarth etc from 07. *The Vicarage, Panteg Road, Aberaeron SA46 0EP* Tel (01545) 570433

LEWIS, The Very Revd John Thomas. b 47. Jes Coll Ox BA69 MA73 St Jo Coll Cam BA72 MA92. Westcott Ho Cam 71. **d** 73 **p** 74. C Whitchurch *Llan* 73-77; C Llanishen and Lisvane 77-80; Asst Chapl Univ of Wales (Cardiff) 80-85; Warden of Ords 81-85; V Brecon St David w Llanspyddid and Llanilltyd *S & B* 85-91; Sec Prov Selection Panel and Bd Ch in Wales 87-94; V Bassaleg *Mon* 91-96; TR 96-00; Bp's Chapl for CME 98-00; Dean Llan from 00; V Llandaff from 00. *The Deanery, The Cathedral Green, Llandaff, Cardiff CF5 2YF* Tel (029) 2056 1545

LEWIS, Joycelyn. See LEWIS-GREGORY, Mrs Joycelyn

LEWIS, Kevin James. b 76. Nottm Univ BA98. St Jo Coll Nottm MTh04 MA(MM)05. **d** 05 **p** 06. C Southgate *Chich* 05-09; C St Helier *S'wark* from 09. *59 Wigmore Road, Carshalton SM5 1RG* Tel (020) 8644 9203 Mobile 07739-139389 E-mail kevinjlewis@btinternet.com

LEWIS, Leslie. b 28. LRAM56. St Aid Birkenhead 61. **d** 63 **p** 64. C Eastham *Ches* 63-66; C W Kirby St Bridget 66-72; V Rainow w Saltersford 72-73; V Rainow w Saltersford and Forest 73-02; Dioc Clergy Widows and Retirement Officer 88-93; rtd 02; Perm to Offic *Ches* from 02. *25 Appleby Close, Macclesfield SK11 8XB* Tel (01625) 616395

LEWIS, Mrs Mary Carola Melton. b 51. LRAM72 S Glam Inst HE CertEd76 Lon Univ BD93. St Mich Coll Llan 97. **d** 98 **p** 99. NSM Aberedw w Llandeilo Graban and Llanbadarn etc *S & B* 98-03. *Brynglocsen, Dolanog, Welshpool SY21 0LJ* Tel (01938) 811202 E-mail marylewis@btinternet.com

LEWIS, Maureen. b 50. Ches Coll of HE BA92. St Jo Coll Nottm 92. **d** 94 **p** 95. C Ellesmere Port *Ches* 94-98; C Prenton 98-00; C New Brighton St Jas w Em 00-05; rtd 05; Perm to Offic *Ches* from 06. *27 Wimborne Avenue, Wirral CH61 7UL* Tel 0151-648 0605

LEWIS, Melville. See LEWIS, William George Melville

LEWIS, Michael. See LEWIS, James Michael

✠**LEWIS, The Rt Revd Michael Augustine Owen.** b 53. Mert Coll Ox BA75 MA79. Cuddesdon Coll 75. **d** 78 **p** 79 **c** 99. C Salfords *S'wark* 78-80; Chapl Thames Poly 80-84; V Welling 84-91; TR Worc SE 91-99; RD Worc E 93-99; Hon Can Worc Cathl 98-99; Suff Bp Middleton *Man* 99-07; Bp Cyprus and the Gulf from 07. *PO Box 22075, CY 1517-Nicosia, Cyprus* Tel (00357) (22) 671220 Fax 674553 E-mail bishop@spidernet.com.cy *or* maolewis_2000@yahoo.com

LEWIS, Canon Michael David Bennett. b 41. Portsm Univ MA01. St Mich Coll Llan 65. **d** 68 **p** 69. C Penarth w Lavernock *Llan* 68-72; Chapl RAF 72-74; C Llanishen and Lisvane 74-77; V Penyfai w Tondu 77-82; Chapl Ardingly Coll 82-90; R Merrow *Guildf* 90-95; RD Guildf 94-95; V Southsea H Spirit *Portsm* from 95; RD Portsm from 06; Hon Can Portsm Cathl from 06. *The Vicarage, 26 Victoria Grove, Southsea PO5 1NY* Tel (023) 9287 3535 Mobile 07808-609912 E-mail fr.lewis@btinternet.com

LEWIS, Michael John. b 37. LLAM86. St Aid Birkenhead 64. **d** 66 **p** 67. C Whitnash *Cov* 66-69; C Nuneaton St Nic 69-73; TV Basildon St Martin w H Cross and Laindon *Chelmsf* 73-79; V W Bromwich St Jas *Lich* 79-85; TV Buxton w Burbage and King Sterndale *Derby* 85-95; P-in-c Brampton St Mark 95-02; rtd 02; Perm to Offic *Lich* from 03. *15 Langley Street, Basford, Stoke-on-Trent ST4 6DX* Tel (01782) 622762

LEWIS, Norman Eric. b 34. SRN55 Open Univ BA77. Roch Th Coll 59 Lich Th Coll 60. **d** 63 **p** 64. C Hope St Jas *Man* 63-67; V Hindsford 67-77; V Bolton SS Simon and Jude 77-90; rtd 90; Perm to Offic *York* from 90. *Millbank Cottage, Kirby Misperton, Malton YO17 6XZ* Tel (01653) 668526 E-mail normanl@btinternet.com

LEWIS, Patrick Mansel. See MANSEL LEWIS, Patrick Charles Archibald

LEWIS, Peter. See LEWIS, Thomas Peter

LEWIS, Peter Andrew. b 67. Pemb Coll Ox MA PhD Univ of Wales (Abth) Bris Univ BA. Trin Coll Bris. **d** 96 **p** 97. C Cardigan w Mwnt and Y Ferwig *St D* 96-98; C Gabalfa *Llan* 98-01; V Aberpergwm and Blaengwrach 01-04; V Vale of Neath from 04. *99A Neath Road, Resolven, Neath SA11 4AN* Tel (01639) 711262 E-mail rev.peterlewis@virgin.net

LEWIS, Peter Richard. b 40. Dur Univ BA62. Qu Coll Birm 62. **d** 64 **p** 65. C Moseley St Mary *Birm* 64-67; C Sherborne w Castleton and Lillington *Sarum* 67-71; P-in-c Bishopstone w Stratford Tony 72-80; V Amesbury 80-02; rtd 02; Perm to Offic

Sarum from 02 and *B & W* from 05. *Rose Cottage, Silton Road, Bourton, Gillingham SP8 5DE*

LEWIS, Miss Rachel Veronica Clare. b 59. St Jo Coll Dur BA80 Man Univ PGCE81 Univ of Wales (Cardiff) MSc. Sarum & Wells Th Coll 86. **d** 86 **p** 94. C Caereithin *S & B* 86-88; Par Dn Bolton St Pet *Man* 88-91; Chapl Bolton Colls of H&FE 88-91; Chapl Trin Coll Carmarthen 91-94; C Yatton Keynell *Bris* 94-97; P-in-c 97-99; C Biddestone w Slaughterford 94-97; P-in-c 97-99; C Castle Combe 94-97; P-in-c 97-99; C W Kington 94-97; P-in-c 97-99; C Nettleton w Littleton Drew 94-97; P-in-c 97-99; P-in-c Grittleton and Leigh Delamere 94-99; TR By Brook 99-02; I Adare and Kilmallock w Kilpeacon, Croom etc *L & K* 02-07; P-in-c Peterston-super-Ely w St Brides-super-Ely *Llan* from 07; P-in-c St Nicholas w Bonvilston and St George-super-Ely from 07; P-in-c Pendoylan w Welsh St Donats from 07. *The Rectory, Peterston-super-Ely, Cardiff CF5 6LH* Tel (01446) 760687 E-mail revlewis@btinternet.com

LEWIS, Ray Arthur. b 63. Oak Hill Th Coll 87. **d** 90 **p** 91. C Holloway St Mary Magd *Lon* 90-93; TV Forest Gate St Sav w W Ham St Matt *Chelmsf* 93-97; St Vincent 97-98; Grenada 98-99. *45 Avenue Road, London E7 0LA*

LEWIS, Raymond James. b 34. Univ of Wales (Cardiff) BA Open Univ BSc. St Mich Coll Llan. **d** 91 **p** 92. C Llanelli *St D* 91-94; rtd 99. *36 Yorath Road, Whitchurch, Cardiff CF14 1QD* Tel (029) 2061 6267

LEWIS, Richard. See LEWIS, The Rt Revd John Hubert Richard

LEWIS, The Very Revd Richard. b 35. Fitzw Ho Cam BA78 MA63. Ripon Hall Ox 58. **d** 60 **p** 61. C Hinckley St Mary *Leic* 60-63; C Sanderstead All SS *S'wark* 63-66; V Merstham 67-72; V S Wimbledon H Trin 72-74; P-in-c S Wimbledon St Pet 72-74; V S Wimbledon H Trin and St Pet 74-79; V Dulwich St Barn 79-90; Chapl Alleyn's Foundn Dulwich 79-90; RD Dulwich *S'wark* 83-90; Hon Can S'wark Cathl 87-90; Dean Wells *B & W* 90-03; Warden of Readers 91-03; rtd 03; Perm to Offic *Worc* 03-08. *1 Monmouth Court, Union Street, Wells BA5 2PX* E-mail dean.lewis@a.btopenworld.com

LEWIS, Canon Richard Charles. b 44. Univ of Wales (Lamp) MA94 Sheff Univ MEd96. ALCD69. **d** 69 **p** 70. C Kendal H Trin *Carl* 69-72; C Chipping Barnet *St Alb* 72-76; V Watford Ch Ch from 76; Chapl Abbots Hill Sch Hemel Hempstead 81-96; Hon Can St Alb Abbey from 90. *Christ Church Vicarage, Leggatts Way, Watford WD24 5NQ* Tel (01923) 672240 Fax 279919 E-mail vicar@ccwatford.u-net.com *or* rts@ccwatford.u-net.com

LEWIS, Robert. b 38. St Pet Coll Ox BA62 MA66. Cuddesdon Coll 62. **d** 64 **p** 65. C Kirkby *Liv* 64-67 and 70-71; TV 71-75; Chapl St Boniface Coll Warminster 68-69; Tutor St Aug Coll Cant 69-70; Abp's Dom Chapl and Dir of Ords *York* 76-79; TR Thirsk 79-92; Chapl Oslo w Bergen, Trondheim, Stavanger etc *Eur* 93-96; P-in-c Danby *York* 96-98; V 98-04; RD Whitby 98-04; rtd 04; Perm to Offic *York* from 04. *19 Long Street, Thirsk YO7 1AW* Tel (01845) 523256

LEWIS, Robert George. b 53. Lanc Univ BEd76. Ripon Coll Cuddesdon. **d** 78 **p** 79. C Liv Our Lady and St Nic w St Anne 78-81; Asst Dir of Educn 81-88; P-in-c Newchurch 88-89; P-in-c Glazebury 88-89; R Newchurch and Glazebury 89-94; R Winwick from 94; R Glazebury w Hollinfare from 04; AD Winwick 01-09; Hon Can Liv Cathl 01-09; Chapl Liv Univ from 09; Chapl Liv Jo Moores Univ from 09. *10 Ladychapel Close, Liverpool L1 7BZ* E-mail thelewises@hotmail.com

LEWIS, Roger Gilbert. b 49. St Jo Coll Dur BA70. Ripon Hall Ox 70. **d** 72 **p** 73. C Boldmere *Birm* 72-76; C Birm St Pet 76-77; TV Tettenhall Regis *Lich* 77-81; V Ward End *Birm* 81-91; rtd 91; Perm to Offic *Birm* from 91. *8 Tudor Terrace, Ravenhurst Road, Birmingham B17 9SB* Tel 0121-427 4915

LEWIS, Simon Wilford. b 66. Westmr Coll Ox BTh94 Roehampton Inst PGCE95. STETS 03. **d** 06 **p** 07. C Ventnor St Cath, Ventnor H Trin and Bonchurch *Portsm* 06-09; P-in-c Brent Knoll, E Brent and Lympsham *B & W* from 09. *The Rectory, 3 Ash Trees, East Brent, Highbridge TA9 4DQ* Tel (01278) 760147 E-mail simonlewis@homecall.co.uk

LEWIS, Stuart William. b 54. Newc Univ BA79 Newc Poly PGCE80. Edin Th Coll 84. **d** 86 **p** 87. C Ledbury w Eastnor *Heref* 86-89; Chapl Malvern Coll 89-96; Chapl and Prec Portsm Cathl 96-97; TV Ross *Heref* 97-01; P-in-c Lower Wharfedale *Ripon* 01-03; R from 03; Chapl St Aid Sch Harrogate 01-05. *The Rectory, Main Street, Kirkby Overblow, Harrogate HG3 1HD* Tel (01423) 872314 E-mail stuartlewis@wyenet.co.uk

LEWIS, Thomas Peter. b 45. Selw Coll Cam BA67 MA. Ripon Hall Ox 68. **d** 70 **p** 71. C Bp's Hatfield *St Alb* 70-74; C Boreham Wood All SS 74-78; Chapl Haileybury Coll 78-85; Chapl Abingdon Sch 86-03; R Narberth w Mounton w Robeston Wathen and Crinow *St D* from 03 *The Rectory, Adams Drive, Narberth SA67 7AE* Tel (01834) 860370

LEWIS, Trevor Arnold. b 55. NEOC 06. **d** 09. NSM Middlesbrough St Martin w St Cuth *York* from 09. *23 Northiam Close, Hemlington, Middlesbrough TS8 9PT* Tel (01642) 595148 E-mail lewist02@sky.com

LEWIS, Vera Elizabeth. b 45. Lon Univ BA66 Univ of Wales (Abth) DipEd67. St As Minl Tr Course 82. **d** 85 **p** 97. NSM Garthbeibio and Llanerfyl and Llangadfan *St As* 85-86; C 87-88; NSM Llanfair Caereinion w Llanllugan 85-86; C 87-88; Dn-in-c Llanrhaeadr-ym-Mochnant etc 88-96; Dn-in-c Llanddulas and Llysfaen 96-97; R 97-03; rtd 03. *Heulwen, Bronwylfa Square, St Asaph LL17 0BU*

LEWIS, Canon Walter Arnold. b 45. NUI BA68 TCD MPhil91. TCD Div Sch 71. **d** 71 **p** 72. C Belfast Whiterock *Conn* 71-73; C Belfast St Mark 73-80; Bp's C Belfast St Andr 80-84; I Belfast St Thos from 84; Can Belf Cathl from 97. *St Thomas's Rectory, 1A Eglantine Avenue, Belfast BT9 6DW* Tel and fax (028) 9066 3332 E-mail walter.lewis@ntlworld.com

LEWIS, William George Melville. b 31. Open Univ BA. S'wark Ord Course. **d** 69 **p** 70. C Coulsdon St Jo *S'wark* 69-71; C Perry Hill St Geo 71-74; V Eltham St Barn 74-80; V Reigate St Mark 80-89; V Ham St Rich 89-97; rtd 97; Hon C Kew *S'wark* 97-00; Perm to Offic from 03. *20 Avenue Court, The Avenue, Tadworth KT20 5BG* Tel (01737) 819748

LEWIS, William George Rees. b 35. Hertf Coll Ox BA59 MA63. Tyndale Hall Bris 61. **d** 63 **p** 64. C Tenby w Gumfreston *St D* 63-66; C Llanelli St Paul 66-69; R Letterston 69-84; R Jordanston w Llanstinan 73-78; R Punchestown and Lt Newc 78-84; R Hubberston w Herbrandston and Hasguard etc 84-90; Prov Officer for Evang and Adult Educn 90-94; V Gabalfa *Llan* 94-00; rtd 00. *5 Westaway Drive, Hakin, Milford Haven SA73 3EG* Tel (01646) 692280

LEWIS, William Rhys. b 20. St Mich Coll Llan 53. **d** 55 **p** 56. C Ystrad Mynach *Llan* 55-58; C Bassaleg *Mon* 58-59; V Cwmtillery 59-62; V Newport St Andr 62-64; TR Ebbw Vale 64-73; R Llangattock and Llangynidr *S & B* 73-78; V Swansea St Luke 78-85; rtd 85; Perm to Offic *Llan* from 85. *6 Beech Avenue, Llantwit Major CF61 1RT* Tel (01446) 796741

LEWIS-ANTHONY, Justin Griffith. b 64. LSE BA86. Ripon Coll Cuddesdon BA91 MA97. **d** 92 **p** 93. C Cirencester *Glouc* 92-98; Prec Ch Ch *Ox* 98-03; R Hackington *Cant* from 03. *The Rectory, St Stephen's Green, Canterbury CT2 7JU* Tel (01227) 765391 E-mail rector@ststephenscanterbury.net

LEWIS-GREGORY, Mrs Joycelyn. b 60. Qu Coll Birm. **d** 08 **p** 09. C Hall Green St Pet *Birm* from 08. *4 Etwall Road, Birmingham B28 0LE* Tel 0121-778 4375 *or* 777 8547

LEWIS-JENKINS, Christopher Robin. b 50. St Mich Coll Llan 94. **d** 96 **p** 97. C Barry All SS *Llan* 96-01; V Dinas and Penygraig w Williamstown from 01; AD Rhondda from 06. *The Vicarage, 1 Llanfair Road, Penygraig, Tonypandy CF40 1TA* Tel (01443) 422677

LEWIS LLOYD, Canon Timothy David. b 37. Clare Coll Cam BA58 MA62. Cuddesdon Coll 58. **d** 60 **p** 61. C Stepney St Dunstan and All SS *Lon* 60-64; C St Alb Abbey 64-67; Prec St Alb Abbey 67-69; V St Paul's Walden 69-78; V Braughing w Furneux Pelham and Stocking Pelham 78-79; P-in-c Lt Hadham 78-79; V Braughing, Lt Hadham, Albury, Furneux Pelham etc 79-82; V Cheshunt 82-95; RD Cheshunt 89-94; Hon Can St Alb 94-01; V Sawbridgeworth 95-01; rtd 01. *c/o M Lewis Lloyd Esq, 219C Goldhawk Road, London W12 8ER* Tel (020) 8576 6122

LEWIS-NICHOLSON, Russell John. b 45. Oak Hill Th Coll 79. **d** 81 **p** 82. C Clayton *Bradf* 81-84; Australia from 84. *Address temp unknown* Tel (0061) 429-358490 (mobile)

LEWISHAM AND GREENWICH, Archdeacon of. *See* HARDMAN, The Ven Christine Elizabeth

LEWORTHY, Graham Llewelyn. b 47. Reading Univ BA69. S Dios Minl Tr Scheme 91. **d** 94 **p** 95. NSM Sark *Win* 94-96; C from 96. *Baleine Studio, La Collenette, Sark, Guernsey GY9 0SB* Tel (01481) 832140

LEYLAND, Derek James. b 34. Lon Univ BSc55. Qu Coll Birm 58. **d** 60 **p** 61. C Ashton-on-Ribble St Andr *Blackb* 60-63; V 80-87; C Salesbury 63-65; V Preston St Oswald 65-67; V Pendleton 67-74; Dioc Youth Chapl 67-69; Ind Youth Chapl 70-74; R Brindle 74-80; V Garstang St Helen Churchtown 87-94; Sec SOSc 90-94; rtd 94; Perm to Offic *Blackb* from 94. *Greystocks, Goosnargh Lane, Goosnargh, Preston PR3 2BP* Tel (01772) 865682

LEYLAND, Tyrone John. b 49. Aston Univ BSc68. St Jo Coll Nottm 89. **d** 91 **p** 92. C Lich St Mary w St Mich 91-94; TV Willenhall H Trin 94-99; P-in-c The Ridwares and Kings Bromley 99-08; R from 08. *The Rectory, Alrewas Road, Kings Bromley, Burton-on-Trent DE13 7HP* Tel and fax (01543) 472932 E-mail t.leyland@btinternet.com

LEYSHON, Philip Alan. b 76. Glam Univ BA. Ripon Coll Cuddesdon BTh03. **d** 03 **p** 04. C Newton Nottage *Llan* 03-07; C Caerphilly 07-09; V Tonypandy w Clydach Vale from 09. *The Vicarage, Richards Terrace, Tonypandy CF40 2LD* Tel (01443) 423037

LEYSHON, Simon. b 63. Trin Coll Carmarthen BA86 Southn Univ BTh89. Sarum & Wells Th Coll. **d** 89 **p** 90. C Tenby *St D* 89-92; TV 92-96; Chapl and Hd RS Llandovery Coll 96-02; Chapl Ld Wandsworth Coll Basingstoke from 02. *Kimbers,*

Lord Wandsworth College, Long Sutton, Hook, Basingstoke RG29 1TB Tel (01256) 862206 E-mail simonleyshon@hotmail.com

LIBBY, Canon John Ralph. b 55. Trin Coll Cam BA83. Ridley Hall Cam 89. **d** 91 **p** 92. C Enfield St Andr *Lon* 91-93; C Northwood Em 93-96; V Denton Holme *Carl* from 96; RD Carl from 04; Hon Can Carl Cathl from 08. *St James's Vicarage, Goschen Road, Carlisle CA2 5PF* Tel (01228) 515639 *or* 810616 Fax 524569 E-mail john.libby@btinternet.com

LICHFIELD, Archdeacon of. *See* LILEY, The Ven Christopher Frank

LICHFIELD, Bishop of. *See* GLEDHILL, The Rt Revd Jonathan Michael

LICHFIELD, Dean of. *See* DORBER, The Very Revd Adrian John

LICHTENBERGER, Miss Ruth Eileen. b 34. NY Th Sem 64 NOC 95. **d** 96 **p** 97. NSM Warrington H Trin *Liv* 96-05; rtd 05. *8 Towers Court, Warrington WA5 0AH* Tel (01925) 656763

LICKESS, Canon David Frederick. b 37. St Chad's Coll Dur BA63. **d** 65 **p** 66. C Howden *York* 65-70; V Rudby in Cleveland w Middleton 70-07; Can and Preb York Minster 90-07; RD Stokesley 93-00; rtd 07; Perm to Offic *York* from 07. *Bridge House, Snape, Bedale DL8 2SZ* Tel (01677) 470077 E-mail david.lickess@tiscali.co.uk

LIDDELL, Mark. b 55. Birm Univ BA00. Coll of Resurr Mirfield 96. **d** 98 **p** 99. C Wednesbury St Jas and St Jo *Lich* 98-00; C Walsall St Andr 00-01; P-in-c 01-05; V 06-08; V Nuneaton St Mary *Cov* from 08. *St Mary's Abbey Vicarage, 99 Bottrill Street, Nuneaton CV11 5JB* Tel (024) 7638 2936

LIDDELL, Canon Peter Gregory. b 40. St Andr Univ MA63 Linacre Ho Ox BA65 MA70 Andover Newton Th Sch DMin75. Ripon Hall Ox 63. **d** 65 **p** 66. C Bp's Hatfield *St Alb* 65-71; USA 71-76; P-in-c Kimpton w Ayot St Lawrence *St Alb* 77-83; Dir of Past Counselling 80-05; Hon Can St Alb 99-05; rtd 05. *The Coach House, Hitchin Road, Kimpton, Hitchin SG4 8EF* Tel (01438) 832266 E-mail petermary.liddell@btinternet.com

LIDDELOW, Peter William. b 33. Oak Hill NSM Course. **d** 82 **p** 83. NSM Finchley Ch Ch *Lon* 82-84; NSM S Mimms Ch Ch from 84; Perm to Offic *St Alb* from 95; Chapl Magic Circle from 02. *23 King's Road, Barnet EN5 4EF* Tel (020) 8441 2968 E-mail chaplain@themagiccircle.co.uk

LIDDLE, George. b 48. NEOC 88. **d** 90 **p** 91. C Auckland St Andr and St Anne *Dur* 90-92; C Crook 92-94; C Stanley 92-94; P-in-c Evenwood 94-96; V 96-03; R Blackhall, Castle Eden and Monksheleden from 03. *The Rectory, The Crescent, Blackhall Colliery, Hartlepool TS27 4LE* Tel 0191-586 4202

LIDDLE, Harry. b 36. Wadh Coll Ox BA57 MA61. Wycliffe Hall Ox 62. **d** 64 **p** 65. C Withington St Paul *Man* 64-68; R Broughton St Jo 68-73; V Balby *Sheff* 73-82; R Firbeck w Letwell 82-94; V Woodsetts 82-94; TV Aston cum Aughton w Swallownest, Todwick etc 94-01; rtd 01; Perm to Offic *Sheff* from 01. *30 Meadow Grove Road, Totley, Sheffield S17 4FF* Tel 0114-236 4941

LIDDLE, Stephen John. b 60. St Jo Coll Ox BA81 PGCE82. Linc Th Coll 88. **d** 91 **p** 92. C Morpeth *Newc* 91-95; P-in-c Byker St Mich w St Lawr 95-98; R Bothal and Pegswood w Longhirst 98-05; P-in-c Billingham St Aid *Dur* from 05. *The Rectory, 12A Tintern Avenue, Billingham TS23 2DE* Tel (01642) 557010

LIDSTONE, Vernon Henry. b 43. SW Minl Tr Course 89. **d** 92 **p** 93. NSM Bovey Tracey SS Pet, Paul and Thos w Hennock *Ex* 92-94; Sub-Chapl HM Pris Channings Wood 92-96; Asst Dioc Chr Stewardship Adv 92-93; Dioc Chr Stewardship Adv 93-96; Dioc Officer for Par Development *Glouc* 96-97; Chapl HM Pris Leyhill 97-03; rtd 03. *The Pike House, Saul, Gloucester GL2 7JD* Tel (01452) 741410 E-mail vernon@lidstone.net

LIDWILL, Canon Mark Robert. b 57. CITC. **d** 87 **p** 88. C Annagh w Drumgoon, Ashfield etc *K, E & A* 87-90; I Urney w Denn and Derryheen from 90; Dioc Youth Adv from 92; Preb Kilmore Cathl from 98. *The Rectory, Keadue Lane, Cavan, Co Cavan, Republic of Ireland* Tel (00353) (49) 436 1016

LIEVESLEY, Mrs Joy Margaret. b 48. Lady Mabel Coll CertEd69. Guildf Dioc Min Course 98. **d** 00 **p** 01. NSM Farnham *Guildf* from 00. *3 Kingfisher Close, Church Crookham, Fleet GU52 6JP* Tel (01252) 690223 E-mail joy.lievesley@ntlworld.com

LIGHT, Mrs Madeline Margaret. b 54. Girton Coll Cam BA77 MA80 Lon Inst of Educn PGCE78. EAMTC 96. **d** 99 **p** 00. C Eaton *Nor* 99-02; P-in-c Nor St Helen 02-09; Chapl Gt Hosp Nor 02-09; P-in-c Nor St Steph from 09. *86 Grove Walk, Norwich NR1 2QH* Tel (01603) 219927 E-mail madelinelight@gmail.com

LIGHT, Mrs Penelope Ann. b 46. Madeley Coll of Educn TCert71 N Lon Poly BEd81. WEMTC 06. **d** 09. NSM Cirencester *Glouc* from 09. *Toad Cottage, 22 Bingham Close, Cirencester GL7 1HJ* Tel (01285) 640125 E-mail jonpen22@tiscali.co.uk

LIGHTFOOT, The Very Revd Vernon Keith. b 34. St Jo Coll Dur BA58. Ripon Hall Ox 58. **d** 60 **p** 61. C Rainhill *Liv* 60-62; C Liv Our Lady and St Nic 62-65; V Stanley 65-75; Chapl St Edm Coll

Liv 66-68; Chapl Rathbone Hosp Liv 70-75; V Mt Albert St Luke New Zealand 75-85; Dean Waikato 85-97; rtd 98. *16C Acacia Crescent, Hamilton 3206, New Zealand* Tel and fax (0064) (7) 843 1381 E-mail keith.jennie@xtra.co.nz

LIGHTOWLER, Joseph Trevor. b 33. **d** 79 **p** 80. Hon C Leverstock Green *St Alb* 79-80; Hon C Chambersbury 80-84; C Woodmansterne *S'wark* 84-88; R Odell and Pavenham *St Alb* 88-97; rtd 97; Perm to Offic *St Alb* from 97. *18 The Dell, Sandpit Lane, St Albans AL1 4HE* Tel (01727) 833422

LIKEMAN, Canon Martin Kaye. b 34. St Mich Coll Llan 55. **d** 57 **p** 58. C Llanwnog w Penstrowed *Ban* 57-60; C Llandudno 60-64; V Llanrhian w Llanhywel and Carnhedryn *St D* 64-73; RD Dewisland and Fishguard 71-73; V Llanstadwel 73-99; Can St D Cathl 88-99; rtd 99. *10 Lawrenny Street, Neyland, Milford Haven SA73 1TB* Tel (01646) 600983

LILES, Malcolm David. b 48. Nottm Univ MA69. St Steph Ho Ox 69. **d** 71 **p** 72. C Corby Epiphany w St Jo *Pet* 71-74; C New Cleethorpes *Linc* 74-76; TV Lt Coates 76-77; TV Gt and Lt Coates w Bradley 78-82; Soc Resp Sec 82-93; Hon C Gt Grimsby St Mary and St Jas 82-93; P-in-c Grimsby All SS 88-93; TV Dronfield w Holmesfield *Derby* 93-98; TR Crawley *Chich* from 98. *The Rectory, 1 Southgate Road, Crawley RH10 6BL* Tel (01293) 535856 *or* 520421
E-mail rectorcrawley@btinternet.com

LILEY, The Ven Christopher Frank. b 47. Nottm Univ BEd70. Linc Th Coll 72. **d** 74 **p** 75. C Kingswinford H Trin *Lich* 74-79; TV Stafford 79-84; V Norton *St Alb* 84-96; RD Hitchin 89-94; V Shrewsbury St Chad w St Mary *Lich* 96-01; P-in-c Shrewsbury St Alkmund 96-01; Adn Lich from 01; Can Res and Treas Lich Cathl from 01. *24 The Close, Lichfield WS13 7LD* Tel (01543) 306145 Fax 306147
E-mail archdeacon.lichfield@lichfield.anglican.org

LILEY, Peter James. b 60. Liv Univ BA82 Westmr Coll Ox PGCE83. Oak Hill Th Coll 91. **d** 93 **p** 94. C Exning St Martin w Landwade *St E* 93-96; V Acton w Gt Waldingfield 96-00; TV Bottesford w Ashby *Linc* 00-05; TR from 05. *The Vicarage, 10 Old School Lane, Bottesford, Scunthorpe DN16 3RD* Tel and fax (01724) 867256 *or* 842732 E-mail peter.liley@ntlworld.com

LILEY, Stephen John. b 65. Liv Univ BA87 MMus88 ARCM93. Wycliffe Hall Ox 97. **d** 99 **p** 00. C Throop *Win* 99-03; V Clapham *St Alb* from 03; RD Elstow from 08. *The Vicarage, Green Lane, Clapham, Bedford MK41 6ER* Tel (01234) 352814
E-mail the.lileys@ukgateway.net

LILLEY, Canon Christopher Howard. b 51. FCA75 FTII83. LNSM course 83 St Jo Coll Nottm 91. **d** 85 **p** 86. OLM Skegness and Winthorpe *Linc* 85-93; C Limber Magna w Brocklesby 93-96; Perm to Offic *S'well* 93-96; P-in-c Middle Rasen Gp *Linc* 96-97; R 97-02; V Scawby, Redbourne and Hibaldstow from 02; P-in-c Bishop Norton, Wadingham and Snitterby from 06; P-in-c Kirton in Lindsey w Manton from 06; RD Yarborough 02-09; Can and Preb Linc Cathl from 05. *St Hybald's Vicarage, Vicarage Lane, Scawby, Brigg DN20 9LX* Tel (01652) 652725 E-mail lilley@btinternet.com

LILLEY, Ivan Ray. b 32. Bps' Coll Cheshunt 58. **d** 61 **p** 62. C Kettering SS Pet and Paul 61-64; C Gt Yarmouth *Nor* 64-75; P-in-c Tottenhill w Wormegay *Ely* 75-83; P-in-c Watlington 76-83; P-in-c Holme Runcton w S Runcton and Wallington 76-83; V Tysoe w Oxhill and Whatcote *Cov* 83-86; C Langold *S'well* 87-91; P-in-c 91-98; rtd 98; Perm to Offic *Nor* from 98. *Linden Lea, 41 Cedar Drive, Attleborough NR17 2EY* Tel and fax (01953) 452710

LILLIAN, Mother. *See* MORRIS, Lillian Rosina

LILLICRAP, Peter Andrew. b 65. Hatf Poly BEng87 CEng93 MIMechE93. Trin Coll Bris 00. **d** 02 **p** 03. C Kineton *Cov* 02-04; C Napton-on-the-Hill, Lower Shuckburgh etc 04-07; V Acton and Worleston, Church Minshull etc *Ches* from 07. *St Mary's Vicarage, Chester Road, Acton, Nantwich CW5 8LG* Tel (01270) 628864 E-mail revlills@homecall.co.uk

LILLICRAP, Stephen Hunter. b 58. Newc Univ MB, BS81 MRCGP85. SEITE 00. **d** 03 **p** 04. C Wye w Brook and Hastingleigh etc *Cant* 03-08; C Stone Street Gp 06-08; C Mersham w Hinxhill and Sellindge 08; P-in-c Teynham w Lynsted and Kingsdown from 08; P-in-c Norton from 08. *The Vicarage, 76 Station Road, Teynham, Sittingbourne ME9 9SN* Tel (01795) 522510 Mobile 07971-224094
E-mail steve.lillicrap@btopenworld.com

LILLIE, Judith Virginia. *See* THOMPSON, Mrs Judith Virginia

LILLIE, Mrs Shona Lorimer. b 49. St Jo Coll Nottm BA03. **d** 03 **p** 04. C Bishopbriggs *Glas* 03-06; Dioc Supernumerary 06-07; Assoc P Glas St Mary 07-09; R Cambuslang from 09; R Uddingston from 09. *5 Brownside Road, Cambuslang G72 8NL* E-mail shonalillie@hotmail.com

LILLINGTON, (née POLLIT), Mrs Ruth Mary. b 65. SS Paul & Mary Coll Cheltenham BA88. St Jo Coll Nottm 88. **d** 90 **p** 94. Par Dn Caverswall *Lich* 90-92; Par Dn Caverswall and Weston Coyney w Dilhorne 92-93; Par Dn Luton St Mary *St Alb* 93-94; C 94-97; Chapl Luton Univ 93-97. *20 Harcourt Road, Bracknell RG12 7JD* Tel (01344) 423025

LILLISTONE, Canon Brian David. b 38. SS Coll Cam BA61 MA65. St Steph Ho Ox 61. **d** 63 **p** 64. C Ipswich All Hallows *St E* 63-66; C Stokesay *Heref* 66-71; P-in-c Lyonshall w Titley 71-76; R Martlesham w Brightwell *St E* 76-03; Hon Can St E Cathl 98-03; rtd 03; Perm to Offic *St E* from 03. *23 Woodland Close, Risby, Bury St Edmunds IP28 6QN* Tel (01284) 811330
E-mail canon.b.lillistone@onetel.net

LIMBERT, Kenneth Edward. b 25. CEng69 MIMechE. S'wark Ord Course 72. **d** 75 **p** 76. NSM Northwood Hills St Edm *Lon* 75-90; Perm to Offic from 90. *55 York Road, Northwood HA6 1JJ* Tel (01923) 825791

LIMBRICK, Gordon. b 36. Open Univ BA88. St Jo Coll Nottm. **d** 87 **p** 91. Hon C Troon *Glas* 87-90; Hon C Yaxley *Ely* 90-97; Hon C Yaxley and Holme w Conington 97-04; rtd 04; Perm to Offic *Pet* from 98 and *Ely* from 04. *271 Broadway, Yaxley, Peterborough PE7 3NR* Tel (01733) 243170
E-mail moandgol@tesco.net

LIMERICK AND ARDFERT, Dean of. *See* SIRR, The Very Revd John Maurice Glover

LIMERICK, Archdeacon of. *See* SHANNON, The Ven Malcolm James Douglas

LIMERICK, ARDFERT, AGHADOE, KILLALOE, KILFENORA, CLONFERT, KILMACDUAGH AND EMLY, Bishop of. *See* WILLIAMS, The Rt Revd Trevor Russell

LINAKER, David Julian John Ramage. b 65. Ripon Coll Cuddesdon BTh95. **d** 95 **p** 96. C Colehill *Sarum* 95-99; V Mere w W Knoyle and Maiden Bradley 99-06; P-in-c Salisbury St Thos and St Edm from 06; RD Salisbury from 07. *Little Bower, Campbell Road, Salisbury SP1 3BG* Tel (01722) 504462 *or* 322537 E-mail david.linaker@ntlworld.com

LINCOLN, Archdeacon of. *See* BARKER, The Ven Timothy Reed

LINCOLN, Bishop of. *See* SAXBEE, The Rt Revd John Charles

LINCOLN, Dean of. *See* BUCKLER, The Very Revd Philip John Warr

LIND-JACKSON, Peter Wilfrid. b 35. Leeds Univ BA67. Linc Th Coll 67. **d** 68 **p** 69. C Heref St Martin 68-71; P-in-c Burghill 71-78; V 78-82; V Barnard Castle *Dur* 82-83; P-in-c Whorlton 82-83; V Barnard Castle w Whorlton 83-00; rtd 00; Perm to Offic *Ripon* from 03. *5 Gill Lane, Barnard Castle DL12 9AS* Tel (01833) 630027 E-mail lindjacksons@googlemail.com

LINDARS, Frank. b 23. Wycliffe Hall Ox 54. **d** 56 **p** 57. C Beeston Hill St Luke *Ripon* 56-59; C Harrogate St Wilfrid 59-61; V Shadwell 61-80; RD Allerton 73-78; V Masham and Healey 80-88; rtd 88; Perm to Offic *Ripon* from 88. *Hope Cottage, Reeth, Richmond DL11 6SF* Tel (01748) 884685

LINDECK, Peter Stephen. b 31. Oak Hill Th Coll 57. **d** 59 **p** 60. C Homerton St Luke *Lon* 59-62; C Salterhebble All SS *Wakef* 62-63; C Islington St Andr w St Thos and St Matthias *Lon* 64-67; Perm to Offic *Derby* and *St Alb* 67-68; V Toxteth Park St Bede *Liv* 68-74; V Kano St Geo Nigeria 74-76; C Netherton *Liv* 76-77; C Ollerton and Boughton *S'well* 77-80; V Whitgift w Adlingfleet and Eastoft *Sheff* 80-86; P-in-c Swinefleet 81-86; V Kilnhurst 86-94; Chapl Montagu Hosp Mexborough 86-94; rtd 94; Perm to Offic *Sheff* 94-06. *1 Stuart Court, High Street, Kibworth, Leicester LE8 0LR* Tel 0116-279 6347
E-mail peter@lindeck.freeserve.co.uk

LINDISFARNE, Archdeacon of. *See* ROBINSON, The Ven Peter John Alan

LINDLAR, Christopher Max Dietrichs. b 55. Leeds Univ BA00 Lon Univ MA06. Coll of Resurr Mirfield 98. **d** 00 **p** 01. C Lancing w Coombes *Chich* 00-04; P-in-c Deal St Andr *Cant* from 04. *St Andrew's Rectory, St Andrew's Road, Deal CT14 6AS* Tel (01304) 374354 Mobile 07710-090195
E-mail c.lindlar@btinternet.com

LINDLEY, Anna Therese. b 42. **d** 09. NSM York St Mich-le-Belfrey from 09. *35 Manor Garth, Wigginton, York YO32 2WZ*

LINDLEY, Geoffrey. b 22. St Jo Coll Ox BA45 MA47. Westcott Ho Cam 47. **d** 47 **p** 48. C E Wickham *S'wark* 47-51; C Welling 51-52; V Lambeth St Phil 52-56; V Ox St Marg 56-72; P-in-c Pyrton w Shirburn 72-79; P-in-c Lewknor 72-79; P-in-c Shipton-under-Wychwood 79-80; P-in-c Milton-under-Wychwood 79-80; V Shipton-under-Wychwood w Milton, Fifield etc 80-85; Perm to Offic from 86; rtd 87. *clo M Woolfson Esq, Monks Walk, Pheasant Copse, Fleet GU51 4LP* Tel (01252) 614118

LINDLEY, Graham William. b 47. CIPFA77. **d** 97 **p** 98. OLM E Crompton *Man* 97-02; NSM Newhey 02-08; P-in-c from 08; P-in-c Belfield from 09. *37 Jordan Avenue, Shaw, Oldham OL2 8DQ* Tel (01706) 845677 E-mail g.lindley7@ntlworld.com

LINDLEY, Harold Thomas. b 28. St Jo Coll Ox BA51 MA73. Wells Th Coll 51. **d** 53 **p** 54. C Normanton *Wakef* 53-57; C-in-c Rawthorpe CD 57-63; P-in-c Longstone *Derby* 63-67; R 64-74; P-in-c Barrow w Twyford 74-84; V Barrow-on-Trent w Twyford and Swarkestone 84-93; rtd 93. *Gorwel, 35 Nant Bychan, Moelfre LL72 8HE* Tel (01248) 410484

LINDLEY, Canon Richard Adrian. b 44. Hull Univ BA65 Man Univ MA79. Cuddesdon Coll 66. **d** 68 **p** 69. C Ingrow cum Hainworth *Bradf* 68-70; Perm to Offic *Birm* 70-74; TV Ellesmere

Port *Ches* 74-79; V Westborough *Guildf* 79-80; TR 80-84; Dir of Educn *Birm* 84-96; Hon Can Birm Cathl 96; Dir of Educn *Win* 96-04; Hon Can Win Cathl 03-04; Perm to Offic from 04. *28 Denham Close, Winchester SO23 7BL* Tel (01962) 621851 E-mail lindleyrs@ntlworld.com

LINDO, Leithland Oscar. b 29. St Aug Coll Cant 57 St Pet Coll Jamaica 53. **d** 56 **p** 57. Jamaica 56-58; C Edmonton St Mary w St Jo *Lon* 58-62; C Heston 62-66; V Staines Ch Ch 66-04; rtd 04. *7 Windmill Close, Waterlooville PO8 0NA* Tel (023) 9259 6675

LINDOP, Andrew John. b 57. Cam Univ MA. Cranmer Hall Dur 80. **d** 82 **p** 83. C Brinsworth w Catcliffe *Sheff* 82-85; C S Shoebury *Chelmsf* 85-89; V Mosley Common *Man* 89-99; V Astley Bridge from 99; AD Walmsley from 02. *St Paul's Vicarage, Sweetloves Lane, Bolton BL1 7ET* Tel and fax (01204) 304119 E-mail andy.lindop@tesco.net

LINDOP, Canon Kenneth. b 45. Linc Th Coll 71. **d** 74 **p** 75. C Leic St Phil 74-77; C Cov H Trin 77-80; P-in-c Cubbington 80-82; V 82-07; RD Warwick and Leamington 91-96; Jt P-in-c Leamington Spa H Trin and Old Milverton 03-07; Hon Can Cov Cathl 04-07; rtd 07. *2 Grove House, Blue Anchor, Minehead TA24 6JU* Tel (01643) 821940 E-mail rev.lindop@btinternet.com

LINDSAY, Alan. *See* LINDSAY, Canon Richard John Alan

LINDSAY, Alexandra Jane (Sandra). b 43. CITC 90. **d** 93 **p** 94. Lic to Offic *K, E & A* 93-94; Aux Min Bailieborough w Knockbride, Shercock and Mullagh 94-05; Aux Min Roscommon w Donamon, Rathcline, Kilkeevin etc from 05. *Clementstown House, Cootehill, Co Cavan, Republic of Ireland* Tel and fax (00353) (49) 555 2207

LINDSAY, Anne. *See* LINDSAY, Mrs Mary Jane Anne

LINDSAY, Anthony. b 38. St Jo Coll Nottm. **d** 89 **p** 90. CMS 76-92; Dioc Admin Bo Sierra Leone 89-92; C Rainham w Wennington *Chelmsf* 93-96; R Quendon w Rickling and Wicken Bonhunt etc 96-03; rtd 03; Perm to Offic *York* 03-07; P-in-c Langtoft w Foxholes, Butterwick, Cottam etc from 07. *The Rectory, Church Lane, Langtoft, Driffield YO15 3TN*

LINDSAY, Ashley. *See* LINDSAY, Robert Ashley Charles

LINDSAY, David Macintyre. b 46. Trin Hall Cam BA68 MA72. Cuddesdon Coll 68. **d** 71 **p** 72. C Gosforth All SS *Newc* 71-74; C Keele *Lich* 74-78; Perm to Offic *St E* 79-80; Chapl Haberdashers' Aske's Sch Elstree 80-06; rtd 06; Perm to Offic *St Alb* 06-07 and *Portsm* from 07. *Chaplaincy, Queen Alexandra Hospital, Southwick Hill Road, Cosham, Portsmouth PO6 3LY* Tel 07769-814165 (mobile)

LINDSAY, Eric Graham. b 30. Witwatersrand Univ BA51 Lon Univ MA80 DipAdEd78. Coll of Resurr Mirfield 55. **d** 57 **p** 59. C Stella *Dur* 57-58; C W Hartlepool St Aid 58-60; C St Geo Grenada 60-61; Perm to Offic *Win* 61-65; *Roch* 65-72; and *Chelmsf* 72-84; C Stepney St Dunstan and All SS *Lon* 84-85; P-in-c Stepney St Dunstan LEP 84-85; R Bridge of Weir *Glas* 85-98; R Kilmacolm 85-98. *1 Woodrow Court, 26-32 Port Glasgow Road, Kilmacolm PA13 4QA* Tel (01505) 874668

LINDSAY, Canon John Carruthers. b 50. Edin Univ MA72 BD82. Edin Th Coll 79. **d** 82 **p** 83. C Broughty Ferry *Bre* 82-84; C Edin St Hilda 84-85; TP 85-88; C Edin St Fillan 84-85; TP 85-88; R N Berwick from 88; R Gullane from 88; Can St Mary's Cathl from 00. *The Rectory, 2 May Terrace, North Berwick EH39 4BA* Tel (01620) 892154 Mobile 07977-520277 E-mail johnlindsay@bigfoot.com

LINDSAY, (née CLEALL), Mrs Mary Jane Anne. b 54. Keele Univ BA77 Herts Univ PGCE92. SAOMC 00. **d** 03 **p** 04. C Chipping Barnet *St Alb* 03-07; Asst Chapl Portsm Hosps NHS Trust from 07. *Chaplaincy, Queen Alexandra Hospital, Southwick Hill Road, Cosham, Portsmouth PO6 3LY* Tel (023) 9228 6000 Mobile 07769-814166 E-mail anne.lindsay@porthosp.nhs.uk

LINDSAY, Richard John. b 36. Sarum & Wells Th Coll 74. **d** 78 **p** 79. C Aldwick *Chich* 78-81; C Almondbury w Farnley Tyas *Wakef* 81-84; V Mossley *Man* from 84. *The Vicarage, Stamford Street, Mossley, Ashton-under-Lyne OL5 0LP* Tel (01457) 832219

LINDSAY, Canon Richard John Alan. b 24. TCD BA46 BD52. **d** 49 **p** 50. C Denton Holme *Carl* 49-52; CMS Burundi 52-64; Chapl and Tutor CMS Tr Coll Chislehurst 65-68; R Chich St Pancras and St Jo 68-74; Chapl Maisons-Laffitte *Eur* 74-82; Can Brussels Cathl 81-88; Chapl The Hague w Leiden and Voorschoten 82-89; rtd 89; Perm to Offic *Heref* 88-01; *Portsm* from 01; *Guildf* from 03. *Flat 24, Manormead, Tilford Road, Hindhead GU26 6RA* Tel (01428) 601524

LINDSAY, Canon Robert. b 16. St Jo Coll Dur BA37 MA40. **d** 39 **p** 40. C Gateshead St Mary *Dur* 39-45; P-in-c Sacriston 43-45; P-in-c Benfieldside 45-46; V Lanercost w Kirkcambeck *Carl* 46-55; V Hawkshead and Low Wray 55-70; R Dean 70-74; RD Derwent 70-81; Hon Can Carl Cathl 72-81; V Loweswater w Buttermere 74-81; rtd 81; Perm to Offic *Ex* from 81. *58 Primley Road, Sidmouth EX10 9LF* Tel (01395) 577882

LINDSAY, Robert Andrew Duqughin. St Mich Coll Llan. **d** 09. C Blaenavon w Capel Newydd *Mon* from 09. *The Vicarage, Vicarage Lane, Abersychan, Pontypool NP4 8PX* Tel (01495) 772213

LINDSAY, Robert Ashley Charles. b 43. Leeds Univ BA66 Ex Univ BPhil81. Coll of Resurr Mirfield 66. **d** 68 **p** 69. C Mill Hill Jo Keble Ch *Lon* 68-72; C Sherborne w Castleton and Lillington *Sarum* 73-78; Chapl Coldharbour Hosp Dorset 73-78; Perm to Offic *Leic* 87-92; rtd 08. *Breezedown Cottage, East Melbury, Shaftesbury SP7 0DS* Tel (01747) 850145

LINDSAY, Sandra. *See* LINDSAY, Alexandra Jane

LINDSAY-PARKINSON, Michael. b 28. Edin Th Coll 66. **d** 67 **p** 68. C Edin Ch Ch 67-70; C Helensburgh *Glas* 70-72; R Lockerbie 72-83; R Annan 72-83; S Africa 83-88; V Alsager St Mary *Ches* 88-93; rtd 93; Perm to Offic *Ches* 93-98. *10 Cherry Tree Avenue, Church Lawton, Stoke-on-Trent ST7 3EL* Tel (01270) 875574

LINDSAY-SMITH, Kevin Roy. b 55. **d** 05 **p** 06. OLM Glascote and Stonydelph *Lich* from 05. *34 Castlehall, Tamworth B77 2EJ* Tel (01827) 251557 E-mail lindsay-smith1@sky.com

LINDSEY, Anna Elizabeth. b 65. Cuddesdon Coll 95. **d** 97 **p** 98. C Limpsfield and Titsey *S'wark* 97-00; C Warlingham w Chelsham and Farleigh 00-03; TV 03-06; rtd 06. *14 Mount Pleasant Road, Caterham CR3 6LP* E-mail anna@heffs.demon.co.uk

LINDSEY, Archdeacon of. *See* SINCLAIR, The Ven Jane Elizabeth Margaret

LINES, Canon Andrew John. b 60. Univ Coll Dur BA82. All Nations Chr Coll 88. **d** 97 **p** 98. Paraguay 91-99; Dir Caleb Bible Cen 91-99; SAMS 97-00; Hon Can Paraguay from 00; Gen Sec Crosslinks from 00. *59 Woodside Road, New Malden KT3 3AW* Tel (020) 8942 2179 *or* 8691 6111 Fax 8694 8023 E-mail gensec@crosslinks.org

LINES, Graham Martin. b 55. St Jo Coll Nottm 97. **d** 99 **p** 00. C Crosby *Linc* 99-02; C Bottesford w Ashby 02-03; TV from 03. *The Rectory, St Paul's Road, Ashby, Scunthorpe DN16 3DL* Tel (01724) 842083 E-mail graham@ml47.sflife.co.uk

LINES, Nicholas David John. b 64. St Jo Coll Nottm 94. **d** 96 **p** 97. C Burton All SS w Ch Ch *Lich* 96-01; P-in-c Rodbourne Cheney *Bris* 01-02; R from 02. *St Mary's Rectory, 298 Cheney Manor Road, Swindon SN2 2PF* Tel (01793) 522379 E-mail nick@linesn.freeserve.co.uk

LINFORD, Preb John Kenneth. b 31. Liv Univ BA52. Chich Th Coll 54. **d** 56 **p** 57. C Stoke upon Trent *Lich* 56-61; V Tunstall Ch 61-70; V Sedgley All SS 70-78; Chapl Chase Hosp Cannock 78-91; TR Cannock *Lich* 78-91; V Hatherton 80-91; Preb Lich Cathl 88-98; rtd 91; Perm to Offic *Lich* 91-00. *16 School Lane, Hill Ridware, Rugeley WS15 3QN* Tel (01543) 492831

LING, Adrian Roger. b 66. Goldsmiths' Coll Lon BA89 Leeds Univ BA02. Coll of Resurr Mirfield 00. **d** 02 **p** 03. C Mill End and Heronsgate w W Hyde *St Alb* 02-06; P-in-c Flegg Coastal Benefice *Nor* 06-08; R from 08. *The Rectory, Somerton Road, Winterton-on-Sea, Great Yarmouth NR29 4AW* Tel (01493) 393227 E-mail adrianrling@btinternet.com

LING, Andrew Joyner. b 35. ACP69 St Luke's Coll Ex TCert63 Open Univ BA80. SWMTC 83. **d** 86 **p** 87. NSM St Dominic, Landulph and St Mellion w Pillaton *Truro* 86-90; C Saltash 90-94; TV 94-97; Chapl Montreux w Gstaad *Eur* 98-03; rtd 03. *Martinets, chemin des Martinets 7, 1872 Troistorrents, Switzerland* Tel (0041) (24) 477 2408

LING, Rebecca (Jordan). b 75. Leic Univ BSc00. St Jo Coll Nottm 04. **d** 08 **p** 09. C Leic St Chris from 08. *20 The Fairway, Leicester LE2 6LN* E-mail jordanling@ntlworld.com

LING, Timothy Charles. b 61. Ex Univ BA85 Selw Coll Cam BA91. Ridley Hall Cam 89. **d** 92 **p** 93. C Gerrards Cross and Fulmer *Ox* 92-96; C Woking St Pet *Guildf* 96-00; V Bathford *B & W* from 00. *The Vicarage, 27 Church Street, Bathford, Bath BA1 7RS* Tel (01225) 858325 E-mail tim.ling@whsmithnet.co.uk

LINGARD, Colin. b 36. Kelham Th Coll 58. **d** 63 **p** 64. C Middlesbrough St Martin *York* 63-66; C Stainton-in-Cleveland 66-71; V Eskdaleside w Ugglebarnby 71-77; P-in-c Redcar w Kirkleatham 77; V Kirkleatham 78-86; RD Guisborough 83-86; V Linc St Botolph 86-89; Dioc Dir of Readers 86-89; R Washington *Dur* 89-93; P-in-c Middleton St George 93-97; rtd 97-01; Chapl Teesside Airport from 97; rtd 01. *29 Belgrave Terrace, Hurworth Place, Darlington DL2 2DW* Tel 07752-179418 (mobile)

LINGARD, Jennifer Mary. *See* ALIDINA, Jennifer Mary

LINGARD, Keith Patrick. b 30. AKC53. **d** 54 **p** 55. C Bedford Park *Lon* 54-56; C Ruislip St Martin 56-58; C Kempston All SS *St Alb* 58-63; Metrop Area Sec UMCA 63-65; V S Farnborough *Guildf* 65-75; R Glaston w Bisbrooke *Pet* 75-76; R Morcott w Glaston and Bisbrooke 77-95; rtd 95. *13 Woodside East, Thurlby, Bourne PE10 0HT* Tel (01778) 425572

LINGS, George William. b 49. Nottm Univ BTh74 Ox Univ PGCE75 Lambeth MLitt93. St Jo Coll Nottm 70. **d** 75 **p** 76. C Harold Wood *Chelmsf* 75-78; C Reigate St Mary *S'wark* 78-85; V Deal St Geo *Cant* 85-97; First Dir CA Sheff Cen for Ch Planting and Evang from 97; NSM Norfolk Park St Leonard CD *Sheff* 97-05. *The Sheffield Centre, 50 Cavendish Street, Sheffield S3 7RZ* Tel 0114-272 7451 E-mail g.lings@sheffieldcentre.org.uk

LINGWOOD, Preb David Peter. b 51. Lon Univ BEd73 Southn Univ BTh80. Sarum & Wells Th Coll 75. d 78 p 79. C Ashford St Hilda Lon 78-81; TV Redditch, The Ridge Worc 81-86; TR Blakenall Heath Lich 86-96; V Rushall 96-04; RD Walsall 98-03; TR Stoke-upon-Trent from 04; RD Stoke from 07; Preb Lich Cathl from 02. Stoke Rectory, 172 Smithpool Road, Stoke-on-Trent ST4 4PP Tel (01782) 747737
E-mail david@dplingwood.freeserve.co.uk
LINKENS, Timothy Martin. b 67. Strathclyde Univ MEng90. Wycliffe Hall Ox BTh99. d 99 p 00. C Blackheath St Jo S'wark 99-03; V Kidbrooke St Nic from 03. 66A Whetstone Road, London SE3 8PZ Tel (020) 8856 6317
LINN, Frederick Hugh. b 37. Em Coll Cam BA61 MA65. Ripon Hall Ox 61. d 63 p 64. C Bramhall Ches 63-68; V Liscard St Mary 68-71; V Liscard St Mary w St Columba 71-74; V Wybunbury 74-82; R Eccleston and Pulford 82-98; rtd 98; Perm to Offic Ches from 98. 4 Stonewalls, Rossett, Wrexham LL12 0LG Tel (01244) 571942 or (01407) 810372
LINNEGAR, George Leonard. b 33. CGA. Kelham Th Coll 63. d 62 p 63. C Wellingborough St Mary Pet 62-65; Lic to Offic Lich 65-69; B & W 69-80; Hon C Lewes All SS, St Anne, St Mich and St Thos Chich 80-86; C 87-99; rtd 99; Perm to Offic Chich from 99. 20 Morris Road, Lewes BN7 2AT Tel (01273) 478145
LINNEY, Barry James. b 64. Spurgeon's Coll BD97 Anglia Poly Univ MA02. Westcott Ho Cam 99. d 01 p 02. C Chingford SS Pet and Paul Chelmsf 01-04; V Cherry Hinton St Andr Ely from 04. The Vicarage, 2 Fulbourn Old Drift, Cherry Hinton, Cambridge CB1 9NE Tel (01223) 247740
E-mail standrews.cherryhinton@btinternet.com
LINNEY, Gordon Charles Scott. b 39. CITC 66. d 69 p 70. C Agherton Conn 69-72; Min Can Down Cathl 72-75; V Dublin St Cath w St Jas D & G 75-80; Preb Tipperkevin St Patr Cathl Dublin 77-80; I Glenageary D & G 80-04; Adn Dublin 88-04; Lect CITC 89-93; rtd 04. 208 Upper Glenageary Road, Glenageary, Co Dublin, Republic of Ireland Tel (00353) (1) 284 8503 Mobile 87-254 1775 E-mail glinney@eircom.net
LINTERN, John. b 61. Linc Th Coll BTh93. d 93 p 94. C Preston on Tees Dur 93-96; Asst Dioc Youth Adv 96-99; P-in-c W Pelton 96-07; P-in-c Pelton 99-07; V Pelton and W Pelton from 07. The Vicarage, West Pelton, Stanley DH9 6RT Tel 0191-370 2146 Fax 07971-114359 E-mail john.lintern@durham.anglican.org
LINTHICUM, James Douglas. b 58. Towson State Univ (USA) BSc81 Leeds Univ MA00. Wesley Th Sem Washington MDiv86. d 01 p 02. Chapl Barnet and Chase Farm Hosps NHS Trust 01-06; NSM Monken Hadley Lon 01-06; Sen Chapl Gt Ormond Street Hosp for Children NHS Trust from 06. Great Ormond Street Hospital, Great Ormond Street, London WC1N 3JH Tel (020) 7813 8232 Mobile 07921-140825
E-mail jlinth5481@aol.com
LINTON, Alan Ross. b 28. St Aid Birkenhead 57. d 60 p 61. C Blundellsands St Nic Liv 60-62; C Southport St Phil 62-63; C Aigburth 63-66; V Glazebury 66-67; C Formby St Pet 67-69; C Douglas Blackb 69-71; P-in-c Appley Bridge All SS CD 71-76; P-in-c Scorton and Calder Vale w Admarsh 76-85; R Hoole 85-93; rtd 93; Perm to Offic Blackb from 93. 12 Clive Road, Penwortham, Preston PR1 0AT Tel (01772) 747813
LINTON, Mrs Angela Margaret. b 45. SAOMC 97. d 00 p 01. NSM Langtree Ox from 00. 10 Yew Tree Court, Goring, Reading RG8 9HF Tel and fax (01491) 874236 Mobile 07884-346552
LINTON, Barry Ian. b 76. Glas Univ DSc98 TCD BTh04 MCIBS01. CITC 01. d 04 p 05. C Enniskillen Clogh 04-08; I Drumcliffe w Lissadell and Munninane K, E & A from 08. The Rectory, Drumcliffe, Co Sligo, Republic of Ireland Tel (00353) (71) 916 3125 E-mail drumcliffe@elphin.anglican.org
LINTON, Joseph Edmund. b 19. St Andr Univ MA46. Sarum Th Coll 46. d 48 p 49. C Monkseaton St Mary Newc 48-53; CF (TA) 50-54; C-in-c Lynemouth St Aid CD Newc 53-59; V Beltingham w Henshaw 59-93; rtd 93; Perm to Offic Newc from 93. 4 Dipton Close, Eastwood Grange, Hexham NE46 1UG Tel (01434) 601457
LINTOTT, William Ince. b 36. St Cath Coll Cam BA58. Ely Th Coll 58. d 60 p 61. C Brighton St Wilfrid Chich 60-62; C Chingford SS Pet and Paul Chelmsf 62-66; Chapl Fulbourn Hosp Cam 66-73; Lic to Offic Ely 66-97; rtd 01. 7 Haverhill Road, Stapleford, Cambridge CB22 5BX Tel (01223) 842008
LINZEY, Prof Andrew. b 52. K Coll Lon BD73 PhD86 AKC73 Lambeth DD01. St Aug Coll Cant 75. d 75 p 76. C Charlton-by-Dover SS Pet and Paul Cant 75-77; Chapl and Lect Th NE Surrey Coll of Tech 77-81; Chapl Essex Univ 81-92; Dir of Studies Cen for Study of Th 87-92; Sen Research Fell Mansf Coll Ox 92-00; Tutor Chr Ethics 93-00; Special Prof Th Nottm Univ 92-96; Special Prof St Xavier Univ Chicago from 96; Hon Prof Birm Univ 97-07; Sen Research Fell Blackfriars Hall Ox 00-06; Dir Ox Cen for Animal Ethics from 06; Hon Prof Win Univ from 07; Hon Res Fell St Steph Ho Ox from 08. 91 Iffley Road, Oxford OX4 1EG Tel (01865) 201565
E-mail andrewlinzey@aol.com
or director@oxfordanimalethics.com
LIONEL, Brother. See PEIRIS, Lionel James Harold

LIPP-NATHANIEL, Julie Christiane. b 41. Melbourne Univ BA63 MA72. d 95 p 95. Tutor United Coll of Ascension Selly Oak 96-99; Lic to Offic Birm 96-99; Regional Desk Officer S Asia & Middle East USPG 99-05; Perm to Offic S'wark 00-05; rtd 05. Frankentobel Strasse 4, 73079 Suessen, Germany Tel (0049) (71) 625846 E-mail julinath@aol.com
LIPPIATT, Michael Charles. b 39. Oak Hill Th Coll BD71. d 71 p 72. C Ardsley Sheff 71-74; C Lenton S'well 74-78; V Jesmond H Trin Newc 78-96; rtd 96. 69 Lansdowne Crescent, Stanwix, Carlisle CA3 9ES Tel (01228) 537080
LIPPIETT, Peter Vernon. b 47. Lon Univ MB, BS73 MRCGP80. Ripon Coll Cuddesdon 86. d 88 p 89. C Pinner Lon 88-91; V Twyford and Owslebury and Morestead Win 91-99; Warden Rydal Hall Carl 99-03; P-in-c Rydal 99-03; Dioc Spirituality Adv Portsm from 03. 50 Penny Street, Portsmouth PO1 2NL Tel (023) 9282 6120
LIPSCOMB, Ian Craig. b 30. Wells Th Coll 61. d 63 p 64. C Feltham Lon 63-65; Australia from 65; rtd 94. South Hill, Garroorigang Road, PO Box 118, Goulburn NSW 2580, Australia Tel and fax (0061) (2) 4821 9591
LIPSCOMB, Timothy William. b 52. Chich Th Coll 82. d 85 p 86. C Sevenoaks St Jo Roch 85-89; C Stanningley St Thos Ripon 89-92; V Armley w New Wortley 92-05; AD Armley 98-05; R Preston St Jo and St Geo Blackb from 05; AD Preston from 08. The Rectory, 13 Ribblesdale Place, Preston PR1 3NA Tel (01772) 252528 E-mail lavish@ermine2.fsnet.co.uk
LIPSCOMBE, Brian. b 37. Bris Univ BA62. Tyndale Hall Bris 62. d 64 p 65. C Eccleston Ch Ch Liv 64-66; C Halliwell St Pet Man 66-69; C Frogmore St Alb 69-72; V Richmond Ch Ch S'wark 72-75; TV Mortlake w E Sheen 76-80; P-in-c Streatham Vale H Redeemer 80-85; V 85-91; R Norris Bank Man 91-96; V Droylsden St Martin 96-02; rtd 02; Perm to Offic Ripon from 02. 15 St Anne's Drive, Leeds LS4 2SA Tel 0113-275 1893 Mobile 07743-168641 E-mail yvonne@ylipscombe.freeserve.co.uk
LISK, Stewart. b 62. Regent's Park Coll Ox BA84 MA88. St Mich Coll Llan 86. d 88 p 89. C Glan Ely Llan 88-92; Chapl Cardiff Inst of HE 92-96; Chapl Welsh Coll of Music and Drama 92-96; Asst Chapl Univ of Wales (Cardiff) 92-96; V Glan Ely 96-06; AD Llan 04-06; V Roath from 06. Roath Vicarage, Waterloo Road, Cardiff CF23 5AD Tel (029) 2048 4808
LISMORE, Dean of. See DRAPER, The Very Revd Paul Richard
LISTER, Anthony Galen. b 27. RIBA54. NEOC 80. d 83 p 84. Hon C Anlaby St Pet York 83-87. Hunter's Colt, Glenborrodale, Ardnamurchan PH36 4JP Tel (01972) 500219
LISTER, Mrs Jennifer Grace. b 44. Totley Hall Coll CertEd65. NOC 87. d 92 p 94. C Cowgate Newc 92-95; C Wall and Lich St Mary w St Mich 95-96; P-in-c Yoxall and Asst P The Ridwares and Kings Bromley 96-07; rtd 07. 81 Kingsley Road, Bishops Tachbrook, Leamington Spa CV33 9RZ Tel (01926) 427922 E-mail jenny.lister@waitrose.com
LISTER (née AISBITT), Mrs Joanne. b 69. St Jo Coll Dur BA91. St Steph Ho Ox 91. d 93. NSM Mill End and Heronsgate w W Hyde St Alb 93-96. Address temp unknown
E-mail listerwilliam@hotmail.com
LISTER, Joseph Hugh. b 38. Tyndale Hall Bris 61. d 64 p 65. C Pemberton St Mark Newtown Liv 64-68; Hon C Braintree Chelmsf 68-71; C Darfield Sheff 71-73; P-in-c Sheff St Swithun 73-76; TV Sheff Manor 76-80; TR Winfarthing w Shelfanger Nor 80-81; P-in-c Burston 80-81; P-in-c Gissing 80-81; P-in-c Tivetshall 80-81; R Winfarthing w Shelfanger w Burston w Gissing etc 81-88; P-in-c Sandon, Wallington and Rushden w Clothall St Alb 88-89; R 89-93; R Nether and Over Seale Derby 93-96; V Lullington 93-96; R Seale and Lullington 96-98; RD Repton 96-98; Dean Ndola Zambia 99-02; rtd 02; Hon C Hartington, Biggin and Earl Sterndale Derby 02-04; C Stoke Canon, Poltimore w Huxham and Rewe etc Ex 05-06. Brooksong, Longmeadow Road, Lympstone, Exmouth EX8 5LF Tel (01395) 266784 E-mail joe@ndolarola.co.uk
LISTER, Miss Mary Phyllis. b 28. St Andr Ho Portsm 52. dss 80 d 87. Inkberrow w Cookhill and Kington w Dormston Worc 80-82; Ancaster Linc 82-87; C 87-88; rtd 88; Perm to Offic Worc 88-00 and Leic from 00. 6 Stuart Court, High Street, Kibworth, Leicester LE8 0LR Tel 0116-279 3763
LISTER, Peter. b 42. Leeds Univ BA64 Newc Univ PGCE75. Coll of Resurr Mirfield 63. d 65 p 66. C Monkseaton St Pet Newc 65-68; C Cramlington 68-70; Hon C 71-78; C Morpeth 79-83; V Shilbottle 83-88; Asst Dioc Dir of Educn 83-88; Dir of Educn 88-95; Hon Can Newc Cathl 88-95; Dioc Dir of Educn Lich 95-06; rtd 07; Perm to Offic Lich from 07. 81 Kingsley Road, Bishops Tachbrook, Leamington Spa CV33 9RZ Tel (01926) 427922 E-mail peter-lister@supanet.com
LISTER, William Bernard. b 67. Keble Coll Ox BA88 MA92. St Steph Ho Ox BA91. d 92 p 93. C Mill End and Heronsgate w W Hyde St Alb 92-96; CF 96-06; Sen CF from 06. c/o MOD Chaplains (Army) Tel (01980) 615804 Fax 615800
E-mail listerwilliam@hotmail.com
LISTON, Scott Carnie. b 62. Edin Univ BD87. Edin Th Coll. d 88 p 88. C Edin St Martin and Edin St Luke 88-91; C Edin St Dav 91-92; Chapl HM YOI Guys Marsh 92-97; Chapl HM YOI

Onley 97-03; Chapl HM Pris Woodhill 03-06; rtd 06. *Address temp unknown*

LITHERLAND, Norman Richard. b 30. Lon Univ BA51 BA52 Man Univ MEd72. NOC 78. **d** 81 **p** 82. NSM Flixton St Mich *Man* 81-94; rtd 94; Perm to Offic *Man* from 94. *1 Overdale Crescent, Urmston, Manchester M41 5GR* Tel 0161-748 4243

LITHERLAND, Terence. b 46. **d** 93 **p** 94. OLM Horwich and Rivington *Man* from 93. *61 Tomlinson Street, Horwich, Bolton BL6 5QR* Tel (01204) 692201

LITJENS, Shan Elizabeth. b 55. **d** 95. C Fareham SS Pet and Paul *Portsm* 95-96; C Fareham H Trin 96-99; NSM Hedge End St Jo *Win* from 00. *11 Abraham Close, Botley, Southampton SO30 2RQ* Tel (01489) 796321 E-mail shanlitjens@aol.com

LITTLE, Andrew. b 27. Open Univ BA83 UEA BA03. AKC51. **d** 52 **p** 53. C Fulham All SS *Lon* 52-54; C Epsom St Barn *Guildf* 54-61; V Northwood *Lich* 61-72; P-in-c Hixon 72-86; V Stowe 72-86; V Hixon w Stowe-by-Chartley 86-89; rtd 89; Perm to Offic *Nor* from 89; Hon PV Nor Cathl from 93. *5 Damocles Court, Norwich NR2 1HN* Tel (01603) 662241

LITTLE, Ms Christine. b 60. Lanc Univ BA83. St Jo Coll Nottm 88. **d** 91 **p** 94. Par Dn Meltham *Wakef* 91-94; C Hatcham St Jas *S'wark* 94-99; P-in-c 99-04; C Nottingham St Pet and All SS *S'well* 04-07; C Nottingham All SS, St Mary and St Pet from 07. *15 Hamilton Drive, Nottingham NG7 1DF* Tel 0115-924 3354

LITTLE, David John. b 65. Oak Hill Th Coll BA94. **d** 94 **p** 95. C Chislehurst Ch Ch *Roch* 94-98; TV Bath Twerton-on-Avon *B & W* 98; Dep Chapl HM Pris Bris 98-99; Chapl HM Pris Reading from 99. *The Chaplain's Office, HM Prison, Forbury Road, Reading RG1 3HY* Tel 0118-908 5000

LITTLE, Derek Peter. b 50. St Jo Coll Dur BA72. Trin Coll Bris. **d** 75 **p** 76. C Bradley *Wakef* 75-78; C Kidderminster St Geo *Worc* 78-82; V Lepton *Wakef* 82-85; E Regional Sec CPAS 85-88; V Canonbury St Steph *Lon* 88-96; R Bedhampton *Portsm* 96-99; rtd 09. *13 Queensland Avenue, London SW19 3AD* Tel (020) 8542 2604 E-mail deepy@blueyonder.co.uk

LITTLE, George Nelson. b 39. CITC 70. **d** 72 **p** 73. C Portadown St Mark *Arm* 72-76; I Newtownhamilton w Ballymoyer and Belleek 76-80; I Aghaderg w Donaghmore *D & D* 80-82; I Aghaderg w Donaghmore and Scarva 82-05; Can Dromore Cathl 93-05; Treas 93-05; Chan 03-05; rtd 05. *22 Willow Dean, Markethill, Armagh BT60 1QG* Tel (028) 3755 2848

LITTLE, Herbert Edwin Samuel. b 21. Lon Univ BA54 BD68. NEOC 79. **d** 80 **p** 81. NSM Dur St Cuth 80-88; rtd 88. *Address temp unknown*

LITTLE, Ian Dawtry Torrance. b 49. Keele Univ BEd72. SW Minl Tr Course 81. **d** 85 **p** 86. NSM St Stythians w Perranarworthal and Gwennap *Truro* 85-97; NSM Chacewater w St Day and Carharrack from 97. *Kernyk, Crellow Fields, Stithians, Truro TR3 7RE*

LITTLE, James Harry. b 57. York Univ BA79. Qu Coll Birm 84. **d** 87 **p** 88. C Wollaton *S'well* 87-90; C N Wheatley, W Burton, Bole, Saundby, Sturton etc 90-93; R E Markham w Askham, Headon w Upton and Grove 93-06; P-in-c Dunham w Darlton, Ragnall, Fledborough etc 04-06; TR Howden *York* from 06. *The Minster Rectory, Market Place, Howden, Goole DN14 7BL* Tel (01430) 432056 E-mail revjlittle@aol.com

LITTLE, Nigel James. b 73. Middx Univ BA93. Oak Hill Th Coll 98. **d** 01 **p** 02. C Highgate St Mich *Lon* 01-07; TV Kirk Ella and Willerby *York* from 07. *St Luke's Vicarage, 2A Chestnut Avenue, Hull HU10 6PA* E-mail nigel_little@uwclub.net

LITTLE, Rebekah Mary. b 70. Oak Hill Th Coll. **d** 97 **p** 03. NSM Chislehurst Ch Ch *Roch* 97-98; NSM Bath Twerton-on-Avon *B & W* 98; Perm to Offic *Ox* 00-04; NSM Reading St Mary w St Laur 04-05. *Address withheld by request*

LITTLE, Canon Stephen Clifford. b 47. Man Univ MEd81. AKC72. **d** 72 **p** 73. C Grange St Andr *Ches* 72-73; C E Runcorn w Halton 73-75; P-in-c Newbold *Man* 75-77; P-in-c Broughton and Milton Keynes *Ox* 77-82; Sector Min Milton Keynes Chr Coun 77-84; TR Warwick *Cov* 84-93; R Harvington and Norton and Lenchwick *Worc* 93-96; R Harvington 96-98; Exec Officer Dioc Bd for Ch and Soc *Man* 98-05; Exec Officer Dioc Bd for Min and Soc 01-05; Hon Can Man Cathl 00-05; Perm to Offic from 05. *12 Redwood, Westhoughton, Bolton BL5 2RU* Tel 0161-832 5253

LITTLEFAIR, David. b 38. ACCA71 FCCA85 Lon Univ BD79. Trin Coll Bris 76. **d** 79 **p** 80. C Bursledon *Win* 79-82; V Charles w Plymouth St Matthias *Ex* 82-89; Warden Lee Abbey Internat Students' Club Kensington 89-94; V Malmesbury w Westport and Brokenborough *Bris* 94-03; rtd 03. *6 Matford Mews, Matford, Exeter EX2 8XP* Tel (01392) 218784

LITTLEFORD, Peter John. b 40. St Mark & St Jo Coll Lon CertEd63 ACP65 Birkbeck Coll Lon BSc70 Lon Inst of Educn DipEd73 MA76. SAOMC 96. **d** 99 **p** 00. NSM Bedf St Mark *St Alb* from 99; Chapl De Montfort Univ from 99. *1 Bindon Abbey, Bedford MK41 0AZ* Tel (01234) 356645 E-mail plittlef@dmu.ac.uk

LITTLEJOHN, Keith Douglas. b 59. Ripon Coll Cuddesdon BTh03. **d** 03 **p** 04. C Horsham *Chich* 03-07; P-in-c Bolney from 07; P-in-c Cowfold from 07. *The Vicarage, Cowfold Road, Bolney,*

Haywards Heath RH17 5QR Tel (01444) 881301 Mobile 07905-595041 E-mail keithdlj@aol.com

LITTLER, Eric Raymond. b 36. AMIC93. Roch Th Coll 65. **d** 68 **p** 69. C Hatfield Hyde *St Alb* 68-73; Chapl Welwyn Garden City Hosp 70-73; TV Pemberton St Jo *Liv* 73-78; Chapl Billinge Hosp Wigan 76-81; V Pemberton St Fran Kitt Green *Liv* 78-81; V White Notley, Faulkbourne and Cressing *Chelmsf* 81-88; V Westcliff St Andr 88-96; Chapl Westcliff Hosp 88-96; Chapl Southend HA 89-96; R E and W Tilbury and Linford *Chelmsf* 96-98; Chapl Orsett Hosp 96-98; RD Thurrock *Chelmsf* 96-98; R Gt Oakley w Wix and Wrabness 98-02; Chapl Essex Rivers Healthcare NHS Trust 98-02; rtd 02; Perm to Offic *Sarum* from 98; *Chelmsf* and *B & W* from 02; Chapl St Jo Hosp Heytesbury 03-08. *Minster Hall, 1 Pound Row, Warminster BA12 8NQ* Tel (01985) 218818 E-mail ericandsuzette@uwclub.net

LITTLER, Keith Trevor. b 35. Lon Univ BSc(Soc)63 TCert64 York Univ MA82 Hull Univ PhD89 Westmr Coll Ox MTh98 Univ of Wales (Bann) DMin06. St D Dioc Tr Course 89 St Mich Coll Llan 94. **d** 92 **p** 93. NSM Betws w Ammanford *St D* 92-94; C 94; R Pendine w Llanmiloe and Eglwys Gymyn w Marros 94-03; RD St Clears 98-03; rtd 03; Hon Research Fell Ban Univ from 06. *Myrtle Hill Cottage, Broadway, Laugharne, Carmarthen SA33 4NS* Tel (01994) 427779

LITTLER, Malcolm Kenneth. b 34. Univ of Wales (Lamp) BA55. **d** 57 **p** 58. C Llanelli *St D* 57-60; C Llandeilo Fawr 60-61; R Puncheston, Lt Newcastle and Castle Bythe 61-64; R Lampeter Velfrey 64-68; V Llanwnda w Goodwick and Manorowen 68-74; V Llanfynydd 74-78; V The Suttons w Tydd *Linc* 87-90; V Graffoe 90-94; rtd 94; Perm to Offic *Linc* 94-97. *Summerdown, Beaumont Fee, Lincoln LN1 1EZ* Tel (01522) 531075

LITTLEWOOD, Alan James. b 51. Man Poly BEd77. **d** 95 **p** 96. OLM Gosberton *Linc* 95-97; OLM Gosberton, Gosberton Clough and Quadring 97-01; C Bourne 01-03; P-in-c Leasingham and Cranwell 03-08; P-in-c Ancaster Wilsford Gp from 08. *The Rectory, 117 Ermine Street, Ancaster, Grantham NG32 3QL* Tel (01400) 231145 E-mail alan@littlewood35.freeserve.co.uk

LITTLEWOOD, Alistair David. b 68. St Cath Coll Ox BA89. Qu Coll Birm 93. **d** 96 **p** 97. C Keyworth and Stanton-on-the-Wolds *S'well* 96-00; Chapl Birm Univ 00-05; P-in-c Edwinstowe *S'well* from 05; P-in-c Perlethorpe from 05. *5 West Lane, Edwinstowe, Mansfield NG21 9QT* Tel (01623) 822430 E-mail vicarofeandp@yahoo.co.uk

LITTLEWOOD, Miss Jacqueline Patricia. b 52. Linc Th Coll 77. **dss** 80 **d** 87 **p** 94. Crayford *Roch* 84-87; Gravesend H Family w Ifield 84-87; Par Dn 87-93; rtd 93; NSM Gravesend St Aid *Roch* from 93. *25 Beltana Drive, Gravesend DA12 4BT* Tel (01474) 560106

LITTLEWOOD, John Richard. b 37. Ridley Hall Cam 69. **d** 72 **p** 73. C Rushden w Newton Bromswold *Pet* 72-75; Chapl Scargill Ho 75-77; V Werrington *Pet* 77-91; V Highbury Ch Ch w St Jo and St Sav *Lon* 91-02; rtd 02; Perm to Offic *York* 03-06. *Panel Pinar Hill Box 33, Calle Azalea 19, 03191 Pinar de Campoverde (Alicante), Spain* Tel (0034) 966 763 933 E-mail johnrlittlewood@hotmail.com

LITTLEWOOD, Mrs Penelope Anne. b 47. WEMTC 05. **d** 08. NSM Burghill *Heref* from 08; NSM Pipe-cum-Lyde and Moreton-on-Lugg from 08; NSM Stretton Sugwas from 08. *Cobwebs, Burghill, Hereford HR4 7HL* Tel (01432) 760835 Mobile 07734-347327 E-mail penny.cobwebs@virgin.net

LITTON, Alan. b 42. Ridley Hall Cam 66. **d** 69 **p** 70. C Bolton St Bede *Man* 69-71; C Ashton St Mich 71-73; V Haslingden St Jo Stonefold *Blackb* 73-77; Ind Chapl *York* 77-81; V Crewe All SS and St Paul *Ches* 81-84; Ind Chapl 81-84; V Spotland *Man* 89-94; R Newchurch *Liv* 94-02; P-in-c Croft w Southworth 99-02; R Newchurch w Croft 02; rtd 02; Perm to Offic *Liv* 03-08; Hon C Burtonwood from 08. *16 Rushton Close, Burtonwood, Warrington WA5 4HB* Tel (01925) 222944

LIVERPOOL, Archdeacon of. See PANTER, The Ven Richard James Graham

LIVERPOOL, Bishop of. See JONES, The Rt Revd James Stuart

LIVERPOOL, Dean of. See WELBY, The Very Revd Justin Portal

LIVERSIDGE, Mrs Linda Sheila. b 48. Oak Hill Th Coll BA98. **d** 98 **p** 99. C Kensal Rise St Mark and St Martin *Lon* 98-01; TV N Wingfield, Clay Cross and Pilsley *Derby* from 01. *The New Vicarage, Morton Road, Pilsley, Chesterfield S45 8EF* Tel and fax (01773) 590529 Mobile 07941-667616 E-mail linda.liversidge.free-online.co.uk

LIVERSUCH, Ian Martin. b 56. St Jo Coll Dur BA79. Wycliffe Hall Ox 79. **d** 83 **p** 84. C Newport St Mark *Mon* 83-85; C Risca 85-88; P-in-c Newport All SS 88-91; Canada from 91; R Hemmingford w Clarenceville 92-98; R La Salle St Lawr from 98. *350 12th Avenue, La Salle QC H8P 3P7, Canada* Tel (001) (514) 364 5718 E-mail islwyn@total.net

LIVESEY, Miss Rachel Elizabeth. b 67. Univ of Wales (Cardiff) BSc89 MBA96 Homerton Coll Cam BTh09 Huddersfield Univ PGCE99. Ridley Hall Cam 07. **d** 09. C Streetly *Lich* from 09.

36 Foley Road East, Streetly, Sutton Coldfield B74 3JL Tel 07977-310049 (mobile) E-mail rachel.livesey@googlemail.com

LIVESLEY, John. b 80. Magd Coll Ox BA02 MSt03 MA07 Leeds Univ MA07. Coll of Resurr Mirfield 04. **d** 07 **p** 08. C Swinton and Pendlebury *Man* from 07. *St Matthew's House, 46 Townsend Road, Pendlebury, Swinton, Manchester M27 6SH* Tel 0161-794 1808 Mobile 07796-117568
E-mail johnlivesley1980@yahoo.co.uk

LIVINGSTON, Bertram. TCD BA56. **d** 57 **p** 58. C Enniscorthy *C & O* 57-61; C Carrickmacross *Clogh* 59-61; I Carrickmacross w Magheracloone 61-63; C-in-c Derryvolgie *Conn* 63-78; I 78-79; I Monaghan *Clogh* 79-86; I Desertlyn w Ballyeglish *Arm* 86-94; rtd 94. *6 The Green, Portadown, Craigavon BT63 5LH* Tel (028) 3835 1859

LIVINGSTON, Richard. b 46. Qu Coll Birm. **d** 83 **p** 84. C Hobs Moat *Birm* 83-87; V Droylsden St Martin *Man* 87-95; P-in-c Wolverton w Norton Lindsey and Langley *Cov* from 95; Chapl to the Deaf 95-03; P-in-c Snitterfield w Bearley from 03; P-in-c Aston Cantlow and Wilmcote w Billesley from 08. *The Rectory, Wolverton, Stratford-upon-Avon CV37 0HF* Tel (01789) 731278
E-mail richard@livingstonr.freeserve.co.uk

LIVINGSTONE, Canon Francis Kenneth. b 26. TCD BA48 MA64. TCD Div Sch Div Test49. **d** 49 **p** 50. C Dublin Santry Union w Coolock *D & G* 49-52; C Dublin St Geo 52-57; I Castledermot Union 57-62; C Arm St Mark 62-66; Hon V Choral Arm Cathl 63-92; I Portadown St Sav 66-78; I Kilmore St Aid w St Saw 78-83; I Donaghmore w Upper Donaghmore 83-92; Preb Yagoe St Patr Cathl Dublin 85-92; rtd 92. *9 Castle Parade, Richhill, Armagh BT61 9QQ* Tel (028) 3887 1574

LIVINGSTONE, Canon John Morris. b 28. Peterho Cam BA53 MA56. Cuddesdon Coll 53. **d** 55 **p** 56. C Hunslet St Mary and Stourton *Ripon* 55-60; Chapl Liddon Ho Lon 60-63; V Notting Hill St Jo *Lon* 63-74; P-in-c Notting Hill St Mark 66-73; P-in-c Notting Hill All SS w St Columb 67-74; P-in-c Notting Hill St Clem 68-74; TR Notting Hill 74-75; Chapl Paris St Geo *Eur* 75-84; Adn N France 79-84; Adn Riviera 84-93; Chapl Nice w Vence 84-93; Chapl Biarritz 93-05; rtd 93. *47 Côte des Basques, 64200 Biarritz, France* Tel and fax (0033) (5) 59 24 71 18
E-mail biarritz.cofe@infonie.fr

LIVINGSTONE, John Philip. b 51. Univ of Wales (Abth) BA PGCE. St D Dioc Tr Course. **d** 96 **p** 97. NSM Maenclochog and New Moat etc *St D* 96-02; V Elerch w Penrhyncoch w Capel Bangor and Goginan from 02. *The Vicarage, 78 Ger y Llan, Penrhyncoch, Aberystwyth SY23 3HQ* Tel (01970) 820998

LIVINGSTONE, Kenneth. See LIVINGSTONE, Canon Francis Kenneth

LIYANAGE, Sylvester. b 78. Kingston Univ BEng01 Surrey Univ MSc03 Cam Univ BTh08. Ridley Hall Cam 05. **d** 08 **p** 09. C Kingston Hill St Paul *S'wark* from 08. *78 Kelvedon Close, Kingston upon Thames KT2 5LF* Tel (020) 8541 0577
E-mail sylvester.liyanage@stpaulskingston.org.uk

LLANDAFF, Archdeacon of. See JACKSON, The Ven Frances Anne

LLANDAFF, Bishop of. See MORGAN, The Most Revd Barry Cennydd

LLANDAFF, Dean of. See LEWIS, The Very Revd John Thomas

✠**LLEWELLIN, The Rt Revd John Richard Allan.** b 38. Fitzw Ho Cam BA64 MA78. Westcott Ho Cam 61. **d** 64 **p** 65 **c** 85. C Radlett *St Alb* 64-68; C Johannesburg Cathl S Africa 68-71; V Waltham Cross *St Alb* 71-79; R Harpenden St Nic 79-85; Hon Can Truro Cathl 85-92; Suff Bp St Germans 85-92; Suff Bp Dover *Cant* 92-99; Bp at Lambeth (Hd of Staff) 99-03; rtd 03; Perm to Offic *Truro* 04-07; Hon Asst Bp Cant from 08. *193 Ashford Road, Canterbury CT1 3XS* Tel (01227) 789515
E-mail rllewellin@clara.co.uk

LLEWELLIN, Brian Michael. b 47. Univ of Wales (Cardiff) LLM99 MRICS73. Sarum & Wells Th Coll 78. **d** 80 **p** 81. C Farncombe *Guildf* 80-83; Chapl RAF 83-87; R Hethersett w Canteloff w Lt and Gt Melton *Nor* 87-95; RD Humbleyard 94-95; P-in-c Smallburgh w Dilham w Honing and Crostwight 95-98; R 98-00; P-in-c Folkestone St Sav *Cant* 00-07; rtd 07. *Le Bourg, 14620 Le Marais-la-Chapelle, France*

LLEWELLYN, Canon Christine Ann. b 46. Univ of Wales (Ban) BA69 DipEd70. **d** 89 **p** 97. NSM Arthog w Fairbourne w Llangelynnin w Rhoslefain *Ban* 90-93; NSM Holyhead w Rhoscolyn w Llanfair-yn-Neubwll 93-94; C 94-95; C Holyhead 95-97; TV 97-04; R from 04; Hon Can Ban Cathl 03-07; Can Cursal from 07. *The Old School, Rhoscolyn, Holyhead LL65 2RQ* Tel (01407) 763001

LLEWELLYN, Neil Alexander. b 55. LWCMD78. Westcott Ho Cam 79 Sarum & Wells Th Coll 83. **d** 84 **p** 85. C Heref St Martin 84-86; Chapl Rotterdam Miss to Seamen *Eur* 86-89; R Docking w The Birchams and Stanhoe w Barwick *Nor* 89-92; Chapl Ypres *Eur* 92-95; Toc H 92-95; CF 95-06; P-in-c Newport w Cilgwyn and Dinas w Llanllawer *St D* 06-07; V Newport w Cilgwyn and Nevern and Y Beifil etc from 07. *The Rectory, Long Street, Newport SA42 0TJ* Tel (01239) 820380

LLEWELLYN, Richard Morgan. b 37. CB91 OBE79 MBE76. FCMI81. Sarum & Wells Th Coll 91. **d** 93 **p** 94. C Brecon

St Mary and Battle w Llanddew *S & B* 93-95; Min Can Brecon Cathl 93-95; Chapl Ch Coll Brecon from 95. *Llangattock Court, Llangattock, Crickhowell NP8 1PH* Tel (01873) 810116

LLEWELLYN-MACDUFF, Ms Lindsay. b 75. Kent Univ BA97. St Mich Coll Llan 97. **d** 99 **p** 00. C Milton next Sittingbourne *Cant* 99-01; C Barham w Bishopsbourne and Kingston 01-03; C Margate All SS 03-05; P-in-c Gt Finborough w Onehouse, Harleston, Buxhall etc *St E* from 05. *The Rectory, Woodlands Close, Onehouse, Stowmarket IP14 3HL* Tel (01449) 616010
E-mail lindsay@hercomputer.fsworld.co.uk

LLEWELYN, Canon Robert John. b 32. Keble Coll Ox BA54 MA58 Cheltenham & Glouc Coll of HE PhD01. Cuddesdon Coll 65. **d** 66 **p** 67. C Bedford St Andr *St Alb* 66-69; C Cheltenham St Luke and St Jo *Glouc* 69-75; V S Cerney w Cerney Wick 75-80; V Glouc St Cath 80-99; P-in-c Glouc St Mark 87-89; Hon Can Glouc Cathl 94-99; rtd 99; Perm to Offic *Glouc* from 99. *10 Beaufort Court, Chesterton Lane, Cirencester GL7 1WJ* Tel (01285) 650526
E-mail robert@llewe4.freeserve.co.uk

LLEWELYN-EVANS, Catherine Ruth. b 55. St Mary's Coll Dur BA76 Southlands Coll Lon PGCE78. STETS 99. **d** 02 **p** 03. NSM Yatton Moor *B & W* from 02. *The Court House, The Triangle, Wrington, Bristol BS40 5LB* Tel (01934) 863269
E-mail cthlle@btinternet.com

LLOYD, Canon Bernard James. b 29. AKC56. **d** 57 **p** 58. C Laindon w Basildon *Chelmsf* 57-65; V E Ham St Geo 65-82; RD Newham 76-82; Hon Can Chelmsf Cathl 82-94; R Danbury 82-94; P-in-c Woodham Ferrers 87-90; rtd 94; Perm to Offic *Chelmsf* from 94. *Chanterelle, 47 Seaview Avenue, West Mersea, Colchester CO5 8HE* Tel (01206) 383892

LLOYD, Bertram John. b 26. St Mich Coll Llan 81. **d** 83 **p** 84. C Malpas *Mon* 83-85; V Blaenavon w Capel Newydd 85-93; rtd 93; Lic to Offic *Mon* 93-96; St Vincent 96-02. *91 Hillside Avenue, Blaenavon, Pontypool NP4 9JL* Tel (01495) 792616
E-mail llwydunion@caribsurf.com

LLOYD, The Ven Bertram Trevor. b 38. Hertf Coll Ox BA60 MA64. Clifton Th Coll 62. **d** 64 **p** 65. C S Mimms Ch Ch *Lon* 64-70; V Wealdstone H Trin 70-84; RD Harrow 77-82; P-in-c Harrow Weald St Mich 80-84; V Harrow Trin St Mich 84-89; Adn Barnstaple *Ex* 89-02; Preb Ex Cathl 91-02; rtd 02. *8 Pebbleridge Road, Westward Ho!, Bideford EX39 1HN* Tel (01237) 424701 E-mail trevor@stagex.fsnet.co.uk

LLOYD, Mrs Carole Barbara. b 53. Sheff Univ BA74 Coll of Ripon & York St Jo MA03 Leeds Metrop Univ PGCE93. NOC 00. **d** 03 **p** 04. C Bolton St Jas w St Chrys *Bradf* 03-06; C Gt Aycliffe and Chilton *Dur* 06-07; TV Gt Aycliffe 07-09; P-in-c Chilton from 09; P-in-c Kelloe and Coxhoe from 08. *1 New South View, Chilton, Ferryhill DL17 0PS* Tel (01388) 722521
E-mail carole.lloyd@amnos.co.uk

LLOYD, David Edgar Charles. b 59. St Mich Coll Llan 97. **d** 99 **p** 00. C Newton Nottage *Llan* 99-03; V Newcastle from 03. *The Vicarage, 1 Walters Road, Bridgend CF31 4HE* Tel (01656) 655999 E-mail revd.lloyd@virgin.net

LLOYD, David Hanbury. b 28. Univ of Wales (Abth) BSc49 Reading Univ PhD70. LNSM course 97. **d** 97 **p** 98. NSM Swanage and Studland *Sarum* 97-98; Perm to Offic 98-06. *Scar Bank House, Russell Avenue, Swanage RH19 2ED* Tel (01929) 426015

LLOYD, David John. b 52. Lon Univ BD82. Burgess Hall Lamp 73. **d** 76 **p** 77. C Pembroke St Mary w St Mich *St D* 76-77; C Llanelli 77-80; V Cil-y-Cwm and Ystrad-ffin w Rhandir-mwyn etc 80-82; Oman 82-84; R Llanllwchaearn and Llanina *St D* 84-88; V Llangennech and Hendy 88-90; Perm to Offic *St Alb* 91-95; V Bampton w Clanfield *Ox* from 96; AD Witney 02-03. *5 Deanery Court, Broad Street, Bampton OX18 2LY* Tel (01993) 851222 E-mail revdjlloyd@aol.com

LLOYD, David John Silk. b 37. Univ of Wales (Lamp) BA62. St Steph Ho Ox 71. **d** 73 **p** 74. C Brentwood St Thos *Chelmsf* 73-77; C Hockley 77-80; C Wickford 80-81; C Wickford and Runwell 81-83; TV 83-88; Chapl Runwell Hosp Wickford 81-88; S Africa from 88; Perm to Offic *Chelmsf* from 88; rtd 97. *D4 Argyll House, Seaforth Road, Westcliff-on-Sea SS0 7SJ*

LLOYD, David Matthew. b 76. SS Hild & Bede Coll Dur BA98. Oak Hill Th Coll 06. **d** 09. C St Helen Bishopsgate w St Andr Undershaft etc *Lon* from 09. *Flat 2, 78 Milson Road, London W14 0LA* Tel 07721-745165 (mobile)
E-mail dmattlloyd@yahoo.co.uk

LLOYD, Dennis John. b 46. BSc70 MSc74 PhD81. S Dios Minl Tr Scheme. **d** 90 **p** 91. C Hamworthy *Sarum* 90-92; Chapl UEA *Nor* 92-97; P-in-c Malvern St Andr *Worc* 97-99; V 99-01; Chapl Defence Evaluation Research Agency 97-01; RD Malvern 98-01; P-in-c Rowlands Castle *Portsm* from 01; Warden of Readers from 01. *The Rectory, 9 College Close, Rowland's Castle PO9 6AJ* Tel (023) 9241 2605 E-mail djlloyd@btinternet.com

LLOYD, Derek James. b 78. Birm Univ BA00 Leeds Univ BA03. Coll of Resurr Mirfield 02. **d** 04 **p** 05. C Burnley St Andr w St Marg and St Jas *Blackb* 04-07; C W Burnley All SS from 07; CMP from 05. *11 Clover Crescent, Burnley BB12 0EX* Tel (01282) 416582

LLOYD

LLOYD, Dyfrig Cennydd. b 80. K Coll Lon BA01. Ripon Coll
Cuddesdon 01. **d** 04 **p** 05. C Llandysul w Bangor Teifi w Henllan
etc *St D* 04-06; C Bro Teifi Sarn Helen 06-07; TV from 07. *Y
Ficerdy, Llanddewi Brefi, Tregaron SY25 6PE*   Tel (01974)
298937 E-mail dyfrigllloyd@hotmail.com
LLOYD, Edward Gareth. b 60. K Coll Cam BA81 MA85 Dur
Univ PhD98. Ridley Hall Cam 85. **d** 88 **p** 89. C Jarrow *Dur*
88-91; C Monkwearmouth St Pet 91-92; P-in-c 92-96; TV
Monkwearmouth 97-99; V Birtley from 99. *6 Ruskin Road,
Birtley, Chester le Street DH3 1AD*   Tel 0191-410 2115
E-mail gareth@dunelm.org.uk
LLOYD, Eileen. *See* TAVERNOR, Mrs Eileen
LLOYD, Canon Elizabeth Jane. b 52. GRIC74 CChem MRIC77.
Linc Th Coll 77. **dss** 80 **d** 87 **p** 94. Linc St Nic w St Jo Newport
80-81; Lic to Offic *Sarum* 81-87; Hon Par Dn Lytchett Matravers
87-92; Chapl Poole Gen Hosp 85-94; Chapl Poole Hosp NHS
Trust from 94; Can and Preb Sarum Cathl from 03; Pres Coll of
Health Care Chapl 02-04. *The Rectory, 19 Springfield Road,
Poole BH14 0LG*   Tel (01202) 748860 *or* 442167
E-mail jane.lloyd@poole.nhs.uk *or* jane@jalloyd.fsnet.co.uk
LLOYD, Gareth. *See* LLOYD, Edward Gareth
LLOYD, Geoffrey. *See* LLOYD, William Geoffrey
LLOYD, Graham. b 36. Brasted Th Coll 62 St Aid Birkenhead 64
Glouc Sch of Min 86. **d** 89 **p** 90. NSM Churchstoke w
Hyssington and Sarn *Heref* 89-97; NSM Lydbury N w Hopesay
and Edgton 97-01; rtd 01; Perm to Offic *Heref* from 01. *The
Pullets Cottage, Church Stoke, Montgomery SY15 6TL*   Tel
(01588) 620285
LLOYD, Gwilym Wyn. b 50. Leic Univ BA72 Birm Univ MSc73
Lon Univ LLB78. Trin Coll Bris 83. **d** 87 **p** 88. C Bexleyheath Ch
Ch *Roch* 87-91; R Darlaston St Lawr *Lich* 91-98. *24 Grosvenor
Avenue, Streetly, Sutton Coldfield B74 3PB*
LLOYD, Hamilton William John Marteine. b 19. Jes Coll Ox
BA41 MA45. Ripon Hall Ox. **d** 43 **p** 44. C Falmouth K Chas
Truro 43-47; R Gerrans w St Anthony in Roseland 47-51; Min
Bournemouth H Epiphany CD 51-53; V Bournemouth H
Epiphany *Win* 53-60; V Whitchurch w Tufton 60-68; V
Whitchurch w Tufton and Litchfield 68-71; V Lyndhurst 71-73;
V Lyndhurst and Emery Down 73-84; rtd 84; Perm to Offic *Win*
from 86. *Post Office House, Litchfield, Whitchurch RG28 7PT*
Tel (01256) 893507
LLOYD, Harry James. b 22. Univ of Wales (Lamp) BA50. **d** 51
p 52. C Hay *S & B* 51-55; C Llanigon 51-55; C Hillingdon St Jo
Lon 55-56; C Marlborough *Sarum* 56-60; V Kingston and Worth
Matravers 60-83; C Milton Abbas, Hilton w Cheselbourne etc
83-87; rtd 87; Perm to Offic *Sarum* 87-00. *Riverside Cottage, 35
Rockbridge Park, Presteigne LD8 2NF*   Tel (01547) 560115
LLOYD, Canon Herbert James. b 31. TD. St D Coll Lamp BA57.
d 58 **p** 59. C Wrexham *St As* 58-65; TV 71-74; R Llanferres
65-67; R Llanferres, Nercwys and Eryrys 67-71; V Rhyl w
St Ann 74-96; CF (TA) 74-06; Can St As Cathl 81-06; Prec St As
Cathl 89-06; rtd 06. *The Orchard, 8 Stoneby Drive, Prestatyn
LL19 9PE*   Tel (01745) 851185
LLOYD, Jane. *See* LLOYD, Canon Elizabeth Jane
LLOYD, John Francis. b 21. **d** 01 **p** 02. OLM Tettenhall Regis *Lich*
from 01. *The Barn, West Trescott Farm, Bridgnorth Road,
Trescott, Wolverhampton WV6 7EU*   Tel (01902) 765612
LLOYD, Jonathan Wilford. b 56. Surrey Univ & City of Lon Poly
BSc80 N Lon Poly MA86 CQSW82 DASS82. S'wark Ord
Course 87. **d** 90 **p** 91. NSM Sydenham St Bart *S'wark* 90-93;
P-in-c 93-94; Dir of Soc Resp 91-95; Bp's Officer for Ch in Soc
95-97; Hon PV S'wark Cathl 91-97; Chapl Team Ldr Bath Univ
97-04; P-in-c Charlcombe w Bath St Steph 04-09; P-in-c
Copenhagen *Eur* from 09; Adn Germany and N Eur from 10.
Tuborgveg 82, 2900 Hellerup, Copenhagen, Denmark   Tel (0045)
(39) 627736 Fax 627735 E-mail jlloyd.uk@btinternet.com
LLOYD, Marc Andrew. b 78. LMH Ox BA99 Middx Univ MA02.
Oak Hill Th Coll 04. **d** 07 **p** 08. C Eastbourne H Trin *Chich* from
07. *20 Chamberlain Road, Eastbourne BN21 1RU*   Tel
07812-054820 (mobile) E-mail marc_lloyd@hotmail.com
LLOYD, Matthew. *See* LLOYD, David Matthew
LLOYD, Michael Francis. b 57. Down Coll Cam BA79 MA82
St Jo Coll Dur BA83 Worc Coll Ox DPhil97. Cranmer Hall Dur
81. **d** 84 **p** 85. C Locks Heath *Portsm* 84-87; Asst Chapl Worc
Coll Ox 89-90; Chapl Ch Coll Cam 90-94; Chapl Fitzw Coll
Cam 95-96; Hon C Westminster St Jas the Less *Lon* 96-03; Tutor
St Steph Ho Ox 03-06; C St Andr Holborn *Lon* from 06; Tutor
St Paul's Th Cen from 06. *134 Clifford's Inn, Fetter Lane, London
EC4A 1BY*   Tel (020) 7583 3913
LLOYD, Canon Nigel James Clifford. b 51. Nottm Univ BTh81
Lambeth STh90. Linc Th Coll 77. **d** 81 **p** 82. C Sherborne w
Castleton and Lillington *Sarum* 81-84; R Lytchett Matravers
84-92; TR Parkstone St Pet w Branksea and St Osmund 92-02;
R Parkstone St Pet and St Osmund w Branksea from 02; Ecum
Officer (Sherborne Area) from 92; Dioc Ecum Officer 00-01; RD
Poole 01-09; Can and Preb Sarum Cathl from 02. *The Rectory, 19
Springfield Road, Poole BH14 0LG*   Tel (01202) 748860 *or*
749085 Fax 08700-558534 E-mail nigel@branksea.co.uk

LLOYD, Mrs Pamela Valpy. b 25. Gilmore Ho 48 St Aug Coll
Cant 76. **dss** 76 **d** 87 **p** 94. Chartham *Cant* 76-78; Cant All SS
78-85; rtd 85; Chapl Asst Kent and Cant Hosp 87; Chapl
Chaucer Hosp Cant 87-90; NSM Elham w Denton and Wootton
Cant 87-93; Sub-Chapl HM Pris Cant 88-96; Hon C Cant
St Martin and St Paul 93-95; Perm to Offic from 96. *Cavendish
House, 9 North Holmes Road, Canterbury CT1 1QJ*   Tel (01227)
457782
LLOYD (née WALMSLEY), Patricia Jane. b 62. Bris Univ
BSc83 PhD87 Trin Coll Cam BTh01. Ridley Hall Cam 99. **d** 01
p 02. C Bowdon *Ches* 01-05; V Over Peover w Lower Peover
from 05. *The Vicarage, The Cobbles, Lower Peover, Knutsford
WA16 9PZ*   Tel (01565) 722304
E-mail jane@janelloyd6.wanadoo.co.uk
LLOYD, Canon Peter John. b 32. TD78. Wells Th Coll 59. **d** 61
p 62. C Walmer *Cant* 61-63; CF (TA) 62-73 and 77-87; C
Maidstone All SS w St Phil *Cant* 63-66; V Milton next
Sittingbourne 66-69; R Brinkley, Burrough Green and Carlton
Ely 69-73; CF 73-77; V Chessington *Guildf* 77-85; RD Epsom
82-87; V Epsom St Martin 85-92; rtd 92; Perm to Offic *B & W*
from 92. *74 Southover, Wells BA5 1UH*   Tel (01749) 672213
LLOYD, Peter Vernon James. b 36. St Jo Coll Dur BA61 MA.
Ridley Hall Cam 60. **d** 62 **p** 63. C Keynsham w Queen Charlton
B & W 62-65; Perm to Offic *Sarum* from 65; NSM Bournemouth
St Jo w St Mich *Win* 87-90; NSM Bournemouth St Pet w
St Swithun, H Trin etc 90-93; Perm to Offic *Win* 93-95; rtd 01.
18 Cornelia Crescent, Branksome, Poole BH12 1LU   Tel and fax
(01202) 741422
LLOYD, Richard Gary. b 75. Ex Coll Ox BA98 St Jo Coll Dur
MA00. Cranmer Hall Dur 98. **d** 00 **p** 01. C Dibden *Win* 00-03;
Asst Chapl Charterhouse Sch Godalming from 04. *Northway
Cottage, Northway, Godalming GU7 2EU*   Tel (01483) 425501
Mobile 07753-835744 E-mail rgl@charterhouse.org.uk
LLOYD, Robert Graham. b 42. St Jo Coll Nottm 82. **d** 84 **p** 85. C
Tonyrefail *Llan* 84-87; V Martletwy w Lawrenny and Minwear
and Yerbeston *St D* 87-91; V Monkton 91-96; V Cymmer and
Porth *Llan* 96-07; AD Rhondda 04-06; rtd 07. *7 Greenhill Park
Drive, Haverfordwest SA61 1LS*   Tel (01437) 783682
LLOYD, Robert James Clifford. b 18. Selw Coll Cam BA41
MA49. Linc Th Coll 46. **d** 47 **p** 48. C Clapham H Trin *S'wark*
47-50; C High Wycombe All SS *Ox* 50-53; CF (TA) 50-53; C
Hampstead St Jo *Lon* 53-55; V Wellington w W Buckland
B & W 55-66; P-in-c Nynehead 56-57; V 57-66; RD Wellington
59-66; R Chartham *Cant* 66-81; RD W Bridge 75-81; Hon C
Elham w Denton and Wootton 81-92; rtd 92; Perm to Offic *Cant*
from 83. *Cavendish House, 9 North Holmes Road, Canterbury
CT1 1QJ*   Tel (01227) 457782
LLOYD, Roger Bernard. b 58. K Coll Lon BA. Cranmer Hall
Dur. **d** 84 **p** 85. C Hornchurch St Andr *Chelmsf* 84-87; C Gt
Parndon 87-94; V Elm Park St Nic Hornchurch 94-99.
494 Heathway, Dagenham RM10 7SH   Tel (020) 8984 9887
Mobile 07703-383176
LLOYD, Ronald. b 37. St Mich Coll Llan. **d** 83 **p** 84. C Penarth All
SS *Llan* 83-85; V Cwmbach 85-91; Perm to Offic from 91.
23 Teilo Street, Cardiff CF11 9JN
LLOYD, Canon Ronald Henry. b 32. Univ of Wales (Lamp) BA52
LTh54. **d** 54 **p** 56. C Manselton *S & B* 54-56; C Sketty 56-59; C
Swansea St Mary 59-63; CF (TA) 59-65; V Elmley Castle w
Netherton and Bricklehampton *Worc* 63-69; Chapl Dragon Sch
Ox 69-82; Chapl St Hugh's Coll Ox 75-80; P-in-c Ox St Marg
75-76; Chapl Magd Coll Ox 75-82; Prec and Chapl Ch Ch *Ox*
82-87; R Alvescot w Black Bourton, Shilton, Holwell etc 87-95;
P-in-c Broughton Poggs w Filkins, Broadwell etc 94-95; R Shill
Valley and Broadshire 95-01; rtd 01; Perm to Offic *Glouc* and *Ox*
from 02. *2 The Farriers, Southrop, Lechlade GL7 3RL*   Tel
(01367) 850071
LLOYD, Mrs Sandra Edith. b 48. Sarum & Wells Th Coll 83.
dss 86 **d** 87 **p** 94. Freshwater *Portsm* 86-87; C 87-89; C Whitwell
89-95; V from 95; C Niton 89-95; P-in-c 95-96; R from 96; R St
Lawrence 96-04. *The Rectory, Pan Lane, Niton, Ventnor
PO38 2BT*   Tel and fax (01983) 730595
E-mail rhadegunde@aol.com
LLOYD, Simon David. b 58. Portsm Poly BA79 RGN91
RSCN95. Wycliffe Hall Ox 80. **d** 83 **p** 84. C Cotmanhay *Derby*
83-85; Chapl Asst Nottm City Hosp 85-87; Chapl Basford Hosp
Nottm 85-87; Perm to Offic *Birm* 91-97; TV Solihull 97-04; P-in-c
Minehead *B & W* from 04. *The Vicarage, 7 Paganel Road,
Minehead TA24 5ET*   Tel (01643) 703530
E-mail fathersi@dsl.pipex.com
LLOYD, Stephen Russell. b 47. Worc Coll Ox BA69 MA77
CertEd. Oak Hill Th Coll 76. **d** 77 **p** 78. C Canonbury St Steph
Lon 77-80; C Braintree *Chelmsf* 80-92; V Braintree St Paul 92-01;
V Ipswich St Andr *St E* from 01. *The Vicarage, 286 Britannia
Road, Ipswich IP4 5HF*   Tel (01473) 714341
E-mail rev.lloyd@tiscali.co.uk
LLOYD, Canon Stuart George Errington. b 49. TCD BA72. **d** 75
p 76. C Cloughfern *Conn* 75-79; C Cregagh *D & D* 79-82; I
Eglantine *Conn* 82-89; I Ballymena w Ballyclug from 89; Can
Conn Cathl from 97; Preb 97-01; Prec from 01. *St Patrick's*

510

Rectory, 102 Galgorm Road, Ballymena BT42 1AE Tel and fax (028) 2565 2253 *or* tel 2563 0741
E-mail ballymena@connor.anglican.org

LLOYD, Timothy David Lewis. *See* LEWIS LLOYD, Canon Timothy David

LLOYD, Trevor. *See* LLOYD, The Ven Bertram Trevor

LLOYD, William Geoffrey. b 48. Man Univ BA70. Oak Hill Th Coll 92. **d** 95 **p** 96. C Plaistow St Mary *Roch* 95-99; TV Ottery St Mary, Alfington, W Hill, Tipton etc *Ex* 99-04; P-in-c Sampford Spiney w Horrabridge from 04; RD Tavistock from 07. *The Rectory, Tor View, Horrabridge, Yelverton PL20 7RE* Tel (01822) 855198 E-mail geofflloyd@ukgateway.net

LLOYD-DAVIES, Arthur (Lloyd). b 31. Univ of Wales BA55. Cuddesdon Coll 55. **d** 57 **p** 58. C Tonypandy w Clydach Vale *Llan* 57-59; C Merthyr Dyfan 59-62; C Amersham *Ox* 62-65; V Tilehurst St Geo 65-73; R Wokingham St Paul 73-84; R Nuthurst *Chich* 84-90; I Fiddown w Clonegam, Guilcagh and Kilmeaden *C & O* 90-96; rtd 96; Hon C Bratton, Edington and Imber, Erlestoke etc *Sarum* 96-99. *The Gatehouse Lodge, Terrys Cross House, Brighton Road, Woodmancote, Henfield BN5 9SX* Tel (01273) 491210

LLOYD HUGHES, Gwilym. *See* HUGHES, Gwilym Lloyd

LLOYD-JAMES, Duncan Geraint. b 66. St Steph Ho Ox BTh94. **d** 94 **p** 96. C St Leonards Ch Ch and St Mary *Chich* 94-96; C Rottingdean 96-99; R Brede w Udimore 99-07; rtd 07; Perm to Offic *Guildf* from 08. *Forge House, Udimore Road, Udimore, Rye TN31 6AY* Tel (01424) 882457
E-mail rectory25@btinternet.com

LLOYD JONES, Ieuan. b 31. St Cath Coll Cam BA51 MA54 FBIM. Sarum & Wells Th Coll 80. **d** 83 **p** 84. NSM Claygate *Guildf* 83-89; Perm to Offic *Ox* 89-06. *Address temp unknown*

LLOYD MORGAN, Richard Edward. b 48. Trin Coll Cam MA70 Ox Univ DipEd71. SEITE 95. **d** 98 **p** 99. NSM Clapham St Paul *S'wark* 98-03; Chapl K Coll Cam from 03. *King's College, Cambridge CB2 1ST* Tel (01223) 331100
E-mail chaplain@kings.cam.ac.uk

LLOYD-RICHARDS, David Robert. b 48. Open Univ BA84 Hull Univ MA87. St D Coll Lamp. **d** 71 **p** 72. C Skewen *Llan* 71-73; C Neath w Llantwit 73-76; Miss to Seamen 76-77; V Pontlottyn w Fochriw *Llan* 77-84; R Merthyr Dyfan 84-90; Chapl Barry Neale-Kent Hosp 84-90; Tutor Open Univ from 85; Sen Chapl Univ Hosp of Wales Cardiff 90-95; Sen Chapl Univ Hosp of Wales and Llandough NHS Trust 95-00; Sen Chapl Cardiff and Vale NHS Trust from 00. *University Hospital of Wales, Heath Park, Cardiff CF14 4XW* Tel (029) 2074 7747 ext 4854
E-mail lloyd-richards@cf.co.uk

LLOYD ROBERTS, Mrs Kathleen Ada May. b 49. Bordesley Coll of Educn CertEd71. Qu Coll Birm 03. **d** 06 **p** 07. NSM Temple Balsall *Birm* 06-09; V from 09. *The Master's House, Temple Balsall, Knowle, Solihull B93 0AL* Tel 0121-684 3844
E-mail klloydr@citycol.ac.uk

LLOYD WILLIAMS, Martin Clifford. b 65. Westmr Coll Lon BEd87. Trin Coll Bris BA93. **d** 93 **p** 94. C Bath Walcot *B & W* 93-97; R Bath St Mich w St Paul from 97. *71 Priory Close, Combe Down, Bath BA2 5AP* Tel (01225) 835490
E-mail martin.lloydwilliams@stmichaelsbath.org.uk

LO, Peter Kwan Ho. b 54. Chinese Univ of Hong Kong BD84 Stirling Univ MBA92 K Coll Lon LLB99 QTS02. **d** 84 **p** 85. Hong Kong 84-91; Perm to Offic *Chich* 02-03; C Uckfield 03-06; R Monterey Park USA from 07. *133 East Graves Avenue, Monterey Park CA 91755-3915, USA* Tel (001) (626) 571 2714
E-mail peterkwanholo@hotmail.com

lo POLITO, Nicola. b 59. Catholic Th Union Chicago MDiv85 MA(Theol)87. Comboni Miss. **d** 85 **p** 86. In RC Ch 85-94; Egypt 86-88; Sudan 88-91; Italy 91-94; Asst Chapl Malta and Gozo *Eur* 94-98; C Castle Bromwich SS Mary and Marg *Birm* 98-01; TV Salter Street and Shirley 01-05; Chapl Birm Univ from 05. *258 Mary Vale Road, Birmingham B30 1PJ* Tel 0121-458 7432 *or* 414 7001 Fax 414 7002 E-mail nlopolito@hotmail.com

LOAT, Canon Andrew Graham. b 61. Aber Univ BD83 Univ of Wales (Ban) MTh00. St Jo Coll Nottm. **d** 87 **p** 88. C Llangynwyd w Maesteg 87-90; C Llansamlet *S & B* 90-91; R Whitton and Pilleth and Cascob etc 91-98; R Llandrindod w Cefnllys and Disserth from 98; Warden of Readers from 02; Can Res Brecon Cathl from 03; AD Maelienydd from 06. *The Rectory, Broadway, Llandrindod Wells LD1 5HT* Tel (01597) 822043
E-mail andrew.loat@googlemail.com

LOBB, Edward Eric. b 51. Magd Coll Ox BA74 MA76. Wycliffe Hall Ox 73. **d** 76 **p** 77. C Haughton St Mary *Man* 76-80; C Rusholme H Trin 80-84; P-in-c Whitfield *Derby* 84-90; V 90-92; V Stapenhill w Cauldwell 92-03; rtd 03; Perm to Offic *Derby* 03-05. *Middleton House, Beith KA15 1HX* Tel (01505) 500232

LOBB, Miss Josephine Mary. b 57. SRN83. **d** 96 **p** 97. OLM St Germans *Truro* from 96. *19 Lowertown Close, Landrake, Saltash PL12 5DG* Tel (01752) 851488

LOCK, Mrs Beverley. b 59. Lougbb Univ BA81 Bris Univ PGCE82. CBDTI 01. **d** 04 **p** 05. C Kendal St Geo *Carl* 04-07; C Beacon 07-08; P-in-c Orton and Tebay w Ravenstonedale etc from 08; P-in-c Shap w Swindale and Bampton w Mardale from

08. *The Vicarage, Orton, Penrith CA10 3RQ* Tel (015396) 24045
E-mail rev.bev@btinternet.com

LOCK, Graham Robert. b 39. Hertf Coll Ox BA63 MA67. Ridley Hall Cam 62. **d** 64 **p** 65. C Bexleyheath St Pet *Roch* 64-66; C Roch St Justus 66-71; C St Mary Cray and St Paul's Cray 71-75; V Chatham St Paul w All SS 75-83; R Lambourne w Abridge and Stapleford Abbotts *Chelmsf* 83-92; V Barkingside St Laur 92-03; rtd 04. *107 Spencer Road, Benfleet SS7 3HS* Tel (01268) 750882

LOCK, Mrs Jacqueline. b 43. **d** 08. OLM High Wycombe *Ox* from 08. *15 Kingsley Crescent, High Wycombe HP11 2UN* Tel (01494) 532216 E-mail jackie@thelocks.org.uk

LOCK, Paul Alan. b 65. St Chad's Coll Dur BA86. Coll of Resurr Mirfield 87. **d** 89 **p** 90. C Upholland *Liv* 89-92; C Teddington SS Pet and Paul and Fulwell *Lon* 92-95; V 95-99; V Wigan St Anne *Liv* 99-04. *151 Mossy Lea Road, Wrightington, Wigan WN6 9RE* Tel (01257) 424817 E-mail paul.a_lock@virgin.net

LOCK, The Ven Peter Harcourt D'Arcy. b 44. AKC67. **d** 68 **p** 69. C Meopham *Roch* 68-72; C Wigmore w Hempstead 72; C S Gillingham 72-77; R Hartley 77-83; R Fawkham and Hartley 83-84; V Dartford H Trin 84-93; Hon Can Roch Cathl 90-01; V Bromley SS Pet and Paul 93-01; RD Bromley 96-01; Adn Roch from 01; Can Res Roch Cathl from 01. *The Archdeaconry, King's Orchard, Rochester ME1 1TG* Tel (01634) 843366 ext 111 Fax 401410 Mobile 07719-737101
E-mail archdeacon.rochester@rochester.anglican.org

LOCK, Thomas. **d** 05 **p** 06. OLM N Poole Ecum Team *Sarum* from 05. *Mount Haven, 61 Albert Road, Corfe Mullen, Wimborne BH21 3QE* Tel (01202) 694325 E-mail thomaslock@fsmail.net

LOCKE, Mrs Jennifer Margaret. b 52. Edin Univ BEd74. Ox Min Course 06. **d** 08. NSM Wexham *Ox* from 08. *Hazeldene House, 20 Seer Mead, Seer Green, Beaconsfield HP9 2QL* Tel (01494) 759734 E-mail jmlocke1@gmail.com

LOCKE, Nigel Richard. *See* HESFORD-LOCKE, Richard Nigel

LOCKE, Robert Andrew. b 62. St Steph Ho Ox 89. **d** 92 **p** 93. C Colchester St Jas, All SS, St Nic and St Runwald *Chelmsf* 92-95; CF 95-00; V Burnham *Chelmsf* 00-04. *331 Broomfield Road, Chelmsford CM1 4DU* Tel (01245) 440745 Mobile 07949-862867 E-mail robert@robertlocke.wanadoo.co.uk

LOCKE, Stephen John. b 60. St Chad's Coll Dur BA82. Sarum & Wells Th Coll 84. **d** 86 **p** 87. C Blackb St Mich w St Jo and H Trin 86-89; C Oswaldtwistle Immanuel and All SS 89-92; V Blackb St Mich w St Jo and H Trin 92-98; Chapl to the Deaf 98-04; V Owton Manor *Dur* from 04. *The Vicarage, 18 Rossmere Way, Hartlepool TS25 5EF* Tel (01429) 290278

LOCKETT, Preb Paul. b 48. Sarum & Wells Th Coll 73. **d** 76 **p** 77. C Horninglow *Lich* 76-78; C Tewkesbury w Walton Cardiff *Glouc* 78-81; P-in-c W Bromwich St Pet *Lich* 81-90; R Norton Canes 90-95; V Longton St Mary and St Chad from 95; Dean's V Lich Cathl from 91; Preb Lich Cathl from 04. *St Mary and St Chad's Presbytery, 269 Anchor Road, Stoke-on-Trent ST3 5DH* Tel (01782) 313142

LOCKETT, Simon David. b 66. Stirling Univ BA96. Wycliffe Hall Ox 00. **d** 02 **p** 03. C Ray Valley *Ox* 02-06; R Madley w Tyberton, Peterchurch, Vowchurch etc *Heref* from 06. *The Vicarage, Madley, Hereford HR2 9LP* Tel (01981) 250245
E-mail simonlizlockett@hotmail.com

LOCKEY, Malcolm. b 45. Sunderland Poly BA67 Newc Univ DipEd68 FRSA75. NEOC 87. **d** 90 **p** 91. NSM Yarm *York* 90-97; C 97-98; TV Whitby w Aislaby and Ruswarp 98-03; Hon Chapl Miss to Seafarers 98-03; Chapl RNLI 00-03, P-in-c Coldstream *Edin* from 04; R Kelso from 05; Offg Chapl RAF and Chapl ATC 02-03. *The Rectory, 6 Forestfield, Kelso TD5 7BX* Tel (01573) 228709 Mobile 07710-467785
E-mail macbrac@hotmail.com

LOCKHART, Clare Patricia Anne (Sister Clare). b 44. Bris Univ BA74 Newc Univ MLitt96. Cranmer Hall Dur 84. **d** 87 **p** 94. Sisters of Charity from 63; Chapl Asst Sunderland Distr Gen Hosp 84-89; Chapl 89-95; NSM N Hylton St Marg Castletown *Dur* 87-95; P-in-c 95-99; NSM Eorropaidh *Arg* from 99; Perm to Offic *Dur* from 02. *The Sisters of Charity, Carmel, 7A Gress, Isle of Lewis HS2 0NB* Tel (01851) 820484
E-mail srlockhart@btinternet.com

LOCKHART, David. b 68. QUB BSc90 TCD BTh93. CITC 90. **d** 93 **p** 94. C Belfast St Mary w H Redeemer *Conn* 93-96; I Belfast St Steph w St Luke 96-03; I Cloughfern from 03. *Cloughfern Rectory, 126 Doagh Road, Newtownabbey BT37 9QR* Tel (028) 9086 2437 E-mail dandblockhart@btinternet.com

LOCKHART, Eileen Ann. b 52. Open Univ BA93 ACII74. EAMTC 95. **d** 98 **p** 99. NSM Shenfield *Chelmsf* from 98. *6 Granary Meadow, Wyatts Green, Brentwood CM15 0QD* Tel and fax (01277) 822537 E-mail eileenlockhart@gmail.com

LOCKHART, Patricia May. b 50. Open Univ BA90 Lon Inst of Educn CertEd73. **d** 06 **p** 07. Hd Teacher Kingussie Primary Sch from 86; NSM Rothiemurchus *Mor* from 07. *Craigentor, Middle Terrace, Kingussie PH21 1EY* Tel (01540) 661873 Mobile 07979-540999 E-mail patricialockhart79@hotmail.com

LOCKHART, Raymond William. b 37. Qu Coll Cam BA58 MA61 LLB60. St Jo Coll Nottm 72. **d** 74 **p** 75. C Aspley *S'well*

74-76; V 81-88; R Knebworth *St Alb* 76-81; Warden Stella Carmel Haifa (CMJ) 88-91; R Jerusalem Ch Ch 91-99; Dir CMJ Israel 99-02; rtd 02; Perm to Offic *B & W* from 03. *2 Paddock Woods, Combe Down, Bath BA2 7AD* Tel (01225) 840432 Mobile 07817-330831 E-mail lockhart@xalt.co.uk

LOCKHART, The Very Revd Robert Joseph Norman. b 24. TCD BA46 MA53. **d** 46 **p** 48. C Belfast St Mary Magd *Conn* 46-49; C Knockbreda *D & D* 49-54; P-in-c Killaney w Carryduff 54-60; I Comber 60-62; I Belfast St Donard 62-70; I Lurgan Ch the Redeemer 70-89; Prec Dromore Cathl 71-75; Dean Dromore 75-89; rtd 89; Lic to Offic *D & D* from 90. *30 Church Road, Belfast BT8 7AQ* Tel (028) 9049 1588

LOCKLEY, Miss Pauline Margaret. b 41. **d** 02. OLM Stoke-upon-Trent *Lich* from 02. *Highfields, 89 Tolkien Way, Stoke-on-Trent ST4 7SJ* Tel (01782) 849806 E-mail plock@cix.co.uk

LOCKWOOD, Richard John. b 46. **d** 01 **p** 02. OLM Glascote and Stonydelph *Lich* from 01. *26 Mossdale, Wilnecote, Tamworth B77 4PJ* Tel (01827) 738105 *or* 330306

LOCKWOOD, Mrs Thelma. b 42. WEMTC 01. **d** 03 **p** 04. OLM Bourton-on-the-Water w Clapton etc *Glouc* 03-07; NSM Wimborne Minster *Sarum* from 07. *82 Merley Ways, Wimborne BH21 1QR* Tel (01202) 882488

LOCKYER, David Ralph George. b 41. Wells Th Coll 65. **d** 67 **p** 68. C Bottesford *Linc* 67-69; C Eling *Win* 69-73; TV Eling, Testwood and Marchwood 73-77; TR Speke St Aid *Liv* 77-84; V Halifax St Jude *Wakef* 84-96; Chapl Halifax R Infirmary 84-96; V Banwell *B & W* 96-06; rtd 06. *The Old Quarry, Stour Provost, Gillingham SP8 5SB* Tel (01747) 839970 E-mail david.r.g.lockyer@btinternet.com

LOCKYER, Desmond Edward Weston. b 18. AKC49. **d** 50 **p** 51. C Norwood St Luke *S'wark* 50-52; C Surbiton St Matt 52-54; Chapl Asst United Sheff Hosps 54-56; C Sheff St Anne and St Phil 54-56; C Eastbourne St Mary *Chich* 56-59; V Hellingly 59-68; V Upper Dicker 62-68; V Eastbourne St Mich 68-75; V Preston 75-87; rtd 87; Perm to Offic *Chich* from 87. *4 Terry's Cross House, Brighton Road, Woodmancote, Henfield BN5 9SX* Tel (01273) 493681

LOCKYER, Peter Weston. b 60. Linc Coll Ox BA80 MA83 PGCE98. St Jo Coll Nottm 84. **d** 87 **p** 88. C Rowner *Portsm* 87-90; C Beaconsfield *Ox* 90-91; TV 91-95; Dep Chapl HM YOI Glen Parva 95; Chapl Wellingborough Sch 96-00; R Ewhurst *Guildf* 00-03; Hd Schs & Youth Chr Aid from 03. *3 King George Avenue, Petersfield GU32 3EU* Tel (01730) 269661 E-mail peterlockyer@btinternet.com

LOCOCK (née MILES), Mrs Jillian Maud. b 33. Lon Univ BSc55. NOC 81. **dss** 84 **d** 87 **p** 95. Didsbury Ch Ch *Man* 84-86; Chapl Asst Man R Infirmary 85-87; Chapl Asst Withington Hosp 86-88; Chapl Asst RN 88-93; NSM Dumbarton *Glas* 93-96; Perm to Offic *Ex* from 02. *2 Glebe Cottage, Dousland, Yelverton PL20 6LU* Tel (01822) 854098 E-mail rjbirtles@aol.com

LODER, Sister Helen. b 43. S'wark Ord Course 91. **d** 94 **p** 95. Soc of St Marg from 70; Hon C S Hackney St Mich w Haggerston St Paul *Lon* 94-01; Hon C Bethnal Green St Matt w St Jas the Gt from 02. *St Saviour's Priory, 18 Queensbridge Road, London E2 8NS* Tel (020) 7613 1464 E-mail helenloder@aol.com

LODGE, Michael John. b 53. Wycliffe Hall Ox 87. **d** 89 **p** 90. C Highworth w Sevenhampton and Inglesham etc *Bris* 89-93; P-in-c Cheltenham St Luke and St Jo *Glouc* 93-05; TR Rayleigh *Chelmsf* from 05; RD Rochford from 08. *The Rectory, 3 Hockley Road, Rayleigh SS6 8BA* Tel (01268) 742151 E-mail mike.lodge@btinternet.com

LODGE, Mrs Patricia Evelyn. b 46. City of Birm Coll CertEd68. **d** 08 **p** 09. OLM Ashton *Man* from 08. *250 Yew Tree Lane, Dukinfield SK16 5DE* Tel 0161-338 5303 E-mail pattery@lodge250.freeserve.co.uk

LODGE, Robin Paul. b 60. Bris Univ BA82 Ch Ch Coll Cant PGCE83. Chich Th Coll 88. **d** 90 **p** 91. C Calne and Blackland *Sarum* 90-94; Asst Chapl St Mary's Sch Calne 90-94; TV Wellington and Distr *B & W* 94-03; V Highbridge from 03. *The Vicarage, 81A Church Street, Highbridge TA9 3HS* Tel (01278) 783671 E-mail rp.lodge@btinternet.com

LODGE, Roy Frederick. b 38. MBE97. BTh DPhil93. Tyndale Hall Bris 63. **d** 66 **p** 67. C Tardebigge *Worc* 66-67; Chapl and Warden Probation Hostel Redditch 67-69; Chapl RAF 69-75; C Kinson *Sarum* 76; Lic to Offic *Pet* 76-77; Asst Chapl HM Pris Stafford 77-78; Chapl HM Pris Ranby 78-84; Chapl HM Pris Long Lartin 84-93; Chapl HM Pris Service Coll 87-93; Chapl HM Pris Hewell Grange 93-98; Chapl HM Pris Brockhill 93-98; rtd 98; Perm to Offic *Cov* from 98 and *Glouc* from 99. *44 Eton Road, Stratford-upon-Avon CV37 7ER*

LODGE, Mrs Sally Nicole. b 61. Keele Univ BA83 St Jo Coll Dur BA09. Cranmer Hall Dur 07. **d** 09. C Halstead Area *Chelmsf* from 09. *47 Tidings Hill, Halstead CO9 1BL* Tel (01787) 475528 Mobile 07747-612817 E-mail sallylodge@ntlworld.com

LODWICK, Canon Brian Martin. b 40. Leeds Univ BA61 MPhil76 Linacre Coll Ox BA63 MA67 Univ of Wales PhD87. St Steph Ho Ox 61. **d** 64 **p** 65. C Aberaman *Llan* 64-66; C Newton Nottage 66-73; R Llansannor and Llanfrynach w

Penllyn etc 73-94; R Llandough w Leckwith 94-04; RD Llantwit Major and Cowbridge 83-94; Warden of Readers 92-03; Chan Llan Cathl 92-02; Treas 02-04; Chapl Llandough Hosp 94-99; Chapl Univ Hosp of Wales and Llandough NHS Trust 99-01; rtd 04. *26 New Road, Neath Abbey, Neath SA10 7NH*

LODWICK, Stephen Huw. b 64. Plymouth Poly BSc85. St Mich Coll Llan. **d** 94 **p** 95. C Clydach *S & B* 94-95; Chapl St Woolos Cathl 95-98; R Grosmont and Skenfrith and Llangattock etc 98-01; CF from 01. *c/o MOD Chaplains (Army)* Tel (01980) 615804 Fax 615860

LOEWE, Jost Andreas. b 73. St Pet Coll Ox BA95 MA99 MPhil97 Selw Coll Cam PhD01. Westcott Ho Cam 97. **d** 01 **p** 02. C Upton cum Chalvey *Ox* 01-04; C Cambridge Gt St Mary w St Mich *Ely* 04-09; Chapl Trin Coll Melbourne Australia from 09. *University of Melbourne, Royal Parade, Parkville Vic 3052, Australia* E-mail jal33@cam.ac.uk

LOEWENDAHL, David Jacob (Jake). b 50. SS Coll Cam BA74 MA77. Ripon Coll Cuddesdon 75. **d** 77 **p** 78. C Walworth *S'wark* 77-80; Chapl St Alb Abbey 80-83; Chapl St Alb Sch 80-83; Team Ldr Community Service Volunteers 84-90; Perm to Offic *Lon* 83-90; R E and W Tilbury and Linford *Chelmsf* 90-95; V Menheniot *Truro* 95-98; RD W Wivelshire 97-98; rtd 98; Perm to Offic *Truro* from 98. *Ashpark House, Ash Park Terrace, Liskeard PL14 4DN* Tel (01579) 348205

LOFT, Edmund Martin Boswell. b 25. St Jo Coll Cam BA49 MA55. Ely Th Coll 49. **d** 51 **p** 52. C Carl H Trin 51-54; C Barrow St Geo 54-56; V Allonby w W Newton 56-62; V Fillongley *Cov* 62-77; V Earlsdon 77-90; rtd 90; Perm to Offic *Sheff* from 90. *10 Quarry Road, Sheffield S17 4DA* Tel 0114-236 0759

LOFTHOUSE, Canon Alexander Francis Joseph. b 30. Keble Coll Ox BA54 MA58. St Steph Ho Ox 54. **d** 56 **p** 57. C Barrow St Jas *Carl* 56-59; C Castleford All SS *Wakef* 59-60; V Airedale w Fryston 60-70; V Maryport *Carl* 70-78; V Helsington 78-95; C Underbarrow 78-95; V Levens 78-95; Hon Can Carl Cathl 85-95; rtd 95; Perm to Offic *Blackb* and *Carl* from 95. *Hazel Grove House, Yealand Redmayne, Carnforth LA5 9RW* Tel (01524) 782405

LOFTHOUSE, Canon Brenda. b 33. RGN60 RM62 RNT69. NOC 84. **d** 87 **p** 94. Hon Par Dn Greengates *Bradf* 87-89; Par Dn Farsley 89-94; V Bolton St Jas w St Chrys 94-00; Hon Can Bradf Cathl 98-00; rtd 00; Perm to Offic *Bradf* from 00. *33 Myrtle Court, Bingley BD16 2LP* Tel (01274) 771476

LOFTUS, Francis. b 52. Newc Univ BA73 St Andr Univ BPhil76 Coll of Ripon & York St Jo PGCE76 FRSA94. NEOC 93. **d** 96 **p** 97. Hd Master Barlby High Sch from 90; NSM Barlby w Riccall *York* from 96; NSM Hemingbrough from 06. *19 Green Lane, North Duffield, Selby YO8 5RR* Tel (01757) 288030 *or* 706161 Fax 213699 E-mail francis-loftus2@supanet.com

LOFTUS, John Michael. b 52. Sheff Univ BSc74 Solicitor 77. **d** 00 **p** 01. OLM Hundred River *St E* from 00. *Keld House, Hulver Street, Henstead, Beccles NR34 7UE* Tel (01502) 476257 Fax 533001 E-mail j.loftus@nortonpeskett.co.uk

LOGAN, Ms Alexandra Jane. b 73. Trin Coll Carmarthen BA94. Ridley Hall Cam 99. **d** 02 **p** 03. C Penwortham St Mary *Blackb* 02-07; V Bethnal Green St Jas Less *Lon* from 07. *St James the Less Vicarage, St James's Avenue, London E2 9JD* Tel and fax (020) 8980 1612 E-mail alexandra.logan@btopenworld.com

LOGAN, Ms Joanne. b 64. Ch Coll Cam BA87 St Jo Coll Dur BA04 MA05. Cranmer Hall Dur 02. **d** 05 **p** 06. C Harrogate St Mark *Ripon* from 05. *30 Halstead Road, Harrogate HG2 8BP* Tel (01423) 870593 E-mail jo_logan@btopenworld.com

LOGAN, Kevin. b 43. Oak Hill Th Coll 73. **d** 75 **p** 76. C Blackb Sav 75-78; C Leyland St Andr 78-82; V Gt Harwood St Jo 82-91; V Accrington Ch Ch 91-08; rtd 08; Perm to Offic *Blackb* from 08. *119 Kingsway, Church, Accrington BB5 5EL*

LOGAN, Samuel Desmond. b 39. TEng. CITC. **d** 78 **p** 79. NSM Belvoir *D & D* 78-85; NSM Knock 85-87; NSM Belfast St Brendan 87-91; Lic to Offic 91-95; C Bangor Abbey 95-97; I Belfast St Clem from 97. *8 Casaeldona Crescent, Belfast BT6 9RE* Tel (028) 9079 5473

LOGUE, Mrs Rosemary Christine. TCD BTh93. CITC 90. **d** 93 **p** 94. C Clooney w Strathfoyle *D & R* 93-96; I Londonderry St Aug 96-03; I Tullyaughnish w Kilmacrennan and Killygarvan 03-05; I Sixmilecross w Termonmaguirke *Arm* 05-08; P-in-c Cambuslang *Glas* 08; P-in-c Uddingston 08. *Address temp unknown* E-mail r.logue@btinternet.com

LOMAS, Anthony David. b 59. Cranfield Inst of Tech BSc81. WEMTC 04. **d** 07 **p** 08. C Sevenhampton w Charlton Abbots, Hawling etc *Glouc* from 07. *The Rectory, Withington, Cheltenham GL54 4BG* Tel 07793-564877 (mobile) E-mail adlomas@aol.com

LOMAS, David Xavier. b 39. St Jo Coll Dur BA78. Cranmer Hall Dur 75. **d** 78 **p** 79. C Chester le Street *Dur* 78-81; C-in-c Newton Hall LEP 81-85; Chapl Scunthorpe Distr HA 85-93; Sen Chapl Linc and Louth NHS Trust 93-01; Sen Chapl Chapl Manager United Lincs Hosps NHS Trust 01-04; rtd 04. *9 Hazel Grove, Welton, Lincoln LN2 3JZ* Tel (01673) 861409 E-mail xavlomas@aol.com

LOMAS, Canon John Derrick Percy. b 58. St Mich Coll Llan 94. **d** 94 **p** 95. C Rhyl w St Ann *St As* 94-00; Chapl RN 00-01; V Holywell *St As* from 01; AD Holywell from 08; Can Cursal St As Cathl from 08. *The Vicarage, Fron Park Road, Holywell CH8 7UT* Tel (01352) 710010

LOMAX, Canon Barry Walter John. b 39. Lambeth STh Lon Coll of Div 63. **d** 66 **p** 67. C Sevenoaks St Nic *Roch* 66-71; C Southport Ch Ch *Liv* 71-73; V Bootle St Matt 73-78; P-in-c Litherland St Andr 76-78; V New Borough and Leigh *Sarum* 78-94; Can and Preb Sarum Cathl 91-02; R Blandford Forum and Langton Long 94-02; rtd 02; Perm to Offic *Sarum* from 03. *Shiloh, 2 Colborne Avenue, Wimborne BH21 2PZ* Tel (01202) 856104 E-mail barry.lomas@virgin.net

LOMAX, Eric John. b 64. St Jo Coll Dur BA93. Cranmer Hall Dur 90. **d** 96 **p** 97. C Goodshaw and Crawshawbooth *Man* 96-00; V Copmanthorpe *York* 00-01. *Address withheld by request*

LOMAX, Mrs Kate Jane. b 73. RGN96. St Jo Coll Nottm BA02. **d** 02 **p** 03. C Luton St Mary *St Alb* 02-04; Asst Chapl Cam Univ Hosps NHS Foundn Trust 04-05; Chapl 05-07; NSM Penn Fields *Lich* from 08. *131 Church Road, Bradmore, Wolverhampton WV3 7EN* Tel (01902) 681298 E-mail katelomax@blueyonder.co.uk

LOMAX, Timothy Michael. b 73. Derby Univ BEd95. Ridley Hall Cam 05. **d** 07 **p** 08. C Penn Fields *Lich* from 07. *131 Church Road, Bradmore, Wolverhampton WV3 7EN* Tel (01902) 681298 E-mail timlomax@blueyonder.co.uk

LONDON (St Paul's), Dean of. *See* KNOWLES, The Rt Revd Graeme Paul

LONDON, Archdeacon of. *See* MEARA, The Ven David Gwynne

LONDON, Bishop of. *See* CHARTRES, The Rt Revd and Rt Hon Richard John Carew

LONEY, Mark William James. b 72. Cen Lancs Univ BSc94 MA97 TCD BTh03. CITC 00. **d** 03 **p** 04. C Larne and Inver *Conn* 03-06; I Ahoghill w Portglenone from 06. *63 Crosskeys Road, Ahoghill, Ballymena BT42 2QX* E-mail rev.loney@btopenworld.com

LONG, Canon Anne Christine. b 33. Leic Univ BA56 Ox Univ DipEd57 Lon Univ BD65 ALBC. **dss** 80 **d** 87 **p** 94. Lect St Jo Coll Nottm 73-84; Acorn Chr Healing Trust 85-98; Stanstead Abbots *St Alb* 85-92; Hon Par Dn 87-92; Hon Par Dn Camberley St Paul *Guildf* 92-94; Hon C 94-03; Hon Can Guildf Cathl 96-03. *3 Chiselbury Grove, Salisbury SP2 8EP* Tel (01722) 341488

LONG, Anthony Auguste. b 45. Linc Th Coll 79. **d** 81 **p** 82. C Kingswinford St Mary *Lich* 81-84; TV Ellesmere Port *Ches* 84-87; V Witton 87-97; P-in-c Wybunbury w Doddington 97-02; V from 02. *The Vicarage, Main Road, Wybunbury, Nantwich CW5 7LS* Tel (01270) 841178 E-mail tojolong@tiscali.co.uk

LONG, Anthony Robert. b 48. SS Mark & Jo Coll Chelsea CertEd70 Southn Univ BTh93 UEA MA96 Lambeth MA04. Chich Th Coll 74. **d** 77 **p** 78. C Chiswick St Nic w St Mary *Lon* 77-80; C Earley St Pet *Ox* 80-85; P-in-c Worstead w Westwick and Sloley *Nor* 85-92; R Worstead, Westwick, Sloley, Swanton Abbot etc from 92; P-in-c Tunstead w Sco' Ruston from 85; Chapl Nor Cathl from 85. *The Vicarage, Withergate Road, Worstead, North Walsham NR28 9SE* Tel (01692) 536000

LONG, Bill. *See* LONG, Edward Percy Eades

LONG, Bradley. b 65. St Jo Coll Dur BA08 Lon Inst of Educn PGCE94. Cranmer Hall Dur 06. **d** 08. C The Hague *Eur* from 08. *Ary van der Spuyweg 1, 2585 HA The Hague, The Netherlands* Tel (0031) (70) 887 6108 Mobile 68-236 6789 E-mail bradley_long@hotmail.com

LONG, The Ven Christopher William. b 47. MBE94. Nottm Univ BTh78 Open Univ BA80. Linc Th Coll 75. **d** 78 **p** 79. C Shiregreen St Jas and St Chris *Sheff* 78-81; V 81-82; Chapl RAF 82-05; I Enniscorthy w Clone, Clonmore, Monart etc *C & O* from 05; Adn Ferns from 08. *The Rectory, 3 Madeira Grove, The Moyne, Enniscorthy, Co Wexford, Republic of Ireland* Tel (00353) (53) 923 9009 E-mail chriswlong1@eircom.net

LONG, David William. b 47. St Aug Coll Cant 70. **d** 72 **p** 73. C Stanley *Liv* 72-73; C W Derby St Luke 73-76; C Cantril Farm 76-79; V Warrington St Barn 79-81; V Westbrook St Jas 82-96; V Ince St Mary from 96; AD Wigan E and Hon Can Liv Cathl 03-05. *St Mary's Vicarage, 240A Warrington Road, Ince, Wigan WN3 4NH* Tel (01942) 864383 E-mail david@scars.org.uk

LONG, Edward Percy Eades (Bill). b 14. Liv Univ BA36 MA38. Linc Th Coll 73. **d** 73 **p** 74. C Sedbergh, Cautley and Garsdale *Bradf* 73-84; rtd 85; Perm to Offic *Bradf* from 85. *4 Derry Cottages, Sedbergh LA10 5SN* Tel (01539) 620577

LONG, Mrs Frances Mary. b 58. SEITE 98. **d** 01 **p** 02. NSM Caterham *S'wark* 01-05; Chapl Surrey and Sussex Healthcare NHS Trust 01-03; C Riddlesdown *S'wark* 05-08; P-in-c Purley St Mark from 08; P-in-c Purley St Swithun from 08. *St Mark's Vicarage, 22 Peaks Hill, Purley CR8 3JE* Tel (020) 8645 0164 E-mail franyb8@hotmail.com

LONG, Frederick Hugh. b 43. EMMTC 90. **d** 90 **p** 91. NSM Grantham *Linc* 90-00; C 00-01; TV 01-02; V Grantham St Anne New Somerby and Spitalgate 02-08; rtd 08; Hon C Drybrook,

Lydbrook and Ruardean *Glouc* from 08. *The Rectory, High Street, Ruardean GL17 9US* Tel (01594) 541070

LONG, Geoffrey Lawrence. b 47. La Sainte Union Coll BTh93 PGCE94. Portsm Dioc Tr Course 88. **d** 89 **p** 98. NSM Whippingham w E Cowes *Portsm* 89-01; Chapl HM Pris Maidstone from 01. *HM Prison, County Road, Maidstone ME14 1UZ* Tel (01622) 755611

LONG, Hermione Jane. b 66. Univ of Wales (Swansea) BSc97 RGN88. St Mich Coll Llan 05. **d** 07 **p** 08. C Bassaleg *Mon* from 07. *St Anne's Church House, 2 High Cross Drive, Rogerstone, Newport NP10 9AB* Tel (01633) 895441

LONG, Canon John Sydney. b 25. Lon Univ BSc49. Wycliffe Hall Ox 50. **d** 51 **p** 52. C Plaistow St Andr *Chelmsf* 51-54; C Keighley *Bradf* 54-57; C-in-c Horton Bank Top CD 57-59; V Buttershaw St Aid 59-64; V Barnoldswick w Bracewell 64-85; Hon Can Bradf Cathl 77-91; RD Skipton 83-90; R Broughton, Marton and Thornton 85-91; rtd 91; Perm to Offic *Bradf* from 91. *1 Church Villa, Carleton, Skipton BD23 3DQ* Tel (01756) 799095

LONG, Kingsley Edward. b 41. CITC 90. **d** 93 **p** 94. NSM Swords w Donabate and Kilsallaghan *D & G* 93-94 and 96-99; NSM Howth 94-96; NSM Holmpatrick w Balbriggan and Kenure 99-01; NSM Dublin Clontarf 02-03; NSM Swords w Donabate and Kilsallaghan from 03. *Crimond, 125 Seapark, Malahide, Co Dublin, Republic of Ireland* Tel (00353) (1) 845 3179

LONG, Canon Michael David Barnby. b 32. AKC55. **d** 56 **p** 57. C Whitby *York* 56-59; C Cottingham 59-61; V Elloughton 61-66; P-in-c Brantingham 61-66; V Sheff St Cecilia Parson Cross 66-68; V Flamborough *York* 68-73; R Litcham w Kempston w E and W Lexham *Nor* 73-75; P-in-c York St Luke 75-77; V 77-80; V Hatton w Haseley and Rowington w Lowsonford *Cov* 80-82; V Derringham Bank *York* 82-85; R Castleacre w Newton, Rougham and Southacre *Nor* 85-86; TV Grantham *Linc* 86-89; V Cayton w Eastfield *York* 89-98; RD Scarborough 94-98; Can and Preb York Minster 97-03; rtd 98; P-in-c York St Clem w St Mary Bishophill Senior 98-03; P-in-c Trowse *Nor* from 03. *19 Ipswich Grove, Norwich NR2 2LU* Tel (01603) 613224 E-mail michael-long@amserve.com

LONG, Peter Ronald. b 48. Cuddesdon Coll 71. **d** 73 **p** 74. Chapl RAFVR 74-99; C Bodmin *Truro* 73-75; C Newquay 75-76; Asst Youth Chapl 75-76; Dioc Youth Chapl 76-79; Perm to Offic *Eur* 76, 78-85 and 87-98; Public Preacher *Truro* 77; P-in-c Mawgan w St Martin-in-Meneage 79-82; Chapl Helston-Meneage Community and Geriatric Hosp 80-95; Miss to Seamen 80-98; P-in-c Cury w Gunwalloe *Truro* 80-82; R Cury and Gunwalloe w Mawgan 83-98; Perm to Offic *Ex* 82-93; Ecum Th in UK Rail Ind from 97; rtd 98. *26 Jubilee Street, Newquay TR7 1LA* Tel 07780-976113 (mobile) Fax (01637) 877060 E-mail ipsn2009@yahoo.co.uk

LONG, Richard John William. b 59. Hull Univ BA80 PGCE81. Cranmer Hall Dur 03. **d** 05 **p** 06. C Beverley St Nic *York* 05-09; TV Marfleet from 09. *St Philip's House, 107 Amethyst Road, Hull HU9 4JG* Tel (01482) 376208 E-mail richard@long6426.freeserve.co.uk

LONG, Roger Eric. b 36. Univ Coll Dur BSc59 PhD62. NEOC 90. **d** 93 **p** 94. C Street *York* 93-97; P-in-c Coxwold and Husthwaite 97-02; rtd 02. *Ivy House, Coxwold, York YO61 4AD* Tel (01347) 868301

LONG, Samuel Allen. b 48. EAMTC 03. **d** 05 **p** 06. NSM Barrow St E 05-08; NSM Pakenham w Norton and Tostock from 08. *16 Drury Close, Rougham, Bury St Edmunds IP30 9JE* Tel (01359) 270972 Mobile 07732-971925 E-mail valerielong16@aol.com

LONG, Canon Samuel Ernest. b 18. JP68. ALCD50 LTh MTh ThD. **d** 49 **p** 50. C Belfast St Clem *D & D* 49-52; C Willowfield 52-56; I Dromara w Garvaghy 56-85; Can Dromore Cathl 81-85; Treas 82-85; rtd 85. *9 Cairnshill Court, Saintfield Road, Belfast BT8 4TX* Tel (028) 9079 3401

LONG, Simon Richard. b 40. Bernard Gilpin Soc Dur 61 Ely Th Coll 62 Coll of Resurr Mirfield 64. **d** 65 **p** 66. C Bournemouth St Fran *Win* 65-68; C Brussels *Eur* 68; V Portales and Fort Sumner USA 69-79; V Lincoln St Mark 79-81; V Martin St Kath 81-83; R Lousville Em 83-86; V Elizabethtown Ch Ch 86-88; P-in-c Medbourne cum Holt w Stockerston and Blaston *Leic* 88-89; P-in-c Bringhurst w St Easton 88-89; R Six Saints circa Holt 90-99; RD Gartree I 93-97; rtd 99. *17C Craft Village, Balnakeil, Durness, Lairg IV27 4PT* Tel (01971) 511777

LONG, William Thomas. b 53. Dur Univ MA88 QUB PhD99. **d** 81 **p** 82. C Orangefield *D & D* 81-84; C Portadown St Mark *Arm* 84-86; I Dromara w Garvaghy *D & D* 86-91; I Aghalurcher w Tattykeeran, Cooneen etc *Clogh* 91-96; I Annalong *D & D* 96-03; I Belfast St Simon w St Phil *Conn* 03-06; I Carnteel and Crilly *Arm* from 06. *St James's Rectory, 22 Carnteel Road, Aughnacloy BT69 6DU* Tel (028) 8555 7682 Mobile 07748 857312 E-mail wlhudhud@bushinternet.com

LONGBOTTOM, Canon Frank. b 41. Ripon Hall Ox 65. **d** 68 **p** 69. C Epsom St Martin *Guildf* 68-72; Asst Chapl St Ebbas Hosp Epsom 68-72; Asst Chapl Qu Mary's Hosp Carshalton 68-72; Asst Chapl Henderson Hosp Sutton 68-72; Chapl Highcroft Hosp Birm 72-94; Chapl Northcroft Hosp Birm

74-94; Dioc Adv for Past Care of Clergy & Families 89-94; Bp's Adv 94-06; Bp's Adv on Health and Soc Care *Birm* 01-06; P-in-c Middleton 99-00; Hon Can Birm Cathl 91-06; rtd 07. *46 Sunnybank Road, Sutton Coldfield B73 5RE* Tel and fax 0121-350 5823

LONGBOTTOM, Canon Paul Edward. b 44. Kent Univ MA02 AKC67. **d** 68 **p** 69. C Rainham *Roch* 68-71; C Riverhead 71-75; C Dunton Green 71-75; V Penge Lane H Trin 75-84; V Chatham St Wm 84-94; V Shorne and Dioc Dir of Ords 94-09; Hon Can Roch Cathl 96-09; rtd 09. *Advent House, Primrose Lane, Bredgar, Sittingbourne ME9 8EH*
E-mail paul.longbottom@rochester.anglican.org

LONGDEN, Lee Paul. b 70. Peterho Cam BA91 MA95 Ches Coll of HE MTh03 FRCO91 LLCM93 ARCM93 LRSM96. Qu Coll Birm 03. **d** 05 **p** 06. C Langley and Parkfield *Man* 05-08; V Ashton Ch Ch from 08. *Christ Church Vicarage, Vicarage Road, Ashton-under-Lyne OL7 9QY* Tel 0161-330 1601
E-mail vicar@christchurch-ashton.org.uk

LONGDON, Anthony Robert James. b 44. STETS 00. **d** 03 **p** 04. OLM N Bradley, Southwick and Heywood *Sarum* 03-08; OLM N Bradley, Southwick, Heywood and Steeple Ashton from 08. *1A Holbrook Lane, Trowbridge BA14 0PP* Tel and fax (01225) 754771 E-mail tony.longdon@homecall.co.uk

LONGE, David John Hastings. b 75. New Coll Edin BD99. Ripon Coll Cuddesdon 07. **d** 09. C N Lambeth *S'wark* from 09. *12 Moat Place, London SW9 0BS* Tel (020) 7735 3403

LONGE, James Robert. b 46. EAMTC 02. **d** 04 **p** 05. NSM Pakenham w Norton and Tostock *St E* 04-07; NSM St Edm Way from 07. *Bush House, Bradfield St Clare, Bury St Edmunds IP30 0EQ*

LONGFELLOW, Erica Denise. b 74. Duke Univ (USA) BA97 Linc Coll Ox MSt98 DPhil01. SEITE 02. **d** 05 **p** 06. NSM Kew St Phil and All SS w St Luke *S'wark* 05-09; NSM Surbiton St Andr and St Mark from 09. *The Coach House, 1 Church Hill Road, Surbiton KT6 4UG* Tel (020) 8390 9129
E-mail e.longfellow@kingston.ac.uk

LONGFOOT, Canon Richard. b 46. Oak Hill Th Coll 76. **d** 78 **p** 79. C Chaddesden St Mary *Derby* 78-81; C Cambridge St Martin *Ely* 81-83; R Folksworth w Morborne 83-89; R Stilton w Denton and Caldecote 83-89; R Stilton w Denton and Caldecote etc from 90; RD Yaxley 02-07; Hon Can Ely Cathl from 04. *The Rectory, Stilton, Peterborough PE7 3RF* Tel (01733) 240282 E-mail richard.lfoot@lineone.net

LONGFORD, Canon Edward de Toesny Wingfield. b 25. Ch Ch Ox BA48 MA53. Wells Th Coll 49. **d** 51 **p** 52. C Stevenage *St Alb* 51-54; PC Chettisham 55-68; Min Can, Prec and Sacr Ely Cathl 55-68; P-in-c Everton w Tetworth 68-71; V 71-73; R Gamlingay 68-80; P-in-c Hatley 78-80; Hon Can Ely Cathl 79-90; R Gamlingay w Hatley St George and E Hatley 80-90; RD St Neots 82-90; rtd 90; Perm to Offic *Ely* from 90. *9 Philippa Close, Ely CB6 1BT* Tel (01353) 667495

LONGMAN, Edward. b 37. Hatf Coll Dur BSc62 Fitzw Coll Cam BA66 MA70. Clifton Th Coll 62. **d** 66 **p** 67. C Lower Homerton St Paul *Lon* 66-72; C Parr *Liv* 72-73; TV 74-85; Perm to Offic *Liv* 87-02 and *Ches* from 96. *21 Canadian Avenue, Hoole, Chester CH2 3HG* Tel (01244) 317544 Fax 400450 Mobile 07779-650791 E-mail elongman@onetel.com

LONGMAN, Edward George. b 35. St Pet Hall Ox BA58 MA62. Westcott Ho Cam 59. **d** 61 **p** 62. C Sheff St Mark Broomhall 61-65; V Brightside St Thos 65-74; V Yardley St Edburgha *Birm* 74-84; RD Yardley 77-84; Hon Can Birm Cathl 81-96; R Sutton Coldfield H Trin 84-96; RD Sutton Coldfield 94-96; Chapl Gd Hope Distr Gen Hosp Sutton Coldfield 84-90; P-in-c Cerne Abbas w Godmanstone and Minterne Magna *Sarum* 96-02; RD Dorchester 00-02; rtd 02; Perm to Offic *B & W* from 04. *5 Old Wells Road, Shepton Mallet BA4 5XN* Tel (01749) 343699
E-mail ted@roseted.co.uk

LONGRIDGE, Richard Nevile. b 15. Sarum Th Coll 46. **d** 48 **p** 49. C Portsea N End St Mark *Portsm* 48-51; R Bourton w Silton *Sarum* 51-63; R Okeford Fitzpaine 63-67; R Spetisbury w Charlton Marshall 67-77; rtd 77; Perm to Offic *Ex* from 78. *The Lodge, 22 Spicer Road, Exeter EX1 1SY* Tel (01392) 493848

LONGUET-HIGGINS, John. b 62. Leeds Univ BA85. St Jo Coll Nottm 88. **d** 91 **p** 92. C Kidlington w Hampton Poyle *Ox* 91-95; TV N Huddersfield *Wakef* 95-01; V Painswick, Sheepscombe, Cranham, The Edge etc *Glouc* from 02. *The Vicarage, Orchard Mead, Painswick, Stroud GL6 6YD* Tel (01452) 812334

LONSDALE, Mrs Gillian. b 36. Qu Mary Coll Lon BA57 MA59 Ex Univ MPhil81 AIMSW61. SWMTC 96. **d** 99 **p** 00. NSM Duloe, Herodsfoot, Morval and St Pinnock *Truro* 99-06; NSM Lansallos and Talland 01-03; RD W Wivelshire 03-06; rtd 06. *Woodhill Manor, Liskeard PL14 6RD* Tel (01579) 340697 Mobile 07801-301031 E-mail gill@glonsdale.freeserve.co.uk

LOOKER, Clare Margaret. *See* FLEMING, Miss Clare Margaret

LOOMES, Gaenor Mary. *See* HOCKEY, Gaenor Mary

✠**LÓPEZ-LOZANO, The Rt Revd Carlos.** b 62. Madrid Univ BA89 Pontifical Univ Salamanca PhD93. United Th Sem Madrid MTh91. **d** 90 **p** 90 **c** 95. Spain from 90; Bp's Chapl 90-91;

R Espiritu Santo 92-95; Adn Cen and N Spain 94-95; Bp in Madrid from 95; Hon Asst Bp Eur from 95. *Calle Beneficencia 18, 28004 Madrid, Spain* Tel (0034) (91) 445 2560 Fax 594 4572
E-mail eclesiae@arrakis.es

LORAINE, Kenneth. b 34. Cranmer Hall Dur 63. **d** 66 **p** 67. C Hartlepool All SS Stranton *Dur* 66-69; C Darlington St Cuth 69-72; V Preston on Tees 72-79; V Staindrop 79-87; P-in-c Haynes *St Alb* 87-96; Dioc Stewardship Adv 87-96; rtd 96; Perm to Offic *York* from 96. *116 Turker Lane, Northallerton DL6 1QD* Tel (01609) 771277

LORD, Alexander. b 13. ALCD43. **d** 43 **p** 44. C Wakef St Mary 43-45; P-in-c Thornham St Jas *Man* 45-47; R Clitheroe St Jas *Blackb* 47-55; V Madeley *Heref* 55-69; R Illogan *Truro* 70-81; C Letton w Staunton, Byford, Mansel Gamage etc *Heref* 81-84. *43 Narrow Lane, Llandudno Junction LL31 9SZ* Tel (01492) 584647

LORD, Andrew Michael. b 66. Warwick Univ BSc87 Birm Univ MA99 Fitzw Coll Cam BA02. Ridley Hall Cam 00. **d** 03 **p** 04. C Long Buckby w Watford *Pet* 03-06; C W Haddon w Winwick and Ravensthorpe 03-06; R Trowell, Awsworth and Cossall *S'well* from 06. *The Rectory, 47 Nottingham Road, Trowell, Nottingham NG9 3PF* Tel 0115-849 5195
E-mail andylord@freenet.co.uk

LORD, Clive Austen. b 69. St Martin's Coll Lanc BA. St Steph Ho Ox BTh. **d** 96 **p** 97. C Penwortham St Leon *Blackb* 96-98; C Blackpool St Mary 98-01; P-in-c 01-04; V 04-06; Chapl Blackpool, Fylde and Wyre Hosps NHS Trust from 06. *Victoria Hospital, Whinney Heys Road, Blackpool FY3 8NR* Tel (01253) 306875 E-mail livecg@aol.com

LORD, Stuart James. b 59. K Coll Lon BD81 AKC81. Sarum & Wells Th Coll 83. **d** 85 **p** 86. C Darwen St Pet w Hoddlesden *Blackb* 85-88; C Otley *Bradf* 88-93; P-in-c Low Moor St Mark 93-02; TV Brighouse and Clifton *Wakef* from 02. *31 Robin Hood Way, Clifton, Brighouse HD6 4LA* Tel (01484) 713290

LORD, Mrs Tanya Marie. b 66. Trin Coll Bris. **d** 09. C Bris St Matt and St Nath from 09. *157 Bishop Road, Bristol BS7 8NA* Tel 07852-928881 (mobile) E-mail tanyalord@aol.com

LORDING, Miss Claire Ann. b 75. Roehampton Inst BA96. Ripon Coll Cuddesdon BTh96. **d** 99 **p** 00. C Ledbury *Heref* 99-02; TV Tenbury 02-08; TR from 08; P-in-c Clee Hill from 09. *The Vicarage, Church Street, Tenbury Wells WR15 8BP* Tel (01584) 810811 E-mail claire.lording@virgin.net

LORIMER, Eileen Jean. b 35. CertEd56. Dalton Ho Bris 62. **dss** 84 **d** 89 **p** 94. Chiddingstone w Chiddingstone Causeway *Roch* 84-04; NSM 89-04; Perm to Offic from 04. *3 Causeway Cottages, Chiddingstone Causeway, Tonbridge TN11 8JR* Tel (01892) 871393

LORT-PHILLIPS, Mrs Elizabeth Priscilla. b 47. STETS 02. **d** 05 **p** 06. NSM Redhorn *Sarum* from 05. *The Cottage on the Green, 1 Manor Farm Lane, Patney, Devizes SN10 3RB* Tel (01380) 840711 E-mail e.lortphillips@btinternet.com

LOSACK, Marcus Charles. b 53. Ch Coll Cam BA76 MA78 MPhil. Sarum & Wells Th Coll 78. **d** 80 **p** 81. C Hattersley *Ches* 80-82; C Dublin Zion Ch *D & G* 83-86; Libya 86-89; CMS Jerusalem 89-92; I Newcastle w Newtownmountkennedy and Calary *D & G* 93-95; Exec Dir Céile Dé from 95. *Céile Dé, Castlekevin, Annamoe, Bray, Co Wicklow, Republic of Ireland* Tel and fax (00353) (404) 45595

LOTHIAN, Iain Nigel Cunningham. b 59. Aber Univ MA84 Bath Univ PGCE86 Leeds Univ MA05. NOC 02. **d** 05 **p** 06. C Sheff St Pet Abbeydale 05-09; C Sheff St Pet and St Oswald from 09. *33 Gatefield Road, Sheffield S7 1RD* Tel 0114-250 9736
E-mail i.lothian@btopenworld.com

LOTT, Eric John. b 34. Lon Univ BA65 Lanc Univ MLitt70 PhD77. Richmond Th Coll BD59. **d** 60 **p** 61. India 60-88; Prof United Th Coll Bangalore 77-88; Wesley Hall Ch and Community Project Leics 88-94; rtd 94; Perm to Offic *Leic* from 94. *16 Main Road, Old Dalby, Melton Mowbray LE14 3LR* Tel (01664) 822405 E-mail eric.lott@breathemail.net

LOUDEN, Canon Terence Edmund. b 48. Ch Coll Cam BA70 MA74. Sarum & Wells Th Coll 72. **d** 75 **p** 76. C Portsea N End St Mark *Portsm* 75-78; C-in-c Leigh Park St Clare CD 78-81; R Chale 81-88; R Niton 81-88; P-in-c Whitwell 82-84; V Cosham 88-96; Hon Can Portsm Cathl from 92; V E Meon from 96; V Langrish from 96; CME Officer 96-03. *The Vicarage, Church Street, East Meon, Petersfield GU32 1NH* Tel (01730) 823221 Mobile 07711-319752 E-mail telouden@cwcom.net

LOUDON (née KING), Mrs Ellen Francis. b 67. Liv Poly BA90 Liv Univ MA96. Trin Coll Bris 06. **d** 08. C Everton St Pet w St Chrys *Liv* from 08. *The Vicarage, St John Chrysostom, Queens Road, Liverpool L6 2NF* Tel 0151-260 8289 Mobile 07718-806891 E-mail ellen@ellenloudon.com

LOUGHBOROUGH, Archdeacon of. *See* HACKWOOD, The Ven Paul Colin

LOUGHEED, Brian Frederick Britain. b 38. TCD BA60. CITC 61. **d** 61 **p** 62. C Glenageary *D & G* 63-66; I Rathmolyon Union *M & K* 66-79; I Killarney w Aghadoe and Muckross *L & K* 79-04; Can Limerick and Killaloe Cathls 87-95; Preb Taney St Patr Cathl Dublin

89-04; Dioc Info Officer (Limerick) *L & K* 90-91; Radio Officer 91-04; rtd 04. *2 Arlington Heights, Park Road, Killarney, Co Kerry, Republic of Ireland* Tel (00353) (64) 21642
E-mail brianlougheed1@eircom.net

LOUGHLIN, Canon Alfred. b 10. Clifton Th Coll 37. **d** 39 **p** 40. C Preston St Mark *Blackb* 39-44; Chapl RAFVR 41-43; Org Sec (SE Area) CPAS 44-48; V Sneinton St Chris *S'well* 48-54; R Kinson *Sarum* 54-81; Can and Preb Sarum Cathl 75-81; rtd 81. *2 Friars Close, Wilmslow SK9 5PP* Tel (01625) 530403

LOUGHLIN, George Alfred Graham. b 43. Clifton Th Coll 65. **d** 69 **p** 70. C Plumstead All SS *S'wark* 69-73; C Bromley Ch Ch *Roch* 73-76; P-in-c Bothenhampton w Walditch *Sarum* 76-79; TV Bridport 79-83; V Heatherlands St Jo 83-08; rtd 08. *239 rue de Florièye, 83460 Taradeau, France* E-mail vicar@gagl.co.uk

LOUGHTON, Michael. b 34. K Coll Lon BD58 AKC58. **d** 59 **p** 60. C Chingford SS Pet and Paul *Chelmsf* 59-62; C Eastbourne St Elisabeth *Chich* 62-65; R Lewes St Jo sub Castro 65-74; Perm to Offic from 87; rtd 99. *Green Woodpecker, 1 Kammond Avenue, Seaford BN25 3JL* Tel (01323) 893506

LOUIS, Ms Emma Christine. b 69. Coll of Ripon & York St Jo BA92 St Jo Coll Dur BA96. Cranmer Hall Dur 94. **d** 97 **p** 98. C Birm St Martin w Bordesley St Andr 97-00; Arts Development Officer 97-00; Asst Chapl Harrogate Health Care NHS Trust 00-02; Chapl Co-ord St Mich Hospice Harrogate 01-02; Asst Chapl Birm Heartlands and Solihull NHS Trust 02-04; Lead Chapl Sandwell Mental Health NHS and Social Care Trust from 04. *Sandwell Mental Health Trust, Delta House, Greets Green Road, West Bromwich B70 9PL* Tel 0121-612 8067 Mobile 07813-015325 E-mail emma.louis@smhsct.nhs.uk

LOUIS, Canon Peter Anthony. b 41. St Cath Coll Ox BA63 MA77 Man Univ MPhil85 Jes Coll Cam CertEd64. Wells Th Coll 66. **d** 68 **p** 70. C E Grinstead St Mary *Chich* 68-75; C Radcliffe-on-Trent *S'well* 75-80; Hd Master Blue Coat Comp Sch Cov 80-85; V Welwyn Garden City *St Alb* 85-08; Chapl Oaklands Coll 93-95; Hon Can St Alb 04-08; rtd 08. *27 Aylesbury Road, Wendover, Aylesbury HP22 6JG* E-mail plouis@ntlworld.com

LOVATT, Bernard James. b 31. Lich Th Coll 64. **d** 65 **p** 66. C Burford III w Lt Heref 65-67; C Cleobury Mortimer w Hopton Wafers 67-68; C Bradford-on-Avon *Sarum* 68-69; C Wootton Bassett 69-72; C Broad Town 69-72; R Bishopstrow and Boreham 72-79; P-in-c Brighton St Geo *Chich* 79-83; V Brighton St Anne 79-83; V Brighton St Geo and St Anne 83-86; P-in-c Kemp Town St Mark and St Matt 85-86; V Brighton St Geo w St Anne and St Mark 86-95; rtd 95; Perm to Offic *Ex* from 95. *7 Cambridge Terrace, Salcombe Road, Sidmouth EX10 8PL* Tel (01395) 514154

LOVATT, James Arthur Roy. b 36. **d** 08 **p** 09. OLM Horton, Lonsdon and Rushton Spencer *Lich* from 08. *25 Kent Drive, Endon, Stoke-on-Trent ST9 9EH* Tel (01782) 504723
E-mail jarl25kd@tiscali.co.uk

LOVATT, Mrs Pamela. b 50. **d** 98 **p** 99. OLM Warrington St Ann *Liv* from 98; Chapl Warrington Community Health Care NHS Trust from 99. *59 Amelia Street, Warrington WA2 7QD* Tel (01925) 650849 *or* 655221 E-mail pam.lovatt@ntlworld.com

LOVATT, William Robert. b 54. SS Coll Cam MA75 K Coll Lon PGCE75 MA78. Oak Hill Th Coll 85. **d** 87 **p** 88. C Devonport St Budeaux *Ex* 87-90; Asst Chapl Paris St Mich *Eur* 90-94; P-in-c Lenton *S'well* 94-00; V 00-04; V Eastbourne All SS *Chich* from 04; RD Eastbourne from 06. *All Saints' Vicarage, 1A Jevington Gardens, Eastbourne BN21 4HR* Tel (01323) 410033 Mobile 07815-138202 E-mail robertlovatt@tiscali.co.uk

LOVE, Ms Anette. b 53. Matlock Coll of Educn CertEd74 Nottm Univ BEd75. St Jo Coll Dur 88. **d** 90 **p** 94. Par Dn Gresley *Derby* 90-92; C Heanor 92-94; C Loscoe 94-02; V Heath from 02. *The Vicarage, Main Road, Heath, Chesterfield S44 5RX* Tel (01246) 850339

LOVE, Richard Angus. b 45. AKC67. **d** 68 **p** 69. C Balham Hill Ascension *S'wark* 68-71; C Amersham *Ox* 71-73; R Scotter w E Ferry *Linc* 73-79; P-in-c Petham w Waltham and Lower Hardres w Nackington *Cant* 79-85; R Petham and Waltham w Lower Hardres etc 85-90; V Sittingbourne H Trin w Bobbing 90-02; P-in-c Aldington w Bonnington and Bilsington etc from 02. *The Rectory, Roman Road, Aldington, Ashford TN25 7EF* Tel (01233) 720898 E-mail revralove@msn.com

LOVE, Robert. b 45. Bradf Univ BSc68 PhD74 NE Lon Poly PGCE89. Trin Coll Bris. **d** 75 **p** 76. C Bowling St Jo *Bradf* 75-79; TV Forest Gate St Sav w W Ham St Matt *Chelmsf* 79-85; P-in-c Becontree St Elisabeth 85-96; V S Hornchurch St Jo and St Matt from 96; AD Havering from 08. *St John's Vicarage, South End Road, Rainham RM13 7XT* Tel (01708) 555260
E-mail stjohns-centre@tiscali.co.uk

LOVEDAY, Joseph Michael. b 54. AKC75. St Aug Coll Cant 75. **d** 78 **p** 79. C Kettering SS Pet and Paul 78 81; C Upper Teddington SS Pet and Paul *Lon* 81-84; CF from 84. *c/o MOD Chaplains (Army)* Tel (01980) 615804 Fax 615800

LOVEDAY, Susan Mary. b 49. Sussex Univ BA70 Surrey Univ MSc81. STETS 94. **d** 97 **p** 98. NSM New Haw *Guildf* 97-03; NSM Egham Hythe from 03; Ecum Co-ord Churches Together in Surrey from 00. *10 Abbey Gardens, Chertsey KT16 8RQ* Tel (01932) 566920 E-mail sue.loveday.ctsurrey@lineone.net

LOVEGROVE, Mrs Anne Maureen. b 44. Oak Hill Th Coll 88. **d** 90 **p** 94. Par Dn Thorley *St Alb* 90-94; C 94-95; V Croxley Green St Oswald 95-02; V Letchworth St Paul w Willian 02-09; rtd 09. *Chenies Lodge, 24 Chenies Avenue, Amersham HP6 6PP* E-mail anne.lovegrove1@ntlworld.com

LOVEGROVE, Michael John Bennett. b 42. FCII FCIPD ACIArb. SEITE. **d** 00 **p** 01. NSM Saffron Walden w Wendens Ambo, Littlebury etc *Chelmsf* 00-08; TV 05-08; rtd 08; Perm to Offic *Chelmsf* from 09. *Craigside, 8 Beck Road, Saffron Walden CB11 4EH* Tel (01799) 528232 Mobile 07980-103541
E-mail lovegrove8@btinternet.com

LOVELESS, Christopher Hugh. b 61. Trin Coll Ox BA84 MA91. Linc Th Coll 89. **d** 91 **p** 92. C Willingdon *Chich* 91-95; C Goring-by-Sea 95-99; V Warnham from 99. *The Vicarage, Church Street, Warnham, Horsham RH12 3QW* Tel (01403) 265041
E-mail nloveless@hotmail.com

LOVELESS, Martin Frank. b 46. N Bucks Coll of Educn CertEd68. Wycliffe Hall Ox 72. **d** 75 **p** 76. C Caversham *Ox* 75-81; V Carterton 81-86; Chapl RAF 86-02; Chapl K Coll Taunton 02-04; Perm to Offic *Heref* 04-05 and from 07; P-in-c Glossop *Derby* 05-07. *Ridge Cottage, Staunton-on-Wye, Hereford HR4 7LP* Tel (01981) 500311 Mobile 07810-002079
E-mail martinloveless@hotmail.com

LOVELESS, Robert Alfred. b 43. Birm Univ BA66. Westcott Ho Cam 66. **d** 68 **p** 69. C Kenilworth St Nic *Cov* 68-72; C Costessey *Nor* 73-75; R Colney 75-80; R Lt w Gt Melton, Marlingford and Bawburgh 75-80; V Lt and Gt Melton w Bawburgh 80-82; P-in-c Westwood *Sarum* 82-83; P-in-c Wingfield w Rowley 82-83; R Westwood and Wingfield 83-87; Chapl Stonar Sch Melksham 82-87; R Paston *Pet* 87-93; V Nassington w Yarwell and Woodnewton 93-07; rtd 07. *93 The Pollards, Bourne PE10 0FR* Tel (01778) 393561

LOVELESS, Canon William Harry. b 21. Lon Univ BSc60. Ridley Hall Cam 61. **d** 63 **p** 64. C Danbury *Chelmsf* 63-65; C Cambridge Gt St Mary w St Mich *Ely* 65-67; V Cambridge St Mark 67-87; RD Cambridge 81-84; Hon Can Ely Cathl 81-87; rtd 87; Perm to Offic *Ely* 87-03. *Langdon House, 20 Union Lane, Cambridge CB4 1QB* Tel (01223) 303279

LOVELL, Charles Nelson. b 34. Oriel Coll Ox BA57 MA61. Wycliffe Hall Ox. **d** 59 **p** 60. C Walsall St Matt *Lich* 59-63; C St Giles-in-the-Fields *Lon* 63; Argentina 64-67; C Cambridge H Trin *Ely* 64; V Esh *Dur* 67-75; V Hamsteels 67-75; Chapl Winterton Hosp Sedgefield 75-83; R Stanhope *Dur* 83-86; Chapl Horn Hall Hosp Weardale 83-97; R Stanhope w Frosterley *Dur* 86-97; V Eastgate w Rookhope 86-97; RD Stanhope 87-97; rtd 97. *10 Riverside, Wolsingham, Bishop Auckland DL13 3BP* Tel (01388) 527038 E-mail charles@thefreeinternet.co.uk

LOVELL, David John. b 38. JP89. Univ of Tasmania BEcon86. Qu Coll Birm 60. **d** 60 **p** 62. C Glouc St Steph 60-64; C Lower Tuffley St Geo 63 64-67; V Sudbrook *Australia* 73-75; Perm to Offic Tas 76-81; rtd 98. *26 Lynden Road, Bonnet Hill Tas 7053, Australia* Tel (0061) (3) 6229 2838

LOVELL, Mrs Gillian Jayne. b 58. Univ of Wales (Ban) BA79 PGCE80. Qu Coll Birm MA04. **d** 04 **p** 05. C Burnham *Ox* 04-08; P-in-c Burghfield from 08. *The Rectory, Hollybush Lane, Burghfield Common, Reading RG7 3JL* Tel 0118-983 4433
E-mail gill.lovell@stmarysburghfield.org

LOVELL, Helen Sarah. *See* HOUSTON, Helen Sarah.

LOVELL, Keith Michael Beard. b 43. K Coll Lon 67. **d** 68 **p** 69. C Romford St Edw *Chelmsf* 68-73; P-in-c Elmstead 73-79; V Tollesbury w Salcot Virley 79-09; rtd 09. *The Vicarage, 12 King's Walk, Tollesbury, Maldon CM9 8XH* Tel (01621) 869393 *or* 868441 E-mail keith@mary.freewire.co.uk

LOVELL, Laurence John. b 31. St D Coll Lamp BA54 Tyndale Hall Bris 54. **d** 56 **p** 57. C Penge Ch Ch w H Trin *Roch* 56-61; C Illogan *Truro* 61-63; V St Keverne 63-68; C-in-c Oatley Australia 68-72; R 72-95; rtd 95. *Donald Robinson Village, 105/81 Flora Street, Kirrawee NSW 2223, Australia*
E-mail ljl01@bigpond.com

LOVELUCK, Canon Allan (Illtyd). b 30. Univ of Qld BSW74 MSocWork79. St D Coll Lamp BA52 St Mich Coll Llan 52. **d** 55 **p** 56. C Dowlais *Llan* 55-58; SSF 58-59; Lic to Offic *Chelmsf* 62-64; Australia from 64; Hon Can Brisbane 92-00; rtd 95. *5/48 Dunmore Terrace, Auchenflower Qld 4066, Australia* Tel (0061) (7) 3719 5342 *or* 3870 2566 Mobile 414-500837

LOVELUCK, Canon Graham David. b 34. Univ of Wales (Abth) BSc55 PhD58 CChem FRSC. St Deiniol's Hawarden 77. **d** 78 **p** 79. NSM Llanfair Mathafarn Eithaf w Llanbedrgoch *Ban* 78-87; NSM Llaneugrad w Llanallgo and Penrhoslligwy etc 87-96; P-in-c 96-03; R 03-04; Dioc Dir of Educn 92-03; Can Cursal Ban Cathl 00-04; rtd 04. *Gwenallt, Marianglas LL73 8PE* Tel (01248) 853741

LOVEMAN, Mrs Ruth. b 45. STETS 01. **d** 04 **p** 05. NSM Portsea N End St Mark *Portsm* 04-09; NSM Cowplain from 09. *3 Cotwell Avenue, Waterlooville PO8 9AP* Tel (023) 9259 1933 E-mail ruthlvm@googlemail.com

LOVERIDGE, Douglas Henry. b 52. Sarum & Wells Th Coll. **d** 84

p 85. C Earley St Pet *Ox* 84-88; V Hurst 88-03; Asst Chapl R Berks NHS Foundn Trust 03-07; Chapl Mid-Essex Hosp Services NHS Trust 07-09; Chapl W Herts Hosps NHS Trust from 09. *All Saints' Vicarage, Churchfields, Hertford SG13 8AE* Tel (01992) 584899 *or* (01923) 217994 E-mail dhloveridge@hotmail.com *or* douglas.loveridge@whht.nhs.uk

LOVERIDGE, Emma Warren. b 65. St Jo Coll Cam BA87 MA90 PhD01. **d** 99 **p** 00. NSM Highbury Ch Ch w St Jo and St Sav *Lon* 99-02; NSM Islington St Mary 03-05; Prin Adv to Abp York 06-07. *6 Prior Bolton Street, London N1 2NX* Tel 07000-777977 (mobile) E-mail eloveridge@windsandstars.co.uk

LOVERIDGE (*née* **RODEN), Ms Joan Margaretha Holland (Jo).** b 57. K Coll Lon BD78 AKC78 Regent's Park Coll Ox MTh98. SAOMC 95. **d** 97 **p** 98. NSM Caversham St Jo *Ox* 97-98; C Earley St Pet 98-03; P-in-c Burghfield 03-07; AD Bradfield 04-07; P-in-c Hertford All SS *St Alb* 07-08; TR Hertford from 08. *All Saints' Vicarage, Churchfields, Hertford SG13 8AE* Tel (01992) 584899 E-mail jonloveridge@hotmail.com

LOVERIDGE, Mrs Jennifer Mary. b 39. Eastbourne Tr Coll CertEd59. Wycliffe Hall Ox 81. **dss** 84 **d** 87 **p** 94. Abingdon w Shippon *Ox* 84-87; Par Dn Abingdon 87-94; C 94-97; rtd 98. *5 Monksmead, Brightwell-cum-Sotwell, Wallingford OX10 0RL* Tel (01491) 825329

LOVERING, Martin. b 35. Imp Coll Lon BScEng57. Wycliffe Hall Ox 82. **d** 84 **p** 85. NSM Abingdon w Shippon *Ox* 84-88; C Abingdon 88-89; TV 89-00; rtd 01. *5 Monks Mead, Brightwell-cum-Sotwell, Wallingford OX10 0RL* Tel (01491) 825329

LOVERN, Mrs Sandra Elaine. b 48. Trin Coll Bris BA07. **d** 07 **p** 08. NSM Chew Magna w Dundry and Norton Malreward *B & W* from 07. *Willow Lodge, Breach Hill Lane, Chew Stoke, Bristol BS40 8YA* Tel (01275) 332657 E-mail sandra.lovern@yahoo.com

LOVESEY, Katharine Patience Beresford. b 62. Trin Coll Bris 01. **d** 03 **p** 04. C Nor Lakenham St Jo and All SS and Tuckswood 03-08; C Stoke H Cross w Dunston, Arminghall etc from 08. *Burnt House Farm, Caistor Lane, Caistor St Edmund, Norwich NR14 8RH* E-mail katelovesey@aol.com

LOVETT, Mrs Frances Mary Anderson. b 46. Plymouth Univ BA92. NOC 00. **d** 03 **p** 04. Ind Chapl *Liv* from 03; NSM Newton in Makerfield St Pet 03-07. *4 Cathedral Close, Liverpool L1 7BR* Tel 0151-708 8071 E-mail franian.lovett@virgin.net

LOVETT, Francis Roland. b 25. Glouc Th Course. **d** 85 **p** 86. NSM Ludlow *Heref* 85-91; rtd 92; Perm to Offic *Heref* 96-05. *7 Poyner Road, Ludlow SY8 1QT* Tel (01584) 872470

LOVETT, Ian Arthur. b 43. NE Lon Poly BSc74. Linc Th Coll 85. **d** 87 **p** 88. C Uppingham w Ayston and Wardley w Belton *Pet* 87-91; R Polebrook and Lutton w Hemington and Luddington 91-04; Asst to RD Corby 05-08; rtd 08. *38 Northbrook, Corby NN18 9AX* Tel (01536) 747644 E-mail ian.lovett@tiscali.co.uk

LOVETT, Canon Ian James. b 49. JP99. CertEd72 BTh89 MA92. S'wark Ord Course 73. **d** 76 **p** 77. NSM Gravesend St Geo *Roch* 76-77; NSM Willesborough w Hinxhill *Cant* 77-83; NSM Landcross, Littleham, Monkleigh etc *Ex* 83-85; C Compton Gifford 85-86; TV Plymouth Em w Efford 86-92; TV Plymouth Em, St Paul Efford and St Aug 93-97; Chapl Aintree Hosps NHS Trust Liv from 97; Bp's Adv for Hosp Chapl *Liv* from 08; Hon Can Liv Cathl from 08. *University Hospital Aintree, Lower Lane, Fazakerley, Liverpool L9 7AL* Tel 0151-525 5980 *or* 529 2203

LOVITT, Gerald Elliott. b 25. St Mich Coll Llan 59. **d** 61 **p** 62. C Aberdare *Llan* 61-66; C Whitchurch 66-71; V Grangetown 71-76; V Rockfield and Llangattock w St Maughan's *Mon* 76-83; V Rockfield and St Maughen's w Llangattock etc 83-93; rtd 93; Perm to Offic *Llan* from 93; Lic to Offic *Mon* from 93. *104B Albany Road, Cardiff CF24 3RT* Tel (029) 2041 1697

LOW, Alastair Graham. b 43. Brunel Univ BSc68 Reading Univ PhD74. Ripon Coll Cuddesdon 90. **d** 92 **p** 93. C Brighton Gd Shep Preston *Chich* 92-96; TV Ifield 96-99; TV Horsham 99-08; Chapl Surrey and Sussex Healthcare NHS Trust 02-08; rtd 08; Perm to Offic *Ox* from 08. *3 Sheepway Court, Iffley, Oxford OX4 4JL* Tel (01865) 777257 E-mail graham@glowpigs.freeserve.co.uk

LOW, Mrs Christine Mabel. b 48. Southlands Coll Lon CertEd69 SS Mark & Jo Univ Coll Plymouth BEd87. SWMTC. **d** 99 **p** 00. NSM Bideford, Northam, Westward Ho!, Appledore etc *Ex* 99-03; P-in-c Thornton in Lonsdale w Burton in Lonsdale *Bradf* 03-08; NSM Bingley All SS from 08; NSM Bingley H Trin from 08. *Winston Grange, Otley Road, Eldwick, Bingley BD16 3DE* Tel (01274) 564694 Mobile 07870-766634 E-mail chris.low@talktalk.net *or* chris.low@bradford.anglican.org

LOW, Canon David Anthony. b 42. AKC66. **d** 67 **p** 68. C Gillingham St Barn *Roch* 67-70; V 82-88; C Wallingford *Ox* 70-73; V Spencer's Wood 73-82; P-in-c Grazeley and Beech Hill 77-82; Chapl Medway Hosp Gillingham 86-88; V Hoo St Werburgh *Roch* 88-02; RD Strood 97-02; Hon Can Roch Cathl 01-02; rtd 02. *12 Stonecrop Close, St Mary's Island, Chatham ME4 3HA*

LOW, Canon David Michael. b 39. Cape Town Univ BA60. Cuddesdon Coll 61. **d** 63 **p** 64. C Portsea St Cuth *Portsm* 63-65; S Africa 65-69; C Havant *Portsm* 69-72; V St Helens 72-88; V Sea View 81-88; V Sandown Ch Ch 88-95; V Lower Sandown St Jo 88-95; R Brading w Yaverland 95-01; Hon Can Portsm Cathl 00-01; rtd 01. *Copeland, Lane End Close, Bembridge PO35 5UF* Tel (01983) 874306

LOW, Mrs Jennifer Anne. b 49. St Anne's Coll Ox MA70 Nottm Univ PGCE71. Trin Coll Bris 01. **d** 03 **p** 04. C Bris St Andr Hartcliffe 03-07; P-in-c Lawrence Weston and Avonmouth from 07; Deanery Growth Officer Bris W from 07. *The Vicarage, 335 Long Cross, Bristol BS11 0NN* Tel 0117-982 5863 E-mail jennilow@yahoo.com

LOW, Peter James. b 52. Nottm Univ BTh89. Linc Th Coll 86. **d** 89 **p** 90. C Dartford H Trin *Roch* 89-92; C Plympton St Mary *Ex* 92-94; TR Devonport St Boniface and St Phil 94-08; V Heybridge w Langford *Chelmsf* from 08. *The Vicarage, 1A Crescent Road, Heybridge, Maldon CM9 4SJ* Tel (01621) 841274 E-mail peter@lowuk.wanadoo.co.uk

LOW, Robbie. *See* LOW, William Roberson

LOW, Stafford. b 42. N Lon Poly BSc65. Trin Coll Bris 82. **d** 85 **p** 86. C Yeovil *B & W* 85-88; C Glastonbury w Meare, W Pennard and Godney 88-92; R Berrow and Breane 92-00; R Wincanton 00-07; R Pen Selwood 00-07; Chapl Voc and Min 97-07; RD Bruton and Cary 03-06; rtd 07. *Les Acacias, route d'Uzès Prolongée, Le Moulinet, 30500 Saint-Ambroix, France* E-mail lowandco@aol.com

LOW, Terence John Gordon. b 37. Oak Hill Th Coll 75. **d** 77 **p** 78. C Kensal Rise St Martin *Lon* 77-79; C Longfleet *Sarum* 79-83; P-in-c Maiden Newton and Valleys 83-84; TV Melbury 84-88; TV Buckhurst Hill *Chelmsf* 88-92; R Gt Hallingbury and Lt Hallingbury 92-01; rtd 01; Perm to Offic *Sarum* from 02. *37 Vicarage Lane, Charminster, Dorchester DT2 9QF* Tel (01305) 260180

LOW, William Roberson (Robbie). b 50. Pemb Coll Cam BA73 MA77. Westcott Ho Cam 76. **d** 79 **p** 80. C Poplar *Lon* 79-83; Chapl St Alb Abbey 83-88; V Bushey Heath 88-03. *3 Trewince Lane, Bodmin Hill, Lostwithiel PL22 0AJ* Tel (01208) 871517

LOWATER, Canon Jennifer Blanche. b 34. Eastbourne Tr Coll TCert54. Sarum & Wells Th Coll 82. **dss** 85 **d** 87 **p** 94. Locks Heath *Portsm* 85-88; Hon C 87-88; NSM Southsea St Pet 88-94; NSM Hook w Warsash 94-01; Asst Dir of Ords 91-99; Hon Can Portsm Cathl 95-97; rtd 97. *Lower Gubbles, Hook Lane, Warsash, Southampton SO31 9HH* Tel (01489) 572156 Fax 572252 E-mail jenny.lowater@care4free.net

LOWDON, Christopher Ian. b 63. Plymouth Univ LLB93 Barrister 94. Aston Tr Scheme 86 St Mich Coll Llan 04. **d** 06 **p** 07. C Chaddesden St Phil *Derby* from 06. *St Mark's Vicarage, 119 Francis Street, Derby DE21 6DE* Tel (01332) 345113 Mobile 07871-087294 E-mail frchris@philipandmark.co.uk

LOWE, Anthony Richard. b 45. York Univ BA66. Qu Coll Birm 66. **d** 69 **p** 70. C Greasbrough *Sheff* 69-71; C Thrybergh 71-75; P-in-c Sheff St Mary w St Simon w St Matthias 75-78; V Shiregreen St Hilda 78-85; V Hoxne w Denham St Jo and Syleham *St E* 85-89; P-in-c Wingfield 86-89; R Hoxne w Denham, Syleham and Wingfield 90-05; rtd 06. *9 Alfred Road, Dover CT16 2AB* Tel (01304) 214047

LOWE, Mrs Brenda June. b 53. Cranmer Hall Dur 75. **d** 88 **p** 94. Chapl to Families Trin Coll and Mortimer Ho Bris 86-91; NSM Clifton Ch Ch w Em *Bris* 88-91; Asst Chapl Southmead Health Services NHS Trust 86-91; NSM Marple All SS *Ches* from 91; Perm to Offic *Man* 91-97; Asst Chapl Wythenshawe Hosp Man 94-96; Chapl Stockport Acute Services NHS Trust 96-98; Sen Chapl Stockport NHS Trust from 98. *4 Greenway Road, Heald Green, Cheadle SK8 3NR* Tel 0161-282 3850 *or* 419 5889 E-mail malowe@mail.com

LOWE, Christopher Alan. b 75. Imp Coll Lon MEng97. Oak Hill Th Coll MTh08. **d** 08 **p** 09. C Cambridge St Andr Less *Ely* from 08. *4 Parsonage Street, Cambridge CB5 8DN* Tel 07962-060786 (mobile) E-mail chris.lowe@christchurchcambridge.org.uk

LOWE, Canon David Charles. b 43. Kelham Th Coll 62. **d** 67 **p** 68. C Wingerworth *Derby* 67-70; C Greenhill St Pet 70-73; TV Eckington 73-74; TV Eckington w Handley and Ridgeway 74-78; V Bury St Edmunds St Geo *St E* 78-86; V Leiston 86-98; RD Saxmundham 88-96; P-in-c Felixstowe St Jo 98-08; Hon Can St E Cathl 98-08; rtd 08; Perm to Offic *St E* from 08. *21 Firebrass Lane, Sutton Heath, Woodbridge IP12 3TS* Tel (01394) 421722 E-mail david_lowechurch@lineone.net

LOWE, David Reginald. b 42. K Coll Lon BD65 AKC65. St Boniface Warminster 65. **d** 66 **p** 67. C Tupsley *Heref* 66-69; C Lewes St Anne *Chich* 69-73; C Heref H Trin 73-77; P-in-c Lyonshall w Titley 77-88; V Lyonshall w Titley, Almeley and Kinnersley 88-96; Perm to Offic *Man* 96-00; rtd 00. *26 Chapel Street, Penzance TR18 4AP* Tel (01736) 331068

LOWE, Donald. b 33. Lich Th Coll 57. **d** 60 **p** 61. C Horwich H Trin *Man* 60; C Wythenshawe St Martin CD 60-62; C Bury St Paul 62-65; S Africa 65-69; V Gannow *Blackb* 70-73; R Virginia St Alb S Africa 73-81; V Colne H Trin 81-89; TV Melbury *Sarum* 89-94; RD Beaminster 93-94; rtd 94; Perm to

Offic *Bradf* from 94. *28 High Bank, Threshfield, Skipton BD23 5BU* Tel (01756) 752344

LOWE, Mrs Elaine Mary. b 55. **d** 98 **p** 99. OLM Bardsley *Man* from 98. *5 Danisher Lane, Bardsley, Oldham OL8 3HU* Tel 0161-633 4535

LOWE, The Ven Frank McLean Rhodes. b 26. ACT 59. **d** 61 **p** 63. Australia 61-86 and from 87; Hon Can Gippsland 73-81; Adn Latrobe Valley 81-86; Adn Gippsland 81-86; P-in-c Kirkby in Ashfield St Thos *S'well* 86-87; C Mansfield Woodhouse 87; rtd 91. *Unit 2, 3 Berg Street, Morwell Vic 3840, Australia* Tel (0061) (3) 5134 1338

LOWE, Mrs Janet Eleanor. b 56. Univ Coll Lon BSc77. NTMTC 98. **d** 01 **p** 02. C Hendon St Paul Mill Hill *Lon* from 01. *12 Frobisher Road, London N8 0QS* Tel (020) 8340 8764
E-mail janlowe@btinternet.com

LOWE, Canon John Bethel. b 30. TCD BA52 BD65. Ridley Hall Cam 55. **d** 55 **p** 56. C Belfast St Mary Magd *Conn* 55-57; Sudan 59-64; Uganda 64-74; Warden CMS Fellowship Ho Foxbury 74-76; V Kippington *Roch* 76-96; Dioc Dir of Ords 82-96; Hon Can Roch Cathl 85-96; rtd 96; Perm to Offic *Ely* from 96. *228 Cambridge Road, Great Shelford, Cambridge CB22 5JU* Tel (01223) 840019

LOWE, John Forrester. b 39. Nottm Univ BA61. Lich Th Coll 61. **d** 64 **p** 65. C N Woolwich *Chelmsf* 64-70; V Marks Gate 70-74; V Moulsham St Jo 74-79; V N Woolwich w Silvertown 79-82; V Birm St Pet 82-86; Gen Sec SOMA UK 86-91; V Heckmondwike *Wakef* 92-98; rtd 98; Perm to Offic *Heref* from 99. *37 Jubilee Close, Ledbury HR8 2XA* Tel (01531) 631890

LOWE, Keith Gregory. b 50. Sarum & Wells Th Coll 91. **d** 93 **p** 94. C Wallasey St Hilary *Ches* 93-94; C W Kirby St Bridget 94-98; V Sandbach Heath w Wheelock 98-01; V High Lane 01-04; Chapl Stockport NHS Trust 01-04; Asst Chapl Sheff Teaching Hosps NHS Trust 04-06; Chapl Sheff Teaching Hosps NHS Foundn Trust from 06. *169 Mortomley Lane, High Green, Sheffield S35 3HT* Tel 0114-284 4076 E-mail keithglowe@mail.com

LOWE, Canon Michael Arthur. b 46. Lon Univ BD67 Hull Univ MA85. Cranmer Hall Dur. **d** 76 **p** 77. C Thorpe Edge *Bradf* 76-79; C N Ferriby *York* 79-84; TV 84-86; Dir Past Studies Trin Coll Bris 86-91; V Marple All SS *Ches* 91-00; RD Chadkirk 95-00; Dir of Miss and Unity 00-05; C Delamere 00-02; C Wilmslow 05-08; Hon Can Ches Cathl 00-08; rtd 08; Dioc Ecum Officer *Ches* from 09. *4 Greenway Road, Heald Green, Cheadle SK8 3NR* Tel 0161-282 3850 E-mail malowe@mail.com

LOWE, Samuel. b 35. St D Coll Lamp. **d** 65 **p** 66. C Tenby w Gumfreston *St D* 65-67; C Lower Mitton *Worc* 67-69; C Halesowen 69-72; R Droitwich St Nic w St Pet 72-73; TV Droitwich 73-77; P-in-c Claines St Geo 77-78; P-in-c Worc St Mary the Tything 77-78; P-in-c Worc St Geo w St Mary Magd 78-84; V 84-00; rtd 00. *57 Camp Hill Road, Worcester WR5 2HG* Tel (01905) 357807

LOWE, Stephen Arthur. b 49. Nottm Univ BSc71. Cuddesdon Coll 71. **d** 74 **p** 75. C Mansfield St Mark *S'well* 74-77; Chapl Martyrs' Sch Papua New Guinea 77-78; P-in-c Nambaiyufa 79; V Kirkby Woodhouse 80-86; V Beeston 86-99; TR Wenlock *Heref* from 99; RD Condover from 06. *The Rectory, New Road, Much Wenlock TF13 6EQ* Tel (01952) 727396
E-mail rector@wenlockchurches.co.uk

✠**LOWE, The Rt Revd Stephen Richard.** b 44. Lon Univ BSc66. Ripon Hall Ox 68. **d** 68 **p** 69 **c** 99. C Gospel Lane St Mich *Birm* 68-72; C-in-c Woodgate Valley CD 72-75; V E Ham w Upton Park *Chelmsf* 75-76; TR E Ham w Upton Park St Alb 76-88; Hon Can Chelmsf Cathl 85-88; Adn Sheff 88-99; Can Res Sheff Cathl 88-99; Suff Bp Hulme *Man* 99-09; rtd 09. *2 Pen y Glyn, Bryn-y-Maen, Colwyn Bay LL28 5EW* Tel (01492) 533510 Mobile 07801-505277 E-mail lowehulme@btinternet.com

LOWE, Mrs Valerie Anne. CBDTI. **d** 07 **p** 08. NSM Skipton Ch Ch w Carleton *Bradf* from 07. *126A Keighley Road, Skipton BD23 2QT* Tel (01756) 790132

LOWELL, Ian Russell. b 53. AKC75. St Aug Coll Cant 75. **d** 76 **p** 77. C Llwynderw *S & B* 76-79; C Swansea St Mary w H Trin and St Mark 79-81; Chapl Ox Hosps 81-83; TV Gt and Lt Coates w Bradley *Linc* 83-88; V Wellingborough St Mark *Pet* 88-02; V Northampton St Alb from 02; Chapl Northants Ambulance Service 92-03; Officer for Major Emergencies from 03. *St Alban's Vicarage, Broadmead Avenue, Northampton NN3 2RA* Tel (01604) 407074
E-mail ianlowell@btinternet.com

LOWEN, Mrs Anne Lois. b 60. DipCOT82. ERMC 03. **d** 06 **p** 07. NSM Basle *Eur* from 06. *Im Wygaertli 15, 4114 Hofstetten, Switzerland* Tel (0041) (61) 731 1485
E-mail anne.lowen@bluewin.ch

LOWEN, David John. b 42. Sussex Univ BSc74 Univ of Wales (Lamp) MA84. Llan Dioc Tr Scheme 86. **d** 88 **p** 89. C Carmarthen St Pet *St D* 88-90; P-in-c Walwyn's Castle w Robeston W 90-92; R 92-08; rtd 08. *The Vicarage, Rock Lane, Llawhaden, Narberth SA67 8HL*

LOWEN, John Michael. b 47. Nottm Univ BTh77. Linc Th Coll 73. **d** 77 **p** 78. C Beeston *S'well* 77-80; C Stratford-on-Avon w Bishopton *Cov* 80-82; V Monkseaton St Mary *Newc* 82-90; V

Ponteland 90-95; Chapl HM Pris Leeds 95; P-in-c Sutton St Mary *Linc* 95-00; R Dunvegan Canada 00-05; rtd 07. *9 Alden Hubley Drive, RR1, Annapolis Royal NS B0S 1A0, Canada*

LOWLES, Martin John. b 48. Thames Poly BSc72. Cranmer Hall Dur. **d** 78 **p** 79. C Leyton St Mary w St Edw *Chelmsf* 78-81; C Waltham Abbey 81-85; V E Ham St Paul 85-95; TR N Huddersfield *Wakef* 95-06; V Birkenshaw w Hunsworth from 06. *The Vicarage, 6 Vicarage Gardens, Birkenshaw, Bradford BD11 2EF* Tel (01274) 683776
E-mail martin.lowles@btinternet.com

LOWMAN, The Ven David Walter. b 48. K Coll Lon BD73 AKC73. St Aug Coll Cant 73. **d** 75 **p** 76. C Notting Hill *Lon* 75-78; C Kilburn St Aug w St Jo 78-81; Selection Sec and Voc Adv ACCM 81-86; TR Wickford and Runwell *Chelmsf* 86-93; Dioc Dir of Ords 93-01; C Chelmsf All SS 93-01; C Chelmsf Ascension 93-01; Hon Can Chelmsf Cathl 93-01; Adn Southend from 01. *The Archdeacon's Lodge, 136 Broomfield Road, Chelmsford CM1 1RN* Tel (01245) 258257 Fax 250845
E-mail a.southend@chelmsford.anglican.org

LOWNDES, Charles. b 22. MISW57 CQSW72. **d** 87 **p** 88. NSM Hanley H Ev *Lich* 87-97; rtd 97. *7 Beacon Rise, Stone ST15 0AL* Tel (01785) 812698

LOWNDES, Harold John (Nobby). b 31. SAOMC 96. **d** 99 **p** 00. OLM Lamp *Ox* from 99. *98 Wolverton Road, Haversham, Milton Keynes MK19 7AB* Tel (01908) 319939
E-mail hlowndes@vivao.net

LOWNDES, Richard Owen Lewis. b 63. Univ of Wales (Ban) BD86. Coll of Resurr Mirfield 87. **d** 89 **p** 90. C Milford Haven *St D* 89-91; C Roath St German *Llan* 91-94; Chapl Cardiff Royal Infirmary 91-94; V Tylorstown w Ynyshir *Llan* 94-96; Asst Chapl St Helier NHS Trust 96-98; Chapl Team Ldr W Middx Univ Hosp NHS Trust 98-03; Chapl Team Ldr Ealing Hosp NHS Trust 01-03; Chapl Team Ldr Southn Univ Hosps NHS Trust from 03. *Trust Management Offices, Southampton General Hospital, Tremona Road, Southampton SO16 6TD* Tel (023) 8077 7222 Fax 8079 4153

LOWRIE, Ronald Malcolm. b 48. Bath Spa Univ MA07. Ripon Hall Ox 70. **d** 72 **p** 73. C Knowle *Birm* 72-75; C Bourton-on-the-Water w Clapton *Glouc* 75-79; R Broadwell, Evenlode, Oddington and Adlestrop 79-81; TV Trowbridge H Trin *Sarum* 81-88; P-in-c Westwood and Wingfield 88-90; R from 90; P-in-c Bradford-on-Avon Ch Ch from 03; Chapl Wilts and Swindon Healthcare NHS Trust 88-05. *The Rectory, Westwood, Bradford-on-Avon BA15 2AF* Tel (01225) 863109 or 867040
E-mail rmlowrie@btinternet.com

LOWRY, Robert Harold. b 19. TCD BA44 MA49. CITC 44. **d** 44 **p** 45. C Belfast St Mary Magd *Conn* 44-48; C Belfast St Donard *D & D* 48-52; I Drumgooland w Kilcoo 52-59; I Aghalee 59-62; I Willowfield 62-75; I Lambeg *Conn* 75-89; Can Conn Cathl 82-89; rtd 90; Lic to Offic *D & D* from 90. *9 Innisfayle Park, Bangor BT19 1DP* Tel (028) 9147 2423

LOWRY, The Very Revd Stephen Harold. b 58. QUB BSc79 CertEd80. CITC 82. **d** 85 **p** 86. C Coleraine *Conn* 85-88; I Greenisland 88-98; I Dromore Cathl from 98; Dean Dromore from 02. *Dromore Cathedral Rectory, 28 Church Street, Dromore BT25 1AA* Tel (028) 9269 2275 or 9269 3968 Mobile 07031 501932 E-mail aathedral@dromore.anglican.org

LOWSON, The Ven Christopher. b 53. AKC75 Heythrop Coll Lon MTh96 Univ of Wales (Cardiff) LLM03. St Aug Coll Cant 76 Pacific Sch of Relig Berkeley STM78. **d** 77 **p** 78. C Richmond St Mary *S'wark* 77-79; C Richmond St Mary w St Matthias and St Jo 79-82; P-in-c Eltham H Trin 82-83; V 83-91; R Buriton *Portsm* 91-99; V Petersfield 91-99; RD Petersfield 95-99; Adn Portsdown 99-06; Bp's Liaison Officer for Pris 00-03; Bp's Adv to Hosp Chapl 03-06; Dir Min Division Abps' Coun from 06; PV Westmr Abbey from 06; Perm to Offic *Lon* from 06. *Church House, Great Smith Street, London SW1P 3AZ* Tel (020) 7898 1391 Fax 7898 1421 Mobile 07957-657312
E-mail christopher.lowson@c-of-e.org.uk

LOWSON, Geoffrey Addison. b 47. Bede Coll Dur BEd70 PGCE70. NEOC 95. **d** 98 **p** 99. NSM Sherburn in Elmet w Saxton *York* 98-04; Fieldworker (NE England) USPG 98-06; P-in-c Tynemouth Priory *Newc* from 06. *Holy Saviour Vicarage, 1 Crossway, North Shields NE30 2LB* Tel 0191-257 1636
E-mail geoffl@freenet.co.uk

LOWTHER, Ms Kareen Anne. b 59. Loughb Univ BSc81. WMMTC 98. **d** 01 **p** 02. C Lich St Mich w St Mary and Wall 01-04; TV Bloxwich from 04. *9 Sanstone Road, Walsall WS3 3SJ* Tel (01922) 711225 Mobile 07940-936033

LOWTHER, Peter Mark. b 56. GTCL77. NTMTC BA08. **d** 08 **p** 09. NSM Pimlico St Pet w Westmr Ch Ch *Lon* from 08. *19 Marlborough Yard, London N19 4ND* Tel (020) 7561 0173 Mobile 07801-258503 E-mail mark.lowther@virgin.net

LOWTON, Nicholas Gerard. b 53. St Jo Coll Ox BA76 FRSA94. Glouc Sch of Min 86. **d** 89 **p** 90. NSM Prestbury *Glouc* 89-94. *Hazelwell, College Road, Cheltenham GL53 7JD* Tel (01242) 265609 or 513540 ext 209 Fax 265688
E-mail ngl@cheltcoll.gloucs.sch.uk

LOXHAM, Edward. b 49. BEd. **d** 04 **p** 05. OLM Birkdale St Pet *Liv* from 04. *34 Alma Road, Southport PR8 4AN* Tel (01704) 568141

LOXHAM, Geoffrey Richard. b 40. Hull Univ BA62. Cranmer Hall Dur. **d** 65 **p** 66. C Darwen St Barn *Blackb* 65-68; C Leyland St Andr 68-72; V Preston St Mark 72-79; V Edgeside *Man* 79-91; P-in-c Heapey and Withnell *Blackb* 91-92; V 92-99; V Grimsargh from 99. *St Michael's Vicarage, 46 Preston Road, Preston PR2 5SD* Tel (01772) 653283

LOXLEY, Mrs Deirdre. b 41. **d** 96 **p** 97. OLM Heacham *Nor* 96-05; NSM Knaresborough *Ripon* 05-08; rtd 08; Perm to Offic *Nor* from 08. *6 Holkham Avenue, Swaffham PE37 7RX* Tel (01760) 723235 E-mail banddloxley@btinternet.com

LOXLEY, Harold. b 43. NOC 79. **d** 82 **p** 83. NSM Sheff St Cecilia Parson Cross 82-87; C Gleadless 87-90; V Sheff St Cath Richmond Road from 90. *St Catherine's Vicarage, 300 Hastilar Road South, Sheffield S13 8EJ* Tel and fax 0114-239 9598

LOXLEY, Ronald Alan Keith. b 26. St Jo Coll Ox BA51 MA55. Wm Temple Coll Rugby 66 Cuddesdon Coll 67. **d** 68 **p** 69. C Swindon Ch Ch *Bris* 68-71; Ind Chapl *Lon* 71-83; Ind Chapl and P-in-c Theydon Garnon *Chelmsf* 83-92; rtd 92; Perm to Offic *Linc* 92-09. *30 Chancellor House, Mount Ephraim, Tunbridge Wells TN4 8BT* Tel (01892) 513330

LOXTON, John Sherwood. b 29. Bris Univ BSc50 Birm Univ BA53. Handsworth Coll Birm 50 Chich Th Coll 80. **d** 80 **p** 81. In Meth Ch 50-80; C Haywards Heath St Wilfrid *Chich* 80-82; TV 82-89; V Turners Hill 89-96; rtd 96; Perm to Offic *Chich* from 96. *3 Ashurst Drive, Worth, Crawley RH10 7FS* Tel (01293) 887762

LOXTON, Mrs Susan Ann. b 57. EAMTC 02. **d** 05 **p** 06. NSM Colchester, New Town and The Hythe *Chelmsf* 05-08; P-in-c Fressingfield, Mendham etc *St E* from 08; C Hoxne w Denham, Syleham and Wingfield from 08. *The Vicarage, 2 Tansy Meadow, Fressingfield, Eye IP21 5RQ* Tel (01379) 586040 E-mail susan.loxton@mypostoffice.co.uk

LOZADA-UZURIAGA, Ernesto. b 61. Wycliffe Hall Ox. **d** 02 **p** 03. C Henley w Remenham *Ox* 02-06; P-in-c Milton Keynes from 06. *1 Cottage Common, Loughton, Milton Keynes MK5 8AE* Tel (01908) 231260 E-mail leon-judah@hotmail.com

LUBBOCK, David John. b 34. S'wark Ord Course. **d** 87 **p** 88. NSM Tulse Hill H Trin and St Matthias *S'wark* 87-04; rtd 04; Perm to Offic *S'wark* from 04. *The Old Vicarage, 107 Upper Tulse Hill, London SW2 2RD* Tel (020) 8674 6146 E-mail lubodj@dircon.co.uk

LUBKOWSKI, Richard Jan. b 51. Westmr Coll Ox BEd75 Warw Univ MA79. St Jo Coll Dur 86. **d** 88 **p** 89. C Duston *Pet* 88-90; C Hellesdon *Nor* 90-91; Perm to Offic *Sheff* 91-94; In RC Ch 94-00; Chapl HM Pris Ashwell from 00. *HM Prison Ashwell, Oakham LE15 7LS* Tel (01572) 884100 ext 4288 Mobile 07449-122406 E-mail richard.lubkowski@hmps.gsi.gov.uk

LUCAS, Anthony Stanley. b 41. Man Univ BA62 K Coll Lon MA99. Qu Coll Birm 63. **d** 65 **p** 66. C N Hammersmith St Kath *Lon* 65-69; C W Wimbledon Ch Ch *S'wark* 69-74; C Caterham 74-78; P-in-c Stockwell St Mich 78-86; V 86-91; R S'wark St Geo the Martyr w St Jude 91-94; P-in-c S'wark St Alphege 92-94; R S'wark St Geo w St Alphege and St Jude 95-06; rtd 06. *23 Clements Road, London SE16 4DW* Tel (020) 7064 9088 E-mail tonyslucas@btinternet.com

LUCAS, Arthur Edgar. b 24. Clifton Th Coll 60. **d** 62 **p** 63. C Hyson Green *S'well* 62-66; V Willoughby-on-the-Wolds w Wysall 66-74; P-in-c Widmerpool 71-74; R Collyhurst *Man* 75-80; V Heapey *Blackb* 80-91; rtd 91; Perm to Offic *Blackb* from 91 and *Liv* 91-00. *18 Parkway, Standish, Wigan WN6 0SJ*

LUCAS, The Ven Brian Humphrey. b 40. CB93. FRSA93 Univ of Wales (Lamp) BA62. St Steph Ho Ox 62. **d** 64 **p** 65. C Llandaff w Capel Llanilltern 64-67; C Neath w Llantwit 67-70; Chapl RAF 70-87; Asst Chapl-in-Chief RAF 87-91; Chapl-in-Chief RAF 91-95; QHC from 88; Perm to Offic *Llan* from 88; Can and Preb Linc Cathl 91-95; P-in-c Caythorpe 96-00; R 00-03. *Pen-y-Coed, 6 Arnhem Drive, Caythorpe, Grantham NG32 3DQ* Tel (01400) 272085 E-mail brian.lucas@savageclub.com

LUCAS, Mrs Carolyn. b 61. Surrey Univ MSc06. SEITE 06. **d** 09. NSM New Malden and Coombe *S'wark* from 09. *10 Presburg Road, New Malden KT3 5AH* E-mail clucas@blueyonder.co.uk

LUCAS, Glyn Andrew. b 63. Oak Hill Th Coll. **d** 09. C Cheadle *Ches* from 09. *39 Oakfield Avenue, Cheadle SK8 1EF*

LUCAS, Mrs Jane Eleanor. b 49. SWMTC 00. **d** 03 **p** 04. NSM N Creedy *Ex* 03-07; NSM Burrington, Chawleigh, Cheldon, Chulmleigh etc 07-08; P-in-c Ashwater, Halwill, Beaworthy, Clawton etc from 08. *The Rectory, Ashwater, Beaworthy EX21 5EZ* Tel and fax (01409) 211205 E-mail jane.e.lucas@btinternet.com

LUCAS, John Kenneth. b 32. LNSM course 92. **d** 95 **p** 96. NSM Deptford St Nic and St Luke *S'wark* 95-97; Perm to Offic 97-00 and from 03. *4 The Colonnade, Grove Street, London SE8 3AY* Tel (020) 8691 3161

LUCAS, John Maxwell. b 34. TD85. Cranmer Hall Dur 59. **d** 62 **p** 63. C Lancaster St Mary *Blackb* 62-65; C Lytham St Cuth 65-68; V Blackb St Aid 68-72; V Sparkhill St Jo *Birm* 72-78; CF

(TAVR) from 73; V Edgbaston St Aug *Birm* 78-85; V Slyne w Hest *Blackb* 85-89; Chapl HM YOI Stoke Heath 89-93; rtd 93. *2 Glendon Close, Market Drayton TF9 1NX* Tel (01630) 652977

LUCAS, Lorna Yvonne. b 48. Bp Lonsdale Coll TCert69. EMMTC 95. **d** 98 **p** 99. NSM Haxey and Owston *Linc* 98-00; NSM Scawby, Redbourne and Hibaldstow 00-04; NSM Lea Gp from 05. *4 Willingham Road, Lea, Gainsborough DN21 5EH* Tel (01427) 811463 E-mail lorna.lucas@virgin.net

LUCAS, Mark Wesley. b 62. Man Univ BSc83. Oak Hill Th Coll BA94. **d** 94 **p** 95. C Harold Wood *Chelmsf* 94-98; Dir Oast Ho Retreat Cen *Chich* 98-00; Co-ord for Adult Educn (E Sussex Area) 98-00; V Polegate from 00. *St John's Vicarage, 1 Church Road, Polegate BN26 5BX* Tel (01323) 483259 Fax 483305 Mobile 07788-100757 E-mail vicar@polegate.org.uk

LUCAS, Maxwell. *See* LUCAS, John Maxwell

LUCAS, Ms Pamela Turnbull. b 68. Westmr Coll Ox BA91 Glas Univ MSW98 Edin Univ MTh99 UNISA MTh05. TISEC 98. **d** 00 **p** 01. C Easington, Easington Colliery and S Hetton *Dur* 00-04; CSC 04-06; Asst Chapl Basingstoke and N Hants NHS Foundation Trust 06-09; Chapl St Mich Hosp Toronto Canada from 09. *St Michael's Hospital, Spiritual Care, room 3-016, 30 Bond Street, Toronto ON M5B 1W8, Canada* Tel (001) (416) 864 5324 E-mail revd_ptlucas@yahoo.co.uk

LUCAS, Paul de Neufville. b 33. Ch Ch Ox BA59 MA59 Cam Univ MA63. Cuddesdon Coll 57. **d** 59 **p** 60. C Westmr St Steph w St Jo *Lon* 59-63; Chapl Trin Hall Cam 63-69; V Greenside *Dur* 69-73; Chapl Shrewsbury Sch 73-77; V Batheaston w St Cath *B & W* 78-88; Preb Wells Cathl 87-88; Can Res and Prec 88-99; rtd 99; Perm to Offic *Sarum* from 01. *11 Fisherton Island, Salisbury SP2 7TG* Tel and fax (01722) 325266

LUCAS, Peter Stanley. b 21. Sarum Th Coll 48. **d** 50 **p** 51. C Gillingham *Sarum* 50-53; Min Heald Green St Cath CD *Ches* 53-58; V Heald Green St Cath 58-62; V Egremont St Jo 62-65; Canada from 66. *404-1241 Fairfield Road, Victoria BC V8V 3B3, Canada* E-mail pmlucas@smartt.com

LUCAS, Preb Ronald Charles. b 25. Trin Coll Cam BA49 MA57. Ridley Hall Cam. **d** 51 **p** 52. C Sevenoaks St Nic *Roch* 51-55; Cand Sec CPAS 55-61; Asst Sec 61-67; R St Helen Bishopsgate w St Martin Outwich *Lon* 61-80; P-in-c St Andr Undershaft w St Mary Axe 77-80; R St Helen Bishopsgate w St Andr Undershaft etc 80-98; Preb St Paul's Cathl 85-98; rtd 98. *16 Merrick Square, London SE1 4JB* Tel (020) 7407 4164

LUCAS, Ronald James. b 38. St Aid Birkenhead 64. **d** 67 **p** 68. C Swindon Ch Ch *Bris* 67-71; C Knowle St Martin 71-74; V Swindon St Jo 74-77; TR Swindon St Jo and St Andr 77-81; V Wroughton 81-83; TV Liskeard w St Keyne, St Pinnock and Morval *Truro* 83-87; R St Ive w Quethiock 87-91; R St Ive and Pensilva w Quethiock 91-01; rtd 01; Perm to Offic *Truro* from 01. *Ough's Folly, Castle Lane, Liskeard PL14 3AH* Tel (01579) 345611 E-mail ronjulialucas@hotmail.com

LUCAS, Ms Susan Catherine. b 59. City of Lon Poly BSc90. STETS 97. **d** 00 **p** 01. C Streetly *Lich* 00-02; C Pheasey 02-04; Chapl HM Pris Albany from 04. *HM Prison Albany, 55 Parkhurst Road, Newport PO30 5RS* Tel (01983) 524055

LUCAS, Susan Joyce. b 61. Bedf Coll Lon BA83 Univ of Wales (Swansea) PGCE90 Birkbeck Coll Lon MPhil95 PhD07. **d** 08. NSM Anfield St Marg *Liv* from 08. *39 Westbury Close, Liverpool L17 5BD* Tel 0151-727 3251 Mobile 07976-901389 E-mail sue.lucas@dsl.pipex.com

LUCAS, Mrs Vivienne Kathleen. b 44. Sarum & Wells Th Coll 84. **d** 87 **p** 94. Chapl Asst W Middx Univ Hosp Isleworth 87-92; Par Dn Whitton St Aug *Lon* 87-94; C Isleworth St Jo 94-97; P-in-c Isleworth St Mary 97-01; P-in-c Pirbright *Guildf* 01-06; rtd 06; Perm to Offic *York* from 07. *36 Harthill Avenue, Leconfield, Beverley HU17 7LN* Tel and fax (01964) 551519

LUCAS, William Wallace. b 29. Sarum Th Coll 56. **d** 59 **p** 60. C Stockton St Jo *Dur* 59-63; V Norton St Mich 63-81; R Broseley w Benthall *Heref* 81-93; P-in-c Jackfield and Linley w Willey and Barrow 81-93; rtd 93; Perm to Offic *Dur* 93-02. *1 Beckwith Mews, Seaham Street, Sunderland SR3 1HN*

LUCK, Benjamin Paul. b 53. BD. St Mich Coll Llan 80. **d** 83 **p** 84. C Blakenall Heath *Lich* 83-87; C Torpoint *Truro* 87-89; V Tuckingmill 89-96; C Knowle St Barn and H Cross Inns Court *Bris* 96-02; V Inns Court H Cross 02-05; C Washfield, Stoodleigh, Withleigh etc *Ex* 05-07; Chapl N Devon Hospice from 07. *The Rectory, Withleigh, Tiverton EX16 8JQ* Tel (01884) 250509

LUCKCUCK, Anthony Michael. b 47. Lon Univ BA70. Wycliffe Hall Ox 70. **d** 77 **p** 78. C Mansfield Woodhouse *S'well* 77-79; C Beeston 79-82; V Harworth 82-85; V Carlton from 85. *St John's Vicarage, 261 Oakdale Road, Carlton, Nottingham NG4 1BP* Tel 0115-987 2216 Mobile 07734-032900 E-mail amleclerc@btinternet.com

LUCKETT, Nicholas Frank. b 43. Ch Ch Ox BA65 DipEd66 MA69. OLM course 95. **d** 98 **p** 99. Hd Master St Edw C of E Middle Sch Leek 94-00; OLM Ipstones w Berkhamsytch and Onecote w Bradnop *Lich* 98-02; NSM Siddington w Preston *Glouc* 02-07; NSM S Cerney w Cerney Wick, Siddington and Preston 07-08; rtd 08; Perm to Offic *Nor* from 09. *Shillingstone,*

Church Road, Beetley, Dereham NR20 4AB Tel (01362) 860738
E-mail nandeluckett@hotmail.com

LUCKMAN, David Thomas William. b 71. Oak Hill Th Coll BA95 K Coll Lon PGCE96. CITC 98. **d** 00 **p** 01. C Portadown St Mark *Arm* 00-02; C Enniskillen *Clogh* 02-03; I Galloon w Drummully and Sallaghy 03-04; N Ireland Field Worker ICM 05-08. *53 Taughrane Lodge, Dollingstown, Craigavon BT66 7UH* Tel (028) 9167 7376 E-mail daveluckman@hotmail.com

LUCKRAFT, Christopher John. b 50. K Coll Lon BD80 AKC80. Ripon Coll Cuddesdon 80. **d** 81 **p** 82. C Sherborne w Castleton and Lillington *Sarum* 81-84; Bermuda 84-87; Chapl RN 87-07; R Merrow *Guildf* from 07. *St John's Rectory, 232 Epsom Road, Guildford GU4 7AA* Tel (01483) 452390
E-mail chrisluckraft@sky.com

LUCKRAFT, Ian Charles. b 47. Qu Coll Ox BA70 BSc81. Ripon Hall Ox 70. **d** 73 **p** 74. C Totteridge *St Alb* 73-77; C Broxbourne w Wormley 77-78; Lect Harrow Tech Coll 78-81; Perm to Offic *Ox* from 06. *4 Willes Close, Faringdon SN7 7DU* Tel (01367) 240135

LUCY CLARE, Sister. *See* WALKER, Margaret

LUDKIN, Miss Linda Elaine. b 50. NEOC 02. **d** 05 **p** 06. NSM Dunnington *York* from 05. *27A Lavender Grove, York YO26 5RX* Tel (01904) 784651
E-mail l.e.ludkin@btinternet.com

LUDLOW, Brian Peter. b 55. Lon Univ MB, BS78 Birm Univ MMedSc90 LRCP90 MRCS90 MRAeS87 AFOM90 MFOM92 FFOM01. WEMTC 01. **d** 04 **p** 05. NSM Winchcombe *Glouc* 04-06; NSM Cainscross w Selsley from 06. *The Rectory, Walkley Hill, Stroud GL5 3TX* Tel (01453) 752659 Mobile 07836-667530 E-mail revbrian@btopenworld.com

LUDLOW, Mrs Lesley Elizabeth. b 43. SEITE 97 OLM course 04. **d** 06 **p** 07. NSM Allington and Maidstone St Pet *Cant* from 06. *37 Tudor Avenue, Maidstone ME14 5HJ* Tel (01622) 673536 Mobile 07778-027031 E-mail lesley.ludlow@blueyonder.co.uk

LUDLOW, Lady Margaret Maude. b 56. WEMTC 98. **d** 01 **p** 02. C Winchcombe *Glouc* 01-05; P-in-c Rodborough from 05. *The Rectory, Walkley Hill, Stroud GL5 3TX* Tel (01453) 751344
E-mail revpeggy@btopenworld.com

LUDLOW, Archdeacon of. *See* MAGOWAN, The Rt Revd Alistair James

LUDLOW, Suffragan Bishop of. *See* MAGOWAN, The Rt Revd Alistair James

LUFF, Canon Alan Harold Frank. b 28. Univ Coll Ox MA54 ARCM77 Hon FGCM93. Westcott Ho Cam 54. **d** 56 **p** 57. C Strctford St Matt *Man* 56-59; C Swinton St Pet 59-61; Prec Man Cathl 61-68; V Dwygyfylchi *Ban* 68-79; Prec and Sacr Westmr Abbey 79-86; Prec 86-92; Can Res Birm Cathl 92-96; rtd 96; Perm to Offic *Llan* from 96. *12 Heol Ty'n-y-Cae, Cardiff CF14 6DJ* Tel and fax (029) 2061 6023

LUFF, Mrs Caroline Margaret Synia. b 44. St Hild Coll Dur BA65 Bris Univ CertEd66. SWMTC 87. **d** 90 **p** 94. NSM Teignmouth, Ideford w Luton, Ashcombe etc *Ex* 90-07; Chapl Trin Sch Teignmouth from 97; C Diptford, N Huish, Harberton, Harbertonford etc *Ex* from 07. *The Vicarage, Harberton, Totnes TQ9 7SA* Tel (01803) 868445
E-mail pgandcmsl@btinternet.com

LUFF, John Edward Deweer. b 46. STETS 04. **d** 07 **p** 08. NSM Guernsey St Peter Port *Win* from 07; Chapl States of Guernsey Bd of Health from 07. *La Neuve Maison Cottage, Rue de la Neuve Maison, St Saviour, Guernsey GY7 9TG* Tel (01481) 264772 E-mail johnluff@cwgsy.net

LUFF, Matthew John. b 70. Brighton Univ BA(QTS)95. Wycliffe Hall Ox 07. **d** 09. C Broadwater *Chich* from 09. *20 Grove Road, Worthing BN14 9DG* Tel 07875-190203 (mobile)
E-mail luff925@hotmail.com

LUFF, Preb Philip Garth. b 42. St Chad's Coll Dur BA63. **d** 65 **p** 66. C Sidmouth St Nic *Ex* 65-69; C Plymstock 69-71; Asst Chapl Worksop Coll Notts 71-74; V Gainsborough St Jo *Linc* 74-80; V E Teignmouth *Ex* 80-89; P-in-c W Teignmouth 85-89; TR Teignmouth, Ideford w Luton, Ashcombe etc 90-07; RD Kenn 01-05; Preb Ex Cathl 02-07; Chapl S Devon Healthcare NHS Trust 85-07; Chapl Trin Sch Teignmouth 88-97; rtd 07. *The Vicarage, Harberton, Totnes TQ9 7SA* Tel (01803) 868445
E-mail pgandcmsl@btinternet.com

LUGG, Donald Arthur. b 31. St Aid Birkenhead 56. **d** 59 **p** 60. C Folkestone H Trin w Ch Ch *Cant* 59-62; V Seasalter 62-66; Iran 67-73; V Cliftonville *Cant* 74-94; rtd 94; Perm to Offic *Cant* from 94. *Redcroft, Vulcan Close, Whitstable CT9 1DF* Tel (01227) 770434

LUGG, Stuart John. b 26. Glouc Th Course 74. **d** 76 **p** 77. NSM Fairford *Glouc* 76-79; P-in-c Kempsford w Welford 80-88; Perm to Offic 88-05. *Content, Station Road, South Cerney, Cirencester GL7 5UB* Tel (01285) 860498

LUKE, Anthony. b 58. Down Coll Cam BA81 MA85. Ridley Hall Cam 82. **d** 84 **p** 85. C Allestree *Derby* 84-87; C Oakham, Hambleton, Egleton, Braunston and Brooke *Pet* 87-88; V Allenton and Shelton Lock *Derby* 88-02; Dir Reader Tr 95-97; Warden of Readers 97-00; R Aston on Trent, Elvaston, Weston on Trent etc from 02; C Ticknall, Smisby and Stanton by Bridge

etc from 07; RD Melbourne from 07. *The Rectory, Rectory Gardens, Aston-on-Trent, Derby DE72 2AZ* Tel (01332) 792658 E-mail tonyluke@lineone.net

LUKE, Denise Elaine. b 60. Wolv Univ BEd92 Leeds Univ BA08. NOC 05. **d** 08 **p** 09. NSM Leesfield *Man* from 08. *11 The Grove, Dobcross, Oldham OL3 5RR* Tel (01457) 875830 Mobile 07894-046606 E-mail deniseluke@btinternet.com

LUMB, David Leslie. b 28. Jes Coll Cam BA52 MA56. Oak Hill Th Coll 52. **d** 54 **p** 55. C Walcot *B & W* 54-58; C Lenton *S'well* 58-60; V Handforth *Ches* 60-74; V Plymouth St Jude *Ex* 74-87; V Southminster *Chelmsf* 87-93; rtd 93; Perm to Offic *Worc* from 93. *13 Glebe Close, Redditch B98 0AW* Tel (01527) 528623

LUMBY, Jonathan Bertram. b 39. Em Coll Cam BA62 MA66 Lon Univ PGCE66. Ripon Hall Ox 63. **d** 64 **p** 65. C Moseley St Mary *Birm* 64-65; Asst Master Enfield Gr Sch 66-67; C Hall Green Ascension 67-70; V Melling *Liv* 70-81; P-in-c Milverton w Halse and Fitzhead *B & W* 81-82; R 82-86; P-in-c Gisburn and Dioc Rural Adv *Bradf* 90-93; P-in-c Easton w Colton and Marlingford *Nor* 95-98; Dioc Missr 95-98; R Eccleston and Pulford *Ches* 98-05; rtd 05; Hon C Redmarley D'Abitot, Bromesberrow, Pauntley etc *Glouc* 05-08. *Valentines Cottage, Hollybush, Ledbury HR8 1ET* Tel (01531) 650641

LUMBY, Simon. b 70. Coll of Resurr Mirfield 99. **d** 02 **p** 03. C Worksop Priory *S'well* 02-06; P-in-c Leic St Aid 06-09; V from 09. *St Aidan's Vicarage, St Oswald's Road, Leicester LE3 6RJ* Tel 0116-287 2342 Mobile 07983-609290
E-mail fathersimonlumby@btinternet.com

LUMBY, Simon John. b 56. Hull Univ BSc80 Open Univ MTh01. St Jo Coll Nottm 99. **d** 01 **p** 04. C Wirksworth *Derby* 01-06; R Clifton Campville w Edingale and Harlaston *Lich* from 06; P-in-c Thorpe Constantine from 06; P-in-c Elford from 06. *The Rectory, 32 Main Street, Clifton Campville, Tamworth B79 0AP* Tel (01827) 373257 E-mail rector@measevalley.org.uk

LUMGAIR, Michael Hugh Crawford. b 43. Lon Univ BD71. Oak Hill Th Coll 66. **d** 71 **p** 72. C Chorleywood Ch Ch *St Alb* 71-74; C Prestonville St Luke *Chich* 74-75; C Attenborough *S'well* 75-80; R Tollerton 80-91; V Bexleyheath St Pet *Roch* 91-06; rtd 06. *11 Bromley College, London Road, Bromley BR1 1PE* Tel (020) 8290 2011 E-mail michael@lumgair.plus.com

LUMLEY (née HATFIELD), Rebecca Alison. b 76. St Andr Univ MTheol99. Cranmer Hall Dur 02. **d** 04 **p** 05. C Haughton le Skerne *Dur* 04-09; V Heworth St Alb from 09. *The Vicarage, Coldwell Park Drive, Gateshead NE10 9BY* Tel 0191-438 1720 Mobile 07930-631936

LUMMIS, Elizabeth Howieson. *See* McNAB, Mrs Elizabeth Howieson

LUMSDON, Keith. b 45. Linc Th Coll 68. **d** 71 **p** 72. C S Westoe *Dur* 71-74; C Jarrow St Paul 74-77; TV Jarrow 77-88; V Ferryhill 88-07; P-in-c Cornforth 03-07; V Cornforth and Ferryhill from 07; AD Sedgefield from 05. *St Luke's Vicarage, Church Lane, Ferryhill DL17 8LT* Tel (01740) 651438

LUND, David Peter. b 46. NOC 88. **d** 91 **p** 92. C Maghull *Liv* 91-94; V Hindley All SS 94-01; V Teddington St Mark and Hampton Wick *Lon* from 01. *The Vicarage, 23 St Mark's Road, Teddington TW11 9DE* Tel (020) 8977 4067 Mobile 07813-493761 E-mail saintseddington@aol.com

LUND, John Edward. b 48. St Jo Coll Dur 78. **d** 80 **p** 81. C Peterlee *Dur* 80-83; C Bishopton w Gt Stainton 83-85; C Redmarshall 83-85; C Grindon and Stillington 83-85; V Hart w Elwick Hall 85-09; Hon Chapl Miss to Seamen 85-99; Chapl Hartlepool and E Durham NHS Trust 94-99; Chapl N Tees and Hartlepool NHS Trust 99-04; rtd 09. *16 Chelker Close, Hartlepool TS26 0QW*

✠**LUNGA, The Rt Revd Cleophus.** b 66. UNISA BTh00. Bp Gaul Th Coll Harare 91. **d** 93 **p** 94 **c** 09. Zimbabwe 94-03; TV Coventry Caludon 03-09; Bp Matabeleland from 09. *PO Box 2422, Bulawayo, Zimbabwe* Tel (00263) (9) 61370 Fax 68353

LUNGLEY, Canon John Sydney. b 41. St Pet Coll Ox BA64 MA70. St Steph Ho Ox 64. **d** 66 **p** 67. C Burslem St Werburgh *Lich* 66-70; C Codsall 70-73; V Ocker Hill 73-88; RD Wednesbury 84-88; V Kingswinford St Mary 88-93; V Kingswinford St Mary *Worc* 93-96; TR 96-07; Hon Can Worc Cathl 94-07; rtd 07; Perm to Offic *Lich* from 07. *Trevethin, 38 Common Road, Wombourne, Wolverhampton WV5 0EZ* Tel (01902) 896292 E-mail johnlungley@btinternet.com

LUNN, Preb Brooke Kingsmill. b 32. TCD BA62 MA66. Chich Th Coll 62. **d** 64 **p** 65. C Northolt Park St Barn *Lon* 64-66; C N St Pancras All Hallows 66-68; P-in-c Hornsey St Luke 68-79; V Stroud Green H Trin 79-02; AD W Haringey 90-95; Preb St Paul's Cathl 96-02; rtd 02; Perm to Offic *Lon* from 02. *The Charterhouse, Charterhouse Square, London EC1M 6AN* Tel (020) 7251 5143

LUNN, Christopher James Edward. b 34. AKC58. **d** 59 **p** 60. C Clapham H Trin *S'wark* 59-62; C Cranleigh *Guildf* 63-64; C Ham St Andr *S'wark* 64-66; V Ham St Rich 66-75; V Coulsdon St Andr 75-96; rtd 96. *24 Penally Heights, Penally, Tenby SA70 7QP* Tel (01834) 845277

LUNN, David. b 47. Bris Univ BSc69. St Jo Coll Dur BA73. **d** 74 **p** 75. C Aigburth *Liv* 74-77; C Slough *Ox* 77-81; P-in-c

Haversham w Lt Linford 81-84; R Haversham w Lt Linford, Tyringham w Filgrave 84-93; RD Newport 86-92; TR Walton Milton Keynes from 93; Dioc Ecum Officer from 00. *The Rectory, Walton Road, Wavendon, Milton Keynes MK17 8LW* Tel (01908) 582839

✠**LUNN, The Rt Revd David Ramsay.** b 30. K Coll Cam BA53 MA57. Cuddesdon Coll 53. **d** 55 **p** 56 **c** 80. C Sugley *Newc* 55-59; C N Gosforth 59-63; Chapl Linc Th Coll 63-66; Sub-Warden 66-70; V Cullercoats St Geo *Newc* 71-72; TR 72-80; RD Tynemouth 75-80; Bp Sheff 80-97; rtd 97; Perm to Offic *York* 97-99; Hon Asst Bp York from 99. *Rivendell, 28 Southfield Road, Wetwang, Driffield YO25 9XX* Tel (01377) 236657

LUNN, Leonard Arthur. b 42. Culham Coll of Educn CertEd64. Trin Coll Bris 69. **d** 72 **p** 73. C Walthamstow St Mary w St Steph *Chelmsf* 72-75; V Collier Row St Jas 75-85; V Collier Row St Jas and Havering-atte-Bower 86-87; Sen Chapl St Chris Hospice Sydenham *S'wark* 87-04; Hon C Redlynch and Morgan's Vale *Sarum* 04-06; Hon C Forest and Avon 06-09. *The Vicarage, Vicarage Road, Lover, Salisbury SP5 2PE* Tel (01725) 510439 E-mail len.lunn@btopenworld.com

LUNN, Maureen Susan. b 48. Middx Univ BSc00. NTMTC BA07. **d** 07. NSM Enfield St Jas *Lon* from 07. *62 First Avenue, Enfield EN1 1BN* Tel (020) 8366 0592

LUNN, Mrs Rosemary Christine. b 51. Bris Univ BA72. Trin Coll Bris 98. **d** 00 **p** 01. NSM Stoke Bishop *Bris* 00-01; C Chippenham St Pet 01-04; Hon Min Can Bris Cathl 02-04; P-in-c Wraxall *B & W* 04-09; R from 09. *The Rectory, 8 School View, Wraxall, Bristol BS48 1HG* Tel (01275) 857086 Mobile 07799-497533

LUNN, Sarah Anne. b 63. Lanc Univ BMus84 Man Metrop Univ MA93. Cranmer Hall Dur 00. **d** 02 **p** 03. C Kirkby Lonsdale *Carl* 02-07; P-in-c Long Marton w Dufton and w Milburn 07-08; TV Heart of Eden from 08. *The Rectory, Long Marton, Appleby-in-Westmorland CA16 6BN* Tel (01768) 361269 E-mail sarahlunn@care4free.net

LUNNEY, Canon Henry. b 31. ACIB57. Wycliffe Hall Ox 73. **d** 74 **p** 75. C Ipswich St Aug *St E* 74-77; P-in-c Westerfield w Tuddenham St Martin 77-83; R Westerfield and Tuddenham w Witnesham 83-97; Asst Dioc Chr Stewardship Adv 78-83; Hon Can St E Cathl 92-97; rtd 97; Perm to Offic *St E* from 98. *6 Karen Close, Ipswich IP1 4LP* Tel (01473) 252876

LUNNON, Canon Robert Reginald. b 31. K Coll Lon BD55 AKC55 Kent Univ MA99. St Boniface Warminster 55. **d** 56 **p** 57. C Maidstone St Mich *Cant* 56-58; C Deal St Leon 58-62; V Sturry 63-68; V Norbury St Steph 68-77; V Orpington All SS *Roch* 77-96; RD Orpington 79-95; Hon Can Roch Cathl 96; rtd 96; Perm to Offic *Cant* from 96. *10 King Edward Road, Deal CT14 6QL* Tel (01304) 364898

LUNT, Colin Peter. b 54. York Univ BA75 Bris Univ MA02. Trin Coll Bris 95. **d** 97 **p** 98. C Westbury-on-Trym H Trin *Bris* 97-00; V Coalpit Heath from 00. *The Vicarage, Beesmoor Road, Coalpit Heath, Bristol BS36 2RP* Tel and fax (01454) 775129 E-mail colin@lunt.co.uk

LUNT, Derek. b 32. St Jo Coll Dur 51. St Aid Birkenhead 55. **d** 57 **p** 58. C Toxteth Park Ch Ch *Liv* 57-59; C Prescot 59-61; R Much Dewchurch w Llanwarne and Llandinabo *Heref* 61-67; R Pembridge 67-74; Chapl Lucton Sch 71-74; rtd 91; Perm to Offic *Worc* from 93. *Olcote, 5 Mansfield Road, Malvern WR14 2WE* Tel (01684) 573932

LUNT, Margaret Joan. b 44. Leeds Univ MB, ChB68. Cranmer Hall Dur 91. **d** 94 **p** 95. C Stanford-le-Hope w Mucking *Chelmsf* 94-97; C Rayleigh 97-00; TV 00-03; TV Rivers Team *Sheff* from 03. *24 Highgate, Tinsley, Sheffield S9 1WL* Tel 0114-244 1740 E-mail robertlunt@luntrfreeserve.co.uk

LURIE, Miss Gillian Ruth. b 42. LRAM62 GNSM63 ACertCM80. Gilmore Ho 68. **dss** 74 **d** 87 **p** 94. Camberwell St Phil and St Mark *S'wark* 74-76; Haddenham *Ely* 76-79; Dioc Lay Min Adv 79-86; Longthorpe *Pet* 79-81; Pet H Spirit Bretton 81-86; Bramley *Ripon* 86-93; C 87-88; TD 88-93; P-in-c Methley w Mickletown 93-98; R 98-01; rtd 02; Perm to Offic *Cant* from 02. *42A Cuthbert Road, Westgate-on-Sea CT8 8NR* Tel and fax (01843) 831698 E-mail gillandjean@hotmail.com

LURY, Anthony Patrick. b 49. K Coll Lon BD71 AKC71. St Aug Coll Cant 71. **d** 72 **p** 73. C Richmond St Mary *S'wark* 72-76; P-in-c Streatham Hill St Marg 76-81; V Salfords 81-90; V Emscote *Cov* 90-01; P-in-c Ascot Heath *Ox* 01-06; NSM The Churn from 06. *The Rectory, Church Lane, South Moreton, Didcot OX11 9AF* Tel (01235) 812042 E-mail anthonyplury@btinternet.com

LUSBY, Dennis John. b 27. Brentwood Coll of Educn CertEd70. **d** 93 **p** 94. NSM Grayshott *Guildf* 93-99; Perm to Offic from 99. *Squirrels Drey, Waggoners Way, Grayshott, Hindhead GU26 6DX* Tel (01428) 604419

LUSCOMBE, John Nickels. b 45. Birm Univ BA99. AKC63 **d** 69 **p** 70. C Stoke Newington St Faith, St Matthias and All SS *Lon* 69-74; V Tottenham St Phil 74-81; Zimbabwe 82-86; V Queensbury All SS *Lon* 86-99; V Estover *Ex* 99-01; Dioc Ecum Officer 99-01; V Norton *St Alb* from 01; RD Hitchin 02-07.

Norton Vicarage, 17 Norton Way North, Letchworth Garden City SG6 1BY Tel (01462) 685059 *or* 678133 E-mail jluscombe@callnetuk.com

✠**LUSCOMBE, The Rt Revd Lawrence Edward (Ted).** b 24. Dundee Univ LLD87 MPhil91 PhD93 ACA52 FSA80 FRSA87. K Coll Lon 63. **d** 63 **p** 64 **c** 75. C Glas St Marg 63-66; R Paisley St Barn 66-71; Provost St Paul's Cathl Dundee 71-75; R Dundee St Paul 71-75; Bp Bre 75-90; Primus 85-90; rtd 90; Perm to Offic *Bre* from 90. *Woodville, Kirkton of Tealing, Dundee DD4 0RD* Tel (01382) 380331

LUSITANIAN CHURCH, Bishop of the. See SOARES, The Rt Revd Fernando da Luz

LUSTED, Jack Andrew. b 58. Sussex Univ BSc79 PGCE81. St Steph Ho Ox 88. **d** 90 **p** 91. C Moulsecoomb *Chich* 90-93; C Southwick St Mich 93-97; R Lurgashall, Lodsworth and Selham 97-07; V Salehurst from 07. *Salehurst Vicarage, Fair Lane, Robertsbridge TN32 5AR* Tel (01580) 880408 E-mail jack.lusted@btinternet.com

LUSTY, Tom Peter. b 71. Glas Univ BD94 Leeds Univ MA06. Coll of Resurr Mirfield 97. **d** 99 **p** 00. C Billingshurst *Chich* 99-02; Asst Chapl Leeds Teaching Hosps NHS Trust 02-06; Chapl Wheatfields Hospice from 06. *Wheatfields Hospice, Grove Road, Leeds LS6 2AE* Tel 0113-278 7249 Fax 230 2778

LUTHER, Canon Richard Grenville Litton. b 42. Lon Univ BD64. Tyndale Hall Bris 66. **d** 68 **p** 69. C Preston St Mary *Blackb* 68-70; C Bishopsworth *Bris* 70-71; C Radipole *Sarum* 72-76; TV Radipole and Melcombe Regis 77-90; TR Hampreston 90-07; Can and Preb Sarum Cathl 00-07; rtd 07. *49 North Street, Charminster, Dorchester DT2 9RN* Tel (01305) 251547

LUTHER THOMAS, The Ven Ilar Roy. b 30. St D Coll Lamp BA51. St Mich Coll Llan 51. **d** 53 **p** 54. C Oystermouth *S & B* 53-56; C Gorseinon 56-59; R Llanbadarn Fawr and Llandegley 59-60; R Llanbadarn Fawr, Llandegley and Llanfihangel etc 60-65; CF (ACF) 62-90; Children's Adv *S & B* 63-77; V Knighton and Norton 65-79; RD Knighton 66-79; V Sketty 79-89; Can Brecon Cathl from 75; Treas 87-88; Chan 88-90; Adn Gower 90-95; rtd 95. *2 Druids Close, Mumbles, Swansea SA3 5TY* Tel (01792) 419455

✠**LUXMOORE, The Rt Revd Christopher Charles.** b 26. Trin Coll Cam BA50 MA54. Chich Th Coll 50. **d** 52 **p** 53 **c** 84. C Newc St Jo 52-55; C-in-c Newsham St Bede CD 55-57; V Newsham 57-58; Trinidad and Tobago 58-66; V Headingley *Ripon* 67-81; Hon Can Ripon Cathl 80-81; Can Res and Prec Chich Cathl 81-84; Bp Bermuda 84-89; Adn Lewes and Hastings *Chich* 89-91; rtd 91; Provost Woodard Corp (S Division) 89-96; Hon Asst Bp Chich from 91. *42 Willowbed Drive, Chichester PO19 8JB* Tel (01243) 784680

LYALL, Canon Graham. b 37. Univ of Wales (Lamp) BA61. Qu Coll Birm 61. **d** 63 **p** 64. C Middlesbrough Ascension *York* 63-67; C Kidderminster St Mary *Worc* 67-72; V Dudley St Aug Holly Hall 72-79; P-in-c Barbourne 79-81; V 81-93; RD Worc E 83-89; TR Malvern Link w Cowleigh 93-04; Hon Can Worc Cathl 85-04; rtd 04; Perm to Offic *Worc* from 04. *44 Victoria Street, Worcester WR3 7BD* Tel (01905) 20511

LYALL, Richard Keith. b 70. Glas Univ BSc92 MSc95 Strathclyde Univ MSc97. Trin Coll Bris BA02. **d** 02 **p** 03. C Gateacre *Liv* 02-06; C Haydock St Mark 06-08; Canada from 08. *Address temp unknown* E-mail rklyall@yahoo.com

LYDDON, David Andrew. b 47. Lon Univ BDS70 LDS70. SW Minl Tr Course 90. **d** 93 **p** 94. NSM Tiverton St Pet *Ex* 93-95; NSM Tiverton St Pet w Chevithorne 95-96; NSM W Exe 96-01; NSM Tiverton St Geo and St Paul from 01. *Hightrees, 19 Patches Road, Tiverton EX16 5AH* Tel (01884) 257250 E-mail dlyddon597@aol.uk

LYDON, Mrs Barbara. b 34. Gilmore Ho 64. **dss** 72 **d** 87 **p** 94. Rastrick St Matt *Wakef* 72-85; Upper Hopton 85-87; Par Dn 87; Dn-in-c Kellington w Whitley 87-94; P-in-c 94-95; rtd 95; Perm to Offic *Wakef* from 95. *17 Garlick Street, Brighouse HD6 3PW* Tel (01484) 722704

LYES-WILSDON, Canon Patricia Mary. b 45. Open Univ BA87 ALA65. Glouc Sch of Min 84 Qu Coll Birm 86. **d** 87 **p** 94. C Thornbury *Glouc* 87-94; P-in-c Cromhall w Tortworth and Tytherington 94-03; Asst Dioc Dir of Ords 90-98; Dioc Voc Officer 94-01; RD Hawkesbury 98-04; Dioc Adv for Women's Min from 01; Hon Can Glouc Cathl from 02; R Cromhall, Tortworth, Tytherington, Falfield etc from 02. *The New Rectory, Rectory Lane, Cromhall, Wotton-under-Edge GL12 8AN* Tel (01454) 294767 E-mail revd.pat@virgin.net

LYMBERY, Peter. b 32. JP73. SAOMC 95. **d** 98 **p** 99. OLM Stewkley w Soulbury and Drayton Parslow *Ox* from 98; Dep Chapl Guild of Servants of the Sanctuary from 00; P Assoc Shrine of Our Lady of Walsingham from 00. *10 Hartwell Crescent, Leighton Buzzard LU7 1NP* Tel (01525) 371235

LYNAS, The Very Revd Norman Noel. b 55. St Andr Univ MTheol78. CITC 78. **d** 79 **p** 80. C Knockbreda *D & D* 79-81; C Holywood 81-85; I Portadown St Columba *Arm* 85-91; Dioc Communications Officer 86-89; Tutor for Aux Min (Arm) 88-91; Radio Officer (Arm) 90-91; I Kilkenny w Aghour and

Kilmanagh *C & O* from 91; Dean Ossory from 91; Can Leighlin Cathl from 91; Dioc Dir of Ords from 05. *The Deanery, Kilkenny, Republic of Ireland* Tel (00353) (56) 772 1516 Fax 775 1817 E-mail normanlynas@eircom.net or dean@ossory.anglican.org

LYNAS, Preb Stephen Brian. b 52. MBE00. St Jo Coll Nottm BTh77. **d** 78 **p** 79. C Penn *Lich* 78-81; Relig Progr Org BBC Radio Stoke-on-Trent 81-84; C Hanley H Ev 81-82; C Edensor 82-84; Relig Progr Producer BBC Bris 85-88; Relig Progr Sen Producer BBC S & W England 88-91; Hd Relig Progr TV South 91-92; Community (and Relig) Affairs Ed Westcountry TV 92-96; Abps' Officer for Millennium 96-01; Dioc Resources Adv *B & W* 01-07; Sen Chapl and Adv to Bps B & W and Taunton from 07; Preb Wells Cathl from 07. *Old Honeygar Cottage, Honeygar Lane, Westhay, Glastonbury BA6 9TS* Tel (01749) 672341 E-mail chaplain@bathwells.anglican.org

LYNCH, Eithne Elizabeth Mary. b 45. CITC BTh94. **d** 97 **p** 98. C Douglas Union w Frankfield *C, C & R* 97-01; Min Can Cork Cathl 98-07; Bp's Dom Chapl from 99; I Kilmoe Union from 01. *Altar Rectory, Toormore, Skibbereen, Co Cork, Republic of Ireland* Tel (00353) (28) 28249 Mobile 86-253 5002 E-mail eithnel@eircom.net

LYNCH, James. b 44. EAMTC 93. **d** 96 **p** 97. NSM High Oak *Nor* 96-97; NSM High Oak, Hingham and Scoulton w Wood Rising 97-99; Asst Chapl Norfolk Mental Health Care NHS Trust 99-03; P-in-c Nor St Steph 99-03; NSM Blanchland w Hunstanworth and Edmundbyers etc *Newc* from 03; NSM Slaley from 03; NSM Healey from 03; NSM Whittonstall from 03. *The Vicarage, Blanchland, Consett DH8 9ST* Tel (01434) 675141

LYNCH, Ms Sally Margaret. b 60. St Jo Coll Dur BA81 UEA MA94 FRSA96. Westcott Ho Cam 04. **d** 08 **p** 09. C Romford St Edw *Chelmsf* from 08. *54 Parkside Avenue, Romford RM1 4ND* Tel (01708) 725462 E-mail sally.lynch@lineone.net

LYNCH, Sheila. b 56. **d** 09. OLM Rossendale Middle Valley *Man* from 09. *70 Fairfield Avenue, Rossendale BB4 9TH* Tel (01706) 217438 Mobile 07711-992004 E-mail sheila.lynch@btinternet.com

LYNCH-WATSON, Graham Leslie. b 30. AKC55. **d** 56 **p** 57. C New Eltham All SS *S'wark* 56-60; C W Brompton St Mary *Lon* 60-62; V Camberwell St Bart *S'wark* 62-66; V Purley St Barn 67-77; C Caversham *Ox* 77-81; C Caversham St Pet and Mapledurham etc 81-85; P-in-c Warwick St Paul *Cov* 85-86; V 86-92; rtd 92; Perm to Offic *Ox* 96-00. *11 Crouch Street, Banbury OX16 9PP* Tel (01295) 263172

LYNE, Peter. b 27. Sheff Univ BA51. Qu Coll Birm 51. **d** 53 **p** 54. C Newland St Aug *York* 53-55; C Harworth *S'well* 55-56; C Burbage *Derby* 56-58; V Horsley Woodhouse 58-62; V Rawcliffe *Sheff* 62-69; V Elvaston and Shardlow *Derby* 69-74; P-in-c Ashbourne St Jo 74-80; P-in-c Kniveton w Hognaston 75-80; P-in-c Fenny Bentley, Thorpe and Tissington 77-78; P-in-c Osmaston w Edlaston 78-80; P-in-c Lt Eaton 80-84; P-in-c Holbrooke 80-84; V Holbrook and Lt Eaton 84-91; rtd 91; Perm to Offic *Derby* from 91. *3 Vicarage Close, High Street, Belper DE56 1TB* Tel (01773) 829188

LYNE, Roger Howard. b 28. Mert Coll Ox BA52 MA56. Oak Hill Th Coll 52. **d** 54 **p** 55. C Rugby St Matt *Cov* 54-58; C Weymouth St Jo *Sarum* 58-61; V Newchapel *Lich* 61-65; C Bucknall and Bagnall 76-81; Perm to Offic *Win* from 82; rtd 88. *21 Copse Road, Burley, Ringwood BH24 4EG* Tel (01425) 402232

LYNESS, Nicholas Jonathan. b 55. Oak Hill Th Coll BA97. **d** 97. C Reading Greyfriars *Ox* 97-98. *3 Roe Green Cottages, Roe Green, Sandon, Buntingford SG9 0QE* Tel (01763) 288172 Mobile 07802-730485

LYNETT, Anthony Martin. b 54. K Coll Lon BD75 AKC75 Darw Coll Cam PGCE76. Sarum & Wells Th Coll 77. **d** 78 **p** 79. C Swindon Ch Ch *Bris* 78-81; C Leckhampton SS Phil and Jas w Cheltenham St Jas *Glouc* 81-83; Asst Chapl HM Pris Glouc 83-88; Chapl 91-98; V Coney Hill *Glouc* 83-88; Chapl HM YOI Deerbolt 88-91; P-in-c Glouc St Mark 91-99; P-in-c Glouc St Mary de Crypt w St Jo, Ch Ch etc 98-99; Chapl HM Pris Wellingborough 99-01; V Wellingborough All SS *Pet* from 01; RD Wellingborough from 07. *The Vicarage, 154 Midland Road, Wellingborough NN8 1NF* Tel (01933) 227101 E-mail tartleknock@aol.com

LYNN, Anthony Hilton. b 44. Golds Coll Lon TCert66 Open Univ BA80. SAOMC 95. **d** 98 **p** 99. NSM Stanford in the Vale w Goosey and Hatford *Ox* 98-00; NSM Cherbury w Gainfield 00-03; TV Hermitage from 03. *The Rectory, Yattendon, Thatcham RG18 0UR* Tel (01635) 201203 E-mail tony@hlynn.fsnet.co.uk

LYNN, Mrs Antonia Jane. b 59. Girton Coll Cam BA80 MA84. St Steph Ho Ox 82. **dss** 84 **d** 87. Portsm Cathl 84-87; Dn-in-c Camberwell St Mich w All So w Em *S'wark* 87-91; Par Dn Newington St Mary 87-91; Perm to Offic 91-94; Chapl Horton Hosp Epsom 91-94; Gen Sec Guild of Health from 94; Hon Par Dn Ewell *Guildf* 94-99. *7 Kingsmead Close, West Ewell, Epsom KT19 9RD* Tel (020) 8786 8983

LYNN, Frank Trevor. b 36. Keble Coll Ox BA61 MA63. St Steph Ho Ox 61. **d** 63 **p** 64. C W Derby St Mary *Liv* 63-65; C Chorley

Ches 65-68; V Altrincham St Jo 68-72; Chapl RN 72-88; Hon C Walworth St Jo *S'wark* 88-90; C Cheam 90-96; rtd 99. *7 Kingsmead Close, West Ewell, Epsom KT19 9RD* Tel (020) 8786 8983

LYNN, Jeffrey. b 39. Moore Th Coll Sydney 67 EMMTC 76. **d** 79 **p** 80. C Littleover *Derby* 79-80; Hon C Allestree 80-85; Chapl HM Pris Man 85-86; Kirkham 86-93; Wakef 93-95; Sudbury and Foston Hall 95-96; rtd 96; Perm to Offic *Blackb* from 98. *48 South Park, Lytham St Annes FY8 4QQ* Tel (01253) 730490

LYNN, Peter Anthony. b 38. Keele Univ BA62 St Jo Coll Cam BA64 MA68 PhD72. Westcott Ho Cam 67. **d** 68 **p** 69. C Soham *Ely* 68-72; Min Can St Paul's Cathl 72-78; Perm to Offic *St Alb* 78-86; Min Can and Sacr St Paul's Cathl 86-88; C Westmr St Matt 89-91; V Glynde, W Firle and Beddingham *Chich* 91-03; rtd 03. *119 Stanford Avenue, Brighton BN1 6FA* Tel (01273) 553361

LYNN, Trevor. *See* LYNN, Frank Trevor

LYNN, Archdeacon of. *See* ASHE, The Ven Francis John

LYNN, Suffragan Bishop of. *See* LANGSTAFF, The Rt Revd James Henry

LYON, Adrian David. b 55. Coll of Resurr Mirfield 84. **d** 87 **p** 88. C Crewe St Andr *Ches* 87-90; C Altrincham St Geo 90-91; TV Accrington *Blackb* 91-00; TR Accrington Ch the King from 00. *St Peter's Vicarage, 151 Willows Lane, Accrington BB5 0LR* Tel and fax (01254) 382173 E-mail lyons@ddens.freeserve.co.uk

LYON, Christopher David. b 55. Strathclyde Univ LLB75 Edin Univ BD81. Edin Th Coll 78. **d** 81 **p** 82. C Dumfries *Glas* 81-84; P-in-c Alexandria 84-88; R Greenock 88-00; R Ayr, Girvan and Maybole 00-02; Chapl Luxembourg *Eur* from 02. *89 rue de Mühlenbach, L-2168 Luxembourg* Tel and fax (00352) 439593 E-mail chris.lyon@escc.lu

LYON, Dennis. b 36. Wycliffe Hall Ox 64. **d** 67 **p** 68. C Woodthorpe *S'well* 67-70; Warden Walton Cen 70-72; V W Derby Gd Shep *Liv* 72-81; V Billinge 81-00; AD Wigan W 89-00; rtd 00; Perm to Offic *Liv* from 01. *10 Arniam Road, Rainford, St Helens WA11 8BU* Tel (01744) 885623

LYON, Canon Donald Robert. b 20. Trin Coll Cam BA41 PhD44 MA45. Linc Th Coll 46. **d** 47 **p** 48. C Dursley *Glouc* 47-51; C Brislington St Luke 51-52; V Glouc St Mark 52-85; Hon Can Glouc Cathl 74-90; RD Glouc City 77-83; rtd 85; Perm to Offic *Glouc* 86-97. *Trevone Care Home, 22 Denmark Road, Gloucester GL1 3HZ* Tel (01452) 529072

LYON, Miss Jane Madeline. b 50. Derby Univ MA05. Ripon Coll Cuddesdon 07. **d** 09. NSM Derby St Andrew St w Osmund from 09. *21 Cedar Close, Ashbourne DE6 1FJ* Tel (01335) 345408 Mobile 07974-806636 E-mail janelyon0910@tiscali.co.uk

LYON, Joan Barace. b 50. Strathclyde Univ BA70. TISEC 94. **d** 96 **p** 00. NSM Glas E End 96-00; Asst Chapl Luxembourg *Eur* from 05. *89 rue de Mühlenbach, L-2168 Luxembourg* Tel and fax (00352) 439593 E-mail joanblyon@hotmail.com

LYON, John Forrester. b 39. Edin Th Coll CertEd95. **d** 95 **p** 96. C Greenock *Glas* 95-98; C Gourock 95-98; Chapl Ardgowan Hospice 95-98; P-in-c Glas Gd Shep and Ascension 98-07; rtd 07. *28 Demondale Road, Arbroath DD11 1TR* E-mail revjohnlyon@btinternet.com

LYON, John Harry. b 51. S Dios Minl Tr Scheme 86. **d** 89 **p** 90. NSM S Patcham *Chich* 89-91; C Chich St Paul and St Pet 91-94; R Earnley and E Wittering 94-04; V E Preston w Kingston from 04. *The Vicarage, 33 Vicarage Lane, East Preston, Littlehampton BN16 2SP* Tel (01903) 783318 E-mail revdjohnlyon@dsl.pipex.com

LYONS, Bruce Twyford. b 37. K Alfred's Coll Win CertEd61. Tyndale Hall Bris. **d** 70 **p** 71. C Virginia Water *Guildf* 70-73; Chapl Ostend w Knokke and Bruges *Eur* 73-78; V E Ham St Paul *Chelmsf* 78-85; V St Alb Ch Ch *St Alb* 85-91; Chapl Wellingborough Sch 92-95; P-in-c Stogumber w Nettlecombe and Monksilver *B & W* 96-98; P-in-c Ostend w Knokke and Bruges *Eur* 98-00; NSM Newbury Deanery *Ox* 01; Chapl Milton Abbey Sch Dorset 01-02; rtd 02; Perm to Offic *Sarum* from 01. *8 Worgret Road, Wareham BH20 4PJ* Tel (01929) 554973 E-mail bruce.lyons1@virgin.net

LYONS, Canon Edward Charles. b 44. Nottm Univ BTh75 LTh. St Jo Coll Nottm 71. **d** 75 **p** 76. C Cambridge St Martin *Ely* 75-78; P-in-c Bestwood Park *S'well* 78-85; R W Hallam and Mapperley *Derby* 85-98; P-in-c Brownsover CD *Cov* 98-02; V Brownsover 02-06; V Clifton upon Dunsmore w Newton and Brownsover from 07; RD Rugby 99-06; Dioc Ecum Officer 03-06; Hon Can Cov Cathl from 07. *43 Bowfell, Brownsover, Rugby CV21 1JF* Tel (01788) 573696 E-mail ted.lyons@btinternet.com

LYONS, Graham Selby. b 29. MBE84. Open Univ BA79. **d** 97 **p** 99. NSM New Eltham All SS *S'wark* 97-04. *56 Cadwallon Road, London SE9 3PY* Tel (020) 8850 6576 E-mail holyons2@aol.com

LYONS, Margaret Rose Marie. b 47. **d** 89. OLM Gainsborough All SS *Linc* 89-91; Hon C Low Moor *Bradf* 04-05; Hon C Oakenshaw, Wyke and Low Moor from 06. *1C Common Road, Low Moor, Bradford BD12 0PN* Tel 07940-558062 (mobile)

LYONS, Paul. b 67. Ulster Univ BA91. TCD Div Sch BTh98. **d** 98 **p** 99. C Seapatrick *D & D* 98-03; I Greenisland *Conn* from 03. *4 Tinamara, Upper Station Road, Greenisland, Carrickfergus BT38 8FE* Tel (028) 9086 3421 *or* 9085 9676 Mobile 07791-472225 E-mail greenisland@connor.anglican.org

LYONS, Paul Benson. b 44. Qu Coll Birm 68. **d** 69 **p** 70. C Rugby St Andr *Cov* 69-70; C Moston St Jo *Man* 70-72; PV Llan Cathl 73-74; C Brookfield St Anne, Highgate Rise *Lon* 74-75; Perm to Offic 76-82; C Westmr St Sav and St Jas Less 82-86; V Gt Cambridge Road St Jo and St Jas from 86. *St John's Vicarage, 113 Creighton Road, London N17 8JS* Tel (020) 8808 4077 E-mail stjohnstjames@hotmail.com

LYONS, William. b 22. LNSM course 78. **d** 80 **p** 81. NSM Glenrothes *St And* 80-81; NSM Kirkcaldy 81-91; NSM Kinghorn 81-91; rtd 91. *24 Auchmithie Place, Glenrothes KY7 4TY* Tel (01592) 630757

LYTTLE, Norma Irene. b 47. CITC. **d** 01 **p** 02. Aux Min Drumachose *D & R* 01-04; Aux Min Dungiven w Bovevagh 04-07; Bp's C Leckpatrick w Dunnalong 07-09; I from 09. *The Rectory, 1 Lowertown Road, Ballymagorry, Strabane BT82 0LE* Tel and fax (028) 7188 3545 Mobile 07742-836688 E-mail leckpatrick@derry.anglican.org

M

MABBS, Miss Margaret Joyce. b 24. St Hilda's Coll Ox BA45 MA47 DipEd46. S'wark Ord Course 79. **dss** 82 **d** 87 **p** 94. Eltham Park St Luke *S'wark* 82-05; NSM 87-05; Perm to Offic from 05. *70 Westmount Road, London SE9 1JE* Tel (020) 8850 4621

McADAM, Gordon Paul. b 66. QUB BSc88 TCD BTh93. CITC 90. **d** 93 **p** 94. C Drumglass w Moygashel *Arm* 93-96; I Dungiven w Bovevagh *D & R* 96-02; I Loughgall w Grange *Arm* from 02. *The Rectory, 2 Main Street, Loughgall, Armagh BT61 8HZ* Tel (028) 3889 1587 E-mail loughgall@armagh.anglican.org

McADAM, Canon Michael Anthony. b 30. K Coll Cam BA52 MA56. Westcott Ho Cam 54. **d** 56 **p** 57. C Towcester w Easton Neston *Pet* 56-59; Chapl Hurstpierpoint Coll 60-68; Bp's Chapl *Lon* 69-73; R Much Hadham *St Alb* 73-95; Hon Can St Alb 89-95; rtd 95; RD Oundle *Pet* 96-97; Perm to Offic *Pet* from 98 and *St Alb* from 03. *Parkers Patch, 55 Barnwell, Peterborough PE8 5PG* Tel (01832) 273451

McALISTER, Canon David. b 39. St Jo Coll Nottm 83. **d** 87 **p** 88. NSM Arpafeelie *Mor* 87-93; NSM Cromarty 87-93; NSM Fortrose 87-93; C Broughty Ferry *Bre* 93-95; P-in-c Nairn *Mor* 95-09; P-in-c Kishorn 08-09; P-in-c Lochalsh 08-09; P-in-c Poolewe 08-09; Chapl Inverness Airport 98-09; Can St Andr Cathl Inverness 01-09; Hon Can from 09; OCF from 03; rtd 09. *36 Feddon Hill, Fortrose IV10 8SP* Tel (01381) 622530 E-mail david.mcalister@tesco.net

McALISTER, Kenneth Bloomer. b 25. TCD BA51. **d** 51 **p** 53. C Cregagh *D & D* 51-54; C Monaghan *Clogh* 54-57; C Portadown St Mark *Arm* 57-62; R Ripley *Ripon* 62-91; rtd 91; Perm to Offic *Ripon* from 91. *31 Wetherby Road, Knaresborough HG5 8LH* Tel (01423) 860705

McALISTER, Margaret Elizabeth Anne (Sister Margaret Anne). b 55. St Mary's Coll Dur BA78 Ex Univ PGCE79. Wycliffe Hall Ox 83 SAOMC 99. **d** 01 **p** 02. ASSP from 91; NSM Cowley St Jas *Ox* 01-04; NSM Cowley St Jo 04-09; NSM Ox St Mary Magd from 09. *All Saints Convent, St Mary's Road, Oxford OX4 1RU* Tel (01865) 200479 Fax 726547 E-mail margaretanne@socallss.co.uk

McALLEN, James. b 38. Lon Univ BD71. Oak Hill Th Coll 63. **d** 66 **p** 67. C Blackheath St Jo *S'wark* 66-69; C Edin St Thos 69-73; V Selby St Jas *York* 73-80; V Wistow 75-80; V Houghton *Carl* 80-91; Gen Sec Lon City Miss 92-03; Hon C Blackheath St Jo *S'wark* 94-04; rtd 04; Perm to Offic *Carl* from 04. *205 Brampton Road, Carlisle CA3 9AX* Tel (01228) 540505

McALLEN, Robert Roy. b 41. Bps' Coll Cheshunt 62. **d** 65 **p** 66. C Seagoe *D & D* 65-67; C Knockbreda 67-70; CF 70-96; Chapl R Memorial Chpl Sandhurst 87-92; Chapl Guards Chpl Lon 92-96; Perm to Offic *Guildf* 96-98; R Ockley, Okewood and Forest Green 98-06; rtd 06. *Maranatha, Church Street, Rudgwick, Horsham RH12 3EG* Tel (01403) 823172 E-mail roy-gill@mcallenr.freeserve.co.uk

MACAN, Peter John Erdley. b 36. Bp Gray Coll Cape Town 58. **d** 60 **p** 61. C Matroosfontein S Africa 60-64; C Maitland Gd Shep 64-67; C S Lambeth St Ann *S'wark* 68-71; V Nunhead

St Silas 72-81; P-in-c Clapham H Spirit 81-87; TV Clapham Team 87-90; V Dulwich St Clem w St Pet 90-02; rtd 02; Perm to Offic *S'wark* from 04; Retirement Officer Croydon Area from 08. *19 The Windings, South Croydon CR2 0HW* Tel (020) 8657 1398 E-mail peter.macan@virgin.net

McARTHUR, Claudette. **d** 08. NSM Norbury St Oswald *S'wark* from 08. *2 Quince House, Hemlock Close, London SW16 5PN* Tel (020) 8715 1341 E-mail claudettemac1@aol.com

McARTHUR, Duncan Walker. b 50. Strathclyde Univ BSc73 Moore Th Coll Sydney ThL80 Melbourne Univ BD82 Newc Univ MA94. **d** 82 **p** 82. C Hornsby Australia 82-85; Asst Min 88-89; Asst Chapl Barker Coll Hornsby 86-88; P-in-c Harraby *Carl* 90-93; R Hurstville Australia 93-95; Hon Asst P Wauchope St Matt from 99; Chapl St Columba Sch Port Macquarie from 02. *43 Narran River Road, Wauchope NSW 2446, Australia* Tel (0061) (2) 6585 1147 *or* 6583 6999 Mobile 412-828341 Fax (2) 6583 6982 E-mail dmcarthe@bigpond.net.au

MACARTHUR, Helen Anne. b 45. Ulster Univ BEd90 QUB MSc96. CITC 05. **d** 08 **p** 09. NSM Derriaghy w Colin *Conn* from 08. *16 Halftown Road, Lisburn BT27 5RD* Tel (028) 9262 1703 E-mail helenmacar@aol.com

McARTHUR-EDWARDS, Mrs Judith Sarah. b 71. Westmr Coll Ox BTh94. Cranmer Hall Dur 97. **d** 99 **p** 00. C Cradley *Worc* 99-02; C Quarry Bank 02-03; Asst Chapl Frimley Park Hosp NHS Trust 04-05; Asst Chapl R Surrey Co Hosp NHS Trust from 05. *The Vicarage, 37 Sturt Road, Frimley Green, Camberley GU16 6HY* Tel (01252) 835179 E-mail scott-edwards@btopenworld.com

MACARTNEY, Gerald Willam. b 52. TCD BTh03. CITC. **d** 03 **p** 04. C Drumglass w Moygashel *Arm* 03-05; I Milltown from 05; Dioc Communications Officer from 09. *10 Derrylileagh Road, Portadown, Craigavon BT62 1TQ* Tel (028) 3885 2626 Mobile 07850-040027 E-mail milltown@armagh.anglican.org

McATEER (née ROBINSON), Katharine Mary. b 51. NUU BA73. CITC 03. **d** 06 **p** 07. NSM Conwal Union w Gartan *D & R* 06-08; NSM Londonderry Ch Ch, Culmore, Muff and Belmont from 08. *27 Northland Road, Londonderry BT48 7NF* Tel (028) 7137 4544 Fax 7127 1991 Mobile 07813-885145 E-mail kmcateer@hotmail.com

MACAULAY (née BRAYBROOKS), Mrs Bridget Ann. b 63. Trin Coll Bris BA92 DipCOT84. TISEC 96. **d** 98 **p** 99. C Edin Old St Paul 98-01; C Edin St Pet 01-06; Dir Coracle Trust from 01. *1F2, 5 Lutton Place, Edinburgh EH8 9PD* Tel 0131-667 6856 E-mail kbmac@gmx.net

MACAULAY, John Roland. b 39. Man Univ BSc61 Liv Inst of Educn PGCE80. Wells Th Coll 61. **d** 63 **p** 64. C Padgate Ch Ch *Liv* 63-66; C Upholland 66-73; TV 73-75; V Hindley St Pet 75-81; Chapl Liv Coll 81-96; Sub-Chapl HM Pris Risley 85-96; R Lowton St Luke *Liv* 96-05; rtd 05. *58 Rectory Road, Ashton-in-Makerfield, Wigan WN4 0QD* Tel (01942) 711336

MACAULAY, Kenneth Lionel. b 55. Edin Univ BD78. Edin Th Coll 74. **d** 78 **p** 79. C Glas St Ninian 78-80; Dioc Youth Chapl 80-87; P-in-c Glas St Matt 80-87; R Glenrothes *St And* 87-89; Chapl St Mary's Cathl 89-92; Min Glas St Mary 89-92; Min Glas St Serf 92-94; Perm to Offic 94-96; NSM Glas St Oswald 96-98; P-in-c 98-01; Chapl HM Pris Glas (Barlinnie) 99-00; P-in-c Dumbarton *Glas* 01-06; R from 06. *The Rectory, 45 St Andrew's Crescent, Dumbarton G82 3ES* Tel (01389) 602261 *or* 734514 Mobile 07734-187250 E-mail frkenny@btinternet.com

MACAULAY, Kenneth Russell. b 63. Strathclyde Univ BSc85. TISEC 95. **d** 98 **p** 99. C Edin Old St Paul 98-01; C Edin St Pet 01-06; Dir Coracle Trust from 01. *1F2, 5 Lutton Place, Edinburgh EH8 9PD* Tel 0131-667 6856 E-mail kbmac@gmx.net

McAULAY, Mark John Simon. b 71. Lanc Univ LLB92 Leeds Univ BA04 Barrister-at-Law (Inner Temple) 93. Coll of Resurr Mirfield 02. **d** 04 **p** 05. C Ruislip St Martin *Lon* 04-07; V New Southgate St Paul from 07. *The Vicarage, 11 Woodland Road, London N11 1PN* Tel (020) 8361 1946 E-mail frmarkmcaulay@hotmail.com

McAUSLAND, Canon William James. b 36. Edin Th Coll 56. **d** 59 **p** 60. C Dundee St Mary Magd *Bre* 59-64; R 71-79; R Glas H Cross 64-71; Chapl St Marg Old People's Home 79-85; R Dundee St Marg *Bre* 79-01; Chapl St Mary's Sisterhood 82-87; Chapl Ninewells Hosp 85-01; Can St Paul's Cathl Dundee 93-01; Hon Can St Paul's Cathl Dundee from 01; rtd 01. *18 Broadford Terrace, Broughty Ferry, Dundee DD5 3EF* Tel (01382) 737721 E-mail billmcausland@talktalk.net

McAVOY, George Brian. b 41. MBE78. TCD BA61 MA72. Div Test 63. **d** 63 **p** 65. C Cork St Luke w St Ann *C, C & R* 63-66; I Timoleague w Abbeymahon 66-68; Chapl RAF 68-88; Asst Chapl-in-Chief RAF 88-95; QHC 91-95; Chapl Fosse Health NHS Trust 95-98; Chapl Oakham Sch 98-03; rtd 03; Perm to Offic *Pet* from 03 and *Leic* from 05; Past Care and Counselling Adv *Pet* from 04. *1 The Leas, Cottesmore, Oakham LE15 7DG* Tel (01572) 812404 Mobile 07967-967803 E-mail gbm@oakham.rutland.sch.uk

McAVOY, Philip George. b 63. Imp Coll Lon BSc85 SS Coll Cam BA90. Westcott Ho Cam 88. **d** 91 **p** 92. C W End *Win* 91-95; TV

Swanage and Studland *Sarum* 95-00; P-in-c Littleton *Lon* 00-06; V Weston *Guildf* from 06. *All Saints' Vicarage, 1 Chestnut Avenue, Esher KT10 8JL* Tel (020) 8972 9118 E-mail pandk.mac@btinternet.com

MACBAIN, Patrick. b 77. G&C Coll Cam BA99. Oak Hill Th Coll BTh06. **d** 09. C Worksop St Anne *S'well* from 09. *27 Sunnyside, Worksop S81 7LN* Tel (01909) 470433 E-mail pmacbain@yahoo.co.uk

McBETH, David Ronald. d 06 **p** 07. C Glendermott *D & R* 06-09. *Address temp unknown*

McBRIDE, Ms Catherine Sarah. b 64. Trent Poly BSc87. Ridley Hall Cam 06. **d** 08 **p** 09. C Meole Brace *Lich* from 08. *7 Dargate Close, Shrewsbury SY3 9QE* Tel (01743) 369322 E-mail cathmcb@yahoo.co.uk

McBRIDE, Murray. b 61. Trin Coll Bris BA00. **d** 00 **p** 01. C S Lawres Gp *Linc* 00-04; V Aspatria w Hayton and Gilcrux *Carl* 04-06; CF 06-09; V Shrewsbury St Geo w Greenfields *Lich* from 09. *The Vicarage, St George's Street, Shrewsbury SY3 8QA* Tel (01743) 235461

McBRIDE, Peter William Frederick. b 66. Trin Coll Ox BA88 MA03 Solicitor 91. SEITE 03. **d** 06 **p** 07. C Guildf H Trin w St Mary 06-09; TV Poplar *Lon* from 09. *St Nicholas' Vicarage, Dee Street, London E14 0PT* Tel (020) 7515 8405 Mobile 07887-551077

McBRIDE, The Ven Stephen Richard. b 61. QUB BSc84 TCD BTh89 MA92 QUB PhD96. CITC 84. **d** 87 **p** 88. C Antrim All SS *Conn* 87-90; I Belfast St Pet 90-95; Bp's Dom Chapl 94-02; I Antrim All SS from 95; Adn Conn from 02; Prec Belfast St Anne from 02. *The Vicarage, 10 Vicarage Gardens, Antrim BT41 4JP* Tel and fax (028) 9446 2186 Mobile 0718-588191 E-mail archdeacon@connor.anglican.org

McCABE, Alan. b 37. Lon Univ BScEng61. Ridley Hall Cam 61. **d** 63 **p** 64. C Bromley SS Pet and Paul *Roch* 63-67; PV Roch Cathl 67-70; V Bromley H Trin 70-77; V Westerham 77-88; V Eastbourne St Jo *Chich* 88-99; rtd 00; Perm to Offic *Chich* from 00. *94 Baldwin Avenue, Eastbourne BN21 1UP* Tel and fax (01323) 643731 E-mail mccabe@talktalk.net

McCABE, Carol. b 49. **d** 03 **p** 04. OLM Blackrod *Man* from 03. *27 Lymbridge Drive, Blackrod, Bolton BL6 5TH* Tel (01204) 669775

McCABE, John Hamilton. b 59. St Edm Hall Ox MA82 PGCE84. Trin Coll Bris MA01. **d** 01 **p** 02. C Burpham *Guildf* 01-05; Lic to Offic 05-06; R Byfleet from 06. *The Rectory, 81 Rectory Lane, Byfleet, West Byfleet KT14 7LX* Tel (01932) 342374 Mobile 07710-094357 E-mail john.h.mccabe@btinternet.com

McCABE, The Ven John Trevor. b 33. RD78. Nottm Univ BA55. Wycliffe Hall Ox 57. **d** 59 **p** 60. C Compton Gifford *Ex* 59-63; P-in-c Ex St Martin, St Steph, St Laur etc 63-66; Chapl RNR 63-03; Chapl Ex Sch 64-66; V Capel *Guildf* 66-71; V Scilly Is *Truro* 71-74; TR Is of Scilly 74-81; Can Res Bris Cathl 81-83; V Manaccan w St Anthony-in-Meneage and St Martin *Truro* 83-96; RD Kerrier 87-90 and 94-96; Chmn Cornwall NHS Trust for Mental Handicap 91-00; Hon Can Truro Cathl from 93; Adn Cornwall 96-99; rtd 00; Non Exec Dir Cornwall Healthcare NHS Trust from 99; Perm to Offic *Truro* from 99. *1 Sunhill, School Lane, Budock Water, Falmouth TR11 5DG* Tel (01326) 378095

McCABE, Terence John. b 46. Sarum Th Coll 71. **d** 74 **p** 75. C Radford *Cov* 74-77; P-in-c Bris St Paul w St Barn 77-80; TV E Bris 80-84; USA 84-90; R Eynesbury *Ely* from 90. *The Rectory, 7 Howitt's Lane, Eynesbury, St Neots PE19 2JA* Tel (01480) 403884 *or* 385364 E-mail mccabe@nildram.co.uk

McCABE, William Alexander Beck. b 27. QUB BA50 PhD65. **d** 74 **p** 74. Sec Sheff Coun of Chs 74-80; Hon C Millhouses H Trin *Sheff* 74-80; TV Sheff Manor 80-83; Mossborough 83; C Portsea St Cuth *Portsm* 83-86; C S w N Hayling 86-87; V Mickleover St Jo *Derby* 87-91; rtd 91; Perm to Offic *Derby* from 91. *4 Rowan House, Flookersbrook, Chester CH2 3AA* Tel (01244) 321623

McCAFFERTY, Andrew. *See* McCAFFERTY, William Andrew

McCAFFERTY, Canon Christine Ann. b 43. FCA76. Gilmore Course 76. **dss** 79 **d** 87 **p** 94. Writtle w Highwood *Chelmsf* 79-94; C 87-94; Chapl to Bp Bradwell 87-92; Dioc NSM Officer 87-94; TR Wickford and Runwell 94-00; Hon C Lt Baddow 00-09; Hon Can Chelmsf Cathl 91-09; rtd 09; Perm to Offic *Chelmsf* from 09. *3 Hanlee Brook, Great Baddow, Chelmsford CM2 8GB* Tel (01245) 476371 E-mail mccafferty@jcmcc.freeserve.co.uk

McCAFFERTY (née BACK), Mrs Esther Elaine. b 52. Saffron Walden Coll CertEd74. Trin Coll Bris 79 Oak Hill Th Coll BA81. **dss** 81 **d** 87 **p** 94. Collyhurst *Man* 81-84; Upton (Overchurch) *Ches* 84-88; Par Dn 87-88; Par Dn Upper Holloway St Pet w St Jo *Lon* 88-90; Min in charge 90-97; P-in-c Pitsea w Nevendon *Chelmsf* 97-02; R Basildon St Martin from 02; RD Basildon 99-04. *The Rectory, St Martin's Square, Basildon SS14 1DX* Tel and fax (01268) 522455 E-mail emccafferty@talk21.com

McCAFFERTY, Keith Alexander. *See* DUCKETT, Keith Alexander

McCAFFERTY, William Andrew. b 49. Open Univ BA93. SWMTC 94. **d** 97 **p** 98. NSM Lapford, Nymet Rowland and Coldridge *Ex* 97-00; CF 00-04; TR Crosslacon *Carl* 04-08; R Forfar *St And* from 08; R Lunan Head from 08. *St John's Rectory, 24 St James Road, Forfar DD8 1LG* Tel (01307) 463440 Mobile 07891-119684 E-mail normandy08@btinternet.com

McCAGHREY, Mark Allan. b 66. Warwick Univ BSc87. St Jo Coll Nottm BTh93. **d** 94 **p** 95. C Byfleet *Guildf* 94-97; V Lowestoft St Andr *Nor* from 97. *The Vicarage, 51 Beresford Road, Lowestoft NR32 2NQ* Tel (01502) 511521 Fax 08701-377567 E-mail mark@romanhill.org.uk

McCALL, Adrienne. b 49. **d** 08 **p** 09. OLM Hawkhurst *Cant* from 08. *Invicta House, Queens Road, Hawkhurst, Cranbrook TN18 4HH* Tel (01580) 754334 E-mail adie.mac@tiscali.co.uk

McCALLA, Robert Ian. b 31. AKC55. St Boniface Warminster 56. **d** 56 **p** 57. C Barrow St Jo *Carl* 56-58; C Penrith St Andr 58-61; R Greenheys St Clem *Man* 61-64; V Glodwick 64-71; R Distington *Carl* 71-73; V Howe Bridge *Man* 73-87; Chapl Atherleigh Hosp 75-98; R Heaton Mersey *Man* 87-92; V Tyldesley w Shakerley 92-98; rtd 98; Perm to Offic *Carl* from 98. *17 Brunswick Square, Penrith CA11 7LW* Tel (01768) 895212

McCALLIG, Darren. b 05 **p** 06. C Monkstown *D & G* 05-07; Dean of Res and Chapl TCD from 07. *House 27, Trinity College, College Green, Dublin 2, Republic of Ireland* Tel (00353) (1) 896 1402 Mobile 87-286 6637 E-mail darrenmccallig@hotmail.com

MacCALLUM, The Very Revd Norman Donald. b 47. Edin Univ LTh70. Edin Th Coll 67. **d** 71 **p** 72. TV Livingston LEP *Edin* 71-82; P-in-c Bo'ness and R Grangemouth 82-00; Syn Clerk 96-00; Can St Mary's Cathl 96-00; Provost St Jo Cathl Oban from 00; R Oban St Jo from 00; R Ardchattan from 00; R Ardbrecknish from 00; Dean Arg from 05. *The Rectory, Ardconnel Terrace, Oban PA34 5DJ* Tel and fax (01631) 562323 E-mail provostoban@argyll.anglican.org

McCAMLEY, Gregor Alexander. b 42. TCD BA64 MA67. CITC 65. **d** 65 **p** 66. C Holywood *D & D* 65-68; C Bangor St Comgall 68-72; I Carnalea 72-80; I Knock 80-07; Stewardship Adv 89-07; Can Down Cathl 90-07; Dioc Registrar 90-95; Adn Down and Chan Belf Cathl 95-07; rtd 07. *1 Rocky Lane, Seaforde, Downpatrick BT30 8PW* Tel (028) 4481 1111

McCAMMON, John Taylor. b 42. QUB BSc65 Lon Univ BD70. Clifton Th Coll 67. **d** 71 **p** 72. C Lurgan Ch the Redeemer *D & D* 71-75; I Kilkeel 75-82; I Lisburn Ch Ch Cathl 82-98; Treas 94-96; Prec 96; Chan 96-98; Can Conn Cathl 85-98; CMS Kenya 98-07. *Address temp unknown* E-mail jmmccammon@hotmail.com

McCANDLESS, John Hamilton Moore. b 24. QUB BA Ulster Poly BEd. **d** 63 **p** 64. C Belfast St Matt *Conn* 63-66; I Termonmaguirke *Arm* 66-69; C Jordanstown *Conn* 69-70; I Ballinderry, Tamlaght and Arboe *Arm* 70-74; I Kilbarron w Rossnowlagh and Drumholm *D & R* 84-87; rtd 87. *4 Greenhill Drive, Ballymoney BT53 6DE* Tel (028) 2766 2078 E-mail jack@theloughan.fsnet.co.uk

McCANN, Alan. *See* McCANN, Thomas Alan George

McCANN, Hilda. b 36. NOC. **d** 03. OLM Parr *Liv* from 03. *25 Newton Road, St Helens WA9 2HZ* Tel (01744) 758759

McCANN, Michael Joseph. b 61. Man Univ BSc84 FCA. **d** 91 **p** 92. C Derryloran *Arm* 91-94; I Dunmurry *Conn* 94-99; I Kilroot and Templecorran from 99. *Kilroot Rectory, 29 Downshire Gardens, Carrickfergus BT38 7LW* Tel (028) 9336 2387

McCANN, Roland Neil. b 39. Serampore Coll BD73. Bp's Coll Calcutta. **d** 70 **p** 73. C Calcutta St Jas 70-73; V Calcutta St Thos 73-74; C Earley St Bart *Ox* 74-77; C-in-c Harlington Ch Ch CD *Lon* 77-99; Perm to Offic *Lon* from 02. *195 Park Road, Uxbridge UB8 1NP* Tel (01895) 259265

McCANN, Stephen Thomas. b 60. Benedictine Coll Kansas BA83 Boston Coll (USA) MA89 Creighton Univ Nebraska MA94. Pontifical Gregorian Univ 96. **d** 97 **p** 98. In RC Ch 97-01; Rydal Hall *Carl* 02-05; C Kendal H Trin from 05. *7 Wattsfield Road, Kendal LA9 5JH* Tel (01539) 729572

McCANN, Thomas Alan George. b 66. Ulster Univ BA90 TCD BTh93 QUB MPhil99. CITC 90. **d** 93 **p** 94. C Carrickfergus *Conn* 93-00; I Woodburn H Trin from 00. *20 Meadow Hill Close, Carrickfergus BT38 9RQ* Tel (028) 9336 2126 E-mail alan@hobbit.fsnet.co.uk

McCARTAN, Mrs Audrey Doris. b 50. Keele Univ CertEd71 BEd72 Lanc Univ MA75 Northumbria Univ MSc99. NEOC 01. **d** 04 **p** 05. NSM Gosforth St Hugh *Newc* 04-07; P-in-c Heddon-on-the-Wall from 07. *St Andrew's Vicarage, The Towne Gate, Heddon-on-the-Wall, Newcastle upon Tyne NE15 0DT* Tel (01661) 853142

McCARTER, Mrs Suzanne. b 63. Hull Univ BA85 PGCE86. CBDTI 04. **d** 07 **p** 08. C Standish *Blackb* from 07. *25 Somerton Close, Standish, Wigan WN6 0RP* Tel (01257) 421523

McCARTHY, Christopher James. b 61. NEOC 04. **d** 06 **p** 07. C Bessingby *York* 06-08; C Bridlington Quay Ch Ch 06-08; V Bridlington Em from 08; P-in-c Skipsea w Ulrome and Barmston w Fraisthorpe from 08. *Emmanuel Vicarage, 72 Cardigan Road, Bridlington YO15 3JT* Tel (01262) 671952 E-mail chrismbrid@aol.com

McCARTHY, David William. b 63. Edin Th Coll BD88. **d** 88 **p** 89. C Edin St Paul and St Geo 88-91; P-in-c S Queensferry 91-95; R Glas St Silas from 95. *77 Southbrae Drive, Glasgow G13 1PU* Tel 0141-954 9368 E-mail david@stsilas.org.uk

MacCARTHY, Denis. b 60. St Patr Coll Maynooth BD85 CITC 05. **d** 85 **p** 86. In RC Ch 85-05; C Bandon Union *C, C & R* 06-08; I Mallow Union from 08. *The Rectory, Lower Bearforest, Mallow, Co Cork, Republic of Ireland* Tel (00353) (22) 21473 E-mail noden1@eircom.net

McCARTHY, The Very Revd John Francis. b 38. TCD BA61 MA72. **d** 62 **p** 63. C Seapatrick *D & D* 62-66; C Seagoe 66-71; I Moira 71-75; I Dundalk *Arm* 75-86; I Enniskillen *Clogh* 86-94; Dean Clogh 89-94; USA from 94. *Address temp unknown*

McCARTHY, Peter James. b 25. OBE. Cranmer Hall Dur. **d** 85 **p** 86. Hon C Farnham w Scotton, Staveley, Copgrove etc *Ripon* 85-87; V Startforth w Bowes 87-92; rtd 92; C Durham *Ab* 92-95; Perm to Offic *Ripon* from 95 and *Newc* from 99. *Manderley, Farnham Lane, Ferrensby, Knaresborough HG5 9JG* Tel (01423) 340503

MacCARTHY, The Very Revd Robert Brian. b 40. TCD BA63 MA66 PhD83 NUI MA65 Ox Univ MA82. Cuddesdon Coll 77. **d** 79 **p** 80. C Carlow w Urglin and Staplestown *C & O* 79-81; Lic to Offic (Cashel, Waterford and Lismore) 81-86; Lib Pusey Ho and Fell St Cross Coll Ox 81-82; C Bracknell *Ox* 82-83; TV 83-86; C Kilkenny w Aghour and Kilmanagh *C & O* 86-88; Bp's V and Lib Kilkenny Cathl 86-88; Chapl Kilkenny Coll 86-88; Bp's Dom Chapl 86-89; I Castlecomer w Colliery Ch, Mothel and Bilboa 88-95; Dioc Info Officer (Ossory and Leighlin) 88-90; Glebes Sec (Ossory and Leighlin) 92-94; Preb Monmohenock St Patr Cathl Dublin 94-99; Provost Tuam *T, K & A* 95-99; I Galway w Kilcummin 95-99; Chapl Univ Coll Galway 95-99; Dean St Patr Cathl Dublin from 99. *The Deanery, Upper Kevin Street, Dublin 8, Republic of Ireland* Tel (00353) (1) 475 5449 *or* 453 9472

McCARTHY, Sandra Ellen. See MANLEY, Mrs Sandra Ellen

MacCARTHY, Stephen Samuel. b 49. ACII81 Univ Coll Chich BA02. **d** 01. NSM Burgess Hill St Edw *Chich* from 01. *St Edward's House, 9 Coopers Close, Burgess Hill RH15 8AN* Tel (01444) 248520 Mobile 07802-734903 E-mail ssmaccarthy@aol.com

McCARTHY, Terence Arthur. b 46. Open Univ BA90. Kelham Th Coll 66. **d** 70 **p** 71. C Gt Burstead *Chelmsf* 70-74; C Wickford 74-76; TV E Runcorn w Halton *Ches* 76-80; V Runcorn H Trin 80-84; Chapl HM Pris Liv 84; Chapl HM Pris Acklington 84-92; Chapl HM Pris Holme Ho from 92. *The Chaplaincy, HM Prison Holme House, Stockton-on-Tees TS18 2QU* Tel (01642) 744115

McCARTNEY, Adrian Alexander. b 57. Stranmillis Coll BEd79 TCD BTh88. CITC 86. **d** 88 **p** 89. C Jordanstown w Monkstown *Conn* 88-91; Bp's C Monkstown 91-94; I 94-96; C Belvoir *D & D* from 02. *94 Comber Road, Dundonald, Belfast BT16 2AG* Tel (028) 9067 3379 Mobile 07970-626384 E-mail adrian@boringwells.org

McCARTNEY, Darren James. b 03. P-in-c Pangnirtung Canada 03-06; C Carrickfergus *Conn* 06-09; I Knocknamuckley *D & D* from 09. *The Rectory, 30 Moss Bank Road, Ballynagarrick, Portadown BT63 5SL*

McCARTNEY, Ellis. b 47. Univ Coll Lon BSc73 Lon Inst of Educn MA82. NTMTC 94. **d** 97 **p** 98. NSM Tollington *Lon* 97-05. *6 Elfort Road, London N5 1AZ* Tel (020) 7226 1533 E-mail macfour@btinternet.com

McCARTNEY, Robert Charles. CITC. **d** 85 **p** 85. C Portadown St Mark *Arm* 85-88; I Errigle Keerogue w Ballygawley and Killeshil 88-89; CF 89-04; I Belfast St Donard *D & D* 04-08; I Aghalee from 08. *The Rectory, 39 Soldierstown Road, Aghalee, Craigavon BT67 0ES* Tel (028) 9265 0407 Mobile 07846-610977 E-mail dunroamin.mccartney@btopenworld.com

McCARTY, Colin Terence. b 46. Loughb Univ BTech68 PhD71 Lon Univ PGCE73 FRSA89. EAMTC 91. **d** 94 **p** 95. NSM Exning St Martin w Landwade *St E* from 94; Perm to Offic *Ely* from 96. *1 Seymour Close, Newmarket CB8 8EL* Tel (01638) 669400 *or* (01223) 552716 Mobile 07711-825157 Fax (01223) 553537 E-mail mccarty.c@ucles.org.uk *or* gjy02@dial.pipex.com

MacCARTY, Paul Andrew. b 34. Sarum & Wells Th Coll 73. **d** 75 **p** 76. Ind Chapl *Win* 75-80; C Bournemouth St Andr 75-84; Hon C Christchurch 80-91; C 91-99; rtd 99; Perm to Offic *Win* from 01. *3 Douglas Avenue, Christchurch BH23 1JT* Tel (01202) 483807 E-mail paulmaccarty@aol.com

McCASKILL, James Calvin. b 73. Wheaton Coll Illinois BA95 Leeds Univ MA02. Coll of Resurr Mirfield 00. **d** 02 **p** 03. C Mt Lebanon St Paul USA 02-04; P-in-c Lundwood *Wakef* from 04. *4 Parkland View, Barnsley S71 5LL* Tel (01226) 711365 *or* 208690 E-mail james@mccaskill.info *or* lundwood@churchlite.co.uk

McCATHIE, Neil. b 62. N Staffs Poly BA84 De Montfort Univ MA00 Huddersfield Univ PGCE93 MAAT96. St Jo Coll Nottm 03. **d** 05 **p** 06. C Shipley St Pet *Bradf* 05-09; TV Parr *Liv* from 09. *St Peter's Vicarage, Broad Oak Road, St Helens WA9 2DZ*

McCAULAY, Stephen Thomas John. b 61. Coll of Resurr Mirfield BA98. **d** 98 **p** 99. C Chaddesden St Phil *Derby* 98-02; V Mackworth St Fran 02-04; CF from 04. *c/o MOD Chaplains (Army)* Tel (01980) 615804 Fax 615800 E-mail mccaulay@ntlworld.com

McCAULEY, Craig William Leslie. b 72. Glam Univ BA95 TCD BTh99. CITC 96. **d** 99 **p** 00. C Seapatrick *D & D* 99-02; C Kill *D & G* 02-04; I Lurgan w Billis, Killinkere and Munterconnaught *K, E & A* from 04. *The Rectory, Virginia, Co Cavan, Republic of Ireland* Tel (00353) (49) 854 8465 E-mail virginia@kilmore.anglican.org

McCAUSLAND, Norman. b 58. TCD BTh89. CITC 89. **d** 89 **p** 90. C Portadown St Columba *Arm* 89-91; P-in-c Clonmel Union *C, C & R* 91-94; Miss to Seamen 91-94; CMS 94-95; Bp's V and Lib Ossory Cathl 96; Chapl and Tutor CITC 96-00; PV Ch Ch Cathl Dublin 96-00; CMS 00-01; Lic to Offic *D & G* from 01. *102 Killiney Hill Road, Killiney, Co Dublin, Republic of Ireland* Tel (00353) (1) 275 1661 E-mail mccausln@tcd.ie

M'CAW, Stephen Aragorn. b 61. Magd Coll Cam BA83 Lon Univ MB, BS86 FRCS90 MRCGP92. Cranmer Hall Dur 97. **d** 99 **p** 00. C Thetford *Nor* 99-02; R Steeple Aston w N Aston and Tackley *Ox* from 02; AD Woodstock from 06. *The Rectory, Fir Lane, Steeple Aston, Bicester OX25 4SF* Tel (01869) 347793 E-mail samcaw@talk21.com

McCLAY, Canon David Alexander. b 59. TCD MA87. **d** 87 **p** 88. C Magherafelt w Dollingstown *D & D* 87-90; I Kilkeel 90-01; I Willowfield from 01; P-in-c Mt Merrion from 07; Can Belf Cathl from 05. *Willowfield Rectory, 149 My Lady's Road, Belfast BT6 8FE* Tel and fax (028) 9046 0105 *or* 9045 7654 E-mail mcclayd@googlemail.com

McCLEAN, Lydia Margaret Sheelagh. See COOK, Mrs Lydia Margaret Sheelagh

McCLEAN, Robert Mervyn. b 38. Greenwich Univ BTh91. Edgehill Th Coll Belf 57. **d** 85 **p** 88. NSM Seapatrick *D & D* 85-99. *2 Kiloanin Crescent, Banbridge BT32 4NU* Tel (028) 4062 7419 E-mail r.m.mcclean@btinternet.com

McCLELLAN, Andrew David. b 71. St Jo Coll Cam BA93 MA96. Oak Hill Th Coll BA05. **d** 05. C Sevenoaks St Nic *Roch* 05-09; P-in-c Bromley St Jo from 09; Chapl St Olave's Gr Sch Orpington from 09. *St John's Vicarage, 9 Orchard Road, Bromley BR1 2PR* Tel (020) 8460 1844 Mobile 07931-731062 E-mail aj_mcc@btinternet.com

McCLENAGHAN, John Mark. b 61. TCD BTh05. CITC 02. **d** 05 **p** 06. C Portadown St Columba *Arm* 05-08; I Keady w Armaghbreague and Derrynoose from 08. *8 Ardmore Close, Portadown, Craigavon BT62 4DX* E-mail jm.mcclenaghan@btinternet.com

MACCLESFIELD, Archdeacon of. See GILLINGS, The Ven Richard John

McCLINTOCK, Darren John. b 77. Hull Univ BA98 Open Univ MA(TS)00. St Jo Coll Nottm 98. **d** 01 **p** 02. C Drypool *York* 01-04; C Bilton *Ripon* 04-06; TV from 06; Dioc Ecum Adv from 08. *8 Pecketts Way, Harrogate HG1 3EW* Tel (01423) 560863 E-mail darren@djmcclintock.freeserve.co.uk

McCLOSKEY, Robert Johnson. b 42. Stetson Univ (USA) AB63. Gen Th Sem NY STB67. **d** 67 **p** 68. C Gd Shepherd USA 67-69; R Somerville W St Jas and Chapl Tufts Univ 69-72; Dioc Adv for Liturgy and Music Massachusetts 71-76; R Westford St Mark 72-76; R Blowing Rock St Mary 76-82; Liturg and Musical Adv and Ecum Officer Dio W N Carolina 76-81; Dio SE Florida 90-93; Ecum Officer Dio Long Is 81-89; R Bay Shore St Pet and St Pet Sch 82-89; R Miami St Steph and St Steph Sch 89-01; Staff Officer Lambeth Conf 98; rtd 01. *Address temp unknown*

McCLURE, Mrs Catherine Abigail. b 63. Birm Univ BA84 SS Hild & Bede Coll Dur PGCE85. Ripon Coll Cuddesdon BTh07. **d** 03 **p** 04. C Cirencester *Glouc* 03-07; Chapl Glos Hosps NHS Foundn Trust from 07. *Cheltenham General Hospital, Sandford Road, Cheltenham GL53 7AN* Tel 08454-224286 ext 4286 *or* (01242) 681139 Fax 08454-221214 Mobile 07824-476505 E-mail katie.mcclure@glos.nhs.uk

McCLURE, John. **d** 07 **p** 08. NSM Skerry w Rathcavan and Newtowncrommelin *Conn* 07-09; NSM Belfast St Mich from 09. *69 Parkgate Road, Kells, Ballymena BT42 3PF* Tel (028) 2589 2324 *or* 9024 1640 E-mail mcclurejohn@hotmail.com *or* belfast@icm-online.ie

McCLURE, Robert (Roy). b 30. Open Univ BA92. TCD Div Sch 68. **d** 70 **p** 71. C Monaghan *Clogh* 70-72; C Belfast St Matt *Conn* 72-76; Chapl HM Pris Liv 76-77; Chapl HM Pris Preston 77-82; V Foulridge *Bradf* 82-88; rtd 88; Perm to Offic *Liv* from 89. *4 Mill Lane Crescent, Southport PR9 7PF* Tel (01704) 27476

McCLURE, The Ven Timothy Elston. b 46. St Jo Coll Dur BA68. Ridley Hall Cam 68. **d** 70 **p** 71. C Kirkheaton *Wakef* 70-73; C Chorlton upon Medlock *Man* 74-79; Chapl Man Poly 74-82; TR Man Whitworth 79-82; Gen Sec SCM 82-92; Bp's Soc and Ind Adv and Dir Chs' Coun for Ind and Soc Resp LEP *Bris* 92-99; Hon Can Bris Cathl from 92; Hon C Cotham St Sav w St Mary 96; Chapl Lord Mayor's Chpl 96-99; Adn Bris from 99. *10 Great*

Brockeridge, Bristol BS9 3TY Tel 0117-962 1433 Fax 962 9438
E-mail tim.mcclure@bristoldiocese.org

McCLUSKEY, Coralie Christine. b 52. Univ of Wales (Cardiff) BEd74. SAOMC 98. **d** 01 **p** 02. C Welwyn w Ayot St Peter *St Alb* 01-04; P-in-c Datchworth 04-05; TV Welwyn from 05; Agric Chapl for Herts from 09. *The Rectory, Brookbridge Lane, Datchworth, Knebworth SG3 6SU* Tel (01438) 813067 *or* 817183
E-mail coralie_mccluskey@yahoo.co.uk

McCLUSKEY, James Terence. b 65. Coll of Resurr Mirfield 01. **d** 03 **p** 04. C Swanley St Mary *Roch* 03-06; V Prittlewell St Luke *Chelmsf* from 06. *The Vicarage, St Luke's Road, Southend-on-Sea SS2 4AB* Tel and fax (01702) 467620 Mobile 07761-632734
E-mail mccluskey@katy-james.freeserve.co.uk

McCLUSKEY, Miss Lesley. b 45. Hull Univ LLB72 Bolton Coll of Educn PGCE77. NOC 89. **d** 92 **p** 94. C Bootle St Mary w St Paul *Liv* 92-94; C Wigan St Anne 94-98; P-in-c Newton in Makerfield Em 98-07; TV Newton 08; Chapl St Helens and Knowsley Hosps NHS Trust 98-08; rtd 09. *9 Mulberry Court, Stockton Heath, Warrington WA4 2DB* Tel (01925) 602286
E-mail lesley-mccluskey@yahoo.co.uk

McCOACH, Jennifer Sara. *See* CROFT, Jennifer Sara

McCOLLUM, Alastair Colston. b 69. Whitelands Coll Lon BA91. Westcott Ho Cam 95. **d** 96 **p** 97. C Hampton All SS *Lon* 96-98; C S Kensington St Aug 98-00; Chapl Imp Coll 98-00; TV Papworth *Ely* 00-08; V Kilmington, Stockland, Dalwood, Yarcombe etc *Ex* from 08. *The Vicarage, Whitford Road, Kilmington, Axminster EX13 7RF* Tel (01297) 32160

McCOLLUM, Charles James. b 41. TCD BTh89. CITC 85. **d** 89 **p** 90. C Larne and Inver *Conn* 89-91; Bp's C Belfast Whiterock 91-96; I Belfast St Pet and St Jas 96-08; I Dunleckney w Nurney, Lorum and Kiltennel *C & O* from 08. *St Mary's Rectory, Dunleckney, Muine Bheag, Co Carlow, Republic of Ireland* Tel and fax (00353) (59) 972 0934 Mobile 87-288 5019
E-mail charlesjmccollum@gmail.com

McCOMB, Samuel. b 33. CITC 70. **d** 71 **p** 72. C Belfast St Mich *Conn* 71-74; C Lisburn Ch Ch 74-79; I Ballinderry *Arm* 79-83; I Lisburn Ch Ch *Conn* 83-04; Can Conn Cathl 98-04; Treas 01-04; rtd 04. *209 Hillsborough Old Road, Lisburn BT27 5QE* Tel (028) 9260 5812

McCONACHIE, Robert Noel. b 40. Goldsmiths' Coll Lon BA86. Oak Hill Th Coll 86. **d** 88 **p** 89. C Larkfield *Roch* 88-93; R Mereworth w W Peckham from 93. *The Rectory, The Street, Mereworth, Maidstone ME18 5NA* Tel (01622) 812214

McCONKEY, Brian Robert. b 62. Carl Dioc Tr Inst 92. **d** 95 **p** 96. C Blackb St Gabr 95-98; Dioc Youth Officer 99-04; V Fulwood Ch Ch from 04; Dioc Voc Team Co-ord from 06; Chapl Preston Coll 05-09. *Christ Church Vicarage, 19 Vicarage Close, Fulwood, Preston PR2 8EG* Tel (01772) 719210
E-mail christchurchfulwood@btinternet.com

McCONKEY, David Benton. b 53. Kansas Wesleyan Univ (USA) BA75 Yale Univ MusM77. Yale Div Sch MDiv79. **d** 83 **p** 84. Dn Ch Cathl Salina USA 83-84; C S Lake Anchorage 84-85; P-in-c Louisville St Luke 85-86; R Warrensburgh H Cross 86-94; Can Capitular All SS Cath Albany 88-93; R Belvedere St Eliz Zimbabwe 94-03; P-in-c Norton St Fran and St Jas 94-99; Lect Bp Gaul Coll 94-01; TR Swindon New Town *Bris* from 03. *18 Park Lane, Swindon SN1 5EL* Tel (01793) 619403
E-mail frdbmcconkey@yahoo.co.uk
or swindonnewtown@btinternet.com

McCONNAUGHIE, Adrian William. b 66. Jes Coll Ox BA89 MA06 Lon Univ PhD93 Cam Univ PGCE96. Trin Coll Bris BA08. **d** 08 **p** 09. C Bath Abbey w St Jas *B & W* from 08. *20A Bellotts Road, Bath BA2 3RT* Tel (01225) 314029
E-mail adrian@bathabbey.org

McCONNELL, Canon Brian Roy. b 46. St Paul's Coll Grahamstown. **d** 71 **p** 72. C Plumstead S Africa 71-74; C St Geo Cathl Cape Town 74-77; C Prestwich St Marg *Man* 77-79; R Sea Point S Africa 79-85; V Liscard St Mary w St Columba *Ches* 85-90; V Altrincham St Geo 90-06; RD Bowdon 95-03; Hon Can Ches Cathl 91-04; P-in-c Sea Carl Cathl from 06. *3 The Abbey, Carlisle CA3 8TZ* Tel (01228) 521834

McCONNELL, Peter Stuart. b 54. Linc Th Coll 89. **d** 91 **p** 92. C N Shields *Newc* 91-95; V Balkwell 95-03; C Killingworth 03-07; P-in-c Longhorsley and Hebron from 08; Sen Chapl Northumbria Police from 98. *The Vicarage, Longhorsley, Morpeth NE65 8UU* Tel (01670) 788218
E-mail mcconnell@balkwell.freeserve.co.uk

McCONNELL, Robert Mark. b 60. Oak Hill Th Coll BA88. **d** 89 **p** 90. C Bedford Ch Ch *St Alb* 89-92; C Bangor St Comgall *D & D* 92-94; I Killyleagh 94-99; I Ballynure and Ballyeaston *Conn* from 99. *The Rectory, 11 Church Road, Ballyclare BT39 9UF* Tel (028) 9332 2350 E-mail s+j-cc@yahoo.co.uk

McCORMACK, Alan William. b 68. Jes Coll Ox BA90 MA94 DPhil94. CITC 93. **d** 96 **p** 97. C Knock *D & D* 96-98; Dean of Res and Chapl TCD 98-07; P-in-c St Botolph without Bishopgate *Lon* from 07; P-in-c St Vedast w St Mich-le-Querne etc from 07. *St Vedast's Rectory, 4 Foster Lane, London EC2V 6HH* Tel (020) 7588 3388 E-mail rector@botolph.org.uk

McCORMACK, Colin. b 47. QUB BSc70 DipEd71. St Jo Coll Nottm BA75. **d** 78 **p** 79. C Carl St Jo 78-81; C Ballynafeigh St Jude *D & D* 81-84; V Harraby *Carl* 84-89; NSM Carl H Trin and St Barn 95-99; Asst Chapl Costa Blanca *Eur* 00-04; Chapl Torrevieja 04-08. *Apartado 3257, 03180 Torrevieja Suc 1, Alicante, Spain* Tel and fax (0034) 966 925 205
E-mail colinmccormack@terra.es

McCORMACK, Canon David Eugene. b 34. Wells Th Coll 66. **d** 68 **p** 69. C Lillington *Cov* 68-71; C The Lickey *Birm* 71-75; V Highters Heath 75-82; V Four Oaks 82-00; Hon Can Birm Cathl 95-00; rtd 00; Perm to Offic *Linc* and *Pet* from 00; *Birm* from 05. *27 Rockingham Close, Market Deeping, Peterborough PE6 8BY* Tel (01778) 347569

McCORMACK, George Brash. b 32. ACIS65 FCIS75. S'wark Ord Course 82. **d** 85 **p** 86. Hon C Crofton St Paul *Roch* 85-89; C Crayford 89-91; R Fawkham and Hartley 91-97; rtd 97; Perm to Offic *Roch* from 98. *11 Turnpike Drive, Pratts Bottom, Orpington BR6 7SJ*

McCORMACK, John Heddon. b 58. Chich Th Coll 85. **d** 88 **p** 89. C Cleobury Mortimer w Hopton Wafers *Heref* 88-90; C Lymington *Win* 90-92; C Portsea N End St Mark *Portsm* 92-95; Chapl St Barn Hospice Worthing 95-06. *10 Columbia Walk, Worthing BN13 2ST* Tel (01903) 263700 Mobile 07974-603518
E-mail humanrites1@sky.com

McCORMACK, Canon Kevan Sean. b 50. Chich Th Coll 77. **d** 80 **p** 81. C Ross *Heref* 80-81; C Ross w Brampton Abbotts, Bridstow and Peterstow 81-83; C Leominster 83; TV 84-87; Chapl R Hosp Sch Holbrook 87-00; R Woodbridge St Mary *St E* from 00; Hon Can St E Cathl from 09. *St Mary's Rectory, Church Street, Woodbridge IP12 1DS* Tel and fax (01394) 610424

McCORMACK, Canon Lesley Sharman. b 50. EAMTC. **d** 88 **p** 94. Hon Par Dn Chevington w Hargrave and Whepstead w Brockley *St E* 88-95; Asst Chapl W Suffolk Hosp Bury St Edm 88-95; Chapl Kettering Gen Hosp NHS Trust 95-09; Chapl Cransley Hospice from 09; NSM Kettering SS Pet and Paul from 09; Bp's Hosp Chapl Adv from 00; Can Pet Cathl from 03. *Barnbrook, Water Lane, Chelveston, Wellingborough NN9 6AP* Tel (01933) 626636

MacCORMACK, Michael Ian. b 54. Kent Univ BA77 Ch Ch Coll Cant MA87 Bris Univ PGCE78. STETS 02. **d** 05 **p** 06. NSM Martock w Ash *B & W* from 05. *12A Middle Street, Montacute TA15 6UZ* Tel (01935) 827823 Mobile 07717-878736
E-mail michael.maccormack@nationaltrust.org.uk

McCORMACK, Mrs Susan. b 60. NEOC 00. **d** 03 **p** 04. C Newburn *Newc* 03-07; P-in-c Fawdon from 07. *St Mary's Vicarage, 7 Fawdon Lane, Newcastle upon Tyne NE3 2RR* Tel 0191-285 5403 E-mail suemc@mccormacks4.fsnet.co.uk

McCORMICK, Mrs Anne Irene. b 67. Sheff Univ BA89 Hull Univ PGCE90. Ripon Coll Cuddesdon 90. **d** 92 **p** 94. C Spalding *Linc* 92-96; C Gt Grimsby St Mary and St Jas 96-01; C Gt and Lt Coates w Bradley from 98; Chapl Doncaster and S Humber Healthcare NHS Trust from 07. *The Glebe House, 11 Church Lane, Limber, Grimsby DN37 8JN* Tel (01469) 561082
E-mail anneoflimber@btinternet.com

McCORMICK, David Mark. b 68. Univ of Wales (Ban) BD89. Ripon Coll Cuddesdon 90. **d** 92 **p** 93. C Holbeach *Linc* 92-96; TV Gt Grimsby St Mary and St Jas 96-01; Prin Linc Min Tr Scheme from 01. *Diocesan Office, Church House, The Old Palace, Minster Yard, Lincoln LN2 1PU* Tel (01522) 504030
E-mail david.mccormick@lincoln.anglican.org

McCOSH, Canon Duncan Ian. b 50. Edin Dioc NSM Course 82. **d** 91 **p** 92. C Dalkeith *Edin* 91-96; C Lasswade 91-96; P-in-c Falkirk 96-97; R 97-03; R Galashiels from 03; Hon Can Cape Coast from 06. *The Rectory, 6 Parsonage Road, Galashiels TD1 3HS* Tel (01896) 753118
E-mail stpeters.gala@btopenworld.com

McCOUBREY, William Arthur. b 36. CEng MIMechE. Sarum & Wells Th Coll 86. **d** 89 **p** 90. C Bedhampton *Portsm* 89-92; V Stokenham w Sherford *Ex* 92-96; R Stokenham w Sherford and Beesands, and Slapton 96-02; rtd 02; Perm to Offic *Chich* and *Portsm* from 02. *19 Warblington Road, Emsworth PO10 7HE* Tel (01243) 374011

McCOULOUGH, David. b 61. Man Univ BA84 St Jo Coll Dur BA88. Cranmer Hall Dur 86. **d** 89 **p** 90. C Man Apostles w Miles Platting 89-92; C Elton All SS 92-94; V Halliwell St Marg 94-98; Min Can Ripon Cathl 98-01; Chapl Univ Coll of Ripon and York St Jo 98-01; Ind Chapl *S'well* 01-07; Chapl Boots PLC 01-07; C Nottingham St Pet and St Jas 01-02; C Nottingham St Pet and All SS 02-07; Assoc Dir Partnerships from 07; P-in-c Edingley w Halam from 07. *15 Adams Row, Southwell NG25 0FF* Tel (01636) 812029

McCOULOUGH, Thomas Alexander. b 32. AKC59. **d** 60 **p** 61. C Norton St Mich *Dur* 60-63; USPG India 63-67; P-in-c Derby St Jas 67-72; Ind Chapl *York* 72-82; P-in-c Sutton on the Forest 82-96; Diec Sec for Local Min 82-89; Lay Tr Officer 89-96; rtd 96; Perm to Offic *Newc* from 96. *1 Horsley Gardens, Holywell, Whitley Bay NE25 0TU* Tel 0191-298 0332

McCRACKEN, William. d 08 p 09. C Camlough w Mullaglass *Arm* from 08. *1 Aughlish Road, Tandragee, Craigavon BT62 2EE* Tel (028) 3884 0655

McCREA, Basil Wolfe. b 21. QUB BA49. Wycliffe Hall Ox 51. d 53 p 54. C Kingston upon Hull H Trin *York* 53-56; C Dundela St Mark *D & D* 56-59; C Cork H Trin w St Paul, St Pet and St Mary *C, C & R* 59-61; I Tullyaughnish *D & R* 61-65; I Rathkeale *L & K* 65-68; I Cork H Trin *C, C & R* 68-72; I Carrigaline Union 72-90; rtd 90. *30 Somerville, Carrigaline, Co Cork, Republic of Ireland* Tel (00353) (21) 437 1538

McCREA, Christina Elizabeth. b 53. d 08 p 09. NSM Glanogwen and Llanllechid w St Ann's and Pentir *Ban* from 08. *2 Bron-y-Waun, Rhiwlas, Bangor LL57 4EX* Tel (01248) 372249 E-mail christinaemcc@aol.com

McCREA, Francis. b 53. BTh. d 91 p 92. C Dundonald *D & D* 91-94; I Belfast St Brendan from 94. *St Brendan's Rectory, 36 Circular Road, Belfast BT4 2GA* Tel (028) 9076 3458

McCREADY, Kennedy Lemar. b 26. Birkbeck Coll Lon BSc59 Sussex Univ MA94 Garnett Coll Lon TCert54 CEng56 FIEE56. Chich Th Coll 91. d 92 p 99. NSM Mayfield *Chich* 92-97; Perm to Offic 97-00; NSM New Groombridge 99-01; Perm to Offic from 01. *Quarry House, Groombridge Road, Groombridge, Tunbridge Wells TN3 9PS* Tel (01892) 864297

McCREADY, Marcus Diarmuid Julian. b 63. NUU BA85 TCD BTh88 MPhil93. CITC 82. d 88 p 89. C Seagoe *D & D* 88-91; I Clonallon w Warrenpoint 91-96; Chapl Liv Coll 96-97; Dep Chapl HM YOI Stoke Heath 97-99; Chapl HM Pris Lindholme 99-06. *Address temp unknown*

McCRORY, Canon Peter. b 34. Chich Th Coll 63. d 67 p 68. C St Marychurch *Ex* 67-72; R Kenn w Mamhead 72-76; R Kenn 76-78; Bp's Dom Chapl *S'wark* 78-81; V Kew 81-00; RD Richmond and Barnes 84-89; Hon Can S'wark Cathl 90-00; rtd 00; Perm to Offic *Nor* from 00. *Dane House, The Street, Kettlestone, Fakenham NR21 0AU* Tel (01328) 878455

McCROSKERY, Andrew. b 74. Glas Univ BD97 TCD MPhil99. CITC 98. d 99 p 00. C Newtownards *D & D* 99-02; Dean's V Cork Cathl 02-04; I Youghal Union 04-08; Chapl Univ Coll Cork 04-08; Bp's Dom Chapl 03-08; Min Can Cork Cathl 04-08; I Dublin St Bart w Leeson Park *D & G* from 08. *The Rectory, 12 Merlyn Road, Ballsbridge, Dublin 4, Republic of Ireland* Tel (00353) (1) 269 4813 E-mail wolfram100@hotmail.com

McCRUM, Michael Scott. b 35. Glas Univ BSc57 UNISA BTh85. d 85 p 85. S Africa 85-89; Asst P Lynnwood 86-87; P-in-c Mamelodi 87; P-in-c Villieria 87-88; Kerygma Internat Chr Min 89-92; Perm to Offic *Nor* 93-94; NSM Chesham Bois *Ox* 94-95; Perm to Offic *St Alb* 95-98 and from 05; Hon C Chorleywood St Andr 98-05. *Cranbrook, 31 South Road, Chorleywood, Rickmansworth WD3 5AS* Tel and fax (01923) 336897 Mobile 07792-621587 E-mail misamccrum@ntlworld.com

McCULLAGH, Elspeth Jane Alexandra. *See* SAVILLE, Mrs Elspeth Jane Alexandra

McCULLAGH, Canon John Eric. b 46. TCD BA68 BTh88 QUB DipEd70. d 88 p 89. C Stillorgan w Blackrock *D & G* 88-91; Chapl and Hd of RE Newpark Sch Dub 90-99; I Clondalkin w Rathcoole 91-99; Sec Gen Syn Bd of Educn 99-08; I Rathdrum w Glenealy, Derralossary and Laragh *D & G* from 08; Can Ch Ch Cathl Dublin from 99; Treas from 09. *The Rectory, Rathdrum, Co Wicklow, Republic of Ireland* Tel (00353) (404) 43814 E-mail rathdrum@glendalough.anglican.org

McCULLAGH, Canon Mervyn Alexander. b 44. TCD BA BAI68. CITC 79. d 79 p 80. C Larne and Inver *Conn* 79-83; C Ballymacash 83-85; C Dublin St Ann w St Mark and St Steph *D & G* 85-88; I Baltinglass w Ballynure etc *C & O* from 88; Warden of Readers 90-05; Can Ossory and Leighlin Cathls 92-96; Treas from 96; P-in-c Kiltegan w Hacketstown, Clonmore and Moyne 00-03. *The Rectory, Baltinglass, Co Wicklow, Republic of Ireland* Tel (00353) (59) 648 1321

McCULLOCH, Alistair John. b 59. Univ of Wales (Lamp) BA81 Leeds Univ BA86 Lon Univ MA07. Coll of Resurr Mirfield 84. d 87 p 88. C Portsm Cathl 87-90; C Portsea St Mary 90-94; V Reading St Matt *Ox* 94-95; Perm to Offic *S'wark* 99; Chapl King's Coll Hosp NHS Trust 00-04; Chapl R Marsden NHS Foundn Trust from 04. *The Royal Marsden Hospital, Fulham Road, London SW3 6JJ* Tel (020) 7808 2818 E-mail alistair.mcculloch@rmh.nhs.uk

McCULLOCH, Mrs Celia Hume. b 53. Leeds Univ BA08. NOC 05. d 08 p 09. C Cheetham *Man* from 08. *Bishopscourt, Bury New Road, Salford, Manchester M7 4LE* Tel 0161-792 2096 Mobile 07943-366331 E-mail celiamcculloch@yahoo.co.uk

MacCULLOCH, Prof Diarmaid Ninian John. b 51. Chu Coll Cam BA72 MA76 PhD77 FSA78 FRHistS81. Ripon Coll Cuddesdon 86. d 87. NSM Clifton All SS w St Jo *Bris* 87-88. *St Cross College, St Giles, Oxford OX1 3LZ* Tel (01865) 270794 Fax 270795 E-mail diarmaid.macculloch@theology.ox.ac.uk

✠**McCULLOCH, The Rt Revd Nigel Simeon.** b 42. Selw Coll Cam BA64 MA69. Cuddesdon Coll 64. d 66 p 67 c 86. C Ellesmere Port *Ches* 66-70; Dir Th Studies Ch Coll Cam 70-75; Chapl 70-73; Dioc Missr *Nor* 73-78; P-in-c Salisbury St Thos and St Edm *Sarum* 78-81; R 81-86; Adn Sarum 79-86; Can and

Preb Sarum Cathl 79-86; Suff Bp Taunton *B & W* 86-92; Preb Wells Cathl 86-92; Bp Wakef 92-02; Bp Man from 02; High Almoner from 97. *Bishopscourt, Bury New Road, Salford, Manchester M7 4LE* Tel 0161-792 2096 Fax 792 6826 E-mail bishop@bishopscourt.manchester.anglican.org

McCULLOCK, Mrs Patricia Ann. b 46. CertEd72. EMMTC 87. d 90 p 94. C Bottesford w Ashby *Linc* 90-95; P-in-c Wragby 95-98; Chapl N Lincs Coll of FE 95-98; Ind Chapl 98-01; rtd 01; Perm to Offic *Linc* from 01. *36 Deepdale Lane, Nettleham, Lincoln LN2 2LT* Tel (01522) 595474 E-mail patricia.mccullock@virgin.net

McCULLOUGH, Mrs Aphrodite Maria. b 47. Derby Univ MSc95. EMMTC 97. d 00 p 01. NSM Kirby Muxloe *Leic* 00-04; TV 04-08; rtd 08. *33 Alton Road, Leicester LE2 8QB* Tel 0116-283 7887 E-mail aphro.mccullough@btinternet.com

McCULLOUGH, Canon Roy. b 46. Brasted Th Coll 69 Linc Th Coll 70. d 73 p 74. Chapl Highfield Priory Sch Lancs 73-77; C Ashton-on-Ribble St Andr *Blackb* 73-77; V Rishton 77-86; V Burnley St Matt w H Trin 86-97; RD Burnley 91-97; Chapl Victoria Hosp Burnley 86-88; V Walton-le-Dale St Leon w Samlesbury St Leon from 97; Hon Can Blackb Cathl from 97. *The Vicarage, Church Brow, Preston PR5 4BH* Tel (01772) 880233 Fax 880289

McCURDY, The Ven Hugh Kyle. b 58. Portsm Poly BA Univ of Wales (Cardiff) PGCE. Trin Coll Bris. d 85 p 86. C Egham *Guildf* 85-88; C Woking St Jo 88-91; V Histon *Ely* 91-05; P-in-c Impington 98-05; RD N Stowe 94-05; Hon Can Ely Cathl 04-05; Adn Huntingdon and Wisbech from 05. *Whitgift House, The College, Ely CB7 4DL* Tel (01353) 658404 or 652735 E-mail archdeacon.handw@ely.anglican.org

McDERMID, The Ven Norman George Lloyd Roberts. b 27. St Edm Hall Ox BA49 MA52. Wells Th Coll 49. d 51 p 52. C Leeds St Pet *Ripon* 51-56; V Bramley 56-64; Dioc Stewardship Adv 64-76; R Kirkby Overblow 64-80; Hon Can Ripon Cathl 72-93; Dioc Stewardship Adv *Wakef* 73-76; Dioc Stewardship Adv *Bradf* 73-76; RD Harrogate *Ripon* 77-83; V Knaresborough 80-83; Adn Richmond 83-93; rtd 93; Perm to Offic *Ripon* from 93. *Greystones, 10 North End, Bedale DL8 1AB* Tel (01677) 422210 Mobile 07704-977035 E-mail norman@gmcdermid.fsbusiness.co.uk

McDERMOTT, Christopher Francis Patrick. b 54. Southeastern Coll USA BA84 Wheaton Coll Illinois MA87. EAMTC. d 95 p 96. C Gt Ilford St Clem and St Marg *Chelmsf* 95-99. *17 Benton Road, Ilford IG1 4AT*

McDERMOTT, Fraser Graeme. b 65. NTMTC 97. d 98 p 00. NSM Oak Tree Angl Fellowship *Lon* 98-02; V N Wembley St Cuth from 02. *St Cuthbert's Vicarage, 214 Carlton Avenue West, Wembley HA0 3QY* Tel (020) 8904 7657 or 8904 8599 E-mail fraser@stcuths.org

MACDONALD, Alan Hendry. b 49. St Steph Ho Ox 86. d 88 p 89. C Heavitree w Ex St Paul 88-91; C Withycombe Raleigh 91-92; TV 92-95; R Silverton, Butterleigh, Bickleigh and Cadeleigh from 95; RD Tiverton 00-02. *The Rectory, 21A King Street, Silverton, Exeter EX5 4JG* Tel (01392) 860350 E-mail almac01@tinyonline.co.uk

MacDONALD, Alastair Douglas. b 48. Cranmer Hall Dur 71. d 74 p 75. C Mottingham St Andr *S'wark* 74-78; C Woolwich St Mary w St Mich 78-81; V S Wimbledon St Andr 81-89; V Brighton St Matthias *Chich* 89-94; Chapl Southn Community Services NHS Trust 94-01; Mental Health Chapl Hants Partnerships NHS Trust 01-04. *Episkopi, Fontwell Avenue, Eastergate, Chichester PO20 3RU* Tel (01243) 542771

MacDONALD, Alastair Robert. b 72. Edin Univ MA94 MTh03. TISEC. d 02 p 03. C Edin St Thos 02-06; Asst Chapl Amsterdam w Den Helder and Heiloo *Eur* from 06. *Christ Church, Groenburgwal 42, 1011 HW Amsterdam, The Netherlands* Tel (0031) (20) 624 8877 E-mail alastair@christchurch.nl

MACDONALD, Cameron. b 59. Open Univ BA89. Wilson Carlile Coll 76 NEOC 89. d 90 p 91. CA from 76; C Nairn *Mor* 90-92; P-in-c 92-95; CF 95-05; Chapl HM YOI Thorn Cross 05-07; Port Chapl Aqaba Jordan from 07. *Church of St Peter and St Paul, PO Box 568, Aqaba 77110, Jordan* Tel (00962) (3) 201 8630 E-mail mtsaqaba@go.com.jo

McDONALD, Carollyn Elisabeth. b 54. Edin Univ BSc76. EMMTC 07. d 09. C Sawley *Derby* from 09. *10 Brecon Close, Long Eaton, Nottingham NG10 4JW* Tel 0115-972 4762 E-mail carollynm@greenfilingcabinet1.fslife.co.uk

MACDONALD, Christopher Kenneth. b 57. Ex Univ BA79 PGCE80. Trin Coll Bris 91. d 93 p 94. C Eastbourne All SS *Chich* 93-96; C Polegate 96-99; Chapl Eastbourne Coll from 99. *14A Grange Road, Eastbourne BN21 4HJ* Tel (01323) 452317 E-mail ckm@eastbourne-college.co.uk

MACDONALD, Colin. b 47. St Jo Coll Nottm 87. d 89 p 90. C Limber Magna w Brocklesby *Linc* 89-92; P-in-c Barrow and Goxhill 92-97; V 97-99; R Hemingby, V Fulletby and R Belchford *Linc* 99-02; TV Wilford Peninsula *St E* 02-09; rtd 09; P-in-c Siddal *Wakef* from 09; P-in-c from 09. *The Vicarage, 15 Whitegate Road, Halifax HX3 9AD* Tel (01422) 364423 E-mail cmacdonald@aol.com

MACDONALD, Canon Donald Courtenay. b 45. Nottm Univ BTh74 St Martin's Coll Lanc CertEd75. Kelham Th Coll 70. **d** 75 **p** 76. C Clifton All SS w Tyndalls Park *Bris* 75-78; C Clifton All SS w St Jo 78-79; Chapl Derby Lonsdale Coll 79-84; V Derby St Andr w St Osmund from 84; RD Derby S 89-99; Dioc Communications Officer 89-93; Hon Can Derby Cathl from 95. *St Osmund's Vicarage, London Road, Derby DE24 8UW* Tel (01332) 571329 E-mail donald.c.macdonald@btinternet.com

MACDONALD, Helen Maria. *See* BARTON, Helen Maria

McDONALD, Ian Henry. b 40. TD. St Aid Birkenhead 65. **d** 68 **p** 69. C Kingston upon Hull H Trin *York* 68-70; C Drumglass *Arm* 70-73; I Eglish w Killylea 73-80; I Maghera w Killelagh *D & R* 80-91; I Killowen 91-98; I Errigal w Garvagh 98-05; Can Derry Cathl 94-00; Preb 00-05; CF (TAVR) 91-05; rtd 05. *4 Ballylagan Lane, Aghadowey, Coleraine BT51 4DD* Tel (028) 7086 9150 Mobile 07740-708402 E-mail ihmcd@hotmail.co.uk

McDONALD, James Damian (Jack). b 66. Pemb Coll Cam BA87 MA91 K Coll Lon MA96 SS Hild & Bede Coll Dur PGCE88 Strasbourg Univ DrTheol07. Qu Coll Birm 90. **d** 92 **p** 93. C Camberwell St Geo *S'wark* 92-95; Chapl G&C Coll Cam 95-99; Fell and Dean 96-06; Sen Proctor Cam Univ 02-03; Headmaster Sancton Wood Sch 06-09. *Le Stift, 1B quai St-Thomas, BP 80022, 67081 Strasbourg, France*

McDONALD, John Richard Burleigh. b 17. TCD BA40 BD41. **d** 41 **p** 42. C Belfast St Pet *Conn* 41-45; Uganda 46-61; Educn Officer Ch of Ireland 61-64; Hd RE Stranmills Coll of Educn Belf 66-86; Dir Post-Ord Tr *Conn* 86-94; rtd 94. *76 Osborne Drive, Belfast BT9 6LJ* Tel (028) 9066 6737

McDONALD, Lawrence Ronald. b 32. St Alb Minl Tr Scheme 84. **d** 87 **p** 88. NSM Sharnbrook and Knotting w Souldrop *St Alb* 87-90; C Bromham w Oakley and Stagsden 90-93; P-in-c Renhold 93-98; rtd 99; P-in-c Stevington *St Alb* 99-02; Perm to Offic from 02. *16 Townsend Road, Sharnbrook, Bedford MK44 1HY* Tel (01234) 782849 E-mail fathermac@ukgateway.net

McDONALD, Malcolm Crawford. b 75. St Andr Univ MA97 MLitt98. Wycliffe Hall Ox BTh05. **d** 05 **p** 06. C Kensington St Barn *Lon* 05-09; R Loughton St Mary *Chelmsf* from 09. *The Rectory, 203 High Road, Loughton IG10 1BB* Tel (020) 8508 7892

MACDONALD, Martin Stanley Harrison. b 51. Dur Univ BSc72 ACA75 FCA82. SAOMC 98. **d** 01 **p** 02. NSM Tring *St Alb* 01-08. *Broad Head End, Cragg Vale, Hebden Bridge HX7 5RT* Tel (01422) 881543 Mobile 07883-091787 E-mail mshmacdonald@ntlworld.com

MACDONALD, Canon Murray Somerled. b 23. Pemb Coll Cam BA46 MA49. Ely Th Coll 47. **d** 48 **p** 49. C Hendon St Mary *Lon* 48-51; C Hanover Square St Geo 51-53; P-in-c Upton and Copmanford *Ely* 53-54; R Sawtry 53-54; R Sawtry, Upton and Copmanford 54-57; V Upwood w Gt and Lt Raveley 57-62; R Wood Walton 57-62; V Fenstanton 62-70; V Hilton 62-70; RD Huntingdon 69-76; R Huntingdon All SS w St Jo 70-82; R Huntingdon St Mary w St Benedict 71-82; Hon Can Ely Cathl 72-82; Can Res 82-88; rtd 89; Perm to Offic *Linc* 89-01 and *Ely* 89-97. *4 Hacconby Lane, Morton, Bourne PE10 0NT* Tel (01778) 570711

MACDONALD (*formerly* **WIFFIN**), **Susan Elizabeth.** b 51. Edin Th Coll 93. **d** 96 **p** 97. NSM Jedburgh *Edin* 96-98; C Galashiels 98-01; P-in-c Fochabers and Dioc Miss Co-ord *Mor* 01-05; Can St Andr Cathl Inverness 03-05; Miss and Min Officer *Ab* 05-07; R Edin Ch Ch from 07. *6A Morningside Road, Edinburgh EH10 4DD* Tel 0131-229 0090 Mobile 07753-684923 E-mail susan@6a.org.uk

MacDONALD, Trevor John. b 33. Hertf Coll Ox BA55 MA59. Chich Th Coll 92. **d** 93 **p** 94. NSM Hove St Barn and St Agnes *Chich* 93-05. *31 Orchard Gardens, Hove BN3 7BH* Tel (01273) 771228

MACDONALD, Warren. Monash Univ Aus BEng Leeds Univ MPhil Gothenburg Univ PhD00 CEng CPEng MIEAust. Trin Coll Bris 93. **d** 95 **p** 96. NSM Iford *Win* 95-98; Perm to Offic from 98. *5 St James's Square, Bournemouth BH5 2BX* Tel (01202) 422131 Fax 422101 Mobile 07774-497872 E-mail warren@warrenmacdonald.com

MACDONALD-MILNE, Canon Brian James. b 35. CCC Cam BA58 MA62 St Pet Coll Ox MA81. Cuddesdon Coll 58. **d** 60 **p** 61. C Fleetwood St Pet *Blackb* 60-63; Solomon Is 64-78; Vanuatu 78-80; Acting Chapl Trin Coll Ox 81; Acting Chapl St Pet Coll Ox 81-82; Relief Chapl HM Pris Grendon and Spring Hill 81-82; Research Fell Qu Coll Birm 82-83; Hon Asst P Bordesley SS Alb and Patr *Birm* 82-83; R Waterbeach *Ely* 83-88; V Waterbeach 83-88; OCF 83-88; R Radwinter w Hempstead *Chelmsf* 88-97; RD Saffron Walden 91-97; P-in-c The Sampfords 95-97; rtd 97; Perm to Offic *Ely* 97 and *Chelmsf* from 02; Dioc Rep Melanesian Miss and Papua New Guinea Ch Partnership from 99; Chapl Ely Chapter Guild of Servants of the Sanctuary from 00; Adv Melanesian Brotherhood from 05; Perm to Offic Melanesia from 07; Can Honiara from 07. *39 Way Lane, Waterbeach, Cambridge CB25 9NQ* Tel (01223) 861631 E-mail bj.macdonaldmilne@homecall.co.uk

McDONNELL, David. CITC. **d** 09. C Dublin Ch Ch Cathl Gp from 09. *32 Shandon Drive, Phibsboro, Dublin 7, Republic of Ireland* Tel (00353) (1) 838 0469 E-mail mcdonndj@tcd.ie

McDONNELL, Mrs Mavis Marian. b 42. **d** 98 **p** 99. OLM Warrington St Ann *Liv* from 98. *32 Shaws Avenue, Warrington WA2 8AX* Tel (01925) 634408 E-mail mmavis@aol.com

McDONOUGH, David Sean. b 55. **d** 89 **p** 90. C Moseley St Mary *Birm* 89-92; TV Glascote and Stonydelph *Lich* from 92. *90 Briar, Tamworth B77 4DZ* Tel (01827) 52754 *or* 330306 E-mail david@dmcdonough.freeserve.co.uk

McDONOUGH, Terence. b 57. St Jo Coll Nottm LTh86. **d** 89 **p** 90. C Linthorpe *York* 89-94; TV Heworth H Trin 94-98; V Heworth Ch Ch from 98; P-in-c York St Thos w St Maurice 06-09. *Christ Church Vicarage, 13 Lawnway, York YO31 1JD* Tel (01904) 425678

McDOUGAL, John Anthony Phelps Standen. *See* STANDEN McDOUGAL, Canon John Anthony Phelps

McDOUGALL, David Robin. b 61. Avery Hill Coll CertEd BEd84. Ridley Hall Cam 85. **d** 87 **p** 88. C Bletchley *Ox* 87-91; C High Wycombe 91-93; C E Twickenham St Steph *Lon* 93-02; P-in-c Upper Sunbury St Sav from 02. *St Saviour's Vicarage, 205 Vicarage Road, Sunbury-on-Thames TW16 7TP* Tel (01932) 782800 E-mail david@st-saviours-sunbury.org.uk

McDOUGALL, Mrs Denise Alma. b 48. Ban Coll TCert69. NOC 00. **d** 03. NSM Waterloo Ch Ch and St Jo Liv 03-09; Chapl St Fran of Assisi City Academy Liv 05-09; NSM Gt Crosby St Faith and Waterloo Park St Mary *Liv* from 09. *27 Mayfair Avenue, Crosby, Liverpool L23 2TL* Tel 0151-924 8870 E-mail denisemcdougall@yahoo.co.uk

MacDOUGALL, Canon Iain William. b 20. TCD BA43 MA59. CITC 43. **d** 43 **p** 44. C Belfast St Steph *Conn* 43-45; C Enniskillen and Trory *Clogh* 45-48; I Drumlane *K, E & A* 48-50; I Ballinaclash *D & G* 51-54; I Moate *M & K* 54-58; I Ballyloughloe 54-58; I Ferbane 54-58; I Mullingar, Portnashangan, Moyliscar, Kilbixy etc 58-85; Can Meath 81-85; rtd 85. *18 Denville Court, Killiney, Co Dublin, Republic of Ireland* Tel (00353) (1) 285 4751

McDOUGALL, Sally-Anne. b 64. Glas Univ BMus86 Edin Univ BD04. TISEC 01. **d** 04. C Glas St Marg 04-06. *Address temp unknown* E-mail sal@mcdougall.gg

McDOUGALL, Stuart Ronald. b 28. Leeds Univ DipAdEd MEd84. Roch Th Coll 64. **d** 66 **p** 67. C Gravesend St Aid *Roch* 66-69; C Wells St Thos w Horrington *B & W* 69-70; TV Tong *Bradf* 70-73; V Cononley w Bradley 73-82; C Thornthwaite w Thruscross and Darley *Ripon* 82-83; P-in-c Dacre w Hartwith 83-86; rtd 86; Perm to Offic *Sarum* 90-08. *35 Sheppard's College, London Road, Bromley BR1 1PF*

MacDOUGALL, William Duncan. b 47. Nottm Univ BTh74 LTh74. St Jo Coll Nottm 69. **d** 74 **p** 75. C Highbury New Park St Aug *Lon* 74-77; SAMS 77-82; Argentina 78-82; V Rashcliffe and Lockwood *Wakef* 83-87; V Tonbridge St Steph *Roch* 87-03; RD Tonbridge 01-03; Dir Past and Evang Studies Trin Coll Bris from 03. *15 Cranleigh Gardens, Bristol BS9 1HD* Tel 0117-968 2028 E-mail billmacdougall@clara.net

McDOWALL, Julian Thomas. b 39. CCC Cam BA62 MA67 Barrister 61. Linc Th Coll 62. **d** 64 **p** 65. C Rugby St Andr *Cov* 64-70; C-in-c Stoke Hill CD *Guildf* 70-72; V Stoke Hill 72-76; R Elstead 76-91; V Thursley 82-91; TV Wellington and Distr *B & W* 91-93; C Lymington *Win* 93-04; rtd 04; Perm to Offic *Win* from 04. *Juniper Cottage, 20 Solent Avenue, Lymington SO41 3SD* Tel (01590) 676750

McDOWELL, Robert Angus (Robin). b 39. AKC66. **d** 67 **p** 68. C Bishopwearmouth St Mich w St Hilda *Dur* 67-69; CF 69-05; Sen CF 80-91; Asst Chapl Gen 91-94; QHC 93-05; rtd 04; Perm to Offic *York* from 05. *c/o Crockford, Church House, Great Smith Street, London SW1P 3AZ* Tel (01482) 862504

McDOWELL, Roger Ian. b 40. AKC64. **d** 65 **p** 66. C Peterlee *Dur* 65-68; C Weaste *Man* 68-70; C Tonge Moor 70-73; V Whitworth St Bart 73-80; TV Torre *Ex* 80-88; V Torre All SS 88-00; Chapl S Devon Tech Coll Torbay 80-00; rtd 04. *1 Dunanellerich, Dunvegan, Isle of Skye IV55 8ZH* Tel (01470) 521271 E-mail mcdowall@lineone.net

McDOWELL, Francis John. b 56. QUB BA78. CITC BTh93. **d** 96 **p** 97. C Antrim *Conn* 96-99; I Ballyrashane w Kildollagh 99-02; I Dundela St Mark *D & D* from 02. *St Mark's Rectory, 4 Sydenham Avenue, Belfast BT4 2DH* Tel (028) 9065 9047 *or* 9065 4090 E-mail dundela@down.anglican.org

McDOWELL, Ian. b 67. Ch Coll Cam MA88 BA92. Westcott Ho Cam 90. **d** 93 **p** 94. C Hackney *Lon* 93-96; Asst Chapl Homerton Hosp NHS Trust Lon 96-98; Chapl Newham Healthcare NHS Trust Lon 98-03. *37 Hemsworth Street, London N1 5LF* Tel (020) 7363 8053 E-mail mcdow@dircon.co.uk

McDOWELL, Ian James. b 37. St Coll Morpeth ACT ThL60 St Aug Coll Cant. **d** 61 **p** 62. C Naracoorte Australia 61-63; P-in-c Elliston Miss 63-66; C S Harrow St Paul *Lon* 66; C Southgate Ch Ch 67; V Ganton *York* 67-71; P-in-c Foxholes and Butterwick 67-68; R 68-71; R Angaston Australia 71-76; R Colonel Light Gardens 76-94; R Gawler 94-98; R Merriwa

98-02; rtd 02. *1516 New England Highway, Harpers Hill NSW 2321, Australia* Tel (0061) (2) 4930 9051

McDOWELL, John. *See* McDOWELL, Francis John

McDOWELL, Peter Kerr. b 69. QUB BA91. CITC BTh94. **d** 94 **p** 95. C Lisburn St Paul *Conn* 94-98; C Arm St Mark 98-99; I Belfast Upper Malone (Epiphany) *Conn* 99-05; I Ballywillan from 05. *The Rectory, 10 Coleraine Road, Portrush BT56 8EA* Tel (028) 7082 4298 Mobile 07724-072944 E-mail revpetermcdowell@hotmail.co.uk

McDOWELL, Sheilah Rosamond Girgis. b 72. **d** 05. NSM Hammersmith H Innocents and St Jo *Lon* from 05. *36 Avenue Gardens, Teddington TW11 0BH* Tel (020) 8943 9259 E-mail rosamond.mcdowell@collyerbristow.com

MACE, Alan Herbert. b 28. Lon Univ BA49 Ex Inst of Educn TCert50. Wycliffe Hall Ox 59. **d** 60 **p** 61. C Disley *Ches* 60-63; C Folkestone H Trin w Ch Ch *Cant* 63-67; Lic to Offic *Win* 67-93; rtd 93; Public Preacher *Win* from 93. *15 Bassett Heath Avenue, Southampton SO16 7GP* Tel (023) 8076 8161

MACE, David Sinclair. b 37. Cam Univ BA61. **d** 95 **p** 96. OLM Godalming *Guildf* 95-07; rtd 07. *Torridon, Grosvenor Road, Godalming GU7 1NZ* Tel (01483) 414646

MACE, Helen Elizabeth. *See* PRIEST, Mrs Helen Elizabeth

MACE, Robert Alfred Beasley. b 16. Leeds Univ BA49. Coll of Resurr Mirfield 48. **d** 50 **p** 51. C Callander *St And* 50-53; C Newc St Mary 53-54; C Penton Street St Silas w All SS *Lon* 54-56; C Aylesbury *Ox* 56-59; P-in-c Glas St Gabr 59-61; R Campbeltown *Arg* 61-65; V Barnsley St Pet *Wakef* 65-72; V Barnsley St Pet and St Jo 72-84; rtd 85; Perm to Offic *Wakef* from 85. *18 Chestnut Court, Barnsley S70 4HW* Tel (01226) 280729

McELHINNEY, Canon Mary Elizabeth Ellen. b 45. TCD BSSc67 BA67. CITC BTh94. **d** 97 **p** 98. C Magheralin w Dollingstown *D & D* 97-01; I Calry *K, E & A* 01-07; Preb Elphin Cathl 04-07; rtd 07. *10 Taughrane Heights, Dollingstown, Craigavon BT66 7RS* Tel (028) 3831 0113 E-mail lizmcelhinney@hotmail.com

McELHINNEY, Robert Stephen. b 70. Aston Univ BSc91. CITC BTh05. **d** 05 **p** 06. C Kill *D & G* 05-08; C Drumglass w Moygashel *Arm* from 08. *Kinore, 84 Killyman Road, Dungannon BT71 6DQ* Tel (028) 8772 7131 E-mail scrap5@eircom.net

McENDOO, Canon Neil Gilbert. b 50. TCD BA72. CITC 75. **d** 75 **p** 76. C Cregagh *D & D* 75-79; C Dublin St Ann *D & G* 79-82; I Dublin Rathmines w Harold's Cross from 82; Can Ch Ch Cathl Dublin 92-02; Preb from 02; Chan from 05. *The Rectory, Purser Gardens, Church Avenue, Rathmines, Dublin 6, Republic of Ireland* Tel (00353) (1) 497 1797 E-mail neil.mcendoo@oceanfree.net

McEUNE, Patrick John. b 55. **d** 04 **p** 05. NSM White Horse *Sarum* from 04; TV from 07; Perm to Offic *Nor* from 08. *82 Danvers Way, Westbury BA13 3UF* Tel 07544-588121 (mobile) E-mail patrickmceune@wiltshire.gov.uk

McEVITT, Canon Peter Benedict. b 58. Coll of Resurr Mirfield 91. **d** 93 **p** 94. C Swinton and Pendlebury *Man* 93-96; TV 96-97; V Darwen St Cuth w Tockholes St Steph *Blackb* 97-02; P-in-c Failsworth H Family *Man* 02-04; R 04-08; AD Oldham 02-08; Dioc Stewardship Officer from 08; Hon Can Man Cathl from 07. *All Saints' Vicarage, Boardman Lane, Middleton, Manchester M24 4TU* Tel 0161-643 2052

MACEY, Preb Anthony Keith Frank. b 46. St Steph Ho Ox 69. **d** 71 **p** 72. C Ex St Thos 71-76; V Wembury 76-88; RD Ivybridge 83-91; V Cockington from 88; RD Torbay 98-03; Preb Ex Cathl from 05. *The Vicarage, 22 Monterey Close, Torquay TQ2 6QW* Tel (01803) 607957 Fax 690338 E-mail smacey@lineone.net *or* cockington@lineone.net

MACEY, Michael David. b 81. Ex Univ BA03 Dur Univ MATM08. Cranmer Hall Dur 03. **d** 05 **p** 06. C Dartmouth and Dittisham *Ex* 05-08; Min Can Westmr Abbey from 08. *7 Little Cloister, Dean's Yard, London SW1P 3PL* Tel (020) 7654 4813 *or* 7654 4855 Fax 7654 4859 E-mail frmacey@hotmail.com *or* michael.macey@westminster-abbey.org

McFADDEN, Canon Ronald Bayle. b 30. TCD BA53 MA55. **d** 54 **p** 55. C Drumglass *Arm* 54-58; S Africa 58-62; Bp's Dom Chapl *D & D* 62-64; C Dundela St Mark 62-64; V Pateley Bridge and Greenhow Hill *Ripon* 64-73; V Knaresborough St Jo 73-79; P-in-c Knaresborough H Trin 78-79; Can Res Ripon Cathl 79-90; rtd 90; Chapl Qu Mary's Sch Baldersby Park 90-00; Perm to Offic *Ripon* from 90 and *York* from 97. *12 Ure Bank Terrace, Ripon HG4 1JG* Tel (01765) 604043

McFADDEN, Terrance. b 61. NTMTC 05. **d** 08 **p** 09. C Greenstead w Colchester St Anne *Chelmsf* from 08. *10 Goldcrest Close, Colchester CO4 3FN*

McFADYAN, Donald Colin Ross. b 63. Wolfs Coll Cam BTh00 Peterho Cam MPhil02. Ridley Hall Cam 97. **d** 01 **p** 02. NSM Haslingfield w Harlton and Gt and Lt Eversden *Ely* 01-05; P-in-c Bassingbourn from 05; P-in-c Whaddon from 05; Course Dir Ridley Hall Cam from 05. *The Vicarage, 21 North End, Bassingbourn, Royston SG8 5NZ* Tel (01763) 244836 Fax 243119 Mobile 07763-401567 E-mail dm240@cam.ac.uk

McFADYEN, Canon Phillip. b 44. K Coll Lon BD69 AKC69 MTh70 ATD. St Aug Coll Cant 69. **d** 71 **p** 72. C Sheff St Mark

Broomhall 71-74; Chapl Keswick Hall Coll of Educn 74-79; V Swardeston *Nor* 79-81; P-in-c E Carleton 79-81; P-in-c Intwood w Keswick 79-81; R Swardeston w E Carleton, Intwood, Keswick etc 81-90; R Ranworth w Panxworth, Woodbastwick etc 90-05; Dioc Clergy Tr Officer 90-98; P-in-c Nor St Geo Colegate from 05; Hon Can Nor Cathl from 97; Bp's Officer for Visual Arts from 01; Relig Adv Anglia TV from 01. *12 The Crescent, Chapel Field Road, Norwich NR2 1SA* Tel (01603) 621570 E-mail phillipmcfadyen@aol.com

McFARLAND, Alan Malcolm. b 24. Lon Univ BA53. Bris Sch of Min 82. **d** 85 **p** 86. NSM Westbury-on-Trym H Trin *Bris* 85-88; Asst Lect Bris Sch of Min 85-88; Perm to Offic *Glouc* 88-89; NSM Lechlade 89-93; Perm to Offic *Sarum* 93-08. *11 The Seahorse, Higher Sea Lane, Charmouth, Bridport DT6 6BB* Tel (01297) 560414

McFARLAND, Darren William. b 71. QUB BA93. CITC BTh96. **d** 96 **p** 97. C Greystones *D & G* 96-98; PV Ch Ch Cathl Dublin 97-99; P-in-c Clydebank *Glas* 99-02; Asst Dioc Miss 21 Co-ord 99-02; R Paisley St Barn from 02; R Paisley H Trin from 02. *The Rectory, 11 Tantallon Drive, Paisley PA2 9JT* Tel (0141) 812359 Mobile 07773-772610 E-mail rector@paisley2.freeserve.co.uk

MACFARLANE, Miss Elizabeth Clare. b 71. St Hugh's Coll Ox BA92. Ripon Coll Cuddesdon BA02. **d** 03 **p** 04. C Watford St Mich *St Alb* 03-06; TV Gt Marlow w Marlow Bottom, Lt Marlow and Bisham *Ox* from 06. *Great Marlow Vicarage, 18 Oak Tree Road, Marlow SL7 3EE* Tel (01628) 488493

MACFARLANE, Iain Philip. b 64. Essex Univ BSc85 W Sussex Inst of HE PGCE88. Trin Coll Bris BA99. **d** 99 **p** 00. C Fishponds St Jo *Bris* 99-03; TV Yate New Town from 03. *The Vicarage, 57 Brockworth, Bristol BS37 8SJ* Tel (01454) 322921 E-mail imacfarlane@ukonline.co.uk

McFARLANE, Iain Scott. b 70. St Jo Coll Nottm 02. **d** 04 **p** 05. C Malvern St Andr and Malvern Wells and Wyche *Worc* 04-07; V Taunton Lyngford *B & W* from 07. *62 Eastwick Road, Taunton TA2 7HD* Tel (01823) 275085 Mobile 07834-191507 E-mail revmcfarlane@gmail.com

McFARLANE, The Ven Janet Elizabeth. b 64. Sheff Univ BMedSci87 St Jo Coll Dur BA92. Cranmer Hall Dur 93. **d** 93 **p** 94. Par Dn Stafford *Lich* 93-94; C 94-96; Chapl and Min Can Ely Cathl 96-99; Dioc Communications Officer *Nor* from 99; Hon PV Nor Cathl 00-09; Bp's Chapl 01-09; Adn Nor from 09. *31 Bracondale, Norwich NR1 2AT* Tel (01603) 620007 E-mail archdeacon.norwich@norwich.anglican.org

MACFARLANE, Katy Antonia. b 69. STETS. **d** 09. NSM Crofton *Portsm* from 09. *20 Shannon Road, Fareham PO14 3RS* Tel (01329) 668920

MACFARLANE, William Angus. b 17. Worc Coll Ox BA39 MA43. Wycliffe Hall Ox 39. **d** 40 **p** 41. C Charles w Plymouth St Luke *Ex* 40-45; C Reading St Jo *Ox* 45-47; CMS Tr Coll Blackheath 47-48; C Brompton H Trin *Lon* 48-49; R Bighton *Win* 49-52; V Bishop's Sutton 49-52; V Southwold *St E* 52-59; V Plaistow St Mary *Roch* 59-71; V Bexleyheath Ch Ch 71-79; Perm to Offic *B & W* 79-95 and 04-07; Chapl Sandhill Park Hosp Taunton 80-87; rtd 82. *Moorlands, Blue Anchor, Minehead TA24 6JZ* Tel (01643) 821564

McGANITY, Canon Steven. b 61. Nottm Univ BTh93. St Jo Coll Nottm 90. **d** 93 **p** 94. C Gateacre *Liv* 93-97; V Clubmoor from 97; AD W Derby from 08; Hon Can Liv Cathl from 08. *St Andrew's Vicarage, 176 Queen's Drive, West Derby, Liverpool L13 0AL* Tel 0151-226 1977 E-mail smcganity@bigfoot.com

McGARAHAN, Kevin Francis. b 51. Oak Hill Th Coll BA84 MA90. **d** 84 **p** 85. C Balderstone *Man* 84-87; C Stoughton *Guildf* 87-89; Par Lect Ashton St Mich *Man* 89-92; TV Madeley *Heref* 92-96; CF 96-99; TV Woughton *Ox* 99-06; rtd 07; Hon C Hanger Hill Ascension and W Twyford St Mary *Lon* from 07. *48 Brentmead Gardens, London NW10 7ED* Tel (020) 8838 2542 E-mail rev_kev@hotmail.com

McGEARY, Peter. b 59. K Coll Lon BD AKC. Chich Th Coll 84. **d** 86 **p** 87. C Brighton St Pet and St Nic w Chpl Royal *Chich* 86-90; C St Marylebone All SS *Lon* 90-95; P-in-c Hayes St Anselm 95-97; V 97-98; V St Geo-in-the-East St Mary from 98; PV Westmr Abbey from 00. *The Clergy House, All Saints Court, 68 Johnson Street, London E1 0BQ* Tel and fax (020) 7790 0973 E-mail mcgeary@pmcg.demon.co.uk

McGEE, The Very Revd Stuart Irwin. b 30. TCD BA53 MA68. **d** 53 **p** 54. C Belfast St Simon *Conn* 53-55; Chapl Miss to Seamen Singapore 55-58; I Drumholm and Rossnowlagh *D & R* 58-65; CF 65-77; Dep Asst Chapl Gen 77-88; Can Achonry Cathl 89-92; I Achonry w Tubbercurry and Killoran 89-92; Dean Elphin and Ardagh and I Sligo w Knocknarea and Rosses Pt *K, E & A* 92-99; rtd 99. *Teach na Mara, Strandhill, Sligo, Republic of Ireland* Tel (00353) (71) 916 8910 Mobile 86-050 9272

MacGEOCH, David John Lamont. b 64. Bath Univ BSc90 CQSW90. Westcott Ho Cam 97. **d** 99 **p** 00. C Midsomer Norton w Clandown *B & W* 99-03; V Puriton and Pawlett 03-08; P-in-c Glastonbury w Meare from 08. *24 Wells Road, Glastonbury BA6 9DJ* E-mail all@macgeoch.fsnet.co.uk

McGHIE, Clinton Adolphus. b 41. Univ of W Indies. d 78 p 79. Jamaica 78-96; Perm to Offic *Chelmsf* 96-97; P-in-c Highams Park All SS 97-02; V from 02. *All Saints' Vicarage, 12A Castle Avenue, London E4 9QD* Tel (020) 8527 3269

McGILL, Francis Leonard. b 31. d 93 p 94. NSM Howell Hill *Guildf* 93-01; Perm to Offic from 02. *27 Hampton Grove, Ewell, Epsom KT17 1LA* Tel (020) 8393 2226

MacGILLIVRAY, Canon Alexander Buchan. b 33. Edin Univ MA55 Aber Univ DipEd67. Edin Th Coll 55. d 57 p 58. Chapl St Ninian's Cathl Perth 57-59; Chapl Aberlour Orphanage 59-62; C Aberlour *Mor* 59-62; R Oldmeldrum and Whiterashes *Ab* 62-07; R Fyvie and Insch 74-81; Can St Andr Cathl 78-07; rtd 07. *Address temp unknown*

MacGILLIVRAY, Jonathan Martin. b 53. Aber Univ MA75. Coll of Resurr Mirfield. d 80 p 81. C Hulme Ascension *Man* 80-84; P-in-c Birch St Agnes 84-85; R 85-91; V Hurst 91-96; Chapl Tameside Gen Hosp 92-96; Dir of Ords and OLM Officer *Man* 96-02; V Carrington *S'well* from 02. *Carrington Vicarage, 6 Watcombe Circus, Nottingham NG5 2DT* Tel 0115-962 1291 E-mail j.macg@virgin.net

McGINLEY, Canon Jack Francis. b 36. ALCD65. d 65 p 66. C Erith St Paul *Roch* 65-70; C Morden *S'wark* 70-74; V New Catton Ch Ch *Nor* 74-94; RD Nor N 84-89; Hon Can Nor Cathl 90-94; R Carlton-in-the-Willows *S'well* 94-02; R Colwick 96-02; rtd 02; Perm to Offic *Nor* from 03. *14 Clovelly Drive, Norwich NR6 5EY* Tel (01603) 788848 E-mail jack.mcginley@talk21.com

McGINLEY, John Charles. b 69. Birm Univ BSocSc90. Trin Coll Bris BA96. d 96 p 97. C Hounslow H Trin w St Paul *Lon* 96-00; TV Hinckley H Trin *Leic* 00-04; TR Leic H Trin w St Jo from 09. *5 Ratcliffe Road, Leicester LE2 3JE* E-mail john.mcginley1@ntlworld.com

McGINTY, Ms Nicola Jane. b 61. Bath Univ BSc83 Warwick Univ MBA06. Qu Coll Birm 06. d 09. NSM Barrow upon Soar w Walton le Wolds *Leic* from 09; NSM Wymeswold and Prestwold w Hoton from 09. *5 Station Road, Rearsby, Leicester LE7 4YX* Tel (01664) 424869 E-mail nicky@njmcginty.co.uk

McGIRR, Canon William Eric. b 43. CITC 68. d 71 p 72. C Carrickfergus *Conn* 71-74; C Mt Merrion *D & D* 74-77; I Donacavey w Barr *Clogh* 77-88; I Ballybeen *D & D* 88-94; I Magheraculmoney *Clogh* from 94; Can Clogh Cathl from 95; Chan from 06. *11 Castle Manor, Kesh, Enniskillen BT93 1RT* Tel (028) 6863 2221

McGLADDERY, David John. b 62. Homerton Coll Cam BEd85 Univ of Wales (Cardiff) MA93. St Mich Coll Llan 02. d 05 p 06. NSM Monmouth w Overmonnow etc 05-09; V from 09; Asst Chapl Mon Sch from 05. *The Vicarage, The Parade, Monmouth NP25 3PA* Tel (01600) 715924

McGLASHAN, Alastair Robin. b 33. Ch Ch Ox BA57 MA58 St Jo Coll Cam BA59 MA63 SAP84. Ridley Hall Cam 58. d 60 p 61. C St Helens St Helen *Liv* 60; C Ormskirk 60-62; CMS India 63-74; USA 74-75; C Lamorbey H Redeemer *Roch* 75-77; Chapl W Park Hosp Epsom 77-85; Chapl Maudsley Hosp Lon 85-87; Perm to Offic *S'wark* 86-06; rtd 98. *102 Westway, London SW20 9LS* Tel (020) 8542 2125

McGLINCHEY, Patrick Gerard. b 59. NUU BA82 Nottm Univ BTh95 MA06. St Jo Coll Nottm 93. d 95 p 96. C Kettering Ch the King *Pet* 95-97; C Gorleston St Andr *Nor* 07-02; Assoc Min Cliff Park Community Ch 99-02; Chapl and Dean of Res QUB from 03. *20 Elmwood Avenue, Belfast BT9 6AY* Tel (028) 9066 7754 Mobile 07799-061718 E-mail paddysoffice@hotmail.com

McGONIGLE, Martin Leo Thomas. b 64. Univ of Greenwich BA94 Anglia Poly Univ MA99. EAMTC 96. d 98 p 99. C Forest Gate All SS and St Edm *Chelmsf* 98-01; Perm to Offic *Lon* 01-02; Chapl Asst Cen Man/Man Children's Univ Hosp NHS Trust 02-03; Lead Chapl 03-07; Spiritual Care Co-ord from 07; Chapl Springhill Hospice from 06. *Springhill Hospice, Broad Lane, Rochdale OL16 4PZ* Tel (01706) 649920 E-mail martin.mcgonigle@springhillhospice.nhs.uk

McGONIGLE, Thomas. b 22. TCD BA45 MA65. TCD Div Sch 43. d 46 p 47. C Drumglass *Arm* 46-50; I Clogherny 50-53; I Magherafelt 53-61 and 74-88; I Portadown St Mark 61-74; Can Arm Cathl 72-88; Treas 79-83; Dean 83-88; Prec 88; rtd 88; Lic to Offic *Arm* from 88. *91 Kernan Gardens, Portadown, Craigavon BT63 5RA* Tel (028) 3833 0892

McGOWAN, Anthony Charles. b 57. Jes Coll Cam BA79 MA83. Coll of Resurr Mirfield 80. d 82 p 83. C Milford Haven *St D* 82-85; C Penistone and Thurlstone *Wakef* 85-88; Asst Chapl Radcliffe Infirmary Ox 91-94; Chapl Radcliffe Infirmary NHS Trust 94-99; Chapl Ox Radcliffe Hosps NHS Trust 99-04; V Northampton H Trin and St Paul *Pet* from 05. *The Vicarage, 24 Edinburgh Road, Northampton NN2 6PH* Tel (01604) 711468 E-mail anthony.mcgowan@tiscali.co.uk

McGOWAN, Daniel Richard Hugh. b 71. Oak Hill Th Coll. d 03 p 04. C Peterlee *Dur* 03-07; TV Morden *S'wark* from 07. *49 Camborne Road, Morden SM4 4JL* Tel (020) 8542 2966

McGOWAN, Timothy Julien. b 68. Wycliffe Hall Ox 05. d 07 p 09. C N Wembley St Cuth *Lon* 07-08; C Fulham St Matt from 08.

2A Clancarty Road, London SW6 3AB Tel (020) 7736 4421 E-mail tmcgowan@tmls.co.uk

McGOWN, Robert Jackson. b 20. Keble Coll Ox BA42 MA46. Linc Th Coll 42. d 45 p 46. C Ipswich St Mary le Tower *St E* 45-47; Chapl Brockhurst Sch 47-49; Perm to Offic *Ox* 49-50; C Astbury *Ches* 50-51; C Glouc St Mary de Lode and St Nic 51-54; Min Can Glouc Cathl 51-54; C W Kirby St Bridget *Ches* 64-71; Perm to Offic from 76; rtd 85. *16 Church Road, West Kirby, Wirral CH48 0RW* Tel 0151-625 9481

McGRANAGHAN, Patrick Joseph Colum. b 46. Glas Univ BSc68 Lanc Univ MA72. St Alb Minl Tr Scheme 82. d 85 p 86. NSM Markyate Street *St Alb* 85-91; NSM Johnstone *Glas* 91-99; NSM Renfrew 97-99; P-in-c Kilmacolm from 99; P-in-c Bridge of Weir from 99. *The Rectory, 4 Balmore Court, Kilmacolm PA13 4LX* Tel (01505) 872733 *or* tel and fax 872961 Mobile 07932-643893 E-mail colum.mcgranaghan@talk21.com

McGRATH, Prof Alister Edgar. b 53. Wadh Coll Ox BA75 Mert Coll Ox MA78 DPhil78 BD83 DD01 FRSA05. Westcott Ho Cam 78. d 80 p 81. C Wollaton *S'well* 80-83; Chapl St Hilda's Coll Ox 83-87; Tutor Wycliffe Hall Ox from 83; Prin 95-04; Prof Systematic Th Regent Coll Vancouver 93-97; Research Lect in Th Ox Univ 93-99; Prof Hist Th 99-08; Dir Ox Cen for Evang and Apologetics 04-08; Hd Cen for Th, Relig and Culture K Coll Lon from 08. *King's College London, Franklin-Wilkins Building, Waterloo Road, London SE1 9NH* Tel (020) 7848 3778

McGRATH, Ian Denver. b 47. Leeds Univ CertEd72. d 87 p 88. OLM Ancaster *Linc* 87-89; OLM Ancaster Wilsford Gp 89-92; C Spilsby w Hundleby 92-95; P-in-c Asterby Gp 95-99; R from 99. *The Rectory, 6 Simons Close, Donington-on-Bain, Louth LN11 9TX* Tel and fax (01507) 343345 E-mail ian@idmcgrath.fsnet.co.uk

McGRATH, Joanna Ruth. See COLLICUTT McGRATH, Joanna Ruth

McGRATH, John. b 49. Salford Univ BSc78 Man Poly CertEd79. NOC 82. d 85 p 86. C Horwich *Man* 85-88; P-in-c Hillock 88-89; V 89-94; V York St Luke 94-97; V Hollinwood *Man* 97-02; P-in-c Oldham St Chad Limeside 97-02; V Hollinwood and Limeside 02-03; TV Turton Moorland Min 03-07; P-in-c Littleborough from 07; P-in-c Calderbrook from 07; P-in-c Shore from 07. *The Vicarage, 4 Stansfield Hall, Littleborough OL15 9RH* Tel (01706) 378055 E-mail john@jmcg.myzen.co.uk

McGRATH, Kenneth David. b 59. Surrey Univ BSc82 QUB PGCE83 TCD BTh03. CITC 00. d 03 p 04. C Lisburn Ch Ch Cathl 03-05; V 05-09; I Kilkeel *D & D* from 09. *The Rectory, 44 Manse Road, Kilkeel, Newry BT34 4BN* Tel (028) 4176 2300 *or* 4176 5994 E-mail revken.mcgrath@btopenworld.com

McGRATH, Patrick Desmond. b 64. Liv Univ LLB86. Wycliffe Hall Ox 92. d 96 p 97. C Netherton *Liv* 96-98; C Ravenhead 98-02; P-in-c Ightham *Roch* 02-07; Perm to Offic *Cant* from 08. *c/o Crockford, Church House, Great Smith Street, London SW1P 3AZ*

MacGREGOR, Alan John. b 31. Jes Coll Ox MA57. S Tr Scheme 94. d 97 p 98. NSM Worting *Win* 97-00; Perm to Offic *Lon* 01 and *Sarum* 03-08. *7 Sterte Avenue, Poole BH15 2AJ* Tel (01202) 667267

McGREGOR, Alexander Scott. b 72. Ch Ch Ox BA95 MA00 Barrister 96. SAOMC 03. d 06 p 07. NSM Harrow St Mary *Lon* 06-09; Legal Adv Legal Office Nat Ch Inst 06-09; Dep Legal Adv Gen Syn and Abps' Coun from 09; Dep Chan *Ox* from 07. *2 Edmunds Mews, Kings Langley WD4 8GB* Tel (01923) 262773 E-mail asmcg@hotmail.com

McGREGOR, Alistair Darrant. b 45. ALCD69. d 69 p 70. C Streatham Immanuel w St Anselm *S'wark* 69-73; C Somerset St Jas Bermuda 73-76; Warden St Mich Cen New Cross 76-80; C Hatcham St Jas *S'wark* 76-80; V Nor Heartsease St Fran 80-87; TR Thetford 87-96; P-in-c Kilverstone 87-90; P-in-c Croxton 87-90; RD Thetford and Rockland 90-96; TR Gt Baddow *Chelmsf* 96-08; rtd 08. *10 Portland Road, West Bridgford, Nottingham NG2 6DL* Tel 0115-981 0689 E-mail asmcgregor@plusnet.co.uk

MacGREGOR, Colin Highmoor. b 19. Lon Univ BSc45 Magd Coll Cam BA47 MA50. Wells Th Coll 54. d 56 p 57. C Camberwell St Giles *S'wark* 56-60; V Clapham St Pet 60-73; V Riddlesdown 73-87; rtd 87; Perm to Offic *S'wark* from 03. *3 Longacre Court, 21 Mayfield Road, South Croydon CR2 0BG* Tel (020) 8651 2615

MacGREGOR, Donald Alexander Thomson. b 52. Loughb Univ BSc75 Nottm Univ MA97 Leic Univ CertEd78. St Jo Coll Nottm 91. d 93 p 94. C Walmley *Birm* 93-96; C Braunstone *Leic* 96-97; TV 97-99; Chapl Loughb Univ 99-04; V Fishguard w Llanychar and Pontfaen w Morfil etc *St D* from 04. *The Vicarage, High Street, Fishguard SA65 9AU* Tel (01348) 872895 E-mail don@macgregors.wanadoo.co.uk

McGREGOR, Mrs Lorraine Louise. b 59. Sarum Th Coll 02. d 05 p 06. OLM Colehill *Sarum* from 05. *Tapiola, Marianne Road, Wimborne BH21 2SQ* Tel (01202) 886519 E-mail lorraine@hayeswood.dorset.sch.uk

McGREGOR, Mrs Lynn. b 61. Ches Coll of HE BTh00. NOC 97. **d** 00 **p** 01. C Colne and Villages *Blackb* 00-03; C Gt Harwood 03-06; P-in-c Wigan St Mich *Liv* 06-07; V from 07. *St Michael's Vicarage, Swinley Road, Wigan WN1 2DN* Tel (01942) 239012 E-mail ian.mcgregor@homecall.co.uk

MacGREGOR, Preb Neil. b 35. Keble Coll Ox BA60 MA80. Wells Th Coll. **d** 65 **p** 66. C Bath Bathwick St Mary w Woolley *B & W* 65-70; R Oare w Culbone 70-74; C Lynton, Brendon, Countisbury and Lynmouth *Ex* 70-74; P-in-c Kenn w Kingston Seymour *B & W* 74-76; R 76-80; R Wem and V Lee Brockhurst *Lich* 80-01; P-in-c Loppington w Newtown 95-01; RD Wem and Whitchurch 95-01; Preb Lich Cathl 97-01; rtd 01; Perm to Offic *Heref* from 01. *19 Castle View Terrace, Ludlow SY8 2NG* Tel (01584) 872671 E-mail juvenal@martial.fsnet.co.uk

McGREGOR, Nigel Selwyn. b 47. FCA69. Sarum & Wells Th Coll 87. **d** 89 **p** 90. C Charlton Kings St Mary *Glouc* 89-92; P-in-c Seale *Guildf* 92-95; P-in-c Puttenham and Wanborough 92-95; R Seale, Puttenham and Wanborough 95-04; R Barming *Roch* from 04. *The Rectory, Church Lane, Barming, Maidstone ME16 9HA* Tel (01622) 726263 E-mail nigel.mcgregor@diocese-rochester.org *or* mcgregorn@aol.com

McGREGOR, Stephen Paul. b 55. **d** 03 **p** 04. OLM Tonge Fold *Man* from 03. *32 Rawcliffe Avenue, Bolton BL2 6JX* Tel (01204) 391205 E-mail steve.mcgregor2@ntlworld.com

McGUFFIE, Duncan Stuart. b 45. Man Univ MA70 Regent's Park Coll Ox DPhil80. S Dios Minl Tr Scheme 84. **d** 85 **p** 85. C Sholing *Win* 85-89; V Clavering and Langley w Arkesden etc *Chelmsf* from 89. *The Vicarage, 54 Pelham Road, Clavering, Saffron Walden CB11 4PQ* Tel (01799) 550703

McGUINNESS, Gordon Baxter. b 57. St Andr Univ BSc79 BNC Ox MSc80. Oak Hill NSM Course 86. **d** 89 **p** 90. NSM Loudwater *Ox* 89-92; C Chilwell *S'well* 92-01; TR Ellesmere Port *Ches* 01-09; R from 09. *The Rectory, Vale Road, Whitby, Ellesmere Port CH65 9AY* Tel 0151-356 8351 *or* 355 2516 E-mail revgordon@supanet.com

McGUIRE, Alec John. b 51. K Coll Cam BA73 MA76 MRSH86 FRSH90. Westcott Ho Cam 74. **d** 78 **p** 79. C Hungerford and Denford *Ox* 78-81; Prec Leeds St Pet *Ripon* 81-86; Perm to Offic from 86; rtd 01. *34 Gledhow Wood Road, Leeds LS8 4BZ* Tel 0113-240 0336

McGUIRE, John. b 31. Oak Hill Th Coll 59. **d** 62 **p** 65. C Tooting Graveney St Nic *S'wark* 62-64; C Normanton *Derby* 64-67; N Area Sec ICM 67-71; Chapl RNR 67-81; R Biddulph Moor *Lich* 71-00; rtd 00; Perm to Offic *Blackb* from 00. *25 Victoria Road, Fulwood, Preston PR2 8NE* Tel (01772) 719549 E-mail jmcguire@argonet.co.uk

McGURK, Michael. b 68. St Jo Coll Nottm 05. **d** 07 **p** 08. C Haughton St Mary *Man* from 07. *Church Farm, Worths Lane, Denton, Manchester M34 7GB* Tel 0161-336 2610 Mobile 07811-360432 E-mail rev.mikemcgurk@hotmail.co.uk

MACHA, David. b 65. Keele Univ BA88 CertEd88 St Jo Coll Dur BA97. **d** 97 **p** 98. C Loughborough Em and St Mary in Charnwood *Leic* 97-01; CMS from 01; Tanzania from 02. *St Margaret's Church, PO Box 306, Moshi, Tanzania* E-mail david@dmacha.idps.co.uk

McHAFFIE, Alistair. b 57. Oak Hill Th Coll 92. **d** 94 **p** 95. C Braintree *Chelmsf* 94-98; R Falkland Is 98-03; V Leyland St Jo *Blackb* from 03. *St John's Vicarage, Leyland Lane, Leyland PR25 1XB* Tel (01772) 621646 E-mail alistair@mchaffie.com

McHALE, John Michael. b 61. Ch Ch Coll Cant BA84 Kingston Univ PGCE89 Univ of Wales (Cardiff) BTh08. St Mich Coll Llan 03. **d** 08 **p** 09. NSM Llandingat w Myddfai *St D* from 08; Asst Chapl Llandovery Coll from 08. *Llandovery College, Llandovery SA20 0EE* Tel (01550) 723009 Fax 723002 Mobile 07912-143374 E-mail john.mchale8@btinternet.com

MACHAM, Miss Anna. b 77. Trin Coll Ox BA98 Cam Univ BA02 MPhil04. Ridley Hall Cam 00. **d** 04 **p** 05. C Cheshunt *St Alb* 04-07; Succ S'wark Cathl from 07; Chapl K Coll Lon from 07. *St Paul's Vicarage, 54 Kipling Street, London SE1 3RU* Tel (020) 7407 8290 E-mail anna.macham@southwark.anglican.org *or* anna.macham@kcl.ac.uk

McHARDY, David William. b 61. Edin Univ BD88 BD90 PhD97. Ab Dioc Tr Course 82 Edin Th Coll 85. **d** 88 **p** 03. C Dumfries *Glas* 88-89; Lect in World Religions Open Univ 97-08; Hon C Oldmeldrum *Ab* 07-08; rtd 08; Chapl Blue Coat Sch Reading from 08. *Reading Blue Coat School, Holme Park, Sonning Lane, Sonning, Reading RG4 6SU* Tel 0118-944 1005 Mobile 07855-581714 E-mail cincture@tiscali.co.uk

MACHELL, Leigh Douglas. b 64. Leic Poly BSc85. St Jo Coll Nottm MTh03. **d** 03 **p** 04. C Beoley *Worc* 03-07; P-in-c Churchill and Langford *B & W* from 07. *Park View, Maysmead Lane, Langford, Bristol BS40 5HX* Tel (01934) 861152 *or* 862000 Mobile 07939-203787 E-mail rev.leigh@ntlworld.com

McHENRY, Brian Edward. b 50. CBE08. New Coll Ox BA73 MA77. SEITE 05. **d** 08. NSM Deptford St Paul *S'wark* from 08. *21 Maude Road, London SE5 8NY* Tel (020) 7701 9350 Mobile 07766-643765 E-mail brian@mchenry.co.uk

MACHIN, Roy Anthony. b 38. BA79. Oak Hill Th Coll 76. **d** 79 **p** 80. C Halliwell St Pet *Man* 79-83; V Eccleston St Luke *Liv* 83-91; V Kendal St Thos and Crook *Carl* 91-99; V Wigan St Barn Marsh Green *Liv* 99-03; rtd 03. *56 Ferndown Road, Harwood, Bolton BL2 3NN* Tel and fax (01204) 362220 E-mail roy.machin@btinternet.com

McHUGH, Brian Robert. b 50. York Univ BA72 Keele Univ CertEd73 IEng92 MIMA98 CMath98. S Dios Minl Tr Scheme 79. **d** 82 **p** 83. NSM Sarisbury *Portsm* 82-86; NSM Shedfield 86-06; NSM Shedfield and Wickham from 07. *28 Siskin Close, Bishops Waltham, Southampton SO32 1RQ* Tel (01489) 896658 E-mail brian.mchugh@bcs.org.uk *or* mchughb@tauntons.ac.uk

McHUGH, Michael. b 57. **d** 88 **p** 88. In RC Ch 88-05; NSM Cley Hill Warminster *Sarum* 05-07; C Salisbury St Thos and St Edm from 07. *22 Castle Road, Salisbury SP1 3RJ* Tel (01722) 414637 Mobile 07977-115551 E-mail mtmch@hotmail.com

McILROY, Sister Honor Margaret. b 24. LRAM44 GRSM45. **d** 98 **p** 99. CSMV from 55. *St Mary's Convent, Challow Road, Wantage OX12 9DJ* Tel (01235) 763141 E-mail sisterscsmv@btinternet.com

McINDOE, Darren Lee. b 76. Univ of Wales (Lamp) BA97. Trin Coll Bris BA05. **d** 06 **p** 07. C Stratford St Jo w Ch Ch and St Jas *Chelmsf* 06-09; C Forest Gate Em w Upton Cross from 09. *29 Maryland Park, London E15 1HB* Tel (020) 8491 6040 *or* 8503 1913 Mobile 07786-5023 E-mail rev.darren.mcindoe@googlemail.com

MACINNES, Canon David Rennie. b 32. Jes Coll Cam BA55 MA59. Ridley Hall Cam 55. **d** 57 **p** 58. C Gillingham St Mark *Roch* 57-61; C St Helen Bishopsgate w St Martin Outwich *Lon* 61-67; Prec Birm Cathl 67-78; Angl Adv ATV 67-82; Angl Adv Cen TV 82-93; Dioc Missr *Birm* 79-87; Hon Can Birm Cathl 81-87; R Ox St Aldate w St Matt 87-94; R Ox St Aldate 95-02; Hon Can Ch Ch 98-02; rtd 02. *Pear Tree Cottage, Milcombe, Banbury OX15 4RS* Tel (01295) 721119

MacINNES, Harry Campbell. b 67. Nottm Poly BA89. Wycliffe Hall Ox BTh94. **d** 97 **p** 98. C E Twickenham St Steph *Lon* 97-00; P-in-c St Margaret's-on-Thames 00-04; R Shill Valley and Broadshire *Ox* from 04. *The Rectory, Church Lane, Shilton, Burford OX18 4AE* Tel (01993) 845954

MACINTOSH, Andrew Alexander. b 36. St Jo Coll Cam BA59 MA63 BD80 DD97. Ridley Hall Cam 60. **d** 62 **p** 63. C S Ormsby Gp *Linc* 62-64; Lect St D Coll Lamp 64-67; Lic to Offic *Ely* from 67; Chapl St Jo Coll Cam 67-69; Asst Dean 69-79; Dean 79-02; Lect Th from 70; Pres 95-99. *St John's College, Cambridge CB2 1TP* Tel (01223) 338709 E-mail aam1003@cus.cam.ac.uk

MacINTOSH, Canon George Grant. b 41. St Jo Coll Dur BA75. Cranmer Hall Dur. **d** 76 **p** 77. C Ecclesall *Sheff* 76-79; Hon C Sheff St Oswald 79-81; Research Fell Sheff Univ 79-81; Dioc Adult Educn Officer 81-88; V Crookes St Tim 81-88; V Abbeydale St Jo 88-97; RD Ecclesall 89-94; P-in-c Cuminestown and Turriff *Ab* 97-06; Dioc Dir Ords 01-03; Can St Andr Cathl 01-06; rtd 06. *9 Millar Street, Carnoustie, Angus DD7 7AS* Tel (01241) 851678 E-mail gmacintosh@onetel.com

McINTOSH, Ian MacDonald. b 64. Jes Coll Cam BA86. Trin Coll Bris BA90. **d** 90 **p** 91. C Belmont *Lon* 90-92; C Pinner 92-95; Chapl Leic Univ 96-02; TV Leic H Spirit 96-02; Co-ord Reader Tr 00-02; Dir Cen for Ecum Studies Westcott Ho Cam 02-04; C Milton Ernest, Pavenham and Thurleigh *St Alb* 02-06; Hon C 06-08; RD Sharnbrook 04-06; Lect and Dir Studies ERMC *Ely* 06-07; Prin from 07. *31 Paddock Close, Clapham, Bedford MK41 6BD* Tel (01234) 302362 *or* (01223) 741740 E-mail mcintosh@ermc.cam.ac.uk

McINTOSH, Mrs Nicola Ann. b 60. Trin Coll Bris 87. **d** 90 **p** 94. Par Dn Queensbury All SS *Lon* 90-93; Par Dn Ruislip Manor St Paul 93-94; C 94-95; NSM Clarendon Park St Jo w Knighton St Mich *Leic* 96-02; Asst Dioc Dir of Ords 00-02; V Milton Ernest, Pavenham and Thurleigh *St Alb* 02-08; Perm to Offic from 08. *31 Paddock Close, Clapham, Bedford MK41 6BD* Tel (01234) 302362

McINTYRE, Robert Mark. b 69. Nottm Univ BA91. Coll of Resurr Mirfield 92. **d** 94 **p** 95. C Wednesbury St Jas and St Jo *Lich* 94-97; TV Wolstanton 97-05; P-in-c Rickerscote from 05; C Stafford from 05; CMP from 97. *St Peter's Vicarage, 16 Chestnut Drive, Stafford ST17 9WE* Tel (01785) 606908 E-mail frmark.mcintyre@ntlworld.com

McINTYRE DE ROMERO, Ms Iris Evelyn. b 60. Worc Coll Ox BA82 MA90. St Steph Ho Ox 82. **dss** 84 **d** 87 **p** 97. Southbroom *Sarum* 84-86; Oakdale 86-88; Par Dn 87-88; Par Dn Ireland Wood *Ripon* 88-89; Area Co-ord (NW) Chr Aid 92-94; Hon C W Derby St Mary *Liv* 94-98; R Bangor Monachorum and Worthenbury *St As* 98-03; Chapl HM Pris Brockhill 03-06; V Stourport and Wilden *Worc* from 06. *The Vicarage, 29 Church Avenue, Stourport-on-Severn DY13 9DD* Tel (01299) 822041 E-mail iris.marco@virgin.net

MACIVER, Donald. b 46. Heriot-Watt Univ BSc69 Nazarene Th Coll Man ThB82 Lon Univ BD82. **d** 08 **p** 09. OLM Heatons *Man* from 08. *20 Withnell Road, Manchester M19 1GH* Tel 0161-431 5814 E-mail dmaciver@eclipse.co.uk

MACK, Mrs Gillian Frances. b 50. SCM72. Cant Sch of Min 84. **d** 87 **p** 94. NSM Deal St Geo *Cant* 87-88; NSM Deal St Leon and St Rich and Sholden 88-92; Par Dn 93-94; C 94-97; rtd 97; Perm to Offic *Cant* 97-06; Hon Chapl Cautley Ho 98-06; Hon C Hurst Green and Mitton *Bradf* 06-07; P-in-c from 07; Hon C Waddington from 06; Fresh Expressions Min Craven Adnry from 08. *The Vicarage, Shire Lane, Hurst Green, Clitheroe BB7 9QR* Tel (01254) 826686 E-mail gillmack@tiscali.co.uk

McKAE, William John. b 42. Liv Univ BSc63 St Mark & St Jo Coll Lon PGCE64. Wells Th Coll 68. **d** 71 **p** 72. C Tranmere St Paul w St Luke *Ches* 71-74; C Midsomer Norton *B & W* 74-75; TV Birkenhead Priory *Ches* 75-80; R Oughtrington 80-91; Chapl Asst Hope, Salford R and Ladywell Hosps Man 91-92; Lic Preacher *Man* 91-92; R Heaton Reddish 92-06; rtd 06; Perm to Offic *Ches* from 06. *3 Grantham Close, Wirral CH61 8SU* Tel 0151-648 0858

MACKARILL, Ian David. b 54. FIBMS86. NEOC 01. **d** 04 **p** 05. NSM Waggoners *York* from 04. *The Old Farmhouse, Fridaythorpe, Driffield YO25 9RT* Tel (01377) 288369 Fax 288459 Mobile 07730-314093 E-mail ianmackarill@btconnect.com

McKAVANAGH, Dermot James. b 51. TCD BA75 MA78 K Coll Lon BD78 AKC78. **d** 78 **p** 79. C Croydon H Sav *Cant* 78-82; Asst Chapl Wellington Coll Berks 82-87; Chapl RAF 87-00; rtd 02. *42 Freshfields, Lea, Preston PR2 1TJ*

McKAY, Brian Andrew. b 39. Sarum Th Coll 69. **d** 71 **p** 72. C Walker *Newc* 71-74; C Wooler Gp 74-77; TV 77-81; V Long Benton St Mary 81-89; TV Bellingham/Otterburn Gp 89-91; TV N Tyne and Redesdale 91-02; rtd 02. *26 Punchards Down, Totnes TQ9 5FB* Tel (01803) 840675

MACKAY, Canon Douglas Brysson. b 27. Edin Th Coll 56. **d** 58 **p** 59. Prec St Andr Cathl Inverness 58-61; P-in-c Fochabers 61-70; R 70-72; Chapl Aberlour Orphanage 64-67; P-in-c Aberlour 64-72; Syn Clerk 65-72; Can St Andr Cathl Inverness 65-72; Hon Can 72; R Carnoustie *Bre* 72-98; Can St Paul's Cathl Dundee 81-97; Hon Can from 98; Syn Clerk 81-97; rtd 97; Tutor Dundee Univ from 97; Chapl St Paul's Cathl Dundee from 99. *24 Philip Street, Carnoustie DD7 6ED* Tel (01241) 852362 E-mail db.mackay@btinternet.com

MACKAY, Hedley Neill. b 27. St Aid Birkenhead 53. **d** 56 **p** 57. C Beverley St Mary *York* 56-59; C Scarborough St Mary 59-60; Nigeria 61-70; C Wawne *York* 70-71; V Sutton St Jas and Wawne 72-76; V Huntington 76-82; TR 82-93; rtd 93; Perm to Offic *York* from 93; Rtd Clergy and Widows Officer (York Adnry) 94-98. *2 Elmfield Terrace, Heworth, York YO31 1EH* Tel (01904) 412971

MACKAY, James Hugh. b 57. Ridley Hall Cam. **d** 09. C Walesby *Linc* from 09. *The Rectory, Beelsby Road, Swallow, Market Rasen LN7 6DG* Tel 07946-054218 (mobile) E-mail jandl.mackay@virgin.net

McKAY, John Andrew. b 38. HDipEd. Chich Th Coll. **d** 74 **p** 75. C Primrose Hill St Mary w Avenue Road St Paul *Lon* 74-77; V Battersea Ch Ch and St Steph *S'wark* 77-82; I Rathkeale w Askeaton and Kilcornan *L & K* 82-85; I Dublin St Bart w Leeson Park *D & G* 85-00; Chapl Venice w Trieste *Eur* 00-03; rtd 03; Chapl Dublin Sandymount *D & G* 05-06. *5 St Peter's Place, Drogheda, Co Louth, Republic of Ireland* Tel (00353) (41) 987 3277 Mobile 87-313 9269

McKAY, Margaret McLeish. *See* HALE, Mrs Margaret McLeish
MACKAY, Neill. *See* MACKAY, Hedley Neill
MACKAY, Paul Douglas. b 60. Trin Coll Bris. **d** 00 **p** 01. C Becontree St Mary *Chelmsf* 00-03; V Mile Cross *Nor* from 03. *St Catherine's Vicarage, Aylsham Road, Norwich NR3 2RJ* Tel (01603) 426767 E-mail vicar@stcatherinesmilecross.org.uk

MACKAY, Rupert. b 61. Oak Hill Th Coll 00. **d** 00 **p** 01. C Knutsford St Jo and Toft *Ches* 00-04; Min Hadley Wood St Paul Prop Chpl *Lon* from 04. *28 Beech Hill, Barnet EN4 0JP* Tel and fax (020) 8449 2572 E-mail rupmac@mac.com

McKEACHIE, The Very Revd William Noble. b 43. Univ of the South (USA) BA66. Trin Coll Cuddesdon STB70. **d** 70 **p** 70. Asst Chapl St Jo Coll Ox 70-72; Dioc Th Toronto Canada 73-78; USA from 78; Dir Ch Relns and Tutor Univ of the South 78-80; R Baltimore St Paul 81-95; Dean S Carolina and R Charleston Cathl from 95. *126 Coming Street, Charleston SC 29403-6151, USA* Tel (001) (843) 722 7345 Fax 722 2105 E-mail cathchlp@dycon.com

McKEARNEY, Andrew Richard. b 57. Selw Coll Cam MA. Edin Th Coll 81. **d** 82 **p** 83. Prec St Ninian's Cathl Perth 82-84; Chapl St Mary's Cath 84-88; R Hardwick and Toft w Caldecote and Childerley *Ely* 88-94; RD Bourn 92-94; V Chesterton Gd Shep 94-06; V Iffley *Ox* from 06. *The Rectory, Mill Lane, Iffley, Oxford OX4 4EJ* Tel (01865) 773516 E-mail theophan@surfaid.org

McKECHNIE, John Gregg. b 30. Em Coll Cam BA54 MA57. Ridley Hall Cam 54. **d** 55 **p** 56. C Morden *S'wark* 55-57; Tutor Clifton Th Coll 57-62; R Chich St Pancras and St Jo 62-68; V Reading St Jo *Ox* 68-85; RD Reading 83-85; V Lindfield *Chich* 85-95; rtd 95; Perm to Offic *Chich* from 95. *3 The Courtyard, Stockbridge Road, Chichester PO19 8GP* Tel (01243) 531703

McKEE, Douglas John Dunstan. b 34. Univ of W Aus BA65. St Mich Th Coll Crafers 54. **d** 57 **p** 58. Australia 57-72 and from 85; SSM from 58; Lic to Offic *S'well* 73-85. *12 Kensington Mews, 69 Maesbury Street, Kensington, SA 5068 Australia* Tel (0061) (8) 8331 3853 E-mail dunstan.mckee@flinders.edu.au

McKEE, Nicholas John. b 71. Nottm Univ MEng94. Ridley Hall Cam 05. **d** 08 **p** 09. C Didsbury St Jas and Em *Man* from 08. *99 Mellington Avenue, Manchester M20 5WF* E-mail nickmckee@stjamesandemmanuel.org

McKEE, Patrick Joseph. b 49. Ripon Coll Cuddesdon 92. **d** 94 **p** 95. C Oakham, Hambleton, Egleton, Braunston and Brooke *Pet* 94-97; V Ryhall w Essendine and Carlby from 97. *The Vicarage, Church Street, Ryhall, Stamford PE9 4HR* Tel (01780) 762398 E-mail pmckee@ryhall.clara.co.uk

McKEEMAN, David Christopher. b 36. AKC58 DipEd76. **d** 60 **p** 61. C Catford St Andr *S'wark* 60-64; P-in-c W Dulwich Em 64-69; Lic to Offic *Win* 70-82; R Silchester 82-01; rtd 01; Perm to Offic *Heref* from 01. *The Maltings, Woodend Lane, Stoke Lacy, Bromyard HR7 4HQ* Tel (01885) 490705 E-mail david.mckeeman@ntlworld.com

McKEGNEY, Canon John Wade. b 47. TCD BA70 MA81. CITC 70. **d** 72 **p** 73. C Ballynafeigh St Jude *D & D* 72-75; C Bangor St Comgall 75-80; I Drumgath w Drumgooland and Clonduff 80-83; I Gilnahirk 83-90; I Arm St Mark from 90; Can Arm Cathl from 01. *St Mark's Rectory, 14 Portadown Road, Armagh BT61 9EE* Tel and fax (028) 3752 2970 *or* tel 3752 3197 Mobile 07801-866555 E-mail john.mckegney@virgin.net *or* armagh@armagh.anglican.org

MacKEITH (née GODFREY), Mrs Ann Veronica. b 35. Bris Univ BSc57 CertEd. Gilmore Course 78. **dss** 79 **d** 87 **p** 94. Bishopwearmouth Ch Ch *Dur* 79-83; Bishopwearmouth St Gabr 83-86; Ryhope 86-88; Par Dn 87-88; Par Dn Darlington H Trin 89-94; C 94-95; Family Life Officer 95-97; rtd 98. *135 Hummersknott Avenue, Darlington DL3 8RR* Tel (01325) 463481 E-mail annmackeith@webportal.co.uk

McKELLAR, John Lorne. b 19. Sarum Th Coll 70. **d** 72 **p** 73. C Warminster St Denys *Sarum* 72-75; USA 75-79 and 81-84; P-in-c Colchester St Barn *Chelmsf* 79-81; rtd 84; Perm to Offic *Sarum* from 84. *Corrie, 105A Clay Street, Crockerton, Warminster BA12 8AG* Tel (01985) 213161

McKELLEN, Pamela Joyce. b 47. Homerton Coll Cam TCert69 BEd70. Cranmer Hall Dur 01. **d** 02 **p** 03. C Ox St Matt 02-04; P-in-c Radley and Sunningwell from 04; AD Abingdon from 07. *The Vicarage, Kennington Road, Radley, Abingdon OX14 2JN* Tel (01235) 554739 E-mail pjmck@compuserve.com

McKELVEY, Mrs Jane Lilian. b 48. Liv Inst of Educn BA94. Nor Bapt Coll 94. **d** 97 **p** 98. C Aughton St Mich *Liv* 97-01; TV Gateacre from 01. *St Mark's Vicarage, Cranwell Road, Liverpool L25 1NZ* Tel 0151-487 9634

McKELVEY, The Very Revd Robert Samuel James Houston. b 42. QVRM00 TD. QUB BA65 MA(Ed)88 Garrett-Evang Th Sem DMin93. CITC 67. **d** 67 **p** 68. C Dunmurry *Conn* 67-70; CF (TAVR) 70-99; P-in-c Kilmakee *Conn* I 77-81; Sec Gen Syn Bd of Educn (N Ireland) 81-01; Preb Newcastle St Patr Cathl Dublin 89-01; Dean Belf from 01. *Belfast Cathedral, Donegal Street, Belfast BT1 2HB* Tel (028) 9032 8332 *or* 9066 0980 Fax 9023 8855 E-mail dean@belfastcathedral.org

McKENDREY, Susan Margaret. b 55. **d** 02 **p** 03. NSM Allonby, Cross Canonby and Dearham *Carl* 02-08; TV Maryport, Netherton and Flimby from 08. *The Vicarage, Church Street, Maryport CA15 6IIE* Tel (01900) 813077 E-mail s.mckendrey@btinternet.com

MACKENNA, Christopher. *See* MACKENNA, Robert Christopher Douglass

McKENNA, Dermot William. b 41. TCD BA63 MA66. CITC 64. **d** 64 **p** 65. C Enniscorthy *C & O* 64-66; I Killeshin 66-84; rtd 84. *20 Sherwood, Pollerton, Carlow, Republic of Ireland* Tel (00353) (59) 913 0915 E-mail mckenna@itcarlow.ie

McKENNA, Edward Patrick. b 48. Liv Univ BTh02. NOC 05. **d** 06 **p** 07. NSM Stretton and Appleton Thorn *Ches* 06-09; Asst Chapl HM Pris Risley from 08; P-in-c Low Marple *Ches* from 09. *15 Brabyns Brow, Marple Bridge, Stockport SK6 5DT* Tel 0161-427 2736 Mobile 07979-624271 E-mail ed1mckenna@aol.com

McKENNA, Lindsay Taylor. b 62. Glas Univ MA83 Aber Univ BD86. Edin Th Coll 87. **d** 87 **p** 88. C Broughty Ferry *Bre* 87-90; C Wantage *Ox* 90-93; V Illingworth *Wakef* 93-99; Dir CARA 99-02; V Hanworth All SS *Lon* 02-08; Provost St Paul's Cathl Dundee 08-09; R Dundee St Paul 08-09. *4 Richmond Terrace, Dundee DD2 1BQ* Tel (01382) 646296 *or* 224486

MACKENNA, Richard William. b 49. Pemb Coll Cam BA71 MA75. Ripon Coll Cuddesdon BA77 MA81. **d** 78 **p** 79. C Fulham St Dionis Parson's Green *Lon* 78-81; C Paddington St Jas 81-85; Tutor Westcott Ho Cam 85-89; V Kingston All SS w St Jo *S'wark* 90-91; Perm to Offic *S'wark* 94-01 and *Nor* 99-04. *Flat 5, 11 Grassington Road, Eastbourne BN20 7BJ* Tel (01323) 730477

MACKENNA, Robert Christopher Douglass. b 44. Oriel Coll Ox BA72 MA75 MBAP85. Cuddesdon Coll 71. **d** 73 **p** 74. C

Farncombe *Guildf* 73-77; C Tattenham Corner and Burgh Heath 77-80; P-in-c Hascombe 80-90; R 90-00; RD Godalming 91-96; Hon Can Guildf Cathl 99-00; Dir St Marylebone Healing and Counselling Cen from 00; NSM St Marylebone w H Trin *Lon* from 00. *37 Clifden Road, Worminghall, Aylesbury HP18 9JR* Tel (01844) 338213 *or* (020) 7935 5066
E-mail cmackenna@stmarylebone.org

MACKENZIE, Andrew John Kett. b 46. Southn Univ BA68. Guildf Dioc Min Course 98. **d** 91 **p** 92. Fullbrook Sch New Haw 76-99; OLM Woodham *Guildf* 91-99; C Aldershot St Mich 99-05; V Effingham w Lt Bookham from 05. *The Rectory, 4 Leewood Way, Effingham, Leatherhead KT24 5JN* Tel (01372) 458314 Mobile 07944-996475 E-mail rectorandy@aol.com

MACKENZIE, Miss Ann. b 54. CertEd76. Trin Coll Bris 82. **dss d** 87 **p** 94. Normanton *Wakef* 85-90; Par Dn 87-90; Par Dn Bletchley *Ox* 94-98; TV W Swindon and the Lydiards *Bris* 98-04; P-in-c E Springfield *Chelmsf* from 04. *The Vicarage, Ashton Place, Chelmsford CM2 6ST* Tel (01245) 462387 E-mail annmackenzie@tregoze.fsnet.co.uk

McKENZIE, Mrs Ann Elizabeth. b 45. Leic Univ BA67 PGCE68. STETS 95. **d** 98 **p** 99. NSM Appleshaw, Kimpton, Thruxton, Fyfield etc *Win* from 98. *The Post House, Thruxton, Andover SP11 8LZ* Tel (01264) 772788
E-mail ann.mckenzie@tinyonline.co.uk

McKENZIE, Cilla. *See* McKENZIE, Mrs Priscilla Ann

MACKENZIE, David Stuart. b 45. Open Univ BA95 FRSA00. Linc Th Coll 66. **d** 69 **p** 70. C Bishopwearmouth St Mary V w St Pet CD *Dur* 69-72; C Pontefract St Giles *Wakef* 72-74; Chapl RAF 74-02; Chapl OHP 02-08; RD Whitby *York* 04-08; QHC from 00; Perm to Offic *Ely* from 09. *57 London Road, Godmanchester, Huntingdon PE29 2HZ* Tel (01480) 413120

MACKENZIE, Duncan. *See* MACKENZIE, Preb Lawrence Duncan

McKENZIE, Ian Colin. b 31. CA56. EMMTC 89. **d** 93. NSM Edin St Mark and Edin St Andr and St Aid 93-94; Perm to Offic *S'well* from 01. *21 Crafts Way, Southwell NG25 0BL* Tel (01636) 815755

MACKENZIE, Ian William. b 46. Trin Coll Bris 93. **d** 95 **p** 96. C Bideford *Ex* 95-96; C Bideford, Northam, Westward Ho!, Appledore etc 96-99; TV Littleham w Exmouth from 99. *The Vicarage, 96 Littleham Road, Littleham, Exmouth EX8 2RD* Tel (01395) 275085

McKENZIE, Jack Llewellyn. b 29. FRSH AMIEHO MAMIT. S'wark Ord Course. **d** 79 **p** 80. Hon C Stonebridge St Mich *Lon* 79-88; Hon C Willesden St Mary 88-91; Perm to Offic *St Alb* 00-08. *2 Becketts Square, Berkhamsted HP4 1BZ* Tel (01442) 874265

MACKENZIE, Miss Janet. b 62. Westmr Coll Ox BEd46. Westcott Ho Cam 04. **d** 06 **p** 07. C Sandy *St Alb* from 06. *14 Pyms Way, Sandy SG19 1BZ* Tel and fax (01767) 683201
E-mail revjanetmackenzie@tiscali.co.uk

MacKENZIE, John Christopher Newman. b 67. Trin Coll Bris 02. **d** 04 **p** 05. C Staplehurst *Cant* 04-07; P-in-c Willesborough from 07; P-in-c Sevington from 07. *The Rectory, 66 Church Road, Willesborough, Ashford TN24 0JG* Tel (01233) 624064
E-mail john@jjsmack.me.uk

MACKENZIE, Preb Lawrence Duncan. b 30. St Aid Birkenhead 52. **d** 55 **p** 56. C Blackb St Gabr 55-58; C Burnley St Pet 58-60; C St Giles-in-the-Fields *Lon* 60-63; V Queensbury All SS 63-85; V Hillingdon St Jo 85-96; Preb St Paul's Cathl 89-96; rtd 96; NSM Gt Stanmore *Lon* 96-99; Perm to Offic *Lon* and *Ely* from 99. *1 Walnut Tree Close, Little Downham, Ely CB6 2SQ* Tel (01353) 698793 E-mail canonmackenzie123@tiscali.co.uk

MACKENZIE, Peter Sterling. b 65. Univ Coll Lon BSc88. Oak Hill Th Coll BA95. **d** 95 **p** 96. C Roxeth *Lon* 95-99; Assoc V 99-00; TV 00-08; V W Ealing St Jo w St Jas from 08. *23 Culmington Road, London W13 9NJ* Tel (020) 8566 3462
E-mail petersmackenzie@btinternet.com

MACKENZIE, Canon Peter Thomas. b 44. Lon Univ LLB67 Westmr Coll Ox MTh97 Univ of E Lon MA01. Cuddesdon Coll 68. **d** 70 **p** 71. C Leigh Park *Portsm* 70-75; P-in-c Sittingbourne St Mary *Cant* 75-82; V Folkestone St Sav 82-90; RD Elham 89-90; R Cant St Martin and St Paul 90-99; RD Cant 95-99; V Goudhurst w Kilndown 99-07; Hon Can Cant Cathl 97-07; AD Cranbrook 01-06; rtd 07. *18 rue Odette d'Auxois, 71250 Salornay-sur-Guye, France* Tel (0033) (3) 85 59 49 91
E-mail canonmack@talk21.com

McKENZIE, Mrs Priscilla Ann. b 47. St Jo Coll Nottm 87. **d** 93 **p** 94. NSM Ellon *Ab* 93-96; NSM Cruden Bay 93-96; Perm to Offic *Roch* 96-99 and from 04; Chapl Medway NHS Trust 99-04. *Iona, Linton Hill, Linton, Maidstone ME17 4AW* Tel (01622) 741318 E-mail johncilla.mckenzie@onetel.net

MACKENZIE, Richard Graham. b 49. St Aug Coll Cant 72. **d** 73 **p** 74. C Deal St Leon *Cant* 73-75; C Deal St Leon w Sholden 75-78; C Herne 78-81; Canada from 81; I Pakenham 81-88; I Richmond 88-90; I Petawawa 90. *1179 Victoria Street, Petawawa ON K8H 2E6, Canada* Tel (001) (613) 687 2218

McKENZIE, Robin Peter. b 61. Sheff Univ BEng82 Birm Univ MSc(Eng)87 Dur Univ BA02 Warwick Univ EngD02 CEng

MIET. Cranmer Hall Dur 00. **d** 03 **p** 04. C Shrewsbury St Chad w St Mary *Lich* 03-07; P-in-c Fenstanton *Ely* from 07; P-in-c Hilton from 07. *The Vicarage, 16 Church Street, Fenstanton, Huntingdon PE28 9JL* Tel (01480) 466162
E-mail mckenzie_robin@hotmail.com

MACKENZIE, Simon Peter Munro. b 52. Univ Coll Ox BA74. Coll of Resurr Mirfield 82. **d** 85 **p** 86. C Tipton St Jo *Lich* 85-91; V Perry Beeches *Birm* from 91. *St Matthew's Vicarage, 313 Beeches Road, Birmingham B42 2QR* Tel 0121-360 2100

McKENZIE, Stephen George. b 58. Leeds Univ BSc80 Imp Coll Lon PhD85. Oak Hill Th Coll 03. **d** 05 **p** 06. C Barton Seagrave w Warkton *Pet* 05-08; P-in-c Swynnerton and Tittensor *Lich* from 08; C Broughton w Croxton and Cotes Heath w Standon from 08. *3 Rectory Gardens, Swynnerton, Stone ST15 0RT* Tel (01782) 796564 Mobile 07986-558861
E-mail stegliverpool@aol.com

MACKENZIE, William. *See* MACKENZIE, Ian William

MACKENZIE MILLS, David Graham. b 75. Bris Univ BA96 St Jo Coll Dur BA01. Cranmer Hall Dur. **d** 01 **p** 02. C Glas St Marg 01-04; Chapl Trin Coll Cam from 04. *12 Bridge Street, Cambridge CB2 1UF* Tel (01223) 741112

McKEON, James Ernest. b 22. TCD BA45 HDipEd49 Div Test. TCD Div Sch. **d** 46 **p** 47. C Dundalk *Arm* 46-48; C Dublin St Geo *D & G* 48-52; I Kilsaran w Drumcar, Dunleer and Dunany *Arm* 52-59; I Drogheda 59-64; P-in-c Termonfeckin and Beaulieu 62-64; Warden Wilson's Hosp Sch Multyfarnham 64-83; Can Kildare Cathl 83-88; Prec 87-88; P-in-c Geashill w Killeigh and Ballycommon 83-88; rtd 88; Dioc Info Officer (Meath) *M & K* 90-91; Radio Officer 91-96. *Araucaria, 200 Bassaleg Road, Newport NP20 3PX* Tel (01633) 661974
E-mail j.mckeon@ntlworld.com

McKEON, Linda. **d** 09. OLM Gentleshaw *Lich* from 09. *17 Bradwell Lane, Rugeley WS15 4RW* Tel (01543) 670739

McKEOWN, Trevor James. b 53. CITC 01. **d** 04 **p** 05. Aux Min Dromore Cathl from 04. *39 Cedar Park, Portadown, Craigavon BT63 5LL* Tel (028) 3832 1217

McKERAN, James Orville. b 71. Kent Univ BA94 K Coll Lon MA06 Leeds Univ MA08. Coll of Resurr Mirfield 06. **d** 08 **p** 09. C Altrincham St Geo *Ches* from 08; C Altrincham St Jo from 08. *18 Hawarden Road, Altrincham WA14 1NG* E-mail james.mckeran@btinternet.com

MACKEY, John. b 34. Lich Th Coll. **d** 64 **p** 65. C Kells *Carl* 64-67; C Barrow St Matt 67-70; R Clayton *Man* 70-75; V Low Marple *Ches* 75-83; R Coppenhall 83-00; rtd 00; Perm to Offic *Ches* from 00. *361 Hungerford Road, Crewe CW1 5EZ* Tel (01270) 254951

McKIBBIN, Gordon. b 29. St Aid Birkenhead 55. **d** 58 **p** 59. C Dundela St Mark *D & D* 58-60; C Knotty Ash St Jo *Liv* 61-64; V Gt Sankey 64-97; rtd 97; Perm to Offic *Liv* from 97. *6 Penmark Close, Warrington WA5 5TG* Tel (01925) 445125

MacKICHAN, Gillian Margaret. b 34. Cam Univ CertEd56 CQSW80. S Dios Minl Tr Scheme 90. **d** 93 **p** 94. NSM Upper Kennet *Sarum* 93-04; TV 95-04; RD Marlborough 02-04; rtd 04; Perm to Offic *Sarum* 04-08. *West Bailey, Lockeridge, Marlborough SN8 4ED* Tel (01672) 861629
E-mail lalmack@globalnet.co.uk

MACKIE, Andrew. b 53. Glas Univ BSc74 CEng MIET. SAOMC 00. **d** 00 **p** 01. OLM Purley *Ox* from 00. *12 Church Mews, Purley-on-Thames, Pangbourne, Reading RG8 8AG* Tel 0118-941 7170
E-mail mackie.family@btinternet.com

MACKIE, Ian William. b 31. Lon Univ BSc53 Ex Univ PGCE54. Linc Th Coll 81. **d** 83 **p** 84. C Market Rasen *Linc* 83-87; V Bracebridge Heath 87-96; RD Christianity 92-96; rtd 96; Perm to Offic *Sheff* 96-02. *57 Bridle Crescent, Chapeltown, Sheffield S35 2QX* Tel 0114-284 4073

MACKIE, Kenneth Johnston. b 20. Univ of NZ BA45 MA46 La Trobe Univ Vic BEd77. St Jo Coll Auckland 46. **d** 47 **p** 48. New Zealand 46-66; C Whangarei 47-51; P-in-c S Hokianga 51-53; V Opotiki 53-56; V Napier St Aug 56-61; Gen Sec NZ Coun for Chr Educn 62-66; Australia 66-72 and 74-94; Chapl Traralgon and Macleod High Schs 66-70; Chapl Univ of Papua New Guinea 72-75; Perm to Offic Melbourne and Gippsland 75-89; Hon P-in-c Nerang 91-94; Perm to Offic *Roch* 97-08. *Address temp unknown*

McKIE, The Very Revd Kenyon Vincent. b 60. Aus Nat Univ BA83 ACT BTh88 K Coll Lon MTh92 Canberra Coll DipEd84. **d** 86 **p** 87. Australia 86-89 and from 91; Dn Queanbeyan 86; C 87; Lucas-Tooth Scholar K Coll Lon 89-91; Hon C Coulsdon St Andr *S'wark* 89-91; R Monaro S 91-94; R Bega 94-99; Adn S Coast and Monaro 96-99; Dean Goulburn from 99. *PO Box 205, Goulburn NSW 2580, Australia* Tel (0061) (2) 4821 9192 *or* 4821 2206 Fax 4822 2639 E-mail mesacgbn@tpgi.com.au *or* deanery@tpgi.com.au

McKILLOP, Mrs Caroline Annis. b 47. Glas Univ MB, ChB72 PhD77. TISEC 95. **d** 98 **p** 99. NSM Glas St Matt 98-01; Chapl Stobhill NHS Trust 99-00; NSM Glas St Mary from 02. *Flat 1, 6 Kirklee Gate, Glasgow G12 0SZ* Tel 0141-339 7000
E-mail caroline.mckillop@yahoo.co.uk

McKINLEY, Canon Arthur Horace Nelson. b 46. TCD BA69 MA79. CITC 70. **d** 70 **p** 71. C Taney Ch Ch *D & G* 71-76; I

Dublin Whitechurch from 76; Preb Dunlavin St Patr Cathl Dublin from 91. *The Vicarage, Whitechurch Road, Rathfarnham, Dublin 16, Republic of Ireland* Tel (00353) (1) 493 3953 *or* 493 4972 E-mail whitechurchparish@ireland.com

McKINLEY, George Henry. b 23. TCD BA44 MA51. **d** 46 **p** 47. C Waterford Ch Ch *C & O* 46-49; I Fiddown 49-51; I Fiddown w Kilmacow 51-54; C S Harrow St Paul *Lon* 54-58; V Stonebridge St Mich 58-65; R Hackney St Jo 65-72; TR Hackney 72-77; V Painswick w Sheepscombe *Glouc* 77-83; Bp's Chapl 83-87; C Sandhurst 83-85; C Twigworth, Down Hatherley, Norton, The Leigh etc 85-87; rtd 88; Perm to Offic *Heref* and *Worc* from 96. *Middlemarch, 2 Old Barn Court, Bircher, Leominster HR6 0AU* Tel (01568) 780795

McKINNEL, Preb Nicholas Howard Paul. b 54. Qu Coll Cam BA75 MA79. Wycliffe Hall Ox BA79 MA86. **d** 80 **p** 81. C Fulham St Mary N End *Lon* 80-83; Chapl Liv Univ 83-87; P-in-c Hatherleigh *Ex* 87-88; R Hatherleigh, Meeth, Exbourne and Jacobstowe 88-94; P-in-c Plymouth St Andr w St Paul and St Geo 94-95; TR Plymouth St Andr and Stonehouse from 95; RD Plymouth Sutton from 01; Preb Ex Cathl from 02. *St Andrew's Vicarage, 13 Bainbridge Avenue, Plymouth PL3 5QZ* Tel (01752) 772139 *or* 661414 E-mail nick@standrewschurch.org.uk

McKINNEY, James Alexander. b 52. Ex Univ BA74 Hull Univ MA87. Ripon Coll Cuddesdon 75. **d** 78 **p** 79. C Wath-upon-Dearne w Adwick-upon-Dearne *Sheff* 78-82; V Doncaster Intake 82-87; Ind Chapl 84-87; Chapl Bramshill Police Coll *Win* 87-92; V Cleator Moor w Cleator *Carl* 92-96; Chapl Cumbria Constabulary 93-96; P-in-c Frizington and Arlecdon 94-96; V Roehampton H Trin *S'wark* from 96. *The Vicarage, 7 Ponsonby Road, London SW15 4LA* Tel (020) 8788 9460 E-mail jim.mckinney@dswark.org

McKINNEY, Canon Mervyn Roy. b 48. St Jo Coll Nottm. **d** 81 **p** 82. C Tile Cross *Birm* 81-84; C Bickenhill w Elmdon 84-89; V Addiscombe St Mary *S'wark* 89-93; V Addiscombe St Mary Magd w St Martin 93-99; P-in-c W Wickham St Fran 99-02; V W Wickham St Fran and St Mary from 02; AD Croydon Addington from 04; Hon Can S'wark Cathl from 05. *The Vicarage, The Avenue, West Wickham BR4 0DX* Tel (020) 8777 5034 E-mail mervmckinney@btinternet.com

MacKINNON, Mrs Karen Audrey. b 63. Ex Univ BA85. Linc Th Coll 92. **d** 92 **p** 94. Par Dn Filton *Bris* 92-93; Par Dn Bris Lockleaze St Mary Magd w St Fran 93-94; C 94-96; P-in-c 96-98; V 98-00; Asst Chapl Southn Univ Hosps NHS Trust 00-03; Chapl 03-04; Dep Team Ldr from 04. *Chaplaincy Department, Southampton General Hospital, Tremona Road, Southampton SO16 6YD* Tel (023) 8079 8517

McKINNON, Neil Alexander. b 46. Wycliffe Hall Ox 71. **d** 74 **p** 75. C Deptford St Nic w Ch Ch *S'wark* 74-76; C St Helier 76-79; Min W Dulwich All SS and Em 79-81; TV Thamesmead 87-95; R S'wark H Trin w St Matt from 95. *The Rectory, Meadow Row, London SE1 6RG* Tel (020) 7407 1707 *or* tel and fax 7357 8532 E-mail neilatelephany@yahoo.com

MACKINTOSH, Canon Robin Geoffrey James. b 46. Rhodes Univ BCom71 Cranfield Inst of Tech MBA78. Ripon Coll Cuddesdon BA85 MA91. **d** 86 **p** 87. C Cuddesdon *Ox* 86; C Cannock *Lich* 86-89; R Girton *Ely* 89-01; Exec Dir The Leadership Inst 01-06; Dir Min and Tr *Cant* from 06; Hon Can Cant Cathl from 09. *4 Loop Court Mews, Sandwich CT13 9HF* Tel (01227) 459401 E-mail rmackintosh@diocant.org

McKINTY, Norman Alexander (Fionn). b 63. St D Coll Lamp BA86. Westcott Ho Cam 97. **d** 99 **p** 00. C Yeovil St Mich *B & W* 99-03; C Gillingham and Milton-on-Stour *Sarum* 03-05; P-in-c Portland All SS w St Andr from 05. *The Rectory, Straits, Portland DT5 1HG* Tel (01305) 861285 E-mail fionn@mckinty.fsworld.co.uk

McKITTRICK, The Ven Douglas Henry. b 53. St Steph Ho Ox 74. **d** 77 **p** 78. C Deptford St Paul *S'wark* 77-80; C W Derby St Jo *Liv* 80-81; TV St Luke in the City 81-89; V Toxteth Park St Agnes and St Pancras 89-97; V Brighton St Pet w Chpl Royal *Chich* 97-02; RD Brighton 98-02; Can and Preb Chich Cathl 98-02; Adn Chich from 02. *2 Yorklands, Dyke Road Avenue, Hove BN3 6RW* Tel (01273) 505330 *or* 421021 E-mail archchichester@diochi.org.uk

McKITTRICK, Noel Thomas Llewellyn. b 28. TCD BA50 MA57 BD71. **d** 51 **p** 53. C Londonderry Ch Ch *D & R* 51-52; C Belfast St Aid *Conn* 52-54; C Knockbreda *D & D* 54-58; C Keynsham w Queen Charlton *B & W* 58-59; V Glastonbury St Benedict 59-82; V Weston-super-Mare St Paul 82-92; rtd 93; Perm to Offic *Ex* from 94. *Priory Lodge, Latimer Road, Exeter EX4 7JP* Tel (01392) 496744

MACKLEY, Robert Michael. b 78. Ch Coll Cam BA99 MA03. Westcott Ho Cam 00. **d** 03 **p** 04. C Clerkenwell H Redeemer and St Mark *Lon* 03-06; C Liv Our Lady and St Nic from 06. *Liverpool Parish Church, Old Churchyard, Liverpool L2 8TZ* Tel 0151-236 5287 E-mail rob_mackley@hotmail.com

MACKLIN, Reginald John. b 29. Bris Univ BA52. Ely Th Coll 54. **d** 55 **p** 56. C W Hackney St Barn *Lon* 55-58; C E Ham St Mary *Chelmsf* 58-61; C Northolt St Mary *Lon* 61-64; Jordan 64-68;

Palma de Mallorca and Balearic Is *Eur* 68-69; P-in-c Hammersmith St Matt *Lon* 69-70; V Stanwell 70-82; V Kimbolton *Ely* 82-88; V Stow Longa 82-88; RD Leightonstone 82-88; P-in-c Keyston and Bythorn 85-88; P-in-c Catworth Magna 85-88; P-in-c Tilbrook 85-88; P-in-c Covington 85-88; R Coveney 88-96; R Downham 88-96; RD Ely 89-96; rtd 96; Perm to Offic *Ely* from 96. *11 Castelhythe, Ely CB7 4BU* Tel and fax (01353) 662205 E-mail macklinrj@aol.com

MACKNESS, Paul Robert. b 73. Univ of Wales (Lamp) BA96 Univ of Wales (Cardiff) BA01. St Mich Coll Llan 98. **d** 01 **p** 02. C Llanelli *St D* 01-04; P-in-c Maenordeifi and Capel Colman w Llanfihangel etc 04-05; R 05-07; R Maenordeifi Gp from 07; AD Cemais and Sub-Aeron from 08. *The Rectory, Manordeifi, Llechryd, Cardigan SA43 2PJ* Tel (01239) 682830 E-mail paulr@pmackness.fsnet.co.uk

MACKNEY, John Pearson. b 17. Univ of Wales BA39 Lon Univ MA81 PGCE73. St D Coll Lamp 39. **d** 41 **p** 42. C Gelligaer *Llan* 41-44; CF 44-47; C Llangeinor 47-49; P-in-c Cardiff All SS 49-58; Chapl HM Pris Cardiff 49-58; V Mountain Ash *Llan* 58-69; Hon C Streatley w Moulsford *Ox* 81-04; Hon C Cholsey and Moulsford 04-07; Perm to Offic from 07. *Merlebank, Moulsford, Wallingford OX10 9JG* Tel (01491) 651347

McKNIGHT, Thomas Raymond. b 48. QUB BEd71. CITC 74. **d** 77 **p** 78. C Lisburn Ch Ch Cathl 77-80; C Carrickfergus 80-82; I Kilcronaghan w Draperstown and Sixtowns *D & R* 82-86; I Magheragall *Conn* 86-91; CF 91-07; I Urney w Sion Mills *D & R* from 07. *The Rectory, 112 Melmount Road, Sion Mills, Strabane BT82 9PY* Tel (028) 8165 8020

MACKRIELL, Peter John. b 64. Mansf Coll Ox BA85 MA93 Man Univ PGCE87. St Jo Coll Nottm BTh93 MA94. **d** 94 **p** 95. C Hale and Ashley *Ches* 94-96; C Marple All SS 96-98; V Brandwood *Birm* 98-01; V Pontblyddyn *St As* 01-05; Chapl to Deaf People from 01; Dioc Communications Officer from 06. *The Rectory, Church Hill, Halkyn, Holywell CH8 8BU* Tel (01352) 781949 E-mail petermackriell@churchinwales.org.uk

MACKRILL, Mrs Deirdre Anne. b 49. ACIS95. SAOMC 01. **d** 05 **p** 06. NSM Hemel Hempstead *St Alb* from 05. *The Old Brewhouse, Chesham Road, Wigginton, Tring HP23 6EH* Tel (01442) 822633 E-mail deirdre@brewhouse4.freeserve.co.uk

MACKRILL, Robert John. b 51. Univ Coll Lon BSc73 RIBA79. EMMTC 92. **d** 93 **p** 94. NSM Stamford All SS w St Jo *Linc* 93-97; P-in-c Stamford Ch Ch from 97; RD Aveland and Ness w Stamford from 09. *110 Lonsdale Road, Stamford PE9 2SF* Tel (01780) 754490 Fax 756212 E-mail bob@mackrill.freeserve.co.uk

MacLACHLAN (née GRIFFITHS), Mrs Margaret. b 44. Birm Poly CertEd81 Open Univ BA82 SRN67. WMMTC 92. **d** 95 **p** 96. NSM Tile Cross *Birm* 95-08; NSM Garretts Green 07-08; NSM Garretts Green and Tile Cross from 08; Chapl Heart of England NHS Foundn Trust from 08. *Wayside, 17 Chester Road, Birmingham B36 9DA* Tel 0121-747 2340

MacLACHLAN, Michael Ronald Frederic. b 39. Wycliffe Hall Ox 75. **d** 75 **p** 76. C Mansfield SS Pet and Paul *S'well* 75-78; P-in-c Newark Ch Ch 78-80; TV Newark w Hawton, Cotham and Shelton 80-86; P-in-c Sparkhill St Jo *Birm* 86-90; P-in-c Sparkbrook Em 86-90; V Sparkhill w Greet and Sparkbrook 90-92; RD Bordesley 90-92; P-in-c Kugluktuk Canada 92-97; R Stoke-next-Guildf 97-05; rtd 05; Hon C Drayton Bassett *Lich* from 05; Hon C Canwell from 09. *35 Moat Drive, Drayton Bassett, Tamworth B78 3UG* Tel (01827) 259730 E-mail mkanddmaclachlan@btinternet.com

McLACHLAN, Canon Sheila Elizabeth. b 52. SRN73 Kent Univ MA89. Wycliffe Hall Ox 80. **dss** 83 **d** 87 **p** 94. Chapl Kent Univ 83-94; Dep Master Rutherford Coll 87-94; Dn-in-c Kingsnorth w Shadoxhurst 94; P-in-c Kingsnorth and Shadoxhurst from 94; AD Ashford from 03; Hon Can Cant Cathl from 08. *The Rectory, Church Hill, Kingsnorth, Ashford TN23 3EG* Tel (01233) 620433 Mobile 07771-691164 E-mail sheila.mclachlan@tesco.net

MacLAREN, Ms Clare. b 67. Edin Univ LLB88. Linc Th Coll BTh95. **d** 95 **p** 96. C Benchill *Man* 95-98; C Bilton *Ripon* 98-03; TV Seacroft from 03. *St Paul's Vicarage, 58 Whinmoor Crescent, Leeds LS14 1EW* Tel 0113-294 0398 E-mail claremac@bigfoot.com

MacLAREN, Duncan Arthur Spencer. b 69. Oriel Coll Ox BA90 MA96 K Coll Lon MA97 PhD03. Oak Hill Th Coll 92. **d** 94 **p** 95. C Ox St Clem 94-97; Chapl St Edm Hall Ox 97-04; Assoc R Edin St Paul and St Geo 04-09; R Edin St Jas from 09. *71 Restalrig Road, Edinburgh EH6 8BG* Tel 0131-538 1053 E-mail rector@stjamesleith.org *or* duncan@maclarens.org

MacLAREN (née ALEXANDER), Mrs Jane Louise. b 69. LMH Ox BA90 MA96. Oak Hill Th Coll BA95. **d** 95 **p** 96. C Ox St Clem 95-98; Chapl St Aug Sch 98-02; Chapl Ox Brookes Univ 02-04; Assoc R Edin St Paul and St Geo 04-09; NSM Edin St Jas from 09. *71 Restalrig Road, Edinburgh EH6 8BG* Tel 0131-466 1800

McLAREN, Mrs Jeanette Moira. b 59. **d** 95 **p** 96. C Dulwich St Clem w St Pet *S'wark* 95-99; P-in-c Brixton St Paul 99-05; P-in-c Brixton St Paul w St Sav 05-08; V Biggin Hill *Roch* from

McLAREN

08. *St Mark's Vicarage, 10 Church Road, Biggin Hill, Westerham TN16 3LB* Tel (01959) 540482 E-mail jmmclaren@tiscali.co.uk
McLAREN, Richard Francis. b 46. S'wark Ord Course 72. **d** 75 **p** 76. C Charlton St Luke w H Trin *S'wark* 75-78; C Kensington St Mary Abbots w St Geo *Lon* 78-81; Hon C St Marylebone w H Trin 82-96; P-in-c 96-97; Development Officer CUF 97; Chmn Art and Christianity Enquiry Trust from 97; Hon C Regent's Park St Mark from 97. *8 Gray's Court, 51-53 Gray's Inn Road, London WC1X 8PP* Tel and fax (020) 7404 5642
E-mail richard@mclaren7.fsnet.co.uk
McLAREN, Robert Ian. b 62. Bris Univ BSc84 St Jo Coll Dur BA87. Cranmer Hall Dur 85. **d** 88 **p** 89. C Birkenhead Ch Ch *Ches* 88-90; C Bebington 90-95; V Cheadle All Hallows 95-05; V Poynton from 05. *The Vicarage, 41 London Road North, Poynton, Stockport SK12 1AF* Tel (01625) 850524 *or* 879277
E-mail vicar@orange.net
McLAREN, Ronald. b 31. Kelham Th Coll. **d** 59 **p** 60. C Redcar *York* 59-62; C Hornsea and Goxhill 62-65; V Middlesbrough St Thos 65-70; Chapl RN 70-73; Australia from 73; rtd 96. *16 Moselle Drive, Thornlands Qld 4164, Australia* Tel (0061) (7) 3821 2069 Mobile 409-039768
E-mail ronanne@ozemail.com.au
McLAREN-COOK, Paul Raymond. b 43. **d** 66 **p** 67. C Mt Lawley Australia 66-67; C Perth Cathl 67-69; R Carnarvon 69-72; V Seremban Malaysia 72-75; Warden Coll of Th 75-76; R Kensington 76-79; R Narrogin 79-84; P-in-c Wellington Australia 84-85; R Eugowra 85-86; P-in-c Berrigan 86-87; P-in-c Hay 87-88; P-in-c Yass 88; R Moruya 88-90; R Heywood 90-92; R Warracknabeal 92-95; Chapl Ballarat Base and St Jo of God Hosps 95-00; R Kansas City St Mary USA 00-03; R Stanway *Chelmsf* from 03. *The Rectory, Church Lane, Stanway, Colchester CO3 5LR* Tel (01206) 210407
E-mail mclarencook@btinternet.com
McLARNON, Mrs Sylvia Caroline Millicent. b 45. S Dios Minl Tr Scheme 92. **d** 95 **p** 96. NSM Burgess Hill St Andr *Chich* 95-99; C 99-09; rtd 09; Asst Chapl St Pet and St Jas Hospice N Chailey from 05. *75 Cants Lane, Burgess Hill RH15 0LX* Tel (01444) 233902
McLAUGHLIN, Adrian. **d** 07 **p** 08. C Bangor Abbey *D & D* from 07. *9 Pinehill Crescent, Bangor BT19 6FS* Tel (028) 9147 7182
E-mail revadrian@nireland.com
McLAUGHLIN, Hubert James Kenneth. b 45. CITC 85. **d** 88 **p** 89. NSM Donagheady *D & R* 88-89; NSM Glendermott 89-98; P-in-c Inver w Mountcharles, Killaghtee and Killybegs 98-02; I from 02. *The Rectory, Inver, Co Donegal, Republic of Ireland* Tel (00353) (74) 973 6013 Mobile 80-254 9380
E-mail inver@raphoe.anglican.org
McLAUGHLIN, Capt Michael Anthony. b 48. **d** 97 **p** 98. C Gt Chart *Cant* 97-01; C-in-c Parkwood CD from 01. *The Vicarage, Wallis Avenue, Maidstone ME15 9JJ* Tel (01622) 764170 Mobile 07977-051649 E-mail macl@blueyonder.co.uk
MACLAURIN, Ms Anne Fiona. b 62. St Andr Univ MA84. Ridley Hall Cam. **d** 99 **p** 00. C Crookes St Thos *Sheff* 99-04; TV 04-05; Miss P Philadelphia St Thos from 05. *St Thomas's Church, Philadelphia Campus, 6 Gilpin Street, Sheffield S6 3BL* Tel 0114-241 9560
E-mail anne.maclaurin@stthomaschurch.org.uk
MACLAY, Christopher Willis. b 64. Stirling Univ BA88 Reading Univ MA92. Trin Coll Bris BA99. **d** 01 **p** 02. C Bedhampton *Portsm* 01-05; P-in-c Ashington, Washington and Wiston w Buncton *Chich* from 05. *The Rectory, Mill Lane, Ashington, Pulborough RH20 3BX* Tel (01903) 893878
McLAY, Robert James. b 49. Cant Univ (NZ) BA71. St Jo Coll Auckland. **d** 73 **p** 74. C Fendalton New Zealand 73-75; Hon C Yardley St Edburgha *Birm* 75-77; V Banks Peninsular New Zealand 77-80; V Marchwiel 80-83; V Huntly 83-89; Lect St Jo Coll 86-88; V Stokes Valley 89-93; V Pauatahanui 93-04; V Brooklyn from 04; Can Wellington Cathl 96-00. *13 Garfield Street, Brooklyn, Wellington 6021, New Zealand* Tel (0064) (4) 389 8003 *or* 389 3470 E-mail stmattes@actrix.gen.nz
MACLEAN, Canon Allan Murray. b 50. Edin Univ MA72. Cuddesdon Coll 72. **d** 76 **p** 77. Chapl St Mary's Cathl 76-81; Tutor Edin Univ 77-80; R Dunoon *Arg* 81-86; R Tighnabruaich 84-86; Provost St Jo Cathl Oban 86-99; R Oban St Jo 86-99; R Ardbrecknish 86-99; R Ardchattan 89-99; Hon Can St Jo Cathl Oban from 99; Perm to Offic *Mor* from 00. *5 North Charlotte Street, Edinburgh EH2 4HR* Tel 0131-225 8609
McLEAN, Bradley Halstead. b 57. McMaster Univ Ontario BSc Toronto Univ MDiv MTh PhD. **d** 83 **p** 84. C Dur St Giles 83-84; Canada from 84. *38 Tweedsmuir Road, Winnipeg MB R3P 1Z2, Canada*
McLEAN, The Ven Donald Stewart. b 48. TCD BA70. CITC 70. **d** 72 **p** 73. C Glendermott *D & R* 72-75; I Castledawson 75-87 and from 03; Dioc Dir of Ords 79-96; I Londonderry Ch Ch 87-03; Can Derry Cathl from 91; Adn Derry from 96. *12 Station Road, Castledawson, Magherafelt BT45 8AZ* Tel (028) 7946 8235 E-mail archdeacon@derry.anglican.org
or dsmclean@iol.ie

McLEAN, Mrs Eileen Mary. b 44. City Univ BSc67. NOC 85. **d** 88 **p** 94. Par Dn Burley in Wharfedale *Bradf* 88-92; Par Dn Nottingham St Pet and St Jas *S'well* 92-94; C 94-02; AD Nottingham Cen 98-02; V Bamburgh *Newc* 02-08; V Ellingham 02-08; rtd 08. *3 The Green, Bewerley, Harrogate HG3 5HU* Tel (01423) 712467
MACLEAN, Kenneth John Forbes. b 31. St Deiniol's Hawarden 80. **d** 81 **p** 82. C Sedgley All SS *Lich* 81-85; V Shareshill 85-90; R Bicton, Montford w Shrawardine and Fitz 90-96; rtd 96; Perm to Offic *Lich* from 99. *7 The Armoury, Wenlock Road, Shrewsbury SY2 6PA* Tel (01743) 243308
MacLEAN, Lawrence Alexander Charles. b 61. K Coll Lon BD84 AKC84. Chich Th Coll 86. **d** 88 **p** 89. C Cirencester *Glouc* 88-91; C Prestbury 91-96; Perm to Offic 01-02; Chapl Florence w Siena *Eur* from 02. *The English Church of St Mark, via Maggio 16/18, 50125 Firenze, Italy* Tel and fax (0039) (055) 294764 Mobile 328-180 4196 E-mail lawrence.maclean@virgilio.it
McLEAN, Ms Margaret Anne. b 62. Birm Univ BA91 Heythrop Coll Lon MA99. Qu Coll Birm 88. **d** 91 **p** 94. Par Dn Bedford All SS *St Alb* 91-94; C 94; Chapl St Alb High Sch for Girls 94-98; Asst Soc Resp Officer *Derby* 98-99; Chapl Huddersfield Univ 99-02; P-in-c Scholes 02-09; P-in-c Cleckheaton St Luke and Whitechapel 02-09; P-in-c Battyeford from 09; Dioc Tr Officer from 09. *Battyeford Vicarage, 107A Stocksbank Road, Mirfield WF14 9QT* Tel (01924) 493277 Mobile 07974-125494
E-mail m.a.mclean@btinternet.com
McLEAN, Canon Michael Stuart. b 32. Dur Univ BA57. Cuddesdon Coll 57. **d** 59 **p** 60. C Camberwell St Giles *S'wark* 59-61; Lic to Offic *Nor* 61-68; R Marsham 68-74; R Burgh 68-74; RD Ingworth 70-74; P-in-c Nor St Pet Parmentergate w St Jo 74-75; TV 75-78; TR 78-86; Hon Can Nor Cathl 82-86; Can Res Nor Cathl 86-94; P-in-c Nor St Mary in the Marsh 87-94; Perm to Offic from 94; rtd 97. *30 Friars Quay, Norwich NR3 1ES* Tel (01603) 630398
McLEAN, Peter. b 50. **d** 94 **p** 95. NSM Mold *St As* 94-02; Perm to Offic 02-03; P-in-c Bodedern w Llanfaethlu *Ban* 03-05; R Llangefni w Tregaean from 05; AD Malltraeth from 06. *Llety'r Llan, 50 Bro Ednyfed, Llangefni LL77 7WB* Tel (01248) 722667
McLEAN, Robert Hedley. b 47. St Jo Coll Dur BA69. Ripon Hall Ox 69. **d** 71 **p** 72. C Redhill St Jo *S'wark* 71-74; C S Beddington St Mich 74-77; C-in-c Raynes Park H Cross CD 77; P-in-c Motspur Park 77-80; V 80-84; V Tadworth 84-00; Asst RD Reigate 92-93; RD Reigate 93-00; R Morpeth *Newc* from 00; AD Morpeth 04-08; Chapl Northd Mental Health NHS Trust from 00; Chapl Northumbria Healthcare NHS Trust from 00. *The Rectory, Cottingwood Lane, Morpeth NE61 1ED* Tel (01670) 513517 E-mail robert@morpeth-rectory.fsnet.co.uk
McLEAN-REID, Robert. b 43. Oak Hill Th Coll 81. **d** 83 **p** 84. C Rainham *Chelmsf* 83-86; R Challoch w Newton Stewart *Glas* 86-87; R Aberdeen St Pet 87-90; P-in-c Aberdeen St Clem 89-90; V Easington Colliery *Dur* 90-95; rtd 95; Hon C Hampsthwaite and Killinghall and Birstwith *Ripon* from 08. *The Vicarage, Wreaks Road, Birstwith, Harrogate HG3 2NJ* Tel (01423) 779790
MacLEAY, Angus Murdo. b 59. Univ Coll Ox BA81 MA86 Man Univ MPhil92 Solicitor 83. Wycliffe Hall Ox 85. **d** 88 **p** 89. C Rusholme H Trin *Man* 88-92; V Houghton *Carl* 92-01; R Sevenoaks St Nic *Roch* from 01. *The Rectory, Rectory Lane, Sevenoaks TN13 1JA* Tel (01732) 740340 Fax 742810
E-mail angus.macleay@diocese-rochester.org
McLELLAN, Eric Macpherson Thompson. b 16. St Jo Coll Dur BA38 MA41. **d** 39 **p** 40. C Byker St Mark *Newc* 39-44; C Fazakerley Em *Liv* 44-45; V Everton Em 45-54; R Sevenoaks St Nic *Roch* 54-70; Hon Can Roch Cathl 68-70; Chapl Br Embassy Ch Paris *Eur* 70-80; RD France 75-79; Adn N France 79-80; Perm to Offic *Chich* 80-99 and *Roch* from 80; rtd 81. *clo I D McLellan Esq, 51 Florida Drive, Exeter EX4 5EX*
MacLEOD, Alan Roderick Hugh (Roddie). b 33. St Edm Hall Ox BA56 MA61 Ox Univ DipEd62. Wycliffe Hall Ox 56. **d** 58 **p** 59. C Bognor St Jo *Chich* 58-61; Chapl Wadh Coll Ox 62; Hd of RE Picardy Boys' Sch Erith 62-68; C Erith St Jo *Roch* 63-69; Dean Lonsdale Coll Lanc Univ 70-72; Hd of RE K Edw VI Sch Totnes 72-73; Dir of Resources St Helier Boys' Sch Jersey 73-84; V Shipton Bellinger *Win* 84-02; rtd 02; Perm to Offic *Win* from 02. *Pippins Toft, Lashmar's Corner, East Preston, Littlehampton BN16 1EZ* Tel (01903) 783523
McLEOD, David Leo Roderick. b 71. Westmr Coll Ox BA92 DipCOT96. **d** 05 **p** 06. OLM Coddenham w Gosbeck and Hemingstone w Henley *St E* from 05; OLM Crowfield w Stonham Aspal and Mickfield from 05; Chapl Team Co-ord Univ Campus Suffolk from 07; Chapl Team Co-ord Suffolk New Coll from 07. *The Chestnuts, The Street, Stonham Aspal, Stowmarket IP14 6AG* Tel (01449) 711457 Mobile 07906-880820 E-mail davidmcleod01@btinternet.com *or* davidmcleod@suffolk.ac.uk
McLEOD, Everton William. b 57. Oak Hill Th Coll 89. **d** 91 **p** 92. C New Ferry *Ches* 91-93; C Moreton 93-98; Chapl R Liv Univ Hosp NHS Trust 98-01; TR Uphill *B & W* from 01. *Uphill*

Rectory, 3 Old Church Road, Uphill, Weston-super-Mare BS23 4UH Tel (01934) 620156 E-mail mcleod@xalt.co.uk

MACLEOD, John Bain Maclennan. b 50. Aber Univ LLB86 Solicitor 89. TISEC 06. **d** 06. NSM Hamilton *Glas* from 06. *Greenrig Barn, Greenrig Road, Lesmahagow, Lanark ML11 9QB* Tel (01555) 664866 E-mail macleod.greenrig@btinternet.com

MacLEOD, John Malcolm (Jay). b 61. Harvard Univ AB84 Pemb Coll Ox BA87 MA91. Linc Th Coll MDiv93. **d** 93 **p** 94. C Chesterfield St Aug *Derby* 93-96; C Stalybridge St Paul *Ches* 96-98; P-in-c Melkilehurst 98-03; P-in-c Bedford All SS *St Alb* from 03; Dioc Interfaith Adv from 03. *All Saints' Vicarage, 1 Cutcliffe Place, Bedford MK40 4DF* Tel (01234) 266945 E-mail macasher@dial.pipex.com

McLEOD, Neil Raymond. b 61. Trin Coll Bris 06. **d** 08 **p** 09. C N w S Wootton *Nor* from 08. *Ambleside, 34 Castle Rising Road, South Wootton, King's Lynn PE30 3JB* Tel (01553) 684064

McLEOD, Paul Douglas. b 66. Cuddesdon Coll BTh95. **d** 98 **p** 99. C Morpeth *Newc* 98-02; V Newbiggin Hall from 02. *St Wilfrid's House, Trevelyan Drive, Newcastle upon Tyne NE5 4DA* Tel 0191-271 4005 E-mail revpaulmcleod@aol.com

MacLEOD, Roderick. *See* MacLEOD, Alan Roderick Hugh

McLEOD, Canon Ronald. b 17. Lon Univ BA39 BA50 BD71 Ex Univ BA56 Man Univ MA59 Ex Univ MPhil01. Bps' Coll Cheshunt 39. **d** 41 **p** 42. C Plymouth St Pet *Ex* 41-44; Chapl RAF 44-69; Prin RAF Chapl Sch and Asst Chapl-in-Chief RAF 69-73; QHC 72-73; R Itchen Abbas cum Avington *Win* 73-91; Hon Can Win Cathl 84-91; rtd 91; Perm to Offic *Ex* from 92. *Melfort, High Wall, Barnstaple EX31 2DP* Tel (01271) 343636

McLEOD, Ms Susan Margaret. b 48. SEN69 Sheff Poly CQSW89. NOC 92. **d** 95 **p** 96. NSM Charlesworth and Dinting Vale *Derby* 95-02; Chapl Asst S Man Univ Hosps NHS Trust 97-02. *Address temp unknown*

MacLEOD-MILLER, Peter Norman. b 66. **d** 91 **p** 91. C Cardiff Australia 91-92; C Hillston 92-94; C Fitzroy 95-97; Perm to Offic Melbourne 97-01; P-in-c Risby w Gt and Lt Saxham *St E* 02-04; V Barrow from 05; Min Can St E Cathl from 05. *The Rectory, Barrow, Bury St Edmunds IP29 5BA* Tel (01284) 810929 E-mail fr_peter@btopenworld.com

McLOUGHLIN, Ian Livingstone. b 38. CEng MICE64. Carl Dioc Tr Course 78. **d** 83 **p** 84. NSM Stanwix *Carl* 83-88; C Barrow St Geo w St Luke 88-90; R Kirkby Thore w Temple Sowerby and Newbiggin 90-01; rtd 01; Perm to Offic *Bradf* and *Carl* from 01. *29 Wordsworth Drive, Kendal LA9 7JW*

McLOUGHLIN, John Robert. b 70. QUB BEng92 Open Univ MSc02. CITC BTh09. **d** 09. C Arm St Mark from 09. *6 Ashley Avenue, Armagh BT60 1HD* Tel (028) 3752 6180 Mobile 07515-353023 E-mail johnnymcloughlin@gmail.com

McLUCKIE, John Mark. b 67. St Andr Univ BD89. Edin Th Coll MTh91. **d** 91 **p** 92. C Perth St Ninian *St And* 91-94; Chapl K Coll Cam 94-96; TV Glas E End 96-00; Assoc R Edin St Jo 00-03; Perm to Offic from 08. *23 Connaught Place, Edinburgh EH6 4RQ* Tel 0131-552 3107 E-mail john.mcluckie@hotmail.co.uk

MACLUSKIE, Mrs Linda. b 55. Lanc Univ MA99. CBDTI 95. **d** 98 **p** 99. NSM Halton w Aughton *Blackb* 98-02; NSM Bolton-le-Sands from 02. *15 Whitendale Drive, Bolton le Sands, Carnforth LA5 8LY* Tel (01524) 822769 E-mail ian@macluskie.freeserve.co.uk

McMAHON, George Ian Robertson. b 23. Monmouth Coll Illinois BA44 Univ of N Carolina BA44 MA49 Ox Univ MLitt61 Birm Univ PhD73. Gen Th Sem NY STB52. **d** 52 **p** 53. P-in-c Roxboro, Yanceyville and Milton USA 52-57; Perm to Offic *Ox* 57-64; Prin Lect Homerton Coll Cam 65-88; P-in-c Cambridge St Clem *Ely* 89-04; Perm to Offic from 04. *44 Grantchester Road, Cambridge CB3 9ED* Tel (01223) 350988

McMAHON, Stephen. b 66. Newc Univ BSc87 MSc89 Leeds Univ BA03 CEng97 MBES97. Coll of Resurr Mirfield 01. **d** 03 **p** 04. C Lancaster St Mary w St John and St Anne *Blackb* 03-07; P-in-c Lowther and Askham and Clifton and Brougham *Carl* from 07; P-in-c Kirkby Thore w Temple Sowerby and Newbiggin from 07. *The Rectory, Clifton, Penrith CA10 2EA* Tel (01768) 210558 E-mail steve1345.mcmahon@virgin.net

McMANN, Duncan. b 34. Jes Coll Ox BA55 MA60. Clifton Th Coll 55. **d** 58 **p** 59. C Newburn *Newc* 58-60; C Bishopwearmouth St Gabr *Dur* 60-62; N Area Sec BCMS 62-66; Midl and E Anglia Area Sec 66-72; Support Co-ord 84-92; Lic to Offic *Man* 62-66 and *Cov* 66-92; C-in-c Answorth w Cossall *S'well* 92-99; Chapl Notts Constabulary 93-99; rtd 99; Perm to Offic *Nor* from 00. *7 Evans Drive, Lowestoft NR32 2RX* Tel (01502) 531337

McMANN, Canon Judith. b 46. Hull Univ BTh96. EMMTC MA98. **d** 98 **p** 99. NSM Gt Grimsby St Mary and St Jas *Linc* 98-08; NSM Caistor Gp from 08; Can and Preb Linc Cathl from 05. *23 Grasby Crescent, Grimsby DN37 9HE* Tel (01472) 887523 E-mail jmcmann@btopenworld.com

McMANNERS, John Roland. b 46. Liv Univ LLB68. Cranmer Hall Dur 99. **d** 01 **p** 02. C Monkwearmouth *Dur* 01-05; P-in-c Bishopwearmouth St Gabr from 05. *The Vicarage, 1 St Gabriel's Avenue, Sunderland SR4 7TF* Tel 0191-567 5200

McMANUS, James Robert. b 33. Wycliffe Hall Ox 56. **d** 58 **p** 59. C Leic H Trin 58-60; C Aylestone 60-63; India 66-79; V Oldham St Barn *Man* 79-83; Asst Regional Sec CMS 83-85; V Wolverhampton St Matt *Lich* 85-93; V Lapley w Wheaton Aston 93-99; P-in-c Blymhill w Weston-under-Lizard 93-99; rtd 99; Perm to Offic *Lich* from 99. *Delamere, McBean Road, Wolverhampton WV6 0JQ* Tel (01902) 833436 Fax 834170 E-mail jimvicar@aol.com

McMANUS-THOMPSON, Elizabeth Gray. *See* THOMPSON, Elizabeth Gray McManus

McMASTER, James Alexander. b 43. **d** 69 **p** 70. C Dundonald *D & D* 69-73; C Antrim All SS *Conn* 73-78; I Tempo and Clabby *Clogh* 78-83; I Knocknamuckley *D & D* 83-95; I Carrickfergus *Conn* 95-08; rtd 08. *18 Glebe Avenue, Derry Keighan, Ballymoney BT53 8AH* Tel (028) 2074 1893

MacMASTER, Mrs Norma. QUB BA DipEd McGill Univ Montreal MEd. **d** 04 **p** 05. NSM Dublin St Geo and St Thos *D & G* 04-07; rtd 07. *1 The Orchard, Tennis Court Lane, Skerries, Co Dublin, Republic of Ireland* Tel (00353) (1) 849 1387 E-mail nmacmaster@eircom.net

McMASTER, Richard Ian. b 32. Edin Th Coll 57. **d** 60 **p** 61. C Carl H Trin 60-63; Chapl St Andr Tr Coll Korogwe Tanzania 63-66; V Broughton Moor 66-69; V Burnley St Steph *Blackb* 69-77; V New Longton 77-89; P-in-c Woodhall Spa and Kirkstead *Linc* 89-91; P-in-c Langton w Woodhall 89-91; P-in-c Bucknall w Tupholme 89-91; P-in-c Horsington w Stixwould 89-91; R Woodhall Spa Gp 92-97; rtd 97; Perm to Offic *Birm* from 97. *18 Marsden Close, Solihull B92 7JR* Tel 0121-707 6208 E-mail bettyandianmc@aol.com

McMASTER, William Keith. b 45. TCD. **d** 82 **p** 84. C Portadown St Columba *Arm* 82-84; C Erdington St Barn *Birm* 84-87; TV Shirley 87-00; TV Salter Street and Shirley 00-02; rtd 02. *38 Lambscote Close, Shirley, Solihull B90 1NS*

MACMATH, Terence Handley. *See* HANDLEY MACMATH, Terence

McMICHAEL, Andrew Hamilton. b 48. Univ of Wales (Ban) BA77. Chich Th Coll 87. **d** 89 **p** 90. C Chorley St Geo *Blackb* 89-92; C Burnley St Andr w St Marg 92-94; Chapl Burnley Health Care NHS Trust 92-94; R Eccleston *Blackb* 94-99; V Lt Marsden w Nelson St Mary 99-04; P-in-c Tain *Mor* 04-07; P-in-c Invergordon St Ninian 04-07; P-in-c Lochinver 04-07; P-in-c Harrington *Carl* from 07. *The Rectory, Rectory Close, Harrington, Workington CA14 5PN* Tel (01946) 830215 E-mail andrew.mcmichael@tesco.net

MacMILLAN, Douglas Middleton. b 41. St Thos Hosp Lon MB, BS66 FRCS70 FTCL82 AMusLCM80 FLCM83. Guildf Dioc Min Course 96. **d** 00. NSM Guildf Cathl 00-02; Perm to Offic 02-04; NSM E and W Clandon from 04. *Rivendell, 50 Speedwell Close, Guildford GU4 7HE* Tel (01483) 533019

✠**McMULLAN, The Rt Revd Gordon.** b 34. ACIS57 QUB BSc61 PhD71 TCD MPhil90 Univ of the South (USA) DMin95. Ridley Hall Cam 61. **d** 62 **p** 63 **c** 80. C Ballymacarrett St Patr *D & D* 62-67; Cen Adv on Chr Stewardship to Ch of Ireland 67-70; C Knock 70-71; I 76-80; I Belfast St Brendan 71-76; Offg Chapl RAF 71-78; Bp's Dom Chapl *D & D* 73-78; Adn Down 79-80; Bp Clogh 80-86; Bp *D & D* 86-97; rtd 97. *26 Wellington Park, Bangor BT20 4PJ* Tel (028) 9146 0821

McMULLEN, Philip Kenneth. b 55. RMN80. St Mich Coll Llan 93. **d** 95 **p** 96. C Coity w Nolton *Llan* 95-98; V Fleur-de-Lis *Mon* 98-04. *29 Clos Coed Bach, Blackwood NP12 1GT* Tel (01495) 220210

McMULLEN, Ronald Norman. b 36. TCD BA61 MA66 California Univ of Integral Studies MA92. Ridley Hall Cam 61. **d** 63 **p** 64. C Fulham St Mary N End *Lon* 63-67; C Cambridge St Sepulchre *Ely* 67-70; C Everton St Ambrose w St Tim *Liv* 70-73; Community Work Course & Research Asst York Univ 73-75; P-in-c Heanor *Derby* 75-79; V 79-88; RD Heanor 76-83; USA 88-93; rtd 98. *Apple Tree Cottage, 38A Main Street, Lowick, Berwick-upon-Tweed TD15 2UA* Tel and fax (01289) 388301

McMULLON, Andrew Brian. b 56. Sheff Univ BSc. St Jo Coll Nottm. **d** 83 **p** 84. C Stainforth *Sheff* 83-86; V Blackb Redeemer 86-90; Chapl RAF from 90. *Chaplaincy Services, Valiant Block, HQ Air Command, RAF High Wycombe HP14 4UE* Tel (01494) 496800 Fax 496343

McMUNN, Lee James. b 78. LSE BSc99. Wycliffe Hall Ox BA04. **d** 05 **p** 06. C Hull St Jo Newland *York* from 05. *32 Riversdale Road, Hull HU6 7HA* Tel (01482) 802611 Mobile 07957-898884 E-mail lee@stjohnnewland.org.uk

McMURRAY, Gary. b 81. QUB BA02. CITC BTh08. **d** 08 **p** 09. C Dundonald *D & D* from 08. *6 Mount Regan Avenue, Dundonald, Belfast BT16 1JA* Tel (028) 9048 1856 E mail garymcmurray@aol.com

McNAB (née LUMMIS), Mrs Elizabeth Howieson. b 44. Lon Univ BDS68 LDS68. St Jo Coll Nottm 85. **d** 88 **p** 95. NSM Lerwick *Ab* from 88; NSM Burravoe from 88. *Waters Edge, Bridge of Walls, Shetland ZE2 9NP* Tel (01595) 809441

MCNAIR SCOTT, Benjamin Guthrie. b 76. K Coll Lon BA98 MA05. Ridley Hall Cam 05. **d** 07 **p** 08. NSM Guildf Ch Ch w

St Martha-on-the-Hill from 07. *3 Newlands Crescent, Guildford GU1 3JS* Tel (01483) 455645 Mobile 07968-617084 E-mail benjaming@lycos.co.uk

McNAMARA, Barbara. *See* SMITH, Mrs Barbara Mary

McNAMARA, Michael Ian. b 59. Van Mildert Coll Dur BA81. Ridley Hall Cam 83. **d** 85 **p** 86. C Bedford Ch Ch *St Alb* 85-89; BCMS Tanzania 89-92; TV Bolton St Paul w Em *Man* 93-97; C Galleywood Common *Chelmsf* 97-03; R Elmswell *St E* from 03. *The Rectory, Church Road, Elmswell, Bury St Edmunds IP30 9DY* Tel (01359) 240512 E-mail mwanza@lineone.net

McNAMEE, William Graham. b 38. Birm Univ BSocSc59. Cranmer Hall Dur BA74. **d** 75 **p** 76. C Tonbridge St Steph *Roch* 75-78; C Fazeley *Lich* 78-87; Chapl Staffs Poly 87-92; Chapl Staffs Univ 92-97; P-in-c Lt Malvern, Malvern Wells and Wyche *Worc* 97-00; P-in-c Malvern Wells and Wyche 00-01; rtd 01. *22 Leadon Road, Malvern WR14 2XF* Tel (01684) 562771

McNAUGHTAN-OWEN, James Thomas (Tom). b 48. Liv Univ MA00. Linc Th Coll 77. **d** 80 **p** 81. C Palmers Green St Jo *Lon* 80-84; C Timperley *Ches* 84-87; C Bramhall 87-92; V Latchford St Jas from 92; RD Gt Budworth 96-03. *St James's Vicarage, Manx Road, Warrington WA4 6AJ* Tel (01925) 631893

MACNAUGHTON, Mrs Diana. b 54. St Hugh's Coll Ox BA76 MA90 Dur Univ PGCE78. NEOC 95. **d** 98 **p** 99. NSM Gosforth All SS *Newc* 98-01; C Willington 01-04; Chapl Team Ldr Northumbria Healthcare NHS Trust from 04. *The Rectory, North Terrace, Wallsend NE28 6PY* Tel 0191-234 0371 Mobile 07950-627799 E-mail dmacnaughton@btinternet.com

MACNAUGHTON, James Alastair. b 54. St Jo Coll Ox BA78 MA82 Fitzw Coll Cam BA80. Ridley Hall Cam 78. **d** 81 **p** 82. C Rounds Green *Birm* 81-85; TV Bestwood Park *S'well* 85-86; TV Bestwood 86-90; V Amble *Newc* 90-97; TR Cramlington 97-07; Jt Newc/Dur Development Officer for Educn for Discipleship from 07. *The Rectory, North Terrace, Wallsend NE28 6PY* Tel 0191-234 0371 E-mail macnaughton@btinternet.com

McNAUGHTON, John. b 29. St Chad's Coll Dur. **d** 54 **p** 55. C Thorney Close CD *Dur* 54-58; C-in-c E Herrington St Chad CD 58-62; PC E Herrington 62-66; CF 66-94; V Hutton Cranswick w Skerne, Watton and Beswick *York* 94-99; rtd 99; Perm to Offic *York* from 99. *47 Southgate, Cranswick, Driffield YO25 9QX* Tel (01377) 270869

MACNAUGHTON, Mrs Pamela. Ox Min Course. **d** 08 **p** 09. NSM Acaster Malbis *York* from 08; NSM Appleton Roebuck w Acaster Selby from 08; NSM Bishopthorpe from 08. *64 Copmanthorpe Lane, Bishopthorpe, York YO23 2RS* Tel (01904) 700141

MACNAUGHTON, William Malcolm. b 57. Qu Coll Cam BA80. Ridley Hall Cam 79. **d** 81 **p** 82. C Haughton le Skerne *Dur* 81-85; P-in-c Newton Hall 85-90; TV Shoreditch St Leon and Hoxton St Jo *Lon* 90-00; AD Hackney 94-99; V Hoxton St Jo w Ch Ch 00-02; R Hambleden Valley *Ox* 02-07; AD Wycombe 05-07; Chief of Staff to Abp York from 07. *The Palace, Bishopthorpe, York YO23 2GE* Tel (01904) 707021 Fax 709204 E-mail malcolm.macnaughton@archbishopofyork.org

McNEE, Canon William Creighton. Ulster Univ MA NUU MA FCIPD. **d** 82 **p** 83. C Larne and Inver *Conn* 82-84; I Donagheady *D & R* 84-91; I Kilwaughter w Cairncastle and Craigy Hill *Conn* 91-93; I Ardstraw w Baronscourt, Badoney Lower etc *D & R* 93-04; P-in-c Londonderry Ch Ch 04-05; I 05-09; I Londonderry Ch Ch, Culmore, Muff and Belmont 08-09; Bp's Dom Chapl 96-07; Can Derry Cathl 00-09; rtd 09. *72 Brookview Glen, Eglinton, Londonderry BT47 3GW* E-mail billmcnee@aol.com

MACNEICE, Alan Donor. b 34. TCD Div Sch 62. **d** 64 **p** 65. C Ballymoney w Finvoy and Rasharkin *Conn* 64-67; R Christiana Jamaica 67-70; C Winchmore Hill H Trin *Lon* 71-76; C Harringay St Paul 76-77; C Kensington St Barn 77-78; P-in-c 78-79; USA 83-06; rtd 99. *29Eo, Street 178, Commond Choychom, nas Distrib Daun Penh, Phnom Penh, Cambodia* Tel (00855) (23) 986064 E-mail donor@online.com.kh

McNEICE, Kathleen Mary. SEITE. **d** 07 **p** 08. NSM Folkestone Trin *Cant* from 07. *19 Beachborough Road, Folkestone CT19 4AA* Tel (01303) 278791

McNEIL, Mrs Ann. b 41. **d** 89 **p** 94. NSM Henfield w Shermanbury and Woodmancote *Chich* 89-99; Perm to Offic from 00. *6 The Daisy Croft, Henfield BN5 9LH* Tel (01273) 492606 E-mail annmcneil@onetel.com

McNEILE, Donald Hugh. b 30. Trin Coll Cam BA53. Coll of Resurr Mirfield 53. **d** 55 **p** 56. C Wigan All SS *Liv* 55-57; C W Derby Gd Shep 57-61; rtd 95. *Monks Barn, North Hinksey Village, Oxford OX2 0NA* Tel (01865) 245473

MACNEILL, Nicholas Terence. b 62. St Steph Ho Ox BTh93. **d** 93 **p** 94. C Ex St Thos and Em 93-97; TV 97-98; V Cople, Moggerhanger and Willington *St Alb* 98-03; R Toddington and Chalgrave 03-06; rtd 07. *20 Black Path, Polegate BN26 5AP* Tel (01323) 485399 E-mail nick.macneill@ntlworld.com

McNELLY, Mrs Nicola. b 62. Cranmer Hall Dur 07. **d** 09. C Edin St Mary from 09. *32 Manor Place, Edinburgh EH3 7EB* Tel 0131-220 2375 Mobile 07825-440580 E-mail nicki.mcnelly@googlemail.com

McNICOL, Andrew Keith. b 45. Westmr Coll of Educn CertEd69 Open Univ BA79 Westmr Coll Ox MA90. Westcott Ho Cam 92. **d** 92 **p** 93. C Whitstable *Cant* 92-95; V Ferring *Chich* 95-00; P-in-c Willesborough *Cant* 00-06; P-in-c Tunstall w Rodmersham from 06. *The Rectory, Tunstall, Sittingbourne ME9 8DU* Tel (01795) 423907 E-mail akmcnicol@tesco.net

McNIVEN, Mrs Betty. b 47. Lanc Univ BA68. NOC 83. **dss** 86 **d** 87 **p** 94. Baguley *Man* 86-87; Hon Par Dn 87-88; Par Dn Newton Heath All SS 88-91; Par Dn E Farnworth and Kearsley 91-94; TV 94-95; P-in-c Spotland 95-02; Hon Can Man Cathl 00-02; TV Cwm Gwendraeth *St D* 02-06; rtd 07; P-in-c Llansteffan and Llan-y-bri etc *St D* 07-08. *12 Longacre Road, Carmarthen SA31 1HL* Tel (01267) 221721 E-mail betty.mcniven@talk21.com

MACONACHIE, Charles Leslie. b 27. TCD BA71 MA74 MDiv85 PhD90. Em Coll Saskatoon 47. **d** 50 **p** 51. C Clooney *D & R* 50-54; P-in-c Lower Tamlaght O'Crilly 54-61; Chapl Newsham Gen Hosp Liv 61-63; Chapl RAF 63-67; C Londonderry Ch Ch *D & R* 69-75; I Belmont 75-78; Warden for Min of Healing 75-96; I Culmore w Muff and Belmont 78-96; Warden Irish Internat Order of St Luke Physician 82-96; Can Derry Cathl 85-96; rtd 96; Chmn Ch's Min of Healing from 96. *3 Broomhill Court, Waterside, Londonderry BT47 6WP* Tel (028) 7134 8942

MACOURT, William Albany. b 19. TCD BA40 MA46. CITC 41. **d** 42 **p** 43. C Ballymena *Conn* 42-46; C Belf Cathl 46-48; I Duneane w Ballyscullion *Conn* 48-51; I Belfast St Mark 51-64; I Ballymacarrett St Patr *D & E* 64-89; Preb Swords St Patr Cathl Dublin 75-89; Adn Down *D & E* 89; Chan Belf Cathl 85-89; rtd 89; Dioc Info Officer *D & E* 89-97. *19 Abbey Court, Abbey Gardens, Belfast BT5 7JE* Tel (028) 9048 2041

McPHATE, The Very Revd Gordon Ferguson. b 50. Aber Univ MB, ChB74 Fitzw Coll Cam BA77 MA81 MD88 Surrey Univ MSc86 Edin Univ MTh94 FRCPEd98. Westcott Ho Cam 75. **d** 78 **p** 79. NSM Sanderstead All SS *S'wark* 78-81; Hon PV S'wark Cathl 81-86; Lect Lon Univ 81-86; Chapl St Andr Univ 86-02; Lect 86-93; Sen Lect 93-02; Dean Ches from 02. *The Deanery, 7 Abbey Street, Chester CH1 2JF* Tel (01244) 500956 or 500971 Fax 341110 E-mail dean@chestercathedral.com

MacPHEE, Canon Roger Hunter. b 43. Leeds Univ BSc65. EAMTC. **d** 86 **p** 87. NSM Trunch *Nor* from 86; Dioc NSM Officer from 97; Hon Can Nor Cathl from 03. *8 Lawn Close, Knapton, North Walsham NR28 0SD* Tel (01263) 720045 E-mail rmacphee4@aol.com

McPHERSON, Andrew Lindsay. b 58. St Jo Coll Dur BA79 MCIPD84. **d** 88 **p** 89. C Bitterne *Win* 88-92; V Weston 92-99; V Holdenhurst and Iford from 99; P-in-c Southbourne St Chris from 07; AD Bournemouth from 08. *The Vicarage, 53A Holdenhurst Avenue, Bournemouth BH7 6RB* Tel (01202) 425978 E-mail andy.mcpherson@ukgateway.net

MACPHERSON, Canon Anthony Stuart. b 56. Qu Coll Birm 77. **d** 80 **p** 81. C Morley St Pet w Churwell *Wakef* 80-84; C Penistone 84-85; P-in-c Thurlstone 85-86; TV Penistone and Thurlstone 86-88; V Grimethorpe 88-95; P-in-c Westgate Common 95-96; V 96-07; P-in-c Horbury Junction 02-07; RD Wakef 99-07; Hon Can Wakef Cathl 06-07; Can Missr from 07. *14 Belgravia Road, Wakefield WF1 3JP* Tel (01924) 275274 Mobile 07780-990354 E-mail tonymacpherson@blueyonder.co.uk

MACPHERSON, Archibald McQuarrie. b 27. Edin Th Coll 50. **d** 52 **p** 53. Asst Chapl St Andr Cathl 52-55; Prec 55-56; P-in-c Airdrie *Glas* 56-63; R Dumbarton 63-92; rtd 92. *29 Bramblehedge Path, Alexandria G83 8PH* Tel (01389) 753981

MacPHERSON, David Alan John. b 42. Lon Univ BD75 Open Univ BA83 Hatf Poly MSc89. Clifton Th Coll 69 Trin Coll Bris 72. **d** 72 **p** 73. C Drypool St Columba w St Andr and St Pet *York* 72-76; Asst Chapl HM Pris Hull 72-76; P-in-c Bessingby and Carnaby *York* 76-78; Chapl RAF 78-83; P-in-c Chedgrave w Hardley and Langley *Nor* 83-87; R 87-97; Chapl Langley Sch Nor 83-97; P-in-c Brington w Whilton and Norton *Pet* 97-98; R Brington w Whilton and Norton etc 98-02; rtd 02; Perm to Offic *Pet* from 02. *24 Coldstream Close, Daventry NN11 9HL* Tel (01327) 704500 E-mail dmacp@compuserve.com

MACPHERSON, Ewan Alexander. b 43. Toronto Univ BA74. Wycliffe Coll Toronto MDiv78. **d** 78 **p** 79. C Toronto St Cuth 78-81; C Toronto Apostles 81-86; V Priddy and Westbury sub Mendip w Easton *B & W* 86-06; rtd 06. *20 Tuddington Gardens, Wells BA5 2EJ* Tel (01749) 675876

MACPHERSON, John. b 28. Lon Univ BSc50 Ex Univ DipEd51 Univ of W Indies HDipEd65. St Alb Minl Tr Scheme 82. **d** 89 **p** 90. NSM Gt Berkhamsted *St Alb* 89-95; Perm to Offic from 00. *Little Tanglewood, Luton Road, Markyate, St Albans AL3 8PZ* Tel (01582) 841219

MACPHERSON, Peter Sinclair. b 44. Lich Th Coll 68. **d** 71 **p** 72. C Honiton, Gittisham and Combe Raleigh *Ex* 71-72; C Bideford 72-74; C Devonport St Mark Ford 74-75; V Thorncombe *Sarum* 75-79; TV Dorchester 79-85; Chapl Jersey Gp of Hosps 85-90; Chapl Derriford Hosp Plymouth 90-98; rtd 98. *Pump Cottage, 1 Rosemary Lane, Musbury, Axminster EX13 6AT* Tel (01297) 552524

MACQUIBAN, Gordon Alexander. b 24. Univ of Wales (Lamp) BA49 Crewe Coll of Educn CertEd72. Ely Th Coll 49. **d** 51 **p** 52. C Christleton *Ches* 51-53; C Disley 53-55; C Heswall and Chapl R Liv Children's Hosp 55-58; V Norley *Ches* 58-64; V Ches Ch Ch 64-71; Hon C Ches H Trin 71-85; Hon C Runcorn All SS 85-87; Hon C Frodsham 87-88; rtd 88; Perm to Offic *B & W* 88-01. *Westlands Residential Home, Reed Vale, Teignmouth TQ14 9EH* Tel (01626) 775843

McQUILLEN, Brian Anthony. b 45. Ripon Hall Ox 73. **d** 75 **p** 76. C Northfield *Birm* 75-78; C Sutton Coldfield H Trin 78-80; V Bearwood 80-89; V Glouc St Geo w Whaddon 89-96; R St Martin w Looe *Truro* from 96; RD W Wivelshire 98-03 and 06-08. *St Martin's Rectory, Barbican Road, Looe PL13 1NX* Tel (01503) 263070 Fax 265550
E-mail revmcq.looe@btopenworld.com

McQUILLEN-WRIGHT, Christopher Charles. b 71. Kent Univ BA92. Westcott Ho Cam 92. **d** 95 **p** 96. C Hayle, St Erth and Phillack w Gwithian and Gwinear *Truro* 95-96; C Godrevy 96-99; TV Bodmin w Lanhydrock and Lanivet 99-02; P-in-c St Columb Minor and St Colan from 02. *The Vicarage, Parkenbutts, Newquay TR7 3HE* Tel (01637) 873496 *or* 877165

McRACRAE, Charles. b 27. RD71. Edin Univ BDS62. S Dios Minl Tr Scheme 88. **d** 91 **p** 92. NSM Heene *Chich* 91-94; NSM Portsea St Alb *Portsm* 94-96; OGS from 96; Perm to Offic *Chich* from 96. *64 Stone Lane, Worthing BN13 2BQ* Tel (01903) 691660

McRAE, Keith Alban. b 44. S'wark Ord Course 68. **d** 73 **p** 74. NSM Crawley *Chich* 73-78; NSM Ifield 78-90. *52 Downsview, Small Dole, Henfield BN5 9YB*

MacRAE, Mrs Rosalind Phyllis. b 41. Sarum & Wells Th Coll 81. **dss** 84 **d** 87 **p** 94. Feltham *Lon* 84-87; Asst Chapl R Cornwall Hosps Trust 87-88; Chapl Mt Edgcumbe Hospice 88-92; Chapl St Austell Hosp 88-92; Chapl Penrice Hosp St Austell 88-92; NSM St Austell *Truro* 88-92; Chapl R Cornwall Hosps Trust 92-95; rtd 95. *16 Rosparc, Probus, Truro TR2 4TJ*

McREYNOLDS, Canon Kenneth Anthony. b 48. **d** 83 **p** 84. C Ballymena w Ballyclug *Conn* 83-86; I Rathcoole 86-90; I Lambeg from 90; Can Conn Cathl from 08. *Lambeg Rectory, 58 Belfast Road, Lisburn BT27 4AT* Tel and fax (028) 9266 3872
E-mail kenmcreynolds@btinternet.com

MacROBERT, Iain. b 49. Wolv Univ BA80 PGCE81 Birm Univ MA85 PhD89. **d** 00 **p** 00. NSM S Queensferry *Edin* from 00. *21 Long Crook, South Queensferry EH30 9XR* Tel and fax 0131-319 1558 *or* tel 244 0651 E-mail iain0macrobert@aol.com

McROBERTS, Ms Tracey. b 68. QUB BTh99 PGCE00 Dub City Univ MA09. CITC 08. **d** 09. C Belfast St Thos *Conn* from 09. *St Thomas's Parish, 1 Eglantine Avenue, Belfast BT9 6DW* Tel 07718-490040 (mobile)
E-mail tracey.mcroberts@btinternet.com

McROSTIE, Mrs Lyn. b 50. Canberra Univ BA77 Portsm Univ MA03 MIInfSc81. STETS 95. **d** 98 **p** 99. C Portsea St Cuth *Portsm* 98-02; P-in-c Shadwell St Paul w Ratcliffe St Jas *Lon* 02-04; Course Ldr NTMTC 04-06; P-in-c Northwood *Portsm* 06-07; R from 07; P-in-c Gurnard 06-07; V from 07; P-in-c Cowes St Faith 06-07; V from 07. *The Rectory, Chawton Lane, Cowes PO31 8PR* Tel (01983) 298370 Mobile 07718-300732
E-mail lyn.mcrostie@mcrostie.info

MACROW-WOOD, Antony Charles. b 60. York Univ BA82 Jes Coll Cam BA91 ACA86. Westcott Ho Cam 89. **d** 92 **p** 93. C Swindon St Jo and St Andr *Bris* 92-96, TV Preston w Sutton Poyntz and Osmington w Poxwell *Sarum* 96-04; P-in-c N Poole Ecum Team 04-06; TR from 06. *The Rectory, 99 Darby's Lane, Poole BH15 3EU* Tel (01202) 660612 Mobile 07775-574971
E-mail amacrowwood@mac.com

McSPARRON, Cecil. b 35. Regent Coll Vancouver MCS87 Trin Th Coll Singapore MMin77 MDiv86. **d** 68 **p** 69. C Glendermott *D & R* 68-70; Singapore 70-77 and 83-89; C Portadown St Mark *Arm* 78-80; UK Regional Dir OMF 80-82; Tutor Miss Studies Lon Bible Coll 90-93. *Cedar House Nursing Home, 39 High Street, Harefield, Uxbridge UB9 6EB* Tel (01895) 820700

MacSWAIN, Robert Carroll. b 69. Liberty Univ USA BA92 Princeton Th Sem MDiv95 Edin Univ MTh96. Virginia Th Sem 99. **d** 01 **p** 02. C Kingston St Mary USA 01-04; OGS from 04; Chapl and Fell St Chad's Coll Dur 05-08. *Address temp unknown*

McTEER, Canon Robert Ian. b 56. Chich Th Coll 90. **d** 92 **p** 93. C S Shields All SS *Dur* 92-95; P-in-c Auckland St Helen 95-97; V from 97; Chapl Bishop Auckland Hospitals NHS Trust 95-98; Chapl S Durham Healthcare NHS Trust 98-02; Hon Can Koforidua from 07. *The Vicarage, 8 Manor Road, St Helen Auckland, Bishop Auckland DL14 9EN* Tel (01388) 604152
E-mail fr.r.mcteer@btinternet.com

MacVANE, Ms Sara Ann Andrew. b 44. Wellesley Coll (USA) BA66 Univ of Wales (Ban) BA05. EAMTC 03. **d** 05 **p** 06. C Rome *Eur* from 05; Asst Dir Angl Cen Rome from 05. *via R Giovagnoli 24, 00152 Rome, Italy* Tel (0039) (06) 5831 0292 *or* 678 0302 Fax 678 0674 E-mail sara@allsaintsrome.org

McVEAGH, Paul Stuart. b 56. Southn Univ BA78. Oak Hill Th Coll BA88. **d** 88 **p** 89. C Bebington *Ches* 88-92; Crosslinks Portugal 92-95; R High Halstow w All Hallows and Hoo St Mary *Roch* 95-02; V Westerham from 02. *The Vicarage, Borde*

Hill, Vicarage Hill, Westerham TN16 1TL Tel and fax (01959) 563127 E-mail paul.mcveagh@diocese-rochester.org *or* pmcveagh@aol.com

McVEETY, Ian. b 46. NOC 82. **d** 85 **p** 86. C Langley and Parkfield *Man* 85-89; V Castleton Moor 89-99; AD Heywood and Middleton 95-99; V Baguley from 99; AD Withington from 06. *St John's Vicarage, 186 Brooklands Road, Sale M33 3PB* Tel 0161-973 5947

McVEIGH, Miss Dorothy Sarah. b 67. QUB BA89 TCD BTh93. CITC 90. **d** 93 **p** 94. C Belfast St Matt *Conn* 93-96; C Carrickfergus 96-99; C Lurgan Ch the Redeemer *D & D* 99-04; I Annaghmore *Arm* from 04. *54 Moss Road, Portadown, Craigavon BT62 1NB* Tel (028) 3885 2751 Mobile 07786-454346

McVEIGH, Canon Samuel. b 49. CITC 77. **d** 79 **p** 80. C Drumragh w Mountfield *D & R* 79-82; I Dromore *Clogh* 82-90; I Drumachose *D & R* from 90; Can Derry Cathl from 01. *49 Killane Road, Limavady BT49 0DJ* Tel (028) 7776 2680

MACVICAR, Miss Mary. b 23. Edin Univ MA44 Ox Univ DipEd45. Ripon Coll Cuddesdon 85. **dss** 86 **d** 87 **p** 94. Bishop's Waltham *Portsm* 86-87; Hon C 87-89; Perm to Offic 89-94; Hon C Portsm Cathl 94-95; Hon Chapl from 94; rtd 95; Perm to Offic *Portsm* from 95. *8/17 Victoria Grove, Southsea PO5 1NF* Tel (023) 9275 1207

McWATT, Glenn Ellsworth. b 48. S'wark Ord Course 89. **d** 92 **p** 93. NSM Tulse Hill H Trin and St Matthias *S'wark* 92-99; C New Malden and Coombe 99-03; C Rayners Lane St Ap 03-08; C Gillingham St Mark *Roch* from 08. *The Garden House, Vicarage Road, Gillingham ME7 5JA* Tel (01634) 575280

McWHIRTER, James Angus. b 58. Portsm Poly BA91 Trin Coll Carmarthen PGCE93. St Steph Ho Ox 00. **d** 02 **p** 03. C Shifnal *Lich* 02-06; CF from 07. *c/o MOD Chaplains (Army)* Tel (01980) 615804 Fax 615800
E-mail revdjames.mcwh@btopenworld.com

MacWILLIAM, The Very Revd Alexander Gordon. b 23. Univ of Wales BA43 Lon Univ BD47 PhD52. St Mich Coll Llan 43. **d** 45 **p** 46. C Llanllyfni *Ban* 46-49; Min Can Ban Cathl 49-55; C Ban St Mary 50-53; C Ban St Jas 53-55; R Llanfaethlu w Llanfwrog 55-56; R Llanfaethlu w Llanfwrog and Llanrhuddlad etc 56-58; Hd of RE Dept Lic to Offic *St D* 60-78; Trin Coll Carmarthen 60-70; Hd Sch of Soc Studies 70-84; Visiting Prof Th Cen Univ Iowa USA 83-84; Can St D Cathl 78-84; Prec, V, and Dean 84-90; rtd 90. *Pen Parc, Smyrna Road, Llangain, Carmarthen SA33 5AD* Tel (01267) 241333

McWILLIAMS, Mrs Laura Jane. b 67. Cranmer Hall Dur 01. **d** 03 **p** 04. C Kingston upon Hull St Aid Southcoates *York* 03-07; V Seamer w East Ayton from 07. *The Vicarage, 3 Stockhill, Seamer, Scarborough YO12 4QG* Tel (01723) 863102 Mobile 07984-003660 E-mail mcwilliams@lmcwilliams.freeserve.co.uk

MADDEN, Kenneth Usher. b 48. St Jo Coll Dur BA70 Lon Inst of Educn PGCE73. WEMTC 06. **d** 09. NSM Newent and Gorsley w Cliffords Mesne *Glouc* from 09. *Plantation Cottage, Ganders Green, May Hill, Longhope GL17 0NJ* Tel (01452) 831401 Mobile 07894-208501 E-mail kenlibby@talktalk.net

MADDERN, James Thomas. b 76. New Coll Edin BD99. Wycliffe Hall Ox MTh07. **d** 02 **p** 03. C Stratford St Jo w Ch Ch and St Jas *Chelmsf* 02-06; Perm to Offic *Ox* 07-09; TV Brize Norton and Carterton from 09. *The Vicarage, 8 Trefoil Way, Carterton OX18 1JQ* Tel (01993) 844175
E-mail vicbrizecarterton@btinternet.com

MADDOCK (née FARLEY), Mrs Claire Louise. b 69. Man Univ BA91 Heythrop Coll Lon MTh99. Westcott Ho Cam 96. **d** 99 **p** 00. C Sherborne w Castleton and Lillington *Sarum* 99-00; C Weymouth H Trin 00-02; Chapl Barts and The Lon NHS Trust 02-03; Chapl Ealing Hosp NHS Trust 03-06; Chapl W Middx Univ Hosp NHS Trust 06-09; Hon C Pimlico St Pet w Westmr Ch Ch *Lon* from 08. *18 Ekarro House, 49A Guildford Road, London SW8 2DT* Tel (020) 7720 6239
E-mail claire@themaddocks.co.uk

MADDOCK, David John Newcomb. b 36. Qu Coll Cam BA60 MA64. Oak Hill Th Coll 60. **d** 62 **p** 63. C Bispham *Blackb* 62-65; R 82-93; RD Blackpool 90-93; Miss Payne Bay Canada 65-69; R Frobisher Bay 70; R Walsoken *Ely* 70-77; V Ore Ch Ch *Chich* 77-82; V Fowey *Truro* 93-02; Chapl Cornwall Healthcare NHS Trust 94-02; rtd 02; Perm to Offic *Truro* from 02. *3 The Moorings, 25 St John's Road, Eastbourne BN20 7NL* Tel (01323) 749172

MADDOCK, Nicholas Rokeby. b 47. ABSM72 Birm Coll of Educn CertEd73. Linc Th Coll 82. **d** 82 **p** 83. C Romford St Edw *Chelmsf* 82-87; V Sway *Win* 87-94; V Taunton St Mary *B & W* 94-04; R Wrington w Butcombe and Burrington from 04. *The Rectory, 3 Alburys, Wrington, Bristol BS40 5NZ* Tel (01934) 862201 E-mail n.maddock@rectory.org.uk

MADDOCK, Philip Arthur Louis. b 47. Open Univ BA82 Lanc Univ MPhil02. Oak Hill Th Coll 75. **d** 78 **p** 79. C New Ferry *Ches* 78-81; C Barnston 81-82; V Over St Jo 82-85; V Norley and Chapl to the Deaf 85-88; P-in-c Treales and Chapl to the Deaf *Blackb* 88-96; Chapl to the Deaf *Lich* 96-02; C Yoxall and The Ridwares and Kings Bromley 98-02; Adv for Deaf and Disabled

People Min Div from 03; NSM Alrewas *Lich* from 03; NSM Wychnor from 03. *23 Jackman Road, Fradley, Lichfield WS13 6PF* Tel (01543) 415088 *or* 306085 Mobile 07984-911488 E-mail philip.maddock@c-of-e.org.uk

MADDOCK, Canon Philip Lawrence. b 20. Bris Univ BA42. Cuddesdon Coll 42. **d** 43 **p** 44. C Kilburn St Aug *Lon* 43-48; C Weston-super-Mare All SS *B & W* 48-57; Chapl Community of the Epiphany Truro 57-60; Sub-Warden 60-63; Chapl HM Pris Wandsworth 63-64; HM Pris Birm 64-67; Ex 67-69; Chapl St Lawr Hosp Bodmin 69-76; Can Res and Treas Truro Cathl 76-88; rtd 88; Perm to Offic Truro from 88. *32A Coinagehall Street, Helston TR13 8EQ*

MADDOCKS, Alison Julie. b 63. Birm Univ BSc84 Loughb Univ MBA92. St Jo Coll Nottm MTh03. **d** 03 **p** 04. C Wollaton *S'well* 03-06; Retail Chapl Birm City Cen 06-08; Ind Chapl *S'well* from 08; C Nottingham All SS, St Mary and St Pet from 08. *The Grange, Church Lane, Thrumpton, Nottingham NG11 0AX* Tel 0115-983 1553 E-mail revmaddocks@aol.com

MADDOX, David John. b 34. AIMLS58. Sarum & Wells Th Coll 92. **d** 81 **p** 93. In RC Ch 81-91; NSM Wimborne Minster and Holt *Sarum* 93-95; NSM Broadstone 95-01; Perm to Offic *Sarum* 00-08 and *Win* from 00. *298 Wimborne Road, Poole BH15 3EG* Tel (01202) 672597

MADDOX, Derek Adrian James. b 64. Kingston Poly BA88. Trin Coll Bris 02. **d** 04 **p** 05. C Mitcham St Mark *S'wark* 04-07; P-in-c S Yardley St Mich *Birm* 07-08; V from 08. *St Michael's Vicarage, 60 Yew Tree Lane, Yardley, Birmingham B26 1AP* Tel 0121-706 7811 E-mail maddoxmob@blueyonder.co.uk

MADDOX, Goronwy Owen. b 23. Univ of Wales (Swansea) BA52 DipEd53. Sarum Th Coll 67. **d** 70 **p** 71. Hd Master H Trin Sch Calne 57-82; NSM Calne and Blackland *Sarum* 70-82; C 82-83; V Llywel and Traean-glas w Llanulid *S & B* 83-92; rtd 92; Perm to Offic *Sarum* 92-08. *4 St Matthew's Close, Rowde, Devizes SN10 2PG* Tel (01380) 728965

MADDOX, Hugh Inglis Monteath. b 37. CCC Cam BA60. Westcott Ho Cam 61. **d** 63 **p** 64. C Attercliffe *Sheff* 63-66; C Maidstone All SS w St Phil *Cant* 66-67; C Folkestone St Mary and St Eanswythe 67-69; C St Martin-in-the-Fields *Lon* 69-73; R Sandwich *Cant* 73-81; V St Peter-in-Thanet 81-84; V Red Post *Sarum* 84-03; rtd 03; Perm to Offic *Sarum* from 03. *36 Corfe Road, Stoborough, Wareham BH20 5AD* Tel (01929) 550872

MADDY, Kevin. b 58. Selw Coll Cam BA83 GRNCM79 FRSA96. Westcott Ho Cam 81. **d** 85 **p** 86. C St Peter-in-Thanet *Cant* 85-88; Perm to Offic *Nor* 88-91; Chapl RAF 88-02; CF 02-07; Regional Chapl Hong Kong Miss to Seafarers from 07. *Yokohama Yamate Sei Ko Kai, 235 Yamate-cho, Naka Ku, Yokohama, Kanagawa 231-0862, Japan* Tel (0081) (45) 628 3319 E-mail seamen@cameo.plala.or.jp

MADELEY, Mark Keith. b 68. AVCM96. Oak Hill Th Coll BA93. **d** 93 **p** 94. C Mickleover All SS *Derby* 93-96; C Charlesworth and Dinting Vale 96-99; Chapl Chr Tours (UK) Ltd 99-00; NSM Moldgreen and Rawthorpe *Wakef* 99-00; V Coley from 00. *Coley Vicarage, 41 Ing Head Terrace, Shelf, Halifax HX3 7LB* Tel and fax (01422) 202292 Mobile 07050-021860 E-mail mark@mibtravel.co.uk

MADGE, Francis Sidney. b 35. AKC58. **d** 59 **p** 60. C York St Mary Bishophill Senior 59-62; C Sutton St Mich 62-64; C Ex St Jas 64-69; R Sutton by Dover w Waldershare *Cant* 69-78; P-in-c W Wickham St Mary 78-81; V 81-02; rtd 02; Perm to Offic *Chich* from 03. *1 Callums Walk, Bexhill-on-Sea TN40 2JF* Tel (01424) 222756

MADGWICK, Mrs Philippa Jane. b 60. Magd Coll Ox BA83 DPhil86. SAOMC 04 ERMC 05. **d** 07 **p** 08. NSM St Alb St Steph *St Alb* from 07. *22 Blenheim Road, St Albans AL1 4NR* Tel (01727) 842449 E-mail pippa.madgwick1@btinternet.com

MADRID, Bishop in. *See* LOPEZ-LOZANO, The Rt Revd Carlos

MADZIMURE, Dominic Makusha. b 52. Middx Univ MA03. **d** 77 **p** 78. Zimbabwe 77-99; Perm to Offic *Carl* 01-03; P-in-c Woodchurch 03-06; P-in-c Byker St Ant *Newc* from 06. *St Anthony's Vicarage, Enslin Gardens, Newcastle upon Tyne NE6 3ST* Tel 0191-265 1605 E-mail dominic@madzimure.fsnet.co.uk

MAGEE, Frederick Hugh. b 33. Yale Univ BA56. Westcott Ho Cam 58. **d** 59 **p** 60. C Bury St Mark *Man* 59-62; USA 63-64 and 87-05; Chapl St Paul's Cathl Dundee 74-79; P-in-c Invergowrie 76-79; R St Andrews St Andr *St And* 79-83; R Forfar 83-87; rtd 05. *17 North Street, St Andrews KY16 9PW* Tel (01334) 470446 E-mail hugh@twomagees.plus.com

MAGEE, Keith Robert. b 60. Bris Univ BA95 PGCE96. Trin Coll Bris 92 Westcott Ho Cam 99. **d** 01 **p** 02. C S Woodham Ferrers *Chelmsf* 01-05; V Moulsham St Jo from 05. *St John's Vicarage, Vicarage Road, Chelmsford CM2 9PH* Tel (01245) 352344 E-mail keith.magee@btinternet.com

MAGILL, Robert James Henderson. b 59. Paisley Coll of Tech BSc81. Sarum & Wells Th Coll 92. **d** 94 **p** 95. C W Moors *Sarum* 94-98; P-in-c Hilperton w Whaddon and Staverton etc 98-05; Community Affairs Chapl 02-05. *The Vicarage, 1A The Weir, Edington, Westbury BA13 4PX*

MAGNESS, Anthony William John. b 37. New Coll Ox BA62 MA65. Coll of Resurr Mirfield 78. **d** 80 **p** 81. C Gt Crosby St Faith *Liv* 80-83; C Newc St Jo 83-85; P-in-c Newc St Luke 85-88; P-in-c Newc St Andr 88; V Newc St Andr and St Luke 89-99; Chapl Hunter's Moor Hosp 89-95; P-in-c Cambois *Newc* 99-00; P-in-c Sleekburn 99-00; V Cambois and Sleekburn 00-03; rtd 03; Perm to Offic *Newc* from 03. *59 Firtree Crescent, Newcastle upon Tyne NE12 7JU* Tel and fax 0191-268 4596

MAGNUSSON, Lisbet Maria. b 50. Mid-Sweden Univ BSc85 Uppsala Univ MDiv93 ML98. Past Inst Uppsala 93. **p** 94. In Ch of Sweden 94-98; C Crosby *Linc* 98-99; TV Gainsborough and Morton 99-04; P-in-c Swallow and Chapl Doncaster and S Humber Healthcare NHS Trust 04-06; Sweden from 06. *Dalhems prästgård, Kyrkoherdebostaden, 622 56 Dalhem, Sweden* Tel (0046) (49) 838186 *or* 838001 E-mail dalhemrectory@hotmail.com

MAGOR, Robert Jolyon. b 47. Sarum & Wells Th Coll 91. **d** 93 **p** 94. C Plaistow *Chelmsf* 93-96; TV Plaistow and N Canning Town 96-99; V Leigh-on-Sea St Aid 99-01; C Thorpe Bay 01-06; R E and W Tilbury and Linford from 06. *The Rectory, Princess Margaret Road, East Tilbury, Tilbury RM18 8PB* Tel (01375) 842220 E-mail bobmagor@btinternet.com

MAGORRIAN, Brian Geoffrey. b 64. St Aid Coll Dur BSc85 York Univ DPhil89. St Jo Coll Nottm. **d** 01 **p** 02. C Bishopwearmouth St Gabr *Dur* 01-04; P-in-c Brough w Stainmore, Musgrave and Warcop *Carl* from 04. *The Rectory, Church Brough, Kirkby Stephen CA17 4EJ* Tel (01768) 341238 E-mail brianmagorrian@tiscali.co.uk

✠**MAGOWAN, The Rt Revd Alistair James.** b 55. Leeds Univ BSc77 Ox Univ MTh02. Trin Coll Bris 78. **d** 81 **p** 82 **c** 09. C Owlerton *Sheff* 81-84; C Dur St Nic 84-89; Chapl St Aid Coll 85-89; V Egham *Guildf* 89-00; RD Runnymede 93-98; Adn Dorset and Can and Preb Sarum Cathl 00-09; Suff Bp Ludlow *Heref* from 09; Adn Ludlow from 09. *Bishop's House, Corvedale Road, Craven Arms SY7 9BT* Tel (01588) 673571 Fax 673585 E-mail bishopofludlow@btinternet.com

MAGOWAN, Harold Victor. b 34. QUB BA55 BSc(Econ)66 DipEd69 ACII69 FCII73. TCD Div Sch Div Test57. **d** 57 **p** 58. C Antrim All SS w Muckamore *Conn* 57-59. *6 Fold Mews, 22 Ballyholme Road, Bangor BT20 5JS* Tel (028) 9146 5091

MAGOWAN, Ian Walter. b 51. St Paul's Cheltenham CertEd73 Ulster Poly BEd82 TCD BTh07. CITC 04. **d** 07 **p** 08. C Killowen *D & R* from 07. *27 Ballycranny Drive, Coleraine BT51 3JX* Tel (028) 7035 2006 Mobile 07810-636167 E-mail iwmagowan@hotmail.co.uk

MAGUIRE, Alan. b 45. CBDTI 03. **d** 06 **p** 07. NSM Croglin *Carl* from 06; NSM Holme Eden and Wetheral w Warwick from 06. *21 Hill Head, Scotby, Carlisle CA4 8BH* Tel (01228) 513638 E-mail alan.maguire@virgin.net

MAGUIRE, Canon Brian William. b 33. Hull Univ BTh84 MA88. Coll of Resurr Mirfield 70. **d** 72 **p** 73. C Guisborough *York* 72-76; TV Haxby w Wigginton 76-77; TR 78-89; V Huddersfield St Pet and All SS *Wakef* 89-00; Hon Can Wakef Cathl 94-00; rtd 00; Perm to Offic *Wakef* from 00; Bp's Dom Chapl 03-04. *Lupset Vicarage, Broadway, Wakefield WF2 8AA* Tel (01924) 373088

MAGUIRE, Michael Timothy Gale (Tim). b 34. Ox Univ Inst of Educn DipEd61. Wycliffe Hall Ox 58. **d** 61 **p** 62. C Southampton St Mary Extra *Win* 61-63; Bp's Youth Chapl 63-66; Perm to Offic *Win* from 97 and Truro from 02; rtd 99. *Mordros, Mullion, Helston TR12 7EP* Tel (01326) 241063

MAGUIRE (formerly GRATTON), Canon Patricia Margaret. b 46. Leeds Univ BTh94 MA96 SRN67 TCert84 CertEd88. EMMTC 89 NOC 96. **d** 97 **p** 98. NSM Shipley St Pet *Bradf* 97-99; C Brighouse and Clifton *Wakef* 99-00; Chapl Wakef Cathl Sch 00-05; P-in-c Lupset *Wakef* from 05; P-in-c Thornes St Jas w Ch Ch from 00; RD Wakef from 08; Hon Can Wakef Cathl from 08. *Lupset Vicarage, Broadway, Wakefield WF2 8AA* Tel (01924) 373088 E-mail revmaguire@tiscali.co.uk

MAGUMBA, Canon Patrick John. b 53. Bp Tucker Coll Mukono BD85 Makerere Univ Kampala PGDE88 Birm Univ MA92 Leeds Univ PhD03. **d** 79 **p** 80. Uganda 79-90 and 93-04; C Kamuli 79-81; V Kaliro 86-90; Sub-Dean Busoga 90; Hon C Harborne Heath *Birm* 91-93; Sen Lect Uganda Chr Univ Mukono 93-04; TV S Rochdale *Man* from 04; Hon Can Th Orlu from 05. *St Luke's Vicarage, 9 Deeplish Road, Rochdale OL11 1NY* Tel (01706) 354628 Mobile 07901-782329 E-mail jmagumba@hotmail.com

MAHER, David James. b 70. St Jo Coll Dur BA01. Cranmer Hall Dur 98. **d** 01 **p** 02. C Hounslow H Trin w St Paul *Lon* 01-04; C Staines 04-07; Chapl to Bp Kensington 04-07; V Chesterton Gd Shep *Ely* from 07. *The Good Shepherd Vicarage, 51 Highworth Avenue, Cambridge CB4 2BQ* Tel (01223) 351844 *or* 312933

MAHONEY, William Denis. b 35. 77. **d** 79 **p** 95. In RC Ch USA 79-87; NSM Egremont and Haile *Carl* 92-93; NSM Kells 93-96; R Cohoes USA 96-98; P-in-c Beckermet St Jo and St Bridget w Ponsonby *Carl* 98-05; rtd 05. *2 Bowden Drive, Huntington Station NY 11746-4218, USA* E-mail vlwd17@aol.com

MAHONY, Conal Martin. b 38. Pontificio Ateneo Antoniano Rome Lic in Sacred Th 64 Lateran Univ Rome ThD66. Franciscan Ho of Studies 57. **d** 62 **p** 63. In RC Ch 62-89; Dir Folkestone Family Care Cen 86-92; Lic to Offic *Cant* 89-92; C Hempnall *Nor* 92-94; TV 94-97; TR 97-08; rtd 08; Perm to Offic *Nor* from 08. *6 Rigby Close, Framingham Earl, Norwich NR14 7TL* Tel (01508) 491646

MAIDEN, Charles Alistair Kingsley. b 60. Trent Poly BSc84. St Jo Coll Nottm LTh88. **d** 89 **p** 90. C Porchester *S'well* 89-93; C Selston 93-96; P-in-c Huthwaite from 96. *The Vicarage, Blackwell Road, Huthwaite, Sutton-in-Ashfield NG17 2QT* Tel (01623) 555053 E-mail charliemaiden@hotmail.com

MAIDMENT, Thomas John Louis. b 43. Lon Univ BSc65. St Steph Ho Ox. **d** 67 **p** 68. C Westmr St Steph w St Jo *Lon* 67-73; P-in-c Twickenham Common H Trin 73-77; V 77-80; V Heston 80-98; V Bolton-le-Sands *Blackb* 98-08; P-in-c Tunstall w Melling and Leck 02-03; AD Tunstall 99-05; rtd 08; Perm to Offic *Blackb* from 08. *69 Aintree Road, Thornton-Cleveleys FY5 5HW* Tel (01253) 829399 E-mail t.j.l.m@btinternet.com

MAIDSTONE, Archdeacon of. *See* DOWN, The Ven Philip Roy

MAIDSTONE, Suffragan Bishop. *Vacant*

MAIN, Mrs Brigid Mary Harvey. b 49. EAMTC 96. **d** 99 **p** 00. NSM Tillingham *Chelmsf* 99-03; NSM Pleshey from 03. *Parsonage Cottage, The Street, Pleshey, Chelmsford CM3 1HA* Tel (01245) 237012 E-mail bmain@chelmsford.anglican.org

MAIN, Clive Timothy. b 53. St Andr Univ MA75 Cam Univ PGCE76. Oak Hill Th Coll BA94. **d** 96 **p** 97. C Alperton *Lon* 96-00; V Highbury New Park St Aug from 00. *St Augustine's Vicarage, 108 Highbury New Park, London N5 2DR* Tel (020) 7226 6870 E-mail clivemain@blueyonder.co.uk

MAIN, Canon David Murray. b 28. Univ Coll Ox BA52 MA56. St Deiniol's Hawarden 73. **d** 73 **p** 74. C Glas St Marg 73-75; R Challoch w Newton Stewart 75-79; R Kilmarnock 79-93; Can St Mary's Cathl 85-93; rtd 93; Hon Can St Mary's Cathl from 93. *Sunnybrae, 50 Abercromby Road, Castle Douglas DG7 1BA* Tel (01556) 504669

MAINA, Simon Mwangi. b 52. Nairobi Univ 85. **d** 80 **p** 81. Kenya 80-95; C Acton St Mary *Lon* 95-97; Worthing Churches Homeless Project from 98; rtd 08. *49 Cambourne Court, Shelley Road, Worthing BN11 4BQ* Tel (01903) 205042

MAINES, Canon Trevor. b 40. Leeds Univ BSc63. Ripon Hall Ox 63. **d** 65 **p** 66. C Speke All SS *Liv* 65-70; C Stevenage St Geo *St Alb* 70-73; V Dorridge *Birm* 73-78; Org Sec CECS *Ex* 79-80; Hon C Tiverton St Pet *Ex* 79-80; Org Sec (Wales) CECS 80-87; Hon C Newton Nottage *Llan* 81-83; Perm to Offic *Mon* 83-87; V Arlesey w Astwick *St Alb* 87-95; RD Shefford 91-95; V Goldington 95-05; RD Bedford 98-05; Hon Can St Alb 04-05; rtd 05; Hon C Beedon and Peasemore w W Ilsley and Farnborough *Ox* 05-07; C Brightwalton w Catmore, Leckhampstead etc 05-07. *1 Adlam Villas, Greenham Road, Newbury RG14 7HX* Tel (01635) 551352 E-mail trevor.maines@tesco.net

MAINEY, Ian George. b 51. CertEd73. Oak Hill Th Coll BA87. **d** 87 **p** 88. C Denton Holme *Carl* 87-91; V Hensingham 91-02; RD Calder 01-02; TR Deane *Man* 02-09; P-in-c Birkdale St Jas *Liv* from 09; P-in-c Birkdale St Pet from 09. *The Vicarage, 26 Lulworth Road, Southport PR8 2BQ* Tel (01704) 566255 E-mail ian.mainey@lineone.net

MAINWARING, Islwyn Paul. b 52. Univ of Wales (Swansea) BD75. St Mich Coll Llan 77. **d** 79 **p** 80. C Llanilid w Pencoed 79-82; C Llanishen and Lisvane 82-85; TV Cwmbran *Mon* 85-88; V Troedyrhiw w Merthyr Vale *Llan* 88-91. *Pennant, 109 Penygroes Road, Blaenau, Ammanford SA18 3BZ* Tel (01269) 850350

MAINWARING (née LANKSHEAR), Jane Frances. b 70. Leeds Univ BA92 Trin Coll Carmarthen MPhil97 PhD99. EAMTC 98. **d** 00 **p** 01. C Sudbury and Chilton *St E* 00-03; TV Hitchin *St Alb* from 03. *St Mark's Vicarage, St Mark's Close, Hitchin SG5 1UR* Tel (01462) 422862 or 434686 E-mail jane@stmarks-hitchin.org.uk

MAIRS, Canon Adrian Samuel. b 43. Oak Hill Th Coll 76. **d** 78 **p** 79. C Rugby St Matt *Cov* 78-82; P-in-c Mancetter 82-84; V 84-08; P-in-c Hartshill 97-01; Hon Can Cov Cathl 03-08; rtd 08. *21 Cleverley Drive, Nuneaton CV10 0JZ* Tel (024) 7639 2852

MAIS, Jeremy Hugh. b 47. **d** 00 **p** 01. NSM Bibury w Winson and Barnsley *Glouc* 00-02; P-in-c 04-08; NSM Stratton, N Cerney, Baunton and Bagendon 02-04; NSM Fairford Deanery from 09. *The Vicarage, Bibury, Cirencester GL7 5NT* Tel (01285) 740387 E-mail jeremy.mais@tiscali.co.uk

MAITIN, Ito. b 36. Open Univ BA. Kelham Th Coll 63. **d** 68 **p** 69. C Longton St Jo *Lich* 68-69; C Leek St Edw 69-71; C Lich St Chad 71-74; C Tamworth 74-81; V Penkhull 81-06; rtd 06; Perm to Offic *Lich* 06-08; C Hanley H Ev from 08. *18 Crescent Grove, Stoke-on-Trent ST4 6EN* Tel (01782) 878788

MAITLAND, The Hon Sydney Milivoje Patrick. b 51. Edin Univ BSc MRTPI. St Jo Coll Nottm. **d** 86 **p** 87. Hon C Glas St Geo 86-01; Hon C Glas St Bride from 03. *14 Kersland Street, Glasgow G12 8BL* Tel 0141-339 4573 E-mail sydney@maitland50.freeserve.co.uk

MAJOR, Richard James Edward. b 54. Trin Coll Bris 78. **d** 81 **p** 82. C Parr *Liv* 81-84; V Burton Fleming w Fordon *York* 84-85; V Grindale and Ergham 84-85; P-in-c Wold Newton 84-85; V Burton Fleming w Fordon, Grindale etc 85-91; V Bilton St Pet from 91. *The Vicarage, 14 Cherry Tree Close, Bilton, Hull HU11 4EZ* Tel (01482) 811441

MAJOR, Richard John Charles. b 63. Massey Univ (NZ) BA85 Ex Coll Ox BA91 MA93 Magd Coll Ox DPhil91. St Steph Ho Ox 92. **d** 94 **p** 95. C Truro Cathl 94-97; C Putney St Mary *S'wark* 97-98; Chapl Florence w Siena *Eur* 98-01; USA from 01. *Nansough Manor, Ladock, Truro TR2 4PB* Tel (01726) 883315 or (001) (718) 442 1589 Fax (001) (718) 442 4555 E-mail email@richardmajor.com

MAKAMBWE, Canon Francis James. b 40. St Jo Sem Lusaka. **d** 65 **p** 67. Zambia 65-91; Miss Partner CMS from 91; C Waterloo St Jo w St Andr *S'wark* 91-96; V Hatcham St Cath from 96; AD Deptford 05-07; Hon Can S'wark Cathl from 03. *St Catherine's Vicarage, 102A Pepys Road, London SE14 5SG* Tel (020) 7639 1050 Fax 7401 3215 E-mail fmakam@aol.com

MAKEL, Arthur. b 39. AKC63. **d** 64 **p** 65. C Beamish *Dur* 64-68; Ind Chapl *York* 68-72; Ind Chapl and P-in-c Scotton w Northorpe *Linc* 72-81; R Epworth 81-89; P-in-c Wroot 81-89; R Epworth and Wroot 89-92; R Sigglesthorne and Rise w Nunkeeling and Bewholme *York* 92-04; P-in-c Aldbrough, Mappleton w Goxhill and Withernwick 98-04; rtd 04; Perm to Offic *York* from 04. *43 Lowfield Road, Beverley HU17 9RF* Tel (01482) 865798

MAKEPEACE, David Norman Harry. b 51. Magd Coll Ox BA74. Trin Coll Bris 83. **d** 85 **p** 86. C Romford Gd Shep *Chelmsf* 85-88; Tanzania 88-89; C York St Paul 89-91; TV Radipole and Melcombe Regis *Sarum* 91-98; V Sandgate St Paul w Folkestone St Geo *Cant* 98-00; Perm to Offic from 01. *10 Limes Road, Folkestone CT19 4AU* Tel (01303) 274011 E-mail dnhm@talk21.com

MAKEPEACE, Preb James Dugard. b 40. Keble Coll Ox BA63 MA67. Cuddesdon Coll 63. **d** 65 **p** 66. C Cullercoats St Geo *Newc* 65-68; Lib Pusey Ho and Chapl Wadh Coll Ox 68-72; V Romford St Edw *Chelmsf* 72-79; V Tettenhall Regis *Lich* 79-80; TR 80-99; RD Trysull 87-97; Preb Lich Cathl 96-99; rtd 00; Perm to Offic *Lich* from 00. *The Retreat, 9 Clive Road, Pattingham, Wolverhampton WV6 7BU* Tel (01902) 701713

✠**MAKHULU, The Most Revd Walter Paul Khotso.** b 35. CMG00. Kent Univ Hon DD88 Gen Th Sem NY Hon DD99. St Pet Rosettenville Selly Oak Coll. **d** 57 **p** 58 **c** 79. S Africa 57-61; Bechuanaland 61-63; C Poplar All SS w St Frideswide *Lon* 64-66; C Pentonville St Silas w Barnsbury St Clem 66-68; V Battersea St Phil *S'wark* 68-73; V Battersea St Phil w St Bart 73-75; Bp Botswana 79-00; Abp Cen Africa 80-00; rtd 00. *Cheyne House, 10 Crondace Road, London SW6 4BB* Tel (020) 7371 9419 E-mail makhulu@btinternet.com

MAKIN, Miss Pauline. b 45. Cranmer Hall Dur 75. **dss** 78 **d** 87 **p** 94. Ashton-in-Makerfield St Thos *Liv* 78-89; Par Dn 87-89; Par Dn Rainford 89-94; C 94-95; C Farnworth from 95; Asst Dioc Chapl to the Deaf from 89. *43 Hampton Drive, Widnes WA8 5DA* Tel, fax and text 0151-423 3900

MAKIN, Valerie Diana. Coll *Ord* Course 86. **d** 88 **p** 94. Hon Par Dn Bryanston Square St Mary w St Marylebone St Mark *Lon* 88-95; Chapl St Marylebone Healing and Counselling Cen 88-94; NSM Godalming *Guildf* 94-95; Perm to Offic *Lon* 95-97 and *Guildf* from 95. *Crowts, Tuesley, Godalming GU7 1UD* Tel (01483) 416613

MÄKIPÄÄ, Tuomas. b 78. Helsinki Univ MTh06. **d** 05. C Helsinki *Eur* from 05. *Rastilantie 5 B 16, Helsinki FI-00980, Finland* Tel (00358) (50) 309 9132 E-mail assistant-curate@anglican.fi

MAKOWER, Canon Malory. b 33. TCD BA61 MA68 St Jo Coll Ox MA64 DPhil64. Ridley Hall Cam 64. **d** 66 **p** 67. C Onslow Square St Paul *Lon* 66-69; Tutor Ridley Hall Cam 69-71; Sen Tutor 71-76; P-in-c Lode and Longmeadow *Ely* 76-84; Warden EAMTC 77-79; Prin 79-84; Dir of Post-Ord Tr for NSM *Nor* 84-90; C Gt Yarmouth 84-89; TV 89-95; Dioc NSM Officer 88-95; Hon Can Nor Cathl 94-97; Prin LNSM Tr Scheme 94-97; rtd 97; Perm to Offic *Nor* from 98. *114 Yarmouth Road, Lowestoft NR32 4AQ* Tel (01502) 574769

MALAN, Victor Christian de Roubaix. b 39. Cape Town Univ BA60 Linacre Coll Ox BA63 MA68. Wycliffe Hall Ox 61. **d** 63 **p** 64. C Springfield *Birm* 63-66; P-in-c 66-67; C New Windsor *Ox* 67-69; Chapl St Jo Coll Cam 69-74; V Northampton All SS w St Kath *Pet* 74-86; V Stockport St Geo *Ches* 86-89; R N Mundham w Hunston and Merston *Chich* 89-06; rtd 06; Perm to Offic *Cant* from 07. *40 St Lawrence Forstal, Canterbury CT1 3PA* Tel (01227) 785752

✠**MALANGO, The Most Revd Bernard Amos.** b 43. TCD MPhil84. St Jo Sem Lusaka. **d** 71 **p** 72 **c** 88. Malawi 71-88 and from 02; Bp N Zambia 88-02; Bp Upper Shire from 02; Abp Cen Africa from 04. *Private Bag 1, Chilema, Zomba, Malawi* Tel and fax (00265) (1) 539203 E-mail angus@malawinet or bernardmalango@hotmail.com

MALBON, Canon John Allin. b 36. Oak Hill Th Coll 62. **d** 65

p 66. C Wolverhampton St Jude *Lich* 65-68; C Hoole *Ches* 68-71; P-in-c Crewe Ch Ch 71-75; V 75-79; V Plemstall w Guilden Sutton 79-01; Hon Can Ches Cathl 96-01; rtd 01; Perm to Offic *Ches* from 02. *22 Hawksey Drive, Nantwick CW5 7GF* Tel (01270) 611584

MALCOLM, Andrew Alexander. b 55. **d** 08 **p** 09. NSM Salesbury *Blackb* from 08. *Townhead Old Barn, 49A Downham Road, Chatburn, Clitheroe BB7 4AU* Tel (01200) 441220

MALCOLM, Brother. See FOUNTAIN, David Roy

MALCOLM, Miss Mercia Alana. b 54. St Andr Univ MA77. S'wark Ord Course 84. **d** 87 **p** 94. C Dartford Ch Ch *Roch* 87-91; Par Dn Stockport St Geo *Ches* 91-94; C Jordanstown *Conn* 95-99; Chapl Ulster Univ 95-03; I Carnmoney *Conn* from 03. *Coole Glebe, 20 Glebe Road, Newtownabbey BT36 6UW* Tel (028) 9083 6337 E-mail carnmoney@connor.anglican.org

MALE, David Edward. b 62. Southn Univ BA84 St Jo Coll Dur BA90. Cranmer Hall Dur 88. **d** 91 **p** 92. C Leic St Chris 91-94; C Kirkheaton *Wakef* 94-98; P Missr Huddersfield 99-06; Dioc Fresh Expressions Adv *Ely* from 06. *130 Hulatt Road, Cambridge CB1 8TH* Tel (01223) 410581 *or* 741102 E-mail dm432@cam.ac.uk

✠**MALECDAN, The Most Revd Edward Pacyaya.** Episc Th Sem of the SW MA93 Hon DD. St Andr Th Sem Manila BTh77 MDiv85. **d** 79 **p** 80 **c**97. Philippines from 79; Dean St Andr Th Sem 94-97; Bp N Philippines 97-09; Prime Bp from 09. *Provincial Office, PO Box 10321, Broadway Centrum, 1112 Quezon City, Philippines* Tel (0063) (2) 722 8478 *or* 722 8481 Fax 721 1923 E-mail ednpvic@hotmail.com

MALEK, Mark Mayool. b 44. Khartoum Univ BSc69 Salford Univ BSc76 Bradf Coll of Educn PGCE93. **d** 03 **p** 04. NSM Horton *Bradf* 03-04; NSM Bradf St Oswald Chapel Green 03-04; NSM Lt Horton from 04. *26 Martlett Drive, Bradford BD5 8QG* Tel (01274) 732712

MALES, Jeanne Margaret. b 49. Reading Univ BA71 Lon Univ MPhil73 Surrey Univ PhD86 AFBPsS75 CPsychol88. S'wark Ord Course 93. **d** 96 **p** 97. NSM Caterham *S'wark* 96-00; C Addington 00-03; V from 03. *Addington Vicarage, Spout Hill, Croydon CR0 5AN* Tel (01689) 841839 *or* 842167 E-mail jeanne@u.genie.co.uk

MALINS, Mrs Judith. b 47. Bris Univ BA69. STETS 97. **d** 00 **p** 01. NSM Wilton w Netherhampton and Fugglestone *Sarum* 00-04; P-in-c Kingston, Langton Matravers and Worth Matravers from 04. *The Rectory, St George's Close, Langton Matravers, Swanage BH19 3HZ* Tel (01929) 422559 E-mail judith.malins@tesco.net

MALINS, Peter. b 18. Down Coll Cam BA40 MA47. Ridley Hall Cam 40. **d** 42 **p** 43. C Earlsdon *Cov* 42-44; CF (EC) 44-47; CF 47-73; QHC 72-73; V Greenwich St Alfege w St Pet and St Paul *S'wark* 73-87; P-in-c Greenwich H Trin and St Paul 76-84; Sub-Dean Greenwich 79-81; rtd 87; Perm to Offic *Guildf* from 87. *12 Ridgeway Drive, Dorking RH4 3AN* Tel (01306) 882035

MALKIN, Thomas Ross. b 64. Hertf Coll Ox BA86. Trin Coll Bris BA98. **d** 99 **p** 00. C Old Trafford St Bride *Man* 99-03; P-in-c Firswood and Gorse Hill from 03. *The Vicarage, 24 Canute Road, Stretford, Manchester M32 0RJ* Tel 0161-865 1802 Mobile 07973-240023 E-mail rev.trm@ntlworld.com

MALKINSON, Canon Christopher Mark. b 47. Chich Th Coll 84. **d** 86 **p** 87. C Stroud and Uplands w Slad *Glouc* 86-89; V Cam w Stinchcombe 89-00; P-in-c Tywardreath w Tregaminion *Truro* 00-02; P-in-c St Sampson 00-02; V Padstow from 02; RD Pydar from 03; Hon Can Truro Cathl from 07; Chapl Miss to Seafarers from 00. *The Vicarage, 46 Treverbyn Road, Padstow PL28 8DN* Tel (01841) 533776 E-mail chrismalk@hotmail.com

MALKINSON, Michael Stephen. b 39. St Steph Ho Ox 65. **d** 68 **p** 69. C New Addington *Cant* 68-71; C Blackpool St Steph *Blackb* 71-74; V Wainfleet St Mary *Linc* 74-81; R Wainfleet All SS w St Thos 74-81; P-in-c Croft 80-81; V Lund *Blackb* 81-93; V Heyhouses on Sea 93-00; R Balcombe *Chich* 00-09; P-in-c Staplefield Common 00-03; rtd 09. *8 Haines Avenue, Wyre Piddle, Pershore WR10 2RQ* Tel (01386) 556102 E-mail malkinson@msn.com

MALLAS, Mrs Wendy Norris. b 42. Cov Coll of Educn CertEd63 Reading Univ MA91. STETS 00. **d** 03 **p** 04. NSM Liss *Portsm* 03-07; NSM Blackmoor and Whitehill from 07; NSM Bordon *Guildf* from 07. *Mayfield, 45 Hogmoor Road, Whitehill, Bordon GU35 9ET* Tel (01420) 478883 E-mail wendy.mallas@mayfieldjays.co.uk

MALLESON, Michael Lawson. b 42. Univ of Wales (Swansea) BA64 Nottm Univ MA92. Linc Th Coll 67. **d** 70 **p** 71. C Wakef St Jo 70-73; C-in-c Holmfield St Andr CD 73-75; V Holmfield 75-80; V Heworth St Alb *Dur* 80-93; V Killingworth *Newc* 93-06; rtd 06. *6 Slingsby Gardens, Newcastle upon Tyne NE7 7RX* Tel 0191-209 2880 E-mail michaelmalleson@aol.com

MALLETT, John Christopher. b 44. EAMTC. **d** 82 **p** 83. NSM Hethersett w Canteloff *Nor* 82-85; NSM Hethersett w Canteloff w Lt and Gt Melton 85-90; Chapl Wayland Hosp Norfolk 88-94; Chapl Norwich Community Health Partnership NHS Trust 94-00; Perm to Offic *Nor* 00-03; NSM Hethersett w Canteloff w

Lt and Gt Melton from 03. *2 Bailey Close, Hethersett, Norwich NR9 3EU* Tel (01603) 811010 E-mail christophersheila@tiscali.co.uk

MALLETT, Marlene Rosemarie. b 59. Sussex Univ BA81 Warwick Univ PhD94. SEITE 01. **d** 04 **p** 05. C Brixton Road Ch Ch *S'wark* 04-07; P-in-c Angell Town St Jo from 07. *St John's Vicarage, 49 Wiltshire Road, London SW9 7NE* Tel (020) 7733 0585 E-mail rosemarie.mallett@btinternet.com

MALLINSON, Peter Albert. b 57. St Jo Coll Nottm 06. **d** 08 **p** 09. NSM Allestree *Derby* from 08; NSM Darley Abbey from 08. *68 High Lane West, West Hallam, Ilkeston DE7 6HQ* Tel 0115-944 3134 E-mail petermallinson@smartemail.co.uk

MALLINSON, Canon Ralph Edward. b 40. Oriel Coll Ox BA63 MA66. St Steph Ho Ox 63. **d** 66 **p** 67. C Bolton St Pet *Man* 66-68; C Elton All SS 68-72; V Bury St Thos 72-76; V Bury Ch King 76-81; P-in-c Goodshaw 81-82; V 82-84; V Goodshaw and Crawshawbooth 84-93; AD Rossendale 83-93; V Unsworth 93-06; Hon Can Man Cathl 92-06; Vice Prin Dioc OLM Scheme 98-06; rtd 06; Perm to Offic *Man* from 06. *18 Woodgate Avenue, Bury BL9 7RU* Tel 0161-797 2006 E-mail ralphandhelen@rmallinson.fsnet.co.uk

MALLON, Allister. b 61. Sheff Univ BA83 TCD BTh89 MA. CITC. **d** 87 **p** 88. C Ballymoney w Finvoy and Rasharkin *Conn* 87-90; C Belfast St Mary w H Redeemer 90-92; Bp's C Belfast St Mary Magd 92-00; Bp's C Stoneyford from 00; Chapl R Group of Hosps Health and Soc Services Trust from 00. *St John's Rectory, 62 Stoneyford Road, Lisburn BT28 3SP* Tel (028) 9264 8300 E-mail bigal@talk21.com

MALLORY, George Henry. b 14. JP. Lon Univ BSc63. St Deiniol's Hawarden. **d** 80 **p** 81. NSM Oaks in Charnwood and Copt Oak *Leic* 80-88; rtd 88; Perm to Offic *Leic* 88-91; Perm to Offic *Worc* from 91. *Claudina, Bewdley Road North, Stourport-on-Severn DY13 8PX* Tel (01299) 827969

MALMESBURY, Archdeacon of. See HAWKER, The Ven Alan Fort

MALONE, Richard Patrick. b 66. Wycliffe Hall Ox BTh03. **d** 03 **p** 04. C Fulham Ch Ch *Lon* 03-06; C Battersea St Pet and St Paul *S'wark* from 06. *29 Winstanley Road, London SW11 2EZ* Tel (020) 7585 3303 Mobile 07973-104941 E-mail patrick.malone@stmarks-battersea.org.uk

MALONEY, Ms Fiona Elizabeth. b 60. Bradf Univ BSc82 St Jo Coll Dur BA91. NOC 91. **d** 92 **p** 94. Par Dn Castleton Moor *Man* 92-94; C 94-96; C Pendlebury St Jo 96-99; C Fatfield *Dur* 99-03; NSM Harrow Trin St Mich *Lon* 03-05; NSM Wealdstone H Trin from 05. *The Vicarage, 39 Rusland Park Road, Harrow HA1 1UN* Tel (020) 8863 5844 *or* 8863 6131 E-mail fiona@cofe.org.uk

MALONEY, Terence Mark. b 63. York Univ BSc84. Cranmer Hall Dur 88. **d** 91 **p** 92. C Blackley St Andr *Man* 91-96; P-in-c Pendlebury St Jo 96-99; P-in-c Fatfield *Dur* 99-03; P-in-c Harrow Trin St Mich *Lon* 03-05; V Wealdstone H Trin from 05. *The Vicarage, 39 Rusland Park Road, Harrow HA1 1UN* Tel (020) 8863 5844 *or* 8863 6131 E-mail mark@cofe.org.uk

MALTBY, Canon Geoffrey. b 38. Leeds Univ BA62. Wells Th Coll 68. **d** 70 **p** 71. C Mansfield St Mark *S'well* 70-73; V Skegby 73-78; V Carrington 78-87; C Rainworth 87-90; Chapl for People w Learning Disability (Mental Handicap) 90-03; Hon Can S'well Minster 99-03; rtd 03; Perm to Offic *S'well* from 03. *18 Beverley Close, Rainworth, Mansfield NG21 0LW* Tel (01623) 474452

MALTBY, Canon Judith Diane. b 57. Illinois Univ BA79 Newnham Coll Cam PhD92 FRHistS99. S Dios Minl Tr Scheme 89. **d** 92 **p** 94. Tutor Sarum & Wells Th Coll 87-93; Hon Par Dn Wilton w Netherhampton and Fugglestone *Sarum* 92-93; Chapl and Fell CCC Ox from 93; Reader Ch Hist Ox Univ from 04; Can Th Leic Cathl from 04; Hon Can Ch Ch *Ox* from 06. *Corpus Christi College, Oxford OX1 4JF* Tel (01865) 276722 E-mail judith.maltby@ccc.ox.ac.uk

MALTIN, Basil St Clair Aston. b 24. Qu Coll Cam BA49 MA54. Westcott Ho Cam 50. **d** 51 **p** 52. C Dursley *Glouc* 51-53; C Bathwick w Woolley *B & W* 53-57; V Frome Ch Ch 57-63; P-in-c Marston Bigot 57-59; V Bishops Lydeard 63-71; R Pulborough *Chich* 71-90; RD Storrington 84-89; rtd 90; Perm to Offic *Chich* from 90. *13 Somerstown, Chichester PO19 6AG* Tel (01243) 786740

MALTON, William Peter Antony. b 33. K Coll Lon AKC56. **d** 57 **p** 58. C N Hammersmith St Kath *Lon* 57-60; C-in-c Blackbird Leys CD *Ox* 60-65; R Pitsford *Pet* 65-66; Canada from 66; rtd 93. *5589 Highway 221, Woodville NS B0P 1V0, Canada*

MAN, Archdeacon of. See SMITH, The Ven Brian

MANCHESTER, Canon John Charles. b 45. Lon Univ BD69. ALCD68. **d** 69 **p** 70. C Scarborough St Martin *York* 69-73; C Selby Abbey 73-76; P-in-c Old Malton 76-79; V from 79; RD Bulmer and Malton 85-91; Can and Preb York Minster 91-03. *The Gannock House, Old Malton, Malton YO17 7HB* Tel (01653) 692121

MANCHESTER, Simon Lorimer. b 53. Univ of NSW BA. Moore Th Coll Sydney ThL79 Melbourne Coll of Div BD80. **d** 80 **p** 80. Australia 80-82 and from 84; C Wollongong Pro-Cathl 80-82; C St Helen Bishopsgate w St Andr Undershaft etc *Lon*

82-84; R Lalor Park 84-89; R N Sydney St Thos from 90. *17 Kitchener Street, PO Box 132, Artarmon NSW 2059, Australia* Tel (0061) (2) 9420 3661 *or* 9929 4807 Fax 9955 5180 E-mail st-thomas@st-thomas.org.au

MANCHESTER, Archdeacon of. *See* ASHCROFT, The Ven Mark David

MANCHESTER, Bishop of. *See* McCULLOCH, The Rt Revd Nigel Simeon

MANCHESTER, Dean of. *See* GOVENDER, The Very Revd Rogers Morgan

MANCO, Gwenda Diane. b 54. NOC 97. **d** 99 **p** 00. NSM Rochdale *Man* 99-02; NSM Dearnley 02-04 and from 06; NSM Spotland 04-06; Asst Chapl HM Pris Buckley Hall 99-03; Chapl HM Pris Styal 03. *5 Stansfield Hall, Littleborough OL15 9RH* Tel (01706) 370264   Mobile 07966-217252 E-mail gwenda.manco@tesco.net

MANCOR, Neil McKay. Univ of BC MA Reading Univ PhD. Wycliffe Hall Ox. **d** 99 **p** 00. C Llandeilo Fawr and Taliaris *St D* 99-02; Canada from 02. *1490 Nanton Avenue, Vancouver BC V6H 2E2, Canada* E-mail neilmancor@hotmail.com

MANDER, Peter John. b 52. Liv Univ BA85. Sarum & Wells Th Coll 85. **d** 87 **p** 88. C Hale and Ashley *Ches* 87-90; TV Grantham *Linc* 90-00; P-in-c Quarrington w Old Sleaford 00-08; P-in-c Silk Willoughby 00-08; RD Lafford 03-07; Can and Preb Linc Cathl 05-08; R Cruden Bay *Ab* from 08; R Ellon from 08. *The Rectory, Craighall, South Road, Ellon AB41 9NP* E-mail peter.mander@gmail.com

MANDER, Canon Thomas Leonard Frederick. b 33. Roch Th Coll 59 Ely Th Coll 60. **d** 62 **p** 63. C Cov St Mary 62-66; V Bishop's Tachbrook 66-70; V Earlsdon 70-76; V Chesterton 76-83; R Lighthorne 76-83; V Newbold Pacey w Moreton Morrell 76-83; Hon Can Cov Cathl 80-92; P-in-c S Leamington St Jo 83-84; V 84-92; rtd 92; Perm to Offic *Cov* from 92. *59 Murcott Road East, Whitnash, Leamington Spa CV31 2JJ* Tel (01926) 339950

MANDERSON, Robert Dunlop (Leslie). b 35. LDS59 FDS65. Ox Min Course 92. **d** 94 **p** 95. NSM Maidenhead St Andr and St Mary *Ox* 94-00; Perm to Offic 00-02; NSM Chipping Norton 02-03; rtd 03; Perm to Offic *Ox* 03-04 and *Ely* from 04. *67 Park Street, Dry Drayton, Cambridge CB23 8DA* Tel (01954) 782388 E-mail lpmanderson@aol.com

MANGA, Amos Morris Yorobama. **d** 06 **p** 07. C Helsinki *Eur* from 06. *The Anglican Church in Finland, Bulevardi 54B, 00120 Helsinki, Finland* Tel (00358) (9) 680 1515 Fax 698 0240

MANHIRE, Ashley Lewin. b 31. AKC55. **d** 56 **p** 57. C Plymouth St Gabr *Ex* 56-59; C Cockington 59-66; V Torquay St Martin Barton 66-83; RD Ipplepen 82-87; V Shaldon 83-01; rtd 01; Perm to Offic *Ex* from 01. *11 Heather Court, Stockbridge Road, Chichester PO19 8HJ*

MANHOOD, Phyllis. *See* DELVES, Canon Phyllis

✠**MANKTELOW, The Rt Revd Michael Richard John.** b 27. Ch Coll Cam BA48 MA52. Chich Th Coll 51. **d** 53 **p** 54 **c** 77. C Boston *Linc* 53-56; Chapl Ch Coll Cam 57-61; Chapl Linc Th Coll 61-63; Sub-Warden 64-66; V Knaresborough St Jo *Ripon* 66-73; RD Harrogate 72-77; V Harrogate St Wilfrid 73-77; P-in-c Harrogate St Luke 75-77; Hon Can Ripon Cathl 75-77; Suff Bp Basingstoke *Win* 77-93; Can Res Win Cathl 77-91; Hon Can 91-93; Vice-Dean 87-93; rtd 93; Hon Asst Bp Chich from 94; Hon Asst Bp Eur from 94; Wiccamical Preb Chich Cathl 97-02. *14 Little London, Chichester PO19 1NZ* Tel (01243) 531096

MANLEY, Mrs Gillian. b 59. St Martin's Coll Lanc BEd80. St Jo Coll Nottm MA04. **d** 00 **p** 01. C Eckington and Ridgeway *Derby* 00-04; TV Wirksworth from 04. *58 Yokecliffe Drive, Wirksworth, Matlock DE4 4EX* Tel (01629) 822896 *or* 826202   Mobile 07949-458383 E-mail gill.manley@supanet.com

MANLEY, Canon Gordon Russell Delpratt. b 33. Ch Coll Cam BA56 MA60. Linc Th Coll 57. **d** 59 **p** 60. C Westbury-on-Trym St Alb *Bris* 59-61; Chapl Ch Coll Cam 61-66; V Radlett *St Alb* 66-75; V Faversham *Cant* 75-99; RD Ospringe 84-90; Hon Can Cant Cathl 90-99; rtd 99; Perm to Offic *Cant* from 99; Retirement Officer (Cant Adnry) from 01. *170 Old Dover Road, Canterbury CT1 3EX* Tel (01227) 784016

MANLEY, Mrs Jane Elizabeth. b 58. Ox Min Course 05. **d** 08 **p** 09. C Bracknell *Ox* from 08. *4 Micheldever Way, Forest Park, Bracknell RG12 0XX* Tel (01344) 420167   Mobile 07711-613057 E-mail johnandjane2@btinternet.com

MANLEY, Canon Michael Alan. b 60. SS Hild & Bede Coll Dur BA82. Trin Coll Bris. **d** 86 **p** 87. C Accrington St Jo w Huncoat *Blackb* 86-90; V Preston St Luke and St Oswald 90-96; V Blackpool St Jo 96-07; Can Res Carl Cathl from 07. *4 The Abbey, Carlisle CA3 8TZ* Tel (01228) 542790 E-mail canonmissioner@carlislecathedral.org.uk

MANLEY (née McCARTHY), Mrs Sandra Ellen. b 56. Man Univ MusB77 Goldsmiths' Coll Lon PGCE79 ARCM75 FRCO77 GRNCM78. S west Min Course 92. **d** 95 **p** 96. C Beckenham St Geo *Roch* 95-99; V Heybridge w Langford *Chelmsf* 99-06; R Creeksea w Althorne, Latchingdon and N Fambridge from 06; P-in-c Purleigh, Cold Norton and Stow

Maries from 08. *The Vicarage, Fambridge Road, Althorne, Chelmsford CM3 6BZ* Tel (01621) 742947   Mobile 07722-425942 E-mail sandra.manley@btinternet.com

MANLEY-COOPER, Simon James. b 46. S Dios Minl Tr Scheme 91. **d** 94 **p** 95. NSM Soho St Anne w St Thos and St Pet *Lon* 94-96; Ind Chapl 94-96; P-in-c Bedford St Mich *St Alb* 96-01; Ind Chapl 96-01; R Bramfield, Stapleford, Waterford etc 01-02; Chapl E and N Herts NHS Trust from 03. *Queen Elizabeth II Hospital, Howlands, Welwyn Garden City AL7 4HQ* Tel (01707) 328111 *or* 365331 E-mail manley-co@ntlworld.com

MANN, Alexandrina Elizabeth. b 67. Westmr Coll Ox BA92 PGCE93 Birm Univ MA95. Trin Coll Bris 01. **d** 03 **p** 04. C Austrey and Warton *Birm* 03-06; V Hanbury, Newborough, Rangemore and Tutbury *Lich* from 06. *The Vicarage, 62 Redhill Lane, Tutbury, Burton-on-Trent DE13 9JW* Tel (01283) 810099 Mobile 07761-263849 E-mail alexandrina.shalom@virgin.net

MANN, Ms Angela. b 58. Bath Univ BA80 Bris Univ PGCE83. Trin Coll Bris 92. **d** 94 **p** 95. C Marlborough *Sarum* 94-97; Perm to Offic *Sarum* 97-98 and *Ox* 98-09; NSM The Claydons and Swan *Ox* from 09. *The Rectory, Grendon Underwood, Aylesbury HP18 0SY* Tel (01296) 770240   Mobile 07982-770161 E-mail angela.mann@o2.co.uk

MANN, Lt Comdr Anthony James. b 34. Open Univ BA76. St Jo Coll Nottm 85. **d** 88 **p** 89. NSM Helensburgh *Glas* 88-01; rtd 01. *Address temp unknown* E-mail didnpud@supanet.com

MANN, Canon Charmlon Anne Montgomery. b 36. Liv Univ BA57 CertEd62 AdDipEd79 Univ of Wales (Lamp) MA06. Trin Coll Bris 80. **dss** 82 **d** 87 **p** 94. Bris St Nath w St Kath 82-84; Bris St Matt and St Nath 84-85; Asst Chapl City Cen Hosps Bris 85-88; Chapl Bris Maternity Hosp 88-94; Chapl Bris R Hosp for Sick Children 88-94; Chapl Bris R Infirmary 88-94; Hon Can Bris Cathl 93-00; P-in-c Lacock w Bowden Hill 94-00; C Gtr Corsham 97-00; rtd 00; Perm to Offic *Bris* 00-06; *Sarum* 01-06; *Ex* from 07. *21 Oak Gardens, Ivybridge PL21 0NB* Tel (01752) 896636 E-mail charmion.mann@danmat.co.uk

MANN, Christopher John. b 57. Glas Univ BSc79. Westcott Ho Cam 83. **d** 86 **p** 87. C Worc SE 86-89; Min Can and Sacr St Paul's Cathl 89-96; R Upminster *Chelmsf* 96-06; Chapl to Bp Bradwell from 06; C Corringham from 07. *The Glebe House, High Road, Fobbing, Stanford-le-Hope SS17 9JN* Tel (01375) 642868 E-mail cmann@chelmsford.anglican.org

MANN, David. b 57. St Jo Coll Dur BA78. Ridley Hall Cam. **d** 82 **p** 83. C Monkwearmouth St Andr *Dur* 82-86; Chapl Sheff Cathl 86-87; C Leeds St Geo *Ripon* 87-94; V Ripon H Trin 94-06; Asst Dir of Ords 02-06; Selection Sec Min Division from 06. *Ministry Division, Church House, Great Smith Street, London SW1P 3AZ* Tel (020) 7898 1593 Fax 7898 1421 E-mail david.mann@c-of-e.org.uk

MANN, Donald Leonard. b 22. Westcott Ho Cam. **d** 47 **p** 48. C S'well Minster 47-49; C Edwinstowe 49-51; C St Alb St Paul *St Alb* 51-54; C Baldock w Bygrave and Clothall 54-56; V Guilden Morden *Ely* 56-59; V Rocester *Lich* 59-63; V Gnosall w Knightley 63-69; V Sheen 69-76; P-in-c Calton 72-76; P-in-c Ellastone 76; rtd 76; Perm to Offic *Ches* from 93. *Bungalow 24, Lyme Green Settlement, Macclesfield SK11 0LD* Tel (01260) 252209

MANN (née WELLS), Ms Gillian Mary. b 46. Bedf Coll Lon BA67 Goldsmiths' Coll Lon TCert68 MCIPD89. EMMTC 99. **d** 01 **p** 02. NSM Wirksworth *Derby* 01-05; P-in-c The Sampfords and Radwinter w Hempstead *Chelmsf* from 05. *The Rectory, Walden Road, Radwinter, Saffron Walden CB10 2SW* Tel (01799) 599332   Mobile 07719-470363 E-mail gillianmann@eidosnet.co.uk

MANN, Ivan John. b 52. Brunel Univ BTech74 Southn Univ BTh80. Sarum & Wells Th Coll 75. **d** 78 **p** 79. C Hadleigh w Layham and Shelley *St E* 78-81; C Whitton and Thurleston w Akenham 81-83; V Leiston 83-86; Perm to Offic 86-89; R Aldringham w Thorpe, Knodishall w Buxlow etc 89-93; V Ipswich St Jo 93-96; Chapl St Mary's Convent Wantage 96-00; Asst Chapl R Berks and Battle Hosps NHS Trust 00; TV Gt Yarmouth *Nor* 00-03; Team Member Loyola Hall Jesuit Spirituality Cen Prescot 03-04; Prec and Hon Can Cumbrae *Arg* 04-06; Can St Jo Cathl Oban 04-06; rtd 06. *18 Paradise Place, Norwich NR1 1QY* Tel (01603) 622465 E-mail ivan@ivanmann.f2s.com

MANN, Mrs Joan. b 42. **d** 98. NSM Eastbourne St Mary *Chich* 98-02; NSM The Hydneye from 02. *39 Cherry Garden Road, Eastbourne BN20 8HF* Tel (01323) 728259

MANN, John. b 35. ISO91. Oak Hill NSM Course 89. **d** 92 **p** 93. NSM Springfield All SS *Chelmsf* 92-05; RD Chelmsf N 99-04; rtd 05; Perm to Offic *Chelmsf* from 05. *18 Humber Road, Chelmsford CM1 7PE* Tel (01245) 259596

MANN, Canon John Owen. b 55. QUB BD77 MTh86 MPhil98. CITC 78. **d** 79 **p** 81. C Cloughfern *Conn* 79-82; C Knock *D & D* 82 85; I Ballyrashane w Kildollagh *Conn* 85-89; R Bentworth and Shalden and Lasham *Win* 89-93; RD Alton 92-93; I Cloughfern *Conn* 93-02; I Belfast Malone St Jo from 02; Preb Clonmethan St Patr Cathl Dublin from 99. *St John's Rectory, 86 Maryville Park, Belfast BT9 6LQ* Tel (028) 9066 6644 *or* 9066 7861 E-mail secstjohns@malo98.freeserve.co.uk

MANN, Julia Corinne. b 52. Open Univ BA92 Anglia Poly Univ BA03 RGN91. **d** 08 **p** 09. OLM Bury St Edmunds All SS w St Jo and St Geo *St E* from 08. *23 Westgate Street, Bury St Edmunds IP33 1QG* Tel (01284) 753984 E-mail jc.mann@btinternet.com

MANN, Julian Farrer Edgar. b 64. Peterho Cam MA90. Oak Hill Th Coll BA93. **d** 96 **p** 97. C Hoole *Ches* 96-00; V Oughtibridge *Sheff* from 00. *The Vicarage, Church Street, Oughtibridge, Sheffield S35 0FU* Tel 0114-286 2317
E-mail julianlisa@oughtimann.freeserve.co.uk

✠**MANN, The Rt Revd Michael Ashley.** b 24. KCVO89. CBIM. Wells Th Coll 55. **d** 57 **p** 58 **c** 74. C Wolborough w Newton Abbot *Ex* 57-59; V Sparkwell 59-62; V Port Harcourt Ch Ch Nigeria 62-67; Home Sec Miss to Seamen 67-69; Can Res Nor Cathl 69-74; Vice-Dean 73-74; Dioc Ind Adv 69-74; Suff Bp Dudley *Worc* 74-76; Dean Windsor and Dom Chapl to The Queen 76-89; rtd 89; Hon Asst Bp Glouc from 89. *Lower End Farm Cottage, Eastington, Northleach, Cheltenham GL54 3PN* Tel (01451) 860767

MANN, Paul William. b 63. Leeds Univ BSc84 CEng MIET. EAMTC 01. **d** 04 **p** 05. NSM Lawford *Chelmsf* from 04. *8 Cherrywoods, Great Bentley, Colchester CO7 8QF* Tel (01206) 252420 E-mail lima3papa-lawford@yahoo.co.uk

MANN, Peter Eric. b 51. St Jo Coll Dur BA73. Westcott Ho Cam 73. **d** 75 **p** 76. C Barrow St Jo *Carl* 75-78; C Egremont 78-80; V Carl St Luke Morton 80-86; TR Egremont and Haile 86-93; P-in-c Barrow St Geo w St Luke 93-99; TR S Barrow 99-01; P-in-c Barrow St Jo 95-96; RD Furness 94-01; RD Barrow 01-06; Hon Can Carl Cathl 95-06; TR Harwich Peninsula *Chelmsf* from 06; RD Harwich from 09. *The Rectory, 51 Highfield Avenue, Harwich CO12 4DR* Tel (01255) 502033
E-mail cookbird@gmail.com

MANN, Philip David. b 78. **d** 08 **p** 09. NSM Guildf St Sav from 08. *16 Cunningham Avenue, Guildford GU1 2PE* Tel (01483) 569603 E-mail philip.mann@st-saviours.org.uk

MANN, Ms Rachel. b 70. Lanc Univ BA91 MA93. Qu Coll Birm 03. **d** 05 **p** 06. C Stretford St Matt *Man* 05-08; P-in-c Burnage St Nic from 08. *The Rectory, 408 Kingsway, Burnage, Manchester M19 1PL* Tel 0161-432 7009 Mobile 07834-403195
E-mail rachel.mann@ntlworld.com

MANN, Ralph Norman. b 27. BNC Ox BA51 MA55 DipEd52. Ox NSM Course 79. **d** 82 **p** 83. NSM Kingham w Churchill, Daylesford and Sarsden *Ox* 82-85; S Area Sec BCMS 82-89; P-in-c Broadwell, Evenlode, Oddington and Adlestrop *Glouc* 89-97; rtd 97; P-in-c Upton St Leonards *Glouc* 97-00. *2 Whittons Close, Hook Norton, Banbury OX15 5QG* Tel (01608) 730327

MANN, Robin. b 45. Fitzw Coll Cam BA76 MA80 MRTPI73. Ridley Hall Cam 73. **d** 77 **p** 78. C Wetherby *Ripon* 77-80; V Hipswell 80-86; V Mamble w Bayton, Rock w Heightington etc *Worc* 86-96; V Avon Valley *Sarum* 96-02; R Selworthy, Timberscombe, Wootton Courtenay etc *B & W* 02-07; rtd 07. *Address withheld by request* E-mail hoarthorns@tiscali.co.uk

MANN, Stephen Paul. b 52. Staffs Univ BA76 Keele Univ PGCE78. Cranmer Hall Dur 96. **d** 98 **p** 99. C Spennymoor, Whitworth and Merrington *Dur* 98-03; Chapl Dur Constabulary 99-03; Chapl Butterwick Hospice Bishop Auckland 00-03; TV Madeley *Heref* 03-04; rtd 05. *42 The Crescent, Montford Bridge, Shrewsbury SY4 1EA* E-mail steve.mann99@lineone.net

MANN, Terence John. b 47. GGSM68 LRSM79 FTCL79 Miami Univ MA80 Lon Univ PGCE69. Ox Min Course 91. **d** 94 **p** 95. NSM Kingham w Churchill, Daylesford and Sarsden *Ox* 94-00; Chapl HM Pris Camp Hill from 00. *HM Prison, Camp Hill, Newport PO30 5PB* Tel (01983) 527661 Fax 520505

MANN, Mrs Tessa. STETS. **d** 08 **p** 09. NSM Bourne Valley *Sarum* from 08; NSM Salisbury St Fran and Stratford sub Castle from 09. *Barton Mead, Tanners Lane, Winterbourne Earls, Salisbury SP4 6HD*

MANNALL, Michael John Frederick. b 37. St Mich Coll Llan 61. **d** 63 **p** 64. C Clapham H Spirit *S'wark* 63-66; C Brighton St Bart *Chich* 66-68; C Willesden St Matt *Lon* 68-69; C-in-c Cricklewood St Pet CD 69-73; R Broughton *Pet* 73-75; Hon C Kingston St Luke *S'wark* 76-84; Perm to Offic Nor from 95. *The Blessings, 55 Sculthorpe Road, Fakenham NR21 9ET* Tel (01328) 863496 E-mail michael.mannall@btinternet.com

MANNERS, Jennifer Helen Edith. b 50. K Coll Lon MB, BS73 AKC73. **d** 06 **p** 07. OLM Bearsted w Thurnham *Cant* from 06. *9 Tilefields, Hollingbourne, Maidstone ME17 1TZ* Tel (01622) 880363 E-mail jhemanners@hotmail.com

MANNERS, Kenneth. b 29. NOC. **d** 84 **p** 85. NSM Brayton *York* 84-00; rtd 00; Perm to Offic *York* from 00. *16 Wistow Road, Selby YO8 3LY* Tel (01757) 702129

MANNING, Adrian Peter. b 63. St Cath Coll Cam MA88 K Coll Lon PGCE88 St Cath Coll Cam BA84. Ridley Hall Cam 92. **d** 95 **p** 96. C Oxhey All SS *St Alb* 95-97; Asst Chapl Bedford Sch 97-02; Chapl St Geo Sch Harpenden from 02. *12 Crecy Gardens, Redbourn, St Albans AL3 7BQ* Tel (01582) 716231

MANNING, Mrs Ann. b 42. Liv Univ CertEd75. St Jo Coll Nottm 93 NOC 94. **d** 95 **p** 96. NSM Grasmere *Carl* 95-96; NSM Delamere *Ches* 96-99; C Middlewich w Byley 99-02; Chapl Mid Cheshire Hosps Trust 99-02; P-in-c Dunton w Wrestlingworth

and Eyeworth *St Alb* 02-05; R 05-08; rtd 08. *27 Barley Croft, Great Boughton, Chester CH3 5SP* Tel (01244) 316781
E-mail revmanning@hotmail.co.uk

MANNING, David Godfrey. b 47. Trin Coll Bris 73. **d** 76 **p** 77. C Richmond H Trin and Ch Ch *S'wark* 76-79; C Anston *Sheff* 79-83; V Blackpool St Mark *Blackb* 83-91; V Creech St Michael *B & W* 91-08. *The Vicarage, Creech St Michael, Taunton TA3 5PP* Tel (01823) 442237

MANNING, Mrs Jean Margaret. b 46. Oak Hill NSM Course 07. **d** 08 **p** 09. NSM Herstmonceux and Wartling *Chich* from 08. *Little Bathurst Farm, Cowbeech Road, Rushlake Green, Heathfield TN21 9QA* Tel and fax (01435) 831105 Mobile 07711-052131 E-mail jmm60@btinternet.com

MANNING, Neville Alexander. b 41. Lon Univ BD68. ALCD68. **d** 68 **p** 69. C Belvedere All SS *Roch* 68-71; C Hollington St Leon *Chich* 71-73; C Hersham *Guildf* 73-77; V Dawley St Jerome *Lon* 77-94; R Denton w S Heighton and Tarring Neville *Chich* 94-06; rtd 06. *7 Salvador Close, Eastbourne BN23 5TB* Tel (01323) 479359

MANNING, Virginia Ann. b 47. Univ of Wales (Ban) BTh07. **d** 07 **p** 08. OLM N Hartismere *St E* from 07. *Fernleigh, Mill Road, Winfarthing, Diss IP22 2DZ* Tel (01379) 644229
E-mail colgin.manning@tesco.net

MANNINGS, Andrew James. b 52. Trent Park Coll of Educn CertEd73. St Jo Coll Nottm 90. **d** 92 **p** 94. C Over St Chad *Ches* 92-93; C Sale St Anne 93-96; C Timperley 96-98; P-in-c Egremont St Jo 98-04; P-in-c Liscard St Mary w St Columba 03-04; V Liscard Resurr from 04; RD Wallasey 02-07. *The Vicarage, 107 Manor Road, Wallasey CH45 7LU* Tel 0151-638 4360 Fax 513 0172 Mobile 07814-878175
E-mail frandrew2004@yahoo.co.uk

MANNS, Edwin Ernest. b 30. Portsm Dioc Tr Course 84. **d** 85. C Paulsgrove *Portsm* 85-95; Chapl St Mary's Hosp Portsm 90-91; Team Chapl Portsm Hosp 91-95; rtd 95. *17 Kelvin Grove, Portchester, Fareham PO16 8LQ* Tel (023) 9232 4818

MANSBRIDGE, The Ven Michael Winstanley. b 32. Southn Univ BA54. Ridley Hall Cam 56. **d** 58 **p** 59. C Ware St Mary *St Alb* 58-60; C Claverdon w Preston Bagot *Cov* 60-62; Kenya 62-65; Asst P Nairobi Cathl and Chapl Nairobi Univ 62-65; V Chilvers Coton w Astley *Cov* 65-75; RD Nuneaton 66-73; V Leamington Priors H Trin 75-83; Chapl Abu Dhabi St Andr UAE 83-97; Adn the Gulf 83-91; Adn Cyprus and the Gulf 91-99; Can Nicosia 86-99; Provost 97-99; Can Bahrain 87-99; rtd 97; Hon Can Nicosia and Bahrain from 99. *Blue Skies, 7 Norman Way, Wootton Bridge, Ryde PO33 4NJ* Tel (01983) 882394
E-mail fiona_mansbridge@compuserve.com

MANSEL LEWIS, Patrick Charles Archibald. b 53. Solicitor 79. St Mich Coll Llan 01. **d** 04 **p** 05. NSM Llandeilo Fawr and Taliaris *St D* from 04. *Capel Isaf, Manordeilo, Llandeilo SA19 7BS* Tel (01558) 822273

MANSELL, The Ven Clive Neville Ross. b 53. Leic Univ LLB74 Solicitor 77. **d** 82 **p** 83. C Gt Malvern St Mary *Worc* 82-85; Min Can Ripon Cathl 85-89; R Kirklington w Burneston and Wath and Pickhill 89-02; AD Wensley 98-02; Adn Tonbridge *Roch* from 02. *3 The Ridings, Blackhurst Lane, Tunbridge Wells TN2 4RU* Tel and fax (01892) 520660
E-mail archdeacon.tonbridge@rochester.anglican.org

MANSELL, Paul John. b 67. Staffs Univ MSc05. Ripon Coll Cuddesdon 05. **d** 07 **p** 08. C Schorne *Ox* from 07. *Maltings Cottage, Lower Road, Hardwick, Aylesbury HP22 4DZ* Tel (01296) 641246 Mobile 07983-707560
E-mail paul@deepblueocean.co.uk

MANSFIELD, Alastair John Fraser. b 60. Ex Univ BA82 Ch Coll Cam PGCE84 City Univ MSc92. SEITE. **d** 99 **p** 00. C Palmers Green St Jo *Lon* 99-02; P-in-c Enfield St Mich 02-07; Chapl RN from 08. *Royal Naval Chaplaincy Service, Mail Point 1-2, Leach Building, Whale Island, Portsmouth PO2 8BY* Tel (023) 9262 5055 Fax 9262 5134 E-mail ajstrawber@aol.com

MANSFIELD, Gordon Reginald. b 35. Lon Univ BA CertEd. Clifton Th Coll 58. **d** 63 **p** 64. C Carl St Jo 63-65; C Westcombe Park St Geo *S'wark* 65-68; C Rashcliffe *Wakef* 68-70; V Woodlands *Sheff* 70-80; V Steeple Bumpstead and Helions Bumpstead *Chelmsf* 80-02; Perm to Offic *Ely* 03-04; *Heref* and *S & B* from 04. *18 Caefelyn, Norton, Presteigne LD8 2UB* Tel (01544) 260380

MANSFIELD, Julian Nicolas (Nick). b 59. K Coll Lon BD AKC. Edin Th Coll 83. **d** 85 **p** 86. C Kirkby *Liv* 85-89; TV Ditton St Mich 89-96; P-in-c Preston St Oswald *Blackb* 96-01; V Penwortham St Leon from 01. *St Leonard's Vicarage, Marshall's Brow, Penwortham, Preston PR1 9HY* Tel (01772) 742367
E-mail nick-vic@fish.co.uk

MANSFIELD, Robert William. b 45. **d** 88 **p** 89. OLM Louth *Linc* from 88. *The Old Railway House, Stewton, Louth LN11 8SD* Tel (01507) 327533 E-mail mansfieldstewton@hotmail.com

MANSFIELD, Simon David. b 55. Brunel Univ BSc81 Lon Univ MA94 Univ of Wales (Ban) MPhil06. Ripon Coll Cuddesdon 88. **d** 90 **p** 91. C N Harrow St Alb *Lon* 90-93; C Birchington w Acol and Minnis Bay *Cant* 93-97; TV Accrington *Blackb* 97-00; TV Accrington Ch the King 00-05; P-in-c Wednesfield St Greg

Lich from 05. *St Gregory's Vicarage, 112 Long Knowle Lane, Wolverhampton WV11 1JQ* Tel (01902) 731677
E-mail smansfeeld@toucansurf.com

MANSFIELD, Stephen McLaren. b 59. FGA. Cranmer Hall Dur 86. **d** 89 **p** 90. C Poynton *Ches* 89-92; C Bromborough 92-94; V Bidston 94-02; C Heswall from 02. *15 Castle Drive, Heswall, Wirral CH60 4RJ* Tel 0151-342 4841
E-mail steve.mansfield@mac.com

MANSHIP, Charmian Margaret. b 45. RCM BMus68 ARCM65 GRSM67 FRCO68. SAOMC 95. **d** 98 **p** 99. NSM Abingdon *Ox* 98-04; Succ and Min Can Worc Cathl from 04. *22 Stanmore Road, Worcester WR2 4PW* Tel (01905) 421147

MANSHIP, Canon David. b 27. ARCO Keble Coll Ox BA52 MA58. Qu Coll Birm 52. **d** 54 **p** 55. C Hackney St Jo *Lon* 54-58; C Preston Ascension 58-61; C St Andr Holborn 61-65; Members' Tr Officer C of E Youth Coun 65-68; Clergy Tr Officer 68-70; Dir of Educn *Win* 70-79; Hon Can Win Cathl 74-79; R Old Alresford 76-79; V Abingdon w Shippon *Ox* 79-89; TR Abingdon 89-93; V Shippon 89; RD Abingdon 87-90; rtd 93; Perm to Offic *Ox* 93-03 and *Worc* from 04. *22 Stanmore Road, Worcester WR2 4PW* Tel (01905) 421147

MANSLEY, Colin Edward. b 56. Edin Univ MA80 BA85. Ripon Coll Cuddesdon 83. **d** 86 **p** 87. C Worle *B & W* 86-89; C Baguley *Man* 89-91; C Radcliffe St Mary 91; TV Radcliffe 91-96; V Bartley Green *Birm* 96-08; R Cefn w Trefnant w Tremeirchion *St As* from 08. *The Rectory, Trefnant, Denbigh LL16 5UG* Tel (01745) 730584 E-mail colin@archangel.clara.co.uk

MANSON-BRAILSFORD, Andrew Henry. b 64. NUU BA86 Liv Univ MPhil98 Sussex Univ DPhil09. Ripon Coll Cuddesdon 87. **d** 90 **p** 91. C Warrington St Elphin *Liv* 90-93; C Torrisholme *Blackb* 93-96; V Brighton St Geo w St Anne and St Mark *Chich* from 96; Chapl St Mary's Hall Brighton from 97. *22 Seymour Square, Brighton BN2 1DW* Tel (01273) 699779 *or* 606061 Fax 620782 E-mail revmanson-brailsford@hotmail.co.uk

MANT, Frances Joy. b 61. Jes Coll Cam BA82 MA86 Lon Univ MB, BS85 Ex Univ BPhil88. Qu Coll Birm BA05. **d** 05 **p** 06. NSM Bromsgrove All SS *Worc* from 05. *107 New Road, Bromsgrove B60 2LJ* Tel (01527) 872040

✠**MANTLE, The Rt Revd John Ambrose Cyril.** b 46. St Andr Univ MTheol74 Kent Univ MA90 Leeds Univ PhD98 FRHistS01. Edin Th Coll 66. **d** 69 **p** 70 **c** 05. C Broughty Ferry *Bre* 69-71; C St Andrews All SS *St And* 71-75; C Edin SS Phil and Jas 75-77; Teacher Royal High Sch Edin 75-77; Chapl and Tutor in Th St Andr Univ 77-80; P-in-c Pittenweem 78-80; P-in-c Elie and Earlsferry 78-80; Chapl and Fell Fitzw Coll Cam 80-86; Tutor Wesley Ho Cam 80-86; Hon C Cambridge Ascension *Ely* 80-86; Tutor and Vice-Prin Cant Sch of Min 86-91; Visiting Lect Th Kent Univ 91-93; C Boxley w Detling 86-93; Dioc Adv for Educn and Tr of Adults *Chich* 94-99; Visiting Lect Th Sussex Univ 95-98; Abps' Adv for Bps' Min *Cant* 99-05; Bp Bre from 05. *Diocesan Office, Unit 14 Prospect 3, Gemini Crescent, Technology Park, Dundee DD2 1SW* Tel (01382) 562244 Fax 220888 E-mail office@brechin.anglican.org

MANTON, Paul Arthur. b 45. Oak Hill Th Coll BD77. **d** 77 **p** 78. C Wolverhampton *Lich* 77-80; Ind Chapl *Lon* 80-87; Hon C St Marylebone All So w SS Pet and Jo 80-87; Perm to Offic from 03. *75 Homefield Gardens, London N2 0XL* Tel (020) 3224 3001 Mobile 07847-425946

MANUEL, Paul. b 55. Univ of Wales (Ban) BA76 ACIS79 FCIS88. SAOMC 97. **d** 00 **p** 01. NSM Luton St Paul *St Alb* 00-03; C Chorleywood Ch Ch 03-07; P-in-c New Milverton *Cov* from 07. *St Mark's Vicarage, 2 St Mark's Road, Leamington Spa CV32 6DL* Tel (01926) 421004
E-mail pmfrompetham@aol.com

MAPES, David. Brunel Univ BSc71 CEng75 MIET74 MIMechE78 EurIng89 FInstD77 MBACP99. NTMTC BA07. **d** 07 **p** 08. NSM Feltham *Lon* from 07. *Candas House, Broadlands Avenue, Shepperton TW17 9DQ* Tel (01932) 224844 Mobile 07885-635378 E-mail davemapes@aol.com

MAPLE, David Charles. b 34. Sarum Th Coll 64. **d** 66 **p** 66. C Buckland in Dover *Cant* 66-67; C St Laur in Thanet 67-71; Chapl RAF 71-75; P-in-c Ivychurch 75-76; P-in-c Newchurch *Cant* 75-78; P-in-c Burmarsh 75-78; P-in-c St Mary in the Marsh 75-76; R Dymchurch 76-78; R Dymchurch w Burmarsh and Newchurch 78-81; Hon Min Can Cant Cathl from 79; Abp's Dioc Chapl 81-91; Chapl St Jo Hosp Cant 91-95; rtd 95; Perm to Offic *Cant* from 98. *1 Mount Pleasant, Blean, Canterbury CT2 9EU* Tel (01227) 459044

MAPLE, John Philip. b 50. Chich Th Coll 71. **d** 74 **p** 79. C Notting Hill St Mich and Ch Ch *Lon* 74-75; Lic to Offic 78-79; C Barnsbury St Dav w St Clem 79-80; C Cotham St Sav w St Mary *Bris* 80-83; TV St Marylebone Ch Ch *Lon* 83-91; R St Marylebone St Paul 91-99; P-in-c Fulham St Alb w St Aug 99-04; P-in-c Fulham St Pet 99-02; Community Min Adv from 04. *London Diocesan House, 36 Causton Street, London SW1P 4AU* Tel (020) 7932 1122
E-mail jack.maple@london.anglican.org

MAPLEY, Mrs Barbara Jean. b 46. Guy's Hosp Medical Sch MCSP69. Oak Hill NSM Course 86. **d** 89 **p** 94. NSM Kelvedon *Chelmsf* 89-93; C Witham 93-94; TV 94-01; R Belbroughton w

Fairfield and Clent *Worc* from 01. *The Rectory, Bradford Lane, Belbroughton, Stourbridge DY9 9TF* Tel (01562) 730531
E-mail barbaramapley@waitrose.com

MAPPLEBECKPALMER, Richard Warwick. b 32. CCC Cam BA56 MA60. Cuddesdon Coll 56. **d** 58 **p** 59. C Redcar *York* 58-60; C Drypool St Jo 61-63; V Pendleton St Ambrose *Man* 63-77; P-in-c Didsbury *Ox* 77; P-in-c Ambrosden w Arncot and Blackthorn 77; P-in-c Merton 77; V Ambrosden w Merton and Piddington 77-88; USA from 88; rtd 97. *472 Dale Road, Martinez CA 94553-4829, USA* Tel (001) (510) 228 5252

MAPSON, Preb John Victor. b 31. Lon Univ BA60. Oak Hill Th Coll 55. **d** 60 **p** 61. C Littleover *Derby* 60-62; C Wandsworth St Mich *S'wark* 62-65; R Willand *Ex* 65-71; P-in-c Axmouth 71-72; V 72-75; V Axmouth w Musbury 75-77; RD Honiton 76-77; V Cullompton 77-89; R Kentisbeare w Blackborough 77-89; RD Cullompton 81-89; P-in-c Sidmouth All SS 89-96; Preb Ex Cathl 91-01; RD Ottery 94-96; rtd 96; Ed *Exeter Diocesan Directory* from 00. *47 Head Weir Road, Cullompton EX15 1NN* Tel (01884) 38037 E-mail jmapson@care4free.net *or* diocesan.news@exeter.anglican.org

MAPSTONE, Trevor Anthony. b 63. Lanc Univ BSc84 MA96. St Jo Coll Nottm 86. **d** 89 **p** 90. C Hoole *Ches* 89-92; C Lancaster St Thos *Blackb* 92-96; V Harrow Trin St Mich *Lon* 96-98; Dir of Ords Willesden Area 98-03; V S Croydon Em *S'wark* from 03. *33 Hurst Way, South Croydon CR2 7AP* Tel (020) 8688 6676
E-mail tmapstone@emmanuelcroydon.org.uk

MARAIS, Rudolph James. b 41. St Bede's Coll Umtata BTh. **d** 81 **p** 82. S Africa 81-85 and from 87; C Belmont *S'wark* 85-87. *PO Box 101, Jefferys Bay, 6300 South Africa* Tel (0027) (42) 291 1659 Mobile 82-578 7522

MARBUS, Alida Janny. *See* WHITTOCK, Alida Janny

MARCER, Graham John. b 52. Ripon Coll Cuddesdon 75. **d** 78 **p** 79. C Sherborne w Castleton and Lillington *Sarum* 78-81; C Christchurch *Win* 81-84; V Southampton St Jude 84-90; P-in-c Moordown 90-91; C Sheff St Cecilia Parson Cross 91-93; V Balby 93-00; RD W Doncaster 97-00; V Radford *Cov* from 00; AD Cov N 01-04. *The Vicarage, 21 Tulliver Street, Coventry CV6 3BY* Tel (024) 7659 8449
E-mail graham.marcer@btinternet.com

MARCETTI, Alvin Julian. b 41. San Jose State Univ BA66 Santa Clara Univ MA76. Cranmer Hall Dur 85. **d** 87 **p** 88. C Stepney St Dunstan and All SS *Lon* 87-91; Chapl City of Lon Poly 91-92; Chapl Lon Guildhall Univ 92-96; Chapl Homerton Univ Hosp NHS Trust Lon 96-03; Chapl City and Hackney Community Services NHS Trust 96-03; rtd 03. *38 Becquerel Court, West Parkside, London SE10 0QQ* Tel (020) 8269 1251
E-mail almarcetti@yahoo.co.uk

MARCH, Alan Mervyn. b 48. Open Univ BA91 CPFA73. EAMTC 00. **d** 03 **p** 04. NSM Northampton St Alb *Pet* 03-06; NSM Northampton Ch Ch from 06. *236 Beech Avenue, Northampton NN3 2LE* Tel (01604) 405722
E-mail alan@march100.freeserve.co.uk

MARCH, Andrew. b 81. UEA BA03. St Jo Coll Nottm MA09. **d** 09. C Werrington and Wetley Rocks *Lich* from 09. *360 Ash Bank Road, Werrington, Stoke-on-Trent ST9 0JS* Tel 07816-998642 (mobile) E-mail revandymarch@googlemail.com

MARCH, Anthony. *See* MARCH, Charles Anthony Maclea

MARCH, Charles Anthony Maclea (Tony). b 32. CCC Cam BA55 MA70. Oak Hill Th Coll 55. **d** 57 **p** 58. C S Croydon Em *Cant* 57-60; C Eastbourne H Trin *Chich* 60-63; V Whitehall Park St Andr Hornsey Lane *Lon* 63-67; V Tunbridge Wells H Trin w Ch Ch *Roch* 67-82; V Prestonville St Luke *Chich* 82-97; rtd 97; Perm to Offic *Roch* from 99. *The Barn, 2 Town Farm Dairy, Brenchley Road, Brenchley, Tonbridge TN12 7PA* Tel (01892) 722802

MARCH, Gerald. b 44. Nottm Univ BA75. Oak Hill Th Coll 92. **d** 95 **p** 96. C Sandgate St Paul w Folkestone St Geo *Cant* 95-99; P-in-c Southampton St Mark *Win* 99-03; V from 03. *St Mark's Vicarage, 54 Archers Road, Southampton SO15 2LU* Tel (023) 8063 6425 E-mail gerald.march@lineone.net

MARCH, Jonathan. b 79. Wycliffe Hall Ox. **d** 05 **p** 06. C Brompton H Trin w Onslow Square St Paul *Lon* from 05. *Basement Flat, 2 Victoria Rise, London SW4 0NY* Tel (020) 7052 0301 E-mail jon.march@htb.org.uk

MARCHAND, Canon Rex Anthony Victor (Toby). b 47. K Coll Lon BD69 AKC69. St Aug Coll Cant 69. **d** 70 **p** 71. C Leigh Park *Portsm* 70-73; C Bp's Hatfield *St Alb* 73-80; R Deal St Leon and St Rich and Sholden *Cant* 80-95; RD Sandwich 91-94; Hon Can Cant Cathl 94-95; V Bishop's Stortford St Mich *St Alb* from 95; RD Bishop's Stortford 03-06. *St Michael's Vicarage, 8 Larkspur Road, Bishop's Stortford CM23 4LL* Tel (01279) 651415 E-mail tandmmarchand@ntlworld.com

MARCHANT, Canon Iain William. b 26. Wells Th Coll 59. **d** 60 **p** 61. C Dalston *Carl* 60-63; V Hawkesbury *Glouc* 63-76; R Newent 76-85; Hon Can Glouc Cathl 84-92; R Newent and Gorsley w Cliffords Mesne 85-92; rtd 92; Perm to Offic *Glouc* from 92. *34 Parklands, Wotton-under-Edge GL12 7LT* Tel (01453) 844779

MARCHANT, John Bennet. b 46. St Jo Coll Nottm. **d** 06 **p** 07. Aux Min Powerscourt w Kilbride *D & G* from 06; Chapl Dublin

City Univ from 07. *276 Harolds Grange Road, Dublin 16, Republic of Ireland* Tel (00353) (1) 494 2408 Mobile 87-239 3682 E-mail revjmarchant@yahoo.ie *or* john.marchant@dcu.ie

MARCHANT, Canon Ronald Albert. b 26. Em Coll Cam BA50 MA52 PhD57 BD64. Ridley Hall Cam 50. **d** 54 **p** 55. C Acomb St Steph *York* 54-57; C Willian *St Alb* 57-59; V Laxfield *St E* 59-92; RD Hoxne 73-78; Hon Can St E Cathl 75-92; P-in-c Wilby w Brundish 86-92; rtd 92; Perm to Offic *York* from 93. *34 The Paddock, Boroughbridge Road, York YO26 6AW* Tel (01904) 798446

MARCUS, Mrs Candice Ann. b 52. FInstLEx80. Trin Coll Bris 05. **d** 07 **p** 08. C Timsbury and Priston *B & W* from 07. *8 The Mead, Timsbury, Bath BA2 0NS* Tel (01761) 479542 Mobile 07788-437063 E-mail candicemarcus@btinternet.com

MARCUSSEN, Mrs Yolande Roberta. b 47. SEITE 98. **d** 01 **p** 02. NSM Bromley Common St Aug *Roch* 01-03; NSM Orpington All SS 03; Asst Chapl HM Pris Roch 01-03; Chapl 03-06; rtd 06. *24 Lucerne Road, Orpington BR6 0EP* Tel (01689) 833599

MARGAM, Archdeacon of. *See* MORRIS, The Ven Philip Gregory

MARGARET ANNE, Sister. *See* McALISTER, Margaret Elizabeth Anne

MARGARET JOY, Sister. *See* HARRIS, Margaret Claire

MARINER, Aris. b 43. Alexandria Univ BSc65. St Alb Minl Tr Scheme 84. **d** 87. NSM Stevenage H Trin *St Alb* from 87. *13 Church Lane, Stevenage SG1 3QS* Tel (01438) 365596

MARION EVA, Sister. *See* RECORD, Sister Marion Eva

MARK, Timothy John. b 34. Bris Univ BA57 PGCE58 MLitt68 MEd71 Leeds Univ PhD79. Didsbury Methodist Coll 54. **d** 59 **p** 61. India 59-69; Perm to Offic *Sheff* 73-08. *Spindrift, 61 Craig-yr-Eos Road, Ogmore-by-Sea, Bridgend CF32 0PH* Tel (01665) 880908 E-mail tjm@timothymark.plus.com

MARKBY, Archibald Campbell. b 15. Em Coll Cam BA37 MA41. Ridley Hall Cam 37. **d** 39 **p** 39. C Bradf St Clem 39-42; C Ox St Aldate 42-46; V Kilburn St Mary *Lon* 46-53; V Hornsey Ch Ch 53-64; R Ickenham 64-68; V Crowfield w Stonham Aspal *St E* 68-71; V Damerham *Sarum* 71-80; V Martin 71-80; rtd 80; Perm to Offic *Sarum* 80-00. *8 Timbermill Court, Church Sreet, Fordingbridge SP6 1RG* Tel (01425) 656141

MARKBY, Ms Jane Elizabeth. b 67. Em Coll Cam BA88 Homerton Coll Cam PGCE89. Ridley Hall Cam 00. **d** 02 **p** 03. NSM Edmonton All SS w St Mich *Lon* 02-06; Chapl Haberdashers' Aske's Sch Elstree from 06. *1A Uvedale Road, Enfield EN2 6HA* Tel (020) 8482 0452 E-mail janemarkby@blueyonder.co.uk

MARKBY, Peter John Jenner. b 38. Em Coll Cam BA60. Clifton Th Coll 62. **d** 64 **p** 65. C Tufnell Park St Geo *Lon* 64-68; C Crowborough *Chich* 68-73; C Polegate 73-77; R Southover 77-02; rtd 02; Perm to Offic *Chich* from 02. *66 Leylands Road, Burgess Hill RH15 8AJ* Tel (01444) 870831 E-mail petermarkby@onetel.com

MARKER, Janet. b 63. WEMTC 02. **d** 06 **p** 07. NSM Bris Lockleaze St Mary Magd w St Fran from 06. *165 Landseer Avenue, Bristol BS7 9YT* Tel 0117-969 3248 E-mail janet.marker@getreal.co.uk

MARKEY, Andrew John. b 73. Univ of Wales (Swansea) BSc96. Westcott Ho Cam BTh02. **d** 02 **p** 03. C Wotton-under-Edge w Ozleworth, N Nibley etc *Glouc* 02-06; Chapl Ox Brookes Univ from 09. *The Chaplaincy, Oxford Brookes University, Headington, Oxford OX3 0BP* Tel (01865) 484690 E-mail chaplaincy@brookes.ac.uk

MARKHAM, Deryck O'Leary. b 28. Oak Hill Th Coll 66. **d** 68 **p** 69. C Purley Ch Ch *S'wark* 68-72; V Budleigh and Bicton *Ex* 72-93; RD Aylesbeare 89-93; rtd 93; Perm to Offic *Ex* 93-03 and *Win* from 03. *8 Milford House, Milford on Sea, Lymington SO41 0QJ* Tel (01590) 643515 E-mail dolm@onetel.com

MARKS, Allan Willi. b 56. Cranmer Hall Dur 92. **d** 94 **p** 95. C Barnoldswick w Bracewell *Bradf* 94-96; C Willington *Newc* 96-98; TV 98-02; V Newc H Cross 02-09; P-in-c Newc Ch Ch w St Ann from 09. *The Vicarage, 11 Gibson Street, Newcastle upon Tyne NE1 6PY* E-mail fatherallan@blueyonder.co.uk

MARKS, Anthony Alfred. b 28. AKC53. **d** 54 **p** 55. C Fleetwood St Pet *Blackb* 54-58; V Burnley St Cuth 58-63; Chapl RN 63-83; QHC from 81; P-in-c Bradninch *Ex* 83-88; R Bradninch and Clyst Hydon 88-90; rtd 90; Perm to Offic *B & W* from 90. *Bryony Cottage, The Combe, Compton Martin, Bristol BS40 6JD* Tel (01749) 221288

MARKS, Anthony Wendt. b 43. G&C Coll Cam BA63 MA67 PhD70 BNC Ox DPhil72. St Steph Ho Ox 70. **d** 72 **p** 73. C Withington St Crispin *Man* 72-75; Chapl Lon Univ Medical Students 75-80; Warden Liddon Ho Lon 80-92; C-in-c Grosvenor Chpl *Lon* 80-92; V Shrewsbury All SS w St Mich *Lich* 92-99; V Fareham SS Pet and Paul *Portsm* 99-09; rtd 09. *94 Throxenby Lane, Scarborough YO12 5HN* Tel (01723) 377504

MARKS, Dennis Ray. b 37. Lon Univ BSc58 PhD67 PGCE59 Univ of Wales (Ban) BTh04 CChem85 MRSC85. **d** 06 **p** 07. OLM Woking St Mary *Guildf* from 06. *Green Tiles, Shaftesbury Road, Woking GU22 7DU* Tel (01483) 762030 E-mail ray@raymarks.fsnet.co.uk

MARKS, Mrs June Margaret. b 49. LCTP. **d** 08. NSM Oakworth *Bradf* from 08. *49 Larkfield Terrace, Oakworth, Keighley BD22 7HJ* Tel (01535) 648328 E-mail emrysandjune@talktalk.net

MARKS, Robert Wesley. b 58. Guelph Univ (Canada) BSc81. Cranmer Hall Dur 03. **d** 05 **p** 06. C Baxenden *Blackb* 05-06; C Anchorsholme 06-09; P-in-c Ribby cum Wrea and Weeton from 09. *The Vicarage, 1 Vicarage Close, Wrea Green, Preston PR4 2PQ* Tel (01772) 687644 Mobile 07906-175379 E-mail wesmarks@supanet.com

MARKS, Timothy John. b 45. Man Univ BA76 Anglia Poly Univ MA97. **d** 88 **p** 89. NSM Burton and Sopley *Win* 88-91; R Croxton and Eltisley *Ely* 91-96; R Graveley w Papworth St Agnes w Yelling etc 91-96; Dir Network Counselling and Tr 96-97; Perm to Offic *B & W* 97-00. *8 Arundell Road, Weston-super-Mare BS23 2QQ* Tel (01934) 415807

MARL, David John. b 42. ARCA67. **d** 01 **p** 02. OLM Okeford *Sarum* from 01. *Bow Cottage, Shute Lane, Iwerne Minster, Blandford Forum DT11 8LZ* Tel (01747) 812048 E-mail burgoyne.marl@tiscali.co.uk

MARLEY, The Very Revd Alan Gordon. b 59. Birm Univ BA89. Qu Coll Birm 87. **d** 89 **p** 90. C Blandford Forum and Langton Long *Sarum* 89-93; Chapl HM YOI Aylesbury 93-97; I Fermoy Union *C, C & R* 97-03; Bp's Dom Chapl 99-03; Dean Cloyne from 03; I Cloyne Union from 03; Dioc Dir of Ords from 05. *The Deanery, Deanery Road, Midleton, Co Cork, Republic of Ireland* Tel (00353) (21) 463 1449 E-mail dean@cloyne.anglican.org

MARLOW, Jonathan James. b 76. SS Hild & Bede Coll Dur MEng99. Wycliffe Hall Ox BTh06. **d** 06 **p** 07. C Elburton *Ex* from 06. *3 Springfield Avenue, Plymouth PL9 8PZ* Tel (01752) 547492 E-mail email@marlow.me.uk

MARLOW (*née* SIBBALD)**, Mrs Olwyn Eileen.** b 57. Aston Tr Scheme 85 Linc Th Coll 87. **d** 89 **p** 94. Par Dn Wythenshawe St Martin *Man* 89-93; Par Dn Baguley 93-94; C 94-95; Asst Chapl Cen Man Healthcare NHS Trust 95-00; NSM Newall Green St Fran *Man* 97-98; rtd 01; NSM Wythenshawe *Man* 01-05; Perm to Offic *Ches* and *Man* from 05. *28 Arcadia Avenue, Sale M33 3SA* Tel 0161-962 9292

MARNHAM, Charles Christopher. b 51. Jes Coll Cam BA73 MA77. Cranmer Hall Dur. **d** 77 **p** 78. C Brompton H Trin *Lon* 77-78; C Brompton H Trin w Onslow Square St Paul 78-80; C Linthorpe *York* 80-84; R Haughton le Skerne *Dur* 84-95; V Ches Square St Mich w St Phil *Lon* from 95. *St Michael's Vicarage, 4 Chester Square, London SW1W 9HH* Tel (020) 7730 8889 Fax 7730 0043 E-mail charles@stmichaelschurch.org.uk

MARNS, Nigel Geoffrey. b 63. Univ of Wales (Abth) BSc(Econ)85 Birm Univ BD92. Qu Coll Birm 90. **d** 93 **p** 94. C Addington *S'wark* 93-96; P-in-c W Bromwich Gd Shep w St Jo *Lich* 96-01; V Bromsgrove St Jo *Worc* 01-09; R Ludgvan, Marazion, St Hilary and Perranuthnoe *Truro* from 09. *The Rectory, Ludgvan, Penzance TR20 8EZ* Tel (01736) 740784

✠**MARONA, The Most Revd Joseph Biringi Hassan.** b 41. Bp Gwynne Th Coll 78. **d** 81 **p** 82 **c** 84. Chapl Rumbek State Secondary Sch Sudan 81-82; Chapl Maridi Teachers' Tr Coll 82-83; Area Bp Maridi 85-89; Bp Maridi 89-00; Dean of Prov from 98; Abp Sudan and Bp Juba from 00. *ECS Liaison Office, PO Box 604, Khartoum, Sudan* Tel (00249) (811) 20040 *or* (11) 485720 Fax (811) 20065 *or* (11) 485717 E-mail ecsprovince@hotmail.com

MARQUEZ, Edilberto. b 57. Bible Sem Alliance Peru BA80 Westmr Coll Ox MTh93. St Steph Ho Ox 92. **d** 94 **p** 95. C Reading St Jo *Ox* 94-98; C New Malden and Coombe *S'wark* 98-01; P-in-c Bucklebury w Marlston *Ox* 01-08; P-in-c Bradfield and Stanford Dingley 04-08; P-in-c Woodley 08-09; V Woodley from 09. *6 Denmark Avenue, Woodley, Reading RG5 4RS* Tel 0118-969 6540 E-mail emarquez@tiscali.co.uk

MARQUIS-FAULKES, Edmund. b 62. Hatf Coll Dur BA85. Ridley Hall Cam 87 Coates Hall Edin 90. **d** 91 **p** 92. C Broughty Ferry *Bre* 91-93; P-in-c Dundee St Ninian 93-02; R Bieldside *Ab* 02-07. *Address temp unknown* E-mail marquisfaulkes@yahoo.com

MARR (*née* PARKER)**, Mrs Anne Elizabeth.** b 46. Hull Univ BSc67 CertEd68. NEOC 91. **d** 96. NSM Whorlton *Newc* 96-97; NSM Chapel House from 97; Chapl Newc City Health NHS Trust 96-01; Chapl Newc Mental Health Unit from 01. *26 The Chesters, Newcastle upon Tyne NE5 1AF* Tel 0191-267 4808

MARR, Derek Paul. b 33. Dur Univ TCert69. **d** 00 **p** 01. OLM Chapel House *Newc* from 00. *26 The Chesters, West Denton, Newcastle upon Tyne NE5 1AF* Tel 0191-267 4808

MARR, Canon Donald Radley. b 37. K Coll Lon 57. St Aid Birkenhead 61. **d** 64 **p** 65. C Macclesfield St Mich *Ches* 64-66; C Sale St Anne 66-67; V Marthall 67-72; C W Kirby St Bridget 72-76; R Waverton 76-83; R Nantwich 83-87; RD Nantwich 86-87; RD Malpas 87-91; V Bunbury 87-91; rtd 91; Dioc Rural Officer *Ches* 91-07; Hon Can Ches Cathl 91-92; Perm to Offic *Truro* from 94 and *Ches* from 07. *St Boniface, 5 Hockenhull Crescent, Tarvin, Chester CH3 8LJ, or The Parsonage, Tresco TR24 0QQ* Tel (01829) 741302 *or* (01720) 423176

MARR, Mrs Joan Mary. b 36. SRN58 SCM75. St Jo Coll Nottm

87. **d** 91. Hon Par Dn Moffat *Glas* 91-97; Hon Par Dn Dumfries 98-03; rtd 03; Perm to Offic *Glas* from 03. *Auburn Cottage, Templand, Lockerbie DG11 1TG* Tel (01387) 810734 Fax 810994 Mobile 07802-823658 E-mail joanmmarr@aol.com

MARR, Mrs Margaret Rose. b 36. JP81. St Mary's Coll Ban TCert56 Open Univ BA00. Ripon Coll Cuddesdon 02. **d** 02 **p** 03. NSM Tarvin *Ches* from 02; Perm to Offic *Truro* from 02. *St Boniface, 5 Hockenhull Crescent, Tarvin, Chester CH3 8LJ, or The Parsonage, Tresco TR24 0QQ* Tel (01829) 741302 *or* (01720) 423176 E-mail david@donaldmarr.wanadoo.co.uk

MARR, Peter. b 36. Reading Univ PhD78. Ox NSM Course 84. **d** 87 **p** 88. NSM Reading St Giles *Ox* 87-89; C Beverley Minster *York* 90-92; P-in-c Beckenham St Barn *Roch* 92-96; V 96-03; rtd 03. *31 Kingsley Road, Mutley, Plymouth PL4 6QP* Tel (01752) 228426 E-mail pbmarr@dircon.co.uk

MARRIAGE, Sophia Briony. b 71. Rob Coll Cam BA93 Edin Univ PhD98 Glas Univ MTh05. TISEC 03. **d** 05 **p** 06. C Edin St Martin from 05. *St Martin's Church, 232 Dalry Road, Edinburgh EH11 2GJ* Tel 0131-337 5493

MARRIOTT (*née* REID), Mrs Amanda Joy. b 63. Nottm Univ BTh92. Linc Th Coll 89. **d** 92 **p** 96. Par Dn Rothwell *Ripon* 92-94; C 94-95; C Manston 95-97; C Wetherby 97-01; P-in-c Water Eaton *Ox* 01-06; AD Milton Keynes 05-06; P-in-c Sherington w Chicheley, N Crawley, Astwood etc 06-09; R from 09. *The Rectory, 21 School Lane, Sherington, Newport Pagnell MK16 9NF* Tel (01908) 610521 E-mail ajmarriott@tiscali.co.uk

MARRIOTT, Frank Lewis. b 29. Lich Th Coll 57. **d** 60 **p** 61. C Earlsdon *Cov* 60-64; R Tysoe w Compton Winyates and Oxhill 64-70; P-in-c Cov St Marg 70-77; R Ufton 77-83; V Long Itchington 77-83; RD Southam 82-89; V Long Itchington and Marton 83-95; rtd 95; Perm to Offic *Heref* from 95. *12 Traherne Close, Ledbury HR8 2JF* Tel (01531) 634576

MARRIOTT, Stanley Richard. b 36. AKC60 Warwick Univ MA92. **d** 61 **p** 62. C Coleshill *Birm* 61-64; C Maxstoke 61-64; V Ansley *Cov* 64-78; Org Sec (E Midl) CECS 79-83; P-in-c Baxterley w Hurley and Wood End and Merevale etc *Birm* 83-84; R 84-87; R Newton Regis w Seckington and Shuttington 87-97; rtd 97; Perm to Offic *B & W* from 97. *Dunkery Pleck, Wootton Courtenay, Minehead TA24 8RH* Tel (01643) 841058

MARRISON, Geoffrey Edward. b 23. Lon Univ BA48 PhD67. Bps' Coll Cheshunt 49 Kirchliche Hochschule Berlin 50. **d** 51 **p** 52. C Wormley *St Alb* 51-52; SPG Miss Selangor Malaya 52-55; C St Andr Cathl Singapore 55-56; C Radlett *St Alb* 56-57; C St Botolph Aldgate w H Trin Minories *Lon* 57-58; V Crookes St Tim *Sheff* 58-61; SPG India 62-64; Perm to Offic *Cant* 64-69; Lic to Offic 69-82; Perm to Offic *Carl* 83-07; Tutor Carl Dioc Tr Course 83-07. *1 Ainsworth Street, Ulverston LA12 7EU* Tel (01229) 586874

MARROW, David Edward Armfield. b 42. Nottm Univ BA65 MA. Tyndale Hall Bris 65. **d** 67 **p** 68. C Clifton Ch Ch w Em *Bris* 67-70; BCMS Ethiopia 70-75; N Area Sec BCMS 75-77; C-in-c Ryde St Jas Prop Chpl *Portsm* 77-84; V Worthing St Geo *Chich* 84-07; rtd 07. *West View, 65 St Michael's Road, St Helens, Ryde PO33 1YJ* Tel (01983) 872729

MARSBURG, John Edward. b 53. Oak Hill Th Coll BA96. Coll of Resurr Mirfield 98. **d** 99 **p** 00. NSM Selby Abbey *York* 99-02; R Lenzie *Glas* 02-06; I Donacavey w Barr *Clogh* from 06. *The Rectory, 247 Tattyreagh Road, Fintona, Omagh BT78 2DA* Tel (028) 8284 1644 E-mail fintona@clogher.anglican.org

MARSDEN, Andrew Philip. b 63. Keble Coll Ox BA85 MA90 Birm Univ MA86. Wycliffe Hall Ox BA90. **d** 91 **p** 92. C Newport St Jo *Portsm* 91-94; C Cowplain *Portsm* 94-97; V Wokingham St Sebastian *Ox* from 97. *St Sebastian's Vicarage, Nine Mile Ride, Wokingham RG40 3AT* Tel (0118) 761050

MARSDEN, Andrew Robert. b 49. AKC71. St Aug Coll Cant 68. **d** 72 **p** 73. C New Addington *Cant* 72-75; C Prudhoe *Newc* 75-77; Asst Chapl HM Pris Wakef 77; Chapl HM Borstal Portland 77-82; Chapl HM YOI Onley 82-89; V Ulceby Gp *Linc* 89-98; Chapl Calderdale Healthcare NHS Trust 98-01; Chapl St Andr Hospice Grimsby 01-05; Community Chapl *Linc* 01-05; Chapl Hull and E Yorks Hosps NHS Trust from 05. *The Chaplain's Office, Castle Hill Hospital, Castle Road, Cottingham HU16 5JQ* Tel (01482) 461227 E-mail andrew.marsden@hey.nhs.uk

MARSDEN, Mrs Carole. b 44. Avery Hill Coll TCert65 Sheff Poly DipEd87. NOC 88. **d** 91 **p** 94. NSM Saddleworth *Man* 91-92; Par Dn 92-94; C 94-95; P-in-c Oldham St Paul 95-02; C Werneth 98-02; P-in-c Shap w Swindale and Bampton w Mardale *Carl* 02-08; P-in-c Orton and Tebay w Ravenstonedale etc 07-08; rtd 08. *Fairfield, Faraday Road, Kirby Stephen CA17 4QL* Tel (017683) 71279 Mobile 07866-006849 E-mail revmothershap@hotmail.com

MARSDEN, Mrs Diana Marion (Dodie). b 53. Deakin Univ Australia BEd88. STETS 00. **d** 03 **p** 04. NSM Hurstbourne Priors, Longparish etc *Win* from 03. *Little Brook House, Church Street, St Mary Bourne, Andover SP11 6BG* Tel (01264) 738211 E-mail dodie.marsden@ukgateway.net

MARSDEN, The Very Revd John Joseph. b 53. York Univ BA74 Nottm Univ MTh81 Kent Univ PhD88. St Jo Coll Nottm 77. **d** 80 **p** 81. C Leigh St Mary *Man* 80-83; Hon C Chatham

St Steph *Roch* 83-91; Ind Chapl 83-91; Lect Systematic Th CITC and TCD from 91; I Newbridge w Carnalway and Kilcullen *M & K* from 97; I Kildare w Kilmeague and Curragh from 06; Dean Kildare from 06. *The Rectory, Morristown, Newbridge, Co Kildare, Republic of Ireland* Tel (00353) (45) 438185 E-mail johnmarsden@eircom.net

MARSDEN, John Robert. b 22. Linc Coll Ox BA48 MA49. Ripon Hall Ox 57. **d** 58 **p** 59. C Dur St Cuth 58-61; Chapl Dur Sch 61-85; rtd 85. *Prebends, High Kilburn, York YO61 4AJ* Tel (01347) 868597

MARSDEN, Canon Joyce. b 47. Eliz Gaskell Coll Man TCert68. Trin Coll Bris 78. **dss** 83 **d** 87 **p** 94. Wavertree H Trin *Liv* 83-85; Much Woolton 85-97; Par Dn 87-94; C 94-97; TV Parr 97-05; C 05-07; Hon Can Liv Cathl 03-07; rtd 07. *4 Mackets Close, Liverpool L25 9NU* Tel 0151-428 2798 E-mail joyceamarsden@hotmail.com

MARSDEN, Michael John. b 59. St Mich Coll Llan 78. **d** 82 **p** 83. C Neath w Llantwit 82-85; Asst Chapl Univ Hosp of Wales Cardiff 85-89; V Graig *Llan* 89-93; P-in-c Cilfynydd 89-93; R Merthyr Tydfil St Dav 93-01; Chapl Gwent Healthcare NHS Trust from 01. *Nevill Hall Hospital, Brecon Road, Abergavenny NP7 7EG* Tel (01873) 732112 E-mail michael.marsden@gwent.wales.nhs.uk

MARSDEN, Robert. b 59. Ch Ch Ox BA81 PGCE82. Oak Hill Th Coll BA92. **d** 92 **p** 93. C Sevenoaks St Nic *Roch* 92-95; Chapl Fettes Coll Edin 95-99; C-in-c Buxton Trin Prop Chpl *Derby* from 99. *37 Temple Road, Buxton SK17 9BA* Tel (01298) 73656 E-mail robert@marsden8833.freeserve.co.uk

MARSDEN, Robert James. b 56. Ch Ch Coll Cant BEd79. Oak Hill Th Coll 90. **d** 94 **p** 95. C Margate H Trin *Cant* 94-98; P-in-c Brinton, Briningham, Hunworth, Stody etc *Nor* 98-08; P-in-c Gressenhall w Longham w Wendling etc from 08. *The Rectory, Bittering Street, Gressenhall, Dereham NR20 4EB* Tel (01362) 860211 E-mail robert@camelhome.co.uk

MARSDEN, Robert William. b 24. TCD BA49 MA52. CITC 50. **d** 50 **p** 51. C Dublin St Jas *D & G* 50-54; Asst Chapl Miss to Seamen 54-58; I Currin w Drum *Clogh* 58-64; I Clones w Killeevan 66-94; Prec Clogh Cathl 86-94; rtd 94. *30 Claremont Park, Sandymount, Dublin 4, Republic of Ireland* Tel (00353) (1) 668 0210

MARSDEN, The Ven Samuel Edward. b 44. Keble Coll Ox BA66 MA85. Linc Th Coll 66. **d** 68 **p** 69. C Liskeard w St Keyne *Truro* 68-72; R Gerrans w St Anthony in Roseland 72-77; Hong Kong 77-81; P-in-c Ingrave *Chelmsf* 81-82; P-in-c Gt Warley w Childerditch 81-82; R Gt Warley w Childerditch and Ingrave 82-89; R Gilgandra Australia 89-93; R Kelso 94-00; R Parkes from 00; Adn Bathurst from 05. *43 Currajong Street, PO Box 86, Parkes NSW 2870, Australia* Tel (0061) (2) 6862 2083 *or* 6862 1868 Fax 6862 1547 E-mail samuelmarsden@hotmail.com

MARSDEN-JONES, Watkin David. b 22. St D Coll Lamp BA48. **d** 49 **p** 50. C Flint *St As* 49-54; C Forest Row *Chich* 54-56; V Copthorne 56-70; RD E Grinstead 66-70; V Bosham 70-86; rtd 86; Perm to Offic *Chich* from 86. *10 Fairfield Road, Bosham, Chichester PO18 8JH* Tel (01243) 575053 E-mail dmj@wdmarjon.go-plus.net

MARSH, Anderson Jason. b 74. STETS 06. **d** 09. NSM Sheet *Portsm* from 09. *12 Rother Close, Petersfield GU31 4DN* Tel (01730) 268156 E-mail amarsh@rotherbank.co.uk

MARSH, Anthony David. b 29. Roch Th Coll 64. **d** 66 **p** 67. C Liskeard w St Keyne *Truro* 66-69; R Wrentham w Benacre and Covehithe *St E* 69-75; R Wrentham w Benacre, Covehithe, Frostenden etc 75-80; P-in-c Beyton and Hessett 80-86; C Felixstowe St Jo 86-88; rtd 88; Perm to Offic *St E* 88-03 and from 07; *B & W* 01-03. *24 Rowland House, Winston Close, Felixstowe IP11 2FA*

MARSH, Carol Ann. See HATHORNE, Mrs Carol Ann

MARSH, Colin Arthur. b 54. Edin Univ PhD02. St Jo Coll Nottm 79. **d** 82 **p** 83. C Kirkby *Liv* 82-86; TV St Luke in the City 86-91; P-in-c Chingola St Barn Zambia 91-95; Perm to Offic *Edin* 95-03; Tutor United Coll of Ascension Selly Oak from 03. *19 St Denis Road, Birmingham B29 4LN* E-mail c.marsh@bham.ac.uk

MARSH, David. b 32. St Jo Coll Dur BA54. Cranmer Hall Dur. **d** 57 **p** 58. C Bilston St Leon *Lich* 57-62; Lic to Offic Dio Maseno Kenya 63-66; Chapl Scargill Ho 67-69; Adn S Maseno 70-72; V Meole Brace *Lich* 72-77; V Westlands St Andr 77-86; V Trentham 86-96; P-in-c Alstonfield, Butterton, Warslow w Elkstone etc 96-99; rtd 99; Perm to Offic *Ches* from 99. Chapl Mid Cheshire Hosps Trust from 02. *31 Spring Gardens, Nantwich CW5 5SH* Tel (01270) 610079 E-mail dlmarsh@btinternet.com

MARSH, Donald. b 35. WMMTC. **d** 90 **p** 91. NSM Wednesbury St Bart *Lich* 90-03; NSM Wednesbury Deanery from 03. *Holly Rise, 19 Trouse Lane, Wednesbury WS10 7HR* Tel and fax 0121-556 0095

MARSH, Mrs Elaine Daphne. b 42. **d** 07 **p** 08. OLM Askerswell, Loders and Powerstock *Sarum* from 07; OLM Symondsbury from 07. *Powerstock Mill Farm, West Milton, Bridport DT6 3SL* Tel (01308) 485213 Fax 485160

MARSH, Francis John. b 47. York Univ BA69 DPhil76 ATCL65 ARCM66 ARCO71. Oak Hill Th Coll 72 Selw Coll Cam 73. **d** 75

p 76. C Cambridge St Matt *Ely* 75-78; C Pitsmoor w Wicker *Sheff* 79; C Pitsmoor w Ellesmere 79-81; C Crookes St Thos 81-85; V S Ossett *Wakef* 85-96; RD Dewsbury 93-96; Adn Blackb 96-01; Bp's Adv on Hosp Chapls 96-01. *137 Edge Lane, Dewsbury WF12 0HB* Tel (01924) 451233
E-mail vendocjon@aol.com

MARSH, Gordon Bloxham. b 25. Cant Sch of Min 82. **d** 85 **p** 86. NSM Loose *Cant* 85-86; NSM New Romney w Old Romney and Midley 86-90; NSM Asst to RD S Lympne 90-94; rtd 94; Perm to Offic *Cant* from 94. *1 Yew Tree House, Ashford Road, Tenterden TN30 7AD*

MARSH, Lawrence Allan. b 36. Sarum Th Coll 66. **d** 67 **p** 68. C Waterlooville *Portsm* 67-70; V Shedfield 70-76; R Fen Ditton *Ely* 76-01; P-in-c Horningsea 83-01; rtd 01; Perm to Offic *Ely* from 01. *The Old Bakery, 22 High Street, Bottisham, Cambridge CB25 9DA* Tel (01223) 811314 E-mail landjmarsh@aol.com

MARSH, Leonard Stuart Alexander. b 55. Hull Univ BA77 SOAS Lon MA00. Linc Th Coll 77. **d** 79 **p** 80. C Eltham St Barn *S'wark* 79-81; C Camberwell St Giles 81-83; Hon C Clifton St Paul *Bris* 83-86; Asst Chapl Bris Univ 83-86; Area Sec (Dio S'wark) USPG 86-91; Chapl Guildhall Sch of Music and Drama *Lon* 91-97; Chapl City Univ 91-98; NSM Clerkenwell H Redeemer and St Mark 94-95; P-in-c Finsbury St Clem w St Barn and St Matt 95-01; P-in-c Upper Norwood All SS *S'wark* 01-08; V from 08. *The Vicarage, 49 Chevening Road, London SE19 3TD* Tel (020) 8653 2820

MARSH, Mrs Margaret Ann. b 37. Nottm Univ BSc59 Ox Univ DipEd60 Lambeth STh87 Newc Univ MA93 Man Univ MPhil95. Carl Dioc Tr Course 86. **d** 87. Asst Chapl Garlands Hosp 87-92; Dn Carl Cathl 87-93; NSM Carl St Luke Morton 93-94; Hon Chapl Carl Hosps NHS Trust 94-00; rtd 00; Perm to Offic *Carl* 00-02 and *St Alb* from 02. *1 The Maltings, Leighton Buzzard LU7 4BS* Tel (01525) 384655

MARSH, Mrs Margaret Evaline. b 47. STETS 96. **d** 99 **p** 00. NSM Tattenham Corner and Burgh Heath *Guildf* 99-03; NSM Epsom St Martin 03-04; P-in-c Walton-on-the-Hill from 04. *The Rectory, Breech Lane, Tadworth KT20 7SD* Tel (01737) 812105 Fax 814333 E-mail margaret.marsh@talk21.com

MARSH, Miss Maxine Dorothy. b 49. Bretton Hall Coll TCert72. Westcott Ho Cam 90. **d** 92 **p** 94. C Kings Norton *Birm* 92-95; P-in-c Kingsbury 95-96; V 96-02; P-in-c Middleton 99; AD Polesworth 99-02; P-in-c Glastonbury w Meare *B & W* 02-07; rtd 07. *7 Millar House, Merchants Road, Clifton, Bristol BS8 4HA* Tel 0117-973 2229 E-mail maxatglastonbury@yahoo.co.uk

MARSH, Michael John. b 47. Reading Univ BA69 DipEd70 York Univ MA91 Leeds Univ BA07. Coll of Resurr Mirfield 05. **d** 07 **p** 08. NSM Castleford *Wakef* from 07. *9 Highland Close, Pontefract WF8 2JZ* Tel (01977) 700533 Mobile 07802-734900 E-mail mikej.marsh@talktalk.net

MARSH, Peter Charles Ernest. b 57. Southn Univ CertEd03 IEng87. WEMTC 04. **d** 06 **p** 07. NSM Wotton-under-Edge w Ozleworth, N Nibley etc *Glouc* from 06. *1 Pitt Court Villas, Pitt Court, North Nibley, Dursley GL11 6EB* Tel (01453) 547521 E-mail pete.marsh@cityofbristol.ac.uk

MARSH, Phillip Edward. b 73. Univ of Wales (Abth) BSc94 Ch Ch Coll Cant PGCE96. Wycliffe Hall Ox BTh02. **d** 02 **p** 03. C Hubberston *St D* 02-05; C Werrington *Pet* 05-09; P-in-c Wilford S'well from 09. *St Wilfrid's New Rectory, Main Road, Wilford, Nottingham NG11 7AJ* Tel 0115-981 7328 Mobile 07766-314957 E-mail revdphilmarsh@aol.com

MARSH, Ralph. b 42. Ches Coll of HE CertEd63 Birm Univ BPhil77 Liv Univ MA00 ACP65. St Deiniol's Hawarden 86. **d** 88 **p** 89. NSM Tranmere St Paul w St Luke *Ches* 88-90; C Guiseley w Esholt *Bradf* 90-92; V Broughton *St As* 92-94; Hon C W Derby St Jo *Liv* 94; C Ribbleton *Blackb* 94-97; NSM Man Victoria Park 98-00; NSM Croxteth *Liv* 00-07; rtd 07. *47 Rolleston Drive, Wallasey CH45 6XE*

MARSH, Richard St John Jeremy. b 60. Keble Coll Ox BA82 MA86 Dur Univ PhD91. Coll of Resurr Mirfield 83. **d** 85 **p** 86. C Grange St Andr *Ches* 85-87; Solway Fell and Chapl Univ Coll Dur 87-92; Abp's Asst Sec for Ecum Affairs *Cant* 92-95; Abp's Sec for Ecum Affairs 95-01; Hon C Westmr St Steph w St Jo *Lon* 94-96; Assoc P Westmr St Matt 96-01; Can Gib Cathl 95-01; Hon Prov Can Cant Cathl 98-01; Can Res Cant Cathl 01-06; Dir of Educn 01-05. *6 Barrack Square, Winchelsea TN36 4EG*

MARSH, Robert Christopher. b 53. Ex Univ BEd76. St Steph Ho Ox 86. **d** 88 **p** 89. C St Leonards Ch Ch and St Mary *Chich* 88-91; TV Crawley 91-00; V Maybridge 00-02. *67 Hythe Crescent, Seaford BN25 3TZ* E-mail rmarsh6204@aol.com

MARSH, Roger Philip. b 44. K Coll Lon BD72 AKC72 Sussex Univ MA95. St Aug Coll Cant 73. **d** 73 **p** 74. C Leagrave *St Alb* 73-76; Asst Youth Officer 76-77; Resources Officer 77-80; Chapl Marlborough Coll 80-86; Master Ardingly Coll Jun Sch Haywards Heath 86-95; Hd Master St Geo Sch Windsor 95-99; Chapl Lancing Coll 99-09; rtd 09. *107 College Road, Deal CT14 6BU* Tel (01304) 362851
E-mail frrogermarsh@hotmail.com

MARSH, Mrs Shelley Ann. b 54. SRN75 SCM76. St Jo Coll Nottm 84. **d** 89 **p** 94. Hon C Glas Gd Shep and Ascension 89-96;

P-in-c Johnstone and Renfrew 96-06; R Bishopbriggs from 06; Chapl Paisley Univ 98-00. *St James's Rectory, 9 Meadowburn, Bishopbriggs, Glasgow G64 3HA* Tel 0141-563 5154
E-mail revshelleymarsh@ntlworld.com

MARSH, Simon Robert. b 59. Sarum & Wells Th Coll 79. **d** 82 **p** 83. C Mottram in Longdendale w Woodhead *Ches* 82-85; Bp's Dom Chapl *Bradf* 85-87; V Ashton Hayes *Ches* 87-90; V Macclesfield St Paul 90-96; V Ringway 96-01; V Bollington St Jo 01-06; V Bramhall from 06. *The Vicarage, 66 St Michael's Avenue, Bramhall, Stockport SK7 2PG* Tel 0161-439 6532
E-mail frsimon@btinternet.com

MARSH, Susan Edith. b 42. Southn Univ BA63 CertEd64. SAOMC 01. **d** 01 **p** 02. NSM Bp's Hatfield *St Alb* 01-05; NSM Bp's Hatfield, Lemsford and N Mymms from 05. *141 Handside Lane, Welwyn Garden City AL8 6TA* Tel (01707) 329744
E-mail susanianmarsh@ntlworld.com

MARSHALL, Alexander John. Leeds Univ BSc. **d** 95 **p** 96. OLM Holbrook, Stutton, Freston, Woolverstone etc *St E* 95-05; Perm to Offic 05-06 and from 09. *Well Cottage, 1 The Street, Freston, Ipswich IP9 1AF* Tel (01473) 780738

MARSHALL, Alexander Robert. b 43. Glouc Sch of Min 84. **d** 87 **p** 88. NSM Newtown w Llanllwchaiarn w Aberhafesp *St As* 87-00; P-in-c Mochdre 00-06. *31 Bromley College, London Road, Bromley BR1 1PE* Tel (020) 8464 9727
E-mail marshall@rhayapow.kc3ltd.co.uk

MARSHALL, Mrs Alison Mary. b 54. Middx Hosp MB, BS79 MRCGP84. SAOMC 98. **d** 01 **p** 02. NSM Reading St Jo *Ox* from 01. *36 Bulmershe Road, Reading RG1 5RJ* Tel 0118-966 8794 Mobile 07740-944102 E-mail ali.marshall@ntlworld.com

MARSHALL, Ms Alison Rose Marie. b 60. Leic Univ BA83 Birkbeck Coll Lon MA86 UEA PGCE87. Ridley Hall Cam. **d** 95 **p** 96. C Whittlesey, Pondersbridge and Coates *Ely* 95-98; Dep Chapl HM Pris Nor 98-99; Chapl HM Pris Northallerton 99-03; TV Sunderland and Chapl Sunderland Univ 03-04; rtd 04. *9 Glamis Avenue, Sunderland SR4 8PB* Tel 0191-520 2580 Mobile 07905-173171

MARSHALL, Andrew Stephen. b 74. UNISA BTh00. Coll of Resurr Mirfield 02. **d** 99 **p** 00. C Port Elizabeth St Hugh S Africa 00-02; V Port Elizabeth St Jo 02; C Easthampstead *Ox* 03-06; Sen Chapl Southn Solent Univ from 06. *St Matthew's Vicarage, 12-14 Kings Park Road, Southampton SO15 2AT* Tel (023) 8033 2153

MARSHALL, Mrs Angela. b 48. Trin Coll Bris 74. **d** 88 **p** 96. Hon Par Dn Newcastle St Geo *Lich* 88-92; Lic to Offic *Eur* 92-94; Dn Versailles 94-96; Asst Chapl 96-04; Perm to Offic *St E* 04-07; Hon C Collier Row St Jas and Havering-atte-Bower *Chelmsf* from 07. *St James's Vicarage, 24 Lower Bedfords Road, Romford RM1 4DG* Tel (01708) 746614 E-mail revdave@dsl.pipex.com

MARSHALL, Basil Eustace Edwin. b 21. OBE69. Westcott Ho Cam 71. **d** 73 **p** 74. C Edenbridge *Roch* 73-78; P-in-c Matfield 78-85; P-in-c Lamberhurst 78-85; C Farnborough 85-86; rtd 86; Perm to Offic *Roch* from 86 and *Chich* from 01. *7 Boyne Park, Tunbridge Wells TN4 8EL* Tel (01892) 521664

MARSHALL, Canon Bryan John. b 40. Chich Th Coll 63. **d** 65 **p** 66. C Poulton-le-Fylde *Blackb* 65-68; C S Shore H Trin 68-70; V Wesham 70-74; PV Chich Cathl 74-82; V Boxgrove 82-91; P-in-c Tangmere 82-84; R 84-91; R Westbourne 91-95; V E Preston w Kingston 95-03; Can and Preb Chich Cathl from 94; rtd 03. *11 Priory Close, Boxgrove, Chichester PO18 0EA* Tel (01243) 536337

MARSHALL, Christine. See MARSHALL, Melinda Christine
MARSHALL, Mrs Christine Anne. b 40. Leeds Univ BSc64. **d** 95 **p** 96. OLM Holbrook, Stutton, Freston, Woolverstone etc *St E* 95-05; Perm to Offic 05-06 and from 09. *Well Cottage, 1 The Street, Freston, Ipswich IP9 1AF* Tel (01473) 780738
E-mail marshall@freston40.freeserve.co.uk

MARSHALL, Christopher John. b 56. BEd79. St Alb Minl Tr Scheme 83. **d** 86 **p** 87. C Biggleswade *St Alb* 86-89; Chapl Asst S Beds Area HA 89-91; Chapl St Helier Hosp Carshalton 91-93; Sen Chapl St Helier NHS Trust 93-98; Gen Office and Bereavement Manager Newham Healthcare NHS Trust from 98; Gen Services Manager from 99. *Newham General Hospital, Glen Road, London E13 8SL* Tel (020) 7363 8462

MARSHALL, Preb Christopher John Bickford. b 32. TD78. AKC56. **d** 57 **p** 58. C Leatherhead *Guildf* 57-60; C Crewkerne *B & W* 60-63; V Long Sutton 63-72; V Long Sutton w Long Load 72-76; V Wiveliscombe 76-93; RD Tone 78-87; Preb Wells Cathl 88-96; P-in-c Chipstable w Huish Champflower and Clatworthy 93; R Wiveliscombe w Chipstable, Huish Champflower etc 93-96; rtd 96; Perm to Offic *B & W* from 96. *Tap Cottage, High Street, Milverton, Taunton TA4 1LL* Tel (01823) 400419

MARSHALL, Christopher Robert. b 49. St Chad's Coll Dur BA71. Sarum & Wells Th Coll 72. **d** 74 **p** 75. C Sheff St Cecilia Parson Cross 74-77; C Walsall St Gabr Fulbrook *Lich* 77-78; C Upper Gornal 78-80; V Walsall St Andr 80-86; V Willenhall St Giles 86-00; V Tividale 00-08; V Tipton St Jo from 08. *St John's Vicarage, Upper Church Lane, Tipton DY4 9ND* Tel 0121-557 1793

MARSHALL, Craig Laurence. b 64. Southn Univ BEd87 Open Univ MA93. St Jo Coll Nottm MTh01. **d** 01 **p** 02. C Staplegrove w Norton Fitzwarren *B & W* 01-04; Chapl K Coll Taunton 04-06; R Aisholt, Enmore, Goathurst, Nether Stowey etc *B & W* from 06. *The Rectory, 25 St Mary Street, Nether Stowey, Bridgwater TA5 1LJ* Tel (01278) 734777
E-mail craig785@btinternet.com

MARSHALL, David. b 66. Liv Univ BA88. Ripon Coll Cuddesdon 89. **d** 92 **p** 93. C Dovecot *Liv* 92-96; P-in-c Westbrook St Jas 96-98; Dioc Communications Officer *Liv* 95-98; *Ches* 98-03; *Man* from 06; Lic to Offic *Ches* 98-06. *Diocesan Church House, 90 Deansgate, Manchester M3 2GJ* Tel 0161-828 1421 E-mail dmarshall@manchester.anglican.org

MARSHALL, David Charles. b 52. St Chad's Coll Dur BA73. Trin Coll Bris 74. **d** 76 **p** 77. C Meole Brace *Lich* 76-78; C W Teignmouth *Ex* 78-80; C Broadwater St Mary *Chich* 80-84; V Newcastle St Geo *Lich* 84-92; Chapl Versailles w Chevry *Eur* 92-04; Min Southgate LEP *St E* 04-07; P-in-c Collier Row St Jas and Havering-atte-Bower *Chelmsf* from 07. *St James's Vicarage, 24 Lower Bedfords Road, Romford RM1 4DG* Tel (01708) 746614 E-mail revdave@dsl.pipex.com

MARSHALL, Canon David Evelyn. b 63. New Coll Ox BA85 Birm Univ MA88 PhD96. Ridley Hall Cam 88. **d** 90 **p** 91. C Roundhay St Edm *Ripon* 90-92; Chapl Ex Coll Ox 95-98; Lect St Paul's United Th Coll Limuru Kenya 98-99; P-in-c Buckden and Hail Weston *Ely* 99-00; Abp's Dom Chapl *Cant* 00-05; Hon Can All SS Cathl Cairo from 02; Perm to Offic *S'wark* 05-09 and *Carl* from 09. *2A Eskin Street, Keswick CA12 4DH* Tel (01768) 772467 E-mail revdem63@yahoo.co.uk

MARSHALL, The Very Revd Geoffrey Osborne. b 48. St Jo Coll Dur BA71. Coll of Resurr Mirfield 71. **d** 73 **p** 74. C Waltham Cross *St Alb* 73-76; C Digswell 76-78; P-in-c Belper Ch Ch and Milford *Derby* 78-86; V Spondon 86-93; Chapl Derby High Sch 87-01; RD Derby N 90-95; Can Res Derby Cathl 93-02; Dioc Dir of Ords 95-00; TR Wrexham *St As* 02-08; AD Wrexham 02-08; Dean Brecon *S & B* from 08; V Brecon St Mary w Llanddew from 08. *The Deanery, Cathedral Close, Brecon LD3 9DP* Tel (01874) 623344 Fax 623716
E-mail admin@breconcathedral.org.uk

MARSHALL, Mrs Gillian Kathryn. b 54. Glouc Sch of Min 84. **d** 87 **p** 97. NSM Newtown w Llanllwchaiarn w Aberhafesp *St As* 87-98; P-in-c Betws Cedewain and Tregynon and Llanwyddelan 98-02; V 02-06. *31 Bromley College, London Road, Bromley BR1 1PE* Tel (020) 8464 9727

MARSHALL, Graham George. b 38. Dur Univ BA60 St Chad's Coll Dur. **d** 65 **p** 66. C Ashton-on-Ribble St Mich *Blackb* 65-67; C Lancaster St Mary 67-71; R Church Eaton *Lich* 71-75; Prec Man Cathl 75-78; R Reddish 78-85; V Chadderton St Luke 87-02; rtd 02; Perm to Offic *Man* from 02. *7 The Woods, Rochdale OL11 3NT* Tel (01706) 642139
E-mail ggm@manutd.com

MARSHALL (née CHADWICK), Mrs Helen Jane. b 63. UEA BA84. St Jo Coll Nottm MTh91. **d** 91 **p** 94. Par Dn Easton H Trin w St Gabr and St Lawr and St Jude *Bris* 91-94; C 94-95; Perm to Offic *Ox* 95-98; Lect St Paul's Th Coll Limuru Kenya 98-99; Perm to Offic *Ely* 99-00; Chapl K Coll Lon 01-05; P-in-c Addiscombe St Mildred *S'wark* 05-06; V 06-09; Perm to Offic *Carl* from 09. *2A Eskin Street, Keswick CA12 4DH* Tel (01768) 772467 E-mail helenmarshall2592@yahoo.co.uk

MARSHALL, Canon Hugh Phillips. b 34. SS Coll Cam BA57 MA61. Linc Th Coll 57. **d** 59 **p** 60. C Westmr St Steph w St Jo *Lon* 59-65; V Tupsley *Heref* 65-74; V Holmwood *S'wark* 74-78; TR 78-87; RD Merton 79-86; V Mitcham SS Pet and Paul 87-90; Hon Can S'wark Cathl 89-90; Perm to Offic 90-96; Chief Sec ABM 90-96; V Wendover *Ox* 96-01; P-in-c Halton 96-01; rtd 01; Hon Can Bulawayo from 96; Perm to Offic *Ox* from 01. *7 The Daedings, Deddington, Banbury OX15 0RT* Tel (01869) 337761 E-mail hughm34@btinternet.com

MARSHALL, James Hudson. b 48. Sheff Univ CertEd70 Open Univ BA74 Cumbria Univ BA08. LCTP 05. **d** 08 **p** 09. NSM Lamplugh w Ennerdale *Carl* from 08. *Iona, Sandwith, Whitehaven CA28 9UG* E-mail j.h.marshall@talk21.com

MARSHALL, Mrs Jean. b 36. SW Minl Tr Course 84. **d** 87 **p** 94. NSM Stratton *Truro* 87-89; NSM Bodmin w Lanhydrock and Lanivet 89-94; P-in-c Lawhitton and S Petherwin w Trewen 94-98; rtd 98; Hon C Bodmin w Lanhydrock and Lanivet *Truro* 00-06; Perm to Offic from 06. *10 Springwell View, Love Lane, Bodmin PL31 2QP* Tel (01208) 79891

MARSHALL, John. b 37. Kelham Th Coll 53. **d** 62 **p** 63. C Winshill *Derby* 62-64; C Chaddesden St Phil 64-65; Chapl HM Borstal Morton Hall 65-75, V Swinderby *Linc* 66-77; R Church Aston *Lich* 77-84; V Auckland St Andr and St Anne *Dur* 84-02; P-in-c Hunwick 88-90; Chapl Bishop Auckland Gen Hosp 84-94; Chapl Bishop Auckland Hospitals NHS Trust 94-98; Chapl S Durham Healthcare NHS Trust 98-00; rtd 02; Perm to Offic *Derby* 02-06; Hon C S Darley, Elton and Winster from 06. *Croft House, West Bank, Winster, Matlock DE4 2DQ* Tel (01629) 650310

MARSHALL, John. b 50. St Luke's Coll Ex CertEd74 W Lon Inst of HE DEHC79. S'wark Ord Course 88. **d** 91 **p** 92. Hon C Brixton Hill St Sav *S'wark* 91-95; Hon C Clapham St Jas from 95. *57A Kingscourt Road, London SW16 1JA* Tel (020) 8769 3665

MARSHALL, John Douglas. b 23. Univ of Wales (Cardiff) BA43. St Alb Minl Tr Scheme 76. **d** 79 **p** 80. Hon C Radlett *St Alb* 79-86; Lic to Offic *Llan* from 86. *Meiros, 3 River Walk, Cowbridge CF71 7DW* Tel (01446) 773930

MARSHALL, John Linton. b 42. Worc Coll Ox BA64 MA68 Bris Univ MLitt75. Wells Th Coll 66. **d** 68 **p** 69. C Bris St Mary Redcliffe w Temple etc 68-71; Tutor Sarum & Wells Th Coll 71-73; Perm to Offic *Pet* 74-77; Lic to Offic *S'well* 77-81; V Choral S'well Minster 79-81; R Ordsall 81-88; P-in-c Grove 84-88; RD Retford 84-88; V Northowram *Wakef* 88-99; P-in-c Glouc St Mark and St Mary de Crypt w St Jo etc 99-00; R Glouc St Mary de Lode and St Mary de Crypt etc 00-09; rtd 09. *166 Calton Road, Gloucester GL1 5ER*
E-mail cyprianus@btopenworld.com

MARSHALL, Mrs Julie. b 62. **d** 08 **p** 09. OLM Bucknall *Lich* from 08. *27 Meadow Avenue, Wetley Rocks, Stoke-on-Trent ST9 0BD* Tel (01782) 550993
E-mail julie.marshall@stokecoll.ac.uk

MARSHALL, Ms Karen Lesley. b 59. Coll of Ripon & York St Jo BA82 Leeds Metrop Univ BSc96 Huddersfield Univ MA05. NEOC 04. **d** 07 **p** 08. C Horsforth *Ripon* from 07. *Kirkstall Vicarage, Vicarage View, Leeds LS5 3HF*
E-mail karenlmarshall@btinternet.com

MARSHALL, Kirstin Heather. See FREEMAN, Kirstin Heather

MARSHALL, Canon Lionel Alan. b 41. TEng. St Deiniol's Hawarden 84 Qu Coll Birm 86. **d** 87 **p** 88. C Llandudno *Ban* 87-90; V Rhayader and Nantmel *S & B* 90-01; P-in-c Llanbister w Llanbadarn Fynydd w Llananno etc 01-06; AD Maelienydd 98-06; Hon Can Brecon Cathl 00-04; Can Res 04-06; rtd 06. *46 Gordon Road, Blackwood NP12 1DW* Tel (01495) 223371

MARSHALL, Mrs Margaret Elizabeth. b 60. New Hall Cam BA81 MA84. EAMTC 01. **d** 04 **p** 05. C St Neots *Ely* 04-09; P-in-c Riversmeet *St Alb* from 09. *The Vicarage, 57 High Street, Great Barford, Bedford MK44 3JJ* Tel (01234) 870363
E-mail riversmeetvicar@ntlworld.com

MARSHALL, Canon Maurice Peter. b 23. Oak Hill Th Coll 59. **d** 61 **p** 62. C Haydock St Mark *Liv* 61-64; V New Ferry *Ches* 64-79; V Hartford 79-89; Hon Can Ches Cathl 87-89; rtd 89; Perm to Offic from 89. *27 East Lane, Sandiway, Northwich CW8 2QQ* Tel (01606) 888591

MARSHALL, Melinda Christine. b 54. Cov Coll of Educn CertEd76. Ridley Hall Cam. **d** 01 **p** 02. C Exning St Martin w Landwade *St E* 01-05; TV Heatons *Man* from 05. *6 Glenfield Road, Stockport SK4 2QP* Tel 0161-432 1227

MARSHALL, Michael David. b 51. BSc. Trin Coll Bris. **d** 84 **p** 85. C Kennington St Mark *S'wark* 84-88; V Streatham Park St Alb 88-96; RD Tooting 93-96; V Blackheath St Jo 96-06; RD Charlton 01-06; Chapl Bishop's Stortford Coll from 06. *96B Hadham Road, Bishop's Stortford CM23 2QF* Tel (01279) 838673 E-mail mikemarshall51@hotmail.com
or mikemarshall@bsc.biblio.net

✠**MARSHALL, The Rt Revd Michael Eric.** b 36. Ch Coll Cam BA58 MA60. Cuddesdon Coll 58. **d** 60 **p** 61 **c** 75. C Birm St Pet 60 62; Tutor Ely Th Coll 62-64; Min Can Ely Cathl 62-64; Chapl Lon Univ 64-69; V St Marylebone All SS 69-75; Suff Bp Woolwich *S'wark* 75-84; Episc Dir Angl Inst Missouri 84-92; Abps' Adv Springboard for Decade of Evang 92-97; Hon Asst Bp Lon 84-07; Hon Asst Bp Chich from 92; Can and Preb Chich Cathl 90-99; Bp in Res Upper Chelsea H Trin *Lon* 97-02; R 02-07; rtd 07. *53 Oakley Gardens, London SW3 5QQ* Tel (020) 7351 0928 Mobile 07710-215131

MARSHALL, Mrs Michèle Jane. b 60. SEN82. NTMTC 05. **d** 08 **p** 09. C Orsett and Bulphan and Horndon on the Hill *Chelmsf* from 08. *Highside, Gordon Road, Horndon-on-the-Hill, Stanford-le-Hope SS17 8NH* Tel (01375) 361599
E-mail mjmarshall@fastmail.co.uk

MARSHALL, Pauline Nikola. b 49. WMMTC 84. **d** 87 **p** 94. C Walsgrave on Sowe *Cov* 87-91; TD Grantham *Linc* 91-94; TV 94-96; Ind Chapl 91-96; Perm to Offic 01-02; C Boston 02-05; TV 05-06; Mental Health Chapl Lincs Partnership NHS Trust 05-06; Lead Chapl Mental Health Beds and Luton Mental Health and Soc Care NHS Trust from 06. *39 Moat Lane, Luton LU3 1UU* Tel (01582) 517824 Mobile 07792-981768
E-mail nikola.marshall@ntlworld.com

MARSHALL, Canon Peter Arthur. b 31. AKC58. **d** 59 **p** 60. C Hutton *Chelmsf* 59-61; C Rickmansworth *St Alb* 61-66; Chapl Orchard View and Kingsmead Court Hosps 66-94; R Lexden *Chelmsf* 66-94; RD Colchester 88-93; Hon Can Chelmsf Cathl 90-94; rtd 94; Perm to Offic *Win* from 94. *21 Manor Close, Wickham, Fareham PO17 5BZ* Tel (01329) 832988

MARSHALL, Peter James. b 48. Qu Coll Birm 78. **d** 80 **p** 81. C Ormskirk *Liv* 80-83; V Dallam from 83. *St Mark's Vicarage, Longshaw Street, Warrington WA5 0DY* Tel (01925) 631193
E-mail pjorm.marshall@btinternet.com

MARSHALL, The Very Revd Peter Jerome. b 40. Westcott Ho Cam 61. **d** 63 **p** 64. C E Ham St Mary *Chelmsf* 63-66; C Woodford St Mary 66-71; C-in-c S Woodford 66-71; V Walthamstow St Pet 71-81; Can Res Chelmsf Cathl 81-85; Dep Dir of Tr 81-84; Can Res Ripon Cathl and Dioc Dir of Tr *Ripon* 85-97; Dean Worc 97-06; rtd 06. *433 Gordon Avenue, Peterborough ON K9J 6G6, Canada* Tel (001) (705) 876 3381 E-mail pmarshall10@cogeco.ca

MARSHALL, Peter John Charles. b 35. Bris Univ BA60. Ridley Hall Cam 60. **d** 62 **p** 63. C Lindfield *Chich* 62-65; Travelling Sec Scripture Union 65-83; Hon C Nottingham St Nic *S'well* 65-67; Hon C Cheadle Hulme St Andr *Ches* 67-83; V Ilkley All SS *Bradf* 83-98; RD Otley 92-97; rtd 98; Perm to Offic *Ches* 00-03 and *St As* from 03. *Creuddyn Barn, Glanwydden, Llandudno Junction LL31 9JL* Tel (01492) 547352 E-mail revmarsh35@yahoo.co.uk

MARSHALL, Richard Albert. b 38. Open Univ BA73 Westmr Coll Ox MTh97 ACIS82. **d** 06 **p** 06. OLM Ray Valley *Ox* from 06. *21 Ancil Avenue, Launton, Bicester OX26 5DL* Tel (01869) 243546 E-mail marshra@aol.com

MARSHALL, Richard Arthur Howard. b 66. Regent's Park Coll Ox BA88 MA92 SS Coll Cam PGCE89. Wycliffe Hall Ox BTh99. **d** 98 **p** 99. C Broughton *Man* 98-02; Asst Chapl Sedbergh Sch 02-03; Sub Chapl HM Pris Man 02-04; Perm to Offic *Man* from 02; V Blackb Redeemer from 04. *2 Kendall Close, Blackburn BB2 4FB* Tel (01254) 51206

MARSHALL, Robert David. b 52. TCD BA75 MA00 Solicitor 77. CITC 99. **d** 02 **p** 03. NSM Stillorgan w Blackrock *D & G* from 02. *The Tontine, 84 The Rise, Mount Merrion, Co Dublin, Republic of Ireland* Tel (00353) (1) 288 6170 or 649 2137 Fax 649 2649 E-mail curate@stillorgan.dublin.anglican.org

MARSHALL, Robert Paul. b 60. Sheff Univ BA81 St Jo Coll Dur MA85. Cranmer Hall Dur 81. **d** 83 **p** 84. C Kirkstall *Ripon* 83-85; C Otley *Bradf* 85-87; Dioc Communications Officer 87-91; P-in-c Embsay w Eastby 87-91; Dioc Communications Officer *Lon* 91-95; P-in-c S Kensington St Aug 95-00; Media Adv to Abp *York* 95-05; Communications Adv *Sheff* from 04; Public Relns Adv Fresh Expressions from 05; Hd of Marketing St Mary's Univ Coll Twickenham 05-07; Hon C Kensington St Mary Abbots w Ch Ch and St Phil from 07. *4 Kensington Church Court, London W8 4SP* Tel 07917-272833 (mobile) E-mail robmarshalluk@gmail.com

MARSHALL, Canon Rodney Henry. b 46. Bernard Gilpin Soc Dur 71 St Steph Ho Ox 72. **d** 75 **p** 76. C Gorton Our Lady and St Thos *Man* 75-78; C Bedford Leigh 78-82; V Goldthorpe w Hickleton *Sheff* 82-90; Dioc Dir of In-Service Tr 88-90; NSM Hemsworth *Wakef* 96-97; P-in-c Athersley 97-98; V from 98; P-in-c Monk Bretton 04-07; Hon Can Wakef Cathl from 07. *St Helen's Vicarage, 27 Laithes Lane, Barnsley S71 3AF* Tel (01226) 245361

MARSHALL, Simon. b 54. Kingston Poly BSc77 Leeds Univ PGCE78 MA(Ed)79. Qu Coll Birm 91. **d** 93 **p** 94. C Gt Clacton *Chelmsf* 93-97; TV Chigwell and Chigwell Row 97-02; C Woodford Wells from 02. *107 Monkhams Avenue, Woodford Green IG8 0ER* Tel (020) 8220 5143 E-mail simon.marshall17@ntlworld.com

MARSHALL, Simon Hardy. b 69. Bp Grosseteste Coll BA92. St Jo Coll Nottm 00. **d** 02 **p** 03. C Bartley Green *Birm* 02-05; TV Solihull from 05. *Oak Cottage, Bryanston Road, Solihull B91 1BS* Tel 0121-704 4730

MARSHALL, Mrs Sonia Margaret Cecilia. b 49. Westf Coll Lon BA71 Nottm Univ MA03. EMMTC 01. **d** 03 **p** 04. NSM Deeping St James *Linc* from 03. *135C Eastgate, Deeping St James, Peterborough PE6 8RB* Tel (01778) 346420 E-mail curate@dsj.org.uk

MARSHALL, Sonya Tolley. b 62. Hull Univ BA84 Lon Inst of Educn PGCE85. NOC 04. **d** 06 **p** 07. NSM Southport Ch Ch *Liv* from 06. *112 Linaker Street, Southport PR8 5DG* Tel 07834-170070 (mobile)

MARSHALL, Susan. *See* PANTER MARSHALL, Canon Susan Lesley

MARSHALL, Timothy John. b 53. GRSM74. Oak Hill Th Coll BA79. **d** 79 **p** 80. C Muswell Hill St Jas w St Matt *Lon* 79-85; V Hammersmith St Simon 85-92; V Bovingdon *St Alb* from 92; RD Rickmansworth 01-06. *The Vicarage, Vicarage Lane, Bovingdon, Hemel Hempstead HP3 0LP* Tel and fax (01442) 833298 E-mail vicartim@btopenworld.com

MARSHALL, William John. b 35. TCD BA57 BD61 PhD75. TCD Div Sch 59. **d** 59 **p** 60. C Ballyholme *D & D* 59-61; India 62-72; Asst Dean of Residence TCD 73-76; I Rathmichael *D & G* 76-92; Can Ch Ch Cathl Dublin 90-02; Chan 91-02; Vice-Prin CITC 92-02; rtd 02. *115 The Elms, Abberley, Killiney, Co Dublin, Republic of Ireland* Tel (00353) (1) 239 0832

MARSHALL, William Michael. b 30. Pemb Coll Ox BA53 MA57 DipEd65 Bris Univ MLitt72 PhD79. Wells Th Coll 63 Sarum & Wells Th Coll 79. **d** 80 **p** 81. Asst Chapl Millfield Sch Somerset 80-96; Hon C Glastonbury St Jo w Godney *B & W* 80-84; Hon C Glastonbury w Meare, W Pennard and Godney

84-96; rtd 96; Perm to Offic *Portsm* and *Win* 96-01 and *Ely* 01-08. *7 The Paddock, Ely CB6 1TP* Tel and fax (01353) 612287 E-mail william.m@ukonline.co.uk

MARSHMAN, Mrs Elizabeth Maryan. b 53. Coll of Ripon & York St Jo BEd75. NEOC 03. **d** 06 **p** 07. C Clifton *York* from 06. *5 Manor Park Close, York YO30 5UZ* Tel 07962-304540 (mobile) E-mail e.m.marshman@talktalk.net

MARSTON, David Howarth. b 48. St Jo Coll Dur BA69. Edin Th Coll 69. **d** 71 **p** 72. C Kendal H Trin *Carl* 71-75; Perm to Offic *Glas* 75-78; NSM Barrow St Matt *Carl* 79-86; Perm to Offic *York* 86-91; *Liv* 91-93 and 99-00; NSM Southport All SS and All So *Liv* 93-99; NSM Southport St Luke from 00. *33 Sandringham Road, Ainsdale, Southport PR8 2NY* Tel (01704) 578303

MARSTON, Neville Charles. b 37. Univ of Wales (Cardiff) BA65 Waterloo Univ (Canada) MA67. Ox Cen for Miss Studies 95. **d** 97 **p** 99. Dioc Dir Tr Seychelles 92-00; C Coven *Lich* 00-02; rtd 02. *8 Appleton Gardens, South Cave, Brough HU15 2EN* Tel (01430) 471093 Mobile 07866-935844 E-mail nevillemarston@aol.com

MARSTON, William Thornton. b 59. Worc Coll Ox BA81 MA85 Cam Univ CertEd83. St Steph Ho Ox BA87. **d** 88 **p** 89. C Beckenham St Geo *Roch* 88-92; TV Ifield *Chich* 92-97; C-in-c Middleton-on-Sea CD 97-99; V Middleton from 99. *The Vicarage, 106 Elmer Road, Middleton-on-Sea, Bognor Regis PO22 6LJ* Tel (01243) 586348 E-mail w.marston@btinternet.com

MART, Terence Eugene. b 47. CertEd76 BA82. St Jo Coll Nottm LTh87. **d** 87 **p** 88. C Prestatyn *St As* 87-91; Chapl Theatr Clwyd Mold 87-91; R Llangystennin 91-01; RD Llanrwst 96-00; V Llanfair DC, Derwen, Llanelidan and Efenechtyd 01-07. *Woodville, Uppergate Street, Conwy LL32 8RF*

MARTIN, Mrs Adele Joan. b 51. BSc74. Cranmer Hall Dur 05. **d** 07 **p** 08. C Seacroft *Ripon* from 07. *Ascension Vicarage, 117 Foundry Mill Street, Leeds LS14 6EJ* Tel 0113-260 1231

MARTIN, Alexander Lewendon. b 26. Em Coll Cam BA47 MA51. Ridley Hall Cam 56. **d** 57 **p** 58. C Ashtead *Guildf* 57-59; Asst Chapl Tonbridge Sch 59-64; Chapl Felsted Sch 64-74; Chapl Sedbergh Sch 74-84; R Askerswell, Loders and Powerstock *Sarum* 84-89; RD Lyme Bay 86-89; rtd 89; Perm to Offic *Ex* from 89. *Thirtover, 7 Alexandra Way, Crediton EX17 2EA* Tel (01363) 776206 E-mail alexmartin777@hotmail.com

MARTIN, Angela Frances. b 66. SEITE 05. **d** 08 **p** 09. C Henfield w Shermanbury and Woodmancote *Chich* from 08. *Glebe House, 41 Furner Mead, Henfield BN5 9JA* Tel (01273) 494509 E-mail ange.martin@virgin.net

MARTIN, Angela Lee. EMMTC 00. **d** 03 **p** 04. NSM Derby St Barn 03-08; P-in-c Hatton from 08. *The Joiners' Arms, 60 Church Road, Quarndon, Derby DE22 5JA* Tel (01332) 552876 Mobile 07967-180531 E-mail hattonlee1968@yahoo.co.uk

MARTIN, Brother. *See* COOMBE, John Morrell

MARTIN, Bryan Robert. b 71. TCD BTh01. CITC 98. **d** 01 **p** 02. C Magherafelt w Dollingstown *D & D* 01-04; C Knockbreda 04-07; I Dromore *Clogh* from 07. *The Rectory, 19 Galbally Road, Dromore, Omagh BT78 3EE* Tel and fax (028) 8289 8246 E-mail brymrtn@aol.com

MARTIN, Canon Cameron Anthony Brian. b 56. Cape Town Univ BA93 Cant Univ (NZ) MBA02 MA05. St Bede's Coll Umtata 82. **d** 84 **p** 85. C Nigel Ch the K S Africa 84-86; R Ennerdale St Nic 87-89; R Eldorado Park Transfiguration 89-90; P-in-c Kenwyn 90-95; R Woodlands 95-02; Adn Mitchell's Plain 98-02; Dioc Admin Kimberley and Kuruman 02-05; Can Kimberley and Kuruman from 03; P-in-c Brumby *Linc* 05-07; TR from 07. *St Hugh's Rectory, 114 Ashby Road, Scunthorpe DN16 2AG* Tel (01724) 343652 E-mail cameron.martin@ntlworld.com

MARTIN, Christopher Edward. b 70. Bris Poly BA92 ACA97. Trin Coll Bris 07. **d** 09. C Newton Flotman, Swainsthorpe, Tasburgh, *etc* Nor from 09. *The New Rectory, Church Hill, Tasburgh, Norwich NR15 1NB* E-mail chris.martin2@blueyonder.co.uk

MARTIN, Christopher John. b 45. Ball Coll Ox BA67 MA87. Wycliffe Hall Ox 86. **d** 88 **p** 89. C Edin St Thos 88-90; R Duns 90-00; Chapl Lyon *Eur* from 00. *38 Chemin de Taffignon, 69110 Ste-Foy-lès-Lyon, France* Tel (0033) (4) 78 59 67 06 E-mail lyonchurch@aol.com

MARTIN, Prof David Alfred. b 29. LSE BSc PhD. Westcott Ho Cam. **d** 83 **p** 84. Hon C Guildf Cathl 83-99; Perm to Offic from 99. *174 St John's Road, Woking GU21 7PQ* Tel (01483) 762134

MARTIN, David Howard. b 47. Worc Coll Ox BEd79. AKC70 St Aug Coll Cant 70. **d** 71 **p** 72. C Sedgley All SS *Lich* 71-75; Dioc Youth Chapl *Worc* 75-81; P-in-c Worc St Andr and All SS w St Helen 75-81; R Newland, Guarlford and Madresfield 81-91; R Alvechurch from 91. *The Rectory, Alvechurch, Birmingham B48 7SB* Tel 0121-445 1087 E-mail davidmartin@lynkserve.net

MARTIN, Donald Philip (Ralph). b 30. Trin Coll Toronto MA55 STB55. **d** 54 **p** 55. Canada 54-57; C Toronto St Simon 55-57; Tutor Kelham Th Coll 57-73; SSM from 60; P-in-c Willen *Ox* 73-81; Japan 81-82; Ghana 83-89; Dir Cleveland Lay Tr Course

89-91; C Middlesbrough All SS *York* 89-91; Kuwait 92-93; Italy 93-94; Canada 94-95; Tutor SAOMC *Ox* 95-96; Chapl OHP 96; Lesotho 97-00; rtd 98. *All Saints Convent, St Mary's Road, Oxford OX4 1RU* Tel (01865) 727276
E-mail ralphssm@yahoo.co.uk

MARTIN, Edward Eldred William. b 37. Cranfield Inst of Tech MSc84 Herts Univ MA88. S'wark Ord Course 65. **d** 68 **p** 69. C Greenwich St Alfege w St Pet *S'wark* 68-71; C Kidbrooke St Jas 71-75; V Peckham St Jo 75-78; P-in-c Peckham St Andr w All SS 76-78; V Peckham St Jo w St Andr 78-81; Hon Chapl S'wark Cathl 81-02; Chapl Guy's Hosp Lon 81-88; rtd 02; Perm to Offic *S'wark* 02-03 and from 07; Hon C Lee St Marg 03-07. *17 Honor Oak Rise, London SE23 3QY* Tel (020) 8699 2303 Mobile 07956-204869 E-mail emartin@fsmail.net

MARTIN, Edward James Russell. b 76. Hull Univ BA98 Leeds Univ BA02 MA06. Coll of Resurr Mirfield 00. **d** 03 **p** 04. C Carrington *S'well* 03-06; P-in-c Chapel St Leonards w Hogsthorpe *Linc* 06-09; R Scartho from 09. *St Giles's Rectory, 44 Waltham Road, Grimsby DN33 2LX* Tel (01472) 239758 Mobile 07736-711360 E-mail fatheredward@ntlworld.com

MARTIN, Mrs Eileen. b 43. City of Portsm Coll of Educn TCert65. **d** 03. OLM Queen Thorne *Sarum* 03-08. *School House, Trent, Sherborne DT9 4SW* Tel (01935) 851078
E-mail rev_eileenm@yahoo.co.uk

MARTIN, Miss Eileen Susan Kirkland. b 45. LCST66. Cranmer Hall Dur 77. **dss** 83 **d** 86. Kilmarnock *Glas* 84-86; Par Dn Heanor *Derby* 87-92; Perm to Offic 92-95. *1 Malin Court, Hardings Close, Hemel Hempstead HP3 9AQ* Tel (01442) 216768

MARTIN, Mrs Elizabeth Anne. b 60. Sheff Univ BMedSci82. ERMC 05. **d** 09. C Gaywood *Nor* from 09. *28 Jermyn Road, King's Lynn PE30 4AE*

MARTIN, George Cobain. b 34. TCD BA57 MA65. **d** 57 **p** 58. C Bangor St Comgall *D & D* 57-64; I Kircubbin 64-74; R Ashby by Partney *Linc* 75-78; R Partney w Dalby 75-78; V Skendleby 75-78; P-in-c Candlesby w Scremby 77-78; R Partney 78-95; rtd 95; Perm to Offic *Linc* 95-98. *Hapstead Cottage, 26 Mill Leat, Baltonsborough, Glastonbury BA6 8HX* Tel (01458) 850590

MARTIN, Glenn. b 52. Qu Coll Birm 84. **d** 86 **p** 87. C Chatham St Wm *Roch* 86-89; Chapl Pastures Hosp Derby 89-94; Chapl Kingsway Hosp Derby 89-94; Sen Chapl S Derbys Mental Health NHS Trust 94-97; Sen Chapl Community Health Sheff NHS Trust 97-01; Professional Development Officer for Chapl and Spiritual Healthcare 01-07; NSM Gilmorton, Peatling Parva, Kimcote etc *Leic* 04-07; NSM Guilsborough w Hollowell and Cold Ashby *Pet* 07-08; NSM Cottesbrooke w Gt Creaton and Thornby 07-08; NSM Spratton 07-08; NSM Ravensthorpe 07-08; P-in-c Sutton Bonington w Normanton-on-Soar *S'well* from 08. *The Rectory, 19A Park Lane, Sutton Bonington, Loughborough LE12 5NQ* Tel (01509) 670757
E-mail glenn.martinrev@btinternet.com

MARTIN, Graham Rowland. b 39. Liv Univ CertEd58 Lon Univ BD70 Bris Univ BEd73 FRSA LCP. Wells Th Coll 71. **d** 71 **p** 72. Hon C Glouc St Cath 71-76; P-in-c Brookthorpe w Whaddon 76-78; Perm to Offic 78-80; Hon C Hucclecote 80-82; Hon C Tuffley 82-89; NSM Hardwicke, Quedgeley and Elmore w Longney 88-89; V Kemble, Poole Keynes, Somerford Keynes etc 89-96; P-in-c Bibury w Winson and Barnsley 96-04; Dioc Ecum Officer 96-04; rtd 04; Perm to Offic *Glouc* from 04. *Wharf Cottage, Wharf Lane, Lechlade GL7 3AU* Tel (01367) 252825

MARTIN, Henry Rowland Felix. b 67. Leeds Univ BA89 SS Coll Cam BA95. Ridley Hall Cam 93. **d** 96 **p** 97. C Becontree St Mary *Chelmsf* 96-00; C Broughton *Man* 00-02; TR from 02. *St James's Vicarage, 396 Great Cheetham Street East, Salford M7 4UH* Tel 0161-792 1208 E-mail h3nrymartin@googlemail.com

MARTIN, James Alwyn. b 47. St Paul's Coll Grahamstown 76. **d** 78 **p** 79. Zimbabwe 78-04; C Highlands St Mary 78-80; P-in-c Lowveld 80-84; R Masvingo St Mich 84-87; Adn Victoria 82-87; R Borrowdale Ch Ch 87-98; Adn Harare S 96-98; Dean Bulawayo 98-04; V Aldershot St Mich *Guildf* from 05. *St Michael's Vicarage, 120 Church Lane East, Aldershot GU11 3SS* Tel (01252) 320108 Mobile 07749-770035
E-mail jamesmartin858@btinternet.com

MARTIN, James Smiley. b 32. MBE98. TCD 65. **d** 67 **p** 68. C Glenavy *Conn* 67-70; C Belfast St Mary 70-73; I Carnmoney 73-74; I Mallusk 74-94; rtd 94. *21 Dundesert Road, Nutts Corner, Crumlin BT29 4SL* Tel (028) 9082 5636

MARTIN, Mrs Jane Juliet. b 56. Warwick Univ BA77 Solicitor 81. ERMC 04. **d** 06 **p** 07. NSM Huntingdon w the Stukeleys *Ely* from 06. *The Old School House, Barham Road, Buckworth, Huntingdon PE28 5AN* Tel (01480) 891543
E-mail jjmandsm@aol.com

MARTIN, Jessica Heloise. b 63. Trin Hall Cam BA86 PhD93 EAMTC 00. **d** 03 **p** 04. NSM Trin Coll Cam from 03. *82 Ditton Walk, Cambridge CB5 8QE* Tel (01223) 411196 Mobile 07780-704006 E-mail jhm28@cam.ac.uk

MARTIN, John Henry. b 42. St Jo Coll Cam BA63 MA67. St Jo Coll Nottm BA73. **d** 73 **p** 74. C Ecclesall *Sheff* 73-77; C Hednesford *Lich* 77-82; V Walsall Pleck and Bescot 82-92; V

Whittington w Weeford 92-08; V Hints 05-08; rtd 08. *Meadowside, Siddington Road, Cirencester GL7 1PE* Tel (01285) 641782

MARTIN, John Hunter. b 42. AKC64. **d** 65 **p** 66. C Mortlake w E Sheen *S'wark* 65-69; C-in-c Bermondsey St Hugh CD 69-72; V Bermondsey St Anne 72-78; P-in-c Lt Ouse *Ely* 78; V Littleport 78-89; V Attercliffe *Sheff* 89-90; P-in-c Darnall 89-90; TR Darnall-cum-Attercliffe 90-96; TR Attercliffe, Darnall and Tinsley 96; R Kirk Sandall and Edenthorpe 96-07; rtd 07. *Salara Haven, Sandgreen, Gatehouse of Fleet, Castle Douglas DG7 2DU* Tel (01557) 815068

MARTIN, Canon John Pringle. b 24. Bris Univ BA50. Clifton Th Coll 50. **d** 52 **p** 53. C Braintree *Chelmsf* 52-56; C St Alb St Paul *St Alb* 56-59; V Congleton St Pet *Ches* 59-81; R Brereton w Swettenham 81-90; RD Congleton 74-85; Hon Can Ches Cathl 80-90; rtd 90; Perm to Offic *B & W* from 90. *49 Parkhouse Road, Minehead TA24 8AD* Tel (01643) 706769

MARTIN, John Stuart. b 11. St Jo Coll Dur BA34. Wycliffe Hall Ox. **d** 35 **p** 36. C Mansfield SS Pet and Paul *S'well* 35-37; C Newhaven *Chich* 37-39; C Barcombe 39-43; V Ox H Trin 43-46; V Leafield w Wychwood 46-51; R Rotherfield Greys 51-63; V Highmore 55-63; R Bow w Broad Nymet *Ex* 63-65; V Upottery 65-72; TV Farway w Northleigh and Southleigh 72-73; rtd 73. *Church Villa, 8 Church Road, Bawdrip, Bridgwater TA7 8PU* Tel (01278) 684092

MARTIN, Canon Jonathan Patrick McLeod. b 55. Leic Univ BA81. Sarum & Wells Th Coll 84. **d** 86 **p** 87. C Southampton Thornhill St Chris *Win* 86-89; Perm to Offic 89-92; C Heatherlands St Jo *Sarum* 92-97; Dioc Link Officer for ACUPA 95-97; Chief Exec Dame Agnes Weston's R Sailors' Rests from 97; Perm to Offic 98-01; NSM Parkstone St Pet and St Osmund w Branksea from 01; Can and Preb Sarum Cathl from 06. *32 Gladstone Road, Poole BH12 2LY* Tel (01202) 733580
E-mail jonathan.martin@poole.gov.uk

MARTIN, Joseph Edward. b 35. Bps' Coll Cheshunt 58. **d** 60 **p** 61. C Short Heath *Birm* 60-62; C Caterham Valley *S'wark* 63-66; R W Hallam and Mapperley *Derby* 66-70; P-in-c Mapperley 66-67; V Wykeham and Hutton Buscel *York* 71-78; Chapl HM Pris Askham Grange 78-82; V Askham Bryan w Askham Richard *York* 78-82; R Amotherby w Appleton and Barton-le-Street 82-84; C Banbury *Ox* 85-88; C Warsop *S'well* 88-90; V Tuxford w Weston and Markham Clinton 90-00; rtd 00; Perm to Offic *Carl* from 03. *Windsmead, Allithwaite Road, Cartmel, Grange-over-Sands LA11 7SB* Tel (01539) 532693

MARTIN, Kenneth. b 20. Univ of Wales (Lamp) BA47. Bp Burgess Hall Lamp. **d** 48 **p** 49. C Rumney *Mon* 48-49; C Griffithstown 49-51; CF (TA) from 52; Perm to Offic *Llan* from 51. *21 Earls Court Road, Penylan, Cardiff CF23 9DE* Tel (029) 2049 3796

MARTIN, Lee. *See* MARTIN, Angela Lee

MARTIN (née BULLEN), Mrs Marilyn Patricia. b 46. Liv Hope Univ Coll BA(Theol)00 MA05. NOC 06. **d** 06 **p** 07. NSM Stretton and Appleton Thorn *Ches* 06-09; Asst Chapl HM YOI Thorn Cross from 06. *Thorn Cross, Arley Road, Appleton Thorn, Warrington WA4 4RL* Tel (01925) 805100
E-mail malmartin@btinternet.com

MARTIN, Miss Marion. b 47. Oak Hill Th Coll 85. **dss** 80 **d** 87. Ditton *Roch* 86-88; C 87-88; Perm to Offic *Glouc* 89-01; rtd 07. *16 Garborough Close, Crosby, Maryport CA15 6RZ* Tel (01900) 810776

MARTIN, Nicholas Roger. b 53. St Jo Coll Dur BA74. Ripon Coll Cuddesdon 75. **d** 77 **p** 78. C Wolvercote w Summertown *Ox* 77-80; C Kidlington 80-82; TV 82-84; V Happisburgh w Walcot *Nor* 84-85; P-in-c Hempstead w Lessingham and Eccles 84-85; R Happisburgh w Walcot, Hempstead, Lessingham etc 85-89; R Blakeney w Cley, Wiveton, Glandford etc 89-97; TR Totnes w Bridgetown, Berry Pomeroy etc *Ex* 97-05; RD Totnes 99-03; Co-ord Chapl HM Pris Channings Wood from 05. *HM Prison, Channings Wood, Denbury, Newton Abbot TQ12 6DW* Tel (01803) 814647 E-mail nick.martin@hmps.gsi.gov.uk

MARTIN, Norman George. b 22. Sarum & Wells Th Coll 74. **d** 77 **p** 78. NSM Long Ashton *B & W* 77-81; NSM Walton in Gordano 81-82; NSM E Clevedon and Walton w Weston w Clapton 82-87; Chapl Barrow Hosp Bris 87-91; Chapl United Bris Healthcare NHS Trust 91-00; Chapl Farleigh Hosp 87-00; Perm to Offic *B & W* 87-00 and *Mon* from 00. *27 Fairview, High Beech, Chepstow NP16 5BX* Tel (01291) 623495

MARTIN, Paul Dexter. b 50. Wabash Coll (USA) BA72 Univ of the South (USA) MDiv75. **d** 75 **p** 76. Educn Tutor Cov Cathl 75-76; C Norbury St Phil *Cant* 76-80; V Salford *Man* 80. *275 Southfield Road, Shreveport LA 71105, USA* Tel (001) (318) 865 8469 E-mail pdmartin@iamerica.net

MARTIN, Canon Penelope Elizabeth. b 44. Cranmer Hall Dur 83. **dss** 86 **d** 87 **p** 94. Seaham w Seaham Harbour *Dur* 86-89; Par Dn 87-89; Par Dn Cassop cum Quarrington 89-93; Par Dn Sherburn w Pittington 93-94; C 94-95; V 95-02; R Shadforth 95-02; R Pittington, Shadforth and Sherburn 02-03; Hon Can Dur Cathl 01-03; rtd 03. *34A Rosemount, Durham DH1 5GA* Tel 0191-386 1742 E-mail penny.martin@charis.co.uk

MARTIN, Preb Peter. b 50. MCIH75. Linc Th Coll 82. **d** 84 **p** 85. C Taunton H Trin *B & W* 84-86; C Bath Bathwick 86-88; R Cannington, Otterhampton, Combwich and Stockland from 88; RD Sedgemoor 00-06; Warden of Readers Taunton Adnry from 06; Chapl Cannington Coll from 89; Preb Wells Cathl from 09. *The Rectory, 27 Brook Street, Cannington, Bridgwater TA5 2HP* Tel (01278) 652953 E-mail revd.petermartin@tiscali.co.uk

MARTIN, Peter. b 66. Univ of Wales (Ban) BD89. Qu Coll Birm 90. **d** 92 **p** 93. C Kingswinford St Mary *Lich* 92-93; C Kingswinford St Mary *Worc* 93-95; Sen Chapl Redbridge Health Care NHS Trust 95-01; Sen Chapl Barking Havering and Redbridge Hosps NHS Trust 01-06; Hd Past Services Lancs Teaching Hosps NHS Trust 06-08. *Address temp unknown*

MARTIN, Philip James. b 58. Cam Univ BA. Coll of Resurr Mirfield. **d** 84 **p** 85. C Pontefract St Giles *Wakef* 84-88; C Wantage *Ox* 88-90; C Didcot All SS 90; V Alderholt *Sarum* from 90. *The Vicarage, Daggons Road, Alderholt, Fordingbridge SP6 3DN* Tel (01425) 653179
E-mail vicar@stjamesalderholt.org.uk

MARTIN, Ralph. *See* MARTIN, Donald Philip

MARTIN, Raymond William. b 32. Lon Univ BSc66 MBIM. Glouc Th Course 73. **d** 76 **p** 76. NSM Glouc St Mary de Lode and St Nic 76-77; NSM Redmarley D'Abitot, Bromesberrow w Pauntley etc 77-84; R 84-91; P-in-c Falfield w Rockhampton 91-98; P-in-c Oldbury-on-Severn 91-98; Chapl HM YOI Eastwood Park 91-92; rtd 98; Perm to Offic *Glouc* 98-00; Clergy Widows' Officer (Glouc Adnry) from 99; P-in-c Shipton Moyne w Westonbirt and Lasborough 00-02; Perm to Offic *Glouc, Heref* and *Worc* from 03. *Tree Tops, 35 Thirlstane Road, Malvern WR14 3PL* Tel (01684) 562714

MARTIN, Rhys Jonathan. b 68. Heythrop Coll Lon BD98. EAMTC 98. **d** 00 **p** 01. C Stansted Mountfitchet w Birchanger and Farnham *Chelmsf* 00-02; C Dovercourt and Parkeston w Harwich 02-04; R Fingringhoe w E Donyland and Abberton etc from 04. *St Lawrence House, Rectory Road, Rowhedge, Colchester CO5 7HR* Tel (01206) 728640
E-mail rhys.martin@zetnet.co.uk

MARTIN, Richard. b 34. Rhodes Univ BA54 Em Coll Cam BA57 MA58. Wells Th Coll 57. **d** 59 **p** 60. C Portsea St Mary *Portsm* 59-60; S Africa 60-87; C Bloemfontein Cathl 60-62; R Wepener 62-64; R Odendaalsrus 64-67; R Newton Park St Hugh 67-76; Chapl St Bede's Coll Umtata 77-79; R Hillcrest 79-87; C Aldershot St Mich *Guildf* 87-94; R Wick *Mor* 94-99; P-in-c Thurso 94-99; rtd 99; Hon C Diptford, N Huish, Harberton, Harbertonford etc *Ex* 99-01; Perm to Offic 01-03; Lic to Offic *Mor* from 03. *10 Royal Oak Drive, Invergordon IV18 0RP* Tel (01349) 853787 E-mail martin@chilledthames.com

MARTIN, Richard Arthur. b 59. Leeds Univ BA91 MA97 Cant Ch Ch Univ Coll PGCE03. SEITE 07. **d** 09. C Gravesend St Aid *Roch* from 09. *81 Laburnum Road, Rochester ME2 2LB* Tel (01634) 721868 Mobile 07789-238627
E-mail ramartin@talktalk.net

MARTIN, Richard Charles de Villeval. b 41. St Jo Coll Ox BA63 MA67. Ox Ord Course. **d** 84 **p** 85. NSM Ox St Thos w St Frideswide and Binsey 84-04; Asst Chapl Highgate Sch Lon 86-92; Asst Master Magd Coll Sch Ox 92-02; Chapl 94-02; rtd 04; Lic to Offic *Ox* from 05. *11 Benson Place, Oxford OX2 6QH* Tel (01865) 510694 E-mail richardcmartin@tiscali.co.uk

MARTIN, Richard Hugh. b 55. Van Mildert Coll Dur BA78 St Jo Coll Nottm BA81 Leeds Univ MA01. Cranmer Hall Dur 79. **d** 82 **p** 83. C Gateshead *Dur* 82-85; C Redmarshall 85-88; V Scarborough St Jas w H Trin *York* 88-96; Chapl R Wolv Hosps NHS Trust 96-02; V Bris St Andr Hartcliffe from 02. *St Andrew's Vicarage, Peterson Square, Bristol BS13 0EE* Tel 0117-964 3554 Mobile 07709-429631
E-mail richardtherev@blueyonder.co.uk

✠**MARTIN, The Rt Revd Robert David Markland.** b 49. Trin Coll Cam BA71 MA74 FCA80. Trin Coll Bris BA91. **d** 91 **p** 92 **c** 08. C Kingswood *Bris* 91-95; V Frome H Trin *B & W* 95-08; RD Frome 03-08; Suff Bp Marsabit Kenya from 08. *ACK Marsabit Mission Area, c/o MAF Kenya, PO Box 21123/00505, Nairobi, Kenya*

MARTIN, Robert Paul Peter. b 58. Chich Th Coll. **d** 83 **p** 84. C Anfield St Columba *Liv* 83-86; C Orford St Marg 86-87; R Blackley H Trin *Man* 87-90; C Oseney Crescent St Luke *Lon* 90-93; C Kentish Town 93-96; V Harringay St Paul from 96; P-in-c W Green Ch Ch w St Pet 04-08; CMP from 01. *St Paul's Vicarage, Wightman Road, London N4 1RW* Tel and fax (020) 8340 5299 E-mail fr.robert@btinternet.com

MARTIN, Robin. *See* MARTIN, Thomas Robin

MARTIN, Robin Hugh. b 35. Rhodes Univ BA56. **d** 58 **p** 59. C Darnall *Sheff* 58-62; C-in-c Kimberworth Park 62-65; Lic to Offic *Sheff* 65-66 and *Newc* 67-71; Perm to Offic *Man* 79-93; *Lich* 97-99; *Heref* from 97; P-in-c Maesbury *Lich* from 99. *Offa House, Treflach, Oswestry SY10 9HQ* Tel (01691) 657090

MARTIN, Roger Allen. b 38. Westmr Coll Lon CertEd59 Birkbeck Coll Lon BA64 FRMetS79. SAOMC 97. **d** 99 **p** 00. NSM Bramfield, Stapleford, Waterford etc *St Alb* 99-06; NSM

Broxbourne w Wormley from 06. *41 The Avenue, Bengeo, Hertford SG14 3DS* Tel (01992) 422441
E-mail roger.martin@ntlworld.com

MARTIN, Canon Roger Ivor. b 42. MCMI. Cant Sch of Min. **d** 85 **p** 86. NSM Saltwood *Cant* 85-90; P-in-c Crundale w Godmersham 90-01; Dioc Exec Officer for Adult Educn and Lay Tr 90-96; CME Officer 94-96; Chapl to Bp Maidstone 96-01; R Saltwood 01-09; Hon Can Cant Cathl 09; rtd 09; Perm to Offic *Cant* from 09. *Kwetu, 23 Tanners Hill Gardens, Hythe CT21 5HY* Tel (01303) 237204 E-mail rogmartin@btinternet.com

MARTIN, Mrs Rosanna Stuart. b 60. Bris Univ BA81. Wycliffe Hall Ox 89. **d** 92 **p** 94. Par Dn Stanford in the Vale w Goosey and Hatford *Ox* 92-94; C 94-96; C Abingdon 96-00; Perm to Offic 00-04; P-in-c Uffington, Shellingford, Woolstone and Baulking from 04. *St Mary's Vicarage, Broad Street, Uffington, Faringdon SN7 7RA* Tel (01367) 820633

MARTIN, Rupert Gresley. b 57. Worc Coll Ox BA78 Ox Univ MA95. Trin Coll Bris 89. **d** 91 **p** 92. C Yateley *Win* 91-95; V Sandal St Helen *Wakef* from 95. *The Vicarage, 333 Barnsley Road, Wakefield WF2 6EJ* Tel (01924) 255441
E-mail office@sandalmagna.fsnet.co.uk

MARTIN, Russell Derek. b 47. St Jo Coll Dur 71. **d** 74 **p** 75. C Hartlepool H Trin *Dur* 74-78; C Swindon St Jo and St Andr *Bris* 78-79; V Penhill 79-91; V Haselbury Plucknett, Misterton and N Perrott *B & W* 91-99. *59 North Street, Martock TA12 6EH* Tel (01935) 829266 Mobile 07770-783893

MARTIN, Scott. b 73. Herts Univ BA99 Leeds Univ BA04 MA05. Coll of Resurr Mirfield 02. **d** 05 **p** 06. C Leagrave *St Alb* 05-09; P-in-c Bishop's Stortford from 09. *Holy Trinity Vicarage, 69 Havers Lane, Bishop's Stortford CM23 3PA* Tel (01279) 656546 Mobile 07766-295678
E-mail scottmar73@hotmail.com

MARTIN, Sean Cal Hugh. b 69. Wycliffe Coll Toronto MDiv04. **d** 04 **p** 05. C Rio Grande St Andr USA 05-06; Asst P ICM 06-08; Canada from 08. *587 Laurel Crescent, Campbell River BC V9W 6K8, Canada*

MARTIN, Steven. b 50. Qu Coll Birm BA08. **d** 08 **p** 09. C Malvern St Andr and Malvern Wells and Wyche *Worc* from 08. *96 Fruitlands, Malvern WR14 4XB* Tel (01684) 893146
E-mail smartin1006@sky.com

MARTIN, Miss Susan. b 56. Nottm Univ BA77. Edin Th Coll 86. **d** 88 **p** 94. C Leigh Park *Portsm* 88-91; C Sandown Ch Ch 91-94; C Portsea St Cuth 94-95; rtd 95; Perm to Offic *Portsm* 95-01 and from 04; NSM Portsea St Geo 01-04. *7 Farthingdale Terrace, Peacock Lane, Portsmouth PO1 2TL* Tel (023) 9229 7994

MARTIN, Mrs Susan Mary. b 49. UEA BEd94. ERMC 04. **d** 09. NSM Gayton, Gayton Thorpe, E Walton, E Winch etc *Nor* from 09. *The Limes, Lynn Road, Gayton, King's Lynn PE32 1QJ* Tel and fax (01553) 636570 Mobile 07801-701677

MARTIN, Sylvia. b 24. **dss** 75 **d** 87 **p** 94. NSM Selsdon St Jo w St Fran *S'wark* 87-99; Perm to Offic 99-07. *17 Frobisher Court, Sydenham Rise, London SE23 3XH* Tel (020) 8699 6247

MARTIN, Sylvia. b 43. Sarum Th Coll 94. **d** 97 **p** 98. NSM Locks Heath *Portsm* 97-02; Perm to Offic 02-04; NSM Fareham H Trin and Chapl Fareham Coll 04-07; rtd 07; Perm to Offic *Portsm* from 07. *9 Harvester Drive, Fareham PO15 5NR* Tel (01329) 312269 E-mail sylvia.martin43@yahoo.com

MARTIN, Thomas Robin. b 40. Bps' Coll Cheshunt 64. **d** 67 **p** 68. C Ripley *Derby* 67-70; C Ilkeston St Mary 70-74; V Chinley w Buxworth 74-83; V Knighton St Mich *Leic* 83-85; V Thurmaston 85-05; rtd 05; C Leic Resurr from 08. *22 Sycamore Road, Birstall, Leicester LE4 4LT* Tel 0116-267 1651

MARTIN, Warrick David. b 71. Stirling Univ BA94. Oak Hill Th Coll BA09. **d** 09. *128 Holwell Road, Welwyn Garden City AL7 3RW* Tel 07738-127587 (mobile)

MARTIN, William Harrison. b 38. Sarum & Wells Th Coll 91. **d** 87 **p** 88. NSM Rushen *S & M* 87-92; C German 92-97; V Lonan and Laxey 97-08; rtd 08. *Crossag Villa, Crossag Road, Ballasalla, Isle of Man IM9 3EF* Tel (01624) 825982
E-mail billmartin@manx.net

MARTIN, William Matthew. b 28. Ch Coll Cam BA52 MA56 TCert81. Ridley Hall Cam 52. **d** 54 **p** 55. C Weaste *Man* 54-56; V 56-61; CF (TA) 58-61; CF 61-82; Dep Asst Chapl Gen 73-82; Asst Master St Jo Southworth RC High Sch Preston 82-88; Lic to Offic *Blackb* 82-93; rtd 93; Perm to Offic *Blackb* from 93. *31 Fosbrooke House, 8 Clifton Drive, Lytham St Annes FY8 5RQ* Tel (01253) 667052

MARTIN-DOYLE, Mrs Audrey Brenda. b 35. Cranmer Hall Dur 80. **dss** 82 **d** 87 **p** 95. The Lye and Stambermill *Worc* 82-86; Chapl Lee Abbey 86-88; Ldr Aston Cottage Community 88-93; C Cheltenham St Mary, St Matt, St Paul and H Trin *Glouc* 94-97; rtd 97; Perm to Offic *Glouc* from 97. *39 Moorend Street, Cheltenham GL53 0EH* Tel (01242) 510352
E-mail audrey@martin-doyle.freeserve.co.uk

MARTIN-SMITH, Paul. b 51. TCD BA64 Lon Univ MSc67 FIPEM88. WMMTC 94. **d** 97 **p** 98. NSM Tile Hill *Cov* 97-99; Perm to Offic *Ex* from 00. *12 Emmasfield, Exmouth EX8 2LS* Tel (01395) 269505

MARTINDALE, Mrs Patricia Ann. b 24. Qu Coll Birm. **dss** 84 **d** 87 **p** 94. Rugby *Cov* 84-94; NSM 87-94; Perm to Offic from 95. *54 Hillmorton Road, Rugby CV22 5AD* Tel (01788) 543038

MARTINEAU, Canon Christopher Lee. b 16. Trin Hall Cam BA38 MA70. Linc Th Coll 39. **d** 41 **p** 42. C Hinckley St Mary *Leic* 41-43; Chapl RNVR 43-46; C St Alb Abbey 46-48; V Balsall Heath St Paul *Birm* 48-54; P-in-c Shard End 54-58; V 58-65; R Skipton H Trin *Bradf* 65-83; Hon Can Bradf Cathl 72-83; rtd 83; Perm to Offic *Bradf* 83-02 and *Heref* from 03. *70 New Street, Ledbury HR8 2EE* Tel (01531) 635454

MARTINEAU, Canon David Richards Durani. b 36. AKC59. **d** 60 **p** 61. C Ches St Jo 60-64; S Africa 64-69; C St Mark's Cathl George 64; C Riversdale 64-66; R Beaufort W and Victoria W 66-69; C Jarrow St Paul *Dur* 69-72; TV 72-75; TR Jarrow 76-85; V Gildersome *Wakef* 85-00; Hon Can Wakef Cathl 94-00; rtd 00; Perm to Offic *Eur* 02-03. *Harlough, St Chad, Barrow-upon-Humber DN19 7AU* Tel (01469) 531475

E-mail david-martineau@harlough.freeserve.co.uk

MARTINEAU, Canon Jeremy Fletcher. b 40. OBE03. K Coll Lon BD65 AKC65. **d** 66 **p** 67. C Jarrow St Paul *Dur* 66-73; Bp's Ind Adv 69-73; P-in-c Raughton Head w Gatesgill *Carl* 73-80; Chapl to Agric 73-80; Ind Chapl *Bris* 80-90; Sec Abps' Commission on Rural Affairs 88-90; Nat Rural Officer Gen Syn Bd of Miss 90-03; Hon Can Cov Cathl 01-03; rtd 04; Lic to Offic *St D* from 05. *11 New Hill Villas, Goodwick SA64 0DT* Tel (01348) 874886

E-mail jeremy.m@onetel.net

MARTINSON, Matthew. b 74. Mattersey Hall BA03. St Jo Coll Nottm. **d** 09. C Beverley St Nic *York* from 09. *7 St Nicholas' Drive, Beverley HU17 0QY* Tel (01482) 862770

E-mail matt@martinson.org.uk

MARTLEW, Andrew Charles. b 50. Nottm Univ BTh76 Lanc Univ MA80. Linc Th Coll 72. **d** 76 **p** 77. C Poulton-le-Fylde *Blackb* 76-79; Hon C Lancaster Ch Ch 79-80; Malaysia 81-83; V Golcar *Wakef* 83-89; Dioc Schs Officer 89-95; V Warmfield 89-95; Dioc Dir of Educn *York* 95-02; CF from 02. *c/o MOD Chaplains (Army),* Tel (01980) 615804 Fax 615800

MARVELL, John. b 32. Lon Univ BD63 Leic Univ MEd73 PhD85. Oak Hill Th Coll 79. **d** 80 **p** 81. NSM Colchester Ch Ch w St Mary V *Chelmsf* 80-85; Perm to Offic 85-87; P-in-c Stisted w Bradwell and Pattiswick 87-98; rtd 98. *3 impasse de Genets, 35800 Dinard, France* Tel (0033) (2) 99 16 56 74

E-mail jmarvell@ctacom.fr

MARVIN, David Arthur. b 51. St Jo Coll Nottm 96. **d** 97 **p** 98. C Mansfield St Jo *S'well* 97-01; P-in-c Greasley from 01. *The Vicarage, 36 Moorgreen, Newthorpe, Nottingham NG16 2FB* Tel (01773) 712509 E-mail dave.marvin1@ntlworld.com

MARWOOD, Canon Timothy John Edmonds. b 51. Whitelands Coll Lon CertEd72 Open Univ BA89 Lon Inst of Educn MA91. S'wark Ord Course 92. **d** 95 **p** 96. NSM Putney St Mary *S'wark* 95-00; Perm to Offic *Ex* 00-07; P-in-c Petersham *S'wark* from 07; Chapl K Coll Sch Wimbledon from 08; Hon Can S'wark Cathl from 08. *The Vicarage, Bute Avenue, Richmond TW10 7AX* Tel (020) 8940 8435 Mobile 07973-518742

E-mail timmarwood@yahoo.co.uk

MARY CLARE, Sister. See FOGG, Cynthia Mary

MARY STEPHEN, Sister. See BRITT, Sister Mary Stephen

MASCALL, Mrs Margaret Ann. b 43. LRAM64 Bris Univ CertEd65 St Jo Coll Dur BA71 MA79. Cranmer Hall Dur 69. **dss** 76 **d** 87 **p** 94. Hertford St Andr *St Alb* 75-79; Herne Bay Ch Ch *Cant* 79-82; Seasalter 82-84; Whitstable 84-90; Par Dn 87-90; Perm to Offic 91-94; Hon C Hackington 94-95; V Newington w Hartlip and Stockbury 95-03; rtd 03; Perm to Offic *Cant* from 03. *48 Holmside Avenue, Minster on Sea, Sheerness ME12 3EY* Tel (01795) 663095 E-mail margaret.mascall@btopenworld.com

MASCARENHAS, Felix Pedro Antonio. b 55. Bombay Univ BA80 Pontifical Univ Rome JCD88. Pilar Major Th Sem Goa BTh81. **d** 82 **p** 82. In RC Ch 82-02; C Chich St Paul and Westhampnett 02-06; P-in-c Brighton Gd Shep Preston from 06. *The Vicarage, 272 Dyke Road, Brighton BN1 5AE* Tel (01273) 882987 Mobile 07814-739312 E-mail felixmas@hotmail.com

MASDING, John William. b 39. Magd Coll Ox BA61 DipEd63 MA65 Univ of Wales (Cardiff) LLM94 FRSA96. Ridley Hall Cam 63. **d** 65 **p** 66. C Boldmere *Birm* 65-71; V Hamstead St Paul 71-97; rtd 97; Perm to Offic *B & W* from 97 and *Bris* from 00. *The Old School House, Norton Hawkfield, Pensford, Bristol BS39 4HB* Tel and fax (01275) 830017

E-mail john.masding@magd.oxon.org

MASH, William Edward John. b 54. Imp Coll Lon BSc75 Open Univ MA00 ARCS. St Jo Coll Nottm 87. **d** 89 **p** 90. C Beverley Minster *York* 89-93; V Elloughton and Brough w Brantingham 93-01; P-in-c Newcastle St Geo *Lich* 01-08; V from 08; P-in-c Knutton 06-08; V from 08; Chapl Town Cen and Newcastle Coll of H&FE from 01. *St George's Vicarage, 28 Hempstalls Lane, Newcastle ST5 0SS* Tel (01782) 710056

E-mail billmash@tiscali.co.uk

MASHEDER, Peter Timothy Charles. b 49. AKC71. St Aug Coll Cant 71. **d** 72 **p** 73. C Barkingside St Fran *Chelmsf* 72-75; C Chingford SS Pet and Paul 75-91; P-in-c High Laver w Magdalen

Laver and Lt Laver etc 91-98; R 98-07; RD Ongar 98-04; R Ray Valley *Ox* from 07; AD Bicester and Islip from 08. *St Mary's Rectory, Church Walk, Ambrosden, Bicester OX25 2UJ* Tel (01869) 247813 E-mail chasmash@ic24.net

MASHEDER, Richard. b 36. AKC59. **d** 60 **p** 61. C Preston St Matt *Blackb* 60-62; C Padiham 62-65; P-in-c Worsthorne 65; V 65-74; CF (TA) 65-67; P-in-c Blackb St Jude 74-78; V Blackb St Thos 76-78; V Blackb St Thos w St Jude 78-82; V Silverdale 82-01; rtd 01; Perm to Offic *Blackb* from 01. *59 Twemlow Parade, Heysham, Morecambe LA3 2AL* Tel and fax (01524) 851151

E-mail revakela@talk21.com

MASHITER, Mrs Marion. b 48. CBDTI 01. **d** 04 **p** 05. NSM Burneside *Carl* 04-07; NSM Beacon from 07. *The Maples, 5 Esthwaite Avenue, Kendal LA9 7NN* Tel (01539) 731957 Mobile 07748-771836 E-mail marionmashiter@lineone.net

MASKELL, John Michael. b 45. Sarum & Wells Th Coll 86. **d** 88 **p** 89. C Swanborough *Sarum* 88-91; Chapl RAF 91-95; P-in-c Ollerton w Boughton *S'well* 95-97; P-in-c Capel *Guildf* 97-02; TV Walton H Trin *Ox* 02-03; Healing Co-ord Acorn Chr Foundn 03-04; rtd 04; Perm to Offic *Chich* from 04. *Fairhaven, Fletching Street, Mayfield TN20 6TH* Tel (01435) 872910 Mobile 07929-134962 E-mail john@maskell.freeserve.co.uk

MASKELL, Miss Rosemary Helen. b 58. Ripon Coll Cuddesdon. **d** 00 **p** 01. C Goodrington *Ex* 00-04; V Littleport *Ely* from 04. *St George's Vicarage, 30 Church Lane, Littleport, Ely CB6 1PS* Tel (01353) 860207 Mobile 07803-499755

E-mail revrose@goodevon.fsnet.co.uk

MASKREY, Mrs Susan Elizabeth. b 43. Cranmer Hall Dur IDC70. **dss** 76 **d** 92 **p** 94. Littleover *Derby* 76-77; Sec to Publicity Manager CMS Lon 77-78; Stantonbury and Willen *Ox* 78-88; Billingham St Aid *Dur* 88-95; C 92-95; Asst Chapl HM Pris Holme Ho 94-95; Asst Chapl HM Pris Preston 95-01; Chapl HM Pris Kirkham 01-05; rtd 05; Perm to Offic *Blackb* from 05. *c/o the Bishop of Blackburn, Bishop's House, Ribchester Road, Blackburn BB1 9EF*

MASLEN, Darren Robert Dunstan. b 71. St Martin's Coll Lanc BA93 Open Univ MA97 Leeds Univ BA99. Coll of Resurr Mirfield 97. **d** 00 **p** 01. C Shaston *Sarum* 00-04; C S Shields All SS *Dur* 04-05; TV from 05. *4 Mitford Road, South Shields NE34 0EQ* Tel 0191-456 1300

MASLEN (formerly CHILD), Mrs Margaret Mary. b 44. ALA76 Open Univ BA79. S Dios Minl Tr Scheme 89. **d** 92 **p** 94. C Portishead *B & W* 92-93; C Ilminster w Whitelackington 93-94; C Ilminster and Distr 94-96; C Tatworth 96-00; TV Chard and Distr 00-05; Chapl Taunton and Somerset NHS Trust 97-05; rtd 05; Hon C Sherston Magna, Easton Grey, Luckington etc *Bris* from 06; Hon C Hullavington, Norton and Stanton St Quintin from 06. *2 Woods Close, Sherston, Malmesbury SN16 0LF* Tel (01666) 840387 E-mail maslens@tiscali.co.uk

MASLEN, Richard Ernest. b 34. S Dios Minl Tr Scheme 89. **d** 92 **p** 93. NSM Sherston Magna, Easton Grey, Luckington etc *Bris* 92-93; NSM Ilminster w Whitelackington *B & W* 93-94; NSM Ilminster and Distr 94-96; P-in-c Tatworth 96-99; TV Chard and Distr 99-00; rtd 00; Perm to Offic *B & W* 00-05. *2 Woods Close, Sherston, Malmesbury SN16 0LF* Tel (01666) 840387

MASLEN, Canon Stephen Henry. b 37. CCC Ox BA62 MA65. Ridley Hall Cam 62. **d** 64 **p** 65. C Keynsham w Queen Charlton *B & W* 64-67; C Cheltenham St Mary *Glouc* 67-71; P-in-c St Mary at Lambeth *S'wark* 72-74; TV N Lambeth 74-79; V Horley 79-84; TR 84-94; RD Reigate 86-91; R Coulsdon St Jo 94-02; Hon Can S'wark Cathl 95-02; rtd 02; Perm to Offic *Worc* from 02. *The Red House, Back Lane, Bredon, Tewkesbury GL20 7LH* Tel (01684) 772575

MASON, Adrian Stanley. b 54. Hatf Poly BSc77 QTS01. Ripon Coll Cuddesdon 77. **d** 80 **p** 81. C Mill End and Heronsgate w W Hyde *St Alb* 80-83; TV Axminster, Chardstock, Combe Pyne and Rousdon *Ex* 83-87; TV Halesworth w Linstead, Chediston, Holton etc *St E* 87-88; R Brandon and Santon Downham 88-91; R Glemsford, Hartest w Boxted, Somerton etc 91-95; Min Can St E Cathl 95-97; P-in-c S Hartismere from 06. *The Rectory, Stanwell Green, Thorndon, Eye IP23 7JL* Tel (01379) 672981

E-mail adrian.s.mason@gmail.com

MASON, Alan Hambleton. b 27. Lon Univ BD59. Wycliffe Hall Ox 56. **d** 59 **p** 60. C Norbiton *S'wark* 59-63; V Thornton St Jas *Bradf* 63-73; V Wavertree St Thos *Liv* 84-92; rtd 92; Perm to Offic *Liv* from 92. *17 Lovelace Road, Liverpool L19 1QE* Tel 0151-427 5678

MASON, Ambrose. See MASON, Canon Thomas Henry Ambrose

MASON, Andrew John. b 77. St Jo Coll Nottm BA06. **d** 06 **p** 07. C Bemerton *Sarum* 06-09; TV Kingswood *Bris* from 09. *60 Lavers Close, Bristol BS15 9ZG* Tel 0117-960 3195

E-mail revandymason06@hotmail.co.uk

MASON, Miss Beverley Anne. Trin Coll Bris BA00. **d** 01 **p** 03. C Rusthall *Roch* 01-02; C Rainham 02-05; V Upper Norwood St Jo *S'wark* from 05. *St John's Vicarage, 2 Sylvan Road, London SE19 2RX* Tel (020) 8653 0378 E-mail revdbev@tiscali.co.uk

MASON, Miss Chantal Marie. b 73. Ex Univ BA96 St Luke's Coll Ex PGCE98. Trin Coll Bris MA08. **d** 08. C Alphington,

Shillingford St George and Ide *Ex* from 08. *13 Sydney Road, Exeter EX2 9AJ* Tel (01392) 427568
E-mail revchantalmason@yahoo.co.uk

MASON, Charles Oliver. b 51. Jes Coll Cam BA73 MA99 St Jo Coll Dur BA79. **d** 80 **p** 81. C Cheltenham St Mary, St Matt, St Paul and H Trin *Glouc* 80-84; C Enfield Ch Ch Trent Park *Lon* 84-88; P-in-c W Hampstead St Cuth 88-93; V 93-01; AD N Camden 98-01; V Braintree *Chelmsf* from 01. *St Michael's Vicarage, 10A Marshalls Road, Braintree CM7 2LL* Tel (01376) 322840 E-mail revdcom@btinternet.com

MASON, Christina Mary. b 42. Univ of Wales BMus63 MA67 BSc(Econ)70 Dundee Univ PhD84 Middx Univ MSc02. St Jo Coll Nottm 81. **d** 83. Lic to Offic *Bre* 83-92; Perm to Offic *Nor* from 09. *44 Long Street, Great Ellingham, Attleborough NR17 1LN* Tel (01953) 451354 E-mail cmason@patsltd.co.uk

MASON, Mrs Christine Mary. b 43. Sarum & Wells Th Coll 91. **d** 93 **p** 94. Par Dn Blakenall Heath *Lich* 93-94; C 94-97; TV Rugeley 97-06; TV Brereton and Rugeley 06-08; rtd 08; Perm to Offic *Lich* from 09. *The Old School, Sutton Maddock, Shifnal TF11 9NQ* Tel (01952) 730442

MASON, Christopher David. b 51. Lanc Univ BA72 Leic Univ MEd82. EAMTC 91. **d** 94 **p** 95. NSM Pet St Mary Boongate 94-00 and 03-05; P-in-c Newborough 00-02; Chapl Pet High Sch from 05. *74 Derby Drive, Peterborough PE1 4NQ* Tel (01733) 700000 E-mail mason.cd@virgin.net

MASON, Clive Ray. b 34. St Chad's Coll Dur BA57. Qu Coll Birm 57. **d** 59 **p** 60. C Gateshead St Mary *Dur* 59-62; C Bishopwearmouth Ch Ch 62-64; V Darlington St Jo 64-74; P-in-c Southwick H Trin 75-84; R 84-89; V Bearpark 89-95; rtd 95; Perm to Offic *Dur* from 95. *41 Harbour View, Littlehaven, South Shields NE33 1LS* Tel 0191-454 0234

MASON, David Gray. b 37. Birm Univ LDS61 K Coll Lon MPhil94. St Alb Minl Tr Scheme 83. **d** 95 **p** 95. NSM Biddenham *St Alb* 95-98; P-in-c Felmersham 98-05; NSM Sharnbrook, Felmersham and Knotting w Souldrop from 05; RD Sharnbrook from 06. *2A Devon Road, Bedford MK40 3DF* Tel and fax (01234) 309737
E-mail david.mason93@ntlworld.com

MASON, Dawn Lavinia. b 53. Ripon Coll Cuddesdon 95. **d** 97 **p** 98. C Wisbech St Aug *Ely* 97-00; V Emneth and Marshland St James 00-09; P-in-c Elm and Friday Bridge w Coldham 04-09; V Fen Orchards from 09. *The Vicarage, 72 Church Road, Emneth, Wisbech PE14 8AF* Tel (01945) 583089

MASON, Dennis Wardell. b 28. Ox NSM Course 83. **d** 86 **p** 87. NSM Ox St Barn and St Paul 86-08. *20 John Lopes Road, Eynsham, Witney OX29 4JR* Tel (01865) 880440

MASON, Edward. *See* MASON, Preb Thomas Edward

MASON, Mrs Elizabeth Ann. b 42. Homerton Coll Cam TCert64 Open Univ BA90. Ox Min Course 91. **d** 94 **p** 95. NSM Worminghall w Ickford, Oakley and Shabbington *Ox* 94-95; NSM Swan 95-98; TV 98-05; rtd 05. *35 Common Road, North Leigh, Witney OX29 6RD* Tel (01993) 883966

MASON, Francis Robert Anthony. b 56. Trin Coll Bris BA90. **d** 90 **p** 91. C Denham *Ox* 90-94; P-in-c Jersey Grouville *Win* 94-98; R 98-04; R Tendring and Lt Bentley w Beaumont cum Moze *Chelmsf* from 07. *The Rectory, The Street, Tendring, Clacton-on-Sea CO16 0BW* Tel (01255) 830586
E-mail francismason@jerseymail.co.uk

MASON, Canon Geoffrey Charles. b 48. K Coll Lon BD74 AKC74. St Aug Coll Cant 74. **d** 75 **p** 76. C Hatcham Park All SS *S'wark* 75-78; V Bellingham St Dunstan 78-87; RD E Lewisham 82-87; C Catford (Southend) and Downham 87-88; Bp's Adv for Min Development 88-00; Dioc Dir of Ords from 00; Hon Can S'wark Cathl from 07. *32 King's Orchard, London SE9 5TJ* Tel (020) 8859 7614 *or* 7378 7506 Fax 7403 6497

✠**MASON, The Rt Revd James Philip.** b 54. Solomon Is Coll of HE TCert73 St Jo Coll Auckland STh86. Bp Patteson Th Coll (Solomon Is) 78. **d** 81 **p** 82 **c** 91. C St Barn Cathl Honiara Solomon Is 81-82; Sec to Abp Melanesia 83-86; Lect Bp Patteson Th Coll 87; Dean Honiara 88-91; Bp Hanuato'o 91-04; P-in-c Plympton St Maurice *Ex* from 05; Hon Asst Bp Ex from 07. *St Maurice's Rectory, 31 Wain Park, Plymouth PL7 2HX* Tel (01752) 346114 Mobile 07875-160159
E-mail jamesphilipmason@stmaurice.eclipse.co.uk

MASON, John Evans. b 32. RD. Linc Th Coll 57. **d** 59 **p** 60. C Putney St Mary *S'wark* 59-62; C Berry Pomeroy *Ex* 62-64; Chapl RN 64-68; V Hopton *Nor* 68-72; Chapl RNR 69-82; P-in-c Roydon St Remigius *Nor* 72-76; R Diss 72-80; Dir YMCA Cam 80-85; Prin YMCA Dunford Coll 85-88; Perm to Offic *Glouc* 88-97 and *Ox* 89-99; rtd 96; Perm to Offic *Nor* 98-02; *Sarum* 02-04; and *B & W* from 05. *Barretts House Farm, Yeovil Road, Halstock, Yeovil BA22 9RP* Tel (01935) 891400

MASON, John Martin. b 41. UMIST BSc63. Glouc Sch of Min 80 Qu Coll Birm 82. **d** 84 **p** 85. C Tuffley *Glouc* 84-87; P-in-c Willersey, Saintbury, Weston-sub-Edge etc 87-92; R 92-96; P-in-c Selling w Throwley, Sheldwich w Badlesmere etc *Cant* 96-06; Dioc Rural Officer 96-06; rtd 06; Perm to Offic *Cant* from 06.

4 Old Garden Court, Chartham, Canterbury CT4 7GA Tel (01227) 733486 Mobile 07951-024355
E-mail ruraljoe@btinternet.com

MASON, Canon Jonathan Patrick. b 55. Edin Th Coll 90. **d** 92 **p** 93. C Edin Ch Ch 92-94; C Edin Old St Paul 94-96; R St Andrews All SS *St And* from 96; Chapl St Andr Univ from 97; Can St Ninian's Cathl Perth from 07. *All Saints' Rectory, North Street, St Andrews KY16 9AQ* Tel and fax (01334) 473193
E-mail jpm2@st-and.ac.uk

MASON, Ms Josephine Margaret. b 41. Edin Univ BMus64. WMMTC 88. **d** 93 **p** 94. Chapl Asst S Birm Mental Health NHS Trust 91-06; C Birm St Jo Ladywood 93-01; C Ladywood St Jo and St Pet 01-06; rtd 06; Perm to Offic *Birm* from 06. *340 Selly Oak Road, Birmingham B30 1HP* Tel 0121-451 1412
E-mail jo.mason@freeuk.com

MASON, Julia Ann. b 43. St Jo Coll Nottm 89. **d** 91 **p** 95. NSM Troon *Glas* 91-93; NSM Ayr, Maybole and Girvan 93-05; Lic to Offic *Edin* from 08; Perm to Offic *Glas* from 08. *13/2 Rocheid Park, Edinburgh EH4 1RU* Tel 0131-343 1165
E-mail revdjuliamason@btinternet.com

MASON, Canon Kenneth Staveley. b 31. ARCS53 Lon Univ BSc53 BD64. Wells Th Coll 56. **d** 58 **p** 59. C Kingston upon Hull St Martin *York* 58-61; C Pocklington w Yapham-cum-Meltonby, Owsthorpe etc 61-63; C Millington w Gt Givendale 61-63; V Thornton w Allerthorpe 63-69; Sub-Warden St Aug Coll Cant 69-76; Abp's Adv in Past Min 76-77; Dir Cant Sch of Min 77-81; Prin 81-89; Sec to Dioc Bd of Min *Cant* 77-87; Six Preacher Cant Cathl 79-84; Hon Can Cant Cathl 84-89; Prin Edin Th Coll 89-95; Can St Mary's Cathl 89-96; rtd 95; Perm to Offic *Ripon* from 96. *2 Williamson Close, Ripon HG4 1AZ* Tel (01765) 607041

MASON, Lesley Jane. b 55. Newnham Coll Cam BA76 FInstD. St Jo Coll Nottm 04. **d** 07 **p** 08. NSM Busbridge and Hambledon *Guildf* from 07. *Russet House, 1 The Paddock, Godalming GU7 1XD* Tel (01483) 423301 E-mail ljmason@btinternet.com

MASON, Matthew. b 74. Man Univ MusB. Oak Hill Th Coll MTh. **d** 05 **p** 06. C Tunbridge Wells St Jo *Roch* from 05. *112 Stephen's Road, Tunbridge Wells TN4 9QA* Tel (01892) 521767 E-mail matthewwmason@gmail.com

MASON, Nigel Frederick. b 60. Wycliffe Hall Ox 93. **d** 95 **p** 96. C Highbury Ch Ch w St Jo and St Sav *Lon* 95-98; C Seaford w Sutton *Chich* 98-01; R Rotherfield w Mark Cross from 01. *The Rectory, Mayfield Road, Rotherfield, Crowborough TN6 3LU* Tel (01892) 852536

MASON, Nigel James. b 56. Culham Coll of Educn BEd78. St Steph Ho Ox 95. **d** 97 **p** 98. C Hove *Chich* 97-00; V Kemp Town St Mary 00-07; Chapl St Mary's Hall Brighton 03-07; V Smethwick *Birm* from 07. *Old Church Vicarage, 93A Church Road, Smethwick B67 6EE* Tel 0121-558 1763

MASON, Paul. b 51. Cranmer Hall Dur 93. **d** 93 **p** 94. C Handforth *Ches* 93-97; V Partington and Carrington 97-04; V Church Hulme from 04. *The Vicarage, 74 London Road, Holmes Chapel, Crewe CW4 7BD* Tel and fax (01477) 533124

MASON, Mrs Pauline. b 49. LCTP. **d** 08 **p** 09. NSM Chorley St Geo *Blackb* from 08. *33 Park Road, Chorley PR7 1QS*

MASON, Peter Charles. b 45. K Coll Lon BD72 AKC72 Birm Univ PGCE89. St Aug Coll Cant 72. **d** 73 **p** 74. C Ilkeston St Mary *Derby* 73-76; C Bridgnorth St Mary *Heref* 76-78; TV Bridgnorth, Tasley, Astley Abbotts, etc 78-88; RE Teacher from 89; Perm to Offic *Heref* 89-04 and *St D* from 04. *63 Nun Street, St Davids, Haverfordwest SA62 6NU* Tel (01437) 721715

MASON, Canon Peter Joseph. b 34. Lon Univ BA58. Coll of Resurr Mirfield 58. **d** 60 **p** 61. C Belhus Park CD *Chelmsf* 60-63; Lic to Offic *Eur* 63-64; Asst Chapl Lon Univ 64-70; Chapl City Univ 66-70; R Stoke Newington St Mary 70-78; V Writtle *Chelmsf* 78-81; P-in-c Highwood 78-81; V Writtle w Highwood 81-86; R Shenfield 86-93; Hon Can Chelmsf Cathl 89-00; P-in-c Maldon All SS w St Pet 93-95; V 95-00; RD Maldon and Dengie 95-00; rtd 00; Perm to Offic *Chelmsf* from 00. *32 Providence, Burnham-on-Crouch CM0 8JU* Tel (01621) 785921
E-mail peter@franknox.demon.co.uk

MASON, Robert Herbert George. b 48. ACII. Oak Hill Th Coll 82. **d** 84 **p** 85. C Ware Ch Ch *St Alb* 84-88; V Eastbourne All So *Chich* 88-98; P-in-c Poole *Sarum* 98-01; R from 01; Chapl Miss to Seafarers from 98. *The Rectory, 10 Poplar Close, Poole BH15 1LP* Tel (01202) 672694 Fax 677117
E-mail revbobmelmason@hotmail.com

MASON, Canon Roger Arthur. b 41. Lon Univ BSc65 K Coll Lon BD68 AKC68. **d** 69 **p** 70. C Enfield St Andr *Lon* 69-72; P-in-c Westbury and Yockleton *Heref* 72-78; P-in-c Gt Wollaston 77-78; V Willesden St Mary *Lon* 78-88; V Prittlewell *Chelmsf* 88-06; P-in-c Prittlewell St Steph 92-04; Hon Can Chelmsf Cathl 01-06; rtd 06; Perm to Offic *Leic* and *Eur* from 07; Hon C Empingham and Exton w Horn w Whitwell *Pet* from 08; Hon C Edith Weston w N Luffenham and Lyndon w Manton from 08; Hon C Preston and Ridlington w Wing and Pilton from 08. *4 Westhorpe Close, Wing, Oakham LE15 8RJ* Tel (01572) 737014 E-mail randjmason@sky.com

MASON, Mrs Sally Lynne. b 52. EMMTC 05. **d** 08 **p** 09. NSM Alfreton *Derby* from 08. *27 Stretton Road, Morton, Alfreton DE55 6GW* Tel (01773) 873508 E-mail sallymason@live.co.uk

MASON (*formerly* **FOALE), Sheila Rosemary.** b 40. Saffron Walden Coll CertEd61 ARCM62. SWMTC 98. **d** 01 **p** 02. NSM Shebbear, Buckland Filleigh, Sheepwash etc *Ex* 01-04; C Cobham and Stoke D'Abernon *Guildf* 04-08; rtd 08. *1 Heron Place, Broughty Ferry, Dundee DD5 3PR* Tel (01382) 350568 Mobile 07712-086540 E-mail rosemary@foale16.fsworld.co.uk

MASON, Simon Ion Vincent. b 60. Birm Univ BA82. Trin Coll Bris BA00. **d** 00 **p** 01. C Nottingham St Nic *S'well* 00-05; P-in-c Newent and Gorsley w Cliffords Mesne *Glouc* from 05. *The Rectory, 43 Court Road, Newent GL18 1SY* Tel (01531) 820248 E-mail mason.simon@ntlworld.com *or* stmarys.church@talk21.com

MASON, Stephen David. b 65. Univ of Wales (Lamp) BA87. Ripon Coll Cuddesdon 89. **d** 92 **p** 93. C Gt Grimsby St Mary and St Jas *Linc* 92-97; V Southborough St Thos *Roch* 97-02; V Paddington St Jo w St Mich *Lon* from 02. *18 Somers Crescent, London W2 2PN* Tel (020) 7706 8101 *or* 7262 1732 Fax 7706 4475 E-mail parishadmin@stjohns-hydepark.com

MASON, Terry Mathew. b 56. Trin Coll Bris 94. **d** 96 **p** 97. C Bexleyheath Ch Ch *Roch* 96-99; P-in-c Stone 99-03; V Broadway w Wickhamford *Worc* from 03; RD Evesham from 05. *The Vicarage, Church Street, Broadway WR12 7AE* Tel (01386) 852352 E-mail broadwayvicarage@tesco.net

MASON, Preb Thomas Edward. b 52. Bris Univ MEd80. Trin Coll Bris BA91. **d** 91 **p** 92. C Glouc St Jas and All SS 91-94; V Churchdown 94-04; RD Glouc N 99-04; R Bath Abbey w St Jas *B & W* from 04; Preb Wells Cathl from 05. *The Rectory, 12 Cleveland Walk, Bath BA2 6JX* Tel (01225) 318267 *or* 422462 E-mail rector@bathabbey.org

MASON, Canon Thomas Henry Ambrose. b 51. Solicitor 75. Oak Hill Th Coll BA86. **d** 86 **p** 87. C W Drayton *Lon* 86-89; Field Officer Oak Hill Ext Coll 89-94; Eur Sec ICS 94-95; Dir of Tr *Eur* 95-03; Dir Min and Dir of Ords 01-03; Can Brussels Cathl 00-03; Hon Can 03-07; R Grosmont and Skenfrith and Llangattock etc *Mon* 03-08; Dioc Dir Min from 06. *The Rectory, Gwernesney, Usk NP15 1HP* Tel (01291) 672152 E-mail ambrose@rectorygwernesney.com

MASON, William Frederick. b 48. Linc Th Coll 75. **d** 78 **p** 79. C Ipswich St Aug *St E* 78-81; TV Dronfield *Derby* 81-88; V Ellesmere St Pet *Sheff* 88-91; V Bedgrove *Ox* 91-00; C Hazlemere 00-07; V Penn Street from 07. *The Vicarage, Penn Street, Amersham HP7 0PX* Tel (01494) 715195 E-mail willfmason@aol.com

MASSEY, Mrs Elizabeth Ann. b 53. N Staffs Poly BSc75. STETS 04. **d** 07 **p** 08. NSM Whitton *Sarum* from 07. *Fairacre, Upavon Road, North Newnton, Pewsey SN9 6JT* Tel (01980) 630256 Mobile 07971-246763 E-mail annmassey@beeb.net

MASSEY, George Douglas. b 44. St Jo Coll Nottm 91. **d** 93 **p** 94. C Higher Bebington *Ches* 93-98; V Messingham *Linc* from 98. *The Vicarage, 12 Holme Lane, Messingham, Scunthorpe DN17 3SG* Tel (01724) 762823 E-mail george.massey@ntlworld.com

MASSEY, Keith John. b 46. Oak Hill Th Coll 69. **d** 72 **p** 73. C Bermondsey St Jas w Ch Ch *S'wark* 72-76; C Benchill Man 76-82; V Clifton Green 82-97; V Flixton St Jo from 97. *St John's Vicarage, Irlam Road, Urmston, Manchester M41 6AP* Tel 0161-748 6754

MASSEY, Michelle Elaine (Shellie). Plymouth Univ BA00. Trin Coll Bris BA04. **d** 04 **p** 05. C Barrowby and Gt Gonerby *Linc* 04-09; P-in-c Saxonwell from 09. *15 Manor Drive, Long Bennington, Newark NG23 5GZ* Tel (01400) 282696 Mobile 07876-645786 E-mail revdmichellem@aol.com

MASSEY, Nigel John. b 60. Birm Univ BA81 MA82. Wycliffe Hall Ox. **d** 87 **p** 88. C Bearwood *Birm* 87-90; C Warley Woods 90; C Tottenham St Paul *Lon* 91-94; USA from 94. *French Church du St Spirit, 111 East 60th Street #4, New York NY 10022, USA* Tel (001) (212) 838 5680 E-mail stesprit@msn.com

MASSEY, Paul Daniel Shaw. b 70. Nottm Univ BA93. Westcott Ho Cam 94. **d** 96 **p** 97. C Ashby-de-la-Zouch St Helen w Coleorton *Leic* 96-01; R Cotgrave *S'well* from 01; P-in-c Owthorpe from 01. *The Rectory, 2 Thurman Drive, Cotgrave, Nottingham NG12 3LG* Tel and fax 0115-989 2223 E-mail pdsmassey@tiscali.co.uk

MASSEY, Peter William. b 45. St Mark & St Jo Coll Lon TCert66 Open Univ BA75. WMMTC 96. **d** 99 **p** 00. Lay Tr Officer *Heref* 97-09; NSM Holmer w Huntington 99-03; NSM Heref St Pet w St Owen and St Jas from 03. *15 Thoresby Drive, Hereford HR2 7RF* Tel and fax (01432) 270248 Mobile 07803-826728 E-mail p.massey@hereford.anglican.org

MASSEY, Shellie. *See* MASSEY, Michelle Elaine

MASSEY, Stephen William. b 56. Hatf Poly BSc79 PhD86 MIMA04. ERMC 06. **d** 09. NSM Watford St Luke *St Alb* from 09. *19 South Riding, Bricket Wood, St Albans AL2 3NG* Tel (01923) 662368 E-mail swmportraits@xalt.co.uk

MASSEY, Wayne Philip. b 74. Brunel Univ BSc97. Wycliffe Hall Ox BA05. **d** 06 **p** 07. C Clifton Ch Ch w Em *Bris* from 06. *2nd*
Floor Flat, Linden Gate, Clifton Down Road, Bristol BS8 4AH Tel 0117-973 5220

MASSEY, Preb William Cyril. b 32. Lich Th Coll 58. **d** 61 **p** 62. C Heref St Martin 61-66; V Kimbolton w Middleton-on-the-Hill 66-75; V Alveley 75-83; P-in-c Quatt 81-83; R Alveley and Quatt 84-85; R Llangarron w Llangrove, Whitchurch and Ganarew 85-97; Preb Heref Cathl 92-97; rtd 97; Perm to Offic *Heref* from 97. *Hollybush Cottage, Pencombe, Bromyard HR7 4RW* Tel (01885) 400713

MASSEY, William Peter. b 50. CITC 96. **d** 99 **p** 00. C Fermoy Union *C, C & R* 99-00; C Carrigrohane Union and Kinsale Union 00-03; Perm to Offic *Eur* from 04. *1801 chemin des Pailles, Lorgues, 83510 France* Tel (0033) (4) 94 73 93 37 E-mail peter@themasseys.fr

MASSHEDAR, Richard Eric. b 57. Nottm Univ BTh86. Linc Th Coll 83. **d** 86 **p** 87. C Cassop cum Quarrington *Dur* 86-89; C Ferryhill 89-91; V Leam Lane 91-94; P-in-c Hartlepool St Paul 94-96; V from 96. *St Paul's Vicarage, 6 Hutton Avenue, Hartlepool TS26 9PN* Tel (01429) 272934 E-mail r.masshedar@ntlworld.com

MASSINGBERD-MUNDY, Roger William Burrell. b 36. TD. Univ of Wales (Lamp) BA59. Ridley Hall Cam 59. **d** 61 **p** 62. C Benwell St Jas *Newc* 61-64; C Whorlton 64-72; TV 73; P-in-c Healey 73-85; Dioc Stewardship Adv 73-85; Hon Can Newc Cathl 82-85; CF (TA) 63-68; CF (TAVR) 71-83; R S Ormsby w Ketsby, Calceby and Driby *Linc* 85-86; P-in-c Harrington w Brinkhill 85-86; P-in-c Haugh 85-86; P-in-c Oxcombe 85-86; P-in-c Ruckland w Farforth and Maidenwell 85-86; P-in-c Somersby w Bag Enderby 85-86; P-in-c Tetford and Salmonby 85-86; R S Ormsby Gp 86-96; RD Bolingbroke 88-96; rtd 96; Chapl Taverham Hall Sch from 03. *The Old Post Office, West Raynham, Fakenham NR21 7AD* Tel (01328) 838611 Fax 838698 E-mail rogermundy@markeaton.co.uk

MASSON, Canon Philip Roy. b 52. Hertf Coll Ox BA75 Leeds Univ MA77. Coll of Resurr Mirfield 75. **d** 78 **p** 79. C Port Talbot St Theodore *Llan* 78-82; V Penyfai w Tondu 82-92; Dioc Dir Post-Ord Tr 85-88; Warden of Ords 88-01; R Newton Nottage from 92; AD Margam 01-06; Can Llan Cathl from 02. *The Rectory, 64 Victoria Avenue, Porthcawl CF36 3HE* Tel and fax (01656) 782042 *or* 786899 E-mail porthcawl.cathl@tiscali.co.uk *or* philipmasson@hotmail.com

MASTERMAN, Malcolm. b 49. City Univ MSc00. K Coll Lon 73 Chich Th Coll 76. **d** 77 **p** 78. C Peterlee *Dur* 77-80; Chapl Basingstoke Distr Hosp 80-85; Chapl Freeman Hosp Newc 85-95; Tr and Development Officer Hosp Chapl Coun 96-00; Sen Chapl N Dur Healthcare NHS Trust 00-02; Sen Chapl Co Durham and Darlington Acute Hosps NHS Trust 02-06; Lead Chapl S Tees Hosps NHS Trust from 06; Bp's Adv on Hosp Chapl (Whitby Area) *York* from 06. *James Cook University Hospital, Marton Road, Middlesbrough TS4 3BW* Tel (01642) 854802 *or* 850850 E-mail malcolm.masterman@stees.nhs.uk

MASTERMAN, Miss Patricia Hope. b 28. St Mich Ho Ox 59. **dss** 79 **d** 87. Asst CF 79-90; rtd 90; Perm to Offic *Chich* from 90. *33 Sea Lane Gardens, Ferring, Worthing BN12 5EQ* Tel (01903) 245231

MASTERS, Kenneth Leslie. b 44. Leeds Univ BA68. Cuddesdon Coll 68. **d** 70 **p** 71. C Wednesbury St Paul Wood Green *Lich* 70-71; C Tettenhall Regis 71-75; TV Chelmsley Wood *Birm* 75-79; R Harting *Chich* 79-87; V Rustington 87-00; TR Beaminster Area *Sarum* from 00. *The Rectory, 3 Clay Lane, Beaminster DT8 3BU* Tel (01308) 862150 E-mail k2masters4@btinternet.com

MASTERS, Stephen Michael. b 52. **d** 87 **p** 88. C Primrose Hill St Mary w Avenue Road St Paul *Lon* 87-90; C Hornsey St Mary w St Geo 90-91; Bp's Dom Chapl *Chich* 91-96; V Brighton St Mich 96-99; C Eastbourne St Andr 00-01; Chapl to Bp Lewes 00-01; Asst to Adn Lewes and Hastings 00-01; P-in-c Alderney Win 01-03; V from 03. *The New Vicarage, La Vallee, Alderney, Guernsey GY9 3XA* Tel (01481) 824866

MASTIN, Brian Arthur. b 38. Peterho Cam BA60 MA63 BD80 Mert Coll Ox MA63. Ripon Hall Ox 62. **d** 63 **p** 64. Asst Lect Hebrew Univ Coll of N Wales (Ban) 63-65; Lect Hebrew 65-82; Sen Lect 82-98; Chapl Ban Cathl 63-65; Lic to Offic 65-98; rtd 98; Perm to Offic *Ely* from 98. *2A Gurney Way, Cambridge CB4 2ED* Tel (01223) 355078

MATABELELAND, Bishop of. *See* LUNGA, The Rt Revd Cleophus

MATANA, Bishop of. *See* NTAHOTURI, The Most Revd Bernard

MATCHETT, Alan William. b 70. TCD BTh01. CITC 98. **d** 01 **p** 02. C Limerick City *L & K* 01-03; C Stillorgan w Blackrock *D & G* 03-05; I Balliehorough w Knockbride, Shercock and Mullagh *K, E & A* 05-08; I Adare and Kilmallock w Kilpeacon, Croom etc *L & K* from 08. *The Rectory, Adare, Co Limerick, Republic of Ireland* Tel (00353) (61) 396227 Mobile 87-964 2054 E-mail alanmatc@mac.com

MATCHETT, Christopher Jonathan. b 65. QUB BSSc TCD BTh98. **d** 98 **p** 99. C Ballynafeigh St Jude *D & D* 98-01; C

Holywood 01-04; I Magheracross *Clogh* from 04. *The Rectory, 27 Craghan Road, Ballinamallard, Enniskillen BT94 2BT* Tel and fax (028) 6638 8238 E-mail magheracross@clogher.anglican.org

MATCHETT, Miss Diane Margaret. b 71. Open Univ BA98. TCD Div Sch BTh05. **d** 05 **p** 06. C Lisburn Ch Ch *Conn* 05-08; I Castlerock w Dunboe and Fermoyle *D & R* from 08. *The Rectory, 52 Main Street, Castlerock, Coleraine BT51 4RA* Tel (028) 7084 8127 Mobile 07853-186509
E-mail revdiane@hotmail.co.uk

MATHER, Cuthbert. b 15. Tyndale Hall Bris 36. **d** 40 **p** 41. C Bebington *Ches* 40-42; C Stapenhill w Cauldwell *Derby* 43-51; C Cambridge St Andr Less *Ely* 51-52; C Dagenham *Chelmsf* 53-57; V Needham w Rushall *Nor* 57-80; rtd 80; Perm to Offic *Nor* from 80. *9 Gorselands, 25 Sandringham Road, Hunstanton PE36 5DP* Tel (01485) 533084

MATHER, David Jonathan. b 65. New Coll Ox BA88 MA95. St Steph Ho Ox BTh95. **d** 95 **p** 96. C Pickering w Lockton and Levisham *York* 95-98; P-in-c Bridlington H Trin and Sewerby w Marton 98-99; V from 99. *Sewerby Vicarage, Cloverley Road, Bridlington YO16 5TX* Tel (01262) 675725

MATHER, Mrs Elizabeth Ann. b 45. CertEd66. Dalton Ho Bris IDC70 St Jo Coll Nottm 92. **d** 94 **p** 95. NSM Littleover *Derby* 94-02; Lic to Offic *St Alb* 02-05; rtd 05; Perm to Offic *York* from 05. *The Rectory, 139 Laburnum Avenue, Garden Village, Hull HU8 8PA* Tel (01482) 377210
E-mail revlib@libbymather.freeserve.co.uk

MATHER, James William. b 63. Sheff Univ BA86. St Steph Ho Ox 88. **d** 91 **p** 92. C Doncaster St Leon and St Jude *Sheff* 91-94; C Cantley 94-95; V Lakenheath *St E* 95-01; P-in-c Downham Market w Bexwell *Ely* 01-02; P-in-c Crimplesham w Stradsett 01-02; R Downham Market and Crimplesham w Stradsett from 02; RD Fincham and Feltwell from 06. *The Rectory, King's Walk, Downham Market PE38 9LF* Tel (01366) 382187

MATHER, Stephen Albert. b 54. Qu Coll Birm 85. **d** 87 **p** 88. C Sutton *Liv* 87-90; TV 90-96; V Abram 96-99; V Bickershaw 96-99; V Hindley St Pet from 99. *St Peter's Vicarage, 122 Wigan Road, Hindley, Wigan WN2 3DF* Tel (01942) 55505

MATHER, William Bernard George. b 45. St Jo Coll Nottm 77. **d** 79 **p** 80. C St Leonards St Leon *Chich* 79-82; TR Netherthorpe *Sheff* 82-90; V Littleover *Derby* 90-02; Assoc Dir SOMA UK 02-05; TR Drypool *York* from 05. *The Rectory, 139 Laburnum Avenue, Garden Village, Hull HU8 8PA* Tel (01482) 786553
E-mail williammather@gmail.com

MATHERS, Alan Edward. b 36. Lon Univ BA FPhS. Oak Hill Th Coll 61. **d** 64 **p** 65. C Ox St Matt 64-66; C Bootle St Leon *Liv* 66-68; C Hampreston *Sarum* 68-70; P-in-c Damerham 70-71; V Queniborough *Leic* 71-76; USA 76-77; V Tipton St Matt *Lich* 77-86; P-in-c Tipton St Paul 77-84; V 85-86; V Sutton Ch Ch *S'wark* 86-95; Chapl Cannes *Eur* 95-98; rtd 98; Perm to Offic *S'wark* and *Chich* from 98. *52 The Meadow, Copthorne, Crawley RH10 3RQ* Tel (01342) 713325

MATHERS, David Michael Brownlow. b 43. Em Coll Cam BA65 MA69. Clifton Th Coll 65. **d** 67 **p** 68. C Branksome St Clem *Sarum* 67-70; C Bromley Ch Ch *Roch* 70-73; V Bures *St E* 73-80; Brazil 80-82; P-in-c Old Newton w Stowupland *St E* 82-86; V 87-90; V Thurston from 90; RD Ixworth 94-03. *The Vicarage, Church Road, Thurston, Bury St Edmunds IP31 3RU* Tel (01359) 230301

MATHERS, Derek. b 48. NOC 82. **d** 85 **p** 86. C Huddersfield St Jo *Wakef* 85-86; C N Huddersfield 86-88; TV Almondbury w Farnley Tyas 88-92; V Marsden 92-02; R Badsworth from 02. *The Rectory, Main Street, Badsworth, Pontefract WF9 1AF* Tel (01977) 643642 E-mail father.derek@badsworth.com

MATHERS, Kenneth Ernest William. b 56. Trin Coll Bris 93. **d** 95 **p** 96. C Bournemouth St Jo w St Mich *Win* 95-99; NSM Darenth *Roch* 99-04; Chapl Dartford and Gravesham NHS Trust 01-04; Chapl N Devon Healthcare NHS Trust from 05. *The Rectory, Newton Tracey, Barnstaple EX31 3PL* Tel (01271) 858292 E-mail revkmathers@btinternet.com

MATHERS, Mrs Kim Deborah. b 61. Southn Univ LLB82. Trin Coll Bris 86. **d** 89 **p** 94. Par Dn Bitterne *Win* 89-93; NSM Stoke Bishop *Bris* 93-95; NSM Bournemouth St Jo w St Mich *Win* 95-99; P-in-c Darenth *Roch* 99-04; TR Newton Tracey, Horwood, Alverdiscott etc *Ex* from 04; RD Torrington from 09. *The Rectory, Newton Tracey, Barnstaple EX31 3PL* Tel (01271) 858292 E-mail revkimmathers@btinternet.com

MATHESON, Alexander John. b 59. Lon Bible Coll BA84 S Tr Scheme 94. **d** 97 **p** 98. NSM Cowplain *Portsm* 97-01; C Portchester 01-04; V Sarisbury from 04. *The Vicarage, 149 Bridge Road, Sarisbury Green, Southampton SO31 7EN* Tel (01489) 572207 E-mail sandy@mathesonuk.com

MATHEW, Laurence Allen Stanfield. b 47. Sarum Th Coll 99. **d** 02 **p** 03. OLM Warminster Ch Ch *Sarum* from 02. *Chalvedune, 25 King Street, Warminster BA12 9AY* Tel (01985) 217282 Mobile 07768-006245 E-mail laurence01@blueyonder.co.uk

MATHEW (née HOLLIS), Rebecca Catherine. b 78. St Martin's Coll Lanc BA99. Ripon Coll Cuddesdon BTh03. **d** 03 **p** 04. C Broughton *Blackb* 03-07; C Mirihana Ch Ch Sri Lanka 07-08;

Chapl St Thos Coll Mt Lavina from 08. *Chaplain's Bungalow, St Thomas' College, Mount Lavina, Sri Lanka*
E-mail revdrebh@hotmail.com

MATHEWS, Richard Twitchell. b 27. Bps' Coll Cheshunt 57. **d** 59 **p** 60. C Leic St Phil 59-62; Chapl Beirut 62-63; Qatar 63-67; V Riddlesden *Bradf* 67-74; Australia 74-78; P-in-c Medbourne cum Holt w Stockerston and Blaston *Leic* 78-82; Chapl Alassio *Eur* 82-83; Chapl San Remo 82-83; Chapl Palma and Balearic Is w Ibiza etc 83-87; P-in-c Witchford w Wentworth *Ely* 87-91; rtd 91; Perm to Offic *Cant* 96-09. *Rosecroft, Church Lane, Ringwould, Deal CT14 8HR* Tel (01304) 367554

MATHEWS, Trevor John. b 50. Goldsmiths' Coll Lon MSc98. St Steph Ho Ox 87. **d** 89 **p** 90. C Cheltenham St Steph *Glouc* 89-91; C Up Hatherley 89-91; Perm to Offic *Chelmsf* from 08; CF from 09. *c/o MOD Chaplains (Army)* Tel (01980) 615804 Fax 615800
E-mail mathews@conflict.co.uk

MATHIAS, John Maelgwyn. b 15. St D Coll Lamp BA38 St Mich Coll Llan 40. **d** 40 **p** 41. C Ban St Mary 40-44; C Swansea St Pet *S & B* 44-49; V Mydroilyn w Dihewyd *St D* 49-54; R Cellan w Llanfair Clydogau 54-83; Lect St Jo Ch Coll Ystrad Meurig 67-77; rtd 83. *Bronallt, Capel Seion Road, Drefach, Llanelli SA14 7BN* Tel (01269) 844350

MATHIAS, Ms Lesley. b 49. Portsm Poly BA72 Nottm Univ MTh90. EMMTC 93. **d** 96 **p** 97. C Oadby *Leic* 96-98; Asst Chapl United Bris Healthcare NHS Trust 98-99; C Pet St Mary Boongate 99-01; V Kings Heath 01-06; Bp's Interfaith Adv 01-05; Perm to Offic *Pet* from 06 and *Ely* from 08. *4 Manor Walk, Hanging Houghton, Northampton NN6 9EP* Tel (01604) 880968 E-mail lesley@lmathias.freeserve.co.uk

MATHIAS-JONES, Edward Lloyd. b 71. Univ of Wales (Lamp) BA93. St Mich Coll Llan BD96. **d** 97 **p** 98. C Llanelli *St D* 97-00; C Milford Haven 00-04; V Newport St Steph and H Trin *Mon* from 04. *St Stephen's Vicarage, Adeline Street, Newport NP20 2HA* Tel (01633) 265192
E-mail frmathias-jones@aol.com

MATHIE, Patricia Jean (Sister Donella). b 22. Worc Coll of Educn CertEd49. **dss** 79 **d** 87. CSA from 74; Asst Superior 82-94; Mother Superior 94-00; Notting Hill St Jo *Lon* 79-80; Abbey Ho Malmesbury 81-82; Notting Hill St Clem and St Mark 82-84; Kensal Town St Thos w St Andr and St Phil 85-87; Hon C 87-96; Perm to Offic 00-09. *34 Reynard Court, Foxley Lane, Purley CR8 3EN* Tel (020) 8668 8401

MATLOOB, Nazir Ahmad Barnabas. b 48. Punjab Univ BA79. Gujranwala Th Sem BTh77 BD81 MDiv85. **d** 78 **p** 78. Pakistan 78-93; Perm to Offic *Chelmsf* 94-97; C Forest Gate All SS and St Edm 98-06; C Lt Ilford St Barn 06; Inter-Faith Worker Newham Deanery from 07. *64 Henderson Road, London E7 8EF* Tel (020) 8552 4280

MATON, Oswald. b 24. St Aug Coll Cant 75. **d** 77 **p** 78. NSM Chatham St Steph *Roch* 77-94; Perm to Offic 94-04. *304 Maidstone Road, Chatham ME4 6JJ* Tel (01634) 843568

MATSON de LAURIER, Mrs Sarah Kennerley. b 46. EMMTC 00. **d** 02 **p** 03. NSM Hilton w Marston-on-Dove *Derby* from 02. *1 Park Way, Etwall, Derby DE65 6HU* Tel (01283) 732859
E-mail pskmdl@aol.com

MATTACKS, Mrs Lesley Anne. b 58. Birm Univ BA79 K Coll Lon MA86 Leeds Univ BA07 W Lon Inst of HE PGCE80. NOC 04. **d** 07 **p** 08. C Birkenshaw w Hunsworth *Wakef* from 07. *10 Southcroft Gate, Birkenshaw, Bradford BD11 2DQ* Tel (01274) 686822 Mobile 07952-375176
E-mail mattacks@blueyonder.co.uk

MATTAPALLY, Sebastian. b 57. N Bengal Univ BA77 Pontifical Salesian Univ BTh84 Pontifical Gregorian Univ LTh98 DTh05. **d** 83 **p** 83. In RC Ch 83-00; Perm to Offic *Eur* 01-04; C Patcham *Chich* 05-07; P-in-c Kirdford from 07. *The Vicarage, Kirdford, Billingshurst RH14 0LU* Tel (01403) 820605
E-mail kirdford_vicar@tiscali.co.uk

MATTEN, Derek Norman William. b 30. Man Univ BA51. Wycliffe Hall Ox 54. **d** 56 **p** 57. C Farnworth *Liv* 56-59; C Walton H Trin *Ox* 59-62; Chapl Kampala and Entebbe Uganda 62-69; Lic to Offic *Eur* 69-93; W Germany 69-90; Germany 90-93; rtd 93; Hon C Modbury, Bigbury, Ringmore w Kingston etc *Ex* 95-00; Perm to Offic from 01. *1 Bramley Meadow, Landkey, Barnstaple EX32 0PB* Tel (01271) 830952
E-mail dnwm@supanet.com

MATTHEWS, Adrian James. b 51. Edge Hill Coll of HE CertEd73. NOC. **d** 87 **p** 88. C Blackley St Andr *Man* 87-90; NSM Tonge w Alkrington 96-01; R Failsworth St Jo from 01. *St John's Rectory, Pole Lane, Manchester M35 9PB* Tel and fax 0161-681 2734

MATTHEWS, The Rt Revd Alan Montague (Dom Basil). b 37. Ex Univ BA86. **d** 02 **p** 02. OSB from 65; Abbot Elmore Abbey from 88. *Elmore Abbey, Church Lane, Speen, Newbury RG14 1SA* Tel (01635) 33080 Fax 580759

MATTHEWS, Anita Kathryn. b 70. Dur Univ BTh91. Ripon Coll Cuddesdon 93. **d** 97 **p** 98. C E Barnet *St Alb* 97-01; Chapl Derby High Sch 01-05; Nat Adv for Children's Work CMS from 05. *5 Bamford Avenue, Derby DE23 8DT* Tel (01332) 270917

MATTHEWS, Mrs Anna Ruth. b 78. Rob Coll Cam BA99 MA03 MPhil03. Westcott Ho Cam 01. **d** 03 **p** 04. C Abbots Langley *St Alb* 03-06; Min Can St Alb Abbey from 06. *1 The Deanery, Sumpter Yard, Holywell Hill, St Albans AL1 1BY* Tel (01727) 890207 Mobile 07534-940582
E-mail mcl@stalbanscathedral.org.uk

MATTHEWS, Barry Alan. b 46. AKC68. St Boniface Warminster 68 St Paul's Coll Grahamstown 69. **d** 69 **p** 70. S Africa 69-74, 77-83 and 01-04; C De Aar 69-72; C Kimberley St Aug 72-74; P-in-c Kimberley St Matt 74-75; C Leeds St Aid *Ripon* 75-77; R Vryburg St Steph 77-81; Dioc Missr 81-82; R Kimberley St Aug 82-83; C Shotton *St As* 83-84; R Hwange St Jas Zimbabwe 84-89; R Bulawayo N St Marg 89-95; R Nkulumane H Family 95-97; Adn N Matabeleland 89-97; Sen P St Mary's Cathl Harare 97-00; rtd 01. *23 Clovelly Drive, Newburgh, Wigan WN8 7LY*

MATTHEWS, Basil. *See* MATTHEWS, The Rt Revd Alan Montague

MATTHEWS, Canon Campbell Thurlow. b 33. Lon Univ BA56 Dur Univ DipEd57. St Jo Coll Nottm 70. **d** 71 **p** 72. C Ryton *Dur* 71-74; Chapl R Victoria Infirmary Newc 74-82; V Greenside *Dur* 74-82; R Wetheral w Warwick *Carl* 82-93; RD Brampton 83-91; P-in-c Farlam and Nether Denton 87-93; P-in-c Gilsland 87-93; Hon Can Carl Cathl 87-00; P-in-c Thornthwaite cum Braithwaite and Newlands 93-00; P-in-c Borrowdale 97-00; rtd 00; Perm to Offic *Carl* from 00 and *Newc* from 01. *The Hayes, Newcastle Road, Corbridge NE45 5LP* Tel (01434) 632010

MATTHEWS, Celia Inger. b 30. St Chris Coll Blackheath 50. **d** 86 **p** 94. Dioc Missr *St And* from 86; rtd 95. *24 Barossa Place, Perth PH1 5HH* Tel (01738) 623578
E-mail cmatthews@toucansurf.com

MATTHEWS, Cilla. *See* MATTHEWS, Mrs Francilla Lacey

MATTHEWS, Canon Colin John. b 44. Jes Coll Ox BA67 MA71 Fitzw Coll Cam BA70 MA74. Ridley Hall Cam 68. **d** 71 **p** 72. C Onslow Square St Paul *Lon* 71-74; C Leic H Apostles 74-78; Bible Use Sec Scripture Union 78-89; Dir Ch Cen Guildf St Sav 89-95; V Burpham from 95; RD Guildf 01-06; Hon Can Guildf Cathl from 02. *272 London Road, Burpham, Guildford GU4 7LF* Tel 07787-575923 (mobile) E-mail vicarage@ntlworld.com

MATTHEWS, David Charles. b 61. TCD BA84 HDipEd86 MA87 BTh95 Lille Univ LèsL85. CITC 95. **d** 95 **p** 96. C Arm St Mark 95-97; Hon V Choral Arm Cathl 96-97; Min Can and Chapl St Woolos Cathl 97-01; V Marshfield and Peterstone Wentloog etc from 01. *The Vicarage, Church Lane, Marshfield, Cardiff CF3 2UF* Tel (01633) 680257
E-mail david@hebron97.freeserve.co.uk

MATTHEWS, David William. b 49. St Paul's Coll Grahamstown 88. **d** 90 **p** 91. S Africa 90-03; C Port Eliz St Sav 90-91; C Port Eliz St Paul 91-94; R Zwartkops River Valley Par 94-00; Chapl Miss to Seafarers 00-03; R Boxford, Edwardstone, Groton etc *St E* 03-09; P-in-c Southn St Anne Bermuda from 09. *St Anne's Rectory, 74 Middle Road, Southampton, Bermuda* Tel (001) (441) 238 0370 E-mail stannesrectory@logic.bm

MATTHEWS, David William Grover. b 73. Acadia Univ (NS) BA93 Toronto Univ MDiv98. Trin Coll Toronto 95. **d** 98 **p** 99. C Newport St Teilo *Mon* 98-00; NSM Cobbold Road St Sav w St Mary *Lon* 00-03; P-in-c Hammersmith H Innocents 03-05; P-in-c Hammersmith H Innocents and St Thomas from 05. *35 Paddenswick Road, London W6 0UA* Tel (020) 8741 6480 E-mail holyinnocentsw6@yahoo.com

MATTHEWS, Mrs Deborah Lynne. b 57. Southn Univ BTh98 MCIPD92. Ripon Coll Cuddesdon MTh01. **d** 00 **p** 01. C Southampton (City Cen) *Win* 00-04; V Clapham St Paul *S'wark* from 04. *St Paul's Vicarage, Rectory Grove, London SW4 0DX* Tel (020) 7622 2128 E-mail revdebmatthews@waitrose.com

MATTHEWS, Mrs Diana Elizabeth Charlotte. b 43. MCSP65. **d** 93 **p** 96. OLM Merrow *Guildf* from 93. *Avila, 13 Wells Road, Guildford GU4 7XQ* Tel (01483) 839738
E-mail diana.matthews@ntlworld.com

MATTHEWS, Mrs Francilla Lacey. b 37. S'wark Ord Course 83. dss 86 **d** 87 **p** 94. Bromley St Mark *Roch* 86-90; Hon Par Dn 87-90; Par Dn Hayes 90-94; C 94-02; rtd 02; Perm to Offic *Roch* from 02. *71 Hayes Road, Bromley BR2 9AE* Tel (020) 8464 4083

MATTHEWS, Frederick Peter. b 45. Grey Coll Dur BA66 MA68 K Coll Lon PGCE68 Lon Univ BSc(Econ)75. Sarum & Wells Th Coll 70. **d** 72 **p** 73. C W Wickham St Jo *Cant* 72-74; C Sholing *Win* 74-77; Lic to Offic 78-79; V Woolston 79-03; P-in-c Over Wallop w Nether Wallop 03-07; Dioc Ecum Officer 03-07; rtd 07; Perm to Offic *Sarum* and *Win* from 07. *19 Berkshire Road, Salisbury SP2 8NY* Tel (01722) 340508
E-mail fpetermatthews@hotmail.com

MATTHEWS, George Charles Wallace. b 27. Sarum Th Coll 58. **d** 60 **p** 61. C Coppenhall St Paul *Ches* 60-63; C Lewes St Anne *Chich* 63-67; V Wheelock *Ches* 67-76; V Mossley 76-93; rtd 93; Perm to Offic *Ches* from 93. *145 Primrose Avenue, Haslington, Crewe CW1 5QB* Tel (01270) 587463

MATTHEWS, Gerald Lancelot. b 31. Bris Univ LLB50. Ripon Hall Ox 55. **d** 57 **p** 58. C The Quinton *Birm* 57-60; C Olton 60-63; V Brent Tor *Ex* 63-72; P-in-c Lydford w Bridestowe and

Sourton 70-72; TR Lydford, Brent Tor, Bridestowe and Sourton 72-78; P-in-c Black Torrington, Bradford w Cookbury etc 78-90; Perm to Offic from 90; rtd 94. *The Larches, Black Torrington, Beaworthy EX21 5PU* Tel (01409) 231228

MATTHEWS, Harold James. b 46. Leeds Univ BSc68 Fitzw Coll Cam BA70 MA74. Westcott Ho Cam 68. **d** 71 **p** 72. C Mossley Hill St Matt and St Jas *Liv* 71-74; C Stanley 74-76; TV Hackney *Lon* 76-78; Chapl Forest Sch Snaresbrook 78-83; Hd Master Vernon Holme Sch Cant 83-88; Perm to Offic *Cant* 83-88; Hd Master Heath Mt Sch Hertf 88-06; Chapl Roedean Sch Brighton from 06. *Roedean School, Roedean Way, Brighton BN2 5RQ* Tel (01273) 676353 E-mail ham@roedean.co.uk

MATTHEWS, Hayley. b 68. Ridley Hall Cam 05. **d** 07 **p** 08. C Lancaster St Mary w St John and St Anne *Blackb* from 07. *Chauntry Cottage, Priory Close, Lancaster LA1 1YZ* Tel (01524) 849123

MATTHEWS, Mrs Heather Ann. b 49. Bris Univ BA71 Lon Univ CertEd72. Trin Coll Bris 87. **d** 89 **p** 94. C Blagdon w Compton Martin and Ubley *B & W* 89-93; Dn-in-c 93-94; R 94-01; R Hodnet w Weston under Redcastle *Lich* 01-03; C Skipton Ch Ch *Bradf* 03-04; rtd 04. *The Sett, Yate Lane, Oxenhope, Keighley BD22 9HL* Tel (01535) 649095

MATTHEWS, Canon Joan Muriel. b 53. NOC 89. **d** 92 **p** 94. C Aughton St Mich *Liv* 92-97; R Wavertree St Mary 97-06; AD Toxteth and Wavertree 04-06; Hon Can Liv Cathl 04-06 and from 07; P-in-c Newton in Makerfield St Pet 06-07; P-in-c Earlestown 06-07; TR Newton from 08; AD Winwick from 09. *8 Parchments, Newton-le-Willows WA12 9SR* Tel (01925) 270795 E-mail revjoan@hotmail.com

MATTHEWS, John Goodman. b 77. Univ of Wales BTh99. St Mich Coll Llan 99. **d** 02 **p** 03. C Lampeter and Llanddewibrefi Gp *St D* 02-05; P-in-c Aberporth w Tremain w Blaenporth and Betws Ifan 05-07; V from 07. *The Rectory, Aberporth, Cardigan SA43 2BX* Tel (01239) 810556

MATTHEWS, Lewis William (Bill). b 29. St Jo Coll Dur BA53 MSc76. **d** 55 **p** 56. C Eston *York* 55-57; Ind Chapl *Sheff* 57-61; V Copt Oak *Leic* 61-64; R Braunstone 64-70; V Thornaby on Tees St Paul *York* 70-72; TR Thornaby on Tees 72-78; Dir Dioc Bd for Soc Resp *Lon* 79-84; Perm to Offic 84-94; Warden Durning Hall Chr Community Cen Forest Gate 84-94; rtd 94; Hon C Jersey Gouray St Martin *Win* 94-06. *2 Malvern, La Ruelle es Ruaux, St Brelade, Jersey JE3 8BB* Tel (01534) 498368 Mobile 07797-731143 E-mail billmatthews@jerseymail.co.uk

MATTHEWS, Liam. *See* MATTHEWS, William Temple Atkinson

MATTHEWS, Canon Melvyn William. b 40. St Edm Hall Ox BA63 MA68. K Coll Lon BD66 AKC67. **d** 67 **p** 68. C Enfield St Andr *Lon* 67-70; Asst Chapl Southn Univ 70-72; Lect Univ of Nairobi Kenya 72-76; V Highgate All SS *Lon* 76-79; P-in-c Clifton St Paul *Bris* 79-87; Sen Chapl Bris Univ 79-87; Dir Ammerdown Cen for Study and Renewal 87-93; V Chew Magna w Dundry *B & W* 93-97; Can and Chan Wells Cathl 97-05; rtd 05; Perm to Offic *B & W* from 05. *Yew Tree House, 22 Beaufort Avenue, Midsomer Norton, Radstock BA3 2TG* Tel (01761) 413630 E-mail mwmatthews@onetel.com

MATTHEWS, Michael Raymond. b 55. JP96. Huddersfield Univ MBA96 Leeds Univ BA04 CQSW82. Coll of Resurr Mirfield 02. **d** 04 **p** 05. C Featherstone and Purston cum S Featherstone *Wakef* 04 07; P-in-c Haslingfield w Harlton and Gt and Lt Eversden *Ely* from 07. *The Vicarage, Broad Lane, Haslingfield, Cambridge CB3 7JF* Tel (01223) 870285
E-mail frmichaelmatthews@yahoo.co.uk

MATTHEWS, Paul. b 47. Brunel Univ BTech70. S Dios Minl Tr Scheme 89. **d** 92 **p** 93. NSM Goring-by-Sea *Chich* from 92. *7 Denton Close, Goring-by-Sea, Worthing BN12 4TZ* Tel (01903) 505859

MATTHEWS, Peter. *See* MATTHEWS, Frederick Peter

MATTHEWS, Peter Henry. b 22. Sarum Th Coll 62. **d** 64 **p** 65. C Wareham w Arne *Sarum* 64-67; P-in-c Houghton 67; C Sholing *Win* 67-69; R Hilperton w Whaddon *Sarum* 70-78; P-in-c Staverton 71-72; V 72-78; P-in-c Milborne St Andrew w Dewlish 78-87; rtd 87; Perm to Offic *B & W* from 87. *Holmlands, Lambrook Road, Shepton Beauchamp, Ilminster TA19 0LZ* Tel (01460) 40938

MATTHEWS, Peter John. b 69. Leic Poly BEng92. Wycliffe Hall Ox 07. **d** 09. C Catterick *Ripon* from 09; Chapl St Fran Xavier Sch Richmond from 09. *1 Wathcote Place, Richmond DL10 7SR* Tel 07590-698333 (mobile) E-mail peterthelong@gmail.com

MATTHEWS, Canon Rodney Charles. b 36. Sarum Th Coll 62. **d** 64 **p** 65. C Gt Clacton *Chelmsf* 64-68; C Loughton St Mary 68-74; TV 74-76; V Goodmayes All SS 76-87; V Woodford Bridge 87-02; Hon Chapl Sail Tr Assn from 89; P-in-c Barkingside St Cedd 90 92; Hon Can Chelmsf Cathl 99-02; rtd 02; Perm to Offic *Chelmsf* from 03. *93 King's Head Hill, London E4 7JG* Tel (020) 8529 4372

MATTHEWS, Canon Roger Charles. b 54. Man Univ BSc75 Nottm Univ MA02 MBCS82 CEng90. Trin Coll Bris 87. **d** 89 **p** 90. C Gt Baddow *Chelmsf* 89-93; P-in-c Chigwell Row 93-94; TV Chigwell and Chigwell Row 94-96; Dioc Miss Officer 96-00;

Millenium Ecum Officer 98-00; Bp's Adv for Miss and Min from 01; Hon C Gt Baddow from 01; Hon Can Chelmsf Cathl from 00. *62 Longmead Avenue, Great Baddow, Chelmsford CM2 7EY* Tel (01245) 478959 *or* 294455 Fax 294477
E-mail rmatthews@chelmsford.anglican.org

MATTHEWS, Canon Roy Ian John. b 27. TD71. St Cath Soc Ox BA52 MA56. St Steph Ho Ox 52. **d** 54 **p** 55. C Barnsley St Mary *Wakef* 54-58; V Staincliffe 58-65; CF (TA) 58-92; V Penistone w Midhope *Wakef* 65-72; V Brighouse 72-84; Hon Can Wakef Cathl 76-92; V Darrington 84-92; Dioc Schs Officer 84-89; Dep Dir of Educn 85-89; rtd 92; Perm to Offic *Wakef* and *York* from 92; P-in-c Selby Abbey *York* 96-97. *14 Spring Walk, Brayton, Selby YO8 9DS* Tel (01757) 707259

MATTHEWS, Canon Royston Peter. b 39. Univ of Wales (Lamp) BA61. St Mich Coll Llan 61. **d** 64 **p** 65. C Fairwater CD *Llan* 64-67; C Cadoxton-juxta-Barry 67-71; V Bettws *Mon* 71-84; V Abergavenny H Trin 84-05; Hon Can St Woolos Cathl 05; rtd 05. *1 Hoburne Gardens, Christchurch BH23 4PP*

MATTHEWS, Canon Stuart James. b 37. St Jo Coll Dur BA60. Bps' Coll Cheshunt 60. **d** 62 **p** 63. C Horsham *Chich* 62-65; C Rednal *Birm* 65-67; Min Brandwood St Bede CD 67-68; C Northfield 68-73; V Thurcroft *Sheff* 73-82; RD Laughton 79-82; R Sprotbrough 82-00; RD Adwick 84-89; Hon Can Sheff Cathl 92-00; rtd 00; Perm to Offic *Sheff* from 00. *43 Dinnington Road, Woodsetts, Worksop S81 8RL* Tel (01909) 560160

MATTHEWS, Terence Leslie. b 35. Handsworth Coll Birm 55. **d** 61 **p** 62. C W Acklam *York* 61-64; V Horden *Dur* 64-72; R Witton Gilbert 72-77; P-in-c Grangetown 77-85; V Cleadon 85-86; V Hebburn St Cuth 86-88; rtd 88; Perm to Offic *Lich* from 08. *22 Bankfield Grove, Scot Hay, Newcastle ST5 6AR*

MATTHEWS, Thomas Bartholomew Hall. *See* HALL, Thomas Bartholomew Berners

MATTHEWS, Timothy John. b 73. Univ of Wales (Cardiff) BScEcon97 PhD00 ACA03. Wycliffe Hall Ox 06. **d** 08 **p** 09. C Brompton H Trin w Onslow Square St Paul *Lon* from 08. *17 Afghan Road, London SW11 2QD* Tel 08456-447533

MATTHEWS, William. *See* MATTHEWS, Lewis William

MATTHEWS, William Andrew. b 44. Reading Univ BA65 MA94. St Steph Ho Ox 65. **d** 67 **p** 68. C Westbury-on-Trym St Alb *Bris* 67-70; C Marlborough *Sarum* 70-73; P-in-c Winsley 73-75; V 75-81; V Bradford-on-Avon 81-09; RD Bradford 84-94; Can and Preb Sarum Cathl 88-09; rtd 09; Chapl to The Queen from 01. *21 Williams Lane, Fernwood, Newark-on-Trent NG24 3FN* Tel (01636) 646927
E-mail wajematthews@gmail.com

MATTHEWS, William John Joseph. **d** 08 **p** 08. NSM Lee-on-the-Solent *Portsm* from 08. *7 Darren Close, Stubbington, Fareham PO14 2LU* E-mail william.matthews@ntlworld.com

MATTHEWS, William Temple Atkinson (Liam). b 47. EMMTC 86. **d** 83 **p** 83. SSF 83-86; C Brinsley w Underwood *S'well* 86-89; TV Hitchin *St Alb* 89-97; R Toddington and Chalgrave 97-03; R N Albury Australia from 03; RD Murray Valley from 05. *St Mark's Rectory, 328 Gulpha Street, North Albury NSW 2640, Australia* Tel (0061) (2) 5794 2443
E-mail liammatthews@bigpond.com

MATTHEWS-LOYDALL, Mrs Elaine. b 63. Bp Otter Coll BA85. St Jo Coll Nottm 87. **d** 90 **p** 94. Par Dn Nottingham All SS *S'well* 90-94; C 94-95; Asst Chapl to the Deaf 91-93; Chapl to the Deaf 93-99; Chapl for Deaf People *Leic* from 99; TV Leic H Spirit from 99. *Pumpkin Cottage, 54 Wilne Road, Long Eaton, Nottingham NG10 3AN* Tel 0115-972 8943
E-mail chaplaincy@cfdleicester.org.uk

MATTHIAE, Canon David. b 40. Fitzw Ho Cam BA63 MA69. Linc Th Coll 63. **d** 65 **p** 66. C New Addington *Cant* 65-70; C Charlton-by-Dover SS Pet and Paul 70-75; V Cant All SS 75-84; P-in-c Tunstall 84-87; R Tunstall w Rodmersham 87-05; RD Sittingbourne 88-94; Hon Can Cant Cathl 99-05; rtd 05; Perm to Offic *Ely* from 06. *7 Bustlers Rise, Duxford, Cambridge CB22 4QU* Tel (01223) 835471 Mobile 07719-716240
E-mail david@matthiae.demon.co.uk

MATTHIAS, George Ronald. b 30. CertEd51. St Deiniol's Hawarden 76. **d** 78 **p** 79. NSM Broughton *St As* 78-83; NSM Wrexham 83-85; C 85-87; V Brymbo 87-95; rtd 95. *Bryn Adref, Pisgah Hill, Pentre Hill, Wrexham LL11 5DB* Tel (01978) 750757

MATTHIAS, John Rex. b 61. St Mich Coll Llan. **d** 94 **p** 95. C Llandrillo-yn-Rhos *St As* 94-98; R Llanfair Talhaearn and Llansannan etc 98-03; V Petryal from 03; P-in-c Betws-yn-Rhos from 03. *The Rectory, Llanfairtalhaiarn, Abergele LL22 8ST* Tel (01745) 720273 E-mail rexmatthias@btinternet.com

MATTHIAS, Paul. b 47. Philippa Fawcett Coll CertEd75 Kent Univ DipEd84. Cant Sch of Min 92. **d** 94 **p** 95. Head RE Hever Sch Maidstone 80-94; Chapl Ch Ch High Sch Ashford 94-07; NSM Gillingham St Aug *Roch* from 94. *33 Malvern Road, Gillingham ME7 4BA* Tel (01634) 576197
E-mail paul.matthias@diocese-rochester.org

MATTOCK, Colin Graham. b 38. Chich Th Coll. **d** 84 **p** 85. C Hove All SS *Chich* 84-87; C Bexhill St Pet 87-90; V Henlow *St Alb* 90-96; V Linslade *Ox* 96-00; P-in-c Pebworth w

Dorsington and Honeybourne *Glouc* 00-02; R Pebworth, Dorsington, Honeybourne etc from 02; AD Campden from 06. *The Vicarage, Stratford Road, Honeybourne, Evesham WR11 7PP* Tel (01386) 830302
E-mail colin.mattock@btinternet.com

MATTOCKS, Mrs Margaret. b 61. **d** 06 **p** 07. C Tettenhall Regis *Lich* 06-09; V Burntwood from 09. *The Vicarage, Church Road, Burntwood, Walsall WS7 9EA* Tel (01543) 675014

MATTY, Horace Anthony (Tony). b 36. Ely Th Coll 61. **d** 63 **p** 64. C Minchinhampton *Glouc* 63-66; C Hunslet St Mary and Stourton *Ripon* 66-69; TV Wendy w Shingay *Ely* 69-71; V Parson Drove 71-74; V Southea cum Murrow 71-74; V Coven *Lich* 74-82; TV Hednesford 82-85; TV Basildon St Martin w Nevendon *Chelmsf* 85-92; P-in-c Basildon St Andr w H Cross 85-92; P-in-c Sandon 92-98; P-in-c E Hanningfield 92-98; rtd 98; Perm to Offic *Truro* 00-01 and 03-04. *7 Calvin Close, Fordhouses, Wolverhampton WV10 6LN* Tel (01902) 781789

MAUCHAN, Andrew. b 44. Hertf Coll Ox BA65 MA69 Man Univ CertEd66. Oak Hill Th Coll 88. **d** 90 **p** 91. C Bridlington Priory *York* 90-94; V Alverthorpe *Wakef* 94-01; R Wombwell *Sheff* 01-07; rtd 07. *Hollins Barn, Top o' the Hill, Slaithwaite, Huddersfield HD7 5UA* Tel (01484) 846731
E-mail andrew.mauchan@yahoo.co.uk

MAUDE, Canon Alan. b 41. Lon Univ BD69 Newc Univ MSc90 Lambeth STh74. Oak Hill Th Coll 66. **d** 69 **p** 70. C Balderstone *Man* 69-73; C Crumpsall St Matt 73-75; Asst Chapl Crumpsall and Springfield Hosps 73-75; Chapl R Victoria Infirmary Newc 75-94; Chapl R Victoria Infirmary and Assoc Hosps NHS Trust 94-98; Chapl Newcastle upon Tyne Hosps NHS Trust 98-06; Hon Can Newc Cathl 88-06; P-in-c Costa del Sol W *Eur* from 06. *Urb Beverly Hill C14, 29680 Estepona (Malga), Spain* Tel (0034) 952 808 605 E-mail alanmarj@hotmail.com

MAUDE, Alexander. b 53. Bingley Coll of Educn TCert74. NOC. **d** 02 **p** 03. NSM Erringden *Wakef* from 02; Chapl Ravenscliffe High Sch from 02. *47 Vicar Park Drive, Norton Tower, Halifax HX2 0NN* Tel (01422) 355856 Mobile 07816-597074
E-mail sandie.maude47@tiscali.co.uk

MAUDE, Gillian Hamer. b 53. St Anne's Coll Ox BA75 MA79 Edin Univ MSc77. St Steph Ho Ox 99. **d** 01 **p** 02. C Hackney Wick St Mary of Eton w St Aug *Lon* 01-05; P-in-c Goodrington *Ex* 05-06; V from 06; RD Torbay from 09. *The Vicarage, 17 Seafields, Paignton TQ4 6NY* Tel (01803) 846335 Mobile 07932-056071 E-mail gillian.maude@btinternet.com

MAUDLIN, David. b 39. EAMTC 92. **d** 95 **p** 96. NSM Bury St Edmunds St Jo *St E* 95-97; NSM Haverhill w Withersfield 97-98; P-in-c The Sampfords and Radwinter w Hempstead *Chelmsf* 98-04; RD Saffron Walden 00-04; rtd 04; Perm to Offic *Leic, Pet* and *Eur* from 04. *3 Goldfinch Road, Uppingham LE15 9UJ* Tel (01572) 820181

MAUDSLEY, Canon George Lambert. b 27. St Jo Coll Nottm 74. **d** 75 **p** 76. C Binley *Cov* 75-77; Chapl Barn Fellowship Winterborne Whitechurch 77-83; V Salford Priors *Cov* 83-94; RD Alcester 87-92; Hon Can Cov Cathl 91-94; rtd 94; Perm to Offic *Cov* and *Worc* from 94. *75 Rawnsley Drive, Kenilworth CV8 2NX* Tel (01926) 512206 E-mail maudsley@tiscali.co.uk

MAUDSLEY, Keith. b 51. York Univ BA72. Ripon Hall Ox 72. **d** 75 **p** 76. C Rugby St Andr *Cov* 75-79; C Cambridge Gt St Mary w St Mich *Ely* 79-82; Chapl Girton Coll 79-82; P-in-c Binley *Cov* 82-89; RD Cov E 87-89; P-in-c Leek Wootton 89-91; Dioc Policy Development Adv 89-91; Dioc Adv on UPA *Liv* 91-97; Soc Resp Officer 91-97; R Lymm *Ches* from 97. *The Rectory, 46 Rectory Lane, Lymm WA13 0AL* Tel (01925) 752164 E-mail keith@maudsley5234.wanadoo.co.uk

MAUDSLEY, Canon Michael Peter. b 38. St Andr Univ BSc61. Oak Hill Th Coll 65. **d** 67 **p** 68. C Blackpool St Mark *Blackb* 67-70; C Hartford *Ches* 70-72; R Balerno *Edin* 72-82; V Stapenhill w Cauldwell *Derby* 82-91; Assoc R Edin St Paul and St Geo 91-95 and 00-03; R 95-00; rtd 03. *44 Buckstone Loan, Edinburgh EH10 6UG*

MAUDSLEY, Richard Leonard. b 55. Trent Park Coll of Educn BEd76. NTMTC 04. **d** 07 **p** 08. NSM Clay Hill St Jo and St Luke *Lon* from 07. *3 Badgers Close, Enfield EN2 7BB* Tel (020) 8367 2841 Fax 8440 8589
E-mail head.whitingshill.barnet@lgfl.net

MAUGHAN, Angela. b 54. Newc Univ BA93. NEOC 94. **d** 97 **p** 98. C Willington *Newc* 97-01; V Weetslade from 01. *Weetslade Vicarage, 59 Kirklands, Burradon, Cramlington NE23 7LE* Tel 0191-268 9366

MAUGHAN, Geoffrey Nigel. b 48. CCC Cam BA69 MA73 Wycliffe Hall Ox MA98. Oak Hill Th Coll 75. **d** 77 **p** 78. C New Malden and Coombe *S'wark* 77-81; C Abingdon w Shippon *Ox* 81-89; TV Abingdon 89-98; Dir of Min and Chapl Wycliffe Hall Ox 98-07; V Cumnor *Ox* from 07. *The Vicarage, 1 Abingdon Road, Cumnor, Oxford OX2 9QN* Tel (01865) 865402

MAUGHAN, John. b 28. Keble Coll Ox BA51 MA55. Linc Th Coll 51. **d** 53 **p** 54. C Heworth St Mary *Dur* 53-56; C Winlaton 56-59; R Penshaw 59-72; V Cleadon Park 72-93; rtd 93. *South Chowdene Care Home, Chowdene Bank, Gateshead NE9 6JE* Tel 0191-491 0861

MAUND, Mrs Margaret Jennifer. b 42. RGN64 RM65. Llan Dioc Tr Scheme 89. **d** 94 **p** 97. NSM Cwmaman and Porth *Llan* 94-97; NSM Pwllgwaun w Llanddewi Rhondda 97-04. *27 Mill Street, Tonyrefail, Porth CF39 8AB* Tel (01443) 670085

MAUNDER, Alan John. b 52. UWIST BSc74. Oak Hill Th Coll 88. **d** 90 **p** 91. C Birkenhead Ch Ch *Ches* 90-95; P-in-c Poulton 95-05; V Cwmaman *St D* from 05. *The Vicarage, 118 Heol Cae Gurwen, Gwaun-cae-Gurwen, Ammanford SA18 1PD* Tel (01269) 822426 E-mail ajmaunder@lineone.net

MAUNDER, Miss Vicky Alexandra. b 73. Leeds Univ BA95. Ripon Coll Cuddesdon BA01. **d** 02 **p** 03. C Swaythling *Win* 02-05; C Pimlico St Pet w Westmr Ch Ch *Lon* 05-07; TV Kingston All SS w St Jo *S'wark* from 07. *30 Bloomfield Road, Kingston upon Thames KT1 2SE* Tel (020) 8546 5964

MAURICE, David Pierce. b 50. Pemb Coll Cam BA72 MA76 BChir76. Dioc OLM tr scheme. **d** 01 **p** 02. OLM Marlborough *Sarum* from 01. *Isbury House, Kingsbury Street, Marlborough SN8 1JA* Tel (01672) 514119
E-mail david.maurice2000@yahoo.com

✠**MAURICE, The Rt Revd Peter David.** b 51. St Chad's Coll Dur BA72. Coll of Resurr Mirfield. **d** 75 **p** 76 **c** 06. C Wandsworth St Paul *S'wark* 75-79; TV Mortlake w E Sheen 79-85; V Rotherhithe H Trin 85-96; RD Bermondsey 91-96; V Tooting All SS 96-03; Adn Wells, Can Res and Preb Wells Cathl 03-06; Suff Bp Taunton from 06. *The Palace, Wells BA5 2PD* Tel (01749) 672341 Fax 679355
E-mail bishop.taunton@bathwells.anglican.org

MAW, Mrs Jacqueline. b 59. Wycliffe Hall Ox 04. **d** 06 **p** 07. C Iwerne Valley *Sarum* from 06. *Glen View, Church Lane, Sutton Waldron, Blandford Forum DT11 8PB* Tel (01747) 812359 Mobile 07747-561375 E-mail jackiemaw@yahoo.co.uk

MAWBEY, Diane. *See* COUTURE, Mrs Diane

MAWDITT, Stephen Donald Harvey. b 56. **d** 96 **p** 97. OLM Ashill w Saham Toney *Nor* 96-05; OLM Watton w Carbrooke and Ovington 00-05; Min Fountain of Life from 05. *43 Cressingham Road, Ashill, Thetford IP25 7DG* Tel (01760) 440363
E-mail themawditts@tiscali.co.uk

MAWER, Canon David Ronald. b 32. Keble Coll Ox BA55 MA58 Dur Univ BA57 McGill Univ Montreal PhD77. Wells Th Coll 58. **d** 59 **p** 60. C Cullercoats St Geo *Newc* 59-61; Canada 61-92; Co-ord Angl Studies St Paul Univ Ottawa 81-92; Can Ottawa from 85; rtd 92; Perm to Offic *Newc* from 93. *Moorside, Church Lane, Thropton, Morpeth NE65 7JA* Tel (01669) 620597

MAWSON, Canon Arthur Cyril. b 35. St Pet Coll Ox BA56 MA61. Wycliffe Hall Ox 61. **d** 62 **p** 63. C Walsall *Lich* 62-66; V Millhouses H Trin *Sheff* 66-73; Selection Sec ACCM 73-79; Can Res and Treas Ex Cathl 79-98; Dioc Dir of Ords 81-87; rtd 99. *4 Woodlands Close, Headington, Oxford OX3 7RY* Tel (01865) 764099

MAWSON, David Frank. b 44. Selw Coll Cam BA65 MA69. Linc Th Coll 79. **d** 80 **p** 81. C Tunstall *Lich* 80-83; C Blakenall Heath 83-84; TV 84-90; Chapl Goscote Hosp Walsall 87-90; V Pelsall *Lich* 90-94; V Tividale 94-99; V Shrewsbury All SS w St Mich 99-07; rtd 07; Perm to Offic *Lich* from 07. *17 Steepside, Shrewsbury SY3 6DS* Tel (01743) 360623
E-mail df.mawson@btinternet.com

MAXFIELD, Roberta. WMMTC. **d** 09. NSM Oxley *Lich* from 09. *53 Swan Bank, Wolverhampton WV4 5PZ* Tel (01902) 834023

MAXTED, Neil Andrew. b 58. Aston Tr Scheme 88 Sarum & Wells Th Coll 90. **d** 92 **p** 93. C Folkestone St Sav *Cant* 92-96; CF 96-05; P-in-c Frome Ch Ch *B & W* from 05. *The Vicarage, 73 Weymouth Road, Frome BA11 1HJ* Tel (01373) 473249
E-mail vicarchchfrome@aol.com

MAXWELL, Alan. b 75. Strathclyde Univ BSc96 Aber Univ MSc97 Selw Coll Cam BTh08. Ridley Hall Cam 05. **d** 08 **p** 09. C Gosforth All SS *Newc* from 08. *1 Northfield Road, Newcastle upon Tyne NE3 3UL* Tel 07790-913581 (mobile)
E-mail alan.maxwell@hotmail.co.uk

MAXWELL, Christopher John Moore (Bill). b 31. Qu Coll Cam MA75 MRCS59 LRCP59. Trin Coll Bris 74. **d** 75 **p** 76. SAMS Chile 75-81; Hon C Homerton St Luke *Lon* 81-94; Chapl Ibiza *Eur* 94-99; rtd 99; Perm to Offic *Chich* 99-08 and *Win* from 08. *Willowbank, Sycamore Close, Milford on Sea, Lymington SO41 0RY* Tel (01590) 643110
E-mail abmaxwell@metronet.co.uk

MAXWELL, Marcus Howard. b 54. Liv Univ BSc76 Man Univ MPhil89. St Jo Coll Nottm BA79. **d** 80 **p** 81. C Chadderton St Matt *Man* 80-84; V Bircle 84-93; P-in-c Heaton Mersey 93-02; TR Heatons from 02; AD Heaton 98-04. *St John's Rectory, 15 Priestnall Road, Stockport SK4 3HR* Tel 0161-432 2165

MAXWELL, Ralph. b 21. CEng MIMechE. **d** 86 **p** 87. NSM Belfast St Mich *Conn* 86-87; Lic to Offic 87-89; NSM Belfast St Jas w St Silas 89-97; NSM Belfast St Pet 97-02; rtd 02. *69 Woodvale Road, Belfast BT13 3BN* Tel (028) 9074 2421

MAY, Charles Henry. b 29. ALCD58. **d** 58 **p** 59. C Bethnal Green St Jas Less *Lon* 58-61; C Woking St Pet *Guildf* 61-64; Area Sec (W Midl) CPAS 64-67; V Homerton St Luke *Lon* 67-80; Home Sec SAMS 80-84; V Fulham Ch Ch *Lon* 84-94; rtd 94; Perm to

Offic *Ely* and *Pet* from 94; *Linc* from 95. *16 Kilverstone, Werrington, Peterborough PE4 5DX* Tel (01733) 328108
E-mail cclergyman@aol.com

MAY, Mrs Deborah Kim. b 60. Trin Coll Bris. **d** 01 **p** 02. C Haughley w Wetherden and Stowupland *St E* 01-04; R Ashwater, Halwill, Beaworthy, Clawton etc *Ex* 04-08; R Melville Australia from 08. *6 Donavon Rise, Murdoch, Perth WA 6150, Australia* Tel (0061) (8) 9310 7767 Mobile 41-817 8688
E-mail revd.debbie@gmail.com

MAY, Donald Charles Leonard. b 25. Chich Th Coll 72. **d** 73 **p** 74. C Barkingside H Trin *Chelmsf* 73-77; V Aldersbrook 77-91; rtd 92; Perm to Offic *Chelmsf* from 92. *236 Prospect Road, Woodford Green IG8 7PQ* Tel (020) 8504 6119

MAY, George Louis. b 27. Selw Coll Cam BA52 MA55 Cam Univ PGCE67 AdDipEd78. Ridley Hall Cam 52. **d** 54 **p** 55. C St Mary Cray and St Paul's Cray *Roch* 54-56; C St Paul's Cray St Barn CD 56-57; C-in-c Elburton CD *Ex* 57-66; Asst Master Guthlaxton Sch Wigston 67-70; Ixworth Sch 70-72; Thurston Upper Sch 73-74; Perias Sch New Alresford 75-85; Hon C Ropley w W Tisted *Win* 78-79; Perm to Offic 79-96; rtd 92; Perm to Offic *Derby* from 07. *Oven House, Water Lane, Eyam, Hope Valley S32 5RG* Tel (01433) 630599

MAY, Janet Isabel. b 51. Lon Univ CertEd72. **d** 00 **p** 01. OLM Gt and Lt Ellingham, Rockland and Shropham etc *Nor* 00-05; Perm to Offic from 05. *The Mill House, Church Street, Great Ellingham, Attleborough NR17 1LE* Tel (01953) 452198
E-mail rev.may@btopenworld.com

MAY, Preb John Alexander Cyril. b 52. K Coll Lon BD77 PhD98 Ch Ch Ox PGCE78. Linc Th Coll 79. **d** 80 **p** 81. C Tynemouth Ch Ch *Newc* 80-82; C Tynemouth Ch Ch w H Trin 82-85; C Tynemouth St Aug 82-85; TV Glendale Gp 85-90; V Wotton-under-Edge w Ozleworth, N Nibley etc *Glouc* 90-07; P-in-c St Endellion w Port Isaac and St Kew *Truro* from 07; P-in-c St Minver from 07; Preb St Endellion from 07. *The Rectory, St Endellion, Port Isaac PL29 3TP* Tel (01208) 881041
E-mail may187@hotmail.com

MAY, Peter Richard. b 43. St Jo Coll Cam BA64 MA68 MICE70. Trin Coll Bris 77. **d** 79 **p** 80. C Lancaster St Thos *Blackb* 79-85; V Darwen St Barn 85-91; Chapl Lyon w Grenoble *Eur* 91-92; Chapl Lyon 92-94; Perm to Offic *S'wark* 94-95; TR Horley 95-02; rtd 03; Perm to Offic *Chich* from 04. *14 Acorn Way, Hurst Green, Etchingham TN19 7QG* Tel (01580) 860441
E-mail rev@petermay.fsnet.co.uk

MAY, Simon George. b 47. Ex Univ BA69 Univ of Wales (Ban) CertEd72 FCA77. Sarum & Wells Th Coll 86. **d** 88 **p** 89. C Tamworth *Lich* 86-88; V Whitchurch *Ex* 92-07; Warden of Readers (Plymouth Adnry) 00-07; RD Tavistock 02-07; TV Barnstaple from 07. *Holy Trinity Vicarage, Victoria Road, Barnstaple EX32 9HP* Tel (01271) 344321

MAY, Stephen Charles Arthur. b 52. Mert Coll Ox BA73 Edin Univ BD78 Aber Univ PhD86. Ridley Hall Cam 84. **d** 86 **p** 87. C Sawley *Derby* 86-88; Lect St Jo Coll Auckland New Zealand 88-01; V Norden w Ashworth *Man* from 01. *St Paul's Vicarage, Heap Road, Rochdale OL12 7SN* Tel (01706) 641001
E-mail smaysfiction@hotmail.com

MAY, Toby Sebastian. b 67. Bris Univ BEng89. St Jo Coll Nottm MTh02. **d** 02 **p** 03. C Kendal St Thos *Carl* 02-06; V Alsager Ch Ch *Ches* from 06. *Christ Church Vicarage, 43 Church Road, Alsager, Stoke-on-Trent ST7 2HS* Tel (01270) 873727
E-mail toby@mays-in-grace.co.uk

MAYBEE, Christine. *See* DALE, Ms Christine

MAYBURY, David Kaines. b 32. G&C Coll Cam BA55 MA59. Ridley Hall Cam 55. **d** 57 **p** 58. C Sydenham H Trin *S'wark* 57-60; C Rainham *Chelmsf* 60-63; R Edin St Jas 63-75; R Jedburgh 75-84; NSM Duns 84-91; Warden Whitchester Conf Cen 84-91; NSM Hawick *Edin* 91-97; Warden Whitchester Chr Guest Ho and Retreat Cen 91-97; Admin from 97; rtd 97. *DaDo Heights, Borthaug, Hawick TD9 7LN* Tel and fax (01450) 370809 *or* tel 377477 Mobile 07941-448402
E-mail dado@maybud.fsnet.co.uk

MAYBURY, Doreen Lorna. b 33. RGN54 SCM56. Edin Th Coll 76. **dss** 81 **d** 95 **p** 95. Jedburgh *Edin* 81-84; Warden Whitchester Conf Cen 84-91; Duns 84-91; Hawick 91-97; NSM 95-97; rtd 97; Chapl Borders Gen Hosp NHS Trust 98-04. *DaDo Heights, Borthaugh, Hawick TD9 7LN* Tel and fax (01450) 370809 Mobile 07801-354134 E-mail dado@maybud.fsnet.co.uk

MAYBURY, Canon John Montague. b 30. G&C Coll Cam BA53 MA57. Ridley Hall Cam 53. **d** 55 **p** 56. C Allerton *Liv* 55-59; C Rowner *Portsm* 59-62; V Wroxall 62-67; V Southsea St Simon 67-78; V Crofton 78-91; Hon Can Portsm Cathl 81-95; C Locks Heath 91-95; rtd 95; Perm to Offic *Portsm* from 95. *19 Netley Road, Titchfield Common, Fareham PO14 4PE* Tel (01489) 584168

MAYBURY, Paul. b 31. St Deiniol's Hawarden 87. **d** 88 **p** 90. NSM Sutton St Geo *Ches* 88-94; Perm to Offic 94-98 and 01-08; P-in-c Towednack *Truro* 98-00. *Address temp unknown*

MAYBURY, Paul Dorian. b 58. Trin Coll Bris 93. **d** 95 **p** 96. C Spondon *Derby* 95-99; V Gawthorpe and Chickenley Heath *Wakef* 99-02; P-in-c Ossett cum Gawthorpe 01-02; V Ossett and

Gawthorpe from 02; RD Dewsbury from 08. *The Vicarage, 12 Fearnley Avenue, Ossett WF5 9ET* Tel (01924) 217379 *or* 263497 Fax 08701-375994 E-mail paul@htossett.org.uk

MAYCOCK, Ms Jane Ellen. b 66. Somerville Coll Ox BA90 MA95 Glas Univ MPhil98. Cranmer Hall Dur 90. **d** 92 **p** 94. Par Dn Harrow Trin St Mich *Lon* 92-94; C 94-95; C Kendal H Trin *Carl* 95-99; Dir of Ords 01-07. *The Rectory, Longlands Road, Bowness-on-Windermere, Windermere LA23 3AS* Tel (01539) 443063 E-mail jemaycock@lineone.net

MAYELL, Howard John. b 50. Bris Sch of Min 81. **d** 84 **p** 88. NSM Patchway *Bris* 84-86; NSM Weston-super-Mare Cen Par *B & W* 87-88; C N Stoneham *Win* 88-91; P-in-c Black Torrington, Bradford w Cookbury etc *Ex* 91-97; C Ledbury w Eastnor *Heref* 97-98; TV Ledbury from 98. *27 Hazle Close, Ledbury HR8 2XX* Tel (01531) 631530

MAYER, Alan John. b 46. AKC70. St Aug Coll Cant 70. **d** 71 **p** 72. C Stanningley St Thos *Ripon* 71-74; C St Helier *S'wark* 74-79; TV Wimbledon 79-85; V Reigate St Luke S Park 85-00; R Oxted and Tandridge from 00. *The Rectory, 29 Chichele Road, Oxted RH8 0AE* Tel (01883) 712955 E-mail revoxted@gmail.com

MAYER, Graham Keith. b 46. St Cath Coll Ox BA68 Nottm Univ PGCE69 Ex Univ MA93. Linc Th Coll 78. **d** 80 **p** 81. C Paignton St Jo *Ex* 80-93; Perm to Offic 93-96; P-in-c Christow, Ashton and Bridford from 96; P-in-c Dunchideock from 97; RD Kenn from 05. *The Rectory, Dry Lane, Christow, Exeter EX6 7PE* Tel (01647) 252845

MAYER, Mrs Paula Denise. b 45. St Hilda's Coll Ox BA68 Nottm Univ CertEd69. SW Minl Tr Course 84. **d** 88 **p** 07. Hon Par Dn Paignton St Jo *Ex* 88-90; Par Dn 90-93; Perm to Offic from 93. *The Haven, 1 Parkside Road, Paignton TQ4 6AE* Tel (01803) 558727 E-mail paula.haven@aniserve.com

MAYERSON, Paul Strom. b 28. PhD MEd MusBac. Ridley Hall Cam 80. **d** 82 **p** 83. C New Romney w Old Romney and Midley *Cant* 82-85; R Eastling w Ospringe and Stalisfield w Otterden 85-90; rtd 90; Perm to Offic *Cant* 90-95. *149 East Side Drive #137, Concord NH 03301-5410, USA* Tel (001) (603) 225 2306 E-mail paulnjoan@pngusa.net

MAYES, Canon Andrew Dennis. b 56. K Coll Lon BD79 AKC79 Man Univ MA97. Armenian Orthodox Sem Jerusalem 79 St Steph Ho Ox 80. **d** 81 **p** 82. C Hendon St Alphage *Lon* 81-84; C Hockley *Chelmsf* 84-87; V Kingstanding St Mark *Birm* 87-92; V Saltdean *Chich* 92-01; P-in-c Ovingdean 01-09; CME Officer 01-09; Course Dir St Geo Coll and C St Geo Cathl Jerusalem from 09; Hon Can Niger Delta from 96. *St George's College Jerusalem, PO Box 1248, Jerusalem 91000, Israel* Tel (00972) (2) 626 4704

MAYES, Aonghus William Alun. **d** 05 **p** 06. C Cregagh *D & D* from 05. *54 Rochester Avenue, Belfast BT6 9JW* Tel (028) 9079 6193

MAYES, John Charles Dougan. b 44. Bps' Coll Cheshunt 63. **d** 67 **p** 68. C Portadown St Mark *Arm* 67-74; I Aghadowey w Kilrea *D & R* 74-86; USPG Area Sec 77-94; I Clooney w Strathfoyle 86-07; Can Derry Cathl 92-96; Preb 94-07; rtd 07. *10 Ebrington Park, Londonderry BT47 6JE* Tel (028) 7131 2973

✠**MAYES, The Rt Revd Michael Hugh Gunton.** b 41. TCD BA62 Lon Univ BD85. TCD Div Sch Div Test64. **d** 64 **p** 65 **c** 93. C Portadown St Columba *Arm* 64-68; USPG Kobe Japan 68-69; Tokyo 69-70; Yokkaichi 70-74; Area Sec USPG *C & O, C, C & R, L & K* and *T, K & A* 75-93; I Cork St Mich Union *C, C & R* 75-86; Adn Cork, Cloyne and Ross 86-93; I Moviddy Union 86-88; I Rathcooney Union 88-93; Bp K, E & A 93-00; Can Elphin Cathl 93-00; Bp L & K 00-08; rtd 08. *4 Langford Place, Langford Row, Cork, Republic of Ireland* Tel (00353) (21) 496 7688

MAYES, Canon Stephen Thomas. b 47. St Jo Coll Nottm 67. **d** 71 **p** 72. C Cullompton *Ex* 71-75; C Cheltenham St Mark *Glouc* 76-84; P-in-c Water Orton *Birm* 84-91; V from 91; AD Coleshill 99-05; Hon Can Birm Cathl from 05. *The Vicarage, Vicarage Lane, Water Orton, Birmingham B46 1RX* Tel 0121-747 2751 Fax 749 7294 E-mail stmayes@yahoo.co.uk

MAYES, Suzanne Janette. b 55. NTMTC 95. **d** 98 **p** 99. NSM E Ham w Upton Park St Alb *Chelmsf* 98-02; Chapl HM Pris Wellingborough 02-04; Perm to Offic *Chelmsf* from 04; Sessional Chapl HM Pris Hollesley Bay from 07. *HM Prison Hollesley Bay, Woodbridge IP12 3JW* Tel (01394) 412400

✠**MAYFIELD, The Rt Revd Christopher John.** b 35. G&C Coll Cam BA57 MA61 Cranfield Inst of Tech MSc83. Wycliffe Hall Ox 61. **d** 63 **p** 64 **c** 85. C Birm St Martin 63-67; Lect 67-71; V Luton St Mary *St Alb* 71-80; RD Luton 74-80; Adn Bedford 80-85; Suff Bp Wolverhampton *Lich* 85-92; Area Bp Wolverhampton 92-93; Bp Man 93-01; rtd 02; Hon Asst Bp Worc from 02. *Harewood House, 54 Primrose Crescent, Worcester WR5 3HT* Tel (01905) 764822

MAYFIELD, Timothy James Edward. b 60. LMH Ox BA82. Trin Coll Bris BA88. **d** 88 **p** 89. C Ovenden *Wakef* 88-92; V Mount Pellon 92-03; V Cheltenham Ch Ch *Glouc* from 03. *Christ Church Vicarage, Malvern Road, Cheltenham GL50 2NU* Tel (01242) 515983

MAYFIELD, Timothy John Joseph. b 59. BA MA. **d** 99 **p** 00. C Battersea Rise St Mark *S'wark* from 99. *93A Bolingbroke Grove, London SW11 6HA* Tel (020) 7924 6833 *or* 7223 6188

MAYHEW, Canon Charles. b 40. K Coll Lon BD64 AKC64. **d** 65 **p** 66. C Nottingham St Mary *S'well* 65-69; R Cawston and P-in-c Felthorpe w Haveringland *Nor* 69-74; R Barnack w Ufford and Bainton *Pet* 74-86; RD Barnack 77-86; V Oakham, Hambleton, Egleton, Braunston and Brooke 86-94; Chapl Catmose Vale and Rutland Memorial Hosps 86-94; Can Pet Cathl 83-94; rtd 94; Perm to Offic *Pet* from 94. *Thorndon Green, Church Road, Lyndon, Oakham LE15 8TU* Tel (01572) 737594

MAYHEW, David Francis. b 51. Ch Ch Ox BA72 MA76 Wycliffe Hall Ox BA75. NEOC 89. **d** 91 **p** 92. NSM High Elswick St Paul *Newc* 91-94; Toc H 91-94; V Mitford *Newc* 94-09; C Longhorsley and Hebron 07-09; Chapl Northgate and Prudhoe NHS Trust 94-09; V Cov H Trin from 09. *Holy Trinity Vicarage, 4 Bishop's Walk, Coventry CV5 6PY* Tel (024) 7671 2114 E-mail dfmayhew@aol.com

MAYHEW, *née* GURNEY), Jean Elizabeth. b 39. OBE97. New Hall Cam BA61 MA85 K Coll Lon BD84 AKC84 PGCE85 Ulster Univ Hon DUniv98 FKC00. SEITE 02. **d** 05 **p** 06. NSM Maidstone St Paul *Cant* from 05. *Twysden, Riseden Lane, Kilndown, Cranbrook TN17 2SG* Tel (01580) 211820 Fax 212232 Mobile 07773-404554 E-mail jean@mayhew.free-online.co.uk

MAYLAND, Mrs Jean Mary. b 36. JP77. LMH Ox BA58 MA61 TCert60. St Deiniol's Hawarden 91. **d** 91 **p** 94. NSM York Minster 91-93; Lect and Tutor NOC 91-93; Lect NEOC 93-96; Dioc Ecum Officer *Dur* 93-96; Local Unity Officer Dur Ecum Relns Gp 93-96; Assoc Sec CCBI 96-99; Co-ord Sec for Ch Life CTBI 99-03; Asst Gen Sec 99-03; rtd 03; Perm to Offic *York* 03-09 and *Newc* from 04. *5 Hackwood Glade, Hexham NE46 1AL* Tel (01434) 6003389

MAYLAND, Canon Ralph. b 27. VRD63. Ripon Hall Ox 57. **d** 59 **p** 60. C Lambeth St Andr w St Thos *S'wark* 59-62; Chapl RNR 61-94; C-in-c Worksop St Paul CD *S'well* 62-68; V Brightside St Marg *Sheff* 68-72; Ind Chapl 68-81; V Ecclesfield 72-81; Can Res and Treas York Minster 82-94; rtd 94; Hon C Brancepeth *Dur* 94-96; Perm to Offic *York* 96-04 and *Chelmsf* 01-03. *5 Hackwood Glade, Hexham NE46 1AL* Tel (01434) 600339

MAYLOR, David Charles. b 59. Lanc Univ BSc80 Edge Hill Coll of HE PGCE81. St Jo Coll Nottm 89. **d** 91 **p** 92. C Hindley All SS *Liv* 91-94; P-in-c Spalding St Paul *Linc* 94-07; Chapl United Lincs Hosps NHS Trust 99-07; Lic Gen Preacher *Linc* from 07; Music Dir Stamford St Geo w St Paul from 07. *St Martin's Rectory, Pinfold Lane, Stamford PE9 2LS* Tel (01780) 767993

MAYLOR, Miles Edward. b 55. St Andr Univ BD85 Glam Univ PhD00 PGCE02. St Mich Coll Llan 03. **d** 05 **p** 06. NSM Mountain Ash and Miskin *Llan* 05; NSM Wheatley *Ox* 06-09; NSM Ox St Barn and St Paul from 09. *30 Skene Close, Headington, Oxford OX3 7XQ* Tel (01865) 769554 Mobile 07967-584670 E-mail miles.maylor@virgin.net

MAYNARD, John William. b 37. Lon Univ BSc58. Ripon Hall Ox 60. **d** 62 **p** 63. C St Laur in Thanet *Cant* 62-67; C S Ashford Ch Ch 67-70; V Pagham *Chich* 70-00; rtd 00. *Two Hedges, Lower Budleigh, East Budleigh, Budleigh Salterton EX9 7DL* Tel (01395) 443869

MAYNARD, Raymond. b 30. S'wark Ord Course 75 Ox Ord Course 76. **d** 77 **p** 78. NSM Hedsor and Bourne End *Ox* 77-80; C Newport Pagnell w Lathbury 80-83; P-in-c Lacey Green 83-89; V 89; Perm to Offic *Guildf* 90-01. *Hardore, Ven Ottery, Ottery St Mary EX11 1RY* Tel (01404) 814307

MAYNARD, Canon Richard Edward Buller. b 42. AKC66. **d** 67 **p** 68. C St Ives *Truro* 67-71; C Falmouth K Chas 71-74; V St Germans 74-85; RD E Wivelshire 81-85; TR Saltash 85-08; Hon Can Truro Cathl 82-08; Chapl St Barn Hosp Saltash 90-93; Chapl Cornwall Healthcare NHS Trust 93-02; Chapl N and E Cornwall Primary Care Trust 02-06; Chapl Cornwall and Is of Scilly Primary Care Trust 06-08; rtd 08. *Harewood, Dunheved Road, Launceston PL15 9JJ* Tel (01752) 843142 E-mail canonrichardmaynard@btinternet.com

MAYNE, Canon Brian John. b 52. Univ of Wales (Cardiff) BA73 LTCL75 MRICS81. NEOC 82 Coll of Resurr Mirfield 84. **d** 85 **p** 86. C Stainton-in-Cleveland *York* 85-89; P-in-c Rounton w Welbury 89-96; Chapl HM YOI Northallerton 89-96; Chapl HM YOI Lanc Farms from 96; Hon Can Blackb Cathl from 09. *HM Young Offender Institution, Lancaster Farms, Stone Row Head, Lancaster LA1 3QZ* Tel (01524) 848745 E-mail brianmayne@tiscali.co.uk *or* brianmayne@lycos.co.uk

MAYNE, John Andrew Brian. b 34. QUB BA55 Lon Univ BD62. TCD Div Sch Div Test 57. **d** 57 **p** 58. C Ballymoney *Conn* 57-60; C Knock *D & D* 60-62; P-in-c Knocknagoney 62-64; P-in-c Belvoir 68-71; I 71-80; Dean Waterford *C & O* 80-84; I Lecale Gp *D & D* 84-01; Can Down Cathl 87-01; Prec 91-00; Dean 00-01; Sec Gen Syn Liturg Cttee 89-99; rtd 01. *114 Ballydugan Road, Downpatrick BT30 8HF* Tel (028) 4461 2521 Mobile 07092-207229 E-mail jab@brianmayne.co.uk *or* editor.bcp@ireland.anglican.org

MAYO, Christopher Paul. b 68. Heythrop Coll Lon BD91 Birm Univ PGCE96. Qu Coll Birm 91. **d** 93 **p** 94. C Wednesfield *Lich*

93-94; C Bilston 94-95. *73 Gorse Road, Wednesfield, Wolverhampton WV11 2PY* Tel (01902) 733163

MAYO, Deborah Ann. *See* MURPHY, Mrs Deborah Ann

MAYO, Inglis John. b 46. FCA. Ripon Coll Cuddesdon 74. **d** 77 **p** 78. C Bitterne Park *Win* 77-81; C Christchurch 81-86; P-in-c Sturminster Marshall *Sarum* 86-89; P-in-c Kingston Lacy and Shapwick 86-89; V Sturminster Marshall, Kingston Lacy and Shapwick 89-00; P-in-c Lilliput 00-06; V 06-08; rtd 08; Perm to Offic *Sarum* from 08. *49B St Catherine's Road, Bournemouth BH6 4AQ* Tel (01202) 424971
E-mail mayofamily@btinternet.com

MAYO, Robert William. b 61. Keble Coll Ox BA83 Trin Coll Carmarthen PhD00. Cranmer Hall Dur 85. **d** 87 **p** 88. C Luton Lewsey St Hugh *St Alb* 87-90; Hd Cam Univ Miss and NSM Bermondsey St Jas w Ch Ch *S'wark* 90-95; Chapl S Bank Univ 95-98; Dir Youth Work Tr Ridley Hall Cam 98-05; V Shepherd's Bush St Steph w St Thos *Lon* from 05. *St Stephen's Vicarage, 1 Coverdale Road, London W12 8JJ* Tel (020) 8743 3166 Mobile 07977-003227 E-mail bobmayo43@gmail.com

MAYO-SMITH, Peter. b 49. Open Univ BA80. Ridley Hall Cam 05. **d** 06 **p** 07. C Greengates *Bradf* from 06; C Idle from 06; C Cottingley from 08. *33 Cavalier Drive, Bradford BD10 0UF* Tel (01274) 620044 Mobile 07880-866222
E-mail peter@mayo-smith.net

MAYOR, Henry William. b 39. Oriel Coll Ox BA62. Westcott Ho Cam 62. **d** 64 **p** 65. C The Quinton *Birm* 64-66; C Dudley St Thos *Worc* 67-71; R Birch St Agnes *Man* 71-83; Community Chapl Aylesbury *Ox* 83-89; Community Chapl Aylesbury w Bierton and Hulcott 89; R Cheetham St Luke and Lower Crumpsall St Thos *Man* 89-96; R Cheetham and Lower Crumpsall 97-01; rtd 01. *57 Hill Street, Manchester M20 3FY* Tel 0161-434 2955 Mobile 07960-767155
E-mail henrywmayor@hotmail.com

MAYOSS, Anthony (Aidan). b 31. Leeds Univ BA55. Coll of Resurr Mirfield 55. **d** 57 **p** 58. C Meir *Lich* 57-62; Lic to Offic *Wakef* 62-72 and from 78; CR from 64; S Africa 73-75; Asst Chapl Lon Univ 76-78; Bursar CR 84-90; rtd 98; Perm to Offic *Lon* 98-07. *House of the Resurrection, Stocks Bank Road, Mirfield WF14 0BN* Tel (01924) 483330
E-mail amayoss@mirfield.org.uk

MAYOSS-HURD, Canon Susan Patricia. b 59. Lanc Univ BA81. Cranmer Hall Dur 82. **dss** 84 **d** 87 **p** 94. Ribbesford w Bewdley and Dowles *Worc* 84-88; Par Dn 87-88; Chapl W Heath Hosp 88-96; C W Heath *Birm* 88-96; V 96-03; V Peachland St Marg Canada from 03. *6146 Turner Avenue, Peachland BC V0H 1X4, Canada* Tel (001) (250) 767 9682 E-mail revsuemh@shaw.ca

MAZUR, Mrs Ann Carol. b 47. St Mich Coll Sarum CertEd69. TISEC 01. **d** 04 **p** 05. NSM St Ninian's Cathl Perth 04-07; Prec from 07; Chapl Craigclowan Sch Perth 04-07. *8 Netherlea, Scone, Perth PH2 6QA* Tel (01738) 551351 E-mail ann@mazur.org.uk

MBALI, Escourt Zolile. b 40. Fort Hare Univ BA68 Ox Univ BA71. St Bede's Coll Umtata 62. **d** 71 **p** 72. S Africa 71-74 and from 93; Botswana 74-81; V Preston on Tees *Dur* 81-83; C Knighton St Mary Magd *Leic* 84-88; P-in-c Church Langton w Tur Langton, Thorpe Langton etc 88-92; Community Relns Officer 88-93; Hon Can Leic Cathl 92-93; rtd 02. *1 Halford Road, Berea, Durban, 4001 South Africa* Tel (0027) (31) 201 6195

MDUMULLA, Jonas Habel. b 50. Nairobi Univ Hull Univ BTh87 MA89. St Phil Coll Kongwa. **d** 74 **p** 75. Tanzania 74-82; C Sutton St Jas and Wawne *York* 82-96; P-in-c Carlton and Drax from 96; Ind Chapl from 96. *The Vicarage, 2 Church Dike Lane, Drax, Selby YO8 8NZ* Tel (01757) 618313

MEACHAM, John David. b 24. AKC51 QTS60 Lambeth STh77 Open Univ MPhil90. **d** 52 **p** 53. C Maidenhead St Luke *Ox* 52-55; Asst Master Linton Ho Maidenhead 52-55; C Croydon St Jo *Cant* 55-58; V Sittingbourne St Mich 58-74; Teacher St Jo Boys' High Sch 64-74; V Brenchley *Roch* 74-83; Teacher Tunbridge Wells Girls' Gr Sch 78-83; P-in-c Gt Wishford and S Newton *Sarum* 83-86; Bp's Chapl and Research Asst 83-86; Sec C of E Doctrine Commn 84-89; rtd 88; Perm to Offic *Sarum* 88-98. *Trewinnard, Grams Road, Walmer, Deal CT14 7NT* Tel (01304) 239613

MEAD, Arthur Hugh. b 39. K Coll Cam BA60 MA64 New Coll Ox BLitt66. St Steph Ho Ox 61. **d** 80 **p** 80. NSM Hammersmith St Jo *Lon* 80-05; NSM Hammersmith H Innocents and St Jo from 05; Chapl St Paul's Sch Barnes 82-97; rtd 97; Dep P in O 85-90 and from 95; P in O 90-95; Reader of The Temple from 95. *11 Dungarvan Avenue, London SW15 5QU* Tel (020) 8876 5833

MEAD, Colin Harvey. b 26. FCA. S Dios Minl Tr Scheme 81. **d** 84 **p** 85 NSM Talbot Village *Sarum* 84-96; rtd 96; Perm to Offic *Sarum* 96-07. *22 Melton Court, 37 Lindsay Road, Poole BH13 6BH* Tel (01202) 763647

MEAD, Canon John Harold. b 37. Wells Th Coll 69. **d** 71 **p** 72. C Charlton Kings St Mary *Glouc* 71-75; R Stratton w Baunton 75-82; R Bishop's Cleeve 82-90; RD Tewkesbury 88-97; Hon Can Glouc Cathl 90-00; rtd 00; Perm to Offic *Glouc* from 00. *13 Cleevemount Close, Cheltenham GL52 3HW* Tel (01242) 241050

MEAD, Mrs Lynda Roberta. b 44. Open Univ BA91. STETS. **d** 99 **p** 00. NSM Hythe *Win* 99-04. *22 Furzedale Park, Hythe, Southampton SO45 3HW* Tel (023) 8084 8901

MEAD, Nicholas Charles. b 50. Newc Univ BEd73 Reading Univ MA76. Ridley Hall Cam 83. **d** 85 **p** 86. C Bilton *Cov* 85-88; C Whittlesey *Ely* 88-89; Hd of Relig Studies Neale-Wade Community Coll March 89-97; Fell Farmington Inst for Chr Studies Ox from 96; Sen Lect RE Westmr Coll Ox 97-00; Sen Lect RE Ox Brookes Univ from 00. *Westminster Institute of Education, Oxford Brookes University, Harcourt Hill, Oxford OX2 9AT* Tel (01865) 488294 E-mail nmead@brookes.ac.uk

MEAD, Peter Tony. b 63. St Jo Coll Dur BA08. Cranmer Hall Dur 06. **d** 08 **p** 09. C Yeovil H Trin w Barwick *B & W* from 08. *19 Foxglove Way, Yeovil BA22 8PU* Tel (01935) 476692 Mobile 07726-959659 E-mail pete.mead@talktalk.net

MEADEN, Philip George William. b 40. Open Univ BA75. Lich Th Coll 63. **d** 66 **p** 67. C Aston SS Pet and Paul *Birm* 66-70; V Lozells St Paul 70-76; Asst Chapl HM Pris Brixton 76-77; Chapl HM Pris Lewes 77-84; Chapl HM Pris Aylesbury 84-88; Chapl HM Pris Wandsworth 88-01; rtd 01; Perm to Offic *St E* 01-05. *2 Waterloo Lane, Fairford GL7 4BP* Tel (01285) 713917

MEADER, Jennifer Lindsay. b 68. UEA BA89. Westcott Ho Cam. **d** 01 **p** 02. C Teversham and Cherry Hinton St Andr *Ely* 01-05; C Westmr St Jas *Lon* from 05. *200 Merrow Street, London SE17 2NP* Tel (020) 7252 7305
E-mail revlindsay@ntlworld.com

MEADER, Philip John. b 44. Oak Hill Th Coll 73. **d** 75 **p** 76. C E Ham St Paul *Chelmsf* 75-77; CMJ 77-90; TV Lowestoft and Kirkley *Nor* 90-94; V Lowestoft St Andr 94-96; R Panfield and Rayne *Chelmsf* 96-09; RD Braintree 06-09; rtd 09. *39 Langdale Avenue, Chichester PO19 8JQ* Tel (01243) 528783
E-mail philip@revdmeader.fsnet.co.uk

MEADOWS, Mrs Freda Angela. b 46. CertEd68. Oak Hill Th Coll 93. **d** 96 **p** 97. NSM N Wembley St Cuth *Lon* 96-01; NSM Roxeth 01-07; rtd 07; Perm to Offic *Lon* from 07. *48 Torrington Drive, Harrow HA2 8NF* Tel (020) 8248 3523
E-mail fam@revfredmead.freeserve.co.uk

MEADOWS, Philip Michael. b 71. Univ of Wales (Lamp) BA95. St Steph Ho Ox BTh01. **d** 01 **p** 03. C W Bromwich St Fran *Lich* 01; C Leeds Belle Is St Jo and St Barn *Ripon* 02-06; Perm to Offic *Ches* from 06; CMP from 04. *13 Naburn Close, Stockport SK5 8JQ* Tel 0161-494 8073 Mobile 09771-035513
E-mail frpmeadows@btinternet.com

MEADS, William Ivan. b 35. Qu Mary Coll Lon BA56 ACIS67 ACMA75. Linc Th Coll 75. **d** 77 **p** 78. C Cheltenham St Luke and St Jo *Glouc* 77-81; Chapl HM Pris Pentonville 81-82; Preston 82-85; Wakef 85-88; P-in-c Wroxton w Balscote and Shenington w Alkerton *Ox* 88-90; R Broughton w N Newington and Shutford etc 90-95; P-in-c Week St Mary w Poundstock and Whitstone *Truro* 95-97; rtd 97; Perm to Offic *B & W* 97-00 and *St E* from 08. *The Meads, Briswell Green, Thorndon, Eye IP23 7JF* Tel (01379) 678670
E-mail nanmeads@whsmithnet.co.uk

MEADWAY, Jeanette Valerie. b 47. Edin Univ MB, ChB69 FRCP87 FRCPEd87. Oak Hill NSM Course 89. **d** 93 **p** 94. NSM Stratford St Jo w Ch Ch and St Jas *Chelmsf* from 93; Perm to Offic *Lon* 99-03. *4 Glebe Avenue, Woodford Green IG8 9HD* Tel (020) 8504 1958 E-mail drjeanettemeadway@btinternet.com

MEAKIN, Canon Anthony John. b 28. TD76. Down Coll Cam BA52 MA56. Westcott Ho Cam 52. **d** 54 **p** 55. C Gosforth All SS *Newc* 54-60; V Alnwick St Paul 60-71; V Edlingham 62-71; CF (TA) 63-83; R Whickham *Dur* 71-88; RD Gateshead W 78-88; Hon Can Dur Cathl 83-93; Bp's Sen Chapl and Exec Officer for Dioc Affairs 88-93; rtd 93. *73 Oakfields, Burnopfield, Newcastle upon Tyne NE16 6PQ* Tel (01207) 270429

MEAKIN, David John. b 61. Hull Univ BA82 Hughes Hall Cam PGCE83 Lambeth STh88. Westcott Ho Cam 86. **d** 88 **p** 89. C Upminster *Chelmsf* 88-92; Prec and Sacr Dur Cathl 92-97; V Ryhope 97-04; P-in-c Schorne *Ox* from 04. *The Rectory, 1 Green Acres Close, Whitchurch, Aylesbury HP22 4JP* Tel (01296) 641606 E-mail d.meakin@btinternet.com

MEANEY, Ashley John. b 67. Ridley Hall Cam 04. **d** 06 **p** 07. C Hammersmith St Paul *Lon* from 06. *4 Margravine Road, London W6 8HJ* Tel (020) 8748 3855 E-mail ash.meaney@sph.org

MEARA, The Ven David Gwynne. b 47. Oriel Coll Ox BA70 MA73. Lambeth STh76 Cuddesdon Coll 71. **d** 73 **p** 74. C Whitley Ch Ch *Ox* 73-77; Chapl Reading Univ 77-82; V Basildon 82-87; P-in-c Aldworth and Ashampstead 85-87; V Basildon w Aldworth and Ashampstead 87-94; RD Bradfield 90-94; V Buckingham w Radclive cum Chackmore 94-97; P-in-c Nash w Thornton, Beachampton and Thornborough 96-97; R Buckingham 97-00; RD Buckingham 95-00; Hon Can Ch Ch 98-00; R St Bride Fleet Street w Bridewell etc *Lon* from 00; Adn Lon from 09. *St Bride's Rectory, Fleet Street, London EC4Y 8AU* Tel (020) 7353 7999 *or* 7427 0133 Fax 7583 4867
E-mail info@stbrides.com
or archdeacon.london@london.anglican.org

MEARDON, Canon Brian Henry. b 44. Reading Univ BSc66 PhD71. Oak Hill Th Coll MPhil84. **d** 79 **p** 80. C Reading St Jo

Ox 79-82; V Warfield 82-90; Hon Can Ch Ch 03-09; rtd 09. *382 Devizes Road, Salisbury SP2 9LY*
E-mail brianmeardon@googlemail.com

MEARDON, Mark James. b 73. Southn Univ BSc94. Trin Th Coll Singapore MTS07 St Jo Coll Nottm MA09. **d** 09. C Hazlemere *Ox* from 09. *Church House, 70 Georges Hill, Widmer End, High Wycombe HP15 6BH* Tel 07905-887125 (mobile) E-mail mark.meardon@gmail.com

MEARNS, Christopher Lee. b 30. Worc Coll Ox BA54 MA58. Ripon Hall Ox BTh56. **d** 57 **p** 58. C Greenhill St Jo *Lon* 57-60; Vice-Prin Qu Coll St John's Canada 60-62; Lect Ripon Coll of Educn 63-75; Sen Lect Coll of Ripon and York St Jo 75-85; Lect New Clairvaux Abbey USA 87 and 89; Tutor Ridley Hall Cam 88; Chapl St Phil Th Coll Seychelles 88-90; Perm to Offic *Ripon* 90-06. *The College of St Barnabas, Blackberry Lane, Lingfield RH7 6NJ* Tel (01342) 872820

MEARS, Mrs Hannah Marie. b 80. St Cuth Soc Dur BA02 St Mary's Ho Dur MA03. Trin Coll Bris 06. **d** 08 **p** 09. NSM Henbury *Bris* 08-09; C St Austell *Truro* from 09. *St Luke's House, 5 Penhaligon Way, St Austell PL25 3AR* Tel (01726) 69857

✠**MEARS, The Rt Revd John Cledan.** b 22. Univ of Wales (Abth) BA43 Univ of Wales MA48. Wycliffe Hall Ox 43. **d** 47 **p** 48 **c** 82. C Mostyn *St As* 47-49; C Rhosllannerchrugog 49-56; V Cwm 56-59; Lic to Offic *Llan* 59-73; Chapl St Mich Coll Llan 59-67; Lect Th Univ of Wales (Cardiff) 59-73; Sub-Warden St Mich Coll Llan 67-73; V Gabalfa *Llan* 73-82; Hon Can Llan Cathl 81-82; Bp Ban 82-92; rtd 92; Perm to Offic *Llan* from 92. *Isfryn, 23 Avonridge, Cardiff CF14 9AU* Tel (029) 2061 5505

MEARS, Oliver Harry John. b 80. Ball Coll Ox BA02. Trin Coll Bris BA08. **d** 09. NSM St Austell *Truro* from 09. *St Luke's House, 5 Penhaligon Way, St Austell PL25 3AR* Tel (01726) 69857 E-mail ollymears@yahoo.co.uk

MEARS, Phillip David. b 40. Dur Univ BA62. **d** 65 **p** 66. C Sandylands *Blackb* 65-68; C Chorley St Geo 68-71; V Leyland St Ambrose 71-81; Chapl Warrington Distr Gen Hosp 81-00; Perm to Offic *Ches* 81-06; Hon C Schorne *Ox* from 06. *The Rectory, Church Street, Quainton, Aylesbury HP22 4AP* Tel (01296) 655237

MEATH AND KILDARE, Bishop of. See CLARKE, The Most Revd Richard Lionel

MEATH, Archdeacon of. See STEVENSON, The Ven Leslie Thomas Clayton

MEATHREL, Timothy James. b 78. **d** 08 **p** 09. C Harborne Heath *Birm* from 08. *33 Margaret Road, Birmingham B17 0EU* Tel 0121-426 2585 Mobile 07818-401372
E-mail timmeathrel@stjohns-church.com

MEATS, Canon Alan John. b 41. Univ of Wales (Cardiff) BA62 DipEd63 Lon Univ BD70. St Mich Coll Llan 68. **d** 70 **p** 71. C Pontypridd St Cath *Llan* 70-73; TV Ystradyfodwg 73-75; Dioc Insp of Schs 73-75 and 83-89; V Llandeilo Tal-y-bont *S & B* 75-83; RD Llwchwr 81-83; V Aberdare St Fagan *Llan* 83-89; V Felin-foel *St D* 89-01; Asst Dioc Dir of Educn 89-92; Dioc Dir of Educn 92-97; V Pen-bre 01-07; Can St D Cathl 94-07; rtd 07; Perm to Offic *St D* from 07. *77 Parc Tyisha, Burry Port SA16 0RR*

MEATYARD, Mrs Christina. b 51. SRN74. STETS 96. **d** 99 **p** 01. NSM S Hayling *Portsm* 99-05; NSM N Hayling St Pet and Hayling Is St Andr 05-06. *38 Staunton Avenue, Hayling Island PO11 0EW* Tel (023) 9234 8886 *or* 9263 7649 Mobile 07979-096779

MECHANIC, Rodney Ian (Roni). b 48. Man Univ MA(Theol)00. **d** 78 **p** 78. S Africa 78-98; P-in-c Shebbear, Buckland Filleigh, Sheepwash etc *Ex* 98-01; Australia 01-02; TV Heatons *Man* 02-08; TV Mildenhall *St E* from 08. *The Vicarage, 1 The Street, Barton Mills, Bury St Edmunds IP28 6AP* Tel (01638) 715112 Mobile 07753-177280 E-mail ronimechanic@googlemail.com

MEDCALF, James Gordon. b 31. CB. Solicitor 63. S'wark Ord Course 87. **d** 90 **p** 91. NSM Shortlands *Roch* 90-00. *15 Losecoat Close, Stamford PE9 1DU* Tel (01780) 482583

MEDCALF, John Edward. b 19. Oak Hill Th Coll 47. **d** 50 **p** 51. C Rugby St Matt *Cov* 50-53; TR Chell *Lich* 53-61; V Wednesfield Heath 61-85; rtd 85; Perm to Offic *Heref* from 86. *9 Richmond Care Village, St Joseph's Way, Nantwich CW5 6TD* Tel (01270) 623244

MEDCALF, William Henry. b 15. TCD BA45 MA49. CITC 46. **d** 46 **p** 47. C Belfast St Mich *Conn* 46-48; C Bedford St Pet *St Alb* 48-50; SE Sec CMJ 50-63; Dir Exhibitions CMJ 63-80; rtd 80; Perm to Offic *Lon* 80-08. *c/o Mrs O H Thompson, Swans View, 26 Wilhelmina Close, Leamington Spa CV32 5JT* Tel (01926) 337577

MEDFORTH, Allan Hargreaves. b 27. Qu Coll Cam BA48 MA52. Westcott Ho Cam 50. **d** 51 **p** 52. C Hexham *Newc* 51-55; PV S'well Minster 55-59; V Farnsfield 59-72; RD S'well 66-72; V St Alb St Pet *St Alb* 72-95; RD St Alb 74-84; rtd 95; Perm to Offic *St Alb* from 95. *62 Cuckmans Drive, St Albans AL2 3AF* Tel (01727) 836437

MEDHURST, Mrs June. b 44. St Hild Coll Dur TCert66. NOC 99. **d** 02 **p** 03. C Silsden *Bradf* 02-06; P-in-c Oxenhope from 06.

The Vicarage, 20 Gledhow Drive, Oxenhope, Keighley BD22 9SA Tel (01535) 642529 E-mail medjune@tiscali.co.uk

MEDHURST, Prof Kenneth Noel. b 38. Edin Univ MA61 Man Univ PhD69. **d** 91 **p** 93. NSM Baildon *Bradf* from 91; Can Th Bradf Cathl from 00. *The Vicarage, 20 Gledhow Drive, Oxenhope, Keighley BD22 9SA* Tel (01535) 642529
E-mail kenmed@btinternet.com

MEDHURST, Leslie John. b 56. TCD BTh90 MA93 Open Univ BA91. **d** 85 **p** 86. C Seapatrick *D & D* 85-90; I Belfast St Mark *Conn* 90-97; I Helen's Bay *D & D* 97-05. *Address temp unknown*

MEDLEY, Canon Philip Roger. b 46. Birm Univ CertEd73 Sheff Univ MA00 FCollP96. SWMTC. **d** 85 **p** 86. NSM Ottery St Mary, Alfington and W Hill *Ex* 85-86; C S Hill w Callington *Truro* 86-89; C Linkinhorne 86-89; V 89-03; Dioc Officer for Evang 93-99; Warden Cornwall Preachers' Coll 93-99; Hon Can Truro Cathl 01-03; Dioc Missr *B & W* from 03. *The Old Deanery, Wells BA5 2UG* Tel (01749) 670777
E-mail roger.medley@bathwells.anglican.org

MEDWAY, Mrs Christine Jean. b 57. Qu Coll Birm 93. **d** 95 **p** 98. C Milton *Win* 95-97; C Southampton St Mary Extra 97-01; P-in-c Haselbury Plucknett, Misterton and N Perrott *B & W* 01-03; rtd 03. *40 Lime Avenue, Southampton SO19 8NZ* Tel (023) 8044 5105

MEDWAY, Daron. b 72. Univ of N Lon BA98. Wycliffe Hall Ox BTh04. **d** 04 **p** 05. C Crofton *Portsm* 04-08; V Penge St Jo *Roch* from 08. *The Vicarage, St Johns Road, London SE20 7EQ* Tel (020) 8778 6176 Mobile 07900-574691
E-mail d.medway@mac.com

MEE, Colin Henry. b 36. Reading Univ BSc58. Bris Sch of Min 83. **d** 85 **p** 86. NSM Stanton St Quintin, Hullavington, Grittleton etc *Bris* 85-87; C Swindon Ch Ch 88-90; TV Washfield, Stoodleigh, Withleigh etc *Ex* 90-95; TR 95-99; Chapl Marie Curie Foundn (Tidcombe Hall) 95-99; rtd 99; Perm to Offic *B & W* from 02. *Rickstones, Burgundy Road, Minehead TA24 5QJ* Tel (01643) 706048

MEEHAN, Cyril Frederick. b 52. St Jo Coll Nottm BTh80. **d** 80 **p** 81. C Keresley and Coundon *Cov* 80-83; P-in-c Linton and Castle Gresley *Derby* 83-90; P-in-c Alvaston 90-00; V 00; Chapl Asst Freeman Gp of Hosps NHS Trust 00-03; Chapl Northumbria Healthcare NHS Trust from 03. *North Tyneside General Hospital, Rake Lane, North Shields NE29 8NH* Tel 0191-259 6660 *or* 237 3416

MEEK, Anthony William. b 45. ACIB. Ox NSM Course 80. **d** 83 **p** 84. NSM Gt Chesham *Ox* 83-01; Perm to Offic *Ex* from 01; Clergy Widow(er)s Officer from 02. *The Willows, Orley Road, Ipplepen, Newton Abbot TQ12 5SA* Tel (01803) 814370
E-mail frtonymeek@aol.com

MEERE, Mrs Alison Elizabeth. b 44. SRN65. Ripon Coll Cuddesdon 85. **d** 87 **p** 94. Par Dn Hengrove *Bris* 87-88; Par Dn Winterbourne 88-91; Par Dn Southmead 91-93; Par Dn Hackney *Lon* 93-94; TV 94-95; Asst Chapl R Berks Hosp Reading 95-96; Asst Chapl Battle Hosp Reading 95-96; Indonesia 02-03; rtd 03. *19 St Elmos Road, London SE16 1SA* Tel 07754-808579 (mobile)

MEERING, Laurence Piers Ralph. b 48. Man Univ BSc70. Trin Coll Bris 79. **d** 81 **p** 82. C Downend *Bris* 81-84; C Crofton *Portsm* 84-87; V Witheridge, Thelbridge, Creacombe, Meshaw etc *Ex* 87-94; TV Southgate *Chich* 94-02; TV Walton H Trin *Ox* 02-07; P-in-c Bedgrove 02-07; P-in-c Newton Longville and Mursley w Swanbourne etc 07-08; R from 08. *1 St Mary's Close, Mursley, Milton Keynes MK17 0HP* Tel (01296) 728055
E-mail laurencemeering@yahoo.co.uk

MEESE, Dudley Noel. b 63. Leic Univ BA86 Nottm Univ PGCE87. Ridley Hall Cam 99. **d** 01 **p** 02. C Sheff St Jo 01-05; Chapl Lee Abbey from 05. *Lee Abbey Fellowship, Lee Abbey, Lynton EX35 6JJ* Tel (01598) 752621

MEGAHEY, Alan John. b 44. Selw Coll Cam BA65 MA69 QUB PhD69. Westcott Ho Cam 69. **d** 70 **p** 71. Asst Chapl Wrekin Coll Telford 70-73; Ho Master Cranleigh Sch Surrey 73-83; Zimbabwe 84-93; Chapl Uppingham Sch 93-01; R Brant Broughton and Beckingham *Linc* from 01; R Leadenham from 01; R Welbourn from 01; RD Loveden from 03. *The Rectory, Church End, Leadenham, Lincoln LN5 0PX* Tel (01400) 273987 E-mail rector.leadenham@btopenworld.com

MEGARRELL, Miss Joanne Myrtle. b 70. QUB BA93 PGCE94. CITC BTh03. **d** 03 **p** 04. C Moira *D & D* from 03. *27 Danesfoot, Moira, Craigavon BT67 0SG* Tel (028) 9261 7346
E-mail jmegarrell@talk21.com *or* joanne@moiraparish.org.uk

✠**MEHAFFEY, The Rt Revd James.** b 31. TCD BA52 MA56 BD56 QUB PhD75 Ulster Univ Hon DLitt99. **d** 54 **p** 55 **c** 80. C Ballymacarrett St Patr *D & D* 54-56; C Deptford St Jo *S'wark* 56-58; C Down Cathl 58-60; C-in-c Ballymacarrett St Chris 60-62; I Kilkeel 62-66; I Cregagh 66-80; Bp's Private Chapl 72-76; Preb Down Cathl 76-80; Dioc Missr 76-80; Bp D & R 80-02; rtd 02. *10 Clearwater, Londonderry BT47 6BE* Tel (028) 7134 2624
E-mail james.mehaffey@btinternet.com

MEHEN, Donald Wilfrid. b 44. Birkbeck Coll Lon BSc72 CertEd66. **d** 00 **p** 01. OLM Sproughton w Burstall, Copdock w

Washbrook etc *St E* from 00. *19 The Link, Bentley, Ipswich IP9 2DJ* Tel (01473) 310383
E-mail don@mehen.freeserve.co.uk

MEIER, Paul. b 64. St Jo Coll Nottm BA98. **d** 98 **p** 99. C Highley w Billingsley, Glazeley etc *Heref* 98-01; C Hildenborough *Roch* 01-07; Storrington Deanery Youth Missr *Chich* from 07. *Cedars, The Driftway, Upper Beeding, Steyning BN44 3JX* Tel (01903) 810049 E-mail paul.meier@diocese-rochester.org *or* paul-meier@virgin.net

MEIKLE, Canon David Skene. b 39. St Cath Coll Cam BA60 MA89. Westcott Ho Cam. **d** 63 **p** 64. C Hawick *Edin* 63-67; C Edin SS Phil and Jas 67-72; C Banbury *Ox* 72-73; TV 74-78; R Ipswich St Matt *St E* 78-91; Hon Can St E Cathl 90-01; TR Mildenhall 91-01; rtd 01; Perm to Offic *St E* from 01. *172 Nacton Road, Ipswich IP3 9JN* Tel (01473) 439113
E-mail dandrmeikle@ntlworld.com

MEIN, The Very Revd James Adlington. b 38. Nottm Univ BA60. Westcott Ho Cam 61. **d** 63 **p** 64. C Edin St Columba 63-67; Bp's Dom Chapl 65-67; Malawi 67-72; R Grangemouth *Edin* 72-82; P-in-c Bo'ness 76-82; TV Livingston LEP 82-90; R Edin Ch Ch 90-04; Can St Mary's Cathl 90-01; Syn Clerk 00-01; Dean Edin 01-04; rtd 04. *Cardhu, Bridgend, Linlithgow EH49 6NH* Tel (01506) 834317 E-mail jim@meins.plus.com

MEIN, Canon Peter Simon. b 27. Nottm Univ BA55 MA59. Kelham Th Coll 48. **d** 55 **p** 56. SSM 54-70; Chapl Kelham Th Coll 55-61; Warden 62-70; Prior 64-70; Chapl St Andr Sch Delaware USA 71-92; Hon Can Delaware 89; rtd 92. *PO Box 13, Odessa DE 19730-0013, USA* Tel (001) (302) 378 9160
E-mail nsmein@earthlink.net

MEIRION-JONES, Dafydd Padrig ap Geraint. b 70. Magd Coll Cam BA91 PGCE92. Oak Hill Th Coll BA01. **d** 01 **p** 02. C Ex St Leon w H Trin 01-05; V Preston All SS *Blackb* from 05. *All Saints' Vicarage, 94 Watling Street Road, Fulwood, Preston PR2 8BP* Tel (01772) 700672 Mobile 07989-390028
E-mail dafandboo@hotmail.com

MEIRION-JONES, Canon Huw Geraint (Gary). b 39. K Coll Lon AKC69 BD71 MA84 MRAC61. St Aug Coll Cant 69. **d** 70 **p** 71. C Harlescott *Lich* 70-73; C Worplesdon *Guildf* 73-77; V Ash Vale 77-85; TR Westborough 85-96; Dioc Press Officer 85-94; P-in-c Shere 96-98; P-in-c Albury 97-98; R Shere, Albury and Chilworth 98-04; Hon Can Guildf Cathl 99-04; Dioc Rural Adv 99-03; RD Cranleigh 00-04; rtd 04; Perm to Offic *Guildf* from 04 and *Ban* 04-06; Lic to Offic *Ban* from 06. *Parc Newydd, Rhosgadfan, Caernarfon LL54 7LF* Tel (01286) 831195 Fax 830141 Mobile 07880-707414

MEIRIONNYDD, Archdeacon of. *See* ROWLANDS, The Ven Emyr Wyn

MELANESIA, Archbishop of. *See* VUNAGI, The Most Revd David

MELANIPHY, Miss Angela Ellen. b 55. SRN79. Cranmer Hall Dur 87. **d** 90 **p** 94. Par Dn Leytonstone St Jo *Chelmsf* 90-94; C 94-95; TV Harlow Town Cen w Lt Parndon 95-06; TV Hackney Marsh *Lon* from 06. *105 Mayola Road, London E5 0RG* Tel (020) 8533 4034 E-mail angels25@ntlworld.com

MELBOURNE, Brian Kenneth. b 45. Trin Coll Toronto 79. **d** 82 **p** 82. R Fogo Is Canada 82-84; R Welland 84-87; C Pembroke Bermuda 88-94; P-in-c Biddenden and Smarden *Cant* 94-97; Hon C Isfield *Chich* 01-06; R Ponoka Canada from 06. *5126 38th Street, Ponoka AB T4J 1C8, Canada* Tel (001) (103) 783 4329
E-mail gandbmelbourne@yahoo.ca *or* stmaryspon@telus.net

MELDRUM, Andrew John Bruce. b 66. Univ of Wales (Abth) LLB89 Lon Univ MA98. Westcott Ho Cam 91. **d** 94 **p** 95. C Paddington St Jas *Lon* 94-99; P-in-c Brookfield St Anne, Highgate Rise 99-02; V from 02; Communications Adv to Bp Edmonton from 00; AD S Camden from 08. *St Anne's Vicarage, 106 Highgate West Hill, London N6 6AP* Tel and fax (020) 8340 5190 E-mail javintner@aol.com

MELDRUM, David Peter John. b 73. St Andr Univ MA95. Oak Hill Th Coll BA01. **d** 01 **p** 02. C Leyton St Mary w Edw and St Luke *Chelmsf* 01-03; C Cranham Park 03-05; C Wandsworth St Steph S'wark 05-06; C Wandsworth St Mich w St Steph from 06. *St Stephen's Vicarage, 2A Oakhill Road, London SW15 2QU* Tel (020) 8870 0561 E-mail davidpjmeldrum@yahoo.com

MELINSKY, Canon Michael Arthur Hugh. b 24. Ch Coll Cam BA47 MA49. Ripon Hall Ox 57. **d** 57 **p** 59. C Wimborne Minster *Sarum* 57-59; C Wareham w Arne 59-61; V Nor St Steph 61-68; Chapl Norfolk and Nor Hosp 61-68; Hon Can Nor Cathl and Can Missr 68-73; Chief Sec ACCM 73-78; Prin NOC 78-88; rtd 88; Perm to Offic *Nor* from 88. *15 Parson's Mead, Norwich NR4 6PG* Tel (01603) 455042

MELLERUP, Miss Eiler Mary. b 37. Saffron Walden Coll CertEd58. **d** 96 **p** 97. OLM Happisburgh, Walcott, Hempstead w Eccles etc *Nor* 96-08; Perm to Offic from 08. *Channings, The Crescent, Walcott, Norwich NR12 0NH* Tel (01692) 651393

MELLING, Canon Leonard Richard. b 13. St Aid Birkenhead 38. **d** 41 **p** 42. C W Acklam *York* 41-45; C Scarborough St Mary 45-48; V Newby 48-54; Borneo 54-59; Area Sec USPG *Ox* 59-64; *York* 64-67; V Osbaldwick w Murton *York* 67-78; RD Bulmer 72-78; Malaysia 78-81; Dean Kuching 78-81; rtd 81;

Perm to Offic *York* from 81. *82 Tranby Avenue, Osbaldwick, York YO10 3NN* Tel (01904) 413796

MELLISH, John. b 26. Cranmer Hall Dur 67. **d** 69 **p** 70. C Ulverston St Mary w H Trin *Carl* 69-72; V Bromfield 72-73; V Bromfield w Waverton 73-79; P-in-c Allonby w W Newton 77-79; V Shap w Swindale 79-86; RD Appleby 82-86; V Bassenthwaite, Isel and Setmurthy 86-90; rtd 90; Perm to Offic *Carl* from 90. *Wyndham, 3 Old Road, Longtown, Carlisle CA6 5TH* Tel (01228) 791441

MELLOR, The Very Revd Kenneth Paul. b 49. Southn Univ BA71 Leeds Univ MA72. Cuddesdon Coll 72. **d** 73 **p** 74. C Cottingham *York* 73-76; C Ascot Heath *Ox* 76-80; V Tilehurst St Mary 80-85; V Menheniot *Truro* 85-94; Hon Can Truro Cathl 90-94 and from 03; Can Res and Treas 94-03; RD W Wivelshire 88-96; R Guernsey St Peter Port *Win* from 03; P-in-c Sark from 03; Dean Guernsey from 03. *The Deanery, Cornet Street, St Peter Port, Guernsey GY1 1BZ* Tel (01481) 720036 Fax 722948 E-mail kpmellor@aol.com

MELLOR, Roy. b 52. Lanc Univ BA92. Cuddesdon Coll 94. **d** 96 **p** 97. C Oakdale *Sarum* 96-00; TV Kingsthorpe w Northampton St Dav *Pet* 00-03; R Blisworth and Stoke Bruerne w Grafton Regis etc from 03. *The Rectory, 37 High Street, Blisworth, Northampton NN7 3BJ* Tel (01604) 879112
E-mail roy_mellor2002@yahoo.co.uk

MELLOR, Sarah Victoria. b 80. St Hilda's Coll Ox BA02 Liv Hope Univ Coll PGCE03 Man Univ MA05. Wycliffe Hall Ox 07. **d** 09. C Dur St Nic from 09. *95 Rochester Road, Durham DH1 5PN* Tel 0191-383 1148
E-mail victoriamellor26@yahoo.co.uk

MELLORS, Derek George. b 38. Bris Univ CertEd60 Lon Univ BSc71 Nottm Univ DipEd74 Liv Univ MEd83. NOC 81. **d** 84 **p** 85. NSM Eccleston Ch Ch *Liv* 84-92; C Lowton St Mary 92-93; V Ashton-in-Makerfield St Thos 93-99; rtd 99; Perm to Offic *Liv* from 00. *20 Millbrook Lane, Eccleston, St Helens WA10 4QU* Tel (01744) 28424

MELLORS, James. b 32. Kelham Th Coll 52. **d** 56 **p** 57. C Horbury *Wakef* 56-61; V Scholes 61-72; V Mirfield 72-88; Hon Can Wakef Cathl 83-88; V Leyburn w Bellerby *Ripon* 88-93; rtd 93; Perm to Offic *Ripon* from 93. *Broomhill, 22 The Shawl, Leyburn DL8 5DG* Tel (01969) 622452 E-mail jj.ww@virgin.net

MELLOWS, Canon Alan Frank. b 23. Qu Coll Cam BA45 MA49. Tyndale Hall Bris 47. **d** 49 **p** 50. C Morden *S'wark* 49-54; V Brimscombe *Glouc* 54-62; R Mileham *Nor* 62-74; P-in-c Beeston next Mileham 62-66; R 66-74; P-in-c Stanfield 62-74; P-in-c Gt w Lt Dunham 70-73; R Ashill 74-79; P-in-c Saham Toney 78-79; R Ashill w Saham Toney 79-88; Hon Can Nor Cathl 82-88; rtd 88; Perm to Offic *Nor* from 88. *8 Smugglers Close, Hunstanton PE36 6JU* Tel (01485) 534271

MELLOWSHIP, Robert John. b 52. St Mich Coll Llan BD92. **d** 92 **p** 93. C Brecon St Mary and Battle w Llanddew *S & B* 92-94; Min Can Brecon Cathl 92-94; C Pontypool *Mon* 94-95; TV 95-97; P-in-c Bressingham w N and S Lopham and Fersfield *Nor* 97-07; P-in-c Roydon St Remigius 04-07; R Upper Waveney from 07. *The Rectory, High Road, Bressingham, Diss IP22 2AT* Tel and fax (01379) 688267 E-mail robmellowship@msn.com

MELLUISH, Mark Peter. b 59. Oak Hill Th Coll 82. **d** 89 **p** 90. C Ashtead *Guildf* 89-93; V Ealing St Paul *Lon* from 93. *St Paul's Vicarage, 102 Elers Road, London W13 9QE* Tel and fax (020) 856/ 4628 *or* tel 8799 3779
E-mail mark.melluish@stpauls-ealing.org

MELLUISH, Stephen. b 60. Trin Coll Bris 91. **d** 93 **p** 94. C Gipsy Hill Ch Ch *S'wark* 93-96; V Wandsworth St Steph 96-06; P-in-c Wandsworth St Mich 01-06; V Wandsworth St Mich w St Steph from 06. *St Michael's Vicarage, 73 Wimbledon Park Road, London SW18 5TT* Tel (020) 8874 5610 or 8877 3003
E-mail smelluish@aol.com

MELLY, Aleck Emerson. b 24. Oak Hill Th Coll 50. **d** 53 **p** 54. C Chadderton Ch Ch *Man* 53-56; C Cheltenham St Mark *Glouc* 56-59; V Tipton St Paul *Lich* 59-68; R Kemberton w Sutton Maddock 68-80; P-in-c Stockton 74-80; R Kemberton, Sutton Maddock and Stockton 81-89; rtd 89; Perm to Offic *Lich* 89-03 and *Heref* from 90. *Bethany, 47 Greenfields Road, Bridgnorth WV16 4JG* Tel (01746) 762711

MELTON, Mrs Anne. b 44. N Riding Coll of Educn CertEd65. St Jo Coll Dur 80. **dss** 83 **d** 87 **p** 94. Newton Aycliffe *Dur* 83-88; Par Dn 87-88; Par Dn Shildon w Eldon 88-94; Asst Dir of Ords 88-94; P-in-c Usworth 94-96; TR 96-06; rtd 06. *4 Lindisfarne, High Shincliffe, Durham DH1 2PH* Tel 0191-416 3533

MELVILLE, Dominic. b 63. Sussex Univ BA84 Southn Univ BTh90. Sarum & Wells Th Coll 87. **d** 90 **p** 91. C Willenhall H Trin *Lich* 90-94; V Wednesfield St Greg 94-99; V Worc St Wulstan from 99. *The Vicarage, Cranham Drive, Worcester WR4 9PA* Tel (01905) 456944

MELVIN, Gordon Thomas. b 55. BA86. Sarum & Wells Th Coll 86. **d** 88 **p** 89. C Linc St Faith and St Martin w St Pet 88-91; TV Horsham *Chich* 91-94; Chapl Horsham Gen Hosp 91-94; Chapl Ipswich Hosp NHS Trust 94-00; Sen Chapl from 00; Chapl Local Health Partnerships NHS Trust 94-00; Sen Chapl from 00;

Perm to Offic *St E* from 04. *The Ipswich Hospital NHS Trust, Heath Road, Ipswich IP4 5PD* Tel (01473) 704100 *or* 712233

MENDEL, Canon Thomas Oliver. b 57. Down Coll Cam BA79 MA82. Cranmer Hall Dur 79. **d** 81 **p** 82. Chapl Down Coll Cam 81-86; Fell 84-86; Hon C Cambridge St Mary Less *Ely* 81-86; V Minsterley *Heref* 86-92; R Habberley 86-92; Chapl Shrewsbury Sch 93-95; Chapl Milan w Genoa and Varese *Eur* 95-96; Chapl Copenhagen w Aarhus 96-04; Sen Chapl Malta and Gozo 04-08; Can and Chan Malta Cathl 04-08; V Eastbourne St Mary *Chich* from 08. *St Mary's Vicarage, 2 Glebe Close, Eastbourne BN20 8AW* Tel (01323) 720420

✠**MENIN, The Rt Revd Malcolm James.** b 32. Univ Coll Ox BA55 MA59. Cuddesdon Coll 55. **d** 57 **p** 58 **c** 86. C Southsea H Spirit *Portsm* 57-59; C Fareham SS Pet and Paul 59-62; V Nor St Jas w Pockthorpe 62-72; P-in-c Nor St Martin 62-74; P-in-c Nor St Mary Magd 68-72; V Nor St Mary Magd w St Jas 72-86; RD Nor E 81-86; Hon Can Nor Cathl 82-86; Suff Bp Knaresborough *Ripon* 86-97; rtd 97; Perm to Offic *Nor* 97-04; Hon Asst Bp Nor from 00. *32C Bracondale, Norwich NR1 2AN* Tel (01603) 627987

MENNISS, Andrew Philip. b 49. Univ of Wales (Swansea) BSc73. Sarum & Wells Th Coll 83. **d** 85 **p** 86. C Horsell *Guildf* 85-89; V Bembridge *Portsm* from 89; RD E Wight 95-00. *The Vicarage, Church Road, Bembridge PO35 5NA* Tel (01983) 872175 Fax 875255 E-mail apmenniss@aol.com

MENON, Nicholas Anthony Thotekat. b 39. Mert Coll Ox BA61 MA65. St Steph Ho Ox 61. **d** 63 **p** 64. C Paddington Ch Ch *Lon* 63-66; Hon C 66-70; V Thorpe *Guildf* 70-76; V Ox SS Phil and Jas w St Marg 76-79; Chapl Surrey Univ 79-82; Chapl and Ho Master Cranleigh Sch Surrey 82-00; Asst Chapl Malvern Coll 00-06; rtd 04-06; Perm to Offic *Worc* from 05 and *Heref* from 06. *Pilgrim Cottage, 187 West Malvern Road, Malvern WR14 4BB* Tel (01684) 577189 E-mail nicholas.menon@ukonline.co.uk

MENSINGH, Gregg Richard. b 69. Portsm Univ BSc94. Westcott Ho Cam 95. **d** 97 **p** 98. C Birchfield *Birm* 97-01; V Gravelly Hill from 01. *All Saints' Vicarage, Broomfield Road, Birmingham B23 7QA* Tel 0121-373 0730 E-mail greggm@onetel.com

MENTZEL, Kevin David. b 60. Reading Univ BSc82 Down Coll Cam BA87 MA91 QUB MTh04. Ridley Hall Cam 85. **d** 88 **p** 89. C Ditton *Roch* 88-91; Asst Chapl Eton Coll 91-93; Asst Chapl R Hosp Sch Holbrook 93-94; Sen C Fulham St Dionis Parson's Green *Lon* 94-97; CF from 97. *c/o MOD Chaplains (Army)* Tel (01980) 615804 Fax 615800

MENZIES, Stanley Hay. b 33. Edin Univ MA55 BD58. New Coll Edin 55. **d** 02 **p** 03. NSM Boston Spa *York* from 02. *Cairn Croft, 2 Crag Gardens, Bramham, Wetherby LS23 6RP* Tel and fax (01937) 541047

MEON, Archdeacon of the. *See* HANCOCK, The Ven Peter

MEPHAM, Alistair. b 75. Trin Coll Bris BA07. **d** 07 **p** 08. C Warminster Ch Ch *Sarum* from 07. *19 Ashley Coombe, Warminster BA12 9QU* Tel (01985) 213150 E-mail alim@sorefeet.org.uk

MEPHAM, Stephen Richard. b 64. K Coll Lon BD85 AKC85. Linc Th Coll 87. **d** 89 **p** 90. C Newark *S'well* 89-92; C Cheshunt *St Alb* 92-95; C-in-c Turnford St Clem CD 95-98; V Rickmansworth 98-06. *46 Thellusson Way, Rickmansworth WD3 8RQ* E-mail sr.mepham@ntlworld.com

MERCER, James John. b 56. Bp Otter Coll Chich BEd79 Lon Inst of Educn MA85. Ridley Hall Cam 00. **d** 02 **p** 03. C Heref St Pet w St Owen and St Jas 02-07; V Harrow Weald All SS *Lon* from 07. *All Saints' Vicarage, 175 Uxbridge Road, Harrow HA3 6TP* Tel (020) 8954 0247 Mobile 07940-506188 E-mail james_ashw@mac.com

MERCER, Canon John James Glendinning. b 20. TCD BA49 MA55. **d** 50 **p** 51. C Newtownards *D & D* 50-53; C Bangor St Comgall 53-55; I Ballyholme 55-90; Can Belf Cathl 76-88; Preb Wicklow St Patr Cathl Dublin 88-90; rtd 90. *6 Hillfoot, Groomsport, Bangor BT19 6JJ* Tel (028) 9147 2979

MERCER, Preb Nicholas Stanley. b 49. Selw Coll Cam BA72 MA76 PGCE73 Spurgeon's Coll BA78 Lon Bible Coll MPhil86. Cranmer Hall Dur 95. **d** 95 **p** 95. C Northwood Hills St Edm *Lon* 95-98; C Pimlico St Mary Bourne Street 98-03; Dir of Min 03-07; V Gen Lon Coll of Bps from 07; Hon C Wilton Place St Paul from 04; Preb St Paul's Cathl from 08. *The Old Deanery, Dean's Court, London EC4V 5AA* Tel (020) 7489 4274 Mobile 07782-250377 E-mail nick.mercer@london.anglican.org

MERCER, Timothy James. b 54. Fitzw Coll Cam BA76 MA80. Westcott Ho Cam 78. **d** 81 **p** 82. C Bromley SS Pet and Paul *Roch* 81-85; R Swanscombe 85-96; Chapl Bromley Hosps NHS Trust 96-09; Chapl S Lon Healthcare NHS Trust from 09. *Princess Royal University Hospital, Farnborough Common, Orpington BR6 8ND* Tel (01689) 863912 *or* 821171 E-mail tim.mercer@diocese-rochester.org

MERCERON, Daniel John. b 58. Lon Univ BA81. Westcott Ho Cam 88. **d** 90 **p** 91. C Clevedon St Jo *B & W* 90-94; CF from 94. *c/o MOD Chaplains (Army)* Tel (01980) 615804 Fax 615800

MERCHANT, Robert Ian. b 73. Keele Univ BA98. Wycliffe Hall Ox BA00. **d** 01 **p** 02. C Harborne Heath *Birm* 01-04; C Cheltenham St Mark *Glouc* 05-06; C Cheltenham St Mich from

06; C Cheltenham St Luke and St Jo from 06. *Garden Flat, 1B Clarence Road, Cheltenham GL52 2AY* Tel (01242) 220190 Mobile 07747-010064 E-mail robmerchant@gmail.com

MERCHANT, Mrs Tamsin Laetitia Rachel. b 70. Wycliffe Hall Ox BTh01. **d** 01 **p** 02. C Harborne Heath *Birm* 01-04; Chapl Glos Univ from 04. *Garden Flat, 1B Clarence Road, Cheltenham GL52 2AY* Tel (01242) 714592 *or* 532735 Mobile 07715-041525 E-mail tmerchant@glos.ac.uk

MERCURIO, Frank James Charles. b 46. Webster Univ (USA) BA73 MA75. St Alb Minl Tr Scheme 87. **d** 89 **p** 90. C Cheshunt *St Alb* 89-93; TV Hitchin 93-00; RD Hitchin 94-00; TR Tring 00-07; P-in-c Alfreton *Derby* from 07; P-in-c Riddings and Ironville from 08. *The Vicarage, 13 Church Street, Alfreton DE55 7AH* Tel (01773) 833280 E-mail frankmercurio@dialstart.net

MEREDITH, Andrew James MacPherson. b 59. St Jo Coll Nottm 91. **d** 93 **p** 94. C Killay *S & B* 93-97; V Waunarllwydd 97-00; V Swansea St Thos and Kilvey from 00. *The Vicarage, Lewis Street, St Thomas, Swansea SA1 8BP* Tel (01792) 652891

MEREDITH, Ian. b 53. Univ of Wales BA85 Lon Univ MTh89 Edin Univ MTh96 Dur Univ PhD07. K Coll Lon 86. **d** 02 **p** 03. Assoc Min Dumfries *Glas* 02-07; R Ayr from 07; R Girvan from 07; R Maybole from 07. *The Rectory, 12 Barns Terrace, Ayr KA7 2DB* Tel (01292) 261145 E-mail rectorayr@yahoo.co.uk

MEREDITH, Robert. b 21. Bps' Coll Cheshunt 56. **d** 58 **p** 59. C Bedford St Andr *St Alb* 58-61; V Luton All SS 61-67; V Kimpton 67-75; RD Wheathampstead 72-76; R Kimpton w Ayot St Lawrence 75-76; R Hunsdon 76-80; R Widford 76-80; R Hunsdon w Widford and Wareside 80-84; P-in-c Braughing, Lt Hadham, Albury, Furneux Pelham etc 84-88; R Braughing w Furneux Pelham and Stocking Pelham 88-90; rtd 90; Perm to Offic *St Alb* 90-97; *Worc* from 98. *57 Ledwych Road, Droitwich WR9 9LA* Tel (01905) 797568

MEREDITH, Canon Roland Evan. b 32. Trin Coll Cam BA55 MA59. Cuddesdon Coll 55. **d** 57 **p** 58. C Bishopwearmouth St Mich *Dur* 57-59; Dioc Chapl *Birm* 59-60; C Knighty Liv 60-63; V Hitchin St Mary *St Alb* 63-72; V Preston St Jo *Blackb* 72-76; TR 76-79; RD Preston 72-79; Hon Can Blackb Cathl 77-79; TR Witney *Ox* 79-94; P-in-c Hailey w Crawley 79-82; RD Witney 89-97; Hon Can Ch Ch 92-97; rtd 94; Perm to Offic *Ox* from 97; *Eur* from 98; *Glouc* from 03. *12 Clover Place, Eynsham, Witney OX29 4QL* Tel (01865) 880210 E-mail roland@canonmeredith.free-online.co.uk

MEREDITH-JONES, Richard. b 26. JP79. K Coll Lon 50. **d** 54 **p** 55. C Perry Hill St Geo *S'wark* 54-56; P-in-c New Charlton H Trin 56-58; V Cinderford St Jo *Glouc* 58-62; Chapl Dilke Hosp Cinderford 58-62; V Richmond St Jo *S'wark* 62-66; Chapl Royal Hosp Richmond 62-66; Ind Chapl *Wakef* 66-70; Chapl Glenside Hosp Bris from 70; Perm to Offic *Glouc* 70-88; CF (TAVR) 78-91; Perm to Offic *Ban* 88-93; rtd 91; Perm to Offic *St D* and *B & W* from 91. *18 Wetlands Lane, Portishead, Bristol BS20 6RA* Tel (01275) 817217

MERIVALE, Charles Christian Robert. b 44. Cranmer Hall Dur 76. **d** 78 **p** 79. C Highbury Ch Ch w St Jo *Lon* 78-81; P-in-c Hawes *Ripon* 81-82; P-in-c Hardrow and St Jo w Lunds 81-82; V Hawes and Hardraw 82-84; Chapl R Cornwall Hosps Trust 85-92; Perm to Offic *B & W* 92-00 and *Ex* 00-02; TV Shebbear, Buckland Filleigh, Sheepwash etc *Ex* 02-08; rtd 08. *35 Hallett Road, Castle Cary BA7 7LG* Tel (01963) 350694 E-mail cjmerivale@milestonenet.co.uk

MERRICK, Canon John. b 51. New Univ of Ulster BA72 DipAdEd75 TCD HDipEd73. CITC 89. **d** 92 **p** 93. Hd Master Sligo Gr Sch from 86; Lic to Offic *K, E & A* from 92; Preb Elphin Cathl from 01. *Pier Lodge, Dunfanaghy PO, Letterkenny, Co Donegal, Republic of Ireland* Tel and fax (00353) (74) 913 6971 Mobile 87-227 4978

MERRIMAN, Stephen Richard. b 74. Leeds Univ BA02. Coll of Resurr Mirfield 99. **d** 02 **p** 03. C Littlehampton and Wick *Chich* 02-06; TV from 08; C Brighton St Matthias 06-08. *St James's House, 12 Cornwall Road, Littlehampton BN17 6EE* Tel (01903) 724311

MERRINGTON, Bill. b 55. Sheff Hallam Univ BSc78 Birm Univ MPhil95 Warwick Univ PhD03. Cranmer Hall Dur 80. **d** 83 **p** 84. C Harborne Heath *Birm* 83-88; V Leamington Priors St Paul *Cov* 88-99; RD Warwick and Leamington 97-99; R Ilmington w Stretton-on-Fosse etc 99-07; R Tredington and Darlingscott 05-07; RD Shipston 99-03; Hon Can Cov Cathl 01-07; Sen Chapl Bournemouth Univ from 07. *Chaplaincy, Bournemouth University, Fern Barrow, Poole BH12 5BB* Tel (01202) 965383 E-mail billmerri@aol.com

MERRY, David Thomas (Tom). b 48. St Chad's Coll Dur BA70. AKC73. **d** 74 **p** 75. C Cirencester *Glouc* 74-78; TV Bridgnorth, Tasley, Astley Abbotts and Oldbury *Heref* 78-83; P-in-c Quatford 81-83; P-in-c Stroud H Trin *Glouc* 83-87; V 87-01; Chapl Stroud Gen Hosp 83-93; Chapl Severn NHS Trust 93-01; Chapl Cheltenham Ladies' Coll from 01. *The Cheltenham Ladies' College, Bayshill Road, Cheltenham GL50 3EP* Tel (01242) 520691

MERRY, Ivor John. b 28. WMMTC 84. **d** 87 **p** 88. NSM Redditch, The Ridge *Worc* 87-94; NSM Astwood Bank 94-98; Perm to Offic from 98. *186 Moorcroft Gardens, Redditch B97 5WQ*

MERRY, Rex Edwin. b 38. AKC67. **d** 68 **p** 69. C Spalding St Jo *Linc* 68-73; C Boxmoor St Jo *St Alb* 73-83; TV Hemel Hempstead 83-95; V Farley Hill St Jo 95-06; rtd 06; Perm to Offic *St Alb* from 06. *4 Wellcroft, Hemel Hempstead HP1 3EG* Tel (01442) 401122

MERRY, Thomas. *See* MERRY, David Thomas

MERRYWEATHER, Mrs Rosalynd. b 50. Hull Coll of Educn CertEd72. NEOC. **d** 00 **p** 01. NSM Beverley St Nic *York* from 00. *10 West Close, Beverley HU17 7JJ* Tel (01482) 867958

MESLEY, Mark Terence. b 59. Plymouth Poly BSc88. St Steph Ho Ox 98. **d** 00 **p** 01. C Bickleigh and Shaugh Prior *Ex* 00-03; P-in-c Llanhilleth *Mon* 03-06; P-in-c Llanhilleth w Six Bells 06-08; P-in-c Penwerris *Truro* from 08; Chapl Miss to Seafarers from 08. *The Vicarage, Pellew Road, Falmouth TR11 2NS* Tel (01326) 218947 E-mail mesleyrev@eurobell.co.uk

MESLEY-SPONG, Terence John. b 32. Roch Th Coll 63. **d** 66 **p** 67. C Forton *Portsm* 66-68; Rhodesia 68-80; Zimbabwe 80-84; R Christow, Ashton, Trusham and Bridford *Ex* 84-86; Chapl Puerto de la Cruz Tenerife *Eur* 86-93; Miss to Seamen 86-93; rtd 93; Perm to Offic *Win* from 93; Chapl R Bournemouth and Christchurch Hosps NHS Trust 97-98. *14B Stuart Road, Highcliffe, Christchurch BH23 5JS* Tel (01425) 277833

MESSAM, Paul James. b 65. Lon Coll of Printing BA87. Cranmer Hall Dur 01. **d** 03 **p** 04. C Market Harborough and The Transfiguration etc *Leic* 03-07; P-in-c Ansty and Shilton *Cov* from 07; Lead Chapl Cov Blue Coat C of E Sch from 07. *St James's Vicarage, School Road, Bulkington, Nuneaton CV12 9JB* Tel (024) 7631 8241 Mobile 07711-098209 E-mail paul.messam@virgin.net

MESSENGER, Paul. b 38. Univ of Wales (Lamp) BA63. Coll of Resurr Mirfield 63. **d** 65 **p** 66. C Battersea St Luke *S'wark* 65-69; C Ainsdale *Liv* 69-71; V Wigan St Steph 71-74; Asst Chapl St Marg Convent E Grinstead 74-76; Chapl Kingsley St Mich Sch W Sussex 74-76; P-in-c Southwater *Chich* 76-81; V 81-97; R Sullington and Thakeham w Warminghurst 97-07; rtd 07. *122 Ninfield Road, Bexhill-on-Sea TN39 5BB* Tel (01424) 220044

MESSER, David Harry. b 61. MCIH93. EAMTC 01. **d** 04 **p** 05. C Stanton, Hopton, Market Weston, Barningham etc *St E* 04-07; R from 07. *The Rectory, Old Rectory Gardens, Stanton, Bury St Edmunds IP31 2JH* Tel (01359) 250239 E-mail david@dmesser.freeserve.co.uk

MESSHAM, Mrs Barbara Lynn. b 52. Bretton Hall Coll CertEd75. STETS 96. **d** 99 **p** 00. C The Bourne and Tilford *Guildf* 99-03; V Guildf All SS from 03; RD Guildf from 06. *All Saints' Vicarage, 18 Vicarage Gate, Guildford GU2 7QJ* Tel (01483) 572006 Mobile 07932-615132 E-mail barbara@messhams.co.uk

METCALF, Preb Michael Ralph. b 37. Clare Coll Cam BA61 MA65. Birm Univ MA80. Ridley Hall Cam 63. **d** 64 **p** 65. C Downend *Bris* 64-67; Perm to Offic *Birm* 68-78 and *Lich* 72-81; Lect W Midl Coll of Educn 72-77; Sen Lect 77-81; Dioc Dir of Educn *Lich* 83-94; V Stafford St Paul Forebridge 94-05; Preb Lich Cathl 91-05; RD Stafford 00-05; Perm to Offic *Heref* from 87; rtd 05. *196 Stone Road, Stafford ST16 1NT* Tel and fax (01785) 600260 E-mail prebmetcalf@hotmail.com *or* berylm@ntlworld.com

METCALF, The Ven Robert Laurence. b 35. Dur Univ BA60. Cranmer Hall Dur 62. **d** 62 **p** 63. C Bootle Ch Ch *Liv* 62-65; C Farnworth 65-67; V Wigan St Cath 67-75; R Wavertree H Trin 75-94; Chapl Blue Coat Sch *Liv* 75-94; Dir of Ords *Liv* 82-94; Hon Can Liv Cathl 87-02; Adn Liv 94-02; rtd 02; P-in-c Garston *Liv* from 04. *32 Storrsdale Road, Liverpool L18 7JZ* Tel 0151-724 3956 Fax 729 0587 E-mail bobmetcalf@ukgateway.net

METCALFE, Alan. b 22. St Aid Birkenhead 49. **d** 52 **p** 53. C Cleckheaton St Jo *Wakef* 52-55; C Todmorden 55-56; C Thornhill Lees 56-58; V Middlestown 58-60; V S Crosland 60-64; V Upwood w Gt and Lt Raveley *Ely* 64-69; Chapl RAF 64-68; V Dewsbury St Matt and St Jo *Wakef* 69-71; Warden Bridgehead Hostel Cardiff 71-73; Field View Hostel Stoke Prior 73-75; McIntyre Ho Nuneaton 75-79; C Southam w Stockton *Cov* 79-84; P-in-c Kinwarton w Gt Alne and Haselor 84-87; rtd 87; Hon C Yarcombe w Membury and Upottery *Ex* 89-92; Perm to Offic *St E* from 92. *3 Mays Court, Garrison Road, Felixstowe IP11 7ST* Tel (01394) 271665

METCALFE, Bernard. *See* METCALFE, Canon William Bernard

METCALFE, Reginald Herbert. b 38. **d** 79. Hon C Aspley Guise *St Alb* 79; Hon C Aspley Guise w Husborne Crawley and Ridgmont 80-84; Hon C Bovingdon 84-03. *30 Manorville Road, Hemel Hempstead HP3 0AP* Tel (01442) 242952 Fax 213137

METCALFE, Canon Ronald. b 41. BA. Edin Th Coll 67. **d** 69 **p** 70. C Saltburn-by-the-Sea *York* 69-72; P-in-c Crathorne 73-77; Youth Officer 73-77; Dioc Adult Tr Officer 78-88; Can Res York Minster 88-00; Sec for Miss and Min 88-00; V Kendal H Trin

Carl 00-07; rtd 07. *50 Carlton Moor Crescent, Darlington DL1 4RF* Tel (01325) 367219

METCALFE, Canon William Bernard. b 47. St Jo Coll Cam BA69 MA73 Ball Coll Ox BA71. Ripon Hall Ox 70. **d** 72 **p** 73. C Caversham *Ox* 72-75; C Aylesbury 75-79; Ind Chapl 75-79; TV Thamesmead *S'wark* 79-84; TR Totton *Win* 84-94; R Gt Bentley and Frating w Thorrington *Chelmsf* from 94; RD St Osyth 99-07; Hon Can Chelmsf Cathl from 06. *The Rectory, Moors Close, Great Bentley, Colchester CO7 8QL* Tel (01206) 250476 E-mail bernard.metcalfe@btinternet.com

METHUEN, Canon Charlotte Mary. b 64. Girton Coll Cam BA85 MA89 New Coll Edin BD91 PhD95. Edin Th Coll 87. **d** 98 **p** 99. C E Netherlands *Eur* 98-01; C Bonn w Cologne 01-03; Hon Asst Chapl 03-05; Dioc Dir of Tr 03-05; Hon C Offenbach (Old Catholic Ch) 05-07; Hon C Bottrop (Old Catholic Ch) from 08; Lect Ecclesiastical Hist Ox 99-01; Dioc Can Th Glouc from 07; Lect Ch Hist and Liturgy Ripon Coll Cuddesdon from 09. *Ripon College, Cuddesdon, Oxford OX44 9EX* Tel (01865) 873760 E-mail charlotte.methuen@theology.ox.ac.uk

METHUEN, John Alan Robert. b 47. BNC Ox BA69 MA74. Cuddesdon Coll 69. **d** 71 **p** 72. C Fenny Stratford *Ox* 71-73; C Fenny Stratford and Water Eaton 74; P-in-c Dorney 74-77; Asst Chapl Eton Coll 74-77; Warden Dorney/Eton Coll Conf Cen 74-77; V Reading St Mark *Ox* 77-83; R Hulme Ascension *Man* 83-95; Dean Ripon 95-05; rtd 06. *Dean's Lodge, 108 Honeypot Lane, London NW9 9QX* Tel (020) 8204 7047 E-mail irmethuen@btinternet.com

METHVEN, Canon George. b 26. Lon Univ BD52 Em Coll Cam BA54 MA58. ACT ThL47 Lon Coll of Div 50. **d** 52 **p** 53. C Cambridge St Andr Less *Ely* 52-54; Chapl RAF 55-60; V Lower Sydenham St Mich *S'wark* 60-67; Australia from 68; rtd 91. *PO Box 494, Belgrave Vic 3160, Australia* Tel (0061) (3) 9754 8056 E-mail agmethven@hotmail.com

METIVIER, Canon Robert John. b 31. Lon Univ BA68. Lambeth STh61 Ch Div Sch of the Pacific (USA) BD66 MDiv69 Codrington Coll Barbados 56. **d** 60 **p** 61. Trinidad and Tobago 61-64 and 68-78; USPG 66-67; C Gt Berkhamsted *St Alb* 78-82; V Goff's Oak St Jas 82-90; V Tokyngton St Mich *Lon* 90-01; Hon Can Trinidad from 98; rtd 01; Perm to Offic *Lon* from 02. *17 Willowcourt Avenue, Kenton, Harrow HA3 8ET* Tel (020) 8909 1371

METRY, Sameh Farid. b 63. **d** 09. C W Ealing St Jo w St Jas *Lon* from 09. *9 Fermoy Road, Greenford UB6 9HX* Tel and fax (020) 8575 0568 Mobile 07971-257287 E-mail smetry@msn.com

METTERS, Anthony John Francis. b 43. AKC65. **d** 68 **p** 69. C Heavitree *Ex* 68-74; V Plymouth Crownhill Ascension 74-79; RD Plymouth 77-79; Chapl RN 79-99; rtd 99. *Knightshayes, 1 De Port Heights, Corhampton, Southampton SO32 3DA*

METZNER (née JEFFREY), Mrs Katrina. b 73. St Jo Coll Ox BA96 MA01. St Steph Ho Ox 97. **d** 99 **p** 00. C Glouc St Geo w Whaddon 99-00; C Parkstone St Pet and St Osmund w Branksea *Sarum* 00-04; Perm to Offic *S'wark* from 05. *All Saints' Vicarage, 84 Franciscan Road, London SW17 8DQ* Tel (020) 8672 3706

METZNER, Simon David. b 64. Magd Coll Ox BA85 K Coll Lon MA93 St Luke's Coll Ex PGCE93. St Steph Ho Ox 88. **d** 00 **p** 01. C Branksome St Aldhelm *Sarum* 00-04; V Tooting All SS *S'wark* from 04. *All Saints' Vicarage, 84 Franciscan Road, London SW17 8DQ* Tel (020) 8672 3706 E-mail simon.metzner@btinternet.com

MEWIS, Canon David William. b 47. Leeds Inst of Educn CertEd68 Leeds Poly BEd83. NOC 87. **d** 90 **p** 91. C Skipton Ch Ch *Bradf* 90-92; R Bolton by Bowland w Grindleton from 92; C Hurst Green and Mitton from 05; C Waddington from 05; RD Bowland 99-08; Hon Can Bradf Cathl from 00. *The Rectory, Sawley Road, Grindleton, Clitheroe BB7 4QS* Tel (01200) 441154 E-mail david.mewis@bradford.anglican.org

MEWS, Stuart Paul. b 44. Leeds Univ BA64 MA67 Trin Hall Cam PhD74 FRHistS75. Westcott Ho Cam 86. **d** 87 **p** 88. Lect Lanc Univ 68-92; NSM Caton w Littledale *Blackb* 87-90; Hon C Lancaster St Mary 88-92; Reader RS Cheltenham and Glouc Coll of HE 92-00; Acting P-in-c Croxton and Eltisley *Ely* 97-98; P-in-c Tilbrook 00-07; P-in-c Keyston and Bythorn 00-07; P-in-c Catworth Magna 00-07; P-in-c Covington 00-07; P-in-c Grantchester from 07. *The Vicarage, 44 High Street, Grantchester, Cambridge CB3 9NF* Tel (01223) 845664

MEXICO, Presiding Bishop of. *See* TOUCHE-PORTER, The Most Revd Carlos

MEYER, Jonathan Peter. b 55. Keble Coll Ox BA76 MA. SAOMC 03. **d** 05 **p** 06. NSM Kintbury w Avington *Ox* 05-08; NSM W Woodhay w Enborne, Hampstead Marshall etc 05-09; P-in-c Ewelme, Brightwell Baldwin, Cuxham w Easington from 09. *The Rectory, Ewelme, Wallingford OX10 6HP* Tel (01491) 837823 E-mail revdjonathan@btinternet.com

MEYER, Malcolm John. b 46. ACIB. Cranmer Hall Dur 83. **d** 85 **p** 86. C Merrow *Guildf* 85-89; V Grayshott 89-98; R Binfield *Ox* from 98. *The Rectory, Terrace Road North, Bracknell RG12 5JG* Tel and fax (01344) 454406 E-mail bill@bmeyer.freeserve.co.uk

MEYNELL, Canon Andrew Francis. b 43. Westcott Ho Cam 70.

MEYNELL

d 73 **p** 74. C Cowley St Jas *Ox* 73-79; TV 79-81; P-in-c Halton 81-95; V Wendover 81-95; P-in-c Monks Risborough 95-98; TV Risborough 98-08; Dir Ords Bucks Adnry 95-08; Hon Can Ch Ch 01-08; rtd 08; Perm to Offic *Ox* from 09. *Pettits House, The Green, Great Milton, Oxford OX44 7NT* Tel (01844) 277912
E-mail andrew.meynell@oxford.anglican.org

MEYNELL, Mrs Honor Mary. b 37. EMMTC 84. **d** 87 **p** 94. NSM Kirk Langley *Derby* 87-03; NSM Mackworth All SS 87-03; NSM Mugginton and Kedleston 87-03; rtd 04; Perm to Offic *Derby* from 04. *The Coachman's Cottage, Meynell Langley, Kirk Langley, Ashbourne DE6 4NT* Tel (01332) 824207

MEYNELL, Mark John Henrik. b 70. New Coll Ox MA93. Ridley Hall Cam MA97. **d** 97 **p** 98. C Fulwood *Sheff* 97-01; Dean Kampala Evang Sch of Th Uganda 01-05; C Langham Place All So *Lon* from 05. *2 St Paul's Court, 56 Manchester Street, London W1U 3AF* Tel (020) 7486 0006 Fax 7436 3019
E-mail mark.meynell@allsouls.org

MEYRICK, The Very Revd Cyril Jonathan. b 52. St Jo Coll Ox BA73 MA77. Sarum & Wells Th Coll 74. **d** 76 **p** 77. C Bicester *Ox* 76-78; Bp's Dom Chapl 78-81; Tutor Codrington Coll Barbados 81-84; TV Burnham w Dropmore, Hitcham and Taplow *Ox* 84-90; TR Tisbury *Sarum* 90-98; Link Officer Black Angl Concerns 90-98; RD Chalke 97-98; Can Res Roch Cathl 98-05; Dean Ex from 05; P-in-c Cen Ex from 06. *The Deanery, 10 Cathedral Close, Exeter EX1 1EZ* Tel (01392) 273509
E-mail dean@exeter-cathedral.org.uk

MEYRICK, Thomas Henry Corfe. b 67. Magd Coll Ox BA88 MA92 Leeds Univ PhD05. St Steph Ho Ox BA94. **d** 95 **p** 96. C Bierley *Bradf* 95-99; Chapl Oriel Coll Ox 99-04; P-in-c Ox St Thos w St Frideswide and Binsey 04-05; P-in-c Newbold de Verdun and Kirkby Mallory *Leic* from 05; P-in-c Barlestone from 09; AD Sparkenhoe W from 08. *The Rectory, 6 The Paddock, Newbold Verdon, Leicester LE9 9NW* Tel (01455) 824986 E-mail tom_meyrick@ekit.com

MIALL, Peter Brian. b 30. Scawsby Coll of Educn TCert69. **d** 89 **p** 89. Hon C Bolsterstone *Sheff* 89-98; Perm to Offic from 98. *Waldershaigh Cottage, Heads Lane, Bolsterstone, Sheffield S36 3ZH* Tel 0114-288 5558

MICHAEL, Canon Ian MacRae. b 40. Aber Univ MA62 Hertf Coll Ox DPhil66. Westcott Ho Cam 77. **d** 79 **p** 80. C Kings Heath *Birm* 79-82; Vice-Provost St Paul's Cathl Dundee 82-88; V Harborne St Faith and St Laur *Birm* 88-03; RD Edgbaston 91-98; Hon Can Birm Cathl 00-03; rtd 03; Perm to Offic *Birm* from 03 and *St And* from 04. *46 Argyle Court, St Andrews KY16 9BW* Tel (01334) 473901

MICHAEL, Stephen David. b 71. Ripon Coll Cuddesdon 01. **d** 03 **p** 04. C St Blazey *Truro* 03-07; C Tywardreath w Tregaminion 03-07; C Lanlivery w Luxulyan 03-07; P-in-c Treverbyn from 07; P-in-c Boscoppa from 07. *The Vicarage, Treverbyn Road, Stenalees, St Austell PL26 8TL* Tel (01726) 851923
E-mail sd.michael@tiscali.co.uk

MICHAELS, David Albert Emmanuel. b 49. Bede Coll Dur BA72 Barrister-at-Law (Inner Temple) 73. Westcott Ho Cam 86. **d** 88 **p** 89. C Hampstead St Jo *Lon* 88-91; TV Wolvercote w Summertown *Ox* 91-04; P-in-c Launceston *Truro* from 04. *The Rectory, Dunheved Road, Launceston PL15 9JE* Tel (01566) 772101 E-mail david.michaels@dunelm.org.uk

MICHELL, Canon Douglas Reginald. b 19. St Jo Coll Dur BA41 MA44. Westcott Ho Cam 41. **d** 43 **p** 44. C Wanstead H Trin Hermon Hill *Chelmsf* 43-45; Chapl St Jo Coll Dur 45-48; R Moss Side St Jas *Man* 48-53; V Horwich H Trin 53-61; V Evington *Leic* 61-80; Hon Can Leic Cathl 67-84; RD Christianity N 74-79; V Billesdon w Goadby and Rolleston 80-82; RD Gartree I 81-84; V Billesdon and Skeffington 82-84; rtd 85; Perm to Offic *St Alb* 85-97 and *Chich* from 97. *9 Ramsay Hall, 11-13 Byron Road, Worthing BN11 3HN* Tel (01903) 207294

MICHELL, Canon Francis Richard Noel. b 42. St Cath Coll Cam BA64 MA68. Tyndale Hall Bris 64. **d** 66 **p** 67. C Northampton St Giles *Pet* 66-69; C Gateacre *Liv* 69-72; V Litherland St Paul Hatton Hill 72-79; V Rainhill 79-88; V Rainford 88-07; Hon Can Liv Cathl 06-07; rtd 07; Hon C Ludgvan, Marazion, St Hilary and Perranuthnoe *Truro* from 07. *The Rectory, St Hilary, Penzance TR20 9DQ* Tel (01736) 710229
E-mail noelmichell@uk7.net

MICKLEFIELD, Andrew Mark. b 71. K Alfred's Coll Win BEd93. Ridley Hall Cam 04. **d** 06 **p** 07. C Alton St Lawr *Win* from 06. *13 Walnut Close, Alton GU34 2BA* Tel (01420) 542288 Mobile 07766-732735 E-mail a.micklefield@btinternet.com

MICKLETHWAITE, Andrew Quentin. b 67. Univ Coll Dur BA89. Trin Coll Bris BA94. **d** 94 **p** 95. C Abington *Pet* 94-97; TV Duston Team 97-04; V Castle Donington and Lockington cum Hemington *Leic* from 04. *The Vicarage, 6 Delven Lane, Castle Donington, Derby DE74 2LJ* Tel (01332) 810364
E-mail revandrew@talk21.com

MICKLETHWAITE, Mrs Dorothy Eileen. b 41. SAOMC 98. **d** 01 **p** 02. NSM Astwell Gp *Pet* from 01; Asst Chapl Ox Radcliffe Hosps NHS Trust 02-09; Perm to Offic *Ox* 02-04. *54 Stuart Road, Brackley NN13 6HZ* Tel (01280) 703697
E-mail dorothymick@aol.com

MICKLETHWAITE, Jane Catherine. b 56. Lanc Univ BSc78. Trin Coll Bris 92. **d** 95 **p** 96. C Kings Heath *Pet* 95-98; Chapl Nene Coll of HE Northn 97-98; Perm to Offic *Pet* 98-01; NSM Kings Heath 01-04; Perm to Offic *Leic* from 04. *The Vicarage, 6 Delven Lane, Castle Donington, Derby DE74 2LJ* Tel (01332) 810364 E-mail j.micklethwaite@talk21.com

MICKLETHWAITE, Peter William. b 62. Peterho Cam BA84 MA88. St Jo Coll Nottm 87. **d** 90 **p** 91. C Leatherhead *Guildf* 90-93; C Wisley w Pyrford 93-97; R Windlesham 97-09. *Address temp unknown*

MIDDLEBROOK, David John. b 61. Newc Univ BSc83 Cranfield Inst of Tech MSc85. Trin Coll Bris BA98. **d** 98 **p** 99. C Chorleywood Ch Ch *St Alb* 98-02; TV Hemel Hempstead 02-08; P-in-c Watford St Luke from 08. *St Luke's Vicarage, Devereux Drive, Watford WD17 3DD* Tel (01923) 231205
E-mail dmiddlebrook@btinternet.com

MIDDLEDITCH, Terry Gordon. b 30. Univ of Wales (Lamp) BA62 St Martin's Coll Lanc PGCE68. St D Coll Lamp 59. **d** 63 **p** 64. C Poulton-le-Fylde *Blackb* 63-65; C-in-c Heysham 65-67; Sch Master 68-88; Hon C Cheltenham St Pet *Glouc* 75-87; Hon C Badgeworth w Shurdington 75-87; Hon C Up Hatherley 75-87; C Poulton-le-Sands w Morecambe St Laur *Blackb* 88-91; V Stalmine 91-00; rtd 00; Perm to Offic *Blackb* from 00. *93 Thornton Road, Morecambe LA4 5PG* Tel (01524) 413378 Mobile 07879-426173

MIDDLEMISS, Fritha Leonora. b 47. Man Univ BA68 CertEd69. Glouc Sch of Min 86. **d** 89 **p** 94. NSM Bengeworth *Worc* 89-94; NSM Stoulton w Drake's Broughton and Pirton etc 94-96; Chapl Malvern Girls' Coll 96-03; Asst Chapl HM Pris Long Lartin 03-08. *1 Ravensdowne, Berwick-upon-Tweed TD15 1HX* Tel (01289) 308553

MIDDLEMISS, Jeffrey Thomas. b 50. Padgate Coll of Educn BEd79 Edge Hill Coll of HE DASE85. NOC 87. **d** 90 **p** 91. C Gateacre *Liv* 90-93; V W Derby Gd Shep 93-94; V Wigan St Cath 94-00; TV Leominster *Heref* from 01; RD Leominster 05-08. *The New Vicarage, Kimbolton, Leominster HR6 0EJ* Tel (01568) 615295 E-mail jeff_middlemiss@lineone.net

MIDDLEMISS, Mrs Justine. b 68. Aston Univ BSc90. Ripon Coll Cuddesdon 00. **d** 02 **p** 03. C Lee St Marg *S'wark* 02-06; P-in-c Beddington 06; R from 06. *The Rectory, 18 Bloxworth Close, Wallington SM6 7NL* Tel (020) 8647 1973

MIDDLESEX, Archdeacon of. See WELCH, The Ven Stephan John

MIDDLETON, Alan Derek. b 46. St Jo Coll Dur BA68 MA85 Bris Univ PGCE70 Sheff Univ MMin00. Qu Coll Birm. **d** 72 **p** 73. C Cannock *Lich* 72-76; Warden St Helen's Youth & Community Cen Bp Auckd 76-79; V Darlington St Jo *Dur* 79-89; TR E Darlington 89-90; V Upper Norwood All SS *S'wark* 90-99; TR Warlingham w Chelsham and Farleigh from 99; Bp's Ecum Adv from 96; AD Caterham from 05. *The Rectory, 35 Dane Road, Warlingham CR6 9NP* Tel (01883) 624125 Fax 624490 E-mail alan.middleton@southwark.anglican.org

MIDDLETON, Arthur. See MIDDLETON, Canon Thomas Arthur

MIDDLETON, Barry Glen. b 41. Lich Th Coll 68. **d** 70 **p** 71. C Westhoughton *Man* 70-73; C Prestwich St Marg 73-74; TV Buxton w Burbage and King Sterndale *Derby* 74-77; Chapl Worc R Infirmary 77-83; Chapl Fairfield Hosp Hitchin 83-85; P-in-c Erpingham w Calthorpe *Nor* 85-86; R Erpingham w Calthorpe, Ingworth, Aldborough etc 86-92; R Badingham w Bruisyard, Cransford and Dennington *St E* 92-96; V Sidcup St Jo *Roch* 96-98; V Gt and Lt Bardfield w Gt and Lt Saling *Chelmsf* 98-00; rtd 00; Perm to Offic *St E* from 00. *20 Lynwood Avenue, Felixstowe IP11 9HS* Tel (01394) 286506

MIDDLETON, David Jeremy. b 68. Ex Univ BSc90. Wycliffe Hall Ox 01. **d** 03 **p** 04. C Ipswich St Jo *St E* 03-06; Hon C Wimbledon Park St Luke *S'wark* from 06. *5 Farquhar Road, London SW19 8DA* Tel (020) 8947 4377

MIDDLETON, Hugh Charles. b 50. Nottm Univ BTh77. Linc Th Coll 73. **d** 77 **p** 78. C New Sleaford *Linc* 77-81; C Grantham 81; TV 81-83; R Caythorpe 83-95; P-in-c Bracebridge Heath 97-00; V from 00; P-in-c Bracebridge from 07. *The Vicarage, 11 Salisbury Drive, Bracebridge Heath, Lincoln LN4 2SW* Tel (01522) 540460

MIDDLETON, Miss Jennifer Ann. b 82. St Jo Coll Dur BA03. St Jo Coll Nottm 06. **d** 08 **p** 09. C Fatfield *Dur* from 08. *80 Rowan Avenue, Washington NE38 9AF* Tel 0191-416 7405

MIDDLETON, Canon Michael John. b 40. Dur Univ BSc62 Fitzw Ho Cam BA66 MA70. Westcott Ho Cam 63. **d** 66 **p** 67. C Newc St Geo 66-69; V 77-85; Chapl St Geo Gr Sch Cape Town 69-72; Chapl K Sch Tynemouth 72-77; R Hexham *Newc* 85-92; Hon Can Newc Cathl 90-92; Adn Swindon *Bris* 92-97; Can and Treas Westmr Abbey 97-04; rtd 04. *37 High Fellside, Kendal LA9 4JG* Tel (01539) 729320

MIDDLETON, Rodney. b 54. St Andr Univ BD80. St Steph Ho Ox 80. **d** 82 **p** 83. C Walton St Mary *Liv* 82-87; C-in-c Kew St Fran CD 87-94; V Kew 94-95; Chapl Southport and Formby Distr Gen Hosp 87-95; V Haydock St Jas from 95. *The Vicarage,*

564

169 Church Road, Haydock, St Helens WA11 0NJ Tel (01942) 727956 E-mail rodmid169@yahoo.co.uk

MIDDLETON, Canon Thomas Arthur. b 36. Dur Univ MLitt95 FRHistS04. K Coll Lon AKC61 St Boniface Warminster 61. **d** 62 **p** 63. C Sunderland *Dur* 62-63; C Auckland St Helen 63-67; C Winlaton 67-70; C-in-c Pennywell St Thos and Grindon St Oswald CD 70-79; Chapl Grindon Hall Hosp 73-79; R Boldon 79-03; Adv in Stewardship Dur Adnry 87-92; Acting Prin St Chad's Coll Dur 97; Hon Can Dur Cathl 98-03; rtd 03. *1 St Mary's Drive, Sherburn Village, Durham DH6 1RL* Tel 0191-372 3436
E-mail thomas@thomas.middleton.wanadoo.co.uk

MIDDLETON, Suffragan Bishop of. *See* DAVIES, The Rt Revd Mark

MIDDLETON-DANSKY, Serge Wladimir. b 45. Cuddesdon Coll 74. **d** 77 **p** 78. C Wisbech SS Pet and Paul *Ely* 77-79; Lic to Offic Adnry Riviera *Eur* from 80; C Ox St Giles and SS Phil and Jas w St Marg 83-86; Perm to Offic *Ox* 86-88 and *Truro* 88-90; P-in-c Zennor and Towednack *Truro* 90-96; Perm to Offic 97-99; Lic to Offic from 99. *The Old Vicarage, Zennor, St Ives TR26 3BY* Tel (01736) 796955

MIDDLEWICK, Robert James. b 44. K Alfred's Coll Win CertEd67 Lon Univ BD76. Ripon Coll Cuddesdon 75. **d** 77 **p** 78. C Bromley SS Pet and Paul *Roch* 77-81; C Belvedere All SS 81-84; P-in-c Lamberhurst 85-88; P-in-c Matfield 85-88; V Lamberhurst and Matfield 88-99. *12 Mill Stream Place, Tonbridge TN9 1QJ* Tel (01580) 212054

MIDGLEY, George William. b 38. NOC. **d** 83 **p** 84. C Penistone and Thurlstone *Wakef* 88-89; TV 89-94; TR 94-04; rtd 04; Perm to Offic *Wakef* from 06. *20 Smithies Moor Lane, Batley WF17 9AR* Tel (01924) 472289

MIDGLEY, Stephen Nicholas. b 60. Jes Coll Cam BA83 MA86 Lon Hosp MB, BS86. Wycliffe Hall Ox. **d** 97 **p** 98. C Hove Bp Hannington Memorial Ch *Chich* 97-01; C Cambridge H Sepulchre *Ely* 01-04; P-in-c Cambridge St Andr Less from 04. *St Andrew the Less Vicarage, Parsonage Street, Cambridge CB5 8DN* Tel (01223) 353794 *or* 362574
E-mail steve.midgley@stag.org

MIDLANE, Colin John. b 50. Qu Mary Coll Lon BA72. Westcott Ho Cam 73 Sarum & Wells Th Coll 77. **d** 78 **p** 79. C Bethnal Green St Pet w St Thos *Lon* 78-82; P-in-c Haggerston All SS 82-88; Chapl Hengrave Hall Ecum Cen 88-89; P Cllr St Botolph Aldgate *Lon* 89-94; C St Botolph Aldgate w H Trin Minories 93-94; TV Haywards Heath St Wilfrid *Chich* 94-97; C Brighton St Geo w St Anne and St Mark 97-01; Chapl Brighton and Sussex Univ Hosps NHS Trust 01-03; rtd 03; Perm to Offic *Lon* from 04. *30 Damien Court, Damien Street, London E1 2HL* Tel (020) 7791 0001

MIDWINTER, Sister Josie Isabel. b 46. Open Univ BA84 Univ of Wales (Lamp) MA98. CA Tr Coll IDC71. **d** 87 **p** 99. CA from 71; CMS 84-93; Uganda 85-91; Kenya 92-96; C Didcot All SS *Ox* 98-05; P-in-c Drayton St Pet (Berks) from 05; rtd 06. *The Vicarage, 8 Gravel Lane, Drayton, Abingdon OX14 4HY* Tel (01235) 531374 E-mail josie.midwinter@lineone.net

MIDWOOD, Canon Peter Stanley. b 47. CertEd69. Linc Th Coll 80. **d** 82 **p** 83. C Garforth *Ripon* 82-85; C-in-c Grinton w Arkengarthdale, Downholme and Marske 85-86; C-in-c Melbecks and Muker 85-86; V Swaledale 86-97; R Romaldkirk w Laithkirk 97-08; R Walkingham Hill from 08; Hon Can Ripon Cathl from 05. *The Rectory, Main Street, Staveley, Knaresborough HG5 9LD* Tel (01423) 340275
E-mail ps.midwood@virgin.net

MIELL, David Keith. b 57. BSc PhD BA. Westcott Ho Cam 83. **d** 86 **p** 87. C Blackbird Leys CD *Ox* 86-89; C Walton 89-90; TV Walton Milton Keynes 90-96; RD Milton Keynes 93-95; TR Upton cum Chalvey 96-05; AD Burnham and Slough 02-05; Perm to Offic 05-08. *73 Barton Drive, Barton on Sea, New Milton BH25 7JH* E-mail drdmiell@surfaid.org

MIER, Ms Catherine Elizabeth. b 60. Bris Univ BSc81 Chelsea Coll Lon MSc84 Dur Univ BA95. Cranmer Hall Dur 93. **d** 96 **p** 97. C Royston *St Alb* 96-00; C Bilton *Cov* 00-04; P-in-c Wellesbourne from 04; P-in-c Walton d'Eiville from 04. *The Vicarage, Church Street, Wellesbourne, Warwick CV35 9LS* Tel (01789) 840262 E-mail kate.mier@virgin.net

MIGHALL, Robert. b 33. St Pet Coll Ox BA57 MA61. Wycliffe Hall Ox 57. **d** 58 **p** 59. C Stoke *Cov* 58-62; C Rugby St Andr 62-64; V Newbold on Avon 64-76; V Combroke w Compton Verney 76-96; V Kineton 76-96; rtd 96; Perm to Offic *Glouc* from 97. *The Dairy House, Quarleston Farm, Clenston Road, Winterborne Stickland, Blandford Forum DT11 0NP* Tel (01258) 881467 E-mail randm@qvalley.tesco.net

MIHILL, Dennis George. b 31. St Alb Minl Tr Scheme 78. **d** 81 **p** 82. NSM Harpenden St Nic *St Alb* 81-86; C Sawbridgeworth 86-89; V Motspur Park *S'wark* 89-96; rtd 96; Perm to Offic *St Alb* 96-98 and 01-08; Hon C Biddenham 98-01; Perm to Offic *Roch* from 06. *7 Bourchier Close, Sevenoaks TN13 1PD* Tel (01732) 459760

MIKHAIL, Stella Frances. *See* JONES, Stella Frances

MILBANK (née LEGG), Alison Grant. b 54. Girton Coll Cam BA78 MA81 PGCE79 Lanc Univ PhD88. EMMTC 05. **d** 06 **p** 07. NSM Lambley *S'well* from 06. *Burgage Hill Cottage, Burgage, Southwell NG25 0EP* Tel (01636) 819224
E-mail alison.milbank@nottingham.ac.uk

MILBURN, John Frederick. b 56. Westmr Coll Ox BA84. Sarum & Wells Th Coll 84. **d** 86 **p** 87. C Leavesden *St Alb* 86-89; C Broxbourne w Wormley 89-93; CF (TA) 90-93; R Inglewood w Texas Australia 93-98; P-in-c Holland Park 98-04; R Bulimba from 04. *171 Oxford Street, PO Box 271, Bulimba Qld 4171, Australia* Tel (0061) (7) 3397 1508 Fax 3397 3253 Mobile 415-838239 E-mail johnmilburn@hotmail.com
or anglicanbulimba@ozemail.com.au

MILES, Mrs Beverley Anne. b 54. **d** 09. NSM Findon Valley *Chich* from 09. *2 Maxwell Cottages, Findon Road, Findon, Worthing BN14 0RA* Tel (01903) 877191

MILES, Damian Stewart. b 76. Fitzw Coll Cam BTh02. Westcott Ho Cam 99. **d** 02 **p** 03. C Willingdon *Chich* 02-06; P-in-c Nork *Guildf* from 06. *St Paul's Vicarage, Warren Road, Banstead SM7 1LG* Tel (01737) 353849 Mobile 07815-848735
E-mail damomiles@btinternet.com

MILES, Gerald Christopher Morgan. b 36. Peterho Cam BA57 MA72 Cranfield Inst of Tech MSc72 CEng MIET. Wycliffe Hall Ox 74. **d** 76 **p** 77. C Tunbridge Wells St Jas *Roch* 76-80; V Leigh 80-90; R Addington w Trottiscliffe 90-91; P-in-c Ryarsh w Birling 90-91; R Birling, Addington, Ryarsh and Trottiscliffe 91-00; Hon Chapl London and SE Region ATC from 96; rtd 00; Perm to Offic *Roch* from 00. *2 Spa Close, Hadlow, Tonbridge TN11 0JX* Tel and fax (01732) 852323
E-mail cmiles@supanet.com

MILES (née HOARE), Ms Janet Francis Mary. b 48. St Aid Coll Dur BA70 Bris Univ MEd84. Sarum & Wells Th Coll 91. **d** 93 **p** 94. C Bruton and Distr *B & W* 93-98; P-in-c Llangarron w Llangrove, Whitchurch and Ganarew *Heref* 98-02; Dixton and Whitchurch w Ganarew 02-04; P-in-c Chewton Mendip w Ston Easton, Litton etc *B & W* 04-08; Dir Studies WEMTC 04-07. *1 Millier Road, Cleeve, Bristol BS49 4NL* Tel (01934) 830276
E-mail jfm2@btinternet.com

MILES, Malcolm Robert. b 36. AKC60. **d** 61 **p** 62. C Northampton St Mary *Pet* 61-63; C E Haddon 63-67; R Broughton 67-73; Asst Chapl Nottm Univ 73-74; V Northampton H Trin *Pet* 75-84; V Painswick w Sheepscombe *Glouc* 84-97; V Painswick w Sheepscombe and Cranham 97-01; RD Bisley 90-94; rtd 01; P-in-c Wensley and W Witton *Ripon* 01-05; Perm to Offic *York* from 06. *32 Turker Lane, Northallerton DL6 1PZ* Tel (01609) 773133
E-mail rachel@milesr.freeserve.co.uk

MILES, Marion Clare. b 41. S Dios Minl Tr Scheme 86. **d** 88 **p** 94. Hon Par Dn Blandford Forum and Langton Long *Sarum* 88-94; Hon C 94-01; Chapl Blandford Community Hosp from 88; NSM Winterborne Valley and Milton Abbas from 01. *153 Salisbury Road, Blandford Forum DT11 7SW* Tel (01258) 452010 E-mail marionclare07@yahoo.co.uk

MILES, Ms Patricia Ellen. b 56. RGN79. STETS 00. **d** 03 **p** 04. NSM Verwood *Sarum* from 03. *4 Firs Glen Road, Verwood BH31 6JB* Tel (01202) 824211 E-mail pe.miles@btinternet.com

MILES, Robert. *See* MILES, Malcolm Robert

MILES, Robert Anthony. b 71. Nottm Univ BSc92 PGCE94 All Nations Chr Coll BA01. Wycliffe Hall Ox M1h08. **d** 08 **p** 09. C Moulton *Pet* from 08. *8 Cubleigh Close, Moulton, Northampton NN3 7BG* Tel (01604) 491062 E-mail 5miles@bigfoot.com

MILES, Canon Robert William. b 27. Magd Coll Cam BA50 MA55. Westcott Ho Cam 50. **d** 52 **p** 53. C Bury St Mary *Man* 52-55; Bp's Dom Chapl *Chich* 55-58; Kenya 58-63; Provost Mombasa 58-63; R Dalmahoy *Edin* 65-70; R Batsford w Moreton-in-Marsh *Glouc* 70-77; rtd 77; Perm to Offic *Glouc* from 79. *Bushingwell, Winchcombe, Cheltenham GL54 5JB* Tel (01242) 603337

MILES, Miss Sharon Elizabeth Ann. b 66. Westcott Ho Cam 00. **d** 02 **p** 03. C Shrub End *Chelmsf* 02-05; P-in-c Rivenhall from 05; Adv for Ordained Women's Min (Colchester Area) from 07. *Swallows, Western Lane, Silver End, Witham CM8 3SA* Tel (01376) 583930 E-mail revdsmiles@btinternet.com

MILES, Stephen John. b 44. Monash Univ Aus BA66 Worc Coll Ox DipEd68 Univ Coll Lon MA75 California Univ PhD80. Melbourne Coll of Div BTheol86. **d** 87 **p** 88. Australia 87-97 and from 03; C E Malvern St Jo 87; C Clifton Hill St Andr 87-89; Chapl Co-ord and Angl Chapl Monash Medical Cen 89-97; Asst Chapl Bonn w Cologne *Eur* 97-00; Chapl 00-03; rtd 03. *67 Caroline Street, South Yarra Vic 3141, Australia* Tel (0061) (3) 9866 1463

MILFORD, Canon Catherine Helena. b 39. LMH Ox BA61 MA65 FRSA92. Gilmore Course 81. **dss** 82 **d** 87 **p** 94. Heaton St Barn *Bradf* 82-88; Par Dn 87-88; Adult Educn Adv *Win* 88-96; TR Barnham Broom *Nor* 96-00; P-in-c Reymerston w Cranworth, Letton, Southburgh etc 96-00; TR Barnham Broom and Upper Yare 00-04; Hon Can Nor Cathl 00-04; rtd 04. *6 Leylands Grove, Bradford BD9 5QP*

MILFORD, Graham Alan. b 57. Trin Coll Bris 00. **d** 02 **p** 03. C Wolborough and Ogwell *Ex* 02-08; P-in-c Newburgh w Westhead *Liv* from 08. *The Vicarage, Back Lane, Newburgh, Wigan WN8 7XB* Tel (01257) 463267
E-mail grahammilford@btinternet.com

MILFORD, Mrs Nicola Claire. b 75. Univ Coll Ches BTh03. Trin Coll Bris 00 NOC 02. **d** 04 **p** 05. C Alphington, Shillingford St George and Ide *Ex* 04-08. *The Vicarage, Back Lane, Newburgh, Wigan WN8 7XB* Tel (01257) 463267
E-mail milford.nicola@virgin.net

MILLAM, Peter John. b 36. Univ of Wales (Lamp) BA58 QTS61 FRSA08. Ridley Hall Cam 58. **d** 63 **p** 64. C Cheltenham Ch Ch *Glouc* 63-66; Sen Chapl Port Stanley Falkland Is and Offg Chapl RN 66-70; V Pulloxhill w Flitton *St Alb* 70-79; V Luton St Paul 79-89; V Chipping Campden w Ebrington *Glouc* 89-94; rtd 94; Perm to Offic *Chich* from 94. *22 Willowhale Avenue, Aldwick, Bognor Regis PO21 4AY* Tel and fax (01243) 268316

MILLAR, Alan Askwith. b 26. Qu Coll Birm 59. **d** 60 **p** 61. C Redcar *York* 60-64; C Kirkleatham 60-64; V Middlesbrough St Aid 64-72; V Cayton w Eastfield 72-88; Chapl to RD of Scarborough 88-89; rtd 89; Perm to Offic *Bradf* from 89. *20 Guardian Court, Wells Promenade, Ilkley LS29 9JT* Tel (01943) 602081

MILLAR, Alan William. b 46. Toronto Univ MDiv. **d** 00 **p** 01. C Drumglass w Moygashel *Arm* 00-02; I Dromara w Garvaghy *D & D* 02-06; I Rathcoole *Conn* from 06. *7 Oaklands Meadow, Newtownabbey BT37 0XN* Tel (028) 9086 7714
E-mail alan.millar3@btinternet.com

MILLAR, Alexander. *See* MILLAR, The Rt Revd John Alexander Kirkpatrick

MILLAR, Andrew Charles. b 48. Hull Univ BSc69. Cuddesdon Coll 71. **d** 73 **p** 74. C Rushmere *St E* 73-76; C Ipswich All Hallows 76-79; Dioc Youth Chapl *Sheff* 79-83; Youth Chapl *Win* 83-92; V Colden 92-08; V Twyford and Owslebury and Morestead etc from 08. *The Vicarage, Colden Common, Winchester SO21 1TL* Tel and fax (01962) 712505

MILLAR, Christine. *See* WHEELER, Mrs Christine

MILLAR, David Glassell. b 43. Dur Univ BSc64 St Cath Coll Cam BA66 MA71 Birkbeck Coll Lon BSc78 Leeds Univ MSc80. Cuddesdon Coll 66. **d** 68 **p** 69. C Pershore w Wick *Worc* 68-72; C Malden St Jas *S'wark* 72-73; V W Dean *Chich* 73-75; rtd 08. *5 Beacon Hill, London N7 9LY* Tel and fax (020) 7607 3809

MILLAR, Gary. b 67. St Mich Coll Llan 88. **d** 91 **p** 92. C Tonyrefail w Gilfach Goch *Llan* 91-93; C Barry All SS 93-95; TV Cowbridge 95-97; I Dromara w Garvaghy *D & D* 97-01; I Kilkeel 01-08; I Belfast St Paul w St Barn *Conn* from 08. *The Rectory, 50 Sunningdale Park, Belfast BT14 6RW* Tel (028) 9071 5413 Mobile 07989-089446 E-mail g.millar@btinternet.com

✠**MILLAR, The Rt Revd John Alexander Kirkpatrick (Sandy).** b 39. Trin Coll Cam BA62 MA66. St Jo Coll Dur 74. **d** 76 **p** 77 **c** 05. C Brompton H Trin w Onslow Square St Paul *Lon* 76-85; V 85-05; Hon C from 05; P-in-c Tollington from 03; AD Chelsea 89-94; Preb St Paul's Cathl from 97; Asst Bp Uganda from 05. *St Mark's Vicarage, 1 Moray Road, London N4 3LD* Tel (020) 7281 7700 *or* 7561 5462
E-mail sandy.millar@tollingtonteam.org.uk

MILLAR, Mrs Julie Ann. b 65. Bris Poly BA87 ACA. SWMTC 02. **d** 05 **p** 06. NSM Penzance St Mary w St Paul and St Jo *Truro* 05-08; Asst Chapl R Cornwall Hosps Trust from 08. *14 Tolver Place, Penzance TR18 2AD* Tel (01736) 333682 Mobile 07719-823600 E-mail revdjulie.pz@btopenworld.com

MILLAR, Sandra Doreen. b 57. Univ of Wales (Cardiff) BA79 Warwick Univ MA94 PhD99. Ripon Coll Cuddesdon 98. **d** 00 **p** 01. C Chipping Barnet w Arkley *St Alb* 00-03; TV Dorchester *Ox* 03-07; Dioc Children's Officer *Glouc* from 07. *18 Overbury Road, Gloucester GL1 4EA* Tel (01452) 382998 Mobile 07787-842674 E-mail revdocsand@aol.com

MILLARD, Canon Jane Mary. b 43. Open Univ BA80. Edin Dioc NSM Course 81. **d** 90 **p** 94. Chapl HIV/AIDS 90-94; NSM Edin St Mary 90-94; C 94-98; Can St Mary's Cathl from 95; Vice Provost from 98. *14 Grosvenor Crescent, Edinburgh EH12 5EL* Tel 0131-346 2469 Mobile 07712-898805
E-mail vice.provost@cathedral.net

MILLARD, Jonathan Neil. b 62. Aston Univ BSc83 Barrister-at-Law (Gray's Inn) 84. Wycliffe Hall Ox 89. **d** 92 **p** 93. C Haddenham w Cuddington, Kingsey etc *Ox* 92-94; R Washington Trin USA 94-00; R Church Stretton *Heref* 00-03; R Pittsburgh Ascension USA from 04. *4729 Ellsworth Avenue, Pittsburgh PA 15213-2888, USA* Tel (001) (412) 621 5378 Fax 621 5746 E-mail jonathan.millard@comcast.net

MILLARD, Malcolm Edoric. b 38. Lon Univ BA60 AKC60 Lon Inst of Educn PGCE61. St Jo Coll Nottm 80. **d** 77 **p** 81. Dn Banjul Cathl The Gambia 77-79; Dn Lamin St Andr 79-81; P-in-c 81-82; P-in-c Fajara St Paul 82-88; V Gen 86-88; P-in-c Farafenni Ch of African Martyrs 89-95; C S Shoebury *Chelmsf* 95-97; C Rainham w Wennington 97-02; P-in-c N Ockendon 02-08; Perm to Offic *Sarum* from 08. *29 Moorcombe Drive, Preston, Weymouth DT3 6NP* Tel (01305) 834060
E-mail weeksmary@gmail.com

MILLARD, Richard Stuart Marsh. b 33. St Pet Coll Ox BA57 MA. Oak Hill NSM Course 90. **d** 93 **p** 94. NSM Laleham *Lon* 93-94; NSM Neatishead, Barton Turf and Irstead *Nor* 94-95; NSM Ashmanhaugh, Barton Turf etc 95-99; rtd 99; Perm to Offic *Nor* from 99. *Semaphore Lodge, 30 Weybourne Road, Sheringham NR25 8HF*

MILLER, Adrian David. b 74. Open Univ BSc02. St Jo Coll Nottm MTh06. **d** 06 **p** 07. C Newton Flotman, Swainsthorpe, Tasburgh, etc *Nor* 06-09; TV from 09. *The Rectory, The Street, Saxlingham Nethergate, Norwich NR15 1AJ* Tel (01508) 498317 Mobile 07871-085013 E-mail aidymiller@i12.com

MILLER, Andrew. *See* MILLER, Ronald Andrew John

MILLER, Anthony. *See* MILLER, Ronald Anthony

MILLER, Anthony Talbot. b 37. Univ of Wales (Lamp) BA59. Coll of Resurr Mirfield. **d** 61 **p** 62. C Panteg w Llanddewi Fach and Llandegfeth *Mon* 61-63; C Monmouth 63-65; V Holme Cultram St Mary *Carl* 65-76; Lic to Offic *Lich* 76-78; P-in-c Wrockwardine Wood 78-80; R 80-94; OCF 92-94; rtd 94. *Smallwythe, 26 Rosemary Lane, Whitchurch SY13 1EG* Tel (01948) 662120

MILLER, Barry. b 42. Bede Coll Dur TCert63 Open Univ BA79 Leic Univ MEd86. Linc Th Coll 63. **d** 65 **p** 66. C Greenside *Dur* 65-68; C Auckland St Andr and St Anne 68-71; Adv in Educn *Leic* 71-77; C Leic St Nic 77-80; Asst Chapl Leic Univ 77-80; Lect RS Leic Poly 77-80; Children's Officer Gen Syn Bd of Educn 80-84; Hd RS W Midl Coll of HE 84-89; Hd Initial Teacher Educn Wolv Poly 89-92; Wolv Univ 92-93; Hd Teacher Educn Bradf Coll from 94. *32 Nab Lane, Shipley BD18 4HH* Tel (01274) 590630 E-mail bm054283@aol.com

MILLER, Charles. *See* MILLER, Ernest Charles

MILLER, Charles Irvine. b 35. Nottm Univ BEd76. Bps' Coll Cheshunt 61. **d** 63 **p** 64. C Anlaby Common St Mark *York* 63-66; C Whitby 66-68; R Ingoldmells w Addlethorpe *Linc* 68-72; P-in-c Bishop Norton 72-76; V Scunthorpe St Jo 76-83; Chapl Manor Hosp Walsall 83-89; rtd 89; Perm to Offic *Ely* 89-98 and from 99; P-in-c Isleham 98-99. *The Old Studio, 6 Chapel Street, Duxford, Cambridge CB22 4RJ*

MILLER, Charles Maitland. b 82. Jes Coll Ox BA04. St Steph Ho Ox 04. **d** 07 **p** 08. C Downham Market and Crimplesham w Stradsett *Ely* from 07. *37 Civray Avenue, Downham Market PE38 9QP* Tel (01366) 383791
E-mail charles.miller@ely.anglican.org

MILLER, Darren Noel. b 67. Birm Univ BSocSc89. Chich Th Coll BTh95 Coll of Resurr Mirfield 94. **d** 95 **p** 96. C Weoley Castle *Birm* 95-98; C Shard End 98-00; V Castle Vale St Cuth 00-06; AD Sutton Coldfield 04-06; TR Cheam *S'wark* from 06. *The Rectory, 33 Mickleham Gardens, Cheam, Sutton SM3 8QJ* Tel (020) 8641 4664 Mobile 07747-858697
E-mail dnmiller@dandsmiller.me.uk

MILLER, Canon David George. b 54. Oriel Coll Ox BA76 MA80. Ripon Coll Cuddesdon 78. **d** 81 **p** 82. C Henfield w Shermanbury and Woodmancote *Chich* 81-84; C Monk Bretton *Wakef* 84-87; V Rastrick St Jo 87-93; TR Helston and Wendron *Truro* from 93; Chapl R Cornwall Hosps Trust 95-01; Chapl W Cornwall Primary Care Trust 01-06; Hon Can Truro Cathl from 06. *St Michael's Rectory, Church Lane, Helston TR13 8PF* Tel (01326) 572516 E-mail millerourrectory@googlemail.com

MILLER, Canon David James Tringham. b 45. AKC70. Sarum & Wells Th Coll 76. **d** 77 **p** 78. C Abington *Pet* 77-80; TV Corby SS Pet and Andr w Gt and Lt Oakley 80-83; V Kettering All SS 83-94; RD Kettering 87-94; V Pet All SS 94-09; rtd 09. *27 Drovers Terrace, Penrith CA11 9EN* Tel (01768) 840406
E-mail djtmiller@o2.co.uk

MILLER, David John. b 37. Louvain Univ Belgium Lic en Sciences Catéchétiques 68. Chich Th Coll 60. **d** 62 **p** 63. C Southsea H Spirit *Portsm* 62-65; C Roehampton H Trin *S'wark* 67-68; Chapl Luxembourg *Eur* 68-72; Chapl Lausanne 72-91; Asst Chapl 91-93; P-in-c Gstaad 82-88; Chapl Le Rosey Sch Switzerland 72-02; rtd 02; Perm to Offic *Eur* from 04. *63 avenue de Savoie, 74500 Publier, France* Tel (0033) (4) 50 26 89 41

MILLER, David Robert. b 47. Middx Univ BA98. ERMC 94. **d** 08 **p** 09. C Eaton Socon *St Alb* from 08. *53 Shakespeare Road, Eaton Socon, St Neots PE19 3HG* Tel (01480) 471132
E-mail davidmiller@care4free.net

MILLER, Ernest Charles. b 56. Franklin & Marshall Coll (USA) BA78 Univ of Michigan MA79 Keble Coll Ox DPhil90. Nashotah Ho MDiv82. **d** 82 **p** 83. C Dallas St Andr USA 82-84; Warden Ho of SS Greg and Macrina 84-90; Asst Chapl Keble Coll Ox 84-88; P-in-c New Marston *Ox* 91-96; Ramsey Prof Th Nashotah Ho Wisconsin USA 96-00; R New York Transfiguration 00-04; Adjunct Prof Ch Hist Gen Th Sem 02-04; TR Abingdon *Ox* from 06. *The Rectory, St Helen's Court, Abingdon OX14 5BS* Tel (01235) 532722 Mobile 07726-743924
E-mail echarlesmiller@yahoo.com

MILLER, Francis Rogers. b 54. Ex Univ BA86. St Steph Ho Ox 86. **d** 88 **p** 89. C Wednesfield *Lich* 88-93; P-in-c Caldmore 93-99; V 99-02; C Walsall St Mary and All SS Palfrey 93-97; P-in-c 97-02; V Caldmore w Palfrey from 02. *St Michael's Vicarage, 12 St Michael's Street, Walsall WS1 3RQ* Tel (01922) 623445

MILLER, Gareth. *See* MILLER, John Gareth

MILLER, Gary Russell. b 58. **d** 07 **p** 08. OLM Wythenshawe *Man* from 07. *77 Mayfair Road, Manchester M22 9ZE* Tel 0161-436 8151 E-mail gary-miller@hotmail.co.uk

MILLER, The Ven Geoffrey Vincent. b 56. Dur Univ BEd78 Newc Univ MA94. St Jo Coll Nottm 81. **d** 83 **p** 84. C Jarrow *Dur* 83-86; TV Billingham St Aid 86-92; Dioc Urban Development Officer 91-97; Community Chapl Stockton-on-Tees 92-94; P-in-c Darlington St Cuth 94-96; V 96-99; Soc Resp Officer 97-99; Can Res Newc Cathl 99-05; Dioc Urban Officer 99-05; Adn Northd and Can Res Newc Cathl from 05. *80 Moorside North, Newcastle upon Tyne NE4 9DU* Tel 0191-273 8245 Fax 226 0286 E-mail g.miller@newcastle.anglican.org

MILLER, The Ven George Charles Alexander. b 20. TCD BA45. CITC Div Test 46. **d** 46 **p** 47. C Wexford w Rathaspeck *C & O* 46-49; Asst Chapl Miss to Seamen Belf 49; Chapl Miss to Seamen Immingham 49-51; Chapl Pernis Miss to Seamen *Eur* 51-55; I Billis w Ballyjamesduff *K, E & A* 55-57; I Knockbride w Shercock 57-65; I Urney w Denn and Derryheen 65-89; Preb Kilmore Cathl 77-87; Adn Kilmore 87-89; rtd 89. *Wavecrest, Blenacup, Cavan, Republic of Ireland* Tel (00353) (49) 436 1270

MILLER, Graham William. b 71. St Andr Univ BD94 Dur Univ MA98. Westcott Ho Cam 99. **d** 01 **p** 02. C Ex St Dav 01-03; C Sunderland St Mary and St Pet *Dur* 03-07; C Sunderland Pennywell St Thos 03-07; C Paddington St Jas *Lon* from 07. *61 Pembroke House, Hallfield Estate, London W2 6HQ* Tel (020) 7706 1248 E-mail grahamwmiller@aol.com

✠**MILLER, The Rt Revd Harold Creeth.** b 50. TCD BA73 MA78. St Jo Coll Nottm BA75. **d** 76 **p** 77 **c** 97. C Carrickfergus *Conn* 76-79; Dir Ext Studies St Jo Coll Nottm 79-84; Chapl QUB 84-89; I Carrigrohane Union *C, C & R* 89-97; Bp's Dom Chapl 91-97; Can Cork and Cloyne Cathls 94-96; Treas Cork Cathl 96-97; Can Cork Cathl 96-97; Preb Tymothan St Patr Cathl Dublin 96-97; Bp D & D from 97. *The See House, 32 Knockdene Park South, Belfast BT5 7AB* Tel (028) 9047 1973 *or* 9023 7602 Fax 9023 1902 E-mail bishop@down.anglican.org

MILLER (*née* BLUNDEN), **Mrs Jacqueline Ann.** b 63. Leic Univ BA86 SS Coll Cam BA90. Ridley Hall Cam 88. **d** 91. Par Dn Bedford St Paul *St Alb* 91-94; C 94-95; Perm to Offic *Lon* from 05. *St Mary's Vicarage, Lansdowne Road, London N17 9XE* Tel (020) 8808 6644

MILLER, James Ivimey. b 33. Trin Hall Cam BA55 MA59. Ridley Hall Cam 56. **d** 61 **p** 62. C Beccles St Mich *St E* 61-63; C Blackpool St Jo *Blackb* 63-67; C Kirk Ella *York* 67-73; R Cockfield *St E* 73-78; rtd 78; Perm to Offic *St E* 78-05. *The College of St Barnabas, Blackberry Lane, Lingfield RH7 6NJ* Tel (01342) 872866

MILLER, Canon John David. b 50. Nottm Univ BTh73 Lanc Univ CertEd74 Newc Univ MA93. Kelham Th Coll 68. **d** 74 **p** 75. C Horden *Dur* 77-80; C Billingham St Aid 79-80; TV 80-84; TR S Shields All SS from 84; Hon Can Dur Cathl from 04. *The Rectory, Tyne Terrace, South Shields NE34 0NF* Tel 0191-456 1851

MILLER, John Douglas. b 24. FCA60. NOC 74. **d** 77 **p** 78. C Prestbury *Ches* 77-80; V Ashton Hayes 80-87; rtd 87; Perm to Offic *Ex* from 87. *35 Branscombe Close, Colyford, Colyton EX24 6RF* Tel (01297) 553581

MILLER, John Forster. b 32. Ox NSM Course. **d** 83 **p** 84. NSM Patcham *Chich* 83-86; NSM Radlett *St Alb* 86-93; Perm to Offic *St Alb* 93-00 and *Sarum* 00-06. *Address temp unknown*

MILLER, John Gareth. b 57. St Jo Coll Dur BA78. Ridley Hall Cam 79 Ven English Coll Rome 80. **d** 81 **p** 82. C Addiscombe St Mary *Cant* 81-84; TV Melbury *Sarum* 84-88; TR 88-91; V Leamington Priors All SS *Cov* 91-94. *Chelwood, Market Street, Charlbury, Chipping Norton OX7 3PL* Tel (01608) 811410 E-mail garethmiller@tiscali.co.uk

MILLER, John Selborne. b 32. RMN70. S'wark Ord Course 64. **d** 71 **p** 72. C Kenton *Lon* 71-74; C Fulham St Etheldreda w St Clem 74-78; Asst at Convent of the Epiphany Truro 79-80; Hon C Pimlico St Sav 80-84; C Shirley *Birm* 84-86; rtd 86; Perm to Offic *Nor* 86-01 and from 08. *28 Knight Street, Walsingham NR22 6DA* Tel (01328) 820824

MILLER, Kenneth Leslie. b 50. Lanc Univ BEd74 Liv Univ BPhil94 FRSA. NOC 78. **d** 80 **p** 81. NSM Formby St Pet *Liv* 80-87; NSM Anfield St Columba from 87; Chapl St Marg C of E High Sch Aigburth Liv from 86. *9 Hampton Road, Liverpool L37 6EJ* Tel (01704) 831256 E-mail jenke_2@hotmail.co.uk

MILLER, Kim Hurst. b 49. Ex Univ PhD89. Canberra Coll of Min BTh82. **d** 82 **p** 83. Australia 82-85 and from 89; C Goulburn Cathl 83-84; P-in-c Koorawatha 84-85; Perm to Offic *Ex* 85-89; R Wagga Wagga St Alb 89-98; Chapl Bathurst Gaol from 98. *3 Oates Place, Eglinton NSW 2795, Australia* Tel (0061) (2) 6337 1841 *or* 6338 3782 E-mail kkmiller@globalfreeway.com.au

MILLER, Luke Jonathan. b 66. SS Coll Cam BA87 MA91. St Steph Ho Ox BA90. **d** 91 **p** 92. C Oxhey St Matt *St Alb* 91-94; C Tottenham St Mary *Lon* 94-95; V from 95; AD E Haringey from 05. *St Mary's Vicarage, Lansdowne Road, London N17 9XE* Tel (020) 8808 6644 E-mail frmiller@stmarystottenham.org

MILLER, Martin Michael. b 55. St Jo Coll Dur BSc78. Trin Coll Bris 94. **d** 96 **p** 97. C Leamington Priors St Paul *Cov* 96-99; C Bermondsey St Anne and St Aug *S'wark* 99-05; R Newhaven *Chich* from 05. *The Rectory, 36 Second Avenue, Newhaven BN9 9HN* Tel (01273) 515251 E-mail martinmrev@aol.com

MILLER, Michael Andrew. b 58. Ripon Coll Cuddesdon 03. **d** 05 **p** 06. C Hockerill *St Alb* 05-08; P-in-c Kensal Town St Thos w St Andr and St Phil *Lon* from 08. *St Thomas's Vicarage, 231 Kensal Road, London W10 5DB* Tel (020) 8960 3703 Mobile 07778-617482 E-mail mmiller363@tiscali.co.uk

MILLER, Michael Daukes. b 46. Qu Coll Cam MA71 Lon Univ BCh70 MB71 MRCGP74. Glouc Th Course 82. **d** 85 **p** 94. NSM Lydney w Aylburton *Glouc* 85-95; NSM Lydney 95-06. *Bowden Hayes, George Nympton, South Molton EX36 4JE*

MILLER, Patrick Figgis. b 33. Ch Coll Cam BA56 MA60 Surrey Univ PhD95. Cuddesdon Coll 56. **d** 58 **p** 59. C Portsea St Cuth *Portsm* 58-61; C Cambridge Gt St Mary w St Mich *Ely* 61-63; Chapl SCM 61-63; Hd RS Man Gr Sch 63-69; Can Res and Lib S'wark Cathl 69-72; Dir of Soc Studies Qu Mary's Coll Basingstoke 72-79; Prin Sunbury Coll 79-80; Prin Esher Coll 81-98; Project Dir Learning for Living 00-05; Chapl London Flotilla from 00; Perm to Offic *Guildf* from 01. *9 Fairfax Avenue, Epsom KT17 2QN* Tel (020) 8394 0970 Mobile 07740-909414 E-mail patrickmiller@ntlworld.com

MILLER, Canon Paul. b 49. Oak Hill Th Coll 71. **d** 74 **p** 75. C Upton *Ex* 74-77; C Farnborough *Guildf* 77-78; P-in-c Torquay St Luke *Ex* 78-81; V 81-86; V Green Street Green *Roch* 86-94; V Green Street Green and Pratts Bottom 94-01; RD Orpington 96-01; V Shortlands from 01; Hon Can Roch Cathl from 00; AD Beckenham from 09; Chapl to The Queen from 05. *The Vicarage, 37 Kingswood Road, Bromley BR2 0HG* Tel (020) 8460 4989 *or* 8460 5682 Fax 8289 7577 Mobile 07940-582040 E-mail canonpmiller@aol.com

MILLER, Paul Richard. b 37. K Coll Lon BSc60 AKC60. Linc Th Coll 60. **d** 62 **p** 63. C Sheff St Geo 62-65; C Bottesford *Linc* 65-67; Bp's Youth Chapl 67-69; C Corringham 67-69; Dioc Youth Officer *Ripon* 69-74; Sec Nat Coun for Voluntary Youth Services 74-79; Hd Youth Nat Coun of Soc Services 74-79; P-in-c Battlesden and Pottesgrove *St Alb* 79-80; P-in-c Eversholt w Milton Bryan 79-80; P-in-c Woburn 79-80; V Woburn w Eversholt, Milton Bryan, Battlesden etc 80-98; rtd 98; Perm to Offic *Heref* from 98 and *Lich* from 03. *6 Elms Paddock, Little Stretton, Church Stretton SY6 6RD* Tel (01694) 724596 E-mail paulmiller@macunlimited.net

MILLER, Canon Philip Harry. b 58. Leeds Univ BA79. Chich Th Coll 80. **d** 82 **p** 83. C Reddish *Man* 82-86; R Lower Broughton Ascension 86-94; P-in-c Cheetwood St Alb 91-94; P-in-c Langley and Parkfield 95-00; TR from 00; Hon Can Man Cathl from 07. *The Rectory, Wood Street, Middleton, Manchester M24 5GL* Tel 0161-643 5013

MILLER, Philip Howard. b 40. Tyndale Hall Bris 67. **d** 72 **p** 73. Argentina 72-73; C Rusholme H Trin *Man* 73-74; SAMS Paraguay 74-77; C Toxteth St Cypr w Ch Ch *Liv* 78-80; V Burscough Bridge 80-85; V Woodbridge St Jo *St E* 85-91; P-in-c Combs 91-92 and 93-96; Chapl Burrswood Chr Cen 92-93; V Yoxford and Peasenhall w Sibton *St E* 96-01; rtd 01; Perm to Offic *St E* from 01. *Salta, 54 Orchard Close, Melton, Woodbridge IP12 1LD* Tel (01394) 388615 E-mail phm91@lineone.net

MILLER, Richard Bracebridge. b 45. Wycliffe Hall Ox 68. **d** 70 **p** /1. C Lee Gd Shep w St Pet *S'wark* 70-74; C Roehampton H Trin 74-77; C Earley St Pet *Ox* 77-80; V Aldermaston w Wasing and Brimpton 80-96; C Newbury 96-01; Perm to Offic from 03. *14 Burcot Park, Burcot, Abingdon OX14 3DH* Tel (01865) 407521 E-mail rbmoxford@breathe.com

MILLER, Robert Stephen. b 71. QUB BSc92. CITC BTh95. **d** 95 **p** 96. C Lurgan Ch the Redeemer *D & D* 95-99; I Tullylish 99-03; I Maghera w Killelagh *D & R* from 03. *The Rectory, 20 Church Street, Maghera BT46 5EA* Tel (028) 7964 2252 *or* 7954 9290 E-mail robsmiller@aol.com *or* maghera@derry.anglican.org

MILLER, Ronald Andrew John. b 46. **d** 96 **p** 97. OLM Heywood *Man* 96-09. *Address temp unknown* E-mail andrew.miller1@virgin.net

MILLER, Ronald Anthony. b 41. CEng CPA MRAeS City Univ BSc63. S'wark Ord Course 69. **d** 72 **p** 80. NSM Crookham *Guildf* 72-73 and 80-85; NSM New Haw 85-95; NSM Effingham w Lt Bookham 95-04. *Glen Anton, Horsley Road, Downside, Cobham KT11 3JZ* Tel and fax (01932) 863394 Mobile 07710-294786

MILLER, Rosamund Joy. *See* SEAL, Mrs Rosamund Joy

MILLER, Mrs Rosslyn Leslie. b 43. St Andr Univ MA65 Ox Univ DipEd66. **dss** 72 **d** 87. Dir of Studies Inst of Chr Studies 72; St Marylebone All SS *Lon* 72; Adult Educn Officer 73-78; Alford w Rigsby *Linc* 86-87; C 87-90; Dioc Dir of Readers 90-03, rtd 03. *59 Malham Drive, Lincoln LN6 0XD* Tel (01522) 831294 E-mail rosslyn.miller@aol.com

MILLER, Roy. b 29. **d** 88 **p** 93. NSM Leic Cathl 88-91; NSM Leic H Apostles 91-97; Perm to Offic 97-99. *5 Bratmyr, Fleckney, Leicester LE8 8BJ* Tel 0116-240 2004

MILLER, Miss Sarah Lydia. b 65. St Andr Univ BD90 Hughes Hall Cam PGCE91. EAMTC 98. **d** 01 **p** 02. NSM Nor St Pet Mancroft w St Jo Maddermarket 01-03; C Wythenshawe *Man* 03-07; C Tewkesbury w Walton Cardiff and Twyning *Glouc* from 07. *The Vicarage, Church End, Twyning, Tewkesbury GL20 6DA* Tel (01684) 290765

MILLER, Stephen Michael. b 63. NE Lon Poly BSc86 Nottm Univ BTh91. Linc Th Coll 88. **d** 91 **p** 92. C Dudley St Fran *Worc* 91-94; V Sedgley St Mary 94-99; Miss to Seafarers from 99; Chapl Rotterdam w Schiedam Miss to Seafarers *Eur* 99-02; Chapl Dubai and UAE from 02. *Address temp unknown* Tel (00971) (4) 398 4918 Fax 398 4918 Mobile 50-552 6044 E-mail flyangel@eim.ae

MILLER, Stuart William. b 71. Univ of Wales (Cardiff) BA92. Trin Coll Bris BA97. **d** 97 **p** 98. C Fordingbridge *Win* 97-98; C Bursledon 98-02; V W Moors *Sarum* 02-05; Chapl Bournemouth and Poole Coll of FE *Win* from 05; C Bournemouth Town Cen from 05. *Bournemouth and Poole College, North Road, Poole BH14 0LS* Tel (01202) 205205 E-mail millersw@bpc.ac.uk

MILLER, William David. b 45. Man Univ BA66. Linc Th Coll 69. **d** 71 **p** 72. C Newc St Geo 71-74; C Corbridge w Halton 74-77; C N Gosforth 77-81; TV Whorlton 81-90; Chapl K Sch Tynemouth 90-09; rtd 09. *7 Strawberry Terrace, Hazlerigg, Newcastle upon Tyne NE13 7AR* Tel 0191-236 5024

MILLETT, Maxwell Roy. b 45. Clare Coll Cam BA67. S Dios Minl Tr Scheme 92. **d** 95 **p** 96. NSM Southsea St Pet *Portsm* 95-03; Perm to Offic from 03. *70 Waverley Road, Southsea PO5 2PR* Tel (023) 9281 7216 E-mail max.millett@ntlworld.com

MILLETT, William Hugh. b 21. AKC49. **d** 50 **p** 51. C Barbourne *Worc* 50-53; V Catshill 53-58; R Richard's Castle *Heref* 58-78; P-in-c Stoke Lacy, Moreton Jeffries w Much Cowarne etc 78-82; Perm to Offic *Worc* from 83; rtd 86; Perm to Offic *Heref* from 93. *18 Shirley Close, Malvern WR14 2NH* Tel (01684) 567056

MILLGATE, Victor Frederick. b 44. St Mich Coll Llan 81. **d** 83 **p** 84. C Pembroke St Mary w St Mich *St D* 83-85; V Manorbier and St Florence w Redberth 85-04; TR Carew from 04; AD Castlemartin from 03. *The Vicarage, Manorbier, Tenby SA70 7TN* Tel (01834) 871617 E-mail esmillgate@yahoo.co.uk

MILLICHAMP, Mrs Penelope Mary. b 39. CertEd60. WMMTC 82. **dss** 85 **d** 87 **p** 94. Wednesfield *Lich* 85-94; Par Dn 87-90; TD 90-94; Perm to Offic 94-95; NSM Wrockwardine Deanery 95-99; rtd 99; Perm to Offic *Lich* 99-00 and from 06. *3 Mathon Lodge, 16 Stockwell Road, Wolverhampton WV6 9PQ* Tel (01902) 741996 Mobile 07971-421562 E-mail penny@millichamp.com

MILLIER, Gordon. b 28. St Aid Birkenhead 63. **d** 65 **p** 66. C Congresbury *B & W* 65-69; P-in-c Badgworth w Biddisham 69-76; R Weare w Badgworth and Biddisham 76-84; R Pilton w Croscombe, N Wootton and Dinder 84-93; rtd 93; Perm to Offic *Ex* from 93. *28 Withy Close, Canal Hill, Tiverton EX16 4HZ* Tel (01884) 253128

MILLIGAN, Peter John. b 52. **d** 01 **p** 02. NSM Putney St Marg *S'wark* 01-06; NSM Angell Town St Jo from 06. *39 Stapleton Road, London SW17 8BA* Tel (020) 8767 3497

MILLIGAN, Canon William John (Barney). b 28. OBE95. Em Coll Cam BA49. Cuddesdon Coll 53. **d** 55 **p** 56. C Portsea N End St Mark *Portsm* 55-62; V New Eltham All SS *S'wark* 62-71; V Roehampton H Trin 71-79; Can Res St Alb 79-86; Chapl Strasbourg *Eur* 86-95; Angl Rep Eur Insts 90-95; rtd 95; Perm to Offic *S'wark* 95-00 and *Sarum* from 98. *3 East Street, Beaminster DT8 3DS* Tel (01308) 862806

MILLING, David Horace. b 29. Oriel Coll Ox BA51 MA54 Cam Univ PhD73. Cuddesdon Coll 54. **d** 56 **p** 57. C Bris St Mary Redcliffe w Temple 56-59; C Fishponds St Jo 59-62; India 62-69; Lect St D Coll Lamp 73-75; C Caversham *Ox* 77-81; C Mapledurham 77-81; C Caversham St Andr 81-86; TV Upper Kennet *Sarum* 86-88; rtd 88; Perm to Offic *Glouc* 90-99 and *Ex* from 00. *14 Matford Mews, Matford, Alphington, Exeter EX2 8XP* Tel (01392) 219718

MILLINGTON, Robert William Ernest. b 51. Sheff Univ BA73 St Jo Coll Dur. **d** 76 **p** 77. C Ormskirk *Liv* 76-79; C Litherland St Paul Hatton Hill 79-81; V Bootle Ch Ch 81-88; Chapl K Edw Sch Witley from 88. *1 South Lodge, Petworth Road, Wormley, Godalming GU8 5SQ* Tel (01428) 685163 *or* 682168 E-mail rwe.millington@virgin.net

MILLINGTON, Stuart. b 45. Lich Th Coll 67. **d** 70 **p** 71. C Boulton *Derby* 70-73; C Moseley St Mary *Birm* 73-76; TV Staveley and Barrow Hill *Derby* 76-82; R Wingerworth 82-99; RD Chesterfield 91-97; P-in-c Elton All SS *Man* 99-09; P-in-c Woolfold 07-09; V Kirklees Valley from 09; AD Bury from 03. *All Saints' Vicarage, 10 Kirkburn View, Bury BL8 1DL* Tel 0161-797 1595 E-mail stuart@revmillington.wanadoo.co.uk

MILLS, Alan Francis. b 29. Ch Coll Cam BA52 MA91. Linc Th Coll 52. **d** 54 **p** 55. C Hucknall Torkard *S'well* 54-58; C Bath Bathwick St Jo *B & W* 58-70; V Drayton 70-76; V Muchelney 70-76; V Alcombe 76-99; rtd 99; Perm to Offic *B & W* from 00. *194 Locking Road, Weston-super-Mare BS23 3LU* Tel (01934) 622679

MILLS, Alexandra. b 56. Univ of Wales (Abth) BMus78 CertEd79. Ripon Coll Cuddesdon 88. **d** 90 **p** 94. Par Dn Earlsfield St Andr *S'wark* 90-94; C Kingston All SS w St Jo 94-99; C Brixton Road Ch Ch 99-00; Perm to Offic from 05. *121A Transmere Road, London SW18 3QP* Tel (020) 8944 1641 Mobile 07900-543068

MILLS, Anne. *See* MILLS, Mrs Leslie Anne

MILLS, Anthony James. b 55. Nottm Univ BA. Linc Th Coll. **d** 84 **p** 85. C Mexborough *Sheff* 84-86; C Howden *York* 86-89; V Fylingdales and Hawsker cum Stainsacre 89-95; V Scarborough St Sav w All SS from 95; P-in-c Scarborough St Martin 02-05; V from 05. *St Martin's Vicarage, Craven Street, Scarborough YO11 2BY* Tel (01723) 360437

MILLS, David Francis. b 51. Oak Hill Th Coll 76. **d** 79 **p** 80. C Rodbourne Cheney *Bris* 79-82; C Wolverhampton St Matt *Lich* 82-85; CF 85-88; TV Braunstone *Leic* 88-95; Past Asst to Adn Leic 95-97; C Barkestone w Plungar, Redmile and Stathern 97-99; C Bottesford and Muston 97-99; C Harby, Long Clawson and Hose 97-99; C Vale of Belvoir Par 00-02; R Winfarthing w Shelfanger w Burston w Gissing etc *Nor* from 02. *The Rectory, Church Lane, Winfarthing, Diss IP22 2EA* Tel (01379) 642543 E-mail dmills@leicester.anglican.org

MILLS, David Graham Mackenzie. *See* MACKENZIE MILLS, David Graham

MILLS (née SHAW), Mrs Elaine Rosemary. b 42. SRN63. **d** 07 **p** 08. OLM Bris Lockleaze St Mary Magd w St Fran from 07. *15 Blake Road, Bristol BS7 9UJ* E-mail elaine.mills@lycos.co.uk

MILLS, Canon Geoffrey Charles Malcolm. b 33. Wycliffe Hall Ox 59. **d** 61 **p** 62. C Buckhurst Hill *Chelmsf* 61-65; C Ecclesall *Sheff* 65-69; V Endcliffe 69-78; R Whiston 78-99; Hon Can Sheff Cathl 96-99; rtd 99; Perm to Offic *Sheff* from 99. *8 Hall Road, Rotherham S60 2BP* Tel (01709) 373863

MILLS, Miss Glenys Christine. b 38. Open Univ BA81. Dalton Ho Bris 64. **d** 87 **p** 94. Par Dn Clifton Ch Ch w Em *Bris* 87-94; C 94-95; P-in-c Gt w Lt Abington *Ely* 95-00; Chapl Arthur Rank Hospice Cam 95-00; Perm to Offic *Bris* from 00. *14 St Bartholomew's Road, Bristol BS7 9BJ* Tel 0117-909 8859

MILLS, Gordon Derek. b 35. Lich Th Coll 60. **d** 63 **p** 64. C W Derby St Mary *Liv* 63-65; C Clifton w Glapton *S'well* 65-67; V N Wilford St Faith 67-72; V Farnsfield and P-in-c Kirklington w Hockerton 77-82; P-in-c Brindle and Asst Dir of Educn *Blackb* 82-86; V Gt Budworth *Ches* 86-88; P-in-c Antrobus 87-88; V Gt Budworth and Antrobus 88-92; V Gt Budworth 92-00; rtd 00; Perm to Offic *Blackb* 01-04; *York* and *Bradf* from 04. *Holmelands House, Raby Lane, East Cowton, Northallerton DL7 0BW* Tel (01325) 378798

MILLS, Canon Hubert Cecil. b 44. TCD BA66 MA71 HDipEd73. CITC 67. **d** 67 **p** 68. C Dublin Rathfarnham *D & G* 67-72; Min Can St Patr Cathl Dublin 69-92; Succ 77-92; Preb Rathmichael St Patr Cathl Dublin 92-01; Treas from 01; C Dublin St Steph and St Ann *D & G* 72-77; I Holmpatrick w Balbriggan and Kenure 77-86; I Killiney H Trin from 86. *Holy Trinity Rectory, Killiney Road, Killiney, Co Dublin, Republic of Ireland* Tel (00353) (1) 285 2695 E-mail cecil.mills@holytrinitykilliney.org

MILLS, Ian Anderson. b 35. Coll of Resurr Mirfield 60 K Coll Lon AKC65. **d** 65 **p** 70. C S'wark St Alphege 65-67; C Hartlepool St Paul *Dur* 69-72; NSM Hartlepool St Hilda 90-95; Perm to Offic from 95. *7 Claypool Farm Close, Hutton Henry, Hartlepool TS27 4QZ* Tel (01429) 836204

MILLS, Jack Herbert. b 14. Selw Coll Cam BA38 MA42. Cuddesdon Coll 39. **d** 40 **p** 41. C Camberwell St Geo *S'wark* 40-42; C Southfields St Barn 42-46; USPG 46-47; Chapl Hurstpierpoint Coll 47-52; Chapl K Coll Auckland New Zealand 52-56; Asst Chapl St Pet Colleg Sch Adelaide 57-59; Chapl St Paul's Colleg Sch Hamilton New Zealand 59-61; Chapl Guildford Gr Sch Perth Australia 62-66; Hd Master Carpentaria Coll Darwin 66-73; Hd Master St Wilfrid's Sch Ex 74-79; Chapl Community of St Wilfrid 74-79; Hon C Ewhurst *Chich* 79-81; Hon C Bodiam 79-81; Perm to Offic *Ex* 81-85 and *Chich* 85-87; rtd 87; New Zealand from 87. *14/28 Maranui Avenue, Point Chevalier 1002, Auckland, New Zealand* Tel (0064) (9) 849 2243

MILLS, Jennifer Clare. *See* TOMLINSON, Mrs Jennifer Clare

MILLS, John Kettlewell. b 53. BA. Cranmer Hall Dur. **d** 84 **p** 85. C Ashton-upon-Mersey St Mary Magd *Ches* 84-87; TV Didsbury St Jas and Em *Man* 87-98; V Styvechale *Cov* from 98. *Styvechale Vicarage, 16 Armorial Road, Coventry CV3 6GJ* Tel (024) 7641 6074 *or* 7669 2299 E-mail jkm@stivichall.freeserve.co.uk

MILLS, Mrs Leslie Anne. b 44. K Alfred's Coll Win CertEd65. SWMTC 99. **d** 02 **p** 03. NSM Kilmington, Stockland, Dalwood, Yarcombe etc *Ex* from 02. *Gorse Bungalow, Cotleigh, Honiton EX14 9JB* Tel (01404) 861430 E-mail anne@stockland.cx

MILLS, Michael Henry. b 51. AKC73. St Aug Coll Cant. **d** 74 **p** 75. C Newton Aycliffe *Dur* 74-78; C Padgate *Liv* 78-79; TV 79-95; V Frodsham *Ches* from 95. *The Vicarage, Vicarage Lane, Frodsham, Warrington WA6 7DU* Tel (01928) 733378 E-mail mikehmills@mac.com

MILLS, Michael John. b 52. St Andr Univ BSc75 Cam Univ PGCE76. Cranmer Hall Dur 97. **d** 99 **p** 00. C Brockmoor *Worc* 99-03; P-in-c St Leonards St Leon *Chich* from 04; P-in-c St Leonards St Ethelburga from 04. *The Rectory, 81A Filsham Road, St Leonards-on-Sea TN38 0PE* Tel (01424) 422199 Mobile 07789-913013 E-mail michael_mills@talktalk.net

MILLS, Pamela Ann. b 44. Southn Univ DAES82. S Tr Scheme 94. **d** 97 **p** 98. NSM Hurstbourne Tarrant, Faccombe, Vernham Dean etc *Win* from 97. *Sunnyside, The Dene, Hurstbourne Tarrant, Andover SP11 0AS* Tel (01264) 736286

MILLS, Peter James. b 32. Univ Coll Lon LLB58. **d** 99 **p** 00. NSM Woodchurch *Ches* 99-03; rtd 03; Perm to Offic *Ches* from 03. *6 West Heath Court, Gerard Road, West Kirby, Wirral CH48 4ES* Tel 0151-625 4459 Mobile 07989-374499 E-mail pjmills@uwclub.net

MILLS, Peter John. b 52. Sarum & Wells Th Coll 87. **d** 89 **p** 90. C Chatham St Wm *Roch* 89-92; V Perry Street 92-95; V E Malling 95-00; CF from 00. *c/o MOD Chaplains (Army)* Tel (01980) 615804 Fax 615800

MILLS, Philippa Jane. b 63. STETS. **d** 09. NSM Hook w Warsash *Portsm* from 09. *Lower Lapstone, Botley Road, Fair Oak, Eastleigh SO50 7AN*

MILLS, Roger Conrad. b 58. Selw Coll Cam BA79 MA83. St Jo Coll Nottm 83. **d** 85 **p** 86. C Jesmond H Trin *Newc* 85-88; C Alnwick 88-91; Chapl Newc Univ 91-00; P-in-c St Barn and St Jude 95-97; V Kingston Park from 00. *12 Shannon Court, Newcastle upon Tyne NE3 2XF* Tel and fax 0191-286 4050 E-mail rogermills123@yahoo.co.uk

MILLS, Timothy John. b 57. Wye Coll Lon BSc79. Trin Coll Bris 01. **d** 03 **p** 04. C Chislehurst Ch Ch *Roch* 03-07; V Ticehurst and Flimwell *Chich* from 07. *The Vicarage, Church Street, Ticehurst, Wadhurst TN5 7AB* Tel (01580) 200316 Mobile 07786-540819 E-mail tim.mills60@ntlworld.com

MILLS-POWELL, Mark Oliver McLay. b 55. Edin Th Sem Virginia. **d** 83 **p** 84. C Huyton St Mich *Liv* 83-86; USA 86-95; P-in-c Basildon w Aldworth and Ashampstead *Ox* 95-02; TR Linton *Ely* 02-08; Warden Guild of St Jo and St Mary Magd from 08. *Address temp unknown* E-mail mark.mills-powell@ely.anglican.org

MILLSON, Brian Douglas. b 53. Univ of W Ontario BA76 Huron Coll MDiv84. Westcott Ho Cam 82. **d** 83 **p** 84. C Walton-on-Thames *Guildf* 83-86; Canada 86-98; R Par of the Six Nations 86-89; Canadian Forces Chapl 89-98; CF from 98. *c/o MOD Chaplains (Army)* Tel (01980) 615804 Fax 615800 E-mail brian.millson@btinternet.com

MILLSON, Mrs Margaret Lily. b 41. CertEd61. EMMTC 83. **dss** 86 **d** 87 **p** 94. NSM Bottesford w Ashby *Linc* 86-01; P-in-c St Tudy w St Mabyn and Michaelstow *Truro* from 01. *The Rectory, Glebe Parc, St Tudy, Bodmin PL30 3AS* Tel and fax (01208) 851691 E-mail mlmillson@aol.com

MILLWARD, Miss Pauline Freda. b 50. AMA74. NOC 89. **d** 92 **p** 94. NSM Warley *Wakef* 92-95; P-in-c Halifax St Hilda from 95; Missr for Halifax Town Cen 95-05. *8 Hill Park Mount, Sowerby Bridge HX6 3JB* Tel (01422) 823576 Fax 354448 Pager 07666-750242

MILLWOOD, Stephen Grant. b 44. Sheff City Coll of Educn CertEd77 Open Univ BA92. St Jo Coll Nottm 92. **d** 94 **p** 95. C Anston *Sheff* 94-98; V Kimberworth Park 98-09; Bp's Urban Adv 05-09; rtd 09. *6 Quarryfield Drive, Sheffield S9 5AG* Tel 0114-243 4948 E-mail steveandjanetm@mac.com

MILLYARD, Alexander John. b 29. St Jo Coll Dur BA53. Qu Coll Birm 53. **d** 54 **p** 55. C Middlesbrough St Aid *York* 54-56; C Pocklington w Yapham-cum-Meltonby, Owsthorpe etc 56-58; C Rickmansworth *St Alb* 58-61; R Wormley 61-65; Asst Chapl HM Pris Pentonville 65-67; Chapl HM Pris Leeds 67-69; Exeter 69-71; Wandsworth 72-73; V Snibston *Leic* 73-75; V Leic All So 75-79; V Blakesley and Adstone *Pet* 79-89; R Blakesley w Adstone and Maidford etc 89-91; rtd 91; Perm to Offic *Chich* from 91. *6 Gainsborough House, Eaton Gardens, Hove BN3 3UA* Tel (01273) 728722

✠**MILMINE, The Rt Revd Douglas.** b 21. CBE83. St Pet Hall Ox BA46 MA46. Clifton Th Coll 47. **d** 47 **p** 48 **c** 73. C Ilfracombe SS Phil and Jas *Ex* 47-50; C Slough *Ox* 50-53; Chile 54-69; Adn N Chile, Bolivia and Peru 63-69; Hon Can Chile from 69; Area Sec SAMS 69-72; Bp Paraguay 73-85; rtd 86. *1C Clive Court, 24 Grand Parade, Eastbourne BN21 3DD* Tel (01323) 734159

MILMINE, Canon Neil Edward Douglas. b 46. Kent Univ BSc70. Wycliffe Hall Ox 80. **d** 82 **p** 83. C Hailsham *Chich* 82-86; C Horsham 86; TV Patcham from 93; Can and Preb Chich Cathl from 00; RD Brighton from 02. *All Saints' Vicarage, 12 Church Hill, Brighton BN1 8YE* Tel (01273) 552157 E-mail n.milmine@yahoo.co.uk

MILNE, Alan. b 54. RMN SRN TCert. Cranmer Hall Dur 89. **d** 91 **p** 92. C Hartlepool St Luke *Dur* 91-94; P-in-c Dalton le Dale 94-00; V 00-05; P-in-c Hawthorn 94-00; R 00-05; R Hawthorn and Murton from 05; AD Easington from 03. *The Vicarage, Church Lane, Murton, Seaham SR7 9RD* Tel 0191-526 2410

MILNE, Miss Christine Helen. b 48. LTCL71. S'wark Ord Course 83. **dss** 86 **d** 87 **p** 90. S Lambeth St Steph *S'wark* 86-89; Par Dn 87-89; New Zealand from 89. *NGA Tawa School, Private Bag 1101, Marton 4741, New Zealand* Tel (0064) (6) 355 4566 Fax 327 7954 E-mail hmilne@xtra.co.nz

MILNE, James Harley. b 73. Univ of Wales (Lamp) BD94 New Coll Edin MTh96. TISEC 95. **d** 98 **p** 99. C Dundee St Mary Magd *Bre* 98-01; Chapl St Marg Res Home Dundee 98-01; R Dundee St Marg 01-09; Chapl Ninewells Hosp Dundee 01-09; R Glas St Bride from 09. *St Bride's Rectory, Flat 1/1, 25 Queensborough Gardens, Glasgow G12 9QP*

MILNE, Norma Campbell. b 45. TISEC 01. **d** 02 **p** 06. OLM Huntly *Mor* 02-03; NSM Aberlour from 05; NSM Dufftown from 05; NSM Elgin w Lossiemouth from 05. *26 Green Road, Huntly AB54 8BE* Tel and fax (01466) 793841 E-mail normamilne@fsmail.com

MILNER, Catherine Mary. *See* MILNER, Catherine Mary

MILNER, Catherine Mary. b 56. **d** 99 **p** 00. OLM Uttoxeter Area *Lich* 99-03; Sub Chapl HM Pris Foston Hall and Werrington YOI 99-03; Chapl Blue Coat Comp Sch Walsall 03-05; Hon Chapl Lich Cathl 99-05; rtd 05. *29 Crown Meadow, Alvechurch, Birmingham B48 7NZ* Tel 0121-445 0477 Mobile 07754-444770

MILNER, Darryl Vickers. b 43. Natal Univ BA63. St Chad's Coll Dur 64. **d** 66 **p** 67. C Oswestry H Trin *Lich* 66-69; S Africa 69-76; New Zealand from 76. *The Vicarage, 47 Church Street, Northcote, North Shore 0627, New Zealand* Tel (0064) (9) 480 7568 Fax 419 7459 E-mail dvmilner@clear.net.nz

MILNER, David. *See* MILNER, William David

MILNER, David. b 38. St Aid Birkenhead 63. **d** 66 **p** 67. C Ulverston H Trin *Carl* 66-68; C Mickleover All SS *Derby* 68-71; C Mickleover St Jo 68-71; V 71-82; P-in-c Sandiacre 82-86; P-in-c Doveridge 86-97; P-in-c Sudbury and Somersal Herbert 92-97; R Doveridge, Scropton, Sudbury etc 98-03; RD Longford 86-96 and 01-03; rtd 03; Perm to Offic *Lich* from 04. *21 Greenwood Park, Hednesford WS12 4DQ* Tel (01543) 428972

✠**MILNER, The Rt Revd Ronald James.** b 27. Pemb Coll Cam BA49 MA52. Wycliffe Hall Ox 51. **d** 53 **p** 54 **c** 88. Succ Sheff Cathl 53-58; V Westwood *Cov* 58-64; V Fletchamstead 64-70; R Southampton St Mary w H Trin *Win* 70-72; P-in-c Southampton St Matt 70-72; Lic to Offic 72-73; TR Southampton (City Cen) 73-83; Hon Can Win Cathl 75-83; Adn Linc 83-88; Can and Preb Linc Cathl 83-88; Suff Bp Burnley *Blackb* 88-93; rtd 93; Hon Asst Bp S'well and Nottm from 94. *7 Crafts Way, Southwell NG25 0BL* Tel (01636) 816256

MILNER, William David. b 52. St Jo Coll Nottm. **d** 93 **p** 94. C Wollaton *S'well* 93-97; P-in-c Daybrook 97; C W Bridgford 98-99; TV Clifton 99-04; P-in-c Collingham w S Scarle and Besthorpe and Girton from 04. *The Rectory, 1 Vicarage Close, Collingham, Newark NG23 7PQ* Tel (01636) 892317

MILNES, David Ian. b 45. Chich Th Coll 74. **d** 76 **p** 77. C Walthamstow St Sav *Chelmsf* 76-80; C Chingford SS Pet and Paul 80-83; P-in-c Gt Ilford St Alb 83-87; V from 87; rtd 09. *Walsingham House, Main Road, Hadlow Down, Uckfield TN22 4ES* Tel (01825) 830076 E-mail frmilnes@aol.com

MILNES, James Clark. b 79. St Chad's Coll Dur BA00 MA01. Westcott Ho Cam 03. **d** 05 **p** 06. C Newbold w Dunston *Derby* 05-08; R Alderley w Birtles *Ches* from 08. *St Mary's Rectory, Congleton Road, Nether Alderley, Macclesfield SK10 4TW* Tel (01625) 585440 E-mail jamesclarkmilnes@yahoo.co.uk

MILROY, Mrs Ethel Doreen. b 33. Bedf Coll Lon BSc54 Bris Univ PGCE69 Nottm Univ MEd79. NOC 88. **d** 91 **p** 94. NSM Tideswell *Derby* 91-95; P-in-c Rowsley 95-02; rtd 02; Perm to Offic *Derby* from 02. *40 Eccles Close, Hope Valley S33 6RG* Tel (01433) 623582

MILSON, Julian James. b 70. De Montfort Univ BEd96. Oak Hill Th Coll BA04. **d** 04 **p** 05. C Bramcote *S'well* 04-07; C Hove Bp Hannington Memorial Ch *Chich* from 07. *43 Hogarth Road, Hove BN3 5RH* Tel (01273) 777020 E-mail jmilson@bigfoot.com

MILTON, Andrew John. b 54. BD. St Steph Ho Ox. **d** 83 **p** 84. C Highfield *Ox* 83-87; TV Banbury 87-95; P-in-c Thorney Abbey *Ely* 95-02; TR Huntingdon 02-07; P-in-c Gt w Lt Stukeley 04-07; TR Huntingdon w the Stukeleys from 07. *The Rectory, 1 The Walks East, Huntingdon PE29 3AP* Tel (01480) 412674 E-mail miltons@walkseast.fsnet.co.uk

MILTON, Miss Angela Daphne. b 50. FInstLEx79. Oak Hill Th Coll 84. **d** 87 **p** 94. NSM Watford *St Alb* 87-95; NSM St Alb St Mary Marshalswick 95-97; C Stevenage St Mary Shephall w Aston 97-02; P-in-c E Molesey St Paul *Guildf* 02-05; V E Molesey from 05. *St Paul's Vicarage, 101 Palace Road, East Molesey KT8 9DU* Tel (020) 8979 1580 E-mail angelamilton@msn.com

MILTON, Claudius James Barton. b 29. K Coll Lon BD52 AKC53. **d** 53 **p** 54. C Sudbury St Andr *Lon* 53-56; Asst Chapl Bedford Sch 57-65; Asst Master 57-65; Chapl Cranbrook Sch Kent 65-74; Asst Master and Housemaster 65-74; Chapl & Asst Master Clayesmore Sch Blandford 74-89; Clayesmore Prep Sch 74-89; rtd 89. *28 Oakwood Drive, Iwerne Minster, Blandford Forum DT11 8QT* Tel (01747) 811792

MILTON-THOMPSON, Jonathan Patrick. b 51. Nottm Univ BA76. Oak Hill Th Coll 86. **d** 88 **p** 89. C Bispham *Blackb* 88-92; C Darfield *Sheff* 92; C-in-c Gt Houghton CD 92-03; P-in-c Livesey *Blackb* from 03. *St Andrew's Vicarage, 112 Full View, Blackburn BB2 4QB* Tel (01254) 59422

MILVERTON, The Revd and Rt Hon Lord (Fraser Arthur Richard Richards). b 30. Bps' Coll Cheshunt. **d** 57 **p** 58. C Beckenham St Geo *Roch* 57-59; C Sevenoaks St Jo 59-60; C Gt Bookham *Guildf* 60-63; V Okewood 63-67; R Christian Malford w Sutton Benger etc *Bris* 67-93; Public Preacher 93-95; rtd 95; Perm to Offic *Sarum* from 96. *7 Betjeman Road, Marlborough SN8 1TL* Tel (01672) 514068

MILVERTON, Frederic Jack. b 15. Lon Univ BSc37 Leeds Univ MEd40. Ripon Hall Ox 56. **d** 57 **p** 58. C Ecclesall *Sheff* 57-60; V Thurcroft 60-61; Lect Nottm Coll of Educn 61-67; Lect Weymouth Coll of Educn 67-76; Hd of Educn 70-76; Dean Educn Dorset Inst of HE 76-79; TV Oakdale St Geo *Sarum* 79-82; rtd 82; Perm to Offic *Sarum* from 82. *4 Compass South, Rodwell Road, Weymouth DT4 8QT* Tel (01305) 788930 E-mail rev.milv.compass@care4free.net

MILVERTON, Mrs Ruth Erica. b 32. Open Univ BA78 Southn Univ MA82. Sarum Th Coll 83. **dss** 86 **d** 87 **p** 95. Weymouth H Trin *Sarum* 86-87; Hon Par Dn 87-95; NSM 95-02; Dioc NSM Officer 89-97; rtd 02; Perm to Offic *Sarum* 02-07. *4 Compass South, Rodwell Road, Weymouth DT4 8QT* Tel (01305) 788930 E-mail rev.milv.compass@care4free.net

MILWARD, Terence George. b 23. Ripon Hall Ox 66. **d** 68 **p** 69. C Selly Oak St Mary *Birm* 68-70; C Edgbaston St Bart 70-75; TV Bournemouth St Pet w St Swithun, H Trin etc *Win* 75-81; R Smannell w Enham Alamein 81-88; rtd 88; Perm to Offic *Guildf* from 88. *Church House Flat, Church Lane, Witley, Godalming GU8 5PN* Tel (01428) 685308

MINALL, Peter. b 26. Lon Univ BSc47. Bps' Coll Cheshunt 51. **d** 53 **p** 54. C Bishop's Stortford St Mich *St Alb* 53-57; C Luton w E Hyde 57-63; C Tuffley *Glouc* 63-65; Asst Youth Chapl 65-69; V Stroud 69-84; RD Bisley 78-84; P-in-c Barnwood 84-91; rtd 91; Chapl Coney Hill Hosp Glouc 86-95; Chapl Severn NHS Trust 95-06; Perm to Offic *Glouc* from 06. *Amberwood, Knapp Lane, Painswick, Stroud GL6 6YE* Tel (01452) 813730 E-mail peter.minall@btinternet.com

MINAY, Francis Arthur Rodney. b 44. Westcott Ho Cam 66. **d** 68 **p** 69. C Edenbridge *Roch* 68-73; C Bromley St Mark 73-75; V Tudeley w Capel 75-79; TV Littleham w Exmouth 79-82; P-in-c Bolton Percy and Asst Chapl to Arts and Recreation in the NE *York* 82-06; rtd 06; Lic to Offic *Mor* from 07; Hon C Kishorn 07-08. *Rosedyke, Achintee, Strathcarron IV54 8YX* Tel (01520) 722144

MINCHER, John Derek Bernard. b 31. **d** 60 **p** 61. OSB 54-80; Lic to Offic *Ox* 60-80; Perm to Offic *St E* 81-87; C Halesworth w Linstead, Chediston, Holton etc 87-90; P-in-c Worlingworth, Southolt, Tannington, Bedfield etc 90-91; R 91-96; rtd 96; Perm to Offic *St E* 96-09. *Flat 7, Manormead, Tilford Road, Hindhead GU26 6RA*

MINCHEW, Donald Patrick. b 48. Univ of Wales (Cardiff) BD76. St Mich Coll Llan 72. **d** 76 **p** 77. C Glouc St Aldate 76-80; P-in-c Sharpness CD 80-81; V Sharpness w Purton and Brookend 81-95; Miss to Seafarers from 81; V Croydon St Mich w St Jas *S'wark* from 95. *St Michael's Vicarage, 39 Oakfield Road, Croydon CR0 2UX* Tel (020) 8680 8413

MINCHIN, Anthony John. b 35. St Cath Coll Cam BA59 MA. Wells Th Coll 59. **d** 61 **p** 62. C Cheltenham St Pet *Glouc* 61-64; C Bushey *St Alb* 64-67; V Cheltenham St Mich *Glouc* 67-74; V Lower Cam 74-82; V Tuffley 82-92; R Huntley and Longhope 92-00; rtd 00; Perm to Offic *Glouc* from 00. *2 Melbourne Drive, Stonehouse GL10 2PJ* Tel (01453) 828899

MINCHIN, Charles Scott. b 51. Trin Coll Cam BA72 MA75. Linc Th Coll 73. **d** 75 **p** 76. C Gt Wyrley *Lich* 75-78; TV Wilnecote 78-82; C Tamworth 82-84; C-in-c Glascote CD 84-88; R Brierley Hill 88-93; R Brierley Hill *Worc* 93-03; P-in-c Stonehouse *Glouc* from 03. *The Vicarage, Elms Road, Stonehouse GL10 2NP* Tel (01453) 822332 E-mail cminchin@lineone.net

MINION, Arthur. b 65. TCD BTh92. CITC 89. **d** 92 **p** 93. C Bandon Union *C, C & R* 92-95; I Taunagh w Kilmactranny, Ballysumaghan etc *K, E & A* 95-99; I Shinrone w Aghancon etc *L & K* 99-08; I Crosspatrick Gp *C & O* from 08. *The Rectory, Churchlands, Tinahely, Co Wicklow, Republic of Ireland* Tel (00353) (402) 28922 Mobile 86-825 1065 E-mail arthurminion@gmail.com

MINION, Hazel Elizabeth Alice. b 47. TCD BA68 HDipEd69. CITC 00. **d** 03 **p** 04. Aux Min Templebreedy w Tracton and Nohoval *C, C & R* 03-04; Aux Min Carrigaline Union from 04; Chapl Ashton Sch Cork 03-07. *22 Inchvale Drive, Shamrock Lawn, Douglas, Cork, Republic of Ireland* Tel (00353) (21) 436 1924 E-mail hminion22@hotmail.com

MINNS, David Andrew. b 59. St Jo Coll Nottm 95. **d** 97 **p** 98. C Burpham *Guildf* 97-00; C Knaphill w Brookwood 00-04; R Ewhurst from 04. *The Rectory, The Street, Ewhurst, Cranleigh GU6 7PX* Tel (01483) 277584 E-mail dlkminns@btinternet.com

MINNS, John Alfred. b 38. Oak Hill Th Coll 63. **d** 68 **p** 69. C Cheadle Hulme St Andr *Ches* 68-72; C Hartford 72-74; V Wharton 74-85; V Halliwell St Paul *Man* 85-87; C Halliwell St Pet 87-91; rtd 91; Perm to Offic *Glouc* 91-97. *39 Hambidge Lane, Lechlade GL7 3BJ* Tel (01367) 253549

MINNS, Canon John Charles. b 42. EAMTC. **d** 85 **p** 86. NSM Heigham St Barn w St Bart *Nor* 85-91; P-in-c Nor St Geo Tombland from 91; Asst Chapl Norfolk and Nor Hosp 92-95; Chapl Nor Sch of Art and Design 99-03; Hon Can Nor Cathl from 05. *18 Thunder Lane, Norwich NR7 0PX* Tel (01603) 437000 Mobile 07951-434485 E-mail john.minns@virgin.net

MINORS, Canon Graham Glyndwr Cavil. b 44. Glouc Sch of Min. **d** 79 **p** 79. NSM Cainscross w Selsley *Glouc* 79-83; C Leckhampton SS Phil and Jas w Cheltenham St Jas 83-89; V Cainscross w Selsley 89-99; RD Stonehouse 97-99; TR Bodmin w Lanhydrock and Lanivet *Truro* from 99; Chapl N and E Cornwall Primary Care Trust 02-06; Hon Can Truro Cathl from 07. *The Rectory, Priory Road, Bodmin PL31 2AB* Tel (01208) 73867 E-mail revgminors@hotmail.com

MINSON, Roger Graham. b 41. Leeds Univ BA64. Coll of Resurr Mirfield 64. **d** 66 **p** 67. C Horfield St Greg *Bris* 66-70; C Southmead 70-73; V Lawrence Weston 74-81; TV Knowle 81-93; V Knowle St Martin 93-95; V Fishponds St Mary 95-06; rtd 06. *2 Box Tree Cottage, Turners Tump, Ruardean GL17 9XG* Tel (01594) 546821

MINTON, Bernard John. b 68. St Chad's Coll Dur BA89 MRICS00. Coll of Resurr Mirfield 00. **d** 04 **p** 05. C Lancing w Coombes *Chich* 04-08; TV Ouzel Valley *St Alb* from 08. *St Barnabas' Vicarage, Vicarage Road, Leighton Buzzard LU7 2LP* E-mail bernardminton@aol.com

MINTY, Kenneth Desmond. b 25. Ch Ch Ox BA48 MA51. Lich Th Coll 71 Qu Coll Birm 72. **d** 73 **p** 74. Asst Chapl Wrekin Coll Telford 73-84; Chapl 84-86; Hon C Lawley *Lich* 74-75; Hon C Cen Telford 75-81; Hon C Longdon-upon-Tern, Rodington, Uppington etc 81-89; V Ercall Magna 89-95; V Rowton 89-95; rtd 95; Perm to Offic *Lich* from 95. *8 Glebelands, High Ercall, Telford TF6 6BB* Tel (01952) 770487

MINTY, Selwyn Francis. b 34. St D Coll Lamp 58. **d** 61 **p** 62. C Tonyrefail *Llan* 61-66; C Pontypridd St Cath 66-69; V Cilfynydd 69-84; V Crynant 84-00; rtd 00. *24 Derwen Fawr, Cilfrew, Neath SA10 8NX*

MIR, Amene Rahman. b 58. Man Univ BA81 PhD93. Coll of Resurr Mirfield 81. **d** 83 **p** 84. C Walton St Mary *Liv* 83-87; Chapl Walton Hosp Liv 83-87; Perm to Offic *Man* 87-90; Asst Chapl Salford Mental Health Unit 90-94; Chapl Salford Mental Health Services NHS Trust 94-96; Chapl R Marsden NHS Trust 96-04. *Address temp unknown*

MIRZANIA, Ms Bassirat Bibi (Bassi). b 43. Tehran Univ MS74 Thames Valley Coll of HE BSc83. **d** 04 **p** 05. Chapl Persian Community from 04; NSM Guildf Ch Ch w St Martha-on-the-Hill from 04. *Shiraz, 11 Nelson Gardens, Guildford GU1 2NZ* Tel (01483) 569316 E-mail bassi.mirzania@btinternet.com

MISTLIN, Mrs Donna Jane. b 68. RGN89. STETS 03. **d** 08 **p** 09. NSM Crookham *Guildf* from 08. *18 Prospect Road, Ash Vale, Aldershot GU12 5ED* Tel (01252) 692720 E-mail djmistl@aol.com

MITCHAM, Andrew Mark. b 66. Kent Univ BA87 Leeds Univ BA90. Coll of Resurr Mirfield 88. **d** 91 **p** 92. C Downham Market w Bexwell *Ely* 91-94; P Shrine of Our Lady of Walsingham 94-96; V W Worthing St Jo *Chich* 96-04; R Eye *St E* from 04. *The Vicarage, 41 Castle Street, Eye IP23 7AW* Tel (01379) 870277 E-mail andrew@redmail.co.uk

MITCHELL, Albert George. b 25. TCD MA. **d** 88 **p** 89. Bp's C Skreen w Kilmacshalgan and Dromard *T, K & A* 88-00; Can Killala Cathl 96-00; rtd 00. *The Glebe, Kilglass, Enniscrone, Co Sligo, Republic of Ireland* Tel (00353) (96) 36258

MITCHELL, Alec Silas. b 52. Man Univ BA75 MPhil95. Nor Bapt Coll 77 Coll of Resurr Mirfield 98. **d** 99 **p** 99. C Ashton *Man* 99-05; TV 05-07; P-in-c Haughton St Anne from 07; Dioc Officer for Racial Justice from 02. *St Anne's Rectory, St Anne's Drive, Denton, Manchester M34 3EB* Tel 0161-336 2374 E-mail fathermit@hotmail.com

MITCHELL, Allan. b 52. Kelham Th Coll 74 Linc Th Coll 78. **d** 78 **p** 79. C Kells *Carl* 78-81; C Upperby St Jo 81-83; V Pennington w Lindal and Marton 83-88; V Westfield St Mary 88-98; P-in-c Dalton-in-Furness 98-02; V Dalton-in-Furness and Ireleth-with-Askam from 02. *The Vicarage, Market Place, Dalton-in-Furness LA15 8AZ* Tel (01229) 462526

MITCHELL, Andrew Patrick (Paddy). b 37. English Coll Valladolid 59 Ripon Coll Cuddesdon 84. **d** 64 **p** 65. In RC Ch 64-85; C Woolwich St Mary w St Mich *S'wark* 85-87; V E Wickham 87-94; P-in-c Walsall St Andr *Lich* 94-00; TV Sedgley All SS *Worc* 00-03; rtd 03; Perm to Offic *Birm* 03-04 and from 05. *714 Pershore Road, Selly Oak, Birmingham B29 7NR* Tel 0121-415 5828

MITCHELL, Anthony. b 54. St Jo Coll Nottm 05. **d** 07 **p** 08. C Plas Newton w Ches Ch Ch from 07. *13 Mannings Lane South, Chester CH2 3RX* Tel (01244) 400064 E-mail tony@tlmitchell.co.uk

MITCHELL, Mrs Brenda Margaret. b 53. Leeds Univ BA06. NOC 03. **d** 06 **p** 07. C Golcar *Wakef* from 06. *24 Banks Avenue, Golcar, Huddersfield HD7 4LZ* Tel (01484) 461699 Mobile 07976-305011 E-mail brenda_m_mitchell@hotmail.com

MITCHELL, Christopher Allan. b 51. Newc Univ BA72. Oak Hill Th Coll 82. **d** 84 **p** 85. C Guisborough *York* 84-87; C Thornaby on Tees 87-88; TV 88-92; V Dent w Cowgill *Bradf* 92-98; R Barney, Fulmodeston w Croxton, Hindringham etc *Nor* 98-03; R Hulland, Atlow, Kniveton, Bradley and Hognaston *Derby* from 03. *The Rectory, 16 Eaton Close, Hulland Ward, Ashbourne DE6 3EX* Tel (01335) 372138 E-mail pennychris@tiscali.co.uk

MITCHELL, Christopher Ashley. b 69. Leeds Univ BA(Econ)91. Ridley Hall Cam 92. **d** 95 **p** 96. Min Can St As Cathl 95-98; CF 98-02; Chapl RAF from 02. *Chaplaincy Services, Valiant Block, HQ Air Command, RAF High Wycombe HP14 4UE* Tel (01494) 496800 Fax 496343

MITCHELL, Christopher Derek. b 61. Univ of Wales (Lamp) BA85 Leic Univ MA86 Qu Coll Cam BA88 MA92 Auckland Univ of Tech MHSc04. Westcott Ho Cam 87. **d** 89 **p** 90. C Streetly *Lich* 89-92; C Brookfield St Mary *Lon* 92-96; Hon C Hornsey St Mary w St Geo 99-02; Lic to Offic Dio Auckland New Zealand 03-07; C Hendon St Mary and Ch Ch 07-08; V Edmonton St Pet w St Martin from 08. *St Peter's Vicarage, St Peter's Road, London N9 8JP* Tel (020) 8807 7431 E-mail fatherchris@btinternet.com

MITCHELL, Clare. *See* GRIFFITHS, Mrs Clare Elizabeth

MITCHELL, Canon David George. b 35. QUB BA56. Sarum Th Coll 59. **d** 61 **p** 62. C Westbury-on-Trym H Trin *Bris* 61-64; C Cricklade w Latton 64-68; V Fishponds St Jo 68-77; RD Stapleton 76-77; TR E Bris 77-87; R Syston 87-94; V Warmley 87-94; P-in-c Bitton 87-94; R Warmley, Syston and Bitton 94-01; RD Bitton 87-93; Hon Can Bris Cathl 87-01; rtd 01; P-in-c Chedworth, Yanworth and Stowell, Coln Rogers etc *Glouc* from 01; AD Northleach from 04; Perm to Offic *Bris* from 01. *The Vicarage, Cheap Street, Chedworth, Cheltenham GL54 4AA* Tel (01285) 720392 E-mail canongeorgemitchell@btinternet.com

MITCHELL, Preb David Norman. b 35. Tyndale Hall Bris 64. **d** 67 **p** 68. C Marple All SS *Ches* 67-70; C St Helens St Helen *Liv* 70-72; V S Lambeth St Steph *S'wark* 72-78; P-in-c Brixton Road Ch Ch 73-75; SE Area Sec CPAS 78-81; R Uphill *B & W* 81-92; TR 92-01; Chapl Weston Area Health Trust 86-01; Preb Wells Cathl from 90; rtd 01; Perm to Offic *B & W* from 02. *3 Pizey Close, Clevedon BS21 7TP* Tel (01275) 349176

MITCHELL, Canon Edwin. b 44. St Jo Coll Nottm BTh74. **d** 74 **p** 75. C Worksop St Jo *S'well* 74-77; C Waltham Abbey *Chelmsf* 77-80; V Whiston *Liv* 80-91; R Wombwell *Sheff* 91-99; V Mortomley St Sav High Green from 99; P-in-c Stocksbridge 06-07; AD Ecclesfield 01-07; Hon Can Sheff Cathl from 07. *The Vicarage, Mortomley Lane, High Green, Sheffield S35 3HS* Tel 0114-284 8231 E-mail edwin.mitchell1@btopenworld.com

MITCHELL, Eric Sidney. b 24. S Dios Minl Tr Scheme 77. **d** 80 **p** 81. NSM Portland All SS w St Pet *Sarum* 80-83; C 88-92; Bermuda 83-88; Chapl HM Pris The Verne 91-92; rtd 92; Perm to Offic *Sarum* from 92. *10 Underhedge Gardens, Portland DT5 2DX* Tel (01305) 821059

MITCHELL, Geoffrey. b 36. SS Coll Cam BA60 MA64 Nottm Univ BA97 CEng66 FIMechE76 FCIT92. EMMTC 88. **d** 91 **p** 92. NSM Oaks in Charnwood and Copt Oak *Leic* 91-94; NSM Loughborough All SS w H Trin 94-00; P-in-c Oaks in Charnwood and Copt Oak 00-03; NSM Shepshed and Oaks in Charnwood 03-04; Dioc NSM Officer 98-02; rtd 04; Perm to Offic *Leic* from 04. *36 Brick Kiln Lane, Shepshed, Loughborough LE12 9EL* Tel (01509) 502280 E-mail mitchell.house@talk21.com

MITCHELL, Geoffrey Peter. b 30. Liv Univ BEng57 Man Univ MSc68. Wells Th Coll 57. **d** 59 **p** 60. C Bradford cum Beswick *Man* 59-61; R Man St Pet Oldham Road w St Jas 61-64; Lic to Offic 64-68; Hon C Unsworth 68-86; V Woolfold 86-95; rtd 95; Perm to Offic *Man* from 95. *14 Redfearn Wood, Rochdale OL12 7GA* Tel (01706) 638180

MITCHELL, George. *See* MITCHELL, Canon David George

MITCHELL, George Alfred. b 23. TCD BA45 MA56. **d** 46 **p** 47. C Belfast St Matt *Conn* 46-48; C Ballymoney 48-51; C Belf Cathl Miss 51-52; I Broomhedge 52-58; I Carrickfergus 59-70; I Bangor St Comgall *D & D* 70-88; Can Belf Cathl 78-88; rtd 88. *2 Glendun Park, Bangor BT20 4UX* Tel (028) 9146 0882

MITCHELL, Geraint Owain. b 71. Lincs & Humberside Univ BA96 Leeds Univ BA. Coll of Resurr Mirfield 99. **d** 02 **p** 03. C Bridlington Em *York* 02-05; V Brigg, Wrawby and Cadney cum Howsham *Linc* from 05. *The Vicarage, 10 Glanford Road, Brigg DN20 8DJ* Tel (01652) 653989 E-mail owain.mitchell@btopenworld.com

MITCHELL, Gordon Frank Henry. b 26. FIFireE. Sarum & Wells Th Coll 74. **d** 77 **p** 78. NSM Alderbury and W Grimstead *Sarum* 77-91; NSM Alderbury Team 91-96; Perm to Offic 96-07. *Seefeld, Southampton Road, Whaddon, Salisbury SP5 3EB* Tel (01722) 710516

MITCHELL, Graham Bell. b 40. Otago Univ BA64 MA65 Worc Coll Ox BA73 MA76. St Chad's Coll Dur 66. **d** 68 **p** 69. C Bris St Agnes w St Simon 68-71; C Bedminster St Mich 73-76; V Auckland St Pet *Dur* 76-78; Vice-Prin Chich Th Coll 78-83; C Brighton St Pet w Chpl Royal and St Jo *Chich* 83-86; P-in-c Scaynes Hill 86-96; V 96-04; rtd 04. *18B Ballin Street, Ellersie, Auckland 1051, New Zealand*

MITCHELL, Ian. *See* MITCHELL, Stuart Ian

MITCHELL, Jolyon Peter. b 64. Selw Coll Cam BA88 MA90 Edin Univ PhD97. St Jo Coll Dur MA93. **d** 93 **p** 94. NSM St Mary's Cathl 93-97; NSM Edin Ch Ch 97-01; NSM Edin St Jas from 01; Lect Edin Univ 93-01; Sen Lect from 01; Visiting Fell Clare Hall Cam 02. *11 Eildon Street, Edinburgh EH3 5JU* Tel 0131-226 1092 *or* 650 8900 E-mail jolyon.mitchell@ed.ac.uk

MITCHELL, Karen Irene. b 68. Westcott Ho Cam 07. **d** 09. C Cheshunt *St Alb* from 09. *156 Churchgate, Cheshunt, Waltham Cross EN8 9DX* Tel (01992) 620659 Mobile 07834-322943

MITCHELL, Kevin. b 49. Newc Univ BSc71 Ox Univ BA83. Ripon Coll Cuddesdon 81. **d** 83 **p** 84. C Cantril Farm *Liv* 83-86; Chapl N Middx Hosp 86-90; C Gt Cambridge Road St Jo and St Jas *Lon* 86-90; P-in-c Cricklewood St Pet 90-96; V Whetstone St Jo from 96. *St John's Vicarage, 1163 High Road, London N20 0PG* Tel (020) 8445 4569 E-mail kevinmitch@onetel.com

MITCHELL, Owain. *See* MITCHELL, Geraint Owain

MITCHELL, Paddy. *See* MITCHELL, Andrew Patrick

MITCHELL, The Very Revd Patrick Reynolds. b 30. FSA81 Mert Coll Ox BA52 MA56. Wells Th Coll 52. **d** 54 **p** 55. C Mansfield St Mark *S'well* 54-57; Chapl Wells Th Coll and PV Wells Cathl 57-61; V Milton *Portsm* 61-67; V Frome St Jo and P-in-c Woodlands *B & W* 67-73; Dir of Ords 70-74; Dean Wells 73-89; Dean Windsor and Dom Chapl to The Queen 89-98; rtd 98; Perm to Offic *Ex* from 98 and *Sarum* from 00. *Wolford Lodge, Dunkeswell, Honiton EX14 4SQ* Tel (01404) 841244

MITCHELL, Richard John Anthony. b 64. St Martin's Coll Lanc BA85 PGCE86. Sarum & Wells Th Coll 88. **d** 91 **p** 92. C Kendal H Trin *Carl* 91-95; TV Kirkby Lonsdale 95-04; P-in-c Badgeworth, Shurdington and Witcombe w Bentham *Glouc* 04-09; R from 09; AD Glouc N from 04. *The Vicarage, School Lane, Shurdington, Cheltenham GL51 4TF* Tel (01242) 702911 E-mail richard.mitchell@talk21.com

MITCHELL, Robert Hugh. b 53. Ripon Coll Cuddesdon. **d** 82 **p** 83. C E Dulwich St Jo *S'wark* 82-86; C Cambridge Gt St Mary w St Mich *Ely* 86-90; Chapl Girton Coll Cam 86-90; Asst Chapl Win Coll 90-91; Assoc Chapl Addenbrooke's Hosp Cam 91-93; Chapl Portsm Hosps NHS Trust 93-95; Chapl St Mary's Hosp Portsm 93-95; Chapl R Free Hampstead NHS Trust from 95. *The Chaplains' Office, The Royal Free Hospital, Pond Street, London NW3 2QG* Tel (020) 7794 0500 ext 3096 *or* 7830 2742 E-mail robert.mitchell@royalfree.nhs.uk

MITCHELL, Robert McFarlane. b 50. Man Univ BA72 Lambeth STh92. Wycliffe Hall Ox 73. **d** 75 **p** 76. C Tonbridge SS Pet and Paul *Roch* 75-80; CF 80-08; P-in-c Tillington *Chich* from 08. *The Rectory, Tillington, Petworth GU28 9AH* Tel (01798) 342827 Mobile 07530-852896 E-mail robert@revbobm.plus.com

MITCHELL, Roger Dalway. b 36. Chich Th Coll 70. **d** 71 **p** 71. C Sidcup St Jo *Roch* 71-74; C Pembury 74-76; Chapl St Lawr Hosp Bodmin 76-96; Chapl Cornwall and Is of Scilly Mental Health Unit 88-96; Chapl Cornwall Healthcare NHS Trust 96-00; TV Bodmin w Lanhydrock and Lanivet *Truro* 97-00; rtd 00. *12 Beacon Road, Bodmin PL31 1AS* Tel (01208) 76357 Mobile 07771-881258

MITCHELL, Miss Sandra Helen. b 47. ERMC 03. **d** 06 **p** 07. NSM Wroxham w Hoveton and Belaugh *Nor* 06-07; NSM Martham and Repps with Bastwick, Thurne etc from 07. *White House Farm, Tower Road, Repps with Bastwick, Great Yarmouth NR29 5JW* Tel (01692) 670439 E-mail shmitch@tiscali.co.uk

MITCHELL, Sarah Rachel. *See* TAN, Mrs Sarah Rachel

MITCHELL, Sheila Rosemary. b 53. Univ Coll Ches CertEd74 AdDipEd80. NOC 93. **d** 96 **p** 97. NSM Plemstall w Guilden Sutton *Ches* 96-98; C New Brighton St Jas w Em 98-00; C New Brighton All SS 98-00; P-in-c Weston 00-02; V 02-07; Perm to Offic from 07. *Casa Robila 21, Calle Jilguero, Mondron, 29710 Periana (Mlaga), Spain* E-mail revsmith@aol.com

MITCHELL, Stephen Andrew John. b 56. Ch Ch Coll Cant CertEd78 K Coll Lon AKC77 BD80 MA02 Lambeth STh90 Heythrop Coll Lon MTh05. Coll of Resurr Mirfield 80. **d** 82 **p** 83. C Chatham St Steph *Roch* 82-87; C Edenbridge 87-91; V from 91; P-in-c Crockham Hill H Trin from 91; Chapl Invicta Community Care NHS Trust from 91. *The Vicarage, Mill Hill, Edenbridge TN8 5DA* Tel (01732) 862258 Fax 864335 E-mail stephen.mitchell@diocese-rochester.org

MITCHELL, Stephen John. b 51. Ex Univ BA73 Fitzw Coll Cam BA78 MA. Ridley Hall Cam 76. **d** 79 **p** 80. C St Malvern St Mary *Worc* 79-81; Prec Leic Cathl 82-85; R Barrow upon Soar w Walton le Wolds 85-02; P-in-c Gazeley w Dalham, Moulton and Kentford *St E* 02-04; V Dalham, Gazeley, Higham, Kentford and Moulton from 05; Min Can St E Cathl from 05;

RD Mildenhall from 08. *All Saints' Vicarage, The Street, Gazeley, Newmarket CB8 8RB* Tel (01638) 552630
E-mail smitch4517@aol.com

MITCHELL, Steven. b 58. St Jo Coll Nottm BTh83. d 83 p 84. C Ovenden *Wakef* 83-87; V Gawthorpe and Chickenley Heath 87-98; V Birkenshaw w Hunsworth 98-05; R Newport w Longford, Chetwynd and Forton *Lich* from 05. *10 Forton Glade, Newport TF10 8BP* Tel (01952) 810089

MITCHELL, Stuart. b 53. Cranmer Hall Dur 01. d 03 p 04. C Pocklington and Owsthorpe and Kilnwick Percy etc *York* 03-06; P-in-c Edith Weston w N Luffenham and Lyndon w Manton *Pet* from 06; P-in-c Preston and Ridlington w Wing and Pilton from 06; C Empingham and Exton w Horn w Whitwell from 06. *The Hollow, 5A Audit Hall Road, Empingham, Oakham LE15 8PH* Tel (01780) 460139

MITCHELL, Stuart Ian. b 50. Wadh Coll Ox BA71 DPhil74. S'wark Ord Course 81. d 85 p 87. NSM Charlton St Luke w H Trin *S'wark* 85-86; NSM Kidbrooke St Jas 86-88; NSM Newbold w Dunston *Derby* 88-94; C 94-96; C Newbold and Gt Barlow 96-97; P-in-c Matlock Bank 97-03; RD Wirksworth 98-03; P-in-c Mackworth All SS from 03; P-in-c Mugginton and Kedleston from 03; P-in-c Kirk Langley from 03. *The Vicarage, 4 Church Lane, Kirk Langley, Ashbourne DE6 4NG* Tel (01332) 824729 E-mail ianandmarym@tiscali.co.uk

MITCHELL, Tim. b 63. Trin Coll Bris 95. d 97 p 98. C Cromer *Nor* 97-01; P-in-c Selston *S'well* 01-05; P-in-c Sutton in Ashfield St Mich from 05. *The Vicarage, 11A Deepdale Gardens, Sutton-in-Ashfield NG17 4ER* Tel (01623) 441743
E-mail timmitchell.t@googlemail.com

MITCHELL, Wendy Mary. b 47. Glas Univ MA70 Callendar Park Coll of Educn Falkirk PGCE71. Trin Coll Bris 99. d 01 p 02. C Yatton Moor *B & W* 01-07; TV Parkham, Alwington, Buckland Brewer etc *Ex* from 07. *The Rectory, Rectory Lane, Parkham, Bideford EX39 5PL* Tel (01237) 451204
E-mail revwendym@aol.com

MITCHELL, William Blanchard. b 26. St Aid Birkenhead 53. d 55 p 56. C Kendal H Trin *Carl* 55-59; C Dalton-in-Furness 59-60; V Nichol Forest 60-61; CF 61-77; V Nicholforest and Kirkandrews on Esk *Carl* 77-84; R Kirkby Thore w Temple Sowerby and Newbiggin 84-89; rtd 89; Perm to Offic *Carl* from 89. *Koi Hai, 23 Longlands Road, Carlisle CA3 9AD* Tel (01228) 546230

MITCHELL-INNES, Charles William. b 47. Pemb Coll Cam BA69 MA73. Sarum Th Coll 83. d 86 p 87. Asst Chapl Sherborne Sch 86-89; Chapl Milton Abbey Sch Dorset 90-96; Conduct Eton Coll 96-07; rtd 07; V of Close Sarum Cathl from 07. *32 The Close, Salisbury SP1 2EJ* Tel (01722) 328361 or 555192 E-mail voc@salcath.org.uk

MITCHELL-INNES, James Alexander. b 39. Ch Ch Ox BA64 MA66. Lon Coll of Div 65. d 67 p 68. C Cullompton *Ex* 67-71; Nigeria 71-75; P-in-c Puddletown w Athelhampton and Burleston *Sarum* 75-78; R Puddletown and Tolpuddle 78-82; V Win Ch Ch 82-92; V Titchfield *Portsm* 92-98; rtd 98; Perm to Offic *Win* from 99. *115 Battery Hill, Winchester SO22 4BH* Tel (01962) 859039 E-mail jamesminness@o2.co.uk

MITCHINSON, Frank. b 37. AKC60. d 61 p 62. C Cross Heath *Lich* 61-64; C Forrabury w Minster and Trevalga *Truro* 64-68; C Harpenden St Nic *St Alb* 68-70; R Southwick St Mich *Chich* 70-83; V Billingshurst 83-88; V Preston 88-02; rtd 02; P-in-c Bolney *Chich* 02-05. *7 St Cyr, 26 Douglas Avenue, Exmouth EX8 2HA* Tel (01395) 268438

MITCHINSON, Canon Ronald. b 35. Westmr Coll Ox MA91. Linc Th Coll 66. d 68 p 69. C Heworth St Mary *Dur* 68-72; C Banbury *Ox* 72-73; TV 73-76; New Zealand 76-82; TR Banbury *Ox* 82-86; RD Deddington 84-86; Ind Chapl 86-92; Hon Can Ch Ch 90-92; TV Brayton *York* 92-96; Sen Chapl Selby Coalfield Ind Chapl 92-96; rtd 96; Perm to Offic *York* from 04. *6 St John's Crescent, York YO31 7QP* Tel (01904) 642382
E-mail rmitchinson@freire.org

MITFORD, Bertram William Jeremy (Bill). b 27. Wells Th Coll 62. d 64 p 65. C Hollinwood *Man* 64-67; C Atherton 67-68; C Frome St Jo *B & W* 68-71; V Cleeve 72-74; V Cleeve w Chelvey and Brockley 74-79; Chapl HM Pris Shepton Mallet 79-92; C Shepton Mallet *B & W* 79-84; C Shepton Mallet w Doulting 84-92; rtd 92. *21 Monkton Road, Honiton EX14 1PZ* Tel (01404) 42632

MITRA, Avijit (Munna). b 53. Keble Coll Ox BA76. Ox NSM Course 84. d 88 p 89. NSM Abingdon *Ox* 88-96; Asst Chapl Abingdon Sch 88-96; Sen Chapl Ch Hosp Horsham 96-09; Hd Classics K Sch Roch from 09. *The Old Archdeaconry Flat, The Precinct, Rochester ME1 1SX*
E-mail munna@amitra.fsnet.co.uk

MITRA, Mrs Nicola Jane. b 54. St Hugh's Coll Ox BA76 MA81 PGCE77. Ox Min Course 92. d 94 p 95. NSM Abingdon *Ox* 94-96; Asst Chapl Ch Hosp Horsham 96-08; Chapl Maidstone and Tunbridge Wells NHS Trust from 08. *Chaplaincy, Maidstone Hospital, Hermitage Lane, Maidstone ME16 9QQ* Tel (01622) 224569

MITSON, Mrs Carol Mae. b 46. SRN SCM. Oak Hill NSM Course 89. d 93 p 94. NSM Lawford *Chelmsf* 93-96; NSM Elmstead 96-98; NSM Harwich 96-98; NSM Dedham 98-00; Perm to Offic from 01. *Drift Cottage, The Drift, Dedham, Colchester CO7 6AH* Tel and fax (01206) 323116 Fax mitson@onetel.net.uk

MITSON, John Dane. b 29. Solicitor 56 SS Coll Cam MA53 LLM54. Oak Hill Th Coll 91 EAMTC 93. d 94 p 95. Dioc Registrar and Legal Sec to Bp St E 75-97; NSM Greenstead *Chelmsf* 94-96; NSM Elmstead 96-98; NSM Dedham 98-00; Perm to Offic from 00. *Drift Cottage, The Drift, Dedham, Colchester CO7 6AH* Tel and fax (01206) 323116
E-mail mitson@onetel.net.uk

MITSON, Miss Joyce. b 37. Man Univ CertEd64. Trin Coll Bris 77. dss 79 d 87 p 94. Wellington w Eyton *Lich* 79-85; Farnworth *Liv* 85-91; Par Dn 87-91; TD Bilston *Lich* 91-94; TV 94; Lich Local Min Adv 91-94; C W Bromwich St Jas 94-97; C W Bromwich St Jas w St Paul 97-98; rtd 98. *13 Birkenhills Drive, Bolton BL3 4TX* Tel (01204) 655081

MITTON, Michael Simon. b 53. Ex Univ BA75. St Jo Coll Nottm 76. d 78 p 79. C High Wycombe *Ox* 78-82; TV Kidderminster St Geo *Worc* 82-89; Dir Angl Renewal Min 89-97; Dep Dir Acorn Chr Foundn 97-03; Renewing Min Project Officer *Derby* 03-06; Miss and Min Development Adv from 06. *25 Church Lane, Darley Abbey, Derby DE22 1EX* Tel (01332) 340088 or 552448 E-mail michael.mitton@derby.anglican.org

MLEMETA, Kedmon Hezron. b 60. CertEd78. CA Tr Coll Nairobi 86. d 89 p 90. Tanzania 89-96 and from 99; P-in-c Loughb Gd Shep *Leic* 96-99. *The Diocese of Mount Kilimanjaro, PO Box 1057, Arusha, Tanzania*

MOAT, Terry. b 61. Nottm Univ BTh92. Aston Tr Scheme 86 Linc Th Coll 88. d 92 p 93. C Caterham *S'wark* 92-96; Hon C Tynemouth Priory *Newc* 04-06; C Morpeth 06-09; V Choppington from 09. *The Vicarage, Scotland Gate, Choppington NE62 5SX*

MOATE, Gerard Grigglestone. b 54. BA FRSA01. Oak Hill Th Coll 79. d 82 p 83. C Mildmay Grove St Jude and St Paul *Lon* 82-85; C Hampstead St Jo 85-88; P-in-c Pinxton *Derby* 88; V Charlesworth and Dinting Vale 88-95; V Dedham *Chelmsf* from 95; RD Dedham and Tey 98-03. *The Vicarage, High Street, Dedham, Colchester CO7 6DE* Tel (01206) 322136
E-mail gerard@moate.org
or vicar@dedham-parishchurch.org.uk

MOATE, Phillip. b 47. RGN70 RNT75. NOC 87. d 90 p 91. NSM Upper Holme Valley *Wakef* 90-92; NSM Almondbury Deanery 92-94; NSM Honley 94-95; P-in-c Roos and Garton w Tunstall, Grimston and Hilston *York* 95-02; R Lockington and Lund and Scorborough w Leconfield 02-09; rtd 09; Perm to Offic *York* from 09. *58 Pilmar Lane, Roos, Hull HU12 0HN* Tel (01964) 671321 E-mail pmoate@tiscali.co.uk

MOATT, Richard Albert. b 54. K Coll Lon BD76 AKC76. Linc Th Coll 80. d 81 p 82. C Egremont and Haile *Carl* 81-85; V Addingham, Edenhall, Langwathby and Culgaith 85-04; P-in-c Skirwith, Ousby and Melmerby w Kirkland 98-04; V Cross Fell Gp from 04; RD Penrith from 09. *1 Low Farm, Langwathby, Penrith CA10 1NH* Tel (01768) 881212
E-mail moatt@btinternet.com

MOBBERLEY, Keith John. b 56. BA. Westcott Ho Cam. d 84 p 85. C Coventry Caludon 84-87; C Kenilworth St Nic 87-92; V Keresley and Coundon 92-98; P-in-c Hatton w Haseley, Rowington w Lowsonford etc 98-00; R from 00. *North Ferncumbe Rectory, Hatton Green, Hatton, Warwick CV35 7LA* Tel (01926) 484332

MOBBERLEY, Mrs Susan. b 57. Kent Univ BA79. Westcott Ho Cam 81. dss 84 d 90 p 94. Coventry Caludon 84-87; Lic to Offic 87-92; NSM Keresley and Coundon 92-98; NSM Hatton w Haseley, Rowington w Lowsonford etc from 98. *North Ferncumbe Rectory, Hatton Green, Hatton, Warwick CV35 7LA* Tel (01926) 484332

MOBBS, Bernard Frederick. b 26. Open Univ BA. S'wark Ord Course 71. d 72 p 73. C Purley St Barn *S'wark* 72-74; Vice-Prin S'wark Ord Course 74-80; P-in-c Sydenham St Bart *S'wark* 80-87; V Dormansland 87-92; rtd 92; Perm to Offic *Chich* from 92. *19 Ramsay Hall, 11-13 Byron Road, Worthing BN11 3HN* Tel (01903) 237663

MOBERLY (née McCLURE), Mrs Jennifer Lynne. b 62. Ball State Univ (USA) BSc84. Cranmer Hall Dur 98. d 01 p 02. C Belmont *Dur* 01-08. *8 Princes Street, Durham DH1 4RP* Tel 0191-386 4255

MOBERLY, Richard Hamilton. b 30. Trin Hall Cam BA53 MA57. Cuddesdon Coll 53. d 55 p 56. C Walton St Mary *Liv* 55-59; C Kensington St Mary Abbots w St Geo *Lon* 59-63; R Chingola Zambia 63-67; V Kennington Cross St Anselm *S'wark* 67-73; TV N Lambeth 74-80; Ind Chapl 80-95; rtd 95; Perm to Offic *S'wark* from 95. *24 Wincott Street, London SE11 4NT* Tel (020) 7735 2233 Fax 7793 9021
E-mail richard@richardmoberly.org.uk

MOBERLY, Robert Walter Lambert. b 52. New Coll Ox MA77 Selw Coll Cam MA80 Trin Coll Cam PhD81. Ridley Hall Cam

74. **d** 81 **p** 82. C Knowle *Birm* 81-85; Lect Dur Univ from 85; Perm to Offic *Dur* from 85. *8 Princes Street, Durham DH1 4RP* Tel 0191-386 4255 *or* 374 2067
E-mail r.w.l.moberly@durham.ac.uk

MOBEY, Jonathan. Wycliffe Hall Ox 05. **d** 08 **p** 09. NSM Ox St Andr from 08. *St Andrew's Church, Linton Road, Oxford OX2 6UG* Tel (01865) 468044
E-mail jonathan.mobey@standrewsoxford.org

MOBSBY, Ian Jonathan. b 68. Leeds Univ BHSc93 SROT93 Anglia Ruskin Univ MA06. EAMTC 00. **d** 04 **p** 05. C Westmr St Matt *Lon* from 04. *Moot Community, St Edmund the King, Lombard Street, London EC3V 9EA* Tel (020) 3239 6350
E-mail ian.mobsby@moot.uk.net

MOCK, David Lawrence. b 64. Whitman Coll Washington BA86 Heythrop Coll Lon MTh01. Trin Coll Bris BA98. **d** 98 **p** 99. C Tadworth *S'wark* 98-01; P-in-c sustm St Geo *Ches* 01-02; C Macclesfield Team 01-02; TV from 02. *St George's Vicarage, 88 Byrons Lane, Macclesfield SK11 7JS* Tel (01625) 432919
E-mail dave@mockcrew.freeserve.co.uk

MOCKFORD (*née* WATKINS), **Mrs Betty Anne.** b 45. Leeds Univ BA66 Nottm Univ CertEd67. EAMTC 94. **d** 97 **p** 98. C Ipswich St Aug *St E* 97-00; P-in-c Charsfield w Debach, Monewden, Hoo etc 01-06; rtd 06; Perm to Offic *St E* from 06. *Mirembe, 10 Castle Brooks, Framlingham, Woodbridge IP13 9SF* Tel (01728) 724193 Mobile 07890-110741

MOCKFORD, Canon John Frederick. b 28. Em Coll Cam BA52 MA56. Ridley Hall Cam 52. **d** 54 **p** 55. C Ardwick St Silas *Man* 54; C Harpurhey Ch Ch 54-57; V Bootle St Leon *Liv* 57-64; CMS 65-73; Uganda 66-73; Can Missr Kampala 72-73; V Bushbury *Lich* 73-77; TR 77-84; Preb Lich Cathl 81-84; Dir Miss and Past Studies Ridley Hall Cam 84-88; V Ipswich St Marg *St E* 88-93; rtd 93; Perm to Offic *St E* from 93. *Mirembe, 10 Castle Brooks, Framlingham, Woodbridge IP13 9SF* Tel (01728) 724193

MOCKFORD, Peter John. b 57. Nottm Univ BSc79 St Jo Coll Dur BA88. Cranmer Hall Dur 86. **d** 89 **p** 90. C Tamworth *Lich* 89-94; V Blurton from 94; P-in-c Dresden from 04; P-in-c Longton Hall from 08. *The Vicarage, School Lane, Stoke-on-Trent ST3 3DU* Tel (01782) 312163
E-mail p.mockford@ukgateway.net

MODY, Rohintan Keki. b 63. New Coll Ox BA85 MA88 Fitzw Coll Cam MPhil05 Aber Univ PhD08. Oak Hill Th Coll BA00. **d** 00 **p** 01. C Wolverhampton St Luke *Lich* 00-03; C Virginia Water *Guildf* from 08. *Santana, Christchurch Road, Virginia Water GU25 4PT* Tel (01344) 843788
E-mail romody@hotmail.com *or* ro@cc-vw.org

MOESEL, Joseph James. b 65. Villanova Univ USA BA90 Harris Man Coll Ox BTh93 Regent's Park Coll Ox MTh03. Ripon Coll Cuddesdon 93. **d** 95 **p** 96. C Twigworth, Down Hatherley, Norton, The Leigh etc *Glouc* 95-98; CF 98-06; Sen CF from 06. *c/o MOD Chaplains (Army)* Tel (01980) 615804 Fax 615800

MOFFAT, Canon George. b 46. Edin Univ BD77 Open Univ BA87 Bradf Univ MA04. Edin Th Coll 67. **d** 72 **p** 73. C Falkirk *Edin* 73-76; C Edin St Pet 76-81; Chapl Edin Univ 77-81; C Heston *Lon* 81-84; V S Elmsall *Wakef* 84-93; TR Manningham *Brad* 93-97; R Bolton Abbey from 07; Chapl to The Queen from 00; Hon Can Bradf Cathl from 02. *The Rectory, Bolton Abbey, Skipton BD23 6AL* Tel (01756) 710326
E-mail george.moffatt@bradford.anglican.org

MOFFATT, Joseph Barnaby. b 72. Fitzw Coll Cam BA96 MA99. Ripon Coll Cuddesdon MTh99. **d** 99 **p** 00. C Cen Wolverhampton *Lich* 99-03; C Chelsea St Luke and Ch Ch *Lon* from 03. *29 Burnsall Street, London SW3 3SR* Tel (020) 7352 5608 E-mail joemoffatt@chelseaparish.org

MOFFATT, Neil Thomas. b 46. Fitzw Coll Cam BA68 MA72. Qu Coll Birm 69. **d** 71 **p** 72. C Charlton St Luke w St Paul *S'wark* 71-74; C Walworth St Pet 74-75; C Walworth 75-77; V Dormansland 77-86; TR Padgate *Liv* 86-96; V Padgate 96-98; TR Thatcham *Ox* from 98; AD Newbury from 02. *The Rectory, 17 Church Gate, Thatcham RG19 3PN* Tel (01635) 862616
E-mail tom@moffatt20.freeserve.co.uk

MOFFETT, Mrs Marie-Louise. b 25. St Andr Univ MA46. **d** 87 **p** 94. St Andr Univ Angl Chapl Team 87-91; C St Andrews All SS *St And* from 91. *10 Queen's Gardens, St Andrews KY16 9TA* Tel (01334) 473678

MOFFITT, Mrs Vivien Louisa. b 37. LSE BSc59. Sarum & Wells Th Coll 90. **d** 91 **p** 94. NSM Chandler's Ford *Win* 91-99; NSM Twyford and Owslebury and Morestead 99-01; rtd 01. *13 Velmore Road, Eastleigh SO53 3HD* Tel (023) 8026 5327

MOGER, Peter John. b 64. Mert Coll Ox BA85 BMus86 MA89 St Jo Coll Dur BA93 ARSCM08. Cranmer Hall Dur 89. **d** 93 **p** 94. C Whitby *York* 93-95; Prec, Sacr and Min Can Ely Cathl 95-01; V Godmanchester 01-05; Nat Worship Development Officer Abps' Coun from 05; Perm to Offic *Ely* from 05; Sec Liturg Commn from 09. *Church House, Great Smith Street, London SW1P 3AZ* Tel (020) 7898 1365 *or* (01480) 392149 Mobile 07970-694021 E-mail peter.moger@c-of-e.org.uk *or* peter.moger@ntlworld.com

MOGFORD, Canon Stanley Howard. b 13. St Pet Hall Ox BA35 MA39. Westcott Ho Cam 36. **d** 37 **p** 38. C Aberdare *Llan* 37-41; C Llan Cathl 41-48; V Cyfarthfa 48-54; V Pontypridd St Cath 54-63; V Llanblethian w Cowbridge 63-66; V Llanblethian w Cowbridge and Llandough etc 66-80; RD Llantwit Major and Cowbridge 69-80; Can Llan Cathl 71-80; rtd 80; Perm to Offic *Llan* from 80. *Fortis Green, 19 Plas Treoda, Cardiff CF14 1PT* Tel (029) 2061 8839

MOGRIDGE, Christopher James. b 31. Culham Coll of Educn CertEd62 LCP70 FCollP86. St Steph Ho Ox 93. **d** 94 **p** 95. NSM Wellingborough St Andr *Pet* 94-98; NSM Ecton 98-02; rtd 02; Perm to Offic *Pet* from 02. *April Cottage, Little Harrowden, Wellingborough NN9 5BB* Tel (01933) 678412

MOIR, Canon David William. b 38. St Aid Birkenhead 64. **d** 67 **p** 68. C Danbury *Chelmsf* 67-70; C Bollington St Jo *Ches* 70-72; V Sutton St Jas 72-81; V Prestbury 81-95; RD Macclesfield 88-98; P-in-c Bosley and N Rode w Wincle and Wildboarclough 95-98; V 98-03; Hon Can Ches Cathl 96-03; Chapl E Cheshire NHS Trust 96-03; rtd 04; Perm to Offic *Heref* from 04. *Dove Top, Bentlawnt, Minsterley, Shrewsbury SY5 0HE* Tel (01743) 891209
E-mail moirdl@compuserve.com

MOIR, Nicholas Ian. b 61. G&C Coll Cam BA82 MA86 Ox Univ BA86 MA91 Lon Univ MTh92. Wycliffe Hall Ox 84. **d** 87 **p** 88. C Enfield St Andr *Lon* 87-91; Bp's Dom Chapl *St Alb* 91-94; Chapl St Jo Coll Cam 94-98; V Waterbeach and R Landbeach *Ely* 98-07; RD N Stowe 05-07; V Chesterton St Andr from 07. *The Vicarage, 10 Lynfield Lane, Cambridge CB4 1DR* Tel (01223) 303469 E-mail nicholas.moir@ntlworld.com

✠**MOKIWA, The Most Revd Valentino.** b 66. **c** 02. Bp Dar-es-Salaam from 02; Abp Tanzania from 08. *PO Box 25016, Ilala, Dar-es-Salaam, Tanzania* Tel (00255) (22) 286 4426 Mobile 755-099 E-mail mokiwa_valentine@hotmail.com

MOLD, Peter John. b 33. **d** 63 **p** 64. C Boston *Linc* 63-66; C Scarborough St Mary w Ch Ch, St Paul and St Thos *York* 67-68; Australia from 68; rtd 91. *Stone Grange, 29 Newcastle Street, PO Box 355, York WA 6302, Australia* Tel (0061) (8) 9641 1965

MOLE, David Eric Harton. b 33. Em Coll Cam BA54 MA58 PhD62. Ridley Hall Cam 55. **d** 59 **p** 59. C Selly Hill St Steph *Birm* 59-62; Tutor St Aid Birkenhead 62-63; Chapl Peterho Cam 63-69; Ghana 69-72; Lect Qu Coll Birm 72-76; Tutor USPG Coll of the Ascension Selly Oak 76-87; C Burton *Lich* 87-93; Chapl Burton Gen Hosp 90-93; Chapl Ostend w Knokke and Bruges *Eur* 93-98; rtd 98; Perm to Offic *Birm* from 99. *48 Green Meadow Road, Selly Oak, Birmingham B29 4DE* Tel 0121-475 1589
E-mail susananddavidmole@yahoo.co.uk

MOLE, Canon Jennifer Vera. b 49. CertEd70. Qu Coll Birm 82. **d** 84 **p** 97. C Pontypool *Mon* 84-87; C Cyncoed 87-88; TV 88-96; C Caerleon 96-99; V Maesglas and Duffryn 99-07; R Panteg w Llanfihangel Pontymoile from 07; AD Pontypool from 08; Can St Woolos Cathl from 07. *Panteg Rectory, The Highway, New Inn, Pontypool NP4 0PH* Tel (01495) 763724

MOLESWORTH, Canon Anthony Edward Nassau. b 23. Pemb Coll Cam BA45 MA48. Coll of Resurr Mirfield 45. **d** 46 **p** 47. C Blyth St Mary *Newc* 46-51; C High Elswick St Phil 51-52; Swaziland 52-68; Can 68-71; Can Zululand 63-68; R Huish Episcopi w Pitney *B & W* 71-78; P-in-c High Ham 76-78; TR Langport Area 78-84; R Charlton Musgrove, Cucklington and Stoke Trister 84-90; RD Bruton 86-90; rtd 90; Perm to Offic *B & W* and *Sarum* from 90. *3 Barrow Hill, Stourton Caundle, Sturminster Newton DT10 2LD* Tel (01963) 362337

MOLL, Christopher David Edward. b 67. St Cath Coll Cam BA89 MA93. Ridley Hall Cam 94. **d** 98 **p** 99. C Byker St Mark and Walkergate St Oswald *Newc* 98-02; C Eastrop *Win* 02-06; V Wembdon *B & W* from 07. *The Vicarage, 12 Greenacre, Wembdon, Bridgwater TA6 7RD* Tel (01278) 423647
E-mail ed@sgw.org.uk

MOLL, Nicola. b 47. Bedf Coll Lon BA69. TISEC 99. **d** 03 **p** 04. C Edin Gd Shep from 03; C Edin St Salvador from 03. *9/3 Forth Street, Edinburgh EH1 3JX* Tel 0131-558 3729 *or* 557 0718
E-mail mollnicola@hotmail.com

MOLL, Randell Tabrum. b 41. Lon Univ BD65. Wycliffe Hall Ox 62. **d** 66 **p** 67. C Drypool St Columba w St Andr and St Pet *York* 66-70; Asst Chapl HM Pris Hull 66-70; Asst Master Hull Gr Sch 66-70; C Netherton *Liv* 70-74; C Sefton 70-72; Ind Chapl 70-74 and 92-99; Belgium 75-76; P-in-c Brockmoor *Lich* 76-81; Team Ldr Black Country Urban Ind Miss 76-81; Dir Chilworth Home Services 81-84; Asst Master Bp Reindorp Sch Guildf 84-90; France and Iraq 91; Chapl Sedbergh Sch 92; Sen Chapl Miss in the Economy (Merseyside) 92-99; Hon Can Liv Cathl 97-99; Chapl Campsfield Ho Immigration and Detention Cen 00-02; Sen Chapl Immigration Detention Services 01-02; Team Ldr Workplace Min *St Alb* 03-07; rtd 08. *Penn Cottage, Green End, Granborough, Buckingham MK18 3NT* Tel and fax (01296) 670970 E-mail randellmoll@yahoo.co.uk

MOLLAN, Patricia Ann Fairbanks. b 44. QUB BSc67 PhD70 BD97. **d** 97 **p** 98. Aux Min *D & D* from 97; Aux Min Lecale Gp 02-04; Dep Dir Ch's Min of Healing from 04. *Echo Sound, 69 Killyleagh Road, Downpatrick BT30 9BN* Tel (028) 4482 1626 Fax 9073 8665 E-mail pat@mollan.net *or* cmhbel@btconnect.com

MOLLAN, Prof Raymond Alexander Boyce. b 43. QUB MB, BCh69 BAO69 MD84 FRCS. CITC 97. **d** 97 **p** 98. Aux Min *D & D* from 97; Aux Min Comber from 02. *Echo Sound, 69 Killyleagh Road, Downpatrick BT30 9BN* Tel (028) 4482 1620 E-mail rab@mollan.net

MOLLER, George Brian. b 35. TCD BA60 MA64 Div Test 61 Lon Univ BD84. **d** 61 **p** 62. C Belfast St Pet *Conn* 61-64; C Larne and Inver 64-68; P-in-c Rathcoole 68-69; I 69-86; Dioc Dir Ords 82-92; I Belfast St Bart 86-01; Chapl Stranmillis Univ Coll Belf 88-01; Preb Conn Cathl 90-96; Treas 96; Prec 96-98; Dean 98-01; rtd 01. *Deneholme, 7 Sunningdale Park, Bangor BT20 4UU* Tel (028) 9145 5903 E-mail gb@moller2.plus.com

MOLLOY, Mrs Heather. b 54. Bradf Univ BTech76. **d** 95 **p** 96. OLM Harwood *Man* from 95. *7 Fellside, Bolton BL2 4HB* Tel (01204) 520395

MOLONEY, Charles Michael Stephen. b 81. Leeds Univ BA03 Cant Ch Ch Univ Coll QTS05. Ridley Hall Cam 07. **d** 09. C Retford *S'well* from 09. *East Retford Vicarage, 1 Chapelgate, Retford DN22 6PL*

MOLONY, Nicholas John. b 43. St Jo Coll Dur BA67 Birm Univ MA78 Fuller Th Sem California DMin06. Qu Coll Birm 67. **d** 70 **p** 71. C Beaconsfield *Ox* 70-75; P-in-c Chesham Ch Ch 75-80; TV Gt Chesham 80-81; P-in-c Weston Turville 81-90; P-in-c Stoke Mandeville 87-89; P-in-c Gt Marlow 90-93; P-in-c Bisham 90-93; TR Gt Marlow w Marlow Bottom, Lt Marlow and Bisham from 93. *The Rectory, The Causeway, Marlow SL7 2AA* Tel (01628) 482660 *or* 481806 E-mail nick.molony@btinternet.com

MONAGHAN, Mrs Hilary Alice. b 78. Edin Univ MA01 Cam Univ BA04. Ridley Hall Cam 02. **d** 06 **p** 07. C Gerrards Cross and Fulmer *Ox* from 06. *Church Office, St James's Church, Oxford Road, Gerrards Cross SL9 7DJ* Tel (01753) 883311 E-mail alice.monaghan@saintjames.org.uk

MONBERG, Ms Ulla Stefan. b 52. Copenhagen Univ BA79. Westcott Ho Cam 88. **d** 90 **p** 94. C Westmr St Jas *Lon* 90-94; Dean Women's Min and Area Dir of Ords Cen Lon 94-99; Dean Women's Min Kensington 94-99; C Paddington St Jo w St Mich 96-98; P-in-c S Kensington H Trin w All SS 98-02; Dir of Ords Two Cities Area 99-02; Denmark from 02; Dioc Adv for Women's Min *Eur* 04-05; Dioc Dir of Tr from 05. *Borgmester Jensens Alle 9, 2th, DK-2100 Copenhagen 0, Denmark* Tel (0045) 3526 0660 E-mail ullamonberg@msn.com

✠**MONDAL, The Rt Revd Barnabas Dwijen.** b 37. Dhaka Univ BA61 Serampore Univ BD64. Bp's Coll Calcutta 61. **d** 64 **p** 65 **c** 75. Barisal Bangladesh 64-67; Khulna 67-69; Rhode Is USA 69-70; Bollorepur 70-71; Thakurpukur 71-72; Prin Coll of Chr Th 72-74; Dhaka St Thos 74-75; Asst Bp Dhaka 75; Bp Dhaka and Moderator Ch of Bangladesh 75-03; rtd 03. *Merlin Apartment, 59/A-1 Barobagh, Dhaka 1216, Bangladesh* Tel (00880) (2) 805 1656 Mobile 172-031350

MONDON, Simon Charles. b 57. WEMTC. **d** 02 **p** 03. OLM Worfield *Heref* 02-09; V Goodrich, Marstow, Welsh Bicknor, Llangarron etc from 09. *The Vicarage, Llangrove, Ross-on-Wye HR9 6EZ* E-mail revsimon@btinternet.com

MONDS, Anthony John Beatty. b 53. Solicitor 77. **d** 97 **p** 00. OLM Queen Thorne *Sarum* 97-04; C Sherborne w Castleton, Lillington and Longburton 04-06; V Piddle Valley, Hilton, Cheselbourne etc from 06. *The Vicarage, Church Lane, Piddletrenthide, Dorchester DT2 7QY* Tel (01300) 348211 E-mail tony.monds@btinternet.com

MONEY, John Charles. b 69. Wycliffe Hall Ox 01. **d** 03 **p** 04. C Porchester *S'well* 03-06; TV Plymouth St Andr and Stonehouse *Ex* from 06. *88 Durnford Street, Stonehouse, Plymouth PL13 3QW* Tel (01752) 223774 Mobile 07711-285217 E-mail john.stjames@ntlworld.com

MONEY, Mrs Lynn Astrid. b 59. St Martin's Coll Lanc BEd80. WEMTC 03. **d** 06 **p** 07. C Letton w Staunton, Byford, Mansel Gamage etc *Heref* from 06. *St Mary's House, Staunton-on-Wye, Hereford HR4 7LT* Tel (01981) 500166 Mobile 07836-295627 E-mail curate@weobleyandstaunton.co.uk

MONGER, John Dennis. b 26. **d** 99 **p** 99. NSM Ewyas Harold w Dulas, Kenderchurch etc *Heref* 99-04; RD Abbeydore 00-02; rtd 04; Perm to Offic *Heref* from 04. *Chapel Cottage, Longtown, Hereford HR2 0LE* Tel (01873) 860306

MONK, Mrs Mary. b 38. CertEd58. S'wark Ord Course 85. **d** 88 **p** 94. NSM Lee Gd Shep w St Pet *S'wark* 88-99; NSM Harpenden St Jo *St Alb* 99-07; Perm to Offic from 07. *3 Hawthorn Close, Harpenden AL5 1HN* Tel (01582) 462057

MONK, Nicholas John. b 32. Westcott Ho Cam 61. **d** 63 **p** 64. C Bris H Cross Inns Court 63-67; C Stoke Bishop 67-69; V Swindon All SS 69-75; V Ashton Keynes w Leigh 75-87; P-in-c Minety w Oaksey 82-87; RD Malmesbury 85-88; V Ashton Keynes, Leigh and Minety 87-91; TR Swindon St Jo and St Andr 91-97; rtd 97; Perm to Offic *Heref* from 97. *The Riddings Cottage, Newcastle on Clun, Craven Arms SY7 8QT* Tel (01686) 670929

MONK, Paul Malcolm Spenser. b 65. Ex Univ BSc86 PhD90 Leeds Univ MA07 CChem MRSC. NOC 05. **d** 07 **p** 08. C

Oldham *Man* from 07. *46 Godson Street, Oldham OL1 2DB* Tel 0161-622 0753 Mobile 07854-776410 E-mail p.monk@mmu.ac.uk

MONK, Stephen David. b 74. Leuven Univ Belgium STB03. Qu Coll Birm 05. **d** 00 **p** 01. C Knighton St Mary Magd *Leic* 06-08; C Wigston Magna from 08. *8 Harrogate Way, Wigston LE18 3YB* Tel 0116-288 8806 Mobile 07967-825277 E-mail rev.stephenmonk@btinternet.com

MONKHOUSE, Henry Alistair. b 34. **d** 99 **p** 00. OLM Quidenham Gp *Nor* 99-05; Perm to Offic from 05. *Wildwood, Mill Road, Old Buckenham, Attleborough NR17 1SG* Tel (01953) 860845 E-mail henrym45@btinternet.com

MONKHOUSE, William Stanley. b 50. Qu Coll Cam BA72 MA76 MB, BChir75 Nottm Univ PhD85 MA06. EMMTC 04. **d** 06 **p** 07. C Wirksworth *Derby* 06-08; P-in-c Old Brampton 08-09; P-in-c Gt Barlow 08-09; P-in-c Old Brampton and Great Barlow from 09; Asst Dir of Ords from 09. *The Rectory, 25 Oldridge Close, Chesterfield S40 4UF* Tel (01246) 558112 Mobile 07739-515895 E-mail stanley.monkhouse@btinternet.com

MONKS, Ian Kay. b 36. K Coll Lon BA60 Lon Inst of Educn PGCE61. Oak Hill NSM Course 90. **d** 93 **p** 94. NSM Woodford Bridge *Chelmsf* 93-06; Perm to Offic from 06. *46 Summit Drive, Woodford Green IG8 8QP* Tel (020) 8550 2390

MONMOUTH, Archdeacon of. *See* PAIN, The Ven Richard Edward

MONMOUTH, Bishop of. *See* WALKER, The Rt Revd Edward William Murray

MONMOUTH, Dean of. *See* FENWICK, The Very Revd Richard David

MONTAGUE (née LAIDLAW), Mrs Juliet. b 52. Nottm Univ BTh82. Linc Th Coll 78. **dss** 82 **d** 87 **p** 94. Gainsborough All SS *Linc* 82-86; Chapl Linc Cathl and Linc Colls of FE 86-92; Dn-in-c Gedney Hill and Whaplode Drove 92-94; P-in-c 94-99; P-in-c Crawley and Littleton and Sparsholt w Lainston *Win* 99-03; R 03-08; R Downs Benefice from 08. *The Rectory, Church Lane, Littleton, Winchester SO22 6QY* Tel (01962) 881898 E-mail revdjuliet@montague.me.uk

MONTAGUE-YOUENS, Canon Hubert Edward. b 30. Ripon Hall Ox 55. **d** 58 **p** 59. C Redditch St Steph *Worc* 58-59; C Halesowen 59-62; V Kempsey 62-69; V Kidderminster St Geo 69-72; R Ribbesford w Bewdley and Dowles 72-81; RD Kidderminster 74-81; Hon Can Worc Cathl 78-81; TR Bridport *Sarum* 81-86; RD Lyme Bay 82-86; V Easebourne *Chich* 86-89; Chapl K Edw VII Hosp Midhurst 86-89; rtd 89; Perm to Offic *Worc* from 89; *Glouc* 89-95 and from 98; P-in-c Twyning *Glouc* 96-98. *6 Harbour View, Bredon Road, Tewkesbury GL20 5AZ* Tel (01684) 292363

MONTEITH, David Robert Malvern. b 68. St Jo Coll Dur BSc89 Nottm Univ BTh92 MA93. St Jo Coll Nottm 90. **d** 93 **p** 94. C Kings Heath *Birm* 93-97; C St Martin-in-the-Fields *Lon* 97-02; P-in-c S Wimbledon H Trin and St Pet *S'wark* 02-09; AD Merton 04-09; Can Res and Chan Leic Cathl from 09. *39 Meadowcourt Road, Leicester LE2 2PF* Tel 0116-248 7400 Mobile 07952-238291 E-mail david.monteith@leccofe.org

MONTGOMERIE, Alexander (Sandy). b 47. St Jo Coll Nottm 89. **d** 94 **p** 96. NSM Irvine St Andr LEP *Glas* from 94; NSM Ardrossan from 94. *105 Sharphill Road, Saltcoats KA21 5QU* Tel and fax (01294) 465193 E-mail sandy.montgomerie@btinternet.com

MONTGOMERIE, Andrew Simon. b 60. Keble Coll Ox BA82. Ridley Hall Cam 83. **d** 85 **p** 86. C Childwall All SS *Liv* 85-87; C Yardley St Edburgha *Birm* 87-90; TV Solihull 90-96; V Balsall Common 96-05; P-in-c Eyam *Derby* from 05; C Baslow w Curbar and Stoney Middleton from 06; RD Bakewell and Eyam from 07. *The Rectory, Church Street, Eyam, Hope Valley S32 5QH* Tel (01433) 630821 E-mail asmontgomerie@hotmail.co.uk

MONTGOMERY, Canon Anthony Alan. b 33. Trin Hall Cam BA56. Edin Th Coll 56. **d** 58 **p** 59. C Dumfries *Glas* 58-63; P-in-c Airdrie 63-66; R 66-68; Asst Chapl Gordonstoun Sch 68-93; Can St Andr Cathl Inverness from 81; rtd 93. *Easter Hillside, Mosstowie, Elgin IV30 8XE* Tel and fax (01343) 850282

MONTGOMERY, Ian David. b 44. St Andr Univ LLB66 Univ of the South (USA) DMin02 FCA69. Wycliffe Hall Ox 71. **d** 75 **p** 76. C Fulham St Dionis Parson's Green *Lon* 75-78; Chapl Amherst Coll USA 78-83; R New Orleans St Phil 83-92; R Nashville St Bart 92-97; R Menasha St Thos 97-09; rtd 09. *26 Gaskill Road, Chester VT 05143, USA* E-mail frianm@aol.com

MONTGOMERY (née YOUATT), Mrs Jennifer Alison. b 49. St Aid Coll Dur BSc70 Homerton Coll Cam PGCE71. NOC 89. **d** 92 **p** 94. NSM Ripon H Trin from 92; Warden of Readers from 99. *Washington House, Littlethorpe, Ripon HG4 3LJ* Tel (01765) 605276 *or* tel and fax 690930 E-mail montgomery@littlethorpe97.freeserve.co.uk

MONTGOMERY, Jennifer Susan. b 54. QUB MB, BCh77 Leeds Univ MA05. NOC 02. **d** 05 **p** 06. NSM Ackworth *Wakef* from 05. *37 Highfield Road, Pontefract WF8 4LL* Tel (01977) 702726 Mobile 07780-764233 E-mail jsm1954@hotmail.com

MONTGOMERY, Laura Alice. b 77. Lon Bible Coll BTh99. St Jo Coll Nottm MTh09. **d** 09. C Newton *Liv* from 09. *St John's Vicarage, 63 Market Street, Newton-le-Willows WA12 9BS* Tel (01925) 223727 Mobile 07511-030948
E-mail la.monty@yahoo.com
MONTGOMERY, Pembroke John Charles. b 24. Codrington Coll Barbados. **d** 53 **p** 55. C St Geo Cathl St Vincent 55-73; R Biabou 56-65; R Calliaqua 65-73; Can Kingstown Cathl 63-73; P-in-c Derby St Jas 73-74; V 74-90; rtd 90. *39 Church Street, Tutbury, Burton-on-Trent DE13 9JE* Tel (01283) 814887
MONTGOMERY, Rachel. *See* TREWEEK, The Ven Rachel
MONTGOMERY, Stanley. b 18. Lich Th Coll. **d** 52 **p** 53. P-in-c Hitcham w Lt Finborough, Kettlebaston etc 93-95; Perm to Offic *St E* 95-05. *34 Drovers Rise, Stanton, Bury St Edmunds IP31 2BW* Tel (01359) 250359
E-mail freddie@fmontgomery.fslife.co.uk
MONTGOMERY, Canon Thomas Charles Osborne. b 59. Edin Univ BD81. Edin Th Coll 77. **d** 82 **p** 83. C Glas St Mary 82-85; C Dumfries 85-88; R Hamilton 88-96; Can St Mary's Cathl from 94; R Glas St Marg from 96. *St Margaret's Rectory, 22 Monreith Road, Glasgow G43 2NY* Tel and fax 0141-632 3292 *or* tel 636 1131 E-mail stmargaretsnewlands@tiscali.co.uk
MONTGOMERY, Canon Timothy Robert. b 59. Hull Univ BA82 Cam Univ PGCE83. EAMTC 90. **d** 93 **p** 94. Dir Romsey Mill Community Cen *Ely* 93-94; NSM Cambridge St Phil 93-96; Warden Kepplewray Cen Broughton-in-Furness 96-00; NSM Kendal St Thos *Carl* 96-00; V from 00; Hon Can Carl Cathl from 06. *St Thomas's Vicarage, South View Lane, Kendal LA9 4QN* Tel (01539) 729617 *or* 730683 Fax 729010
E-mail vicar@saintthomaskendal.net
MONTGOMERY, Archdeacon of. *See* THELWELL, The Ven John Berry
MONTROSE, Michelle Ann. b 57. NOC 05. **d** 08. NSM W Derby St Mary *Liv* 08-09; NSM W Derby St Mary and St Jas from 09. *1 Highfield View, Liverpool L13 3BP* Tel 0151-220 1746 Mobile 07528-331316 E-mail michelleamontrose@yahoo.co.uk
MOODY, Christopher John Everard. b 51. New Coll Ox BA72 Lon Univ MSc90. Cuddesdon Coll BA74. **d** 75 **p** 76. C Fulham All SS *Lon* 75-79; C Surbiton St Andr and St Mark *S'wark* 79-82; Chapl K Coll Lon 82-87; V S Lambeth St Anne and All SS *S'wark* 87-95; RD Lambeth 90-95; P-in-c Market Harborough *Leic* 95-97; P-in-c Market Harborough Transfiguration 95-97; V Market Harborough and The Transfiguration and The 95-97; Hon Can Leic Cathl 04-05; V Greenwich St Alfege *S'wark* from 05. *The Vicarage, Park Vista, London SE10 9LZ* Tel (020) 8858 6828
E-mail chrisjemoody@btinternet.com
MOODY, Colin John. b 36. Chich Th Coll 61. **d** 63 **p** 64. C Hove All SS *Chich* 63-69; C Dulwich St Barn *S'wark* 69-70; Perm to Offic *Bris* 70-71; *Chich* 72-78 and from 90; Lic to Offic *Ely* 78-89; rtd 01. *11 Hewitts, Henfield BN5 9DT* Tel and fax (01273) 495062
MOODY, Ms Elizabeth Jane. b 61. Hull Univ BA82 Westmr Coll Ox PGCE84. Ridley Hall Cam 00. **d** 02 **p** 03. C Uxbridge *Lon* 02-05; C Hanwell St Mary w St Chris from 05. *St Christopher's Vicarage, 4 Hillyard Road, London W7 1BH* Tel (020) 8578 2796 Mobile 07796-988302 E-mail lizmoody@blueyonder.co.uk
MOODY, Preb George Henry. b 27. ACIS56 ARCA68. Cranmer Hall Dur 69. **d** 71 **p** 72. C Marske in Cleveland *York* 71 74; Chapl to the Deaf *Lich* 74-89; Preb Lich Cathl 83-89; rtd 89; Perm to Offic *York* from 90. *21 Priestcrofts, Marske-by-the-Sea, Redcar TS11 7HW* Tel (01642) 489660
MOODY, Canon Ivor Robert. b 57. K Coll Lon BD80 AKC Anglia Ruskin Univ MA03. Coll of Resurr Mirfield. **d** 82 **p** 83. C Leytonstone St Marg w St Columba *Chelmsf* 82-85; C Leigh-on-Sea St Marg 85-88; V Tilbury Docks 88-96; Chapl Anglia Ruskin Univ from 96; Hon Can Chelmsf Cathl from 09. *4 Bishops Court Gardens, Chelmsford CM2 6AZ* Tel (01245) 261700 *or* 08451-967722 E-mail ivor.moody@anglia.ac.uk
MOODY, John Kelvin. b 30. St Fran Coll Brisbane ThL55. **d** 56 **p** 57. C Warwick Australia 56-57; C Southport 57-58; C Dalby 58-61; C Earl's Court St Cuth w St Matthias *Lon* 61-64; Chapl Ankara *Eur* 64-69; Chapl Istanbul 64-66; Chapl Palma 69-75; Chapl Tangier 75-79; Can Gib Cathl 74-79; Hon Can from 79; Australia from 79; rtd 01. *1 Short Street, Watson's Bay NSW 2030, Australia* Tel (0061) (2) 9337 2871
E-mail jm986672@bigpond.net.au
MOOKERJI, Michael Manoje. b 45. Baring Union Coll Punjab BSc69. Ridley Hall Cam 83. **d** 85 **p** 86. C Heanor *Derby* 85-92; V Codnor and Loscoe 92-93; V Codnor 93-02; V Winshill from 02. *The Vicarage, 54 Mill Hill Lane, Burton-on-Trent DE15 0BB* Tel (01283) 545043
MOON, Arthur Thomas. b 22. ACP53 LCP56. Sarum Th Coll 65. **d** 66 **p** 67. C Fulwood Ch Ch *Blackb* 66-71; Hon C Bispham 71-80; C 80-87; rtd 87; Perm to Offic *Blackb* from 87. *15 Kirkstone Drive, Thornton-Cleveleys FY5 1QQ* Tel (01253) 853521
MOON, Sister Catherine Joy. b 48. LRAM68 ARCM69. Gen Th Sem NY 84. **d** 84 **p** 85. USA 84-02; CSF from 87; Chapl

Ashworth Hosp Maghull from 04. *Liverpool Parish Church, Old Churchyard, Liverpool L2 8TZ* Tel 07906-365962 (mobile)
MOON, John Charles. b 23. Sarum Th Coll 49. **d** 51 **p** 52. C Bottesford *Linc* 51-54; C Habrough 54-55; V Immingham 55-61; V Weaste *Man* 61-67; V Spalding St Jo *Linc* 67-82; V Spalding St Jo w Deeping St Nicholas 82-86; rtd 86; Perm to Offic *Linc* 87-02. *14 Harrox Road, Moulton, Spalding PE12 6PR* Tel (01406) 370111
MOON, Philip. b 59. CCC Ox BA80 Warwick Univ PhD92. Wycliffe Hall Ox BA82. **d** 01 **p** 02. C Otley *Bradf* 01-05; V Lt Aston *Lich* from 05. *The Vicarage, 3 Walsall Road, Little Aston, Sutton Coldfield B74 3BD* Tel 0121-353 0798
E-mail familyofmoon@aol.com
MOON, Philip Russell. b 56. Em Coll Cam BA78 MA81 Reading Univ PGCE79. Wycliffe Hall Ox BA82. **d** 85 **p** 86. C Crowborough *Chich* 85-87; Hd of CYFA (CPAS) 87-94; V Lowestoft Ch Ch *Nor* 94-04; P-in-c Hove Bp Hannington Memorial Ch *Chich* 04-06; V from 06; RD Hove 05-08. *82 Holmes Avenue, Hove BN3 7LD* Tel (01273) 732821
MOON, Thomas Arnold. b 24. Lon Univ BA51. Oak Hill Th Coll 49. **d** 52 **p** 53. C Fazakerley Em *Liv* 52-56; V Everton St Benedict 56-70; V Formby St Luke 70-95; rtd 95; Perm to Offic *Liv* from 95. *8 Harington Road, Formby, Liverpool L37 1NU* Tel (01704) 872249
MOONEY, Canon Paul Gerard. b 58. St Patr Coll Maynooth BD84 Asian Cen for Th Studies and Miss Seoul ThM92 Protestant Th Faculty Brussels DrTheol02. **d** 84 **p** 85. In RC Ch 84-90; Chapl Miss to Seamen Korea 90-94; Hon Can Pusan from 94; Chapl Antwerp Miss to Seamen 94-97; Asst Chapl Antwerp St Boniface *Eur* 94-97; C Galway w Kilcummin *T, K & A* 97-98; I New w Old Ross, Whitechurch, Fethard etc *C & O* 98-07; Hon Chapl New Ross and Waterford Miss to Seamen 98-07; Prec Ferns Cathl 01-07; Adn Ferns 02-07; Chapl Seoul Cathl Korea from 07. *3 Chong-dong, Jung-Ku, Seoul 120-100, South Korea* Tel (0082) (2) 739 0785 E-mail pgmoon@hotmail.com
MOOR, Simon Alan. b 65. Nottm Univ BTh93. Linc Th Coll 90. **d** 93 **p** 94. C Skegness and Winthorpe *Linc* 93-96; C Airedale w Fryston *Wakef* 96-98; V Hoylandswaine and Silkstone w Stainborough from 98; Bp's Adv for Ecum Affairs from 08. *The Vicarage, 12 High Street, Silkstone, Barnsley S75 4JN* Tel and fax (01226) 790232 E-mail samoor@onetel.com
MOORCROFT, Steven James. b 73. Wye Coll Lon BSc95. Cranmer Hall Dur 05. **d** 07 **p** 08. C Kendal St Thos *Carl* 07-09. *Little Pendene, Fore Street, Grampound, Truro TR2 4RS* Tel (01726) 882242 E-mail s.j.moorcroft@btinternet.com
MOORE, Albert William (Bill). b 47. WMMTC 91. **d** 94 **p** 95. C Hobs Moat *Birm* 94-98; V Dosthill 98-06; V Hill from 06. *61 Mere Green Road, Sutton Coldfield B75 5BW* Tel 0121-308 0074
MOORE, Andrew Jonathan. b 57. York Univ BA82 Wycliffe Hall Ox BA84 MA89 Worc Coll Ox DPhil99. **d** 86 **p** 86. C Camberwell St Jo Australia 86-87; Assoc P S Yarra Ch Ch 87-90; Asst/Acting Chapl Worc Coll Ox 91-94; Chapl Jes Coll Ox 94-99; Voc Adv *Ox* 98-04; Dir of Ords from 04; Hon Chapl Cen for Mediaeval and Renaissance Studies Ox 99-04; Research Fell Regent's Park Coll Ox 01-04; Chapl St Pet Coll Ox 04-07. *Theology Faculty, 41 St Giles, Oxford OX1 3LW* Tel (01865) 270731 E-mail andrew.moore@spc.ox.ac.uk
MOORE, Anthony Harry. b 34. Westcott Ho Cam 88. **d** 90 **p** 91. C Eyke w Bromeswell, Rendlesham, Tunstall etc *St E* 90 93; V Aldeburgh w Hazlewood 93-02; rtd 02; Perm to Offic *St E* and *Chelmsf* from 02. *5 Kings Meadow, Great Cornard, Sudbury CO10 0HP* Tel (01787) 377967
MOORE, Anthony Michael. b 71. Ex Univ BA94 Leeds Univ BA98 MA99. Coll of Resurr Mirfield 96. **d** 99 **p** 00. C Carnforth *Blackb* 99-03; Fell and Past Tutor Coll of Resurr Mirfield 03-04; C Wilton Place St Paul *Lon* 04-07; Chapl R Academy of Music 04-07; Chapl and Fell St Cath Coll Cam from 07; CMP from 07. *St Catharine's College, Trumpington Street, Cambridge CB2 1RL* Tel (01223) 338300 E-mail amm217@cam.ac.uk
MOORE, Anthony Richmond. b 36. Clare Coll Cam BA59 MA63. Linc Th Coll 59. **d** 61 **p** 62. C Roehampton H Trin *S'wark* 61-66; C New Eltham All SS 66-70; P Missr Blackbird Leys CD *Ox* 70-81; Dioc Ecum Officer 80-98; TV Dorchester 81-93; V Enstone and Heythrop 93-01; rtd 01; Perm to Offic *Ox* from 01. *13 Cobden Crescent, Oxford OX1 4LJ* Tel (01865) 244673 E-mail moore.t@which.net
MOORE, Arlene. b 64. Dundee Univ BSc87 N Coll of Educn PGCE90 TCD BTh95. CITC 92. **d** 95 **p** 96. C Portadown St Mark *Arm* 95-99; Perm to Offic *Sheff* 99-02 and 03-09; C Crookes St Thos 02-03; Chapl Belfast Health and Soc Care Trust from 09; C Monkstown *Conn* from 09. *Musgrave Park Hospital, 20 Stockman's Lane, Belfast BT9 7JB* Tel (028) 9090 2000
MOORE, Arthur Lewis. b 33. Dur Univ BA58 PhD64. Cranmer Hall Dur. **d** 62 **p** 63. C Stone *Roch* 62-66; C Clevedon St Andr *B & W* 66-68; Chapl Wycliffe Hall Ox 68-70; Vice-Prin 70-83; P-in-c Ampfield *Win* 83-84; V Hursley and Ampfield 84-92; TV Ewyas Harold w Dulas, Kenderchurch etc *Heref* 92-94; P-in-c

94-98; rtd 98. *2 Tollstone Way, Grosmont, Abergavenny NP7 8ER* Tel (01981) 240473

MOORE, Canon Bernard Geoffrey. b 27. New Coll Ox BA47 MA52. Ely Th Coll 49. **d** 51 **p** 52. C Chorley St Pet *Blackb* 51-54; Bp's Dom Chapl 54-55; C-in-c Blackpool St Mich CD 55-67; Chapl Victoria Hosp Blackpool 58-67; V Morecambe St Barn *Blackb* 67-81; R Standish 81-88; Hon Can Blackb Cathl 86-92; RD Chorley 86-92; V Charnock Richard 88-92; rtd 92; Perm to Offic *Ex* from 92; *Carl* from 01; *Win* from 00. *29 Wiltshire Close, Exeter EX4 1LU* Tel (01392) 258686

MOORE, Bernard George. b 32. Qu Coll Birm 57. **d** 60 **p** 62. C Middlesbrough St Columba *York* 60-62; S Africa 62-70; Chapl RN 70-74; C Milton *Portsm* 74-76; New Zealand from 76; rtd 97. *45 Feasegate Street, Manurewa, Manukau 2102, New Zealand* Tel (0064) (9) 267 6924 E-mail freesaxon2000@yahoo.com

✠**MOORE, The Rt Revd Bruce Macgregor.** b 31. Univ of NZ BA55. Coll of Resurr Mirfield. **d** 57 **p** 58 **c** 92. C Blackpool St Steph *Blackb* 57-61; New Zealand from 61; Hon Can Auckland 78-96; Adn Manukau 81-90; Asst Bp Auckland 92-97. *5 Pokaka Crescent, Taupo 3330, New Zealand* Tel (0064) (7) 378 4849 E-mail brucemoore@xtra.co.nz

MOORE, Caroline Judith. *See* FALKINGHAM, Mrs Caroline Judith

MOORE, Charles David. b 59. Dundee Univ BSc82 BArch85 Open Univ MA96 RIBA86. St Jo Coll Nottm 91. **d** 93 **p** 94. C Deane *Man* 93-97; Crosslinks 98-02; R and Sub Dean Mutare Zimbabwe 98-02; R Bermondsey St Mary w St Olave, St Jo etc *S'wark* from 02. *The Rectory, 193 Bermondsey Street, London SE1 3UW* Tel (020) 7357 0984

MOORE, Christopher Kevin William. b 69. Ox Brookes Univ BSc92 Bris Univ BA01 MRICS95. Bris Bapt Coll 04. **d** 09. C Tenbury *Heref* from 09. *Deepcroft Cottage, Worcester Road, Newnham Bridge, Tenbury Wells WR15 8JA* Tel (01584) 781157 E-mail chris@cm5j.com

MOORE, Preb Clive Granville. b 31. St Pet Hall Ox BA54 MA58. Wycliffe Hall Ox 54. **d** 55 **p** 56. C Newbarns w Hawcoat *Carl* 55-57; CF 57-61; Chapl Joyce Green Hosp Dartford 61-69; R Stone 61-69; R Radstock *B & W* 69-71; P-in-c Writhlington 69-71; R Radstock w Writhlington 71-83; RD Midsomer Norton 81-83; R S Petherton w the Seavingtons 83-95; RD Crewkerne 83-92; RD Crewkerne and Ilminster 93; Preb Wells Cathl 90-95; rtd 95; Perm to Offic *B & W* from 95. *Mowries Stable, West Street, Somerton TA11 6NA* Tel (01458) 274649

MOORE, Canon Colin Frederick. b 49. CITC 69. **d** 72 **p** 73. C Drumglass w Moygashel *Arm* 72-80; I Newtownhamilton w Ballymoyer and Belleek from 80; Hon V Choral Arm Cathl 85-96; Can and Preb from 97; Asst Dioc and Prov Registrar 96-09; Dioc and Prov Registrar from 09. *71 Ballymoyer Road, Whitecross, Armagh BT60 2LA* Tel (028) 3750 7256

MOORE, Darren Lee. b 73. Kingston Univ BEng95. Oak Hill Th Coll BA01. **d** 01 **p** 02. C Camberwell All SS *S'wark* 01-04; P-in-c Tranmere St Cath *Ches* 04-07; V from 07. *St Catherine's Vicarage, 39 Westbank Road, Birkenhead CH42 7JP* Tel 0151-652 7379 E-mail darren@stcatherinestranmere.co.uk

MOORE, Darren Richard. b 70. Univ of Wales (Abth) BD91 Hull Univ PGCE97 St Jo Coll York MA(Ed)03 Leeds Univ MA04. Coll of Resurr Mirfield 02. **d** 04 **p** 05. C Scarborough St Martin *York* 04-07; R Brayton 07-09; Chapl Ranby Ho Sch Retford from 09. *Ranby House School, Retford DN22 8HX* Tel (01777) 703138 Mobile 07745-296406 E-mail chaplain@ranbyhouseschool.co.uk

MOORE, David James Paton. b 60. Sheff Univ BEng82. Cranmer Hall Dur 88. **d** 91 **p** 92. C Pemberton St Mark Newtown *Liv* 91-94; C St Helens St Helen 94-97; V Canonbury St Steph *Lon* 97-07; NSM Easton H Trin w St Gabr and St Lawr and St Jude *Bris* from 08. *St Michael's Vicarage, St Michael's Court, Kingswood, Bristol BS15 1BE* Tel 0117-967 9446

MOORE, David Leonard. b 51. **d** 80 **p** 82. Hon C Brixton St Matt *S'wark* 80-82; C 82-84; TV Bris St Agnes and St Simon w St Werburgh 84-86; Perm to Offic *Bris* 86-88 and *Blackb* from 88. *154 Victoria Road, Fulwood, Preston PR2 8NQ*

MOORE, David Metcalfe. b 41. Hull Univ BA64 PhD69. Trin Coll Bris 76. **d** 78 **p** 79. C Marple All SS *Ches* 78-82; V Loudwater *Ox* 82-90; V Chilwell *S'well* 90-93; rtd 93; Perm to Offic *Ely* from 05. *12 Rhugarve Gardens, Linton, Cambridge CB21 4LX* Tel (01223) 894315

MOORE, David Roy. b 39. Clare Coll Cam BA61. Ripon Hall Ox 61. **d** 63 **p** 64. C Melton Mowbray w Thorpe Arnold *Leic* 63-66; C St Steph Walbrook and St Swithun etc *Lon* 66-72; Dep Dir The Samaritans 66-72; Public Preacher *S'wark* 72-77; C Daybrook 77-80; V 80-87; V Ham St Andr *S'wark* 87-99; P-in-c Rothbury *Newc* 99-04; rtd 04; P-in-c Kneesall w Laxton and Wellow *S'well* 04-07. *Lily Cottage, Far Back Lane, Farnsfield, Newark NG22 8JX*

MOORE, Donald John. b 31. Chich Th Coll 86. **d** 87 **p** 88. C Uckfield *Chich* 87-88; C Southwick St Mich 88-90; Bermuda from 90; Asst P St Geo 90-97; P-in-c St Dav 90-97; Chapl

Brendan's Psychiatric Hosp 92-97; rtd 97. *PO Box FL 239, Flatts FL BX, Bermuda* Tel (001) (441) 236 8360

MOORE, Douglas Gregory. b 49. Bris Univ BA71 CertEd72. Coll of Resurr Mirfield 87. **d** 89 **p** 90. C Hessle *York* 89-93; P-in-c Micklefield w Aberford 93-95; V Aberford w Micklefield 95-04; P-in-c Darwen St Cuth w Tockholes St Steph *Blackb* from 04. *21 The Meadows, Darwen BB3 0PF* Tel (01254) 771196

MOORE, Edward James. b 32. TD85. TCD BA54 MA59. **d** 56 **p** 57. C Belfast St Luke *Conn* 56-59; CF 59-62; C Dunmurry *Conn* 62-64; P-in-c Kilmakee 64-70; I Belfast H Trin 70-80; I Jordanstown w Monkstown 80-91; I Jordanstown 91-97; Chapl Ulster Poly 80-84; Chapl Ulster Univ 84-88; CF (ACF) 66-70 and 88-97; CF (TAVR) 70-88; Can Belf Cathl 89-97; rtd 97. *16 Langford Close, Carrickfergus BT38 8HG* Tel (028) 9336 7209 E-mail ejm@ejmoore.plus.com

MOORE, James. *See* MOORE, Edward James

MOORE, Geoffrey David. b 51. Poly Cen Lon BA73. ERMC 04. **d** 07 **p** 08. NSM Brackley St Pet w St Jas from 07. *61 Westfield Avenue, Deanshanger, Milton Keynes MK19 6LH* Tel (01908) 563530 E-mail geoff@ccvp.co.uk

MOORE, Geoffrey Robert. b 46. WEMTC 03. **d** 06 **p** 07. NSM Upton-on-Severn, Ripple, Earls Croome etc *Worc* from 06. *12 Hill View Gardens, Upton-upon-Severn WR8 0QJ* Tel (01684) 594531 Mobile 07876-162402

MOORE, Mrs Gillian Mary. NTMTC. **d** 09. NSM Harwich Peninsula *Chelmsf* from 09. *15 Lushington Road, Manningtree CO11 1EE*

MOORE, Henry James William. b 33. TCD BA55 MA70. **d** 56 **p** 57. C Mullabrack *Arm* 56-61; C Drumglass 61-63; I Clogherny 63-81; I Ballinderry, Tamlaght and Arboe 81-08; Can Arm Cathl 90-08; Chan 98-01; Prec 01-08; rtd 08. *20 Laragh Road, Beragh, Omagh BT79 0TH*

✠**MOORE, The Rt Revd Henry Wylie.** b 23. Liv Univ BCom50 Leeds Univ MA72. Wycliffe Hall Ox 50. **d** 52 **p** 53. C Farnworth *Liv* 52-54; C Middleton *Man* 54-56; CMS 56-60; Iran 57-60; R Burnage St Marg *Man* 60-63; R Middleton 60-74; Home Sec CMS 74-80; Exec Sec CMS 80-83; Bp Cyprus and the Gulf 83-86; Gen Sec CMS 86-90; rtd 90; Asst Bp Dur 90-94; Perm to Offic *Heref* from 94. *Fern Hill Cottage, Hopesay, Craven Arms SY7 8HD* Tel (01588) 660248

MOORE, Preb Hugh Desmond. b 37. St Cath Soc Ox BA58 MA64. St Steph Ho Ox 58. **d** 61 **p** 62. C Kingston St Luke *S'wark* 61-68; Asst Chapl Lon Univ 68-70; Chapl Edgware Community Hosp 70-92; Chapl Wellhouse NHS Trust 92-99; V Hendon St Alphage *Lon* from 70; AD W Barnet 85-90; Preb St Paul's Cathl from 95. *The Vicarage, Montrose Avenue, Edgware HA8 0DN* Tel (020) 8952 4611 E-mail hugh.moore@tesco.net

MOORE, Ivan. MA BTh. **d** 90 **p** 91. C Knock *D & D* 90-93; I Taney *D & G* 97-99; Chapl Bancroft's Sch Woodford Green from 99. *41 Wynndale Road, London E18 1DY* Tel (020) 8559 2791 *or* 8505 4821 Fax 8559 0032

MOORE, Canon James Kenneth. b 37. AKC62. St Boniface Warminster 62. **d** 63 **p** 64. C W Hartlepool St Oswald *Dur* 63-66; C-in-c Manor Park CD *Sheff* 66-76; TV Sheff Manor 76-78; R Frecheville and Hackenthorpe 78-87; V Bilham 87-91; V Sheff St Oswald 91-02; Hon Can Sheff Cathl 93-02; rtd 02; Perm to Offic *Sheff* from 02. *115 Greenhill Main Road, Sheffield S8 7RG* Tel 0114-283 9634

MOORE (formerly BEVAN), Ms Janet Mary. b 46. Bris Poly CertEd86. WMMTC. **d** 98 **p** 99. C Bishop's Cleeve *Glouc* 98-02; V Overbury w Teddington, Alstone etc *Worc* 02-08; Faith Co-ord Surrey Police *Guildf* from 08. *3 Southbury, Lawn Road, Guildford GU2 4DD* E-mail therevjan@btinternet.com

MOORE, Janis. **d** 05 **p** 06. OLM Bridport *Sarum* from 05. *61 North Allington, Bridport DT6 5DZ* Tel (01305) 425644

MOORE, John. ERMC. **d** 08 **p** 09. C Paris St Mich *Eur* from 08. *32 avenue Bugeaud, 75116 Paris, France*

MOORE, John. b 22. St Aid Birkenhead 54. **d** 57 **p** 58. C Glenavy w Tunny and Crumlin *Conn* 57-59; I Kingscourt w Syddan *M & K* 60-63; C Carnmoney *Conn* 63-65; P-in-c Templepatrick w Donegore 65-68; I Templepatrick 68-85; rtd 85. *13 Brookhill House, 2 Newmills Road Lower, Coleraine BT52 2JR* Tel (028) 7032 6753 E-mail jack@cuthona.fsnet.co.uk

MOORE, John. b 26. Univ of Wales (Lamp) BA51. Oak Hill Th Coll 51. **d** 53 **p** 54. C Illogan *Truro* 53-57; C Margate H Trin *Cant* 57-58; C Abingdon w Shippon *Ox* 58-67; V Retford St Sav *S'well* 67-73; R Aspenden and Layston w Buntingford *St Alb* 73-86; V Stanstead Abbots 86-91; rtd 91; Perm to Offic *Ox* from 95. *20 Radley Road, Abingdon OX14 3PQ* Tel (01235) 532518

MOORE, John Arthur. b 33. Cuddesdon Coll 70. **d** 71 **p** 72. Hon C Gt Burstead *Chelmsf* 71-74; Chapl Barnard Castle Sch 74-97; ‚rtd 97; Perm to Offic *Dur* from 97 and *Ripon* from 02. *39 Woodside, Barnard Castle DL12 8DY* Tel (01833) 690947

MOORE, John Cecil. b 37. TCD BA61 MA67 BD69. CITC 62. **d** 62 **p** 63. C Belfast St Matt *Conn* 62-65; C Holywood *D & D* 65-70; I Ballyphilip w Ardquin 70-77; I Mt Merrion 77-79; I Donaghcloney w Waringstown 79-02; Treas Dromore Cathl

90-93; Chan 93-02; rtd 02. *22 Kensington Court, Dollingstown, Craigavon BT66 7HU* Tel (028) 3832 1606
E-mail johncmoore@talktalk.net

MOORE, John David. b 30. St Chad's Coll Dur BA54 DipEd56. **d** 56 **p** 57. C Wallsend St Pet *Newc* 56-60; C Leamington Priors All SS *Cov* 60-62; V Longford 62-75; P-in-c Nuneaton St Mary 75-77; V 77-83; V St Ives *Ely* 83-00; rtd 00; Perm to Offic *Chelmsf* from 01. *25 Felmongers, Harlow CM20 3DH* Tel (01279) 436496 Mobile 07890-976056 E-mail frjdavid@aol.com

MOORE, John Henry. b 35. Nottm Univ BMus56 CertEd57 MA61. EMMTC 87. **d** 90 **p** 91. NSM Gotham *S'well* 90-95; NSM Kingston and Ratcliffe-on-Soar 90-95; NSM Bunny w Bradmore 95-00; P-in-c 97-00; rtd 00. *19 Hall Drive, Gotham, Nottingham NG11 0JT* Tel 0115-983 0670
E-mail john@moorerev.freeserve.co.uk

MOORE, John Keith. b 26. Sarum & Wells Th Coll 78. **d** 81 **p** 82. NSM Guildf All SS 81-86; NSM Guildf H Trin w St Mary 86-94; Dean of Chapter 90-94; Perm to Offic *Chich* 94-06 and *Guildf* from 94. *4 Grover's Manor, Wood Road, Hindhead GU26 6JP* Tel (01428) 605871

MOORE, John Michael. b 48. Em Coll Cam BA70 MA73. Cuddesdon Coll 72. **d** 74 **p** 75. C Almondbury *Wakef* 74-78; TV Basingstoke *Win* 78-88; P-in-c Southampton St Alb 88-91; V Swaythling 91-99; rtd 99; Chapl St Jo Win Charity from 99. *13 Priors Way, Winchester SO22 4HQ* Tel (01962) 862341 *or* 854226 Fax 840602 E-mail office@stjohnswinchester.co.uk

MOORE, Canon John Richard. b 35. Lambeth MA01. St Jo Coll Nottm 56. **d** 59 **p** 60. C Northwood Em *Lon* 59-63; V Burton Dassett *Cov* 63-66; Dioc Youth Chapl 63-71; Dir Lindley Lodge Educn Trust Nuneaton 71-82; TR Kinson *Sarum* 82-88; Gen Dir CPAS 88-96; Hon Can Cov Cathl 95-01; Internat Dir ICS 96-01; rtd 01; Perm to Offic *Cov* from 01. *26 Jourdain Park, Heathcote, Warwick CV34 6FJ* Tel (01926) 429299

MOORE, John Richard. b 45. Linc Th Coll 80. **d** 82 **p** 83. C Gt Grimsby St Mary and St Jas *Linc* 82-86; V Skirbeck Quarter 86-95; P-in-c Coningsby w Tattershall 95-99; R 99-06; R Bain Valley Gp from 06. *The Rectory, 22 High Street, Coningsby, Lincoln LN4 4RA* Tel (01526) 342223

MOORE, Mrs Joyce. b 48. TCD BA70 HDipEd71 ARIAM68. CITC 98. **d** 01 **p** 02. NSM Camlough w Mullaglass *Arm* 01-07; NSM Drogheda w Ardee, Collon and Termonfeckin from 07. *Dundalk Road, Dunleer, Co Louth, Republic of Ireland* Tel (00353) (41) 685 1327
E-mail am.drogheda@armagh.anglican.org

MOORE, Leonard Richard. b 22. Leeds Univ BA47. Coll of Resurr Mirfield 47. **d** 49 **p** 50. C Hendon St Mary *Lon* 49-54; C Stevenage *St Alb* 54-60; V Bedford All SS 60-68; Lic to Offic 68-70; P-in-c Bedford H Trin 70-74; rtd 87; Hon C Cardington *St Alb* 87-91; Perm to Offic from 92. *22 Dart Road, Bedford MK41 7BT* Tel (01234) 357536
E-mail leonard@moore9926.fsnet.co.uk

MOORE, Margaret Louise. b 62. DipOT85. SAOMC 04. **d** 06 **p** 07. C Bp's Hatfield, Lemsford and N Mymms *St Alb* from 06. *69 Hardings, Welwyn Garden City AL7 2HA* Tel (01707) 375333 Mobile 07729-385830 E-mail louisemoore85@btinternet.com

MOORE, Matthew Edward George. b 38. Oak Hill Th Coll 77. **d** 77 **p** 78. C Larne and Inver *Conn* 77-80; I Desertmartin w Termoneeny *D & R* 80-84; I Milltown *Arm* 84-96; I Culmore w Muff and Belmont *D & R* 96-06, Dioc Warden for Min of Healing 97-06; Can Derry Cathl 04-06; rtd 06. *9 Glen House Mews, Main Street, Eglinton, Londonderry BT47 3AA* Tel (028) 7181 1238 Mobile 07720-036211
E-mail mmoore9@toucansurf.com

MOORE, Canon Michael Mervlyn Hamond. b 35. LVO99. Pemb Coll Ox BA60 MA63. Wells Th Coll 60. **d** 62 **p** 63. C Bethnal Green St Matt *Lon* 62-66; Chapl Bucharest w Sofia and Belgrade *Eur* 66-67; Asst Gen Sec C of E Coun on Foreign Relns 67-70; Gen Sec 70-72; Abp's Chapl on Foreign Relns *Cant* 72-82; Hon C Walworth St Pet *S'wark* 67-80; Hon Can Cant Cathl 74-90; Chapl Chpl Royal Hampton Court Palace 82-99; Dep P in O 92-99; rtd 99. *The College of St Barnabas, Blackberry Lane, Lingfield RH7 6NJ* Tel (01342) 872859

MOORE, Michael Peter John. b 60. Qu Coll Birm 05. **d** 08 **p** 09. C Pet St Mary Boongate from 08. *21 College Park, Peterborough PE1 4AW* Tel (01733) 554815 E-mail revmichael@tiscali.co.uk

MOORE, Paul Henry. b 59. Ball Coll Ox BA82 DPhil86. Wycliffe Hall Ox 87. **d** 89 **p** 90. C Ox St Andr 89-93; V Kildwick *Bradf* 93-01; V Cowplain *Portsm* from 01; RD Havant from 04. *The Vicarage, Padnell Road, Cowplain, Waterlooville PO8 8DZ* Tel (023) 9226 2295 E-mail p.h.moore@btinternet.com

MOORE, Philip. b 49. York Univ MA71 Leeds Univ MA05 PGCE72. NOC 02. **d** 05 **p** 06. NSM Heworth Ch Ch *York* 05-09; P-in-c York St Thos w St Maurice from 09. *14 Whitby Avenue, York YO31 1ET* Tel (01904) 425250
E-mail philip.moore@britishlibrary.net

MOORE, Raymond. b 47. QUB BSc70. **d** 87 **p** 88. Aux Min Belfast All SS *Conn* 87-95; NSM 95-96; Aux Min Kilmakee 96-04; P-in-c Drung w Castleterra, Larah and Lavey etc

K, E & A from 04. *Drung Vicarage, Drung, Co Cavan, Republic of Ireland* Tel (00353) (49) 433 8204 Mobile 87-278 8226
E-mail rmoore@rmoore.uklinux.net

MOORE, Richard William Robert. b 39. UCD BA70 TCD HDipEd71. CITC 98. **d** 01 **p** 02. Aux Min Drogheda w Ardee, Collon and Termonfeckin *Arm* 01-05; Aux Min Dundalk w Heynestown from 05; Aux Min Ballymascanlan w Creggan and Rathcor from 05. *Dundalk Road, Dunleer, Co Louth, Republic of Ireland* Tel (00353) (41) 685 1327 E-mail richwmoore@yahoo.ie

MOORE, Richard Noel. b 34. TCD BA56 MA60. **d** 57 **p** 58. C Derry Cathl 57-60; I Clondehorkey 60-66; I Stranorlar w Meenglas and Kilteevogue 66-76; I Glendermott 76-00; Can Derry Cathl 89-00; rtd 00. *Evergreen House, 37 Mullanahoe Road, Dungannon BT71 5AT* Tel (028) 8673 7112

MOORE, Richard Norman Theobald. b 39. St Andr Univ BSc62 Lon Univ BD66. Clifton Th Coll. **d** 66 **p** 67. C Stowmarket *St E* 66-69; C New Humberstone *Leic* 69-72; P-in-c Leic Martyrs 73; V 73-84; Chapl Manor Hosp Epsom 84-94; Chapl Surrey Oaklands NHS Trust 94-00; rtd 00; Perm to Offic *Guildf* 02-07 and *St E* from 07. *9 Cranmer Cliff Gardens, Felixstowe IP11 7NH* Tel (01394) 273889

MOORE, Robert Allen. b 32. Univ of the Pacific BA54 Boston Univ STB58 STM59. **d** 63 **p** 63. USA 63-80; V Farington *Blackb* 80-83; TV Preston St Jo 83-85; P-in-c Fleetwood St Pet 85-87; V Leyland St Jas 87-97; rtd 97; Perm to Offic *Blackb* from 97. *19 Lea Road, Whittle-le-Woods, Chorley PR6 7PF* Tel (01257) 265701 E-mail rmoore1980@aol.com

MOORE, Mrs Roberta. b 46. CITC 03. **d** 06 **p** 07. Aux Min Drung w Castleterra, Larah and Lavey etc *K, E & A* from 06. *Drung Vicarage, Drung, Co Cavan, Republic of Ireland* Tel (00353) (49) 433 8204 Mobile 87-693 6444
E-mail bobbie@rmoore.uklinux.net

MOORE, Robin Hugh. b 52. CertEd BEd QUB BD. **d** 84 **p** 85. C Derryloran *Arm* 84-86; C Knock *D & D* 86-89; Bp's C Belfast St Steph w St Luke *Conn* 89-94; I 94-96; I Whitehouse 96-03; Bp's C Belfast St Mary Magd 03-07; I Belfast St Mark from 07. *9 Sycamore Park, Newtownabbey BT37 0NR* Tel (028) 9086 9569

MOORE, Shaun Christopher. b 52. Open Univ BA92 NE Lon Poly CertEd75. NTMTC BA08. **d** 08 **p** 09. NSM Leyton St Mary w St Edw and St Luke *Chelmsf* from 08. *17 Rayfield, Epping CM16 5AD* Tel (01992) 570684
E-mail shaunmoore@freeola.com

MOORE, Simon Quentin. b 61. Sheff Univ BA83 PGCE84. St Jo Coll Nottm MA99. **d** 00 **p** 01. C St Alb St Paul *St Alb* 00-03; TV Digswell and Panshanger from 03. *69 Hardings, Welwyn Garden City AL7 2HA* Tel (01707) 375333
E-mail sqmoore@btinternet.com

MOORE, Thomas Sydney. b 50. St Paul's Coll Grahamstown 77. **d** 79 **p** 80. C Rondebosch St Thos S Africa 79-82 and 83-84; C Bredasdorp 82-83; R Green Pt 84-88; C Bushey *St Alb* 97-08; C Aldershot St Mich *Guildf* from 08. *Ascension House, Ayling Hill, Aldershot GU11 3LL* Tel (01252) 330224
E-mail ts.moore@virgin.net

MOORE, Mrs Wendy. b 44. Westcott Ho Cam 92. **d** 94 **p** 95. C Rotherham *Sheff* 94-97; V Laughton w Throapham 97-01; V Bromsgrove All SS *Worc* 01-09; rtd 09; TV Saffron Walden w Wendens Ambo, Littlebury etc *Chelmsf* from 09. *Ashdown Vicarage, Radwinter Road, Ashdown, Saffron Walden CB10 2ET* Tel (01799) 584171 E-mail wendywmoor@aol.com

MOORE, William. *See* MOORE, Albert William

MOORE, William Henry. b 14. K Coll Lon 34. **d** 38 **p** 39. C Mill End *St Alb* 38-41; C Tring 41-44; C Gt Yarmouth *Nor* 44-46; New Zealand 46-52; R Houghton Conquest *St Alb* 52-56; Canada 56-59; R Filby w Thrigby *Nor* 60-62; P-in-c Mautby 60-62; Perm to Offic 62-71; Asst Master Mildenhall Sec Sch 68-73; Heartsease Sch Nor 73-75; C Mildenhall *St E* 71-73; rtd 79; Perm to Offic *Nor* from 88. *21 Green Court, Avenue Green, Norwich NR7 0DN* Tel (01603) 432758

MOORE, William Morris. b 33. QUB BSc55 TCD. **d** 61 **p** 62. C Belfast St Mich *Conn* 61-64; I 70-80; I Belfast All SS 64-70; I Ballynafeigh St Jude *D & D* 80-03; Can Belf Cathl 95-03; rtd 03. *10 Hollygate Park, Carryduff, Belfast BT8 8DZ* Tel (028) 9081 4896

MOORE-BICK, Miss Elizabeth Mary. b 77. Qu Coll Cam BA99 MA03 Anglia Poly Univ BA04. Westcott Ho Cam 02. **d** 05 **p** 06. C Hillingdon St Jo *Lon* 05-09; TV Clarendon *Sarum* from 09. *The Rectory, 5 The Copse, Alderbury, Salisbury SP5 3BL* Tel (01722) 711144 Mobile 07803-044217
E-mail lizmoore_bick@yahoo.co.uk *or* emm25@cam.ac.uk

MOORE BROOKS, Dorothy Anne. b 66. York Univ BA87 Hughes Hall Cam PGCE88. Ridley Hall Cam 96. **d** 98 **p** 99. C S Kensington St Jude *Lon* 98-01; Perm to Offic 02-08; Chapl Gt Ormond Street Hosp for Children NHS Trust 02-08; NSM Hoddesdon *St Alb* from 01; Chapl Isabel Hospice from 08. *11 Oxenden Drive, Hoddesdon EN11 8QF* Tel (01992) 464335 E-mail moorebrooks@ntlworld.com

MOORGAS, Geoffrey Gordon. b 30. Sarum & Wells Th Coll 80. **d** 81 **p** 82. C Brixton St Matt *S'wark* 81-84; C Clapham Old

Town 84-87; Namibia 87-94; rtd 95; NSM Limpsfield and Titsey *S'wark* 95-05; Perm to Offic from 05. *St Silvan's House, Red Lane, Oxted RH8 0RS* Tel (01883) 723452

MOORHEAD, Michael David. b 52. BSc BA. St Steph Ho Ox. **d** 83 **p** 84. C Kilburn St Aug w St Jo *Lon* 83-87; C Kenton 87-89; Chapl Cen Middx Hosp NHS Trust from 89; V Harlesden All So *Lon* from 89; P-in-c Willesden St Matt 92-02. *All Souls' Vicarage, 3 Station Road, London NW10 4UJ* Tel and fax (020) 8965 4988 E-mail michael@allsoulschurch.fsnet.co.uk

MOORHOUSE, Christine Susan. b 49. K Coll Lon BD71 AKC71. WMMTC. **dss** 86 **d** 87 **p** 94. NSM Stourbridge St Thos *Worc* 86-99; Perm to Offic 02-07. *Address temp unknown*

MOORHOUSE, Humphrey John. b 18. Oak Hill Th Coll 37. **d** 41 **p** 42. C Dalston St Mark w St Bart *Lon* 41-42; C Chadwell Heath *Chelmsf* 42-45; R Vange 45-83; rtd 83; Perm to Offic *Chelmsf* from 83. *12 Waverley Road, Benfleet SS7 4AZ* Tel (01268) 754952

MOORHOUSE, Peter. b 42. Liv Univ BSc64 Hull Univ CertEd. Linc Th Coll 79. **d** 81 **p** 82. C Horsforth *Ripon* 81-85; R Ackworth *Wakef* 85-96; Dep Chapl HM Pris Leeds 96-97; Chapl HM Pris Stocken 97-98; Chapl HM Pris Everthorpe 98-07; rtd 07; Perm to Offic *York* from 07. *65 Eastfield Lane, Dunnington, York YO19 5ND* Tel (01904) 481055

MOORSE, Michael William. b 36. Culham Coll of Educn TCert63. Guildf Dioc Min Course 96. **d** 98 **p** 99. OLM Woking St Pet *Guildf* 98-06; Perm to Offic from 06. *4 Bonners Close, Woking GU22 9RA* Tel (01483) 767460

MOORSOM, Christopher Arthur Robert. b 55. Ox Univ BA. Sarum & Wells Th Coll 79. **d** 82 **p** 83. C Bradford-on-Avon *Sarum* 82-85; R Broad Town, Clyffe Pypard and Tockenham 85-89; V Banwell *B & W* 89-96; R Upper Stour *Sarum* from 96. *The Rectory, Portnells Lane, Zeals, Warminster BA12 6PG* Tel (01747) 840221 E-mail chrisliz.moorsom@btopenworld.com

MORAN, Adrian. CITC. **d** 09. NSM Cork St Ann's Union *C, C & R* from 09. *Address temp unknown*

MORAY, ROSS AND CAITHNESS, Bishop of. *See* STRANGE, The Rt Revd Mark Jeremy

MORAY, ROSS AND CAITHNESS, Dean of. *See* PIPER, The Very Revd Clifford John

MORBY, Canon Helen Mary. b 62. Wolv Univ BA99. Ripon Coll Cuddesdon 99. **d** 01 **p** 02. C Lich St Chad 01-04; V Farnworth *Liv* from 04; AD Widnes 05-07; Hon Can Liv Cathl from 05. *The Vicarage, Coroners Lane, Widnes WA8 9HY* Tel 0151-424 2735 E-mail helen@morby.freeserve.co.uk

MORDECAI, Mrs Betty. b 27. Birm Univ BA48 Cam Univ CertEd49. Wycliffe Hall Ox 85. **dss** 86 **d** 87 **p** 94. Leamington Priors All SS *Cov* 86-89; Hon Par Dn 87-89; C Worc City St Paul and Old St Martin etc 89-94; rtd 94; Perm to Offic *Cov* from 00. *8 Swain Crofts, Leamington Spa CV31 1YW* Tel (01926) 882001 E-mail bettyhoward@btinternet.com

MORDECAI, Thomas Huw. b 59. Bris Univ BA81 St Jo Coll Dur BA85 MA92. Cranmer Hall Dur 83. **d** 87 **p** 88. C Gillingham St Mary *Roch* 87-90; Chapl Warw Sch 90-96; Chapl Gigglesswick Sch 96-98; Chapl Westmr Sch and PV Westmr Abbey 98-01; Chapl Geelong Gr Sch Australia 02-04; Chapl Malvern Coll 05-07; Chapl K Wm's Coll Is of Man from 07. *King William's College, Castletown, Isle of Man IM9 1TP* Tel (01624) 820400

MORE, Canon Richard David Antrobus. b 48. St Jo Coll Dur BA70. Cranmer Hall Dur 70. **d** 72 **p** 73. C Macclesfield St Mich *Ches* 72-77; Chapl Lee Abbey 77-82; V Porchester *S'well* 82-96; RD Gedling 90-96; Bp's Dom Chapl *Chelmsf* 96-01; Dioc Dir of Ords from 01; Dioc NSM Officer from 01; Hon Can Chelmsf Cathl from 96. *25 Roxwell Road, Chelmsf CM1 2LY* Tel (01245) 264187 Fax 348789 E-mail ddo@chelmsford.anglican.org

MORETON, Ann Louise. b 32. **d** 02 **p** 03. OLM Whitstable *Cant* from 02. *Church House, 24 Freemans Close, Seasalter, Whitstable CT5 4BB* Tel (01227) 277140 E-mail annmoreton@hotmail.com

MORETON, Harley. *See* MORETON, Philip Norman Harley

MORETON, Preb Mark. b 39. Jes Coll Cam BA64 MA68. Westcott Ho Cam 63. **d** 65 **p** 66. C Portsea All SS *Portsm* 65-70; C St Martin-in-the-Fields *Lon* 70-72; Chapl Jes Coll Cam 72-77; R Stafford St Mary and St Chad *Lich* 77-79; P-in-c Stafford Ch Ch 77-79; TR Stafford 79-91; P-in-c Marston w Whitgreave 77-79; V W Bromwich All SS 91-04; Preb Lich Cathl 99-04; rtd 04. *Rosemont, Dry Mill Lane, Bewdley DY12 2BL* Tel (01299) 401965

MORETON, Michael Bernard. b 44. St Jo Coll Cam BA66 MA70 Ch Ch Ox BA66 MA69 DPhil69. St Steph Ho Ox 66. **d** 68 **p** 69. C Banstead *Guildf* 68-74; R Alburgh *Nor* 74-75; R Denton 74-75; R Middleton Cheney w Chacombe *Pet* 75-87; Perm to Offic *Cant* from 00. *Waterloo House, 56-58 High Street, Rolvenden, Cranbrook TN17 4LN* Tel (01580) 241287

MORETON, Preb Michael Joseph. b 17. Univ Coll Lon BA40 Ch Ch Ox BA47 MA53. Wells Th Coll 47. **d** 48 **p** 49. C Rowbarton *B & W* 48-52; C Ilfracombe H Trin *Ex* 52-59; Lect Th Ex Univ 57-86; R Ex St Mary Steps 59-86; P-in-c 86-92; RD Christianity

83-89; Preb Ex Cathl 85-86; rtd 86; Perm to Offic *Ex* from 86. *3 Glenthorne Road, Duryard, Exeter EX4 4QU* Tel (01392) 438083

MORETON, Philip Norman Harley. b 28. Linc Th Coll. **d** 57 **p** 58. C Howden *York* 57-60; C Bottesford *Linc* 60-65; V Linc St Giles 65-70; V Bracebridge Heath 71-77; V Seasalter *Cant* 77-84; TV Whitstable 84-88; rtd 88; Perm to Offic *York* 96-06. *112 Grantham Road, Bracebridge Heath, Lincoln LN4 2QF* Tel (01522) 534672 Mobile 07851-717891

MORETON, Rupert Robert James. b 66. TCD BA89. CITC BTh92. **d** 92 **p** 93. C Dublin Ch Ch Cathl Gp 92-96; Asst Chapl Costa Blanca *Eur* 96-98; Chapl Helsinki from 98. *Mannerheimintie 19 A7, 00250 Helsinki, Finland* Tel (00358) (9) 490424 *or* 680 1515 Fax 698 6302 E-mail rupert.moreton@icon.fi

MORFILL, Mrs Mary Joanna. b 46. Seaford Coll of Educn TCert67. STETS 01. **d** 04 **p** 08. NSM Swanmore St Barn *Portsm* from 04. *Whistlers, New Road, Swanmore, Southampton SO32 2PF* Tel (01489) 878227 Mobile 07906-755145 E-mail mary@swanmore.net

✠**MORGAN, The Rt Revd Alan Wyndham.** b 40. OBE05. Univ of Wales (Lamp) BA62. St Mich Coll Llan 62. **d** 64 **p** 65 **c** 89. C Llangyfelach and Morriston *S & B* 64-69; C Swansea St Pet 69-72; C Cov E 72-73; TV 73-83; Bp's Officer for Soc Resp 78-83; Adn Cov 83-89; Suff Bp Sherwood *S'well* 89-04; rtd 04. *10 Station Road, Alcester B49 5ET* Tel (01789) 762486

MORGAN, Alison Jean. b 59. Girton Coll Cam BA82 MA85 Darw Coll Cam PhD86. EMMTC 93. **d** 96 **p** 97. NSM Oadby *Leic* 96; NSM Leic H Trin w St Jo 98-08; Thinker and writer ReSource from 04. *10 Dairy Close, Wells BA5 2ND* Tel (01749) 600341 E-mail alisonmorgan@resource-arm.net

MORGAN, Anthony Hogarth. b 42. St Josef Missiehuis Holland 60 St Jos RC Coll Lon 62. **d** 65 **p** 66. In RC Ch 66-93; NSM Handsworth Woodhouse *Sheff* 93-94; C Sheff St Leon Norwood 94-97; P-in-c Shiregreen St Hilda 97-05; C Shiregreen St Jas and St Chris 05-07; rtd 07; Perm to Offic *York* from 09. *30 Dulverton Hall, Esplanade, Scarborough YO11 2AR* Tel (01723) 340130

MORGAN, Anthony Paul George. b 57. Sarum & Wells Th Coll 89. **d** 91 **p** 92. C Plymstock *Ex* 91-95; P-in-c Wolborough w Newton Abbot 95-00; V York St Hilda 01-06; rtd 06; Perm to Offic *Derby* from 07. *Silver Birches, 91 Alfreton Road, Westhouses, Alfreton DE55 5AJ* E-mail tony@thefms.fsnet.co.uk

✠**MORGAN, The Most Revd Barry Cennydd.** b 47. Lon Univ BA69 Selw Coll Cam BA72 MA74 Univ of Wales PhD86. Westcott Ho Cam 70. **d** 72 **p** 73 **c** 93. Chapl Bryn-y-Don Community Sch 72-75; C St Andrews Major w Michaelston-le-Pit *Llan* 72-75; Ed *Welsh Churchman* 75-82; Lect Th Univ of Wales (Cardiff) 75-77; Chapl and Lect St Mich Coll Llan 75-77; Warden Ch Hostel Ban 77-84; Chapl and Lect Th Univ of Wales (Ban) 77-84; In-Service Tr Adv *Ban* 78-84; Dir of Ords 82-84; Can Ban Cathl 83-84; TR Wrexham *St As* 84-86; Adn Meirionnydd *Ban* 86-93; R Criccieth w Treflys 86-93; Bp Ban 93-99; Bp Llan from 99; Abp Wales from 03. *Llys Esgob, The Cathedral Green, Llandaff, Cardiff CF5 2YE* Tel (029) 2056 2400 Fax 2057 7129 E-mail archbishop@churchinwales.org.uk

MORGAN, Miss Beryl. b 30. **dss** 63 **d** 87 **p** 94. Rickerscote *Lich* 63-69; Hd Dss 70-87; Dioc Lay Min Adv 70-93; Willenhall H Trin 80-93; Par Dn 87-93; rtd 93; Hon C Penn *Lich* 94-01; Perm to Offic *Lich* 01-04 and *Leic* from 05. *12 Stuart Court, High Street, Kibworth, Leicester LE8 0LR* Tel 0116-279 6345

MORGAN, Charles Nicholas Brendan. b 55. MBE91. Open Univ BSc94 Leeds Univ BA08. NOC 05. **d** 08 **p** 09. C Derwent Ings *York* from 08. *The Rectory, Church Lane, Elvington, York YO41 4AD* Tel 07902-033174 (mobile) E-mail dadintheditch@hotmail.com

MORGAN, Christopher. b 66. Wycliffe Hall Ox 02. **d** 04 **p** 05. C Brackley St Pet w St Jas 04-07; Chapl Chadwick Lodge Secure Hosp 05-07; R Reepham, Hackford w Whitwell, Kerdiston etc *Nor* from 07. *The Rectory, Station Road, Reepham, Norwich NR10 4LJ* Tel (01603) 870220

✠**MORGAN, The Rt Revd Christopher Heudebourck.** b 47. Lanc Univ BA73 Heythrop Coll Lon MTh91. Kelham Th Coll 66. **d** 73 **p** 74 **c** 01. C Birstall *Leic* 73-76; Asst Chapl Brussels *Eur* 76-80; P-in-c Redditch St Geo *Worc* 80-81; TV Redditch, The Ridge 81-85; V Sonning 85-96; Prin Berks Chr Tr Scheme 85-89; Dir Past Studies Ox Min Course 92-96; Dioc Can Res Glouc Cathl and Officer for Min 96-01; Area Bp Colchester *Chelmsf* from 01. *1 Fitzwalter Road, Colchester CO3 3SS* Tel (01206) 576648 Fax 763868 E-mail b.colchester@chelmsford.anglican.org

MORGAN, Christopher John. b 46. Brasted Th Coll 68 Linc Th Coll 70. **d** 72 **p** 73. C Earley St Pet *Ox* 72-76; C Epsom St Martin *Guildf* 76-79; V Stoneleigh 79-83; Ind Chapl *York* 83-92; NACRO 87-91; V York St Hilda 92-96; TV E Greenwich *S'wark* 96-03; P-in-c Norbury St Oswald 03-05; V from 05. *The Vicarage, 2B St Oswald's Road, London SW16 3SB* Tel (020) 8764 2853

MORGAN, Clive. b 41. **d** 02. Par Dn Blaina and Nantyglo *Mon* from 02. *26 Victoria Street, Blaina, Abertillery NP13 3BG* Tel (01495) 291637

MORGAN, David Farnon Charles. b 43. Leeds Univ BA68. Coll of Resurr Mirfield 68. **d** 70 **p** 71. C Swinton St Pet *Man* 70-73; C Langley All SS and Martyrs 73-75; R Salford St Clem w St Cypr Ordsall 75-76; R Salford Ordsall St Clem 76-86; V Adlington *Blackb* from 86; AD Chorley 98-04. *St Paul's Vicarage, Railway Road, Adlington, Chorley PR6 9QZ* Tel (01257) 480253 E-mail morgvvic@tinyworld.co.uk

MORGAN, David Joseph (Joe). b 47. Bp Burgess Hall Lamp 66 St Deiniol's Hawarden 74. **d** 74 **p** 75. C Pembroke Dock *St D* 74-77; C Burry Port and Pwll 77-80; Miss to Seafarers from 80; Sen Chapl and Sec Welsh Coun from 85. *25 Glanmor Park Road, Sketty, Swansea SA2 0QG* Tel (01792) 206637

MORGAN, Deiniol Tudur. d 02 **p** 03. Min Can Ban Cathl 02-04; P-in-c Llanberis, Llanrug and Llandinorwig 04-05; Min Can and Prec Westmr Abbey 05-08; CF from 08. *c/o MOD Chaplains (Army)* Tel (01980) 615804 Fax 615800

MORGAN, Sister Enid May. b 37. St Luke's Coll Ex CertEd69 Ex Univ DipEd76 Univ of Wales (Lamp) BA04. **d** 07 **p** 07. NSM Llanfrechfa and Llanddewi Fach w Llandegfeth *Mon* 07-08. *Llety'r Pererin, Whitchurch, Solva, Haverfordwest SA62 6UD* E-mail enidmorgan@onetel.com

MORGAN, Canon Enid Morris Roberts. b 40. St Anne's Coll Ox BA61 Univ of Wales (Ban) MA73. United Th Coll Abth BD81. **d** 84 **p** 97. C Llanfihangel w Llanafan and Llanwnnws etc *St D* 84-86; Dn-in-c 86-93; Dir Bd of Miss Ch in Wales 93-00; V Llangynwyd w Maesteg 00-05; Hon Can Llan Cathl 02-05; rtd 05. *Rhiwlas, Cliff Terrace, Aberystwyth SY23 2DN* Tel (01970) 624648

MORGAN, Gareth Morison Kilby. b 33. Bris Univ BA56. Cuddesdon Coll 57 Bangalore Th Coll. **d** 61 **p** 62. C St Helier *S'wark* 61-65; Chapl Scargill Ho 65-70; Dir RE *Linc* 71-74; Dioc Dir of Educn *St E* 74-81; TR Hanley H Ev *Lich* 81-89; TR Cen Telford 89-92; Warden Glenfall Ho *Glouc* 92-98; rtd 98; Perm to Offic *Win* from 00; Chapl Hants Partnership NHS Trust from 08. *St Neots, Kanes Hill, Southampton SO19 6AH* Tel (023) 8046 6509 E-mail geejaymo@aol.com

MORGAN, Gary. b 61. Westmr Inst of Educn BA03. St Steph Ho Ox 04. **d** 06 **p** 07. C Spilsby Gp *Linc* from 06. *The Curate's House, 3 Woodlands View, Spilsby PE23 5GD* Tel (01790) 755615 Mobile 07879-068196 E-mail fathergaz@yahoo.co.uk

MORGAN, Geoffrey. See MORGAN, James Geoffrey Selwyn

MORGAN, Gerwyn. See MORGAN, William Charles Gerwyn

MORGAN, Glyn. b 21. Oak Hill Th Coll 73. **d** 76 **p** 77. NSM Barton Seagrave w Warkton *Pet* 76-00; Perm to Offic from 00. *St Edmund's House, Warkton, Kettering NN15 5AB* Tel (01536) 520610

MORGAN, Glyn. b 33. Univ of Wales (Ban) BA55 MA69. Coll of Resurr Mirfield 55. **d** 57 **p** 58. C Dolgellau *Ban* 57-60; C Conway 60-63; V Corris 63-68; Hd of RE Friars' Sch Ban 69-70; Lic to Offic 70-71; Hd of RE Oswestry Boys' Modern Sch 70-74; Hd of RE Oswestry High Sch for Girls 74-79; Hon C Oswestry H Trin *Lich* 71-79; Hd of RE Fitzalan Sch Oswestry 79-88; V Meifod and Llangynyw *St As* 88-01; RD Caereinion 89-01; rtd 01. *Crib y Gwynt Annexe, Trefnanney, Meifod SY22 6XX* Tel (01938) 500066

MORGAN, Graham. b 47. Kt00. S'wark Ord Course. **d** 83 **p** 84. NSM S Kensington St Steph *Lon* 83-90; NSM Hammersmith H Innocents 90-02; NSM Bedford Park from 02. *24 Charleville Court, Charleville Road, London W14 9JG* Tel (020) 7381 3211 E-mail graham.morgan@nwlh.nhs.uk

MORGAN, Henry. b 45. Hertf Coll Ox BA68. Westcott Ho Cam 68. **d** 70 **p** 71. C Lee St Marg *S'wark* 70-73; C Newington St Paul 73-76; V Camberwell St Mich w All So w Em 76-84; V Kingswood 84-93; Perm to Offic *S'wark* 93-03 and *Sheff* from 03. *St Helen's, Grange Lane, Burghwallis, Doncaster DN6 9JL* Tel (01302) 700227 E-mail henry.morgan1@virgin.net

MORGAN, Mrs Hilary. WEMTC. **d** 09. NSM Tenbury *Heref* from 09. *The Steps, Bleathwood, Ludlow SY8 4LR* E-mail hilsandbern@btinternet.com

MORGAN, Hogarth. See MORGAN, Anthony Hogarth

MORGAN, Canon Ian David John. b 57. Hull Univ BA78 LTCL75. Ripon Coll Cuddesdon 80. **d** 83 **p** 84. C Heref H Trin 83-86; C New Shoreham *Chich* 86-88; Researcher, Producer & Presenter BBC Local Radio 88-92; V Ipswich All Hallows *St E* 92-95; TR Ipswich St Mary at Stoke w St Pet 95-97; TR Ipswich St Mary at Stoke w St Pet and St Fran from 97; CUF Link Officer from 06; RD Ipswich from 08; Hon Can St E Cathl from 09. *1 Salmet Close, Ipswich IP2 9BA* Tel (01473) 601895 Fax 683303 E-mail ianmorgan@aol.com

MORGAN, Ian Stephen. b 50. Open Univ BA88. Sarum & Wells Th Coll. **d** 88 **p** 89. C Baldock w Bygrave *St Alb* 88-91; C S Elmham and Ilketshall *St E* 91-95; V Bungay H Trin w St Mary 95-05; R Lt Barningham, Blickling, Edgefield etc *Nor* from 05. *The Rectory, The Street, Itteringham, Norwich NR11 7AX* Tel (01263) 584262 Mobile 07808-451350 E-mail smorganciho@aol.com

MORGAN, James Geoffrey Selwyn. b 59. Ex Univ BA81 PGCE82 Open Univ MPhil97. Cranmer Hall Dur 88. **d** 91 **p** 92. C Reading St Agnes w St Paul *Ox* 91-93; C Bromham w Oakley and Stagsden *St Alb* 94-95; Perm to Offic *Pet* 96-98; C Epsom St Martin *Guildf* 98-01; Ox Cen for Miss Studies from 01. *Oxford Centre for Mission Studies, PO Box 70, Oxford OX2 6HB* Tel (01865) 556071 Fax 510823 E-mail jgs_morgan@tiscali.co.uk

MORGAN, Joe. See MORGAN, David Joseph

MORGAN, John. See MORGAN, William John

MORGAN, John Geoffrey Basil. b 21. Wells Th Coll 59. **d** 60 **p** 61. C Oakdale St Geo *Sarum* 60-64; C Talbot Village 64-67; C-in-c Ensbury St Thos CD 67-69; V Ensbury 69-82; C W Parley 82-86; rtd 86; Perm to Offic *Sarum* 01-05. *Widgery, 32 Church Road, Ferndown BH22 9EU* Tel (01202) 861207

MORGAN, John Laurence. b 41. Melbourne Univ BA62 Oriel Coll Ox BA69 MA73 DPhil76. **d** 68 **p** 69. Acting Chapl Oriel Coll Ox 69 and 70-76; USA 77-78; Australia from 78. *St John's College, College Road, St Lucia Qld 4067, Australia* Tel (0062) (7) 3371 3741 *or* 3842 6600 Fax 3870 5124 E-mail john.morgan@mailbox.uq.edu.au

MORGAN, John Roland. b 31. Birm Univ BA54. Bps' Coll Cheshunt 54. **d** 55 **p** 56. C Selly Oak St Mary *Birm* 55-57; C Yardley Wood 57-58; C Hamstead St Paul 58-61; V Smethwick St Chad 61-68; V Balsall Common 68-82; V N Leigh *Ox* 82-95; RD Woodstock 87-92; rtd 95; Perm to Offic *Ely* from 95. *Dyn Caryn, 2 Hayling Close, Godmanchester, Huntingdon PE29 2XB* Tel (01480) 459522

MORGAN, John William Miller. b 34. Lon Univ BSc56. Wycliffe Hall Ox 61. **d** 63 **p** 64. C St Alb Ch Ch *St Alb* 63-68; V Luton St Matt High Town 68-79; V Mangotsfield *Bris* 79-90; P-in-c Stanton St Quintin, Hullavington, Grittleton etc 90-95; R Hullavington, Norton and Stanton St Quintin 95-99; rtd 99; Perm to Offic *Bris* from 00. *3 Bouverie Park, Stanton St Quintin, Chippenham SN14 6EE* Tel (01666) 837670 E-mail johnwmmorgan@compuserve.com

MORGAN, Mrs Judith. b 62. CBDTI 96. **d** 99 **p** 00. C Brigham and Gt Broughton and Broughton Moor *Carl* 99-04; P-in-c Doxford St Wilfrid *Dur* from 04. *2 Whitebark, Sunderland SR3 2NX* Tel 0191-522 7639 E-mail morgjud@aol.com

MORGAN, Katharine. b 41. **d** 91 **p** 97. NSM Loughor *S & B* from 91. *68 Borough Road, Loughor, Swansea SA4 6RT*

MORGAN, Kathleen Irene. b 52. St Martin's Coll Lanc CertEd74. WEMTC 93. **d** 96 **p** 97. NSM Barnwood *Glouc* 96-99; C Coney Hill 99-02; V Churchdown St Jo and Innsworth from 02. *The Vicarage, St John's Avenue, Churchdown, Gloucester GL3 2DA* Tel (01452) 713421 E-mail revkaty@aol.com

MORGAN, Linda Marianne. b 48. Bris Univ BSc69 Surrey Univ MSc72 Lon Univ PhD77 FRCPath01. STETS 99. **d** 02 **p** 03. NSM Claygate *Guildf* from 02. *8 Melbury Close, Claygate KT10 0EX* Tel (01372) 462911 E-mail lindamorgan@holytrinityclaygate.org.uk

MORGAN, Mrs Marian Kathleen Eleanor. b 38. Birm Univ MA94 FCMI82. WEMTC. **d** 00 **p** 01. NSM Cusop w Blakemere, Bredwardine w Brobury etc *Heref* 00-03; P-in-c New Radnor and Llanfihangel Nantmelan etc *S & B* 03-07; rtd 08. *Trefechan, Aberedw, Builth Wells LD2 3UH* Tel (01982) 560702 Mobile 07977-477212 E-mail mkemorgan@btinternet.com

MORGAN, Mark Anthony. b 58. LLB. Chich Th Coll. **d** 84 **p** 85. C Thorpe St Andr *Nor* 84-87; C Eaton 87-90; V Southtown 90-92; Perm to Offic from 92. *Nethergate End, The Street, Saxlingham, Nethergate, Norwich NR15 1AJ* Tel (01603) 762850

MORGAN, Mark Steven Glyn. b 60. Essex Univ BSc83 RGN86. Ridley Hall Cam 95. **d** 97 **p** 99. C Herne Bay Ch Ch *Cant* 97-02; TV Ipswich St Mary at Stoke w St Pet and St Fran *St E* from 02. *St Peter's Church House, Stoke Park Drive, Ipswich IP2 9TH* Tel (01473) 601438 E-mail hama.morgan-@tinyworld.co.uk

MORGAN, Martin Paul. b 46. St Steph Ho Ox 71. **d** 73 **p** 74. C Kettering St Mary *Pet* 73-76; C Fareham SS Pet and Paul *Portsm* 76-80; V Portsea Ascension 80-94; V Rottingdean *Chich* from 94. *The Vicarage, Steyning Road, Rottingdean, Brighton BN2 7GA* Tel (01273) 309216 E-mail martin.morgan43@ntlworld.com

MORGAN, Mrs Melanie Jane. b 54. RMN. Qu Coll Birm 98. **d** 02 **p** 03. NSM Derby St Andr w St Osmund 02-05. *16 Brading Close, Alvaston, Derby DE24 0UW* Tel (01332) 754419 E-mail clifden@btinternet.com

MORGAN, Michael. b 32. Lon Univ BSc57 MSc67 PhD63. **d** 74 **p** 75. NSM Portsdown *Portsm* 74-98; Perm to Offic from 98. *12 East Cosham Road, Cosham, Portsmouth PO6 2JS* Tel (023) 9237 7442

MORGAN, Michael John. b 45. Nottm Univ BA66 MEd71. Linc Th Coll 80. **d** 82 **p** 83. C Bulkington *Cov* 82-83; C Bulkington w Shilton and Ansty 83-85; V Longford 85-89; R Norton *Sheff* 89-99; R Lapworth *Birm* 99-09; R Baddesley Clinton 99-09; rtd 09; Perm to Offic *Birm* from 09. *77 Tiverton Drive, Nuneaton CV11 6XJ*

MORGAN, Morley Roland. b 47. Univ of Wales (Lamp) BA76. St Steph Ho Ox 76. **d** 77 **p** 78. C Merthyr Dyfan *Llan* 77-78; C Llantrisant 78-80; TV Coventry Caludon 80-86; Chapl N Man

MORGAN

Gen Hosp 86-93; Chapl N Man Health Care NHS Trust 93-02; Chapl Pennine Acute Hosps NHS Trust 02-07; Hon C Bury St Jo w St Mark *Man* 05-07; rtd 07; Perm to Offic *Man* from 08. *14 Rectory Road, Manchester M8 5EA* Tel 0161-740 9925

MORGAN, Canon Nicholas John. b 50. K Coll Lon BD71 AKC71 CertEd. St Aug Coll Cant 72. **d** 73 **p** 74. C Wythenshawe Wm Temple Ch *Man* 73-76; C Southam w Stockton *Cov* 76-79; V Brailes from 79; R Sutton under Brailes from 79; P-in-c Tysoe w Oxhill and Whatcote from 06; RD Shipston 90-98; Hon Can Cov Cathl from 03. *The Vicarage, Brailes, Banbury OX15 5HT* Tel (01608) 685230

MORGAN, Nicola. b 64. Nottm Univ BA86. Linc Th Coll BTh95. **d** 95 **p** 96. C Lillington *Cov* 95-98; C Gospel Lane St Mich *Birm* 98-01; P-in-c Gt Paxton *Ely* 01-05; P-in-c Lt Paxton 01-05; P-in-c Diddington 01-05; V The Paxtons w Diddington 05; Perm to Offic *Pet* from 05; P-in-c Hallaton and Allexton, w Horninghold, Tugby etc *Leic* from 08. *The Rectory, 19 Churchgate, Hallaton, Market Harborough LE16 8TY* Tel (01858) 555363

MORGAN, Peter Neville. b 36. Univ of Wales (Cardiff) BSc60 BD63 Sussex Univ PGCE82. S Wales Bapt Coll 60. **d** 98 **p** 99. NSM Ardingly *Chich* 98-06; P-in-c 04-06; P-in-c Poynings w Edburton, Newtimber and Pyecombe 06-09. *The Rectory, The Street, Poynings, Brighton BN45 7AQ* Tel (01273) 857494 E-mail revpnm98@aol.com

MORGAN, Philip. b 51. Lon Univ BSc75 Univ of Wales (Cardiff) BD78. St Mich Coll Llan 75. **d** 78 **p** 79. C Swansea St Nic *S & B* 78-81; C Morriston 81-83; C Swansea St Mary w H Trin 83-84; USA from 84. *17476 Hawthorne Avenue, Culpeper VA 22701-8003, USA* E-mail padre4u@hotmail.com

MORGAN, Canon Philip Brendan. b 35. G&C Coll Cam BA59 MA63. Wells Th Coll 59. **d** 61 **p** 62. C Paddington Ch Ch *Lon* 61-66; C Trunch w Swafield *Nor* 66-68; P-in-c Nor St Steph 68-72; Sacr Nor Cathl 72-74; Can Res and Sub-Dean St Alb 74-81; Hon Can St Alb 81-94; R Bushey 81-94; RD Aldenham 91-94; Can Res and Treas Win Cathl 94-01; rtd 01; Perm to Offic *Win* from 01. *9 Clifton Hill, Winchester SO22 5BL* Tel (01962) 867549

MORGAN, Canon Philip Reginald Strange. b 27. St D Coll Lamp BA51 Keble Coll Ox BA53 MA57. Wells Th Coll 57. **d** 57 **p** 58. C Fleur-de-Lis *Mon* 57-59; C Bassaleg 59-62; CF (TA) 62-74; V Dingestow and Wanastow *Mon* 62-65; V Dingestow and Penrhos 65-66; R Machen and Rudry 66-75; R Machen 75-76; V Caerleon 76-95; Can St Woolos Cathl 84-95; rtd 95; Lic to Offic *Mon* from 95. *4 Anthony Drive, Caerleon, Newport NP18 3DS* Tel (01633) 422238

MORGAN, Philip Richard Llewelyn. b 27. Wadh Coll Ox BA50 MA52. St Steph Ho Ox 53. **d** 55 **p** 56. C Warlingham w Chelsham and Farleigh *S'wark* 55-58; Chapl Haileybury Coll 58-73; Hd Master Haileybury Jun Sch Berks 73-87; R The Deverills *Sarum* 87-94; rtd 94; Perm to Offic *Guildf* and *Win* from 95. *6 Phillips Close, Headley, Bordon GU35 8LY* Tel and fax (01428) 712194 E-mail philipmorgan@msn.com

MORGAN, Canon Reginald Graham. b 25. St D Coll Lamp BA46 LTh48. **d** 48 **p** 49. C Chirk *St As* 48-50; C Llangollen and Trevor 50-55; R Llanwyddelan w Manafon 55-66; V Rhuddlan 66-94; RD St As 78-94; Hon Can St As Cathl 83-89; Can from 89; rtd 94. *Manafon, 49 Ffordd Ffynnon, Rhuddlan, Rhyl LL18 2SP* Tel (01745) 591036

MORGAN, The Ven Reginald Graham Tharle. b 46. St Jo Coll Nottm LTh75. **d** 75 **p** 76. C Oadby *Leic* 75-78; S Africa from 79; R Greytown St Jas from 88; Adn Estcourt from 95. *PO Box 112, Greytown, Natal, 3250 South Africa* Tel and fax (0027) (334) 71240 *or* tel 71241 E-mail beehive@cybertrade.co.za

MORGAN, Rhys Bryn. b 65. E Lon Univ BA94. St Mich Coll Llan 00. **d** 02 **p** 03. C Carmarthen St Pet *St D* 02-05; P-in-c Cil-y-Cwm and Ystrad-ffin w Rhandir-mwyn etc 05-09. *Rhiwlas, Cliff Terrace, Aberystwyth SY23 2DN* Tel (01970) 624648 Mobile 07973-254062 E-mail rhys.morgan1@btinternet.com

MORGAN, Richard Mervyn. b 50. Wadh Coll Ox BA73 MA75 K Alfred's Coll Win PGCE74. **d** 92 **p** 93. CMS 85-94; Kenya 88-94; Perm to Offic *S'wark* 95-96; R Therfield w Kelshall *St Alb* from 96; Tutor ERMC *Ely* from 99. *The Rectory, Church Lane, Therfield, Royston SG8 9QD* Tel (01763) 287364 E-mail rm@therfieldrectory.freeserve.co.uk

MORGAN, Richard Thomas. b 70. Peterho Cam BA91 MA95. Wycliffe Hall Ox 94. **d** 96 **p** 97. C Bath Twerton-on-Avon *B & W* 96-99; Chapl Lee Abbey 99-01; R Marks Tey and Aldham *Chelmsf* 01-08; C Fisherton Anger *Sarum* from 08. *14 Wyndham Park, Salisbury SP1 3BA* Tel (01722) 333808 E-mail richardtmorgan@i24.net

MORGAN, Robert Chowen. b 40. St Cath Coll Cam BA63 MA67. St Chad's Coll Dur 64. **d** 66 **p** 67. C Lancaster St Mary *Blackb* 66-76; Lect Th Lanc Univ 67-76; Fell Linacre Coll Ox from 76; Lect Th Ox Univ 76-97; Reader from 97; P-in-c Sandford-on-Thames *Ox* from 87. *Lower Farm, Sandford-on-Thames, Oxford OX4 4YR* Tel (01865) 748848 E-mail robert.morgan@theology.oxford.ac.uk

MORGAN, Canon Robert Harman. b 28. OBE94. Univ of Wales (Cardiff) BA55. Coll of Resurr Mirfield 55. **d** 57 **p** 58. C Penarth w Lavernock *Llan* 57-61; C Caerau w Ely 61-67; V Glan Ely 67-95; Hon Can Llan Cathl 94-95; rtd 95; Perm to Offic *St D* and *Llan* from 95. *Y Felin Wynt, St Davids, Haverfordwest SA62 6QS* Tel (01437) 720130

MORGAN, Canon Roger William. b 40. Mert Coll Ox BA62 Cam Univ MA67. Ridley Hall Cam 80. **d** 81 **p** 82. NSM Cambridge St Paul *Ely* 81-84; V Corby St Columba *Pet* 84-90; V Leic H Trin w St Jo 90-08; C-in-c Leic St Leon CD 01-08; Hon Can Leic Cathl 06-08. *10 Dairy Close, Wells BA5 2ND* Tel (01749) 679865 Mobile 07799-403346 E-mail rogermorgan@resource-arm.net

MORGAN, Simon John. b 58. Univ of Wales (Swansea) BA81 Univ of Wales (Cardiff) BD86 MA94 FRGS03 FRSA07. St Mich Coll Llan 83. **d** 86 **p** 87. C Penarth All SS *Llan* 86-87; C Port Talbot St Theodore 87-89; C Gelligaer 89-91; R Dowlais 91-96; Asst P Peacehaven and Telscombe w Piddinghoe and Southease *Chich* 96; P-in-c E Dean w Friston and Jevington 96-99; NSM Hellingly and Upper Dicker 99-05; NSM Fairwarp 05-08; Chapl St Bede's Sch Upper Dicker 99-07. *The Vicarage, Back Lane, Fairwarp, Uckfield TN22 3BL* Tel (01825) 712277 E-mail simon.morgan@stbedesschool.org

MORGAN, Stephen. *See* MORGAN, Ian Stephen

MORGAN, Stephen John. b 67. UEA BA89 SS Coll Cam BA02. Westcott Ho Cam 99. **d** 02 **p** 03. C Pitlochry and Kilmaveonaig *St And* 02-04; P-in-c E Knoyle, Semley and Sedgehill *Sarum* 05-08; P-in-c St Bartholomew 08-09; R from 09. *The Rectory, Semley, Shaftesbury SP7 9AU* Tel (01747) 830174 E-mail revstevemorgan@tiscali.co.uk

MORGAN, Canon Steve Shelley. b 48. St Mich Coll Llan 67. **d** 71 **p** 72. C Llanharan w Peterston-super-Montem 71; C Llandaff w Capel Llanilltern 71-74; C Neath w Llantwit 74-77; TV Merthyr Tydfil and Cyfarthfa 77-91; V Merthyr Tydfil Ch Ch from 91; RD Merthyr Tydfil 93-04; Can Llan Cathl from 98. *24 Pen y Bryn View, Incline Top, Merthyr Tydfil CF47 0GB* Tel (01685) 723272 E-mail christchurch737@btinternet.com

MORGAN, Mrs Susan Dianne. b 53. Univ of Wales (Lamp) BA74 Westmr Coll Ox PGCE75. NOC 03. **d** 05 **p** 06. C Droylsden St Martin *Man* 05-07; P-in-c Kirkholt from 08. *St Thomas's Vicarage, Cavendish Road, Rochdale OL11 2QX* Tel (01706) 649373 Mobile 07837-706037 E-mail sue_morgan14@hotmail.com

MORGAN, Teresa Jean. b 68. Clare Coll Cam BA90 MA94 PhD95 Oriel Coll Ox MA98 BA01 LRAM91. SAOMC 00. **d** 02 **p** 03. NSM Littlemore *Ox* from 02. *Oriel College, Oxford OX1 4EW* Tel (01865) 276579 E-mail teresa.morgan@classics.ox.ac.uk

MORGAN, Trevor. b 45. **d** 01 **p** 05. C Fleur-de-Lis *Mon* 01-06; P-in-c from 06; AD Bedwellty from 08. *The Tidings, Woodfieldside, Blackwood NP12 0PJ* Tel and fax (01495) 222198 E-mail tmo1036014@aol.com

MORGAN, Verna Ireta. b 42. NEOC. **d** 89 **p** 94. NSM Potternewton *Ripon* 89-92; Par Dn Longsight St Luke *Man* 92-94; C 94-95; P-in-c Gorton St Phil 95-02; rtd 02. *Butler's Village, St James's Parish, Nevis, St Kitts and Nevis*

MORGAN, William Charles Gerwyn. b 30. Univ of Wales (Lamp) BA52. St Mich Coll Llan 52. **d** 56 **p** 57. C Hubberston *St D* 56-62; V Ambleston w St Dogwells 62-68; Miss to Seamen 68-93; V Fishguard w Llanychar *St D* 68-85; V Fishguard w Llanychar and Pontfaen w Morfil etc 85-93; Can St D Cathl 85-93; Chan 91-93; rtd 93. *Wrth y Llan, Pontycleifion, Cardigan SA43 1DW* Tel (01239) 613943

MORGAN, William John. b 38. Selw Coll Cam BA62 MA66. Cuddesdon Coll 62. **d** 65 **p** 66. C Stratford St Jo *Llan* 65-68; Asst Chapl Univ of Wales (Cardiff) 68-70; Perm to Offic *Lon* 70-73; C Albany Street Ch Ch 73-78; P-in-c E Acton St Dunstan 78-80; V E Acton St Dunstan w St Thos 80-95; V Isleworth All SS 95-04; P-in-c St Margaret's-on-Thames 95-00; rtd 04. *Marvol, 24310 Bourdeilles, France* Tel (0033) (5) 53 54 18 90 E-mail marvol24@orange.fr

MORGAN, William Stanley Timothy. b 41. Univ of Wales (Lamp) BA63. Wycliffe Hall Ox 63. **d** 66 **p** 67. C Aberystwyth St Mich *St D* 66-69; V Ambleston w St Dogwells 69-70; V Ambleston, St Dogwells, Walton E and Llysyfran 70-74; V Llannon 74-80; V Lampeter 80-87; V Lampeter Pont Steffan w Silian 87-01; V Llanbadarn Fawr 01-08; rtd 08. *12 Devon Place, Cardiff CF11 6PR*

MORGAN-CROMAR, Christopher. *See* MORGAN, Christopher

MORGAN-GUY, John Richard. b 44. St D Coll Lamp BA65 Univ of Wales PhD85 ARHistS80 FRHistS05 FRSM81. St Steph Ho Ox 65. **d** 67 **p** 68. C Canton St Cath *Llan* 67-68; C Roath St Sav 68-70; Chapl Llandough Hosp 70-71; C Machen and Rudry *Mon* 71-74; R Wolvesnewton w Kilgwrrwg and Devauden 74-80; Perm to Offic *B & W* 80-93; V Betws Cedewain and Tregynon and Llanwyddelan *St As* 93-97; RD Cedewain 97; Lect Univ of Wales (Lamp) 98-03; Research Fell from 04; Research Fell Cen for Adv Welsh & Celtic Studies 99-04; Tutor

580

Welsh Nat Cen for Ecum Studies Carmarthen from 00. *Tyngors, Silian, Lampeter SA48 8AS* Tel (01570) 422710

MORGAN-JONES, Canon Christopher John. b 43. Bris Univ BA66 Chicago Univ MBA68 McMaster Univ Ontario MA69. Cuddesdon Coll 70. **d** 73 **p** 74. C Folkestone St Sav *Cant* 73-76; P-in-c Swalecliffe 76-82; V Addington 82-84; V Addington *S'wark* 85-92; RD Croydon Addington 85-90; V Maidstone All SS and St Phil w Tovil *Cant* from 92; Hon Can Cant Cathl from 99. *The Vicarage, Priory Road, Maidstone ME15 6NL* Tel (01622) 756002 Fax 692320

E-mail vicar@maidstoneallsaints.wanadoo.co.uk

MORGANNWG, Archdeacon of. *See* SMITH, The Ven Christopher Blake Walters

MORGANS, Paul Hywel. b 61. LWCMD83. Chich Th Coll 86. **d** 90 **p** 91. C Johnston w Steynton *St D* 90-92; C Caerau w Ely *Llan* 92-95; V Pentre 95-99; Hon C Roath St German 99-00. *Address temp unknown*

MORIARTY, Mrs Susan Margaret. b 43. Cartrefle Coll of Educn TCert65. St As Minl Tr Course. **d** 02. Par Dn Gorsedd w Brynford, Ysgeifiog and Whitford *St As* from 02. *7 St Michael's Drive, Caerwys, Mold CH7 5BS* Tel (01352) 720874

MORING, Sally Margaret. b 61. St Martin's Coll Lanc BEd84 Middx Univ BA06. NTMTC 03. **d** 06 **p** 07. NSM Northolt St Mary *Lon* 06-09; V Hayes St Edm from 09. *St Edmund's Vicarage, 1 Edmund's Close, Hayes UB4 0HA* Tel (020) 8573 6913 Mobile 07932-616203 E-mail sallymoring@hotmail.com

MORISON, John Donald. b 34. ALCD60. **d** 61 **p** 62. C Rayleigh *Chelmsf* 61-64; C St Austell *Truro* 64-67; V Meltham Mills *Wakef* 67-71; Youth Chapl *Cov* 71-76; S Africa 76-82; Can Port Elizabeth 80-82; Bardsley Missr 82-86; Lic to Offic *S'wark* 82-86; Dioc Missr *Derby* 86-99; V Quarndon 86-99; rtd 99; Perm to Offic *Sarum* from 01. *Flat 1, Canford Place, 59 Cliff Drive, Canford Cliffs, Poole BH13 7JX* Tel (01202) 709377

E-mail kayandjohn@waitrose.com

MORLEY, Athelstan John. b 29. Linc Coll Ox BA52 MA56. Ridley Hall Cam. **d** 54 **p** 55. C Surbiton St Matt *S'wark* 54-57; Succ Chelmsf Cathl 57-60; R Mistley w Manningtree 60-69; R Hadleigh St Jas 69-94; rtd 94; Hon C Prittlewell *Chelmsf* 94-97; Perm to Offic from 94; P-in-c St Martin Ludgate *Lon* 01-04. *38 Bridgwater Drive, Westcliff-on-Sea SS0 0DH* Tel (01702) 339335

MORLEY, Georgina Laura (George). b 63. Dur Univ BA84 Nottm Univ MTh95 PhD99. Cranmer Hall Dur. **d** 03 **p** 03. Dir Studies NEOC 99-04; NSM Osmotherley w Harlsey and Ingleby Arncliffe *York* 03-08; Lect Cranmer Hall Dur from 07. *Cranmer Hall, St John's College, 3 South Bailey, Durham DH1 3RJ* Tel 0191-334 3858 E-mail georgina.morley@durham.ac.uk

MORLEY, Miss Gillian Dorothy. b 21. Greyladies Coll 49. **dss** 70 **d** 87. Lewisham St Swithun *S'wark* 70-82; Sturry w Fordwich and Westbere w Hersden *Cant* 82-87; Perm to Offic from 87. *28 Glen Iris Avenue, Canterbury CT2 8HP* Tel (01227) 459992

MORLEY, John. *See* MORLEY, Athelstan John

MORLEY, John. b 43. AKC67. St Deiniol's Hawarden 67. **d** 68 **p** 69. C Newbold on Avon *Cov* 69-73; C Solihull *Birm* 73-77; C-in-c Elmdon Heath CD 76-77; Chapl RAF 77-93; TR Wallingford *Ox* 93-99; RD Wallingford 95-99; Dean St Paul's Cathl and Chapl Nicosia 99-02; V Henlow and Langford *St Alb* 02-08; RD Shefford 06-08; rtd 08; Perm to Offic *Pet* from 08 and *Lich* from 09. *31 Walcot Road, Market Harborough LE16 9DL* Tel (01858) 419714 Mobile 07900-892566

E-mail revjmorley@ntlworld.com

MORLEY, Keith. b 44. St Chad's Coll Dur BA66 Open Univ BSc93. **d** 67 **p** 68. C S Yardley St Mich *Birm* 67-70; C Solihull 70-73; V Shaw Hill 73-77; P-in-c Burton Coggles *Linc* 77-79; P-in-c Boothby Pagnell 77-79; V Lenton w Ingoldsby 77-79; P-in-c Bassingthorpe w Bitchfield 77-79; R Ingoldsby 79-87; RD Beltisloe 84-87; P-in-c Old Dalby and Nether Broughton *Leic* 87-94; RD Framland 88-90; Perm to Offic *Linc* from 03; rtd 04. *11 Swallow Close, Quarrington, Sleaford NG34 7UU*

MORLEY, Canon Leslie James. b 45. K Coll Lon BD67 AKC67 MTh68. St Boniface Warminster 68. **d** 69 **p** 70. C Birm St Pet 69-72; C W Brompton St Mary *Lon* 72; C W Brompton St Mary w St Pet 73-74; Chapl Nottm Univ 74-80; Dir Post-Ord Tr 80-85; Can Res and Vice-Provost S'well Minster 80-85; Can 85-99; Chapl Bluecoat Sch Nottm 85-90; R Nottingham St Pet and St Jas *S'well* 85-99; AD Nottingham Cen 90-93; Dioc Rural Officer *Ripon* from 99; Perm to Offic *York* from 00; Hon Chapl Yorks Agric Soc from 09. *Beacon Hill, High Street, Low Pittington, Durham DH6 1BE* Tel 0191-372 0385 Mobile 07879-470752

E-mail leslie.morley@virgin.net

MORLEY, Peter. b 36. St Jo Coll Nottm 81. **d** 83 **p** 84. C Sheff St Jo 83-87; Chapl The Shrewsbury Hosp *Sheff* 85-87; V Worsbrough Common *Sheff* 87-93; Chapl Mt Vernon Hosp Barnsley 87-93; R Harthill and Thorpe Salvin *Sheff* 93-99; rtd 99. *39 Hallcroft Road, Retford DN22 7LE* Tel (01777) 719081

MORLEY, Terence Martin Simon. b 49. SS Hild & Bede Coll Dur CertEd78. St Steph Ho Ox 71. **d** 74 **p** 75. C Kingston upon Hull St Alb *York* 74-76; C Middlesbrough All SS 76-77; Perm to Offic

Dur 77-78; Hon C Worthing St Andr *Chich* 78-80; C Brighton Ch Ch 80-82; C Hove St Patr 80-82; C Ayr *Glas* 83-86; C Maybole 83-84; P-in-c Coatbridge 86-88; R 88-92; P-in-c 92; V Plymouth St Jas Ham *Ex* 93-09; Chapl Plymouth Community Services NHS Trust 96-98; rtd 09. *St James's Presbytery, Ham Drive, Plymouth PL2 2NJ* Tel (01752) 362485

MORLEY, Trevor. b 39. Man Univ BSc62 MPS62 MRSH84. Ripon Hall Ox 65. **d** 67 **p** 68. C Compton Gifford *Ex* 67-70; Chapl Hammersmith Hosp Lon 70-83; Hon C N Hammersmith St Kath *Lon* 70-83; Chapl Univ Coll Hosp Lon 83-94; Chapl Univ Coll Lon Hosps NHS Trust 94-99; Hon Chapl St Luke's Hosp for the Clergy 89-99; V Linthwaite *Wakef* 99-06; rtd 06; Perm to Offic *Sheff* from 06. *19 Queenswood Road, Sheffield S6 1RR* Tel 0114-232 5232 E-mail tmqwr@tiscali.co.uk

MORLEY-BUNKER, John Arthur. b 27. Wells Th Coll 67. **d** 68 **p** 69. C Horfield H Trin *Bris* 68-71; P-in-c Easton All Hallows 71-75; V 75-82; RD Bris City 74-79; V Horfield St Greg 82-93; rtd 93; Perm to Offic *Bris* from 93. *1 Knoll Court, Knoll Hill, Bristol BS9 1QX* Tel 0117-968 5837

MORLEY-JONES, Anthony Roger. St Mich Coll Llan. **d** 04 **p** 05. NSM Cydweli and Llandyfaelog *St D* from 04. *11 Westhill Crescent, Cydweli SA17 4US* Tel (01554) 890458

MORLING, David Arthur. b 45. Saltley Tr Coll Birm CertEd66 Open Univ BA78. S Dios Minl Tr Scheme 83 Linc Th Coll. **d** 85 **p** 86. NSM Chich 85-97; P-in-c Doncaster Intake *Sheff* 97-02; P-in-c Doncaster H Trin 97-02; rtd 02; Perm to Offic *Bradf* from 02. *Lorindell, 61 Layton Lane, Rawdon, Leeds LS19 6RA* Tel 0113-250 3488 E-mail david.morling@bradford.anglican.org *or* david@morling.co.uk

MORONEY, Kevin John. b 61. Valley Forge Chr Coll Pennsylvania BS86. Gen Th Sem NY MDiv92. **d** 92 **p** 93. Asst Pastor Metuchen St Luke USA 92-94; R Metuchen All SS 94-98; Chapl St James Sch St James Maryland 98-00; Chapl and Tutor CITC 00-05; P-in-c Dublin Sandymount *D & G* 01-05; Dir Educn Radnor St Dav USA from 05. *St James School, 17641 College Road, St James MD 21781, USA* Tel (001) (301) 733 9330 E-mail kjmcoi@yahoo.com

MORPHY, George David. b 49. Birm Univ BEd71 Lon Univ BA75 Warwick Univ MA90. WMMTC. **d** 89 **p** 90. NSM Ribbesford w Bewdley and Dowles *Worc* 89-06; NSM Barbourne from 06; Dioc Dir of Educn from 99. *41 Hallow Road, Worcester WR2 6BX* Tel (01905) 422207 *or* 732825 Mobile 07867-525779 E-mail dmorphy@cofe-worcester.org

MORPHY, Canon Michael John. b 43. Newc Univ BSc65 Dur Univ MSc66 QUB PhD73. Ripon Coll Cuddesdon 82. **d** 84 **p** 85. C Halifax *Wakef* 84-86; V Luddenden w Luddenden Foot 86-97; V Corbridge w Halton and Newton Hall *Newc* 97-08; Hon Can Newc Cathl 07-08; rtd 08. *7 Mallard Drive, Montrose DD10 9NB* Tel (01674) 675277 E-mail mj.morphy@tiscali.co.uk

MORRELL, Mrs Jennifer Mary. b 49. NOC 84. **d** 87 **p** 94. Par Dn Crewe All SS and St Paul *Ches* 87-90; Par Dn Padgate *Liv* 90-94; C 94-95; TV Kirkby 95-00; V Croxteth Park 00-02. *24 Oak Tree Close, Kingsbury, Tamworth B78 2JF* Tel (01827) 874445

MORRELL, Canon Nigel Paul. b 38. S'wark Ord Course 73. **d** 76 **p** 77. C Letchworth St Paul w Willian *St Alb* 76-85; V Farley Hill St Jo 85-95; RD Luton 90-94; V Cardington 95-03; Hon Can St Alb 01-03; RD Elstow 03-08; rtd 03. *22 Sunderland Place, Shortstown, Bedford MK42 0FD* Tel and fax (01234) 743202 E-mail nigel.morrell@btopenworld.com

MORRELL, Paul Rodney. b 49. SRN70. SWMTC 91. **d** 93 **p** 94. C Heavitree w Ex St Paul 93-02; C Heavitree and St Mary Steps 02-05; TV from 05. *1A St Loyes Road, Exeter EX2 5HA* Tel (01392) 273430

MORRELL, His Honour Peter Richard. b 44. Univ Coll Ox MA71 Solicitor 70 Barrister-at-Law (Gray's Inn) 74. ERMC 06. **d** 08 **p** 09. NSM Uppingham w Ayston and Wardley w Belton *Pet* from 08. *New Sulehay Lodge, Nassington, Peterborough PE8 6QT* Tel (01780) 782281 Mobile 07860-573597 E-mail pmorrell@btinternet.com

MORRELL, Robin Mark George. b 29. Cuddesdon Coll 58. **d** 60 **p** 61. C Petersfield w Sheet *Portsm* 60-63; C-in-c Stockwood CD *Bris* 63-71; Lic to Offic 71-72; R Honiton, Gittisham and Combe Raleigh *Ex* 72-78; Lay Tr Officer *S'wark* 78-81; Asst Chapl HM Pris Brixton 81-85; Past Cllr from 85; Hon C Hatcham St Cath *S'wark* 91-97; rtd 94; Perm to Offic *Chich* from 96. *57 Bousfield Road, London SE14 5TP*

MORRELL, Mrs Susan Marjorie. b 46. Open Univ BA94. SEITE 93. **d** 96 **p** 97. NSM E Peckham and Nettlestead *Roch* from 96; Chapl Kent Coll Pembury 99-00. *7 Pippin Road, East Peckham, Tonbridge TN12 5BT* Tel (01622) 871150

MORRIS, Alan Ralph Oakden. b 29. Roch Th Coll 59. **d** 61 **p** 62. C Riverhead *Roch* 61-62; C Roch St Pet w St Marg 62 66; C Wrotham 66-74; V Biggin Hill 74-82; R Kingsdown 82-88; V Seal St Pet 88-92; rtd 92; P-in-c Renhold *St Alb* 92-93; Perm to Offic *Roch* from 93. *268 Woolwich Road, London SE2 0DW* Tel (020) 8310 7860

MORRIS, Miss Alison Mary. b 58. W Midl Coll of Educn BEd81 Wolv Univ PGCE00 MA02. Qu Coll Birm 06. **d** 09. NSM Pelsall *Lich* from 09. *32 Chestnut Road, Leamore, Walsall WS3 1BD* Tel (01922) 477734 Mobile 07837-649756
E-mail a.morris125@btinternet.com

MORRIS, Andy. *See* MORRIS, Edward Andrew

MORRIS, Mrs Ann. b 52. N Co Coll Newc CertEd73. WEMTC 00. **d** 03 **p** 04. C Churchdown St Jo and Innsworth *Glouc* 03-07; P-in-c Barnwood from 07. *The Vicarage, 27A Barnwood Avenue, Gloucester GL4 3AB* Tel (01452) 619531

MORRIS, Mrs Ann Veronica Marsham. b 46. Open Univ BA83. WEMTC 99. **d** 01 **p** 02. NSM Amberley *Glouc* from 01. *Cotswold, Amberley, Stroud GL5 5AB* Tel (01453) 872587
E-mail annmorris@cotswold85@btinternet.com

MORRIS, Anne. *See* MORRIS, Ms Margaret Anne

MORRIS (*née* SHAW)**, Mrs Anne.** b 47. LMH Ox BA69 MA72 Lon Univ BD82. NOC 01. **d** 03 **p** 04. NSM Leamington Priors All SS *Cov* from 03; NSM Leamington Spa H Trin and Old Milverton from 03. *20 Hayle Avenue, Warwick CV34 5TW* Tel (01926) 403512

MORRIS, Anthony David. b 61. Aston Univ BSc83. Qu Coll Birm 06. **d** 09. NSM Droitwich Spa *Worc* from 09. *15 Elgar Crescent, Droitwich WR9 7SP* Tel (01905) 771040
E-mail david.morris@droitwich777.freeserve.co.uk

MORRIS, Bernard Lyn. b 28. St Aid Birkenhead 55. **d** 58 **p** 59. C-in-c Hartcliffe St Andr CD *Bris* 58-61; C Bishopston 61-63; R Ardwick St Thos *Man* 63-69; R Aylton w Pixley, Munsley and Putley *Heref* 69-79; P-in-c Tarrington w Stoke Edith 72-77; R 77-79; P-in-c Queen Camel, Marston Magna, W Camel, Rimpton etc *B & W* 79-80; R 80-87; R Queen Camel w W Camel, Corton Denham etc 87-95; rtd 95; Perm to Offic *B & W* from 95 and *Ex* from 01. *Canterbury Bells, Ansford Hill, Castle Cary BA7 7JL* Tel (01963) 351154
E-mail revblmorris@supanet.com

MORRIS, Beti Elin. b 36. CertEd57. Sarum & Wells Th Coll 87. **d** 89 **p** 97. C Llangeitho and Blaenpennal w Betws Leucu etc *St D* 89-92; C-in-c Pencarreg and Llanycrwys 92-97; V 97-05; rtd 05. *Bro Mihangel, Maes y Tren, Felinfach, Lampeter SA48 8AH*

MORRIS, Brian. *See* MORRIS, Reginald Brian

MORRIS, Brian Michael Charles. b 32. S Dios Minl Tr Scheme 82. **d** 85 **p** 86. NSM Denmead *Portsm* 85-89; C S w N Hayling 89-96; P-in-c Shalfleet 96-97; rtd 97; Perm to Offic *Portsm* from 97. *Ashleigh, 5 Ashwood Close, Hayling Island PO11 9AX* Tel (023) 9246 7292 E-mail rev_b_morris@talk21.com

MORRIS, Ms Catharine Mary. b 75. Regent's Park Coll Ox BA96 MA00. Ridley Hall Cam 99. **d** 01 **p** 02. C Malpas *Mon* 01-06; C Reading Greyfriars *Ox* from 06. *93 York Road, Reading RG1 8DU* Tel 0118-957 1585
E-mail catharine.morris@greyfriars.org.uk

MORRIS, Canon Christopher John. b 45. K Coll Lon AKC67 BD68. **d** 68 **p** 69. C W Bromwich All SS *Lich* 68-72; C Porthill 72-74; Min Can Carl Cathl 74-77; Ecum Liaison Officer BBC Radio Carl 74-77; Dioc Communications Officer *Carl* 77-83; V Thursby 77-83; Angl Adv Border TV from 82; V Upperby St Jo *Carl* 83-91; P-in-c Lancercost w Kirkcambeck and Walton 91-99; P-in-c Gilsland w Nether Denton 96-99; R Lanercost, Walton, Gilsland and Nether Denton from 99; RD Brampton 98-05; Hon Can Carl Cathl from 98. *The Vicarage, Lanercost, Brampton CA8 2HQ* Tel (01697) 72478
E-mail chris@ca8morris.fsnet.co.uk

MORRIS, Prof Colin. b 28. Qu Coll Ox BA48 BA51 MA53 FRHistS71. Linc Th Coll 51. **d** 53 **p** 54. Fell and Chapl Pemb Coll Ox 53-69; Prof Medieval Hist Southn Univ 69-92; rtd 92; Public Preacher *Win* from 69. *12 Bassett Crescent East, Southampton SO16 7PB* Tel (023) 8076 8176

MORRIS, Preb David Meeson. b 35. Trin Coll Ox BA56 MA60. Chich Th Coll 57. **d** 60 **p** 61. C Westmr St Steph w St Jo *Lon* 60-65; Lib Pusey Ho 65-68; Chapl Wadh Coll Ox 67-68; C Sheff St Leon Norwood 68-69; Ind Chapl 68-72; C Brightside St Marg 69-72; R Adderley *Lich* 72-82; V Drayton in Hales 72-82; RD Tutbury 82-95; Chapl Burton Gen Hosp 82-90; P-in-c Burton St Modwen *Lich* 82; V Burton 82-99; Preb Lich Cathl 93-99; P-in-c Shobnall 94-99; rtd 99; Perm to Offic *Heref* and *Lich* from 99. *Watling House, All Stretton, Church Stretton SY6 6HH* Tel (01694) 722243

MORRIS, David Michael. b 59. Ox Univ MA84 Cam Univ PGCE91. Sarum & Wells Th Coll 82. **d** 84 **p** 85. C Angell Town St Jo *S'wark* 84-87; C Mitcham SS Pet and Paul 87-90; V Llandygwydd and Cenarth w Cilrhedyn etc *St D* 90-98; Lect Th St D Coll Lamp from 90; Hd RE Lampeter Comp Sch from 98. *Bronant, Rhydargaeau, Carmarthen SA32 7DR*

MORRIS, Canon David Pryce. b 39. St Mich Coll Llan 62. **d** 63 **p** 64. C Colwyn Bay *St As* 63-70; R St George 70-76; Dioc Children's Adv 75-87; V Bodelwyddan and St George 76-79; V Connah's Quay 79-95; St As Dioc Adult Lay Tr Team 88-05; Ed *St Asaph Diocesan News* from 89; Dioc Communications Officer 90-06; V Shotton 95-06; Hon Can St As Cathl 96-00; Can Cursal

St As Cathl 00-06; rtd 07. *7 Rhuddlan Road, Buckley CH7 3QA* Tel (01244) 540779 Mobile 07711-519752
E-mail david@dandpmorris.net

MORRIS, David Thomas. St Mich Coll Llan. **d** 09. C Merthyr Tydfil St Dav *Llan* from 09. *4 Lancaster Terrace, Merthyr Tydfil CF47 8SL* Tel (01685) 386072
E-mail fr.davidmorris@hotmail.co.uk

MORRIS, Dennis Gordon. b 41. ALCM58. St D Coll Lamp. **d** 67 **p** 68. C Neath w Llantwit 67-92; V Troedrhiwgarth from 92. *Garth Vicarage, 72 Bridgend Road, Maesteg CF34 0NL* Tel (01656) 732441

MORRIS, Edward. b 42. **d** 72 **p** 73. C Darlington H Trin *Dur* 72-75; Tutor St Steph Ho Ox 75-82; Sen Tutor 79-82; R Shadforth *Dur* 82-86; Chapl Hammersmith Hosp Lon 86-94; Chapl Qu Charlotte's Hosp Lon 86-94; Hd Chapl Hammersmith Hosps NHS Trust 94-07; rtd 07. *64 Shepherds Pool, Evesham WR11 4JG* E-mail morristed@hotmail.com

MORRIS, Edward Andrew (Andy). b 57. St Jo Coll Nottm BTh93. **d** 96 **p** 97. C Conisbrough *Sheff* 96-01; Perm to Offic *S'well* 01-04; V Bestwood St Matt w St Phil from 04. *St Matthew's Vicarage, Padstow Road, Nottingham NG5 5GH* Tel 0115-927 7229 Mobile 07775-925297 E-mail andy-morris@ntlworld.com

MORRIS, Canon Edwin Alfred. b 32. Wells Th Coll 62. **d** 64 **p** 65. C Wood End *Cov* 64-66; Lic to Offic 66-68; Ind Chapl 68-85; P-in-c Churchover w Willey 74-85; RD Rugby 78-85; R City of Bris 85-97; Hon Can Bris Cathl 89-97; RD Bris City 91-94; rtd 97; Perm to Offic *Cov* 97-00. *c/o Mrs G Morgan, 27 Booth Road, Banbury OX16 1EG* Tel (01295) 268432

MORRIS, Mrs Elizabeth Anne. b 59. BA05. **d** 00 **p** 01. OLM Darsham and Westleton w Dunwich *St E* 00-04; C Hadleigh, Layham and Shelley 04-06; C Yoxmere 08-09. *Maison Neuve, Plaisance, 24560 Issigeac, France* Tel (0033) (5) 53 58 71 90 E-mail cookingcurate@tiscali.co.uk

MORRIS, Canon Frank Leo. b 20. St Steph Ho Ox 50. **d** 53 **p** 54. C Bickley *Roch* 53-55; C Letchworth *St Alb* 55-61; V Wareside 61-65; R Wyddial 65-79; P-in-c 79-82; V Gt w Lt Hormead 65-79; RD Buntingford 68-75; V Gt w Lt Hormead, Anstey, Brent Pelham etc 79-82; V Hormead, Wyddial, Anstey, Brent Pelham etc 82-89; Hon Can St Alb 85-89; rtd 89; Perm to Offic *St Alb* from 00. *9 Manland Avenue, Harpenden AL5 4RG* Tel (01582) 462348 E-mail leo@harpenden9.freeserve.co.uk

MORRIS, Geoffrey. *See* MORRIS, Canon Martin Geoffrey Roger

MORRIS, Geoffrey David. b 43. Fitzw Coll Cam BA65 MA69 Westmr Coll Ox DipEd67. NOC. **d** 82 **p** 83. C Man Clayton St Cross w St Paul 82-85; V Lower Kersal 85-03; P-in-c Priors Hardwick, Priors Marston and Wormleighton *Cov* 03-08; Asst Chapl HM Pris Rye Hill 03-07; rtd 08. *20 Hayle Avenue, Warwick CV34 5TW* Tel (01926) 403512

MORRIS, Graham Edwin. b 60. Sarum & Wells Th Coll 83. **d** 86 **p** 87. C Coalbrookdale, Iron-Bridge and Lt Wenlock *Heref* 86-90; TV Bilston *Lich* 90-99; R Northwood *Portsm* 99-05; V Gurnard 99-05; P-in-c Ventnor H Trin 05-06; V from 06; P-in-c Ventnor St Cath 05-06; V from 06; P-in-c Bonchurch 05-06; R from 06; RD E Wight from 05. *The Vicarage, Maples Drive, Ventnor PO38 1NR* Tel (01983) 853729
E-mail graham.morris@btinternet.com

MORRIS, Henry James. b 47. Lon Univ BSc69. Wycliffe Hall Ox MA. **d** 79 **p** 80. C Woodford Wells *Chelmsf* 79-82; C Gt Baddow 82-87; R Siddington w Preston *Glouc* 87-01; RD Cirencester 97-01; TR Madeley *Heref* from 01. *St Michael's Vicarage, Church Street, Madeley, Telford TF7 5BN* Tel and fax (01952) 586645 *or* tel 585718 E-mail henrym@dircon.co.uk

MORRIS, Ian Henry. b 42. Sarum & Wells Th Coll 73. **d** 75 **p** 76. C Lawrence Weston *Bris* 75-78; C St Buryan, St Levan and Sennen *Truro* 78-81; P-in-c Lanteglos by Fowey 81-84; V 84-85; R Lanteglos by Camelford w Advent 85-95; RD Trigg Minor and Bodmin 93-95; TR Probus, Ladock and Grampound w Creed and St Erme 95-07; RD Powder 01-04; rtd 07. *43 Abbots Way, West Kirby, Wirral CH48 6EH* Tel 0151-625 8474

MORRIS, Ivor Leslie. b 50. Chich Th Coll 82. **d** 84 **p** 85. C Southend *Chelmsf* 84-87; C Somers Town *Lon* 87-90; P-in-c Chelmsf Ascension 90-96; V from 96; P-in-c Chelmsf All SS 92-96. *The Vicarage, 57 Maltese Road, Chelmsford CM1 2PB* Tel (01245) 353914 E-mail il.morris@virgin.net

MORRIS, Miss Jane Elizabeth. b 50. York Univ BA71 CertEd72 MSc80. NEOC 92. **d** 92 **p** 94. NSM York St Mich-le-Belfrey 92-95; C Leeds St Geo *Ripon* 95-05; V Cricklewood St Gabr and St Mich *Lon* from 05. *St Gabriel's Vicarage, 156 Anson Road, London NW2 6BH* Tel (020) 8452 6305
E-mail janemorris@ntlworld.com

MORRIS, Jeremy Nigel. b 60. Ball Coll Ox MA81 DPhil86 Clare Coll Cam BA92. Westcott Ho Cam 90. **d** 93 **p** 94. C Battersea St Mary *S'wark* 93-96; Dir Studies Westcott Ho Cam 96-01; Vice-Prin 97-01; Dean and Chapl Trin Hall Cam from 01. *Trinity Hall, Cambridge CB2 1TJ* Tel (01223) 332500
E-mail jnm20@cam.ac.uk

MORRIS, Mrs Joanna Elizabeth. b 60. N Riding Coll of Educn CertEd81. Qu Coll Birm 07. **d** 09. C Riddings and Ironville

Derby from 09. *The Vicarage, Vicarage Lane, Ironville, Nottingham NG16 5PT* Tel (01773) 528136
E-mail jomorris17@googlemail.com

MORRIS, Canon John. b 25. Westcott Ho Cam. **d** 65 **p** 66. C St Alb St Mich *St Alb* 65-68; V Leverstock Green 68-80; TR Chambersbury 80-82; V N Mymms 82-90; RD Hatfield 83-88; Hon Can St Alb 89-90; rtd 90; Perm to Offic *St Alb* 90-02; *Nor* 92-94 and from 95; P-in-c Barney, Fulmodeston w Croxton, Hindringham etc *Nor* 94-95. *Elba, Croxton Road, Fulmodeston, Fakenham NR21 0NJ* Tel (01328) 878685

MORRIS, John Douglas. b 37. Cam Univ BA58 Lon Inst of Educn PGCE60 Univ of E Africa MEd67 Ex Univ PhD87. S Dios Minl Tr Scheme 94. **d** 95 **p** 96. NSM Twyford and Owslebury and Morestead *Win* 95-01; Perm to Offic from 01; Chapl Twyford Sch Win from 96. *Gifford House, St Giles Hill, Winchester SO23 0JH* Tel (01962) 869720
E-mail johnmarymorris@btopenworld.com

MORRIS, John Dudley. b 33. Ball Coll Ox BA57 MA61. Wycliffe Hall Ox 58. **d** 60 **p** 61. C Tonbridge SS Pet and Paul *Roch* 60-65; C Enfield Ch Ch Trent Park *Lon* 65-69; Chapl Elstree Sch Woolhampton 70-74; Hd Master Handcross Park Sch W Sussex 74-89; V Rudgwick *Chich* 89-98; RD Horsham 93-98; rtd 98; Perm to Offic *Chich* from 98. *13 Hoadlands, Handcross, Haywards Heath RH17 6HB* Tel (01444) 400184

MORRIS, John Edgar. b 20. Keble Coll Ox BA42 MA50. Wycliffe Hall Ox 42. **d** 44 **p** 45. C Eccleston St Thos *Liv* 44-48; C Warrington H Trin 48-50; V Newton-le-Willows 50-57; R Wavertree H Trin 57-66; V Ainsdale 66-82; R Broadwell, Evenlode, Oddington and Adlestrop *Glouc* 82-88; rtd 89; Perm to Offic *Glouc* 89-97 and 01-07. *Pen y Dref, Rhosneigr, Anglesey LL64 5JH* Tel (01407) 810202

MORRIS, John Owen. b 56. Nottm Univ BCom82. Linc Th Coll 79. **d** 82 **p** 83. C Morriston *S & B* 82-84; C Kingstone w Clehonger and Eaton Bishop *Heref* 84-87; P-in-c Lugwardine w Bartestree and Weston Beggard 87-92; Chapl RN from 92. *Royal Naval Chaplaincy Service, Mail Point 1-2, Leach Building, Whale Island, Portsmouth PO2 8BY* Tel (023) 9262 5055 Fax 9262 5134

MORRIS, Jonathan Richard. b 57. Lanc Univ BA78 Trin Coll Ox MSc84. WEMTC 99. **d** 02 **p** 03. C Taunton St Andr *B & W* 02-06; C Wulfric Benefice from 06. *The Rectory, New Street, North Perrott, Crewkerne TA18 7ST* Tel (01460) 72356
E-mail jonbea@supanet.com

MORRIS, Kevin John. b 63. Univ of Wales (Ban) BMus84. Westcott Ho Cam 85. **d** 88 **p** 89. C Roath *Llan* 88-91; C Holborn St Alb w Saffron Hill St Pet *Lon* 91-96; V Bedford Park from 96; Dir Post-Ord Tr from 99. *The Vicarage, Priory Gardens, London W4 1TT* Tel (020) 8994 0139 *or* 8994 1380
E-mail kevin.john.morris@ukgateway.net

MORRIS, Kirsteen Helen Grace. b 44. STETS 99. **d** 02 **p** 03. NSM Cowes H Trin and St Mary *Portsm* from 02. *35 Granville Road, Cowes PO31 7JF* Tel (01983) 289585 Fax 292919
E-mail morris.scawfell@onwight.net

MORRIS, Leo. *See* MORRIS, Canon Frank Leo

MORRIS, Leslie Heber. b 26. Ox Univ MA47. Qu Coll Birm 83. **d** 84 **p** 93. NSM W Leigh *Portsm* 84-85; NSM Warblington w Emsworth 86-96. *Mermaid Cottage, 7 Slipper Road, Emsworth PO10 8BS* Tel (01243) 373389

MORRIS, Lilliau Rosina (Mother Lillian). b 29. **dss** 70 **d** 87. CSA 68-97; Mother Superior 82-94 and from 00; Sherston Magna w Easton Grey *Bris* 71-73; Notting Hill All SS w St Columb *Lon* 74-82. *34 Reynard Court, Foxley Lane, Purley CR8 3EN* Tel (020) 8668 8401

MORRIS, Lyn. *See* MORRIS, Bernard Lyn

MORRIS, Mrs Lynne Margaret. b 53. SEN. WMMTC 95. **d** 98 **p** 99. NSM Wrockwardine Wood *Lich* 98-01; Chapl Birm Specialist Community Health NHS Trust from 01. *5 Kingston Road, Trench, Telford TF2 7HT* Tel (01952) 618158 *or* 0121-442 4321 E-mail lynne.morris@southbirminghampct.nhs.uk

MORRIS, Ms Margaret Anne. b 61. Man Univ BA82 MA91. NOC 94. **d** 96 **p** 97. C Bury St Pet *Man* 96-98; C Accrington St Jo w Huncoat *Blackb* 98-01; V Knuzden from 01. *St Oswald's Vicarage, 68 Bank Lane, Blackburn BB1 2AP* Tel (01254) 698321
E-mail annemorris@gn.apc.org

MORRIS, Canon Margaret Jane. Ox Univ MTh96 Leic Univ Hon LLM96. EMMTC 86. **d** 89 **p** 94. NSM Quorndon *Leic* 89-96; Chapl for People affected by HIV 94-05; NSM Loughborough All SS w H Trin 96-98; Hon Can Leic Cathl from 97; Chapl Asst Leic R Infirmary NHS Trust 98-00; Chapl Asst Univ Hosps Leic NHS Trust from 00. *10 Toller Road, Quorn, Loughborough LE12 8AH* Tel and fax (01509) 412092
E-mail morris@rog15.freeserve.co.uk

MORRIS, Canon Martin Geoffrey Roger. b 41. Trin Coll Cam BA63 MA67. St D Coll Lamp 63. **d** 64 **p** 65. C Newport St Paul *Mon* 66-72; R Lampeter Velfrey *St D* 72-74; R Lampeter Velfrey and Llanddewi Velfrey 74-08; RD St Clears 83-98; Can St D Cathl 92-08; Chan St D 08-08; rtd 08. *Greenfield Cottage, Gilfach Hill, Lampeter Velfrey, Narberth SA67 8UL*

MORRIS, Ms Mary. b 27. Birm Univ BA49 CertEd50 MA56. **dss** 68 **d** 87 **p** 94. Kinver *Lich* 83-87; Hon Par Dn Kinver and

Enville 87-94; Hon C from 94. *12 Pavilion End, Prestwood, Stourbridge DY7 5PF* Tel (01384) 877245
E-mail marymorris12@tiscali.co.uk

MORRIS, Michael Alan. b 46. Jes Coll Cam BA70 MA74. Coll of Resurr Mirfield 79. **d** 81 **p** 82. C Leamington Priors All SS *Cov* 81-83; C Milton *Portsm* 83-88; R Petworth *Chich* 88-90; R Egdean 88-90; Chapl St Pet Hosp Chertsey 90-95; Hon C Thorpe *Guildf* 90-95; P-in-c Harbledown *Cant* 95-97; R from 97; Chapl St Nic Hosp Cant from 95. *The Rectory, Summer Hill, Harbledown, Canterbury CT2 8NW* Tel (01227) 464117 Fax 760530 E-mail michael@summer-hill.freeserve.co.uk

MORRIS, Michael James. b 70. Univ of Wales (Abth) BScEcon92. Qu Coll Birm BA. **d** 00 **p** 01. C Tupsley w Hampton Bishop *Heref* 00-04; TV Watling Valley *Ox* from 04. *21 Edzell Crescent, Westcroft, Milton Keynes MK4 4EU* Tel (01908) 507123 E-mail mike.morris@wvep.org

MORRIS (née ROBERTS), Nia Wyn. b 64. Univ of Wales (Ban) BA86 PGCE87 CQSW90 Anglia Poly Univ MA00. Westcott Ho Cam 98. **d** 00 **p** 01. C Rhyl w St Ann *St As* 00-03; R Bala from 03. *Y Rheithordy, 13 Heol-y-Castell, Bala LL23 7YA* Tel (01678) 521047 Mobile 07833-302312

MORRIS, Norman Foster Maxwell. b 46. Ex Univ BA68 MA71 Leic Univ PGCE69 K Coll Lon MTh85 Univ of Wales (Cardiff) MA91 Cheltenham & Glouc Coll of HE MA98. S'wark Ord Course 75. **d** 78 **p** 79. C Hackbridge and N Beddington *S'wark* 78-81; Chapl Tonbridge Sch 81-85; Chapl Mon Sch 85-00; Asst Warden Jones Almshouses Mon 89-00; R Wentnor w Ratlinghope, Myndtown, Norbury etc *Heref* from 00; P-in-c Churchstoke w Hyssington from 04; CF (ACF) from 02. *The Rectory, Wentnor, Bishops Castle SY9 5EE* Tel (01588) 650244 Mobile 07974-771069 E-mail revnorm@btinternet.com

MORRIS, Paul David. b 56. St Jo Coll Nottm BTh79. **d** 80 **p** 81. C Billericay and Lt Burstead *Chelmsf* 80-84; C Luton Lewsey St Hugh *St Alb* 84-89; Dioc Adv on Evang *S'well* 89-00; Dioc Millennium Officer 97-01; Min Tommy's (ch for the unchurched) 96-01; C Barton in Fabis 01-02; C Thrumpton 01-02; C Thrumpton 01-02; C Kingston and Ratcliffe-on-Soar 01-02; C Sutton Bonington w Normanton-on-Soar 01-02; Dir Evang Chr Associates Internat 02-04; Assoc Eur Dir 04-06; Eur Dir 06-08; Brussels Team 08-09; P-in-c Derby St Pet and Ch w H Trin from 09. *St Peter's Vicarage, 16 Farley Road, Derby DE23 6BX* Tel (01332) 204686 E-mail paul@stpetersderby.org.uk

MORRIS, Peter. b 45. Leeds Univ CertEd66. Tyndale Hall Bris 68. **d** 71 **p** 72. C Southport SS Simon and Jude *Liv* 71-74; Min-in-c Ch Ch Netherley LEP 74-76; V Bryn 76-91; R Redenhall, Harleston, Wortwell and Needham *Nor* 91-05; rtd 05. *6 Bromley College, London Road, Bromley BR1 1PE* Tel (020) 8460 3455

MORRIS, Canon Peter Arthur William. b 23. Bps' Coll Cheshunt 57. **d** 58 **p** 59. C Croxley Green All SS *St Alb* 58-62; V Sawbridgeworth 62-74; V S Gillingham *Roch* 74-79; Warden Pleshey Retreat Ho 79-85; P-in-c Pleshey *Chelmsf* 79-85; Hon Can Chelmsf Cathl 81-85; P-in-c Rumburgh w S Elmham w the Ilketshalls *St E* 85-89; rtd 89; Perm to Offic *St E* from 90. *The Cottage on the Common, Bakers Lane, Westleton, Saxmundham IP17 3AZ* Tel (01728) 648788

MORRIS, The Ven Philip Gregory. b 50. Leeds Univ BA71 MPhil74. Coll of Resurr Mirfield 71. **d** 73 **p** 74. C Aberdare *Llan* 74-77; C Neath w Llantwit 77-80; V Cymmer and Porth 80-88; TV Llantwit Major 88-01; Dioc Missr 88-99; Can Res Llan Cathl 00-01; Adn Margam from 02; TV Aberavon 02; P-in-c Kenfig Hill 02-05; P-in-c Ewenny w St Brides Major from 05. *The Vicarage, Southerndown Road, St Brides Major, Bridgend CF32 0SD* Tel (01656) 880108 E-mail pmorri@globalnet.co.uk

MORRIS, Philip John. b 50. FCIPD96. St Mich Coll Llan 97. **d** 99 **p** 00. NSM Builth and Llanddewi'r Cwm w Llangynog etc *S & B* 99-04; NSM Aberedw w Llandeilo Graban and Llanbadarn etc from 04. *Lochaber, 22 North Road, Builth Wells LD2 3BU* Tel (01982) 552390

MORRIS, Raymond. b 48. Open Univ BA88. NOC 80. **d** 83 **p** 84. C Tonge w Alkrington *Man* 83-86; R Blackley St Paul 86-91; V Heyside from 91; AD Tandle 02-09. *St Mark's Vicarage, Perth Street, Royton, Oldham OL2 6LY* Tel (01706) 847177

MORRIS, Raymond Arthur. b 42. Trin Coll Ox BA64 MA66 Lon Univ LLB71 CQSW72. Clifton Th Coll 66. **d** 67 **p** 91. C Greenstead *Chelmsf* 67-68; Perm to Offic *York* 69-91; NSM Linthorpe from 91. *3 Medina Gardens, Middlesbrough TS5 8BN* Tel (01642) 593726 E-mail raykate@themorrises.freeserve.co.uk

MORRIS, Raymond John Walton. b 08. OBE69. Em Coll Cam BA33 MA37. Coll of Div 33. **d** 34 **p** 35. C E Twickenham St Steph *Lon* 34-37; C Bradf Cathl 37-40; V Plymouth Em *Ex* 40-45; V E Twickenham St Steph *Lon* 45-56; Chapl Br Embassy Ch Paris *Eur* 56-69; RD France 56-69; V Brompton H Trin *Lon* 69-75; rtd 75; Perm to Offic *Sarum* 75-99. *The Malt House, Ray Road, Gillingham SP8 4EN* Tel (01747) 821973

MORRIS, Reginald Brian. b 31. St Mich Coll Llan 56. **d** 59 **p** 60. C St Jo in Bedwardine *Worc* 59-61; P-in-c Tolladine 61-62; CF 62-78; V Cheswardine *Lich* 78-84; V Hales 78-84; Perm to Offic 84-86; C Cen Telford 86-89; rtd 89; Perm to Offic *Heref* 90-07

and *Lich* from 07. *Woodside Cottage, School Lane, Prees, Whitchurch SY13 2BU* Tel (01948) 840090

MORRIS, Canon Robert John. b 45. Leeds Univ BA67. Coll of Resurr Mirfield 74. **d** 76 **p** 77. C Beeston Hill St Luke *Ripon* 76; C Holbeck 76-78; C Moseley St Mary *Birm* 78-83; P-in-c Handsworth St Jas 83-88; V 88-99; P-in-c Handsworth St Mich 86-87; AD Handsworth 92-99; TR Kings Norton from 99; Hon Can Birm Cathl from 97. *The Rectory, 273 Pershore Road South, Kings Norton, Birmingham B30 3EX* Tel 0121-459 0560 Fax 486 2825 Mobile 07973-389427 E-mail morrisrob4@aol.com

MORRIS, Robert Lee. b 47. W Virginia Univ BA69. Gen Th Sem (NY) MDiv73. **d** 73 **p** 74. USA 73-74 and from 84; Community of Celebration 75-84; P-in-c Cumbrae (or Millport) *Arg* 75-76 and 79-84. *St Dunstan's Episcopal Church, 14301 Stuebner Airline Road, Houston TX 77069 USA* Tel (001) (281) 440 1600

MORRIS, Canon Robin Edward. b 32. St Jo Coll Ox BA55 MA60. Westcott Ho Cam 55. **d** 57 **p** 58. C Halliwell St Thos *Man* 57-61; V Castleton Moor 61-71; V Stalybridge 71-80; R Heswall *Ches* 80-97; Hon Can Ches Cathl 91-97; RD Wirral N 93-97; rtd 97; Perm to Offic *Man* from 97. *122 Kiln Lane, Milnrow, Rochdale OL16 3HA* Tel (01706) 642846

MORRIS, The Ven Roger Anthony Brett. b 68. Imp Coll Lon BSc89 Trin Coll Cam BA92 MA08 ARCS89. Ridley Hall Cam 90. **d** 93 **p** 94. C Northleach w Hampnett and Farmington etc *Glouc* 93-96; P-in-c Sevenhampton w Charlton Abbotts and Hawling etc 96-00; P-in-c Dowdeswell and Andoversford w the Shiptons etc 96-00; R Sevenhampton w Charlton Abbots, Hawling etc 00-03; Dioc Dir Par Development and Evang *Cov* 03-08; Adn Worc from 08. *The Archdeacon's House, Walkers Lane, Whittington, Worcester WR5 2RE* Tel 07590-696212 (mobile) E-mail roger.morris@me.com

MORRIS (née GILES), Ms Sarah Jayne. b 76. Aston Univ BSc98. St Jo Coll Nottm MTh06. **d** 06 **p** 07. C Telford *Lich* from 06. *40 Eleanor Crescent, Newcastle ST5 3SA* Tel (01782) 505108 E-mail morris.sarah33@btinternet.com

MORRIS, Shaun Anthony. b 64. Keele Univ BSocSc85. Oak Hill Th Coll 04. **d** 06 **p** 07. C Westlands St Andr *Lich* from 06. *40 Eleanor Crescent, Newcastle ST5 3SA* Tel (01782) 638054 E-mail morris.shaun@btinternet.com

MORRIS, Simon John. b 83. St Jo Coll Dur BA05. St Steph Ho Ox BA07. **d** 08 **p** 09. C Tottenham St Mary *Lon* from 08. *The Cottage, Kemble Road, London N17 9UE* Tel (020) 8808 5027

MORRIS, Stephen Bryan. b 54. Linc Th Coll 88. **d** 90 **p** 91. C Glouc St Geo w Whaddon 90-94; Chapl for the Deaf from 94; C Glouc St Mary de Crypt w St Jo, Ch Ch etc 94-99; C Glouc St Mark and St Mary de Crypt w St Jo etc 00-02; C Barnwood 02-03. *The Vicarage, 27A Barnwood Avenue, Gloucester GL4 3AB* Tel (01452) 610450

MORRIS, Stephen Francis. b 52. St Jo Coll Nottm BTh79. **d** 79 **p** 80. C N Hinksey *Ox* 79-82; C Leic H Apostles 82-85; TV Shenley and Loughton *Ox* 85-88; TV Watling Valley 88-95; V Chatham St Wm *Roch* 95-98; TR S Chatham H Trin 98-00; Lect Nottingham St Mary and St Cath *S'well* 00-07; Lect Nottingham All SS, St Mary and St Pet from 07; AD Nottingham Cen 02-08. *21 Private Road, Sherwood, Nottingham NG5 4DD* Tel 0115-960 4477 *or* 947 2476 E-mail parishoffice@stmarysnottingham.org

MORRIS, Canon Stuart Collard. b 43. AKC66. St Boniface Warminster 66. **d** 67 **p** 68. C Hanham *Bris* 67-71; C Whitchurch 71-74; P-in-c Westerleigh and Wapley w Codrington and Dodington 74-77; P-in-c Holdgate w Tugford *Heref* 77-82; P-in-c Abdon w Clee St Margaret 77-82; R Diddlebury w Bouldon and Munslow 77-82; P-in-c Sotterley, Willingham, Shadingfield, Ellough etc *St E* 82-87; RD Beccles and S Elmham 83-94; P-in-c Westhall w Brampton and Stoven 86-88; P-in-c Flixton w Homersfield and S Elmham 86-92; Hon Can St E Cathl 87-99; V Bungay H Trin w St Mary 87-94; P-in-c Hadleigh w Layham and Shelley 94-96; R Hadleigh 96-99; Dean Bocking 94-99; RD Hadleigh 94-98; rtd 99; Perm to Offic *Ely* from 07. *Black Bank Farm, Ringmore Road, Southery, Downham Market PE38 0NL* Tel (01366) 377567

MORRIS, Canon Timothy David. b 48. Lon Univ BSc69. Trin Coll Bris. **d** 75 **p** 76. C Edin St Thos 75-77; R Edin St Jas 77-83; R Troon *Glas* 83-85; R Galashiels *Edin* 85-02; R Edin Gd Shep 02-08; Dean Edin 92-01; Hon Can St Mary's Cathl from 01; rtd 08. *2 The Firs, Foulden Newton, Berwick-upon-Tweed TD15 1UL* Tel (01289) 386615 E-mail timdmorris@blueyonder.co.uk

MORRIS, Mrs Valerie Ruth. b 46. St Hugh's Coll Ox BA68 MA72. Gilmore Course 76. **dss** 78 **d** 87 **p** 05. Drayton in Hales *Lich* 82-87; Burton 82-90; Par Dn 87-91; Perm to Offic *Heref* 04-05; Hon C Church Stretton from 05. *Watling House, All Stretton, Church Stretton SY6 6HH* Tel (01694) 722243 E-mail valerieanddavid@caradoc-as.fsnet.co.uk

MORRIS, William Hazlitt. b 62. Trin Coll Cam BA84 MA88 Virginia Univ LLM89 Solicitor 88. NTMTC BA09. **d** 09. NSM St Martin-in-the-Fields *Lon* from 09. *St Martin-in-the-Fields, 6 St Martin's Place, London WC2N 4JH* Tel (020) 7766 1100 E-mail william.morris@smitf.org

MORRIS, William Humphrey Francis. b 29. Univ of Wales BA54 MA72 Trin Coll Cam BA62 MA66 PhD75 Man Univ MEd76 PhD80 Ox Univ DPhil85 DD88 FRAS84 FInstP92. Qu Coll Birm 56. **d** 58 **p** 59. C Prestbury *Ches* 58-60; C Neston 60-65; V Sandbach Heath 65-68; Lic to Offic 69-93; rtd 84; Lic to Offic *Lich* from 93; Perm to Offic *Ches* from 93. *Stonyflats Farm, Smallwood, Sandbach CW11 2XH* Tel (01477) 500354

MORRIS, William James. b 23. St Deiniol's Hawarden 72. **d** 73 **p** 74. NSM Brecon Adnry 73-78; NSM Crickhowell w Cwmdu and Tretower *S & B* 78-98; rtd 98. *The School House, Cwmdu, Crickhowell NP8 1RU* Tel (01874) 730355

MORRIS, William Richard Price. b 23. FCollP82. Glouc Sch of Min 86. **d** 88 **p** 89. Hon C Bussage *Glouc* 88-90; Perm to Offic 90-91; Hon C France Lynch 91; Hon C Chalford and France Lynch 91-93; rtd 93; Perm to Offic *Glouc* from 93. *Langendun House, Manor Close, Michinhampton, Stroud GL6 9DG* Tel (01453) 886382

MORRISON, Barbara Anne. b 29. St Andr Univ BSc50. **d** 95 **p** 96. NSM Eorropaidh *Arg* from 95; P-in-c 00-04; rtd 04. *46 Upper Coll, Back, Isle of Lewis HS2 0LT* Tel and fax (01851) 820559 E-mail barbara.stmoluag@care4free.net

MORRISON, Barry John. b 44. Pemb Coll Cam BA66 MA70. ALCD69. **d** 69 **p** 70. C Stoke Bishop *Bris* 69-72; C Edgware *Lon* 72-76; Chapl Poly Cen Lon 76-83; Hon C Langham Place All So 76-83; P-in-c W Hampstead St Luke 83-88; V 88-98; Chapl Westf Coll 84-92; R Rushden St Mary w Newton Bromswold *Pet* 98-08; rtd 08; Perm to Offic *Pet* from 09. *The Stable Cottage, Mill Lane, Wadenhoe, Peterborough PE8 5XD* Tel (01832) 720254 E-mail ganbmorrison@btinternet.com

MORRISON, Bryony Clare. b 47. Lon Univ CertEd77 Brentwood Coll of Educn BEd86. NTMTC 96. **d** 99 **p** 00. C Epping Distr *Chelmsf* 99-05; TV from 05; Chapl Epping Forest Primary Care Trust 02-05. *Theydon Garnon Vicarage, Fiddlers Hamlet, Epping CM16 7PQ* Tel (01992) 573672 Mobile 07850-876304 E-mail revbry@dibleyhouse.com

MORRISON, Mrs Caroline. b 63. SEITE. **d** 09. C Bexleyheath Ch Ch *Roch* from 09. *50 Martin Dene, Bexleyheath DA6 8NA* Tel 07765-244724 (mobile) E-mail carol.morrison@ntlworld.com

MORRISON, Diana Mary (Sister Diana). b 43. St Kath Coll Liv CertEd64. EAMTC 02. **d** 05 **p** 06. NSM Breadsall *Derby* from 05. *The Convent of the Holy Name, Morley Road, Chaddesden, Derby DE21 4QZ* Tel (01332) 671716 Fax 669712 E-mail dianachn@tiscali.co.uk

MORRISON, Iain Edward. b 36. St Steph Ho Ox 76. **d** 78 **p** 79. C Brighton St Aug and St Sav *Chich* 78-81; C Felpham w Middleton 81-83; P-in-c Barnham and Eastergate 83-85; R Aldingbourne, Barnham and Eastergate 85-91; V Jarvis Brook 91-98; R Hastings St Clem and All SS 98-03; rtd 03; P-in-c Arlington, Folkington and Wilmington *Chich* from 03. *The Vicarage, The Street, Wilmington, Polegate BN26 5SL* Tel (01323) 870268 E-mail iain@hafodty.demon.uk

MORRISON, Preb James Wilson Rennie. b 42. Aber Univ MA65. Linc Th Coll 76. **d** 78 **p** 79. C Whitley Ch Ch *Ox* 78-81; R Burghfield 81-87; CF 87-97; P-in-c Burghill *Heref* 97-03; V from 03; P-in-c Stretton Sugwas 97-03; R from 03; P-in-c Pipe-cum-Lyde 97-03; P-in-c Pipe-cum-Lyde and Moreton-on-Lugg from 03; Preb Heref Cathl from 08. *The Vicarage, Burghill, Hereford HR4 7SG* Tel (01432) 760246

MORRISON, The Ven John Anthony. b 38. Jes Coll Cam BA60 MA64 Linc Coll Ox MA68. Chich Th Coll 61. **d** 64 **p** 65. C Birm St Pet 64-68; C Ox St Mich 68-71; Chapl Linc Coll Ox 68-74; C Ox St Mich w St Martin and All SS 71-74; V Basildon 74-82; RD Bradfield 78-82; V Aylesbury 82-89; RD Aylesbury 85-89; TR Aylesbury w Bierton and Hulcott 89-90; Adn Buckingham 90-98; P-in-c Princes Risborough w Ilmer 96-97; Adn Ox and Can Res Ch Ch 98-05; rtd 05; Perm to Offic *Ox* from 05. *39 Crown Road, Wheatley, Oxford OX33 1UJ* Tel (01865) 876625 E-mail morrison039@btinternet.com

MORRISON, Keith Charles. b 63. Wycliffe Hall Ox. **d** 01 **p** 02. C Ipswich St Aug *St E* 01-04; Asst Chapl Cam Univ Hosps NHS Foundn Trust from 04. *Addenbrooke's Hospital, Hills Road, Cambridge CB2 0QQ* Tel (01223) 245151 Mobile 07798-965651 E-mail keith.morrison@addenbrookes.nhs.uk

MORRISON, Raymond. *See* MORRISON, Walter John Raymond

MORRISON, Richard James. b 55. Sarum & Wells Th Coll 87. **d** 89 **p** 90. C Boston *Linc* 89-93; P-in-c Digby 93-99; V Whaplode Drove from 99; V Gedney Hill from 99. *The Vicarage, 1 Broadgate, Whaplode Drove, Spalding PE12 0TN* Tel (01406) 330392

MORRISON, Canon Robin Victor Adair. b 45. Nottm Univ BA67. Bucharest Th Inst 67 Ripon Hall Ox 68. **d** 70 **p** 71. C Hackney St Jo *Lon* 70-73; Chapl Newc Univ 73-76; P-in-c

Teversal *S'well* 76-78; Chapl Sutton Cen 76-78; Asst Hd Deans Community Sch Livingston *Edin* 78-80; R Edin St Columba 80-81; Chapl Birm Univ 81-88; Prin Soc Resp Officer *Derby* 88-96; TV Southampton (City Cen) *Win* 96-01; Ind Chapl 96-01; Non Exec Dir Southampton and SW Hants HA 00-01; Officer for Ch and Soc Ch in Wales Prov Coun from 01; Hon Can Llan Cathl from 09. *1 Dannog y Coed, Barry CF63 1HF* Tel (01446) 741900 E-mail robin@sparticus.net

MORRISON, Walter John Raymond (Ray). b 30. Jes Coll Cam BA55 MA58. Westcott Ho Cam 55. **d** 57 **p** 58. C Dalston St Mark w St Bart *Lon* 57-60; C Totteridge *St Alb* 60-63; V Letchworth St Paul 63-71; RD Hitchin 70-71; R Ludlow *Heref* 72-83; RD Ludlow 78-83; Preb Heref Cathl 78-83; P-in-c Ludlow, Ludford, Ashford Carbonell etc 80-83; Chapl St Thos Hosp Lon 83-86; Chapl Eastbourne Distr Gen Hosp 86-95; rtd 95; Perm to Offic *Worc* from 95. *190 Farleigh Road, Pershore WR10 1LY* Tel (01386) 556542
E-mail ray_morrison@tiscali.co.uk

MORROW, Daniel Ross. b 77. Oklahoma Bapt Univ BA01. Claremont Sch of Th MDiv06. **d** 07 **p** 08. C San Clemente USA 07-08; Asst Chapl Zürich *Eur* from 08. *St Andrew, Promenadengasse 9, 8001 Zürich, Switzerland* Tel and fax (0041) (1) 252 6024 E-mail zurich@anglican.ch
or revdanmorrow@gmail.com

MORROW, David. b 63. NUU BSc86 TCD BTh89. CITC 86. **d** 89 **p** 90. C Portadown St Mark *Arm* 89-91; C Ballymena w Ballyclug *Conn* 91-94; I Tempo and Clabby *Clogh* 94-01; I Kilcronaghan w Draperstown and Sixtowns *D & R* from 01; Bp's Dom Chapl from 07. *Kilcronaghan Rectory, 12 Rectory Road, Tobermore, Magherafelt BT45 5QP* Tel (028) 7962 8823 Mobile 07784-738217 E-mail davidmorrow763@btinternet.com

MORROW, Canon Henry Hugh. b 26. TCD BA49 MA67 Flinders Univ Aus BSocAdmin76. TCD Div Sch Div Test49. **d** 49 **p** 50. C Dublin St Thos *D & G* 49-53; I Rathmolyon *M & K* 53-58; I Killoughter *K, E & A* 58-63; C Portadown St Columba *Arm* 63-65; I Ballinderry w Tamlaght 65-70; Australia from 70; Hon Can Adelaide from 84. *5 Allendale Grove, Stonyfell SA 5066, Australia* Tel (0061) (8) 8332 5890

MORROW, Canon Joseph John. b 54. JP87. Edin Univ BD79 Dundee Univ LLB92 NY Th Sem DMin87. Edin Th Coll 76. **d** 79 **p** 80. Chapl St Paul's Cathl Dundee 79-82; P-in-c Dundee St Martin 82-85; R 85-90; P-in-c Dundee St Jo 85-08; P-in-c Dundee St Ninian 02-07; Can St Paul's Cathl Dundee 00-08; Dioc Chan from 08. *Milton Haugh, Tealing, Dundee DD4 0QZ* Tel (01382) 380501 E-mail j.j.morrow@btinternet.com

MORROW, Nigel Patrick. b 68. Dur Univ BA94 TCD MPhil02 Anglia Ruskin Univ MA05. Westcott Ho Cam 03. **d** 05 **p** 06. C Linc St Botolph and Linc St Pet-at-Gowts and St Andr 05-08; C Camberwell St Giles w St Matt *S'wark* from 08; Chapl K Coll Lon from 08. *St Matthew's House, 77 Coldharbour Lane, London SE5 9NS* Tel (020) 7733 4247 Mobile 07515-770440
E-mail patrickmorrow@live.co.uk

MORSE, Mrs Elisabeth Ann. b 51. New Hall Cam MA73 Qu Eliz Coll Lon MSc74 Heythrop Coll Lon MA97. S'wark Ord Course 91. **d** 94 **p** 95. C Wimbledon *S'wark* 94-99; C Fulham All SS *Lon* 99-08; V Battersea St Luke *S'wark* from 08. *52 Thurleigh Road, London SW12 8UD* Tel (020) 8673 6506
E-mail morseelisabeth@yahoo.co.uk

MORSHEAD, Ivo Francis Trelawny. b 27. ACA52 FCA63. Cuddesdon Coll 61. **d** 63 **p** 64. C Bris St Mary Redcliffe w Temple etc 63-68; C Wimbledon *S'wark* 68-73; V Elham *Cant* 73-78; V Whitchurch *Ex* 78-91; rtd 91; Perm to Offic *Lon* from 91. *28 Edge Street, London W8 7PN* Tel (020) 7727 5975

MORSON, Mrs Dorothy Mary. b 29. Linc Th Coll 71. **d** 87. Par Dn Cen Telford *Lich* 87-89; rtd 89; Perm to Offic *Lich* 89-00. *Ashleigh, Hunter Street, Shrewsbury SY3 8QN* Tel (01743) 369225

MORSON, Mrs Eleanor. b 42. CA Tr Coll 63 TISEC 95. **d** 96 **p** 96. NSM Kirkwall *Ab* 96-01; R Edin St Mark 01-05. *2 Royal Oak Court, Kirkwall KW15 1US* Tel (01856) 870862

MORSON, John. b 41. CA Tr Coll 62. **d** 88 **p** 92. NSM Duns *Edin* 88-89; CF 89-92; R Kirkwall *Ab* 92-01; R Stromness 92-01; NSM Edin St Mark 01-05; rtd 06. *2 Royal Oak Court, Kirkwall KW15 1US* Tel (01856) 870862

MORT, Alister. b 52. BSc BA. Oak Hill Th Coll. **d** 82 **p** 83. C Cheadle Hulme St Andr *Ches* 82-85; C Rodbourne Cheney *Bris* 86-87; TV 87-90; V New Milverton *Cov* 90-05; Perm to Offic from 05. *11 Eglamour Way, Heathcote, Warwick CV34 6GE* Tel (01926) 337260 E-mail alister.mort@ntlworld.com

MORT, Ivan Laurence (Laurie). b 61. Nottm Univ BTh87. Linc Th Coll 84. **d** 87 **p** 88. C Aston cum Aughton and Ulley *Sheff* 87-90; C Greenstead *Chelmsf* 90-94; Chapl Toulouse *Eur* 94-05. *19 rue Bel Soulhel, 31700 Cornebarrieu, France*
E-mail laurie.mort@tiscali.fr

MORT, Canon Margaret Marion. b 37. Edin Univ MA. S Tr Scheme 94. **d** 97 **p** 98. NSM Swanmore St Barn *Portsm* 97-07; Hon Can Portsm Cathl 01-07; rtd 07; Perm to Offic *Portsm* from

07. *Rivendell, High Street, Shirrell Heath, Southampton SO32 2JN* Tel and fax (01329) 832178 Mobile 07761-225222 E-mail marian@colinholy.f2s.com

MORTER, Preb Ian Charles. b 54. AKC77. Coll of Resurr Mirfield 77. **d** 78 **p** 79. C Colchester St Jas, All SS, St Nic and St Runwald *Chelmsf* 78-82; C Brixham w Churston Ferrers *Ex* 82-83; TV 84-86; TV Sidmouth, Woolbrook, Salcombe Regis, Sidbury etc 86-95; P-in-c Exminster and Kenn 95-00; TR Littleham w Exmouth from 00; RD Aylesbeare from 07; Preb Ex Cathl from 08. *The Rectory, 1 Maer Road, Exmouth EX8 2DA* Tel (01395) 272227

MORTIBOYS, John William. b 45. K Coll Lon BD69 AKC69. Sarum Th Coll 71. **d** 71 **p** 72. C Reading All SS *Ox* 71-95; Perm to Offic *Portsm* from 97. *13 Oyster Street, Portsmouth PO1 2HZ* Tel (023) 9275 6676 Fax 9266 2626

MORTIMER, Aileen Jane. b 46. Edin Univ MA67 CQSW69. ERMC 05. **d** 08 **p** 09. NSM E Bergholt and Brantham *St E* from 08. *20 Leggatt Drive, Bramford, Ipswich IP8 4ET* Tel (01473) 747419 E-mail ajmortimer@hotmail.co.uk

MORTIMER, Anthony John. b 42. Sarum & Wells Th Coll 68. **d** 71 **p** 72. C Heref St Martin 71-79; V Kingstone 79-85; P-in-c Clehonger and Eaton Bishop 80-85; TR Pinhoe and Broadclyst *Ex* 85-05; rtd 05. *97 Egremont Road, Exmouth EX8 1SA* Tel (01395) 271390 E-mail themortimers@totalise.co.uk

MORTIMER, Charles Philip. b 38. Linc Th Coll 68. **d** 70 **p** 71. C Penistone w Midhope *Wakef* 70-74; V Luddenden 74-77; P-in-c Luddenden Foot 74-77; Chapl RAF 77-91; Asst Chapl-in-Chief RAF 91-93; V Staincliffe *Wakef* 93-99; rtd 99; Perm to Offic *Wakef* from 99. *15 Park Avenue, Liversedge Hall Lane, Liversedge WF15 7EQ* Tel (01924) 510051

MORTIMER, Mrs Elizabeth Anne. b 69. RGN92. Ripon Coll Cuddesdon 05. **d** 07 **p** 08. C Minehead *B & W* from 07. *75 Summerland Avenue, Minehead TA24 5BW* Tel (01643) 708858

MORTIMER, Jonathan Michael. b 60. Bris Univ BA83. Oak Hill Th Coll BA92. **d** 92 **p** 93. C Rugby St Matt *Cov* 92-96; C Southgate *Chich* 96-98; TR 98-07; Through Faith Miss Ev from 07. *1 Hyde Cottages, London Road, Handcross, Haywards Heath RH17 6EZ* Tel (01444) 401089
E-mail mortimerj@btinternet.com

MORTIMER, Canon Lawrence George. b 45. St Edm Hall Ox BA67 MA71. St Chad's Coll Dur. **d** 70 **p** 71. C Rugby St Andr *Cov* 70-75; V Styvechale 75-89; Dioc Broadcasting Officer 80-89; Dioc Communications Officer 89-03; P-in-c Wootton Wawen from 95; P-in-c Claverdon w Preston Bagot from 03; Hon Can Cov Cathl from 96. *The Vicarage, Stratford Road, Wootton Wawen, Henley-in-Arden B95 6BD* Tel and fax (01564) 792659 *or* tel 795545 E-mail l.mortimer@btinternet.com

MORTIMER, Canon Peter Jackson. b 41. MBE95 TD73. St Jo Coll York CertEd63 Essex Univ MA71 FRSA97. EAMTC 97. **d** 98 **p** 99. NSM Needham Market w Badley *St E* 98-02; NSM Ringshall w Battisford, Barking w Darmsden etc 98-02; Bp's Ecum Adv from 02; Chapl to Suffolk Fire Service from 03; Hon Can St E Cathl from 06. *20 Leggatt Drive, Bramford, Ipswich IP8 4ET* Tel (01473) 747419

MORTIMER, Philip. *See* MORTIMER, Charles Philip.

MORTIMER, Richard James. b 63. Ex Univ BSc85 Lon Bible Coll BA97. Oak Hill Th Coll. **d** 01 **p** 02. C Ore St Helen and St Barn *Chich* 01-05; Chapl Hastings Univ from 05; C Hastings H Trin from 05. *4 Gresham Way, St Leonards-on-Sea TN38 0UE* Tel (01424) 440093 E-mail richard@rmortimer.freeserve.co.uk

MORTIMER, William Raymond. b 31. MIET66. St Deiniol's Hawarden 68. **d** 69 **p** 70. C Flint *St As* 69-71; Lic to Offic 72-73; V Llanwddyn and Llanfihangel-yng-Nghwynfa etc 73-85; RD Llanfyllin 83-84; R Llanrwst and Llanddoget and Capel Garmon 85-96; rtd 96. *1 Coed Masarn, Woodlands Estate, Abergele LL22 7EE* Tel (01745) 822306

MORTIMORE, David Jack. b 42. Master Mariner 69. St Mich Coll Llan 90. **d** 91 **p** 92. C Pembroke St Mary w St Mich *St D* 91-92; C Bargoed and Deri w Brithdir *Llan* 92-97; Perm to Offic 98-02; P-in-c Llangeinor 02-04; P-in-c Llangeinor and the Garw Valley from 04. *The Vicarage, St Davids Street, Pontycymer, Bridgend CF32 8LT* Tel (01656) 870280
E-mail cleddau@tesco.net

MORTIMORE, Robert Edward. b 39. Kelham Th Coll 61 Wells Th Coll 66. **d** 69 **p** 70. C Byfleet *Guildf* 69-72; C Fitzroy New Zealand 72-75; C Remuera 76-78; Min Bell Block 77-79; V Te Kuiti 79-85; Offic Min Auckland 86-89; Sen Asst P Whangarei 89-92; V Avondale 92-98; V Milford 98-04; Offic Min from 04. *69 Crawford Crescent, Kamo, Whangarei 0112, New Zealand* Tel and fax (0064) (9) 435 1285 E-mail b.jmortimore@xtra.co.nz

MORTIS, Lorna Anne. b 54. Moray Ho Coll of Educn DipEd76 Open Univ BA88. TISEC 95. **d** 98 **p** 99. NSM Gullane and N Berwick *Edin* 98-02; P-in-c Edin St Marg 02-08; Hon C Musselburgh from 08; Hon C Prestonpans from 08. *Rosebank, 2 Main Street, Athelstaneford, North Berwick EH39 5BE* Tel (01620) 880505 Mobile 07779-553807 E-mail anrola@aol.com

MORTON, Adrian Ian. b 65. Brighton Poly BSc87 Brunel Univ MSc93. Ridley Hall Cam 98. **d** 00 **p** 01. C Kettering Ch the King

Pet 00-04; P-in-c Bozeat w Easton Maudit 04-06; P-in-c Wollaston and Strixton 04-06; V Wollaston w Strixton and Bozeat etc from 06. *The Vicarage, 81 Irchester Road, Wollaston, Wellingborough NN29 7RW* Tel (01933) 664256
E-mail adrian-morton@supanet.com

MORTON, Albert George. b 34. Saskatchewan Univ BA61 McGill Univ Montreal MA73. Em Coll Saskatoon 56. **d** 61 **p** 61. Canada 61-65; C Stanford-le-Hope *Chelmsf* 66-69; V Linc St Geo Swallowbeck 69-82; R Lt Munden w Sacombe *St Alb* 82-89; R The Mundens w Sacombe 89-96; rtd 96; Perm to Offic *Sarum* from 00. *10 Church Green, Bishop's Caundle, Sherborne DT9 5NN* Tel (01963) 23383

MORTON, Andrew Edward. b 51. Lon Univ BA72 BD74 AKC74 Univ of Wales (Cardiff) MPhil93. St Aug Coll Cant 75. **d** 76 **p** 77. C Feltham *Lon* 76-79; C Pontlottyn w Fochriw *Llan* 79-81; V Ferndale w Maerdy 81-88; V Tylorstown w Ynyshir 88-93; Dir of Studies Llan Ord Course 91-93; R Llangybi and Coedypaen w Llanbadoc *Mon* from 93; Chapl Coleg Gwent from 93; Dioc FE Officer from 93; Prov HE Officer from 01; Dioc Dir NSM Studies from 00. *The Rectory, Parc Road, Llangybi, Usk NP15 1NL* Tel (01633) 450214 E-mail mortonae@hotmail.com

MORTON, Mrs Christine Mary. b 39. Linc Th Coll 78. **dss** 80 **d** 87 **p** 94. Ore St Helen and St Barn *Chich* 80-84; Southwick St Mich 84-85; Winchmore Hill St Paul *Lon* 85-87; Par Dn 87-94; C 94-99; Hon C 00-02; rtd 00; Perm to Offic *Lon* from 02. *122 Bourne Hill, London N13 4BD* Tel (020) 8886 3157

MORTON, Clive Frederick. b 47. Lon Univ BA70 Birm Univ MA98. Cranmer Hall Dur 78. **d** 80 **p** 81. C Countesthorpe w Foston *Leic* 80-83; C Glen Parva and S Wigston 83-86; Asst Chapl HM Youth Cust Cen Glen Parva 83-86; V Birm St Pet 86-98; Miss Partner CMS 99-02; Chapl St Petersburg *Eur* 99-02; Lect St Petersburg Th Academy and Sem 99-02; V Kingsbury H Innocents *Lon* from 02. *Kingsbury Vicarage, 54 Roe Green, London NW9 0PJ* Tel (020) 8204 7531 Mobile 07447-883559 E-mail holyinnocents.kingsbury@virgin.net

MORTON, Derek. *See* MORTON, Canon William Derek

MORTON, Howard Knyvett. b 30. St Jo Coll Cam BA51 MA67. Linc Th Coll 55. **d** 57 **p** 58. C Hatfield Hyde *St Alb* 57-60; Hd RE Heaton Gr Sch Newc 60-66 and 72-75; CMS 66-72; Heworth Grange Sch Dur 75-83; Regional Org Oxfam 88-91; Grainger Gr Sch Newc 91-94; Lic to Offic *Newc* 73-93; Dioc World Development Officer 94-95; rtd 95; Perm to Offic *Dur* 95-98 and *Newc* from 96. *Daisy Cottage, Hawthorn Lane, Rothbury, Morpeth NE65 7TL* Tel (01665) 577958

MORTON, Mrs Jacqueline Mavis. b 46. UEA BSc67 York Univ BSc82. EMMTC 97. **d** 00 **p** 01. NSM Sibsey w Frithville *Linc* from 00. *8 Lucan Close, Sibsey, Boston PE22 0SH* Tel (01205) 751378 E-mail jacqui.morton@care4free.net

MORTON, Jennifer. b 50. Bedf Coll Lon BA72 Leic Univ PGCE73. EMMTC 87. **d** 90 **p** 94. C New Mills *Derby* 90-94; Chapl Asst Nottm City Hosp NHS Trust 94-98; Chapl Basford Hosp Nottm 94-98; Chapl S Derbyshire Acute Hosps NHS Trust 98-02; Vice Prin EMMTC *S'well* from 02. *56 Marshall Drive, Beeston, Nottingham NG9 3LD* Tel 0115-939 5784 *or* 951 4427 Fax 951 4817 E-mail jenny.morton@nottingham.ac.uk

MORTON, Mrs Judith. b 58. St Jo Coll Nottm 04. **d** 06 **p** 07. C Shaston *Sarum* from 06. *1 Gower Road, Shaftesbury SP7 8RU* Tel (01747) 855969 Mobile 07932-630232
E-mail bosie.morton@tiscali.co.uk

MORTON, Mark Paul. b 58. Univ of Wales (Swansea) BA79 Univ of Wales (Lamp) MA99 Cardiff Univ MTh08. Ridley Hall Cam 90. **d** 92 **p** 93. C Daventry, Ashby St Ledgers, Braunston etc *Pet* 92-95; Chapl Danetre Hosp 93-94; CF (TA) 93-95; CF 95-03; Sen CF from 03. *c/o MOD Chaplains (Army)* Tel (01980) 615804 Fax 615800 E-mail revmpmorton@hotmail.com

MORTON, Michelle. b 67. Ripon Coll Cuddesdon 00. **d** 02 **p** 03. C Buckingham *Ox* 02-05; P-in-c Stewkley w Soulbury and Drayton Parslow from 05. *The Vicarage, High Street North, Stewkley, Leighton Buzzard LU7 0HH* Tel (01525) 240287 E-mail squarenalo@hotmail.com

MORTON, Rex Gerald. b 61. St Jo Coll Nottm 96. **d** 98 **p** 99. C Bury St Edmunds All SS *St E* 98-01; C Woodside Park St Barn *Lon* 01-07; V Golders Green from 07. *The Vicarage, 3 St Alban's Close, London NW11 7RA* Tel (020) 8455 4525 Mobile 07968-088714 E-mail sj@morton4.swinternet.co.uk

MORTON, Sister Rita. b 34. Wilson Carlile Coll. **dss** 85 **d** 87 **p** 94. CA from 76; Par Dn Harlow New Town w Lt Parndon *Chelmsf* 87-89; C Harold Hill St Geo 89-94; rtd 94; NSM Elm Park St Nic Hornchurch *Chelmsf* from 94. *16 Cheviot Road, Hornchurch RM11 1LP* Tel (01708) 709842

MORTON, Robert Hart. b 28. Moray Ord Course 91. **d** 94. Hon C St Andr Cathl Inverness from 94. *75 Fairfield Road, Inverness IV3 5LJ* Tel (01463) 223525

MORTON, Miss Rosemary Grania. b 65. Qu Coll Birm BA05. **d** 05 **p** 06. C Kings Heath *Birm* 05-07; C Handsworth St Mary from 07. *43 St Christophers, Birmingham B20 1BP* Tel 0121-544 2551 E-mail rosie_morton@yahoo.co.uk

MORTON, Mrs Sheila. b 44. Leeds Univ. Sarum & Wells Th Coll 79. **dss** 84 **d** 87 **p** 94. HM Forces Düsseldorf 84-86; Cov St Mary

86-89; Par Dn 87-89; Par Dn Boston Spa *York* 89-92; C Flitwick *St Alb* 93-00; R Wilden w Colmworth and Ravensden from 00. *The New Rectory, High Street, Wilden, Bedford MK44 2PB* Tel (01234) 772895 E-mail revsheila@vicarage727freeserve.co.uk

MORTON, Canon William Derek. b 28. Wells Th Coll 67. **d** 69 **p** 70. C Kibworth Beauchamp *Leic* 69-72; Ind Chapl *Nor* 72-93; Hon Can Nor Cathl 90-93; RD Nor E 90-93; rtd 93; Perm to Offic *Nor* from 93. *55 Cameron Green, Taverham, Norwich NR8 6UA* Tel (01603) 861240

MORTON, The Very Revd William Wright. b 56. ALAM TCD BTh88 MA95 QUB PhD96. CITC. **d** 88 **p** 89. C Drumachose *D & R* 88-91; I Conwal Union w Gartan 91-97; Bp's Dom Chapl 92-97; Can Raphoe Cathl 94-97; Dean Derry from 97; I Templemore from 97. *The Deanery, 30 Bishop Street, Londonderry BT48 6PP* Tel (028) 7126 2746
E-mail dean@derry.anglican.org

MOSEDALE, Jonathan Ralph. b 69. Imp Coll Lon BSc90 York Univ MSc91 Trin Coll Ox DPhil95. Protestant Th Inst Montpellier Lic99 Ripon Coll Cuddesdon 07. **d** 09. C St Endellion w Port Isaac and St Kew *Truro* from 09; C St Minver from 09. *The Vicarage, Churchtown, St Minver, Wadebridge PL27 6QH* Tel (01208) 862398 Mobile 07760-275087 E-mail mosedale@metanoia.com

MOSELEY, David John Reading. b 30. Univ Coll Ox BA54 MA58. Wells Th Coll 54. **d** 56 **p** 57. C Farnworth and Kearsley *Man* 56-59; Trinidad and Tobago 59-63; V Bedminster St Paul *Bris* 63-75; TV Bedminster 75-78; V Kilmington w Shute *Ex* 78-95; P-in-c Stockland w Dalwood 90; rtd 95; Perm to Offic *Ex* from 95. *3 Nevada Court, Havenview Road, Seaton EX12 2PF* Tel (01297) 24174

MOSELEY, Canon Hugh Martin. b 47. St Jo Coll Dur BA70. Westcott Ho Cam 71. **d** 73 **p** 74. C Hythe *Cant* 73-77; P-in-c Eythorne w Waldershare 77-83; V Ringmer *Chich* 83-99; RD Lewes and Seaford 93-97; P-in-c E Dean w Friston and Jevington 99-00; R 00-03; TR Rye from 03; RD Rye from 03; Can and Preb Chich Cathl from 07. *St Mary's Rectory, Gungarden, Rye TN31 7HH* Tel (01797) 222430
E-mail hugh@rabbitwarren13.freeserve.co.uk

MOSELEY, Michael. b 45. Oak Hill Th Coll 02. **d** 04 **p** 05. NSM Forty Hill Jes Ch *Lon* 04-07; P-in-c Murston w Bapchild and Tonge *Cant* from 07. *Bapchild Rectory, School Lane, Sittingbourne ME9 9NL* Tel (01795) 474557
E-mail michaelmoseley07@googlemail.com

MOSELEY, Roger Henry. b 38. Edin Th Coll 60. **d** 63 **p** 64. C Friern Barnet All SS *Lon* 63-66; C Grantham St Wulfram *Linc* 66-69; P-in-c Swaton w Spanby 69-73; P-in-c Horbling 69-73; V Soberton w Newtown *Portsm* 73-80; V Sarisbury 80-03; rtd 03; Perm to Offic *Portsm* from 03. *53B St Michael's Road, St Helens, Ryde PO33 1YJ* Tel (01983) 875203
E-mail roger.moseley@tesco.net

MOSELING, Peter. b 48. WMMTC 92. **d** 95 **p** 96. C Daventry, Ashby St Ledgers, Braunston etc *Pet* 95-97; P-in-c Northampton H Trin 97-99; P-in-c Northampton St Paul 98-99; V Northampton H Trin and St Paul 99-05; Chapl Univ Coll Northn 99-05; P-in-c Bletchingley *S'wark* 05-06; R Bletchingley and Nutfield from 06. *The Rectory, Outwood Lane, Bletchingley, Redhill RH1 4LR* Tel (01883) 743252
E-mail p.moseling@tiscali.co.uk

MOSES, The Very Revd John Henry. b 38. KCVO06. Nottm Univ BA59 PhD65. Linc Th Coll 62. **d** 64 **p** 65. C Bedford St Andr *St Alb* 64-70; P-in-c Cov St Pet 70-73; P-in-c Cov St Mark 71-73; TR Cov E 73-77; RD Cov E 73-77; Adn Southend *Chelmsf* 77-82; Provost Chelmsf 82-96; Chmn Coun of Cen for Th Study Essex Univ 87-96; Dean St Paul's *Lon* 96-06; rtd 06. *Chestnut House, Burgate, Southwell NG25 0EP* Tel (01636) 814880

MOSES, Leslie Alan. b 49. Hull Univ BA71 Edin Univ BD76. Edin Th Coll 73. **d** 76 **p** 77. C Edin Old St Paul 76-79; R Leven *St And* 79-85; R Edin Old St Paul 85-95; P-in-c Edin St Marg 86-92; V St Marylebone All SS *Lon* from 95; AD Westmr St Marylebone from 01. *All Saints' Vicarage, 7 Margaret Street, London W1W 8JG* Tel (020) 7636 1788 *or* 7636 9961 Fax 7436 4470 E-mail alan@asms.org.uk

MOSFORD, Canon Denzil Huw Erasmus. b 56. Florida State Univ MTh04 AKC78. Sarum & Wells Th Coll 77. **d** 79 **p** 80. C Clydach *S & B* 79-82; V 87-97; Jamaica 82-85; V Ystalyfera *S & B* 85-87; Dioc World Miss Officer from 91; RD Cwmtawe 93-97; V Gorseinon from 97; AD Llwchwr from 00; Hon Can Brecon Cathl 01-04; Can Res from 04. *The Vicarage, 42 Princess Street, Gorseinon, Swansea SA4 4US* Tel (01792) 892849
E-mail huw.mosford@ntlworld.com

MOSLEY, Edward Peter. b 38. Clifton Th Coll 62. **d** 67 **p** 68. C Mirehouse *Carl* 67-69; C Newbarns w Hawcoat 69-72; R Aikton and Orton St Giles 72-77; V Silloth 77-78; CF 78-94; Hon C Rothiemurchus and Grantown-on-Spey *Mor* 94-95; rtd 98; P-in-c Strathnairn St Paul *Mor* 03-09. *52 Castle Heather Crescent, Inverness IV2 4BF* Tel (01463) 232552
E-mail epmos@onetel.com

MOSLEY, Robin Howarth. b 46. Birm Univ LLB67 Leeds Univ BA09 Solicitor 71. NOC 06. **d** 09. NSM Ches St Mary from 09.

Brookside, Sandy Lane, Higher Kinnerton, Chester CH4 9BJ Tel (01244) 661097 E-mail robinm243@btinternet.com

MOSS, Barbara Penelope. b 46. St Anne's Coll Ox BA66 MA70 Lon Univ BD97 Middx Univ MA00. EAMTC 95. **d** 97 **p** 98. NSM Leytonstone H Trin Harrow Green *Chelmsf* 97-00; C Cambridge Gt St Mary w St Mich *Ely* 00-05; P-in-c Gothenburg w Halmstad, Jönköping etc *Eur* from 05; Chapl Gothenburg Univ and Chalmers Univ of Tech from 05. *St Andrew's Church Flat, Norra Liden 15, S411-18 Gothenburg, Sweden* Tel and fax (0046) (31) 711 1915 E-mail bar@barmoss.demon.co.uk *or* st.andrews.got@telia.com

MOSS, Catherine. b 53. ERMC. **d** 09. NSM Guilsborough w Hollowell and Cold Ashby *Pet* from 09. *Dripwell House, High Street, Guilsborough, Northampton NN6 8PY*

MOSS (née BELL), Mrs Catherine Ann. b 63. Trin Coll Bris BA88. **d** 89 **p** 94. Par Dn Southsea St Jude *Portsm* 89-94; C 94-97; C Luton St Mary *St Alb* from 97; Chapl Luton Univ 97-02. *2 Saxtead Close, Luton LU2 9SQ* Tel (01582) 391125

MOSS, Christopher Ashley. b 52. Ex Univ BA73 Southn Univ DASS78 CQSW78. Wycliffe Hall Ox 89. **d** 91 **p** 92. C Malvern H Trin and St Jas *Worc* 91-96; V Longdon, Castlemorton, Bushley, Queenhill etc from 96. *The Vicarage, Longdon, Tewkesbury GL20 6AT* Tel and fax (01684) 833256 E-mail cmoss@holyplace.feeserve.co.uk

MOSS, David Glyn. b 62. St Anne's Coll Ox BA83 Em Coll Cam BA89. Westcott Ho Cam 87. **d** 90 **p** 91. C Halesowen *Worc* 90-93; Tutor St Steph Ho Ox 93-03; Dioc Prin 00-03; Dioc Tr Officer *Ex* 03-04; Prin SWMTC from 04. *SWMTC Office, Amory Building, University of Exeter, Rennes Drive, Exeter EX4 4RJ* Tel (01392) 264403 E-mail principal@swmtc.org.uk

MOSS, David Sefton. b 59. Sunderland Poly BSc80 Anglia Poly Univ MA05 MRPharmS81. Ridley Hall Cam 91. **d** 93 **p** 94. C Highworth w Sevenhampton and Inglesham etc *Bris* 93-97; V Bedminster St Mich from 97. *St Michael's Vicarage, 153 St John's Lane, Bedminster, Bristol BS3 5AE* Tel and fax 0117-977 6132 E-mail david.moss@iname.com

MOSS, Canon Denis. b 32. St Jo Coll Auckland LTh83. **d** 74 **p** 75. New Zealand 74-92; Chapl Budapest *Eur* from 92; Hon Can Malta Cathl from 01. *The Rectory, 2092 Budakeszi, Pf 25, Hungary* Tel (0036) (23) 452023 Fax 457123 E-mail st.marg.anglicanch@mail.datanet.hu

MOSS, James Wilfred. b 15. Oak Hill Th Coll 75. **d** 76 **p** 77. Hon C Frogmore *St Alb* 76-78 and 81-93; Hon C Watford St Luke 78-81; Perm to Offic 93-08. *8A The Rise, Park Street, St Albans AL2 2NT* Tel (01727) 872467

MOSS, Preb Kenneth Charles. b 37. Imp Coll Lon BSc59 PhD62 ARCS59. **d** 66 **p** 67. Canada 66-73; Chapl Ex Univ 73-83; V St Marychurch 83-02; RD Ipplepen 87-93; Preb Ex Cathl from 92; rtd 02. *3 Mondeville Way, Northam, Bideford EX39 1DQ* Tel (01237) 422251

MOSS, The Ven Leonard Godfrey. b 32. K Coll Lon BD59 AKC59. **d** 60 **p** 61. C Putney St Marg *S'wark* 60-63; C Cheam 63-67; R Much Dewchurch w Llanwarne and Llandinabo *Heref* 67-72; Dioc Ecum Officer 69-83; V Marden w Amberley 72-80; V Marden w Amberley and Wisteston 80-84; P-in-c 92-94; Preb Heref Cathl 79-97; Can Heref Cathl 84-91; Dioc Ecum Resp Officer 84-91; Adn Heref 91-97; rtd 97; Perm to Offic *Heref* from 97. *10 Saxon Way, Ledbury HR8 2QY* Tel (01531) 631195

MOSS, Leslie. b 52. **d** 02 **p** 03. OLM Ditton St Mich w St Thos *Liv* from 02. *105 Heath Road, Widnes WA8 7NU* Tel 0151-423 1100

MOSS, Miss Lindsey. b 70. St Jo Coll Nottm 07. **d** 09. C Standon and The Mundens w Sacombe *St Alb* from 09. *Parish Office, Standon Vicarage, Kents Lane, Standon, Ware SG11 1PJ* Tel 07974-823727 (mobile) E-mail lindseymoss822@yahoo.co.uk

MOSS, Mrs Nelva Elizabeth. b 44. Bp Grosseteste Coll TCert66 Sussex Univ BEd73. S Dios Minl Tr Scheme 90. **d** 93 **p** 94. NSM Bincombe w Broadwey, Upwey and Buckland Ripers *Sarum* 93-96; NSM Langtree *Ox* 96-98; TV from 98. *The Vicarage, Reading Road, Woodcote, Reading RG8 0QX* Tel (01491) 680979

MOSS, Peter Hextall. b 34. Clare Coll Cam BA59 MA62. Linc Th Coll 59. **d** 61 **p** 62. C Easington Colliery *Dur* 61-63; C Whickham 63-65; C-in-c Town End Farm CD 65-72; TV Mattishall *Nor* 72-75; P-in-c Welborne 75-84; P-in-c Mattishall w Mattishall Burgh 75-84; P-in-c Yaxham 80-84; TR Hempnall 84-89. *High House Cottage, Gunn Street, Foulsham, Dereham NR20 5RN* Tel (01362) 683823

MOSS, Peter John. b 41. K Coll Cam BA64 MA67. Westcott Ho Cam 63. **d** 84 **p** 85. NSM Leighton Buzzard w Eggington, Hockliffe etc *St Alb* 84-93; NSM Luton St Sav 93-98; NSM Houghton Regis 03-05; P-in-c Devizes St Pet *Sarum* from 05. *St Peter's Vicarage, Bath Road, Devizes SN10 2AP* Tel (01380) 722621 E-mail peter.moss87@ntlworld.com

MOSSE, Mrs Barbara Ann. b 51. CertEd73 Open Univ BA77 Univ of Wales (Lamp) MA99 Lambeth STh83. CA Tr Coll IDC81. **d** 90 **p** 95. CA 81-91; NSM Southbourne w W Thorney *Chich* 90-93; Community Mental Health Chapl Fareham/Gosport 94-97; NSM Purbrook *Portsm* 95-03; Team Chapl Portsm Hosps NHS Trust from 01; Asst Dioc Spirituality

Adv *Portsm* from 05. *Drogo, 1 Grenfield Court, Emsworth PO10 7SA* Tel (01243) 376155 E-mail barbaramosse@btinternet.com

MOSSLEY, Iain Stephen. b 72. Univ of Wales (Ban) BTh94. St Steph Ho Ox 95. **d** 98 **p** 99. C Ribbleton *Blackb* 98-01; C Marton Moss 01-03; V Burnley St Matt w H Trin 03-08; P-in-c Leyland St Jas from 08. *St James's Vicarage, 201 Slater Lane, Leyland PR26 7SH* Tel (01772) 421034 E-mail fatheriain@blueyonder.co.uk

MOSSMAN, Mrs Margaret. b 46. NOC 97. **d** 00 **p** 01. NSM Beighton *Sheff* 00-02; C 02-04; V Owston from 04. *The Vicarage, 11 Crabgate Lane, Skellow, Doncaster DN6 8LE* Tel (01302) 337101

MOSSOP, Patrick John. b 48. Solicitor St Jo Coll Cam MA LLB. Linc Th Coll BTh93. **d** 93 **p** 94. C Halstead St Andr w H Trin and Greenstead Green *Chelmsf* 93-97; Assoc Chapl Essex Univ 97-99; Chapl 99-04; V Forest Gate Em w Upton Cross from 04. *Emmanuel Vicarage, 2B Margery Park Road, London E7 9JY* Tel (020) 8534 8780 *or* 8522 1900 E-mail pat.mos@btinternet.com

MOTE, Gregory Justin. b 60. Oak Hill Th Coll BA83. **d** 86 **p** 87. C W Ealing St Jo w St Jas *Lon* 86-90; C St Helen Bishopsgate w St Andr Undershaft etc 90-95; V Poulton Lancelyn H Trin *Ches* 96-04; Perm to Offic *Blackb* from 04. *22 Evergreen Avenue, Leyland PR25 3AW* E-mail gjmote@aol.com

MOTH, Miss Susan. b 44. Leic Univ BA65 K Coll Lon CertEd66. Linc Th Coll 83. **dss** 85 **d** 87 **p** 94. Churchdown St Jo *Glouc* 85-93; C 87-93; Dn-in-c The Rissingtons 93-94; P-in-c 94-05; rtd 05. *19 Cunliffe Close, Oxford OX2 7BJ*

MOTHERSDALE, Paul John. b 52. NOC 94. **d** 97 **p** 98. C Kirkleatham *York* 97-00; V Middlesbrough St Agnes 00-05; R Thornton Dale w Allerston, Ebberston etc from 05; RD Pickering from 06. *The Rectory, High Street, Thornton Dale, Pickering YO18 7QW* Tel (01751) 474244 E-mail paulmothersdale@bigfoot.com

MOTHERSOLE, John Robert. b 25. Lon Univ MA99. Chich Th Coll. **d** 84 **p** 85. NSM Hayes St Anselm *Lon* 84-93; NSM Hayes St Edm 93-98; P-in-c St Mary Aldermary from 98. *116 Nestles Avenue, Hayes UB3 4QD* Tel (020) 8848 0626 E-mail john@stmaryaldermary.co.uk

MOTT, Julian Ward. b 52. Loughb Univ BSc77. Ripon Coll Cuddesdon 78. **d** 81 **p** 82. C Aylestone *Leic* 81-84; C Gt Ilford St Mary *Chelmsf* 84-88; R Chevington w Hargrave and Whepstead w Brockley *St E* 88-99; V Lower Gornal *Worc* from 99. *The Vicarage, Church Street, Lower Gornal, Dudley DY3 2PF* Tel (01902) 882023

MOTT, Peter John. b 49. Ch Coll Cam BA70 MA75 Dundee Univ PhD73. St Jo Coll Nottm BA79. **d** 80 **p** 81. C Hull St Jo Newland *York* 80-83; C Selly Park St Steph and St Wulstan *Birm* 83-87; C Mosbrough *Sheff* 87-92; R Colne St Bart *Blackb* 92-98; TV Colne and Villages 98-01; P-in-c Keighley St Andr *Bradf* from 01; Dioc Ecum Officer from 04. *The Rectory, 13 Westview Grove, Keighley BD20 6JJ* Tel (01535) 601499 E-mail peter.mott@bradford.anglican.org

✠**MOTTAHEDEH, The Rt Revd Iraj Kalimi.** b 32. United Th Coll Bangalore 56. **d** 59 **p** 60 **c** 86. C Isfahan St Luke Iran 59-62; V Shiraz St Simon 62-66; V Tehran St Paul 67 75; V Isfahan St Luke 75-83; Adn Iran 83-86; Asst Bp Iran 86-90; Bp Iran 90-02; Pres Bp Episc Ch Jerusalem and Middle E 00-02; rtd 02; Interim Bp Iran 02-04, Hon Asst Bp Birm and Lich from 05. *2 Highland Road, Newport TF10 7QE* Tel (01952) 813615 E-mail bishraj@btinternet.com

MOTTERSHEAD, Derek. b 39. Open Univ BA74 BEd. Chich Th Coll 65. **d** 69 **p** 70. C Walthamstow St Barn and St Jas Gt *Chelmsf* 69-72; C Chelmsf All SS 72-77; P-in-c Cold Norton w Stow Maries 77-80; V Leytonstone St Andr 80-92; V Eastbourne St Sav and St Pet *Chich* 92-04; Miss to Seafarers 92-04; rtd 04; Perm to Offic *Cant* 05-06; Hon C Preston next Faversham, Goodnestone and Graveney from 06. *Sherwood, 25B The Paddock, Spring Lane, Canterbury CT1 1SX* Tel (01227) 453118 E-mail de@dmotters.fsnet.co.uk

MOTTRAM, Andrew Peter. b 53. AKC77. Ripon Coll Cuddesdon 77. **d** 78 **p** 79. C E Bedfont *Lon* 78-81; C Bp's Hatfield *St Alb* 81-84; V Milton Ernest 84-91; V Thurleigh 84-91; P-in-c Heref All SS 91-06; RD Heref City 02-03; Perm to Offic from 06. *Ecclesiastical Property Solutions, Mulberry Dock, Pencombe, Bromyard HR7 4SH* Tel (01885) 400311 Mobile 07960-726717 E-mail andrew@abetterview.co.uk

MOTYER, John Alexander. b 24. TCD BA46 MA51 BD51 Lambeth DD97. Wycliffe Hall Ox 47. **d** 47 **p** 48. C Penn Fields *Lich* 47-50; C Bris H Trin and Tutor Clifton Th Coll 51-54; Vice-Prin 54-65; Tutor Tyndale Hall Bris 52-54; V W Hampstead St Luke *Lon* 54-70; Dep Prin Tyndale Hall Bris 70-71; Prin and Dean Trin Coll Bris 71-81; Min Westbourne Ch Ch Prop Chpl *Win* 81-89; rtd 89; Perm to Offic *Ex* from 90. *27 Georges Road West, Poynton, Stockport SK12 1JY*

MOTYER, Stephen. b 50. Pemb Coll Cam BA73 MA77 Bris Univ MLitt79 K Coll Lon PhD93. Trin Coll Bris 73. **d** 76 **p** 77. Lect Oak Hill Th Coll 76-83; C Braughing, Lt Hadham, Albury,

Furneux Pelham etc *St Alb* 83-87; Lect Lon Sch of Th from 87; Perm to Offic *Lon* and *St Alb* from 87. *7 Hangar Ruding, Watford WD19 5BH* Tel (020) 8386 6829 *or* (01923) 826061
E-mail s.motyer@londonbiblecollege.ac.uk

MOUGHTIN, Ross. b 48. St Cath Coll Cam BA70 St Jo Coll Dur BA75. **d** 76 **p** 77. C Litherland St Paul Hatton Hill *Liv* 76-79; C Heswall *Ches* 79-84; Chapl Edw Unit Rochdale Infirmary 83-92; V Thornham w Gravel Hole *Man* 84-92; V Aughton Ch Ch *Liv* from 92; Chapl W Lancashire NHS Trust from 94. *Christ Church Vicarage, 22 Long Lane, Aughton, Ormskirk L39 5AT* Tel (01695) 422175 E-mail ross.moughtin@lineone.net

MOUGHTIN-MUMBY, Andrew Denis Paul. b 78. Birm Univ BA00 SS Coll Cam BA05. Westcott Ho Cam 03. **d** 06 **p** 07. C Walworth St Chris *S'wark* from 06. *76 Tatum Street, London SE17 1QR* Tel (020) 7277 4875 Fax 7703 3803
E-mail andrewmoughtinmumby@gmail.com

MOUGHTIN-MUMBY, Sharon. b 76. St Jo Coll Dur BA97 MA98 Worc Coll Ox DPhil04. Westcott Ho Cam 05. **d** 06 **p** 07. C Walworth St Pet *S'wark* from 06. *76 Tatum Street, London SE17 1QR* Tel 07980-611347 (mobile)
E-mail sharon.mm@btinternet.com

MOUL, Russell Derek. b 56. Reading Univ BA83. Oak Hill Th Coll 97. **d** 99 **p** 00. C Harold Wood *Chelmsf* 99-02; C Harold Hill St Paul 02-03; V from 03. *St Paul's Vicarage, Redcar Road, Romford RM3 9PT* Tel (01708) 341225
E-mail russell@themouls.fslife.co.uk

MOULAND, Norman Francis. b 38. OLM course 98. **d** 99 **p** 00. OLM Verwood *Sarum* from 99. *13 Park Drive, Verwood BH31 7PE* Tel (01202) 825320

MOULD, Mrs Jacqueline. b 66. QUB BD88. CITC BTh91. **d** 91 **p** 92. C Belfast St Aid *Conn* 91-94; C Drumragh w Mountfield *D & R* 94-96; NSM Kinross *Sarum* 97-00; C Belvoir *D & R* from 03. *10A Ballyclough Road, Lisburn BT28 3UY* Tel (028) 9264 7912 *or* 9049 1436 E-mail jjmould@hotmail.com

MOULD, James Michael. b 46. SEITE 95. **d** 98 **p** 99. NSM Wallington *S'wark* 98-03; NSM W Wittering and Birdham w Itchenor *Chich* from 03. *Quinneys, Itchenor Road, Itchenor, Chichester PO20 7DD* Tel (01243) 513600
E-mail revd.jim@btinternet.com

MOULD, Jeremy James. b 63. Nottm Univ BA85 TCD BTh91. CITC 88. **d** 91 **p** 92. C Mossley *Conn* 91-94; C Drumragh w Mountfield *D & R* 94-96; C Kinson *Sarum* 97-00. *10A Ballyclough Road, Lisburn BT28 3UY* Tel (028) 9264 7912

MOULDEN, David Ivor. b 52. Cant Ch Univ BA02. SEITE 05. **d** 08. C Madeley *Heref* from 08. *7 Mellor Close, Madeley, Telford TF7 5SS* Tel (01952) 275287
E-mail davidmoulden@hotmail.com

MOULDER, John William Michael Cornock. b 39. City of Lon Poly ACIB67. Glouc Sch of Min 82. **d** 86 **p** 86. C Hopton Hill Australia 86-88; P-in-c Berrigan 88-94; P-in-c Edenhope 94-98; C Tividale *Lich* 98-01; P-in-c W Bromwich St Pet 01-04; rtd 04; Hon Asst P Cobram Australia from 04. *Goldwick, 130 Jerilderie Street, Berrigan NSW 2712, Australia* Tel and fax (0061) (3) 5885 2913 E-mail fatherm@dragnet.com.au

MOULDER, Kenneth. b 53. Lon Univ BEd75. Ridley Hall Cam 78. **d** 81 **p** 82. C Harold Wood *Chelmsf* 81-84; C Darfield *Sheff* 84-88; V Walkergate *Newc* 88-92; P-in-c Byker St Mark 90-92; V Byker St Mark and Walkergate St Oswald from 92. *St Oswald's Parsonage, Woodhead Road, Newcastle upon Tyne NE6 4RX* Tel 0191-263 6249

MOULT, Jane Elizabeth Kate. b 61. Trin Coll Bris 91. **d** 94 **p** 95. C St Jo in Bedwardine *Worc* 94-97; NSM Bilton *Cov* 97-99; Chapl Staunton Harold Hosp 00; Sen Chapl Leics Partnership NHS Trust 01-07; Perm to Offic *Leic* from 07. *17 The Leascroft, Ravenstone, Coalville LE67 2BL* Tel (01530) 833160
E-mail jane.moult@btinternet.com

MOULT, Simon Paul. b 66. Trin Coll Bris BA94. **d** 94 **p** 95. C St Jo in Bedwardine *Worc* 94-97; C Bilton *Cov* 97-99; P-in-c Thringstone St Andr *Leic* 99-05; RD Akeley S 03-05; Chapl N Warks NHS Trust from 05; Chapl Geo Eliot Hosp NHS Trust Nuneaton from 05. *The Chaplaincy, George Eliot Hospital, College Street, Nuneaton CV10 7DJ* Tel (024) 7686 5046 *or* 7635 1351

MOULTON, Canon Paul Oliver. b 43. NOC 77. **d** 80 **p** 81. C Wilmslow *Ches* 80-85; V Knutsford St Cross 85-92; Chapl Mary Dendy Hosp Knutsford 86-92; V Gatley *Ches* 92-01; Chapl Cen Man Healthcare NHS Trust 92-01; P-in-c Capesthorne w Siddington and Marton *Ches* from 01; Hon Can Ches Cathl from 07. *The Vicarage, School Lane, Marton, Macclesfield SK11 9HD* Tel (01260) 224447
E-mail paulo.moulton@btinternet.com

MOUNCER, David Peter. b 65. Univ of Wales (Abth) BA86. Oak Hill Th Coll BA94. **d** 94 **p** 95. C Foord St Jo *Cant* 94-98; Min Grove Green LEP 98-03; R Brampton St Thos *Derby* 03-07; C Walton St Jo from 07. *5 Foxbrook Drive, Chesterfield S40 3JR*

MOUNSEY, William Lawrence Fraser. b 51. St Andr Univ BD75. Edin Th Coll 76. **d** 78 **p** 79. C Edin St Mark 78-81; Chapl RAF 81-90 and 96-06; R Dalmahoy and Chapl Heriot-Watt Univ 90-96; Perm to Offic *Eur* from 96; Hon C Roslin (Rosslyn

Chpl) *Edin* from 96. *33 Manor Place, Edinburgh EH3 7EB* Tel 07967-322651 (mobile) E-mail williamlfm@tiscali.co.uk

MOUNSTEPHEN, Philip Ian. b 59. Southn Univ BA80 Magd Coll Ox MA87 PGCE. Wycliffe Hall Ox 85. **d** 88 **p** 89. C Gerrards Cross and Fulmer *Ox* 88-92; V W Streatham St Jas *S'wark* 92-98; Hd Pathfinders CPAS 98-02; Dir CY Network 01-02; Hd Min 02-07; Dep Gen Dir 04-07; Chapl Paris St Mich *Eur* from 07. *St Michael's Church, 5 rue d'Aguesseau, 75008 Paris, France* Tel (0033) (1) 47 42 70 88 Fax 47 42 74 75
E-mail office@saintmichaelsparis.org

MOUNT, Canon Judith Mary. b 35. Bedf Coll Lon BA56 Lon Univ CertEd57. Ripon Coll Cuddesdon 81. **dss** 83 **d** 87 **p** 94. Carterton *Ox* 83-85; Charlton on Otmoor and Oddington 85-87; Dioc Lay Min Adv and Asst Dir of Ords 86-89; Par Dn Islip w Charlton on Otmoor, Oddington, Noke etc 87-94; C 94-95; Assoc Dioc Dir Ords and Adv for Women in Ord Min 89-95; Hon Can Ch Ch 92-95; rtd 95; Hon C Shill Valley and Broadshire *Ox* from 95; Perm to Offic *Glouc* from 99. *The Owl House, Bell Lane, Poulton, Cirencester GL7 5JF* Tel (01285) 850242

MOUNTFORD, Canon Brian Wakling. b 45. Newc Univ BA66 Cam Univ MA73 Ox Univ MA90. Westcott Ho Cam 66. **d** 68 **p** 69. C Westmr St Steph w St Jo *Lon* 68-69; C Paddington Ch Ch 69-73; Chapl SS Coll Cam 73-78; V Southgate Ch Ch *Lon* 78-86; V Ox St Mary V w St Cross and St Pet from 86; Chapl St Hilda's Coll Ox from 89; Hon Can Ch Ch *Ox* from 98. *9A Norham Gardens, Oxford OX2 6PS* Tel (01865) 515778 *or* 279111 E-mail brian.mountford@oriel.ox.ac.uk

MOUNTFORD, Ian David. b 65. St Jo Coll Nottm BTh93. **d** 96 **p** 97. C Chilwell *S'well* 96-00; TV Thame *Ox* from 00. *22 Stuart Way, Thame OX9 3WP* Tel (01844) 216508

MOUNTNEY, Frederick Hugh. b 14. St Chad's Coll Dur BA36 MA39. Lich Th Coll 36. **d** 37 **p** 38. C Beighton *Derby* 37-39; C Spondon 39-40; C Byker St Laur *Newc* 40-44; C Backworth St Jo 44-48; V N Gosforth 48-51; R Lillingstone Dayrell w Lillingstone Lovell *Ox* 51-56; V Heref All SS 56-75; Chapl Victoria Eye Hosp Heref 56-75; Dioc Ecum Officer 63-69; Chapl Bonn w Cologne *Eur* 75-79; rtd 79; Perm to Offic *Heref* 79-90; *Nor* 82-00; St *E* 82-02; *Eur* 90-02. *The Grange, 3 Church Road, Rennington, Alnwick NE66 3RR* Tel (01665) 577344

MOURANT, Julia Caroline. b 58. Sheff Univ BA79. St Jo Coll Nottm 82. **dss** 84 **d** 92 **p** 94. Cropwell Bishop w Colston Bassett, Granby etc *S'well* 84-86; Marple All SS *Ches* 86-89; Harlow St Mary and St Hugh w St Jo the Bapt *Chelmsf* 89-92; NSM 92-04; Asst Dir of Min 98-04; CME Officer 00-02; Perm to Offic *Win* from 04; Lay Tr Officer 05-07; Voc, Recruitment and Selection Officer from 07. *The Vicarage, Knapp Lane, Ampfield, Romsey SO51 9BT* Tel (01794) 367195

MOURANT, Sidney Eric. b 39. Lon Univ BD73. Oak Hill Th Coll. **d** 89 **p** 90. C Oxton *Ches* 89-92; V Douglas All SS and St Thos *S & M* 92-96; I Rathkeale w Askeaton, Kilcornan and Kilnaughtin *L & K* 96-00; I Nenagh 00-04; rtd 04. *12 Breezemount, Hamiltonsbawn, Armagh BT61 9SB* Tel (00353) (48) 3887 2203 Mobile 87-239 9785
E-mail sid@sidneymourant.wanadoo.co.uk

MOURANT, Stephen Philip Edward. b 54. St Jo Coll Nottm BTh83. **d** 83 **p** 84. C Cropwell Bishop w Colston Bassett, Granby etc *S'well* 83-86; C Marple All SS *Ches* 86-89; P-in-c Harlow St Mary and St Hugh w St Jo the Bapt *Chelmsf* 89-90; V 90-04; P-in-c Bitterne *Win* 04-08; C Fair Oak from 08. *The Vicarage, Knapp Lane, Ampfield, Romsey SO51 9BT* Tel (01794) 367195
E-mail stephen.mourant@btinternet.com

MOUSIR-HARRISON, Stuart Nicholas. b 68. SW Poly Plymouth BSc89 Nottm Univ MSc92 St Martin's Coll Lanc PhD99 St Jo Coll Dur BA99. Cranmer Hall Dur. **d** 00 **p** 01. C Oadby *Leic* 00-03; C W Malling w Offham *Roch* 03-07; C Mereworth w W Peckham 03-07; P-in-c Dallington *Pet* from 07; Chapl Northn Univ from 07. *The Vicarage, The Bartons Close, Northampton NN5 7HQ* Tel (01604) 751478
E-mail rev.moose@mousir.org

MOVERLEY, Ruth Elaine. b 55. K Alfred's Coll Win CertEd76. St Mich Coll Llan. **d** 90 **p** 91. C Llangynwyd w Maesteg 90-95; C Glan Ely 95-97; V Llanharan w Peterston-super-Montem 97-05; V Tonyrefail w Gilfach Goch from 05. *The Vicarage, High Street, Tonyrefail, Porth CF39 8PL* Tel (01443) 670330

MOWAT, Robert Alexander Laird (Sandy). b 50. CD80 and Bar 90. Univ Coll of Em and St Chad Saskatoon BTh96. **d** 96 **p** 96. C Saskatchewan Gateway Canada 96-01; P-in-c Kinnerley w Melverley and Knockin w Maesbrook *Lich* 01-08; P-in-c Big Country Canada from 08. *PO Box 1765, Kindersley SK S0L 1S0, Canada* E-mail smowat@sk.sympatico.ca

MOWBRAY, David. b 38. Fitzw Ho Cam BA60 MA64 Lon Univ BD62. Clifton Th Coll. **d** 63 **p** 64. C Northampton St Giles *Pet* 63-66; Lect Watford St Mary *St Alb* 66-70; V Broxbourne 70-77; R Broxbourne w Wormley 77-84; V Hertford All SS 84-91; V Darley Abbey *Derby* 91-03; Asst Chapl Derby R Infirmary 91-94; Chapl Derbyshire Mental Health Services NHS Trust 99-03; rtd 03. *Blackbird Cottage, 169 Newport, Lincoln LN1 3DZ* Tel (01522) 546753

MOWBRAY, James Edward. b 78. Univ of Wales (Abth) BTh00 Leeds Univ BA03. Coll of Resurr Mirfield 01. **d** 03 **p** 04. C Perry Street *Roch* 03-07; V Swanley St Mary from 07. *St Mary's Vicarage, London Road, Swanley BR8 7AQ* Tel (01322) 662201 E-mail vicarofswanley@sky.com

MOWBRAY, Ms Jill Valerie. b 54. Sussex Univ BEd76 Lon Inst of Educn MA86 Anglia Poly Univ MA01. Ridley Hall Cam 99. **d** 01 **p** 02. C Tufnell Park St Geo and All SS *Lon* 01-04; V Whitton SS Phil and Jas from 04. *The Vicarage, 205 Kneller Road, Twickenham TW2 7DY* Tel (020) 8894 1932 Mobile 07761-236910 E-mail jill.mowbray@virgin.net

MOWER, Miss Marguerite Mary. b 36. Bris Univ BA57. Cant Sch of Min 90. **d** 93 **p** 94. NSM Eythorne and Elvington w Waldershare etc *Cant* 93-03; NSM Denholme and Harden and Wilsden *Bradf* 04-07; Perm to Offic *Cant* from 07. *Meadow Bank, Eythorne Road, Shepherswell, Dover CT15 7PN*

MOWLL, John William Rutley. b 42. Sarum Th Coll 63. **d** 66 **p** 67. C Oughtibridge *Sheff* 66-69; C Hill *Birm* 69-73; Ind Chapl and V Upper Arley *Worc* 73-78; P-in-c Upton Snodsbury and Broughton Hackett etc 78-81; R 81-83; V Boughton under Blean w Dunkirk *Cant* 83-89; V Boughton under Blean w Dunkirk and Hernhill 89-07; RD Ospringe 95-01; Hon Min Can Cant Cathl 96-07; rtd 07; Chapl to The Queen from 00; Perm to Offic *Cant* from 07. *Holly Cottage, Water Lane, Ospringe, Faversham ME13 8TS* Tel (01795) 597597

MOXLEY, Mrs Elizabeth Jane. b 52. St Jo Coll Nottm. **d** 05 **p** 06. C Aston Clinton w Buckland and Drayton Beauchamp *Ox* 05-08; R from 08. *The Rectory, 23 New Road, Aston Clinton, Aylesbury HP22 5JD* Tel (01296) 632488 E-mail elizabethmoxley@hotmail.com

MOXON, John. **d** 02 **p** 03. NSM Birm St Luke 02-04. *41 Mariner Avenue, Birmingham B16 9DF* Tel 0121-456 1628 *or* 472 0726 Mobile 07887-573122 E-mail john.moxon@birminghamchristiancollege.ac.uk

MOXON, Michael Anthony. b 42. LVO98. Lon Univ BD78 Heythrop Coll Lon MA96. Sarum Th Coll 67. **d** 70 **p** 71. C Kirkley *Nor* 70-74; Min Can St Paul's Cathl 74-81; Sacr 77-81; Warden Coll of Min Canons 79-81; V Tewkesbury w Walton Cardiff *Glouc* 81-90; Chapl to The Queen 86-98; Can Windsor and Chapl in Windsor Gt Park 90-98; Dean Truro and R Truro St Mary 98-04; Chapl Cornwall Fire Brigade HQ 98-04; rtd 04. *36 Trelawney Avenue, Treskerby, Redruth TR15 1RH* Tel (01209) 313823 Mobile 07745-120453

MOY, Mrs Joy Patricia. b 35. Cant Sch of Min 87. **d** 90 **p** 94. NSM Cranbrook *Cant* 90-96; Perm to Offic *Win* 96-02. *16 Hillside Avenue, Purley CR8 2DP*

MOY (née PLUMB), Mrs Nicola Louise. b 80. Birm Univ BA01 Bris Univ MA03 PGCE04. St Jo Coll Nottm 06. **d** 08 **p** 09. C Wolverhampton St Jude *Lich* from 08. *21 St Jude's Road, Wolverhampton WV6 0EB* Tel (01902) 653942 E-mail nicolamoy@hotmail.com

MOY, Richard John. b 78. St Cath Coll Cam BA99. Trin Coll Bris MA03. **d** 04 **p** 05. C Wolverhampton St Jude *Lich* 04-07; Pioneer Min Wolv City Cen from 07. *21 St Jude's Road, Wolverhampton WV6 0EB* Tel (01902) 653942 Mobile 07811-336910 E-mail notintheratrace@yahoo.co.uk

MOYES (née WATSON), Mrs Stephanie Abigail. b 61. Heriot-Watt Univ BA84. Cranmer Hall Dur 86. **d** 90 **p** 94. C Bishop's Castle w Mainstone *Heref* 90-93; Dep Chapl HM Pris Dur 93-95; Chapl HM Rem Cen Low Newton 95-98; V Chilton and Cornforth *Dur* 98-02; Chapl Wrekin Coll Telford 02-04; Perm to Offic *Worc* from 04. *7 Birchanger Green, Worcester WR4 0DW* Tel (01905) 619181

MOYNAGH, David Kenneth. b 46. LRCP70 MRCS70 MRCGP76 Lon Univ MB, BS70. S Dios Minl Tr Scheme 88. **d** 91 **p** 92. NSM Ore St Helen and St Barn *Chich* 91-99; Perm to Offic *Win* from 01. *White Cottage, Jordan's Lane, Sway, Lymington SO41 6AR* Tel (01590) 682475

MOYNAGH, Michael Digby. b 50. Southn Univ BA73 Lon Univ MA74 Aus Nat Univ PhD78 Bris Univ MA85. Trin Coll Bris. **d** 85 **p** 86. C Northwood Em *Lon* 85-89; P-in-c Wilton *B & W* 89-90; TR 90-96; Dir Cen for Futures Studies St Jo Coll Nottm 96-04; Co-Dir Tomorrow Project from 04. *Templeton College, Oxford OX1 5NY* Tel (01865) 422713 E-mail michael.moynagh@templeton.ox.ac.uk

MOYNAN, Canon David George. b 53. **d** 86 **p** 87. C Seagoe *D & G* 86-88; C Taney *D & G* 88-89; I Arklow w Inch and Kilbride 89-94; Dioc Stewardship Adv from 92; Dioc Ch of Ireland Bps' Appeal Rep from 92; I Kilternan from 94; Dioc Dir for Decade of Evang from 96; Can Ch Ch Cathl Dublin from 97. *Kilternan Rectory, Kilternan, Dublin 18, Republic of Ireland* Tel and fax (00353) (1) 295 5603 *or* tel 295 2643 E-mail moynandg@gmail.com

MOYO, Edmore Illingworth. b 71. Bedfordshire Univ MSc08. Bp Gaul Th Coll Harare 99. **d** 02. NSM Luton St Mary *St Alb* 06-08. *Address temp unknown* Tel 07909-671876 (mobile) E-mail edmorei@yahoo.co.uk

MOYSE, Mrs Pauline Patricia. b 42. Ex Univ CertEd62. S Dios Minl Tr Scheme 88. **d** 91 **p** 94. NSM Fleet *Guildf* 91-92; C 93-97;

Chapl Farnborough Coll of Tech 96-97; P-in-c Stoneleigh *Guildf* 97-02; Warden of Readers 97-07; Dioc Adv Lay Min 01-07; Tr Officer for Past Assts 07-09; rtd 07. *Beechend, 2 Hillcrest, Fleet GU51 4PZ* Tel (01252) 671382 E-mail pauline.moyse1@ntlworld.com

✠**MPALANYI-NKOYOYO, The Rt Revd Livingstone.** b 37. **d** 69 **p** 70. c 80. Kasubi Uganda 69-75; Nsangi 75-77; Adn Namirembe 77-79; Suff Bp 80-81; Suff Bp Mukono 81-94; Abp Uganda and Bp Kampala 94-03; rtd 03. *PO Box 14123, Kampala, Uganda* E-mail couab@uol.co.ug

MPUNZI, Nduna Ananias. b 46. Federal Th Coll S Africa 69. **d** 71 **p** 72. C Galeshewe St Jas S Africa 71-74; C Taung 74-75; C Vaal Hartz 75-77; R Vryburg St Phil 77-78; Lic to Offic *Glas* 82-84; C Bilston *Lich* 84-86; TV 86-90; P-in-c Walsall St Mary and All SS Palfrey 90-97; P-in-c Caldmore 90-93; P-in-c Shobnall 02-04; TV Worc St Barn w Ch Ch 04-08. *Address temp unknown*

✠**MTETEMELA, The Most Revd Donald Leo.** b 47. St Phil Th Coll Kongwa Wycliffe Hall Ox 75. **p** 71 **c** 82. Asst Bp Cen Tanganyika 82-90; Bp Ruaha from 90; Abp Tanzania 98-08. *Box 1028, Iringa, Tanzania* Tel (00255) (262) 270 1211 Fax 270 2479 E-mail ruaha@anglican.or.tz

MUDD, Mrs Linda Anne. b 59. WMMTC 00. **d** 03 **p** 04. C Exhall *Cov* 03-07; Chapl Geo Eliot Hosp NHS Trust Nuneaton from 07. *19 Falmouth Close, Nuneaton CV11 6GB* Tel (024) 7638 6146 E-mail muddie@mudda.freeserve.co.uk

MUDDIMAN, John Bernard. b 47. Keble Coll Ox BA67 MA72 DPhil76 Selw Coll Cam BA71 MA75. Westcott Ho Cam 69. **d** 72 **p** 73. Hon C Ox St Giles 72-83; Chapl New Coll Ox 72-76; Tutor St Steph Ho Ox 76-83; Vice-Prin 80-83; Lect Th Nottm Univ 83-90; Fell Mansf Coll Ox from 90; Chapl from 97; Lic to Offic *Ox* 90-02; NSM Littlemore from 97. *Mansfield College, Oxford OX1 3TF* Tel (01865) 270999 E-mail john.muddiman@mansfield.ox.ac.uk

MUDGE, Frederick Alfred George. b 31. Leeds Univ BSc58 Univ of Wales BD67. St Mich Coll Llan 58. **d** 61 **p** 62. C Cwmavon *Llan* 61-64; PV Llan Cathl 64-70; R Llandough w Leckwith 70-88; V Penarth All SS 88-96; rtd 96. *Pathways, 6 Fairwater Road, Llandaff, Cardiff CF5 2LD*

MUDIE, Martin Bruce. b 54. Goldsmiths' Coll Lon BA76. Sarum & Wells Th Coll 92. **d** 92 **p** 93. C Bromley St Mark *Roch* 92-95; rtd 95; Perm to Offic *B & W* 02-03; Hon C Glastonbury w Meare from 03. *20 Oriel Road, Street BA16 0JL* Tel (01458) 448034

MUFFETT, Mrs Sarah Susan. b 53. STETS 02. **d** 05 **p** 06. NSM Okeford *Sarum* from 05. *Prides Cottage, High Street, Child Okeford, Blandford Forum DT11 8EH* Tel (01258) 860010 E-mail sarahmuffett@btopenworld.com

MUGAN, Miriam Ruth. b 56. RNMH77. Oak Hill Th Coll 93. **d** 96 **p** 97. NSM St Alb St Sav *St Alb* 96-07; P-in-c Croxley Green All SS from 07. *All Saints' Vicarage, The Green, Croxley Green, Rickmansworth WD3 3HJ* Tel (01923) 772109 E-mail miriam.mugan@btopenworld.com

MUGGLETON, James. b 55. Bris Univ BA80. Chich Th Coll 81 EAMTC 99. **d** 01 **p** 02. NSM E Leightonstone *Ely* 01-03; C 03-04; C Buckworth and Alconbury cum Weston 04; R Barney, Fulmodeston w Croxton, Hindringham etc *Nor* from 04. *The Rectory, The Street, Hindringham, Fakenham NR21 0AA* Tel (01328) 878159 E-mail jamiemuggs@aol.com

MUGGLETON, Major George. b 25. Chich Th Coll 55. **d** 57 **p** 58. C Oldham St Mary *Man* 57-59; C Ashton St Mich 59-61; V Croydon H Trin *Cant* 61-68; R Stisted *Chelmsf* 68-69; P-in-c Pattiswick 68-69; P-in-c Bradwell 68-69; R Stisted w Bradwell and Pattiswick 69-87; rtd 87. *Curvalion House, Creech St Michael, Taunton TA3 5QF* Tel (01823) 443842

MUGHAL, Dominic Jacob. b 55. Asian Soc Inst Manila MSc88 Edin Univ MTh93 Leeds Univ MPhil05. St Jo Coll Nottm 05. **d** 07 **p** 08. C Fairweather Green *Bradf* 07-09; Community Outreach P from 09; C Thornbury from 09; C Woodhall from 09; C Bradf St Aug Undercliffe from 09; C Bradf St Clem from 09. *11 Daleside Road, Pudsey LS28 8EX* Tel 07821-246891 (mobile) E-mail dominic_moghal@hotmail.com

MUGRIDGE, Mrs Gloria Janet. b 45. R Holloway Coll Lon BA66. S Dios Minl Tr Scheme 92. **d** 95 **p** 96. NSM Dorchester *Sarum* 95-97; Asst Chapl Weymouth Coll 95-97; Chapl 97-04; NSM Melbury *Sarum* 97-02; NSM Stour Vale 04-06. *3 Hedgehog Path, Gillingham SP8 4GD* Tel (01747) 821562 E-mail janetmug@aol.com

MUIR, David Murray. b 49. Glas Univ MA70. St Jo Coll Nottm BA72. **d** 76 **p** 77. C Fulham St Mary N End *Lon* 76-80; C Aspley *S'well* 80; India 81-85; Dir Ext Studies St Jo Coll Nottm 85-02; C Upton (Overchurch) *Ches* 02-04; Adult Educn and Par Development Adv *Ex* 04-08; Pioneer Min Okehampton Deanery from 08. *The Rectory, South Tawton, Okehampton EX20 2LQ* Tel (01837) 840867 Mobile 07854-845067 E-mail david.muir@exeter.anglican.org

MUIR, David Trevor. b 49. TCD MA MLitt93. CITC 75. **d** 78 **p** 79. C Dublin Clontarf *D & G* 78-80; C Monkstown St Mary 80-83; I Kilternan 83-94; I Delgany 94-97; Can Ch Ch Cathl Dublin 95-97; Chapl to Ch of Ireland Assn of Deaf People from

97. Luogh North, Doolin, Co Clare, Republic of Ireland Tel (00353) (65) 707 4778 Fax 707 4871

MUIR, John William. b 38. Dur Univ BA59 Mansf Coll Ox MA65. Chich Th Coll 78. **d** 78 **p** 79. In Congr Ch 62-70; United Ch of Zambia 70-78; C Brighouse *Wakef* 78-80; V Northowram 80-87; V Sowerby 87-01; rtd 01; Perm to Offic *Wakef* from 02. *8 Whitley Drive, Holmfield, Halifax HX2 9SJ* Tel (01422) 244163 Mobile 07733-152089 E-mail jmuir@msn.com

MUIR, Peter Robert James. b 49. Ex Univ BSc71. **d** 09. OLM Thursley *Guildf* from 09; OLM Elstead from 09. *Yew Cottage, Thursley, Godalming GU8 6QA* Tel (01252) 702360 Mobile 07747-793253 E-mail peter@cellarworld.co.uk

MUKHERJEE (or MUKHOPADHYAY), Supriyo. b 42. Calcutta Univ BA70 Serampore Th Coll BD76 Derby Univ MA97. Bp's Coll Calcutta 70. **d** 75 **p** 76. India 75-91; C Crook *Dur* 91-92; V Nelson in Lt Marsden *Blackb* 92-95; Dioc Community Relns Officer *Cov* 95-02; TV Cov E 95-02; rtd 02; Perm to Offic *Cov* from 02. *16 Nunts Lane, Coventry CV6 4HB* Tel (024) 7636 3064 E-mail samukh@lineone.net

MUKHOLI, Eshuchi Patrick. b 60. Nairobi Univ BSc86. Nairobi Evang Graduate Sch of Th MDiv98. **d** 98 **p** 99. Dioc Youth Adv Mombasa Kenya 98-02; Dioc Miss and Communications Officer 99-02; Chapl St Aug Prep Sch 99-02; NSM Blackbird Leys *Ox* 02-08. *88 Blackbird Leys Road, Oxford OX4 6HS* Tel (01865) 748284 Mobile 07781-489070 E-mail pmukholi@yahoo.com

MUKUNGA, James. b 74. Univ of Zimbabwe BA00. Bp Gaul Th Coll Harare 95. **d** 97 **p** 99. Zimbabwe 97-04; R Kadoma All SS 01-02; R Mabelreign St Pet and Lect Bp Gaul Coll 02-04; Perm to Offic *Ox* 04-06; C High Wycombe 06-07; C Peckham St Sav *S'wark* from 07. *173 Choumert Road, London SE15 4AW* Tel (020) 7639 5072 Mobile 07886-235698 E-mail jamesmukunga@yahoo.com

MULCAHY, Richard Patrick. b 67. SW Poly Plymouth BSc90. St Mich Coll Llan 02. **d** 05 **p** 06. NSM Bassaleg *Mon* from 05. *9 High Cross Drive, Rogerstone, Newport NP10 9AB* Tel (01633) 894641 E-mail richard-mulcahy@ntlworld.com

MULFORD, Robert. b 57. Middx Poly CertEd79 Open Univ BA87 MA93. Oak Hill Th Coll BA03 ERMC 05. **d** 07 **p** 08. C Billing *Pet* from 07. *80 Worcester Close, Northampton NN3 9GD* Tel 07768-960896 (mobile) E-mail robert@mulford.me.uk

MULHALL, James Gerard. b 60. NUI DipSW92 CQSW92. Carlow Coll BA95. **d** 86 **p** 87. NSM Clonmel w Innislounagh, Tullaghmelan etc *C & O* from 09. *Mulfai House, Coolnahorna, Carrick-on-Suir, Co Waterford, Republic of Ireland* Tel (00353) (51) 646984 Mobile 87-240 1913 E-mail jamesgmulhall@eircom.net

MULHOLLAND, Canon Nicholas Christopher John. b 44. Chich Th Coll 77. **d** 79 **p** 80. C Thornbury *Glouc* 79-83; R Boxwell, Leighterton, Didmarton, Oldbury etc from 83; RD Tetbury 00-03; Hon Can Glouc Cathl from 06. *The Vicarage, Badminton GL9 1ET* Tel (01454) 218427

MULKERN, Richard Neville. b 39. S'wark Ord Course 88. **d** 91 **p** 92. NSM Leytonstone St Andr *Chelmsf* 91-93; Min Sec and Welfare Officer Miss to Seamen 91-93; Welfare Sec 93-94; Dir N Region 94-00; Perm to Offic *Wakef* 93-06; NSM Oulton w Woodlesford *Ripon* 96-99; rtd 00. *120 Norwood Road, Birkby, Huddersfield HD2 2XX* Tel (01484) 480864

MULLALLY, Dame Sarah Elisabeth. b 62. DBE05. S Bank Univ BSc84 MSc92 Bournemouth Univ Hon DSc01 Wolv Univ Hon DSc04 Herts Univ Hon DSc05 RGN84. SEITE 03. **d** 01 **p** 02. C Battersea Fields *S'wark* 01-06; TR Sutton from 06. *The Rectory, 34 Robin Hood Lane, Sutton SM1 2RG* Tel (020) 8642 3499 Mobile 07909-595752 E-mail sarah.mullally@btinternet.com

MULLANEY, Mrs Jane Megan. b 48. Kingston Poly BA72. **d** 04 **p** 05. OLM Kenilworth St Jo *Cov* from 04. *5 Knightlow Close, Kenilworth CV8 2PX* Tel (01926) 850723 E-mail jane_m_mullaney@tiscali.co.uk

MULLEN, Canon Charles William. b 60. CITC BTh92. **d** 92 **p** 93. C Lecale Gp *D & D* 92-95; I Gorey w Kilnahue, Leskinfere and Ballycanew *C & O* 95-00; Dean's V St Patr Cathl Dublin from 00; Preb Rathmichael St Patr Cathl Dublin from 08. *258 Circular Road South, Dublin 8, Republic of Ireland* Tel (00353) (1) 453 9472 Mobile 87-261 8878 E-mail deans.vicar@stpatrickscathedral.ie

MULLEN, Lee Ross. b 73. Cranmer Hall Dur 05. **d** 07 **p** 08. C Chelmsf St Andr from 07. *8 Wickfield Ash, Chelmsford CM1 4UT* Tel (01245) 440516 E-mail tdyp@msn.com

MULLEN, Peter John. b 42. Liv Univ BA70 Middx Univ PhD00. St Aid Birkenhead 66. **d** 70 **p** 71. C Manston *Ripon* 70-72; C Stretford All SS *Man* 72-73; C Oldham St Mary w St Pet 73-74; Lic to Offic 74-77; V Tockwith and Bilton w Bickerton *York* 77-89; Perm to Offic 97-98; P-in-c St Mich Cornhill w St Pet le Poer etc *Lon* from 98; P-in-c St Sepulchre w Ch Ch Greyfriars etc from 98; Chapl City Inst Stock Exchange from 98. *The Watch House, Giltspur Street, London EC1A 9DE* Tel and fax (020) 7248 3826 E-mail citychurches@pmullen.freeserve.co.uk

MULLENGER, William. b 44. Linc Th Coll 68. **d** 69 **p** 70. C Clapham St Jo *S'wark* 69-73; C Hook 73-81; P-in-c Camberwell St Phil and St Mark 81-85; V Hackbridge and N Beddington

85-93; rtd 93; Perm to Offic *Roch* from 93. *30 Constance Crescent, Bromley BR2 7QJ*

MULLER, Vernon. b 40. Natal Univ BA62 Birm Univ MPhil93. St Chad's Coll Dur 62. **d** 64 **p** 65. S Africa 64-76; C Durban N St Martin 64-68; R Queensburgh 68-76; C Hendon St Mary *Lon* 76-77; Chapl Friern Hosp Lon 77-91; Chapl R Berks Hosp and Battle Hosp Reading 91-95; Dep Dir Bodey Ho Counselling Cen 95-05; rtd 05; Perm to Offic *Chelmsf* from 95. *8 Ruskin Road, Chelmsford CM2 6HN* Tel (01245) 345865 E-mail vernonmuller@aol.com

MULLETT, John St Hilary. b 25. St Cath Coll Cam BA47 MA49. Linc Th Coll. **d** 50 **p** 51. C Tottenham All Hallows *Lon* 50-52; R Que Que S Rhodesia 52-61; V Bollington St Jo *Ches* 61-69; V Oxton 69-77; R Ashwell *St Alb* 77-90; RD Buntingford 82-88; rtd 90; Fell St Cath Coll Cam from 90; Perm to Offic *Ely* from 90. *13 Church Lane, Madingley, Cambridge CB23 8AF* Tel (01954) 211670

MULLEY, Mrs Margery Ann Oclanis. b 38. **d** 07 **p** 08. OLM Iwerne Valley *Sarum* from 07. *Hellum Farmhouse, Iwerne Courtney, Blandford Forum DT11 8QF*

MULLIGAN, Colin Arthur. b 42. Llan Ord Course 96. **d** 96 **p** 97. NSM Neath w Llantwit 96-01; NSM Neath 01-07; rtd 07. *12 Chestnut Road, Cimla, Neath SA11 3PB* Tel (01639) 630409

MULLIGAN, Ronald Leslie. b 53. LCTP. **d** 08 **p** 09. NSM Haslingden w Grane and Stonefold *Blackb* from 08. *3 Chatburn Close, Rossendale BB4 8UT* Tel (01706) 220749

MULLIN, Horace Boies (Dan). b 44. **d** 00 **p** 01. OLM Mildenhall *St E* from 00. *47 Oak Drive, Beck Row, Bury St Edmunds IP28 8UA* Tel (01638) 718200 E-mail dan-martha@mullin47.freeserve.co.uk

MULLINER, Denis Ratliffe. b 40. BNC Ox BA62 MA66. Linc Th Coll 70. **d** 72 **p** 73. C Sandhurst *Ox* 72-76; Chapl Bradfield Coll Berks 76-99; Chapl Chpl Royal Hampton Court Palace from 00; Dep P in O from 00. *Chapel Royal, Hampton Court Palace, East Molesey KT8 9AU* Tel (020) 3166 6515

MULLINGS, Paulette Patricia Yvonne. b 53. **d** 07 **p** 08. NSM Cobbold Road St Sav w St Mary *Lon* from 07. *53A Melina Road, London W12 9HY* Tel (020) 7386 1262 Mobile 07751-374857 E-mail pmullings@aol.com

MULLINS, Caroline Anne. b 56. Ex Univ BA78 St Anne's Coll Ox CertEd79. SEITE 04. **d** 07 **p** 08. NSM Wandsworth St Paul *S'wark* from 07. *8 Highbury Road, London SW19 7PR* Tel (020) 8286 9693 E-mail caroline.mullins@blueyonder.co.uk

MULLINS, Joe. b 20. MC45. Trin Coll Ox BA49 MA59. Ridley Hall Cam 48. **d** 50 **p** 51. C Portman Square St Paul *Lon* 50-52; India 52-74; Australia from 74; rtd 86. *33/31 Cockcroft Avenue, Monash ACT 2904, Australia* Tel (0061) (2) 6291 0345 E-mail emullins@autarmetro.com.au

MULLINS, Malcolm David. b 42. St Edm Hall Ox BA63. St Steph Ho Ox 63. **d** 65 **p** 66. C Kirkby *Liv* 65-69; C Lamorbey H Redeemer *Roch* 69-75; C Solihull *Birm* 75-77; Perm to Offic *Lon* from 06. *843 Field End Road, Ruislip HA4 0QN* Tel (020) 8864 8733 Mobile 07710-313922

MULLINS, Mrs Margaret. b 49. Southn Univ CertEd70. Sarum & Wells Th Coll 94. **d** 94 **p** 95. C Bishopstoke *Win* 94-98; TV Bicester w Bucknell, Caversfield and Launton *Ox* from 98. *The Vicarage, The Spinney, Launton, Bicester OX25 6EP* Tel and fax (01869) 252377 E-mail mgt.mullins@tiscali.co.uk

MULLINS, Canon Peter Matthew. b 60. Ch Ch Ox BA82 MA86 Irish Sch of Ecum MPhil90. Qu Coll Birm 82. **d** 84 **p** 85. C Caversham St Pet and Mapledurham etc *Ox* 84-88; Perm to Offic *D & G* 88-89; TV Old Brumby *Linc* 89-94; Clergy Tr Adv 94-99; TR Gt and Lt Coates w Bradley from 99; Can and Preb Linc Cathl from 02; RD Grimsby and Cleethorpes from 05. *The Rectory, 23 Littlecoates Road, Grimsby DN34 4NG* Tel (01472) 346986 E-mail p.m.mullins@virgin.net

MULLINS, Timothy Dougal. b 59. Wycliffe Hall Ox 83. **d** 85 **p** 86. C Reading Greyfriars *Ox* 85-89; C Haughton le Skerne *Dur* 89-95; Chapl Eton Coll 95-05; Chapl Radley Coll from 05. *Radley College, Radley, Abingdon OX14 2HR* Tel (01235) 543190 E-mail tdm@radley.org.uk

MULLIS, Robert Owen. b 49. Bris Univ BA71 CertEd71. St Mich Coll Llan 93. **d** 93 **p** 94. NSM Llangenni and Llanbedr Ystrad Yw w Patricio *S & B* from 93. *16 Chestnut Drive, Abergavenny NP7 5JZ* Tel (01873) 851613

MULRAINE, Miss Margaret Haskell. b 24. Birm Univ BA45 DipEd46. Sarum Th Coll 83. **dss** 86 **d** 87 **p** 94. Wareham *Sarum* 86-93; Hon Par Dn 87-93; Perm to Offic 93-08. *9 Turnworth Close, Broadstone BH18 8LS* Tel (01202) 640292

MULRYNE, Thomas Mark. b 70. St Cath Coll Cam BA91 MA95 Lon Inst of Educn PGCE93. Oak Hill Th Coll BA02. **d** 02 **p** 03. C W Streatham St Jas *S'wark* 02-06; C Gt Clacton *Chelmsf* from 06. *112 Woodlands Close, Clacton-on-Sea CO15 4RU* Tel (01255) 425159 E-mail mark_and_caroline_mulryne@hotmail.com

MUMBY, Andrew. *See* MOUGHTIN-MUMBY, Andrew Denis Paul

MUMFORD, Clare. *See* VAN DEN BOS, Mrs Clare

MUMFORD, David. *See* MUMFORD, Michael David

MUMFORD, David Bardwell. b 49. MRCPsych86 St Cath Coll Cam BA71 MA75 Bris Univ MB, ChB81 MD92 Edin Univ MPhil89. Bp's Coll Calcutta 71 Cuddesdon Coll 73. **d** 75. C Bris St Mary Redcliffe w Temple etc 75-76; NSM 76-82; NSM Edin St Columba 82-86; NSM Calverley *Bradf* 86-92; Perm to Offic *B & W* 92-06. *14 Clifton Vale, Clifton, Bristol BS8 4PT* Tel 0117-927 2221 E-mail david.mumford@bristol.ac.uk

MUMFORD, The Very Revd David Christopher. b 47. Mert Coll Ox BA68 MA74 York Univ MSW CQSW81. Linc Th Coll 84. **d** 86 **p** 87. C Shiremoor *Newc* 86-89; C N Shields 89-91; V Byker St Ant 91-97; RD Newc E 96-97; V Cowgate 97-02; Internat Co-ord Internat Fellowship of Reconciliation 02-07; R Brechin from 07; R Tarfside from 07; Dean Bre from 08. *St Andrew's Rectory, 9 Castle Street, Brechin DD9 6JW* Tel (01356) 622708 E-mail dmumford3@btinternet.com

MUMFORD, Geoffrey Robert. b 70. York Univ BSc92 St Jo Coll Nottm MA00. **d** 00 **p** 01. C Rowley Regis *Birm* 00-03; TV Darwen St Pet w Hoddlesden *Blackb* 03-08; P-in-c Copmanthorpe *York* from 08; P-in-c Askham Bryan from 08; P-in-c Bolton Percy from 08. *The Vicarage, 17 Sutor Close, Copmanthorpe, York YO23 3TX* Tel (01904) 705937

MUMFORD, Grenville Alan. b 34. Richmond Th Coll. **d** 78 **p** 78. C Witham *Chelmsf* 78-81; C-in-c Gt Ilford St Marg CD 81-85; V Gt Ilford St Marg 85-87; P-in-c Everton and Mattersey w Clayworth *S'well* 87-89; R 89-96; RD Bawtry 93-96; rtd 96; Perm to Offic *Ches* from 96. *146 Audlem Road, Nantwich CW5 7EB* Tel (01270) 610221

MUMFORD, Canon Hugh Raymond. b 24. Oak Hill Th Coll 50. **d** 53 **p** 54. C Bethnal Green St Jas Less *Lon* 53-57; C Watford St Mary *St Alb* 57-59; R Thetford St Pet w St Nic *Nor* 59-69; RD Thetford 68-69; V Nether Cerne *Sarum* 69-71; R Godmanstone 69-71; R Cerne Abbas w Upcerne 69-71; R Minterne Magna 69-71; V Cerne Abbas w Godmanstone and Minterne Magna 71-89; RD Dorchester 75-79; Can and Preb Sarum Cathl 77-89; rtd 89; Perm to Offic *Sarum* from 89. *10 South Walks Road, Dorchester DT1 1ED* Tel (01305) 264971

MUMFORD, Michael David. b 29. **d** 79 **p** 80. Chapl Lister Hosp Stevenage 79-83; C Preston 79-87; P-in-c Kelshall and Therfield 83-88; C Barkway, Reed and Buckland w Barley 87-88; V Bodiam and R Ewhurst *Chich* 88-94; RD Rye 90-91; rtd 94; Perm to Offic *Chich* 94-09. *The College of St Barnabas, Blackberry Lane, Lingfield RH7 6NJ* Tel (01342) 872861 Mobile 07803-004492

MUNBY, Canon David Philip James. b 52. Pemb Coll Ox BA75 MA80. St Jo Coll Nottm 76. **d** 78 **p** 79. C Gipsy Hill Ch Ch *S'wark* 78-82; C-in-c W Dulwich Em CD 82-88; V Barnsley St Geo *Wakef* from 88; Asst Dioc Ecum Officer 99-01; Can Bungoma from 04. *St George's Vicarage, 100 Dodworth Road, Barnsley S70 6HL* Tel (01226) 203870 E-mail david.munby@bigfoot.com

MUNCEY, William. b 49. Oak Hill Th Coll BA80. **d** 80 **p** 81. C Wandsworth St Mich *S'wark* 80-84; C Morden 84-88; TV 88-01; RD Merton 00-01; P-in-c Croydon Ch Ch 01-04; V from 04. *Christ Church Vicarage, 34 Longley Road, Croydon CR0 3LH* Tel (020) 8665 9664

MUNCH, Philip Douglas. b 55. Witwatersrand Univ BMus. Cranmer Hall Dur. **d** 88 **p** 89. C Walvis Bay Namibia 88-89; P-in-c 89-92; Warden Ho of Prayer Luderitz 92-99; Prec Port Elizabeth S Africa 99-02; Warden Emmaus Ho of Prayer Northampton from 02; NSM Northampton St Mich w St Edm Pet from 02. *Emmaus House of Prayer, St Michael's Church, Perry Street, Northampton NN1 4HL* Tel (01604) 627669 Fax 230316

MUNCHIN, David Leighfield. b 67. Imp Coll Lon BSc88 K Coll Lon MA00 Heythrop Coll Lon PhD09. Ripon Coll Cuddesdon 89. **d** 92 **p** 93. C Golders Green *Lon* 92-96; Prec and Min Can St Alb Abbey 96-02; P-in-c Hatfield Hyde from 02. *St Mary Magdalene Vicarage, Hollybush Lane, Welwyn Garden City AL7 4JS* Tel and fax (01707) 322313 Mobile 07787-567747 E-mail davidmunchin@tiscali.co.uk

MUNCHIN, Ysmena Rachael. *See* PENTELOW, Mrs Ysmena Rachael

MUNDAY, Mrs Sandra Anne. b 61. St Jo Sem Wonersh BTh89 Ripon Coll Cuddesdon 97. **d** 99 **p** 00. C Esher *Guildf* 99-02; Team Chapl R United Hosp Bath NHS Trust 02-03; Perm to Offic *B & W* from 03. *18 Chestnut Walk, Saltford, Bristol BS31 3BG* Tel (01225) 342740 E-mail sandy.munday@fastblue.net

MUNDELL, Mrs Christine Elizabeth. b 49. WEMTC 01. **d** 04 **p** 05. C Ledbury *Heref* 04-08; TV Leominster from 08. *118 Buckfields Road, Leominster HR6 8SQ* Tel (01568) 615514

MUNDEN, Alan Frederick. b 43. Nottm Univ BTh74 Birm Univ MLitt80 Dur Univ PhD87. St Jo Coll Nottm. **d** 74 **p** 75. C Cheltenham St Mary *Glouc* 74-76; C Cheltenham St Mary, St Matt, St Paul and H Trin 76; Hon C Jesmond Clayton Memorial *Newc* 76-80; C 80-83; V Cheylesmore *Cov* 83-01; R Weddington and Caldecote 01-03; rtd 03; Hon C Jesmond Clayton Memorial *Newc* from 03. *11 The Crescent, Benton, Newcastle upon Tyne NE7 7ST* Tel 0191-266 1227

MUNGAVIN, David Stewart. b 60. Stirling Univ BA80. Edin Th Coll 87. **d** 90 **p** 91. C Glas St Marg 90-92; P-in-c Airdrie 92-96; R 96-99; P-in-c Coatbridge 92-96; R 96-99; P-in-c Gartcosh 92-96; R 96-99; R Troon from 99. *70 Bentinck Drive, Troon KA10 6HZ* Tel (01292) 313731 E-mail davidmungavin@wightcablenorth.net

MUNGAVIN, Canon Gerald Clarence. b 27. Edin Th Coll 51. **d** 54 **p** 55. C Dunfermline *St And* 54-55; C Glas Gd Shep 55-57; CF 57-60; C Stanwix *Carl* 60-62; Chapl RAF 62-75; R Turriff *Ab* 75-81; R Cuminestown 75-81; R Banff 75-81; R Banchory 81-92; R Kincardine O'Neil 81-92; Can St Andr Cathl 89-92; Hon Can from 92; rtd 92. *5 Lade Court, Lochwinnoch PA12 4BT* Tel (01505) 843972

MUNN, Canon Carole Christine. b 45. EMMTC 83. **d** 90 **p** 94. NSM Long Bennington w Foston *Linc* 90-95; NSM Saxonwell 95-98; NSM Claypole 98-08; Asst Chapl HM Pris Line 94-01; Chapl HM Pris Morton Hall from 01; Gen Preacher *Linc* from 01; Can and Preb Linc Cathl from 05. *HM Prison, Morton Hall, Swinderby, Lincoln LN6 9PT* Tel (01522) 666739

MUNN, George. b 44. Master Mariner 72. Linc Th Coll 85. **d** 87 **p** 88. C Boston *Linc* 87-90; R Claypole 90-08; rtd 08. *15 The Meadow, Caistor, Market Rasen LN7 6XD* E-mail g.munn@tiscali.co.uk

MUNN, Richard Probyn. b 45. Selw Coll Cam BA67 MA69. Cuddesdon Coll 67. **d** 69 **p** 70. C Cirencester *Glouc* 69-71; USPG Zambia 71-79; Chapl St Mark's Sch Mapanze 72-74; R Livingstone 75-79; Adn S Zambia 79; P-in-c Kings Stanley *Glouc* 80-83; R Lezant w Lawhitton and S Petherwin w Trewen *Truro* 84-92; Lesotho from 93; rtd 01. *Reavenall, PO Box 249, Leribe 300, Lesotho* Tel (00266) 877 8553

MUNNS, John Millington. b 76. Univ Coll Dur BA99 MA00 Bris Univ MPhil07 FRSA04. Westcott Ho Cam 01. **d** 03 **p** 04. C Bridgwater St Mary and Chilton Trinity *B & W* 03-06; Asst Chapl Em Coll Cam from 06. *Emmanuel College, Cambridge CB2 3AP* Tel (01223) 311751 E-mail j.m.munns@dunelm.org.uk *or* jmm89@cam.ac.uk

MUNNS, Stuart Millington. b 36. OBE77. St Cath Coll Cam BA58 MA62 MCIPD91. Cuddesdon Coll 58. **d** 60 **p** 61. C Allenton and Shelton Lock *Derby* 60-63; C Brampton St Thos 63-65; C-in-c Loundsley Green Ascension CD 65-66; Bp's Youth Chapl 66-72; Nat Dir of Community Industry 72-77; Hon C Hornsey Ch Ch *Lon* 72-77; Dioc Missr *Liv* 77-82; V Knowsley 77-82; P-in-c Stramshall *Lich* 82-88; V Uttoxeter w Bramshall 82-88; RD Uttoxeter 82-87; P-in-c Kingstone w Gratwich 84-88; P-in-c Marchington w Marchington Woodlands 84-88; P-in-c Checkley 86-88; Perm to Offic *B & W* 88-90; NSM Wells St Thos w Horrington 90-94; P-in-c Fosse Trinity 94-02; rtd 02; Dioc Pre-Th Educn Co-ord *B & W* 02-03; Perm to Offic from 03. *Applewood House, Ham Street, Baltonsborough, Glastonbury BA6 8PX* Tel (01458) 851443 E-mail munns@ukonline.co.uk

MUNOZ-TRIVINO, Daniel. b 75. Hatf Coll Dur BA99. Wycliffe Hall Ox MTh01. **d** 01 **p** 02. C Hazlemere *Ox* 01-04; TV Gt Marlow w Marlow Bottom, Lt Marlow and Bisham from 04. *165 Marlow Bottom, Marlow SL7 3PL* Tel (01628) 472816 Mobile 07866-678766 E-mail daniel.munoz@haciendalosolivos.org

MUNRO, Basil Henry. b 40. Ripon Hall Ox 73. **d** 75 **p** 76. C N Mymms *St Alb* 75-78; C St Alb St Steph 78-80; V 80-87; R Aston-on-Trent and Weston-on-Trent *Derby* 87-99; P-in-c Elvaston and Shardlow 98-99; R Aston on Trent, Elvaston, Weston on Trent etc 99-01; Chapl Aston Hall Hosp Derby 87-93; Chapl S Derbyshire Community Health Services NHS Trust 93-01; rtd 01; Perm to Offic *Derby* from 01. *40 Brisbane Road, Mickleover, Derby DE3 9JZ*

MUNRO, Duncan John Studd. b 50. Magd Coll Ox BA72 MA76 Warwick Univ MBA96 CDir05. Wycliffe Hall Ox 73. **d** 76 **p** 77. C Ecclesall *Sheff* 76-77; C Sheff St Barn and St Mary 78-80; Lic to Offic 80-86; Perm to Offic 97-05; Lic to Offic *Edin* 06-08; NSM Musselburgh from 08; NSM Prestonpans from 08. *Little Acre, Westerdunes Park, North Berwick EH39 5HJ* Tel (01620) 890513

MUNRO, Ingrid Phyllis. b 51. Herts Univ BEd80. St Jo Coll Nottm MA96 St Alb Minl Tr Scheme 83. **d** 98 **p** 99. NSM Walbrook Epiphany *Derby* 98-01 and 05-09; NSM Alvaston from 09. *40 Brisbane Road, Mickleover, Derby DE3 9JZ*

MUNRO, Robert. b 40. Leeds Univ BA62 Bris Univ PGCE63. SWMTC 95. **d** 98 **p** 99. NSM Saltash *Truro* 98-03; NSM Calstock from 03. *15 Valley Road, Saltash PL12 4BT* Tel (01752) 844731 E-mail bobmu@valley151.fsnet.co.uk

MUNRO, Robert Speight. b 63. Bris Univ BSc84 Man Univ PGCE87. Oak Hill Th Coll BA93. **d** 93 **p** 94. C Hartford *Ches* 93-97; R Davenham 97-03; R Cheadle from 03. *The Rectory, 1 Depleach Road, Cheadle SK8 1DZ* Tel 0161-428 3440 *or* 428 8050 E-mail rob@munro.org.uk

MUNRO, Canon Terence George. b 34. Jes Coll Cam BA56 MA60. Linc Th Coll 59. **d** 61 **p** 62. C Far Headingley St Chad *Ripon* 61-64; Jamaica 64-70; R Methley w Mickletown *Ripon* 70-79; V Hunslet Moor St Pet and St Cuth 79-85; R Barwick in Elmet 85-93; V Woodhouse and Wrangthorn 93-99; Dioc Ecum Officer 93-99; Hon Can Ripon Cathl 94-99; rtd 99; Perm to Offic

York from 00. *45 Laburnum Drive, Beverley HU17 9UQ* Tel (01482) 861237

MUNRO, Teresa Frances. b 51. Leeds Poly CertEd73 Leeds Univ BEd74. SEITE 03. **d** 06 **p** 07. NSM Coulsdon St Andr *S'wark* from 06. *Burach, 23 Purley Knoll, Purley CR8 3AF* Tel (020) 8763 2927

MUNRO-SMITH, Alison Jean. *See* WATERS, Alison Jean

MUNT, Cyril. b 27. AKC52. **d** 53 **p** 54. C Ashford *Cant* 53-56; C Dorking w Ranmore *Guildf* 56-60; R Cheriton w Newington *Cant* 60-68; R Harbledown 68-83; R Porlock w Stoke Pero *B & W* 83-92; rtd 92; Perm to Offic *B & W* from 92. *Applegarth, 26 Hood Close, Glastonbury BA6 8ES* Tel (01458) 831842

MUNT, Mrs Linda Christine. b 55. NEOC 92. **d** 95 **p** 96. C Beverley St Nic *York* 95-98; Chapl E Yorkshire Hosps NHS Trust 97-99; V Bridlington Em *York* 99-03; P-in-c Skipsea w Ulrome and Barmston w Fraisthorpe 02-03; Chapl Martin House Hospice for Children Boston Spa 03-05; Hon C Boston Spa, Thorp Arch w Walton etc 03-05; V Market Weighton *York* from 05; V Sancton from 05; R Goodmanham from 05. *The Vicarage, 38 Cliffe Road, Market Weighton, York YO43 3BN* Tel (01430) 873230 E-mail l.munt@btinternet.com

MUNYANGAJU, Canon Jerome Cassian. b 53. Serampore Univ BD85 Open Univ MA97. St Phil Coll Kongwa 73. **d** 75 **p** 76. Tanzania 75-80 and 85-95; India 80-85; Hon Can Kagera from 91; Overseas Resource Person *D & D* 95-97; C Bangor Abbey *D & D* 98-00; I Killyleagh from 00. *The Rectory, 34 Inishbeg, Killyleagh, Downpatrick BT80 9TR* Tel and fax (028) 4482 8231 E-mail jmunyangaju@yahoo.co.uk

MURCH, Canon Robin Norman. b 37. Wells Th Coll. **d** 67 **p** 68. C Wisbech St Aug *Ely* 67-70; C Basingstoke *Win* 70-73; C Whitstable All SS *Cant* 73-76; V Queenborough 76-99; Hon Can Cant Cathl 96-99; rtd 99; Perm to Offic *Ex* from 00. *Flat 3, Narenta, 2 Barton Crescent, Dawlish EX7 9QL* Tel (01626) 863532 Mobile 07836-514528

MURDOCH, Alexander Edward Duncan. b 37. Oak Hill Th Coll 68. **d** 71 **p** 72. C Kensington St Helen w H Trin *Lon* 71-72; C Kensington St Barn 73-74; CF 74-78; C W Kirby St Bridget *Ches* 78-84; V N Shoebury *Chelmsf* 84-87; V W Poldens *B & W* 87-96; R Gayhurst w Ravenstone, Stoke Goldington etc *Ox* 96-07; rtd 07. *Hopp House, Back Lane, Old Bolingbroke, Spilsby PE23 4EU* Tel (01790) 763603

MURDOCH, David John. b 58. Birm Univ BSocSc81 Leeds Univ MA03. Ripon Coll Cuddesdon 81. **d** 84 **p** 85. C Penwortham St Leon *Blackb* 84-87; C Wirksworth w Alderwasley, Carsington etc *Derby* 87-89; R Shirland 89-97; Dioc World Development Officer 96-00; P-in-c New Mills 97-01; V 01-05; RD Glossop 04-05; TR Wilford Peninsula *St E* from 05. *The Rectory, 109A Front Street, Orford, Woodbridge IP12 2LN* Tel (01394) 450336 E-mail murdochs@btopenworld.com

MURDOCH, Mrs Lucy Eleanor. b 41. STETS BTh99. **d** 99 **p** 00. NSM Warbleton and Bodle Street Green *Chich* 99-02; NSM Rye from 02; TV from 03. *The Vicarage, 39 Lydd Road, Camber, Rye TN31 7RN* Tel (01797) 225386 E-mail lucy@murdoch26.fsnet.co.uk

MURFET, Edward David. b 36. Qu Coll Cam BA59 MA63. Chich Th Coll 59. **d** 61 **p** 62. C Croydon St Mich *Cant* 61-64; C Hunslet St Mary and Stourton *Ripon* 64-65; C Hackney Wick St Mary of Eton w St Aug *Lon* 65-69; Chapl Berne *Eur* 69-71; Chapl Naples 71-74; Chapl Rome 74-77; Lic to Offic *Bris* 78-81; Gen Sec CEMS 81-86; C Leeds St Pet *Ripon* 87-89; P-in-c 89-90; C Leeds City 91-93; Min Can Ripon Cathl 93-03; rtd 03; Perm to Offic *Ripon* from 03. *3 Old Deanery Close, St Marygate, Ripon HG4 1LZ* Tel (01765) 608422

MURFET, Gwyn. b 44. Linc Th Coll 71. **d** 74 **p** 75. C Scalby w Ravenscar and Staintondale *York* 74-77; P-in-c S Milford 77-83; R 83-84; V Kirkby Ireleth *Carl* 84-05; rtd 05. *75 Portsmouth Street, Walney, Barrow-in-Furness LA14 3AJ* Tel (01229) 471157

MURFITT, Mrs Ruth Margaret. b 48. **d** 09. NSM St Goran w Caerhays *Truro* from 09. *Haven Cottage, Gorran, St Austell PL26 6HN* Tel (01726) 844891 E-mail ruthmurfitt@hotmail.com

MURPHIE, Andrew Graham. b 65. Reading Univ BA86. St Jo Coll Nottm BTh91 MA92. **d** 92 **p** 93. C Boulton *Derby* 92-96; C Marston on Dove w Scropton 96-97; V Hilton w Marston-on-Dove from 98; RD Longford from 04. *The Vicarage, 28 Back Lane, Hilton, Derby DE65 5GJ* Tel (01283) 733433 E-mail andymurphie@btinternet.com

MURPHY, Alexander Charles. b 28. St Edm Coll Ware 50. **d** 55 **p** 56. NSM Edin St Jas 88-90; TV Edin St Mark 90-93; TV Edin St Andr and St Aid 90-93; TV Edin St Marg 93-96; rtd 96. *Ardleven, 48 Victoria Street, Dumbarton G82 1HP* Tel (01389) 733755 E-mail almagda328@hotmail.com

MURPHY, Andrew John. b 46. Edin Univ LLB67 MA68. **d** 95. NSM Aberdeen St Marg 95-98; NSM Fraserburgh 98-01; Hon Asst C Bridge of Don St Luke's Miss from 01. *Old Schoolhouse, Logie, Crimond, Fraserburgh AB43 8SQ* Tel (01346) 532711

MURPHY, Mrs Deborah Ann. b 67. Newc Univ BA89. Qu Coll Birm BD92. **d** 93 **p** 94. C Bloxwich *Lich* 93-97; TV Gt Grimsby

St Mary and St Jas *Linc* 97-00; Chapl N Lincs and Goole Hosps NHS Trust 99-00; Perm to Offic *St Alb* 01-05; Asst Chapl Walsall Hosps NHS Trust 05-08; TV Blakenall Heath *Lich* from 08. *St Aidan's Vicarage, 78A Chestnut Road, Walsall WS3 1AP* Tel (01922) 494655 E-mail deborahamurphy@tiscali.co.uk

MURPHY, Gerry. *See* MURPHY, Canon John Gervase Maurice Walker

MURPHY, Ms Hilary Elizabeth. b 57. St Martin's Coll Lanc BSc00. St Jo Coll Nottm MTh05. **d** 05 **p** 06. C S Shore H Trin *Blackb* 05-08; C Bloemfontein Cathl S Africa from 08. *St Andrew's Cathedral, PO Box 1523, Bloemfontein, 9300 South Africa* Tel (0027) (51) 448 3010

MURPHY, Jack. b 27. NOC 83. **d** 86 **p** 87. C Armley w New Wortley *Ripon* 86-90; C Hawksworth Wood 90-94; rtd 94; Perm to Offic *York* from 96. *70 Avocet Way, Bridlington YO15 3NT* Tel (01262) 609477

MURPHY, James Royse. b 54. Bris Univ MB, ChB77 MRCGP81. Glouc Sch of Min 89. **d** 92 **p** 94. NSM Glouc St Cath 92-98; NSM Glouc St Paul from 98. *52 Lansdown Road, Gloucester GL1 3JD* Tel (01452) 505080 E-mail jrmurphy@supanet.com

MURPHY, Canon John Gervase Maurice Walker (Gerry). b 26. LVO87. TCD BA52 MA55. **d** 52 **p** 53. C Lurgan Ch the Redeemer *D & D* 52-55; CF 55-73; Asst Chapl Gen 73-77; V Ranworth w Panxworth *Nor* 77-79; RD Blofield 79; Dom Chapl to The Queen 79-87; Chapl to The Queen 87-96; R Sandringham w W Newton *Nor* 79-87; RD Heacham and Rising 85-87; Hon Can Nor Cathl 86-87; Chapl ICS 87-91; R Ch Ch Cathl Falkland Is 87-91; Miss to Seamen 87-91; rtd 91; Chapl St Pet-ad-Vincula at HM Tower of Lon 91-96; Dep P in O 92-96; Extra Chapl to The Queen from 96; Perm to Offic *Nor* from 98. *Saffron Close, 17 Ringstead Road, Heacham, King's Lynn PE31 7JA* Tel (01485) 572351

MURPHY, Ms Julia Mary. b 58. Essex Univ BA81 Lon Bible Coll BTh00. Wycliffe Hall Ox MTh07. **d** 07 **p** 08. C Thetford *Nor* from 07. *44 Nunsgate, Thetford IP24 3EL* Tel 07779-266034 (mobile) E-mail julesthepoet@hotmail.com

MURPHY, Owen. b 52. Open Univ BA85 Liv Univ MA04. Chich Th Coll 92. **d** 94 **p** 95. C Oxhey St Matt *St Alb* 94-96; C Watford St Mich 96-98; P-in-c Shinfield *Ox* 98-05; V Barnehurst *Roch* 05-07; Dir St Columba's Retreat and Conf Cen from 07. *70 Sandy Lane, Woking GU22 8BH* Tel (01483) 750739 *or* 766498 Fax 776208 E-mail omurphy@globalnet.co.uk *or* director@stcolumbashouse.org.uk

MURPHY, Peter Frederick. b 40. AKC65. **d** 67 **p** 68. C Paddington St Jo w St Mich *Lon* 67-72; P-in-c Basingstoke *Win* 72-76; TV 76-81; V Hythe 81-92; V Lyndhurst and Emery Down 92-99; P-in-c Minstead 95-99; V Lyndhurst and Emery Down and Minstead 99-05; rtd 05; Hon C Fordingbridge and Breamore and Hale etc *Win* from 05. *Smuggler's Cottage, 20 Shaftesbury Street, Fordingbridge SP6 1JF* Tel (01425) 650209 Mobile 07815-050096 E-mail petermurf@gmail.com

MURPHY, Philip John Warwick. b 65. Kent Univ BA87 Southn Univ BTh93. Chich Th Coll 88. **d** 91 **p** 92. C Broadstone *Sarum* 91-94; C Teddington SS Pet and Paul and Fulwell *Lon* 94-96; V Leytonstone St Marg w St Columba *Chelmsf* 96-01; P-in-c Leytonstone St Andr 96-97; Australia from 01; R Benalla 01-04; V Fitzroy from 04. *268 George Street, PO Box 124, Fitzroy Vic 3065, Australia* Tel (0061) (3) 9419 4587 E-mail pjwm@bigpond.net.au

MURPHY, Ronald Frederick. b 38. **d** 84 **p** 85. NSM Swindon Dorcan *Bris* 84-87; P-in-c N Cerney w Bagendon *Glouc* 87-90. *Flat 2, 7 Hulham Road, Exmouth EX8 3HR* Tel (01395) 224375

MURPHY, Rosalyn Frances Thomas. b 55. Marquette Univ (USA) BA85 Ustinov Coll Dur MTh00 Union Th Sem Virginia MDiv99 St Jo Coll Dur PhD05. Cranmer Hall Dur 04. **d** 05 **p** 06. C Dur St Nic 05-08; P-in-c Blackpool St Thos *Blackb* from 08. *St Thomas's Vicarage, 80 Devonshire Road, Blackpool FY3 8AE* Tel (01253) 392544 Mobile 07730-466782 E-mail murphyfamuk@aol.com

MURPHY, Royse. *See* MURPHY, James Royse

MURPHY, Canon William Albert. b 43. MBE98. Lon Univ BD73 QUB MTh78. **d** 73 **p** 74. C Lisburn Ch Ch *Conn* 73-79; Supt & Chapl Ulster Inst for the Deaf 79-98; Chapl HM Pris Maze from 82; Dioc Dir Ords *Conn* from 92; Chapl Ch of Ireland Min to Deaf people from 98; Can Belf Cathl from 04. *2 Maghaberry Manor, Moira, Craigavon BT67 0JZ* Tel (028) 9261 9140 E-mail murphy43@btinternet.com

MURPHY, Mrs Yvonne Letita. b 52. Brunel Univ BA90 PGCE91. SEITE. **d** 98 **p** 99. NSM Hampton St Mary *Lon* 98-01; NSM Staines St Mary and St Pet 01-04; Chapl Bp Wand Sch 98-04; P-in-c Kennington *Cant* 04-09; TV High Wycombe *Ox* from 09. *175 Dashwood Avenue, High Wycombe HP12 3DB* Tel (01494) 474996 E-mail ylm.bwm@virgin.net

MURRAY, Alan. b 61. St Jo Coll Nottm BTh92. **d** 92 **p** 93. C Wombwell *Sheff* 92-95; C Mortomley St Sav High Green 95-99; P-in-c Doncaster St Jas 99-01; V from 01. *The Vicarage, 54 Littlemoor Lane, Doncaster DN4 0LB* Tel (01302) 365544

MURRAY, Mrs Anne. b 53. MCSP75. NOC 03. **d** 06 **p** 07. NSM Fairfield *Liv* from 06. *75 Priorsfield Road, Liverpool L25 8TL* Tel 0151-428 2254 E-mail annel25@yahoo.co.uk

MURRAY, Christine Jean. *See* MEDWAY, Mrs Christine Jean

MURRAY, Christopher James. b 49. Open Univ BA78. St Jo Coll Nottm 79. **d** 81 **p** 82. C Heatherlands St Jo *Sarum* 81-84; C Hamworthy 84-90; R Passenham *Pet* from 90. *The Rectory, Wicken Road, Deanshanger, Milton Keynes MK19 6JP* Tel (01908) 262371

MURRAY, David McIlveen. b 36. ALCD61. **d** 61 **p** 62. C Mortlake w E Sheen *S'wark* 61-64; C Lyncombe *B & W* 64-67; C Horsham *Chich* 67-73; V Devonport St Bart *Ex* 73-79; R Chalfont St Peter *Ox* 79-95; RD Amersham 86-89; R Lower Windrush 95-03; rtd 03; Perm to Offic *Glouc* from 03. *Collum End Farm, 88 Church Road, Leckhampton, Cheltenham GL53 0PD* Tel (01242) 528008

MURRAY, Elaine Mary Edel. b 58. TCD BTh05 MICS97. CITC 02. **d** 05 **p** 06. Bp's V and C Kilkenny w Aghour and Kilmanagh *C & O* from 05. *The Vicar's Residence, St Canice's Library, Cathedral Close, Kilkenny, Republic of Ireland* Tel (00353) (56) 777 1998 E-mail vicar.cathedral@ossory.anglican.org

MURRAY, Elizabeth Ruth. **d** 03 **p** 04. C Antrim All SS *Conn* 03-06; I Woodschapel w Gracefield *Arm* from 06. *The Rectory, 140 Ballyronan Road, Magherafelt BT45 6HU* Tel (028) 7941 8311 E-mail ruth@mdroll.fsnet.co.uk

MURRAY, Gordon John. b 33. St Cath Coll Cam BA57 MA61. Clifton Th Coll 57. **d** 59 **p** 60. C Heref St Jas 59-61; C Uphill *B & W* 62-65; C-in-c Reading St Mary Castle Street Prop Chpl *Ox* 65-68; Ed *English Churchman* 65-71; Prin Kensit Coll Finchley 68-75; Hd of RE Sandown High Sch 76-78; rtd 98. *18 Longcroft, Felixstowe IP11 9QH* Tel (01394) 273372

MURRAY, Gordon Stewart. b 33. Birkbeck Coll Lon BSc72. Ripon Coll Cuddesdon 76. **d** 78 **p** 79. C Kenilworth St Nic *Cov* 78-81; V Pottersbury w Furtho and Yardley Gobion *Pet* 81-83; V Pottersbury, Furtho, Yardley Gobion and Cosgrove 84; TV Wolvercote w Summertown *Ox* 84-90; P-in-c Walworth *S'wark* 90-95; TR Walworth St Pet 95-98; rtd 98; P-in-c Tillington, Duncton and Up Waltham *Chich* 98-01. *26 Burton Stone Lane, York YO30 6BU* Tel (01904) 330401 E-mail gordon.murray11@ntlworld.com

MURRAY, Heather. b 62. RGN82. NEOC 04. **d** 07 **p** 08. NSM Burnopfield *Dur* from 07. *33 Church Street, Castleside, Consett DH8 9QW* Tel (01207) 581156 E-mail heather.murray0@btinternet.com

MURRAY, Ian Hargraves. b 48. Man Univ BSc71. St Jo Coll Nottm 79. **d** 81 **p** 82. C Erith St Paul *Roch* 81-84; C Willenhall H Trin *Lich* 84-87; TV 87-92; P-in-c Moxley 92-00; C Darlaston St Lawr 99-00; TR Glascote and Stonydelph from 00; RD Tamworth 04-09. *20 Melmerby, Wilnecote, Tamworth B77 4LP* Tel (01827) 737326 *or* 330306 E-mail rockin.rev@ntlworld.com

MURRAY, Ian William. b 32. Lon Univ BA53 PGCE54. Oak Hill NSM Course 80. **d** 83 **p** 84. NSM Pinner *Lon* 83-03; Perm to Offic from 03. *4 Mansard Close, Pinner HA5 3FQ* Tel (020) 8866 2984 E-mail bimurray@talk21.com

MURRAY, James Beattie. b 67. Goldsmiths' Coll Lon BMus87 Southlands Coll Lon PGCE89. Oak Hill Th Coll 01. **d** 03 **p** 04. C Upper Holloway *Lon* 03-07; C Chesham Bois *Ox* from 07. *The Vicarage, 22 Green Lane, Chesham Bois, Amersham HP6 5LQ* E-mail jamiebmurray@yahoo.co.uk

MURRAY, The Ven John Grainger. b 45. CITC 67. **d** 70 **p** 71. C Carlow *C & O* 70-72; C Limerick St Mary *L & K* 72-77; I Rathdowney w Castlefleming, Donaghmore etc *C & O* from 77; Can Leighlin Cathl 83-88; Treas 88-89; Chan 89-90; Prec 90-92; Preb Ossory Cathl 83-88; Treas 88-89; Chan 89-90; Prec 90-92; Adn Ossory and Leighlin from 92; Adn Cashel, Waterford and Lismore from 94. *The Rectory, Rathdowney, Portlaoise, Co Laois, Republic of Ireland* Tel (00353) (505) 46314 Fax 46540 E-mail venjgm@iol.ie *or* archdeacon@cashel.anglican.org

MURRAY, John Louis. b 47. Keble Coll Ox BA67 MA69. **d** 82 **p** 83. Asst Chapl Strasbourg *Eur* 82-05; P-in-c 05-09. *Aumônerie Anglicane, 2 Quai Mathiss, 67000 Strasbourg, France* Tel and fax (0033) (3) 88 36 93 90 E-mail john.murray@coe.int

MURRAY, Mrs Kim Margaret. b 58. OLM Camberley St Mich Yorktown *Guildf* from 07. *190 Upper College Ride, Camberley GU15 4HD* Tel (01276) 28213 E-mail k.murray208@btinternet.com

MURRAY, Mrs Margaret Janice. b 46. Carl Dioc Tr Course. **dss** 86 **d** 87 **p** 94. Walney Is *Carl* 86-87; Hon Par Dn 87-89; Par Dn Carl H Trin and St Barn 89-94; Chapl Cumberland Infirmary 90-94; C Harraby *Carl* 94-97; P-in-c 97-00; V 00-02; Chapl to the Deaf and Hard of Hearing 94-02; rtd 02; Perm to Offic *Carl* from 02. *6 Follyskye Cottages, Tindale Fell, Brampton CA8 2QR* Tel (01697) 746400

MURRAY, Paul Ridsdale. b 55. BEd. St Steph Ho Ox 80. **d** 83 **p** 84. C Hartlepool St Oswald *Dur* 83-86; C S Shields All SS 86-88; V Sacriston and Kimblesworth 88-94; P-in-c Waterhouses 94-98; P-in-c Chopwell from 98; Perm to Offic *Newc* from 99. *St John's Vicarage, Derwent View, Chopwell, Newcastle upon Tyne*

NE17 7AN Tel (01207) 561248 Fax 563850 Mobile 07803-906727 E-mail p.r.murray@durham.anglican.org

MURRAY, Roy John. b 47. Open Univ BA92 Wolv Poly CertEd89 RGN75 RMN77. WMMTC 01. **d** 04 **p** 05. NSM Solihull *Birm* 04-08; C Torquay St Jo and Ellacombe *Ex* from 08. *3 Redgate Close, Torquay TQ1 3UG* Tel (01803) 313042 Mobile 07768-436363 E-mail roy.j.murray@btinternet.com

MURRAY, Ruth. *See* MURRAY, Elizabeth Ruth

MURRAY, Mrs Ruth Elizabeth. b 55. Dur Univ BA77 Man Coll of Educn CertEd78. BA. **d** 94 **p** 95. NSM Alloa *St And* 94-98; Chapl Stirling Univ 94-99. *2 Wallace Street, Alloa FK10 3RZ* Tel (01259) 217432 E-mail ruthemurray@lineone.net

MURRAY (*née* GOULD), Mrs Susan Judith. b 61. Poly of Wales BSc83 Open Univ MA95. St Jo Coll Nottm 90. **d** 91 **p** 94. Par Dn Stokesley *York* 91-94; CMS 94-95; Argentina 95-03; P-in-c Haddlesey w Hambleton and Birkin *York* 03-09; TV Crawley *Chich* from 09. *St Richard's Vicarage, 1 Crossways, Crawley RH10 1QF* Tel (01293) 533727

MURRAY, Canon William Robert Craufurd. b 44. St Chad's Coll Dur BA66. **d** 68 **p** 69. C Workington St Mich *Carl* 68-71; C Harrogate St Wilfrid *Ripon* 71-74; P-in-c Sawley 74; V Winksley cum Grantley and Aldfield w Studley 74; R Fountains 75-81; V Hutt New Zealand 81-87; V Fendalton and Chapl Medbury Sch 87-00; V Merivale 00-09; Can Christchurch Cathl 91-09; rtd 09. *28 High Street, Waddington 7500, New Zealand* Tel (0064) (3) 318 3068 E-mail craufurd@xtra.co.nz

MURRAY-LESLIE, Adrian John Gervase. b 46. Lich Th Coll 67. **d** 69 **p** 70. C Sheff St Cuth 69-73; C Mosbrough 73-75; C-in-c Mosborough CD 75-80; P-in-c Edale *Derby* from 80; Warden The Peak Cen from 80. *The Vicarage, Edale, Hope Valley S33 7ZA* Tel (01433) 670254 E-mail warden@peakcentre.org.uk

MURRAY, THE, Bishop of. *See* DAVIES, The Rt Revd Ross Owen

MURRELL, Canon John Edmund. b 28. Westcott Ho Cam. **d** 66 **p** 67. C Ivychurch w Old Romney and Midley *Cant* 66-70; R Bardwell *St E* 70-75; Perm to Offic *Ely* 75-77; V Wenhaston w Thorington and Bramfield w Walpole *St E* 77-86; V Thorington w Wenhaston and Bramfield 86-92; P-in-c Walberswick w Blythburgh 86-92; V Thorington w Wenhaston, Bramfield etc 92-93; RD Halesworth 85-90; Hon Can St E Cathl 89-93; rtd 93; Perm to Offic *St E* from 93. *Strickland Cottage, 12 Lorne Road, Southwold IP18 6EP* Tel (01502) 722074

MURRIE, Clive Robert. b 44. Ripon Coll Cuddesdon 77. **d** 79 **p** 80. C Kenton Ascension *Newc* 79-80; C Prudhoe 80-83; V Burnopfield *Dur* 83-87; R Stella 87-91; V Coalpit Heath *Bris* 91-95; P-in-c Sittingbourne St Mich *Cant* 95-98; Chapl HM Pris Stocken 98-03; Chapl HM YOI Castington 03-04; rtd 04; Perm to Offic *Pet* 04-08; P-in-c Publow w Pensford, Compton Dando and Chelwood *B & W* 08-09. *1 Kingsway Cottages, Corston, Malmesbury SN16 0HW* Tel (01666) 838887 E-mail c.murrie@btinternet.com

MURRIN, Robert Staddon. b 42. Reading Univ BA68 Open Univ MA96. WMMTC 90. **d** 93 **p** 95. NSM Peterchurch w Vowchurch, Turnastone and Dorstone *Heref* 93-95; NSM Tupsley w Hampton Bishop 95-97; Chapl Kemp Hospice Kidderminster 97-05; Perm to Offic *Heref* from 06. *Albion Cottage, Peterchurch, Hereford HR2 0RP* Tel (01981) 550656 *or* 550467 Fax 550432

✠**MURSELL, The Rt Revd Alfred Gordon.** b 49. BNC Ox BA70 MA73 BD87 Birm Univ Hon DD05 ARCM74. Cuddesdon Coll 71. **d** 73 **p** 74. C 05. C Walton St Mary *Liv* 73-77; V E Dulwich St Jo *S'wark* 77-86; Tutor Sarum Th Coll 87-91; TR Stafford *Lich* 91-99; Provost Birm 99-02; Dean Birm 02-05; Area Bp Stafford *Lich* from 05. *Ash Garth, Broughton Crescent, Barlaston, Stoke-on-Trent ST12 9DD* Tel (01782) 373308 E-mail bishop.stafford@lichfield.anglican.org

MUSGRAVE, James Robert Lord. b 20. MBE97. TCD BA43 MA51. **d** 44 **p** 45. C Belfast St Andr *Conn* 44-46; C Derriaghy 46-51; R Duneane w Ballyscullion 51-54; I Belfast St Steph 54-64; I Magheragall 64-85; Can Conn Cathl 82-85; Bp's C Killead w Gartree 87-95; rtd 95. *14 Earlsfort, Moira, Craigavon BT67 0LY* Tel (028) 9261 2047

MUSHEN, Canon Francis John. b 34. Birm Univ BA60. Ripon Hall Ox 60. **d** 62 **p** 63. C Foleshill St Laur *Cov* 62-65; C Halesowen *Worc* 65-69; V Stourbridge St Mich Norton 69-81; Hon Can Worc Cathl 81-99; P-in-c Bromsgrove St Jo 81-87; V 87-92; R Kempsey and Severn Stoke w Croome d'Abitot 92-99; rtd 99; Perm to Offic *Worc* from 99. *16 Longheadland, Ombersley, Droitwich WR9 0JB* Tel (01905) 621461

MUSINDI, Mrs Beatrice Nambuya Balibali. b 64. Birm Univ MA94. Bp Tucker Coll Mukono BD90. **d** 03 **p** 04. C Caerleon w Llanhennock *Mon* 03-07; C Malpas 07-08. *The Vicarage, 1 Brookfield Close, Llyswerry, Newport NP19 4LA* Tel (01633) 783912 Mobile 07899-469938

MUSINDI, Philip. b 63. Bp Tucker Coll Mukono BD91 Univ of Wales (Cardiff) MA94. **d** 87 **p** 90. Uganda 87-92; C Builth and Llanddewi'r Cwm w Llangynog etc *S & B* 92-94; C Newport

St Teilo *Mon* 94-97; P-in-c Newport St Matt 97-04; V Newport St Andr from 04. *The Vicarage, 1 Brookfield Close, Llyswerry, Newport NP19 4LA* Tel (01633) 783912

✠**MUSK, The Rt Revd Bill Andrew.** b 49. Ox Univ BA70 MA75 Fuller Th Sem California ThM80 UNISA D Litt et Phil84. Trin Coll Bris. **d** 81 **p** 82 **c** 08. Egypt 81-86; CMS 88-89; TV Maghull *Liv* 89-97; V Tulse Hill H Trin and St Matthias *S'wark* 97-08; Hon Can S'wark Cathl 07-08; Area Bp N Africa and R Tunis St Geo from 08. *5 rue Ahmed Beylem, 1006 Tunis Bab Souika, Tunisia* Tel (00216) 7133 5493 E-mail billmusk@gmail.com

MUSKETT, David John. b 63. Southn Univ BA85. Ripon Coll Cuddesdon 87. **d** 90 **p** 91. C Kempston Transfiguration *St Alb* 90-93; C Ampthill w Millbrook and Steppingley 93-96; V Milford *Guildf* 96-06; C Stoughton from 06. *41 Ashenden Road, Guildford GU2 7XE* Tel (01483) 454083
E-mail associate.minister@emmanuelchurch.co.uk

MUSSER, Ms Christine. b 55. Ex Univ 96. **d** 00 **p** 01. C Torpoint *Truro* 00-03; P-in-c Boscastle w Davidstow 03-07; P-in-c Pirbright *Guildf* from 07. *The Vicarage, The Green, Pirbright, Woking GU24 0JE* Tel (01483) 473332
E-mail revdchrismusser@aol.com

MUSSON, David John. b 46. Open Univ BA86 Univ of Wales (Lamp) MPhil96 Univ of Wales (Ban) PhD00. Linc Th Coll 70. **d** 73 **p** 74. C New Sleaford *Linc* 73-76; C Morton 76-80; P-in-c Thurlby 80-86; R Quarrington w Old Sleaford 86-99; P-in-c Silk Willoughby 86-87; R 87-99; Perm to Offic *Chich* from 01. *Flat 9, Regency Court 4-5, South Cliff, Eastbourne BN20 7AE* Tel (01323) 723345 E-mail davidmusson@tiscali.co.uk

MUSSON, Mrs Joanne Chatterley. b 60. Qu Coll Birm 07. **d** 09. C Redditch Ch the K *Worc* from 09. *2 Compton Close, Redditch B98 7NL* Tel (01527) 551996 Mobile 07590-514115

MUSSON, John Keith. b 39. Nottm Univ BSc61 PhD66 CEng MIMechE. St As Minl Tr Course 85. **d** 88 **p** 89. Assoc Prin NE Wales Inst of HE 80-93; NSM Holywell *St As* 88-93; C 93-95; R Caerwys and Bodfari 95-02; rtd 02; Perm to Offic *Lich* from 02. *4 Hayes View, Oswestry SY11 1TP* Tel (01691) 656212

MUSSON, William John. b 58. UMIST BSc80 Open Univ MA02. St Jo Coll Nottm 88. **d** 91 **p** 92. C Nantwich *Ches* 91-94; C Finchley Ch Ch *Lon* 94-97; V Lynchmere and Camelsdale *Chich* from 97. *The Vicarage, School Road, Camelsdale, Haslemere GU27 3RN* Tel (01428) 642983
E-mail stpandp@btinternet.com

MUST, Albert Henry. b 27. Clifton Th Coll 61. **d** 63 **p** 64. C Becontree St Mary *Chelmsf* 63-68; V Highbury Vale St Jo *Lon* 68-78; V Highbury New Park St Aug 78-84; V Walthamstow St Jo *Chelmsf* 84-93; rtd 93; Perm to Offic *Cant* from 93. *24 Nightingale Avenue, Whitstable CT5 4TR* Tel and fax (01227) 772160

MUST, Mrs Shirley Ann. b 35. St Mich Ho Ox 61. **dss** 82 **d** 87 **p** 94. Highbury New Park St Aug *Lon* 82-84; Walthamstow St Jo *Chelmsf* 84-93; Hon Par Dn 87-93; Perm to Offic *Cant* 93-94; Hon C Herne Bay Ch Ch 94-05; Perm to Offic from 05. *24 Nightingale Avenue, Whitstable CT5 4TR* Tel and fax (01227) 772160

MUSTARD, James Edmond Alexander. b 74. Ex Univ BA95 Clare Coll Cam BA04 MA08. Westcott Ho Cam 02 Berkeley Div Sch 04. **d** 05 **p** 06. C Nor St Pet Mancroft w St Jo Maddermarket 05-08; C Pimlico St Pet w Westmr Ch Ch *Lon* from 08. *3 St Peter's House, 119 Eaton Square, London SW1W 9AL* Tel (020) 7235 4480 E-mail curate@stpetereatonsquare.co.uk

MUSTOE, Alan Andrew. b 52. Man Univ BA74. Qu Coll Birm. **d** 78 **p** 79. C Chatham St Wm *Roch* 78-82; R Burham and Wouldham 82-88; Dioc Info Officer 83-88; V Strood St Nic w St Mary 88-99; V Orpington All SS from 99; AD Orpington from 05. *The Vicarage, 1A Keswick Road, Orpington BR6 0EU* Tel and fax (01689) 824624
E-mail alan.mustoe@diocese-rochester.org

MUSTON, David Alan. b 33. Nottm Univ BA60. Ridley Hall Cam 62. **d** 64 **p** 65. C Tankersley *Sheff* 64-67; C Goole 67-70; Sec Ind Cttee of Gen Syn Bd for Soc Resp 70-76; Asst Gen Sec Bd for Soc Resp 74-76; Ind Chapl *Win* 77-79; V Leigh St Mary *Man* 79-83; R Otham w Langley *Cant* 83-97; rtd 97; Perm to Offic *Ox* from 01. *7 The Homestead, Bladon, Woodstock OX20 1XA* Tel (01993) 812650 E-mail musto33@tiscali.co.uk

MUSTON, James Arthur. b 48. Open Univ BA92 Derby Univ MA. EMMTC 89. **d** 91 **p** 92. NSM Chaddesden St Mary *Derby* 91-95; Community Min E Marsh Grimsby *Linc* 95-99; V Gresley *Derby* 99-04; rtd 04; Perm to Offic *Derby* from 04. *20 Whitmore Road, Chaddesden, Derby DE21 6HR* Tel (01332) 678073 Mobile 07946-575563

MUTCH, Canon Sylvia Edna. b 36. St Mich Ho Ox 57. **dss** 79 **d** 87 **p** 94. Clifton *York* 79-95; Par Dn 87-94; C 94-95; Chapl Clifton Hosp York 81-94; R Elvington w Sutton on Derwent and E Cottingwith *York* 95-01; Can and Preb York Minster 98-01; rtd 01; Perm to Offic *York* from 01. *18 Waite Close, Pocklington, York YO42 2YU* Tel (01759) 307894

MUTETE, Lameck. b 61. Bp Gaul Th Coll Harare 94. **d** 96 **p** 97. C Harare St Luke Zimbabwe 96-97; Asst P Harare Cathl 97-01; P-in-c 01; Adn Harare E 01; Can Harare 01-04; Perm to Offic

Bradf 04; P-in-c Tattenhall and Handley *Ches* from 04. *The Rectory, 4 Rean Meadow, Tattenhall, Chester CH3 9PU* Tel (01829) 770245 Mobile 07940-512748
E-mail lameckmutete@yahoo.co.uk

MUTHALALY, Verghese Malayil Lukose (Saju). b 79. S Asia Bible Coll Bangalore BTh01. Wycliffe Hall Ox BTh08. **d** 08 **p** 09. C Lancaster St Thos *Blackb* from 08. *6 Jackson Close, Lancaster LA1 5EY* Tel (01524) 590418 E-mail sajudoj@yahoo.com

MUXLOW, Judy Ann. b 47. Univ of Wales (Cardiff) BSc69 St Luke's Coll Ex CertEd73. SEITE. **d** 00 **p** 01. Chapl Ch Ch High Sch Ashford 00-03; Bp's Officer for NSM *Cant* 03-07; NSM Biddenden and Smarden 00-06; NSM Appledore w Brookland, Fairfield, Brenzett etc 06-08; NSM Wittersham w Stone-in-Oxney and Ebony 06-08; NSM Woodchurch 06-08; Perm to Offic *Roch* from 00 and *Cant* from 09. *29 The Meadows, Biddenden, Ashford TN27 8AW* Tel (01580) 291016
E-mail judy@mucat.eclipse.co.uk

MWANGI, Capt Joel Waweru. b 59. CA Tr Coll Nairobi 81. **d** 93 **p** 94. Kenya 93-96 and from 00; C Sheff St Mary Bramall Lane 96-99. *PO Box 57227, Nairobi, Kenya*

MWAURA, Nicholas Chege. b 65. **d** 90 **p** 91. Nairobi 91-95; NSM Limehouse *Lon* 99-00. *75 Harold Road, London E11 4QX*

MYANMAR, Archbishop of. *See* SAN SI HTAY, The Most Revd Samuel

MYATT, Edwin Henry. b 54. MA. Ripon Coll Cuddesdon. **d** 84 **p** 85. C W Bromwich St Fran *Lich* 84-88; C Sedgley All SS 88-93; V Trent Vale 93-94. *The Conifers, 5 Prestwick Road, Kingswinford ST4 6JY*

MYATT, Francis Eric. b 60. St Jo Coll Nottm 89. **d** 92 **p** 93. C W Derby St Luke *Liv* 92-95; TV Sutton 95-98; V Liv St Chris Norris Green 98-01; CF from 01. *c/o MOD Chaplains (Army)* Tel (01980) 615804 Fax 615800

MYATT, Philip Bryan. b 29. Wycliffe Hall Ox 54. **d** 57 **p** 58. C Fareham St Jo *Portsm* 57-61; C Westgate St Jas *Cant* 61-64; R Woodchester *Glouc* 64-70; R Bath Walcot *B & W* 70-91; R The Edge, Pitchcombe, Harescombe and Brookthorpe *Glouc* 91-94; rtd 94; Perm to Offic *Glouc* from 94. *West Cottage, Littleworth, Amberley, Stroud GL5 5AL*

MYCOCK, Geoffrey John Arthur. b 22. Open Univ BA76. St Deiniol's Hawarden 76. **d** 77 **p** 78. Hon C Ches H Trin 77-79; Bp's Dom Chapl 79-80; P-in-c Hargrave 79-80; V Sandbach Heath 80-82; Chapl and Lect St Deiniol's Lib Hawarden 82-85; V Holt *St As* 85-90; rtd 90; Perm to Offic *St A* from 90 and *Ches* from 91. *20 Eaton Close, Broughton, Chester CH4 0RF* Tel (01244) 531214

MYERS, Mrs Alison Margaret. b 66. Bris Univ BSc88. SEITE 04. **d** 07 **p** 08. NSM Cambourne *Ely* from 07. *37 Foxhollow, Great Cambourne, Cambridge CB23 5HT* Tel (01954) 718528 Mobile 07884-370933 E-mail alison@cambournechurch.org.uk

MYERS, Andrew Thomas Christopher. b 57. Leeds Univ BA81 Ches Coll of HE MTh05. NOC 02. **d** 04 **p** 05. C Leeds St Aid *Ripon* 04-08; P-in-c Middleton St Cross from 08; P-in-c Middleton St Mary from 08. *St Cross Vicarage, Middleton Park Avenue, Leeds LS10 4HT* Tel 0113-271 6398 Mobile 07876-431183 E-mail andymyers@elmet4.freeserve.co.uk

MYERS, Duncan Frank. b 57. Warwick Univ BSc. St Jo Coll Nottm 81. **d** 84 **p** 85. C Upton cum Chalvey *Ox* 84-86; C Farnborough *Guildf* 86-90; Chapl Nottm Poly *S'well* 90-92; Chapl Nottm Trent Univ 92-95; Sen Past Adv 95-02; Hon Min Can Dur Cathl 04-08; Chapl Hatf Coll Dur 06-08; Chapl Salford Univ from 08. *2 Booth Clibborn Court, Salford M7 4PJ* Tel 0161-792 0979 E-mail duncanmyers@ymail.com

MYERS, Canon Gillian Mary. b 57. Warwick Univ BSc78 Nottm Univ MA96. St Jo Coll Nottm 83. **d** 95 **p** 97. NSM Nottingham St Jude *S'well* 95-97; NSM Gedling 97-00; NSM Nottingham All SS 00-02; Succ, Sacr and Min Can Dur Cathl 02-08; Can Res Man Cathl from 08. *2 Booth Clibborn Court, Salford M7 4PJ* Tel 0161-792 0979 E-mail gilly@myers.uk.net

MYERS, John Bulmer. b 19. Worc Ord Coll 64. **d** 66 **p** 67. C Linthorpe *York* 66-68; NSM Huddersfield St Jo *Wakef* 74-76; C 76-79; V Cornholme 79-88; rtd 88; Perm to Offic *Wakef* 88-04. *2 Pine Close, Redcar TS10 3BL*

MYERS, Paul Henry. b 49. ALA72. Qu Coll Birm 74. **d** 77 **p** 78. C Baildon *Bradf* 77-80; C W Bromwich All SS *Lich* 80-83; Chapl RAF 83-86; V Milton *Lich* 87-92; C Baswich 96-99; C Hixon w Stowe-by-Chartley 96-99; V Mid Trent 02-05; TR Blakenall Heath from 05. *Christ Church Rectory, Blakenall Heath, Walsall WS3 1HT* Tel (01889) 270418

MYERS, Peter John. b 60. St Jo Coll Dur BA81. Linc Th Coll 84. **d** 84 **p** 85. C Bulwell St Mary *S'well* 84-88; C Shrewsbury H Cross *Lich* 88-92; rtd 92. *15 Winchelsea Street, Dover CT17 9ST* Tel (01304) 204354

MYERS, Robert William John. b 57. Aus Nat Univ BSc80 Newc Univ Aus DipEd82. Trin Coll Bris 93. **d** 95 **p** 96. C Addiscombe St Mary Magd w St Martin *S'wark* 95-98; C Surbiton St Matt 98-03; P-in-c Blayney Australia from 04. *88 Adelaide Street, PO Box 125, Blayney NSW 2799, Australia* Tel (0061) (2) 6368 2065 Fax 6368 4185 E-mail rwjmyers@netscape.net

MYERS, Sally Ann. b 65. Leic Univ BA86 Nottm Univ MA06. EMMTC 02. **d** 06 **p** 07. C Grantham *Linc* 06-08; Vice-Prin Dioc Min Tr Course from 08. *15 Wain Well Mews, Lincoln LN2 4BF* Tel (01522) 567804 *or* 504050
E-mail sally.myers@lincoln.anglican.org

MYERSCOUGH, Robin Nigel. b 44. K Coll Lon BD69 Nottm Univ PGCE70. Coll of Resurr Mirfield 69. **d** 81 **p** 82. Hon C Diss *Nor* 81-84; Chapl Nor Sch 81-84; Hd RS Sedbergh Sch 84-85; Chapl and Hd RS Dur Sch 85-92; Chapl Gresham's Sch Holt 92-01; Asst Chapl 01-04; rtd 04; Perm to Offic *Nor* from 04. *Hamer, The Street, Bodham, Holt NR25 6NW* Tel (01263) 588859 E-mail robin@myerscough3.freeserve.co.uk

MYLNE, Mrs Christine. b 44. Open Univ BA76 Univ of Wales (Lamp) MA03. St Alb Minl Tr Scheme 89 NEOC 04. **d** 04 **p** 05. NSM Norham and Duddo *Newc* 04-06; NSM Cornhill w Carham 04-06; NSM Branxton 04-06; P-in-c Challoch *Glas* from 06. *All Saints' Rectory, Challoch, Newton Stewart DG8 6RB* Tel (01671) 402101

MYLNE, Denis Colin. b 31. Kelham Th Coll 69. **d** 71. Perm to Offic *Glas* 74-84 and *Ab* 84-88; C Bedford All SS *St Alb* 88-91; C Harpenden St Jo 91-96; rtd 96; Perm to Offic *Newc* 96-06; Hon C Kelso *Edin* 99-03. *All Saints' Rectory, Challoch, Newton Stewart DG8 6RB* Tel (01671) 402101

MYNETT, Colin. b 25. Roch Th Coll 61. **d** 63 **p** 64. C Liskeard w St Keyne *Truro* 63-66; R Lifton and Kelly w Bradstone *Ex* 66-71; TV Devonport St Aubyn 71-75; V Cinderford St Jo *Glouc* 75-84; P-in-c Pittville All SS 84-89; rtd 89. *11 Gracey Court, Woodland Road, Broadclyst, Exeter EX5 3GA*

MYNETT, John Alan. b 37. Bris Univ BSc59 MSc61 CEng MIMechE67. NOC 82. **d** 85 **p** 86. NSM Poynton *Ches* 85-90; NSM Macclesfield Team 90-01; P-in-c Sutton St Geo 98-01; Perm to Offic 01-05. *Address temp unknown*
E-mail johanne@mynett46.freeserve.co.uk

MYNORS, James Baskerville. b 49. Peterho Cam BA70 MA74. Ridley Hall Cam 70 St Jo Coll Nottm 77. **d** 78 **p** 80. Hon C Leic H Apostles 78-79; C Virginia Water *Guildf* 79-83; C Patcham *Chich* 83-88; P-in-c Fowlmere and Thriplow *Ely* 88-01; Sen Tutor EAMTC 88-90; Vice-Prin 90-97; P-in-c Gt w Lt Abington 01-07; P-in-c Hildersham 01-07; Dioc Rural Miss Officer 04-07; R Aldwincle, Clopton, Pilton, Stoke Doyle etc *Pet* from 07. *The Rectory, Main Street, Aldwincle, Kettering NN14 3EP* Tel (01832) 720613 E-mail jim@mynors.me.uk

N

NADEN, Anthony Joshua. b 38. Jes Coll Ox BA62 MA64 SOAS Lon PhD73. Wycliffe Hall Ox 60. **d** 62 **p** 63. C Rowner *Portsm* 62-66; C Fisherton Anger *Sarum* 69-72; Ghana from 72. *PO Box TM524, 1echman, B-A/R, Ghana*
E-mail tanddbusiness@yahoo.com

NADIN, Dennis Lloyd. b 37. St D Coll Lamp BA60 Man Univ MEd81. Ridley Hall Cam 60. **d** 64 **p** 65. C Childwall All SS *Liv* 64-67; P-in-c Seacroft *Ripon* 67-69; Project Officer Grubb Inst 69-70; Lect CA Tr Coll Blackheath 70-72; Community Educn Essex Co Coun 73-80; Public Preacher *Chelmsf* from 73; Perm to Offic *St Alb* 01-03. *The Hermitage, 201 Willowfield, Harlow CM18 6RZ* Tel (01279) 325904

NAGEL, Canon Lawson Chase Joseph. b 49. Univ of Michigan BA71 K Coll Lon PhD82 ARHistS75. Sarum & Wells Th Coll 81. **d** 83 **p** 84. C Chiswick St Nic w St Mary *Lon* 83-86; Sec Gen Confraternity of the Blessed Sacrament from 85; C Horsham *Chich* 86; TV 86-91; V Aldwick from 91; Hon Can Popondota from 95. *The Vicarage, 25 Gossamer Lane, Aldwick, Bognor Regis PO21 3AT* Tel (01243) 262049
E-mail nagel@aldwick.demon.co.uk

NAIDU, Michael Sriram. b 28. Univ of the South (USA) 81. Ridley Hall Cam 86. **d** 80 **p** 85. Acting Chapl Stuttgart *Eur* 85-91; Chapl 91-00; rtd 00. *Kloster Kinchberg, 72172 Sulz am Neckar, Stuttgart, Germany* Tel (0049) (7454) 883136 *or* 87418 Fax 883250

NAIRN, Frederick William. b 43. TCD 64. Luther NW Th Sem DMin88. **d** 67 **p** 68. C Larne and Inver *Conn* 67-70; Chapl RAF 70 74; P in c Harmston *Linc* 75-77; V 77-84; V Coleby 78-84; USA from 84; rtd 04. *5895 Stoneybrook Drive, Minnetonka MN 55345-6434, USA*

NAIRN, Canon Stuart Robert. b 51. K Coll Lon BD75 AKC75 Univ of Wales (Lamp) MTh04 FRSA01. St Aug Coll Cant 75. **d** 76 **p** 77. C E Dereham *Nor* 76-80; TV Hempnall 80-88; V Narborough w Narford 88-99; R Pentney St Mary Magd w W Bilney 88-99; R Narborough w Narford and Pentney from 99; P-in-c Castleacre, Newton, Westacre and Southacre from 97; RD Lynn 91-99; RD Breckland from 06; Hon Can Nor Cathl from 03. *The Rectory, Main Road, Narborough, King's Lynn PE32 1TE* Tel (01760) 338552 *or* 338562
E-mail nairn@narvalleygroup.freeserve.co.uk

NAIRN-BRIGGS, The Very Revd George Peter. b 45. AKC69. St Aug Coll Cant 69. **d** 70 **p** 71. C Catford St Laur *S'wark* 70-73; C Raynes Park St Sav 73-75; V Salfords 75-81; V St Helier 81-87; Dioc Soc Resp Adv *Wakef* 87-97; Can Res Wakef Cathl 92-97; Provost Wakef 97-00; Dean Wakef 00-07; rtd 07. *Abbey House, 2 St James Court, Park Avenue, Wakefield WF2 8DN* Tel (01924) 291029 Mobile 07770-636840
E-mail nairnbriggs@btinternet.com

NAISH, Miss Annie Claire. b 65. St Jo Coll Dur BA04. Cranmer Hall Dur. **d** 05 **p** 06. C Gorleston St Andr *Nor* 05-09; Dioc Ecum Miss Enabler *B & W* from 09. *Diocesan Office, The Old Deanery, Wells BA5 2UG* Tel (01749) 670777 Mobile 07800-866494

NAISH, Mrs Hilary Marilyn. b 43. Edin Univ MA04. TISEC 04. **d** 05 **p** 07. NSM Edin Gd Shep and Edin St Salvador 05-09. *51 Lauderdale Street, Edinburgh EH9 1DE* Tel 0131-447 2068
E-mail hmnaish@talk21.com

NAISH, Mrs Joanna Mary. b 60. Bris Univ BA81 Southn Univ MA92 Sheff Univ PGCE82. STETS 06. **d** 09. NSM Woodford Valley *Sarum* from 09. *44 Balmoral Road, Salisbury SP1 3PX* Tel (01722) 504934 Mobile 07810-810231
E-mail joanna.naish@ntlworld.com

NAISH, Timothy James Neville. b 57. St Jo Coll Ox BA80 MA88 Bris Univ PhD05. WMMTC 86. **d** 87 **p** 88. CMS 81-00; C Cov H Trin 87; Dir Th Formation (Shaba) Zaïre 88-91; Research Fell, Tutor, and Lect Qu Coll Birm 92-93; Tutor and Lect Bp Tucker Th Coll Uganda 93-00; R Hanborough and Freeland *Ox* 00-06; Dir Studies Ox Min Course from 06. *307 London Road, Headington, Oxford OX3 9EJ* Tel (01865) 766627

NAISMITH, Mrs Carol. b 37. St Andr Univ MA59 Edin Univ MTh98. Edin Dioc NSM Course 85. **d** 90 **p** 94. NSM Edin Old St Paul from 90; Hon C Edin St Salvador 00-03. *38 Castle Avenue, Edinburgh EH12 7LB* Tel 0131-334 4486
E-mail carol.naismith@tiscali.co.uk

✠**NALEDI, The Rt Revd Theophilus Tswere.** b 36. UNISA BTh82 K Coll Lon MTh84. St Bede's Coll Umtata LTh59. **d** 59 **p** 60 **c** 87. S Africa 59-70; R Kimberley St Jas 67-70; Botswana 71-83 and 85-87; R Gaborone 71-73; Adn and R Lobatse 74-83; C Wimbledon *S'wark* 83-85; Prov Sec Ch of the Prov of Cen Africa 86-87; Bp Matabeleland Zimbabwe 87-01; Bp Botswana 01-04; rtd 04. *PO Box 237, Gaborone, Botswana*

NALL, Sheila Ann. b 48. Univ of Wales (Ban) BA69. WMMTC 00. **d** 03 **p** 04. NSM Worc St Wulstan 03-07; Chapl HM Pris Blakenhurst from 07. *HM Prison Blakenhurst, Hewell Lane, Redditch B97 6QS* Tel (01527) 400500
E-mail nall@simplesurveys.freeserve.co.uk

NANCARROW, Mrs Rachel Mary. b 38. Cam Inst of Educn TCert59. EAMTC 87. **d** 90 **p** 94. NSM Girton *Ely* 90-95; P-in-c Foxton 95-01; P-in-c Shepreth 98-01; C Fulbourn and Gt and Lt Wilbraham 01-03; rtd 03; Perm to Offic *Pet* from 04. *Thimble Cottage, 11 Geeston, Ketton, Stamford PE9 3RH* Tel (01780) 729382 E-mail r.m.nancarrow@skogen.co.uk

NANKIVELL, Christopher Robert Trevelyan. b 33. Jes Coll Ox BA55 MA63 Birm Univ MSocSc79. Linc Th Coll 56. **d** 58 **p** 59. C Bloxwich *Lich* 58-60; C Stafford St Mary 60-64; P-in-c Malins Lee 64-72; Soc Welfare Sector Min to Milton Keynes Chr Coun 73-76; Tutor Qu Coll Birm 76-81; rtd 96. *77 Pereira Road, Birmingham B17 9JA* Tel 0121-427 1197

NAPIER, Graeme Stewart Patrick Columbanus. b 66. Magd Coll Ox BA MA MPhil LRSM. St Steph Ho Ox. **d** 95 **p** 96. C Inverness St Andr *Mor* 95-98; Asst P St Laurence Ch Ch Australia 98-02; Min Can and Succ Westmr Abbey from 02. *4B Little Cloister, Westminster Abbey, London SW1P 3PL* Tel (020) 7654 4850 E-mail graeme.napier@westminster-abbey.org

NAPIER, Lady (Jennifer Beryl). *See* BLACK, Jennifer Beryl

NARUSAWA, Masaki Alec. b 53. K Coll Lon BD77 AKC77. Linc Th Coll 77. **d** 78 **p** 79. C Hendon St Alphage *Lon* 78-81; C Eastcote St Lawr 81-84; V Glodwick *Man* 84-99; P-in-c Withington St Crispin 99-03; Perm to Offic *Blackb* from 03. *21 Regency Gardens, Blackpool FY2 0WX* Tel (01253) 593336 Fax 594606 E-mail masaki.narusawa@lineone.net

NASCIMENTO COOK, Mrs Anesia. b 62. Mogidas Cruces Univ BA86. Porto Allegre Th Sem BTh91. **d** 91 **p** 93. Brazil 91-94; Lic to Offic *St Alb* 96-97; C Dinnington *Sheff* 97-99; P-in-c Shiregreen St Jas and St Chris 99-07; P-in-c Shiregreen St Hilda 05-07; V Shiregreen 07-08; C Rotherham from 08. *7 Oxley Court, Rotherham S60 2RE* Tel (01709) 365145

NASH, Alan Frederick. b 46. Sarum & Wells Th Coll 72. **d** 75 **p** 76. C Foley Park *Worc* 75-79; P-in-c Mildenhall *Sarum* 79-82; Wilts Adnry Youth Officer 79-82; TV N Wingfield, Pilsley and Tupton *Derby* 82-85. *17 Chapel Road, Astwood Bank, Redditch B96 6AL* Tel (01527) 894294 E-mail alan.nash@bigfoot.com

NASH, David. b 25. K Coll Lon BD51 AKC51. **d** 52 **p** 53. C Buckhurst Hill *Chelmsf* 52-58; Min St Cedd CD Westcliff 58-66; R Rivenhall 66-83; P-in-c Boscastle w Davidstow *Truro* 83-85; TR 85-90; rtd 90; Perm to Offic *Truro* from 90. *9 Boscundle Avenue, Falmouth TR11 5BU*

NASH, Preb David John. b 41. Pemb Coll Ox BA64 MA70. Wells Th Coll 65. **d** 67 **p** 68. C Preston Ascension *Lon* 67-70; TV Hackney 70-75; TV Clifton *S'well* 76-82; V Winchmore Hill St Paul *Lon* 82-98; AD Enfield 87-91; R Monken Hadley 98-08; AD Cen Barnet 00-04; Preb St Paul's Cathl 96-08; rtd 08; Perm to Offic from 08. *36 Birkbeck Road, Enfield EN2 0DX* Tel (020) 8367 6873 E-mail prebdjnash@yahoo.co.uk

NASH, Mrs Ingrid. b 36. SRN57 RNT80 BEd78. S'wark Ord Course 91. **d** 94 **p** 95. NSM Eltham Park St Luke *S'wark* 94-06; Perm to Offic *Roch* from 97 and *S'wark* from 06. *13 Crookston Road, London SE9 1YH* Tel (020) 8850 0750 E-mail ingrid.nash@btopenworld.com

NASH, James Alexander. b 56. St Jo Coll Nottm BA94. **d** 97 **p** 98. C Trunch *Nor* 97-01; R Stratton St Mary w Stratton St Michael etc from 01. *The Rectory, Flowerpot Lane, Long Stratton, Norwich NR15 2TS* Tel (01508) 530238 E-mail james.nash8@btopenworld.com

NASH, James David Gifford. b 76. New Coll Ox MEng98. Wycliffe Hall Ox BTh03. **d** 03 **p** 04. C Plymouth St Andr and Stonehouse *Ex* 03-07; Hon C Preston All SS *Blackb* from 07. *50 St Andrews Avenue, Ashton-on-Ribble, Preston PR2 1JN* E-mail james.nash@wycliffe.ox.ac.uk

NASH, Mrs Jane. b 58. ERMC 05. **d** 08 **p** 09. C Kempston All SS *St Alb* from 08; C Biddenham from 08. *The Vicarage, 57 Church End, Biddenham, Bedford MK40 4AS* Tel (01234) 351265 E-mail janenash@hotmail.co.uk

NASH, Paul. See NASH, William Paul

NASH, Paul. b 59. WMMTC 94. **d** 97 **p** 98. C Aston SS Pet and Paul *Birm* 97-02; Asst Chapl Birm Children's Hosp NHS Trust from 02; Tutor St Jo Coll Nottm from 02. *13 Jaffray Road, Birmingham B24 8AZ* Tel 0121-384 6034 *or* 0333 8526 Fax 333 8527 E-mail paulandsal@msn.com *or* p.nash@bch.nhs.uk

NASH, Paul Alexander. b 20. Glouc Th Course 73. **d** 76 **p** 76. NSM Coleford w Staunton *Glouc* 76-88; Perm to Offic from 98. *16 Orchard Road, Coleford GL16 8AU* Tel (01594) 832758

NASH, Penelope Jane. b 71. Trin Coll Bris 04. **d** 06 **p** 07. C Downend *Bris* from 06. *15 Glendale, Downend, Bristol BS16 6EQ* Tel 0117-956 8859 E-mail penny@jeznash.co.uk

NASH, Robin Louis. b 51. Open Univ BA87. Aston Tr Scheme 80 Chich Th Coll 82. **d** 84 **p** 85. C Lymington *Win* 84-86; C Andover w Foxcott 86-90; R Kegworth *Leic* 90-01; P-in-c Bournemouth St Alb *Win* from 01. *St Alban's Vicarage, 17 Linwood Road, Bournemouth BH9 1DW* Tel (01202) 534193 E-mail vicar@saintalban.org.uk

NASH, Thomas James. b 82. SS Hild & Bede Coll Dur BA03 MA04. Wycliffe Hall Ox 04. **d** 09. C St Helen Bishopsgate w St Andr Undershaft etc *Lon* from 09. *64 Arbery Road, London E3 5DD* Tel (020) 7283 2231

NASH, The Ven Trevor Gifford. b 30. Clare Coll Cam BA53 MA57. Cuddesdon Coll 53. **d** 55 **p** 56. C Cheshunt *St Alb* 55-57; CF (TA) 56-61; C Kingston All SS *S'wark* 57-61; C Stevenage *St Alb* 61-63; V Leagrave 63-67; Dir Luton Samaritans 66-67; Chapl St Geo Hosp Lon 67-73; R Win St Lawr and St Maurice w St Swithun 73-82; Bp's Adv Min of Healing 73-98; P-in-c Win H Trin 77-82; RD Win 75-82; Hon Can Win Cathl 80-90; Adn Basingstoke 82-90; Exec Co-ord Acorn Chr Healing Trust 90-97; Pres Guild of Health 92-97; Warden Guild of St Raphael 95-98; Perm to Offic *Win* from 95; rtd 97; Hon Chapl Win Cathl from 98. *The Corner Stone, 50B Hyde Street, Winchester SO23 7DY* Tel (01962) 861759

NASH, William Henry. b 31. Oak Hill Th Coll 58. **d** 61 **p** 62. C New Milverton *Cov* 61-64; C Toxteth Park St Philemon w St Silas *Liv* 64-67; V Bryn 67-76; NW Area Sec CPAS 76-82; V Penn Fields *Lich* 82-99; rtd 99; Perm to Offic *Lich* from 01. *29 Peterdale Drive, Penn, Wolverhampton WV4 5NY* Tel (01902) 344745

NASH, William Paul. b 48. St Mich Coll Llan 86. **d** 87 **p** 88. C Pembroke Dock *St D* 87-89; P-in-c Llawhaden w Bletherston and Llanycefn 89-90; V 90-92; P-in-c E Brixton St Jude *S'wark* 92-96; V 96-99; V Cwmaman *St D* 99-04; R Pendine w Llanmiloe and Eglwys Gymyn w Marros from 04. *The Rectory, Pendine, Carmarthen SA33 4PD* Tel (01994) 453405

NASH-WILLIAMS, Mrs Barbara Ruth. b 66. St Martin's Coll Lanc BA88 Anglia Poly Univ MA03. EAMTC 96. **d** 99 **p** 00. C Tettenhall Wood and Perton *Lich* 99-02; NSM Cheswardine, Childs Ercall, Hales, Hinstock etc 04-06; Dioc Development Officer for Youth Work *Newc* from 06. *The Vicarage, Stamfordham, Newcastle upon Tyne NE18 0QQ* Tel (01661) 886853 E-mail bar@nash-williams.name

NASH-WILLIAMS, Mark Christian Victor. b 64. Trin Hall Cam BA86 MA90 PGCE87. Qu Coll Birm BD01. **d** 02 **p** 03. C Edgmond w Kynnersley and Preston Wealdmoors *Lich* 02-06; P-in-c Stamfordham w Matfen *Newc* from 06. *The Vicarage,*

Stamfordham, Newcastle upon Tyne NE18 0QQ Tel (01661) 886456 E-mail mark@nash-williams.name

NASH-WILLIAMS, Canon Piers le Sor Victor. b 35. Trin Hall Cam BA57 MA61. Cuddesdon Coll 59. **d** 61 **p** 62. C Milton *Win* 61-64; Asst Chapl Eton Coll 64-66; Perm to Offic *Chich* 66-68; C Furze Platt *Ox* 69-72; V Newbury St Geo Wash Common 72-73; TV Newbury 73-91; R Ascot Heath 91-01; Hon Can Ch Ch 01; rtd 01; Perm to Offic *Ox* from 02. *18 Chiltern Close, Newbury RG14 6SZ* Tel (01635) 31762 E-mail pnashwilliams@tesco.net

NASON, Canon Thomas David. b 44. Open Univ BA92 ACA68 FCA78. Ripon Coll Cuddesdon 84. **d** 86 **p** 87. C Banstead *Guildf* 86-89; Chapl Prebendal Sch Chich from 89; PV Chich Cathl from 89; Can and Preb Chich Cathl from 06. *1 St Richard's Walk, Canon Lane, Chichester PO19 1QA* Tel (01243) 775615 Mobile 07732-114279 E-mail d.nason@tesco.net

NASSAR, Nadim. b 64. Near E Sch of Th BTh88. **d** 03 **p** 04. Prin Trin Foundn for Christianity and Culture 03-05; Dir from 05; Hon C Upper Chelsea H Trin *Lon* from 03. *Holy Trinity Church, Sloane Street, London SW1X 9DF* Tel (020) 7730 8830 Mobile 07961-968193 E-mail director@tfcinternational.com

NATHANAEL, Brother. See THOMPSON, Kenneth

NATHANAEL, Martin Moses. b 43. Lon Univ BEd73 K Coll Lon MTh77. Ripon Coll Cuddesdon 77. **d** 79 **p** 80. C Hampton All SS *Lon* 79-82; P-in-c Kensal Town St Thos w St Andr and St Phil 82-83; Hd Div Bp Stopford Sch Lon 83-91; TV Tring *St Alb* 91-00; rtd 00. *5 Carvers Croft, Woolmer Green, Knebworth SG3 6LX* Tel (01438) 815853 E-mail martinascend@aol.com

NATHANIEL, Garth Edwin Peter. b 61. Brunel Univ BTh99. Lon Bible Coll 96. **d** 98 **p** 99. NSM Hanwell St Mary w St Chris *Lon* 98-99; C Lt Stanmore St Lawr 99-01; P-in-c Brockmoor *Worc* 02-07; TV Brierley Hill from 07. *5 Leys Road, Brockmoor, Brierley Hill DY5 3UR* Tel (01384) 263327 Fax 573382 Mobile 07949-490265 E-mail gn004d6359@blueyonder.co.uk

NATHANIEL, Ivan Wasim. Punjab Univ MA65. Bp's Coll Calcutta 59. **d** 62 **p** 64. India 62-68; C Newland St Aug *York* 68-70; Hon C Crawley *Chich* 70-98; Chapl H Trin Sch Crawley 76-97; Hd RS 76-97; Perm to Offic *Chich* from 97. *13 Haywards, Crawley RH10 3TR* Tel (01293) 882932 E-mail i.nathaniel@btopenworld.com

NATHANIEL, Leslie Satianathan. b 54. Bangalore Univ BA74 Jawaharlal Nehru Univ Delhi BA79 Birm Univ PhD08. **d** 01 **p** 02. Interchange Adv CMS 99-04; Germany from 04; Abp's Dep Sec Ecum Affairs and Eur Sec Coun for Chr Unity from 09. *Frankentobelstrasse 4, 73079 Suessen, Germany* Tel (020) 7898 1474 E-mail leslie.nathaniel@c-of-e.org.uk

NATTRASS, Elizabeth Jane. b 59. CBDTI 97. **d** 00 **p** 01. C Dalston w Cumdivock, Raughton Head and Wreay *Carl* 00-03; TV S Barrow 03-08; P-in-c 08; TR from 08. *St Aidan's Vicarage, 31 Middle Hill, Barrow-in-Furness LA13 9HD* Tel (01229) 830445 E-mail nattrassjane@aol.com

NATTRASS, Michael Stuart. b 41. CBE98. Man Univ BA62. Cuddesdon Coll 62. **d** 64 **p** 65. C Easington Colliery *Dur* 64-65; C Silksworth 65-68; Perm to Offic *S'well* 68-72; Lic to Offic *Dur* 72-76; Perm to Offic *Lon* 76-78 and from 05; Hon C Pinner 78-05; rtd 05. *36 Waxwell Lane, Pinner HA5 3EN* Tel (020) 8866 0217 Fax 8930 0622 E-mail msnattrass@btinternet.com

NAUDÉ, John Donald. b 62. Ridley Hall Cam 95. **d** 97 **p** 98. C Kettering Ch the King *Pet* 97-00; C Wellingborough All Hallows 00-06; Dioc Disability Officer 06-06; V Cowplain *Portsm* from 06. *The Vicarage, 87 Perseus Place, Waterlooville PO7 8AW* Tel (023) 9226 7647 E-mail john@naudeuk.com

NAUMANN, Canon David Sydney. b 26. Ripon Hall Ox 54. **d** 55 **p** 56. C Herne Bay Ch Ch *Cant* 55-58; Asst Chapl United Sheff Hosps 58-60; V Reculver *Cant* 60-64; Dioc Youth Chapl 63-70; R Eastwell w Boughton Aluph 65-67; V Westwell 65-67; Warden St Gabr Retreat Ho Westgate 68-70; V Littlebourne 70-82; RD E Bridge 78-82; Hon Can Cant Cathl 81-00; R Sandwich 82-91; RD Sandwich 85-90; rtd 91; Perm to Offic *Cant* from 91. *2 The Forrens, The Precincts, Canterbury CT1 2ER* Tel (01227) 458939

NAUNTON, Hugh Raymond. b 38. Whitelands Coll Lon CertEd69 Open Univ BA75. Bernard Gilpin Soc Dur 59 Chich Th Coll 60. **d** 63 **p** 64. C Stanground *Ely* 63-66; NSM Woolwich St Mary w H Trin *S'wark* 66-67; NSM Wandsworth St Anne 67-69 and 71-73; NSM Paddington St Sav *Lon* 69-71; NSM Cuddington *Guildf* 73-78; Hd RE Raynes Park High Sch 69-76; Hd RE Paddington Sch 76-78; Sen Teacher and Hd RE Ch Sch Richmond 79-93; Hon C Cheam Common St Phil *S'wark* 79-95; C Cheam 95-02; Perm to Offic *Guildf* 97-02; TV Selsdon St Jo w St Fran *S'wark* 02-03; rtd 03; Perm to Offic *S'wark* from 04. *35 Farm Way, Worcester Park KT4 8RZ* Tel (020) 8395 1748 E-mail hugh.naunton@blueyonder.co.uk

NAY, Ms Imogen Joyce. b 79. York Univ BA00 Warwick Univ MA02 Cam Univ BA08. Westcott Ho Cam 06. **d** 09. C Surbiton St Andr and St Mark *S'wark* from 09. *1 The Mall, Surbiton KT6 4EH* Tel (020) 8399 6806 Mobile 07828-064710 E-mail imogen.nay1@btinternet.com

NAYLOR, Alison Louise. See CHESWORTH, Mrs Alison Louise

NAYLOR, Barry. See NAYLOR, Canon James Barry

NAYLOR, Fiona. b 68. CQSW93. St Jo Coll Nottm 02. **d** 05 **p** 08. C Len Valley *Cant* 05-06; Hon C Lower Darwen St Jas *Blackb* from 07. *28 Aintree Drive, Lower Darwen, Blackburn BB3 0QW* Tel (01254) 263710 E-mail revfionanaylor@btinternet.com

NAYLOR, Canon Frank. b 36. Lon Univ BA58 Liv Univ MA63. NW Ord Course 75. **d** 75 **p** 76. NSM Eccleston Ch Ch *Liv* 75-92; Asst Dioc Chapl to the Deaf 92-94; Sen Chapl from 94; Hon Can Liv Cathl from 01. *27 Daresbury Road, Eccleston, St Helens WA10 5DR* Tel (01744) 757034

NAYLOR, Ian Frederick. b 47. AKC70 Open Univ BA92 Heythrop Coll Lon MA00. St Aug Coll Cant 70. **d** 71 **p** 72. C Camberwell St Giles *S'wark* 71-74; OSB 74-86; Chapl RN 86-04; rtd 04; P-in-c Pau *Eur* from 08. *Appt 23, 3 bis rue Pasteur, 64000 Pau, France* Tel (0033) (5) 59 30 91 84 Mobile (6) 81 20 80 03 E-mail if.naylor@ntlworld.com

NAYLOR, Ian Stuart. b 63. Wycliffe Hall Ox. **d** 01 **p** 02. C Ipswich St Marg *St E* 01-04; P-in-c Martlesham w Brightwell from 04. *The Rectory, 17 Lark Rise, Martlesham Heath, Ipswich IP5 3SA* Tel (01473) 622424 Mobile 07712-309848 E-mail inaylor17@aol.com

NAYLOR, Canon James Barry. b 50. Wadham Coll Ox BSc71 St Benet's Hall Ox BA75. Wycliffe Hall Ox 72. **d** 76 **p** 76. C Catford (Southend) and Downham *S'wark* 76-79; TV 79-82; P-in-c Lewisham St Swithun 82-87; V E Dulwich St Jo 87-97; RD Dulwich 90-97; P-in-c Blythburgh w Reydon *St E* 97-99; P-in-c Frostenden, Henastead, Covehithe etc 97-99; P-in-c Southwold 97-99; P-in-c Uggeshall w Sotherton, Wangford and Henham 97-99; TR Sole Bay 99-02; Chapl Supervisor St Felix Sch Southwold 99-02; Can Res Leic Cathl from 02; C The Abbey Leic 02-08; P-in-c from 08; C Leic H Spirit 02-08; P-in-c from 08. *St Andrew's House, 53B Jarrom Street, Leicester LE2 7DH* Tel 0116-255 0031 *or* 248 7471 E-mail barry.naylor@leccofe.org

NAYLOR, Miss Jean. b 29. Linc Th Coll 77. **dss** 79 **d** 87. Charlton St Luke w H Trin *S'wark* 79-84; Crofton Park St Hilda w St Cypr 84-89; Par Dn 87-89; rtd 89; Perm to Offic *Wakef* from 89. *12 Winter Terrace, Barnsley S75 2ES* Tel (01226) 204767

NAYLOR, John Watson. b 26. Trin Hall Cam BA52 MA56. Ripon Hall Ox 64. **d** 66 **p** 67. C Newc St Andr 66-69; C Otterburn w Elsdon and Horsley w Byrness 69-72; R Husborne Crawley w Ridgmont *St Alb* 72-76; Chapl Caldicott Sch Farnham Royal 76-80; P-in-c Chollerton w Thockrington *Newc* 80-82; R Chollerton w Birtley and Thockrington 82-91; rtd 91; Perm to Offic *Newc* from 91. *1 Mitchell House, Abbeyfield, Gillings Court, Thirsk YO7 1SZ* Tel (01845) 524335

NAYLOR, Canon Peter Aubrey. b 33. Kelham Th Coll 54 Ely Th Coll 57. **d** 58 **p** 59. C Shepherd's Bush St Steph *Lon* 58-62; C Portsea N End St Mark *Portsm* 62-64; Chapl HM Borstal Portsm 64-66; V Foley Park *Worc* 66-74; V Maidstone All SS w St Phil and H Trin *Cant* 74-81; P-in-c Tovil 79-81; V Maidstone All SS and St Phil w Tovil 81-91; Hon Can Cant Cathl 79-93; RD Sutton 80-86; R Biddenden and Smarden 91-93; P-in-c Leic St Marg and All SS 93-96; P-in-c Leic St Aug 93-96; TR The Abbey Leic 96; rtd 98; Perm to Offic *Chich* 98-02; P-in-c Crowborough St Jo from 02. *St John's Vicarage, St John's Road, Crowborough TN6 1RZ* Tel and fax (01892) 654660

NAYLOR, Peter Edward. b 30. Linc Th Coll 58. **d** 61 **p** 62. C S Beddington St Mich *S'wark* 61-64; V S Lambeth St Ann 64-77; V Nork *Guildf* 77-90; R Ecton *Pet* 90-97; Warden Ecton Ho 90-97; rtd 97; Perm to Offic *Ely* 97-01 and *Eur* from 03. *51 avenue du Bezet, 64000 Pau, France* Tel (0033) (5) 59 62 41 68 E-mail peternaylor30@hotmail.com

NAYLOR, Peter Henry. b 41. MIMechE. Chich Th Coll 64. **d** 67 **p** 68. C Filton *Bris* 67-70; C Brixham *Ex* 70-72; C Leckhampton St Pet *Glouc* 72-76; V Brockworth 76-94; P-in-c Gt Witcombe 91-94; RD Glouc N 91-94; P-in-c The Ampneys w Driffield and Poulton 94-95; R 95-99; P-in-c Cheltenham Em w St Steph 99-07; rtd 07. *11 The Yarnolds, Shurdington, Cheltenham GL51 4SJ* Tel (01242) 861329

NAYLOR, Robert James. b 42. CQSW66. NOC 74. **d** 77 **p** 78. C Aigburth *Liv* 77-80; Soc Resp Officer *Glouc* 80-85; Leonard Cheshire Foundn (Lon) 85-91; Dir The Stable Family Home Trust (Hants) 91-07; NSM The Lulworths, Winfrith Newburgh and Chaldon *Sarum* 98-00; P-in-c 00-07; RD Purbeck 02-07; R Jersey St Mary *Win* from 07. *The Rectory, La route de Ste Marie, St Mary, Jersey JE3 3DB* Tel (01534) 484678 E-mail rjn-rectory@tiscali.co.uk

NAYLOR, Russell Stephen. b 45. Leeds Univ BA70. St Chad's Coll Dur 70. **d** 72 **p** 73. C Chapel Allerton *Ripon* 72-75; Ind Chapl *Liv* 75-81; P-in-c Burtonwood 81-83; V 83-05; rtd 05; Perm to Offic *Ches* from 05. *6 Hillside Avenue, Runcorn WA7 4BW* Tel (01928) 835139 E-mail russnaylor@ntlworld.com

NAYLOR, Mrs Shelagh. b 47. I M Marsh Coll of Physical Educn Liv CertEd68 MBACP. Ban Ord Course 06. **d** 07 **p** 08. NSM Ardudwy Ban from 07. *Tanyffridd, Heol y Bryn, Harlech LL46 2TU* Tel (01766) 780922 Mobile 07855-057037

NAYLOR, Vivien Frances Damaris. See BRADLEY, Ms Vivien Frances Damaris

✠NAZIR-ALI, The Rt Revd Michael James. b 49. Karachi Univ BA70 St Edm Hall Ox BLitt74 MLitt81 Fitzw Coll Cam MLitt77 ACT ThD85 Bath Univ Hon DLitt03 Greenwich Univ Hon DLitt03 Kent Univ Hon DD04 Westmr Coll Penn (USA) DHumLit04 Lambeth DD05. Ridley Hall Cam 70. **d** 74 **p** 76 **c** 84. C Cambridge H Sepulchre w All SS *Ely* 74-76; Tutorial Supervisor Th Cam Univ 74-76; Sen Tutor Karachi Th Coll Pakistan 76-81; Provost Lahore 81-84; Bp Raiwind 84-86; Asst to Abp Cant 86-89; Co-ord of Studies and Ed Lambeth Conf 86-89; Hon C Ox St Giles and SS Phil and Jas w St Marg 86-89; Gen Sec CMS 89-94; Asst Bp S'wark 89-94; Hon C Limpsfield and Titsey 89-94; Can Th Leic Cathl 92-94; Bp Roch 94-09; Visiting Prof Th and RS Univ of Greenwich from 96; Hon Fell St Edm Hall Ox from 99. *PO Box 54, Orpington BR5 9RT*

✠NDUNGANE, The Most Revd Winston Hugh Njongonkulu. b 41. K Coll Lon BD78 AKC78 MTh. St Pet Coll Alice 71. **d** 73 **p** 74 **c** 91. C Atholone S Africa 73-75; C Mitcham St Mark *S'wark* 75-76; C Hammersmith St Pet *Lon* 76-77; C Primrose Hill St Mary w Avenue Road St Paul 77-79; Asst Chapl Paris St Geo *Eur* 79; R Elsies River S Africa 80-81; Prov Liaison Officer 81-84; Prin St Bede's Th Coll Umtata 85-86; Prov Exec Officer 87-91; Bp Kimberley and Kuruman 91-96; Abp Cape Town from 96. *Bishopscourt, 16-20 Bishopscourt Drive, Claremont, 7708 South Africa* Tel (0027) (21) 761 2531 Fax 797 1298 *or* 761 4193 E-mail archbish@bishopscourt-cpsa.org.za

NEAL, Alan. b 27. Trin Coll Bris 82. **d** 84 **p** 85. Hon C Broughty Ferry *Bre* 84-85; P-in-c Dundee St Ninian 85-86; R Lockerbie and Annan *Glas* 86-94; rtd 94. *c/o Mr and Mrs Graham Rew, 3 Vallance Drive, Lockerbie DG11 2DU*

NEAL, Canon Anthony Terrence. b 42. BA CertEd. Chich Th Coll 65. **d** 68 **p** 69. C Cross Green St Sav and St Hilda *Ripon* 68-73; NSM Hawksworth Wood 73-78; Asst Chapl and Hd RE Abbey Grange High Sch Leeds 73-81; NSM Farnley *Ripon* 78-81; Dioc Adv in RE *Truro* 81-85; Children's Officer 85-87; Stewardship Adv 87-88; P-in-c St Erth 81-84; V 84-96; P-in-c Phillack w Gwithian and Gwinear 94-96; P-in-c Hayle 94-96; TR Godrevy 96-06; Hon Can Truro Cathl 94-06; rtd 06. *11 Adelaide Street, Camborne TR14 8HH* Tel (01209) 712733 E-mail steamerneal@tiscali.co.uk

NEAL, Canon Christopher Charles. b 47. St Pet Coll Ox BA69. Ridley Hall Cam 69. **d** 72 **p** 73. C Addiscombe St Mary *Cant* 72-76; C Camberley St Paul *Guildf* 76-83; TV Thame w Towersey *Ox* 86-98; TR Thame 98-03; Hon Can Ch Ch 98-03; Dir Miss and Community CMS from 03. *Church Mission Society, Watlington Road, Cowley, Oxford OX4 6BZ* Tel 08456-201799 Fax (01865) 776375 E-mail chris.neal@cms-uk.org

NEAL, Miss Frances Mary. b 37. BEd76. S'wark Ord Course 94. **d** 96 **p** 97. NSM Catford (Southend) and Downham *S'wark* 96-07; Perm to Offic 07-08. *29 Ballamore Road, Downham, Bromley BR1 5LN* Tel (020) 8698 6616

NEAL, Gary Roy. b 57. St Jo Coll Nottm 03. **d** 05 **p** 06. C Kinson *Sarum* 05-09; TV Broadwater *Chich* from 09. *St Stephen's Vicarage, 37 Angola Road, Worthing BN14 8DU* Tel (01903) 235054 E-mail gary@cofekinson.org.uk

NEAL, Canon Geoffrey Martin. b 40. AKC63. **d** 64 **p** 65. C Wandsworth St Paul *S'wark* 64-66; USA 66-68; C Reigate St Mark *S'wark* 68-70; P-in-c Wandsworth St Faith 70-72; V 72-75; V Houghton Regis *St Alb* 75-95; Hon Can St Alb 93-95; rtd 00; Perm to Offic *St Alb* from 00. *63 The Moor, Carlton, Bedford MK43 7JS* Tel (01234) 720938

NEAL, John Edward. b 44. Nottm Univ BTh74. Linc Th Coll 70. **d** 74 **p** 75. C Lee St Marg *S'wark* 74-77; C Clapham St Jo 77; C Clapham Ch Ch and St Jo 77-81; P-in-c Eltham St Barn 81-83; V 83-98; Sub-Dean Eltham 89-91; Sub-Dean Greenwich S 91-97; RD Greenwich S 97-01; V Eltham St Jo from 98. *The Vicarage, Sowerby Close, London SE9 6HB* Tel (020) 8850 2731 *or* 8859 1242

NEAL, Stephen Charles. b 44. K Coll Lon BSc66. NOC 90. **d** 93 **p** 94. C Walmsley *Man* 93-96; P-in-c Bolton St Matt w St Barn 96-98; TV Halliwell 98-02; Chapl Bolton Hospice 02-05; Perm to Offic *Man* 05-08 and *Derby* from 08. *40 Trusley Brook, Hilton, Derby DE65 5LA*

NEALE, Alan James Robert. b 52. LSE BSc(Econ)73. Wycliffe Hall Ox BA76 MA81. **d** 77 **p** 78. C Plymouth St Andr w St Paul and St Geo *Ex* 77-80; C Portswood Ch Ch *Win* 80-82; V Stanstead Abbots *St Alb* 82-85; Asst Master Chelmsf Hall Sch Eastbourne 85-88; R Brookings St Paul USA 88-90; R Middletown St Columba 91-04; R Philadelphia H Trin from 04. *316 S 16th Street, Philadelphia PA 19102, USA* Tel (001) (215) 567 1267 Fax 567 3766

NEALE, Andrew Jackson. b 58. Oak Hill Th Coll 97. **d** 99 **p** 00. C Harold Hill St Geo *Chelmsf* 99-02; C Bentley Common, Kelvedon Hatch and Navestock 02-03; TV Chigwell and Chigwell Row from 03. *The Vicarage, Romford Road, Chigwell IG7 4QD* Tel (020) 8501 5150 E-mail andy.neale2pray@btopenworld.com

NEALE, David. b 50. Lanchester Poly Cov BSc72. St Mich Coll

Llan BD83. **d** 83 **p** 84. Min Can St Woolos Cathl 83-87; Chapl St Woolos Hosp Newport 85-87; R Blaina and Nantyglo *Mon* 87-91; Video and Tech Officer Bd of Miss 91-01; TV Cyncoed 99-01; Creative Resources Officer 01-03; V Maindee Newport from 03. *St John's Vicarage, 25 St John's Road, Newport NP19 8GR* Tel (01633) 674155 E-mail dneale@ntlworld.com

NEALE, Edward. *See* NEALE, Canon James Edward McKenzie

NEALE, Geoffrey Arthur. b 41. Brasted Th Coll 61 St Aid Birkenhead 63. **d** 65 **p** 66. C Stoke *Cov* 65-68; C Fareham H Trin *Portsm* 68-71; TV 71-72; R Binstead 72-77; TR Bottesford w Ashby *Linc* 77-80; V Horncastle w Low Toynton 80-90; V Brigg 90-95; V Blockley w Aston Magna and Bourton on the Hill *Glouc* 95-01; Local Min Officer 95-01; V Heath and Reach *St Alb* 01-05; TV Billington, Egginton, Hockliffe etc 06; RD Dunstable 02-04; rtd 06; Perm to Offic *Cant* from 06. *46 Cavendish Road, Herne Bay CT6 5BB* Tel (01227) 360717 Mobile 07703-174761 E-mail revd.geoffn@gmail.com

NEALE, Hannah. b 40. SEITE. **d** 99 **p** 00. NSM Mitcham St Mark *S'wark* 99-00; NSM Merton St Jo 00-09; NSM Merton Priory from 09. *42 Palestine Grove, London SW19 2QN* Tel (020) 8648 5405

NEALE, Canon James Edward McKenzie (Eddie). b 38. MBE04. Selw Coll Cam BA61 Nottm Trent Univ Hon DLitt00 Nottm Univ Hon DD03. Clifton Th Coll 61. **d** 63 **p** 64. C Everton St Ambrose w St Tim *Liv* 63-72; Relig Adv BBC Radio Merseyside 72-76; V Bestwood St Matt *S'well* 76-86; Dioc Urban Officer 86-91; V Nottingham St Mary and St Cath 91-03; Hon Can S'well Minster 91-03; rtd 03; Perm to Offic *S'well* from 03. *Church Cottage, Church Lane, Maplebeck, Nottingham NG22 0BS* Tel (01636) 636559 E-mail eddie@neale007.freeserve.co.uk

NEALE, Mrs Jan Celia. b 42. EMMTC 92. **d** 92 **p** 94. C Gt and Lt Coates w Bradley *Linc* 92-96; TV 96-01; TV Chambersbury *St Alb* 01-07; rtd 07. *1 Dickens Close, St Albans AL3 5PP* Tel (01727) 853936

✠**NEALE, The Rt Revd John Robert Geoffrey.** b 26. AKC54 St Boniface Warminster 54. **d** 55 **p** 56 **c** 74. C St Helier *S'wark* 55-58; Chapl Ardingly Coll 58-62; Recruitment Sec CACTM 63-66; ACCM 66-68; R Hascombe *Guildf* 68-74; Can Missr and Dir Post-Ord Tr 68-74; Hon Can Guildf Cathl 68-74; Adn Wilts *Sarum* 74-80; Suff Bp Ramsbury 74-81; Area Bp Ramsbury 81-88; Can and Preb Sarum Cathl 74-88; Sec Partnership for World Miss 89-91; Hon Asst Bp Lon and S'wark 89-91; rtd 91; Hon Asst Bp B & W 91-08; Bris from 92; Glouc from 94. *26 Prospect, Corsham SN13 9AF* Tel (01249) 712557

NEALE, Martyn William. b 57. G&C Coll Cam BA78 MA82. Ripon Coll Cuddesdon 78. **d** 81 **p** 82. C Perry Hill St Geo *S'wark* 81-83; C Purley St Mark 83-85; V Abbey Wood 85-97; V Hawley H Trin *Guildf* from 97; V Minley from 97. *The Vicarage, Hawley, Blackwater, Camberley GU17 9BN* Tel (01276) 35287 E-mail frmartyn@aol.com

NEALE, Paul Edward. b 46. Portsm Coll of Tech BSc68. **d** 07 **p** 08. OLM Cromer *Nor* from 07. *30 Fulcher Avenue, Cromer NR27 9SG* Tel (01263) 513563 E-mail paulneale127@btinternet.com

NEARY (née TAYLOR), Mrs Joanna Beatrice. b 74. Warwick Univ BA96 Homerton Coll Cam PGCE97. St Jo Coll Nottm 04. **d** 06 **p** 07. C Northolt St Jos *Lon* 06-09. *7 Cedar Road, Charlton Down, Dorchester DT2 9UL* Tel (01305) 267708 Mobile 07939-062409 E-mail jo@joneary.com

NEAUM, David Andrew. b 79. Trin Coll Melbourne BA01 SS Coll Cam BA06 Em Coll Cam MPhil08. Westcott Ho Cam 04 Yale Div Sch 06. **d** 07 **p** 08. NSM Cambridge St Mary Less *Ely* 07-08; C Marnhull *Sarum* from 08. *The Round House, 23 Drovers, Sturminster Newton DT10 1QZ* Tel (01258) 475533 E-mail david.neaum@gmail.com

NEAVE, Garry Reginald. b 51. Leic Univ BA72 MA73 PGCE74 MCMI. S'wark Ord Course. **d** 82 **p** 83. NSM Harlow St Mary Magd *Chelmsf* 82-87 and from 92; NSM St Mary-at-Latton 87-92; Chapl and Asst Prin Harlow Tertiary Coll 84-99; Dir Student Services and Admin W Herts Coll 99-04; Educn Dir Girls' Day Sch Trust from 04. *35 Perry Spring, Harlow CM17 9DQ* Tel (01279) 411775

NEECH, Canon Alan Summons. b 15. Dur Univ LTh37. Tyndale Hall Bris 34. **d** 39 **p** 40. BCMS 39-81; India 39-66; Can Lucknow 64-66; Overseas Sec BCMS 64-66; Gen Sec 66-81; Hon Can Tanganyika from 72; Hon C Slough *Ox* 75-81; rtd 80; RD Loddon *Nor* 85-90; Perm to Offic from 90. *The Gardens Cottage, Rockland St Mary, Norwich NR14 7HQ* Tel (01508) 538519

NEED, The Very Revd Philip Alan. b 54. AKC75. Chich Th Coll 76. **d** 77 **p** 78. C Clapham Ch Ch and St Jo *S'wark* 77-79; C Luton All SS w St Pet *St Alb* 80-83; V Harlow St Mary Magd *Chelmsf* 83-89; P-in-c Chaddesden St Phil *Derby* 89-91; Bp's Dom Chapl *Chelmsf* 91-96; R Bocking St Mary from 96; Dean Bocking from 96; Bp's Adv Braintree 00-06 and from 09; Hon Can Chelmsf Cathl from 07. *The Deanery, Deanery Hill, Braintree CM7 5SR* Tel (01376) 324887 *or* 553092 E-mail thedeanofbocking@tiscali.co.uk

NEED, Stephen William. b 57. K Coll Lon BD79 MTh83 PhD93 AKC79 FRSA95. **d** 08 **p** 08. Dean St Geo Coll Jerusalem from 05; Perm to Offic *Chelmsf* from 09. *St George's College, PO Box 1248, Jerusalem 91000, Israel* Tel (00972) (2) 626 4704 Fax 626 4703

NEEDHAM, Mrs Marian Ruth. b 52. Birm Univ BMus74 City Univ MA96. NOC 06. **d** 08 **p** 09. NSM Ches H Trin from 08. *14 Roselands Court, Chester Road, Rossett, Wrexham LL12 0DD* Tel (01244) 610339 Fax 571857 E-mail marianruthmailbox-rev@yahoo.co.uk

NEEDHAM, Brother Peter Douglas. b 56. Chich Th Coll 86. **d** 88 **p** 88. SSF from 80; C S Moor *Dur* 88-90; Chapl RN 91-93; Lic to Offic *Newc* 91-96 and *Lon* 97-99; C Ealing Ch the Sav *Lon* 99-02; P-in-c Grimethorpe *Wakef* 02-05; V Grimethorpe w Brierley from 05. *St Luke's Vicarage, High Street, Grimethorpe, Barnsley S72 7JA* Tel (01226) 717561

NEEDLE, Mrs Jill Mary. b 56. Matlock Coll of Educn TCert77 BEd78. St Jo Coll Nottm 03. **d** 05 **p** 06. NSM Allestree St Nic *Derby* from 05; NSM Quarndon from 05. *117 Hazelwood Road, Duffield, Belper DE56 4AA* Tel (01332) 840746 E-mail jill.needle@btinternet.com

NEEDLE, Paul Robert. b 45. Oak Hill Th Coll 67. **d** 70 **p** 71. C Gt Horton *Bradf* 70-74; C Pudsey St Lawr 74-77; Hon C Horton and Chapl St Luke's Hosp Bradf 78-80; NSM Irthlingborough *Pet* 87-90; NSM Gt w Lt Addington 90-98; Bp's Media Adv 94-02; NSM Higham Ferrers w Chelveston 02-06; Bp's Communications Officer *Eur* from 05; P-in-c Costa Azahar from 07; Perm to Offic *Pet* from 07. *Apdo Correos 136, 12579 Alcossebre, Spain,* or *Countess Gardens, Bell Street, Henley-on-Thames RG9 2BN* Tel (0034) (964) 413166 Mobile 07833-372439 E-mail paulneedle@aol.com

NEEDLE, Richard John. b 57. Bath Univ BPharm78 PhD83 MRPharmS79. ERMC 04. **d** 07 **p** 08. NSM Sproughton w Burstall, Copdock w Washbrook etc *St E* from 07. *Meadowside, Gandish Road, East Bergholt, Colchester CO7 6UR* Tel (01206) 298859 E-mail richard.needle@btinternet.com

NEEDS, Michael John. b 42. Open Univ BA82 Univ of Wales (Swansea) MSc84 PhD87. Wycliffe Hall Ox 91. **d** 93 **p** 94. C Aberystwyth *St D* 93-96; R Llanllwchaearn and Llanina 96-06; rtd 07; P-in-c Martletwy w Lawrenny and Minwear etc *St D* 07-09. *2 Llanwonno Close, Pontypridd CF37 2EB* Tel (01443) 405773 E-mail michaeljohnneeds@aol.com

NEELY, William George. b 32. Lon Univ BD62 QUB PhD. **d** 56 **p** 57. C Cregagh *D & D* 56-62; C-in-c Mt Merrion 62-68; I 68-76; Dioc Missr (Down) 70-76; Can Down Cathl 74-76; I Kilcooley w Littleton, Crohane and Killenaule *C & O* 76-84; P-in-c Fertagh 79-84; I Keady w Armaghbreague and Derrynoose 84-06; Tutor for Aux Min (Arm) 86-06; Dir Post-Ord Tr 86-06; Preb Swords St Patr Cathl Dublin 97-06; rtd 06. *c/o B J MacKey Esq, 16 North Circular Road, Lisburn BT28 3AH*

NEIL, Prof Peter Sydney. b 62. Edin Univ MA83 MEd86 QUB PhD95 MDiv03. **d** 08 **p** 09. NSM Elerch w Penrhyncoch w Capel Bangor and Goginan *St D* from 08. *2 Erw Goch, Waunfawr, Aberystwyth SY23 3AZ* Tel (01970) 624263 Mobile 07801-458694 E-mail psn@aber.ac.uk

NEILAND, Paul Andrew. b 62. CITC 00. **d** 01 **p** 02. Aux Min Enniscorthy w Clone, Clonmore, Monart etc *C & O* 01-05; Aux Min Wexford w Ardcolm and Killurin from 05. *Butlerstown, Killinick, Co Wexford, Republic of Ireland* Tel (00353) (53) 913 5701 Mobile 87-242 2842

NEILL, Barbara June. b 39. St Jo Coll Nottm. **d** 00 **p** 01. NSM Bestwood Park w Rise Park *S'well* from 00. *17 Harvest Close, Nottingham NG5 9BW* Tel 0115-975 3378 E-mail barbjn@btopenworld.com

NEILL, James Purdon. b 41. Oak Hill Th Coll 60. **d** 64 **p** 65. C Kendal St Thos *Carl* 64-68; Chapl Park Hill Flats Sheff 68-71; P-in-c Mansfield St Jo *S'well* 71-77; V Nottingham St Ann w Em 77-09; rtd 09. *7 Thomas Close, Nottingham NG3 1PA* E-mail rev.jimneill@tiscali.co.uk

✠**NEILL, The Most Revd John Robert Winder.** b 45. TCD BA66 MA69 Jes Coll Cam BA68 MA72 NUI Hon LLD03. Ridley Hall Cam 67. **d** 69 **p** 70 **c** 86. C Glenageary *D & G* 69-71; Lect CITC 70-71 and 82-84; Dioc Registrar (Ossory, Ferns and Leighlin) *C & O* 71-74; Bp's V, Lib and Chapter Registrar Kilkenny Cathl 71-74; I Abbeystrewry *C, C & R* 74-78; I Dublin St Bart w Leeson Park *D & G* 78-84; Chapl Community of St Jo the Ev 78-84; Dean Waterford *C & O* 84-86; Hon Can Cork 84-86; Adn Waterford 84-86; I Waterford w Killea, Drumcannon and Dunhill 84-86; Bp T, K & A 86-97; Bp C & O 97-02; Abp Dublin *D & G* from 02; Preb Cualaun St Patr Cathl Dublin from 02. *The See House, 17 Temple Road, Dartry, Dublin 6, Republic of Ireland* Tel (00353) (1) 497 7849 Fax 497 6355 E-mail archbishop@dublin.anglican.org

NEILL, Richard Walter. b 67. Wadh Coll Ox BA89 Em Coll Cam BA92. Westcott Ho Cam 90. **d** 93 **p** 94. C Abbots Langley *St Alb* 93-97; C Wisley w Pyrford *Guildf* 97-00; V Winkfield and Cranbourne *Ox* 00-08; V Wedmore w Theale and Blackford *B & W* from 08. *The Vicarage, Manor Lane, Wedmore BS28 4EL* Tel (01934) 713566 E-mail neill.hall@care4free.net

NEILL, Canon Robert Chapman. b 51. Lon Univ BD82. CITC 77. d 77 p 78. C Lurgan Ch the Redeemer *D & D* 77-82; I Tullylish 82-88; I Mt Merrion 88-98; I Drumbo from 98; Can Down Cathl from 07. *Drumbo Rectory, 5 Pinehill Road, Ballylesson, Belfast BT8 8LA* Tel (028) 9082 6225
E-mail rc.neill@talktalk.net

NEILL, Canon Stephen Mahon. b 69. TCD BA91. CITC 91. d 93 p 94. C Monkstown *D & G* 93-95; Dom Chapl to Bp of Killaloe and Clonfert *L & K* from 95; C Limerick City 95-98; I Cloughjordan w Borrisokane etc from 98; Can Limerick Cathl from 04. *Modreeny Rectory, Cloughjordan, Co Tipperary, Republic of Ireland* Tel and fax (00353) (505) 42183 Mobile 87-232 8172 E-mail paddyanglican@eircom.net

NEILL, The Ven William Barnet. b 30. TCD BA61. d 63 p 64. C Belfast St Clem *D & D* 63-66; C Dundonald 66-72; I Drumgath 72-80; I Drumgooland 76-80; I Mt Merrion 80-83; I Dromore Cathl 83-97; Adn Dromore 85-97; rtd 97. *10 Cairnshill Court, Saintfield Road, Belfast BT8 4TX* Tel (028) 9079 2969

NEILL, Canon William Benjamin Alan. b 46. Open Univ BA76. CITC 68. d 71 p 72. C Dunmurry *Conn* 71-74; C Coleraine 75-77; C Dublin St Ann w St Steph *D & G* 77-78; I Convoy w Monellan and Donaghmore *D & R* 78-81; I Faughanvale 81-86; I Waterford w Killea, Drumcannon and Dunhill *C & O* 86-97; Dean Waterford 86-97; Prec Lismore Cathl 86-97; Prec Cashel Cathl 87-97; Can Ossory and Leighlin Cathls 96-97; I Dalkey St Patr *D & G* from 97; Can Ch Ch Cathl Dublin from 04. *The Rectory, Barnacoille Park, Church Road, Dalkey, Co Dublin, Republic of Ireland* Tel (00353) (1) 280 3369

NELLIST, Canon Valerie Ann. b 48. SRN69 SCM71. St And Dioc Tr Course 87. d 90 p 94. NSM W Fife Team Min *St And* 90-99; Hon Can St Ninian's Cathl Perth from 97; R Aberdour from 99; R Burntisland from 99; R Inverkeithing from 99. *28 Glamis Gardens, Dalgety Bay, Dunfermline KY11 9TD* Tel (01383) 824066 Fax 824668 E-mail atgn02@dsl.pipex.com

NELMES, Mrs Christine. b 41. St Mary's Coll Chelt Dip Teaching63 UWE BA97. S Dios Minl Tr Scheme 92. d 95 p 96. NSM Winscombe *B & W* 95-99; Perm to Offic 00-03; P-in-c Mark w Allerton 03-08. *Yarrow Farm, Yarrow Road, Mark, Highbridge TA9 4LW* Tel (01278) 641650
E-mail revcnelmes@btinternet.com

NELSON, Christopher James. b 57. Lanc Univ MA91. Aston Tr Scheme 83 St Jo Coll Nottm BTh88. d 88 p 89. C Blackpool St Thos *Blackb* 88-90; C Altham w Clayton le Moors 90-92; V Knuzden 92-01; V Penwortham St Mary from 01; AD Leyland from 04. *St Mary's Vicarage, 14 Cop Lane, Penwortham, Preston PR1 0SR* Tel (01772) 743143 E-mail kitnel@btinternet.com

NELSON, Gibson. *See* NELSON, Robert Gibson

NELSON, Graham William. b 61. St Jo Coll Nottm BA91. d 91 p 92. C Pype Hayes *Birm* 91-93; C Lancaster St Mary *Blackb* 94-97; Chapl HM Pris Lanc Castle 94-97; P-in-c Preston St Jude w St Paul *Blackb* 97-06; P-in-c Preston St Oswald 01-06; P-in-c Preston St Oswald w St Jude from 06. *Deepdale Vicarage, 97 Garstang Road, Preston PR1 1LD* Tel (01772) 252987
E-mail gw.nelson@btinternet.com

NELSON, Hugh Edmund. b 72. Worc Coll Ox BA94. Ripon Coll Cuddesdon 07. d 09. C Upchurch w Lower Halstow *Cant* from 09; C Iwade from 09; C Newington w Hartlip and Stockbury from 09. *The Vicarage, Church Lane, Newington, Sittingbourne ME9 7JU* Tel (01795) 844345
E-mail revhughnelson@googlemail.co.uk

NELSON, Jane. b 42. d 94 p 99. Par Dn Muchalls *Bre* 94-99; C 99-04; Asst Chapl Grampian Healthcare NHS Trust 93-97; NSM Brechin from 04; NSM Tarfside from 05. *4 St Michael's Road, Newtonhill, Stonehaven AB39 3RW* Tel (01569) 730967
E-mail nelson.jane1@btinternet.com

NELSON, Mrs Julie. b 52. St Aid Coll Dur BA73 Ex Univ MA95. SW Minl Tr Course 92. d 95 p 96. NSM Tavistock and Gulworthy *Ex* 95-01; Germany 01-04; P-in-c Kirklington w Burneston and Wath and Pickhill *Ripon* from 04; AD Wensley from 08. *The Rectory, Kirklington, Bedale DL8 2NJ* Tel (01845) 567429 E-mail revjulie@tiscali.co.uk

NELSON, Michael. b 44. Newc Univ Aus BSc68 BA72 St Jo Coll Cam BA74 Cam Univ MA78. Westcott Ho Cam 74. d 75 p 76. Perm to Offic *Newc* 75; Australia from 77. *185 Burbong Street, Chapel Hill Qld 4069, Australia* Tel (0061) (7) 3720 1283 Fax 3720 1620 E-mail mnelson@hradvantage.com.au

NELSON, Canon Michael. b 44. Lon Univ BD62. Coll of Resurr Mirfield 66. d 68 p 69. C Newbold w Dunston *Derby* 68-72; C N Gosforth *Newc* 72-77; V Seaton Hirst 77-83; V Blyth St Mary 83-93; P-in-c Horton 86-87; RD Bedlington 88-93; R Hexham 93-03; Hon Can Newc Cathl from 94; P-in-c Ovingham from 03; RD Corbridge 03-09. *St Mary's Vicarage, 2 Burnside Close, Ovingham, Prudhoe NE42 6BS* Tel (01661) 832273
E-mail canon.michael.nelson@care4free.net

NELSON, Sister Norma Margaret. b 34. Liv Univ DASS91 CQSW77. CA Tr Coll IDC60. d 93 p 94. TD Kirkby *Liv* 93-94; TV 94-95; rtd 95; Perm to Offic *Liv* from 95. *15 Pateley Close, Kirkby, Liverpool L32 4UT* Tel 0151-292 0255

NELSON, Canon Paul John. b 52. Nottm Univ BCombStuds84. Linc Th Coll 81. d 84 p 85. C Waltham Cross *St Alb* 84-87; C Sandridge 87-90; V 90-98; R Hundred River *St E* from 98; C Wainford from 06; RD Beccles and S Elmham from 03; Hon Can St E Cathl from 08. *The Rectory, Moll's Lane, Brampton, Beccles NR34 8DB* Tel (01502) 575859

NELSON, Peter Joseph. b 46. Nottm Poly BSc73. Nor Bapt Coll 82 NEOC 99. d 99 p 99. In Bapt Min 85-99; Chapl R Hull Hosps NHS Trust 94-99; Chapl Hull and E Yorks Hosps NHS Trust 99-02; Sen Chapl from 02; NSM Sutton St Mich *York* 99-06. *Cobblestones, 1 Low Street, Sancton, York YO43 4QZ* Tel (01430) 828779 *or* (01482) 674427

NELSON, Ralph Archbold. b 27. St Cuth Soc Dur BA50. Bps' Coll Cheshunt 50. d 52 p 53. C Penwortham St Mary *Blackb* 52-57; C Eglingham *Newc* 57-58; V Featherstone *Wakef* 58-80; V Kirkham *Blackb* 80-92; RD Kirkham 88-91; rtd 92; Perm to Offic *Blackb* from 92. *6 Blundell Lane, Penwortham, Preston PR1 0EA* Tel (01772) 742573

NELSON, Robert Gibson. b 34. ALCD61. d 61 p 62. C Isleworth St Mary *Lon* 61-64; C-in-c Reading St Barn CD *Ox* 64-69; R Margaret River Australia 69-72; V Guernsey St Jo *Win* 72-78; R Guernsey Ste Marie du Castel 78-86; V Guernsey St Matt 84-86; rtd 86; Perm to Offic *Win* from 86. *Le Petit Feugre, Clos des Mielles, Castel, Guernsey GY5 7XB* Tel (01481) 52726

NELSON, Robert Towers. b 43. MSOSc Liv Coll of Tech BSc65. NW Ord Course 76. d 79 p 80. NSM Liv Our Lady and St Nic w St Anne 79-83; NSM Liscard St Thos *Ches* 83-87; P-in-c from 87; Ind Missr from 87; Asst Sec SOSc from 89; Perm to Offic *Liv* 89-98; Chapl Wirral and W Cheshire Community NHS Trust 98-03. *5 Sedbergh Road, Wallasey CH44 2BR* Tel 0151-630 2830

NELSON, Roger Charles. b 44. ATII74 Newc Univ LLB66 Solicitor 69. Cant Sch of Min 88. d 91 p 92. NSM Deal St Leon and St Rich and Sholden *Cant* 91-96; NSM Northbourne and Gt Mongeham w Ripple and Sutton by Dover 96-97; Perm to Offic *Cant* 97-00 and *Wakef* from 01. *26 Meal Hill Road, Holme, Holmfirth HD9 2QQ* Tel (01484) 680309
E-mail nelsontrap@aol.com

NELSON, Warren David. b 38. TCD BA67. d 68 p 69. C Belfast St Mich *Conn* 68-70; I Kilcooley w Littleton, Crohane, Killenaule etc *C & O* 70-76; Chapl Coalbrook Fellowship Hosp Ho Thurles 76-94; Perm to Offic (Cashel, Waterford and Lismore) 93-94; I Lurgan w Billis, Killinkere and Munterconnaught *K, E & A* 94-98; rtd 98. *6 Mucklagh, Tullamore, Co Offaly, Republic of Ireland* Tel (00353) (57) 932 4218 E-mail wnelson@eircom.net

NELSON, William. b 38. Oak Hill Th Coll 74. d 76 p 77. C Hensingham *Carl* 76-81; V Widnes St Paul *Liv* 81-89; R Higher Openshaw *Man* 89-03; AD Ardwick 96-00; rtd 03; Perm to Offic *S'well* from 03. *215 Stapleford Road, Trowell, Nottingham NG9 3QE* Tel 0115-932 2910

NENER, Canon Thomas Paul Edgar. b 42. Liv Univ MB, ChB FRCSEd71 FRCS71. Coll of Resurr Mirfield 78. d 80 p 81. C Warrington St Elphin *Liv* 80-83; V Haydock St Jas 83-95; V W Derby St Jo from 95; Hon Can Liv Cathl from 95. *The Vicarage, 1A Snaefell Avenue, Liverpool L13 7HA* Tel 0151-228 2023

NENO, David Edward. b 62. SS Mark & Jo Univ Coll Plymouth BA85. Ripon Coll Cuddesdon 85. d 88 p 89. C Chapel Allerton *Ripon* 88-91; C Acton St Mary *Lon* 91-94; V Kingsbury H Innocents 94-02; R Brondesbury Ch Ch and St Laur from 02. *The Rectory, Chevening Road, London NW6 6DU* Tel (020) 8969 5961 Mobile 07976-905294 E-mail d.s.neno@dial.pipex.com

NESBITT, Heather Hastings. b 48. S'wark Ord Course 88. d 90 p 94. Par Dn Camberwell St Luke *S'wark* 90-94; C Addiscombe St Mary Magd w St Martin 94-01; TV Sutton St Jas and Wawne *York* from 01. *Sutton Rectory, 25 Church Street, Sutton-on-Hull, Hull HU7 4TL* Tel (01482) 782154
E-mail h.nesbitt@tinyworld.co.uk

NESBITT, Patrick Joseph. b 72. St Martin's Coll Lanc BA96. St Jo Coll Nottm 00. d 03 p 04. C Blackpool St Thos *Blackb* 03-07; TV Kinson and W Howe *Sarum* from 07. *St Andrew's Rectory, 51 Milhams Road, Bournemouth BH10 7LJ* Tel (01202) 571996 Mobile 07879-660100 E-mail patricknesbitt72@hotmail.com

NESBITT, Canon Ronald. b 58. Sheff Univ LLB. CITC 82. d 85 p 86. C Ballymena w Ballyclug *Conn* 85-88; C Holywood *D & D* 88-90; I Helen's Bay 90-96; I Bangor Abbey from 96; Can Belf Cathl from 04. *The Abbey Rectory, 5 Downshire Road, Bangor BT20 3TW* Tel (028) 9146 0173 E-mail ronnienesbitt@aol.com

NESBITT, Miss Wilhelmina. b 65. Qu Coll Birm 98. d 00 p 01. C Bridgnorth, Tasley, Astley Abbotts, etc *Heref* 00-04; TV Saddleworth *Man* 04-08; I Fanlobbus Union *C, C & R* from 08. *The Rectory, Sackville Street, Dunmanway, Co Cork, Republic of Ireland* Tel and fax (00353) (23) 45151

NETHERWAY, Diana Margaret. b 47. Bp Otter Coll 94. d 96. NSM Northwood *Portsm* from 96; NSM Gurnard from 96; Asst Chapl Isle of Wight NHS Primary Care Trust from 09. *138 Bellevue Road, Cowes PO31 7LD* Tel (01983) 298505
E-mail revdiana@onwight.net

NETHERWAY, Robert Sydney. b 37. Bp Otter Coll 94. **d** 96. NSM Cowes St Faith *Portsm* 96-07; Perm to Offic from 07. *138 Bellevue Road, Cowes PO31 7LD* Tel (01983) 298505 E-mail revbob@onwight.net

NETHERWOOD, Mrs Anne Christine. b 43. Liv Univ BArch66 Lon Univ BD92 ARIBA68. St Deiniol's Hawarden 88. **d** 91 **p** 94. NSM Ellesmere and Welsh Frankton *Lich* 91-94; C Dudleston 94-97; C Criftins 94-97; C Criftins w Dudleston and Welsh Frankton 97; P-in-c Criftins w Dudleston and Welsh Frankton from 97. *The Vicarage, Criftins, Ellesmere SY12 9LN* Tel (01691) 690401 Fax 690778 E-mail anne_netherwood@talk21.com

NEUDEGG, Mrs Joan Mary. b 36. Cant Sch of Min 81. **dss** 84 **d** 87 **p** 94. Chalk *Roch* 84-86; Hon C Dean Forest H Trin *Glouc* 87-90; Hon C Woolaston w Alvington 90-95; Hon C Woolaston w Alvington and Aylburton 95-96; rtd 96; Perm to Offic *Ex* from 96. *48 Marker Way, Honiton EX14 2EN* Tel (01404) 43957

NEUPERT, Douglas Alan. b 46. Chris Newport Univ (USA) BA78. Dioc OLM tr scheme 97. **d** 99 **p** 00. OLM Blackbourne *St E* from 99. *Hall Farm, Troston, Bury St Edmunds IP31 1EZ* Tel (01359) 269614 Mobile 07944-214417 E-mail doug_neupert@eu.odedodea.edu

NEVILL, James Michael. b 50. Cranmer Hall Dur 84. **d** 86 **p** 87. C Sowerby Bridge w Norland *Wakef* 86-91; CF 91-94; TV Broadwater *Chich* 94-99; Chapl St Mich Hospice Hereford 99-05; Spiritual Care Co-ord St Cath Hospice from 05. *St Catherine's Hospice, Malthouse Road, Crawley RH10 6BH* Tel (01293) 447333 Fax 611977

NEVILL, Mavis Hetty. b 45. Bradf Univ BEd95. NOC 92. **d** 95 **p** 96. NSM Mount Pellon *Wakef* 95-99; P-in-c Mixenden 99-04; rtd 04; Hon C Harden and Wilsden *Bradf* 06-07; P-in-c Steeton from 07. *The Vicarage, 2 Halsteads Way, Steeton, Keighley BD20 6SN* Tel (01535) 652877 E-mail mh.nevill@btinternet.com

NEVILLE, Alfred John. b 21. K Coll Lon BA40. Sarum & Wells Th Coll 80. **d** 83 **p** 84. NSM Weston-super-Mare St Paul *B & W* 83-93; Perm to Offic from 93. *10 Clarence House, 17 Clarence Road North, Weston-super-Mare BS23 4AS* Tel (01934) 631176

NEVILLE, David Bruce. b 61. Ravensbourne Coll of Art & Design BA83. St Jo Coll Nottm 87. **d** 91 **p** 92. C Broxtowe *S'well* 91-94; C Attenborough 94-95; Perm to Offic 95-97; C Carrington 97-99; C Bulwell St Mary 99-02; Perm to Offic from 02. *3 Inham Road, Beeston, Nottingham NG9 4FL* Tel 0115-854 5648 E-mail rev.dnev@virgin.net

NEVILLE, Michael Robert John. b 56. Hatf Coll Dur BA80 Hughes Hall Cam PGCE81. Wycliffe Hall Ox 82. **d** 85 **p** 86. C E Twickenham St Steph *Lon* 85-88; Asst Dir Proclamation Trust 88-93; R Fordham *Chelmsf* from 93. *Fordham Hall, Church Road, Fordham, Colchester CO6 3NL* Tel (01206) 240221 E-mail mike.neville@fordhamchurch.org.uk

NEVILLE, Paul Stewart David. b 61. Wycliffe Hall Ox 98. **d** 00 **p** 01. C Chester le Street *Dur* 00-03; R Middleton St George from 03; R Sadberge from 03. *17 Hunters Green, Middleton St George, Darlington DL2 1DZ* Tel (01325) 332017

NEVIN, Alan Joseph. b 51. Univ Coll Galway BA72 MCIPD80. CITC 87. **d** 92 **p** 93. Aux Min Youghal Union *C, C & R* 92-94; Aux Min Waterford w Killea, Drumcannon and Dunhill *C & O* 94-95; C 95-98; I Bunclody w Kildavin, Clonegal and Kilrush 98-04; I Clonfert Gp *L & K* from 04. *The Rectory, Banagher, Birr, Co Offaly, Republic of Ireland* Tel and fax (00353) (57) 915 1269 Mobile 87-285 8251 E-mail clonfert@clonfert.anglican.org

NEVIN, Graham Harold. b 45. QUB BSc68 MSc72 Ulster Poly CertEd74 FGS75. St Jo Coll Nottm 06. **d** 09. NSM Billy w Derrykeighan *Conn* from 09. *11 Carthall Crescent, Coleraine BT51 3LT* Tel (028) 7035 3713 E-mail graham@carthall.fsnet.co.uk

NEW, David John. b 37. Lon Univ BScEng58. Chich Th Coll 65. **d** 67 **p** 68. C Folkestone St Mary and St Eanswythe *Cant* 67-72; C Kings Heath *Birm* 72-74; V S Yardley St Mich 74-83; V Moseley St Agnes 83-00; rtd 00; Perm to Offic *Worc* from 00. *6 Falmouth, Worcester WR4 0TE* Tel (01905) 458084 E-mail david@revnew.freeserve.co.uk

NEW, Derek. b 30. **d** 86 **p** 87. NSM Brondesbury St Anne w Kilburn H Trin *Lon* 86-98; NSM Willesden St Matt 99-02; Perm to Offic from 02. *20 Lynton Road, London NW6 6BL* Tel (020) 7912 0640

NEW, Canon Thomas Stephen. b 30. K Coll Cam BA52 MA56. Cuddesdon Coll 52. **d** 54 **p** 55. C Greenford H Cross *Lon* 54-55; C Old St Pancras w Bedford New Town St Matt 55-58; C Woodham *Guildf* 58-64; V Guildf All SS 64-72; V Banstead 72-93; RD Epsom 76-80; Hon Can Guildf Cathl 79-93; Sub-Chapl HM Pris Downview 88-93; rtd 93; Perm to Offic *Ex* from 94. *St Katharine's, North Street, Denbury, Newton Abbot TQ12 6DJ* Tel (01803) 813775

NEW ZEALAND, Archbishop of. See TUREI, The Most Revd William Brown

NEWALL, Arthur William. b 24. Univ of Wales (Lamp) BA49. Chich Th Coll 49. **d** 51 **p** 52. C Hulme St Phil *Man* 51-53; C

Fallowfield 53-55; V Oldham St Barn 55-60; V Aspull *Liv* 60-68; R Foots Cray *Roch* 68-78; V Henlow St Alb 78-89; rtd 89; Perm to Offic *Liv* from 89. *38 Fairhaven Road, Southport PR9 9UH* Tel (01704) 26045

NEWALL, Richard Lucas. b 43. K Coll Lon AKC66. **d** 66 **p** 67. C Roby *Liv* 66-69; C Douglas St Geo and St Barn *S & M* 69-71; Lic to Offic *Man* 72-75; C Ban St Mary 75-77; R Newborough w Llangeinwen w Llangaffo etc 77-97; R Newborough w Llanidan and Llangeinwen etc 98-07; AD Tindaethwy and Menai 03-07; V Llanilar w Rhostie and Llangwyryfon etc *St D* 07-09; rtd 09. *Himmelbjerg, 18 Maesydderwen, Cardigan SA43 1PE* Tel (01239) 623816

NEWARK, Archdeacon of. See PEYTON, The Ven Nigel

NEWBOLD, Stephen Mark. b 60. Trin Coll Bris 01. **d** 03 **p** 04. C Roxeth *Lon* 03-09; V Ealing St Steph Castle Hill from 09. *St Stephen's Vicarage, Sherborne Gardens, London W13 8AQ* Tel (020) 8864 4929

NEWBON, Kenneth. b 29. Wells Th Coll 67. **d** 69 **p** 70. C Church Stretton *Heref* 69-72; P-in-c Cressage w Sheinton 72-75; R Braunstone *Leic* 75-81; TR 81-84; P-in-c Eardisley w Bollingham and Willersley *Heref* 84-88; P-in-c Brilley w Michaelchurch on Arrow 84-88; P-in-c Whitney w Winforton 84-88; RD Kington and Weobley 87-95; R Eardisley w Bollingham, Willersley, Brilley etc 88-96; rtd 96; Perm to Offic *Heref* from 96. *Grace Dieu House, Staunton-on-Wye, Hereford HR4 7LT* Tel (01981) 500188

NEWBON, Michael Charles. b 59. Oak Hill Th Coll 92. **d** 94 **p** 95. C Bedford St Jo and St Leon *St Alb* 94-99; V Luton St Fran from 99. *The Vicarage, 145 Hollybush Road, Luton LU2 9HQ* Tel (01582) 753919 E-mail lutonstfrancis@aol.com

NEWBORN, Carol Margaret. b 45. **d** 05 **p** 06. OLM Styvechale *Cov* from 05. *76 The Park Paling, Coventry CV3 5LL* Tel (024) 7650 3707 E-mail rev.carol@newborn.org.uk

NEWBY, Mrs Ailsa Ballantyne. b 56. Collingwood Coll Dur BA78. St Steph Ho Ox 98. **d** 98 **p** 99. C Streatham Ch Ch *S'wark* 98-01; V S Lambeth St Anne and All SS from 01. *The Vicarage, 179 Fentiman Road, London SW8 1JY* Tel (020) 7735 3191 E-mail ailsanewby@f2s.com

NEWBY, Peter Gordon. b 23. **d** 64 **p** 65. C Leic St Phil 64-69; R Lt Bowden St Nic 69-72; V Jersey Gouray St Martin *Win* 72-77; Chapl Jersey Gp of Hosps 78-80; R Much Birch w Lt Birch, Much Dewchurch etc *Heref* 80-88; rtd 89; Perm to Offic *Ex* from 90. *The Shippen, Lower Hampton Farm, Shute, Axminster EX13 7PA*

NEWBY, Mrs Susan. b 48. Lady Spencer Chu Coll of Educn CertEd70 BEd71. **d** 04 **p** 05. OLM Adderbury w Milton *Ox* from 04. *2 Meadow View, Adderbury, Banbury OX17 3LZ* Tel 07766-716659 (mobile) E-mail susan@newby4448.freeserve.co.uk

NEWCASTLE (AUSTRALIA), Assistant Bishop of. See RUTHERFORD, The Rt Revd Graeme Stanley

NEWCASTLE (AUSTRALIA), Dean of. See RIGNEY, The Very Revd James Thomas

NEWCASTLE, Bishop of. See WHARTON, The Rt Revd John Martin

NEWCASTLE, Dean of. See DALLISTON, The Very Revd Christopher Charles

NEWCOMBE, Andrew Charles. b 70. Melbourne Univ BA92 BMus93 Monash Univ Aus DipEd96 LTCL93. St Steph Ho Ox 03. **d** 05 **p** 06. C Tottenham St Mary *Lon* 05-08; C Edmonton St Alphege from 08; C Ponders End St Matt from 08. *St Matthew's Vicarage, 1 Church Road, Enfield EN3 4NT* Tel (020) 8443 2255 Mobile 07931-700675 E-mail andrewnewcombe@yahoo.co.uk

NEWCOMBE, John Adrian. b 61. Univ of Wales (Lamp) BA83 SS Paul & Mary Coll Cheltenham PGCE85. Ripon Coll Cuddesdon 90. **d** 92 **p** 93. C Stroud and Uplands w Slad *Glouc* 92-96; C Nailsworth 96-01; P-in-c Childswyckham w Aston Somerville, Buckland etc 01-05; TV Winchcombe from 05. *New Vicarage, Buckland Road, Childswickham, Broadway WR12 7HH* Tel (01386) 853824

NEWCOMBE, John Charlie. BSc. Ridley Hall Cam. **d** 07 **p** 08. NSM Wimbledon Em Ridgway Prop Chpl *S'wark* from 07. *Emmanuel Church, 24 Ridgway, London SW19 4QL* E-mail admin@wimbledon.org.uk

NEWCOMBE, Canon Timothy James Grahame. b 47. AKC75. St Aug Coll Cant 75. **d** 76 **p** 77. C Heref St Martin 76-79; C Hitchin *St Alb* 79-85; R Croft and Stoney Stanton *Leic* 85-91; P-in-c Launceston *Truro* 91-92; V Launceston 92-97; TR Launceston 97-03; Hon Can Truro Cathl 01-03; Chapl Cornwall Healthcare NHS Trust 96-03; V Wotton St Mary *Glouc* from 03. *Holy Trinity Vicarage, Church Road, Longlevens, Gloucester GL2 0AJ* Tel (01452) 524129 E-mail tnewco@tiscali.co.uk

✠**NEWCOME, The Rt Revd James William Scobie.** b 53. Trin Coll Ox BA74 MA78 Selw Coll Cam BA77 MA81. Ridley Hall Cam 75. **d** 78 **p** 79 **c** 02. C Leavesden *St Alb* 78-82; P-in-c Bar Hill LEP *Ely* 82-92; V Bar Hill 92-94; Tutor Ridley Hall Cam 83-88; P-in-c Dry Drayton *Ely* 89-94; RD N Stowe 93-94; Can

Res Ches Cathl and Dioc Dir of Ords 94-02; Dir of Educn and Tr 96-02; Suff Bp Penrith *Carl* 02-09; Bp Carl from 09. *Holm Croft, 13 Castle Road, Kendal LA9 7AU* Tel (01539) 727836 Fax 734380 E-mail bishop.carlisle@carlislediocese.org.uk

NEWELL, Aubrey Francis Thomas. b 20. St D Coll Lamp BA43. **d** 45 **p** 46. C Rhosddu *St As* 45-49; C Llanwnog *Ban* 49-50; C Gabalfa *Llan* 50-53; C Gt Marlow *Ox* 53-57; R Lavendon w Cold Brayfield 57-62; V Gawcott and Hillesden 62-77; P-in-c Radclive 69-72; RD Buckingham 70-76 and 82-84; P-in-c Padbury w Adstock 72-77; V Lenborough 77-87; rtd 87; Perm to Offic *Ox* 89-00 and *St D* from 07. *Station House, Glandyfi, Machynlleth SY20 8SS* Tel (01654) 781307

NEWELL, Christopher David. b 53. Ex Univ MA03. S'wark Ord Course 84. **d** 87 **p** 88. C Stockwell St Mich *S'wark* 87-90; Asst Chapl R Lon Hosp (Whitechapel) 90-92; Asst Chapl R Lon Hosp (Mile End) 90-92; R Birch St Agnes *Man* 92-96; P-in-c Longsight St Jo w St Cypr 94-96; R Birch St Agnes w Longsight St Jo w St Cypr 97; R Lansallos and V Talland *Truro* 97-98; Asst P Liskeard and St Keyne 00-02; C Duloe, Herodsfoot, Morval and St Pinnock 02-03; P-in-c 03-05; C Lansallos and Talland 02-03; Chapl Cornwall Partnership NHS Trust from 02. *4 Russell Street, Liskeard PL14 4BP* Tel (01579) 349617 E-mail christopher.newell@cpt.cornwall.nhs.uk

NEWELL, David Walter. b 37. Nottm Univ BSc57. WEMTC 01. **d** 03 **p** 04. OLM Painswick, Sheepscombe, Cranham, The Edge etc *Glouc* from 03. *Woodside, Kingsmill Lane, Painswick, Stroud GL6 6SA* Tel (01452) 812083 E-mail d.newell083@btinternet.com

NEWELL, Canon Edmund John. b 61. Univ Coll Lon BSc83 Nuff Coll Ox DPhil88 MA89 FRHistS98 FRSA08. Ox Min Course 89 Ripon Coll Cuddesdon 92. **d** 94 **p** 95. C Deddington w Barford, Clifton and Hempton *Ox* 94-98; Bp's Dom Chapl 98-01; Chapl Headington Sch 98-01; Can Res St Paul's Cathl 01-08; Chan 03-08; Can Res and Sub-Dean Ch Ch *Ox* from 08. *Christ Church, Oxford OX1 1DP* Tel (01865) 276278 E-mail edmund.newell@chch.ox.ac.uk

NEWELL, Jack Ernest. b 26. CEng FIChemE ARCS BSc. Glouc Th Course 80. **d** 83 **p** 84. NSM Hempsted *Glouc* 83-96; Perm to Offic from 96. *Hempsted House, Rectory Lane, Hempsted, Gloucester GL2 5LW* Tel (01452) 523320

NEWELL, Kenneth Ernest. b 22. S Dios Minl Tr Scheme 77. **d** 79 **p** 80. NSM Lynton, Brendon, Countisbury, Lynmouth etc *Ex* 79-85; TR 85-89; RD Shirwell 84-89; rtd 89; Perm to Offic *Ex* from 89. *Mole End, Lydiate Lane, Lynton EX35 6HE*

NEWELL, Samuel James. b 28. TCD BA MA63. TCD Div Sch Div Test54. **d** 54 **p** 55. C Belfast St Mary *Conn* 54-57; C Derriaghy 57-60; C Reading St Mary V *Ox* 60-63; V Chesham Ch Ch 63-74; P-in-c Wraysbury 74-78; TV Riverside 78-94; rtd 94; Perm to Offic *Ox* 97-07. *41 Redford Road, Windsor SL4 5ST* Tel (01753) 862300

NEWELL OF STAFFA, Gerald Frederick Watson. b 34. Sarum Th Coll 56. **d** 59 **p** 61. C Southampton SS Pet and Paul w All SS *Win* 59-61; C Overton w Laverstoke and Freefolk 61-63; CF (TA) 61-63; CF 63-66; R Spennithorne *Ripon* 66-68; R Finghall 66-68; R Hauxwell 66-68; Hon C Steyning *Chich* 74-78; Perm to Offic *Ex* 93-95 and 99-00; P-in-c Breamore *Win* 95-98; rtd 99; P-in-c Palermo w Taormina *Eur* 99-00; R Glencarse *Bre* 00-03; Perm to Offic *Ox* 04-06. *Church Cottage, Compton Beauchamp, Swindon SN6 8NN* Tel (01738) /10334

NEWELL PRICE, John Charles. b 29. SS Coll Cam BA50 MA MB, BChir MRCGP. **d** 91 **p** 94. OLM Frensham *Guildf* 91-99; rtd 99; Perm to Offic *Guildf* from 99. *The Linney, Clamoak, Bere Alston, Yelverton PL20 7BU* Tel (01822) 841126

NEWEY, Edmund James. b 71. Linc Coll Ox BA95 MA97 Em Coll Cam BA99 Man Univ PhD08. Westcott Ho Cam 97. **d** 00 **p** 01. C Birch w Fallowfield *Man* 00-03; R Newmarket St Mary w Exning St Agnes *St E* 03-07; V Handsworth St Andr *Birm* from 07. *St Andrew's Vicarage, 55 Laurel Road, Handsworth, Birmingham B21 9PB* Tel 0121-551 2097 Mobile 07986-530511 E-mail ejnewey@waitrose.com

NEWHAM, Simon Frank Eric. b 65. Sheff Univ BSc87 MSc89. Trin Coll Bris BA00. **d** 00 **p** 01. C Horsham *Chich* 00-04; P-in-c Wisborough Green 04-09; V from 09. *The Vicarage, Billingshurst Road, Wisborough Green, Billingshurst RH14 0DZ* Tel (01403) 700339 E-mail simon_newham@revd.fsbusiness.co.uk

✠**NEWING, The Rt Revd Dom Kenneth Albert.** b 23. Selw Coll Cam BA53 MA57. Coll of Resurr Mirfield 53. **d** 55 **p** 56 **c** 82. C Plymstock *Ex* 55-63; R Plympton St Maurice 63-82; RD Plympton 71-76; Preb Ex Cathl 75-82; Adn Plymouth 78-82; Suff Bp Plymouth 82-88; Lic to Offic *Ex* 88-93; OSB from 89; rtd 93. *Elmore Abbey, Church Lane, Newbury RG14 1SA* Tel (01635) 33080

NEWING, Peter. b 33. Birm Univ CertEd55 Dur Univ BA63 Bris Univ BEd76 State Univ NY BSc85 EdD88 FRSA60 FSAScot59 ACP67 FCollP86 FCollP95 APhS63 FVCM01. Cranmer Hall Dur 63. **d** 65 **p** 66. C Blockley w Aston Magna *Glouc* 65-69; P-in-c Taynton 69-75; P-in-c Tibberton 69-75; R Brimpsfield w Elkstone and Syde 75-83; R Brimpsfield, Cranham, Elkstone

and Syde 83-97; P-in-c Daglingworth w the Duntisbournes and Winstone 95-97; R Brimpsfield w Birdlip, Syde, Daglingworth etc 97-01; C Redmarley D'Abitot, Bromesberrow, Pauntley etc 01-02; NSM from 02; rtd 02; Perm to Offic *Heref* from 02 and *Worc* from 04. *The Rectory, Albright Lane, Bromesberrow, Ledbury HR8 1RU* Tel (01531) 650898

NEWITT, Mark Julian. b 76. Bradf Univ BSc97 St Jo Coll Dur BA02. Cranmer Hall Dur 00. **d** 03 **p** 04. C Billing *Pet* 03-06; Asst Chapl Sheff Teaching Hosps NHS Foundn Trust from 06. *Chaplaincy Services, Royal Hallamshire Hospital, Glossop Road, Sheffield S10 2JF* Tel 0114-271 1900

NEWLAND, Mrs Patricia Frances. b 35. Edin Univ MA56. EAMTC 96. **d** 97 **p** 98. NSM Duxford *Ely* 97-02; NSM Hinxton 97-02; NSM Ickleton 97-02; rtd 02; Perm to Offic *Ely* from 02. *Ickelton Lodge, 14 Frogge Street, Ickleton, Saffron Walden CB10 1SH* Tel (01799) 530268 Fax 531146 E-mail tricia.newland@ukgateway.net

NEWLANDS, Christopher William. b 57. Bris Univ BA79. Westcott Ho Cam 81. **d** 84 **p** 85. C Bishop's Waltham *Portsm* 84-87; Hon C Upham 85-87; Prec, Sacr and Min Can Dur Cathl 87-92; Chapl Bucharest w Sofia *Eur* 92-95; V Shrub End *Chelmsf* 96-04; Bp's Chapl from 04. *The Vicarage, Penny's Lane, Margaretting, Ingatestone CM4 0HA* Tel (01277) 356277 E-mail cnewlands@chelmsford.anglican.org

NEWLANDS, Prof George McLeod. b 41. Edin Univ MA63 Heidelberg Univ BD66 PhD70 Ch Coll Cam MA73. **d** 82 **p** 82. Lect Cam Univ 73-86; Fell and Dean Trin Hall Cam 82-86; Prof Div Glas Univ 86-08; Perm to Offic *Glas* from 86. *12 Jamaica Street Lane, Edinburgh EH3 6HQ,* or *The University, Glasgow G12 8QQ* Tel 0131-225 2545 *or* 0141-330 5297 Mobile 07979-691966 Fax 0141-330 4943 E-mail g.newlands@arts.gla.ac.uk

NEWLYN, Canon Edwin. b 39. AKC64. **d** 65 **p** 66. C Belgrave St Mich *Leic* 65-68; Miss to Seamen 68-81; Chapl Santos Brazil 68-69; Asst Chapl Glas and C Glas St Gabr 69-73; Chapl E Lon S Africa 73-76; R W Bank St Pet 75-76; V Fylingdales *York* 81; P-in-c Hawsker 81; V Fylingdales and Hawsker cum Stainsacre 81-88; RD Whitby 85-92; Sec Dioc Adv Cttee for Care of Chs 87-01; P-in-c Goathland 88-99; Can and Preb York Minster 90-08; rtd 01; Perm to Offic *York* from 01. *The Garden Flat, 12 Royal Crescent, Whitby YO21 3EJ* Tel (01947) 604533 E-mail edwin.newlyn@btinternet.com

NEWMAN, The Very Revd Adrian. b 58. Bris Univ BSc80 MPhil89. Trin Coll Bris 82. **d** 85 **p** 86. C Forest Gate St Mark *Chelmsf* 85-89; V Hillsborough and Wadsley Bridge *Sheff* 89-96; RD Hallam 94-96; R Birm St Martin w Bordesley St Andr 96-05; Hon Can Birm Cathl 01-05; Dean Roch from 05. *The Deanery, Prior's Gate House, The Precinct, Rochester ME1 1SR* Tel (01634) 843366 *or* 857330 Fax 410410 E-mail deanspa@rochestercathedraluk.org

NEWMAN, Alan George. b 18. Lich Th Coll 41. **d** 44 **p** 45. C Twerton *B & W* 44-52; V Clandown 52-56; V Bradford-on-Avon Ch Ch *Sarum* 56-76; R Monkton Farleigh w S Wraxall 76-84; rtd 84; Perm to Offic *Sarum* from 84 and *B & W* 00-04. *The Old Vicarage, Staverton, Trowbridge BA14 6NX* Tel (01225) 782019

NEWMAN, Alfred John Gordon. b 10. Qu Coll Birm 71. **d** 74 **p** 74. NSM Hall Green St Pet *Birm* 74-84; Perm to Offic *St E* 84-96 and *Chich* 96-07. *Address temp unknown*

NEWMAN, Mrs Alison Myra. b 55. K Coll Lon BD77. SEITE 99. **d** 02 **p** 03. C Bromley SS Pet and Paul *Roch* 02-06; C Shortlands 06-08; C Farnborough from 08. *Church House, Leamington Avenue, Orpington BR6 9QB* Tel (01689) 854451 E-mail alison@st-nicks.org.uk

NEWMAN, David. See NEWMAN, Richard David

NEWMAN, David Malcolm. b 54. FSAScot81 Aber Univ BTh. St Steph Ho Ox 89. **d** 91 **p** 92. C St Mary-at-Latton *Chelmsf* 91-94; R Weeley and Lt Clacton from 94. *The Vicarage, 2 Holland Road, Little Clacton, Clacton-on-Sea CO16 9RS* Tel (01255) 860241

NEWMAN, Canon David Maurice Frederick. b 54. Hertf Coll Ox BA75 MA79. St Jo Coll Nottm. **d** 79 **p** 80. C Orpington Ch Ch *Roch* 79-83; C Bushbury *Lich* 83-86; V Ockbrook *Derby* 86-97; TR Loughborough Em and St Mary in Charnwood *Leic* from 97; RD Akeley E 99-06; Hon Can Leic Cathl from 06. *Emmanuel Rectory, 47 Forest Road, Loughborough LE11 3NW* Tel and fax (01509) 263264 *or* tel 261773 E-mail davidnewman@emmanuel.fsnet.co.uk

NEWMAN, Mrs Diana Joan. b 43. Sarum Th Coll 81. dss 84 **d** 87 **p** 94. Parkstone St Pet and St Osmund w Branksea *Sarum* from 84; NSM from 87; TV 96-02. *62 Vale Road, Poole BH14 9AU* Tel and fax (01202) 745136 E-mail diana.n@ntlworld.com

NEWMAN, Ms Elizabeth Ann. b 57. K Coll Lon BD79 Hull Univ CQSW81. **d** 05 **p** 06. OLM Charlton *S'wark* from 05. *66 Annandale Road, London SE10 0DB* Tel (020) 8305 0642 E-mail newman66@btopenworld.com

NEWMAN, Geoffrey Maurice. b 22. Ox NSM Course 77. **d** 80 **p** 81. NSM Binfield *Ox* 80-84; Chapl St Geo Sch Ascot 82-84; V Teynham *Cant* 84-87; rtd 87; Perm to Offic *Cant* 87-05. *c/o Mrs*

A M L Newman, 55 St Mildred's Road, Westgate-on-Sea CT8 8RJ Tel (01843) 833837

NEWMAN, Mrs Helen Margaret. b 58. York Univ BA80 Nottm Univ MA02. EMMTC 99. **d** 02 **p** 03. NSM Thorpe Acre w Dishley *Leic* 02-05; NSM Loughborough Em and St Mary in Charnwood from 05. *Emmanuel Rectory, 47 Forest Road, Loughborough LE11 3NW* Tel (01509) 216652
E-mail helen@astad.org

NEWMAN, James Edwin Michael. b 59. Nottm Univ BA80 Ox Univ BA90. Wycliffe Hall Ox 88. **d** 91 **p** 92. C Bidston *Ches* 91-95; C Cheadle from 95. *4 Cuthbert Road, Cheadle SK8 2DT* Tel 0161-428 3983 E-mail mike@stcuthberts.org

NEWMAN, John Humphrey. b 17. ALCD49. **d** 49 **p** 50. C Hove Bp Hannington Memorial Ch *Chich* 49-52; V Welling *Roch* 52-64; V Penge St Jo 64-74; R Knockholt 74-82; rtd 82; Perm to Offic *Chich* from 82. *Stonegarth, Pett Level Road, Fairlight, Hastings TN35 4EA* Tel (01424) 812518

NEWMAN, Kevin Richard. b 74. Warwick Univ BSc95 PGCE96. Oak Hill Th Coll BA06. **d** 06 **p** 07. C Crowborough *Chich* from 06. *Ghyll Farm Annex, Sweethaws Lane, Crowborough TN6 3SS* Tel (01892) 662542 E-mail kev@kevandfran.co.uk

NEWMAN, Michael Alan. b 40. Chich Th Coll 67. **d** 70 **p** 71. C Kilburn St Aug *Lon* 70-73; C St Geo-in-the-East St Mary 75-78; rtd 78. *April Cottage, Georges Lane, Storrington, Pulborough RH20 3JH* Tel (01903) 744354 E-mail tcepriest@tiscali.co.uk

NEWMAN, Preb Michael John. b 50. Leic Univ BA72 MA75. Cuddesdon Coll 73. **d** 75 **p** 76. C Tettenhall Regis *Lich* 75-79; C Uttoxeter w Bramshall 79-82; R Norton Canes 82-89; TR Rugeley 89-06; TR Brereton and Rugeley from 06; Preb Lich Cathl from 02. *The Rectory, 20 Church Street, Rugeley WS15 2AB* Tel (01889) 582149

NEWMAN, Canon Michael Robert. b 30. K Coll Lon BD61. St Jo Coll Auckland LTh53. **d** 54 **p** 55. New Zealand 54-58; C Hampstead St Jo *Lon* 58-61; New Zealand from 61; Can Auckland 81-93. *2/26 Alfriston Road, Manurewa East, Manukau 2102, New Zealand* Tel (0064) (9) 267 4357
E-mail bobnewman@xtra.co.nz

NEWMAN, Paul. b 65. St Martin's Coll Lanc BA90. Oak Hill Th Coll. **d** 00 **p** 01. C Poynton *Ches* 00-04; V Barnton from 04. *The Vicarage, Church Road, Barnton, Northwich CW8 4JH* Tel (01606) 74358 E-mail scallyvic@yahoo.com

NEWMAN, Paul Anthony. b 48. Lon Univ BSc70. Coll of Resurr Mirfield 73. **d** 76 **p** 77. C Catford St Laur *S'wark* 76-81; TV Grays All SS *Chelmsf* 81-83; TV Lt Thurrock St Mary 81-83; Youth Chapl W Ham Adnry 83-87; P-in-c Forest Gate All SS 83-89; V 89-91; Dep Chapl HM Pris Wormwood Scrubs 91-92; Chapl HM Pris Downview 92-02; Chapl HM Pris Win 02-07; Chapl HM Pris Kingston (Portsm) from 07. *HM Prison Kingston, 122 Milton Road, Portsmouth PO3 6AS* Tel (023) 9295 3229 E-mail paul.anthony.newman@hmps.gsi.gov.uk

NEWMAN, Richard David. b 38. BNC Ox BA60 MA63. Lich Th Coll 60. **d** 62 **p** 63. C E Grinstead St Swithun *Chich* 62-66; C Gt Grimsby St Jas *Linc* 66-69; C Gt Grimsby St Mary and St Jas 69-73; TV 73-74; V St Nicholas at Wade w Sarre *Cant* 74-75; P-in-c Chislet w Hoath 74-75; V St Nicholas at Wade w Sarre and Chislet w Hoath 75-81; V S Norwood H Innocents 81-84; V S Norwood H Innocents *S'wark* 85-04; rtd 04; Perm to Offic *B & W* from 04. *10 Hardy Court, Lang Road, Crewkerne TA18 8JE* Tel (01460) 271496

NEWMAN, William Nigel Edward. b 61. St Jo Coll Dur BA83 Bris Univ PGCE86. Westcott Ho Cam 99. **d** 01 **p** 02. C Halstead Area *Chelmsf* 01-04; Chapl St Jo Cathl Hong Kong from 04; P-in-c Stanley St Steph from 04. *Bungalow 5, St Stephen's College, 22 Tung Tau Wan Road, Stanley, Hong Kong, China*
E-mail willanddot@netvigator.org

NEWNHAM, Eric Robert. b 43. FCA. Sarum & Wells Th Coll 70. **d** 75 **p** 76. NSM Blackheath Ascension *S'wark* 75-06; NSM Deptford St Jo w H Trin and Ascension from 06. *27 Morden Hill, London SE13 7NN* Tel (020) 8692 6507 or 8691 6559

NEWPORT, Derek James. b 39. Acadia Univ (NS) BA82 MEd84. Sarum & Wells Th Coll 74. **d** 76 **p** 77. C Tavistock and Gulworthy *Ex* 76-78; Canada 78-86; V Malborough w S Huish, W Alvington and Churchstow *Ex* 86-95; TR Widecombe-in-the-Moor, Leusdon, Princetown etc 95-04; rtd 04. *Woodland Cottage, Southdown Woods, Yarnscombe, Barnstaple EX31 3LZ* Tel (01271) 858685

E-mail dereknewport@dnewport.fsnet.co.uk

NEWPORT, Prof Kenneth George Charles. b 57. Columbia Union Coll (USA) BA83 Andrews Univ (USA) MA84 Linacre Coll Ox MSt85 St Hugh's Coll Ox DPhil88. NOC 98. **d** 00 **p** 01. Reader Chr Thought Liv Hope 99-01; Prof Th and RS Liv Hope Univ from 01; Asst Vice Chan from 05; Hon Research Fell Man Univ from 98; NSM Bolton St Pet from 00; Perm to Offic *Liv* from 00. *Theology and Religious Studies, Liverpool Hope, Hope Park, Taggart Avenue, Liverpool L16 9JD* Tel 0151-291 3510 Fax 291 3772 E-mail knewport@hope.ac.uk

NEWPORT, Archdeacon of. *See* HACKETT, The Ven Ronald Glyndwr

NEWSOME, David Ellis. b 55. St Jo Coll Dur BA77. Westcott Ho Cam 80. **d** 82 **p** 83. C Finchley St Mary *Lon* 82-85; C Fulham All SS 85-87; Bp's Dom Chapl *Birm* 87-91; V Gravelly Hill 91-00; P-in-c Stockland Green 93-96; AD Aston 95-00; TR Tettenhall Regis *Lich* 00-08; Dioc Dir of Ords from 08. *10 The Brambles, Lichfield WS14 9SE* Tel (01543) 306220

NEWSOME, Canon John Keith. b 49. Mert Coll Ox BA73 MA76. Ripon Coll Cuddesdon 73. **d** 76 **p** 77. C Bywell *Newc* 76-78; C Berwick H Trin 78-82; Chapl Bonn w Cologne *Eur* 86-93; Chapl Hamburg 93-00; Chapl Zürich from 00; Can Brussels Cathl from 98. *Promenadengasse 9, 8001 Zürich, Switzerland* Tel (0041) (44) 252 6024 or 261 2241 Fax 252 6042
E-mail jknewsome@anglican.ch

NEWSOME, Monica Jane. b 55. WMMTC 96. **d** 99 **p** 00. NSM Kingshurst *Birm* 99-00; Asst Chapl HM YOI Stoke Heath from 00. *HM Young Offender Institution, Stoke Heath, Market Drayton TF9 2LJ* Tel (01630) 636000

NEWSON, Julie. b 60. Southn Univ BA97. Bp Otter Coll 00. **d** 03. NSM Brighton St Pet w Chpl Royal *Chich* 03-09; NSM Brighton Chpl Royal from 09. *77 Wilson Avenue, Brighton BN2 5PA* Tel (01273) 570978 Mobile 07803-750147
E-mail julie.newson@btinternet.com

NEWSTEAD, Dominic Gerald Bruno. b 65. Wycliffe Hall Ox BTh95. **d** 95 **p** 96. C Windlesham *Guildf* 95-00; Asst Chapl Fontainebleau *Eur* 00-05; V Southwater *Chich* 05-09; C Bebington *Ches* from 09. *2 Wellington Road, Bebington, Wirral CH63 7NF*

NEWSUM, Alfred Turner Paul. b 28. Coll of Resurr Mirfield 52. **d** 53 **p** 54. C Roath St German *Llan* 53-59; C Westmr St Matt *Lon* 59-60; C Washwood Heath *Birm* 60-68; P-in-c Small Heath St Greg 68-78; V Birm St Aid Small Heath 72-80; V Stockland Green 80-93; rtd 93; Perm to Offic *Llan* and *Mon* from 93. *Ty'r Offeiriad, 18 Almond Drive, Cardiff CF23 8HD*

NEWTH, Barry Wilfred. b 33. Bris Univ BA56. ALCD58. **d** 58 **p** 59. C Upton (Overchurch) *Ches* 58-62; C Kimberworth *Sheff* 62-63; V Clifton *Man* 63-72; V Radcliffe St Thos 72-74; V Radcliffe St Thos and St Jo 74-81; R Heaton Mersey 81-86; V Kirkby Malham *Bradf* 86-87; P-in-c Coniston Cold 86-87; V Kirkby-in-Malhamdale w Coniston Cold 87-97; rtd 97; Perm to Offic *Man* from 00. *1 Higher Ridings, Bromley Cross, Bolton BL7 9HP* Tel (01204) 451927

NEWTON, Angela Margaret. b 48. RGN70. Ripon Coll Cuddesdon 06. **d** 07 **p** 08. NSM Luton St Aug Limbury *St Alb* from 07. *The Rectory, 2 Manor Farm Close, Barton-le-Clay, Bedford MK45 4TB* Tel (01582) 881873 Mobile 07940-824206 E-mail angela.m.newton@talktalk.net

NEWTON, Miss Ann. b 46. Trin Coll Bris 75. **d** 87 **p** 94. Par Dn Rothley *Leic* 87-91; Par Dn Becontree St Mary *Chelmsf* 91-94; C 94-01; V Canley *Cov* 01-08; rtd 08. *35 Mossford Street, London E3 4TH* Tel (020) 8981 5764 E-mail revanew@aol.com

NEWTON, Barrie Arthur. b 38. Dur Univ BA61. Wells Th Coll 61. **d** 63 **p** 64. C Walton St Mary *Liv* 63-67; C N Lynn w St Marg and St Nic *Nor* 67-69; Chapl Asst The Lon Hosp (Whitechapel) 69-71; Chapl K Coll Hosp *Lon* 72-77; P-in-c Bishops Sutton w Stowey *B & W* 77-81; P-in-c Compton Martin w Ubley 79-81; P-in-c Bridgwater St Jo w Chedzoy 81-83; Chapl St Mary's Hosp Praed Street Lon 83-94; Chapl St Mary's NHS Trust Paddington 94-99; rtd 00; Perm to Offic *Lon* from 04. *10 Brondesbury Park Mansions, 132 Salusbury Road, London NW6 6PD* Tel and fax (020) 7328 0397

NEWTON, Brian Karl. b 30. Keble Coll Ox BA55 MA59. Wells Th Coll 56. **d** 58 **p** 59. C Barrow St Geo *Carl* 58-61; Trinidad and Tobago 61-69 and 71-77; Gen Ed Trinidad *Guild* 69-71; P-in-c Gt Coates *Linc* 77; TV Gt and Lt Coates w Bradley 78-88; V Burgh le Marsh 88-94; R Bratoft w Irby-in-the-Marsh 88-94; V Orby 88-94; R Welton-le-Marsh w Gunby 88-94; rtd 94; Perm to Offic *Linc* 94-97. *27 Somersby Way, Boston PE21 9PQ* Tel (01205) 362433

NEWTON, Canon Christopher Wynne. b 25. Trin Hall Cam BA46. Westcott Ho Cam 48. **d** 50 **p** 51. C Gateshead Ch Ch *Dur* 50-52; Canada 52-55; C Harrow Weald All SS *Lon* 55-58; V Radlett *St Alb* 58-66; RD St Alb 63-66; TR Hemel Hempstead 66-72; RD Milton Keynes *Ox* 72-77; TV Swan 78-84; RD Claydon 78-84; Dioc Ecum Officer 79-84; Hon Can Ch Ch 80-83; P-in-c Lt Gaddesden *St Alb* 84-86; rtd 86; Perm to Offic *St Alb* from 86. *24 Slade Court, Watling Street, Radlett WD7 7BT* Tel (01923) 859131

NEWTON, David Ernest. b 42. Sarum & Wells Th Coll 72. **d** 74 **p** 75. C Wigan All SS *Liv* 74-80; V Choral York Minster 80-85; R Ampleforth w Oswaldkirk 85-86; P-in-c E Gilling 85-86; R Ampleforth and Oswaldkirk and Gilling E 86-97; V Ampleforth w Oswaldkirk, Gilling E etc 98-01; RD Helmsley 94-99; P-in-c Overton *Blackb* from 01. *St Helen's Vicarage, Chapel Lane, Overton, Morecambe LA3 3HU* Tel (01524) 858234
E-mail davidnoot@aol.com

NEWTON, Derek. b 50. NEOC 89. **d** 92 **p** 93. NSM Houghton le Spring *Dur* 92-96; C 06-09; NSM Deanery of Houghton 97-06; P-in-c Chilton Moor from 09. *Pine Lodge, Warwick Drive, Houghton le Spring DH5 8JR*

NEWTON, Mrs Fiona Olive. b 46. GTCL67. WMMTC 96. **d** 99 **p** 00. C Southam and Ufton *Cov* 99-03; P-in-c Laxfield, Cratfield, Wilby and Brundish *St E* 03-04; R from 04; C Hoxne w Denham, Syleham and Wingfield from 06; RD Hoxne from 07. *The Vicarage, 15 Noyes Avenue, Laxfield, Woodbridge IP13 8EB* Tel (01986) 798998
E-mail fionanewton@rmplc.co.uk

NEWTON, George Peter Howgill. b 62. Pemb Coll Cam BA84 MA88. Oak Hill Th Coll BA93. **d** 93 **p** 94. C Blackpool St Thos *Blackb* 93-99; P-in-c Aldershot H Trin *Guildf* 99-03; V from 03; Chapl Farnborough Coll of Tech from 00. *2 Cranmore Lane, Aldershot GU11 3AS* Tel (01252) 320618
E-mail g@gjsk.prestel.co.uk

NEWTON, Gerald Blamire. b 30. Lich Th Coll. **d** 69 **p** 70. C Leeds Halton St Wilfrid *Ripon* 69-73; C Gt Yarmouth *Nor* 73-74; P-in-c Cattistock w Chilfrome and Rampisham w Wraxall *Sarum* 74-77; V Coney Hill *Glouc* 77-79; V Bryneglwys and Llandegla *St As* 79-80; R Llandegla and Bryneglwys and Llanarmon-yn-Ial 80-86; P-in-c Burythorpe, Acklam and Leavening w Westow *York* 86-95; rtd 95; Perm to Offic *York* 95-09. *9 Ropery Walk, Malton YO17 7JS* Tel (01653) 698980

NEWTON, Gordon. b 81. Cant Ch Ch Univ Coll BA03. Coll of Resurr Mirfield 07. **d** 09. C Armley w New Wortley *Ripon* from 09. *7 Stephenson Drive, Leeds LS12 5TN*
E-mail gnewton@mirfield.org.uk

NEWTON, Graham Hayden. b 47. AKC69. St Aug Coll Cant 70. **d** 70 **p** 71. C St Mary-at-Lambeth *S'wark* 70-73; TV Catford (Southend) and Downham 73-78; P-in-c Porthill *Lich* 78-79; TV Wolstanton 79-86; V Stevenage H Trin *St Alb* 86-96; TR Dunstable 96-04; RD Dunstable 96-02; R Barton-le-Cley w Higham Gobion and Hexton from 04. *The Rectory, 2 Manor Farm Close, Barton-le-Clay, Bedford MK45 4TB* Tel (01582) 881873 E-mail rectorofbarton@talktalk.net

NEWTON, Ian. b 66. Westmr Coll Ox BEd89 Leeds Univ BA03. Coll of Resurr Mirfield 01. **d** 03 **p** 04. C Horninglow *Lich* 03-06; V W Bromwich St Pet from 06. *17 Gough Drive, Tipton DY4 7AL* Tel 0121-520 3182 E-mail fatheriannewton@yahoo.co.uk

NEWTON, John. b 66. AKC63. **d** 66 **p** 67. C Whipton *Ex* 66-68; C Plympton St Mary 68-74; V Broadwoodwidger 74-81; R Kelly w Bradstone 74-81; R Lifton 74-81; Chapl All Hallows Sch Rousdon 81-94; Lic to Offic *Ex* 81-94; rtd 99. *Flat 2, 5 Eyewell Green, Seaton EX12 2BN* Tel (01297) 625887

NEWTON, John Richard. b 25. FBIM. St Jo Coll Dur 76 Cranmer Hall Dur. **d** 78 **p** 79. C Cottingham *York* 78-80; R Beeford w Frodingham and Foston 80-86; R Todwick *Sheff* 86-92; rtd 92; Perm to Offic *Linc* from 92. *Quiet Corner, 12 Pelham Close, Sudbrooke, Lincoln LN2 2SQ* Tel (01522) 595123

✠**NEWTON, The Rt Revd Keith.** b 52. K Coll Lon BD73 AKC73 Ch Ch Coll Cant PGCE75. St Aug Coll Cant 74. **d** 75 **p** 76 **c** 02. C Gt Ilford St Mary *Chelmsf* 75-78; TV Wimbledon *S'wark* 78-85; Malawi 85-91; Dean Blantyre 86-91; Can S Malawi from 86; P-in-c Knowle *Bris* 91-93; V Knowle H Nativity 93-02; P-in-c Easton All Hallows 97-02; RD Brislington 95-99; AD Bris S 99-01; Hon Can Bris Cathl 00-02; Suff Bp Richborough (PEV) *Cant* from 02; Hon Asst Bp St E from 09. *Richborough House, 6 Mellish Gardens, Woodford Green IG8 0BH* Tel (020) 8505 7259 Fax 8504 3349 E-mail pev@btinternet.com

NEWTON, Miles Julius Albert. b 69. K Alfred's Coll Win BA91. Qu Coll Birm BTh96. **d** 97 **p** 98. C Sholing *Win* 97-01; C Bitterne Park 01-03; V Woolston from 03. *St Mark's Vicarage, 117 Swift Road, Southampton SO19 9ER* Tel (023) 8044 1124 *or* 8032 6908

NEWTON, Canon Nigel Ernest Hartley. b 38. St Jo Coll Nottm 87. **d** 89 **p** 90. C Largs *Glas* 89-92; Angl Chapl Ashbourne Home Largs 89-92; P-in-c Eyemouth *Edin* 92-95; Chapl Miss to Seamen 92-95; P-in-c Challoch *Glas* 95-04; R 04-06; Can St Mary's Cathl 04-06; Hon Can from 06; rtd 06. *Glenairlie, 7 Wigtown Road, Newton Stewart DG8 6JZ* Tel (01671) 401228 Mobile 07885-436892 E-mail glenairlie@btinternet.com

NEWTON, Miss Pauline Dorothy. b 48. Southn Univ BA70 PGCE71 MPhil79. Sarum Th Coll 79. **dss** 82 **d** 87 **p** 94. Bemerton *Sarum* 82-06; Hon C 87-06; Dep Hd Malvern Girls' Coll 86-06; rtd 06; Perm to Offic *Heref* from 07. *16 Weston Park, Weston under Penyard, Ross-on-Wye HR9 7FR* Tel (01989) 564414 E-mail pnewton48@hotmail.com

NEWTON, Peter. b 39. St Jo Coll Nottm 73. **d** 75 **p** 76. C Porchester *S'well* 75-79; R Wilford 79-99; rtd 99; Perm to Offic *S'well* and *Leic* from 00; Warden Advent Ho Healing Min Birmingham USA from 99. *Advent House, 2317 Arlington Avenue, Birmingham AL 35205 USA,* or, *20 Main Street, Eaton, Grantham NG32 1SE* Tel (001) (205) 918 0124 *or* (01476) 870024

NEWTON, Richard. b 47. Trin Coll Bris 72. **d** 73 **p** 74. C Fareham St Jo *Portsm* 73-76; C Cheltenham St Mark *Glouc* 76-83; P-in-c Malvern St Andr *Worc* 83-95; TR Upton-upon-Severn 95-99, Master St Jo Hosp Bath 00-07; rtd 07. *61 Columba Drive, Worcester WR2 4DB* Tel (01905) 426702
E-mail evergreenric@tiscali.co.uk

NEWTON, Richard John Christopher. b 60. Bris Univ BSc81. Qu Coll Birm 85. **d** 88 **p** 89. C Bris Ch the Servant Stockwood 88-92; C Dorking w Ranmore *Guildf* 92-96; P-in-c Hagley *Worc* 96-00;

R from 00. *The Rectory, 6 Middlefield Lane, Hagley, Stourbridge DY9 0PX* Tel (01562) 882442 *or* 886363 Fax 887833
E-mail richard.kathy@yescomputers.co.uk
or hagley.pcc@freeuk.com

NGOY, Lusa. *See* NSENGA-NGOY, Lusambo

NGURURI, Miss Naomi. b 73. St Jo Coll Nottm 07. **d** 09. C Hackney Marsh *Lon* from 09. *Basement Flat, 306A Amhurst Road, London N16 7UE* Tel 07896-970367 (mobile)
E-mail naomingururi02@yahoo.com

NIASSA, Bishop of. *See* VAN KOEVERING, The Rt Revd Mark Allan

NIBLOCK, Mark. b 78. Fitzw Coll Cam MA03 Milltown Inst Dub MA08. CITC 06. **d** 08 **p** 09. C Agherton *Conn* from 08. *23 Cappaghmore Manor, Portstewart BT55 7RD* Tel and fax (028) 7083 4606 E-mail curate.agherton@connor.anglican.org

NICE, Canon John Edmund. b 51. Univ of Wales (Ban) BA73. Coll of Resurr Mirfield 74. **d** 76 **p** 77. C Oxton *Ches* 76-79; C Liscard St Mary w St Columba 79-82; V Latchford St Jas 82-92; R Holyhead w Rhoscolyn w Llanfair-yn-Neubwll *Ban* 92-95; R Holyhead 95-04; RD Llifon and Talybolion 97-01; AD 01-04; R Llandudno from 04; Can Cursal Ban Cathl 02-04; Can and Preb Ban Cathl from 04. *The Rectory, Church Walks, Llandudno LL30 2HL* Tel (01492) 876624
E-mail john.nice2@btopenworld.com

NICHOL, William David. b 58. Hull Univ BA84. Ridley Hall Cam 84. **d** 87 **p** 88. C Hull St Jo Newland *York* 87-90; C Kirk Ella 90-92; TV 92-98; P-in-c Powick *Worc* 98-99; R Powick and Guarlford and Madresfield w Newland 99-05; V Malvern H Trin and St Jas from 05; RD Malvern from 07. *Holy Trinity Vicarage, 2 North Malvern Road, Malvern WR14 4LR* Tel (01684) 561126 E-mail david@trinityandthewest.wanadoo.co.uk

NICHOLAS, Ernest Milton. b 25. ACP50 Newc Univ DipAdEd69 Lanc Univ MA78. NEOC 85. **d** 86 **p** 87. NSM Hexham *Newc* 86-96; Perm to Offic from 96. *Hillside, Eilansgate, Hexham NE46 3EW* Tel (01434) 603609

NICHOLAS, Malcolm Keith. b 46. FIBMS71 Open Univ BA79. S Dios Minl Tr Scheme 81. **d** 84 **p** 85. NSM Gatcombe *Portsm* 84-92; NSM Shorwell w Kingston 88-92; C Hartley Wintney, Elvetham, Winchfield etc 92-96; TV Grantham *Linc* 96-02; V Grantham, Harrowby w Londonthorpe 02-03; V Carr Dyke Gp from 03. *The Vicarage, 6 Walcott Road, Billinghay, Lincoln LN4 4EH* Tel (01526) 861746 E-mail revmalc14@yahoo.co.uk

NICHOLAS, Maurice Lloyd. b 30. Kelham Th Coll 54. **d** 58 **p** 59. C Stepney St Dunstan and All SS *Lon* 58-60; C Sevenoaks St Jo *Roch* 60-65; Chapl RADD 65-75; C Northolt St Mary *Lon* 75-85; rtd 85; Hon C Upper Teddington SS Pet and Paul *Lon* 85-90; Perm to Offic from 91. *c/o N C Ward Esq, 23 Thames Haven, Portsmouth Road, Surbiton KT6 4JA* Tel (020) 8399 5003

NICHOLAS, Milton. *See* NICHOLAS, Ernest Milton

NICHOLAS, Patrick. b 37. Selw Coll Cam BA60 MA65. Wells Th Coll 60. **d** 62 **p** 63. C Camberwell St Giles *S'wark* 62-63; C Warlingham w Chelsham and Farleigh 63-65; C Oxted 65-68; Hong Kong 68-74; C Portsea St Mary *Portsm* 75; Hd of Ho St Chris Fellowship Chiswick 76-79; Dept of Soc Services Glos Co Coun 79-92; Probation Officer Glouc Probation Service 92-97; rtd 97; Chapl St Jo Coll Hong Kong 97-00; Perm to Offic *Glouc* from 02. *35 Norwich Drive, Cheltenham GL51 3HD* Tel (01242) 510007 E-mail patnic@btinternet.com

NICHOLAS, Paul James. b 51. Univ of Wales (Lamp) BA. Coll of Resurr Mirfield 73. **d** 74 **p** 75. C Llanelli *St D* 74-78; C Roath *Llan* 78-84; P-in-c Leic St Pet 84-87; V Shard End *Birm* 87-96; rtd 96; Perm to Offic *Birm* from 96. *50 Delrene Road, Shirley, Solihull B90 2HJ* Tel 0121-745 7339
E-mail frpaul@oikos.screaming.net

NICHOLAS ALAN, Brother. *See* WORSSAM, Brother Nicholas Alan

NICHOLL, Mrs Karen. b 65. Bradf Univ BA99 Leeds Univ BA07. Coll of Resurr Mirfield 05. **d** 07 **p** 08. C Lindley *Wakef* from 07. *38 Holly Grove, Lindley, Huddersfield HD3 3NS*

NICHOLLS, Brian Albert. b 39. LBIPP LMPA. WMMTC 90. **d** 93 **p** 94. NSM Oakham, Hambleton, Egleton, Braunston and Brooke *Pet* 93-96; R Edith Weston w N Luffenham and Lyndon w Manton 96-05; P-in-c Empingham w Whitwell 02-05; rtd 05; Perm to Offic *Pet* and *Leic* from 05. *28 Heron Road, Oakham LE15 6BN* Tel (01572) 759657
E-mail whollynich@ewrut.fsnet.co.uk

NICHOLLS (née HUMPHRIES), Mrs Catherine Elizabeth. b 53. Anglia Poly Univ MA97. Trin Coll Bris BA87. **d** 87 **p** 94. C Bath Twerton-on-Avon *B & W* 87-90; Personnel Manager and Tr Officer TEAR Fund 90-95; Hon C Norbiton *S'wark* 91-95; Perm to Offic *Ely* 95-97; Dir Past Studies EAMTC 97-03; Vice Prin 01-03; Min Can Can Pet Cathl 97-03; Perm to Offic *Nor* 03-05; Dioc Dir CME from 05. *North Cottage, Church Lane, Hethel, Norwich NR14 8HE* Tel (01508) 570557
E-mail cathynicholls@norwich.anglican.org

NICHOLLS, Irene. **d** 09. OLM Penkridge *Lich* from 09. *79 Croydon Drive, Penkridge, Stafford ST19 5DW* Tel (01785) 714686

✠**NICHOLLS, The Rt Revd John.** b 43. AKC66. **d** 67 **p** 68 **c** 90. C Salford St Clem Ordsall *Man* 67-69; C Langley All SS and Martyrs 69-72; V 72-78; Dir Past Th Coll of Resurr Mirfield 78-83; Can Res Man Cathl 83-90; Suff Bp Lancaster *Blackb* 90-97; Bp Sheff 97-08; rtd 08; Hon Asst Bp Derby from 09. *77 Rowton Grange Road, Chapel-en-le-Frith, High Peak SK23 0LD*

NICHOLLS, Keith Barclay. b 57. Nottm Univ BA78. Wycliffe Hall Ox 03. **d** 05 **p** 06. C Bisley and W End *Guildf* 05-09; V Burchetts Green *Ox* from 09. *The Vicarage, Burchetts Green Road, Burchetts Green, Maidenhead SL6 6QS* Tel (01623) 828822 E-mail kbnicholls@hotmail.com

NICHOLLS, Mark Richard. b 60. LSE BSc(Econ)82 Leeds Univ BA88. Coll of Resurr Mirfield 86. **d** 89 **p** 90. C Warrington St Elphin *Liv* 89-92; V Wigan St Andr 92-96; R North End St Marg Zimbabwe 96-00; Shrine P Shrine of Our Lady of Walsingham 00-02; V Mill End and Heronsgate w W Hyde *St Alb* 02-07; P-in-c Rotherhithe St Mary w All SS *S'wark* from 07. *483B Southwark Park Road, London SE16 2JP* Tel (020) 7394 3394 Mobile 07909-546659
E-mail mmarini2001@aol.com

NICHOLLS, Mark Simon. b 57. Down Coll Cam MA79. Ripon Coll Cuddesdon 92. **d** 94 **p** 95. C Farnham *Guildf* 94-98; P-in-c Crookham 98-03; V from 03. *The Vicarage, 14 Gally Hill Road, Church Crookham, Fleet GU52 6LH* Tel (01252) 617130 E-mail office@christchurch.crookham.org.uk

NICHOLLS, Michael Stanley. b 34. AKC59. St Boniface Warminster 59. **d** 60 **p** 61. C Torquay St Martin Barton CD *Ex* 60-63; C E Grinstead St Mary *Chich* 63-66; C-in-c Salfords CD *S'wark* 66-68; V Salfords 68-75; V Tunbridge Wells St Barn *Roch* 75-97; rtd 97; Perm to Offic *Cant* 98-99 and *Chich* from 99. *30 St Itha Road, Selsey, Chichester PO20 0AA* Tel (01243) 603837

NICHOLLS, Neil David Raymond. b 65. Univ Coll Lon BA86. Wycliffe Hall Ox BA90. **d** 91 **p** 92. C Westmr St Steph w St Jo *Lon* 91-94; C Islington St Mary 94-96; Chapl LSE 96-00; C St Bride Fleet Street w Bridewell etc 99-00; V Ealing St Barn 00-05; V Hatcham St Jas *S'wark* from 05; AD Deptford from 07. *St James's Vicarage, St James's, London SE14 6AD* Tel (020) 8691 2167 E-mail rev.neil@tiscali.co.uk

NICHOLLS, Rachel. b 62. BA MPhil. **d** 00 **p** 01. NSM Chesterton St Geo *Ely* 00-04; Perm to Offic 04-07; NSM Cambridge St Benedict from 07. *5 Eachard Road, Cambridge CB3 0HZ* Tel (01223) 359167

NICHOLLS, Robert Graham. b 56. Sheff Univ BEng77 CEng MIET07. STETS 05. **d** 08 **p** 09. NSM Fair Oak *Win* from 08. *20 The Spinney, Eastleigh SO50 8PF* Tel (023) 8069 3716 Mobile 07837-804366 E-mail bob.nicholls@dsl.pipex.com

NICHOLLS, Roger. b 43. Ox Univ MA Cam Univ DipEd. **d** 01 **p** 02. OLM Kenwyn w St Allen *Truro* 01-04; NSM Truro St Paul and St Clem 04-08; NSM Truro St Geo and St Jo 04-08; P-in-c Mylor w Flushing from 08. *17 Olivey Place, Mylor Bridge, Falmouth TR11 5RX* Tel (01326) 374408
E-mail rognicholls@tesco.net

NICHOLLS, Simon James. b 53. Anglia Ruskin Univ MA08 Trent Park Coll of Educn CertEd76. Ridley Hall Cam. **d** 00 **p** 01. C Nuneaton St Nic *Cov* 00-04; R Markfield, Thornton, Bagworth and Stanton etc *Leic* from 04. *The Rectory, 3A The Nook, Markfield LE67 9WE* Tel (01530) 242844
E-mail markfield.rector@virgin.net

NICHOLLS, Barry Edward. b 40. ACA63 FCA73. S'wark Ord Course 66. **d** 69 **p** 70. NSM Surbiton St Andr and St Mark *S'wark* 69-92; Dean for MSE Kingston 90-92; Hon Can S'wark Cathl 90-92; Perm to Offic 99-01; NSM Upper Tooting H Trin 01-04; NSM Upper Tooting H Trin w St Aug from 04. *19 Arterberry Road, London SW20 8AF* Tel and fax (020) 8879 0154 E-mail barrynichols@btinternet.com

NICHOLLS, Dennis Harry. b 25. Kelham Th Coll 47. **d** 52 **p** 53. C Oakham *Pet* 52-55; C Kettering St Mary 55-57; P-in-c Spalding St Paul *Linc* 57-61; V Bury H Trin *Man* 61-81; V St Gluvias *Truro* 81-90; RD Carnmarth S 85-90; rtd 90; Perm to Offic *Truro* 90-08. *15 Ramsay Hall, 9-13 Byron Road, Worthing BN11 3HN*

NICHOLLS, Mrs Elizabeth Margaret. b 45. WEMTC 00. **d** 00 **p** 03. NSM Ledbury *Heref* 02-05; NSM Boxwell, Leighterton, Didmarton, Oldbury etc *Glouc* from 05. *The Rectory, The Meads, Leighterton, Tetbury GL8 8UW* Tel (01666) 890635 E-mail reverend.elizabeth@cotswoldwireless.co.uk

NICHOLLS, Frank Bernard. b 43. Kelham Th Coll 64. **d** 68 **p** 69. C Luton St Andr *St Alb* 68-72; C Cheshunt 72-76; C-in-c Marsh Farm CD 76-81; Australia from 05; Perm to Offic Brisbane from 08. *Unit 1, 28 Hill View Crescent, Carina Heights, Brisbane Qld 4152, Australia* Tel (0061) (7) 3398 7435 Mobile 42-488 8169 E-mail frank.nichols2@bigpond.com

NICHOLLS, Howard Keith. b 41. CCC Ox BA64 MA68 CEng86 FIEE92 EurIng94. WEMTC 98. **d** 01 **p** 02. NSM Ledbury *Heref* 01-04; NSM Boxwell, Leighterton, Didmarton, Oldbury etc *Glouc* from 04. *The Rectory, The Meads, Leighterton, Tetbury GL8 8UW* Tel (01666) 890635
E-mail reverend.howard@cotswoldwireless.co.uk

NICHOLS, Mark Steven. b 68. Lon Bible Coll BA94 Ridley Hall Cam 95. **d** 97. C Balham Hill Ascension *S'wark* 97-99. *37 Harrier Court, Fenton Street, Lancaster LA1 1AE*
E-mail markn1968uk@yahoo.co.uk

NICHOLS, Canon Raymond Maurice. b 22. ALCD53. **d** 53 **p** 54. C Childwall All SS *Liv* 53-56; Kenya 56-64; Home Sec SPCK 64-71; Overseas Sec 67-73; Publisher 73-74; P-in-c Dorchester *Ox* 74-78; P-in-c Newington 77-78; TR Dorchester 78-87; V Warborough 78-87; Hon Can Ch Ch 84-87; rtd 87; Perm to Offic *Sarum* 91-08 and *Ox* from 09. *14 Augustine Way, Oxford OX4 4DG* Tel (01865) 747772

NICHOLS, Robert Warren. b 54. Biola Univ (USA) BA77 Fuller Th Sem California MA81. SAOMC 93. **d** 96 **p** 97. C Headington Quarry *Ox* 96-00; Sen Asst P Wymondham *Nor* 00-05; Lect 01-05; R Caston, Griston, Merton, Thompson etc from 05. *The Rectory, 4 Hunters Ride, Caston, Attleborough NR17 1DE* Tel (01953) 483222 E-mail revbobnichols@gmail.com

NICHOLS, Stephen Robert Chamberlain. b 73. Ch Coll Cam BA96 MA00. Wycliffe Hall Ox BA06. **d** 09. *18 Glenhurst Road, Plymouth PL3 5LT* Tel (01752) 267025 Mobile 07960-063174

NICHOLSON, Andrew John. b 69. Leeds Univ BA93 MA00. St Jo Coll Nottm MTh04. **d** 05 **p** 06. C E Richmond *Ripon* 05-09; P-in-c Barwick in Elmet from 09; P-in-c Thorner from 09. *The Vicarage, Church View, Thorner, Leeds LS14 3ED* Tel 0113-289 2437 Mobile 07723-345917
E-mail andydebbie80@hotmail.com

NICHOLSON, Mrs Barbara Ruth. b 39. Nor City Coll TCert59. Dioc OLM tr scheme 99. **d** 02 **p** 03. OLM Reculver and Herne Bay St Bart *Cant* from 02. *34 Cliff Avenue, Herne Bay CT6 6LZ* Tel (01227) 364606 Fax 365384

NICHOLSON, Brian Warburton. b 44. ALCD73 LTh74. St Jo Coll Nottm 70. **d** 73 **p** 74. C Canford Magna *Sarum* 73-77; C E Twickenham St Steph *Lon* 77-80; V Colchester St Jo *Chelmsf* 80-96; R Oakley w Wootton St Lawrence *Win* 96-09; rtd 09. *16 St Vigor Way, Colden Common, Winchester SO21 1UU*

NICHOLSON, Christina. d 08. OLM Mossley Hill *Liv* from 08. *9 Mossville Road, Liverpool L18 7JN*
E-mail christinanic099@aol.com

NICHOLSON, Miss Clare. b 46. RMN80 Keele Univ BA70 CertEd70. St Jo Coll Nottm 83. **dss** 85 **d** 87 **p** 94. Bletchley *Ox* 85-89; Par Dn 87-89; Par Dn Milton Keynes 89-90; Par Dn Prestwood and Gt Hampden 90-94; C 94-99; P-in-c E Springfield *Chelmsf* 99-03; V Aldborough Hatch from 03. *The Vicarage, 89 St Peter's Close, Ilford IG2 7QN* Tel (020) 8599 0524
E-mail revdclare@stpetersah.org.uk *or* revclare46@aol.com

NICHOLSON, David. b 57. Sarum & Wells Th Coll 80. **d** 83 **p** 84. C Trevethin *Mon* 83-85; C Ebbw Vale 85-87; V Newport St Steph and H Trin 87-95; V Abertillery w Cwmtillery w Six Bells 95-97; Hon Chapl Miss to Seamen 87-97; P-in-c Cudworth *Wakef* 97-98; V from 98; P-in-c Lundwood 01-04; Dioc Urban Officer from 08. *The Vicarage, St John's Road, Cudworth, Barnsley S72 8DE* Tel (01226) 710279
E-mail fr_d_pp_cudworth@hotmail.com

NICHOLSON, Mrs Diane Maureen. b 45. Birm Coll of Educn CertEd68. **d** 97 **p** 98. OLM Ludham, Potter Heigham, Hickling and Catfield *Nor* from 97. *25 Latchmoor Park, Ludham, Great Yarmouth NR29 5RA* Tel (01692) 678683

NICHOLSON, Dorothy Ann. b 40. Surrey Univ Roehampton MSc04. S'wark Ord Course 81. **dss** 84 **d** 87 **p** 94. Carshalton Beeches *S'wark* 84-88; Par Dn 87-88; Par Dn Brixton Road Ch Ch 88-89; C Malden St Jo 89-95; V Balham St Mary and St Jo 95-05; rtd 05. *13 Tebbs Close, Countesthorpe, Leicester LE8 5XG* Tel 0116-277 5737 E-mail nicholsonda@btopenworld.com

NICHOLSON, Eric. b 33. **d** 01 **p** 02. OLM W Wycombe w Bledlow Ridge, Bradenham and Radnage *Ox* 01-07; Lic to Offic *Mor* from 07. *Gordon Chapel Rectory, 40 Castle Street, Fochabers IV32 7DW* Tel (01343) 820337
E-mail eric@torrington67.freeserve.co.uk

NICHOLSON, Prof Ernest Wilson. b 38. Comdr OM (Italy)90. TCD BA60 MA64 Glas Univ PhD64 Cam Univ MA67 BD71 DD78 Ox Univ DD79 FBA87. Westcott Ho Cam 69. **d** 69 **p** 70. Lect Div Cam Univ 67-79; Fell, Chapl and Dir of Th Studies Pemb Coll Cam 69-79; Dean 73-79; Prof of Interpr of H Scripture Oriel Coll Ox 79-90; Provost from 90; Pro-Vice-Chan Ox Univ from 93; Lic to Offic *Ox* from 84. *The Provost's Lodgings, Oriel College, Oxford OX1 4EW* Tel (01865) 276533

NICHOLSON, Gary. b 62. Open Univ BA89. Cranmer Hall Dur 91 NEOC 92. **d** 95 **p** 96. NSM Whitworth w Spennymoor *Dur* 95-97; NSM Spennymoor, Whitworth and Merrington 97-00; C Coundon and Eldon 00-02; P-in-c from 02. *St James's Vicarage, 2A Collingwood Street, Coundon, Bishop Auckland DL14 8LG* Tel (01388) 603312 E-mail frgary@hotmail.com

NICHOLSON, Harold Sydney Leonard. b 35. Garnett Coll Lon PGCE67 Open Univ BA77. Oak Hill NSM Course 92. **d** 94 **p** 95. NSM Stanwell *Lon* 94-00; NSM Sunbury 98-00; NSM Shepperton 00-05; Perm to Offic from 05. *7 Academy Court, Fordbridge Road, Sunbury-on-Thames TW16 6AN* Tel (01932) 787690 E-mail hslnicholson@onetel.com

NICHOLSON, James Benjamin. NEOC. **d** 08 **p** 09. NSM Helmsley *York* from 08; NSM Upper Ryedale from 08. *5 Bells Court, Helmsley, York YO62 5BA* Tel (01439) 772150

NICHOLSON, John Paul. b 57. Sarum Th Coll. **d** 82 **p** 83. C Kirkby *Liv* 82-85; TV Speke St Aid 85-95; Ind Chapl *Ox* 95-04; Chapl Cambs & Pet Mental Health Partnerships NHS Trust from 04. *Chaplaincy Office, Kent House, Fulbourn Hospital, Cambridge CB21 5EF* Tel (01223) 218598
E-mail john.nicholson@cambsmh.nhs.uk

NICHOLSON, Kevin Smith. b 47. CQSW76. Edin Th Coll 89. **d** 91 **p** 92. C TV Fife Team Min *St And* 91-94; P-in-c 94-95; R Kinross 95-03; rtd 03. *Oldshoremore, 3A West Huntingtower, Perth PH1 3NU* Tel (01738) 583555
E-mail keith.nicholson@virgin.net
or keithsnicholson@yahoo.co.uk

NICHOLSON, Canon Nigel Patrick. b 46. DL07. Sarum & Wells Th Coll 72. **d** 75 **p** 76. C Farnham *Guildf* 75-78; C Worplesdon 78-81; CF (ACF) from 80; P-in-c Compton *Guildf* 81-85; R Compton w Shackleford and Peper Harow 85-89; R Cranleigh from 89; RD Cranleigh 95-00; Hon Can Guildf Cathl from 01. *The Rectory, High Street, Cranleigh GU6 8AS* Tel (01483) 273620 E-mail stnicoloff@aol.com

NICHOLSON, Miss Pamela Elizabeth. b 47. Ripon Coll Cuddesdon. **d** 92 **p** 94. C Balsall Heath St Paul *Birm* 92-95; V Smethwick St Matt w St Chad from 95. *1 St Matthew's Road, Smethwick, Warley B66 3TN* Tel 0121-558 1653
E-mail pamela.nicholson1@btinternet.com

NICHOLSON, Paul Shannon. b 52. York Univ BA74 Middx Univ BA02 ARCO74 ARCM75. NTMTC 99. **d** 02 **p** 03. C Primrose Hill St Mary w Avenue Road St Paul *Lon* 02-06; P-in-c S Hampstead St Sav from 06; P-in-c Belsize Park from 06. *St Saviour's Vicarage, 30 Eton Villas, London NW3 4SQ* Tel (020) 7586 6522 Mobile 07971-223764
E-mail nicholsongarrison@hotmail.com

NICHOLSON, Canon Peter Charles. b 25. OBE92. Lambeth Hon MA89 Chich Th Coll 57. **d** 59 **p** 60. C Sawbridgeworth *St Alb* 59-62; Min Can, Prec and Sacr Pet Cathl 62-67; V Wroxham w Hoveton *Nor* 67-74; V Lyme Regis *Sarum* 74-80; Gen Sec St Luke's Hosp for the Clergy 80-93; NSM Harlington *Lon* 80-87; Hon Chapl S'wark Cathl from 87; Can and Preb Chich Cathl 89-93; rtd 93. *St Luke's Cottage, 13 Brearley Close, Uxbridge UB8 1JJ* Tel (01895) 233522

NICHOLSON, Peter Charles. b 44. Oak Hill Th Coll 74. **d** 76 **p** 77. C Croydon Ch Ch Broad Green *Cant* 76-80; C Gt Baddow *Chelmsf* 80-88; TV 88-96; V Westcliff St Mich from 96. *St Michael's Vicarage, 5 Mount Avenue, Westcliff-on-Sea SS0 8PS* Tel (01702) 478462 E-mail pedinic@tiscali.co.uk

NICHOLSON, Canon Rodney. b 45. Mert Coll Ox BA68 MA71. Ridley Hall Cam 69. **d** 72 **p** 73. C Colne St Bart *Blackb* 72-75; C Blackpool St Jo 75-78; V Ewood 78-90; V Clitheroe St Paul Low Moor from 90; P-in-c Chatburn and Downham from 03; Hon Can Blackb Cathl from 06. *The Vicarage, St Paul's Street, Clitheroe BB7 2LS* Tel and fax (01200) 458019
E-mail rodnic@btopenworld.com

NICHOLSON, Roland. b 40. Sarum & Wells Th Coll 72. **d** 74 **p** 75. C Morecambe St Barn *Blackb* 74-78; V Feniscliffe 78-90; V Sabden and Pendleton 90-02; C Poulton-le-Fylde 02-04; C Poulton Carleton and Singleton 04-07; rtd 08. *13 Laurel Bank Terrace, Feniscowles, Blackburn BB2 5JA*

NICHOLSON, Mrs Samantha. b 69. St Jo Coll York BA92. St Jo Coll Nottm MA95 LTh93. **d** 96 **p** 97. C Toxteth St Cypr w Ch Ch *Liv* 96-01; P-in-c W Derby St Luke 01-08; P-in-c Ince Ch Ch 08-09; P-in-c Wigan St Cath 08-09; V Ince Ch Ch w Wigan St Cath from 09. *The Vicarage, 70 Belle Green Lane, Ince, Wigan WN2 2EP* Tel (01942) 495831

NICHOLSON, Stephen Lee. b 65. St Jo Coll Cam BA87 MA91 PhD94 Ox Univ MTh01. St Steph Ho Ox 98. **d** 00 **p** 01. C Middlesbrough All SS *York* 00-05; Asst Chapl HM Pris Holme Ho 00-05; Chapl York Univ 05-08. *Address temp unknown* Tel 07875-909792 (mobile)

NICHOLSON, Trevor Parry. b 35. St Edm Hall Ox BA58 MA. Wycliffe Hall Ox 58. **d** 60 **p** 61. C Eastbourne Ch Ch *Chich* 60-63; V Ifield 63-67; Asst Youth Chapl *Win* 67-73; Chapl Shoreham Gr Sch 73-78; P-in-c Capel *Guildf* 78-85; V 85-90; Chapl Qu Anne's Sch Caversham 90-00; rtd 00; P-in-c N Chapel w Ebernoe *Chich* from 00. *Lexham, Dodsley Lane, Easebourne, Midhurst GU29 9BB* Tel (01730) 810452

NICHOLSON, Miss Velda Christine. b 44. Charlotte Mason Coll of Educn TCert65. Cranmer Hall Dur 81. **dss** 82 **d** 87 **p** 94. Gt and Lt Driffield *York* 82-86; Newby 86-88; Par Dn 87-88; TD Cramlington *Newc* 88-93; TV 94-96; Perm to Offic from 96; rtd 04. *24 Glendale, Amble, Morpeth NE65 0RG* Tel (01665) 713796

NICHOLSON, Veronica Mary. *See* WILSON, Mrs Veronica Mary

NICKLAS-CARTER, Derath May. *See* DURKIN, Mrs Derath May

NICKLESS, Christopher John. b 58. Univ of Wales BA79. Coll of Resurr Mirfield 79. **d** 81 **p** 82. C Bassaleg *Mon* 81-85; TV

Ebbw Vale 85-93; V Newport St Teilo 93-99. *c/o Bishopstow, Stow Hill, Newport NP9 4EA* Tel (01633) 263510

NICKLIN, Ivor. b 41. FRSA68 BEd MTh73 PhD76 MA84. Wycliffe Hall Ox. **d** 84 **p** 85. NSM Weaverham *Ches* 84-89; P-in-c Kings Walden *St Alb* 89-91; P-in-c Offley w Lilley 89-91; V King's Walden and Offley w Lilley 91-93; V Basford *Lich* 93-98; rtd 98; Perm to Offic *Ches* from 99 and *Lich* from 00. *232 Manor Way, Crewe CW2 6PH* Tel (01270) 669080

NICKOLS, James Alexander. b 75. Regent's Park Coll Ox BA96. Ridley Hall Cam 98. **d** 00 **p** 01. C Plymouth St Jude *Ex* 00-04; C Camberwell All SS *S'wark* 04-08; Hon C Camberwell Ch Ch from 09. *Christ Church, 676-680 Old Kent Road, London SE15 1JF* Tel 07968-062339 (mobile)
E-mail jamesnkls@aol.com

NICKOLS-RAWLE, Peter John. b 44. St Luke's Coll Ex CertEd73. Sarum & Wells Th Coll 76. **d** 78 **p** 79. C Ex St Thos 78-80; Old and New Shoreham *Chich* 80-86; P-in-c Donnington 86-90; Chapl RAF 90-92; TV Ottery St Mary, Alfington, W Hill, Tipton etc *Ex* 92-97; V Breage w Germoe and Godolphin *Truro* 98-01; rtd 01; Perm to Offic *Truro* 01-05. *14 The Copse, Exmouth EX8 4EY* Tel (01395) 270068

NICKSON, Ann Louise. b 58. New Hall Cam BA80 Fitzw Coll Cam BA95 Solicitor 81. Ridley Hall Cam PhD98. **d** 98 **p** 99. C Sanderstead All SS *S'wark* 98-01; P-in-c Norbury St Steph and Thornton Heath 01-05; V from 05; AD Croydon N from 06. *St Stephen's Vicarage, 9 Warwick Road, Thornton Heath CR7 7NH* Tel (020) 8684 3820 E-mail annnickson@aol.com

NICOL, David Christopher. b 56. Westmr Coll Ox BEd84 Ox Univ Inst of Educn 91. SAOMC 95. **d** 98 **p** 99. NSM Deddington w Barford, Clifton and Hempton *Ox* 98-01; V Longnor, Quarnford and Sheen *Lich* 01-08. *6 Hill View, Leek ST13 5TA* E-mail fr.david@tinyworld.co.uk

NICOL, Ernest. b 25. S'wark Ord Course 71. **d** 74 **p** 75. NSM Hornsey Ch Ch *Lon* 74-75; NSM Hornsey St Geo 76-84; C Hendon Ch Ch 85-90; rtd 90; C Steeton *Bradf* 90-96; Asst Chapl Airedale Hosp Bradf 90-96; Perm to Offic *Lon* from 96. *75 Nightingale Lane, London N8 7RA* Tel (020) 8341 5496

NICOL, Harvie Thomas. b 61. Aston Tr Scheme 95 St Jo Coll Nottm 97. **d** 99 **p** 00. C Balderstone *Man* 99; C S Rochdale 00-03; TV Ashton 03-08; P-in-c Ashton St Pet 03-08; V Formby St Luke *Liv* from 08. *St Luke's Vicarage, St Luke's Church Road, Liverpool L37 2DF* Tel (01704) 877655

NICOLE, Bruce. b 54. K Coll Lon MA96 ACIB. Wycliffe Hall Ox 89. **d** 91 **p** 92. C Headley All SS *Guildf* 91-95; V Camberley St Mich Yorktown from 95; RD Surrey Heath 02-06. *The Vicarage, 286 London Road, Camberley GU15 3JP* Tel (01276) 23602 E-mail revbrucenicole@aol.com

NICOLL, Alexander Charles Fiennes Jack. b 34. Lon Coll of Div 66. **d** 68 **p** 69. C Trentham *Lich* 68-71; C Hednesford 72-74; P-in-c Quarnford 74-84; V Longnor 74-84; P-in-c Sheen 80-84; V Longnor, Quarnford and Sheen 85-00; RD Alstonfield 96-00; Perm to Offic from 00; rtd 00. *110 Stone Road, Uttoxeter ST14 7QW* Tel (01889) 569361

NICOLL, Miss Angela Olive Woods. b 50. Linc Th Coll 77. **dss** 79 **d** 87 **p** 94. Catford St Laur *S'wark* 79-83; Peckham St Jo w St Andr 83-88; Par Dn 87-88; Par Dn New Addington 88-94; C 94-02; S Africa 02-06; Perm to Offic *Ely* from 06. *Fair Hill Cottage, 9 Globe Street, Methwold, Thetford IP26 4PQ*

NICOLLS, Andrew John. b 67. Regents Th Coll BA03. Trin Coll Bris MA05. **d** 05 **p** 06. C Higher Bebington *Ches* 05-08; P-in-c Bulwell St Mary *S'well* from 08. *Bulwell Rectory, Station Road, Nottingham NG6 9AA* Tel 0115-927 8468

NICOLSON, Paul Roderick. b 32. Cuddesdon Coll 65. **d** 67 **p** 68. C Farnham Royal *Ox* 67-68; Lic to Offic *St Alb* 69-82; C Hambleden Valley *Ox* 82-99; rtd 99. *93 Campbell Road, London N17 0AX* Tel (020) 8376 5455 Fax 8376 5319 Mobile 07961-177889 E-mail paul@nicolson.com

NIEMIEC, Paul Kevin. b 56. EAMTC 03. **d** 05 **p** 06. Youth Officer *Pet* 97-08; NSM Thrapston, Denford and Islip 05-08; TV Barnstaple *Ex* from 08. *The Vicarage, 40 Chichester Road, Newport, Barnstaple EX32 9EH* Tel (01271) 376285

NIGER, Bishop on the. *See* OKEKE, The Rt Revd Ken Sandy Edozie

NIGERIA, Archbishop of. *See* AKINOLA, The Most Revd Peter Jasper

NIGHTINGALE, Catherine. b 72. **d** 01 **p** 02. C Birchencliffe *Wakef* 01-04; C to Dioc Chapl among Deaf People 01-04; TV E Farnworth and Kearsley *Man* 04-08; P-in-c Roughtown from 08; Chapl among Deaf People from 04. *The Vicarage, Carrhill Road, Mossley, Ashton-under-Lyne OL5 0BL* Tel (01457) 832250
E-mail cathy.nightingale@clearclergy.info

NIGHTINGALE, Mrs Jennifer. b 66. Wolv Univ BA99. Qu Coll Birm **d** 04 **p** 05. C Walsall St Paul *Lich* 04-07; C Holdenhurst and Iford *Win* from 07; Chapl Bp Win Comp Sch from 07. *13 Brackendale Road, Bournemouth BH8 9HY* Tel (01202) 533356 Mobile 07703-558668

NIGHTINGALE, Canon John Brodie. b 42. Pemb Coll Ox BA64 Qu Coll Cam BA67. Westcott Ho Cam 65. **d** 67 **p** 68. C Wythenshawe St Martin *Man* 67-70; Nigeria 70-76; P-in-c

Amberley w N Stoke *Chich* 76-79; Adult Educn Adv 76-79; Asst Home Sec Gen Syn Bd for Miss and Unity 80-84; Miss Sec 84-87; P-in-c Wolverton w Norton Lindsey and Langley *Cov* 87-95; Dioc Miss Adv 87-95; V Rowley Regis *Birm* 95-07; Hon Can Birm Cathl 01-07; Warden of Readers 03-07; rtd 07; Perm to Offic *Birm* from 07. *19 Berberry Close, Birmingham B30 1TB* Tel 07811-128831 (mobile)
E-mail john.nightingale@btinternet.com

NIGHTINGALE, Susan Kay. b 44. Keele Univ BA66 Seabury-Western Th Sem DMin99. S'wark Ord Course 90. **d** 93 **p** 94. NSM St Giles Cripplegate w St Bart Moor Lane etc *Lon* 93-99; Perm to Offic *York* 93-99; Asst Chapl H Trin Geneva *Eur* 99-02; P-in-c Sutton on the Forest *York* 03-06. *Westfield Farm, Sheriff Hutton, York YO60 6QQ* Tel (01347) 878423

NIMMO, The Very Revd Alexander Emsley. b 53. Aber Univ BD76 PhD97 Edin Univ MPhil83 FSAScot93. Edin Th Coll 76. **d** 78 **p** 79. Prec St Andr Cathl Inverness 78-81; P-in-c Stornoway *Arg* 81-83; R 84; R Edin St Mich and All SS 84-90; Chapl HM Pris Saughton 87-90; R Aberdeen St Marg from 90; Can St Andr Cathl from 96; Syn Clerk 01-08; Dean Ab from 08. *St Margaret's Clergy House, Gallowgate, Aberdeen AB25 1EA* Tel (01224) 644969 Fax 630767 E-mail alexander306@btinternet.com

NIND, Robert William Hampden. b 31. Ball Coll Ox BA54 MA60. Cuddesdon Coll 54. **d** 56 **p** 57. C Spalding *Linc* 56-60; Jamaica 60-67; P-in-c Battersea St Bart *S'wark* 67-70; V Brixton St Matt 70-82; Lic to Offic 82-84; Ind Chapl 84-89; Ind Chapl *Ox* 89-95; rtd 95. *19 Binswood Avenue, Headington, Oxford OX3 8NY* Tel (01865) 66604
E-mail bawalker@rwhnind.freeserve.co.uk

NINEHAM, Prof Dennis Eric. b 21. Qu Coll Ox BA43 MA46 Cam Univ BD64 Birm Univ Hon DD72. Linc Th Coll 44. **d** 44 **p** 45. Asst Chapl Qu Coll Ox 44-46; Chapl 46-54; Prof Bibl and Hist Th K Coll Lon 54-58; Prof Div Lon Univ 58-64; Regius Prof Div Cam Univ 64-69; Warden Keble Coll Ox 69-79; Hon Can Bris Cathl 80-86; Prof Th Bris Univ 80-86; rtd 86; Perm to Offic *Ox* from 87. *9 Fitzherbert Close, Iffley, Oxford OX4 4EN* Tel (01865) 715941

NINIS, The Ven Richard Betts. b 31. Linc Coll Ox BA53 MA62 Derby Univ Hon DUniv99. Linc Th Coll 53. **d** 55 **p** 56. C Poplar All SS w St Frideswide *Lon* 55-62; V Heref St Martin 62-71; V Upper and Lower Bullinghope w Grafton 68-71; R Dewsall w Callow 68-71; Dioc Missr 69-74; Preb Heref Cathl 70-74; Telford Planning Officer *Lich* 70-74; Can Res and Treas Lich Cathl 74-98; Adn Stafford 74-80; Adn Lich 80-98; rtd 98; Perm to Offic *B & W* from 00. *Hill View, 32 Robert Street, Williton, Taunton TA4 4QL* Tel and fax (01984) 634987

NISBECK, Peter. b 51. SOAS Lon BA73 Aston Univ MSc94. NOC 03. **d** 06 **p** 07. NSM Newcastle w Butterton *Lich* from 06. *210 Seabridge Lane, Newcastle ST5 3LS* Tel (01782) 662379

NISBET, Gillian Ruth. b 65. NOC 00. **d** 03 **p** 04. NSM Childwall St Dav *Liv* 03-06; NSM Abu Dhabi St Andr UAE from 06. *PO Box 60534, Al Bateen PO, Abu Dhabi, UAE* Tel (00971) 508-173234 E-mail gilliannisbet@hotmail.co.uk

NISBETT, Canon Thomas Norman. b 25. OBE91. Codrington Coll Barbados. **d** 62 **p** 63. Barbados 62-64; Bermuda from 65; Hon Can Bermuda Cathl from 81; rtd 97. *2 Shelton Road, Pembroke HM 20, Bermuda* Tel and fax (001441) 236 0537

NIXON, David John. b 59. St Chad's Coll Dur BA81 Ex Univ PhD02. St Steph Ho Ox 88. **d** 91 **p** 92. C Plymouth St Pet *Ex* 91-94; Chapl Ex Univ 94-03; P-in-c Stoke Damerel 03-09; P-in-c Devonport St Aubyn 03-09; R Stoke Damerel and Devonport St Aubyn from 09. *The Rectory, 6 Underhill Road, Plymouth PL3 4BP* Tel (01752) 562348 E-mail rev.dave@virgin.net

NIXON, Frances (Isobel). b 34. TCD BA62. **d** 94 **p** 95. NSM Rossorry *Clogh* from 94. *Honiara, 61 Granshagh Road, Enniskillen BT92 2BL* Tel (028) 6634 8723 Mobile 07710-307263 E-mail isobel@honiara.fsnet.co.uk

NIXON, John David. b 38. Leeds Univ BSc60 CEng70 MICE. Linc Th Coll 76. **d** 78 **p** 79. C Rugby *Cov* 78-83; TV 83-86; TV Bicester w Bucknell, Caversfield and Launton *Ox* 86-98; USA from 98; rtd 03. *1209 W 21st Street, Lawrence KS 66046-2833, USA* E-mail frjdn@hotmail.com
or allsaintskcrector@juno.com

NIXON, Ms Naomi Jane. b 75. Keele Univ BA97. St Jo Coll Nottm MA00. **d** 01 **p** 02. C Ludlow, Ludford, Ashford Carbonell etc *Heref* 01-04; Chapl N Warks and Hinckley Coll of FE from 04. *St Philip's Vicarage, Ringwood Highway, Coventry CV2 2GF* Tel (024) 7661 7706

NIXON, Pauline Margaret. b 49. **d** 05 **p** 06. NSM Perranzabuloe *Truro* from 05; NSM Crantock w Cubert from 09. *3 Dorrington House, Grannys Lane, Perranporth TR6 0HB* Tel (01872) 571697 *or* 552340 E-mail paulinenixon@btinternet.com

NIXON, Canon Phillip Edward. b 48. Ch Ch Ox MA73 DPhil73 Trin Coll Cam BA80 K Coll Lon MA00. Westcott Ho Cam 78. **d** 81 **p** 82. C Leeds Halton St Wilfrid *Ripon* 81-84; V Goring *Ox* 84; V Goring w S Stoke 84-03; RD Henley 94-02; Hon Can Ch Ch 00-03; P-in-c Northampton St Jas *Pet* from 03; Warden of

Readers from 05. *St James's Vicarage, Vicarage Road, Northampton NN5 7AX* Tel (01604) 751164
E-mail phillipn@btopenworld.com

NIXON, Miss Rosemary Ann. b 45. Bp Grosseteste Coll CertEd66 Dur Univ MA83 Edin Univ MTh95. Dalton Ho Bris BD73. **d** 87 **p** 94. Tutor St Jo Coll w Cranmer Hall Dur 75-89; Dir St Jo Coll Ext Progr 82-89; NSM Chester le Street *Dur* 87-89; TD Gateshead 89-92; Dir Cranmer Hall Urban Studies Unit 89-92; Staff Member Edin Th Coll 92-95; Prin TISEC 95-99; Can St Mary's Cathl 96-99; V Cleadon *Dur* 99-07; rtd 07. *6 Wearside Drive, Durham DH1 1LE* Tel 0191-384 6558

NIXON, Mrs Tonya. b 69. Plymouth Univ BSc93 St Mark & St Jo Coll Lon PGCE94. Qu Coll Birm 06. **d** 09. C Farmborough, Marksbury and Stanton Prior *B & W* from 09. *The Gables, Stanton Prior, Bath BA2 9HT*
E-mail tonya39n@btinternet.com

NIXON, William Samuel. Reading Univ BSc94 TCD BTh00. **d** 00 **p** 01. C Lisburn St Paul *Conn* 00-02; C Hillsborough *D & D* 02-06; P-in-c Edin Clermiston Em 06-08; I Killaney w Carryduff *D & D* from 08. *The Rectory, 700 Saintfield Road, Carryduff, Belfast BT8 8BU* Tel (028) 9081 2342 Mobile 07764-277771
E-mail cazza-willie@hotmail.com

NIXSON, Peter. b 27. Ball Coll Ox BA51 MA59 Ex Univ PGCE67 DipEd72. Coll of Resurr Mirfield 51. **d** 53 **p** 54. C Babbacombe *Ex* 53-56; C Swindon New Town *Bris* 56-57; C Boyne Hill *Ox* 57-60; C-in-c Bayswater St Mary CD 60-66; Perm to Offic *Ex* 66-67 and 70-85; Perm to Offic *Lich* 67-69; Hd RE Oswestry Boys' High Sch 67-69; Hon C Oswestry H Trin 69-70; Sch Coun Tiverton 70-75; Newton Abbot 75-85; V Winkleigh *Ex* 85-92; R Ashreigney 85-92; R Broadwoodkelly 85-92; V Brushford 85-92; RD Chulmleigh 87-93; rtd 93; Perm to Offic *Ex* from 93. *40 Lidford Tor Avenue, Paignton TQ4 7ED* Tel (01803) 522698

NIXSON, Rosemary Clare. *See* WARD, Mrs Rosemary Clare

NJENGA, Kennedy Samuel. b 60. Oak Hill Th Coll Qu Coll Birm. **d** 01 **p** 02. C Old Trafford St Jo *Man* 01-04; P-in-c Pheasey *Lich* from 04. *St Chad's Vicarage, 88 Hillingford Avenue, Birmingham B43 7HN* Tel 0121-360 6098 E-mail njambinjenga@aol.com

✠**NJOJO, The Rt Revd Patrice Byankya.** b 38. BA76. Montreal Dioc Th Coll 78. **d** 70 **p** 80 **c** 80. Bp Boga from 80; Abp Congo 92-02. *PO Box 25586, Kampala, Uganda* Tel (00256) 77-647495
E-mail eac-mags@infocom.co.uk

NJOKA, Stanley. b 80. St Andr Coll Kabare 01 Lon Sch of Th 06. **d** 04 **p** 05. Kenya 04-06; Perm to Offic *Lon* 06-07 and *S'wark* from 08. *89 Highlever Road, London W10 6PW* Tel (020) 8969 0243 Mobile 07846-759133 E-mail sknjoka@yahoo.co.uk

NJOKU, Chinenye Ngozi. b 63. Trin Coll Bris. **d** 09. C Goldington *St Alb* from 09. *1 Atholl Walk, Bedford MK41 0BG* Tel 07515-171579 (mobile) E-mail gozy78@hotmail.com

NJUGUNA, Daniel Cahira. b 73. St Jo Coll Nottm BA04. **d** 00 **p** 01. Kenya 00-03; C Balderton and Barnby-in-the-Willows *S'well* 04-06; TV Hucknall Torkard from 06. *St Peter and Paul's Vicarage, Ruffs Drive, Hucknall, Nottingham NG15 6JG* Tel 0115-963 3640 Mobile 07817-577436
E-mail dcahira@yahoo.co.uk

NJUGUNA, Timothy. b 49. St Paul's Coll Limuru BD84 Presbyterian Th Coll Seoul ThM89 San Francisco Th Sem DMin03. **d** 83 **p** 84. V Nairobi St Mary Kenya 84-86; V Karura 86-87; V Kirangari 89-90; Dioc Sec Mt Kenya S 91-93; P-in-c San Bruno USA 99-03; Perm to Offic *S'wark* 05-07; Chapl Forth Valley NHS Trust from 07; Hon C Falkirk *Edin* from 07. *NHS Forth Valley, 33 Spittal Street, Stirling FK8 1DX* Tel (01786) 463031 Mobile 07950-536215 E-mail tegssa@hotmail.com

NOAH, Michael John. b 44. WEMTC 00. **d** 02 **p** 03. NSM Hucclecote *Glouc* 02-05; NSM Malmesbury w Westport and Brokenborough *Bris* from 05. *1 Athelstan Court, Malmesbury SN16 0FD* Tel (01666) 826564 E-mail mikenoah@supanet.com

NOAKES, Mrs Dorothy. b 35. Derby Coll of Educn CertEd55 Ex Univ BEd85 BPhil(Ed)92. **d** 96 **p** 97. OLM Helston and Wendron *Truro* from 96. *6 Tenderah Road, Helston TR13 8NT* Tel (01326) 573239 E-mail dorothy@dorothy1.wanadoo.co.uk

NOBBS, Charles Henry ffrench. b 67. Hatf Coll Dur BSc89 St Jo Coll Dur BA99 CEng96. Cranmer Hall Dur 97. **d** 99 **p** 00. C Northampton St Giles *Pet* 99-02; C Collingtree w Courteenhall and Milton Malsor from 02; Police Chapl Co-ord from 03. *10 Foxglove Close, Grange Park, Northampton NN4 5DD* Tel (01604) 875188 E-mail charlie@dunelm.org.uk

NOBBS, John Ernest. b 35. Tyndale Hall Bris 60. **d** 63 **p** 64. C Walthamstow St Mary *Chelmsf* 63-66; C Braintree 66-69; C Wakef St Andr and St Mary 69-71; C Tooting Graveney St Nic *S'wark* 71-74; C Woking St Pet *Guildf* 74-78; C Worthing St Geo *Chich* 78-88; C Rayleigh *Chelmsf* 88-94; rtd 94; Perm to Offic *Chelmsf* from 00. *89 Panfield Lane, Braintree CM7 5RP* Tel (01376) 322901

NOBEL, Johannes. b 81. Evang Th Faculty Leuven BA03 Utrecht Univ MA05 St Jo Coll Dur MA08. Cranmer Hall Dur 06. **d** 08 **p** 09. C Norton St Mary *Dur* from 08; C Stockton St Chad from

08. *St Chad's Vicarage, Ragpath Lane, Stockton-on-Tees TS19 9JN* Tel (01642) 672502
E-mail johannes.nobel@gmail.com

NOBLE, Alexander Frederick Innes (Sandy). b 30. Selw Coll Cam BA53 MA58. Lon Coll of Div ALCD55. **d** 55 **p** 56. C Stratton St Margaret *Bris* 55-57; C Brislington St Luke 57-59; Chapl Pierrepont Sch Frensham 59-61; Asst Chapl Repton Sch Derby 61-63; Chapl 63-66; Chapl Blundell's Sch Tiverton 66-72; St Jo C of E Sch Cowley 73-77; Chapl Cranbrook Sch Kent 77-81; Chapl St Geo Sch Harpenden 81-90; Hon C Herriard w Winslade and Long Sutton etc 90-94; rtd 95; P-in-c Oare w Culbone *B & W* 95-99; Perm to Offic from 00. *Upway, Church Street, Minehead TA24 5JU* Tel (01643) 708976

NOBLE, Anne Valerie. b 60. Univ Coll Ox BA82 Toronto Univ MSc84 PhD91. St Jo Coll Nottm 04. **d** 07 **p** 08. C Wollaton *S'well* from 07. *73 Torvill Drive, Nottingham NG8 2BR* Tel 0115-928 8622 E-mail nobles1@btinternet.com

NOBLE, Christopher John Lancelot. b 58. Oak Hill Th Coll 88. **d** 90 **p** 91. C Tonbridge SS Pet and Paul *Roch* 90-95; P-in-c Stansted w Fairseat and Vigo 95-98; R from 98. *The Rectory, 9 The Coach Drive, Meopham, Gravesend DA13 0SZ* Tel (01732) 822494

NOBLE, David. b 37. S Dios Minl Tr Scheme 84. **d** 87 **p** 88. C Alverstoke *Portsm* 87-89; R Jerramungup Australia 90-93; R Bridgetown 93-97; R Willetton 97-02; rtd 02. *Quill Studio, 9 Chaparral Crescent, Willetton WA 6155, Australia* Tel and fax (0033) (8) 9259 0323 Mobile 41-717 2542
E-mail thenobles@surak.com.au

NOBLE, Mrs Eileen Joan. b 45. NEOC 90. **d** 93 **p** 94. C Gosforth All SS *Newc* 93-96; C Cramlington 96-97; TV 97-01; V Ashington 01-06; rtd 06; Hon C Monkseaton St Mary *Newc* from 07. *34 Gorsedene Road, Whitley Bay NE26 4AH*
E-mail revnoble2000@yahoo.com

NOBLE, Canon Graham Edward. b 49. Open Univ BA74 SS Paul & Mary Coll Cheltenham CertEd71. EAMTC 85. **d** 88 **p** 89. C Kesgrave *St E* 88-90; P-in-c Gt and Lt Blakenham w Baylham and Nettlestead 90-95; P-in-c Debenham w Aspall and Kenton 95-04; P-in-c Helmingham w Framsden and Pettaugh w Winston 99-04; R Debenham and Helmingham 04-05; RD Loes 99-05; Hon Can St E Cathl 03-05; rtd 05; Perm to Offic *St E* from 05. *36 Gracechurch Street, Debenham, Stowmarket IP14 6RE* Tel (01728) 861008 E-mail graham@noblefamily.fsnet.co.uk

NOBLE, Paul Vincent. b 54. Leeds Univ BA75 PGCE76 Ox Univ BA81 MA85. St Steph Ho Ox 79. **d** 82 **p** 83. C Prestbury *Glouc* 82-85; P-in-c Avening w Cherington 85-90; V The Suttons w Tydd *Linc* 90-98; R Skirbeck St Nic from 98. *The Rectory, Fishtoft Road, Skirbeck, Boston PE21 0DJ* Tel (01205) 362734 E-mail frpnoble@skirbeckrectory.freeserve.co.uk

NOBLE, Canon Philip David. b 46. Glas Univ BSc67 Edin Univ BD70. Edin Th Coll 67. **d** 70 **p** 71. C Edin Ch Ch 70-72; Papua New Guinea 72-75; R Cambuslang *Glas* 76-83; R Uddingston 76-83; Ev Prestwick 83-85; R Prestwick from 85; Can St Mary's Cathl from 99. *56 Ayr Road, Prestwick KA9 1RR* Tel (01292) 477108

NOBLE, Robert. b 43. TCD BA66 BD73. **d** 68 **p** 69. C Holywood *D & D* 68-71; Chapl Holmewood Ho Sch Tunbridge Wells 98-04; Perm to Offic *Chich* 01-08 and *Heref* from 08. *Temperance Cottage, Weston under Penyard, Ross-on-Wye HR9 7NX* Tel (01989) 566 /48
E-mail rjnobles@tiscali.co.uk

NOBLES, Mrs Mary Joy. b 37. WEMTC 04. **d** 05 **p** 06. NSM Malvern Link w Cowleigh *Worc* from 05. *4 Hamilton Close, Powick, Worcester WR2 4NH* Tel (01905) 831925
E-mail m.nobles@btopenworld.com

NOBLET, David. b 62. Cranmer Hall Dur 97. **d** 99 **p** 00. C Standish *Blackb* 00-03; P-in-c Langho Billington from 03; Chapl HM Pris Kirkham from 08. *The Vicarage, 11 Whalley New Road, Billington, Blackburn BB7 9NA* Tel (01254) 822246

NOBLETT, The Ven William Alexander. b 53. Southn Univ BTh78 Westmr Coll Ox MTh99. Sarum & Wells Th Coll 74. **d** 78 **p** 79. C Sholing *Win* 78-80; I Ardamine w Kiltennel, Glascarrig etc *C & O* 80-82; Chapl RAF 82-84; V Middlesbrough St Thos *York* 84-87; Asst Chapl HM Pris Wakef 87-89; Chapl 89-92; Chapl HM Pris Nor 92-97; Chapl HM Pris Full Sutton 97-01; Chapl Gen of Pris and Adn to HM Pris from 01; Can and Preb York Minster from 01; Lic to Offic from 01; Chapl to The Queen from 05; Hon Can Liv Cathl from 09. *HM Prison Service Chaplaincy, Room 310, Abell House, John Islip Street, London SW1P 4LH* Tel (020) 7217 8960 or 7217 8678 Fax 7217 8980

NOCK, Peter Arthur. b 15. Keble Coll Ox BA36 MA42. Bps' Coll Cheshunt 37. **d** 39 **p** 40. C Gt Harwood St Bart *Blackb* 39-40; C Lancaster Priory Ch 40-45; V Over Wyresdale 45-50; V Darwen St Cuth 50-64; V Sparkhill St Jo *Birm* 64-71; RD Bordesley 67-71; V Maney 71-81; rtd 81; Perm to Offic *Carl* from 81. *Westlands, Linden Fold, Grange-over-Sands LA11 7AY* Tel (01539) 535139

NOCK, Roland George William. b 62. St Andr Univ BSc84 BD89. Edin Th Coll 91. **d** 91 **p** 92. C Dunfermline *St And* 91-93;

C W Fife Team Min 91-93; R Cupar 93-96; CF 96-99. *46 Heol Y Parc, Cefneithin, Llanelli SA14 7DL* Tel (01269) 845847
E-mail roland@nock.screaming.net

NOCKELS, John Martin. b 46. Lich Th Coll Qu Coll Birm 73. **d** 73 **p** 74. C Eccleshill *Bradf* 73-76; C Fawley *Win* 76-78; V Southampton St Jude 78-84; R Tadley St Pet 84-98; P-in-c Gt and Lt Massingham and Harpley *Nor* 98-99; P-in-c S Raynham, E w W Raynham, Helhoughton, etc 98-99; R Gt w Lt Massingham, Harpley, Rougham etc 99-06; rtd 06. *96 Church Lane, Beeston Regis, Sheringham NR26 8EY* Tel (01263) 825404

NODDER, Marcus Charles Colmore. b 67. Pemb Coll Cam BA89 PGCE90. Oak Hill Th Coll BA01. **d** 01 **p** 02. C Denton Holme *Carl* 01-04; C Limehouse *Lon* from 04. *13 Storers Quay, London E14 3BZ* Tel (020) 7515 7947 E-mail mnodder@hotmail.com *or* marcus@nodder.fsbusiness.co.uk

NODDER, Thomas Arthur (Brother Arnold). b 20. K Coll Lon 58. **d** 60 **p** 61. Brotherhood of the H Cross from 49; C Rotherhithe St Mary w All SS *S'wark* 60-63; SSF from 63; Lic to Offic *Chelmsf* 63-66; C Plaistow St Andr 69-70; Lic to Offic *Newc* 69-70 and *Birm* 70-83; Perm to Offic *Birm* 90-98; Lic to Offic *Sarum* 83-89; rtd 90; Perm to Offic *Chelmsf* from 98. *Society of St Francis, 42 Balaam Street, London E13 8AQ* Tel (020) 7476 5189

NODDINGS, John Henry. b 39. Chich Th Coll 80. **d** 81 **p** 82. C Southborough St Pet w Ch Ch and St Matt *Roch* 81-83; C Prittlewell *Chelmsf* 83-86; V Clay Hill St Jo *Lon* 86-88; V Clay Hill St Jo and St Luke 88-02; Chapl Chase Farm Hosp Enfield 88-94; Chapl Chase Farm Hosps NHS Trust 94-95; rtd 03; P-in-c Gt Coxwell w Buscot, Coleshill etc *Ox* from 03. *The Vicarage, Great Coxwell, Faringdon SN7 7NG* Tel (01367) 240665

NOKE, Christopher. b 48. Ex Coll Ox BA69 MA79 LSE MSc78 ACA72 FCA79. SEITE 03. **d** 06 **p** 07. NSM Raynes Park St Sav *S'wark* from 06; NSM S Wimbledon All SS from 06. *Cedar Lodge, Church Road, Ham, Richmond TW10 5HG* Tel (020) 8948 7986

NOKES, Michael David Patrick. b 44. CA MCMI. **d** 02 **p** 03. NSM Heworth Ch Ch *York* 02-08; Perm to Offic *Bradf* from 02; *Ripon* from 03; *York* from 08. *5 Fox Covert, York YO31 9EN* Tel (01904) 620411 *or* 674879 Mobile 07776-252440
E-mail mnokes@cpas.org.uk

NOKES, Peter Warwick. b 48. Leic Univ BA71. Westcott Ho Cam 79. **d** 81 **p** 82. C Northfield *Birm* 81-84; C Ludlow *Heref* 84-87; P-in-c Writtle w Highwood *Chelmsf* 87-91; V 91-92; P-in-c Epping St Jo 92-95; P-in-c Coopersale 93-95; TR Epping Distr 95-99; R Nor St Pet Mancroft w St Jo Maddermarket from 99. *37 Unthank Road, Norwich NR2 2PB* Tel (01603) 627816 *or* 610443 Fax 766652 Mobile 07711-384009
E-mail pwnokes@aol.com

NOKES, Robert Harvey. b 39. Keble Coll Ox BA61 MA65. Qu Coll Birm 61. **d** 63 **p** 64. C Totteridge *St Alb* 63-67; C Dunstable 67-73; V Langford 73-90; R Braughing w Furneux Pelham and Stocking Pelham 90-04; Perm to Offic *Ox* from 04. *92 Western Drive, Hanslope, Milton Keynes MK19 7LE* Tel (01908) 337939 E-mail nokes@easykey.com

NOLAN, James Charles William. b 44. Chich Th Coll 75. **d** 77 **p** 78. C Crewe St Andr *Ches* 77-79; C Sale St Anne 79-83; R Holme Runcton w S Runcton and Wallington *Ely* from 83; V Tottenhill w Wormegay from 83; R Watlington from 83. *The Rectory, Downham Road, Watlington, King's Lynn PE33 0HS* Tel (01553) 810305

NOLAN, Marcus. b 54. Bris Univ BEd. Ridley Hall Cam. **d** 83 **p** 84. C Dagenham *Chelmsf* 83-86; C Finchley St Paul and St Luke *Lon* 86-90; V W Hampstead Trin 90-98; rtd 99; Perm to Offic *Derby* 00-06. *55 Blanch Croft, Melbourne, Derby DE73 8GG*

NOLES, Jeremy Andrew. b 67. St Jo Coll Nottm 02. **d** 04 **p** 05. C Southchurch Ch Ch *Chelmsf* 04-07; C Colchester St Jo from 07. *6 Baronia Croft, Colchester CO4 9EE* Tel 07719-652333 (mobile)

NOLLAND, John Leslie. b 47. New England Univ (NSW) BSc67 Clare Coll Cam PhD78. Moore Th Coll Sydney ThL70 BD71. **d** 71 **p** 72. Australia 71-78; Canada 78-86; Asst Prof NT Studies Regent Coll Vancouver 78-86; Tutor Trin Coll Bris from 86; Vice Prin 91-97. *Trinity College, Stoke Hill, Bristol BS9 1JP* Tel 0117-968 2083 *or* 968 4053 Fax 968 7470
E-mail john.nolland@trinity-bris.ac.uk

NOLLER, Hilda Elizabeth Mary (Sister Elizabeth Mary). b 26. MSR47 FSR53. **d** 95 **p** 96. Lic to Offic *Chelmsf* 96-02; Sister Superior CSD from 00. *Retired Nurses Home, Riverside Avenue, Bournemouth BH7 7EE* Tel (01202) 397014

NOON, Canon Edward Arthur. b 16. Selw Coll Cam BA38 MA42. Bps' Coll Cheshunt 38. **d** 40 **p** 41. C Kingston St Jo *S'wark* 40-43; C Dulwich St Barn 43-48; P-in-c S Wimbledon St Pet 48-50; V 50-55; V Mitcham St Mark 55-65, V Horley 65-77; RD Reigate 72-76; Hon Can S'wark Cathl 72-83; P-in-c Purley St Barn 77-83; rtd 83; Hon C Overbury w Teddington, Alstone etc *Worc* 83-86; Perm to Offic *Glouc* 86-95. *40 Shepherds Leaze, Wotton-under-Edge GL12 7LQ* Tel (01453) 844978

NOORDANUS, Francis Peter. b 61. Cant Univ (NZ) BA82 ACT BTh90. **d** 92 **p** 93. New Zealand 92-02; C Ashburton 92-94; V Masterton St Matt 94-02; Chapl Eindhoven *Eur* from 02. *Paradijslaan 76, 5611 KR Eindhoven, The Netherlands* Tel (0031) (40) 245 0601 E-mail f.p.noordanus@planet.nl

NORBURN, Christopher Richard. b 62. Cov Poly BSc85. Aston Tr Scheme 92 Ridley Hall Cam 94. **d** 96 **p** 97. C Exning St Martin w Landwade *St E* 96-99; P-in-c Redgrave cum Botesdale w Rickinghall 99-01; R from 01. *The Rectory, Bury Road, Rickinghall, Diss IP22 1HA* Tel (01379) 898685

NORBURN, The Very Revd Richard Evelyn Walter. b 21. Witwatersrand Univ BA44 TDip44. St Paul's Coll Grahamstown 49. **d** 51 **p** 53. Vice-Prin Dioc Tr Coll Pretoria S Africa 51-56; Dioc Dir RE and R Potgietersrus 56-62; C Croydon St Sav *Cant* 63-64; V Norbury St Phil 65-75; V Addington 75-81; Hon Can Cant Cathl 79-81; RD Croydon Addington 81; Dean Botswana 81-88; rtd 89; Perm to Offic *Cant* 98-05. *The College of St Barnabas, Blackberry Lane, Lingfield RH7 6NJ* Tel (01342) 872839

NORBURN, Canon Richard Henry. b 32. MBE97. St Edm Hall Ox BA57. Wycliffe Hall Ox 57. **d** 59 **p** 59. C Sudbury St Greg and St Pet *St E* 59-65; Dioc Youth Officer 65-74; P-in-c Gt Livermere 74-81; R Ampton w Lt Livermere and Ingham 74-81; RD Thingoe 78-88; Hon Can St E Cathl 81-97; R Ingham w Ampton and Gt and Lt Livermere 81-92; TV Blackbourne 92-97; rtd 97; Perm to Offic *St E* from 97. *69 Churchgate Street, Bury St Edmunds IP33 1RL* Tel (01284) 702644 E-mail richardhnorburn@btopenworld.com

NORBURY, Robert John. b 60. Southn Univ BA83 Univ of Wales (Ban) BTh07. **d** 04 **p** 05. OLM Eltham Park St Luke *S'wark* 04-07; Perm to Offic *Chich* 07-08; NSM Crowborough St Jo from 08; Chapl Wandsworth Primary Care Trust from 09. *Oak House, 4 Eridge Drive, Crowborough TN6 2TJ* Tel (01892) 668188 E-mail frrobnorbury@aol.com

NORFIELD, David Jonathan. b 67. Humberside Univ BA89. Linc Th Coll MA94 Westcott Ho Cam 95. **d** 97 **p** 98. C Halstead St Andr w H Trin and Greenstead Green *Chelmsf* 97-01; V Moulsham St Jo 01-04; Chapl RAF from 04. *Chaplaincy Services, Valiant Block, HQ Air Command, RAF High Wycombe HP14 4UE* Tel (01494) 496800 Fax 496343 E-mail davidnorfield@hotmail.com

NORFOLK, The Ven Edward Matheson. b 21. Leeds Univ BA44. Coll of Resurr Mirfield 41. **d** 46 **p** 47. C Greenford H Cross *Lon* 46-47; C S Mymms K Chas 47-50; C Bushey *St Alb* 50-53; PC Waltham Cross 53-59; V Welwyn Garden City 59-69; R Gt Berkhamsted 69-81; Hon Can St Alb 72-82; V Kings Langley 81-82; Adn St Alb 82-87; rtd 87; Perm to Offic *Ex* from 87. *5 Fairlawn Court, Sidmouth EX10 8UR* Tel (01395) 514222

NORFOLK, Archdeacon of. *See* HAYDEN, The Ven David Frank

NORGATE, Norman George. b 32. Qu Coll Cam BA55 MA58. Ridley Hall Cam. **d** 57 **p** 58. C Erith St Paul *Roch* 57-60; C E Twickenham St Steph *Lon* 60-63; V Bexleyheath St Pet *Roch* 63-71; V Woking St Mary *Guildf* 71-83; V Tunbridge Wells St Jas *Roch* 83-92; TR Tunbridge Wells St Jas w St Phil 92-97; rtd 97; Perm to Offic *St E* from 97. *Crathie, 52 Sexton Meadows, Bury St Edmunds IP33 2SB* Tel (01284) 767363

NORKETT, Alan. b 45. Sarum & Wells Th Coll 85. **d** 87 **p** 88. C Shrewsbury St Giles w Sutton and Atcham *Lich* 87-90; V Mow Cop 90-94; NSM Astbury and Smallwood *Ches* 96-97; NSM Sandbach Heath w Wheelock 97-98; C Castleford All SS and Whitwood *Wakef* 98-01; C Glass Houghton 98-01; R Shrawley, Witley, Astley and Abberley *Worc* from 01. *The Rectory, Shrawley, Worcester WR6 6TS* Tel (01905) 620489 E-mail vicaralan@aol.com

NORMAN, Canon Andrew Herbert. b 54. K Coll Lon BD77 AKC77 Lon Univ PhD88. St Steph Ho Ox 77. **d** 78 **p** 79. C Deal St Leon w Sholden *Cant* 78-81; C Maidstone All SS and St Phil w Tovil 81-84; V Tenterden St Mich 84-93; Chapl Benenden Hosp 86-91; Dir Post-Ord Tr *Cant* 91-93; R Guildf St Nic from 93; Hon Can Guildf Cathl from 05. *The Rectory, 3 Flower Walk, Guildford GU2 4EP* Tel (01483) 504895 E-mail fr-andrew@st-nicholas.freeserve.co.uk

NORMAN, Canon Andrew Robert. b 63. Univ Coll Ox BA84 MA99 Selw Coll Cam BA94 MA99 Birm Univ MPhil08 AIL89. Ridley Hall Cam 92. **d** 95 **p** 96. Asst Chapl Paris St Mich *Eur* 95-00; C Clifton Ch Ch w Em *Bris* 00-02; Abp's Asst Sec for Ecum and Angl Affairs *Cant* 02-05; Abp's Prin Sec for Internat, Ecum and Angl Communion Affairs 05-08; Prin Ridley Hall Cam from 09; Hon Prov Can Cant Cathl from 06. *Ridley Hall, Cambridge CB3 9HG* Tel (01223) 741060 Fax 741081 E-mail arn1000@cam.ac.uk

NORMAN, Catherine. b 51. Nottm Univ BSc73 N Counties Coll Newc CertEd74. Linc Th Coll. **d** 95 **p** 96. C Scartho *Linc* 95-99; V Ulceby Gp 99-02; TV Guiseley w Esholt *Bradf* 02-08; P-in-c Rawdon from 08; RD Otley from 09. *The Vicarage, Layton Avenue, Rawdon, Leeds LS19 6QQ* Tel 0113-250 3263 E-mail caytenorman@aol.com *or* office@stpetersrawdon.co.uk

NORMAN, Canon Edward Robert. b 38. Selw Coll Cam BA61 PhD64 MA65 BD67 DD78 FRHistS72 FRSA88. Linc Th Coll 65. **d** 65 **p** 71. Fell Jes Coll Cam 64-71; Lect Cam Univ 65-88; Dean Peterho Cam 71-88; Dean of Chpl Ch Ch Coll of HE Cant 88-95; Six Preacher Cant Cathl 84-90; Can Res York Minster 95-04; Treas 95-99; Chan 99-04; Hon Prof York Univ from 96; Hon C St Andr-by-the-Wardrobe w St Ann, Blackfriars *Lon* from 05; Hon C St Jas Garlickhythe w St Mich Queenhithe etc from 05. *Peterhouse, Cambridge CB2 1RD*

NORMAN, Mrs Elizabeth Ann. b 43. SAOMC 95. **d** 98 **p** 99. OLM Amersham *Ox* 98-04. *Lamorna, Main Road, Bickington, Barnstaple EX31 2NA* Tel (01271) 859314

NORMAN, The Ven Garth. b 38. St Chad's Coll Dur BA62 MA68 UEA MEd84 Cam Inst of Educn PGCE68. **d** 63 **p** 64. C Wandsworth St Anne *S'wark* 63-66; C Trunch w Swafield *Nor* 66-71; R Gimingham 71-77; TR Trunch 77-83; RD Repps 75-83; Prin Chiltern Chr Tr Course *Ox* 83-87; C W Wycombe w Bledlow Ridge, Bradenham and Radnage 83-87; Dir of Tr *Roch* 88-94; Adn Bromley and Bexley 94-03; Hon Can Roch Cathl 91-03; rtd 03; Perm to Offic *S'well* from 03; Chapl to Retired Clergy from 04. *5 Riverside, Southwell NG25 0HA* Tel (01636) 815209 E-mail gnorman@southwell.anglican.org

NORMAN, Gary. b 64. Newc Univ BA87. Ripon Coll Cuddesdon 02. **d** 04 **p** 05. C Spennymoor and Whitworth *Dur* 04-09; P-in-c Croxdale and Tudhoe from 08; P-in-c Merrington from 09. *The Vicarage, 21 York Villas, Spennymoor DL16 6LP* Tel (01388) 811108

NORMAN, Jillianne Elizabeth. b 59. Ridley Hall Cam 85. **d** 88 **p** 94. Par Dn Fishponds St Jo *Bris* 88-92; Perm to Offic 92-94; Hon C Warmley, Syston and Bitton from 94; Chapl Univ Hosps Bris NHS Foundn Trust from 02. *74 Blackhorse Road, Mangotsfield, Bristol BS16 9AY* Tel 0117-956 1551 Fax 904 6894 E-mail jilliannenorman@blueyonder.co.uk

NORMAN, Linda Mary. b 48. Man Univ BSc69 CertEd70 St Jo Coll Dur BA82. dss 83 **d** 87. York St Mich-le-Belfrey 83-88; Par Dn 87-88; rtd 88. *23 Ainsty Avenue, Dringhouses, York YO24 1HH* Tel (01904) 706152

NORMAN, Lynette Dianne. b 52. Sussex Univ CertEd73 Univ of Wales (Ban) BEd89. Ripon Coll Cuddesdon 00. **d** 02 **p** 03. C Welshpool w Castle Caereinion *St As* 02-04; R LLanrwst from 04. *The Rectory, Llanddoged Road, Llanrwst LL26 0DW* Tel (01492) 640223 Mobile 07889-184517

NORMAN, Michael John. b 59. Southn Univ LLB82. Wycliffe Hall Ox 82. **d** 85 **p** 86. C Woodley St Jo the Ev *Ox* 85-89; C Uphill *B & W* 89-92; TV 92-98; R Bath St Sav w Swainswick and Woolley from 98. *St Saviour's Rectory, Claremont Road, Bath BA1 6LX* Tel (01225) 311637 E-mail michael@stsaviours.org.uk

NORMAN, Michael John. b 62. St Jo Coll Ox BSc83 Univ Coll Lon MSc84. Aston Tr Scheme 89 St Jo Coll Nottm 91. **d** 93 **p** 94. C Haughton le Skerne *Dur* 93-97; R Sapcote and Sharnford w Wigston Parva *Leic* from 97; RD Sparkenhoe W 02-07. *The Rectory, 4 Sharnford Road, Sapcote, Leicester LE9 4JN* Tel (01455) 272215 E-mail micknorman@msn.com

NORMAN, Peter John. b 42. Culham Coll of Educn TCert66 Lon Inst of Educn DipEd83 MA86. STETS 95. **d** 98 **p** 99. NSM Bath Weston All SS w N Stoke and Langridge *B & W* from 98. *5 Rockliffe Avenue, Bathwick, Bath BA2 6QP* Tel (01225) 463348

NORMAN, Peter John. b 59. Chich Th Coll 84. **d** 87 **p** 88. C Farncombe *Guildf* 87-91; C Cockington *Ex* 91-94; V Winkleigh from 94; R Ashreigney from 94; R Broadwoodkelly from 94; V Brushford from 94. *The Vicarage, Torrington Road, Winkleigh EX19 8HR* Tel (01837) 83719

NORMAN, Canon Richard Hudson. b 58. Louisiana State Univ BS84 MA88. Gen Th Sem NY MDiv93 STM93. **d** 92 **p** 93. C Southgate St Andr *Lon* 92 and 97-98; USA 92-97 and from 02; Assoc New York City St Matt and St Tim 92-93; R Abbeville St Paul 93-95; Assoc R Chevy Chase All SS 95-97; V Mill Hill St Mich *Lon* 98-02; R Greenville Redeemer 02-05; Sen Can St Mark's Cathl Minneapolis from 05. *St Mark's Cathedral, 519 Oak Grove Street, Minneapolis MN 55403, USA* Tel (001) (612) 870 7800 Fax 870 7802

NORMAN, Timothy. b 68. Jes Coll Cam BA91 Univ Coll Lon PhD95. Spurgeon's Coll 95 Wycliffe Hall Ox BA00. **d** 01 **p** 02. C Chipping Norton *Ox* 01-04; Asst Chapl Paris St Mich *Eur* 04-06; Perm to Offic 06-08; C Rugby W *Cov* from 09. *58 Park Road, Rugby CV21 2QH* E-mail tim.norman@bigfoot.com

NORMAN, Canon William Beadon. b 26. Trin Coll Cam BA49 MA55. Ridley Hall Cam 52. **d** 52 **p** 53. C Beckenham St Jo *Roch* 52-54; CMS Miss and Tutor Buwalasi Th Coll Uganda 55-65; Hon Can Mbale 63-65; V Alne *York* 65-74; RD Warley *Birm* 74-79; V Blackheath 74-79; Hon Can Birm Cathl 78-91; TR Kings Norton 79-91; RD Kings Norton 82-87; Warden Dioc Readers Bd 84-91; rtd 91; Perm to Offic *S'wark* from 91; Preacher Lincoln's Inn 94-06. *37 Cloudesdale Road, London SW17 8ET* Tel (020) 8673 9134 Fax 8675 6890 E-mail bbnorman@hotmail.com

NORMAN-WALKER, Mrs Anna Elizabeth. b 67. RGN89. St Jo Coll Nottm BA03. **d** 03 **p** 04. C Cullompton, Willand, Uffculme,

Kentisbeare etc *Ex* 03-06; TV from 06. *The Rectory, Old Village, Willand, Cullompton EX15 2RH* Tel (01884) 33249 Fax 08701-645107 Mobile 07986-450330
E-mail anna@norman-walker.fsnet.co.uk

NORMAND, Stephen Joseph William. b 48. N Texas State Univ BSEd80. Sarum & Wells Th Coll 90. **d** 92 **p** 93. C Norton *St Alb* 92-94; C St Alb St Pet 95-97; Chapl Canadarm Coll 95-97; TV Horsham *Chich* 97-01; R Wimbotsham w Stow Bardolph and Stow Bridge etc *Ely* 01-04; rtd 04; Perm to Offic *Ely* from 05. *3 Fincham Road, Stow Bardolph, King's Lynn PE34 3HX* Tel (01366) 387037 E-mail normasteph@aol.com

NORRINGTON, Paul Richard. b 57. Brighton Poly BSc80. Trin Coll Bris 96. **d** 98 **p** 99. C Prittlewell St Pet w Westcliff St Cedd *Chelmsf* 98-02; R Colchester Ch Ch w St Mary V from 02. *The Rectory, 21 Cambridge Road, Colchester CO3 3NS* Tel (01206) 563478 E-mail pnozzer@tesco.net

NORRIS, Mrs Alison. b 55. St Andr Univ MTheol77 Dur Univ PGCE78. Cant Sch of Min 80. **dss** 82 **d** 87 **p** 94. Warlingham w Chelsham and Farleigh *S'wark* 82-85; Willingham *Ely* 85-90; Hon Par Dn 87-90; Hon Par Dn Worle *B & W* 90-94; NSM Milverton w Halse and Fitzhead 94-02; P-in-c Deane Vale from 02. *6 Cole Close, Cotford St Luke, Taunton TA4 1NZ* Tel (01823) 432625

NORRIS, Allan Edward. b 43. St Jo Coll Dur BA72. Cranmer Hall Dur 69. **d** 73 **p** 74. C Plumstead St Jo w St Jas and St Paul *S'wark* 73-78; C Battersea Park St Sav 78-82; C Battersea St Geo w St Andr 78-82; V Grain w Stoke *Roch* 82-92; V Sissinghurst w Frittenden *Cant* from 92. *The Rectory, Oakleaves, Frittenden, Cranbrook TN17 2DD* Tel (01580) 852275
E-mail revco@amserve.com

NORRIS, Andrew David. b 54. St Andr Univ BSc78 Lon Univ MPhil80 CPsychol. EAMTC 87. **d** 90 **p** 91. C Worle *B & W* 90-94; R Milverton w Halse and Fitzhead 94-08; RD Tone 01-07; Nat Chapl Adv Methodist Homes for the Aged from 08. *6 Cole Close, Cotford St Luke, Taunton TA4 1NZ* Tel (01823) 432625
E-mail revnog@tinyonline.co.uk

NORRIS, Andrew Peter. b 62. Aston Univ BSc83. St Jo Coll Nottm BA86. **d** 87 **p** 88. C Mountsorrel Ch Ch and St Pet *Leic* 87-90; C Harborne Heath *Birm* 90-91; P-in-c Edgbaston St Germain 91-92; V 92-99; P-in-c Hook w Warsash *Portsm* 99-00; V from 00. *The Vicarage, 113 Church Road, Warsash, Southampton SO31 9GF* Tel and fax (01489) 572324

NORRIS, Barry John. b 46. Nottm Univ CQSW75 MTh86 Open Univ BA80 K Coll Lon PhD95. St Jo Sem Wonersh. **d** 70 **p** 71. In RC Ch 70-72; C Wisbech SS Pet and Paul *Ely* 76-78; TV E Ham w Upton Park St Alb *Chelmsf* 78-81; Chapl RAF 81-87; V N Tadley St Mary *Win* from 87. *St Mary's Vicarage, Bishopswood Road, Tadley, Basingstoke RG26 4HQ* Tel 0118-981 4435 E-mail baz.norris@btinternet.com

NORRIS, Canon Clifford Joseph. b 29. Codrington Coll Barbados. **d** 61 **p** 68. Antigua 61-62; C Penton Street St Silas w All SS *Lon* 68-70; C Stepney St Dunstan and All SS 70-73; P-in-c Bethnal Green St Jas the Gt w St Jude 73-82; V Aveley and Purfleet *Chelmsf* 82-98; Hon Can NE Caribbean from 95; rtd 98; Perm to Offic *Chelmsf* from 98. *20 Hayhouse Road, Earls Colne, Colchester CO6 2PD* Tel (01787) 222015

NORRIS, Eric Richard. b 43. MICFM86. Bernard Gilpin Soc Dur 65 Ripon Hall Ox 66. **d** 69 **p** 70. C Huyton St Mich *Liv* 69-72; C Mexborough *Sheff* 72-74; V Dalton 74-78; Org Sec CECS *Carl* 78-89; Area Appeals Manager N Co 89-93; TR Thirsk *York* 93-02; RD Mowbray 00-02; V Boosbeck w Moorsholm 02-06; Abp's Adv in Tourism 02-06; rtd 06; Perm to Offic *York* from 06. *39 Upleatham Street, Saltburn-by-the-Sea TS12 1JX* Tel (01287) 280940

NORRIS, Mrs Helen. b 53. Univ of Wales (Abth) LLB74 Univ Coll Lon LLM76 Solicitor 78. **d** 04 **p** 05. OLM Coddenham w Gosbeck and Hemingstone w Henley *St E* from 04; OLM Crowfield w Stonham Aspal and Mickfield from 04. *The Villa, The Street, Stonham Aspal, Stowmarket IP14 6AQ* Tel (01449) 711395 E-mail helen.norris@btinternet.com

NORRIS, Julie Mary. b 63. Westmr Coll Ox BA84 Fitzw Coll Cam MPhil88 Birm Univ PhD03. Wesley Ho Cam 86. **d** 06 **p** 06. C Orwell Gp *Ely* 06-09; P-in-c Gt w Lt Abington from 09; P-in-c Hildersham from 09; TV Linton from 09. *The Vicarage, 35 Church Lane, Little Abington, Cambridge CB1 6BQ* Tel (01223) 891350 E-mail julienorris1323@aol.com

NORRIS, Keith David. b 47. E Lon Univ BA89 MIAM76 MBIM80. NTMTC 95. **d** 98 **p** 02. NSM Cranham Park *Chelmsf* 98-99; NSM S Hornchurch St Jo and St Matt 01-06; NSM Rainham w Wennington from 06. *Still Waters, 8 Hesselyn Drive, Rainham RM13 7EJ* Tel (01708) 780767
E-mail keithdnorris@hotmail.co.uk

NORRIS, Mark. b 68. Brunel Univ BEng90. Oak Hill Th Coll BA93. **d** 93 **p** 94. C Roby *Liv* 93-97; C St Helens St Helen 97-00; TV Gateacre 00-09; asst Dioc Dir of Ords 05-09; Leadership Development Adv (Voc) CPAS from 09. *CPAS, Athena Drive, Tachbrook Park, Warwick CV34 6NG* Tel (01926) 458461 E-mail mnorris@cpas.org.uk

NORRIS, Michael Charles Latham. b 69. Reading Univ LLB. Wycliffe Hall Ox 99. **d** 01 **p** 02. C Bryanston Square St Mary w St Marylebone St Mark *Lon* 01-03; V Symonds Street St Paul New Zealand from 04. *PO Box 6349, Wellesley Street, Auckland 1141, New Zealand* Tel (0064) (9) 373 3268
E-mail mikenorris1@hotmail.com

NORTH, Barry Albert. b 46. **d** 82 **p** 83. C Brampton St Thos *Derby* 82-84; C Chesterfield St Aug 84-88; P-in-c Derby St Mark 88-91; R Coalbrookdale, Iron-Bridge and Lt Wenlock *Heref* 91-97; Ch and Community Worker (Manlake Deanery) *Linc* 97-00; Adv for Ch in Soc *Chich* from 00; C Brighton St Mich from 00. *2 Windlesham Road, Brighton BN1 3AG* Tel (01273) 269274 *or* 725806 E-mail barry.north@diochi.org.uk

NORTH, Christopher David. b 69. Trin Coll Bris BA01. **d** 01 **p** 02. C Bathampton w Claverton *B & W* 01-05; P-in-c Chilcompton w Downside and Stratton on the Fosse from 05. *The Rectory, The Street, Chilcompton, Radstock BA3 4HN* Tel (01761) 232219
E-mail chris.north1@tesco.net

NORTH, Preb David Roland. b 45. Lich Th Coll 70 Qu Coll Birm 72. **d** 73 **p** 74. C Salesbury *Blackb* 73-76; C Marton 76-79; C Penwortham St Leon 79-87; R Whittington St Jo *Lich* from 87; P-in-c W Felton from 96; RD Oswestry from 02; Chapl Robert Jones/Agnes Hunt Orthopaedic NHS Trust 00-01; Preb Lich Cathl from 07. *The Rectory, Castle Street, Whittington, Oswestry SY11 4DF* Tel (01691) 652222
E-mail davidnorth@micro-plus-web.net

NORTH, Lyndon Percival. b 55. Lon Bible Coll BA77. NTMTC. **d** 00 **p** 01. NSM Sudbury St Andr *Lon* 00-04 and from 05; C Roxbourne St Andr 04-05. *143 Abbotts Drive, Wembley HA0 3SH* Tel (020) 8904 2408 Mobile 07774-685906
E-mail lyndonnorth@hotmail.com

NORTH, Mark Richard. b 71. St Steph Ho Ox 03. **d** 05 **p** 06. C Sevenoaks St Jo *Roch* from 05. *14 Quakers Hall Lane, Sevenoaks TN13 3TR* Tel (01732) 741691 Mobile 07776-231681
E-mail mark.north@ssho.ox.ac.uk

NORTH, Philip John. b 66. York Univ BA88. St Steph Ho Ox BA91 MA01. **d** 92 **p** 93. C Sunderland St Mary and St Pet *Dur* 92-96; V Hartlepool H Trin 96-02; AD Hartlepool 00-02; P Admin Shrine of Our Lady of Walsingham 02-08; P-in-c Hempton and Pudding Norton 04-07; TR Old St Pancras *Lon* from 08; CMP from 97. *The Rectory, 191 St Pancras Way, London NW1 9NH* Tel (020) 7485 5791 *or* 7485 0724 Mobile 07919-180788 E-mail fr.philip@posp.co.uk

NORTH, Preb Robert. b 54. Lon Univ BSc77. Ripon Coll Cuddesdon 78. **d** 81 **p** 82. C Leominster *Heref* 81-86; TV Heref St Martin w St Fran, Dewsall etc 86-92; P-in-c Heref St Nic 92-97; TR W Heref from 97; Dir of Ords 92-00; Preb Heref Cathl from 94; Dioc Chapl MU from 05. *St Nicholas's Rectory, 76 Breinton Road, Hereford HR4 0JY* Tel (01432) 273810 Pager 07623-476523

NORTH, Canon Vernon Leslie. b 26. Bps' Coll Cheshunt 61. **d** 63 **p** 64. C N Holmwood *Guildf* 63-65; C Dunstable *St Alb* 65-68; V Stotfold 68-91; V Stotfold and Radwell 91-92; RD Shefford 79-91; Hon Can St Alb 89-92; rtd 92; Perm to Offic *Ely* from 96 and *St Alb* from 00. *Hunters Moon, 10 High Street, Little Paxton, St Neots PE19 6HA* Tel (01480) 471146

NORTH, William Walter. b 77. Ox Brookes Univ BA03. St Jo Coll Nottm 07. **d** 09. C N Farnborough *Guildf* from 09. *14 Wilton Court, Farnborough GU14 7EL* Tel 07766-560793 (mobile) E-mail wilnorth@hotmail.com

NORTH INDIA, Moderator of the Church of. *See* LYNGDOH, The Rt Revd Purely

NORTH SYDNEY, Bishop of. *See* DAVIES, The Rt Revd Glenn Naunton

NORTH WEST EUROPE, Archdeacon of. *See* DE WIT, The Ven John

NORTHALL, Malcolm Walter. b 26. Cheshunt Coll Cam 59 Ely Th Coll 63. **d** 64 **p** 65. C Bromsgrove St Jo *Worc* 64-67; V Blockley w Aston Magna *Glouc* 67-82; P-in-c Churchdown 82; V 82-92; rtd 92; Perm to Offic *Ban* from 92. *5 Maethlon Close, Tywyn LL36 0BN* Tel (01654) 710123

NORTHAM, Cavell Herbert James Cavell. *See* CAVELL-NORTHAM, Canon Cavell Herbert James

NORTHAM, Mrs Susan Jillian. b 36. Oak Hill Th Coll 87. **d** 89. NSM Enfield Ch Ch Trent Park *Lon* 89-91; Par Dn 91-94; C 94-97; rtd 97; Perm to Offic *Lon* from 02. *5 Beech Hill Avenue, Barnet EN4 0LW* Tel and fax (020) 8440 2723
E-mail jillandjohn.northam@btinternet.com

NORTHAMPTON, Archdeacon of. *See* ALLSOPP, The Ven Christine

NORTHCOTT, Canon Michael Stafford. b 55. St Chad's Coll Dur BA76 MA77 Sunderland Univ PhD81. St Jo Coll Dur 80. **d** 81 **p** 82. C Chorlton-cum-Hardy St Clem *Man* 81-84; USPG 84-89; Malaysia 84-89; Sen Lect Chr Ethics New Coll Edin Univ 89-91; NSM Edin Old St Paul 89-91; NSM Edin St Jas from 91; TV Edin St Marg 93-96; Can Th Liv Cathl from 05. *8 Dudley Gardens, Edinburgh EH6 4PY* Tel 0131-554 1651
E-mail m.northcott@ed.ac.uk

NORTHCOTT, William Mark. b 36. Clifton Th Coll 61. **d** 64 **p** 65. C Walthamstow St Luke *Chelmsf* 64-68; C Idle *Bradf* 68-70; N Sec CMJ 70-79; V Withnell *Blackb* 79-90; P-in-c Glenrothes *St And* 90-91; Asst Dioc Supernumerary 90-91; Perm to Offic *Blackb* and *Liv* from 91. *34 Welsby Road, Leyland PR25 1JB* Tel (01772) 493932

NORTHERN, Mrs Elaine Joy. b 54. Leic Univ BSc75. SEITE 00. **d** 03 **p** 04. C Snodland All SS w Ch Ch *Roch* 03-08. *Address temp unknown*

NORTHERN LUZON, Bishop of. See SOLIBA, The Most Revd Ignacio Capuyan

NORTHEY (née GANT), Mrs Joanna Elizabeth. b 75. Dur Univ BSc96 Ox Univ PGCE97. Trin Coll Bris BA09. **d** 09. NSM Swindon Ch Ch *Bris* from 09. *58 Upham Road, Swindon SN3 1DN* Tel 07807-188912 (mobile) E-mail joannagant@yahoo.co.uk

NORTHFIELD, Stephen Richmond. b 55. Lon Univ BSc77 Southn Univ BTh84. Sarum & Wells Th Coll 79. **d** 82 **p** 83. C Colchester St Jas, All SS, St Nic and St Runwald *Chelmsf* 82-85; C Chelmsf All SS 85-89; V Ramsey w Lt Oakley and Wrabness 89-95; V Hatfield Peverel w Ulting from 95. *The Vicarage, Church Road, Hatfield Peverel, Chelmsford CM3 2LE* Tel (01245) 380958 E-mail srnorthfield@aol.com

NORTHING, Ross. b 58. St Steph Ho Ox 92. **d** 94 **p** 95. CA from 87; C Up Hatherley *Glouc* 94-98; C Cheltenham St Steph 94-95; C Cheltenham Em w St Steph 95-98; V Stony Stratford *Ox* from 98; R Calverton from 98. *St Mary and St Giles Vicarage, 14 Willow Lane, Stony Stratford, Milton Keynes MK11 1FG* Tel (01908) 562148 Fax 565132 E-mail r.northing@btinternet.com

NORTHOLT, Archdeacon of. See TREWEEK, The Ven Rachel

NORTHOVER, Kevin Charles. b 57. Coll of Resurr Mirfield 89. **d** 91 **p** 92. C Kingston upon Hull St Alb *York* 91-94; V Moorends *Sheff* 94-00; R Guernsey St Michel du Valle *Win* from 00; Vice-Dean Guernsey from 07; Chapl HM Pris Guernsey from 00; CMP from 99. *The Rectory, L'Abbaye, Vale, Guernsey GY3 5SF* Tel (01481) 244088 E-mail frkevin@cwgsy.net

NORTHRIDGE, Herbert Aubrey Hamilton. b 16. TCD BA40 MA43. **d** 41 **p** 42. C Londonderry Ch Ch *D & R* 41-45; P-in-c Convoy 45-47; I 47-50; I Derg 50-70; I Derg w Termonamongan 70-81; Can Derry Cathl 72-81; rtd 81. *Goblusk, Ballinamallard BT94 2LW* Tel (028) 6638 8676

NORTHUMBERLAND, Archdeacon of. See MILLER, The Ven Geoffrey Vincent

NORTHWOOD, Michael Alan. b 36. Lon Univ BSc60 MInstP69. Wells Th Coll 62. **d** 64 **p** 65. C Eastbourne St Mary *Chich* 64-66; C Sanderstead All SS *S'wark* 66-68; P-in-c Alton Barnes w Alton Priors etc *Sarum* 69-75; Lic to Offic 76-86; Perm to Offic *Ox* 86-09; rtd 10. *The Garth, 31 Mill Road, Marlow SL7 1QB* Tel (01628) 488646 Fax 488649 Mobile 07836-372021 E-mail michael@mmsolutions.com

NORTON, Andrew. See NORTON, John Colin

NORTON, Anthony Bernard. b 40. Man Univ BA62. Linc Th Coll 63. **d** 65 **p** 66. C Westbury-on-Trym H Trin *Bris* 65-68; C Bris St Agnes w St Simon 68-70; P-in-c Bris St Werburgh 70-72; TV Bris St Agnes and St Simon w St Werburgh 72-77; V Lakenham St Alb *Nor* 77-85; TV Trunch 85-93; TV Halesworth w Linstead, Chediston, Holton etc *St E* 93-99; TV Blyth Valley 99-05; RD Halesworth 98-01; rtd 05; Perm to Offic *St E* 06-08; P-in-c Heveningham from 08. *6 Bramblewood Way, Halesworth IP19 8JT* Tel (01986) 875374 E-mail anthonynorton@btinternet.com

NORTON, Benjamin James. b 80. Hull Univ BTh05. St Jo Coll Nottm 06. **d** 07 **p** 08. C Bridlington Em *York* from 07. *40 Georgian Way, Bridlington YO15 3TB* Tel (01262) 678133 Mobile 07780-606314 E-mail thepartycanstart@yahoo.co.uk

NORTON, Howard John. b 41. Fitzw Coll Cam BA64 MA68. S'wark Ord Course 78 St Jo Coll Nottm 79. **d** 80 **p** 81. C Sutton Ch Ch *S'wark* 80-82; C Morden 82-84; V Motspur Park 84-88; Perm to Offic *Chich* from 03. *Gladstone House, 8 Coburg Place, Hastings TN34 3HY*

NORTON, James Herbert Kitchener. b 37. Qu Coll Birm 78. **d** 81 **p** 82. NSM Donnington Wood *Lich* 81-83; C Matson *Glouc* 83-86; V New Mills *Derby* 86-96; RD Glossop 93-96; TR Buxton w Burbage and King Sterndale 96-02; RD Buxton 99-02; rtd 02; Perm to Offic *Derby* from 02; P-in-c Lt Drayton *Lich* from 04. *Heather Glen, 11 Ellis Peter's Drive, Telford TF3 1AW* Tel (01952) 595343 Mobile 07879-470172 E-mail jhknorton@lineone.net

NORTON, John Colin (Andrew). b 25. Magd Coll Ox BA50 MA54. Cuddesdon Coll 50. **d** 52 **p** 53. C Bris St Mary Redcliffe w Temple 52-57; C Bitterne Park *Win* 57-63; C-in-c Bishopwearmouth St Mary V w St Pet CD *Dur* 63-68; V Clifton All SS w Tyndalls Park *Bris* 68-78; Hon Can Bris Cathl 77-80; V Clifton All SS w St Jo 78-80; V Penistone *Wakef* 80-83; CR from 85; rtd 95. *House of the Resurrection, Stocks Bank Road, Mirfield WF14 0BN* Tel (01924) 494318

NORTON, Mrs Lesley Gillian. b 47. STETS 99. **d** 02 **p** 03. NSM Kinson *Sarum* 02-06; TV Harlow Town Cen w Lt Parndon

Chelmsf from 06. *The Vicarage, 4A The Drive, Harlow CM20 3QD* Tel (01279) 439721 E-mail blgnorton@btinternet.com

NORTON (or HARCOURT-NORTON), Michael Clive Harcourt. b 34. Selw Coll Cam BA58 MA60 Union Th Sem (NY) STM69 Univ of NSW MCom81 MACE84. Wells Th Coll 56 Bossey Ecum Inst Geneva 57. **d** 58 **p** 59. C Gt Ilford St Jo *Chelmsf* 58-62; NSW Sec Aus Coun Chs Australia 62-68; C Manhattan St Steph USA 68-69; C-in-c Mortdale Australia 69-77; R 77-79; Assoc Chapl and Hd RS Cranbrook Sch Sydney 79-85; R Hunter's Hill 85-00; rtd 00. *7 Dulwich Road, Chatswood NSW 2067, Australia* Tel (0061) (2) 9411 8606 Fax 9410 2069 Mobile 417-041719 E-mail chnorton@bigpond.com

NORTON, Michael James Murfin. b 42. Lich Th Coll 66. **d** 67 **p** 68. C W Bromwich St Fran *Lich* 67-70; C Wellington Ch Ch 70-72; C Norwood All SS *Cant* 72-76; V Elstow *St Alb* 76-82; Asst Chapl HM Pris Wakef 82-83; Chapl HM Pris Camp Hill 83-86; Parkhurst 86-88; Win 88-93; V Somborne w Ashley *Win* 93-03; rtd 03. *Bryneirian, Penparc, Cardigan SA43 1RG* Tel (01239) 623512 E-mail revmnorton@aol.com

NORTON, Paul James. b 55. Oak Hill Th Coll BA86. **d** 86 **p** 87. C Luton St Fran *St Alb* 86-89; C Bedworth *Cov* 89-95; TV Hitchin *St Alb* 95-02; V Portsdown *Portsm* 03-07; rtd 07. *23 Oxford Road, Southsea PO5 1NP*

NORTON, Canon Peter Eric Pepler. b 38. TCD BA61 G&C Coll Cam PhD64. Cranmer Hall Dur 78. **d** 80 **p** 81. C Ulverston St Mary w H Trin *Carl* 80-83; P-in-c Warcop, Musgrave, Soulby and Crosby Garrett 83-84; R 84-90; OCF 83-90; V Appleby and R Ormside *Carl* 90-04; P-in-c Kirkby Thore w Temple Sowerby and Newbiggin 01-04; RD Appleby and Hon Can Carl Cathl 00-04; rtd 04; Perm to Offic *Nor* 05-08. *Ard na Cree, Church Hill, Wicklow, Co Wicklow, Republic of Ireland* Tel (00353) (404) 62648 Mobile 07802-334575 E-mail pepnorton@gmail.com

NORTON, Sam Charles. b 70. Trin Coll Ox BA92 MA99 Heythrop Coll Lon MA00. Westcott Ho Cam 97. **d** 99 **p** 00. C Stepney St Dunstan and All SS *Lon* 99-02; R W w E Mersea *Chelmsf* from 03; P-in-c Peldon w Gt and Lt Wigborough from 03. *93 Kingsland Road, West Mersea, Colchester CO5 8AG* Tel (01206) 385635 E-mail elizaphanian@hotmail.com

NORTON (née FISHER), Mrs Susan Alexandra. b 54. Man Univ BA75 Hughes Hall Cam PGCE76. NEOC 01. **d** 04 **p** 05. NSM York St Olave w St Giles from 04; NSM York St Helen w St Martin from 04. *21 Wentworth Road, York YO24 1DG* Tel (01904) 634911 E-mail e.norton@tinyworld.co.uk

NORTON, William Fullerton. b 23. Selw Coll Cam BA46 MA52. Wycliffe Hall Ox 46. **d** 48 **p** 49. C Leic H Apostles 48-52; C Singapore St Matt 52-54; Miss Selangor Malaya 54-56; Miss Kampong Tanas 56-60; V Ipoh St Pet 60-63; R Manila St Steph Philippines 63-66; C Homerton St Luke *Lon* 67; C Tooting Graveney St Nic *S'wark* 68-71; V Hanley Road St Sav w St Paul *Lon* 71-89; rtd 89. *Charlesworth Nursing Home, 37 Beaconsfield Villas, Brighton BN1 6HB* Tel (01273) 565561

NORWICH, Archdeacon of. See McFARLANE, The Ven Janet Elizabeth

NORWICH, Bishop of. See JAMES, The Rt Revd Graham Richard

NORWICH, Dean of. See SMITH, The Very Revd Graham Charles Morell

NORWOOD, Andrew David. b 65. Lon Bible Coll BA91. Cranmer Hall Dur 92. **d** 94 **p** 95. C Headingley *Ripon* 94-97; C Handsworth St Mary *Birm* 97-00; Perm to Offic *Lon* 01-02; Chapl Chelsea Coll from 02; Perm to Offic *S'wark* from 06. *11 Ormonde Mansions, 106 Southampton Row, London WC1B 4BP* Tel (020) 7242 7533 or 7514 6230 E-mail a.norwood@arts.ac.uk or a.norwood@csm.linst.ac.uk

NORWOOD, David John. b 40. SS Paul & Mary Coll Cheltenham BEd82. Linc Th Coll 65. **d** 68 **p** 69. C Hitchin St Mary *St Alb* 68-71; P-in-c Luanshya Zambia 72-76; C Littlehampton St Jas *Chich* 76-77; P-in-c Chacewater *Truro* 77-79; Chapl N Cornwall Hosp Treliske 77-79; Hd RE Red Maids Sch Bris 82-85; Appeals Organiser Children's Soc 86-94; P-in-c Clarkston *Glas* 94-96; R 96-99; R Dalbeattie 99-05; rtd 05. *Dove Cottage, Wellfield Terrace, Ferryside SA17 5DD* Tel (01267) 267125 E-mail norwoods@talktalk.net

NORWOOD, Paul James. b 71. **d** 08. OLM S Lynn *Nor* from 08. *46 Tennyson Avenue, King's Lynn PE30 2QJ* Tel (01553) 777455 Mobile 07720-806318 E-mail pjandcas.norwood@virgin.net

NORWOOD, Canon Philip Geoffrey Frank. b 39. Em Coll Cam BA62 MA66. Cuddesdon Coll 63. **d** 65 **p** 66. C New Addington *Cant* 65-69; Abp's Dom Chapl 69-72; V Hollingbourne 72-78; P-in-c Wormshill and Huckinge 74-78; V St Laur in Thanet 78-88; RD Thanet 86-88; V Spalding *Linc* 88-98; RD Elloe W 96-98; R Blakeney w Cley, Wiveton, Glandford etc *Nor* 98-05; RD Holt 02-05; Hon Can Nor Cathl 03-05; rtd 05. *30 Home Close Road, Houghton-on-the-Hill, Leicester LE7 9GT* Tel 0116-241 0255 E-mail philipandannenorwood@hotmail.com

NORWOOD, Robert William. b 38. Keble Coll Ox BA71 MA71 Lon Univ TCert64 Lambeth STh83. **d** 01 **p** 03. NSM St Pancras

H Cross w St Jude and St Pet *Lon* from 01; Perm to Offic *Chelmsf* from 08. *Carlton Court, 11A Hermon Hill, London E11 2AR* Tel (020) 8530 2493

NORWOOD, Timothy. b 70. Aber Univ BD94. Westcott Ho Cam 95. **d** 97 **p** 98. C Upton cum Chalvey *Ox* 97-00; TV Watling Valley from 00; AD Milton Keynes from 06. *3 Daubeney Gate, Shenley Church End, Milton Keynes MK5 6EH* Tel (01908) 505812 E-mail tim@thenorwoods.fsnet.co.uk

NOTLEY, Michael James. b 41. St Edm Hall Ox BA63 MA68 DipEd64. EMMTC 84. **d** 87 **p** 88. NSM Oadby *Leic* 87-96; P-in-c Holbeach Marsh *Linc* 96-06; P-in-c Lutton w Gedney Drove End, Dawsmere 96-06; rtd 06. *38 St John's Drive, Corby Glen, Grantham NG33 4NG* Tel (01476) 550721

NOTT, Canon George Thomas Michael. b 34. Ex Coll Ox BA58 MA62 Birm Univ MEd88 Cov Univ PhD95. Coll of Resurr Mirfield. **d** 60 **p** 61. C Solihull *Birm* 60-69; Chapl K Sch Worc and Min Can Worc Cathl 69-77; P-in-c Worc St Nic and Children's Officer 77-87; P-in-c Worc St Andr and All SS w St Helen 82-84; Droitwich Spa 87-89; V Broadheath, Crown East and Rushwick 89-04; Chapl Worc Coll of HE 89-96; RD Martley and Worc W 95-03; Hon Can Worc Cathl 99-04; P-in-c Worc St Mich 00-01; rtd 04. *17 Wirlpiece Avenue, Worcester WR4 0NF* Tel (01905) 729494
E-mail mnott17@btinternet.com

✠**NOTT, The Rt Revd Peter John.** b 33. Fitzw Ho Cam BA61 MA65. Westcott Ho Cam 58. **d** 61 **p** 62 **c** 77. C Harpenden St Nic *St Alb* 61-64; Chapl Fitzw Coll Cam 64-69; Fell 66-69; Chapl New Hall Cam 66-69; R Beaconsfield *Ox* 69-76; TR 76-77; Preb Wells Cathl 77-85; Suff Bp Taunton 77-85; Bp Nor 85-99; rtd 99; Hon Asst Bp Ox from 99. *Westcot House, Westcot, Wantage OX12 9QA* Tel (01235) 751233
E-mail peternott@btinternet.com

NOTT, Philip James. b 69. Nottm Trent Univ BA92. Ridley Hall Cam 95. **d** 98 **p** 99. C Kersal Moor *Man* 98-01; C Ealing St Mary *Lon* 01-04; Chapl Thames Valley Univ 01-04; P-in-c Broxtowe *S'well* 04-06; P-in-c Easton H Trin w St Gabr and St Lawr and St Jude *Bris* from 06; Min Inner City Partnership from 06. *The Vicarage, 69 Stapleton Road, Bristol BS5 0QQ* Tel 0117-955 4255 E-mail rev@ecfc.org.uk

NOTTAGE, Preb Terence John. b 36. Oak Hill Th Coll 62. **d** 65 **p** 66. C Finchley St Paul Long Lane 65-68; C Edgware 68-72; V Harlesden St Mark 72-86; V Kensal Rise St Mark and St Martin 86; TR Plymouth Em w Efford *Ex* 86-92; P-in-c Laira 88-92; TR Plymouth Em, St Paul Efford and St Aug 93-96; Preb Ex Cathl from 96; Adv for Voc and Dioc Dir of Ords 96-01; rtd 01. *4 Keyberry Close, Newton Abbot TQ12 1DA* Tel (01626) 332277
E-mail terry.nottage@tesco.net

NOTTINGHAM, Archdeacon of. *See* HILL, The Ven Peter

NOVELL, Jill. b 49. Bris Univ BA72 Open Univ MA89 St Martin's Coll Lanc PGCE77. CBDTI 01. **d** 04 **p** 05. NSM Silverdale *Blackb* from 04. *29 Hall Park, Lancaster LA1 4SH* Tel (01524) 381046

NOVIS, Timothy Wellington George. b 70. Trin Coll Toronto BA93 MDiv96. **d** 96 **p** 96. C Guelph St Geo Canada 96-98; R Hornby St Steph 98-05; Chapl Ridley Coll 05-08; Chapl Wellington Coll Berks from 08. *Chapel Hill, Wellington College, Crowthorne RG45 7PT* Tel (01344) 444104
E-mail twgn@wellingtoncollege.org.uk

NOWAK, Jurek Anthony (George). b 47. N I M TC 04. **d** 07. NSM Edmonton St Mary w St Jo *Lon* from 07. *138 Dysons Road, London N18 2DJ* Tel (020) 8884 0903 Mobile 07944-854617
E-mail jurek-n@dysons.demon.co.uk

NOWELL, Canon John David. b 44. AKC67. **d** 68 **p** 69. C Lindley *Wakef* 68-70; C Lightcliffe 70-72; V Wyke *Bradf* 72-80; V Silsden 80-92; V Baildon from 92; Hon Can Bradf Cathl from 00. *The Vicarage, Baildon, Shipley BD17 6BY* Tel and fax (01274) 594941

NOWÉN, Lars Fredrik. b 71. Summit Pacific Coll BC BTh93 Regent Coll Vancouver MCS98. **d** 98 **p** 99. Dn Halifax St Geo Canada 98-99; P-in-c Meadow Lake and Loon Lake 99-04; C Pelton and W Pelton *Dur* 04-07; P-in-c St Bees *Carl* from 07; Chapl St Bees Sch Cumbria from 07. *The Priory, St Bees CA27 0DR* Tel (01946) 822279
E-mail lars_nowen@hotmail.com

NOY, Frederick William Vernon. b 47. Sarum Th Coll 67. **d** 71 **p** 72. C Swindon St Jo *Bris* 71-75; Chapl to the Deaf *Sarum* 75-80; P-in-c Stinsford, Winterborne Came w Whitcombe etc 76-80; Perm to Offic 80-08. *54 Casterbridge Road, Dorchester DT1 2AG* Tel (01305) 264269

NOYCE, Colin Martley. b 45. Brasted Th Coll 73 Ridley Hall Cam 74. **d** 76 **p** 77. C Cambridge St Jas *Ely* 76-78; Chapl RN 78-82; R Mistley w Manningtree *Chelmsf* 82-86; Miss to Seamen Kenya 86-89; Trinidad and Tobago 89-90; V Four Marks *Win* 90-99; Chapl Pilgrims Hospices E Kent 99-01; Chapl and Dir Ch Ch and Ras Morbat Clinics Yemen 01-03; Chapl Limassol St Barn and Miss to Seafarers 03-05; rtd 05; Perm to Offic *Chelmsf* 06-09 and *Portsm* from 08. *64 Whitwell Road, Southsea PO4 0QS* Tel (023) 9275 3517 E-mail candinoyce@sky.com

NOYCE, Graham Peter. b 62. Bedf Coll Lon BSc84. Trin Coll Bris BA92. **d** 92 **p** 93. C Sketty *S & B* 92-94; C Swansea St Jas 94-96; C Kensal Rise St Mark and St Martin *Lon* 96-04; TV from 04. *26 Ashburnham Road, London NW10 5SD* Tel (020) 8960 6211 E-mail graham@noycefamily.co.uk

NOYES, Roger. b 39. Linc Th Coll 65. **d** 67 **p** 68. C Adel *Ripon* 67-70; Chapl Aldenham Sch Herts 70-74; V Aldborough w Boroughbridge and Roecliffe *Ripon* 74-89; Rural Min Adv 89-90; Perm to Offic from 91; rtd 04. *Rose Cottage, Moor End, Nun Monkton, York YO26 8EN* Tel (01423) 330846
E-mail r.noyes1@btinternet.com

NSENGA-NGOY, Lusambo. b 77. Cranmer Hall Dur. **d** 08 **p** 09. C Staplehurst *Cant* from 08. *5 Oliver Road, Staplehurst, Tonbridge TN12 0TE* Tel (01580) 892324
E-mail lusansenga@gmail.com

NSHIMYE, Stephen Kamegeri. b 60. Bp Lutaya Th Coll Uganda 88. **d** 90 **p** 91. C Kamusemene Uganda 90-91; C Kigalama 92-93; C Nyagatovu Rwanda 94-99; Perm to Offic *S'wark* 02-05. *58 Hickin Close, London SE7 8SH* Tel (020) 8858 0624 Mobile 07950-346477

✠**NTAHOTURI, The Most Revd Bernard.** b 48. St Jo Coll Cam MA. Bp Tucker Coll Mukono 68. **d** 73 **c** 97. Burundi from 73; Bp Matana from 97; Abp Burundi from 05. *BP 447, Bujumbura, Burundi* Tel (00257) (2) 70361 Fax 29129
E-mail ntahober@cbinf.com

NTEGE, Nathan Kasolo. b 59. **d** 87 **p** 89. C St Paul's Cathl Namirembe Uganda 87-91; Bp Tucker Coll Mukono 91-94; V Luzira and Kabowa 94-96; Perm to Offic *S'wark* 97-02; P-in-c Thornton Heath St Jude w St Aid 02-07; V from 07. *St Jude's Vicarage, 11 Dunheved Road North, Thornton Heath CR7 6AH* Tel (020) 8665 5564 Mobile 07904-197329

NTOYIMONDO, Samuel. b 54. Wolv Univ BA05. Butare Th Sch Rwanda 80 All Nations Chr Coll BA02. **d** 84 **p** 87. Pastor Mutunda Rwanda 84-87; Pastor Butare 87-92; Dioc Sec Kigeme 92-94; Germany 96-99; Perm to Offic *Birm* from 08. *173 Perrywood Road, Great Barr, Birmingham B42 2BL* Tel 0121-358 6474 Mobile 07908-207085
E-mail finasando@yahoo.co.uk

NUDDS, Douglas John. b 24. St Aid Birkenhead 48. **d** 51 **p** 52. C E Dereham w Hoe *Nor* 51-55; C Birstall *Leic* 55-58; V Bardon Hill 58-62; V Belgrave St Mich 62-68; Chapl Leic R Infirmary 68-72; High Royds Hosp Menston 72-79; V Bradf St Wilfrid Lidget Green 79-84; Lic to Offic *St Alb* 84-93; Chapl Shenley Hosp Radlett Herts 84-89; rtd 89; Perm to Offic *Nor* from 89. *Longview, Southgate Close, Wells-next-the-Sea NR23 1HG* Tel (01328) 711926

NUGENT, Canon Alan Hubert. b 42. Dur Univ BA65 MA78. Wycliffe Hall Ox 65 United Th Coll Bangalore 66. **d** 67 **p** 68. C Mossley Hill St Matt and St Jas *Liv* 67-71; C Bridgnorth St Mary *Heref* 71-72; Chapl Dur Univ 72-78; P-in-c Bishopwearmouth Ch 78-85; P-in-c Brancepeth 85-94; Dioc Dir of Educn 85-97; Hon Can Dur Cathl 86-97; Dir of Miss and Tr Development Forum *Linc* 97-03; Can and Preb Linc Cathl 98-03; Can Res and Subdean Linc Cathl from 03. *The Subdeanery, 18 Minster Yard, Lincoln LN2 1RU* Tel (01522) 521932 or 523113 E-mail subdean@lincolncathedral.com

NUGENT, David Richard. b 54. MInstPS84 Liv Poly BA87. Oak Hill Th Coll BA95. **d** 95 **p** 96. C Birkenhead St Jas w St Bede *Ches* 95-99; V Blundellsands St Mich *Liv* 99-02; Asst Chapl Wirral and W Cheshire Community NHS Trust 02-03; Asst Chapl Cheshire and Wirral Partnerships NHS Trust from 03. *Chaplains' Office, Clatterbridge Hospital, Clatterbridge Road, Wirral CH63 4JY* Tel 0151-334 4000
E-mail dave.nugent@whnt.nhs.uk

NUGENT, Eric William. b 26. Bps' Coll Cheshunt 56. **d** 58 **p** 59. C Rochford *Chelmsf* 58-61; C Eastwood 61-62; C-in-c Eastwood St Dav CD 62-66; V Eastwood St Dav 66-79; P-in-c Weeley 79-81; V Lt Clacton 80-81; R Weeley and Lt Clacton 81-93; rtd 93; Perm to Offic *Chelmsf* from 93. *1 King's Court, King's Road, Dovercourt, Harwich CO12 4DS* Tel (01255) 552640

NUNN, Ms Alice Candida. b 52. Ripon Coll Cuddesdon 95. **d** 97 **p** 98. C Margate St Jo *Cant* 97-01; V Winterton Gp *Linc* from 01. *The Vicarage, High Street, Winterton, Scunthorpe DN15 9PU* Tel (01724) 732262

NUNN, Canon Andrew Peter. b 57. Leic Poly BA79 Leeds Univ BA82. Coll of Resurr Mirfield 80. **d** 83 **p** 84. C Manston *Ripon* 83-87; C Leeds Richmond Hill 87-91; Chapl Agnes Stewart C of E High Sch Leeds 87-95; V Leeds Richmond Hill *Ripon* 91-95; Personal Asst to Bp S'wark 95-99; Hon PV S'wark Cathl 95-99; Sub-Dean, Prec and Can Res S'wark Cathl from 99; Dioc Warden of Readers from 01. *73 St George's Road, London SE1 6ER* Tel (020) 7735 8322 or 7367 6727 Fax 7367 6725 Mobile 07961-332051
E-mail andrew.nunn@southwark.anglican.org

NUNN, Mrs Christine Jane. b 47. **d** 05 **p** 06. NSM Kesgrave *St E* from 05. *37 Bracken Avenue, Kesgrave, Ipswich IP5 2PP* Tel (01473) 622363

NUNN, Peter. b 32. Kelham Th Coll 53. **d** 57 **p** 58. C Wigan St Geo *Liv* 57-60; C Warrington St Elphin 60-62; V Warrington

St Pet 62-65; Chapl Winwick Hosp Warrington 65-90; rtd 90; Perm to Offic *Liv* from 90. *9 Derby House, Scholes, Wigan WN1 3RN* Tel (01942) 235407

NUNN, Canon Peter Michael. b 38. MBE98. Sarum Th Coll 64. **d** 66 **p** 67. C Hornsey St Geo *Lon* 66-71; C Cleator Moor w Cleator *Carl* 71-72; V Carl St Luke Morton 72-79; V Wotton St Mary *Glouc* 79-02; Offg Chapl RAF 80-97; RD Glouc City 88-94; Hon Can Glouc Cathl 90-02; rtd 02; Perm to Offic *Chich* from 02. *87 South Street, Tarring, Worthing BN14 7ND* Tel (01903) 233748

NUNN, Peter Rawling. b 51. St Cath Coll Ox BA73 Sheff Univ MSc74. Oak Hill Th Coll BA85. **d** 85 **p** 86. C Bispham *Blackb* 85-87; C-in-c Anchorsholme 87-89; V 89-08; P-in-c Preston Risen Lord from 08. *St Matthew's Vicarage, 20 Fishwick View, Preston PR1 4YA*

NUNN, Richard Ernest. b 38. SAOMC 96. **d** 99 **p** 00. NSM Maidenhead St Luke *Ox* 99-02; NSM Waltham St Lawrence 02-07; rtd 07; Perm to Offic *Ox* from 07 and *Win* from 08. *5 Glebe Fields, Milford on Sea, Lymington SO41 0WW* Tel (01590) 643118

NUNNERLEY, William John Arthur. b 27. Univ of Wales (Lamp) BA54. St Chad's Coll Dur. **d** 56 **p** 57. C Tredegar St Geo *Mon* 56-60; Chapl RN 60-81; QHC from 79; R Barnoldby le Beck *Linc* 81-92; R Waltham 81-92; rtd 92; Perm to Offic *B & W* from 00. *Juniper Cottage, 82B Lower Street, Merriott TA16 5NW* Tel (01460) 76049

NUNNEY, Sheila Frances. b 49. SRN74 RSCN74 SCM75. Oak Hill Th Coll BA92. **d** 92 **p** 94. C Swaffham *Nor* 92-96; Chapl Asst Norfolk and Nor Health Care NHS Trust 96-00; Chapl 00-01; Chapl Norfolk Community Health and Care 01-09; Chapl Norfolk & Waveney Mental Health NHS Foundn Trust 03-09; rtd 09; Perm to Offic *Nor* from 09. *43A Chestnut Hill, Eaton, Norwich NR4 6NL* Tel (01603) 507110
E-mail sfn60@btinternet.com

NURSER, Canon John Shelley. b 29. Peterho Cam BA50 MA54 PhD58. Wells Th Coll 58. **d** 58 **p** 59. C Tankersley *Sheff* 58-61; Dean Trin Hall Cam 61-68; Australia 68-74; R Freckenham w Worlington *St E* 74-76; Can Res and Chan Linc Cathl 76-92; Can and Preb Linc Cathl 92-94; P-in-c Shudy Camps *Ely* 92-94; rtd 94; Perm to Offic *St E* from 94 and *Ely* from 00. *68 Friars Street, Sudbury CO10 2AG* Tel (01787) 378595

NURSEY (née HYLTON), Mrs Jane Lois. b 56. Leeds Univ BA78. **d** 07 **p** 08. OLM Dereham and Distr *Nor* from 07. *34 Allwood Avenue, Scarning, Dereham NR19 2TF* Tel (01362) 697058 E-mail nursey1@btinternet.com

NURTON, Robert. b 44. Univ of Wales (Lamp) BA67. Ridley Hall Cam 67. **d** 69 **p** 70. C Bris St Andr Hartcliffe 69-73; C Ipswich St Mary at Stoke w St Pet etc *St E* 73-77; Chapl RN 77-99; Chapl Morden Coll Blackheath 99-09; rtd 09. *The Thatched Cottage, High Road, Great Finborough, Stowmarket IP14 3AQ* Tel (01449) 674396

NUTH, Stephen William. b 55. St Jo Coll Nottm 93. **d** 95 **p** 96. C Wadhurst and Stonegate *Chich* 95-99; R Marks Tey and Aldham *Chelmsf* 99-01; Perm to Offic *St E* 01-04; P-in-c Woburn w Eversholt, Milton Bryan, Battlesden etc *St Alb* 04-08; V from 08. *The Vicarage, Park Street, Woburn, Milton Keynes MK17 9PG* Tel (01525) 290225
E-mail stephen.nuth@googlemail.com

NUTT, Susan Mary. b 45. **d** 99 **p** 00. OLM Blackbourne *St E* from 99. *Portelet, Blacksmith Lane, Barnham, Thetford IP24 2NE* Tel (01842) 890409 E-mail revdsuenutt@hotmail.com

NUTTALL, George Herman. b 31. St Jo Coll Dur BA59. Cranmer Hall Dur 59. **d** 61 **p** 62. C Eccleshill *Bradf* 61-65; V Oldham St Barn *Man* 65-70; Area Sec CMS *Derby* and *Lich* 70-81; V Derby St Aug 81-84; Chapl Bournemouth and Poole Coll of FE *Sarum* 85-97; Chapl Dorset Inst of HE 85-90; Chapl Bournemouth Poly *Win* 90-92; Chapl Bournemouth Univ 92-97; rtd 97; Perm to Offic *Sarum* 97-03 and *Carl* from 03. *Orchard End, 91 Silverdale Road, Arnside, Carnforth LA5 0EH* Tel (01524) 760001

NUTTALL, Michael John Berkeley. b 36. K Coll Lon AKC60. St Boniface Warminster 61. **d** 61 **p** 62. C Chapel Allerton *Ripon* 61-64; C Stanningley St Thos 64-68; V Leeds Gipton Epiphany 68-76; P-in-c Stainby w Gunby *Linc* 76-83; R N Witham 76-83; R S Witham 76-83; TV Bottesford w Ashby 83-88; I Adare w Kilpeacon and Croom *L & K* 88-94; I Adare and Kilmallock w Kilpeacon, Croom etc 94-01; Chapl Limerick Univ 88-95; Adn Limerick 92-01; rtd 01. *11 Cluaindara, Anglesborough, Kilmallock, Co Limerick, Republic of Ireland* Tel (00353) (62) 46280 Mobile 87-904 5738
E-mail adnmichaelnuttall@yahoo.com

NUZUM, Daniel Robert. b 73. RGN94 TCD BTh99. **d** 99 **p** 00. C Bandon Union *C, C & R* 99-01; I Templebreedy w Tracton and Nohoval 02-09; Chapl Cork Univ Hosp from 09. *Cork University Hospital, Wilton, Cork, Republic of Ireland* Tel (00353) (21) 454 6400

NWAEKWE, Augustine Ugochukwu. b 75. Leuven Univ Belgium MA07. St Paul's Univ Coll Awka Nigeria 95. **d** 98 **p** 00. Lic to Offic Dio Mbaise Nigeria 98-04; Asst Chapl Brussels *Eur* from

06. *rue Capitaine Crespel 29, 1050 Brussels, Belgium* Tel (0032) (2) 511 7183 Fax 511 1028 Mobile 48-499 5790
E-mail augustine.nwaekwe@htbrussels.com

NYATSANZA, Petros Hamutendi. b 69. Redcliffe Coll Glouc BA04. Bp Gaul Th Coll Harare 95. **d** 95 **p** 96. Zimbabwe 95-01; C Greendale St Luke 95-96; C Highfields St Paul 96-97; R Mufakose St Luke 97-01; Perm to Offic *Glouc* 02-04; P-in-c Rounds Green *Birm* 04-08; V Goodmayes All SS *Chelmsf* from 08. *All Saints' Vicarage, 38 Broomshill Road, Ilford IG3 9SJ* Tel (020) 8590 1476 Mobile 07877-841643
E-mail petrosnyatsanza@yahoo.co.uk

NYE, Canon David Charles. b 39. K Coll Lon BD65 Glos Univ MA01. **d** 63 **p** 64. C Charlton Kings St Mary *Glouc* 63-67; C Yeovil St Jo w Preston Plucknett *B & W* 67-70; V Lower Cam *Glouc* 70-74; Min Can Glouc Cathl 74-79; Dir of Ords 74-79; Prin Glouc Th Course 74-79; V Glouc St Mary de Lode and St Nic 74-76; V Maisemore 76-79; Chapl Grenville Coll Bideford 79-81; V Leckhampton SS Phil and Jas w Cheltenham St Jas *Glouc* 81-95; Hon Can Glouc Cathl 88-04; RD Cheltenham 89-95; P-in-c Northleach w Hampnett and Farmington 95-00; P-in-c Cold Aston w Notgrove and Turkdean 95-00; R Northleach w Hampnett and Farmington etc 00-04; RD Northleach 99-04; rtd 04. *2 Old Burford Road, Bledington, Chipping Norton OX7 6US* Tel (01608) 659140
E-mail tisnyes@tiscali.co.uk

O

OADES, Debbie Gaynor. b 63. Middx Univ BA06. NTMTC 03. **d** 06 **p** 07. C Hounslow W Gd Shep *Lon* 06-08; NSM Hampton Hill from 08. *41 Brightside Avenue, Staines TW18 1NE* Tel (01784) 490186 E-mail debbieoades@hotmail.com

OADES, Michael Anthony John. b 45. Brasted Th Coll 69 Sarum & Wells Th Coll 71. **d** 73 **p** 74. C Eltham Park St Luke *S'wark* 73-78; C Coulsdon St Andr 78-81; P-in-c Merton St Jas 81-86; V 86-87; V Benhilton from 87. *All Saints' Vicarage, All Saints' Road, Sutton SM1 3DA* Tel (020) 8644 9070

OADES, Canon Peter Robert. b 24. Fitzw Ho Cam BA47 CertEd48 MA53. **d** 67 **p** 67. C Warblington w Emsworth *Portsm* 67-68; V Choral Sarum Cathl 68-74; Chapl Salisbury Cathl Sch 68-74; P-in-c Sturminster Newton and Hinton St Mary *Sarum* 74-75; V Stock and Lydlinch 75-81; RD Blackmore Vale 78-81; V Woodford Valley 81-89; Can and Preb Sarum Cathl 85-89; rtd 89; Hon Chapl to the Deaf *Sarum* 82-92; Perm to Offic *Sarum* and *Win* from 89. *28 Mulberry Gardens, Fordingbridge SP6 1BP* Tel (01425) 657113

OAKE, Canon Barry Richard. b 47. MRICS71. Ripon Coll Cuddesdon 83. **d** 85 **p** 86. C Wantage *Ox* 85-88; C Warlingham w Chelsham and Farleigh *S'wark* 88-91; R N w S Wootton *Nor* 91-05; R Thorpe St Andr from 05; Asst Chapl among Deaf and Hearing-Impaired People from 01; Hon Can Nor Cathl from 07. *The Rectory, 56A Thunder Lane, Norwich NR7 0JW* Tel (01603) 433578

OAKES, Graham. b 42. Chich Th Coll 68. **d** 70 **p** 71. C Hulme Ascension *Man* 70-74; C Clifton All SS w Tyndalls Park *Bris* 74-76; P-in-c Chadderton St Mark *Man* 76-79; V 79-82; V King Cross *Wakef* 82-95; R Bath H Trin *B & W* 95-07; Chapl R United Hosp Bath NHS Trust 99-07; rtd 07. *3 Friary Close, Clevedon BS21 7QA* Tel (01275) 343822
E-mail revd@goakes.fsbusiness.co.uk

OAKES, Miss Jennifer May. b 43. Trin Coll Bris 78. **dss** 82 **d** 87 **p** 94. Wilncote *Lich* 82-85; Stoneydelph St Martin CD 82-85; Bentley 85-89; Par Dn 87-89; Par Dn Hixon w Stowe-by-Chartley 89-94; C 94-98; Par Dn Fradswell, Gayton, Milwich and Weston 93-94; C 94-98; P-in-c Standon and Cotes Heath 98-00; rtd 03; Hon C Alfrick, Lulsley, Suckley, Leigh and Bransford *Worc* 03-04; Perm to Offic *Lich* from 05. *Willow Rise, Ashbourne Road, Whiston, Stoke-on-Trent ST10 2JE* Tel (01538) 260013 E-mail oaklud@supanet.com

OAKES, Canon Jeremy Charles. b 51. ACA75 FCA81. Westcott Ho Cam 75. **d** 78 **p** 79. C Evington *Leic* 78-81; C Ringwood *Win* 81-84; P-in-c Thurnby Lodge *Leic* 84-89; TV Oakdale *Sarum* 89-95; P-in-c Canford Cliffs and Sandbanks 95-03; V from 03; Can and Preb Sarum Cathl from 03. *The Vicarage, 14 Flaghead Road, Canford Cliffs, Poole BH13 7JW* Tel and fax (01202) 700341 E-mail jeremy.oakes@virgin.net

OAKES, John Cyril. b 49. AKC71. St Aug Coll Cant 71. **d** 72 **p** 73. C Broseley w Benthall *Heref* 72-76; C Cannock *Lich* 76-79; TV 79-83; V Rough Hills 83-09; P-in-c Wolverhampton St Steph

94-09; rtd 09; Perm to Offic *Lich* from 09. *Glendower, Bull Street, Gornal Wood, Dudley DY3 2NQ* Tel (01384) 232097 E-mail classfortyseven@hotmail.com

OAKES, Canon Leslie John. b 28. AKC53. **d** 54 **p** 55. C Bedford Leigh *Man* 54-58; C Walsall St Matt *Lich* 58-60; Chapl Selly Oak Hosp Birm 60-64; V Longbridge *Birm* 64-93; Hon Can Birm Cathl 84-93; rtd 93; Perm to Offic *Birm* from 93. *108 Hole Lane, Birmingham B31 2DF* Tel 0121-476 8514

OAKES, Melvin. b 36. Linc Th Coll 77. **d** 79 **p** 80. C Lt Ilford St Mich *Chelmsf* 79-82; V Highams Park All SS 82-96; rtd 96; Perm to Offic *Chelmsf* from 99. *115 Richmond Avenue, London E4 9RR* Tel (020) 8527 0457

OAKES, Robert. b 47. Chan Sch Truro 79. **d** 82 **p** 83. NSM Probus, Ladock and Grampound w Creed and St Erme *Truro* 82-84; TV Bodmin w Lanhydrock and Lanivet 85-88; R S Hill w Callington 88-03; RD E Wivelshire 95-00; Bp's Adv on Healing Min 98-03; Hon Can Truro Cathl 01-03; C Calstock from 06; Chapl Cornwall and Is of Scilly Primary Care Trust from 09. *48 Boconnoc Avenue, Callington PL17 7TW* Tel (01579) 389109 Mobile 07890-099248
E-mail robert@oakesrobert.wanadoo.co.uk

OAKEY-JONES, Ms Angela Jean. b 71. Keele Univ BA93. NTMTC BA08. **d** 08 **p** 09. C Rushmere *St E* from 08. *15 Adelaide Road, Ipswich IP4 5PS* Tel (01473) 273027
E-mail angela.oj@btinternet.com

OAKHAM, Archdeacon of. *See* PAINTER, The Ven David Scott

OAKLAND, Mrs Sarah Marie. b 54. UEA BEd85. EAMTC 99. **d** 02 **p** 03. C Diss *Nor* 02-06; V Chessington *Guildf* from 06. *The Vicarage, Garrison Lane, Chessington KT9 2LB* Tel (020) 8391 4855 E-mail sarahoakland@hotmail.com

OAKLEY, Barry Wyndham. b 32. TD72. SS Coll Cam BA53 MA57. Ridley Hall Cam 56. **d** 58 **p** 59. C Alverstoke *Portsm* 58-61; C Bermondsey St Mary w St Olave and St Jo *S'wark* 61-63; V Crofton *Portsm* 63-78; V Edmonton All SS *Lon* 78-82; P-in-c Edmonton St Mich 80-82; V Edmonton All SS w St Mich 82-97; rtd 97; Perm to Offic *Lon* from 98. *25 Queen's Road, Enfield EN1 1NF* Tel (020) 8363 3199

OAKLEY, Hilary Robert Mark. b 53. Univ of Wales (Ban) BSc75 Ox Univ BA78 MA81 MCIPD91. Ripon Coll Cuddesdon 76. **d** 79 **p** 80. C Birm St Pet 79-82; C Cambridge Gt St Mary w St Mich *Ely* 82-86; Chapl Girton Coll Cam 82-86; Chapl Zürich w St Gallen and Winterthur *Eur* 86-88; NSM Lon 88-92; Perm to Offic *St Alb* from 92. *55 Southdown Road, Harpenden AL5 1PQ* Tel (01582) 761514
E-mail hilary.oakley@talk21.com

OAKLEY, James Robert. b 75. St Edm Hall Ox BA96. Oak Hill Th Coll BA05. **d** 05 **p** 06. C Audley *Lich* 05-09; P-in-c Kemsing w Woodlands *Roch* from 09. *The Vicarage, High Street, Kemsing, Sevenoaks TN15 6NA* Tel (01732) 762556 Mobile 07827-299342
E-mail vicar@kemsing.org

OAKLEY, Jeremy Steven. b 52. Birm Univ BA99. Trin Coll Bris 95. **d** 97 **p** 98. C Walsall *Lich* 97-02; V Penn Fields from 02. *St Philip's Vicarage, Church Road, Bradmore, Wolverhampton WV3 7EJ* Tel (01902) 332749
E-mail jeremy@pennfieldsparish.co.uk

OAKLEY, Canon Mark David. b 68. K Coll Lon BD90 AKC90 FRSA96. St Steph Ho Ox 90. **d** 93 **p** 94. C St John's Wood *Lon* 93-96; Bp's Chapl 96-00; P-in-c Covent Garden St Paul 00-03; R 03-05; AD Westmr St Marg 04-05; Chapl RADA 03-05; Chapl Copenhagen and Adn Germany and N Eur 05-08; P-in-c Grosvenor Chpl *Lon* from 08; Dep P in O from 96. *24 South Audley Street, London W1K 2PA* Tel (020) 7499 1684
E-mail mark.chaplain@gmail.com

OAKLEY, Richard John. b 46. AKC69 St Aug Coll Cant 69. **d** 70 **p** 71. C Wythenshawe Wm Temple Ch *Man* 70-75; V Ashton H Trin 75-80; CR 80-93; Lic to Offic *Lon* 88-93; V Cantley *Sheff* 93-99; V Carl St Aid and Ch Ch from 99. *St Aidan's Vicarage, 6 Lismore Place, Carlisle CA1 1LX* Tel (01228) 522942
E-mail fr.oakley.staidan@virgin.net

OAKLEY, Robert Paul. b 51. Sheff Univ BScTech72 PGCE74. St Jo Coll Nottm. **d** 89 **p** 90. C Heatherlands St Jo *Sarum* 89-92; V Burton All SS w Ch Ch *Lich* 92-99; V Gt Wyrley 99-07; Tutor Wilson Carlile Coll of Evang from 07. *Wilson Carlile College of Evangelism, 50 Cavendish Street, Sheffield S3 7RZ* Tel 0114-279 5863 E-mail p.oakley@churcharmy.org.uk

OAKLEY, Robin Ian. b 37. Ripon Hall Ox 68. **d** 70 **p** 71. C Leighton Buzzard *St Alb* 70-73; C Watford St Mich 73-76; R Ickleford 76-80; R Ickleford w Holwell 80-02; rtd 02; Perm to Offic *St Alb* from 02 and *Win* from 03. *13 Anders Road, South Wonston, Winchester SO21 3EL* Tel (01962) 880613

OAKLEY, Susan Mary. *See* HENWOOD, Mrs Susan Mary

OAKLEY, Timothy Crispin. b 45. Qu Coll Cam BA66 MA70 Bris Univ PGCE69. St Jo Coll Nottm 73. **d** 76 **p** 77. C Bromley Common St Aug *Roch* 76-79; C Fairfield *Liv* 79-81; CMS Kenya 82-90; P-in-c Beaford, Roborough and St Giles in the Wood *Ex* 91-96; Chapl St Andr Sch Turi Kenya 96-98; V Woodford Halse w Eydon *Pet* from 99; RD Brackley 03-05. *The New Vicarage, Parsons Street, Woodford Halse, Daventry NN11 3RE* Tel (01327) 261477 E-mail tim@revoakley.freeserve.co.uk

OATES, Alan. b 32. S'wark Ord Course 79. **d** 80 **p** 81. NSM Rayleigh *Chelmsf* 80-87; TV Jarrow *Dur* 87-92; P-in-c Stella 92-95; R 95-97; rtd 97; Perm to Offic *Dur* from 98 and *Newc* from 00. *1 The Haven, North Shields NE29 6YH* Tel 0191-258 6984

OATES, Alexander John. b 38. Clifton Th Coll 63. **d** 67 **p** 68. C Brixton Hill St Sav *S'wark* 67-68; C Westcombe Park St Geo 68-71; C Stechford *Birm* 71-74; R Greenhithe St Mary *Roch* 74-77; Soc worker 77-02; rtd 03. *1 Fairlight Villas, North Road, Havering-atte-Bower, Romford RM4 1PP* Tel (01708) 760252

OATES, Douglas. b 39. Bolton Coll of Educn CertEd74 Ches Coll of HE BTh97. NOC 94. **d** 97 **p** 98. NSM Balderstone *Man* 97-01; NSM Oldham St Barn 01-06; P-in-c 03-06; P-in-c Waterhead 05-06; TV Medlock Head 06-09; rtd 09; Perm to Offic *Man* from 09. *43 Devonport Crescent, Royton, Oldham OL2 6JX* Tel (01706) 849929 E-mail doug@oates400.freeserve.co.uk

OATES, Jeanette Linda. b 50. SEN70. NEOC 05. **d** 08 **p** 09. NSM Bridlington Priory *York* from 08. *77 St Alban Road, Bridlington YO16 7SY* Tel (01262) 678534
E-mail jeanetteoates@tiscali.co.uk

OATES, Canon John. b 30. Kelham Th Coll 53. **d** 57 **p** 58. C Hackney Wick St Mary of Eton w St Aug *Lon* 57-60; Development Officer C of E Youth Coun 60-64; Sec C of E Coun Commonwealth Settlement 64-65; Gen Sec 65-72; Sec C of E Cttee on Migration & Internat Affairs 68-72; Hon Can Bunbury from 69; V Richmond St Mary *S'wark* 70-79; P-in-c Richmond St Jo 76-79; V Richmond St Mary w St Matthias and St Jo 79-84; RD Richmond and Barnes 79-84; R St Bride Fleet Street w Bridewell etc *Lon* 84-00; AD The City 97-00; Preb St Paul's Cathl 97-00; rtd 00; Perm to Offic *Lon* from 01 and *S'wark* from 03. *27 York Court, Albany Park Road, Kingston upon Thames KT2 5ST* Tel (020) 8974 8821
E-mail john.oates@blueyonder.co.uk

OATES, Michael Graham. b 62. Leic Poly BSc84. Aston Tr Scheme 87 Cranmer Hall Dur 89. **d** 92 **p** 93. C Enfield St Andr *Lon* 92-96; TV N Poole Ecum Team *Sarum* 96-07; Perm to Offic 07-08. *51 Ringwood Road, Poole BH14 0RE*

OATES (née ADAMS), Mrs Ruth. b 47. Bris Univ BSc69. SEITE 97. **d** 00 **p** 01. C Rainham *Roch* 00-03; V Gravesend St Mary from 03; RD Gravesend from 09. *The Vicarage, 57 New House Lane, Gravesend DA11 7HJ* Tel (01474) 740565
E-mail ruth.oates@diocese-rochester.org

OBAN, Provost of. *See* MacCALLUM, The Very Revd Norman Donald

OBEDOZA, William. b 58. NTMTC 05. **d** 08 **p** 09. NSM Walthamstow St Sav *Chelmsf* from 08. *212 Markhouse Road, London E17 8EP* Tel (020) 8988 6323 Fax 3006 6394 Mobile 07916-281227 E-mail fr.williamobedoza@yahoo.com

O'BENEY, Robin Mervyn. b 35. Ely Th Coll 61. **d** 64 **p** 65. C Liss *Portsm* 64-65; C Portsea St Cuth 65-68; Hon C Wymondham *Nor* 74-76; R Swainsthorpe w Newton Flotman 76-80; NSM Sparkenhoe Deanery *Leic* 87-90; V Billesdon and Skeffington 90-91; rtd 95. *19 Bridge Street, Kington HR5 3DL* Tel (01544) 230416

OBIN, Raymond Clive. b 63. Girton Coll Cam BA85 MA89. Wycliffe Hall Ox BTh. **d** 04 **p** 05. NSM Bucklebury w Marlston *Ox* from 04; NSM Bradfield and Stanford Dingley from 04. *Solfonn, Enborne Row, Wash Water, Newbury RG20 0LY* Tel (01635) 38212 E-mail raymond@2bsd.org.uk

OBIORA, Arthur Cuenyem. b 42. JP91. **d** 95 **p** 95. OLM Hatcham St Cath *S'wark* from 95. *126 Perry Hill, London SE6 4EY*

OBORNE, Mrs Martine Amelia. b 57. St Hilda's Coll Ox MA80. SEITE BA09. **d** 09. C Islington St Mary *Lon* from 09. *Corner House, 12 Highbury Place, London N5 1QZ* Tel (020) 7359 8701 Mobile 07842-199556 E-mail maoborne@hotmail.com

O'BOYLE, Liam Patrick Butler. b 66. Nottm Univ BA90 MA98. EMMTC 98. **d** 01 **p** 02. C Cinderhill *S'well* 01-06; TV Clifton from 06. *23 Fellows Road, Beeston, Nottingham NG9 1AQ* Tel 0115-943 1032

O'BRIEN, Andrew David. b 61. Nottm Univ BTh88. Linc Th Coll 85. **d** 88 **p** 89. C Clare w Poslingford *St E* 88-89; C Clare w Poslingford, Cavendish etc 89-91; V Belton *Linc* 91-97; P-in-c Melbourn *Ely* 97-99; V from 99; P-in-c Meldreth 97-99; V from 99. *The Vicarage, Vicarage Close, Melbourn, Royston SG8 6DY* Tel (01763) 260295 E-mail revobrien@ntlworld.com

O'BRIEN, David. b 62. Moorlands Th Coll BA99. CBDTI 01. **d** 04 **p** 05. C Bispham *Blackb* 04-08; C S Shore H Trin from 08. *92 Watson Road, Blackpool FY4 2DE*

O'BRIEN, Donogh Smith. b 34. St Pet Hall Ox BA56 MA60. Ripon Hall Ox 56. **d** 57 **p** 58. C Gt Sankey *Liv* 57-63; C Farnworth 63-66; Lic to Offic 66-03; Asst Master Wade Deacon Gr Sch Widnes 66-99; rtd 99; Perm to Offic *Liv* from 03. *Fourways, 178 Lunts Heath Road, Widnes WA8 5AZ* Tel 0151-424 0147

O'BRIEN, Mrs Elaine. b 55. CITC 94. **d** 97 **p** 98. Aux Min Killyman *Arm* 97-00; Aux Min Gilnahirk *D & D* 00-06; Bp's C Clogherny w Seskinore and Drumnakilly *Arm* 06-08; P-in-c 08. *96 Church Road, Clogherney Glebe Lower, Sixmilecross, Omagh BT79 0SA* Tel (028) 8075 7016 Mobile 07912-950690 E-mail rvelaine49@aol.com

O'BRIEN, George Edward. b 32. Clifton Th Coll 61. **d** 64 **p** 65. C Denton Holme *Carl* 64-68; V Castle Town *Lich* 68-88; Chapl St Geo Hosp Stafford 88-94; Chapl Kingsmead Hosp Stafford 88-94; Chapl Foundation NHS Trust Stafford 94-99; rtd 99; Perm to Offic *Lich* from 99. *Abily, 185 Tixall Road, Stafford ST16 3XJ* Tel (01785) 244261

O'BRIEN, Kevin Michael. b 60. Herts Univ BA82. St Steph Ho Ox BTh05. **d** 01 **p** 02. C Uppingham w Ayston and Wardley w Belton *Pet* 01-04; Asst Chapl Wellington Coll Berks 04-06; Bp's Chapl and Office Manager *Eur* from 06. *Bishop's Lodge, Church Road, Worth, Crawley RH10 7RT* Tel (01293) 883051 Fax 884479 E-mail bishops.chaplain@dioceseineurope.org

O'BRIEN, Mary. *See* GUBBINS, Mrs Mary

O'BRIEN, Shelagh Ann. *See* STACEY, Mrs Shelagh Ann

OCHOLA, George Otieno. b 58. Lon Sch of Th BTh02. St Jo Sch of Miss Kokise. **d** 88 **p** 89. Kenya 88-99; Perm to Offic *Lon* 00-08; NSM Watford St Mich *St Alb* from 08. *157 Vicarage Road, Watford WD18 0HA* Tel (01923) 239567 Mobile 07866-359120 E-mail georgeochola@hotmail.com

OCKFORD, Paul Philip. b 46. St Chad's Coll Dur BA67. St Steph Ho Ox 68. **d** 70 **p** 71. C Streatham St Pet *S'wark* 70-74; C Cheam 74-77; P-in-c Eastrington *York* 77-79; TV Howden 80-83; R Sherburn and W and E Heslerton w Yedingham 83-92; V Bampton, Morebath, Clayhanger and Petton *Ex* 92-98; R Goodmanham *York* 98-04; V Market Weighton 98-04; V Sancton 98-04; rtd 04. *78 Wold Road, Pocklington, York YO42 2QG*

OCKWELL, Canon Herbert Grant. b 12. Kelham Th Coll 30. **d** 36 **p** 37. C Newington St Matt *S'wark* 36-40; CF (EC) 40-46; V Lambeth St Phil *S'wark* 46-52; V Surbiton St Andr 52-62; V Balham Hill Ascension 62-70; Hon Can S'wark Cathl 64-70; R Blendworth, Chalton and Idsworth *Portsm* 70-81; rtd 81; Perm to Offic *Portsm* 81-07 and *Chich* 82-07. *Manormead Nursing Home, Tilford Road, Hindhead GU26 6RA* Tel (01428) 602500

O'CONNELL, Miss Mary Joy. b 49. York Univ BA71 Leeds Univ CertEd74. Chich Th Coll 84. **dss** 86 **d** 87 **p** 94. Cinderhill *S'well* 86-87; Par Dn 87-94; C 94; P-in-c 94-98; V Linc St Giles from 98. *The Vicarage, 25 Shelley Drive, Lincoln LN2 4BY* Tel (01522) 527655 E-mail mjoconnell@lineone.net

O'CONNOR, Alfred Stanley. b 20. TCD BA43 MA60. **d** 43 **p** 44. C Belfast St Mich *Conn* 43-45; C Urney Union *K, E & A* 45-49; I Killesher 49-54; I Roscrea *L & K* 54-62; I Camlough w Killeavy *Arm* 62-65; I Drumglass 65-85; Can Arm Cathl 83-85; rtd 85. *25 West Street, Stewartstown, Dungannon BT71 5HT* Tel (028) 8773 8784

O'CONNOR, Canon Brian Michael McDougal. b 42. St Cath Coll Cam BA67 MA69. Cuddesdon Coll 67. **d** 69 **p** 70. C Headington *Ox* 69-71; Sec Dioc Past and Redundant Chs Uses Cttees 72-79; P-in-c Merton 72-76; V Rainham *Roch* 79-97; RD Gillingham 81-88; Hon Can Roch Cathl 89-97; Dean Auckland New Zealand 97-00; Hon Can from 00; Perm to Offic *Ox* 00-02; P-in-c Lt Missenden 02-04; rtd 04. *1 Steadys Lane, Stanton Harcourt, Witney OX29 5RL* Tel (01865) 882776 Mobile 07740-702161 E-mail canonmichaeloc@aol.com

O'CONNOR, Canon Daniel. b 33. Univ Coll Dur BA54 MA67 St Andr Univ PhD81. Cuddesdon Coll 56. **d** 58 **p** 59. C Stockton St Pet *Dur* 58-62; C W Hartlepool St Aid 62-63; Cam Miss to Delhi 63-70; USPG India 70-72; Chapl St Andr Univ 72-77; R Edin Gl Shep 77-82; Prin Coll of Ascension Selly Oak 82-90; Dir Scottish Chs Ho (Chs Together in Scotland) 90-93; Can Res Wakef Cathl 93-96; Bp's Adv on Inter-Faith Issues 93-96; rtd 96. *15 School Road, Balmullo, St Andrews KY16 0BA* Tel (01334) 871326 E-mail danoconnor@btinternet.com

O'CONNOR, John Goodrich. b 34. Keble Coll Ox BA58 MA60. Lich Th Coll. **d** 61 **p** 62. C Blackpool St Steph *Blackb* 61-66; C Holbeck *Ripon* 66-68; C Hendon St Mary *Lon* 68-73; TV Thornaby on Tees *York* 73-79; TR 79-89; V Blyth St Cuth *Newc* 89-96; Chapl Wellesley Nautical Sch 89-96; V Feniscliffe *Blackb* 96-04; rtd 04; Hon C Lightbowne *Man* from 04. *The Rectory, 173 Kenyon Lane, Manchester M40 5HS* Tel 0161-681 1308

O'CONNOR, Michael. *See* O'CONNOR, Canon Brian Michael McDougal

O'CONNOR, Rosemary Irene. b 43. St Gabr Coll Lon TCert65. WMMTC 96. **d** 99 **p** 00. NSM Cannock *Lich* 99-01; TV 01-09; rtd 09. *Windyridge, 25 The Leasowe, Lichfield WS13 7HD* Tel (01543) 252675

ODA-BURNS, John Macdonald. b 31. AKC56. **d** 57 **p** 58. C St Marychurch *Ex* 57-59; S Africa 59-64; Bahamas 64-67; USA from 67; rtd 96. *611 La Mesa Drive, Portola Valley CA 94028-7416, USA* Tel and fax (001) (650) 854 2831 E-mail bussels@batnet.com

ODDY, Canon Frederick Brian. b 29. Univ of Wales (Lamp) BA50. Linc Th Coll 50. **d** 52 **p** 53. C Preston Em *Blackb* 52-55; C St Annes St Thos 55-57; V Chorley St Jas 57-64; V Warton St Oswald 64-76; P-in-c Yealand Conyers 74-76; V Warton St Oswald w Yealand Conyers 76-98; RD Tunstall 84-90; Hon Can Blackb Cathl 89-98; rtd 98; Perm to Offic *Blackb* from 98. *9 Main Road, Nether Kellet, Carnforth LA6 1HG*

ODDY, Joan Winifred. b 34. **d** 97 **p** 98. OLM Kessingland w Gisleham *Nor* 97-99; OLM Kessingland, Gisleham and Rushmere 99-04; rtd 04; Perm to Offic *Nor* from 04. *Rose Cottage, Wash Lane, Kessingland, Lowestoft NR33 7QY* Tel (01502) 742001

ODDY, Mrs Julie Louise. b 61. SRN82 SCM85. Ridley Hall Cam 04. **d** 06 **p** 07. C Watton w Carbrooke and Ovington *Nor* 06-07; C Ashill, Carbrooke, Ovington and Saham Toney 07-09; P-in-c Gillingham w Geldeston, Stockton, Ellingham etc from 09. *The Rectory, 60 The Street, Geldeston, Beccles NR34 0LN* Tel (01502) 712255 Mobile 07944-226869 E-mail jlo32@tiscali.co.uk

O'DELL, Colin John. b 61. WEMTC 03. **d** 06 **p** 07. C Bishop's Cleeve *Glouc* from 06. *2A Orchard Road, Bishops Cleeve, Cheltenham GL52 8LX* Tel (01242) 675471 Mobile 07779-126050

ODEN, Mark. b 74. Ex Univ BA97. Oak Hill Th Coll BA09. **d** 09. C Sevenoaks St Nic *Roch* from 09. *40 South Park, Sevenoaks TN13 1EJ* Tel (01732) 454221 Mobile 07840-180395 E-mail mjoden@tiscali.co.uk

ODEWOLE, Israel Oluwagbemiga Omoniyi. b 68. Immanuel Coll Ibadan 95 W Africa Th Sem Lagos MA02. **d** 97 **p** 98. Nigeria 97-06; Chapl and Co-ord Boys' Brigade and Girls' Guild 98-06; Sec Youth Bd Dioc Ondo 99-06; Perm to Offic *Man* 06-08. *Address temp unknown* Tel 07786-858657 (mobile) E-mail jesuoluwaobami340@yahoo.com

ODLING-SMEE, George William. b 35. K Coll Dur MB, BS59 FRCS68 FRCSI86. **d** 77 **p** 78. NSM Belfast St Thos *Conn* 77-90; NSM Belfast St Geo 90-02. *The Boathouse, 24 Rossglass Road South, Killough, Downpatrick BT30 7RA* Tel (028) 4484 1868 Fax 4484 1143 E-mail wodlingsmee@aol.com

O'DONNELL, Mrs Mollie. b 39. Portsm Poly BA91. STETS 97. **d** 00 **p** 03. NSM Calbourne w Newtown *Portsm* from 00; NSM Shalfleet from 00. *1 Mill Green Cottages, Newbridge, Yarmouth PO41 0TZ* Tel (01983) 531320

O'DONOGHUE, Mark Ronald. b 69. St Aid Coll Dur BA91 Solicitor 93. Oak Hill Th Coll BA04. **d** 04 **p** 05. C St Helen Bishopsgate w St Andr Undershaft etc *Lon* from 04. *22 Chisenhale Road, London E3 5QZ* Tel (020) 8980 9150 E-mail odonoghue_mark@hotmail.com

O'DONOVAN, Canon Oliver Michael Timothy. b 45. Ball Coll Ox BA68 MA71 DPhil75. Wycliffe Hall Ox 68. **d** 72 **p** 73. Tutor Wycliffe Hall Ox 72-77; Prof Systematic Th Wycliffe Coll Toronto 77-82; Regius Prof Moral and Past Th Ox Univ 82-06; Can Res Ch Ch *Ox* 82-06; Prof Chr Ethics Edin Univ from 06. *New College, Mound Place, Edinburgh EH1 2LX* Tel 0131-650 8900 E-mail oliver.odonovan@ed.ac.uk

O'DOWD SMYTH, Christine. CITC. **d** 09. NSM Lismore w Cappoquin, Kilwatermoy, Dungarvan etc *C & O* from 09. *Address temp unknown*

O'DWYER, John Francis Joseph. b 61. NOC 00. **d** 03 **p** 04. C Bury St Jo w St Mark *Man* 03-06; P-in-c Bury St Pet from 06. *St Peter's Vicarage, St Peter's Road, Bury BL9 9QZ* Tel 0161-764 1187 E-mail johntricia2000@yahoo.co.uk

OEHRING, Canon Anthony Charles. b 56. Sheff City Poly BA79 CQSW79 Kent Univ MA02. Ridley Hall Cam 86. **d** 88 **p** 89. C Gillingham *Sarum* 88-91; TV S Gillingham *Roch* 91-00; P-in-c Faversham *Cant* from 00; C Preston next Faversham, Goodnestone and Graveney from 02; P-in-c The Brents and Davington w Oare and Luddenham 03-06; AD Ospringe from 02; Hon Can Cant Cathl from 06. *The Vicarage, 16 Newton Road, Faversham ME13 8DY* Tel (01795) 532592 E-mail anthonyoehring@aol.com

OEPPEN, Canon John Gerard David. b 44. St D Coll Lamp. **d** 67 **p** 68. C-in-c Cwmmer w Abercregan CD *Llan* 67-70; TV Glyncorrwg w Afan Vale and Cymmer Afan 70-71; C Whitchurch 71-74; V Aberavon H Trin 74-78; V Bargoed and Deri w Brithdir 78-86; R Barry All SS 86-08; Can Llan Cathl 04-08; rtd 08. *Oak Cottage, 5 Heol Leubren, Barry CF63 1HG*

OESTREICHER, Canon Paul. b 31. OM(Ger)95. Univ of NZ BA53 MA56 Cov Poly Hon DLitt91 Sussex Univ Hon LLD05 Lambeth DD08 Otago Univ Hon DD09. Linc Th Coll 56. **d** 59 **p** 60. C Dalston H Trin w St Phil *Lon* 59-61; C S Mymms K Chas 61-68; Asst in Relig Broadcasting BBC 61-64; Assoc Sec Internat Affairs Dept BCC 64-69; V Blackheath Ascension *S'wark* 68-81; Dir of Tr 69-72; Hon Can S'wark Cathl 78-81; Asst Gen Sec BCC 81-86; Can Res Cov Cathl 86-97; Dir of Internat Min 86-97; Humboldt Fell Inst of Th Free Univ of Berlin 92-93; rtd 98; Perm to Offic *Cov* from 98 and *Chich* from 03; Hon Chapl Sussex Univ from 04. *97 Furze Croft, Furze Hill, Hove BN3 1PE* Tel (01273) 728033 E-mail paul_oestreicher@yahoo.co.uk

O'FARRELL, Anne Marie. **d** 08 **p** 09. NSM Dublin Sandford w Milltown *D & G* from 08. *138 Meadow Grove, Dundrum, Dublin 14, Republic of Ireland* Tel (00353) (1) 296 6222

O'FERRALL, Patrick Charles Kenneth. b 34. New Coll Ox BA58 MA60. **d** 00 **p** 01. OLM Godalming *Guildf* 00-04; Perm to Offic from 04. *Catteshall Grange, Catteshall Road, Godalming GU7 1LZ* Tel (01483) 410134 Fax 414161 E-mail pof59@hotmail.com

OFFER, The Ven Clifford Jocelyn. b 43. Ex Univ BA67 FRSA97. Westcott Ho Cam 67. **d** 69 **p** 70. C Bromley SS Pet and Paul *Roch* 69-74; TV Southampton (City Cen) *Win* 74-83; TR Hitchin *St Alb* 83-94; Adn Nor and Can Res Nor Cathl 94-08; rtd 08. *Chase House, Peterstow, Ross-on-Wye HR9 6JX* Tel (01989) 567874

OFFER, Mrs Jill Patricia. b 44. CertEd65. **d** 03 **p** 04. OLM Salisbury St Mark *Sarum* from 03. *11 Netheravon Road, Salisbury SP1 3BJ* Tel (01722) 334455
E-mail jill.offer@osser.wanadoo.co.uk

OGADA, John Ochieng. b 56. Nairobi Univ LLB83 Univ of Wales (Cardiff) LLM89. **d** 01. Perm to Offic *York* 01-02; NSM Hull St Martin w Transfiguration 02-03. *44 Kingston Road, Willerby, Hull HU10 6BH* Tel (01482) 653592

O'GARRO, Henry Roland Furlonge. b 30. Leeward Is TCert52. St Steph Ho Ox 00. **d** 00. NSM Kilburn St Aug w St Jo *Lon* 00-05; NSM Willesden St Mary from 05. *32 Cedar Road, London NW2 6SR* Tel (020) 8452 4530

OGBEDE, Ms Olufunke Oladunni. b 48. Lon Inst of Educn MA81. **d** 05 **p** 06. OLM S Lambeth St Anne and All SS *S'wark* from 05. *98 Plummer Road, London SW4 8HJ* Tel (020) 8678 7387 Mobile 07944-424931 E-mail fundunni@aol.com

OGDEN, Eric. b 34. NW Ord Course 73. **d** 76 **p** 77. NSM Lydgate St Anne *Man* 76-92; NSM Lydgate w Friezland 92-01; rtd 01; Perm to Offic *Man* from 01. *40 Burnedge Lane, Grasscroft, Oldham OL4 4EA* Tel (01457) 873661

OGDEN, Harry. b 30. AKC57. **d** 58 **p** 59. C Hollinwood *Man* 58-60; C Langley St Aid CD 60-61; R Lightbowne 61-69; V Farnworth and Kearsley 69-72; V Oldham St Steph and All Martyrs 72-79; R Moss Side Ch Ch 79-95; rtd 95; Perm to Offic *Man* 95-98; *Worc* 01-05; *Blackb* from 06. *1 Park Avenue, Lytham St Annes FY8 5QU* Tel (01253) 796723

OGILVIE, The Ven Gordon. b 42. Glas Univ MA64 Lon Univ BD67. ALCD66. **d** 67 **p** 68. C Ashtead *Guildf* 67-72; V New Barnet St Jas *St Alb* 72-80; Dir Past Studies Wycliffe Hall Ox 80-87; P-in-c Harlow New Town w Lt Parndon *Chelmsf* 87-89; R 89-94; TR Harlow Town Cen w Lt Parndon 94-96; Hon Can Chelmsf Cathl 94-96; Chapl Princess Alexandra Hosp Harlow 88-96; Adn Nottingham *S'well* 96-06; rtd 07; Lic to Offic *St And* from 07. *49 Argyle Street, St Andrews KY16 9BX* Tel (01334) 470185 E-mail gordon.ogilvie@virgin.net

OGILVIE, Ian Douglas. b 37. Em Coll Cam BA59 MA63. Linc Th Coll 59. **d** 61 **p** 62. C Clapham H Trin *S'wark* 61-63; C Cambridge Gt St Mary w St Mich *Ely* 63-66; Chapl Sevenoaks Sch 66-77; Hon C Sevenoaks St Nic *Roch* 67-77; Chapl Malvern Coll 77-84; Hd Master St Geo Sch Harpenden 84-87; Lic to Offic *St Alb* 84-87; Bp's Dom Chapl 87-89; P-in-c Aldenham 87-91; Appeals Dir Mind 89-91; Fund Raising Dir Br Deaf Assn 91-94; NSM Tring *St Alb* 92-94; Perm to Offic from 94; Fund Raising Dir R Nat Miss to Deep Sea Fishermen from 94. *The White House, 19 Lower Icknield Way, Marsworth, Tring HP23 4LN* Tel (01296) 661479

OGILVIE, Pamela. b 56. Brunel Univ MA89 CQSW82. Qu Coll Birm 01. **d** 03 **p** 04. C Hill *Birm* 03-07; V Billesley Common from 07. *Holy Cross Vicarage, 29 Beauchamp Road, Birmingham B13 0NS* Tel 0121-444 1737 Mobile 07789-911576
E-mail church@holycrossbillesley.co.uk

OGLE, Canon Catherine. b 61. Leeds Univ BA82 MPhil85 MA91 Fitzw Coll Cam 83. Westcott Ho Cam 85. **d** 88 **p** 94. C Middleton St Mary *Ripon* 88-91; Relig Progr Ed BBC Radio Leeds 91-95; NSM Leeds St Marg and All Hallows 91-95; P-in-c Woolley *Wakef* 95-01; P-in-c Huddersfield St Pet and All SS 01-03; V Huddersfield St Pet from 03; RD Huddersfield from 09; Chapl Huddersfield Univ 03-06; Hon Can Wakef Cathl from 08. *59 Lightridge Road, Fixby, Huddersfield HD2 2HF* Tel (01484) 544558 Fax 427964 E-mail cogleathome@aol.com

OGLESBY, Ms Elizabeth Jane. b 73. Roehampton Inst BA95 Man Univ BPhil98. Westcott Ho Cam 00. **d** 03 **p** 04. C S Dulwich St Steph *S'wark* 03-06; P-in-c Camberwell St Mich w All So w Em 06-07; V from 07. *St Michael's Vicarage, 128 Bethwin Road, London SE5 0YY* Tel (020) 7703 8686 Mobile 07790-219725

OGLESBY, Canon Leslie Ellis. b 46. Univ Coll Ox BA69 MA73 City Univ MPhil73 Fitzw Coll Cam BA73 MA77. Ripon Coll Cuddesdon 77. **d** 78 **p** 79. C Stevenage St Mary Shephall *St Alb* 78-80; Dir St Alb Minl Tr Scheme 80-87; V Markyate Street *St Alb* 80-87; Dir CME 87-94; Hon Can St Alb 93-01; TR Hitchin 94-01; Adult Educn and Tr Officer *Ely* from 01; Hon Can Ely Cathl from 04. *1A Church Road, Everton, Sandy SG19 2JY* Tel (01767) 699165
E-mail les.oglesby@ely.anglican.org

OGLEY, James Edward. b 76. St Jo Coll Nottm BA07. **d** 07 **p** 08. C Bursledon *Win* from 07. *13 Redcroft Lane, Bursledon, Southampton SO31 8GS* Tel (023) 8040 4220 Mobile 07968-083744 E-mail james@jamesthevicar.com

OGLEY, John. b 40. Oak Hill Th Coll 62. **d** 65 **p** 66. C Ardsley *Sheff* 65-68; C Carlton-in-the-Willows *S'well* 68-71; P-in-c Tollerton 71-79; V Skegby 79-93; R Carlton in Lindrick 93-01;

P-in-c Langold 98-01; rtd 01; Perm to Offic *S'well* from 01. *Shalom, 39 Sparken Dale, Worksop S80 1BL* Tel (01909) 479462

O'GORMAN, Paul Anthony. b 46. Portsm Poly BSc79. Oak Hill Th Coll 79. **d** 81 **p** 82. C Leyton St Mary w St Edw *Chelmsf* 81-83; C Rayleigh 83-84; CF 84-87; R Northiam *Chich* 87-93; V Hastings Em and St Mary in the Castle 93-99; rtd 99; NSM Southsea St Simon *Portsm* from 99. *2 Dorothy Court, 16 Wilson Grove, Southsea PO5 1PD* Tel (023) 9283 9323

OGRAM, Mrs Ann. b 44. WEMTC 04. **d** 06 **p** 07. NSM Clun w Bettws-y-Crwyn and Newcastle *Heref* from 06. *Highbeech House, Mount Pleasant, Llwyn Road, Clun, Craven Arms SY7 8JJ* Tel (01588) 640830 Mobile 07970-072836
E-mail ann@ogram.com

OGSTON, Russell James. b 71. La Sainte Union Coll BA94. Qu Coll Birm BD97. **d** 98 **p** 99. C Andover w Foxcott *Win* 98-01; C Southampton Maybush St Pet 01-03; Asst Chapl Homerton Univ Hosp NHS Trust Lon 03-05; Chapl 05-08; Chapl Pilgrims Hospice Thanet 08-09; Chapl Newham Univ Hosp NHS Trust from 09. *Newham University Hospital, Glen Road, London E13 8SL* Tel (020) 7476 4000
E-mail russell.ogston@newhamhealth.nhs.uk

OGUGUO, Barnabas Ahuna. b 47. Rome Univ BA70 BD74 Glas Univ MTh84 PhD90 Strathclyde Univ PGCE93. **d** 73 **p** 74. Nigeria 73-93; RE Teacher Lenzie Academy *Glas* 93-96; Bearsden Academy from 96; Hon C Lenzie 95-05; P-in-c Cumbernauld from 07. *32 Carron Crescent, Lenzie, Glasgow G66 5PJ* Tel 0141-776 1321 *or* 942 2297 Fax 578 9802
E-mail boguguo@lycos.co.uk

OGUNSANYA, Olumuyiwa Adegboyega. b 67. Lagos Angl Dioc Sem 01. **d** 03 **p** 04. C Alapere Ch Ch Nigeria 04-05; Perm to Offic *S'wark* from 07. *222 Seabrook Rise, Grays RM17 6BL* Tel (01375) 369415 Mobile 07946-488595
E-mail revoolord2005@yahoo.com

OGUNYEMI, Dele Johnson. b 56. Obafemi Awolowo Univ BA90. SEITE 04. **d** 07 **p** 08. NSM Plumstead All SS *S'wark* from 07. *4 Chiltern Close, Bexleyheath DA7 6SA* Tel and fax (01322) 349790 Mobile 07957-425113
E-mail djogunyemi@tiscali.co.uk

OHEN, John. b 42. **d** 06 **p** 07. NSM Clapham St Jas *S'wark* from 06. *47 Kirkstall Gardens, London SW2 4HR* Tel (020) 8671 0028

OHS, Lt Comdr Douglas Fredrick. b 49. Saskatchewan Univ BA74. Em Coll Saskatoon LTh75. **d** 74 **p** 75. C Bridgwater St Mary w Chilton Trinity *B & W* 75-77; Canada from 77. *14-3505 Willowdale Crescent, Brandon MB R7B 3C5, Canada*

OJI, Erasmus Oluchukwu. b 43. Lon Univ BSc66 LRCP70 MRCS70 FRCS76. Oak Hill Th Coll 75. **d** 78 **p** 79. C Ealing Dean St Jo *Lon* 78-80; Nigeria 80-90; Asst Chapl Rotherham Distr Gen Hosp 90-91; Perm to Offic *Sheff* from 92. *369 Fulwood Road, Sheffield S10 3BS* Tel and fax (07092) 147747
E-mail erasmus@doctors.org.uk

OKE, Mrs Elizabeth Mary. b 43. SAOMC 96. **d** 99 **p** 00. NSM Woolhampton w Midgham and Beenham Valance *Ox* 99-08; NSM Aldermaston w Wasing and Brimpton 05-08; NSM Aldermaston and Woolhampton from 08. *Gladstone Cottage, 18 Windmill Road, Mortimer, Reading RG7 3RN* Tel 0118-933 2829

OKE, Michael John. b 42. Ox Min Course 89. **d** 92 **p** 93. NSM Stratfield Mortimer *Ox* 92-99; NSM Stratfield Mortimer and Mortimer W End etc 99-03; NSM Tilehurst St Geo from 03; NSM Tilehurst St Mary from 03. *Gladstone Cottage, 18 Windmill Road, Mortimer, Reading RG7 3RN* Tel 0118-933 2829

OKECHI, Patrick Otosio. b 62. Chas Univ Prague MTh94. **d** 95 **p** 98. Perm to Offic *Eur* 95-02; Asst P Angl Episc Congregation Czech Republic 02; V W Bromwich Gd Shep w St Jo *Lich* 02-08. *Address temp unknown* E-mail pokechi@btopenworld.com

OKEKE, Christian. b 71. **d** 05 **p** 06. C Avondale Zimbabwe 05; C Glas St Silas 05-08; P-in-c Glas Gd Shep and Ascension from 08; Chapl Strathclyde Univ from 08. *31 Westfield Drive, Glasgow G52 2SG* Tel 0141-882 4996

✠**OKEKE, The Rt Revd Ken Sandy Edozie.** b 41. Nigeria Univ BSc67 Man Univ MA94. Igbaja Sem Nigeria. **d** 76 **p** 76 **c** 00. Nigeria 76-80 and 87-89; Chapl to Nigerians in UK and Irish Republic 80-87; Hon Can Kwara from 85; Hon Adn from 98; C Man Whitworth 89-95; Chapl Inst of Higher Learning Man 89-95; CMS 95-01; Perm to Offic *S'wark* 96-02; Bp on the Niger from 00. *PO Box 42, Onitsha, Nigeria* Tel (00234) (46) 411282 *or* 410337

OKELLO, Modicum. b 53. Trin Coll Bris BA90. St Paul's Coll Limuru 76 Wycliffe Hall Ox 86. **d** 78 **p** 79. Kenya 78-80; Uganda 80-86; NSM Goodmayes All SS *Chelmsf* 91-92; C Barking St Marg w St Patr 92-96; C Stratford St Jo and Ch Ch w Forest Gate St Jas 96-99; TV Forest Gate St Sav w W Ham St Matt from 99. *St Matthew's Vicarage, Dyson Road, Stratford E15 4JX* Tel (020) 8519 2524
E-mail modicumokello@okello8726modicum.freeserve.co.uk

OKWUOSA, Canon Amaechi Chukwudube. b 64. Anambra State Univ LLB89 Nigerian Law Sch Lagos BL90. Faith Th Sem 94. **d** 96 **p** 97. Nigeria 96-98; Hon Can Nnewi from 01; Perm to Offic

Lon 98-01; NSM Gt Ilford St Jo *Chelmsf* from 01. *2 Applegate, Brentwood CM14 5PL* Tel (01277) 374710
E-mail dubem@okwuosa.com

OLADUJI, Christopher Temitayo. b 57. Awosika Th Coll Nigeria 84. **d** 87 **p** 88. Nigeria 87-89; C Ilutitun Ebenezer 87; Asst P Ondo Cathl 88; NSM W Ham *Chelmsf* 89-93; NSM Peckham St Jo w St Andr *S'wark* 97-98; NSM E Ham St Geo *Chelmsf* 99-01; NSM Hackney Wick St Mary of Eton w St Aug *Lon* 02-04; NSM Smithfield St Bart Gt from 04. *Church House, Cloth Fair, London EC1A 7JQ* Tel (020) 7606 1575 Mobile 07985-465401 E-mail coladuji@yahoo.com

OLANCZUK, Jonathan Paul Tadeusz. b 49. EAMTC 94. **d** 96 **p** 97. C Haverhill w Withersfield *St E* 96-00; P-in-c Badingham w Bruisyard, Cransford and Dennington 00-04; P-in-c Rendham w Sweffling 00-04; R Upper Alde from 04. *The Rectory, 5 Orchard Rise, Badingham, Woodbridge IP13 8LN* Tel and fax (01728) 638823 Mobile 07766-953558 *or* 07944-186526
E-mail olanczuk@suffolkonline.net *or* jolanczuk@aol.com

OLD, Arthur Anthony George (Tony). b 36. Clifton Th Coll 69. **d** 71 **p** 72. C Clitheroe St Jas *Blackb* 71-73; C Bispham 73-77; V Haslingden St Jo Stonefold 77-81; TV Lowestoft and Kirkley *Nor* 81-83; Chapl to the Deaf *Cant* 83-01; P-in-c Hernhill 83-85; C Preston next Faversham, Goodnestone and Graveney 85-01; rtd 01; Perm to Offic *Cant* from 01. *62 Knaves Acre, Headcorn, Ashford TN27 9TJ* Tel (01622) 891498

OLDFIELD, Jonathan Thomas. b 54. Bede Coll Dur TCert76. NEOC 04. **d** 07 **p** 08. NSM Patrick Brompton and Hunton *Ripon* from 07; NSM Crakehall from 07; NSM Hornby from 07. *12 St Mary's Mount, Leyburn DL8 5JB* Tel (01969) 622958
E-mail jonathan@jonathanoldfield.wanadoo.co.uk

OLDFIELD, Canon Roger Fielden. b 45. Qu Coll Cam BA67 MA71 Lon Univ BD75. Trin Coll Bris 75. **d** 75 **p** 76. C Halliwell St Pet *Man* 75-80 and from 03; V 80-03; AD Bolton 93-02; Hon Can Man Cathl from 00. *505 Church Road, Bolton BL1 5RE* Tel (01204) 849412 E-mail rogerandruth@3strands.net

OLDHAM, Dale Raymond. b 40. NZ Coll of Pharmacy MPS63 Cant Univ (NZ) MA87. Ridley Hall Cam 64. **d** 67 **p** 68. C Woking St Mary *Guildf* 67-70; C Papanui New Zealand 71-73; CMS Miss Dodoma Tanzania 74-81; Sec Home CMS New Zealand 81-85; C Burnside 85-88; V Shirley St Steph 89-06; rtd 06. *58 Pitcairn Crescent, Papanui, Christchurch 8053, New Zealand* E-mail d.oldham@xtra.co.nz

OLDNALL, Frederick Herbert. b 16. Ripon Hall Ox 56. **d** 57 **p** 58. C Radford *Cov* 57-59; C Stratford-on-Avon 59-62; V Rosliston w Coton in the Elms *Derby* 62-83; rtd 83; Perm to Offic *Cov* from 93. *4 Margetts Close, Kenilworth CV8 1EN* Tel (01926) 852417

OLDROYD, Preb Colin Mitchell. b 30. Down Coll Cam BA54 MA60. Wells Th Coll 60. **d** 61 **p** 62. C Elton All SS *Man* 61-63; C Ex St Dav 63-66; P-in-c Neen Sollars w Milson *Heref* 66-78; P-in-c Coreley and Doddington 66-78; R Cleobury Mortimer w Hopton Wafers 66-78; RD Ludlow 75-78; P-in-c Eastnor 78-81; R Ledbury 78-81; RD Ledbury 78-81; Chapl Ledbury Cottage Hosp Heref 79-95; R Ledbury w Eastnor *Heref* 81-95; Preb Heref Cathl 84-95; P-in-c Lt Marcle 85-95; rtd 95; Perm to Offic *Heref* from 96. *2 Hampton Manor Close, Hereford HR1 1TG* Tel (01432) 340569

OLDROYD, David Christopher Leslie. b 42. FRICS. S Dios Minl Tr Scheme. **d** 85 **p** 86. NSM Four Marks *Win* 85-90; Perm to Offic *Portsm* from 06 and *Guildf* from 08. *18 Rozeldene, Grayshott, Hindhead GU26 6TW* Tel (01428) 606620

OLDROYD, Mrs Sheila Margaret. b 40. Liv Univ BSc63. St Steph Ho Ox 98. **d** 99 **p** 00. NSM Cotgrave *S'well* 99-03; NSM Keyworth and Stanton-on-the-Wolds and Bunny etc 03-08; rtd 08. *27 Lowlands Drive, Keyworth, Nottingham NG12 5HG* Tel 0115-937 6344 Mobile 07974-785242
E-mail margaretoldroyd@aol.com

OLDROYD, Trevor. b 33. Hatf Coll Dur BA55 Lon Univ BD60. Wycliffe Hall Ox 60. **d** 61 **p** 62. C Barnes St Mary *S'wark* 61-65; C Wimbledon 65-68; W Germany 68-73; Chapl Dudley Sch 73-80; Asst Chapl Wellington Coll Berks 80-82; P-in-c Rendcomb *Glouc* 82-86; Chapl Rendcomb Coll 82-86; Chapl Wrekin Coll Telford 86-90; V Deptford St Jo w H Trin *S'wark* 91-94; rtd 94; Perm to Offic *Sarum* 94-00 and *Guildf* from 02. *4 The Larches, Woking GU21 4RE* Tel (01483) 720398

OLEY, Mrs Carolyn Joan Macdonald. b 44. Ox Min Course 05. **d** 08 **p** 09. NSM Lambfold *Pet* from 08. *10 The Green, Evenley, Brackley NN13 5SQ* Tel (01280) 701311 Mobile 07808-776751
E-mail carolyn.oley@btinternet.com

OLHAUSEN, William Paul. b 67. Wycliffe Hall Ox BA97. **d** 98 **p** 99. C Reading Greyfriars *Ox* 98-01; Sub Chapl HM YOI Reading 98-01; C Cambridge H Trin *Ely* 01-04; I Carrigrohane Union *C, C & R* 04-08; Chapl Monkton Combe Sch Bath from 08. *Monkton Combe School, Monkton Combe, Bath BA2 7HG* Tel (01225) 721102 E-mail wpo@oceanfree.net

OLIVE, Dan. b 29. ARIBA54. Sarum & Wells Th Coll 79. **d** 82 **p** 83. NSM Wells St Cuth w Wookey Hole *B & W* 82-85; C Yatton Moor 86-88; R Mells w Buckland Dinham, Elm, Whatley etc 88-97; RD Frome 93-97; rtd 97; Perm to Offic

B & W from 97. *Roseleigh, Woodcombe, Minehead TA24 8SA* Tel (01643) 702218

OLIVER, Bernard John. b 31. CEng65 MIMechE. S'wark Ord Course 75. **d** 78 **p** 79. NSM Chipping Ongar *Chelmsf* 78-81; C Waltham Abbey 81-85; C High Ongar w Norton Mandeville 85-87; C Somerton w Compton Dundon, the Charltons etc *B & W* 87-88; rtd 96; Perm to Offic *Sarum* from 01. *1 Orchard Way, Mosterton, Beaminster DT8 3LT* Tel (01308) 868037

OLIVER, Canon David Ryland. b 34. Univ of Wales (Lamp) BA56 St Cath Coll Ox BA58 MA62. Wycliffe Hall Ox 56. **d** 58 **p** 59. C Carmarthen St Pet *St D* 58-61; C Llangyfelach and Morriston *S & B* 61-63; R Aberedw w Llandeilo Graban etc 63-66; R Llanbadarn Fawr, Llandegley and Llanfihangel etc 66-67; Lic to Offic *Llan* 68-70 and *Ban* 70-73; V Nefyn w Pistyll w Tudweiliog w Llandudwen etc *Ban* 73-74; V Abercraf and Callwen *S & B* 74-77; V Llangyfelach 77-79; R Llanllwchaearn and Llanina *St D* 79-83; V Cwmaman 83-94; Can St D Cathl from 90; RD Dyffryn Aman 93-94; V Cynwyl Gaeo w Llansawel and Talley 94-99; rtd 99. *Maes y Gelynen, 40 Heol Bryngwili, Cross Hands, Llanelli SA14 6LR* Tel (01269) 840146

OLIVER, Gordon. *See* OLIVER, Canon Thomas Gordon

OLIVER, Graham Frank. b 42. St Barn Coll Adelaide. **d** 68 **p** 69. Australia 68-86; C Ealing Ch the Sav *Lon* 86-93; Perm to Offic 94-97 and 00-08; Asst Chapl Ypres *Eur* 97-99; P-in-c 99-00; rtd 07. *Flat 1, 4 High Street, London NW10 4LX* Tel (020) 8963 0477

OLIVER, John Andrew George. b 28. OBE83. St Jo Coll Dur BA53. **d** 55 **p** 56. C Bermondsey St Mary w St Olave and St Jo *S'wark* 55-58; C Dulwich St Barn 58-61; Chapl RN 61-83; QHC 79-83; R Guisborough *York* 83-89; Tutor and Chapl Whittington Coll Felbridge 89-93; rtd 93; Perm to Offic *Carl* from 93. *Allandale, Thacka Lane, Penrith CA11 9HX* Tel (01768) 892096

OLIVER, John Graham Wyand. b 47. Ridley Hall Cam 76. **d** 78 **p** 79. C Shortlands *Roch* 78-81; C Hammersmith St Paul *Lon* 81-85; V Mazabuka Zambia 85-91; Adn S Zambia 89-91; R Cape Town St Mark S Africa from 95. *The Rectory, 35 Beresford Road, University Estate, Cape Town, 7925 South Africa* Tel (0027) (21) 705 5502 *or* 448 1006 Fax 448 8500 Mobile 82-733 3500 E-mail revjohn@iafrica.com

✠**OLIVER, The Rt Revd John Keith.** b 35. G&C Coll Cam BA59 MA63 MLitt65. Westcott Ho Cam 59. **d** 64 **p** 65 **c** 90. C Hilborough w Bodney *Nor* 64-68; Chapl Eton Coll 68-72; R S Molton w Nymet St George *Ex* 73-75; P-in-c Filleigh w E Buckland 73-75; P-in-c Warkleigh w Satterleigh and Chittlehamholt 73-75; P-in-c High Bray w Charles 73-75; TR S Molton, Nymet St George, High Bray etc 75-82; P-in-c N Molton w Twitchen 77-79; RD S Molton 74-80; TR Cen Ex 82-85; Adn Sherborne *Sarum* 85-90; P-in-c w Stafford w Frome Billet 85-90; Can Res Sarum Cathl 85-90; Bp Heref 90-03; rtd 03; Hon Asst Bp *S & B* from 04; Perm to Offic *Heref* from 05. *The Old Vicarage, Glascwm, Llandrindod Wells LD1 5SE* Tel and fax (01982) 570771

OLIVER, John Kenneth. b 47. Brunel Univ MA92 ALBC70. EAMTC 98. **d** 00 **p** 01. C E Ham St Paul *Chelmsf* 00-03; V Stratford New Town St Paul 03-05; TV Totton *Win* from 05. *Calmore Vicarage, Cooks Lane, Calmore, Southampton SO40 2RU* Tel (023) 8081 2702 E-mail j.k.oliver@tesco.net

OLIVER, The Ven John Michael. b 39. Univ of Wales (Lamp) BA62. Ripon Hall Ox 62. **d** 64 **p** 65. C High Harrogate St Pet *Ripon* 64-67; C Bramley 67-72; V Low Harrogate St Mary 72-78; V Beeston 78-92; RD Armley 86-92; Adn Leeds 92-05; Hon Can Ripon Cathl 87-05; rtd 05; Perm to Offic *Ripon* from 05. *42A Chapel Lane, Barwick in Elmet, Leeds LS15 4EJ* Tel 0113-393 5019

OLIVER, The Ven John Rodney. b 31. Melbourne Univ BA53 Lon Univ MTh73. Bps' Coll Cheshunt 54. **d** 56 **p** 57. C Much Hadham *St Alb* 56-57; Chapl Ballarat Gr Sch Australia 58-69; C Thorley and Bishop's Stortford H Trin *St Alb* 70-73; V Aberfeldie Australia 74-77; Chapl Trin Coll Melbourne 77-81; I Dandenong 81-91; Adn Box Hill 87-00; I East Kew St Paul 91-00; rtd 00. *27 Asquith Street, Box Hill South Vic 3128, Australia* Tel (0061) (3) 9888 7517 Fax 9888 7598
E-mail rodley@smartchat.net.au

OLIVER, Mrs Josephine May. b 48. Cranmer Hall Dur. **d** 01 **p** 02. C Buckrose Carrs *York* 01-04; P-in-c Bubwith w Skipwith from 04. *The Vicarage, 2 Highfield Road, Bubwith, Selby YO8 6LY* Tel (01757) 289129 Mobile 07885-448331
E-mail jo@j-oliver.freeserve.co.uk

OLIVER (née TROMANS), Mrs Judith Anne. b 54. Liv Univ BSc76 Lanc Univ PGCE77 Birm Univ MA07. WMMTC. **d** 96 **p** 97. C Old Swinford Stourbridge *Worc* 96-99; C Pennsett 99-01; Asst to Suff Bp Dudley 99-01; P-in-c Dudley Wood 01-08; V from 08. *The Vicarage, 57 Lantern Road, Dudley DY2 0DL* Tel (01384) 832164 Mobile 07903-104862
E-mail juditholiver@blueyonder.co.uk

OLIVER, Canon Paul Robert. b 41. Tyndale Hall Bris 63. **d** 66 **p** 67. C Virginia Water *Guildf* 66-70; Scripture Union (E Region) 70-74; TV Thetford *Nor* 75-83; V Earlham St Anne 83-98; RD

Nor S 94-98; Hon Can Nor Cathl 96-98; rtd 98; Perm to Offic *Nor* from 98. *Cherry Tree Cottage, 91 High Road, Needham, Harleston IP20 9LF* Tel (01379) 852892

OLIVER, Canon Philip Maule. b 38. Birm Univ LLB59. Wells Th Coll 62. **d** 64 **p** 65. C Chesterton *Lich* 64-67; C Tettenhall Wood 67-71; V Milton 71-78; V Ixworth and Bardwell *St E* 78-92; P-in-c Honington w Sapiston and Troston 81-92; TR Blackbourne 92-08; RD Ixworth 85-94; Hon Can St E Cathl 00-08; rtd 08; Perm to Offic *St E* from 08. *25 Millfield Road, Barningham, Bury St Edmunds IP31 1DX*

OLIVER, Rodney. *See* OLIVER, The Ven John Rodney

OLIVER, Ryland. *See* OLIVER, Canon David Ryland

OLIVER, Simon Andrew. b 71. Mansf Coll Ox BA93 MA98 Peterho Cam BA97 MA00 PhD03. Westcott Ho Cam 95. **d** 98 **p** 99. NSM Teversham *Ely* 98-01; NSM Cherry Hinton St Andr 98-01; Chapl Hertf Coll Ox 01-05; Perm to Offic *St D* from 05; Lect Univ of Wales (Lamp) 05; Sen Lect from 06. *Department of Theology, University of Wales Lampeter, College Street, Lampeter SA48 7ED* Tel (01570) 424959
E-mail s.oliver@lamp.ac.uk

✠**OLIVER, The Rt Revd Stephen John.** b 48. AKC69. St Aug Coll Cant 70. **d** 71 **p** 72 **c** 03. C Clifton w Glapton *S'well* 71-75; P-in-c Newark Ch Ch 75-79; R Plumtree 79-85; Sen Producer BBC Relig Broadcasting Dept Lon 85-87; Chief Producer 87-91; TR Leeds City *Ripon* 91-97; Can Res and Prec St Paul's Cathl 97-03; Area Bp Stepney from 03. *63 Coborn Road, London E3 2DB* Tel (020) 8981 2323 Fax 8981 8015
E-mail bishop.stepney@london.anglican.org

OLIVER, Mrs Susan Jacqueline. b 54. Univ Coll Lon LLB78 CQSW86. Qu Coll Birm 03. **d** 05 **p** 06. C Fladbury w Wyre Piddle and Moor etc *Worc* 05-09; TV Louth *Linc* from 09. *St Michael's Vicarage, Little Lane, Louth LN11 9DU* Tel (01507) 601250 Mobile 07740-460313
E-mail suejoliver@tiscali.co.uk

OLIVER, Suzanne Marie. *See* PATTLE, Mrs Suzanne Marie

OLIVER, Canon Thomas Gordon. b 48. Nottm Univ BTh72 DipAdEd80. St Jo Coll Nottm 68 ALCD82. **d** 72 **p** 73. C Thorpe Edge *Bradf* 72-76; C Woodthorpe *S'well* 76-80; V Huthwaite 80-85; Dir Past Studies St Jo Coll Nottm 85-94; Dir of Min and Tr *Roch* from 94; Hon Can Roch Cathl from 95. *18 King's Avenue, Rochester ME1 3DS* Tel (01634) 841232 *or* 830333 Fax 829463 E-mail gordon.oliver@rochester.anglican.org

OLIVER, Ms Wendy Louise. b 54. Aston Tr Scheme 93 Oak Hill Th Coll 94. **d** 96 **p** 97. C Walmsley *Man* 96-99; P-in-c Goodshaw and Crawshawbooth 99-08; AD Rossendale 04-08; V Harwood from 08. *The Vicarage, Stitch mi Lane, Bolton BL2 4HU* Tel (01204) 525196 E-mail wendyloliver@hotmail.com

OLIVEY, Hugh Charles Tony. b 35. St Mich Coll Llan 77. **d** 79 **p** 80. C St Winnow *Truro* 79-81; C Lanhydrock 81-82; C Lostwithiel 81-82; C Lanivet 81-82; P-in-c 82-83; TV Bodmin w Lanhydrock and Lanivet 84-89; P-in-c St Neot 89-90; P-in-c Warleggan 89-90; R St Neot and Warleggan 90-99; P-in-c Cardynham 97-99; rtd 99; Perm to Offic *Truro* from 99; Hon Chapl Duchy Hosp Truro from 04. *The Bungalow, 2 Lower Hugus Road, Threemilestone, Truro TR3 6BD* Tel (01872) 223103

OLIVIER, Bertrand Maurice Daniel. b 62. Ecole des Cadres Paris BA84. S'wark Ord Course 93. **d** 96 **p** 97. C Walworth St Jo *S'wark* 96-00; V Southfields St Barn 00-05; RD Wandsworth 03-05; V All Hallows by the Tower etc *Lon* from 05. *The Residence, 43 Trinity Square, London EC3N 4DJ* Tel (020) 7488 4772 Mobile 07958-411529 E-mail bertrand@ahbtt.org.uk

OLLIER, Mrs Jane Sarah. b 60. Leeds Univ BA81 Ex Univ MA05. SWMTC 02. **d** 05 **p** 06. NSM Seaton and Beer *Ex* 05-07; C Ottery St Mary, Alfington, W Hill, Tipton etc from 07. *The Vicarage, Bendarroch Road, West Hill, Ottery St Mary EX11 1UW* Tel (01404) 811716

OLLIER, Canon Timothy John Douglas. b 44. Trin Hall Cam BA66 MA69. Cuddesdon Coll 66. **d** 68 **p** 69. C Silksworth *Dur* 68-71; C St Marylebone w H Trin *Lon* 71-74; C Winlaton *Dur* 74-77; R Redmarshall and V Bishopton w Gt Stainton 77-88; P-in-c Grindon and Stillington 83-88; V Gainford and R Winston 88-00; AD Barnard Castle 88-00; P-in-c Egglescliffe 00-03; R from 03; AD Stockton 01-07; Hon Can Dur Cathl from 94. *The Rectory, 10 Butts Lane, Egglescliffe, Stockton-on-Tees TS16 9BT* Tel (01642) 780185 Fax 791886
E-mail timollier@onyxnet.co.uk

OLLIFF, Roland. b 61. Ex Coll Ox MA98. Coll of Resurr Mirfield 93. **d** 95 **p** 96. C Bickleigh and Shaugh Prior *Ex* 95-98; CF 98-07; Sen CF from 07. *c/o MOD Chaplains (Army)* Tel (01980) 615804 Fax 615800 E-mail olliff@hotmail.com

OLLIVE, Mrs Patricia Ann. b 55. St Luke's Coll Ex BA91. Ripon Coll Cuddesdon DTh05. **d** 05 **p** 06. C Backwell w Chelvey and Brockley *B & W* 05-09; P-in-c Shapwick w Ashcott and Burtle from 09; P-in-c W Poldens from 09. *The Vicarage, Vicarage Lane, Shapwick, Bridgwater TA7 9LR* Tel (01458) 210260 Mobile 07840-387121 E-mail trishollive@hotmail.com

OLNEY, Dorian Frederick. b 50. Kingston Poly BA71 Anglia Poly Univ MA03 MIL88 MCIPD88. Ridley Hall Cam 96. **d** 98

p 99. C Glenfield *Leic* 98-02; Chapl ATC 99-01; TV Newark *S'well* 02-07; P-in-c Shenstone *Lich* from 07; P-in-c Stonnall from 07. *The Vicarage, St John's Hill, Shenstone, Lichfield WS14 0JB* Tel (01543) 480286
E-mail fred.olney@webleicester.co.uk

O'LOUGHLIN, Mrs Kathryn. b 60. Man Univ BSc81 Win Univ MA08. STETS 96. **d** 99 **p** 00. NSM Basing *Win* 99-03; Perm to Offic 03-08; C N Hants Downs from 08; Tutor STETS from 08. *Manor Lodge, Froyle Lane, South Warnborough, Hook RG29 1SG* Tel 07796-411511 (mobile)
E-mail kathy.oloughlin@gmail.com

OLSEN, Arthur Barry. b 37. Univ of NZ BA61 Melbourne Coll of Div BD73. ACT ThL64. **d** 64 **p** 64. New Zealand 64-67; C Nelson All SS 64-67; V Ahuara 67-69; V Motupiko 69-70; V Amuri 70-73; Maori Miss and C Dunedin St Matt 73-76; V Brooklyn 77-81; C Hersham *Guildf* 81-84; P-in-c Botleys and Lyne 84-95; V 95-03; P-in-c Long Cross 95-03; Chapl NW Surrey Mental Health Partnership NHS Trust 85-03; rtd 03; Hon C Rotherfield Peppard and Kidmore End etc *Ox* from 03. *2 Priory Copse, Peppard Common, Henley-on-Thames RG9 5LH* Tel 0118-924 2812 E-mail barry.o22@virgin.net

OLSWORTH-PETER, Edward James. b 77. UWE BA99. Wycliffe Hall Ox BTh04. **d** 04 **p** 05. C Guildf Ch Ch w St Martha-on-the-Hill 04-07; C Upper Chelsea *Lon* from 07. *The Parish Office, St Saviour's Church, Walton Place, London SW3 1SA* Tel (020) 7823 8979
E-mail ed_olsworth@hotmail.com

OLUKANMI, Miss Stella Grace Oluwafunmilayo Olanrewaju. b 57. St Jo Coll Nottm BTh95 LTh92. **d** 96 **p** 97. C Gt Ilford St Jo *Chelmsf* 96-01; V Barkingside St Cedd from 01. *The Vicarage, 10 Marston Road, Ilford IG5 0LY* Tel (020) 8551 3406 E-mail revdsolukanmi@btinternet.com

OLUMIDE, The Ven Oluseye Abiola Abisogun Okikiade ('Seye. b 42. Bradf Univ BA89 MSc92. Clifton Th Coll 68. **d** 71 **p** 72. C Halliwell St Pet *Man* 71-72; C Salford St Phil w St Steph 72; P-in-c Wood Green St Mich *Lon* 73; C Stanmer w Falmer and Moulsecoomb *Chich* 73-76; C Hulme Ascension *Man* 76-77; Chapl Asst N Man Gen Hosp 77-80; Chapl St Bernard's and Ealing Hosps 80-86; Chapl Bradf R Infirmary 86-91; Chapl Lynfield Mt Hosp Bradf 86-91; Chapl St Luke's Hosp Bradf 86-91; Chapl Bradf Hosps NHS Trust 91-96; Chapl Co-ord Parkside Community NHS Trust Lon 96-01; rtd 01; Can Lagos Cathl from 98; Adn in Egba from 00. *7 St Brides Close, Pontarddulais, Swansea SA4 1LE* Tel (01792) 882823 Mobile 07799-471301

O'MALLEY, Canon Brian Denis Brendan. b 40. Univ of Wales (Lamp) MA97 MHCIMA60. Oscott Coll (RC) 74 Coll of Resurr Mirfield 82. **d** 77 **p** 83. In RC Ch 77-81; Warden St Greg Retreat Rhandirmwyn *St D* 80-83; Chapl and Min Can St D Cathl 83-85; V Wiston w Ambleston, St Dogwells, Walton E etc 85-89; V Wiston w Clarbeston and Walton E 89; R Walton W w Talbenny and Haroldston W 89-98; Chapl Pembrokeshire Coll of FE 93-98; Chapl St D Coll Lamp 98-07; Can St D Cathl 01-07; rtd 07. *Millbank, North Road, Lampeter SA48 7HZ* Tel (01570) 422148

O'MEARA, Colette Margaret Mary. *See* THORNBOROUGH, Ms Colette Margaret Mary

OMOLE, Oluremi Richard. b 63. **d** 05 **p** 07. NSM Dur N from 05. *7 Frensham Way, Meadowfield, Durham DH7 8UR* Tel 0191-378 9756

OMOYAJOWO, Justus Akinwale. b 65. Obafemi Awolowo Univ BA87 Ibadan Univ Nigeria MA90 Bayreuth Univ PhD99. Vining Coll of Th 90. **d** 92 **p** 93. Nigeria 92-94; C Akure St Andr 92; Chapl Ondo-State Pris 93; Chapl Ondo-State Univ 94; Asst Lect Bayreuth Univ Germany 95-97; Perm to Offic *S'wark* 98-99 and 00-01; C Hatcham St Jas 99-00; Chapl Goldsmiths' Coll Lon 99-00; P-in-c Sutton New Town St Barn 01-03; Perm to Offic *S'wark* 07-08; Hon C Morden *S'wark* from 08. *4 Litchfield Avenue, Morden SM4 5QS* Tel (020) 8640 7311 Mobile 07790-593392
E-mail precious.omuku@yahoo.com

O'NEILL, Mrs Caroline Lois. b 55. CQSW. Trin Coll Bris BA00. **d** 00 **p** 01. C Bath St Sav w Swainswick and Woolley *B & W* 00-03; C Charlcombe w Bath St Steph 03-08; Chapl K Edw Sch Bath from 09; Chapl Partis Coll Bath from 09. *28 Pera Place, Bath BA1 5NX*

O'NEILL, Christopher John. b 53. Worc Coll Ox BA75 MA80 Surrey Univ PhD03 CertEd91 ALAM LGSM. Ripon Coll Cuddesdon 77. **d** 78 **p** 79. Asst Chapl Rugby Sch 78-80; Chapl Charterhouse Sch Godalming 81-98; Hd of Counselling from 98. *14 Chapelfields, Charterhouse Road, Godalming GU7 2BF* Tel (01483) 414437 E-mail cbenedictoneill@hotmail.com

O'NEILL, Edward Daniel. b 42. Man Univ BA62 Bradf Univ MSc76. NOC 89. **d** 92 **p** 93. NSM Prenton *Ches* 92-94; NSM

Newton 94-95; Perm to Offic *Liv* 97-98; NSM W Derby Gd Shep 98-99; C 99-02; V Stockbridge Village from 02. *1 The Cross, Stanley Road, Huyton, Liverpool L36 9XL* Tel 0151-449 3800 E-mail eddieoneill@blueyonder.co.uk

O'NEILL, Gary. b 57. K Coll Lon BD79 AKC79. Westcott Ho Cam 80. **d** 81 **p** 82. C Oldham *Man* 81-84; C Birch w Fallowfield 84-87; R Moston St Chad 87-97; Can Res Birm Cathl 97-07; Dir Studies for Ords *Ches* from 07. *10 Neston Close, Helsby, Frodsham WA6 0FH* Tel (01928) 723327 Mobile 07976-729449 E-mail gary.oneill@chester.anglican.org

O'NEILL, Irene. *See* CARTER, Mrs Irene

O'NEILL, Robert Patrick. b 66. Herts Univ BA96. Ridley Hall Cam 06. **d** 08. NSM Lt Berkhamsted and Bayford, Essendon etc *St Alb* from 08. *41 Hillcrest, Hatfield AL10 8EZ* Tel (01707) 695141 E-mail rob.oneill@ntlworld.com

ONIONS, Mrs Angela Ann. b 33. STETS 01. **d** 02. NSM Bradford-on-Avon *Sarum* 02-08. *27 Berryfield Road, Bradford-on-Avon BA15 1SX* Tel (01225) 309001 Mobile 07719-726461 E-mail r.a.onions@btinternet.co.uk

ONIONS, Martin Giles. b 63. Bp Otter Coll Chich BA99 Univ Coll Chich MA02. Chich Th Coll 85. **d** 88 **p** 89. C Eastbourne St Mary *Chich* 88-91; C-in-c The Hydneye CD 91-96; V The Hydneye 96-97; V Findon Valley 97-01; V Willingdon from 01. *The Vicarage, 35A Church Street, Willingdon, Eastbourne BN20 9HR* Tel and fax (01323) 502079 E-mail martin.onions@btinternet.com

ONSLOW, Sister Denzil Octavia. b 19. dss 61 **d** 87 **p** 94. CSA from 56; Novice Guardian 68-73 and 90-94; R Foundn of St Kath in Ratcliffe 73-79; Notting Hill St Jo and St Pet *Lon* 80-87; Hon Par Dn 87-94; Hon C 94-01; Perm to Offic from 01. *St Mary's Convent and Nursing Home, Burlington Lane, London W4 2QE* Tel (020) 8995 1019

ONUNWA, The Ven Udobata Rufus. b 47. Univ of Nigeria BA78 MA82 PhD85. Trin Coll Umuahia 72. **d** 74 **p** 75. Chapl Owerri Cathl Nigeria 74-75; Chapl Univ of Nigeria 75-78 and 82-84; Chapl to Abp Nigeria and P-in-c Okebola St Paul 78-79; Lect Trin Th Coll Umuahia 79-81; Hon Can Okigwe-Orlu 84-89; Can Res Calabar 90-91; V Calabar St Jude 92-96; Adn Calabar 94-96; Tutor Crowther Hall CMS Tr Coll Selly Oak 97-02; NW Regional Dir Crosslinks 03-05; P-in-c Grange St Andr *Ches* from 05. *The Vicarage, 37 Lime Grove, Runcorn WA7 5JZ* Tel (01928) 574411 Mobile 07967-965161 E-mail u.onunwa@btinternet.com

ONYEKWELU, Mrs Ada. b 54. Ibadan Univ Nigeria BSc83 SEN98. **d** 07 **p** 08. NSM Selsdon St Fran CD *S'wark* from 07. *80 Tedder Road, South Croydon CR2 8AQ* Tel (020) 8657 4018 E-mail a_onye@yahoo.co.uk

OOSTERHOF, Ms Liesbeth. b 61. Ripon Coll Cuddesdon 02. **d** 04 **p** 05. C E Bergholt and Brantham *St E* 04-07; R Shoreline from 07. *The Rectory, Rectory Field, Chelmondiston, Ipswich IP9 1HY* Tel (01473) 781902 E-mail l.oosterhof@btinternet.com

OPPERMAN, Graham William. b 40. Th Ext Educn Coll 98. **d** 00 **p** 03. C Linden St Thos S Africa 00-04; NSM Aberdour *St And* 04; NSM Burntisland 04; NSM Inverkeithing 04; TV Jarrow *Dur* from 05. *St John the Baptist House, Iona Road, Jarrow NE32 4HY* Tel 0191-489 2043 Mobile 07792-451622 E-mail graham.opperman@btinternet.com

ORAM, Canon Geoffrey William James. b 14. Em Coll Cam BA37 MA40. Ridley Hall Cam 36. **d** 38 **p** 39. C Tooting Graveney St Nic *S'wark* 38-40; C Rugby St Andr *Cov* 40-41; V Ipswich St Thos *St E* 41-49; R E Bergholt 49-64; Bp's Chapl 54-67; Hon Can St E Cathl 59-80; RD Samford 59-64; V Aldeburgh w Hazlewood 64-80; rtd 80; Perm to Offic *St E* 80-81 and from 86; P-in-c Ipswich St Mich 81-86. *2B Clarkson Court, Ipswich Road, Woodbridge IP12 4BF* Tel (01394) 380269

ORAM, John Ernest Donald. b 34. Open Univ BA74. Tyndale Hall Bris. **d** 61 **p** 62. C Cheetham Hill *Man* 61-64; C Gt Baddow *Chelmsf* 64-67; V Blackb St Barn 67-72; Bp's Chapl for Soc Resp *Sheff* 72-86; Chapl Psychotherapist 79-86; Perm to Offic from 86; rtd 99. *12 Montgomery Road, Sheffield S7 1LQ* Tel 0114-221 4982

ORAM, Roland Martin David. b 45. Trin Coll Cam BA68 ARCM70. Cranmer Hall Dur. **d** 78 **p** 79. C Aspley *S'well* 78-81; Chapl Alleyn's Sch Dulwich 81-88; Chapl Versailles w Grandchamp and Chevry *Eur* 88-92; Chapl Denstone Coll Uttoxeter 92-01; Assoc V Hanford *Lich* from 01; Assoc V Trentham from 02. *Hanford Vicarage, 76 Church Lane, Stoke-on-Trent ST4 4QD* Tel (01782) 657848

ORAM, Stephen John. b 58. **d** 84 **p** 85. C Kidderminster St Jo *Worc* 84-88; Chapl RAF 88-92; P-in-c Brislington St Anne 92-97; V Cricklade w Latton 97-04; Co-ord Chapl N Bris NHS Trust from 04. *North Bristol NHS Trust, Frenchay Park Road, Bristol BS16 1LE* Tel 0117-970 1212 E-mail stephen.oram@ntlworld.com

ORAM, Vincent Charles. b 55. Rhodes Univ BA78 Fort Hare Univ BTh84. St Paul's Coll Grahamstown. **d** 81 **p** 82. C King Williams Town H Trin S Africa 81-85; R Barkly East St Steph 85-90; Can Grahamstown Cathl 96; Adn East London South

97-99; P-in-c Shenley *St Alb* 00-05; TV Aldenham, Radlett and Shenley from 05; RD Aldenham 03-08. *The Rectory, 63 London Road, Shenley, Radlett WD7 9BW* Tel (01923) 855383 E-mail vincent.oram@ntlworld.com

ORAMS, Ronald Thomas. b 49. ACMA80. **d** 08 **p** 09. NSM Laxfield, Cratfield, Wilby and Brundish *St E* from 08. *Crane Lodge, Bickers Hill, Laxfield, Woodbridge IP12 8DP* Tel (01986) 798901 Mobile 07721-682183 E-mail ron.orams@care4free.net

O'RAW, Canon Neal John. **d** 02 **p** 03. C Killala w Dunfeeny, Crossmolina, Kilmoremoy etc *T, K & A* 02-05; Bp's C from 05; Can Tuam Cathl from 09. *The Rectory, The Boreen, Crossmolina, Co Mayo, Republic of Ireland* Tel (00353) (96) 31384 Mobile 87-292 2405 E-mail revdoraw@hotmail.com

ORCHARD, Canon George Richard. b 41. Ex Coll Ox BA62 BA64 MA66. Ripon Hall Ox 62. **d** 65 **p** 66. C Greenhill St Pet *Derby* 65-70; Member Ecum Team Min Sinfin Moor 70-78; V Sinfin Moor 76-78; TR Dronfield 78-86; Can Res Derby Cathl 86-92; Hon Can 92-06; P-in-c Baslow 92-93; P-in-c Curbar and Stoney Middleton 92-93; V Baslow w Curbar and Stoney Middleton 93-06; rtd 06; Perm to Offic *Cant* and *Chich* from 07. *7 Love Lane, Rye TN31 7NE* Tel (01797) 225916 E-mail richardorchard41@yahoo.co.uk

ORCHARD, Harry Frank. b 23. Roch Th Coll. **d** 63 **p** 64. C Sturminster Newton *Sarum* 63-65; Argentina 65-67; V Preston *Sarum* 67-71; R Teffont Evias and Teffont Magna 71-73; V Dinton 71-73; C Fovant w Compton Chamberlayne etc 76-78; Lic to Offic 78-02; RD Chalke 80-82; rtd 88. *49 Highfields, Ashby Meadows, Spilsby PE23 5DN* Tel (01790) 753044

ORCHARD, Helen Claire. b 65. Sheff Univ BA87 PhD96 Em Coll Cam MPhil02. Westcott Ho Cam 01. **d** 03 **p** 04. C Merrow *Guildf* 03-06; Chapl and Fell Ex Coll Ox from 06. *Exeter College, Oxford OX1 3DP* Tel (01865) 279600 E-mail helen.orchard@exeter.ox.ac.uk

ORCHARD, Nigel John. b 56. CertEd78. St Steph Ho Ox 82. **d** 85 **p** 86. C Tottenham St Paul *Lon* 85-89; C Is of Dogs Ch Ch and St Jo w St Luke 89-90; TV 90-92; P-in-c Southall Ch Redeemer 92-99; V from 99. *Christ The Redeemer Vicarage, 299 Allenby Road, Southall UB1 2HE* Tel (020) 8578 2711 E-mail nigel.orchard1@btinternet.com

ORCHARD, Richard. *See* ORCHARD, Canon George Richard

ORCHARD, Mrs Tryphena Jane. b 35. Westf Coll Lon BA57. S'wark Ord Course 87. **d** 92 **p** 94. NSM Shaston *Sarum* 92-01; rtd 01; Perm to Offic *Sarum* 01-08. *Dunscar Fold, Hawkesdene Lane, Shaftesbury SP7 8NU* Tel (01747) 855228

O'REILLY, Brian. **d** 07 **p** 08. C Seagoe *D & D* from 07. *24 The Glebe, Portadown, Craigavon BT63 5HN*

O'REILLY, Clare Maria. *See* KING, Clare Maria

O'REILLY, Philip Jonathon. b 66. Portsm Poly BSc87 Kent Univ MA97 MRICS. Westcott Ho Cam 93. **d** 93 **p** 94. C Selsdon St Jo w St Fran *S'wark* 93-96; TV Staveley and Barrow Hill *Derby* 96-01; V Wistow *Leic* from 01. *The Vicarage, 12 Saddington Road, Fleckney, Leicester LE8 8AW* Tel 0116-240 2215 E-mail philiporeilly@leicester.anglican.org

ORFORD, Barry Antony. b 49. Univ of Wales (Ban) BA71 MTh97 PhD01. St Steph Ho Ox 71. **d** 73 **p** 74. C Monmouth 73-77; V Choral St As Cathl 77-81; CR 83-96; Perm to Offic *St As* from 97; Hon Asst Chapl Univ of Wales (Ban) 99-01; Lib Pusey Ho from 01. *Pusey House, St Giles, Oxford OX1 3LZ* Tel (01865) 278415

ORFORD, Canon Keith John. b 40. FCIT. EMMTC 76. **d** 79 **p** 80. NSM Matlock Bank *Derby* 79-99; NSM Wirksworth from 99; Hon Can Derby Cathl from 00. *27 Lums Hill Rise, Matlock DE4 3FX* Tel and fax (01629) 55349 E-mail keith.orford@btinternet.com

ORGAN, Mrs Alma. b 45. Bordesley Coll of Educn CertEd66. WEMTC 08. **d** 09. NSM Worc St Barn w Ch Ch from 09. *14 Ongrils Close, Pershore WR10 1QE* Tel (01386) 554248 Mobile 07531-461810 E-mail piglet1723@btinternet.com

ORGAN, Peter. b 73. K Coll Lon BA97 Birm Univ MA01. Qu Coll Birm 99. **d** 01 **p** 02. C E Wickham *S'wark* 01-05; TV Thamesmead from 05. *5 Finchale Road, London SE2 9PG* Tel (020) 8310 5614 E-mail revpeterorgan@yahoo.co.uk

ORLAND, Canon Ernest George. b 28. Lich Th Coll 61. **d** 62 **p** 63. C Northampton St Mich *Pet* 62-65; R Gayton w Tiffield 65-69; R Corby SS Pet and Andr 69-72; TR Corby SS Pet and Andr w Gt and Lt Oakley 72-81; RD Corby 79-81; V Pet All SS 81-93; Can Pet Cathl 79-93; rtd 93; Perm to Offic *Pet* from 93 and *Linc* 95-02. *43 Godsey Lane, Market Deeping, Peterborough PE6 8HY* Tel (01778) 380724

ORME, Christopher Malcolm. b 60. City Univ BSc83. Wycliffe Hall Ox 03. **d** 05 **p** 06. C Shrewsbury H Cross *Lich* 05-08; P-in-c Meanwood *Ripon* from 08. *Meanwood Vicarage, 9 Parkside Green, Leeds LS6 4NY* Tel 0113-275 7885 E-mail chris.orme@holytrinitymeanwood.org.uk

ORME, Mrs Delia. b 57. STETS 01. **d** 08 **p** 09. NSM Haslemere and Grayswood *Guildf* from 08. *Tarn House, 17 Critchmere Hill, Haslemere GU27 1LS* Tel (01428) 644853 E-mail dj.orme@btconnect.com

ORME, Edward John Gilbert. b 42. Man Univ BSc64. Ox Min Course 04. **d** 07 **p** 08. NSM Reading St Agnes w St Paul and St Barn *Ox* from 07. *288 Wokingham Road, Reading RG6 1JU* Tel 07901-528971 (mobile) E-mail eddie.orme@yahoo.co.uk

ORME, John. b 29. Sarum Th Coll 58. **d** 60 **p** 61. C Heald Green St Cath *Ches* 60-64; C Ellesmere Port 64-67; Chapl Harperbury Hosp Radlett 67-73; P-in-c Luton All SS w St Pet *St Alb* 73-79; V 79-87; V Oxhey St Matt 87-96; rtd 97; Perm to Offic *St Alb* from 97. *1 Alzey Gardens, Harpenden AL5 5SZ* Tel (01582) 761931 E-mail john@orme117.freeserve.co.uk

ORME, Sydney. b 27. Oak Hill Th Coll 54. **d** 58 **p** 59. C Halliwell St Pet *Man* 58-61; V Friarmere 61-73; V Knypersley *Lich* 73-92; rtd 92; Perm to Offic *Ches* from 92. *10 Elworth Road, Sandbach CW11 9HQ* Tel (01270) 759233

ORMEROD, Henry Lawrence. b 35. Pemb Coll Cam BA58 MA63. Qu Coll Birm. **d** 60 **p** 61. C Chigwell *Chelmsf* 60-64; C Thundersley 64-68; C Canvey Is 68-72; V Stanground *Ely* 72-77; TR Stanground and Farcet 77-81; TR Swindon St Jo and St Andr *Bris* 81-90; TR N Wingfield, Clay Cross and Pilsley *Derby* 90-97; rtd 97; Hon C Ironstone *Ox* 98-03; Perm to Offic from 03. *5 Waterloo Drive, Banbury OX16 3QN* Tel (01295) 278483 E-mail henryormerod@aol.com

ORMESHER, David Rodney. b 39. **d** 05 **p** 06. OLM Delaval *Newc* from 05. *14 The Crest, Seaton Sluice, Whitley Bay NE26 4BG* Tel 0191-237 1104 E-mail david@ormesher.fslife.co.uk

ORMISTON, Albert Edward. b 26. AMCT46. Oak Hill Th Coll 53. **d** 56 **p** 57. C Worksop St Jo *S'well* 56-58; P-in-c Everton St Polycarp *Liv* 58-59; V 59-63; Org Sec SAMS 63-67; R Gateacre *Liv* 67-73; V Tonbridge St Steph *Roch* 73-86; V Dent w Cowgill *Bradf* 86-91; rtd 91; Perm to Offic *Ches* 91-00; *Glouc* from 02. *30 Capel Court, The Burgage, Prestbury, Cheltenham GL52 3EL* Tel (01242) 518625

ORMROD, Paul William. b 57. Liv Univ BA80 MTh08. Westcott Ho Cam 80. **d** 83 **p** 84. C Prescot *Liv* 83-86; TV Padgate 86-95; V Formby St Pet from 95. *St Peter's Vicarage, Cricket Path, Formby, Liverpool L37 7DP* Tel (01704) 873369

ORMSBY, Robert Daly. b 22. CCC Ox BA42 MA48. Sarum & Wells Th Coll 77. **d** 78 **p** 79. Hon C Lydford and Brent Tor *Ex* 78-96; Hon C Peter Tavy, Mary Tavy, Lydford and Brent Tor from 96. *Lipscliffe, Coryton, Okehampton EX20 4AB* Tel (01822) 860344

ORMSTON, Derek. b 43. **d** 67 **p** 68. C Ogley Hay *Lich* 67-70; C Tettenhall Regis 70-74; P-in-c Leek All SS 74-79; TV Leek and Meerbrook 79-83; Youth Chapl *Bris* 83-87; R Brinkworth w Dauntsey from 87; Chapl New Coll Swindon from 87. *The Rectory, Brinkworth, Chippenham SN15 5AF* Tel (01666) 510207

ORMSTON, Canon Richard Jeremy. b 61. Southlands Coll Lon BA83 Brunel Univ MTh98. Oak Hill Th Coll BA87. **d** 87 **p** 88. C Rodbourne Cheney *Bris* 87-91; R Collingtree w Courteenhall and Milton Malsor *Pet* 91-01; RD Wootton 96-01; R Oundle w Ashton and Benefield w Glapthorn from 01; Can Pet Cathl from 03; RD Oundle from 03. *The Vicarage, 12 New Street, Oundle, Peterborough PE8 4EA* Tel (01832) 273595 E-mail ormston4@aol.com

✠**OROMBI, The Most Revd Henry Luke.** b 49. Bp Tucker Coll Mukono 75 St Jo Coll Nottm BTh83. **d** 79 **p** 79 **c** 93. Dioc Youth Officer Madi/W Nile Uganda 79-86; Adn Goli 87-93; Bp Nebbi 93-03; Abp Uganda and Bp Kampala from 03. *PO Box 14123, Kampala, Uganda* Tel (00256) (41) 270218, 270219 or 271138 Mobile 77-476476 Fax (41) 251925 or 245597 E-mail orombih@yahoo.com or couab@uol.co.ug

O'ROURKE, Brian Joseph Gerard. b 58. TCD BA82 HDipEd83. CITC 89. **d** 92 **p** 93. Chapl Glendalough Sch 90-96; C Newcastle w Newtownmountkennedy and Calary *D & G* 92-96; Bp's C 96-98; I 98-00; I Cork St Ann's Union *C, C & R* from 00; Hon Chapl Miss to Seafarers from 00. *The Rectory, 49 Ard na Laoi, Montenotte, Co Cork, Republic of Ireland* Tel and fax (00353) (21) 450456 or 455 2605 Mobile 86-807 9452 E-mail shandonrector@eircom.net

O'ROURKE, Shaun. b 58. NOC 02. **d** 05 **p** 06. C Gorton and Abbey Hey *Man* 05-08; P-in-c Heaton Reddish from 08. *The Rectory, 8 St Mary's Drive, Stockport SK5 7AX* Tel 0161-477 6702 E-mail sorourke@freezone.co.uk

ORPIN, Mrs Gillian. b 32. SRN53. Oak Hill Th Coll 82. **d** 87 **p** 95. Par Dn Passenham *Pet* 87-92; rtd 92; NSM Oban St Jo *Arg* 92-95; Dioc Chapl 95-98; Perm to Offic *St Alb* from 98. *11 Berwick Way, Sandy SG19 1TR* Tel (01767) 680629

ORR, Andrew Dermot Harman. b 66. Sheff Univ BSc89. CITC BTh92. **d** 92 **p** 93. C Ballymacash *Conn* 92-95; I Castlecomer w Colliery Ch, Mothel and Bilbo *C & O* 95-00; Dioc Registrar 95-00; I Castleknock and Mulhuddart w Clonsilla *D & G* 00-09; I Tullow w Shillelagh, Aghold and Mullinacuff *C & O* from 09. *The Rectory, Tullow, Co Carlow, Republic of Ireland* Tel and fax (00353) (59) 915 1481 E-mail greenorr@esatclear.ie

ORR, David Cecil. b 33. TCD BA56 MA68. **d** 57 **p** 58. C Drumragh *D & R* 57-60; I Convoy 60-70; I Maghera 70-80; I Drumragh w Mountfield 80-84; Dean Derry 84-97; I Templemore 84-97; Miss to Seamen 84-97; rtd 97. *Kilrory, 11*

Broomhill Court, Londonderry BT47 6WP Tel (028) 7134 8183 E-mail dcecilorr@btopenworld.com

ORR, Donald Macrae. b 50. Humberside Poly BA73 Glas Univ BD02 MTh04 PhD08. TISEC 02. **d** 04 **p** 05. C Greenock *Glas* 04-07; P-in-c Johnstone from 07; P-in-c Renfrew from 07. *16 Neilston Road, Barrhead, Glasgow G78 1TY* Tel 0141-881 1372 E-mail donaldorr@lycos.co.uk

ORR, Robert Vernon. b 50. Westmr Univ 80 MIQA89. Wycliffe Hall Ox 96. **d** 98 **p** 99. C Cowley St Jo *Ox* 98-01; P-in-c Reading St Agnes w St Paul 01-02; R Reading St Agnes w St Paul and St Barn from 02. *The Vicarage, 290 Northumberland Avenue, Reading RG2 8DD* Tel 0118-987 4448 E-mail vernon.orr@lineone.net

ORR, William James Craig. TCD BTh01. CITC 98. **d** 01 **p** 02. C Lurgan Ch the Redeemer *D & D* 01-07; I Muckamore *Conn* from 07; I Killead w Gartree from 07. *2 Greenmill, Muckamore, Antrim BT41 4SR* Tel (028) 9442 9019 E-mail william-orr@sky.com

ORR-EWING, Francis Ian Lance (Frog). b 75. Regent's Park Coll Ox BA97. Wycliffe Hall Ox MTh00. **d** 00 **p** 01. C Ox St Aldate 00-03; V Camberwell All SS *S'wark* from 03. *All Saints' Church, Blenheim Grove, London SE15 4QS* Tel (020) 7639 3052 Mobile 07979-594762 E-mail vicar@allsaintspeckham.co.uk

ORRIDGE, Harriet Grace. b 72. St Jo Coll Nottm. **d** 09. C Ironstone Villages *Leic* from 09. *18 Windsor Road, Waltham on the Wolds, Melton Mowbray LE14 4AS* Tel (01664) 464452

ORTON, Peter Joseph. b 57. **d** 03 **p** 04. OLM Burton St Chad *Lich* from 03. *237 Wetmore Road, Burton-on-Trent DE14 1RB* Tel (01283) 537574 E-mail lightcommunity@yahoo.co.uk

ORTON, Canon Richard. b 33. Keble Coll Ox BA56 MA60 Leeds Univ. Lich Th Coll 60. **d** 61 **p** 64. C Penistone w Midhope *Wakef* 61-62; Hon C Meltham 62-69; Hon C Horsforth *Ripon* 69-72; C Far Headingley St Chad 72-75; V Hellifield *Bradf* 75-80; RD Bowland 78-80; R Hutton *Chelmsf* 80-87; R Wallasey St Hilary *Ches* 87-00; Dioc Ecum Officer 92-99; RD Wallasey 96-99; Hon Can Ches Cathl 97-00; rtd 00; C Gt Sutton *Ches* 01-05; Perm to Offic from 05. *137 Brimstage Road, Barnston, Wirral CH60 1XF* Tel 0151-348 4911

OSBORN, Miss Anne. b 40. Reading Univ BA62 MA64 Lon Univ PGCE67. Oak Hill NSM Course 87. **d** 92. Chapl Lon Univ 92-94; Chapl Lon Guildhall Univ 94-96; Chapl Univ of Westmr 94-95; Assoc Tutor NTMTC 97-03; Adv on Women's Min Edmonton Area *Lon* from 03. *8 Beaufort House, Talbot Road, London N15 4DR* Tel (020) 8801 0115

OSBORN, David Ronald. b 42. Bris Univ BA66 Leeds Univ CertEd77 Bath Univ MEd80. Clifton Th Coll 62. **d** 66 **p** 67. C Farndon *S'well* 66-69; P-in-c W Bridgford 69-72; Asst Dioc Dir Educn *Carl* 72-77; P-in-c Kirkandrews-on-Eden w Beaumont and Grinsdale 72-77; Hd RE and Chapl Dauntsey's Sch Devizes 77-83; V Southbroom *Sarum* 83-86; Hd RE Bexhill High Sch 86-93; TV Langtree *Ox* 93-95; TR 95-97; TR Bracknell 97-06; rtd 06; P-in-c Llantilio Crossenny w Penrhos, Llanvetherine etc *Mon* from 06. *The Vicarage, Llantilio Crossenny, Abergavenny NP7 8SU* Tel (01600) 780240 Mobile 07803-618464 E-mail davidosborn@ntlworld.com

OSBORN, David Thomas. b 58. K Coll Lon BD79 AKC79 PGCE80. Linc Th Coll 82. **d** 83 **p** 84. C Bearsted w Thurnham *Cant* 83-86; Chapl RAF 86-90; R Bassingham *Linc* 90-91; V Aubourn w Haddington 90-91; V Carlton-le-Moorland w Stapleford 90-91; R Thurlby w Norton Disney 90-91; Chapl RAF from 91. *Chaplaincy Services, Valiant Block, HQ Air Command, RAF High Wycombe HP14 4UE* Tel (01494) 496800 Fax 496343

OSBORN, Mrs Diana Marian. b 52. R Holloway Coll Lon BSc74 Birm Univ PGCE75. NEOC 81. **dss** 84 **d** 87 **p** 94. Malden St Jo *S'wark* 84-89; Par Dn 87-89; Par Dn Brampton *Ely* 89-92; Par Dn Richmond H Trin and Ch Ch *S'wark* 92-93; Chapl Ridley Hall Cam 94-96; Chapl Milton Children's Hospice 96-98; Chapl E Anglia's Children's Hospices 98-01; Perm to Offic *Ely* 01-07 and *Guildf* from 08. *25 Beech Hanger End, Grayshott, Hindhead GU26 6LS* Tel (01428) 606308

OSBORN, Preb John Geoffrey Rowland. b 33. Jes Coll Cam BA55 MA59. Wells Th Coll 63. **d** 65 **p** 66. C Easthampstead *Ox* 65-68; Lic to Offic *Blackb* 68-70; Brunei 70-75; Asst Dir RE *Blackb* 75-77; V Tockholes 75-77; Dir RE *B & W* 77-83; Dir and Sec Lon Dioc Bd for Schs 83-95; Preb St Paul's Cathl 86-95; rtd 96. *4 Musson Close, Abingdon OX14 5RE* Tel (01235) 528701

OSBORNE, Alexander Deas. b 34. Liv Univ BSc54 PhD57. Oak Hill NSM Course 78. **d** 81 **p** 82. NSM Redbourn *St Alb* 81-98; rtd 98; Perm to Offic *Ely* from 00 and *St Alb* 00-08. *6 Cam Farm, North End, Meldreth, Royston SG8 6NT* Tel (01763) 260456

OSBORNE, Anthony Russell. b 47. Sarum & Wells Th Coll 77. **d** 79 **p** 80. C Heref St Martin 79-81; TV 82-86; TV Hanley H Ev *Lich* 86-92; Can Heref Cathl and Dioc Soc Resp Officer *Heref* 92-97; TR Cannock and V Hatherton *Lich* 97-06; V Penkhull 06-07; P-in-c Hartshill 06-07; P-in-c Trent Vale 06-07; TR Hartshill, Penkhull and Trent Vale from 07. *Trent Vale Vicarage, Crosby Road, Stoke-on-Trent ST4 6JY* Tel (01782) 747669 E-mail anthony@osbornex.plus.com

OSBORNE, Canon Brian Charles. b 38. St Andr Univ MA61. Clifton Th Coll 61. **d** 63 **p** 64. C Skirbeck H Trin *Linc* 63-68; V 80-03; P-in-c New Clee 68-71; V 71-75; V Derby St Aug 75-80; Chapl Pilgrim Hosp Boston 84-88; RD Holland E *Linc* 85-95; Can and Preb Linc Cathl 92-03; rtd 03; Chapl to The Queen 97-08. *3 Newlands Road, Haconby, Bourne PE10 0UT* Tel (01778) 570818 E-mail revbrianosborne@ukonline.co.uk

OSBORNE, Christopher Hazell. b 60. Aston Tr Scheme 89 Sarum & Wells Th Coll 91. **d** 93 **p** 94. C Paignton St Jo *Ex* 93-96; C Hooe 96-97; TV Plymstock and Hooe 97-01; V Ivybridge w Harford from 01. *The Vicarage, Blachford Road, Ivybridge PL21 0AD* Tel (01752) 690193
E-mail osborne@btinternet.com

OSBORNE, David Robert. b 50. Birm Univ BSc71 MEd86 Bris Univ PGCE73. St Jo Coll Dur 78. **d** 80 **p** 81. C Penkridge w Stretton *Lich* 80-85; R Longdon-upon-Tern, Rodington, Uppington etc 85-94; R Pilton w Croscombe, N Wootton and Dinder *B & W* from 94; RD Shepton Mallet 01-07. *The Rectory, Pilton, Shepton Mallet BA4 4DX* Tel (01749) 890423
E-mail osbornepilton@ukonline.co.uk

OSBORNE, David Victor. b 36. Dur Univ BA59 Univ of Wales MA99. Cranmer Hall Dur. **d** 62 **p** 63. C Kennington Cross St Anselm *S'wark* 62-66; C Sandal St Helen *Wakef* 66-67; R Ancoats *Man* 67-73; V Claremont H Angels 73-80; R Breedon cum Isley Walton and Worthington *Leic* 80-87; V Beaumont Leys 87-92; V Billesdon and Skeffington 92-01; rtd 01; Perm to Offic *Leic* and *Pet* from 02. *Rose Cottage, 12 Barlows Lane, Wilbarston, Market Harborough LE16 8QB* Tel (01536) 770400

OSBORNE, Canon Derek James. b 32. Tyndale Hall Bris 53. **d** 57 **p** 58. C Weymouth St Mary *Sarum* 57-60; C Southgate *Chich* 60-63; V Croydon Ch Ch Broad Green *Cant* 63-71; V Cromer *Nor* 71-83; P-in-c Gresham w Bessingham 71-83; Hon Can Nor Cathl 77-83; V Northwood Em *Lon* 83-94; Chapl Lee Abbey 94-97; rtd 97; Perm to Offic *Nor* from 97. *50 Clifton Park, Cromer NR27 9BG* Tel (01263) 511272

OSBORNE, Gerald Edward Richard. b 63. Ch Ch Ox MA85 Wye Coll Lon MSc86. **d** 99 **p** 00. OLM Pewsey and Swanborough *Sarum* from 99. *Lawn Farm, Milton Lilbourne, Pewsey SN9 5LQ* Tel (01672) 563459 Fax 564271 Mobile 07798-942118
E-mail gerald.osborne@farmline.com

OSBORNE, Gillian Margaret. b 54. Open Univ BA90 UEA PGCE93. **d** 07 **p** 08. OLM Stratton St Mary w Stratton St Michael etc *Nor* from 07. *5 Welford Court, The Street, Long Stratton, Norwich NR15 2XL*
E-mail d-gosborne@btinternet.com

OSBORNE, Graham Daking. b 51. City Univ ACII74 FCII77. Cuddesdon Coll 94. **d** 96 **p** 97. C Cirencester *Glouc* 96-00; V Glouc St Cath from 00; AD Glouc City 03-08. *St Catharine's Vicarage, 29 Denmark Road, Gloucester GL1 3JQ* Tel and fax (01452) 524497 E-mail gdosborne@bigfoot.com

OSBORNE, The Ven Hayward John. b 48. New Coll Ox BA70 MA73. Westcott Ho Cam 71. **d** 73 **p** 74. C Bromley SS Pet and Paul *Roch* 73-77; C Halesowen *Worc* 77-80; TV 80-83; TR Worc St Barn w Ch Ch 83-88; V Moseley St Mary *Birm* 88-01; AD Moseley 94-01; Hon Can Birm Cathl 00-01; Adn Birm from 01; P-in-c Allens Croton from 08. *23 Carisbrooke Road, Birmingham B17 8NN* Tel 0121-420 3299 *or* 426 0441 Fax 428 1114
E-mail archdeaconofbham@birmingham.anglican.org

OSBORNE, Jonathan Lloyd. b 62. Ripon Coll Cuddesdon 95. **d** 97 **p** 98. C Mill End and Heronsgate w W Hyde *St Alb* 97-00; Asst Chapl Ealing Hosp NHS Trust 00-03; Chapl Team Ldr from 03; Asst Chapl W Middx Univ Hosp NHS Trust 00-03; Chapl Team Ldr from 03; Chapl Team Ldr Meadow House Hospice from 03; Chapl W Lon Mental Health NHS Trust from 03; Hon Chapl S'wark Cathl from 03. *West Middlesex University Hospital NHS Trust, Twickenham Road, Isleworth TW7 6AF* Tel (020) 8321 5447
E-mail jonathan.osborne@wmuh-tr.nthames.nhs.uk

OSBORNE, The Very Revd June. b 53. Man Univ BA74. St Jo Coll Nottm. **dss** 80 **d** 87 **p** 94. Birm St Martin 80-84; Old Ford St Paul and St Mark *Lon* 84-95; Par Dn Old Ford St Paul w St Steph and St Mark 87-94; P-in-c Old Ford St Paul and St Mark 94-95; Can Res and Treas Sarum Cathl 95-04; Bp's Dom Chapl 95-97; Dean Sarum from 04. *The Deanery, 7 The Close, Salisbury SP1 2EF* Tel (01722) 555176 Fax 555177
E-mail thedean@salcath.co.uk

OSBORNE, Malcolm Eric (Max). b 64. EN(G)87 RMN92. St Jo Coll Nottm 94. **d** 96 **p** 97. C Walton *St E* 96-99; C Ipswich St Matt 99-02; Soc Resp Adv 99-02; V Newmarket All SS from 02. *All Saints' Vicarage, 32 Warrington Street, Newmarket CB8 8BA* Tel (01638) 662514
E-mail max.osborne@stedmundsbury.anglican.org

OSBORNE, Mrs Marianne Lily-May. b 64. St Mich Coll Llan. **d** 09. C Tenby *St D* from 09. *The Vicarage, Penally, Tenby SA70 7PN* Tel (01834) 849141

OSBORNE, Mark William. b 67. Univ of Wales BA89 Lon Univ MTh06. Coll of Resurr Mirfield 94. **d** 94 **p** 95. C Goldthorpe w Hickleton *Sheff* 94-97; C-in-c Southey Green St Bernard CD 97-01; P-in-c Walham Green St Jo w St Jas *Lon* from 01. *The*

Vicarage, 40 Racton Road, London SW6 1LP Tel and fax (020) 7385 3676 *or* 7385 7634 E-mail mark.osborne5@btinternet.com

OSBORNE, Norma. b 36. **d** 97 **p** 03. NSM Upper Tooting H Trin *S'wark* 02-03; NSM Tooting St Aug 02-03; NSM Wandsworth St Mich 03-06; NSM Wandsworth St Mich w St Steph 06-07; Perm to Offic from 07. *Garden Flat, 21A Trinity Crescent, London SW17 7AG* Tel (020) 8682 0423

OSBORNE, Ralph. b 38. Bernard Gilpin Soc Dur 62 Clifton Th Coll 63. **d** 66 **p** 67. C Harpurhey Ch Ch *Man* 66-68; C Chorlton on Medlock St Sav 68-71; C Wilmington *Roch* 71-74; V St Mary Cray and St Paul's Cray 74-85; P-in-c Bath St Steph *B & W* 85-88; P-in-c Charlcombe 86-88; R Charlcombe w Bath St Steph 88-03; rtd 03. *406 Bath Road, Saltford, Bristol BS31 3DH* Tel (01225) 872536 E-mail ralph.osborne@ic24.net

OSBORNE, Canon Robin Orbell. b 29. Leeds Univ BA54. Coll of Resurr Mirfield 52. **d** 54 **p** 55. C Wellingborough All Hallows *Pet* 54-58; C Oxhey St Matt *St Alb* 60-61; V Woburn and Battlesden and Pottesgrove 61-65; V Cheshunt 65-82; RD Cheshunt 70-81; Hon Can St Alb 76-82; V Penzance St Mary w St Paul *Truro* 82-88; Can Res and Treas Truro Cathl 88-94; rtd 94; Perm to Offic *B & W* from 94 and *S'wark* from 05. *The College of St Barnabas, Blackberry Lane, Lingfield RH7 6NJ* Tel (01342) 872833 Mobile 07776-081564
E-mail orbellosborne@gmail.com

OSBOURNE, David John. b 56. Linc Th Coll 78. **d** 79 **p** 80. C Houghton le Spring *Dur* 79-82; C Spalding St Jo *Linc* 82-83; C Spalding St Jo w Deeping St Nicholas 83-84; V Swineshead 84-94; RD Holland W 86-92; P-in-c Boultham 94-01; R from 01; RD Christianity from 08. *The Rectory, 2A St Helen's Avenue, Lincoln LN6 7RA* Tel and fax (01522) 682026
E-mail davidosbourne@tiscali.co.uk

OSBOURNE, Steven John. b 59. St Jo Coll Nottm 92. **d** 94 **p** 95. C Bushbury *Lich* 94-98; C Tamworth 98-03; V Caverswall and Weston Coyney w Dilhorne from 03; RD Cheadle from 07. *8 Vicarage Crescent, Caverswall, Stoke-on-Trent ST11 9EW* Tel (01782) 388037 *or* 312570
E-mail steve.osbourne@btopenworld.com

OSEI, Robert Emmanuel. b 56. **d** 96 **p** 77. Ghana 76-83; C Hangleton *Chich* 83-84; Perm to Offic *S'wark* 00-02. *8 Plummer Court, London SE13 6RA*

OSGERBY, John Martin. b 34. Sheff Univ BSc56 PhD59. Linc Th Coll 75. **d** 77 **p** 78. C Rotherham *Sheff* 77-80; C-in-c W Bessacarr CD 80-84; V W Bessacarr 84-87; Warden of Readers 86-99; R Fishlake w Sykehouse and Kirk Bramwith etc 87-99; RD Snaith and Hatfield 93-99; rtd 99; Perm to Offic *Sheff* from 99 and *Linc* 00-02. *4 Marlborough Avenue, Haxey, Doncaster DN9 2HL* Tel (01427) 754815
E-mail jmosgerby.hax@virgin.net

OSGOOD, Graham Dean. b 39. Lon Univ BSc62 ALCD71. St Jo Coll Nottm 71. **d** 71 **p** 72. C Bebington *Ches* 71-76; V Gee Cross 76-05; rtd 05. *4 Lower Close, Bodicote, Banbury OX15 4DZ* Tel (01295) 266848 E-mail graham.btsc@btinternet.com

OSGOOD, Sylvia Joy. b 47. QUB BSc68 Lon Univ BD78 Man Univ PhD92. St Jo Coll Nottm MA98. **d** 97 **p** 98. NSM Bredbury St Mark *Ches* 97-01; Tutor and Chapl Spurgeon's Coll from 01. *4 Lower Close, Bodicote, Banbury OX15 4DZ* Tel (01295) 266848 E-mail j.osgood@spurgeons.ac.uk

O'SHAUGHNESSY, Mrs Janice Florence. b 51. STETS 95. **d** 98 **p** 99. NSM Bembridge *Portsm* 98-02; Asst Chapl Isle of Wight Healthcare NHS Trust 99-02; C Catherington and Clanfield *Portsm* 02-07; P-in-c Newchurch from 07; P-in-c Arreton from 07; P-in-c Gatcombe from 07. *The Vicarage, High Street, Newchurch, Sandown PO36 0NN*

O'SHEA, Mrs Helen Mary. b 55. Univ of Wales (Abth) BA77 SRN79. Llan Ord Course 94. **d** 98 **p** 99. NSM Skewen *Llan* 98-01; C Llangynwyd w Maesteg 01-02; P-in-c Cwmafan from 02. *The Vicarage, 11 Tabernacle Terrace, Cwmavon, Port Talbot SA12 9HS* Tel (01639) 681890

OSLER, Philip. b 55. SEITE 99. **d** 02 **p** 03. NSM Staplehurst *Cant* 02-07; C Thurlestone, S Milton, W Alvington etc *Ex* 07-09; P-in-c from 09. *The Vicarage, Townsend Close, West Alvington, Kingsbridge TQ7 3QA* Tel (01548) 560967
E-mail philip.osler@btinternet.com

OSMAN, David Thomas. b 49. Bradf Univ BTech72 Newc Univ MA93. Trin Coll Bris 75. **d** 78 **p** 79. C Stranton *Dur* 78-81; C Denton Holme *Carl* 81-84; V Preston on Tees *Dur* 84-97; P-in-c Hebburn St Jo from 97; P-in-c Jarrow Grange from 00. *St Mary's Vicarage, 23 St John's Avenue, Hebburn NE31 2TZ* Tel 0191-422 7505

OSMAN, Ernest. b 35. St Aid Birkenhead 61. **d** 64 **p** 65. C Heaton Ch Ch *Man* 64-68; V Farnworth St Pet 68-77; V St Martin's *Lich* 77-85; V Endon w Stanley 85-00; rtd 00; Hon C Llanyblodwel and Trefonen *Lich* 01-05; Perm to Offic from 05. *The Paddock, Silverdale Drive, Trefonen, Oswestry SY10 9DW* Tel (01691) 654184 E-mail paddock6@btinternet.com

OSMAN, Stephen William. b 53. Matlock Coll of Educn CertEd74 Teesside Poly CQSW80. St Jo Coll Dur 88. **d** 90 **p** 91. C Newbarns w Hawcoat *Carl* 90-93; TV Marfleet *York* 93-00; P-in-c Gotham *S'well* from 00; P-in-c Barton in Fabis from 02;

P-in-c Thrumpton from 02; P-in-c Kingston and Ratcliffe-on-Soar from 02. *The New Rectory, 39 Leake Road, Gotham, Nottingham NG11 0JL* Tel 0115-983 0608
E-mail steveosman500@aol.com

OSMASTON, Canon Amiel Mary Ellinor. b 51. Ex Univ BA73 St Jo Coll Dur BA84. Cranmer Hall Dur 82. **dss** 84 **d** 87 **p** 94. Chester le Street *Dur* 84-88; Par Dn 87-88; Dir Miss and Past Studies Ridley Hall Cam 89-96; Min Development Officer *Ches* 96-03; C Lache cum Saltney 00-03; Min Development Officer *Carl* from 03; C Penrith w Newton Reigny and Plumpton Wall from 03; Hon Can Carl Cathl from 05. *The New Vicarage, Plumpton, Penrith CA11 9PA* Tel (01768) 885756 *or* (01228) 522573 Fax (01768) 885773
E-mail ministry.dev@carlislediocese.org.uk

✠**OSMERS, The Rt Revd John Robert.** b 35. Cant Univ (NZ) MA58. Coll of Resurr Mirfield 59. **d** 61 **p** 62 **c** 95. C Rawmarsh w Parkgate *Sheff* 61-65; Lesotho 65-81; Par P Quthing 65-73; R Masite Miss 73-81; Botswana 81-88; Asst P H Cross Cathl 82-87; R Mpolopole 82-88; Zambia from 88; Chapl ANC 88-91; Dioc Tr Chapl Lusaka 90-95; Bp E Zambia 95-03; Asst Bp Lusaka 03-07; R St Jo Angl Sem Kitwe from 07. *St John's Anglican Seminary, Mindolo Ecumenical Foundation, PO Box 20369, Kitwe, Zambia* Tel (00260) (2) 210960 Mobile 97-841215
E-mail josmers@zamnet.zm

OSMOND, Andrew Mark. b 62. Leeds Univ LLB85. Wycliffe Hall Ox 02. **d** 02. C Cheltenham St Mary, St Matt, St Paul and H Trin *Glouc* 02-03; NSM Cheltenham St Mark from 09. *40 Priors Road, Cheltenham GL52 5AA* Tel (01242) 253859 Mobile 07906-314463
E-mail andysueosmond@googlemail.com

OSMOND, David Methuen. b 38. Qu Coll Birm 75. **d** 77 **p** 78. C Yardley St Edburgha *Birm* 77-80; V Withall 80-89; R W Coker w Hardington Mandeville, E Chinnock etc *B & W* 89-95; Perm to Offic 96-98; rtd 98; Hon C Castle Town *Lich* 01-03; Perm to Offic *Blackb* from 05. *7 Lowerfield, Langho, Blackburn BB6 8HE* Tel (01254) 246146

OSMOND, Mrs Heather Christine. b 44. ABSM64 ARCM65 Birm Poly CertEd65. Qu Coll Birm 83. **dss** 84 **d** 87 **p** 97. Brandwood *Birm* 84-85; Withall 85-89; Par Dn 87-89; Perm to Offic *B & W* 89-01; P-in-c Castle Town *Lich* 01-03; rtd 04; Perm to Offic *Blackb* 05-09. *25 Franklin Gardens, Hitchin SG4 0BS*

OSMOND, Oliver Robert. b 44. Ch Coll Cam BA66 MA70. Cuddesdon Coll 66 Trin Coll Toronto STB69. **d** 69 **p** 70. C Toronto St Jo York Mills 69-71; R N Essa 71-74; R Westmorland 74-77; P-in-c Lower Sackville 77-81; V Mill Hill Jo Keble Ch *Lon* 81-09; rtd 09. *PO Box 211, Lunenburg NS B0J 2C0, Canada* Tel (001) (902) 766 4318

OSMOND, Tobias Charles. b 74. Plymouth Univ BSc96. Ripon Coll Cuddesdon BTh99. **d** 99 **p** 00. C Wilton *B & W* 99-02; C Bath Abbey w St Jas 02-05; I Craighurst, Midhurst and Minesing Canada from 05. *St Paul's Church, 5 Noraldine Avenue, Midhurst ON L0L 1X1, Canada* Tel (001) (705) 721 9722 Fax 721 7744

OSSORY AND LEIGHLIN, Archdeacon of. *See* MURRAY, The Ven John Grainger

OSSORY, Dean of. *See* LYNAS, The Very Revd Norman Noel

OSTLER, Mrs Christine Anne. b 46. Bp Otter Coll CertEd68. Westcott Ho Cam 07. **d** 09. NSM Gt w Lt Harrowden and Orlingbury and Isham etc *Pet* from 09. *19B Castle Street, Wellingborough NN8 1LW* Tel (01933) 226730
E-mail c.ostler@btinternet.com

OSTLI-EAST (*formerly* **EAST), Peter Alan.** b 61. Southn Univ LLB82 ACIB89. Cranmer Hall Dur 90. **d** 93 **p** 94. C Combe Down w Monkton Combe and S Stoke *B & W* 93-97; Perm to Offic *Bris* 06-09; TV Bourne Valley *Sarum* from 09; C Salisbury St Fran and Stratford sub Castle from 09. *The Vicarage, Winterbourne Earls, Salisbury SP4 6HA* Tel (01980) 611350

O'SULLIVAN, Mrs Hazel. b 50. S Dios Minl Tr Scheme 91. **d** 94 **p** 95. C Cove St Jo *Guildf* 94-98; TV Headley All SS 98-02; V Bordon 02-04; Chapl Whiteley Village from 04. *21 West Mount, The Mount, Guildford GU2 4HL* Tel (01932) 827428
E-mail hazel@revd.fsnet.co.uk

O'SULLIVAN, Helen Louise. b 68. Westmr Coll Ox BTh96. St Steph Ho Ox 06. **d** 08 **p** 09. C Chinnor, Sydenham, Aston Rowant and Crowell *Ox* from 08. *11 Elm Drive, Chinnor OX39 4HQ* Tel (01844) 354821
E-mail helenosullivan@o2.co.uk

O'SULLIVAN, Richard Norton. b 59. Glas Coll of Tech BSc80. Gregorian Univ Rome PhB85 STB88 STL90. **d** 89 **p** 90. In RC Ch 89-96; NSM Clarkston *Glas* 00-02; P-in-c Glas St Oswald 02-06; P-in-c Peterhead *Ab* from 06. *19 York Street, Peterhead AB42 1SN* Tel (01779) 472217
E-mail dick@osullivan53.fsnet.co.uk

OSWALD, John Edward Guy. b 39. Qu Coll Cam BA63 MA67. Ridley Hall Cam. **d** 68 **p** 69. C Chippenham St Paul w Langley Burrell *Bris* 68-72; C Hengrove 72-75; P-in-c Hardenhuish 75-79; P-in-c Kington St Michael 75-79; TV Chippenham St Paul w Hardenhuish etc 79-82; P-in-c Gt w Lt Somerford and Seagry 82-86; P-in-c Corston w Rodbourne 84-86; R Gt Somerford, Lt Somerford, Seagry, Corston etc 86-09; rtd 09. *The Rectory, Frog Lane, Great Somerford, Chippenham SN15 5JA* Tel (01249) 720220

OSWIN, Frank Anthony (Tony). b 43. Chich Th Coll 69. **d** 71 **p** 72. C Radford *Cov* 71-74; C Shrub End *Chelmsf* 74-76; V Layer de la Haye 76-80; V Eastwood St Dav 80-93; TR Withycombe Raleigh *Ex* from 93. *The Rectory, 74 Withycombe Village Road, Exmouth EX8 3AE* Tel (01395) 264182

OTTAWAY, Michael John. b 17. Mert Coll Ox BA40 MA44. Cuddesdon Coll 40. **d** 41 **p** 42. C Leytonstone St Marg *Chelmsf* 41-45; C Kettering SS Pet and Paul 45-48; C Kibworth Beauchamp *Leic* 48-49; V Wolvercote *Ox* 49-76; TV Wolvercote w Summertown 76-83; rtd 83; Perm to Offic *Chich* from 84. *3 Lower Drive, Seaford BN25 3AR* Tel (01323) 899179

OTTER, Anthony Frank. b 32. Kelham Th Coll 54. **d** 59 **p** 60. C Bethnal Green St Jo w St Simon *Lon* 59-63; C Aylesbury *Ox* 63-68; V Hanslope w Castlethorpe 68-77; P-in-c N w S Moreton 77-79; P-in-c Aston Tirrold w Aston Upthorpe 77-79; R S w N Moreton, Aston Tirrold and Aston Upthorpe 79-97; rtd 97; Perm to Offic *Ox* from 97. *4 Emden House, Barton Lane, Headington, Oxford OX3 9JU* Tel (01865) 765447

OTTEY, Canon John Leonard. b 34. AKC60 Nottm Univ BA70. **d** 61 **p** 62. C Grantham St Wulfram *Linc* 61-64; R Keyworth *S'well* 76-83; P-in-c Stanton-on-the-Wolds 71-85; P-in-c E Retford 85-87; V 87-99; P-in-c W Retford 85-87; R 87-99; Hon Can S'well Minster 93-99; rtd 99; Perm to Offic *Linc* from 00 and *S'well* from 04. *1 The Orchards, Grantham NG31 9GW* Tel (01476) 578762

OTTLEY, David Ronald. b 57. Lanc Univ BA78. Sarum & Wells Th Coll 79. **d** 81 **p** 82. C Urmston *Man* 81-85; Lect Bolton St Pet 85-87; P-in-c Halliwell St Thos 87-88; V Bolton St Thos 88-98; TR Halliwell 98-03; P-in-c Goostrey *Ches* 03-05; V Goostrey w Swettenham from 05. *The Vicarage, Blackden Lane, Goostrey, Crewe CW4 8PG* Tel (01477) 532109

OTTO, Andrew James. b 63. St Pet Coll Ox BA86 MA90 Bris Univ BA01. Trin Coll Bris 98. **d** 01 **p** 02. C Trowbridge H Trin *Sarum* 01-05. *25 Cockhill, Trowbridge BA14 9BG* Tel (01225) 769791

OTTO, Francis James Reeve. b 42. New Coll Ox BA64 BA68. St Steph Ho Ox 66 Wells Th Coll 68. **d** 69 **p** 70. C St Stephen by Saltash *Truro* 69-72; C Newquay 72-73; V Lanteglos by Fowey 73-79; V St Goran w Caerhays 79-82; Chapl St Mary's Hall Brighton 82-88; Chapl Reading Sch 88-90; Chapl Lic Victuallers' Sch Ascot 91-93; Lic to Offic *Ox* 89-95; C Boyne Hill 95; P-in-c Cocking, Bepton and W Lavington *Chich* 95-99; Chapl Heathfield Sch Ascot 99-05; Perm to Offic *Ox* 05-06; C Parkham, Alwington, Buckland Brewer etc *Ex* from 06. *10 Thornton Close, Bideford EX39 3ND* Tel (01237) 477227
E-mail corporaljones@tiscali.co.uk

OUGH, John Christopher. b 51. Lon Univ CertEd74 Open Univ BA82. SW Minl Tr Course 91. **d** 94 **p** 95. C Plymouth Em, St Paul Efford and St Aug *Ex* 94-97; P-in-c Diptford, N Huish, Harberton and Harbertonford 97-01; P-in-c Halwell w Moreleigh 97-01; R Diptford, N Huish, Harberton, Harbertonford etc from 01. *The Rectory, Diptford, Totnes TQ9 7NY* Tel (01548) 821148
E-mail john@diptfordough.freeserve.co.uk

OULD, Julian Charles. b 57. MHCIMA77. Coll of Resurr Mirfield 80. **d** 83 **p** 84. C Hebburn St Cuth *Dur* 83-86; C Pet H Spirit Bretton 86-90; R Peakirk w Glinton 90 95; R Peakirk w Glinton and Northborough 95-96; TR Is of Scilly *Truro* 96-98; R 98-06; TR Totnes w Bridgetown, Berry Pomeroy etc *Ex* from 06. *The Rectory, Northgate, Totnes TQ9 5NX* Tel (01803) 865615
E-mail ypj69@dial.pipex.com

OULD, Peter. b 74. Man Univ BA96. Wycliffe Hall Ox BTh05. **d** 05 **p** 06. C Ware Ch Ch *St Alb* from 05. *10 Cromwell Road, Ware SG12 7JZ* Tel (01920) 467918
E-mail mail@peter-ould.net

OULESS, John Michael. b 22. AKC49. Ridley Hall Cam 49. **d** 50 **p** 51. C Dallington *Pet* 50-55; C Evesham *Worc* 55-56; R Halewood *Liv* 56-62; V Southwick w Glapthorn *Pet* 62-71; Chapl Glapthorn Road Hosp Oundle 63-71; R Cogenhoe *Pet* 71-89; R Whiston 71-89; rtd 89; Perm to Offic *Win* 92-06 and *Pet* from 07. *15 St Peters Way, Cogenhoe, Northampton NN7 1NU* Tel (01604) 891104

OULTON, Anthony Martin. b 81. Keble Coll Ox BA05. St Steph Ho Ox MSt06. **d** 06 **p** 07. C Haydock St Jas *Liv* from 06. *27 Homestead Avenue, Haydock, St Helens WA11 0ND* Tel (01744) 633312

OUTEN (*née* **BAILEY), Mrs Joyce Mary Josephine.** b 33. St Gabr Coll Lon CertEd69. S'wark Ord Course 80. **dss** 83 **d** 87 **p** 94. Par Dn Woolwich St Mary w St Mich *S'wark* 87-89; Par Dn Rusthall *Roch* 89-94; C 94-97; rtd 97; Asst Chapl Kent and Cant Hosps NHS Trust 97-99; Asst Chapl E Kent Hosps NHS Trust 99-00; TV Whitstable *Cant* 00-07; Perm to Offic from 07. *10 Foxgrove Road, Whitstable CT5 1PB* Tel (01227) 273643
E-mail joyceouten@tiscali.co.uk

OUTHWAITE, Stephen Anthony (Tony). b 35. Wells Th Coll 62. **d** 64 **p** 65. C Bitterne Park *Win* 64-67; C-in-c N Tadley CD 67-71;

R Milton 71-93; RD Christchurch 82-90; V Win St Cross w St Faith 93-04; Master St Cross Hosp 93-04; rtd 04; Perm to Offic *B & W* from 05. *Wason House, Upper High Street, Castle Cary BA7 7AT* Tel (01963) 350302 Mobile 07940-389946

OUTRAM, David Michael. b 42. Univ of Wales (Ban) BA77 BD79. Coll of Resurr Mirfield 79. **d** 80 **p** 81. C Llandegfan and Beaumaris w Llanfaes w Penmon etc *Ban* 80-82; Chapl Prebendal Sch Chich 82-86; PV Chich Cathl 82-86; Asst Chapl Wellington Coll Berks 86-89; Hd Div 87-03; Chapl 89-03; V Dwygyfylchi *Ban* from 03; Hon Succ Ban Cathl from 08. *The Vicarage, Church Road, Penmaenmawr LL34 6BN* Tel (01492) 621276

OVENDEN, Canon John Anthony. b 45. LVO07. Open Univ BA80 BA93 K Coll Lon MA96. Sarum & Wells Th Coll 71. **d** 74 **p** 75. C Handsworth *Sheff* 74-77; C Isfield *Chich* 77-80; C Uckfield 77-80; P-in-c Stuntney *Ely* 80-85; Min Can, Prec and Sacr Ely Cathl 80-85; V Primrose Hill St Mary w Avenue Road St Paul *Lon* 85-98; Dir English Hymnal Co from 93; Can Windsor and Chapl in Windsor Gt Park from 98; Chapl to The Queen from 02. *Chaplain's Lodge, Windsor Great Park, Windsor SL4 2HP* Tel (01784) 432434

OVEREND, Alan. b 53. Sheff Univ BA75. Oak Hill Th Coll 84. **d** 86 **p** 87. C Aughton St Mich *Liv* 86-89; P-in-c Eccleston Park 89-92; V 92-99; V Billinge 99-07; V Billinge from 07. *5 Lostock Close, Billinge, Wigan WN5 7TQ* Tel (01744) 892210

OVEREND, Barry Malcolm. b 49. K Coll Lon BD71 AKC71. St Aug Coll Cant 71. **d** 72 **p** 73. C Nailsworth *Glouc* 72-74; C High Harrogate Ch Ch *Ripon* 75-78; V Collingham w Harewood 78-87; V Far Headingley St Chad from 87. *St Chad's Vicarage, Otley Road, Leeds LS16 5JT* Tel 0113-275 2224 *or* 274 4322 E-mail bmochad@aol.com

OVEREND, Paul. b 66. Coll of Ripon & York St Jo BA88 Hull Univ MA97 Univ of Wales (Cardiff) PhD04. Coll of Resurr Mirfield 88. **d** 93 **p** 94. C Cayton w Eastfield *York* 93-96; Asst Chapl Univ of Wales (Cardiff) *Llan* 96; Sen Chapl 97-03; Tutor 03-04; Tutor St Mich Coll Llan 03-04; Teaching Fell Liv Hope Univ 04-05; Dir Initial Minl Formation *Sarum* 05-07; Vice Prin Sarum OLM Scheme 05-07; Prin OLM 07-08; Tutor STETS and Co-ord for Locally Deployable Ord Min from 08. *Russell House, Stratford Road, Stratford sub Castle, Salisbury SP1 3LG* Tel (01722) 411944 E-mail paul.overend@salisbury.anglican.org

OVERINGTON, Canon David Vernon. b 34. ALCD60. **d** 60 **p** 61. C Penge Ch Ch w H Trin *Roch* 60-62; C Lenton *S'well* 62-65; PC Brackenfield w Wessington *Derby* 65-71; P-in-c Cubley w Marston Montgomery 71-76; R Bridgetown Australia 76-79; Par P Denmark 79-85; Can Bunbury 84-85; R E Fremantle w Palmyra 85-90; Field Officer Angl Dept of Educn 90-93; R Wembley 93-99; Hon Can Perth from 96; rtd 99; P-in-c Longside *Ab* 99-03; P-in-c New Pitsligo 99-03; P-in-c Old Deer 99-03; P-in-c Strichen 99-03; Perm to Offic *Roch* from 04. *223 Ralph Perring Court, Stone Park Avenue, Beckenham BR3 3LX* Tel (020) 8650 5291
E-mail david.overington@diocese-rochester.org

OVERTHROW, Royston John. b 45. Southn Univ BTh94. Portsm Dioc Tr Course 84. **d** 85. NSM Portsm Cathl 85-91; Perm to Offic 91-94; Bp's Dom Chapl *Sarum* 94-02; NSM Marlborough 02-04; rtd 04. *19 Bratton Avenue, Devizes SN10 5BA* Tel (01380) 722404 E-mail liznroyuk@supanet.com

OVERTON, Charles Henry. b 51. CCC Ox BA74 MA77 Fitzw Coll Cam PGCE75 BA79 MA85. Ridley Hall Cam 77. **d** 80 **p** 81. C Tonbridge SS Pet and Paul *Roch* 80-84; Asst Chapl St Lawr Coll Ramsgate 84-87; P-in-c Aythorpe w High and Leaden Roding *Chelmsf* 88-95; P-in-c Hucklington *Ox* 95-07; P-in-c Chalfont St Peter 05-08; R from 08. *The Vicarage, 4 Austenway, Chalfont St Peter, Gerrards Cross SL9 8NW* Tel (01753) 882389 E-mail charlesoverton@hotmail.com

OVERTON, David Malcolm. b 52. Surrey Univ BA97. Chich Th Coll. **d** 84 **p** 85. C Ches H Trin 84-86; C Woodchurch 86-88; C Coppenhall 88-91; C Croydon St Jo *S'wark* 91-94; Perm to Offic *Lon* 97-00; C Selsey *Chich* 98-02; Miss P Ribbleton *Blackb* 02-07; Hon C Preston St Jo and St Geo from 07. *Glebe House, Bairstow Street, Preston PR1 3TN* Tel (01772) 884921

OVERTON, Keith Charles. b 28. EAMTC 78. **d** 81 **p** 82. NSM Duxford *Ely* 81-84; NSM Whittlesford 84-88; P-in-c 88-94; P-in-c Pampisford 88-90; Perm to Offic *Bris* from 94. *86 Pittsfield, Cricklade, Swindon SN6 6AW* Tel (01793) 750321 E-mail keith@overton.org.uk

OVERTON, Thomas Vincent Edersheim. b 34. New Coll Ox BA58 MA61. Wycliffe Hall Ox 58. **d** 60 **p** 61. C W Hampstead Trin *Lon* 60-63; C Leeds St Geo *Ripon* 63-67; Perm to Offic *Lon* 68-71; Thailand 71-78; R Knossington and Cold Overton *Leic* 78-81; V Owston and Withcote 78-81; R Bedford St Jo and St Leon *St Alb* 81-90; V Leigh Rock 91-99; rtd 99; Perm to Offic *B & W* 90-91 and *Lon* from 99. *14 The Broadwalk, Northwood HA6 2XD* Tel (01923) 829612

OVERTON-BENGE, Mrs Angela Margaret. b 46. UEA BA99 Anglia Poly Univ MA04. EAMTC 94. **d** 97 **p** 98. NSM Moulsham St Jo *Chelmsf* 97-01; Ind Chapl 01-04; C Aveley and Purfleet 01-04; Bp's Soc and Ind Adv *Bris* from 04; C Swindon All SS w St Barn from 06; C Swindon St Aug from 06. *St Augustine's Vicarage, Morris Street, Swindon SN2 2HT* Tel (01793) 618986

OVERY, Arthur William. b 19. JP. Nor Ord Course 73. **d** 76 **p** 77. NSM Lowestoft St Marg *Nor* 76-78; NSM Lowestoft and Kirkley 79-89; Perm to Offic from 89. *The Hollies, Warren Road, Lowestoft NR32 4QD* Tel (01502) 561289
E-mail bill@wovery.fsnet.co.uk

OVEY, Michael John. b 58. Ball Coll Ox BA81 BCL82 ACT MTh00 Lon Univ PhD04. Ridley Hall Cam 88. **d** 91 **p** 92. C Crowborough *Chich* 91-95; Australia 95-98; Kingham Hill Fell Oak Hill Th Coll 98-07; Prin from 07. *Oak Hill Theological College, Chase Side, London N14 4PS* Tel (020) 8449 0467 ext 248 E-mail mikeo@oakhill.ac.uk

OWEN, Bryan Philip. b 47. Keswick Hall Coll CertEd70. Cant Sch of Min 83. **d** 86 **p** 87. NSM Deal St Geo Cant 86-87; C Herne 87-89; R Clarkston *Glas* 89-93; Warden Scottish Chs Ho (Chs Together in Scotland) 93-96; V Cuddington *Guildf* 96-01; rtd 01; Perm to Offic *Glas* from 01. *Columcille, 10 Waverley Park, Kirkintilloch, Glasgow G66 2BP* Tel 0141-776 0407 Mobile 07796-155560 E-mail owen.owen@virgin.net

OWEN, Mrs Carole Janice. b 55. **d** 01 **p** 02. NSM Cley Hill Warminster *Sarum* 01-07; NSM Warminster St Denys and Upton Scudamore from 07. *11 Stuart Green, Warminster BA12 9NU* Tel (01985) 214849
E-mail richardowen50@hotmail.com

OWEN, Caroline Ann. b 59. Univ of Wales (Abth) BA80 PGCE81. St Mich Coll Llan 03. **d** 05 **p** 06. NSM Bangor 05-09; V Cadoxton-juxta-Neath and Tonna *Llan* from 09. *St Catwg's Vicarage, Glebeland Street, Cadoxton, Neath SA10 8AY* Tel (01639) 643777

OWEN, Christine Rose. b 62. Univ of Wales (Ban) BA83 PGCE84. Qu Coll Birm 86. **d** 88 **p** 94. C Ynyscynhaearn w Penmorfa and Porthmadog *Ban* 88-90; Chapl Lon Univ 90-96; Hon C St Marylebone w H Trin 94-96; Min Can and Prec Worc Cathl 96-00; R Llansantffraid Glan Conwy and Eglwysbach *St As* from 00. *The Rectory, 16 Y Bryn, Glan Conwy, Colwyn Bay LL28 5NJ* Tel (01492) 583099 E-mail rectorgc@lineone.net

OWEN, Clifford. *See* OWEN, Phillip Clifford

OWEN, Dafydd Gwyn. b 62. St Steph Ho Ox 95. **d** 97 **p** 98. C Whitchurch *Bris* 97-01; V Bris Ch the Servant Stockwood from 01; AD Bris S from 06; Hon Min Can Bris Cathl from 04. *The Vicarage, Goslet Road, Stockwood, Bristol BS14 8SP* Tel (01275) 831138 E-mail christtheservant@blueyonder.co.uk

OWEN, Daniel James. b 71. Anglia Poly Univ BSc94 TCD BTh00. CITC 97. **d** 00 **p** 01. C Belfast St Donard *D & D* 00-03; I Rathcooney Union *C, C & R* from 03. *The Rectory, Fota View, Glounthaune, Cork, Republic of Ireland* Tel (00353) (21) 435 5208 E-mail danielsonja@eircom.net

OWEN, David Cadwaladr. b 56. Grey Coll Dur BSc77 Univ Coll Worc PGCE99. WEMTC 00. **d** 03 **p** 04. NSM Pershore w Pinvin, Wick and Birlingham *Worc* 03-07; TV Droitwich Spa from 07. *1 Ombersley Close, Droitwich WR9 8JY* Tel (01905) 771516 Mobile 07837-800009 E-mail dc.owen@dunelm.org.uk

OWEN, Canon David William. b 31. Down Coll Cam BA55 MA58. Linc Th Coll 55. **d** 57 **p** 58. C Salford St Phil w St Steph *Man* 57-61; C Grantham St Wulfram *Linc* 61-65; V Messingham 65-70; V Spilsby w Hundleby 70-77; R Aswardby w Sausthorpe 71-77; R Langton w Sutterby 71-77; R Halton Holgate 73-77; P-in-c Firsby w Gt Steeping 75-77; P-in-c Lt Steeping 75-77; TR Louth 77-92; Chapl Louth Co Hosp 77-92; RD Louthesk *Linc* 82-89; Can and Preb Linc Cathl 85-92; TR Swan *Ox* 92-97; RD Claydon 94-96; rtd 97. *19 Stephen Road, Headington, Oxford OX3 9AY* Tel (01865) 766585

OWEN, Derek Malden. b 29. Oak Hill Th Coll 74. **d** 76 **p** 77. C Eastbourne H Trin *Chich* 76-78; C Walthamstow St Mary w St Steph *Chelmsf* 78-81; R Ditcheat w E Pennard and Pylle *B & W* 81-83; Warden Shaftesbury Housing Assn 86-94; rtd 94; Hon C Fairlight, Guestling and Pett *Chich* 94-97; P-in-c Llanishen w Trelleck Grange and Llanfihangel etc *Mon* from 00. *The Vicarage, Llanishen, Chepstow NP16 6QE* Tel (01600) 860845

OWEN, Edgar. b 26. WMMTC. **d** 82 **p** 83. NSM Garretts Green Birm 82-88; NSM Stechford 88-94; rtd 94; Perm to Offic *Birm* from 94. *36 Colbourne Court, 116 Frederick Road, Stechford, Birmingham B33 8AE* Tel 0121-783 5603

OWEN, Emyr. b 69. Lancs Poly BSc91. Westcott Ho Cam BA94. **d** 95 **p** 96. C Llanbeblig w Caernarfon and Betws Garmon etc *Ban* 95-96; C Llanberis w Llanrug 96-98; TV Bangor 98-02; P-in-c Llandygai and Maes y Groes 98-02; V Nefyn w Tudweiliog w Llandudwen w Edern 02-07. *Westview House, Hanmer, Whitchurch SY13 3BS*
E-mail emyr.owen@hotmail.com

OWEN, Eric Cyril Hammersley. b 46. Liv Univ LLB68 Barrister 69. St As Minl Tr Course 95. **d** 97 **p** 98. NSM Gresford w Holt *St As* 97-03; NSM Rhosymedre w Penycae 03-04. *Thistle Patch, 28 Wynnstay Lane, Marford, Wrexham LL12 8LG* Tel (01978) 856495 E-mail eowen@lineone.net

OWEN, Gary John. b 72. City Univ BSc93. Ridley Hall Cam BA97. **d** 98 **p** 99. C Welshpool w Castle Caereinion *St As* 98-01; TV Wrexham from 01. *The Vicarage, 160 Borras Road, Wrexham LL13 9ER* Tel (01978) 350202

OWEN, Geoffrey Neill. b 55. Chich Th Coll. **d** 85 **p** 86. C Streatham St Pet *S'wark* 85-89; C Battersea Ch Ch and St Steph 89-91; TV Surbiton St Andr and St Mark 91-97; V Merton St Jas 97-08; V Battersea Ch Ch and St Steph from 08. *Christ Church Vicarage, Candahar Road, London SW11 2PU* Tel (020) 7228 1225

OWEN, Glyn John. b 56. Open Univ BA91 Nottm Univ MSc93 St Jo Coll Dur BA05. Cranmer Hall Dur 01. **d** 03 **p** 04. C Whiston *Sheff* 03-07; V Rudston w Boynton, Carnaby and Kilham *York* from 07; P-in-c Burton Fleming w Fordon, Grindale etc from 07. *The Vicarage, Rudston, Driffield YO25 4XA* Tel (01262) 420313 E-mail revglynowen@btinternet.com

OWEN, Graham Anthony. b 54. Birm Univ BA77. Trin Coll Bris 92. **d** 94 **p** 95. C Wiveliscombe w Chipstable, Huish Champflower etc *B & W* 94-98; R 98-09; V Frome H Trin from 09. *Holy Trinity Vicarage, Orchard Street, Frome BA11 3BX* Tel (01373) 462586 E-mail graham-owen@hotmail.co.uk

OWEN, Graham Wynne. b 46. Lon Inst of Educn MA81 GTCL67 FTCL70. Cant Sch of Min 90. **d** 93 **p** 94. C Eltham H Trin *S'wark* 93-97; P-in-c Shooters Hill Ch Ch 97-00; V 00-01; TV Sole Bay *St E* 01-04; P-in-c Framlingham w Saxtead from 04; RD Loes from 05. *The Rectory, St Michael's Close, Framlingham, Woodbridge IP13 9BJ* Tel and fax (01728) 621082 E-mail gowen.mowen@btinternet.com

OWEN, Gwyn. *See* OWEN, Dafydd Gwyn

OWEN, Harry Dennis. b 47. Oak Hill Th Coll 73. **d** 76 **p** 77. C Fulham Ch Ch *Lon* 76-81; V Byker St Mark *Newc* 81-89; V Plumstead All SS *S'wark* from 89; RD Plumstead from 03. *All Saints' Vicarage, 106 Herbert Road, London SE18 3PU* Tel (020) 8854 2995 E-mail h.d.owen@talk21.com

OWEN, James Thomas. *See* McNAUGHTAN-OWEN, James Thomas

OWEN, John Edward. b 52. Middx Poly BA75. Sarum & Wells Th Coll BTh81. **d** 81 **p** 82. C S Ashford Ch Ch *Cant* 81-85; TV Bemerton *Sarum* 85-91; V St Leonards and St Ives *Win* 91-95; R N Stoneham 95-09; V Steep and Froxfield w Privett *Portsm* from 09. *The Vicarage, 77 Church Road, Steep, Petersfield GU32 2DF* Tel (01730) 264282 *or* 260169 E-mail revjohnnowen@gmail.com

OWEN, Keith Robert. b 57. Warwick Univ BA Ox Univ BA MA85 Hull Univ MA(Ed)89. St Steph Ho Ox 79. **d** 82 **p** 83. C Headingley *Ripon* 82-85; Chapl Grimsby Colls of H&FE 85-90; Chapl for Educn *Linc* 85-90; P-in-c Linc St Botolph 90-95; Chapl to Caring Agencies Linc City Cen 90-95; V Steeton *Bradf* 95-01; Chapl Airedale NHS Trust 95-01; P-in-c Penzance St Mary w St Paul *Truro* 01-02; P-in-c Penzance St Jo 01-02; TR Penzance St Mary w St Paul and St Jo from 02. *St Mary's Vicarage, Chapel Street, Penzance TR18 4AP* Tel (01736) 363079 E-mail keith@gresley.f9.co.uk

OWEN, Kenneth Phillip. b 56. Liv Univ BA77 PGCE78. NOC 92. **d** 95 **p** 96. C Heswall *Ches* 95-01; V Frankby w Greasby from 01. *The Vicarage, 14 Arrowe Road, Greasby, Wirral CH49 1RA* Tel 0151-678 6155 E-mail greasby@office.fsworld.co.uk

OWEN, Mark. b 63. RMN. St Mich Coll Llan 03. **d** 05 **p** 06. C Tredegar *Mon* 05-08; V Rhymney from 08. *7 Rhymney Walk, Rhymney, Tredegar NP22 5BL* Tel (01685) 840500

OWEN, Paul Jonathan. b 59. S Bank Poly BSc81. Ridley Hall Cam 00. **d** 02 **p** 03. C Seaford w Sutton *Chich* 02-06; R Denton w S Heighton and Tarring Neville from 06. *The Rectory, 6 Heighton Road, Newhaven BN9 0RB* Tel (01273) 514319 E-mail paulowen@freenet.co.uk

OWEN, Peter Russell. b 35. St Mich Coll Llan. **d** 63 **p** 64. C Wrexham *St As* 63-64; C Connah's Quay Asst Master Miss to Seamen 66-69; P-in-c Upper Norwood All SS w St Marg *Cant* 69-72; C Hawarden *St As* 72-75; V Cilcain and Nannerch 75-79; R Cilcain and Nannerch and Rhydymwyn 79-83; V Brymbo and Bwlchgwyn 83-87; R Llangynhafal and Llanbedr Dyffryn Clwyd 87-99; P-in-c Llanychan 87-99; rtd 00. *Telpyn Forge, Rhewl, Ruthin LL15 1TP* Tel (01824) 704051

OWEN, Phillip Clifford. b 42. G&C Coll Cam BA65 MA69 Birm Univ PhD07. Ridley Hall Cam 71. **d** 73 **p** 74. C Stowmarket *St E* 73-76; C Headley All SS *Guildf* 76-81; TV 81-89; P-in-c Clifton-on-Teme, Lower Sapey and the Shelsleys *Worc* 89-97; rtd 97-02; Dioc Ecum Officer 89-02; P-in-c Corfu *Eur* 03-08; P-in-c Ostend from 08. *The English Church, Langestraat 101, 8400 Oostende, Belgium* Tel 07887-745632 (mobile) E-mail clavis@hotmail.com

OWEN, Mrs Phyllis Elizabeth. b 48. NTMTC. **d** 05 **p** 06. NSM Southend *Chelmsf* from 05. *42 Harcourt Avenue, Southend-on-Sea SS2 6IIU* Tel (01702) 313312 E mail thephiz@blueyonder.co uk

OWEN, Raymond Philip. b 37. Man Univ BScTech60 AMCST60. Chich Th Coll 65. **d** 67 **p** 68. C Elland *Wakef* 67-70; C Lindley 70-73; V Bradshaw 73-80; Ind Chapl *Dur* 80-91; TR Hanley H Ev *Lich* 91-99; Bp Stafford's Past Aux 03-04; rtd 04; Perm to Offic *Lich* 04-07; C Mayfield from 07; C Denstone w Ellastone

and Stanton from 07; C Alton w Bradley-le-Moors and Oakamoor w Cotton from 07. *The Vicarage, Church Lane, Mayfield, Ashbourne DE6 2JR* Tel 07747-601379 (mobile) E-mail revrayowen@hotmail.com

OWEN, Canon Richard Llewelyn. b 27. Univ of Wales (Lamp) BA51. St Mich Coll Llan 51. **d** 53 **p** 54. C Holyhead w Rhoscolyn w Llanfair-yn-Neubwll *Ban* 53-57; C Porthmadog 57-59; R Llanfechell w Bodewryd, Rhosbeirio etc 59-67; Youth Chapl 66-67; V Penrhyndeudraeth and Llanfrothen 67-77; R Llangefni w Tregaean and Llangristiolus etc 77-89; Can Ban Cathl 82-93; Hon Can from 93; Treas 86-93; Can Missr and V Bangor Cathl Par 89-93; RD Arfon 92-93; rtd 93; Perm to Offic *Ban* from 93. *Bodowen, Great Orme's Road, Llandudno LL30 2BF* Tel (01492) 872765

OWEN, Richard Matthew. b 49. Sheff Univ BA70 Leeds Univ CertEd73. NOC 84. **d** 87 **p** 88. NSM Chorlton-cum-Hardy St Werburgh *Man* 87-89; C N Reddish 89-91; Perm to Offic *York* 91-96 and 97-03; NSM York St Olave w St Giles 96-97. *12 Sandrock House, Sandrock Road, Tunbridge Wells TN2 3PZ* Tel (01892) 516106 E-mail owen_rm@hotmail.com

OWEN, Robert Glynne. b 33. St Mich Coll Llan 56. **d** 58 **p** 59. C Machynlleth and Llanwrin *Ban* 58-62; C Llanbeblig w Caernarfon 62-65; V Carno and Trefeglwys 65-69; Hon C Dorking w Ranmore *Guildf* 69-75; Perm to Offic *St As* 75-94; V Broughton from 99. rtd 99. *Briarcroft, Minera Road, Cefn y Bedd, Wrexham LL12 9TR* Tel (01978) 750134

OWEN, Robert Lee. b 56. Univ of Wales (Cardiff) BD79. Qu Coll Birm 79. **d** 81 **p** 82. C Holywell *St As* 81-84; Perm to Offic *Birm* 85-87; Chapl Blue Coat Sch Birm 85-87; Chapl St Elphin's Sch Matlock 87-94; Chapl Qu Marg Sch York from 94. *Queen Margaret's School, Escrick Park, Escrick, York YO19 6EU* Tel (01904) 728261

OWEN, Ronald Alfred. b 44. Wilson Carlile Coll 73 Sarum & Wells Th Coll 80. **d** 81 **p** 82. C Wotton St Mary *Glouc* 81-83; CF 83-97; P-in-c Salcombe *Ex* 97-02; V Salcombe and Malborough w S Huish 02-06; RD Woodleigh 00-03; rtd 07; Perm to Offic *B & W* from 07. *9 Reedmoor Gardens, Bridgwater TA6 3SL* Tel (01278) 433801 Mobile 07917-853901 E-mail ronowen517@gmail.com

OWEN, Canon Stanley Alfred George. b 17. Worc Ord Coll 57. **d** 59 **p** 60. C Bickenhill w Elmdon *Birm* 59-60; R 60-86; rtd 86; Perm to Offic *Birm* from 86; Chmn and Sec Assn Ch Fellowships from 88. *Bickenhill House, 154 Lode Lane, Solihull B91 2HP* Tel 0121-704 9281

OWEN, Stuart James. b 68. Sunderland Poly BA91. Ripon Coll Cuddesdon BTh00. **d** 00 **p** 01. C Hendon St Mary *Lon* 00-01; C Hendon St Mary and Ch Ch 01-04; P Missr Edmonton St Mary w St Jo 04-08; V Edmonton All SS w St Mich from 08. *All Saints' Vicarage, 43 All Saints' Close, London N9 9AT* Tel (020) 8803 9199 E-mail fr_stuart@hotmail.com

OWEN, Mrs Susan Margaret. b 38. St Andr Univ MA61 Univ of Wales (Swansea) MPhil91 Univ of Wales (Ban) BD93. Qu Coll Birm 94. **d** 95 **p** 96. NSM Shrewsbury St Geo *Lich* 95-98; P-in-c Penrhyndeudraeth w Llanfrothen w Beddgelert *Ban* 98-99; V 99-06; V Penrhyndeudraeth and Llanfrothen w Maentwrog etc 06-07; rtd 08. *Coed Helyg, Lower Moranedd, Criccieth LL52 0LA*

OWEN-JONES, Peter Charles. b 57. Ridley Hall Cam 92. **d** 94 **p** 95. C Leverington and Wisbech St Mary *Ely* 94-97; R Haslingfield w Harlton and Gt and Lt Eversden 97-05; P-in-c Glynde, W Firle and Beddingham *Chich* from 05. *The Vicarage, The Street, Firle, Lewes BN8 6NP* Tel (01273) 858005 Mobile 07973-265953 E-mail poj@lineone.net

OWEN-JONES, Peter John. b 47. RMCS BScEng68 CEng84 MIMechE84 MBIM87. EMMTC 85. **d** 88 **p** 89. NSM Holbrook and Lt Eaton *Derby* 88-00; NSM W Hallam and Mapperley w Stanley from 01. *Bridge Cottage, 63 Derby Road, Stanley, Ilkeston DE7 6EX* Tel and fax 0115-932 0764 E-mail jowenjones@aol.com

OWEN-MOORE, Ms Petra Davine. b 65. Liv Univ BA87 Lanc Univ PGCE88. St Jo Coll Nottm MA97 MA98. **d** 98 **p** 99. C Brampton St Thos *Derby* 98-01; C Federal Way Gd Shep USA 01-05; NSM Ecclesall Deanery *Sheff* 06-08; TV N Wingfield, Clay Cross and Pilsley *Derby* 08-09. *Address temp unknown*

OWENS, Mrs Ann Lindsay. b 47. St Hild Coll Dur CertEd68 Man Univ BA94. NOC 92. **d** 95 **p** 96. Chapl St Jas Sch Farnworth 94-97; NSM New Bury *Man* 95-97; C Heywood St Luke w All So 97-98; C Heywood 98-99; P-in-c Chadderton St Matt 99-04; P-in-c Chadderton St Luke 03-04; V Chadderton St Matt w St Luke 04-05; V Hurst from 05. *St John's Vicarage, 155 Kings Road, Ashton-under-Lyne OL6 8EZ* Tel 0161-330 1935 E-mail ann-lindsay.owens@virgin.net

OWENS, Christopher Lee. b 42. SS Mark & Jo Coll Chelsea 61 Lon Inst of Educn 1Cert. Linc Th Coll 66. **d** 69 **p** 70. C Dalston H Trin w St Phil *Lon* 69-72; C Portsea N End St Mark *Portsm* 72-81; TV E Ham w Upton Park St Alb *Chelmsf* 81-92; C Is of Dogs Ch Ch and St Jo w St Luke *Lon* 92-98; P-in-c Chingford St Edm *Chelmsf* 98-02; V 02-07; rtd 07; Perm to Offic *Chelmsf* from 08. *67 Disraeli Road, London E7 9JU* Tel (020) 8555 6337 E-mail christopher@owenseaster.freeserve.co.uk

OWENS, Mrs Margaret Jean. b 49. Man Univ BSc70 Birm Univ MSc72. St Jo Coll Nottm 99. **d** 01 **p** 02. NSM Hurdsfield *Ches* 01-07; V Disley from 07. *Disley Vicarage, Red Lane, Disley, Stockport SK12 2NP* Tel (01663) 762068 Mobile 07775-801613 E-mail mowens44@hotmail.com

OWENS, Patricia Margaret. d 07 **p** 08. NSM Buckley *St As* from 07. *The Clappers, Pont-y-Capel Lane, Gresford, Wrexham LL12 8RS* Tel (01978) 854855 E-mail p.owens@liv.ac.uk

OWENS, Philip Roger. b 47. Wells Th Coll 71. **d** 71 **p** 72. C Colwyn Bay *St As* 71-74; C Wrexham 74-77; TV 77-80; P-in-c Yoxford *St E* 80-85; Asst Stewardship and Resources Adv 80-85; R Bangor Monachorum and Worthenbury *St As* 85-98; Sec Dioc Stewardship Cttee 89-98; RD Bangor Isycoed 92-98; R Flint 98-03; AD Holywell 02-03; rtd 06. *101 Thingwall Road, Wirral CH61 3UD* Tel 0151-648 3940 Mobile 07808-167147 E-mail philipowens653@btinternet.com

OWENS, Stephen Graham Frank. b 49. Ch Coll Cam BA71 MA75 CertEd72. Qu Coll Birm 73. **d** 75 **p** 76. C Stourbridge St Mich Norton *Worc* 75-80; Tanzania 80-88; V Dudley Wood *Worc* 88-99; P-in-c Mamble w Bayton, Rock w Heightington etc 99-02; V from 02. *The Vicarage, Church Lane, Rock, Kidderminster DY14 9TT* Tel (01299) 266580 E-mail stephen.owens@ffvicarage.fsnet.co.uk

OWERS, Ian Humphrey. b 46. Em Coll Cam BA68 MA72. Westcott Ho Cam 71. **d** 73 **p** 74. C Champion Hill St Sav *S'wark* 73-77; V Peckham St Sav 77-82; P-in-c E Greenwich Ch Ch w St Andr and St Mich 82-83; V 83-94; P-in-c Westcombe Park St Geo 85-94; RD Greenwich 92-94; Perm to Offic *St E* 01-07; *Bradf* from 03; *Ripon* from 05. *St Margaret's Vicarage, Newlay Lane, Leeds LS13 2AJ* Tel 0113-257 4811 Mobile 07808-613252 E-mail ianowers.co.uk

OXBROW, Canon Mark. b 51. Reading Univ BSc72 Fitzw Ho Cam BA75 MA79. Ridley Hall Cam 73. **d** 76 **p** 77. C Luton Ch Ch *Roch* 76-80; TV Newc Epiphany 80-88; Chapl Newc Mental Health Unit 80-88; Regional Sec Eur CMS from 88; Communication Resources Sec from 94; Internat Miss Dir from 01; Hon Can Brussels Cathl from 98. *10 Nettleden Avenue, Wembley HA9 6DP*, or *CMS, Partnership House, 157 Waterloo Road, London SE1 8UU* Tel (020) 8900 2485 *or* 7928 8681 Fax 7401 3215 E-mail markoxbrow@aol.com

OXENFORTH, Colin Bryan. b 45. St Chad's Coll Dur BA67. **d** 69 **p** 70. C Bromley St Andr *Roch* 69-72; C Nunhead St Antony *S'wark* 72-76; V Toxteth St Marg *Liv* 76-89; V Brixton St Matt *S'wark* 89-00; V Pemberton St Jo *Liv* from 00. *2 Shelley Drive, Orrell, Wigan WN5 8HW* Tel and fax (01942) 222237 E-mail oxenforth@3tc4u.net

OXFORD (Christ Church), Dean of. *See* LEWIS, The Very Revd Christopher Andrew

OXFORD, Archdeacon of. *See* HUBBARD, The Ven Julian Richard Hawes

OXFORD, Bishop of. *See* PRITCHARD, The Rt Revd John Lawrence

OXLEY, Christopher Robert. b 51. Sheff Univ BA73 PGCE74. Wycliffe Hall Ox BA78 MA83. **d** 79 **p** 80. C Greasbrough *Sheff* 79-82; C Doncaster St Leon and St Jude 82-84; Asst Chapl Brussels *Eur* 84-87; V Humberstone *Leic* 87-93; V Beaumont Leys 93-05; RD Christianity S 98-01; P-in-c Leic St Anne 05-09; P-in-c Leic St Paul and St Aug 05-09; V Leic St Anne, St Paul and St Aug from 09; Dir Post-Ord Tr from 04. *St Anne's Vicarage, 76 Letchworth Road, Leicester LE3 6FH* Tel 0116-285 8452 E-mail oxley@leicester.anglican.org *or* oxleycr@btopenworld.com

OXLEY, David William. b 63. TCD BA85 BTh89. CITC 85. **d** 89 **p** 90. C Dublin Ch Ch Cathl Gp 89-92; Clerical V Ch Ch Cathl Dublin 90-92; I Templebreedy w Tracton and Nohoval *C, C & R* 92-96; Min Can Cork Cathl 95-96; I Tullow w Shillelagh, Aghold and Mullinacuff *C & O* 96-02; I Dublin Santry w Glasnevin and Finglas *D & G* from 02. *The Rectory, Church Street, Finglass, Dublin 11, Republic of Ireland* Tel (00353) (1) 834 1015 Mobile 86-881 6486 E-mail revdwo@hotmail.com

OXLEY, Martin Neil. b 65. Birm Univ BA86 Edin Univ BD95. Edin Th Coll 92. **d** 95 **p** 96. C Glas St Mary 95-97; C Glas St Matt 95-97; C Clydebank 95-97; P-in-c Glas St Matt 97-00; Dir Studies Edin Th Coll 97-00; R Lerwick *Ab* 00-05; P-in-c Burravoe 00-05. *1 Churant Avenue, Beckenham BR3 1DT* Tel (020) 8658 1846 Mobile 07970-266578 E-mail frmartin@globalnet.co.uk

OXLEY, Paul. b 80. Chelt & Glouc Coll of HE BSc01 Glos Univ PGCE02. Trin Coll Bris BTh09. **d** 09. C Upper Sunbury St Sav *Lon* from 09. *41 Wolsey Road, Sunbury-on-Thames TW16 7TY* Tel 07985-937117 (mobile) E-mail pauloxo@gmail.com

OXLEY, Mrs Paula Jane. b 51. Sheff Univ BA74 Nottm Univ MA00 PGCE75. EMMTC 93. **d** 93 **p** 94. NSM Birstall and Wanlip *Leic* 93-95; C Beaumont Leys 95-05; NSM Leic St Anne, St Paul and St Aug from 05. *St Anne's Vicarage, 76 Letchworth Road, Leicester LE3 6FH* Tel 0116-285 8452 E-mail oxleyp@btopenworld.com

OYET, The Ven Julius Isotuk. b 34. Concordia Coll (USA) MA79. Immanuel Coll Ibadan 66. **d** 70 **p** 72. Nigeria 70-90 and from 96; Provost St Steph Cathl Bonny 81-85; Hon Can Ondo from 88; Miss Partner CMS 91-96; C Warblington w Emsworth *Portsm* 91-95; C Kirkby *Liv* 95-96; V Port Harcourt St Cypr 97-99; rtd 99; Dioc Dir Tr Niger Delta 97-05; Adn Bonny 01-05. *1 Panama Street, Abuloma GRA, Trans-Amadi Annex, PO Box 13608, Port Harcourt, Nigeria* Tel (00234) (803) 338 7403 (mobile) E-mail jisotuawaji@yahoo.com

P

PACEY, Graham John. b 52. Open Univ BA81 Leeds Univ CertEd74 Teesside Poly AdDipEd85. NEOC 90. **d** 93 **p** 94. C Kirkleatham *York* 93-96; V Middlesbrough St Agnes 96-00; R Skelton w Upleatham 00-09; V Boosbeck and Lingdale 07-09; R Guisborough from 09. *The Rectory, Church Street, Guisborough TS14 6BS* Tel (01287) 650329 E-mail graham.pacey@ntlworld.com

PACEY, Michael John. b 28. **d** 96 **p** 97. NSM Tamworth *Lich* 96-09; Perm to Offic from 09. *1 Benson View, Tamworth B79 8TD* Tel (01827) 700410

PACKER, Catherine Ruth. *See* PICKFORD, Mrs Catherine Ruth

PACKER, Prof James Innell. b 26. CCC Ox BA48 MA52 DPhil55. Wycliffe Hall Ox 49. **d** 52 **p** 53. C Harborne Heath *Birm* 52-54; Lect Tyndale Hall Bris 55-61; Lib Latimer Ho Ox 61-62; Warden 62-69; Prin Tyndale Hall Bris 70-72; Assoc Prin Trin Coll Bris 72-79; Prof Hist Th Regent Coll Vancouver 79-89; Prof Th from 89; rtd 91. *6017 Holland Street, Vancouver BC V6N 2B2, Canada* Tel (001) (604) 266 6722

✠**PACKER, The Rt Revd John Richard.** b 46. Keble Coll Ox BA67 MA. Ripon Hall Ox 67. **d** 70 **p** 71 **c** 96. C St Helier *S'wark* 70-73; Chapl Abingdon St Nic *Ox* 73-77; Tutor Ripon Hall Ox 73-75; Tutor Ripon Coll Cuddesdon 75-77; V Wath-upon-Dearne w Adwick-upon-Dearne *Sheff* 77-86; RD Wath 83-86; TR Sheff Manor 86-91; RD Attercliffe 90-91; Adn W Cumberland *Carl* 91-96; P-in-c Bridekirk 95-96; Suff Bp Warrington *Liv* 96-00; Bp Ripon and Leeds from 00. *Hollin House, Weetwood Avenue, Headingley, Leeds LS16 5NG* Tel 0113-224 2789 Fax 230 5471 E-mail bishop@riponleeds-diocese.org.uk

PACKER, Peter Aelred. b 48. St Jo Coll Dur BA70 St Chad's Coll Dur PhD79 Strathclyde Univ MBA00. Ven English Coll Rome 95. **d** 96 **p** 99. SSM 93-99; Hon C S Lambeth St Anne and All SS *S'wark* 96-98; Lic to Offic *Ox* 97-99; Bp's Adv in Miss and Resources *Glas* 99-00; Perm to Offic *S'wark* 08-09; Hon C Deptford St Paul from 09. *104 St Donatt's Road, London SE14 6NT* Tel 07932-648034 (mobile) E-mail packer@ppacker.co.uk

PACKER, Preb Roger Ernest John. b 37. ARCO59 Pemb Coll Cam BA60 MA64. Cuddesdon Coll 60. **d** 62 **p** 63. C Chippenham St Andr w Tytherton Lucas *Bris* 62-65; C Caversham *Ox* 65-70; R Sandhurst 70-91; V Bridgwater St Mary, Chilton Trinity and Durleigh *B & W* 91-00; RD Bridgwater 94-00; Preb Wells Cathl 96-00; rtd 00; Perm to Offic *Chelmsf* from 00. *3 Kreswell Grove, Harwich CO12 3SZ* Tel (01255) 502239

PACKHAM, Ms Elizabeth Daisy. b 33. Goldsmiths' Coll Lon BSc54 CertEd55. NOC. **dss** 83 **d** 87 **p** 94. Fairfield *Derby* 83-84; Buxton w Burbage and King Sterndale 84-95; Par Dn 87-94; C 94-95; P-in-c Chinley w Buxworth 95-98; Perm to Offic from 98; rtd 98. *100 Manchester Road, Chapel-en-le-Frith, Stockport SK23 9TP* Tel (01298) 812921

PACKMAN, James Morley. b 76. SS Hild & Bede Coll Dur MSci99. Oak Hill Th Coll BA04. **d** 04 **p** 05. C Eastbourne All SS *Chich* 04-08; R Frant w Eridge from 08. *The Rectory, Church Lane, Frant, Tunbridge Wells TN3 9DX*

PADDICK, Graham. b 47. S'wark Ord Course. **d** 89 **p** 90. C St Helier *S'wark* 89-93; P-in-c Thornton Heath St Paul 93-96; V 96-98; V Dormansland from 98; Chapl MU 03-08; AD Godstone from 08; Dir Ords Croydon Area from 08. *St John's Vicarage, The Platt, Dormansland, Lingfield RH7 6QU* Tel (01342) 832391 E-mail stjohndor@btinternet.com

PADDISON, Mrs Jennifer Sheila. b 70. Cranmer Hall Dur. **d** 07 **p** 08. C Newc H Cross from 07. *2A Lancercost Drive, Newcastle upon Tyne NE5 2DE* Tel 0191-274 9574 E-mail jenny@paddisons.plus.com

PADDISON, Canon Michael David William. b 41. Oak Hill Th Coll 75. **d** 77 **p** 78. C Gt Warley Ch Ch *Chelmsf* 77-80; C Rayleigh 80-83; R Scole, Brockdish, Billingford, Thorpe Abbots etc *Nor* 83-95; RD Redenhall 89-94; R Reepham, Hackford w Whitwell, Kerdiston etc 95-06; RD Sparham 00-05; Hon Can Nor Cathl 02-06; rtd 06; Perm to Offic *Nor* from 06. *4 North Street, Castle Acre, King's Lynn PE32 2BA*

PADDISON, Robert Michael. b 70. Cranmer Hall Dur. **d** 07 **p** 08. C Whorlton *Newc* from 07. *2A Lanercost Drive, Newcastle upon Tyne NE5 2DE* Tel 0191-274 9574
E-mail jenny@paddisons.plus.com

PADDOCK, The Very Revd John Allan Barnes. b 51. Liv Univ BA74 MA91 Ox Univ BA77 MA81 Glas Univ PhD05 Man Univ PGCE75 FRSA94. St Steph Ho Ox 75. **d** 80 **p** 81. C Matson *Glouc* 80-82; Asst Chapl Madrid *Eur* 82-83; Chapl R Gr Sch Lanc 83-86; Hon C Blackb Ch Ch w St Matt 83-86; Chapl RAF 86-91; Offg Chapl RAF 92-94; Chapl St Olave's Gr Sch Orpington 91-94; Perm to Offic *Blackb* 94-97; Chapl R Russell Sch Croydon 97-00; Hon C Bickley *Roch* 97-00; V Folkestone St Pet *Cant* 00-03; Hon Min Can Cant Cathl 01-03; V Glouc St Geo w Whaddon 03-08; Dean Gib *Eur* from 08. *The Deanery, Bomb House Lane, Gibraltar* Tel (00350) 200 78377 Fax 78463
E-mail deangib@gibraltar.gi

PADDOCK, Susan. b 54. NTMTC 03. **d** 06 **p** 07. NSM Upper Holloway *Lon* from 06. *53 Morland Mews, London N1 1HN* Tel (020) 7609 1299 E-mail susie.paddock@lcbroadband.co.uk

PADFIELD, Stephen James. b 68. Ex Univ BA90 Univ Coll Dur PGCE92. Trin Coll Bris BA00 MA01. **d** 01 **p** 02. C Luton Ch Ch *Roch* 01-05; Chapl R Russell Sch Croydon from 05. *The Royal Russell School, Coombe Lane, Croydon CR9 5BX* Tel (020) 8657 4433 Mobile 07747-775385 E-mail stevepadfield@tiscali.co.uk

PADLEY, Miss Karen. b 68. RGN89. St Jo Coll Nottm MA00. **d** 00 **p** 01. C Broxtowe *S'well* 00-04; V Marlpool *Derby* from 04. *All Saints' Vicarage, 85 Ilkeston Road, Heanor DE75 7BP* Tel (01773) 712097 E-mail karen@hpadley.fsnet.co.uk

PADLEY, Kenneth Peter Joseph. b 78. Ex Coll Ox BA00 MA04 Ox Univ MSt04. Ripon Coll Cuddesdon BA03. **d** 04 **p** 05. C Cen Swansea *S & B* 04-07; Warden of Ch Hostel and Chapl Ban Univ from 07. *Church Hostel, Prince's Road, Ffordd y Tyw, Bangor LL57 2BD* Tel (01248) 370566
E-mail kenneth_padley@hotmail.com

PADMORE, Lynn Beverley. b 51. EMMTC. **d** 06 **p** 07. NSM Beaumont Leys *Leic* from 06. *122 Colby Drive, Thurmaston, Leicester LE4 8LB* Tel 0116-260 1584
E-mail lynnpadmore@btopenworld.com

PAGAN, Canon Keith Vivian. b 37. St Jo Coll Dur BA60 MA66. Chich Th Coll 60. **d** 62 **p** 63. C Clacton St Jas *Chelmsf* 62-64; C Wymondham *Nor* 64-70; P-in-c Guestwick 70-80; P-in-c Kettlestone 70-79; V Hindolveston 70-80; R Islay *Arg* 80-98; R Campbeltown 80-98; Miss to Seamen 80-98; Can St Jo Cathl Oban 85-98; Can Cumbrae 85-98; Hon Can from 99; rtd 98. *Mariefield, Southend, Campbeltown PA28 6RW* Tel (01586) 830310

PAGE, Alan Richard Benjamin. b 38. Univ of Wales (Lamp) BA60 BSc. St Mich Coll Llan 60. **d** 62 **p** 63. C Cardiff St Andr and St Teilo *Llan* 62-64; C Newport St Julian *Mon* 64-67; C Hoxton H Trin w St Mary *Lon* 67-69; C Winchmore Hill H Trin 69-71; V Camden Town St Mich w All SS and St Thos 71-98; Public Preacher 98-02; rtd 02. *7 Four Ash Street, Usk NP15 1BW*

PAGE, David. b 48. Bris Univ BA70 Leic Univ MA74 Southn Univ PGCE74. St Jo Coll Nottm 81. **d** 83 **p** 84. C Morden *S'wark* 83-86; V Wimbledon St Luke 86-91, P-in-c Clapham Common St Barn 91-92; V 92-08; rtd 08. *Rye View, The Strand, Winchelsea TN36 4JY* Tel (01797) 226524
E-mail david@ryeview.net

PAGE, David James. b 62. Liv Univ BSc83 Qu Coll Ox DPhil87. Trin Coll Bris BA93 MA95. **d** 96 **p** 97. C Knutsford St Jo and Toft *Ches* 96-99; R Elworth and Warmingham from 99. *The Rectory, 38 Roman Way, Sandbach CW11 9EW* Tel (01270) 762415 E-mail page.stpeter@tinyworld.co.uk

PAGE, Mrs Dorothy Jean. b 29. Portsm Poly CertEd50. Ox NSM Course 84. **d** 87 **p** 94. NSM Wantage Downs *Ox* from 87. *11 North Street, Marcham, Abingdon OX13 6NG* Tel (01865) 391462

PAGE, The Ven Gilbert Alfred Derek. b 35. **d** 93 **p** 94. C Launceston St Jo Australia 94-95; P-in-c George Town 95-98; Chapl Miss to Seamen Bell Bay 95-98; Adn Burnie 97-00; R Devonport 98-01; Miss Support Officer 01; rtd 01. *Unit 32/4 Brereton Street, Nowra NSW 2541, Australia* Tel (0061) (02) 4422 3403 Mobile 41-924 1950
E-mail gandrpage@shoal.net.au

PAGE, Mrs Irene May. b 38. Birm Univ BA58. NEOC 85. **d** 87 **p** 94. Par Dn Cockfield *Dur* 87-90; Par Dn Waterloo St Jo w St Andr *S'wark* 90-94; C 94-95; R Old Charlton St Thos 95-02; C Charlton 02-03; rtd 03. *40 Wolverton Road, Rednal, Birmingham B45 8RN* Tel 0121-460 1745

PAGE, Jacqueline Anne. b 57. SAOMC 96. **d** 99 **p** 00. NSM Stevenage H Trin *St Alb* 99-03; NSM Benington w Walkern 03-06; P-in-c Ardeley and Cottered w Broadfield and Throcking 06-08; Perm to Offic from 08. *5 Sinfield Close, Stevenage SG1 1LQ* Tel (01438) 368502

PAGE, Jean. *See* PAGE, Mrs Dorothy Jean

PAGE, John Jeremy. b 56. Keble Coll Ox BA79 MA82 New Coll Edin BD86. Edin Th Coll 83. **d** 86 **p** 87. C Wetherby *Ripon* 86-89; TV Wrexham *St As* 89-92; Chapl Hymers Coll Hull 92-98; Chapl Charterhouse Sch Godalming 98-03; TR Hale w Badshot Lea *Guildf* from 03. *The Rectory, 25 Upper Hale Road, Farnham GU9 0NX* Tel (01252) 716469 Fax 713862
E-mail john@padblack.co.uk

PAGE, John Laurence Howard. b 40. ALCD. **d** 65 **p** 66. C Spitalfields Ch Ch w All SS *Lon* 65-69; C Win Ch Ch 69-72; C Ringwood 72-76; V Lockerley and E Dean w E and W Tytherley 76-89; V Lord's Hill 89-97; P-in-c Darby Green 97-02; V 02-05; RD Romsey 85-89; rtd 05. *2 Champions Close, Fowlmere, Royston SG8 7TR* Tel (01763) 208214
E-mail page@web-hq.com

PAGE, Jonathan Michael. b 58. Ripon Coll Cuddesdon 97. **d** 99 **p** 00. C Littlemore *Ox* 99-02; V Chaddesden St Phil *Derby* from 02; P-in-c Derby St Mark from 07; RD Derby N from 06. *St Philip's Vicarage, Taddington Road, Chaddesden, Derby DE21 4JU* Tel (01332) 660072
E-mail frjonathan@philipandmark.org.uk

PAGE, Judy. b 42. Keele Univ DipEd63 BA63 Westmr Coll Ox BTh02. TISEC 03. **d** 05 **p** 06. C Paisley H Trin *Glas* from 05; C Paisley St Barn from 05. *36 Langside Drive, Kilbarchan, Johnstone PA10 2EW* Tel (01505) 703122
E-mail judypage@btinternet.com

PAGE, Lynda Christina. b 55. STETS 04. **d** 07 **p** 08. NSM Blackmoor and Whitehill *Portsm* from 07. *Willow Bank, Hawkley, Liss GU33 6NF* Tel (01730) 827334 Mobile 07790-494296 E-mail lyn.page@eds.com

PAGE, Mathew James. b 77. WEMTC. **d** 09. NSM Cainscross w Selsley *Glouc* from 09. *23 Regent Street, Stonehouse GL10 2AA*

PAGE, Canon Michael John. b 42. K Coll Lon BD66 AKC66. **d** 67 **p** 68. C Rawmarsh w Parkgate *Sheff* 67-72; C-in-c Gleadless Valley CD 72-74; TR Gleadless Valley 74-77; V Lechlade *Glouc* 77-86; RD Fairford 81-86; V Winchcombe, Gretton, Sudeley Manor etc 86-02; Hon Can Glouc Cathl 91-02; RD Winchcombe 94-99; Chapl E Glos NHS Trust 94-02; rtd 02; Perm to Offic *Sheff* from 03. *18 Brocco Bank, Sheffield S11 8RR* Tel 0114-266 3798 E-mail pages.brocco18@btinternet.com

PAGE, Owen Richard. b 53. FIBMS83. Linc Th Coll 89. **d** 91 **p** 92. C Gt Bookham *Guildf* 91-94; V Kings Heath *Pet* 94-99; TR Daventry, Ashby St Ledgers, Braunston etc 99-07; RD Daventry 00-07; ACUPA Link Officer 00-07; CUF Project Officer 00-05; Can Pet Cathl 07; V Todmorden *Wakef* from 07. *The Vicarage, 7 Fern Valley Chase, Todmorden OL14 7HB* Tel (01706) 813180
E-mail owen@owenpage.plus.com

PAGE, Canon Richard Dennis. b 23. G&C Coll Cam BA48 MA50. Ridley Hall Cam 48. **d** 50 **p** 51. C Ecclesfield *Sheff* 50-52; Chapl St Lawr Coll Ramsgate 52-58; Chapl Dean Close Sch Cheltenham 58-60 and 62-64; Chapl Netherton Tr Sch Morpeth 60-62; V Ecclesfield *Sheff* 64-71; RD Ecclesfield 66-71; P-in-c Holkham w Egmere and Waterden *Nor* 71-78; R Wells next the Sea 71-78; RD Burnham and Walsingham 72-78; V Hemsby 78-83; P-in-c Brooke w Kirstead 83-85; P-in-c Mundham w Seething 83-05; P-in-c Thwaite 82-85; R Brooke, Kirstead Mundham w Seething and Thwaite 85-89; Hon Can Nor Cathl 87-89; rtd 90; Perm to Offic *Nor* from 90. *39 Bircham Road, Reepham, Norwich NR10 4NG* Tel (01603) 870886

PAGE, Robert William Charles. b 67. St Steph Ho Ox 90. **d** 93 **p** 94. C Hockerill *St Alb* 93-95; C Kilburn St Aug w St Jo *Lon* 95-02; V Leytonstone St Marg w St Columba *Chelmsf* from 02; CMP from 96. *St Margaret's Vicarage, 15 Woodhouse Road, London E11 3NG* Tel (020) 8519 0813
E-mail rob@stmandstc.fsnet.co.uk

PAGE, Teehan Dawson. b 61. Ch Ch Ox BA83 MA87 K Coll Lon MA96. St Steph Ho Ox 91. **d** 93 **p** 94. C Surbiton St Andr and St Mark *S'wark* 93-96; Chapl Reed's Sch Cobham 96-99; Asst Chapl Tonbridge Sch 99-00; Sen Chapl from 00. *1 Dry Hill Road, Tonbridge TN9 1LT* Tel (01732) 353468
E-mail tdp@tonbschl.demon.co.uk

PAGE, Thomas William. b 57. Sarum & Wells Th Coll 84. **d** 87 **p** 88. C Caterham *S'wark* 87-91; C Cheam 91-95; P-in-c Cranham *Chelmsf* 95-04; Dioc NSM Officer from 99; R Chingford SS Pet and Paul from 04. *The Rectory, 2 The Green Walk, London E4 7ER* Tel (020) 8529 1291
E-mail frtompage@priest.com

PAGE, Canon Trevor Melvyn. b 41. Dur Univ BA63 Fitzw Coll Cam BA67 MA72. Westcott Ho Cam 64. **d** 67 **p** 68. C Millhouses H Trin *Sheff* 67-69; Chapl Sheff Univ 69-74; V Doncaster Intake 74-82; Can Res Sheff Cathl 82-00; Dioc Dir of In-Service Tr 82-95; Dioc Dir of Ords and Post-Ord Tr 82-00; R Bradfield 00-06; Hon Can Sheff Cathl 01-06; rtd 06. *39 Benty Lane, Sheffield S10 5NF* Tel 0114-268 3879

PAGE, William George. b 42. Linc Th Coll 83. **d** 85 **p** 86. C Boston *Linc* 85-89; V Sibsey w Frithville 89-97; RD Holland E 95-97; rtd 07; Perm to Offic *York* from 08. *20 Marshall Drive, Pickering YO18 7JT* Tel (01751) 476915

PAGE-CHESTNEY, Michael William. b 47. Linc Th Coll 80. **d** 82 **p** 83. C Barton upon Humber *Linc* 82-85; TV Gt Grimsby St Mary and St Jas 85-91; V E Stockwith 91-96; V Blyton w Pilham and Laughton w Wildsworth 91-93; V Corringham and Blyton Gp 93-03; P-in-c Immingham from 03; P-in-c Habrough Gp from 03; P-in-c Keelby Gp from 08. *The Vicarage, 344 Pelham Road, Immingham DN40 1PU* Tel (01469) 572560 E-mail mike@page-chestney.co.uk

PAGE-CHESTNEY, Mrs Susan Valerie. b 49. EMMTC. **dss** 86 **d** 87 **p** 94. NSM Gt Grimsby St Mary and St Jas *Linc* 86-91; NSM Blyton w Pilham and Laughton w Wildsworth 91-93; NSM Corringham and Blyton Gp 93-03; Chapl W Lindsey NHS Trust 94-99; Chapl Linc and Louth NHS Trust 99-01; Chapl United Lincs Hosps NHS Trust 01-03; NSM Immingham *Linc* from 03; NSM Habrough Gp from 03. *The Vicarage, 344 Pelham Road, Immingham DN40 1PU* Tel (01469) 572560 E-mail sue@heavenlyhugs.com

PAGE-CLARK, Howard David. b 53. Fitzw Coll Cam MA77. **d** 97 **p** 98. OLM Lytchett Minster *Sarum* from 97. *37 Gorse Lane, Poole BH16 5RR* Tel (01202) 620239 E-mail hdpc@talktalk.net

PAGE DAVIES, David John. b 36. St Cath Soc Ox BA58 MA62. St D Coll Lamp 58. **d** 60 **p** 61. C Rhosddu *St As* 60-68; Chr Aid Area Sec (Glos, Herefords and Worcs) 68-85; Midl Regional Co-ord 78-85; Area Co-ord (Devon and Cornwall) 85-01; Lic to Offic *Truro* 86-01; Perm to Offic from 01; rtd 01. *3 Chyenhal Cottages, Buryas Bridge, Penzance TR19 6AN* Tel (01736) 732466 E-mail johnp-d@tiscali.co.uk

PAGE-TURNER, Canon Edward Gregory Ambrose Wilford. b 31. Qu Coll Birm 57. **d** 60 **p** 61. C Helmsley *York* 60-64; C Kensington St Phil Earl's Court *Lon* 64-67; C Walton-on-Thames *Guildf* 67-70; V Seend *Sarum* 70-71; V Seend and Bulkington 71-79; R Bladon w Woodstock *Ox* 79-87; P-in-c Begbroke 80-86; P-in-c Shipton-on-Cherwell 80-86; P-in-c Hampton Gay 80-85; RD Woodstock 84-87; P-in-c Wootton by Woodstock 85-87; R Patterdale *Carl* 87-89; R Askerswell, Loders and Powerstock *Sarum* 89-01; RD Lyme Bay 92-98; RD Beaminster 94-98; Can and Preb Sarum Cathl 99-01; rtd 01; Perm to Offic *Sarum* from 01; *B & W* 02-05; *Eur* 02-06. *The Old School House, 9 School House Close, Beaminster DT8 3AH* Tel (01308) 861410

PAGET, Alfred Ivor. b 24. St Aid Birkenhead 56. **d** 59 **p** 60. C Hoylake *Ches* 59-62; Chapl Miss to Seamen Hong Kong 62-63; Melbourne Australia 63-64; C Hyde St Geo *Ches* 64-66; R Gt and Lt Henny w Middleton *Chelmsf* 66-74; C Gt Holland 74-79; V Holland-on-Sea 79-92; rtd 92; Perm to Offic *S'wark* 92-98; *Lon* 96-02; *Chelmsf* 99-05. *6 Bary Close, Cheriton Fitzpaine, Crediton EX17 4JY* Tel (01363) 860069

PAGET, Richard Campbell. b 54. Collingwood Coll Dur BA76 Rob Coll Cam BA87. Ridley Hall Cam 85. **d** 88 **p** 89. C Gipsy Hill Ch Ch *S'wark* 88-92; R Chatham St Mary w St Jo *Roch* 92-98; P-in-c Brenchley 99-00; V from 00; RD Paddock Wood from 06. *The Vicarage, 8 Broadoak, Brenchley, Tonbridge TN12 7NN* Tel (01892) 722140

PAGET, Robert James Innes. b 35. AKC59. **d** 60 **p** 61. C Attenborough w Bramcote *S'well* 60-63; C Cheltenham St Mark *Glouc* 63-72; P-in-c Pilsley *Derby* 72-73; TV N Wingfield, Pilsley and Tupton 73-89; R Pinxton 89-97; P-in-c Ambergate and Heage 97-05; rtd 06; Perm to Offic *Derby* from 06. *1A Jeffries Lane, Crich, Matlock DE4 5DT* Tel (01773) 852072

PAGET-WILKES, The Ven Michael Jocelyn James. b 41. ALCD69. **d** 69 **p** 70. C Wandsworth All SS *S'wark* 69-74; V Hatcham St Jas 74-82; V Rugby St Matt *Cov* 82-90; Adn Warwick 90-09; rtd 09. *64 Tarlton, Cirencester GL7 6PA* Tel (01285) 770553 E-mail michael.pw@btinternet.com

PAGETT, Andrew Stephen. b 45. Bris & Glouc Tr Course. **d** 82 **p** 83. NSM Swindon New Town *Bris* 82-01; C Paignton St Jo *Ex* 01-04; V Lifton, Broadwoodwidger, Stowford etc from 04. *The Rectory, Parsonage Court, Lifton PL16 0BJ* Tel (01566) 784008

PAICE, Alan. b 26. AKC53. **d** 55 **p** 56. C Leek St Edw *Lich* 55-59; C Haslemere *Guildf* 59-63; C Eton w Boveney *Ox* 63-74; P-in-c Hawridge w Cholesbury 74-83; P-in-c The Lee 74-83; V 83-86; P-in-c Aston Clinton St Leon 79-83; R Hawridge w Cholesbury and St Leonard 83-86; rtd 86. *2 The Poplars, Park Lane, Pinhoe, Exeter EX4 9HH* Tel (01392) 464741

PAICE, Michael Antony. b 35. Kelham Th Coll 55. **d** 60 **p** 61. C Skegby *S'well* 60-62; C Carlton 62-66; V Misterton and W Stockwith 66-81; V Olveston and P-in-c Littleton on Severn w Elberton *Bris* 81-83; Deputation Appeals Org CECS *Bris* and *Glouc* 83-84; *Bris, Glouc* and *B & W* 84-89; R Sutton St Nicholas w Sutton St Michael *Heref* 89-96; R Withington w Westhide 89-96; rtd 96. *Frankhurst, Sutton St Nicholas, Hereford HR1 3BN* Tel (01432) 880279 Mobile 07713-906554

PAICE, Richard James Rowland. b 72. Ch Ch Ox BA94 MA99. Oak Hill Th Coll BA00. **d** 00 **p** 01. C Eastbourne All So *Chich* 00-03; Chapl Bp Bell Sch 00-03; P-in-c Warbleton and Bodle Street Green *Chich* 03-08; V Wimbledon Park St Luke *S'wark*

from 08. *St Luke's Vicarage, 28 Farquhar Road, London SW19 8DA* Tel (020) 8946 3396 E-mail warblebodle@yahoo.co.uk

PAILING, Crispin Alexander. b 75. Qu Coll Ox BA98 MA01 Birm Univ PhD08. Ripon Coll Cuddesdon BA02. **d** 03 **p** 04. C Four Oaks *Birm* 03-06; P-in-c Perry Barr from 06. *The Vicarage, Church Road, Perry Barr, Birmingham B42 2LB* Tel 0121-356 7998 E-mail crispin.pailing@queens.oxon.org

PAILING, Rowena Fay. b 77. Qu Coll Ox BA99 MA02 Birm Univ PhD08. Ripon Coll Cuddesdon BA02. **d** 03 **p** 04. C Four Oaks *Birm* 03-04; C Gravelly Hill 04-07; P-in-c Handsworth St Mich from 07. *The Vicarage, Church Road, Perry Barr, Birmingham B42 2LB* Tel 0121-356 7998 E-mail rowena.pailing@queens.oxon.org

PAIN, Canon David Clinton. b 36. K Coll Lon 56. **d** 64 **p** 64. Lic to Offic Benin 64-67; Lic to Offic Accra Ghana 67-86; Hon Can Accra from 67; V Kemp Town St Mary *Chich* 86-93; Chapl St Mary's Hall Brighton 88-93; V Billingshurst *Chich* 93-05; RD Horsham 98-02; rtd 05; P-in-c Chidham *Chich* from 05. *The Vicarage, Cot Lane, Chidham, Chichester PO18 8TA* Tel (01243) 573147

PAIN, Michael Broughton George. b 37. Dur Univ BA61. Wycliffe Hall Ox 61. **d** 63 **p** 64. C Downend *Bris* 63-67; C Swindon Ch Ch 67-70; V Alveston 70-78; V Guildf Ch Ch 78-90; TR Melksham *Sarum* 90-98; Chapl Melksham Hosp 90-98; TR Redhorn *Sarum* 98-03; rtd 03; Perm to Offic *Sarum* from 03. *Rickety Cottage, 70 Bradenstoke, Chippenham SN15 4EL* Tel (01249) 890727

PAIN, The Ven Richard Edward. b 56. Bris Univ BA79 Univ of Wales (Cardiff) BD84. St Mich Coll Llan 81. **d** 84 **p** 85. C Caldicot *Mon* 84-86; P-in-c Cwmtillery 86-88; V 88-91; V Six Bells 88-91; V Risca 91-98; V Overmonnow w Wonastow and Michel Troy 98-03; V Monmouth w Overmonnow etc 03-08; Adn Mon from 08; P-in-c Mamhilad w Monkswood and Glascoed Chapel from 08; Dioc Warden of Ord from 01; Can St Woolos Cathl from 03. *The Archdeaconry, 7 Lansdown Drive, Abergavenny NP7 6AW* Tel (01873) 856742 E-mail archdeacon.monmouth@churchinwales.org.uk

PAINE, Alasdair David MacConnell. b 60. Trin Coll Cam BA82 MA86 MSc84. Wycliffe Hall Ox 94. **d** 96 **p** 97. C Ex St Leon w H Trin 96-01; V Westbourne Ch Ch Chpl *Win* from 02. *134 Alumhurst Road, Bournemouth BH4 8HU* Tel (01202) 762164 E-mail alasdair@claranet.co.uk

PAINE, Peter Stanley. b 46. K Coll Lon BD69 AKC69. Cuddesdon Coll 69. **d** 71 **p** 72. C Leeds St Aid *Ripon* 71-74; C Harrogate St Wilfrid 74-78; V Beeston Hill H Spirit 78-82; TV Seacroft 82-90; V Martham w Repps w Bastwick *Nor* 90-94; V Martham and Repps with Bastwick, Thurne etc 94-04; P-in-c Foremark and Repton w Newton Solney *Derby* 04-08; V from 08. *St Wystan's Vicarage, Willington Road, Repton, Derby DE65 6FH* Tel (01283) 703317

PAINE, William Barry. b 58. CITC. **d** 84 **p** 85. C Glendermott *D & R* 84-86; C Lurgan St Jo *D & D* 86-88; I Kilbarron w Rossnowlagh and Drumholm *D & R* 88-91; CF 91-00; I Tynan w Middletown and Aghavilly *Arm* from 00. *The Rectory, 16 Derryhaw Road, Tynan BT60 4SS* Tel (028) 3756 8619 E-mail bpaine.888@hotmail.co.uk

PAINE DAVEY, Nathan Paul. b 64. Barrister-at-Law 88 Birm Poly LLB86. St Steph Ho Ox 89. **d** 92 **p** 93. C Palmers Green St Jo *Lon* 92-95; C Kentish Town St Silas 95-98; C Haverstock Hill H Trin w Kentish Town St Barn 95-98; C Kentish Town St Silas and H Trin w St Barn 98-01; Perm to Offic 01-05. *Address temp unknown*

PAINTER, Christopher Mark. b 65. Cranmer Hall Dur. **d** 00 **p** 01. C Melksham *Sarum* 00-03; Chapl Wilts and Swindon Healthcare NHS Trust 02-03; TV Eccles *Man* 03-07. *Address temp unknown* E-mail ckpainter@blueyonder.co.uk

PAINTER, The Ven David Scott. b 44. Worc Coll Ox BA68 MA72 LTCL65. Cuddesdon Coll 68. **d** 70 **p** 71. C Plymouth St Andr *Ex* 70-73; Chapl Plymouth Poly 71-73; C St Marylebone All SS *Lon* 73-76; Abp's Dom Chapl and Dir of Ords *Cant* 76-80; V Roehampton H Trin *S'wark* 80-91; RD Wandsworth 85-90; PV Westmr Abbey 81-91; Can Res and Treas S'wark Cathl 91-00; Dioc Dir of Ords 91-00; Adn Oakham *Pet* from 00; Can Res Pet Cathl from 00. *7 Minster Precincts, Peterborough PE1 1XS* Tel (01733) 891360 Fax 554524 E-mail david.painter@peterborough-cathedral.org.uk

PAINTER, John. b 25. Selw Coll Cam BA48 MA53. Ripon Hall Ox 48. **d** 50 **p** 51. C Stoke Newington St Mary *Lon* 50-55; C Woodside Park St Barn 55-56; C Llangiwg *S & B* 56-59; C-in-c Swansea St Jo 59-60; R Chipstable w Raddington *B & W* 61-64; V Audenshaw St Steph *Man* 64-66; V Sandown Ch Ch *Portsm* 66-72; R Keinton Mandeville *B & W* 72-77; P-in-c Lydford-on-Fosse 76-77; R Keinton Mandeville w Lydford on Fosse 77-90; RD Cary 81-90; RD Bruton 82-85; rtd 90; Perm to Offic *B & W* 90-05 and *Sarum* from 96. *2 Juniper Gardens, Gillingham SP8 4RF* Tel (01747) 823818

PAINTING, Stephen Nigel. b 60. Trin Coll Bris 01. **d** 03 **p** 04. C Heanton Punchardon w Marwood *Ex* 03-08; TV Beaconsfield

Ox from 08. *St Thomas's House, Mayflower Way, Beaconsfield HP9 1UF* Tel (01496) 672750
E-mail s.painting@btinternet.com

PAIRMAN, David Drummond. b 47. GGSM CertEd. Chich Th Coll 82. **d** 84 **p** 85. C Cowes St Mary *Portsm* 84-87; C Marshwood Vale *Sarum* 87-90; C Hawkchurch 87-90; C Marshwood Vale 90-95; rtd 95. *Chestnut Cottage, Old Pinn Lane, Exeter EX1 3RF* Tel (01392) 464488

PAISEY, Gerald Herbert John. b 31. Wm Booth Memorial Coll 51 Leic Univ CertEd62 Nottm Univ DipAdEd70 MPhil77 Lanc Univ MA78 K Coll Lon PhD91. St Alb Minl Tr Scheme 80. **d** 88 **p** 90. NSM Montrose *Bre* 88-90; NSM Inverbervie 88-90; Lect Robert Gordon Univ 89-97; P-in-c Stonehaven and Catterline *Bre* 90-01; rtd 01; Tutor Open Univ 90-05; Perm to Offic *Bre* 03-07; Lic to Offic *Edin* from 08. *40 South Middleton, Uphall, Broxburn EH52 5GB* Tel (01506) 865937

PAISEY, Canon Jeremy Mark. b 58. Aber Univ LLB81 Solicitor 83. Coates Hall Edin 92. **d** 94 **p** 95. C Turriff *Ab* 94-97; C Buckie 94-97; C Banff 94-97; C Cuminestown 94-97; C Portsoy 94-97; P-in-c Buckie from 97; P-in-c Portsoy from 97; P-in-c Banff from 98; Can St Andr Cathl from 08. *All Saints' Rectory, 14 Cluny Square, Buckie AB56 1HA* Tel (01542) 832312 Mobile 07817-261435 E-mail jpaisey@aol.com

PAISLEY, Canon Samuel Robinson (Robin). b 51. Man Univ BSc72. Edin Th Coll BD91. **d** 91 **p** 92. C St Mary's Cathl 91-95; P-in-c Bishopbriggs 95-06; Teaching Consultant Glas Univ 95-99; Chapl Stobhill NHS Trust 95-99; Bp's Adv in Min *Glas* 99-07; R Dumfries from 06; Chapl NHS Dumfries and Galloway from 06; Can St Mary's Cathl from 06. *8 Newall Terrace, Dumfries DG1 1LW* Tel (01387) 254126
E-mail rector@episcopaldumfries.org

PAJUNEN, Mika Kari Tapani. b 76. Helsinki Univ MTh00. **p** 01. C Helsinki *Eur* 02-04; Asst Chapl from 05. *Kivikarintie 3, 21570 Sauvo, Finland* E-mail mika.pajunen@helsinki.fi

PAKENHAM, Charles Wilfrid. b 18. Trin Coll Ox BA40 MA52. Wycliffe Hall Ox 40. **d** 41 **p** 42. C Sutton *Liv* 41-44; CMS 44-49; Nigeria 44-49; C Cheltenham St Mary *Glouc* 49-52; V Litherland Ch Ch *Liv* 52-84; rtd 84; Perm to Offic *Sarum* from 90; P-in-c W Woodhay w Enborne, Hampstead Marshall etc *Ox* 91-92; Perm to Offic 92-00. *15 Cook Road, Marlborough SN8 2EG* Tel (01672) 540531

PALIN, Roy. b 34. Man Univ BA56. Ripon Hall Ox 65. **d** 67 **p** 68. C Ilkeston St Mary *Derby* 67-70; C Wollaton *S'well* 70-71; V Harby w Swinethorpe 71-79; V Thorney w Wigsley and Broadholme 71-79; P-in-c N Clifton 75-79; R Harby w Thorney and N and S Clifton 79-80; V Tuxford 80-81; P-in-c Laxton 80-81; P-in-c Markham Clinton 80-81; P-in-c Weston 80-81; V Tuxford w Weston and Markham Clinton 81-90; R Nuthall 90-99; rtd 99; Perm to Offic *Nor* from 00. *31 Pine Walk, Weybourne, Holt NR25 7HJ* Tel (01263) 588144

PALK, Mrs Deirdre Elizabeth Pauline. b 41. Reading Univ BA63 Lon Univ MA94 AIL77 FIOSH96. S'wark Ord Course 81. **dss** 84 **d** 87. Wanstead H Trin Hermon Hill *Chelmsf* 84-88; Hon Par Dn 87-88; Hon Par Dn Walthamstow St Pet 88-93; Hon Chapl UPA Projects 93-97; Tutor NTMTC 97-05. *12 rue Max Blondat, 89000 Auxerre, France* Tel (0033) (3) 86 51 77 46

PALLANT, Canon Roger Frank. b 35. Trin Coll Cam BA57 MA61. Wells Th Coll 57. **d** 59 **p** 60. C Stafford St Mary *Lich* 59-62; C Ipswich St Mary le Tower *St E* 62-65; Dioc Youth Chapl 62-65; Development Officer C of E Youth Coun 65-70; Hon C Putney St Mary *S'wark* 66-71; Org Sec New Syn Gp 70-71; R Hintlesham w Chattisham *St E* 71-80; V Ipswich All Hallows 80-88; Hon Can St E Cathl 85-00; P-in-c Sproughton w Burstall 88-00; Dioc Officer for OLM 88-00; RD Samford 93-99; rtd 00; Perm to Offic *St E* from 00. *163 Fircroft Road, Ipswich IP1 6PT* Tel (01473) 461148

PALLENT, Ian. b 70. Newc Poly BA91. Ridley Hall Cam 05. **d** 07 **p** 08. C Bayston Hill *Lich* from 07. *15 Glebe Road, Bayston Hill, Shrewsbury SY3 0PJ* Tel 07870-630433 (mobile)
E-mail ianpallent@hotmail.com

PALLETT, Ian Nigel. b 59. Leeds Univ BA80. Linc Th Coll 81. **d** 84 **p** 85. C Halesowen *Worc* 84-88; C Mansfield Woodhouse *S'well* 88-91; R Morton and Stonebroom *Derby* 91-98; P-in-c Heanor 98-01; V 01-03; P-in-c Dingwall *Mor* from 03; P-in-c Strathpeffer from 03. *The Parsonage, 4 Castle Street, Dingwall IV15 9HU* Tel (01349) 862204
E-mail pallett3000@btinternet.com

PALLIS, Mrs Maria. b 60. NOC 96. **d** 99 **p** 00. C Chapel Allerton *Ripon* 99-03; P-in-c Collingham w Harewood from 03; P-in-c Spofforth w Kirk Deighton from 07. *The Vicarage, Church Lane, Collingham, Wetherby LS22 5AU* Tel (01937) 573975
E-mail mariapallis@hotmail.com

PALMER, Alister Gordon. b 46. Univ of Tasmania BA73 DipEd74. Trin Coll Bris 76 Ridley Hall Cam 78. **d** 80 **p** 81. C Patchway *Bris* 80-83; C Bushbury *Lich* 83-86; V Wednesfield Heath 86-93; NSM Independent Ch Community Work 93-98; Dioc Officer for Min Tas Australia 98-02; Dir Angl Miss 99-02; C Smestow Vale *Lich* 02-03; V Knowle St Barn *Bris* 03-07; P-in-c

Inns Court H Cross 05-07; V Filwood Park from 07. *St Barnabas' Vicarage, Daventry Road, Bristol BS4 1DQ* Tel 0117-966 4139 E-mail agpal46@btopenworld.com

PALMER, Angus Douglas. b 40. St Chad's Coll Dur BA62. **d** 63 **p** 64. C Wallsend St Pet *Newc* 63-66; C Newc H Cross 66-69; C Bottesford *Linc* 69-70; R Penicuik *Edin* 70-84; R W Linton 77-84. *6 Hackworth Gardens, Wylam NE41 8EJ* Tel (01661) 853786

PALMER, Christopher. b 71. **d** 98 **p** 99. C Emscote *Cov* 98-02; TV Mortlake w E Sheen *S'wark* from 02; AD Richmond and Barnes from 05. *86 East Sheen Avenue, London SW14 8AU* Tel (020) 8487 8208 E-mail christopherpalmer@talk21.com

PALMER, David Michael. b 53. QUB BA95 MSc. CITC 95. **d** 97 **p** 98. C Glenageary *D & G* 97-99; C Agherton *Conn* 99-00; I Ramoan w Ballycastle and Culfeightrin from 00. *Ramoan Rectory, 12 Novally Road, Ballycastle BT54 6HB* Tel (028) 2076 2461 E-mail ramoan@connor.anglican.org

PALMER, David Philip. b 50. Sarum & Wells Th Coll. **d** 84 **p** 85. C St Ives *Ely* 84-86; V Luton All SS w St Pet *St Alb* 86-88; V Stocksbridge *Sheff* 88-97; P-in-c Seaton Hirst *Newc* 97-98; TR 98-08; R from 08; Chapl Northd Coll from 99. *The Vicarage, Newbiggin Road, Ashington NE63 0TQ* Tel (01670) 813218
E-mail davidseahirst@aol.com

PALMER, David Roderick. b 34. St Jo Coll Dur BA56. Qu Coll Birm 56. **d** 60 **p** 61. C Loughton St Jo *Chelmsf* 60-63; C Pimlico St Gabr *Lon* 63-64; Miss to Seamen 64-67; CF 67-74; Chapl Luxembourg *Eur* 74-80; P-in-c Exton and Winsford and Cutcombe w Luxborough *B & W* 80-82; P-in-c Wrington w Butcombe 82-84; Dep Dir of Tr Inst Wednesbury St Jas *Lich* 84-86; C Gt Wyrley 86-89; V Wilshamstead and Houghton Conquest *St Alb* 90-00; rtd 01. *14B Place du Marché, 61330 Céaucé, France*

PALMER, Derek James. b 54. Man Univ BA77. Qu Coll Birm 77. **d** 79 **p** 80. C Leek *Lich* 79-83; CF 83-92; R Riviera Beach St Geo USA 92-95; C S Ockendon and Belhus Park *Chelmsf* 95-98; V Walthamstow St Mich 98-00; Chapl Salford Univ 00-06; AD Salford 02-03; P-in-c Droylsden St Andr 06-09; TR Oldham from 09; Bp's Adv on New Relig Movements from 02. *The Rectory, Prince Charlie Street, Oldham OL1 4HJ* Tel 0161-633 4847 Mobile 07504-953670
E-mail derek_palmer@hotmail.co.uk

PALMER, Elizabeth. See BLATCHLEY, Ms Elizabeth

PALMER, Preb Francis Harvey. b 30. Jes Coll Cam BA52 MA56. Wycliffe Hall Ox 53. **d** 55 **p** 56. C Knotty Ash St Jo *Liv* 55-57; C Southgate *Chich* 58-60; Chapl Fitzw Ho Cam 60-64; V Cambridge H Trin *Ely* 64-71; Chapl to Cam Pastorate 64-71; Prin Ridley Hall Cam 71-72; R Worplesdon *Guildf* 72-80; Bp's Ecum Officer 74-80; P-in-c Blymhill w Weston-under-Lizard *Lich* 80-82; Dioc Missr and Sec to Bd for Miss and Unity 80-90; Preb Lich Cathl 86-89; TV Walsall 87-90; rtd 90; Perm to Offic *Lich* 90-99; *Heref* 93-09; *Glouc* from 93. *The Old Vicarage, Claverley, Wolverhampton WV5 7DT* Tel (01746) 710746
E-mail francis@palmerfh.freeserve.co.uk

PALMER, Graham. b 31. Em Coll Cam BA53 MA57. Qu Coll Birm 56. **d** 58 **p** 59. C Camberwell St Giles *S'wark* 58-61; C Kilburn St Aug *Lon* 61-67; P-in-c Fulham St Alb 67-73; V 73-92; V Fulham St Alb w St Aug 92-97; rtd 97; Perm to Offic *Lon* 97-04. *7 Wellington Court, 116 Knightsbridge, London SW1X 7PL* Tel (020) 7584 4036

PALMER, Hugh. b 50. Pemb Coll Cam BA72 MA76. Ridley Hall Cam 73. **d** 76 **p** 77. C Heigham H Trin *Nor* 76-80; Bp's Chapl for Tr and Miss 80-84; C St Helen Bishopsgate w St Andr Undershaft etc *Lon* 85-95; C Fulwood *Sheff* 95-97; V 97-05; Hon Can Sheff Cathl 01-05; R Langham Place All So *Lon* from 05. *12 Weymouth Street, London W1W 5BY* Tel (020) 7580 6029
E-mail hugh.palmer@allsouls.org

PALMER, Hugh Maurice Webber. b 28. Magd Coll Cam BA51 MA55. Cuddesdon Coll 51. **d** 53 **p** 54. C Bitterne Park *Win* 53-57; N Rhodesia 57-62; V Owslebury w Morestead *Win* 62-65; Rhodesia 65-70; C Headbourne Worthy *Win* 70-71; P-in-c Stratton Strawless *Nor* 72-77; R Hainford 72-77; R Haynford w Stratton Strawless 77-80; Chapl HM Pris Stafford 80-82; Chapl HM Pris Standford Hill 82-89; Sub-Chapl HM Pris Nor 89-91; rtd 91. *29 Mayfield Way, North Walsham NR28 0DQ* Tel (01692) 403664

PALMER, Ian Stanley. b 50. K Coll Lon BD71. Cranmer Hall Dur 73. **d** 75 **p** 76. C Huyton St Mich *Liv* 75-78; Chapl Dur Univ 78-83; V Collierley w Annfield Plain 83-90; Dir Evang Newc Australia 90-92; R Belmont N and Redhead 93-00; Adn Upper Hunter and R Muswellbrook 00-05; R Queanbeyan from 05. *39 Rutledge Street, PO Box 103, Queanbeyan NSW 2620, Australia* Tel (0061) (2) 6299 2924 or 6299 3917 Fax 6299 1360 Mobile 411-242596 E-mail palmeris@hunterlink.net.au

PALMER, John Richard Henry. b 29. AKC52. **d** 53 **p** 54. C Englefield Green *Guildf* 53-57; P-in-c Brewarrina Australia 57-62; C Wareham w Arne *Sarum* 62-63; PC Derby St Jo 63-66; Chapl Holloway Sanatorium Virginia Water 66-70; Chapl Brookwood Hosp Woking 70-94; rtd 94; Perm to Offic *Truro*

from 94. *Lightning Ridge, Pentreath Road, The Lizard, Helston TR12 7NY* Tel (01326) 290654
E-mail vsp@oldlizardhead.freeserve.co.uk

PALMER, Judith Angela. b 47. Bris Univ MB, ChB71. NOC 02. **d** 05 **p** 06. NSM Strensall *York* from 05. *20 Bedern, York YO1 7LP* Tel (01904) 637629
E-mail j.palmer@britishlibrary.net

PALMER, Mrs Julia Elizabeth. b 57. Hull Univ BA80. St Jo Coll Nottm MA98. **d** 99 **p** 00. C Snodland All SS w Ch Ch *Roch* 99-03; P-in-c Sutton Bonington w Normanton-on-Soar *S'well* 03-08; P-in-c Sutton in Ashfield St Mary from 08. *St Mary's Vicarage, Church Avenue, Sutton-in-Ashfield NG17 2EB* Tel (01623) 554509 E-mail revjuliap@msn.com

PALMER, Kevin Anthony. b 59. St Steph Ho Ox. **d** 01 **p** 02. C Tunstall *Lich* 01-04; CMP from 02; R Wednesbury St Jas and St Jo *Lich* from 04. *The Rectory, 1 Hollies Drive, Wednesbury WS10 9EQ* Tel 0121-505 1188 *or* 505 1568

PALMER, Malcolm Leonard. b 46. Sarum & Wells Th Coll 80. **d** 82 **p** 83. C Cannock *Lich* 82-85; Chapl RAF 85-89; Asst Chapl HM Pris Dur 89-90; Chapl HM YOI Hewell Grange 90-93; Chapl HM Rem Cen Brockhill 90-93; Chapl HM Pris Blakenhurst 93-01; Miss P Kugluktuk Canada 01-04; R Meadows from 04. *Box 3631, RR 2, Corner Brook NL A2H 6B9, Canada* Tel (001) (709) 783 2194 Fax 783 3093
E-mail atanck@excite.com

PALMER, Marc Richard. b 72. St Jo Coll Dur BA96. Cranmer Hall Dur 93. **d** 98 **p** 99. C Chester le Street *Dur* 98-03; TV Bensham 03-08; V Bensham and Teams from 08. *St Chad's Vicarage, Dunsmuir Grove, Gateshead NE8 4QL* Tel 0191-478 6338 E-mail marcr.palmer@virgin.net

PALMER, Marion Denise. b 42. Open Univ BA82 SRN64 SCM66. Linc Th Coll 84. **dss** 86 **d** 87 **p** 94. Poplar *Lon* 86-90; Par Dn 87-90; Par Dn Gillingham St Mary *Roch* 90-94; C 94-96; C Farnborough 96-02; rtd 02; Perm to Offic *St E* from 04. *14 Prestwick Avenue, Felixstowe IP11 9LF* Tel (01394) 671588

PALMER, Canon Maureen Florence. b 38. Qu Eliz Coll Lon BSc60 PhD64. Ripon Coll Cuddesdon. **dss** 85 **d** 87 **p** 94. Tupsley *Heref* 85-88; C 87-88; Par Dn Talbot Village *Sarum* 88-91; Chapl Birm Cathl 91-96; Can Pastor and Can Res Guildf Cathl 96-06; Sub-Dean 99-06; rtd 06; Perm to Offic *Heref* from 06. *28A Green Street, Hereford HR1 2QG* Tel (01432) 353771
E-mail drmaureenpalmer@btinternet.com

PALMER, Michael Christopher. b 43. MBE00. AKC67 CQSW76. **d** 68 **p** 69. C Easthampstead *Ox* 68-71; Miss to Seamen 71-73; Hong Kong 73; Lic to Offic *Ox* 76-79 and *Truro* 79-83; Dioc Soc Resp Adv Truro 83-98; Bp's Dom Chapl 85-87; V Devoran 87-98; rtd 98; Perm to Offic *Truro* 98-08. *5 Little Drove, Singleton, Chichester PO18 0HD* Tel (01243) 811540

PALMER, Norman Ernest. b 28. Lon Univ BD59. Roch Th Coll 66. **d** 67 **p** 67. C Chipping Norton *Ox* 67-69; V Bozeat w Easton Maudit *Pet* 69-90; rtd 90; Perm to Offic *Chich* 90-94. *6 Abbeyfield House, 22 Falmouth Road, Truro TR1 2HX* Tel (01872) 273846

PALMER, Mrs Patricia. STETS. **d** 09. NSM Basingstoke *Win* from 09. *97 Packenham Road, Basingstoke RG21 8YA* Tel (01256) 412986 E-mail pat.palmer@ntlworld.com

PALMER, Canon Peter Malcolm. b 31. Chich Th Coll 56. **d** 59 **p** 60. C Leighton Buzzard *St Alb* 59-63; C Apsley End 63-65; C Hitchin H Sav 65-69; R Ickleford 69-76; V Oxhey St Matt 76-86; V Kensworth, Studham and Whipsnade 86-96; Hon Can St Alb 94-96; rtd 97; Perm to Offic *St Alb* from 97; Bishop's Retirement Officer from 97. *4 Sefton Close, St Albans AL1 4PF* Tel (01727) 763196

PALMER, Peter Parsons. b 27. **d** 59 **p** 61. SSJE from 59; Miss to Bracebridge Canada 59-79; Perm to Offic *Leic* 80-86 and *Lon* 86-94; Lic to Offic *Lon* 94-02. *The College of St Barnabas, Blackberry Lane, Lingfield RH7 6NJ*

PALMER, Philip Edward Hitchen. b 35. St Jo Coll Cam MA61 DipAdEd74. Ridley Hall Cam 61 EAMTC 87. **d** 90 **p** 91. NSM Gt Oakley w Wix *Chelmsf* 90-96; NSM Gt Oakley w Wix and Wrabness 96-00; Perm to Offic from 00. *Glebe House, Wix Road, Great Oakley, Harwich CO12 5BJ* Tel (01255) 880737

PALMER, Robert William. b 28. Wells Th Coll 63. **d** 65 **p** 66. C Earlsdon *Cov* 65-69; P-in-c Cov St Mark 69-71; Chapl Cov and Warks Hosp 69-71; Hon C Binley *Cov* 72-76; V Sheff St Paul 76-84; V Deepcar 84-93; rtd 93; Perm to Offic *Sheff* from 93. *Moorlands, 26 Coal Pit Lane, Stocksbridge, Sheffield S36 1AW*

PALMER, Canon Stephen Charles. b 47. Portsm Univ PhD04 FRGS98 FLS01. Oak Hill Th Coll 71. **d** 74 **p** 75. C Crofton *Portsm* 74-77; Bp's Dom Chapl 77-80; Chapl RNR 78-91; R Brighstone and Brooke w Mottistone *Portsm* 80-91; P-in-c Shorwell w Kingston 82-86; RD W Wight 87-91; R Falkland Is 91-96; V Portsdown *Portsm* 96-02; V Newport St Jo 02-09; V Newport St Thos 02-09; Bp's Ecological Adv 00-07; Hon Can Portsm Cathl 91-09; rtd 09; Chapl to The Queen from 08. *Fintry Schoolhouse, Fintry, Turriff AB53 5RN* Tel (01888) 551367 Mobile 07799-412512 E-mail palmers@fintry.plus.com

PALMER, Steven Roy. b 51. Birm Univ BSc71. WMMTC 91. **d** 94 **p** 95. C Sheldon *Birm* 94-97; P-in-c Duddeston w Nechells 97-99; V Nechells 99-03; R Billing *Pet* from 03; RD Northn

06-07. *The Rectory, 25 Church Walk, Great Billing, Northampton NN3 4ED* Tel (01604) 788508 Fax 401641
E-mail stevenrpalmer@hotmail.com

PALMER, Canon Terence Henry James. b 34. Univ of Wales (Lamp) BA55 LTh57 St Edm Hall Ox BA65 MA69 FRSA08. **d** 57 **p** 58. C Griffithstown *Mon* 57-60; Min Can and C St D Cathl 60-63; Perm to Offic *B & W* and *Ox* 63-65; C Monmouth 65-69; C-in-c St Hilary Greenway CD 69-72; R Roggiett w Llanfihangel Roggiett 72-80; R Portskewett and Rogiet w Llanfihangel Rogiet 80-00; RD Netherwent 89-00; Dir NSM Studies 91-99; Can St Woolos Cathl 96-00; rtd 00; Perm to Offic *Eur* from 99; Lic to Offic *Mon* from 00; P-in-c Newport St Teilo from 03. *Terleen, 12 Windsor Park, Magor, Caldicot NP26 3NJ* Tel (01633) 881927

PALMER FINCH, Barry Marshall. b 23. Hertf Coll Ox BA47 MA48. Westcott Ho Cam 47. **d** 49 **p** 50. C Alrewas *Lich* 49-52; C Wychnor 49-52; C Birchington w Acol *Cant* 52-56; R Harrietsham 56-66; Chapl Westmr Hosp Lon 66-73; V Chipping Sodbury and Old Sodbury *Glouc* 73-88; rtd 88; Perm to Offic *Glouc* and *Bris* 88-96; *Lon* 90-00. *Finch's Folly, 45 Hay Street, Marshfield, Chippenham SN14 8PF* Tel (01225) 891096

PAMMENT, Gordon Charles. b 31. TCD BA54. Linc Th Coll 56. **d** 58 **p** 60. C Hemel Hempstead *St Alb* 58-63; C Gedney Drove End *Linc* 63-65; I Macroom Union *C, C & R* 65-72; I Rathcormac Union 72-78; I Fermoy Union 78-91; Can Ross Cathl 89-91; Can Cork Cathl 89-91; rtd 91. *Magoola, Dripsey, Co Cork, Republic of Ireland* Tel (00353) (21) 451 6532

PAMPLIN, Canon Richard Lawrence. b 46. Lon Univ BScEng68 Dur Univ BA75 NY Th Sem DMin85. Wycliffe Hall Ox 75. **d** 77 **p** 78. C Greenside *Dur* 77-80; C Sheff St Barn and St Mary 80-84; R Wombwell 84-90; P-in-c Madeley *Heref* 90-91; TR 91-01; Chapl Berne w Neuchâtel *Eur* 01-07; Can Gib Cathl 04-07; Chapl Via del Mar w Valparaiso Chile from 07. *Casilla 676, Via del Mar, Chile* Tel (0056) (32) 239 7771
E-mail richard.l.pamplin@gmail.com

PANG, Wing-On. b 43. Manitoba Univ BA67 SOAS Lon MA70. Oak Hill Th Coll 85. **d** 87 **p** 88. C Pennycross *Ex* 87-91; TV Mildenhall *St E* 91-96; Assoc P Kowloon St Andr Hong Kong 96-08; rtd 08. *20 Oakland Drive, Wirral CH49 6JL* Tel 0151-677 2690 E-mail wingonheather@gmail.com

PANGBOURNE, John Godfrey. b 36. Ridley Hall Cam 82. **d** 84 **p** 85. C Ashtead *Guildf* 84-88; V Ore Ch Ch *Chich* 88-03; rtd 03; Perm to Offic *Ex* 04-06; Hon C Ottery St Mary, Alfington, W Hill, Tipton etc from 06. *Meon Croft, Toadpit Lane, West Hill, Ottery St Mary EX11 1TR* Tel (01404) 812393

PANKHURST, Donald Araunah. b 28. Qu Coll Birm. **d** 64 **p** 65. C Pemberton St Jo *Liv* 64-68; V Aspull 68-76; R Newchurch 76-88; R Winwick 88-94; rtd 94; Perm to Offic *Carl* from 94. *Hunters Hill, Spooner Vale, Windermere LA23 1AU* Tel (01539) 446390

PANKHURST, Ian Charles. b 50. Trin Coll Cam BA72 Lon Inst of Educn PGCE88. SAOMC 01. **d** 04 **p** 05. C Watford St Luke *St Alb* from 04. *2 Albert Road North, Watford WD17 1QE* Tel (01923) 249139 E-mail sueandian.pankhurst@virgin.net

PANNETT, Philip Anthony. b 36. Brighton Poly MPS59 MRPharmS59. K Coll Lon AKC63 St Boniface Warminster 63. **d** 64 **p** 65. C Stanmer w Falmer and Moulsecoomb *Chich* 64-68; C Hangleton 68-72; Teacher Finchden Manor Sch Tenterden 72-74; Teacher Bodiam Manor Sch 74-76; Perm to Offic from 76; rtd 01. *1 Fitzjohns Road, Lewes BN7 1PP* Tel (01273) 472804

PANTER, The Ven Richard James Graham. b 48. Oak Hill Th Coll 73. **d** 76 **p** 77. C Rusholme H Trin *Man* 76-80; C Toxteth St Cypr w Ch Ch *Liv* 80-85; V Clubmoor 85-96; P-in-c Litherland St Jo and St Jas 96-02; AD Bootle 99-02; Can Liv from 02; V Orrell Hey St Jo and St Jas from 02. *St John and St James Vicarage, 2A Monfa Road, Bootle L20 6BQ* Tel and fax 0151-922 3758 E-mail archdeaconricky@blueyonder.co.uk

PANTER MARSHALL, Canon Susan Lesley. b 49. Portsm Poly BSc72. S Dios Minl Tr Scheme 88. **d** 91 **p** 94. NSM Southover *Chich* 91-95; C Iford w Kingston and Rodmell 95-98; C Hollington St Jo 98-02; P-in-c Herstmonceux and Wartling 02-07; R from 07; Can and Preb Chich Cathl from 07. *The Rectory, West End, Herstmonceux, Hailsham BN27 4NY* Tel (01323) 833124

PANTLING, Rosemary Caroline. b 60. Ex Coll Ox BA83 MA89 Anglia Poly Univ MA03 Birm Univ PGCE84. EAMTC 98. **d** 01 **p** 02. NSM Bishop's Tachbrook *Cov* 01-08; P-in-c Cubbington from 08. *22 Touchstone Road, Heathcote, Warwick CV34 6EE* Tel 07846-220974 (mobile)

PANTON, Alan Edward. b 45. K Coll Lon BD67 AKC67. **d** 68 **p** 69. C Eltham St Jo *S'wark* 68-73; C Horley 73-78; V Dallington *Pet* 78-07; rtd 07. *16 Kimble Close, Northampton NN4 0RF* Tel (01604) 709552 E-mail rev.panton@virgin.net

PANTRY, John Richard. b 46. Oak Hill NSM Course 90. **d** 93 **p** 94. NSM Alresford *Chelmsf* 93-04; NSM W w E Mersea from 04. *48 Empress Avenue, West Mersea, Colchester CO5 8EX* Tel and fax (01206) 386910 E-mail johnpantry@fsmail.net

PAPADOPULOS, Nicholas Charles. b 66. G&C Coll Cam BA88 MA92 Barrister-at-Law (Middle Temple) 90. Ripon Coll Cuddesdon. **d** 99 **p** 00. C Portsea N End St Mark *Portsm* 99-02;

Bp's Dom Chapl *Sarum* 02-07; Hon Chapl from 07; V Pimlico St Pet w Westmr Ch Ch *Lon* from 07. *1 St Peter's House, 119 Eaton Square, London SW1W 9AL* Tel (020) 7235 4242 Mobile 07903-620018 E-mail vicar@stpeteratonsquare.co.uk

PAPANTONIOU, Ms Frances Caroline. b 52. S Dios Minl Tr Scheme 89. **d** 92 **p** 94. Par Dn Harrow Weald All SS *Lon* 92-94; C 94-95; C Preston Ascension 95-98; Assoc V Wembley Park 98-99; TV 99-04; V Horton Kirby and Sutton-at-Hone *Roch* from 04. *The Vicarage, 51A Main Road, Sutton at Hone, Dartford DA4 9HQ* Tel (01322) 862253
E-mail fran.papantoniou@diocese-rochester.org

PAPE, David. b 54. **d** 98 **p** 99. OLM S'wark St Geo w St Alphege and St Jude from 98; OLM Waterloo St Jo w St Andr from 98. *10 Stopher House, Webber Street, London SE1 0RE* Tel (020) 7928 3503

PAPE, Timothy Vernon Francis. b 39. OBE. Lon Univ BSc63. Wells Th Coll 63. **d** 65 **p** 66. C Pershore w Wick *Worc* 65-69; Perm to Offic *Birm* 69-73; NSM Southbroom *Sarum* 75-08; Hd Master Chirton Primary Sch Wilts from 81; Dir Gen Shaw Trust from 90. *Mallards, Chirton, Devizes SN10 3QX* Tel (01380) 840593

PAPUA NEW GUINEA, Archbishop of. *See* AYONG, The Most Revd James Simon

PAPWORTH, Daniel John. b 69. Plymouth Poly BSc90. Trin Coll Bris BA98 MA00. **d** 99 **p** 00. C Gabalfa *Llan* 99-02; Perm to Offic *B & W* 03-04; Asst Chapl Dudley Gp of Hosps NHS Trust 04-07; Chapl R Devon and Ex NHS Foundn Trust 07-08; TV N Cheltenham *Glouc* from 08. *The Rectory, Tatchley Lane, Prestbury, Cheltenham GL52 3DQ* Tel (01242) 575649

PAPWORTH, John. b 21. Lon Univ BSc(Econ). **d** 75 **p** 76. Zambia 76-81; Hon C Paddington St Sav *Lon* 81-83; Hon C St Marylebone St Mark Hamilton Terrace 85-97; Perm to Offic *Bris* from 01. *The Fourth World, The Close, 26 High Street, Purton, Swindon SN5 4AE* Tel (01793) 772214 Fax 772521

PAPWORTH, Miss Shirley Marjorie. b 33. CA Tr Coll. **d** 88 **p** 94. Par Dn Hornchurch H Cross *Chelmsf* 88-93; rtd 93; Chapl Havering Primary Care Trust 93-08; NSM Hornchurch St Andr *Chelmsf* 93-08; Perm to Offic from 08. *4 Gosport Drive, Hornchurch RM12 6NU* Tel (01708) 524348

PARAGUAY, Bishop of. *See* BARTLETT, The Rt Revd Peter

PARBURY, Mrs Heather Christina Winifred. b 56. **d** 01 **p** 02. C Long Compton, Whichford and Barton-on-the-Heath *Cov* 01-05; C Barcheston 01-05; C Cherington w Stourton 01-05; C Wolford w Burmington 01-05; TV Cherwell Valley *Ox* 05-08; P-in-c Pangbourne w Tidmarsh and Sulham from 08. *The Rectory, St James's Close, Pangbourne, Reading RG8 7AP* Tel 0118-984 2928 E-mail parbury@btinternet.com

PARE, Stephen Charles. b 53. Sussex Univ BEd75. St Mich Coll Llan 78. **d** 80 **p** 81. C Cardiff St Jo *Llan* 80-83; P-in-c Marcross w Monknash and Wick 83; TV Llantwit Major 83-91; V Penmark w Porthkerry 91-06; P-in-c Llansantffraid, Bettws and Aberkenfig from 06; Chapl Cardiff Wales Airport from 93. *St Bride's Rectory, Heol Persondy, Sarn, Bridgend CF32 9RH* Tel (01656) 720274 E-mail stephen.pare@homecall.co.uk

PARFFETT, Allan John. b 51. Open Univ BA97 CQSW76. Qu Coll Birm MA00. **d** 98 **p** 99. C Hall Green Ascension *Birm* 98-00; Soc Worker 00-09; rtd 09. *20 Kiln Close, Corfe Mullen, Wimborne BH21 3UR* Tel (01202) 690164

PARFITT, Anthony Colin. b 44. Ox Univ Inst of Educn CertEd66 Open Univ BA71 Plymouth Poly MPhil84. SW Minl Tr Course 93. **d** 96 **p** 97. NSM Langport Area *B & W* 96-00; NSM Bruton and Distr 01-06; Perm to Offic from 07. *Tile Hill Cottage, North Brewham, Bruton BA10 0JT* Tel (01749) 850177
E-mail tonyparfitt@btinternet.com

PARFITT, Brian John. b 49. Ex Coll Ox BA71 MA76. Wycliffe Hall Ox 71. **d** 74 **p** 75. C Newport St Mark *Mon* 74-78; R Blaina 78-83; R Blaina and Nantyglo 83-86; Chapl Blaina and Distr Hosp Gwent 83-86; Regional Consultant (W Midlands and Wales) CPAS 86-95; V Magor w Redwick and Undy *Mon* 95-98; TR Magor 98-06; Local Min Officer *Glouc* from 06. *62 Roman Road, Abbeymead, Gloucester GL4 5HR* Tel (01452) 621979
E-mail brianparfitt@btinternet.com

PARFITT, David George. b 65. De Montfort Univ Leic BA87. Wycliffe Hall Ox BTh92. **d** 95 **p** 96. C Malpas *Mon* 95-98; C Bassaleg 98-00; TV 00-01; V Malpas from 01. *The Vicarage, Malpas Road, Newport NP20 6GQ* Tel (01633) 852047

PARFITT, George Rudolf William. b 54. WMMTC 96. **d** 99 **p** 00. OLM Highnam, Lassington, Rudford, Tibberton etc *Glouc* 99-08; NSM Hardwicke and Elmore w Longney from 08. *8 Hillcrest, Highnam, Gloucester GL2 8LS* Tel (01452) 301635
E-mail george.parfitt@btinternet.com

PARFITT, Graeme Stanley. b 36. Qu Coll Birm 77. **d** 79 **p** 80. C Fishponds St Jo *Bris* 79-82; V Southmead 82-91; V Stockwell St Mich *S'wark* 91 01; rtd 01; Perm to Offic *Bris* from 02. *Brook End, Rectory Gardens, Bristol BS10 7AQ* Tel 0117-959 0293

PARFITT, Preb John Hubert. b 29. Southn Univ MA72 BPhil. Qu Coll Birm 78. **d** 80 **p** 81. C Fladbury, Wyre Piddle and Moor *Worc* 80-82; C Malvern Link w Cowleigh 82; V Hanley Castle, Hanley Swan and Welland 82-83; Dir RE *B & W* 84-93; Preb Wells Cathl from 85; rtd 93; Perm to Offic *B & W* from 93;

Master Hugh Sexey's Hosp Bruton 95-05. *3 Willow Farm Cottages, Brister End, Yetminster, Sherborne DT9 6NH* Tel (01935) 873260 E-mail passitatwillow@btinternet.com

PARFITT, Canon Keith John. b 44. K Coll Lon BD68 AKC68. St Aug Coll Cant 69. **d** 70 **p** 71. C Kettering St Andr *Pet* 70-74; Asst Soc and Ind Adv *Portsm* 74-89; RD Alverstoke 79-86; C-in-c Bridgemary CD 81-82; V Bridgemary 82-89; Dioc UPA Officer *Blackb* 89-97; Can Res Blackb Cathl 94-97; Dir Is of Wight Rural Community Coun from 97. *Downsview, Farriers Way, Shorwell, Newport PO30 3JP* Tel (01983) 740434

PARFITT, Susan Mary. b 42. Bris Univ BA63 CertEd68. Bris Minl Tr Scheme 82. **dss** 84 **d** 87 **p** 94. Assoc Dir of Ords *Bris* 84-86; CME Officer 87-91; Dir Past Care and Counselling *S'wark* 91-01; rtd 01; Perm to Offic *Bris* from 02. *Brook End, Rectory Gardens, Bristol BS10 7AQ* Tel 0117-959 0293

PARGETER, Canon Muriel Elizabeth. b 28. St Mich Ho Ox 53. **dss** 82 **d** 87 **p** 95. Hd Dss *Roch* 82-87; Dioc Dir of Ords 87-90; Hon Can Roch Cathl 87-90; rtd 90; Hon C Worthing Ch the King *Chich* 95-03; Perm to Offic from 03. *63 Pavilion Road, Worthing BN45 7EE* Tel (01903) 214476

PARISH, Mrs Mary Eileen. b 48. Nottm Univ BA70. STETS BTh98. **d** 98 **p** 99. NSM Worthing Ch the King *Chich* 98-08; NSM Worthing St Matt from 08. *The Heritage, 10 Winchester Road, Worthing BN11 4DJ* Tel (01903) 236909
E-mail frmary@theheritage.freeserve.co.uk

PARISH, Canon Nicholas Anthony. b 58. Oak Hill Th Coll BA84 Kingston Univ MA97. Ridley Hall Cam 84. **d** 86 **p** 87. C Eltham H Trin *S'wark* 86-89; C Barnes St Mary 89-91; V Streatham St Paul 91-96; Ind Chapl *Ox* 96-07; P-in-c Bracknell from 07; AD Bracknell from 04; Hon Can Ch Ch from 08. *1 Old Lands Hill, Bracknell RG12 2QX* Tel and fax (01344) 641498 *or* tel 867383 E-mail nick.parish@ntlworld.com

PARISH, Stephen Richard. b 49. Liv Univ MTh05. Oak Hill Th Coll 74. **d** 77 **p** 78. C Chadderton Ch Ch *Man* 77-81; C Chell *Lich* 81-82; TV 82-88; V Warrington St Ann *Liv* from 88; P-in-c Warrington H Trin from 06. *St Ann's Vicarage, 1A Fitzherbert Street, Warrington WA2 7QG* Tel (01925) 631781
E-mail bloovee@ntlworld.com

PARK, Christopher John. b 62. Sheff Poly BA83. Cranmer Hall Dur 00. **d** 02 **p** 03. C Didsbury St Jas and Em *Man* 02-08; P-in-c Alne from 08; P-in-c Brafferton w Pilmoor, Myton-on-Swale etc from 08. *Monk Green House, Main Street, Alne, York YO61 1TB* Tel (01347) 833449
E-mail pasta@cjparko.freeserve.co.uk

PARK, John Charles. b 55. St Pet Coll Ox BA77 St Mary's Coll Newc PGCE81. Cranmer Hall Dur 00. **d** 02 **p** 03. C Morpeth *Newc* 02-06; R Bothal and Pegswood w Longhirst from 06. *Bothal Rectory, Longhirst Road, Pegswood, Morpeth NE61 6XF* Tel (01670) 510793 E-mail jjat@parks2002.fsnet.co.uk

PARK, Tarjei Erling Alan. b 64. W Lon Inst of HE BA88 Lanc Univ MA89 Pemb Coll Ox DPhil96. Ripon Coll Cuddesdon 92. **d** 94 **p** 95. C Lancaster St Mary *Blackb* 94-98; V Enfield St Mich *Lon* 98-01; Asst Dir Post-Ord Tr 98-03; V Golders Green 01-06; C St Pancras w St Jas and Ch Ch 06-08; rtd 09. *30A Hadley Street, London NW1 8SS* Tel (020) 7482 1170
E-mail tarjeipark@aol.co.uk

PARK, Trevor. b 38. MBE05. Lon Univ BA64 Open Univ PhD90 Lambeth STh81. Linc Th Coll 64. **d** 66 **p** 67. C Crosthwaite Kendal *Carl* 66-68; Asst Chapl Solihull Sch 69-71; Chapl St Bees Sch and V St Bees *Carl* 71-77; V Dalton-in-Furness 77-84; V Natland 84-97; Hon Can Carl Cathl 86-97; RD Kendal 89-94; Chapl Oslo w Bergen, Trondheim and Stavanger *Eur* 97-05; rtd 05; P-in-c St Petersburg *Eur* 06-07. *20 Seacroft Drive, St Bees CA27 0AF*

PARKER, Alfred. b 20. Man Univ BA47. Wycliffe Hall Ox 47. **d** 49 **p** 50. C Droylsden St Mary *Man* 49-53; C New Bury 53-54; P-in-c Bolton St Bart 54-56; V 56-61; P-in-c Gt Lever 59-61; R 61-65; V Belmont 65-87; rtd 87. *21 Edgeley Road, Whitchurch SY13 1EU*

PARKER, Angus Michael Macdonald. b 53. Bris Univ BSc74. St Jo Coll Nottm 80. **d** 83 **p** 84. C Northampton St Giles *Pet* 83-86; C Attenborough *S'well* 86-96; V Pennycross *Ex* 96-09; P-in-c Bitterne *Win* from 09. *The Vicarage, 2 Bursledon Road, Bitterne, Southampton SO19 7LW*
E-mail angus@mmparker.wanadoo.co.uk

PARKER, Miss Anika Lois. b 74. BMus BMin. **d** 06 **p** 07. NSM Redland *Bris* from 06. *9 Hatherley Road, Bristol BS7 8QA* Tel 0117-946 4690 Mobile 07885-666878
E-mail anika@redland.org.uk

PARKER, Mrs Ann Jacqueline. b 41. Dur Inst of Educn TCert63 Sunderland Poly TCert65 Open Univ BA82. WEMTC 91. **d** 95 **p** 96. NSM Pilning w Compton Greenfield *Bris* 95-98; NSM Almondsbury and Olveston 98-03; Asst Chapl N Bris NHS Trust from 98. *Wyngarth, Easter Compton, Bristol BS35 5RA* Tel (01454) 632329 E-mail annatdibley@aol.com

PARKER, Anne Margaret. *See* HINDLE, Anne Margaret

PARKER, Mrs Brenda. b 36. **d** 00 **p** 01. OLM Eccleston Ch Ch *Liv* 00-06; rtd 06. *22 Selkirk Drive, Eccleston, St Helens WA10 5PE* Tel (01744) 757495

PARKER, Brian William. b 39. Ulster Univ BA88. CITC 99. **d** 01 **p** 02. NSM Knock *D & D* 01-02; NSM Glencraig from 02. *7 Cairnsville Park, Bangor BT19 6EW* Tel (028) 9145 4549 Fax 9147 1804 E-mail bwparker@ukgateway.net

PARKER, Carole Maureen. *See* PROUSE, Ms Carole Maureen

PARKER, David Anthony. b 38. St Chad's Coll Dur BA62. **d** 64 **p** 65. C Palmers Green St Jo *Lon* 64-65; C Kenton 65-71; C W Hyde St Thos *St Alb* 71-75; P-in-c Brinksway *Ches* 76-80; V 80-83; V Weston 83-92; NSM Cheadle Hulme All SS 97-98; C Offerton 98-00; TV Crosslacon *Carl* 00-02; rtd 02; C Cheadle Hulme All SS *Ches* from 02; Perm to Offic *Man* from 02. *77 Station Road, Cheadle Hulme, Cheadle SK8 7BG* Tel 0161-485 4451

PARKER, David Charles. b 53. St Andr Univ MTheol75 Univ of Leiden DTh90. Ridley Hall Cam 75. **d** 77 **p** 78. C Hendon St Paul Mill Hill *Lon* 77-80; C Bladon w Woodstock *Ox* 80-85; C-in-c Shipton-on-Cherwell 80-85; C-in-c Begbroke 80-85; C-in-c Hampton Gay 80-85; Lect Qu Coll Birm 85-93 and 89-93; Lect Birm Univ 93-96; Sen Lect 96-98; Reader in NT Textual Criticism and Palaeography from 98. *Dumbleton Cottage, 24 Church Street, Bromyard HR7 4DP* Tel 0121-415 2415 E-mail d.c.parker@bham.ac.uk

PARKER, Canon David John. b 33. St Chad's Coll Dur BA55 Hull Univ MA85. Linc Th Coll 57. **d** 59 **p** 60. C Tynemouth Ch Ch *Newc* 59-60; C Ponteland 60-63; C Byker St Mich 63-64; C-in-c Byker St Martin CD 64-69; V Whorlton 69-73; TR 73-80; Ind Chapl *Linc* 80-84; Master Newc St Thos Prop Chpl 84-89; Exec Officer Dioc Bd for Ch and Soc *Man* 90-98; Lic Preacher 90-98; Hon Can Man Cathl 97-98; rtd 98; Perm to Offic *Newc* from 98. *4 The Kylins, Morpeth NE61 2DJ* Tel (01670) 516218 E-mail d.j.parker@tesco.net

PARKER, Canon David Louis. b 47. Lon Univ LLB70. Wycliffe Hall Ox BA79 MA82. **d** 80 **p** 81. C Broadwater St Mary *Chich* 80-84; TR Ifield 84-97; R Lavant from 97; RD Chich 01-06; Can and Preb Chich Cathl from 03. *The Rectory, Pook Lane, Lavant, Chichester PO18 0AH* Tel (01243) 527313

PARKER, David William. b 21. SEN CQSW MBASW. Glouc Th Course 77 Sarum & Wells Th Coll 81. **d** 81 **p** 81. Chapl HM Pris Leyhill 81-84; NSM Cromhall w Tortworth *Glouc* 81-83; NSM Wickwar w Rangeworthy 83-87; Perm to Offic 88-01. *22 Durham Road, Charfield, Wotton-under-Edge GL12 8TH* Tel (01454) 260253

PARKER, George William. b 29. Univ of K Coll Halifax NS BS53 BD57 Lon Univ PGCE67. **d** 53 **p** 54. C Calgary Cathl 53-55; I Cardston 55-59; C W Hackney St Barn *Lon* 59-61; V Haggerston St Mary w St Chad 61-68; Teacher St Adele Canada 68-71; C Portsea N End St Mark *Portsm* 72-75; V Darlington St Jo *Dur* 75-78; R Des Monts Canada 78-81; R Digby 81-87; R Rawdon 87-91; rtd 91. *c/o T Parker Esq, 7 McNeil Street, Dartmouth NS B2Y 2H2, Canada*

PARKER, Hugh James. b 30. ACP55 TCD MA57 Ulster Univ DASE74. **d** 63 **p** 64. Lic to Offic *Conn* 63-70 and 96-01; Dioc C 70-96; Hd Master Larne High Sch 71-92; rtd 96. *25 Ballykillaire Terrace, Bangor BT19 1GS* Tel (028) 9185 7142

PARKER, Janet Elizabeth. b 54. Cranmer Hall Dur 05. **d** 07 **p** 08. C Sale St Anne *Ches* from 07. *3 Windermere Avenue, Sale M33 3FP* Tel 0161-962 8981 Mobile 07707-601263 E-mail janetparker1@homecall.co.uk

PARKER, Mrs Joanna Caroline. b 63. UEA BA95 Leeds Univ MA07 RGN85 RM92. NOC 04. **d** 07 **p** 08. C Pocklington and Owsthorpe and Kilnwick Percy etc *York* from 07. *110 Wold Road, Pocklington, York YO42 2QG* Tel (01759) 306966 Mobile 07981-858853 E-mail joanna.parker@tinyworld.co.uk

PARKER, John. *See* PARKER, Linsey John Owen

PARKER, John Bristo. b 26. Edin Th Coll 61. **d** 64 **p** 65. C Barrow St Jo *Carl* 64-68; V Sledmere *York* 68-74; V Sledmere and Wetwang w Cowlan 74-79; R Cowlam 68-74; P-in-c Wetwang 69-74; V Kirkby Ireleth *Carl* 79-83; V Rillington w Scampston, Wintringham etc *York* 83-87; R Bishop Wilton w Full Sutton, Kirby Underdale etc 87-91; rtd 91; Perm to Offic *York* from 91. *East Lodge, Sledmere, Driffield YO25 3XQ* Tel (01377) 86325

PARKER, John David. b 61. Ridley Hall Cam 00. **d** 02 **p** 03. C Aston cum Aughton w Swallownest and Ulley *Sheff* 02-06; TV Rugby *Cov* from 06. *The Vicarage, 63A Lower Hillmorton Road, Rugby CV21 3TQ* Tel (01788) 544381 E-mail jdparkeruk@aol.com

PARKER, Julian Roderick. b 57. Essex Univ BA80. Sarum & Wells Th Coll 91. **d** 93 **p** 94. C Gillingham *Sarum* 93-97; V N Bradley, Southwick and Heywood 97-08; V N Bradley, Southwick, Heywood and Steeple Ashton from 08. *The Vicarage, 62 Church Lane, North Bradley, Trowbridge BA14 0TA* Tel (01225) 752635 E-mail julian@roderick17.freeserve.co.uk

PARKER, Linsey John Owen. b 70. Oriel Coll Ox BA91 Lon Univ PGCE94. Oak Hill Th Coll 02. **d** 05 **p** 06. C Arborfield w Barkham *Ox* from 05. *7 Sheerlands Road, Arborfield, Reading RG2 9ND* Tel 0118-976 0245 E-mail johnandmim@bigfoot.com

PARKER, Lynn. b 54. SS Mark & Jo Univ Coll Plymouth BEd94. SWMTC 04. **d** 07 **p** 08. NSM S Hill w Callington *Truro* from 07. *30 Tamar Close, Callington PL17 7PW* Tel (01579) 382900 E-mail parker30@hotmail.com

PARKER, Miss Margaret. b 27. Lightfoot Ho Dur 54. **dss** 60 **d** 87 **p** 94. Ryhope *Dur* 56-61; Monkwearmouth St Andr 61-79; Adv for Accredited Lay Min 74-87; Adv for Accredited Lay Min *Newc* 79-87; Newc St Geo 79-87; C 87; rtd 87; Perm to Offic *Dur* and *Newc* from 87; Tutor Cranmer Hall Dur 87-92; Hon C Dur Cathl 87-94; Min Can Dur Cathl 94-97; Chapl St Mary's Coll Dur 95-98. *53 Devonshire Road, Durham DH1 2BJ* Tel 0191-386 3233

PARKER, Margaret Grace. *See* TORDOFF, Mrs Margaret Grace

PARKER, Matthew John. b 63. Man Univ BA85 SS Coll Cam BA88. Ridley Hall Cam 85. **d** 88 **p** 89. C Twickenham St Mary *Lon* 88-91; Chapl Stockport Gr Sch 91-94; C Stockport St Geo *Ches* 91-93; P-in-c Stockport St Mark 93-94; TV Stockport SW 94-00; TR Leek and Meerbrook *Lich* from 00; RD Leek from 07. *St Edward's Vicarage, 24 Ashenhurst Way, Leek ST13 5SB* Tel (01538) 382515 *or* 388134 E-mail matpark01@aol.com

PARKER, Michael. b 54. **d** 07. C Ebbw Vale *Mon* 07-09; Hon C Llanhilleth w Six Bells from 09. *43 Drysiog Street, Ebbw Vale NP23 6DE* Tel (01495) 304193 E-mail naso.01@btinternet.com

PARKER, Michael Alan. b 70. St Jo Coll Dur BA91. CITC BTh93. **d** 96 **p** 97. C Dundela St Mark *D & D* 96-00; I Carnalea from 00. *St Gall's Rectory, 171 Crawfordsburn Road, Bangor BT19 1BT* Tel (028) 9185 3366 *or* 9185 3810 E-mail carnalea@down.anglican.org *or* stgall@fish.co.uk

PARKER, Michael John. b 54. Cam Coll of Art and Tech BA76 Lon Univ BD85. Trin Coll Bris 82. **d** 85 **p** 86. C Leic H Trin w St Jo 85-88; P-in-c Edin Clermiston Em 88-90; R Edin St Thos 90-03; Can St Mary's Cathl 94-03; NSM Edin St Paul and St Geo 03-06; Gen Sec Evang Alliance Scotland 03-06; Middle E Dir Middle E Chr Outreach 06-09; Sen Min All SS Cathl Cairo from 09. *Middle East Christian Outreach, 22 Culverden Park Road, Tunbridge Wells TN4 9RA* Tel (01892) 521541 E-mail mikeparker@f2s.com

PARKER, Canon Michael John. b 57. BSc Nottm Univ MA04. Wycliffe Hall Ox 80. **d** 83 **p** 84. C Heigham H Trin *Nor* 83-86; C Muswell Hill St Jas w St Matt *Lon* 86-90; R Bedford St Jo and St Leon *St Alb* 90-98; V Knowle *Birm* from 98; AD Solihull from 04; Hon Can Birm Cathl from 05. *The Vicarage, 1811 Warwick Road, Knowle, Solihull B93 0DS* Tel and fax (01564) 773666 *or* tel 778802 Fax 779123 E-mail vicar@knowleparishchurch.org.uk

PARKER, Nigel Howard. b 69. St Jo Coll Dur BSc90. CITC BTh97. **d** 97 **p** 98. C Holywood *D & D* 97-00; Outreach Development Officer Think Again 00-04; I Bangor St Comgall from 04. *The Rectory, 2 Raglan Road, Bangor BT20 3TL* Tel (028) 9146 0712 E-mail bangorparish@btconnect.com

PARKER, Peter Edward. b 32. Edin Univ MA55 Lon Univ PGCE56 FRSA. Sarum & Wells Th Coll 73. **d** 74 **p** 75. C Kirkby Lonsdale w Mansergh *Carl* 74-76; C Kingston All SS w St Jo *S'wark* 76-80; Chapl S Bank Poly 80-85; Ind Chapl *Chelmsf* 85-90; Chapl Chelmsf Cathl 85-90; R Mistley w Manningtree and Bradfield 90-97; rtd 97; Perm to Offic *Ely* from 97. *2 Waterside, Ely CB7 4AZ* Tel (01353) 614103

PARKER, Philip Vernon. b 60. Birm Univ BSc82 PGCE83. Wycliffe Hall Ox BA89. **d** 90 **p** 91. C Walkergate *Newc* 90-93; Chapl Shiplake Coll Henley 93-96; V Lindfield *Chich* 97-99; Scripture Union 99-04; Chapl Cranleigh Sch Surrey from 04; CF (TA) from 97. *Cranleigh School, Horseshoe Lane, Cranleigh GU6 8QQ* Tel (01483) 542028 E-mail pvp@cranleigh.org

PARKER, Ramon Lewis (Brother Raphael). b 36. Kelham Th Coll 56. **d** 61 **p** 62. C Tonge Moor *Man* 61-64; C Clerkenwell H Redeemer w St Phil *Lon* 64-65; V Prestwich St Hilda *Man* 65-71; SSF from 71; Chapl Univ of Wales (Lamp) *St D* 81-86; Lic to Offic *Sarum* from 87; rtd 97. *c/o Brother Samuel SSF, The Friary, Hilfield, Dorchester DT2 7BE* Tel (01300) 341345 Fax 341293

PARKER, Richard Bryan. b 64. Sheff Poly BA87. Coll of Resurr Mirfield 92. **d** 95 **p** 96. C Norton *Sheff* 95-98; C Hoyland 98-00; V Moorends 00-08; V Hoyland from 08. *The Vicarage, 104 Hawshaw Lane, Hoyland, Barnsley S74 0HH* Tel (01226) 749231 E-mail r.b.parker@btinternet.com

PARKER, Richard Frederick. b 36. Oak Hill Th Coll 72. **d** 74 **p** 75. C Wootton *St Alb* 74-76; C Hove Bp Hannington Memorial Ch *Chich* 76-81; R Northwood *Portsm* 81-88; V W Cowes H Trin 81-88; V Aldershot H Trin *Guildf* 88-98; R Spaxton w Charlynch, Goathurst, Enmore etc *B & W* 98-03; rtd 03. *47 Banneson Road, Nether Stowey, Bridgwater TA5 1NS* Tel (01278) 733883

PARKER, Robert. b 43. Lon Univ BSc65. Cuddesdon Coll. **d** 67 **p** 68. C Sheff St Cuth 67-70; Asst Chapl Cheltenham Coll 70-74; R Yate *Glouc* 74-76; R Yate *Bris* 76-77; TR Yate New Town 77-80; C of E Development Officer 80-83; NSM Pool Quay *St As* 99-07; P-in-c 99-04; Perm to Offic *Lich* from 08. *Tedsmore Hall, Tedsmore, West Felton, Oswestry SY11 4HD* Tel (01691) 610628 E-mail rgparker@tedsmorehall.co.uk

PARKER, Robert Lawrence. b 34. ALCD59. **d** 59 **p** 60. C Chippenham St Paul *Bris* 59-61; C Swindon Ch Ch 61-63; New Zealand 63-71; P-in-c Over Stowey w Aisholt *B & W* 71-73; V Nether Stowey 71-73; V Nether Stowey w Over Stowey 73-93; RD Quantock 87-93; V Pitminster w Corfe 93-99; rtd 99; Perm to Offic *B & W* from 00. *Oratia, 9 Brookfield Way, Street BA16 0UE* Tel (01458) 442906

PARKER, Robert Nicolas. b 71. Nottm Univ BA93 PGCE95. Ridley Hall Cam 95. **d** 98 **p** 99. C Yardley St Edburgha *Birm* 98-02; Asst P Eugene St Mary USA 02-05; P-in-c Coleshill *Birm* 05-08; V from 08; P-in-c Maxstoke 05-08; V from 08. *The Vicarage, High Street, Coleshill, Birmingham B46 3BP* Tel (01675) 462188 E-mail nickthevicparker@btinternet.com

PARKER, Robert William. b 18. Linc Th Coll 81. **d** 81 **p** 82. NSM Mablethorpe w Trusthorpe *Linc* 81-83; NSM Alford w Rigsby 83-86; NSM Bilsby w Farlesthorpe 83-86; NSM Ford and Alberbury w Cardeston *Heref* 87-90; NSM Westbury 87-88; Perm to Offic *Linc* 90-99 and *Derby* 06-08. *Tedsmore Hall, West Felton, Oswestry SY11 4HD* Tel (01691) 610628 E-mail rgparker@tedsmorehall.co.uk

PARKER, Roger Thomas Donaldson. b 55. Simon Fraser Univ BC BA80 Univ of Wales (Cardiff) LLB84 Univ Coll Lon LLM85. Coll of Resurr Mirfield 95. **d** 95 **p** 96. C Swinton and Pendlebury *Man* 95-02; V Burnley St Cath w St Alb and St Paul *Blackb* from 02. *St Catherine's Parsonage, 156 Todmorden Road, Burnley BB11 3ER* Tel (01282) 424587 Mobile 07977-291166 E-mail frrogerparker@aol.com

PARKER, Roland John Graham. b 48. AKC72 Hull Univ BA(Ed)83. St Aug Coll Cant 71. **d** 74 **p** 75. C Linc St Faith and St Martin w St Pet 74-78; V Appleby 78-84; Ind Chapl 78-84; V N Kelsey 84-92; V Cadney 84-92; P-in-c Waddington 92-97; R from 97. *The Rectory, Rectory Lane, Waddington, Lincoln LN5 9RS* Tel (01522) 720323 E-mail rolapark2@btinternet.com

PARKER, Russell Edward. b 48. Man Univ BA80. St Jo Coll Nottm MTh82. **d** 81 **p** 82. C Walmsley *Man* 81-85; V Coalville and Bardon Hill *Leic* 85-90; Dir Acorn Chr Foundn from 90. *Acorn Christian Foundation, Whitehill Chase, Bordon GU35 0AP* Tel (01420) 478121 E-mail rparker@acornchristian.org

PARKER, Stephen George. b 65. Birm Univ BEd89 MA97 PhD03. Qu Coll Birm 96. **d** 98. Teaching Asst Westhill Coll of HE Birm 98-01; Sen Lect Th Univ Coll Ches 01-04; Hd RS Cadbury Sixth Form Coll 04-08; Hd Postgraduate Studies in Educn Worc Univ from 08. *University of Worcester, Henwick Grove, Worcester WR2 6AJ* Tel (01905) 542165 E-mail s.parker@worc.ac.uk

PARKER, Thomas Henry Louis. b 16. Em Coll Cam BA38 MA42 BD50 DD61. Lon Coll of Div 38. **d** 39 **p** 40. C Chesham St Mary *Ox* 39-42; C Cambridge St Phil *Ely* 42-43; C Cambridge St Andr Less 43-45; C Luddesdowne *Roch* 45-48; V Brothertoft *Linc* 48-55; R Lt Ponton w Stroxton 55-59; R Lt Ponton 59-61; R Gt Ponton 58-61; V Oakington *Ely* 61-71; Lect Dur Univ 71-81; rtd 81; Perm to Offic *Ely* 90-00. *Ceriogh, Flaggoners Green, Bromyard HR7 4QR* Tel (01885) 489307

PARKER, Thomas Richard. b 52. Imp Coll Lon BScEng73 Keele Univ MEd83. Cranmer Hall Dur. **d** 94 **p** 95. C Chadkirk *Ches* 94-08; RD Chadkirk 04-08; P-in-c Stalybridge H Trin and Ch Ch from 08. *The Vicarage, 18 Chadkirk Road, Romiley, Stockport SK6 3JY* Tel 0161-430 8709 E-mail tom_parker@ntlworld.com

PARKER, Timothy Percy. b 58. Man Univ BA. St Jo Coll Nottm. **d** 85 **p** 86. C Pitsmoor Ch Ch *Sheff* 85-87; C Kimberworth 87-89; C Brightside w Wincobank 89-91; C Upper Armley *Ripon* 91-95; TV Billingham St Aid *Dur* 95-97; V Billingham St Luke from 97. *17 Shadforth Drive, Billingham TS23 3PW* Tel (01642) 561870 E-mail timparker@ntlworld.com

PARKERSON, Trevor Richard. b 46. Qu Coll Birm 06. **d** 08 **p** 09. NSM Ashby-de-la-Zouch and Breedon on the Hill *Leic* from 08. *36 Ashby Road, Woodville, Swadlincote DE11 7BY* Tel (01283) 225408 E-mail trp@gofast.co.uk

PARKES, Mrs Celia Anne. b 50. STETS 06. **d** 09. NSM Bursledon *Win* from 09. *5 Cambrian Close, Bursledon, Southampton SO31 8GW* Tel (023) 8040 6363

PARKES, Kevin. b 62. Trent Poly BA84. Sarum & Wells Th Coll BTh90. **d** 88 **p** 89. C Wandsworth St Anne *S'wark* 88-92; USPG 92-95; Trinidad and Tobago 93-95; Kingston Area Miss Team *S'wark* 95-01; V Wandsworth Common St Mary from 01; AD Tooting from 07. *The Vicarage, 291 Burntwood Lane, London SW17 0AP* Tel (020) 8874 4804

PARKHILL, Alan John. b 43. TCD BA66. CITC 68. **d** 67 **p** 68. C Knockbreda *D & G* 67-70; Asst Warden Elswick Lodge Newc 71-72; C Bangor St Comgall 73-78; Bp's C Kilmore 78-82; I Kilmore and Inch 82-86; I Clonfeacle w Derrygortreavy *Arm* from 86. *4 Clonfeacle Road, Benburb, Dungannon BT71 7LQ* Tel and fax (028) 3754 8239 E-mail aparkhill@talktalk.net

PARKIN, George David. b 37. Cranmer Hall Dur BA60. **d** 62 **p** 63. C Balderstone *Man* 62-65; C Tunstead 65-67; C Gateshead Fell *Dur* 69-73; CMS Nigeria 74-76; V Walton Breck *Liv* 80-92; V Rawtenstall St Mary *Man* 92-07; P-in-c Constable Lee 02-07;

rtd 07; Perm to Offic *Man* from 08. *16 Ambleside Avenue, Rossendale BB4 6RY* Tel (01706) 831195 E-mail pamandco@googlemail.com

PARKIN, Mrs Jennifer Anne. b 47. Nene Coll Northn BEd85. WMMTC 95. **d** 98 **p** 99. C Northampton St Alb *Pet* 98-02; P-in-c Ecton 02-07; P-in-c Wootton w Quinton and Preston Deanery from 07; Chapl Cynthia Spencer Hospice 02-07; Warden of Past Assts *Pet* from 06. *The Rectory, 67 Water Lane, Wootton, Northampton NN4 6HH* Tel (01604) 761891 E-mail parkinjen@btinternet.com

PARKIN, Canon John Edmund. b 44. Open Univ BA73. St Jo Coll Nottm 83. **d** 85 **p** 86. C Aberavon *Llan* 85-90; R Eglwysilan 90-01; P Missr Merthyr Tydfil Ch Ch from 01; Hon Can Llan Cathl from 09. *12 Heol Scwrfa, Merthyr Tydfil CF48 1HE*

PARKIN, John Francis. b 40. Linc Th Coll 65. **d** 68 **p** 69. C Cullercoats St Geo *Newc* 68-72; C Stony Stratford *Ox* 72-73; TV Lt Coates *Linc* 73-76; Perm to Offic 88-93; NSM Horncastle w Low Toynton 93-06; NSM High Toynton 93-06; NSM Horncastle Gp from 06. *The Firs, 68 Louth Road, Horncastle LN9 5LJ* Tel (01507) 523208

PARKIN, Jonathan Samuel. b 73. La Sainte Union Coll BTh95 Birm Univ MA97. Qu Coll Birm 98. **d** 98 **p** 99. C Skegness and Winthorpe *Linc* 98-01; Chapl Leic Coll of FE 01-03; Chapl De Montfort Univ 04-07; Chapl Leic Cathl 01-07; TV Market Harborough and The Transfiguration etc from 07; P-in-c Welham, Glooston and Cranoe and Stonton Wyville from 07. *The Vicarage, Dingley Road, Great Bowden, Market Harborough LE16 7ET* Tel (01858) 469109 E-mail parkin@tiscali.co.uk

PARKIN, Melvyn Christopher. b 57. NEOC 99. **d** 02 **p** 03. NSM Boston Spa *York* 02-03; C Elvington w Sutton on Derwent and E Cottingwith 03-06; R Howardian Gp from 06. *The Rectory, Terrington, York YO60 6PU* Tel (01653) 648226

PARKIN, Canon Trevor Kinross. b 37. MCMI. Cranmer Hall Dur 63. **d** 66 **p** 67. C Kingston upon Hull St Martin *York* 66-69; C Reading St Jo *Ox* 69-73; Ind Chapl *Lon* 73-80; Hon C Langham Place All So 73-80; Ind Chapl *Ely* 80-82; V Maidenhead St Andr and St Mary *Ox* 82-02; Hon Can Butare from 00; rtd 02; Perm to Offic *Guildf* 03-07. *5 Hardwick Road, Eastbourne BN21 4NY* Tel (01323) 642287 E-mail trevorparkin@fsmail.net

PARKINSON, Alan. *See* PARKINSON, Thomas Alan

PARKINSON, Andrew. b 56. Keble Coll Ox BA77 MA80. Westcott Ho Cam 78. **d** 80 **p** 81. C S Shore H Trin *Blackb* 80-85; V Lea 85-94; V Longton from 94. *Longton Vicarage, Birchwood Avenue, Hutton, Preston PR4 5EE* Tel (01772) 612179 E-mail aparkinson@longtonvicarage.freeserve.co.uk

PARKINSON, Andrew. b 74. St Steph Ho Ox. **d** 01 **p** 02. C Lancaster Ch Ch *Blackb* 01-04; P-in-c Yarnton w Begbroke and Shipton on Cherwell *Ox* 04-05; TV Blenheim from 05. *The Rectory, 26 Church Lane, Yarnton, Kidlington OX5 1PY* Tel (01865) 375749

PARKINSON, Miss Brenda. b 40. Lancs Poly CQSW. Dalton Ho Bris 65. **dss** 74 **d** 87 **p** 94. Ribbleton *Blackb* 75-80; Ingol 82-88; Par Dn 87-88; Par Dn Ashton-on-Ribble St Mich 89-92; Par Dn Gt Marsden 92-94; C 94-98; C Gt Marsden w Nelson St Phil 99-00; rtd 00; Perm to Offic *Blackb* from 01. *18 Thorn Hill Close, Blackburn BB1 1YE* Tel (01254) 678367

PARKINSON, David Thomas. b 42. Linc Th Coll 77. **d** 79 **p** 80. C Yate New Town *Bris* 79-82; TV Keynsham *B & W* 82-88; R Bleadon 88-07; rtd 07. *3 Rockville, Bridge Road, Bleadon, Weston-super-Mare BS24 0AU* Tel (01934) 631183 E-mail dtparkinson@aol.com

PARKINSON, Derek Leslie. b 29. Ripon Hall Ox 64. **d** 66 **p** 67. C Guildf Ch Ch 66-69; P-in-c Preston St Sav *Blackb* 69-74; P-in-c Preston St Jas 69-74; P-in-c Fontmell Magna *Sarum* 74-81; P-in-c Ashmore 74-81; P-in-c Sutton Waldron w Alderley and Hillesley *Glouc* 81-82; R 82-94; rtd 94. *25 Fountain Crescent, Wotton-under-Edge GL12 7LD*

PARKINSON, Francis Wilson. b 37. Open Univ BA80 MBACP. St Aid Birkenhead 59. **d** 62 **p** 63. C Monkwearmouth St Andr *Dur* 62-64; C Speke All SS *Liv* 64-67; CF 67-92; Perm to Offic *Ox* from 92. *9 Priory Mead, Longcot, Faringdon SN7 7TJ* Tel (01793) 784406

PARKINSON, George Stanley. b 20. St Jo Coll Dur BA47. **d** 48 **p** 49. C Widnes St Paul *Liv* 48-51; C Bradf Cathl Par 51-55; V Greengates 55-58; V Pennington *Man* 58-71; V Eccles St Mary 71-80; V Churt *Guildf* 80-82; RD Farnham 82-88; rtd 90; Perm to Offic *Worc* from 90. *12 Bevere Court, Bevere, Worcester WR3 7RE* Tel (01905) 457106 E-mail revgsp@yahoo.co.uk

PARKINSON, Ian Richard. b 58. Dur Univ BA79 Lon Univ BD84. Wycliffe Hall Ox 80. **d** 83 **p** 84. C Hull St Jo Newland *York* 83-86; C Linthorpe 86-92; V Saltburn-by-the-Sea 92-01; V Marple All SS *Ches* from 01. *The Vicarage, 155 Church Lane, Marple, Stockport SK6 7LD* Tel and fax 0161-449 0950 *or* tel 427 2378 E-mail ian.parkinson7@ntlworld.com

PARKINSON, John Reginald. b 32. Qu Coll Birm 79. **d** 81 **p** 82. NSM Catshill *Worc* 81-85; C Knightwick w Doddenham, Broadwas and Cotheridge 85-88; C Martley and Wichenford 85-88; P-in-c Berrow w Pendock and Eldersfield 88-89; R Berrow w Pendock, Eldersfield, Hollybush etc 89-97; RD Upton 95-97; rtd 97; Perm to Offic *Glouc* and *Worc* from 97. *8 Glebe Close, Stow on the Wold, Cheltenham GL54 1DJ* Tel (01451) 830822

PARKINSON, Leslie. *See* PARKINSON, Derek Leslie

PARKINSON, Nicholas John. b 46. FCCA75 Cranfield Inst of Tech MBA85. St Alb Minl Tr Scheme 92. **d** 95 **p** 96. NSM Woburn Sands *St Alb* 95-98; NSM Westoning w Tingrith 98-01; NSM Woburn Sands from 01. *Thornbank House, 7 Church Road, Woburn Sands, Milton Keynes MK17 8TE* Tel (01908) 583397

PARKINSON, Peter. b 23. Roch Th Coll 61. **d** 63 **p** 64. C Linc St Mary-le-Wigford w St Martin 63-65; C Skegness 65-68; R Kettlethorpe 68-73; V Newton-on-Trent 68-73; V Grainthorpe w Conisholme 74-83; V Marshchapel 74-83; R N Coates 74-83; V Bicker 83-88; rtd 88. *11 Waltham Road, Lincoln LN6 0SD* Tel (01522) 680604

PARKINSON, Richard. ERMC. **d** 07 **p** 08. NSM Leverington, Newton and Tydd St Giles *Ely* from 07. *166 Leverington Common, Leverington, Wisbech PE13 5BP* Tel (01945) 465818

PARKINSON, Mrs Sarah Kathryn Rachel. b 80. Trin Coll Ox MMath02. Ripon Coll Cuddesdon BA06. **d** 07 **p** 08. NSM Steeple Aston w N Aston and Tackley *Ox* from 07; Chapl HM Pris Bullingdon 05-08; Manager Relig Affairs Campsfield Ho Immigration Removal Cen from 08. *Campsfield House, Langford Lane, Kidlington OX5 1RE* Tel (01865) 233000 E-mail sparkinson@thegeogroupinc.co.uk

PARKINSON, Simon George Denis. b 39. Univ of Wales (Lamp) BA66. Westcott Ho Cam 65. **d** 67 **p** 68. C Rothwell *Ripon* 67-70; Chapl RAF 70-73; C Leeds St Pet *Ripon* 74-75; V Horbury Junction *Wakef* 76-83; V Hanging Heaton 83-92; P-in-c Upper Hopton 92; V Eastthorpe and Upper Hopton 92-02; rtd 02. *126 Edge Lane, Dewsbury WF12 0HB* Tel (01924) 508885

PARKINSON, Thomas Alan. b 40. St Jo Coll York CertEd61. NW Ord Course 75. **d** 78 **p** 79. NSM Sheff St Cecilia Parson Cross 78-82; NSM Goldthorpe w Hickleton 82-90; C Cantley 90-01; Dioc RE and Worship Adv 93-04; V Ryecroft St Nic from 02; CMP from 00. *St Nicolas' Presbytery, Kilnhurst Road, Rawmarsh, Rotherham S62 5NG* Tel (01709) 522596

PARKINSON, Vivian Leslie. b 54. St Luke's Coll Ex CertEd76 Brighton Poly BEd87. St Jo Coll Nottm. **d** 94 **p** 95. C Cowbridge *Llan* 94-97; V Llantrisant from 97; AD Pontypridd from 06. *The Vicarage, Coed yr Eglob, Llantrisant, Pontyclun CF72 8EL* Tel (01443) 223356 *or* 237983 Fax 230631 E-mail vivparkinson@parishofllantrisant.org.uk

PARKMAN, Mrs Michelle Joy. b 77. SS Mark & Jo Univ Coll Plymouth BA00. Trin Coll Bris BA08. **d** 08 **p** 09. C Nailsea H Trin *B & W* from 08. *26 St Mary's Grove, Nailsea, Bristol BS48 4NQ* Tel 07740-366597 (mobile) E-mail mparkman@hotmail.co.uk

PARKS, Paul. b 59. K Coll Lon BA96. St Jo Coll Nottm MA97. **d** 98 **p** 99. C S Molton w Nymet St George, High Bray etc *Ex* 98-04; P-in-c Hurst *Ox* 04-05; C Wokingham St Sebastian 05-07; TV Wednesfield *Lich* from 07. *St Alban's House, Griffiths Park, Wolverhampton WV11 2LJ* Tel (01902) 723317 E-mail revpaulparks@tiscali.co.uk

PARMENTER, Canon Deirdre Joy. b 45. EAMTC 91. **d** 94 **p** 95. C Ipswich St Aug *St E* 94-97; P-in-c Haughley w Wetherden 97-00; V Haughley w Wetherden and Stowupland 00-07; RD Stowmarket 99-05; Bp's Chapl from 07; Dioc Adv for Women's Min from 08; Hon Can St E Cathl from 03. *The Bishop's House, 4 Park Road, Ipswich IP1 3ST* Tel (01473) 252829 Fax 232552 E-mail deirdre@stedmundsbury.anglican.org

PARNELL, Bryan Donald. b 38. JP. DipEd88. Chich Th Coll 66. **d** 69 **p** 70. C Lewisham St Jo Southend *S'wark* 69-72; Asst Chapl Colleg Sch of St Pet Australia 72-76; R Angaston 76-78; Chapl RAN 78-88; R Edwardstown 89-02; rtd 02. *PO Box 6619, Halifax Street, Adelaide SA 5000, Australia* Tel (0061) (8) 4100337 Mobile 414-692340 E-mail trinitas@senet.com.au

PARNELL-HOPKINSON, Clive. b 46. FRSA01. Sarum & Wells Th Coll 75. **d** 78 **p** 79. C Maldon All SS w St Pet *Chelmsf* 78-81; C Chandler's Ford *Win* 81-84; Chapl RAF 84-01; P-in-c Cliddesden and Ellisfield w Farleigh Wallop etc *Win* from 01; Dioc Adv in Tourism from 01. *The Rectory, Church Lane, Ellisfield, Basingstoke RG25 2QR* Tel (01256) 381217 E-mail halo.cph@ukonline.co.uk

PARR, Mrs Anne Patricia. b 38. Nottm Univ CertEd59. **d** 07 **p** 08. OLM Penistone and Thurlstone *Wakef* from 07. *7 Rydal Close, Penistone, Sheffield S36 8HN* Tel (01226) 764490 Mobile 07971-513301 E-mail mail@anneparr.co.uk

PARR, Clive William. b 41. FCIS. WEMTC 02. **d** 03 **p** 04. NSM Evesham w Norton and Lenchwick *Worc* 03-07; NSM Hampton w Sedgeberrow and Hinton-on-the-Green from 07; Bp's Health Service Adv from 08. *Grace Cottage, Mill Lane, Elmley Castle, Pershore WR10 3HP* Tel (01386) 710700 Fax 761214 Mobile 07801-820006

PARR, David Jonathan. b 77. Chelt & Glouc Coll of HE BA98. Trin Coll Bris BA04. **d** 04 **p** 05. C Whitchurch *Ex* 04-08; C Shepton Mallet w Doulting *B & W* from 08. *35 Society Road, Shepton Mallett BA4 5GF* Tel 07816-752990 (mobile) E-mail davejparr@yahoo.co.uk

PARR, Frank. b 35. Nottm Univ BCombStuds82 Lanc Univ MA86. Linc Th Coll 79. **d** 82 **p** 83. C Padiham *Blackb* 82-85; P-in-c Accrington St Andr 85-88; V Oswaldtwistle Immanuel and All SS 88-96; V Tunstall w Melling and Leck 96-01; rtd 01; Perm to Offic *Blackb* from 01 and *Bradf* from 04. *1 Bank View, Burton Road, Lower Bentham, Lancaster LA2 7DZ* Tel (015242) 61159 E-mail frank_parr@lineone.net

PARR, Jeffrey John. b 48. FCA73. EMMTC 03. **d** 06 **p** 07. NSM Bassingham Gp *Linc* from 06. *The Beeches, Sands Lane, Carlton-le-Moorland, Lincoln LN5 9HJ* Tel and fax (01522) 789947 Mobile 07785-281215 E-mail jparr@chesapeake.co.uk

PARR, John. b 53. St Edm Hall Ox BA74 MA87 Lon Univ BD79 Sheff Univ PhD90. Trin Coll Bris 75. **d** 79 **p** 80. C Gt Crosby St Luke *Liv* 79-82; C Walton St Mary 82-84; V Ince St Mary 84-87; Tutor and Lect Ridley Hall Cam 87-95; Chapl 87-93; Dir Studies 93-95; CME Officer *Ely* 95-99; P-in-c Harston w Hauxton 95-99; P-in-c Newton 97-99; Can Res and CME Officer *St E* 99-00; Perm to Offic 06-09; TR Bury St Edmunds All SS w St Jo and St Geo from 09. *All Saints' Vicarage, 59 Bennett Avenue, Bury St Edmunds IP33 3JJ* Tel (01284) 701063 E-mail parr28@btinternet.com

PARR, Mabel Ann. b 37. CBDTI 07. **d** 07 **p** 08. NSM Bentham *Bradf* from 07. *1 Bank View, Burton Road, Lower Bentham, Lancaster LA2 7DZ* E-mail f.parr207@btinternet.com

PARR, Miss Vanessa Caroline. b 78. Lanc Univ BA00. Trin Coll Bris BA07. **d** 08 **p** 09. C Hoddesdon *St Alb* from 08. *134 Plomer Avenue, Hoddesdon EN11 9FS* Tel 07811-444435 (mobile) E-mail vanessa_parr@yahoo.com

PARRATT, Dennis James. b 53. Glos Coll of Art & Design BA74. St Steph Ho Ox 82. **d** 84 **p** 85. C Cainscross w Selsley *Glouc* 84-88; C Old Shoreham and New Shoreham *Chich* 88-91; Perm to Offic *Glouc* 01-08. *11 Millbrook Gardens, Cheltenham GL50 3RQ* Tel (01242) 525730 E-mail djparratt@hotmail.co.uk

PARRATT, Mrs Mary Margaret. b 42. Shenstone Coll of Educn DipEd63. St Alb Minl Tr Scheme 86. **d** 98 **p** 99. NSM Barton-le-Cley w Higham Gobion and Hexton *St Alb* 98-06; Perm to Offic from 06. *49 Manor Road, Barton-le-Clay, Bedford MK45 4NP* Tel (01582) 883089

PARRETT, Mrs Rosalind Virginia. b 43. Ox Brookes Univ MTh02. Cant Sch of Min 84. **d** 87 **p** 94. NSM Selling w Throwley, Sheldwich w Badlesmere etc *Cant* 87-91; Asst Chapl Cant Hosp 87-91; Par Dn Stantonbury and Willen *Ox* 91-94; TV 94-96; P-in-c Owlsmoor 96-98; V 98-03; rtd 03; Perm to Offic *Cant* 03-04; Hon C Faversham from 04. *16 Hilton Close, Faversham ME13 8NN* Tel (01795) 530380 Mobile 07881-788155 E-mail revros@talktalk.net

PARRETT, Simon Christopher. b 60. Sarum & Wells Th Coll. **d** 87 **p** 88. C Ifield *Chich* 87-91; Chapl to the Deaf *Sarum* 91-94; NSM Bournemouth H Epiphany *Win* 94-96; Asst Chapl Poole Hosp NHS Trust 96-03; Chapl Dorothy House Hospice Winsley 01-04. *252 The Common, Holt, Trowbridge BA14 6QN* Tel (01225) 783163

PARRETT, Stanley Frederick Donald. b 24. **d** 78 **p** 79. NSM Whitchurch w Ganarew *Heref* 78-83; C Goodrich w Welsh Bicknor and Marstow 83-86; C Walford w Bishopswood 83-86; R Pembridge w Moorcourt, Shobdon, Staunton etc 86-89; rtd 89. *4 Manley Lane, Pembridge, Leominster HR6 9DR* Tel (01544) 388815

PARRETT, Stephen. b 65. Cant Ch Ch Univ Coll BA96. **d** 07 **p** 08. OLM Herne Bay Ch Ch *Cant* from 07. *1 Birkdale Gardens, Herne Bay CT6 7TS* Tel (01227) 360139 Mobile 07742-439563 E-mail stephenparrett@lycos.co.uk

PARRI, Emyr. Univ of Wales BA96 FRAS. Ban & St As Minl Tr Course 98. **d** 98 **p** 99. NSM Tregarth *Ban* 98-04; Bp's Chapl 04-07. *The Rectory, Llanllechid, Bangor LL57 3SD* Tel (01248) 602176

PARRISH, Ian Robert. b 62. SEITE. **d** 09. C Kingsnorth and Shadoxhurst *Cant* from 09. *24 Bramble Walk, Kingsnorth, Ashford TN23 3GF*

PARRISH, Robert Carey. b 57. St Steph Ho Ox 89. **d** 91 **p** 92. C Abington *Pet* 91-94; C Leckhampton SS Phil and Jas w Cheltenham St Jas *Glouc* 94-97; PV Llan Cathl 97-02; R Merthyr Dyfan from 02. *Merthyr Dyfan Rectory, 10 Buttrills Road, Barry CF62 8EF* Tel (01446) 735943

PARROTT, David Wesley. b 58. Univ of Wales (Cardiff) LLM01. Oak Hill Th Coll BA. **d** 84 **p** 85. C Thundersley *Chelmsf* 84-87; C Rainham 87-89; P-in-c Heydon w Gt and Lt Chishill 89-90; P-in-c Chrishall 89-90; P-in-c Elmdon w Wendon Lofts and Strethall 89-90; R Heydon, Gt and Lt Chishill, Chrishall etc 91-96; R Rayleigh 96-00; TR 00-04; RD Rochford 02-04; Barking Area CME Adv 04-09; C Hornchurch St Andr 05-09; Hon Can Chelmsf Cathl 07-09; V St Lawr Jewry *Lon* from 09. *St Lawrence Jewry Vicarage, Church Passage, London EC2V 5AA* Tel (020) 7600 9478 E-mail dwparrott01@aol.com

PARROTT, George. b 37. Leeds Univ BA61. Bps' Coll Cheshunt 61. **d** 63 **p** 64. C Lower Mitton *Worc* 63-65; C-in-c Fairfield St Rich CD 65-68; Zambia 68-70; C Cleethorpes *Linc* 70-75; R Withern 75-80; P-in-c Gayton le Marsh 76-80; P-in-c Strubby

76-80; P-in-c Authorpe 76-80; P-in-c Belleau w Aby and Claythorpe 76-80; P-in-c N and S Reston 76-80; P-in-c Swaby w S Thoresby 76-80; R Withern 80-90; V Reston 80-90; V Messingham 90-93; P-in-c Fincham *Ely* 95-02; P-in-c Marham 95-02; P-in-c Shouldham 95-02; P-in-c Shouldham Thorpe 95-02; rtd 02; Perm to Offic *Linc* from 03. *8 Anson Close, Skellingthorpe, Lincoln LN6 5TH* Tel (01522) 694417

PARROTT, Canon Gerald Arthur. b 32. St Cath Coll Cam BA56 MA60. Chich Th Coll. **d** 58 **p** 59. C Ashington *Newc* 58-61; C Brighton St Pet *Chich* 61-63; V Leeds St Wilfrid *Ripon* 63-68; R Lewisham St Jo Southend *S'wark* 69-73; TR Catford (Southend) and Downham 73-77; RD E Lewisham 75-77; Can Res and Prec S'wark Cathl 77-88; TR Wimbledon 88-95; rtd 95; Perm to Offic *Chich* from 95. *10 Palings Way, Fernhurst, Haslemere GU27 3HJ* Tel (01428) 641533

PARROTT, Martin William. b 57. Keele Univ BA79 Lon Univ PGCE80. Ripon Coll Cuddesdon 82. **d** 85 **p** 86. C Birchfield *Birm* 85-88; Chapl Lon Univ 88-93; P-in-c Univ Ch Ch the K Lon 90-93; V Hebden Bridge *Wakef* 93-01; Asst Chapl Pinderfields and Pontefract Hosps NHS Trust 01-02; Chapl Calderdale and Huddersfield NHS Trust from 02. *The Royal Infirmary, Acre Street, Lindley, Huddersfield HD3 3EA* Tel (01484) 342000 E-mail martin.parrott@cht.nhs.uk

PARRY, Canon Alfred Charles Ascough. b 37. Natal Univ BA58. Westcott Ho Cam 59. **d** 61 **p** 62. C E Ham w Upton Park *Chelmsf* 61-63; C Durban N St Martin S Africa 63-64; R Newcastle H Trin 64-70; Dir Chr Educn Kloof 70-76; Sub Dean Pietermaritzburg 76-81; R Estcourt 81; Adn N Natal 81-85; R Kloof 86-93; R Berea 93-98; Hon Can Pietermaritzburg from 86; Sen Asst Min Hornchurch St Andr *Chelmsf* 99-04; C Furze Platt *Ox* 04-05; Hon C 05-07; rtd 05. *45 Windmill Drive, Croxley Green, Rickmansworth WD3 3FF* Tel (01923) 771037

PARRY, Andrew Martyn. b 61. Witwatersrand Univ BA81 MBA91 Open Univ BSc04. Ox Min Course 06. **d** 09. *2 Pennylets Green, Stoke Poges, Slough SL2 4BT* Tel (01753) 644239 E-mail andrew@vamparry.eclipse.co.uk

PARRY, Canon Bryan Horace. b 33. St Mich Coll Llan 65. **d** 67 **p** 68. C Holyhead w Rhoscolyn w Llanfair-yn-Neubwll *Ban* 67-71; TV 71-73; P-in-c Small Heath St Greg *Birm* 73-78; V 78-80; V Perry Barr 80-94; RD Handsworth 83-91; P-in-c Kingstanding St Luke 86-92; Hon Can Birm Cathl 87-94; rtd 94; Perm to Offic *Nor* from 94. *St Seiriol, Old Crown Yard, Walsingham NR22 6BU* Tel (01328) 820019

PARRY, Charles. *See* PARRY, Canon Alfred Charles Ascough

PARRY, David Allan. b 62. Bris Univ BSc83 Univ of Wales (Cardiff) CQSW88. Trin Coll Bris. **d** 94 **p** 95. C Withywood *Bris* 94-98; P-in-c Litherland St Phil *Liv* 98-02; V 02-06; Hon Chapl to the Deaf 00-05; AD Bootle 02-05; Hon Can Liv Cathl 03-05; Dioc Dir of Ords from 05; V Toxteth Park Ch Ch and St Mich w St Andr from 06. *St Michael's Vicarage, St Michael's Church Road, Liverpool L17 7BD* Tel 0151-286 2411

PARRY, David Thomas Newton. b 45. Selw Coll Cam BA67 MA71. Lambeth STh76 Cuddesdon Coll 67. **d** 69 **p** 70. C Oldham St Mary w St Pet *Man* 69-73; C Baguley 73-74; Tutor Sarum & Wells Th Coll 74-78; V Westleigh St Pet *Man* 78-88; TR E Farnworth and Kearsley 88-97; TR Chambersbury *St Alb* 97-03; V Blackbird Leys *Ox* from 03. *Church House, 5 Cuddesdon Way, Oxford OX4 6JH* Tel (01865) 778728 E-mail dtnparrv@parsonage.u-net.com

PARRY, Denis. b 34. Sarum & Wells Th Coll 83. **d** 85 **p** 86. C Hubberston w Herbrandston and Hasguard etc *St D* 85-89; P-in-c Herbrandston and Hasguard w St Ishmael's 89-90; R 90-99; Dioc RE Adv 89-99; rtd 99; Perm to Offic *Heref* from 99. *Mayfield, 33 Mill Street, Kington HR5 3AL* Tel (01544) 230550

PARRY, Canon Dennis John. b 38. Univ of Wales (Lamp) BA60. St Mich Coll Llan 60. **d** 62 **p** 63. C Caerphilly *Llan* 62-64; C Aberdare St Fagan 64-67; Miss at Povungnituk Canada 67-69; R Gelligaer *Llan* 69-75; V Llanwnnog and Caersws w Carno *Ban* 75-89; V Llanidloes w Llangurig 89-01; RD Arwystli 89-01; Hon Can Ban Cathl 90-01; Can Cursal 97-01; rtd 01; Perm to Offic *Ban* from 02. *Lock Cottage, Groesfford, Brecon LD3 7UY* Tel (01874) 665400 E-mail dj519@btinternet.com

PARRY, Derek Nugent Goulding. b 32. Ely Th Coll 60. **d** 63 **p** 64. C Fareham SS Pet and Paul *Portsm* 63-67; C Portsea N End St Mark 67-74; P-in-c Piddletrenthide w Plush, Alton Pancras etc *Sarum* 74-92; rtd 92; Perm to Offic *Sarum* from 92. *Farthing Cottage, 12 Fordington Green, Dorchester DT1 1LU* Tel (01305) 269794

PARRY, Gordon Martyn Winn. b 47. Down Coll Cam BA68 MA70 Univ Coll Chich MA02. **d** 04 **p** 05. NSM Turners Hill *Chich* 04-07; NSM E Grinstead St Swithun from 07. *8 Hoathly Hill, West Hoathly, East Grinstead RH19 4SJ* Tel and fax (01342) 810618 Mobile 07802-432398 E-mail gordonmwparry@btinternet.com

PARRY, Jane. *See* PARRY, Mrs Patricia Jane

PARRY, John Gareth. b 61. Univ of Wales (Abth) BA83 Univ of Wales (Ban) PGCE84. Westcott Ho Cam 94. **d** 96 **p** 97. C Holyhead *Ban* 96-99; C-in-c Llandinorwig w Penisa'r-waen 99-00; Perm to Offic from 00; Asst Master Bodedern Secondary

Sch 00-01; Hd RE Pensby High Sch for Boys Wirral 02; Chapl and Hd RE Tettenhall Coll Wolv 03-09; Chapl Prestfelde Sch Shrewsbury from 09. *34 Merton Park, Penmaenmawr LL34 6DH,* or *Prestfelde School, London Road, Shrewsbury SY2 6NZ* Tel (01492) 622671 *or* (01743) 245400 E-mail merton34@uku.co.uk

PARRY, Keith Melville. b 31. MRICS65. S'wark Ord Course 80. **d** 83 **p** 84. NSM Bexley St Jo *Roch* 83-88; C Orpington All SS 88-96; rtd 96; Perm to Offic *Roch* from 96. *5 Greenside, Bexley DA5 3PA* Tel (01322) 555425

PARRY, Canon Kenneth Charles. b 34. Ripon Hall Ox 56. **d** 58 **p** 59. C Stoke *Cov* 58-61; Chapl RN 61-65; V Cradley *Worc* 65-70; V Gt Malvern H Trin 70-83; RD Malvern 74-83; Hon Can Worc Cathl 80-83; V Budleigh Salterton *Ex* 83-91; Can Res and Prec Ex Cathl 91-00; rtd 00. *Brook Cottage, Pye Corner, Kennford, Exeter EX6 7TB* Tel (01392) 832767 E-mail kcparry@ic24.net

PARRY, Ms Manon Ceridwen. b 69. Poly of Wales BA90 Selw Coll Cam BA93 MA97. Ridley Hall Cam. **d** 94 **p** 97. C Llandudno *Ban* 94-98; P-in-c Glanogwen w St Ann's w Llanllechid 98-99; V 99-05; V Pentir 04-05; Dir of Ords 02-05; C Llanrhos *St As* 05-07; Dioc Dir Lifelong Learning 05-08; R Llanddulas and Llysfaen from 08. *The Rectory, 2 Rhoddfa Wen, Llysfaen, Colwyn Bay LL29 8LE* Tel (01492) 516728 E-mail manon.parry@sky.com

PARRY, Canon Marilyn Marie. b 46. W Coll Ohio BA68 Man Univ MA77 PhD00. Episc Th Sch Cam Mass 68 Gilmore Ho 76. **dss** 79 **d** 87 **p** 94. Westleigh St Pet *Man* 78-85; Chapl Asst N Man Gen Hosp 85-90; Tutor NOC 90-97; Dir Studies 91-97; Lic Preacher *Man* 90-94; Hon C E Farnworth and Kearsley 94-97; Nat Adv for Pre-Th Educn and Selection Sec Min Division Abps' Coun 97-01; Public Preacher *St Alb* 98-01; Can Res Ch Ch *Ox* from 01; Dioc Dir of Ords from 01. *Diocesan Church House, North Hinksey, Oxford OX2 0NB* Tel (01865) 276215 *or* 208289 Mobile 07712-834973 Fax (01865) 790470 *or* 208246 E-mail marilyn.parry@oxford.anglican.org

PARRY, Nicholas John Sinclair. b 56. Sarum & Wells Th Coll 82. **d** 85 **p** 86. C Hendon St Mary *Lon* 85-87; C Verwood *Sarum* 87-90; TV Witney *Ox* 90-96; V Costessey *Nor* from 96. *The Vicarage, Folgate Lane, Costessey, Norwich NR8 5DP* Tel (01603) 742818 E-mail nicholas.parry@btinternet.com

PARRY, Mrs Olwen Margaret. b 45. Cardiff Coll of Educn CertEd67. Llan Dioc Tr Scheme 88. **d** 92 **p** 97. NSM Newcastle *Llan* 92-04; NSM Llansantffraid, Bettws and Aberkenfig from 04. *17 Wernlys Road, Bridgend CF31 4NS* Tel (01656) 721860

PARRY, Owen Benjamin. b 42. St As Minl Tr Course 99. **d** 01 **p** 02. C Llangollen w Trevor and Llantysilio *St As* 01-07; rtd 07; C-in-c Pradoe *Lich* from 09. *Fairways, Halton, Chirk, Wrexham LL14 5BD* Tel (01691) 778484

PARRY, Mrs Patricia Jane. b 54. Liv Univ BTh99. NOC 97. **d** 99 **p** 00. C Wilmslow *Ches* 99-03; V Baddiley and Wrenbury w Burleydam 03-08; V Alderley Edge from 08. *The Vicarage, Church Lane, Alderley Edge SK9 7UZ* Tel (01625) 583249 E-mail formidocornicarum@hotmail.com

PARRY, Peter John. b 42. Westmr Coll Ox BTh99. EAMTC 99. **d** 01 **p** 02. NSM Montreux w Gstaad *Eur* 01-06; Perm to Offic *Pet* from 05. *Forge House, Church Road, Hargrave, Wellingborough NN9 6BQ* E-mail pparry@compuserve.com

PARRY, Richard Neil. **d** 98 **p** 99. C Glan Ely *Llan* 98-00; C Merthyr Dyfan 00-02; TV Canton Cardiff 02-06. *Address temp unknown*

PARRY, Miss Violet Margaret. b 30. Selly Oak Coll 53. **dss** 82 **d** 87. W Kilburn St Luke w St Simon and St Jude *Lon* 82-83; St Marylebone St Mary 83-86; Stamford All SS w St Jo *Linc* 86-90; C 87-90; rtd 90; Perm to Offic *Linc* 90-01 and *Leic* from 03. *2 Stuart Court, High Street, Kibworth, Leicester LE8 0LR* Tel 0116-279 6858

PARRY-JENNINGS, Christopher William. b 34. Lon Coll of Div 57. **d** 60 **p** 62. C Claughton cum Grange *Ches* 60-63; C Folkestone H Trin w Ch Ch *Cant* 63-67; New Zealand from 67; V Lincoln 67-72; Chapl Cant Univ 68-72; V Riccarton St Jas 72-88; V Heathcote Mt Pleasant 88-96; First Gen Sec SPCK (NZ) 89-90; P Asst Upper Riccarton St Pet from 96. *22 Ambleside Drive, Burnside, Christchurch 8053, New Zealand* Tel and fax (0064) (3) 358 9304 E-mail chpj@globe.net.nz

PARRY JONES, Leonard. b 29. Univ of Wales (Ban) BA52. St Mich Coll Llan 52. **d** 54 **p** 55. C Newtown w Llanllwchaiarn w Aberhafesp *St As* 54-58; C Abergele 58-60; V Pennant, Hirnant and Llangynog 60-65; V Llanynys w Llanychan 65-71; V Brynymaen w Trofarth 71-94; RD Rhos 77-94; rtd 94. *The Cottage, Kerry, Newtown SY16 4NU* Tel (01686) 670822

PARSELL, Howard Vivian. b 60. Univ of Wales (Lamp) BA87 Univ of Wales (Swansea) PGCE88. St Mich Coll Llan 93. **d** 94 **p** 95. C Builth and Llanddewi'r Cwm w Llangynog etc *S & B* 94-96; C Swansea St Thos and Kilvey 96-98; P-in-c Swansea St Jude 98-09; V Swansea St Jude w St Nic from 09; Chapl to the Deaf from 98; AD Swansea from 04. *St Nicholas' Vicarage, 58A Dyfed Avenue, Townhill, Swansea SA1 6NG* Tel (01792) 473154

PARSELLE, Stephen Paul. b 53. Univ of Wales (Cardiff) MTh06. St Jo Coll Nottm. **d** 82 **p** 83. C Boscombe St Jo *Win* 82-86; CF 86-05; Dir of Ords 02-05; Chapl RN 05-08. *11 Southbourne Overcliff Drive, Bournemouth BH6 3TE* Tel (01202) 433858 Mobile 07711-017282 E-mail parselle@aol.com

PARSONAGE, Robert Hugh. b 55. Nottm Trent Univ BSc78. Trin Coll Bris BA97. **d** 97 **p** 98. C Chell *Lich* 97-01; R Poringland *Nor* from 01. *The Rectory, Rectory Lane, Poringland, Norwich NR14 7SL* Tel (01508) 492215 E-mail robert@hparsonage.freeserve.co.uk

PARSONS, Andrew David. b 53. UEA BA74 Fitzw Coll Cam BA77 MA81. Westcott Ho Cam 75. **d** 78 **p** 79. C Hellesdon *Nor* 78-82; C Eaton 82-85; P-in-c Burnham Thorpe w Burnham Overy 85-87; R Burnham Sutton w Burnham Ulph etc 85-87; R Burnham Gp of Par 87-93; P-in-c Wroxham w Hoveton and Belaugh 93; R 93-07; RD St Benet 99-07; V Old Catton from 07. *St Margaret's Vicarage, 1 Parkside Drive, Norwich NR6 7DP* Tel (01603) 425615 E-mail 2andrew@andrewparsons.fsnet.co.uk

PARSONS, Bernard. b 26. Ely Th Coll 60. **d** 62 **p** 63. C Bourne *Linc* 62-64; V W Pinchbeck 64-71; V Sutton Bridge 71-83; R Coningsby w Tattershall 83-93; rtd 93; Perm to Offic *Linc* from 93. *12 St Peter's Drive, Woodhall Spa LN10 6SY* Tel (01526) 353027

PARSONS, Christopher James Hutton. b 54. Univ of Wales (Ban) BA75. Qu Coll Birm. **d** 79 **p** 80. C Crowthorne *Ox* 79-83; V Tilehurst St Cath 83-88; P-in-c Wrentham w Benacre, Covehithe, Frostenden etc *St E* 89-91; R 91-94. *Address temp unknown*

PARSONS, Christopher Paul. b 58. EAMTC 01. **d** 04 **p** 05. C Pakefield *Nor* 04-08; P-in-c Kenwyn w St Allen *Truro* from 08. *The Vicarage, Kenwyn Church Road, Truro TR1 3DR* Tel (01872) 263015 E-mail chris@cpp1.freeserve.co.uk

PARSONS, David Norman. b 39. FCIB83. Trin Coll Bris 92. **d** 94 **p** 95. NSM Swindon Dorcan *Bris* 94-03; Perm to Offic *Glouc* from 03. *31 Couzens Close, Chipping Sodbury, Bristol BS37 6BT* Tel (01454) 323070 E-mail david.parsons1@virgin.net

PARSONS, Mrs Deborah Anne. b 66. Surrey Univ BA87. STETS 04. **d** 07. C Goodrington *Ex* from 07. *40 Steed Close, Paignton TQ4 7SN* Tel (01803) 845325 E-mail d.a.parsons@btinternet.com

PARSONS, Desmond John. b 25. Coll of Resurr Mirfield 65. **d** 66 **p** 67. C Purley St Mark *S'wark* 66-70; V W Dulwich All SS and Em 71-83; R Limpsfield and Titsey 83-95; rtd 95; Perm to Offic *Guildf* and *S'wark* from 96. *Priors House, The Court, Croft Lane, Crondall, Farnham GU10 5QF* Tel (01252) 851137

PARSONS, Geoffrey Fairbanks. b 35. Trin Coll Cam BA58 MA68. Ridley Hall Cam 59. **d** 61 **p** 62. C Over St Chad *Ches* 61-64; C Heswall 64-69; V Congleton St Steph 69-75; V Weaverham 75-94; P-in-c Backford and Capenhurst 94-00; R 00-01; rtd 01; Perm to Offic *Ches* from 02. *28 Springcroft, Parkgate, South Wirral CH64 6SE* Tel 0151-336 3354

PARSONS, George Edward. b 35. St D Coll Lamp BA60 Ripon Hall Ox 60. **d** 62 **p** 63. C Leominster *Heref* 62-66; NSM Bromfield 67-72; NSM Culmington w Onibury 67-72; NSM Stanton Lacy 67-72; NSM Ludlow 72-77; P-in-c Caynham 77-79; NSM Bishop's Cleeve *Glouc* 79-91; Sub-Chapl HM Pris Glouc 88-91; P-in-c Hartley w Tirley and Ashleworth 91-00; P-in-c Maisemore 91-00; rtd 00; Perm to Offic *Glouc* 00-02 and *Blackb* from 02. *Ballalona, 2 The Meadows, Hollins Lane, Forton, Preston PR3 0AF* Tel (01524) 792656

PARSONS, George Horace Norman. b 19. S'wark Ord Course 65. **d** 68 **p** 69. C Hatcham St Cath *S'wark* 68-72; C Horley 72-76; P-in-c S Wimbledon All SS 76-78; P-in-c Caterham 78-81; C Caterham and Chapl St Lawr Hosp Caterham 82-84; RAChD 72-84; rtd 85; Perm to Offic *S'wark* from 85. *8 Whitgift House, 76 Brighton Road, Croydon CR2 6AB* Tel (020) 8680 0028

PARSONS, Canon Jennifer Anne. b 53. Univ of Wales (Lamp) BA76 MA78 Jes Coll Cam PhD90. Westcott Ho Cam 92. **d** 94 **p** 95. C Halesowen *Worc* 94-97; TV Worc St Barn w Ch Ch 97-04; R Matson *Glouc* from 04; Hon Can Glouc Cathl from 07; Dean of Women Clergy from 09. *The Rectory, Matson Lane, Gloucester GL4 6DX* Tel (01452) 522598 E-mail jeni@hencity.fsnet.co.uk

PARSONS, Jeremy. Ridley Hall Cam. **d** 09. NSM Cambridge St Martin *Ely* from 09. *8A Saxon Street, Cambridge CB2 1HN*

PARSONS, Canon John Banham. b 43. Selw Coll Cam BA65 MA68. Ridley Hall Cam 65. **d** 67 **p** 68. C Downend *Bris* 67-71; Public Preacher Withywood LEP 71-77; P-in-c Hengrove 77-78; V 78-85; V Letchworth St Paul w Willian *St Alb* 85-94; P-in-c Barking w St Marg w St Patr *Chelmsf* 94-98; TR 98-04; RD Barking and Dagenham 00-04; P-in-c Hornchurch H Cross 04-09; RD Havering 04-08; Hon Can Chelmsf Cathl 01-09; rtd 09. *8 Pound Close, Upper Caldecote, Biggleswade SG18 9AU* Tel (01767) 315285 E-mail j.parsons986@btinternet.com

PARSONS, Laurie. b 19. Keble Coll Ox BA41. Wells Th Coll 41. **d** 43 **p** 44. C Westwood *Cov* 43-49; C-in-c Galley Common Stockingford CD 49-57; V Priors Marston 57-69; V Radford

Semele 70-83; V Radford Semele and Ufton 83-84; rtd 84. *c/o I Reid Esq, Inwood House, New Road, Alderminster, Stratford-upon-Avon CV37 8PE*

PARSONS, Canon Marlene Beatrice. b 43. Wilson Carlile Coll. **dss** 76 **d** 87 **p** 94. Coulsdon St Jo *S'wark* 76-79; Hill *Birm* 79-86; Dioc Lay Min Adv 80-90; Vice Prin WMMTC 86-90; Dioc Dir of Ords *Birm* 90-04; Dean of Women's Min 90-04; Hon Can Birm Cathl 89-04; rtd 04; Perm to Offic *Birm* from 04. *20 Copperbeech Close, Birmingham B32 2HT* Tel 0121-427 2632

PARSONS, Miss Mary Elizabeth. b 43. Wilson Carlile Coll 65. **dss** 78 **d** 87 **p** 94. Chapl Asst Chu Hosp Ox 78-89; Chapl 89-93; rtd 93; NSM Sandford-on-Thames *Ox* 94-00. *20 Copperbeech Close, Birmingham B32 2HT* Tel 0121-426 4527

PARSONS, Michael. b 46. Open Univ BA84. SWMTC 05. **d** 08 **p** 09. NSM Boscastle w Davidstow *Truro* from 08. *2 Penally Terrace, Boscastle PL35 0HA* Tel (01840) 250625 E-mail mike@2penally.co.uk

PARSONS, Canon Michael William Semper. b 47. St Cath Coll Ox BA69 MA74 DPhil74 Selw Coll Cam BA77 MA81. Ridley Hall Cam 75. **d** 78 **p** 79. C Edmonton All SS *Lon* 78-81; SPCK Research Fell Dur Univ 81-84; Hon Lect Th 84-85; SPCK Fell N of England Inst for Chr Educn 84-85; P-in-c Derby St Aug 85-95; TR Walbrook Epiphany 95-96; Dioc Voc Adv 86-96; P-in-c Hempsted *Glouc* 96-00; Dir of Ords 96-04; Dir Curates' Tr 00-04; Prin WEMTC from 04; Prin Lect Glos Univ from 09; Hon Can Glouc Cathl from 03. *6 Spa Villas, Montpellier, Gloucester GL1 1LB* Tel (01452) 524550 *or* (01242) 714846 E-mail mparsons@wemtc.org.uk *or* mwsp@btinternet.com

PARSONS, Canon Robert Martin. b 43. Qu Coll Cam BA65 MA69. ALCD68. **d** 68 **p** 69. C Chapeltown *Sheff* 68-71; C Sheff St Jo 71-75; V Swadlincote *Derby* 75-91; RD Repton 81-91; P-in-c Gresley 82-86; R Etwall w Egginton 91-93; Can Res Derby Cathl 93-98; Hon Can 98-09; P-in-c Belper 98-03; V 03-09; Jt P-in-c Ambergate and Heage 06-09; rtd 09; Hon C Bicton, Montford w Shrawardine and Fitz *Lich* from 09; Hon C Leaton and Albrighton w Battlefield from 09. *The Vicarage, Baschurch Road, Bomere Heath, Shrewsbury SY4 3PN* Tel (01939) 291494 E-mail canonparsons@tiscali.co.uk

PARSONS, Roger John. b 37. Sarum Th Coll 62. **d** 65 **p** 66. C Bitterne Park *Win* 65-69; C Clerkenwell H Redeemer w St Phil *Lon* 69-72; C Willesden St Andr 72-76; C St Laur in Thanet *Cant* 76-81; Chapl Luton and Dunstable Hosp 81-86; Chapl St Mary's Hosp Luton 81-86; C Luton All SS w St Pet *St Alb* 81-86; TV E Dereham *Nor* 86-88; TV E Dereham and Scarning 89; Perm to Offic 89-93. *6 Ellastone Court, 1 Salisbury Road, Sheringham NR26 8EA* Tel (01263) 821241

PARSONS, Stephen Christopher. b 45. Keble Coll Ox BA67 MA72 BLitt78. Cuddesdon Coll 68. **d** 70 **p** 71. C Whitstable All SS *Cant* 70-71; C Croydon St Sav 71-74; Perm to Offic *Ox* 74-76; C St Laur in Thanet *Cant* 76-79; V Lugwardine w Bartestree and Weston Beggard *Heref* 79-87; V Lechlade *Glouc* 87-03; R Edin St Cuth from 03. *St Cuthbert's Rectory, 6 Westgarth Avenue, Edinburgh EH13 0BD* Tel 0131-441 3557 E-mail stephen@parsons252262.freeserve.co.uk

PARSONS, Stephen Drury. b 54. Qu Mary Coll Lon BSc76 CCC Cam MSc79. Westcott Ho Cam 79. **d** 82 **p** 83. C Stretford All SS *Man* 82-85; C Newton Heath All SS 85-86; V Ashton St Jas 86-90; Perm to Offic from 01. *150 Henrietta Street, Ashton-under-Lyne OL6 8PH* Tel 0161-308 2852

PARSONS, Mrs Susan Catherine. b 60. SWMTC 06 ERMC 08. **d** 09. NSM Oakham, Hambleton, Egleton, Braunston and Brooke *Pet* from 09. *4 Quorn Crescent, Cottesmore, Oakham LE15 7NB* Tel (01572) 813848 E-mail susie.parsons@hotmail.co.uk

PARSONS, Thomas James. b 74. K Coll Lon BMus97 LRAM96. Oak Hill Th Coll BA06. **d** 06 **p** 07. C Hensingham *Carl* from 06. *13 West View, Hensingham, Whitehaven CA28 8QY* Tel (01946) 67030 *or* 591599 Mobile 07960-944287 E-mail thomasjparsons@yahoo.co.uk

PARTINGTON, The Ven Brian Harold. b 36. OBE02. St Aid Birkenhead 60. **d** 63 **p** 64. C Barlow Moor *Man* 63-66; C Deane 66-68; V Patrick *S & M* 68-96; Bp's Youth Chapl 68-77; RD Peel 76-96; P-in-c German St Jo 77-78; V 78-96; P-in-c Foxdale 77-78; V 78-96; Can St German's Cathl 85-96; Adn Man 96-05; V Douglas St Geo 96-04 and 04. *Brambles, Patrick Village, Peel, Isle of Man IM5 3AH* Tel (01624) 844173 E-mail archd-sodor@mcb.net

PARTINGTON, John. *See* PARTINGTON, Peter John

PARTINGTON, Kenneth. b 41. Lanc Univ MA86. Ripon Hall Ox. **d** 70 **p** 71. C Atherton *Man* 70-72; C Kippax *Ripon* 72-75; V Cartmel Fell *Carl* 75-95; V Crosthwaite Kendal 75-95; V Witherslack 75-95; V Winster 78-95; rtd 01; Perm to Offic *Carl* from 01 and *Blackb* from 03. *Kilvert Heights, 9 Castle Park, Kendal LA9 7AX* Tel (01539) 723963

PARTINGTON, Canon Kevin. b 51. Huddersfield Poly BA73. St Jo Coll Nottm 91. **d** 93 **p** 94. C Salterhebble All SS *Wakef* 93-96; V Pontefract All SS 96-03; TR Dewsbury from 03; Hon

Can Wakef Cathl from 07. *The Rectory, 16A Oxford Road, Dewsbury WF13 4JT* Tel (01924) 465491 *or* 457057 E-mail kevin.partington@btopenworld.com

PARTINGTON, Peter John. b 57. Peterho Cam MA. St Jo Coll Nottm 79. **d** 81 **p** 82. C Cov H Trin 81-85; C Woking St Jo *Guildf* 85-87; C 94-99; R Busbridge 87-94; Dir of Ords 94-03; P-in-c Winchcombe, Gretton, Sudeley Manor etc *Glouc* 03-05; TR Winchcombe from 05. *The Rectory, Langley Road, Winchcombe, Cheltenham GL54 5QP* Tel (01242) 602368 E-mail revpjp@aol.com

PARTON, John Michael. b 44. Bradf & Ilkley Community Coll MA93. **d** 04 **p** 05. NSM Horbury w Horbury Bridge *Wakef* from 04. *106 Lennox Drive, Wakefield WF2 8LF* Tel and fax (01924) 360395 E-mail johnmparton@btinternet.com

PARTRIDGE, Alan Christopher. b 55. Thames Poly BA77 Ex Univ PGCE78. St Jo Coll Nottm MA00. **d** 00 **p** 01. C Woking St Jo *Guildf* 00-03; C Ely 03-08; TV Ely 08-09; P-in-c Sawston from 09; P-in-c Babraham from 09. *The Vicarage, Church Lane, Sawston, Cambridge CB22 3JR* E-mail a.partridge7@ntlworld.com

PARTRIDGE, Anthony John. b 38. Univ of Wales (Lamp) BA61 Linacre Ho Ox BA63 K Coll Lon PhD77. St Steph Ho Ox 61. **d** 64 **p** 65. C Sydenham All SS *S'wark* 64-67; Hon C 68-74; Lic to Offic 74-08; Perm to Offic from 08; Lect Woolwich Poly 67-70; Thames Poly 70-74; Prin Lect 75-92; Greenwich Univ 92-03; rtd 03. *40 Upwood Road, London SE12 8AN* Tel (020) 8318 9901

PARTRIDGE, Canon David John Fabian. b 36. Ball Coll Ox BA60 MA. Westcott Ho Cam 60. **d** 62 **p** 63. C Halliwell St Thos *Man* 62-65; C St Martin-in-the-Fields *Lon* 65-69; R Warblington w Emsworth *Portsm* 69-01; Hon Can Portsm Cathl 84-01; rtd 01. *7 Wensley Gardens, Emsworth PO10 7RA* Tel (01865) 558630

PARTRIDGE, Ian Starr. b 36. Linc Th Coll 87. **d** 89 **p** 90. C Barton upon Humber *Linc* 89-92; P-in-c Barkwith Gp 92-97; R 97-02; rtd 02; Perm to Offic *Linc* from 02; RD Calcewaithe and Candleshoe 03-05. *Altair, 4 Thames Street, Louth LN11 7AD* Tel (01507) 600398 E-mail ian@altair.org.uk

PARTRIDGE, Miss Margaret Edith. b 35. Gilmore Ho 63. **dss** 85 **d** 87 **p** 94. Amblecote *Worc* 85-89; Par Dn 87-89; C Borehamwood *St Alb* 89-94; TV 94-00; rtd 00; Perm to Offic *Birm* from 01. *4 Cornerstone, Maryland Drive, Birmingham B31 2AT* Tel 0121-476 0854

PARTRIDGE, Martin David Waud. b 38. Ox NSM Course 86. **d** 89 **p** 90. NSM Wargrave *Ox* 89-97; NSM Schorne 97-05; rtd 05; Perm to Offic *Ox* from 05. *Barnes House, St James Street, Eastbury, Hungerford RG17 7JL* Tel (01488) 670281

PARTRIDGE, Michael John. b 61. St Edm Hall Ox BA83 MA89 St Jo Coll Dur BA86. Cranmer Hall Dur 84. **d** 87 **p** 88. C Amington *Birm* 87-90; C Sutton Coldfield H Trin 90-93; P-in-c W Exe 93-01; RD Tiverton 96-00; V Tiverton St Geo and St Paul 01-06; P-in-c Pinhoe and Broadclyst from 06; P-in-c Aylesbeare, Rockbeare, Farringdon etc from 06. *The Rectory, 9 Church Hill, Pinhoe, Exeter EX4 9ER* Tel (01392) 466257 E-mail m.partridge@tesco.net

PARTRIDGE, Ronald Malcolm. b 49. Bris Bapt Coll LTh74 Cuddesdon Coll 74. **d** 75 **p** 76. C Bris St Andr Hartcliffe 75-78; C E Bris 78-82; V Easton All Hallows 82-85; TV Brighton St Pet w Chpl Royal and St Jo *Chich* 85-86; TV Brighton St Pet and St Nic w Chpl Royal 86-88; C-in-c Bermondsey St Hugh CD *S'wark* 88-90; Asst Chapl Gt Ormond Street Hosp for Sick Children Lon 91-94; Asst Chapl Gt Ormond Street Hosp for Children NHS Trust 94-97. *29 All Saints Street, Hastings TN34 3BJ* Tel (01424) 715219

PARTRIDGE, Ronald William. b 42. Shimer Coll Illinois BA64. Cant Sch of Min 93. **d** 96 **p** 97. NSM Upchurch w Lower Halstow *Cant* from 96. *4 The Green, Lower Halstow, Sittingbourne ME9 7DT* Tel (01795) 842007 Mobile 07779-789039 E-mail revdron.partridge@virgin.net

PARTRIDGE, Mrs Sarah Mercy. b 59. SEITE 04. **d** 07 **p** 08. NSM Tunbridge Wells K Chas *Roch* from 07. *Long Hedges, Station Road, Rotherfield, Crowborough TN6 3HP* Tel (01892) 853451 E-mail spartridge@partridges59.fsnet.co.uk

PARTRIDGE, Canon Timothy Reeve. b 39. Lon Univ BSc60 AKC60. Wells Th Coll 60. **d** 62 **p** 63. C Glouc St Cath 62-65; C Sutton St Nicholas *Linc* 65-74; R Bugbrooke *Pet* 74-95; R Bugbrooke w Rothersthorpe 95-04; RD Daventry 81-88; Can Pet Cathl 83-04; Warden of Par Ev 96-02; rtd 04. *54 Thorney Leys, Witney OX28 5LS* Tel (01993) 864926 E-mail tim.partridge39@tiscali.co.uk

PASCHAL, Brother. *See* WORTON, David Reginald

PASCOE, Mrs Caroline Elizabeth Alice. **d** 08 **p** 09. NSM Ewenny w St Brides Major *Llan* from 08. *3A Park Road, Barry CF62 6NU* Tel (01446) 701814

PASCOE, Michael Lewis. b 43. **d** 99 **p** 00. OLM Crowan and Treslothan *Truro* 99-02; C from 02; OLM Penponds 01-02; C from 02. *Genesis, Bosparva Lane, Leedstown, Hayle TR27 6DN* Tel (01736) 850425 E-mail revdmike@supanet.com

PASHLEY, Howard Thomas. b 47. Kent Univ MSc85 Keele Univ PGCE71 ARIC70. **d** 06 **p** 07. OLM Sandwich *Cant* from

06. *8 Dover Road, Sandwich CT13 0BN* Tel (01304) 612018 E-mail howardpashley@yahoo.co.uk

PASK, Howard. b 54. St Jo Coll Nottm. **d** 99 **p** 00. C Todmorden *Wakef* 99-02; P-in-c Hebden Bridge 02-03; P-in-c Heptonstall 02-03; V Hebden Bridge and Heptonstall from 03. *The Vicarage, 12 Becketts Close, Heptonstall, Hebden Bridge HX7 7LJ* Tel (01422) 842138 Mobile 07779-243176 E-mail howardpask@btinternet.com

PASKETT, Ms Margaret Anne. b 45. Northd Coll of Educn CertEd67 York Univ BSc81 Leeds Univ MEd83. NEOC 84. **d** 87 **p** 94. Par Dn Marske in Cleveland *York* 87-91; C 92-96; Dioc Adv for Diaconal Mins 92-96; P-in-c Hemingbrough and Tr Officer (York Adnry) 96-05; rtd 06. *15 Hubert Street, York YO23 1EF* Tel (01904) 626521 E-mail annepaskett62@btinternet.com

PASKINS, David James. b 52. Univ of Wales (Lamp) BA73 Trin Hall Cam BA76 MA81. Westcott Ho Cam 74. **d** 77 **p** 78. C St Peter-in-Thanet *Cant* 77-80; C Swanage *Sarum* 80-82; R Waldron *Chich* 82-92; R Bere Ferrers *Ex* 92-96; V Lockerley and E Dean w E and W Tytherley *Win* 96-03; R Cranborne w Boveridge, Edmondsham etc *Sarum* from 03. *The Rectory, Grugs Lane, Cranborne, Wimborne BH21 5PX* Tel (01725) 517232

PASSANT, Keith. b 39. St Jo Coll Dur BA62 CertEd70. St Alb Minl Tr Scheme 77. **d** 87 **p** 88. C Hatfield Hyde *St Alb* 87-93; rtd 93; Perm to Offic *St Alb* from 93. *26 Monk's Rise, Welwyn Garden City AL8 7NF* Tel (01707) 332869

PASSEY, Miss Rhona Margaret. b 52. St Jo Coll Nottm BTh96. EMMTC 06. **d** 09. NSM Hugglescote w Donington, Ellistown and Snibston *Leic* from 09. *14 Atherstone Road, Measham, Swadlincote DE12 7EG* Tel (01530) 270823 Mobile 07787-573731 E-mail rhona.passey@btinternet.com

PATCH, Simon John. b 63. Aus Nat Univ BA87. Chich Th Coll BTh95. **d** 95 **p** 96. C Ifield *Chich* 95-99; TV 99-03; C Stepney St Dunstan and All SS *Lon* 03-06. *Address temp unknown* E-mail simon_patch@lineone.net

PATCHELL, Miss Gwendoline Rosa. b 49. Goldsmiths' Coll Lon BA69 TCert70. Trin Coll Bris 90. **d** 92 **p** 94. C Ashton-upon-Mersey St Mary Magd *Ches* 92-98; TV Hemel Hempstead *St Alb* 98-06; P-in-c Kirkby in Ashfield *S'well* from 06. *The Rectory, 12 Church Street, Kirkby-in-Ashfield, Nottingham NG17 8LE* Tel (01623) 720030

PATCHING, Colin John. b 47. Linc Th Coll 84. **d** 86 **p** 87. C Farnley *Ripon* 86-89; C Didcot St Pet *Ox* 89-92; P-in-c Steventon w Milton from 92. *The Vicarage, 73 Field Gardens, Steventon, Abingdon OX11 6TF* Tel (01235) 831243

PATE, Barry Emile Charles. b 50. NE Lon Poly BA80 CQSW80. S'wark Ord Course 85. **d** 88 **p** 89. NSM E Dulwich St Jo *S'wark* 88-92; C Farnborough *Roch* 92-94; C Broxbourne w Wormley *St Alb* 94-00; V Wilbury from 00. *Church House, 103 Bedford Road, Letchworth Garden City SG6 4DU* Tel and fax (01462) 623119 E-mail b.pate@ntlworld.com

PATEMAN, Edward Brian. b 29. Leeds Univ BA51. Qu Coll Birm 51. **d** 53 **p** 54. C Stockton St Pet *Dur* 53-57; Lect Bolton St Pet 57-58; V Coxhoe 58-65; V Dalton le Dale 65-93; RD Houghton 72-75; R Hawthorn 88-93; rtd 93. *27 Atherton Drive, Houghton le Spring DH4 6TA* Tel 0191-385 3168

PATEN, Richard Alfred. b 32. Ch Coll Cam BA56 MA60 CEng60 MICE60. Ripon Hall Ox 61. **d** 63 **p** 64. C Oadby *Leic* 63-67; C Pet St Mark 67-71; Chapl Community Relns 71-95; Bp's Dioc Chapl 73-85; rtd 97; Perm to Offic from 93. *19 The Lindens, 86 Lincoln Road, Peterborough PE1 2SN* Tel (01733) 562089

PATERNOSTER, Canon Michael Cosgrove. b 35. Pemb Coll Cam BA59 MA63. Cuddesdon Coll 59. **d** 61 **p** 62. C Surbiton St Andr *S'wark* 61-63; Chapl Qu Coll Dundee 63-68; Dioc Supernumerary of SS Alb and Sergius 68-71; R Dollar *St And* 71-75; R Stonehaven *Bre* 75-90; Hon Can St Paul's Cathl Dundee from 81; R Aberdeen St Jas 90-00; rtd 00; Perm to Offic *B & W* from 00. *12 Priest Row, Wells BA5 2PY*

PATERSON, Alan (Brother Alan Michael). **d** 06 **p** 07. NSM Bartley Green *Birm* from 06. *St Clare's House, 2 Fourlands Road, Birmingham B31 1EX*

PATERSON (née SOAR), Mrs Angela Margaret. b 59. Aston Univ MSc81 MCIPD82. SAOMC 97. **d** 00 **p** 01. NSM Icknield *Ox* from 00. *86 Hill Road, Watlington OX49 5AF* Tel (01491) 614034 E-mail angela@patersonlink.co.uk

PATERSON, David. b 33. Ch Ch Ox BA55 MA58. Linc Th Coll 56. **d** 58 **p** 59. C Kidderminster St Mary *Worc* 58-60; C Wolverhampton St Geo *Lich* 60-64; V Loughborough St Pet *Leic* 64-04; rtd 04; Perm to Offic *Ox* from 05. *487 Marston Road, Marston, Oxford OX3 0JQ* Tel (01865) 726842 E-mail davidpaterson129@hotmail.com

PATERSON, Douglas Monro. b 30. Em Coll Cam BA54 MA57. Tyndale Hall Bris 55. **d** 57 **p** 58. C Walcot *B & W* 57-60; C Portman Square St Paul *Lon* 60-62; Lect Oak Hill Th Coll 60-62; Min Hampstead St Jo Downshire Hill Prop Chpl *Lon* 62-65; Lect All Nations Chr Coll Ware 62-65; Rwanda 67-73; C Edin

St Thos 73-75; Lect Northumbria Bible Coll 73-94; Perm to Offic *Edin* 75-94; Lic to Offic *Newc* 76-94; rtd 94; Perm to Offic *Ox* from 94. *3 Penn Mead, Church Road, Penn, High Wycombe HP10 8NY* Tel (01494) 812496

PATERSON, Geoffrey Gordon. b 45. Cant Univ (NZ) LTh69. **d** 69 **p** 70. New Zealand 69-74 and from 80; C Belfast-Redwood 70-74; V Mayfield Mt Somers 75-78; P-in-c Astwood Bank w Crabbs Cross *Worc* 78-80; V Halswell-Prebbleton from 80. *19 Ridder Place, Christchurch 8003, New Zealand* Tel (0064) (3) 322 7787 *or* 365 3211

PATERSON, Gordon Ronald (Ron). b 16. MBE57. Ripon Hall Ox 58. **d** 59 **p** 60. C Warblington w Emsworth *Portsm* 59-62; V Swanmore St Barn 62-85; RD Bishop's Waltham 79-82; rtd 85; Perm to Offic *Win* 85-95 and *Portsm* from 85. *28 Eastways, Bishops Waltham, Southampton SO32 1EX* Tel (01489) 895671

PATERSON, James Beresford. b 21. DSC42. St Andr Univ MPhil85 FRSA93. Westcott Ho Cam 59. **d** 61 **p** 62. C Woodbridge St Mary *St E* 61-64; R Broughty Ferry *Bre* 64-72; Dioc Supernumerary 72-75; Sec Scottish Ch Action for World Development 72-79; P-in-c Glencarse 76-84; Dioc Sec 79-84; Hon Can St Paul's Cathl Dundee 79-89; rtd 84; Perm to Offic *Bre* and *St E* from 84. *67 Ipswich Road, Woodbridge IP12 4BT* Tel (01394) 383512

PATERSON, Mrs Jennifer Ann. b 49. Brooklands Tech Coll 69. S Dios Minl Tr Scheme 85. **d** 88 **p** 95. C Hale *Guildf* 88-92; NSM Seale, Puttenham and Wanborough 95-01; rtd 01; Perm to Offic *Guildf* 94-95 and from 01. *4 St George's Close, Badshot Lea, Farnham GU9 9LZ* Tel (01252) 316775 E-mail buao91@exchange.uk.com

✠**PATERSON, The Rt Revd John Campbell.** b 45. Auckland Univ BA66. St Jo Coll Auckland. **d** 69 **p** 70 **c** 95. C Whangarei New Zealand 69-71; V Waimate Maori N Pastorate 71-76; Co-Missr Auckland Maori Miss 76; Chapl Qu Victoria Sch 76-82; CF 76-84; Sec Bishopric of Aotearoa 78-87; Prov Sec 86-92; Gen Sec Angl Ch in Aotearoa, NZ and Polynesia 92-95; Bp Auckland from 95; Presiding Bp and Primate New Zealand 98-04. *PO Box 37-242, Parnell, Auckland 1033, New Zealand* Tel (0064) (9) 302 7202 Fax 302 7217 E-mail bishop.auckland@xtra.co.nz

PATERSON, Michael Séan. b 61. Heythrop Coll Lon BD89 MA95 Univ of Wales (Lamp) MMin04. **d** 04 **p** 05. C Stonehaven *Bre* 04-05; C Arbroath 05-06; C Edin Ch Ch 06-08; Chapl St Andr Hospice Airdrie from 08. *St Andrew's Hospice, 1 Henderson Street, Airdrie ML6 6DJ* Tel (01236) 766951 Fax 748787 E-mail rev.pilgrim@btinternet.com

PATERSON, Nigel John Merrick. b 53. Lanc Univ BEd75 Open Univ MA89. **d** 01 **p** 02. OLM N Walsham and Edingthorpe *Nor* from 01. *Marshgate Cottage, Marshgate, North Walsham NR28 9LG* Tel (01692) 406259 Mobile 07786-381361 E-mail nigel-paterson@tiscali.co.uk

PATERSON, Rex Douglas Trevor. b 27. AKC54. **d** 55 **p** 56. C Maidenhead St Luke *Ox* 55-58; C Littlehampton St Mary *Chich* 58-62; V Woodingdean 62-73; V Ferring 73-94; rtd 94; Perm to Offic *Chich* from 94. *14 Hurst Avenue, Worthing BN11 5NY* Tel (01903) 504252

✠**PATERSON, The Rt Revd Robert Mar Erskine.** b 49. St Jo Coll Dur BA71 MA82. Cranmer Hall Dur. **d** 72 **p** 73 **c** 08. C Harpurhey St Steph and Harpurhey Ch Ch *Man* 72-73; C Sketty *S & B* 73-78; R Llangattock and Llangynidr 78-83; V Gabalfa *Llan* 83-94; TR Cowbridge 94-00; Prin Officer Ch in Wales Coun for Miss and Min 00-06; Metrop Can from 04; Abp's Chapl and Researcher *York* 06-08; Bp S & M from 08. *The yn Aspick, The Falls, Tromode Road, Douglas, Isle of Man IM4 4PZ* Tel (01624) 622108 Fax 672890 E-mail bishop-sodor@iommail.com

PATERSON, Robin Fergus (Robert). b 32. Moore Th Coll Sydney 83. **d** 87 **p** 89. Singapore 87-88; NSM Crieff *St And* 88-92; NSM Comrie 88-92; R Dunkeld 93-98; R Strathtay 93-98; rtd 98; Lic to Offic *St And* and *Eur* from 98. *1 Corsiehill House, Corsiehill, Perth PH2 7BN* Tel (01738) 446621 E-mail robinatcorsie@talktalk.net

PATERSON, Robin Lennox Andrew. b 43. NOC 84. **d** 87 **p** 88. C Manston *Ripon* 87-91; P-in-c Leeds All So 91-95; V 95-98; V Middleton St Mary 98-08; rtd 08. *22 Manston Way, Leeds LS15 8BR* Tel 07778-860178 (mobile) E-mail rlap@ntlworld.com

PATERSON, Rodney John. b 62. Keele Univ BA84. St Jo Coll Nottm MA98. **d** 98 **p** 99. C Huddersfield H Trin *Wakef* 98-01; P-in-c Charlton Kings H Apostles *Glouc* from 01. *The Vicarage, Langton Grove Road, Charlton Kings, Cheltenham GL52 6JA* Tel (01242) 512254

PATERSON, Ron. See PATERSON, Gordon Ronald

PATERSON, Stuart Maxwell. b 37. Kelham Th Coll 57 Lich Th Coll 58. **d** 60 **p** 61. C Ilkeston St Mary *Derby* 60-64; V Somercotes 64-70; R Wingerworth 70-73; P-in-c Hawick *Edin* 92-95; R 95-00; rtd 00; Perm to Offic *Ab* 05-08; P-in-c Aberdeen St Jas from 08. *31 Gladstone Place, Aberdeen AB10 6UX* Tel (01224) 321714 E-mail max.stjames@btinternet.com

PATERSON, Mrs Susan Ann. b 57. St Hilda's Coll Ox MA84. EMMTC 92. **d** 95 **p** 96. NSM Evington *Leic* 95-98; C Humberstone 98-03; TV Melton Mowbray 03-09; P-in-c Ab

Kettleby and Holwell w Asfordby from 09. *The Rectory, 2 Church Lane, Asfordby, Melton Mowbray LE14 3RU* Tel (01664) 813130 E-mail spaterson@leicester.anglican.org

PATIENT, Terence Ian. b 35. Open Univ BA83. **d** 96 **p** 97. OLM Old Catton *Nor* 96-05; Perm to Offic from 05. *8 Players Way, Norwich NR6 7AU* Tel (01603) 427899 E-mail mandt.patient@virgin.net

PATO, Luke Luscombe Lungile. b 49. Fort Hare Univ BA76 Manitoba Univ MA80. St Bede's Coll Umtata. **d** 73 **p** 75. S Africa 73-81 and from 92; Canada 81-90; Tutor Coll of Ascension Selly Oak 90-92. *PO Box 62098, Marshalltown, 2107 South Africa* Tel (0027) (11) 763 2510 *or* 492 1380 Mobile 83-367 3961 E-mail luke@cpsa.org.za

PATON, David. *See* PATON, Preb John David Marshall

PATON, George Hemsell. b 23. Wadh Coll Ox MA49. Oak Hill Th Coll 50. **d** 52 **p** 53. C Earlham St Anne *Nor* 52-54; C Darfield *Sheff* 54-56; Area Sec CMS *Ely* 56-62; *St E* and *Nor* 56-66; P-in-c Kemp Town St Mark *Chich* 66-67; V Kemp Town St Mark and St Matt 67-71; R Ripe w Chalvington 71-76; R Laughton w Ripe and Chalvington 77-78; V Iford w Kingston and Rodmell 78-90; rtd 90; Perm to Offic *Chich* from 90. *70 Clevedown, Barons Down Road, Lewes BN7 1EY*

PATON, Canon Ian James. b 57. Jes Coll Cam MA78 PGCE79. Westcott Ho Cam MA81. **d** 82 **p** 83. C Whitley Ch Ch *Ox* 82-84; Bp's Dom Chapl 84-86; Chapl Wadh Coll Ox 86-90; C Ox St Mary V w St Cross and St Pet 86-90; Can and Vice Provost St Mary's Cathl Edin 90-94; R Edin St Mary 90-94; R Haddington and Dunbar 94-97; R Edin Old St Paul from 97; Can St Mary's Cathl from 04. *Lauder House, 39 Jeffrey Street, Edinburgh EH1 1DH* Tel 0131-556 3332 Mobile 07751-510594 E-mail rector@osp.org.uk

PATON, Preb John David Marshall. b 47. Barrister-at-Law (Middle Temple) 71. St Steph Ho Ox 81. **d** 83 **p** 84. C Bethnal Green St Matt w St Jas the Gt *Lon* 83-86; P-in-c St Geo-in-the-East St Mary 86-89; V 89-92; P-in-c Bethnal Green St Barn 92-96; AD Tower Hamlets 92-96; Dir Post-Ord Tr 92-99; P-in-c St Vedast w St Mich-le-Querne etc 97-06; P-in-c St Botolph without Bishopsgate 97-06; AD The City 00-06; Preb St Paul's Cathl from 04; Master R Foundn of St Kath in Ratcliffe from 06. *The Royal Foundation of St Katharine, 2 Butcher Row, London E14 8DS* Tel (020) 7790 3540 Fax 7702 7603 E-mail enquiries@stkatharine.org.uk

PATON, John William Scholar. b 52. Mert Coll Ox BA74 MA95. St Steph Ho Ox 93. **d** 95 **p** 96. C Sherborne w Castleton and Lillington *Sarum* 95-98; Succ S'wark Cathl 98-01; Chapl Medical and Dental Students K Coll Lon 98-01; P-in-c Purley St Mark 01-07; P-in-c Purley St Swithun 05-07; Prec Ch Ch Ox from 07. *Christ Church, Oxford OX1 1DP* Tel (01865) 276150 E-mail john_w_s_paton@msn.com

PATON, The Ven Michael John Macdonald. b 22. Magd Coll Ox BA49 MA54. Linc Th Coll 52. **d** 54 **p** 55. C Gosforth All SS *Newc* 54-57; V Norton Woodseats St Chad *Sheff* 57-67; Sen Chapl Sheff United Hosps 67-70; Chapl Weston Park Hosp Sheff 70-78; V Sheff St Mark Broomhall 70-78; Adn Sheff 78-87; Can Res Sheff Cathl 78-87; rtd 88; Perm to Offic *Sheff* from 88. *947 Abbeydale Road, Sheffield S7 2QD* Tel 0114-236 6148

PATON-WILLIAMS, David Graham. b 58. Warwick Univ BA81 Selw Coll Cam BA86 MA90 Newc Univ MA92. Ridley Hall Cam 84. **d** 87 **p** 88. C S Westoe *Dur* 87-90; C Newton Aycliffe 90-91; TV 91-93; Chapl Univ Coll of Ripon and York St Jo 93-98; Min Can Ripon Cathl 93-98; R Bedale 98-02; P-in-c Leeming 98-02; R Bedale and Leeming 03-08; P-in-c Thornton Watlass 07-08; R Bedale and Leeming and Thornton Watlass 08; AD Wensley 05-08; V Roundhay St Edm from 08. *St Edmund's Vicarage, 5A North Park Avenue, Leeds LS8 1DN* Tel 0113-266 2550 E-mail davidpw@onetel.net

PATRICIA, Sister. *See* PERKINS, Patricia Doris

PATRICIA ANN, Sister. *See* GORDON, Sister Patricia Ann

PATRICK, Charles. *See* PATRICK, Peter Charles

PATRICK, Hugh Joseph. b 37. TCD BA62 MA66. **d** 63 **p** 64. C Dromore Cathl 63-66; C Lurgan Ch the Redeemer 66-70; C Rothwell *Ripon* 70-73; V Thurnscoe St Hilda *Sheff* 73-78; V Wales 78-02; P-in-c Thorpe Salvin 78-82; RD Laughton 93-98; rtd 02; Perm to Offic *Sheff* from 02. *5 Fairfax Avenue, Worksop S81 7RH* Tel (01909) 477622 E-mail hughpatrick@sky.com

PATRICK, James Harry Johnson. b 67. Birm Poly LLB88 Barrister 89. STETS 96 St Steph Ho Ox 99. **d** 99 **p** 00. Hon C Clifton All SS w St Jo *Bris* from 99. *4 Clifton Park Road, Bristol BS8 3HL* Tel 0117-908 0460 Fax 930 3813 Mobile 07768-340344 E-mail jp@guildhallchambers.co.uk

PATRICK, Canon John Andrew. b 62. St Jo Coll Dur BA84. Ripon Coll Cuddesdon 87. **d** 89 **p** 90. C Frankby w Greasby *Ches* 89-92; Lect Boston *Linc* 92-95; P-in-c Graffoe Gp 95-97; V 97-02; P-in-c New Sleaford from 02; Can and Preb Linc Cathl from 07; RD Lafford from 08. *The Vicarage, Market Place, Sleaford NG34 7SH* Tel (01529) 302177 E-mail japatrick1@btinternet.com

PATRICK, John Peter. b 23. AKC. d 52 p 53. C S Westoe *Dur* 52-55; C Woodhouse *Wakef* 55-58; C Batley All SS 58-59; V Upperthong 59-75; V Slaithwaite w E Scammonden 75-80; V Donington *Linc* 80-92; rtd 92; Perm to Offic *Linc* 92-01. *Little Paddock, 140 Main Road, Hundleby, Spilsby PE23 5NQ* Tel (01790) 752304

PATRICK, Peter Charles. b 64. Leeds Univ BA86 Fitzw Coll Cam BA91 MA95. Ridley Hall Cam 89. d 92 p 93. C Barton upon Humber *Linc* 92-96; TV Gt Grimsby St Mary and St Jas 96-03; RD Grimsby and Cleethorpes 99-03; R Middle Rasen Gp from 03; P-in-c Barkwith Gp from 07. *The Vicarage, North Street, Middle Rasen, Market Rasen LN8 3TS* Tel (01673) 842249 E-mail charles.patrick@talk21.com

PATSTON, Raymond Sidney Richard. b 26. Kelham Th Coll 47. d 51 p 52. C Hammersmith H Innocents *Lon* 51-53; C Acton Green St Pet 53-56; Area Sec E Counties UMCA 56-62; C Chesterton St Luke *Ely* 56-59; R Downham Market w Bexwell 61-71; V Clee *Linc* 71-97; rtd 97. *Ashlea Court Care Home, Church Lane, Waltham, Grimsby DN37 0ES* Tel (01472) 822666

PATTEN (née STARNS), Mrs Helen Edna. b 43. St Hilda's Coll Ox BA65 Maria Grey Coll Lon CertEd70. Trin Coll Bris 73 Oak Hill Th Coll 81. dss 82 d 87 p 94. Tunbridge Wells St Jo *Roch* 82-86; Patcham *Chich* 86-91; Par Dn 87-91; Par Dn Eckington w Handley and Ridgeway *Derby* 91-94; C 94-95; TV 95-98; Chapl St Mich Hospice 98-03; rtd 03; Hon C Fairlight, Guestling and Pett *Chich* from 04. *Holyoak, Workhouse Lane, Westfield, Hastings TN35 4QJ* Tel (01424) 752052

PATTENDEN, Mrs Alison Margaret. b 53. Eastbourne Tr Coll CertEd75 Sussex Univ BEd76. St Steph Ho Ox 04. d 06 p 07. C Goring-by-Sea *Chich* from 06. *19 Angus Road, Goring-by-Sea, Worthing BN12 4BL* Tel (01903) 700284 E-mail alison.pattenden@btinternet.com

PATTERSON, Alfred Percy. d 85 p 87. NSM Aghalee *D & D* 85-91; C Gilford 91-93; Bp's C 93-95; I 95-00; rtd 00. *Brookdale, 723 Upper Newtownards Road, Belfast BT4 3NU* Tel (028) 9029 4741 E-mail revap.patterson@ntlworld.com

PATTERSON, Andrew John. b 56. Master Mariner 85. Qu Coll Birm 85. d 88 p 89. C Newc St Phil and St Aug 88-92; Chapl Hunter's Moor Hosp 91-92; Asst Chapl R Victoria Infirmary Newc 92-96; V Whitley *Newc* from 96; Chapl Hexham Gen Hosp from 96. *The Vicarage, Whitley, Hexham NE46 2LA* Tel (01434) 673379

PATTERSON, Anthony. b 43. Moore Th Coll Sydney BTh82. d 83 p 83. Australia 83-91; C Darfield *Sheff* 91-94; TR Marfleet *York* 94-99; TV Heeley and Gleadless Valley *Sheff* 99-04; TR from 04; AD Attercliffe from 04. *Heeley Vicarage, 151 Gleadless Road, Sheffield S2 3AE* Tel 0114-255 7718 E-mail tony@yahoo.co.uk

PATTERSON, Charles David Gilliat. b 40. Oak Hill Th Coll 71. d 74 p 75. C Brompton H Trin *Lon* 74-77; C Spring Grove St Mary 77-80; V Bures *St E* 80-92; R Bath Weston St Jo w Kelston *B & W* 92-01; rtd 01; Perm to Offic *Ox* from 02. *Grove Mill, Mill Lane, Grove, Wantage OX12 7HU* Tel (01235) 772013

PATTERSON, Colin Hugh. b 52. St Pet Coll Ox MA77 Univ of Wales (Cardiff) MPhil90 CertEd75. Trin Coll Bris. d 87 p 88. C Blackb Sav 87-90; C Haughton le Skerne *Dur* 90-93; Adult Educn Adv 93-05; Asst Dir Bridge Builders from 05; NSM Dur St Nic from 05. *24 Monks Crescent, Durham DH1 1HD* Tel 0191-386 1691 E-mail colinpatterson@menno.org.uk

PATTERSON, Colin Peter Matthew. b 62. Newc Poly BA84. St Steph Ho Ox 92. d 94 p 95. C Cullercoats St Geo *Newc* 94-97; Shrine P Shrine of Our Lady of Walsingham 97-99; P-in-c Harlow St Mary Magd *Chelmsf* 99-00; V 00-09; V Willesden Green St Andr and St Fran *Lon* from 09; CMP from 97. *The Clergy House, St Andrew's Road, London NW10 2QS* Tel (020) 8459 2670 E-mail cpmp1@btinternet.com

PATTERSON, Mrs Diane Rosemary. b 46. WMMTC 88. d 91 p 94. C Hill *Birm* 91-95; Perm to Offic 95-96; C Shottery St Andr *Cov* 96-01; C Hunningham from 01; C Wappenbury w Weston under Wetherley from 01; C Long Itchington and Marton from 01; C Offchurch from 01; RD Southam 02-08. *The Vicarage, School Lane, Hunningham, Leamington Spa CV33 9DS* Tel (01926) 633630

PATTERSON, Hugh John. b 38. Southn Univ MPhil76. AKC63. d 64 p 65. C Epsom St Martin *Guildf* 64-65; Chapl Ewell Coll 65-68; Asst Chapl and Lect Bp Otter Coll Chich 68-71; Lect Dudley Coll of Educn 71-77; Lect Wolv Poly 77-92; Wolv Univ 92-00; Chapl 89-00; rtd 01; Hon C Morville w Aston Eyre *Heref* from 82; Hon C Upton Cressett w Monk Hopton from 82; Hon C Acton Round from 82. *6 Victoria Road, Bridgnorth WV16 4LA* Tel (01746) 765298

PATTERSON, John. *See* PATTERSON, Norman John

PATTERSON, John. b 27. MRTM76. Bps' Coll Cheshunt 60. d 61 p 62. C Maidenhead St Luke *Ox* 61-65; Chapl RAF 65-72; V Ashton St Jas *Man* 72-78; USA 78-90; R Somercotes and Grainthorpe w Conisholme *Linc* 90-92; rtd 92; Perm to Offic *Linc* from 92. *9 Simpson Close, Barrow-upon-Humber DN19 7BL* Tel (01469) 30867

PATTERSON, John Norton. b 39. TCD BA64 MA68. d 65 p 66. C Belfast St Paul *Conn* 65-68; C Larne and Inver 68-72; I Ballintoy w Rathlin and Dunseverick 72-05; Miss to Seafarers 72-05; Can Belf Cathl 97-05; Adn Dalriada *Conn* 01-05; rtd 05. *31 Moycraig Road, Dunseverick, Bushmills BT57 8TB* Tel (028) 2073 0654

PATTERSON, Marjorie Jean. *See* BROWN, Mrs Marjorie Jean

PATTERSON, Neil Sydney. b 79. BNC Ox BA00 MA04. Ripon Coll Cuddesdon BA03. d 04 p 05. C Cleobury Mortimer w Hopton Wafers etc *Heref* 04-08; TV Ross 08; V Ariconium from 08. *The Rectory, Weston under Penyard, Ross-on-Wye HR9 7QA* Tel (01989) 567229 E-mail pattersonneil@hotmail.com

PATTERSON, Norman John. b 47. Peterho Cam BA69 ALCD. St Jo Coll Nottm 70. d 73 p 74. C Everton St Ambrose w St Tim *Liv* 73-74; C Everton St Pet 74-78; TV 79-84; C Aigburth and Dioc Adv for Past Care and Counselling 84-92; V Gt Crosby All SS 92-05; Crosslinks Uganda from 05. *PO Box 20, Hoima, Uganda* E-mail patterson@crosslinks.org

PATTERSON, Patric Douglas MacRae. b 51. Wycliffe Hall Ox 73. d 76 p 77. C Bebington *Ches* 76-79; Canada from 79. *The Rectory, PO Box 10, Milford ON K0K 2P0, Canada*

PATTERSON, The Ven Philip Fredrick. b 56. Ulster Univ BSc QUB BD. d 82 p 83. C Lurgan Ch the Redeemer *D & D* 82-86; I Carrowdore w Millisle 86-89; I Knockbreda from 89; Preb Down Cathl from 00; Dioc Registrar 00-07; Adn Down from 07. *Knockbreda Rectory, 69 Church Road, Newtownbreda, Belfast BT8 4AN* Tel and fax (028) 9064 1493 E-mail pfpatterson@hotmail.com

PATTERSON, Scott Robert. b 71. GTCL92. Oak Hill Th Coll 07. d 09. C Newton Tracey, Horwood, Alverdiscott etc *Ex* from 09. *The Rectory, Beaford, Winkleigh EX19 8NN* Tel 07973-139092 (mobile) E-mail scottr.patterson@btinternet.com

PATTERSON, The Very Revd Susan Margaret. b 48. Otago Univ BA71 BD89 PhD92. Knox Coll Dunedin 84. d 88 p 89. New Zealand 88-91 and 92-97; C Dunedin St Martin 88-91; Tutor Otago Univ and Knox Coll 89-91; USA 91-92; Assoc P Hawke's Bay 92-96; Lect Trin Coll Bris 97-00; I Kildallon w Newtowngore and Corrawallen *K, E & A* 00-04; I Killala w Dunfeeny, Crossmolina, Kilmoremoy etc *T, K & A* from 04; Dean Killala from 05. *St Michael's Rectory, Church Road, Ballina, Co Mayo, Republic of Ireland* Tel (00353) (96) 77894 Mobile 86-605 7829 E-mail kilmoremoy@killala.anglican.org

PATTERSON, Trevor Harold. b 60. QUB BA82 Stranmillis Coll PGCE83. Trin Coll Bris 91. d 93 p 94. C Ashtead *Guildf* 93-98; V Richmond H Trin and Ch Ch *S'wark* from 98. *Holy Trinity Vicarage, Sheen Park, Richmond TW9 1UP* Tel (020) 8404 1114 E-mail trevor.patterson@htrichmond.org.uk

PATTIMORE, Daniel James. b 64. Nottm Univ MEng88 Lon Bible Coll BA94. Wycliffe Hall Ox 97. d 99 p 00. C Charlesworth and Dinting Vale *Derby* 99-03; NSM Norley, Crowton and Kingsley *Ches* 03-04; P-in-c Heanor *Derby* from 04. *The Vicarage, 1A Mundy Street, Heanor DE75 7EB* Tel (01773) 719800 Mobile 07973-406022 E-mail dan.pattimore@tiscali.co.uk

PATTIMORE (née GORDON), Mrs Kristy. b 72. Leeds Univ BA94 Newc Univ PGCE95. Wycliffe Hall Ox 98. d 01 p 02. C Hallwood *Ches* 01-04; NSM Heanor *Derby* from 04. *The Vicarage, 1A Mundy Street, Heanor DE75 7EB* Tel (01773) 719800

PATTINSON, Christine Brodie. b 43. Darlington Tr Coll CertEd64. d 06 p 07. OLM Chertsey, Lyne and Longcross *Guildf* from 06. *28 Moorfields Close, Staines TW18 3LU* Tel (01784) 457260 E-mail cbpattinson@btinternet.com

PATTINSON, Richard Clive. b 46. Keble Coll Ox BA68 MA84. CBDTI 98. d 00 p 01. C Hesket-in-the-Forest and Armathwaite *Carl* 00-04; C Inglewood Gp 04-05; P-in-c Dacre from 05; TV Penrith w Newton Reigny and Plumpton Wall from 05. *Dacre Vicarage, 12 Keld Close, Stainton, Penrith CA11 0EJ* Tel (01768) 890530

PATTINSON, Robert James. St Mich Coll Llan. d 04 p 05. C Llanelli *St D* 04-07; TV Dewisland from 07; Min Can St D Cathl from 07. *Whitchurch Vicarage, Solva, Haverfordwest SA62 6UD* Tel (01437) 721281

PATTISON, Anthony. b 50. Heriot-Watt Univ BSc72 MRPharmS73. Sarum & Wells Th Coll 85. d 87 p 88. C Cullercoats St Geo *Newc* 87-89; Ind Chapl 89-99; C Cramlington 89-91; TV 91-99; TR Benwell 99-07; V Killingworth from 07. *The New Vicarage, West Lane, Killingworth Village, Newcastle upon Tyne NE12 6BL* Tel 0191-268 3242 E-mail pattison@lineone.net

PATTISON, Prof George Linsley. b 50. Edin Univ MA72 BD77 Dur Univ PhD89. Edin Th Coll 74. d 77 p 78. C Benwell St Jas *Newc* 77-80; P-in-c Kimblesworth *Dur* 80-83; R Badwell Ash w Gt Ashfield, Stowlangtoft etc *St E* 83-91; Dean of Chpl K Coll Cam 91-01; Lect Aarhus Univ Denmark 01-04; Lady Marg Prof Div Ox Univ from 04; Can Res Ch Ch *Ox* from 04. *Christ Church, Oxford OX1 1DP* Tel (01865) 276247 E-mail george.pattison@theology.ox.ac.uk

PATTISON, Stephen Bewley. b 53. Selw Coll Cam BA76. Edin Th Coll 76. **d** 78 **p** 80. C Gosforth All SS *Newc* 78-79; NSM St Nic Hosp Newc 78-82; Hon C Newc St Thos Prop Chpl 80-82; Chapl Edin Th Coll 82-83; Lect Past Studies Birm Univ 83-88; Perm to Offic *Birm* 83-86 and 87-00; Hon C Moseley St Mary 86-87. *11A Salisbury Road, Moseley, Birmingham B13 8JS* Tel 0121-449 3023

PATTLE (née OLIVER), Mrs Suzanne Marie. b 66. LMH Ox BA88 SSEES Lon MA91. Trin Coll Bris BTS03. **d** 03 **p** 04. C Rainham *Roch* 03-07; P-in-c Gillingham St Mary from 07. *The Vicarage, 27 Gillingham Green, Gillingham ME7 1SS* Tel (01634) 850529 Mobile 07971-073093
E-mail suzanne.pattle@diocese-rochester.org

PATTMAN, Andrew. b 53. Didsbury Coll Man BEd75. Westcott Ho Cam. **d** 95 **p** 96. C Washington *Dur* 95-98; Children's Work Adv *St Alb* 98-02; Perm to Offic 04-05. *110 Marshalswick Lane, St Albans AL1 4XE* Tel (01727) 841201

PAUL, Brother. *See* SINGLETON, Ernest George

PAUL, Ian Benjamin. b 62. St Jo Coll Ox BA84 MA88 Southn Univ MSc85 Nottm Univ BTh91 PhD98. St Jo Coll Nottm 89. **d** 96 **p** 97. C Longfleet *Sarum* 96-00; NSM 00-04; Visiting Lect Trin Coll Bris 00-01; Th Adv Dioc Bd of Min *Sarum* 00-04; Tutor Sarum OLM Scheme 00-04; Visiting Lect STETS 00-04; Dir Partnership Development St Jo Coll Nottm 04-05; Dean of Studies from 05. *St John's College, Chilwell Lane, Bramcote, Nottingham NG9 3DS* Tel 0115-925 1114 ext 254
E-mail ian.paul@stjohns-nottm.ac.uk
or ian.paul@grovebooks.co.uk

PAUL, Canon John Douglas. b 28. Edin Univ MA52. Ely Th Coll 52. **d** 54 **p** 55. C Portsea Ascension *Portsm* 54-56; Nyasaland 56-60; Portuguese E Africa 60-70; Adn Metangula 65-70; R Castle Douglas *Glas* 70-75; R Edin St Mark 75-80; R Elgin w Lossiemouth *Mor* 80-92; Syn Clerk 89-91; Hon Can St Andr Cathl Inverness from 89; Dean Mor 91-92; rtd 92. *2 The Avenue, Gifford, Haddington EH41 4QX* Tel (01620) 810547

PAUL, John Matthew. b 61. K Coll Lon BA82 Fitzw Coll Cam BA88 MA92. Westcott Ho Cam 86. **d** 89 **p** 90. C Writtle w Highwood *Chelmsf* 89-94; Min Can and Chapl St Paul's Cathl 94-96; Min Can and Sacr St Paul's Cathl 96-99; V Winchmore Hill St Paul from 99; AD Enfield from 04. *St Paul's Vicarage, Church Hill, London N21 1JA* Tel (020) 8886 3545
E-mail john.paul@london.anglican.org

PAUL, Naunihal Chand (Nihal). b 40. Allahabad Univ MA. Bangalore Th Coll BD. **d** 69 **p** 70. C Simla Ch Ch India 69-70; V Kangra w Dharamsala 70-74; C Urmston *Man* 75-77; Perm to Offic Farnworth St Pet 77-80; TV E Farnworth and Kearsley 80-83; TV Laindon St Martin and St Nic w Nevendon *Chelmsf* 83-90; R Laindon w Dunton 90-05; rtd 05; Perm to Offic *Chelmsf* from 06. *3 Wellstye Green, Basildon SS14 2SR*
E-mail rupriwas@aol.com

PAUL, Roger Philip. b 53. Clare Coll Cam BA74 MA88 CertEd76 Open Univ PhD98. Westcott Ho Cam 78. **d** 81 **p** 82. C Coventry Caludon 81-85; R Warmington w Shotteswell and Radway w Ratley 85-98; R Kirkby Stephen w Mallerstang etc *Carl* 98-08; Nat Adv (Unity in Miss) Coun for Chr Unity from 08. *Council for Christian Unity, Church House, Great Smith Street, London SW1P 3AZ* Tel (020) 7898 1473
E-mail roger.paul@c-of-e.org.uk

PAUL, Rosalind Miranda. b 53. Man Univ BA74 Bris Univ PGCE77 Paris Univ LèsL86 Open Univ MBA95. Ripon Coll Cuddesdon 05. **d** 07 **p** 08. C Budock *Truro* from 07; C Mawnan from 07; R Higham, Holton St Mary, Raydon and Stratford *St E* from 09. *The Rectory, Raydon, Ipswich IP7 5LH* Tel 07715-535748 (mobile) E-mail rosalind.paul@yahoo.co.uk

PAUL, Simon Nicholas. b 56. Hull Univ BA81 PGCE82. Trin Coll Bris BA95. **d** 95 **p** 96. C Cranleigh *Guildf* 95-99; P-in-c Broughton and Duddon *Carl* 99-04; Chapl Ranby Ho Sch Retford from 04. *Ranby House School, Retford DN22 5HX* Tel (01777) 703138

PAVEY, Canon Angela Mary. b 55. Hull Univ BA77 Nottm Univ BCommStuds84 Univ of Wales (Lamp) MA06. Linc Th Coll 81. **dss** 84 **d** 87 **p** 94. Linc St Faith and St Martin w St Pet 84-86; Chapl Boston Coll of FE 87-95; Asst Min Officer *Linc* 89-95; C Birchwood 95-97; Dioc Dir of Ords 97-07; P-in-c Linc St Faith and St Martin w St Pet from 07; Chapl Lincs Partnership NHS Trust from 07; Can and Preb Linc Cathl from 00. *The Vicarage, 165C Carholme Road, Lincoln LN1 1RU* Tel (01522) 829385
E-mail a.pavey1@ntlworld.com

PAVEY, John Bertram. b 51. Keele Univ BA73 Hull Univ PGCE74 MEd95. Linc Th Coll 81. **d** 83 **p** 84. C Boultham *Linc* 83-86; R Fishtoft 86-95; P-in-c Birchwood 95-01; V from 01. *St Luke's Vicarage, Jasmin Road, Lincoln LN6 0YR* Tel (01522) 688665 E-mail j.pavey@ntlworld.com

PAVLOU, Michael. b 55. St Jo Coll Nottm BA. **d** 06 **p** 07. C Woodside Park St Barn *Lon* from 06. *Oakleigh Community Church, 168/170 Oakleigh Road North, London N20 0UB* Tel (020) 8368 4021 Mobile 07956-573217
E-mail mike@pavi.freeserve.co.uk

PAVYER, Miss Jennifer Elizabeth. b 75. Ex Univ BSc96 Cam Univ BTh02. Westcott Ho Cam 99. **d** 02 **p** 03. C Stevenage St Andr and St Geo *St Alb* 02-05; C Harpenden St Nic from 05. *86 Tufnells Way, Harpenden AL5 3HG* Tel (01582) 762485
E-mail jenny.pavyer@ukgateway.net

PAWSEY, Jack Edward. b 35. Trin Coll Ox BA59 MA65. Westcott Ho Cam 64. **d** 66 **p** 67. Sec Coun Soc Aid *S'wark* 66-75; Race Relns Worker 75-78; Acting Sec Coun Soc Aid 78-82; Perm to Offic 84-86 and from 98; Hon C Camberwell St Geo 86-98; Staff Cllr Westmr Past Foundn 87-97. *20 Addington Square, London SE5 7JZ* Tel (020) 7701 8920

PAWSON (née ROYLE), Mrs Gillian Mary. b 57. Kingston Univ BA79 Roehampton Inst PGCE82. SEITE 99. **d** 02 **p** 03. C Wimbledon *S'wark* 02-06; P-in-c Merton St Jo 06-09; P-in-c Colliers Wood Ch Ch 06-09; TV Merton Priory from 09. *St John's Vicarage, 135 High Path, London SW19 2JY* Tel (020) 8542 3283 E-mail gillypawson@blueyonder.co.uk

PAWSON, John. b 66. Moorlands Th Coll BA00. Wycliffe Hall Ox. **d** 02 **p** 03. C Bursledon *Win* 02-06; P-in-c Sway from 06. *The Vicarage, Station Road, Sway, Lymington SO41 6BA* Tel (01590) 682358 Mobile 07762-246947
E-mail john@pawson1.wanadoo.co.uk

PAWSON, Preb John Walker. b 38. Kelham Th Coll 58. **d** 63 **p** 64. C N Hull St Mich *York* 63-67; C Lower Gornal *Lich* 67-70; V Tipton St Jo 70-78; V Meir Heath 78-03; RD Stoke 88-98; Preb Lich Cathl 93-03; rtd 03; Perm to Offic *Nor* from 03. *39 Runton Road, Cromer NR27 9AT* Tel (01263) 511715
E-mail pawson.meirton@virgin.net

PAXON, Robin Michael Cuninghame. b 46. St Jo Coll Dur BA69. Westcott Ho Cam 69. **d** 71 **p** 72. C Croydon St Pet S End *Cant* 71-77; C Saffron Walden w Wendens Ambo and Littlebury *Chelmsf* 77-80; P-in-c Plaistow St Mary 80-83; TV Plaistow 83-89; TV Dovercourt and Parkeston 90-95; rtd 95. *20 Park Road, Harwich CO12 3BJ* Tel (01255) 551139

PAXTON, John Ernest. b 49. Ex Univ BA71. Westcott Ho Cam 74. **d** 74 **p** 75. C Redditch St Steph *Worc* 74-77; UAE 77-81; C Bolton St Pet *Man* 81-91; Ind Missr 81-91; TV Southampton (City Cen) *Win* 91-96; R S'wark Ch Ch 96-03; Sen Chapl S Lon Ind Miss 96-03; Adv to Bd of Soc Resp *Worc* from 03. *57 Drovers Way, Worcester WR3 8QD* Tel (01905) 456793 *or* 732819
E-mail jpaxton@cofe-worcester.org.uk

PAXTON, William Neil. b 60. Brunel Univ BSc88 MA90. Ripon Coll Cuddesdon 02. **d** 04 **p** 05. C Camberwell St Geo *S'wark* 04-08; TV Southend *Chelmsf* from 08. *All Saints' Vicarage, 1 Sutton Road, Southend-on-Sea SS2 5PA* Tel (01702) 613440
E-mail neil.paxton@blueyonder.co.uk

PAY, Norman John. b 50. St Jo Coll Dur BA72. Cranmer Hall Dur. **d** 74 **p** 75. C S Moor *Dur* 74-78; C Rawmarsh w Parkgate *Sheff* 78-80; C-in-c New Cantley CD 80-82; V New Cantley 82-89; V Doncaster St Leon and St Jude from 89; Asst Clergy In-Service Tr Officer 90-93. *St Leonard's Vicarage, Barnsley Road, Doncaster DN5 8QE* Tel (01302) 784858

PAYN, Peter Richard. b 33. Moore Th Coll Sydney LTh59. **d** 60 **p** 60. C Pittwater Australia 60-61; C Kensington St Matt 61-63; C Melbourne St Jas w St Jo 63-65; V E Geelong St Matt 65-79; C Blackfr Ch Ch w St Matt 79-81; V Lowestoft Ch Ch *Nor* 81-92; P-in-c Tunbridge Wells St Pet *Roch* 92-96; V 96-03; rtd 03. *Vincent, 24190 Neuvic, France* Tel (0033) (5) 53 81 13 56
E-mail richardpayn@aol.com

PAYNE, Alan. *See* PAYNE, Canon Kenneth Alan

PAYNE, Arthur Edwin. b 37. K Alfred's Coll Win TCert59. St Mich Coll Llan 86. **d** 87 **p** 88. C Swansea St Gabr *S & B* 87-90; Chapl Univ of Wales (Swansea) 87-90; V Brynmawr 90-91; TV Wickford and Runwell *Chelmsf* 91-94; Chapl Runwell Hosp Wickford 91-94; P-in-c Wraxall *B & W* 94-95; Perm to Offic 95-97; V Rhymney *Mon* 97-98; rtd 98. *10 Wickham Court, Sunnyside Road, Clevedon BS21 7TN* Tel (01275) 342653

PAYNE, Cyril Gordon. b 26. Bris Univ BA53. Linc Th Coll 53. **d** 55 **p** 56. C Southall H Trin *Lon* 55-58; C Christchurch *Win* 58-63; V Otterbourne 63-75; V Milford 75-90; rtd 90; Perm to Offic *Win* from 90. *11 Oaklands, Lymington SO41 3TH* Tel (01590) 671274

PAYNE, David Charles. b 62. Univ of Wales (Abth) BLib84. St Jo Coll Nottm MA95. **d** 95 **p** 96. C Horncastle w Low Toynton *Linc* 95-99; V Metheringham w Blankney and Dunston 99-04; Chapl Sherwood Forest Hosps NHS Trust 04-06; R Standon and The Mundens w Sacombe *St Alb* from 06. *The Vicarage, Kents Lane, Standon, Ware SG11 1PJ* Tel (01920) 821390
E-mail davidandjoanna.payne@virgin.net

PAYNE, David James. b 31. Clare Coll Cam BA54 MA61. Wycliffe Hall Ox 60. **d** 62 **p** 63. C Gt Faringdon w Lt Coxwell *Ox* 62-63; C Guildf Ch Ch 63-66; R Shackleford 66-73; R Peper Harow 66-73; R Odell *St Alb* 73-78; Warden Home of Divine Healing Crowhurst 78-84; R Wraxall *B & W* 84-92; rtd 92; Perm to Offic *Glouc* 92-08; *Bris* 00-08; *Ely* from 07; Hon C Finchley St Mary *Lon* 93-95. *29 Hatley Drive, Burwell, Cambridge CB25 0AY* Tel (01638) 741448

PAYNE, David Ronald. b 49. Open Univ BA87. St Mich Coll Llan 88. **d** 90 **p** 91. C Oystermouth *S & B* 90-93; V Penllergaer 93-02;

TV Llanelli *St D* from 02. *The Vicarage, Swiss Valley, Felinfoel, Llanelli SA14 8BS* Tel (01554) 773559

PAYNE, Elizabeth. b 50. Univ Coll Lon BSc92. St Mich Coll Llan 96. d 98 p 99. C Cyncoed *Mon* 98-03; TV 03-04. *7A Cader Idris Close, Risca, Newport NP11 6RP* Tel (01633) 619004

PAYNE, Frederick Gates (Eric). b 19. Jes Coll Cam BA40 MA43. Lon Coll of Div 40. d 42 p 43. C Walcot *B & W* 42-45; CF (EC) 45-48; Hd CMJ Miss Ethiopia 48-67; SW Org Sec CMJ 68-85; rtd 84; Perm to Offic *B & W* from 85 and *Truro* from 91. *83 Penn Lea Road, Bath BA1 3RQ* Tel (01225) 423092

PAYNE, James John Henry. b 26. MBE69. St Pet Hall Ox BA53 MA59. Tyndale Hall Bris 48 Linc Th Coll 53. d 53 p 54. Asst Chapl Mersey Miss to Seamen 53-55; C Stoneycroft All SS *Liv* 55-57; Chapl Igbobi Coll Yaba Nigeria 57-62; Chapl Lagos St Sav 62-88; Dir Lagos Ord Course 81-87; Hon Can Lagos 71-88; rtd 88; Perm to Offic *Ox* 88-93 and from 04; Hon C Uffington, Shellingford, Woolstone and Baulking 93-04. *1 Timberyard Cottages, Church Street, Shellingford, Faringdon SN7 7QA* Tel (01367) 710274
E-mail james@payne2277.freeserve.co.uk

PAYNE, Jeffery Mark. b 68. Lon Sch of Th BTh99. Wycliffe Hall Ox 06. d 08 p 09. C Southall St Geo *Lon* from 08. *St Christopher's Vicarage, 4 Hillyard Road, London W7 1BH* Tel (020) 8578 2796 Mobile 07896-586511
E-mail jeff.payne5@btinternet.com

PAYNE, John. *See* PAYNE, Victor John

PAYNE, John Percival. b 49. Nottm Univ BA70. Cuddesdon Coll 70. d 72 p 73. C Tilehurst St Mich *Ox* 72-76; C Cross Green St Sav and St Hilda *Ripon* 76-79; Chapl St Hilda's Priory Whitby 79-83; V Leeds Belle Is St Jo and St Barn *Ripon* 83-88; Chapl St Hilda's Sch Whitby 88-97; R Loftus and Carlin How w Skinningrove *York* 97-99; Chapl OHP 99-01; Teacher Qu Mary's Sch Thirsk from 02; Chapl from 03. *Queen Mary's School, Baldersby Park, Topcliffe, Thirsk YO7 3BZ* Tel (01765) 609786 *or* 575000 E-mail johnp-virgil@connectfree.co.uk

PAYNE, John Rogan. b 44. Episc Th Coll São Paulo. d 78 p 79. Brazil 78-86; C Ilkley All SS *Bradf* 86-88; R Elvington w Sutton on Derwent and E Cottingwith *York* 88-94. *Manor Farm House, East Flotmanby Road, Muston, Filey YO14 0HX* Tel (01723) 513969

PAYNE, Canon Joseph Marshall. b 17. TCD BA38 MA52. d 40 p 41. C Belfast St Aid *Conn* 40-43; C Ballynafeigh St Jude *D & D* 43-44; Chapl RAF 44-65; Asst Chapl-in-Chief RAF 65-72; QHC 70-72; V Malew *S & M* 72-82; RD Castletown 77-82; Can St German's Cathl 78-84; Treas 80-84; rtd 82; Perm to Offic *S & M* from 84. *4B Milner Towers, Port Erin, Isle of Man IM9 6AG* Tel (01624) 832039

PAYNE, Julia Kathleen. *See* PEATY, Julia Kathleen

PAYNE, Canon Kenneth Alan. b 45. Pemb Coll Ox BA68 MA71. Qu Coll Birm 71. d 74 p 74. Hon C Perry Barr *Birm* 74-78; Hon C Ruislip Manor St Paul *Lon* 78-79; C Hawksworth Wood *Ripon* 79-84; R Stanningley St Thos 84-94; TR Kippax w Allerton Bywater 94-00; AD Whitkirk 95-00; P-in-c Lambley *S'well* from 00; Dioc Min Development Adv from 00; Dioc Dir of Min from 02; Hon Can S'well Minster from 06. *The Rectory, 2 Cocker Beck, Lambley, Nottingham NG4 4QP* Tel 0115-931 3531 *or* (01636) 814331 E-mail alanp@southwell.anglican.org

PAYNE, Leonard John. b 49. St Jo Coll Nottm 93. d 95 p 96. C Trimley St Mary *St E* 95-98; V Sole Bay 98-09, P-in-c Wrentham, Covehithe w Benacre etc from 09. *The Vicarage, 59 Southwold Road, Wrentham, Beccles NR34 7JE* Tel (01502) 675208 Mobile 07879-457902 E-mail leonard.payne@ireverend.com

PAYNE, Mark James Townsend. b 69. Van Mildert Coll Dur BA90. Ridley Hall Cam 92. d 94 p 95. C Angmering *Chich* 94-98; Dioc Ev and C Prestonville St Luke 98-04; P-in-c Scaynes Hill from 04. *The Vicarage, Vicarage Lane, Scaynes Hill, Haywards Heath RH17 7PB* Tel (01444) 831265

PAYNE, Matthew Charles. b 62. Ex Univ LLB85 All Nations Chr Coll BA95 Solicitor 89. Oak Hill Th Coll 99. d 01 p 02. C Angmering *Chich* 01-05; V Lowestoft Ch Nor from 05. *The Vicarage, 16 Corton Road, Lowestoft NR32 4PL* Tel (01502) 572444 E-mail matthew@christ-church.info

PAYNE, Michael Frederick. b 49. St Jo Coll Nottm 81. d 83 p 84. C Hyson Green *S'well* 83-86; P-in-c Peckham St Mary Magd *S'wark* 86-90; V 90-05; Hon C Chenies and Lt Chalfont, Latimer and Flaunden *Ox* from 05. *The Rectory, Latimer, Chesham HP5 1UA* Tel (01494) 764196
E-mail mikefpayne@hotmail.com

PAYNE, Mrs Norma. b 48. Bris Univ BA70 Homerton Coll Cam PGCE71. STETS 98. d 01 p 02. NSM Cley Hill Warminster *Sarum* 01-04; TV 04-07; R Cley Hill Villages from 07. *The Vicarage, 6 Homefields, Longbridge Deverill, Warminster BA12 7DQ* Tel (01985) 841371

PAYNE, Mrs Penelope Kenward. b 42. LGSM64. Bp Otter Coll 94. d 94 p 98. NSM Portsea N End St Mark *Portsm* 94-05; NSM S Hayling from 05. *35 Saltmarsh Lane, Hayling Island PO11 0JT* Tel and fax (023) 9246 5259 *or* tel 9266 5753
E-mail pennie@ppayne.f9.co.uk

PAYNE, Mrs Priscilla Mary. b 40. d 04 p 05. NSM Ditton *Roch* from 04. *7 Cobdown Close, Ditton, Aylesford ME20 6SZ* Tel (01732) 841257 E-mail priscilla.payne@diocese-rochester.org

PAYNE, Preb Robert Christian. b 42. St Mich Coll Llan. d 65 p 66. C Charlton Kings St Mary *Glouc* 65-69; C Waltham Cross *St Alb* 69-71; V Falfield *Glouc* 71-72; P-in-c Rockhampton 71-72; V Falfield w Rockhampton 72-76; Chapl HM Det Cen Eastwood Park 71-76; Chapl HM Borstal Everthorpe 76-79; Chapl HM YOI Glen Parva 79-85; Pris Service Chapl Tr Officer 85-88; Chapl HM Pris Swinfen Hall 85-88; Asst Chapl Gen of Pris 88-02; rtd 02; Sessional Chapl HM YOI Stoke Heath 02-06; Sessional Chapl HM Pris Swinfen Hall from 05; Sessional Chapl HM Pris Foston Hall 06-08; Preb Lich Cathl from 05. *HM Prison Swinfen Hall, Swinfen, Lichfield WS14 9QS* Tel (01543) 484125 E-mail bob.payne@ukgateway.net
or bob.payne@hmps.gsi.gov.uk

PAYNE, Robert Harold Vincent. b 44. St Jo Coll York CertEd69. St Jo Coll Nottm 77. d 79 p 80. C Didsbury St Jas *Man* 79-80; C Didsbury St Jas and Em 80-83; V Southchurch Ch Ch *Chelmsf* 83-90; P-in-c Charles w Plymouth St Matthias *Ex* 90-94; Warden Lee Abbey 94-02; R Thorley *St Alb* from 02. *The Rectory, Vicerons Place, Bishop's Stortford CM23 4EL* Tel (01279) 659152 Fax 755179
E-mail bobpayne@stjamesthorley.freeserve.co.uk

PAYNE, Robert Sandon. b 48. Reading Univ BSc69 MRICS72. Ripon Coll Cuddesdon 77. d 80 p 81. C Bridgnorth, Tasley, Astley Abbotts and Oldbury *Heref* 80-83; P-in-c Wistanstow 83-92; P-in-c Acton Scott 86-92; P-in-c Dorrington 92-94; P-in-c Leebotwood w Longnor 92-94; P-in-c Smethcott w Woolstaston 92-94; R Dorrington w Leebotwood, Longnor, Stapleton etc from 94. *The Rectory, Church Road, Dorrington, Shrewsbury SY5 7JL* Tel (01743) 718578

PAYNE, Rosemary Ann. b 46. LSE LLB68. SAOMC 97. d 00 p 01. NSM Wooburn *Ox* 00-05; NSM Hedsor and Bourne End from 05; Bp's NSM Officer (Bucks) 05-09. *30 Goddington Road, Bourne End SL8 5TZ* Tel (01628) 521677

PAYNE, Stephen Michael. b 55. d 03 p 04. C Plymouth Em, St Paul Efford and St Aug *Ex* from 03. *1 Yeo Close, Efford, Plymouth PL3 6ER* Tel (01752) 785576

PAYNE, Mrs Trudy. b 48. K Coll Lon BA66 Lon Inst of Educn PGCE73. d 04 p 05. OLM Clapham Park St Steph *S'wark* 04-06; Hon C Telford Park 06-09; Hon C Mitcham St Barn from 09. *6 Clarence Road, Croydon CR0 2EN* Tel (020) 8689 5857
E-mail paynetrudy@hotmail.com

PAYNE, Victor John. b 45. Open Univ BA81. St Mich Coll Llan. d 70 p 71. C Ystrad Mynach *Llan* 70-72; C Whitchurch 72-75; CF (TA) 74-75; CF 75-93; V Talgarth and Llanelieu *S & B* 85-87; Chapl Mid-Wales Hosp 85-87; C Bassaleg *Mon* 93-96; TV 96-01; V Tongwynlais *Llan* from 01; AD Llan from 08. *The Vicarage, 1 Merthyr Road, Tongwynlais, Cardiff CF15 7LE* Tel (029) 2081 0437 E-mail jaypay777@live.co.uk

PAYNE, Warwick Martin. b 26. AKC51. d 52 p 53. C Mansfield SS Pet and Paul *S'well* 52-56; P-in-c Kristi Kunda The Gambia 56-58; C Winlaton *Dur* 59-62; R Qacha's Nek Lesotho 63-77; P-in-c Butterworth S Africa 77-80; P-in-c Swartberg 80-83; P-in-c Ugie 83-92; rtd 92; Hon C Eshowe Cathl 92-96. *Murambi, Wellington Avenue, Wynberg, Cape Town, 7800 South Africa*

PAYNE COOK, Canon John Andrew Somerset. b 43. St Pet Coll Ox BA65 MA65. Coll of Resurr Mirfield 65. d 68 p 69. C St Mary-at-Latton *Chelmsf* 68-71; C St Barnhamsted *St Alb* 71-76; C-in-c N Brickhill CD 76-82; V N Brickhill and Putnoe 83-85; TR Tring 85-99; RD Berkhamsted 92-97; Hon Can St Alb 98-99; USPG 99-03; P-in-c Sandy Pt St Anne St Kitts-Nevis 00-03; P-in-c Ickleford w Holwell *St Alb* 03 05; P-in-c Pirton 03-05; R Holwell, Ickleford and Pirton from 05; Hon Can St Alb from 03. *The Vicarage, Crabtree Lane, Pirton, Hitchin SG5 3QE* Tel (01462) 712230 Fax 713597
E-mail jaspc@h-i-p.freeserve.co.uk

PAYNTER, Stephen Denis. b 59. Bath Univ BSc82 CertEd82. Trin Coll Bris BA89. d 89 p 90. C Nailsea Ch Ch *B & W* 89-92; C Farnborough *Guildf* 92-97; TV N Farnborough 97-98; V Ealing St Mary *Lon* from 98. *11 Church Place, London W5 4HN* Tel (020) 8567 0414 *or* 8579 7134 Fax 8840 4534
E-mail stevejen@lineone.net

PAYNTON, Paul Alexander. b 42. Linc Th Coll 72. d 74 p 75. C Uppingham w Ayston *Pet* 74-77; R Teigh w Whissendine 77-79; P-in-c Market Overton w Thistleton 77-79; R Teigh w Whissendine and Market Overton 79-95; V Irchester 95-00; rtd 04. *11 Mount Street, Lincoln LN1 3JE* Tel (01522) 560428

PAYTON, Paul John. b 59. Middx Poly MA90 LRAM79 GRSM80. Ripon Coll Cuddesdon. d 05 p 06. C Lancaster St Mary w St John and St Anne *Blackb* 05 08; P-in-c Leeds Gipton Epiphany *Ripon* from 08. *Epiphany Vicarage, 227 Beech Lane, Leeds LS9 6SW* E-mail paytonpj@hotmail.com

PEABODY, Anthony John. b 43. St Cuth Soc Dur BSc64 MSc67 Surrey Univ PhD82 MIBiol82 CBiol82. Cuddesdon Coll 08. d 08. NSM Sulhamstead Abbots and Bannister w Ufton Nervet

Ox from 08. *Blackberries, 29 Woodlands Avenue, Burghfield Common, Reading RG7 3HU* Tel 0118-983 2491
E-mail pisumcorporum@tinyworld.co.uk

PEACE, Brian. b 38. St Jo Coll Nottm 90. **d** 92 **p** 93. C Huddersfield H Trin *Wakef* 92-95; R Cheswardine, Childs Ercall, Hales, Hinstock etc *Lich* 95-00; TR 00-03; RD Hodnet 00-03; rtd 03; Perm to Offic *Ches* from 03. *2 Mouldsworth Close, Northwich CW9 8FT* Tel (01606) 333013
E-mail brian@peaceb.freeserve.co.uk

PEACE, Stuart Vaughan. **d** 04 **p** 05. OLM Dorking w Ranmore *Guildf* from 04. *95 Ashcombe Road, Dorking RH4 1LW* Tel (01306) 883002 E-mail stuart@peaces.freeserve.co.uk

PEACH, Malcolm Thompson. b 31. St Chad's Coll Dur BA56. Sarum Th Coll 56. **d** 58 **p** 59. C Beamish *Dur* 58-61; Chapl Dur Univ 61-65; NE England Sec SCM 61-65; C-in-c Stockton St Mark CD *Dur* 65-72; P-in-c Bishopwearmouth St Nic 72-81; V 81-85; V S Shields St Hilda w St Thos 85-95; Hon Chapl Miss to Seamen 85-95; P-in-c S Shields St Aid w St Steph *Dur* 92-95; rtd 95; Perm to Offic *Dur* from 95. *116 Mount Road, Sunderland SR4 7QD* Tel 0191-522 6216

PEACHELL, David John. b 45. Oak Hill Th Coll 85. **d** 86 **p** 87. C Prescot *Liv* 86-89; CF 89-98; P-in-c Hockering, Honingham, E and N Tuddenham *Nor* 98-02; rtd 02. *21 Brentwood, Eaton, Norwich NR4 6PN* Tel (01603) 880121

PEACOCK, Canon David. b 39. Liv Univ BA61 Lanc Univ MA71 Univ of the South (USA) Hon DD00 FRSA95. Westcott Ho Cam 84. **d** 84 **p** 85. Prin Lect St Martin's Coll Lanc 81-85; Hon C Lancaster St Mary *Blackb* 84-85; Prin Whitelands Coll 85-00; Pro Rector Surrey Univ 93-00; Hon C Roehampton H Trin *S'wark* 85-92; Hon C Putney St Mary 92-00; Hon Can S'wark Cathl 97-00; Perm to Offic *Blackb* from 00. *The Old Dairy, Keerside, Arkholme, Carnforth LA6 1AP* Tel (01524) 221706 E-mail keersidecowshed@aol.com

PEACOCK, John. b 34. ALCD60. **d** 60 **p** 61. C Addiscombe St Mary *Cant* 60-62; C Felixstowe St Jo *St E* 62-65; Chapl RAF 65-70; C Panania Australia 71-74; R Strathfield 74-80; Chapl Gladesville Hosp Sydney 81-94; Chapl Angl Retirement Villages Sydney 94-99; rtd 99. *51/16 Tarragal Glen Avenue, Erina NSW 2250, Australia* Tel (0061) (2) 4367 0936

PEACOCK, Mrs Kate Rebecca. b 78. Hatf Coll Dur BA00. Westcott Ho Cam 01. **d** 03 **p** 04. C Cambridge Ascension *Ely* 03-07; C Three Rivers Gp from 07. *The Vicarage, 24 Mildenhall Road, Fordham, Ely CB7 5NR* Tel (01638) 723960
E-mail kate.peacock@btopenworld.com

PEACOCK, Nicholas James. b 76. CCC Cam BA99 MA02. Ripon Coll Cuddesdon BA06. **d** 07 **p** 08. C Clapham Ch Ch and St Jo *S'wark* from 07. *49 Voltaire Road, London SW4 6DD* Tel 07837-425792 (mobile) E-mail revd.nick@btinternet.com

PEAD, Charles Henry. b 31. **d** 87 **p** 88. NSM Llanfrechfa and Llanddewi Fach w Llandegfeth *Mon* 87-92; NSM Mamhilad and Llanfihangel Pontymoile 92-95; Lic to Offic from 96. *Jasmine, Caerleon Road, Llanfrechfa, Cwmbran NP44 8DQ* Tel (01633) 482685

PEAKE, Robert Ernest. b 27. Univ Coll Lon BSc51 FSS. Coll of Resurr Mirfield 83. **d** 85 **p** 86. C Linslade *Ox* 85-88; TV Gt Chesham 88-89; rtd 89; Hon C Princes Risborough w Ilmer *Ox* 93-98; Hon C Risborough 98-00. *Butley Cottage, Chestnut Way, Longwick, Princes Risborough HP27 9SD* Tel (01844) 344952

PEAKE, Ms Sue. b 42. K Coll Lon BA63. SEITE 99. **d** 02 **p** 03. NSM Clapham Ch Ch and St Jo *S'wark* from 02. *20 Gauden Road, London SW4 6LT* Tel (020) 7627 4060

PEAL, Jacqueline. b 46. MCSP70. Cant Sch of Min 88. **d** 91 **p** 94. NSM Bexley St Jo *Roch* 91-97; NSM Crayford 91-94; C 94-97 and 00-01; C Dartford H Trin 97-00; Hon C Ash from 01; Asst Chapl Thames Gateway NHS Trust from 01; Chapl Wisdom Hospice from 04. *The Rectory, The Street, Ash, Sevenoaks TN15 7HA* Tel and fax (01474) 872209
E-mail jacquie.peal@diocese-rochester.org

PEAL, John Arthur. b 46. K Coll Lon BD70 AKC. **d** 71 **p** 72. C Portsea All SS w St Jo Rudmore *Portsm* 71-74; C Westbury *Sarum* 74-77; V Borstal *Roch* 77-82; Chapl HM Pris Cookham Wood 78-82; V Erith Ch Ch *Roch* 82-91; P-in-c Erith St Jo 86-91; V Bexley St Jo 91-00; Chapl Erith and Distr Hosp 82-90; R Ash *Roch* from 00; R Ridley from 00. *The Rectory, The Street, Ash, Sevenoaks TN15 7HA* Tel and fax (01474) 872209
E-mail peal@btinternet.com
or john.peal@diocese-rochester.org

PEAL, William John. b 26. K Coll Lon BSc47 AKC PhD52. St Jo Coll Nottm 79. **d** 80 **p** 81. C Coalville and Bardon Hill *Leic* 80-83; TV Melton Mowbray w Thorpe Arnold 83-86; TV Melton Gt Framland 86-90; rtd 90; Perm to Offic *Lich* from 91 and *Ches* 91-99. *20 Conway Road, Knypersley, Stoke-on-Trent ST8 7AL* Tel (01782) 513580

PEALL, Mrs Linda Grace. b 66. Westmr Coll Ox BEd88. EAMTC 99. **d** 02 **p** 03. NSM Blackwell All SS and Salutation *Dur* 02-04; C Darlington H Trin 04-07; Chapl Co Durham and Darlington NHS Foundn Trust from 05. *3 Westfield Drive,*

Darlington DL3 9BB Tel (01325) 469300, (01325) 743029 *or* 0191-333 2183 E-mail linda.peall@btopenworld.com
or linda.peall@cddft.nhs.uk

PEARCE, Adrian Francis. b 55. Westmr Coll Ox BTh05. S Dios Minl Tr Scheme 92. **d** 95 **p** 96. NSM Jersey St Jas *Win* from 95; NSM Jersey St Luke from 95; NSM Jersey St Mary from 01. *2 La Carriethe, Les Vaux, St Saviour, Jersey JE2 7US* Tel (01534) 873115 E-mail afpear@jerseymail.co.uk

PEARCE, Andrew John. b 66. Ex Univ BA89 Homerton Coll Cam PGCE93. St Mich Coll Llan 94. **d** 96 **p** 97. C Llansamlet *S & B* 96-99; C Clydach 99-00; P-in-c Knighton, Norton, Whitton, Pilleth and Cascob 00-02; V 02-06; V Bishopston w Penmaen and Nicholaston from 06. *The Rectory, 4 Portway, Bishopston, Swansea SA3 3JR* Tel (01792) 232140

PEARCE, Mrs Angela Elizabeth. b 36. K Coll Lon BSc58 CertEd59 BD79 AKC79. **dss** 79 **d** 87. Chapl Raines Sch 79-87; Homerton St Barn w St Paul *Lon* 79-85; Upper Chelsea St Simon 85-89; Hon Par Dn 87-89; Hon Par Dn Limehouse 89-97; Perm to Offic *St E* from 97. *50 Crown Street, Bury St Edmunds IP33 1QX* Tel (01284) 760016

PEARCE, Canon Brian Edward. b 39. Kelham Th Coll 59. **d** 64 **p** 65. C Smethwick St Matt *Birm* 64-68; C Kings Norton 68-72; TV 73-80; TR Swindon Dorcan *Bris* 80-91; Min Withywood CD 91-94; V Withywood 94-98; V Fishponds All SS 98-05; RD Bedminster 92-98; Hon Can Bris Cathl 97-05; rtd 05. *32 Brook Estate, Monmouth NP25 5AW* Tel (01600) 716057
E-mail rev.pearce@tesco.net

PEARCE, Preb Clive. b 40. Univ of Wales (Lamp) BA63 Heythrop Coll Lon MA01. St Steph Ho Ox 63. **d** 65 **p** 66. C Acton Green St Pet *Lon* 65-67; C Eastcote St Lawr 67-73; V Hatch End St Anselm from 73; Preb St Paul's Cathl from 08. *Hatch End Vicarage, 50 Cedar Drive, Pinner HA5 4DE* Tel and fax (020) 8428 4111 Mobile 07710-900545
E-mail ecclesiaenavis@aol.com

PEARCE, Colin James. b 51. Trin Coll Bris 94. **d** 96 **p** 97. C Kingswood *Bris* 96-00; TV Bedminster 00-07; Canada from 07. *189 Lafferty Avenue, Lasalle, Windsor ON N9J 1K1, Canada* Tel (001) (519) 734 1476 E-mail colinjpearce@hotmail.com

PEARCE, Daniel. *See* PEARCE, William Philip Daniel

PEARCE, Desmond. b 30. Univ of Wales (Abth) BA52. EMMTC 85. **d** 88 **p** 89. NSM Chellaston *Derby* 88-90; NSM Walsall St Gabr Fulbrook *Lich* 90; C Stoke Lacy, Moreton Jeffries w Much Cowarne etc *Heref* 91-97; Perm to Offic *Mon* 98-00; P-in-c New Tredegar 00-03. *56 Bedwellty Road, Cefn Forest, Blackwood NP12 3HB* Tel (01443) 833015

PEARCE, Elizabeth. *See* PEARCE, Mrs Janet Elizabeth

PEARCE, Preb Eustace Kenneth Victor. b 13. Univ Coll Lon BSc65 FRAI64. ALCD37. **d** 37 **p** 38. C Toxteth Park St Clem *Liv* 37-40; R Sutton 40-42; C Fordington *Sarum* 42-44; V Camberwell All SS *S'wark* 44-50; R Bucknall and Bagnall *Lich* 50-71; CF (TA) 66-81; V Audley *Lich* 71-81; Preb Lich Cathl 67-81; rtd 81; Chief Exec Evidence for Truth Broadcasting Assn from 83; Perm to Offic *Ches* from 83; *Chich* 83-97; *Lich* 83-95. *15 Kinnersley Avenue, Kidsgrove, Stoke-on-Trent ST7 1AP, or 13 Lismore Road, Eastbourne BN21 3AY* Tel (01782) 773325, (01323) 725231 *or* (01782) 642000 Fax (01782) 641121
E-mail ucb@ucb.co.uk

PEARCE, Canon Gerald Nettleton. b 25. St Jo Coll Dur BA49. **d** 51 **p** 52. C Bury St Edmunds St Mary *St E* 51-54; C Attenborough w Bramcote and Chilwell *S'well* 54-56; V Selston 56-61; R Wilford 61-73; RD Bingham 73-84; P-in-c Holme Pierrepont w Adbolton 73-84; V Radcliffe-on-Trent 73-84; V Shelford 73-84; Hon Can S'well Minster 77-84; R Sigglesthorne and Rise w Nunkeeling and Bewholme *York* 84-91; RD N Holderness 86-90; Perm to Offic from 91; rtd 91; Rtd Clergy and Widows Officer (E Riding) *York* from 91. *Sutherland Bridge, Cropton, Pickering YO18 8EU* Tel (01751) 417420

PEARCE, Mrs Iris Rose. b 27. **d** 00 **p** 03. OLM Parkstone St Pet and St Osmund w Branksea *Sarum* 00-03; Chapl Asst Poole Hosp NHS Trust 00-03; Hon Asst Chapl from 03. *Flat 1 Pelham, 34 Lindsay Road, Poole BH13 6AY* Tel (01202) 769301
E-mail iris1pelham@aol.com

PEARCE, Mrs Janet Elizabeth. b 49. Somerville Coll Ox BA72 MA76 CertEd74. NOC 85. **d** 88 **p** 94. Par Dn Helsby and Dunham-on-the-Hill *Ches* 88-94; C 94-96; C Norley, Crowton and Kingsley 96-06; Dioc Adv in Spirituality 02-06; R Llanfair Mathafarn Eithaf w Llanbedrgoch *Ban* from 06. *The Rectory, 3 Swn y Don, Benllech, Tyn-y-Gongl LL74 8PR* Tel (01248) 853744

PEARCE, Preb John Frederick Dilke. b 32. Ex Coll Ox BA55 MA59. Westcott Ho Cam. **d** 57 **p** 58. C Dalston St Mark w St Bart *Lon* 57-60; C Chelsea Ch Ch 60-63; R Lower Homerton St Paul 63-81; P-in-c Clapton Park All So 72-77; V 77-84; RD Hackney 74-79; R Homerton St Barn w St Paul 81-85; TR Hackney Marsh 85; P-in-c Upper Chelsea St Simon 85-89; AD Chelsea 88-89; R Limehouse 89-97; Preb St Paul's Cathl 70-97; rtd 97; Perm to Offic *St E* from 97. *50 Crown Street, Bury St Edmunds IP33 1QX* Tel (01284) 760016 Fax 756306
E-mail john@jfdp.freeserve.co.uk

PEARCE, Jonathan. b 55. St Jo Coll Nottm BTh85. **d** 85 **p** 86. C Gt Chesham *Ox* 85-89; C Newport Pagnell w Lathbury and Moulsoe 89-93; TV Waltham H Cross *Chelmsf* 93-07; R Gt Totham and Lt Totham w Goldhanger from 07. *The Vicarage, 1 Hall Road, Great Totham, Maldon CM9 8NN* Tel and fax (01621) 893150 E-mail revdjpearce@aol.com

PEARCE, Kenneth Jack. b 25. CIPFA. Linc Th Coll 62. **d** 63 **p** 64. C Wootton Bassett *Sarum* 63-66; C Broad Town 63-66; P-in-c Derby St Andr 66-68; V Derby St Mark 68-87; rtd 87; Perm to Offic *St Alb* from 91. *117 Oaks Cross, Stevenage SG2 8LT* Tel (01438) 317385

PEARCE, Michael Hawkins. b 29. Sarum Th Coll 61. **d** 62 **p** 63. C Bedminster St Aldhelm *Bris* 62-65; C Bishopston 65-68; R Jacobstow w Warbstow *Truro* 68-74; V Treneglos 68-74; V St Teath 74-94; rtd 94; Perm to Offic *Truro* from 94. *32 Trenant Road, Tywardreath, Par PL24 2QJ* Tel (01726) 813658

PEARCE, Neville John Lewis. b 33. CBIM88 Leeds Univ LLB53 LLM54. Trin Coll Bris 90. **d** 91 **p** 92. NSM Bath Walcot *B & W* 91-93; P-in-c Swainswick w Langridge and Woolley 93-98; Perm to Offic from 98. *Penshurst, Weston Lane, Bath BA1 4AB* Tel (01225) 426925 E-mail nevillepearce@tiscali.co.uk

PEARCE, Robert John. b 47. GLCM LLCM72 Birm Univ PGCE73. Ripon Coll Cuddesdon 79. **d** 82 **p** 83. C Broseley w Benthall *Heref* 82-83; C Kington w Huntington, Old Radnor, Kinnerton etc 83-85; R Westbury 85-94; V Yockleton 85-94; V Gt Wollaston 85-94; V Gwersyllt *St As* 94-99; V Northop 99-03; P-in-c Cerrigydrudion w Llanfihangel Glyn Myfyr etc from 08. *The Rectory, Cerrigydrudion, Corwen LL21 0RU* Tel (01490) 420313

PEARCE, Sacha Jane. b 64. Reading Univ BA92. RGN86 Ripon Coll Cuddesdon. **d** 00 **p** 01. C Tisbury *Sarum* 00-01; C Nadder Valley 01-04; V Seend, Bulkington and Poulshot 04-09; Chapl Plymouth Hosps NHS Trust from 09. *Derriford Hospital, Derriford Road, Plymouth PL6 8DH* Tel (01752) 202082 E-mail sacha.pearce@phnt.swest.nhs.uk

PEARCE, Mrs Susan Elizabeth. b 44. NEOC 03. **d** 06 **p** 07. NSM Pannal w Beckwithshaw *Ripon* from 06. *56 Beckwith Crescent, Harrogate HG2 0BH* Tel (01423) 565954 E-mail sue.pearce56@btopenworld.com

PEARCE, Trevor John. b 27. FSR57. Roch Th Coll 65. **d** 67 **p** 68. C Cheriton Street *Cant* 67-69; C Willesborough w Hinxhill 69-73; V Devonport St Barn *Ex* 73-79; Chapl N Devon Healthcare NHS Trust 79-83; V Derby St Andr w St Osmund 83-84; Chapl Derbyshire R Infirmary 83-92; Lic to Offic *Derby* 84-92; rtd 92; Perm to Offic *Derby* from 92. *4 Morrell Wood Drive, Belper DE56 0JD* Tel (01773) 828450

PEARCE, Valerie Olive. b 46. Whitelands Coll Lon CertEd67. SEITE 96. **d** 97 **p** 98. CSC 77-04; Lic to Offic *S'wark* 97-04. *13 Helder Street, South Croydon CR2 6HT* Tel (020) 8688 4082 E-mail v.pearce@homecall.co.uk

PEARCE, Victor. *See* PEARCE, Preb Eustace Kenneth Victor

PEARCE, William Philip Daniel. b 26. Stanford Univ BA48 Leeds Univ CertEd64 MA75. Cuddesdon Coll 54. **d** 56 **p** 57. USA 56-60; CR 60-84; C St Geo-in-the-East w St Paul *Lon* 84-86; USA from 86; rtd 02. *1037 Olympic Lane, Seaside CA 93955-6226, USA* Tel (001) (831) 393 2176 E-mail danielp@mbay.net

PEARKES, Nicholas Robin Clement. b 49. Ex Univ BA. Linc Th Coll. **d** 82 **p** 83. C Plymstock *Ex* 82-85; P-in-c Weston Mill 85-86; TV Devonport St Boniface and St Phil 86-99; R Broadhempston, Woodland, Staverton etc from 99. *The Rectory, Broadhempston, Totnes TQ9 6AU* Tel (01803) 813754 E-mail platypus@wordoflife.fsnet.co.uk

PEARMAIN, Andrew Neil. b 55. K Coll Lon BD79 AKC79. Ridley Hall Cam 79. **d** 81 **p** 82. C Cranleigh *Guildf* 81-84; P-in-c Frimley 85-86; C 86-87. *4 Laurel Close, Farnborough GU14 0PT*

PEARMAIN, Brian Albert John. b 34. Lon Univ BD68. Roch Th Coll 63. **d** 66 **p** 67. C Shirley St Jo *Cant* 66-69; C Selsdon St Jo w St Fran 69-73; P-in-c Louth H Trin *Linc* 73-75; TV Louth 75-79; R Scartho 79-97; RD Grimsby and Cleethorpes 89-94; Can and Preb Linc Cathl 94-97; rtd 97; Perm to Offic *Linc* 00-07. *20 Red Lion Street, Earby, Barnoldswick BB18 6RD* Tel (01282) 842680 Mobile 07944-675321

PEARMAN, Mrs Barbara Elizabeth Anne. b 48. RGN69 RHV72. ERMC 07. **d** 09. NSM E Marshland *Ely* from 09. *Rambles, 8 School Road, Tilney All Saints, King's Lynn PE34 4RS* Tel (01553) 828808 Mobile 07946-348744 E-mail barbarapearman@hotmail.com

PEARS, Anthony John. b 58. Ripon Coll Cuddesdon 00. **d** 02 **p** 03. C Watton w Carbrooke and Ovington *Nor* 02-05; R Northanger *Win* from 05. *The Rectory, Gaston Lane, Upper Farringdon, Alton GU34 3EE* Tel (01420) 588398 E-mail tony.pears@virgin.net

PEARSE, Andrew George. b 46. Wycliffe Hall Ox 71. **d** 74 **p** 75. C Homerton St Luke *Lon* 74-77; C Chadderton Em *Man* 77-81; R Collyhurst 81-89; Area Sec (NE, E Midl and Scotland) SAMS 89-03; rtd 03; Chapl Co-ord St Leon Hospice York from 03. *9 Troutsdale Avenue, Rawcliffe, York YO30 5TR* Tel (01904) 332373 E-mail andrew.stleonards@virgin.net

PEARSE, Ronald Thomas Hennessy. b 26. AKC52. **d** 53 **p** 54. C Leic St Pet 53-55; C Hanwell St Thos *Lon* 55-58; R Asfordby *Leic* 58-84; P-in-c Scalford w Wycombe and Chadwell 75-76; R Thurcaston 84-89; rtd 89; Perm to Offic *Leic* 89-90. *15 Burton Street, Loughborough LE11 2DT* Tel (01509) 215478

PEARSON, Canon Andrew George Campbell. b 41. Qu Coll Ox BA63 BA66. Wycliffe Hall Ox 63. **d** 71 **p** 72. C Gillingham St Mark *Roch* 71-72; C Billingshurst *Chich* 72-77; C Ches Square St Mich w St Phil *Lon* 77-82; Co-ord Busoga Trust 82-02; Dir from 02; Hon Can Busoga from 98; P-in-c St Marg Pattens *Lon* 90-06; Hon C Kensington St Mary Abbots w St Geo 96-06; rtd 06. *Denecroft, Little East Street, Billingshurst RH14 9PN* Tel (01403) 782080 E-mail busogatrust@hotmail.com

PEARSON, Andrew John. b 59. Westcott Ho Cam 86. **d** 89 **p** 90. C Knaresborough *Ripon* 89-92; C Wetherby 92-94; P-in-c Hunslet Moor St Pet and St Cuth 94-96; V 96-01; V Hawksworth Wood 01-06; Dioc Environment Officer 97-06; P-in-c Oulton w Woodlesford from 06; P-in-c Methley w Mickletown from 06. *The Vicarage, 46 Holmsley Lane, Woodlesford, Leeds LS26 8RY* Tel 0113-282 0411 E-mail lindrew@pearley.fsnet.co.uk

PEARSON, Andrew Michael. b 54. Solicitor 77. **d** 07 **p** 08. OLM Shere, Albury and Chilworth *Guildf* from 07. *Owl House, Shophouse Lane, Albury, Guildford GU5 9ET* Tel (01483) 203220 Mobile 07815-049950 E-mail rev.a.m.pearson@btinternet.com

PEARSON, Ms Brenda Elizabeth Frances (Brandy). b 51. SEITE 00. **d** 03 **p** 04. NSM Finsbury Park St Thos *Lon* 03-07; C Acton Green from 07. *276 Osborne Road, London W3 8SR* Tel (020) 8993 3237 E-mail brandy@brandypearson.wanadoo.co.uk

PEARSON, Canon Brian Robert. b 35. Leeds Univ BA59. Coll of Resurr Mirfield 59. **d** 61 **p** 62. C Chesterfield St Mary and All SS *Derby* 61-66; P-in-c Derby St Jo 66-72; P-in-c Derby St Anne 66-72; R Thorpe St Andr *Nor* 72-90; Hon Can Nor Cathl 85-90; RD Nor E 86-90; V Harrogate St Wilfrid *Ripon* 90-00; rtd 00; Perm to Offic *York* from 00 and *Bradf* from 04. *Green Garth, 13 Cedar Glade, Dunnington, York YO19 5QZ* Tel (01904) 481232

PEARSON, Canon Brian William. b 49. FHSM Brighton Poly BSc71 City Univ MSc80 Westmr Coll Ox MTh94. S'wark Ord Course & Clapham Ord Scheme 76. **d** 79 **p** 80. Hon C Plumstead All SS *S'wark* 79-81; Perm to Offic *Chich* 81-83; Hon C Broadwater St Mary 83-88; Bp's Research and Dioc Communications Officer *B & W* 88-90; Dioc Missr 91; Abp's Officer for Miss and Evang and Tait Missr *Cant* 91-97; Abp's Dioc Chapl 91-97; Hon Prov Can Cant Cathl 92-97; Gen Dir CPAS 97-00; P-in-c Leek Wootton and Dioc Officer for OLM *Cov* 00-06. *Woodspring, Northfields, Somerton TA11 6SL* Tel (01458) 274360 E-mail brian@bwpvic.fslife.co.uk

PEARSON, Mrs Béatrice Levasseur. b 53. Sorbonne Univ Paris LèsL74 MèsL75 Lon Inst of Educn PGCE76. Ripon Coll Cuddesdon 01. **d** 03 **p** 04. C Easthampstead *Ox* 03-06; TV Loddon Reach from 06. *The Vicarage, 11 Clares Green Road, Spencers Wood, Reading RG7 1DY* Tel 0118-988 3215 Mobile 07981-462145 E-mail bea.acumen@zetnet.co.uk

PEARSON, Christian David John (Brother Christian). b 42. Open Univ BA76 CCC Cam BA79 MA83. AKC65. **d** 66 **p** 67. C Pallion *Dur* 66-68; C Peterlee 68-71; SSF from 71; Lic to Offic *Sarum* 71-73; Tanzania 74-75; Lic to Offic *Ely* 75-90; Asst Chapl Keble Coll Ox 82-83; Chapl St Cath Coll Cam 83-86; Chapl Down Coll Cam 86-90; Lic to Offic *Lon* from 90; Dep Warden and Chapl Lon Goodenough Trust 90-95. *66 Warwick Way, London SW1V 1RZ* Tel (020) 7828 0271

PEARSON, Christopher Ian. b 65. Thames Poly BA91 K Coll Lon MA96. Coll of Resurr Mirfield 91. **d** 93 **p** 94. C Newington St Mary *S'wark* 93-95; C Streatham St Pet 95-97; V Kennington Park St Agnes from 97. *The Vicarage, 37 St Agnes Place, London SE11 4BB* Tel (020) 7735 3860 E-mail vicar@saintagnes.org.uk

PEARSON, Christopher John. b 49. GRSM LRAM ARCM. Oak Hill NSM Course 81. **d** 84 **p** 85. NSM Barton Seagrave w Warkton *Pet* 84-86; C Kettering St Andr 86-88; V Nassington w Yarwell and Woodnewton 88-91; V Pet St Mark 91-03; P-in-c Gt Doddington and Wilby from 03; P-in-c Ecton from 07. *The Vicarage, 72 High Street, Great Doddington, Wellingborough NN29 7TH* Tel and fax (01933) 226711 E-mail c.pearson@homecall.co.uk

PEARSON, Christopher William. b 56. Univ Coll Ox MA. St Jo Coll Nottm 07. **d** 09. C Norton St Mary *Dur* from 09; C Stockton St Chad from 09. *243 Darlington Lane, Stockton-on-Tees TS19 8AA* Tel (01642) 350430 E-mail cwpearson@fastmail.fm

PEARSON, Colin Graham. b 58. St Jo Coll Nottm 01. **d** 04 **p** 05. C Mickleover All SS *Derby* 04-09; C Breadsall from 09. *28 Earlswood Drive, Mickleover, Derby DE3 5LN* Tel (01332) 674604 E-mail colin_pearson@tiscali.co.uk

PEARSON, David. *See* PEARSON, James David

PEARSON, David. b 57. Man Poly BA78. Trin Coll Bris 85. **d** 88 **p** 89. C Shawbury *Lich* 88-91; C Morton 88-91; C Stanton on Hine Heath 88-91; R Mattishall w Mattishall Burgh, Welborne etc *Nor* 91-00; RD Dereham in Mitford 98-00; Asst P Tawa

Linden New Zealand 00-04; V Levin from 04. *120 Cambridge Street, Levin 5500, New Zealand* (0064) (6) 368 5955
E-mail vicar.levinanglicans@xtra.co.nz

PEARSON, Edgar. b 13. Tyndale Hall Bris 37. d 41 p 42. C Handforth *Ches* 41; Burma 42; India 42-47; Hon CF 47; Chapl Valparaiso Chile 50-55; C St Paul's Cathl Melbourne Australia 55-56; R Eureka 56-59; P-in-c Dunoon 60-61; P-in-c Adaminaby 61-65; R Dallinghoo and Pettistree *St E* 65-83; P-in-c Bredfield w Boulge 74-86; rtd 83; P-in-c Dallinghoo and Pettistree *St E* 83-86; Perm to Offic *Mon* 86-08. *Manormead, Tilford Road, Hindhead GU26 6RA*

PEARSON, Fergus Tom. b 58. Middx Poly BA81 Moore Th Coll Sydney MA98. Oak Hill Th Coll BA95. d 92 p 93. C Mildmay Grove St Jude and St Paul *Lon* 92-95; Australia 96-98; C Heatherlands St Jo *Sarum* 98-03; V Hensingham *Carl* from 03. *St John's Vicarage, Egremont Road, Hensingham, Whitehaven CA28 8QW* Tel (01946) 692822
E-mail fpe@rson.justbrowsing.com

PEARSON, Geoffrey Charles. b 49. Imp Coll Lon BSc70 ARCS. Oak Hill Th Coll 80. d 82 p 83. C Foord St Jo *Cant* 82-86; V Ramsgate St Luke 86-93; Chapl to People at Work in Cam *Ely* 93-01; Co-ord Chapl HM Pris Chelmsf 01-07; Perm to Offic *Cant* from 08. *99 Cherry Drive, Canterbury CT2 8ER* Tel and fax (01227) 379451 Mobile 07890-808739
E-mail pearson.geoff@yahoo.com

✠**PEARSON, The Rt Revd Geoffrey Seagrave.** b 51. St Jo Coll Dur BA72. Cranmer Hall Dur 72. d 74 p 75 c 06. C Kirkheaton *Wakef* 74-77; C-in-c Blackb Redeemer 77-82; V 82-85; Asst Home Sec Gen Syn Bd for Miss and Unity 85-89; Hon C Forty Hill Jes Ch *Lon* 85-89; Exec Sec BCC Evang Cttee 86-89; V Roby *Liv* 89-06; AD Huyton 02-06; Hon Can Liv Cathl 03-06; Suff Bp Lancaster *Blackb* from 06; C Ellel w Shireshead from 08. *Shireshead Vicarage, Whinney Brow, Forton, Preston PR3 0AE* Tel (01524) 799900 Fax 799901
E-mail bishoplancaster@btconnect.com

PEARSON, George Michael. b 31. FCA FBCS MIMC. Qu Coll Birm 86 Coll of Resurr Mirfield 89. d 88 p 90. NSM Solihull *Birm* 88-95; Perm to Offic from 95. *The Parsonage, 67A Hampton Lane, Solihull B91 2QD* Tel 0121-705 0288

PEARSON, Canon Henry Gervis. b 47. Mansf Coll Ox BA72 MA76. St Jo Coll Nottm 72. d 74 p 75. C Southgate *Chich* 74-76; TV 76-82; V Debenham w Aspall and Kenton *St E* 82-91; Chapl to Suffolk Fire Service 88-91; RD Loes 89-91; TR Marlborough *Sarum* 91-02; RD Marlborough 94-02; Can and Preb Sarum Cathl from 99; Chapl Savernake Hosp Marlborough 91-94; Chapl E Wilts Health Care NHS Trust from 94; R Queen Thorne *Sarum* from 02; RD Sherborne from 04. *The Rectory, Trent, Sherborne DT9 4SL* Tel (01935) 851049
E-mail canonhenry@btinternet.com

PEARSON, Ian. b 49. Liv Univ BA71. S'wark Ord Course 79. d 82 p 83. Archivist USPG 82-85; Archivist Nat Soc 85-91; NSM Lavender Hill Ascension *S'wark* 82-84; Lic to Offic *Lon* 84-86 and 88-90; NSM Westmr St Matt 86-88; Perm to Offic *S'wark* 85-90 and *St Alb* 90-91; C Chesterfield St Mary and All SS *Derby* 91-95; R Bengeo *St Alb* 95-04; P-in-c Worc City St Paul and Old St Martin etc 04-06; R Worc City from 06. *18 Shrubbery Avenue, Worcester WR1 1QH* Tel (01905) 734833
E-mail ianandlizpearson@waitrose.com

PEARSON, James David. b 51. Cape Town Univ BSocSc74. St Paul's Coll Grahamstown 76. d 78 p 79. C St Geo Cathl Cape Town 78-80; R Caledon H Trin 80-84; R Tristan da Cunha St Mary 84-86; R Camps Bay St Pet 86-89; R Kuruman St Mary-le-Bourne w Wrenchville St Pet 89-91; R Amalinda Ch 92-96; Asst P Cambridge St Mark 96-98; Asst P-in-c Kidds Beach St Mary and St Andr 99; C Prittlewell St Steph *Chelmsf* 00-04; TV Barking St Marg w St Patr from 04. *Christ Church Vicarage, Bastable Avenue, Barking IG11 0NG* Tel (020) 8594 1976 E-mail david_pearson@dsl.pipex.com

PEARSON, James William. b 20. FCA59. Qu Coll Birm 75. d 78 p 79. NSM Beoley *Worc* 78-90; Perm to Offic from 90. *Ringwood, Rowney Green, Alvechurch, Birmingham B48 7QE* Tel (01527) 66952

PEARSON, Miss Joanna Ruth. b 76. St Hilda's Coll Ox BA97 PGCE98 St Jo Coll Dur BA05. Cranmer Hall Dur 03. d 06 p 07. C Leeds St Geo *Ripon* from 06. *46 Vesper Lane, Leeds LS5 3NR* Tel 0113-368 5914 E-mail jopearson@supanet.com

PEARSON, The Very Revd Kevin. b 54. Leeds Univ BA75 Edin Univ BD79. Edin Th Coll 76. d 79 p 80. C Horden *Dur* 79-81; Chapl Leeds Univ 81-87; R Edin St Salvador 87-93; Chapl Napier Poly 88-92; Chapl Napier Univ 92-94; Dioc Dir of Ords 90-95; Prov Dir of Ords from 91; Assoc R Edin Old St Paul 93-94; P-in-c Linlithgow 94-95; R Edin St Mich and All SS from 95; Can St Mary's Cathl from 03; Dean Edin from 04. *The Rectory, 203 Gilmore Place, Edinburgh EH3 9PN* Tel 0131-229 6368 *or* 225 6357 E-mail pdo@scotland.anglican.org

PEARSON, Mrs Lindsey Carole. b 61. Cov Poly BA85 CQSW85. Westcott Ho Cam 86. d 89 p 94. Par Dn High Harrogate St Pet *Ripon* 89-93; Par Dn Moor Allerton 93-96; C 94-96; TV Seacroft 96-04; World Development Officer 99-04; Area Co-ord (N and

W Yorks) Chr Aid 04-07; P-in-c Swillington *Ripon* from 07. *The Vicarage, 46 Holmsley Lane, Woodlesford, Leeds LS26 8RY* Tel 0113-282 0411 E-mail lindrew@pearley.fsnet.co.uk

PEARSON, Michael Carden. b 38. Guy's Hosp Medical Sch MB63 BChir63 Down Coll Cam MA64 Lon Univ MSc94 FRCR75 FRCP94. St Steph Ho Ox 96. d 98 p 99. NSM Horsted Keynes *Chich* 98-99; NSM Worth 99-00; Chapl Gtr Athens *Eur* 00-01; Perm to Offic *Chich* 04-05; P-in-c Staplefield Common 05-08; rtd 08. *Bleak House, Station Road, Horsted Keynes, Haywards Heath RH17 7ED* Tel (01825) 790617
E-mail michaelpearson@coxlesspair.demon.co.uk

PEARSON, Michael John. b 53. Southn Univ BTh78. Sarum Th Coll 74. d 78 p 79. C Paignton St Jo *Ex* 78-82; TV Ilfracombe, Lee, Woolacombe, Bittadon etc 82-86; TV Barnstaple 86-08; Chapl N Devon Healthcare NHS Trust 86-96; RD Barnstaple *Ex* 97-01; C Shaldon, Stokeinteignhead, Combeinteignhead etc 08-09; rtd 09. *Mira Ceti, Salty Lane, Shaldon, Teignmouth TQ14 0AP* Tel (01626) 872443
E-mail fathermichaelpearson@googlemail.com

PEARSON, Nigel Hetley Allan. b 45. Fitzw Coll Cam BA67 MA87. EMMTC 04. d 06 p 07. NSM Papworth *Ely* from 06. *Manor Farm House, 53 Ermine Street, Caxton, Cambridge CB23 3PQ* Tel (01954) 719750 Fax 718566 Mobile 07713-639928 E-mail njfarm@gmail.com

PEARSON, Pauline Hilary. b 54. BA77 PhD88 RN77 RHV79. NEOC 02. d 05 p 06. NSM Denton *Newc* from 05. *3 Belle Grove Place, Newcastle upon Tyne NE2 4LH* Tel 0191-232 5980 Mobile 07050-105918 E-mail p.h.pearson@ncl.ac.uk

PEARSON, Mrs Priscilla Dawn. b 45. Oak Hill Th Coll BA90. d 90 p 94. Par Dn Stanford-le-Hope w Mucking *Chelmsf* 90-94; C 94; C Colchester St Jo 94-96; Hon C Woking St Jo *Guildf* 03-05. *Address temp unknown*

PEARSON, Raymond Joseph. b 44. AKC71. St Aug Coll Cant 71. d 72 p 73. C Wetherby *Ripon* 72-75; C Goring-by-Sea *Chich* 75-77; C Bramley *Ripon* 77-82; V Patrick Brompton and Hunton 82-94; V Crakehall 82-94; V Hornby 82-94; World Miss Officer 88-94; RD Wensley 92-94; V Bardsey 94-09; rtd 09; Perm to Offic *York* from 09. *7 St George's Croft, Bridlington YO16 7RW* Tel (01262) 424332

PEARSON, Robert James Stephen. b 52. Cov Poly BA74. St Steph Ho Ox 85. d 87 p 88. C Stoke Newington St Mary *Lon* 87-90; C Haggerston All SS 90-97; C Dalston H Trin w St Phil and Haggerston All SS 97-98; Chapl HM Pris Wandsworth 98-02; Chapl HM Pris Pentonville 02-07; Perm to Offic *Lon* from 07. *276 Osborne Road, London W3 8SR* Tel (020) 8993 3237

PEARSON, Robert Lyon. b 57. St Jo Coll Nottm 90. d 92 p 93. C Netherton *Liv* 90-94; V Woolston 96-02; V Highfield from 02. *St Matthew's Vicarage, Billinge Road, Wigan WN3 6BL* Tel (01942) 222121 Fax 211332
E-mail vicar@stmatthewhighfield.org.uk

PEARSON, Preb Roy Barthram. b 35. K Coll Lon 56. d 60 p 61. C Brookfield St Mary *Lon* 60-64; C St Marylebone St Cypr 64-70; V Tottenham All Hallows from 70; AD E Haringey 95-00; Preb St Paul's Cathl from 96. *The Priory, Church Lane, London N17 7AA* Tel (020) 8808 2470

PEARSON-GEE, William Oliver Clinton. b 61. Wycliffe Hall Ox 04. d 06 p 07. C Ox St Andr from 06. *37 Hamilton Road, Oxford OX2 7PY* Tel (01865) 314855
E-mail will.pearson.gee@standrewsoxford.org

PEARSON-MILES, David. b 37. St Jo Coll Nottm 74. d 76 p 77. C Hazlemere *Ox* 76-79; R Waddesdon w Over Winchendon and Fleet Marston 79-82; CF 82-92; P-in-c Barcombe *Chich* 92-94; R 94-00; rtd 00. *The Coach House, Holme Place, Oakford, Tiverton EX16 9DH* Tel (01398) 351495

PEART, John Graham. b 36. Bps' Coll Cheshunt 65. d 68 p 69. C Cheshunt *St Alb* 68-70; C St Alb St Pet 70-73; R Hunsdon and Widford 73-76; Ind Chapl 76-82; Chapl St Geo Hosp and Distr Gen Hosp Stafford 82-87; Chapl Qu Eliz Hosp and Bensham Hosp Gateshead 87-89; Chapl Garlands Hosp 89-94; P-in-c Cotehill and Cumwhinton *Carl* 89-94; V Irthington, Crosby-on-Eden and Scaleby 94-98; rtd 98; Chapl Douglas MacMillan Hospice Stoke-on-Trent 98-01; P-in-c Salt and Sandon w Burston *Lich* 01-02; TV Mid Trent 02-03; Perm to Offic *Lich* 04-07 and *Eur* from 07. *Taljovagen 2, SE-184-92 Taljo, Akersberga, Sweden* Tel (0046) (8) 5402 1214
E-mail johnpeart@hotmail.co.uk

PEART, Patricia Isidora. b 55. Westcott Ho Cam 97. d 99. C Holland-on-Sea *Chelmsf* 99-00; C Shrub End 00-01. *6 Whitsand Road, Manchester M22 4ZA*

PEAT, Mrs Ann Kathleen. b 40. TCert60. d 98 p 99. OLM Brumby *Linc* from 98. *36 Glover Road, Scunthorpe DN17 1AS* Tel (01724) 852609

PEAT, David James. b 62. Leeds Univ BA84 Dur Univ MA91. Cranmer Hall Dur 86. d 89 p 90. C Wetherby *Ripon* 89-92; C Beeston 92-95; Chapl St Lawr Coll Ramsgate 95-06; Hd Relig Educn Eastbourne Coll from 06. *Eastbourne College, Old Wish Road, Eastbourne BN21 4JY* Tel (01323) 452244
E-mail djpeat@eastbourne-college.co.uk

PEAT, David William. b 37. Clare Coll Cam MA59 PhD62 FRAS63. Westcott Ho Cam 72. **d** 75 **p** 76. C Chesterton St Andr *Ely* 75-77; Chapl Univ Coll of Ripon and York St Jo 77-83; V E Ardsley *Wakef* 83-87; Prin Willesden Min Tr Scheme 87-94; NSM Headingley *Ripon* from 94; Perm to Offic from 06; Research Lect Leeds Univ from 94. *12 North Grange Mews, Headingley, Leeds LS6 2EW* Tel 0113-275 3179
E-mail phy6dwp@phys-iric.leeds.ac.uk

PEAT, The Ven Lawrence Joseph. b 28. Linc Th Coll 55. **d** 58 **p** 59. C Bramley *Ripon* 58-61; V 65-73; R Heaton Norris All SS *Man* 61-65; P-in-c Stockton St Erkenwald *Chelmsf* 73-74; TR Southend St Jo w St Mark, All SS w St Fran etc 74-79; V Skelsmergh w Selside and Longsleddale *Carl* 79-86; RD Kendal 84-89; TV Kirkby Lonsdale 86-89; Hon Can Carl Cathl 88-95; Adn Westmorland and Furness 89-95; rtd 95; Perm to Offic *Carl* from 95. *32 White Stiles, Kendal LA9 6DJ* Tel (01539) 733829

PEAT, Matthew. b 71. Bradf and Ilkley Coll BA97. Ripon Coll Cuddesdon BTh03. **d** 03 **p** 04. C Walney Is *Carl* 03-06; C Barrow St Matt 06-08; TR from 08. *St Matthew's Vicarage, Highfield Road, Barrow-in-Furness LA14 5NZ* Tel (01229) 823569

PEATMAN (née HUGHES), Mrs Debbie Ann. b 62. SS Hild & Bede Coll Dur BA83 St Jo Coll Dur BA89. Cranmer Hall Dur 87. **d** 90 **p** 94. C Edin Old St Paul 90-91; NSM Greasley *S'well* 92-94; NSM Whitley *Cov* 94-02; C Lancaster St Thos *Blackb* 02-09; Co Ecum Development Officer for Churches Together in Lancs from 09. *The Rectory, Church Walk, Morecambe LA4 5PR* E-mail debbie.peatman@ctlancashire.org.uk

PEATMAN, Michael Robert. b 61. Keble Coll Ox BA85 MA89 St Jo Coll Dur BA89 Lanc Univ MA06. Cranmer Hall Dur 87. **d** 90 **p** 91. C Greasley *S'well* 90-94; P-in-c Whitley *Cov* 94-02; Dio Stewardship Adv 94-02; Sen Chapl St Martin's Coll *Blackb* 02-07; Sen Chapl Cumbria Univ 07-09; P-in-c Poulton-le-Sands w Morecambe St Laur from 09. *The Rectory, Church Walk, Morecambe LA4 5PR*
E-mail mike.peatman@cumbria.ac.uk

PEATTIE, The Ven Colin Hulme Reid. b 39. Natal Univ BSc59. Ripon Hall Ox 61. **d** 63 **p** 64. C Belmont *Lon* 63-65; S Africa 65-83 and from 85; R Durban St Columba 65-69; R Dundee St Jas 69-72; Chapl St Andr Sch Bloemfontein 72-76; R Pietermaritzburg St Alphege 76-83; V S Ossett *Wakef* 83-85; R York-cum-Ravensworth 85-93; R Stanger All SS 93-96; R Umhlali All So from 96; Adn N Coast from 01. *PO Box 222, Salt Rock, 4391 South Africa* Tel and fax (0027) (32) 947 2001 Mobile 82-413 8650 E-mail cpeattie@absamail.co.za

PEATY, Julia Kathleen. b 53. Salford Univ BSc75. STETS 96. **d** 99 **p** 00. NSM E Grinstead St Swithun *Chich* from 99. *15 Overton Shaw, East Grinstead RH19 2HN* Tel (01342) 322386 E-mail julia@peaty.net

PEBERDY (née GARNETT), Mrs Alyson Susan. b 48. Trevelyan Coll Dur BA69 Reading Univ MA75. Ox Min Course 95. **d** 96 **p** 97. C New Windsor *Ox* 96-99; V Brockley Hill St Sav *S'wark* from 99; P-in-c Perry Hill St Geo 00-01; P-in-c Forest Hill St Aug 00-02. *St Saviour's Vicarage, 5 Lowther Hill, London SE23 1PZ* Tel (020) 8690 2499 E-mail alysonpeberdy@aol.com

PECK, David Warner. b 66. American Univ (Washington) BA88 Jclw Coll Cam DA91 MA99. Westcott Ho Cam 92. **d** 95 **p** 96. C Weybridge *Guildf* 95-99; Bp's Chapl 99-05; Abp's Sec for Internat Development *Cant* 05-08; R Lancaster St Jas USA from 08. *The Rectory, 115 North Duke Street, Lancaster PA 17602, USA* Tel and fax (001) (717) 397 4858

PECK, Kay Margaret. b 51. Milton Keynes Coll of Ed BEd76. Ox Min Course 04. **d** 07 **p** 08. NSM Swan *Ox* 07-09; NSM The Claydons and Swan from 09. *21 Beamish Way, Winslow, Buckingham MK18 3EU* E-mail kmpeck@btinternet.com

PECK, Robert John. b 49. Bath Univ BSc72. STETS 00. **d** 03 **p** 04. NSM Stoke-next-Guildf 03-08; V Camberley St Martin Old Dean from 08. *St Martin's Vicarage, 2A Hampshire Road, Camberley GU15 4DW* Tel (01276) 23958
E-mail bob@stmartinolddean.com or rpeck@btinternet.com

PECKETT, Desmonde Claude Brown. b 19. Ex & Truro NSM Scheme. **d** 77 **p** 78. NSM Charlestown *Truro* 77-89; Perm to Offic from 89. *Smugglers, Porthpean, St Austell PL26 6AY* Tel (01726) 72768

PECKHAM, Richard Graham. b 51. Sarum & Wells Th Coll 84. **d** 86 **p** 87. C Bishop's Cleeve *Glouc* 86-89; TV Ilfracombe, Lee, Woolacombe, Bittadon etc *Ex* 89-96; TV Sidmouth, Woolbrook, Salcombe Regis, Sidbury etc from 96; RD Ottery 98-02; Hon Chapl ATC from 98. *The Vicarage, Harcombe Lane, Sidford, Sidmouth EX10 9QN* Tel (01395) 514522
E-mail rikpeckham@lineone.net or rikpeckham@hotmail.com

PEDDER, Brian. b 38. Carl Dioc Tr Inst 88. **d** 91 **p** 92. NSM Wigton *Carl* 91-93; C Cleator Moor w Cleator 93-96; P-in-c Grayrigg, Old Hutton and New Hutton 96-04; rtd 04. *5 Scholars Green, Wigton CA7 9QW* Tel (016973) 45344

PEDLAR, Canon John Glanville. b 43. Ex Univ BA68 De Montfort Univ Hon MA06. St Steph Ho Ox 68. **d** 70 **p** 71. C Tavistock and Gulworthy *Ex* 70-73; Prec Portsm Cathl 74-77; Prec St Alb Abbey 77-81; V Redbourn 81-98; V Bedford St Paul from 98; PV Westmr Abbey 87-04; Hon Can St Alb from 06.

St Paul's Vicarage, 12 The Embankment, Bedford MK40 3PD Tel (01234) 364638 E-mail johnpedlar@btinternet.com

PEDLEY, Canon Betty. b 49. Ripon Coll of Educn CertEd70 Leeds Univ BEd71 ALCM78. NOC 85. **d** 88 **p** 03. Par Dn Sowerby *Wakef* 88-92; Par Educn Adv and Youth Chapl 92-03; P-in-c Luddenden w Luddenden Foot 03-08; P-in-c Norland 06-08; Hon Can Wakef Cathl 00-08; rtd 08; Perm to Offic *Wakef* from 08. *7 Ogden View Close, Halifax HX2 9LY*

✠**PEDLEY, The Rt Revd Geoffrey Stephen.** b 40. Qu Coll Cam BA64 MA67. Cuddesdon Coll 64. **d** 66 **p** 67 **c** 98. C Liv Our Lady and St Nic 66-69; C Cov H Trin 69-71; P-in-c Kitwe Zambia 71-77; P-in-c Stockton H Trin *Dur* 77-83; V Stockton St Pet 77-88; Chapl to The Queen 84-98; R Whickham *Dur* 88-93; Can Res Dur Cathl 93-98; Suff Bp Lancaster *Blackb* 98-05; Hon Can Blackb Cathl 98-05; rtd 05. *The Blue House, Newbrough, Hexham NE47 5AN* Tel (01434) 674238

PEDLEY, Nicholas Charles. b 48. CQSW75. Qu Coll Birm 88. **d** 90 **p** 91. C Stafford St Jo and Tixall w Ingestre *Lich* 90-93; C Kingswinford St Mary *Worc* 93-96; TV 96-97; C Cheswardine, Childs Ercall, Hales, Hinstock etc *Lich* 97-99; Chapl HM YOI Stoke Heath 97-99; rtd 99; Perm to Offic *Worc* from 00. *33 Comber Grove, Kinver, Stourbridge DY7 6EN* Tel (01384) 877219 E-mail nick@npedley48.freeserve.co.uk

PEDLOW, Henry Noel. b 37. QUB BA59. **d** 61 **p** 62. C Belfast St Phil *Conn* 61-66; C Belfast St Nic 66-70; I Eglantine 70-82; I Kilkeel *D & D* 82-89; I Belfast St Donard 89-03; rtd 03. *8 Old Mill Dale, Dundonalad, Belfast BT16 1WG* Tel (028) 9048 5416

PEEBLES, David Thomas. b 64. Bris Univ BSc St Chad's Coll Dur PGCE86 Man Univ MA94. Coll of Resurr Mirfield 90. **d** 90 **p** 91. C Crewe St Andr *Ches* 90-93; Lect and Asst Dir Studies Mirfield 93-95; Chapl Qu Mary and Westf Coll *Lon* 95-00; P-in-c Bethnal Green St Matt w St Jas the Gt 97-99; Chapl LSE from 00; Bp's Adv on New Relig Movements from 01. *3 Bristol House, 80A Southampton Row, London WC1B 4BA* Tel (020) 7242 4794 or 7980 1204 E-mail d.peebles@lse.ac.uk

PEEK, Alan Nicholas. b 65. Ridley Hall Cam 02. **d** 04 **p** 05. C Much Woolton *Liv* 04-08; I Derg w Termonamongan *D & R* from 08. *The Rectory, 13 Strabane Road, Castlederg BT81 7HZ* Tel (028) 8167 1362 E-mail rev.al@sky.com

PEEK, John Richard. b 51. Bris Univ BSc72 Nottm Univ BA75. St Jo Coll Nottm. **d** 76 **p** 77. C Hebburn St Jo *Dur* 76-78; C Dunston 78-81; R Armthorpe *Sheff* 81-86; RE Teacher K Edw VI Sch Southn 87-88; Chapl and Hd RE Casterton Sch Cumbria 89; Teacher Furze Platt Comp Sch Berks 89-90; Perm to Offic *Portsm* 90-96; Chapl Bearwood Coll Wokingham 96-98; Hd Mathematics Stowford Coll Sutton 98-08; Teacher Ryde Sch w Upper Chine from 08; Perm to Offic *Portsm* from 08. *St Lawrence House, 59 Albert Street, Ventnor PO38 1EU* Tel (01983) 853328

PEEL, Mrs Christine Mary. b 44. Whitelands Coll Lon CertEd66. Portsm Dioc Tr Course. **d** 90. NSM Sheet *Portsm* 90-03; Perm to Offic *York* from 03. *11 Whiteoak Avenue, Easingwold, York YO61 3GB* Tel (01347) 823548

PEEL, Canon David Charles. b 41. AKC75. St Aug Coll Cant 75. **d** 76 **p** 77. C Tynemouth Cullercoats St Paul *Newc* 76-79; C Tynemouth St Jo 79-84; Ldr Cedarwood Project 84-88 and from 91; Warden Communicare Ho 89-91; Min Killingworth 89-91; Hon Can Newc Cathl from 08. *116 Grey Street, North Shields NE30 2AG* Tel 0191-272 8743 or 259 0245

PEEL, Derrick. b 50. Open Univ BA82. Linc Th Coll 75. **d** 78 **p** 79. C Otley *Bradf* 78-82; V Shelf 82-94; P-in-c Buttershaw St Aid 89-94; TR Shelf w Buttershaw St Aid 94-95; V E Crompton *Man* 95-05; V Ware St Mary *St Alb* from 05. *St Mary's Vicarage, 31 Thunder Court, Ware SG12 0PT* Tel (01920) 464817

PEEL, John Bruce. b 30. TCD BA54 MA68. Wells Th Coll 69. **d** 70 **p** 71. C Wilmslow *Ches* 70-75; V Weston 75-83; V Henbury 83-95; Chapl Parkside Hosp Ches 83-95; rtd 95; Perm to Offic *Ches* from 95. *Winneba, 29 Hungerford Terrace, Crewe CW1 6HF* Tel (01270) 587464

PEEL, Capt Jonathan Sidney. b 37. CBE95 MC57 DL75. St Jo Coll Cam BA70 MA75. **d** 00 **p** 01. NSM Ashmanhaugh, Barton Turf etc *Nor* 00-07; rtd 07; Perm to Offic *Nor* from 07. *Barton Hall, Barton Turf, Norwich NR12 8AU* Tel (01692) 536250 Fax 536135

PEEL, Michael Jerome. b 31. Bris Univ BA55 MLitt73 Man Univ BD65 K Coll Lon PhD88. Wycliffe Hall Ox 57. **d** 59 **p** 60. C Stretford St Matt *Man* 59-61; C Chorlton upon Medlock 61-62; Chapl Man Univ 61-62; C Chorlton-cum-Hardy St Clem 62-65; V Chirbury *Heref* 65-68; P-in-c Marton 65-68; R Iver Heath *Ox* 68-87; V Linslade 87-95; rtd 95; Warden Coll of St Barn Lingfield 95-00; Perm to Offic *S'wark* 95-00; Perm to Offic *Chich* and *Roch* 95-00; *St E* from 00; *Chelmsf* from 01. *Poplar Meadow, Thedwastre Road, Thurston, Bury St Edmunds IP31 3QY* Tel (01359) 270296

PEELING, Mrs Pamela Mary Alberta. b 44. Oak Hill Th Coll 83. **dss** 86 **d** 87 **p** 94. NSM Moulsham St Luke *Chelmsf* 86-88; NSM N Springfield 88-95; C Basildon St Martin 95-97; TV Grays

Thurrock 97-05; rtd 05; Perm to Offic *St E* from 05. *4 Heron Road, Saxmundham IP17 1WR* Tel (01728) 604584
E-mail phil@ppeeling.freeserve.co.uk

PEER, Charles Scott. b 69. Bris Univ BSc91 PGCE94. Trin Coll Bris BA02. **d** 02 **p** 03. C Dawlish *Ex* 02-05; P-in-c Kea *Truro* from 05. *The Vicarage, Killiow, Truro TR3 6AE* Tel (01872) 272850 E-mail charlespeer@aol.com

PEERS, John Edward. b 39. Bps' Coll Cheshunt 60. **d** 63 **p** 64. C Crayford *Roch* 63-67; C Beckenham St Jas 67-69; C Winlaton *Dur* 69-72; P-in-c Silksworth 72-81; R Lt Bowden St Nic *Leic* 81-86; P-in-c Lt Bowden St Hugh 83-86; RD Gartree I 84-88; R Market Harborough Transfiguration 86-88; V Skipton Ch Ch *Bradf* 88-99; V Hambleton w Out Rawcliffe *Blackb* 99-03; rtd 03; Perm to Offic *Heref* from 08. *9 Holland Road, Leominster HR6 8PF* Tel (01568) 614794
E-mail johnepeers@totalise.co.uk

✠**PEERS, The Most Revd Michael Geoffrey.** b 34. Univ of BC BA56. Trin Coll Toronto LTh59 Hon DD78. **d** 59 **p** 60 **c** 77. C Ottawa St Thos 59-61; C Ottawa Trin 61-65; Chapl Carleton Univ 61-66; R Winnipeg St Bede 66-72; R Winnipeg St Martin w Middlechurch St Paul 72-74; Adn Winnipeg 69-74; R St Paul's Cathl Regina and Dean Qu'Appelle 74-77; Bp Qu'Appelle 77-82; Abp Qu'Appelle and Metrop Rupert's Land 82-86; Primate Angl Ch of Canada 86-04; rtd 04. *195 Westminster Avenue, Toronto ON M6R 1N9, Canada*

PEERS, Michael John. b 65. SS Paul & Mary Coll Cheltenham BA86. Ripon Coll Cuddesdon 88. **d** 91 **p** 92. C Birstall and Wanlip *Leic* 91-94; C Leic St Marg and All SS 94-96; TV The Abbey Leic 96-00; P-in-c Langley Park *Dur* 00-01; V from 01; P-in-c Esh 00-01; V from 01; P-in-c Hamsteels 00-01; V from 01; P-in-c Waterhouses 00-01; V from 01. *The Vicarage, Church Street, Langley Park, Durham DH7 9TZ* Tel 0191-373 3110
E-mail mjpeers@aol.com

PEERS, Richard Charles. b 65. K Alfred's Coll Win BEd88 Lon Inst of Educn MA05. Chich Th Coll BTh93. **d** 93 **p** 94. C Grangetown *York* 93-95; C Portsea St Mary *Portsm* 95-97; Dep Hd Emsworth Primary Sch 97-01; Hon Chapl Portsm Cathl 01-03; Chapl St Luke's Sch Southsea 01-03; Dep Hd Ch Sch Richmond 03-06; Chapl Abp Tenison's Sch Kennington 06-08; Headmaster Northbrook C of E Sch Lewisham from 08; Hon C Earlsfield St Andr *S'wark* from 06. *1 Glebe House, Waynflete Street, London SW18 3QG* Tel (020) 8879 7298
E-mail richard.peers1@btopenworld.com

PEET, Derek Edwin. b 26. Sheff Univ BA51 DipEd52. Qu Coll Birm 66. **d** 67 **p** 68. C Hebden Bridge *Wakef* 67-70; V Darton 70-79; TR Gleadless Valley *Sheff* 79-85; V Kirk Hallam *Derby* 85-96; rtd 96; Perm to Offic *Ripon* from 96. *44 Parkways Grove, Woodlesford, Leeds LS26 8TP* Tel 0113-282 3079 Mobile 07960-450038

PEET, John Christopher. b 56. Oriel Coll Ox BA80 MA83 Clare Coll Cam BA82 MA87. Ridley Hall Cam 80. **d** 83 **p** 84. C Menston w Woodhead *Bradf* 83-86; C Cononley w Bradley from 97. *The Vicarage, 3 Meadow Close, Cononley, Keighley BD20 8LZ* Tel (01535) 634369
E-mail john.peet@bradford.anglican.org

PEET, John Michael. b 44. AKC67. **d** 68 **p** 72. C Battersea St Pet *S'wark* 68-69; C Sutton St Nic 69-74; C Perry Hill St Geo 74-78; TV Stepney St Dunstan and All SS *Lon* 78-81; P-in-c Stamford Hill St Bart 81-86; V 87-89; P-in-c Mile End Old Town H Trin 89-90; P-in-c Bromley All Hallows 89-90; TR Bow H Trin and All Hallows 90-03; V Mile End H Trin 03-09; R Bow w Bromley St Leon from 09. *28 Coborn Street, London E3 2AB* Tel (020) 8980 2074 Fax 8980 2247 E-mail michael@mpeet.fsnet.co.uk

PEGG, Brian Peter Richard (Bill). b 30. Ox NSM Course 77 Sarum & Wells Th Coll 82. **d** 83 **p** 84. C Furze Platt *Ox* 83-85; V Ashbury, Compton Beauchamp and Longcot w Fernham 85-94; Chapl Mlaga *Eur* 94-97; rtd 97; Hon C Shere, Albury and Chilworth *Guildf* 98-02; Perm to Offic *Eur* from 98 and *Linc* from 03. *31 King Street, Winterton, Scunthorpe DN15 9TP* Tel (01724) 734860

PEGLER, Mrs Eve Charlotte. b 73. Cheltenham & Glouc Coll of HE BSc95. Ridley Hall Cam 05. **d** 07 **p** 08. C Hullavington, Norton and Stanton St Quintin *Bris* from 07; C Sherston Magna, Easton Grey, Luckington etc from 07. *The Vicarage, Green Lane, Sherston, Malmesbury SN16 0NP* Tel and fax (01666) 840654 E-mail evepegler@tiscali.co.uk

PEGLER, Frederic Arthur. b 19. Selw Coll Cam BA46 MA48. Qu Coll Birm 46. **d** 47 **p** 48. C Crawley *Chich* 47-49; C Rickmansworth *St Alb* 49-50; V Sark *Win* 50-52; PV S'well Minster 52-55; Canada 55-84 and from 86; rtd 84; Perm to Offic *St Alb* 84-85. *302 Goodwin Manor, 1148 Goodwin Street, Victoria BC V8S 5H2, Canada* Tel (001) (250) 370 9300

PEILOW, Lynda Elizabeth Anne. b 74. CITC BTh97. **d** 97 **p** 98. C Castleknock and Mulhuddart w Clonsilla *D & G* 97-00; C Dublin St Ann and St Steph 00-01; Min Can St Patr Cathl Dublin 00-01; I Clonsast w Rathangan, Thomastown etc *M & K*

from 01. *The Rectory, Monasteroris, Edenderry, Co Offaly, Republic of Ireland* Tel (00353) (46) 973 1585
E-mail lpeilow@oceanfree.net
or edenderry@kildare.anglican.org

PEIRCE, John. b 35. Worc Coll Ox BA59 MA64 Kent Univ MA96. Wycliffe Hall Ox 59. **d** 61 **p** 62. C Brompton H Trin *Lon* 61-64; C Wareham w Arne *Sarum* 64-68; V Sturminster Newton and Hinton St Mary 68-74; V Kingswood *Bris* 74-79; Dir Coun Chr Care *Ex* 79-89; Public Preacher 89-92; NSM Hackney *Lon* 90-94; NSM St Botolph Aldgate w H Trin Minories from 94; Co-ord Ch Action on Disability 90-98; Perm to Offic *Ex* 92-98. *3 Mile End Place, London E1 4BH* Tel (020) 7790 9418

PEIRCE, Canon John Martin. b 36. Jes Coll Cam BA59 MA65. Westcott Ho Cam 65. **d** 66 **p** 67. C Croydon St Jo *Cant* 66-70; C Fareham H Trin *Portsm* 70-71; TV 71-76; TR Langley Marish *Ox* 76-85; RD Burnham 78-82; Dir of Ords and Post-Ord Tr 85-01; Can Res Ch Ch 87-01; rtd 01. *8 Burwell Meadow, Witney, Oxford OX28 5JQ*

PEIRIS, Lionel James Harold (Brother Lionel). b 45. Serampore Coll BD71. Bp's Coll Calcutta 67. **d** 70 **p** 71. P Lect Colombo Coll Sri Lanka 71-76 and 78-95; C Shirley *Birm* 76-78; P Brother SSF Auckland New Zealand 96-97; Asst Chapl and Past Asst Annerley Hosp Australia 97-98; Hon C Annerley St Phil 97-98; P-in-c from 99. *115 Cornwall Street, Annerley Qld 4103, Australia* Tel (0061) (7) 3391 3915 Fax 3391 3916

PELHAM, John. b 36. New Coll Ox BA61 MA65. **d** 79 **p** 80. NSM Balerno *Edin* 79-91; NSM W Linton and Penicuik 91-94; Dioc Supernumerary from 94; NSM Lanark *Glas* 03-07; Lic to Offic *Edin* from 08. *2 Horsburgh Bank, Balerno EH14 7DA* Tel 0131-449 3934 E-mail john@pelham21.fsnet.co.uk

PELL, Charles Andrew. b 54. Leeds Univ CertEd77. Aston Tr Scheme 87 St Jo Coll Nottm 87. **d** 89 **p** 90. C Mottram in Longdendale w Woodhead *Ches* 89-90; C Handforth 90-93; P-in-c Walton Breck *Liv* 93-94; V 94-96; P-in-c Glyndyfrdwy and Llansantffraid Glyn Dyfrdwy *St As* 96-01; V Rhodes *Man* 01-07; CF (ACF) 93-07; rtd 07; Perm to Offic *Man* from 09. *32 Harden Drive, Bolton BL2 5BX* Tel 07831-279429 (mobile)
E-mail padre@milnet.uk.net

PELLEY, John Lawless. b 34. Oak Hill Th Coll 67. **d** 69 **p** 70. C Fareham St Jo *Portsm* 69-72; C Frogmore *St Alb* 72-76; V Standon 76-96; RD Bishop's Stortford 91-95; rtd 96; Perm to Offic *Ely* from 96. *7 Home Close, Histon, Cambridge CB24 9JL* Tel (01223) 234636

PELLING, Nicholas Philip. b 48. EMMTC 05. **d** 07 **p** 08. C S Cluster S'well Deanery from 07. *9 Bartley Gardens, Calverton, Nottingham NG14 6RG* Tel 0115-965 2545 Mobile 07804-326416 E-mail nickandjuliepelling@hotmail.com

PELLY, Mrs Elizabeth Wigram (Lulu). b 52. Bris Univ BA73. ERMC 05. **d** 08 **p** 09. NSM Towcester w Caldecote and Easton Neston etc *Pet* from 08. *Home Farm, Wakefield Lodge, Potterspury, Towcester NN12 7QX* Tel (01327) 811218 Mobile 07723-604316 E-mail lulu.pelly@farming.co.uk

PELLY, Raymond Blake. b 38. Worc Coll Ox BA61 MA63 Geneva Univ DTh71. Linc Th Coll 61 Bossey Ecum Inst Geneva 62. **d** 63 **p** 64. C Gosforth All SS *Newc* 63-65; C N Lynn w St Marg and St Nic *Nor* 69-70; Vice-Prin Westcott Ho Cam 71-76; Warden St Jo Coll Auckland New Zealand 77-85; Visiting Lect Univ of Mass Boston USA 86-88 and 96; Chapl Victoria Univ of Wellington New Zealand 90-94; Asst P Wellington St Pet 92-94 and from 96; rtd 03. *12 Kio Crescent, Hataitai, Wellington 6021, New Zealand* Tel (0064) (4) 386 3972 Mobile 21-486200 Fax (4) 386 3729 E-mail raymond.pelly@xtra.co.nz

PEMBERTON, Anthony Thomas Christie (Chris). b 57. BA. Cranmer Hall Dur 82. **d** 84 **p** 85. C Maidstone St Luke *Cant* 84-88; Chapl Ox Pastorate 88-98; V Cant St Mary Bredin 98-09; Perm to Offic from 09. *Address temp unknown*

PEMBERTON, Carrie Mary. b 55. St Hilda's Coll Ox BA78 Cam Univ PGCE82 Leeds Univ MA92 Newnham Coll Cam PhD98. Cranmer Hall Dur 83 NEOC 84. **dss** 86 **d** 87 **p** 94. NSM Leeds St Geo *Ripon* 86-87; Miss Partner CMS and Dir Women's Studies Angl Th Inst Zaïre 87-91; Perm to Offic *Pet* 92-94; NSM Bourn and Kingston w Caxton and Longstowe *Ely* 94-99; TV Elsworth w Knapwell 99; Min Cambourne LEP 00-01; Perm to Offic 01-07; Cen Chapl Yarlswood Immigration and Detention Cen 01-03; Chief Exec CHASTE 04-08; Development Officer Cam Cen for Applied Research in Human Trafficking from 08. *9 South End, Bassingbourn, Royston SG8 5NJ* Tel (01763) 252866 E-mail carrie@ccarht.org

PEMBERTON, Crispin Mark Rugman. b 59. St Andr Univ MTheol83. St Steph Ho Ox 84. **d** 86 **p** 87. C Acton Green *Lon* 86-90; C Leckhampton SS Phil and Jas w Cheltenham St Jas *Glouc* 90-93; V Tuffley 93-97; RE Teacher Cheltenham Coll Jun Sch 97-00. *3 Langdon Road, Cheltenham GL53 7NZ* Tel (01242) 526188

PEMBERTON, Elizabeth Joan. b 70. Univ of W Aus BA90. ACT. **d** 98. Field Officer Bible Soc Australia 98-09; Perm to Offic *Lich* from 09. *17 The Spinney, Finchfield, Wolverhampton WV3 9HE*

PEMBERTON, Canon Jeremy Charles Baring. b 56. Mert Coll Ox MA77 Fitzw Ho Cam BA80 Leeds Univ MA92. Ridley Hall Cam 78. **d** 81 **p** 82. C Stranton *Dur* 81-84; C Leeds St Geo *Ripon* 84-87; CMS Miss Partner and Dir Angl Th Inst Zaïre 87-91; V Irchester *Pet* 92-94; R Bourn and Kingston w Caxton and Longstowe *Ely* 94-00; P-in-c Elsworth w Knapwell 99-00; P-in-c Boxworth 99-00; TR Papworth 00-07; RD Bourn 98-03; Hon Can Ely Cathl 05-07; Community Chapl Notts Co Teaching Primary Care Trust from 08; Hon Can Boga from 05. *47 Easthorpe, Southwell NG25 0HY* Tel (01636) 815998 E-mail jeremy.pemberton@live.co.uk

PEMBERY, Gerald Marcus. b 29. Glouc Sch of Min 89. **d** 90 **p** 91. NSM Bream *Glouc* 90-97; rtd 97; Perm to Offic *Glouc* 97-05. *Kings Wood, The Tufts, Bream, Lydney GL15 6HW* Tel (01594) 562750

PENBERTHY, Canon Joanna Susan. b 60. Newnham Coll Cam BA81 MA85. St Jo Coll Nottm MTh84 St Jo Coll Dur 83. **dss** 84 **d** 87 **p** 97. Haughton le Skerne *Dur* 84-85; Llanishen and Lisvane *Llan* 85-87; NSM 87-89; NSM Llanwddyn and Llanfihangel-yng-Nghwynfa etc *St As* 89-93; NSM Llansadwrn w Llanwrda and Manordeilo *St D* 93-95; Officer Div for Par Development Ch in Wales 95-99; P-in-c Cynwyl Gaeo w Llansawel and Talley *St D* 99-01; V from 01; Can St D Cathl from 07. *The Vicarage, Llanwrda SA19 8HD* Tel (01550) 777343 E-mail jspenberthy@tiscali.co.uk

PENDLEBURY, Stephen Thomas. b 50. ACA78 Southn Univ BSc73. Ridley Hall Cam 86. **d** 88 **p** 89. C Birkenhead St Jas w St Bede *Ches* 88-91; V 91-00; V Ches St Paul from 00. *St Paul's Vicarage, 10 Sandy Lane, Chester CH3 5UL* Tel (01244) 351377 E-mail stpendleby@aol.com

PENDORF, Canon James Gordon. b 45. Drew Univ New Jersey BA67. Episc Th Sch Cam Mass STB71. **d** 71 **p** 71. V Newark St Greg USA 71-76; V Colne H Trin *Blackb* 76-80; Sen Dioc Stewardship Adv *Chelmsf* 80-83; Dioc Sec *Birm* 83-95; P-in-c Highgate 95-97; V 97-04; Dioc Stewardship Adv 95-04; AD Birm City Cen 96-02; Hon Can Birm Cathl 90-04; Par Resources Adv and Chapl St Nic Ch Cen *St E* from 04; NSM Holbrook, Stutton, Freston, Woolverstone etc from 05. *Little Park, Main Road, Woolverstone, Ipswich IP9 1AR* Tel (01473) 780295 *or* 298501 Mobile 07943-265037 E-mail jim@stedmundsbury.anglican.org

PENFOLD, Brian Robert. b 54. Lon Univ BSc75 Bris Univ PGCE77. Oak Hill Th Coll BA84. **d** 84 **p** 85. C Norwood St Luke *S'wark* 84-88; C Rayleigh *Chelmsf* 88-92; V New Barnet St Jas *St Alb* 92-08; V Worthing St Geo *Chich* from 08. *14 Pendine Avenue, Worthing BN11 2NB* Tel (01903) 203309 Mobile 07753-680839 E-mail brian@brpenfold.freeserve.co.uk

PENFOLD, Colin Richard. b 52. St Pet Coll Ox BA74 MA78. Ridley Hall Cam 81. **d** 84 **p** 85. C Buckhurst Hill *Chelmsf* 84-87; C Greenside *Dur* 87-90; V Cononley w Bradley *Bradf* 90-97; P-in-c Shipley St Paul and Frizinghall 97; V Shipley St Paul 98-08; P-in-c Gt Harwood *Blackb* from 08. *St Bartholomew's Vicarage, Church Lane, Great Harwood, Blackburn BB6 7PU* Tel (01254) 884039 E-mail colin@thepenfolds.org.uk

PENFOLD, Marion Jean. b 49. NEOC 96. **d** 99 **p** 00. NSM Lesbury w Alnmouth *Newc* 99-02; C 02-03; NSM Longhoughton w Howick 99-02; C 02-03; TV N Tyne and Redesdale from 03. *The Vicarage, Otterburn, Newcastle upon Tyne NE19 1NP* Tel (01830) 520212 *or* (01665) 712698 E-mail marion.penfold@btinternet.com

PENFOLD, Canon Susan Irene. b 52. York Univ BA73 Bris Univ PhD77 Selw Coll Cam BA83 MA87. Ridley Hall Cam 81. **dss** 84 **d** 87 **p** 94. Buckhurst Hill *Chelmsf* 84-87; Hon C Greenside *Dur* 87-90; Hon C Cononley w Bradley *Bradf* 90-97; Assoc Dioc Dir of Ords 96-01; Hon C Shipley St Paul 97-00; Perm to Offic from 00; Dir of Ords and CME Officer *Wakef* 01-03; Dir of Ords and Dean of Min 03-08; Hon Can Wakef Cathl 04-08; Can Res Blackb Cathl from 08; Dir of Min from 08. *The Vicarage, Church Lane, Great Harwood, Blackburn BB6 7PU* Tel (01254) 503085 Mobile 07753-987977 E-mail sue.penfold@blackburn.anglican.org

PENGELLEY, Peter John. b 22. Sarum & Wells Th Coll 72. **d** 74 **p** 75. C Midsomer Norton *B & W* 74-78; R Stogursey w Fiddington 78-88; Ind Chapl 80-88; rtd 88; Perm to Offic *B & W* from 89. *Rosslyn Cottage, Roadwater, Watchet TA23 0RB* Tel (01984) 640798

PENGELLY, Canon Geoffrey. b 50. Oak Hill Th Coll 86. **d** 88 **p** 89. C Redruth w Lanner and Treleigh *Truro* 88-91; TV Bolventor 91-92; V Egloskerry, N Petherwin, Tremaine and Tresmere from 92; C Lezant w Lawhitton and S Petherwin w Trewen from 03; Hon Can Truro Cathl from 03; RD Trigg Major from 04. *The Vicarage, Egloskerry, Launceston PL15 8RX* Tel (01566) 785365

PENISTAN, Richard Luke. *See* PENNYSTAN, Richard Luke

PENMAN, John Bain. b 67. Aber Univ BD89 New Coll Edin MTh93. Edin Th Coll 91. **d** 93 **p** 94. C Glas St Ninian 93-96; C Ealing Ch the Sav *Lon* 96-98; P-in-c Kirkcaldy and Kinghorn *St And* 98-04; R Falkirk *Edin* from 04. *55 Kerse Lane, Falkirk FK1 1RX* Tel (01324) 623709 Mobile 07713-254660 E-mail jpenmanfct@btconnect.com

PENMAN, Miss Margaret Heather. b 50. St Martin's Coll Lanc CertEd71 Lanc Univ DipEd82 FRSA95. Carl Dioc Tr Inst 90. **d** 93 **p** 94. Headteacher Hesketh w Becconsall All SS C of E Sch 85-00; RE/Schools Adv *Liv* from 00; NSM Lostock Hall *Blackb* 93-95; NSM Leyland St Jas from 95. *9 Oakfield Drive, Leyland, Preston PR5 3XE* Tel (01772) 435927 *or* 812630 Fax 814721 E-mail heatherpenman@onetel.com

PENN, Robert George. b 42. St Jo Coll Auckland LTh66. **d** 65 **p** 66. C Mt Roskill New Zealand 65-68; C Henderson 69-70; V Glen Innes 71-72; C Alverstoke *Portsm* 73-74; CF 74-77; C Bridgwater St Mary w Chilton Trinity *B & W* 77-80; P-in-c Haselbury Plucknett w N Perrott 80-81; P-in-c Misterton 80-81; V Haselbury Plucknett, Misterton and N Perrott 81-89; P-in-c Appleton *Ox* 89-07; P-in-c Besselsleigh w Dry Sandford 89-00; P-in-c Besselsleigh 00-07; rtd 07; Perm to Offic *Ox* from 07. *31 High Street, Sherington, Newport Pagnell MK16 9NU* Tel (01908) 611838 E-mail penman298@btinternet.com

PENN, Barry Edwin. b 46. Univ of Wales (Swansea) BA72. St Jo Coll Nottm 77. **d** 79 **p** 80. C New Barnet St Jas *St Alb* 79-83; TV Preston St Jo *Blackb* 83-92; V Patchway *Bris* 92-01; Perm to Offic from 01. *50 Eastfield Road, Westbury-on-Trym, Bristol BS9 4AG* Tel 0117-962 2862

PENN, Christopher Francis. b 34. ACII63. Wells Th Coll 68. **d** 70 **p** 71. C Andover w Foxcott *Win* 70-72; C Odiham w S Warnborough 72-75; C Keynsham *B & W* 75-76; TV 76-82; R Chilcompton w Downside and Stratton on the Fosse 82-87; RD Midsomer Norton 84-86; V Bathford 87-90; V Avonmouth St Andr *Bris* 90-96; Ind Chapl 90-96; rtd 96; Perm to Offic *B & W* and *Bris* from 96. *53 Caernarvon Road, Keynsham, Bristol BS31 2PF* Tel 0117-986 2367

PENN, Christopher Wilson. b 60. Cranmer Hall Dur 98. **d** 00 **p** 01. C Wrockwardine Deanery *Lich* 00-03; P-in-c Llanblodwel and Trefonen 03-07; P-in-c Llanymynech 03-07; P-in-c Morton 03-07; R Llanblodwel, Llanymynech, Morton and Trefonen from 07; Rural Officer (Salop Adnry) from 08. *The Rectory, Rectory Lane, Pant, Oswestry SY10 9RA* Tel (01691) 831211 E-mail bordergroupadmin@hotmail.co.uk

PENN, Clive Llewellyn. b 12. Oak Hill Th Coll 47. **d** 48 **p** 49. C Deptford St Luke *S'wark* 48-50; C Guernsey St Sampson *Win* 50-54; P-in-c Cummins Australia 55-56; Miss Chapl Somerton Park and Warradale 56-59; R Port Elliot w Goolwa 59-65; V Jersey Gouray St Martin 66-71; rtd 77; Lic to Offic *Win* 71-86. *PO Box 679, Williamstown SA 5351, Australia*

PENN, Mrs Jennifer Anne. b 61. Imp Coll Lon BEng84 Leeds Univ BA07. NOC 04. **d** 07 **p** 08. C Halliwell St Pet *Man* from 07. *9 Capitol Close, Bolton BL1 6LU* E-mail j.penn@homecall.co.uk

PENNAL, David Bernard. b 37. Ripon Hall Ox 64. **d** 67 **p** 68. C Moseley St Mary *Birm* 67-71; C Bridgwater St Mary w Chilton Trinity *B & W* 71-73; P-in-c Hilton w Cheselbourne and Melcombe Horsey *Sarum* 73-76; R Milton Abbas, Hilton w Cheselbourne etc 76-78; P-in-c Spetisbury w Charlton Marshall 78-88; R Spetisbury w Charlton Marshall etc 89-00; rtd 00. *11 High Street, Wicken, Ely CB7 5XR*

PENNANT, David Falconer. b 51. Trin Coll Cam MA73. Trin Coll Bris BD84 PhD88 **d** 86 **p** 87. C Bramcote *S'well* 86-88; C Woking St Jo *Guildf* 88-93. *30 Oriental Road, Woking GU22 7AW* Tel (01483) 768055 E-mail david.pennant@ntlworld.com

PENNELL (formerly COFFIN), Ms Pamela. b 45. EAMTC 94. **d** 97 **p** 98. NSM Moulsham St Luke *Chelmsf* 97-98; NSM Writtle w Highwood 98-00; Perm to Offic 01-04; NSM Gt Waltham w Ford End 04-06; Perm to Offic 06-08; P-in-c Sandon from 08; P-in-c E Hanningfield from 08. *33 Birch Lane, Stock, Ingatestone CM4 9NA* Tel (01277) 841270 E-mail pencof.pam@btinternet.com

PENNEY, David Richard John. b 39. St Jo Coll Dur BA63. Cranmer Hall Dur 63. **d** 67 **p** 68. C Chilvers Coton w Astley *Cov* 67-70; C Styvechale 70-72; P-in-c Shilton w Ansty 72-77; P-in-c Withybrook 74-77; R Easington w Liverton *York* 77-85; Dir Soc Resp *Sarum* 85-93; Perm to Offic *Blackb* 93-02; rtd 01. *Noyna House, 2 Noyna Street, Colne BB8 0PE* Tel (01282) 870076 Mobile 07966-157697

PENNEY, William Affleck. b 41. MBIM75 FRSA91. K Coll Lon BD63 AKC63 St Boniface Warminster 65. **d** 66 **p** 67. C Chatham St Steph *Roch* 66-70; Ind Chapl 70-77; P-in-c Bredhurst 70-72; Hon C S Gillingham 72-74; Hon C Eynsford w Farningham and Lullingstone 74-77; Bp's Dom Chapl 74-88; Hon Ind Chapl 77-88; Hon C Balham St Mary and St Jo *S'wark* 89-91; Perm to Offic *St Alb* 91-94; Hon C Bushey 94-05; rtd 05. *6 Devonshire Court, 26A Devonshire Street, London W1G 6PJ* Tel (020) 7486 1227 E-mail wpenney@btconnect.com

PENNICEARD, Clifford Ashley. b 42. Monash Univ Aus BA65 DipEd71 Linacre Coll Ox BA67 Ox Univ MA70. St Steph Ho Ox 65. **d** 68 **p** 69. C S Leamington St Jo *Cov* 68-70; P-in-c

Wantirna Australia 74; Assoc P N Brighton 76-80; P-in-c Euroa 84-91; P-in-c Nagumbie 93-95; P-in-c Cudal 96-98; R Manly St Paul 98-04; P-in-c Cen Goulburn from 04. *RMB 5400, Strathbogie Vic 3666, Australia* Tel (0061) (3) 5790 5331 Mobile 416-177732 E-mail cliffpenn@dodo.com.au

PENNIECOOKE, Dorothy Victoria. b 45. Dioc OLM tr scheme 97. **d** 00 **p** 01. NSM Balham Hill Ascension *S'wark* from 00. *56 Lysias Road, London SW12 8BP* Tel (020) 8673 0037

PENNINGTON, Mrs Catherine Prudence. b 56. Man Poly BSc82 Sussex Univ MSc87 Flinders Univ Aus BTh00. Adelaide Coll of Div 96. **d** 00 **p** 01. C Glenelg Australia 00-01; NSM American Cathl Paris 01-02; C Is of Dogs Ch Ch and St Jo w St Luke *Lon* 02-03; C De Beauvoir Town St Pet 03-04; P-in-c Nazeing *Chelmsf* from 05; P-in-c Roydon from 05. *The Vicarage, Betts Lane, Nazeing, Waltham Abbey EN9 2DB* Tel (01992) 893167 Mobile 07800-822297 E-mail pennington@hotmail.com

PENNINGTON, Edward Francis Quentin. b 76. G&C Coll Cam BA97 MA01 Birm Univ MSc98. Oak Hill Th Coll BTh04. **d** 04 **p** 05. C Moulton *Pet* 04-07; C Fulwood *Sheff* from 07. *23 Hallamshire Close, Sheffield S10 4FJ* Tel 0114-230 2234 Mobile 07743-942931 E-mail efqpennington@hotmail.com

PENNINGTON, Emma Louise. b 71. Ex Univ BA92 Kent Univ MA96. Ripon Coll Cuddesdon BA00. **d** 00 **p** 01. C Shepperton *Lon* 00-03; Chapl Worc Coll Ox 03-08; TV Wheatley *Ox* from 08. *Garsington Rectory, 17 Southend, Garsington, Oxford OX44 9DH* Tel (01865) 361381 E-mail emma.pennington@worc.ox.ac.uk

PENNINGTON, Frederick William. b 71. K Coll Lon. **d** 55 **p** 56. C Tiverton St Pet *Ex* 55-58; R Bradford 58-66; R Thornbury 58-66; V N Molton w Twitchen 66-77; P-in-c Molland 68-77; rtd 77; Lic to Offic *Ex* 77-95; Perm to Offic from 95. *6 Meadow Road, Budleigh Salterton EX9 6JL*

PENNINGTON, John Kenneth. b 27. Man Univ LLB48. Linc Th Coll 51. **d** 52 **p** 53. C Wavertree H Trin *Liv* 52-56; C Rotherham *Sheff* 56-59; P-in-c Kanpur All So India 59-63; V Nelson St Phil *Blackb* 64-66; Area Sec USPG *Derby, Leic* and *S'well* 66-71; *Derby* and *Sheff* 71-75; C Nottingham St Mary *S'well* 75-78; C Nottingham St Mary and St Cath 78-92; rtd 93; Perm to Offic *S'well* from 93. *3 St Jude's Avenue, Nottingham NG3 5FG* Tel 0115-962 3420

PENNINGTON, John Michael. b 32. Em Coll Cam BA54 MA58 IEng MIET MIHEEM. Wells Th Coll 58. **d** 60 **p** 61. C Stockport St Geo *Ches* 60-64; V Congleton St Steph 64-68; Chapl Nor Sch 68-70; V Hattersley *Ches* 70-72; C-in-c Upton Priory CD 72-75; V Upton Priory 75-79; Perm to Offic *Newc* 83-87; V Tynemouth St Jo 87-94; P-in-c Cambois 94-97; Chapl Northd HA 94-97; Ashington and Wansbeck Hosps 94-97; rtd 97; Perm to Offic *Newc* from 97. *297 Wingrove Road North, Fenham, Newcastle upon Tyne NE4 9EE* Tel and fax 0191-274 5281

PENNOCK, Mrs Christine. b 48. Bp Grosseteste Coll BEd71 Leeds Univ PGCE94 Teesside Univ PGDE95. NEOC 98. **d** 01 **p** 02. C Crowland *Linc* 01-05; P-in-c Ruskington Gp from 05. *The Rectory, All Saints' Close, Ruskington, Sleaford NG34 9FP* Tel (01526) 832463 Mobile 07813-954043 E-mail chris@cpennock.fsnet.co.uk

PENNY, Alexander Stuart Egerton. b 52. Wolv Art Coll BA75. Ridley Hall Cam MA00. **d** 00 **p** 01. C Uttoxeter Area *Lich* 00-03; V Crosthwaite Keswick *Carl* from 03. *Crosthwaite Vicarage, Vicarage Hill, Keswick CA12 5QB* Tel (01768) 772509 E-mail stuartpenny@onetel.com

PENNY, David Roy. b 67. Wilson Carlile Coll 89 NOC 00. **d** 03 **p** 04. C Hey and Waterhead *Man* 03-05; V Chadderton St Matt w St Luke from 05; AD Oldham W from 09. *St Matthew's Vicarage, Mill Brow, Chadderton, Oldham OL1 2RT* Tel 0161-624 8600 E-mail dpennyca@aol.com

PENNY, Diana Eleanor. b 51. Open Univ BA87 Birm Univ DipEd96. Nor Ord Course 87. **d** 89 **p** 94. NSM Gillingham w Geldeston, Stockton, Ellingham etc *Nor* 89-93; NSM Upton St Leonards *Glouc* 93-97; NSM Stiffkey and Cockthorpe w Morston, Langham etc *Nor* 97-03; NSM Stiffkey and Bale 03-04; C Lowestoft St Marg 04-06; V E Marshland *Ely* from 06. *The Vicarage, 37 Church Road, Tilney St Lawrence, King's Lynn PE34 4QQ* Tel (01945) 880259 E-mail dep@dialstart.net

PENNY, Edwin John. b 43. Leeds Univ BA64. Coll of Resurr Mirfield 64. **d** 66 **p** 67. C Acocks Green *Birm* 66-69; C Wombourne *Lich* 69-71; C Wednesbury St Paul Wood Green 71-74; V Kingshurst *Birm* 74-79; Chapl All Hallows Convent Norfolk 79-82; Hon Chapl Overgate Hospice Yorkshire 82-84; Hon C Raveningham *Nor* 84-90; All Hallows Hosp Nor Past Team 90-93; P-in-c Upton St Leonards *Glouc* 93-97; Dioc Communications Officer 93-97; P-in-c Stiffkey and Cockthorpe w Morston, Langham etc *Nor* 97-03; P-in-c Gunthorpe w Bale w Field Dalling, Saxlingham etc 99-03; R Stiffkey and Bale 03-04; rtd 04; Perm to Offic *Nor* from 04 and *Ely* from 08; RD Wisbech Lynn Marshland *Ely* from 09. *The Vicarage, 37 Church Road, Tilney St Lawrence, King's Lynn PE34 4QQ* Tel (01945) 880259 E-mail noakhillpupil@dialstart.net

PENNY, Michael John. b 36. Linc Th Coll 78. **d** 80 **p** 81. C Knighton St Mary Magd *Leic* 80-83; TV Leic Resurr 83-85; V Blackfordby 85-95; V Blackfordby and Woodville 95-00; RD

Akeley W 88-93; rtd 00; Perm to Offic *Nor* from 00. *15 Sarah's Road, Hunstanton PE36 5PA* Tel (01485) 534957

PENNY, Stuart. *See* PENNY, Alexander Stuart Egerton

PENNYSTAN, Richard Luke. b 74. Newc Univ BA97 St Jo Coll Cam BA02. Ridley Hall Cam 00. **d** 03 **p** 04. C E Twickenham St Steph *Lon* 03-06; C Fulham Ch Ch from 06. *55 Clancarty Road, London SW6 3AH* Tel (020) 7736 3302 Mobile 07971-663129

PENRITH, Suffragan Bishop of. *Vacant*

PENTELOW, Mrs Ysmena Rachael. b 73. St Andr Univ BD96 MLitt99. EAMTC 01. **d** 03 **p** 04. C Stevenage H Trin *St Alb* 03-06; P-in-c Langleybury St Paul from 06; Dioc CME Officer from 06. *The Vicarage, 1 Langleybury Lane, Kings Langley WD4 8QQ* Tel (01923) 270634 Mobile 07798-654194 E-mail pentelow@waitrose.com

PENTLAND, The Ven Raymond Jackson. b 57. Wm Booth Memorial Coll CertEd79 Open Univ BA90 Westmr Coll Ox MTh02. St Jo Coll Nottm 86. **d** 88 **p** 89. C Nottingham St Jude *S'well* 88-90; Chapl RAF 90-05; Command Chapl RAF 05-06; Adn RAF from 06; QHC from 06; Can and Preb Linc Cathl from 06. *Chaplaincy Services, Valiant Block, HQ Air Command, RAF High Wycombe HP14 4UE* Tel (01494) 497595 Fax 496343 E-mail ray.pentland929@mod.uk

PENTREATH, Canon Harvey. b 29. Wells Th Coll 54. **d** 57 **p** 58. C Bris St Ambrose Whitehall 57-60; C Leatherhead *Guildf* 60-63; C Haslemere 63-65; R Elstead 65-72; V Cuddington 73-80; Hon Can Guildf Cathl 80; V Helston *Truro* 80-85; RD Kerrier 84-86; C Helston and Wendron 85-92; Hon Can Truro Cathl 88-92; rtd 93; Perm to Offic *Truro* from 93. *Penmarr, 15 Penarwyn Crescent, Heamoor, Penzance TR18 3JU* Tel (01736) 360133

PEOPLES, James Scott. b 59. TCD BA HDipEd90. **d** 85 **p** 86. C Carlow w Urglin and Staplestown *C & O* 85-90; Chapl Kilkenny Coll 90-91; I Portarlington w Cloneyhurke and Lea *M & K* 91-99; Dioc Youth Officer (Kildare) 92-99; I Lucan w Leixlip *D & G* from 99. *5 Uppercross, Ballyowen Lane, Ballydowd, Lucan, Co Dublin, Republic of Ireland* Tel (00353) (1) 624 9147

PEOPLES, Mervyn Thomas Edwards. b 53. Open Univ BA88. CITC 03. **d** 06 **p** 07. Aux Min Raphoe w Raymochy and Clonleigh *D & R* from 06. *29 Dunnalong Road, Magheramason, Londonderry BT47 2RU* Tel (028) 7184 1416 E-mail mervynpeoples@hotmail.com

PEPPER, David Reginald. b 50. Lon Bible Coll. St Alb Minl Tr Scheme 89. **d** 92 **p** 93. NSM Cheshunt *St Alb* 92-95; NSM Bengeo 06-08; NSM Hertford from 08. *36 Salisbury Road, Hoddesdon EN11 0HX* Tel (01992) 410544 E-mail davidpepper2@yahoo.co.uk

PEPPER, Leonard Edwin. b 44. Ex Univ BA71. Ripon Hall Ox 71. **d** 73 **p** 74. C Cottingham *York* 73-76; C Kingshurst *Birm* 76-79; Dir Past Studies St Steph Ho Ox 80-89; TV Aylesbury w Bierton and Hulcott *Ox* 89-91; TV High Wycombe 91-96; rtd 96. *19 Gardiner Street, Oxford OX3 7AW* Tel (01865) 66191

PEPPIATT, Martin Guy. b 33. Trin Coll Ox BA57 MA60. Wycliffe Hall Ox 57. **d** 59 **p** 60. C St Marylebone All So w SS Pet and Jo *Lon* 59-63; Kenya 65-69; V E Twickenham St Steph *Lon* 69-96; rtd 96. *Pipers Cottage, East End, North Leigh, Witney OX29 8ND* Tel (01993) 883001

PEPPIATT, Quintin Brian Duncombe. b 63. Ex Univ BSc85 St Luke's Coll Ex PGCE86. Ripon Coll Cuddesdon 89 Ch Div Sch of the Pacific (USA) 90. **d** 92 **p** 93. C Gt Ilford St Clem and St Marg *Chelmsf* 92-95; TV E Ham w Upton Park St Alb from 95. *1 Norman Road, London E6 6HN* Tel (020) 8471 8751 E-mail quintinpeppiatt@aol.com

PERCIVAL, Brian Sydney. b 37. Univ of Wales (Ban) BA61. NOC 81. **d** 84 **p** 85. NSM Norbury *Ches* 84-88; P-in-c Werneth 88-04; RD Chadkirk 00-04; rtd 04; Perm to Offic *Ches* from 04. *21 Holly Road, High Lane, Stockport SK6 8HW* Tel (01663) 810217

PERCIVAL, Geoffrey. b 46. Ridley Hall Cam 73. **d** 76 **p** 77. C Eccleshill *Bradf* 76-79; C Otley 79-82; V Windhill 82-02; P-in-c Oakenshaw cum Woodlands 03-05; P-in-c Oakenshaw, Wyke and Low Moor 06-07. *27 Lane Side Close, Wyke, Bradford BD12 8EH* Tel (01274) 414925 E-mail geoff@microrey.co.uk

PERCIVAL, James Edward Charles. b 50. NOC 92. **d** 95 **p** 96. C Broughton *Blackb* 95-99; P-in-c Blackb St Steph 99-03; P-in-c Freckleton from 03; Chapl Blackb, Hyndburn and Ribble Valley NHS Trust 99-03. *Holy Trinity Vicarage, 3 Sunnyside Close, Freckleton, Preston PR4 1YJ* Tel (01772) 632209

PERCIVAL, James Frederick. b 74. New Coll Ox BA96 MA01 Barrister-at-Law (Middle Temple) 99. Ripon Coll Cuddesdon MA02. **d** 03 **p** 04. C Redhill St Matt *S'wark* 03-06; TV Sanderstead from 06. *St Mary's Vicarage, 85 Purley Oaks Road, South Croydon CR2 0NY* Tel (020) 8657 1725 E-mail james@sanderstead-parish.org.uk

PERCIVAL, Joanna Vera. b 52. Univ of San Francisco BA87. Ch Div Sch of Pacific MDiv94. **d** 94 **p** 94. Asst R Almaden USA 94-95; NSM Ockham w Hatchford *Guildf* 95-96; C Cobham 96-00; Dioc Spirituality Adv 00-02; V Weston 02-06; Perm to Offic *Lon* 06-07 and *S'wark* 06-07; Chapl Southn Univ Hosps

NHS Trust from 08. *Southampton General Hospital, Tremona Road, Shirley, Southampton SO16 6 YD* Tel (023) 8077 7222 E-mail joanna.percival@btinternet.com

PERCIVAL, Martin Eric. b 45. Lon Univ BSc66 Linacre Coll Ox BA70 MA74. Wycliffe Hall Ox 67. **d** 70 **p** 71. C Anfield St Marg *Liv* 70-73; C Witney *Ox* 73-74; TV Bottesford w Ashby *Linc* 74-76; TV Grantham 76-80; R Coningsby w Tattershall 80-82; P-in-c Coleford w Holcombe *B & W* 82-83; V 83-84; Chapl Rossall Sch Fleetwood 84-88; Chapl Woodbridge Sch 88-02; R Downham w S Hanningfield *Chelmsf* 02-05; P-in-c Ramsden Bellhouse 02-05; P-in-c Leiston *St E* from 05. *St Margaret's Vicarage, 2 King Edward Road, Leiston IP16 4HQ* Tel (01728) 833408 E-mail revmepercival@lycos.co.uk

PERCIVAL, Patricia Anne. b 52. SEITE 03. **d** 06 **p** 07. NSM Footscray w N Cray *Roch* from 06. *31 Collindale Avenue, Sidcup DA15 9DN* Tel (020) 8302 9754 E-mail pat@thepercies.freeserve.co.uk

PERCIVAL, Richard Thomas. b 33. MRICS59 MRTPI67 FRICS71. Edin Dioc NSM Course 88. **d** 91 **p** 98. S Africa 91-94; RD Adnry of Kokstad 93-94; NSM Edin St Ninian 94-01; rtd 01; Perm to Offic *Edin* from 01. *2/1 Fettes Rise, Edinburgh EH4 1QH* Tel 0131-552 5271 E-mail rpercival@freeukisp.co.uk

PERCIVAL, Robert Standring. b 27. Sheff Univ BA55. Qu Coll Birm 57. **d** 59 **p** 60. C Lightbowne *Man* 59-62; C Prestwich St Marg 62-63; V Pendlebury St Aug 63-68; Lect Glos Coll of Arts and Tech 68-93; NSM Glouc St Mary de Crypt w St Jo and Ch Ch 68-82; Perm to Offic 82-97 and from 01; rtd 92. *5 Firwood Drive, Gloucester GL4 0AB* Tel (01452) 522739

PERCY, Brian. b 34. **d** 93 **p** 94. OLM Walton *St E* 93-00; OLM Walton and Trimley 00-04; rtd 04; Perm to Offic *St E* from 04. *16 Lynwood Avenue, Felixstowe IP11 9HS* Tel (01394) 286782

PERCY, Christopher. *See* HEBER PERCY, Canon Christopher John

PERCY, Mrs Emma Margaret. b 63. Jes Coll Cam BA85 MA89 St Jo Coll Dur BA89. Cranmer Hall Dur 87. **d** 90 **p** 94. C Bedford St Andr *St Alb* 90-94; Chapl Anglia Poly Univ 94-97; P-in-c Millhouses H Trin *Sheff* 97-03; V 03-04; Chapl Trin Coll Ox from 05. *2 Orchard View, High Street, Cuddesdon, Oxford OX44 9HP* Tel (01865) 876211 E-mail emma.percy@pmb.ox.ac.uk

PERCY, Gordon Reid. b 46. St Jo Coll Dur BA68. Cranmer Hall Dur 69. **d** 71 **p** 72. C Flixton St Jo *Man* 71-76; C Charlesworth *Derby* 76-77; P-in-c 77-87; P-in-c Dinting Vale 80-87; V Long Eaton St Jo 87-98; RD Ilkeston 92-98; R Torquay St Matthias, St Mark and H Trin *Ex* from 98. *The Rectory, Wellswood Avenue, Torquay TQ1 2QE* Tel (01803) 293280 *or* 214175 E-mail gordonpercy@minister.com *or* stmathiaschurch@minister.com

PERCY, Prof Martyn William. b 62. Bris Univ BA84 K Coll Lon PhD92 Sheff Univ MEd. Cranmer Hall Dur 88. **d** 90 **p** 91. C Bedford St Andr *St Alb* 90-94; Chapl and Dir Th and RS Ch Coll Cam 94-97; Dir Th and RS SS Coll Cam 95-97; Dir Linc Th Inst 97-04; Hon C Millhouses H Trin *Sheff* 97-04; Hon Can Sheff Cathl 97-04; Can Th from 04; Sen Lect Relig and Soc Sheff Univ 97-00; Reader 00-02; Reader Man Univ 02-04; Prof Th and Min Hartford Sem Connecticut 02-07; Prin Ripon Coll Cuddesdon from 04; Prof Th Educn K Coll Lon from 04; Prin Ox Min Course from 06. *Ripon College, Cuddesdon, Oxford OX44 9FX* Tel (01865) 874404 Fax 875431 Mobile 07941-072542 E-mail mpercy@ripon-cuddesdon.ac.uk

PERDUE, Ernon Cope Todd. b 30. TCD BA52 MA BD56 MEd73 UCD MPsychSc80. TCD Div Sch 53. **d** 54 **p** 55. C Dublin Drumcondra w N Strand *D & G* 54-58; C Dublin Booterstown w Carysfort 58-60; Dean of Res TCD 60-68; C-in-c Dublin St Mark *D & G* 66-68; C-in-c Dublin St Steph 68-69; I Rathmichael 69-76; Careers Counsellor Wicklow Voc Sch 76-82; I Limerick *L & K* 82-87; Can Limerick Cathl 82-87; Dean Killaloe, Kilfenora and Clonfert 87-95; I Killaloe w Stradbally 87-95; rtd 95. *18 The Mageough, Cowper Road, Rathmines, Dublin 6, Republic of Ireland* Tel and fax (00353) (1) 491 4867 Mobile 86-278 0354 E-mail ernonandheather@hotmail.com

PEREIRA, Melvyn Christopher. b 52. Oak Hill Th Coll BA04. **d** 04 **p** 05. C Kettering Ch the King *Pet* 04-07; Min Gleneagles CD from 07. *20 Ribble Close, Wellingborough NN8 5XJ* Tel (01933) 679688 Mobile 07810-816744 E-mail melvyn02@yahoo.co.uk

PERERA, Ms Chandrika Kumudhini. b 61. Qu Coll Birm. **d** 03 **p** 04. C Luton All SS w St Pet *St Alb* 03-07; TV Hemel Hempstead from 07. *St Paul's Vicarage, 23 Saturn Way, Hemel Hempstead HP2 5NY* Tel (01442) 255023 E-mail chandy.perera@btinternet.com

PERERA, George Anthony. b 51. Edin Univ BD74. Linc Th Coll 74. **d** 76 **p** 77. Chapl Mabel Fletcher Tech Coll Liv 76-79; C Wavertree H Trin *Liv* 76-79; TV Maghull 79-94; V Hunts Cross 94-04; Chapl Park Lane Hosp Maghull 79-89; Asst Chapl Ashworth Hosp Maghull 89-94; Chapl R Liverpool and Broadgreen Univ Hosps NHS Trust from 05. *Broadgreen Hospital, Thomas Drive, Liverpool L14 3LB* Tel 0151-282 6000 Fax 254 2070

✠**PERHAM, The Rt Revd Michael Francis.** b 47. Keble Coll Ox BA74 MA78. Cuddesdon Coll 74. **d** 76 **p** 77 **c** 04. C Addington *Cant* 76-81; Bp's Dom Chapl *Win* 81-84; Sec C of E Doctrine Commn 79-84; TR Oakdale *Sarum* 84-92; Prec and Can Res Nor Cathl 92-98; Provost Derby 98-00; Dean Derby 00-04; Bp Glouc from 04. *Bishopscourt, Pitt Street, Gloucester GL1 2BQ* Tel (01452) 410022 ext 271 Fax 308324 E-mail bshpglos@glosdioc.org.uk

PERKES, Brian Robert Keith. b 46. St Andr Univ BSc68. NOC 91. **d** 94 **p** 95. NSM Witton *Ches* 94-98; Bp's Chapl 98-00; P-in-c Ashton Hayes from 98; P-in-c Delamere from 00. *The Vicarage, Church Road, Ashton, Chester CH3 8AB* Tel (01829) 751265 E-mail brkperkes@tinyworld.co.uk

PERKIN, David Arthur. b 30. Pemb Coll Ox BA54 MA58. Linc Th Coll 54. **d** 56 **p** 57. C St John's Wood *Lon* 56-61; Chapl Loughb Univ 61-84; V Paddington St Jas *Lon* 84-92; rtd 92. *14 Englewood Road, London SW12 9NZ*

PERKIN, Jonathan Guy. b 52. Westmr Coll Ox BEd76. Trin Coll Bris 89. **d** 91 **p** 92. C Cullompton *Ex* 91-96; C Ashtead *Guildf* 96-01; V Egham 01-05; V Churchdown *Glouc* from 05. *The Vicarage, 5 Vicarage Close, Churchdown, Gloucester GL3 2NE* Tel (01452) 713203 E-mail jjperkin@btconnect.com

PERKIN, Paul John Stanley. b 50. Ch Ch Ox BA71 MA75 CertEd. Wycliffe Hall Ox 78. **d** 80 **p** 81. C Gillingham St Mark *Roch* 80-84; C Brompton H Trin w Onslow Square St Paul *Lon* 84-87; P-in-c Battersea Rise St Mark *S'wark* 87-92; V from 92; P-in-c Battersea St Pet and St Paul from 00. *St Mark's Vicarage, 7 Elsynge Road, London SW18 2HW* Tel (020) 8874 6023 *or* 7223 6188 E-mail mark.mail@ukonline.co.uk

PERKINS, Colin Blackmore. b 35. FCII65. Lon Coll of Div 68. **d** 70 **p** 71. C Hyson Green *S'well* 70-73; V Clarborough w Hayton 73-79; P-in-c Cropwell Bishop 79-84; P-in-c Colston Bassett 79-84; P-in-c Granby w Elton 79-84; P-in-c Langar 79-84; V Tithby w Cropwell Butler 79-84; R Cropwell Bishop w Colston Bassett, Granby etc 84-94; P-in-c Sutton Bonington w Normanton-on-Soar 94-01; rtd 01; Perm to Offic *Newc* from 01. *6 Ravensmede, Alnwick NE66 2PX* Tel (01665) 510445 E-mail cperk68836@aol.com

PERKINS, Canon David. b 51. Sarum & Wells Th Coll. **d** 87 **p** 88. C New Mills *Derby* 87-90; V Marlpool 90-95; P-in-c Turnditch 95-02; Min in charge Belper Ch Ch and Milford 95-02; V Belper Ch Ch w Turnditch 02-09; Jt P-in-c Ambergate and Heage 06-09; RD Duffield 97-09; Chapl Derbyshire Mental Health Services NHS Trust 95-09; Can Res Derby Cathl from 09. *24 Kedleston Road, Derby DE22 2GU* Tel (01332) 343523 E-mail revdaveperkins@aol.com

PERKINS, David John Elmslie. b 45. Dur Univ BA66 ATII75. Cranmer Hall Dur 66. **d** 69 **p** 70. C Wadsley *Sheff* 69-71; C Shortlands *Roch* 71-73; Perm to Offic *Lon* 76-78; *B & W* 78-80 and from 02; Lic to Offic 80-02; rtd 02. *Rainbow's End, Montacute Road, Stoke-sub-Hamdon TA14 6UQ* Tel (01935) 823314

PERKINS, John Everard. b 47. SEITE 04. **d** 06 **p** 07. NSM Speldhurst w Groombridge and Ashurst *Roch* from 06. *25 Northfields, Speldhurst, Tunbridge Wells TN3 0PN* Tel (01892) 863239

PERKINS, Miss Julia Margaret. b 49. Linc Th Coll 85. **d** 87 **p** 94. Par Dn Owton Manor *Dur* 87-89; Par Dn Leam Lane 89-94; C 94; P-in-c Stockton St Chad 94-96; V 96-00; C Eppleton and Hetton le Hole 00-06; C Heworth St Mary from 06. *19 Lauder Way, Gateshead NE10 0BG* Tel 0191-469 2866

PERKINS, Julian John. b 67. Southn Univ BSc90 MSc92. Trin Coll Bris BA00 MPhil03. **d** 01 **p** 02. C Thornbury *Glouc* 01-04; C Tewkesbury w Walton Cardiff and Twyning 04-07; P-in-c Crosland Moor *Wakef* 07-08; P-in-c Linthwaite 07-08; V Crosland Moor and Linthwaite from 08. *The Vicarage, Church Avenue, Crosland Moor, Huddersfield HD4 5DF* Tel (01484) 422381 E-mail julian.perkins@zen.co.uk

PERKINS, Malcolm Bryan. b 20. SS Coll Cam BA41 MA45. Wycliffe Hall Ox 41. **d** 43 **p** 44. C Rainham *Roch* 43-47; C Bexley St Jo 47-50; P-in-c Chalk 50-51; V 51-56; V Borstal 56-61; Chapl St Bart Hosp *Roch* 59-74; P-in-c Strood St Mary *Roch* 61-65; R Wouldham 65-73; Chapl Medway Hosp Gillingham 65-67; Toc H Staff Padre (SE Region) 73-85; Hon C Roch 74-85; rtd 85; Perm to Offic *Roch* 85-05 and *Cant* 85-04. *Roke Cottage, 3 Belgrave Terrace, Laddingford, Maidstone ME18 6BP* Tel (01622) 871774

PERKINS, Patricia Doris (Sister Patricia). b 29. Gilmore Ho 60. dss 67. CSA from 71; Sherston Magna w Easton Grey *Bris* 73-75; Cant St Martin and St Paul 76-78; Kilburn St Aug w St Jo *Lon* 80-84; Abbey Ho Malmesbury 84-87; Hon Par Dn Bayswater 87-94; Chapl St Mary's Hosp Praed Street Lon 88-89; Chapl St Chas Hosp Ladbroke Grove 88-89; Dean of Women's Min *Lon* from 89; Dioc Dir of Ords 90-94; Hon Par Dn St Olave Hart Street w All Hallows Staining etc 94-01. *St Mary's Convent and Nursing Home, Burlington Lane, London W4 2QF*

PERKINS, Sheila Barbara. b 50. SEITE BA07. **d** 07 **p** 08. NSM Tonbridge St Steph *Roch* from 07. *25 Northfields, Speldhurst,*

Tunbridge Wells TN3 0PN Tel (01892) 863239 Mobile 07952-354478 E-mail perkins25@btinternet.com

PERKINSON, Neil Donald. b 46. Wycliffe Hall Ox 84. **d** 85 **p** 86. C Workington St Jo *Carl* 85-88; TV Cockermouth w Embleton and Wythop 88-93; TV St Laur in Thanet *Cant* 93-01; P-in-c Darlaston All SS *Lich* 01-08; Ind Chapl Black Country Urban Ind Miss 01-08; rtd 08; V Whangamata New Zealand from 08. *203B Rangi AU6, Whangamata, New Zealand* E-mail neil@perkinson.org.uk

PERKINTON, Keith Glyn. b 61. Humberside Poly BA83 Leeds Univ BA92. Coll of Resurr Mirfield 93. **d** 93 **p** 94. C Knowle H Nativity *Bris* 93-97; TV Brighton Resurr *Chich* 97-05; P-in-c Hangleton 05-07; V from 07. *The Vicarage, 127 Hangleton Way, Hove BN3 8ER* Tel (01273) 413044

PERKS, David Leonard Irving. b 38. Avery Hill Coll TCert61 Sussex Univ MA76. S Dios Minl Tr Scheme 84. **d** 87 **p** 88. NSM Lewes All SS, St Anne, St Mich and St Thos *Chich* 87-91; Chapl HM Pris Lewes 91-94; NSM Deanery of Lewes and Seaford *Chich* 94-96; C Peacehaven and Telscombe Cliffs 96-00; C Telscombe w Piddinghoe and Southease 96-00; rtd 00; Asst to RD Lewes and Seaford *Chich* from 00; Chapl S Downs Health NHS Trust from 01. *45 Fitzjohns Road, Lewes BN7 1PR* Tel (01273) 478719 E-mail danddperks@btopenworld.com

PERKS, Edgar Harold Martin. b 31. Open Univ BA87. Glouc Sch of Min 85. **d** 88 **p** 89. NSM Bromfield *Heref* 88-89; NSM Culmington w Onibury 88-89; NSM Stanton Lacy 88-89; NSM Culmington w Onibury, Bromfield etc 90-98; Perm to Offic from 98. *The Oaklands, Bromfield Road, Ludlow SY8 1DW* Tel (01584) 875525

PERRENS, Everard George. b 15. St Cath Coll Cam BA37 MA42. Linc Th Coll 40. **d** 42 **p** 43. C Rugby St Andr *Cov* 42-44; CF 44-47; CMS 47-65; Uganda 47-65; Chapl St Marg Sch Bushey 65-74; Hon C Earlsdon *Cov* 75-79 and 80-83; C Allesley Park 79-80; rtd 80; Perm to Offic *Cov* from 83. *2 Beechwood Court, Rochester Road, Earlsdon, Coventry CV5 6AE* Tel (024) 7671 2821 E-mail perrenseg@hotmail.com

PERRETT, David Thomas. b 48. Cranmer Hall Dur 80. **d** 82 **p** 83. C Stapleford *S'well* 82-86; V Ollerton 86-87; P-in-c Boughton 86-87; V Ollerton w Boughton 87-93; V Winklebury 93-05; P-in-c Gresley *Derby* from 05. *The Vicarage, 120 Church Street, Church Gresley, Swadlincote DE11 9NR* Tel (01283) 222966 E-mail dtp@dperrett.freeserve.co.uk

PERRETT, Mrs Jill. b 59. Trent Poly BA80 CQSW82. STETS 99. **d** 02 **p** 03. C Mere w W Knoyle and Maiden Bradley *Sarum* 02-07; P-in-c Atworth w Shaw and Whitley from 07; C Broughton Gifford, Gt Chalfield and Holt from 07; C Melksham from 07. *The Vicarage, Corsham Road, Shaw, Melksham SN12 8EH* Tel (01225) 703498 E-mail revjperrett@tiscali.co.uk

PERRETT (*formerly* ROWE), **Mrs Carol Sheila.** b 63. STETS 95. **d** 98 **p** 99. C Marlborough *Sarum* 98-01; TV Pewsey and Swanborough 01-06; TR Bourne Valley from 06; C Salisbury St Fran and Stratford sub Castle from 09; RD Alderbury from 06. *The Rectory, High Street, Porton, Salisbury SP4 0LH* Tel (01980) 610305 E-mail rev.vandaperrett@googlemail.com

PERRICONE, Vincent James. b 50. Connecticut Univ BA74 Pontifical Univ Rome STB88 STL90 Glas Univ PhD98. **d** 90 **p** 90. In RC Ch 89-94; C Glas St Mary 94-95; P-in-c Glas All SS and Glas H Cross 95-03; USA 03-08; Asst Chapl Florence w Siena *Eur* 08-09. *Address temp unknown*

PERRIN, Bruce Alexander. b 72. Birm Univ BSc94 MSc96. St Jo Coll Nottm 08. **d** 09. C Marple All SS *Ches* from 09. *66 Brindley Avenue, Marple, Stockport SK6 7NH* Tel 0161-427 6273 Mobile 07914-211376 E-mail bruce.perrin7@ntlworld.com

PERRIN, Michael Leonard. b 47. Shenstone Coll of Educn CertEd66 Lanc Univ BEd71. Dioc OLM tr scheme 97. **d** 01 **p** 02. OLM Aspull St Eliz *Liv* 01-06; OLM Haigh and Aspull from 06. *21 Firs Park Crescent, Aspull, Wigan WN2 2SJ* Tel (01942) 257418 E-mail mikeperrin99@hotmail.com

PERRINS, Christopher Neville. b 68. St Steph Ho Ox 01. **d** 03 **p** 04. C Warrington St Elphin *Liv* 03-08; TV Walton-on-the-Hill from 08. *51 Queens Drive, Walton, Liverpool L4 6SF* Tel 0151-521 5276 E-mail revdcnperrins@aol.com

PERRINS, Harold. b 21. Kelham Th Coll 38. **d** 44 **p** 45. C Fenton *Lich* 44-49; C Talke 49-53; R Armitage 53-61; V Lapley w Wheaton Aston 61-65; V Priorslee 65-69; R Harlaston and V Edingale 69-77; V Shobnall 77-86; rtd 86; Perm to Offic *Lich* from 86. *20 Meadow Rise, Barton under Needwood, Burton-on-Trent DE13 8DT* Tel (01283) 713515

PERRINS, Mrs Lesley. b 53. St Hugh's Coll Ox BA74. S Dios Minl Tr Scheme 90. **d** 93 **p** 95. NSM Stoneleigh *Guildf* 93-94; NSM Haxby w Wigginton *York* 94-00; Asst Chapl York Health Services NHS Trust 99-00. *37 St John's Rise, Woking GU21 7PN* Tel (01483) 761427

PERRIS, Anthony. b 48. Univ of Wales (Abth) BSc69 Selw Coll Cam BA76 MA79. Ridley Hall Cam 74. **d** 77 **p** 78. C Sandal St Helen *Wakef* 77-80; C Plymouth St Andr w St Paul and St Geo *Ex* 80-87; TV Yeovil *B & W* 87-88; V Preston Plucknett

from 88; RD Yeovil from 06. *St James's Vicarage, 1 Old School Close, Yeovil BA21 3UB* Tel (01935) 429398 E-mail antonyperris@yahoo.com

PERRIS, John Martin. b 44. Liv Univ BSc66. Trin Coll Bris 69. **d** 72 **p** 73. C Sevenoaks St Nic *Roch* 72-76; C Bebington *Ches* 76-79; V Redland *Bris* 79-97; RD Horfield 91-97; R Barton Seagrave w Warkton *Pet* from 97. *The Rectory, St Botolph's Road, Barton Seagrave, Kettering NN15 6SR* Tel and fax (01536) 513629 *or* tel 414052 E-mail stbotolphschurch@btopenworld.com

PERROTT, John Alastair Croome. b 36. Univ of NZ LLB60. Clifton Th Coll 62. **d** 64 **p** 65. C Tunbridge Wells St Pet *Roch* 64-67; C Stanford-le-Hope *Chelmsf* 67-78; R Elmswell *St E* 78-02; rtd 02; Perm to Offic *St E* from 02. *7 Millfield Road, Barningham, Bury St Edmunds IP31 1DX* Tel (01359) 221909

PERRY, Alan David. b 64. Avery Hill Coll BA86 Lon Inst of Educn PGCE87 Greenwich Univ MA99. NTMTC 01. **d** 03 **p** 04. NSM Romford St Edw *Chelmsf* 03-08; Hd Teacher St Edw C of E Sch Havering from 08; Public Preacher from 08. *1A Lyndhurst Drive, Hornchurch RM11 1JL* Tel (01708) 437852 Mobile 07946-730291 E-mail alan.perry80@ntlworld.com

PERRY, Andrew John. b 65. St Steph Ho Ox BTh00. **d** 00 **p** 01. C Southwick St Mich *Chich* 00-03; P-in-c Upper St Leonards St Jo 03; R from 03. *St John's Rectory, 53 Brittany Road, St Leonards-on-Sea TN38 0RD* Tel (01424) 423367 Mobile 07900-981345 E-mail perry.rickard@virgin.net

PERRY, Andrew Nicholas. b 62. Westmr Coll Ox BA86. Trin Coll Bris MA91. **d** 91 **p** 92. C Bath Weston All SS w N Stoke *B & W* 91-93; C Bath Weston All SS w N Stoke and Langridge 93-95; P-in-c Longfleet *Sarum* 95-00; V from 00. *The Vicarage, 2 Twemlow Avenue, Poole BH14 8AN* Tel (01202) 723359 *or* tel and fax 253527 E-mail andrew.perry@smlpoole.org.uk

PERRY, Andrew William. b 44. MRAC65. WMMTC 91. **d** 94 **p** 95. NSM Redmarley D'Abitot, Bromesberrow, Pauntley etc *Glouc* from 94; Perm to Offic *Heref* from 05. *Rye Cottage, Broomsgreen, Dymock GL18 2DP* Tel (01531) 890489 E-mail aw@perry.net

PERRY, Anthony Henry. b 54. Leic Univ BA76. Aston Tr Scheme 89 Linc Th Coll 93. **d** 93 **p** 94. C Bartley Green *Birm* 93-97; V Bearwood from 97; AD Warley from 06. *St Mary's Vicarage, 27 Poplar Avenue, Birmingham B17 8EG* Tel 0121-429 2165 E-mail trinity20@btopenworld.co.uk

PERRY, Anthony Robert. b 21. Birkbeck Coll Lon 39 Natal Univ 40. Kelham Th Coll 48. **d** 52 **p** 53. SSM 52-01; C Sheff St Cecilia Parson Cross 52-56; S Africa 56-59 and 70-88; Min Modderpoort St Aug 56-58 and 83-88; Lesotho 59-70; Min Ha Chooko St Jas 59; Min Teyateyaneng St Agnes 60; Min Morija 66-67 and 76; Chapl Natal Univ 70-74 and 76-77; Melbourne Australia 75; Asst P Durban St Paul 78; Chapl Addington Hosp Durban 79-82; Chapl Chich Th Coll 88-90; Willen Priory 90-92; St Ant Priory 92-97; Vassall Road Priory 98-99; Warminster Priory 99; Perm to Offic *S'wark* from 98 and *Sarum* from 01. *2 Saxon's Acre, Warminster BA12 8HT* Tel (01985) 212510 *or* tel and fax 308818 E-mail awap@blueyonder.co.uk

PERRY, Christopher Richard. b 78. St Jo Coll Dur BA00 Leeds Univ MA02. Coll of Resurr Mirfield 00. **d** 02 **p** 03. C Penzance St Mary w St Paul and St Jo *Truro* 02-07; P-in-c Marsh Farm *St Alb* from 07. *The Vicarage, 40 Purway Close, Luton LU3 3RT* Tel (01582) 575757 E-mail father.perry@btopenworld.com

PERRY, Canon Colin Charles. b 16. K Coll Cam BA38 MA42. Westcott Ho Cam 39. **d** 40 **p** 41. C Champion Hill St Sav *S'wark* 40-42; C Redhill St Jo 42-44; Ghana 45-56; V Aldbourne *Sarum* 56-64; V Baydon 57-64; PC Salisbury St Fran 64-69; V 69-71; V Preston 71-81; RD Weymouth 75-79; Can and Preb Sarum Cathl 77-82; TR Preston w Sutton Poyntz and Osmington w Poxwell 81-82; rtd 82; Perm to Offic *Sarum* from 82. *Avon Cliff Nursing Home, 50 Christchurch Road, Bournemouth BH1 3PE* Tel (01202) 789998

PERRY, David William. b 42. St Chad's Coll Dur BA64. **d** 66 **p** 67. C Middleton St Mary *Ripon* 66-69; C Bedale 69-71; C Marton-in-Cleveland *York* 71-75; V Skirlaugh w Long Riston, Rise and Swine 75-07; N Humberside Ecum Officer 75-07; RD N Holderness 06-07; rtd 07. *11 Middle Garth Drive, South Cave, Brough HU15 2AY* Tel (01964) 562259 E-mail david@perryskirlaugh.karoo.co.uk

PERRY, Edward John. b 35. AKC62. **d** 63 **p** 64. C Honicknowle *Ex* 63-65; C Ashburton w Buckland-in-the-Moor 65-70; V Cornwood 70-92; Asst Dir of Educn 71-92; Chapl Moorhaven Hosp 91-93; V Ermington and Ugborough *Ex* 92-00; rtd 00; Perm to Offic *Ex* from 01. *32 Finches Close, Elburton, Plymouth PL9 8DP* Tel (01752) 405364

PERRY, Mrs Elizabeth Ann. b 59. WEMTC 04. **d** 07 **p** 08. NSM Soundwell *Bris* from 07. *228 Station Road, Kingswood, Bristol BS15 4XR* Tel 0117-976 1729 Mobile 07900-150649

PERRY, James Marcus. b 71. Ridley Hall Cam 02. **d** 04 **p** 05. C Cen Wolverhampton *Lich* 04-07; TV Tettenhall Regis from 07. *St Paul's Vicarage, 1 Talaton Road, Wolverhampton WV9 5LS* E-mail jimperry@operamail.com

PERRY, Mrs Joanna Teresa. b 60. K Coll Lon BD82. Trin Coll Bris. d 96 p 00. C Thornbury *Glouc* 96-97; C Winchcombe, Gretton, Sudeley Manor etc 97-99; Sub Chapl HM Pris and YOI New Hall 99-06; Chapl HM Pris and YOI Warren Hill from 06; Chapl HM Pris Hollesley Bay from 06. *HM Prison Hollesley Bay, Hollesley, Woodbridge IP12 3JW* Tel (01394) 412400

✠**PERRY, The Rt Revd John Freeman.** b 35. Lon Coll of Div MPhil86 ALCD59. d 59 p 60 c 89. C Woking Ch Ch *Guildf* 59-62; C Chorleywood Ch Ch *St Alb* 62; Min Chorleywood St Andr CD 63-66; V Chorleywood St Andr 66-77; RD Rickmansworth 72-77; Warden Lee Abbey 77-89; RD Shirwell *Ex* 80-84; Hon Can Win Cathl 89-96; Suff Bp Southampton 89-96; Bp Chelmsf 96-03; rtd 03. *Foxbury, Gutch Common, Shaftesbury SP7 9AZ* Tel (01747) 828416

PERRY, John Neville. b 20. Leeds Univ BA41. Coll of Resurr Mirfield 41. d 43 p 44. C Poplar All SS w St Frideswide *Lon* 43-50; V De Beauvoir Town St Pet 50-63; V Feltham 63-75; RD Hounslow 67-75; Adn Middx 75-82; R Orlestone w Snave and Ruckinge w Warehorne *Cant* 82-86; rtd 86; Perm to Offic *Chich* from 90. *73 Elizabeth Crescent, East Grinstead RH19 3JG* Tel (01342) 315446

PERRY, John Walton Beauchamp. b 43. Ex Coll Ox BA64 Sussex Univ MA67. EAMTC 82 Westcott Ho Cam 84. d 85 p 86. C Shrewsbury St Chad w St Mary *Lich* 85-89; V Batheaston w St Cath *B & W* 89-99; V Milborne Port w Goathill etc from 99. *The Vicarage, Bathwell Lane, Milborne Port, Sherborne DT9 5AN* Tel (01963) 250248 E-mail jwbperry@hotmail.com

PERRY, Jonathan Robert. b 55. Cranmer Hall Dur. d 82 p 83. C Filey *York* 82-84; C Rayleigh *Chelmsf* 84-88; Asst Chapl St Geo Hosp Linc 88-90; Chapl Gateshead Hosps NHS Trust 90-98; Chapl Gateshead Health NHS Trust from 98. *Queen Elizabeth Hospital, Sheriff Hill, Gateshead NE9 6SX* Tel 0191-403 2072 *or* 482 0000 ext 2072

PERRY, Lesley Anne. b 52. K Coll Lon BA73 MIPR99. SEITE 96. d 99 p 00. NSM Fulham All SS *Lon* 99-07; NSM Kensington St Mary Abbots w Ch Ch and St Phil from 07. *Flat 3, 76 Philbeach Gardens, London SW5 9EY* Tel (020) 7373 3085 *or* 7419 5404 E-mail lesley.perry@universitiesuk.ac.uk

PERRY, Mrs Lynne Janice. b 48. d 90 p 97. NSM Llanfair Mathafarn Eithaf w Llanbedrgoch *Ban* 90-97; C Bangor 97-99; TV 99-05; V Tregarth 04-05; V Tregarth and Llandygai and Maes y Groes from 05; AD Ogwen 02-07. *Cwm Collen, 39 Tal-y-Cae, Tregarth, Bangor LL57 4AE* Tel (01248) 600997

PERRY, Martin Herbert. b 43. Cranmer Hall Dur 66. d 70 p 71. C Millfield St Mark *Dur* 70-74; C Haughton le Skerne 74-77; V Darlington St Matt 77-79; V Darlington St Matt and St Luke 79-84; TR Oldland *Bris* 84-91; V 91-01; rtd 01. *Address withheld by request*

PERRY, Martyn. b 57. Coll of Resurr Mirfield 89. d 90 p 91. In Bapt Ch 85-89; C Hornsey St Mary w St Geo *Lon* 90-93; V Pontlottyn w Fochriw *Llan* 93-97; R Cilybebyll from 97. *The Rectory, 7 Cwmnantllwyd Road, Gellinudd, Pontardawe, Swansea SA8 3DT* Tel (01792) 862118
E-mail father_martyn@tiscali.co.uk

PERRY, Canon Michael Charles. b 33. Trin Coll Cam BA55 MA59 Lambeth DD03. Westcott Ho Cam 56. d 58 p 59. C Baswich *Lich* 58-60; Chapl Ripon Hall Ox 61-63; Chief Asst Home Publishing SPCK 63-70; Can Res Dur Cathl 70-98; Adn Dur 70-93; Bp's Sen Chapl 93-98, rtd 98. *57 Ferens Park, Durham DH1 1NU* Tel 0191-386 1891
E-mail mandmperry@totalserve.co.uk

PERRY, Michael James Matthew. b 66. Bris Univ BSc87 MSc89 PhD93. Trin Coll Bris BA99. d 99 p 00. C Keynsham *B & W* 99-03; R Cam Vale from 03. *The Rectory, Englands Lane, Queen Camel, Yeovil BA22 7NN* Tel (01935) 850326
E-mail mikepqc-crockfords@yahoo.co.uk

PERRY, Nicholas Charles. b 07 p 08. NSM Ebbw Vale *Mon* from 07. *26 Bailey Street, Cwm, Ebbw Vale NP23 7RT* Tel (01495) 370188 E-mail nick.perry1@btinternet.com

PERRY, The Very Revd Robert Anthony. b 21. Leeds Univ BA47. Coll of Resurr Mirfield 47. d 49 p 50. C Middlesbrough St Jo the Ev *York* 49-54; Prin St Aug Sch Betong Malaysia 54-60; Provost Kuching 60-66; R Hasfield w Tirley *Glouc* 66-69; Asst Chapl HM Pris Man 69; Chapl HM Pris Gartree 70-73; P-in-c Mottingham St Edw *S'wark* 73-75; P-in-c Miri St Columba Malaysia 75-77; Warden Coll of Epiphany Kuching 77-79; P-in-c Presteigne w Discoed *Heref* 80-83; R Presteigne w Discoed, Kinsham and Lingen 83-86; rtd 86; Perm to Offic *Heref* 87-93; Linc and Pet from 93; Chapl Laslett's *Worc* 91-92; P-in-c Ryhall w Essendine *Pet* 94-95; P-in-c Ryhall w Essendine and Carlby 95-96. *7 Balk Road, Ryhall, Stamford PE9 4HT* Tel (01780) 763938

PERRY, Russell Lee. b 38. Worc Coll Ox BA60 MA64. CBDTI 98. d 98 p 99. NSM Grasmere *Carl* 98-01; rtd 01; Perm to Offic *S'well* from 01. *Dumble Howe, 3 Byron Gardens, Southwell NG25 0DW* Tel (01636) 815813

PERRY, Timothy Richard. b 64. Trin Coll Bris BA93. d 93 p 95. C Abingdon *Ox* 93-97; New Life Outreach/Fit Lives 97-01;

Mountaintop Life Coaching Canada from 01. *363 Stellar Drive, Kelowna BC V1W 4K4, Canada* Tel (001) (250) 764 2881
E-mail timperry@mountaintopcoach.com

PERRY, Valerie Evelyn. b 39. Southn Univ CertEd59. S'wark Ord Course 82. dss 85 d 87 p 94. NSM Romford St Edw *Chelmsf* 85-89; Par Dn 89-91; Asst Chapl Middx Hosp Lon 92-94; Chapl S Kent Hosps NHS Trust 94-98; Hon C Aylesham w Adisham *Cant* 98-00; Hon C Nonington w Wymynswold and Goodnestone etc 98-00; rtd 99; Perm to Offic *Truro* from 01. *115 Century Close, St Austell PL25 3UZ* Tel (01726) 68075

PERRY, William Francis Pitfield. b 61. Keble Coll Ox BA84 MA87. Ripon Coll Cuddesdon 94. d 96 p 97. C Brockworth *Glouc* 96-01; P-in-c Millbrook *Win* from 01. *58 Shirley Avenue, Shirley, Southampton SO15 5NJ* Tel (023) 8070 1896
E-mail fr.will@icxc.org

PERRY-GORE, Canon Walter Keith. b 34. Univ of Wales (Lamp) BA59. Westcott Ho Cam 60. d 61 p 62. C St Austell *Truro* 61-64; R H Innocents Barbados 64-71; Canada from 71; R New Carlisle 71-74; R N Hatley 74-96; rtd 96. *1115 Rue Massawippi, North Hatley QC J0B 2C0, Canada* Tel (001) (819) 842 4665 Fax 842 2176

PERRYMAN, Preb David Francis. b 42. Brunel Univ BSc64. Oak Hill Th Coll 74. d 76 p 77. C Margate H Trin *Cant* 76-80; R Ardingly *Chich* 80-90; V Bath St Luke *B & W* 90-07; RD Bath 96-03; Preb Wells Cathl 01-07; rtd 07. *Treetops, Upper Froyle, Alton GU34 4JH* Tel (01420) 520647
E-mail david@perrypeople.co.uk

PERRYMAN, Graham Frederick. b 56. Southn Univ BA78 Reading Univ PGCE80. Aston Tr Scheme 90 Trin Coll Bris 92. d 94 p 95. C Hamworthy *Sarum* 94-98; P-in-c Moreton and Woodsford w Tincleton 98-02; R 02-04; TV Melbury 04-06; TR from 06. *The Rectory, Tollerford Lane, Higher Frome Vauchurch, Dorchester DT2 0AT* Tel and fax (01300) 320284
E-mail revgfp@btopenworld.com

PERRYMAN, James Edward. b 56. Lon Bible Coll BA85. Oak Hill Th Coll 86. d 88 p 89. C Gidea Park *Chelmsf* 88-91; C Becontree St Mary 91-94; Chapl Lyon *Eur* 94-00; R Allington and Maidstone St Pet *Cant* 00-08; Dioc Ecum Officer 02-08; P-in-c Stoneleigh w Ashow *Cov* from 08. *The Vicarage, 4 Hill Wootton Road, Leek Wootton, Warwick CV35 7QL* Tel (01926) 854832 E-mail jim@me16.com

PERRYMAN, Canon John Frederick Charles. b 49. Mert Coll Ox BA71 MA74 MInstGA98. Ridley Hall Cam 72. d 74 p 75. C Shortlands *Roch* 74-78; Asst Chapl St Geo Hosp Lon 78-82; Chapl Withington Hosp Man 83-94; Chapl S Man Univ Hosps NHS Trust from 94; Hon Can Man Cathl from 00. *Withington Hospital, Nell Lane, Manchester M20 2LR,* or *24 Alan Road, Withington, Manchester M20 4WG* Tel 0161-291 4800 *or* 445 8111

PERSSON, Matthew Stephen. b 60. Dundee Univ BSc82 Bris Univ MA98. Wycliffe Hall Ox 88. d 91 p 92. C Bath Twerton-on-Avon *B & W* 91-94; Chapl HM Pris Shepton Mallet 94-97; Perm to Offic *B & W* 97-98; C Shepton Mallet w Doulting 98-00. *Grange Farm, Fair Place, West Lydford, Somerset TA11 7DN* Tel (01963) 240024

✠**PERSSON, The Rt Revd William Michael Dermot.** b 27. Oriel Coll Ox BA51 MA55. Wycliffe Hall Ox 51. d 53 p 54 c 82. C S Croydon Em *Cant* 53-55; C Tunbridge Wells St Jo *Roch* 55-58; V S Mimms Ch Ch *Lon* 58-67; R Bebington *Ches* 67-79; V Knutsford St Jo and Toft 79-82; Suff Bp Doncaster *Sheff* 82-92; rtd 93; Hon Asst Bp B & W from 93. *Ryalls Cottage, Burton Street, Marnhull, Sturminster Newton DT10 1PS* Tel (01258) 820452

PERTH, Dean of. See SHEPHERD, The Very Revd John Harley

PERTH, Provost of. See FARQUHARSON, The Very Revd Hunter Buchanan

PERU, Bishop of. See GODFREY, The Rt Revd Harold William

PERUMBALATH, John. b 66. Calicut Univ BA86 Union Bibl Sem Pune BD90 Osmania Univ Hyderabad MA93 NW Univ S Africa PhD07. Serampore Th Coll MTh93. d 94 p 95. C Calcutta St Jo India 94-95; V Calcutta St Jas 95-00; V Calcutta St Thos 00-01; C Beckenham St Geo *Roch* 02-05; TV Northfleet and Rosherville 05-08; V Perry Street from 08; Dioc CUF Link Officer from 08. *All Saints' Vicarage, Perry Street, Gravesend DA11 8RD* Tel (01474) 534398
E-mail jperumbalath@btopenworld.com

PESCOD, John Gordon. b 44. Leeds Univ BSc70. Qu Coll Birm. d 72 p 73. C Camberwell St Geo *S'wark* 72-75; Chapl R Philanthropic Soc Sch Redhill 75-80; P-in-c Nunney w Wanstrow and Cloford *B & W* 80-84; R Nunney and Witham Friary, Marston Bigot etc 84-87; R Milverton w Halse and Fitzhead 87-93; V Frome St Jo and St Mary 93-00; V Frome St Jo 01; V Woodlands 01; RD Frome 97-01; V Castle Cary w Ansford from 01. *The Vicarage, Church Street, Castle Cary BA7 7EJ* Tel (01963) 351615

PESKETT, Richard Howard. b 42. Selw Coll Cam BA64 MA67. Ridley Hall Cam 64. d 68 p 69. C Jesmond H Trin *Newc* 68-71; Lect Discipleship Tr Cen Singapore 71-76; Dean 76-86; Lect Coll of SS Paul and Mary Cheltenham 86-87; Research Dir OMF

88-91; Tutor Trin Coll Bris 91-06; Vice-Prin 98-06; rtd 07; Perm to Offic *Truro* 06-08; Hon C Penzance St Mary w St Paul and St Jo from 08; RD Penwith from 08. *7 North Parade, Penzance TR18 4SH* Tel (01736) 362913
E-mail howard.peskett@btinternet.com

PESKETT, Timothy Lewis. b 64. St Kath Coll Liv BA86. Chich Th Coll BTh90. **d** 90 **p** 91. C Verwood *Sarum* 90-91; C Southsea H Spirit *Portsm* 91-95; TV Burgess Hill St Jo w St Edw *Chich* 95-00; V Burgess Hill St Edw 00-05; R Felpham from 05. *The Rectory, 24 Limmer Lane, Felpham, Bognor Regis PO22 7ET* Tel (01243) 842522

PESTELL, Robert Carlyle. b 54. Aston Tr Scheme 89 Linc Th Coll 91. **d** 93 **p** 94. C Matson *Glouc* 93-97; P-in-c Charfield 97-01; R Charfield and Kingswood 02-06; P-in-c Cheltenham St Mich from 06; P-in-c Cheltenham St Luke and St Jo from 06. *St Michael's Vicarage, 1 Severn Road, Cheltenham GL52 5QA* Tel (01242) 694985
E-mail stmichaelsvicarage@blueyonder.co.uk

PETCH, Canon Douglas Rodger. b 57. Nottm Univ BSc79. St Jo Coll Nottm MA96. **d** 94 **p** 94. C Vom Nigeria 94-95; C Pendleton *Man* 96-98; P-in-c Werneth and C Oldham St Paul 98-03; CMS Nigeria 03-07; Hon Can Jos from 05; TV Halliwell *Man* from 07. *101 Cloister Street, Bolton BL1 3HA* Tel (01204) 842627 Mobile 07837-423501 E-mail rodgerpetch@yahoo.co.uk

PETER, Christopher Javed. b 51. Peshawar Univ BA75. Qu Coll Birm 94. **d** 96 **p** 97. C Darwen St Pet w Hoddlesden *Blackb* 96-98; C Accrington 98-99; C Burnley St Andr w St Marg and St Jas 99-05; Chapl R Liverpool and Broadgreen Univ Hosps NHS Trust from 05. *Royal Liverpool University Hospital, Prescot Street, Liverpool L7 8XP* Tel 0151-706 2826
E-mail christopher.peter@rlbuht.nhs.uk

PETER DOUGLAS, Brother. *See* NEEDHAM, Brother Peter Douglas

PETERBOROUGH, Bishop of. *Vacant*

PETERBOROUGH, Dean of. *See* TAYLOR, The Very Revd Charles William

PETERKEN, Canon Peter Donald. b 28. K Coll Lon BD51 AKC51. **d** 52 **p** 53. C Swanley St Mary *Roch* 52-55 and 62-65; C Is of Dogs Ch Ch and St Jo w St Luke *Lon* 55-57; R S Perrott w Mosterton and Chedington *Sarum* 57-59; Br Guiana 59-62; R Killamarsh *Derby* 65-70; V Derby St Luke 70-90; RD Derby N 79-90; Hon Can Derby Cathl 85-95; R Matlock 90-95; rtd 95; Perm to Offic *Derby* from 95. *64 Brayfield Road, Littleover, Derby DE23 6GT* Tel (01332) 766285

PETERS, Bill. *See* PETERS, Canon Cyril John

PETERS, Carl Richard. b 62. Ripon Coll Cuddesdon 95. **d** 97 **p** 98. C Coventry Caludon 97-01; V Gt Grimsby St Andr w St Luke and All SS *Linc* 01-02; TV Leek and Meerbrook *Lich* from 02. *All Saints Vicarage, Compton, Leek ST13 5PT* Tel (01538) 382588 E-mail carljackie@petersc.freeserve.co.uk

PETERS, Miss Carole Jean. b 61. Ripon Coll Cuddesdon 07. **d** 09. C Ivinghoe w Pitstone and Slapton and Marsworth *Ox* from 09. *5 The Crescent, Marsworth, Tring HP23 4LP* Tel (01296) 668238 Mobile 07710-128859
E-mail carolepeters@aol.com

PETERS, The Very Revd Christopher Lind. b 56. Oak Hill Th Coll. **d** 82 **p** 83. C Knockbreda *D & D* 82-84; C Lisburn Ch Ch Cathl 84-87; I Kilmocomogue Union *C, C & R* 87-93; P-in-c Beara 92-93; I Killiney Ballybrack *D & G* 93-98; Dean Ross *C, C & R* from 98; Chan Cork Cathl from 98; I Ross Union from 98. *The Deanery, Rosscarbery, Co Cork, Republic of Ireland* Tel (00353) (23) 48166 E-mail candjpeters@eircom.net

PETERS, Canon Cyril John (Bill). b 19. Fitzw Ho Cam BA42 MA45. Chich Th Coll 40. **d** 42 **p** 43. C Brighton St Mich *Chich* 42-45 and 47-50; CF (EC) 45-47; Hon CF from 47; Chapl Brighton Coll 50-69; R Uckfield *Chich* 69-96; R Isfield 69-96; R Lt Horsted 69-96; RD Uckfield 73-96; Can and Preb Chich Cathl 81-89; rtd 96; Perm to Offic *Chich* from 96. *Canon's Lodge, 9 Calvert Road, Uckfield TN22 2DB* Tel (01825) 766397

PETERS, David Alexander. b 72. K Coll Lon BA94. St Steph Ho Ox BA98 MA08. **d** 99 **p** 00. C Paddington St Jas *Lon* 99-03; PV Westmr Abbey from 01; V Reading H Trin and Reading St Mark *Ox* 03-08; Asst Chapl Tonbridge Sch from 08. *20 Manor Grove, Tonbridge TN10 3DT* Tel (01732) 364476
E-mail frpeters@hotmail.com

PETERS, David Lewis. b 38. Ch Ch Ox BA62 MA66. Westcott Ho Cam 63. **d** 65 **p** 66. C Oldham St Mary w St Pet *Man* 65-69; C Stand 70-74; P-in-c Hillock 70-74; V 74-82; V Haslingden w Haslingden Grane *Blackb* 82-88; rtd 88; Perm to Offic *Blackb* and *Man* 88-09. *37 Cyprus Road, Faversham ME13 8HB* Tel (01795) 537917

PETERS, Geoffrey John. b 51. BCom BSc MDiv MInstC(Glas). Oak Hill Th Coll 85. **d** 87 **p** 88. C Forest Gate St Sav w W Ham St Matt *Chelmsf* 87-90; C Wembley St Jo *Lon* 90-92; Chapl Wembley Hosp 90-92; TV Manningham *Bradf* 92-97; Res Scheme Manager Anchor Trust 02-04; NSM York St Clem w St Mary Bishophill from 07. *15 Cameron Walker Court, Bishopthorpe Road, York YO23 1LD* Tel (01904) 638632 Mobile 07990-644779 E-mail geoffpeters04@aol.com

PETERS, Mrs Jane Elisabeth. b 48. Kent Univ BA08. **d** 08 **p** 09. NSM Shortlands *Roch* from 08. *27 The Gardens, Beckenham BR3 5PH* Tel (020) 8650 5986
E-mail jane@beckenham.eclipse.co.uk

PETERS, John Peter Thomas. b 63. Keble Coll Ox BL85. Wycliffe Hall Ox BA91. **d** 95 **p** 96. C Brompton H Trin w Onslow Square St Paul *Lon* 95-99; P-in-c Bryanston Square St Mary w St Marylebone St Mark 00-04; R from 04. *13 Chomeley Crescent, London N6 5EZ* Tel (020) 7258 5042

PETERS, John Thomas. b 58. Connecticut Univ BA80. St Jo Coll Nottm 84. **d** 87 **p** 88. C Virginia Water *Guildf* 87-93; R Grand Rapids Ch Ch USA 93-00; R Eden Prairie St Alb from 00. *14434 Fairway Drive, Eden Prairie MN 557344-1904, USA* E-mail johnpeters@isd.net

PETERS, Canon Kenneth. b 54. Newport Univ Tokyo MBA88 Greenwich Univ MA02 MIW96. St Mich Coll Llan 74. **d** 77 **p** 78. C Mountain Ash *Llan* 77-80; Asst Chapl Mersey Miss to Seamen 80-82; Chapl Miss to Seamen Japan 82-89; Hon Can Kobe from 85; Chapl Supt Mersey Miss to Seamen 89-93; Justice and Welfare Sec from 94; Hon C St Mich Paternoster Royal *Lon* from 94. *The Mission to Seafarers, St Michael Paternoster Royal, College Hill, London EC4R 2RL* Tel (020) 7248 5202 Fax 7248 4761 E-mail justice@missiontoseafarers.org

PETERS, Malcolm John. b 71. Leic Univ BA92. Oak Hill Th Coll BA03. **d** 03 **p** 04. C Braintree *Chelmsf* 03-06; C Hull St Jo Newland *York* from 06. *892 Beverley Road, Hull HU6 7DG* Tel (01482) 854526 E-mail malcolm.peters@ukgateway.net

PETERS, Marilyn Ann. b 49. Open Univ BA90. Qu Coll Birm 96. **d** 98 **p** 99. C Blakenall Heath *Lich* 98-01; TV Cen Telford 01-05; TR from 05. *The Rectory, 20 Burlington Close, Dawley, Telford TF4 3TD* Tel (01952) 595915 Mobile 07754-435272
E-mail marilyn.peters1@virgin.net

PETERS, Canon Michael. b 41. Chich Th Coll 75. **d** 77 **p** 78. C Redruth *Truro* 77-79; TV 79-80; TV Redruth w Lanner 80-82; R St Mawgan w St Ervan and St Eval 82-86; Chapl HM Pris Liv 86-87; Chapl HM Pris Bris 87-01; Hon Can Bris Cathl 96-01; P-in-c Middlezoy and Othery and Moorlinch *B & W* 01-08; rtd 08. *Archway House, Lane Othery, Bridgwater TA7 0QG* Tel (01823) 690208 E-mail mikesandra@ukgateway.net

PETERS, Rebecca Ann. b 76. St Hilda's Coll Ox MPhys98 St Cross Coll Ox PGCE99. Wycliffe Hall Ox 06. **d** 08 **p** 09. C Roxeth *Lon* from 08. *69 Southdown Crescent, Harrow HA2 0QT* Tel (020) 8422 2520 Mobile 07967-598115
E-mail curate@ccrharrow.org

PETERS, Canon Robert David. b 54. BA76. Oak Hill Th Coll 78. **d** 79 **p** 80. C Hyde St Geo *Ches* 79-83; C Hartford 83-86; V Lindow 86-96; V Throop *Win* from 96; P-in-c Bournemouth H Epiphany from 08; AD Bournemouth 03-08; Hon Can Win Cathl from 08. *St Paul's Vicarage, 1 Chesildene Avenue, Bournemouth BH8 0AZ* Tel (01202) 531064
E-mail rob.peters@tiscali.co.uk

PETERS, Stephen Eric. b 45. Westcott Ho Cam 74. **d** 77 **p** 78. C Wanstead St Mary *Chelmsf* 77-79; C Leigh-on-Sea St Marg 79-81; P-in-c Purleigh 81-82; P-in-c Cold Norton w Stow Maries 81-82; R Purleigh, Cold Norton and Stow Maries 83-84; V Bedford Park *Lon* 84-87; Perm to Offic *Ex* 87-88 and from 93; TR Totnes and Berry Pomeroy 88-90; Chapl Ex Sch and St Marg Sch 91-93. *Address temp unknown*

PETERS-WOTHERSPOON, Ann Margaret. b 48. Lon Univ BD84 Open Univ MA95 UEA EdD05. ERMC 05. **d** 07 **p** 08. NSM Somersham w Pidley and Oldhurst *Ely* from 07. *14 Twentypence Road, Cottenham, Cambridge CB24 8SP* Tel (01954) 250694 E-mail ann_m_peters@hotmail.com

PETERSEN, Miss Jennifer Elizabeth. b 55. Aus Nat Univ BA78. Moore Th Coll Sydney BTh82 Wycliffe Hall Ox 92. **d** 94 **p** 95. C Elloughton and Brough w Brantingham *York* 94-96; C Ealing St Mary *Lon* 96-00; Chapl Thames Valley Univ 96-00; Chapl Qu Mary and Westf Coll from 00. *24 Sidney Square, London E1 2EY* Tel (020) 7791 1973 *or* 7882 3179
E-mail j.e.petersen@qmul.ac.uk

PETERSON, David Gilbert. b 44. Sydney Univ BA65 MA74 Lon Univ BD68 Man Univ PhD78. Moore Th Coll Sydney ThL68. **d** 68 **p** 69. C Manly St Matt Australia 68-70; Lect Moore Th Coll 71-75; C Cheadle *Ches* 75-78; Sen Can and R Wollongong Cathl Australia 80-84; Lect Moore Th Coll 84-96; Prin Oak Hill Th Coll 96-07; Perm to Offic *Lon* and *St Alb* 96-07; Research Fell Moore Th Coll Australia from 07. *1 King Street, Newtown NSW 2042, Australia*

PETERSON, Dennis. b 25. Oak Hill Th Coll 51. **d** 54 **p** 55. C Leyton All SS *Chelmsf* 54-56; C Leeds St Geo *Ripon* 56-58; V E Brixton St Jude *S'wark* 58-91; rtd 91; Perm to Offic *Chelmsf* from 91. *79 Cavendish Gardens, Westcliff-on-Sea SS0 9XP* Tel (01702) 334400

PETERSON, Canon John Louis. b 42. Concordia Coll (USA) BA65 Harvard Div Sch STB68 Chicago Th Sem ThD76 Virginia Th Sem Hon DD93. **d** 76 **p** 77. V Plainwell St Steph USA 76-82; Dean St Geo Coll Jerusalem 82-94; Can Res 82-94; Hon Can from 95; Hon Can Kalamazoo from 82; Hon Prov Can Cant Cathl from 95; Sec Gen ACC 95-04; Hon Can Kaduna from 99;

Hon Can St Paul's Cathl 00-05. *Episcopal Church House, Mount St Alban, Washington DC 20016, USA*

PETERSON, Paul John. b 67. Trin Coll Bris 94. **d** 97 **p** 98. C Burney Lane *Birm* 97-01; C-in-c Bradley Stoke N CD *Bris* from 01. *106 Cooks Close, Bradley Stoke, Bristol BS32 0BB* Tel (01454) 856947 E-mail paul@petersonp.freeserve.co.uk

PETFIELD, Bruce le Gay. b 34. FHA. NEOC 76. **d** 79 **p** 80. NSM Morpeth *Newc* 79-86; C Knaresborough *Ripon* 86-87; V Flamborough *York* 87-94; V Bempton 87-94; rtd 94; Perm to Offic *York* from 94. *36 Maple Road, Bridlington YO16 6TE* Tel (01262) 676028 E-mail bruce.petfield@btinternet.com

PETIT, Andrew Michael. b 53. Em Coll Cam MA78. Trin Coll Bris. **d** 83 **p** 84. C Stoughton *Guildf* 83-87; C Shirley *Win* 87-92; V Cholsey *Ox* 92-04; C Streatley w Moulsford 03-04; V Cholsey and Moulsford from 04; Chapl W Berks Priority Care Services NHS Trust 92-03. *The Vicarage, Church Road, Cholsey, Wallingford OX10 9PP* Tel (01491) 651216 Mobile 07986-005618 E-mail apetit@lineone.net

PETIT, Michael David. b 53. BCombStuds. Linc Th Coll 79. **d** 82 **p** 83. C Arnold *S'well* 82-86; Asst Chapl HM Youth Cust Cen Glen Parva 86-87; V Blaby *Leic* 87-94; V Leagrave *St Alb* 94-98; R Badby w Newham and Charwelton w Fawsley etc *Pet* 98-08; Dioc Voc Adv 00-08; Dir Tr for Past Assts 01-03; P-in-c Guilsborough w Hollowell and Cold Ashby from 08; P-in-c Cottesbrooke w Gt Creaton and Thornby from 08; C W Haddon w Winwick and Ravensthorpe from 08; P-in-c Spratton from 08. *The Vicarage, 15 Church Mount, Guilsborough, Northampton NN6 8QA* Tel (01604) 743508 E-mail michael.dp@virgin.net

PETRIE, Alistair Philip. b 50. Fuller Th Sem California DMin99. Oak Hill Th Coll 76. **d** 76 **p** 77. C Eston *York* 76-79; P-in-c Prestwick *Glas* 79-81; R 81-82; Canada from 82. *1224 Mission Ridge Road, Kelowna BC V1W 3B2, Canada* Tel (001) (250) 764 8590 Fax 764 0683 E-mail alistair@partnershipministries.org

PETRIE, Ian Robert (Eric). b 53. Avery Hill Coll PGCE84 Oak Hill Th Coll BA83. Qu Coll Birm 93. **d** 95 **p** 96. C Sedgley All SS *Worc* 95-98; P-in-c Salwarpe and Hindlip w Martin Hussingtree 98-08; Co-ord Chapl W Mercia Police 98-08; rtd 08. *100 Highbridge Road, Burnham-on-Sea TA8 1LW* Tel (01278) 787402 E-mail eric@petrierev.freeserve.co.uk

PETRINE, Andrei Anatolievich. b 73. St Jo Coll Dur BA05. Cranmer Hall Dur 02. **d** 05 **p** 06. C Hounslow H Trin w St Paul *Lon* 05-08; Perm to Offic 08-09; P-in-c Greensted-juxta-Ongar w Stanford Rivers etc *Chelmsf* from 09; Chapl Russian Community *Lon* from 09. *52 Epping Road, Toot Hill, Ongar CM5 9SQ* Tel 07723-026925 (mobile) E-mail a.petrine@mac.com

PETTENGELL, Ernest Terence. b 43. Ex Univ MA98. K Coll Lon 65. **d** 69 **p** 70. C Chesham St Mary *Ox* 69-72; C Farnborough *Guildf* 72-75; Asst Master K Alfred Sch Burnham-on-Sea 75-78; C Bishop's Cleeve *Glouc* 78-80; Chapl Westonbirt Sch 80-85; P-in-c Shipton Moyne w Westonbirt and Lasborough *Glouc* 80-85; V Berkeley w Wick, Breadstone and Newport 85-92; TV Weston-super-Mare Cen Par *B & W* 92-95; P-in-c Weston super Mare Em 96-99; Chapl Staffs Univ 99-03; V Douglas All SS and St Thos *S & M* 03-07; rtd 07. *3 Rushall Road, Thame OX9 3TR* Tel (01844) 216298

PETTERSEN, Canon Alvyn Lorang. b 51. TCD BA73 Dur Univ BA75 PhD81. Sarum & Wells Th Coll 78. **d** 81 **p** 82. Chapl Clare Coll Cam 81-85; Fell and Chapl Ex Coll Ox 85-92; Research Fell Linc Coll Ox 92-93; V Frensham *Guildf* 93-02; Can Res Worc Cathl from 02. *2 College Green, Worcester WR1 2LH* Tel (01905) 732900
E-mail alvynpettersen@worcestercathedral.org.uk

PETTET, Christopher Farley. b 54. Ou Univ BEd78. St Jo Coll Nottm 87. **d** 90 **p** 91. C Luton St Mary *St Alb* 90-93; C Fawley *Win* 93-97; P-in-c Amport, Grateley, Monxton and Quarley 97-09; TV Portway and Danebury from 09. *The Vicarage, Amport, Andover SP11 8BE* Tel (01264) 772950
E-mail cpettet@btinternet.com

PETTIFER, Bryan George Ernest. b 32. Qu Coll Cam BA55 MA59 Bris Univ MEd74. Wm Temple Coll Rugby 56 Ridley Hall Cam 57. **d** 59 **p** 60. C Attercliffe w Carbrook *Sheff* 59-61; C Ecclesall 61-65; Chapl City of Bath Tech Coll 65-74; Adult Educn Officer *Bris* 75-80; Dir Past Th Sarum & Wells Th Coll 80-85; Can Res St Alb 85-92; Prin St Alb Minl Tr Scheme 85-92; Prin Ox Area Chr Tr Scheme 92-94; Min and Deployment Officer/Selection Sec ABM 94-97; rtd 97; Perm to Offic *Glouc* 98-00; *Sarum* and *Bris* from 98; *B & W* 02-05; Rtd Clergy Officer Malmesbury Adnry *Bris* from 04. *23 Curlew Drive, Chippenham SN14 6YG* Tel (01249) 659823

PETTIFER, John Barrie. b 38. Linc Th Coll 63. **d** 65 **p** 66. C Stretford St Matt *Man* 65-67; C Stand 67-71; V Littleborough 71-00; rtd 00. *Littleborough Christian Centre, 43 Todmorden Road, Littleborough OL15 9EL* Tel (01706) 374074

PETTIFOR, Canon David Thomas. b 42. Ripon Coll Cuddesdon 78. **d** 81 **p** 82. C Binley *Cov* 81-84; P-in-c Wood End 84-88; V 88-92; V Finham 92-98; TV Coventry Caludon 98-07; Hon Can Cov Cathl 04-07; rtd 07. *8 Austin Edwards Drive, Warwick CV34 5GW* Tel (01926) 498736
E-mail david@dtpettifor.fsnet.co.uk

PETTIGREW, Stanley. b 27. TCD BA49 MA62. Div Test. **d** 50 **p** 51. C Newcastle *D & D* 50-53; C Dublin Clontarf *D & G* 53-57; I Derralossary 57-62; Miss to Seamen 62-92; I Wicklow w Killiskey *D & G* 62-92; Can Ch Ch Cathl Dublin 87-92; rtd 92. *Corr Riasc, Bollarney South, Wicklow, Republic of Ireland* Tel (00353) (404) 69755

PETTINGELL, Hubert. b 32. ACA54 FCA65 AKC58. **d** 59 **p** 60. C Mansfield SS Pet and Paul *S'well* 59-61; CMS Iran 61-66; C Wellington w W Buckland and Nynehead *B & W* 67-68; Warden Student Movement Ho Lon 68-69; R Holywell w Needingworth *Ely* 69-71; Dir Finance WCC 80-96; Perm to Offic *Eur* from 94; rtd 97. *chemin du Pommier 22, CH-1218 Le Grand Saconnex, Geneva, Switzerland* Tel (0041) (22) 798 8586
E-mail hpettingell@hotmail.com

PETTIT, Anthony David. b 72. Univ of Cen England in Birm BA94 MA95 St Jo Coll Dur BA01. Cranmer Hall Dur 98. **d** 01 **p** 02. C Gt Malvern St Mary *Worc* 01-04; P-in-c Cradley 04-05; TV Halas from 05. *34 Beecher Road, Halesowen B63 2DJ* Tel (01384) 566928

PETTIT, James. b 78. Lon Bible Coll BA01 MA03. Ox Min Course 07. **d** 09. C Faversham *Cant* from 09. *Heronsmere, 19 Nobel Court, Faversham ME13 7SD* Tel (01795) 533153
E-mail jamesthemonk@gmail.com

PETTITT, Maurice. b 13. Clare Coll Cam BA35 MA57 MusBac37. Lich Th Coll 56. **d** 57 **p** 58. Asst Chapl Wellingborough Sch 57-62; R Rounton w Welbury *York* 62-69; V Riccall 69-78; RD Escrick 73-78; rtd 78; Perm to Offic *York* from 78. *Holbeck House, Low Street, Lastingham, York YO62 6TJ* Tel (01751) 417517

PETTITT, Robin Adrian. b 50. MRTPI79 Newc Univ BA77. St Steph Ho Ox 81. **d** 83 **p** 84. C Warrington St Elphin *Liv* 83-87; C Torrisholme *Blackb* 87-93; P-in-c Charnock Richard 93-00; Dioc Par Development Officer 93-98; Sec Dioc Adv Cttee for the Care of Chs 98-99; C Broughton 00-01; rtd 01; Perm to Offic *Liv* from 03. *The Vicarage, 169 Church Road, Haydock, St Helens WA11 0NJ* Tel (01942) 727956

PETTITT, Canon Simon. b 50. Nottm Univ BTh74 CertEd. Kelham Th Coll 70. **d** 75 **p** 76. C Penistone *Wakef* 75-78; Dioc Youth Officer 78-80; Dioc Schs Officer *St E* 80-86; P-in-c Hintlesham w Chattisham 80-86; V Bury St Edmunds St Jo 86-93; RD Thingoe 88-92; Dioc Communications Officer 93-00; P-in-c Exning St Martin w Landwade 00-01; V 01-08; RD Mildenhall 01-08; R Horringer from 08; Hon Can St E Cathl from 93. *The Rectory, Manor Lane, Horringer, Bury St Edmunds IP29 5PY* Tel (01284) 735946 Mobile 07786-922384
E-mail canonsimon@btinternet.com

PETTMAN, Mrs Hilary Susan. b 45. STETS 99. **d** 02 **p** 03. NSM Shottermill *Guildf* 02-08. *Stacey's Farm Cottage, Thursley Road, Elstead, Godalming GU8 6DG* Tel (01252) 703217
E-mail hilarypettman@tiscali.co.uk

PETTS, Mrs Anna Carolyn. b 44. St Mich Coll Sarum CertEd65. STETS 00. **d** 03 **p** 04. NSM Hordle *Win* from 03. *65 Ferndale Road, New Milton BH25 5EX* Tel (01425) 620856
E-mail carolyn.petts@ukgateway.net

PETTY, Alicia Christina Margaret. b 64. Wycliffe Hall Ox 01. **d** 03 **p** 04. C Ockbrook *Derby* 03-07; P-in-c Sawley from 07. *The Rectory, 561 Tamworth Road, Long Eaton, Nottingham NG10 3FB* Tel 0115-973 4900
E-mail sawleyrector-alicia@yahoo.co.uk

PETTY, Brian. b 34. Man Univ BA90. St Aid Birkenhead 59. **d** 62 **p** 63. C Meole Brace *Lich* 62-65; Chapl RAF 65-69; Australia 70-75; P-in-c Kimbolton w Middleton-on-the-Hill *Heref* 76-79; P-in-c Pudleston-cum-Whyle w Hatfield, Docklow etc 76-79; P-in-c Haddenham *Ely* 79-80; V 80-84; V Fairfield *Derby* 84-90; Chapl St Geo Sch Ascot 90-93; TR Sampford Peverell, Uplowman, Holcombe Rogus etc *Ex* 93-99; RD Cullompton 95-99; rtd 99; Perm to Offic *Ex* 99-02; Hon C Diptford, N Huish, Harberton, Harbertonford etc from 02. *Woodrising, Fortescue Road, Sidmouth EX10 9QB* Tel (01395) 514203

PETTY, Duncan. See PETTY, William Duncan

PETTY, The Very Revd John Fitzmaurice. b 35. Trin Hall Cam BA59 MA65. Cuddesdon Coll 64. **d** 66 **p** 67. C Sheff St Cuth 66-69; C St Helier *S'wark* 69-75; V Hurst *Man* 75-88; AD Ashton-under-Lyne 83-87; Hon Can Man Cathl 86-88; Provost Cov 88-00; Dean Cov 00; rtd 00; Perm to Offic from 01. *4 Granville Street, Copthorne, Shrewsbury SY3 8NE* Tel (01743) 231513

PETTY, Neil. b 40. Coll of Resurr Mirfield 04. **d** 04 **p** 05. NSM N Thornaby *York* from 04. *28 Bader Avenue, Thornaby, Stockton-on-Tees TS17 0HQ* Tel (01642) 761588 Mobile 07985-760490
E-mail neilpetty@hotmail.com

PETTY, Capt Stuart. b 56. Chich Th Coll 91. **d** 93 **p** 94. CA from 88; C W Bromwich St Andr w Ch Ch *Lich* 93-96; Asst Chapl Walsall Hosps NHS Trust 96-00; Sen Chapl 00-03; Chapl Team Ldr R Wolv Hosps NHS Trust 03-08; Sen Chapl York Hosps NHS Foundn Trust from 08. *York Hospital, Wigginton Road, York YO31 8HE* Tel (01904) 631313

PETTY, William Duncan. b 55. Ex Univ BSc76 Leic Univ PGCE77. Oak Hill Th Coll 97. **d** 99 **p** 00. C Burscough Bridge

Liv 99-04; Min Tanhouse The Oaks CD from 04. *121 Ennerdale, Skelmersdale WN8 6AQ* Tel (01704) 892444
E-mail duncan@thepettys.freeserve.co.uk

PETZER, Garth Stephen. MBE99. Rhodes Univ BTh95. St Paul's Coll Grahamstown. **d** 88 **p** 91. C Queenstown St Mich S Africa 88-89; C E London St Sav 90-93; R E London St Martin 93-95; Chapl RN 96-03 and 04-07; CF 03-04; rtd 07; Perm to Offic *Nor* 04-07. *Address temp unknown* Tel 07801-637205 (mobile) E-mail polgear@btopenworld.com

PETZSCH, Hugo Max David. b 57. Edin Univ MA79 BD83 PhD95 FSAScot91. Edin Th Coll 80. **d** 83 **p** 84. C Dollar *St And* 83-86; New Zealand 86-90; P-in-c Alyth, Blairgowrie and Coupar Angus *St And* 90-91; Chapl Glenalmond Coll 91-98; Dep Headmaster Benenden Sch from 99. *Benenden School, Cranbrook Road, Benenden, Cranbrook TN17 4AA* Tel (01580) 240592

PEVERELL, Canon Paul Harrison. b 57. Hull Univ BA80. Ripon Coll Cuddesdon. **d** 82 **p** 83. C Cottingham *York* 82-85; V Middlesbrough St Martin 85-93; V Gt Ayton w Easby and Newton under Roseberry from 93; Hon Can Ho Ghana from 04. *The Vicarage, Low Green, Great Ayton, Middlesbrough TS9 6NN* Tel (01642) 722333 E-mail revpev@btinternet.com

PEYTON, The Ven Nigel. b 51. JP87. Edin Univ MA73 BD76. Union Th Sem (NY) STM77 Edin Th Coll 73. **d** 76 **p** 77. Chapl St Paul's Cathl Dundee 76-82; Dioc Youth Chapl 76-85; Chapl Invergowrie 79-82; P-in-c 82-85; Chapl Univ Hosp Dundee 82-85; V Nottingham All SS *S'well* 85-91; P-in-c Lambley 91-99; Chapl Bluecoat Sch Nottm 90-92; Dioc Min Development Adv *S'well* 91-99; Adn Newark from 99. *Dunham House, Westgate, Southwell, NG25 0JL,* or *4 The Woodwards, Newark NG24 3GG* Tel (01636) 817206 *or* 612249 Fax 815882 Mobile 07917-690576 E-mail archdeacon-newark@southwell.anglican.org

PEYTON JONES, Mrs Dorothy Helen. b 58. LMH Ox BA79 MPhil82 DipSW02. Trin Coll Bris 84. **dss** 86 **d** 87 **p** 94. W Holloway St Luke *Lon* 86-89; Par Dn 87-89; C Glas St Oswald 89-92; NSM Drumchapel 92-98; Perm to Offic *Ely* 98-03; NSM Chesterton St Andr from 03; Ind Chapl from 09. *71 Humberstone Road, Cambridge CB4 1JD* Tel (01223) 523485 E-mail dorothypj@ntlworld.com

PHAIR, Neal David Stewart. b 70. Limerick Univ BA98 UCD HDipEd99 TCD MPhil02. CITC 99. **d** 02 **p** 03. C Ballymena w Ballyclug *Conn* 02-05; I Ballintoy w Rathlin and Dunseverick 05-07; Chapl Dub Inst of Tech from 07. *96 Lower Drumcondra Road, Dublin 9, Republic of Ireland* Tel (00353) (1) 4024112 Mobile 87-614 3951 E-mail nealphair@hotmail.com

PHARAOH, Carol Helen. b 63. Preston Poly BTech84. St Jo Coll Dur 96. **d** 98 **p** 99. C Heaton Ch Ch *Man* 98-02; TV Walkden and Lt Hulton 02-09; P-in-c E Farnworth and Kearsley from 09. *The Rectory, 55 Church Street, Farnworth, Bolton BL4 8AQ* Tel (01204) 572819 E-mail pharaohingham@freenetname.co.uk

PHARAOH, Douglas William. b 18. MSHAA56. Worc Ord Coll 68. **d** 69 **p** 70. C Gt Malvern Ch Ch *Worc* 69-71; Area Sec Leprosy Miss 71-72; P-in-c Gateshead St Cuth *Dur* 72-73; V New Seaham 73-76; P-in-c Wymeswold *Leic* 76-78; V Wymeswold and Prestwold w Hoton 78-80; P-in-c Grandborough w Willoughby and Flecknoe *Cov* 80-81; V 81-83; rtd 83; Perm to Offic *Cov* from 83. *11 Margetts Close, Kenilworth CV8 1EN* Tel (01926) 779026

PHEELY, William Rattray. b 35. EN(M)88. Edin Th Coll 57. **d** 60 **p** 61. C Glas St Mary 60-63; C Salisbury St Martin *Sarum* 63-66; Guyana 66-82; V Bordesley St Oswald *Birm* 82-86; Perm to Offic *Birm* 86-00 and *Ex* 00-03; rtd 00. *Flat 2, 16 Westcliffe Road, Birkdale, Southport PR8 2BN* Tel (01704) 563346

PHELAN, Thomas Sylvester Patrick. b 36. CQSW79. Chich Th Coll 72. **d** 94 **p** 95. C Somers Town *Lon* 94-96; C Old St Pancras w Bedford New Town St Matt 96-97; Chapl Camden and Islington Community Health NHS Trust 96-97; OSB from 97; Lic Preacher *Ox* 97-02; Hon C Nor St Jo w St Julian 02-06; Perm to Offic from 06. *7 Chaplain's House, The Great Hospital, Bishopgate, Norwich NR1 4EL* Tel (01603) 305522

PHELPS, Canon Arthur Charles. b 26. St Cath Coll Cam BA50 MA55. Ridley Hall Cam 51. **d** 53 **p** 54. C Kirkdale St Lawr *Liv* 53-56; C Rainham *Chelmsf* 56-60; Min Collier Row St Jas CD 60-65; V Collier Row St Jas 65-75; R Thorpe Morieux w Preston and Brettenham *St E* 75-84; R Rattlesden w Thorpe Morieux and Brettenham 84-90; Hon Can St E Cathl 89-90; rtd 90; Perm to Offic *Truro* 90-00 and *St E* from 01. *8 Northfield Court, Aldeburgh IP15 5LU* Tel (01728) 454772

PHELPS, Ian James. b 29. Oak Hill Th Coll 53. **d** 56 **p** 57. C Peckham St Mary *S'wark* 56-59; R Gaddesby w S Croxton *Leic* 59-67; R Beeby 59-67; Asst Dioc Youth Chapl and Rural Youth Adv 65-67; CF (TA) 60-67; CF (R of O) 67-84; Youth Chapl *Leic* 67-85; Dioc Adult Educn Officer 85-91; Past Asst to Bp and Adn *Leic* 91-94; rtd 94; Perm to Offic *Leic* 94-99 and *S'wark* from 99. *6 Montague Graham Court, Kidbrooke Gardens, London SE3 0PD* Tel (020) 8305 2150

PHELPS, Ian Ronald. b 28. Lon Univ BScS3 PhD57 FLS58. Chich Th Coll 57. **d** 59 **p** 60. C Brighton Gd Shep Preston *Chich* 59-61; C Sullington 62-64; C Storrington 62-64; R Newtimber w

Pyecombe 64-68; V Brighton St Luke 68-74; TV Brighton Resurr 74-76; V Peacehaven 76-94; rtd 94; Perm to Offic *Chich* from 94. *2 Kingston Green, Seaford BN25 4NB* Tel (01323) 899511

PHENNA, Timothy Peter. b 69. Ridley Hall Cam BTh01. **d** 01 **p** 02. C Woodseats St Chad *Sheff* 01-04; USA from 04. *2051 Braun Drive, Golden CO 80401, USA*
E-mail tpphenna@aol.com

PHILBRICK, Canon Gary James. b 57. Southn Univ BA78 K Alfred's Coll Win CertEd79 ACertCM84 MA(Theol)00 Edin Univ BD86. Edin Th Coll 83. **d** 86 **p** 87. C Southampton Maybush St Pet *Win* 86-90; R Fawley 90-00; P-in-c Swaythling 00-04; V from 04; AD Southampton from 07; Hon Can Win Cathl from 09. *Swaythling Vicarage, 357 Burgess Road, Southampton SO16 3BD* Tel (023) 8055 4231 *or* 8067 9787 E-mail gary.philbrick@dsl.pipex.com

PHILIP, Mathew. b 54. Leeds Univ BSc77 MSc78 PhD83 Surrey Univ BA05. STETS 02. **d** 05 **p** 06. NSM Patcham *Chich* from 05. *Hillside Lodge, 76 Redhill Drive, Brighton BN1 5FL* Tel (01273) 883726 Mobile 07760-158043 E-mail paluvalil@aol.com

PHILIP, Peter Wells. b 35. Ridley Hall Cam 64. **d** 67 **p** 68. C Tollington Park St Mark w St Anne *Lon* 67-70; C Battersea St Pet *S'wark* 70-72; Hon C Kennington St Mark 72-73; V Titirangi New Zealand 74-80; Hon C Blockhouse Bay 80-92; Past Dir Chr Advance Min 80-84; Dir Evang Fellowship of NZ 87-90; C Finchley Ch Ch *Lon* 92-93; V Frankton New Zealand 94-00; rtd 00. *608 Rolleston Street, Thames 3500, New Zealand* Tel (0064) (7) 868 5028 E-mail peterphilip@paradise.net.nz

PHILIP BARTHOLOMEW, Brother. See KENNEDY, Brother Philip Bartholomew

PHILIPPINES, Prime Bishop of the Episcopal Church in the. See MALECDAN, The Most Revd Edward Pacyaya

PHILLIP, Isaiah Ezekiel. b 59. Univ of W Indies BA88. Codrington Coll Barbados 85. **d** 88 **p** 89. C St Jo Cathl Antigua 88-91; R St Geo Dominica 91-96; R All SS Antigua 96-01; P-in-c Handsworth St Mich *Birm* 02-05; V Basseterre St Kitts from 05. *St Peter's Rectory, PO Box 702, Basseterre, St Kitts, West Indies* Tel (001869) (465) 2774 E-mail phillipisaiah@hotmail.com

PHILLIPS, Mrs Adele. b 59. Newc Univ LLB84. NEOC 04. **d** 07 **p** 08. NSM Gateshead *Dur* from 07. *47 Blackstone Court, Blaydon NE21 4HH* Tel 0191-414 0955 Mobile 07752-325736 E-mail jophillips06@aol.com

PHILLIPS, Andrew Graham. b 58. Ex Univ BSc79. Chich Th Coll 84. **d** 87 **p** 88. C Frankby w Greasby *Ches* 87-89; C Liv St Chris Norris Green 89-92; CF 92-97; Chapl RN from 97. *Royal Naval Chaplaincy Service, Mail Point 1-2, Leach Building, Whale Island, Portsmouth PO2 8BY* Tel (023) 9262 5055 Fax 9262 5134

PHILLIPS, Canon Anthony Charles Julian. b 36. Lon Univ BD63 AKC63 G&C Coll Cam PhD67 St Jo Coll Ox MA75 DPhil80. Coll of Resurr Mirfield 66. **d** 66 **p** 67. C-in-c Chesterton Gd Shep CD *Ely* 66-69; Dean, Chapl and Fell Trin Hall Cam 69-74; Hon Bp's Chapl *Nor* 70-71; Chapl and Fell St Jo Coll Ox 75-86; Lect Th Jes Coll Ox 75-86; Lect Th Hertf Coll Ox 84-86; Hd Master K Sch Cant 86-96; Hon Can Cant Cathl 87-96; Can Tr Truro Cathl 86-02; Perm to Offic from 02; rtd 01. *10 St Peter's Road, Flushing, Falmouth TR11 5TP* Tel (01326) 377217

PHILLIPS, Mrs Audrey Katherine. b 32. Lorain Coll Ohio BS73. Ox Min Course 88. **d** 91 **p** 94. NSM Princes Risborough w Ilmer *Ox* 91-94; P Assoc Marco Is St Mark USA 94-98; NSM Akeman *Ox* 98-00; Perm to Offic from 08. *1 The Chestnuts, Kirtlington, Kidlington OX5 3UB* Tel (01869) 350194

PHILLIPS, Benjamin Guy. b 75. Wycliffe Hall Ox. **d** 02 **p** 03. C Cockermouth w Embleton and Wythop *Carl* 02-05; V Stanwix from 05. *Stanwix Vicarage, Dykes Terrace, Carlisle CA3 9AS* Tel (01228) 514600 *or* 511430 E-mail benphillips@uk2k.com

PHILLIPS, Benjamin Lambert Meyrick. b 64. K Coll Cam BA86 MA90. Ridley Hall Cam 87. **d** 90 **p** 91. C Wareham *Sarum* 90-94; C Chipping Barnet w Arkley *St Alb* 94-96; V Bodicote *Ox* from 96; AD Deddington from 05. *The Vicarage, Wykham Lane, Bodicote, Banbury OX15 4BW* Tel (01295) 270174

PHILLIPS, Beryl. See PHILLIPS, Mrs Elizabeth Beryl

PHILLIPS, Bill. See PHILLIPS, Edward Leigh Bill

PHILLIPS, Mrs Brenda. b 41. St Hugh's Coll Ox BA63 MA68. **d** 04 **p** 05. OLM Sherborne w Castleton, Lillington and Longburton *Sarum* from 04. *100 Lenthay Road, Sherborne DT9 6AG* Tel (01935) 812738
E-mail brendaphillips@courthousedairyfarm.freeserve.co.uk

PHILLIPS, Brian Edward Dorian William. b 36. Bris Univ BA58. Ripon Hall Ox 58. **d** 60 **p** 61. C Ross *Heref* 60-64; Chapl RAF 64-68; Hon C Fringford w Hethe and Newton Purcell *Ox* 68-73; Chapl Howell's Sch Denbigh 73-76; C Cleobury Mortimer w Hopton Wafers *Heref* 76-80; V Dixton 80-02; rtd 02; Perm to Offic *Heref* from 02. *37 Duxmere Drive, Ross-on-Wye HR9 5UW* Tel (01989) 562993 Mobile 07712-071558
E-mail brianphillips@u-genie.com

PHILLIPS, Canon Brian Robert. b 31. Clare Coll Cam BA53 MA57. Linc Th Coll 54. **d** 56 **p** 57. C Tuffley *Glouc* 56-59; C

Southgate Ch Ch *Lon* 59-62; R Luckington w Alderton *Bris* 62-69; V Highworth w Sevenhampton and Inglesham etc 69-84; Hon Can Bris Cathl 84-90; P-in-c Long Newnton 84-87; P-in-c Crudwell w Ashley 84-87; R Ashley, Crudwell, Hankerton, Long Newnton etc 87-90; rtd 90; Perm to Offic *Portsm* and *Win* from 90. *Hannington, Hospital Road, Shirrell Heath, Southampton SO32 2JR* Tel (01329) 834547

PHILLIPS, The Very Revd Christopher John. b 46. **d** 79 **p** 80. Hong Kong 79-04; Chapl Hong Kong Cathl 83-87; Dean Hong Kong 88-04; Perm to Offic *Ely* 04. *Address temp unknown* E-mail cjphil@netvigator.com

PHILLIPS, David Arthur. b 36. S Dios Minl Tr Scheme 90. **d** 94 **p** 95. NSM Canford Magna *Sarum* 94-06; rtd 06. *32 Lynwood Drive, Wimborne BH21 1UG* Tel (01202) 880262

PHILLIPS, David Keith. b 61. New Coll Ox MA90. St Jo Coll Dur BA90. **d** 91 **p** 92. C Denton Holme *Carl* 91-94; C Chadderton Ch Ch *Man* 94-98; Sec Ch Soc from 98; Public Preacher *St Alb* from 98. *The Flat, 16 Rosslyn Road, Watford WD18 0JY* Tel (01923) 235111 Fax 800362 E-mail director@churchsociety.org

PHILLIPS, David Thomas. b 47. NEOC 03. **d** 05 **p** 06. NSM Gt and Lt Driffield *York* 05-06; C Elloughton and Brough w Brantingham from 06. *55 Stockbridge Park, Elloughton, Brough HU15 1JQ* Tel (01482) 662734 E-mail dphill9590@hotmail.com

PHILLIPS, Edward Leigh Bill. b 12. St Edm Hall Ox BA34 MA47. Wycliffe Hall Ox 33. **d** 35 **p** 36. Asst Chapl Dean Close Sch Cheltenham 35-37; C Highfield *Ox* 37-38; C-in-c Patcham Chr the K CD *Chich* 39-41; CF (EC) 41-46; R Ide Hill *Roch* 46-49; V Moulsecoomb *Chich* 49-52; V Kingston w Iford 52-75; V Iford w Kingston and Rodmell 75-78; RD Lewes 65-77; rtd 78; Perm to Offic *Glouc* from 78. *35 Woodland Green, Upton St Leonards, Gloucester GL4 8BD* Tel (01452) 619894

PHILLIPS, Edwin George. b 35. N Wales Baptist Coll 64. **d** 03. NSM Morriston *S & B* 03-08; rtd 09. *146 Lingfield Avenue, Port Talbot SA12 6QA* Tel (01639) 886784 Mobile 07815-969913

PHILLIPS, Mrs Elizabeth Beryl. b 34. **d** 94 **p** 95. C N Farnborough *Guildf* 94-99; rtd 99; Perm to Offic *Sarum* from 00. *8 Byron Road, Wimborne BH21 1NX* Tel (01202) 883328

PHILLIPS, Mrs Emma Catharine. b 62. St Anne's Coll Ox BA84. Trin Coll Bris BA99. **d** 99 **p** 00. C Shawbury *Lich* 99-01; C Moreton Corbet 99-01; C Stanton on Hine Heath 99-01; C Cen Telford 01-02; TV 03-07; Perm to Offic 07-09; NSM Cen Telford from 09; Chapl Severn Hospice from 09. *11 Stocking Park Road, Lightmoor, Telford TF4 3QZ* Tel (01952) 502878

PHILLIPS, Geoffrey Clarke. b 50. SWMTC 94. **d** 96 **p** 97. NSM Georgeham *Ex* 96-98; Chapl HM YOI Huntercombe and Finnamore 99-00; Chapl HM Pris Shepton Mallet 01-03; Chapl Children's Hospice SW from 07. *Children's Hospice South West, Little Bridge House, Redlands Road, Fremington, Barnstaple EX31 2PZ* Tel (01271) 325270

PHILLIPS, Canon Geoffrey John. b 23. BNC Ox BA47 MA56. Ridley Hall Cam 54. **d** 56 **p** 57. C Kettering St Andr *Pet* 56-59; C Tideswell *Derby* 59-62; Ceylon 62-65; R Gillingham w Geldeston and Stockton *Nor* 65-70; V Eaton 70-81; RD Nor S 71-81; Hon Can Nor Cathl 78-81; Chapl Vienna w Budapest and Prague *Eur* 81-87; rtd 87; Perm to Offic *Nor* from 87. *Fieldside, Threadneedle Street, Bergh Apton, Norwich NR15 1BJ* Tel (01508) 480656

PHILLIPS, Ivor Lynn. b 44. Leeds Univ BA70. Cuddesdon Coll 69. **d** 71 **p** 72. C Bedlinog *Llan* 71-73; C Roath 73-77; TV Wolverhampton All SS *Lich* 77-78; TV Wolverhampton 78-81; Chapl Charing Cross Hosp *Lon* 81-91; Chapl Milan w Genoa and Lugano *Eur* 91-94; C Hampstead St Jo *Lon* 95-00; V Whitton St Aug 00-09; rtd 09. *Brooklyn Cottage, Church Street, East End, Earlston TD4 6HS* E-mail i.lyn@virgin.net

PHILLIPS, Mrs Janet Elizabeth. b 37. Bp Grosseteste Coll CertEd57. EMMTC 81. **dss** 84 **d** 87 **p** 94. Wisbech St Aug *Ely* 84-86; Cambridge St Jas 86-91; Par Dn 87-91; Par Dn Wisbech SS Pet and Paul 91-94; C 94-02; rtd 02; Hon C Elm and Friday Bridge w Coldham *Ely* 03-07; Hon C Leverington, Newton and Tydd St Giles from 07. *The Rectory, Chapel Lane, Newton, Wisbech PE13 5EX* Tel (01945) 871387

PHILLIPS, Jason Paul. b 73. Man Metrop Univ BA95 CertEd95 PhD05. Ripon Coll Cuddesdon 07. **d** 09. C Mid Trent *Lich* from 09. *St Basil's House, 20 Sandalwood Drive, Stafford ST16 3FX* E-mail paxstbasils@fastmail.co.uk

PHILLIPS (née LANGLEY), Mrs Jean. b 52. St Mary's Coll Chelt CertEd73. WEMTC 03. **d** 06 **p** 07. NSM Bishop's Cleeve *Glouc* 06-08; NSM Bishop's Cleeve and Woolstone w Gotherington etc from 08. *3 St Nicholas Drive, Cheltenham GL50 4RY* Tel (01242) 237683 E-mail bcparishoffice@btinternet.com

PHILLIPS, Jeffery Llewellyn. b 32. Sarum & Wells Th Coll. **d** 87 **p** 88. C Ringwood *Win* 87-90; V Somborne w Ashley 90-93; rtd 93; Perm to Offic *Win* from 93. *Queen's Acre, 3 Solent Avenue, Lymington SO41 3SD* Tel (01590) 673955

PHILLIPS, Mrs Jennifer Jean. b 36. Guildf Dioc Min Course 98. **d** 01 **p** 02. OLM New Haw *Guildf* 01-07; Perm to Offic from 07.

20 Lindsay Road, New Haw, Addlestone KT15 3BD Tel (01932) 429689 E-mail jennifer.phillips73@ntlworld.com

PHILLIPS, John. b 50. ACIB74. NOC 01. **d** 04. NSM Wavertree H Trin *Liv* from 04. *12 Montclair Drive, Liverpool L18 0HA* Tel 0151-722 2542 E-mail jpipps@hotmail.com

PHILLIPS, John David. b 29. G&C Coll Cam BA50 MA54 CertEd69. SW Minl Tr Course 85. **d** 87 **p** 88. NSM St Martin w E and W Looe *Truro* 87-88; NSM St Merryn 88-94; rtd 94; Perm to Offic *Truro* from 94. *Restings, Plaidy, Looe PL13 1LF* Tel (01503) 262121

PHILLIPS, John Eldon. b 50. Univ of Wales (Cardiff) BEd85 MEd92. St Mich Coll Llan. **d** 90 **p** 91. NSM Merthyr Cynog and Dyffryn Honddu etc *S & B* 90-94; Lic to Offic *St D* 94-99; NSM Ystradgynlais *S & B* 95-99; Chapl Trin Coll Carmarthen 95-99; P-in-c Llanrhidian w Llanmadoc and Cheriton *S & B* 99-05; Dioc Press Officer from 02; NSM Burry Port and Pwll *St D* from 07. *2 Gerddi Glasfryn, Llanelli SA15 3LL* Tel (01554) 744770 E-mail reveldon@btinternet.com

PHILLIPS, John Reginald. b 64. St Steph Ho Ox BTh93. **d** 96 **p** 97. C Bognor *Chich* 96-99; TV Moulsecoomb 99-00; C Hove 00-05; P-in-c Mackworth St Fran *Derby* from 05. *St Francis's Vicarage, 78 Collingham Gardens, Derby DE22 4FQ* Tel (01332) 224264 E-mail frjohnphillips@aol.com

PHILLIPS, John William Burbridge. b 39. Dur Univ BSc60 Lon Univ BD68. Tyndale Hall Bris 65. **d** 68 **p** 69. C Barton Seagrave *Pet* 68-71; C Northampton All SS w St Kath 71-75; R Irthlingborough 75-88; V Weedon Lois w Plumpton and Moreton Pinkney etc 88-95; rtd 95; Perm to Offic *Pet* 95-96. *Finca Morito 8, 12579 Alcocebre (Castellon), Spain* Tel and fax (0034) 964 412 329

PHILLIPS, Judith Mary. b 46. Reading Univ BA67 Cardiff Coll of Educn PGCE86. St Mich Coll Llan 93. **d** 95 **p** 97. Lect Neath Coll 84-00; NSM Clydach *S & B* 95-00; Dep Chapl HM Pris Bris 00-01; Chapl HM Pris Eastwood Park from 01. *HM Prison, Eastwood Park, Falfield, Wotton-under-Edge GL12 8DB* Tel (01454) 382105 or 382100 Fax 382101 E-mail judith.phillips@hmps.gsi.gov.uk

PHILLIPS, Canon Kenneth John. b 37. Coll of Resurr Mirfield 67. **d** 67 **p** 68. C Blackb St Jas 67-69; C-in-c Lea CD 70-80; V Lea 80-84; P-in-c Priors Hardwick, Priors Marston and Wormleighton *Cov* 85-02; Sec Dioc Adv Cttee 85-99; RD Southam 89-95; Hon Can Cov Cathl 94-02; Dioc Rural Chs Officer 00-02; rtd 02; Hon C Gisburn *Bradf* from 02; Hon C Hellifield from 02. *7 Temperance Square, Hellifield, Skipton BD23 4LG* Tel (01729) 850340 E-mail kcanonic@aol.com

PHILLIPS, Lamont Wellington Sanderson. b 33. S'wark Ord Course 73. **d** 76 **p** 78. NSM Tottenham St Paul *Lon* 76-83; P-in-c Upper Clapton St Matt 83-88; V 88-97; rtd 98. *24 Berkshire Gardens, London N18 2LF* Tel (020) 8807 7025

PHILLIPS, Lynn. *See* PHILLIPS, Ivor Lynn

PHILLIPS, Canon Martin Nicholas. b 32. Em Coll Cam BA57 MA61. Linc Th Coll 57. **d** 59 **p** 60. C Stocking Farm CD *Leic* 59-63; V Sheff Gillcar St Silas 63-71; V Birstall *Leic* 72-82; R Wanlip 72-82; V Birstall and Wanlip 82-88; TR Loughborough Em and St Mary in Charnwood 88-96; Hon Can Leic Cathl 90-96; rtd 96; Perm to Offic *Leic* from 96. *Foxhollow, 40A Lodge Close, Barrow upon Soar, Loughborough LE12 8ZL* Tel (01509) 416361

PHILLIPS, Mary Alice. b 53. Ripon Coll Cuddesdon 97. **d** 99 **p** 00. C Addiscombe St Mildred *S'wark* 99-02; TV Basingstoke *Win* from 02. *219 Paddock Road, Basingstoke RG22 6QP* Tel (01256) 464393 E-mail map13@tinyworld.co.uk

PHILLIPS, Michael John. b 54. JP. Trent Poly BA77. Sarum & Wells Th Coll 78. **d** 81 **p** 82. C Killay *S & B* 81-83; C Trebeoth 83-85; Hong Kong 85-88; Japan 88-91; TR Is of Scilly *Truro* 91-95; TR Cwmbran *Mon* from 95. *The Rectory, Clomendy Road, Cwmbran NP44 3LS* Tel (01633) 489719

PHILLIPS, Michael Thomas. b 46. CQSW81. Linc Th Coll 89. **d** 90 **p** 91. C Hyson Green *S'well* 90-91; C Basford w Hyson Green 91-93; Chapl HM Pris Gartree 93-99; Chapl HM Pris Nottm 99-08; Hon C Radford St Pet *S'well* from 08; Hon C Radford All So w Ch Ch and St Mich from 08. *12 Edgbaston Gardens, Aspley, Nottingham NG8 5AY* Tel 0115-929 7029

PHILLIPS, Mrs Patricia. b 45. Glouc Sch of Min 83. **dss** 86 **d** 87 **p** 94. Newent and Gorsley w Cliffords Mesne *Glouc* 86-95; C 87-95; P-in-c Childswyckham w Aston Somerville, Buckland etc 95-97; R 97-00; R Redmarley D'Abitot, Bromesberrow, Pauntley etc from 00. *The Rectory, Redmarley, Gloucester GL19 3HS* Tel and fax (01531) 620715 E-mail revpp@tesco.net

PHILLIPS, Patrick Noble Stowell. b 22. Edin Univ MA50 CertEd63. ALCD52. **d** 52 **p** 53. CMS 52-55; St Mark Nibo Nisi Niger 52-55; St Paul Awka 52-55; C Mossley Hill St Matt and St Jas *Liv* 55-57; V Milverton, Milbank and Elma Canada 57-60; Hd Ang Grammar Sch Benin 60-63; R Moresby *Carl* 63-66, V Mapleton and Clandeboye Canada 66-71; R Arthuret 71-88; rtd 88. *14 Gipsy Lane, Reading RG6 7HB* Tel 0118-926 4654

PHILLIPS, Miss Pauline. b 54. **d** 96 **p** 97. OLM Mossley *Man* from 96. *32 Mountain Street, Mossley, Ashton-under-Lyne OL5 0EZ* Tel (01457) 832363

PHILLIPS, Percy Graham. b 26. St Aid Birkenhead 46. **d** 51 **p** 52. C Wallasey St Hilary *Ches* 51-54; C Thrybergh *Sheff* 54-58; C Guernsey St Michel du Valle *Win* 58-60; V Heytesbury w Tytherington and Knook *Sarum* 60-65; V Stonebridge St Mich *Lon* 65-70; R Vernham Dean w Linkenholt *Win* 70-78; C Farnham *Guildf* 78-82; TV Cove St Jo 82-89; rtd 89. *22 Charts Close, Cranleigh GU6 8BH*

PHILLIPS, Peter. b 26. Oak Hill Th Coll 63. **d** 65 **p** 66. C Eastbourne All SS *Chich* 65-69; C St Alb St Paul *St Alb* 69-73; V Riseley w Bletsoe 73-84; R Arley *Cov* 84-91; rtd 91; Perm to Offic *B & W* 91-04; Clergy Retirement and Widows' Officer 99-04; Perm to Offic *Guildf* from 09. *Flat 1, Manormead, Tilford Road, Hindhead GU26 6RA* Tel (01428) 601501

PHILLIPS, Peter Miles Lucas. b 44. Reading Univ BA66 QUB DipEd69 Univ of Wales (Cardiff) MEd88 Bris Univ MA07. St Mich Coll Llan 90. **d** 92 **p** 93. Dep Hd Teacher Dynevor Sch 82-96; NSM Llangyfelach *S & B* 92-96; Dep Chapl HM Pris Liv 96-97; Chapl HM Pris Usk and Prescoed 97-01; Chapl HM Pris Bris 01-04; rtd 04. Perm to Offic *Bris* from 07. *7 St Lucia Close, Bristol BS7 0XS* Tel 0117-952 5859 E-mail revdpeterphillips@yahoo.co.uk

PHILLIPS, Ms Rachel Susan. b 64. Newnham Coll Cam BA86 MA90 Solicitor 89. St Jo Coll Nottm 04. **d** 07 **p** 08. C Eastcote St Lawr *Lon* from 07. *1 Farthings Close, Pinner HA5 2QR* Tel (020) 8429 1131 E-mail rachelphillips64@yahoo.co.uk

PHILLIPS, Robin Michael. b 33. AKC58. **d** 59 **p** 60. C Hanwell St Mellitus *Lon* 59-61; C St Margaret's-on-Thames 61-64; C Hangleton *Chich* 64-68; V Mellor *Derby* 68-95; RD Glossop 89-93; rtd 95; Hon C Bridekirk *Carl* 95-96. *87 George Lane, Bredbury, Stockport SK6 1DH*

PHILLIPS, Mrs Sandra Georgina. b 49. STETS 01. **d** 04 **p** 05. NSM Portsdown *Portsm* from 04. *14 Forest End, Waterlooville PO7 7AB* Tel (023) 9226 7740 Mobile 07778-921624

PHILLIPS, Canon Stephen. b 38. QUB BA60. Linc Th Coll 60. **d** 62 **p** 63. C Waddington *Linc* 62-65; C Gt Grimsby St Jas 65-72; V Kirmington 72-97; V Limber Magna w Brocklesby 73-97; V Brocklesby Park and R Croxton 97-04; RD Yarborough 92-00; Can and Preb Linc Cathl from 98; rtd 04. *The Stables, 14 Church Lane, Keelby, Grimsby DN41 8ED* Tel (01469) 561395 E-mail canstephil@glimreho.freeserve.co.uk

PHILLIPS, Thomas Wynford. b 15. Univ of Wales BA37 BD40. St Mich Coll Llan. **d** 43 **p** 44. C Shotton *St As* 43-46; C Rhyl 46-50; C Hall Green Ascension *Birm* 50-52; R Shustoke 52-55; P-in-c Maxstoke 52-55; V Clay Cross *Derby* 55-68; R Upton Magna *Lich* 68-73; V Withington 68-73; R Roche *Truro* 73-80; R Withiel 73-80; RD St Austell 76-80; rtd 80; Perm to Offic *Truro* from 80. *Brynawelon, Wheal Quoit Avenue, St Agnes TR5 0SJ* Tel (01872) 552862

PHILLIPS, Timothy Leo. b 72. Bris Univ BSc95 PhD99. Trin Coll Bris BA01 MA02. **d** 02 **p** 03. C Leic H Trin w St Jo 02-05; TV Ashby-de-la-Zouch and Breedon on the Hill from 05. *Holy Trinity Vicarage, 1 Trinity Close, Ashby-de-la-Zouch LE65 2GQ* Tel (01530) 412339

PHILLIPS-SMITH, Edward Charles. b 50. AKC71. **d** 73 **p** 74. C Wolverhampton *Lich* 73-76; Chapl St Pet Colleg Sch Wolv 77-87; Hon C Wolverhampton *Lich* 78-87; V Stevenage St Pet Broadwater *St Alb* 87-89; Chapl Millfield Jun Sch Somerset 89-95; Chapl Papplewick Sch 95-08. *5 Hampton Drive, Kings Sutton, Banbury OX17 3QR* Tel (01295) 811220 E-mail email@ecp-s.eclipse.co.uk

PHILLIPSON (née MACKAY), Alison. b 62. Teesside Univ BA00. NEOC 01. **d** 04 **p** 05. C Stokesley w Seamer *York* 04-08; P-in-c Cosby *Leic* 08-09; P-in-c Whetstone 08-09; V Cosby and Whetstone from 09. *The Vicarage, Church Lane, Whetstone, Leicester LE8 6BA* Tel 0116-284 9935 E-mail alisonphillipson@aol.com

PHILLIPSON, Hugh Brian. b 41. Birm Univ BSc62 Qu Univ Kingston Ontario MSc64. **d** 96 **p** 97. Chapl Hong Kong Cathl 96-04; Perm to Offic *Ox* 05-06; NSM Ox St Mary V w St Cross and St Pet 06-08. *Address temp unknown* E-mail huruphillipson@yahoo.co.uk

PHILLIPSON-MASTERS, Miss Susan Patricia. b 52. Sussex Univ CertEd73 K Alfred's Coll Win BEd81 Leeds Univ MA04 Glos Univ MA09 FIST76 ACP80 ACertCM99. Trin Coll Bris 86. **d** 89 **p** 95. C Saltford w Corston and Newton St Loe *B & W* 89-94; C Uphill 94-97; C Nailsea Ch Ch w Tickenham 97-98; P-in-c Tredington and Darlingscott w Newbold on Stour *Cov* 98-00; P-in-c The Stanleys *Glouc* from 00; Chapl Wycliffe Prep Sch from 07. *The Rectory, Church Road, Leonard Stanley, Stonehouse GL10 3NP* Tel (01453) 826698 Fax 826712 E-mail suepm@f2s.com

PHILLPOT, Donald John. b 27. St Jo Coll Dur BA53. **d** 55 **p** 56. C Southmead *Bris* 55-60; C Brislington St Luke 60-63; R Stapleton *Heref* 63-68; V Dorrington 63-68; P-in-c Astley Abbotts 68-78; R Bridgnorth w Tasley 68-78; V Lillington *Cov* 78-92; rtd 92; Perm to Offic *Glouc* from 92. *22 Williams Orchard, Highnam, Gloucester GL2 8EL* Tel (01452) 386844

PHILP (née NOBLE), Canon Ann Carol. b 42. Sarum Dioc Tr Coll CertEd63 Southn Univ MA(Ed)89 MCIPD. S Dios Minl Tr Scheme 93. **d** 95 **p** 96. Dir Sarum Chr Cen 93-98; Chapl Sarum Cathl 95-02; Dioc NSM Officer 98-02; P-in-c Woodford Valley from 02; Dioc Dir of Ords 02-07; Bp's Dom Chapl from 07; Can and Preb Sarum Cathl from 05. *The Vicarage, Middle Woodford, Salisbury SP4 6NR* Tel (01722) 782310 *or* 411944 E-mail ann.philp@tiscali.co.uk

PHILPOTT, Barbara May. *See* WILKINSON, Canon Barbara May

PHILPOTT, Canon John David. b 43. Leic Univ BA64. Trin Coll Bris 69. **d** 72 **p** 73. C Knutsford St Jo *Ches* 72-75; C Toft 72-75; C Bickenhill w Elmdon *Birm* 75-79; V Birm St Luke 79-91; RD Birm City 83-88; Hon Can Birm Cathl 89-91; V Chilvers Coton w Astley *Cov* 91-00; RD Nuneaton 95-00; Hon Can Cov Cathl 96-00; P-in-c Prague *Eur* 00-08; rtd 08. *2 Portland Court, 1 Portland Avenue, Exmouth EX8 2DJ* Tel (01395) 225044 E-mail jamphilpott@yahoo.com

PHILPOTT, John Wilfred. b 44. K Coll Lon BD67 AKC67. **d** 68 **p** 69. C Norbury St Steph *Cant* 68-71; C Addiscombe St Mildred 71-75; V Whitfield w Guston 75-01; rtd 02; Perm to Offic *Cant* from 02. *9 Mannering Close, River, Dover CT17 0UD* Tel (01304) 825875

PHILPOTT, Jonathan Mark. b 76. Chelt & Glouc Coll of HE BA98. Trin Coll Bris BA06. **d** 07 **p** 08. C Lydney *Glouc* from 07. *12 Almond Walk, Lydney GL15 5LP* Tel (01594) 845767 E-mail jonathan_philpott@yahoo.co.uk

PHILPOTT, Ronald. b 38. IPFA69. Cranmer Hall Dur 88. **d** 89 **p** 90. NSM S Ossett *Wakef* 89-93; R Clitheroe St Jas *Blackb* 93-03; rtd 03; Perm to Offic *York* from 03. *8 Headland Close, Haxby, York YO32 3HW* Tel (01904) 758697

PHILPOTT, Preb Samuel. b 41. Kelham Th Coll 60. **d** 65 **p** 66. C Swindon New Town *Bris* 65-70; C Torquay St Martin Barton *Ex* 70-73; TV Withycombe Raleigh 73-76; V Shaldon 76-78; P-in-c Plymouth St Pet 78-80; V 80-09; V Plymouth St Pet and H Apostles from 09; RD Plymouth Devonport 86-93 and 95-01; Preb Ex Cathl from 91. *St Peter's Vicarage, 23 Wyndham Square, Plymouth PL1 5EG* Tel (01752) 222007 Fax 257973 E-mail frphilpott@aol.com

PHILPOTT-HOWARD, John Nigel. b 54. Univ of Wales Coll of Medicine MB, BCh77 FRCPath83. SEITE 99. **d** 02 **p** 03. NSM Shooters Hill Ch Ch *S'wark* from 02. *80 Charlton Road, London SE7 7EY* Tel (020) 8858 4692 E-mail jphilpoth@cs.com

PHILPS, Mark Seymour. b 51. Worc Coll Ox BA73 MA78 Lon Univ MA75 Nottm Univ BA79. St Jo Coll Nottm 77. **d** 80 **p** 81. C Chadwell Heath *Chelmsf* 80-83; V Broxtowe *Southw* 83-87; V Tipton St Matt *Lich* 87-02; TV Roxeth *Lon* 02-03; TR from 03. *Christ Church Vicarage, Roxeth Hill, Harrow HA2 0JN* Tel (020) 8423 3168 E-mail mark.philps@roxethteam.org

PHILSON, James Alexander Summers (Hamish). b 20. Edin Th Coll 48. **d** 51 **p** 52. C Falkirk *Edin* 51-53; R Dunblane *St And* 53-62; Australia from 62; R Beverley 62-64; R Victoria Park 64-75; R Cottesloe 75-85; rtd 85. *38 Allenswood Road, Greenwood WA 6024, Australia* Tel (0061) (8) 9447 9523 Mobile 0416-001620 E-mail jasp@smartchat.net.au

PHIPPS, David John. b 46. Bris Univ BSc68 Ex Univ PhD94 Nottm Univ PGCE69. Trin Coll Bris 75. **d** 78 **p** 79. C Madron w Morvah *Truro* 78-80; C Kenilworth St Jo *Cov* 80-83; TV Barnstaple *Ex* 83-95; I Abercraf w Callwen w Capel Coelbren *S & B* 95-02; P-in-c Gulval and Madron *Truro* 02-05; rtd 05. *11 Walton Way, Barnstaple EX32 8AE* Tel (01271) 349746 E-mail phippsdv@dialstart.net

PHIPPS, David Frederick George. b 30. Kelham Th Coll 50. **d** 54 **p** 55. C Staveley *Derby* 54-59; Korea 59-65; Australia from 65; Can Ballarat Ch Ch Cathl 84-95; rtd 95. *240 Lava Street, PO Box 297, Warrnambool Vic 3280, Australia* Tel (0061) (3) 5562 6738

PHIZACKERLEY, The Ven Gerald Robert. b 29. Univ Coll Ox BA52 MA56. Wells Th Coll 52. **d** 54 **p** 55. C Carl St Barn 54-57; Chapl Abingdon Sch 57-64; R Gaywood, Bawsey and Mintlyn *Nor* 64-78; RD Lynn 68-78; Hon Can Nor Cathl 75-78; Hon Can Derby Cathl 78-96; P-in-c Ashford w Sheldon 78-90; Adn Chesterfield 78-96; rtd 96; Perm to Offic *Derby* and *Cov* from 96. *Archway Cottage, Hall Road, Leamington Spa CV32 5RA* Tel (01926) 332740 E-mail phizleam@yahoo.co.uk

PHOEBE, Sister. *See* HANMER, Sister Phoebe Margaret

PHYPERS, David John. b 39. Leic Univ CertEd61 Lon Univ BD65. Linc Th Coll 76. **d** 78 **p** 79. NSM Normanton *Derby* 78-80; NSM Sinfin 80-87; Lic to Offic 87-88; P-in-c Denby and Horsley Woodhouse 88-00; P-in-c Wormhill, Peak Forest w Peak Dale and Dove Holes 00-07; Adv for Chr Giving 00-07; rtd 07; Perm to Offic *Derby* from 07. *15 Albert Road, Chaddesden, Derby DE21 6SL* Tel (01332) 239134 E-mail david@phypers.co.uk

PICK, David. b 44. Linc Th Coll 85. **d** 87 **p** 88. C Howden *York* 87-90; P-in-c Sledmere and Cowlam w Fridaythorpe, Fimer etc 90-91; V 91-96; rtd 96; Perm to Offic *York* from 96. *Westwood Close, 16 North Street, Nafferton, Driffield YO25 4JW* Tel (01377) 240360

PICK, William Harry. b 23. Open Univ BA77. St Aid Birkenhead 51. **d** 54 **p** 55. C Wigan St Geo *Liv* 54-57; V Newton-le-Willows 57-67; V Stoneycroft All SS 67-79; R N Meols 79-88; rtd 88;

Perm to Offic *Liv* from 88. *8 Morley Road, Southport PR9 9JS* Tel (01704) 541428

PICKARD, Canon Frank Eustace. b 31. Lon Univ BScEcon52 St Cath Soc Ox BA56 MA63. St Steph Ho Ox. **d** 57 **p** 58. C Haydock St Jas *Liv* 57-59; C Davenham *Ches* 59-60; Asst Master St Dunstan's Sch Lon 60-63; Min Can Pet Cathl 63-72; P-in-c Newborough 67-68; V 68-72; R Isham w Pytchley 72-76; R Abington 76-96; Can Pet Cathl 86-02; rtd 96; P-in-c Wappenham w Weedon Lois and Plumpton 96-02; Perm to Offic *Pet* from 02. *19 Watersmeet, Northampton NN1 5SQ* Tel (01604) 239667

PICKARD, Mrs Patricia Anne. b 44. **d** 04 **p** 05. NSM Ovenden *Wakef* from 04. *46 Crag Lane, Halifax HX2 8NU* Tel (01422) 346948 E-mail ap.pickard@tiscali.co.uk

PICKARD, Stephen Kim. b 52. Newc Univ Aus BCom74 Van Mildert Coll Dur PhD90. Melbourne Coll of Div BD79 St Jo Coll Morpeth 77. **d** 80 **p** 80. C Singleton Australia 80-82; C Dur St Cuth 82-84; Chapl Van Mildert Coll Dur 84-90; Chapl Trev Coll Dur 84-90; Australia from 91; Lect United Th Coll Sydney 91-97; Dir St Mark's Nat Th Cen from 98; Assoc Prof and Hd Th Chas Sturt Univ from 99. *St Mark's National Theological Centre, 15 Blackall Street, Barton ACT 2607, Australia* Tel (0061) (2) 6249 8647 *or* 6273 1572 Fax 6273 4067 Mobile 419-638020 E-mail spickard@csu.edu.au

PICKARD, William Priestley. b 31. MCIPD72. Clifton Th Coll 56. **d** 59 **p** 60. C Upper Tulse Hill St Matthias *S'wark* 59-63; Asst Warden Shaftesbury Crusade Bris from 64; rtd 96. *45 Totterdown Road, Weston-super-Mare BS23 4LJ* Tel (01934) 628994

PICKEN, David Anthony. b 63. Lon Univ BA84 Kent Univ PGCE85 Nottm Univ MA96. Linc Th Coll 87. **d** 90 **p** 91. C Worth *Chich* 90-93; TV Wordsley *Worc* 93-97; TR 97-04; RD Kingswinford 01-04; TR High Wycombe *Ox* from 04; AD Wycombe from 07. *The Rectory, 6 Priory Avenue, High Wycombe HP13 6SH* Tel (01494) 525602 E-mail dap@dircon.co.uk

PICKEN, James Hugh. b 51. Victoria Univ (BC) BMus75 ARCT73. Ripon Coll Cuddesdon BA79 MA94. **d** 80 **p** 81. C Jarrow *Dur* 80-83; SSF 83-93; Perm to Offic *Sarum* 86-92; Guardian Alnmouth Friary 92-94; Lic to Offic *Newc* 92-94; Canada from 94. *929 4th Street NW, Calgary AB T2N 1P4, Canada* Tel (001) (403) 270 9661

PICKERING, Alastair David. b 72. Newc Univ BA94. Wycliffe Hall Ox 03. **d** 05 **p** 06. C Silverhill St Matt *Chich* from 05. *98 Sedlescombe Gardens, St Leonards-on-Sea TN38 0YW* Tel (01424) 720809 Mobile 07976-449896 E-mail al@thepickerings.net

PICKERING, David Arthur Ashley. b 67. G&C Coll Cam BA89. Wycliffe Hall Ox BTh06. **d** 06 **p** 07. C Hornchurch H Cross *Chelmsf* 06-09; P-in-c Fyfield w Tubney and Kingston Bagpuize *Ox* from 09. *The Vicarage, Fyfield, Abingdon OX13 5LR* Tel (01865) 390803 Mobile 07955-057479 E-mail picklesnpip@mac.com

PICKERING, Canon David Colville. b 41. Kelham Th Coll 61. **d** 66 **p** 67. C Chaddesden St Phil *Derby* 66-70; C New Mills 70-72; C Buxton 72-74; V Chesterfield St Aug 74-90; R Whittington 90-99; P-in-c Hathersage 99; P-in-c Bamford 99; R Hathersage w Bamford and Derwent 00-06; Hon Can Derby Cathl 05-06; rtd 06; Perm to Offic *Derby* from 06. *Les Chênes Verts, Chemin de St Laurent, Le Rang, 84750 Viens, France* Tel (0033) (4) 90 74 68 55 Mobile (6) 33 84 95 86 E-mail david@pickport.eu

PICKERING, The Ven Fred. b 19. St Pet Hall Ox BA41 MA45. St Aid Birkenhead 41. **d** 43 **p** 44. C Leyland St Andr *Blackb* 43-46; C Islington St Mary *Lon* 46-48; NE Area Sec CPAS 48-51; V Burton All SS *Lich* 51-56; V Carl St Jo 56-63; V Chitts Hill St Cuth *Lon* 63-74; RD E Haringey 68-73; Adn Hampstead 74-84; rtd 84; Perm to Offic *Pet* 84-93 and Ex 94-96. *8 Fosbrooke House, 8 Clifton Drive, Lytham St Annes FY8 5RQ* Tel (01253) 667052

PICKERING, Geoffrey Craig. b 40. Leic Univ CertEd62. S Dios Minl Tr Scheme 90. **d** 93 **p** 94. C Horsham *Chich* 93-97; V Heathfield 97-08; rtd 08. *3 Bedlam Green, West End, Hertsmonceux, Hailsham BN27 4NW* Tel (01323) 833325 E-mail pickeringgeoff@aol.com

PICKERING, John Alexander. b 41. TCD BA63 MA66. CITC 65. **d** 65 **p** 66. C Magheralin *D & D* 65-67; C-in-c Outeragh *K, E & A* 67-68; I 68-71; Deputation Sec Hibernian Bible Soc 71-74; C-in-c Drumgoon and Ashfield 74-80; I Keady w Armaghbreague and Derrynoose 80-83; I Drumcree 83-07; rtd 07. *25 Twinem Court, Portadown, Craigavon BT63 5FH* Tel 07752-339558 (mobile)

PICKERING, John David. b 38. **d** 86 **p** 86. NSM Ellon *Ab* 86-88; NSM Cruden Bay 86-88; Ind Chapl *Dur* 88-97; TV Jarrow 91-97; P-in-c Newton Hall 97-02; TV Ind Chapl 97-03. *14 Denholm Avenue, Cramlington NE23 3FT* Tel (01670) 716619

PICKERING, John Michael Staunton. b 34. Sarum & Wells Th Coll 71. **d** 72 **p** 73. C Gaywood, Bawsey and Mintlyn *Nor* 72-77; P-in-c Foulsham 77-81; R Foulsham w Hindolveston and Guestwick 81-88; P-in-c Bacton w Edingthorpe w Witton and Ridlington 88-98; rtd 98; Perm to Offic *Nor* from 04. *The*

Brambles, School Lane, Neatishead, Norwich NR12 8XH Tel (01692) 630818

PICKERING, Malcolm. b 37. Sarum Th Coll 65. **d** 68 **p** 69. C Milton *Portsm* 68-70; C Stanmer w Falmer and Moulsecoomb *Chich* 70-75; Chapl Brighton Coll of Educn 71-75; V Hooe and R Ninfield *Chich* 75-80; V Ventnor H Trin and Ventnor St Cath *Portsm* 80-88; Chapl St Cath Sch Ventnor 87-88; V Marton *Blackb* 88-97; P-in-c Badingham w Bruisyard, Cransford and Dennington *St E* 97-99; V Leiston 99-04; rtd 04; Perm to Offic *B & W* 04-07; Hon C Drybrook, Lydbrook and Ruardean *Glouc* 07-08. *38 Lethbridge Road, Wells BA5 2FW* Tel (01749) 676526 E-mail malcolm@totland-a.freeserve.co.uk

PICKERING, Mark Penrhyn. b 36. Liv Univ BA59 St Cath Coll Ox BA62 MA67. Wycliffe Hall Ox 60. **d** 63 **p** 64. C Claughton cum Grange *Ches* 63-67; C Newland St Jo *York* 67-72; TV Marfleet 72-76; V Kingston upon Hull St Nic 76-85; V Elloughton and Brough w Brantingham 85-88; Chapl R Hull Hosps NHS Trust 88-01; Perm to Offic *York* from 01. *14 Sykes Close, Swanland, North Ferriby HU14 3GD* Tel (01482) 634834

PICKERING, Mrs Maureen Anne. b 46. Man Univ CertEd67 Open Univ BA88 MA93 Leeds Univ MA07. NOC 04. **d** 07 **p** 08. NSM Ches St Mary from 07. *Curzon Cottage, 2A Curzon Park South, Chester CH4 8AB* Tel (01244) 677352 Mobile 07966-409404

PICKERING, Michael. See PICKERING, John Michael Staunton

PICKERING, William Stuart Frederick. b 22. K Coll Lon BD49 AKC49 PhD58 Manitoba Univ Hon DCL81. **d** 50 **p** 51. C Frodingham *Linc* 50-53; Lic to Offic Guildf & Linc 55-56; Tutor K Coll Lon 53-56; Canada 58-66; Lic to Offic *Newc* 66-87; rtd 87; Perm to Offic *Ely* 87-97 and from 03. *1 Brookfield Road, Coton, Cambridge CB23 7PT* Tel (01954) 210525

PICKETT, Brian Laurence. b 48. Reading Univ BA70 Qu Coll Birm BA73 MA77. Ripon Coll Cuddesdon. **d** 88 **p** 88. C Highcliffe w Hinton Admiral *Win* 88-91; P-in-c Colbury 91-01; P-in-c W End 01-04; V from 04. *St James's Vicarage, Elizabeth Close, Southampton SO30 3LT* Tel (023) 8047 2180 Fax 8047 7661

PICKETT, Ms Joanna Elizabeth. b 53. Leic Univ BA74 MA80 Lon Univ MTh95. Wycliffe Hall Ox 87. **d** 89 **p** 94. Chapl Southn Univ 89-94; C N Stoneham 94-95; NSM Colbury 97-01; NSM W End from 01. *St James's Vicarage, Elizabeth Close, Southampton SO30 3LT* Tel (023) 8047 2180 Fax 8047 7661

PICKETT, Mark William Leslie. b 60. Westhill Coll Birm BEd84. Trin Coll Bris 93. **d** 95 **p** 96. C Hellesdon *Nor* 95-98; TV Thetford 98-03; R Clitheroe St Jas *Blackb* from 03. *The Rectory, Woone Lane, Clitheroe BB7 1BJ* Tel (01200) 423608 E-mail cloverfieldchurch@talk21.com

PICKETT, Peter Leslie. b 28. Guy's Hosp Medical Sch LDS52. S Dios Minl Tr Scheme 83. **d** 86 **p** 87. NSM Eastbourne H Trin *Chich* 86-88; P-in-c Danehill 88-93; rtd 93; Perm to Offic *Chich* from 93. *Springfield, 76 Meads Road, Eastbourne BN20 7QJ* Tel (01323) 731709 Mobile 07733-090957 E-mail pjpickett@btinternet.com

PICKFORD (née PACKER), Mrs Catherine Ruth. b 76. Nottm Univ BA97 Anglia Poly Univ MA00. Westcott Ho Cam MA00. **d** 00 **p** 01. C Gosforth All SS *Newc* 00-04; TV Benwell 04-09; TR from 09. *56 Dunholme Road, Newcastle upon Tyne NE4 6XE* Tel 0191-273 5356 E-mail catherine.p@blueyonder.co.uk

PICKLES, Mark Andrew. b 62. Edin Univ BA83. Cranmer Hall Dur 85. **d** 88 **p** 89. C Rock Ferry *Ches* 88-91; C Hartford 91-93; V Wharton 93-00; P-in-c Duffield *Derby* 00-05; V Duffield and Lt Eaton from 05. *St Alkmund's Vicarage, Vicarage Lane, Duffield, Belper DE56 4EB* Tel (01332) 841168 *or* 840536 Fax 842595 E-mail pickles465@btinternet.com

PICKSTONE, Charles Faulkner. b 55. BNC Ox BA77 MA81 Leeds Univ BA80. Coll of Resurr Mirfield 78. **d** 81 **p** 82. C Birkenhead Priory *Ches* 81-84; Chapl Paris St Geo *Eur* 84; C Camberwell St Giles w St Matt *S'wark* 84-89; V Catford St Laur from 89; Asst RD E Lewisham 92-99. *St Laurence's Vicarage, 31 Bromley Road, London SE6 2TS* Tel (020) 8698 2871 *or* 8698 9706 E-mail charlston@mailbox.co.uk

PICKTHORN, Canon Charles Howard. b 25. Linc Coll Ox BA48 MA52. Sarum Th Coll 48. **d** 50 **p** 51. C High Harrogate Ch Ch *Ripon* 50-54; C Cheam *S'wark* 54-60; R Bourton-on-the-Water w Clapton *Glouc* 60-91; Chapl RAF 60-76; RD Stow *Glouc* 67-90; P-in-c Gt Rissington 68-81; Hon Can Glouc Cathl from 77; rtd 91; Perm to Offic *Glouc* from 91. *clo Mrs S P Stiggers, 23 Sutherland Close, Warwick CV34 5UJ*

PICKUP, Harold. b 17. St Pet Hall Ox BA39 MA46. Ridley Hall Cam 46. **d** 47 **p** 48. C Middleton *Man* 47-50; V Gravesend St Mary *Roch* 51-57; Australia from 57; rtd 82. *7 Farview Avenue, Riverside Tas 7250, Australia* Tel (0061) (3) 6327 4891

PIDGEON, Warner Mark. b 68. Trin Coll Bris 00. **d** 02 **p** 03. C Fair Oak *Win* 02-06; TV Billericay and Lt Burstead *Chelmsf* from 06. *10 Chestwood Close, Billericay CM12 0PB* Tel (01277) 652659 Mobile 07876-085054 E-mail warner@billericaychurches.org

PIDOUX, Ian George. b 32. Univ Coll Ox BA55 MA60. Coll of Resurr Mirfield 54. **d** 57 **p** 58. C Middlesbrough All SS *York* 57-60; C Haggerston St Aug w St Steph *Lon* 60-62; C Aylesford *Roch* 80-81; TV Rye *Chich* 81-84; P-in-c Bridgwater St Jo *B & W* 84-86; V 86-98; Chapl Bridgwater Hosp 91-98; rtd 98; Perm to Offic *B & W* from 98. *18 Alexandra Road, Bridgwater TA6 3HE* Tel (01278) 452882 E-mail igsepidoux@btinternet.com

PIDSLEY, Preb Christopher Thomas. b 36. ALCD61. **d** 61 **p** 62. C Enfield Ch Ch Trent Park *Lon* 61-66; C Rainham *Chelmsf* 66-70; V Chudleigh *Ex* 70-98; RD Moreton 86-91; Preb Ex Cathl 92-98; rtd 98. *Bellever, Shillingford Abbot, Exeter EX2 9QF* Tel (01392) 833588

PIENAAR, Joseph. b 77. Birm Chr Coll MA09. **d** 09. C Chadkirk *Ches* from 09. *6 Etherow Avenue, Romiley, Stockport SK6 4HA* Tel 0161-427 6731 Mobile 07854-179087 E-mail joe@romileylifecentre.co.uk

PIERARD, Canon Beaumont Harold. b 21. MBE72 JP68. St Jo Coll Auckland. **d** 46 **p** 51. New Zealand 46-53; Chapl Hurstpierpoint Coll 53-54; Chapl Worksop Coll Notts 54-57; New Zealand from 57; Hon Can St Peter's Cathl Waikato 64-82. *287 Peachgrove Road, Hamilton 3214, New Zealand* Tel (0064) (7) 855 7000

PIERCE, Alan. b 46. St Mark & St Jo Coll Lon TCert68 Southlands Coll Lon BEd75 K Coll Lon MA85. NOC 89. **d** 92 **p** 93. NSM Bolton St Thos *Man* 92-98; NSM Halliwell 98-00; NSM Bolton Breightmet St Jas 00-06; NSM Leverhulme from 06. *3 Astley Road, Bolton BL2 4BR* Tel (01204) 300071 Fax 401556

✠**PIERCE, The Rt Revd Anthony Edward.** b 41. Univ of Wales (Swansea) BA63 Linacre Coll Ox BA65 MA71. Ripon Hall Ox 63. **d** 65 **p** 66 **c** 99. C Swansea St Pet *S & B* 65-67; C Swansea St Mary and H Trin 67-74; Chapl Univ of Wales (Swansea) 71-74; V Llwynderw 74-92; P-in-c Swansea St Barn 92-96; Dioc Dir of Educn 93-96; Can Brecon Cathl 93-99; Adn Gower 95-99; V Swansea St Mary w H Trin 96-99; Bp S & B 99-08; rtd 08. *2 Coed Ceirios, Swansea Vale, Swansea SA7 0NU* Tel (01792) 790258

PIERCE, Brian William. b 42. St Steph Ho Ox 86. **d** 88 **p** 89. C Cudworth *Wakef* 88-93; TV Manningham *Bradf* 93-98; V Tipton St Jo *Lich* 98-07; rtd 07; Perm to Offic *Blackb* from 08. *53 St Patricks Road North, Lytham St Annes FY8 2HB* Tel (01253) 711247 E-mail loggos@btinternet.com

PIERCE, Bruce Andrew. b 58. TCD BBS80 BTh89 Dub City Univ MA99 MA02. CITC 86. **d** 89 **p** 90. C Raheny w Coolock *D & G* 89-92; C Taney 92-93; I Lucan w Leixlip 93-98; Chapl Adelaide and Meath Hosp Dublin 98-02; C Haarlem *Eur* 02-03; Chapl Toronto Gen Hosp Canada 03-04; Chapl Princess Marg Hosp Toronto 04-05; Supervisor (Assoc) Kerry Gen Hosp 06-08; Dir Educn St Luke's Home Mahon from 08. *6 East Avenue, Frankfield, Douglas, Cork, Republic of Ireland* Tel (00353) (21) 489 7511 *or* 435 9444 ext 507 Fax 435 9450 E-mail brupierce@hotmail.com *or* bruce.pierce@stlukeshome.ie

PIERCE, David. *See* PIERCE, Thomas David Benjamin

PIERCE, Jeffrey Hyam. b 29. Chelsea Coll Lon BSc51 FBIM80. Ox NSM Course 86. **d** 88 **p** 89. NSM Gt Missenden w Ballinger and Lt Hampden *Ox* 88-93; NSM Penn 93-97; rtd 97; Perm to Offic *Ox* from 97. *Glebe Cottage, Manor Road, Penn, High Wycombe HP10 8HY* Tel (01494) 817179

PIERCE, Jonathan Douglas Marshall. b 70. UCD BA91. CITC BTh96. **d** 96 **p** 97. C Knockbreda *D & D* 96-99; L'Arche Community Dublin 99-00; C Taney *D & G* 00-03; I Kilmore and Inch *D & D* 03-09; I Cregagh from 09. *St Finnian's Rectory, 3 Upper Knockbreda Road, Belfast BT6 9QH* Tel (028) 9079 3822

PIERCE, Neil David. b 42. Cant Univ (NZ) BA63 MA64 Ch Ch Coll Cant Dip Teaching65. Coll of Resurr Mirfield. **d** 70 **p** 71. C Huddersfield SS Pet and Paul *Wakef* 70-74; Prec St Jo Cathl Bulawayo Zimbabwe 75-81; Hd Master Cyrene Sch 82-99; P-in-c Figtree, Marula and Plumtree 82-99; Dioc Sec Matabeleland and R Barham Green St Fran 00-04; rtd 04; Perm to Offic *Lich* from 05. *20 Poplar Avenue, Walsall WS5 4EX* Tel (01922) 632888 Mobile 07833-530111 E-mail pierceneil@aol.com

PIERCE, Roderick Martin. b 52. ACIB74. **d** 06 **p** 07. OLM Guildf H Trin w St Mary from 06. *Appledore, 18 Blackwell Avenue, Guildford GU2 8LU* Tel (01483) 505816 E-mail ann.rodpierce@ntlworld.com

PIERCE, Stephen Barry. b 60. Birm Univ BA81 MA82. Cranmer Hall Dur. **d** 85 **p** 86. C Huyton St Mich *Liv* 85-89; V Walton Breck Ch Ch 89-00; P-in-c Walton Breck 98-00; Resources Officer 00-08; Perm to Offic from 01. *39 Duke Street, Formby, Liverpool L37 4AP* Tel (0704) 833725

PIERCE, Thomas David Benjamin. b 67. Ulster Univ BA88. Oak Hill Th Coll BA94. **d** 94 **p** 95. C Cromer *Nor* 94-97; C Belfast St Donard *D & D* 97-99; C Holywood 99-00; I Kilwarlin Upper w Kilwarlin Lower from 00. *Kilwarlin Rectory, 9 St John's Road, Hillsborough BT26 6ED* Tel (028) 9268 3299

PIERCE, William Johnston. b 32. NOC. **d** 89 **p** 90. NSM Gt Crosby St Luke *Liv* 89-96; Perm to Offic from 96. *1 Forton Lodge, Blundellsands Road East, Liverpool L23 8SA* Tel 0151-924 2400

PIERCE-JONES, Alan. b 74. Coll of Ripon & York St Jo BA98. St Mich Coll Llan 98. **d** 00 **p** 01. C Port Talbot St Theodore *Llan* 00-02; TV Neath 02-05; V Lt Marsden w Nelson St Mary and Nelson St Bede *Blackb* from 05. *St Paul's Vicarage, Bentley Street, Nelson BB9 0BS* Tel (01282) 615888 E-mail fr.alan@apj.org.uk

PIERCY, Elizabeth Claire. *See* FRANCE, Mrs Elizabeth Claire

PIERPOINT, The Ven David Alfred. b 56. **d** 86 **p** 88. NSM Athboy w Ballivor and Killallon *M & K* 86-88; NSM Killiney Ballybrack *D & G* 88-89; NSM Narraghmore and Timolin w Castledermot etc 89-91; Chan V St Patr Cathl Dublin 90-96; C Dublin St Patr Cathl Gp 92-95; V Dublin Ch Ch Cathl Gp from 95; Can Ch Ch Cathl Dublin from 95; Adn Dublin from 04. *The Vicarage, 30 Phibsborough Road, Dublin 7, Republic of Ireland* Tel (00353) (1) 830 4601 Mobile 87-263 0402 E-mail dpier@iol.ie

PIGGOT, Alan Robert Lennox. b 62. Peterho Cam BA84 MA88. Westcott Ho Cam 00. **d** 02 **p** 03. C Dalston H Trin w St Phil and Haggerston All SS *Lon* 02-04; C Stoke Newington St Mary 04-05; P-in-c Hackney Wick St Mary of Eton w St Aug from 05. *6 Meynell Road, London E9 7AP* Tel (020) 8986 7655 Mobile 07743-294532 E-mail alan.piggot@btinternet.com

PIGGOTT, The Ven Andrew John. b 51. Qu Mary Coll Lon BSc(Econ)72. St Jo Coll Nottm 83. **d** 86 **p** 87. C Dorridge *Birm* 86-89; TV Kidderminster St Geo *Worc* 89-94; V Biddulph *Lich* 94-99; Min and Voc Adv CPAS 99-01; Patr Sec 01-05; Adn Bath and Preb Wells Cathl from 05. *56 Grange Road, Saltford, Bristol BS31 3AG* Tel (01225) 873609 Fax 874110 E-mail adbath@bathwells.anglican.org

PIGGOTT, Clive. b 47. St Luke's Coll Ex CertEd69. **d** 96 **p** 97. OLM Malden St Jas *S'wark* from 96. *84 Manor Drive North, New Malden KT3 5PA* Tel (020) 8337 0801

PIGOTT, Graham John. b 44. Lon Bible Coll BD73 Nottm Univ MPhil84 MEd94 Lon Inst of Educn PGCE74. St Jo Coll Nottm 79. **d** 81 **p** 82. C Beeston *S'well* 81-84; P-in-c W Bridgford 84-88; V Wilford Hill 88-00; AD W Bingham 97-04; Hon Can S'well Minster 04-09; rtd 09; Perm to Offic *Derby* from 09. *Tanner's House, 5A Goatscliff Cottages, Grindleford, Hope Valley S32 2HG* Tel (01433) 639641 E-mail graham.pigott@btinternet.com

PIGOTT, Canon John Drummond. b 26. TCD Div Test50 BA50 MA56. **d** 51 **p** 52. C Belfast St Phil *Conn* 51-54; C Jordanstown 54-56; Chapl RAF 56-59; R Upper Clatford w Goodworth Clatford *Win* 59-65; V Warley Woods *Birm* 65-74; RD Warley 72-74; V Boldmere 74-97; Hon Can Birm Cathl 81-97; RD Sutton Coldfield 88-93; rtd 97; Perm to Offic *B & W* from 97. *Clatford House, 41 Farriers Green, Monkton Heathfield, Taunton TA2 8PP* Tel (01823) 413552

PIGOTT, Nicholas John Capel. b 48. Qu Coll Birm 75. **d** 78 **p** 79. C Belmont *Dur* 78-79; C Folkestone St Sav *Cant* 79-82; C Birm St Geo 82-85; V Stevenage St Hugh and St Jo *St Alb* 85-91; TV Totnes w Bridgetown, Berry Pomeroy etc *Ex* 91-02; Asst P 02-04; rtd 04. *27 Croft Road, Ipplepen, Newton Abbot TQ12 5SS* Tel (01803) 813664 E-mail njsa@pigott.freeserve.co.uk

PIGREM, Terence John (Tim). b 39. Middx Univ BA97 MA01. Oak Hill Th Coll 66. **d** 69 **p** 70. C Islington St Andr w St Thos and St Matthias *Lon* 69-73; C Barking St Marg w St Patr *Chelmsf* 73-75; TV 75-76; C W Holloway St Luke *Lon* 76-79; V 79-95; P-in-c Abbess Roding, Beauchamp Roding and White Roding *Chelmsf* 95-96; R S Rodings 96-07; RD Dunmow 97-02; rtd 07; Perm to Offic *Chelmsf* from 08. *96 Vicarage Lane, Great Baddow, Chelmsford CM2 8JB* Tel (01245) 471878 E-mail pigrem@btinternet.com

PIIR, The Very Revd Gustav Peeter. b 61. St Olaf Coll Minnesota BA83 Saskatchewan Univ MDiv86. **p** 88. Asst Toronto St Pet Canada 88-92; Asst Chas Ch Tallinn Estonia 92-95; R Tallinn H Spirit from 95; Dean Tallinn from 99; P-in-c Tallinn SS Tim and Titus *Eur* from 00. *Pühavaimu 2, Tallinn 10123, Estonia* Tel (00372) 646 4430 Mobile 51-76159 Fax 644 1487 E-mail praost@hot.ee

PIKE, Mrs Amanda Shirley Gail. b 69. Cranmer Hall Dur 99. **d** 01 **p** 02. C Boston Spa *York* 01-03; C Elloughton and Brough w Brantingham 03-05; P-in-c Eggleston and Middleton-in-Teesdale w Forest and Frith *Dur* 05-08; TV Bosworth and Sheepy Gp *Leic* from 08. *The Rectory, Church Lane, Sheepy Magna, Atherstone CV9 3QS* Tel (01827) 880301 Mobile 07968-543569 E-mail amanda@ichthos.me.uk

PIKE, David Frank. b 35. BA Lon Univ TCert CEng MIMechE. S Dios Minl Tr Scheme 82. **d** 85 **p** 86. NSM Lancing w Coombes *Chich* 85-88; R Albourne w Sayers Common and Twineham 88-94; V Woolsdown Green 94-04; rtd 04. *42 Greenoaks, Lancing BN15 0HE* Tel (01903) 766209

PIKE, George Richard. b 38. Birm Univ BSc57. WMMTC 79. **d** 82 **p** 83. NSM Edgbaston St Bart *Birm* 82-89; NSM S Yardley St Mich 89-06; Perm to Offic from 06. *138 Charlbury Crescent, Birmingham B26 2LW* Tel and fax 0121-783 2818 E-mail kepi@geopi.fsnet.co.uk

PIKE, Paul Alfred. b 38. Bognor Regis Coll of Educn CertEd58 MIL88. Wycliffe Hall Ox 83. **d** 84 **p** 85. C Penn Fields *Lich* 84-89; OMF Internat Japan 89-03; rtd 03; Perm to Offic *Bris* from 03. *18 Silverlow Road, Nailsea, Bristol BS48 2AD* Tel (01275) 856270 E-mail papike@attglobal.net

PIKE, Peter John. b 53. Southn Univ BTh86 Lanc Univ PhD00. Sarum & Wells Th Coll 81. **d** 84 **p** 85. C Broughton *Blackb* 84-88; V Woodplumpton 88-93; Asst Dir of Ords and Voc Adv 89-93; P-in-c Barnacre w Calder Vale 93-98; Tutor CBDTI 93-98; V Briercliffe *Blackb* 98-04; AD Burnley 01-04; V Bempton w Flamborough, Reighton w Speeton *York* from 04; RD Bridlington from 08. *The Vicarage, Church Street, Flamborough, Bridlington YO15 1PE* Tel (01262) 851370 E-mail revpeterpike@hotmail.com

PIKE, Robert James. b 47. Kelham Th Coll 66. **d** 70 **p** 71. C Cov St Pet 70-74; C Bilton 74-76; P-in-c Southall St Geo *Lon* 76-81; V S Harrow St Paul 81-86; C Hillingdon St Jo 86-88; Chapl Hillingdon Hosp & Mt Vernon Hosp Uxbridge 88-90; Perm to Offic 91-96. *6 Salt Hill Close, Uxbridge UB8 1PZ* Tel (01895) 235212

PIKE, Timothy David. b 68. Collingwood Coll Dur BA90 Leeds Univ BA94. Coll of Resurr Mirfield 92. **d** 95 **p** 96. C Owton Manor *Dur* 95-98; C Old St Pancras w Bedford New Town St Matt *Lon* 98-03; CMP from 98; Warden from 05; CR 03-04; P-in-c Hornsey H Innocents *Lon* 04-07; V from 07; C Stroud Green H Trin from 04; AD W Haringey from 06. *99 Hillfield Avenue, London N8 7DG* Tel (020) 8340 1300 E-mail fathertimpike@hotmail.com

PILCHER, Mrs Jennifer. b 42. **d** 04 **p** 05. OLM Eastry and Northbourne w Tilmanstone etc *Cant* from 04. *1 Long Drive, Church Street, Eastry, Sandwich CT13 0HN* Tel (01304) 611472 E-mail jennifer.p@torview1.freeserve.co.uk

PILDITCH, Miss Patricia Desiree. b 21. dss 82 **d** 87 **p** 94. Barnstaple *Ex* 82-87; NSM Barnstaple 87-01; Asst Chapl N Devon Healthcare NHS Trust 82-01; Perm to Offic *Ex* from 01. *4 The Mews, Bydown, Swimbridge, Barnstaple EX32 0QB* Tel (01271) 830770

PILGRIM, Canon Colin Mark. b 56. BA77. Westcott Ho Cam 81. **d** 84 **p** 85. C Chorlton-cum-Hardy St Clem *Man* 84-87; C Whitchurch *Bris* 87-89; V Bedminster Down 89-95; Dioc Youth Officer 95-01; Hon C Stoke Bishop 96-01; V Henleaze from 01; AD Bris W from 06; Hon Can Bris Cathl from 09. *St Peter's Vicarage, 17 The Drive, Henleaze, Bristol BS9 4LD* Tel 0117-962 0636 *or* 962 3196 E-mail markpilgrimis@aol.com

PILGRIM, Donald Eric. b 55. Cant Univ (NZ) BA80 LTh87. St Jo Coll Auckland 81. **d** 81 **p** 82. New Zealand 81-85 and from 86; C Southampton Maybush St Pet *Win* 85-86. *212 Hoon Hay Road, Hoon Hay, Christchurch 8025, New Zealand* Tel and fax (0064) (3) 338 4277 E-mail pilgrimspalace@paradise.net.nz

PILGRIM, Ms Judith Mary. b 44. Westcott Ho Cam 88. **d** 90 **p** 94. C Probus, Ladock and Grampound w Creed and St Erme *Truro* 90-94; C Nottingham All SS *S'well* 94-97; Asst Chapl to the Deaf 94-97; Perm to Offic *S'well* 97-00 and *Ox* 00-01; P-in-c Zennor and Towednack *Truro* 02-06; rtd 06. *6 Cape Terrace, St Just, Penzance TR19 7JF* Tel (01736) 787371

PILGRIM, Kenneth George. b 49. Lon Univ BEd77 Kent Univ MA94. **d** 01 **p** 02. OLM Alkham w Capel le Ferne and Hougham *Cant* 01-03; Perm to Offic *Nor* 04-05; NSM E Dereham and Scarning 05-06; NSM Swanton Morley w Beetley w E Bilney and Hoe 05-06; NSM Dereham and Distr from 06. *Sunny Oak, 27 Fakenham Road, Beetley, Dereham NR20 4BT* Tel (01362) 861265 E-mail ken@prilgrim12.freeserve.co.uk

PILGRIM, Mark. *See* PILGRIM, Canon Colin Mark

PILKINGTON, Miss Anne. b 57. Aston Tr Scheme 88 NOC 90. **d** 93 **p** 94. C Wythenshawe Wm Temple Ch *Man* 93-96; P-in-c 96-99; TV Wythenshawe 99-06; P-in-c Didsbury Ch Ch 06; P-in-c Withington St Chris 06; R W Didsbury and Withington St Chris from 06. *Christ Church Rectory, 35 Darley Avenue, Manchester M20 2ZD* Tel 0161-445 4152 E-mail anne@christchurchdidsbury.org.uk

PILKINGTON, Charles George Willink. b 21. Trin Coll Cam BA42 MA64. Westcott Ho Cam. **d** 63 **p** 64. C Pendleton St Thos *Man* 63-65; C Brindle Heath 63-65; C Chorlton-cum-Hardy St Clem 65-68; R Withington St Chris 68-88; rtd 88; Perm to Offic *Man* from 88. *32 Rathen Road, Withington, Manchester M20 9GH* Tel 0161-434 5365

PILKINGTON, Edward Russell. b 39. ALCD65. **d** 65 **p** 66. C Eccleshill *Bradf* 65-68; C Billericay St Mary *Chelmsf* 68-72; V New Thundersley 72-78; R Theydon Garnon 78-82; V Gidea Park 82-04; rtd 04. *19 Tryon Close, Swindon SN3 6HG* Tel (01793) 433495

PILKINGTON, John Rowan. b 32. Magd Coll Cam BA55 MA59. Ridley Hall Cam 57. **d** 59 **p** 60. C Ashtead *Guildf* 59-61; C Wimbledon *S'wark* 62-65; R Newhaven *Chich* 65-75; R Farlington *Portsm* 75-89; V Darlington St Mark w St Paul *Dur* 89-97; rtd 97; Perm to Offic *Portsm* from 98. *38 Main Road, Emsworth PO10 8AU* Tel (01243) 375830

PILKINGTON, Canon Timothy William. b 54. Nottm Univ BA85 Univ of Wales (Lamp) MA09. Linc Th Coll 82. **d** 85 **p** 86.

C Newquay *Truro* 85-88; C Cockington *Ex* 88-91; R St John w Millbrook *Truro* 91-97; V Northampton St Matt *Pet* 97-02; TR Solihull *Birm* from 02; Hon Can Birm Cathl from 06. *The Rectory, St Alphege Close, Church Hill Road, Solihull B91 3RQ* Tel 0121-705 0069 *or* 705 5350 Fax 704 0646 E-mail rector@solihullparish.org.uk

PILKINGTON OF OXENFORD, The Revd Canon Lord (Peter). b 33. Jes Coll Cam BA55 MA59. Westcott Ho Cam 58. **d** 59 **p** 60. C Bakewell *Derby* 59-62; Chapl Eton Coll 62-75; Hd Master K Sch Cant 75-85; Hon Can Cant Cathl 75-90; High Master St Paul's Sch Barnes 86-92; Chmn Broadcasting Complaints Commn 92-96; Hon C Pimlico St Mary Bourne Street *Lon* 92-05. *Oxenford House, Dowlish Wake, Ilminster TA19 0PP* Tel (01460) 52813 Fax 55280

✠**PILLAR, The Rt Revd Kenneth Harold.** b 24. Qu Coll Cam BA48 MA53. Ridley Hall Cam 48. **d** 50 **p** 51 **c** 82. C Childwall All SS *Liv* 50-53; Chapl Lee Abbey 53-57; V New Beckenham St Paul *Roch* 57-62; V Cant St Mary Bredin 62-65; Warden Lee Abbey 65-70; V Waltham Abbey *Chelmsf* 70-82; RD Chigwell 76-78; RD Epping Forest 78-82; Suff Bp Hertford *St Alb* 82-89; rtd 89; Asst Bp Sheff from 89. *75 Dobcroft Road, Sheffield S7 2LS* Tel 0114-236 7902

PIMENTEL, Peter Eric. b 55. Lon Bible Coll BA79 MA94. Ridley Hall Cam. **d** 82 **p** 83. C Gt Ilford St Andr *Chelmsf* 82-85; Chapl Basingstoke Distr Hosp 85-88; TV Grays Thurrock *Chelmsf* 88-96; P-in-c Barton *Portsm* 96-99; V from 99; Dioc Ecum Officer 96-02. *St Paul's Vicarage, Staplers Road, Newport PO30 2HZ* Tel (01983) 522075 Mobile 07949-366625 Fax 08701-303386 E-mail peter@pimentel.freeserve.co.uk

PIMM, Robert John. b 57. Bris Univ BA78 ACIB82. Trin Coll Bris 92. **d** 94 **p** 95. C Long Benton *Newc* 94-98; TV Bath Twerton-on-Avon *B & W* from 98. *Ascension Vicarage, 35A Claude Avenue, Bath BA2 1AG* Tel (01225) 405354 E-mail robertpimm@tiscali.co.uk

PINCHBECK, Miss Caroline Rosamund. b 70. Hatf Coll Dur BA93. Wesley Ho Cam MA00. **d** 02 **p** 03. C Mawnan *Truro* 02-06; C Budock 03-06; P-in-c Eastling w Ospringe and Stalisfield w Otterden *Cant* from 06; Rural Life Adv *Cant* and Roch from 06. *The Rectory, Newnham Lane, Eastling, Faversham ME13 0AS* Tel (01795) 890487 E-mail caroline.pinchbeck575@btinternet.com

PINCHES, Donald Antony. b 32. Pemb Coll Cam BA55 MA60 Linacre Coll Ox BA67. Wycliffe Hall Ox 64. **d** 67 **p** 68. C Aylesbury *Ox* 67-71; C Compton Gifford *Ex* 71-74; TV Lydford, Brent Tor, Bridestowe and Sourton 74-77; V Shiphay Collaton 77-97; rtd 97; Perm to Offic *Ex* from 98. *3 Malderek Avenue, Preston, Paignton TQ3 2RP* Tel (01803) 698003

PINDER, Canon John Ridout. b 43. Peterho Cam BA65 MA69. Cuddesdon Coll 65. **d** 73 **p** 74. C Leavesden *St Alb* 73-76; Gen Sec Melanesian Miss 77-89; P-in-c Harpsden *Ox* 82-89; R Farlington *Portsm* 89-02; R Liss 02-09; RD Portsm 96-01; Hon Can Portsm Cathl 01-09; rtd 09; P-in-c Stapleford *Ely* from 09. *The Vicarage, 43 Mingle Lane, Stapleford, Cambridge CB22 5SY* Tel (01223) 840256 E-mail johnpinder@waitrose.com

PINDER-PACKARD, John. b 47. Lon Univ BSc. NOC 81. **d** 84 **p** 85. NSM Mosbrough *Sheff* 84-85; C Norton 85-88; V New Whittington *Derby* 88-04; P-in-c Newbold and Gt Barlow 99-00; Chapl Whittington Hall Hosp 88-04; R Barlborough and Renishaw *Derby* from 04; P-in-c Clowne from 05. *The New Rectory, Church Street, Barlborough, Chesterfield S43 4EP* Tel (01246) 570621 E-mail packards@tiscali.co.uk

PINE, David Michael. b 41. Lich Th Coll 68. **d** 71 **p** 72. C Northam *Ex* 71-74; R Toft w Caldecote and Childerley *Ely* 74-80; R Hardwick 74-80; V Ipswich St Andr *St E* 80-84; P-in-c Hazelbury Bryan w Stoke Wake etc *Sarum* 84-91; R Hazelbury Bryan and the Hillside Par 91-93; V Steep and Froxfield w Privett *Portsm* 93-00; rtd 00; Perm to Offic *Portsm* from 07. *Amberley, High Road, Nettlestone, Seaview PO34 5DZ* Tel (01983) 563734

PINES, Christopher Derek. b 65. Lon Univ MB, BS89. Oak Hill Th Coll BA93 MA01. **d** 93 **p** 94. C Heref St Pet w St Owen and St Jas 93-97; Min Can and Chapl St Alb Abbey 97-03; Chapl St Alb Sch from 03. *1 Fishpool Street, St Albans AL3 4RS* Tel (01727) 846508 E-mail cdpines@st-albans.herts.sch.uk

PINFIELD, Leslie Arthur. b 57. Birm Univ BMus79. St Steph Ho Ox 92. **d** 94 **p** 95. C Bath Bathwick *B & W* 94-98; TV Swindon New Town *Bris* 98-07; P-in-c Huddersfield All SS and St Thos *Wakef* from 07; Bp's Adv on Inter-Faith Issues from 07. *The Vicarage, 17 Cross Church Street, Paddock, Huddersfield HD1 4SN* Tel (01484) 428253 E-mail frleslie@btopenworld.com

PINK, Canon David. b 34. Qu Coll Cam BA58 MA62. Linc Th Coll 58. **d** 60 **p** 61. C Lt Ilford St Mich *Chelmsf* 60-63; Lect Boston 63-65; V Kirton in Holland *Linc* 65 71; V Spittlegate 71-77; Ecum Officer Lincs and S Humberside 77-85; P-in-c Canwick 77-87; R Washingborough w Heighington 87-88; R Washingborough w Heighington and Canwick 88-90; Can and Preb Linc Cathl 77-05; rtd 90; Perm to Offic *Linc* from 90. *The Old School, Swarby, Sleaford NG34 8TG*

PINKERTON, Ms Patricia Edith. b 38. California Univ BA72 MA75 BTh80. Ch Div Sch of the Pacific (USA). d 81 p 82. USA 81-88; C Coleford w Staunton *Glouc* 88-92; Dn-in-c St Briavels w Hewelsfield 92-94; P-in-c 94-97; rtd 97; Perm to Offic *Glouc* from 97. *Lammas Cottage, 7 Stephens Place, Broadwell, Coleford GL16 7BJ* Tel (01594) 810321

PINNELL *(formerly ALLEN)*, **Ms Beverley Carole.** b 52. Ch Ch Coll Cant CertEd74 Open Univ BA91. Sarum Th Coll 93. d 96 p 97. NSM Ruislip Manor St Paul *Lon* from 96. *127 Cobden Close, Uxbridge UB8 2YH* E-mail revbev@tiscali.co.uk

PINNELL, George. b 39. NTMTC 96. d 99 p 00. NSM Hillingdon St Jo *Lon* from 99; Chapl Heathrow Airport from 08. *127 Cobden Close, Uxbridge UB8 2YH* Tel 07951-124976 (mobile) E-mail pinneg@tiscali.co.uk

PINNER, John Philip. b 37. K Coll Lon BA59 AKC59 Lon Inst of Educn PGCE60. Westcott Ho Cam 69. d 71 p 72. C Dover St Mary *Cant* 71-74; Chapl Felsted Sch 74-81; Chapl Rathkeale Coll New Zealand 81-02; rtd 02. *PO Box 133, Greytown, Wairarapa 5953, New Zealand* Tel (0064) (6) 304 8301 E-mail cheri.john.pinner@xtra.co.nz

PINNER, Canon Terence Malcolm William. b 35. Southn Univ MA89. AKC59. d 60 p 61. C Eltham St Barn *S'wark* 60-64; S Africa 64-67 and 69-74; USPG 67-69; Sec for Home Affairs Conf of Br Miss Socs 74-76; P-in-c Hinstock *Lich* 76-79; Adult Educn Officer 76-79; Adult RE Officer 79-83; Chapl Southn Univ 83-88; Tutor S Dios Minl Tr Scheme 88-92; Dioc Dir of Ords *Win* 88-98; Hon Can Win Cathl 92-00; P-in-c Old Alresford and Bighton 93-00; rtd 00; Perm to Offic *Win* from 01. *47 Buriton Road, Winchester SO22 6JF* Tel (01962) 884215 Mobile 07889-177203

PINNINGTON, Mrs Gillian. b 59. St Kath Coll Liv BEd81 Ches Coll of HE BTh02. NOC 99. d 02 p 03. C Roby *Liv* 02-06; TV Speke St Aid from 06. *62 East Millwood Road, Liverpool L24 6SQ* Tel 0151-425 3388 E-mail pinny@supanet.com

PINNINGTON, Suzanne Jane. b 66. Trevelyan Coll Dur BA89. St Steph Ho Ox 95. d 97 p 98. C Oakham, Hambleton, Egleton, Braunston and Brooke *Pet* 97-00; V Cottingley *Bradf* 00-08; Hon Can Bradf Cathl 04-08; R Houghton le Spring *Dur* from 08. *The Rectory, 5 Lingfield, Houghton le Spring DH5 8QA* Tel 0191-584 3487 E-mail rectorstmichaels@btinternet.com

PINNOCK, Giles Antony. b 67. Leic Univ BA88 MA93. St Steph Ho Ox BTh04. d 02 p 03. C Stony Stratford and Calverton *Ox* 02-06; V Kenton *Lon* from 06; Hon Chapl ATC from 07. *St Mary's Vicarage, 3 St Leonard's Avenue, Harrow HA3 8EJ* Tel (020) 8907 2914 Mobile 07792-971375 Fax 08714-332362 E-mail parishpriest@stmaryskenton.org

PINNOCK, Martyn Elliott. b 47. Linc Th Coll 93. d 93 p 94. C Fordingbridge *Win* 93-97; V St Minver *Truro* 97-01; P-in-c Luray Ch Ch USA 01-02; V Steeton *Bradf* 02-05; P-in-c Scottsville USA 05-08; rtd 09. *26 Kirby Road, Truro TR1 3PH* Tel (01872) 273553 E-mail martynpinnock@aol.com

PINSENT, Ewen Macpherson. b 30. Edin Th Coll 67. d 69 p 70. C Holt *Nor* 69-72; R Kelso *Edin* 72-82; R Blendworth w Chalton w Idsworth etc *Portsm* 82-90; R Blendworth w Chalton w Idsworth 90-92; rtd 92; Perm to Offic *Sarum* from 94. *The Cross House, The Cross, Child Okeford, Blandford Forum DT11 8ED* Tel (01258) 860803

PIPER, Canon Andrew. b 58. Magd Coll Ox BA79 MA83. Chich Th Coll 83. d 83 p 84. C Eastbourne St Mary *Chich* 83-88; TV Lewes All SS, St Anne, St Mich and St Thos 88-93; TR Worth 93-03; Can Res and Prec Heref Cathl from 03. *1 The Close, Hereford HR1 2NG* Tel (01432) 266193 Fax 374220 E-mail piperandrew@herefordcathedral.org

PIPER, The Very Revd Clifford John. b 53. Moray Ord Course 91. d 93 p 94. C Invergordon St Ninian *Mor* 93-96; P-in-c 00-03; NSM Tain 96-98; P-in-c 98-03; P-in-c Forres from 03; Can St Andr Cathl Inverness 00-09; Dean Mor from 09. *St John's Rectory, Victoria Road, Forres IV36 3BN* Tel (01309) 672856 Fax 08712-422221 Mobile 07895-105104 E-mail cliffpiper@tiscali.co.uk

PIPER, Gary Quentin David. b 42. Nottm Coll of Educn TCert65 Maria Grey Coll Lon DipEd71. Oak Hill Th Coll 75. d 78 p 79. NSM Fulham St Matt *Lon* 78-85; V from 85; AD Hammersmith 86-92; AD Hammersmith and Fulham from 06. *St Matthew's Vicarage, 2 Clancarty Road, London SW6 3AB* Tel (020) 7731 3272 E-mail revgarypiper@hotmail.com

PIPER, Graham. b 58. Southn Univ BTh91. Chich Th Coll 88. d 91 p 92. C Horsham *Chich* 91-94; TV Haywards Heath St Wilfrid 94-99; Dioc Voc Adv 96-99; V Bamber Bridge St Aid *Blackb* 99-04; V Hawes Side and Marton Moss from 04. *The Vicarage, Hawes Side Lane, Blackpool FY4 5AH* Tel (01253) 697937 Mobile 07816-525843

PIPER, John Howard. b 09. St Chad's Coll Dur BA31. d 32 p 34. Asst Chapl Denstone Coll Uttoxeter 32-34; C Knowle H Nativity *Bris* 34-41; C Sidmouth St Nic *Ex* 41-44; Chapl RAFVR 44-46; C Cov St Mark and St Jas 46-49; C Paignton St Jo *Ex* 49-55; C Devonport St Budeaux 55-57; V Whiteleigh 57-68; R Rearsby w Ratcliffe on the Wreake *Leic* 68-78; P-in-c Thrussington 77-78; R Rearsby w Ratcliffe-on-the-Wreake etc

78-82; rtd 82; Perm to Offic *Leic* from 82. *52 Avenue Road, Queniborough, Leicester LE7 3FA* Tel 0116-260 6603

PIPER, Kenneth John. b 29. St Luke's Coll Ex TCert53 Leeds Univ DipEd67. S Dios Minl Tr Scheme 79. d 82 p 83. NSM Bradford w Oake, Hillfarrance and Heathfield *B & W* 82-87; Chapl to Norway and Scandinavia Lay Tr Officer *Eur* 87-89; R Durrington *Sarum* 90-94; P-in-c Antony w Sheviock *Truro* 94-00; rtd 00; Perm to Offic *Truro* 01-03 and *B & W* from 03. *5 Manor Ride, Brent Knoll, Highbridge TA9 4DY* Tel (01278) 760347

PIPPEN, Canon Brian Roy. b 50. St D Coll Lamp. d 73 p 74. C Maindee Newport *Mon* 73-77; TV Cwmbran 77-84; V Newport Ch Ch 84-90; R Pontypool from 90; AD Pontypool 98-08; Can St Woolos Cathl from 01. *The Vicarage, Trevethin, Pontypool NP4 8JF* Tel (01495) 762228

PIRET, Michael John. b 57. State Univ NY BA79 Univ of Michigan MA80 PhD91 Mert Coll Ox MLitt89. Edin Th Coll 90. d 92 p 93. C St Andr Cathl Inverness 92-94; Dean of Div and Chapl Magd Coll Ox from 94. *Magdalen College, Oxford OX1 4AU* Tel (01865) 276027

PIRRIE, Stephen Robin. b 56. Kent Univ BA79 Cam Univ MA83 Barrister 80. EAMTC 94. d 97 p 98. C King's Lynn St Marg w St Nic *Nor* 97-99; C Bideford, Northam, Westward Ho!, Appledore etc *Ex* 99-00; TV 00-03. *Address withheld by request*

PITCHER, Canon David John. b 33. Ely Th Coll 55. d 58 p 59. C Kingswinford St Mary *Lich* 58-61; C Kirkby *Liv* 61-66; R Ingham w Sutton *Nor* 66-72; V Lakenham St Jo 72-76; R Framlingham w Saxtead *St E* 76-91; RD Loes 82-89; Hon Can St E Cathl 85-99; R Woodbridge St Mary 91-99; rtd 99; Perm to Offic *St E* from 00. *25 Coucy Close, Framlingham, Woodbridge IP13 9AX* Tel (01728) 621580

PITCHER, George Martell. b 55. Birm Univ BA77 Middx Univ BA05. NTMTC 02. d 05 p 06. NSM St Bride Fleet Street w Bridewell etc *Lon* from 05. *Culverwood, Little London Road, Cross in Hand, Heathfield TN21 0AX* Tel (01435) 865377 Mobile 07778-917182 E-mail george@pitcher.com

PITCHER, Robert Philip. b 47. Westhill Coll Birm DipEd70. Trin Coll Bris 90. d 92 p 93. C Llansamlet *S & B* 92-96; V Caereithin 96-02; V Llanidloes w Llangurig *Ban* from 02; AD Arwystli from 04. *The Vicarage, Trefeglwys Road, Llanidloes SY18 6HZ* Tel (01686) 412370 E-mail bob.pitcher@openworld.com

PITCHER, Ronald Charles Frederick. b 21. AKC50. d 51 p 52. C Burnage St Marg *Man* 51-53; C Heywood St Jas 53-55; C Newall Green CD 55-61; V Newall Green St Fran 61-73; Chapl Wythenshawe Hosp Man 64-73; C-in-c Danesholme CD *Pet* 73-81; V Estover *Ex* 81-91; rtd 91; Perm to Offic *Sarum* from 92. *18 East Wyld Road, Weymouth DT4 0RP* Tel (01305) 771916

PITCHER, Simon John. b 63. Reading Univ BA85. Ridley Hall Cam 00. d 02 p 03. C Lightcliffe *Wakef* 02-05; P-in-c Heckmondwike from 05; C Liversedge w Hightown from 05; C Roberttown w Hartshead from 05; RD Birstall from 08. *The Vicarage, Church Street, Heckmondwike WF16 0AX* Tel (01924) 405881 E-mail sjp@ukgateway.net

PITCHFORD, Herbert John. b 34. Dur Univ BA60. Ridley Hall Cam 60. d 62 p 63. C Heref St Martin 62-68; R Much Birch w Lt Birch 68-78; P-in-c Much Dewchurch w Llanwarne and Llandinabo 73-78; R Much Birch w Lt Birch, Much Dewchurch etc 78-80; V Grange Park St Pet *Lon* 80-91; V Wylde Green *Birm* 91-01; rtd 01; Perm to Offic *Glouc* and *Worc* from 03. *Woodlands, Eaton Road, Malvern WR14 4PE* Tel (01684) 575893 Mobile 07870-841150 E-mail revjpitchford@woodlands45.freeserve.co.uk

PITHERS, Canon Brian Hoyle. b 34. Chich Th Coll 63. d 66 p 67. C Wisbech SS Pet and Paul *Ely* 66-70; V Fenstanton 70-75; V Hilton 70-75; V Habergham Eaves St Matt *Blackb* 75-85; P-in-c Habergham Eaves H Trin 78-85; V Burnley St Matt w H Trin 85-86; TR Ribbleton 86-92; V Torrisholme 92-00; Hon Can Blackb Cathl 97-00; rtd 01; Perm to Offic *Blackb* from 01. *37 Dallam Avenue, Morecambe LA4 5BB* Tel (01524) 424786 E-mail brianpithers@talktalk.net

PITKIN, James Mark. b 62. Man Univ BSc83 MRAeS90 CEng90 Glos Univ BA(Theol)03. STETS. d 99 p 00. C Chilworth w N Baddesley *Win* 99-03; V Lockerley and E Dean w E and W Tytherley from 03. *The Vicarage, The Street, Lockerley, Romsey SO51 0JF* Tel (01794) 340635 Fax 08701-674661 Mobile 07931-736166 E-mail jamespitkin@priest.com

PITKIN, Mrs Susan Margaret. b 60. Man Univ BA84 Surrey Univ BA03. STETS 00. d 03 p 04. C Southampton Maybush St Pet *Win* 03-06; C Maybush and Southampton St Jude from 06. *The Vicarage, The Street, Lockerley, Romsey SO51 0JF* Tel (01794) 340635 Mobile 07906-027042 E-mail suepitkin@minister.com

PITMAN, Roger Thomas. b 64. St Mich Coll Llan BTh00. d 00 p 01. C Caerphilly *Llan* 00-02; C Coity w Nolton 02-07; P-in-c Llanharry from 07; Chapl Pontypridd and Rhondda NHS Trust from 07. *The Rectory, Llanharry, Pontyclun CF72 9LH* Tel (01443) 223140 E-mail way-follower@hotmail.com

PITT, Mrs Beatrice Anne. b 50. I M Marsh Coll of Physical Educn Liv CertEd71 Open Univ BA01. Trin Coll Bris 80. d 82

p 97. C Rhyl w St Ann *St As* 82-86; CMS 86-92; Jt Co-ord Dioc Bible Schs Bukavu Zaïre 88-92; NSM Penycae *St As* 92-98; Hon Rep for CMS *St As* and *Ban* 93-98; NSM Killesher *K, E & A* 98-01; P-in-c Killinagh w Kiltyclogher and Innismagrath 98-01; P-in-c Firbank, Howgill and Killington *Bradf* 04-05; rtd 05. *20 Thornsbank, Sedbergh LA10 5LF* Tel (01539) 622095
E-mail anne@pitt.euro1net.com

PITT, George. b 52. QUB BD79 MTh88. CITC 81. **d** 81 **p** 82. C Belfast St Mary *Conn* 81-86; CMS 86-92; Zaïre 88-92; V Penycae *St As* 92-98; I Killesher *K, E & A* 98-01; Educn Adv Ch of Ireland Bps' Appeal 01-03; Perm to Offic *Bradf* 04-06; Chapl HM Pris Moorland from 06. *HM Prison Moorland, Bawtry Road, Hatfield Woodhouse, Doncaster DN7 6BW* Tel (01302) 523000

PITT, Karen Lesley Finella. *See* TIMMIS, Mrs Karen Lesley Finella

PITT, Robert Edgar. b 37. Chich Th Coll 70. **d** 73 **p** 74. C Knowle *Bris* 73-77; C Wells St Cuth w Coxley and Wookey Hole *B & W* 77-81; TV Wellington and Distr 81-94; V Burnham 94-02; Chapl Taunton and Somerset NHS Trust 94-02; rtd 02; Perm to Offic *Sarum* from 03. *Redmaye, 119 High Street, Burbage, Marlborough SN8 3AA* Tel (01672) 810651

PITT, Canon Trevor. b 45. Hull Univ BA66 MA69 Open Univ DipEd91. Linc Th Coll 68 Union Th Sem (NY) STM70. **d** 70 **p** 71. C Sheff St Geo 70-74; TV Gleadless Valley 74-78; TR 78-79; P-in-c Elham *Cant* 79-82; V Elham w Denton and Wootton 82-91; Vice Prin Cant Sch of Min 81-91; Six Preacher Cant Cathl 85-91; Prin NEOC *Newc* from 91; Can Newc Cathl from 91; Perm to Offic *Ripon* and *York* from 91. *Greenview House, Hamsterley, Bishop Auckland DL13 3QF,* or *NEOC, Ushaw College, Durham DH7 9RH* Tel and fax (01388) 488898 *or* tel 0191-373 7600 Fax 0191-373 7601
E-mail trevorpitt@aol.com *or* tpitt@neoc.org.uk

PITT, Mrs Valerie. b 55. Liv Univ BA77. STETS 02. **d** 05 **p** 06. NSM Oxshott *Guildf* from 05. *166 Manor Green Road, Epsom KT19 8LL* Tel (01372) 721776
E-mail curate@standrewsoxshott.org.uk

PITTAM, Matthew Richard. b 78. Cov Univ BA01 DipSW01. St Jo Coll Nottm 07. **d** 09. C Leamington Priors All SS *Cov* from 09; C Leamington Spa H Trin and Old Milverton from 09. *3 Sheepcote Close, Leamington Spa CV32 5YD* Tel (01926) 421223 E-mail matthewpittam@yahoo.co.uk

PITTARD, Roger. **d** 05 **p** 06. OLM Bridport *Sarum* from 05. *Rogaels, 32 Maple Gardens, Bothenhampton, Bridport DT6 4DR* Tel (01308) 456481

PITTARIDES, Renos. b 62. Surrey Univ BA85. **d** 07 **p** 08. OLM Cobham and Stoke D'Abernon *Guildf* from 07. *46 Freelands Road, Cobham KT11 2ND* Tel and fax (01932) 887996
E-mail renosp@gmail.com

PITTIS, Canon Stephen Charles. b 52. Sheff Univ MA01. Oak Hill Th Coll. **d** 76 **p** 77. C Win Ch Ch 76-79; Chapl Dorset Inst of HE and Bournemouth and Poole Coll of FE *Sarum* 79-84; V Woking St Paul *Guildf* 84-97; Dir of Faith Development *Win* 97-09; Dioc Missr and Can Res Win Cathl from 09. *60 Upper Brook Street, Winchester SO23 8DG* Tel (01962) 854133

PITTS, Canon Evadne Ione (Eve). b 50. Qu Coll Birm. **d** 89 **p** 94. C Bartley Green *Birm* 89-93; TD Kings Norton 93-94; TV 94-98; P-in-c Highters Heath 98-00; V from 00; Hon Can Birm Cathl from 05. *Immanuel Vicarage, Pickenham Road, Birmingham B14 4TG* Tel 0121-430 7578

PITTS, The Very Revd Michael James. b 44. Worc Coll Ox BA67. Qu Coll Birm 67. **d** 69 **p** 70. C-in-c Pennywell St Thos and Grindon St Oswald CD *Dur* 69-72; C Darlington H Trin 72-74; Chapl Dunkerque w Lille Arras etc Miss to Seamen 74-79; V Tudhoe *Dur* 79-81; Chapl Helsinki w Moscow *Eur* 81-85; Chapl Stockholm 85-88; Hon Can Brussels Cathl 87-88; Hon Chapl Miss to Seafarers Canada from 88; Dean and R Ch Ch Cathl Montreal 91-09; rtd 09. *3279 Gapiepy, Sainte Julienne QC J0K 2T0, Canada* Tel (001) (450) 834 2956
E-mail michael.pitts@worc.oxon.org

PITYANA, Prof Nyameko Barney. b 45. K Coll Lon BD81 Cape Town Univ PhD95 Trin Coll Hartford (USA) Hon DD96. Ripon Coll Cuddesdon 82. **d** 82 **p** 83. C Woughton *Ox* 82-85; V Highters Heath *Birm* 85-88; Dir Progr to Combat Racism WCC 88-92; Hon C Geneva *Eur* 88-92; S Africa from 93; Sen Lect RS Cape Town Univ 93-95; Chair Human Rights Commission 95-01; Prin and Vice Chan UNISA from 01. *PO Box 69334, Bryanston, 2021 South Africa* Tel and fax (0027) (12) 341 5583 Mobile 83-379 1329 E-mail pityanb@mweb.co.za

PIX, Mrs Sarah Anne Louise. b 71. Southn Univ BSc92 Birkbeck Coll Lon MSc97. Ridley Hall Cam 02. **d** 06 **p** 07. C W Slough *Ox* 06-08; C Britwell from 08. *8 Lovegrove Drive, Slough SL2 2LS* Tel (01753) 521820 E-mail revsarahpix@yahoo.co.uk

PIX, Stephen James. b 42. Ex Coll Ox BA64 MA68 Univ of Wales (Cardiff) LLM97. Clifton Th Coll 66. **d** 68 **p** 69. C St Helens St Helen *Liv* 68-71; Lic to Offic *S'wark* 71-76; Hon C Wallington 76-84; V Osmotherley w E Harlsey and Ingleby Arncliffe *York* 84-89; V Ox St Mich w St Martin and All SS 89-01; rtd 01; Perm

to Offic *St E* 01-07 and *Ox* from 07. *10 Cadogan Park, Woodstock OX20 1UW* Tel (01993) 812473

PIZZEY, Canon Lawrence Roger. b 42. Dur Univ BA64. Westcott Ho Cam 65. **d** 67 **p** 68. C Bramford *St E* 67-71; Tutor Woodbridge Abbey 71-77; Asst Chapl Woodbridge Sch 71-77; P-in-c Flempton w Hengrave and Lackford *St E* 77-85; P-in-c Culford, W Stow and Wordwell 77-85; P-in-c Acton w Gt Waldingfield 85-89; V 89-95; P-in-c Sudbury and Chilton 95-98; R 98-07; RD Sudbury 96-06; Hon Can St E Cathl 00-07; rtd 07; Perm to Offic *St E* from 07. *9 Constable Road, Bury St Edmunds IP33 3UQ* Tel (01284) 762863 E-mail lrp.sudbury@virgin.net

PLACE, Rodger Goodson. b 37. St Chad's Coll Dur BA60. **d** 62 **p** 63. C Pontesbury I and II *Heref* 62-65; C Heref St Martin 65-68; V Ditton Priors 68-75; R Neenton 68-75; P-in-c Aston Botterell w Wheathill and Loughton 68-75; P-in-c Burwarton w N Cleobury 69-75; P-in-c Dacre w Hartwith *Ripon* 75-76; V 76-82; V Wyther 82-92; P-in-c Roundhay St Jo 92-97; V 97-00; rtd 00; Perm to Offic *York* from 00. *72 Field Lane, Thorpe Willoughby, Selby YO8 9FL* Tel (01757) 703174

PLACE, Thomas Richard. b 59. Ridley Hall Cam 93. **d** 93 **p** 94. C Huyton St Geo *Liv* 93-97; CF 97-07; Sen CF from 07. *clo MOD Chaplains (Army)* Tel (01980) 615804 Fax 615800

PLAISTER, Keith Robin. b 43. K Coll Lon BD65 AKC65. **d** 66 **p** 67. C Laindon w Basildon *Chelmsf* 66-71; V Gt Wakering 71-78; V Gt Wakering w Foulness 78-90; C Witham 91-94; TV 94-99; P-in-c Sandon and E Hanningfield 99-08; rtd 08. *118 Maldon Road, Great Baddow, Chelmsford CM2 7DH* Tel (01245) 473135 E-mail keithplaister@hotmail.com

PLANT, Caroline Mary. b 56. Ripon Coll Cuddesdon 01. **d** 03 **p** 04. C Gnosall *Lich* 03-06; C Gnosall and Moreton 06-07; TV Penkridge from 07. *The Vicarage, Top Road, Acton Trussell, Stafford ST17 0RQ* Tel (01785) 711154
E-mail carolineplant@yahoo.co.uk

PLANT, Mrs Edith Winifred Irene (Ewith). b 31. Liv Univ BEd71. Cranmer Hall Dur 81. **dss** 83 **d** 87. Countesthorpe w Foston *Leic* 83-86; Loughborough All SS and H Trin 86-90; Par Dn 87-90; Par Dn Thurnby Lodge 90-91; rtd 91; Perm to Offic *Leic* 91-96 and *Ab* from 97. *clo Mrs J Wallis, Upper Braikley Cottage, Methlick, Ellon AB41 7HD* Tel (01651) 806209

PLANT, Miss Elizabeth Bowers. b 48. Westf Coll Lon BA70 Man Univ PGCE71. **d** 08 **p** 09. OLM Deane *Man* from 08. *25 Kintyre Drive, Bolton BL3 4PE* Tel (01204) 63730
E-mail eplant@supanet.com

PLANT, Mrs Glenys. b 49. ALA71. EMMTC 95. **d** 98 **p** 99. C Allestree *Derby* 98-01; rtd 01; Perm to Offic *Derby* from 01. *3 Stoodley Pike Gardens, Allestree, Derby DE22 2TN* Tel (01332) 552697

PLANT, John Frederick. b 61. Man Univ BA82 MEd95. Qu Coll Birm 83. **d** 85 **p** 86. C Kersal Moor *Man* 85-88; Chapl Aston Univ 88-94; TR Market Bosworth, Cadeby w Sutton Cheney etc *Leic* 94-00; P-in-c The Sheepy Gp 98-00; TR Bosworth and Sheepy Gp from 00; P-in-c Nailstone and Carlton w Shackerstone from 04. *The Rectory, Park Street, Market Bosworth, Nuneaton CV13 0LL* Tel (01455) 290239
E-mail jplant@leicester.anglican.org

PLANT, Michael Ian. b 47. Man Univ MEd85 GNSM68. St Jo Coll Nottm 97. **d** 99 **p** 00. NSM St D Cathl 99-01; NSM Dewisland from 01. *Lower Treginnis, St Davids, Haverfordwest SA62 6RS* Tel (01437) 720840 Fax 721350

PLANT, Michelle. NEOC. **d** 08. NSM Burley *Ripon* from 08. *20 Lakeland Crescent, Leeds LS17 7PR* Tel 0113-261 4757

PLANT, Nicholas. *See* PLANT, Richard George Nicholas

PLANT, Nicholas. b 58. MAAT87. SAOMC 95. **d** 98 **p** 99. OLM W Slough *Ox* 98-04; OLM Burnham w Dropmore, Hitcham and Taplow 04-08; OLM Taplow and Dropmore 08-09; NSM The Cookhams from 09. *The Pines, 6A Green Lane, Burnham, Slough SL1 8DR* Tel (01628) 604532 Mobile 07802-363835 Pager 07625-349908 E-mail fr.nick@ymail.com

PLANT, Richard. b 41. Open Univ BSc93. Qu Coll Birm 88. **d** 90 **p** 91. C Skelmersdale St Paul *Liv* 90-93; R Golborne 93-00; R Hesketh w Becconsall *Blackb* 00-07; rtd 07; Perm to Offic *Blackb* from 07. *12 Grangeville Avenue, Hesketh Bank, Preston PR4 6AH* Tel (01772) 815257 E-mail richard.plant1@btinternet.com

PLANT, Richard George Nicholas. b 45. Man Univ BA67. Coll of Resurr Mirfield 68. **d** 71 **p** 72. C Cleckheaton St Jo *Wakef* 71-74; P-in-c Adel *Ripon* 74-78; V Ireland Wood 78-82; V Armley w New Wortley 82-92; R Garforth 92-08; rtd 08; Perm to Offic *York* from 08. *3 Holman Avenue, Garforth, Leeds LS25 1HU* Tel 0113-287 6064 E-mail nick.plant@tiscali.co.uk

PLANT, Robert David. b 28. Birm Univ BSc49 Ch Ch Coll Cant MA98. St Deiniol's Hawarden 74. **d** 76 **p** 80. NSM Llandrillo-yn-Rhos *St As* 76-79; NSM St Nicholas at Wade w Sarre and Chislet w Hoath *Cant* from 79. *4 Sandalwood Drive, St Nicholas-at-Wade, Birchington CT7 0PE* Tel (01843) 847276

PLATT, Andrew Martin Robert. b 41. Oak Hill Th Coll 74. **d** 76 **p** 77. C St Alb St Paul *St Alb* 76-79; V Gazeley w Dalham and Moulton *St E* 79-85; V Gazeley w Dalham, Moulton and Kentford 85-86; RD Mildenhall 84-86; P-in-c Saxmundham 86-89; R 89-97; P-in-c Sudbury w Ballingdon and Brundon

97-98; V 98-04; rtd 04; Co Ecum Officer *Nor* 04-09; Perm to Offic *Nor* and *St E* from 04. *21 Homefield Paddock, Beccles NR34 9NE* Tel (01502) 717744

PLATT, Anthea Kate Helen. b 71. d 08 p 09. NSM Thorley *St Alb* from 08. *St Barnabas Centre, Church Lane, Thorley, Bishop's Stortford CM23 4BE* Tel (01279) 506753
E-mail antheaplatt@hotmail.com

PLATT, David. *See* PLATT, William David

PLATT, Mrs Jane Marie. b 54. Westhill Coll Birm CertEd76 Open Univ BA90. Qu Coll Birm 05. d 08 p 09. NSM Quinton Road W St Boniface *Birm* from 08. *39 Richmond Road, Rubery, Rednal, Birmingham B45 9UN* Tel 0121-453 3035
E-mail janeplatt@onetel.com

PLATT, John Dendy. b 24. Magd Coll Cam BA49 MA55. Wells Th Coll 50. d 52 p 53. C Headley All SS *Guildf* 52-56; C Haslemere 56-58; R Skelton w Hutton-in-the-Forest *Carl* 59-71; rtd 89. *17 Primula Drive, Norwich NR4 7LZ* Tel (01603) 504272

PLATT, John Emerson. b 36. Pemb Coll Ox BA59 MA65 DPhil77 Hull Univ MTh72. Cuddesdon Coll 59. d 61 p 62. C Adlington *Blackb* 61-64; C Sutton St Mich *York* 64-68; C Ox St Giles 68-71; Asst Chapl Pemb Coll Ox 68-69; Chapl 69-02; rtd 02. *Apple Tree Cottage, 2 Church Road, Wilmcote, Stratford-upon-Avon CV37 9XD* Tel (01789) 770127

PLATT, Mrs Katherine Mary. b 29. ARIBA51 Sheff Univ BA51. Westcott Ho Cam 76. dss 79 d 87. Chesterton Gd Shep *Ely* 78-84; Whitton St Aug *Lon* 84-86; Dean of Women's Min 86-94; Hampton St Mary 86-94; Par Dn 87-94; rtd 94; Perm to Offic *Ches* from 94. *56 Mereheath Park, Knutsford WA16 6AU* Tel (01656) 651192

PLATT, Michael Robert. b 39. SS Coll Cam BA61 MA85 Nottm Univ PGCE62. Cuddesdon Coll 62. d 64. C Far Headingley St Chad *Ripon* 64-65; Asst Master Belmont Coll Barnstaple 65-68; Asst Master Qu Coll Taunton 68-00; Ho Master 72-83; Hd Geography 89-00; rtd 00. *8 Court Hill, Taunton TA1 4SX* Tel and fax (01823) 270687

PLATT, William David. b 31. St Chad's Coll Dur BA54. Coll of Resurr Mirfield 54. d 56 p 57. C Bethnal Green St Jo w St Simon *Lon* 56-60; C Pinner 60-65; V N Hammersmith St Kath 65-72; V Woodham *Guildf* 72-88; Chapl Community of St Mary V Wantage 88-96; rtd 96; NSM Blewbury, Hagbourne and Upton *Ox* 96-03. *14 Radley House, Marston Ferry Road, Oxford OX2 7EA* Tel (01865) 556019

PLATTEN, Aidan Stephen George. b 76. Ripon Coll Cuddesdon BTh03. d 03 p 04. C Woodbridge St Mary *St E* 03-06; Bp's Chapl *Glouc* from 06. *4A Millers Green, Gloucester GL1 2BN* Tel (01452) 525242 *or* 410022 ext 268
E-mail aplatten@glosdioc.org.uk

PLATTEN, Gregory Austin David. b 78. Worc Coll Ox BA00 Ox Univ MTh05. Ripon Coll Cuddesdon 01. d 03 p 04. C St John's Wood *Lon* 03-07; Chapl Linc Coll Ox from 07; Hon C Ox St Mich w St Martin and All SS from 07. *14 Newton Road, Oxford OX1 4PT* E-mail gregoryplatten@ukonline.co.uk

✠**PLATTEN, The Rt Revd Stephen George.** b 47. Lon Univ BEd72 Trin Coll Ox BD03 UEA Hon DLitt03. Cuddesdon Coll 72. d 75 p 76 c 03. C Headington *Ox* 75-78; Chapl and Tutor Linc Th Coll 78-83; Can Res Portms Cathl and Dir of Ords 83-89; Abp's Sec for Ecum Affairs *Cant* 90-95; Hon Can Cant Cathl 90-95; Dean *Nor* 95-03; Bp Wakef from 03; Hon Can Musoma from 08. *Bishop's Lodge, Woodthorpe Lane, Wakefield WF2 6JL* Tel (01924) 255349 Fax 250202
E-mail bishop@bishopofwakefield.org.uk

PLATTIN, Miss Darleen Joy. b 63. Oak Hill Th Coll BA94. ERMC 04. d 07 p 08. C Barnham Broom and Upper Yare *Nor* from 07. *The Vicarage, Honingham Road, Barnham Broom, Norwich NR9 4DB* Tel (01603) 757744

PLATTS, Anthony Russell. b 41. Qu Coll Birm. d 08 p 09. NSM Hill *Birm* from 08. *Tree Tops, 200 Hill Village Road, Sutton Coldfield B75 5JN* Tel 0121-308 4478

PLATTS, Mrs Hilary Anne Norrie. b 60. K Coll Lon BD85 AKC85 SRN81. Ripon Coll Cuddesdon 86. d 88 p 94. C Moulsham St Jo *Chelmsf* 88-90; Chapl Reading Univ 90-99; C Calcot 90-92; NSM Reading Deanery 99-00; Perm to Offic *Birm* 00-07; Chapl Birm Specialist Community Health NHS Trust 01-07; Chapl N Warks NHS Trust 03-07; Perm to Offic *Chelmsf* from 07; Adv for Women's Min (Colchester Area) from 08; Chapl Colchester Hosp Univ NHS Foundn Trust from 09. *The Vicarage, Church Road, Elmstead, Colchester CO7 7AW* Tel (01206) 822431 E-mail hilaryplatts@googlemail.com

PLATTS, Timothy Caradoc. b 61. LMH Ox BA83 MA88 St Cross Coll Ox DPhil88. Ripon Coll Cuddesdon 87. d 89 p 90. C Whitley Ch Ch *Ox* 89-95; P-in-c Earley St Nic 95-98; V 98-00; V Four Oaks *Birm* 00-07; P-in-c Elmstead *Chelmsf* from 07; Chapl to Bp Colchester from 07. *The Vicarage, Church Road, Elmstead, Colchester CO7 7AW* Tel (01206) 822431
E-mail timatthevicarage@tiscali.co.uk

PLAXTON, Canon Edmund John Swithun. b 36. AKC60. d 61 p 62. C Crofton Park St Hilda w St Cypr *S'wark* 61-65; C Coulsdon St Jo 65-69; V Forest Hill St Paul 69-80; V Belmont

80-93; V Lingfield and Crowhurst 93-01; Hon Can S'wark Cathl 97-01; rtd 01. *Tynymaes, Y Fron, Upper Llandwrog, Caernarfon LL54 7BW* Tel (01286) 880188
E-mail edmundrachel@aol.com

PLAYER, Leslie Mark. b 65. Ridley Hall Cam 92. d 95 p 96. C Belper *Derby* 95-98; C Hamworthy *Sarum* 98-03; R W Downland from 03. *The Rectory, 97 Mill End, Damerham, Fordingbridge SP6 3HU* Tel (01725) 518642

PLAYLE, Ms Merrin Laura. b 58. Univ of Wales (Swansea) BSc79. Ridley Hall Cam 99. d 01 p 02. C Haslemere and Grayswood *Guildf* 01-05; V E Ham St Paul *Chelmsf* from 05. *St Paul's Vicarage, 227 Burges Road, London E6 2EU* Tel (020) 8472 5531 E-mail merrin.playle@btopenworld.com

PLEDGER, Miss Alison Frances. b 56. Univ of Wales (Cardiff) BA79 K Alfred's Coll Win PGCE80. Linc Th Coll 89. d 91 p 94. Par Dn Soham *Ely* 91-94; C Ely 94-96; C Rusthall *Roch* 97-00; V Alkborough *Linc* from 00; P-in-c Flixborough w Burton upon Stather from 09. *The Vicarage, Back Street, Alkborough, Scunthorpe DN15 9JJ* Tel (01724) 721126

PLEDGER, Mrs Nicola. b 55. Lon Bible Coll BA94. SAOMC 99. d 01 p 02. C Ware Ch Ch *St Alb* 01-05; Perm to Offic from 05. *132 Quickley Lane, Chorleywood, Rickmansworth WD3 5PQ* Tel (01923) 283220 *or* 447111 E-mail nicky@thepledgers.co.uk

PLESSIS, John Kenneth. b 69. Univ of Wales (Cardiff) BSc91 BA05 Univ of Wales (Swansea) PhD03 PGCE92. St Mich Coll Llan 03. d 05 p 06. C Haverfordwest St Mary and St Thos w Haroldston *St D* 05-08; C Abergavenny St Mary w Llanwenarth Citra *Mon* from 08. *4 Holywell Close, Abergavenny NP7 5LN* Tel (01873) 850128 Mobile 07868-750228

PLIMLEY, Canon William. b 17. St Aid Birkenhead 50. d 52 p 53. C Norbury *Ches* 52-55; V Laisterdyke *Bradf* 55-83; RD Calverley 65-78; Hon Can Bradf Cathl 67-83; rtd 83; Perm to Offic *Bradf* from 83. *465 Bradford Road, Pudsey LS28 8ED* Tel (01274) 664862

PLIMMER, Wayne Robert. b 64. St Chad's Coll Dur BA85 Leeds Univ MA07. St Steph Ho Ox 86. d 88 p 89. C Cockerton *Dur* 88-91; C Poulton-le-Fylde *Blackb* 91-93; V Darton *Wakef* 93-06; P-in-c Cawthorne 04-06; V Beeston *S'well* from 06. *The Vicarage, Middle Street, Beeston, Nottingham NG9 1GA* Tel 0115-925 4571 E-mail wplimmer@tiscali.co.uk

PLOWMAN, Richard Robert Bindon. b 38. Solicitor 61. Ridley Hall Cam 76. d 78 p 79. C Combe Down w Monkton Combe *B & W* 78-81; C Combe Down w Monkton Combe and S Stoke 81-83; V Coxley w Godney, Henton and Wookey 83-03; RD Shepton Mallet 95-01; rtd 03; Perm to Offic *B & W* from 04. *Hyland House, Lower Rudge, Frome BA11 2QE* Tel (01373) 831316

PLOWS, Jonathan. b 57. Warwick Univ BA79 Homerton Coll Cam PGCE80 Birkbeck Coll Lon MSc85. STETS BA07. d 07 p 08. NSM Salisbury St Thos and St Edm *Sarum* from 07. *171 Castle Road, Salisbury SP1 3RX* Tel (01722) 331647 Fax 410941 E-mail jonplows@aol.com

PLUCK, Richard. b 60. Southn Univ BTh90. Aston Tr Scheme 84 Sarum & Wells Th Coll 86. d 90 p 91. C Harpenden St Nic *St Alb* 90-94; CF from 94. *c/o MOD Chaplains (Army)* Tel (01980) 615804 Fax 615800

PLUMB, Gordon Alan. b 42. Leeds Univ BA. Sarum & Wells Th Coll. d 82 p 83. C Biggleswade *St Alb* 82-86; TV Grantham *Linc* 86-95; P-in-c Saxby All Saints 95-97; R 97-07; P-in-c Bonby 95-97; V 97-07; P-in-c Horkstow 95-97; V 97-07; P-in-c S Ferriby 95-97; R 97-07; P-in-c Worlaby 95-97; V 97-07; rtd 07. *Ingham House, High Street, Barton-upon-Humber DN18 5BT* Tel (01652) 636445 E-mail gplumb2000@aol.com

PLUMB, Miss Valerie Isabelle Dawn Frances. b 69. Ripon Coll Cuddesdon BTh02. d 01 p 02. C Newport St Andr *Mon* 01-03; C Monmouth w Overmonnow etc 03-06; TV By Brook *Bris* from 06; TV Colerne w N Wraxall from 06. *The Rectory, Market Place, Colerne, Chippenham SN14 8DF* Tel and fax (01225) 742742 E-mail revd_val@yahoo.co.uk

PLUMLEY, Paul Jonathan. b 42. St Jo Coll Nottm 71. d 74 p 75. C Mile Cross *Nor* 74-77; P-in-c Wickham Skeith *St E* 77-79; P-in-c Stoke Ash, Thwaite and Wetheringsett 77-79; Assoc Min Woodbridge St Jo 80-81; Chapl RAF 81-86; Perm to Offic *Roch* 86-95; R Hever, Four Elms and Mark Beech 95-00; Sen Chapl Maidstone and Tunbridge Wells NHS Trust 00-07; rtd 07; Perm to Offic *Roch* from 04. *4 Cedar Ridge, Tunbridge Wells TN2 3NX* Tel (01892) 514499 Mobile 07925-615601
E-mail paul.plumley@tiscali.co.uk

PLUMMER, Miss Anne Frances. b 36. Bedf Coll Lon BA57. S'wark Ord Course 79. dss 82 d 87 p 94. NSM Salfords *S'wark* 82-06; Dean MSE (Croydon) 97-02; Perm to Offic 06-07. *50 Park View Road, Salfords, Redhill RH1 5DN* Tel (01293) 785852

PLUMMER, Mrs Deborah Ann. b 49. St Hugh's Coll Ox BA71 MA75. St Alb Minl Tr Scheme 82. dss 85 d 87 p 94. Ickenham *Lon* 85-88; Par Dn 87-88; C Northolt St Mary 88-92; Chapl Lee Abbey 92-95; P-in-c Kintbury w Avington *Ox* 95-01; Lect Bolton St Pet *Man* 01-07; P-in-c Prestwich St Marg from 07; AD Radcliffe and Prestwich from 09. *St Margaret's Vicarage, 2*

St Margaret's Road, Prestwich, Manchester M25 2QB   Tel 0161-773 2698   Mobile 07939-916315
E-mail prestwichplummers@btinternet.com

PLUMMER, Miss June Alice. b 29. Bris Univ BA50 CertEd51. Sarum & Wells Th Coll 89. **d** 89 **p** 94. NSM Hanham Bris 89-97; rtd 97; Perm to Offic Bris from 97. 11 Glenwood Drive, Oldland Common, Bristol BS30 9RZ   Tel 0117-949 8667

PLUMPTON, Paul. b 50. Keble Coll Ox BA72 MA76. St Steph Ho Ox 72. **d** 74 **p** 75. C Tonge Moor Man 74-76; C Atherton 76-79; V Oldham St Jas 79-99; V Oldham St Jas w St Ambrose from 99. The Vicarage, Yates Street, Oldham OL1 4AR   Tel 0161-633 4441

PLUNKETT, Michael Edward. b 38. MBE04. Leeds Univ BSc61. Ely Th Coll 61. **d** 63 **p** 64. C Kirkby Liv 63-68; Lect Stockton-on-Tees 68-72; Lic to Offic Dur 72-73; TV Stockton 73-75; V Cantril Farm Liv 75-81; Soc Resp Officer 81-89; V Melling 81-91; TR Speke St Aid 91-04; rtd 04; Perm to Offic Heref from 04. 1 The Ridge, Bishops Castle SY9 5AB   Tel (01588) 630018

PLUNKETT, Canon Peter William. b 30. Oak Hill Th Coll. **d** 61 **p** 62. C Fazakerley Em Liv 61-64; C St Helens St Mark 64-68; V Kirkdale St Paul N Shore 68-79; P-in-c Bootle St Mary w St Jo 77-79; V Bootle St Mary w St Paul 79-81; V Goose Green 81-89; V W Derby St Jas 89-98; Hon Can Liv Cathl 97-98; rtd 98. 50 Trinity Crescent, West Shore, Llandudno LL30 2PQ   Tel (01492) 872109

PLYMING, Philip James John. b 74. Rob Coll Cam BA96 St Jo Coll Dur BA00 Edin Univ PhD08. Cranmer Hall Dur 98. **d** 01 **p** 02. C Chineham Win 01-06; V Claygate Guildf from 06. The Vicarage, Church Road, Claygate, Esher KT10 0JP   Tel (01372) 463603   E-mail philipplyming@holytrinityclaygate.org.uk

PLYMOUTH, Archdeacon of. See WILDS, The Ven Anthony Ronald

PLYMOUTH, Suffragan Bishop of. See FORD, The Rt Revd John Frank

PNEMATICATOS, Nicholas Peter Anthony. b 59. N Lon Univ BA92 Lon Univ MA93. Ripon Coll Cuddesdon 93. **d** 95 **p** 96. C Yeovil St Mich B & W 95-98; Chapl Yeovil Coll 95-96; Chapl RN 98-02; Chapl RAF 02-08; P-in-c Mill End and Heronsgate w W Hyde St Alb from 08. St Peter's Vicarage, Berry Lane, Mill End, Rickmansworth WD3 7HQ   Tel and fax (01923) 770369   Mobile 07703-566787   E-mail delvillewood@aol.com

POARCH, Canon John Chilton. b 30. Bris Univ BA54. Ridley Hall Cam 54. **d** 56 **p** 57. C Swindon Ch Ch Bris 56-59; C Corsham 59-61; R Praslin Seychelles 61-63; V Brislington St Cuth 63-69; Adn Seychelles and R St Paul's Cathl Mahé 69-72; V Warmley 72-86; R Syston 72-86; RD Bitton 79-85; P-in-c Bitton 80-86; Hon Can Bris Cathl 82-95; P-in-c Langley Fitzurse 86-94; Dioc Dir of Ords 86-94; Dir Ord Tr 94-95; P-in-c Draycot Cerne 87-94; rtd 95; Perm to Offic Bris from 95 and B & W 98-01; Officer for the Welfare of Rtd Mins Bris Adnry from 01; Dioc Convenor Rtd Clergy Assn from 01. 86 Stanshaws Close, Bradley Stoke, Bristol BS32 9AF   Tel (01454) 619053

POCOCK, Mrs Gillian Margaret. b 35. Nottm Univ BA57. Cranmer Hall Dur 82. **dss** 83 **d** 87 **p** 94. Bearpark Dur 83-88; Hon Par Dn 87-88; Par Dn S Hetton w Haswell 88; Asst RD Dur 89-90; Chapl St Aid Coll Dur 89-93; Par Dn Esh Dur 90-92; P-in-c 92-99; P-in-c Hamsteels 97-99; P-in-c Langley Park 98-99; rtd 99. 11 Cooke's Wood, Broom Park, Durham DH7 7RL   Tel 0191-386 1140   E-mail gillian.pocock@lineone.net

POCOCK, Lynn Elizabeth. b 48. Coll of Wooster Ohio BA69 CertEd71. Qu Coll Birm 73. **dss** 82 **d** 87 **p** 94. Gleadless Sheff 82-85; Thorpe Hesley 85-92; Par Dn 87-92; NSM Ribbesford w Bewdley and Dowles Worc 92-03; Perm to Offic from 03. 2 Waterworks Road, Worcester WR1 3EX   Tel (01905) 612634

POCOCK, Canon Nigel John. b 47. Lon Univ BSc68 Birm Univ MA83 Lambeth STh78. Oak Hill Th Coll 69. **d** 72 **p** 73. C Tunbridge Wells St Jas Roch 72-75; C Heatherlands St Jo Sarum 75-78; V Leic St Chris 78-83; R Camborne Truro 83-97; RD Carnmarth N 91-96; Hon Can Truro Cathl 92-97; V Old Windsor Ox 97-09; rtd 09. 23 Culm Valley Way, Uffculme, Cullompton EX15 3XZ   Tel (01884) 849198   E-mail njpoc@tiscali.co.uk

PODGER, Richard Philip Champeney. b 38. K Coll Cam BA61 MA66. Cuddesdon Coll 62. **d** 64 **p** 65. C Doncaster St Geo Sheff 64-68; C Orpington All SS Roch 68-74; W Germany 76-88; Chapl Kassel Eur 83-88; TV Whitstable Cant 88-94; Perm to Offic from 95; Chapl E Kent NHS and Soc Care Partnership Trust 02-06; Chapl Kent & Medway NHS and Soc Care Partnership Trust from 06. 3 Alcroft Grange, Tyler Hill, Canterbury CT2 9NN   Tel and fax (01227) 462038 or tel (01233) 616082   E-mail podger@centrespace.freeserve.co.uk

POGMORE, Canon Edward Clement. b 52. Sarum & Wells Th Coll 76. **d** 79 **p** 80. C Calne and Blackland Sarum 79-82; TV Oakdale 82-89; Min Creekmoor LEP 82-89; Chapl Geo Eliot Hosp Nuneaton 89-94; Chapl Nuneaton Hosps 89-94; Chapl Geo Eliot Hosp NHS Trust Nuneaton from 94; Chapl Co-ord for N Warks from 94; Perm to Offic Leic from 91; Hon Can Cov Cathl from 00. The Chaplaincy, George Eliot Hospital, College Street, Nuneaton CV10 7DJ   Tel (024) 7686 5046, 7686 5281 or 7635 1351 ext 3528   E-mail edpog@hotmail.com or edward.pogmore@geh-tr.wminds.nhs.uk

✠**POGO, The Most Revd Sir Ellison Leslie.** b 47. KBE01. St Jo Coll Auckland LTh. **d** 79 **p** 79 **c** 81. Asst P Anderson's Bay New Zealand 79-81; Solomon Is from 81; Bp Ysabel 81-94; Abp Melanesia and Bp Cen Melanesia 94-08; rtd 08. Address temp unknown   E-mail epogo@comphq.org.sb

POIL, Canon Ronald Wickens. b 30. AKC56. **d** 57 **p** 58. C Willesborough Cant 57-60; Chapl RAF 60-76; P-in-c Edith Weston w Normanton Pet 65-67; V Southbourne Chich 76-80; P-in-c W Thorney 76-80; RD Westbourne 78-91; V Southbourne w W Thorney 80-96; Can and Preb Chich Cathl 90-96; rtd 96; Perm to Offic Portsm from 97. 33 Mays Lane, Stubbington, Fareham PO14 2EW

POINTS, John David. b 43. Qu Coll Birm 78. **d** 80 **p** 81. C Wednesbury St Paul Wood Green Lich 80-85; V 93-01; V Sedgley St Mary 85-93; TR Wednesfield 01-08; AD Wolverhampton 03-08; rtd 08. 13 Oldcastle Avenue, Guilsfield, Welshpool SY21 9PA   Tel (01938) 552092

POLASHEK, Miss Stella Christine. b 44. Leic Poly MA85. EMMTC 92. **d** 95 **p** 96. NSM Appleby Gp Leic 95-08; NSM Woodfield Team from 08; Chapl Leic Gen Hosp NHS Trust 99-00; Chapl Univ Hosps Leic NHS Trust from 00. 38 Mawbys Lane, Appleby Magna, Swadlincote DE12 7AA   Tel (01530) 272707   E-mail polashek@applebymagna.freeserve.co.uk

POLE, David John. b 46. Bath Academy of Art BA72. Trin Coll Bris 84. **d** 86 **p** 87. C Bris St Mary Redcliffe w Temple etc 86-90; V Alveston 90-98; V Alveston and Littleton-on-Severn w Elberton from 98. The Vicarage, Gloucester Road, Alveston, Bristol BS35 3QT   Tel and fax (01454) 414810   E-mail david.pole@dial.pipex.com

POLE, Francis John Michael. b 42. FRSA64 MInstTA00 CQSW74 MCMI99. St Jo Sem Wonersh 62. **d** 67 **p** 68. In RC Ch 67-75; NSM Walthamstow St Pet Chelmsf 75; NSM Penge Lane H Trin Roch 76-77; NSM Shirley St Jo Cant 77-79; Assoc Chapl The Hague Eur 79-83; V Norbury St Steph and Thornton Heath Cant 83-84; S'wark 85-00; Sen Dioc Police Chapl 95-00; Sen Chapl Sussex Police 00-03; Nat Co-ord Chapl Pool 00-04; Sen Chapl Sussex Ambulance Service 04-06; Co-ord Chapl SE Coast Ambulance Service from 06; TV Crawley Chich from 00; Chapl to People at Work from 00. 35 Turnpike Place, Crawley RH11 7UA   Tel (01293) 513264   Mobile 07764-752608   E-mail francis.pole@virgin.net

POLHILL, Mrs Christine. b 46. Nottm Coll of Educn CertEd67 Qu Coll Birm BA00. St Alb Minl Tr Scheme 81. **dss** 84 **d** 87 **p** 94. St Alb St Mary Marshalswick St Alb 84-94; Hon Par Dn 87-94; C Cottered w Broadfield and Throcking 94-96; P-in-c 96-99; C Ardeley 94-96; P-in-c 96-99; C Weston 94-96; Perm to Offic Lich 99-10; C Lich St Mich w St Mary and Wall 00-06; rtd 06; Lic to Offic Lich from 06. Little Hayes, Beaudesert Park, Cannock Wood, Rugeley WS15 4JJ   Tel (01543) 674474

POLITT, Robert William. b 47. ARCM LGSM68. Oak Hill Th Coll 73. **d** 76 **p** 77. C Bexleyheath St Pet Roch 76-82; TV Southgate Chich 82-90; Chapl N Foreland Lodge Sch Basingstoke 90-98; R Sherfield-on-Loddon and Stratfield Saye etc Win from 98. The Rectory, 33 Northfield Road, Sherfield-on-Loddon, Hook RG27 0DR   Tel (01256) 882209   E mail 113225.103@compuserve.com

POLKINGHORNE, Canon John Charlton. b 30. KBE97. Trin Coll Cam BA52 PhD55 MA56 ScD74 FRS74. Westcott Ho Cam 79. **d** 81 **p** 82. NSM Chesterton St Andr Ely 81-82; C Bedminster St Mich Bris 82-84; V Blean Cant 84-86; Dean Trin Hall Cam 86-89; Pres Qu Coll Cam 89-96; Can Th Liv Cathl from 94; rtd 96; Six Preacher Cant Cathl from 96; Perm to Offic Ely from 96. 74 Hurst Park Avenue, Cambridge CB4 2AF   Tel (01223) 360743

POLL, Martin George. b 61. Kent Univ BA83. Ripon Coll Cuddesdon 84. **d** 87 **p** 88. C Mill Hill Jo Keble Ch Lon 87-90; Chapl RN from 90. Royal Naval Chaplaincy Service, Mail Point 1-2, Leach Building, Whale Island, Portsmouth PO2 8BY   Tel (023) 9262 5055 Fax 9262 5134

POLLAK, Canon Peter Henry. b 18. Worc Ord Coll 67. **d** 69 **p** 70. C Claines St Jo Worc 69-73; R Grimley w Holt 73-88; RD Martley and Worc W 84-88; Hon Can Worc Cathl 85-88; rtd 88; Perm to Offic Worc from 88. 2 Tweenways, Main Road, Kempsey, Worcester WR5 3JY   Tel (01905) 820351

POLLARD, Mrs Ann Beatrice. b 46. **d** 03 **p** 04. OLM Mirfield Wakef from 03. 9 Manor Drive, Mirfield WF14 0ER   Tel (01924) 495322   Mobile 07751-630609
E-mail annrich@pollard5910fsnet.co.uk

POLLARD, Mrs Christine Beryl. b 45. NOC 86. **d** 89 **p** 94. Par Dn Ingrow cum Hainworth Bradf 89-94; C Nuneaton St Nic Cov 94-98; P-in-c Bourton w Frankton and Stretton on Dunsmore etc 98-07; C Leam Valley 06-07; rtd 07. 9 Overberry Orchard, Leamington Spa CV33 9SJ   Tel (01926) 832053

POLLARD, Canon Clifford Francis. b 20. AKC49. **d** 50 **p** 51. C Leominster Heref 50-53; C Luton St Mary St Alb 53-56; V

Stopsley 56-60; Chapl Toc H (Kent and Sussex) 60-64; R Mersham *Cant* 64-68; Asst Dir of Educn 68-69; Dir of Educn 69-87; Hon Can Cant Cathl 72-91; rtd 87; Perm to Offic *Cant* from 03. *6 Lady Wootton's Green, Canterbury CT1 1NG* Tel (01227) 761674

POLLARD, David. b 55. LSE BSc77. Trin Coll Bris 78. **d** 80 **p** 81. Canada 81-84; C-in-c Hillsfield and Monkspath LEP *Birm* 85-89; BCMS 89-93; Crosslinks 93-95; Spain 89-94; V Doncaster St Jas *Sheff* 95-98; rtd 98. *6 Mulberry Way, Armthorpe, Doncaster DN3 3UE* Tel (01302) 833404

POLLARD, David John Athey. b 44. ACP74 Culham Coll Ox CertEd69. St Jo Coll Nottm LTh88. **d** 88 **p** 89. C Illogan *Truro* 88-91; R Roche and Withiel 91-95; TV Maidstone St Martin *Cant* 95-97; C Parkwood CD 95-97; R Lanreath *Truro* 97-99; V Pelynt 97-99; R Lanreath, Pelynt and Bradoc 99-03; rtd 03. *Melyn Brea, 11 Mill Hill, Lostwithiel PL22 0HB* Tel (01208) 871541 E-mail david.pollard@totalise.co.uk

POLLARD, Eric John. b 43. Chich Th Coll 83. **d** 85 **p** 86. C Brighton St Matthias *Chich* 85-90; C E Grinstead St Swithun 90-96; C Hove 96-00; P-in-c Brighton St Matthias from 00. *St Matthias's Vicarage, 45 Hollingbury Park Avenue, Brighton BN1 7JQ* Tel and fax (01273) 508178 E-mail eric.pollard@btinternet.com

POLLARD, John Edward Ralph. b 40. ALCD68. **d** 67 **p** 68. C Ollerton *S'well* 67-71; C Walton H Trin *Ox* 71-74; P-in-c Cuddington w Dinton 74-77; V Haddenham 74-77; V Kingsey 75-77; V Haddenham w Cuddington and Kingsey 77-85; RD Aylesbury 80-85; V Haddenham w Cuddington, Kingsey etc 85-87; V Furze Platt 87-96; rtd 97. *113 Thame Road, Haddenham, Aylesbury HP17 8EH* Tel (01844) 290582

POLLARD, Matthew Rupert. b 66. St Jo Coll Nottm. **d** 03 **p** 04. C Huddersfield St Pet *Wakef* 03-07; Asst Chapl Huddersfield Univ 03-07; P-in-c Rastrick St Matt 07-08; P-in-c Rastrick St Jo 07-08; V Rastrick from 08. *St Matthew's Vicarage, 1 Vicarage Gardens, Ogden Lane, Brighouse HD6 3HD* Tel (01484) 713386 E-mail matthewpollard@btinternet.com

POLLARD, Mrs Patricia Julie. b 46. Open Univ BA97. Cant Sch of Min 93. **d** 96 **p** 97. NSM Eastling w Ospringe and Stalisfield w Otterden *Cant* 96-04; rtd 04; Perm to Offic *Cant* from 04. *7 Arthur Salmon Close, Faversham ME13 7PS* Tel (01795) 535407 E-mail norman.pollard@tesco.net

POLLARD, Roger Frederick. b 32. Sheff Univ BSc52 K Coll Lon PGCE55 Lanc Univ MA78. Linc Th Coll 56. **d** 58 **p** 59. C Catford St Laur *S'wark* 58-63; Ghana 63-66; C Fulford *York* 66-67; C Camberwell St Geo *S'wark* 67; Asst Master Roch Valley Sch Milnrow 68-69; S Craven Sch Cross Hills 69-91; rtd 91; Perm to Offic *Bradf* 69-93 and *B & W* 93-06. *Little Garth, Rectory Lane, Dowlish Wake, Ilminster TA19 0NX* Tel (01460) 52594

POLLARD, Stephen. b 59. Coll of Resurr Mirfield 96. **d** 98 **p** 99. C Lt Lever *Man* 98-02; P-in-c Westleigh St Pet from 02; P-in-c Westleigh St Paul from 08. *St Peter's Vicarage, 6 Malham Close, Leigh WN7 4SD* Tel (01942) 673626

POLLARD (née RAMSBOTTOM), Mrs Susan Elizabeth. b 56. Trin Coll Bris BD79. Qu Coll Birm 06. **d** 09. NSM Warndon St Nic *Worc* from 09. *5 Falmouth, Worcester WR4 0TE* Tel (01905) 759214 E-mail suepollard2610@hotmail.com

POLLARD, Vaughan. b 59. Aston Tr Scheme 88 Trin Coll Bris 90. **d** 92 **p** 93. C Nailsea H Trin *B & W* 92-95; C Acomb St Steph *York* 95-97; P-in-c Moldgreen *Wakef* 97-99; P-in-c Rawthorpe 97-99; V Moldgreen and Rawthorpe 99-07; C Spalding St Paul *Linc* from 07; C Spalding from 07. *18 Maple Grove, Spalding PE11 2LE* Tel (01775) 725637 E-mail pollard247@ntlworld.com

POLLINGER (née WHITFORD), Mrs Judith. b 41. Ex Univ TCert78 BEd79 Plymouth Univ 95. SW Minl Tr Course 92. **d** 95 **p** 96. NSM St Endellion w Port Isaac and St Kew *Truro* from 95; NSM St Minver from 07; Convenor Bp's Gp for Min of Healing from 04. *4 Marshalls Way, Trelights, Port Isaac PL29 3TE* Tel (01208) 880181 E-mail rev.judith@btinternet.com

POLLINGTON, Miss Ann Elizabeth Jane. b 56. Univ Coll Chich BA00. Ripon Coll Cuddesdon 00. **d** 02 **p** 03. C Honiton, Gittisham, Combe Raleigh, Monkton etc *Ex* 02-07; P-in-c St Ippolyts *St Alb* from 07; P-in-c Gt and Lt Wymondley from 07. *The Vicarage, Stevenage Road, St Ippolyts, Hitchin SG4 7PE* Tel (01462) 457552 E-mail annpolly@freeuk.com

POLLIT, Preb Michael. b 30. Worc Coll Ox BA54 MA58. Wells Th Coll 54. **d** 56 **p** 57. C Cannock *Lich* 56-59; C Codsall 59-62; V W Bromwich St Pet 62-67; R Norton in the Moors 67-76; RD Leek 72-76; V Shrewsbury St Chad 76-87; V Shrewsbury St Chad w St Mary 87-95; Preb Lich Cathl 81-95; P-in-c Shrewsbury St Alkmund 91-95; rtd 95; Perm to Offic *Heref* from 96. *Pentreheyling House, Churchstoke, Montgomery SY15 6HU* Tel (01588) 620273

POLLIT, Ruth Mary. *See* LILLINGTON, Mrs Ruth Mary

POLLITT, Graham Anthony. b 48. BA79. Oak Hill Th Coll 76. **d** 79 **p** 80. C Rusholme H Trin *Man* 79-82; TV Southgate *Chich* 82-83; C Burgess Hill St Andr 83-86; Chapl St Martin's Coll of Educn *Blackb* 86-90; Chapl Cheltenham and Glouc Coll of HE

90-98; Perm to Offic *Glouc* 98-99; C Bispham *Blackb* 99-04; P-in-c Caton w Littledale from 04. *The Vicarage, 153 Brookhouse Road, Brookhouse, Lancaster LA2 9NX* Tel (01524) 770300

POLLOCK, Christopher John. b 62. TCD BTh89 QUB BD. CITC 86. **d** 89 **p** 90. C Agherton *Conn* 89-91; C Ballymoney w Finvoy and Rasharkin 91-93; I Derryvolgie 93-03; I Saintfield *D & D* from 03. *The Vicarage, 11 Lisburn Road, Saintfield, Ballynahinch BT24 7AL* Tel (028) 9751 0286 E-mail chriswenda@talk21.com

POLLOCK, Duncan James Morrison. b 54. MBE95 QGM75. Nottm Univ BCombStuds83. Linc Th Coll 80. **d** 83 **p** 84. C Folkestone St Mary and St Eanswythe *Cant* 83-85; CF 85-98; R Broughton, Bossington, Houghton and Mottisfont *Win* 98-00; I Groomsport *D & D* from 00. *22 Sandringham Drive, Bangor BT20 5NA* Tel (028) 9146 4476 E-mail duncanjmpollock@btinternet.com

POLLOCK, Hugh Gillespie. b 36. Oak Hill Th Coll 61. **d** 64 **p** 65. C Maidstone St Luke *Cant* 64-68; C Washfield *Ex* 68-71; C Washfield, Stoodleigh, Withleigh etc 71-73; Chapl Lee Abbey 73-76; V Dersingham *Nor* 76-80; P-in-c Anmer 79-80; P-in-c Shernbourne 79-80; R Dersingham w Anmer and Shernborne 80-89; RD Heacham and Rising 87-89; C Barnstaple *Ex* 89-94; P-in-c Atherington and High Bickington 94-96; P-in-c Burrington 94-96; TV Newton Tracey, Horwood, Alverdiscott etc 96-98; rtd 99; Perm to Offic *Ex* 99-01; C Diptford, N Huish, Harberton, Harbertonford etc 01-07. *74A Fair View, Barnstaple EX31 1JR*

POLLOCK, James Colin Graeme. b 53. St Chad's Coll Dur BA76. Ripon Coll Cuddesdon 77. **d** 78 **p** 79. C Hartlepool St Oswald *Dur* 78-81; C Hartlepool St Aid 81-84; V Dawdon 84-05; V Seaham Harbour 03-05; TV S Shields All SS from 05. *The Vicarage, St Oswin's Street, South Shields NE33 4SE* Tel 0191-455 3072

POLLOCK, John Charles. b 23. Trin Coll Cam BA46 MA48 Samford Univ (USA) Hon DLitt02. Ridley Hall Cam 49. **d** 51 **p** 52. C Portman Square St Paul *Lon* 51-53; Ed *The Churchman* 53-58; R Horsington *B & W* 53-58; Perm to Offic *Ex* 61-98 and from 00; rtd 88. *Rose Ash House, Rose Ash, South Molton EX36 4RB* Tel (01769) 550403

POLOMSKI, Elias Robert Michael. b 42. **d** 85 **p** 86. In RC Ch 85-90; C Headington Quarry *Ox* 91-94; Chapl St Alb Abbey 94-97; Chapl St Alb Sch 94-97; P-in-c Streatley w Moulsford *Ox* 97-03; C 03-04; P-in-c Streatley 04-07; rtd 07. *The Hermitage, 1 Bremilham Road, Malmesbury SN16 0DQ* Tel (01666) 825607

POMERY, David John. b 45. SS Mark & Jo Coll Chelsea CertEd67. Chich Th Coll 75. **d** 77 **p** 78. C Coseley Ch Ch *Lich* 77-79; C Stocksbridge *Sheff* 79-81; V Bentley 81-87; Asst Master Radlett Prep Sch 87-03; P-in-c Barton Bendish w Beachamwell and Shingham *Ely* 03-09; P-in-c Fincham 03-09; P-in-c Marham 03-09; P-in-c Shouldham 03-09; P-in-c Shouldham Thorpe 03-09; V Edstaston, Fauls, Prees, Tilstock and Whixall *Lich* from 09. *The Vicarage, Church Street, Prees, Whitchurch SY13 2EE* Tel (01948) 840243 E-mail rev-djpomery@supanet.com

POMFRET, Albert. b 23. Univ of Wales (Cardiff) BSc57 MTh95 Lon Univ MA69 FCP83 Potchefstroom Univ PhD02. Oak Hill NSM Course 72. **d** 75 **p** 76. NSM Dartford Ch Ch *Roch* 75-80; Perm to Offic 80-92; Perm to Offic *Ex* 92-08. *8 Wilshere Court, 43 Queen Street, Hitchin SG4 9TT* Tel (01462) 420821

POND, Geraldine Phyllis. b 53. SRN74 HVCert75. St Jo Coll Nottm MA97. **d** 97 **p** 98. C Ancaster Wilsford Gp *Linc* 97-01; P-in-c Harlaxton Gp 01-07; Chapl Linc Distr Healthcare NHS Trust 01-07; P-in-c Ashbourne w Mapleton *Derby* from 07; P-in-c Clifton from 09; P-in-c Norbury w Snelston from 09; Asst Dir of Ords 08-09; Dioc Dir of Ords from 09. *The Vicarage, 61 Belle Vue Road, Ashbourne DE6 1AT* Tel (01335) 343129 E-mail geraldine@geraldinepond.com

POND, Nigel Peter Hamilton. b 40. AKC65. **d** 66 **p** 67. C E Dereham w Hoe *Nor* 66-69; C Chapl RN 69-85; TR Woughton *Ox* 85-93; Chapl Milton Keynes Gen Hosp 85-93; RD Milton Keynes *Ox* 90-93; R Olney w Emberton 93-97; R Olney 97-03; rtd 03. *11 Gippingstone Road, Bramford, Ipswich IP8 4DR* Tel (01473) 741887 E-mail nigel@npond.freeserve.co.uk

PONSONBY, Simon Charles Reuben. b 66. Bris Univ MLitt96. Trin Coll Bris BA94. **d** 95 **p** 96. C Thorpe Edge *Bradf* 95-98; Pastorate Chapl Ox St Aldate from 98. *St Aldate's Parish Centre, 40 Pembroke Street, Oxford OX1 1BP* Tel (01865) 254800 Fax 201543 E-mail simon.ponsonby@staldates.org.uk

PONT, Gordon John Harper. b 35. Glas Univ BSc56 BD65. Edin Th Coll 56. **d** 59 **p** 60. C Dunfermline *St And* 59-62; C Motherwell *Glas* 62-65; R Largs 65-68; Dioc Supernumerary *Bre* 68-71; Chapl Dundee Univ 68-73; R Dundee St Luke 71-74; NSM Dundee St Paul and Hon Chapl St Paul's Cathl Dundee 74-99; Dioc Sec 90-02; rtd 02. *Dalhouzie, 11 West Moulin Road, Pitlochry PH16 5EA* Tel (01796) 472745 E-mail gordon.pont1@tesco.net

PONTEFRACT, Archdeacon of. *See* TOWNLEY, The Ven Peter Kenneth

PONTEFRACT, Suffragan Bishop of. *See* ROBINSON, The Rt Revd Anthony William

PONTER, John Arthur. b 37. Univ of Wales (Abth) BA61 Linacre Coll Ox BA63 MA68 UEA PhD81. Wycliffe Hall Ox 61. **d** 63 **p** 64. C Gidea Park *Chelmsf* 63-67; C-in-c Colchester St Anne CD 67-69; V Colchester St Anne 69-72; Chapl UEA *Nor* 72-78; Chapl Chelmsf Cathl 78-79; Chapl Chelmsf Cathl Cen 78-84; V Moulsham St Jo 79-85; Dir Man Chr Inst and Chr Leadership Course 85-92; Educn Officer N Federation for Tr in Min 85-92; TR Stantonbury and Willen *Ox* 92-02; rtd 02. *3 The Croft, 43A East Street, Wareham BH20 4NW* Tel (01929) 558286 E-mail ponter@msn.com

PONTIN, Colin Henry. b 37. Trin Coll Bris. **d** 83 **p** 84. C Downend *Bris* 83-86; C Riverside *Ox* 86-88; V Eton w Eton Wick and Boveney 88-90; TV Riverside 91-95; V Churt *Guildf* 95-02; rtd 02; Perm to Offic *Win* from 03. *22 Shearsbrook Close, Bransgore, Christchurch BH23 8HF* Tel (01425) 673918 Mobile 07989-173259 E-mail colinpontin@lineone.net

POOBALAN, Canon Isaac Munuswamy. b 62. RGN84 Edin Univ BD94 MTh97 Aber Univ MPhil98. Edin Th Coll 91. **d** 94 **p** 95. C Edin St Pet 94-97; P-in-c Aberdeen St Clem 97-01; R Aberdeen St Jo from 01; P-in-c Aberdeen St Pet from 04; Can St Andr Cathl from 06. *The Rectory, 15 Ashley Road, Aberdeen AB10 6RU* Tel (01224) 591527 E-mail aipoobalan@btinternet.com *or* rector@st-johns-aberdeen.org

POODHUN, Canon Lambert David. b 30. Natal Univ BA53. Edin Th Coll 54. **d** 56 **p** 57. C Durban St Aidan 56-60; P-in-c Pietermaritzburg St Paul 60-64; R 64-67; R Overport 67-76; Adn Durban 75-76; C Upton cum Chalvey *Ox* 77-80; Chapl Kingston Hosp Surrey 80-81; Chapl Tooting Bec Hosp Lon 81-84; Chapl Hurstwood Park Hosp Haywards Heath 84-01; Chapl St Fran Hosp Haywards Heath 84-94; Chapl Mid Sussex NHS Trust 94-01; Can and Preb Chich Cathl from 93; Hon C Haywards Heath St Rich from 01. *8 Nursery Close, Haywards Heath RH16 1HP* Tel (01444) 440938 E-mail lambertpoodhun@aol.com

POOLE, Andrew John. b 52. EMMTC 98. **d** 01 **p** 02. NSM Scraptoft *Leic* from 01. *64 Scalborough Close, Countesthorpe, Leicester LE8 5XH* Tel 0116-277 4949 E-mail andrew@aptrainingonline.co.uk

POOLE, Clifford George. b 36. Keble Coll Ox BA61 MA65 Lon Univ PGCE75. S'wark Ord Course 83. **d** 86 **p** 87. C W Dulwich All SS and Em *S'wark* 86-90; Chapl Luxembourg *Eur* 90-02; rtd 02; P-in-c Alderton, Gt Washbourne, Dumbleton etc *Glouc* 02-05; TV Winchcombe 05-08. *11 Berwyn Road, London SE24 9BD* Tel (020) 8674 3369 E-mail poole_clifford@yahoo.co.uk

POOLE, David. b 54. **d** 02 **p** 04. OLM Chase Terrace *Lich* from 02. *435 Littleworth Road, Cannock WS12 1HZ* Tel (01543) 422218 E-mail dave.poole54@sky.com

POOLE, Canon Denise June. b 49. Leic Univ BSc70 Bradf and Ilkley Coll DipAdEd85. NOC 90. **d** 93 **p** 94. C Horton and Bradf St Oswald Chapel Green 93-97; Chapl Co-ord Bradf Hosps NHS Trust 97-00; V Bradf St Aug Undercliffe 00-06; Dioc Dir of Ords 01-06; Bp's Dom Chapl from 06; Hon Can Bradf Cathl from 07. *23 Leylands Lane, Bradford BD9 5PX* Tel (01274) 401679 E-mail denise.poole@bradford.anglican.org

POOLE, Edward John. b 53. Hull Univ BA81 Heythrop Coll Lon MA04. St Steph Ho Ox 81. **d** 83 **p** 84. C Stevenage St Andr and St Geo *St Alb* 83-86; Tutor St Paul's Th Coll Madagascar 86-88; V Weston and P-in-c Ardeley *St Alb* 88-96; P-in-c Cottered w Broadfield and Throcking 94-96; Chapl Bucharest w Sofia *Eur* 96-98; Chapl HM Pris Lewes 98-03; Chapl HM Pris Featherstone 03-09; R York, Beverley-Brookton and Quairading Australia from 09. *St Mary's Rectory, 64 John Street, Beverley WA 6304, Australia* Tel (0061) (8) 9646 1112 Mobile 43-704 0950 E-mail jpoole4@bigpond.com

POOLE, Helen Margaret. b 39. SRN. SWMTC. **d** 94 **p** 95. NSM Ludgvan *Truro* 94-97; NSM Paul 97-02; NSM St Buryan, St Levan and Sennen 02-04; rtd 04. *Underhill Farmhouse, St Levan, Penzance TR19 6JS* Tel (01736) 810842 Fax 810858

POOLE, Ian Richard Morley. b 62. Birm Univ MB, ChB85 MRCGP90. St Jo Coll Nottm MTh02. **d** 02 **p** 03. C Willenhall H Trin *Lich* 02-06; TV Bushbury from 06. *131 Taunton Avenue, Wolverhampton WV10 6PN* Tel (01902) 788151 E-mail woodchipper@blueyonder.co.uk

POOLE, James Christopher. b 73. Peterho Cam BA94 MA98. Aston Tr Scheme 96 Wycliffe Hall Ox 97. **d** 00 **p** 01. C Wimbledon Park St Luke *S'wark* 00-04; Miss Partner Crosslinks 04-07; Kenya 05-07; C Cambridge H Sepulchre *Ely* from 07. *64 St Albans Road, Cambridge CB4 2HG* E-mail james@realfire.org

POOLE, Miss Joan Wendy. b 37. Sarum Dioc Teacher Tr Coll CertEd57 Trin Coll Bris 86. **d** 87 **p** 94. Par Dn Longfleet *Sarum* 87-89; Par Dn Hamworthy 89-94; C 94-97; rtd 97; Perm to Offic *Sarum* from 97. *35 Borley Road, Poole BH17 7DT* Tel (01202) 256377

POOLE, John. See POOLE, Edward John

POOLE, Martin Bryce. b 59. Reading Univ BSc80. St Jo Coll Nottm 81. **d** 87 **p** 88. NSM Tulse Hill H Trin and St Matthias

S'wark 87-99; NSM Hove *Chich* 00-01; Perm to Offic from 01. *14 Pembroke Avenue, Hove BN3 5DA* Tel and fax (01273) 747919 E-mail mb.poole@ntlworld.com

POOLE, Martin Ronald. b 59. Aston Univ BSc81 Leeds Univ BA86. Coll of Resurr Mirfield 84. **d** 87 **p** 88. C Sheff St Cath Richmond Road 87-90; C W Hampstead St Jas *Lon* 90-94; V Colindale St Matthias 94-06; V Munster Square Ch Ch and St Mary Magd from 06. *8 Laxton Place, London NW1 3PT* Tel (020) 7388 3095 Fax 08701-289048 E-mail martin@mpoole57.freeserve.co.uk

POOLE, Peter William. b 35. St Pet Hall Ox BA59 MA63. Wells Th Coll 59. **d** 61 **p** 62. C Cheriton Street *Cant* 61-64; C Birchington w Acol 64-67; V Newington 67-73; P-in-c Lower Halstow 72-73; V Bearsted 73-76; V Lane End w Cadmore End *Ox* 84-89; R Chalfont St Giles 89-99; rtd 99; Perm to Offic *Guildf* from 01. *Primrose Cottage, St Nicholas Avenue, Cranleigh GU6 7AQ* Tel (01483) 272703

POOLE, Richard Eric. b 65. Huddersfield Poly BEng87. Trin Coll Bris BA98. **d** 98 **p** 99. C Sandal St Helen *Wakef* 98-01; TV Southgate *Chich* from 01. *St Andrew's Vicarage, Weald Drive, Crawley RH10 6NU* Tel (01293) 531828

POOLE, Roy John. b 26. Lon Univ BD54. St Jo Coll Lon LTh54. **d** 54 **p** 55. C Benwell St Aid *Newc* 54-57; Australia 57-61; R Bradford cum Beswick *Man* 61-66; Area Sec Chr Aid Dept BCC 66-68; Regional Supervisor (S and E England) Chr Aid 68-74; Australia from 74; rtd 91. *14 Chungking Grove, Stratton WA 6056, Australia* Tel (0061) (8) 9250 2652 E-mail roy@poole.com.au

POOLE, Stuart. b 33. Lon Univ BScEng55 Man Univ MSc76 CEng65 FIEE85. **d** 91 **p** 92. NSM Cheadle *Ches* 91-03; Perm to Offic from 03. *1 Dene House, Green Pastures, Stockport SK4 3RB* Tel and fax 0161-432 6426 E-mail stuart.poole@ukgateway.net

POOLE, Wendy. See POOLE, Miss Joan Wendy

POOLEY, Peter Owen. b 32. Kelham Th Coll 54. **d** 58 **p** 59. C Paddington St Mary Magd *Lon* 58-62; R Rockland St Mary w Hellington *Nor* 62-67; Asst Master Thos Lethaby Sch 67-70; St Phil Gr Sch Edgbaston 70-74; Lordswood Gr Sch 74-80; Hon C Edgbaston St Geo *Birm* 77-80; R Elton *Ely* 80-01; P-in-c Stibbington and Water Newton 80-01; R Elton w Stibbington and Water Newton 01-02; rtd 02; Perm to Offic *Linc* from 03. *1 Warrenne Keep, Stamford PE9 2NX* Tel (01780) 751646

POOLMAN, Alfred John. b 46. K Coll Lon BD69 AKC69. St Aug Coll Cant 69. **d** 70 **p** 71. C Headingley *Ripon* 70-74; C Moor Allerton 75-78; C Monk Bretton *Wakef* 78-80; V Copley and Chapl Halifax Gen Hosp 80-90; R Llanfynydd *St As* 90-06; P-in-c from 06. *The Rectory, Llanfynydd, Wrexham LL11 5HH* Tel (01978) 762304 E-mail john.poolman@tesco.net

POOLMAN, Mrs Carole Margaret. b 53. St As & Ban Minl Tr Course 98. **d** 01 **p** 02. NSM Pontblyddyn *St As* 01-06; P-in-c from 06. *The Rectory, Llanfynydd, Wrexham LL11 5HH* Tel (01978) 762304 E-mail carole.poolman@tesco.net

POOLTON, Martin Ronald. b 60. Kingston Poly BSc81 Salford Univ MSc83 Bp Grosseteste Coll PGCE85 FRGS81. Cuddesdon Coll 95. **d** 97 **p** 98. C Penzance St Mary w St Paul *Truro* 97-99; C Northampton St Matt *Pet* 99-01; R Jersey St Pet *Win* from 01. *The Rectory, La Rue du Presbytèrè, St Peter, Jersey JE3 7ZH* Tel and fax (01534) 481805 E-mail pooton@onetel.com

POPE, Preb Charles Guy. b 48. AKC70. St Aug Coll Cant 70. **d** 71 **p** 72. C Southgate Ch Ch *Lon* 71-74; C N St Pancras All Hallows 74-77; C Hampstead St Steph 74-77; V New Southgate St Paul 77-86; V Brookfield St Mary from 86; P-in-c Brookfield St Anne, Highgate Rise 88-99; AD S Camden 95-00; Preb St Paul's Cathl from 04. *St Mary's Vicarage, 85 Dartmouth Park Road, London NW5 1SL* Tel (020) 7267 5941 Fax 7482 2136 Mobile 07770-693435 E-mail guypope@blueyonder.co.uk

POPE, Canon Colin. b 51. Brasted Place Coll 74. Linc Th Coll 75. **d** 78 **p** 79. C W Derby Gd Shep *Liv* 78-81; C-in-c Westbrook St Phil CD 81-82; V Westbrook St Phil 82-87; V Orrell and Chapl Billinge Hosp Wigan 87-96; V Southport Em *Liv* from 96; P-in-c Birkdale St Pet 04-08; AD N Meols from 00; Hon Can Liv Cathl from 03. *Emmanuel Vicarage, 12 Allerton Road, Southport PR9 9NJ* Tel and fax (01704) 532743

POPE, David Allan. b 20. Oriel Coll Ox BA45 MA72. Ely Th Coll 45. **d** 47 **p** 48. C Folkestone St Mary and St Eanswythe *Cant* 47-51; V Tovil 51-54; R E Horsley *Guildf* 54-63; R Ivychurch w Old Romney and Midley *Cant* 63-65; P-in-c Brenzett w Snargate and Snave 64-65; P-in-c Newchurch 64-65; P-in-c St Mary in the Marsh 64-65; P-in-c Burmarsh 64-65; R Broadstairs 65-73; P-in-c Berwick *Chich* 73-76; P-in-c Arlington 73-75; P-in-c Selmeston w Alciston 74-76; R Berwick w Selmeston and Alciston 76; P-in-c Rusper 76-79; R Colsterworth *Linc* 79-81; P-in-c Ingworth 81-85; P-in-c Alby w Thwaite *Nor* 81-85; P-in-c Erpingham w Calthorpe 81-85; P-in-c Aldborough w Thurgarton 83-85; rtd 85; Perm to Offic *Nor* from 85. *Burgate Lodge, Saddle Bow, King's Lynn PE34 3AR* Tel (01553) 617599

POPE, Donald Keith. b 35. Sarum & Wells Th Coll 61. **d** 76 **p** 77. Hon C Caerleon *Mon* 76-82; C 82-83; V Pontypool 83-86; R Grosmont and Skenfrith and Llangattock etc 86-98; RD

Abergavenny 93-98; rtd 98. *24 Incline Way, Ridgewood Gardens, Saundersfoot SA69 9LX* Tel (01834) 812089

POPE, Miss Elizabeth Mercy. b 51. Man Univ BSc73 Ex Univ PGCE74. Trin Coll Bris 99. **d** 01 **p** 02. C Bardsley *Man* 01-05; P-in-c Oldham St Paul 05-08; P-in-c Denton St Lawr from 08. *St Lawrence's Rectory, 131 Town Lane, Denton, Manchester M34 2DJ* Tel 0161-320 4895
E-mail elizabeth@mpope.plus.com

POPE, Guy. *See* POPE, Preb Charles Guy

POPE, Michael John. b 37. Sarum Th Coll 62. **d** 65 **p** 66. C Broseley w Benthall *Heref* 65-68; C Shrewsbury St Giles *Lich* 68-71; P-in-c Shrewsbury St Geo 71-75; V 75-79; V Gnosall 79-00; RD Eccleshall 92-00; rtd 00; Perm to Offic *Lich* from 01. *Rivendell, 2 Dark Lane, Broseley TF12 5LH* Tel (01952) 883960

POPE, Michael Ronald. b 41. Bps' Coll Cheshunt 65. **d** 68 **p** 69. C Lyonsdown H Trin *St Alb* 68-72; C Seaford w Sutton *Chich* 72-76; R Hurstpierpoint 76-80; rtd 99. *34 Wilton Road, Shanklin PO37 7BZ* Tel (01983) 863602

POPELY, David Charles. K Coll Lon BA00. SEITE 00. **d** 03. NSM Catford St Laur *S'wark* 03-05. *83 Bower Hinton, Martock TA12 6LA* Tel (01935) 829376 Mobile 07957-825714
E-mail davidcpopely@hotmail.co.uk

POPHAM, Neil Andrew. b 69. Trin Coll Ox BA91 DPhil96 MA05 St Jo Coll Dur BA05. Cranmer Hall Dur 03. **d** 05 **p** 06. C Quarry Bank *Worc* 05-07; C Brierley Hill from 07. *71 New Street, Quarry Bank, Brierley Hill DY5 2AZ* Tel (01384) 561350

POPP, Miss Julia Alice Gisela. b 45. Univ of BC BA71. St Jo Coll Nottm 78. **dss** 81 **d** 87 **p** 94. Woking St Mary *Guildf* 81-83; Hornsey Rise St Mary w St Steph *Lon* 83-87; Par Dn Hornsey Rise Whitehall Park Team 87-91; Par Dn Sutton St Nic *S'wark* 91-94; C 94-98; Missr Sutton Town Cen 91-98; TV Hackney Marsh *Lon* 98-05; rtd 05. *32 Regatta Court, Oyster Row, Cambridge CB5 8NS* Tel (01223) 350164
E-mail j.popp@btinternet.com

POPPLE, The Ven Dennis. b 31. Master Mariner 58. Vancouver Sch of Th LTh72 San Francisco Th Sem DMin89 St Aid Birkenhead 59. **d** 62 **p** 63. C Walkden Moor *Man* 62-65; Canada from 65; Admin Adn 87-96; rtd 96. *8580 General Currie Road, Suite 113, Richmond BC V6Y 3V5, Canada*

POPPLETON, Julian George. b 63. St Chad's Coll Dur BA85 PGCE86 Surrey Univ BA02. STETS 99. **d** 02 **p** 03. NSM Harnham *Sarum* from 02; Chapl K Edw VI Sch Southn from 02. *19 Thompson Close, Salisbury SP2 8QU* Tel (01722) 334272 *or* (023) 8070 4561 E-mail jge.hants.sch.uk

POPPLEWELL, Andrew Frederick. b 53. St Jo Coll Dur BA75. Wycliffe Hall Ox 76. **d** 78 **p** 79. C Clifton York 78-81; C Lich St Chad 82-84; V Laisterdyke *Bradf* 84-99. *Clifton, 210A Leeds Road, Eccleshill, Bradford BD2 3JU* Tel (01274) 637651

PORT MORESBY, Bishop of. *See* RAMSDEN, The Rt Revd Peter Stockton

PORTEOUS, Michael Stanley. b 35. S'wark Ord Course 70. **d** 73 **p** 74. C Barnes St Mich *S'wark* 73-76; Chapl Greycoat Hosp Sch 76-78; C Brighton Annunciation *Chich* 78-80; Chapl Ch Hosp Horsham 80-85; TV Moulsecoomb *Chich* 85-88; R W Blatchington 88-99; rtd 99; Perm to Offic *Chich* from 99. *15 Mariners Close, Shoreham-by-Sea BN43 5LU*

PORTER, Andrew William. b 69. Bris Univ BSc91 BA01 PGCE94. Trin Coll Bris 98. **d** 01 **p** 02. C Ipsley *Worc* 01-04; V Fairfield *Liv* from 04; P-in-c Liv St Phil w St Dav from 08. *St John's Vicarage, 19 Lockerby Road, Liverpool L7 0HG* Tel 0151-263 4001 E-mail anne.porter@bigfoot.com

PORTER, Anthony. *See* PORTER, Canon David Anthony

✠**PORTER, The Rt Revd Anthony.** b 52. Hertf Coll Ox BA74 MA78 Fitzw Ho Cam BA76 MA80. Ridley Hall Cam 74. **d** 77 **p** 78 **c** 06. C Edgware *Lon* 77-80; C Haughton St Mary *Man* 80-83; P-in-c Bacup Ch Ch 83-87; V 87-91; R Rusholme H Trin 91-06; Hon Can Man Cathl 04-06; Suff Bp Sherwood *S'well* from 06; Hon Can S'well Minster from 06. *Dunham House, Westgate, Southwell NG25 0JL* Tel (01636) 819133 Fax 819085
E-mail bishopsherwood@southwell.anglican.org

PORTER, Arthur William. b 29. St Deiniol's Hawarden 70. **d** 70 **p** 71. C Ruislip St Martin *Lon* 70-80; V Kingsbury H Innocents 80-94; rtd 94; Perm to Offic *Sarum* from 94. *24 Belle Vue Road, Salisbury SP1 3YG* Tel (01722) 331314
E-mail rev.porter@tesco.net

PORTER, Barbara Judith. *See* JEAPES, Mrs Barbara Judith

PORTER, Brian John Henry. b 33. SWMTC 78. **d** 81 **p** 82. NSM Plymouth St Andr w St Paul and St Geo *Ex* 81-85; Perm to Offic 85-87; NSM Devonport St Barn 87-90; C Brampton St Thos *Derby* 90-95; Asst Chapl Amsterdam w Den Helder and Heiloo *Eur* 95-97; rtd 97; Perm to Offic *Glouc* 99-00 and 05-08; *Ex* from 09. *Cornerstone, Burrator Road, Dousland, Yelverton PL20 6NE* Tel (01822) 853851

PORTER, Brian Meredith. b 39. Monash Univ Aus BA66 Trin Hall Cam BA75 MA79 New England Univ NSW BLitt79 MLitt85 ACT ThD01. Cuddesdon Coll 68. **d** 68 **p** 71. C Kew Australia 68-69; K Sch Parramatta 70-73; Perm to Offic *Ely* 73-75; Chapl Canberra Gr Sch Australia 75-82; Chapl Ivanhoe Gr Sch 83-97; Sen Chapl Melbourne Gr Sch 98-05; Chapl

Brighton Gr Sch from 05. *4 Fairholme Grove, Camberwell Vic 3124, Australia* Tel (0061) (3) 9882 8740
E-mail bmporter@comcen.com.au

PORTER (née RICHARDSON), Mrs Catherine Elisabeth. b 75. Edge Hill Coll of HE BA96 Trin Coll Bris BA99 MA01. SNWTP 07. **d** 08. NSM Fairfield *Liv* from 08. *St John's Vicarage, 19 Lockerby Road, Liverpool L7 0HG* Tel 0151-263 2681
E-mail cathy.porter@bigfoot.com

PORTER, Damian Michael. b 66. Linc Th Coll BTh92. **d** 92 **p** 93. C Pelsall *Lich* 92-96; V Greenlands *Blackb* 96-00; V St Annes St Anne 00-09; AD Kirkham 06-09; P-in-c Warton St Oswald w Yealand Conyers from 09. *St Oswald's Vicarage, Warton, Carnforth LA5 9PG* Tel (01524) 732946
E-mail fatherd@btinternet.com

PORTER, Canon David Anthony (Tony). b 34. Wycliffe Hall Ox 73. **d** 75 **p** 76. C Watford St Luke *St Alb* 75-78; C Worting *Win* 78-81; V Snettisham *Nor* 81-82; P-in-c Ingoldisthorpe 81-82; C Fring 81-82; R Snettisham w Ingoldisthorpe and Fring 82-84; Chapl Asst Colchester Gen Hosp 87-88; Chapl Maidstone Hosp 88-94; Chapl Mid Kent Healthcare NHS Trust 94-98; Hon Can Cant Cathl 97-98; rtd 98; Perm to Offic *Nor* and *Ely* from 98. *The Greys, 12 Hawthorn Close, Watlington, King's Lynn PE33 0HD* Tel (01553) 811301

PORTER, David Michael. b 37. Coll of Ripon & York St Jo BA88. Ely Th Coll 61. **d** 64 **p** 65. C Clun w Chapel Lawn *Heref* 64-67; C Scarborough St Mary w Ch Ch, St Paul and St Thos *York* 67-69; C Fulford 69-71; V Strensall 71-78; Chapl Claypenny and St Monica's Hosps 78-91; V Easingwold w Raskelfe *York* 78-91; TR York All SS Pavement w St Crux and St Martin etc 91-97; R York All SS Pavement w St Crux and St Mich 97-02; rtd 02; Perm to Offic *York* from 02. *10 Hall Rise, Haxby, York YO32 3LP* Tel (01904) 769823

PORTER, David Michael. b 46. Nottm Univ BMedSci80 BM82 BS82. EMMTC 94. **d** 97 **p** 98. NSM Edwinstowe *S'well* 97-99. *Gorsethorpe Cottage, Edwinstowe, Mansfield NG21 9HJ* Tel (01623) 844657

PORTER, David Rowland Shelley. b 46. City of Liv Coll of HE CertEd69. STETS 00. **d** 03 **p** 04. NSM Whitehawk *Chich* from 03. *33 Warleigh Road, Brighton BN1 4NT* Tel (01273) 703499
E-mail davejanera@aol.com

PORTER, Howard. b 56. S Glam Inst HE CertEd78. St Mich Coll Llan 99. **d** 01 **p** 02. C Maindee Newport *Mon* 01-05; TV Aberystwyth *St D* from 05. *Fronheulog, Piercefield Lane, Penparcau, Aberystwyth SY23 1RX* Tel (01970) 617819

PORTER, James Richard. b 73. Lon Univ BMedSci97 MB, BS98. Oak Hill Th Coll MTh05. **d** 05 **p** 06. C Cromer *Nor* 05-09; R W Horsley *Guildf* from 09. *The Rectory, 80 East Lane, West Horsley, Leatherhead KT24 6LQ* Tel (01483) 283783
E-mail jamesthecurate@yahoo.co.uk

PORTER, John Dudley Dowell. b 33. St Edm Hall Ox BA60 MA61. Qu Coll Birm 57. **d** 59 **p** 60. C Londonderry *Birm* 59-62; C Tettenhall Regis *Lich* 62-65; Chapl RAF 65-69; V Wombourne *Lich* 69-75; V Rickerscote 75-81; P-in-c Chapel Chorlton 81-85; P-in-c Maer 81-85; P-in-c Whitmore 81-85; R Chapel Chorlton, Maer and Whitmore 85-92; TR Wednesfield 92-00; rtd 00; P-in-c Haughton St Anne *Man* 00-03; P-in-c Nord Pas de Calais *Eur* 04-06. *37 Rue Principale, 62130 Framecourt, France* Tel (0033) (3) 21 04 36 35 E-mail jddporter@hotmail.co.uk

PORTER, Malcolm Derek. b 53. BSc. NTMTC. **d** 05 **p** 06. C Woodford Wells *Chelmsf* 05-09. *Address temp unknown*
E-mail thoseporters@aol.com

PORTER, Mrs Marie-Jeanne. b 60. EMMTC 95. **d** 98 **p** 99. NSM Warsop *S'well* 98-04. *Gorsethorpe Cottage, Edwinstowe, Mansfield NG21 9HJ* Tel (01623) 844657

PORTER, Matthew James. b 69. Nottm Univ BA90. Wycliffe Hall Ox BTh93. **d** 96 **p** 97. C Dore *Sheff* 96-00; V Woodseats St Chad 00-09; C York St Mich-le-Belfrey from 09. *13 Hempland Drive, York YO31 1AY* Tel (01904) 427802 Mobile 07985-645844 E-mail matthew.porter@stmichaelsyork.org

PORTER, Canon Michael Edward. b 44. Trin Coll Bris 75. **d** 77 **p** 78. C Corby St Columba *Pet* 77-81; C Rainham *Chelmsf* 81-82; TV 82-92; P-in-c S Hornchurch St Jo and St Matt 92-95; V Anerley *Roch* 95-09; TR 09; AD Beckenham 05-09; Hon Can Roch Cathl 09; rtd 09. *20 Park Lane, Wymondham NR18 9BG* E-mail mike@porterfamily.freeuk.com

PORTER, Raymond John. b 43. Worc Coll Ox BA66 MA70 Wycliffe Hall Ox MPhil93 FRAS93. **d** 06 **p** 07. Dir World Miss Studies Oak Hill Th Coll from 06; Perm to Offic *St Alb* from 07. *24 Bevington Way, Eynesbury, St Neots PE19 2HQ* Tel (01480) 211839 *or* (020) 8449 0467 Mobile 07976-753822
E-mail ray@wiradanuprojo.f2s.com *or* rayp@oakhill.ac.uk

PORTER, Mrs Susan Patricia June. b 53. STETS 00. **d** 03. NSM Wilton w Netherhampton and Fugglestone *Sarum* 03-05; NSM Sarum Cathl 05-08; Perm to Offic from 08. *24 Belle Vue Road, Salisbury SP1 3YG* Tel (01722) 331314
E-mail rev.porter@tesco.net

PORTER, William Albert. b 28. Univ of NZ BA51 MA52. Coll of Resurr Mirfield 53. **d** 55 **p** 56. C Perry Barr *Birm* 55-58; V Port Chalmers NZ 59-61; V Warrington 61-62; Tutor St Jo Coll Suva

Fiji 62-63; Asst Supt Melanesian Miss 62-64; Supt 64-67; Can and Prec H Trin Cathl Suva 65-67; C Wimbledon *S'wark* 68; Asst Chapl HM Pris Liv 69-70; Chapl HM Pris Brixton 70-74; Long Lartin 74-79; Liv 79-87; Nottm 87-90; P-in-c Sneinton St Matthias *S'well* 90-93; rtd 94; Perm to Offic *Glouc* from 01. *40 Duke Street, Cheltenham GL52 6BP* Tel (01242) 262198

PORTER-PRYCE, Ms Julia Frances. b 57. Man Univ BA78 Leic Univ MPhil94. NTMTC 93. **d** 96 **p** 97. C Stoke Newington Common St Mich *Lon* 96-99; C Is of Dogs Ch Ch and St Jo w St Luke 99-02; V De Beauvoir Town St Pet from 02; AD Hackney from 09. *St Peter's Vicarage, 86 De Beauvoir Road, London N1 5AT* Tel (020) 7254 5670 E-mail juliap@freeuk.com

PORTEUS, Canon James Michael. b 31. Worc Coll Ox BA55 MA58. Cuddesdon Coll. **d** 57 **p** 58. C Fleetwood St Pet *Blackb* 57-60; C Ox St Mary V 60-62; Staff Sec SCM Ox 60-62; Chapl Univ of Chicago USA 62-69 and 86-91; Chapl Lon Univ 69-74; V Hampstead Garden Suburb 74-86; Min Livingston LEP *Edin* 91-96; rtd 96; P-in-c Portree *Arg* 96-05; Hon Can Cumbrae from 06. *Triskele, Rinsey, Ashton, Helston TR13 9TS* Tel (01736) 761870

PORTEUS, Canon Robert John Norman. b 50. TCD BA72 MA76. CITC 75. **d** 75 **p** 76. C Portadown St Mark *Arm* 75-79; I Ardtrea w Desertcreat 79-83; I Annaghmore 83-98; I Derryloran from 98; Can Arm Cathl from 98; Preb from 01. *Derryloran Rectory, 13 Loy Street, Cookstown BT80 8PZ* Tel and fax (028) 8676 2261 E-mail rector@derryloran.com

PORTHOUSE, Canon John Clive. b 32. Lon Univ BD58. Tyndale Hall Bris 55 Oak Hill Th Coll 58. **d** 60 **p** 61. C Leyton All SS *Chelmsf* 60-62; C Kendal St Thos *Carl* 62-64; V Flimby 64-68; V Sidcup St Andr *Roch* 68-74; V Beckenham St Jo 74-86; RD Beckenham 80-86; V Southborough St Pet w Ch Ch and St Matt 86-96; TR 96-97; Hon Can Roch Cathl 96-97; rtd 97; Perm to Offic *Carl* from 98. *148 Stainbank Road, Kendal LA9 5BE* Tel (01539) 736106 E-mail clive.porthouse@virgin.net

PORTHOUSE, Roger Gordon Hargreaves. b 39. Tyndale Hall Bris 66. **d** 69 **p** 70. C Wellington w Eyton *Lich* 69-71; C Cheadle *Ches* 71-75; R Frettenham w Stanninghall *Nor* 75-81; R Spixworth w Crostwick 75-81; V Hailsham *Chich* 81-04; RD Dallington 96-03; rtd 05. *19 Cornmill Gardens, Polegate BN26 5NJ* Tel (01323) 487372 E-mail rporthouse@btclick.com

PORTLOCK, John Anthony. b 37. RIBA. WMMTC 96. **d** 99 **p** 00. NSM Lyddington w Stoke Dry and Seaton etc *Pet* 99-07; NSM Bulwick, Blatherwycke w Harringworth and Laxton 05-07; rtd 07; Perm to Offic *Pet* from 08. *7 Chestnut Close, Uppingham, Oakham LE15 9TQ* Tel (01572) 823225 E-mail portlocklydd@aol.com

PORTSDOWN, Archdeacon of. *See* READER, The Ven Trevor Alan John

PORTSMOUTH, Bishop of. *Vacant*

PORTSMOUTH, Dean of. *See* BRINDLEY, The Very Revd David Charles

PORTWOOD, Prof Derek. b 31. Keele Univ MA69 PhD79. ALCD57. **d** 57 **p** 58. C Laisterdyke *Bradf* 57-60; C-in-c Westlands St Andr CD *Lich* 60-66; V Westlands St Andr 66-69; rtd 96; Perm to Offic *Ely* 96-00. *51 River Lane, Cambridge CB5 8HP* Tel and fax (01223) 311044

POSKITT, Mark Sylvester. b 63. Loughb Univ BSc84. St Jo Coll Nottm MA95. **d** 97 **p** 98. C Brigg, Wrawby and Cadney cum Howsham *Linc* 97-00; TV Howden *York* 00-09; P-in-c Barnsley St Edw *Wakef* from 09; P-in-c Gawber from 09. *The Vicarage, Church Street, Gawber, Barnsley S75 2RL* Tel (01226) 207140 E-mail rev.markp@tiscali.co.uk

POST, David Charles William. b 39. Jes Coll Cam BA61 MA65. Oak Hill Th Coll 61. **d** 63 **p** 64. C Orpington Ch Ch *Roch* 63-66; C Fulwood *Sheff* 66-68; V Lathom *Liv* 68-70; V Poughill *Truro* 75-78; V Braddan and Santan *S & M* 78-79; Dioc Missr 78-79; V Sherburn in Elmet *York* 79-91; P-in-c Kirk Fenton 84-85; V Thornthwaite cum Braithwaite and Newlands *Carl* 91-93; R Wheldrake w Thorganby *York* 93-04; P-in-c Elvington w Sutton on Derwent and E Cottingwith 03-04; rtd 04. *Cheviot, 5 Mayfield Crescent, Middle Rasen, Market Rasen LN8 3UA* Tel (01673) 843388

POST, Oswald Julian. b 48. Derby Lonsdale Coll BEd79. EMMTC. **d** 84 **p** 85. Travelling Sec Ruanda Miss 79-89; Hon C Hulland, Atlow, Bradley and Hognaston *Derby* 84-89; V Wormhill, Peak Forest w Peak Dale and Dove Holes 89-99; P-in-c Youlgreave, Middleton, Stanton-in-Peak etc 99-09; rtd 09. *Rose Cottage, Hulland Village, Ashbourne DE6 3EP* Tel (01335) 370285 E-mail ossiepost@hotmail.com

POSTILL, John Edward. b 35. Oak Hill Th Coll 64. **d** 67 **p** 68. C Southgate *Chich* 67-70; C Bowling St Jo *Bradf* 70-74; TV Winfarthing w Shelfanger *Nor* 74-79; R Slaugham *Chich* 79-97; C Busbridge and Hambledon *Guildf* 97-03; rtd 03. *Dora Cottage, Beech Hill, Hambledon, Godalming GU8 4HL* Tel (01428) 687968 E-mail jandjpostill@talk21.com

POSTILL, Canon Richard Halliday. b 37. Hull Univ BSc59. Westcott Ho Cam 66. **d** 68 **p** 69. C Wylde Green *Birm* 68-72; C Kingswinford St Mary *Lich* 72-76; V Yardley Wood *Birm* 76-86;

V Acocks Green 86-02; AD Yardley 93-00; Hon Can Birm Cathl 99-02; rtd 02; Perm to Offic *Birm* from 03. *32 Longmore Road, Shirley, Solihull B90 3DY* Tel 0121-744 6217 E-mail richardh@postill.fsbusiness.co.uk

POSTLES, Donald. b 29. MPS51 Birm Univ MA65. Qu Coll Birm 56. **d** 59 **p** 60. C Southport H Trin *Liv* 59-62; C Prescot 62-63; V Wigan St Steph 63-71; V Farnworth 71-84; V Mossley Hill St Barn 84-92; rtd 93. *43 The Broadway, Abergele LL22 7DD* Tel (01745) 826165

POSTON, Jonathan David. b 59. Ches Coll of HE MTh05. NOC 01. **d** 04 **p** 05. C Prestwich St Mary *Man* 04-07; C Prestwich St Marg from 07. *49 Cromwell Road, Prestwich, Manchester M25 1HR* Tel and fax 0161-798 6352 Mobile 07754-517797 E-mail revjp@poston.org.uk

POTHEN, Canon Simon John. b 60. Westmr Coll Ox BA86. Ripon Coll Cuddesdon 86. **d** 88 **p** 89. C Southgate Ch Ch *Lon* 88-91; C Tottenham St Mary 91-93; TV Gt Grimsby St Mary and St Jas *Linc* 93-96; R Friern Barnet St Jas *Lon* 96-02; V Pinner 02-07; Prec and Can Res Chelmsf Cathl from 07. *1A Harlings Grove, Chelmsford CM1 1YQ* Tel (01245) 491599 Mobile 07939-523366 E-mail precentor@chelmsfordcathedral.org.uk

POTIPHER, John Malcolm Barry. b 42. St Alb Minl Tr Scheme 79. **d** 82 **p** 83. Chapl Herts Fire Brigade 82-91; NSM Chambersbury *St Alb* 82-84; NSM Hemel Hempstead 84-86; NSM Digswell and Panshanger 86-92; P-in-c Pirton 92-95; rtd 95; Perm to Offic *St Alb* from 95. *66 Peartree Lane, Welwyn Garden City AL7 3UH* Tel (01707) 886953 E-mail jmbpot@ntlworld.com

POTTER, Charles Elmer. b 42. Georgetown Univ (USA) BS65 Valparaiso Univ JD73. Wycliffe Coll Toronto MDiv81. **d** 81 **p** 82. C Southport Ch Ch *Liv* 81-84; Chapl Lee Abbey 84-87; P-in-c Westmeadows and Bulla Australia 87-93; P-in-c Aldingham and Dendron and Rampside *Carl* 93-96; P-in-c Aldingham, Dendron, Rampside and Urswick 96-99; V Bexley St Mary *Roch* 99-07; rtd 07. *20 Bromley College, London Road, Bromley BR1 1PE* Tel 07951-780869 (mobile) E-mail charles.potter@tiscali.co.uk

POTTER, The Very Revd Christopher Nicholas Lynden. b 49. Leeds Univ BA71. St As Minl Tr Course 90. **d** 93 **p** 94. C Flint *St As* 93-96; V Llanfair DC, Derwen, Llanelidan and Efenechtyd 96-01; Dean and Lib St As Cathl from 01; V St As 01-03; TR from 03. *The Deanery, Upper Denbigh Road, St Asaph LL17 0RL* Tel (01745) 583597 E-mail chris_potter@btinternet.com

POTTER, Clive Geoffrey. b 55. Aston Tr Scheme 88 Sarum & Wells Th Coll 90. **d** 92 **p** 93. C Epsom Common Ch Ch *Guildf* 92-97; TV Westborough 97-98; TR 98-07; V Milford from 07. *The New Vicarage, Milford Heath, Milford, Godalming GU8 5BX* Tel (01483) 414710 E-mail milfordvicarage@gmail.com

POTTER, Desmond. b 54. St Paul's Coll Grahamstown 85. **d** 88 **p** 88. C Benoni S Africa 88-90; C Springs 90-91; C Linden 91-93; R Kempton Park 93-97; V Newton *Ches* 98-06; Australia from 06. *76 Kariboe Street, PO Box 69, Biloela Qld 4715, Australia* E-mail thesapotters@bigpond.com

POTTER, Harry Drummond. b 54. Em Coll Cam BA76 MA79 MPhil81 LLB92 Barrister 93. Westcott Ho Cam 79. **d** 81 **p** 82. C Deptford St Paul *S'wark* 81-84; Chapl Selw Coll Cam 84-87; Chapl Newnham Coll Cam 84-87; Chapl HM Pris Wormwood Scrubs 87-88; Chapl HM YOI Aylesbury 88-93; NSM Camberwell St Giles w St Matt *S'wark* 93-03; Perm to Offic 03-07. *19 Dobell Road, London SE9 1HE* Tel (020) 7067 1500 E-mail tuahousis@hotmail.com

POTTER, Canon James David. b 35. AKC66. **d** 67 **p** 68. C Longbridge *Birm* 67-70; Lic to Offic 71-73; V N Harborne 73-78; V Smethwick H Trin w St Alb 78-83; V Blurton *Lich* 83-90; V Dordon *Birm* 90-98; RD Polesworth 91-96; Hon Can Birm Cathl 96-98; rtd 98; Perm to Offic *Birm* from 98. *49 Wanstley Road, Stechford, Birmingham B33 8UH* Tel 0121-783 2734

POTTER, John Daniel. b 29. Sydney Univ BA50. St Jo Coll Morpeth ThL51. **d** 51 **p** 53. Australia 52-65 and from 71; C High Harrogate Ch Ch *Ripon* 65-66; Chapl St Mary's Sch Wantage 66-68; Chapl St Jo Sch and NSM St Andr Cathl Singapore 68-71; OCF 68-71; rtd 95; Lic to Offic *Eur* 95-97. *200 Castella Road, Toolangi Vic 3777, Australia* Tel (0061) (3) 5962 9449

POTTER, John Dennis. b 39. Ealing Tech Coll. S Dios Minl Tr Scheme 92. **d** 94 **p** 95. NSM Box w Hazlebury and Ditteridge *Bris* 94-98; Perm to Offic *B & W* from 06. *87A Southdown Road, Bath BA2 1HL* Tel (01225) 316656 E-mail johnpotter@tinyworld.co.uk

POTTER, John Ellis. b 45. Sarum & Wells Th Coll 82. **d** 84 **p** 85. C Wootton Bassett *Sarum* 84-88; TV Swindon New Town *Bris* 88-96; V Milber *Ex* from 96. *St Luke's Vicarage, 10 Laburnum Road, Newton Abbot TQ12 4LQ* Tel (01626) 365837

POTTER, Canon John Henry. b 26. Lon Univ BA50. Oak Hill Th Coll 50. **d** 52 **p** 53. C Islington St Mary *Lon* 52-55; C Kinson *Sarum* 55-58; V Upper Holloway St Jo *Lon* 58-65; R Illogan *Truro* 65-69; P-in-c Ilfracombe SS Phil and Jas *Ex* 69-72; V

72-76; R Poole *Sarum* 76-87; RD Poole 80-85; Can and Preb Sarum Cathl 83-91; P-in-c Charmouth and Catherston Leweston 87-91; rtd 91; Perm to Offic *Sarum* 91-99 and *Win* 91-00. *11 Park Terrace, Tenby SA70 7LY* Tel (01834) 843647

POTTER, Mrs Judith Anne. b 46. Rolle Coll CertEdd8. **d** 05 **p** 06. OLM Shere, Albury and Chilworth *Guildf* 05-08; Chapl Birtley Ho Bramley from 08. *3 Bank Terrace, Gomshall Lane, Shere, Guildford GU5 9HB* Tel (01483) 203352 Fax 202077
E-mail judyp@btopenworld.com

POTTER, Kenneth Benjamin. b 39. Open Univ BA GLCM. NEOC 84. **d** 87 **p** 88. NSM Ryton w Hedgefield *Dur* 87-95; P-in-c Harby w Thorney and N and S Clifton *S'well* from 95. *The Rectory, Front Street, South Clifton, Newark NG23 7AA* Tel (01522) 778258 E-mail kenneth.b.potter@btinternet.com

POTTER, Mrs Linda. b 47. Cranmer Hall Dur 92. **d** 94 **p** 95. C Shildon w Eldon *Dur* 94-98; P-in-c Castleside 98-04; TR Gt Aycliffe from 04. *St Clare's Rectory, St Cuthbert's Way, Newton Aycliffe DL5 5NT* Tel (01325) 313613
E-mail linda.potter@durham.anglican.org

POTTER, Malcolm Emmerson. b 48. Bedf Coll Lon BSc70. St Jo Coll Nottm 72. **d** 76. C Upton (Overchurch) *Ches* 76-78; CPAS Staff 78-84; Development Officer St Jo Coll Nottm 84-86; P-in-c Wellington All SS w Eyton *Lich* 86-95; V 95-06; Preb Lich Cathl 99-06; Membership Development Manager Age Concern 06-07; Chapl Shropshire Co Primary Care Trust from 07. *2 Barns Green, Shrewsbury SY3 9QB* Tel (01743) 641251
E-mail malcolm.potter@blueyonder.co.uk

POTTER, The Ven Peter Maxwell. b 46. Univ of Wales (Swansea) BA69 Univ of BC MA71. Sarum & Wells Th Coll 83. **d** 85 **p** 86. C Bradford-on-Avon *Sarum* 85-88; C Harnham 88-91; P-in-c N Bradley, Southwick and Heywood 91-96; V Sale St Anne *Ches* 96-00; R Largs *Glas* 00-08; Chapl Berne w Neuchâtel *Eur* from 08; Adn Switzerland from 09. *St Ursula, Jubiläumsplatz 2, 3005 Berne, Switzerland* Tel (0041) (31) 352 8567 Fax 351 0548 E-mail peshar@bluewin.ch
or berne@anglican.ch

POTTER, Canon Phillip. b 54. Stirling Univ BA75. Trin Coll Bris 82. **d** 84 **p** 85. C Yateley *Win* 84-88; V Haydock St Mark *Liv* 88-07; Dir Pioneer Min from 07; C Haydock St Mark from 07; Hon Can Liv Cathl from 03. *St Mark's Vicarage, 2 Stanley Bank Road, St Helens WA11 0UW* Tel (01744) 23957 Fax 602641
E-mail info@stmarkshaydock.org

POTTER, Richard Antony. b 36. K Coll Cam BA60 MA64. Ridley Hall Cam 60. **d** 62 **p** 63. C Luton w E Hyde *St Alb* 62-72; V Lyonsdown H Trin 72-85; R Broxbourne w Wormley 85-02; rtd 02; C Thorverton, Cadbury, Upton Pyne etc *Ex* 02-09. *Rivermead, 6 Colyford Road, Seaton EX12 2DF* Tel (01297) 21178

POTTER, Miss Sharon Jane. b 63. Suffolk Coll BSc96 K Coll Lon MSc00 RGN91. **d** 04 **p** 05. OLM Ipswich All Hallows *St E* 04-06; OLM Ipswich St Helen, H Trin, and St Luke from 07. *9 Norman Crescent, Ipswich IP3 9JY* Tel (01473) 421087 Mobile 07795-168600
E-mail sharon.jane@potterdome.fsnet.co.uk

POTTER, Stephen Michael. b 55. Oak Hill Th Coll 93. **d** 95 **p** 96. C Chesterfield H Trin and Ch Ch *Derby* 95-99; P-in-c S Normanton from 99. *The Rectory, Church Street, South Normanton, Alfreton DE55 2BT* Tel (01773) 811273
E-mail stephen@potter55.fsnet.co.uk

POTTER, Canon Timothy John. b 49. Bris Univ BSc71. Oak Hill Th Coll 73. **d** 76 **p** 77. C Wallington *S'wark* 76-79; C Hampreston *Sarum* 79-81; TV Stratton St Margaret w S Marston etc *Bris* 81-87; P-in-c Hatfield Heath *Chelmsf* 87-89; P-in-c Sheering 87-89; R Hatfield Heath and Sheering 90-09; P-in-c Gt Hallingbury and Lt Hallingbury 06-09; RD Harlow 07-09; Hon Can Chelmsf Cathl 07-09; rtd 09. *3 Richmond Court, High Road, Broxbourne EN10 7BN*
E-mail tim.potter1@btinternet.com

POTTIER, Ronald William. b 36. S'wark Ord Course 73. **d** 76 **p** 77. NSM Lower Sydenham St Mich *S'wark* 76-98; NSM Sydenham All SS 98-05; Perm to Offic from 05. *12 Neiderwald Road, London SE26 4AD* Tel (020) 8699 4375

POTTINGER, Justin Charles Edward. b 82. Keble Coll Ox BA03 Ox Brookes Univ PGCE04. STETS 05 Ripon Coll Cuddesdon 07. **d** 08 **p** 09. C Devizes St Jo w St Mary *Sarum* from 08. *52 Queen's Road, Devizes SN10 5HW* Tel (01380) 829931
E-mail justinpottinger@msn.com

POTTS, Heather Dawn. *See* BUTCHER, Heather Dawn

POTTS, James. b 30. K Coll Lon BD56 AKC56. **d** 57 **p** 58. C Brighouse *Wakef* 57-59; Tanganyika 59-64; Tanzania 64-71; C-in-c Athersley and New Lodge CD *Wakef* 71-73; V Athersley 73-77; V Madeley *Lich* 77-85; V Baswich 85-93; RD Stafford 88-95; rtd 93. *16A Christchurch Lane, Lichfield WS13 8BA* Tel (01543) 418808

POTTS, Mrs Jill. b 46. Open Univ BA89. STETS 02. **d** 05 **p** 06. NSM Corfe Mullen *Sarum* 05-07; NSM Grantham, Manthorpe *Linc* from 07. *104 Longcliffe Road, Grantham NG31 8DY* Tel (01476) 578553 E-mail jill@jpotts.me.uk

POULARD, Christopher. b 39. FCA64. Ridley Hall Cam 82. **d** 84

p 85. C N Walsham w Antingham *Nor* 84-86; C Oulton Broad 86-90; TV Ravenningham 90-94; R Raveningham Gp 94-99; RD Loddon 98-99; Perm to Offic *Chelmsf* from 99; rtd 04. *Cuddington, Colam Lane, Little Baddow, Chelmsford CM3 4SY* Tel (01245) 224221 Fax 221394 E-mail chris@poulard.org.uk

POULSON, Anna Louise. b 73. Univ Coll Dur BA94 K Coll Lon MA97 PhD06. Ridley Hall Cam 98. **d** 02 **p** 03. C Ealing St Mary *Lon* 02-06. *St John's Vicarage, Church Avenue, Southall UB2 4DH* Tel (020) 8571 3027 Mobile 07929-348621
E-mail annapoulson@btinternet.com

POULSON, Mark Alban. b 63. Bath Coll of HE BEd86 Anglia Poly Univ MA03. Ridley Hall Cam. **d** 00 **p** 01. C Alperton *Lon* 00-03; P-in-c Southall Green St Jo 03-06; V from 06. *St John's Vicarage, Church Avenue, Southall UB2 4DH* Tel (020) 8574 2055

POULTNEY, Andrew Timothy. b 68. K Coll Lon MA03. St Paul's Th Cen Lon 06. **d** 08 **p** 09. NSM Collier Row St Jas and Havering-atte-Bower *Chelmsf* from 08. *56 Parkside Avenue, Romford RM1 4ND* Tel (01708) 734418 Mobile 07903-112599
E-mail andy.poultney@ntlworld.com

POULTNEY, David Elis. b 73. Loughb Univ BEng96 CEng97 Trin Coll Bris 07. **d** 09. C Luton Lewsey St Hugh *St Alb* from 09. *247 Leagrave High Street, Luton LU4 0ND* Tel 07712-005449 (mobile) E-mail david_poultney@hotmail.com

POULTNEY, Wilfred Howard. b 25. Qu Coll Birm 71. **d** 73 **p** 74. NSM S Leamington St Jo *Cov* 73-85; NSM Holbrooks 85-95; NSM Walsall St Gabr Fulbrook *Lich* 95-04. *80 Coppice Road, Whitnash, Leamington Spa CV31 2JB* Tel (01926) 882077

POULTON, Arthur Leslie. b 28. K Coll Lon BA53 AKC53 BD60 Leic Univ MA85. Tyndale Hall Bris 53. **d** 55 **p** 56. C New Catton St Luke *Nor* 55-56; C Earlham St Anne 56-58; C Chorleywood Ch Ch *St Alb* 58-61; R E Barnet 61-64; Ches Coll of HE 64-87; Chapl 64-84; Sen Lect 66-87; Dir of Studies Course in Chr Studies *Chelmsf* 87-94; P-in-c Gt Canfield 87-94; rtd 94; Perm to Offic *Ches* from 96. *2 The Cloisters, Rhos on Sea, Colwyn Bay LL28 4PW* Tel (01493) 549473

POULTON, Ian Peter. b 60. Lon Univ BSc(Econ)83 Open Univ BA94. **d** 86 **p** 87. C Newtownards *D & D* 86-89; I Bright w Ballee and Killough 89-96; Relig Adv Downtown Radio 91-96; I Larne and Inver *Conn* 96-99; I Killiney Ballybrack *D & G* from 99. *The Rectory, Killiney Avenue, Killiney, Co Dublin, Republic of Ireland* Tel and fax (00353) (1) 285 2228 E-mail poulton@oceanfree.net

POULTON, Canon Katharine Margaret. b 61. Man Univ BA83. **d** 87 **p** 91. C Bangor St Comgall *D & D* 87-91; C Seagoe 91-96; C Kilwaughter w Cairncastle and Craigy Hill *Conn* 96-99; C Greystones *D & G* 99-00; Bp's C Dublin St Geo and St Thos from 00; Can Ch Ch Cathl Dublin from 07. *The Rectory, Killiney Avenue, Killiney, Co Dublin, Republic of Ireland* Tel and fax (00353) (1) 285 2228 E-mail katharinepoulton@gmail.com

POULTON, Neville John. b 48. STETS. **d** 02. NSM Portsea St Cuth *Portsm* 02-07. *18 Belgravia Road, Portsmouth PO2 0DX* Tel (023) 9236 1104 Mobile 07768-661796

POUNCE, Alan Gerald. b 34. Lon Univ BSc55. Wycliffe Hall Ox 57. **d** 59 **p** 60. C Wednesfield Heath *Lich* 59-61; C Heref St Pet w St Owen 61-63; R Gt w Lt Dunham *Nor* 63-69; Asst Master Windsor Boys' Sch 69-94; rtd 94; Perm to Offic *Ox* 99-99; Lic to Offic from 99. *38 Longdown Road, Sandhurst GU47 8QG* Tel (01344) 772870

POUNCEY, Christopher Michael Godwin. b 52. Reading Univ BSc74 Wycliffe Hall Ox BA77 MA. SWMTC 03. **d** 04 **p** 05. NSM S Molton w Nymet St George, High Bray etc *Ex* from 04. *Brightley Barton, Umberleigh EX37 9AL* Tel (01769) 540405 Mobile 07977-930045 E-mail cmgpouncey@hotmail.com

POUND, Canon Keith Salisbury. b 33. St Cath Coll Cam BA54 MA58. Cuddesdon Coll 55. **d** 57 **p** 58. C St Helier *S'wark* 57-61; Tr Officer Hollowford Tr and Conf Cen Sheff 61-64; Warden 64-67; R S'wark H Trin 68-74; P-in-c Newington St Matt 68-74; R S'wark H Trin w St Matt 74-78; RD S'wark and Newington 73-78; TR Thamesmead 78-86; Sub-Dean Woolwich 84-86; RD Greenwich 85-86; Hon Can S'wark Cathl 85-86; Chapl Gen of Pris 86-93; Chapl to The Queen 88-03; Chapl HM Pris Grendon and Spring Hill 93-98; rtd 98; Perm to Offic *Chich* from 99. *Adeleine, Pett Road, Pett, Hastings TN35 4HE* Tel (01424) 813873

POVEY, William Peter. b 36. JP85. Man Univ MSc82 MRCS61 LRCP61 FFPH79 FRIPH HonFChS. NOC 90. **d** 93 **p** 94. Dioc Drug Liaison Officer *Ches* 93-01; NSM Latchford Ch Ch 93-00; NSM Daresbury 00-03; rtd 03; Perm to Offic *Ches* from 03 and *Ex* from 04. *Applebrook House, 4 Trinnicks Orchard, Ugborough, Ivybridge PL21 0NX* E-mail povey.peter@googlemail.com

POW, Miss Joyce. b 29. RGN55 SCM57 RSCN60 RNT73. St Jo Coll Nottm 88. **d** 88 **p** 94. Hon Par Dn Largs *Glas* 88-94; Hon C 94-00. *15 Shuma Court, Skelmorlie PA17 5EJ* Tel (01475) 520289 E-mail joycepow@yahoo.co.uk

POWE, David James Hector. b 50. Wycliffe Hall Ox 88. **d** 90 **p** 91. C Ventnor St Cath *Portsm* 90-92; Chapl HM Pris Belmarsh 93-94; Chapl 98-04; Chapl HM Pris Lewes 94-97; Chapl HM Pris Bris from 04. *The Chaplain's Office, HM Prison, Cambridge Road, Bristol BS7 8PS* Tel 0117-372 3246 *or* 372 3100

POWELL, Canon Anthony James. b 51. Sarum & Wells Th Coll 78. d 79 p 80. C Larkfield *Roch* 79-83; C Leybourne 79-83; V Borough Green from 83; Hon Can Roch Cathl from 04. *The Vicarage, 24 Maidstone Road, Borough Green, Sevenoaks TN15 8BD* Tel and fax (01732) 882447

POWELL, Charles **David**. b 38. St Pet Coll Saltley CertEd61 ACP74. SAOMC 96. d 99 p 00. NSM Ampthill w Millbrook and Steppingley *St Alb* 99-04; Perm to Offic from 05; RD Ampthill 03-08. *33 Putnoe Heights, Bedford MK41 8EB* Tel (01234) 345020 Mobile 07811-260675
E-mail rev.davidpowell@btinternet.com

POWELL, Christopher John. b 71. K Coll Lon BA94 AKC94. Coll of Resurr Mirfield 95. d 97 p 98. C Botley *Portsm* 97-01; C Portsea N End St Mark 01-05; P-in-c Clayton w Keymer *Chich* from 05. *The Rectory, 1 The Crescent, Hassocks BN6 8RB* Tel (01273) 843570 E-mail christopherpowl@supanet.com

POWELL, Colin Arthur. b 32. Hatf Coll Dur BA53. Oak Hill Th Coll 56. d 58 p 59. C Leyland St Andr *Blackb* 58-61; C Lancaster St Thos 61-64; C Tranmere St Cath *Ches* 64-65; R Cheetham Hill *Man* 65-81; TV Oldham 81-86; TV Rochdale 86-97; Chapl Rochdale Healthcare NHS Trust 94-97; rtd 97; Perm to Offic *Man* 00-03. *103 Parsonage Road, Withington, Manchester M20 4NU* Tel 0161-434 2409

POWELL, David. *See* POWELL, Charles David

POWELL, Mrs Diane. b 41. SW Minl Tr Course 85. d 88 p 94. Hon C St Merryn *Truro* 88-92; Dn-in-c Gerrans w St Anthony in Roseland 92-94; P-in-c 94-00; Asst Chapl R Cornwall Hosps Trust 00-05; rtd 05; Perm to Offic *Truro* from 05. *Windsway, Sandy Common, Constantine Bay, Padstow PL28 8JL* Tel (01841) 521610 E-mail diannick@msn.com

POWELL, Dudley John. b 44. Tyndale Hall Bris 65. d 69 p 70. C Blackb Sav 69-71; C Rodbourne Cheney *Bris* 71-74; P-in-c Kingsdown 74-79; V 79-80; V Stoke Gifford 80-90; TR 90-91; Ancient World Outreach Albania 91-03; Perm to Offic *Bris* 91-03 and *Win* from 03. *30 Homechurch House, 31 Purewell, Christchurch BH23 1EH* Tel (01202) 481379
E-mail dudleyberat@tesco.net

POWELL, Eleanor Ann. b 55. Univ of Wales BA82 Leeds Univ MA06 Gwent Coll Newport CertEd76. Qu Coll Birm 82. d 83 p 94. C Caereithin *S & B* 83-86; C Bishopston 86-88; Dioc Children's Officer *Glouc* 88-94; Dioc Adv for Women's Min 94-01; P-in-c The Edge, Pitchcombe, Harescombe and Brookthorpe 94-00; V Churchdown St Jo 00-01; Hon Can Glouc Cathl 94-01; Chapl United Bris Healthcare NHS Trust 01-06; Chapl N Glam NHS Trust from 06. *Park Farm Lodge, The Legar, Langattock, Crickhowell NP8 1HH* Tel (01873) 811355
E-mail eleanor.powell@nglam-tr.wales.nhs.uk

POWELL, Elizabeth Mary. d 09. OLM The Bourne and Tilford *Guildf* from 09. *13 Woodcut Road, Wrecclesham, Farnham GU10 4QF* Tel (01252) 725933 E-mail powellliz@hotmail.com

POWELL, Eric **Michael**. b 46. St As Minl Tr Course. d 04. NSM Gwersyllt *St As* 04-06; NSM Welshpool w Castle Caereinion 06-08; NSM Welshpool, Castle Caereinion and Pool Quay from 08. *The Vicarage, Llansantffraid SY22 6TZ* Tel (01691) 828244
E-mail empowell@tiscali.co.uk

POWELL, Preb Frank. b 29. AKC52. d 53 p 54. C Stockingford *Cov* 53-56; C Netherton St Andr *Worc* 56-60; P-in-c W Bromwich St Jo *Lich* 60-66; C W Bromwich Gd Shep w St Jo 60-66; V 66-69; V Bilston St Leon 69-76; P-in-c Hanbury 76-82; V Hanbury w Newborough 83-86; V Basford 86-92; Preb Lich Cathl 87-92; rtd 92; Perm to Offic *Ches* from 92. *Pippins, 15 Jubilee Terrace, Nantwich CW5 7BT* Tel (01270) 610688
E-mail frank@fjpowell.fsnet.co.uk

POWELL, Gary Charles. b 62. UWIST BSc84. Coll of Resurr Mirfield 92. d 95 p 96. C Roath *Llan* 95-00; V Llansawel, Briton Ferry from 00. *The Vicarage, 251 Neath Road, Briton Ferry, Neath SA11 2SL* Tel (01639) 812200

POWELL, John. b 44. St Luke's Coll Ex CertEd66 Univ of Wales (Lamp) MA02. Glouc Sch of Min 81. d 84 p 85. NSM Stroud and Uplands w Slad *Glouc* 84-89; Chapl Eliz Coll Guernsey 89-92; C Llandudno *Ban* 92-93; TV 94-96; V Dwygyfylchi 96-02; V Cardigan w Mwnt and Y Ferwig w Llangoedmor *St D* from 02. *The Vicarage, Napier Gardens, Cardigan SA43 1EG* Tel (01239) 612722 E-mail parchjohnpowell@lycos.co.uk

POWELL, John **Keith** Lytton. b 52. S Dios Minl Tr Scheme 91. d 94 p 95. NSM Bridgwater H Trin *B & W* 94-97; P-in-c Hatch Beauchamp w Beercrocombe, Curry Mallet etc 97-02; P-in-c Staple Fitzpaine, Orchard Portman, Thurlbear etc 97-02; R Beercrocombe w Curry Mallet, Hatch Beauchamp etc 02-05; P-in-c Exford, Exmoor, Hawkridge and Withypool 05-09; P-in-c Greinton from 06. *Homefields House, Paynes Lane, Othery, Bridgwater TA7 0QB* Tel (01823) 698619 E-mail jill.powell3@googlemail.com

POWELL, **Miss** Katherine. b 56. Sydney Univ BSS79. Wycliffe Hall Ox 84. dss 86 d 87 p 94. Broadwater St Mary *Chich* 86-87; Par Dn 87-91; Asst Chapl Ch Hosp Horsham 91-96; Australia from 96; Chapl Glennie Sch from 97. *The Glennie School, Herries Street, Toowoomba Qld 4350, Australia* Tel (0061) (7) 4637 9359 or 4688 8808 Fax 4688 8848 E-mail powellk@glennie.qld.edu.au

POWELL, Kelvin. b 49. Wycliffe Hall Ox 71. d 74 p 75. C Prescot Liv 74-77; C Ainsdale 77-79; V Bickershaw 79-85; R Hesketh w Becconsall *Blackb* 85-99; Perm to Offic *Ox* from 03. *43 Sharman Beer Court, Southern Road, Thame OX9 2DD*

POWELL, Llewellyn. b 28. Glouc Th Course 67. d 70 p 71. C Quinton *Glouc* 70-73; P-in-c 74-76; V Church Honeybourne w Cow Honeybourne 76-83; R Pebworth w Dorsington and Honeybourne 83-87; rtd 87; Perm to Offic *St D* from 87. *Bodathro Bungalow, Llangynin, St Clears, Carmarthen SA33 4LD* Tel (01994) 448301

POWELL, Mark. b 57. Bath Univ BSc78 PhD81. Ripon Coll Cuddesdon BA84 MA88. d 85 p 86. C Evesham *Worc* 85-88; V Exhall *Cov* 88-96; V Leavesden *St Alb* 96-00; V Ealing St Pet Mt Park *Lon* from 00. *St Peter's Vicarage, 56 Mount Park Road, London W5 2RU* Tel and fax (020) 8997 1620
E-mail mark.powell4@btinternet.com

POWELL, Martin. b 71. St Steph Ho Ox BTh00. d 00 p 01. C Caterham *S'wark* 00-03; V New Addington from 03. *St Edward's Vicarage, Cleves Crescent, Croydon CR0 0DL* Tel (01689) 845588

POWELL, Michael. *See* POWELL, Eric Michael

POWELL, Pamela. b 56. Univ of Wales BEd79 Goldsmiths' Coll Lon MA82. St As Minl Tr Course 00. d 03 p 04. C Wrexham *St As* 03-06; P-in-c Llansantffraid-ym-Mechain and Llanfechain 06-08; V from 08. *The Vicarage, Llansantffraid SY22 6TZ* Tel (01691) 828244 Mobile 07711-053565

POWELL, Patricia. STETS. d 03 p 04. NSM Woodford Valley *Sarum* from 03. *Hawthorn Cottage, Great Durnford, Salisbury SP4 6AZ* Tel (01722) 782546
E-mail patricia_powell@btinternet.com

POWELL, Ralph Dover. b 49. ARMCM70. Chich Th Coll 71. d 74 p 75. C Coppenhall *Ches* 74-77; C Heref H Trin 77-80; V Crewe St Barn *Ches* from 80. *St Barnabas' Vicarage, West Street, Crewe CW1 3AX* Tel (01270) 212418

POWELL, Richard Penry. b 15. Dur Univ LTh38. St Aid Birkenhead 34. d 38 p 39. C Brierley Hill *Lich* 38-42; C Derby St Chad 42-45; C Uttoxeter w Bramshall *Lich* 45-47; V Alton 47-60; V Bradley-in-the-Moors 48-60; R Drayton Bassett 60-64; Min Canwell CD 60-64; V Wrockwardine 64-80; V Uppington 64-80; rtd 80; Perm to Offic *Lich* from 80. *34 Herbert Avenue, Wellington, Telford TF1 2BS* Tel (01952) 242528

POWELL, Robert John. b 65. Trin Coll Bris BA92. d 92 p 93. C Biggin Hill *Roch* 92-95; C Edgware *Lon* 95-01; Area Sec SAMS (NW England and N Wales) 01-04; TV Upper Holloway *Lon* from 04. *The Vicarage, 43 Dresden Road, London N19 3BG* Tel (020) 7686 2293

POWELL, Roger Roy. b 68. Thames Poly BSc91. Ripon Coll Cuddesdon BA. d 94 p 95. C Leic St Jas 94-98; C The Abbey Leic 98-00; TV 00-05; P-in-c Leic St Paul 01-05; Youth Chapl 98-05; P-in-c Ridgeway *Sarum* from 05. *The Rectory, 3 Butts Road, Chiseldon, Swindon SN4 0NN* Tel (01793) 740369
E-mail revd.rpowell@btopenworld.com

POWELL, Stuart William. b 58. K Coll Lon BD80 AKC80. Ripon Coll Cuddesdon 86. d 88 p 89. C Horden *Dur* 88-90; C Northolt Park St Barn *Lon* 90-93; V Stockland Green from 00. *The Vicarage, Bleak Hill Road, Birmingham B23 7EL* Tel and fax 0121-373 0130 Mobile 07889-881358 Pager 07336-734456 E-mail spowell@talk21.com

POWER, Alan Edward. b 26. Worc Coll Ox BA50 MA53. Lich Th Coll. d 57 p 58. C Summerfield *Birm* 57-60; C Oldbury 60-63; V Short Heath 63-97; rtd 97; Perm to Offic *Birm* from 97. *8 Southam Drive, Sutton Coldfield B73 5PD* Tel 0121-355 8923

POWER, David Michael. b 56. BA81 BEd. Oak Hill Th Coll. d 81 p 82. C Warblington w Emsworth *Portsm* 81-84; C-in-c Hartplain CD 84-88; V Hartplain 88-91; Adv in Evang 91-97; V Portsea St Cuth from 97. *St Cuthbert's Vicarage, 2 Lichfield Road, Portsmouth PO3 6DE* Tel and fax (023) 9282 7071

POWER, Ivor Jonathan. b 43. Lambeth STh87. CITC 66. d 69 p 70. C Dromore Cathl 69-71; C Enniscorthy *C & O* 71-74; I Youghal *C, C & R* 74-78; I Youghal Union 78-81; I Athlone w Benown, Kiltoom and Forgney *M & K* 81-98; Can Meath 87-98; Dir of Ords (Meath) 91-97; I Dublin Crumlin w Chapelizod *D & G* 98-08; Can Ch Ch Cathl Dublin 05-08; rtd 08. *62 Maudlin Street, Kilkenny, Republic of Ireland*

POWER, James Edward. b 58. Nottm Univ BSc81 Leeds Univ BA85. Coll of Resurr Mirfield 83. d 86 p 87. C Cadoxton-juxta-Barry *Llan* 86-89; Chapl Harrow Sch from 89. *35 West Street, Harrow HA1 3EG* Tel (020) 8872 8234
E-mail jep@harrowschool.org.uk

POWER, Mrs Jeanette. b 57. Oak Hill Th Coll BA81. dss 82 d 87 p 94. Warblington w Emsworth *Portsm* 82-84; Hartplain CD 84-87; Hon C Hartplain 87-91; Community Mental Health Chapl Havant and Petersfield from 91; NSM Wickham 93-97; NSM Portsea St Cuth from 97; Team Chapl Portsm Hosps NHS Trust from 01. *St Cuthbert's Vicarage, 2 Lichfield Road, Portsmouth PO3 6DE* Tel and fax (023) 9282 7071
E-mail jeanettepower@ntlworld.com

POWIS, Michael Ralph. b 63. St Jo Coll Nottm BTh95. **d** 95 **p** 96. C Dibden *Win* 95-00; V Hedge End St Luke 00-09; Adult Discipleship and Evang Tr Officer from 09. *8 Juniper Close, Winchester SO22 4LU* Tel (01962) 621471
E-mail mike.powis@ukgateway.net

POWLES, Charles Anthony. b 39. EAMTC. **d** 88 **p** 89. NSM Hemsby *Nor* 88-93; NSM Bradwell 01-07; Perm to Offic from 07. *94 Winifred Way, Caister-on-Sea, Great Yarmouth NR30 5PE* Tel (01493) 720096 E-mail charles.powles@btinternet.com

POWLES, Michael Charles. b 34. Reading Univ BSc56 Lon Univ PGCE83. Qu Coll Birm. **d** 60 **p** 61. C Goodmayes All SS *Chelmsf* 60-65; C Surbiton St Matt *S'wark* 65-78; Lect Woolwich Coll 79-99; rtd 99. *Spring Cottage, 3 Rushett Close, Thames Ditton KT7 0UR* Tel (020) 8398 9654

POWLEY, Miss Julia Hodgson. b 55. St Andr Univ MA77 FCA80. Ridley Hall Cam 87. **d** 09. C Carl H Trin and St Barn from 09. *Holy Trinity Vicarage, 25 Wigton Road, Carlisle CA2 7BB* Tel (01228) 522938 Mobile 07765-217335
E-mail julia@powley.plus.com

POWLEY, Mark Thomas. b 75. Nottm Univ BA96 Birm Univ PGCE98. Wycliffe Hall Ox 01. **d** 03 **p** 04. C Addiscombe St Mary Magd w St Martin *S'wark* 03-06; C Hammersmith St Paul *Lon* from 06. *30 Rannoch Road, London W6 9SR* Tel (020) 8746 5260 E-mail mark.powley@sph.org

POWLEY, Canon Robert Mallinson. b 39. Fitzw Coll Cam MA65. Ridley Hall Cam 61. **d** 63 **p** 64. C Bermondsey St Mary w St Olave, St Jo etc *S'wark* 63-67; C Moseley St Anne *Birm* 67-69; Lic to Offic *Man* 72-77; Hon C Walshaw Ch Ch 77-88; V Prestwich St Gabr 88-94; Bp's Dom Chapl 88-94; P-in-c Hargrave *Ches* 94-05; Exec Officer Bd for Soc Resp 94-05; Hon Can Ches Cathl 00-05; rtd 05. *4 Bron y Cae, Terrace Walk, Llanfairfechan LL33 0EW* Tel (01248) 689200

POWNALL, Lydia Margaret. *See* HURLE, Mrs Lydia Margaret

POWNALL, Stephen. b 56. St Jo Coll Nottm BA02. **d** 02 **p** 03. C Herne Hill *S'wark* 02-06; TV Westborough *Guildf* from 06. *St Clare's Vicarage, 242 Cabell Road, Guildford GU2 8JW* Tel (01483) 301349 E-mail steve@sbpownall.fsworld.co.uk

POWNALL-JONES, Timothy William. b 79. Univ of Wales (Cardiff) BD00 MTh02. Trin Coll Bris 04. **d** 06 **p** 07. C Newark *S'well* from 06. *All Saints' Vicarage, 1 Newark Road, Coddington, Newark NG24 2QF* Tel (01636) 700617
E-mail t_pownall_jones@hotmail.com

POWNE, Peter Rebbeck Lamb. b 23. Sarum & Wells Th Coll 80. **d** 83 **p** 84. C Calne and Blackland *Sarum* 83-86; V Netheravon w Fittleton and Enford 86-93; rtd 93; Perm to Offic *Sarum* from 93. *2 Oak Lane, Figheldean, Salisbury SP4 8JS* Tel (01980) 670356

✠**POYNTZ, The Rt Revd Samuel Greenfield.** b 26. TCD BA48 MA51 BD53 PhD60 Ulster Univ Hon DLitt95. TCD Div Sch Div Test50. **d** 50 **p** 51 **c** 78. C Dublin St Geo *D & G* 50-52; C Bray 52-55; C Dublin St Michan w St Paul 55-59; Sec and Sch Insp Ch Educn Soc for Ireland 56-75; I Dublin St Steph 59-67; I Dublin St Ann 67-70; I Dublin St Ann w St Steph 70-78; Adn Dublin 74-78; Bp C, C & R 78-87; Bp Conn 87-95; rtd 95. *3 The Gables, Ballinteer Road, Dundrum, Dublin 16, Republic of Ireland* Tel (00353) (1) 296 6748

PRADELLA, Henry. b 54. St Mary's Coll Twickenham BEd78. NTMTC 97. **d** 00 **p** 01. NSM Hainault *Chelmsf* 00-04; C Romford Gd Shep 04-06; R Rainham w Wennington from 06. *The Vicarage, 73 Lake Avenue, Rainham RM13 9SG* Tel (01708) 559157 E-mail pradfam@btinternet.com

PRAGNELL, John William. b 39. Lon Univ BD65. Lambeth STh87 LTh88. **d** 65 **p** 66. C Bitterne *Win* 65-68; C Hatfield Hyde *St Alb* 68-73; Kuwait 73-75; Chapl Leavesden Hosp and Abbots Langley Hosp 75-88; Chapl Watford Gen Hosp 86-88; V St Alb St Steph *St Alb* 88-95; RD St Alb 91-95; P-in-c Copythorne *Win* 95-02; Dioc Ecum Officer 95-02; Hosp Chapl Adv (Bournemouth Adnry) 00-02; rtd 02; Perm to Offic *Sarum* 03-07. *10 Palmers Court, Southwell NG25 0JG*

PRAGNELL, Michael John. b 40. Down Coll Cam BA62 PhD65 MA66 FIQA81 MRSC CChem MSOSc88. Ox NSM Course 81. **d** 84 **p** 85. NSM High Wycombe *Ox* 84-98; C Beercrocombe w Curry Mallet, Hatch Beauchamp etc *B & W* 98-05; rtd 05; Perm to Offic *B & W* from 05. *2 Listers Court, Listers Hill, Ilminster TA19 0DP* Tel (01460) 54212

PRAGNELL, Ms Sandra Ann. b 53. Hull Univ BA75 TCD BTh01 Dub City Univ MA04. CITC 98. **d** 01 **p** 02. C Castleknock and Mulhuddart w Clonsilla *D & G* 01-05; PV Ch Ch Cathl Dublin 03-05; I Dundalk w Heynestown *Arm* from 05; I Ballymascanlan w Creggan and Rathcor from 05. *The Rectory, Old Golf Links Road, Blackrock, Co Louth, Republic of Ireland* Tel (00353) (42) 932 1402 Mobile 87-265 8592
E-mail dundalk@armagh.anglican.org

PRAILL, David William. b 57. York Univ BA79 FRGS90. Cranmer Hall Dur 81. **d** 82 **p** 83. C Digswell and Panshanger *St Alb* 82-84; CMS 84-89; Course Dir St Geo Coll Jerusalem 85-89; Dir McCabe Educn Trust 90-91; Dir St Luke's Hospice Harrow and Wembley 91-98; Chief Exec Help the Hospices from 98. *Hospice House, 34-44 Britannia Street, London WC1X 9JG* Tel (020) 7520 8200 Fax 7278 1021

PRANCE, Jeremy Roy. b 64. St Jo Coll Nottm BA99. **d** 99 **p** 00. C Bramcote *S'well* 99-04; C Bestwood Em w St Mark 04-05; Perm to Offic 05-06. *Address temp unknown*

PRANCE, Nicholas David. b 55. St Luke's Coll Ex CertEd77 RMN83. EMMTC 95. **d** 98 **p** 99. NSM Radford St Pet *S'well* 98-99. *Address temp unknown*

PRANCE, Robert Penrose. b 47. Southn Univ BTh73. Sarum & Wells Th Coll 69. **d** 72 **p** 73. C Gillingham and Fifehead Magdalen *Sarum* 72-76; P-in-c Edmondsham 76-80; P-in-c Woodlands 76-80; P-in-c Wimborne St Giles 76-80; P-in-c Cranborne 77-80; R Cranborne w Boveridge, Edmondsham etc 80-83; Chapl Sherborne Sch 83-93; Asst Dir of Ords *Sarum* 76-86; V Stoke Gabriel and Collaton *Ex* 93-99; Dep PV Ex Cathl 95-99; Chapl Shiplake Coll Henley 99-09; Chapl St Edm Sch Cant from 09. *St Edmund's School, St Thomas' Hill, Canterbury CT2 8HU* Tel (01227) 475600

PRASAD, Andrew. b 53. Ewing Coll, Allahabad BA75. Bp's Coll Calcutta BD81 Presbyterian Th Coll Seoul ThM88. **d** 79 **p** 81. *48 Ederline Avenue, London SW16 4SA* Tel (020) 8764 0633
E-mail a.prasad@pgen.net

PRASADAM, Goruganthula Samuel Narayanamurthy. b 34. Andhra Univ India BA57. Bangalore Th Coll BD65 Union Th Sem (NY) STM68. **d** 62 **p** 65. In Ch of S India 62-74; C Llanbeblig w Caernarfon and Betws Garmon etc *Ban* 75-76; C Norbury *Ches* 77-78; V Aberaman and Abercwmboi *Llan* 78-83; N Sec CMS 83-87; V Luton All SS w St Pet *St Alb* 87-96; rtd 99. *c/o Mr S Prasadam, 3 Campden Terrace, Linden Gardens, London W4 2EP*

PRASADAM, Canon Jemima. b 39. MBE05. BD61 BA87. Cranmer Hall Dur 86. **d** 87 **p** 94. Par Dn Luton All SS w St Pet *St Alb* 87-94; C 94-96; P-in-c Lozells St Paul and St Silas *Birm* 96-07; V from 07; Hon Can Birm Cathl from 05. *St Silas's Vicarage, 103 Heathfield Road, Birmingham B19 1HE* Tel 0121-523 5645

PRASADAM, Madhu Smitha. b 64. Qu Coll Birm. **d** 03 **p** 04. C Blackheath *Birm* 03-07; V Hamstead St Paul from 07. *Hamstead Vicarage, 840 Walsall Road, Birmingham B42 1ES* Tel 0121-357 8941

PRASADAM, Samuel. *See* PRASADAM, Goruganthula Samuel Narayanamurthy

PRATT, Basil David. b 38. Ripon Hall Ox 64. **d** 67 **p** 68. C Lewisham St Jo Southend *S'wark* 67-68; C Caterham Valley 68-70; CF 70-93; Perm to Offic *Glas* from 08. *St Michael's, Bankend Road, Dumfries DG1 4AL* Tel (01387) 267933

PRATT, Christine Fiona. *See* BLACKMAN, Christine Fiona

PRATT, Edward Andrew. b 39. Clare Coll Cam BA61 MA65. Clifton Th Coll 63. **d** 66 **p** 67. C Southall Green St Jo *Lon* 66-69; C Drypool St Columba w St Andr and St Pet *York* 69-71; P-in-c Radbourne *Derby* 71-74; R Kirk Langley 71-78; V Mackworth All SS 71-78; V Southsea St Simon *Portsm* 78-97; rtd 97; Perm to Offic *Sarum* from 97. *7 Bay Close, Swanage BH19 1RE*

PRATT, Mrs Janet Margaret. b 40. Herts Coll BEd78. St Alb Minl Tr Scheme 78. **dss** 81 **d** 87 **p** 94. High Wych and Gilston w Eastwick *St Alb* 81-89; Hon Par Dn 87-89; Par Dn Histon *Ely* 89-94; C 94-97; Par Dn Impington 89-94; C 94-97; R Bardney *Linc* 97-07; rtd 07; Perm to Offic *Ely* from 08. *26 Stamford Avenue, Royston SG8 7DD* Tel (01763) 243508
E-mail janet@jmpratt.freeserve.co.uk

PRATT, John. b 37. **d** 99 **p** 00. OLM St Enoder *Truro* 99-05; rtd 06. *Chyteg, Newquay Road, St Columb Road, St Columb TR9 6PY* Tel and fax (01726) 860747

PRATT, John Anthony. b 38. Selw Coll Cam BA61 MA65. Qu Coll Birm. **d** 66 **p** 67. C Harrow Weald All SS *Lon* 66-69; C St Pancras w St Jas and Ch Ch 69-74; C Saffron Walden *Chelmsf* 74-75; St Mary-at-Latton 79-88; Chapl Princess Alexandra Hosp Harlow 82-88; RD Harlow *Chelmsf* 83-88; R Tolleshunt Knights w Tiptree and Gt Braxted 88-03; rtd 03; Perm to Offic *Cov* from 03. *2 Erica Drive, Whitnash, Leamington Spa CV31 2RS* Tel (01926) 428609

PRATT, Michael. *See* HARRIS, Michael

PRATT, The Ven Richard David. b 52. Linc Coll Ox BA77 MA81 Birm Univ PhD01 Nottm Univ BCombStuds84. Linc Th Coll 81. **d** 84 **p** 85. C Wellingborough All Hallows *Pet* 84-87; TV Kingsthorpe w Northampton St Dav 87-92; V Northampton St Benedict 92-97; Dioc Communications Officer *Carl* from 97; P-in-c Carl St Cuth w St Mary 97-08; Hon Can Carl Cathl 02-08; Adn W Cumberland from 09. *50 Stainburn Road, Stainburn, Workington CA14 1SN* Tel (01900) 66190
E-mail archdeacon.west@carlislediocese.org.uk

PRATT, Samuel Charles. b 40. ALAM59. Oak Hill Th Coll 69. **d** 71 **p** 72. C Upper Holloway St Jo *Lon* 71-73; C Bucknall and Bagnall *Lich* 73-76; V Liv St Mich 76-80; Chapl R Liv Hosp 80-94; Chapl R Liv Univ Hosp NHS Trust 94-01; V Billinge *Liv* 01-06; rtd 06. *15 Billinge Road, Wigan WN5 9JW* Tel (01942) 731346 Mobile 07957-367114
E-mail sp001f3678@blueyonder.co.uk

PRATT, Stephen Samuel. b 67. Univ Coll Ches BA88 Keele Univ PGCE89. Oak Hill Th Coll BA00. **d** 00 **p** 01. C Goodmayes All

SS *Chelmsf* 00-03; TV Chell *Lich* 03-07; P-in-c 07-08; V from 08. *The Rectory, 203 St Michael's Road, Stoke-on-Trent ST6 6JT* Tel (01782) 838708 E-mail stephen_pratt@sky.com

PRATT, Canon William Ralph. b 47. Keble Coll Ox BA69 MA73. Linc Th Coll 70. **d** 72 **p** 73. C Ifield *Chich* 72-78; TV 78; C Brighton St Pet w Chpl Royal and St Jo 79-83; P-in-c Hove St Jo 83-87; Dioc Communications Officer 87-00; V Ringmer from 00; Can and Preb Chich Cathl from 03. *The Vicarage, Vicarage Way, Ringmer, Lewes BN8 5LA* Tel (01273) 812243 E-mail wrpratt@btinternet.com

PREBBLE, The Ven Albert Ernest. b 08. Univ of NZ BA31 MA32. St Jo Coll Auckland 32. **d** 32 **p** 33. C Remuera St Mark New Zealand 32-35; V Pukekohe 36-42; V Whangarei 42-49; Adn Waimate 44-49; V Remuera St Mark 49-63; Adn Manukau 49-56; V Gen and Adn Auckland 56-63; V Greenhill St Jo *Lon* 63-72; rtd 73. *clo J M Prebble Esq, 11 Greenhill, Sherborne DT9 4EW*

PRECIOUS, Sally Joanne. *See* WRIGHT, Sally Joanne

PREECE, Barry Leslie. b 48. Lich Th Coll 68. **d** 71 **p** 72. C Ewell *Guildf* 71-74; C York Town St Mich 75-77; P-in-c Ripley 77-81; Chapl HM Det Cen Send 77-81; V Cuddington *Guildf* 81-88; V Cobham 88-03; R E and W Clandon from 03. *The Rectory, The Street, West Clandon, Guildford GU4 7RG* Tel and fax (01483) 222573 E-mail rev.preece@btinternet.com

PREECE, Canon Colin George. b 51. Bernard Gilpin Soc Dur 71 Chich Th Coll 72. **d** 75 **p** 76. C Upper Gornal *Lich* 75-78; C Wednesbury St Paul Wood Green 78-81; V Oxley 81-89; V Kennington *Cant* 89-03; RD E Charing 92-98; P-in-c Ashford from 03; Hon Can Cant Cathl from 08. *The College, Church Yard, Ashford TN23 1QG* Tel (01233) 620672 E-mail cpreece@globalnet.co.uk

PREECE, Joseph. b 23. Univ of Wales (Ban) BA50. NW Ord Course 73. **d** 73 **p** 74. C Claughton cum Grange *Ches* 73-74; C Barnston 74-75; R Aldford and Bruera 75-80; V Wincle and Wildboarclough 80-82; P-in-c Cleeton w Silvington *Heref* 82-86; P-in-c Farlow 82-86; V Stottesdon 82-86; R Stottesdon w Farlow, Cleeton and Silvington 86-88; rtd 88; Perm to Offic *Heref* from 91. *Lingholm, Woodhall Drive, Hanwood, Shrewsbury SY5 8JU* Tel (01743) 860946

PREECE, Mark Richard. b 61. St Paul's Cheltenham BA85. Linc Th Coll 85. **d** 87 **p** 88. C Coity w Nolton *Llan* 87-89; C Penarth w Lavernock 89-92; V Ewenny w St Brides Major 92-99; V Canton St Luke 99-02; TR Canton Cardiff from 02; AD Cardiff from 08. *Canton Rectory, 12 Thompson Avenue, Cardiff CF5 1EY* Tel and fax (029) 2056 2022 E-mail mp@mandm6162.plus.com

PREECE, Roger Martin Howell. b 64. Imp Coll Lon BSc86 FRSA96. St Steph Ho Ox BA05. **d** 06 **p** 07. C Marple All SS *Ches* 06-08; V Bowdon from 08. *The Vicarage, Church Brow, Bowdon, Altrincham WA14 2SG* Tel 0161-928 2468 E-mail preece@europe.com

PREECE, Ronald Alexander. b 29. Lon Univ BD56. ALCD55. **d** 56 **p** 57. C Rusholme H Trin *Man* 56-59; Teacher Kidbrooke Sch Lon 59-60; Chapl Pernambuco Brazil 60-63; Perm to Offic *Cant* 63-70; Teacher Abp's Sch Cant 64-70; OMF 70-94; SW Regional Dir 76-94; rtd 94; Perm to Offic *Cant* from 98. *5 Tonford Lane, Canterbury CT1 3XU* Tel (01227) 471061

PREMRAJ, Deborah Devashanthy. b 66. Bangalore Univ BSc87 BEd92 Serampore Univ BD91. United Th Coll Bangalore 87. **d** 96 **p** 97. Deacon Vedal India 96-97; Presbyter Madurantakam 97-02; Perm to Offic *S'wark* 02-05; C Battersea Fields 05-06; Presbyter St Geo Cathl Chennai India from 06. *St George's Cathedral, 224 Cathedral Road, Chennai 600 086, India* (0091) (44) 2811 4261 E-mail premraj@csistgeorgescathedral.org

PREMRAJ, Dhanaraj Charles. b 63. Madras Univ BA86 MA88 Heythrop Coll Lon MTh03. United Th Coll Bangalore BD92. **d** 93 **p** 94. India 93-02; Perm to Offic *S'wark* 02-05; C Battersea Fields 05-06; Presbyter St Geo Cathl Chennai India from 06. *St George's Cathedral, 224 Cathedral Road, Chennai 600 086, India* Tel (0091) (44) 2811 4261 E-mail premraj@csistgeorgescathedral.org

PRENTICE, Brian. b 40. St Jo Coll Nottm 81. **d** 83 **p** 84. C W Bromwich All SS *Lich* 83-86; C Tettenhall Wood 86-89; TV 89-90; V Essington 90-98; TR Willenhall H Trin 98-05; P-in-c Bentley 05; AD Wolverhampton 03-05; rtd 05; Perm to Offic *Lich* from 05. *3 Hamilton Gardens, Bushbury, Wolverhampton WV10 8AX* Tel (01902) 564603

PRENTICE, Mark Neil. b 73. Ex Univ BA94. Wycliffe Hall Ox MTh00. **d** 00 **p** 01. C Tulse Hill H Trin and St Matthias *S'wark* 00-04; C Langham Place All So *Lon* from 04. *25 Fitzroy Street, London W1T 6DR* Tel (020) 7387 1360 or 7580 3745

PRENTICE, Paul Frederick. b 68. SEITE 04. **d** 07 **p** 08. C Bromley SS Pet and Paul *Roch* from 07. *13 Rochester Avenue, Bromley BR1 3DB* Tel (020) 8464 9532 Mobile 07949-059993 E-mail paul.prentice2@btinternet.com

PRENTIS, Calvert Clayton. b 62. Aston Tr Scheme 93 St Jo Coll Nottm 95. **d** 97 **p** 98. C Wood End *Cov* 97-00; TV Leeds St Geo *Ripon* 00-05; Asst Dioc Dir of Ords 02-05; P-in-c Huddersfield H Trin *Wakef* 05-07; V from 07; Asst Dioc Dir of Ords from 09.

Holy Trinity Vicarage, 132 Trinity Street, Huddersfield HD1 4DT Tel (01484) 422998 E-mail ccp@talktalk.net

PRENTIS, Richard Hugh. b 36. Ch Coll Cam BA60 MA64. Sarum Th Coll 69. **d** 71 **p** 72. C Bath Bathwick St Mary *B & W* 71-76; Bp's Dom Chapl *Lich* 76-80; PV Lich Cathl 76-80; V Longton St Mary and St Chad 80-84; V Shifnal 84-94; P-in-c Badger 84-85; P-in-c Ryton 84-85; P-in-c Beckbury 84-85; rtd 94. *23A The Close, Lichfield WS13 7LD* Tel (01543) 411234

PRESCOTT, David Anthony. b 62. Univ of Wales (Lamp) BA84 Coll of Ripon & York St Jo PGCE85. Ripon Coll Cuddesdon MTh07. **d** 07 **p** 08. C W Heref from 07. *79 Bridle Road, Hereford HR4 0PW* Tel and fax (01432) 273708 Mobile 07779-588619 E-mail david.prescott@ripon.soton.org

PRESCOTT, David John. b 51. St Kath Coll Liv BEd73. NOC 00. **d** 03 **p** 04. C Southport Em *Liv* 03-07; P-in-c Birchwood from 07. *The Vicarage, Admiral's Road, Birchwood, Warrington WA3 6QG* Tel (01925) 811906 Mobile 07762-943138

PRESCOTT, Thomas Robert. b 41. St Mich Coll Llan 93. **d** 95 **p** 96. C Abertillery w Cwmtillery w Six Bells *Mon* 95-99; V Llanhilleth 99-03; rtd 03. *70 Glandwr Street, Abertillery NP13 1TZ* Tel (01495) 216782

PRESCOTT, William Allan. b 57. ACIS87. Sarum & Wells Th Coll 91. **d** 93 **p** 94. C Horsell *Guildf* 93-98; R Guernsey St Sav *Win* 98-08; P-in-c Guernsey St Marguerite de la Foret 98-08; Chapl Guernsey Airport 08; R Compton, Hursley, and Otterbourne from 08. *The Rectory, Kiln Lane, Otterbourne, Winchester SO21 2EJ* Tel (01962) 714551

PRESS, Richard James. b 45. Southn Univ CertEd67. Sarum & Wells Th Coll 92. **d** 92 **p** 93. C Bradford-on-Avon *Sarum* 92-95; P-in-c Rowde and Poulshot 95-98; R Rowde and Bromham 98-01; Chapl Wilts and Swindon Healthcare NHS Trust 98-00; P-in-c Chickerell w Fleet *Sarum* 01-07; R from 07; P-in-c Abbotsbury, Portesham and Langton Herring from 09. *The Rectory, East Street, Chickerell, Weymouth DT3 4DS* Tel (01305) 784915 E-mail revrichardpress@yahoo.co.uk

PRESS, William John. b 72. QUB MEng94 BTh. **d** 99 **p** 00. C Knockbreda *D & D* 99-03; C Dundonald 03-05; I Annalong from 05. *Kilhorne Rectory, 173 Kilkeel Road, Annalong, Newry BT34 4TN* Tel (028) 4376 8246

PRESTIDGE, Colin Robert. b 58. W Sussex Inst of HE BEd86 Open Univ BA01. STETS 01. **d** 04 **p** 05. NSM Crofton *Portsm* from 04; Asst Chapl E Hants Primary Care Trust from 04. *96 Titchfield Road, Stubbington, Fareham PO14 2JB* Tel (01329) 664375 E-mail colin@prestidge.org.uk

PRESTNEY, Canon Patricia Christine Margaret. b 49. UEA BEd94. Oak Hill Th Coll 84. **d** 87 **p** 94. NSM Lawford *Chelmsf* 87-95; Chapl Benenden Sch 95-97; Chapl St Jo Coll Ipswich 97-00; R Lawford *Chelmsf* from 00; Hon Can Chelmsf Cathl from 09. *The Rectory, Church Hill, Lawford, Manningtree CO11 2JX* Tel (01206) 392659 Fax 396039 E-mail patprestney@yahoo.com

PRESTON, David Francis. b 50. BNC Ox BA72 MA78. St Steph Ho Ox 72. **d** 74 **p** 75. C Beckenham St Jas *Roch* 74-79; C Hockley *Chelmsf* 81-83; C Lamorbey H Redeemer *Roch* 83-89; V Gillingham St Barn 89-00; Perm to Offic from 00. *17 Hermitage Road, Higham, Rochester ME3 7DB* Tel (01474) 823824

PRESTON, Mrs Deborah Anne. b 46. GTCL67. CBDTI 01. **d** 04 **p** 06. OLM Kirkby Lonsdale *Carl* 04-06; NSM Old Hutton and New Hutton from 06; NSM Crosscrake from 06. *The Old Schoolhouse, Kirkby Lonsdale, Carnforth LA6 2DX* Tel (015242) 72509 Mobile 07749-246380 E-mail deborah@jpreston83.freeserve.co.uk

PRESTON, Donald George. b 30. St Alb Minl Tr Scheme 77. **d** 80 **p** 81. NSM Elstow *St Alb* 80-95; NSM Goldington 87-94; Perm to Offic from 95. *106 Putnoe Street, Bedford MK41 8HJ* Tel (01234) 267313

PRESTON, Frederick John. b 32. MBE72. Oak Hill Th Coll 54. **d** 57 **p** 58. C Hove Bp Hannington Memorial Ch *Chich* 57-59; C-in-c Knaphill *Guildf* 60-62; CF 62-69; V Otterton *Ex* 69-71; CF 71-79; NSM 79-84; Chapl ICS 84-89; rtd 89; Perm to Offic *Nor* 96-98 and *Chich* from 98. *24 Patcham Mill Road, Stone Cross, Pevensey BN24 5PA* Tel (01323) 766644

PRESTON, James Martin. b 31. Trin Coll Cam MA55 Ch Ch Ox MA57. Virginia Th Sem 57 S'wark Ord Course 87. **d** 88 **p** 88. NSM Blackheath Ascension *S'wark* 88-95; NSM Lewisham St Mary 95-97; NSM Catford St Laur 97-99; Perm to Offic *Chich* 99-08 and *S'wark* from 08. *14 Curness Street, London SE13 6JY* Tel (020) 8690 0993 E-mail prestonjm@btopenworld.com

PRESTON, John Baker. b 23. Lon Univ BA49. Oak Hill Th Coll 46. **d** 51 **p** 52. C Fazakerley Em *Liv* 51-55; C Eastbourne H Trin *Chich* 55-57; V Blackheath St Jo *S'wark* 57-65; Perm to Offic *Cant* 69-91; rtd 88. *43 Wedgwood Drive, Poole BH14 8ES*

PRESTON, John Michael. b 40. K Coll Lon BD63 AKC63 Lon Univ BA81 Southn Univ PhD91. St Boniface Warminster. **d** 65 **p** 66. C Heston *Lon* 65-69; C Northolt St Mary 67-72; Trinidad and Tobago 72-74; P-in-c Aveley *Chelmsf* 74-78; V 78-82; C Eastleigh *Win* 82-84; C-in-c Boyatt Wood CD 84-87; V W End 87-00; P-in-c Newton Valence, Selborne and E Tisted w

Colemore 00-03; rtd 03; Perm to Offic *Portsm* from 03; Chapl
SSB from 03. *29 Selsmore Road, Hayling Island PO11 9JZ* Tel
(023) 9263 7673 E-mail john.preston@ukgateway.net
PRESTON, Mrs Junko Monica. b 38. Aoyama Gakuin Tokyo
BA. **d** 92 **p** 93. C St Paul's Cathl Wellington from 92. *60A
Messines Road, Karori, Wellington 6012, New Zealand* Tel
(0064) (4) 476 7902
PRESTON, Martin. *See* PRESTON, James Martin
PRESTON, Michael Christopher. b 47. Hatf Coll Dur BA68.
Ripon Coll Cuddesdon 75. **d** 78 **p** 79. C Epsom St Martin *Guildf*
78-82; C Guildf H Trin w St Mary 82-86; V Epsom St Barn from
86. *St Barnabas' Vicarage, Hook Road, Epsom KT19 8TU* Tel
(01372) 722874 E-mail rev@m-c-preston.org.uk
PRESTON, Canon Percival Kenneth. b 16. Ch Ch Ox BA38
MA48. Cuddesdon Coll 38. **d** 40 **p** 45. C Jersey St Helier *Win*
40-46; C Ox SS Phil and Jas 46-48; C Westbury-on-Trym H Trin
Bris 48-50; Min Lawrence Weston CD 50-55; V Horfield St Greg
55-81; Hon Can Bris Cathl 74-82; RD Horfield 76-81; rtd 81;
Perm to Offic *Bris* from 82 and *Glouc* from 83. *56 Gloucester
Road, Rudgeway, Bristol BS35 3RT* Tel (01454) 612794
PRESTON, Reuben James. b 65. York Univ BSc86 MEng87 Birm
Univ PGCE97. Westcott Ho Cam 88. **d** 91 **p** 92. C Weoley Castle
Birm 91-94; TV Malvern Link w Cowleigh *Worc* 94-96; Perm to
Offic *Birm* 96-99; C Bordesley St Benedict 99-07; Perm to Offic
Portsm 07-08; Hon C Portsea St Sav and Portsea St Alb 08;
P-in-c Bridgemary from 08; Chapl Bridgemary Community
Sports Coll from 08; Chapl HM Pris Kingston (Portsm) from 08.
St Matthew's Vicarage, 7 Duncton Way, Gosport PO13 0FD Tel
(01329) 829883 E-mail rjp@reubenjamespreston.co.uk
PRESTON, William. b 25. St Cath Coll Cam BA46 MA50
Reading Univ MSc79. Oak Hill Th Coll 48. **d** 50 **p** 51. C Hyson
Green *S'well* 50-52; C Lenton 52-55; Lic to Offic Kenya 55-59;
Asst Master Thika High Sch 59-62; Bethany Sch Goudhurst
62-69; Cranbrook Sch Kent 69-90; Perm to Offic *Cant* from 64
and *Roch* from 66; rtd 90. *29 Orchard Way, Horsmonden,
Tonbridge TN12 8LA* Tel (01892) 722616
PRESTON-THOMAS, Canon Colin Barnabas Rashleigh. b 28.
K Coll Lon 48 Edin Th Coll 51. **d** 53 **p** 54. C Edin St Dav 53-54;
Chapl St Ninian's Cathl Perth 54-55; Prec St Ninian's Cathl
Perth 55-60; Chapl HM Pris Perth 55-60; P-in-c Inverkeithing
St And 60; R 61-72; P-in-c Rosyth 60; R 61-72; Syn Clerk 68-93;
Can St Ninian's Cathl Perth 68-93; R Forfar 72-82; Dioc Sec
80-90; R Kilmaveonaig 82-93; R Pitlochry 82-93; rtd 93; Hon
Can St Ninian's Cathl Perth from 93. *14 Muirend Grove, Perth
PH1 1JW* Tel (01738) 627807
PRESTWOOD, Ms Jayne Marie. b 64. Man Univ BA86 Nottm
Univ MA93. Linc Th Coll MA94. **d** 94 **p** 95. C Reddish *Man*
94-98; Dioc Drugs Misuse Project Worker 98-00; P-in-c N
Reddish 00-04; P-in-c Haughton St Anne 04-06; Tr Officer for
Reader Tr 04-06; Vice Prin Dioc Reader and OLM Schemes
from 06. *Church House, 90 Deansgate, Manchester M3 2GH* Tel
0161-828 1456 E-mail jprestwood@manchester.anglican.org
PRETT, Alan. b 39. **d** 05 **p** 06. OLM Styvechale *Cov* from 05.
55 Watercall Avenue, Coventry CV3 5AX Tel (024) 7641 5357
E-mail alanprett@btinternet.com
PREVETT, Mark Norman. b 59. Univ of Wales (Cardiff) BD88.
St Mich Coll Llan 85. **d** 88 **p** 89. C Brynmawr *S & B* 88-90; C
Bassaleg *Mon* 90-92; R Blaina and Nantyglo 92-97; TV Halas
Worc 97-04; RD Dudley 00-04; TR Totton *Win* from 04. *The
Rectory, 92 Salisbury Road, Totton, Southampton SO40 3JA* Tel
(023) 8086 5103 E-mail prevtherev@btopenworld.com
PREVITÉ, Anthony Michael Allen. b 41. CITC 85. **d** 88 **p** 89. C
Galway w Kilcummin *T, K & A* 88-91; I Omey w Ballynakill,
Errislannan and Roundstone 91-93; Dean Tuam 93-96; I Tuam
w Cong and Aasleagh 93-96; Adn Tuam and Can Tuam Cathl
96-06; I Omey w Ballynakill, Errislannan and Roundstone
96-06; rtd 06. *Oldchapel, Oughterard, Co Galway, Republic of
Ireland* Tel and fax (00353) (91) 552126
PREWER, Dennis. b 30. Kelham Th Coll 50. **d** 54 **p** 55. C
Stockport St Thos *Ches* 54-58; C Gt Grimsby St Mary and
St Jas *Linc* 58-62; V Gt Harwood St Jo *Blackb* 62-64; V Scarcliffe
Derby 64-70; Org Sec CECS 70-92; Dios Liv, Ban and St As
70-78; Dio Man 78-92; Lic to Offic *Ches* 70-92; Perm to Offic
Man 78-96; rtd 92; Perm to Offic *Ches* from 92. *19 Alan Drive,
Marple, Stockport SK6 6LN* Tel 0161-427 2827
PRICE, Alan John. b 48. Wilson Carlile Coll 69. **d** 08 **p** 08. P-in-c
Charlesworth and Dinting Vale *Derby* from 08. *The Vicarage,
Marple Road, Charlesworth, Glossop SK13 5DA* Tel (01457)
852440 Mobile 07785-723952 E-mail alan@alanprice.me.uk
PRICE, Alison Jane. *See* DOBELL, Mrs Alison Jane
PRICE, Alison Jean. b 50. Man Univ BSc71 Open Univ MA93
Kellogg Coll Ox DPhil01 PGCE89. Ox Min Course 06. **d** 09.
NSM Marston w Elsfield *Ox* from 09. *The Vicarage, Elsfield
Road, Marston, Oxford OX3 0PR* Tel (01865) 721399
E-mail aprice@brookes.ac.uk
PRICE, Mrs Alison Mary. b 48. K Alfred's Coll Win CertEd69.
d 01. Par Dn Magor *Mon* from 01. *Greenwillow, Church Road,
Undy, Caldicot NP26 3EN* Tel (01633) 880557

PRICE, Alun. b 60. Bradf Univ BSc82 Loughb Univ MSc88 Univ
Coll Ches BTh04 CSci. NOC 01. **d** 04 **p** 05. NSM Bramley *Sheff*
04-05; NSM Wath-upon-Dearne 05-07; P-in-c Wadworth w
Loversall from 07. *The Vicarage, Vicarage Drive, Wadworth,
Doncaster DN11 9AN* Tel (01302) 851974 Mobile
07958-685393 E-mail fatheralun@hotmail.com
PRICE, Alun Huw. b 47. MBE91. St D Coll Lamp. **d** 70 **p** 71. C
Carmarthen St Dav *St D* 70-73; V Betws Ifan 73-77; CF 77-03.
Bryn Seion, Llynyfran Road, Llandysul SA44 4JW
PRICE, Anthony Ronald. b 49. Linc Coll Ox BA71 MA83 St Jo
Coll Dur BA78. **d** 79 **p** 80. C St Alb St Paul *St Alb* 79-81; C
Wootton 81-85; C Lydiard Millicent w Lydiard Tregoz *Bris*
85-86; TV The Lydiards 86-91; V Marston *Ox* 91-95; V Marston
w Elsfield from 95; RD Cowley 97-02. *The Vicarage, Elsfield
Road, Marston, Oxford OX3 0PR* Tel (01865) 247034
E-mail tony@godspell.org.uk
PRICE, Carol Ann. b 46. St Jo Coll Nottm 02. **d** 03 **p** 04. NSM
Derby St Alkmund and St Werburgh 03-04; NSM Charlesworth
and Dinting Vale from 04. *The Vicarage, Marple Road,
Charlesworth, Glossop SK13 5DA* Tel (01457) 852440 Mobile
07787-522127 E-mail carol@carolprice.me.uk
PRICE, Christine. b 66. Leic Univ BA94. EAMTC 98. **d** 01 **p** 02.
C Jersey St Helier *Win* 01-06. *7 Le Geyt Close, La Rue de
Deloraine, St Saviour, Jersey JE2 7NY* Tel (01534) 737575
Mobile 07971-026711 E-mail christinenriss@jerseymail.co.uk
PRICE, Mrs Christine Janice. b 45. Sarum & Wells Th Coll 83.
dss 86 **d** 87 **p** 94. Roxbourne St Andr *Lon* 86-90; NSM 87-90;
NSM Roxeth Ch Ch and Harrow St Pet 90-93; C Roxeth 93-96;
C Costessey *Nor* 96-98; rtd 98; Perm to Offic *Nor* 98-05.
31 Russell Court, Chesham HP5 3JH Tel (01494) 773263
E-mail chrisjpri@aol.com
PRICE, Canon Clive Stanley. b 42. ALCD69. **d** 69 **p** 70. C Chenies
and Lt Chalfont *Ox* 69-75; R Upper Stour *Sarum* 75-79; C-in-c
Panshanger CD *St Alb* 79-82; TV Digswell and Panshanger
82-86; P-in-c St Oswald in Lee w Bingfield *Newc* 86-07; Dioc
Ecum Officer 86-07; Hon Can Newc Cathl 97-07; AD
Bellingham 00-06; rtd 07. *Ubbanford Bank Cottage, Norham,
Berwick-upon-Tweed TD15 2JZ* Tel (01289) 382051
PRICE, David. b 27. Wycliffe Hall Ox 61. **d** 63 **p** 64. C Bucknall
and Bagnall *Lich* 63-67; C Abingdon w Shippon *Ox* 67-76;
Warden Stella Carmel Conf Cen Haifa Israel 76-80; Dir Israel
Trust of the Angl Ch and R Jerusalem 80-84; V S Kensington
St Luke *Lon* 84-92; Hon C Hordle *Win* 92-97; Perm to Offic *Win* 97-98 and *Worc*
98-07. *16 Masefield Avenue, Ledbury HR8 1BW* Tel (01531)
634831
PRICE, David Gareth Michael. b 64. Ex Univ BA86 Kent Univ
MA87 FSS. Wycliffe Hall Ox BTh94. **d** 97 **p** 98. C Godalming
Guildf 97-00; C-in-c Elvetham Heath LEP 00-02; Min from 02.
Church House, 30 Chineham Close, Fleet GU51 1BF Tel (01252)
695067 Fax 695068 E-mail minister@churchontheheath.org.uk
PRICE, Canon David Rea. b 39. St Aid Birkenhead 61. **d** 63 **p** 64.
C Green Street Green *Roch* 63-66; C Gillingham St Mary 66-69;
C New Windsor St Jo *Ox* 69-72; V Winkfield 72-80; RD
Bracknell 78-86; V Sunningdale 80-86; TR Wimborne Minster
and Holt *Sarum* 86-96; R Wimborne Minster 96-01; Chapl
Wimborne Hosp 86-01; RD Wimborne 88-98; Can and Preb
Sarum Cathl 92-01; P-in-c Witchampton, Stanbridge and Long
Crichel etc 00-01; rtd 01; Perm to Offic from 01. *14 The
Broadway, Exmouth EX8 2NW* Tel (01395) 269811
E-mail rea@14broadway.eclipse.co.uk
PRICE, Canon David Trevor William. b 43. Keble Coll Ox BA65
MA69 MEHS79 FRHistS79 FSA95. Sarum & Wells Th Coll 72.
d 72 **p** 73. Lect Univ of Wales (Lamp) *St D* 70-87; Sen Lect
87-97; Chapl 79-80; Dean of Chpl 90-91; Public Preacher 72-86;
Dioc Archivist 82-98; P-in-c Betws Bledrws 86-97; Hon Can
St D Cathl 90-92; Can 92-00; V Cydweli and Llandyfaelog 97-00;
P-in-c Myddle and Broughton *Lich* 00-08; P-in-c Loppington w
Newtown 02-08; rtd 08; Perm to Offic *St As* from 01 and *Lich*
from 08. *57 Kynaston Drive, Wem, Shrewsbury SY4 5DE* Tel
(01939) 234777 Mobile 07811-712911
E-mail williamprice@talktalk.net
PRICE, Dawson. b 31. OBE. Peterho Cam BA52. Oak Hill NSM
Course 88. **d** 91 **p** 92. NSM Harpenden St Nic *St Alb* 91-99; rtd
99; Perm to Offic *Win* from 99. *8 Kimberley Close, Fair Oak,
Eastleigh SO50 7EE* Tel (023) 8069 2273
PRICE, Derek Henry. b 51. Trin Coll Bris BA98. **d** 98 **p** 99. C
Bayston Hill *Lich* 98-02; R Barrow St Paul *Carl* from 02.
St Paul's Rectory, 353 Abbey Road, Barrow-in-Furness LA13 9JY
Tel (01229) 821546 E-mail dh.price@virgin.net
PRICE, Canon Derek William. b 27. St Pet Hall Ox BA51 MA55.
Qu Coll Birm 51. **d** 53 **p** 54. C St Marylebone St Mark Hamilton
Terrace *Lon* 53-57; C Stevenage *St Alb* 57-63; Jamaica 63-67; R
Bridgham and Roudham *Nor* 67-80; R E w W Harling 69-80;
Hon Can Nor Cathl 75-92; RD Thetford and Rockland 76-86;
P-in-c Kilverstone 80-87; P-in-c Croxton 80-87; TR Thetford
80-87; R Castleacre w Newton, Rougham and Southacre 87-92;
Perm to Offic 92-99 and from 00; P-in-c Easton w Colton and

Marlingford 99-00. *Fourways, King's Road, Dereham NR19 2AG* Tel (01362) 691660

PRICE, Chan Desmond. b 23. St D Coll Lamp BA50. **d** 51 **p** 52. C Llwynypia *Llan* 51-52; C Ystradyfodwg 52-54; C Watford Ch Ch *St Alb* 54-56; Chapl RAF 56-68; R Dinas and Llanllawer *St D* 68-72; V Llandeilo Fawr w Llandyfeisant 72-79; V Llandeilo Fawr and Taliaris 79-91; Can St D Cathl 83-91; Chan 89-91; RD Llangadog and Llandeilo 90-91; rtd 91; Hon Can St D Cathl from 91. *24 Diana Road, Llandeilo SA19 6RS* Tel (01558) 824039

PRICE, Canon Edward <u>Glyn</u>. b 35. Univ of Wales (Lamp) BA55. Ch Div Sch of the Pacific (USA) BD58. **d** 58 **p** 59. C Denbigh *St As* 58-65; V Llanasa 65-76; V Buckley 76-91; Dioc RE Adv 77-88; RD Mold 86-91; Can St As Cathl from 87; Preb and Sacr from 95; V Llandrillo-yn-Rhos 91-00; rtd 00. *7 Rhodfa Criccieth, Bodelwyddan, Rhyl LL18 5WL* Tel (01745) 571286

PRICE, Frank Lea. b 69. SS Coll Cam BA92 Solicitor 96. Oak Hill Th Coll BA99. **d** 99 **p** 00. C Hinckley H Trin *Leic* 99-04; C Cambridge H Sepulchre *Ely* 04-08; P-in-c Cambridge St Matt from 08. *St Matthew's Vicarage, 24 Geldart Street, Cambridge CB1 2LX* E-mail frank.price@stag.org

PRICE, Frederick <u>Leslie</u>. b 30. Oak Hill Th Coll 59. **d** 61 **p** 62. C Hougham in Dover Ch Ch *Cant* 61-64; R Plumbland and Gilcrux *Carl* 64-95; rtd 95; Perm to Offic *Carl* from 98. *1 Beech Hill, Oughterside, Aspatria, Carlisle CA7 2QA* Tel (01697) 320255

PRICE, Geoffrey David Gower. b 46. Oak Hill Th Coll. **d** 83 **p** 84. C Gt Baddow *Chelmsf* 83-86; C Hampreston *Sarum* 86-88; TV 88-93; P-in-c Drayton in Hales *Lich* 93-97; V 97-99; P-in-c Adderley and Moreton Say 93-97; R Ipswich St Helen, H Trin, and St Luke *St E* 99-05; V E Bedfont *Lon* from 05. *St Mary's Vicarage, 9 Hatton Road, Bedfont, Feltham TW14 8JR* Tel (020) 8751 0088

PRICE, Gerald Andrew. b 31. NEOC. **d** 84 **p** 85. C Monkseaton St Mary *Newc* 84-87; V Cowgate 87-94; C Beltingham w Henshaw 94-96; C Haydon Bridge 94-96; rtd 96; Perm to Offic *Newc* from 96. *39 Primlea Court, Aydon Road, Corbridge NE45 5ES* Tel (01434) 634919

PRICE, Glyn. See PRICE, Canon Edward Glyn

PRICE, Iorweth. b 68. WEMTC. **d** 08. C Heref S Wye from 08. *2 Nelson Street, Hereford HR1 2NZ* Tel (01432) 379696

PRICE, Mrs Jean Amelia. b 44. SAOMC 99. OLM N Buckingham *Ox* 02-06; NSM Beercrocombe w Curry Mallet, Hatch Beauchamp etc *B & W* from 06. *The Rectory, Station Road, Hatch Beauchamp, Taunton TA3 6AB* Tel (01823) 481236 E-mail jeanaprice@aol.com

PRICE, John Francis. b 32. Qu Coll Cam BA54 MA. Ridley Hall Cam 54. **d** 56 **p** 57. C Leic H Apostles 56-60; V Forest Gate St Mark *Chelmsf* 60-71; V Harold Hill St Geo 72-79; R Loughton St Mary 79-83; TR Loughton St Mary and St Mich 83-88; R Kirby-le-Soken w Gt Holland 88-92; rtd 92; Perm to Offic *Chelmsf* from 00. *97 Kings Parade, Holland-on-Sea, Clacton-on-Sea CO15 5JH* Tel (01255) 813202

PRICE, John Joseph. b 44. Ridley Hall Cam 89. **d** 92 **p** 93. C Glenfield *Leic* 92-97; Relig Affairs Adv BBC Radio Leics 93-97; Midl Regional Co-ord Crosslinks 97-05; NSM Werrington *Pet* 04-05; P-in-c Pet St Mark and St Barn from 05. *Copper Beeches, 59A Peterborough Road, Castor, Peterborough PE5 7AL* Tel (01733) 380025 E-mail jprice@onetel.net

PRICE, John Newman. b 32. St Alb Minl Tr Scheme 80. **d** 83 **p** 84. NSM Bedford St Pet w St Cuth *St Alb* 83-88; C Lt Berkhamsted and Bayford, Essendon etc 88-92; P-in-c Benington w Walkern 92-99; rtd 99; Perm to Offic *St Alb* from 00. *21 Wendover Drive, Bedford MK41 9QY* Tel (01234) 313373

PRICE, Canon John Richard. b 34. Mert Coll Ox BA58 MA62. Westcott Ho Cam 58. **d** 60 **p** 61. C Man St Aid 60-63; C Bramley *Ripon* 63-67; V Leeds All Hallows w St Simon 67-74; P-in-c Wrangthorn 73-74; V Claughton cum Grange *Ches* 74-78; V Mottram in Longdendale w Woodhead 78-88; R Nantwich 88-99; RD Mottram 89-99; Hon Can Ches Cathl 86-99; rtd 99; Perm to Offic *Bradf* from 99. *21 Mill Croft, Cowling, Keighley BD22 0AJ* Tel (01535) 637699

PRICE, Joseph <u>Roderick</u>. b 45. St Mich Coll Llan 74. **d** 75 **p** 76. C Fleur-de-Lis *Mon* 75-79; CF 79-99; Rtd Officer Chapl RAChD 99-05; Chapl Limassol St Barn Cyprus 06-08; rtd 08; Perm to Offic Cyprus and the Gulf from 08. *Flamingo Villa, Pine Bay Villas, PO Box 59246, Pissouri Village, 4607 Limassol, Cyprus* Tel (00357) (25) 222213 Mobile 99-965663 E-mail rodberyl@hotmail.com

PRICE, Preb Lawrence Robert. b 43. LICeram71. St Jo Coll Dur 76. **d** 78 **p** 79. C Harlescott *Lich* 78-80; C Cheddleton 80-83; P-in-c Calton, Cauldon, Grindon and Waterfall 83-84; R 85-88; P-in-c Kingsley 95-01; R Kingsley and Foxt-w-Whiston 01-07; C Alton w Bradley-le-Moors and Oakamoor w Cotton 06-07; RD Cheadle 98-07; Preb Lich Cathl 00-08; rtd 08; P-in-c Cheddleton *Lich* from 07. *The Vicarage, Hollow Lane, Cheddleton, Leek ST13 7HP* Tel (01538) 360226 E-mail preblrprice@btinternet.com

PRICE, Leslie. See PRICE, Frederick Leslie

PRICE, Mari Josephine. b 43. St Hugh's Coll Ox BA65 Ox Univ MA69 DipEd66. Llan Dioc Tr Scheme 93. **d** 97 **p** 98. NSM Lisvane *Llan* 97-02; NSM Roath 02-03; Hon Chapl Llan Cathl from 03. *23 Ty Draw Road, Roath, Cardiff CF23 5HB* Tel (029) 2045 6757 Mobile 07850-019883

PRICE, Martin Randall Connop. b 45. Lon Univ BSc71 Fitzw Coll Cam BA75 MA79 Univ of Wales (Swansea) PhD02. Ridley Hall Cam 73. **d** 76 **p** 77. C Keynsham *B & W* 76-79; Ind Chapl *Sheff* 79-83; V Wortley 79-83; R Hook Norton w Gt Rollright, Swerford etc *Ox* 83-91; V Shiplake w Dunsden 91-03; P-in-c Harpsden 02-03; R Shiplake w Dunsden and Harpsden from 03. *The Rectory, Shiplake, Henley-on-Thames RG9 4BS* Tel 0118-940 1306

PRICE (née ALDERTON), Mrs Mary Louise. b 54. Nottm Univ BSc75 IPFA87. EAMTC 02. **d** 05 **p** 06. NSM Melbourn *Ely* from 05; NSM Meldreth from 05. *4 Barrons Green, Shepreth, Royston SG8 6QN* Tel (01763) 261569 E-mail mary@price10051.fsnet.co.uk

PRICE, Michael Graham. b 62. Ex Coll Ox BA84. Linc Th Coll 84. **d** 86 **p** 87. C Salford St Phil w St Steph *Man* 86-90; R Man Gd Shep 90-95; V Netherton St Andr *Worc* 95-99; Chapl Bloxham Sch from 00. *Bloxham School, Bloxham, Banbury OX15 4PQ* Tel (01295) 720222

PRICE, Morris John. b 39. **d** 03 **p** 04. OLM Gt Wyrley *Lich* from 03. *42 Huthill Lane, Walsall WS6 6PB* Tel (01922) 412846 E-mail normoss@talktalk.net

PRICE, Norman. See PRICE, William Norman

PRICE, Canon Norman Havelock. b 28. Univ of Wales (Lamp) BA52. St Mich Coll Llan 52. **d** 54 **p** 55. C Maindee Newport *Mon* 54-58; V Llantilio Crossenny and Llanfihangel Ystern etc 58-64; V Mon St Thos-over-Monnow 64-65; V Mon St Thos-over-Monnow and Wonastow 65-71; V Overmonnow w Wonastow and Michel Troy 71-93; RD Monmouth 84-93; Can St Woolos Cathl 91-93; rtd 93; Hon Can St Woolos Cathl 93-96; Lic to Offic from 93. *17 Cinderhill Street, Monmouth NP25 5EY* Tel (01600) 714587

✠**PRICE, The Rt Revd Peter Bryan.** b 44. Redland Coll of Educn CertEd66. Oak Hill Th Coll 72. **d** 74 **p** 75 **c** 97. C Portsdown *Portsm* 74-78; Chapl Scargill Ho 78-80; P-in-c Addiscombe St Mary *Cant* 80-81; V 81-84; V Addiscombe St Mary *S'wark* 85-88; Can Res and Chan S'wark Cathl 88-92; Gen Sec USPG 92-97; Area Bp Kingston *S'wark* 97-02; Bp B & W from 02. *The Palace, Wells BA5 2PD* Tel (01749) 672341 Fax 679355 E-mail bishop@bathwells.anglican.org

PRICE, Peter Charles. b 27. Angl Th Coll (BC). **d** 61 **p** 62. Canada 61-66; C St Mary-at-Latton *Chelmsf* 66-68; C Bearsted *Cant* 68-74; TV Ebbw Vale *Mon* 74-77; V Llanfihangel Crucorney w Oldcastle etc 77-87; V St Paul's Cathl St Helena 87-90; V Llanishen w Trelleck Grange and Llanfihangel etc *Mon* 90-94; rtd 94; Perm to Offic *Heref* from 95. *1 Kynaston, Much Marcle, Ledbury HR8 2PD* Tel (01531) 670687

PRICE, Canon Philip. b 24. Tyndale Hall Bris 50. **d** 55 **p** 56. Kenya 55-75; R Gt Horkesley *Chelmsf* 75-89; rtd 89; Perm to Offic *Chelmsf* from 89; Hon Can Kitale from 02. *229 Meadgate Avenue, Great Baddow, Chelmsford CM2 7NJ* Tel (01245) 251499 E-mail rev.pip@talktalk.net

PRICE, Raymond Francklin. b 30. Wycliffe Hall Ox 61. **d** 62 **p** 63. C Bilston St Leon *Lich* 62-67; C Keighley *Bradf* 67-70; V Mangotsfield *Bris* 70-79; Ind Chapl *Birm* 79-86; C Birm St Martin 84-85, C Birm St Martin w Bordesley St Andr 85-86; V Edgbaston St Aug 86-99; rtd 99; Perm to Offic *Birm* from 00. *35 Middle Park Road, Selly Oak, Birmingham B29 4BH* Tel 0121-475 4458

PRICE, Roderick. See PRICE, Joseph Roderick

PRICE, Roland Kendrick. b 41. Cam Univ MA64 Essex Univ PhD69. SAOMC 92. **d** 95 **p** 96. NSM Cholsey *Ox* 95-97; Asst Chapl The Hague *Eur* from 99. *Bentinckstraat 129, 2582 ST Den Haag, The Netherlands* Tel (0031) (15) 215 1871 *or* (70) 355 5359 Fax (70) 354 1023 E-mail rolandprice@orange.nl

PRICE, Stanley George. b 32. FRICS69. Trin Coll Bris 84. **d** 85 **p** 86. C Newport w Longford and Chetwynd *Lich* 85-88; V Ipstones w Berkhamsytch and Onecote w Bradnop 88-97; rtd 98; Perm to Offic *B & W* 98-03; P-in-c Rodney Stoke w Draycott 03-08. *St Aidan, Rectory Way, Lympsham, Weston-super-Mare BS24 0EN* Tel (01934) 750323 E-mail rev.price@tiscali.co.uk

PRICE, Steven Albert. b 68. Brunel Univ BSc90 CEng95. Oak Hill Th Coll BTh06. **d** 06 **p** 07. C New Borough and Leigh *Sarum* 06-09; C Loose *Cant* from 09. *The Vicarage, 17 Linton Road, Loose, Maidstone ME15 0AG* Tel (01622) 743513 E-mail steveandhelenprice@yahoo.co.uk

PRICE, Timothy Fry. b 51. CQSW. St Jo Coll Nottm 85. **d** 87 **p** 88. C Church Stretton *Heref* 87-91; V Sinfin *Derby* 91-00; Regional Adv (SW) CMJ 00-03; Nat Field Co-ord 03-05; Perm to Offic *B & W*, *Bris* and *Glouc* 01-05; V Chaffcombe, Cricket Malherbie etc *B & W* from 06. *The Vicarage, 3 Home Farm, Tatworth, Chard TA20 2SH* Tel (01460) 220237 *or* tel and fax 220404 E-mail pricetf@aol.com

PRICE, Victor John. b 35. Oak Hill Th Coll 62. **d** 65 **p** 66. C Rainham *Chelmsf* 65-70; V Dover St Martin *Cant* 70-78; V

Madeley *Heref* 78-90; P-in-c Derby St Pet and Ch Ch w H Trin 90-91; V 91-96; P-in-c Morley w Morley 96-00; rtd 00; Perm to Offic *S'well* from 03. *4 Holmefield, Farndon, Newark NG24 3TZ* Tel (01636) 611788

PRICE, William. *See* PRICE, Canon David Trevor William

PRICE, William Norman. b 52. GRNCM73. NOC 86. d 89 p 90. C Lower Broughton Ascension *Man* 89-91; Min Can and Succ St E Cathl 92-96; Prec 94-96; V Par *Truro* 96-00; V Musbury *Blackb* 00-06; rtd 06; Perm to Offic *Man* from 06. *5 Lower Drake Fold, Westhoughton, Bolton BL5 2RE* Tel 07071-299999 E-mail golfsierra999@rcsb.co.uk

PRICE-ROBERTS, Mervyn. b 29. Trin Coll Carmarthen TCert51 Univ of Wales BEd79. Ban Ord Course 84. d 87 p 88. NSM Bangor 87-89; V Llandygai w Tregarth 89-97; rtd 97; Perm to Offic *Ban* from 97. *17 Parc Hen Blas Estate, Llanfairfechan LL33 0RW* Tel (01248) 680305

PRICHARD, Canon Thomas John. b 16. Univ of Wales (Ban) BA38 MA72 Keele Univ PhD81 FRHistS82. Chich Th Coll 38. d 39 p 40. C Blaenau Ffestiniog *Ban* 39-41; C Machynlleth *Ban* 41-42; C Llanfabon 42-44; C Ystradyfodwg 44-50; V Dinas w Penygraig 50-69; RD Rhondda 64-69; Can Llan Cathl 66-84; R Neath w Llantwit 69-84; Dioc Archivist 70-84; rtd 84; Perm to Offic *Ban* from 97. *Tros yr Afon, Llangwnnadl, Pwllheli LL53 8NS* Tel (01758) 770393

PRIDAY, Gerald Nelson. b 35. Glouc Th Course. d 85 p 88. NSM Eardisland *Heref* 85-91; NSM Aymestrey and Leinthall Earles w Wigmore etc 85-91; NSM Kingsland 85-91; NSM Eye, Croft w Yarpole and Lucton 91-94; NSM Heref All SS 94-96; NSM Letton w Staunton, Byford, Mansel Gamage etc 96-98; rtd 98; Perm to Offic *Heref* from 99. *4 Lime Close, Ludlow SY8 2PP* Tel (01584) 876910

PRIDDIN, Mrs Maureen Anne. b 46. Leeds Univ BA67 Nottm Univ DipEd68. EMMTC 82. dss 85 d 87 p 94. Mickleover St Jo *Derby* 85-87; Hon Par Dn 87-94; Hon C 94-06; P-in-c from 06; Hon C Mickleover All SS from 06; Dioc World Development Officer 87-90. *7 Portland Close, Mickleover, Derby DE3 9BZ* Tel (01332) 513672 E-mail mpriddin@ntlworld.com

✠**PRIDDIS, The Rt Revd Anthony Martin.** b 48. CCC Cam BA69 MA73 New Coll Ox MA75. Cuddesdon Coll 69. d 72 p 73 c 96. C New Addington *Cant* 72-75; Chapl Ch Ch Ox 75-80; TV High Wycombe *Ox* 80-86; P-in-c Amersham 86-90; R 90-96; RD Amersham 92-96; Hon Can Ch Ch 95-96; Suff Bp Warw *Cov* 96-04; Hon Can Cov Cathl 96-04; Bp Heref from 04. *The Bishop's House, The Palace, Hereford HR4 9BN* Tel (01432) 271355 Fax 373346 E-mail bishop@hereford.anglican.org

PRIDEAUX, Humphrey Grevile. b 36. CCC Ox BA59 MA63 Birm Univ CertEd66 Lon Univ DipEd73 Open Univ BA87. Linc Th Coll 59. d 61 p 62. C Northampton St Matt *Pet* 61-62; C Milton *Portsm* 62-65; Perm to Offic *Birm* 65-66; Hd of RE Qu Mary's Gr Sch Walsall 66-69; Lect St Martin's Coll Lanc 69-80; Perm to Offic *Portsm* 80-86; Hon C Fareham H Trin 86-87; Hon C Bishop's Waltham 87-94; NSM Fawley w W Meon and Warnford 94-03. *6 Rectory Close, Alverstoke, Gosport PO12 2HT* Tel (023) 9250 1794

PRIDGEON, Paul Garth Walsingham. b 45. Sussex Univ BA69 CertEd. Glouc Sch of Min 87. d 87 p 88. NSM Cirencester *Glouc* 87-97; NSM Northleach w Hampnett and Farmington etc 97-03; Perm to Offic from 03. *4 Abbey Way, Cirencester GL7 2DT* Tel (01285) 656860

PRIDIE, William Raleigh. b 49. Bris Univ BEd72 ACP82 FCollP83. SWMTC 90. d 93 p 94. C Kingstone w Clehonger, Eaton Bishop etc *Heref* 93-96; P-in-c Kimbolton w Hamnish and Middleton-on-the-Hill 96-97; P-in-c Bockleton w Leysters 96-97; CME Officer 96-00; TV Leominster 99-00; R Fownhope w Mordiford, Brockhampton etc from 00. *The Rectory, Fownhope, Hereford HR1 4PS* Tel (01432) 860365

PRIDMORE, John Stuart. b 36. Nottm Univ BA62 MA67 Lon Inst of Educn PhD00. Ridley Hall Cam 62. d 65 p 66. C Camborne *Truro* 65-67; Tutor Ridley Hall Cam 67-68; Chapl 68-71; Asst Chapl K Edw Sch Witley 71-75; Chapl 75-86; Tanzania 86-88; Angl Chapl Hengrave Hall Cen 88-89; C St Martin-in-the-Fields *Lon* 89-95; TR Hackney 95-03; R St John-at-Hackney 03-06; rtd 06. *Flat 2, 3 Palmeira Square, Hove BN3 2JA* Tel (01273) 720654 E-mail john.pridmore@btinternet.com

PRIEST (*formerly* MACE), Mrs Helen Elizabeth. b 31. Ox Univ MA52 Solicitor 56. Coll of Ascension 62. dss 74 d 87 p 94. Tadcaster *York* 77-84; Asst Chapl Leeds Gen Infirmary 84-94; C Woodhouse and Wrangthorn *Ripon* 94-96; Perm to Offic from 96. *25 Grosvenor Park Gardens, Leeds LS6 2PL* E-mail hppriest@cstone.net

PRIEST, Richard Mark. b 63. Oak Hill Th Coll BA90. d 90 p 91. C Okehampton w Inwardleigh *Ex* 90-94; C Okehampton w Inwardleigh, Bratton Clovelly etc 94; CF from 94. *c/o MOD Chaplains (Army)* Tel (01980) 615804 Fax 615800

PRIESTLEY, Canon Alan Charles. b 41. Lon Univ BD69. Kelham Th Coll 64 Wm Temple Coll Rugby 65. d 65 p 66. C Edgbaston St Aug *Birm* 65-68; C Chelmsley Wood 68-72; TV 72-76; V Hazelwell from 76; Dioc Communications Officer

83-94; Bp's Press Officer from 85; Hon Can Birm Cathl from 87. *The Vicarage, 316 Vicarage Road, Birmingham B14 7NH* Tel 0121-444 4469 Fax 444 8184 Mobile 07720-936729 E-mail apriestley@waitrose.com

PRIESTLEY, Richard Allan. b 63. Ridley Hall Cam 07. d 09. C Broughton w Loddington and Cransley etc *Pet* from 09. *The Maples, 15 Loddington Way, Mawsley, Kettering NN14 1GE* Tel (01536) 790140 Mobile 07725-190782 E-mail rpriestley@mac.com

PRIESTLEY, Rosemary Jane. *See* LAIN-PRIESTLEY, Ms Rosemary Jane

PRIESTNER, Hugh. b 45. Nottm Univ BTh75. Linc Th Coll 71. d 75 p 76. C Seaton Hirst *Newc* 75-78; C Longbenton St Bart 78-81; P-in-c Glendale Gp 81-82; TV 83-88; Chapl Stafford Acute Hosps 88-89; Tr Co-ord W Cumberland Hosp 89-92; Chapl Fair Havens Hospice 94-98; Chapl Walsgrave Hosps NHS Trust 98-00; Chapl Team Ldr Univ Hosps Cov and Warks NHS Trust from 00. *Walsgrave General Hospital, Clifford Bridge Road, Coventry CV2 2DX* Tel (024) 7696 7515 E-mail hugh.priestner@uhcw.nhs.uk

PRIGG, Patrick John. b 53. K Coll Lon BD82. Sarum & Wells Th Coll 89. d 92 p 93. C Wavertree St Mary *Liv* 92-96; Chapl Sandown Coll 92-96; P-in-c Glemsford, Hartest w Boxted, Somerton etc *St E* 96-99; R from 99. *The Rectory, 6 Lion Road, Glemsford, Sudbury CO10 7RF* Tel (01787) 282164 E-mail revpat@glem-valley.org.uk

PRIME, Geoffrey Daniel. b 12. Lich Th Coll 32. d 35 p 36. C Uttoxeter w Bramshall *Lich* 35-42; P-in-c Newborough w Ch Ch on Needwood 42-43; V Pattingham 43-55; V Longstone *Derby* 55-62; Org Sec CECS *Derby, Linc, Sheff* and *S'well* 62-65; Perm to Offic *Derby* 62-00; rtd 77. *Westside Mill Farm, Hulme End, Buxton SK17 0EY* Tel (01298) 84461

PRIMROSE, David Edward Snodgrass. b 55. St Jo Coll Cam MA80. Trin Coll Bris BA92. d 87 p 92. Pakistan 87-89; C Glouc St Paul 92-96; R Badgeworth, Shurdington and Witcombe w Bentham 96-03; V Thornbury and Oldbury-on-Severn w Shepperdine from 03; AD Hawkesbury 04-09. *The Vicarage, 27 Castle Street, Thornbury, Bristol BS35 1HQ* Tel (01454) 413209 or 281900 E-mail primrose@blueyonder.co.uk

PRINCE, Alastair. b 76. Nottm Univ BSc99 SS Coll Cam BTh06. Westcott Ho Cam 03. d 06 p 07. C Toxteth Park Ch Ch and St Mich w St Andr *Liv* from 06. *Flat 4, 5 Linnet Lane, Liverpool L17 3BE* Tel 0151-222 7243 Mobile 07732-489424 E-mail alastairprince@hotmail.com

PRINCE (*née* RUMBLE), Mrs Alison Merle. b 49. Surrey Univ BSc71. Trin Coll Bris BA89. d 89 p 94. Par Dn Willesden Green St Gabr *Lon* 89-91; Par Dn Cricklewood St Gabr and St Mich 92; Par Dn Herne Hill *S'wark* 92-94; C 94-95; Chapl Greenwich Healthcare NHS Trust 95-96; TV Sanderstead All SS *S'wark* 97-03; TV Kegworth, Hathern, Long Whatton, Diseworth etc *Leic* from 04. *The Rectory, Presents Lane, Belton, Loughborough LE12 9UN* Tel (01530) 223447

PRINCE (*née* GRIFFITHS), Caroline Heidi Ann. b 66. Ex Univ BA88. Linc Th Coll 90. d 90 p 97. C Newport St Woolos and Chapl St Woolos Cathl 90-94; C Abergavenny Deanery 94-96; TV Cwmbran 96-97; V Llantilio Crossenny w Penrhos, Llanvetherine etc 97-06. *24 Cae Porth, Llangynidr, Crickhowell NP8 1NL*

PRINCE, Helena. b 23. Lightfoot Ho Dur 59. dss 66 d 87 p 94. W Derby St Mary *Liv* 65-85; rtd 85; Perm to Offic *Liv* 85-04. *5 Dominic Close, Liverpool L16 1JZ* Tel 0151-722 0263

PRINCE, Mrs Melanie Amanda. b 71. St D Coll Lamp BA92 Univ of Wales (Cardiff) MPhil93. St Mich Coll Llan 96. d 98 p 99. C Aberavon *Llan* 98-01; C Gabalfa 01-08; TV Llantwit Major from 08. *The Rectory, 1 Rectory Drive, St Athan, Barry CF62 4PD* Tel (01446) 751241

PRINCE, Penelope Ann. b 46. SWMTC 96. d 99 p 00. NSM Halsetown *Truro* 99-02; P-in-c Breage w Godolphin and Germoe from 02. *The Vicarage, Breage, Helston TR13 9PN* Tel (01326) 573449 Mobile 07929-152234

PRING, Althon Kerrigan (Kerry). b 34. AKC58. d 59 p 60. C Limehouse St Anne *Lon* 59-61; C Lt Stanmore St Lawr 61-64; C Langley Marish *Ox* 64-68; P-in-c Radnage 68-72; P-in-c Ravenstone w Weston Underwood 72-75; P-in-c Stoke Goldington w Gayhurst 72-75; R Gayhurst w Ravenstone, Stoke Goldington etc 75-85; P-in-c 85-86; RD Newport 78-80; TV Woughton 86-90; P-in-c Nash w Thornton, Beachampton and Thornborough 90-94; R 94-96; rtd 96; Perm to Offic *Ox* 99-07. *Kingsmead, 9 Malting Close, Stoke Goldington, Newport Pagnell MK16 8NX* Tel (01908) 551345

PRINGLE, The Ven Cecil Thomas. b 43. TCD BA65. CITC 66. d 66 p 67. C Belfast St Donard *D & D* 66-69; I Cleenish *Clogh* 69-80; I Mullaghdun 78-80; I Rossorry 80-08; P-in-c Drumkeeran w Templecarne and Muckross from 08; Preb Clogh Cathl 86-89; Adn Clogh from 89. *31 Station Road, Letterbreen, Enniskillen BT74 9FD* Tel 07742-516188 (mobile)

PRINGLE, Graeme Lindsley. b 59. St Cath Coll Cam BA81 MA85. St Jo Coll Nottm 92. d 94 p 95. C Binley *Cov* 94-99; V Allesley Park and Whoberley from 99. *St Christopher's Vicarage,*

99 Buckingham Rise, Coventry CV5 9HF Tel (024) 7667 2879
E-mail graeme@stchristopher.org.uk

PRINGLE, Miss Janyce Mary. b 32. ARCM53 LRAM54 Ex Univ DipAdEd70 MPhil85. SW Minl Tr Course 83. **dss** 86 **d** 87 **p** 94. NSM Torquay St Matthias, St Mark and H Trin *Ex* 86-98; Chapl Asst Torbay Hosp Torquay 86-89; Perm to Offic *Ex* from 98. *Pendower, Wheatridge Lane, Torquay TQ2 6RA* Tel (01803) 607136

PRINGLE, Margaret Brenda. b 49. CITC. **d** 05 **p** 06. NSM Clogh w Errigal Portclare from 05. *Rawdeer Park, Clones, Co Monaghan, Republic of Ireland* Tel (00353) (47) 51439
E-mail margaretpringle@eircom.net

PRINGLE, Richard John. b 55. Lon Univ AKC76 CertEd77 Open Univ BA84. Chich Th Coll 78. **d** 78 **p** 79. C Northampton St Matt *Pet* 78-81; C Delaval *Newc* 81-84; V Newsham from 84; RD Bedlington 93-98. *St Bede's Vicarage, Newcastle Road, Newsham, Blyth NE24 4AS* Tel and fax (01670) 352391

PRINS, Canon Stanley Vernon. b 30. TD76. Dur Univ BSc54 MA69. Ripon Hall Ox 56. **d** 58 **p** 59. C Benwell St Jas *Newc* 58-61; Asst Chapl Newc Univ 61-65; CF (TA) from 64; C-in-c Whorlton H Nativity Chpl Ho Estate *Newc* 65-72; TV Whorlton 73-76; V Humshaugh 76-83; P-in-c Simonburn 82-83; P-in-c Wark 82-83; RD Bellingham 83-93; R Humshaugh w Simonburn and Wark 83-96; Hon Can Newc Cathl 88-96; rtd 96; Perm to Offic *Newc* from 96. *Woodside Cottage, Scrogwood, Bardon Mill, Hexham NE47 7AA* Tel (01434) 344876

PRIOR, Adam Phillip. b 72. **d** 08. NSM Watford St Pet *St Alb* from 08. *Soul Survivor, 5 Greycaine Road, Watford WD24 7GP* Tel (01923) 337000

PRIOR, David Clement Lyndon. b 40. Trin Coll Ox BA63 MA66. Ridley Hall Cam 65. **d** 67 **p** 68. C Reigate St Mary *S'wark* 67-72; C Kenilworth Ch Ch S Africa 72-76; R Wynberg 76-79; Can Cape Town 76-79; C Ox St Aldate w H Trin 79-82; C Ox St Aldate w St Matt 82-84; USA 84-85; V Ches Square St Mich w St Phil *Lon* 85-95; P-in-c Mayfair Ch Ch 85-95; Public Preacher 95-97; P-in-c St Botolph without Aldersgate 97-00; rtd 05; Perm to Offic *Chich* from 05. *2 North Lane, Wiston, Steyning BN44 3DQ* Tel (01903) 893566
E-mail dclraprior@hotmail.com

PRIOR (née CHIUMBU), Esther Tamisa. b 73. Univ of Zimbabwe BSc95. Trin Coll Bris BA02 MA07. **d** 03 **p** 04. NSM Redland *Bris* 03-05; C Deptford St Jo w H Trin and Ascension *S'wark* 05-08; Chapl Blackheath Bluecoat C of E Sch from 08. *The Vicarage, 76 Borstal Street, Rochester ME1 3HL* Tel (01634) 845948 E-mail esthertj@yahoo.com

PRIOR, Gregory Stephen. b 68. Geo Whitfield Coll S Africa BTh90. **d** 95 **p** 96. In C of E in S Africa 95-01; Min for Miss Muswell Hill St Jas w St Matt *Lon* 01-04; P-in-c Wandsworth All SS *S'wark* 04-06; V from 06. *Wandsworth Vicarage, 11 Rusholme Road, London SW15 3JX* Tel (020) 8788 7400
E-mail greg@wandsworthparish.co.uk

PRIOR, Canon Ian Graham. b 44. Lon Univ BSc(Econ)71. Oak Hill Th Coll 78. **d** 80 **p** 81. C Luton Ch Ch *Roch* 80-83; TV Southgate *Chich* 83-93; V Burgess Hill St Andr 93-09; RD Hurst 98-04; Can and Preb Chich Cathl 03-09; rtd 09. *5 Chestnut Walk, Worthing BN13 3QL* Tel (01903) 830127
E-mail ian@priorjane.wanadoo.co.uk

PRIOR, Ian Roger Lyndon. b 46. St Jo Coll Dur BA68. Lon Coll of Div 68. **d** 70 **p** 71. C S Croydon Em *Cant* 70-73; Perm to Offic *S'wark* 73-85; Dir Overseas Personnel TEAR Fund 73-79; Dep Dir 79-83; Fin and Admin Dir CARE Trust and CARE Campaigns 85-92; NSM New Malden and Coombe *S'wark* from 85; Dir Caredrose from 92. *39 Cambridge Avenue, New Malden KT3 4LD* Tel (020) 8949 0912 *or* 8942 3331

PRIOR, James Murray. b 39. Edin Univ BCom64. St And Dioc Tr Course 85. **d** 90 **p** 91. NSM Kirriemuir *St And* 90-02; NSM Forfar 90-02; NSM Dundee St Jo *Bre* from 02; NSM Dundee St Ninian from 02. *Naughton Lodge, Balmerino, Newport-on-Tay DD6 8RN* Tel (01382) 330132 E-mail ham.prior@tiscali.co.uk

PRIOR, John Gilman Leathes. b 15. Qu Coll Cam BA37 MA41. Ridley Hall Cam 37. **d** 39 **p** 40. C Ipswich St Marg *St E* 39-41; CF 41-46; V Springfield H Trin *Chelmsf* 46-49; V Guildf Ch Ch 49-63; V Camberley St Paul 63-74; V Crondall 75-77; V Crondall and Ewshot 77-80; rtd 80; Perm to Offic *Win* from 80; *Guildf* 82-96; *Portsm* from 84. *Bungalow 116, Clare Park, Farnham GU10 5DT* Tel (01252) 855088

PRIOR, Preb John Miskin. b 27. Lon Univ BSc(Econ)48. Westcott Ho Cam 49. **d** 51 **p** 52. C Bedminster St Fran *Bris* 51-55; C Sherston Magna w Easton Grey 55-57; C Yatton Keynell 57-61; C Castle Combe 57-61; C Biddestone w Slaughterford 57-61; V Bishopstone w Hinton Parva 61-66; V Marshfield w Cold Ashton 66-82; P-in-c Tormarton w W Littleton 68 82; RD Bitton 73-79; P Trull w Angersleigh *B & W* 82 91; RD Taunton 84-90; Preb Wells Cathl 90-91; Chapl Huggens Coll Northfleet 91-97; rtd 92; Hon PV Roch Cathl from 98; Perm to Offic from 99. *21 St Catherines Court, Star Hill, Rochester ME1 1GA* Tel (01634) 403499

PRIOR, Jonathan Roger Lyndon. b 74. Trin Coll Ox BA95 MA99 K Coll Lon PGCE96. Wycliffe Hall Ox 07. **d** 09. C Elworth and

Warmingham *Ches* from 09. *80 Abbey Road, Elworth, Sandbach CW11 3AB* Tel (01270) 762555 E-mail j.prior@yahoo.co.uk

PRIOR, Canon Kenneth Francis William. b 26. St Jo Coll Dur BA49. Oak Hill Th Coll 46. **d** 49 **p** 50. C S Mimms Ch Ch *Lon* 49-52; C Eastbourne H Trin *Chich* 52-53; V Onslow Square St Paul *Lon* 53-65; V Hove Bp Hannington Memorial Ch *Chich* 65-70; R Sevenoaks St Nic *Roch* 70-87; Hon Can Roch Cathl 82-87; C-in-c Hampstead St Jo Downshire Hill Prop Chpl *Lon* 87-90; rtd 89; Perm to Offic *Ex* from 01. *22 Barnfield Road, Torquay TQ2 6TN* Tel (01803) 606760

PRIOR, Canon Kenneth George William. b 17. Bris Univ BA39. Bible Churchmen's Coll Bris 35. **d** 40 **p** 41. C Toxteth Park St Clem *Liv* 40-43; C Edge Hill St Cypr 43-45; C Garston 45-48; V Plymouth St Jude *Ex* 48-55; V Longfleet *Sarum* 55-82; Chapl Poole Gen Hosp 55-76; RD Poole *Sarum* 75-80; Can and Preb Sarum Cathl 77-82; rtd 82; Perm to Offic *Sarum* 82-00. *22 Ramsay Hall, 11-13 Byron Road, Worthing BN11 3HN* Tel (01903) 214880 E-mail kgwprior@aol.com

PRIOR, Matthew Thomas. b 74. Rob Coll Cam BA97 MA00. Trin Coll Bris BA04 MA05. **d** 05 **p** 06. C Deptford St Jo w H Trin and Ascension *S'wark* 05-08; P-in-c Borstal *Roch* from 08. *The Vicarage, 76 Borstal Street, Rochester ME1 3HL* Tel (01634) 845948 E-mail prior@esthermatt.freeserve.co.uk

PRIOR, Nigel John. b 56. Bris Univ BA78. Westcott Ho Cam 79. **d** 81 **p** 82. C Langley All SS and Martyrs *Man* 81-82; C Langley and Parkfield 82-84; C Bury St Jo w St Mark 84-87; R Man Clayton St Cross w St Paul 87-99; P-in-c Mark Cross *Chich* 99-00; V Mayfield from 99. *The Vicarage, High Street, Mayfield TN20 6AB* Tel (01435) 873180

PRIOR, Stephen Kenneth. b 55. Rhode Is Coll (USA) BA78. Wycliffe Hall Ox 79. **d** 82 **p** 83. C Aberavon *Llan* 82-85; P-in-c New Radnor and Llanfihangel Nantmelan etc *S & B* 85-86; R 86-90; V Llansamlet 90-94; P-in-c Chester le Street *Dur* 94-96; R 96-01; R Caldbeck, Castle Sowerby and Sebergham *Carl* 01-09; Dir of Ords 04-08; R Rushden St Mary w Newton Bromswold *Pet* from 09. *The Rectory, Rectory Road, Rushden NN10 0HA* Tel (01933) 312554 E-mail sprior@toucansurf.com

PRIORY, Barry Edwin. b 44. FCIS Open Univ BA81. Qu Coll Birm 84. **d** 86 **p** 87. C Boldmere *Birm* 86-89; C Somerton w Compton Dundon, the Charltons etc *B & W* 89-93; R Porlock and Porlock Weir w Stoke Pero etc 93-08; RD Exmoor 97-03; rtd 08. *Dove Cottage, Moor Road, Minehead TA24 5RX* Tel (01643) 706808 E-mail barry.priory@virgin.net

PRISTON, David Leslie. b 28. Lon Bible Coll 49 Oak Hill Th Coll 66. **d** 66 **p** 67. C Heref St Pet w St Owen 66-71; R Beeby *Leic* 72-88; R Gaddesby w S Croxton 72-88; R S Croxton Gp 88-93; rtd 93; Perm to Offic *S'well* 93-08. *14 Gracey Court, Woodland Road, Broadclyst, Exeter EX5 3GA*

PRITCHARD, Andrew James Dunn. b 57. Van Mildert Coll Dur BSc79 Ch Ch Ox PGCE80. Wycliffe Hall Ox 07. **d** 09. C Cogges and S Leigh *Ox* from 09. *7 Barleyfield Way, Witney OX28 1AA* Tel 07944-522098 (mobile) E-mail andrewjdp@yahoo.co.uk

PRITCHARD, Antony Robin. b 53. Van Mildert Coll Dur BSc74 SS Paul & Mary Coll Cheltenham CertEd75. St Jo Coll Nottm. **d** 84 **p** 85. C Desborough *Pet* 84-87; C Rushden w Newton Bromswold 87-91; R Oulton St Mich *Nor* from 91. *The Rectory, Christmas Lane, Oulton, Lowestoft NR32 3JX* Tel (01502) 565722 E-mail robinpritchard925@btinternet.com

PRITCHARD, Brian James. Open Univ BA05 ACIS85. SAOMC 99. **d** 01 **p** 02. NSM Newbury *Ox* 01 06; V Billingshurst *Chich* from 06; Perm to Offic *St D* from 05. *The Vicarage, East Street, Billingshurst RH14 9PY* Tel (01403) 785303 *or* 782332
E-mail vicar.billingshurst@gmail.com

PRITCHARD, Brian James Pallister. b 27. CCC Cam BA51 MA66. Westcott Ho Cam 51. **d** 53 **p** 54. C Attercliffe w Carbrook Sheff 53-58; V New Bentley 58-60; Chapl Park Hill Flats Sheff 60-67; P-in-c Sheff St Swithun 67-72; V Welton *Linc* 72-92; RD Lawres 86-92; rtd 92; Perm to Offic *Derby* from 92. *Bridgeways, Milford Lane, Bakewell DE45 1DX* Tel (01629) 813553

PRITCHARD, Mrs Carol Sandra. b 52. St Aid Coll Dur BA74 Bris Univ PGCE75. EAMTC 96. **d** 99 **p** 00. NSM Oulton St Mich *Nor* from 99. *The Rectory, Christmas Lane, Oulton, Lowestoft NR32 3JX* Tel (01502) 565722
E-mail carolpritchard3@btinternet.com

PRITCHARD, Colin Wentworth. b 38. K Coll Lon 59 St Boniface Warminster 59. **d** 63 **p** 64. C Putney St Marg *S'wark* 63-67; C Brixton St Matt 67-70; C Milton *Portsm* 70-74; V Mitcham St Mark *S'wark* 74-82; R Long Ditton 82-94; V Earlsfield St Andr 94-03; RD Wandsworth 98-03; rtd 03. *38 Hartfield Road, Seaford BN25 4PW* Tel (01323) 894899
E-mail colin@loavesandfishes.f2s.com

PRITCHARD, Mrs Coral. b 37. F L Calder Coll Liv TCert58 Lanc Univ BA97. CBDTI 99. **d** 02 **p** 03. OLM Stalmine w Pilling *Blackb* 02-07; NSM from 07. *Heyswood House, Head Dyke Lane, Pilling, Preston PR3 6SJ* Tel (01253) 790335
E-mail pritchard@heyswood.freeserve.co.uk

PRITCHARD, Canon David Paul. b 47. Newc Univ BA68 Em Coll Cam PGCE69 LTCL70 FRCO72. Wycliffe Hall Ox 80. **d** 82

p 83. C Kidlington *Ox* 82-84; P-in-c Marcham w Garford 84-85; V 86-96; RD Abingdon 91-96; R Henley w Remenham 96-04; Can Res Ely Cathl from 04; Vice Dean and Pastor from 08. *The Black Hostelry, The College, Ely CB7 4DL* Tel (01353) 660302 E-mail david.pritchard@cathedral.ely.anglican.org

PRITCHARD, Donald Oliver. b 22. Qu Coll Birm 73. **d** 75 **p** 76. Hon C Dunchurch *Cov* 75-83; P-in-c Mells w Buckland Dinham, Elm, Whatley etc *B & W* 83-84; R 84-88; rtd 88; Perm to Offic *Truro* from 88. *Moonrakers, Pengelly, Callington PL17 7DZ* Tel (01579) 84329

PRITCHARD, John Anthony. b 74. Ripon Coll Cuddesdon BTh07. **d** 07 **p** 08. C Gt Berkhamsted, Gt and Lt Gaddesden etc *St Alb* from 07. *6 Severns Close, Berkhamsted HP4 2FY* Tel (01442) 870016 E-mail johnapritchard@hotmail.co.uk

✠**PRITCHARD, The Rt Revd John Lawrence.** b 48. St Pet Coll Ox MA73 Dur Univ MLitt93. Ridley Hall Cam 70. **d** 72 **p** 73 **c** 02. C Birm St Martin 72-76; Asst Dir RE *B & W* 76-80; Youth Chapl 76-80; P-in-c Wilton 80-88; Dir Past Studies Cranmer Hall Dur 89-93; Warden 93-96; Adn Cant and Can Res Cant Cathl 96-02; Suff Bp Jarrow *Dur* 02-07; Bp Ox from 07. *Bishop's House, 27 Linton Road, Oxford OX2 6UL* Tel (01865) 208222 E-mail bishopoxon@oxford.anglican.org

PRITCHARD, Jonathan Llewelyn. b 64. Edin Univ MA87 Leeds Univ MA89 PhD99. Ripon Coll Cuddesdon 98. **d** 00 **p** 01. C Skipton H Trin *Bradf* 00-04; P-in-c Keighley All SS from 04; P-in-c Thwaites Brow from 06. *All Saints' Vicarage, 21 View Road, Keighley BD20 6JN* Tel (01535) 665312 E-mail jonathan.pritchard@bradford.anglican.org

PRITCHARD, Miss Kathryn Anne. b 60. St Cath Coll Ox MA. St Jo Coll Dur. **d** 87. Par Dn Addiscombe St Mary *S'wark* 87-90; CPAS Staff 90-92; Perm to Offic *Cov* 92-95; Producer Worship Progr BBC Relig Broadcasting 94-99; Publicity Manager Hodder & Stoughton Relig Books 99-01; Commissioning and Product Development Manager Ch Ho Publishing from 01. *Church House, Great Smith Street, London SW1P 3AZ* Tel (020) 7898 1485 E-mail kathryn.pritchard@c-of-e.org.uk

PRITCHARD, Kenneth John. b 30. Liv Univ BEng51. NW Ord Course 72. **d** 74 **p** 75. C Ches 74-78; Miss to Seamen 78-84; V Runcorn St Jo Weston *Ches* 78-84; V Gt Meols 84-98; rtd 98; Perm to Offic *Ches* and *Liv* from 99. *13 Fieldlands, Scarisbrick, Southport PR8 5HQ* Tel (01704) 514600 E-mail kjp@talk21.com

PRITCHARD, Malcolm John. b 55. Bradf Univ BA85 CQSW85. St Jo Coll Nottm 86. **d** 88 **p** 89. C Peckham St Mary Magd *S'wark* 88-93; V Luton St Matt High Town *St Alb* from 93. *St Matthew's Vicarage, 85 Wenlock Street, Luton LU2 0NN* Tel (01582) 732320 E-mail b4mjp2c@ntlworld.com

PRITCHARD, Michael Owen. b 49. Trin Coll Carmarthen CertEd71. St Mich Coll Llan 71. **d** 73 **p** 74. C Conwy w Gyffin *Ban* 73-76; TV Dolgellau w Llanfachreth and Brithdir etc 76-78; Dioc Children's Officer 77-86; V Betws y Coed and Capel Curig 78-83; CF (TAVR) from 79; V Betws-y-Coed and Capel Curig w Penmachno etc *Ban* 83-86; Chapl Claybury Hosp Woodford Bridge 86-96; Chapl Team Leader Forest Healthcare NHS Trust Lon 96-01; Chapl Team Leader NE Lon Mental Health Tr from 01. *The Chaplaincy, Whipps Cross Hospital, Whipps Cross Road, London E11 1NR* Tel (020) 8539 5522 ext 5005 *or* 8989 3813 E-mail mopritchard@hotmail.com

PRITCHARD, Mrs Norma Kathleen. b 32. Birm Univ BA53 CertEd54. EMMTC 81. **dss** 84 **d** 87 **p** 94. Derby St Alkmund and St Werburgh 84-90; Par Dn 87-90; Par Dn Derby St Andr w St Osmund 90-94; C 94-96; Assoc Min Alvaston 96-02; rtd 02; Perm to Offic *Derby* and *S'wark* from 02. *44 Evans Avenue, Allestree, Derby DE22 2EN* Tel (01332) 557702

PRITCHARD, Peter Benson. b 30. FPhS60 LCP68 Univ of Wales (Lamp) BA51 Lon Univ PGCE68 DipEd70 Liv Univ MEd74 PhD81. Ripon Hall Ox 55. **d** 58 **p** 59. C Wavertree H Trin *Liv* 58-60; C Sefton 60-61; C-in-c Thornton CD 61-64; Chapl Liv Coll Boys' Sch 64-70; Hon C Wavertree St Bridget 70-89; Lect CF Mott Coll of Educn 70-76; Sen Lect Liv Coll of HE 76-83; Liv Poly 83-87; Perm to Offic *Liv* 90-96 and *Ches* from 90; Chapl St Jo Hospice Wirral from 93; Tutor Open Univ 90-95; rtd 95. *68 Gleggside, West Kirby, Wirral CH48 6EA* Tel 0151-625 8093

PRITCHARD, Peter Humphrey. b 47. Univ of Wales (Ban) BA70 MA98 Liv Univ PGCE73. Qu Coll Birm 85. **d** 87 **p** 88. C Llanbeblig w Caernarfon and Betws Garmon etc *Ban* 87-90; R Llanberis w Llanrug 90-94; R Llanfaethlu w Llanfwrog and Llanrhuddlad etc 94-99; R Llanfair Mathafarn Eithaf w Llanbedrgoch 99-05; rtd 05. *4 Penlon Gardens, Bangor LL57 1AQ*

PRITCHARD, Simon Geraint. b 61. Coll of Ripon & York St Jo BA85 Ex Univ PGCE88. Cranmer Hall Dur 98. **d** 00 **p** 01. C Heysham *Blackb* 00-01; C Morecambe St Barn 01-03; C Standish 03-06; V Haigh and Aspull *Liv* from 06. *The Vicarage, Copperas Lane, Haigh, Wigan WN2 1PA* Tel (01942) 830356

PRITCHARD, Thomas James Benbow. b 47. St Paul's Cheltenham CertEd69 Univ of Wales (Cardiff) BEd79 MSc85 Ex Univ BTh08. SWMTC 96. **d** 99 **p** 00. NSM St Enoder *Truro* 99-01; P-in-c Roche and Withiel 01-05; V Llangollen w Trevor

and Llantysilio *St As* 05-06; P-in-c Mylor w Flushing *Truro* 06-07; rtd 07. *Suncot, Short Cross Road, Mount Hawke, Truro TR4 8DU* Tel (01209) 891766 E-mail thms_pritchard@yahoo.co.uk

PRITCHARD, The Ven Thomas William. b 33. Keele Univ BA55 DipEd55 Univ of Wales (Cardiff) LLM94. St Mich Coll Llan 55. **d** 57 **p** 58. C Holywell *St As* 57-61; C Ruabon 61-63; V 77-87; R Pontfadog 63-71; R Llanferres, Nercwys and Eryrys 71-77; Dioc Archivist 76-98; Can St As Cathl 84-98; RD Llangollen 86-87; Adn Montgomery 87-98; V Berriew and Manafon 87-98; rtd 98. *4 Glynne Way, Hawarden, Deeside CH5 3NL* Tel (01244) 538381

PRITCHETT, Antony Milner. b 63. Kent Univ BA86. Westcott Ho Cam 96. **d** 98 **p** 99. C Broughton Astley and Croft w Stoney Stanton *Leic* 98-02; V Gawber *Wakef* 02-08; Chapl Barnsley Hospice 02-08; P-in-c Pickering w Lockton and Levisham *York* from 08. *The Vicarage, Whitby Road, Pickering YO18 7HL* Tel (01751) 472983 E-mail antonypritchett@btinternet.com

PRITCHETT, Mrs Beryl Ivy. b 48. Worc Coll of Educn TCert69. WMMTC 02. **d** 05 **p** 06. NSM Brockmoor *Worc* 05-07; NSM Brierley Hill from 07. *7 Muirville Close, Wordsley, Stourbridge DY8 5NR* Tel (01384) 271470 Mobile 07790-563479 E-mail beryl.pritchett@btinternet.com

PRIVETT, Peter John. b 48. Qu Coll Birm 75. **d** 78 **p** 79. C Moseley St Agnes *Birm* 78-81; V Kingsbury 81-87; P-in-c Dilwyn and Stretford *Heref* 87-90; Dioc Children's Adv 87-01; TV Leominster 90-98; NSM 98-05; Dioc Millennium Officer 98-01; Perm to Offic 05-07. *38 Oakfield Road, Rugby CV22 6AU* Tel (01788) 570332 E-mail pet.ros@btopenworld.com

PROBART, Raymond. b 21. Sarum Th Coll 49. **d** 51 **p** 52. C Padiham *Blackb* 51-54; C Burnley St Pet 54-56; V Heyhouses 56-60; V Douglas 60-88; rtd 88; Perm to Offic *B & W* 88-98; *Glouc* from 03. *6 Capel Court, The Burgage, Prestbury, Cheltenham GL52 3EL* Tel (01242) 235771

PROBERT, Beverley Stuart. b 42. **d** 01 **p** 02. OLM Canford Magna *Sarum* from 01. *Blaenafon, 102 Knights Road, Bournemouth BH11 9SY* Tel (01202) 571731

PROBERT, Christopher John Dixon. b 54. Univ of Wales (Ban) BTh95 MTh97. St Mich Coll Llan 74. **d** 78 **p** 79. C Aberdare St Fagan *Llan* 78-79; C Cadoxton-juxta-Barry 79-81; R Llanfynydd *St As* 81-84; V Gosberton Clough and Quadring *Linc* 84-86; TV Coventry Caludon 86-88; V Llanrhian w Llanhywel and Llanrheithan *St D* 88-91; V Tregaron w Ystrad Meurig and Strata Florida 91-93; Chapl Tregaron Hosp 91-93; Tutor St D NSM Course 89-93; V Betws-y-Coed and Capel Curig w Penmachno etc *Ban* 93-98; Warden of Readers 96-98; V Lt Drayton *Lich* 98-04; P-in-c North Hill and Lewannick *Truro* from 04; C Lezant w Lawhitton and S Petherwin w Trewen from 04; OCF from 01. *The Rectory, North Hill, Launceston PL15 7PQ* Tel (01566) 786976 Mobile 07718-667177 E-mail christopher.probert@homecall.co.uk

PROBERT, Canon Edward Cleasby. b 58. St Cath Coll Cam BA80 MA84. Ripon Coll Cuddesdon BA84. **d** 85 **p** 86. C Esher *Guildf* 85-89; V Earlsfield St Andr *S'wark* 89-94; V Belmont 94-04; Can Res and Chan Sarum Cathl from 04. *24 The Close, Salisbury SP1 2EH* Tel (01722) 555193 E-mail chancellor@salcath.co.uk

PROBETS, Canon Desmond. b 26. AKC50. **d** 51 **p** 52. C Finsbury St Clem *Lon* 51-52; C Kenton 52-62; Sub Warden St Pet Th Coll Siota Solomon Is 62-64; Hd Master All Hallows Sch Pawa Ugi 64-69; Hon Can Honiara from 67; Dean 69-72; V Timperley *Ches* 72-92; RD Bowdon 77-87; Hon Can Ches Cathl 82-92; rtd 92; Perm to Offic *Wakef* from 92. *24 Shelley Close, Penistone, Sheffield S36 6GT* Tel (01226) 766402

PROCTER, Andrew David. b 52. St Jo Coll Ox BA74 MA BA86. Trin Coll Bris 74. **d** 77 **p** 78. C Barnoldswick w Bracewell *Bradf* 77-80; P-in-c Kelbrook 80-82; V 82-87; V Heaton St Barn 87-93; V Swanley St Paul *Roch* 93-07; R Shipbourne w Plaxtol from 07. *The Rectory, The Street, Plaxtol, Sevenoaks TN15 0QG* Tel (01732) 811081 Mobile 07963-943524 E-mail a.procter@live.co.uk

PROCTER, Nicholas Jonathan. b 59. Liv Univ BVSc84 MRCVS84. LCTP 06. **d** 09. NSM Leyland St Jo *Blackb* from 09. *23 Regents Way, Euxton, Chorley PR7 6PG* Tel (01257) 241927

PROCTER, Robert Hendy. b 31. Trin Hall Cam BA54 MA58. Edin Dioc NSM Course 88. **d** 93 **p** 94. NSM Edin Ch Ch 93-94; TV 94-07. *2 Braid Avenue, Edinburgh EH10 6DR* Tel 0131-447 1140 E-mail hendy@procters.plus.com

PROCTOR, Kenneth Noel. b 33. St Aid Birkenhead 61. **d** 63 **p** 64. C Oldham St Paul *Man* 63-66; C Davyhulme St Mary 66-69; V Norden w Ashworth 69-00; rtd 00. *4 Bankscroft, Hopwood, Heywood OL10 2NG* Tel (01706) 364197

PROCTOR, Michael John. b 59. Cranmer Hall Dur 93. **d** 93 **p** 94. C Leatherhead *Guildf* 93-98; V Henlow and Langford *St Alb* 98-01; V Marton-in-Cleveland *York* from 01; Min Coulby Newham LEP from 03. *The Vicarage, Stokesley Road, Marton-in-Cleveland, Middlesbrough TS7 8JU* Tel (01642) 326305 E-mail mlm.proctor@virgin.net

PROCTOR, Canon Michael Thomas. b 41. Ch Ch Ox BA65 MA67. Westcott Ho Cam 63. **d** 65 **p** 66. C Monkseaton St Mary *Newc* 65-69; Pakistan 69-72; C Willington *Newc* 72-77; TV Willington 77-79; Ed Sec Nat Soc 79-84; P-in-c Roxwell *Chelmsf* 79-84; Bp's Ecum Officer 85-00; Dir of Miss and Unity 85-94; P-in-c Gt Waltham w Ford End 94-00; Hon Can Chelmsf Cathl 85-00; rtd 00; Dir Chelmsf Counselling Foundn from 00. *Claremont, South Street, Great Waltham, Chelmsford CM3 1DP* E-mail mtproctor@lineone.net

PROCTOR, Nicholas Jonathan. See PROCTER, Nicholas Jonathan

PROCTOR, Canon Noel. b 30. MBE93. St Aid Birkenhead 62. **d** 64 **p** 65. C Haughton le Skerne *Dur* 64-67; R Byers Green 67-70; Chapl HM Pris Eastchurch 70-74; Dartmoor 74-79; Man 79-95; Hon Can Man Cathl 91-95; rtd 95; Perm to Offic *Man* from 95. *222 Moor Lane, Salford M7 3PZ* Tel 0161-792 1284

PROCTOR, Canon Susan Katherine. b 44. **d** 89 **p** 94. Par Dn Beighton *Sheff* 89-91; Par Dn Aston cum Aughton and Ulley 91-93; Par Dn Aston cum Aughton w Swallownest, Todwick etc 93-94; TV 94-96; P-in-c Aston cum Aughton w Swallownest and Ulley 01-02; TR 02-05; R Dinnington 96-01; AD Laughton 98-03; Hon Can Sheff Cathl 98-05; rtd 05. *69 Ings Mill Avenue, Clayton West, Huddersfield HD8 9QG* Tel (01484) 866189 Mobile 07768-293588 E-mail sueproctor@lineone.net

PROFIT, David Hollingworth. b 17. Man Univ BA38. Cuddesdon Coll 40. **d** 41 **p** 42. C Kings Heath *Birm* 41-43; S Africa from 43. *Braehead House, 1 Braehead Road, Kenilworth, 7708 South Africa* Tel (0027) (21) 762 6041

PROSSER, Gillian Margaret. b 40. Lon Inst of Educn TCert61. **d** 99. OLM Cwmbran *Mon* from 99. *25 Forest Close, Coed Eva, Cwmbran NP44 4TE* Tel (01633) 866716

PROSSER, Hugh. See PROSSER, Richard Hugh Keble

PROSSER, Jean. b 40. Open Univ BA84 Surrey Univ PhD94. **d** 02 **p** 05. NSM Grosmont and Skenfrith and Llangattock etc *Mon* from 02; P-in-c from 09. *Yew Tree Farm, Llangattock Lingoed, Abergavenny NP7 8NS* Tel (01873) 821405 E-mail jean.prosser@talk21.com

PROSSER, Canon Rhys. b 51. BA74 Southn Univ BTh83 Hull Univ MA93 Bris Univ CertEd75. Sarum & Wells Th Coll 77. **d** 80 **p** 81. C Wimbledon *S'wark* 80-83; C St Helier 83-88; TV Gt and Lt Coates w Bradley *Linc* 88-95; P-in-c Saxilby Gp 95-97; R from 97; RD Corringham from 00; Can and Preb Linc Cathl from 03. *The Rectory, 1 Westcroft Drive, Saxilby, Lincoln LN1 2PT* Tel (01522) 702427 E-mail rs.prosser@virgin.net

PROSSER, Richard Hugh Keble. b 31. Trin Coll Cam BA53 MA57 Leeds Univ PGCE63. Cuddesdon Coll 55. **d** 57 **p** 58. C Wigan All SS *Liv* 57-60; CR 62-87; St Aug Miss Penhalonga Zimbabwe 64-90; R Pocklington and Owsthorpe and Kilnwick Percy etc *York* 90-00; rtd 00; Perm to Offic *Sarum* from 02. *26 Fleur de Lis, Middlemarsh Street, Poundbury, Dorchester DT1 3GX* Tel (01305) 260329

PROSSER, Stephanie. b 42. Linc Th Coll 94. **d** 96 **p** 99. NSM Linc St Nic w St Jo Newport 96-99; NSM Saxilby Gp from 99. *The Rectory, 1 Westcroft Drive, Saxilby, Lincoln LN1 2PT* Tel (01522) 702427

PROTHERO, Brian Douglas. b 52. St Andr Univ MTheol75 Dundee Univ CertEd77. Linc Th Coll 84. **d** 86 **p** 87. C Thornbury *Glouc* 86-89; V Goodrington *Ex* 89-04; R Weybridge *Guildf* from 04; Chapl Sam Beare Hospice from 06. *The Rectory, 3 Churchfields Avenue, Weybridge KT13 9YA* Tel (01932) 842566 Mobile 07715-364389 E-mail brianprothero@btinternet.com

PROTHERO, David John. b 43. St Pet Coll Ox BA66 MA70. St Steph Ho Ox 68. **d** 70 **p** 71. C Kirkby *Liv* 70-72; C St Marychurch *Ex* 72-74; V Marldon 74-83; Chapl HM Pris Channings Wood 78-83; V Torquay St Martin Barton *Ex* 83-91; P-in-c Bath Bathwick *B & W* 91-93; R from 93. *Bathwick Rectory, Sham Castle Lane, Bath BA2 6JL* Tel (01225) 460052 E-mail david@djprothero.fsnet.co.uk

PROTHERO, John Martin. b 32. Oak Hill Th Coll 64. **d** 66 **p** 67. C Tipton St Martin *Lich* 66-69; C Wednesfield Heath 69-72; Distr Sec BFBS 72-85; Lic to Offic *S'well* 73-86; Hon C Gedling 73; V Willoughby-on-the-Wolds w Wysall and Widmerpool 86-97; rtd 98. *The Elms, Vicarage Hill, Aberaeron SA46 0DY* Tel (01545) 570568

PROTHEROE, Rhys Illtyd. b 50. St D Coll Lamp. **d** 74 **p** 75. C Pen-bre *St D* 74-76; C Carmarthen St Dav 76-78; V Llanegwad 78-79; V Llanegwad w Llanfynydd 79-82; V Gors-las 82-95; RD Dyffryn Aman 94-95; V Llan-llwch w Llangain and Llangynog from 95. *The New Vicarage, Millbank Lane, Johnstown, Carmarthen SA31 3HW* Tel (01267) 236805

PROTHEROE, Canon Robin Philip. b 33. St Chad's Coll Dur BA54 MA60 Nottm Univ MPhil75 Ox Univ DipEd62. **d** 57 **p** 58. C Roath *Llan* 57 60; Asst Chapl Culham Coll Abingdon 60-64; Sen Lect RS Trent (Nottm) Poly *S'well* 64-84; Perm to Offic 64-66; Lic to Offic 66-84; P-in-c Barton in Fabis 70-73; P-in-c Thrumpton 70-73; Dir of Educn *Bris* 84-98; Hon Can Bris Cathl 85-98; Selector for ACCM 88-91; ABM from 91; Bp's Insp of Th Colls from 88; Perm to Offic from 98; Capitular Can Bris

Cathl 01-07. *29 Barley Croft, Bristol BS9 3TG* Tel 0117-968 3245 Fax 968 4826 E-mail robinprotheroe@aol.com

✠**PROUD, The Rt Revd Andrew John.** b 54. K Coll Lon BD79 AKC79 SOAS Lon MA01. Linc Th Coll 79. **d** 80 **p** 81 **c** 07. C Stansted Mountfitchet *Chelmsf* 80-83; TV Borehamwood *St Alb* 83-90; C Bp's Hatfield 90-92; R E Barnet 92-01; Chapl Adis Ababa St Matt Ethiopia 02-07; Area Bp Ethiopia and Horn of Africa from 07. *PO Box 14601, Adis Ababa, Ethiopia* Tel (00251) (91) 140 5587 *or* (11) 662 3578 E-mail anglican.church@ethionet.et

PROUD, David John. b 56. Leeds Univ BA77 Dur Univ CertEd78. Ridley Hall Cam 85. **d** 88 **p** 89. C Lindfield *Chich* 88-91; TV Horsham 91-97; V Ware th Ch *St Alb* from 97; RD Hertford and Ware from 04; Chapl E Herts NHS Trust 97-00; Chapl E and N Herts NHS Trust 00-06. *The Vicarage, 15 Hanbury Close, Ware SG12 7BZ* Tel and fax (01920) 463165 E-mail vicar@ccware.org

PROUDFOOT (née BLACKBURN), Mrs Jane Elizabeth. b 66. Lanc Univ BA88 St Martin's Coll Lanc PGCE73 Leeds Univ BA09. NOC 06. **d** 09. C Stockton Heath *Ches* from 09. *36 Senna Lane, Comberbach, Northwich CW9 6BQ* Tel (01606) 892418 E-mail janeproudfoot@tiscali.co.uk

PROUDLEY, Sister Anne. b 38. Edin Univ BSc60. SAOMC 97. **d** 00 **p** 01. CSJB from 00; NSM Blackbird Leys *Ox* 00-04; Lic to Offic from 04; Chapl to the Homeless from 05. *The Priory, 2 Springhill Road, Begbroke, Kidlington OX5 1RX* Tel (01865) 855331 E-mail annecsjb@csjb.org.uk

PROUDLOVE, Lee Jason. b 70. Lon Bible Coll BA94. Trin Coll Bris MA01. **d** 01 **p** 02. C Morden *S'wark* 01-04; CMS Philippines 05-08; P-in-c W Bridgford *S'well* from 08. *The Rectory, 86 Bridgford Road, West Bridgford, Nottingham NG2 6AX* Tel 0115-981 1112

PROUDMAN, Canon Colin Leslie John. b 34. K Coll Lon BD60 MTh63. Wells Th Coll 60. **d** 61 **p** 62. C Radlett *St Alb* 61-64; Canada from 64; Hon Can Toronto from 86; Dean Div Toronto Div Coll 90-92. *1802-77 Maitland Place, Toronto ON M4Y 2V6, Canada* Tel (001) (416) 923 4235

PROUSE, Ms Carole Maureen. b 45. NOC. **dss** 86 **d** 87 **p** 95. NSM Coalville and Bardon Hill *Leic* 87-90; Perm to Offic 90-95; NSM Thorpe Acre w Dishley 95-96; P-in-c Packington w Normanton-le-Heath 96-01; Chapl HM Pris Low Newton 01-04; Asst Chapl from 04. *HM Prison Low Newton, Finchale Avenue, Brasside, Durham DH1 5YA* Tel 0191-386 1141

PROUT, Mrs Joan. b 42. Gipsy Hill Coll of Educn TCert63. **d** 97 **p** 98. OLM Whitton *Sarum* 97-06. *22 Ermin Close, Baydon, Marlborough SN8 2JQ* Tel (01672) 540465 E-mail joan.prout@genie.co.uk

PROVOST, Ian Keith. b 47. CA Tr Coll IDC73 Ridley Hall Cam 91. **d** 93 **p** 94. C Verwood *Sarum* 93-97; P-in-c Redlynch and Morgan's Vale 97-02; TV Plymstock and Hooe *Ex* from 02. *The Vicarage, 9 St John's Drive, Hooe, Plymouth PL9 9SD* Tel (01752) 403076 E-mail ian.provost@virgin.net

PROWSE, Mrs Barbara Bridgette Christmas. b 41. R Holloway Coll Lon BA62. **d** 91 **p** 94. C Kingsthorpe w Northampton St Dav *Pet* 91-97; V Northampton St Jas 97-02; rtd 02; Perm to Offic *Truro* from 02. *36 Carn Basavern, St Just, Penzance TR19 7QX* Tel (01736) 787994 E-mail bbc@prowseb.freeserve.co.uk

PRUDOM, William Haigh. b 26. STh79 APhS81 Hull Univ MPhil88. St D Coll Lamp 60. **d** 62 **p** 63. C Aylesford *Roch* 62 63; C Margate St Jo *Cant* 63-66; V Long Preston *Bradf* 66-73; C Darlington St Cuth *Dur* 73-75; V Ticehurst *Chich* 75-79; P-in-c Flimwell 78-79; V Ticehurst and Flimwell 79-81; R Spennithorne w Finghall and Hauxwell *Ripon* 81-91; rtd 91; Perm to Offic *Ripon* from 91. *9 Sydall's Way, Catterick Village, Richmond DL10 7ND* Tel (01748) 818604

PRUEN, Canon Edward Binney. b 56. K Coll Lon BD77 AKC77. St Jo Coll Nottm 78. **d** 79 **p** 80. C Kidderminster St Mary *Worc* 79-82; C Woking St Jo *Guildf* 82-84; Chapl Asst R Marsden Hosp Lon and Surrey 84-86; C Stapleford *S'well* 86-88; Min Winklebury CD 88; V Winklebury 88-93; Chapl Ld Mayor Treloar Coll Alton from 93; Hon Can Win Cathl from 05. *2 St Joseph's Cottage, Upper Froyle, Alton GU34 4JY* Tel (01420) 23893 *or* 526400 Fax 526426 E-mail ed.pruen@treloar.org.uk

PRUST, Mrs Judith Ann. b 46. St Mich Coll Llan 05. **d** 07. NSM Llanrhaeadr ym Mochnant etc *St As* from 07. *Minffordd, Llangynog, Oswestry SY10 0HD* Tel (01691) 860420 E-mail judithprust@yahoo.co.uk

PRYCE, Donald Keith. b 36. Man Univ BSc. Linc Th Coll 69. **d** 71 **p** 72. C Heywood St Jas *Man* 71-74; P-in-c 74-75; V 75-86; R Ladybarn 86-06; Chapl S Man Coll 87-06; Chapl Christie Hosp NHS Trust Man 93-06; rtd 06; Perm to Offic *Ches* from 06. *62 Belmont Road, Gatley, Cheadle SK8 4AQ* E-mail donaldpryce@hotmail.com

PRYCE, Robin Mark. b 60. Sussex Univ BA82 Cam Univ MA94. Westcott Ho Cam 84 United Th Coll Bangalore 85. **d** 87 **p** 88. C W Bromwich All SS *Lich* 87-90; Chapl Sandwell Distr Gen Hosp 90; Chapl and Fell CCC Cam 90-02; Tutor 92-02; Dean of Chpl

PRYCE

96-02; V Smethwick *Birm* 02-06; Bp's Adv for Clergy CME from 06. *175 Harborne Park Road, Birmingham B17 0BH* Tel 0121-426 0430 E-mail m.pryce@birmingham.anglican.org

PRYCE, William Robert. b 28. MBE91. **d** 79 **p** 80. NSM Leverstock Green *St Alb* 79-80; Perm to Offic *Sheff* 80-84; NSM Sheff St Barn and St Mary 84-90; NSM Alveley and Quatt *Heref* 91-93; Perm to Offic 93-03. *5 Wren Way, Bicester OX26 6UJ*

PRYKE, Jonathan Justin Speaight. b 59. Trin Coll Cam BA80 MA85. Trin Coll Bris BD85. **d** 85 **p** 86. C Corby St Columba *Pet* 85-88; C Jesmond Clayton Memorial *Newc* from 88. *15 Lily Avenue, Newcastle upon Tyne NE2 2SQ* Tel 0191-281 9854

PRYOR, Derek John. b 29. Lon Univ BD63 Birm Univ MEd74. Linc Th Coll 79 Chich Th Coll 79. **d** 80 **p** 81. Hon C Youlgreave *Derby* 80-82; Hon C Stanton-in-Peak 80-82; Hon C Ingham w Cammeringham w Fillingham *Linc* 82-87 and 92-99; Chapl Bp Grosseteste Coll Linc 83-84; Dioc Schs Officer *Linc* 87-92; rtd 92. *Walnut Cottage, Chapel Lane, Fillingham, Gainsborough DN21 5BP* Tel (01427) 668276 Fax 667956 E-mail john.pryor@btinternet.com

PRYOR, William Lister Archibald. b 39. Trin Coll Cam BA67 MA69 DipEd68. Ox NSM Course 72. **d** 75 **p** 90. NSM Summertown *Ox* from 75; Perm to Offic *Nor* 93-04. *23 Harbord Road, Oxford OX2 8LH* Tel and fax (01865) 515102

PRYS, Deiniol. b 53. Univ of Wales (Ban) BTh91. St Mich Coll Llan 82. **d** 83 **p** 84. C Llanbeblig w Caernarfon and Betws Garmon etc *Ban* 83-86; TV Amlwch 86-88; V Llanerch-y-medd 89-92; R Llansadwrn w Llanddona and Llaniestyn etc from 92. *The Rectory, Llansadwrn, Porthaethwy LL59 5SL* Tel (01248) 810534 Mobile 07740-541316

PRYSE, Hugh Henry David. b 58. St Chad's Coll Dur BA81 SS Coll Cam PGCE82 K Coll Lon MA96. St Steph Ho Ox 94. **d** 96 **p** 97. C Branksome St Aldhelm *Sarum* 96-00; TV Hove *Chich* 00-05; R Ex St Jas from 05. *The Rectory, 45 Thornton Hill, Exeter EX4 4NR* Tel (01392) 431297 *or* 420407

PRYSOR-JONES, John Glynne. b 47. Heythrop Coll Lon MA94 Leeds Metrop Univ BSc05 Liv Univ CQSW73. Westcott Ho Cam 88. **d** 90 **p** 91. C Mitcham St Mark *S'wark* 90-93; V Dudley St Fran *Worc* 93-99; R Woodchurch *Ches* 99-01; Hd Past Care Services Chorley and S Ribble NHS Trust and Preston Acute Hosps NHS Trust 01-02; Hd Past Care Services Lancs Teaching Hosps NHS Trust 02-06. *Bryn-y-Mor, St John's Park, Penmaenmawr LL34 6NE* Tel (01492) 622515

PRYTHERCH, David. b 30. Down Coll Cam BA54 MA58 Lon Univ CertEd68 DipAdEd71. Coll of Resurr Mirfield 54. **d** 56 **p** 57. C Blackpool St Steph *Blackb* 56-61; R Matson *Glouc* 61-65; Chapl St Elphin's Sch Matlock 65-85; V Thornton-le-Fylde *Blackb* 85-94; RD Poulton 91-94; rtd 94; Perm to Offic *Ches* from 96. *8A Dunraven Road, West Kirby, Wirral CH48 4DS*

PRZYWALA, Karl Andrzej. b 63. Sturt Univ NSW BTh04. St Mark's Nat Th Cen Canberra 01. **d** 04 **p** 05. C Houghton le Spring *Dur* 04-05; C Chester le Street 05-07; P-in-c Whatton w Aslockton, Hawksworth, Scarrington etc *S'well* from 07. *The Vicarage, Main Street, Aslockton, Nottingham NG13 9AL* Tel (01949) 850523 E-mail karl_sydney@yahoo.co.uk

PUCKRIN, Christopher. b 47. Oak Hill Th Coll. **d** 82 **p** 83. C Heworth H Trin *York* 82-84; C Sherburn in Elmet 84-85; P-in-c Kirk Fenton 85-86; P-in-c Kirkby Wharfe 85-86; V Kirk Fenton w Kirkby Wharfe and Ulleskelfe 86-87; C York St Mich-le-Belfrey 87-94; P-in-c Barnstaple *Ex* 94-97; TV 97-00; V Woodside *Ripon* 00-07; C Holbeck from 07. *St James's Vicarage, 1 Scotland Close, Horsforth, Leeds LS18 5SG* Tel 0113-258 2433

PUDDEFOOT, John Charles. b 52. St Pet Coll Ox BA74 Edin Univ BD78. Edin Th Coll 76. **d** 78 **p** 79. C Darlington H Trin *Dur* 78-81; Ind Chapl *Chich* 81-84; Asst Master Eton Coll from 84; Hd Mathematics from 93. *Eton College, Windsor SL4 6DB* Tel (01753) 671320 E-mail j.puddefoot@etoncollege.org.uk

PUDGE, Mark Samuel. b 67. K Coll Lon BD90 AKC90 Heythrop Coll Lon MA99. Ripon Coll Cuddesdon 91. **d** 93 **p** 94. C Thorpe Bay *Chelmsf* 93-96; TV Wickford and Runwell 97-00; Management Consultant Citizens' Advice Bureau from 00; Hon C Paddington St Jo w St Mich *Lon* from 03. *Flat 2, 12 Connaught Street, London W2 2AF*

PUDNEY, Malcolm Lloyd. b 48. SEITE 99. **d** 01 **p** 02. NSM S Nutfield w Outwood *S'wark* 01-06; P-in-c Woodham Mortimer w Hazeleigh *Chelmsf* from 06; P-in-c Woodham Walter from 06. *St Margaret's Rectory, Maldon Road, Woodham Mortimer, Maldon CM9 6SN* Tel (01621) 843373 Mobile 07860-464836 E-mail yenduptoo@madasafish.com

PUERTO RICO, Bishop of. *See* ALVAREZ-VELAZQUEZ, The Rt Revd David Andres

PUGH, Brian. *See* PUGH, William Bryan

PUGH, Geoffrey William. b 47. Ox Min Course 09. **d** 09. NSM Ruscombe and Twyford *Ox* from 09. *3 Willow Drive, Twyford, Reading RG10 9DD* Tel 0118-934 5482 Mobile 07934-420303 E-mail revgeoff@familypugh.co.uk

PUGH, Harry. b 48. K Coll Lon BD70 AKC71 Lanc Univ MA89. **d** 72 **p** 73. C Milnrow *Man* 72-75; P-in-c Rochdale Gd Shep

75-78; TV Rochdale 78-79; Perm to Offic *Liv* 79-82; C Darwen St Cuth *Blackb* 82-85; C Darwen St Cuth w Tockholes St Steph 85-86; V Burnley St Steph 86-93; R Hoole 93-01; P-in-c Porthleven w Sithney *Truro* from 01. *The Vicarage, Pendeen Road, Porthleven, Helston TR13 9AL* Tel (01326) 562419

PUGH, Lynda. b 49. Man Univ BSocSc93 MA96 PhD04. Ripon Coll Cuddesdon 07. **d** 09. C Glen Gp *Linc* from 09. *78 Gallery Walk, Pinchbeck, Spalding PE11 3XJ* Tel (01775) 710904 Mobile 07775-660081 E-mail lynda.pugh@hemscott.net

PUGH, Ronald Keith. b 32. Jes Coll Ox BA54 MA57 DPhil57. Ripon Hall Ox 56. **d** 59 **p** 60. C Bournemouth St Mich *Win* 59-61; Asst Chapl Bryanston Sch 61-66; Chapl Cranleigh Sch Surrey 66-68; Lect K Alfred Coll Winchester 68-97; rtd 97; Hon Sec and Treas Win and Portsm Dioc Clerical Registry 97-06. *6 Windermere Gardens, Alresford SO24 9NL* Tel (01962) 732879 E-mail rk.pugh@btinternet.com

PUGH, Stephen Gregory. Southn Univ BEd77. Linc Th Coll 85. **d** 87 **p** 88. C Harpenden St Nic *St Alb* 87-90; C Stevenage All SS Pin Green 90-93; V Stotfold and Radwell 93-00; V Gt Ilford St Marg and St Clem *Chelmsf* from 00. *The Vicarage, 70 Brisbane Road, Ilford IG1 4SL* Tel (020) 8554 7542 Mobile 07910-395925 E-mail stephenpugh@waitrose.com

PUGH, Miss Wendy Kathleen. b 48. Newnham Coll Cam BA69 MA75. Trin Coll Bris 93. **d** 95 **p** 96. C Hailsham *Chich* 95-99; C Frimley *Guildf* 99-07; Hon C Chertsey, Lyne and Longcross from 07. *The Vicarage, Lyne Lane, Lyne, Chertsey KT16 0AJ* Tel (01932) 874405 E-mail wkpugh@aol.com

PUGH, William Bryan (Brian). b 34. Ridley Hall Cam 59. **d** 61 **p** 62. C Oseney Crescent St Luke w Camden Square St Paul *Lon* 61-64; C N Wembley St Cuth 64-67; CF 67-88; QHC 85-88; Chapl Heathfield Sch Ascot 88-95; rtd 99; Perm to Offic *Ox* and *Guildf* from 99. *3 College Close, Camberley GU15 4JU* Tel (01276) 503702 E-mail w.pugh@ntlworld.com

PUGMIRE, Canon Alan. b 37. Tyndale Hall Bris 61. **d** 64 **p** 65. C Islington St Steph w St Bart and St Matt *Lon* 64-66; C St Helens St Mark *Liv* 66-71; R Stretford St Bride *Man* 71-82; R Burnage St Marg 82-02; AD Heaton 88-98; Hon Can Man Cathl 98-02; rtd 02; Perm to Offic *Man* from 02. *20 Shortland Crescent, Manchester M19 1SZ* Tel and fax 0161-431 3476 E-mail alan.pugmire@tiscali.co.uk

PUGSLEY, Anthony John. b 39. ACIB. Oak Hill Th Coll 89. **d** 90 **p** 91. C Chadwell *Chelmsf* 90-94; P-in-c Gt Warley Ch 94-01; V Warley Ch Ch and Gt Warley St Mary 01-04; rtd 04. *3 Southcliffe Court, Southview Drive, Walton on the Naze CO14 8EP* Tel (01255) 850967 E-mail revtony@aol.com

PULESTON, Mervyn Pedley. b 35. K Coll Lon BD60 AKC60. **d** 61 **p** 62. C Gt Marlow *Ox* 61-65; P Missr Blackbird Leys CD 65-70; V Kidlington 70-85; R Hampton Poyle 70-85; TR Kidlington w Hampton Poyle 85-86; Chapl Geneva *Eur* 86-92; TV Dorchester *Ox* 92-00; rtd 00. *55 Benmead Road, Kidlington OX5 2DB* Tel (01865) 372360 E-mail mpuleston@aol.com

PULFORD, Christopher. b 59. Pemb Coll Ox BA81 MA87. Trin Coll Bris 82. **d** 84 **p** 85. C Parr *Liv* 84-87; Chapl Berkhamsted Colleg Sch Herts 87-92; Development Dir React from 92. *c/o React, St Luke's House, 270 Sandycombe Road, Kew, Richmond TW9 3NA* Tel (020) 8940 2575 Fax 8940 2050

PULFORD, John Shirley Walter. b 31. Jes Coll Cam BA55 MA59. Cuddesdon Coll 55. **d** 57 **p** 58. C Blackpool St Steph *Blackb* 57-60; N Rhodesia 60-63; V Newington St Paul *S'wark* 63-68; C Seacroft *Ripon* 68-70; Chapl HM Pris Liv 70-72; Chapl HM Pris Linc 72-73; Student Cllr Linc Colls of Art and Tech 73-79; Cam Univ Counselling Service 79-96; Dir 82-96; rtd 96. *59 Cromer Road, North Walsham NR28 0HB* Tel (01692) 404320

PULFORD, Canon Stephen Ian. b 25. Clifton Th Coll 53. **d** 56 **p** 57. C Heref St Jas 56-58; R Coberley w Cowley *Glouc* 58-94; P-in-c Colesborne 75-94; Hon Can Glouc Cathl 84-94; RD Cirencester 88-89; rtd 94; Perm to Offic *Glouc* from 94. *16 Bafford Grove, Charlton Kings, Cheltenham GL53 9JE* Tel (01242) 524261

PULLAN, Ben John. b 43. Univ of Wales (Cardiff) MSc(Econ)83. Bris Minl Tr Scheme 74. **d** 77 **p** 78. NSM Westbury-on-Trym St Alb *Bris* 77-91; NSM Henleaze 91-03; NSM Bishopston and St Andrews from 05. *28 Hobhouse Close, Bristol BS9 4LZ* Tel 0117-962 4190 E-mail ben@bpullan.wanadoo.co.uk

PULLAN, Lionel Stephen. b 37. Keble Coll Ox BA58 MA62 ARCO58 FIST77. Cuddesdon Coll 58. **d** 60 **p** 61. C Tranmere St Paul *Ches* 60-63; C Higher Bebington 63-64; Perm to Offic 64-70; Hon C Luton St Chris Round Green *St Alb* 70-72; Hon C Hitchin H Sav 72-73; Hon C Welwyn 73-75; Hon C Welwyn w Ayot St Peter 75-78; Hon C Kimpton w Ayot St Lawrence 78-82; Hon C Stevenage St Andr and St Geo 82-85; Deputation Appeals Org CECS 85-90; V Sundon *St Alb* 90-03; rtd 03; Perm to Offic *St Alb* from 03; Chapl ATC from 92. *139 Turnpike Drive, Luton LU3 3RB* Tel (01582) 573236

PULLEN, Adam William. b 73. Univ of Wales (Abth) BSc97. St Jo Coll Nottm 03. **d** 06 **p** 07. C Swansea St Pet *S & B* 06-09; C

Swansea St Thos and Kilvey from 09. *76 Danygraig Road, Port Tennant, Swansea SA1 8NA*
E-mail adam.pullen@googlemail.com

PULLEN, James Stephen. b 43. Lon Univ BSc64 PGCE65 Linacre Coll Ox BA68. St Steph Ho Ox 66. **d** 68 **p** 69. C Chorlton-cum-Hardy St Clem *Man* 68-71; C Doncaster St Leon and St Jude *Sheff* 72-73; Chapl St Olave's Gr Sch Orpington 73-75; Chapl Haileybury Coll 75-01; Second Master 99-01; V St Ives *Ely* from 01. *The Vicarage, Westwood Road, St Ives PE27 6DH* Tel (01480) 463254
E-mail james.pullen@ely.anglican.org

PULLEN, Roger Christopher. b 43. Lon Univ BSc65 PGCE90. Wells Th Coll 65. **d** 67 **p** 68. C S w N Hayling *Portsm* 67-69; C Farlington 69-73; V Farington *Blackb* 73-80; V Chorley All SS 80-83; V Kingsley *Ches* 83-92; R Cilcain and Nannerch and Rhydymwyn *St As* 92-99; Dioc MU Animation *Guildf* 99-02; Hon C Bramley and Grafham 99-00; Perm to Offic *Guildf* 00-02 and *Chich* from 03. *Ewhurst, 6 Chichester Way, Selsey, Chichester PO20 0PJ* Tel (01243) 601684 Mobile 07989-732729
E-mail roger_pullen@lineone.net

PULLEN, Canon Timothy John. b 61. BNC Ox BA84 St Jo Coll Dur MA96. Cranmer Hall Dur 93. **d** 96 **p** 97. C Allesley *Cov* 96-00; V Wolston and Church Lawford 00-08; Can Res Cov Cathl from 08. *18 Ranulf Croft, Coventry CV3 5FB* Tel (024) 7650 2844 *or* 7652 1230 Mobile 07974-007665
E-mail tim.pullen@coventrycathedral.org.uk

PULLIN, Andrew Eric. b 47. Kelham Th Coll 67 Linc Th Coll 71. **d** 73 **p** 74. C Pershore w Pinvin, Wick and Birlingham *Worc* 73-77; TV Droitwich 77-80; V Woburn Sands *St Alb* 80-85; Perm to Offic *B & W* 85-87. *85 Weymouth Road, Frome BA11 1HJ* Tel (01373) 472170 E-mail a.pullin@talktalk.net

PULLIN, Canon Christopher. b 56. St Chad's Coll Dur BA77 Heythrop Coll Lon MA04. Ripon Coll Cuddesdon 78 Ch Div Sch of Pacific 79. **d** 80 **p** 81. C Tooting All SS *S'wark* 80-85; V New Eltham All SS 85-92; V St Jo in Bedwardine *Worc* 92-08; RD Martley and Worc W 03-08; Hon Can Worc Cathl 07-08; Can Res and Chan Heref Cathl from 08. *2 Cathedral Close, Hereford HR1 2NG* Tel (01432) 341905 Fax 374220
E-mail chancellor@herefordcathedral.org

PULLIN, Kathleen Jean Rebecca. b 58. Qu Coll Birm BA07. **d** 07 **p** 08. C Kings Norton *Birm* from 07. *6 Butter Walk, Birmingham B38 8JQ* Tel 0121-458 2950 Fax 486 3954
E-mail parishoffice@kingsnorton.org.uk

PULLIN, Peter Stanley. b 29. MA MSc CEng. Trin Coll Bris 87. **d** 88 **p** 89. NSM Rugby *Cov* 88-90; NSM Aylesbeare, Rockbeare, Farringdon etc *Ex* 90-98; Perm to Offic *Ex* 99-04 and *B & W* from 05. *25 Ashley Road, Bathford, Bath BA1 7TT* Tel (01225) 852050

PULLIN, Stephen James. b 66. S Bank Univ BEng89 Open Univ MBA98. Trin Coll Bris BA04. **d** 04 **p** 05. C Soundwell *Bris* 04-07; P-in-c Stapleton from 07; C Frenchay and Winterbourne Down from 07. *The Rectory, 21 Park Road, Stapleton, Bristol BS16 1AZ* Tel 0117-958 4714 Mobile 07866-700881
E-mail stephenjpullin@aol.com

PULLINGER, Mrs Catherine Ann. b 54. York Univ BA76. Oak Hill Th Coll 91. **d** 93 **p** 97. NSM Luton St Paul *St Alb* 93-99; NSM Luton Lewsey St Hugh from 99. *52 Wheatfield Road, Luton LU4 0TR* Tel (01582) 606996 Fax 472726
E-mail cathy@pullinger.net

PULLINGER, Ian Austin. b 61. Oak Hill Th Coll. **d** 96 **p** 97. C Weston *Win* 96-00; TV The Ortons, Alwalton and Chesterton *Ely* from 00. *Christ Church House, 1 Benstead, Orton Goldhay, Peterborough PE2 5JJ* Tel (01733) 394185
E-mail ianpullinger@bigfoot.com

PULLINGER, Peter Mark. b 53. Heythrop Coll Lon MA97. Ridley Hall Cam 01. **d** 03 **p** 04. C Clapham Park St Steph *S'wark* 03-06; C Telford Park 06-07; TV Sutton from 07. *Christ Church Vicarage, 14C Christchurch Park, Sutton SM2 5TN* Tel (020) 8642 2757 Mobile 07796-956774 E-mail mark@pullinger.net

PULMAN, John. b 34. EMMTC 78. **d** 81 **p** 82. NSM Mansfield SS Pet and Paul *S'well* 81-83; C Mansfield Woodhouse 83-86; V Flintham 86-99; R Car Colston w Screveton 86-99; Chapl HM YOI Whatton 87-90; Chapl HM Pris Whatton 90-99; rtd 99; Perm to Offic *S'well* from 99 and *Derby* from 00. *101 Ling Forest Road, Mansfield NG18 3NQ* Tel (01623) 474707

PUMFREY (née CERRATTI), Christa Elisabeth. b 54. Wycliffe Hall Ox 94. **d** 97 **p** 98. C Chipping Norton *Ox* 97-00; P-in-c Lavendon w Cold Brayfield, Clifton Reynes etc 00-08; R from 08; R Gayhurst w Ravenstone, Stoke Goldington etc from 08; Deanery Youth Co-ord from 00; AD Newport from 06. *The New Rectory, 7A Northampton Road, Lavendon, Olney MK46 4EY* Tel (01234) 240013

PUMPHREY, Norman John Albert. b 21. Nor Ord Course 76. **d** 77 **p** 78. NSM Aylsham *Nor* 77-94; Chapl St Mich Hosp Aylsham 88-99; Perm to Offic *Nor* from 94. *12 Buxton Road, Aylsham, Norwich NR11 6JD* Tel (01263) 733207

PUNSHON, Carol Mary. See BRENNAND, Ms Carol Mary

PUNSHON, George Wilson. b 30. Bris Univ BSc Michigan State Univ MSc DipEd. Ripon Hall Ox 71. **d** 73 **p** 74. C Knighton

St Mary Magd *Leic* 73-76; V Donisthorpe and Moira w Stretton-en-le-Field 76-82; R Gt Bowden w Welham, Glooston and Cranoe 82-86; Zimbabwe 87-89 and 00-04; Perm to Offic *Pet* 96-00; V Ascension Is 97-98; Chapl Peterho Sch Marondera 00-04. *101 The Downs, Nottingham NG11 7EA*

PUNSHON, Canon Keith. b 48. JP. Jes Coll Cam BA69 MA73 Birm Univ MA77. Qu Coll Birm 71. **d** 73 **p** 74. C Yardley St Edburgha *Birm* 73-76; Chapl Eton Coll 76-79; V Hill *Birm* 79-86; CF (TA) from 79; V S Yardley St Mich *Birm* 86-96; Can Res Ripon Cathl from 96. *St Peter's House, Minster Close, Ripon HG4 1QP* Tel (01765) 604108
E-mail postmaster@riponcathedral.org.uk

PURCHAS, Canon Catherine Patience Ann. b 39. St Mary's Coll Dur BA61. St Alb Minl Tr Scheme 77. **dss** 80 **d** 87 **p** 94. RE Resource Cen 80-81; Relig Broadcasting Chiltern Radio 81-87; Wheathampstead *St Alb* 81-00; Hon Par Dn 87-94; Hon C 94-00; Relig Broadcasting Beds Radio from 88; Bp's Officer for Women 93-07; Bp's Officer for NSMs and Asst Dir of Ords 93-00; Assoc Dioc Dir of Ords 00-03; Hon Can St Alb 96-00; rtd 03. *14 Horn Hill, Whitwell, Hitchin SG4 8AS* Tel and fax (01438) 871668 E-mail patience@purchas.fsworld.co.uk

PURCHAS, Canon Thomas. b 35. Qu Coll Birm 59. **d** 62 **p** 63. C Bp's Hatfield *St Alb* 62-71; R Blunham 71-78; P-in-c Tempsford w Lt Barford 71-78; R Blunham w Tempsford and Lt Barford 78-80; R Wheathampstead 80-00; RD Wheathampstead 92-99; Hon Can St Alb 99-00; rtd 00; RD Hitchin 00-02; Perm to Offic *St Alb* from 00. *14 Horn Hill, Whitwell, Hitchin SG4 8AS* Tel and fax (01438) 871668

PURDY, Canon John David. b 44. Leeds Univ BA65 MPhil76. Coll of Resurr Mirfield 72. **d** 75 **p** 76. C Marske in Cleveland *York* 75-78; C Marton-in-Cleveland 78-80; V Newby 80-87; V Kirkleatham 87-95; V Kirkbymoorside w Gillamoor, Farndale etc from 95; Can and Preb York Minster from 98; RD Helmsley from 99. *The Vicarage, Kirkbymoorside, York YO62 6AZ* Tel (01751) 431452

PURNELL, Marcus John. b 75. Ridley Hall Cam 07. **d** 09. C Northampton St Benedict *Pet* from 09. *44 Barn Owl Close, East Hunsbury, Northampton NN4 0UA* Tel (01604) 765060 Mobile 07535-639915 E-mail marcuspurnell@hotmail.com

PURSER, Alan Gordon. b 51. Leic Univ BSc73. Wycliffe Hall Ox 74. **d** 77 **p** 78. C Beckenham Ch Ch *Roch* 77-81; TV Barking St Marg w St Patr *Chelmsf* 81-84; R Kensington S Africa 84-88; Min Hadley Wood St Paul Prop Chpl *Lon* 88-03; UK Team Ldr Crosslinks from 03. *18 Salmon Lane, London E14 7LZ* Tel (020) 7702 8741 Mobile 07802-888439
E-mail apurser@crosslinks.org

PURVEY-TYRER, Neil. b 66. Leeds Univ BA87 MA88. Westcott Ho Cam 88. **d** 90 **p** 91. C Denbigh and Nantglyn *St As* 90-92; Chapl Asst Basingstoke Distr Hosp 92-95; TV Cannock *Lich* 95-99; V Northampton H Sepulchre w St Andr and St Lawr *Pet* 99-02; Dioc Co-ord for Soc Resp 99-03; TR Duston Team 02-08; Chapl St Andr Hosp Northn from 08. *St Andrew's Healthcare, Billing Road, Northampton NN1 5DG* Tel (01604) 616000
E-mail ntyrer@standrew.co.uk

PURVIS, Canon Colin. b 19. Kelham Th Coll 37. **d** 44 **p** 45. C Hebburn St Cuth *Dur* 44-47; C Sunderland 47-50; C Darlington St Cuth 50-53; C-in-c Humbledon St Mary V CD 53-58; C-in-c Bishopwearmouth St Mary V w St Pet CD 58-62; V Heworth St Mary 62-76; RD Gateshead 69-76; R Egglescliffe 76-84; Hon Can Dur Cathl 83-92, rtd 84. *4 Duke's Drive, Newcastle upon Tyne NE3 5NT* Tel 0191-236 6394

PURVIS, Lynn. b 58. St Jo Coll Dur BA97. Cranmer Hall Dur 94. **d** 98 **p** 99. C Gt Aycliffe *Dur* 98-02; Chapl N Tees and Hartlepool NHS Trust from 02. *University Hospital of North Tees, Hardwick Road, Stockton-on-Tees TS19 8PE* Tel (01642) 624714
E-mail lpurvis@nth.nhs.uk

PURVIS, Ms Sandra Anne. b 56. Univ Coll Ches BTh01. NOC 98. **d** 01 **p** 02. C Blackpool St Jo *Blackb* 01-06; P-in-c Gt Harwood 06-08; Chapl Pennine Acute Hosps NHS Trust from 08. *North Manchester General Hospital, Delaunays Road, Crumpsall, Manchester M8 5RB* Tel 0161-795 4567 Mobile 07967-136992 E-mail sandraapurvis@aol.com

PURVIS, Canon Stephen. b 48. AKC70. **d** 71 **p** 72. C Peterlee *Dur* 71-75; Dioc Recruitment Officer 75-79; V Stevenage All SS Pin Green *St Alb* 79-88; TR Borehamwood 88-00; RD Aldenham 94-98; V Leagrave from 00; Hon Can St Alb from 02; RD Luton from 07. *St Luke's Vicarage, High Street, Leagrave, Luton LU4 9JY* Tel and fax (01582) 572737
E-mail stephen.purvis@yahoo.co.uk

PUSEY, Canon Ian John. b 39. Sarum Th Coll 69. **d** 71 **p** 72. C Waltham Abbey *Chelmsf* 71-75; TV Stantonbury *Ox* 75-80; P-in-c Bletchley 80-84; R 84-00; RD Milton Keynes 96-00; P-in-c Lamp 00-06; AD Newport 04-06; Hon Can Ch Ch 06; rtd 06. *16 Gussiford Lane, Exmouth EX8 2SF* Tel (01395) 275549
E-mail ian.pusey@virgin.net

PUTNAM, Mrs Gillian. b 43. WEMTC 00. **d** 02 **p** 03. NSM Milton *B & W* from 02. *6 Miller Close, Weston-super-Mare BS23 2SQ* Tel (01934) 416917
E-mail gillianputnam@yahoo.co.uk

✠**PWAISIHO, The Rt Revd William Alaha.** b 48. Bp Patteson Th Coll (Solomon Is) 71. **d** 74 **p** 75 **c** 81. Solomon Is 74-76; New Zealand 78-79; Solomon Is 79-95; Dean Honiara 80-81; Bp Malaita 81-89; Hon Asst Bp Ches from 97; C Sale St Anne 97-99; R Gawsworth from 99. *The Rectory, Church Lane, Gawsworth, Macclesfield SK11 9RJ* Tel (01260) 223201 Mobile 07711-241625 E-mail bishop.gawsworth@virgin.net

PYATT, Noel Watson. b 34. AKC57. **d** 58 **p** 59. C Prenton *Ches* 58-61; C Cheadle Hulme All SS 61-63; P-in-c Hattersley 63-66; V 66-70; V Ches St Paul 70-99; rtd 99; Perm to Offic *Sheff* 99-02. *273 School Road, Sheffield S10 1GQ* Tel 0114-266 9944

PYBURN, Canon Alan. b 29. G&C Coll Cam BA51 MA55. Westcott Ho Cam 53. **d** 55 **p** 56. C Barnard Castle *Dur* 55-57; Chapl G&C Coll Cam 57-60; V Dallington *Pet* 60-72; V Ox St Giles 72-79; P-in-c Remenham 79-94; R Henley 79-94; RD Henley 84-94; Hon Can Ch Ch 90-95; R Henley w Remenham 94-95; rtd 95. *Pippin Cottage, Well Hill, Finstock, Chipping Norton OX7 3BU* Tel (01993) 868651

PYBUS, Antony Frederick. b 54. Birm Univ BA77. St Jo Coll Dur 78. **d** 81 **p** 82. C Ches H Trin 81-84; C W Hampstead St Jas *Lon* 84-89; V Alexandra Park St Andr 89-93; V Alexandra Park from 93. *The Vicarage, 34 Alexandra Park Road, London N10 2AB* Tel (020) 8883 3181 *or* 8444 6898 E-mail office@alexandrapark.org *or* vicar@alexandrapark.org

PYE, Alexander Frederick. b 61. St Mich Coll Llan 93. **d** 95 **p** 96. C Griffithstown *Mon* 95-97; P-in-c Bistre *St As* 97-99; P-in-c Penmaen and Crumlin *Mon* 99-00; V 00-02; R Govilon w Llanfoist w Llanelen from 02. *The Rectory, Merthyr Road, Govilon, Abergavenny NP7 9PT* Tel (01873) 832703

PYE, Canon Allan Stephen. b 56. Univ of Wales (Lamp) BA78 Lanc Univ MA85 MPhil87. Westcott Ho Cam 79. **d** 81 **p** 82. C Scotforth *Blackb* 81-85; C Oswaldtwistle All SS 85-87; V Wrightington 87-91; Chapl Wrightington Hosp 87-91; P-in-c Hayton St Mary *Carl* 91-93; V Hayton w Cumwhitton 93-98; RD Brampton 96-98; Hon Can Carl Cathl from 97; P-in-c Hawkshead and Low Wray w Sawrey 98-03; V Hawkshead and Low Wray w Sawrey and Rusland etc 03-06; V Keswick St Jo from 06. *St John's Vicarage, Ambleside Road, Keswick CA12 4DD* Tel (017687) 72130 E-mail stephen.pye@virgin.net

PYE, Mrs Gay Elizabeth. b 46. RN67 RM68. Trin Coll Bris BD73. **d** 96 **p** 96. NSM Castle Church *Lich* 96-00; Asst Chapl HM Pris Stafford 96-97; Chapl HM Pris Shrewsbury 97-00; Regional Manager Bible Soc 00-06; NSM Upper Derwent *Carl* from 06. *The Vicarage, Borrowdale, Keswick CA12 5XQ* Tel (017687) 77238 Mobile 07901-837813 E-mail gay.pye@gmail.com

PYE, James Timothy. b 58. Oak Hill Th Coll BA90. **d** 90 **p** 91. C Normanton *Derby* 90-94; R Talke *Lich* 94-04; R Knebworth *St Alb* from 04. *The Rectory, 15 St Martin's Road, Knebworth SG3 6ER* Tel (01438) 817396 E-mail jim@jimpye.plus.com

PYE, Joseph Terence Hardwidge. b 41. MRICS64. Trin Coll Bris 70. **d** 73 **p** 74. C Blackb Ch Ch 73-76; OMF 77-90; Korea 77-90; V Castle Church *Lich* 90-06; rtd 06. *The Vicarage, Borrowdale, Keswick CA12 5XQ* Tel (017687) 77238 E-mail terry.pye@gmail.com

PYE, Michael Francis. b 53. New Coll Ox BA75 MA78 DPhil78. STETS 97. **d** 00 **p** 01. C Fareham H Trin *Portsm* 00-07; V Portsea All SS from 07. *All Saints' Vicarage, 51 Staunton Street, Portsmouth PO1 4EJ* Tel (023) 9287 2815 E-mail mike@pye229.freeserve.co.uk

PYE, Nicholas Richard. b 62. Univ Coll Lon BA84 Man Univ PGCE87 Anglia Poly Univ MA03. Ridley Hall Cam 95. **d** 98 **p** 99. C Epsom Common Ch Ch *Guildf* 98-01; C Harrow Trin St Mich *Lon* 01-03; V Finchley St Paul and St Luke from 03. *St Paul's Vicarage, 50 Long Lane, London N3 2PU* Tel (020) 8346 8729 E-mail revpye@xalt.co.uk

PYE, Mrs Paula Jayne. b 67. St Jo Coll Dur BA09 RGN90. Cranmer Hall Dur 07. **d** 09. C Cockermouth Area *Carl* from 09. *139 The Parklands, Cockermouth CA13 0XJ* Tel 07805-411936 (mobile) E-mail thepyes@hotmail.co.uk

PYE, Sandra Anne. *See* ELLISON, Ms Sandra Anne

PYE, Stephen. *See* PYE, Canon Allan Stephen

PYKE, Alan. b 37. Trin Coll Bris BA87. **d** 87 **p** 88. CA 58-87; C Ipswich St Mary at Stoke w St Pet *St E* 87-90; R Creeting St Mary, Creeting St Peter etc 90-98; C S Trin Broads *Nor* 98-02; rtd 03; Perm to Offic *Nor* 03-08. *29 Stuart Court, High Street, Kibworth, Leicester LE8 0LR* Tel 0116-279 0113 E-mail alanpyke@scs-datacom.co.uk

PYKE, Barry John. b 62. Qu Mary Coll Lon BSc84 Southn Univ BTh94 Open Univ BA96 FGS84. Sarum & Wells Th Coll 91. **d** 94 **p** 95. C Bengeworth *Worc* 94-96; C Worc City St Paul and Old St Martin etc 96-99; R Chipping Ongar w Shelley *Chelmsf*

99-06; RD Ongar 04-06; R Hinderwell, Roxby and Staithes etc *York* from 06. *The Rectory, 1 The High Street, Hinderwell, Saltburn-by-the-Sea TS13 5JX* Tel (01947) 840249 E-mail bpyke@care4free.net

PYKE, Richard Ernest. b 50. Sarum & Wells Th Coll. **d** 82 **p** 83. C Bushey *St Alb* 82-85; C Gt Berkhamsted 85-89; V St Alb St Mary Marshalswick 89-00; TR Bp's Hatfield 00-05; TR Bp's Hatfield, Lemsford and N Mymms from 05; RD Welwyn Hatfield from 03. *The Rectory, 1 Fore Street, Hatfield AL9 5AN* Tel and fax (01707) 262072 E-mail richard50pyke@tiscali.co.uk

PYKE, Mrs Ruth Cheryl. b 56. Bath Coll of HE BA78 W Lon Inst of HE PGCE80. SAOMC 95. **d** 98 **p** 99. C Leavesden *St Alb* 98-02; C St Alb St Steph 02-06; P-in-c Caddington from 06; Bedfordshire Area Children's Work Adv from 06. *The Vicarage, Collings Wells Close, Caddington, Luton LU1 4BG* Tel (01582) 731692 E-mail ruth.pyke@tesco.net

PYKE, Thomas Fortune. b 62. St Chad's Coll Dur BA85 Fitzw Coll Cam BA88. Ridley Hall Cam 86. **d** 89 **p** 90. C Hitchin *St Alb* 89-94; Chapl Aston Univ 94-99; V Birm St Paul 99-00; Ind Chapl 01-06; Th Ecum Officer Birm Bd for Miss 01-06; V Is of Dogs Ch Ch and St Jo w St Luke *Lon* from 06. *Christ Church Vicarage, Manchester Road, London E14 3BN* Tel (020) 7538 1766 Mobile 07753-616499 E-mail tom.pyke@virgin.net

PYLE, John Alan. b 31. Qu Coll Birm. **d** 69 **p** 70. C Fenham St Jas and St Basil *Newc* 69-72; C Monkseaton St Pet 72-74; C Morpeth 74-78; R Bothal 78-83; TV Willington 83-91; R Chollerton w Birtley and Thockrington 91-97; rtd 97; Perm to Offic *Newc* from 97. *37 Ullswater Drive, Killingworth, Newcastle upon Tyne NE12 6GX* Tel 0191-268 6044

PYM, David Pitfield. b 45. Nottm Univ BA65 Ex Coll Ox DPhil68. Ripon Hall Ox 66. **d** 68 **p** 69. C Nottingham St Mary *S'well* 68-72; Chapl RN 72-76 and 79-84; Chapl Worksop Coll Notts 76-79; R Avon Dassett w Farnborough and Fenny Compton *Cov* 84-07; rtd 07; Perm to Offic *Ox* from 07. *Sunrise, Bury Court Lane, Shotteswell, Banbury OX17 1JA* Tel (01295) 738948 E-mail davidpym@lineone.net

PYM, Francis Victor. b 24. ARIBA52. St Jo Coll Dur 74. **d** 76 **p** 77. C Keighley *Bradf* 76-79; Chapl Bethany Fellowship 79-87; Lic to Offic *Chich* from 87; Dir Joshua Chr Trust from 88; Research Asst Ho of Lords from 89; Dir Gp Apologetics Initiative from 92. *Bolney House, Bolney, Haywards Heath RH17 5QR* Tel (01444) 881877

PYM, Gordon Sydney. b 19. Worc Ord Coll 59. **d** 61 **p** 62. C Highweek *Ex* 61-63; C Plymouth Em 63-66; V Kilnhurst *Sheff* 66-69; V Owston 69-72; V Hensall 72-75; rtd 75; Perm to Offic *Sheff* from 75. *6 Greno Road, Swinton, Mexborough S64 8RP* Tel (01709) 586884

PYNE, Robert Leslie. b 51. Lanchester Poly Cov BA72 Solicitor 75. Coll of Resurr Mirfield 76. **d** 79 **p** 80. C Clifton All SS w St Jo *Bris* 79-81; Bp's Dom Chapl *Ox* 81-84; TV High Wycombe 84-90; Chapl RN from 90. *Royal Naval Chaplaincy Service, Mail Point 1-2, Leach Building, Whale Island, Portsmouth PO2 8BY* Tel (023) 9262 5055 Fax 9262 5134

PYNN, Catherine. b 45. Reading Univ BSc67. SAOMC 93. **d** 96 **p** 97. NSM Caversham St Pet and Mapledurham etc *Ox* 96-03; NSM Aldermaston w Wasing and Brimpton 03-06; NSM Woolhampton w Midgham and Beenham Valance 05-06; Chapl Bradfield Coll Berks 00-06; NSM Kintbury w Avington *Ox* from 06; NSM W Woodhay w Enborne, Hampstead Marshall etc from 06. *The Vicarage, 3 Elizabeth Gardens, Kintbury, Newbury RG17 9TB* Tel (01488) 658243 Mobile 07717-726410

PYNN, David Christopher. b 47. Trin Coll Cam MA70 Cam Inst of Educn CertEd69. NOC 06. **d** 08 **p** 09. NSM Scalby *York* from 08; NSM Scarborough St Luke from 08. *6 Stepney Drive, Scarborough YO12 5DH* Tel 07530-753187 (mobile) E-mail davidpynn12@aol.com

✠**PYTCHES, The Rt Revd George Edward David.** b 31. Bris Univ BA54 Nottm Univ MPhil84. Tyndale Hall Bris 51. **d** 55 **p** 56 **c** 70. C Ox St Ebbe 55-58; C Wallington *S'wark* 58-59; Chile 59-77; Suff Bp Valparaiso 70-72; Bp Chile, Bolivia and Peru 72-77; V Chorleywood St Andr *St Alb* 77-96; rtd 96; Perm to Offic *St Alb* from 96. *Red Tiles, Homefield Road, Chorleywood, Rickmansworth WD3 5QJ* Tel (01923) 283763 Fax 283762

PYTCHES, Preb Peter Norman Lambert. b 32. Lon Univ BD57 Bris Univ MLitt67 Southn Univ PhD81 K Coll Lon MA00 Potchefstroom Univ MTh03 Open Univ MPhil06 Lambeth STh74. Tyndale Hall Bris 53. **d** 57 **p** 58. C Heatherlands St Jo *Sarum* 57-61; C Cromer *Nor* 61-63; V Plymouth St Jude *Ex* 63-71; V Heatherlands St Jo *Sarum* 71-76; Dir Past Tr Oak Hill Th Coll 76-81; V Finchley Ch Ch *Lon* 81-91; AD Cen Barnet 86-91; V Forty Hill Jes Ch 91-97; Preb St Paul's Cathl 92-97; rtd 97; Perm to Offic *Lon* from 98. *25 Weardale Gardens, Enfield EN2 0BA* Tel and fax (020) 8366 5126

Q

QUANCE, John David. b 42. Kelham Th Coll 61. **d** 67 **p** 68. C Southgate Ch Ch *Lon* 67-70; C Norbury St Phil *Cant* 70-73; Asst Chapl Middx Hosp Lon 73-80; R Failsworth St Jo *Man* 80-95; Australia 84-85; P-in-c Healey *Man* 95-04; V Islamabad Pakistan 00-01; rtd 07. *4 Elm Grove, Rochdale OL11 3RZ* Tel (01706) 343473 Mobile 07876-742189

QUARMBY, David John. b 43. St Jo Coll Dur BA64 Lon Univ CertEd70 Man Univ MEd89 Sheff Univ MA99. Ridley Hall Cam 65. **d** 67 **p** 68. C Bournville *Birm* 67-71; V Erdington St Chad 71-73; Lic to Offic *Blackb* 73-83; Perm to Offic *Man* 83-90 and from 98; C Oldham St Paul 90-98; Hon C from 98; Cllr Huddersfield Poly 90-92; Huddersfield Univ 92-01; Prin Adult Psychotherapist Hyndburn Community Mental Health Team from 00; Sen Cllr Blackb and Darwen Primary Care Trust 01-08. *30 College Avenue, Oldham OL8 4DS* Tel 0161-626 2771 E-mail david.quarmby@zen.co.uk

QUARRELL, John Beck. b 39. Hull Coll of Educn CertEd59. Chich Th Coll 67. **d** 70 **p** 71. C Horbury *Wakef* 70-71; C Sowerby 71-73; V Brotherton 74-80; Chapl Pontefract Gen Hosp 78-80; V Staincliffe *Wakef* 80-88; Chapl Staincliffe Hosp 82-88; R Farndon w Thorpe, Hawton and Cotham *S'well* 89-09; rtd 09. *The Rectory, 3 Marsh Lane, Farndon, Newark NG24 3SS* Tel (01636) 705048 E-mail jbq339@yahoo.co.uk

QUARTON, Robert Edward. b 43. Wilson Carlile Coll 64 EMMTC 84. **d** 87 **p** 88. C Gresley *Derby* 87-88; C Clay Cross 88-90; C N Wingfield, Clay Cross and Pilsley 90-91; R Darley from 91; P-in-c S Darley, Elton and Winster from 03; RD Wirksworth 03-08. *The Rectory, 15 Hall Rise, Darley Dale, Matlock DE4 2HD* Tel (01629) 734257 E-mail robertquarton@ctlmail.co.uk

QUASH, Canon Jonathan Ben. b 68. Peterho Cam BA90 MA94 PhD99. Westcott Ho Cam 91. **d** 95 **p** 96. NSM Cambridge St Mary Less *Ely* 95-96; Asst Chapl Peterho Cam 95-96; Chapl Fitzw Coll Cam 96-99; Fell 98-99; Tutor Wesley Ho Cam 96-99; Fell and Dean Peterho Cam 99-07; Prof K Coll Lon from 07; Can Th Cov Cathl from 04. *King's College London, Strand, London WC2R 2LS* Tel (020) 7848 2336 Fax 7848 2255 E-mail ben.quash@kcl.ac.uk

✠**QUASHIE, The Rt Revd Kobina Adduah.** b 34. ACIS60 Univ of Ghana LLB71 LLM74. **d** 78 **p** 78 **c** 92. Ghana 78-80 and 92-02; Chapl Middx Hosp Lon 80; Funding Officer USPG 80-92; Hon Can Kumasi from 86; Hon Can Koforidua from 86; Hon Can Accra from 87; Bp Cape Coast 92-02; rtd 02. *32 Chandos Road, London NW2 4LU* Tel (020) 8452 5721

QUAYLE, Margaret Grace. b 28. Gipsy Hill Coll of Educn TCert48 Lon Univ BA53 Liv Univ MPhil78. **d** 98 **p** 99. OLM Gt Crosby St Luke *Liv* 98-03; Perm to Offic from 03. *Clwyd, 9 Myers Road West, Liverpool L23 0RS* Tel 0151-924 1659

QUIBELL, Edward Villiers. b 71. Anglia Poly BSc93 Hughes Hall Cam PGCE94. Trin Coll Bris BA03. **d** 03 **p** 04. C Swindon Ch Ch *Bris* 03-06; Perm to Offic *Lon* 06-08; TV Broadwater *Chich* from 08. *The Vicarage, 53 Lavington Road, Worthing BN14 7SL* Tel (01903) 236363 E-mail revted@hotmail.co.uk

QUIBELL, Mrs Susan Elizabeth. b 50. **d** 03 **p** 04. OLM Aldridge *Lich* from 03. *29 Lingmoor Grove, Aldridge, Walsall WS9 8BY* Tel (01922) 744205 E-mail s.quibell@googlemail.com

QUICK, John Michael. b 46. N Counties Coll Newc TCert68 Birkbeck Coll Lon BSc73 FRGS70. SAOMC 97. **d** 00 **p** 01. OLM New Windsor *Ox* from 00. *White Roses, 45 York Road, Windsor SL4 3PA* Tel (01753) 865557 Mobile 07977-754822 E-mail littlefrquick@aol.com

QUICK, Roger Aelfred Melvin Tricquet. b 55. Leeds Univ BA79 PGCE81. Coll of Resurr Mirfield BA94. **d** 96 **p** 97. C Chapel Allerton *Ripon* 96-00; C Ireland Wood 00-03; Hon C 03-04; Chapl Strathallan Sch from 04. *Jacaranda, Strathallan School, Forgandenny, Perth PH2 9EN* Tel (01738) 813509 Mobile 07762-159047 E-mail father@priest.com

QUIGLEY, Adam. b 03 **p** 04. NSM Castlerock w Dunboe and Fermoyle *D & R* from 03. *41 Queens Park, Coleraine BT51 3JS* Tel (028) 7035 5191

QUIGLEY, Andrew. b 72. New Coll Ox BA96 Bris Univ PGCE98. St Jo Coll Nottm MTh03. **d** 04 **p** 05. C Burbage w Aston Flamville *Leic* 04-07; TV Market Harborough and The Transfiguration etc from 07. *The Vicarage, 49 Ashley Road, Market Harborough LE16 7XD* Tel (01858) 463441 E-mail a.quigley@ntlworld.com

QUIGLEY, Donna Maree. Ulster Univ BEd BTh. **d** 01 **p** 02. C Portadown St Columba *Arm* 01-03; I Derryvolgie *Conn* from 04. *The Rectory, 35 Kirkwoods Park, Lisburn BT28 3RR* Tel (028) 9260 7370 E-mail donna_quigley@yahoo.co.uk

QUIGLEY, John Christopher. b 33. Pontifical Lateran Univ STL68. **d** 67 **p** 68. P-in-c N Bersted *Chich* 03-08; rtd 08. *31 Worthing Road, Rustington, Littlehampton BN16 3JU* Tel 07792-718875 (mobile) E-mail john.quigley4@btinternet.com

QUIGLEY, William. b 46. Ulster Univ BA86. CITC BTh98. **d** 98 **p** 99. C Ballymoney w Finvoy and Rasharkin *Conn* 98-01; I Eglish w Killylea *Arm* from 01. *154 Killylea Road, Armagh BT60 4LN* Tel and fax (028) 3756 8320 E-mail williamquigley@btinternet.com

QUILL, Andrew Thomas Edward. b 67. Heriot-Watt Univ BArch91. Uganda Chr Univ 05. **d** 05 **p** 07. Dioc HE Co-ord Luweero Uganda 05-06; C Drumragh w Mountfield *D & R* from 06. *12 Crevenagh Way, Omagh BT79 0JE* Tel (028) 8224 1527 Mobile 07738-960707 E-mail quills155@btinternet.com

QUILL, Walter Paterson. b 35. **d** 60 **p** 61. C Glendermott *D & R* 60-63; I Kilbarron 63-66; I Kilcronaghan w Ballynascreen 66-81; I Derg w Termonamongan 81-07; Can Derry Cathl 89-07; Preb Howth St Patr Cathl Dublin 94-07; rtd 07. *1 University Gardens, Coleraine BT52 1JT* Tel (028) 7035 2114 E-mail wquill@btinternet.com

QUILLIAM, Miss Anne Eleanor Scott. b 31. Bedf Coll Lon BA54 CertEd55. Dalton Ho Bris 59. **d** 87. Par Dn Toxteth St Philemon w St Gabr and St Cleopas *Liv* 87-92; rtd 92; Perm to Offic *S & M* from 92. *13 Raad ny Gabbil, Castletown, Isle of Man IM9 1HH* Tel (01624) 822375

QUIN, David Christopher. b 42. SAOMC 97. **d** 00 **p** 01. NSM Blunham, Gt Barford, Roxton and Tempsford etc *St Alb* 00-06; rtd 06. *16 Beceshore Close, Moreton-in-Marsh GL56 9NB* Tel (01608) 651571 Mobile 07867-664924 E-mail davidcquin@aol.com

QUIN, Eric Arthur. b 22. Magd Coll Cam BA46 MA48 Lon Univ BD56. Bps' Coll Cheshunt 46. **d** 48 **p** 49. C Luton St Andr *St Alb* 48-50; C Barnoldswick w Bracewell *Bradf* 50-52; PC Bradf St Sav 52-57; P-in-c Gt w Lt Wymondley *St Alb* 57-58; P-in-c St Ippolyts 57-58; V 58-70; RD Hitchin 68-70; V Haynes 70-87; rtd 87; Perm to Offic *Ches* from 87. *Annabel's Cottage, The Lydiate, Wirral CH60 8PR* Tel 0151-342 8650

QUIN, John James Neil. b 31. Ox Univ MA DipEd53. Qu Coll Birm 61. **d** 63 **p** 64. C Cannock *Lich* 63-68; V Sneyd Green 68-78; V Stafford St Paul Forebridge 78-90; TV Tettenhall Regis 90-98; rtd 98; Perm to Offic *Ex* from 00. *Watcombe House, 28 Barnpark Road, Teignmouth TQ14 8PN* Tel (01626) 772525

QUINBY, Mrs Janice Mary. b 51. Liv Univ MB, ChB75 FRCSEd81 FRCS82. **d** 08. OLM Mitford *Newc* from 08; OLM Longhorsley and Hebron from 08. *Black Close House, Black Close Bank, Ashington NE63 8TF* Tel (01670) 811480 Mobile 07947-140831 E-mail janice.quinby@btinternet.com

QUINE, Christopher Andrew. b 38. St Aid Birkenhead 61. **d** 64 **p** 65. C Hunts Cross *Liv* 64-67; C Farnworth and C-in-c Widnes St Jo 67-71; V Clubmoor 71-78; V Formby H Trin 78-99; V Arbory and Santan *S & M* 99-03; rtd 03. *17 Fieldlands, Southport PR8 5HQ* Tel (01704) 540569

QUINE, David Anthony. b 28. Qu Coll Cam BA52 MA59. Ridley Hall Cam 53. **d** 55 **p** 56. C Beckenham Ch Ch *Roch* 55-59; C Normanton *Derby* 59-60; V Low Elswick *Newc* 60-66; V Houghton *Carl* 66-68; Lic to Offic *York* 68-71; Chapl Monkton Combe Sch Bath 71-85; rtd 85; Perm to Offic *Carl* from 85. *Briar Cragg, Gale Rigg, Ambleside LA22 0AZ* Tel (01539) 433563

QUINE, Canon Ernest Kendrick Leigh. b 21. St Jo Coll Dur BA50 MA55 Nottm Univ DPhil68. **d** 51 **p** 52. C Grassendale *Liv* 51-52; C Shrewsbury St Alkmund *Lich* 52-54; C-inc Park Estate St Chris CD *Leic* 54-61; V Belgrave St Pet 61-93; Hon Can Leic Cathl 67-93; rtd 93; Perm to Offic *Leic* from 93. *63 Somerset Drive, Glenfield, Leicester LE3 8QW* Tel 0116-232 1994

✠**QUINLAN, The Rt Revd Alan Geoffrey.** b 33. Kelham Th Coll 54. **d** 58 **p** 59 **c** 88. C Bedford Leigh *Man* 58-61; S Africa from 61; Suff Bp Cape Town (Cen Region) 88-98; rtd 98. *132 Woodley Road, Plumstead, Cape Town, 7800 South Africa*

QUINN, Canon Arthur Hamilton Riddel. b 37. TCD BA60 MA64 BD67. **d** 61 **p** 62. C Belfast H Trin *Conn* 61-63; C Belfast St Mary Magd 63-64; Chapl Hull Univ 64-69; Chapl Keele Univ 69-74; P-in-c Keele 72-74; V Shirley St Jo *Cant* 74-84; V Shirley St Jo *S'wark* 85-86; RD Croydon Addington 95-04; Hon Can S'wark Cathl 03-06; rtd 06; Perm to Offic *S'wark* from 06. *23 Eden Road, Croydon CR0 1BB* E-mail quinncanon@aol.com

QUINN, Canon Derek John. b 55. TCD BTh88. **d** 88 **p** 89. C Mossley *Conn* 88-91; I Cappagh w Lislimnaghan *D & R* from 91; Bp's Dom Chapl from 00; Dioc Warden of Readers from 04; Can Derry Cathl from 07. *Erganagh Rectory, 1 Erganagh Road, Omagh BT79 7SX* Tel (028) 8224 2572

QUINN, Eugene Frederick. b 35. Allegheny Coll (USA) AB57 Univ of California MA66 MA69 PhD70. Vancouver Sch of Th 71. **d** 74 **p** 75. C Washington St Columba USA 74-75 and 78-81; Chapl Prague *Eur* 75-78; C Chevy Chase All SS USA 81-82 and 86-90; Chapl Nat Cathl Washington 81-82 and from 95; C Washington Epiphany 82 and 86-88; V Bowie St Jas 83-84; Chapl Warsaw 93-95. *5702 Kirkside Drive, Chevy Chase MD 20815-7116, USA* E-mail etquinn@msn.com

QUINN, George Bruce. b 23. MBE05. **d** 82 **p** 83. NSM Douglas St Ninian *S & M* 82-05. *85 Port-e-Chee Avenue, Douglas, Isle of Man IM2 5EZ* Tel (01624) 674080

QUINN, John James. b 46. TCD BA70 PhD76. St Jo Coll Nottm. **d** 81 **p** 82. C Gorleston St Andr *Nor* 81-84; R Belton 84-90; R

Burgh Castle 84-90; R Belton and Burgh Castle from 90. *The Rectory, Beccles Road, Belton, Great Yarmouth NR31 9JQ* Tel (01493) 780210

QUINN, Kenneth Norman. b 40. QUB BSc62 CEng MICE. CITC 80. d 85 p 86. NSM Seapatrick *D & D* 85-91; Lic to Offic from 91. *4 Knollwood, Seapatrick, Banbridge BT32 4PE* Tel (028) 4062 3515 E-mail ken.quinn@nireland.com

QUINN, Marjorie. d 94 p 97. NSM Hawarden *St As* 94-05; Lic to Offic from 05. *21 Hawarden Way, Mancot, Deeside CH5 2EL* Tel (01244) 531639

QUINNELL, Peter Francis. b 48. St Steph Ho Ox 93. d 95 p 96. C Tewkesbury w Walton Cardiff *Glouc* 95-99; R Stratton, N Cerney, Baunton and Bagendon 99-08; AD Cirencester 06-08; R Whitewater *Win* from 08. *The Rectory, London Road, Hook RG27 9EG* Tel (01256) 760377 E-mail quinnell708@btinternet.com

QUINT, Mrs Patricia Mary. b 51. Milton Keynes Coll of Ed CertEd76 Open Univ BA77 Lon Univ MA99. St Alb Minl Tr Scheme 90. d 93 p 94. C Hertford St Andr *St Alb* 93-96; C Bromham w Oakley and Stagsden 96-00; V Stotfold and Radwell from 00. *The Vicarage, 61 Church Road, Stotfold, Hitchin SG5 4NE* Tel and fax (01462) 730218 E-mail revquint@ntlworld.com

QUIREY, Mrs Edith. b 56. CITC 98. d 01 p 02. Aux Min Belfast St Mich *Conn* 01-05; P-in-c Belfast St Steph w St Luke 05-07; Bp's C 07-09; I from 09. *92 Lansdowne Road, Belfast BT15 4AB* Tel (028) 9077 4119 E-mail edith.quirey@tesco.net

QUIST, Ms Frances Buckurel. NTMTC BA09. d 09. C E Ham w Upton Park St Alb *Chelmsf* from 09. *2 Norman Road, London E6 6HN* Tel (020) 8471 3214 Mobile 07734-711929 E-mail francesquist@btinternet.com

R

✠**RABENIRINA, The Rt Revd Remi Joseph.** b 38. Antananarivo Univ LèsL83. St Paul's Coll Ambatoharanana 61 St Chad's Coll Dur 64 Bossey Ecum Inst Geneva. d 67 p 68 c 84. Dn Toamasina St Jas Madagascar 67; R St Matt Pro-Cathl Antsiranana 68-73; R Ambohimangakely St Jo 73-84; Angl Chapl Antananarivo Univ 73-84; Bp Antananarivo 84-08; Abp Indian Ocean 95-06; rtd 08. *Address temp unknown* Tel (00261) 3311-20827 (mobile)

RABIN, Peter David. b 62. Southlands Coll Lon BA86. Aston Tr Scheme 88 Ripon Coll Cuddesdon BTh93. d 93 p 94. C Hornsey St Mary w St Geo *Lon* 93-97; V Cricklewood St Pet 97-07; C S Ockendon and Belhus Park *Chelmsf* from 07. *The Rectory, North Road, South Ockendon RM15 6QJ* Tel (01708) 855321 E-mail frrabin@dsl.pipex.com

RABJOHNS, Alan. b 40. Leeds Univ BA62. Coll of Resurr Mirfield 62. d 64 p 65. C Ashington *Newc* 64-67; C Upton cum Chalvey *Ox* 67-76; V Roath St Sav *Llan* 76-08; AD Cardiff 03-08; rtd 08. *40 Cwmgelli Close, Treboeth, Swansea SA5 9BY* Tel (01792) 561157

RABLEN, Antony Ford. b 52. St Jo Coll Nottm. d 82 p 83. C Clifton *York* 82-85; TV Marfleet 85-92; P-in-c Welton w Melton 92-00; TR Sutton St Jas and Wawne 00-05; Chapl R Brompton and Harefield NHS Trust 05-08; Chapl Oxon & Bucks Mental Health Partnership NHS Trust from 06. *St Andrew's Vicarage, Malvern Avenue, Harrow HA2 9ER* Tel (020) 8422 3633 E-mail antonym@rablen.fsnet.co.uk

RABLEN, Mrs Christine Mary. b 52. Trevelyan Coll Dur BA74 Hull Univ BA92 Leeds Univ MA94. NOC 00. d 02 p 03. C Sutton St Mich *York* 02-05; V Roxbourne St Andr *Lon* from 05. *St Andrew's Vicarage, Malvern Avenue, Harrow HA2 9ER* Tel (020) 8422 3633 Fax 8422 2009 E-mail christine@rablen4394.fsnet

RABY, Malcolm Ernest. b 47. St Jo Coll York BEd73. NOC 81. d 84 p 85. NSM Chadkirk *Ches* 84-88; Consultant E England CPAS 88-94; C Ely 94-96; TV Ely 96-98; P-in-c Over from 98; Dioc Adv in Miss and Evang from 98; P-in-c Long Stanton w St Mich from 02. *The Vicarage, Horseware, Over, Cambridge CB24 5NX* Tel and fax (01954) 230329 E-mail mission@ely.anglican.org

RACE, Canon Alan. b 47. St Jo Coll York BEd73 Birm Univ MA82. Ripon Coll Cuddesdon 73. d 76 p 77. C Tupsley *Heref* 76-79; Asst Chapl Kent Univ 79-84; Dir Studies S'wark Ord Course 84-94; R Aylestone St Andr w St Jas *Leic* 94-07; P-in-c Leic

St Phil from 07; Hon Can Leic Cathl from 07. *2 Westminster Road, Leicester LE2 2EG* Tel 0116-212 0627 E-mail alan.race@ntlworld.com

RACE, Christopher Keith. b 43. St Paul's Coll Grahamstown 76. d 78 p 80. Angl Chapl Stellenbosch Univ S Africa 79-81; R Kalk Bay 81-83; Dioc Admin Botswana and Personal Asst to Abp Cen Africa 83-86; P-in-c E Kalahari 83-86; V Tanworth St Patr Salter Street *Birm* 86-96; P-in-c Rothiemurchus *Mor* 96-01; Perm to Offic *Glouc* 02-03; P-in-c Kemble, Poole Keynes, Somerford Keynes etc 03-04; R 04-06; Prin Tutor and Lect Cant Ch Ch Univ 06-08; rtd 08. *c/o the Revd S P Race, The Vicarage, Green Road, Dodworth, Barnsley S75 3RT* Tel 07866-585973 (mobile) E-mail ck.race@gmail.com

RACE, John Arthur. b 37. SAOMC 95. d 98 p 99. OLM Haddenham w Cuddington, Kingsey etc *Ox* 98-08; Perm to Offic from 08. *8 The Closes, Haddenham, Aylesbury HP17 8JN* Tel (01844) 290180

RACE, Stephen Peter. b 69. SS Hild & Bede Coll Dur BA93. St Steph Ho Ox 00. d 02 p 03. C Wigton *Carl* 02-05; V Dodworth *Wakef* from 05; Asst Dioc Dir of Ords 05-09; Dir from 09; RD Barnsley from 09. *The Vicarage, Green Road, Dodworth, Barnsley S75 3RT* Tel (01226) 206276 E-mail stephen.race@wakefield.anglican.org

RACTLIFFE, Dudley John. b 38. Man Univ BA62. Ridley Hall Cam 63. d 66 p 67. C Radford *Cov* 66-68; C Haslemere *Guildf* 69-73; V Perry Beeches *Birm* 73-78; V Worle *B & W* 78-88; Dioc Ecum Officer and R Dowlishwake w Kingstone, Chillington etc 88-93; TR Swanage and Studland *Sarum* 93-01; rtd 01; Perm to Offic *B & W* from 02. *12 Sid Lane, Sidmouth EX10 9AN* Tel (01395) 579712

RADCLIFFE, Canon Albert Edward. b 34. Lon Univ BD63. St Aid Birkenhead Ch Div Sch of the Pacific (USA) 61. d 62 p 63. C Knotty Ash St Jo *Liv* 62-64; C Blundellsands St Nic 64-66; Chapl Haifa St Luke Israel 66-69; V Tonge w Alkrington *Man* 69-77; R Ashton St Mich 77-91; AD Ashton-under-Lyne 87-91; Can Res Man Cathl 91-00; rtd 00; Perm to Offic *Man* from 01. *26 St Chad's Road, Withington, Manchester M20 4WH* Tel 0161-445 1327

RADCLIFFE, David Jeffrey. b 52. Linc Th Coll 77. d 79 p 80. C Poulton-le-Fylde *Blackb* 79-84; V Ingol 84-88; R Lowther and Askham *Carl* 88-96; R Lowther and Askham and Clifton and Brougham 96-06; R Upton-on-Severn, Ripple, Earls Croome etc *Worc* from 06. *The Rectory, Old Street, Upton-upon-Severn, Worcester WR8 0JQ* Tel (01684) 591241 E-mail revradcliffe@btinternet.com

RADCLIFFE, Eileen Rose (Rosie). b 54. Carl Dioc Tr Inst 92. d 95 p 96. NSM Gt Salkeld w Lazonby *Carl* 95-96; NSM Dacre 99-02; Perm to Offic *Carl* 02-06 and *Worc* 06-08; NSM Upton-on-Severn, Ripple, Earls Croome etc *Worc* from 08. *The Rectory, Old Street, Upton-upon-Severn, Worcester WR8 0JQ* Tel (01684) 591241

RADCLIFFE, James. b 75. Rob Coll Cam MA98. Oak Hill Th Coll BA08. d 08 p 09. C Hove Bp Hannington Memorial Ch *Chich* from 08. *7 Church Court, Nevill Avenue, Hove BN3 7NS* Tel (01273) 739770 Mobile 07941-248213 E-mail radders@eb1000.fsnet.co.uk

RADCLIFFE, John Frederick. b 39. d 01 p 02. OLM Meltham *Wakef* from 01. *13 Orchard Close, Meltham, Huddersfield HD9 4EG* Tel (01484) 348806

RADCLIFFE, Robert Mark. b 63. Cranmer Hall Dur 05. d 08 p 09. C Welling *Roch* from 08. *52 Clifton Road, Welling DA16 1QD* Tel (020) 8306 1829 E-mail markradcliffe@msn.com

RADCLIFFE, Mrs Rosemary. b 45. SW Minl Tr Course 87. d 90 p 94. NSM Devoran *Truro* 90-93; Dn-in-c N Newton w St Michaelchurch, Thurloxton etc *B & W* 93-96; P-in-c 94-00; Chapl to the Deaf 93-96; P-in-c Whipton *Ex* 00-01; rtd 01; Perm to Offic *Truro* from 03. *76 Upland Crescent, Truro TR1 1NE* Tel (01872) 273906

RADCLIFFE, Rosie. See RADCLIFFE, Eileen Rose

RADFORD, Vincent Arthur. b 45. Ches Coll of HE CertEd69. d 05 p 06. OLM Westhoughton and Wingates *Man* from 05. *64 Molyneux Road, Westhoughton, Bolton BL5 3EU* Tel (01942) 790091 E-mail vincent.radford@ntlworld.com

RADLEY, Mrs Jean Frances. b 40. Man Univ RGN62 Univ Coll Lon RSCN65 Cen Lancs Univ BSc95. d 00 p 01. OLM Kendal St Geo *Carl* 00-07; OLM Beacon from 07. *7 Castle Grove, Kendal LA9 7AY* Tel (01539) 740811 Mobile 07714-020189 E-mail jeanradley@btconnect.com

RADLEY, Richard Brian. b 68. St Jo Coll Nottm 02. d 04 p 05. C Utley *Bradf* 04-08; P-in-c Doncaster St Mary *Sheff* from 09; P-in-c Wheatley Park from 09. *St Mary's Vicarage, 59 St Mary's Road, Doncaster DN1 2NR* Tel (01302) 342565 E-mail radley@radleyfamily.fsnet.co.uk

RADLEY, Stephen John. b 68. St Jo Coll Nottm BTh96. d 96 p 97. C Boulton *Derby* 96-00; Chapl RAF from 00. *Chaplaincy Services, Valiant Block, HQ Air Command, RAF High Wycombe HP14 4UE* Tel (01494) 496800 Fax 496343 E-mail steve.radley@cwcom.net

RAE, Stephen Gordon. b 65. AGSM87. Oak Hill Th Coll BA09. **d** 09. C Danehill *Chich* from 09. *Marten Cottage, Coach and Horses Lane, Danehill, Haywards Heath RH17 7JF* Tel 07776-147212 (mobile) E-mail stephen@raefamily.net

RAE SMITH, Tristram Geoffrey. b 57. Clare Coll Cam BA79 MA83 St Jo Coll Dur BA04. Cranmer Hall Dur 02. **d** 04 **p** 05. C Bradford-on-Avon Ch Ch *Sarum* 04-08; C Westwood and Wingfield 04-08; R Camelot Par *B & W* from 08; C Bruton and Distr from 08. *The Rectory, 6 The Close, North Cadbury, Yeovil BA22 7DX* Tel (01963) 440585 Mobile 07751-306272

RAFFAY, Julian Paul. b 60. Stirling Univ BSc84. Cranmer Hall Dur BA90. **d** 90 **p** 91. C Adel *Ripon* 90-93; C Leeds Halton St Wilfrid 93-95; Asst Chapl S Derbys Mental Health NHS Trust 95-97; TV Gleadless *Sheff* 97-01; V Deepcar 01-07; Chapl Team Ldr Sheff Care Trust from 07. *Chaplaincy, Sheffield Care Trust, Longley Centre, Longley Grange Drive, Sheffield S5 7AU* Tel 0114-226 1675 E-mail julian.raffay@sct.nhs.uk

RAGAN, Mrs Jennifer Mary. b 39. Linc Th Coll 71. **dss** 80 **d** 87 **p** 94. Hackney 80-84; Hornchurch St Andr *Chelmsf* 84-88; Par Dn 87-88; Par Dn Ingrave St Steph CD 88-90; Par Dn Gt Parndon 90-94; C 94-99; TV 99-07; rtd 07; Perm to Offic *Chelmsf* and *St E* from 07. *18 Holme Oaks Court, 50 Cliff Lane, Ipswich IP3 0PE* Tel (01473) 213577
E-mail revjenniferragan@btinternet.com

RAGBOURNE, Miss Pamela Mary. b 27. CertEd47. Dalton Ho Bris 53. **dss** 76 **d** 87 **p** 94. CPAS Staff 68-79; Tottenham St Jo *Lon* 79-81; Gt Cambridge Road St Jo and St Jas 82-84; Camberley St Paul *Guildf* 84-86; rtd 87; Perm to Offic *Glouc* 87-93 and 97-05; NSM Winchcombe, Gretton, Sudeley Manor etc 93-97. *14 Crispin Close, Winchcombe, Cheltenham GL54 5JY* Tel (01242) 603469

RAGGETT, Anita Jane. b 56. NOC. **d** 07 **p** 08. C Gomersal *Wakef* from 07; C Cleckheaton St Jo from 08. *26 Burnleys Mill Road, Gomersal, Cleckheaton BD19 4PQ* Tel (01274) 879551
E-mail daragett@hotmail.com

RAHI, Hakim Banta Singh. b 36. Union Bibl Sem Yavatmal BD71. **d** 74 **p** 74. India 74-83; In URC 83-88; Perm to Offic *Birm* 88-93; Ecum Evang Asian Community 88-93. *Flat 5, 12 Taverners Gree, Birmingham B20 2JJ*

RAHILLY, Philip James. b 54. Univ of Wales (Cardiff) BD86. Wycliffe Hall Ox 86. **d** 88 **p** 89. C Knightwick w Doddenham, Broadwas and Cotheridge *Worc* 88; C Martley and Wichenford, Knightwick etc 89-91; C Worc St Barn w Ch Ch 91-92; TV Kidderminster St Mary and All SS w Trimpley etc 92-95; P-in-c Childe Okeford, Okeford Fitzpaine, Manston etc *Sarum* 95-00; P-in-c Shilling Okeford 99-00; R Okeford 00-06; P-in-c Stogursey w Fiddington *B & W* 06-07; R Quantock Coast from 07. *The Rectory, High Street, Stogursey, Bridgwater TA5 1PL* Tel (01278) 732884

RAI, Mrs Mary Anne. b 61. La Sainte Union Coll BTh83 PGCE84. Trin Coll Bris 85. **dss** 86 **d** 87 **p** 99. Bury St Edmunds St Mary *St E* 86-89; Par Dn 87-89; Perm to Offic 90-93; Perm to Offic *Cov* 94-99 and from 02; NSM Styvechale 99-01. *61 Malthouse Lane, Kenilworth CV8 1AD* Tel (01926) 732223
E-mail kal.rai@virgin.net

RAIKES, Miss Gwynneth Marian Napier. b 51. Somerville Coll Ox MA72 Lon Univ BD81. Trin Coll Bris 79. **dss** 81 **d** 98 **p** 98. Asst Chapl Bris Poly 81-86; Beckenham Ch Ch *Roch* 86-98; C 98-00; Dean of Women and Dir Past Tr Oak Hill Th Coll from 00; Perm to Offic *Lon* from 03 and *Ely* from 07. *Oak Hill College, Chase Side, London N14 4PS* Tel (020) 8449 0467 Mobile 07866-651272 E-mail marianr@oakhill.ac.uk

RAIKES, Canon Peter. b 37. St Mich Coll Llan 78. **d** 80 **p** 81. C Roath *Llan* 80-82; V Resolven 82-86; V Resolven w Tonna 86-92; RD Neath 89-01; V Skewen 92-02; Can Llan Cathl 97-02; rtd 02. *2 Kennedy Drive, Pencoed, Bridgend CF35 6TW* Tel (01656) 862317

RAIKES, Robert Laybourne. b 32. Wells Th Coll 59. **d** 61 **p** 62. C Poplar All SS w St Frideswide *Lon* 61-66; C Grendon Underwood w Edgcott *Ox* 66-68; C Swan 68-71; V Whitchurch Canonicorum w Wooton Fitzpaine etc *Sarum* 71-81; P-in-c Branksome St Aldhelm 81-82; V 82-91; V Pitminster w Corfe *B & W* 91-92; rtd 92; Chapl Madeira *Eur* 93-95; Perm to Offic *Glouc* 95-98; Hon C Broadwell, Evenlode, Oddington, Adlestrop etc 98-01; Lic to Offic *Eur* from 02; Perm to Offic *Chelmsf* from 09. *44 Quakers Court, Abingdon OX14 3PY* Tel (01235) 524068

RAILTON, David James. b 66. Bradf Univ BPharm89. EMMTC 06. **d** 08 **p** 09. C Melbourne *Derby* from 08. *1 Blackthorn Close, Melbourne, Derby DE73 8LY* Tel (01332) 862383
E-mail davidrailton@gmail.com

RAILTON, John Robert Henry. b 45. Reading Univ BSc68 PhD82 FCIB79. S Dios Minl Tr Scheme 82. **d** 85 **p** 86. NSM Wickham *Portsm* 85-89; C Bridgemary 89-90; V 90-96; TR Ridgeway *Sarum* 96-02; TR Whitton 02-08; rtd 08. *20 Baileys Way, Wroughton, Swindon SN4 9AH* Tel (01793) 814162
E-mail john.railton@btinternet.com

RAILTON, Sandra. b 46. S Dios Minl Tr Scheme 82. **dss** 85 **d** 87 **p** 94. Catherington and Clanfield *Portsm* 85-86; Lee-on-the-Solent 86-89; C 87-89; Par Dn Burnham w Dropmore, Hitcham

and Taplow *Ox* 89-94; TV Wallingford w Crowmarsh Gifford etc 94-98; Dioc Dir Ords (OLM) Berks 96-99; TV Ridgeway *Sarum* 98-02; Dioc Voc Adv 99-02; TV Whitton 02-08; RD Marlborough 04-08; rtd 08. *20 Baileys Way, Wroughton, Swindon SN4 9AH* Tel (01793) 814162

RAILTON-CROWDER, Mrs Mary. b 51. Luton Univ BA96 RN72 RM91 MIOSH93. SAOMC 98. **d** 01 **p** 02. NSM Elstow *St Alb* 01-04; Chapl De Montford Univ 02-04; C Douglas All SS and St Thos *S & M* 04-07; P-in-c Birchencliffe *Wakef* 07-08; V Birkby and Birchencliffe from 08. *The Vicarage, 4 Brendon Drive, Huddersfield HD2 2DF* Tel (01484) 546966
E-mail revmrc@yahoo.com

RAINBIRD, Ms Ruth Patricia. b 40. SRN62. OLM course 98. **d** 01 **p** 02. OLM Limpsfield and Titsey *S'wark* from 01. *73 Stoneleigh Road, Oxted RH8 0TP* Tel (01883) 713683

RAINBOW, Preb Gerald Anton Hayward. b 15. St Edm Hall Ox BA38 MA41. Linc Th Coll 38. **d** 39 **p** 40. C Monkwearmouth St Andr *Dur* 39-43; Chapl RAFVR 43-47; V Claverley *Heref* 47-57; V Leominster 57-80; RD Leominster 60-80; Preb Heref Cathl 67-95; P-in-c Eyton 69-80; rtd 80; Perm to Offic *Heref* 89-01. *Whingate Cottage, Corby Hill, Carlisle CA4 8PN* Tel (01228) 562586

RAINE, Alan. b 49. NEOC 92. **d** 95 **p** 96. NSM Jarrow *Dur* 95-05; Chapl S Tyneside Coll 95-05; V Leam Lane *Dur* from 05. *St Andrew's Vicarage, Whinbrooke, Gateshead NE10 8HR* Tel 0191-489 3042 E-mail alanraine49@aol.com

RAINE, David. b 58. Dur Univ MBA96 Open Univ BA96 MCIM99 MCIPD03. NEOC 01. **d** 04 **p** 05. NSM N Wearside *Dur* 04-06; NSM Millfield St Mary from 06; NSM Bishopwearmouth Gd Shep from 06. *5 Maydown Close, Sunderland SR5 3DZ* Tel 0191-549 7262
E-mail davidraine@dunelm.org.uk

RAINE, Patrick John Wallace. b 21. DFC. Sarum & Wells Th Coll 72. **d** 74 **p** 75. C Chandler's Ford *Win* 74-76; R Highclere and Ashmansworth w Crux Easton 76-84; R Copythorne and Minstead 84-87; rtd 87; P-in-c Breamore *Win* 91-95; Perm to Offic *Win* 95-03; *Sarum* 98-03; *Cov* from 03. *23 Willis House, Hilditch Way, Nuneaton CV11 4LW* Tel (024) 7634 9871

RAINE, Stephen James. b 49. Sheff Poly BA80. NOC 85. **d** 86 **p** 87. C Cottingham *York* 86-90; V Dunscroft Ch Ch *Sheff* 90-92; V Dunscroft St Edwin 92-96; V Kettering St Mary *Pet* 96-08; P-in-c Ipswich St Mary at the Elms *St E* from 08; Chapl Ipswich Hosp NHS Trust from 08. *The Vicarage, 68 Black Horse Lane, Ipswich IP1 2EF* Tel (01473) 216484
E-mail evangelist24@aol.com

RAINER, John Charles. b 54. Ex Univ BA76 CertEd78 Hull Univ MBA02. St Jo Coll Nottm 86. **d** 88 **p** 89. C Fletchamstead *Cov* 88-94; V Leic H Apostles 94-03; V Shipley St Pet *Bradf* from 03. *The Vicarage, 2 Glenhurst Road, Shipley BD18 4DZ* Tel (01274) 584488 E-mail john.rainer@bradford.anglican.org

RAINES, Mrs Gisela Rolanda. b 58. Groningen Univ Kandidaats 80. K Coll Lon BD83. **dss** 84 **d** 87 **p** 94. Charlton St Luke w H Trin *S'wark* 84-87; Par Dn 87; Chapl Imp Coll *Lon* 87-91; Hon C Birch w Fallowfield *Man* 94-95; P-in-c Withington St Chris 95-03; C Man St Ann from 03. *197 Old Hall Lane, Manchester M14 6HJ* Tel 0161-224 6643
E-mail associate_rector@stannsmanchester.com

RAINES, William Guy. b 46. Lon Univ BSc69 MSc70 Ox Univ BA80. Ripon Coll Cuddesdon 78. **d** 81 **p** 82. C W Drayton *Lon* 81-84; C Charlton St Luke w H Trin *S'wark* 84-87; Chapl K Coll Lon 87-94; Chapl Imp Coll 91-94; P-in-c Birch w Fallowfield *Man* 94-95; R from 95. *197 Old Hall Lane, Manchester M14 6HJ* Tel 0161-224 1310 E-mail wraines@emmental.demon.co.uk

RAINEY, Graeme Norman. b 66. Van Mildert Coll Dur BA88 Reading Univ MA01. Ridley Hall Cam 93. **d** 93 **p** 94. C Maltby *Sheff* 93-96; Chapl Reading Univ 96-04; Chapl Downe Ho Sch Berks from 04. *Pickering, St Mary's Paddock, The Ridge, Cold Ash, Thatcham RG18 9JX* Tel (01635) 865112 or 204771
E-mail chaplain@downehouse.net

RAINFORD, Robert Graham. b 56. Lanc Univ CertEd76 BEd77. St Steph Ho Ox 81. **d** 83 **p** 84. C Burnley St Cath w St Alb and St Paul *Blackb* 83-86; C-in-c Hawes Side St Chris CD 86-89; V Hawes Side 89-03; P-in-c Marton Moss 01-03; AD Blackpool 00-03; Hon Can Blackb Cathl 01-03; Sen Chapl to Bp Dover *Cant* 03-05; P Admin Upper Chelsea H Trin *Lon* 05-08; Asst P from 08; Perm to Offic from 08. *Holy Trinity Church, Sloane Street, London SW1X 9BZ* Tel (020) 7730 7270
E-mail priest@holytrinitysloanesquare.co.uk

RAINSBERRY, Edward John. b 24. TCD BA48 MA58. TCD Div Sch Div Test49. **d** 49 **p** 50. C Abbeystrewry Union *C, C & R* 49-52; Chapl RAF 52-58; V Long Compton *Cov* 58-84; R Whichford 58-84; V Long Compton, Whichford and Barton-on-the-Heath 84-95; rtd 95; Perm to Offic *Cov* 95-01; *Ox* and *Pet* from 95. *12 Portway Gardens, Aynho, Banbury OX17 3AR* Tel (01869) 810417

RAINSBURY, Mark James. b 56. NE Lon Poly BA79. Oak Hill Th Coll BA87. **d** 88 **p** 89. C Tonbridge St Steph *Roch* 88-95; C Hampreston *Sarum* 95-97; TV 97-99; Perm to Offic *Win* from 03.

Old Orchard, Church Lane, West Parley, Ferndown BH22 8TS Tel (01202) 590042

RAINSFORD, Peter John. b 31. FCP72. Qu Coll Birm 75. **d** 77 **p** 78. Hon C Lich St Chad 77-81; C 82; C Coseley Ch Ch 82-84; V Wednesbury St Bart 84-91; Chapl Sandwell Distr Gen Hosp 89-91; rtd 91; Perm to Offic *Lich* from 91. *157 Broadway, Walsall WS1 3HD* Tel (01922) 624526
E-mail p.j.rainsford@tinyonline.co.uk

RAISTRICK, Brian. b 38. St Paul's Cheltenham TCert60 Ex Univ AdDipEd68 Newc Univ MEd76 Univ Hull PhD86. Westcott Ho Cam 92. **d** 93 **p** 94. C Haverhill w Withersfield, the Wrattings etc *St E* 93-95; P-in-c Horringer cum Ickworth 95-02; P-in-c Risby w Gt and Lt Saxham and Westley 99-02; P-in-c Chevington w Hargrave and Whepstead w Brockley 00-02; R Horringer 02; RD Thingoe 99-01; rtd 03; Perm to Offic *St E* from 03. *Greenways, Westwood, Great Barton, Bury St Edmunds IP31 2SF* Tel (01284) 787372 *or* 747372
E-mail brian@raistrick.freeserve.co.uk

RAITT, Derek. b 41. K Coll Lon BD63 AKC63. **d** 64 **p** 65. C Blackb St Jas 64-67; C Burnley St Pet 67-69; V Foulridge 69-74; V Euxton 74-91; V Penwortham St Mary 91-00; P-in-c Halton w Aughton 00-06; rtd 06; Perm to Offic *Blackb* from 06. *84 Lymm Avenue, Lancaster LA1 5HR*

RAJ-SINGH, Reji. b 52. Sidney Webb Coll of Educn CertEd79 N Lon Poly BEd90 Heythrop Coll Lon MA02. SAOMC 02. **d** 05 **p** 06. NSM Paddington St Jas *Lon* from 05. *27 Kendal Steps, St Georges Fields, London W2 2YE* Tel (020) 7262 4261 Mobile 07983-430050

RAJA, John Joshva. b 65. Serampore Coll MTh93 Leic Univ MA96 New Coll Edin 96. **d** 93 **p** 94. India 93-95; Hon C Leic H Spirit 95-96; Hon C Edin H Cross 96-99. *43 Scotland Street, Edinburgh EH3 6PY* Tel and fax 0131-557 3797
E-mail j.raja@sms.ed.ac.uk

RAJKOVIC, Michael. b 52. Sheff Univ BMet74 MMet75 PhD79 St Jo Coll Nottm MA95 Lon Bible Coll MPhil03. Cranmer Hall Dur 93. **d** 95 **p** 96. C Harrow Weald All SS *Lon* 95-98; C Woodford Wells *Chelmsf* 98-02; V Bricket Wood *St Alb* from 02. *20 West Riding, Bricket Wood, St Albans AL2 3QP* Tel (01923) 681107 E-mail mrajk30852@aol.com

RAJKUMAR, Peniel Jesudason Rufus. b 77. Sri Venkateswara Univ India BA98 MA02 BD03. **d** 05 **p** 06. NSM Upper Holloway *Lon* 05-08; Tutor United Th Coll Bangalore from 08. *63 Millers Road, Benson Town Post, Bangalore, 560 046, India* E-mail rufus_peniel@rediffmail.com

RAKE, David John. b 47. Nottm Univ BA68 PhD73. Wycliffe Hall Ox 73. **d** 74 **p** 75. C Radcliffe-on-Trent *S'well* 74-77; P-in-c Upwell St Pet *Ely* 77-79; P-in-c Outwell 77-79; Chapl Warw Univ 79-86; V Kenilworth St Nic 86-98; P-in-c Tintagel *Truro* 98-08; Bp's Adv on Spiritual Formation 98-03; Dioc Adv 03-08; Perm to Offic from 09. *The Old Vicarage, Zennor, St Ives TR26 3BY* Tel (01736) 796955

RALPH, Brian Charles. b 66. St Steph Ho Ox 89. **d** 92 **p** 93. C Yeovil St Mich *B & W* 92-95; TV St Jo on Bethnal Green *Lon* 95-01; P-in-c Bethnal Green St Barn 01-03; V from 03. *12 Chisenhale Road, London E3 5TG* Tel (020) 8983 3426, 8806 4130 *or* 7247 1448 E-mail brianralph@btinternet.com

RALPH, Ms Caroline Susan. b 60. Birm Univ BA81 UWE LLM98. Westcott Ho Cam 04. **d** 06 **p** 07. C Crediton, Shobrooke and Sandford etc *Ex* from 06. *50 Beech Park, Crediton EX17 1HW* Tel (01363) 777924
E-mail csralph@ukonline.co.uk

RALPH, Canon Nicholas Robert. b 63. Lanc Univ BSc85 Trin Coll Cam BA91. Westcott Ho Cam 89. **d** 92 **p** 93. C Fareham H Trin *Portsm* 92-95; C Portsea St Cuth 95-96; V Hayling Is St Andr 96-03; V N Hayling St Pet 96-03; Soc Resp Adv 03-06; Hd Miss and Soc from 06; Hon Can Portsm Cathl from 06. *100 St Thomas's Street, Portsmouth PO1 2HE* Tel (023) 9289 9674 E-mail nick@ralphy.org
or nick.ralph@portsmouth.anglican.org

RALPH, Richard Gale. b 51. Pemb Coll Ox BA73 MA78 DPhil78 FRSA90. S Dios Minl Tr Scheme 84. **d** 87 **p** 88. NSM St Leonards Ch Ch and St Mary *Chich* from 87; NSM St Pancras H Cross w St Jude and St Pet *Lon* 87-94; Prin Westmr Coll Ox 96-00. *St Alban, 11 The Mount, St Leonards-on-Sea TN38 0HR* Tel (01424) 422722 E-mail wea@nildram.co.uk

RALPHS, John Eric. b 26. St Cath Coll Ox BA52 MA56 MBAP66. Wycliffe Hall Ox 53. **d** 53 **p** 54. C Wolvercote *Ox* 53-55; Chapl Asst Radcliffe Infirmary Ox 54-62; Chapl Dragon Sch Ox 55-68; Asst Chapl HM Pris Ox 58-61; Jun Chapl Mert Coll Ox 59-62; Chapl St Hugh's Coll Ox 62-67; Priest-Psychotherapist from 68; Lic to Offic *Ox* from 83; rtd 91. *209 Woodstock Road, Oxford OX2 7AB* Tel (01865) 515550

RALPHS, Robert Brian. b 31. Qu Coll Birm 75. **d** 78 **p** 79. Hon C Wednesbury St Jo *Lich* 78-80; Hon C Wednesbury St Paul Wood Green 80-81; Perm to Offic 81-96 and from 97; Hon C W Bromwich Gd Shep w St Jo 96. *204 Bromford Lane, West Bromwich B70 7HX* Tel 0121-553 0119

RALPHS, Sharon Ann. *See* SIMPSON, Mrs Sharon Ann

RAMPTON, Paul Michael. b 47. St Jo Coll Dur BA69 MA73 K Coll Lon PhD85 Westmr Coll Ox MTh99. Wycliffe Hall Ox 72. **d** 73 **p** 74. C Folkestone H Trin w Ch Ch *Cant* 73-77; P-in-c Ringwould w Oxney 77-79; P-in-c Kingsdown 77-79; R Ringwould w Kingsdown 79-83; V Maidstone St Paul 83-88; V Maidstone St Martin 88-95; V Steyning *Chich* from 95; R Ashurst from 95; RD Storrington 99-03. *St Andrew's Vicarage, Station Road, Steyning BN44 3YL* Tel and fax (01903) 813256

RAMPTON, Canon Valerie Edith. b 41. Nottm Univ BSc63 MSc66 BA79. Gilmore Course 78. **dss** 82 **d** 87 **p** 94. Sneinton St Chris w St Phil *S'well* 80-87; Par Dn 87-88; Par Dn Stapleford 88-93; Dioc Adv on Women in Min 90-01; Dn-in-c Kneesall w Laxton and Wellow 93-94; V 94-02; Hon Can S'well Minster 97-02; rtd 02; Perm to Offic *Linc* and *S'well* from 02. *Tansy Cottage, Hillside, Beckingham, Lincoln LN5 0RQ* Tel (01636) 626665 E-mail valerie.rampton@btinternet.com

RAMSARAN (or COOPER), Susan Mira. b 49. K Coll Lon BA70 Univ Coll Lon MA72 PhD78. Ripon Coll Cuddesdon BA92. **d** 93 **p** 94. C Selling w Throwley, Sheldwich w Badlesmere etc *Cant* 93-97; P-in-c Shipbourne *Roch* 97-99; C Plaxtol 97-99; R Shipbourne w Plaxtol 99-06; RD Shoreham 01-06; TR N Tyne and Redesdale *Newc* from 06; AD Bellingham from 06. *The Rectory, Bellingham, Hexham NE48 2JS* Tel (01434) 220019 E-mail smramsaran@aol.com

RAMSAY, Canon Alan Burnett. b 34. AKC62. **d** 63 **p** 64. C Clapham H Trin *S'wark* 63-67; C Warlingham w Chelsham and Farleigh 67-71; P-in-c Stockwell St Mich 71-78; V Lingfield 78-85; P-in-c Crowhurst 83-85; V Lingfield and Crowhurst 85-92; RD Godstone 88-92; V Mitcham St Mark 92-00; Hon Can S'wark Cathl 93-00; rtd 00; Perm to Offic *Cant* from 00. *Kent House, 9 Scotton Street, Wye, Ashford TN25 5BU* Tel (01233) 813730 E-mail aramsay@talktalk.net

RAMSAY, Preb Carl Anthoney St Aubyn. b 55. WMMTC 88. **d** 90 **p** 91. C Wednesfield Heath *Lich* 90-94; V Willenhall St Anne 94-03; V Pelsall from 03; Preb Lich Cathl from 04. *The Vicarage, 39 Hall Lane, Pelsall, Walsall WS3 4JN* Tel (01922) 682098 E-mail spreeboy@talk21.com

RAMSAY, Christopher. b 68. St Jo Coll Dur BA90. Wycliffe Hall Ox BTh94. **d** 97 **p** 98. C Cricklewood St Gabr and St Mich *Lon* 97-01; P-in-c Southall St Geo 01-06; V from 06. *1 Lancaster Road, Southall UB1 1NP* Tel (020) 8574 1876
E-mail christopher.ramsay@btinternet.com

RAMSAY, Eric Nicolson. b 29. **d** 94 **p** 95. C Forfar *St And* 94-99 and 00-09; C Kirriemuir 94-99 and 00-09; Asst Chapl Gtr Athens *Eur* 99-00. *4 Beechwood Place, Kirriemuir DD8 5DZ* Tel (01575) 572029 E-mail ericaileenramsay@tinyworld.co.uk

RAMSAY, James Anthony. b 52. Wadh Coll Ox BA75 MA. **d** 86 **p** 87. C Olney w Emberton *Ox* 86-89; V Blackbird Leys 89-02; Chapl Bucharest w Sofia *Eur* 02-05; P-in-c Lt Ilford St Barn *Chelmsf* from 05; Chapl E Lon Univ from 05. *St Barnabas' Vicarage, Browning Road, London E12 6PB* Tel (020) 8472 2777

RAMSAY, Kenneth William. b 18. ALCD48. **d** 52 **p** 53. C Southall Green St Jo *Lon* 52-57; Asst Chapl Lee Abbey 57-60; Perm to Offic *Portsm* 69-80 and *Sarum* 77-87; rtd 87; Hon C Burstow *S'wark* 87-98; Perm to Offic from 98. *3 Park Close, Strood Green, Betchworth RH3 7JB* Tel (01737) 843470
E-mail ramsay@iname.com

RAMSAY, Kerry. b 59. Heythrop Coll Lon MA94. Westcott Ho Cam 92. **d** 94 **p** 96. V Westville St Eliz S Africa 95-96; C Charlton St Luke w H Trin *S'wark* 96-99; C Cambridge St Mary w St Mich *Ely* 99-04; V Sunninghill *Ox* 04-08; P-in-c S Ascot 07-08; Perm to Offic from 08. *c/o Crockford's Clerical Directory, Church House, Great Smith Street, London SW1P 3AZ* E-mail kerry.ramsay@virgin.net

RAMSAY, Max Roy MacGregor. b 34. Ball Coll Ox MA58. Qu Coll Birm 82. **d** 84 **p** 85. C Hale *Ches* 84-86; C Nantwich 87; V Haslington w Crewe Green 87-91; P-in-c Dunham Massey St Marg and St Mark 92-95; rtd 95; Perm to Offic *Ches* from 95. *6 Comber Way, Knutsford WA16 9BT* Tel (01565) 632362 E-mail max@rmramsay.fsnet.co.uk

RAMSBOTTOM, Mrs Julie Frances. b 54. Trevelyan Coll Dur BA76. S'wark Ord Course 88. **d** 91 **p** 94. Dur Dn Bray and Braywood *Ox* 91-94; C 94-97; R W Woodhay w Enborne, Hampstead Marshall etc from 97; P-in-c Kintbury w Avington from 05. *The Rectory, Enborne, Newbury RG20 0HD* Tel (01635) 34427 E-mail julie.ramsbottom@talk21.com

RAMSBURY, Area Bishop of. *See* CONWAY, The Rt Revd Stephen David

RAMSDEN, Canon Arthur Stuart. b 34. Kelham Th Coll 56. **d** 61 **p** 62. C Featherstone *Wakef* 61-63; C Barnsley St Pet 63-67; V Charlestown 67-70; V Middlestown 70-77; V Purston cum S Featherstone 77-04; Hon Can Wakef Cathl 95-04; rtd 04. *31 Barnsley Road, Cawthorne, Barnsley S75 4HW* Tel (01226) 790696

✠**RAMSDEN, The Rt Revd Peter Stockton.** b 51. Univ Coll Lon BSc74 Leeds Univ MA92. Coll of Resurr Mirfield 74. **d** 77 **p** 78 **c** 07. C Houghton le Spring *Dur* 77-80; C S Shields All SS 80-83; Papua New Guinea 83-90 and 93-96; P-in-c Micklefield *York* 90-93; V Long Benton *Newc* 96-07; Bp Port Moresby from 07.

PO Box 6491, Boroko, NCD, Papua New Guinea Tel (00675) 323 2489 E-mail psramsden.pomanglican@gmail.com

RAMSDEN, Raymond Leslie. b 49. Open Univ BA86. **d** 78 **p** 79. C Greenhill St Jo *Lon* 78-85; C Staines St Mary and St Pet 85-90; V Hounslow St Steph from 90. *St Stephen's Vicarage, Parkside Road, Hounslow TW3 2BP* Tel (020) 8570 3056
E-mail revrramsden@hotmail.com

RAMSDEN, Stuart. *See* RAMSDEN, Canon Arthur Stuart

RAMSEY, Alan Edward. b 72. Wycliffe Hall Ox. **d** 08 **p** 09. C Ox St Aldate from 08. *19 Lamarsh Road, Oxford OX2 0LD* Tel (01865) 254800 E-mail alanramsey@yahoo.com

RAMSEY, Christopher John. b 76. St Jo Coll Nottm BA07. **d** 07 **p** 08. C Saxmundham w Kelsale cum Carlton *St E* from 07. *7 Gull Road, Saxmundham IP17 1WN* Tel (01728) 652916
E-mail revchrisramsey@googlemail.com

RAMSEY-HARDY, Stuart John Andrew. b 46. St Jo Coll Dur BA69. Wycliffe Hall Ox 69. **d** 74 **p** 75. C Stoke Newington St Mary *Lon* 74-77; C Hersham *Guildf* 78-79; Hon C Thames Ditton 79-83. *Address temp unknown*

RAMSHAW, Marcus John. b 71. St Andr Univ MTheol93 York Univ MA94. Cranmer Hall Dur 94. **d** 96 **p** 97. C Hythe *Cant* 96-00; Chapl Down Coll Cam 01-03; NSM Cam St Edw *Ely* from 03. *19 Grantchester Road, Cambridge CB3 9ED* Tel 07793-064455 (mobile)

RANCE, Miss Eleanor Jane. b 72. K Coll Lon BA93 AKC93 St Jo Coll Dur MA96. Cranmer Hall Dur 94. **d** 96 **p** 97. C Barnes St Mary *S'wark* 96-97; C Barnes 97-99; Chapl RAF from 99. *Chaplaincy Services, HQ Personnel and Training Command, RAF High Wycombe HP14 4UE* Tel (01494) 496800 Fax 496343

RANDALL, Anthony. *See* RANDALL, James Anthony

RANDALL, Bernard Charles. b 72. St Andr Univ MA95 Edin Univ MSc97 Man Univ PhD04. St Steph Ho Ox BA06. **d** 06 **p** 07. C Bury St Mary *Man* 06-07; C Atherton and Hindsford w Howe Bridge from 07. *271 North Road, Atherton, Manchester M46 0RF* Tel (01942) 874274

RANDALL, Colin Antony. b 57. SS Paul & Mary Coll Cheltenham BEd78. Trin Coll Bris BD84. **d** 84 **p** 85. C Denton Holme *Carl* 84-87; C Brampton Rch 87-90; R Hanborough and Freeland *Ox* 90-99; P-in-c Croglin *Carl* 99-09; P-in-c Holme Eden 99-05; P-in-c Wetheral w Warwick 99-05; R Holme Eden and Wetheral w Warwick 05-09; RD Brampton 05-09; Hon Can Carl Cathl 08-09; P-in-c Barrow *Ches* from 09; Dioc Worship Adv from 09. *The Rectory, Mill Lane, Great Barrow, Chester CH3 7JF* Tel (01829) 740263 E-mail carandall@freeuk.com

RANDALL, Preb Colin Michael Sebastian. b 50. Aston Univ BSc72. Qu Coll Birm 72. **d** 75 **p** 76. C Tonge w Alkrington *Man* 75-78; C Elton All SS 78-82; P-in-c Bridgwater H Trin *B & W* 82-86; V 86-90; V Bishops Hull 90-00; TR Wellington and Distr from 00; Preb Wells Cathl from 05. *The Rectory, 72 High Street, Wellington TA21 8RF* Tel (01823) 662248
E-mail colinms.randall@virgin.net

RANDALL, Elizabeth. *See* BILLETT, Mrs Elizabeth Nicola

RANDALL, Gareth John. b 49. Southn Univ BA72 PGCE73 ACP80. Oak Hill Th Coll 90. **d** 93 **p** 94. Dir of Studies Dame Alice Owen's Sch Potters Bar 84-95; Dir of Personnel 95-00; Asst Hd 00-07; NSM S Mymms K Chas *St Alb* 93-98; NSM Potters Bar 98-07; P-in-c Dinard *Eur* from 07. *No 7 Residence Victor Hugo, 6 ave Georges Clemenceau, 35800 Dinard, France* Tel (0033) (2) 99 46 77 00

RANDALL, Ian Neville. b 39. Oriel Coll Ox BA62 MA65. St Steph Ho Ox 62. **d** 65 **p** 66. C Perivale *Lon* 65-68; C Fulham St Jo Walham Green 68-73; C Cowley St Jas *Ox* 73-79; TV 79-82; V Didcot St Pet 82-93; P-in-c Clewer St Andr 93-04; rtd 04. *12 Westmead Road, Fakenham NR21 8BL* Tel (01328) 862443

RANDALL, James Anthony. b 36. ACIB69. Ridley Hall Cam 68. **d** 70 **p** 71. C Rusthall *Roch* 70-74; V Shorne 74-79; V Bexleyheath Ch Ch 79-89; R Stone 89-98; rtd 98; Perm to Offic *Roch* from 99. *6 Sandling Way, St Mary's Island, Chatham ME4 3AZ* Tel (01634) 890603

RANDALL, Canon John Terence. b 29. St Cath Coll Cam BA52 MA59. Ely Th Coll 52. **d** 54 **p** 55. C Luton Ch St Alb 54; C Dunstable 54-57; C Ely 57-60; C March St Jo 60-62; Area Sec (S Midl) UMCA 62-64; Area Sec USPG *Birm* and *Cov* 65-76; P-in-c Avon Dassett w Farnborough *Cov* 76-78; P-in-c Fenny Compton 76-78; R Avon Dassett w Farnborough and Fenny Compton 78-84; V New Bilton 84-94; RD Rugby 89-94; Hon Can Cov Cathl 93-94; rtd 94; Perm to Offic *Cov* and *Pet* from 94; *Leic* from 96. *52 Cymbeline Way, Rugby CV22 6LA* Tel (01788) 816659

RANDALL, Jonathan Aubrey. b 64. Bris Univ BSc85. Ridley Hall Cam 04. **d** 06 **p** 07. C Hemingford Grey and Hemingford Abbots *Ely* 06-09; V Yaxley and Holme w Conington from 09; P-in-c Farcet Hampton from 09. *The Vicarage, Church Street, Yaxley, Peterborough PE7 3LH* Tel (01733) 240339

RANDALL, Julian Adrian. b 45. Open Univ BA78 Stirling Univ MSc94 St Andr Univ PhD01 MCIPD. St Jo Sem Wonersh 68. **d** 70 **p** 71. Asst P Mortlake w E Sheen *S'wark* 71-72; Asst P Welling 72-74; Asst P Tunbridge Wells H Trin w Ch Ch *Roch*

74-79; NSM Dunfermline *St And* 96-98; P-in-c Elie and Earlsferry 98-03; P-in-c Pittenweem 98-03; Asst P St Andrews St Andr 03-05; Dir Progr Business Sch St Andr Univ 03-05; Sen Lect Aber Univ from 05. *Flat D, 10 Shearwater Crescent, Dunfermline KY11 8JX* Tel (01382) 554345
E-mail jrandall@randall.co.uk *or* julian.randall@abdn.ac.uk

RANDALL, Kelvin John. b 49. JP80. K Coll Lon BD71 AKC71 Birm Univ PGCE72 Trin Coll Carmarthen MPhil97 Univ of Wales (Ban) PhD00. St Jo Coll Nottm 73. **d** 74 **p** 75. C Peckham St Mary Magd *S'wark* 74-78; C Portsdown *Portsm* 78-81; C-in-c Crookhorn Ch Cen CD 81-82; R Bedhampton 82-90; Bp's Chapl for Post-Ord Tr 84-89; RD Havant 87-89; P-in-c Bournemouth St Jo w St Mich *Win* 90-94; V 94-97; Chapl Talbot Heath Sch Bournemouth 90-94; Research Fell Trin Coll Carmarthen 97-00; C Portswood St Denys *Win* from 00. *The Vicarage, 54 Whitworth Crescent, Southampton SO18 1GD* Tel (023) 8067 2108 Fax 8067 1757 E-mail st.denys@tiscali.co.uk

RANDALL, Mrs Lynda Lorraine. b 44. Sarum & Wells Th Coll 89. **d** 91 **p** 94. Par Dn Chesterton St Andr *Ely* 91-94; C 94-95; C Linton 95-96; TV Linton 96-99; R Byfield w Boddington and Aston le Walls *Pet* from 99. *The Rectory, 55 Church Street, Byfield, Daventry NN11 6XN* Tel (01327) 260204
E-mail lynda@chrislyn.demon.co.uk

RANDALL, Miss Marian Sally. b 49. Trin Coll Bris 75. **dss** 80 **d** 87 **p** 94. Peckham St Mary Magd *S'wark* 80-87; C Sutton Ch 83-97; Par Dn 87-94; C 94-97; P-in-c S Merstham 97-08; rtd 08; Perm to Offic *Cant* from 09. *5 Cheeselands, Biddenden, Ashford TN27 8HJ* Tel (01580) 291684

RANDALL, Martin Trevor. b 51. St Jo Coll Dur BA74. Trin Coll Bris 74. **d** 77 **p** 78. C Ashton-upon-Mersey St Mary Magd *Ches* 77-80; C Everton St Sav w St Cuth *Liv* 80-82; V W Derby Gd Shep 82-91; P-in-c Toxteth Park Ch Ch 91-94; P-in-c Toxteth Park St Bede 91-94; V Toxteth Park Ch Ch w St Bede 95-97; Chapl HM Pris Altcourse 97-07; Perm to Offic *Liv* from 07. *HM Prison Altcourse, Higher Lane, Liverpool L9 7LH* Tel 0151-522 2000 ext 2397 E-mail martin.randall@gslglobal.com

RANDALL, Canon Samuel Paul. b 59. Leeds Univ MA90. Ridley Hall Cam 84. **d** 87 **p** 88. C Kingston upon Hull St Nic *York* 87-89; CF 89-93; TV Bramley *Ripon* 93-96; Dioc Ecum Officer *Dur* 97-01; P-in-c Holmside 97-01; Bp's Officer for Ch in the World *Bradf* from 02; Hon Can Bradf Cathl from 04. *The Vicarage, Morton Lane, East Morton, Keighley BD20 5RS* Tel (01274) 561640 Mobile 07967-120070
E-mail sam.randall@bradford.anglican.org
or sam@bede.u-net.com

RANDELL, David Peter. b 48. Trin Coll Bris BA88. **d** 92 **p** 93. C Wells St Cuth w Wookey Hole *B & W* 92-95; TV Wellington and Distr 95-05; R Chenderit *Pet* from 05. *The Rectory, Marston St Lawrence, Banbury OX17 2DB* Tel (01295) 712279
E-mail revrandell@supanet.com

RANDELL, John Harrison. b 35. Lon Univ BD62. Chich Th Coll 77. **d** 78 **p** 78. C Ribbleton *Blackb* 78-82; V Barton 82-00; rtd 00; Perm to Offic *Blackb* from 00. *6 Royds Avenue, Morecambe LA3 1PA* Tel (01524) 850269

RANDELL, Phillip John. b 45. Lon Univ BD73 CertEd. Linc Th Coll 67. **d** 68 **p** 69. C Henbury *Bris* 68-71; C Summertown *Ox* 71-73; C Liskeard w St Keyne *Truro* 73-75; Chapl Coll of SS Mark and Jo Plymouth 75-79; Tutor St Mark's Th Coll Dar es Salaam 80-82; R Alvescot w Black Bourton, Shilton, Holwell etc *Ox* 82-87; R St Gennys, Jacobstow w Warbstow and Treneglos *Truro* 87-97; rtd 97; Perm to Offic *Truro* from 01. *14 Merlin's Way, Tintagel PL34 0BP* Tel (01840) 770559

RANDOLPH-HORN, David Henry. b 47. Nottm Univ BA69 CQSW71. Qu Coll Birm 80. **d** 82 **p** 83. C Hamstead St Paul *Birm* 82-84; V Sutton St Jas 84-94; Hon C Leytonstone H Trin Harrow Green *Chelmsf* 93-99; Sec Inner Cities Relig Coun 94-99; Assoc Dir Leeds Ch Inst 99-07; P-in-c Heptonstall *Wakef* 99-02; Hon C Farnley *Ripon* 03; Hon C Leeds St Marg and All Hallows from 07. *23 Spencer Place, Leeds LS7 4DQ* Tel 0113-229 7546
E-mail david.hrh@virgin.net

RANGER, Keith Brian. b 34. Down Coll Cam BA58 MA63. Glas NSM Course 58. **d** 81 **p** 84. OMF Internat 81-99; Ethnic Min Co-ord 90-99; Hong Kong 81-89; Perm to Offic *Ches* 89-93 and from 99; *Man* 93-99; rtd 99. *144 Newton Street, Macclesfield SK11 6RW* Tel (01625) 439184
E-mail keithcath@ranger144.fsnet.co.uk

RANKIN, John. *See* RANKIN, Canon William John Alexander

RANKIN, John Cooper. b 24. Glas Univ MA44 Lon Univ BD53. Edin Th Coll 48. **d** 50 **p** 51. C Dundee St Mary Magd *Bre* 50-52; Chapl R Merchant Navy Sch Bearwood 53-60; Min Can Bris Cathl 60-66; Lic to Offic *Lich* 66-69; Prin Lect Bp Otter Coll Chich 69-84; rtd 84. *Address temp unknown*
E-mail johnrankin@cs.com

RANKIN, Joyce. **d** 03 **p** 04. C Dublin St Ann and St Steph *D & G* 03-09; I Bailieborough w Knockbride, Shercock and Mullagh *K, E & A* from 09. *The Rectory, Bailieborough, Co Cavan, Republic of Ireland* Tel (00353) (42) 966 6794
E-mail fejoycer@eircom.net

RANKIN, Stephen Brian. b 65. Salford Univ BSc88. Trin Coll Bris 95. **d** 97 **p** 98. C Ashton-upon-Mersey St Mary Magd *Ches* 97-06; V from 06. *St Mary's Vicarage, 20 Beeston Road, Sale M33 5AG* Tel 0161-973 5118 E-mail srankin@uk2.net

RANKIN, Canon William John Alexander. b 45. Van Mildert Coll Dur BA68 Fitzw Coll Cam BA73 MA77. Westcott Ho Cam 71. **d** 74 **p** 75. C St John's Wood *Lon* 74-78; Chapl Clifton Coll Bris 78-86; P-in-c The Claydons *Ox* 86-91; R 91-93; R Clare w Poslingford, Cavendish etc *St E* 93-04; R Stour Valley from 04; Hon Can St E Cathl from 05. *The Vicarage, 14 High Street, Clare, Sudbury CO10 8NY* Tel (01787) 278501

RANKINE, Christopher Barry. b 66. Portsm Poly BA88. Linc Th Coll BTh93. **d** 93 **p** 95. C Farlington *Portsm* 93-96; C Alverstoke 96-98; C Romsey *Win* 98-00; P-in-c W Andover 00-09; TR Portway and Danebury from 09. *The Vicarage, 17 Millway Road, Andover SP10 3EU* Tel (01264) 392541
E-mail chris.rankine@lineone.net

RANN, Preb Harry Harvey. b 18. Sarum Th Coll 47. **d** 50 **p** 51. C Victoria Docks Ascension *Chelmsf* 50-52; C Christchurch *Win* 52-56; C Mill Hill Jo Keble Ch *Lon* 56-57; V Woolfold *Man* 57-62; Dean's Chapl and PV Ex Cathl 62-77; Sacr 65-77; Succ 73-77; V Colyton 77-84; R Colyton and Southleigh 84-86; RD Honiton 84-86; Preb Ex Cathl 84-87; TR Colyton, Southleigh, Offwell, Widworthy etc 86-87; rtd 87; Perm to Offic *Ex* from 87. *All Saints' House, Kenton, Exeter EX6 8NG* Tel (01626) 890451

RANN, Ruth Margaret. b 32. Bris Univ BA54. **d** 03 **p** 04. NSM Exminster and Kenn 03-04; C Kenton, Mamhead, Powderham, Cofton and Starcross from 04. *All Saints' House, Kenton, Exeter EX6 8NG* Tel (01626) 890451

RANSFORD, Elizabeth Ann. b 49. Sussex Univ BSc70 Leeds Univ MA99 Whitelands Coll Lon PGCE71. Cranmer Hall Dur 07. **d** 08 **p** 09. OLM York St Thos w St Maurice from 08. *17 St Mary's, York YO30 7DD* Tel (01904) 672332 Mobile 07525-210572 E-mail liz.ransford@ntlworld.com

RANSOME, Arthur. b 21. St Jo Coll Nottm 71. **d** 72 **p** 72. Israel 72-76; C Virginia Water *Guildf* 76-79; P-in-c Peper Harow 79-82; P-in-c Shackleford 79-82; P-in-c Seale 82-89; rtd 89; Perm to Offic *Truro* 89-99. *Tudor Lodge, 60 East Church Street, Xenia OH 45385-3002, USA* Tel (001) (937) 372 2339

RANSON, Canon Arthur Frankland. b 50. St Jo Coll Dur BA73. Wycliffe Hall Ox 73. **d** 75 **p** 76. C Bare *Blackb* 75-78; C Scotforth 78-81; V Leyland St Ambrose 81-02; AD Leyland 96-02; P-in-c Blackb St Silas from 02; Hon Can Blackb Cathl from 00. *St Silas's Vicarage, Preston New Road, Blackburn BB2 6PS* Tel (01254) 671293 E-mail arthur.ranson@ntlworld.com

RANSON, George Sidney. b 28. Open Univ BA78. NEOC 85. **d** 86 **p** 87. NSM Acomb H Redeemer *York* 86-88; C Warton St Oswald w Yealand Conyers *Blackb* 88-90; V Pilling 90-95; rtd 95; Perm to Offic *Blackb* 95-06. *2 The Ridings, Bourne PE10 0FS*

RANSON, Terence William James. b 42. AKC64 MTh87 STM88 AFAIM91. St Boniface Warminster 64. **d** 65 **p** 66. C Walton St Mary *Liv* 65-69; C Ipswich St Mary le Tower *St E* 69-71; Chapl Mersey Miss to Seamen 71-74; V N Keyham *Ex* 74-79; Australia 79-91; Sen Chapl and State Sec Fremantle Miss to Seamen 79-91; V N Mymms *St Alb* 91-04; rtd 04; Perm to Offic *Heref* from 04. *23 Pennine Close, Hereford HR4 0TE* Tel and fax (01432) 278363

RANYARD, Michael Taylor. b 43. Nottm Univ BTh74. Linc Th Coll 71. **d** 74 **p** 75. C Sutton in Ashfield St Mary *S'well* 74-76; Hon C Lewisham St Mary *S'wark* 76-77; C Rushmere *St E* 77-79; R Hopton, Market Weston, Barningham etc 79-83; Chr Educn and Resources Adv *Dur* 83-93; Perm Adv to Dioc Bd of Educn *Blackb* 93-98; Asst P Blackb Cathl 98-99; rtd 99; Perm to Offic *Heref* from 99. *72 Wyedean Rise, Belmont, Hereford HR2 7XZ* Tel and fax (01432) 355452
E-mail smranyard@xalt.co.uk

RAO, Norma Ruoman. b 63. Westmr Coll Ox BTh97. Westcott Ho Cam 99. **d** 01 **p** 02. C Endcliffe *Sheff* 01-04; C Rotherham 04-08; R Rossington from 08. *The Rectory, Sheep Bridge Lane, Rossington, Doncaster DN11 0EZ* Tel (01302) 867597
E-mail normarowe@btinternet.com

RAPHAEL, Brother. See PARKER, Ramon Lewis

RAPHAEL, The Ven Timothy John. b 29. Leeds Univ BA53. Coll of Resurr Mirfield. **d** 55 **p** 56. C Westmr St Steph w St Jo *Lon* 55-60; V Welling *S'wark* 60-63; New Zealand 63-72; Dean Dunedin 65-72; V St John's Wood *Lon* 72-83; AD Westmr St Marylebone 82-83; Adn Middx 83-96; rtd 96; Perm to Offic *Glouc* from 96. *121 Hales Road, Cheltenham GL52 6ST* Tel (01242) 256075

RAPHOE, Archdeacon of. See HARTE, The Ven Matthew Scott

RAPHOE, Dean of. See HAY, The Very Revd John

RAPKIN, Kevern. b 39. St D Coll Lamp BA62 Univ of Wales BD72. Lich Th Coll 63. **d** 65 **p** 66. C Hanley w Hope *Lich* 65-68; C Woodchurch *Ches* 68-70; C Abbots Langley *St Alb* 70-73; R Mt Pleasant Australia 73-80; R Rockingham and Safety Bay 80-90; R Lesmurdie 90-00; C Sholing *Win* 00-04; rtd 04; Australia from 04. *15 Gamage Way, Lockridge WA 6054, Australia* Tel (0061) (8) 9377 0332

RAPLEY, Frederick Arthur. b 27. Roch Th Coll 67. **d** 69 **p** 70. C Tenterden St Mildred w Smallhythe *Cant* 69-75; P-in-c Sittingbourne H Trin w Bobbing 75-85; V 85-89; rtd 89; Hon C Luton St Andr *St Alb* 89-92; Perm to Offic *St Alb* 92-98; *Cant* 98-02; *St E* from 02. *26 Angela Close, Martlesham, Woodbridge IP12 4TG* Tel (01473) 622922

RAPLEY, Mrs Joy Naomi. b 41. Portsm Poly CertEd63 Open Univ BA79. Sarum & Wells Th Coll 87. **d** 89 **p** 94. Par Dn Welwyn Garden City *St Alb* 89-92; Chapl S Beds Community Healthcare Trust 92-98; C Wilbury *St Alb* 94-95; NSM St Mary's Bay w St Mary-in-the-Marsh etc *Cant* 98-02; NSM New Romney w Old Romney and Midley 98-02; Asst Chapl E Kent NHS and Soc Care Partnership Trust 99-02; P-in-c Clopton w Otley, Swilland and Ashbocking *St E* 02-08; Perm to Offic from 08. *26 Angela Close, Martlesham, Woodbridge IP12 4TG* Tel (01473) 622922 E-mail revraps@aol.com

RAPSEY, Preb Peter Nigel. b 46. K Coll Lon BD68 AKC68. St Boniface Warminster. **d** 69 **p** 70. C Walton-on-Thames *Guildf* 69-73; C Fleet 73-77; P-in-c The Collingbournes and Everleigh *Sarum* 77-79; TV Wexcombe 79-84; R Wokingham St Paul *Ox* 84-93; Chapl Warminster Sch 93-96; V Frome Ch Ch *B & W* 96-04; P-in-c Evercreech w Chesterblade and Milton Clevedon from 04; RD Frome 01-03; Dir of Ords from 03; Preb Wells Cathl from 04. *The Vicarage, Church Lane, Evercreech, Shepton Mallet BA4 6HU* Tel (01749) 830322
E-mail peter.rapsey@btinternet.com

RASHBROOK, Alan Victor. b 42. S'wark Ord Course. **d** 75 **p** 76. Hon C Woking St Mary *Guildf* 75-83. *Hope Cottage, Robin Hood Lane, Sutton Green, Guildford GU4 7QG* Tel (01483) 762760

RASON, Frederick George. b 26. Qu Coll Birm 68. **d** 69 **p** 70. C Weymouth H Trin *Sarum* 69-72; P-in-c Yatesbury 72-73; P-in-c Cherhill 72-73; R Oldbury 73-76; R W Parley 76-91; rtd 91; Perm to Offic *Sarum* from 91 and *Win* from 92. *4 Knoll Gardens, St Ives, Ringwood BH24 2LW* Tel (01425) 475761

RASON, Stuart Paul. Trin Coll Bris BA08. **d** 08 **p** 09. C Downs Benefice *Win* from 08. *The Rectory, The Street, Chilbolton, Stockbridge SO20 6BA* Tel (01264) 860258
E-mail stuartrason@hotmail.com

RASTALL, Preb Thomas Eric. b 19. St Aid Birkenhead 62. **d** 63 **p** 64. C Leek St Luke *Lich* 64-67; V Brown Edge 67-74; P-in-c Croxden 74-78; V Denstone 74-81; P-in-c Ellastone 78-81; V Denstone w Ellastone and Stanton 81-91; RD Uttoxeter 87-91; Preb Lich Cathl 89-91; rtd 91; Perm to Offic *Cov* 91-01. *10 Vicarage Close, Burton, Carnforth LA6 1NP* Tel (01524) 782386

RATCLIFF, Canon David William. b 37. Edin Th Coll 59. **d** 62 **p** 63. C Croydon St Aug *Cant* 62-65; C Selsdon St Jo w St Fran 65-69; V Motspur Park *S'wark* 69-75; Hon Min Can Cant Cathl 75-91; Asst Dir of Educn 75-91; Dioc Adv in Adult Educn and Lay Tr 75-91; Hon Pres Protestant Assn for Adult Educn in Eur 82-88; Chapl Frankfurt-am-Main 91-98; Adn Scandinavia *Eur* 96-05; Chapl Stockholm w Gävle and Västerås 98-02; rtd 05; Perm to Offic *Cant* from 02. *9 The Orchards, Elham, Canterbury CT4 6TR* Tel (01303) 840624 Fax 840871

RATCLIFF, Paul Ronald. b 62. Univ Coll Lon BSc83 Leic Univ MSc84 PhD89 FRAS MInstP. SEITE 05. **d** 09. C Cant St Martin and St Paul from 09. *Glebe House, Military Road, Canterbury CT1 1PA* Tel (01227) 463505
E-mail pr.ratcliff@googlemail.com

RATCLIFFE, Canon Michael David. b 43. Lon Univ BSc65 Southn Univ PGCE67 Lon Univ BA75 Lanc Univ MA84. Cranmer Hall Dur 75. **d** 77 **p** 78. C Blackpool St Thos *Blackb* 77-81; V Oswaldtwistle St Paul from 81; RD Accrington 97-03; Hon Can Blackb Cathl from 00. *29 Mayfield Avenue, Oswaldtwistle, Accrington BB5 3AA* Tel (01254) 231038 Fax 390273 E-mail mratossy@tiscali.co.uk

RATCLIFFE, Peter Graham Bruce. St Mich Coll Llan. **d** 08 **p** 09. C Carmarthen St Pet *St D* from 08. *St Peter's Clergy House, 10A The Parade, Carmarthen SA31 1LY* Tel (01267) 237303

RATCLIFFE, Peter William Lewis. b 30. Birm Univ BSc55 Lon Univ BD58. Tyndale Hall Bris 55. **d** 58 **p** 59. C Cambridge St Andr Less *Ely* 58-61; R Wistow 61-74; R Bury 61-74; V Rainham *Chelmsf* 74-85; R Wennington 75-85; V Heacham *Nor* 85-87; P-in-c Sedgeford w Southmere 85-87; V Heacham and Sedgeford 87-95; rtd 95; Perm to Offic *Nor* from 95. *22 Birchfield Gardens, Mulbarton, Norwich NR14 8BT* Tel (01508) 570511
E-mail p&mratcliffe@mulb.fsnet.co.uk

RATCLIFFE, Mrs Roosevelta (Rosie). b 60. K Coll Lon BA97 MA99. SEITE 98. **d** 01 **p** 02. C Croydon St Matt *S'wark* 01-04; Hon C Sanderstead 05-06; Chapl S Lon and Maudsley NHS Foundn Trust from 04. *Bethlem Royal Hospital, Monks Orchard Road, Beckenham BR3 3BX* Tel (020) 8777 6611 Fax 8777 1668

RATHBAND, The Very Revd Kenneth William. b 60. Edin Univ BD86. Edin Th Coll 82. **d** 86 **p** 87. C Dundee St Paul *Bre* 86-88; TV Dundee St Martin 88-89; C Edin SS Phil and Jas 90-91; R Alyth *St And* from 91; R Blairgowrie from 91; R Coupar Angus

from 91; Dean St Andr from 07. *10 Rosemount Park, Blairgowrie PH10 6TZ* Tel (01250) 872431 *or* 874583
E-mail krathband@btinternet.com

RATHBONE, Mrs Elizabeth. b 51. Lon Univ MB, BS76 MRCGP80. WMMTC 03. **d** 03 **p** 04. C Tettenhall Regis *Lich* 03-06; TV from 06. *76 Tyninghame Avenue, Wolverhampton WV6 9PW* Tel (01902) 753562
E-mail liz.rathbone@blueyonder.co.uk

RATHBONE, Mrs Isobel. b 48. Girton Coll Cam MA70 Leeds Univ MA02 Solicitor 81. NEOC 02. **d** 05 **p** 06. NSM Moor Allerton *Ripon* 05-08; NSM Hooe *Chich* 08-09; NSM Ninfield 08-09. *44 Wealden Way, Bexhill-on-Sea TN39 4NY* Tel 07775-656257 (mobile) E-mail rathbone.i@sky.com

RATHBONE, Paul. b 36. BNC Ox BA58 MA62. Wycliffe Hall Ox 58. **d** 60 **p** 61. C Carl St Jo 60-63; C Heworth w Peasholme St Cuth *York* 63-68; V Thorganby w Skipwith and N Duffield 68-83; V Bishopthorpe and Acaster Malbis 83-01; rtd 01; Perm to Offic *York* from 01. *12 Whitelass Close, Thirsk YO7 1FG* Tel (01845) 523347

RATHBONE, Stephen Derek. b 61. Wycliffe Hall Ox. **d** 00 **p** 01. C W Kirby St Bridget *Ches* 00-03; P-in-c Rainow w Saltersford and Forest from 03. *The Vicarage, Rainow, Macclesfield SK10 5TZ* Tel (01625) 572013 E-mail steve.rathbone@virgin.net

RATINGS, Canon John William. b 37. St Pet Coll Ox BA62 MA71. Cuddesdon Coll 62. **d** 64 **p** 65. C Langley All SS and Martyrs *Man* 64-68; C Easthampstead *Ox* 68-71; V Wargrave 71-02; V Wargrave w Knowl Hill 02-08; RD Sonning 88-98; Hon Can Ch Ch from 97; Provost Woodard Corp (S Division) 00-06; rtd 08; Perm to Offic *Ox* from 08. *18 Autumn Walk, Wargrave, Reading RG10 8BS* Tel 0118-940 1363
E-mail jratings@sky.com

RATTENBERRY, Christopher James. b 59. York Univ BA80 Solicitor. St Jo Coll Nottm 91. **d** 93 **p** 94. C Porchester *S'well* 93-98; P-in-c Daybrook 98-04; V 04-06; AD Nottingham N 01-05; P-in-c Ravenshead from 06. *St Peter's Vicarage, 55 Sheepwalk Lane, Ravenshead, Nottingham NG15 9FD* Tel (01623) 405203 E-mail chris.rattenberry@ntlworld.com

✠**RATTERAY, The Rt Revd Alexander Ewen.** b 42. Codrington Coll Barbados 61. **d** 65 **p** 66 **c** 96. C S Kirkby *Wakef* 66-68; C Sowerby St Geo 68-71; V Airedale w Fryston 71-80; Bermuda 80-08; Adn Bermuda 94-96; Bp Bermuda 96-08; rtd 08. *PO Box HM 2021, Hamilton HM CX, Bermuda*
E-mail bishopratteray@ibl.bm

RATTIGAN, Paul Damian. b 61. Reading Univ BSc87 Liv Hope MA00 Sussex Univ PGCE88. Qu Coll Birm 93. **d** 95 **p** 96. C Parr *Liv* 95-99; P-in-c St Helens St Matt Thatto Heath 99-01; V 01-05; Dioc Voc Adv 02-05; P-in-c Boldmere *Birm* 05-08; V from 08. *209 Station Road, Sutton Coldfield B73 5LE* Tel 0121-354 4501
E-mail paul@stmichaels.org.uk

RATTUE, James. b 69. Ball Coll Ox BA91 MA04 Leic Univ MA93. St Steph Ho Ox 03. **d** 05 **p** 06. C Weybridge *Guildf* 05-08 and from 09; C Englefield Green 08-09. *87 Greenlands Road, Weybridge KT13 8PS* Tel (01932) 821196 Mobile 07952-615499 E-mail jamesrattue@hotmail.com

RAVALDE, Canon Geoffrey Paul. b 54. St Cuth Soc Dur BA76 SS Coll Cam BA80 MA90 Lon Univ MTh01 Barrister 78 Westcott Ho Cam 84. **d** 87 **p** 88. C Spalding *Linc* 87-91; P-in-c Wigton *Carl* 91-92; V from 92; RD Carl 95-00; Hon Can Carl Cathl from 96. *The Vicarage, Longthwaite Road, Wigton CA7 9JR* Tel (01697) 342337

RAVEN, Ann. *See* GURNER, Mrs Margaret Ann

RAVEN, Barry. b 48. Sarum & Wells Th Coll 69. **d** 72 **p** 73. C Henbury *Bris* 72-76; P-in-c S Marston w Stanton Fitzwarren 76-78; TV Stratton St Margaret w S Marston etc 78-80; P-in-c Coalpit Heath 80-84; V 84-91; R Ashley, Crudwell, Hankerton and Oaksey from 91; P-in-c Ashton Keynes, Leigh and Minety from 07; RD N Wilts 99-06. *The Rectory, 1 Days Court, Crudwell, Malmesbury SN16 9HG* Tel (01666) 577118
E-mail barry@deanery.org.uk

RAVEN, Margaret Hilary. b 45. Dur Univ BA67 Man Univ MEd73. Wesley Th Sem Washington MDiv95. **d** 96 **p** 97. USA 96-01; Asst R Martinsburg Trin Ch 96-99; Assoc R Toms River Ch Ch 99-00; Perm to Offic *Edin* 02-06; NSM Edin Ch Ch from 06. *32 Montpelier Park, Edinburgh EH10 4NJ* Tel 0131-228 4790
E-mail mthrraven@btopenworld.com

RAVEN, Tony. b 39. Garnett Coll Lon CertEd65 CEng72 MIET72. SAOMC 94. **d** 97 **p** 98. NSM Lt Berkhamsted and Bayford, Essendon etc *St Alb* 97-01; P-in-c Lt Hadham w Albury 01-05; rtd 05; Hon C Hazelbury Bryan and the Hillside Par *Sarum* from 07. *1 Church View, Wonston, Hazelbury Bryan, Sturminster Newton DT10 2DF*
E-mail t_raven@btopenworld.com

RAVENS, David Arthur Stanley. b 30. Jes Coll Ox BA53 MA61 Lon Univ BD63. Wells Th Coll 61. **d** 63 **p** 64. C Seacroft *Ripon* 63-70; TV 70-73; Teacher Sir Wm Borcase's Sch Marlow 73-87; rtd 95. *44 Arthursdale Grange, Scholes, Leeds LS15 4AW* Tel 0113-273 6648

RAVENSCROFT, The Ven Raymond Lockwood. b 31. Leeds Univ BA53. Coll of Resurr Mirfield 54. **d** 55 **p** 56. C Goodwood

S Africa 55-57; C St Jo Cathl Bulawayo S Rhodesia 57-59; R Francistown Bechuanaland 59-62; C St Ives *Truro* 62-64; V Falmouth All SS 64-68; V St Stephens by Launceston 68-73; P-in-c Launceston St Thos 68-73; V Launceston St Steph w St Thos 73-74; TR Probus, Ladock and Grampound w Creed and St Erme 74-88; RD Powder 77-81; Hon Can Truro Cathl 82-88; P-in-c St Erme 84-85; Adn Cornwall and Can Lib Truro Cathl 88-96; rtd 96; Perm to Offic *Truro* from 96 and *Ex* from 00. *19 Montpelier Court, St David's Hill, Exeter EX4 4DP* Tel (01392) 430607

RAVENSDALE, Jonathan Christopher. b 56. Aston Tr Scheme 90 Chich Th Coll 92. **d** 94 **p** 95. C Leytonstone St Marg w St Columba *Chelmsf* 94-97; P-in-c Leytonstone St Andr 97-01; Voc Adv Richborough *Cant* and Barking from 97; V Walthamstow St Mich from 01. *St Michael's Vicarage, 9 Palmerston Road, London E17 6PQ* Tel (020) 8520 6328

✠**RAWCLIFFE, The Rt Revd Derek Alec.** b 21. OBE71. Leeds Univ BA42. Coll of Resurr Mirfield 42. **d** 44 **p** 45 **c** 74. C Claines St Geo *Worc* 44-47; Solomon Is 47-58; New Hebrides 58-80; Adn S Melanesia 59-74; Asst Bp Melanesia 74-75; Bp New Hebrides 75-80; Bp Glas 81-91; rtd 91; Asst Bp Ripon 91-96; Lic to Offic from 96. *7 Dorset Avenue, Leeds LS8 3RA* Tel 0113-249 2670 E-mail derek@derekrawcliffe.me.uk

RAWDING, Andrew. b 70. Cranmer Hall Dur 00. **d** 02 **p** 03. C Enfield St Andr *Lon* 02-05; Hon C Arm St Mark 05-07; Chapl RN from 08. *Royal Naval Chaplaincy Service, Mail Point 1-2, Leach Building, Whale Island, Portsmouth PO2 8BY* Tel (023) 9262 5055 Fax 9262 5134

RAWDON-MOGG, Timothy David. b 45. St Jo Coll Dur BA76. Cuddesdon Coll 75. **d** 77 **p** 78. C Wotton St Mary *Glouc* 77-80; C Ascot Heath *Ox* 80-82; V Woodford Halse w Eydon *Pet* 82-88; V Shrivenham w Watchfield and Bourton *Ox* 88-00; R Horsted Keynes *Chich* 00-08; rtd 08. *Stone Cottage, The Bog, Minsterley, Shrewsbury SY5 0NJ* Tel (01743) 792073

RAWE, Alan Charles George. b 29. ALCD56. **d** 56 **p** 57. C W Kilburn St Luke w St Simon and St Jude *Lon* 56-59; Lect Watford St Mary *St Alb* 59-61; R Ore St Helen and St Barn *Chich* 61-69; R Moreton *Ches* 69-80; V Coppull *Blackb* 80-83; Miss to Seamen 83-94; Felixstowe Seafarers' Cen 88-94; rtd 94; Perm to Offic *Blackb* from 94. *15 Starfield Close, Lytham St Annes FY8 4QA* Tel (01253) 733647

RAWLING, Miss Jane Elizabeth. b 51. Birm Univ BSc73 St Jo Coll York CertEd75. St Jo Coll Nottm 81. **dss** 84 **d** 87 **p** 94. Southsea St Jude *Portsm* 84-88; C 87-88; C St Paul's Cray St Barn *Roch* 88-91; Hon C from 91; SE Regional Co-ord BCMS Crosslinks 91-01; Sec for Bps' Selection Conf and CME Sec Min Division 01-07. *50 Batchwood Green, Orpington BR5 2NF* Tel (01689) 871467

RAWLING, Preb Stephen Charles. b 43. Man Univ BSc64 Bris Univ MSc71. Sarum & Wells Th Coll 71. **d** 73 **p** 74. C Bris St Andr Hartcliffe 73-76; C Westlands St Andr *Lich* 76-78; R Darlaston St Lawr 78-90; TR Bloxwich 90-08; Preb Lich Cathl 07-08; rtd 08. *31 Stowe Street, Lichfield WS13 6AQ* Tel (01543) 262917

RAWLINGS, Canon Brenda Susan. b 48. Sussex Univ CertEd69. Oak Hill Th Coll 83. **d** 07 **p** 94. Par Dn Green Street Green *Roch* 87-90; Par Dn Collier Row St Jas and Havering-atte-Bower *Chelmsf* 90-94; C Greenstead 94-98; R 98-00; TR Greenstead w Colchester St Anne 00-06; Hon Can Chelmsf Cathl 05-06; rtd 06; Perm to Offic *Nor* and *St E* from 07. *10 Sorrel Drive, Thetford IP24 2YJ* Tel (01842) 752881

RAWLINGS, Elizabeth. b 66. Nottm Univ BSc96 RGN87. St Jo Coll Nottm 04. **d** 06 **p** 07. C Derby St Alkmund and St Werburgh 06-07; C Walbrook Epiphany from 07. *25 Queen Mary Court, Derby DE22 1BB* Tel (01332) 200551
E-mail lizrawlings66@yahoo.co.uk

RAWLINGS, Gayle Ann Mary. b 53. Toronto Univ MD76 BA88 K Coll Lon MA89 FRCP(C)81. Westcott Ho Cam 01. **d** 03 **p** 04. C Ex St Thos and Em 03-07; Chapl Univ Coll of SS Mark and Jo Plymouth 07-09; Canada from 09. *Address temp unknown*

RAWLINGS, The Ven John Edmund Frank. b 47. AKC69. St Aug Coll Cant 69. **d** 70 **p** 71. C Rainham *Roch* 70-73; C Tattenham Corner and Burgh Heath *Guildf* 73-76; Chapl RN 76-92; V Tavistock and Gulworthy *Ex* 92-05; Chapl Kelly Coll Tavistock 93-02; RD Tavistock *Ex* 97-02; Preb Ex Cathl from 99; Adn Totnes from 06. *Blue Hills, Bradley Road, Bovey Tracey, Newton Abbot TQ13 9EU* Tel (01626) 832064 Fax 834947
E-mail archdeacon.of.totnes@exeter.anglican.org

RAWLINGS, Canon Philip John. b 53. St Jo Coll Nottm BTh83. **d** 83 **p** 84. C Blackley St Andr *Man* 83-87; C Halliwell St Pet 87-93; R Old Trafford St Bride from 93; AD Stretford 98-05; Hon Can Man Cathl from 04. *St Bride's Rectory, 29 Shrewsbury Street, Old Trafford, Manchester M16 9BB* Tel 0161-226 6064 E-mail philjr@zetnet.co.uk

RAWLINGS, Susan. *See* RAWLINGS, Canon Brenda Susan

RAWLINS, Clyde Thomas. b 28. **d** 02. NSM Leeds St Aid *Ripon* from 02. *26 Gledhow Wood Close, Leeds LS8 1PN* Tel 0113-266 7731

RAWLINSON, Curwen. b 32. MBE73. Leeds Univ CertEd55 Man Univ DipEd56 Open Univ BA80. Sarum Th Coll 59. **d** 61 **p** 62. C Wigan St Mich *Liv* 61-63; CF 63-78; Dep Asst Chapl Gen 78-80; Asst Chapl Gen 80-85; QHC 83-98; R Uley w Owlpen and Nympsfield *Glouc* 85-98; RD Dursley 89-96; rtd 98; Perm to Offic *Glouc* from 98; Sub Chapl HM Pris Glouc from 02. *Cark House, 6 Groves Place, Fairford GL7 4BJ* Tel (01285) 711009

RAWLINSON, James Nigel. b 56. Em Coll Cam BA77 MB, BCh80 FRCSE86 FFAEM98. WMMTC 95. **d** 98 **p** 99. NSM Bath Weston All SS w N Stoke and Langridge *B & W* from 98; Perm to Offic *Bris* from 98; Consultant Bris R Infirmary from 99. *Glen Boyd House, 38 Court View, Wick, Bristol BS30 5QP* Tel 0117-303 9220 E-mail nigel.rawlinson@bristol.ac.uk

RAWLINSON, John. b 47. Guy's Hosp Medical Sch BSc67 MB, BS71 MRCS. EAMTC 89. **d** 92 **p** 93. NSM Tilbrook *Ely* 92-05; NSM Covington 92-05; NSM Catworth Magna 92-05; NSM Keyston and Bythorn 92-05; Chapl Chu Coll Cam from 98. *The Malt House, 42 Stonely, Huntingdon PE28 0EH* Tel (01480) 860263 Fax 861590 E-mail dingleberry@lineone.net *or* jr338@cam.ac.uk

RAWSON, Canon Michael Graeme. b 62. York Univ BA84. St Steph Ho Ox BA88. **d** 89 **p** 90. C Brighouse St Martin *Wakef* 89-92; C Brighouse and Clifton 92-93; V Gomersal 93-04; Bp's Dom Chapl and Publicity Officer 04-07; Can Res Wakef Cathl from 07. *3 Cathedral Close, Margaret Street, Wakefield WF1 2DP* Tel (01924) 379743 *or* 373923 E-mail michael.rawson@wakefield-cathedral.org.uk

RAY, Mrs Joanna Zorina. b 55. AIMLS78 K Coll Lon BSc77 Garnett Coll Lon PGCE80 Lon Inst of Educn MA92. S'wark Ord Course 84. **d** 87 **p** 94. NSM Carshalton *S'wark* 87-91; NSM Sutton New Town St Barn 91-93; NSM Knighton St Mary Magd *Leic* 93-94; C Leic H Spirit 94-98; Chapl for Deaf People 94-98; Chapl St Andr Hosp Northn 99-03; Perm to Offic *S'well* from 04. *37 Torvill Drive, Nottingham NG8 2BU* Tel 07802-300799 (mobile) E-mail revdjoannaray@aol.com

RAY, John Mead. b 28. OBE79. St Andr Univ MA50 DipEd51. CMS Tr Coll Chislehurst 60. **d** 70 **p** 71. Miss Partner CMS 70-95; C Sparkhill St Jo *Birm* 87-90; C Sparkbrook Em 87-90; C Sparkhill w Greet and Sparkbrook 90; Deanery Missr 90-95; rtd 95; Perm to Offic *Birm* from 95. *190 Sarehole Road, Birmingham B28 8EF* Tel 0121-777 6143 E-mail cath.john@lycos.co.uk

RAY, Robin John. b 44. Sarum & Wells Th Coll 72. **d** 74 **p** 75. C Bourne Valley *Sarum* 74-78; P-in-c Dilton's-Marsh 78-82; V 82-87; V Taunton Lyngford *B & W* 87-93; R Exford, Exmoor, Hawkridge and Withypool 93-04; ACORA Link Officer and Rural Affairs Officer 93-04; rtd 04; Perm to Offic *B & W* from 04. *Leigholt Farm, Somerton Road, Street BA16 0SU* Tel (01458) 841281

RAYBOULD, James Clive Barham. b 37. Wolv Univ BSc62 Anglia Poly Univ MBA94 PhD01. Cranmer Hall Dur 81. **d** 83 **p** 84. C Cannock *Lich* 83-86; P-in-c Leek Wootton *Cov* 86-89; Dioc Tr Adv 86-89; TV Cannock *Lich* 89; Assoc Lect Anglia Ruskin Univ from 90; rtd 00. *73 Eastwood Old Road, Leigh-on-Sea SS9 4RS* Tel (01702) 522277

✠**RAYFIELD, The Rt Revd Lee Stephen.** b 55. Southn Univ BSc78 Lon Univ PhD81 SOSc95. Ridley Hall Cam 93. **d** 93 **p** 94 **c** 05. C Woodford Wells *Chelmsf* 93-97; P-in-c Furze Platt *Ox* 97-05; AD Maidenhead and Windsor 00-05; Suff Bp Swindon *Bris* from 05. *Mark House, Field Rise, Swindon SN1 4HP* Tel (01793) 538654 Fax 525181 E-mail bishop.swindon@bristoldiocese.org

RAYMENT, Andrew David. b 45. Univ of Wales (Lamp) BA68 Univ of Wales (Abth) MA70 Nottm Univ PhD06. Ridley Hall Cam 78. **d** 80 **p** 81. C Costessey *Nor* 80-83; C Earlham St Anne 83-90; V Old Catton 90-96; Perm to Offic *Pet* from 00; Min Partnership Development Officer from 04; Adult Educn Officer (CME and Min Partnership) from 05. *Diocese of Peterborough, Bouverie Court, 6 The Lakes, Northampton NN4 7YD* Tel (01604) 887047 *or* (01327) 340359 E-mail andrew.rayment@peterborough-diocese.org.uk

RAYMENT, Mrs Helen Elizabeth. b 46. Keswick Hall Coll CertEd67. EAMTC 92. **d** 95 **p** 96. NSM Old Catton *Nor* 95-96; Perm to Offic *Pet* 01-02; P-in-c Weedon Bec w Everdon and Dodford 02-03; V from 03. *The Vicarage, Church Street, Weedon, Northampton NN7 4PL* Tel (01327) 340359 E-mail revdh@hrayment.wanadoo.co.uk

RAYMER, Victoria Elizabeth. b 46. Wellesley Coll (USA) BA68 Harvard Univ MA69 JD78 PhD81. St Steph Ho Ox BA86 Qu Coll Birm 88. **d** 89 **p** 94. Par Dn Bushey *St Alb* 89-94; C Eaton Socon 94-98; V Milton Ernest, Pavenham and Thurleigh 98-01; Dir Studies Westcott Ho Cam from 01. *1 Short Street, Cambridge CB1 1LB* Tel (01223) 352922 *or* tel and fax 741011 E-mail ver21@cam.ac.uk

RAYMOND, The Very Revd Walter. b 49. **d** 92 **p** 93. OGS from 93; C Willowdale All So Canada 92-94; Chapl H Trin Sch Toronto 94-99; Dean and R H Trin Cathl Quebec 99-07; Chapl Monte Carlo *Eur* from 08. *St Paul's House, 22 avenue de Grande-*

Bretagne, 98000 Monte Carlo, Monaco Tel (00377) 9330 7106 Fax 9330 5039 E-mail wraymond@ogs.net

RAYMONT, Philip Richard. b 56. Univ of Qld BA79 BEdSt86 Melbourne Univ MEd00 Cam Univ PhD05 MACE. **d** 04 **p** 09. Asst Chapl Selw Coll Cam 04-07; Perm to Offic *Ely* from 07. *Hughes Hall, Wollaston Road, Cambridge CB1 2EW* E-mail prr22@cam.ac.uk

RAYNER, Canon George Charles. b 26. Bps' Coll Cheshunt 50. **d** 52 **p** 53. C Rowbarton *B & W* 52-56; V Taunton H Trin 56-63; Chapl Taunton and Somerset Hosp 60-63; V Lower Sandown St Jo *Portsm* 63-69; R Wootton 69-89; Hon Can Portsm Cathl 84-89; rtd 89; Perm to Offic *B & W* 89-92 and *Portsm* from 98; P-in-c Six Pilgrims *B & W* 93-02. *The Bungalow, 1 Alresford Road, Shanklin PO37 6HX* Tel (01983) 867304

RAYNER, Paul Anthony George. b 39. Dur Univ BA60 Lon Univ BD68 Cape Town Univ MA79. Lon Coll of Div 65. **d** 68 **p** 69. C Crookes St Thos *Sheff* 68-72; S Africa 72-79; P-in-c S Shoebury *Chelmsf* 80-84; R 84-97; V Loughton St Mich 97-04; rtd 04; Perm to Offic *Chelmsf* from 04. *36 Amberley Road, Buckhurst Hill IG9 5QW* Tel (020) 8504 7434 E-mail prayner@globalnet.co.uk

RAYNER, Richard Noel. b 24. Lon Univ BD51. Oak Hill Th Coll 50. **d** 52 **p** 53. C Plymouth St Jude *Ex* 52-55; V Walthamstow St Luke *Chelmsf* 55-61; V Romford Gd Shep 61-65; V Slough *Ox* 65-72; V Heworth w Peasholme St Cuth *York* 72-75; V Heworth H Trin 75-81; V Okehampton w Inwardleigh *Ex* 81-89; RD Okehampton 87-89; rtd 89; Perm to Offic *Ex* 90-98 and *B & W* 90-06. *Redlands, 5 Ladymeade, Ilminster TA19 0EA* Tel (01460) 52491

RAYNER, Mrs Shirley Christine. b 54. SEITE BA08. **d** 05 **p** 06. C S Croydon St Pet and St Aug *S'wark* from 05; NSM 05-07. *59 Ewhurst Avenue, South Croydon CR2 0DL* Tel (020) 8651 2266 E-mail revshirley@btinternet.com

RAYNER, Stewart Leslie. b 39. St Jo Coll Dur BA61 MA73. Cranmer Hall Dur. **d** 67 **p** 68. C Whiston *Sheff* 67-70; C Doncaster St Geo 70-74; Chapl Doncaster R Infirmary 70-74; R Adwick-le-Street *Sheff* 74-85; V Totley 85-91; Asst Chapl Pastures Hosp Derby 91-94; Asst Chapl Kingsway Hosp Derby 91-94; Asst Chapl S Derby Mental Health Services 91-94; P-in-c Etwall w Egginton *Derby* 94-99; R 99-08; RD Longford 96-01; rtd 09. *26 Lawn Avenue, Etwall, Derby DE65 6JB* Tel (01283) 736079 E-mail stewart.rayner37@googlemail.com

RAYNES, Andrew. b 60. R Holloway Coll Lon BA83. Wycliffe Hall Ox 93. **d** 95 **p** 96. C Crowborough *Chich* 95-99; V Blackb Ch Ch w St Matt from 99; AD Blackb and Darwen from 03. *The Vicarage, Brandy House Brow, Blackburn BB2 3EY* Tel (01254) 56292 E-mail andrewraynes@btopenworld.com

RAYNHAM, Mrs Penelope Anne. b 44. SWMTC 97. **d** 00 **p** 01. OLM S Hill w Callington *Truro* from 00. *Bramblings, Honicombe Corner, Harrowbarrow, Callington PL17 8JN* Tel (01822) 833065 E-mail penny@bramvista.co.uk

RAYNOR, Duncan Hope. b 58. Ex Coll Ox MA80 MA82 Birm Univ PGCE88 MLitt93. Qu Coll Birm 82. **d** 84 **p** 85. C Kings Heath *Birm* 84-87; Perm to Offic from 87; Hd of RE Alderbrook Sch Solihull 88-94; Chapl K Edw Sch Birm from 94. *134 Addison Road, Birmingham B14 7EP* Tel 0121-684 3407 *or* 472 1672 E-mail dhr@kes.bham.sch.uk

RAYNOR, Michael. b 53. Lanc Univ BA74 MSc75. Ripon Coll Cuddesdon BA84 MA99. **d** 85 **p** 86. C Gt Crosby St Faith *Liv* 85-88; V Warrington St Barn 88-97; V Orford St Andr from 97; AD Warrington 99-05; Hon Can Liv Cathl 03-05. *St Andrew's Vicarage, Poplars Avenue, Orford, Warrington WA2 9UE* Tel (01925) 631903 E-mail mjraynor@care4free.net

RAZZALL, Charles Humphrey. b 56. Worc Coll Ox BA76 MA81 Qu Coll Cam BA78. Westcott Ho Cam 76. **d** 79 **p** 80. C Catford (Southend) and Downham *S'wark* 79-83; V Crofton Park St Hilda w St Cypr 83-87; UPA Officer 87-92; TV Oldham *Man* 87-01; AD Oldham 92-99; Hon Can Man Cathl 98-01; R Coppenhall *Ches* from 01. *The Rectory, 198 Ford Lane, Crewe CW1 3TN* Tel (01270) 215151

REA, Simon William John. b 60. G&C Coll Cam MA Victoria Univ Wellington MA Liv Univ BTh07 Univ of Wales (Ban) PGCE. Ridley Hall Cam 02. **d** 04 **p** 05. C Moreton *Ches* 04-08; C Edgware *Lon* from 08. *St Peter's Vicarage, Stonegrove, Edgware HA8 8AB* Tel 07905-699185 (mobile) E-mail simonrea@gmx.net

READ, Andrew Gordon. b 40. Nottm Univ BA69 MRICS63 FRICS86. Cuddesdon Coll 70. **d** 70 **p** 71. C E Retford *S'well* 70-72; C Woodthorpe 72-76; P-in-c Newark St Leon 76-78; Perm to Offic *Roch* 79-91. *The Gables, 148 Hastings Road, Battle TN33 0TW* Tel (01424) 773044

READ, Charles William. b 60. Man Univ BA81 MPhil95 Man Poly PGCE82. St Jo Coll Nottm 86. **d** 88 **p** 89. C Oldham *Man* 88-90; C Urmston 90-94; P-in-c Broughton St Jas w St Clem and St Matthias 94-96; TV Broughton 96-99; Lect Cranmer Hall Dur 99-06; Dir Studies Dioc Min Scheme Dur 00-06; Teacher Dur Sch 06; Vice-Prin and Dir Studies Nor Dioc Min Course from 07. *42 Heigham Road, Norwich NR2 3AU* Tel (01603) 660824 E-mail charlesread@norwich.anglican.org

READ, Geoffrey Philip. b 61. Bris Univ LLB82 Spurgeon's Coll MTh04. Wycliffe Hall Ox 85. **d** 88 **p** 89. C Dorking St Paul *Guildf* 88-92; TV Westborough 92-97; TR 97-98; Chapl Basle *Eur* from 98; P-in-c Freiburg-im-Breisau 98-01. *St Johanns-Ring 92, CH-4056 Basle, Switzerland* Tel (0041) (61) 321 7477 Fax 321 7476 E-mail admin@anglicanbasel.ch

READ, James Arthur. b 51. Nottm Coll of Educn BEd74. EMMTC 84. **d** 87 **p** 88. C Weoley Castle *Birm* 87-91; C W Smethwick 91-92; TV Atherton *Man* 92-97; P-in-c Facit 97-00; C Whitworth w Facit 00-08; P-in-c Royton St Anne from 08. *St Anne's Vicarage, St Anne's Avenue, Royton, Oldham OL2 5AD* Tel 0161-624 2249 E-mail revjames.read@btinternet.com

READ, John. b 33. Worc Coll Ox BA56 MA60. Chich Th Coll 56. **d** 58 **p** 59. C Babbacombe *Ex* 58-60; C Heavitree 60-63; V Swimbridge 63-69; V Ex St Matt 69-80; P-in-c Ex St Sidwell 79-80; R Ex St Sidwell and St Matt 80-83; Chapl Warneford Hosp Leamington Spa 83-89; Chapl S Warks Hosps 83-89; Chapl Dur and Ches le Street Hosps 89-95; Chapl Dryburn Hosp 89-95; rtd 95; NSM Tamworth *Lich* 95-98; Perm to Offic *Cov* from 02. *8 Newsholme Close, Warwick CV34 5XF* Tel (01926) 411598

READ, John du Sautoy. **d** 66 **p** 67. V Choral Derry Cathl 66-67; Dean's V Derry Cathl 67; S Africa from 69. *33 Town Street, Potchefstroom, 2520 South Africa* Tel (0027) (148) 297 8580

READ, John Samuel. b 33. Fitzw Ho Cam BA56. Clifton Th Coll 62. **d** 64 **p** 65. C Sneinton St Chris w St Phil *S'well* 64-67; C Huyton St Geo *Liv* 67-70; Lic to Offic *Blackb* 70-72; V Moldgreen *Wakef* 72-84; V Rawtenstall St Mary *Man* 84-91; Chapl Rossendale Gen Hosp 84-91; R Earsham w Alburgh and Denton *Nor* 91-98; P-in-c Ditchingham, Hedenham and Broome 94-98; rtd 98; Perm to Offic *Nor* and *St E* from 98. *7 Pine Tree Close, Worlingham, Beccles NR34 7EE* Tel (01502) 712585

READ, Mrs Julie Margaret. b 61. Keble Coll Ox BA82 Univ of Wales (Ban) PGCE83. WEMTC 97. **d** 00 **p** 01. C Bishop's Castle w Mainstone, Lydbury N etc *Heref* 00-03; R Pembridge w Moor Court, Shobdon, Staunton etc from 03. *The Rectory, Manley Crescent, Pembridge, Leominster HR6 9EB* Tel (01544) 388998

READ, Maureen Elizabeth. b 52. Man Metrop Univ BEd93 Ches Coll of HE BTh99. NOC 95. **d** 98 **p** 99. NSM Leesfield *Man* 98-99; C 99-02; TV Heywood 02-09; V Meltham *Wakef* from 09. *The Vicarage, 150 Huddersfield Road, Meltham, Holmfirth HD9 4AL* Tel (01484) 850050

READ, Michael Antony. b 75. Lanc Univ BA99 St Jo Coll Dur BA01. Cranmer Hall Dur 99. **d** 02 **p** 03. C Stanley *Liv* 02-05; P-in-c Lowton St Luke from 05. *The Rectory, 246 Slag Lane, Lowton, Warrington WA3 2ED* Tel (01942) 728434

READ, Nicholas George. b 51. Chelsea Coll Lon BSc72 PhD81. SEITE 97. **d** 00 **p** 01. NSM Beckenham St Jo *Roch* 00-03; P-in-c Penge Lane H Trin from 03. *Holy Trinity Vicarage, 64 Lennard Road, London SE20 7LX* Tel (020) 8778 8113 Mobile 07904-317488 E-mail nicholas.read@diocese-rochester.org *or* hancompro@aol.com

READ, Nicholas John. b 59. OBE99. Keble Coll Ox BA81 MSc82 MA85. Ox Min Course 92. **d** 95 **p** 96. NSM Charlbury w Shorthampton *Ox* 95-98; Dir Rural Stress Information Network 96-00; Chapl for Agric *Heref* from 98. *The Rectory, Manley Crescent, Pembridge, Hereford HR6 9EB* Tel (01544) 388998

READ, Canon Robert Edgar. b 47. Kelham Th Coll 66. **d** 70 **p** 71. C Harton Colliery *Dur* 70-75; C Wilmslow *Ches* 76-80; V Gatley 80-92; V Offerton 92-06; RD Stockport 00-05; V Newton 06-07; P-in-c Gatley from 07; Hon Can Ches Cathl from 03. *14 Elm Road, Gatley, Cheadle SK8 4LY* Tel 0161-428 4764 E-mail reread@btinternet.com

READ, Victor. b 29. Lon Univ BD58. ALCD57. **d** 58 **p** 59. C Wimbledon *S'wark* 58-61; C Lt Marlow *Ox* 61-64; V Wootton *Linc* 64-67; R Croxton 64-67; V Ulceby 64-67; V Linc St Pet in Eastgate w St Marg 67-73; V W Wimbledon Ch Ch *S'wark* 73-94; rtd 94; Perm to Offic *Pet* from 94. *27 Nightingale Drive, Towcester NN12 6RA* Tel (01327) 352027

READ-SMITH, Troy Justin Nathan. b 76. **d** 08 **p** 09. C Ealing St Mary *Lon* from 08. *38 Airedale Road, London W5 4SD* Tel (020) 8354 2709 *or* 8579 7134 Mobile 07590-669546 E-mail tjustinreadsmith@gmail.com

✠**READE, The Rt Revd Nicholas Stewart.** b 46. Leeds Univ BA70. Coll of Resurr Mirfield 70. **d** 73 **p** 74 **c** 04. C Coseley St Chad *Lich* 73-75; C Codsall 75-78; V Upper Gornal 78-82; V Mayfield *Chich* 82-88; RD Dallington 82-88; V Eastbourne St Mary 88-97; RD Eastbourne 88-97; Can and Preb Chich Cathl 90-97; Can 97-04; Min The Hydneye CD 91-93; Adn Lewes and Hastings 97-04; Bp Blackb from 04. *Bishop's House, Ribchester Road, Blackburn BB1 9EF* Tel (01254) 248234 Fax 246668 E-mail bishop@bishopofblackburn.org.uk

READE, Richard Barton. b 66. Wolv Poly BA88. Ripon Coll Cuddesdon BA91 MA97. **d** 92 **p** 93. C Wilnecote *Lich* 92-96; C Penkridge 96-98; P-in-c Basford 98-04; P-in-c Matlock Bank *Derby* from 04. *All Saints' Vicarage, Smedley Street, Matlock DE4 3JG* Tel (01629) 584107 E-mail richardreade3@supanet.com

READER, Christine Sarah. b 44. STETS. **d** 00 **p** 01. NSM N Waltham and Steventon, Ashe and Deane *Win* from 00. *5 Church Farm Close, North Waltham, Basingstoke RG25 2BN* Tel (01256) 397503

READER, John. b 53. Trin Coll Ox BA75 MA79 Man Univ MPhil87 Univ of Wales (Ban) PhD02. Ripon Coll Cuddesdon 76. **d** 78 **p** 79. C Ely 78-80; C Baguley *Man* 80-83; TV Kirkby Lonsdale *Carl* 83-86; V Lydbury N *Heref* 86-89; P-in-c Hopesay w Edgton 86-89; R Lydbury N w Hopesay and Edgton 89-90; Tutor Glouc Sch for Min 86-88; Vice-Prin 88-90; Dir Past Th Sarum & Wells Th Coll 90-92; P-in-c Elmley Lovett w Hampton Lovett and Elmbridge etc *Worc* 92-07; Assoc Tr and Educn Officer 92-02; Ind Chapl 01-07; P-in-c Chelford w Lower Withington *Ches* from 07; Dioc Rural Officer from 07. *The New Vicarage, Chelford, Macclesfield SK11 9AH* Tel (01625) 861231 E-mail drjohnreader@hotmail.co.uk

READER, The Ven Trevor Alan John. b 46. Lon Univ BSc68 MSc70 Portsm Poly PhD72. S Dios Minl Tr Scheme 83. **d** 86 **p** 87. C Alverstoke *Portsm* 86-89; P-in-c Hook w Warsash 89-95; V 95-98; P-in-c Blendworth w Chalton w Idsworth 98-03; Dioc Dir NSM 98-04; Adn Is of Wight 03-06; Adn Portsmouth from 06; Bp's Liaison Officer for Pris from 03. *5 Brading Avenue, Southsea PO4 9QJ* Tel and fax (023) 9229 8788 *or* tel 9243 2693

READER-MOORE, Anthony. b 43. Kent Univ BA80 Hull Univ MA83. Linc Th Coll. **d** 82 **p** 83. C Addiscombe St Mildred *Cant* 82-84; C Addiscombe St Mildred *S'wark* 85-86; R N Wheatley, W Burton, Bole, Saundby, Sturton etc *S'well* 86-89; Rural Officer 89-93; P-in-c Alford w Rigsby *Linc* 93-97; V 97-00; P-in-c Bilsby w Farlesthorpe 93-97; V 97-00; P-in-c Hannah cum Hagnaby w Markby 93-97; R 97-00; P-in-c Well 93-97; R 97-00; P-in-c Saleby w Beesby and Maltby 93-97; R 97-00; V Wellingborough All Hallows *Pet* 00-09; rtd 09. *8 Knights Close, Earls Barton, Northampton NN6 0JD* Tel (01604) 812073 E-mail tonyreadermoore@yahoo.co.uk

READING, Glenn Thomas. b 76. Staffs Univ BSc98. Ripon Coll Cuddesdon 07. **d** 09. C Horninglow *Lich* from 09. *10 Field Rise, Burton-on-Trent DE13 0NR* Tel 07964-282278 (mobile) E-mail glenn.reading@googlemail.com

READING, Mrs Lesley Jean. b 49. GNSM70 Trent Park Coll of Educn CertEd71. NOC 98. **d** 01 **p** 02. NSM Eccles *Man* 01-05; P-in-c Heywood St Jas from 05. *St James's Vicarage, 46 Bury Old Road, Heywood OL10 3JD* Tel (01706) 369754 E-mail readinglesley@hotmail.com

READING, Miss Siân Jacqueline Mary. b 64. Westcott Ho Cam 92. **d** 95 **p** 96. C Northampton St Alb *Pet* 95-98; TV Duston Team 98-05; P-in-c Gretton w Rockingham and Cottingham w E Carlton from 05. *The Vicarage, Station Road, Gretton, Corby NN17 3BU* Tel (01536) 770237 E-mail sianreading@tinyonline.co.uk

READING, Area Bishop of. See COTTRELL, The Rt Revd Stephen Geoffrey

REAGON, Darrol Franklin. b 46. St Mich Coll Llan 74. **d** 76 **p** 77. C Llandrillo-yn-Rhos *St As* 76-78; C Hawarden 78-81; V Northwich St Luke and H Trin *Ches* 81-85; V Moulton *Linc* 85-91; V Scunthorpe Resurr 91-92; P-in-c Branston 92-94; R Branston w Nocton and Potterhanworth 94-07; rtd 07. *17 Wessex Avenue, New Milton BH25 6NG* Tel (01425) 613622 E-mail revddarrol@btinternet.com

REAKES, Richard Frank. b 68. STETS 02. **d** 05 **p** 06. NSM Shepton Mallet w Doulting *B & W* 05-09; NSM Evercreech w Chesterblade and Milton Clevedon from 09. *Ashdene, Frome Road, Doulting, Shepton Mallet BA4 4QQ* Tel (01749) 880086 Fax 880105 E-mail richard@trotmanfuneral.co.uk

REAKES-WILLIAMS, Gordon Martin. b 63. St Cath Coll Cam BA86 MA89. St Jo Coll Dur BA90. **d** 91 **p** 92. C Harold Wood *Chelmsf* 91-94; Chapl Leipzig *Eur* from 95. *Hillerstrasse 3, 04109 Leipzig, Germany* Tel (0049) (341) 302 7951 Fax 215 3666 Mobile 177-240 4207 E-mail earwig@t-online.de

REALE, Mrs Kathleen. b 38. Carl Dioc Tr Course 83. **dss** 86 **d** 87 **p** 94. Dalston *Carl* 86-87; Par Dn 87-90; Par Dn Westward, Rosley-w-Woodside and Welton 87-90; Par Dn Thursby 89-90; Dn-in-c Gt Salkeld w Lazonby 90-94; P-in-c 94-97; rtd 97; Perm to Offic *Carl* from 98. *4 Low Moorlands, Carlisle CA5 7NX* Tel (01228) 711749

REANEY, Mrs Beverly Jane. b 58. Nottm Univ BA81. S Wales Ord Course 00. **d** 03 **p** 04. NSM Llanharry from 03. *The Rectory, High Street, Nelson, Treharris CF46 6HA* Tel and fax (01443) 450335 E-mail beverly.j.reaney@rhondda-cynon-taf.gov.uk

REANEY, Christopher Thomas. b 60. Univ of Wales (Lamp) BA82. St Mich Coll Llan. **d** 85 **p** 86. C Maindee Newport *Mon* 85-87; C Griffithstown 88-89; V Treherbert w Treorchy *Llan* 89-99; V Treorchy and Treherbert 99-02; R Llanfabon from 02. *The Rectory, High Street, Nelson, Treharris CF46 6HA* Tel and fax (01443) 450335 E-mail chris.reaney@virgin.net

REAST, Eileen Joan. See BANGAY, Mrs Eileen Joan

REAVLEY, Cedric. b 35. Lon Univ BPharm73. **d** 05 **p** 06. OLM Burford w Fulbrook, Taynton, Asthall etc *Ox* from 05. *124 High Street, Burford OX18 4QR* Tel (01993) 823957 Fax 824887 E-mail cedric_reavley@lineone.net

RECORD, John. b 47. St Chad's Coll Dur BA71. Westcott Ho Cam 71. **d** 73 **p** 74. C Paddington St Jo w St Mich *Lon* 73-75; C Witney *Ox* 75-78; P-in-c Lt Compton and Chastleton 78-80; R Lt Compton w Chastleton, Cornwell etc 80-83; V Hawkhurst *Cant* 83-97; RD W Charing 89-95; Hon Can Cant Cathl 96-97; P-in-c Devizes St Jo w St Mary *Sarum* 97-07; P-in-c Devizes St Pet 00-04; RD Devizes 98-07; Can and Preb Sarum Cathl 02-07; V Hammersmith St Pet *Lon* from 07. *17 Ravenscourt Road, London W6 0UH* Tel (020) 8748 1781
E-mail vicar@stpetersw6.org

RECORD, Sister Marion Eva. b 25. MRCS50 LRCP50 Leeds Univ FFARCS57 Lon Univ BD79. **dss** 78 **d** 87 **p** 94. OHP from 72; Chapl Hull Univ 72-78; Chapl York Univ 78-80; Lic to Offic 80-95; Perm to Offic from 95; rtd 96. *St Hilda's Priory, Sneaton Castle, Whitby YO21 3QN* Tel (01947) 602079

REDDIN, Mrs Christine Emily. b 46. Essex Univ BA67. STETS 01. **d** 04 **p** 05. NSM Burpham *Guildf* from 04. *The Corner House, Sutton Green Road, Guildford GU4 7QD* Tel (01483) 714708 Mobile 07764-677898 E-mail c.reddin@sky.com

REDDING, Benjamin James. b 73. K Coll Lon BSc94 PGCE95. Oak Hill Th Coll BA05. **d** 05 **p** 06. C Angmering *Chich* from 05. *7 Beech View, Angmering, Littlehampton BN16 4DE* Tel (01903) 784459 E-mail benjamesredding@yahoo.co.uk

REDDING, Roger Charles. b 45. Chich Th Coll 87. **d** 89 **p** 90. C Yeovil St Mich *B & W* 89-93; P-in-c Salisbury St Mark *Sarum* 93-94; Lic to Offic 94-96; TV Chalke Valley from 96; Chapl to Travelling People from 02. *The Vicarage, May Lane, Ebbesbourne Wake, Salisbury SP5 5JL* Tel (01722) 780408

REDDINGTON, Gerald Alfred. b 34. S'wark Ord Course 76. **d** 79 **p** 79. NSM St Vedast w St Mich-le-Querne etc *Lon* 79-85; Dir Past Support Gp Scheme 83-86; Hon C St Marylebone All SS 85-90; V Ealing St Barn 90-99; rtd 99; Perm to Offic *Portsm* from 88 and *Lon* from 02. *The Orange Tree, Madeira Road, Seaview PO34 5BA* Tel (01983) 617026 E-mail rev.redd@btinternet.com

REDEYOFF, Neil Martyn. b 69. St Jo Coll Nottm BA01. **d** 01 **p** 02. C Grange St Andr and Runcorn H Trin *Ches* 01-04; R Darfield *Sheff* 04-08; P-in-c Finningley w Auckley from 08. *The Rectory, Rectory Lane, Finningley, Doncaster DN9 3DA* Tel (01302) 770240 E-mail neilredeyoff1@btinternet.com

REDFEARN, James Jonathan. b 62. Newc Univ BA83 PGCE89. Cranmer Hall Dur 95. **d** 95 **p** 96. C Kidsgrove *Lich* 95-97. *56 Holly Avenue, Jesmond, Newcastle upon Tyne NE2 2QA* Tel 0191-281 9046 E-mail jaredfearn@compuserve.com

REDFEARN, Michael. b 42. Open Univ BA78 Hull Univ MA84 BA86. St Aid Birkenhead 64. **d** 68 **p** 69. C Bury St Pet *Man* 68-71; C Swinton St Pet 71-74; Ind Chapl *Bris* 74-79 and 80-81; Ind Chapl Australia 79-80; Ind Chapl *York* 81-86; V Southill and Course Dir St Alb Minl Tr Scheme 86-93; Dep Chapl HM Pris Wandsworth 94; Chapl HM YOI and Rem Cen Feltham 94-97; Chapl HM YOI Aylesbury 97-02; rtd 02; Asst Chapl Palma de Mallorca *Eur* from 04. *Calle Xarxes Los Ciclamens 7, El Pinaret, 07470 Puerto Pollensa (Mallorca), Spain* Tel (0034) 971 866 689 Mobile 696 391 584 E-mail michaelredfearn18@hotmail.com

REDFEARN, Ms Tracy Anne. b 66. Heythrop Coll Lon BD88. Ripon Coll Cuddesdon 91. **d** 93 **p** 94. C Haslemere *Guildf* 93-97; TV Gt Grimsby St Mary and St Jas *Linc* 97-00; P-in-c Legbourne 00-01; P-in-c Raithby 00-01; P-in-c Wold-Marsh Gp 00-01; V Legbourne and Wold Marsh 01-05; C Brumby 05-08; rtd 08. *674 Firskill Crescent, Sheffield S4 7DR* E-mail tracy.redfearn@btopenworld.com

✠**REDFERN, The Rt Revd Alastair Llewellyn John.** b 48. Ch Ch Ox BA70 MA74 Trin Coll Cam BA74 MA79 Bris Univ PhD01. Westcott Ho Cam 72 Qu Coll Birm 75. **d** 76 **p** 77 **c** 97. C Tettenhall Regis *Lich* 76-79; Tutor Ripon Coll Cuddesdon 79-87; Hon C Cuddesdon *Ox* 83-87; Can Res Bris Cathl 87-97; Dioc Dir Tr 91-97; Suff Bp Grantham *Linc* 97-05; Dean Stamford 98-05; Can and Preb Linc Cathl 00-05; Bp Derby from 05. *The Bishop's House, 6 King Street, Duffield, Belper DE56 4EU* Tel (01332) 840132 Fax 842743 E-mail bishop@bishopofderby.org

REDFERN, Paul. b 48. Ulster Univ BA88. CITC BTh94. **d** 94 **p** 95. C Belfast St Aid *Conn* 94-97; I Belfast St Mark 97-03; I Kilbride from 03. *Kilbride Rectory, 7 Rectory Road, Doagh, Ballyclare BT39 0PT* Tel (028) 9334 0225

REDGERS, Brian. b 42. St Jo Coll Dur BA65 Keswick Hall Coll PGCE75. Westcott Ho Cam 65. **d** 67 **p** 68. C Rushmere *St E* 67-73; Lic to Offic from 73. *44 Belvedere Road, Ipswich IP4 4AB* Tel (01473) 273829

REDGRAVE, Canon Christine Howick. b 50. AIAT73. Trin Coll Bris 75. **dss** 78 **d** 87 **p** 94. Watford *St Alb* 78-83; Maidenhead St Andr and St Mary *Ox* 83-85; Bracknell 85-96; Par Dn 87-94; TV 94-96; P-in-c Woolhampton w Midgham and Beenham Valance 96-04; Asst Dir of Ords 95-04; Dir of Ords (Reading and Dorchester) from 04; Hon Can Ch Ch from 00. *41 North Street, Marcham, Abingdon OX13 6NQ* Tel (01865) 391756 E-mail ordberk@oxford.anglican.org

REDHEAD, Edward. b 30. St Deiniol's Hawarden 60. **d** 63 **p** 64. C Mottram in Longdendale w Woodhead *Ches* 63-67; V Rivington *Man* 67-72; V Bloxwich *Lich* 72-75; Hon C Lich St Chad 82-84; P-in-c Bromfield w Waverton *Carl* 84-85; V 85-90; P-in-c W

Newton 84-85; V 85-90; R Harrington 90-93; rtd 93. *Tigh-na-Mara, 2-3 Caroy, Struan, Isle of Skye IV56 8FQ* Tel (01470) 572338

REDHOUSE, Mark David. b 67. Oak Hill Th Coll BA94. **d** 94 **p** 95. C Fulham St Mary N End *Lon* 94-96; C Hove Bp Hannington Memorial Ch *Chich* 96-01; V Horam from 01; RD Dallington 04-07. *The Vicarage, Horebeech Lane, Horam, Heathfield TN21 0DT* Tel (01435) 812563
E-mail markredhouse@aol.com

REDKNAP, Clive Douglas. b 53. Trin Coll Bris BA95. **d** 95 **p** 96. C Patcham *Chich* 95-00; C Wadhurst and Stonegate 00-03; P-in-c Hollington St Jo 03-05; V from 05. *The Vicarage, 94 Lower Glen Road, St Leonards-on-Sea TN37 7AR* Tel (01424) 751103

REDMAN, Anthony James. b 51. Reading Univ BSc72 Anglia Ruskin Univ MA05 FRICS95. EAMTC 01. **d** 03 **p** 04. NSM Bury St Edmunds All SS w St Jo and St Geo *St E* 03-06; NSM Blackbourne from 06. *The Cottage, Great Livermere, Bury St Edmunds IP31 1JG* Tel (01359) 269335 Fax (01284) 704734 E-mail tony@theredmans.co.uk

REDMAN, Canon Arthur Thomas. b 28. Dur Univ BA52 PGCE. Ridley Hall Cam 62. **d** 63 **p** 64. C Heaton St Barn *Bradf* 63-66; C Hitchin St Mary *St Alb* 66-70; P Missr 72-75; Hd RE Stopsley High Sch Luton 66-70; Hd Humanities and Modern Studies Hewett Sch Nor 70-72; Perm to Offic *Nor* 70-72; V Swannick and Pentrich *Derby* 75-80; Warden of Readers 78-97; Dir Bp's Cert 78-88; V Allestree 80-96; P-in-c Morley 82-85; Hon Can Derby Cathl 86-96; RD Duffield 88-96; rtd 96; Hon C Bretby w Newton Solney *Derby* 96-97; Chapl and Development Officer Children in Distress 97-01; Dir St Barn Project Romania from 01. *9 Ludgate Walk, Mackworth, Derby DE22 4HQ* Tel (01332) 521733 Fax 551569

REDMAN, Canon Douglas Stuart Raymond. b 35. MCIOB64. Roch Th Coll 66. **d** 68 **p** 69. C Shortlands *Roch* 68-71; V 80-00; R Kingsdown 71-76; R Chatham St Mary w St Jo 76-80; RD Beckenham 90-00; Hon Can Roch Cathl 93-00; rtd 00; Perm to Offic *Cant* from 01. *25 Hovendens, Sissinghurst, Cranbrook TN17 2LA* Tel and fax (01580) 714600

REDMAN, Julia Elizabeth Hithersay. *See* WHITE, Mrs Julia Elizabeth Hithersay

REDMAN, Michael John. b 52. St Jo Coll Ox BA74 Solicitor 86. NTMTC 04. **d** 06 **p** 07. NSM St Marylebone St Paul *Lon* from 06. *8 Bryanston Mews West, London W1H 2DD* Tel (020) 7723 7407

REDPARTH, Paul Robert. b 58. Open Univ BSc97 K Coll Lon PhD01. Westcott Ho Cam 04. **d** 06 **p** 07. C Roughey *Chich* from 06. *3 Rowlands Road, Horsham RH12 4LH* Tel (01403) 260865

REDVERS HARRIS, Jonathan Francis. b 60. Solicitor 87 Southn Univ LLB81 Univ of Wales (Cardiff) LLM94. Ridley Hall Cam 87. **d** 90 **p** 91. C Enfield St Jas *Lon* 90-93; PV Llan Cathl 93-96; Succ 94-96; V Houghton Regis *St Alb* 96-03; V Ryde All SS *Portsm* from 03. *14 Argyll Street, Ryde PO33 3BZ* Tel (01983) 565953 E-mail j.redvers_harris@virgin.net

REDWOOD, Canon David Leigh. b 32. Glas Univ DipSW78. Edin Th Coll 57. **d** 59 **p** 60. C Stirling *Edin* 59-61; C Glas Ch Ch 61-64; P-in-c Glas Ascension 64-66; R 66-69; R Hamilton 69-74; R Callander *St And* 74-76; Hon C Perth St And 76-76; R Lochearnhead 74-76; R Killin 74-76; Hon C Doune 76-78; Hon C Aberfoyle 78-85; R Dunfermline 85-97; TR W Fife Team Min 85-97; Can St Ninian's Cathl Perth 90-97; Syn Clerk 93-97; rtd 97. *8 Strathmore Avenue, Dunblane FK15 9HX* Tel and fax (01786) 825493 E-mail david.redwood1@btinternet.com

REDWOOD, Marion. b 47. **d** 00 **p** 09. NSM Abercarn and Cwmcarn *Mon* from 00. *30 John Street, Cwmcarn, Crosskeys, Newport NP11 7EH* Tel (01495) 271910

REECE, Donald Malcolm Hayden. b 36. CCC Cam BA58 MA62. Cuddesdon Coll 58. **d** 60 **p** 61. C Latchford St Jas *Ches* 60-63; C Matlock and Tansley *Derby* 63-67; C-in-c Hackenthorpe Ch Ch CD 67-70; C Salisbury Cathl Rhodesia 70-73; V Leic St Pet 74-82; V Putney St Marg *S'wark* 82-91; Home Sec Coun for Chr Unity 92-97; Hon C Wandsworth St Anne 94-97; V Shepherd's Bush St Steph w St Thos *Lon* 97-04; rtd 04; Perm to Offic *Ox* from 05. *8 Lamarsh Road, Oxford OX2 0LD* Tel (01865) 792678

REECE, Paul Michael. b 60. Southn Univ BA81. Coll of Resurr Mirfield 83. **d** 85 **p** 86. C Borehamwood *St Alb* 85-89; C Potters Bar 89-92; R Lt Stanmore St Lawr *Lon* from 92; AD Harrow 97-02; Chapl R Nat Orthopaedic Hosp NHS Trust from 92. *Whitchurch Rectory, St Lawrence Close, Edgware HA8 6RB* Tel (020) 8952 0019 Fax 8537 0547 Mobile 07860-690503 E-mail paul.reece@london.anglican.org

REECE, Roger Walton Arden. b 56. **d** 00 **p** 01. OLM Chadderton St Luke *Man* 00-04; OLM Chadderton St Matt w St Luke 04-08; NSM 08-09; C Ashton from 09; Chapl HM Pris Buckley Hall from 08. *HM Prison Buckley Hall, Buckley Hall Road, Rochdale OL12 9DP* Tel (01706) 514300 Mobile 07904-078901 E-mail roger.reece@ntlworld.com

REED, Adam Michael Frederick. b 73. Humberside Univ BA95. Cranmer Hall Dur 96. **d** 99 **p** 00. C Northallerton w Kirby Sigston *York* 99-03; R Middleton, Newton and Sinnington from

03. *St Andrew's House, 15 Carr Lane, Middleton, Pickering YO18 8PU* Tel (01751) 474858

REED, Alan Ronald. b 44. Sarum Th Coll 66. **d** 68 **p** 70. C Ifield *Chich* 68-71; C Perivale *Lon* 71-72; C Ruislip St Martin 72-75; C Burgess Hill St Jo *Chich* 76-78; V Shoreham Beach 78-80; V Roughey 80-97; P-in-c Rusper 84-86; V Hove St Barn and St Agnes from 97. *St Barnabas' Vicarage, 88 Sackville Road, Hove BN3 3HE* Tel (01273) 732427

REED, Ms Annette Susan. b 54. Birm Univ BA76 CQSW78. Qu Coll Birm 84. **d** 87 **p** 94. C Churchover w Willey *Cov* 89-92; C Clifton upon Dunsmore and Newton 89-92; C Walsgrave on Sowe 92-95; C Cov E 92-95; C Burbage w Aston Flamville *Leic* 95-98; C Hinckley St Mary 95-98; C The Sheepy Gp 98-00; TV Bosworth and Sheepy Gp 00-06; V The Paxtons w Diddington *Ely* from 06; RD St Neots from 07. *The Vicarage, 24 St James's Road, Little Paxton, St Neots PE19 6QW* Tel (01480) 211048 E-mail rev.reed@btinternet.com

REED, Brian. b 43. Bris Univ BSc65. Linc Th Coll 73. **d** 76 **p** 77. C S Ashford Ch Ch *Cant* 76-78; C Spring Park 78-83; V Barming Heath from 83. *St Andrew's Vicarage, 416 Tonbridge Road, Maidstone ME16 9LW* Tel (01622) 726245 Mobile 07759-620502

REED, Christopher John. b 42. Selw Coll Cam BA64 MA68. Cranmer Hall Dur 64. **d** 67 **p** 68. C Gt Ilford St Andr *Chelmsf* 67-70; P-in-c Bordesley St Andr *Birm* 70-72; V 72-80; V Crofton St Paul *Roch* 80-98; V Yalding w Collier Street 98-08; RD Paddock Wood 01-06; rtd 08; Perm to Offic *Roch* from 09. *66 Willow Park, Otford, Sevenoaks TN14 5NG* Tel (01959) 523439 E-mail chris.reed@diocese-rochester.org

REED, Colin. *See* REED, Matthew Colin

REED, Colin Bryher. b 58. York Univ BA80 RGN86. Ridley Hall Cam 93. **d** 95 **p** 96. C Grays North *Chelmsf* 95-99; Chapl Plymouth Hosps NHS Trust 99-02; Hd Chapl Services Norfolk and Nor Univ Hosp NHS Trust from 02. *The Chaplaincy, Norfolk and Norwich University Hosp, Colney Lane, Norwich NR4 7UZ* Tel (01603) 286286 *or* 287470 E-mail colin.reed@norfolk-norwich.thenhs.com

REED, Colin Charles Gilmour. b 40. LCP75 FCP86 St Luke's Coll Ex TCert63 La Trobe Univ Vic MA94 ACT ThD06. Tyndale Hall Bris 67. **d** 69 **p** 70. C Weston-super-Mare Ch Ch *B & W* 69-71; Asst Master St Andr Sch Turi Kenya 71-79; Chapl Brighton Coll Jun Sch 79-80; Australia 80-99 and from 06; R Corrimal 80-84; Educn Sec CMS 84-99; Lect Amani Inst Tanzania 99-06; rtd 06. *7 Camden Street, Wingello NSW 2579, Australia* Tel (0061) (2) 4884 4551 E-mail wendyreed2@hotmail.com *or* cwreed@cms.org.au

REED, David. *See* REED, Richard David

REED, Mrs Elizabeth Christine. b 43. Lon Bible Coll Lon Univ BD65. WMMTC 95. **d** 97 **p** 98. NSM Lingdale *Heref* from 97; Chapl Bromsgrove Sch 99-06. *The Old Barn, Perrystone Hill, Ross-on-Wye HR9 7QX* Tel (01989) 780439

REED, Ethel Patricia Ivy. *See* WESTBROOK, Mrs Ethel Patricia Ivy

REED, Geoffrey Martin. b 51. Univ of Wales (Cardiff) BA73 Open Univ PGCE98. Oak Hill Th Coll 73. **d** 76 **p** 77. C Swansea St Nic *S & B* 76-78; C Sketty 78-84; V Glasbury and Llowes 84-86; V Glasbury and Llowes w Clyro and Betws 86-01; R Teme Valley S *Worc* 01-04. *Address temp unknown*

REED, Mrs Gillian Yvonne. b 44. CBDTI 04. **d** 07. NSM Blackb St Thos w St Jude 07-09; NSM Blackb St Mich w St Jo and H Trin 07-09. *18 Four Horseshoes Park, Seasalter Road, Graveney, Faversham ME13 9DE* E-mail gill.pete@tesco.net

REED, Harvey. *See* REED, William Harvey

REED, The Ven John Peter Cyril. b 51. BD78 AKC78. Ripon Coll Cuddesdon 78. **d** 79 **p** 80. C Croydon St Jo *Cant* 79-82; Prec St Alb Abbey 82-86; R Timsbury and Priston *B & W* 86-93; Chapl Rural Affairs Bath Adnry 87-93; P-in-c Ilminster w Whitelackington 93-94; TR Ilminster and Distr 94-99; Adn Taunton from 99. *4 Westerkirk Gate, Staplegrove, Taunton TA2 6BQ* Tel (01823) 323838 Fax 325420 E-mail adtaunton@bathwells.anglican.org

REED, John William. b 57. Sussex Univ BSc79. NOC 95. **d** 97 **p** 98. C Padgate *Liv* 97-99; C Orford St Marg 99-01; V 01-08; P-in-c Golborne from 08. *St Thomas's Rectory, Church Street, Golborne, Warrington WA3 3TH* Tel (01942) 728305 E-mail john@scobiem.freeserve.co.uk

REED, Martin. *See* REED, Geoffrey Martin

REED, Matthew Colin. b 50. Edin Univ BD82. Edin Th Coll 72. **d** 84 **p** 85. C Edin St Pet 84-87; P-in-c Linlithgow 87-94; P-in-c Bathgate 87-91; Chapl HM Pris Polmont 91-94; R Motherwell *Glas* 94-97; R Wishaw 94-97; Hon Asst P Edin St Fillan from 00; Chapl HM Pris Edin from 02. *HM Prison Edinburgh, 33 Stenhouse Road, Edinburgh EH11 3LN* Tel 0131-444 3115 E-mail colin.reed@sps.gov.uk

REED, Matthew Graham. b 68. Nottm Univ BEng89 Roehampton Inst MSc03. Ripon Coll Cuddesdon BA92 MA97. **d** 93 **p** 94. C Oxton *Ches* 93-97; TV Gt Marlow w Marlow Bottom, Lt Marlow and Bisham *Ox* 97-02; Hd Lon and SE Team Chr Aid 02-04; C and Community Dir 04-08; Marketing

Dir from 08. *Interchurch House, 35 Lower Marsh, London SE1 7RL* Tel (020) 7523 2325 E-mail mreed@christian-aid.org

REED, Canon Pamela Kathleen. b 38. EMMTC. **dss** 84 **d** 87 **p** 94. Cambridge Ascension *Ely* 84-88; Par Dn 87-88; Par Dn Cherry Hinton St Andr 88-90; C 91-95; C Teversham 91-95; V Chesterton St Geo 95-04; Hon Can Ely Cathl 00-04; rtd 04; Perm to Offic *Ely* from 04. *17 Woodland Road, Sawston, Cambridge CB22 3DT* Tel (01223) 832571 E-mail pamk.reed@hotmail.com

REED, Richard David. b 32. K Alfred's Coll Win CertEd54 Ex Univ MA02. Trin Coll Carmarthen. **d** 91 **p** 92. NSM Dale and St Brides w Marloes *St D* 91-96; P-in-c Blisland w St Breward *Truro* 96-99; rtd 99; Perm to Offic *Truro* from 99 and *St D* from 02. *5 Smokehouse Quay, Milford Haven SA73 3BD* Tel (01646) 663819 E-mail davidreed456@btinternet.com

REED, Canon Robert Chase. b 47. Emerson Coll Boston (USA) BSc70 TCD HDipEd72. **d** 87 **p** 88. Aux Min Taney *D & G* 87-97; Res Hd Master Wesley Coll Dub from 87; Succ St Patr Cathl Dublin 93-97; Treas 96-01; Prec from 01. *Embury House, Wesley College, Dublin 16, Republic of Ireland* Tel and fax (00353) (1) 296 8010 *or* 299 1140 E-mail canrcr@gmail.com

REED, Simon John. b 63. Trin Coll Ox BA86 MA90. Wycliffe Hall Ox BA90. **d** 91 **p** 92. C Walton H Trin *Ox* 91-96; P-in-c Hanger Hill Ascension and W Twyford St Mary *Lon* 96-01; V from 01. *The Ascension Vicarage, Beaufort Road, London W5 3EB* Tel and fax (020) 8566 9920 E-mail coa@surfaid.org

REED, William Harvey. b 47. K Coll Lon BD69 AKC69. St Aug Coll Cant 69. **d** 70 **p** 71. C Stockton St Mark CD *Dur* 70-72; C Billingham St Cuth 72-76; C S Westoe 76-79; V Chilton Moor 79-87; R Hutton *Chelmsf* 87-95; V Hullbridge from 95; C Rawreth w Rettendon from 06. *The Vicarage, 93 Ferry Road, Hullbridge, Hockley SS5 6EL* Tel (01702) 232017 E-mail revharveyreed@whsmithnet.co.uk

REEDE, Samuel William. b 24. TCD BA48 MA52 BD55. CITC 50. **d** 50 **p** 51. C Waterford Ch Ch *C & O* 50-54; C Cregagh *D & D* 54-59; Hd S Ch Miss Ballymacarrett 59-67; Chapl Stranmillis Coll Belf 64-68; Can Raphoe Cathl 67-92; I Raphoe w Raymochy 67-68; I Raphoe w Raymochy and Clonleigh 68-92; Dean Raphoe 80-92; rtd 92. *c/o the Revd Canon H Gilmore, The Rectory, Moville, Co Donegal, Republic of Ireland*

REEDER, Angela Lilian. **d** 99 **p** 00. OLM Eastington, Frocester, Haresfield etc *Glouc* 99-04; Perm to Offic from 04. *St Loy Cottage, West End, Stonehouse GL10 3SL* Tel (01453) 827446

REEDER, Michael William Peter. b 58. Wilson Carlile Coll 84. **d** 09. Chapl St Luke's Hospice Sheff from 07; Hon C Sheff Cathl from 09. *St Luke's Hospice, Little Common Lane, Sheffield S11 9NE* Tel 0114-236 9911 Mobile 07947-706256 E-mail m.reeder@hospicesheffield.co.uk

REES (née HOLDER), Ms Adèle Claire. b 76. Luton Univ BSc97 Sheff Univ MTh03. Ripon Coll Cuddesdon 04. **d** 07 **p** 08. C Hill *Birm* from 07. *3 Dower Road, Sutton Coldfield B75 6UA* Tel 0121-308 0759 Mobile 07841-640974 E-mail adelerees@yahoo.co.uk

REES, Andrew Richard Akeroyd. b 76. Sydney Univ BEc. Moore Th Coll Sydney BD. **d** 04. C Kellyville Australia 04-06; C Fulwood *Sheff* from 07. *50 Brooklands Crescent, Sheffield S10 4GG* Tel 0114-230 1588 *or* 229 5567

REES, Anthony John. b 49. St Jo Coll Dur BA72 MA77 Man Univ MEd89. **d** 74 **p** 75. C Smethwick St Matt w St Chad *Birm* 74-77, C Bolton St Pet *Man* 77 80; R Cheetham St Mark 80-88; V Mottram in Longdendale w Woodhead *Ches* 88-93; V Mottram in Longdendale 93-02; V Chirk *St As* from 02. *The Vicarage, Trevor Road, Chirk, Wrexham LL14 5HD* Tel (01691) 778519

REES, Antony. *See* REES, Percival Antony Everard

REES, Brian. b 48. McGill Univ Montreal BA74 St Andr Univ BD76 PhD80. Montreal Dioc Th Coll 76. **d** 80 **p** 81. Canada 80-85; C Montreal St Jas and Chapl Concordia Univ 80-82; R Rawdon Ch Ch 82-85; Chapl Bedford Sch 85-92; Hd Master Bedford Prep Sch 92-97; Hd Master Pilgrims' Sch from 97. *The Pilgrims' School, 3 The Close, Winchester SO23 9LT* Tel (01962) 854189 E-mail hmsecretary@pilgrims-school.co.uk

REES, Celia Pamela. b 48. St D Coll Lamp BA70. **d** 98 **p** 99. OLM Leominster *Heref* from 98. *Rivendell, 50 Oldfields Close, Leominster HR6 8TL* Tel (01568) 616581 *or* 612124

REES, Mrs Christine Deryn Irving. b 57. Nottm Univ BSc Sheff Univ MA. Qu Coll Birm. **d** 00 **p** 01. NSM Astwood Bank *Worc* 00-01; C 01-03; TV Dronfield w Holmesfield *Derby* from 03. *43 Firthwood Road, Dronfield S18 3BW* Tel (01246) 411251 *or* 413893 E-mail christine.rees@dwhparish.org.uk

REES, Christopher John. b 40. Dur Univ BA62. Ridley Hall Cam 62. **d** 64 **p** 65. C Wilmslow *Ches* 64-70; C Birkenhead St Pet w St Matt 70-75; V Lostock Gralam 75-83; R Davenham 83-96; P-in-c Aldford and Bruera 96-05; rtd 05; Perm to Offic *Ches* from 05. *15 Chapel Close, Comberbach, Northwich CW9 6BA* Tel (01606) 891366 E-mail cjrees@surfaid.org

REES, Canon David Frederick. b 21. SS Coll Cam BA48 MA52. Sarum Th Coll 48. **d** 50 **p** 51. C Blackb St Luke 50-53; C St Annes St Thos 53-55; V Choral York Minster 55-62; V

Penwortham St Mary *Blackb* 62-90; RD Leyland 70-84; Hon Can Blackb Cathl 79-90; rtd 90; Perm to Offic *Blackb* from 91. *24 Fosbrooke House, 8 Clifton Drive, Lytham St Annes FY8 5RQ* Tel (01253) 667024

REES, David Grenfell. b 18. St D Coll Lamp BA40 Qu Coll Birm 42. **d** 43 **p** 44. C Llangeinor *Llan* 43-47; C Cadoxton-juxta-Barry 47-53; C St Andrews Major 53-60; V Dyffryn 60-84; rtd 84; Perm to Offic *Llan* from 84. *10 Tyn-yr-Heol Road, Bryncoch, Neath SA10 7EA* Tel (01639) 644488

REES, Canon David Philip Dunn Hugh. b 38. Jes Coll Ox BA60 MA64 Ox Univ DipEd67. Westcott Ho Cam 62. **d** 64 **p** 65. C Salford St Phil w St Steph *Man* 64-66; Perm to Offic *St A* 66-67 and *Derby* 67-74; Chapl St Marg C of E High Sch Aigburth Liv 74-83; V Meliden and Gwaenysgor *St As* 84-08; Dioc Adv for Schs 85-91; Warden of Readers 89-91; Dioc Dir of Ords 91-00; Hon Can St As Cathl 93-95; Can Cursal 95-08; Chan 96-08; rtd 08. *Y Cae Gwyn, Ffordd Teilia, Gwaenysgor, Rhyl LL18 6EW*

REES, David Richard. b 60. St Mich Coll Llan. **d** 84 **p** 85. C Llanstadwel *St D* 84-86; C Carmarthen St Dav 86-91; V Llanrhian w Llanhywel and Carnhedryn etc 91-99; V Spittal w Trefgarn and Ambleston w St Dogwells from 99. *The Vicarage, Spittal, Haverfordwest SA62 5QP* Tel (01437) 741505

REES, Ms Diane Eluned. b 61. Univ of Wales (Ban) BSc82 Em Coll Cam PGCE83 Univ of Wales (Swansea) MEd87 CPsychol AFBPsS. St Jo Coll Nottm BTh95 MA96. **d** 96 **p** 97. C Hall Green St Pet *Birm* 96-00; P-in-c Bozeat w Easton Maudit *Pet* 00-03; C Putney St Mary *S'wark* 03-04; TV 04-05; Asst Dir of Min and Tr *Roch* 06-09. *59 Hayes Wood Avenue, Bromley BR2 7BG* E-mail dereeswdt@aol.com

REES, Glyn. b 63. St Bede's Coll Umtata 85. **d** 87 **p** 87. C Turffontein S Africa 87-88; Chapl S African Defence Force 89-90; P-in-c Nigel 91-92; C Kempton Park and Edenvale 92-93; TR Secunda 94-98; R Brakpan 99-00; R Whitwell *Derby* 00-05; R Wodonga Australia from 05. *225 Beechworth Road, Wodonga Vic 3690, Australia* Tel (0061) (2) 6056 5795 *or* tel and fax 6024 2053

REES, Grenfell. *See* REES, David Grenfell

REES, Gruffydd Nicholas. b 23. Univ of Wales (Lamp) BA46. Wycliffe Hall Ox 46. **d** 48 **p** 49. C Fishguard *St D* 48-51; C Betws w Ammanford 51-53; C Carmarthen St Dav 53-57; C Epsom St Martin *Guildf* 57-62; V Llanbister and Llanbadarn Fynydd w Llananno *S & B* 62-75; R New Radnor and Llanfihangel Nantmelan etc 75-84; R Llangenni and Llanbedr Ystrad Yw w Patricio 84-88; rtd 88. *Trefilan, 26 Lakeside Avenue, Llandrindod Wells LD1 5NT* Tel (01597) 825451

REES, Mrs Helen. b 78. Univ of Wales (Cardiff) BD99. St Mich Coll Llan 07. **d** 09. NSM Penarth All SS *Llan* from 09. *The Vicarage, Pyle Road, Pyle, Bridgend CF33 6PG* Tel (01656) 740500 E-mail helenv.rees@virgin.net

REES, Ian Kendall. b 66. St Mich Coll Llan 98. **d** 00 **p** 01. C Barry All SS *Llan* 00-03; Assoc P Grangetown 03-05; P-in-c Pyle w Kenfig from 05. *The Vicarage, Pyle Road, Pyle, Bridgend CF33 6PG* Tel (01656) 740500 E-mail ian.rees2@virgin.net

REES, Ivor. *See* REES, The Rt Revd John Ivor

REES, Jennifer Mary. *See* MORRELL, Mrs Jennifer Mary

REES, Joanna Mary. *See* STOKER, Canon Joanna Mary

REES, John. *See* REES, Canon Vivian John Howard

✠**REES, The Rt Revd John Ivor.** b 26. Univ of Wales (Abth) BA50. Westcott Ho Cam 50. **d** 52 **p** 53 **c** 88. C Fishguard w Llanychar *St D* 52-55; C Llangathen w Llanfihangel Cilfargen 55-57; P-in-c Uzmaston and Boulston 57-59; V Slebech and Uzmaston w Boulston 59-65; V Llangollen and Trevor *St As* 65-74; RD Llangollen 70-74; TR Wrexham 74-76; Can St As Cathl 75-76; Dean Ban 76-88; V Ban Cathl 79-88; Asst Bp St D 88-91; Adn St D 88-91; Bp St D 91-95; rtd 95; Hon Fell Trin Coll Carmarthen from 96. *Llys Dewi, 45 Clover Park, Haverfordwest SA61 1UE* Tel (01437) 764846

REES, John Martin Rawlins Gore. b 30. St D Coll Lamp BA53. **d** 55 **p** 57. C Mold *St As* 55-56; C Broughton 56-59; C Newtown 59-61; V Penycae 61-73; V Northop 73-83; V Bickerton w Bickley *Ches* 83-91; Lic to Offic 91-95; rtd 95. *Hafod, 9 High Park, Gwernaffield, Mold CH7 5EE* Tel (01352) 740412

REES, John Nigel. b 58. Derby Lonsdale Coll BCombStuds79 Coll of Ripon & York St Jo PGCE80. STETS 03. **d** 06 **p** 07. NSM Highworth w Sevenhampton and Inglesham etc *Bris* from 06; NSM Broad Blunsdon from 06. *13 Priory Green, Highworth, Swindon SN6 7NU* Tel (01793) 764026 Mobile 07912-503267 E-mail reesfam@btinternet.com

REES, Canon John Philip Walford. b 41. St D Coll Lamp BA62 Linacre Coll Ox BA64 MA69 Univ of Wales (Cardiff) BD72. Wycliffe Hall Ox 62. **d** 64 **p** 65. C Reading St Jo *Ox* 64-67; V Patrick *S & M* 67-68; C Pontypool *Mon* 68-70; Area Sec CMS *Glouc, Heref* and *Worc* 70-75; V Bream *Glouc* 75-91; Team Ldr Ichthus Chr Fellowship 91-96; TV Glyncorrwg w Afan Vale and Cymmer Afan *Llan* 96-99; R Llandogo and Tintern *Mon* 99-00; R Llandogo w Whitebrook Chpl and Tintern Parva 00-07; AD Monmouth 02-06; Hon Can St Woolos Cathl 05-07; rtd 07. *Sparrow Cottage, The Narth, Monmouth NP25 4QG* Tel (01600) 869194

REES, Canon Judith Margaret. b 39. Southn Univ BTh89. **dss** 86 **d** 87 **p** 94. Sanderstead All SS *S'wark* 86-87; Par Dn 87; Dir Cottesloe Chr Tr Progr *Ox* 89-99; Par Dn Gt Horwood 89-91; Par Dn Winslow w Gt Horwood and Addington 91-94; C 94-99; RD Claydon 96-99; Hon Can Ch Ch 97-99; rtd 99; Perm to Offic *Sarum* from 01. *Sidney Cottage, 111 Lower Road, Salisbury SP2 9NH* Tel (01722) 410050

REES, Leslie. b 49. Leeds Univ LLB72. NOC 03. **d** 06 **p** 07. NSM Swinton H Rood *Man* 06-08; NSM Eccles 08-09; NSM Hanbury, Newborough, Rangemore and Tutbury *Lich* from 09. *The New Vicarage, Church Lane, Hanbury, Burton-on-Trent DE13 8TF* Tel (01283) 813357 E-mail leslie.rees@virgin.net

✠**REES, The Rt Revd Leslie Lloyd.** b 19. Kelham Th Coll 36. **d** 42 **p** 43 **c** 80. C Roath St Sav *Llan* 42-45; Asst Chapl HM Pris Cardiff 42-45; Chapl HM Pris Dur 45-48; V Princetown *Ex* 48-55; Chapl HM Pris Dartmoor 48-55; Chapl HM Pris Win 55-62; Chapl Gen of Pris 62-80; Hon Can Cant Cathl 66-80; Chapl to The Queen 71-80; Suff Bp Shrewsbury *Lich* 80-86; rtd 86; Hon Asst Bp Win from 87. *c/o G H Rees Esq, 31 Collin Road, Kendal LA9 5LH*

REES, Matthew Haydn Brinley. b 69. Wycliffe Hall Ox. **d** 03 **p** 04. C Ox St Aldate 03-06; C Ox St Clem 06-08; Lic to Offic from 08. *11 Duke Street, Oxford OX2 0HX* Tel (01865) 728866 *or* 254811 Mobile 07811-149305 E-mail matt@home-online.org

REES, Michael. *See* REES, Canon Richard Michael

REES, Michael Lloyd. b 51. St D Coll Lamp. **d** 74 **p** 75. C Cardigan w Mwnt and Y Ferwig *St D* 74-77; Min Can St D Cathl 77-81; TV Aberystwyth 81-83; Dioc Children's Adv 83-92; V Pen-boyr 83-88; V Henfynyw w Aberaeron and Llanddewi Aberarth 88-99; RD Glyn Aeron 95-99; V Gors-las from 99; AD Dyffryn Aman from 07. *The Vicarage, 56 Black Lion Road, Cross Hands, Llanelli SA14 6RU* Tel (01269) 842561

REES (*née* CURREY), **Mrs Pauline Carol.** b 46. WMMTC 94. **d** 98 **p** 99. OLM Leominster *Heref* from 98. *Crossways Cottage, Leysters, Leominster HR6 0HR* Tel (01568) 750300 *or* 612124 E-mail rees.crossways@btinternet.com

REES, Percival Antony Everard. b 35. Pemb Coll Ox BA56 MA59. Clifton Th Coll 58. **d** 60 **p** 61. C Heatherlands St Jo *Sarum* 60-65 and 69-70; India 65-69; V W Hampstead St Luke *Lon* 70-82; Lect Oak Hill Th Coll 82-86; V Enfield Ch Ch Trent Park *Lon* 87-00; rtd 00; Perm to Offic *Chelmsf* from 00. *10 Winchester Road, Frinton-on-Sea CO13 9JB* Tel (01255) 852464

REES, Philip. *See* REES, Canon John Philip Walford

REES, Canon Richard John Edward Williams. b 36. Univ of Wales (Lamp) BA58. St Mich Coll Llan 58. **d** 60 **p** 61. C St Issells *St D* 60-64; C Llanedy 64-67; V Whitchurch w Solva and St Elvis 67-77; V Whitchurch w Solva and St Elvis w Brawdy etc 77-01; RD Dewisland and Fishguard 73-01; Can St D Cathl 87-01; Treas 97-01; rtd 01. *The Smithy, Cheriton, Stackpole, Pembroke SA71 5BZ* Tel (01646) 672235

REES, Canon Richard Michael. b 35. St Pet Hall Ox BA57 MA61. Tyndale Hall Bris 57. **d** 59 **p** 60. C Crowborough *Chich* 59-62; C Clifton Ch Ch w Em *Bris* 62-64; V Clevedon Ch Ch *B & W* 64-72; V Cambridge H Trin *Ely* 72-84; Chief Sec CA 84-90; Can Res Ches Cathl 90-00; Vice-Dean 93-00; Dioc Missr 90-00; Cheshire Co Ecum Officer 91-99; rtd 00; Perm to Offic *Nor* from 01. *65 Tennyson Avenue, King's Lynn PE30 2QJ* Tel (01553) 691982

REES, Ronald Benjamin Dennis. b 44. Univ of Wales (Ban) BTh00. St Mich Coll Llan 00. **d** 00 **p** 01. C Llanbedrog w Llannor and Llangian *Ban* 00-02; P-in-c Llanllyfni 02-03; R 03-05; R Dolgellau w Llanfachreth and Brithdir etc from 05. *The Rectory, Pencefn Road, Dolgellau LL40 2YW* Tel (01341) 422275

REES, Stephen Philip. b 70. St Luke's Coll Ex BA. Oak Hill Th Coll BA03. **d** 03 **p** 04. C Moreton-in-Marsh w Batsford, Todenham etc *Glouc* 03-06; P-in-c Lt Heath *St Alb* from 06. *The Vicarage, Thornton Road, Potters Bar EN6 1JJ* Tel (01707) 654414 E-mail zipyzac@globalnet.com

REES, Miss Susan Mary. b 61. Univ of Wales (Cardiff) BSc82. Ripon Coll Cuddesdon 00. **d** 02 **p** 03. C Penarth All SS *Llan* 02-05; C Roath 05-08; P-in-c Eglwysilan from 08. *The Rectory, Brynhafod Road, Abertridwr, Caerphilly CF83 4BH* Tel (029) 2083 0220 E-mail susanmrees@hotmail.com

REES, Canon Vivian John Howard. b 51. Southn Univ LLB72 Ox Univ BA79 MA84 Leeds Univ MPhil84. Wycliffe Hall Ox 76. **d** 79 **p** 80. C Moor Allerton *Ripon* 79-82; Sierra Leone 82-86; Lic to Offic *Ox* from 86; Jt Dioc Reg from 98; Dep Prov Reg 98-00; Prov Reg from 00; Legal Adv ACC from 98; Hon Prov Can Cant Cathl from 01. *Oxford Diocesan Registry, 16 Beaumont Street, Oxford OX1 2LZ* Tel (01865) 241974 Fax 726274 E-mail oxford@winckworths.co.uk

REES, William David Cledwyn. b 25. FRGS54 Qu Coll Cam BA49 DipEd50 MA52 Univ of Wales MA75 PhD81. St Deiniol's Hawarden 63. **d** 65 **p** 66. Hon C Rhyl w St Ann *St As* 65-72; Chapl and Lect St Mary's Coll Ban 72-77; Lic to Offic *Ban* 72-77; Lect Ban Univ from 77; Chapl Univ of Wales

(Ban) 77-84; Sec Dioc Schs Cttee 84-86. *Anwylfa, Fron Park Avenue, Llanfairfechan LL33 0AS* Tel (01248) 680054

REES-JONES, Diana Mary. b 58. Ridley Hall Cam. **d** 07 **p** 08. C Ness Gp *Linc* 07-09; Asst Chapl Oundle Sch from 09. *Oundle School, Oundle, Peterborough PE8 4GH*
E-mail dandh.reesjones@btinternet.com

REESE, Preb John David. b 49. Cuddesdon Coll 73. **d** 76 **p** 77. C Kidderminster St Mary *Worc* 76-81; Malaysia 81-85; V Bishop's Castle w Mainstone *Heref* 85-91; RD Clun Forest 87-91; V Tupsley 91-93; P-in-c Hampton Bishop and Mordiford w Dormington 91-93; V Tupsley w Hampton Bishop 93-08; RD Heref City 96-02; TR Heref S Wye from 08; Preb Heref Cathl from 96. *1 Prinknash Close, Belmont, Hereford HR2 7XA*

REEVE, Canon Brian Charles. b 36. Lon Univ BSc57 BD60. Tyndale Hall Bris 58. **d** 61 **p** 62. C Eccleston St Luke *Liv* 61-63; C Upton (Overchurch) *Ches* 63-65; C Pemberton St Mark Newtown *Liv* 65-68; V Macclesfield Ch Ch *Ches* 68-74; V Stone Ch Ch *Lich* 74-84; RD Trentham 77-84; V Hoole *Ches* 84-94; Chapl Ches City Hosp 84-91; P-in-c Alderley *Ches* 94-01; Dioc Warden of Readers 94-00; Hon Can Ches Cathl 94-01; rtd 01; Perm to Offic *Ches* from 02. *73 Spring Gardens, Leek ST13 8DD* Tel (01538) 387321

REEVE, David Michael. b 44. St Cath Coll Cam BA67 MA71. Coll of Resurr Mirfield 68. **d** 70 **p** 71. C Willingdon *Chich* 70-73; C Hove All SS 73-76; C Moulsecoomb 76-80; R Singleton and V E and W Dean 80-90; R Hurstpierpoint 90-99; R Kingston Buci 99-05; rtd 05; Perm to Offic *Cant* from 06; Clergy Widows Officer Cant Adnry from 09. *11 Wells Avenue, Canterbury CT1 3YB* Tel (01227) 478446

REEVE, John Richard. b 65. Southn Univ BA86 La Sainte Union Coll PGCE88. Ripon Coll Cuddesdon 95. **d** 97 **p** 98. C Hale w Badshot Lea *Guildf* 97-00; TV Totton *Win* from 00. *The Vicarage, Ringwood Road, Woodlands, Southampton SO40 7GX* Tel (023) 8066 3267 E-mail johnreeve6@aol.com

REEVE, Kenneth John. b 42. Sarum & Wells Th Coll 91. **d** 93 **p** 94. C Thorpe St Matt *Nor* 93-96; P-in-c S Lynn 96-99; Perm to Offic 03-04; P-in-c Gt and Lt Ellingham, Rockland and Shropham etc from 04. *The Rectory, Rectory Lane, Great Ellingham, Attleborough NR17 1LD* Tel (01953) 457644
E-mail kenrevreeve@hotmail.com

REEVE, Kenneth Robert. b 23. St Cath Coll Ox BA49 MA53. Sarum Th Coll 64. **d** 68 **p** 69. Hon C Farleigh Hungerford w Tellisford *B & W* 68-71; Perm to Offic Virgin Is 71-72; Hon C Norton St Philip 72-74; Hon C Hinton Charterhouse 72-74; Seychelles 74-76; Perm to Offic *B & W* 77-89 and *Chich* 78-82. *10 Kent's Yard, Littlebury, Saffron Walden CB11 4XU* Tel (01799) 528829

REEVE, Michael. *See* REEVE, David Michael

REEVE, Richard Malcolm. b 64. Reading Univ BSc85. Trin Coll Bris BA92. **d** 92 **p** 93. C Northolt St Mary *Lon* 92-95; C Acton Green 95-98; V Hayes St Edm 98-08; TR Tettenhall Regis *Lich* from 08. *The Rectory, 2 Lloyd Road, Tettenhall, Wolverhampton WV6 9AU* Tel (01902) 742801 E-mail richardmreeve@aol.com

REEVE, Richard Noel. b 29. MB, ChB. St Deiniol's Hawarden. **d** 84 **p** 85. Hon C Norton *Ches* 84-85; C Filey *York* 85-87; TV Brayton 87-90; rtd 90; Perm to Offic *Man* 90-93 and *Lich* from 99; Res Min Bicton, Montford w Shrawardine and Fitz *Lich* 97-99. *26 Windsor Road, Stafford ST17 4PA* Tel (01785) 252607

REEVE, Preb Roger Patrick. b 42. Fitzw Coll Cam BA65 MA68. Coll of Resurr Mirfield. **d** 67 **p** 68. C Barnstaple St Pet w H Trin *Ex* 67-74; V Ernesettle 74-78; V Braunton 78-05; RD Barnstaple 85-93 and 01-03; Preb Ex Cathl from 92; rtd 05. *27 Westacott Meadow, Barnstaple EX22 8QX* Tel (01271) 326927
E-mail rogerreeve@cwcom.net

REEVES, Christopher. b 30. Nottm Univ BA53. Wells Th Coll 53. **d** 55 **p** 56. C Rowbarton *B & W* 55-59; C Cant St Greg 59-61; Chapl Schiedam Miss to Seamen *Eur* 61-67; V Barkingside H Trin *Chelmsf* 67-97; rtd 97; Perm to Offic *Truro* from 00. *3 Albany Close, Goonown, St Agnes TR5 0XE* Tel (01872) 552976

REEVES, David Eric. b 46. Sarum Th Coll 68. **d** 71 **p** 72. C Guildf H Trin w St Mary 71-74; C Warmsworth *Sheff* 74-78; V Herringthorpe 78-90; V Cleveleys *Blackb* from 90; RD Poulton 94-00. *The Vicarage, Rough Lea Road, Thornton-Cleveleys FY5 1DP* Tel (01253) 852153

REEVES, Donald St John. b 34. Qu Coll Cam BA57 MA61 Lambeth MLitt03. Cuddesdon Coll 62. **d** 63 **p** 64. C Maidstone All SS w St Phil *Cant* 63-65; Bp's Dom Chapl *S'wark* 65-68; V St Helier 69-80; R Westmr St Jas *Lon* 80-98; Dir Soul of Eur Project from 98; rtd 98; Perm to Offic *Ex* from 00. *The Coach House, Church Street, Crediton EX17 2AQ* Tel (01363) 775100 Fax 773911 E-mail donalreeve@aol.com

REEVES, Elizabeth Anne. *See* THOMAS, Mrs Elizabeth Anne

REEVES, Gillian Patricia. b 46. S'wark Ord Course 87. **d** 90 **p** 94. Par Dn Shirley St Geo *S'wark* 90-94; C 94-96; C Caterham 96-98; TV from 98. *St Luke's Vicarage, 8 Whyteleafe Hill, Whyteleafe CR3 0AA* Tel (020) 8660 4015

REEVES, Graham. b 65. Southn Univ BTh94 Univ Coll Chich MA04. Chich Th Coll 91. **d** 94 **p** 95. C Cardiff St Mary and

St Steph w St Dyfrig etc *Llan* 94-95; C Roath 95-98; Chapl Sussex Weald and Downs NHS Trust 98-02; Chapl W Sussex Health and Soc Care NHS Trust from 02. *45 Abbottsbury, Bognor Regis PO21 4RT* Tel (01243) 815310 *or* 623576

REEVES, John Graham. b 44. Kelham Th Coll 64. **d** 69 **p** 71. C Aston cum Aughton *Sheff* 69-71; C Ribbleton *Blackb* 72-74; C Cleveleys 74-75; P-in-c Huncoat 75-77; V 77-82; V Knuzden 82-92; V Sandylands 92-09; rtd 09. *51 Parkfield Drive, Lancaster LA1 4BT* Tel (01524) 411299 E-mail revjgr@tiscali.co.uk

REEVES, Ms Karen Susan. b 56. Bris Univ BA78. Ripon Coll Cuddesdon 02. **d** 05 **p** 07. C De Beauvoir Town St Pet *Lon* 05-06; C Islington St Jas w St Pet 06-08; Chapl Frimley Park Hosp NHS Foundn Trust 08-09; NSM Frimley *Guildf* 08-09; Chapl Milton Keynes Hosp NHS Foundn Trust from 09. *Milton Keynes Hospital NHS Foundation Trust, Standing Way, Eaglestone, Milton Keynes MK6 5LD* Tel (01908) 660033
E-mail karen.reeves6@btinternet.com

REEVES, Kenneth William. b 38. TCD 67. **d** 69 **p** 70. C Killowen *D & R* 69-70; I Ardara 70-76; TV Quidenham *Nor* 76-81; V Swaffham 81-86; Chapl Nor Coll of Educn 86-91; P-in-c Lakenham St Alb *Nor* 86-91; rtd 92; Perm to Offic *Nor* 92-98 and from 05; P-in-c Trowse 99-03; P-in-c Nerja and Almuécar *Eur* 03-04. *15 Morris Close, Stoke Holy Cross, Norwich NR14 8LL* Tel (01508) 494583 E-mail revkenn@aol.com

REEVES, Maria Elizabeth Ann. *See* COULTER, Mrs Maria Elizabeth Ann

REEVES, Michael Richard Ewert. b 74. Girton Coll Cam MA00. Oak Hill Th Coll 98. **d** 02 **p** 03. NSM Langham Place All So *Lon* 02-05; Th Adv UCCF from 05. *UCCF, 38 De Montfort Street, Leicester LE1 7GP* Tel 0116-255 1700 Fax 255 5672
E-mail mreeves@dsl.pipex.com

REEVES, Nicholas John Harding. b 44. Open Th Coll BA99 Nottm Univ MA02. ALCD69. **d** 69 **p** 70. C Upton (Overchurch) *Ches* 69-72; C Woodlands *Sheff* 72-74; C-in-c Cranham Park CD *Chelmsf* 74-79; V Cranham Park 79-88; R Aldridge *Lich* 88-02; Dioc Officer for Evang *Carl* from 03; C Eden, Gelt and Irthing from 03. *The New Vicarage, Irthington, Carlisle CA6 4NJ* Tel (01697) 741864 Mobile 07714-245506
E-mail the7reeves@aol.com

✠**REEVES, The Rt Revd Sir Paul Alfred.** b 32. ONZ07 GCMG85 GCVO86 QSO90. Univ of NZ BA55 MA56 St Pet Coll Ox BA61 MA65 Hon DCL85 Wellington Univ (NZ) Hon LLD89 Gen Th Sem NY Hon DD92. St Jo Coll Auckland LTh58. **d** 58 **p** 60 **c** 71. New Zealand 58-59 and from 64; C Ox St Mary V 59-61; C Kirkley *Nor* 61-63; C Lewisham St Mary *S'wark* 63-64; Bp Waiapu 71-79; Bp Auckland 79-85; Abp New Zealand 80-85; Gov Gen NZ 85-90; ACC Rep at United Nations 91-93; Asst Bp New York 91-94; Dean Te Rau Kahikatea Th Coll Auckland 94-95. *14B Victoria Avenue, Remuera, Auckland 1005, New Zealand* E-mail sirpaulreeves@xtra.co.nz

REGAN, Brian. b 46. MBIM80. WMMTC 88. **d** 91 **p** 92. C Cov St Jo 91-94; V Tile Hill 94-09; rtd 09; Perm to Offic *Cov* from 09. *160 Ansley Road, Nuneaton CV10 8LZ* Tel 07766-721837 (mobile) E-mail brianregan32@hotmail.com

REGAN, Noel Henry Likely. b 49. **d** 99 **p** 00. Aux Min Cloonclare w Killasnett, Lurganboy and Drumlease *K, E & A* 99-06; Dioc C Garrison w Slavin and Belleek *Clogh* from 06. *Gurteen Farm, Cliffoney, Co Sligo, Republic of Ireland* Tel (00353) (71) 916 6253 Mobile 86 887 5714 E-mail revnoelregan@hotmail.com

REGAN, Paul John. b 67. Southn Univ BA88 PhD96 St Jo Coll Dur BA98. Cranmer Hall Dur 96. **d** 99 **p** 00. C St Alb St Pet *St Alb* 99-03; TV Smestow Vale *Lich* 03-09; Chapl Trevelyan Coll *Dur* from 09; Chapl Van Mildert Coll from 09; C Dur St Oswald and Shincliffe from 09. *6 Trevelyan College Houses, Elvet Hill Road, Durham DH1 3LW* Tel 0191-334 7037

REGAN, Philip. b 49. Qu Mary Coll Lon BSc MSc. Wycliffe Hall Ox 81. **d** 83 **p** 84. NSM Scotforth *Blackb* 83-89; P-in-c Combe St Nicholas w Wambrook *B & W* 89-01; V 01-08; P-in-c Whitestaunton 89-01; R 01-08; rtd 08. *5 Mill Court, Tudor Park, Priorswood, Taunton TA2 8TD* Tel (01823) 354247
E-mail pregan@ukonline.co.uk

REGINALD, Brother. *See* BOX, Reginald Gilbert

REID, Amanda Joy. *See* MARRIOTT, Mrs Amanda Joy

REID, Andrew John. b 47. Birm Univ BEd70 Man Univ MEd76. S'wark Ord Course 88. **d** 88 **p** 89. NSM Westerham *Roch* 88-90; Chapl Abp Tenison's Sch Kennington 90-05; Perm to Offic *Roch* from 05. *12 Westways, Westerham TN16 1TT* Tel (01959) 561428

REID, Christopher Jason. b 69. Trin Coll Bris 01. **d** 03 **p** 04. C Woodley *Ox* 03-07; V Selby St Jas *York* from 07. *St James's Vicarage, 14 Leeds Road, Selby YO8 4HX* Tel (01757) 702861 E-mail cjasonreid@hotmail.com

REID, Canon Colin Guthrie. b 30. **d** 56 **p** 57. C Kendal St Thos *Carl* 56-59; C Crosthwaite Keswick 59-60; R Caldbeck w Castle Sowerby 60-76; RD Wigton 69-70; P-in-c Sebergham 75-76; R Caldbeck, Castle Sowerby and Sebergham 76-93; Hon Can Carl Cathl 88-93; rtd 93; Perm to Offic *Carl* from 93. *Mellbreak, Longthwaite Road, Wigton CA7 9JR* Tel (01697) 345625

REID, David Graham. b 78. Hatf Coll Dur BSc00. Wycliffe Hall Ox BTh09. **d** 09. NSM Ox St Ebbe w H Trin and St Pet from 09. *24 East Avenue, Oxford OX4 1XP* Tel (01865) 240438
E-mail dave.reid@stebbes.org.uk

REID, Mrs Diane Mary. b 73. Lanc Univ BMus94 Huddersfield Univ PGCE98. Trin Coll Bris BA04. **d** 04 **p** 05. C Reading St Agnes w St Paul and St Barn *Ox* 04-07. *St James's Vicarage, 14 Leeds Road, Selby YO8 4HX* Tel (01757) 702861
E-mail dianem_clark@hotmail.com

REID, Donald. b 58. Glas Univ LLB79 Pemb Coll Ox MPhil81 Edin Univ BD85. Edin Th Coll 82. **d** 85 **p** 86. C Greenock *Glas* 85-88; C Baillieston 88-91; R 91-95; C Glas St Serf 88-91; R 91-95; Chapl Glas Univ 89-00; Chapl Glas Caledonian Univ 89-00; Chapl Strathclyde Univ 89-00; TP Glas St Mary 95-00; Assoc P 00-04; C Edin St Jo from 04. *11A Cornwall Street, Edinburgh EH1 2EQ* Tel 0131-466 2461 *or* 229 7565
E-mail donald.reid@stjohns-edinburgh.org.uk

✠**REID, The Rt Revd Gavin Hunter.** b 34. OBE00. K Coll Lon BA56. Oak Hill Th Coll 56. **d** 60 **p** 61 **c** 92. C E Ham St Paul *Chelmsf* 60-63; C Rainham 63-66; Publications Sec CPAS 66-71; Hon C St Paul's Cray St Barn *Roch* 68–71; Ed Scc USCL 71-74; Hon C Woking St Jo *Guildf* 72-92; Sec for Evang CPAS 74-92; Consultant Missr CPAS and BMU Adv 90-92; Suff Bp Maidstone *Cant* 92-00; Six Preacher Cant Cathl 92-97; rtd 00; Perm to Offic *Nor* and *St E* from 00; Hon Asst Bp St E from 08. *Furzefield, 17 Richard Crampton Road, Beccles NR34 9HN* Tel (01502) 717042 Fax 710739 Mobile 07941-770549
E-mail gavin@reids.org

REID, Geraldine Felicity (Jo). b 47. RGN69. EMMTC 95. **d** 98 **p** 99. NSM Skellingthorpe w Doddington *Linc* 98-02; NSM Hykeham from 02. *Tol Peden, Monson Park, Skellingthorpe, Lincoln LN6 5UE* Tel (01522) 828402 *or* 828403
E-mail tolpedn@ntlworld.com

REID, Gordon. *See* REID, Canon William Gordon

REID, Herbert Alan. b 31. AKC55. **d** 56 **p** 57. C Penwortham St Mary *Blackb* 56-59; C-in-c Penwortham St Leon CD 59-63; V Brierfield 63-72; V Warton St Paul 72-79; V Read in Whalley 79-98; rtd 98; Perm to Offic *Blackb* from 98. *Paslew House, 6 The Sands, Whalley, Blackburn BB7 9TL* Tel (01254) 824620

REID, James. b 46. Strathclyde Univ BSc69. WMMTC 88. **d** 91 **p** 92. C Attleborough *Cov* 91-95; V Walsall Pleck and Bescot *Lich* 95-99; TR Chell 99-06; rtd 06. *22 St Ives Way, Nuneaton CV11 6FR* Tel (024) 7634 2264

REID, Jason. *See* REID, Christopher Jason

REID, Jo. *See* REID, Geraldine Felicity

REID, Lucinda Jane. b 57. Dur Univ BA78. Ripon Coll Cuddesdon 79. **dss** 81 **d** 85 **p** 85. Birtley *Dur* 81-84; Canada from 84. *5551 West Saanich Road, Victoria BC V9E 2G1, Canada* E-mail lreid@uoguelpha.ca

REID, Mark. **d** 07 **p** 08. NSM Glenavy w Tunny and Crumlin *Conn* from 07. *12B Carmavy Road, Nutts Corner, Crumlin BT29 4TF* Tel (028) 9445 4725

REID, Mrs Pauline Ann. b 57. EAMTC 00. **d** 03 **p** 04. C Silverstone and Abthorpe w Slapton etc *Pet* 03-07; P-in-c Raddesley Gp *Ely* from 07. *The Rectory, 23 Stetchworth Road, Dullingham, Newmarket CB8 9UJ* Tel (01638) 507786 Mobile 07812-831869 E-mail p.reid@tiscali.co.uk

REID, Peter Ivor. b 30. Qu Coll Cam BA53 MA72. St Mich Coll Llan 78. **d** 80 **p** 81. C Llantwit Major and St Donat's 80-83; C Llantwit Major 83-84; V Laleston w Tythegston 84; V Laleston w Tythegston and Merthyr Mawr 84-88; V Roath 88-98; rtd 98. *18 Woolaston Avenue, Cardiff CF23 5AD* Tel (029) 2075 3306

REID, Robert. *See* McLEAN-REID, Robert

REID, Stewart Thomas. b 45. Liv Hope MA01. Oak Hill Th Coll 66. **d** 70 **p** 71. C Normanton *Derby* 70-73; C Leyland St Andr *Blackb* 73-78; V Halliwell St Luke *Man* 78-95; V Southport Ch *Liv* from 95. *The Vicarage, 12 Gloucester Road, Southport PR8 2AU* Tel (01704) 565120

REID, Canon William Gordon. b 43. Edin Univ MA63 Keble Coll Ox BA66 MA72. Edin Th Coll 63 Cuddesdon Coll 66. **d** 67 **p** 68. C Edin St Salvador 67-69; Chapl and Tutor Sarum Th Coll 69-72; R Edin St Mich and All SS 72-84; Provost St Andr Cathl Inverness 84-87; Chapl Ankara *Eur* 87-89; Chapl Stockholm w Gävle and Västerås 89-92; V Gen to Bp Eur 92-02; Can Gib Cathl 92-98; Adn in Eur 96-98; P-in-c St Mich Cornhill w St Pet le Poer etc *Lon* 97-98; Dean Gib *Eur* 98-00; Adn Italy and Malta 00-03; Chapl Milan w Genoa and Varese 00-03; R Philadelphia St Clem USA from 04. *2013 Appletree Street, Philadelphia PA 19103-1409, USA* Tel (001) (215) 563 1876 Fax 563 7627
E-mail gordonrr@earthlink.net

REIDE, Susannah Louise Court. b 69. Clare Coll Cam BA91. Trin Coll Bris BA04. **d** 04 **p** 05. C Marlborough *Sarum* 04-08; TV Cowley St Jas *Ox* from 08. *27 Don Bosco Close, Oxford OX4 2LD*

REIGATE, Archdeacon of. *See* KAJUMBA, The Ven Daniel Steven Kimbugwe

REILLY, Frederick James. b 29. CITC 70. **d** 73 **p** 74. C Agherton *Conn* 73-75; C Ballymena 75-82; I Ballyscullion *D & R* 82-04;

Can Derry Cathl 03-04; rtd 04. *11 Swilly Drive, Portstewart BT55 7FJ* Tel (028) 7083 5788

REILLY, Thomas Gerard. b 38. **d** 64 **p** 64. In RC Ch 64-73; Hon C Clapton Park All So *Lon* 73-76; Hon C Haggerston All SS 76-78; Hon C Walthamstow St Sav *Chelmsf* 79-85; P-in-c Forest Gate Em w Upton Cross 85-89; V 89-92; V Chaddesden St Phil *Derby* 92-01; RD Derby N 95-00; rtd 01; Perm to Offic *B & W* from 01. *8 Victoria Square, Poples Well, Crewkerne TA18 7ES* Tel (01460) 72613 E-mail ger_mon@totalise.co.uk

REILY, Paul Alan. b 59. UEA BA81. St Jo Coll Nottm MA92. **d** 92 **p** 93. C Westcliff St Mich *Chelmsf* 92-96; P-in-c Barkingside St Cedd 96-98; V 98-01; V Leyton St Cath and St Paul from 01; AD Waltham Forest 04-07. *St Catherine's Vicarage, Fairlop Road, London E11 1BL* Tel (020) 8539 6361
E-mail paul@reily.co.uk

REINDORP, David Peter Edington. b 52. TD05. Trin Coll Cam BA82 MA86 CQSW77. Westcott Ho Cam 79. **d** 83 **p** 84. C Chesterton Gd Shep *Ely* 83-85; C Hitchin *St Alb* 85-88; R Landbeach and V Waterbeach *Ely* 88-97; OCF 88-97; CF(V) from 92; RD Quy *Ely* 94-97; V Cherry Hinton St Jo 97-06; RD Cambridge 04-06; Hon Can Ely Cathl 05-06; V Chelsea All SS *Lon* from 06. *2 Old Church Street, Crewkerne SW3 5DQ* Tel (020) 7352 5627 E-mail david.reindorp@talk21.com

REINDORP, Canon Michael Christopher Julian. b 44. Trin Coll Cam BA67 MA70 K Coll Lon MA99. Cuddesdon Coll 67 United Th Coll Bangalore 68. **d** 69 **p** 70. C Poplar *Lon* 69-74; V Chatham St Wm *Roch* 74-84; R Stantonbury *Ox* 84-87; TR Stantonbury and Willen 87-92; P-in-c Richmond St Mary w St Matthias and St Jo *S'wark* 92-95; TR from 96; Hon Can S'wark Cathl from 03. *The Vicarage, Ormond Road, Richmond TW10 6TH* Tel and fax (020) 8940 0362
E-mail rector@richmondteam.freeserve.co.uk

REISS, Prof Michael Jonathan. b 58. Trin Coll Cam BA78 MA82 PhD82 PGCE83 FIBiol90 Open Univ MBA02. EAMTC 87. **d** 90 **p** 91. Lect Cam Univ 88-94; Reader 94-00; NSM Comberton *Ely* 90-94; NSM Deanery of Bourn 94-96 and 99-00; P-in-c Boxworth and Elsworth w Knapwell 96-99; Perm to Offic 99-03; Prof Science Educn Inst of Educn Lon Univ from 01; NSM Toft w Caldecote and Childerley *Ely* from 03. *Institute of Education, University of London, 20 Bedford Way, London WC1H 0AL* Tel (020) 7947 9522 E-mail m.reiss@ioe.ac.uk

REISS, Peter Henry. b 62. Hertf Coll Ox BA85 MA91 Natal Univ MA95. St Jo Coll Nottm 95. **d** 95 **p** 96. C Sherwood *S'well* 95-00; TV Bestwood 00-03; V Bestwood Park w Rise Park 03-04; Tr Officer CME and Laity Development *Man* 04-06; Dir Discipleship and Min Tr from 06. *Discipleship and Ministry Training, 5th Floor, Church House, 90 Deansgate, Manchester M3 2GJ* Tel 0161-828 1455 Fax 828 1485
E-mail preiss@manchester.anglican.org

REISS, Canon Robert Paul. b 43. Trin Coll Cam BA67 MA71. Westcott Ho Cam 67. **d** 69 **p** 70. C St John's Wood *Lon* 69-73; Bangladesh 73; Chapl Trin Coll Cam 73-78; Selection Sec ACCM 78-85; Sen Selection Sec 83; TR Grantham *Linc* 86-96; RD Grantham 92-96; Adn Surrey and Hon Can Guildf Cathl 96-05; Can Westmr Abbey from 05. *1 Little Cloister, London SW1P 3PL* Tel (020) 7654 4804 Fax 7654 4811
E-mail robert.reiss@westminster-abbey.org

REITH, Robert Michael. b 55. Oak Hill Th Coll BA83. **d** 83 **p** 84. C Kendal St Thos *Carl* 83-87; C Leyland St Andr *Blackb* 87-92; V Leyland St Jo 92-94; TR Dagenham *Chelmsf* 94-03; V from 03. *The Vicarage, Church Lane, Dagenham RM10 0JU* Tel (020) 8592 1339 Mobile 07595-303023 E-mail mikereith@me.com

RENDALL, Canon John Albert. b 43. Hull Univ BTh84 MA89. Ripon Hall Ox 65. **d** 68 **p** 69. C Southsea St Simon *Portsm* 68-71; C Wallington *S'wark* 71-77; P-in-c Rufforth w Moor Monkton and Hessay *York* 77-79; R 79-08; P-in-c Long Marston 77-79; R 79-08; RD New Ainsty 85-97; P-in-c Healaugh w Wighill, Bilbrough and Askham Richard 02-08; P-in-c Tockwith and Bilton w Bickerton 03-08; Can and Preb York Minster 94-08; Chapl Purey Cust Nuffield Hosp 82-04; rtd 08; Perm to Offic *York* from 09. *Kingfisher Cottage, 3 Corn Mill Court, Leeds LS13 4HW* Tel 0113-239 3871 E-mail nata@supanet.com

RENDALL, Richard John. b 54. Wadh Coll Ox BA76 LLB76 MA92 Solicitor 78. Wycliffe Hall Ox 90. **d** 92 **p** 93. C Heswall *Ches* 92-98; R High Ongar w Norton Mandeville *Chelmsf* 98-04; R Broadwell, Evenlode, Oddington, Adlestrop etc *Glouc* from 04. *The Rectory, Broadwell, Moreton-in-Marsh GL56 0TU* Tel (01451) 831866 E-mail rendalls@talk21.com

RENDELL, Jason. b 68. **d** 05 **p** 09. Chapl to Bp Stepney *Lon* 05-07; NSM Clerkenwell H Redeemer 06-07; NSM Clerkenwell St Mark 06-07; Min Can and Succ St Paul's Cathl from 07. *8A Amen Court, London EC4M 7BU* Tel (020) 7246 8338
E-mail succentor@stpaulscathedral.org.uk

RENDLE, Graham Barton. b 40. **d** 99 **p** 00. OLM Rougham, Beyton w Hessett and Rushbrooke *St E* from 99. *Appletrees, Bury Road, Beyton, Bury St Edmunds IP30 9AB* Tel (01359) 270924

RENFREY, Edward Donald John-Baptist. b 53. ACT. **d** 76 **p** 77. C Naracoorte Australia 76-77; P-in-c Kingston w Robe 78-81; R

81-84; Chapl RN 84-99; Chapl R Aus Navy from 99. *5/7 Bayview Street, Fannie Bay NT 0820, Australia* Tel (0061) (8) 409-662823 (mobile) E-mail edwardrenfrey@hotmail.com.au

RENGERT, Keith Alan Francis. b 67. RGN92. Ripon Coll Cuddesdon 07. **d** 09. C N Walsham and Edingthorpe *Nor* from 09. *8 Plumbly Close, North Walsham NR28 9YB* Tel (01692) 500028 Mobile 07796-607649
E-mail k.rengert@btinternet.com

RENISON, Gary James. b 62. SS Hild & Bede Coll Dur BA83. Ridley Hall Cam 84. **d** 86 **p** 87. C Stapenhill w Cauldwell *Derby* 86-89; C Cheadle Hulme St Andr *Ches* 89-92; Min Cheadle Hulme Em CD 92-95; P-in-c Bar Hill *Ely* 95-05; V Childwall All SS *Liv* from 05. *All Saints' Vicarage, Childwall Abbey Road, Liverpool L16 0JW* Tel 0151-737 2169
E-mail vicar.allsaints@uwclub.net

RENNARD, Edward Lionel. b 51. CertEd72 Nottm Univ BTh80. Linc Th Coll 76. **d** 80 **p** 81. C Old Brumby *Linc* 80-82; C-in-c Gt Grimsby St Matt Fairfield CD 82-86; V Fairfield St Matt 86-88; V Hykeham 88-91; TR 91-00; TR Blyth Valley *St E* from 00. *The Rectory, Highfield Road, Halesworth IP19 8SJ* Tel (01986) 872602 Mobile 07958-191975
E-mail edward.rennard@btinternet.com

RENNARD, Margaret Rose. b 49. CertEd75. Linc Th Coll 76. **dss** 80 **d** 87 **p** 94. C Fairfield St Matt *Linc* 87-88; C Hykeham 88-00; Chapl HM Pris Morton Hall 91-00; Asst Chapl HM Pris Blundeston 00-01; Asst Chapl HM Pris Hollesley Bay from 01; Chapl Allington NHS Trust 00-01; Perm to Offic *St E* from 00. *The Rectory, Highfield Road, Halesworth IP19 8SJ* Tel (01986) 872602 E-mail edward.rennard@btinternet.com

RENNIE, Iain Hugh. b 43. Ripon Coll Cuddesdon 88. **d** 90 **p** 91. C Poulton-le-Sands w Morecambe St Laur *Blackb* 90-94; V Hornby w Claughton 94-02; V Hornby w Claughton and Whittington etc from 02. *The Vicarage, Main Street, Arkholme, Carnforth LA6 1AX* Tel (015242) 21238

RENNIE, John Aubery. b 47. Lon Univ MB, BS70 FRCS75. SEITE 04. **d** 06 **p** 07. NSM Melbury *Sarum* from 06. *Rectory House, 2 Fore Street, Evershot, Dorchester DT2 0JW* Tel (01935) 83698 Mobile 07792-502299
E-mail johnrennie40@aol.com

RENNIE, Paul Antony. b 58. Heriot-Watt Univ BSc82 Edin Univ LTh. **d** 87 **p** 88. C Nairn *Mor* 87-90; C Forres 87-90; C Edin St Pet 90-92; Dep Chapl HM Pris Leeds 92; Chapl HM YOI Hindley 93-95; Chapl HM Pris Liv 95-97; Chapl RAF from 97. *Chaplaincy Services, HQ Personnel and Training Command, RAF High Wycombe HP14 4UE* Tel (01494) 496800 Fax 496343

RENNIX, Raymond Latham. b 37. QUB BTh02. CITC 00. **d** 03 **p** 04. NSM Killaney w Carryduff *D & D* 03-08; NSM Glencraig from 08. *5 Brompton Court, Dromara, Dromore BT25 2DQ* Tel (028) 9753 3167 Mobile 07977-584053
E-mail r.rennix@btinternet.com

RENSHAW, Mrs Anne-Marie Louise. b 71. St Hilda's Coll Ox MA96 Fitzw Coll Cam BA97. Ridley Hall Cam 95. **d** 98 **p** 99. C Norton *St Alb* 98-02; TV Borehamwood 02-05; TV Elstree and Borehamwood from 05. *Holy Cross Vicarage, 1 Warren Grove, Borehamwood WD6 2QU* Tel (020) 8953 2183
E-mail amlrenshaw@tiscali.co.uk

RENSHAW, Anthony. b 40. Montreal Dioc Th Coll 83. **d** 87 **p** 88. Canada 87-90; P-in-c Ainsdale *Liv* 90-91; V 91-98; V Singleton w Weeton *Blackb* 98-03; rtd 03. *20 The Windrush, Rochdale OL12 6DY* Tel (01706) 341420
E-mail tonyrenshaw@tiscali.co.uk

RENSHAW, David William. b 59. Oak Hill Th Coll BA85. **d** 85 **p** 86. C Shawbury *Lich* 85-88; V Childs Ercall and R Stoke upon Tern 88-92; V Stoneleigh *Guildf* 92-97; RD Epsom 95-97; Chapl Scarborough and NE Yorks Healthcare NHS Trust 97-99; Chapl St Cath Hospice Scarborough 97-99; R Meppershall w Campton and Stondon *St Alb* 99-01; C Bedford St Andr 02; rtd 02; Perm to Offic *Chich* 05-06; Hon C Bexhill St Pet 06. *35 Mendip Avenue, Eastbourne BN23 8HP* Tel (01323) 461153
E-mail renshaw221@btinternet.com

RENSHAW, Peter Selwyn Kay. b 29. Keble Coll Ox BA52 MA64. St Steph Ho Ox 52. **d** 64 **p** 65. Lic to Offic *Ox* 64-66; Chapl RN 66-70; Chapl Br Emb and Athens St Paul *Eur* 71-74; Gothenburg 74-75; Chapl RN Haslemere 75-81; Costa Blanca *Eur* 81-82; R Ewelme *Ox* 83-85; R Ewelme, Brightwell Baldwin, Cuxham w Easington 85-92; rtd 92. *Lovedays House, Painswick, Stroud GL6 6QB* Tel (01452) 812811

RENSHAW, Susan Kathryn. b 55. Shenstone Coll of Educn CertEd77. WMMTC 99. **d** 02 **p** 03. C Sedgley All SS *Worc* 02-05; C Gornal and Sedgley 05-06; V Eckington from 06; V Defford w Besford from 06. *The Vicarage, Drakes Bridge Road, Eckington, Pershore WR10 3JW* Tel (01386) 750203
E-mail rcvsusan@btinternet.com

RENSHAW, Timothy John. b 65. Trin Coll Carmarthen BA86. St Jo Coll Nottm MA97. **d** 97 **p** 98. C Calverton *S'well* 97-01; C Epperstone 97-01; C Gonalston 97-01; C Oxton 97-01; P-in-c Shireoaks 01-05; Dioc Adv on Notts Coalfield 01-05; Project Manager Cathl Breakfast and Archer Projects *Sheff* from 05.

The Cathedral, 4-7 East Parade, Sheffield S1 2ET Tel 0114-275 1650 *or* 279 7042

RENWICK, Canon Colin. b 30. St Aid Birkenhead. **d** 59 **p** 60. C Drypool St Columba w St Andr and St Pet *York* 59-62; C Wigan St Cath *Liv* 62-64; Min Thornton CD 64-77; V Thornton 77-97; RD Bootle 83-89; Hon Can Bauchi from 93; rtd 97; Perm to Offic *Ches* from 97. *27 Briar Drive, Heswall, Wirral CH60 5RN* Tel 0151-342 3308

RENYARD, Christopher. b 52. Open Univ BA87. Coll of Resurr Mirfield 81. **d** 84 **p** 85. C Heckmondwike *Wakef* 84-88; C Harpenden St Nic *St Alb* 88-95; Asst Chapl Salisbury Health Care NHS Trust 95-01; Chapl Team Ldr from 01. *The Chaplain's Office, Salisbury District Hospital, Salisbury SP2 8BJ* Tel (01722) 429271
E-mail chaplains.department@shc-tr.swest.nhs.uk

RENYARD, Paul Holmwood. b 42. K Coll Lon BD65 AKC65. **d** 66 **p** 67. C Croydon St Aug *Cant* 66-69; C Farnham *Guildf* 69-72; V Capel 72-78; Asst Dir RE 72-78; Asst Dir RE *Roch* 78-83; Hon C Roch 78-83; V Holdenhurst *Win* 83-95; V Pennington 95-07; rtd 07. *53 Scarf Road, Poole BH17 8QJ* Tel (01202) 682460 E-mail renyard@tiscali.co.uk

REPATH, George David. b 43. Kellogg Coll Ox MSt96. St D Coll Lamp. **d** 68 **p** 69. C Cardiff St Jo *Llan* 68-73; C Gt Stanmore *Lon* 73-77; V Stratfield Mortimer *Ox* 77-85; RD Bradfield 82-85; P-in-c Mortimer W End w Padworth 83-85; V Bray and Braywood 85-07; rtd 07. *8 Summerfields, Findon, Worthing BN14 0TU* Tel (01903) 877366

REPATH, John Richard. b 48. St Mich Coll Llan 72. **d** 75 **p** 76. C Canton St Jo *Llan* 75-79; C Burghclere w Newtown and Ecchinswell w Sydmonton *Win* 80-83; R Bewcastle and Stapleton *Carl* 83-88; P-in-c Kirklinton w Hethersgill and Scaleby 86-88; R Bewcastle, Stapleton and Kirklinton etc 88-97; rtd 97; P-in-c New Galloway *Glas* from 97. *The Rectory, Kenbridge Road, New Galloway, Castle Douglas DG7 3RP* Tel (01644) 420235

REPTON, Suffragan Bishop of. See SOUTHERN, The Rt Revd Humphrey Ivo John

RESCH, Colin Ernst. b 67. Trin Coll Bris 04. **d** 06 **p** 07. C Highley w Billingsley, Glazeley etc *Heref* from 06. *43 Yew Tree Grove, Highley, Bridgnorth WV16 6DG* Tel (01746) 862588
E-mail colin@godstuff.org.uk

RESCH, Michael Johann. b 63. NTMTC 96. **d** 99 **p** 00. C Cullompton *Ex* 99-01; C Cullompton, Willand, Uffculme, Kentisbeare etc 01-03; P-in-c Sittingbourne H Trin w Bobbing *Cant* from 03. *88 Albany Road, Sittingbourne ME10 1EL* Tel (01795) 473393 Mobile 07967-771231
E-mail mikeresch@aol.com

RESTALL, Miss Susan Roberta. b 45. MSc. Sarum & Wells Th Coll 79. **dss** 82 **d** 87 **p** 94. Dorchester *Sarum* 82-84; Portland All SS w St Pet 84-87; Par Dn 87; TD Yate New Town *Bris* 87-94; TV 94-95; Chapl Birm Heartlands and Solihull NHS Trust 95-01; rtd 01; Perm to Offic *Birm* from 03. *12 Croft Road, Yardley, Birmingham B26 1SG* Tel 0121-783 3325

REVELEY, James Stewart. b 69. Goldsmiths' Coll Lon BMus92. Ch Div Sch of the Pacific (USA) 95 Ripon Coll Cuddesdon BA97. **d** 90 **p** 97. C Oddington *St Alb* 96 00; C Harpenden St Nic 00-04; V Boxmoor St Jo from 04. *St John's Vicarage, 10 Charles Street, Hemel Hempstead HP1 1JH* Tel and fax (01442) 255382 E-mail revjumble@aol.com

REVELEY, Mrs Valerie Mary. b 39. Lon Inst of Educn BEd77. SAOMC 96. **d** 99 **p** 00. OLM Olney *Ox* 99-05. *Address temp unknown*

REVELL, Patrick Walter Millard. b 32. Wells Th Coll 65. **d** 67 **p** 68. C Leic St Jas 67-74; V Quorndon 74-82; TR Camelot Par *B & W* 82-90; RD Cary and Bruton 90-96; V Castle Cary w Ansford 90-97; rtd 97; Perm to Offic *B & W* and *Sarum* from 97. *80 Sheepland Lane, Sherborne DT9 4BP* Tel (01935) 813083

REVERA, Susan Mary. See LEATHLEY, Susan Mary.

REW, Eric Malcolm. b 63. UEA BSc84 PGCE89. Qu Coll Birm 98. **d** 00 **p** 01. C Shepshed *Leic* 00-03; C Shepshed and Oaks in Charnwood 03-04; TV Kingsthorpe w Northampton St Dav *Pet* from 04. *The Vicarage, 42 Fallow Walk, Northampton NN2 8DE* Tel (01604) 471948

REX, Keith Leslie Herbert. b 30. K Coll Lon 53. **d** 55 **p** 56. C Shepton Mallet *B & W* 55-58; C Cheshunt *St Alb* 58-60; V Weston-super-Mare St Andr Bournville *B & W* 60-67; R Charlton Adam w Charlton Mackrell 67-69; rtd 90. *46 Perrett Gardens, Hengrove, Bristol BS14 9BS*

REYNISH, David Stuart. b 52. Nottm Univ BEd75. Linc Th Coll 72. **d** 77 **p** 78. C Boston *Linc* 77-80; C Chalfont St Peter *Ox* 80-84; V Thursby *Carl* 84-88; R Iver Heath *Ox* 88-03; V Kelvedon and Feering *Chelmsf* from 03. *The Vicarage, Church Street, Kelvedon, Colchester CO5 9AL* Tel (01376) 571172

REYNOLDS, Alan Martin. b 53. Sarum & Wells Th Coll 73. **d** 77 **p** 78. C Glan Ely *Llan* 77-84; V Pontyclun w Talygarn 84-97; Perm to Offic from 97. *The Orchards, Stow Hill, Newport NP20 4EA* Tel (01633) 215841
E-mail martin.reynolds1@virgin.net

REYNOLDS, Alan Thomas William. b 43. Lon Univ BSc64. Linc Th Coll 64. **d** 66 **p** 67. C Leic St Pet 66-70; C Huntington *York* 70-72; R Darliston Jamaica 72-76; V Stechford *Birm* 76-83; Chapl E Birm Hosp 76-83; P-in-c Hampton in Arden *Birm* 83-86; V 87-93; Chapl Parkway Hosp Solihull 83-93; V Moseley St Anne *Birm* 93-02; Chapl Moseley Hall Hosp Birm 93-02; V Kerry, Llanmerewig, Dolfor and Mochdre *St As* 02-08; AD Cedewain 03-08; rtd 08; Perm to Offic *Lich* from 08. *49 Gittin Street, Oswestry SY11 1DU* Tel (01691) 680416
E-mail robbie.reynolds1@btinternet.com

REYNOLDS, Mrs Angela Heather. b 44. Wye Coll Lon BSc66 Birm Univ CertEd67. EAMTC 94. **d** 97 **p** 98. NSM Barnham Broom *Nor* 97-99; C Easton w Colton and Marlingford 99-00; P-in-c Easton, Colton, Marlingford and Bawburgh 00-09; rtd 09. *26 Clickers Road, Norwich NR3 2DD*
E-mail angela@ecmb.wanadoo.co.uk

REYNOLDS, David Hammerton. b 39. St Jo Coll Dur BA62. Qu Coll Birm 63. **d** 65 **p** 66. C N Ormesby *York* 65-68; C Hessle 68-71; V Sherburn in Elmet 71-79; V Fulford 79-87; Resp for Clergy In-Service Tr York Area 82-87; TV Bolventor *Truro* 87-90; TR Brayton *York* 90-06; RD Selby 04-06; rtd 06; Perm to Offic *Sheff* from 06 and *York* from 08. *42A George Street, Snaith, Goole DN14 9HZ* Tel (01405) 869352
E-mail dhrey@btopenworld.com

REYNOLDS, David James. b 48. St Jo Coll Dur BA72 Lanc Univ MA85. Cranmer Hall Dur 69. **d** 73 **p** 74. C Formby H Trin *Liv* 73-77; P-in-c Widnes St Paul 77-80; V Southport St Paul 80-87; P-in-c Mawdesley *Blackb* 87-91; R from 91; P-in-c Croston and Bretherton from 06; Chapl Derian Ho Children's Hospice 93-97. *Mawdesley Rectory, Green Lane, Ormskirk L40 3TH* Tel (01704) 822203 E-mail davidreynolds@tinyworld.co.uk

REYNOLDS, Gordon. b 42. Sarum & Wells Th Coll 71. **d** 72 **p** 73. C Tunstall *Lich* 72-74; USPG Zambia 75-88; C Southmead *Bris* 88-90; rtd 07. *78 William Bentley Court, Graiseley Lane, Wolverhampton WV11 1QW* Tel (01902) 730381

REYNOLDS, Hannah Claire. b 67. Kingston Univ MBA95. St Steph Ho Ox BTh09. **d** 06 **p** 07. C Twickenham All Hallows *Lon* 06-09; P-in-c Hanworth All SS from 09. *All Saint's Vicarage, Uxbridge Road, Feltham TW13 5EE* Tel (020) 8894 9330 Mobile 07981-981493 E-mail hcreynolds@hotmail.co.uk

REYNOLDS, Ms Helen Tracy. b 65. Huddersfield Univ BA. Cranmer Hall Dur 03. **d** 06 **p** 07. C Ryton *Dur* from 06. *19 Willow Court, Ryton NE40 3PE* Tel 0191-413 1299
E-mail tracyreynolds@gmail.com

REYNOLDS, Canon John Lionel. b 34. JP. Westmr Coll Ox MTh00. Chich Th Coll 58. **d** 61 **p** 62. C Whitkirk *Ripon* 61-64; C Tong *Bradf* 64-68; V Chisledon and Draycot Foliatt *Sarum* 68-74; TR Ridgeway 74-76; RD Marlborough 74-76; V Calne and Blackland 76-89; RD Calne 77-84; Can and Preb Sarum Cathl 80-02; V Woodford Valley 89-02; rtd 02; Perm to Offic *Sarum* from 02 and *Win* from 03. *Rose Court, Church Hill, Lover, Salisbury SP5 2PL* Tel (01725) 512311

REYNOLDS, John Stewart. b 19. St Edm Hall Ox BA42 MA45 BLitt50 FSA81. Ridley Hall Cam 42. **d** 44 **p** 45. C Ox St Clem 44-46; C-in-c Ox All SS w St Martin 46-49; R Easton-on-the-Hill *Pet* 49-56; R Besselsleigh w Dry Sandford *Ox* 56-85; Lect Wycliffe Hall Ox 71-78; rtd 85; Perm to Offic *Ox* from 85. *Linden Lodge, 59 St Mary's Road, Oxford OX4 1PZ* Tel (01865) 727386

REYNOLDS, Mandy Elizabeth. b 59. NTMTC 99. **d** 02 **p** 03. NSM Wembley St Jo *Lon* 02-04; CF from 04. *c/o MOD Chaplains (Army)* Tel (01980) 615804 Fax 615800
E-mail mandyreynoldsuk@yahoo.co.uk

REYNOLDS, Marion. b 49. Chelmer Inst of HE CertEd84. STETS 04. **d** 06 **p** 07. NSM Quantock Towers *B & W* 06-07; NSM Shelswell *Ox* from 07. *10C St Michael's Close, Fringford, Bicester OX27 8DW* Tel (01869) 278972 Mobile 07834-062268 E-mail marion.reynolds2@btopenworld.com

REYNOLDS, Martin. See REYNOLDS, Alan Martin

REYNOLDS, Michael. See REYNOLDS, Richard Michael

REYNOLDS, Mrs Michelle Angela. b 70. Ridley Hall Cam 02. **d** 04 **p** 05. C Hoddesdon *St Alb* 04-07; TV Grays Thurrock *Chelmsf* from 07. *Wendover Vicarage, College Avenue, Grays RM17 5UW* Tel (01375) 373468
E-mail michellea_reynolds@hotmail.com

REYNOLDS, Paul Andrew. b 57. Bath Univ BA86. Trin Coll Bris 83. **d** 86 **p** 87. C Reading St Jo *Ox* 86-90; C Dorridge *Birm* 90-95; TV Riverside *Ox* 95-06; R Beercrocombe w Curry Mallet, Hatch Beauchamp etc *B & W* from 06. *The Rectory, Stoke St Mary, Taunton TA3 5BX* Tel (01823) 444023

REYNOLDS, Paul Frederick. b 56. St Jo Coll Nottm 90. **d** 92 **p** 93. C Hyde St Geo *Ches* 92-96; P-in-c Delamere 96-00; Asst Dir Par Support and Development 96-98; Acting Dir 98-00; V Handforth 00-07; P-in-c Bramcote *S'well* from 07. *The Vicarage, Moss Drive, Bramcote, Beeston NG9 3NF* Tel 0115-922 9600
E-mail vicar@bramcoteparishchurch.com

REYNOLDS, Philip Delamere. b 53. Leeds Univ CertEd74 Nottm Univ BCombStuds82. Linc Th Coll 79. **d** 82 **p** 83. C Huddersfield St Jo *Wakef* 82-85; C Barkisland w W Scammonden 85-87; P-in-c Skelmanthorpe from 87. *St Aidan's*

Vicarage, Radcliffe Street, Skelmanthorpe, Huddersfield HD8 9AF Tel (01484) 863232
E-mail northmist@thales.demon.co.uk

REYNOLDS, Raymond Ernest. b 29. Nottm Univ MPhil89. Lambeth STh84 CA Tr Coll 50 Chich Th Coll 58. **d** 60 **p** 61. C Leeds St Marg *Ripon* 60-62; C Beeston *S'well* 62-64; R Farnley *Ripon* 64-76; R Higham-on-the-Hill w Fenny Drayton *Leic* 76-81; R Higham-on-the-Hill w Fenny Drayton and Witherley 81-90; V Sutton *Ely* 90-94; R Witcham w Mepal 90-94; rtd 94; C Nantwich *Ches* 94-96; Perm to Offic from 96. *4 St Alban's Drive, Nantwich CW5 7DW* Tel (01270) 623534

REYNOLDS, Richard Michael. b 42. St Steph Ho Ox 65. **d** 67 **p** 68. C Kidderminster St Mary *Worc* 67-70; Guyana 70-73; TV N Creedy *Ex* 73-80; R Holsworthy w Hollacombe 80-86; R Holsworthy w Hollacombe and Milton Damerel from 86; Chapl N Devon Healthcare NHS Trust from 94. *The Rectory, Bodmin Street, Holsworthy EX22 6BH* Tel (01409) 253435
E-mail michael@rnlds85.freeserve.co.uk

REYNOLDS, Roderick Bredon (Rory). b 58. Man Univ BA80. Ripon Coll Cuddesdon 93. **d** 95 **p** 96. C Hitchin *St Alb* 95-98; C Stevenage St Andr and St Geo 98-00; P-in-c High Wych and Gilston w Eastwick 00-06; TV Plaistow and N Canning Town *Chelmsf* from 06. *St Martin's Vicarage, 34 St Martins Avenue, London E6 3DX* Tel (020) 8552 6991 Mobile 07515-353456 E-mail roryreynolds@mac.com

REYNOLDS, Mrs Rosemary Joan. b 46. WMMTC 00. **d** 03 **p** 04. NSM Brandwood *Birm* from 03. *23 Chanston Avenue, Birmingham B14 5BD* Tel 0121-444 7015
E-mail hello@frankandrosemary.freeserve.co.uk

REYNOLDS, Simon Andrew. b 65. UEA MA00 ARCM85. Westcott Ho Cam 98. **d** 00 **p** 01. C Ex St Thos and Em 00-03; Min Can and Succ St Paul's Cathl 03-07; Warden Coll Min Cans 04-07; P-in-c Darton *Wakef* from 07; P-in-c Cawthorne from 07. *The Vicarage, 6 Jacob's Hall Court, Darton, Barnsley S75 5LY* Tel (01226) 384596 E-mail frsimonreynolds@btinternet.com

REYNOLDS, Stephen Paul. b 08 **p** 09. NSM Cannock *Lich* from 08. *4 Harebell Close, Cannock WS12 5XA* Tel (01543) 270940 E-mail stevereyno@tiscali.co.uk

REYNOLDS, Tracy. See REYNOLDS, Ms Helen Tracy

RHAM, Canon John Theodore. b 27. Magd Coll Cam BA50 MA65. Sarum Th Coll 50. **d** 52 **p** 53. C Harborne St Pet *Birm* 52-54; C Coleshill 54-56; C Falmouth K Chas *Truro* 56-59; R St Ewe 59-68; RD St Austell 65-68; V Budock 68-93; RD Carnmarth S 77-84; Hon Can Truro Cathl 80-93; rtd 93; France from 94. *Villa Budoc, 136 route de Bernis, 30980 Langlade, France*

RHOADES, Andrew Craig. b 56. Hatf Poly BSc79 CEng84 MIEE84. St Jo Coll Nottm MTh09. **d** 09. C Hexagon *Leic* from 09. *The Rectory, Dag Lane, North Kilworth, Lutterworth LE17 6HA* Tel (01858) 882099 Mobile 07531-121145 E-mail acrhoades@cheerful.com

RHODES, Adrian Michael. b 48. K Coll Lon BD71 AKC71. Qu Coll Birm 71. **d** 72 **p** 73. C Bury St Jo *Man* 72-75; Chapl N Man Gen Hosp 75-77; C Crumpsall *Man* 75-77; Chapl Walsall Manor and Bloxwich Hosps 77-83; Chapl Walsall Gen Hosp 81-83; Chapl Man R Infirmary 83-94; Chapl St Mary's Hosp Man 83-94; Chapl Man R Eye Hosp 83-94; Chapl Cen Man Healthcare NHS Trust 94-00; Perm to Offic *Man* from 00. *58 Errwood Road, Burnage, Manchester M19 2QH* Tel 0161-224 1739 E-mail adrian@rhodes.net

RHODES, Mrs Amanda Louise. b 63. Leeds Univ BA07. NOC 04. **d** 07 **p** 08. C Kippax w Allerton Bywater *Ripon* from 07. *21 Old Garth Croft, Fairburn, Knottingley WF11 9HD* Tel (01977) 670938 Mobile 07971-998621
E-mail macrho21@aol.com

RHODES, Anthony John. b 27. Mert Coll Ox BA50 MA53. St Steph Ho Ox 52. **d** 54 **p** 55. C Northampton St Alb *Pet* 54-57; C Oakham 57-60; P-in-c S Queensferry *Edin* 60-74; V Mitcham St Olave *S'wark* 74-81; V Owston *Linc* 81-92; V W Butterwick 81-92; rtd 92. *1 Trentside, Owston Ferry, Doncaster DN9 1RS* Tel (01427) 728237

RHODES, Arthur. b 31. Dur Univ BA58. Cranmer Hall Dur 57. **d** 59 **p** 60. C Kirkdale St Lawr *Liv* 59-61; C Litherland St Phil 61-64; V St Helens St Matt Thatto Heath 64-67; V Samlesbury *Blackb* 67-79; Lic to Offic 80-01; Perm to Offic from 01. *88 Deborah Avenue, Fulwood, Preston PR2 9HU* Tel (01772) 712212

RHODES, Benjamin. b 71. Portsm Univ BSc93. Westcott Ho Cam 94. **d** 97 **p** 98. C Upminster *Chelmsf* 97-01; Asst Chapl Lewisham Hosp NHS Trust 01-05; Sen Chapl Barts and The Lon NHS Trust from 05; NSM St Bart Less Lon from 05. *The Royal London Hospital, Whitechapel Road, London E1 1BB* Tel (020) 7377 7385 E-mail ben.rhodes@bartsandthelondon.nhs.uk

RHODES, Christine. See RHODES, Lois Christine

RHODES, David George. b 45. Univ of Wales (Abth) BA66. Trin Coll Bris 83. **d** 85 **p** 86. C Brinsworth w Catcliffe *Sheff* 85-89; V Mortomley St Sav 89-90; V Mortomley St Sav High Green 90-99; V Totley from 99. *All Saints' Vicarage, 37 Sunnyvale Road, Sheffield S17 4FA* Tel 0114-236 2322
E-mail drhodes@toucansurf.com

RHODES, David Grant. b 43. Ex Univ BA66 Leeds Univ DipAdEd75. Sarum & Wells Th Coll 69. d 72 p 73. C Mirfield *Wakef* 72-75; V Batley St Thos 75-80; Dioc Adult Educn Officer 76-80; Hon C Huddersfield St Jo 85-86; Dir BRF 86-87; V Robert Town *Wakef* 87-94; Project Worker 'Faith in Leeds' 94-99; Hon C Potternewton *Ripon* 95-99; Chapl Missr Children's Soc 99-03; Hon C Leeds City *Ripon* 99-03; rtd 03; Perm to Offic *York* from 00. *2 Moorland Road, York YO10 4HF* Tel (01904) 651749 Mobile 07712-006930 E-mail rhodes@freeuk.com

RHODES, Duncan. b 35. Leeds Univ BSc56. d 93 p 94. OLM Saddleworth *Man* 93-05; rtd 05; Perm to Offic *Man* from 06. *Holden Cottage, 21 Spurn Lane, Diggle, Oldham OL3 5QP* Tel (01457) 872399 E-mail dunrhodes@aol.com

RHODES, Mrs Heather. b 32. d 88. Par Dn Purley St Mark *S'wark* 89-94; C 94-98; rtd 98; Hon C Purley St Mark *S'wark* 00-05; Perm to Offic from 05. *24 Highfield Road, Purley CR8 2JG* Tel (020) 8660 1486

RHODES, Canon John Lovell. b 33. MBE81. Lon Univ BD59. St Aid Birkenhead 55. d 59 p 60. C Bradf St Clem 59-61; C Heeley *Sheff* 61-66; Ind Chapl *Linc* 66-81; Sen Ind Chapl 81-98; RD Grimsby and Cleethorpes 76-83; Can and Preb Linc Cathl 77-98; Chapl Franklin Coll 92-98; rtd 98; Perm to Offic *Linc* 98-01. *19 Augusta Close, Grimsby DN34 4TQ* Tel (01472) 343167

RHODES, Jonathan Peter. b 69. Coll of Ripon & York St Jo BA96. NOC 01. d 04 p 05. C High Harrogate Ch Ch *Ripon* 04-08; P-in-c Hartlepool St Aid *Dur* from 08. *39 Chichester Close, Hartlepool TS25 2QT* Tel (01429) 871009

RHODES, Lois Christine. b 34. Lon Univ BSc61. Glouc Sch of Min 84. d 87 p 94. NSM Weobley w Sarnesfield and Norton Canon *Heref* 87-92; NSM Letton w Staunton, Byford, Mansel Gamage etc 87-92; Chapl Asst Heref Hosps NHS Trust from 93. *Bellbrook, Bell Square, Weobley, Hereford HR4 8SE* Tel (01544) 318410 *or* (01432) 355444

RHODES, Matthew Ivan. b 66. Bris Univ BA89 Birm Univ MPhil95. Qu Coll Birm BD93. d 94 p 95. C Willenhall H Trin *Lich* 94-97; Chapl Maadi St Jo Egypt 97-00; P-in-c Middleton *Birm* 00-07; P-in-c Wishaw 00-07; P-in-c Curdworth 05-07; R Curdworth, Middleton and Wishaw from 07; AD Sutton Coldfield from 06. *The Rectory, Glebe Fields, Curdworth, Sutton Coldfield B76 9ES* Tel (01675) 470384 E-mail catmat30@hotmail.com

RHODES, Robert George. b 41. Man Univ BSc62. Ripon Hall Ox 72. d 74 p 75. C Banbury *Ox* 74-77; TV Banbury 77-81; P-in-c Long Horsley and Adult Educn Adv *Newc* 81-86; TR Wolverton *Ox* 86-97; P-in-c Bledlow w Saunderton and Horsenden 97-98; TV Risborough 98-02; Warden of Readers 97-02; USPG Miss Belize 02-06; rtd 06; Perm to Offic *Derby* from 07. *3 China House Yard, St Mary's Gate, Wirksworth, Matlock DE4 4DQ* Tel (01629) 823623 E-mail bandjrhodes@hotmail.com

RHODES-WRIGLEY, James. b 35. AKC59. d 60 p 61. C S Harrow St Paul *Lon* 60-66; V Hendon Ch Ch 66-71; V Northolt Park St Barn 71-92; rtd 92; Hon C Whyke w Rumboldswhyke and Portfield *Chich* from 96. *4 Gordon Avenue, Donnington, Chichester PO19 8QY* Tel (01243) 781664

RHYDDERCH, David Huw. b 48. St Mich Coll Llan 70. d 73 p 74. C Gelligaer *Llan* 73-76; C Penarth All SS 76-78; V Resolven /8-81; V Ystrad Rhondda w Ynyscynon 81-93; RD Rhondda 89-93; R St Andrews Major w Michaelston-le-Pit from 93. *The Rectory, Lettons Way, Dinas Powys CF64 4BY* Tel (029) 2051 2555

RICE, David. b 57. Nottm Univ BA79. Ripon Coll Cuddesdon 80. d 82 p 83. C Cirencester *Glouc* 82-86; R Theale and Englefield *Ox* 86-00; TR Wallingford from 00. *The Rectory, 22 Castle Street, Wallingford OX10 8DW* Tel (01491) 202188

RICE, Franklin Arthur. b 20. FRICS49. St Alb Minl Tr Scheme 77. d 80 p 81. NSM Hoddesdon *St Alb* 80-84; Perm to Offic *Guildf* from 85. *27 Mead Court, 281 Station Road, Addlestone KT15 2PR* Tel (01932) 846462

RICE, John Leslie Hale. b 38. Lon Univ BScEng60 BD68 FCMI. EMMTC 73. d 76 p 77. NSM Allestree St Nic *Derby* 76-90; Lic to Offic from 90. *14 Gisborne Crescent, Allestree, Derby DE22 2FL* Tel (01332) 557222

RICE, Lt Cdr Peter Langford. b 49. STETS 97. d 00 p 01. NSM Salisbury St Fran and Stratford sub Castle *Sarum* 00-03; P-in-c W Highland Region *Arg* 03-08. *The Old Manse, Lochgair, Argyll PA31 8SB* Tel (01546) 886674 Mobile 07776-105279 E-mail fynesinbosun@aol.com

RICE-OXLEY, John Richard. b 44. Keble Coll Ox BA66 MA69 Dur Univ MA85. Lon Coll of Div 68. d 70 p 71. C Eastwood *S'well* 70 73; Youth Adv CMS 73-78; V Mansfield St Jo *S'well* 78-82; P-in-c Thornley *Dur* 82-85; P-in-c Darlington St Matt and St Luke 85-87; V Hornsea w Atwick *York* 98-06; P-in-c Aldbrough, Mappleton w Goxhill and Withernwick 05-06; rtd 06; Perm to Offic *York* from 07. *The Vicarage, Carlton Drive, Aldbrough, Hull HU11 4SF* Tel (01964) 529032 E-mail richardriceoxley@gmail.com

RICE-OXLEY, Mrs Sylvia Jeanette Kathleen. b 48. d 08 p 09. C Aldbrough, Mappleton w Goxhill and Withernwick *York* from 08. *The Vicarage, Carlton Drive, Aldbrough, Hull HU11 4SF* Tel (01964) 529032

RICH, Brian John. b 49. Reading Univ BSc70. Guildf Dioc Min Course 94. d 97 p 98. OLM Stoke Hill *Guildf* from 97. *Roewen, 1 Trentham Crescent, Woking GU22 9EW* Tel (01483) 829541 E-mail btrich@ntlworld.com

RICH, Canon Christopher Robin. b 49. LSE MSc(Econ)95. Brasted Th Coll 70 Sarum & Wells Th Coll 72. d 74 p 75. C Sholing *Win* 74-76; C Southampton Maybush St Pet 76-79; R Fawley 79-90; Ind Chapl 83-90; Dir Soc Resp 90-99; Hon Can Win Cathl 96-99; Dir Soc Resp *Blackb* 99-05; Dir Soc Resp *Guildf* from 06. *Diocesan House, Quarry Street, Guildford GU1 3XG* Tel (01483) 571826 E-mail chris.rich@cofeguildford.org.uk

RICH, Nicholas Philip. b 49. St Cuth Soc Dur BA74 PGCE75 Coll of Ripon & York St Jo CertEd83. Linc Th Coll 86. d 88 p 89. C W Acklam *York* 88-91; Chapl St Geo Sch Harpenden 91-95; rtd 95. *36 Park Hill, Ampthill, Bedford MK45 2LP* Tel (01525) 403445 E-mail maggie.rich@phonecoop.coop

RICH, Paul Michael. b 36. OBE87. Sarum Th Coll 62. d 65 p 66. C Woodbridge St Mary *St E* 65-68; C W Wycombe *Ox* 68-70; CF 70-88; Lic to Offic *S & B* 88-90; V Crondall and Ewshot *Guildf* 91-05; rtd 05. *The Firs, The Street, Binsted, Alton GU34 4PF* Tel (01420) 525302

RICH, Peter Geoffrey. b 45. Oak Hill Th Coll 74. d 77 p 78. C Blackheath St Jo *S'wark* 77-80; C Surbiton St Matt 80-87; V St Alb St Luke *St Alb* 87-98; V Gravesend St Aid *Roch* from 98. *The Vicarage, St Gregory's Crescent, Gravesend DA12 4JL* Tel (01474) 352500 E-mail peter.rich@diocese-rochester.org

RICH, Thomas. b 52. St Jo Coll Nottm 86. d 88 p 89. C Netherton *Liv* 88-91; P-in-c Bootle Ch Ch 91-93; V from 93. *Christ Church Vicarage, 1 Breeze Hill, Bootle L20 9EY* Tel 0151-525 2565 Mobile 07958-784313 E-mail tom@richchurch.freeserve.co.uk

RICHARDS, Alan Grenville. b 41. Kelham Th Coll 64. d 69 p 70. C Northolt St Mary *Lon* 69-75; V Fatfield *Dur* 75-84; V Beighton *Sheff* 84-91; V Endcliffe 91-94; Deputation Appeals Org Children's Soc 94-98; V Cheriton All So w Newington *Cant* 98-06; rtd 06; Hon C Cheriton All So w Newington *Cant* 06-07; Hon C Cheriton St Martin 06-07; Perm to Offic from 07. *82 Capel Street, Capel-le-ferne, Folkestone CT18 7HF* Tel (01303) 243999

RICHARDS, Andrew David Thomas. b 55. St Jo Coll Dur BA76 Roehampton Inst PGCE84 FRSA96. St Steph Ho Ox 76. d 78 p 79. C Shirley *Birm* 78-80; C Cowley St Jo *Ox* 80-82; Perm to Offic *Win* 84-88 and *Sarum* 88-92; NSM Hazelbury Bryan and the Hillside Par *Sarum* 92-94; Chapl Rossall Sch Fleetwood 94-99; Hon Can Ely Cathl and Chapl K Sch Ely 99-03; Sen Chapl and Hd RS Wellington Coll Berks 03-08; Chapl Duke of York's R Mil Sch Dover from 08. *Duke of York's Royal Military School, Dover CT15 5EQ* Tel (01304) 245023 Mobile 07757-601244 E-mail andrew.richards@doyrms.com

RICHARDS, Anthony Francis. b 26. Edin Univ 45 Wadh Coll Ox BA51 MA54. Ridley Hall Cam 50. d 52 p 53. C Finchley Ch Ch *Lon* 52-55; C Maidenhead St Andr and St Mary *Ox* 55-59; Lect All Nations Chr Coll Ware 58-59; V High Wycombe Ch Ch *Ox* 59-63; P-in-c 63-66; V Terriers 63-73; USA 70-71; V Cinderford St Steph w Littledean *Glouc* 73-80; V Clacton St Paul *Chelmsf* 80-93; New Zealand 88 89; rtd 93. *Mont, Ouroux-en-Morvan, 58230 Montsauche-les-Settons, France* Tel (0033) (3) 86 78 24 44 E-mail anthony.richards@libertysurf.fr

RICHARDS, Mrs April Deborah. b 42. Man Univ BSc63. S Dios Minl Tr Scheme 82. dss 85 d 87 p 94. Catherington and Clanfield *Portsm* 85-89; C 87-89; C E Meon and Langrish 89-95; Chapl Portsm Hosps NHS Trust 92-95; P-in-c Blackmoor and Whitehill *Portsm* 95-98; V 98-05; RD Petersfield 99-04; rtd 05; Perm to Offic *Pet* 06-08; Hon C Brington w Whilton and Norton etc from 08. *6 Burrows Vale, Brixworth, Northampton NN6 9US* Tel (01604) 882230

RICHARDS, Brian. b 39. Open Univ BA78 BSc05. St Deiniol's Hawarden 94. d 94 p 94. C St Mellons and Michaelston-y-Fedw *Mon* 94-96; P-in-c Michaelston-y-Fedw 96-02; P-in-c Haarlem *Eur* 02-06; rtd 06; P-in-c Llangwm Uchaf and Llangwm Isaf w Gwernesney etc *Mon* 06-07. *32 Monnow Keep, Monmouth NP25 3EX* Tel (01600) 772824

RICHARDS, Brian William. b 45. Spurgeon's Coll Lon BA88 MTh99. Guildf Dioc Min Course 01. d 03 p 04. NSM Howell Hill w Burgh Heath *Guildf* from 03. *2 Canford Court, 88A Epsom Road, Sutton SM3 9ES* Tel (020) 8330 1196 E-mail brianr@saintpauls.co.uk

RICHARDS, Christopher Mordaunt. b 40. New Coll Ox BA63 MA72 Bris Univ MB, ChB72. Cuddesdon Coll 63. d 65 p 81. C Bris St Mary Redcliffe w Temple etc 65-66; Perm to Offic 66-72; Hon C Keynsham *B & W* 81-90; Perm to Offic 90 93. *4 St Ronans Avenue, Bristol BS6 6EP* Tel 0117-974 4062

RICHARDS, Daniel James. b 40. St D Coll Lamp. d 66 p 67. C Kingswinford H Trin *Lich* 66-69; C Banbury *Ox* 69-71; C Aylesbury 71-73; C-in-c Stoke Poges St Jo Manor Park CD

73-78; R W Slough 78-80; R Ilchester w Northover, Limington, Yeovilton etc *B & W* 80-90; RD Ilchester 81-91; RD Martock 89-91; TR Bruton and Distr 90-97; R Axbridge w Shipham and Rowberrow 97-04; rtd 04; Perm to Offic *B & W* from 05; Co-ord Clergy Retirement and Widows' Officer from 06. *1 Quaperlake Street, Bruton BA10 0HA* Tel (01749) 812386
E-mail revdanrich@mbzonline.net

RICHARDS, Daniel Michael Hamilton. b 79. Man Univ BA02. Cranmer Hall Dur 05. **d** 07 **p** 08. C Bury St Jo w St Mark *Man* 07-08; C Tonge w Alkrington from 08. *21 Pebworth Close, Middleton, Manchester M24 1QH* Tel 0161-643 5757
E-mail dogcollar@tiscali.co.uk

RICHARDS, Canon David. b 30. Bris Univ BA52. St Mich Coll Llan 52. **d** 54 **p** 55. C Llangynwyd w Maesteg 54-56; Iran 57-61 and 62-66; C Skewen *Llan* 61-62; V Cwmbach 66-76; Warden of Ords 71-77; R Coity w Nolton 76-96; Can Llan Cathl 88-96; rtd 96; Perm to Offic *Llan* and *Mon* from 96. *Inglewood, 5 Hopewell Close, Bulwark, Chepstow NP16 5ST* Tel (01291) 628912

RICHARDS, David Arnold. b 56. Wycliffe Hall Ox 76. **d** 81 **p** 82. C Skewen *Llan* 81-84; C Barking St Marg w St Patr *Chelmsf* 84-85; TV 85-90; Chapl Barking Hosp 87-88; P-in-c Stratford St Jo and Ch Ch w Forest Gate St Jas *Chelmsf* 90-97; V Stratford St Jo w Ch Ch and St Jas from 97. *Stratford Vicarage, 20 Deanery Road, London E15 4LP* Tel (020) 8534 8388 *or* 8503 1913
E-mail office@stjohnse15.freeserve.co.uk

RICHARDS, David Gareth. b 60. Hull Univ BA83. Qu Coll Birm 89. **d** 92 **p** 93. C Knowle *Birm* 92-96; Assoc R Edin St Paul and St Geo 96-00; R from 00. *11 East Fettes Avenue, Edinburgh EH4 1DN* Tel 0131-332 3904 *or* 556 1355 Fax 556 0492
E-mail dave@pandgchurch.org.uk

RICHARDS, Dennis. b 48. St Mich Coll Llan 95. **d** 97 **p** 98. C Cwmbran *Mon* 97-00; TV 00-06; TV Caldicot from 06. *The Rectory, 19 Main Road, Portskewett, Caldicot NP26 5SG* Tel (01291) 420313 E-mail den.richards@btinternet.com

RICHARDS, Mrs Glenys Heather. b 51. SEN73. **d** 06 **p** 07. OLM Heatons *Man* from 06. *61 All Saints Road, Heaton Norris, Stockport SK4 1QA* Tel 0161-477 2157 E-mail ghr@f25.com

RICHARDS, Gwilym David Marshall. b 56. SEITE. **d** 09. NSM Southgate *Chich* from 09. *11 Duncton Close, Crawley RH11 0AX* Tel (01293) 547809

RICHARDS, James Johnston. b 59. Solicitor 84 Lon Bible Coll BA90 Dur Univ MA97. Cranmer Hall Dur 90. **d** 92 **p** 93. C Harrow Trin St Mich *Lon* 92-95; C Kendal H Trin *Carl* 95-99; R Windermere from 99. *The Rectory, Longlands Road, Bowness-on-Windermere, Windermere LA23 3AS* Tel (01539) 443063
E-mail rector@stmartin.org.uk

RICHARDS, Mrs Jane Valerie. b 43. Westf Coll Lon BA64 Birm Univ CertEd65. S Dios Minl Tr Scheme 84. **d** 87 **p** 94. NSM Locks Heath *Portsm* 87-90; Asst Chapl Qu Alexandra Hosp Portsm 90-92; Chapl Portsm Hosps NHS Trust 92-95; Asst to RD Fareham *Portsm* 95-96; C Locks Heath 95-96; Chapl Southn Univ Hosps NHS Trust 96-03; rtd 03; Perm to Offic *Portsm* from 97 and *Win* 03-06. *16 Lodge Road, Locks Heath, Southampton SO31 6QY* Tel (01489) 573891
E-mail revjane.richards@btinternet.com

RICHARDS, Preb John Francis. b 37. Dur Univ BA61. Wells Th Coll 61. **d** 63 **p** 64. C Sherwood *S'well* 63-67; C Bishopwearmouth St Mich *Dur* 67-69; C Egg Buckland *Ex* 69-75; CF (ACF) 72-02; V Plymouth St Jas Ham *Ex* 75-83; V Plympton St Mary 83-02; RD Plymouth Moorside 88-93 and 96-01; Preb Ex Cathl 91-07; rtd 02; Clergy Widow(er)s Officer *Ex* from 02. *24 Trewithy Drive, Plymouth PL6 5TY* Tel (01752) 214442 E-mail jfr-sjr@blueyonder.co.uk

RICHARDS, John George. b 48. Qu Coll Birm 87. **d** 89 **p** 90. C Acocks Green *Birm* 89-92; TV Shirley 92-96; P-in-c Yardley Wood 96-00; V from 00. *Christ Church Vicarage, School Road, Yardley Wood, Birmingham B14 4EP* Tel 0121-436 7726
E-mail rev.johnrichards@btinternet.com

RICHARDS, John Henry. b 34. CCC Cam BA57 MA75. St Mich Coll Llan BD77. **d** 77 **p** 78. C Llangynwyd w Maesteg 77-79; C Cardiff St Jo 79-82; Asst Chapl Univ of Wales (Cardiff) 79-82; V Penmark w Porthkerry 82-83; R Stackpole Elidor w St Petrox *St D* 83-85; R St Petrox w Stackpole Elidor and Bosherston etc 85-99; rtd 99. *20 Williamson Street, Pembroke SA71 4ER* Tel (01646) 672472

RICHARDS, John Michael. b 53. Coll of Ripon & York St Jo TCert76 Open Univ BA81. Cranmer Hall Dur 93. **d** 93 **p** 94. C Wath-upon-Dearne *Sheff* 93-95; R Warmsworth 95-01; R Sprotbrough from 01. *The Rectory, 42A Spring Lane, Sprotborough, Doncaster DN5 7QG* Tel and fax (01302) 853203

RICHARDS, John Stanley. b 39. St Jo Coll Dur BA60. Ridley Hall Cam 61. **d** 64 **p** 65. C Fordingbridge w Ibsley *Win* 64-67; CF (TA) 64-68; C Bitterne Park *Win* 67-68; C Pokesdown All SS 68-70; Fell Qu Coll Birm 70-71; C Chesterton St Andr *Ely* 71-73; Asst Chapl Canford Sch Wimborne 73-77; Assoc Dir Fountain Trust 77-80; NSM New Haw *Guildf* 81-84; Dir Renewal Servicing from 81. *Crossover Cottage, Riverside, Staines TW18 8NH, or PO Box 463, Staines TW18 3WL*

RICHARDS, John William. b 29. Southn Univ BSc55. Sarum & Wells Th Coll 78. **d** 81 **p** 82. NSM Woking St Mary *Guildf* 81-85; C Addlestone 85-87; C S Gillingham *Roch* 87-89; Hon C W Byfleet *Guildf* 91-95; rtd 94; Perm to Offic *Sarum* from 95. *16 Normandy Way, Poundbury Whitfield, Dorchester DT1 2PP* Tel (01305) 251529

RICHARDS, Julian. b 25. Wycliffe Hall Ox 71. **d** 73 **p** 74. C Hessle *York* 73-76; P-in-c Rowley 76-82; Chapl HM Pris Hull 79-82; P-in-c Boldre *Win* 82-83; P-in-c Boldre w S Baddesley 83; V 83-93; rtd 93; RD Alton *Win* 93-98; Perm to Offic *Portsm* and *Win* from 98; Clergy Widows Officer (Win Adnry) 00-04. *Manor End, Worldham Hill, East Worldham, Alton GU34 3AX* Tel (01420) 86894 E-mail julian.richards@manorend.fsnet.co.uk

RICHARDS (née WOOLLEY), Mrs Justine Clare. b 73. Plymouth Univ BSc95 SS Mark & Jo Coll Chelsea PGCE98. Cranmer Hall Dur 03. **d** 05 **p** 06. C Dulverton and Brushford *B & W* from 05. *Yearnor Farm, Porlock, Minehead TA24 8JL* Tel (01643) 862678 Mobile 07891-807932
E-mail yarnergarner@hotmail.co.uk

RICHARDS, Keith David. b 50. Didsbury Coll of Educn CertEd72. S'wark Ord Course 79. **d** 82 **p** 83. NSM Walworth *S'wark* 82-85; Chapl Derbyshire Coll of HE 85-87; V Rottingdean *Chich* 87-93; TR Crawley 93-97; V Arundel w Tortington and S Stoke 97-07; RD Arundel and Bognor 04-07; Can and Preb Chich Cathl 07; V Selby Abbey *York* from 07. *The Abbey Vicarage, 32A Leeds Road, Selby YO8 4HX* Tel (01757) 709128

RICHARDS, Kelvin. b 58. Univ of Wales (Abth) BSc80 MA88. Ripon Coll Cuddesdon BA82. **d** 83 **p** 84. C Killay *S & B* 83-86; C Morriston 86-89; R Llangattock and Llangynidr from 89; AD Crickhowell from 02. *The Rectory, Llangattock, Crickhowell NP8 1PH* Tel (01873) 810270

RICHARDS, Llewelyn. b 15. St Deiniol's Hawarden 73. **d** 75 **p** 76. NSM Corwen and Llangar *St As* 75-85; Past Care Gwyddelwern 78-85; rtd 85. *120 Maesyfallen, Corwen LL21 9AD* Tel (01490) 412195

RICHARDS, Mrs Mary Edith. b 33. SW Minl Tr Course 85. **d** 87 **p** 94. NSM Kea *Truro* 87-88; Asst Chapl Bris Poly 88-91; C E Clevedon and Walton w Weston w Clapton *B & W* 91-96; rtd 96; Hon C Probus, Ladock and Grampound w Creed and St Erme *Truro* from 97; Mental Health Chapl Cornwall Healthcare NHS Trust 97-01. *62 Midway Drive, Uplands Park, Truro TR1 1NQ* Tel (01872) 277556

RICHARDS, Norman John. b 47. BSc. Ridley Hall Cam. **d** 83 **p** 84. C Luton St Fran *St Alb* 83-86; R Aspenden and Layston w Buntingford 86-95; P-in-c Westmill 94-95; R Aspenden, Buntingford and Westmill 95-08; rtd 09; Hon Chapl Stansted Airport *Chelmsf* from 09. *Gardners Cottage, Hare Street, Buntingford SG9 0DY* Tel (01763) 289720
E-mail nrichardsvic@aol.com

RICHARDS, Robert Graham. b 42. St Jo Coll Nottm 77. **d** 80 **p** 81. C Radipole and Melcombe Regis *Sarum* 80-83; TV Billericay and Lt Burstead *Chelmsf* 84-91; UK Dir CMJ 91-95; Chief Exec Nat Bibl Heritage Cen Ltd Trust 95-97; C Chorleywood St Andr *St Alb* 97-00; Chapl Lee Abbey 02-05; rtd 05; Perm to Offic *Sarum* from 05. *33 Stowell Crescent, Wareham BH20 4PT* Tel (01929) 552174
E-mail robandannar@tiscali.co.uk

RICHARDS, Shaun. b 62. St Steph Ho Ox 95. **d** 97 **p** 98. C Willesden Green St Andr and St Fran *Lon* 97-01; P-in-c Pentonville St Silas w All SS and St Jas 01; V from 02. *St Silas House, 45 Cloudesley Road, London N1 0EL* Tel (020) 7278 1101 E-mail father.sr@talktalk.net

RICHARDS, Simon Granston. b 47. St Jo Coll Nottm BTh72 ALCD72. **d** 72 **p** 73. C Waltham Abbey *Chelmsf* 72-77; TV Basildon St Martin w H Cross and Laindon etc 77-80; V Grayshott *Guildf* 80-88; V Eccleston Ch Ch *Liv* 88-92; V Berkeley w Wick, Breadstone and Newport *Glouc* 92-02; P-in-c Stone w Woodford and Hill 99-02; V Berkeley w Wick, Breadstone, Newport, Stone etc 02-05; RD Dursley 96-02; Chapl Severn NHS Trust 94-05; V Bisley, Chalford, France Lynch, and Oakridge *Glouc* from 05; AD Bisley 06-08. *The Vicarage, Cheltenham Road, Bisley, Stroud GL6 7BJ* Tel (01452) 770056
E-mail simongr@tiscali.co.uk

RICHARDS, Stuart Anthony. b 70. K Coll Lon BA92 AKC92 Keble Coll Ox BA97 MA02. St Steph Ho Ox MTh02. **d** 99 **p** 00. C Reading All SS *Ox* 99-02; C Solihull *Birm* 02-06; Deanery P Handsworth 06-07; CF from 07. *c/o MOD Chaplains (Army)* Tel (01980) 615804 Fax 615800

RICHARDS, Terence David. b 43. Trin Coll Carmarthen DipEd64 Open Univ BA73 Magd Coll Ox MSc83. Ox Min Course 04. **d** 07 **p** 08. NSM Chenderit *Pet* from 07. *11 Portway Drive, Croughton, Brackley NN13 5NA* Tel (01869) 811251
E-mail tasker1@btinternet.com

RICHARDS, Canon Thomas John Wynzie. b 25. St D Coll Lamp BA49. **d** 51 **p** 52. C Llandybie *St D* 51-53; V 71-87; C Llandegai *Ban* 53-56; R Llanymawddwy 56-57; Chapl Nat Nautical Sch Portishead 57-71; RD Dyffryn Aman *St D* 78-85; Can St D Cathl 83-92; Treas St D Cathl 89-92; V Pencarreg and

Llanycrwys 87-92; rtd 92. *Maes Teifi, Cwmann, Lampeter SA48 8DT* Tel (01570) 423354

RICHARDS, Tony Benjamin. b 48. STETS. d 09. NSM Sandown Ch Ch *Portsm* from 09; NSM Lower Sandown St Jo from 09. *Abbotsford Lodge, Cliff Bridge, Shanklin PO37 6QJ* Tel (01983) 863607

RICHARDS, Canon William Hughes. b 37. St D Coll Lamp BA58. d 60 p 61. C Llandysul *St D* 60-63; C Llanelli 63-65; V Llanddewi Brefi w Llanbadarn Odwyn 65-73; V Pen-bre 73-83; V Llangunnor w Cwmffrwd 83-88; V Cardigan w Mwnt and Y Ferwig 88-99; V Cardigan w Mwnt and Y Ferwig w Llangoedmor 99-01; Can St D Cathl 89-01; Treas 01; rtd 01. *Hafan Gobaith, 6 Cwrt y Gloch, Peniel, Carmarthen SA32 7HW* Tel (01267) 235995

RICHARDS, Canon William Neal. b 38. ALCD63. d 63 p 64. C Otley *Bradf* 63-65; C Leamington Priors St Mary *Cov* 65-67; CMS 67-69; Kenya 69-74; Asst Provost and Can Res Nairobi 70-74; V Gt Malvern St Mary *Worc* 74-86; Chapl Kidderminster Health Distr 86-91; RD Kidderminster 89-91; R Martley and Wichenford, Knightwick etc 91-01; rtd 01; Perm to Offic *Worc* from 01. *Bay Tree Cottage, 32 Pump Street, Malvern WR14 4LU* Tel (01684) 569658

RICHARDSON, Aidan. *See* RICHARDSON, James Aidan

RICHARDSON, Ms Alison Mary. b 63. Leic Univ BSc84 St Jo Coll Dur BA09. Cranmer Hall Dur 07. d 09. C Spennymoor and Whitworth *Dur* from 09. *34 Bluebell Drive, Spennymoor DL16 7YF* Tel (01388) 814277 Mobile 07873-596164 E-mail arichardson2@btinternet.com

RICHARDSON, Andrew Edward John. b 75. St Andr Univ BD97. TISEC 04. d 06 p 07. C Dundee St Mary Magd *Bre* 06-09; Hon Chapl Dundee Univ 07-09; P-in-c Glas S End from 09. *Flat 1/1, 25 Queensborough Gardens, Glasgow G12 9QP* E-mail aejrichardson@hotmail.com

RICHARDSON, Andrew John. b 44. Ex Univ CertEd69. Trin Coll Bris 83. d 82 p 83. Kenya 82-87; Dioc Educn Sec *Maseno N* 83-87; Chapl Brentwood Sch Essex 88; Chapl Scarborough Coll 88-01; TV Parkham, Alwington, Buckland Brewer etc *Ex* 01-09; RD Hartland 03-09; rtd 09. *La Retraite, 3 Park Avenue, Bideford EX39 2QH* Tel (01237) 478324 E-mail rev.andy-ros@care4free.net

RICHARDSON, Aubrey. *See* RICHARDSON, John Aubrey

RICHARDSON, Charles Leslie Joseph. b 54. St Jo Coll Dur BA76. Coll of Resurr Mirfield 76. d 79 p 80. C Folkestone St Mary and St Eanswythe *Cant* 79-83; C Maidstone St Martin 83-86; Selection Sec and Voc Adv ACCM 86-91; PV Westmr Abbey 87-91; R Hastings St Clem and All SS *Chich* 91-98; RD Hastings 92-97; V E Dulwich St Jo *S'wark* from 98; Dioc Voc Adv from 99. *St John's Vicarage, 62 East Dulwich Road, London SE22 9AU* Tel (020) 7639 3807 *or* 8693 3897 E-mail stjohnsse22@hotmail.com

RICHARDSON, Clive John. b 57. Oak Hill Th Coll BA83 Bris Univ MA00. d 83 p 84. C Woking St Pet *Guildf* 83-86; C Worplesdon 86-90; V Rowledge 90-03; V Rowledge and Frensham from 03. *The Vicarage, Church Lane, Rowledge, Farnham GU10 4EN* Tel (01252) 792402 E-mail rowvicar@aol.com

RICHARDSON, David. b 71. Edin Univ MA93 Stranmillis Coll PGCE94 QUB PhD98. CITC BTh02. d 02 p 03. C Coleraine *Conn* 02-06; Chapl RAF from 06. *Chaplaincy Services, Valiant Block, HQ Air Command, RAF High Wycombe HP14 4UE* Tel (01494) 496800 Fax 496343 E-mail richardsons05@hotmail.co.uk

RICHARDSON, David Anthony. b 41. Kelham Th Coll 57. d 66 p 67. C Tong *Bradf* 66-68; C Richmond St Mary *S'wark* 68-71; C Sanderstead All SS 71-74; TV 74-78; R Beddington 78-92; V Dormansland 92-98; RD Godstone 95-98; Assoc R Tucson St Phil in the Hills USA 98-03; R Lake Havasu City from 04. *3111 Silver Saddle Drive, Lake Havasu City AZ 86406-6284, USA* Tel (001) (928) 855 5397 Fax 855 2508 E-mail medart1@frontiernet.net

RICHARDSON, Canon David Gwynne. b 39. AMIMinE. K Coll Lon 60. d 64 p 65. C Battersea St Mary *S'wark* 64-67; Bp's Soc and Ind Adv 67-77; TV Brayton *York* 78-92; Ind Chapl 78-92; Chapl IMinE from 85; R Monk Fryston and S Milford 92-04; RD Selby 93-04; Can and Preb York Minster 03-04; rtd 04; Perm to Offic *York* from 04. *14 Beechcroft, Brayton, Selby YO8 9EP* Tel (01757) 704121 E-mail d.grich@freeuk.com

RICHARDSON, David John. b 50. MA LLB FCIArb. S'wark Ord Course. d 85 p 86. NSM S Croydon Em *S'wark* 85-06; Perm to Offic 06-07. *20 Hurst View Road, South Croydon CR2 7AG* Tel (020) 8688 4947 *or* 8688 6676 E-mail richardsonhome@blueyonder.co.uk

RICHARDSON, The Very Revd David John Leyburn. b 46. Univ of Qld BA69. St Barn Coll Adelaide ACT ThL70 Melbourne Coll of Div BD75. d 70 p 71. C Maryborough Australia 71-73; C Ipswich and C-in-c E Heights 74-75; Perm to Offic *Birm* 75-76; C Cambridge Gt St Mary w St Mich *Ely* 76-79; Tutor St Barn Th Coll Adelaide 79-80; Sub-Warden 80-82; R St Lucia 82-88; R Adelaide Cathl 88-89; Dean Adelaide 89-99; Dean Melbourne

99-08; Dir Angl Cen Rome from 08. *Palazzo Doria Pamphilj, Piazza del Collegio Romano 2, 00186 Rome, Italy* Tel (0039) 066 780 302 Fax 066 780 674 E-mail director@anglicancentre.it

RICHARDSON, Preb Douglas Stanley. b 23. Bps' Coll Cheshunt 55. d 57 p 58. C Hampton St Mary *Lon* 57-61; V W Twyford 61-69; V Notting Hill St Pet 69-78; V Staines St Pet 78-83; P-in-c Staines St Mary 81-83; V Staines St Mary and St Pet 83-92; AD Spelthorne 83-92; Preb St Paul's Cathl 92; rtd 92; Perm to Offic *Win* from 92. *22 Rooks Down Road, Badgers Farm, Winchester SO22 4LT* Tel (01962) 863687

RICHARDSON, Edward John. b 39. Westmr Coll Ox MTh98. Lich Th Coll 62. d 65 p 66. C Chessington *Guildf* 65-70; TV Trunch *Nor* 70-75; V Stoneleigh *Guildf* 75-79; Perm to Offic *S'wark* 92-94; Hon C Kingston All SS w St Jo 94-99; C 99-04; rtd 04; Perm to Offic *S'wark* 04-05; P-in-c Burpham *Chich* 05-09. *3 Westways, Epsom KT19 0PH* Tel (0208) 393 3648 E-mail rev.johnrichardson@tiscali.co.uk

RICHARDSON *(née* WOOD*)*, **Elaine Mary.** b 51. SRN74. SEITE 00. d 03 p 04. C Hythe *Cant* 03-06; C Folkestone Trin 06-07; V Herne from 07. *The New Vicarage, Herne Street, Herne Bay CT6 7HE* Tel (01227) 374328 E-mail elaine.longview@virgin.net

RICHARDSON, Mrs Elizabeth Rosalind. b 54. STETS 05. d 08 p 09. NSM Ewell St Fran *Guildf* from 08. *1 Stewart, Tadworth KT20 5TU* Tel (01737) 379859 E-mail liz@servercity.co.uk

RICHARDSON, Canon Eric Hatherley Humphrey. b 12. Qu Coll Ox BA35 MA46. Westcott Ho Cam 35. d 36 p 37. C Stoke Newington St Mary *Lon* 36-39; S Africa from 39. *PO Box 2289, Cramerview, 2060 South Africa* Tel (0027) (11) 787 7813 E-mail ceric@kon.co.za

RICHARDSON, Geoffrey Stewart. b 47. St Jo Coll Ox BA69 MA73. St Steph Ho Ox 70. d 72 p 73. C Roxbourne St Andr *Lon* 72-75; C Woodford St Barn *Chelmsf* 75-80; V Goodmayes St Paul 80-87; R Stow in Lindsey *Linc* 87-92; P-in-c Coates 87-92; P-in-c Willingham 87-92; R Stow Gp 92-01; RD Corringham 93-00; R Shaldon, Stokeinteignhead, Combeinteignhead etc *Ex* from 01. *The Rectory, Torquay Road, Shaldon, Teignmouth TQ14 0AX* Tel (01626) 872396

RICHARDSON, Graeme James. b 75. Oriel Coll Ox BA97. Ripon Coll Cuddesdon MPhil02. d 03 p 04. C Hatfield Hyde *St Alb* 03-06; Chapl BNC Ox from 06. *Brasenose College, Oxford OX1 4AJ* Tel (01865) 277833 Fax 277822 E-mail graeme.richardson@theology.ox.ac.uk

RICHARDSON, Gwynne. *See* RICHARDSON, Canon David Gwynne

RICHARDSON, James Aidan. b 28. St Chad's Coll Dur BA51. d 54 p 55. C Ferryhill *Dur* 54-56; C Stirling *Edin* 56-58; P-in-c Bo'ness 58-64; P-in-c Linlithgow 58-64; V Linthwaite *Wakef* 64-79; RD Blackmoorfoot 77-79; V Clifton 79-92; P-in-c Hartshead 83-88; rtd 92; Perm to Offic *Wakef* 92-04. *10B Brooke Street, Cleckheaton BD19 3RY* Tel (01274) 874587

RICHARDSON, James Horner. b 19. De Coll Cam BA42 MA45. Ridley Hall Cam 41. d 43 p 44. C Normanton *Derby* 43-47; C Far Headingley St Chad *Ripon* 47-48; C High Harrogate St Pet 48-50; CF 50-53; Hon CF from 53; V Chadderton Em *Man* 53-59; V Huyton St Mich *Liv* 59-70; V Ormskirk 70-80; Hon Chapl ATC 71-80; V Giggleswick *Bradf* 80-82; P-in-c Rathmell 80-82; V Giggleswick and Rathmell w Wigglesworth 82-84; rtd 84; Hon Chapl Spennithorne Hall *Ripon* 84-97; Hon C Aysgarth and Bolton cum Redmire 84-97; Perm to Offic *Bradf* 97-08. *27 Fosbrooke House, Clifton Drive, Lytham St Annes FY8 5RQ* Tel (01253) 667052

RICHARDSON, Canon James John. b 41. OBE07. Hull Univ BA63 Sheff Univ DipEd64 FRSA91. Cuddesdon Coll 66. d 69 p 70. C Wolverhampton St Pet *Lich* 69-72; P-in-c Hanley All SS 72-75; R Nantwich *Ches* 75-82; Hon Can Ripon Cathl 82-88; V Leeds St Pet 82-88; Exec Dir Coun of Chrs and Jews 88-92; P-in-c Brington w Whilton and Norton *Pet* 93-96; P-in-c Church Brampton, Chapel Brampton, Harlestone etc 94-96; TR Bournemouth St Pet w St Swithun, H Trin etc *Win* 96-08; P-in-c Bournemouth St Aug 01-08; rtd 09; Hon C Sherborne w Castleton, Lillington and Longburton *Sarum* from 09. *67 Acreman Street, Sherborne DT9 3PH* Tel (01935) 814984 E-mail canonrichardson@btinternet.com

RICHARDSON, John. *See* RICHARDSON, Edward John

RICHARDSON, John. b 41. Qu Coll Birm 69. d 72 p 73. C Ormskirk *Liv* 72-74; C Doncaster St Geo *Sheff* 74-77; R Hemsworth *Wakef* 77-79; V Penallt *Mon* 79-85; R Amotherby w Appleton and Barton-le-Street *York* 85-89; P-in-c Hovingham 86-89; P-in-c Slingsby 86-89; TR Street 89-90; R Skelton w Shipton and Newton on Ouse 90-93; V Alsager St Mary *Ches* 93-96; V Grangetown *York* 96-00; V E Coatham 00-02; V Coatham and Dormanstown 02-04; P-in-c York St Lawr w St Nic 04-06; rtd 06; Chapl Castle Howard from 06. *Beech House, Coneysthorpe, York YO60 7DD* Tel (01653) 648359 E-mail johnrichardson02@aol.com

RICHARDSON, John. b 47. Linc Th Coll 78. d 80 p 81. C Keighley St Andr *Bradf* 80-83; V Hugglescote w Donington *Leic* 83-84; V Hugglescote w Donington-le-Heath and Ellistown

84-86; TR Hugglescote w Donington, Ellistown and Snibston 86-97; RD Akeley S 87-96; Chapl ATC 84-97; R Hallaton w Horninghold, Allexton, Tugby etc *Leic* 97-00; Rural Officer (Leic Adnry) 97-00; rtd 00; Perm to Offic *Pet* 04-05; P-in-c Fylingdales and Hawsker cum Stainsacre *York* 05-09; C Alton w Bradley-le-Moors and Oakamoor w Cotton *Lich* from 09; C Denstone w Ellastone and Stanton from 09; C Mayfield from 09. *The Vicarage, Bennion Grove, Denstone, Uttoxeter ST14 5EZ* Tel (01889) 590266

RICHARDSON, John. b 55. Lon Univ BEd BD Kent Univ MA. St Steph Ho Ox. d 83 p 84. C Thornbury *Glouc* 83-86; C Sheff St Cecilia Parson Cross 86-87; C Clacton St Jas *Chelmsf* 87-90; R Gt and Lt Tey w Wakes Colne and Chappel from 90. *The Rectory, Brook Road, Great Tey, Colchester CO6 1JF* Tel (01206) 211481 E-mail revjohn.richardson@virgin.net

RICHARDSON, John Aubrey. b 33. NEOC 90. d 93 p 94. NSM Warkworth and Acklington *Newc* 93-03; Perm to Offic from 03. *Harvest Lodge, 27 Acklington Village, Morpeth NE65 9BL* Tel (01670) 760761

RICHARDSON, John Hedley. b 45. Leeds Univ BA72. Qu Coll Birm 72. d 74 p 75. C Chaddesden St Phil *Derby* 74-76; Perm to Offic 76-86; TV Old Brampton and Loundsley Green 86-91; R Caston w Griston, Merton, Thompson etc *Nor* 91-95; RD Breckland 94-99; P-in-c Hockham w Shropham Gp of Par 94-95; R Caston, Griston, Merton, Thompson etc 95-02; P-in-c Clifton St Jas *Sheff* 02-03; V 03-08; rtd 08. *2 Admirals Court, Swaffham PE37 7TE* E-mail hedleyrichardson@aol.com

✠**RICHARDSON, The Rt Revd John Henry.** b 37. Trin Hall Cam BA61 MA65. Cuddesdon Coll 61. d 63 p 64 c 94. C Stevenage *St Alb* 63-66; C Eastbourne St Mary *Chich* 66-68; V Chipperfield St Paul *St Alb* 68-75; V Rickmansworth 75-86; RD Rickmansworth 77-86; V Bishop's Stortford St Mich 86-94; Hon Can St Alb 87-94; Suff Bp Bedford 94-02; rtd 02; Hon Asst Bp Carl from 03; Hon Asst Bp Newc from 03. *The Old Rectory, Bewcastle, Carlisle CA6 6PS* Tel (01697) 748389

RICHARDSON, John Humphrey. b 33. Dur Univ BA57. Chich Th Coll 57. d 59 p 60. C Bexhill St Barn *Chich* 59-61; C Stanmer w Falmer and Moulsecoomb 61-64; C Ifield 64-70; R Earnley and E Wittering 70-79; V Stamford All SS w St Pet *Linc* 79-81; R Stamford St Jo w St Clem 79-81; V Stamford All SS w St Jo 81-92; RD Aveland and Ness w Stamford 80-87; P-in-c Metheringham w Blankney 92-94; V Metheringham w Blankney and Dunston 94-98; rtd 98; Perm to Offic *Chich* from 99. *68 Bishopsgate Walk, Chichester PO19 6FQ* Tel (01243) 536864

RICHARDSON, John Malcolm. b 39. Glas Univ MA60 BD63 Andover Newton Th Coll STM65. Edin Th Coll 84. d 84 p 85. C Edin Old St Paul 84-86; R Leven *St And* 86-90; R Newport-on-Tay 90-96; R Tayport 90-96; R Forfar 96-07; Can St Ninian's Cathl Perth 93-07; rtd 07; Lic to Offic *St And* from 07. *14 Chewton Road, Thornton, Kirkcaldy KY1 4AZ* Tel and fax (01592) 775133

RICHARDSON, John Peter. b 50. Keele Univ BA72. St Jo Coll Nottm 73. d 76 p 77. C Blackheath *Birm* 76-81; P-in-c Sparkbrook Ch Ch 81-83; Chapl NE Lon Poly *Chelmsf* 83-92; Chapl E Lon Univ 92-99; Hon C Stratford St Jo w Ch Ch and St Jas 83-99; C 99-00; C Henham and Elsenham w Ugley from 00. *39 Oziers, Elsenham, Bishop's Stortford CM22 6LS* Tel (01279) 813743 Mobile 07931-506913 E-mail john.richardson@heuchurch.f9.co.uk

RICHARDSON, John Stephen. b 50. Southn Univ BA71. St Jo Coll Nottm 72. d 74 p 75. C Bramcote *S'well* 74-77; C Radipole and Melcombe Regis *Sarum* 77-80; P-in-c Stinsford, Winterborne Came w Whitcombe etc 80-83; Asst Dioc Missr 80-83; V Nailsea Ch Ch *B & W* 83-90; Adv on Evang 86-90; Provost Bradf 90-00; Dean Bradf 00-01; V Wye w Brook and Hastingleigh etc *Cant* 01-09; P-in-c Eastwell w Boughton Aluph 04-09; C Mersham w Hinxhill and Sellindge 08-09; AD W Bridge 03-09; Chapl Wye Coll Kent *Lon* 01-09; P-in-c Margate H Trin *Cant* from 09. *The Vicarage, 5 Devonshire Gardens, Cliftonville, Margate CT9 3AF* Tel (01843) 294129 E-mail vicarjohnsrichardson@googlemail.com

RICHARDSON, Canon John Stuart. b 46. Trin Coll Ox BA68 MA71 DPhil73 FRSE96. d 79 p 80. NSM St Andrews St Andr *St And* 79-87; Chapl St Andr Univ 80-87; Prof Classics Edin Univ from 87; TV Edin St Columba from 87; Hon Can St Mary's Cathl from 00. *29 Merchiston Avenue, Edinburgh EH10 4PH* Tel 0131-228 3094 E-mail j.richardson@ed.ac.uk

RICHARDSON, John Thandule. b 49. Bradf and Ilkley Coll BSc80 Lanc Univ MA97. CBDTI 94. d 97 p 98. NSM Lea *Blackb* 97-02; NSM Broughton 02-04; NSM Lanercost, Walton, Gilsland and Nether Denton *Carl* 04-05; Perm to Offic *Blackb* 06-09; C Preston Risen Lord from 09; Chapl Preston Coll from 09. *65 Lower Bank Road, Fulwood, Preston PR2 8NU* Tel (01772) 787689 Mobile 07769-716861 E-mail johntr123@aol.com

RICHARDSON, John William. b 56. Bp Otter Coll BA85 Chich Th Coll 85. d 87 p 88. C E Preston w Kingston *Chich* 87-89; C Goring-by-Sea 89-90; TV Aldrington 91-92; V Sompting 92-02; P-in-c Margate All SS *Cant* 02-08; P-in-c Westgate St Sav 02-08;

P-in-c St Peter-in-Thanet from 08. *The Vicarage, 14 Vicarage Street, Broadstairs CT10 2SG* Tel (01843) 869169 E-mail jwrichardson@dsl.pipex.com

RICHARDSON, Mrs Kathleen Beatrice. b 50. CBDTI 02. d 04 p 05. NSM Kirkby Thore w Temple Sowerby and Newbiggin *Carl* 04-06; C Distington 06-08; P-in-c from 08. *The Rectory, Church Road, Distington, Workington CA14 5TE* Tel (01946) 833737 E-mail katmalric@aol.com

RICHARDSON, Laurence Leigh. b 71. Trin Coll Carmarthen BA92 PGCE93 Univ of Wales (Cardiff) BTh97 FGMS04. St Mich Coll Llan 94. d 97 p 98. C Carmarthen St Pet *St D* 97-01; Chapl Carmarthenshire Coll 99-01; P-in-c Abergwili w Llanfihangel-uwch-Gwili etc *St D* 01-03; V from 03; AD Carmarthen from 09; CF(V) from 01. *The Vicarage, Wellfield Road, Abergwili, Carmarthen SA31 2JQ* Tel (01267) 234189 E-mail landcat10a@aol.com

RICHARDSON, Mrs Linda Joan. b 58. Univ of Wales BSc80. SAOMC 01. d 04 p 05. NSM W Wycombe w Bledlow Ridge, Bradenham and Radnage *Ox* from 04. *Long Acre, Greenend Road, Radnage, High Wycombe HP14 4BY* Tel (01494) 484607 Fax 484608 E-mail linda.richardson@long-acre.co.uk

RICHARDSON, Malcolm. *See* RICHARDSON, John Malcolm

RICHARDSON, Preb Neil. b 46. Southn Univ BTh83. Sarum & Wells Th Coll 71. d 74 p 75. C Oldham St Mary w St Pet *Man* 74-77; C-in-c Holts CD 77-82; R Greenford H Cross *Lon* from 82; Preb St Paul's Cathl from 02. *The Rectory, Oldfield Lane South, Greenford UB6 9JS* Tel (020) 8578 1543 E-mail neil@holycross.ndo.co.uk

✠**RICHARDSON, The Rt Revd Paul.** b 47. Qu Coll Ox BA68 BA70 MA75. Harvard Div Sch 70 Cuddesdon Coll 71. d 72 p 73 c 87. C Earlsfield St Jo *S'wark* 72-75; Asst Chapl Oslo St Edm *Eur* 75-77; Miss P Nambaiyufu Papua New Guinea 77-79; Lect Newton Th Coll 79-81; Prin 81-85; Dean Port Moresby 85-86; Bp Aipo Rongo 87-95; Bp Wangaratta Australia 95-97; Asst Bp Newc from 98. *Close House, St George's Close, Jesmond, Newcastle upon Tyne NE2 2TF* Tel 0191-281 2556 *or* 285 2220 Fax 284 6933

RICHARDSON, Canon Paul. b 58. Univ of Wales (Cardiff) BSc80. Ridley Hall Cam 81. d 84 p 85. C Stanwix *Carl* 84-87; Ind Chapl 87-89; Staff P Dalton-in-Furness 87-89; V Marton Moss *Blackb* 89-95; P-in-c Prestwich St Gabr *Man* 95-00; Bp's Dom Chapl 95-00; V Westbury *Sarum* 00-02; TR White Horse 02-07; RD Heytesbury 04-07; R Devizes St Jo w St Mary from 07; Can and Preb Sarum Cathl from 07. *The Rectory, 39 Long Street, Devizes SN10 1NS* Tel (01380) 723705 E-mail paul.richardson8@btinternet.com

RICHARDSON, Pauline Kate. *See* JENKINS, Pauline Kate

RICHARDSON, Robin John. b 71. Bris Univ BA01 Loughb Univ BEng92 PGCE93. Trin Coll Bris 98. d 01 p 02. C Sidmouth, Woolbrook, Salcombe Regis, Sidbury etc *Ex* 01-04; CF from 04. *c/o MOD Chaplains (Army)* Tel (01980) 615804 Fax 615800 E-mail strangways@xalt.co.uk

RICHARDSON, Simon James. b 51. Loughb Univ BSc82 Nottm Univ MA99. EMMTC 96. d 99 p 00. C Market Harborough and The Transfiguration etc *Leic* 99-02; C Loughborough All SS w H Trin 02-04; Chapl Loughb Univ from 02. *13 Spinney Hill Drive, Loughborough LE11 3LB* Tel (01509) 237761 *or* 223741 Fax 223740 E-mail s.j.richardson@lboro.ac.uk

RICHARDSON, Simon John. b 56. Univ of Wales (Ban) BA77. Ridley Hall Cam 81. d 84 p 85. C Luton St Mary *St Alb* 84-88; C Middleton *Man* 88-91; Sweden from 91. *Enebacken, Racksätter, 732 97 Arboga, Sweden* Tel (0046) (589) 70103

RICHARDSON, Simon Kay Caoimhín. b 74. St Jo Coll Dur BA96. Wycliffe Hall Ox 01. d 03 p 04. C Folkestone Trin *Cant* 03-06; C Hillsborough *D & D* 06-08; I from 08. *The Rectory, 17 Dromore Road, Hillsborough BT26 6HS* Tel (028) 9268 8284 *or* 9268 8839 Mobile 07530-570299 E-mail simonkcr@aol.com *or* rector@hillsboroughparish.org.uk

RICHARDSON, Miss Susan. b 58. Cranmer Hall Dur. d 87 p 94. Par Dn Stokesley *York* 87-91; Par Dn Beverley St Nic 91-94; P-in-c Cloughton 94-97; Tr Officer E Riding Adnry from 94; V Cloughton and Burniston w Ravenscar etc 97-99; V Middlesbrough St Oswald from 99. *St Oswald's Vicarage, Lambton Road, Middlesbrough TS4 2RG* Tel (01642) 816156

RICHBOROUGH, Suffragan Bishop of (Provincial Episcopal Visitor). *See* NEWTON, The Rt Revd Keith

RICHENS, Canon Geoffrey Roger. b 23. ALCD52. d 52 p 53. C St Helens St Helen *Liv* 52-56; V Widnes St Mary 56-80; V Skelmersdale St Paul 80-93; Hon Can Liv Cathl 89-93; rtd 93; Perm to Offic *Liv* from 93 and *Blackb* from 98. *43 West View, Parbold, Wigan WN8 7NT* Tel (01257) 463143

RICHERBY, Canon Glynn. b 51. K Coll Lon BD73 AKC73. St Aug Coll Cant 73. d 74 p 75. C Weston Favell *Pet* 74-78; Prec Leic Cathl 78-81; V Glen Parva and S Wigston 81-93; V Leic St Jas from 93; Dir Post-Ord Tr 86-95; Dir CME from 95; Hon Can Leic Cathl from 98. *St James the Greater Vicarage, 216 London Road, Leicester LE2 1NE* Tel 0116-254 4113 E-mail vicar.stjames@ntlworld.com

RICHES, Canon John Kenneth. b 39. CCC Cam BA61 MA65. Kirchliche Hochschule Bethel 61 Westcott Ho Cam 62. **d** 65 **p** 66. C Costessey *Nor* 65-69; Chapl and Fell SS Coll Cam 68-72; Lect Glas Univ 72-86; Sen Lect 86-91; Prof Div and Bibl Criticism Glas Univ 91-02; Hon Research Prof from 03; Lic to Offic *Glas* from 85; Can St Mary's Cathl from 01. *Viewfield House, Balmore, Torrance, Glasgow G64 4AE* Tel (01360) 620254 E-mail randj.riches@virgin.net *or* j.riches@divinity.gla.ac.uk

RICHES, Malcolm Leslie. b 46. St Jo Coll Nottm 92. **d** 94 **p** 95. C Swaythling *Win* 94-97; P-in-c Boldre w S Baddesley 97-01; V 01-03; V Ellingham and Harbridge and Hyde w Ibsley from 03. *The Vicarage, Frogham Hill, Stuckton, Fordingbridge SP6 2HH* Tel (01425) 650853 E-mail malcolm.riches@tiscali.co.uk

RICHES, Nichola. b 72. Homerton Coll Cam BEd95 R Holloway & Bedf New Coll Lon MA96. SEITE 05. **d** 08. NSM Purley St Mark *S'wark* from 08; NSM Purley St Swithun from 08. *5 Hambledon Road, Caterham CR3 5EZ*

RICHEUX, Marc Stephen. b 66. Man Univ BA89. Trin Coll Bris BA00. **d** 00 **p** 01. C Plumstead St Jo w St Jas and St Paul *S'wark* 00-04; V Streatham Park St Alb from 04. *St Alban's Vicarage, 5 Fayland Avenue, London SW16 1SR* Tel (020) 8677 4521 *or* 8769 5415 E-mail mricheux@clara.co.uk

✠RICHMOND, The Rt Revd Francis Henry Arthur. b 36. TCD BA59 MA66 Strasbourg Univ BTh60 Lincoln Coll Ox MLitt64. Wycliffe Hall Ox 60. **d** 63 **p** 64 **c** 86. C Woodlands *Sheff* 63-66; Chapl Sheff Cathl 66-69; V Sheff St Geo 69-77; Chapl Sheff Univ 74-77; Warden Linc Th Coll 77-86; Can and Preb Linc Cathl 77-86; Suff Bp Repton *Derby* 86-98; Hon Can Derby Cathl 86-98; rtd 98; Hon Asst Bp Ox from 99. *39 Hodges Court, Oxford OX1 4NZ* Tel (01865) 790466

RICHMOND, Gordon Hazlewood. b 33. Launde Abbey 77. **d** 79 **p** 80. C Leic St Paul 79-81; C Shepshed 81-84; V Ryhall w Essendine *Pet* 84-91; RD Barnack 89-91; V Gretton w Rockingham 91-98; rtd 98; Perm to Offic *Pet* from 98 and *Leic* from 99. *Malvern, 2 Linwal Avenue, Houghton-on-the-Hill, Leicester LE7 9HD* Tel 0116-241 7638

RICHMOND, Patrick Henry. b 69. Ball Coll Ox BA90 Green Coll Ox MA94 DPhil94. Wycliffe Hall Ox BA96. **d** 97 **p** 98. C Leic Martyrs 97-01; Chapl and Fell St Cath Coll Cam 01-07; Dean of Chpl 06-07; V Eaton Ch Ch *Nor* from 07. *161 Newmarket Road, Norwich NR4 6SY* Tel (01603) 250844 E-mail phr@eatonparish.com

RICHMOND, Peter James. b 54. Ex Univ PGCE95 Cant Ch Ch Univ MSc07. St Jo Coll Nottm. **d** 80 **p** 81. C Ogley Hay *Lich* 80-83; C Trentham 83-85; P-in-c Wolverhampton St Jo 85-89; P-in-c Loppington w Newtown 89-93; P-in-c Edstaston 89-93; Perm to Offic *Ex* 94-95; P-in-c Weston Zoyland w Chedzoy *B & W* 95-03; Chapl Somerset Partnership NHS and Soc Care Trust 97-03; Lead Chapl E Kent NHS and Soc Care Partnership Trust 03-06; Lead Chapl Kent & Medway NHS and Soc Care Partnership Trust from 06; Hon C St Nicholas at Wade w Sarre and Chislet w Hoath *Cant* from 04. *St Martin's Hospital, Littlebourne Road, Canterbury CT1 1TD* Tel (01227) 812047 E-mail peter.richmond@ekentmht.nhs.uk

RICHMOND, Canon Yvonne Lorraine. b 63. Sheff Univ MA07. WEMTC 96. **d** 99 **p** 00. NSM Magor *Mon* 99-00; NSM Kenilworth St Jo *Cov* 00-05; Chapl for Evang Cov Cathl 05-06; Can Res for Miss 06-09; Can for Development Birm Cathl from 09. *Hope House, Sixpence Close, Coventry CV4 8HL* Tel 0121-262 1840 E-mail canonfordevelopment@birminghamcathedral.com

RICHMOND, Archdeacon of. *See* HENDERSON, The Ven Janet

RICKARDS, Bruce Walter. b 69. NTMTC 98. **d** 01 **p** 02. NSM St Marg Lothbury and St Steph Coleman Street etc *Lon* 01-06; NSM Wimbledon *S'wark* from 06. *85A Toland Square, London SW20 8SJ* Tel (020) 8540 4150 Mobile 07850-655102 E-mail byrickards@btinternet.com

RICKETTS, Allan Fenn. b 46. Open Univ BA76. Cranmer Hall Dur 68. **d** 71 **p** 72. C Rowley Regis *Birm* 71-72; C The Quinton 72-74; C Brierley Hill *Lich* 74-77; TV Chelmsley Wood *Birm* 77-82; TV Ross w Brampton Abbotts, Bridstow and Peterstow *Heref* 82-88; R Linton w Upton Bishop and Aston Ingham 88-96; rtd 06. *13 Falaise Close, Ross-on-Wye HR9 5UT* Tel (01989) 565077 E-mail allanricketts@fsmail.net

RICKETTS, Mrs Diane. b 54. NTMTC 98. **d** 01 **p** 02. NSM Nazeing and Roydon *Chelmsf* 01-06; R Laindon w Dunton from 06. *38 Claremont Road, Basildon SS15 5PZ* Tel (01268) 411190 E-mail revd_diane_ricketts@hotmail.com

RICKETTS, Canon Kathleen Mary. b 39. Southlands Coll Lon TCert59 Univ of W Aus BA79. Westcott Ho Cam 81. **dss** 83 **d** 87 **p** 94. All Hallows by the Tower etc *Lon* 83-88; C 87-88; C Hall Green Ascension *Birm* 88-91; Chapl Birm Children's Hosp 91-94; Chapl Birm Children's Hosp NHS Trust 94-99; Hon Can Birm Cathl 96-99; rtd 99; Perm to Offic *Birm* from 00. *22 Holly Drive, Birmingham B27 7NF* Tel 0121-706 1087

RICKETTS, Mrs Linda Elizabeth. b 52. RNMH85. EAMTC 98. **d** 01 **p** 02. C Loddon, Sisland, Chedgrave, Hardley and Langley *Nor* 01-05; V Gorleston St Mary from 05. *The Vicarage, 41*

Nuffield Crescent, Gorleston, Great Yarmouth NR31 7LL Tel (01493) 661741 E-mail l.ricketts787@btinternet.com

RICKMAN, Peter Alan. b 68. Ripon Coll Cuddesdon BTh97. **d** 97 **p** 98. C Bitterne Park *Win* 97-01; Chapl St Paul's Colleg Sch Hamilton NZ 01-04; Sub Chapl HM Pris Win 04-05; P-in-c Bransgore *Win* 05-09; P-in-c Bransgore and Hinton Admiral from 09. *St Mary's Vicarage, Ringwood Road, Bransgore, Christchurch BH23 8JH* Tel (01425) 672327 Mobile 07789-684481 E-mail pizzarev@aol.com

RIDDEL, Robert John. b 37. CITC 65. **d** 68 **p** 69. C Derryloran *Arm* 68-74; I Keady w Armaghbreague and Derrynoose 74-80; I Mullaghdun *Clogh* 80-84; I Cleenish 80-84; I Fivemiletown 84-05; Can Clogh Cathl 91-05; Preb Donaghmore St Patr Cathl Dublin 95-05; rtd 05. *9 Coolcrannel Square, Maguiresbridge, Enniskillen BT94 4RE* Tel (028) 6772 3199 E-mail riddel.r.j@btinternet.com

RIDDELL, Morris Stroyan. b 34. Lon Univ BD69. Tyndale Hall Bris 57. **d** 60 **p** 60. S Africa 60-63; C Mowbray 60-62; V Addington Ch Ch 62-63; V N Grimston w Wharram Percy and Wharram-le-Street *York* 63-67; V Kirby Grindalythe 63-67; P-in-c Weaverthorpe w Helperthorpe and Luttons 65-67; P-in-c Settrington 65-67; P-in-c Wintringham 65-67; P-in-c Thorpe Bassett 65-67; R Bris St Jo w St Mary-le-Port 67-70; Dir Bris Samaritans 67-70; Chapl HM Pris Long Lartin 71-74; Chapl HM Pris Brixton 74-78; Chapl Cane Hill Hosp Coulsdon 78-85; Chapl HM Rem Cen Latchmere Ho 85-89; rtd 95. *Flat 5, 30 Montpelier Crescent, Brighton BN1 3JJ* Tel (01273) 329229

RIDDELSDELL, Canon John Creffield. b 23. Selw Coll Cam BA47 MA52 Lon Univ BD70. Ridley Hall Cam 47. **d** 49 **p** 50. C Kilburn St Mary *Lon* 49-52; Kenya 52-77; V Gt Ilford St Andr *Chelmsf* 77-88; rtd 88; Perm to Offic *Chelmsf* from 88. *Waverley, Mill Lane, Walton on the Naze CO14 8PE* Tel (01255) 850213

RIDDING, George. b 24. Oriel Coll Ox BA50 MA57. Wells Th Coll 60. **d** 61 **p** 62. C Countess Wear *Ex* 61-62; Chapl Ex Sch 62-64; India 64-68; Hd Master W Buckland Sch Barnstaple 68-78; USPG 78-82; P-in-c Broadhembury w Payhembury *Ex* 82-83; P-in-c Plymtree 82-83; R Broadhembury, Payhembury and Plymtree 83-89; rtd 89; Perm to Offic *Sarum* 89-09. *The College of St Barnabas, Blackberry Lane, Lingfield RH7 6NJ* Tel (01342) 872821

RIDDING, William Thomas. b 54. Southn Univ BTh. Sarum & Wells Th Coll 80. **d** 83 **p** 84. C Verwood *Sarum* 83-86; TV Gillingham 86-01; RD Blackmore Vale 95-01; P-in-c Stalbridge 01-02; R Stalbridge and Stock 02-07; R Spire Hill from 07; C Hazelbury Bryan and the Hillside Par from 08; C Okeford from 08. *The Rectory, Church Hill, Stalbridge, Sturminster Newton DT10 2LR* Tel (01963) 362859

RIDDLE, Kenneth Wilkinson. b 20. St Cath Soc Ox BA42 MA46. Ripon Hall Ox 42. **d** 43 **p** 44. C Lowestoft St Marg *Nor* 43-47; C Luton St Mary *St Alb* 47-49; V Sundon w Streatley 49-52; R Pakefield *Nor* 52-59; V Nor St Pet Mancroft 59-60; R E w W Harling 60-65; P-in-c Bridgham and Roudham 60-61; R 61-65; R Lowestoft St Marg 65-68; rtd 85. *9 Clare Court, Clarence Road, Fleet GU51 3XX* Tel (01252) 617450

RIDEOUT, Canon Gordon Trevor. b 38. BA87 Westmr Coll Ox MTh96. Lon Coll of Div 58. **d** 62 **p** 63. C Southgate *Chich* 62-65; Chapl Dr Barnardo's Barkingside and Woodford Bridge 65-67; CF 67-73; V Nutley *Chich* 73-79; V Eastbourne All SS and Chapl Moira Ho Sch 79-03; Chapl Brighton Poly 80-92; Chapl Brighton Univ 92-03; rtd 03; Can and Preb Chich Cathl from 90; RD Eastbourne 97-06. *9 Filching Close, Polegate BN26 5NU* Tel (01323) 482660 Fax 640033

RIDER, Andrew. b 62. RMN85 Nottm Univ BTh90 K Coll Lon MA96. Aston Tr Scheme 85 St Jo Coll Nottm 87. **d** 90 **p** 91. C Luton Ch Ch *Roch* 90-93; C w resp for Clubhouse Langham Place All So *Lon* 93-03; P-in-c Spitalfields Ch Ch w All SS 03-04; R from 04. *The Rectory, 2 Fournier Street, London E1 6QE* Tel (020) 7247 0790 *or* 7247 7202 Fax 7247 5921 E-mail arider@clara.co.uk

RIDER, Canon Dennis William Austin. b 34. St Aid Birkenhead 58. **d** 61 **p** 62. C Derby St Aug 61-64; C Sutton *Liv* 64-67; R Stiffkey w Morston, Langham Episcopi etc *Nor* 67-71; V Buxton w Oxnead 71-79; R Lammas w Lt Hautbois 72-79; R Gaywood, Bawsey and Mintlyn 79-91; RD Lynn 89-91; Hon Can Nor Cathl 90-99; R E Dereham and Scarning 91-98; TR 98-99; RD Dereham in Mitford 95-98; rtd 99; Perm to Offic *Nor* 01-08; C Litcham w Kempston, E and W Lexham, Mileham etc from 08; C Gt and Lt Dunham w Gt and Lt Fransham and Sporle from 08. *37A Holt Road, Fakenham NR21 8BW* Tel (01328) 856018

RIDER, Geoffrey Malcolm. b 29. Selw Coll Cam BA53 MA56 Lon Inst of Educn PGCE68. Coll of Resurr Mirfield 53. **d** 55 **p** 56. C S Elmsall *Wakef* 55-60; C Barnsley St Mary 60-63; V Cleckheaton St Jo 63-67; Public Preacher *S'wark* 67-92; rtd 92; Succ Kimberley Cathl S Africa 92-95; Perm to Offic *S'wark* 95-03; Chapl and Hon Min Can Ripon Cathl from 04. *35 Kirkby Road, Ripon HG4 2EY* Tel (01765) 690517 E-mail geoffrey.rider@btinternet.com

RIDER, Neil Wilding. b 35. St Jo Coll Dur BA59 Univ of Wales (Lamp) MA00. Cranmer Hall Dur 59. **d** 62 **p** 63. C Blackb

St Barn 62-64; C Chadderton Em *Man* 64-69; C Deane 69-72; V Coldhurst 72-75; Perm to Offic *Ely* 76-78; C Didsbury Ch Ch *Man* 78-80; Perm to Offic *St D* from 80; rtd 00. *Caergrawnt, Llandovery Road, Cwmann, Lampeter SA48 8EL* Tel (01570) 422921

RIDGE, Aubrey. b 25. Oak Hill Th Coll 67. **d** 68 **p** 69. C Gorleston St Andr *Nor* 68-70; C Hamworthy *Sarum* 70-75; P-in-c Pitsea *Chelmsf* 75-78; R *78*-81; P-in-c Stoke Ash, Thwaite and Wetheringsett *St E* 81-85; P-in-c Bedingfield and Thorndon w Rishangles 81-85; P-in-c Thorndon w Rishangles, Stoke Ash, Thwaite etc 85-86; P-in-c Risby w Gt and Lt Saxham and Westley 86-90; rtd 90; Perm to Offic *Sarum* 90-93; Hon C Milford *Win* 93-96; Perm to Offic *Win* 96-99. *7 Cherry Tree Court, Station Road, New Milton BH25 6LP*

RIDGE, Haydn Stanley. b 24. Univ of Wales (Lamp) BA51 Bris Univ CertEd52. Qu Coll Birm 56. **d** 56 **p** 57. C Blackheath *Birm* 56-60; Div Master Guernsey Gr Sch 57-60; Perm to Offic *Win* 60-62; Hon C Guernsey St Steph 62-96; Dep Hd Master St Peter Port Sch 75-80; Hd Master St Sampson Sch 75-87; rtd 91; Perm to Offic *Win* 96-00. *St David, Les Cherfs, Castel, Guernsey GY5 7HG* Tel (01481) 56209

RIDGE, James Scott. b 77. Ex Univ BSc99 Selw Coll Cam BTh05. Westcott Ho Cam 02. **d** 05 **p** 06. C Halstead Area *Chelmsf* 05-09; C Bocking St Pet from 09. *The Manse, Chapel Lane, West Bergholt, Colchester CO6 3EF* Tel 07796-647343 (mobile) E-mail jamessridge@gmail.com

RIDGE, Michael Anthony. b 70. Collingwood Coll Dur BSc91 Dur Sch of Educn PGCE93. St Jo Coll Nottm 07. **d** 09. C Formby St Luke *Liv* from 09. *17 Moor Coppice, Liverpool L23 2XJ* Tel 07980-242401 (mobile) E-mail michaelridge@hotmail.co.uk

RIDGEWAY, David. b 59. St Chad's Coll Dur BSc80 Cam Univ CertEd81. Ripon Coll Cuddesdon 84. **d** 87 **p** 88. C Kempston Transfiguration *St Alb* 87-90; C Radlett 90-95; P-in-c Heath and Reach 95-98; V St Alb St Steph from 01; RD St Alb from 05. *St Stephen's Vicarage, 14 Watling Street, St Albans AL1 2PX* Tel (01727) 862598 Fax 07092-109111 E-mail davidridgeway@btinternet.com

RIDGEWELL, Miss Mary Jean. b 54. Dur Univ BA76 PGCE77. Ridley Hall Cam 89. **d** 91 **p** 94. Par Dn Trowbridge St Jas *Sarum* 91-94; C 94-95; Chapl Lee Abbey 95-96; NSM Bradford Peverell, Stratton, Frampton etc *Sarum* 96-97; Chapl HM Pris and YOI Guys Marsh from 97. *HM Prison and YOI, Guy's Marsh, Shaftesbury SP7 0AH* Tel (01747) 853344 ext 325 Fax 851584 E-mail mary@jridgewell.fsnet.co.uk

RIDGWAY, David. b 28. Trin Hall Cam BA54 MA58. Westcott Ho Cam 54. **d** 56 **p** 57. C Milton *Portsm* 56-59; CF 59-63; R Gosforth *Carl* 63-70; V Walney Is 70-76; P-in-c Irthington 76-78; P-in-c Crosby-on-Eden 77-78; V Irthington, Crosby-on-Eden and Scaleby 79-93; rtd 93. *11 Woodleigh, Walton, Brampton CA8 2DS* Tel (01697) 73252

RIDGWAY, Mrs Janet Elizabeth Knight. b 40. St Alb Minl Tr Scheme 83. **dss** 86 **d** 87 **p** 94. Tring *St Alb* 86-87; Hon Par Dn 87-94; Hon C 94-05; rtd 05. *Barlecombe, Trooper Road, Aldbury, Tring HP23 5RW* Tel and fax (01442) 851303 E-mail rev.j.ridgway@breathemail.net

RIDGWELL, Graham Edgar Charles. b 46. LGSM71 Open Univ BA82 Leeds Univ MA04. **d** 02 **p** 03. NSM Whitby w Aislaby and Ruswarp *York* 02-05; Hon TV Linton *Ely* from 05. *The Vicarage, Park Lane, Castle Camps, Cambridge CB21 4SR* Tel (01799) 584545 E-mail ridgwell@onetel.com

RIDING, Pauline Alison. *See* BICKNELL, Mrs Pauline Alison

RIDINGS, Neil Arthur. b 66. Man Poly BEd90. St Jo Coll Nottm 01. **d** 01 **p** 02. C Holyhead *Ban* 01-05; TV 05-07; R Valley w Llechylched and Caergeiliog from 07. *The Rectory, London Road, Valley, Holyhead LL65 3DP* Tel (01407) 741242

RIDLEY, Alfred Forbes. b 34. Bps' Coll Cheshunt 62. **d** 65 **p** 66. C Prittlewell St Mary *Chelmsf* 65-69; R Paulerspury *Pet* 69-73; P-in-c Wicken 71-73; V W Haddon w Winwick 73-83; RD Brixworth 80-83; R Guernsey St Philippe de Torteval *Win* 83-92; R Guernsey St Pierre du Bois 83-92; R Blakesley w Adstone and Maidford etc *Pet* 92-99; rtd 99; Perm to Offic *Pet* 99-07. *7 Alchester Court, Towcester NN12 6RL* Tel (01327) 358664

RIDLEY, Andrew Roy. b 55. St Pet Coll Ox BA77. Ripon Coll Cuddesdon 78. **d** 79 **p** 80. C Bollington St Jo *Ches* 79-83; V Runcorn St Mich 83-94; Dioc Chapl to MU 92-98; RD Frodsham 94-98; V Helsby and Dunham-on-the-Hill 94-98; P-in-c Alvanley 94-98; R Whitchurch *Lich* from 98; RD Wem and Whitchurch 01-06. *The Rectory, Church Street, Whitchurch SY13 1LB* Tel and fax (01948) 662342 E-mail arceridley@btinternet.com

RIDLEY, David Gerhard. b 60. Southn Univ BSc82 Bath Univ PGCE83. Qu Coll Birm 91. **d** 93 **p** 94. C Faversham *Cant* 93-97; Min Folkestone St Aug CD 97-01; V Dover St Mary from 01; P-in-c Guston from 02; AD Dover from 06. *The Vicarage, Taswell Street, Dover CT16 1SE* Tel and fax (01304) 206842 Mobile 07887-880272 E-mail davidridley@bigfoot.com

RIDLEY, Derek. b 40. Newc Univ BSc74. Cranmer Hall Dur 75. **d** 78 **p** 79. C Upperby St Jo *Carl* 78-81; C Penrith w Newton

Reigny 81; C Penrith w Newton Reigny and Plumpton Wall 81-82; TV 82-86; V Cadishead *Man* 86-99; R Asfordby and P-in-c Ab Kettleby Gp *Leic* 99-02; P-in-c Old Dalby and Nether Broughton 99-01; rtd 02. *32 Carleton Place, Penrith CA11 8LW* Tel (01768) 890676

RIDLEY, Jay. b 41. Birm Univ BA63. St Steph Ho Ox 63. **d** 65 **p** 66. C Woodford St Mary *Chelmsf* 65-67; C Prittlewell St Mary 67-70; C-in-c Dunscroft CD *Sheff* 70-74; Asst Chapl HM Pris Wormwood Scrubs 75-77; Chapl HM Rem Cen Ashford 77-84; Chapl HM YOI Feltham 84-91; Chapl HM Pris Ashwell 91-00; C Oakham, Hambleton, Egleton, Braunston and Brooke *Pet* from 00. *45 Trent Road, Oakham LE15 6HE* Tel (01572) 756086 E-mail j.ridley@zetnet.co.uk

RIDLEY, Mrs Lesley. b 46. Cranmer Hall Dur 75. **dss** 78 **d** 87 **p** 94. Upperby St Jo *Carl* 78-81; Penrith w Newton Reigny and Plumpton Wall 81-86; Cadishead *Man* 86-99; Par Dn 87-94; C 94-99; C Asfordby and Ab Kettleby Gp *Leic* 99-02; rtd 02. *32 Carleton Place, Penrith CA11 8LW* Tel (01768) 890676

RIDLEY, Louise. *See* COLLINS, Louise Ridley

RIDLEY, Canon Michael Edward. b 37. Ex Univ MA90. St Boniface Warminster AKC62. **d** 63 **p** 64. C Chapel Allerton *Ripon* 63-67; C Epsom St Martin *Guildf* 67-70; C Claxby w Normanby-le-Wold etc *Linc* 70-72; V Leake 72-75; R Harlaxton w Wyville and Hungerton 75-80; R Stroxton 76-80; Dioc Stewardship Adv *Portsm* 80-86; P-in-c Rowlands Castle 80-82; C Blendworth w Chalton w Idsworth etc 83-86; TV N Creedy *Ex* 86-90; R W Downland *Sarum* 90-02; RD Chalke 92-97 and 98-00; Can and Preb Sarum Cathl 00-02; rtd 02; Perm to Offic *Truro* from 03. *6 Cole Moore Meadow, Tavistock PL19 0ES* Tel (01822) 610799

RIDLEY, Michael Laurence. b 59. BA81. Ripon Coll Cuddesdon 81. **d** 83 **p** 84. C Bollington St Jo *Ches* 83-88; V Thelwall 88-95; V Weaverham 95-05; RD Middlewich 99-05; V Stockton Heath from 05. *The Vicarage, 91 Walton Road, Stockton Heath, Warrington WA4 6NR* Tel (01925) 261396

RIDLEY, Peter John. b 39. Keble Coll Ox BA61. Tyndale Hall Bris 61. **d** 63 **p** 64. C Clifton Ch Ch w Em *Bris* 63-67; C Lambeth St Andr w St Thos *S'wark* 67-69; V W Hampstead St Cuth *Lon* 69-77; V Eynsham *Ox* 77-85; RD Woodstock 82-84; V Nicholforest and Kirkandrews on Esk *Carl* 85-96; P-in-c E Knoyle, Semley and Sedgehill *Sarum* 96-04; rtd 04. *The Castle, Castle Street, Hilton, Appleby-in-Westmorland CA16 6LX* Tel (017683) 51682

RIDLEY, Simon. b 33. Magd Coll Ox BA54 MA58 BD66. Linc Th Coll 54. **d** 57 **p** 58. C St John's Wood *Lon* 57-60; Abp's Dom Chapl *Cant* 60-61; V N Wootton *B & W* 61-66; Lect Wells Th Coll 61-65; Hong Kong 66-70; TR Basingstoke *Win* 70-73; rtd 96; Perm to Offic *Cant* from 96. *Oxney House, The Street, Wittersham, Tenterden TN30 7ED* Tel (01797) 270215

RIDLEY, Stephen James. b 57. St Pet Coll Ox MA83. Ripon Coll Cuddesdon 80. **d** 82 **p** 83. C Heald Green St Cath *Ches* 82-85; Chapl Ches Coll 85-90; Dioc Press Officer 85-90; Chapl Birkenhead Sch Merseyside 90-96; Lic to Offic *Ches* 90-96; Chapl Barnard Castle Sch from 96. *3 Old Courts, Barnard Castle School, Newgate, Barnard Castle DL12 8UN* Tel (01833) 690222

RIDLEY, Stewart Gordon. b 47. K Coll Lon AKC72. St Aug Coll Cant 72. **d** 73 **p** 74. C Armley w New Wortley *Ripon* 73-77; C Hawksworth Wood 77-79; C Rothwell w Lofthouse 79-81; R Whitwood *Wakef* 81-87; R Ingoldmells w Addlethorpe *Linc* 87-92; RD Calcewaithe and Candleshoe 89-92; V Settle *Bradf* 92-05; C Bolton by Bowland w Grindleton 05-07; P-in-c Hurst Green and Mitton 05-07; P-in-c Waddington 05-07; rtd 07; Perm to Offic *York* from 09. *12 Bramblefields, Northallerton DL6 1ST* Tel (01609) 775857 E-mail stewartridley@uwclub.net

RIDLEY, Vic. *See* RIDLEY, David Gerhard

RIDOUT, Canon Christopher John. b 33. K Coll Lon BD57 AKC57 MA92. **d** 58 **p** 59. C Roxeth Ch Ch *Lon* 58-62; CMS 62-63; Kenya 63-75; C Gt Malvern St Mary *Worc* 75-79; R Bredon w Bredon's Norton 79-98; RD Pershore 91-97; Hon Can Worc Cathl 92-98; rtd 98; Perm to Offic *Glouc* from 98. *5 Belworth Drive, Hatherley, Cheltenham GL51 6EL* Tel (01242) 231765

RIDYARD, Preb John Gordon. b 33. St Aid Birkenhead 59. **d** 62 **p** 63. C Lancaster St Mary *Blackb* 62-65; C Bushbury *Lich* 65-68; V Darlaston All SS 68-76; TV Wolverhampton St Mark 76-78; TV Wolverhampton 78-82; V Bishopswood 82-89; V Brewood 82-89; RD Penkridge 83-89; R Newcastle w Butterton 89-98; Preb Lich Cathl 82-03; rtd 98; V in The Close and Perm to Offic *Lich* from 98. *Upper Flat, Vicars' Hall, Beacon Street, Lichfield WS13 7AD* Tel (01543) 306297

RIDYARD, Malcolm Charles. b 32. St D Coll Lamp BA54 Wycliffe Hall Ox 54. **d** 56 **p** 57. C Widnes St Paul *Liv* 56-59; C Ashton-in-Makerfield St Thos 59-61; India 62-71; Area Sec CMS *B & W*, Bris and *Sarum* 71-80; P-in-c Church Coniston *Carl* 80-87; P-in-c Torver 80-87; R Bootle, Corney, Whicham and Whitbeck 87-97; rtd 98; Perm to Offic *Birm* from 98. *140 Quinton Road West, Quinton, Birmingham B32 2RH* Tel 0121-422 3895

RIEM, Canon Roland Gerardus Anthony. b 60. St Chad's Coll Dur BSc82 Kent Univ PhD86 Heythrop Coll Lon MA99. St Jo

Coll Nottm 86. **d** 89 **p** 90. C Deal St Leon and St Rich and Sholden *Cant* 89-92; Sen Chapl Nottm Univ 92-98; Dir Min STETS 98-05; Can Res Win Cathl from 05. *5A The Close, Winchester SO23 9LS* Tel (01962) 857216 *or* 857239 Fax 857201 E-mail roland.riem@winchester-cathedral.org.uk

RIESS, Trevor William. b 54. Down Coll Cam MA76 CertEd77. St Jo Coll Nottm 84. **d** 86 **p** 87. C Stainforth *Sheff* 86-88; Chapl St Jas Choir Sch Grimsby 89; C Lowestoft and Kirkley *Nor* 89-90; TV 90-94; TV Lowestoft St Marg 94-95; Chapl Lothingland Hosp 90-95; V Gorleston St Mary *Nor* 95-05; P-in-c Scole, Brockdish, Billingford, Thorpe Abbots etc from 05. *The Rectory, Norwich Road, Scole, Diss IP21 4DB* Tel (01379) 742762

RIGBY, Francis Michael. b 29. Glouc Sch of Min. **d** 90 **p** 91. NSM Alvescot w Black Bourton, Shilton, Holwell etc *Ox* 90-92; P-in-c Gt w Lt Tew 92-95; P-in-c Bishop's Frome w Castle Frome and Fromes Hill *Heref* 96-99; Perm to Offic 00-07. *Address temp unknown*

RIGBY, Harold. b 34. Nottm Univ BA56 St Cath Soc Ox BA58 MA62 Man Poly PGCE77. Ripon Hall Ox 56. **d** 58 **p** 59. C Didsbury St Jas and Em *Man* 58-61; C Bury St Jo 61-64; P-in-c Lostock St Thos and St Jo 64-76; Hon C Davyhulme St Mary 76-79; Lic Preacher from 79; rtd 99. *17 Atwood Road, Didsbury, Manchester M20 0TA* Tel 0161-445 7454

RIGBY, Joseph. b 37. Open Univ BA72. Ox NSM Course. **d** 78 **p** 79. NSM Earley St Pet *Ox* 78-80; C Penzance St Mary w St Paul *Truro* 80-82; V Mevagissey 82-83; P-in-c St Ewe 83; R Mevagissey and St Ewe 83-90; rtd 90; Perm to Offic *Truro* from 90. *5 The Close, Truro TR1 1LY* Tel (01872) 240440

RIGBY, Michael. *See* RIGBY, Francis Michael

RIGBY, William. b 51. Leic Univ BSc(Econ)72 Newc Poly BSc82. Cranmer Hall Dur 86. **d** 88 **p** 89. C Morpeth *Newc* 88-92; R St John Lee 92-00; Chapl to the Deaf 92-08; P-in-c Chapel House 00-08; V Bywell and Mickley from 08. *Bywell Vicarage, Meadowfield Road, Stocksfield NE43 7PY* Tel (01661) 842272 E-mail bill.rigby1@btopenworld.com

RIGELSFORD, Mrs Anne Catharina (Ank). b 44. EAMTC 99. **d** 02 **p** 03. NSM Cambridge H Cross *Ely* 02-06; NSM Cambridge Ascension from 06. *19 Clare Street, Cambridge CB4 3BY* Tel (01223) 368150 Mobile 07932-846395 E-mail ank@rigelsford.freeserve.co.uk

RIGGS, Sidney James. b 39. Bps' Coll Cheshunt 62. **d** 63 **p** 64. C S'wark St Geo 63-66; C Plymouth Crownhill Ascension *Ex* 66-69; Asst Youth Chapl *Glouc* 69-71; Hon Min Can Glouc Cathl 71-74; Min Can Glouc Cathl 74-76; V Glouc St Mary de Lode and St Nic 76-92; R Rodborough 92-04; RD Stonehouse 94-96; rtd 04; Perm to Offic *Glouc* from 05. *6 Severn Road, Stonehouse GL10 2DL* Tel (01453) 824682

RIGLIN, Keith Graham. b 57. Lon Inst of Educn BEd80 Regent's Park Coll Ox BA83 MA86 Heythrop Coll Lon MTh85 Birm Univ ThD08 FRSA09. Westcott Ho Cam 06. **d** 08 **p** 08. In Bapt Union 83-96; in URC 97-08; C Notting Dale St Clem w St Mark and St Jas *Lon* from 08. *St Clement's Vicarage, 95 Sirdar Road, London W11 4EQ* Tel (020) 7313 4674 E-mail kgr23@cam.ac.uk

RIGNEY, Mrs Cindy Joanne. b 65. Coll of Ripon & York St Jo BA89. CBDTI 03. **d** 06 **p** 07. C Poulton Carleton and Singleton *Blackb* from 06. *24 Roylen Avenue, Poulton-le-Fylde FY6 7PH* Tel (01253) 884535 E-mail cinders@hibernian1973.fsnet.co.uk

RIGNEY, The Very Revd James Thomas. b 59. Sydney Univ BA82 MA88 Pemb Coll Ox DPhil95 CCC Cam BA00 MA04. Westcott Ho Cam 98. **d** 01 **p** 02. C Cambridge St Jas *Ely* 01-04; Chapl and Fell Magd Coll Cam 05-09; Dean Newcastle Australia from 09. *The Deanery, 46 Newcomer Street, Newcastle NSW 2300, Australia* E-mail jamesrigney@hotmail.com

RILEY, David Leo. b 51. S Bank Univ MSc95. Dioc OLM tr scheme 97. **d** 00 **p** 01. NSM Bellingham St Dunstan *S'wark* from 00. *117 Whitefoot Lane, Bromley BR1 5SB* Tel (020) 8516 4544 E-mail driley3020@aol.com

RILEY, John Graeme. b 55. St Jo Coll Dur BA78. Trin Coll Bris 79. **d** 81 **p** 82. C Hensingham *Carl* 81-84; C Preston St Cuth *Blackb* 84-87; V Blackb Ch Ch w St Matt 87-98; Chapl Qu Park Hosp Blackb 87-94; V Shevington *Blackb* 98-04; V Euxton from 04. *The Vicarage, Wigan Road, Euxton, Chorley PR7 6JH* Tel (01257) 262102

RILEY, Canon John Martin. b 37. St D Coll Lamp BA62. **d** 63 **p** 64. C Conwy w Gyffin *Ban* 63-68; P-in-c Llanfachraeth 68-70; TV Dolgellau, Llanfachreth, Brithdir etc 70-72; V Beddgelert and Dioc Youth Chapl 72-78; V Tywyn 78-82; V Tywyn w Aberdyfi 82-95; V Llanegryn w Aberdyfi w Tywyn 95-03; AD Ystumaner 87-03; Can Ban Cathl 90-97; Preb 97-03; rtd 03; Perm to Offic *Ban* from 03. *Llwyncelyn, Chapel Street, Corris, Machynlleth SY20 9SP* Tel (01654) 761769

RILEY, The Very Revd Kenneth Joseph. b 40. OBE03. Univ of Wales BA61 Linacre Ho Ox BA64 MA68. Wycliffe Hall Ox 61. **d** 64 **p** 65. C Fazakerley Em *Liv* 64-66; Chapl Brasted Place Coll Westerham 66-69; Chapl Oundle Sch 69-74; Chapl Liv Cathl 74-75; Chapl Liv Univ 74-93; V Mossley Hill St Matt and St Jas 75-83; RD Childwall 82-83; Can Res Liv Cathl 83-93; Treas

83-87; Prec 87-93; Dean Man 93-05; rtd 05. *145 Turning Lane, Southport PR8 5HZ*

RILEY, Mrs Lesley Anne. b 54. Totley Thornbridge Coll TCert75. Trin Coll Bris. **dss** 81 **d** 87 **p** 98. Hensingham *Carl* 81-84; Preston St Cuth *Blackb* 84-87; Hon Par Dn Blackb Ch Ch w St Matt 87-98; Asst Dir of Ords 96-00; Dir of Ords 00-05; Hon C Shevington 98-04; Hon C Whittle-le-Woods 06-07; Resources Co-ord Dioc Bd of Educn from 07. *The Vicarage, Wigan Road, Euxton, Chorley PR7 6JH* Tel (01257) 262102

RILEY, Linda. *See* RILEY-DAWKIN, Mrs Linda

RILEY, Martin. *See* RILEY, Canon John Martin

RILEY, Martin Shaw. b 47. Selw Coll Cam BA71 MA75 Cam Univ CertEd72. Sarum & Wells Th Coll 85. **d** 87 **p** 88. C Tuffley *Glouc* 87-91; Hon Min Can Glouc Cathl from 88; P-in-c Barnwood 91-94; V 94-99; P-in-c Highnam, Lassington, Rudford, Tibberton etc 99-04; R 04-06; Chapl Glos Hosps NHS Foundn Trust from 06. *61 Kingsholm Road, Gloucester GL1 3BA,* or *Gloucestershire Royal Hospital, Great Western Road, Gloucester GL1 3NN* Tel (01452) 417337 *or* 08454-222222

RILEY, Michael Charles. b 57. Ball Coll Ox BA79 MA83 Ex Univ CertEd80. Edin Th Coll 84. **d** 86 **p** 87. C Newc St Geo 86-89; C Chiswick St Nic w St Mary *Lon* 89-90; V Chiswick St Paul Grove Park from 90. *St Paul's Vicarage, 64 Grove Park Road, London W4 3SB* Tel (020) 8987 0312 E-mail michaelc.riley@virgin.net

RILEY, Preb Patrick John. b 39. Leeds Univ BA62. Coll of Resurr Mirfield 62. **d** 64 **p** 65. C Rowbarton *B & W* 64-72; P-in-c Farleigh Hungerford w Tellisford 72-73; P-in-c Rode, Rode Hill and Woolverton 72-73; R Rode Major 73-85; RD Frome 78-85; V Glastonbury w Meare and W Pennard 85-01; Preb Wells Cathl 90-01; rtd 01; Perm to Offic *Sarum* from 02. *24 Tanyard Lane, Shaftesbury SP7 8HW* Tel (01747) 850361

RILEY, Peter Arthur. b 23. Kelham Th Coll 40. **d** 51 **p** 52. C Aston cum Aughton *Sheff* 51-53; C Doncaster Ch Ch 53-55; Trinidad and Tobago 55-59; C-in-c Leic St Chad CD 59-62; Jamaica 62-77; V Abertillery *Mon* 77-83; R Panteg 83-88; rtd 88; Hon C Dartmouth *Ex* 88-99; Lic to Offic *Mon* from 99. *The Bungalow, Clewer Court, Newport NP20 4LQ* Tel (01633) 766870

RILEY, Sidney David. b 43. Birm Univ BA. Ridley Hall Cam 69. **d** 71 **p** 72. C Herne Bay Ch Ch *Cant* 71-74; C Croydon St Sav 74-77; C-in-c Aylesham CD 77; P-in-c Aylesham 77-78; V 78-82; V Tudeley w Capel *Roch* 82-97; Asst Chapl Pembury Hosp 83-86; P-in-c Morley St Paul *Wakef* 97-00; rtd 00; Perm to Offic *York* from 00. *18 Wheatlands Drive, Beverley HU17 7HR*

RILEY, Canon William. b 24. St Aid Birkenhead 48. **d** 51 **p** 52. C Edgehill St Dunstan *Liv* 51-53; C Halsall 53-57; V Prestolee *Man* 57-62; P-in-c Ringley 60-62; R Tarleton *Blackb* 62-92; RD Leyland 84-89; Hon Can Blackb Cathl 90-92; rtd 92; Perm to Offic *Blackb* from 92. *114 Liverpool Road, Hutton, Preston PR4 5SL* Tel (01772) 614267

RILEY-BRALEY, Robert James. b 57. Ch Ch Ox BA82 Ch Ch Ox MA82 Down Coll Cam BA83 MA87 K Coll Lon MA98 Surrey Univ PGCE92. Ridley Hall Cam 81. **d** 84 **p** 85. C Thames Ditton *Guildf* 84-87; C Gravesend St Geo *Roch* 87-91; Perm to Offic *Lon* 91-92; *Blackb* 92-95; *S'wark* 95-02; C Stevenage St Mary Shephall w Aston *St Alb* 02-08; P-in-c Croxley Green St Oswald from 08. *St Oswald's Vicarage, 159 Baldwins Lane, Croxley Green, Rickmansworth WD3 3LL* Tel (01923) 332244 E-mail ril.bral@virgin.net

RILEY-DAWKIN, Mrs Linda. b 67. St Jo Coll Nottm BA00. **d** 00 **p** 01. C Ince Ch Ch *Liv* 00-06; Chapl Knowsley Community Coll 06-08; V Ditton St Mich w St Thos *Liv* from 08. *339 Ditchfield Road, Widnes WA8 8XR* Tel 0151-420 4963 Mobile 07932-038443 E-mail revlin.riley@btinternet.com

RIMELL, Gilbert William. b 22. Llan Dioc Tr Scheme 76. **d** 81 **p** 82. NSM Laleston w Tythegston and Merthyr Mawr *Llan* 81-94; rtd 94; Perm to Offic *Llan* from 94. *75 Bryntirion Hill, Bridgend CF31 4BY* Tel (01656) 658002

RIMMER, Andrew Malcolm. b 62. Magd Coll Cam BA84 MA88. Wycliffe Hall Ox 86. **d** 88 **p** 89. C Romford Gd Shep *Chelmsf* 88-92; C Hazlemere *Ox* 92-97; V Crookhorn *Portsm* 97-05; TV Canford Magna *Sarum* from 05. *The Vicarage, 359 Sopwith Crescent, Wimborne BH21 1XQ* Tel (01202) 883630 E-mail a.rimmer@tesco.net

RIMMER, Clive. *See* RIMMER, John Clive

RIMMER, Canon David Henry. b 36. Ex Coll Ox BA60 MA65. Linc Th Coll 62. **d** 64 **p** 65. C Liv Our Lady and St Nic 64-66; C Daybrook *S'well* 66-69; Chapl St Mary's Cathl 69-71; R Kirkcaldy *St And* 71-78; R Haddington *Edin* 78-83; R Dunbar 79-83; R Edin Gd Shep 83-01; Hon Can St Mary's Cathl 98-01; rtd 01; Lic to Offic *Edin* from 01. *3 Southbank Court, Easter Park Drive, Edinburgh EH4 6SH* Tel 0131-539 0283 E-mail rimmerdh@blueyonder.co.uk

RIMMER, Janet. *See* SPICER, Dorothy Janet Rosalind

RIMMER, John Clive. b 25. Oak Hill Th Coll 63. **d** 65 **p** 66. C Earlestown *Liv* 65-69; C-in-c Dallam CD 69-74; V Southport SS Simon and Jude 74-83; V Westhead 83-90; Chapl Ormskirk

Hosp Liv 84-90; rtd 90; Perm to Offic *Liv* from 90. *14 Hurlston Drive, Ormskirk L39 1LD* Tel (01695) 570838

RIMMER, Mrs Margaret. b 55. St Jo Coll Dur BA05 SRN77 SCM78. Cranmer Hall Dur 00. **d** 02 **p** 03. C Aysgarth and Bolton cum Redmire *Ripon* 02-06; V Gt and Lt Ouseburn w Marton cum Grafton etc from 06. *The Vicarage, Main Street, Great Ouseburn, York YO26 9RQ* Tel (01423) 330928 E-mail margaret.rimmer1@tesco.net

RIMMER, Paul Nathanael. b 25. Jes Coll Ox BA48 MA50. Wycliffe Hall Ox 48. **d** 50 **p** 51. C Douglas St Thos *S & M* 50-52; C Windermere St Martin *Carl* 52-55; Ch of S India 55-59; V Marston *Ox* 59-90; RD Cowley 69-73; rtd 90. *32 Ulfgar Road, Wolvercote, Oxford OX2 8AZ* Tel (01865) 352567

RIMMER, Peter Anthony. b 39. St As Minl Tr Course 90. **d** 96 **p** 97. NSM Abergele *St As* 96-00; C Bodelywddan from 00. *St Mary's, 25 Lon Caradog, Abergele LL22 7DE* Tel (01745) 833222

RIMMINGTON, Gerald Thorneycroft. b 30. Lon Univ BSc56 PhD64 Leic Univ MA59 Nottm Univ MEd72 PhD75 FCP66. **d** 76 **p** 78. C Sackville and Dorchester Canada 76-79; Prof of Educn Mt Allison Univ 76-79; Lic to Offic *Leic* 79-80; R Paston *Pet* 81-86; V Cosby *Leic* 86-90; Dir CME 87-90; R Barwell w Potters Marston and Stapleton 90-95; rtd 95; Perm to Offic *Leic* from 95; RD Guthlaxton I 03-04. *7 Beechings Close, Countesthorpe, Leicester LE8 5PA* Tel 0116-277 7155

RINDL, Antony William. b 64. St Jo Coll Nottm 97. **d** 99 **p** 00. C Syston *Leic* 99-03; TV Colne and Villages *Blackb* 03-08; TR from 08; AD Pendle from 05. *The Vicarage, Skipton Road, Foulridge, Colne BB8 7NP* Tel (01282) 870959

RINGER, Philip James. b 47. Ox Min Course 88. **d** 91 **p** 92. NSM Chalfont St Peter *Ox* 91-95; TV Combe Martin, Berrynarbor, Lynton, Brendon etc *Ex* 96-03; R Wriggle Valley *Sarum* 03-08; rtd 08; Perm to Offic *Sarum* from 08. *7 Wanderwell Farm Lane, Bridport DT6 4JW* Tel (01308) 425774 E-mail philipringer@aol.com

RINGLAND, Tom Laurence. b 61. SS Hild & Bede Coll Dur BSc83. Trin Coll Bris BA89. **d** 89 **p** 90. C Southgate *Chich* 89-92; C Polegate 92-96; P-in-c Coalville and Bardon Hill *Leic* 96-98; V 98-06; TR Kirby Muxloe from 06. *The Rectory, 6 Station Road, Kirby Muxloe, Leicester LE9 2EJ* Tel 0116-238 6822 *or* 238 6811 E-mail tringland@aol.com

RINGROSE, Brian Sefton. b 31. Clare Coll Cam BA54 MA58 Lon Univ PGCE55. Tyndale Hall Bris 56. **d** 58 **p** 59. C Ox St Ebbe 58-60; C Erith St Paul *Roch* 60-61; India 61-75; P-in-c Ox St Matt 75-78; Interserve (Scotland) 78-96; Perm to Offic *Glas* 78-96; rtd 96; Lic to Offic *Edin* from 96. *1 Napier Road, Edinburgh EH10 5BE* Tel 0131-447 2012 E-mail brianringrose@aol.com

RINGROSE, The Ven Hedley Sidney. b 42. Open Univ BA79. Sarum Th Coll 65. **d** 68 **p** 69. C Bishopston *Bris* 68-71; C Easthampstead *Ox* 71-75; V Glouc St Geo w Whaddon 75-88; RD Glouc City 83-88; Hon Can Glouc Cathl from 86; V Cirencester 88-98; RD Cirencester 89-97; Adn Cheltenham from 98. *The Sanderlings, Thorncliffe Drive, Cheltenham GL51 6PY* Tel (01242) 522923 Fax 253259 E-mail archdchelt@star.co.uk

RINTAMÄKI, Juha Matti Sakari. b 69. **d** 02. Chapl Finnish Ch in Lon from 03; Lic to Offic *S'wark* from 04. *The Finnish Church in London, 33 Albion Street, London SE16 7HZ* Tel (020) 7237 1261 Fax 7237 1245 Mobile 07768-870614 E-mail juha.rintamaki@finnishchurch.org.uk

RIOCH, Mrs Wenda Jean. b 35. Sarum & Wells Th Coll 84. **d** 87 **p** 94. Par Dn Basingstoke *Win* 87-91; Par Dn Catshill and Dodford *Worc* 91-94; C 94-98; TV Ottery St Mary, Alfington, W Hill, Tipton etc *Ex* 98-05; rtd 05. *76 Gardeners Green, Shipton Bellinger, Tidworth SP9 7TA* Tel (01980) 842334 E-mail wrioch@aol.com

RIORDAN, Sean Charles. b 67. Loughb Univ BA89. St Jo Coll Nottm MA98 LTh99. **d** 99 **p** 00. C Ockbrook *Derby* 99-03; Asst Chapl Tervuren *Eur* 03-08; C Woodley *Ox* from 08. *171 Hurricane Way, Woodley, Reading RG5 4UH* Tel 0118-375 3718 E-mail sean.riordan907@gmail.com

RIPLEY, Preb Geoffrey Alan. b 39. Dur Univ BA62. St Aid Birkenhead. **d** 64 **p** 65. C E Herrington *Dur* 64-67; Hon C Hodge Hill CD *Birm* 68-70; Youth Chapl *Liv* 70-75; Chapl Liv Cathl 70-78; Bp's Dom Chapl 75-78; V Wavertree St Bridget 78-87; Lay Tr Adv *B & W* 87-95; Dioc Chapl MU 92-01; R S Petherton w the Seavingtons 95-01; Chapl E Somerset NHS Trust 95-01; Preb Wells Cathl 97-01; rtd 02; Perm to Offic *B & W* from 02. *20 Overleigh, Street BA16 0TL* Tel (01458) 446766

RIPLEY, Gordon. b 48. SWMTC 03. **d** 06 **p** 07. NSM Torquay St Matthias, St Mark and H Trin *Ex* from 06. *80 Exe Hill, Torquay TQ2 7RG* Tel (01803) 401608 E-mail gordonripley@blueyonder.co.uk

RIPON AND LEEDS, Bishop of. *See* PACKER, The Rt Revd John Richard

RIPON, Dean of. *See* JUKES, The Very Revd Keith Michael

RISBY, John. b 40. Lambeth STh82. Oak Hill Th Coll 64. **d** 67 **p** 68. C Fulham Ch Ch *Lon* 67-68; C Ealing St Mary 68-70; C Chitts Hill St Cuth 70-73; C Hove Bp Hannington Memorial Ch

---

Chich 73-76; V Islington St Jude Mildmay Park *Lon* 76-82; P-in-c Islington St Paul Ball's Pond 78-82; V Mildmay Grove St Jude and St Paul 82-84; R Hunsdon w Widford and Wareside *St Alb* 84-05; RD Hertford 91-96; rtd 05; Perm to Offic *Chelmsf* from 06. *1 Pilgrim Close, Great Chesterford, Saffron Walden CB10 1QG* Tel (01799) 530232 E-mail jjrisby@tiscali.co.uk

RISDON, John Alexander. b 42. Clifton Th Coll 66. **d** 68 **p** 69. C Ealing Dean St Jo *Lon* 68-72; C Heref St Pet w St Owen 72-74; Ord Cand Sec CPAS and Hon C Bromley Ch Ch *Roch* 74-77; TV Cheltenham St Mary, St Matt, St Paul and H Trin *Glouc* 77-86; R Stapleton *Bris* 86-00; R Bedhampton *Portsm* from 00; rtd 06. *10 St Margarets Road, Gloucester GL3 3PB* Tel 07719-430991 (mobile) E-mail sue.risdon@care4free.net

RISHTON, Mrs Tracy Jane. b 67. St Jo Coll Nottm 01. **d** 04 **p** 05. C Earby *Bradf* 04-07; C Kelbrook 04-07; C Cross Roads cum Lees 07-09; Area Missr S Craven Deanery 07-09. *Hovland, 4389 Vikesa, Norway* E-mail tracy@rishton.info

RITCHIE, Angus William Mark. b 74. Magd Coll Ox BA94 BPhil96 MA98. Westcott Ho Cam 96. **d** 98 **p** 99. C Plaistow and N Canning Town *Chelmsf* 98-02; TV 02-04; Dir Contextual Th Cen R Foundn of St Kath in Ratcliffe from 05; Hon C Gt Ilford St Luke from 05; Fells' Chapl Magd Coll Ox from 05; Chapl E Lon Univ from 08. *The Royal Foundation of St Katharine, 2 Butcher Row, London E14 8DS* Tel (020) 7790 3540 Fax 7702 7603 E-mail director@theology-centre.org

RITCHIE, Brian Albert. b 34. Open Univ BA80 Birm Univ MA84. Qu Coll Birm 60. **d** 63 **p** 64. C S Leamington St Jo *Cov* 63-67; C-in-c Canley CD 67-70; Perm to Offic 71-80; Hon C Cov H Trin 82-88; R Hatton w Haseley, Rowington w Lowsonford etc 88-97; rtd 97; Perm to Offic *Cov* from 98. *10 Margetts Close, Kenilworth CV8 1EN*

RITCHIE, David John Rose. b 48. St Jo Coll Dur BA72. Cranmer Hall Dur. **d** 74 **p** 75. C Harold Wood *Chelmsf* 74-79; TV Ipsley *Worc* 79-84; Chapl Vevey w Château d'Oex and Villars *Eur* 84-93; V Stoke Bishop *Bris* from 93. *The Vicarage, Mariner's Drive, Bristol BS9 1QJ* Tel 0117-968 1858 *or* 968 7449 E-mail churchmanager@stmarymagdalenestokebishop.org.uk

RITCHIE, Canon David Philip. b 60. Hatf Coll Dur BA85. Wycliffe Hall Ox 85. **d** 87 **p** 88. C Chadwell *Chelmsf* 87-90; C Waltham H Cross 90-94; TV Becontree W 94-98; TR 98-01; Lay Tr Officer from 01; C Lt Waltham 02-05; C Gt and Lt Leighs and Lt Waltham from 05; Hon Can Chelmsf Cathl from 09. *Glebelands, Boreham Road, Great Leighs, Chelmsford CM3 1PP* Tel (01245) 362644 *or* 294449 E-mail pritchie@chelmsf.anglican.org

RITCHIE, Miss Jean. b 30. Lon Univ CertEd51. Trin Coll Bris 77. **dss** 79 **d** 87 **p** 94. Ox St Ebbe w H Trin and St Pet 79-87; Par Dn 87-91; rtd 91; Perm to Offic *B & W* 91-94 and from 96; NSM Clevedon St Andr and Ch Ch 94-96. *63 Holland Road, Clevedon BS21 7YJ* Tel (01275) 871702

RITCHIE, Philip. *See* RITCHIE, Canon David Philip

RITCHIE, Philip Simon James. b 68. Man Univ BA90 Sussex Univ MA98 Leeds Univ MA01 Man Metrop Univ PGCE92. Coll of Resurr Mirfield 99. **d** 01 **p** 02. C Brighton St Nic *Chich* 01-04; P-in-c Chich St Wilfrid 04-08; P-in-c Hove from 08. *The Vicarage, Wilbury Road, Hove BN3 3PB* Tel (01273) 733331 E-mail allsaintshove@tiscali.co.uk

RITCHIE, Robert Peter. b 57. St Pet Coll Ox BA81 St Jo Coll Cam MPhil83. SEITE 97. **d** 00 **p** 01. NSM Kingston All SS w St Jo *S'wark* from 00. *7 Gibbon Road, Kingston upon Thames KT2 6AD* Tel (020) 8546 5964 E-mail robert@rsritchie.freeserve.co.uk

RITCHIE, Canon Samuel. b 31. Lon Coll of Div 65. **d** 67 **p** 68. C Westlands St Andr *Lich* 67-70; V Springfield H Trin *Chelmsf* 70-82; Chapl HM Pris Chelmsf 70-82; Brixton 82-84; Hull 84-86; Sen Chapl HM Prison Wymott 86-95; NW Area Chapl Co-ord 86-95; rtd 95; P-in-c Helmingham w Framsden and Pettaugh w Winston *St E* 96-97; Perm to Offic from 03. *Hillcrest, 3 Highfield Drive, Claydon, Ipswich IP6 0EY* Tel (01473) 833798

RITCHIE, William James. b 62. TCD MA84. CITC. **d** 86 **p** 87. C Enniscorthy *C & O* 86-89; Asst Chapl Alexandria Egypt 89-91; Bp's C Kells Gp *C & O* 91-92; I Kells Union *M & K* 92-99; Warden of Readers 93-97; Dioc Ecum Officer 97-99; Min Can St Patr Cathl Dublin 97-99; I Clondehorkey w Cashel *D & R* 99-00; I Dublin St Bart w Leeson Park *D & G* 00-04; I Tullow w Shillelagh, Aghold and Mullinacuff *C & O* 04-08; Warden of Readers 05-08; Perm to Offic *Lon* from 08. *St Alban's Clergy House, 18 Brooke Street, London EC1N 7RD* Tel (020) 7405 1831

RITSON, Canon Gerald Richard Stanley (Bill). b 35. CCC Cam BA59 MA63. Linc Th Coll 59. **d** 61 **p** 62. C Harpenden St Jo *St Alb* 61-65; C Goldington 65-69; R Clifton 69-76; Sec to Dioc Past Cttee and P-in-c Aldenham 76-87; Hon Can St Alb 80-87; Can Res St Alb 87-00; rtd 00; Perm to Offic *S'wark* from 00 and *Lon* from 04. *97 Mitre Road, London SE1 8PT* Tel (020) 7633 0012

RIVERS, Arthur. b 20. Oak Hill Th Coll 52. **d** 53 **p** 54. C Wigan St Cath *Liv* 53-56; V Parr Mt 56-60; V Burscough Bridge 60-79; V Holmesfield *Derby* 79-86; rtd 86; Hon C Warton St Oswald w

Yealand Conyers *Blackb* 86-88; Perm to Offic *Blackb* from 88 and *Carl* 88-04. *125A Thelwall New Road, Thelwall, Warrington WA4 2HR* Tel (01925) 600442

RIVERS, David John. b 51. St Jo Coll Nottm. **d** 84 **p** 85. C Woodthorpe *S'well* 84-88; C Hyson Green St Paul w St Steph 88; Asst Chapl Colchester Gen Hosp 89-91; Chapl Leeds Teaching Hosps NHS Trust 91-05; rtd 05; Perm to Offic *Ripon* from 05. *28 Palace Road, Ripon HG4 1ET* Tel (01765) 606227 Mobile 07810-430245 E-mail woollrivers@msn.com

RIVERS, John Arthur. b 21. EAMTC 79. **d** 81 **p** 82. NSM Blakeney w Cley, Wiveton, Glandford etc *Nor* 81-86; Hon C Cromer 86-87; Perm to Offic 87-06. *28 Compit Hills, Cromer NR27 9LJ* Tel (01263) 513051

RIVETT, Peter John. b 42. St Jo Coll Dur BA71. Cranmer Hall Dur 68. **d** 72 **p** 73. C Newland St Jo *York* 72-76; TV Marfleet 76-82; V Oxhey All SS *St Alb* 82-93; TR Swanborough *Sarum* 93-98; TV Pewsey and Swanborough 98-01; USPG Zambia from 01; rtd 07. *St Mark's Secondary School, Mapanza, Private Bag IXC Choma, Zambia* Tel (00260) (3) 250319 Mobile 977-604474 E-mail peterjrivett@hotmail.com

RIVIERE, Jonathan Byam Valentine. b 54. Cuddesdon Coll. **d** 83 **p** 84. C Wymondham *Nor* 83-88; TV Quidenham 88-94; P-in-c Somerleyton w Ashby, Fritton and Herringfleet 94; R Somerleyton, Ashby, Fritton, Herringfleet etc 95-03; R Sandringham w W Newton and Appleton etc from 03; P-in-c Castle Rising from 03; P-in-c Hillington from 03; Dom Chapl to The Queen from 03; Chapl to The Queen from 07. *The Rectory, Sandringham PE35 6EH* Tel (01485) 540587 E-mail jonathan@riviere.org.uk

RIVIERE, Mrs Tanagra June. b 41. S Dios Minl Tr Scheme 88. **d** 91. NSM Medstead w Wield *Win* 91-94; NSM Bishop's Sutton and Ropley and W Tisted 94-96. *The Drey, Paice Lane, Medstead, Alton GU34 5PT* Tel and fax (01420) 563330

RIX, Patrick George. b 30. Magd Coll Ox BA54 MA57 DipEd55. Ridley Hall Cam 58. **d** 60 **p** 61. C Dur St Nic 60-62; Asst Chapl Wrekin Coll Telford 62-70; Asst Chapl Gresham's Sch Holt 70-80; Chapl Bloxham Sch 80-86; rtd 86; P-in-c Swanton Abbott w Skeyton *Nor* 89; Perm to Offic 89-08. *c/o Miss C Rix, 195 Earlham Road, Norwich NR2 3RQ*

ROACH, Kenneth Thomas. b 43. St Andr Univ BD69 Fitzw Coll Cam BA71 MA76. Westcott Ho Cam 69. **d** 71 **p** 72. C Glas St Marg 71-73; CF 73-76; R Johnstone *Glas* 76-85; R Bearsden 85-96; TR Bearsden w Milngavie 96-08; CF (TA) 86-08; rtd 08. *34 Roman Road, Bearsden, Glasgow G61 2SQ* Tel 0141-942 0386 Fax 08701-336109 E-mail kenroach@freeuk.co.uk

ROACH, Lynne Elisabeth. *See* DAVIES, Mrs Lynne Elisabeth

ROACHE, Anthony. b 60. Nazarene Th Coll Man BA78. **d** 99 **p** 00. C Bury St Mary *Man* 99-02; P-in-c Ringley w Prestolee 02-06; Voc Adv 04-06; CF(V) 03-06; CF from 06. *c/o MOD Chaplains (Army)* Tel (01980) 615804 Fax 615800 E-mail roachefamily@ntlworld.com

ROAKE, Anthony Richard Garrard. b 52. Keble Coll Ox BA75 MA80. Wycliffe Hall Ox 75. **d** 77 **p** 78. C Clifton *S'well* 77-80; V Lapley w Wheaton Aston *Lich* 80-86; V Bournemouth St Andr *Win* 86-98; V Fernhurst *Chich* 98-07; Chapl The Hague *Eur* from 07. *Riouwstraat 2, 2585 HA Den Haag, The Netherlands* Tel (0031) (70) 355 5359 E-mail tonyrgr@gmail.com

ROAN, Canon William Forster. b 21. St Chad's Coll Dur BA47. **d** 49 **p** 50. C Barrow St Jas *Carl* 49-52; C-in-c Westf St Mary CD 52-58, V Westfield St Mary 58-61; R Greystoke 61-69; V Workington St Jo 70-86; Hon Can Carl Cathl 72-86; RD Solway 77-84; rtd 86; Perm to Offic *Carl* from 86. *41 Chiswick Street, Carlisle CA1 1HJ* Tel (01228) 521756

ROBARTS, Mrs Freda Margaret. b 43. Open Univ BA86. St As Minl Tr Course 98. **d** 04 **p** 06. NSM Berriew *St As* 04-06; P-in-c Llansilin w Llangadwaladr and Llangedwyn from 06. *The Vicarage, Llansilin, Oswestry SY10 7PX* Tel (01691) 791207

ROBB, Ian Archibald. b 48. K Coll Lon 68. **d** 72 **p** 73. C E Ham w Upton Park *Chelmsf* 72-74; C Leckhampton SS Phil and Jas w Cheltenham St Jas *Glouc* 74-79; P-in-c Cheltenham St Mich 79-90; V Lower Cam w Coaley from 90. *St Bartholomew's Vicarage, 99 Fairmead, Cam, Dursley GL11 5JR* Tel (01453) 542679 E-mail ia_jdr@lineone.net

ROBB, Robert Hammond Neill. b 46. Open Univ BA89 Man Univ 66. St Deiniol's Hawarden 87. **d** 87 **p** 88. C Lache cum Saltney *Ches* 87-89; V Norley and Crowton 89-97; P-in-c Kingsley 95-97; V Norley, Crowton and Kingsley 97-98; V Neston from 98. *The Vicarage, High Street, Neston CH64 9TZ* Tel 0151-353 1000 E-mail celtic.robb@btopenworld.com

ROBB, Timothy Simon. b 72. Cant Univ (NZ) BMus94 LTCL94 Lon Bible Coll BTh98. Trin Coll Bris MA03. **d** 03 **p** 04. C Bedford Ch Ch *St Alb* 03-07; Chapl De Montford Univ 05-07; V Eaton Socon from 07. *St Mary's Vicarage, 34 Drake Road, Eaton Socon, St Neots PE19 8IIS* Tel (01480) 212219 E-mail vicar@stmaryseatonsocon.org.uk

ROBBIE, James Neil. b 68. Strathclyde Univ BEng90. Oak Hill Th Coll BTh02. **d** 05 **p** 06. C Wolverhampton St Luke *Lich* 05-09; V Bromwich H Trin from 09. *Holy Trinity Vicarage, 1 Burlington Road, West Bromwich B70 6LF* Tel 0121-525 3595 E-mail rev.robbie@btinternet.com

ROBBINS, Angela Mary. *See* WEAVER, Canon Angela Mary

ROBBINS, David Leslie. b 43. Univ Coll Lon BSc65 Nottm Univ CertEd66. EMMTC 96. **d** 00 **p** 01. NSM Newark *S'well* 00-04; NSM S'well H Trin from 04. *21 Woodland View, Southwell NG25 0AG* Tel (01636) 812641 Mobile 07773-361042 E-mail dlrobbins1@hotmail.com

ROBBINS, David Ronald Walter. b 47. Sarum & Wells Th Coll 85. **d** 87 **p** 88. C Meir Heath *Lich* 87-89; C Collier Row St Jas and Havering-atte-Bower *Chelmsf* 89-93; C Tamworth *Lich* 93-97; P-in-c Hulland, Atlow, Bradley and Hognaston *Derby* 97-98; P-in-c Kniveton 97-98; R Hulland, Atlow, Kniveton, Bradley and Hognaston 98-02; R Widford *Chelmsf* from 02. *The Rectory, 3 Canuden Road, Widford, Chelmsford CM1 2SU* Tel (01245) 346329 Fax 346365 E-mail robbinsdrw@btinternet.com

ROBBINS, Mrs Janet Carey. b 41. Ox Univ BA63 MA95 PGCE81 Univ of Wales (Lamp) 92. St D Dioc Tr Course 96. **d** 98 **p** 99. NSM Llanfihangel Ystrad and Cilcennin w Trefilan etc *St D* 98-01; NSM Quantock Towers *B & W* 02-03; rtd 03; Hon C Bro Teifi Sarn Helen *St D* from 08. *Rhydyfran, Cribyn, Lampeter SA48 7NH* Tel (01570) 470349 E-mail revdjanet@tiscali.co.uk

ROBBINS, Martin Charles. b 68. Thames Valley Univ BA91. Ripon Coll Cuddesdon BTh00. **d** 00 **p** 01. C Thatcham *Ox* 00-03; CF 03-08; Chapl Heathfield St Mary's Sch Ascot from 08. *55 Arkley Court, Holyport, Maidenhead SL6 2HR* Tel (01628) 778136 *or* (01344) 898343

ROBBINS, Peter Tyndall. b 25. Magd Coll Ox BA46 MA51. Westcott Ho Cam 48. **d** 50 **p** 51. C Bury St Paul *Man* 50-53; C Swinton St Pet 53-55; V Prestwich St Hilda 55-59; V Lower Halstow *Cant* 59-63; V Charing w Lt Chart 63-73; V Basing *Win* 73-83; V Kingsclere 83-90; rtd 90; Perm to Offic *Birm* 91-00; Asst RD Tamworth *Lich* 91-95; Perm to Offic from 95. *St John's Hospital, St John Street, Lichfield WS13 6PB* Tel (01543) 415197 E-mail robbinspt@tiscali.co.uk

ROBBINS, The Ven Stephen. b 53. K Coll Lon BD74 AKC74. St Aug Coll Cant 75. **d** 76 **p** 77. C Tudhoe Grange *Dur* 76-80; C-in-c Harlow Green CD 80-84; V Gateshead Harlow Green 84-87; CF 87-97; Sen CF 97-01; Chapl R Memorial Chpl Sandhurst 01-02; Asst Chapl Gen 02-07; Dep Chapl Gen from 07; Adn for the Army from 04; QHC from 05; Can and Preb Sarum Cathl from 07. *c/o MOD Chaplains (Army)* Tel (01980) 615804 Fax 615800

ROBBINS, Walter. b 35. **d** 72 **p** 73. Argentina 73-82; Adn N Argentina 80-82; C Southborough St Pet w Ch Ch and St Matt *Roch* 82-86; V Sidcup St Andr 86-95; V Grain w Stoke 95-00; rtd 00; Perm to Offic *Roch* from 00 and *Cant* 01-09. *Mariners, Imperial Avenue, Minster on Sea, Sheerness ME12 2HG* Tel (01795) 876588

ROBBINS-COLE, Adrian Peter. b 62. LSE BSc(Econ)84 K Coll Lon MA96. Ch Div Sch of the Pacific (USA) 90 Ripon Coll Cuddesdon BA92. **d** 93 **p** 94. C S Dulwich St Steph *S'wark* 93-97; V Motspur Park 97-04; RD Merton 01-04; R Peterborough All SS USA from 04. *49 Concord Street, Peterborough NH 03458-1510, USA* Tel (001) (603) 924 3202 E-mail allsaintsnh@verizon.net

ROBBINS-COLE, Ms Sarah Jane. b 68. Vermont Univ BA90 K Coll Lon MA00. Ch Div Sch of the Pacific (USA) 92 Ripon Coll Cuddesdon BA95. **d** 95 **p** 96. C W Dulwich All SS *S'wark* 95-98; Chapl K Coll Sch Wimbledon 98-04; Hon C Motspur Park *S'wark* 98-04; Asst P Peterborough All SS USA from 04. *49 Concord Street, Peterborough NH 03458-1510, USA* Tel (001) (603) 924 3202 E-mail allsaintsnh@verizon.net

ROBERT, Brother. *See* ATWELL, The Rt Revd Robert Ronald

ROBERT HUGH, Brother. *See* KING-SMITH, Philip Hugh

ROBERTS, Aelwyn. *See* ROBERTS, Joseph Aelwyn

ROBERTS, Alan Moss. b 39. CEng68 MIMechE68 MIMarEST68. St Jo Coll Nottm 77. **d** 79 **p** 80. C Bromsgrove St Jo *Worc* 79-83; C Edgbaston St Germain *Birm* 83-89; R Broadhembury, Payhembury and Plymtree *Ex* 89-06; rtd 06. *8 Oakleigh, Sheldon, Honiton EX14 4QT* Tel (01404) 841358 E-mail alanmossroberts@lineone.net

ROBERTS, Allen. b 47. Trin Coll Ox MA72 Warwick Univ MA73 PhD79 Wolv Univ LLM99. Qu Coll Birm 06. **d** 07 **p** 09. NSM Tettenhall Regis *Lich* from 07. *11 Grosvenor Court, Lime Tree Avenue, Wolverhampton WV6 8HB* Tel (01902) 765741 Mobile 07885-341540 E-mail allen.roberts@btinternet.com

ROBERTS, Mrs Andrea Joan. b 46. Liv Poly ALA68 St Jo Coll Dur BA73 PGCE74. Cranmer Hall Dur 70 CBDTI 03. **d** 04 **p** 05. NSM Garstang St Thos *Blackb* from 04. *The Vicarage, 5 Lancaster Road, Cockerham, Lancaster LA2 0EB* Tel and fax (01524) 791390 E-mail michael.andrea.r@ukonline.co.uk

ROBERTS, Preb Andrew Alexander. b 49. Open Univ BA75. Bp Otter Coll CertEd70 Sarum & Wells Th Coll 76. **d** 80 **p** 81. NSM Dorchester *Sarum* 80-85; C Swanage and Studland 85-87; TV 87-94; TR Bridgnorth, Tasley, Astley Abbotts, etc *Heref* from 94; P-in-c Morville w Aston Eyre from 08; P-in-c Acton Round from 08; P-in-c Upton Cressett w Monk Hopton from 08; Preb Heref Cathl from 03; RD Bridgnorth 05-09. *The Rectory, 16 East*

Castle Street, Bridgnorth WV16 4AL Tel (01746) 763256 *or* 767174 E-mail andyaroberts@talk21.com

ROBERTS, Andrew John. b 55. Newc Univ BA77. EMMTC 00. d 03 p 04. NSM Church Langton cum Tur Langton etc *Leic* 03-07; Chapl HM Pris Linc from 07. *The Chaplains' Office, HM Prison, Greetwell Road, Lincoln LN2 4BD* Tel (01522) 663090 E-mail andrewroberts28@aol.com

ROBERTS, Anne Judith. b 44. CertEd65 DipEd78 Open Univ BA82. S Dios Minl Tr Scheme 86. d 89 p 94. Hon Par Dn S Kensington H Trin w All SS *Lon* 89-92; NSM Barnes *S'wark* from 92; S'wark OLM Scheme 98-04. *5 Avenue Gardens, London SW14 8BP* Tel (020) 8878 5642 E-mail revjr@blueyonder.co.uk

ROBERTS, Mrs Anne Marie. b 55. York Univ BA77. St Jo Coll Nottm 80 WMMTC 93. d 96 p 97. NSM Meole Brace *Lich* 96-08; Chapl Robert Jones/Agnes Hunt Orthopaedic NHS Trust 98-00; Chapl Prestfelde Sch Shrewsbury 99-08. *2 The Abbey, Carlisle CA3 8TZ*

ROBERTS, Anthony. *See* ROBERTS, John Anthony Duckworth

ROBERTS, Barrie Moelwyn Antony. b 43. RN Coll Dartmouth 63 Trin Coll Carmarthen CertEd70 Birm Poly BA83. Qu Coll Birm 00. d 04 p 05. NSM Bartley Green *Birm* from 04. *34 Wheats Avenue, Harborne, Birmingham B17 0RJ* Tel 0121-426 2501 E-mail b.roberts@lineone.net

ROBERTS, Barry. *See* ROBERTS, Ronald Barry

ROBERTS, Bernard John. b 21. Ox NSM Course 79. d 82 p 83. NSM Wendover *Ox* 82-01; NSM Wendover and Halton from 01. *19 The Paddocks, Wendover, Aylesbury HP22 6HE* Tel (01296) 623445

ROBERTS, Brian David. b 44. Ball Coll Ox BA66 Univ of Wales (Ban) BTh06 FRSA00. d 03 p 04. OLM Guildf H Trin w St Mary from 03. *Risby, Upper Guildown Road, Guildford GU2 4EZ* Tel (01483) 570556 Fax (020) 7631 6224 Mobile 07979-766471 E-mail b.roberts44@ntlworld.com

ROBERTS, Bryan Richard. b 55. Univ of Wales (Cardiff) BD80. St Mich Coll Llan 78. d 80 p 81. C Finham *Cov* 80-83; Asst Youth Officer *Nor* 83-86; R N and S Creake w Waterden 86-91; P-in-c E w N and W Barsham 86-91; Chapl Epsom Coll 91-01; Chapl Gresham's Sch Holt from 01. *10 Kelling Road, Holt NR25 6RT* Tel (01263) 713234

ROBERTS, Carol Susan Butler. b 63. Univ of Wales (Ban) BA84 MTh99 MPhil02 PhD05. Ban Ord Course 06. d 07 p 08. NSM Bangor from 07. *Tu Hwnt I'r Afon, 55 Braichmelyn, Bethesda, Bangor LL57 3RD* Tel (01248) 600420 E-mail davecas@tesco.net

ROBERTS, Charles Richard Meyrick. b 53. Huddersfield Poly BA75 ARCM75. St Paul's Coll Grahamstown 89. d 92 p 92. C Lansdowne St Aidan S Africa 92-93; C Claremont St Sav 93-94; C Bath Abbey w St Jas *B & W* 94-98; P-in-c Chew Magna w Dundry 98-00; R Chew Magna w Dundry and Norton Malreward from 00; P-in-c Chew Stoke w Nempnett Thrubwell from 03. *The Rectory, Tunbridge Close, Chew Magna, Bristol BS40 8SU* Tel (01275) 332199 E-mail chewrector@hotmail.com

ROBERTS, Christopher Michael. b 39. Man Univ DipAE79. Qu Coll Birm 62. d 64 p 65. C Milton next Gravesend Ch Ch *Roch* 64-68; C Thirsk w S Kilvington *York* 68-69; V Castleton *Derby* 69-75; TV Buxton w Burbage and King Sterndale 75-79; Perm to Offic 84-87; NSM Marple All SS *Ches* 87-90; Chapl Asst St Helens Hosp Liv 90-91; Chapl Asst Whiston Co Hosp Prescot 90-91; Chapl Asst Rainhill Hosp Liv 90-91; Chapl R United Hosp Bath 91-94; Chapl R United Hosp Bath NHS Trust 94-99; Sen Chapl Birm Children's Hosp NHS Trust 99-04; rtd 04; Perm to Offic *Birm* from 04. *6 Myring Drive, Sutton Coldfield B75 7RZ* Tel 0121-329 2547 E-mail chrismirob@aol.com

ROBERTS, Colin Edward. b 50. Sarum & Wells Th Coll. d 83 p 84. C Harton *Dur* 83; C S Shields All SS 83-85; C Thamesmead *S'wark* 85-87; TV 87-89; C Streatham St Pet 89-90 and 92; Zimbabwe 90-92; V Earlsfield St Jo *S'wark* from 92. *St John's Vicarage, 40 Atheldene Road, London SW18 3BW* Tel (020) 8874 2837 Fax 08088-742816 E-mail vicar@stjohnthedivine.freeserve.co.uk

ROBERTS, Canon Cyril. b 41. St Deiniol's Hawarden. d 84 p 85. C Maltby *Sheff* 84-86; TR Gt Snaith from 86; AD Snaith and Hatfield from 03; Hon Can Sheff Cathl from 05. *The Orchard, Pontefract Road, Snaith, Goole DN14 9JS* Tel (01405) 860866 Mobile 07702-004870 E-mail cyril@holyburrows.fsnet.co.uk

ROBERTS, David. b 44. Ex Univ BA65. St Steph Ho Ox 65. d 67 p 68. C Southwick St Columba *Dur* 67-72; C-in-c Southwick St Cuth CD 72-79; R Alyth *St And* 79-84; R Blairgowrie 79-84; R Coupar Angus 79-84; P-in-c Taunton St Jo *B & W* from 84; Chapl Somerset Coll of Arts and Tech from 84. *17 Henley Road, Taunton TA1 5BW* Tel (01823) 284176 E-mail scat.chap@virgin.net

ROBERTS, David Alan. b 38. Open Univ BA82. Ripon Hall Ox 71. d 73 p 74. C W Bridgford *S'well* 73-77; V Awsworth w Cossall 77-82; V Oxclose *Dur* 82-94; P-in-c New Seaham 94-04; rtd 04. *8 Hazel Road, Gateshead NE8 2EP* Tel 0191-460 9919

ROBERTS, David Charles. b 53. Poly of Wales CertEd76 Open Univ BA82 BA93 Univ of Wales MEd87. St Mich Coll Llan 96.

d 98 p 99. C Whitchurch *Llan* 98-00; Chapl Univ of Wales Inst Cardiff 00-05; Mental Health Chapl Gwent Healthcare NHS Trust from 05. *6 Gwaun Llwyfen, Nelson, Treharris CF46 6HY* Tel (01443) 450995

ROBERTS, Preb David Henry. b 38. St Chad's Coll Dur BA60. Qu Coll Birm. d 62 p 63. C Stonehouse *Glouc* 62-65; C Hemsworth *Wakef* 65-69; V Newsome 69-76; R Pontesbury I and II *Heref* 76-03; RD Pontesbury 83-93; Preb Heref Cathl from 85; rtd 03; Perm to Offic *Heref* from 03. *14 Beaconsfield Park, Ludlow SY8 4LY* Tel (01584) 878568 E-mail dhroberts@lineone.net

ROBERTS, Canon David John. b 36. Man Univ BSc58. St D Coll Lamp 65. d 67 p 68. C Rhosllannerchrugog *St As* 67-70; R Cerrigydrudion w Llanfihangel Glyn Myfyr etc 70-75; R Llanrwst and Llanddoget 75-77; R Llanrwst and Llanddoget and Capel Garmon 77-84; RD Llanrwst 77-84; V Abergele 84-01; RD Rhos 94-00; Hon Can St As Cathl 95-96; Can Cursal St As Cathl 96-01; rtd 01. *Brithdir, Abergele Road, Bodelwyddan, Rhyl LL18 5SR* Tel (01745) 585807

ROBERTS, Mrs Deryn Anne. b 49. Nottm Univ TCert70 BEd71. SWMTC 04. d 07 p 08. NSM Lanteglos by Camelford w Advent *Truro* from 07; NSM St Teath from 07. *11 Cambeak Close, Crackington Haven, Bude EX23 0PE* Tel (01840) 230493 Mobile 07977-318589

ROBERTS, Dewi. b 57. LWCMD77 Cyncoed Coll CertEd78. St Mich Coll Llan. d 84 p 85. C Clydach *S & B* 84-88; V Glantawe 88-94; V Loughor 94-06; V Gowerton from 06. *The Vicarage, 14 Church Street, Gowerton, Swansea SA4 3EA* Tel (01792) 872266

ROBERTS, Dewi James Llewelyn. b 63. United Th Coll Abth 83. d 96 p 97. C Llandudno *Ban* 96-02; C Bodedern w Llanfachraeth and Llechgynfarwy 99-02; C Llanfaethlu w Llanfwrog and Llanrhuddlad etc 99-02; V Newcastle Emlyn w Llandyfriog and Troedyraur etc *St D* from 02. *The Vicarage, Terra Cotta, Station Road, Newcastle Emlyn SA38 9BX* Tel (01239) 710154 E-mail d.roberts10@btinternet.com

ROBERTS, Diane. b 45. Bris Univ CertEd66 BEd82. STETS 02. d 05 p 06. NSM Kinson and W Howe *Sarum* from 05. *21 Highfield Road, Bournemouth BH9 2SE* E-mail robertsdiane1@aol.com

ROBERTS, Dilwyn Carey. b 38. St Deiniol's Hawarden 74. d 76 p 77. C Glanadda *Ban* 76-77; TV Amlwch, Rhosybol, Llandyfrydog etc 77-81; V Llanllechid 81-85; V Caerhun w Llangelynin 85-87; V Caerhun w Llangelynin w Llanbedr-y-Cennin 87-92; rtd 93. *67 St Georges Drive, Conwy LL31 9PR*

ROBERTS, Donald James. b 26. Sarum & Wells Th Coll 83. d 86 p 87. NSM Corfe Castle, Church Knowle, Kimmeridge etc *Sarum* 86-88 and 91-95; C Broadstone 88-91; rtd 91; Perm to Offic *Sarum* 95-98 and *St E* from 01. *42 Priory Court, Nacton, Ipswich IP10 0JU* Tel (01473) 711242

ROBERTS, Edward. *See* ROBERTS, Canon Henry Edward

ROBERTS, Edward John Walford. b 31. Trin Coll Carmarthen CertEd. St D Dioc Tr Course. d 79 p 80. NSM Burry Port and Pwll *St D* 79-98; NSM Swansea St Jas *S & B* 98-02; Lic to Offic from 02. *1A Woodlands Terrace, Uplands, Swansea SA1 6BR*

ROBERTS, Edward Mark. b 84. d 07 p 08. OLM Droylsden St Mary *Man* from 07. *20 Drayfields, Droylsden, Manchester M43 7ET*

ROBERTS, Canon Edward Owen. b 38. K Coll Lon BD63 AKC63. d 64 p 65. C Auckland St Andr and St Anne *Dur* 64-67; C Cheltenham St Paul *Glouc* 67-68; Asst Master Colne Valley High Sch Linthwaite 69-71; V Meltham Mills *Wakef* 71-75; R Emley 75-88; RD Kirkburton 80-88; V Huddersfield H Trin 88-04; RD Huddersfield 89-99; Hon Can Wakef Cathl 92-04; rtd 04; Perm to Offic *York* from 04. *2B Queen Street, Filey YO14 9HB* Tel (01723) 515535

ROBERTS, Eric. b 40. Ban Ord Course 90 St Mich Coll Llan 92. d 93 p 94. Min Can Ban Cathl 93-97; R Llanllyfni 97-02; V Llandysul w Bangor Teifi w Henllan etc *St D* from 02; AD Emlyn from 04. *The Vicarage, Tanyfron, Well Street, Llandysul SA44 4DR* Tel (01559) 362277

ROBERTS, Graham Miles. b 59. Open Univ BA95. Trin Coll Bris 90. d 92 p 93. C Charles w Plymouth St Matthias *Ex* 92-96; Chapl Plymouth Univ 92-94; TV Liskeard, St Keyne, St Pinnock, Morval etc *Truro* 96-99; P-in-c Bournemouth St Andr *Win* from 04. *St Andrew's Vicarage, 53 Bennett Road, Bournemouth BH8 8QQ* Tel (01202) 396022 E-mail graham_roberts@ntlworld.com

ROBERTS, Canon Henry Edward (Ted). b 28. Oak Hill Th Coll 53. d 56 p 57. C Edgware *Lon* 56-58; C Bedworth *Cov* 58-61; V Bethnal Green St Jas Less *Lon* 61-73; V Old Ford St Mark Victoria Park 61-73; V Bethnal Green St Jas Less w Victoria Park 73-78; RD Tower Hamlets 76-78; Can Res Bradf Cathl 78-82; Dioc Dir Soc Resp 78-82; V Bermondsey St Jas w Ch Ch *S'wark* 82-90; P-in-c Bermondsey St Anne 82-90; Hon Can S'wark Cathl 90-93; Gen Adv for Inner City Min 90-93; rtd 93. *12 Bromeswell Road, Ipswich IP4 3AS* Tel (01473) 288956

ROBERTS, James. *See* ROBERTS, William James

ROBERTS, Jane Elizabeth. b 53. SEITE 98. **d** 01 **p** 02. NSM Mitcham Ascension *S'wark* from 01. *39 Castleton Road, Mitcham CR4 1NZ* Tel (020) 8764 6423 Mobile 07790-703710 E-mail janeroberts@nasuwt.net

ROBERTS, Miss Janet Lynne. b 56. Trin Coll Bris 76. **dss** 82 **d** 87 **p** 94. Dagenham *Chelmsf* 82-86; Huyton St Mich *Liv* 86-91; Par Dn 87-91; C Aughton Ch Ch 91-98; TV Parr 98-05; TR from 05. *St Paul's Vicarage, 75 Chain Lane, St Helens WA11 9QF* Tel and fax (01744) 734335
E-mail church@stpaulschainlane.freeserve.co.uk

ROBERTS, Mrs Jasmine Cynthia. b 46. Cant Sch of Min 88. **d** 91. NSM Sandwich *Cant* from 91; Asst Dir of Ords from 02. *The Rectory, Knightrider Street, Sandwich CT13 9ER* Tel and fax (01304) 613138 E-mail jasmineroberts@supanet.com

ROBERTS, Ms Jeanette. b 67. RMHN00. Cranmer Hall Dur 07. **d** 09. C Todmorden *Wakef* from 09. *12 Phoenix Court, Todmorden OL14 5SJ* Tel (01706) 813165
E-mail jay.roberts@hotmail.co.uk

ROBERTS, John Anthony Duckworth. b 43. K Coll Lon BD65 AKC65. St Boniface Warminster 65. **d** 66 **p** 67. C Wythenshawe Wm Temple Ch CD *Man* 66-69; C Bradford-on-Avon *Sarum* 69-72; Chapl Dauntsey's Sch Devizes 72-73; CF 73-77; P-in-c Verwood *Sarum* 77-81; V 81-86; V Clitheroe St Mary *Blackb* 86-97; R Paget St Paul Bermuda 97-03; rtd 03. *The Old Coach House, Forwood, Minchinhampton, Stroud GL6 9AB* Tel (01453) 835811

ROBERTS, John Charles Welch. b 39. UMIST BSc60. Oak Hill NSM Course 91 SW Minl Tr Course 92. **d** 94 **p** 95. NSM Washfield, Stoodleigh, Withleigh etc *Ex* from 94. *East Sidborough, Loxbeare, Tiverton EX16 8DA* Tel and fax (01884) 256302 E-mail john@sidborough.freeserve.co.uk

ROBERTS, Canon John Hugh. b 42. K Alfred's Coll Win CertEd72 Open Univ BA75. Wells Th Coll 65. **d** 67 **p** 68. C Wareham w Arne *Sarum* 67-70; C Twyford *Win* 70-72; Asst Teacher Rawlins Sch Leics 72-74; V Nassington w Yarwell *Pet* 74-77; Asst Teacher Sponne Sch Towcester 78-92; RD Brackley 94-03; P-in-c Helmdon w Stuchbury and Radstone etc 93-03; P-in-c Weedon Lois w Plumpton and Moreton Pinkney etc 02-03; R Astwell Gp 03-05; Can Pet Cathl 01-05; rtd 05; Perm to Offic *Pet* from 05; Chapl to Retired Clergy and Clergy Widows' Officer from 08. *Pimlico House, Pimlico, Brackley NN13 5TN* Tel (01280) 850378 E-mail rev.roberts@virgin.net

ROBERTS, Canon John Mark Arnott. b 54. AKC75 CertEd76. Chich Th Coll 77. **d** 77 **p** 78. C Ashford *Cant* 77-82; V St Mary's Bay w St Mary-in-the-Marsh etc 82-91; R Sandwich from 91; AD Sandwich 00-06; Hon Can Cant Cathl from 03; C Woodnesborough w Worth and Staple from 04. *The Rectory, Knightrider Street, Sandwich CT13 9ER* Tel and fax (01304) 613138 E-mail revdmarkroberts@supanet.com

ROBERTS, Canon John Victor. b 34. St Edm Hall Ox BA58 MA62. Tyndale Hall Bris 58. **d** 60 **p** 61. C Southport Ch Ch *Liv* 60-62; C Pemberton St Mark Newtown 62-65; V Blackb Sav 65-71; Chapl Blackb and Lancs R Infirmary and Park Lee Hosp 65-71; V Parr *Liv* 71-73; TR 73-80; R Much Woolton 80-02; RD Childwall 84-89; AD Liv S 89-00; Hon Can Liv Cathl 95-02; rtd 02; Perm to Offic *Liv* from 02; Hon Chapl Liv Cathl from 04. *8 Cherry Vale, Liverpool L25 5PX* Tel and fax 0151-428 8290 E-mail canonjvr@hotmail.com

ROBERTS, John Victor. b 40. GIPE61. Qu Coll Birm 83. **d** 85 **p** 86. C Ludlow *Heref* 85-89 and 92-93; P-in-c Coreley and Doddington 89-92; P-in-c Knowbury 89-92; TV Ludlow, Ludford, Ashford Carbonell etc 93-02; rtd 02; Perm to Offic *Heref* from 02. *Carwood, 16 Stretton Farm Road, Church Stretton SY6 6DX* Tel (01694) 723164

ROBERTS, Jonathan George Alfred. b 60. Lon Univ BD. Qu Coll Birm. **d** 84 **p** 85. C Shepshed *Leic* 84-86; C Braunstone 86-87; Dioc Youth Adv *Dur* 88-92; Nat Youth Officer Gen Syn Bd of Educn 92-94; P-in-c Washington *Dur* 94-95; R 95-99; Regional Co-ord for Community Work Assessment Consortium for the NE 99-03; Sen Lect Teesside Univ from 03; Perm to Offic *Dur* from 99 and *Newc* from 01. *10 Brierville, Durham DH1 4QE* Tel 0191-383 9148 E-mail j.roberts@tees.ac.uk

ROBERTS, Joseph Aelwyn. b 18. Univ of Wales (Lamp) BA40. St Mich Coll Llan 41. **d** 42 **p** 43. C Llanllyfni *Ban* 42-44; Min Can Ban Cathl 44-52; V Llandegai 52-88; Dioc Dir for Soc Work 73-88; rtd 88; Perm to Offic *Ban* from 88. *The Vicarage, Llandygai, Bangor LL57 4LA* Tel (01248) 353711

ROBERTS, Judith. *See* ROBERTS, Anne Judith

ROBERTS, Ms Judith. b 55. Collingwood Coll Dur BA76 Goldsmiths' Coll Lon PGCE77. SWMTC 00. **d** 03 **p** 04. C Burrington, Chawleigh, Cheldon, Chulmleigh etc *Ex* 03-06; C Axminster, Chardstock, All Saints etc from 06. *The Vicarage, Chardstock, Axminster EX13 7BY* Tel (01460) 220005
E-mail judith75@yahoo.com

ROBERTS, Mrs Kathleen Marie. b 50. Th Ext Educn Coll 94. **d** 00 **p** 01. S Africa 00-02; C Crediton, Shobrooke and Sandford etc *Ex* 03-05; P-in-c Black Torrington, Bradford w Cookbury etc from 05. *The Rectory, Black Torrington, Beaworthy EX21 5PU* Tel (01409) 231279

ROBERTS, Canon Keith Mervyn. b 55. St Pet Coll Birm CertEd76 LGSM78 GMus78. Qu Coll Birm 89. **d** 91 **p** 92. C Hall Green St Pet *Birm* 91-95; TV Warwick *Cov* 95-00; P-in-c Bishop's Tachbrook from 00; Dioc Communications Officer 03-04; Dir Communications from 04; Relig Affairs Correspondent BBC Radio Cov and Warw 95-01; Presenter/Producer from 01; Hon Can Cov Cathl from 07. *The Vicarage, 24 Mallory Road, Bishops Tachbrook, Leamington Spa CV33 9QX* Tel and fax (01926) 426922
E-mail mervynrob@aol.com *or* mervyn.roberts@covcofe.org

ROBERTS, Canon Kenneth William Alfred. b 26. Roch Th Coll 63. **d** 65 **p** 66. C Waterlooville *Portsm* 65-67; C Honicknowle *Ex* 67-68; C Christchurch *Win* 68-69; C Shiphay Collaton *Ex* 70-71; CF 71-74; R Bassingham *Linc* 74-75; V Carlton-le-Moorland w Stapleford 74-75; R Thurlby w Norton Disney 74-75; V Aubourn w Haddington 74-75; Chapl R Hosp Sch Holbrook 75-78; P-in-c Copdock w Washbrook and Belstead *St E* 78-79; P-in-c Brandeston w Kettleburgh 79-82; Chapl Brandeston Hall Sch 79-84; Chapl Lisbon *Eur* 84-86; Can and Chan Malta Cathl 86-89; R Wimbotsham w Stow Bardolph and Stow Bridge etc *Ely* 89-91; rtd 91; Perm to Offic *St E* 91-98. *2 Valley Farm Bungalows, Combs Lane, Stowmarket IP14 2NL* Tel (01449) 674746

ROBERTS, The Ven Kevin Thomas. b 55. Qu Coll Cam BA78 MA82 Nottm Univ BA82. St Jo Coll Nottm 80. **d** 83 **p** 84. C Beverley Minster *York* 83-86; C Woodley St Jo the Ev *Ox* 86-91; V Meole Brace *Lich* 91-09; RD Shrewsbury 98-08; Preb Lich Cathl 02-08; Adn Carl and Can Res Carl Cathl from 09. *2 The Abbey, Carlisle CA3 8TZ* Tel (01228) 523026
E-mail archdeacon.north@carlislediocese.org.uk

ROBERTS, Laurence James. b 51. Sussex Univ BEd73. Sarum & Wells Th Coll 75. **d** 78 **p** 79. C Rotherhithe St Mary w All SS *S'wark* 78-81; Public Preacher 81-84; Ind Chapl 81-84; Hon P Nunhead St Silas 82-84; TV Plaistow *Chelmsf* 84-89; Chapl Newham Gen Hosp and Plaistow Hosp 84-96; Tutor Community Nursing Services 89-96; Tutor Westmr Past Foundn from 90; Lect E Lon Univ from 92. *40 Boleyn Road, London E7 9QE* Tel (020) 8472 2430
E-mail laurence.roberts@virgin.net

ROBERTS, Ms Leanne Kelly. b 74. St Hilda's Coll Ox BA95 MA02 Em Coll Cam BA01. Westcott Ho Cam 99. **d** 02 **p** 03. C Hampton All SS *Lon* 02-05; Chapl Hertf Coll Ox from 05. *Hertford College, Catte Street, Oxford OX1 3BW* Tel (01865) 279400 E-mail leanneroberts_uk@yahoo.co.uk

ROBERTS, Miss Marguerite Mary Grace. b 43. Keswick Hall Coll CertEd65 Sussex Univ BEd74 UEA MA86. EAMTC 97. **d** 00 **p** 01. Hon C Cambridge St Mark *Ely* from 00. *5 Eachard Road, Cambridge CB3 0HZ* Tel (01223) 359167

ROBERTS, Mark. *See* ROBERTS, Canon John Mark Arnott

ROBERTS, Martin Meredith Edward. b 62. Univ of Wales (Abth) BSc85. **d** 06 **p** 07. OLM Woodbridge St Jo and Bredfield *St E* from 06. *64 Victoria Road, Woodbridge IP12 1EL* Tel (01394) 388140 E-mail martin.me.roberts@bt.com

ROBERTS, Martin Vincent. b 53. Birm Univ BA76 MA77 PhD82 LRAM72. Ripon Coll Cuddesdon 76. **d** 78 **p** 79. C Perry Barr *Birm* 78-81; Sen Chapl and Lect W Sussex Inst of HE 81-86; Leic Poly 86-92; Sen Chapl De Montfort Univ 92-95; TV Leic H Spirit 86-89; TR 89-95; V Baswich *Lich* 95-01; V Selly Oak St Mary *Birm* 01-08; rtd 08. *89 Sargent House, Symphony Court, Birmingham B16 8AF* Tel 0121-472 0250
E-mail martin@mroberts48.fsnet.co.uk

ROBERTS, Matthew Garnant. b 13. St D Coll Lamp BA37. **d** 37 **p** 38. C St Brides Minor *Llan* 37-39; C Iford *Win* 39-43; C Bournemouth St Alb 43-46; Chapl RAF 47-68; P-in-c Hinton Ampner w Bramdean *Win* 68-70; R 70-74; R Hinton Ampner w Bramdean and Kilmeston 74-78; rtd 78; Lic to Offic *B & W* 79-96. *19 Sexey's Hospital, Bruton BA10 0AS* Tel (01749) 812545

ROBERTS, Mervyn. *See* ROBERTS, Canon Keith Mervyn

ROBERTS, Michael Brian. b 46. Oriel Coll Ox BA68 MA72 St Jo Coll Dur BA73. Cranmer Hall Dur 71. **d** 74 **p** 75. C St Helens St Helen *Liv* 74-76; C Goose Green 76-78; C Blundellsands St Nic 78-80; V Fazakerley St Nath 80-87; V Chirk *St As* 87-01; V Cockerham w Winmarleigh and Glasson *Blackb* from 01. *The Vicarage, 5 Lancaster Road, Cockerham, Lancaster LA2 0EB* Tel and fax (01524) 791390
E-mail michael.andrea.r@ukonline.co.uk

ROBERTS, Michael Frederick. b 46. Sarum Th Coll 86. **d** 88 **p** 89. C Reading St Matt *Ox* 88-91; NSM Douglas St Geo and St Barn *S & M* 91-93; V Malew from 93. *Malew Vicarage, Crossag Road, Ballasalla, Isle of Man IM9 3EF* Tel (01624) 822469 E-mail malew@globalnet.co.uk

ROBERTS, Michael Graham Vernon. b 43. Keble Coll Ox BA65. Cuddesdon Coll 65 Ch Div Sch of the Pacific (USA) BD67. **d** 67 **p** 68. C Littleham w Exmouth 67-70; Chapl Clare Coll Cam 70-74; V Bromley St Mark *Roch* 74-79; Tutor Qu Coll Birm 79-85; TR High Wycombe *Ox* 85-90; Vice-Prin Westcott Ho

Cam 90-93; Prin 93-06; Hon Can Ely Cathl 04-06; rtd 06. *La Herviais, 22100 Trévron, France* Tel 08446-176806
E-mail michael.su.roberts@orange.fr

ROBERTS, Nia Wyn. *See* MORRIS, Nia Wyn

ROBERTS, Nicholas John. b 47. Lon Univ BD70 AKC70 MTh78 Surrey Univ MSc93. St Aug Coll Cant 70. **d** 71 **p** 72. C Tividale *Lich* 71-74; C St Pancras H Cross w St Jude and St Pet *Lon* 74-76; C Camberwell St Giles *S'wark* 76-78; Chapl Ch Coll Cam 78-82; V Kingstanding St Luke *Birm* 82-85; Chapl St Chas Hosp Ladbroke Grove 85-96; Chapl Princess Louise Hosp Lon 85-96; Chapl Paddington Community Hosp 85-96; Chapl Cen Middx Hosp NHS Trust 96-99; Chapl St Mary's NHS Trust Paddington 99-04; Chapl CSC from 04. *32 Burnell Avenue, Richmond TW10 7YE* Tel (020) 8549 1060 Mobile 07984-892635
E-mail nick@norlon.freeserve.co.uk

ROBERTS, Mrs Patricia Frances. b 62. Roehampton Inst BEd85. Trin Coll Bris 93. **d** 96 **p** 97. NSM Buckhurst Hill *Chelmsf* 96-99; NSM Gt Baddow 99-07. *The Vicarage, The Butts, Lydiard Millicent, Swindon SN5 3LR* Tel (01793) 772417
E-mail tudorandtricia@btinternet.com

ROBERTS, Paul Carlton. b 57. Worc Coll Ox BA78 MA86 CertEd. St Jo Coll Nottm 84. **d** 87 **p** 88. C Hazlemere *Ox* 87-91; C Woodley St Jo the Ev 91-92; TV Woodley 92-03; R Coulsdon St Jo *S'wark* from 03. *The Rectory, 232 Coulsdon Road, Coulsdon CR5 1EA* Tel and fax (01737) 552152
E-mail proberts8@toucansurf.com

ROBERTS, Paul John. b 60. Man Univ BA82 PhD91 Man Poly PGCE83. St Jo Coll Nottm 83. **d** 85 **p** 86. C Burnage St Marg *Man* 85-88; Tutor Trin Coll Bris 88-00; R Cotham St Sav w St Mary and Clifton St Paul *Bris* 00-08; Hon Can Bris Cathl 06-08; Dean Non-Res Tr St Mich Coll Llan from 09. *St Michael and All Angels' College, 54 Cardiff Road, Llandaff, Cardiff CF5 2YJ* Tel (029) 2083 8006 Mobile 07941-968422
E-mail pr@stmichaels.ac.uk

ROBERTS, Peter Francis. b 59. N Illinois Univ BSc81 Leeds Univ BA87. Coll of Resurr Mirfield 85. **d** 88 **p** 89. C Leeds All So *Ripon* 88-92; Asst Dioc Youth Chapl 91-92; USPG Belize 92-94; V Collingham w Harewood *Ripon* 95-01; World Miss Officer 95-01; Chapl Dubai and Sharjah w N Emirates 01-03; R Merritt Is USA from 03. *PO Box 541025, Merritt Island FL 32953, USA* Tel (001) (321) 452 5260 E-mail stlukes1@bellsouth.net

ROBERTS, Peter Gwilym. b 42. NOC 78. **d** 81 **p** 82. NSM Seaforth *Liv* 81-83; TV Kirkby 83-88; Dioc Adv on UPA 88-91; P-in-c Southport H Trin 91-94; S Africa from 94; rtd 00. *PO Box 44108, Linden, Gauteng, 2104 South Africa* Tel (0027) (11) 475 4439 *or* 475 1314 Fax 475 8284

ROBERTS, Peter Reece. b 43. Chich Th Coll 73. **d** 75 **p** 76. C Cadoxton-juxta-Barry *Llan* 75-79; C Brixham w Churston Ferrers *Ex* 79-81; C Bexhill St Pet *Chich* 81-84; R Heene from 84; RD Worthing 89-97. *Heene Rectory, 4 Lansdowne Road, Worthing BN11 4LY* Tel (01903) 202312
E-mail revp.roberts@btinternet.com

ROBERTS, Philip Alan. b 59. Chich Th Coll 85. **d** 88 **p** 89. C Friern Barnet St Jas *Lon* 88-93; C Farnham Royal w Hedgerley *Ox* 93-02; TV Southend *Chelmsf* from 02. *39 St John's Road, Westcliff-on-Sea SS0 7JY* Tel (01702) 433327

ROBERTS, Philip Anthony. b 50. St Jo Coll Dur BA73. Wycliffe Hall Ox 75. **d** 77 **p** 78. C Roby *Liv* 77-79; C Ainsdale 79-80; C Pershore w Pinvin, Wick and Birlingham *Worc* 80-83; Chapl Asst Radcliffe Infirmary Ox 83-88; John Radcliffe and Littlemore Hosps Ox 83-88; Chapl R Victoria and Bournemouth Gen Hosps 88-91; Chapl Heref Co Hosp 91-94; Chapl Heref Hosps NHS Trust from 94. *The County Hospital, Union Walk, Hereford HR1 2ER* Tel (01432) 364139 *or* 355444

ROBERTS, Canon Phillip. b 21. Sarum Th Coll 55. **d** 57 **p** 58. C Salisbury St Mich *Sarum* 57-60; Australia 60-63; V Westbury *Sarum* 63-73; TR Dorchester 73-80; Can and Preb Sarum Cathl 75-87; R Upper Chelsea H Trin *Lon* 80-87; rtd 87; Perm to Offic *Sarum* from 87; V of Close Sarum Cathl 89-95. *112 Harnham Road, Salisbury SP2 8JW* Tel (01722) 323291

ROBERTS, The Ven Raymond Harcourt. b 31. CB84. St Edm Hall Ox BA54 MA58. St Mich Coll Llan 54. **d** 56 **p** 57. C Bassaleg *Mon* 56-59; Chapl RNR 57-59; Chapl RN 59-84; Chapl of the Fleet and Adn for the RN 80-84; QHC 80-84; Hon Can Gib Cathl 80-84; Gen Sec JMECA 85-89; C Hale *Guildf* 85-89; Hon Chapl Llan Cathl 90-95; Lic to Offic from 95. *8 Baynton Close, Llandaff, Cardiff CF5 2NZ* Tel (029) 2057 8044

ROBERTS, Miss Rebecca Mary. b 71. Glam Univ BA92 Chelt & Glouc Coll of HE PGCE93. Qu Coll Birm BA02. **d** 03 **p** 04. C Greenstead w Colchester St Anne *Chelmsf* 03-06; Perm to Offic *Win* from 06. *10 Amport Close, Winchester SO22 6LP*
E-mail bricklanebek@hotmail.com

ROBERTS, Richard. b 23. Univ of Wales BA48. St Mich Coll Llan 48. **d** 50 **p** 51. C Pwllheli *Ban* 50-53; C Llangelynnin 53-57; V Llanwnog w Penstrowed 57-68; R Llanrwst and Llanddoget *St As* 68-75; RD Llanrwst 73-75; V Llandrillo-yn-Rhos 75-90; rtd 91; Perm to Offic *Ban* from 91 and *St A* from 97. *2 Bryn Ithel, Abergele LL22 8QB* Tel (01745) 826353

ROBERTS, Canon Richard Stephanus Jacob (Steph). b 28. TCD BA51 MA57. TCD Div Sch Div Test51. **d** 51 **p** 52. C Orangefield *D & D* 51-54; Miss to Seamen 51-94; Portuguese E Africa 51-65; Ceylon 65-68; Chapl Miss to Seamen Dublin 68-72; Chapl Miss to Seamen Southn 72-94; Sen Chapl Ch on the High Seas 72-94; Hon Can Win Cathl 82-94; rtd 94; Perm to Offic *Win* from 94. *25 Bassett Crescent West, Southampton SO16 7EB* Tel (023) 8079 0734

ROBERTS, Ronald Barry. b 40. S Dios Minl Tr Scheme 80. **d** 83 **p** 85. NSM Wedmore w Theale and Blackford *B & W* 83-85; C Odd Rode *Ches* 85-87; V Eaton and Hulme Walfield 87-04; rtd 04; Perm to Offic *Ches* from 04. *Iona, 8 Belmont Avenue, Sandbach CW11 1BX* Tel (01270) 766124
E-mail barryroberts@uwclub.net

ROBERTS, Mrs Rosamunde Mair. b 59. RN80. STETS 98. **d** 01 **p** 02. C Farnham *Guildf* 01-04; C Fleet 04-08; P-in-c Lenborough *Ox* from 08. *The Vicarage, Thornborough Road, Padbury, Buckingham MK18 2AH* Tel (01280) 813162
E-mail rosm.roberts@dsl.pipex.com

ROBERTS, Mrs Rosanne Elizabeth. b 51. Glouc Sch of Min 85. **d** 88 **p** 94. NSM Charlton Kings St Mary *Glouc* 88-93; C Leckhampton SS Phil and Jas w Cheltenham St Jas 93-96; R Ashchurch 96-08; R Ashchurch and Kemerton from 08. *The Rectory, Ashchurch Road, Tewkesbury GL20 8JZ* Tel (01684) 293729

ROBERTS, Miss Sandra June. b 58. Univ Coll Ches BA96. Qu Coll Birm 98. **d** 98 **p** 99. C Mold *St As* 98-01; V Llandrillo and Llandderfel from 01; P-in-c Betws Gwerful Goch w Llangwm w Llawrybetws from 05; AD Penllyn and Edeirnion from 04. *The Vicarage, Llandrillo, Corwen LL21 0SW* Tel (01490) 440224

ROBERTS, Stephanus. *See* ROBERTS, Canon Richard Stephanus Jacob

ROBERTS, Stephen Bradley. b 66. K Coll Lon BD90 Wycliffe Hall Ox 89. **d** 91 **p** 92. C W Hampstead St Jas *Lon* 91-94; TV Uxbridge 94-98; Chapl Brunel Univ 98-04; Vice Prin St Mich Coll Llan from 04. *St Michael's College, 54 Cardiff Road, Llandaff, Cardiff CF5 2YJ* Tel (029) 2083 8004 *or* 2055 1780
E-mail sr@stmichaels.ac.uk

ROBERTS, The Ven Stephen John. b 58. K Coll Lon BD81 Heythrop Coll Lon MTh99. Westcott Ho Cam. **d** 83 **p** 84. C Riverhead w Dunton Green *Roch* 83-86; C St Martin-in-the-Fields *Lon* 86-89; Warden Trin Coll Cen Camberwell 89-99; V Camberwell St Geo *S'wark* 89-99; RD Camberwell 97-99; Treas and Can Res S'wark Cathl 00-05; Sen Dioc Dir of Ords 00-05; Adn Wandsworth from 05. *2 Alma Road, London SW18 1AB* Tel (020) 8874 8567 *or* 8545 2440 Fax 8545 2441
E-mail stephen.roberts@southwark.anglican.org

ROBERTS, Preb Susan Emma. b 60. La Sainte Union Coll BTh93. St Steph Ho Ox 94. **d** 96 **p** 97. C Petersfield *Portsm* 96-00; P-in-c Ashprington, Cornworthy and Dittisham *Ex* 00-04; TV Totnes w Bridgetown, Berry Pomeroy etc 04-06; RD Totnes 03-06; TR Honiton, Gittisham, Combe Raleigh, Monkton etc from 06; Preb Ex Cathl from 06; RD Honiton from 07. *The Rectory, Rookwood Close, Honiton EX14 1BH* Tel (01404) 42925 E-mail revdsue@btinternet.com

ROBERTS, Sydney Neville Hayes. b 19. K Coll Lon 38. Cuddesdon Coll 45. **d** 47 **p** 48. C Aylesbury *Ox* 47-52; CF 52-69; R Theale w N Street *Ox* 69-76; R Theale and Englefield 76-85; rtd 85; Perm to Offic *Ox* from 89. *34 Stonebridge Road, Steventon, Abingdon OX13 6AU* Tel (01235) 834777

ROBERTS, Mrs Sylvia Ann. b 40. Stockwell Coll Lon TCert60. S Dios Minl Tr Scheme 81. **dss** 84 **d** 87 **p** 94. Crookhorn *Portsm* 84-88; Hon Par Dn Bedhampton 88-89; Par Dn Southampton (City Cen) *Win* 89-91; TD 91-94; TV 94-96; V Merton St Jo *S'wark* 96-06; P-in-c Colliers Wood Ch Ch 01-06; rtd 06; Perm to Offic *Portsm* from 07. *16 Bramble Road, Petersfield GU31 4HL*
E-mail sylkenco@hotmail.com

ROBERTS, Canon Tegid. b 47. **d** 87 **p** 88. Lic to Offic *Ban* 87-93; NSM Llandinorwig w Penisa'r-waen 93-99; Lic to Offic 99-00; Dioc Officer for Children and Schs from 00; Min Can Ban Cathl 00-05; V Llandwrog and Llanwnda from 05; Hon Can Ban Cathl from 07. *Arwel, Llanrug, Caernarfon LL55 3BA* Tel (01286) 870760 E-mail tr@roberts485.freeserve.co.uk

ROBERTS, Terry Harvie. b 45. Sarum & Wells Th Coll 87. **d** 89 **p** 90. C Weymouth H Trin *Sarum* 89-93; TV Basingstoke *Win* 93-98; P-in-c Win St Barn from 98. *St Barnabas' Vicarage, Trussell Crescent, Winchester SO22 6DY* Tel and fax (01962) 882728 E-mail stbarnabas.winchester@ukgateway.net

ROBERTS, Tudor Vaughan. b 58. Newc Univ BA81. All Nations Chr Coll 91 Trin Coll Bris BA94. **d** 96 **p** 97. C Buckhurst Hill *Chelmsf* 96-99; TV Gt Baddow 99-07; TV W Swindon and the Lydiards *Bris* from 07. *The Vicarage, The Butts, Lydiard Millicent, Swindon SN5 3LR* Tel (01793) 772417
E-mail tudorandtricia@btinternet.com

ROBERTS, Tunde. *See* ROBERTS, Vincent Akintunde

ROBERTS, Vaughan Edward. b 65. Selw Coll Cam BA88 MA91. Wycliffe Hall Ox 89. **d** 91 **p** 92. C Ox St Ebbe w H Trin and St Pet

91-95; Student Pastor 95-98; R from 98. *St Ebbe's Rectory, 2 Roger Bacon Lane, Oxford OX1 1QE* Tel (01865) 248154
E-mail vroberts@stebbes.org.uk

ROBERTS, Vaughan Simon. b 59. Univ of Wales (Ban) BA80 Bath Univ PhD99. McCormick Th Sem Chicago MA82 Westcott Ho Cam 83. **d** 85 **p** 86. C Bourne *Guildf* 85-89; Chapl Phyllis Tuckwell Hospice Farnham 88-89; NSM Bath Ch Ch Prop Chpl 90-96; P-in-c 92-96; P-in-c Chewton Mendip w Ston Easton, Litton etc 96-03; Dioc Voc Adv 96-99; Dir of Ords 99-03; TR Warwick *Cov* from 03. *St Mary's Vicarage, The Butts, Warwick CV34 4SS* Tel and fax (01926) 492909 E-mail vaughan.roberts@btinternet.com

ROBERTS, Vincent Akintunde (Tunde). b 55. Kingston Poly BA(Econ)81. S'wark Ord Course. **d** 91 **p** 92. Hon C Brixton Road Ch Ch *S'wark* 91-96; C Mitcham St Barn 96-99; P-in-c Stoke Newington St Olave *Lon* 99-03; V from 03; P-in-c Stoke Newington St Andr from 06; P-in-c Upper Clapton St Matt from 08. *St Olave's Vicarage, Woodberry Down, London N4 2TW* Tel and fax (020) 8800 1374 E-mail tunde.roberts@talk21.com

ROBERTS, Vivian Phillip. b 35. Univ of Wales BD78. St D Coll Lamp 57. **d** 60 **p** 61. C Cwmaman *St D* 60-64; R Puncheston, Lt Newcastle and Castle Bythe 64-72; V Brynamman 72-77; V Brynaman w Cwmllynfell 77-83; V Pen-bre 83-00; rtd 00. *40 New Road, Llanelli SA15 3DR* Tel (01554) 755506

ROBERTS, Wallace Lionel. b 31. Univ of Wales (Lamp) BA58. St D Coll Lamp 55. **d** 59 **p** 60. C Astley Bridge *Man* 59-61; Asst Master Stand Gr Sch 61-66; Hon C Stand 61-66; Hon CF Aden 66-67; Lect Stockport Tech Coll 67-70; Hon C Heaton Moor *Man* 67-70; Chapl Qu Sch Rheindahlen 70-76; Hon CF 70-76; Swaziland 76-85; Chapl Oporto *Eur* 86-89; Chapl Hordle Ho Sch Milford-on-Sea 89-90; C Portishead *B & W* 91-96; rtd 96; Perm to Offic *B & W* from 96. *44 Hallett's Way, Portishead, Bristol BS20 6BT* Tel (01275) 817484

ROBERTS, William James (Jim). b 55. Lon Bible Coll BA77 Hughes Hall Cam PGCE78. NEOC 92. **d** 94 **p** 95. NSM York St Mich-le-Belfrey from 94; Chapl Pocklington Sch from 06. *12 Bishop's Way, York YO10 5JG* Tel (01904) 413479

ROBERTS, Wynne. b 61. Univ of Wales (Ban) BTh92. Ridley Hall Cam 85. **d** 87 **p** 88. Min Can Bath Cathl and C Ban Cathl 87-90; V Ynyscynhaearn w Penmorfa and Porthmadog 90-94; TV Bangor 94-04; Chapl NW Wales NHS Trust from 99. *North West Wales NHS Trust, Ysbyty Gwynedd, Penrhosgarnedd, Bangor LL57 2PW* Tel (01248) 384384 Fax 370629
E-mail wynne.roberts@nww-tr.wales.nhs.uk

ROBERTSHAW, John Sean. b 66. Cranmer Hall Dur 90. **d** 93 **p** 94. C Morley St Pet w Churwell *Wakef* 93-96; TV Upper Holme Valley 96-01; TR from 01; CF (TA) from 98. *The Vicarage, Kirkroyds Lane, New Mill, Holmfirth HD9 1LS* Tel and fax (01484) 683375 Mobile 07980-289727
E-mail revsean@tiscali.co.uk

ROBERTSHAW, Jonothan Kempster Pickard Sykes. b 41. AKC65. **d** 66 **p** 67. C Perranzabuloe *Truro* 66-69; Miss to Seamen 69-76; Hong Kong 69-72; Namibia 73-76; TV Probus, Ladock and Grampound w Creed and St Erme *Truro* 76-79; TV N Hill w Altarnon, Bolventor and Lewannick 79-80; P-in-c Lansallos 80-84; R 84-96; P-in-c Talland 80-84; V 84-96; V Madron 96-01; P-in-c Gulval 99-01; V Gulval and Madron 01; rtd 01; Hon C Penzance St Mary w St Paul and St Jo *Truro* from 09; Hon Chapl R Cornwall Hosps Trust from 09; Hon Chapl Miss to Seafarers from 09. *38 Treassowe Road, Penzance TR18 2AU* Tel (01736) 330612

ROBERTSON, Agnes Muriel Hodgson. b 20. Edin Univ MA41. St And NSM Tr Scheme. **d** 91 **p** 94. NSM Lochgelly *St And* 91-92; Par Dn Glenrothes 92-94; NSM 94-98; NSM Leven 94-01; NSM St Andrews St Andr 94-01; NSM Lochgelly 94-01; rtd 98; P Cupar *St And* 01-04. *8 Bathgate Court, Cupar KY15 4LP* Tel (01334) 653543

ROBERTSON, Ms Beverley Ann. b 57. Qu Coll Birm 98. **d** 01 **p** 02. C Sutton Coldfield H Trin *Birm* 01-05; C Portsea N End St Mark *Portsm* 05-06; TV from 06. *90A Compton Road, Portsmouth PO2 0SR* Tel (023) 9266 5317
E-mail bev_robertson@yahoo.com

ROBERTSON, Brian Ainsley. b 50. Warwick Univ BSc72. St Jo Coll Nottm 94. **d** 94 **p** 95. C Leic Martyrs 94-97; C Oadby 97-98; TV 98-02; P-in-c Ashby-de-la-Zouch St Helen w Coleorton 02-05; P-in-c Breedon cum Isley Walton and Worthington 03-05; TR Ashby-de-la-Zouch and Breedon on the Hill from 05; RD NW Leics from 07. *The Rectory, 4 Upper Packington Road, Ashby-de-la-Zouch LE65 1EF* Tel (01530) 414404
E-mail barobertson@tesco.net

ROBERTSON, Charles Kevin. b 64. Virginia Poly & State Univ BA85 Dur Univ PhD99. Virginia Th Sem MDiv93 **d** 93 **p** 94. P-in-c USA 93-96; NSM Neville's Cross St Jo CD *Dur* 96-97; NSM Esh 97-99; R Milledgeville St Steph USA from 99. *Box 309, Milledgeville GA 31059-0309, USA*
E-mail rector@ststephensga.org

ROBERTSON, Charles Peter. b 57. Aston Tr Scheme 92 Linc Th Coll 94. **d** 96 **p** 97. C Holbeach *Linc* 96-99; C S Lafford 01-03;

P-in-c from 03. *The Rectory, 16 West Street, Folkingham, Sleaford NG34 0SW* Tel (01529) 497617

ROBERTSON, David. See ROBERTSON, Thomas John

ROBERTSON, David John. b 54. Sheff Univ BA76. Ridley Hall Cam 77. **d** 79 **p** 80. C Downend *Bris* 79-83; C Yate New Town 83-85; TV 85-87; TV High Wycombe *Ox* 87-97; RD Wycombe 91-97; P-in-c Haley Hill *Wakef* 97-99; V Ovenden from 97. *St George's Vicarage, 2 Bracewell Drive, Wheatley, Halifax HX3 5HY* Tel (01422) 354153

ROBERTSON, Douglas Laurence. b 52. St Edm Hall Ox MA75. SEITE 04. **d** 07 **p** 08. C Roch from 07. *67 Hathaway Court, Esplanade, Rochester ME1 1QY*
E-mail dlrobertson@btinternet.com

ROBERTSON, Edward Macallan. b 28. Aber Univ MA49 Qu Coll Ox BLitt51. Coll of Resurr Mirfield 53. **d** 55 **p** 56. C Swindon New Town *Bris* 55-60; R Hawick *Edin* 60-69; R Alloa *St And* 70-73; Lic to Offic *Edin* 74-78; P-in-c Bathgate 78-82; P-in-c Linlithgow 78-82; Hon C Strathtay *St And* 82-90; P-in-c Auchterarder 90-93; P-in-c Muthill 90-93; rtd 93. *Pitculdees Cottage, Back Dykes, Abernethy, Perth PH2 9JU* Tel (01738) 850095

ROBERTSON, Mrs Elizabeth Mary. b 60. Cam Univ BA82 MA86 ACA85 FCA95. SEITE 03. **d** 06 **p** 07. NSM Fawkham and Hartley *Roch* from 06. *58 Redhill Wood, New Ash Green, Longfield DA3 8QP* Tel (01474) 874144
E-mail robertem@supanet.com

ROBERTSON, Miss Fiona Jane. b 76. Birm Univ BA98. Wycliffe Hall Ox BA05. **d** 06 **p** 07. C Aston and Nechells *Birm* from 08. *68 Manor Road, Aston, Birmingham B6 6QT* Tel 0121-326 7390 E-mail fionajanerobertson@yahoo.co.uk

ROBERTSON, Iain Michael. b 67. Trin Coll Bris 03. **d** 05 **p** 06. C E Clevedon w Clapton in Gordano etc *B & W* 05-09; TV Salter Street and Shirley *Birm* from 09. *68 Tythe Barn Lane, Shirley, Solihull B90 1RW* Tel 0121-733 6658

ROBERTSON, Canon James Alexander. b 46. Ox Univ MTh99. Sarum & Wells Th Coll 72. **d** 75 **p** 76. C Monksearton St Pet *Newc* 75-78; C Prudhoe 78-79; TV Brayton *York* 79-84; V Redcar 84-93; V Selby Abbey 93-96; V Monkseaton St Pet *Newc* from 96; AD Tynemouth 98-09; Hon Can Newc Cathl from 05. *St Peter's Vicarage, 6 Elmwood Road, Whitley Bay NE25 8EX* Tel and fax 0191-252 1991
E-mail jim.a.robertson@blueyonder.co.uk

ROBERTSON, James Macaulay. b 51. St Jo Coll Dur BA73. Oak Hill Th Coll. **d** 00 **p** 01. C Holdenhurst and Iford *Win* 00-04; V Marden *Cant* from 04. *The Vicarage, Haffenden Close, Marden, Tonbridge TN12 9DR* Tel (01622) 831379
E-mail james@mardenchurch.org.uk

ROBERTSON, John Charles. b 61. St Pet Coll Ox BA81 Trin Coll Cam BA89. Ridley Hall Cam 87. **d** 90 **p** 91. C Kenilworth St Jo *Cov* 90-94; Chapl York Univ 94-00; V Grove *Ox* from 00; RD Wantage from 09. *The Vicarage, Main Street, Grove, Wantage OX12 7LQ* Tel (01235) 766484
E-mail vicargrove@tiscali.co.uk

ROBERTSON (née PEGG), Mrs Josephine Anne. b 51. Lon Univ CertEd72. Ch Ch Coll Cant BSc91. **d** 02 **p** 03. OLM Folkestone H Trin w Ch Ch Cant 02-06; Chapl Dover Coll 02-05; C Sandgate St Paul w Folkestone St Geo *Cant* 05-06; C Folkestone Trin from 06. *100 Surrenden Road, Folkestone CT19 4AQ* Tel (01303) 277330 Mobile 07905-954504
E-mail jo.robertson@ntlworld.com

ROBERTSON, Kathryn. b 58. Leeds Univ BA05. NOC 02. **d** 05 **p** 06. C Dewsbury *Wakef* 05-08; TV from 08. *The Vicarage, 68 Staincliffe Road, Dewsbury WF13 4ED* Tel (01924) 438302
E-mail kathycurate@drobertson99.wanadoo.co.uk

ROBERTSON, Mrs Linda Margaret. b 50. Somerville Coll Ox BA71 MA76 Aber Univ MSc72. STETS 00. **d** 03 **p** 04. NSM Ampfield *Win* 03-08; NSM Totton from 08. *35 Winnington, Fareham PO15 6HP* Tel (01329) 239857
E-mail revlindarob@yahoo.co.uk

ROBERTSON, Muriel. See ROBERTSON, Agnes Muriel Hodgson

ROBERTSON, Canon Paul Struan. b 45. St Jo Coll Dur BA73 Newc Univ Aus BEdSt79 MA95. **d** 72 **p** 73. C Chester le Street *Dur* 72-73; Australia 73-88 and from 89; C Hamilton 73-77; C Cessnock 77-79; R Scone 79-88; V Collierley w Annfield Plain *Dur* 88-89; R New Lambton from 89; AD Newc W from 96; Lect St Jo Coll Morpeth from 97; Can Newc Cathl from 01. *122 St James Road, PO Box 292, New Lambton NSW 2305, Australia* Tel (0061) (2) 4957 1173 or 4952 2218 Fax 4957 1788 E-mail saints@idl.net.au

ROBERTSON, Philip Stuart. b 55. Newc Univ BA77 BArch80. Oak Hill Th Coll BA07. **d** 07 **p** 08. C Woking St Jo *Guildf* from 07. *13 Ashley Road, Woking GU21 8SR* Tel (01483) 721244
E-mail philip_r_is@hotmail.com

ROBERTSON, Mrs Priscilla Biddulph. b 25. St And Dioc Tr Course 87. **d** 90 **p** 91. C St Andrews St Andr *St And* from 90; P-in-c Pittenweem 04-06. *8 Balrymonth Court, St Andrews KY16 8XT* Tel (01334) 474976

ROBERTSON, Scott. b 64. Edin Univ BD90 Open Univ MA02 Glas Univ PhD08. Edin Th Coll 86. **d** 90 **p** 91. C Glas Gd Shep and Ascension 90-92; P-in-c 92-97; P-in-c Ardrossan from 97; P-in-c Irvine St Andr LEP from 97; P-in-c Dalry from 97. *31 Milgarholm Avenue, Irvine KA12 0EL* Tel and fax (01294) 278341 Mobile 07703-709176
E-mail revscottrobertson@btinternet.com

ROBERTSON, Mrs Sheila Jean. b 40. **d** 99 **p** 01. OLM Chase *Sarum* 99-09; rtd 09. *Church Mead, Harley Lane, Gussage All Saints, Wimborne BH21 5HD* Tel (01258) 840182
E-mail ross@churchmead.wanadoo.co.uk

ROBERTSON, Stephen Andrew. b 60. Strathclyde Univ BSc82. Trin Coll Bris 90. **d** 92 **p** 93. C Vange *Chelmsf* 92-96; R Creeksea w Althorne, Latchingdon and N Fambridge 96-06; R Downham w S Hanningfield from 06. *The Rectory, Castledon Road, Downham, Billericay CM11 1LD* Tel (01268) 710370
E-mail stephen.r@quista.net

ROBERTSON, Stuart Lang. b 40. Glas Univ MA63 Edin Univ MTh97. St Jo Coll Nottm 72. **d** 75 **p** 76. C Litherland St Jo and St Jas *Liv* 75-78; C Edin St Thos 78-81; Chapl Edn Univ and C Edin St Pet 81-83; R Edin St Jas 83-91; Miss to Seamen 83-91; Crosslinks 91-05; Hon Chapl St Petersburg *Eur* 93-98; Chapl Warsaw 98-04; Asst Chapl Barcelona 04-05; rtd 05. *3 Pentland Villas, Juniper Green EH14 5EQ* Tel 0131-453 4755
E-mail stur067@yahoo.co.uk

ROBERTSON, Thomas John (David). b 15. Univ of Wales BA38 Lon Univ DipEd66. St Steph Ho Ox 38. **d** 40 **p** 41. C Welshpool *St As* 40-42; C Shotton 42-45; C Colwyn Bay 45-48; V Choral St As Cathl 48-49; R Newmarket 49-53; V Woolfold *Man* 53-57; V Bury St Thos 57-61; Hd RE Bramhall Gr Sch 61-74; V Taddington and Chelmorton *Derby* 74-80; rtd 80; Perm to Offic *Derby* 80-87; *Ches* and *Man* 80-95; *S'wark* 95-03; *Roch* 01-03. *c/o G W Robertson Esq, 2 Clifton Villas, London W9 2PH*

ROBERTSON, William Robert Wilson. b 48. Glas Univ MA71 MPhil74 Strathclyde Univ PGCE72. TISEC 03. **d** 05 **p** 06. C Edin St Mich and All SS 05-08; Chapl Dioc Boys' Sch Kowloon Hong Kong from 08. *Diocesan Boys' School, 131 Argyle Street, Mongkok, Kowloon, Hong Kong, China* Tel (00852) 2711 5191 *or* 2711 5192 E-mail bill.robertson1@tiscali.co.uk

ROBIN, Peter Philip King. b 23. Trin Coll Cam BA48 MA81. Cuddesdon Coll 49. **d** 51 **p** 52. C Bethnal Green St Matt *Lon* 51-54; Papua New Guinea 54-75; R Elsing w Bylaugh *Nor* 76-85; R Lyng w Sparham 76-85; P-in-c Holme Cultram St Mary *Carl* 85-88; rtd 88; Perm to Offic *Carl* 88-99 and from 02. *191 Brampton Road, Carlisle CA3 9AX* Tel (01228) 545293

ROBINS, Christopher Charles. b 41. St Mich Coll Llan 66. **d** 68 **p** 69. C Bideford *Ex* 68-71; C Dawlish 71-74; V Laira 74-81; P-in-c Dodbrooke 81-83; P-in-c Churchstow w Kingsbridge 81-83; R Kingsbridge and Dodbrooke 83-06; rtd 07. *26 Brownings Walk, Ogwell, Newton Abbot TQ12 6YR* Tel (01626) 331366

ROBINS, Canon Douglas Geoffrey. b 45. Open Univ BA90. Ex & Truro NSM Scheme. **d** 81 **p** 83. NSM Kenwyn *Truro* 81-84; Public Preacher 84-00; NSM Truro St Paul and St Clem 00-04; P-in-c Gerrans w St Anthony-in-Roseland and Philleigh 04-08; P-in-c Veryan w Ruan Lanihorne from 08; Hon Can Truro Cathl from 09. *The Vicarage, Veryan, Truro TR2 5QA* Tel (01872) 501618 E-mail fatherdougrobins@talktalk.net

ROBINS, Ian Donald Hall. b 28. K Coll Lon BD51 AKC51 Lanc Univ MA74. **d** 52 **p** 53. C Heyhouses on Sea *Blackb* 52-55; C Clitheroe St Mary 55-57; V Trawden 57-67; Hd of RE St Chris C of E Sch Accrington 67-76; P-in-c Hugill *Carl* 76-82; Asst Adv for Educn 76-82; Chapl St Martin's Coll of Educn *Blackb* 82-86; V St Annes St Marg 86-91; rtd 91; Perm to Offic *Blackb* from 91. *20 Painter Wood, Billington, Blackburn BB7 9JD* Tel (01254) 824930

ROBINS, Mrs Mary Katherine. b 34. FRGS Bris Univ BSc55 CertEd56. St Alb Minl Tr Scheme. **dss** 84 **d** 87 **p** 94. N Mymms *St Alb* 84-92; Hon Par Dn 87-92; NSM Northaw 92-95; Hon C Westmr St Jas *Lon* 95-00; Perm to Offic *St Alb* from 95. *15 Bluebridge Road, Brookmans Park, Hatfield AL9 7UW* Tel (01707) 656670 E-mail maryrob@eclipse.co.uk

ROBINS, Terrence Leslie. b 38. CEng67 FIMechE78. NOC 99. **d** 00 **p** 01. Bp's Adv for Elderly People in Res Care *Wakef* 98-01; Hon C Cumberworth, Denby and Denby Dale 00-03; P-in-c 03-08; rtd 08; Perm to Offic *Wakef* from 08. *Cruck Cottage, Cumberworth Lane, Denby Dale, Huddersfield HD8 8RU* Tel and fax (01484) 866000 E-mail robinslt@aol.com

ROBINS, Canon Wendy Sheridan. b 56. Lanc Univ BA77. EAMTC 93. **d** 93 **p** 94. Dir Communications and Resources *S'wark* from 92; NSM Walthamstow St Pet *Chelmsf* 93-02; Hon C S'wark Cathl from 02; Hon Can S'wark Cathl from 08. *17 Hillcrest Road, London E17 4AP, or Trinity House, 4 Chapel Court, Borough High Street, London SE1 1HW* Tel (020) 8523 0016 *or* 7403 8686 Fax 7403 4770
E-mail wendy.robins@southwark.anglican.org

ROBINSON, Alan Booker. b 27. Keble Coll Ox BA51 MA56. Sarum Th Coll 51. **d** 53 **p** 54. C Leeds All So *Ripon* 53-56; C Ilkley St Marg *Bradf* 57-59; V Carlton *Wakef* 59-66; OCF 66-92;

V Hooe *Ex* 66-95; RD Plympton 81-83; RD Plymouth Sutton 86-91; rtd 95; Perm to Offic *Ripon* from 95. *1 Charlton Court, Knaresborough HG5 0BZ* Tel (01423) 860884
E-mail robalb@ntlworld.com

ROBINSON, Alison Jane. b 55. WEMTC 99. **d** 02 **p** 03. C Bishop's Cleeve *Glouc* 02-06; P-in-c Meysey Hampton w Marston Meysey and Castle Eaton 06-08; NSM Fairford Deanery from 09. *Orchard House, High Street, Meysey Hampton, Cirencester GL7 5JT* Tel 07773-721238 (mobile)
E-mail alisonjane.robinson@btinternet.com

ROBINSON, Andrew David. b 61. St Cath Coll Ox BA84 MA01 RMN89. Trin Coll Bris 97. **d** 02 **p** 08. C Southmead *Bris* 02-03; C Kington St Michael and Chippenham St Paul w Hardenhuish etc 03-04; NSM Barlby w Riccall *York* from 05. *13 The Crescent, Riccall, York YO19 6PL* Tel (01757) 249248
E-mail room_2_live@yahoo.co.uk

ROBINSON, Canon Andrew Nesbitt. b 43. AKC67. **d** 68 **p** 69. C Balsall Heath St Paul *Birm* 68-71; C Westmr St Steph w St Jo *Lon* 71-75; Chapl Sussex Univ from 75; Chapl Brighton Poly 75-92; Chapl Brighton Univ 92-93; P-in-c Stanmer w Falmer from 80; Can and Preb Chich Cathl from 98. *St Laurence House, Park Street, Brighton BN1 9PG* Tel (01273) 606928 *or* 606755
E-mail goretti_uk@yahoo.co.uk

ROBINSON, Andrew Stephen. b 49. Lanc Univ BA71 Worc Coll of Educn PGCE72. St Mich Coll Llan 90. **d** 95 **p** 96. NSM Llangattock and Llangynidr *S & B* 95-04; P-in-c Llanfeugan w Llanthetty etc from 04. *17 Pencommin, Llangynidr, Crickhowell NP8 1LT* Tel (01874) 730034

✠**ROBINSON, The Rt Revd Anthony William.** b 56. CertEd. Sarum & Wells Th Coll. **d** 82 **p** 83 **c** 02. C Tottenham St Paul *Lon* 82-85; TV Leic Resurr 85-89; TR 89-97; RD Christianity N 92-97; P-in-c Belgrave St Pet 94-95; Hon Can Leic Cathl 94-97; Adn Pontefract *Wakef* 97-03; Suff Bp Pontefract from 02; Can Res Wakef Cathl from 05. *Pontefract House, 181A Manygates Lane, Sandal, Wakefield WF2 7DR* Tel (01924) 250781 Fax 240490 E-mail bishop.pontefract@wakefield.anglican.org

ROBINSON, Arthur Robert Basil. b 32. ACP67 St Jo Coll Dur BA56 Bradf Univ MA84. Wycliffe Hall Ox 56. **d** 58 **p** 59. C Pemberton St Mark Newtown *Liv* 58-62; CF 62-65; Asst Master Colne Valley High Sch Linthwaite 65-69; Asst Chapl HM Pris Man 69; Chapl HM Borstal Roch 69-74; Peru 74-77; V Golcar *Wakef* 77-83; Admin Sheff Fam Conciliation Service 84-91; Warden St Sampson's Cen York 91-00; rtd 00. *Morangie, 2A Brecksfield, Skelton, York YO30 1YD* Tel (01904) 470558

ROBINSON, Arthur William. b 35. Dur Univ BSc60. Clifton Th Coll 60. **d** 62 **p** 63. C Ox St Clem 62-65; Chile 65-77; V Hoxton St Jo w Ch Ch *Lon* 78-88; TV Gateacre *Liv* 88-00; rtd 00; Perm to Offic *Liv* from 00. *86 Kingsthorne Park, Liverpool L25 0QS* Tel 0151-486 2588 E-mail arthelrob@aol.com

ROBINSON, Brian John Watson. b 33. St Cath Coll Cam BA56 MA60. Westcott Ho Cam 57. **d** 58 **p** 59. C Whitworth w Spennymoor *Dur* 58-62; India 62-66; P-in-c Preston St Steph *Blackb* 66-72; V Ashton-on-Ribble St Andr 72-79; Lic to Offic 79-82; V Preston St Jude w St Paul 82-97; Chapl N Tyneside Health Care NHS Trust 94-97; rtd 97; Perm to Offic *Blackb* from 97. *50 Greenacres, Fulwood, Preston PR2 7DB* Tel (01772) 861516

ROBINSON, Canon Bryan. b 32. Fitzw Ho Cam BA56. Ely Th Coll 56. **d** 58 **p** 59. C Fleetwood St Pet *Blackb* 58-65; V Burnley St Andr 65-74; V Burnley St Marg 65-74; V Burnley St Andr w St Marg 74-97; RD Burnley 85-91; P-in-c Burnley St Jas 92-97; Hon Can Blackb Cathl 94-97; rtd 97; Perm to Offic *Blackb* from 97. *50 Fountains Avenue, Simonstone, Burnley BB12 7PY* Tel (01282) 776518

ROBINSON, Mrs Christine. b 50. Nottm Univ BA71. EAMTC 01. **d** 04 **p** 05. NSM Prittlewell St Pet w Westcliff St Cedd *Chelmsf* from 04. *Pasadena, St John's Road, Benfleet SS7 2PT* Tel (01702) 557000 E-mail crrob75@aol.com

ROBINSON (née KILCOOLEY), Mrs Christine. b 59. K Coll Lon BA05. SEITE 06. **d** 07 **p** 08. C Notting Hill St Pet *Lon* from 07. *7 Gaumont Terrace, Lime Grove, London W12 8HR* Tel (020) 8740 0863 E-mail xtinerob@googlemail.com

ROBINSON, Christopher Gordon. b 49. Ridley Hall Cam. **d** 82 **p** 83. C Stanton *St E* 82-85; C Lawshall 85-86; P-in-c Lawshall w Shimplingthorne and Alpheton 86-89; TV Oakdale *Sarum* 89-99; V Easton H Trin w St Gabr and St Lawr and St Jude *Bris* 99-05; C S Molton w Nymet St George, High Bray etc *Ex* from 05. *The Rectory, Parsonage Lane, South Molton EX36 3AX* Tel (01769) 572411

ROBINSON, Christopher James. b 52. St Pet Coll Birm CertEd74. OLM course 97. **d** 99 **p** 00. OLM Wilnecote *Lich* from 99. *55 Sycamore, Wilnecote, Tamworth B77 5HB* Tel (01827) 282331 E-mail chrisrobinson55@hotmail.co.uk

ROBINSON, Christopher Mark Scott. b 83. Warwick Univ BSc04. Ridley Hall Cam 06. **d** 09. C S Hartismere *St E* from 09. *4 Yaxley Road, Mellis, Eye IP23 8DP* Tel (01379) 788430 Mobile 07789-772024 E-mail tifferrobinson@gmail.com

ROBINSON, Daffyd Charles. b 48. Qu Coll Birm 77. **d** 80 **p** 85. C Abington *Pet* 80-82; C Immingham *Linc* 85-90; R Willoughby

from 90. *The Rectory, Station Road, Willoughby, Alford LN13 9NA* Tel and fax (01507) 462045
E-mail rector@willoughby-lincs.org.uk

ROBINSON, Mrs Danielle Georgette Odette. b 47. SEITE 98. **d** 01 **p** 02. NSM Reigate St Mary *S'wark* from 01; Chapl Surrey and Sussex Healthcare NHS Trust from 01; Perm to Offic *Chich* from 01. *1 Chandler Way, Dorking RH5 4GA* Tel (01306) 883947 *or* (01293) 600300 ext 3141
E-mail daniellerobinson@uwclub.net
or danielle.robinson@sash.nhs.uk

ROBINSON, David. b 42. Sarum & Wells Th Coll. **d** 82 **p** 83. C Billingham St Cuth *Dur* 82-86; V Longwood *Wakef* 86-94; C Athersley 94-97; P-in-c Brotherton 97-02; rtd 02; Perm to Offic *York* from 03. *The Vicarage, Market Weighton Road, Holme-on-Spalding-Moor, York YO43 4AG* Tel (01430) 860379

ROBINSON, Canon David Hugh. b 47. Linc Th Coll 76. **d** 79 **p** 80. C Bulkington *Cov* 79-82; P-in-c Whitley 82-87; Chapl Whitley, Gulson & Cov and Warks Hosp 82-87; Chapl Walsgrave Hosp Cov 87-97; Hon Can Cov Cathl 92-98; Succ 00-05; Perm to Offic 97-00 and 05-07; P-in-c Cov St Mary from 07. *95 Potters Green Road, Coventry CV2 2AN* Tel (024) 7662 2683 Mobile 07947-023888 E-mail drx2robinson@talktalk.net

ROBINSON, David Mark. b 55. Univ Coll Dur BSc76 Leic Univ MA80 CQSW80. Cranmer Hall Dur 86. **d** 88 **p** 89. C Shipley St Pet *Bradf* 88-92; P-in-c Ingrow cum Hainworth 92-97; V Bramhope *Ripon* 97-05; V Chapel Allerton from 05. *The Vicarage, Wood Lane, Chapel Allerton, Leeds LS7 3QF* Tel 0113-268 3072

ROBINSON, David Michael Wood. *See* WOOD-ROBINSON, David Michael

ROBINSON, Deborah Veronica. b 73. St Andr Univ MTheol95 Hull Univ MA97. NEOC 05. **d** 08 **p** 09. NSM Darlington St Hilda and St Columba *Dur* from 08. *37 Acacia Street, Darlington DL3 6QD* Tel (01325) 265434 Mobile 07971-549439 E-mail deborah.robinson5@ntlworld.com

ROBINSON, Capt Denis Hugh. b 53. SS Mark & Jo Univ Coll Plymouth CertEd75. Sarum & Wells Th Coll 88. **d** 91 **p** 92. NSM Bisley and W End *Guildf* from 91; Asst Chapl Gordon's Sch Woking 91-94; Chapl from 94. *2A Queen's Road, Bisley, Woking GU24 9AN* Tel (01276) 857624 E-mail steviedenrob@aol.com

ROBINSON, Canon Dennis Winston. b 42. QUB BScEng68. CITC. **d** 88 **p** 89. NSM Mullavilly *Arm* 88-92; NSM Arm St Mark 92-95; C Portadown St Mark 95-98; I Aghavea *Clogh* from 98; Preb Clogh Cathl from 06. *The Rectory, Brookeborough, Enniskillen BT94 4EE* Tel (028) 8953 1210
E-mail dw.robinson@btopenworld.com
or aghavea@clogher.anglican.org

ROBINSON, Derek Charles. b 43. S'wark Ord Course 91. **d** 94 **p** 95. NSM Abbey Wood *S'wark* from 94. *19 Silverdale Road, Bexleyheath DA7 5AB* Tel (01322) 523870

ROBINSON, Dorothy Ann. b 50. Cranmer Hall Dur 05. **d** 07 **p** 08. NSM Tynemouth Priory *Newc* from 07. *57 Millview Drive, North Shields NE30 2QD* Tel and fax 0191-257 9980
E-mail dottirobinson@hotmail.com

ROBINSON, Douglas. b 48. Nottm Univ BEd70 Lon Univ BD74 Union Th Sem Virginia MA75. **d** 75 **p** 76. C Southport Ch Ch *Liv* 75-78; V Clubmoor 78-85; Chapl Epsom Coll 85-88; Chapl Dauntsey's Sch Devizes 89-95; Perm to Offic *Eur* from 95. *Im Grunen Weg 1, Hungen Wieshcim 55234, Germany* Tel (0049) (6375) 941575 E-mail reverendrobinson@t-online.de

ROBINSON, Elizabeth Carole Lesley. b 67. CITC 99. **d** 02 **p** 03. Aux Min Clonfert Gp *L & K* 02-06; Aux Min Roscrea w Kyle, Bourney and Corbally from 06. *St Cronan's Rectory, Roscrea, Co Tipperary, Republic of Ireland* Tel and fax (00353) (505) 21725 Mobile 87-909 1561 E-mail kandlrobinson@eircom.net

ROBINSON, Eric Charles. b 47. Lon Univ BD71 Lanc Univ MA97. CBDTI 94. **d** 97 **p** 98. NSM Carl St Cuth w St Mary 97-99; C Kendal H Trin 99-01; P-in-c Arthuret 01-07; P-in-c Nicholforest and Kirkandrews on Esk 01-07; R Arthuret w Kirkandrews-on-Esk and Nicholforest 07-08; P-in-c Kendal H Trin from 08. *Holy Trinity Vicarage, 2 Lynngarth Drive, Kendal LA9 4JA* Tel (01539) 721541

ROBINSON, Frank. *See* ROBINSON, John Francis Napier

ROBINSON, George. b 27. Oak Hill Th Coll 59. **d** 61 **p** 62. C Branksome St Clem *Sarum* 61-64; Australia from 64; rtd 80. *24 Abingdon Road, Roseville NSW 2069, Australia* Tel (0061) (2) 9416 4330 Fax 9416 9936
E-mail mandgrobinson@ozemail.com.au

ROBINSON, Mrs Gillian Dawn. b 69. Edin Univ BD91. Trin Coll Bris 94. **d** 96 **p** 97. C Totton *Win* 96-00; P-in-c Roughtown *Man* 00-07. *Address temp unknown*
E-mail gill@robinson.camnews.net

ROBINSON, Mrs Hazel. b 61. RGN83 RSCN83. St Jo Coll Nottm 02. **d** 04 **p** 05. C Toton *S'well* 04-09; P-in-c Blidworth w Rainworth from 09. *The Vicarage, 27 St Peter's Drive, Rainworth, Mansfield NG21 0BE* Tel (01623) 475135 Mobile 07944-440941 E-mail haze.rob@btinternet.com

ROBINSON, Canon Ian. b 57. Nottm Univ BTh87 MA97. Linc Th Coll 84. **d** 87 **p** 88. C Bottesford w Ashby *Linc* 87-90; TV

90-95; P-in-c Caistor w Clixby 95-00; P-in-c Grasby 95-00; P-in-c Searby w Owmby 95-00; V Caistor Gp from 00; RD W Wold from 01; Can and Preb Linc Cathl from 07. *3 Spa Top, Caistor, Market Rasen LN7 6RB* Tel (01472) 851339
E-mail revianrobinson@tiscali.co.uk

ROBINSON, Ian Cameron. b 19. OBE72. Em Coll Cam BA40 MA44. Linc Th Coll 71. **d** 72 **p** 73. C Ipswich St Aug *St E* 72-74; V Darsham 74-84; V Westleton w Dunwich 74-84; RD Saxmundham 79-83; rtd 84; Perm to Offic *St E* 84-03. *Corner House, Rectory Street, Halesworth IP19 8BS* Tel (01986) 873573

ROBINSON, Ian Morgan. b 53. Lanc Univ BA08 CEng86 MCIBSE86. CBDTI 05. **d** 08 **p** 09. NSM Askrigg w Stallingbusk *Ripon* from 08. *Tom Gill House, Thoralby, Leyburn DL8 3SU* Tel (01969) 663159 Mobile 07801-657988
E-mail revrobbo@btinternet.com

ROBINSON, Mrs Jane Hippisley. b 41. Somerville Coll Ox MA66 K Coll Lon PGCE. S Dios Minl Tr Scheme 88. **d** 91. NSM Ealing St Pet Mt Park *Lon* 91-96; NSM N Acton St Gabr 96-00; Perm to Offic from 00. *40 Brentham Way, London W5 1BE* Tel (020) 8991 0206

ROBINSON, Mrs Janet. b 34. Milton Keynes Coll of Ed CertEd77 Open Univ BA78. WMMTC 89. **d** 92 **p** 94. NSM Roade and Ashton w Hartwell *Pet* 92-94; NSM Potterspury, Furtho, Yardley Gobion and Cosgrove 94-99; rtd 99; Perm to Offic *Pet* from 99. *73 Eastfield Crescent, Yardley Gobion, Towcester NN12 7TT* Tel (01908) 542331

ROBINSON, Mrs Jean Anne. b 50. Lon Univ BPharm72 MRPharmS73 Southn Univ BTh98. STETS 95. **d** 98 **p** 99. NSM Frimley *Guildf* 98-03; NSM Worplesdon 03-05; NSM Egham Hythe 05-07; C Woodham from 07; Chapl Surrey and Borders Partnership NHS Trust from 05; Chapl Alpha Hosp Woking from 06. *4 Chequer Tree Close, Knaphill, Woking GU21 2PB* Tel (01483) 481825 E-mail revjar@yahoo.co.uk

ROBINSON, Jennifer Elizabeth. b 53. Sheff Hallam Univ BA96. NOC 01. **d** 04 **p** 06. NSM Fishlake w Sykehouse and Kirk Bramwith etc *Sheff* 04-08; Perm to Offic from 08. *The Fold, 5 Old School Close, Armthorpe, Doncaster DN3 2SA* Tel (01302) 830087 E-mail jenny@ardyne.freeserve.co.uk

ROBINSON, John Francis Napier (Frank). b 42. St Edm Hall Ox BA64 MA68. Clifton Th Coll 65. **d** 68 **p** 69. C Southport Ch Ch *Liv* 68-71; C Coleraine *Conn* 71-74; Deputation Sec (Ireland) BCMS 74-76; TV Marfleet *York* 76-81; V Yeadon St Jo *Bradf* 81-95; P-in-c Rounds Green *Birm* 95-00; V 00-02; rtd 02; Perm to Offic *Derby* and *S'well* from 03. *61 Clumber Avenue, Beeston, Nottingham NG9 4BH* Tel 0115-922 1704

ROBINSON, The Very Revd John Kenneth. b 36. K Coll Lon BD61 AKC61. **d** 62 **p** 63. C Poulton-le-Fylde *Blackb* 62-65; C Lancaster St Mary 65-66; Chapl HM Pris Lanc 65-66; Chapl St Jo Sch Singapore 66-68; V Colne H Trin *Blackb* 68-71; Dir Educn Windward Is 71-74; V Skerton St Luke *Blackb* 74-81; Area Sec (E Anglia) USPG 81-91; Hon Min Can St E Cathl 82-91; Chapl Gtr Lisbon *Eur* 91-00; Adn Gib 94-02; Can Gib Cathl 94-00; Dean Gib 00-03; rtd 03; Perm to Offic *Blackb* from 03. *9 Poplar Drive, Coppull, Chorley PR7 4LS* Tel (01257) 470042

ROBINSON, John Leonard William. b 23. Lon Univ BA50. Bps' Coll Cheshunt 50. **d** 52 **p** 53. C Victoria Docks Ascension *Chelmsf* 52-55; C Kilburn St Aug *Lon* 55-63; C Westmr St Jas 63-81, V Compton, the Mardens, Stoughton and Racton *Chich* 81-93; V Stansted 85-93; rtd 93; Perm to Offic *St Alb* from 93 and *Lon* from 96. *19 Greenhill Park, Barnet EN5 1HQ* Tel (020) 8449 3984

ROBINSON, Jonathan William Murrell. b 42. Univ of Wales (Lamp) MA01. Sarum Th Coll 65. **d** 68 **p** 69. C Tooting All SS *S'wark* 68-71; C Bourne *Guildf* 71-76; Dir Grail Trust from 76; Dir Grail Trust Chr Community Cen Burtle *B & W* 78-82; Hon C Willesden Green St Gabr *Lon* 78-82; V Stoke St Gregory w Burrowbridge and Lyng *B & W* 82-90; Dir Grail Retreat Cen from 90; NSM Aymestrey and Leinthall Earles w Wigmore etc *Heref* 92-96; rtd 01; Perm to Offic *Heref* from 01 and *St D* 05-07. *Grail Barn, Church Stoke, Montgomery SY15 6TH* Tel (01588) 620779

ROBINSON, Kathryn Elizabeth. b 55. Hull Univ BA76 K Coll Lon MSc86 St Hilda's Coll Ox PGCE77. NTMTC 03. **d** 05 **p** 06. NSM Leytonstone St Jo *Chelmsf* from 05. *54 Corbett Road, London E17 3JZ* Tel (020) 8503 6023
E-mail kthrynrbnsn@aol.com

ROBINSON, Keith. b 48. Lon Univ BA75 BD77 AKC77. Westcott Ho Cam 77. **d** 78 **p** 79. C Bow w Bromley St Leon *Lon* 78-81; C Leighton Buzzard w Eggington, Hockliffe etc *St Alb* 81-88; PV Westmr Abbey 82-90; V Bulkington w Shilton and Ansty *Cov* 90-95; P-in-c Salisbury St Martin *Sarum* 95-00; P-in-c Laverstock 95-00; R Salisbury St Martin and Laverstock from 00; RD Salisbury 98-03. *The Rectory, Tollgate Road, Salisbury SP1 2JJ* Tel (01722) 504813 *or* tel and fax 503123
E-mail frkeithssm@yahoo.co.uk

ROBINSON, Kenneth. *See* ROBINSON, The Very Revd John Kenneth

ROBINSON, Kenneth Borwell. b 37. Lon Univ BA62. Ridley Hall Cam 68. **d** 70 **p** 71. C Walthamstow St Jo *Chelmsf* 70-74; P-in-c Becontree St Alb 74-78; P-in-c Heybridge w Langford 78-84; TV Horley *S'wark* 84-98; C Oxted and Tandridge 98-02; rtd 02; Perm to Offic *Portsm* from 03. *49 Osborne Road, East Cowes PO32 6RZ* Tel (01983) 295736

ROBINSON, Lesley. *See* ROBINSON, Elizabeth Carole Lesley

ROBINSON, Leslie. b 31. St Aid Birkenhead 56. **d** 59 **p** 60. C Hugglescote w Donington *Leic* 59-61; C Greenside *Dur* 61-63; C-in-c New Cantley CD *Sheff* 63-66; V Choral Heref Cathl 66-67; R Easton-on-the-Hill *Pet* 67-69; Hon Min Can Pet Cathl 68-69; C Weston-super-Mare St Jo *B & W* 69-70; V Winkleigh *Ex* 70-72; V Thorpe Acre w Dishley *Leic* 72-78; V Cloughton *York* 78-79; V Hedon w Paull 79-81; V Bywell *Newc* 81-86; V Wymeswold and Prestwold w Hoton *Leic* 86-97; rtd 97; Perm to Offic *Leic* 97-98. *16 Victoria Road, Oundle, Peterborough PE8 4AY* Tel (01832) 275048

ROBINSON, Miss Margaret. b 32. S'wark Ord Course 83. **dss** 86 **d** 87 **p** 94. Finsbury St Clem w St Barn and St Matt *Lon* 86-87; Par Dn St Giles Cripplegate w St Bart Moor Lane etc 87-94; C 94-95; rtd 95; Perm to Offic *Win* 95-00; Hon Chapl Win Cathl 98-00. *10 Barnfield Road, Petersfield GU31 4DQ* Tel (01730) 268056

ROBINSON, Monica Dorothy. b 40. SAOMC 99. **d** 01 **p** 02. NSM Bedford St Andr *St Alb* from 01. *Shoyswell, Radwell Road, Milton Ernest, Bedford MK44 1RY* Tel (01234) 824366 E-mail mdrobinson@btopenworld.com

ROBINSON, The Ven Neil. b 29. St Jo Coll Dur BA52. **d** 54 **p** 55. C Kingston upon Hull H Trin *York* 54-58; V Glen Parva and S Wigston *Leic* 58-68; Hon Can Leic Cathl 68-83; RD Sparkenhoe I 69-83; R Market Bosworth w Shenton 69-83; Can Res Worc Cathl 83-87; Adn Suffolk *St E* 87-94; rtd 94; Perm to Offic *Ripon* from 94. *16 Mallorie Court, Ripon HG4 2QG* Tel (01765) 603075

ROBINSON, Norman Leslie. b 50. Liv Univ BSc71. Lon Bible Coll BA78 Wycliffe Hall Ox 78. **d** 80 **p** 81. C Bebington *Ches* 80-83; C St Helens St Helen *Liv* 83-90; P-in-c Westward, Rosley-w-Woodside and Welton *Carl* from 90; P-in-c Thursby from 98. *The Vicarage, Rosley, Wigton CA7 8AU* Tel (01697) 343723 E-mail normalrevs@aol.com

ROBINSON, Paul Andrew. b 68. Hull Univ MBA09. **d** 09. OLM Royton St Anne *Man* from 09. *19 Dorchester Drive, Royton, Oldham OL2 5AU* Tel 0161-628 9019 Mobile 07984-938393 E-mail paul@nomoreproblems.co.uk

ROBINSON, Canon Paul Leslie. b 46. Dur Univ BA67. Linc Th Coll 71. **d** 74 **p** 75. C Poynton *Ches* 74-76; C Prenton 76-78; V Seacombe 78-88; V Stalybridge St Paul 88-00; P-in-c Wallasey St Hilary 00-04; R from 04; Urban Min Officer 96-00; Hon Can Ches Cathl from 98. *St Hilary's Rectory, Church Hill, Wallasey CH45 3NH* Tel 0151-638 4771 E-mail paul@canonrobinson.plus.com

ROBINSON, Paul Leslie. b 65. St Steph Ho Ox 95. **d** 97 **p** 98. C Upholland *Liv* 97-01; V Lydiate and Downholland 01-08; P-in-c Halsall 04-08; R Halsall, Lydiate and Downholland from 08. *The Vicarage, Church Lane, Lydiate, Liverpool L31 4HL* Tel 0151-526 0512 E-mail frpaul.robinson@btopenworld.com

ROBINSON, Paula Patricia. b 50. Man Univ MEd83 TCD BTh94. **d** 94 **p** 95. C Killala w Dunfeeny, Crossmolina, Kilmoremoy etc *T, K & A* 94-97; I Crosspatrick Gp *C & O* 97-00; R Leonardtown St Andr USA 00-09; P-in-c Healaugh w Wighill, Bilbrough and Askham Richard *York* from 09; P-in-c Long Marston from 09; P-in-c Rufforth w Moor Monkton and Hessay from 09; P-in-c Tockwith and Bilton w Bickerton from 09. *The Vicarage, Wetherby Road, Rufforth, York YO23 3QF* E-mail revpaula@olg.com

ROBINSON, Canon Peter Charles. b 53. Open Univ BA83. Oak Hill Th Coll 85. **d** 87 **p** 88. C Nottingham St Ann w Em *S'well* 87-89; C Worksop St Anne 89-92; V S Ramsey St Paul *S & M* 92-99; Can St German's Cathl 98-99; P-in-c Goostrey and Dioc Dir of Ords *Ches* 99-03; P-in-c Aldeburgh w Hazlewood *St E* 03-04; C Arbory *S & M* 05-06; V from 06; C Santan 05-06; V from 06; C Castletown 05-06; V from 06; RD Castletown and Peel from 08; Hon Can St German's Cathl from 09. *The Vicarage, Arbory Road, Castletown, Isle of Man IM9 1ND* Tel (01624) 823509 Mobile 07941-202524 E-mail pcrwoodbridge@aol.com

ROBINSON, Peter Edward Barron. b 40. Open Univ BSc99. Sarum & Wells Th Coll 76. **d** 78 **p** 79. C Petersfield w Sheet *Portsm* 78-82; R Bentworth and Shalden and Lasham *Win* 82-88; R W Horsley *Guildf* 88-00; rtd 00; Perm to Offic *B & W* from 01. *Byways, Kingstone, Ilminster TA19 0NT* Tel (01460) 259016 E-mail peb.robinson@ntlworld.com

ROBINSON, The Ven Peter John Alan. b 61. St Jo Coll Cam BA83 MA87 St Jo Coll Dur BA92 PhD97. Cranmer Hall Dur 90. **d** 95 **p** 96. C N Shields *Newc* 95-99; P-in-c Byker St Martin 99-08; P-in-c Byker St Mich w St Lawr 01-08; Hon Can Newc Cathl 07-08; Adn Lindisfarne from 08. *4 Acomb Close, Morpeth NE61 2YH* Tel (01670) 503810 Fax 510469 E-mail p.robinson@newcastle.anglican.org

ROBINSON, Peter McCall. b 24. Worc Coll Ox BA48 MA50. Wells Th Coll 48. **d** 50 **p** 51. S Africa 50-54; C Stoke Poges *Ox* 55-57; S Africa 57-71; V Payhembury *Ex* 71-79; R Cheriton Tichborne and Beauworth *Win* 79-81; S Africa 81-82; V Marystowe, Coryton, Stowford, Lewtrenchard etc *Ex* 82-85; V Blackawton and Stoke Fleming 85-88; rtd 88; Perm to Offic *Ex* from 89. *2 Langwells Court, Blackawton, Totnes TQ9 7BG* Tel (01803) 712827

ROBINSON, Philip. b 38. S Dios Minl Tr Scheme 88. **d** 91 **p** 92. NSM Ickenham *Lon* 91-95; P-in-c 95-04; P-in-c Hayes St Anselm 98-99; P-in-c Harlington 98-00; AD Hillingdon 97-03; rtd 04; Perm to Offic *Lon* and *Eur* from 04. *5 Preston Court, 4 Fairfield Road, Uxbridge UB8 1DQ* Tel (01895) 200303 *or* (0033) (4) 93 04 75 11 E-mail philip@stjean.fslife.co.uk

ROBINSON, Philip John. b 50. St Luke's Coll Ex CertEd71. NOC 04. **d** 06 **p** 07. NSM Macclesfield Team *Ches* from 06. *6 Sevenoaks Close, Macclesfield SK10 3BE* Tel (01625) 610579 E-mail p.robinson233@ntlworld.com

ROBINSON, Raymonde Robin. b 43. St Jo Coll Dur BA66. Chich Th Coll 67. **d** 70 **p** 71. C Ealing St Barn *Lon* 70-72; C Pinner 72-75; C Clerkenwell H Redeemer w St Phil 75-80; TV Kingsthorpe w Northampton St Dav *Pet* 80-89; R Letchworth *St Alb* 89-95; V Noel Park St Mark *Lon* 95-06; rtd 06. *12 West Hill Street, Brighton BN1 3RR* Tel (01273) 728778

ROBINSON, Richard Hugh. b 35. St Jo Coll Cam BA58 MA62. Ridley Hall Cam 58. **d** 60 **p** 81. C Cheadle Hulme St Andr *Ches* 60-62; Hon C Alvanley 62-64; Perm to Offic *York* 64-80; Hon C Elloughton and Brough w Brantingham 80-86; C 86-87; Ext Dir CMJ 87-88; NSM Appleby *Carl* 91-93; Perm to Offic *Carl* and *York* 93-98; *Ely* 01-04; rtd 00. *26 Paradise Street, Cambridge CB1 1DR* Tel (01223) 328833 Fax 328838

ROBINSON, Canon Roger George. b 24. Qu Coll Cam BA46 MA50. Ridley Hall Cam 46. **d** 48 **p** 49. C Gorleston St Andr *Nor* 48-51; C Drypool St Andr and St Pet *York* 51-54; P-in-c Kingston upon Hull St Aid Southcoates 54-55; V 55-60; V Clifton 60-70; Chapl Clifton Hosp York 61-70; V Far Headingley St Chad *Ripon* 70-81; RD Headingley 72-81; Hon Can Ripon Cathl 81; R Drayton w Felthorpe *Nor* 81-91; rtd 91; Perm to Offic *Ripon* from 91. *24 St Matthew's Walk, Leeds LS7 3PS* Tel 0113-269 6307

ROBINSON, Ronald Frederick. b 46. Brasted Place Coll 72. Oak Hill Th Coll 74. **d** 76 **p** 77. C Pennington *Man* 76-77; C Bedhampton *Portsm* 77-79; C Portsea N End St Mark 79-82; V 90-92; R Rowner 82-90; Perm to Offic *Portsm* 93-02; P-in-c Bury and Houghton *Chich* 96-97; P-in-c Coldwaltham and Hardham 96-97; P-in-c Bury w Houghton and Coldwaltham and Hardham 97-98; V 98; Past Sec Ch Union 98-02; P-in-c Portsea Ascension *Portsm* 02-05; V from 05. *The Vicarage, 98 Kirby Road, Portsmouth PO2 0PW* Tel (023) 9266 0123 Fax 9266 7499 E-mail fr.robinson@talk21.com

ROBINSON, Roy David. b 35. AKC59. **d** 60 **p** 61. C Acocks Green *Birm* 60-62; C Shirley 62-65; C Haslemere *Guildf* 65-70; R Headley w Box Hill 70-85; V Hinchley Wood 85-00; rtd 00; Perm to Offic *Guildf* from 02. *1 Park Road, Slinfold, Horsham RH13 0SD* Tel (01403) 791640

ROBINSON, Prof Simon John. b 51. Edin Univ MA72 PhD89 Ox Univ BA77. Wycliffe Hall Ox 75. **d** 78 **p** 79. C Haughton le Skerne *Dur* 78-81; Chapl Asst N Tees Hosp Stockton-on-Tees 81-83; C Norton St Mary 81-83; Chapl Heriot-Watt Univ 83-90; R Dalmahoy 83-90; Chapl Leeds Univ 90-04; P-in-c Leeds Em 90-04; Prof Ethics Leeds Metrop Univ from 04; NSM Leeds City from 05. *42 Woodside Avenue, Meanwood, Leeds LS7 2UL* Tel 0113-283 7440 Mobile 07931-916381 E-mail s.j.robinson@leedsmet.ac.uk

✠**ROBINSON, The Rt Revd Stuart Peter.** b 59. Moore Th Coll Sydney BTh85. ACT. **d** 87 **p** 87 **c** 09. C Miranda Australia 87-89; Asst Min Doonside and Quakers Hill 89-91; C-in-c Quakers Hill 91-97; Perm to Offic *Ox* 96; Chapl Tervuren *Eur* 98-01; P-in-c Liège 98-00; Sen Assoc Ev Dept Evang Min Australia 01-09; R Chatswood 05-09; Bp Canberra and Goulburn from 09. *GPO Box 1981, Canberra ACT 2601, Australia* Tel (0061) (2) 6248 0811 Fax 6247 6829

ROBINSON, Mrs Teresa Jane. b 56. SAOMC 98. **d** 01 **p** 02. OLM The Cookhams *Ox* 01-08; NSM Maidenhead St Luke from 08. *7 Golden Ball Lane, Maidenhead SL6 6NW* Tel (01628) 634107 E-mail terrie@7goldenball.freeserve.co.uk

ROBINSON, Canon Thomas Fisher. b 20. St Jo Coll Dur BA49. **d** 50 **p** 51. C Pendlebury St Jo *Man* 50-54; C Davyhulme St Mary 54-56; V Litherland St Andr *Liv* 56-62; V Wigan St Cath 62-67; V Garston 67-88; Hon Can Liv Cathl 85-88; rtd 88; Perm to Offic *Liv* from 88. *208 Mather Avenue, Liverpool L18 9TG* Tel 0151-475 7870

ROBINSON, Tiffer. *See* ROBINSON, Christopher Mark Scott

ROBINSON, Timothy. b 56. Hull Univ BSc78 Liv Univ PhD83 St Jo Coll Dur BA07 FGA86. Cranmer Hall Dur 05. **d** 07 **p** 08. C Nantwich *Ches* from 07. *22 Beatty Road, Nantwich CW5 5JP* Tel (01270) 623620 Mobile 07981-108779 E-mail timrobbo@aol.com

ROBINSON, Timothy James. b 59. Middx Poly BA84 Coll of Ripon & York St Jo PGCE00. St Steph Ho Ox 88. **d** 91 **p** 92. C W Acklam *York* 91-95; P-in-c N Ormesby 95-96; V 96-99; Teacher Hall Garth Sch Middlesbrough from 00; Perm to Offic *Ripon* 99-02; Tutor NEOC from 02. *Manor Farm, Watermill Lane, North Stainley, Ripon HG4 3HT* Tel (01765) 635067
E-mail tim.robinson@north-stainley.net

ROBINSON, Miss Tracy. b 75. Univ of Zimbabwe BSc98. Wycliffe Hall Ox 03 Ripon Coll Cuddesdon MA09. **d** 09. C Fordingbridge and Breamore and Hale etc *Win* from 09. *19 Falconwood Close, Fordingbridge SP6 1TB* Tel (01425) 657516 *or* 653112 E-mail team.curate@googlemail.com

ROBINSON-MULLER, Mrs Ank. b 75. Radboud Univ Nijmegen MA04. ERMC 07. **d** 09. C E Netherlands *Eur* from 09. *Adolf van Nieuwenaarlaan 3A, 6824 AM Arnhem, The Netherlands* Tel (0031) (26) 322 9531
E-mail ank_muller@yahoo.com

ROBOTTOM, David Leonard Douglas. b 40. Qu Coll Birm 80 Sarum & Wells Th Coll 81. **d** 83 **p** 84. C Uppingham w Ayston and Wardley w Belton *Pet* 83-87; TV Sidmouth, Woolbrook and Salcombe Regis *Ex* 87-91; TV Sidmouth, Woolbrook, Salcombe Regis, Sidbury etc 91-95; R Bradninch and Clyst Hydon from 95; RD Cullompton from 03. *The Rectory, 27 West End Road, Bradninch, Exeter EX5 4QS* Tel (01392) 881264
E-mail su2312@eclipse.co.uk

ROBSON, Alan. *See* ROBSON, Gilbert Alan.

ROBSON, Angus William. b 13. Kelham Th Coll 32. **d** 38 **p** 39. C Regent Square St Pet *Lon* 38-40; CM Mill End *St Alb* 40-45; CF 43-45; P-in-c Luton St Pet 45; Perm to Offic *St Alb* 45-46; V Sark *Win* 46-50; V Jersey St Jas 50-75; Chapl HM Pris Jersey 60-75; rtd 78; Perm to Offic *Win* 78-98. *Flat 1, La Petite Carrière, Wellington Road, St Helier, Jersey JE2 4RJ* Tel (01534) 31656

ROBSON, Claire English. b 62. Middx Poly BEd88. Westcott Ho Cam 96. **d** 99 **p** 00. C Dorchester *Sarum* 99-02; C Kilburn St Mary w All So and W Hampstead St Jas *Lon* 02-04; Min Can and Chapl St Paul's Cathl from 04. *7B Amen Court, London EC4M 7BU* Tel (020) 7246 8323
E-mail chaplain@stpaulscathedral.org.uk

ROBSON, Gilbert Alan. b 30. St Pet Hall Ox BA53 MA57. Linc Th Coll 56. **d** 57 **p** 58. C Chatham St Mary w St Jo *Roch* 57-59; Sub Warden Roch Th Coll 59-62; Min Can Roch Cathl 59-62; Bp's Dom Chapl 61-64; Chapl Roch Th Coll 62-64; R Wouldham *Roch* 62-64; Chapl Nor Coll of Educn 65-68; Sen Lect in Div 68-72; V Shotwick *Ches* 72-74; Dioc Dir of Ords 72-74; Bp's Dom Chapl 72-74; Hd of Div Eton Coll Windsor 74-89; R Wrotham *Roch* 89-95; rtd 95; Perm to Offic *Nor* from 95. *3 Staden Park, Trimingham, Norwich NR11 8HX* Tel (01263) 834887

ROBSON, Howard. *See* ROBSON, John Howard

ROBSON, Preb Ian Leonard. b 32. K Coll Lon MA00. Bps' Coll Cheshunt 61. **d** 63 **p** 64. C Croxley Green All SS *St Alb* 63-65; C Harpenden St Nic 65-68; V Redbourn 68-72; V Ashford St Matt *Lon* 72-77; V Kensington St Mary Abbots w St Geo 77-97; AD Kensington 94-97; Preb St Paul's Cathl 96-97; rtd 97; Perm to Offic *Chich* from 97. *Wepham Lodge, Wepham, Arundel BN18 9RA* Tel (01903) 884667 E-mail robsonoblate@aol.com

ROBSON, James Edward. b 65. Pemb Coll Ox BA88 Middx Univ PhD05. Wycliffe Hall Ox 91. **d** 94 **p** 95. C Enfield Ch Ch Trent Park *Lon* 94-98; C Oakwood St Thos 98-00; Tutor Oak Hill Th Coll 00-09; Tutor Wycliffe Hall Ox from 09. *Wycliffe Hall, 54 Banbury Road, Oxford OX2 6PW* Tel (01865) 274200

ROBSON, John Howard. b 60. Newc Univ BA81 ACIB87. Cranmer Hall Dur 98. **d** 00 **p** 01. C Hethersett w Canteloff w Lt and Gt Melton *Nor* 00-04; R Brooke, Kirstead, Mundham w Seething and Thwaite from 04. *The Vicarage, 105 The Street, Brooke, Norwich NR15 1JU* Tel (01508) 550378

ROBSON, John Phillips. b 32. LVO99. St Edm Hall Ox. AKC58. **d** 59 **p** 60. C Huddersfield SS Pet and Paul *Wakef* 59-62; Asst Chapl Ch Hosp Horsham 62-65; Chapl 65-80; Sen Chapl Wellington Coll Berks 80-89; Chapl to RVO and Qu Chpl of the Savoy 89-02; Chapl to The Queen 93-02; rtd 02; Extra Chapl to The Queen from 02. *A2 Odhams Walk, London WC2H 9SA* Tel (020) 7240 7662

ROBSON, Mrs Margery June. b 44. Darlington Tr Coll CertEd65. St Steph Ho Ox 92. **d** 94 **p** 95. C Tuffley *Glouc* 94-98; V Darlington St Mark w St Paul *Dur* 98-03; Chapl Metro Cen Gateshead 03-06; rtd 06. *23 Carr House Mews, Consett DH8 6FD* Tel (01207) 581270

ROBSON, Martin Douglas. b 62. St Andr Univ MTheol85 Cam Univ PGCE88 Edin Univ MTh94. Edin Th Coll 92. **d** 94 **p** 95. C Perth St Ninian *St And* 94-97; P-in-c Lockerbie *Glas* 97-01; P-in-c Moffat 97-01; R Edin St Fillan from 01. *St Fillan's Rectory, 8 Buckstone Drive, Edinburgh EH10 6PD* Tel 0131-445 2942 E-mail stfillan@blueyonder.co.uk

ROBSON, Pamela Jean. b 44. STETS 94. **d** 97 **p** 98. NSM W Ewell *Guildf* 97-01; NSM Wotton and Holmbury St Mary from 02. *The Rectory, Horsham Road, Holmbury St Mary, Dorking RH5 6NL* Tel (01306) 730285
E-mail pamrobson@waitrose.com

ROBSON, Canon Patricia Anne. b 40. MBE99. CertEd60. SW Minl Tr Course 85. **d** 87 **p** 94. Dioc Youth Officer *Truro* 87-92; Hon C Paul 87-92; Hon C Kenwyn St Geo 88-92; Dn-in-c St Enoder 92-94; P-in-c 94-05; P-in-c Newlyn St Newlyn 03-05; Hon Can Truro Cathl 98-05; RD Pydar 02-03; rtd 05; P-in-c St Goran w Caerhays *Truro* from 06. *The Vicarage, Gorran, St Austell PL26 6HN* Tel (01726) 844457
E-mail intercelt@aol.com

ROBSON, Paul Coutt. b 37. Leeds Univ BA60. Coll of Resurr Mirfield 63. **d** 64 **p** 65. C Stokesay *Heref* 64-66; C St Geo Cathl Cape Town 66-68; R Roodebloem All SS 68-70; Chapl HM Pris Man 70-71; Chapl HM Borstal Feltham 71-74; Hollesley Bay 74-78; Chapl HM Pris Grendon and Spring Hill 78-85; Norwich 85-92; Chapl HM YOI and Remand Cen Brinsford 92-99; rtd 99; Perm to Offic *Heref* 00-01 and from 04; P-in-c Wistanstow 01-04. *Pilgrims, Henley Common, Church Stretton SY6 6RS* Tel (01694) 781221 E-mail smrpcr@lineone.net

ROBSON, Peter. b 58. Leeds Univ BEd80. Cranmer Hall Dur 05. **d** 07 **p** 08. C Bishopwearmouth St Gabr from 07. *35 Charter Drive, Sunderland SR3 3PG* Tel 0191-528 2848
E-mail peterpoprobson@aol.co.uk

ROBSON, Peter Cole. b 45. Clare Coll Cam BA66 MA70 Oriel Coll Ox BLitt69 MLitt70. Coll of Resurr Mirfield 70. **d** 71 **p** 72. C Gt Grimsby St Mary and St Jas *Linc* 71-73; Chapl BNC Ox 73-76; R Timsbury *B & W* 76-79; P-in-c Blanchland w Hunstanworth *Newc* 80-83; rtd 87. *c/o J W T Robson Esq, 54 Linkfield Road, Mountsorrel, Leicester LE12 7DL*

ROBSON, Stephen Thomas. b 54. Chich Th Coll 84. **d** 86 **p** 87. C Newc St Fran 86-89; C Gateshead St Cuth w St Paul *Dur* 89-91; TV Stanley 91-96; V Sugley *Newc* from 96. *Sugley Vicarage, Lemington, Newcastle upon Tyne NE15 8RD* Tel 0191-267 4633

ROBSON, William. b 34. FCIS66 FCCA80. Sarum & Wells Th Coll 77. **d** 79 **p** 80. C Lymington *Win* 79-81; CF 81-93; V Barton Stacey and Bullington etc *Win* 93-98; rtd 98; Hon C Knaresborough *Ripon* 98-01; Perm to Offic *Newc* 03-04; Hon C Barrow upon Soar w Walton le Wolds *Leic* 04-07; Hon C Wymeswold and Prestwold w Hoton 04-07. *5 Churchill Way, Painswick, Stroud GL6 6RQ* Tel (01452) 814540
E-mail knotsbarn@talktalk.net

ROBUS, Keith Adrian. b 59. Heythrop Coll Lon MA01 MHCIMA82. Chich Th Coll 85. **d** 88 **p** 89. C Greenhill St Jo *Lon* 88-92; C Willesden St Matt 92-02; V N Acton St Gabr from 02; Chapl RN from 09. *Royal Naval Chaplaincy Service, Mail Point 1-2, Leach Building, Whale Island, Portsmouth PO2 8BY* Tel (023) 9262 5055 Fax 9262 5134
E-mail keith@robus.demon.co.uk

ROBY, Richard James. b 33. Imp Coll Lon BSc54 Lon Inst of Educn PGCE55. St Alb Minl Tr Scheme 82. **d** 85 **p** 86. NSM Bushey *St Alb* 85-92; NSM Wootton 92-00; rtd 00; Perm to Offic *St Alb* from 00. *5 Powis Mews, Flitwick, Bedford MK45 1SU* Tel (01525) 718529 E-mail richard.roby@ntlworld.com

ROCHDALE, Archdeacon of. *See* VANN, The Ven Cherry Elizabeth

ROCHE, Miss Alison Mary. b 70. Man Univ BSc91 Nottm Univ PGCE94. St Jo Coll Nottm MA00. **d** 01 **p** 02. C Leic Martyrs 01-05; P-in-c Leic St Chris 05-09; V from 09. *256 Milligan Road, Leicester LE2 8FD* Tel 0116-283 0510 Mobile 07918-642567
E-mail vicar@stchristophers.info

ROCHE, Barry Robert Francis. b 40. Lon Univ BD66 Ox Univ MTh93. Clifton Th Coll 63. **d** 68 **p** 69. C Beckenham Ch Ch *Roch* 68-72; C Chester le Street *Dur* 72-74; C-in-c N Bletchley CD *Ox* 74-78; R Luton Ch Ch *Roch* 78-92; Chapl All SS Hosp Chatham 78-92; TR Glascote and Stonydelph *Lich* 92-99; RD Tamworth 95-99; V Oulton Broad *Nor* 99-05; rtd 05. *24 Lakeside Close, Nantyglo, Ebbw Vale NP23 4EG* Tel (01495) 311048

ROCHESTER, Thomas Robson. b 33. NEOC 85. **d** 90 **p** 91. NSM Glendale Gp *Newc* 90-03; rtd 03; Perm to Offic *Newc* from 03. *Cushat Law, Thropton, Morpeth NE65 7HX* Tel (01669) 62079
E-mail trochester2@aol.com

ROCHESTER, Archdeacon of. *See* LOCK, The Ven Peter Harcourt D'Arcy

ROCHESTER, Bishop of. *Vacant*

ROCHESTER, Dean of. *See* NEWMAN, The Very Revd Adrian

ROCK, Mrs Jean. b 37. Gilmore Course 76. **dss** 79 **d** 87 **p** 97. Douglas St Matt *S & M* 79-81; Marown 81-83; Chapl Asst Oswestry and Distr Hosp 83-87; Oswestry St Oswald *Lich* 83-90; Par Dn 87-90; C-in-c Pont Robert and Pont Dolanog *St As* 90-97; V 97; rtd 97; Perm to Offic *Lich* from 99. *10 Wharf Cottages, Rhoswiel, Weston Rhyn, Oswestry SY10 7TD* Tel (01691) 773766

ROCKALL, Miss Valerie Jane. b 42. City of Cov Coll CertEd63. St Alb Minl Tr Scheme 78. **dss** 81 **d** 87 **p** 94. Asst Hd Wigginton Sch Tring 73-90; Boxmoor St Jo *St Alb* 81-87; NSM Hemel Hempstead 87-90; Par Dn Ampthill w Millbrook and Steppingley 90-93; TD Southampton (City Cen) *Win* 93-94; TV 94-99; P-in-c Aveley and Purfleet *Chelmsf* from 99. *The Vicarage, Mill Road, Aveley, South Ockendon RM15 4SR* Tel (01708) 891242

ROCKEY, Antony Nicolas. b 65. Kingston Poly BEng89 CEng94 MICE94 MCIWEM95. CBDTI 02. **d** 05 **p** 06. C Cockermouth Area *Carl* 05-09; P-in-c Fernhurst *Chich* from 09. *The Vicarage, Church Road, Fernhurst, Haslemere GU27 3HZ* Tel (01428) 652229

RODD, Philip Rankilor. b 60. Ex Univ BA79 K Coll Lon PGCE85. Ridley Hall Cam 03. **d** 05 **p** 06. C Heigham H Trin *Nor* 05-08; V Eaton St Andr from 08. *The Vicarage, 210 Newmarket Road, Norwich NR4 7LA* Tel (01603) 250915

RODDY, Keith Anthony. b 67. Leic Univ BA89. Oak Hill Th Coll BA09. **d** 09. C Chesterton *Lich* from 09. *17 Checkley Road, Newcastle ST5 7TN* Tel (01782) 560721 Mobile 07986-903110 E-mail keitharoddy@googlemail.com

RODE, Margaret. d 08. NSM Hedsor and Bourne End *Ox* from 08. *Address temp unknown* Tel 07855-952237 (mobile) E-mail maggie.rode@ntlworld.com

RODE, Nigel. d 08. NSM Chalfont St Peter *Ox* from 08. *Address temp unknown* E-mail nigel.rode@ntlworld.com

RODEL, Mark Neil. b 71. Southn Univ BA96. STETS 02. **d** 05 **p** 06. C Southsea St Jude *Portsm* 05-08; C Portsea St Luke from 08. *39 St Andrews Road, Portsmouth PO5 1ER* Tel 07748-272360 (mobile) Pager 07654-325425 E-mail curate@stjudes-southsea.org.uk

RODEN, Jo. *See* LOVERIDGE, Ms Joan Margaretha Holland

RODEN, John Michael. b 37. St Jo Coll York CertEd64 Open Univ BA82 MA92 York Univ DPhil96. Ripon Hall Ox 71. **d** 73 **p** 74. C Saltburn-by-the-Sea *York* 73-77; Chapl St Pet Sch York 77-82; Warden Marrick Priory *Ripon* 83; Hon C Appleton Roebuck w Acaster Selby *York* 84-85; P-in-c 86-03; Youth Officer 86-91; Sen Chapl Selby Coalfield Ind Chapl 96-03; rtd 03; Perm to Offic *York* from 03. *Ebor Cottage, 8 Copmanthorpe Grange, Copmanthorpe, York YO23 3TN* Tel (01904) 744826 E-mail rodenjohn@lineone.net

RODEN, Michael Adrian Holland. b 60. Ripon Coll Cuddesdon 82. **d** 85 **p** 86. C S Lambeth St Anne and All SS *S'wark* 85-88; C Wandsworth St Paul 88-90; C St Mary V w St Cross and St Pet 90-94; Chapl Wadh Coll Ox 90-94; R Steeple Aston w N Aston and Tackley *Ox* 94-02; TR Hitchin *St Alb* from 02; RD Hitchin from 07. *The Rectory, 21 West Hill, Hitchin SG5 2HZ* Tel (01462) 434017 *or* 452758 E-mail michaelroden@btinternet.com

RODERICK, Philip David. b 49. Univ of Wales (Swansea) BA70 Univ of Wales (Abth) BD77 Lon Univ CertEd71. Linc Th Coll 80. **d** 80 **p** 81. C Llanfair-is-gaer and Llanddeiniolen *Ban* 80-82; TV Holyhead w Rhoscolyn w Llanfair-yn-Neubwll 82-84; Chapl and Lect Th Univ of Wales (Ban) 84-88; Warden Angl Chapl Cen 84-88; Prin Bucks Chr Tr Scheme *Ox* 88-94; Dir Chiltern Chr Tr Progr 88-94; Dir Quiet Garden Trust from 92; Dir The Wells Inst from 96; V Amersham on the Hill *Ox* 96-04; Ldr Contemplative Fire from 04; Perm to Offic from 04. *21 Elm Close, Weston Turville, Aylesbury HP22 5SS* Tel (01296) 614597 E-mail philiproderick@btinternet.com

RODFORD, Canon Brian George. b 50. Hatf Poly BEd84. **d** 79 **p** 80. NSM St Alb St Steph *St Alb* 79-85; Chapl St Mary's Sch 81-90; Sen Teacher 83-90; Hon C Hendon St Mary and Golders Green *Lon* 85-90; Hon C Winchmore Hill H Trin 90-95; V Ponders End St Matt 95-02; Dir Chain Foundn Uganda from 02; Can All SS Cathl Kampala from 02; Perm to Offic *St Alb* 04-05. *Simon's Acre, 17 Pagasvlei Road, Constantia, 7806 South Africa* Tel (0027) (21) 794 8940 *or* (01727) 850382 E-mail brodford_chain@hotmail.com

RODGER, Canon Raymond. b 39. Westmr Coll Ox MTh93. Bps' Coll Cheshunt 62. **d** 63 **p** 64. C Frodingham *Linc* 63-66; Asst Chapl St Geo Hosp Lon 66-69; C Waltham *Linc* 69-73; V Nocton 73-86; P-in-c Potter Hanworth 74-86; P-in-c Dunston 77-86; RD Graffoe 81-92; Can and Preb Linc Cathl from 85; V Nocton w Dunston and Potterhanworth 86-92; Bp's Dom Chapl 92-05; Gen Preacher 92-05; rtd 05. *13 Lupin Road, Lincoln LN2 4GB* Tel (01522) 536723 Mobile 07803-123975 E-mail canrod@hotmail.com

RODGERS, Canon Cyril George Hooper. b 20. Qu Coll Birm 50. **d** 52 **p** 53. C Bishop's Cleeve *Glouc* 52-56; V Nailsworth 56-61; Chapl Longford's Approved Sch Minchinhampton 56-57; (TA) 58-62; R Upwell Christchurch *Ely* 61-66; CF (TA - R of O) 62-87; V Wiggenhall St Germans and Islington *Ely* 66-76; RD Lynn Marshland 68-76; R Woolpit *St E* 76-84; RD Lavenham 78-87; Hon Can St E Cathl 84-87; R Woolpit w Drinkstone 84-87; rtd 87; Perm to Offic *St E* from 87. *Fox Farm, Wetherden, Stowmarket IP14 3NE* Tel (01359) 40364

RODGERS, David. b 26. Sarum Th Coll 63. **d** 65 **p** 66. C Combe Down *B & W* 65-68; V Leigh Woods 68-76; R Wellow w Foxcote and Shoscombe 76-79; C Wells St Cuth w Coxley and Wookey Hole 79-82; P-in-c Wookey w Henton 79-82; V Ercall Magna *Lich* 82-89; V Rowton 82-89; RD Wrockwardine 84-89; rtd 89; Perm to Offic *B & W* from 98. *6 The Cloisters, South Street, Wells BA5 1SA*

RODGERS, Eamonn Joseph. b 41. QUB BA63 PhD70. TISEC 04. **d** 05 **p** 06. NSM Glas St Ninian from 05. *4 Albert Drive,*

Glasgow G73 3RT Tel 0141-583 6949 Mobile 07910-262983 E-mail eamonn.rodgers@mac.com *or* curate@stniniansglasgow.org.uk

RODGERS, Preb Frank Ernest. b 46. Tyndale Hall Bris 68. **d** 71 **p** 72. C Madeley *Heref* 71-74; C Littleover *Derby* 74-77; V Clodock and Longtown w Craswell and Llanveyno *Heref* 77-79; P-in-c St Margaret's w Michaelchurch Eskley and Newton 77-79; V Clodock and Longtown w Craswell, Llanveynoe etc from 79; RD Abbeydore 90-96; Preb Heref Cathl from 96. *The Vicarage, Longtown, Hereford HR2 0LD* Tel (01873) 860289

RODGERS, John Terence Roche. b 28. TCD BA53 MA57 ACII. Bps' Coll Cheshunt. **d** 57 **p** 58. C Templecorran *Conn* 57-60; C Derriaghy 60-61; C Antrim All SS 62-64; I Belfast St Steph 64-79; I Dunmurry 79-94; Can Belf Cathl 92-94; rtd 94. *8 Aberdelghy Park, Lambeg, Lisburn BT27 4QF* Tel (028) 9266 0430

RODGERS, Richard Thomas Boycott. b 47. Lon Univ MB, BS70 FRCS81. St Jo Coll Nottm. **d** 77 **p** 78. C Littleover *Derby* 77-80; Lect Birm St Martin w Bordesley St Andr 89-90; Perm to Offic from 90. *63 Meadow Brook Road, Birmingham B31 1ND* Tel 0121-476 0789

RODHAM, Morris. b 59. Hatf Coll Dur BA81 St Jo Coll Dur PGCE85. Trin Coll Bris MA93. **d** 93 **p** 94. C New Milverton *Cov* 93-97; V Leamington Priors St Mary from 97; RD Warwick and Leamington from 06. *The Vicarage, 28 St Mary's Road, Leamington Spa CV31 1JP* Tel (01926) 778507 *or* tel and fax 778505 E-mail morris/helen@stmaryschurch.swinternet.co.uk

RODLEY, Ian Tony. b 48. Open Univ BA08. Qu Coll Birm 77. **d** 80 **p** 81. C Baildon and Dioc Children's Adv *Bradf* 80-85; V Bradf St Wilfrid Lidget Green 85-90; Chapl to the Deaf 88-90; V Otley 90-98; C Wolverton *Ox* 98-03; TR Bramley *Ripon* from 03. *St Peter's Vicarage, 8 Hough Lane, Leeds LS13 3NE* Tel 0113-255 5180 E-mail ianrod@clara.co.uk

RODLEY, James William Eric. b 66. SS Hild & Bede Coll Dur BA86 ACA89. St Steph Ho Ox 07. **d** 09. C Pokesdown All SS *Win* from 09; C Bournemouth St Clem from 09. *The Vicarage, St Clement's Road, Bournemouth BH1 4DZ* E-mail jwerodley@yahoo.co.uk

RODRIGUEZ-VEGLIO, Francis Bonny. b 33. Sarum Th Coll 62. **d** 64 **p** 65. C Alnwick St Paul *Newc* 64-68; V Horton w Piddington *Pet* 68-79; P-in-c Preston Deanery 68-79; CF (ACF) 75-82; TV Is of Scilly *Truro* 79-82; Hon Chapl Miss to Seamen 79-82; Perm to Offic *Pet* 86-88; C Leic Ch Sav 88-91; V Kirkwhelpington, Kirkharle, Kirkheaton and Cambo *Newc* 91-95. *Gemacq Cottage, 14 Daventry Road, Norton, Daventry NN11 2ND* Tel (01327) 872030 E-mail francis.andree@tiscali.co.uk

RODWELL, Barry John. b 39. Birm Univ CertEd59 Cam Univ DipAdEd77. Ridley Hall Cam 67. **d** 70 **p** 71. C Sudbury St Greg and St Pet *St E* 70-73; Hd RE Hedingham Sch 73-80; R Sible Hedingham *Chelmsf* 80-85; RE Adv 85-93; V Gt Burstead 93-00; rtd 00; Perm to Offic *Nor* 00-07. *The Nutshell, 11 Filbert Road, Loddon, Norwich NR14 6LW* Tel (01508) 522949 E-mail nutshell@tesco.net

RODWELL, Mrs Helen. WEMTC. **d** 09. NSM Forest of Dean Ch Ch w English Bicknor *Glouc* from 09. *The Other House, English Bicknor, Coleford GL16 7PD* Tel (01594) 860205

RODWELL (née VINCENT), Mrs Jacqueline Margaret. b 59. Glos Univ BA04. WEMTC 01. **d** 04 **p** 05. NSM Cheltenham St Mark *Glouc* 04-08; NSM Cheltenham Em w St Steph from 08. *27 Hatherley Court Road, Cheltenham GL51 3AG* Tel (01242) 697541 E-mail emmanuel.church@btconnect.com

RODWELL, Canon John Stanley. b 46. Leeds Univ BSc68 Southn Univ PhD74. Cuddesdon Coll 71. **d** 74 **p** 75. Hon C Horfield H Trin *Bris* 74-75; Hon C Skerton St Luke *Blackb* 75-77; Lic to Offic from 77; Hon Can Blackb Cathl from 03. *7 Derwent Road, Lancaster LA1 3ES* Tel (01524) 62726

ROE, Mrs Caroline Ruth. b 57. Birm Univ BA80 PGCE93. Wycliffe Hall Ox 81. **dss** 84 **d** 87 **p** 96. Olveston *Bris* 84-87; Par Dn 87; NSM Alveley and Quatt *Heref* 87-94; Bp's Voc Officer 90-94; Hon C Loughborough Em and St Mary in Charnwood *Leic* 97-98; C Hathern, Long Whatton and Diseworth w Belton etc 98-00; Perm to Offic 01-04; Chapl Univ Hosps Leic NHS Trust 04-07; Lead Chapl from 07. *4 John's Lee Close, Loughborough LE11 3LH* Tel (01509) 260217 *or* 0116-258 5487

ROE, Frank Ronald. b 31. Brasted Th Coll Westcott Ho Cam 55. **d** 57 **p** 58. C S w N Hayling *Portsm* 57-61; Hong Kong 61-77; Sen Chapl St Jo Cathl 61-66; Asst Chapl 77; Sen Chapl Miss to Seamen 66-69; Hon Chapl Miss to Seamen Australia 77-06; rtd 96. *2004-699 Cardero Street, Vancouver BC V6G E3H, Canada* Tel (001) (604) 325 5591 E-mail revfrank@bigpond.com

ROE, Canon Joseph Thorley. b 22. AKC49 DipAdEd Hull Univ PhD90. K Coll Lon 46. **d** 50 **p** 51. C Methley *Ripon* 50-53; C Richmond 53-55; V Leeds Gipton Epiphany 55-60; C of E Youth Coun Tr Officer 60-64; Sec Youth Dept BCC 64-67; Prin Lect Bretton Hall Coll Wakef 67-74; Sec for Miss and Unity *Ripon* 74-78; Dioc Missr and Bp's Dom Chapl 75-78; Can Res Carl Cathl 78-82; Dioc Dir of Tr 78-82; Dioc Adult Educn Officer *Wakef* 82-88; Hon Can Wakef Cathl 83-88; Dir Educn

85-88; rtd 88; Perm to Offic *Wakef* 88-08. *2 Fosbrook House, 8 Clifton Drive, Lytham St Annes FY8 5RQ* Tel (01253) 667052

ROE, Peter Harold. b 37. K Coll Lon BD62 AKC62. **d** 63 **p** 64. C Knowle St Barn *Bris* 63-65; C Leckhampton St Pet *Glouc* 65-68; V Shaw Hill *Birm* 68-73; V Hobs Moat 73-90; V Packwood w Hockley Heath 90-99; rtd 99; Perm to Offic *Blackb* from 99. *14 Worcester Avenue, Garstang, Preston PR3 1EY* Tel (01995) 605775

ROE, Robert Henry. b 22. LCP57. Westcott Ho Cam 72. **d** 74 **p** 75. Hd Master St Mary's Primary Sch Saffron Walden 74-83; NSM Saffron Walden w Wendens Ambo and Littlebury *Chelmsf* 75-86; Perm to Offic *Nor* from 86. *Larchmount, High Street, Cley, Holt NR25 7RG* Tel (01263) 740369
E-mail robertroe@ukf.net

ROE, Robin. b 28. CBE MC68. TCD BA52 MA55. **d** 53 **p** 54. C Dublin Sandford *D & G* 53-55; CF 55-81; QHC 77-81; R Merrow *Guildf* 81-89; rtd 89; Perm to Offic *Guildf* from 89. *Lansdowne, 6 Mitchells Close, Shalford, Guildford GU4 8HY* Tel (01483) 563852

ROE, Thorley. *See* ROE, Canon Joseph Thorley

ROEMMELE, Michael Patrick. b 49. TCD BA72 MA76. **d** 73 **p** 74. C Portadown St Columba *Arm* 73-77; C Drumachose *D & R* 77-80; Bahrain 79-83; Cyprus 79-83; Chapl RAF 83-00; CF 00-07; I Camus-juxta-Bann *D & R* from 07. *30 Drumrane Road, Limavady BT49 9LB* Tel (028) 7776 3554 Mobile 07977-239863 E-mail mproemmele@googlemail.com *or* macosquin@derry.anglican.org

ROESCHLAUB, Robert Friedrich. b 39. Purdue Univ BSc63. Berkeley Div Sch MDiv66. **d** 66 **p** 66. USA 66-77; Hon C Tilehurst St Cath *Ox* 78-79; Hon C Tilehurst St Mich 79-82; P-in-c Millom H Trin w Thwaites *Carl* 82-85; P-in-c Millom 85-89; R Dunstall w Rangemore and Tatenhill *Lich* 89-93; rtd 94; Perm to Offic *Carl* from 98. *20 Pannatt Hill, Millom LA18 5DB* Tel (01229) 772185

ROEST, Wilma. b 62. Utrecht Univ MA88 Roehampton Inst PGCE92. SEITE 96. **d** 99 **p** 00. C Merton St Mary *S'wark* 99-02; TV N Lambeth 02-06; P-in-c Balham St Mary and St Jo from 06. *St Mary's Vicarage, 35 Elmfield Road, London SW17 8AG* Tel (020) 8673 1188 E-mail wilma.roest@virgin.net

ROFF, Andrew Martin. b 42. Bede Coll Dur BSc65. Westcott Ho Cam 65. **d** 70 **p** 71. C Ches St Mary 70-73; Min Can Blackb Cathl 73-76; P-in-c Blackb St Jo 74-75; V Longton 76-81; Chapl Trin Coll Glenalmond 82-83; R Allendale w Whitfield *Newc* 83-92; V Gosforth St Nic 92-97; Dioc Supernumerary *Mor* 01-07; Lic to Offic from 08. *Rowan Glen, Upper Braefindon, Culbokie, Dingwall IV7 8GY* Tel (01349) 877762
E-mail martin@roff-rowanglen.co.uk

ROFF, Canon John Michael. b 47. St Chad's Coll Dur BSc69. Westcott Ho Cam 70. **d** 72 **p** 73. C Lancaster St Mary *Blackb* 72-75; C Dronfield *Derby* 75-76; TV 76-80; TR N Wingfield, Pilsley and Tupton 80-85; V Ilkeston St Mary 85-90; V Stockport St Geo *Ches* 90-94; TR Stockport SW 94-00; RD Stockport 95-00; Dioc Ecum Officer 92-99; Hon Can Ches Cathl 98-00; Can Res 00-04; rtd 04; Perm to Offic *Ches* and *Blackb* from 05. *14 Westbourne Road, Lancaster LA1 5DB* Tel (01524) 841621 E-mail roff@roff.org.uk

ROGAN, Canon John. b 28. St Jo Coll Dur BA49 MA51 Open Univ BPhil81. **d** 54 **p** 55. C Ashton St Mich *Man* 54-57; C Sharrow St Andr *Sheff* 57-61; Ind Chapl 57-61, Sec C of E Ind Cttee 61-66; V Leigh St Mary *Man* 66-78; RD Leigh 71-78; Hon Can Man Cathl 75-78; Provost St Paul's Cathl Dundee 78-83; R Dundee St Paul 78-83; Soc Resp Adv *Bris* 83-93; Can Res Bris Cathl 83-93; rtd 93; Perm to Offic *Bris* from 93. *84 Concorde Drive, Bristol BS10 6PX* Tel 0117-950 5803

ROGERS, Mrs Angela. b 52. **d** 00 **p** 01. OLM Bridgnorth, Tasley, Astley Abbotts, etc *Heref* 00-08; TV from 08. *18 St Nicholas Road, Bridgnorth WV15 5BW* Tel (01746) 762013
E-mail angelam@rogers4949.freeserve.co.uk

ROGERS, Brian Robert. b 36. Open Univ BA80. St Jo Coll Nottm 70. **d** 72 **p** 73. C Ealing St Mary *Lon* 72-74; C Greenside *Dur* 74-75; Lic to Offic 75-85; Perm to Offic *Lich* 85-95; rtd 97; Perm to Offic *Sarum* from 97. *71 Alderney Avenue, Poole BH12 4LF* Tel (01202) 772103

ROGERS, Brian Victor. b 50. Trin Coll Bris 75. **d** 78 **p** 79. C Plumstead St Jo w St Jas and St Paul *S'wark* 78-83; P-in-c Gayton *Nor* 83-85; P-in-c Gayton Thorpe w E Walton 83-85; P-in-c Westacre 83-85; P-in-c Ashwicken w Leziate 83-85; R Gayton Gp of Par 85-91; R Rackheath and Salhouse 91-96; P-in-c Warmington, Tansor, Cotterstock and Fotheringhay *Pet* 96-97; V Warmington, Tansor and Cotterstock etc from 97. *The Vicarage, Church Street, Warmington, Peterborough PE8 6TE* Tel (01832) 280263 E-mail brian.rogers@boltblue.net

ROGERS, Christopher Antony. b 47. NOC 79. **d** 81 **p** 82. C Chesterfield St Aug *Derby* 81-84; C Chaddesden St Phil 84-86; R Whitwell 86-95; V W Burnley All SS *Blackb* 95-01; V Ashford St Hilda *Lon* from 01. *St Hilda's Vicarage, 8 Station Crescent, Ashford TW15 3HH* Tel (01784) 254237 *or* 245712
E-mail christopher.rogers@london.anglican.org

ROGERS, Christopher Ian. b 79. **d** 07 **p** 08. NSM Roxeth *Lon* from 07. *58 Drury Road, Harrow HA1 4BW* Tel (020) 8423 1152 *or* 8422 9867 E-mail cris@soulsurvivorharrow.com

ROGERS, Clive Trevor Thorne. b 49. SAOMC 02. **d** 05 **p** 06. NSM Beaconsfield *Ox* from 05. *23 Stratton Road, Beaconsfield HP9 1HR* Tel (01494) 675298
E-mail clive_rogers@btinternet.com

ROGERS, Clive William. b 62. Selw Coll Cam BA83 MA87 MEng93 Southn Univ BTh90. Chich Th Coll 87. **d** 90 **p** 91. C Leic St Aid 90-93; P-in-c Ryhall w Essendine *Pet* 93-94; Lic to Offic *Ely* 94-03; Perm to Offic 00-04; Lic to Offic *Sarum* from 04. *4 The Sidings, Downton, Salisbury SP5 3QZ* Tel (01725) 512141 Mobile 07909-992548 E-mail bill@billrogers.info

ROGERS, Cyril David. b 55. Birm Univ BA76 BTheol. Sarum & Wells Th Coll 80. **d** 83 **p** 84. C Leagrave *St Alb* 83-87; TV Langtree *Ox* 87-97; R Ballaugh *S & M* from 97. *The Rectory, Ballacrosha, Ballaugh, Isle of Man IM7 5AQ* Tel (01624) 897873

ROGERS, Damon. b 66. Cov Univ BEng92 Wolv Univ PGCE94 Warwick Univ BPhil02. Cranmer Hall Dur 01. **d** 03 **p** 04. C Heigham St Thos *Nor* 03-06; R Freethorpe, Wickhampton, Halvergate etc from 06. *The Rectory, Church Road, Reedham, Norwich NR13 3TZ* Tel (01493) 700268
E-mail therogers5@ukonline.co.uk

ROGERS, Canon David. b 48. Univ of Wales (Ban) BA69. Westcott Ho Cam 70. **d** 72 **p** 73. C Rainbow Hill and Tolladine *Worc* 72-75; C Astwood Bank w Crabbs Cross 75-79; V Cradley 79-90; V Beoley 90-08; RD Bromsgrove 00-06; TR Redditch H Trin from 08; Hon Can Worc Cathl from 07. *The Vicarage, Church Hill, Beoley, Redditch B98 9AR* Tel (01527) 63976
E-mail davidrogers@santiago.plus.com

ROGERS, David Alan. b 55. City of Lon Poly BA77 MCIT82. Linc Th Coll 88. **d** 90 **p** 91. C Kingston upon Hull St Nic *York* 90-93; P-in-c Kingston upon Hull St Mary 93-96; N Humberside Ind Chapl 93-02; Dir Leeds Ch Inst *Ripon* 02-04; Chief Officer Hull Coun for Voluntary Service from 04; Perm to Offic *York* from 07. *Hull Council for Voluntary Service, 29 Anlaby Road, Hull HU1 2PG* Tel (01482) 324474 Fax 580565

ROGERS, The Ven David Arthur. b 21. Ch Coll Cam BA47 MA52. Ridley Hall Cam 47. **d** 49 **p** 50. C Stockport St Geo *Ches* 49-53; R Levenshulme St Pet *Man* 53-59; V Sedbergh *Bradf* 59-74; P-in-c Cautley w Dowbiggin 59-60; V 60-74; P-in-c Garsdale 59-60; V 60-74; V Sedbergh, Cautley and Garsdale 74-79; P-in-c Firbank, Howgill and Killington 73-77; RD Sedbergh 59-73; RD Ewecross 73-77; Hon Can Bradf Cathl 67-77; Adn Craven 77-86; rtd 86; Lic to Offic *Bradf* 86-06; Perm to Offic *Blackb* 87-06 and *Carl* 89-06. *24 Towns End Road, Sharnbrook, Bedford MK44 1HY* Tel (01234) 782560

ROGERS, David Barrie. b 46. S Dios Minl Tr Scheme 89. **d** 93. NSM Old Alresford and Bighton *Win* 93-96; Dep Warden Dioc Retreat Ho (Holland Ho) Cropthorne *Worc* 96-98; Warden Stacklands Retreat Ho W Kingsdown 98-03; Hon C Kingsdown *Roch* 98-03; Warden St Pet Bourne Cen from 03. *St Peter's Bourne Centre, 40 Oakleigh Park South, London N20 9JU*

ROGERS, David Martyn. b 56. Univ of Wales (Lamp) BA77 K Coll Lon BD79 AKC79 St Kath Coll Liv DipEd86 Liv Univ BPhil94 MA07. Chich Th Coll 79. **d** 80 **p** 81. C Hockerill *St Alb* 80-85; Perm to Offic *St As* 85-87; C Kilburn St Mary *Lon* 87-90; V New Longton *Blackb* from 90; Chapl Lancs Constabulary from 90. *All Saints' Vicarage, Station Road, New Longton, Preston PR4 4LN* Tel (01772) 613347

ROGERS, George Hutchinson. b 51. Windsor Univ Ontario BSW75. Wycliffe Coll Toronto MDiv78. **d** 78 **p** 78. C Victoria St Matthias Canada 78-81; R Cobble Hill and Cowichan Station 81-86; I Vancouver St Matthias 86-97; Hon C Vancouver St Helen 97-98; C Tonbridge SS Pet and Paul *Roch* 99-03; V Werrington *Pet* from 03. *The Vicarage, 51 The Green, Werrington, Peterborough PE4 6RT* Tel (01733) 571649
E-mail ghrogers@nildram.co.uk

ROGERS, Ian Colin. b 73. Wolv Univ BA95. Coll of Resurr Mirfield BA99. **d** 00 **p** 01. C Lon Docks St Pet w Wapping St Jo 00-03; P-in-c Hammersmith St Luke 03-08; P-in-c Tangmere and Oving *Chich* from 08. *St Andrew's Vicarage, 21 Gibson Road, Tangmere, Chichester PO20 2JA* Tel (01243) 785089
E-mail fr.ianrogers@ntlworld.com

ROGERS, The Very Revd John. b 34. Univ of Wales (Lamp) BA55 Oriel Coll Ox BA58 MA61. St Steph Ho Ox 57. **d** 59 **p** 60. C Roath St Martin *Llan* 59-63; Br Guiana 63-66; Guyana 66-71; V Caldicot *Mon* 71-77; V Monmouth 77-84; RD Monmouth 81-84; TR Ebbw Vale 84-93; RD Blaenau Gwent 86-93; Can St Woolos Cathl 88-93; Dean Llan 93-99; V Llandaff w Capel Llanilltern 93-99; rtd 99. *Fron Lodge, Llandovery SA20 0LJ* Tel (01550) 720089

ROGERS, John. b 61. St Jo Coll Nottm 03. **d** 05 **p** 06. C Otley *Bradf* 05-08; V Oakworth from 08. *The Vicarage, 18 Sunhurst Drive, Oakworth, Keighley BD22 7RG* Tel (01274) 408354
E-mail jollyjohnrogers@tiscali.co.uk

ROGERS, John Arthur. b 47. MBIM. Edin Dioc NSM Course 90. **d** 92. C Middlesbrough St Martin *York* 92-93; NSM The Trimdons *Dur* 00-05; NSM Upper Skerne 05-07; R Tilehurst

St Mich *Ox* from 07. *Tilehurst Rectory, Routh Lane, Reading RG30 4JY* Tel 0118-941 1127 E-mail rogj8@aol.com

ROGERS, John Robin. b 36. St Alb Minl Tr Scheme 78. **d** 81 **p** 82. NSM Digswell and Panshanger *St Alb* 81-84; C Welwyn w Ayot St Peter 85-92; R Wilden w Colmworth and Ravensden 92-99; rtd 99; Perm to Offic *St Alb* 99-02 and *Heref* from 03. *37 The Birches, Shobdon, Leominster HR6 9NG* Tel (01568) 708903

ROGERS, John William Trevor. b 28. Qu Coll Birm. **d** 85 **p** 86. NSM Dunchurch *Cov* 85-95; Perm to Offic 95-07. *15 Hillyard Road, Southam, Leamington Spa CV47 0LD* Tel (01926) 813469

ROGERS, Mrs Kathleen. b 54. **d** 08 **p** 09. C Machynlleth w Llanwrin and Penegoes *Ban* from 08. *30 Tregarth, Machynlleth SY20 8HU* Tel (01654) 702061
E-mail kathleenrogers@hotmail.co.uk

ROGERS, Mrs Kathleen. b 56. Open Univ BA93 Leeds Univ BA07. NOC 04. **d** 07 **p** 08. NSM Formby H Trin *Liv* from 07; Sen Resources Officer from 93. *St James's House, 20 St James Road, Liverpool L1 7BY* Tel 0151-705 2180

ROGERS, Canon Kenneth. b 33. Cuddesdon Coll 68. **d** 69 **p** 70. C Perranzabuloe *Truro* 69-71; C Truro St Paul 71-74; P-in-c Kenwyn St Geo 74-87; RD Powder 81-88; Hon Can Truro Cathl 87-98; TR Bodmin w Lanhydrock and Lanivet 87-98; RD Trigg Minor and Bodmin 89-93; rtd 98; Perm to Offic *Truro* from 98. *25 Pauls Row, Truro TR1 1HH* Tel (01872) 261007

ROGERS, Leon James. b 83. St Andr Univ MTheol06. Qu Coll Birm 07. **d** 09. C E Darlington *Dur* from 09. *239 Parkside, Darlington DL1 5TG* Tel 07714-354771 (mobile)
E-mail lnrgrs@gmail.com

ROGERS, Canon Llewelyn. Univ of Wales (Lamp) BA59. St Mich Coll Llan. **d** 61 **p** 62. C Holywell *St As* 61-64; C Hawarden 64-70; R Bodfari 70-73; V Rhosymedre 73-78; V Llansantffraid-ym-Mechain 77-83; V Llansantffraid-ym-Mechain and Llanfechain 83-98; RD Llanfyllin 84-88; V Pont Robert, Pont Dolanog, Garthbeibio etc 98-01; Can St As Cathl 98-01; rtd 01; Perm to Offic *Lich* from 02. *17 Maes-y-Berllan, Llanymynech SY22 6PJ* Tel (01691) 839920

ROGERS, Mrs Lynne Rosemary. b 49. CITC 00. **d** 03 **p** 04. Aux Min Ferns w Kilbride, Toombe, Kilcormack etc *C & O* 03-06; Aux Min Gorey w Kilnahue, Leskinfere and Ballycanew 06-07; P-in-c New w Old Ross, Whitechurch, Fethard etc from 07. *The Rectory, College Road, New Ross, Co Wexford, Republic of Ireland* Tel (00353) (51) 425004 Mobile 87-677 4408
E-mail lynnerogers@eircom.net *or* newross@ferns.anglican.org

ROGERS, Malcolm Dawson. b 63. SS Hild & Bede Coll Dur BA84 Selw Coll Cam BA88. Ridley Hall Cam 86. **d** 89 **p** 90. C Ipswich St Jo *St E* 89-93; CMS Russia 93-95; C Holloway St Mary Magd *Lon* 95-97; V 97-05; V Bury St Edmunds St Mary *St E* from 05. *St Mary with St Peter Vicarage, 78 Hardwick Lane, Bury St Edmunds IP33 2RA* Tel (01284) 763416
E-mail malcolmrogers@onetel.com

ROGERS, Malcolm Kenneth. b 72. Liv Inst of Educn BA93. St Jo Coll Nottm MA95 LTh96. **d** 96 **p** 97. C W Derby St Luke *Liv* 96-00; V Huyton Quarry from 00. *St Gabriel's Vicarage, 2 St Agnes Road, Huyton, Liverpool L36 5TA* Tel 0151-489 2688
E-mail malcolm.rogers@huytondeanery.org

ROGERS, Mark James. b 64. Univ of Wales (Lamp) BA. Qu Coll Birm. **d** 89 **p** 90. C Dudley St Aug Holly Hall *Worc* 89-93; C Worc St Barn w Ch Ch 93-94; TV 94-97; USPG Belize 97-00; R Montreal St Columba Canada from 00. *4020 Hingston Avenue, Montreal QC H4A 2J7, Canada* Tel (001) (514) 486 1753
E-mail mrogers@montreal.anglican.ca

ROGERS, Martin Brian. b 53. **d** 92 **p** 93. OLM Collyhurst *Man* from 92. *8 Greenford Road, Crumpsall, Manchester M8 0NW* Tel 0161-740 4614

ROGERS, Maurice George Walden. b 23. AKC51. **d** 52 **p** 53. C Bedford All SS *St Alb* 52-56; C Southfields St Barn *S'wark* 56-58; C Chingford SS Pet and Paul *Chelmsf* 58-61; V Gt Ilford St Luke 61-72; V Woodford St Barn 72-89; rtd 89; Perm to Offic *Chelmsf* from 89 and *Win* from 93. *The Coach House, 13 Bodorgan Road, Bournemouth BH2 6NQ* Tel (01202) 291034

ROGERS, Michael Andrew. b 47. OBE96. FRAeS96. Ripon Coll Cuddesdon. **d** 01 **p** 02. C Bromsgrove St Jo *Worc* 01-04; R Berrow w Pendock, Eldersfield, Hollybush etc from 04. *The Vicarage, Berrow, Malvern WR13 6JN* Tel (01684) 833230
E-mail mandmrogers@btinternet.com

ROGERS, Michael Ernest. b 34. Sarum & Wells Th Coll 83. **d** 85 **p** 86. C Roehampton H Trin *S'wark* 85-88; V Ryhill *Wakef* 88-94; V S Elmsall 94-00; rtd 00; Perm to Offic *Derby* from 00. *The Willows, 49 Main Street, Weston-on-Trent, Derby DE72 2BL* Tel (01332) 700273

ROGERS, Michael Hugh Walton. b 52. K Coll Lon BD73 AKC73. St Aug Coll Cant 74. **d** 75 **p** 76. C Eastbourne St Andr *Chich* 75-78; C Uppingham w Ayston *Pet* 78-82; V Eye 82-90; R Cottesmore and Barrow w Ashwell and Burley 90-04; C 04-09; C Greetham and Thistleton w Stretton and Clipsham 01-05; P-in-c Empingham and Exton w Horn w Whitwell 06-09; RD Rutland 95-09; Can Pet Cathl 01-09; Bp's Adv for Min of Healing 05-09; P-in-c Ilfracombe SS Phil and Jas w W Down *Ex*

from 09. *St James's Vicarage, Kingsley Avenue, Ilfracombe EX34 8ET* Tel (01271) 863519
E-mail mhwrogers@btinternet.com

ROGERS, Mrs Pamela Rose. b 46. Keswick Hall Coll CertEd68. S Dios Minl Tr Scheme 92. **d** 95 **p** 96. NSM Axbridge w Shipham and Rowberrow *B & W* from 95; Bp's Officer for Ord NSM (Wells Adnry) from 02. *28 Beech Road, Shipham, Winscombe BS25 1SB* Tel (01934) 842685

ROGERS, Mrs Patricia Anne. b 54. Lon Univ BD. Trin Coll Bris. **d** 87 **p** 94. Hon C Gayton Gp of Par *Nor* 87-91; Hon C Rackheath and Salhouse 91-96; Chapl to the Deaf 91-96; Chapl to the Deaf *Pet* 96-00; Visual Communications from 00. *1-2 Lees Cottages, Poole Lane, Thornton-le-Moors, Chester CH2 4JE*
E-mail visiblecommunication@lineone.net

ROGERS, Philip John. b 52. Univ of Wales CertEd74 Nottm Univ BTh79. St Jo Coll Nottm 76. **d** 79 **p** 80. C Stretford St Bride *Man* 79-84; P-in-c Plumstead St Jo w St Jas and St Paul *S'wark* 84-85; V from 85. *St John's Vicarage, 176 Griffin Road, London SE18 7QA* Tel (020) 8855 1827
E-mail philipjrogers@ukonline.co.uk

ROGERS (née GOLDER), Mrs Rebecca Marie (Beki). b 71. Brunel Univ BA94. Trin Coll Bris BA02. **d** 02 **p** 03. C Short Heath *Birm* 02-05; Dir Faith Willesden Area *Lon* from 05; NSM Roxeth from 05. *58 Drury Road, Harrow HA1 4BW* Tel (020) 8423 1152 E-mail bekirogers@hotmail.com

ROGERS, Richard Anthony. b 46. Ex Coll Ox BA69. Qu Coll Birm 70. **d** 71 **p** 72. C Shirley *Birm* 71-74; Chapl Solihull Sch 74-78; Hon C Cotteridge *Birm* 78-84; Hon C Hill 84-93; Hd RE Kings Norton Girls' Sch 93-05; Perm to Offic *Birm* from 93. *48 Jordan Road, Sutton Coldfield B75 5AB* Tel 0121-308 0310

ROGERS, Richard Jonathan. b 64. Trin Coll Bris BTh96. **d** 96 **p** 97. C Carterton *Ox* 96-00; Crosslinks 00-03; Perm to Offic *B & W* 00-06. *11 East End Avenue, Warminster BA12 9NF* Tel (01985) 214123

ROGERS, Canon Robert. b 42. Bernard Gilpin Soc Dur 66 St Aid Birkenhead 67 Ridley Hall Cam 69. **d** 70 **p** 71. C Childwall St Dav *Liv* 70-73; C Huntington *York* 73-76; TR Brayton 76-89; RD Selby 84-89; V New Malton 89-98; RD Bulmer and Malton 97-98; Asst Chapl York Health Services NHS Trust 98-99; Sen Chapl York Hosps NHS Foundn Trust 99-08; Can and Preb York Minster 03-08; rtd 08; Perm to Offic *York* from 08. *Tabgha, 9 Middlecave Drive, Malton YO17 7BB* Tel (01653) 699469

ROGERS, Robert Charles. b 55. St Pet Coll Birm CertEd77 Warwick Univ MA99. St Jo Coll Nottm 87. **d** 89 **p** 90. C Wellesbourne *Cov* 89-93; R Bourton w Frankton and Stretton on Dunsmore etc 93-97; Behaviour Support Teacher Warks LEA from 98; Lic to Offic 98-07; NSM Rugby from 07. *18 Waring Way, Dunchurch, Rugby CV22 6PH* Tel (01788) 817361
E-mail rob.rogers@talktalk.net

ROGERS, Robin. *See* ROGERS, John Robin

ROGERS, Ryder Rondeau. b 44. Lon Bible Coll 62. **d** 08 **p** 08. In Bapt Min 68-04; NSM Bride Valley *Sarum* from 08. *Stonehaven, 25 Bindbarrow Road, Burton Bradstock, Bridport DT6 4RG* Tel (01308) 897780

ROGERS, Ms Sally Jean. b 54. Univ of Wales (Lamp) BA77 Nottm Univ BTh87. Linc Th Coll 88. **d** 87 **p** 94. Par Dn Bris St Mary Redcliffe w Temple etc 87-90; Par Dn Greenford H Cross *Lon* 90-94; C 94-96; TV Hemel Hempstead *St Alb* 96-02; Development Worker Changing Attitude 03-06; Chapl R Holloway and Bedf New Coll *Guildf* from 06; Perm to Offic *St Alb* 02-05 and *Chelmsf* from 06. *10 Willow Walk, Englefield Green, Egham TW20 0DQ* Tel (01784) 443070
E-mail sally.rogers@rhul.ac.uk

ROGERS, Sarah Ann. b 73. York Univ BSc94 Univ of Wales (Cardiff) PhD98. St Mich Coll Llan BA09. **d** 09. C Caerphilly *Llan* from 09. *Church House, 71 Bartlett Street, Caerphilly CF83 1JT* Tel (029) 2088 2695

ROGERS, Trevor. *See* ROGERS, John William Trevor

ROGERS, William. *See* ROGERS, Clive William

ROGERS, William Arthur. b 41. Lon Univ BA64 CertEd. Chich Th Coll 78. **d** 81 **p** 82. C Chandler's Ford *Win* 81-84; R Bentley and Binsted 84-94; P-in-c The Lulworths, Winfrith Newburgh and Chaldon *Sarum* 94-99; rtd 99. *Greenways, 6 Shaves Lane, New Milton BH25 5DJ* Tel (01425) 638751

ROGERSON, Anthony Carroll. b 37. Trin Coll Ox BA59 MA63 MCIPD92. SAOMC 96. **d** 98 **p** 99. NSM Radley and Sunningwell *Ox* 98-02; Perm to Offic from 02. *Noggins, 35 Lower Radley, Abingdon OX14 3AY* Tel (01235) 550214
E-mail tonyrogerson@cygnet.org.uk

✠**ROGERSON, The Rt Revd Barry.** b 36. Leeds Univ BA60 Bris Univ Hon LLD93. Wells Th Coll 60. **d** 62 **p** 63 **c** 79. C S Shields St Hilda w St Thos *Dur* 62-65; C Bishopwearmouth St Nic 65-67; Lect Lich Th Coll 67-71; Vice-Prin 71-72; Lect Sarum & Wells Th Coll 72-74; V Wednesfield St Thos *Lich* 75-79; TR Wednesfield 79; Suff Bp Wolverhampton 79-85; Bp Bris 85-02; rtd 02; Hon Asst Bp *B & W* from 03. *Flat 2, 30 Albert Road, Clevedon BS21 7RR* Tel (01275) 541964
E-mail barry.rogerson@blueyonder.co.uk

ROGERSON, Colin Scott. b 30. St Andr Univ MA55. Edin Th Coll. **d** 57 **p** 58. C Byker St Ant *Newc* 57-59; C Newc St Geo 59-63; C Wooler 63-67; V Tynemouth St Aug 67-75; C Dur St Marg 75-88; P-in-c Hebburn St Jo 88-95; rtd 95; Perm to Offic *Dur* from 95. *6 Edlingham Road, Durham DH1 5YS* Tel 0191-386 1956

ROGERSON, Canon Ian Matthew. b 45. Bede Coll Dur CertEd67 Open Univ BA76. Oak Hill Th Coll. **d** 83 **p** 84. C Haughton St Mary *Man* 83-86; V Ramsbottom St Andr 86-05; P-in-c Edenfield and Stubbins 04-05; TR Ramsbottom and Edenfield from 05; AD Bury 96-05; Hon Can Man Cathl from 04. *St Andrew's Vicarage, 2 Henwick Hall Avenue, Ramsbottom, Bury BL0 9YH* Tel and fax (01706) 826482

ROGERSON, Prof John William. b 35. Man Univ BD61 DD75 Linacre Ho Ox BA63 MA67 Aber Univ Hon DD98 Friedrich Schiller Univ DrTheol05 Freiburg Univ DrTheol06. Ripon Hall Ox 61. **d** 64 **p** 66. C Dur St Oswald 64-67; Lect Th Dur Univ 64-75; Sen Lect 75-79; Lic to Offic *Dur* 67-79; Lic to Offic *Sheff* from 79; Prof Bibl Studies Sheff Univ 79-96; Hd of Dept 79-94; Hon Can Sheff Cathl 82-95. *60 Marlborough Road, Sheffield S10 1DB* Tel 0114-268 1426

ROLAND, Andrew Osborne. b 45. Mert Coll Ox BA66 St Jo Coll Dur BA84. Cranmer Hall Dur. **d** 84 **p** 85. C Streatham St Leon *S'wark* 84-87; C Kingston All SS w St Jo 87-94; P-in-c Hackbridge and Beddington Corner 94-06; V from 06. *All Saints' Vicarage, New Road, Mitcham CR4 4JL* Tel (020) 8648 3650

ROLFE, Charles Edward. b 34. Wells Th Coll 68. **d** 70 **p** 71. C Bath Twerton-on-Avon *B & W* 70-79; TV Wellington and Distr 79-85; P-in-c Frome Ch Ch 85-89; V 89-94; Chapl Victoria Hosp Frome 85-94; Chapl St Adhelm's Hosp Frome 88-94; rtd 94; NSM Fordingbridge and Breamore and Hale etc *Win* 95-05. *29 Ayleswade Road, Salisbury SP2 8DW* Tel (01722) 335601 E-mail charles@rolfe14.freeserve.co.uk

ROLFE, Joseph William. b 37. Qu Coll Birm 78. **d** 81 **p** 82. NSM Tredington and Darlingscott w Newbold on Stour *Cov* 81-91; NSM Brailes from 91; NSM Sutton under Brailes from 91; NSM Shipston Deanery from 98. *35 Manor Lane, Shipston-on-Stour CV36 4EF* Tel (01608) 661737

ROLFE, Paul Douglas. b 46. MIBC90. NOC 90. **d** 93 **p** 94. C Urmston *Man* 93-96; V Lawton Moor 96-03; P-in-c Burnage St Nic 03-07; Sen Chapl Costa Blanca *Eur* 07-08. *Address temp unknown* E-mail paul.d.rolfe@btinternet.com

ROLFE, Mrs Susan Margaret. b 58. Man Univ BA81. ERMC 05. **d** 08 **p** 09. NSM Pet Ch Carpenter from 08. *1 Woodfield Road, Peterborough PE3 6HD* Tel (01733) 567509

ROLLETT, Robert Henry. b 39. Leeds Univ BA61 Leic Univ CertEd62. Linc Th Coll 77. **d** 79 **p** 80. C Littleport *Ely* 79-82; P-in-c Manea 82-83; V 83-85; P-in-c Wimblington 82-83; R 83-85; V Thorney Abbey 85-93; P-in-c The Ramseys and Upwood 93-94; TR 94-99; rtd 99; P-in-c Scalford w Goadby Marwood and Wycombe etc *Leic* 99-00. *2 Stockerston Crescent, Uppingham, Oakham LE15 9UB* Tel (01572) 823685

ROLLINS, David. b 65. De Montfort Univ BA98. St Steph Ho Ox 99. **d** 01 **p** 02. C Leic St Aid 01-05; P-in-c Corringham *Chelmsf* from 05; P-in-c Fobbing from 05. *The Rectory, Church Road, Corringham, Stanford-le-Hope SS17 9AP* Tel (01375) 673074 E-mail drollins@drollins.freeserve.co.uk

ROLLS, Peter. b 40. Leeds Inst of Educn CertEd. NOC 80. **d** 83 **p** 84. NSM Meltham *Wakef* from 83. *14 Heather Road, Meltham, Huddersfield HD7 3EY* Tel (01484) 340342

ROLPH, Reginald Lewis George. b 29. Open Univ BA74. Bps' Coll Cheshunt 55. **d** 58 **p** 59. C Perivale *Lon* 58-61; C Wokingham St Paul *Ox* 61-63; C Letchworth St Alb 63-78; Perm to Offic from 78; rtd 93. *22 Souberie Avenue, Letchworth Garden City SG6 3JA* Tel (01462) 684596

ROLSTON, Cyril Willis Matthias. b 29. CITC 66. **d** 68 **p** 69. C Portadown St Mark *Arm* 68-71; I Loughgilly w Clare 71-81; Dir of Ords from 72; Asst Chapl Craigavon Area Hosp Gp Trust 80-96; I Moy w Charlemont *Arm* 81-96; Preb Arm Cathl 92-96; rtd 96; Chapl Armagh and Dungannon Health and Soc Services from 96. *19 Lower Parklands, Dungannon BT71 7JN* Tel (028) 8772 5910 Mobile 07718-864242 E-mail cyril.rolston@btinternet.com

ROLSTON, John Ormsby. b 28. TCD BA51 MA59 BD63. CITC 51. **d** 51 **p** 52. C Belfast St Mary Magd *Conn* 51-55; C Knock *D & D* 55-59; P-in-c Gilnahirk 59-63; I 63-66; I Belfast St Jas *Conn* 66-79; I Belfast St Jas w St Silas 79-96; Can Belf Cathl 82-96; Prec Belf Cathl 88-96; Adn Conn 88-96; rtd 96; Dioc C Conn 96-98. *5 Springburn Park, Lisburn BT27 5QZ* Tel (028) 9267 8932 E-mail j.o.rolston@lineone.net

ROLT (*formerly* **SHARPLES**), **Mrs Jean.** b 37. Padgate Coll of Educn TCert58. **d** 04 **p** 05. NSM Gerrans w St Anthony-in-Roseland and Philleigh *Truro* 04-08; NSM St Just-in-Roseland and St Mawes 05-08; rtd 08. *Tregear Vean Farmhouse, St Mawes, Truro TR2 5AB* Tel (01326) 270954 Mobile 07840-567933 E-mail revjeanrolt@mac.com

ROLTON, Patrick Hugh. b 49. Sarum & Wells Th Coll 72. **d** 74 **p** 75. C Roch 74-79; C Edenbridge 79-81; R N Cray 81-97; rtd 97. *45 Chalk Pit Avenue, Orpington BR5 3JJ* Tel (01689) 872916

ROM, Norman Charles. b 24. S'wark Ord Course 63. **d** 66 **p** 67. C Leatherhead *Guildf* 66-71; Chapl HM Pris Cant 71-74; Pentonville 74-85; Stocken 85-87; P-in-c Empingham *Pet* 85-87; R Empingham and Exton w Horn w Whitwell 87-94; rtd 94; Perm to Offic *Pet* 94-09 and *Linc* 03-09. *6 Church View, Clowne, Chesterfield S43 4LN* Tel (01246) 575795

ROMANIS, Adam John Aidan. b 57. Pemb Coll Ox BA78 MA83. Westcott Ho Cam 81. **d** 84 **p** 85. C Northfield *Birm* 84-88; TV Seaton Hirst *Newc* 88-93; V Newc Ch Ch w St Ann 93-99; V Cowley St Jo *Ox* from 99. *The Vicarage, 271 Cowley Road, Oxford OX4 2AJ* Tel (01865) 242396 E-mail adamox4@aol.com

ROMANO, Paul. b 56. Glas Univ MA77 LLB79 Open Univ BA91. TISEC. **d** 05. NSM Glas St Marg from 05. *63 Westfield Drive, Glasgow G52 2SG* Tel 0141-882 7026 E-mail paul.romano@btinternet.com

ROMER, William Miller. b 35. Brown Univ Rhode Is BA57. MDiv60. **d** 60 **p** 60. P-in-c Lake Luzerne St Mary USA 60-64; Asst Min Hanover St Andr 64-65; V New York St Boniface 65-70; P-in-c Troy St Luke 70-71; R Rochester Redeemer 98-03; P-in-c Rathkeale w Askeaton, Kilcornan and Kilnaughtin *L & K* 03-08; rtd 08. *Address temp unknown* Tel (00353) 87-236 8552 (mobile) E-mail molroms@aol.com

ROMO-GARCIA, Brother Gerardo. b 66. **d** 04 **p** 05. Mexico 04-07; SSF from 08; Perm to Offic *Cant* from 09. *The Master's Lodge, 58 St Peter's Street, Canterbury CT1 2BE* Tel (01227) 479364 E-mail amici_91401@hotmail.com

RONAYNE, Peter Henry. b 34. FCA68. Oak Hill Th Coll 64. **d** 66 **p** 67. C Chesham St Mary *Ox* 66-69; C Worthing H Trin *Chich* 69-74; V Shoreditch St Leon w St Mich *Lon* 74-82; P-in-c Norwood St Luke *S'wark* 82-85; V 85-94; V W Norwood St Luke 94-99; RD Streatham 87-91; rtd 99; Perm to Offic *S'wark* 00-04. *54 Maywater Close, South Croydon CR2 0LS* Tel (020) 8651 9743 E-mail pronayne@onetel.com

RONCHETTI, Quentin Marcus. b 56. Ripon Coll Cuddesdon 79. **d** 80 **p** 81. C Eastbourne St Mary *Chich* 80-83; C Moulsecoomb 83-85; TV 85-90; V Findon Valley 90-97; V Shoreham Beach 97-07; V Midhurst from 07. *The Vicarage, June Lane, Midhurst GU29 9EW* Tel (01730) 813339

RONE, The Ven James. b 35. St Steph Ho Ox 79. **d** 80 **p** 81. C Stony Stratford *Ox* 80-82; P-in-c Fordham St Pet *Ely* 82-83; V 83-89; P-in-c Kennett 82-83; R 83-89; Can Res Ely Cathl 89-95; Treas 92-95; Adn Wisbech 95-02; Hon Can Ely Cathl 95-02; Bp's Adv for Hosp Chapl 96-02; rtd 03; Perm to Offic *Ely* from 03. *Little Housing, 32 Lumley Close, Ely CB7 4FG* Tel (01353) 667088

RONGONG, Tembu Namderr. b 76. St Andr Univ MA98. TISEC. **d** 06. C Dunfermline *St And* 06-08; R Edin SS Phil and Jas from 08. *Church of St Philip and St James, 57B Inverleigh Road, Edinburgh EH5 5PX* Tel 0131-624 7777 E-mail tembu.rongong@btinternet.com

ROOKE, James Templeman. b 43. Saltley Tr Coll Birm CertEd65. EMMTC 79. **d** 84 **p** 85. NSM Bassingham *Linc* 84-89; NSM Hykeham 89-94; Sub Chapl HM Pris Morton Hall 94; P-in-c Borrowdale *Carl* 94-97; Chapl Keswick Sch 94-95; NSM Hykeham *Linc* 97-02; Sub Chapl HM Pris Morton Hall 97-00; NSM Swinderby *Linc* from 02; CF (ACF) from 00. *The Chestnuts, Main Street, Norton Disney, Lincoln LN6 9JU* Tel (01522) 788315

ROOKE, John George Michael. b 47. St Jo Coll Dur BA72. Cranmer Hall Dur 71. **d** 74 **p** 75. C Skelmersdale St Paul *Liv* 74-78; TV Speke St Aid 78-81; Ind Chapl 81-85; V Knotty Ash St Jo 85-08; rtd 08. *c/o Fairway Golf Shops Ltd, Units 1 & 2, Victoria Forge, Victoria Street, Windermere LA23 1AD*

ROOKE, The Very Revd Patrick William. b 55. Open Univ BA85. Sarum & Wells Th Coll 75. **d** 78 **p** 79. C Mossley *Conn* 78-81; C Ballywillan 81-83; I Craigs w Dunaghy and Killagan 83-88; I Ballymore *Arm* 88-94; Asst Prov and Dioc Registrar 92-94; Hon V Choral Arm Cathl 93-94; I Agherton *Conn* 94-06; Preb and Can Conn Cathl 01-06; Adn Dalriada 05-06; Dean Arm and Keeper of Public Lib from 06. *The Library, 43 Abbey Street, Armagh BT61 7DY* Tel (028) 3752 3142 *or* 3751 8447 Fax 3752 4177 E-mail dean@armagh.anglican.org *or* rooke59@hotmail.com

ROOKWOOD, Colin John. b 40. TCD BA64 MA66 SS Mark & Jo Coll Chelsea PGCE66. Clifton Th Coll 67. **d** 70 **p** 71. C Eccleston Ch Ch *Liv* 70-75; V Penge St Jo *Roch* 75-82; V Childwall All SS *Liv* 82-91; Chapl Bethany Sch Goudhurst 91-03; rtd 03; Perm to Offic *Roch* from 01. *3 Spout Lane, Brenchley, Tonbridge TN12 7AP* Tel (01892) 725547 E-mail carolrookwood@aol.com

ROOM, Canon Frederick John. b 24. St Jo Coll Ox BA49 MA53. Wells Th Coll 49. **d** 51 **p** 52. C Bradford cum Beswick *Man* 51-54; C Halliwell St Marg 54-56; C Farnham Royal *Ox* 56-58; C-in-c Farnham Royal S CD 58-70; TV Thetford *Nor* 70-89; Sen Ind Missr 75-89; Hon Can Nor Cathl 77-89; rtd 89; Perm to Offic

Nor from 89. *61 Beechwood Drive, Thorpe St Andrew, Norwich NR7 0LN* Tel (01603) 435930

ROOME, Mrs Alison Morag Venessa. b 48. Bp Lonsdale Coll TCert71. EMMTC 98. **d** 01 **p** 02. NSM Alfreton *Derby* 01-07; P-in-c 05-07; NSM Belper Ch Ch w Turnditch from 07. *55 Dovedale Crescent, Belper DE56 1HJ* Tel (01773) 825635 E-mail aliroome@lineone.net

ROOMS (*née* JONES), **Mrs Karen Sheila Frances.** b 61. Bris Univ BA82. St Jo Coll Nottm MTh06. **d** 06 **p** 07. C Hyson Green and Forest Fields *S'well* from 06. *8 Austen Avenue, Nottingham NG7 6PE* Tel 0115-978 4333 E-mail vyumba@yahoo.co.uk

ROOMS, Canon Nigel James. b 60. Leeds Univ BSc81 Nottm Univ MA95 Birm Univ ThD08 CEng84 MIChemE86. St Jo Coll Nottm 87. **d** 90 **p** 91. C Chell *Lich* 90-94; Min Moshi St Marg Tanzania 94-01; Dir Th Educn by Ext 94-01; Hon Can Arusha from 01; Dioc Dir of Tr *S'well* 02-07; Assoc Dir Practical Th from 07; P-in-c Basford St Leodegarius from 07. *8 Austen Avenue, Nottingham NG7 6PE* Tel 0115-978 4333 E-mail nigel.rooms@southwell.anglican.org

ROOSE-EVANS, James Humphrey. b 27. St Benet's Hall Ox BA52 MA56. **d** 81 **p** 81. NSM Kington and Weobley *Heref* 81-05; NSM Primrose Hill St Mary w Avenue Road St Paul *Lon* 82-97; Perm to Offic *Lon* from 97; *Heref* from 05; *S & B* from 07. *Waterloo Lodge, Knighton LD7 1NA*

ROOT, Preb John Brereton. b 41. Lon Univ BA64 Em Coll Cam BA66 MA. Ridley Hall Cam 64. **d** 68 **p** 69. C Harlesden St Mark *Lon* 68-73; C Lower Homerton St Paul 73-76; Chapl Ridley Hall Cam 76; Vice-Prin 76-79; V Alperton *Lon* from 79; AD Brent 95-00; Preb St Paul's Cathl from 01. *The Vicarage, 34 Stanley Avenue, Wembley HA0 4JB* Tel and fax (020) 8902 1729 *or* tel 8900 0222 Fax 8902 6231 E-mail stjames2000@breathemail.net

ROOTES, William Brian. b 44. St And NSM Tr Scheme 88. **d** 91. NSM Auchterarder *St And* 91-97; NSM Muthill 91-97; Dioc Sec 98-00; Treas Action of Chs Together in Scotland 01-06; Lic to Offic from 06. *Drummond Park Farm, Logiealmond, Perth PH1 3TJ* Tel (01738) 880477 Fax 880709 E-mail w.rootes77@btinternet.com

ROOTHAM, Gerald Raymond. b 47. **d** 02 **p** 03. OLM Mattishall and the Tudd Valley *Nor* from 02. *Norfolk Wing, Letton Hall, Shipdham, Thetford IP25 7SA* Tel (01362) 820886

ROPER, Canon David John. b 53. St Steph Ho Ox 93. **d** 95 **p** 96. C Hunstanton St Mary w Ringstead Parva etc *Nor* 95-98; TV E Dereham and Scarning 98-00; R Barham w Bishopsbourne and Kingston *Cant* 00-08; C Nonington w Wymynswold and Goodnestone etc 00-08; AD E Bridge 01-08; P-in-c Broadstairs from 08; AD Thanet from 08; Hon Min Can Cant Cathl 03-08; Hon Can from 08. *The Rectory, Nelson Place, Broadstairs CT10 1HQ* Tel (01843) 862921 E-mail roper995@btinternet.com

ROPER, Glenn. b 51. York Univ MA91 Caerleon Coll of Educn CertEd73. **d** 04 **p** 05. NSM Ovenden *Wakef* from 04. *113 Meadow Drive, Halifax HX3 5JZ* Tel (01422) 368086 E-mail glsroper@lineone.net

ROPER, Michael Darwin Alston. b 66. Leeds Univ BA03. Coll of Resurr Mirfield 01. **d** 03 **p** 04. C Mortlake w E Sheen *S'wark* 03-07; P-in-c Egham Hythe *Guildf* from 07. *St Paul's Vicarage, 214 Wendover Road, Staines TW18 3DF* Tel (01784) 453625 E-mail gore_lodge@yahoo.co.uk

ROPER, Neil Vincent James. b 35. **d** 98 **p** 99. C Port Talbot St Theodore *Llan* 98-00; C Newton Nottage 00-03; C Treorchy and Treherbert 03; Chapl Quainton Hall Sch Harrow from 04. *Quainton Hall School, Hindes Road, Harrow HA1 1RX* Tel (020) 8427 1304

ROPER, Terence Chaus. b 35. K Coll Lon 56. St Boniface Warminster 59. **d** 60 **p** 61. C Forton *Portsm* 60-63; C Arlington St Alban USA 63-65; C Dallas St Thos 65-67; R Dallas Our Lady of Grace 67-73; R Irving Redeemer 73-76; R Dallas Transfiguration 76-99; R Philadelphia H Trin from 99. *1815 John F Kennedy Boulevard #2308, Philadelphia PA 19103-1731, USA* Tel (001) (215) 587 6873 *or* 567 1267

ROPER, Canon Timothy Hamilton. b 34. Qu Coll Cam BA57 MA61. Sarum Th Coll 57. **d** 59 **p** 60. C Kingsthorpe *Pet* 59-62; C Kirkby *Liv* 62-65; Chapl Rossall Sch Fleetwood 65-84; R Arthingworth, Harrington w Oxendon and E Farndon *Pet* 84-99; RD Brixworth 89-94; Can Pet Cathl 94-99; rtd 99. *47 Cromwell Crescent, Market Harborough LE16 8JN* Tel (01858) 468032

ROSAMOND, Derek William. b 49. Linc Th Coll 87. **d** 89 **p** 90. C Coventry Caludon 89-93; Urban Regeneration Chapl S Tyneside *Dur* 93-96; TV Sunderland 96-04; Community P SW Stockton from 04; P-in-c Stockton St Paul from 04. *65 Bishopton Road, Stockton-on-Tees TS18 4PE* Tel (01642) 895868 E-mail derekrosamond@hotmail.com

ROSBOROUGH, Mrs Rachel. b 76. Anglia Poly Univ BA00. St Jo Coll Nottm 06. **d** 08 **p** 09. C Charlton Kings H Apostles *Glouc* from 08. *Ashley Cottage, Overbury Street, Charlton Kings, Cheltenham GL53 8HJ* Tel (01242) 539462 E-mail rachel.rosborough@holyapostles.org.uk

ROSCOE, David John. b 64. UEA BA87 Selw Coll Cam BA93. Aston Tr Scheme 89 Westcott Ho Cam 91. **d** 94 **p** 95. C Ditton St Mich *Liv* 94-98; TV Kirkby 98-99; V Wigan St Steph 99-03; Jt P-in-c Aspull and New Springs 02-03; V New Springs and Whelley from 03; Chapl Wrightington Wigan and Leigh NHS Trust from 03. *St Stephen's Vicarage, 141 Whelley, Wigan WN2 1BL* Tel (01942) 242579

ROSCOE, Simon Nicolas. b 51. SEITE 02. **d** 04 **p** 06. C Whitstable *Cant* 04-05; C Faversham 05-09; V Southchurch Ch Ch *Chelmsf* from 09. *Christ Church Vicarage, 58 Colbert Road, Southend-on-Sea SS1 3BP* Tel (01702) 582585 E-mail simonsccc@aol.com

ROSE, Andrew David. b 45. BA81. Oak Hill Th Coll 78. **d** 81 **p** 82. C Northwood Em *Lon* 81-86; V Iver *Ox* 86-95; R Frinton *Chelmsf* 95-07; TV Washfield, Stoodleigh, Withleigh etc *Ex* from 07. *The Rectory, Withleigh, Tiverton EX16 8JQ* Tel (01884) 250509

ROSE (*née* ARDLEY), **Annette Susan.** b 68. SEITE 01. **d** 04 **p** 05. C Barham w Bishopsbourne and Kingston *Cant* 04-07; P-in-c Wingham w Elmstone and Preston w Stourmouth 07-09; P-in-c New Eltham All SS *S'wark* from 09. *All Saints' Vicarage, 22 Bercta Road, London SE9 3TZ* Tel (020) 8850 0374 E-mail revannette.rose@btinternet.com

ROSE, Anthony James. b 47. Trin Coll Bris BD72. **d** 73 **p** 74. C Halliwell St Pet *Man* 73-76; CF 76-94; R Colchester Ch Ch w St Mary V *Chelmsf* 94-01; RD Colchester 98-01; P-in-c Boreham 01-06; rtd 06; Perm to Offic *Chelmsf* from 06. *19 Holm Oak, Colchester CO2 8QA* Tel (01206) 576532 E-mail ajrose@dsl.pipex.com

ROSE, Anthony John. b 53. Birm Univ BA79. Trin Coll Bris 84. **d** 86 **p** 87. C The Quinton *Birm* 86-90; R Abbas and Templecombe w Horsington *B & W* 90-98; V New Thundersley *Chelmsf* from 98. *St George's Vicarage, 89 Rushbottom Lane, Benfleet SS7 4DN* Tel (01268) 792088 E-mail anthony.rose@ukonline.co.uk

ROSE, Canon Barry Ernest. b 35. Chich Th Coll 58. **d** 61 **p** 62. C Forest Gate St Edm *Chelmsf* 61-64; Antigua 64-66; Dominica 66-69; V St Mary-at-Latton *Chelmsf* 69-79; V Stansted Mountfitchet 79-88; V Halstead St Andr w H Trin and Greenstead Green 88-00; RD Halstead and Coggeshall 91-95; RD Hinckford 95-98; Hon Can Chelmsf Cathl 96-00; rtd 00; Perm to Offic *Chelmsf* from 00. *26 Gurton Road, Coggeshall CO6 1QA* Tel (01376) 563988 Mobile 07984-546638 E-mail jbrose@talk21.com

ROSE, Canon Bernard Frederick. b 47. **d** 91 **p** 92. OLM Ipswich St Thos *St E* 91-09; P-in-c Somersham w Flowton and Offton w Willisham from 09; P-in-c Ringshall w Battisford, Barking w Darmsden etc from 09; Hon Can St E Cathl from 05. *The Rectory, Main Road, Willisham, Ipswich IP8 4SP* Tel (01473) 657153 E-mail holy-rose@supanet.com

ROSE, Charles. *See* ROSE, Westmoreland Charles Edward

ROSE, Christopher John. b 66. Edin Univ BSc88. EAMTC 97. **d** 00 **p** 01. NSM Cambridge St Paul *Ely* 00-07; NSM All Hallows Lon Wall from 07. *6 Montreal Road, Cambridge CB1 3NP* Tel (01223) 511241 *or* (020) 7588 8922 Fax 566092 E-mail chris@amostrust.org

ROSE, David. *See* ROSE, John David

ROSE, Eve. b 63. Leeds Univ BA85. Qu Coll Birm 99. **d** 01 **p** 02. C Seacroft *Ripon* 01-04; Chapl Hull and E Riding Community Health NHS Trust 04-06; Mental Health Chapl Humber Mental Health Teaching NHS Trust from 06; Hon C Hessle *York* from 06. *Humber Mental Health NHS Trust, Trust HQ, Beverley Road, Willerby, Hull HU10 6ED* Tel (01482) 223191 Fax 303900 Mobile 07771-851725

ROSE, Miss Geraldine Susan. b 47. Trin Coll Bris BD78. dss 78 **d** 87 **p** 94. Tonbridge St Steph *Roch* 78-80; Littleover *Derby* 80-88; Par Dn 87-88; Par Dn Wombwell *Sheff* 88-94; C 94-96; rtd 96; Perm to Offic *Sheff* from 96. *5 Wheatcroft, Conisbrough, Doncaster DN12 2BL* Tel (01709) 867761 E-mail sroserhodon@onetel.net.uk

ROSE, Harry. *See* ROSE, Lionel Stafford Harry

ROSE, Ingrid Elizabeth. b 57. Univ of Wales (Abth) BA78 DipEd79. Trin Coll Carmarthen 84. **d** 87 **p** 01. NSM Ysbyty Cynfyn w Llantrisant and Eglwys Newydd *St D* 87-90 and 92-95; NSM to Adn Cardigan 00-03; NSM Grwp Bro Ystwyth a Mynach from 06. *Ystwyth Villa, Pontrhydygroes, Ystrad Meurig SY25 6DF* Tel (01974) 282398

ROSE, John Clement Wansey. b 46. New Coll Ox BA71 MA72. Ripon Hall Ox 70. **d** 72 **p** 73. C Harborne St Pet *Birm* 72-76; TV Kings Norton 76-81; V Maney 81-02; R Condover w Frodesley, Acton Burnell etc *Heref* from 02. *The Vicarage, Condover, Shrewsbury SY5 7AA* Tel (01743) 872251

ROSE, John David. b 40. Dioc OLM tr scheme 97. **d** 00 **p** 01. OLM Prescot *Liv* from 00. *18 Eccleston Gardens, St Helens WA10 3BL* Tel (01744) 736168 Mobile 07808-350859 Fax 0151-426 5121

ROSE, Judith Barbara. b 51. TCert72. SAOMC 98. **d** 99 **p** 00. OLM Stantonbury and Willen *Ox* from 99. *16 Runnymede,*

Giffard Park, Milton Keynes MK14 5QL Tel and fax (01908) 618634

ROSE, The Ven Kathleen Judith. b 37. Lon Bible Coll BD73 St Mich Ho Ox 64. **dss** 76 **d** 87 **p** 94. Leeds St Geo *Ripon* 76-81; Bradf Cathl 81-85; S Gillingham *Roch* 85-87; Par Dn 87-90; RD Gillingham 88-90; Bp's Dom Chapl 90-95; Asst Dir of Ords 90-95; Hon Can Roch Cathl 93-02; Acting Adn Tonbridge 95-96; Adn Tonbridge 96-02; rtd 02; Perm to Offic *B & W* from 03. *4 Glebelands Close, Cheddar BS27 3XP* Tel (01934) 741708 Mobile 07736-616382

ROSE, Lionel Stafford Harry. b 38. MBE93. Wells Th Coll 69. **d** 71 **p** 72. C Minchinhampton *Glouc* 71-73; C Thornbury 73-75; R Ruardean 75-80; V Whiteshill 80-84; CF 84-93; Chapl HM Pris Kirkham 93-95; Wymott 95-01; Rye Hill 01; rtd 01; Perm to Offic *Ely* from 02. *4 Samian Close, Highfield, Caldecote, Cambridge CB23 7GP*

ROSE, Mrs Lynda Kathryn. b 51. Barrister-at-Law (Gray's Inn) 81 Ex Univ BA73 Ox Univ BA86. Wycliffe Hall Ox 87. **d** 87 **p** 94. C Highfield *Ox* 87-88; C Ox St Clem 89-93; Dir Anastasis Min 93-99; NSM Ambrosden w Merton and Piddington 94-99; Pres Assn Chr Writers from 99. *95 Staunton Road, Oxford OX3 7TR* Tel (01865) 768774

ROSE, Michael Mark. b 63. Hull Univ BA04. Westcott Ho Cam 07. **d** 09. C Linc St Nic w St Jo Newport from 09. *Flat 1, 2 Greenstone Place, Lincoln LN2 1PP* Tel 07846-601141 (mobile) E-mail mikeredrose63@hotmail.com

ROSE, Mrs Pamela Inneen. b 49. Hull Univ BSc71 Moray Ho Coll of Educn PGCE72. **d** 06 **p** 07. OLM Stow Gp *Linc* from 06. *Daisy Cottage, 16-18 Grange Lane, Willingham by Stow, Gainsborough DN21 5LB* Tel (01427) 787578 E-mail pamrose@worldshare.org.uk

ROSE, Canon Paul Rosamond. b 32. Trin Hall Cam BA56 MA60. Westcott Ho Cam 57. **d** 59 **p** 60. C Wandsworth St Anne *S'wark* 59-61; C Tormohun *Ex* 61-64; P-in-c Daramombe Rhodesia 64-67; Min Can, Prec and Sacr Pet Cathl 67-72; V Paddington St Jo w St Mich *Lon* 72-79; PV Westmr Abbey 74-79; Min Can and Prec Cant Cathl 79-84; V Rothwell w Orton *Pet* 84-87; R Rothwell w Orton, Rushton w Glendon and Pipewell 87-97; Can Pet Cathl 94-97; rtd 97; Heidelberg *Eur* 98; Perm to Offic *Pet* from 97; *Lon* and *Eur* from 98; *Ely* from 03. *15 Standish Court, Campaign Avenue, Peterborough PE2 9RR* Tel (01733) 553272 E-mail canons.rose@virgin.net

ROSE, Robert Alec Lewis. b 41. Man Univ BSc64. Wycliffe Hall Ox 85. **d** 87 **p** 88. C Vange *Chelmsf* 87-91; C Langdon Hills 91-94; P-in-c Bentley Common 94-00; P-in-c Kelvedon Hatch 94-00; P-in-c Navestock 94-00; R Bentley Common, Kelvedon Hatch and Navestock 00-08; rtd 08; Perm to Offic *St E* from 09. *47 High Street, Wickham Market, Woodbridge IP13 0HE* Tel (01728) 748199 E-mail robdaphnerose@btinternet.com

ROSE, Susan. *See* ROSE, Miss Geraldine Susan

ROSE, Mrs Susan Margaret. b 59. Westmr Coll of Educn BEd81. SAOMC 95. **d** 98 **p** 99. C N Petherton w Northmoor Green *B & W* 98-01; P-in-c 01-03; P-in-c N Newton w St Michaelchurch, Thurloxton etc 01-03; R Alfred Jewel 03-09; RD Sedgemoor 06-09; P-in-c Cheddar from 09; P-in-c Rodney Stoke w Draycott from 09. *The Vicarage, Station Road, Cheddar BS27 3AH* Tel (01934) 740394 E-mail rev.suerose@virgin.net

ROSE, Miss Susan Mary. b 36. TCert56. Dalton Ho Bris 68 Trin Coll Bris 74. **dss** 81 **d** 87 **p** 94. Brinsworth w Catcliffe *Sheff* 75-77; Scargill Ho 77-83; Netherthorpe *Sheff* 83-87; Tutor Trin Coll Bris 87-96; V Normanton *Wakef* 96-01; rtd 01; Perm to Offic *Sheff* from 01 and *Wakef* from 02. *23 Kendal Vale, Worsborough Bridge, Barnsley S70 5NL* Tel (01226) 771590

ROSE, Timothy Edward Francis. b 72. Univ of Wales (Cardiff) BD93 MA95 K Coll Lon PhD98. Wycliffe Hall Ox MTh03. **d** 01 **p** 02. C Jesmond H Trin and Newc St Barn and St Jude 01-04; Chapl R Holloway and Bedf New Coll Lon 04-06; C Farnham *Guildf* from 06. *6 High Park Road, Farnham GU9 7JL* Tel (01252) 737771 Mobile 07709-722325 E-mail tim.rose1@btinternet.com

ROSE, Westmoreland Charles Edward. b 32. St Jo Coll Nottm 85. **d** 87 **p** 88. C Fairfield *Derby* 87-90; V Linton and Castle Gresley 90-01; rtd 01; Perm to Offic *Derby* 01-08. *Lavender Lodge Nursing Home, 48-50 Stafford Street, Derby DE1 1JL* Tel (01332) 298388

ROSE-CASEMORE, Claire Pamela. b 63. St Paul's Cheltenham BA84 St Luke's Coll Ex PGCE85 Anglia Poly Univ MA02. Ridley Hall Cam 95. **d** 97 **p** 98. Par Dn Kingsthorpe w Northampton St Dav *Pet* 97-98; C 98-01; TV Daventry, Ashby St Ledgers, Braunston etc from 01. *The Rectory, 71 High Street, Braunston, Daventry NN11 7HS* Tel (01788) 890235 E-mail clairerc@btopenworld.com

ROSE-CASEMORE, John. b 27. Chich Th Coll. **d** 55 **p** 56. C Epsom Common Ch Ch *Guildf* 55-58; C Hednesford *Lich* 58-60; V Dawley 60-65; R Puttenham and Wanborough *Guildf* 65-72; R Frimley 72-83; RD Surrey Heath 76-81; R Ludgershall and Faberstown *Sarum* 83-86; R Tidworth, Ludgershall and Faberstown 86-92; rtd 92; Perm to Offic *Ex* from 93. *5 Culvery Close, Woodbury, Exeter EX5 1LZ* Tel (01395) 233426

ROSE-CASEMORE, Miss Penelope Jane. b 56. Bris Univ CertEd77 BEd78. Westcott Ho Cam 83. **dss** 85 **d** 87 **p** 94. Waterloo St Jo w St Andr *S'wark* 85-87; Par Dn 87-88; Asst Chapl Gt Ormond Street Hosp for Sick Children Lon 88-90; Par Dn Balham St Mary and St Jo *S'wark* 90-94; C 94-96; Par Dn Upper Tooting H Trin 90-94; C 94-96; TV Clapham Team 96-01; V Clapham Ch Ch and St Jo from 02; AD Lambeth N from 05. *Christchurch Vicarage, 39 Union Grove, London SW8 2QJ* Tel and fax (020) 7622 3552

ROSEDALE, John Richard. b 54. NOC 02. **d** 05 **p** 06. NSM Hadfield *Derby* from 05. *43 Spire Hollin, Glossop SK13 7BJ* Tel (01457) 857441 E-mail john@glossop.org

ROSENTHAL, Canon James Milton. b 51. **d** 07. Dir Communications Angl Communion Office 89-09; NSM All Hallows by the Tower etc *Lon* from 07. *8 Margaret Street, London W1W 8JG* Tel 07595-888751 (mobile) E-mail james.rosenthal@gmail.com

ROSENTHAL, Sheila. b 57. Warwick Univ BA81 MA95. Ripon Coll Cuddesdon 04. **d** 06 **p** 07. C Worc SE from 06. *24 Albert Road, Worcester WR5 1EB* Tel (01905) 356656 E-mail mrsr@quista.net

ROSEWEIR, Clifford John. b 43. Glas Univ MA64 MCIPD81. S'wark Ord Course 83. **d** 84 **p** 85. NSM Redhill H Trin *S'wark* 84-89; P-in-c Croydon St Martin 89-92; Perm to Offic 92-93; Hon C Warlingham 93-94; V Croydon Ch Ch 94-97; Perm to Offic from 06. *206 Bridle Road, Croydon CR0 8HL* Tel (020) 8777 2820 Mobile 07850-480058 E-mail rosewec@hotmail.com

✠**ROSIER, The Rt Revd Stanley Bruce.** b 28. Univ of W Aus BSc48 Ox Univ BA52 MA56. Westcott Ho Cam 53. **d** 54 **p** 55 **c** 67. C Ecclesall *Sheff* 54-57; R Wyalkatchem Australia 57-64; R Kellerberrin 64-67; Can Perth 66-67; Adn Northam 67-70; Bp Willochra 70-87; Asst Bp 90-92; R Parkside 87-94; rtd 94. *5A Fowler's Road, Glenunga SA 5064, Australia* Tel (0061) (8) 8379 5213 E-mail bfrosier@senet.com.au

ROSKELLY, James Hereward Emmanuel. b 57. BSc ACSM80. Cranmer Hall Dur 83. **d** 86 **p** 87. C Dunster, Carhampton and Withycombe w Rodhuish *B & W* 86-90; C Ealing St Mary *Lon* 90-93; Chapl R Marsden Hosp Lon and Surrey 93-95; CF 95-03; TV Rayleigh *Chelmsf* from 03. *St Michael's House, 13 Sir Walter Raleigh Drive, Rayleigh SS6 9JB* Tel (01268) 785043 Mobile 07989-442434 E-mail jamesroskelly@aol.com

ROSKILLY, John Noel. b 33. Man Univ MB, ChB58 MRCGP68. St Deiniol's Hawarden 74. **d** 75 **p** 76. NSM Bramhall *Ches* 75-86; V Capesthorne w Siddington and Marton 86-91; Dioc Dir of Counselling 84-93; Bp's Officer for NSM 87-93; NSM Macclesfield St Paul 92-93; rtd 93; Perm to Offic *Ches* from 93. *North View, Hawkins Lane, Rainow, Macclesfield SK10 5TL* Tel (01625) 501014

ROSKROW, Neil. b 27. FBCO80. St Alb Minl Tr Scheme 82. **d** 85 **p** 86. NSM Digswell and Panshanger *St Alb* 85-90; P-in-c Gt Gaddesden 90-95; P-in-c Lt Gaddesden 92-95; rtd 96; Perm to Offic *St Alb* 96-05. *Jevinda, 5 Phillips Terrace, North Roskear, Camborne TR14 8PJ* Tel (01209) 711761

ROSKROW, Mrs Pamela Mary. b 25. St Alb Minl Tr Scheme. **dss** 85 **d** 87 **p** 94. Digswell and Panshanger *St Alb* 85-90; Hon Par Dn 87-90; Hon Par Dn Gt Gaddesden 90-94; Hon C 94-95; Hon Par Dn Lt Gaddesden 92-94; Hon C 94-95; Perm to Offic 96-05. *Jevinda, 5 Phillips Terrace, North Roskear, Camborne TR14 8PJ* Tel (01209) 711761

ROSS, Alexander. *See* ROSS, David Alexander

ROSS, Canon Anthony McPherson. b 38. OBE. Univ of Wales (Lamp) BA60 Lon Univ BD63. St Mich Coll Llan 60. **d** 61 **p** 62. C Gabalfa *Llan* 61-65; Chapl RN 65-93; QHC 89-93; P-in-c Coln St Aldwyns, Hatherop, Quenington etc *Glouc* 93-95; V 95-08; RD Fairford 96-04; rtd 08; Bp's Adv on Deliverance Min *Glouc* from 08; Hon Can Glouc Cathl from 02. *Rowan Tree Cottage, Ampney Crucis, Cirencester GL7 5RY* Tel (01285) 851410 E-mail tonyrosstsst@talktalk.net

ROSS, Mrs Audrey Ruth. b 42. Herts Coll BA86. SAOMC 99. **d** 02 **p** 03. NSM Leavesden *St Alb* 02-06; NSM Storrington *Chich* from 06. *9 Longland Avenue, Storrington, Pulborough RH20 4HY* Tel (01903) 746231 E-mail revross@supanet.com

ROSS, David Alexander. b 46. Oak Hill Th Coll 73. **d** 75 **p** 76. C Northwood Em *Lon* 75-80; R Eastrop *Win* 80-86; V Hove Bp Hannington Memorial Ch *Chich* 86-93; V Muswell Hill St Jas w St Matt *Lon* 93-07; rtd 07; Hon C S Tottenham St Ann *Lon* from 07. *18 Wroxham Gardens, London N11 2BA* Tel (020) 8292 8981 E-mail alexlynne.ross@googlemail.com

ROSS, Preb Duncan Gilbert. b 48. Lon Univ BSc70. Westcott Ho Cam 75. **d** 78 **p** 79. C Stepney St Dunstan and All SS *Lon* 78-84; V Hackney Wick St Mary of Eton w St Aug 84-95; P-in-c Bow Common 95-03; V from 03; Preb St Paul's Cathl from 95. *St Paul's Vicarage, Leopold Street, London E3 4LA* Tel and fax (020) 7987 4941 E-mail duncan.ross5@btinternet.com

ROSS, Frederic Ian. b 34. Man Univ BSc56. Westcott Ho Cam 58. **d** 62 **p** 63. C Oldham *Man* 62-65; Sec Th Colls Dept SCM 65-69; Teacher Man Gr Sch 69-84; V Shrewsbury H Cross *Lich* 84-02; rtd 02; Perm to Offic *Heref* and *Lich* from 02. *The Paddock,*

Plealey Road, Annscroft, Shrewsbury SY5 8AN Tel (01743) 860327

ROSS, Henry Ernest. b 40. NW Ord Course 70. **d** 73 **p** 74. NSM Litherland St Phil *Liv* 73-75; C Newton-le-Willows 75-77; P-in-c Walton St Luke 77-79; V from 79; RD Walton 84-89. *46 Somerset Drive, Southport PR8 3SN* Tel (01704) 571287
E-mail harry.ross@rossfamily.fsnet.co.uk

ROSS, John. b 41. Wells Th Coll 66. **d** 69 **p** 70. C Newc St Gabr 69-71; C Prudhoe 71-75; Hon C Shotley 75-87; Hon C Whittonstall 75-87; P-in-c Wallsend St Pet 93-94. *11 Weston Avenue, Whickham, Newcastle upon Tyne NE16 5TS* Tel 0191-488 1546 E-mail rossj41@blueyonder.co.uk

ROSS, John Colin. b 50. Oak Hill Th Coll 84. **d** 86 **p** 87. C Stowmarket *St E* 86-89; C Wakef St Andr and St Mary 89-91; R Gt and Lt Whelnetham w Bradfield St George *St E* 91-94; V Newmarket All SS 94-02; V Erith St Paul *Roch* 02-04; P-in-c Combs and Lt Finborough *St E* from 04. *The Rectory, 135 Poplar Hill, Combs, Stowmarket IP14 2AY* Tel (01449) 612076 Mobile 07904-124227 E-mail revjohnross@dsl.pipex.com

ROSS (née YOUNG), Mrs Karen Heather. b 66. Nottm Univ BA01. Westcott Ho Cam 02. **d** 05 **p** 07. C Airedale w Fryston *Wakef* 05-06; Hon C Ravenshead *S'well* 07-09; Mental Health Chapl Notts Healthcare NHS Trust 08-09. *Address temp unknown*

ROSS, Malcolm Hargrave. b 37. Dur Univ BSc58. Westcott Ho Cam 63. **d** 64 **p** 65. C Armley St Bart *Ripon* 64-67; USPG 67-71; Trinidad and Tobago 67-71; V New Kensington *Sheff* 71-75; Bp's Missr in E Lon 75-82; P-in-c Haggerston All SS 75-82; V Bedford Leigh *Man* 82-85; Area Sec USPG *Bris* and *Glouc* 85-90; Bp's Officer for Miss and Evang *Bris* 90-94; P-in-c Lacock w Bowden Hill 90-94; V Sherston Magna, Easton Grey, Luckington etc 94-06; rtd 06. *132 Larecombe Road, St Austell PL25 3EZ* E-mail m-eross@tiscali.co.uk

ROSS, Oliver Charles Milligan. b 58. Lon Univ BA80 St Edm Ho Cam BA85. Ridley Hall Cam 84. **d** 87 **p** 88. C Preston St Cuth *Blackb* 87-90; C Paddington St Jo w St Mich *Lon* 90-95; V Hounslow H Trin w St Paul 95-06; P-in-c Isleworth St Mary 01-02; R St Olave Hart Street w All Hallows Staining etc from 06; P-in-c St Kath Cree from 06; AD The City from 09. *St Olave's Rectory, 8 Hart Street, London EC3R 7NB* Tel (020) 7702 0244 E-mail oliver.ross@london.anglican.org

ROSS, Mrs Rachel Anne. b 64. York Univ BSc85 SS Coll Cam PGCE86 Sheff Univ MA97 Coll of Ripon & York St Jo MA00. NOC 97. **d** 00 **p** 01. C Pendleton *Man* 00-04; P-in-c Salford Ordsall St Clem 03-04; P-in-c Salford St Ignatius and Stowell Memorial 03-04; R Ordsall and Salford Quays 04-07; P-in-c Loughborough All SS w H Trin *Leic* 07-08; R Loughborough All SS w H Trin from 08. *The Rectory, 60 Westfield Drive, Loughborough LE11 3QL* Tel (01509) 212780 Mobile 07884-371688 E-mail rachelross@tiscali.co.uk

ROSS, Canon Raymond John. b 28. Trin Coll Cam BA52 MA57. St Steph Ho Ox 52. **d** 54 **p** 55. C Clifton All SS *Bris* 54-58; C Solihull *Birm* 58-66; C-in-c Hobs Moat CD 66-67; V Hobs Moat 67-72; R Newbold w Dunston *Derby* 72-95; RD Chesterfield 78-91; Hon Can Derby Cathl 86-95; rtd 96; Perm to Offic *Derby* from 96. *Threeways, Bridge Hill, Belper DE56 2BY* Tel (01773) 825876

ROSS (née FAIRWEATHER), Mrs Sally Helen. b 69. St Hilda's Coll Ox BA91. Cranmer Hall Dur 94. **d** 97 **p** 98. C Illingworth *Wakef* 97-01; Warden H Rood Ho and C Thirsk *York* 01-02; Chapl Northallerton Health Services NHS Trust 01-02; C Sheff St Mark Broomhill 02-04; Mental Health Chapl Sheff Care Trust from 04. *40 Bents Drive, Sheffield S11 9RP* Tel 0114-235 1652 E-mail sh.ross@tiscali.co.uk

ROSS, Vernon. b 57. Portsm Poly BSc79 RGN86. Trin Coll Bris 89. **d** 91 **p** 92. C Fareham St Jo *Portsm* 91-94; P-in-c Witheridge, Thelbridge, Creacombe, Meshaw etc *Ex* 94-00; TR Barnstaple 00-08; P-in-c Fyfield, Moreton w Bobbingworth etc *Chelmsf* from 08. *6 Forest Drive, Fyfield, Ongar CM5 0TP* Tel (01277) 899886 E-mail vfsd.ross1@btinternet.com

ROSS-McCABE, Mrs Philippa Mary Seton. b 63. Natal Univ BA83 HDipEd86 Bris Univ BA01. Trin Coll Bris 99. **d** 01 **p** 02. C Burpham *Guildf* 01-05; Lic to Offic 05-06; C Wisley w Pyrford 06-08; Tutor Local Min Progr from 06; Hon C Byfleet from 09. *The Rectory, 81 Rectory Lane, Byfleet, West Byfleet KT14 7LX* Tel (01932) 342374 E-mail p.rossmccabe@btinternet.com

ROSS, Dean of. See PETERS, The Very Revd Christopher Lind

✠**ROSSDALE, The Rt Revd David Douglas James.** b 53. Westmr Coll Ox MA91 Surrey Univ MSc01. K Coll Lon 72 Chich Th Coll 80. **d** 81 **p** 82 **c** 00. C Upminster *Chelmsf* 81-86; V Moulsham St Luke 86-90; V Cookham *Ox* 90-00; RD Maidenhead 94-00; Hon Can Ch Ch 99-00; Suff Bp Grimsby *Linc* from 00; Can and Preb Linc from 00. *Bishop's House, Church Lane, Irby, Grimsby DN37 7JR* Tel (01472) 371715 Fax 371716 E-mail rossdale@btinternet.com

ROSSETER, Miss Susan Mary. b 46. Man Univ BA67 Edin Univ DASS71. St Jo Coll Nottm LTh84. **d** 87 **p** 94. Par Dn Bromley Common St Aug *Roch* 87-88; C Pudsey St Lawr and St Paul *Bradf* 88-95; C Haughton le Skerne *Dur* 95-00; C Wilnecote *Lich*

from 00. *5 Avill, Hockley, Tamworth B77 5QE* Tel (01827) 701075 E-mail s.rosseter@ntlworld.com

ROSSITER, Donald William Frank. b 30. **d** 80 **p** 81. NSM Abergavenny St Mary w Llanwenarth Citra *Mon* 80-96; NSM Govilon w Llanfoist w Llanelen 92-05; Perm to Offic from 05. *10 Meadow Lane, Abergavenny NP7 7AY* Tel (01873) 855648

ROSSITER, Gillian Alice. b 56. SRN75 RSCN75. NOC 98. **d** 01 **p** 02. C Neston *Ches* 01-06; P-in-c Gt Meols 06-09; V from 09; RD Wirral N from 08. *St John's Vicarage, 142 Birkenhead Road, Meols, Wirral CH47 0LF* Tel 0151-632 1661

ROSSITER, Paul Albert. b 55. Leeds Univ BA06. NOC 03. **d** 06 **p** 07. NSM Wallasey St Nic w All SS *Ches* from 06. *St John's Vicarage, 142 Birkenhead Road, Meols, Wirral CH47 0LF* Tel 0151-632 1661 E-mail p.a.rossiter@liverpool.ac.uk

ROSSITER, Raymond Stephen David. b 22. MBE99. St Deiniol's Hawarden 75. **d** 76 **p** 77. NSM Sale St Anne *Ches* 76-90; Perm to Offic rtd 91. *75 Temple Road, Sale M33 2FQ* Tel 0161-962 3240

ROSSLYN SMITH, Mrs Katherine Dorothy Nevill. b 40. STETS 97. **d** 00 **p** 01. NSM Tisbury *Sarum* 00-01; NSM Nadder Valley 01-03; NSM Chalke Valley 03-06; rtd 06. *The Old School House, Church Street, Bowerchalke, Salisbury SP5 5BE* Tel (01722) 780011

ROSSLYN-SMITH, Mrs Kirsten Louise. b 73. Nottm Trent Univ BA96. St Jo Coll Nottm MTh05. **d** 05 **p** 06. C Tunbridge Wells St Jas *Roch* from 05. *3 Andrews Close, Tunbridge Wells TN2 3PA* Tel (01892) 531297

ROSTILL, Brian. b 50. K Alfred's Coll Win BTh00. Cranmer Hall Dur 01. **d** 03 **p** 04. C Knight's Enham and Smannell w Enham Alamein *Win* 03-07; P-in-c Boyatt Wood from 07. *St Peter's Church House, 53 Sovereign Way, Eastleigh SO50 4SA* Tel (023) 8064 2188 E-mail rostill@tiscali.co.uk

ROSTRON, Derek. b 34. St Mich Coll Llan 65. **d** 67 **p** 68. C Morecambe St Barn *Blackb* 67-70; C Ribbleton 70-72; V Chorley All SS 72-79; C Woodchurch *Ches* 79-80; V Audlem 80-03; RD Nantwich 87-97; rtd 04; Perm to Offic *Lich* 01-06 and *Ches* 04-06. *30 St Matthew's Drive, Derrington, Stafford ST18 9LU* Tel (01785) 246349

ROTHERAM, Eric. b 36. Clifton Th Coll 63. **d** 67 **p** 68. C Gt Crosby St Luke *Liv* 67-69; C Sutton 69-71; V Warrington St Paul 72-79; Lic to Offic 79-80; Perm to Offic *Ches* and *Liv* from 80. *7 Paul Street, Warrington WA2 7LE* Tel (01925) 633048

ROTHERY, Jean. b 44. **d** 98 **p** 99. NSM Purley *Ox* from 98. *Oak Lea, Tidmarsh Road, Tidmarsh, Reading RG8 8ER* Tel 0118-984 3625

ROTHERY, Robert Frederick (Fred). b 34. Lon Coll of Div 67. **d** 69 **p** 70. C Burscough Bridge *Liv* 69-72; C Chipping Campden *Glouc* 72-75; P-in-c Didmarton w Oldbury-on-the-Hill and Sopworth 75-77; R Boxwell, Leighterton, Didmarton, Oldbury etc 77-83; R Stow on the Wold 83-00; RD Stow 90-99; rtd 00. *12 Phillips Road, Marnhull, Sturminster Newton DT10 1LF* Tel (01258) 820668

ROTHWELL, Canon Bryan. b 60. St Edm Hall Ox BA81 MA85. Trin Coll Bris. **d** 85 **p** 86. C Carl St Jo 85-88; C Ulverston St Mary w H Trin 88-90; P-in-c Preston St Mary *Blackb* 90-96; P-in-c St John's in the Vale w Wythburn *Carl* 96-99; R St John's-in-the-Vale, Threlkeld and Wythburn from 99; Warden Dioc Youth Cen from 96; RD Derwent from 05; Hon Can Carl Cathl from 08. *The Rectory, Threlkeld, Keswick CA12 4RT* Tel (017687) 79714 E-mail bryan.rothwell@btinternet.com

ROTHWELL, Edwin John. b 53. Lanc Univ BA74 PhD79. Sarum & Wells Th Coll 88. **d** 90 **p** 91. C Malvern Link w Cowleigh *Worc* 90-94; R Bowbrook N 94-00; Asst Chapl Swindon and Marlborough NHS Trust 00-03; Chapl E Somerset NHS Trust from 03. *Chaplain's Office, Yeovil District Hospital, Higher Kingston, Yeovil BA21 4AT* Tel (01935) 475122 E-mail john.rothwell@ydh.nhs.uk

ROTHWELL, Harold. b 34. AKC58. K Coll Lon St Boniface Warminster. **d** 59 **p** 60. C Old Brumby *Linc* 59-62; P-in-c Sheff St Steph w St Phil and St Ann 62-64; V Caistor w Holton le Moor and Clixby *Linc* 67-77; Chapl Caistor Hosp 67-77; Org Sec CECS *Ex* and *B & W* 77-81; P-in-c Deeping Fen *Linc* 78-81; C Boston 86-88; C Spilsby w Hundleby 88-91; C Bracebridge Heath 91-94; rtd 94; Perm to Offic *Linc* 94-05. *47 Ridgeway, Nettleham, Lincoln LN2 2TL* Tel (01522) 751610

ROTHWELL, Michael John Hereward. See HEREWARD-ROTHWELL, Canon Michael John

ROTHWELL, Steven. b 68. Roehampton Inst BA99 Cam Univ MA02. Westcott Ho Cam 00. **d** 02 **p** 03. C Chesterton Gd Shep *Ely* 02-06; R Gamlingay and Everton from 06. *The Rectory, Stocks Lane, Gamlingay, Sandy SG19 3JP* Tel (01767) 650568 E-mail srothwell@hotmail.com

ROTHWELL-JACKSON, Christopher Patrick. b 32. St Cath Soc Ox BA58 MA61 Bris Univ PGCE66. St Steph Ho Ox 55. **d** 59 **p** 60. C E Clevedon All SS *B & W* 59-62; C Midsomer Norton 62-65; Asst Teacher St Pet Primary Sch Portishead 66-68; Clevedon Junior Sch 68-72; Dep Hd Clevedon All SS Primary Sch 72-75; Hd Master Bp Pursglove Sch Tideswell

75-90; rtd 90; Perm to Offic *Ex* from 95. *Rosedale, Hookway, Crediton EX17 3PU* Tel (01363) 772039

ROUCH, David Vaughan. b 36. Oak Hill Th Coll 67. **d** 69 **p** 70. C Denton Holme *Carl* 69-74; V Litherland St Jo and St Jas *Liv* 74-95; V Pemberton St Mark Newtown 95-96; P-in-c Wigan St Barn Marsh Green 03-06; rtd 06; Perm to Offic *Lich* from 07. *16 Parrs Lane, Bayston Hill, Shrewsbury SY3 0JS* Tel (01743) 873800 E-mail drouchatjennyr@blueyonder.co.uk

ROUCH, Peter Bradford. b 66. BNC Ox MA87 Peterho Cam MA99 Man Univ PhD05. Westcott Ho Cam 96. **d** 99 **p** 00. C E Dulwich St Jo *S'wark* 99-02; Jun Research Fell St Steph Ho Ox 02-04; Chapl St Jo Coll Ox 03-04; P-in-c Man Apostles w Miles Platting from 05; Hon Research Fell Man Univ from 07. *St George's Rectory, 10 Redacre Road, Manchester M18 8RU* Tel 0161-202 6891 Mobile 07952-262616 E-mail revrouch@aol.com

ROULSTON, Joseph Ernest. b 52. BNC Ox BA74 MA78 Lon Univ PhD81 FRSC86 FLS94 FIBiol01 FRCPath01 CSci04. Edin Dioc NSM Course 83. **d** 86 **p** 87. C Edin St Hilda 86-88; C Edin St Fillan 86-88; NSM Edin St Mich and All SS 88-97; Dioc Chapl Gen from 96; Assoc P Roslin (Rosslyn Chpl) 99-07; P-in-c from 07. *16 Summerside Street, Edinburgh EH6 4NU* Tel 0131-554 6382 *or* 242 9225 Mobile 07903-969698 E-mail j.e.roulston@ed.ac.uk

ROUND, Keith Leonard. b 49. Sarum & Wells Th Coll 88. **d** 90 **p** 91. C Meir *Lich* 90-95; V Burslem St Werburgh from 95. *The Presbytery, Haywood Road, Stoke-on-Trent ST6 7AH* Tel (01782) 837582

ROUND, Malcolm John Harrison. b 56. Lon Univ BSc77 BA81. Oak Hill Th Coll. **d** 81 **p** 82. C Guildf St Sav w Stoke-next-Guildford 81-85; C Hawkwell *Chelmsf* 85-88; R Balerno *Edin* from 88. *53 Marchbank Drive, Balerno EH14 7ER* Tel 0131-449 4127

ROUNDHILL, Andrew (John). b 65. CCC Cam BA87. Ripon Coll Cuddesdon BTh93. **d** 93 **p** 94. C Lancaster Ch Ch w St Jo and St Anne *Blackb* 93-97; Chapl Loretto Sch Musselburgh 97-02; Chapl Hong Kong Cathl from 02. *D2 On Lee, 2 Mount Davis Road, Pok Fu Lam, Hong Kong, China* Tel (00852) 2817 8774 *or* 2523 4157 E-mail roundhill@netvigator.com

ROUNDTREE, James Clabern (Clay). b 75. Oklahoma Univ BFA98 York Univ MA00. St Steph Ho Ox BA02. **d** 03 **p** 04. C Yarm *York* 03-07; V Ingleby Barwick from 07. *St Francis's House, Barwick Way, Ingleby Barwick, Stockton-on-Tees TS17 0WD* Tel (01642) 760171 E-mail clayroundtree@hotmail.com

ROUNDTREE, Samuel William. b 19. TCD BA42 MA54. CITC 43. **d** 43 **p** 44. C Waterford Ch Ch *C & O* 44-47; I Tallow w Kilwatermoy 47-51; I Kiltegan w Stratford (and Rathvilly from 60) 51-62; Treas Leighlin Cathl 62-78; Preb Ossory Cathl 62-78; I Dunleckney 62-82; Chan Ossory and Leighlin Cathls 78-80; Prec 80-82; I New w Old Ross, Whitechurch, Fethard etc 82-88; Adn Ferns 86-88; rtd 88. *Greystones Nursing Home, Church Road, Greystones, Co Wicklow, Republic of Ireland*

ROUNTREE, The Ven Richard Benjamin. b 52. NUI BA73. CITC 76. **d** 76 **p** 77. C Orangefield *D & D* 76-80; C Dublin Zion Ch *D & G* 80-83; I Dalkey St Patr 83-97; I Powerscourt w Kilbride from 97; Dioc Dir Decade of Evang 90-96; Can Ch Ch Cathl Dublin from 92; Treas from 04; Dioc Dir Lay Min 05-09; Adn Glendalough from 09. *Powerscourt Rectory, Enniskerry, Bray, Co Wicklow, Republic of Ireland* Tel and fax (00353) (1) 286 3534 Mobile 87-276 7564 E-mail rbrountree@eircom.net

ROUSE, Graham. b 58. Sheff City Coll of Educn CertEd79 Leic Univ DipEd84. Cranmer Hall Dur 90. **d** 92 **p** 93. C Longridge *Blackb* 92-96; P-in-c Fairhaven 96-97; V 97-07; P-in-c Blackpool St Mary from 07; P-in-c S Shore St Pet from 07; P-in-c S Shore H Trin from 08. *1 Windermere Road, Blackpool FY4 2BX* Tel (01253) 349911

ROUTH, Canon Eileen Rosemary. b 41. Cant Sch of Min 82. **dss** 85 **d** 87 **p** 94. Folkestone St Sav *Cant* 85-90; Par Dn 87-90; Par Dn Woodnesborough w Worth and Staple 90-91; Dn-in-c 91-94; V 94-96; V Maidstone St Martin 96-99; Hon Can Cant Cathl 99; rtd 99; Perm to Offic *Cant* from 00. *31 Tile Kiln Hill, Blean, Canterbury CT2 9EE* Tel (01227) 464052

ROUTH, William John. b 60. Magd Coll Ox BA81 MA92. Ripon Coll Cuddesdon 93. **d** 95 **p** 96. C Longton *Blackb* 95-99; V Sutton Coldfield St Chad *Birm* 99-06; P-in-c from 06; P-in-c Sutton Coldfield H Trin from 06. *Holy Trinity Rectory, 5 Broome Gardens, Sutton Coldfield B75 7JE* Tel 0121-311 0474 E-mail john.routh@btinternet.com

ROUTLEDGE, Christopher Joseph. b 78. Keele Univ BSc99 SS Mark & Jo Univ Coll Plymouth PGCE01. Oak Hill Th Coll DA08. **d** 08. C Tiverton St Geo and St Paul *Ex* from 08. *St George's Vicarage, St Andrew Street, Tiverton EX16 6PH*

ROW, Mrs Pamela Anne. b 54. Open Univ BA86 MA92 Homerton Coll Cam BEd75. NOC 94. **d** 96 **p** 97. NSM Neston *Ches* 96-01; Chapl Heref Cathl Sch from 02; Min Can Heref Cathl from 04. *4 Harley Court, Hereford HR1 2NA* Tel (01432) 363508 *or* 363522 Fax 363525

ROWAN, Nicholas Edward. b 76. Essex Univ BA. Trin Coll Bris. **d** 06 **p** 07. C Rayleigh *Chelmsf* from 06. *15 The Limes, Rayleigh SS6 8TH* E-mail nick@rowan1129.freeserve.co.uk

ROWBERRY, Christopher Michael. b 58. Univ of Wales (Lamp) MA04 Plymouth Univ CQSW85. Qu Coll Birm 94. **d** 96 **p** 97. C Lytchett Minster *Sarum* 96-00; TV Totton *Win* from 00. *The Vicarage, Eling Hill, Totton, Southampton SO40 9HF* Tel (023) 8086 6426 E-mail stmarythevirgin@btinternet.com

ROWBERRY, Michael James. b 46. Sussex Univ BA74. Edin Th Coll 85. **d** 87 **p** 92. C Wolvercote w Summertown *Ox* 87-88; NSM Cov St Fran N Radford 91-95; Perm to Offic 95-98; C Doncaster Intake and Doncaster H Trin *Sheff* 98-00; C-in-c St Edm Anchorage Lane CD 00-06; C Doncaster St Geo from 06. *69 Chequer Road, Doncaster DN1 2AN* Tel (01302) 323392

ROWDON, John Michael Hooker. b 27. Witwatersrand Univ BA52. Ridley Hall Cam 52. **d** 54 **p** 55. C Broadwater St Mary *Chich* 54-56; C Streatham Immanuel w St Anselm *S'wark* 56-59; Nigeria 60-62; C All Hallows Lon Wall 62-66; Warden Toc H Tower Hill 64-66; Australia from 66; rtd 92. *PO Box 678, Ballarat Vic 3350, Australia*

ROWE, Andrew Gidleigh Bruce. b 37. AKC62. St Boniface Warminster. **d** 63 **p** 64. C Midsomer Norton *B & W* 63-68; Chapl RN 68-84; Chapl Heathfield Sch Ascot 84-86; Hon C Winkfield and Cranbourne *Ox* 84-86; TV Wellington and Distr *B & W* 86-95; R Chewton Mendip w Ston Easton, Litton etc 95-96; Perm to Offic *Ex* from 96; rtd 99. *19 Greenway, Crediton EX17 3LP* Tel (01363) 772262

ROWE, Andrew Robert. b 64. Westmr Coll Ox BA85 PGCE86. Ridley Hall Cam 93. **d** 95 **p** 96. C Broadheath *Ches* 95-99; V Ardsley *Wakef* 99-06; Chapl HM Pris Wakef from 06. *HM Prison, 5 Love Lane, Wakefield WF2 9AG* Tel (01924) 246000 Pager 01523-472096 E-mail andyrowe@uwclub.net

ROWE, Canon Bryan. b 50. Carl Dioc Tr Course 87. **d** 90 **p** 91. C Kells *Carl* 90-93; P-in-c Aspatria w Hayton 93-02; R Workington St Mich from 02; P-in-c Distington 06-08; RD Solway 99-08; Hon Can Carl Cathl from 99. *St Michael's Rectory, Dora Crescent, Workington CA14 2EZ* Tel (01900) 602311

ROWE, Christine Elizabeth. b 55. Southn Univ BEd77. Ripon Coll Cuddesdon 83. **dss** 86 **d** 87 **p** 94. Denham *Ox* 86-87; Par Dn 87-89; Par Dn Aylesbury 89; Par Dn Aylesbury w Bierton and Hulcott 89-93; NSM Caversham St Jo 93-99; Chapl HM Pris Reading 93-98; Chapl MU 95-00; Chapl R Berks and Battle Hosps NHS Trust 96-00; P-in-c Vancouver St Thos Canada 00-01; R 01-04; Adn Burrard 04-06; R N Vancouver St Cath from 06. *1062 Ridgewood Drive, North Vancouver BC V7R 1H8, Canada* Tel (001) (604) 987 6307 *or* 985 0666 Fax 980 3868 E-mail stcatherinecr@aol.com

ROWE, David Brian. b 58. Trin Coll Bris 80. **d** 83 **p** 84. C Radipole and Melcombe Regis *Sarum* 83-86; C Cranham Park *Chelmsf* 86-88; Assoc Min and Par Missr Eastrop *Win* 88-92; P-in-c Arborfield w Barkham *Ox* 92-97; Asst Dioc Adv in Evang *S'well* 97-02; P-in-c Wilford 00-06; R 06-08; Warden Lee Abbey from 08. *Garden Lodge, Lee Abbey, Lynton EX35 6JJ* Tel (01598) 752621 *or* 754204 Fax 752619 E-mail warden@leeabbey.org.uk

ROWE, Geoffrey Lewis. b 44. Univ of Wales (Lamp) BA. Ripon Coll Cuddesdon 80. **d** 82 **p** 83. C Milber *Ex* 82-84; TV Withycombe Raleigh 84-90; R Clyst St Mary, Clyst St George etc 90-08; rtd 08. *Odle Hill Cottage, Abbotskerswell, Newton Abbot TQ12 5NW* Tel (01626) 366143

ROWE, George William. b 36. K Alfred's Coll Win CertEd64 BEd82. **d** 07 **p** 08. NSM Week St Mary Circle of Par *Truro* from 07. *Tanglewood, Long Park Drive, Widemouth Bay, Bude EX23 0AN* Tel (01288) 361712 Mobile 07970-186038 E-mail george@rowe.gs.go-plus.net

ROWE, Miss Joan Patricia. b 54. Trin Coll Bris BA87. **d** 88 **p** 94. C Radstock w Writhlington *B & W* 88-92; C Nailsea H Trin 92-96; P-in-c Shapwick w Ashcott and Burtle 96-07; Master St Jo Hosp Bath from 07. *6 West Lea Road, Bath BA1 3RL* Tel (01225) 334023 E-mail joanrowe@ic24.net

ROWE, John Goring. b 23. McGill Univ Montreal BA48 BD51 Selw Coll Cam BA53. Montreal Dioc Th Coll LTh51. **d** 51 **p** 52. C N Clarendon Canada 51; C Trumpington *Ely* 51-53; Chapl NC Bow Common *Lon* 53-84; rtd 88. *10 Cordelia Street, London E14 6DZ* Tel (020) 7515 4681

ROWE, Peter Anthony. b 46. Univ Coll Dur BA68 Birkb Coll Lon MA91 Heythrop Coll Lon MTh02 Barrister 78 Solicitor 85. SEITE 95. **d** 98 **p** 99. NSM Ashford *Cant* 98-03; Perm to Offic from 04. *1 Woodside Villas, Ashford Road, Hamstreet, Ashford TN26 2DT* Tel (01233) 732172 *or* 664711 Fax 664722 E-mail peterrowe@madasafish.com

ROWE, Peter Farquharson. b 19. Selw Coll Cam BA41. Westcott Ho Cam 41. **d** 43 **p** 44. C Putney St Mary *S'wark* 43-47; C Lewisham St Jo Southend 47-54; V Mitcham Ascension 54-65; V Eltham Park St Luke 65-77; V Ravensthorpe w E Haddon and Holdenby *Pet* 77-84; rtd 84; Perm to Offic *Ex* 84-89; *Sarum* 89-92; *Win* 92-08. *Flat 12, Manormead, Tilford Road, Hindhead GU26 6RA* Tel (01428) 601512

ROWE, Philip William. b 57. Southn Univ BSc78 Lambeth STh86. Trin Coll Bris 82. **d** 85 **p** 86. C Tooting Graveney St Nic

S'wark 85-89; V Abbots Leigh w Leigh Woods *Bris* 89-96; V Almondsbury 96-98; P-in-c Littleton on Severn w Elberton 96-98; V Almondsbury and Olveston from 98; AD Bris W 00-06. *The Vicarage, Sundays Hill, Almondsbury, Bristol BS32 4DS* Tel (01454) 613223 E-mail philip.w.rowe@btopenworld.com

ROWE, Shiela. *See* JOHNSON, Mrs Shiela

ROWE, Canon Stanley Hamilton. b 18. St Pet Hall Ox BA48 MA52. ALCD50. **d** 50 **p** 51. C Leyton St Paul *Chelmsf* 50-52; CMS Nigeria 52-65; P-in-c Becontree St Cedd *Chelmsf* 65-67; Hd of RE Jo Hampden Sch High Wycombe 67-83; Perm to Offic *Ox* 67-84 and from 86; rtd 83; Hon P-in-c Aston Rowant w Crowell *Ox* 84-86; Hon Can Oke-Osun from 94. *37 Greenwood Avenue, Chinnor OX39 4HW* Tel (01844) 351278

ROWE, The Ven Stephen Mark Buckingham. b 59. SS Mark & Jo Univ Coll Plymouth BA81. Ripon Coll Cuddesdon 83. **d** 86 **p** 87. C Denham *Ox* 86-89; C Aylesbury w Bierton and Hulcott 89-90; TV 90-93; V Caversham St Jo 93-00; Canada from 00; Sen Chapl Miss to Seafarers 00-01; P-in-c Surrey Epiphany 01-02; R 02-07; Adn Fraser from 07. *1062 Ridgewood Drive, North Vancouver BC V7R 1H8, Canada* Tel (001) (604) 987 6307 *or* tel and fax 588 4511 E-mail rowesmb@aol.com

ROWE, Vanda Sheila. *See* PERRETT, Mrs Vanda Sheila

ROWELL, Canon Alan. b 50. Lon Univ BSc71 AKC71. Trin Coll Bris. **d** 75 **p** 76. C W Hampstead St Cuth *Lon* 75-78; C Camborne *Truro* 78-81; V Pendeen w Morvah from 81; Hon Can Truro Cathl from 03. *The Vicarage, Pendeen, Penzance TR19 7SE* Tel (01736) 788777

✠**ROWELL, The Rt Revd Douglas Geoffrey.** b 43. CCC Cam BA64 MA68 PhD68 Keble Coll Ox DD97. Cuddesdon Coll. **d** 68 **p** 69 **c** 94. Asst Chapl New Coll Ox 68-72; Chapl Keble Coll Ox 72-94; Wiccamical Preb Chich Cathl 81-01; Suff Bp Basingstoke *Win* 94-01; Bp Eur from 01. *Bishop's Lodge, Church Road, Worth, Crawley RH10 7RT, or 14 Tufton Street, London SW1P 3QZ* Tel (01293) 883051 *or* (020) 7898 1155 Fax (01293) 884479 *or* (020) 7898 1166
E-mail bishop@dioceseineurope.org.uk

ROWELL, Mrs Gillian Margaret. b 56. Lon Bible Coll BA96. SAOMC 97. **d** 99 **p** 00. NSM The Lee *Ox* 99-04; NSM Hawridge w Cholesbury and St Leonard 99-04. *81 Eskdale Avenue, Chesham HP5 3AY* Tel (01494) 772833

ROWELL, Canon William Kevin. b 51. Reading Univ BSc71. Linc Th Coll 78. **d** 80 **p** 81. C Cannock *Lich* 80-83; Ind Chapl 83-86; C Ketley and Oakengates 83-86; R Norton in the Moors 86-93; RD Leek 92-93; P-in-c Minsterley and Habberley *Heref* 93-01; RD Pontesbury 99-01; Miss Adv USPG *Heref, Worc* and *Glouc* 01-03; NSM Wenlock *Heref* 02-03; R Llandysilio and Penrhos and Llandrinio etc *St As* 04-08; R Welshpool, Castle Caereinion and Pool Quay from 08; Can Cursal St As Cathl from 08. *The Vicarage, Church Street, Welshpool SY21 7DP* Tel (01938) 553164 E-mail bilkro@btinternet.com

ROWETT, David Peter. b 55. Univ Coll Dur BA76. Ripon Coll Cuddesdon 82. **d** 84 **p** 85. C Yeovil *B & W* 84-88; C Yeovil St Mich 88-89; V Fairfield St Matt *Linc* 89-05; P-in-c Barton upon Humber from 05. *The Vicarage, Beck Hill, Barton-upon-Humber DN18 5EY* Tel (01652) 632202
E-mail david.rowett@aol.com

ROWETT, Mrs Margaret Pettigrew Coupar. b 33. Sarum & Wells Th Coll 84. **dss** 86 **d** 87 **p** 95. Widley w Wymering *Portsm* 86-88; C 87-88; Par Dn Plympton St Mary *Ex* 88-91; rtd 91; NSM St Mewan *Truro* 94-96; Perm to Offic from 97. *Epiphany Cottage, 9 Socotra Drive, Trewoon, St Austell PL25 5SQ* Tel (01726) 71450

ROWLAND, Andrew John William. b 60. STETS 98. **d** 01 **p** 02. C Verwood *Sarum* 01-06; V W Moors from 06. *The Vicarage, 57 Glenwood Road, West Moors, Ferndown BH22 0EN* Tel (01202) 893197

ROWLAND, Barry William. b 59. St Jo Coll Nottm BA95. **d** 95 **p** 96. C Welling *Roch* 95-98; C Green Street Green and Pratts Bottom 98-02; V New Beckenham St Paul from 02. *St Paul's Vicarage, Brackley Road, Beckenham BR3 1RB* Tel (020) 8650 3400 Mobile 07969-428519
E-mail barry.rowland@diocese-rochester.org

ROWLAND, Prof Christopher Charles. b 47. Ch Coll Cam BA69 MA73 PhD75. Ridley Hall Cam 72. **d** 75 **p** 76. Lect RS Newc Univ 74-79; Hon C Benwell St Jas 75-78; Hon C Gosforth All SS 78-79; Dean Jes Coll Cam 79-91; Asst Lect Div Cam Univ 83-85; Lect Div 85-91; Lic to Offic *Ely* 79-91; Prof of Exegesis of H Scripture Ox Univ from 91; Fell Qu Coll Ox from 91; Can Th Liv Cathl from 05. *Queen's College, Oxford OX1 4AW* Tel (01865) 279120

ROWLAND, Ms Dawn Jeannette. b 38. RSCN61 RGN63. S'wark Ord Course 81. **dss** 84 **d** 87 **p** 94. Par Dn Croydon H Sav *S'wark* 84-89; NSM Riddlesdown 89-08; Perm to Offic from 08. *9 Hartley Hill, Purley CR8 4EP* Tel (020) 8660 6270

ROWLAND, Derek John. b 47. St Jo Coll Nottm 84. **d** 86 **p** 87. C Porchester *S'well* 86-89; V Fairfield *Liv* 89-96; V Buckfastleigh w Dean Prior *Ex* from 96. *The Vicarage, Glebelands, Buckfastleigh TQ11 0BH* Tel (01364) 644228

ROWLAND, Eric Edward James. b 35. Leeds Univ BA62. Coll of Resurr Mirfield 61. **d** 63 **p** 64. C S Kirkby *Wakef* 63-65; C Headingley *Ripon* 65-70; V Osmondthorpe St Phil 70-79; R Sandy *St Alb* 79-00; RD Biggleswade 85-94; rtd 00; Perm to Offic *Ely* from 01. *3 Tower Road, Ely CB7 4HW* Tel (01353) 664359

ROWLAND, Geoffrey Watson. b 17. **d** 55 **p** 56. BCMS Burma 55-65; C Blackheath Park St Mich *S'wark* 65-71; V W Bromwich St Paul *Lich* 71-76; Chapl Community Relns *Lon* 77-83; C Southall Green St Jo 83; rtd 83; Perm to Offic *Lon* 83-05. *3 Amber Court, Longford Avenue, Southall UB1 3QR* Tel (020) 8574 3442

ROWLAND, Jennifer Norah. b 48. Worc Coll of Educn CertEd70 Open Univ BA83 ACIB. WMMTC 96. **d** 99 **p** 00. C Stratford-upon-Avon, Luddington etc *Cov* 99-03; P-in-c Ditton Priors w Neenton, Burwarton etc *Heref* from 03. *The Vicarage, Ditton Priors, Bridgnorth WV16 6SQ* Tel (01746) 712636
E-mail jenny@rowland.entadsl.org

ROWLAND, Mrs June Mary. b 46. SRN67. EMMTC 03. **d** 05 **p** 06. NSM Grantham *Linc* from 05. *The Vicarage, The Grove, Grantham NG31 7PU* Tel (01476) 572380
E-mail junerowlandhome@aol.com

ROWLAND, Canon Robert William. b 51. Birm Univ BA72. St Mich Coll Llan 72. **d** 74 **p** 75. C Connah's Quay *St As* 74; C Shotton 74-75; C Llanrhos 76-81; V Dyserth and Trelawnyd and Cwm from 81; AD St As from 94; Hon Can St As Cathl from 08. *The Vicarage, Dyserth, Rhyl LL18 6DB* Tel (01745) 570750

ROWLAND, Stanley George. b 48. Middx Univ BA86. NTMTC 95. **d** 98 **p** 99. NSM Enfield St Geo *Lon* 98-02; C Grantham *Linc* 02-03; V Grantham, Earlesfield from 03. *The Vicarage, The Grove, Grantham NG31 7PU* Tel (01476) 572380
E-mail sgrathome@aol.com

ROWLAND JONES, Sarah Caroline. b 59. LVO93 OBE97. Newnham Coll Cam BA80 MA84. St Jo Coll Nottm BTh98. **d** 99 **p** 00. C Wrexham *St As* 99-02; S Africa from 02. *Bishopsharm, PO Box 420, Malmesbury, 7299 South Africa* E-mail sarahrj@surfaid.org

ROWLANDS, Mrs Alison Mary. b 51. **d** 06 **p** 07. OLM Redland *Bris* from 06. *24 Northumberland Road, Bristol BS6 7BB* Tel 0117-924 3528 Mobile 07749-044041
E-mail alisrow@blueyonder.co.uk

ROWLANDS, The Ven Emyr Wyn. b 42. St Mich Coll Llan 69. **d** 70 **p** 71. C Holyhead w Rhoscolyn *Ban* 70-74; V Bodedern w Llechgynfarwy and Llechylched etc 74-88; R Machynlleth and Llanwrin 88-97; R Machynlleth w Llanwrin and Penegoes from 97; AD Cyfeiliog and Mawddwy from 96; Can Ban Cathl 97-03; Can and Preb Ban Cathl from 03; Adn Meirionnydd from 04. *The Rectory, Newtown Road, Machynlleth SY20 8HE* Tel (01654) 702261

ROWLANDS, Forrest John. b 25. LSE BSc(Econ)51. Chich Th Coll 54. **d** 56 **p** 57. C Hove St Phil *Chich* 56-58; C Haywards Heath St Wilfrid 58-62; R Kingston by Sea 62-74; rtd 90. *11 Granville Terrace, Yeadon, Leeds LS19 7UW* Tel 0113-250 0208

ROWLANDS, Gareth Richard. b 70. Univ of Wales BA93. St Steph Ho Ox BTh93. **d** 96 **p** 97. C Shotton *St As* 96-00; TV Wrexham and Chapl Maelor Hosp 00-03; Chapl Co-ord Ches and Ellesmere Port Hosps 03-05; Lead Chapl Princess Alexandra Hosp NHS Trust 05-07; Chapl Papworth Hosp NHS Foundn Trust from 07; Bp's Adv for Health Chapl *Ely* from 09. *Papworth Hospital, Papworth Everard, Cambridge CB3 8RE* Tel (01480) 830541

ROWLANDS, Graeme Charles. b 53. K Coll Lon BD74 AKC74. St Aug Coll Cant 75. **d** 76 **p** 77. C Higham Ferrers w Chelveston *Pet* 76-79; C Gorton Our Lady and St Thos *Man* 79-81; C Reading H Trin *Ox* 81-89; P-in-c Kentish Town St Silas *Lon* 89-92; V 92-98; P-in-c Haverstock Hill H Trin w Kentish Town St Barn 93-98; V Kentish Town St Silas and H Trin w St Barn from 98. *St Silas's House, 11 St Silas's Place, London NW5 3QP* Tel (020) 7485 3727 E-mail ssmktw@gmail.com

ROWLANDS, Mrs Jacqueline Adèle. b 43. Golds Coll Lon CertEd65 BEd72. St Alb Minl Tr Scheme 82. **dss** 85 **d** 87 **p** 05. Bromham w Oakley *St Alb* 85-88; Par Dn 87-88; Par Dn Bromham w Oakley and Stagsden 88-89; Perm to Offic 04-05; Hon C Bedford St Andr from 05. *2A Rosemary Drive, Bromham, Bedford MK43 8PL* Tel (01234) 403841

ROWLANDS, Canon John Henry Lewis. b 47. Univ of Wales (Lamp) BA68 Magd Coll Cam BA70 MA74 Dur Univ MLitt86. Westcott Ho Cam 70. **d** 72 **p** 73. C Aberystwyth *St D* 72-76; Chapl Univ of Wales (Lamp) 76-79; Youth Chapl 76-79; Dir Academic Studies St Mich Coll Llan 79-84; Sub-Warden 84-88; Warden 88-97; Lect Univ of Wales (Cardiff) *Llan* 79-97; Asst Dean 81-83; Dean 93-97; Dean of Div Univ of Wales 91-95; Dir of Ords 85-88; V Whitchurch 97-02; TR from 02; Hon Can Llan Cathl 90-97; Can from 97; Chan from 02; Chapl Cardiff Community Healthcare NHS Trust from 97. *The Vicarage, 6 Pennline Road, Cardiff CF14 2AD* Tel and fax (029) 2062 6072 E-mail office@parishofwhitchurch.freeserve.co.uk

ROWLANDS, Canon Joseph Haydn. b 36. Univ of Wales (Lamp) BA61. **d** 63 **p** 64. C Llanfairisgaer *Ban* 63-68; R Maentwrog w

Trawsfynydd 68-75; V Henfynyw w Aberaeron and Llanddewi Aberarth *St D* 75-80; R Trefdraeth *Ban* 80-84; V Llandysul *St D* 84-98; V Llandysul w Bangor Teifi w Henllan etc 98-01; Hon Can St D Cathl 88-90; Can St D Cathl from 90; RD Emlyn 92-01; rtd 01. *1 Llys Ystrad, Johnstown, Carmarthen SA31 3PU*

ROWLANDS, Kenneth Albert. b 41. MA DipAE. NW Ord Course 70. **d** 73 **p** 74. NSM Hoylake *Ches* 73-80; NSM Oxton 80-82; Perm to Offic 82-00; C Stoneycroft All SS *Liv* 92-94; V Mossley Hill St Barn 94-03; rtd 03. *77 Queens Avenue, Meols, Wirral CH47 0LT* Tel 0151-632 3033

ROWLANDS, Marc Alun. b 62. Univ of Wales (Abth) BSc84 St D Coll Lamp MPhil89 PhD95. Wycliffe Hall Ox 97. **d** 99 **p** 00. C Betws w Ammanford *St D* 99-01; C Carmarthen St Pet 01-02; P-in-c Llanpumsaint w Llanllawddog 02-05; TV Cwm Gwendraeth from 06. *The Vicarage, 32A Heol y Bryn, Upper Tumble, Llanelli SA14 6DR* Tel (01269) 841358
E-mail marc_rowlands@hotmail.com

ROWLANDS, Michael Huw. b 62. Birm Univ BA85 Univ of Wales (Cardiff) BD88. St Mich Coll Llan 85. **d** 88 **p** 89. C Penarth All SS *Llan* 88-91; V Martletwy w Lawrenny and Minwear etc *St D* 91-99; CF 99-02; P-in-c Nolton w Roch *St D* 02-04; R Nolton w Roch and St Lawrence w Ford etc from 04. *Calbern, Simpson Cross, Haverfordwest SA62 6EP* Tel (01437) 710209

ROWLANDS, Robert. b 31. Roch Th Coll. **d** 68 **p** 69. C Hooton *Ches* 68-71; V Stretton 71-88; P-in-c Appleton Thorn and Antrobus 87-88; V Stretton and Appleton Thorn 88-00; rtd 00; Perm to Offic *Carl* from 01. *Uplands, Redhills Road, Arnside, Carnforth LA5 0AS* Tel (01524) 761612

ROWLANDS, Simon David. b 66. **d** 99 **p** 00. C St Peter-in-Thanet *Cant* 99-03; Chapl Cant Ch Ch Univ 03-06; V Bridge *Cant* from 07. *The Vicarage, 23 High Street, Bridge, Canterbury CT4 5JZ* Tel (01227) 830250

ROWLANDS, Mrs Valerie Christine. b 54. St As Minl Tr Course 99. **d** 02 **p** 03. NSM Llanbedr DC w Llangynhafal, Llanychan etc *St As* 02-04; Chapl St As Cathl from 04; TV St As from 06. *Cefn Coed, Upper Denbigh Road, St Asaph LL17 0RR*

ROWLES, Mrs Carol. d 06 **p** 07. NSM Worcester Park Ch Ch w St Phil *S'wark* from 06. *23 Delcombe Avenue, Worcester Park KT4 8NY* Tel (020) 8330 2068

ROWLEY, Christopher Francis Elmes. b 48. St Jo Coll Dur BA70 St Luke's Coll Ex PGCE71. St Steph Ho Ox 76. **d** 78 **p** 79. C Parkstone St Pet w Branksea and St Osmund *Sarum* 78-81; TV 82-85; P-in-c Chard Gd Shep Furnham *B & W* 85-89; P-in-c Dowlishwake w Chaffcombe, Knowle St Giles etc 88-89; R Chard, Furnham w Chaffcombe, Knowle St Giles etc 89-91; V Stoke St Gregory w Burrowbridge and Lyng 91-04; RD Taunton 01-04; TV Wellington and Distr from 04; RD Tone from 07. *All Saints' Vicarage, 62 Rockwell Green, Wellington TA21 9BX* Tel (01823) 662742 E-mail christopherrowley@uwclub.net

ROWLEY, David Michael. b 39. NOC 87. **d** 90 **p** 91. C Stainland *Wakef* 90-93; V Hayfield *Derby* 93-99; P-in-c Chinley w Buxworth 98-99; V Glossop 99-04; RD Glossop 99-04; rtd 04; Perm to Offic *Derby* from 04. *8 Weavers Close, Belper DE56 0HZ* Tel (01773) 882690

ROWLEY, Jennifer Jane Elisabeth. b 61. LMH Ox BA84 MA92. EAMTC 99. **d** 02 **p** 03. C Kingsthorpe w Northampton St Dav *Pet* 02-04; C Kettering SS Pet and Paul 04-06; P-in-c Nettleham *Linc* from 06. *The Vicarage, 2 Vicarage Lane, Nettleham, Lincoln LN2 2RH* Tel (01522) 754752
E-mail jenny@peterandpaul.org.uk

ROWLEY, John. b 47. **d** 05 **p** 06. OLM Mitford *Newc* from 05. *Thistledene, Fulbeck, Morpeth NE61 3JU* Tel (01670) 515915
E-mail john_rowley1@btinternet.com

ROWLEY, Mrs Susan. b 49. **d** 01 **p** 02. OLM Fazeley *Lich* from 01. *76 Reindeer Road, Fazeley, Tamworth B78 3SW* Tel (01827) 250431 *or* 289414 E-mail s.rowley2@sky.com

ROWLEY-BROOKE, Mrs Marie Gordon. b 46. ARIAM69. Ripon Coll Cuddesdon 00. **d** 02 **p** 03. C Leckhampton SS Phil and Jas w Cheltenham St Jas *Glouc* 02-05; I Nenagh *L & K* from 05. *St Mary's Rectory, Church Road, Nenagh, Co Tipperary, Republic of Ireland* Tel (00353) (67) 32598
E-mail revdmarie@eircom.net

ROWLING, Canon Catherine. b 55. Man Poly BEd77. Westcott Ho Cam 83 NEOC 85. **dss** 86 **d** 87 **p** 94. Gt Ayton w Easby and Newton-in-Cleveland *York* 86-89; Par Dn 87-89; Chapl Teesside Poly 89-92; Chapl Teesside Univ 92-96; Dioc Adv for Diaconal Mins 96-98; Dean of Women's Min 98-08; Co Dir of Ords 98-05; Dioc Dir of Ords 05-09; Dioc Moderator Reader Tr 99-04; Dir Reader Studies 05-09; Prin Lindisfarne Regional Tr Partnership from 09; Can and Preb York Minster from 01. *The Rectory, Cemetery Road, Thirsk YO7 1PR* Tel (01845) 523183
E-mail cathyrowling@aol.com

ROWLING, Richard Francis. b 56. BA. Westcott Ho Cam. **d** 84 **p** 85. C Stokesley *York* 84-87; C Stainton-in-Cleveland 87-90; V New Marske 90-96; V Wilton 92-96; P-in-c Ingleby Greenhow w Bilsdale Priory, Kildale etc 96-98; V 98-03; TR Thirsk from 03; Abp's Adv for Rural Affairs from 98; RD Mowbray from 04. *The*

Rectory, Cemetery Road, Thirsk YO7 1PR Tel (01845) 523183
E-mail rfrowling@aol.com

ROWNTREE, Peter. b 47. St D Coll Lamp BA68 Univ of Wales (Cardiff) MA70. St Steph Ho Ox 70. **d** 72 **p** 73. C Stanwell *Lon* 72-75; C Northolt St Mary 75-79; Chapl Ealing Gen Hosp 79-83; Chapl Cherry Knowle Hosp Sunderland 83-87; Chapl Ryhope Hosp Sunderland 83-87; Chapl Ealing Gen Hosp 87-94; Chapl Ealing Hosp NHS Trust 94-99; Chapl W Lon Healthcare NHS Trust 94-99; Sen Co-ord Chapl Univ Coll Lon Hosps NHS Foundn Trust 99-08; rtd 08; Perm to Offic *Nor* from 08. *4 Chapel Court, Chapel Street, King's Lynn PE30 1EG*

ROWSELL, Canon John Bishop. b 25. Jes Coll Cam BA49 MA55. Ely Th Coll 49. **d** 51 **p** 52. C Hackney Wick St Mary of Eton w St Aug *Lon* 51-55; C Is of Dogs Ch Ch and St Jo w St Luke 55-56; C Reading St Mary V *Ox* 56-59; V Hightown *Wakef* 59-69; R Harlton *Ely* 69-81; V Haslingfield 69-81; V Methwold 81-95; RD Feltwell 81-95; R Northwold 82-95; Hon Can Ely Cathl 84-99; P-in-c Hockwold w Wilton 95-99; P-in-c Weeting 95-99; Perm to Offic from 00. *Reed House, High Street, Hilgay, Downham Market PE38 0LH* Tel (01366) 387662

ROWSON, Frank. b 40. CEng67 MIStructE67. Sarum & Wells Th Coll 87. **d** 90 **p** 91. NSM Ore Ch Ch *Chich* 90-98; NSM Fairlight, Guestling and Pett 98-00; rtd 00; Perm to Offic *Chich* from 01. *149 Priory Road, Hastings TN34 3JD* Tel (01424) 439802

ROWSON, Mrs Rhoda Lyn. b 63. RGN86. Qu Coll Birm 06. **d** 09. NSM Coseley Ch Ch *Worc* from 09. *54 Grenville Road, Dudley DY1 2NE* Tel (01384) 829868 E-mail lyn63@blueyonder.co.uk

ROWSTON, Geoffrey. b 34. Sarum Th Coll 59. **d** 62 **p** 63. C Ashburton w Buckland-in-the-Moor *Ex* 62-65; C Basingstoke *Win* 65-68; V Netley 68-78; V W End 78-87; R Alderbury and W Grimstead *Sarum* 87-91; P-in-c Whiteparish 89-91; TR Alderbury Team 91-99; rtd 99; Perm to Offic *Cov* from 99. *34 Oldbutt Road, Shipston-on-Stour CV36 4EG* Tel (01608) 663024

✠**ROWTHORN, The Rt Revd Jeffery William.** b 34. Ch Coll Cam BA57 MA62 Union Th Sem (NY) BD61 Oriel Coll Ox BLitt72 Berkeley Div Sch DD87. Cuddesdon Coll 61. **d** 62 **p** 63 **c** 87. C Woolwich St Mary w H Trin *S'wark* 62-65; R Garsington *Ox* 65-68; Chapl and Dean Union Th Sem NY USA 68-73; Assoc Prof Past Th Yale and Berkeley Div Schs 73-87; Suff Bp Connecticut 87-93; Bp in Charge Convocation of American Chs in Eur 94-01; Asst Bp Eur 95-01; Asst Bp Spain 97-01; Asst Bp Portugal 97-01; rtd 01. *17 Woodland Drive, Salem CT 06420-4023, USA* Tel (001) (860) 859 3377
E-mail jefferyrowthorn@yahoo.com

ROXBY, Gordon George. b 39. Lon Univ BSc61. Coll of Resurr Mirfield 61. **d** 63 **p** 64. C Fleetwood St Pet *Blackb* 63-66; C Kirkham 66-68; V Runcorn St Jo Weston *Ches* 68-78; R Moston St Chad *Man* 78-86; V Bury St Pet 86-99; AD Bury 86-96; Hon Can Man Cathl 97-99; V Sandiway *Ches* 99-05; Initial Minl Tr Officer 99-04; rtd 05; Perm to Offic *Ches* from 05. *16 St Joseph's Way, Nantwich CW5 6TE* Tel (01270) 619898
E-mail gordon@roxbylife.org.uk

ROY, Jennifer Pearl. See DREW, Mrs Jennifer Pearl

ROYALL, Preb Arthur Robert. b 19. Lambeth MA. Qu Coll Birm 51. **d** 53 **p** 54. C Ashford St Matt *Lon* 53-56; V Heap Bridge *Man* 56-59; V Whitton St Aug *Lon* 59-64; R Poplar All SS w St Frideswide 64-71; P-in-c Bromley St Mich 64-71; P-in-c Poplar St Sav w St Gabr and St Steph 68-71; R Poplar 71-73; R Bow w Bromley St Leon 73-76; P-in-c Mile End Old Town H Trin 73-76; P-in-c Bethnal Green St Barn 73-75; RD Poplar 65-66; RD Tower Hamlets 68-76; Preb St Paul's Cathl 73-86; Clergy Appts Adv 76-85; Perm to Offic *Nor* 77-98, *Ely* 78-98 and *Lon* 86-91; rtd 86. *4 Manormead Nursing Home, Tilford Road, Hindhead GU26 6RA* Tel (01428) 608755
E-mail arthur@royall.co.uk

ROYDEN, Charles. b 60. Wycliffe Hall Ox BA86 MA91. **d** 87 **p** 88. C Bidston *Ches* 87-91; V N Brickhill and Putnoe *St Alb* 91-92; V Bedf St Mark from 93. *The Vicarage, Calder Rise, Bedford MK41 7UY* Tel and fax (01234) 342613 *or* tel 309175 Mobile 07973-113861 E-mail vicar@thisischurch.com

ROYDEN, Eric Ramsay. b 29. St Deiniol's Hawarden 75. **d** 77 **p** 78. Hon C Tranmere St Paul w St Luke *Ches* 77-81; C Eastham 81; V New Brighton All SS 81-95; P-in-c 95-97; rtd 95; Perm to Offic *Ches* 97-07. *84 Asgard Drive, Bedford MK41 0UT* Tel (01234) 294496 E-mail eroyden@googlemail.com

ROYDEN, Ross Eric. b 55. Lon Bible Coll BA77 Nottm Univ MTh82. Wycliffe Hall Ox 79. **d** 81 **p** 82. C Moreton *Ches* 81-84; Chapl and Tutor Bedf Coll of HE *St Alb* 84-93; R Banchory *Ab* 93-00; R Kincardine O'Neil 93-00; V Kowloon Tong Ch Ch Hong Kong from 00\ *Christ Church Vicarage, 2 Derby Road, Kowloon Tong, Kowloon, Hong Kong* Tel (00852) 2338 4433 Fax 2338 8422 E-mail rossroyden@aol.com

ROYDS, John Caress. b 20. Qu Coll Cam BA47 MA52. **d** 74 **p** 75 C Kettering St Andr *Pet* 74-76; Dioc Dir of Educn and R Loddington w Cransley 76-81; V Northampton St Jas 81-85; CMS Pakistan 85-86; rtd 87; Perm to Offic *Sarum* from 90. *16B Donaldson Road, Salisbury SP1 3AD* Tel (01722) 332293

ROYLANCE, Mrs Margaret. b 47. St Mary's Coll Chelt CertEd68. Cant Sch of Min 93. **d** 96 **p** 97. NSM Tenterden St Mildred w Smallhythe *Cant* from 96; NSM Tenterden St Mich from 07; Chapl Ashford Sch from 96. *5 Southgate Road, Tenterden TN30 7BS* Tel (01580) 762332 Fax 765267
E-mail johnsroylance@btopenworld.com

ROYLE, Antony Kevan. b 50. Lon Univ BSc71 FIA76. Trin Coll Bris 76. **d** 79 **p** 80. C Chell *Lich* 79-82; C Leyland St Andr *Blackb* 82-86; V Blackb Sav 86-95; Chapl Blackb R Infirmary and Park Lee Hosp 86-95; Chapl E Lancs Hospice 86-95; TR Walton H Trin *Ox* 95-01; NSM Wendover Deanery from 01. *4 Darley Close, Aylesbury HP21 7EA* Tel (01296) 582470 Mobile 07796-143905

ROYLE, Michael Arthur. b 38. Univ of Wales (Ban) BSc61. St Jo Coll Nottm 81. **d** 82 **p** 83. C Boulton *Derby* 82-85; C Belper 85-87; P-in-c Smalley and Morley 87-95; RD Heanor 89-94; V Charlesworth and Dinting Vale 95-02; rtd 02; Perm to Offic *Ches* from 02 and *Derby* from 03. *Kaiama, 55 Cross Lane, Marple, Stockport SK6 7PZ* Tel 0161-427 6453

ROYLE, Canon Peter Sydney George. b 34. K Coll Lon BD57 AKC57. **d** 58 **p** 59. C St Helier *S'wark* 58-62; C Alice Springs Australia 62-63; R 63-68; Can Darwin 68; P-in-c Sydenham St Phil *S'wark* 69-72; V Leigh Park *Portsm* 72-85; RD Havant 77-82; V S w N Hayling 85-96; V S Hayling 96-97; Hon Can Portsm Cathl 95-97; rtd 97; Perm to Offic *Ex* 97-06 and *Sarum* from 06. *12 Jackson Close, Devizes SN10 3AP* Tel (01380) 720405

ROYLE, Canon Roger Michael. b 39. AKC61 Lambeth MA90. **d** 62 **p** 63. C Portsea St Mary *Portsm* 62-65; C St Helier *S'wark* 65-68; Succ S'wark Cathl 68-71; Warden Eton Coll Dorney Par Project *Ox* 71-74; Conduct Eton Coll 74-79; Lic to Offic *S'wark* 79-90; Chapl Ld Mayor Treloar Coll Alton 90-92; Hon C Froyle and Holybourne *Win* 90-92; Hon Can and Chapl S'wark Cathl 93-99; Perm to Offic from 99; rtd 04. *Address withheld by request*

ROYLE, Canon Stanley Michael. b 43. K Coll Lon BD69 AKC69 Man Univ MA75. St Aug Coll Cant 71. **d** 72 **p** 73. C Timperley *Ches* 72-76; Perm to Offic 76-81; R Milton Abbas, Hilton w Cheselbourne etc *Sarum* 81-86; Dir of Ords 86-01; Adv on CME 86-98; Can and Preb Sarum Cathl from 89; Bp's Dom Chapl 98-01; Lic to Offic from 01. *Three Firs, Blandford Road, Sturminster Marshall, Wimborne BH21 4AF* Tel (01258) 857326

RUAHA, Bishop of. *See* MTETEMELA, The Most Revd Donald Leo

RUCK, John. b 47. Bris Univ BSc68 Birm Univ MPhil92. All Nations Chr Coll MA03. **d** 80 **p** 83. OMF Internat from 78; Indonesia 80-86 and 87-91; Perm to Offic *Birm* 86-87 and 91-98; Lic to Offic from 03; Lect Crowther Hall CMS Tr Coll Selly Oak 00-04; CMS from 04. *121 Bournbrook Road, Birmingham B29 7BY* Tel 0121-415 4036
E-mail johnanne@ruckja.freeserve.co.uk

RUDALL, Mark Edward. b 53. Regent's Park Coll Ox BA80 MA84. Ripon Coll Cuddesdon 00. **d** 01 **p** 02. In Bapt Min 80-00; C Wallingford *Ox* 01-03; Dioc Dir Communications *Guildf* from 04. *Diocesan House, Quarry Street, Guildford GU1 3XG* Tel (01483) 790310 Fax 790311 Mobile 07779-654975
E-mail mark.rudall@cofeguildford.org.uk
or mark.rudall@ntlworld.com

RUDD, Carl Nigel. b 71. Salford Univ BSc93 PhD97. Trin Coll Bris BA06. **d** 06 **p** 07. C Whitstable Cant from 06. *69B Herne Bay Road, Whitstable CT5 2LP* Tel (01227) 273909
E-mail carl.rudd@googlemail.com

RUDD, Charles Robert Jordeson. b 34. TCD BA56 MA65 BD65. **d** 57 **p** 58. C Lurgan Redeemer *D & D* 57-61; C Lisburn Ch Ch Cathl 61-62; C Willowfield *D & D* 62-66; I Drumgooland w Kilcoo 66-75; I Moira 75-95; I Magherally w Annaclone 95-02; Can Belf Cathl 90-02; rtd 02. *12 Thorn Heights, Banbridge BT32 4BF* Tel (028) 4062 8995

RUDD, Colin Richard. b 41. AKC64. **d** 65 **p** 66. C N Stoneham *Win* 65-70; V Rotherwick, Hook and Greywell 70-74; R Hook w Greywell 74-78; Toc H 78-89; V Buckland *Ox* 89-98; V Littleworth 89-98; R Pusey 89-98; RD Vale of White Horse 96-99; rtd 99; Perm to Offic *B & W* from 06. *Alcudia, Bilbrook, Minehead TA24 6HE* Tel (01984) 640021

RUDD, Canon Julian Douglas Raymond. b 19. Leeds Univ BA40. Coll of Resurr Mirfield 40. **d** 42 **p** 43. C Bury St Edmunds St Jo *St E* 42-46; C Holborn St Alb w Saffron Hill St Pet *Lon* 46-49; V Bournemouth St Fran *Win* 49-60; RD Bournemouth 56-60; R Old Alresford 60-70; RD Alresford 60-70; Hon Can Win Cathl 62-70; V Warwick St Mary *Cov* 70-76; V Warwick St Mary w St Nic 76-83; Hon Can Cov Cathl 76-84; TR Warwick 83-84; RD Warwick 77-79; rtd 84. *The College of St Barnabas, Blackberry Lane, Lingfield RH7 6NJ* Tel (01342) 872840

RUDD, Robert. *See* RUDD, Charles Robert Jordeson

RUDD, Robert Arthur. b 33. ALCD60. **d** 60 **p** 61. C Blackb Sav 60-63; C Huyton St Geo *Liv* 63-65; V Bickershaw 65-72; Asst Chapl HM Pris Liv 72-73; Birm 73-78; Parkhurst 78-86; Camp Hill 86-92; Chapl St Mary's Hosp Newport 92-95; rtd 95; Perm

to Offic *Portsm* from 95. *The Elms, 13 Horsebridge Hill, Newport PO30 5TJ* Tel (01983) 524415

RUDD, Mrs Sonia Winifred. b 44. Nottm Univ BSc66 Leeds Univ MSc68. Ox Min Course 92. **d** 94 **p** 95. NSM Ox St Andr 94-95; C Buckland 96-98; C Gainfield 98-99; Perm to Offic *B & W* from 06. *Alcudia, Bilbrook, Minehead TA24 6HE* Tel (01984) 640021 Mobile 07930-558882

RUDDICK, David Mark. b 76. Pemb Coll Cam BA98 Homerton Coll Cam PGCE99. Oak Hill Th Coll BA09. **d** 09. C Elmswell *St E* from 09. *25 Crown Mill, Elmswell, Bury St Edmunds IP30 9GF* Tel 07761-320736 (mobile)
E-mail davidruddick.online@googlemail.com

RUDDLE, Canon Donald Arthur. b 31. MBE04. Linc Th Coll 64. **d** 66 **p** 67. C Kettering SS Pet and Paul 66-70; V Earlham St Anne *Nor* 70-79; V E Malling *Roch* 79-95; RD Malling 84-93; Hon Can Roch Cathl 88-95; Chapl Nord Pas de Calais *Eur* 95-98; rtd 98; Perm to Offic *Eur* from 98 and *Cant* from 05. *Sycamore Lodge, 5 Windmill Lane, Faversham ME13 7GT* Tel (01795) 533461 E-mail don.ruddle@tiscali.co.uk

RUDDOCK, Brian John. b 45. Dur Univ BA66 Nottm Univ MEd91. Westcott Ho Cam 67. **d** 69 **p** 70. C Ross *Heref* 69-72; C Kettering SS Pet and Paul 72-75; P-in-c Colchester St Steph *Chelmsf* 75-77; TR Colchester St Leon, St Mary Magd and St Steph 77-84; R March St Pet *Ely* 84-89; R March St Mary 84-89; RD March 87-89; Dioc Unemployment Officer *Sheff* 89-94; Resource and Development Officer CCWA 96-02. *46 Tanners Field, Amesbury, Salisbury SP4 7SF* Tel (01980) 623072 E-mail brianjruddock@btinternet.com

RUDDOCK, Bruce. *See* RUDDOCK, Canon Reginald Bruce

RUDDOCK, Charles Cecil. b 28. TCD Div Sch. **d** 57 **p** 58. C Belfast St Mary *Conn* 57-59; C Carnmoney 59-61; C Belfast St Aid 61-63; I Kiltegan w Rathvilly *C & O* 63-69; C Newtownards *D & D* 69-72; R Beaconsfield w Exeter Australia 72-77; R Sandford 77-83; I Mallow Union *C, C & R* 83-89; I Fenagh w Myshall, Aghade and Ardoyne *C & O* 89-95; Can Ossory and Leighlin Cathls 92-95; rtd 95; Perm to Offic *Glouc* 95-05. *11 Bevis Court, Bibra Lake, Perth WA 6163, Australia*

RUDDOCK, Edgar Chapman. b 48. St Jo Coll Dur BA70 MA76. Cranmer Hall Dur 70. **d** 74 **p** 75. C Birm St Geo 74-78; R 78-83; S Africa 83-91; Dir Tr Dio St Jo 83-86; P-in-c Mandini 86-87; Prov Dir Tr 88-91; TR Stoke-upon-Trent *Lich* 91-02; Internat Relns Sec USPG from 03. *USPG, 200 Dover Street, London SE1 4YB* Tel (020) 7378 5678 E-mail edrud@cix.co.uk

RUDDOCK, Kenneth Edward. b 30. TCD BA52 QUB MTh79. CITC 53 Div Test. **d** 53 **p** 54. C Ballymena *Conn* 53-56; C Belfast St Thos 56-60; I Tomregan w Drumlane *K, E & A* 60-68; I Belfast St Luke *Conn* 68-80; Miss to Seamen 80-95; I Whitehead and Islandmagee *Conn* 80-96; Can Lisburn Cathl 90-96; Dioc Info Officer from 90; Chan Conn Cathl 96; rtd 96; Dioc C *Conn* from 98. *24 Fourtowns Manor, Ahoghill, Ballymena BT42 1RS* Tel (028) 2587 8966 Mobile 07970-639067

RUDDOCK, Leonard William. b 58. CITC 90. **d** 94 **p** 95. NSM Roscrea w Kyle, Bourney and Corbally *L & K* 94-06; C Stillorgan w Blackrock *D & G* 06-08; I Blessington w Kilbride, Ballymore Eustace etc from 08. *The Rectory, 13 Ashton, Blessington, Co Wicklow, Republic of Ireland* Tel (00353) (45) 865178 Mobile 87-764 3296
E-mail leonardruddock@gmail.com

RUDDOCK, Canon Reginald Bruce. b 55. AGSM77. Chich Th Coll. **d** 83 **p** 84. C Felpham w Middleton *Chich* 83-86; C Portsea St Mary *Portsm* 86-88; P-in-c Barnes St Mich *S'wark* 88-95; Dir Angl Cen Rome 95-99; Hon Can American Cathl Paris from 96; Can Res Worc Cathl 99-04; Can Res Pet Cathl from 04; Liturg Officer from 04; Chapl to The Queen from 04. *The Chapter Office, Minster Precincts, Peterborough PE1 1XS* Tel (01733) 343342 *or* 355310
E-mail bruce.ruddock@peterborough-cathedral.org.uk

RUDEN, Lars Olav. b 43. **d** 00 **p** 01. OLM Bamford *Man* 00-05; P-in-c Healey from 05. *Healey Vicarage, 10 Healey Avenue, Rochdale OL12 6EG* Tel (01706) 657386 Mobile 07743-509193
E-mail larsruden.norge@virgin.net

RUDIGER, David John. b 42. MCMI91. Ox Min Course 91. **d** 94 **p** 95. NSM Woughton *Ox* from 94. *56 Kirtlington, Downhead Park, Milton Keynes MK15 9AZ* Tel (01908) 668474
E-mail david@rudiger2.freeserve.co.uk

RUDKIN, Simon David. b 51. Bradf Univ BA74 K Coll Lon BD77 AKC77. Coll of Resurr Mirfield 77. **d** 78 **p** 79. C Flixton St Mich *Man* 78-81; C Atherton 81-84; V Lever Bridge 84-91; P-in-c Pennington w Lindal and Marton *Carl* 91-96; P-in-c Pennington w Lindal w Marton and Bardsea 96-00; V Morland, Thrimby, Gt Strickland and Cliburn 00-09; P-in-c Kirkby Thore w Temple Sowerby and Newbiggin 04-07; P-in-c Bolton 05-09; P-in-c Crosby Ravensworth 05-09; R Bedale and Leeming and Thornton Watlass *Ripon* from 09. *The Rectory, North End, Bedale DL8 1AF* Tel (01677) 422103
E-mail sd.rudkin@btinternet.com

RUDMAN, David Walter Thomas. b 48. Oak Hill Th Coll BD72. **d** 72 **p** 73. C Plymouth St Jude *Ex* 72-75; C Radipole *Sarum* 76-77; Warden St Geo Ho Braunton 77-03; R Georgeham *Ex*

88-03; Dioc Adv in Adult Tr 97-03; TV S Molton w Nymet St George, High Bray etc from 03; Dioc Adv in OLM from 03. *The Rectory, Kingsnympthon, Umberleigh EX37 9ST* Tel (01769) 580457 E-mail davidrudman@ntlworld.com

RUEHORN, Eric Arthur. b 33. St Aid Birkenhead 58. **d** 61 **p** 62. C Harpurhey Ch *Man* 61-65; V Roughtown 65-74; V Hawkshaw Lane 74-99; rtd 99; Perm to Offic *Man* from 00. *29 Hunstanton Drive, Bury BL8 1EG* Tel 0161-761 3983

RUFF, Brian Chisholm. b 36. Lon Univ BD66 ACA60 FCA70. Oak Hill Th Coll 63. **d** 67 **p** 68. C Cheadle *Ches* 67-72; Educn and Youth Sec CPAS 72-76; V New Milverton *Cov* 76-90; V Westbourne Ch Ch Chpl *Win* 90-01; rtd 02; Perm to Offic *Win* from 02 and *Sarum* from 03. *19 Hardy Road, West Moors, Wimborne BH22 0EX* Tel (01202) 868733 E-mail bcr@ruffys.fsnet.co.uk

RUFF, Michael Ronald. b 49. K Coll Lon BD72 AKC72 Ch Ch Coll Cant PGCE77. St Aug Coll Cant 72. **d** 73 **p** 74. C Old Shoreham *Chich* 73-76; Chapl Ellesmere Coll 77-81; Chapl Grenville Coll Bideford 81-87; Chapl Stamford Sch 87-06; P-in-c Stamford St Mary and St Martin *Linc* from 06. *9 Vence Close, Stamford PE9 2LZ* Tel (01780) 766567

RUFFLE, Preb John Leslie. b 43. ALCD66. **d** 66 **p** 67. C Eastwood *S'well* 66-70; C Keynsham w Queen Charlton *B & W* 70-75; P-in-c Weston-super-Mare Em 75; TV Weston-super-Mare Cen Par 75-84; V Yatton Moor 84-91; TR 91-98; P-in-c Chew Stoke w Nempnett Thrubwell 98-03; Dioc Adv in Past Care and Counselling 03-06; rtd 06; Perm to Offic *B & W* from 06; Preb Wells Cathl from 97. *52 Highbridge Road, Burnham-on-Sea TA8 1LN* Tel (01278) 788322 E-mail john@vicpress01.freeserve.co.uk

RUFFLE, Peter Cousins. b 19. Lon Univ BD42. ALCD42. **d** 42 **p** 43. C Highbury Ch Ch *Lon* 42-46; CMS Missr Bihar India 46-52; Youth Adv CMS 52-57; Hon C Bromley St Jo *Roch* 54-57; V Walton Breck *Liv* 57-60; V Aigburth 60-66; Prin Wilson Carlile Coll of Evang 66-74; Can Res Blackb Cathl 74-78; V Meole Brace *Lich* 78-85; rtd 85; Perm to Offic *Portsm* and *Win* 85-03; *York* from 03. *20 Dulverton Hall, Esplanade, Scarborough YO11 2AR* Tel (01723) 340120

RUFLI, Alan John. b 63. TCD BA89. **d** 91 **p** 92. C Donaghcloney w Waringstown *D & D* 91-94; C Knock 94-95; I Rathcoole *Conn* 95-01; I Holmpatrick w Balbriggan and Kenure *D & G* from 01. *Holmpatrick Rectory, Miller's Lane, Skerries, Co Dublin, Republic of Ireland* Tel (00353) (1) 849 2247 E-mail rufrev@aol.com

RUGEN, Peter. b 60. Crewe & Alsager Coll BEd86. Trin Coll Bris MA00. **d** 00 **p** 01. C Shipley St Pet *Bradf* 00-04; P-in-c Riddlesden and Morton St Luke 04-08; P-in-c Norley, Crowton and Kingsley *Ches* from 08. *St John's House, Pike Lane, Kingsley, Frodsham WA6 8EH* Tel (01928) 787180 E-mail peter.rugen1@tiscali.co.uk

RUGG, Andrew Philip. b 47. Kent Univ BA82. Sarum & Wells Th Coll 83. **d** 85 **p** 86. C Harlesden All So *Lon* 85-90; TV Benwell *Newc* 90-97; V Weetslade 97-00; rtd 00; Perm to Offic *York* from 00. *36 Whenby Grove, York YO31 9DS* Tel and fax (01904) 652567 Mobile 07980-390051

RUGG, Christopher James McTeer. b 75. St Jo Coll Dur BSc97. Trin Coll Bris 06. **d** 08 **p** 09. C Week St Mary Circle of Par *Truro* from 08. *1 Market Place, Week St Mary, Holsworthy EX22 6XT* Tel (01288) 341089 E-mail cjmrugg@gmail.com

RUGMAN, Mrs Hazel. b 47. R Holloway Coll Lon BA68 ACIS89. NOC 01. **d** 03 **p** 04. NSM Sandbach *Ches* 03-06; NSM Crewe St Andr w St Jo from 06; NSM Crewe Ch Ch from 07. *High Trees, 157 Sandbach Road North, Alsager, Stoke-on-Trent ST7 2AX* Tel (01270) 876386 Fax 883737 Mobile 07762-706120 E-mail hazelrugman@btinternet.com

✠**RUHUMULIZA, The Rt Revd Jonathan.** b 56. Makumira Univ Coll Tanzania BD89. Butare Th Sch Rwanda 78. **d** 82 **p** 83 **c** 91. C Kigeme Rwanda 82-84; Manager and Chapl Kigeme High Sch 83-86 and 90-91; Manager and Chapl Kigeme Hosp 89-90; Asst Bp Butare 91-92; Prov Sec 92-93; Asst Bp Kigali 93; Coadjutor Bp 93-95; Bp 95-97; Miss Bp Cameroon 98-04; C Droitwich Spa *Worc* 05-06; Hon Asst Bp Worc from 05. *6 Riverside Way, Droitwich, Worcester WR9 8UP* Tel (01905) 799329 E-mail bspjrmuliza@yahoo.co.uk

RUITERS, Ivan John. b 61. Coll of Transfiguration Grahamstown 94. **d** 96 **p** 97. C Berea S Africa 96-00; R Maidstone 00-01; R Newlands 02-07; I Killesher *K, E & A* from 07. *The New Rectory, Unity, Enniskillen BT92 1FN* Tel (028) 6634 8235 Mobile 07902-174219 E-mail ivanruiters@yahoo.com

✠**RUMALSHAH, The Rt Revd Munawar Kenneth (Mano).** b 41. Punjab Univ BSc60 Serampore Coll BD65 Karachi Univ MA68 Homerton Coll Cam PGCE88. Bp's Coll Calcutta 62. **d** 65 **p** 66 **c** 94. C H Trin Cathl Karachi Pakistan 65-69; C Roundhay St Edm *Ripon* 70-73; Area Sec and Asst Home Sec CMS 73-78; Educn Sec BCC 78-81; P-in-c Southall St Geo *Lon* 81-88; Lect Edwardes Coll Peshawar Pakistan 89-94; Bp Peshawar 94-99 and

03-07; Gen Sec USPG and Hon Asst Bp S'wark 99-03; rtd 07. *62 Stapleton Close, Marlow SL7 1TZ* Tel (01628) 475889 E-mail bishopmanodop@hotmail.com

RUMBALL, William Michael. b 41. Surrey Univ BSc63 Birm Univ PhD66 Open Univ BA75 MIM66 MINucE73 FIMMM03. Wycliffe Hall Ox 78. **d** 80 **p** 81. C S Molton, Nymet St George, High Bray etc *Ex* 80-83; V S Hetton w Haswell *Dur* 83-90; V S Wingfield and Wessington *Derby* 90-99; rtd 99; Hon C Brailsford w Shirley and Osmaston w Edlaston *Derby* 01-03; Perm to Offic *Derby* from 03 and *Lich* from 08. *4 Hawthorn Close, Ashbourne DE6 1HW* Tel (01335) 343203 E-mail wm.rumball@virgin.net

RUMBLE, Alison Merle. See PRINCE, Mrs Alison Merle

RUMBOLD, Bernard John. b 43. **d** 73 **p** 75. Hon C Alotau Papua New Guinea 73-76; C Gt Burstead *Chelmsf* 76-77; Chapl RAF 77-93; Chapl HM Pris Featherstone 93-95; C Wordsley *Worc* 95-96; TV 96-99; Chapl Dudley Gp of Hosps NHS Trust 96-99; R Teme Valley N *Worc* 99-02; rtd 02; P-in-c Brompton Regis w Upton and Skilgate *B & W* 03-08; P-in-c Gt w Lt Tew *Ox* from 08; P-in-c Over w Nether Worton from 08. *The Vicarage, New Road, Great Tew, Chipping Norton OX7 4AG* E-mail bernardrumbold@btinternet.com

RUMBOLD, Graham Charles. b 44. Open Univ BA79. S Dios Minl Tr Scheme 76. **d** 79 **p** 80. NSM Widley w Wymering *Portsm* 79-82; Chapl Cynthia Spencer Unit Manfield Hosp 82-94; Chapl Northampton Community Healthcare NHS Trust 94-01; Chapl Northants Healthcare NHS Trust 01-04; NSM Weston Favell *Pet* 93-95; NSM Northampton St Matt from 98. *3 Calstock Close, Northampton NN3 3BA* Tel (01604) 627389

RUMENS, Canon John Henry. b 21. AKC49. **d** 50 **p** 51. C Wareham w Arne *Sarum* 50-54; V Alderholt 54-59; R Salisbury St Edm 59-72; RD Salisbury 69-72; R Trowbridge H Trin 72-79; P-in-c Sturminster Marshall 79-83; V 83-85; Can and Preb Sarum Cathl 72-85; rtd 85; Perm to Offic *Sarum* from 85. *20 Constable Way, Salisbury SP2 8LN* Tel (01722) 334716

RUMENS, Ms Katharine Mary. b 53. UEA BEd76. Westcott Ho Cam 90. **d** 92 **p** 94. Par Dn E Ham w Upton Park St Alb *Chelmsf* 92-94; C 94-95; C Waterloo St Jo w St Andr *S'wark* 95-00; Chapl S Bank Cen and Chapl Lon Weekend TV 95-00; R St Giles Cripplegate w St Bart Moor Lane etc *Lon* from 00. *The Rectory, 4 The Postern, Wood Street, London EC2Y 8BJ* Tel and fax (020) 7588 3013 or tel 7638 1997 E-mail rumens@stgileschurch.com

RUMING, Canon Gordon William. b 27. Kelham Th Coll 45. **d** 52 **p** 53. C Baildon *Bradf* 52-55; C Prestbury *Glouc* 55-60; C Penzance St Mary *Truro* 60-61; R Calstock 61-92; Hon Can Truro Cathl 79-92; RD E Wivelshire 85-91; rtd 92; Perm to Offic *Truro* from 92 and *Ex* from 99. *3 Derry Avenue, Plymouth PL4 6BH* Tel (01752) 661986

RUMSEY, Andrew Paul. b 68. Reading Univ BA89. Ridley Hall Cam MA98. **d** 97 **p** 98. C Harrow Trin St Mich *Lon* 97-01; V Gipsy Hill Ch Ch *S'wark* from 01. *Christ Church Vicarage, 1 Highland Road, London SE19 1DP* Tel (020) 8670 0385 E-mail vicar@gipsyhill.org.uk

RUMSEY, Ian Mark. b 58. Van Mildert Coll Dur BSc79 St Jo Coll Dur BA89. Cranmer Hall Dur 87. **d** 90 **p** 91. C Dalston *Carl* 90-94; C Wreay 92-94; TV Cockermouth w Embleton and Wythop 94-04; Adv for Post-Ord Tr 97-00; V Hurdsfield *Ches* from 04. *197A Hurdsfield Road, Macclesfield SK10 2PX* Tel (01625) 424587

RUNCORN, David Charles. b 54. BA77. St Jo Coll Nottm 77. **d** 79 **p** 80. C Wealdstone H Trin *Lon* 79-82; Chapl Lee Abbey 82-87; C Ealing St Steph Castle Hill *Lon* 89-90; V 90-96; Dir Past and Evang Studies Trin Coll Bris 96-03; Dir Min Development *Lich* 03-08; Perm to Offic *Derby* from 08. *The Vicarage, 35 Church Street, Littleover, Derby DE23 6GF* Tel (01332) 272184 Mobile 07870-331337 E-mail davidruncorn@mac.com

RUNCORN, Jacqueline Ann. See SEARLE, Jacqueline Ann

RUNDELL, Simon Philip. b 67. Univ of N Lon BSc95 Leeds Univ BA01 RGN90. Coll of Resurr Mirfield 99. **d** 01 **p** 02. C Southsea H Spirit *Portsm* 01-04; P-in-c Elson from 04. *St Thomas's Vicarage, 21 Elson Road, Gosport PO12 4BL* Tel (023) 9258 2824 E-mail simon@rundell.org.uk

RUNDLE, Mrs Beryl Rosemary. b 28. Bris Univ BA49 CertEd50. S Dios Minl Tr Scheme 83. **dss** 86 **d** 87. Tangmere *Chich* 86-87; Hon Par Dn 87-92; Boxgrove 86-87; Hon Par Dn 87-92; Hon Par Dn Eastbourne St Sav and St Pet 92-98; Perm to Offic *Portsm* from 98. *22 Sovereign Drive, Southsea PO4 8XX* Tel (01705) 826859

RUNDLE, Hilary. See WONG, Hilary

RUNDLE, Nicholas John. b 59. Southn Univ BA80. St Steph Ho Ox BTh84. **d** 84 **p** 85. C E Preston w Kingston *Chich* 84-87; Chapl RAF 87-91; Australia from 91, Assoc P Magill 91 93; R Grange 93-98; R Hawthorn 98-02; Chapl and Past Care Co-ord Mission Australia from 03. *Mission Australia, PO Box 6626, Adelaide SA 5000, Australia* Tel (0061) (8) 8370 3583 or 8223 5428 Fax 8223 6425 Mobile 403-183005 E-mail rundlen@mission.com.au

RUNDLE, Penelope Anne. b 36. St Hugh's Coll Ox MA59. S Dios Minl Tr Scheme 85. **d** 88 **p** 94. Hon Par Dn Mere w W Knoyle and Maiden Bradley *Sarum* 88-91; Hon Par Dn Upper Stour 91-94; Hon C 94-02; rtd 02; Perm to Offic *Sarum* 02-08. *7 Prospect Place, Ann Street, Salisbury SP1 2EA* Tel (01722) 411774

RUNNACLES, Ms Jasmine Celine Leweston. b 47. Lon Bible Coll BA75 RN68. STETS 05. **d** 08 **p** 09. NSM Burpham *Guildf* from 08. *Chydham Cottage, Maybury Hill, Woking GU22 8AF* Tel and fax (01483) 765239 Mobile 07774-171818 E-mail jclrunnacles@tiscali.co.uk

RUSCHMEYER, Henry Cassell. b 44. Union Coll NY BA66 Bank St Coll of Ed NY MEd73 NY Univ MA88. Gen Th Sem (NY) MD78. **d** 78 **p** 79. USA 78-89 and from 97; NSM Wilton Place St Paul *Lon* 89-97. *PO Box 25012, Sarasota FL 34277-2012, USA*

RUSCOE, Canon John Ernest. b 32. Dur Univ BA57. Qu Coll Birm 57. **d** 59 **p** 60. C Jarrow St Paul *Dur* 59-63; C Whitburn 63-65; V S Hylton from 65; Hon Can Dur Cathl from 85. *The Vicarage, Vicarage Lane, Sunderland SR4 0QB* Tel 0191-534 2325

RUSDELL-WILSON, Arthur Neville. b 43. Lon Univ BScEng65 Linacre Coll Ox BA70 MA74. St Steph Ho Ox 68. **d** 71 **p** 72. C Whitton St Aug *Lon* 71-73; C Chiswick St Nic w St Mary 73-76; C Littlehampton St Jas *Chich* 76-81; C Littlehampton St Mary 76-81; C Wick 76-81; V Whitworth St Bart *Man* 81-88; V Shaw 88-98; rtd 03. *21 Fairview Avenue, Goring-by-Sea, Worthing BN12 4HT* Tel (01903) 242561

RUSH, Paul Andrew. b 57. Lon Bible Coll BA79 Anglia Poly Univ MA03. Ridley Hall Cam 98. **d** 00 **p** 01. C Bar Hill *Ely* 00-03; Dioc Evang Officer *Leic* 03-06; Adv in Evang and Par Development *Bris* from 06. *5 Gold View, Swindon SN5 8ZG* Tel (01793) 872853 E-mail rev.paul.rush@ntlworld.com

RUSHER, James Victor Francis. b 28. RMA. Ridley Hall Cam 58. **d** 60 **p** 61. C Kensington St Helen w H Trin *Lon* 60-63; C Edgbaston St Bart *Birm* 63-66; V Summerfield 66-71; V Knowle 71-82; Perm to Offic from 82; Chapl Parkway Hosp Solihull 85-93; rtd 93. *4 Froxmere Close, Solihull B91 3XG* Tel 0121-705 4514

RUSHFORTH, Richard Hamblin. b 40. Keble Coll Ox BA62 MA71. Chich Th Coll 62. **d** 64 **p** 65. C St Leonards Ch Ch *Chich* 64-79; Org Sec Fellowship of St Nic 79-81; V Portslade St Nic and St Andr from 81; Min Portslade Gd Shep CD 88-89. *The Vicarage, South Street, Portslade, Brighton BN41 2LE* Tel (01273) 418090

RUSHTON, David William. b 70. St Chad's Coll Dur BA96. St Steph Ho Ox. **d** 98 **p** 99. C Hornsey St Mary w St Geo *Lon* 98-01; C Thamesmead *S'wark* 01-02; Asst Chapl King's Coll Hosp NHS Trust 02-04; Chapl from 04. *The Chaplain's Office, King's College Hospital, Denmark Hill, London SE5 9RS* Tel (020) 3299 3522 E-mail rev.rushton@kingsch.nhs.uk

RUSHTON, Canon James David. b 39. Dur Univ BA61. Cranmer Hall Dur. **d** 64 **p** 65. C Upper Armley *Ripon* 64-67; C Blackpool Ch Ch *Blackb* 67-70; V Preston St Cuth 70-79; V Denton Holme *Carl* 79-96; P-in-c Preston All SS *Blackb* 96-00; V 00-04; AD Preston 98-03; Hon Can Blackb Cathl 00-04; rtd 04; Perm to Offic *Blackb* from 04. *1 Stable Mews, Fleetwood Road, Thornton-Cleveleys FY5 1SQ* Tel (01253) 820402 E-mail james@jamesrushton.wanadoo.co.uk

RUSHTON, Ms Janet Maureen. b 46. Keele Univ BA68 Leic Univ PGCE69. Wycliffe Hall Ox BTh94. **d** 94 **p** 95. C Harrow St Mary *Lon* 94-98; C Putney St Mary *S'wark* 98-02; P-in-c Wolvercote w Summertown *Ox* 02-07; P-in-c Summertown from 07. *The Vicarage, 37 Lonsdale Road, Oxford OX2 7ES* Tel (01865) 556079 E-mail janrushton@lineone.net

RUSHTON, Malcolm Leslie. b 47. Bris Univ BSc69 Birm Univ PhD72 Fitzw Coll Cam BA74. Ridley Hall Cam 72. **d** 75 **p** 76. C Cullompton *Ex* 75-79; Chapl Univ Coll Lon 79-87; Chapl R Veterinary Coll Lon 87-90; Chapl R Free Medical Sch 87-90. *Flat 3, 13 Belsize Grove, London NW3 4UX* Tel and fax (020) 7722 1989

RUSHTON, Matthew John. b 75. St Anne's Coll Ox BA96 MA01 Solicitor 01. Ripon Coll Cuddesdon 07. **d** 09. C Nettleham *Linc* from 09. *23 Kingsway, Nettleham, Lincoln LN2 2QA*

RUSHTON, Philip William. b 38. Open Univ BA87. Clifton Th Coll 62. **d** 65 **p** 66. C Brixton St Paul *S'wark* 65-67; C Aldridge *Lich* 67-69; C Bushbury 69-71; Chapl Nat Nautical Sch Portishead 71-72; Chapl RAF 72-79; P-in-c Bolton on Swale *Ripon* 79-87; P-in-c The Cowtons 80-82; V 82-89; CF (TA) from 88; R Litcham, Kempston, Lexham, Mileham, Beeston etc *Nor* 89-95; P-in-c Tittleshall w Godwick 93-95; R Litcham w Kempston, E and W Lexham, Mileham etc 95-96; P-in-c Scole, Brockdish, Billingford, Thorpe Abbots etc 96-98; R 98-01; rtd 01; Perm to Offic *St E* and *Carl* from 01. *Helm Lea, Kirkby Thore, Penrith CA10 1UA* Tel and fax (01768) 361597 E-mail philipwrushton@hotmail.com

RUSHTON, Mrs Samantha Jayne. b 65. St Hilda's Coll Ox MA87. Trin Coll Bris BA05. **d** 05 **p** 06. C Highworth w Sevenhampton and Inglesham etc *Bris* 05-08; C Broad Blunsdon 05-08; Dioc Adv for Lic Min from 08; C Chippenham St Paul w Hardenhuish etc from 08; C Kington St Michael from 08. *33 Fallow Field, Chippenham SN14 6YA* Tel (01249) 660451 E-mail sam.rushton@bristoldiocese.org

RUSHTON, Mrs Susan Elizabeth. b 44. Univ of Wales (Cardiff) BA65. Bris Sch of Min 83. **dss** 86 **d** 87 **p** 94. Westbury-on-Trym H Trin *Bris* 86-91; Hon Par Dn 87-91; C Wotton St Mary *Glouc* 91-94; P-in-c Frampton Cotterell *Bris* 94-07; Chapl United Bris Healthcare NHS Trust 94-98; P-in-c Iron Acton 98-07; rtd 07; Perm to Offic *York* from 08. *9 Lime Avenue, Heworth, York YO31 1BT* Tel (01904) 410363 E-mail susan.rushton@onetel.net

RUSHTON, Mrs Valerie Elizabeth Wendy. b 40. Birm Univ BSocSc62. WMMTC 86. **d** 89 **p** 94. C Nuneaton St Nic *Cov* 89-93; C Stockingford 93-96; TV Watling Valley *Ox* 96-01; rtd 02; Perm to Offic *Ox* from 02. *106 Moreton Road, Buckingham MK18 1PW* Tel (01280) 824942

RUSK, The Very Revd Frederick John. b 28. QUB BA50 TCD 52. **d** 53 **p** 54. C Ballymoney *Conn* 53-56; C Belfast St Nic 56-59; I Broomhedge 59-65; RE Insp 64-66; I Belfast St Simon 65-78; I Ballylesson w Ballyclug 78-88; I Belfast St Nic 88-98; Preb Conn Cathl 84-86; Treas 86-90; Prec 90; Chan Conn Cathl 90-95; Dean Conn 95-98; rtd 98. *28 Banbridge Road, Lurgan, Craigavon BT66 7EQ* Tel (028) 3832 9763

RUSK, Canon Michael Frederick. b 58. Cam Univ BA MA Dur Univ MA98. Westcott Ho Cam 81. **d** 84 **p** 85. C Altrincham St Geo *Ches* 84-87; Chapl Collingwood and Grey Coll *Dur* 87-90; Lect Dur Univ 89-99; C-in-c Neville's Cross St Jo CD 90-99; TR Oadby *Leic* from 99; RD Gartree II from 00; RD Gartree I from 07; Hon Can Leic Cathl from 06. *The Rectory, 31 Hill Field, Oadby, Leicester LE2 4RW* Tel 0116-271 2135 E-mail m.f.rusk@leicester.anglican.org

RUSS, Canon Timothy John. b 41. AKC64. Sarum Th Coll 66. **d** 66 **p** 67. C Walthamstow St Pet *Chelmsf* 66-70; C Epping St Jo 70-73; C Stepney St Dunstan and All SS *Lon* 73-75; Youth Officer 75-79; Tutor YMCA Nat Coll Walthamstow 79-84; Hon C St Botolph Aldgate w H Trin Minories *Lon* 82-89; Selection Sec ACCM 84-89; Dir St Marylebone Healing and Counselling Cen 89-92; Gen Sec Inst of Relig and Medicine 89-92; Hon C Hoxton St Anne w St Columba *Lon* 90-92; P-in-c St Dennis *Truro* 92-06; Par Development Adv 92-99; Dioc Dir Minl Tr 99-06; Hon Can Truro Cathl 01-06; rtd 06. *Russet Cottage, 26 St Francis Meadow, Mitchell, Newquay TR8 5DB* Tel (01872) 519142 E-mail timruss@tesco.net

RUSSELL, Adrian Camper. b 45. Chich Th Coll 79. **d** 81 **p** 82. C Marton *Blackb* 81-84; C Haslemere *Guildf* 84-85; V Hartlepool H Trin *Dur* 85-89; P-in-c Cornforth 89-94; R Auchterarder and Muthill *St And* 94-97; P-in-c Kenton Ascension *Newc* 97-07; rtd 07. *23 Lambley Avenue, North Shields NE30 3SL* Tel 0191-280 9552 E-mail acr26682@blueyonder.co.uk

RUSSELL, Alexandra Blaise. b 58. St Steph Ho Ox 96. **d** 98 **p** 99. C Gt Bookham *Guildf* 98-03; R Long Ditton 03-07; Perm to Offic *Win* 07-08; P-in-c Pennington from 08. *19 Stanley Road, Lymington SO41 3SJ* Tel (01590) 610963 E-mail revdalexrussell@hotmail.co.uk

✠**RUSSELL, The Rt Revd Anthony John.** b 43. St Chad's Coll Dur BA65 Trin Coll Ox DPhil71. Cuddesdon Coll 65. **d** 70 **p** 71 **c** 88. C Hilborough w Bodney *Nor* 70-73; P-in-c Preston-on-Stour w Whitchurch *Cov* 73-76; P-in-c Atherstone on Stour 73-76; V Preston on Stour and Whitchurch w Atherstone 77-88; Can Th Cov Cathl 77-88; Chapl Arthur Rank Cen 73-82; Dir 83-88; Chapl to The Queen 88-00; Area Bp Dorchester *Ox* 88-00; Bp Ely from 00. *The Bishop's House, Ely CB7 4DW* Tel (01353) 662749 Fax 669437 E-mail bishop@ely.anglican.org

RUSSELL, The Ven Brian Kenneth. b 50. Trin Hall Cam BA73 MA76 Birm Univ MA77 PhD83. Cuddesdon Coll 74. **d** 76 **p** 77. C Redhill St Matt *S'wark* 76-79; Dir Studies NEOC 79-83; P-in-c Merrington *Dur* 79-83; Dir of Studies and Lect Linc Th Coll 83-86; Selection Sec and Sec Cttee for Th Educn ABM 86-93; Bp's Dir for Min *Birm* 93-05; Adn Aston from 05; Hon Can Birm Cathl from 99. *26 George Road, Edgbaston, Birmingham B15 1PJ* Tel 0121-454 5525 or 426 0437 Fax 455 6085 or 428 1114 E-mail b.russell@birmingham.anglican.org

RUSSELL, Brian Robert. b 61. QUB BA BD92. CITC. **d** 85 **p** 86. C Dublin Drumcondra w N Strand *D & G* 85-87; C Carrickfergus *Conn* 87-90; I Kilmegan w Maghera *D & D* 90-96; I Bailieborough w Knockbride, Shercock and Mullagh *K, E & A* 96-00; I Kilbarron w Rossnowlagh and Drumholm *D & R* from 00. *The Rectory, Lisminton, Ballintra, Co Donegal, Republic of Ireland* Tel and fax (00353) (74) 973 4025 E-mail bestrussell@eircom.net

RUSSELL, Bruce Harley. b 57. Ch Ch Ox BA79 Roehampton Inst PGCE80. Ripon Coll Cuddesdon. **d** 99 **p** 00. C Bracknell *Ox* 99-03; TV Langley Marish from 03. *St Francis's Vicarage, 21 Lynward Avenue, Slough SL3 7BJ* Tel (01753) 557150 E-mail bhrussell@supanet.com

RUSSELL, Christopher Ian. b 68. St Jo Coll Dur BA91 St Edm Coll Cam MPhil96. Ridley Hall Cam 93. **d** 96 **p** 97. C Deptford St Jo w H Trin *S'wark* 96-99; Soul Survivor Watford *St Alb*

99-01; C Reading St Mary w St Laur *Ox* from 01. *9 Mansfield Road, Reading RG1 6AL* Tel 0118-956 0559
E-mail chris@belindarussell.freeserve.co.uk

RUSSELL, Clive Phillip. b 61. Ridley Hall Cam 04. **d** 06 **p** 07. C High Ongar w Norton Mandeville *Chelmsf* from 06. *49 Kettlebury Way, Ongar CM5 9HA* Tel (01277) 364482

RUSSELL, David John. b 57. Sarum & Wells Th Coll BTh94. **d** 94 **p** 95. C Glouc St Geo w Whaddon 94-98; P-in-c Wickwar w Rangeworthy 98-01; R Wickwar, Rangeworthy and Hillesley from 02. *The Rectory, 75 High Street, Wickwar, Wotton-under-Edge GL12 8NP* Tel (01454) 294267
E-mail davidrussell@gmx.com

RUSSELL, David John Timothy. b 75. Oak Hill Th Coll. **d** 09. C Padiham w Hapton and Padiham Green *Blackb* from 09. *5 St John's Road, Padiham, Burnley BB12 7BN* Tel (01282) 773219

RUSSELL, David Robert. b 43. Brasted Th Coll 66 Sarum Th Coll 68. **d** 70 **p** 71. C Leintwardine *Heref* 70-73; C Bridgnorth w Tasley 73-75; R Lockridge and Eden Hill Australia 75-80; R Bellevue and Darlington 80-87; Asst Chapl Dept of Corrective Services 87-93; Sen Chapl 93-95; R Carlisle and Rivervale 95-03; E Deanery Miss Development P 03-04; R Kondinin and Corrigin 05-08; rtd 08. *PO Box 3036, 98 Oat Street, Carlisle WA 6101, Australia* Tel (0061) 42-754 5560 (mobile)
E-mail drussl@westnet.com.au

RUSSELL, Canon Derek John. b 30. St Pet Hall Ox BA54 MA58. Qu Coll Birm 54. **d** 56 **p** 57. C Boxley *Cant* 56-59; C Whitstable All SS 59-63; Chapl HM Pris Wormwood Scrubs 63-65 and 71-89; Chapl HM Pris Stafford 65-69; Pentonville 70; SE Regional Chapl 74-81; Chapl HM Rem Cen Latchmere Ho 74-77; Asst Chapl Gen of Pris 81-83; Dep 83-90; Hon Can Cant Cathl 86-90; rtd 90; Perm to Offic *Cant* from 90. *25 Pier Avenue, Whitstable CT5 2HQ* Tel (01227) 276654

RUSSELL, Ms Elizabeth Marilyn Vivia. b 50. LRAM70 GRSM72. Westcott Ho Cam 95. **d** 97 **p** 98. C Alton St Lawr *Win* 97-01; C St Martin-in-the-Fields *Lon* 01-08; P-in-c S Kensington H Trin w All SS from 08; Dir of Ords Two Cities Area from 08. *5 Aldwyn House, Davidson Gardens, London SW8 2HX* Tel (020) 7766 1108

RUSSELL, Eric Watson. b 39. FCA76. Clifton Th Coll 66. **d** 69 **p** 70. C Kinson *Sarum* 69-73; C Peckham St Mary Magd *S'wark* 73-77; TV Barking St Marg w St Patr *Chelmsf* 77-82; V Lozells St Paul and St Silas *Birm* 82-95; RD Aston 89-94; P-in-c Barston and C Knowle 95-04; I Kells Union *M & K* 04-09; rtd 09. *20 Slater Road, Bentley Heath, Solihull B93 8AG* Tel (01564) 779709 E-mail ericandjoan@uwclub.net

RUSSELL, Gary William Algernon. b 64. Ripon Coll Cuddesdon 04. **d** 06 **p** 07. C Harpenden St Nic *St Alb* from 06; Chapl ATC from 07. *37 St James Road, Harpenden AL5 4PB* Tel (01582) 713830 E-mail moreteavicar@hotmail.co.uk

RUSSELL, The Ven Harold Ian Lyle. b 34. Lon Coll of Div ALCD59 BD60. **d** 60 **p** 61. C Iver *Ox* 60-63; C Fulwood *Sheff* 63-67; V Chapeltown 67-75; RD Tankersley 73-75; V Nottingham St Jude *S'well* 75-89; AD Nottingham Cen 86-89; Hon Can S'well Minster 88-89; Adn Cov 89-01; rtd 01; Chapl to The Queen 97-01; Perm to Offic *S'well* from 01. *5 Old Acres, Woodborough, Nottingham NG14 6ES* Tel 0115-965 3543

RUSSELL, Ms Isoline Lucilda (Lyn). b 41. **d** 03 **p** 04. OLM Camberwell St Giles w St Matt *S'wark* from 03. *124 Hindman's Road, London SE22 9NH* Tel (020) 8299 4431

RUSSELL, James Anthony Tomkins. b 67. Oak Hill Th Coll BA99. **d** 99 **p** 00. C Chadwell *Chelmsf* 99-03; C Patcham *Chich* 03-07; P-in-c N Mundham w Hunston and Merston from 07. *The Rectory, Church Lane, Hunston, Chichester PO20 1AJ* Tel (01243) 782003 E-mail jamesandannabel@aol.com

RUSSELL, Mrs Janet Mary. b 53. Univ of Wales BSc74 BArch76. Ox Min Course 91. **d** 94 **p** 95. C Watlington w Pyrton and Shirburn *Ox* 94-97; C Icknield 97-98; TV Wallingford 98-05; Par Development Adv (Berks) from 05. *The Rectory, Marsh Baldon, Oxford OX44 9LS* Tel (01865) 343215
E-mail revrussell@btopenworld.com

RUSSELL, Canon John Arthur. b 29. AKC62. **d** 63 **p** 64. C Fareham H Trin *Portsm* 63-67; R Greatham w Empshott 67-79; V Ham St Andr *S'wark* 79-87; P-in-c Battersea St Luke 87-92; V 92-96; Hon Can S'wark Cathl 95-96; rtd 97; Perm to Offic *S'wark* 97-03. *Toni Llido 4, 2, apt 5, 03730 Puerto de Javea (Alicante), Spain* Tel (0034) 965 790 587 E-mail jarussell@ya.com

RUSSELL, John Bruce. b 56. Ripon Coll Cuddesdon. **d** 95 **p** 96. C Newport Pagnell w Lathbury and Moulsoe *Ox* 95-98; P-in-c Wing w Grove 98-03; AD Mursley 02-03; Hon C Gt Berkhamsted, Gt and Lt Gaddesden etc *St Alb* from 08. *49 Tring Road, Aylesbury HP20 1LD* Tel (01296) 423022
E-mail john.karen.russell@ntlworld.com

RUSSELL, John Graham. b 35. G&C Coll Cam BA58 MA62. Westcott Ho Cam 59. **d** 61 **p** 62. C Durleigh *B & W* 61-66; C Bridgwater St Mary w Chilton Trinity 61-66; C Far Headingley St Chad *Ripon* 66-72; P-in-c Leeds St Matt Lt London 72-79; V Rowley Regis *Birm* 79-84; V Hall Green Ascension 84-95; Deanery P Warley Deanery 95-00; rtd 01; Perm to Offic *Birm*

from 01. *1 Stapylton Avenue, Harborne, Birmingham B17 0BA* Tel 0121-426 4529 E-mail pmr@russellp21.fsnet.co.uk

RUSSELL, John Richard. b 53. Westmr Coll Ox MTh01 FRSA02. Spurgeon's Coll 77 Ripon Coll Cuddesdon 01. **d** 01 **p** 02. Hon C St Mary le Strand w St Clem Danes *Lon* 01-02; Chapl RAF 02-08; Perm to Offic *Chelmsf* from 09. *18 Wambrook, Shoeburyness, Southend-on-Sea SS3 8BW* Tel (01702) 580545

RUSSELL, Canon Jonathan Vincent Harman. b 43. K Coll Lon 68. **d** 69 **p** 70. C Addington *Cant* 69-73; C Buckland in Dover w Buckland Valley 73-76; P-in-c Selling 76-85; P-in-c Throwley w Stalisfield and Otterden 79-85; R Selling w Throwley, Sheldwich w Badlesmere etc 85-95; Hon Min Can Cant Cathl 83-94; RD Ospringe 90-95; P-in-c Elham w Denton and Wootton 95-01; V 01-08; Hon Can Cant Cathl 94-08; rtd 08; Perm to Offic *Cant* from 08. *Kirkella, Goodwin Road, St Margaret's Bay, Dover CT15 6ED* Tel (01304) 852811 Mobile 07702-314865

RUSSELL, Jonathan Wingate. b 55. Newc Univ BSc76. St Jo Coll Nottm BA83. **d** 84 **p** 85. C Southsea St Jude *Portsm* 84-87; P-in-c Shorwell w Kingston 87-92; V 92-06; P-in-c Gatcombe 87-92; R 92-06; P-in-c Chale 89-92; R 92-06; RD W Wight 96-01; R Allendale w Whitfield *Newc* from 06. *The Rectory, 16 Forstersteads, Allendale, Hexham NE47 9AS* Tel and fax (01434) 618607 E-mail rector@allendalechurch.co.uk

RUSSELL, Lloyd George Winkler. b 19. Hatf Coll Dur BA49. **d** 45 **p** 46. C Kingston St Mich Jamaica 45-47; P-in-c Lucea and Green Is 48; Perm to Offic *Dur* 48-50; R Black River Kings and Lacovia etc Jamaica 51-52; Perm to Offic *Lon* 53-58; *S'wark* 53-59; *Roch* 58-81; R Port Maria Jamaica 82-85; rtd 85; Perm to Offic *S'wark* and *Roch* 85-03. *39 Pembroke Road, Bromley BR1 2RT* Tel (020) 8460 1498

RUSSELL, Lyn. *See* RUSSELL, Ms Isoline Lucilda

RUSSELL, Madeleine. b 41. Pargau Teacher Tr Coll Switzerland TDip62. **d** 04 **p** 05. NSM Halifax H Trin and St Jude *Wakef* from 04. *Holy Trinity Vicarage, 9 Love Lane, Halifax HX1 2BQ* Tel (01422) 352446

RUSSELL, Mrs Marion. b 54. Glas Univ BEd75 Jordanhill Coll Glas TCert75. CBDTI 03. **d** 06 **p** 07. NSM Altham w Clayton le Moors *Blackb* from 06. *407 Revidge Road, Blackburn BB1 8DF* Tel (01254) 692252 E-mail mrussell.lcc@btopenworld.com

RUSSELL, Martin Christopher. b 48. St Jo Coll Dur BA70. Coll of Resurr Mirfield 72. **d** 74 **p** 75. C Huddersfield St Pet *Wakef* 74-77; Trinidad and Tobago 78-85; V S Crosland *Wakef* 86-00; P-in-c Helme 86-00; P-in-c Halifax H Trin 00-02; P-in-c Halifax St Jude 00-02; V Halifax H Trin and St Jude from 02. *Holy Trinity Vicarage, 9 Love Lane, Halifax HX1 2BQ* Tel (01422) 352446

RUSSELL, Michael John. b 38. Clifton Th Coll 68. **d** 68 **p** 69. C Cranham Park CD *Chelmsf* 68-70; C Bucknall and Bagnall *Lich* 70-77; P-in-c Tintwistle *Ches* 77-79; V Nassam from 86; rtd 03. *144 Winchester Street, Ashhurst 4810, New Zealand* Tel (0064) (6) 326 8547

RUSSELL, Canon Neil. b 47. EMMTC 78. **d** 81 **p** 82. NSM Wyberton *Linc* 81-84; C 84-85; V Frampton 85-93; Agric Chapl and Countryside Officer 89-93; P-in-c Stamford All SS w St Jo 93-97; V 97-08; RD Aveland and Ness w Stamford 00-06; Warden Sacrista Prebend Retreat Ho *S'well* from 00; Can and Preb Linc Cathl from 02. *11 Gleneagles Drive, Greylees, Sleaford NG34 8GH* Tel (01529) 488225 *or* (01636) 816833 Mobile 07730-403630 E-mail canonneilrussell@yahoo.co.uk

RUSSELL, Mrs Noreen Margaret. b 39. Man Univ BA60 Lon Univ PGCE61 BD66. WMMTC 90. **d** 91 **p** 94. NSM Swynnerton and Tittensor *Lich* 91-97; C Draycott-le-Moors w Forsbrook 97-06; rtd 06; Perm to Offic *Lich* from 06. *40 Old Road, Barlaston, Stoke-on-Trent ST12 9EQ* Tel (01782) 372992

RUSSELL, The Ven Norman Atkinson. b 43. Chu Coll Cam BA65 MA69 Lon Univ BD70. Lon Coll of Div 67. **d** 70 **p** 71. C Clifton Ch Ch w Em *Bris* 70-74; C Enfield Ch Ch Trent Park *Lon* 74-77; R Harwell w Chilton *Ox* 77-84; P-in-c Gerrards Cross 84-88; P-in-c Fulmer 85-88; R Gerrards Cross and Fulmer 88-98; Hon Can Ch Ch 95-98; RD Amersham 96-98; Adn Berks from 98. *Foxglove House, Love Lane, Donnington, Newbury RG14 2JG* Tel (01635) 552820 Fax 522165
E-mail archdber@oxford.anglican.org

RUSSELL, Peter Richard. b 60. Ch Ch Coll Cant BA99. SEITE 02. **d** 05 **p** 06. NSM Margate All SS and Westgate St Sav *Cant* 05-08; Chapl St Lawr Coll Ramsgate from 09. *St Lawrence College, College Road, Ramsgate CT11 7AE* Tel (01843) 572900 E-mail minnisbay@hotmail.com

RUSSELL, Ralph Geoffrey Major. b 19. St Aug Coll Cant 47 Sarum Th Coll 48. **d** 50 **p** 51. C Redruth *Truro* 50-55; C Hayes St Mary *Lon* 55-56; C W Wycombe *Ox* 56-62; V New Bradwell w Stantonbury 62-73; P-in-c Gt Linford w Willen and Gt and Lt Woolstone 62-64; P-in-c Linslade 74-75; V 75-87; rtd 87; Perm to Offic *Ox* 87-04 and *Pet* 89-04. *Churchill House, 46 Beaumont Village, Alexandra Road, Aldershot GU11 1BB* Tel (01252) 346746

RUSSELL, Richard Alexander. b 44. Univ of Wales (Abth) BA65 McMaster Univ Ontario MA67 Bris Univ MA73 PGCE74

MEd76. Trin Coll Bris 79. **d** 82 **p** 83. C Hartlepool St Paul *Dur* 82-85; P-in-c Bath Widcombe *B & W* 85-88; V 88-00; rtd 00. *76 Waterside Way, Radstock, Bath BA3 3YQ* Tel (01761) 433217 E-mail 113135.2044@compuserve.com

RUSSELL, Roger Geoffrey. b 47. Worc Coll Ox BA69 MA73. Cuddesdon Coll 70. **d** 72 **p** 73. C Anlaby Common St Mark *York* 72-75; C Wilton Place St Paul *Lon* 75-86; R Lancing w Coombes *Chich* from 86; RD Worthing 97-05. *The Vicarage, 63 Manor Road, Lancing BN15 0EY* Tel (01903) 753212

RUSSELL, Canon William Warren. b 52. QUB BSocSc74. CITC 74. **d** 77 **p** 78. C Agherton *Conn* 77-79; C Lisburn Ch Ch Cathl 79-83; I Magheradroll *D & D* from 83; Treas Dromore Cathl from 08. *The Rectory, 18 Church Road, Ballynahinch BT24 8LP* Tel (028) 9756 2289 Mobile 07810-222906 E-mail rev_wwrussell@hotmail.com

RUSSELL-SMITH, Mark Raymond. b 46. New Coll Edin MTh91. St Jo Coll Dur BA71 Cranmer Hall Dur. **d** 72 **p** 73. C Upton (Overchurch) *Ches* 72-75; C Deane *Man* 75-77; UCCF Travelling Sec 77-80; Lic to Offic *York* 78-81; BCMS 81-92; Kenya 81-92; P-in-c Slaidburn *Bradf* from 92; P-in-c Long Preston w Tosside from 97. *The Rectory, Slaidburn, Clitheroe BB7 3ER* Tel (01200) 446238

RUST, Jonathan Kenneth. b 62. Reading Univ BSc84. Ridley Hall Cam. **d** 00 **p** 01. C Holloway St Mary Magd *Lon* from 00. *59 Bride Street, London N7 8RN* Tel (020) 7607 1316 E-mail j.rust@tiscali.co.uk

RUSTED, Mrs Mary Elizabeth. b 44. **d** 00 **p** 01. OLM Mildenhall *St E* from 00. *Spring Hall Farm, Cooks Drove, West Row, Bury St Edmunds IP28 8QL* Tel (01638) 715054

RUSTELL, Anthony Christopher. b 77. Ch Ch Ox BA98 MSt01 MA02 Keble Coll Ox DPhil07. St Steph Ho Ox 98. **d** 01 **p** 02. NSM Ox St Barn and St Paul 01-04; P-in-c N Hinksey and Wytham from 04. *The Vicarage, 81 West Way, Oxford OX2 9JY* Tel (01865) 242345 E-mail acrustell@tiscali.co.uk

✠**RUSTON, The Rt Revd John Harry Gerald.** b 29. SS Coll Cam BA52 MA56. Ely Th Coll 52. **d** 54 **p** 55 **c** 83. C Leic St Andr 54-57; OGS from 55; C Cuddesdon and Tutor Cuddesdon Coll 57-61; C Sekhukhuniland S Africa 62-70; Prin St Fran Coll 67-70; Can Pretoria 68-76; Sub Dean 71-76; Adn Bloemfontein 76-83; Suff Bp Pretoria 83-91; Bp St Helena 91-99; rtd 99; Perm to Offic *Roch* from 99. *The College of St Barnabas, Blackberry Lane, Lingfield RH7 6NJ* Tel (01342) 872865

RUTHERFORD, Anthony Richard. b 37. Culham Coll Ox TCert62 Sussex Univ MA77. S'wark Ord Course 83. **d** 86 **p** 87. Hon C Tunbridge Wells St Luke *Roch* 86-88; C Bromley SS Pet and Paul 88-90; V Wragby *Linc* 90-94; Asst Min Officer 90-94; V Penge Lane H Trin *Roch* 94-02; rtd 02; Perm to Offic *Roch* from 03. *6 Ashley Gardens, Tunbridge Wells TN4 8TY* Tel (01892) 541009 E-mail arrutherford@f2s.com

RUTHERFORD, Arthur Ernest. b 26. Saltley Tr Coll Birm CertEd53 Loughb Coll of Educn DipEd54. Sarum & Wells Th Coll 91. **d** 92 **p** 93. NSM Lilliput *Sarum* 92-96; Perm to Offic 96-08. *9 Park View, 53 Parkstone Road, Poole BH15 2NX* Tel (01202) 669019

RUTHERFORD, Daniel Fergus Peter. b 65. Hatf Coll Dur BA86 CertEd87. Ridley Hall Cam 88. **d** 90 **p** 91. C Harold Wood *Chelmsf* 90-94; C Hove Bp Hannington Memorial Ch *Chich* 94-97; Chapl City of Lon Freemen's Sch from 97. *City of London Freemen's School, Park Lane, Ashtead KT21 1ET* Tel (01372) 277933 Fax 276728

✠**RUTHERFORD, The Rt Revd Graeme Stanley.** b 43. Cranmer Hall Dur BA77 MA78 ACT 66. **d** 66 **p** 67 **c** 00. Australia 66-73 and from 77; C Bendigo St Paul 66-70; V Pyramid Hill 70-73; C Holborn St Geo w H Trin and St Bart *Lon* 73-74; C Dur St Nic 74-77; R Kyabram 77-82; I Malvern 82-87; I Camberwell St Jo 87-00; Can Melbourne Cathl 91-00; Asst Bp Newcastle from 00. *10 Pangari Place, PO Box 9095, Wyoming NSW 2250, Australia* Tel (0061) (2) 4329 2902 Fax 4329 5501 E-mail bishopgraeme@bigpond.com

RUTHERFORD, Ian William. b 46. Univ of Wales (Lamp) BA68. Cuddesdon Coll 68. **d** 70 **p** 71. C Gosforth All SS *Newc* 70-72; C Prestbury *Glouc* 73-76; Chapl RAF 76-93; CMP from 93; TV Redruth w Lanner and Treleigh *Truro* 93-94; V Paulsgrove *Portsm* 94-99; V Leeds Belle Is St Jo and St Barn *Ripon* from 99. *The Vicarage, 30 Low Grange View, Leeds LS10 3DT* Tel 0113-271 7821 E-mail fatherian@onetel.com

RUTHERFORD, Janet Elizabeth. b 37. S'wark Ord Course 86. **d** 89. NSM Plaistow St Mary *Roch* 89-90; NSM Linc St Botolph 91-93. *6 Ashley Gardens, Tunbridge Wells TN4 8TY* Tel (01892) 541009

RUTHERFORD, Canon John Bilton. b 23. Qu Coll Birm 49. **d** 52 **p** 53. C Newc H Cross 52-57; C Longbenton St Bart 57-60; V High Elswick St Phil 60-66; V Walker 66-74; I Benwell St Jas 74-81; Hon Can Newc Cathl 80-90; V Lesbury w Alnmouth 81-90; RD Alnwick 86-89; Perm to Offic from 90; rtd 90. *68 Worcester Way, Woodlands Park, Wideopen, Newcastle upon Tyne NE13 6JD* Tel 0191-236 4785

RUTHERFORD, Peter George. b 34. Nor Ord Course 73. **d** 76 **p** 77. NSM New Catton Ch Ch *Nor* 76-79; NSM Eaton 79-80;

NSM Nor St Steph 81-92; Perm to Offic 92-94 and from 99; P-in-c Earlham St Mary 94-99; RD Nor S 98-99; rtd 99. *126 Colman Road, Norwich NR4 7AA* Tel and fax (01603) 457629 E-mail pgr457629@aol.com

RUTHERFORD, Peter Marshall. b 57. St Andr Univ MTheol81 Ulster Univ MA96. CITC 83. **d** 83 **p** 84. C Stormont *D & D* 83-85; CF 85-01; Asst Chapl Gen 01-02; Asst Chapl Milan w Genoa and Varese *Eur* 03-04; I Castlepollard and Oldcastle w Loughcrew etc *M & K* from 04; Dioc Dir of Ords from 05. *St Michael's Rectory, Castlepollard, Mullingar, Co Westmeath, Republic of Ireland* Tel and fax (00353) (44) 966 1123 E-mail peterrutherford@me.com

RUTHERFORD (née ERREY), Ms Rosalind Elisabeth. b 52. St Hugh's Coll Ox BA74 Surrey Univ BA02 Goldsmiths' Coll Lon PGCE78. STETS 99. **d** 02 **p** 03. C Earley St Pet *Ox* 02-06; TV Basingstoke *Win* from 06. *45 Beaconsfield Road, Basingstoke RG21 3DG* Tel (01256) 464616 E-mail rosalind@rutherfords.fsnet.co.uk

RUTLEDGE, Canon Christopher John Francis. b 44. Lon Univ BSc67 Univ of Wales MPhil94 PhD99 TCert80. Sarum Th Coll 67. **d** 70 **p** 71. C Birm St Pet 70-73; C Calne and Blackland *Sarum* 73-76; P-in-c Derry Hill 76-78; V 78-81; P-in-c Talbot Village 81-82; V from 82; Can and Preb Sarum Cathl from 95; Chapl Talbot Heath Sch Bournemouth 04-09. *The Vicarage, 20 Alton Road, Bournemouth BH10 4AE* Tel (01202) 513646 *or* 529349 E-mail christopher.rutledge@ntlworld.com

RUTLEDGE, Francis George. b 62. TCD BA83 BTh90. **d** 86 **p** 87. C Holywood *D & D* 86-89; C Willowfield 89-91; I Kilmakee *Conn* 91-97; I Carrigrohane Union *C, C & R* 97-04; I Donacavey w Barr *Clogh* 04-05; Bp's C Bangor Primacy *D & D* from 05. *4 Glendowan Way, Bangor BT19 7SP* Tel (028) 9185 9731 E-mail francis.rutledge@btinternet.com

RUTT, Mrs Celia Mary Avril. b 43. Cranmer Hall Dur. **d** 02 **p** 03. NSM Heworth H Trin *York* 02-05; NSM Acomb St Steph 05-09; NSM Clifton from 09. *226 Shipton Road, York YO30 5RZ* Tel (01904) 627384 E-mail celia.rutt@tiscali.co.uk

RUTT, Canon Denis Frederic John. b 17. Kelham Th Coll 34. **d** 41 **p** 42. C Luton Ch Ch *St Alb* 41-44; Bp's Youth Chapl 44-48; R Empangeni S Africa 48-54; R Yaxham and Welborne *Nor* 54-61; R Kirkley 61-71; RD Lothingland 65-71; R N Lynn w St Marg and St Nic 71-76; Can Res and Prec Lich Cathl 76-83; rtd 83; Perm to Offic *Bradf* 83-99. *5 Manormead, Tilford Road, Hindhead GU26 6RA* Tel (01428) 604415

RUTT-FIELD, Benjamin John. b 48. Chich Th Coll. **d** 90 **p** 91. C Wickford and Runwell *Chelmsf* 90-94; V Goodmayes St Paul from 94. *St Paul's Vicarage, 20 Eastwood Road, Ilford IG3 8XA* Tel (020) 8590 6596 E-mail bjrf@nildram.co.uk

RUTTER, Canon Allen Edward Henry (Claude). b 28. Qu Coll Cam BA52 MA56. Cranmer Hall Dur. **d** 59 **p** 60. C Bath Abbey w St Jas *B & W* 59-60; C E Dereham w Hoe *Nor* 60-64; R Cawston 64-69; Chapl Cawston Coll 64-69; P-in-c Felthorpe w Haveringland 64-69; R Gingindhlovu S Africa 69-73; P-in-c Over and Nether Compton, Trent etc *Sarum* 73-80; RD Sherborne 77-87; P-in-c Oborne w Poyntington 79-80; P-in-c Queen Thorne 80-96; Can and Preb Sarum Cathl 86-96; rtd 96; Perm to Offic *B & W* 98-99 and from 00; P-in-c Thorncombe w Winsham and Cricket St Thomas 99; C Chard and Distr 99-00. *Home Farm, Chilson, South Chard, Chard TA20 2NX* Tel (01460) 221368

RUTTER, Graham Piers. b 77. St Jo Coll Dur BSc98 PhD03 Liv Univ MSc99. St Jo Coll Nottm 06. **d** 08 **p** 09. C Wellington All SS w Eyton *Lich* from 08. *1 Stile Rise, Telford TF5 0LR* Tel (01952) 641229 E-mail graham_rutter@yahoo.co.uk

RUTTER, John Edmund Charles. b 53. Qu Coll Cam MA76. St Jo Coll Nottm MA93. **d** 93 **p** 94. C Penge St Jo *Roch* 93-97; Bp's C Bangor Primacy *D & D* 97-04; I Glenavy w Tunny and Crumlin *Conn* from 04. *The Vicarage, 30 Crumlin Road, Glenavy, Crumlin BT29 4LG* Tel and fax (028) 9442 2361 E-mail glenavy@connor.anglican.org

RUTTER, John Smiles. b 49. Hertf Coll Ox BA71 PGCE72. NEOC 02. **d** 07 **p** 08. NSM Ripon H Trin from 07. *17 Church Lane, Ripon HG4 2ES* Tel (01765) 605638

RUTTER, Martin Charles. b 54. Wolv Poly BSc75 Southn Univ BTh81. Sarum & Wells Th Coll 76. **d** 79 **p** 80. C Cannock *Lich* 79-82; C Uttoxeter w Bramshall 82-86; V W Bromwich St Jas 86-97; P-in-c W Bromwich St Paul 89-97; V W Bromwich St Jas w St Paul 97-02; RD W Bromwich 94-02; V Gt Barr from 02. *St Margaret's Vicarage, Chapel Lane, Great Barr, Birmingham B43 7BD* Tel 0121-357 1390

RUTTER, Michael. b 75. Trin Coll Bris BA06. **d** 07 **p** 08. C Dudley Wood *Worc* from 07. *2 Stadium Drive, Dudley DY2 0DD*

RUTTER, Ronald. b 47. SS Hild & Bede Coll Dur TCert71 Open Univ BA81 CMath MIMA. CBDTI. **d** 00 **p** 01. NSM Heversham and Milnthorpe *Carl* from 00. *Ellerslie, Woodhouse Lane, Heversham, Milnthorpe LA7 7EW* Tel and fax (01539) 564260 E-mail ron_rutter@hotmail.com

RUXTON, Charles. b 58. Van Mildert Coll Dur BSc79 CGeol FGS MCIWEM. **d** 06 **p** 07. OLM Meole Brace *Lich* from 06.

New Place, Westbury, Shrewsbury SY5 9RY Tel (01743) 891636
E-mail c.ruxton@btinternet.com

RWANDA, Archbishop of. *See* KOLINI, The Most Revd Emmanuel Musaba

RYALL, John Francis Robert. b 30. New Coll Ox BA52 MA57. Westcott Ho Cam 52. **d** 54 **p** 55. C Petersfield w Sheet *Portsm* 54-56; C Portsea St Mary 56-62; C Warblington w Emsworth 62-65; C Freshwater 65-67; R Frating w Thorrington *Chelmsf* 67-73; R Gt Yeldham 74-76; P-in-c Lt Yeldham 75-76; R Gt w Lt Yeldham 76-80; P-in-c Thorley *Portsm* 80-82; P-in-c Shalfleet 80-82; V Calbourne w Newtown 82-95; rtd 95; Perm to Offic *Portsm* from 95. *Weald House, Main Road, Wellow, Yarmouth PO41 0SZ* Tel (01983) 760783

RYALL, Michael Richard. b 36. TCD BA58 MA65. TCD Div Sch Div Test58. **d** 58 **p** 59. C Dublin St Geo *D & G* 58-62; CF 62-65 and 68-90; CF (TAVR) 67-68; C Dublin Rathmines *D & G* 65-66; Asst Master Dungannon Secondary Sch 66-68; R Yardley Hastings, Denton and Grendon etc *Pet* 90-01; rtd 01; Perm to Offic *Chich* from 02; *Pet* 06-09; *St D* from 07; P-in-c Mayland *Chelmsf* from 08. *31 Imperial Avenue, Mayland, Chelmsford CM3 6AH* Tel (01621) 740943 Mobile 07968-111258
E-mail michaelryall@waitrose.com

RYALLS, Craig James. b 74. Bris Univ BA96 Peterho Cam BA01. Ridley Hall Cam 99. **d** 02 **p** 03. C Bearsted w Thurnham *Cant* 02-06; C Woking Ch Ch *Guildf* from 06. *4 Orchard Drive, Woking GU21 4BN* Tel (01483) 771551 *or* 740897
E-mail craig.ryalls@christchurchwoking.org

RYAN, Alan John. b 57. SWMTC. **d** 09. C Fremington *Ex* from 09. *19 Lane End Close, Instow, Bideford EX39 4LG* Tel (01271) 860822

RYAN, David Peter. b 64. Aston Univ BSc86. Linc Th Coll BTh94. **d** 94 **p** 95. C Horsforth *Ripon* 94-97; C Bedale 97-98; P-in-c Startforth and Bowes and Rokeby w Brignall 98-00; V 00-04; P-in-c Warndon St Nic *Worc* from 04; Dioc Ecum Officer from 04. *The Vicarage, 4 Daty Croft, Home Meadow, Worcester WR4 0JB* Tel (01905) 616109
E-mail davidryannow@netscapeonline.co.uk

RYAN, Graham William Robert (Gregg). b 51. CITC 90. **d** 93 **p** 94. NSM Clonsast w Rathangan, Thomastown etc *M & K* 93-97; Dioc Communications Officer 96-97; Press Officer from 97; Dioc C from 97. *Millicent Hall, Millicent South, Sallins, Naas, Co Kildare, Republic of Ireland* Tel (00353) (45) 879464 Fax 875173 E-mail gregg.ryan@irishrail.ie

RYAN, James Francis. b 47. Surrey Univ BSc. St Jo Coll Nottm. **d** 83 **p** 84. C Littleover *Derby* 83-86; C Chipping Sodbury and Old Sodbury *Glouc* 86-89; V Pype Hayes *Birm* 89-99; R W Winch w Setchey, N Runcton and Middleton *Nor* from 99. *The Rectory, Rectory Lane, West Winch, King's Lynn PE33 0NR* Tel (01553) 840835

RYAN, Canon Maureen. **d** 98 **p** 99. C Tuam w Cong and Aasleagh *T, K & A* from 98; Preb Kilmactalway St Patr Cathl Dublin from 01; Can Tuam Cathl from 05. *Marshal's Park, Rinville, Oranmore, Galway, Republic of Ireland* Tel and fax (00353) (91) 794599 E-mail ryans@iol.ie

RYAN, Robert Lloyd. b 65. Warwick Univ BA(QTS)87. SEITE 05. **d** 08 **p** 09. C Roch Cathl from 08. *68 Montrose Avenue, Chatham ME5 7HX* Tel (01634) 856098
E-mail robryan8@blueyonder.co.uk

RYAN, Roger John. b 47. Lon Bible Coll BA79 Surrey Univ MA00 St Pet Coll Ox DPhil06. Oak Hill Th Coll 79. **d** 80 **p** 81. C Luton St Fran *St Alb* 80-83; R Laceby *Linc* 83-88; V Summerstown *S'wark* from 88. *St Mary's Vicarage, 46 Wimbledon Road, London SW17 0UQ* Tel (020) 8946 9853

RYAN, Canon Stephen John. b 49. Univ of Wales (Swansea) BA70. Sarum & Wells Th Coll 70. **d** 73 **p** 74. C Llantrisant *Llan* 73-77; V Treherbert w Treorchy 77-89; Youth Chapl 80-85; RD Rhondda 84-89; V Aberdare St Fagan 89-02; RD Cynon Valley 97-02; TR Neath from 02; Can Llan Cathl from 02; AD Neath from 04. *The Rectory, 23 London Road, Neath SA11 1LE* Tel (01639) 644612

RYCRAFT, Andrew George. b 48. FRICS94. Wycliffe Hall Ox 02 SAOMC 04. **d** 06 **p** 07. NSM Ray Valley *Ox* 06-07. *18 Bronte Close, Aylesbury HP19 8LF* Tel (01296) 381599

RYCRAFT, Mrs Rosemary Ives Stewart. b 49. Westmr Coll Ox BTh00 SRN72 SCM74. SAOMC 00. **d** 03 **p** 04. NSM New Marston *Ox* 03-07; TV Aylesbury w Bierton and Hulcott from 07. *18 Bronte Close, Aylesbury HP19 8LF* Tel (01296) 381599

RYCROFT, Alistair John. b 79. St Cath Coll Ox BA01 Fitzw Coll Cam BA08 Ox Brookes Univ PGCE02. Ridley Hall Cam 06. **d** 09. C York St Mich-le-Belfrey from 09. *157 Haxby Road, York YO31 8JL*

RYDER, Canon Derek Michael. b 36. St Cath Coll Cam BA60 MA64. Tyndale Hall Bris 61. **d** 63 **p** 64. C Hampreston *Sarum* 63-66; Asst Chapl Brentwood Sch Essex 66-72; Chapl Ipswich Sch 72-77; Home Sec CMJ 77-87; TR Wexcombe *Sarum* 87-99; RD Pewsey 89-99; Can and Preb Sarum Cathl 97-99; rtd 99; Perm to Offic *Ox* and *Sarum* from 00. *31 The Green, Calne SN11 8DJ* Tel (01249) 821797

RYDER, Jennifer Ann. *See* HAYNES, Mrs Jennifer Ann

RYDER, John Merrick. b 55. Natal Univ BA75 BA77. St Pet Coll Natal 81. **d** 82 **p** 83. S Africa 84-88; St Helena 88-91; C Havant *Portsm* 91-95; P-in-c Godshill 95-99; V from 99; P-in-c Wroxall 99-02. *The Vicarage, Church Hill, Godshill, Ventnor PO38 3HY* Tel (01983) 840895 E-mail johnmryder@btinternet.com

RYDER, Lisle Robert Dudley. b 43. Selw Coll Cam BA68 MA72. Sarum Th Coll 69. **d** 71 **p** 72. C Lowestoft St Marg *Nor* 71-75; Chapl Asst Oxon Area HA 76-79; C Littlehampton St Jas *Chich* 79-85; C Littlehampton St Mary 79-85; C Wick 79-85; Chapl Worc R Infirmary 85-94; Chapl Worc R Infirmary NHS Trust 94-00; Chapl Worcs Acute Hosps NHS Trust 00-03; Hon Can Worc Cathl 89-04; P-in-c Pyworthy, Pancrasweek and Bridgerule *Ex* 04-08; rtd 08. *Little Appleton, 3 Lumley Terrace, Newton le Willows, Bedale DL8 1SS* Tel (01677) 450180
E-mail lisle@safehaven.me.uk

RYDER, Oliver Hugh Dudley. b 74. UEA BA98. Ridley Hall Cam 05. **d** 07 **p** 08. C Tollington *Lon* from 07. *Top Flat, St Mark's Vicarage, 1A Moray Road, London N4 3LD* Tel 07963-580242 (mobile) E-mail oliver.ryder@gmail.com

RYDER-WEST, Keith. b 63. Sunderland Poly BSc86 Leeds Univ BTh95. Chich Th Coll 92 Coll of Resurr Mirfield. **d** 95 **p** 96. C Rawmarsh w Parkgate *Sheff* 95-96; C Armley w New Wortley *Ripon* 96-99; V Altofts *Wakef* 99-06; V Sheff St Cecilia Parson Cross from 06. *St Cecilia's Priory, 98 Chaucer Close, Sheffield S5 9QE* Tel 0114-232 1084

RYDINGS, Donald. b 33. Jes Coll Ox BA57 MA61. Linc Th Coll 57. **d** 59 **p** 60. C Poulton-le-Fylde *Blackb* 59-62; C Ox St Mary V 62-66; Staff Sec SCM 62-66; C-in-c Bourne End St Mark CD *Ox* 66-74; R Hedsor and Bourne End 74-76; P-in-c Gt Missenden w Ballinger and Lt Hampden 76-93; RD Wendover 79-89; V Gt Missenden w Ballinger and Lt Hampden 93-02; rtd 02. *16 Marroway, Weston Turville, Aylesbury HP22 5TQ* Tel (01296) 612281

RYE, David Ralph. b 33. AKC59. **d** 60 **p** 61. C Rushmere *St E* 60-64; C Barnham Broom w Kimberley, Bixton etc *Nor* 64-76; TV Barnham Broom 76-82; TR 82-95; P-in-c Reymerston w Cranworth, Letton, Southburgh etc 85-95; rtd 95; Perm to Offic *Nor* from 95. *5A Yarmouth Road, Norwich NR7 0EA* Tel (01603) 439717

RYELAND, John. b 58. K Coll Lon BD80 AKC80. Linc Th Coll 80. **d** 81 **p** 82. C Enfield St Jas *Lon* 81-84; C Coulsdon St Andr *S'wark* 84-87; C-in-c Ingrave St Steph CD *Chelmsf* 87-97; Dir Chr Healing Miss from 97; NSM Paddington St Steph w St Luke *Lon* 97-99. *8 Cambridge Court, 210 Shepherd's Bush Road, London W6 7NJ* Tel (020) 7603 8118 Fax 7603 5224
E-mail chm@healingmission.org

RYLANDS, Preb Amanda Craig. b 52. Homerton Coll Cam CertEd75. Trin Coll Bris 83. **dss** 85 **d** 87 **p** 94. Chippenham St Andr w Tytherton Lucas *Bris* 85-87; Par Dn Stockport St Geo *Ches* 87-91; Par Dn Acton and Worleston, Church Minshull etc 91-94; C 94-97; Dioc Adv for Min Among Children 95-97; NSM Langport Area *B & W* 97-98 and 99-01; TV 98-99; Asst Dioc Voc Adv 00-01; Perm to Offic *Ex* 02-03; C Tedburn St Mary, Whitestone, Oldridge etc 04-05; Dioc Dir of Ords 05-09; 05; Bp's Adv for Women in Min 06-09; Preb Ex Cathl from 08. *Athlone House, 68 London Road, Shrewsbury SY2 6PG*

✠ **RYLANDS, Canon Mark James.** b 61. SS Hild & Bede Coll Dur BA83. Trin Coll Bris BA87. **d** 87 **p** 88 **c** 09. C Stockport St Geo *Ches* 87-91; V Acton and Worleston, Church Minshull etc 91-97; TR Langport Area *B & W* 97-02; Dioc Missr *Ex* 02-09; Can Res Ex Cathl 02-09; Area Bp Shrewsbury *Lich* from 09. *Athlone House, 68 London Road, Shrewsbury SY2 6PG* Tel (01743) 235867 Fax 243296
E-mail bishop.shrewsbury@lichfield.anglican.org

RYLE, Denis Maurice. b 16. OBE70. St Aid Birkenhead 35. **d** 39 **p** 40. C Parr *Liv* 39-42; C Widnes St Paul 42-44; C Much Woolton 44-45; CF 45-58; Sen CF 58-65; Dep Asst Chapl Gen 65-73; P-in-c Latimer w Flaunden *Ox* 73-85; rtd 85; Perm to Offic *York* from 90. *5 Church Close, Wheldrake, York YO19 6DP* Tel (01904) 898124

RYLEY, Canon Patrick Macpherson. b 30. Pemb Coll Ox BA54 Lon Univ BD56. Clifton Th Coll 54. **d** 56 **p** 57. C Ox St Clem 56-59; Burma 60-66; Kenya 68-75; V Lynn St Jo *Nor* 76-92; V King's Lynn St Jo the Ev 92-95; RD Lynn 90-92; Hon Can Nor Cathl 90-95; rtd 95; Perm to Offic *Bradf* from 95. *106 Little Lane, Ilkley LS29 8JJ* Tel (01943) 817026

RYLEY, Timothy Patrick. b 64. Man Univ BA86. St Jo Coll Nottm MA93. **d** 93 **p** 94. C Pendlebury St Jo *Man* 93-97; P-in-c Norris Bank 97-01; Age Concern from 01; Perm to Offic *Man* from 09. *12 Green End, Denton, Manchester M34 7PU*

RYMER, David John Talbot. b 37. Chich Th Coll 63. **d** 66 **p** 67. C Tuffley *Glouc* 66-69; Rhodesia 69-79; P-in-c S Kensington St Jude *Lon* 79-82; V 82-88, P-in-c Ambergate *Derby* 88-91; P-in-c Heage 88-91, R Ambergate and Heage 91-96; P-in-c Findern 96-01; V 01-03; P-in-c Willington 96-01; V 01-03; rtd 03; Perm to Offic *Derby* from 03. *2 Glebe Close, Long Lane, Dalbury Lees, Ashbourne DE6 5BJ* Tel (01332) 824165
E-mail david.rymer@amserve.net

RYRIE, Alexander Crawford. b 30. Edin Univ MA52 BD55 Glas Univ MLitt75. New Coll Edin 52 Union Th Sem (NY) STM56. d 83 p 83. Hon C Edin St Mary 83-85; R Jedburgh 85-95; rtd 95. *Boisils, Bowden, Melrose TD6 0ST* Tel (01835) 823226 E-mail sandyryrie@googlemail.com

RYRIE, Mrs Isabel. b 31. Edin Univ MA51 Glas Univ MEd70 ABPsS73 CPsychol88. d 89 p 94. Bp's Dn *Edin* 89-91; NSM Edin St Mary 91-98; rtd 98. *Boisils, Bowden, Melrose TD6 0ST* Tel (01835) 823226 E-mail isabel.ryrie@virgin.net

S

SABAN, Ronald Graham Street. b 28. Bps' Coll Cheshunt 60. d 62 p 63. C Maidstone St Martin *Cant* 62-66; C Croydon St Sav 66; rtd 94. *34 Kingsway, Caversham, Reading RG4 6RA* Tel 0118-947 9454

SABELL, Michael Harold. b 42. Open Univ BA78 Surrey Univ MSc. Sarum & Wells Th Coll 77. d 80 p 81. NSM Shirley *Win* 80-82; NSM Finham *Cov* 82-85; Chapl to the Deaf *Win* 81-82; *Cov* 82-85; *Sheff* 85-89; *Lich* 89-96; P-in-c Gt and Lt Wymondley *St Alb* 96-01; R Ingoldsby *Linc* 01-04; R Old Somerby 01-04; R Ropsley 01-04; R Sapperton w Braceby 01-04; rtd 04; Perm to Offic *Lich* 05-08; P-in-c Muchalls *Bre* from 08. *St Ternan's Rectory, Muchalls, Stonehaven AB39 3PP* Tel (01569) 730625 E-mail michaelhsabell@btinternet.com

SABEY-CORKINDALE, Charmaine Clare. b 58. SROT87. SAOMC. d 02 p 03. NSM St Ippolyts *St Alb* 02-03; C Hitchin 03-05; TV from 05. *5 Lavender Way, Hitchin SG5 2LU* Tel (01462) 435497

SABINE WILLIS, Anthony Charles. See WILLIS, Anthony Charles Sabine

SACH, Andrew. b 75. Oak Hill Th Coll. d 07. C St Helen Bishopsgate w St Andr Undershaft etc *Lon* from 07. *St Helen's Church, Great St Helen's, London EC3A 6AT* Tel (020) 7283 2231

SACHS, Andrew James. b 73. Reading Univ BSc94 Kingston Univ PGCE96. Wycliffe Hall Ox BTh05. d 05 p 06. C Upper Sunbury St Sav *Lon* 05-08; C E Twickenham St Steph from 08. *308 Richmond Road, Twickenham TW1 2PD* Tel (020) 8892 5258 E-mail andysachs@freeuk.com

SACKLEY (née WITT), Mrs Caroline Elizabeth. b 51. Surrey Univ BSc04. STETS 02. d 05 p 06. C Grayfice Gp *Linc* 05-08; P-in-c W Meon and Warnford *Portsm* from 08. *The Rectory, Doctors Lane, West Meon, Petersfield GU32 1LR* Tel (01730) 829226 E-mail sackleys@btopenworld.com

SADDINGTON, Mrs Jean. b 53. Bournemouth Univ BSc02 Cant Ch Ch Univ PGCE04. STETS 05. d 08. Lic to RD Dorchester from 08. *9 Conway Walk, Dorchester DT1 2EJ* Tel (01305) 250334 E-mail jean.saddington@hotmail.co.uk

SADDINGTON, Peter David. b 42. Cranmer Hall Dur. d 84 p 85. C Tudhoe Grange *Dur* 84-86; C Monkwearmouth St Andr 86-88; V Burnopfield 88-94; P-in-c Greenside 94-96; V 96-04; rtd 04. *19 The Lawns, Ryton Village, Ryton NE40 3QN* Tel 0191-413 6881

SADGROVE, The Very Revd Michael. b 50. Ball Coll Ox BA71 MA75. Trin Coll Bris 72. d 75 p 76. C St Helen's *Ox* 75-77; Tutor Sarum & Wells Th Coll 77-82; Vice-Prin 80-82; V Alnwick *Newc* 82-87; Vice-Provost, Can Res and Prec Cov Cathl 87-95; Provost Sheff 95-00; Dean Sheff 00-03; Dean Dur from 03. *The Deanery, The College, Durham DH1 3EQ* Tel 0191-384 7500 Fax 386 4267 E-mail michael.sadgrove@durhamcathedral.co.uk

SADLER, The Ven Anthony Graham. b 36. Qu Coll Ox BA60 MA64. Lich Th Coll 60. d 62 p 63. C Burton St Chad *Lich* 62-65; V Rangemore and Dunstall 65-72; V Abbots Bromley 72-79; V Pelsall 79-90; RD Walsall 82-90; P-in-c Uttoxeter w Bramshall 90-97; P-in-c Stramshall 90-97; P-in-c Marchington w Gratwich 90-97; P-in-c Checkley 90-97; P-in-c Marchington w Marchington Woodlands 90-97; P-in-c Leigh 93-97; TR Uttoxeter Area 97; Adn Walsall 97-04; Preb Lich Cathl 87-04; rtd 04. *Llidiart Newydd, Llanrhaeadr-ym-Mochnant, Oswestry SY10 0ED* Tel (01691) 780276

SADLER, Canon John Ernest. b 45. Nottm Univ BTh78. Linc Th Coll 74. d 78 p 79. C Brampton St Thos *Derby* 78-81; TV Coventry Caludon 81-85; V Newc St Phil and St Aug 86-94; P-in-c Newc Epiphany 94-99; Perm to Offic from 00; Ch Development Worker from 01; Hon Can Newc Cathl from 04. *26 Crompton Road, Heaton, Newcastle upon Tyne NE6 5QL* Tel 0191-262 1680 E-mail jjsadler@btinternet.com or john@umtp.org

SADLER, Michael Stuart. b 57. Wycliffe Hall Ox 78. d 81 p 82. C Henfynyw w Aberaeron and Llanddewi Aberarth *St D* 81-88; V Llanddewi Rhydderch w Llangattock-juxta-Usk etc *Mon* from 88. *The Vicarage, Llanddewi Rhydderch, Abergavenny NP7 9TS* Tel (01873) 840373

SAFFORD, Jeremy. b 66. Ox Brookes Univ BA02. Ridley Hall Cam 08. d 09. C Collingtree w Courteenhall and Milton Malsor Pet from 09. *The Rectory, Barn Corner, Collingtree, Northampton NN4 0NF* Tel (01604) 705620 Mobile 07512-856732 E-mail jez.safford@ntlworld.com

SAGAR, Brian. b 39. Sarum & Wells Th Coll 78. d 80 p 81. C Radcliffe St Thos and St Jo *Man* 80-82; P-in-c Charlestown 82-85; R Gt Lever 85-89; Chapl Cov Ch Housing Assn 89-92; V Wing w Grove *Ox* 92-97; P-in-c Diddington, Lt Paxton and Southoe *Ely* 97-00; P-in-c Lever Bridge *Man* 00-05; rtd 05; Perm to Offic *Man* from 05. *6 Loweswater Road, Farnworth, Bolton BL4 0PL* Tel (01204) 574200 E-mail b.sagar@ntlworld.com

SAGE, Canon Andrew George. b 58. Univ Coll Chich BA99. Chich Th Coll 83. d 85 p 86. C Rawmarsh w Parkgate *Sheff* 85-87; C Fareham SS Pet and Paul *Portsm* 87-89; C Southsea H Spirit 89-91; P-in-c Nuthurst *Chich* 91-93; R 93-95; V Hangleton 95-04; Chapl Worthing and Southlands Hosps NHS Trust 01-04; V Blackpool St Steph *Blackb* from 04; Warden Whalley Abbey from 08; Hon Can Blackb Cathl from 08. *The Vicarage, St Stephen's Avenue, Blackpool FY2 9RB* Tel (01253) 351484 E-mail andrewsage@aol.com

SAGE, Canon Jesse. b 35. Trin Hall Cam BA61 MA65. Chich Th Coll 61. d 63 p 64. C Feltham *Lon* 63-67; S Africa 67-72 and from 96; R Abbas and Temple Combe *B & W* 72-75; R Abbas and Templecombe w Horsington 76-77; Chapl Agric and Rural Soc in Kent *Cant* 78-95; Hon Can Cant Cathl 90-95; R Gonubie St Martin by the Sea 96-00; P-in-c Komga St Paul 98-00; Hon Can Grahamstown from 02; rtd 00. *30 Hazy Ridge, Swallow Lane, Gonubie, 5257 South Africa* Tel (0027) (43) 732 1298 Fax 732 1317 Mobile 82-651 6698 E-mail jessesage@qwest.co.za

SAGE, John Arthur. b 32. MInstP Lon Univ BSc54. St Alb Minl Tr Scheme 78. d 81 p 82. NSM Stevenage St Mary Shephall *St Alb* 81-86; NSM Stevenage St Mary Shephall w Aston 86-87; C St Peter-in-Thanet *Cant* 87-98; rtd 98; Perm to Offic *Cant* from 99. *3 West Cliff Road, Broadstairs CT10 1PU* Tel (01843) 603471

SAGOVSKY, Canon Nicholas. b 47. CCC Ox BA69 St Edm Ho Cam PhD81. St Jo Coll Nottm BA73. d 74 p 75. C Newc St Gabr 74-77; C Cambridge Gt St Mary w St Mich *Ely* 81; Vice-Prin Edin Th Coll 82-86; Dean of Chpl Clare Coll Cam 86-97; Wm Leech Prof Fell Newc Univ 97-02; Liv Hope Univ Coll 02-04; Can Westmr Abbey from 04. *3 Little Cloister, Westminster Abbey, London SW1P 3PL* Tel (020) 7654 4808 Fax 7654 4809 E-mail nicholas.sagovsky@westminster-abbey.org

SAID, Yazeed. b 75. Hebrew Univ Jerusalem BA96 CCC Cam BA99 MA03 MPhil05. Westcott Ho Cam 97. d 99 p 01. Chapl Ch Ch Sch Nazareth 99-00; Chapl to Bp Jerusalem 00-02; C St Geo Cathl 00-04; Acting Dean 02-04; Asst Chapl CCC Cam 04-08; Perm to Offic *Ely* from 08. *Corpus Christi College, Cambridge CB2 1RH* Tel (01223) 302995 Mobile 07847-503902 E-mail ys215@cam.ac.uk

SAIET, Timothy Robin. b 65. Wycliffe Hall Ox 06. d 08 p 09. NSM Ealing St Paul *Lon* from 08. *23 Littlewood Close, London W13 9XH* Tel (020) 8579 9444 E-mail tim.saiet@stpauls-ealing.org

SAINSBURY, Peter Donald. b 67. K Coll Lon MA04. Ridley Hall Cam 98. d 00 p 01. C Longfleet *Sarum* 00-04; Chapl Glos Univ 04-08; V Summerfield *Birm* from 08. *Christ Church Vicarage, 64 Selwyn Road, Birmingham B16 0SW* Tel 0121-454 2689 E-mail cc.summerfield@yahoo.co.uk

✠SAINSBURY, The Rt Revd Roger Frederick. b 36. Jes Coll Cam BA58 MA62. Clifton Th Coll. d 60 p 61 c 91. C Spitalfields Ch Ch w All SS *Lon* 60-63; Missr Shrewsbury Ho Everton *Liv* 63-74; P-in-c Everton St Ambrose w St Tim 63-74; Warden Mayflower Family Cen Canning Town *Chelmsf* 74-81; P-in-c Victoria Docks St Luke 78-81; V Walsall *Lich* 81-87; TR 87-88; Adn W Ham *Chelmsf* 88-91; Area Bp Barking 91-02; Moderator Ch's Commn for Racial Justice 99-02; rtd 02; Hon Asst Bp B & W from 03. *Abbey Lodge, Battery Lane, Portishead, Bristol BS20 7JD* Tel (01275) 847082 E-mail bishoproger.abbey@btopenworld.com

SAINT, David Gerald. b 45. Sarum & Wells Th Coll 72. d 75 p 76. C Wellingborough All Hallows *Pet* 75-79; R Kislingbury w Rothersthorpe 79-83; V Kings Heath 83-85; Relig Progr Producer BBC Radio Northn from 85; Perm to Offic *Pet* from 86. *71 Stanwell Way, Wellingborough NN8 3DD* Tel (01933) 675995

ST ALBANS, Archdeacon of. See SMITH, The Ven Jonathan Peter

ST ALBANS, Bishop of. See SMITH, The Rt Revd Alan Gregory Clayton

ST ALBANS, Dean of. See JOHN, The Very Revd Jeffrey Philip Hywel

ST ANDREWS, DUNKELD AND DUNBLANE, Bishop of. See CHILLINGWORTH, The Rt Revd David Robert

ST ANDREWS, DUNKELD AND DUNBLANE, Dean of. See RATHBAND, The Very Revd Kenneth William

ST ASAPH, Archdeacon of. *See* THOMAS, The Ven Elwyn Bernard

ST ASAPH, Bishop of. *See* CAMERON, The Rt Revd Gregory Kenneth

ST ASAPH, Dean of. *See* POTTER, The Very Revd Christopher Nicholas Lynden

ST DAVIDS, Archdeacon of. *See* HOLDSWORTH, The Ven John Ivor

ST DAVIDS, Bishop of. *See* EVANS, The Rt Revd John Wyn

ST DAVIDS, Dean of. *See* LEAN, The Very Revd David Jonathan Rees

ST EDMUNDSBURY AND IPSWICH, Bishop of. *See* STOCK, The Rt Revd William Nigel

ST EDMUNDSBURY, Dean of. *See* COLLINGS, The Very Revd Neil

ST GERMANS, Suffragan Bishop of. *See* SCREECH, The Rt Revd Royden

ST HELENA, Bishop of. *See* SALT, The Rt Revd John William

ST JOHN-CHANNELL, Canon Michael Alister Morrell. b 53. Bris Univ BEd76 MA01. Ripon Coll Cuddesdon 76. **d** 78 **p** 79. C Portsea St Mary *Portsm* 78-81; PV Linc Cathl 82-85; P-in-c Linc St Mary-le-Wigford w St Benedict etc 82-85; R Cranford *Lon* 85-92; V Staines St Mary and St Pet 92-99; V Cirencester *Glouc* 99-06; RD Cirencester 01-06; Can Res Win Cathl from 06. *8 The Close, Winchester SO23 9LS* Tel (01962) 856236 *or* 857211 E-mail mstjc@hotmail.com

ST JOHN NICOLLE, Jason Paul. b 66. Mert Coll Ox BA88 Called to the Bar (Inner Temple) 95. Ripon Coll Cuddesdon 01. **d** 04 **p** 05. C Kidlington w Hampton Poyle *Ox* 04-08; R The Churn from 08. *The Rectory, Church End, Blewbury, Didcot OX11 9QH* Tel (01235) 850267

SALA, Kuabuleke Meymans. b 68. **d** 08. C Edmonton All SS w St Mich *Lon* from 08. *60 Tillotson Road, London N9 9AH* Tel (020) 8887 9369 E-mail smeymans@hotmail.com

SALES, Canon Patrick David. b 43. K Coll Lon AKC68 BD74 Kent Univ MA00. **d** 69 **p** 70. C Maidstone All SS w St Phil *Cant* 69-72; C Chart next Sutton Valence 72-74; C Birchington w Acol 75-77; V Boughton under Blean w Dunkirk 77-83; V Herne 83-03; P-in-c Hoath 98-03; TV Whitstable 03-06; Hon Min Can Cant Cathl 83-01; Hon Can 01-06; RD Reculver 86-92; AD 01-06; Dioc Adv in Liturgy 00-06; rtd 06. *The Well House, South Lane, Dallington, Heathfield TN21 9NJ* Tel (01435) 830194 Mobile 07803-257283 E-mail patrick@sales64.freeserve.co.uk

SALISBURY, Anne Ruth. b 37. Dalton Ho Bris 63. **d** 87 **p** 94. C Harrow Trin St Mich *Lon* 87-98; C Paddington Em and W Kilburn St Luke w St Simon and St Jude 99-03; rtd 03. *c/o Crockford, Church House, Great Smith Street, London SW1P 3AZ* Tel 07986-868667 (mobile)

SALISBURY, Harold Gareth. b 21. St Pet Hall Ox BA42 MA46. Wycliffe Hall Ox 42. **d** 44 **p** 45. C Pet St Mark 44-46; India 47-63; Lect Bp's Coll Calcutta 47-49; Chapl St Andr Cathl Nasik 49-51; Chapl Aurangabad 51-53; Chapl Thana and Agripada 53-57; Chapl Union Th Coll Poona 58-62; V Norham *Newc* 63-70; V Duddo 63-70; V Norham and Duddo 70-78; V Snaith *Sheff* 78-86; P-in-c Cowick 78-86; TR Gt Snaith 86; rtd 86; Perm to Offic *Pet* from 87. *33 Nightingale Drive, Towcester NN12 6RA* Tel (01327) 353674

SALISBURY, Peter Brian Christopher. b 58. UMIST BSc80 MBCS85. Sarum & Wells Th Coll BTh92. **d** 92 **p** 93. C Stanmore *Win* 92-95; V Chilworth w N Baddesley 95-05; V Lymington from 05. *The Vicarage, Grove Road, Lymington SO41 3RF* Tel (01590) 673847

SALISBURY, Canon Roger John. b 44. Lon Univ BD67. Lon Coll of Div 66. **d** 68 **p** 69. C Harold Wood *Chelmsf* 68-73; V Dorking St Paul *Guildf* 73-82; R Rusholme H Trin *Man* 82-90; TR Gt Chesham *Ox* 90-06; RD Amersham 98-04; Hon Can Ch Ch 02-06; C Langham Place All So *Lon* from 06; Sec Ch Patr Trust from 06. *12 De Walden Street, London W1G 8RN* Tel (020) 7935 9811 Fax 7436 3019 E-mail roger.salisbury@allsouls.org

SALISBURY, Canon Tobias. b 33. Em Coll Cam BA60. Ripon Hall Ox 60. **d** 62 **p** 63. C Putney St Mary *S'wark* 62-65; C Churchdown St Jo *Glouc* 65-67; V Urchfont w Stert *Sarum* 67-73; R Burton Bradstock w Shipton Gorge and Chilcombe 73-79; P-in-c Long Bredy w Lt Bredy and Kingston Russell 75-79; TR Bride Valley 79-86; V Gt and Lt Bedwyn and Savernake Forest 86-97; Can and Preb Sarum Cathl 92-98; rtd 98; Perm to Offic *B & W* from 98. *Anfield, Hayes Lane, Compton Dundon, Somerton TA11 6PB* Tel (01458) 274459

SALISBURY, Bishop of. *See* STANCLIFFE, The Rt Revd David Staffurth

SALISBURY, Dean of. *See* OSBORNE, The Very Revd June

SALMON, Alan Clive. b 63. Bris Univ BA84. St Mich Coll Llan 84. **d** 86 **p** 87. C Llanelli St D 86 88; C Roath St German *Llan* 88-90; V Nevern and Y Beifil w Eglwyswrw and Meline etc *St D* 90-92; In RC Ch 92-99; Perm to Offic *S'wark* 99-00; Hon C Lavender Hill Ascension etc 00-01; TP Glas E End 01-03; P-in-c Mathry w St Edren's and Grandston etc *St D* from 08. *The Rectory, St Nicholas, Goodwick SA64 0LG* Tel (01348) 891230 Mobile 07763-133775

SALMON, Andrew Ian. b 61. St Jo Coll Nottm BTh88. **d** 88 **p** 89. C Collyhurst *Man* 88-92; P-in-c Pendleton St Ambrose 92-95; TV Pendleton 95-99; TR 99-04; P-in-c Salford Sacred Trin and St Phil from 04; AD Salford 06. *St Philip's Rectory, 6 Encombe Place, Salford M3 6FJ* Tel 0161-834 2041 E-mail rev.andy@btinternet.com

SALMON, Andrew Meredith Bryant. b 30. Jes Coll Cam BA54 MA58. Ridley Hall Cam 54. **d** 56 **p** 57. C Enfield Ch Ch Trent Park *Lon* 56-58; Chapl Monkton Combe Sch Bath 58-71; Chapl Milton Abbey Sch Dorset 71-89; TV Bride Valley *Sarum* 89-96; rtd 97; Perm to Offic *Sarum* from 97. *1 Barnhill Road, Wareham BH20 5BD* Tel (01929) 554039

SALMON, Anthony James Heygate. b 30. CCC Ox BA53 MA57. Cuddesdon Coll 54. **d** 56 **p** 57. C S Norwood St Mark *Cant* 56-59; S Africa 59-69; Chapl USPG Coll of the Ascension Selly Oak 69-74; P-in-c Frinsted 74-78; R Harrietsham *Cant* 74-85; P-in-c Ulcombe 81-85; V Chobham w Valley End *Guildf* 85-95; rtd 95; Perm to Offic *St Alb* from 95. *24 Elmwood, Welwyn Garden City AL8 6LE* Tel (01707) 333694

SALMON, Mrs Constance Hazel. b 25. R Holloway Coll Lon BSc46. Lon Bible Coll 66 Gilmore Course 71. **dss** 80 **d** 87 **p** 96. Sidcup St Andr *Roch* 80-88; NSM 87-88; Perm to Offic 88-96; NSM Eynsford w Farningham and Lullingstone from 96. *43 Old Mill Close, Eynsford, Dartford DA4 0BN* Tel (01322) 866034

SALMON, Jonathan. b 66. Univ Coll of Swansea BSc(Econ)88 Sussex Univ MA95 MPhil95. Wycliffe Hall Ox 01. **d** 03 **p** 04. C Bowling St Jo *Bradf* 03-07; P-in-c Earley Trin *Ox* from 07. *Trinity Church House, 15 Caraway Road, Earley, Reading RG6 5XR* Tel 0118-986 9798 Mobile 07840-494072 E-mail salmonj@btinternet.com

SALMON, Mrs Margaret Penny. b 37. Leeds Univ BA59 CertEd60. SW Minl Tr Course 85. **d** 88 **p** 94. NSM Yelverton, Meavy, Sheepstor and Walkhampton *Ex* from 88. *Hinnies, Leg-o-Mutton Corner, Yelverton PL20 6DJ* Tel (01822) 853310 E-mail peggysalmon@compuserve.com

SALMON, Mark Harold. b 62. Trin Coll Bris. **d** 00 **p** 01. C Bath Weston All SS w N Stoke and Langridge *B & W* 00-04; P-in-c Harlescott *Lich* 04-07; V from 07. *Harlescott Vicarage, Meadow Farm Drive, Shrewsbury SY1 4NG* Tel (01743) 362883 E-mail mark.salmon@xalt.co.uk

SALMON, Paul Richard. **d** 06 **p** 07. OLM Humberston *Linc* from 06. *47 Tetney Road, Humberstone, Grimsby DN36 4JQ* Tel (01472) 814550 E-mail paulsal@stayfree.co.uk

SALMON, Philip John. b 63. Oak Hill Th Coll 96. **d** 98 **p** 99. C Kington w Huntington, Old Radnor, Kinnerton etc *Heref* 98-02; TV Radipole and Melcombe Regis *Sarum* from 02. *The Vicarage, 74 Field Barn Drive, Weymouth DT4 0EF* Tel (01305) 778995 Mobile 07771-688226 E-mail vicar@emmanuelwey.co.uk

SALMON, Richard Harold. b 35. Fitzw Ho Cam BA57. Clifton Th Coll 57. **d** 59 **p** 60. C Blackheath Park St Mich *S'wark* 59-61; C St Alb St Paul *St Alb* 61-63; Malaysia 63-75; OMF 63-65; C Telok Anson St Luke 63-65; V Kuantan Pehang Epiphany 65-75; P-in-c March St Wendreda *Ely* 75-76; R 76-85; V Congresbury w Puxton and Hewish St Ann *B & W* 85-00; rtd 00; Perm to Offic *Truro* 00-01 and *B & W* from 02. *2 Wisteria Avenue, Hutton, Weston-super-Mare BS24 9QF* Tel (01934) 813750 E-mail richard.salmon@talk21.com

SALMON, The Very Revd Thomas Noel Desmond Cornwall. b 13. TCD BA35 MA49 BD42 TCD Div Sch 35. **d** 37 **p** 38. C Bangor St Comgall *D & D* 37-40; C Belfast St Jas *Conn* 40-41; C Larne and Inver 42-44; Clerical V Ch Ch Cathl Dublin 44-45; Lect TCD 45-89; C Dublin Rathfarnham *D & G* 45-50; Hon Clerical V Ch Ch Cathl Dublin 45-63; I Tullow 50-62; I Dublin St Ann 62-67; Preb Dunlavin St Patr Cathl Dublin 63-67; Dean Ch Ch Cathl Dublin 67-89; I Dublin Ch Ch Cathl Gp 76-89; rtd 89. *c/o Mrs I Sherwood, Hillcrest, Kilmolin, Enniskerry, Co Wicklow, Republic of Ireland*

SALMON, William John. b 50. Lon Univ BSc72 DipEd73. Cranmer Hall Dur 76. **d** 79 **p** 80. C Summerstown *S'wark* 79-81; C Hampreston *Sarum* 81-86; V Sundon *St Alb* 86-90; Dep Chapl HM Young Offender Inst Glen Parva 90-91; Chapl HM Pris Whitemoor 91-95; Chapl HM Pris Blundeston 95-04 and from 07; Chapl HM Pris Belmarsh 04-07. *HM Prison Blundeston, Lowestoft NR32 5BG* Tel (01502) 734500 Fax 734501 E-mail william.salmon@hmps.gsi.gov.uk

SALMON, Mrs Yvonne Delysia. b 40. Cant Sch of Min 00. **d** 03 **p** 04. OLM Boughton Monchelsea *Cant* from 03. *Elderden Farm Cottage, Maidstone Road, Staplehurst, Tonbridge TN12 0RN* Tel (01622) 842598 E-mail y.salmon@tesco.net

SALONIA, Ivan. b 38. Open Univ BA81 N Lon Poly MA85 CQSW78. Milan Th Coll (RC) 60. **d** 63 **p** 64. In RC Ch Hong Kong 64-73; Hon C Woolwich St Thos *S'wark* 89-91; C Greenwich St Alfege w St Pet and St Paul 91-93; C Kidbrooke St Jas 93-95; TV 95-02, rtd 02; Perm to Offic *S'wark* from 03. *247 Hook Lane, Welling DA16 2NZ* Tel (020) 8306 2862 *or* 8298 1309 Fax 8306 6859 Mobile 07946-085065 E-mail ivanus_magnus@hotmail.com

SALOP, Archdeacon of. *See* HALL, The Ven John Barrie

SALT, Canon David Christopher. b 37. Univ of Wales (Lamp) BA59. Sarum Th Coll 59. **d** 61 **p** 62. C Kidderminster St Mary *Worc* 61-66; Ind Chapl 66-72; R Knightwick w Doddenham, Broadwas and Cotheridge 72-82; Chapl Worc Coll of HE 72-82; V Redditch St Steph *Worc* 82-02; P-in-c Tardebigge 84-88; RD Bromsgrove 91-00; Hon Can Worc Cathl 92-02; rtd 02; Perm to Offic *Worc* from 03 and *Cov* from 05. *7 Longmoor Close, Redditch B97 6SX* Tel (01527) 68735

SALT, David Thomas Whitehorn. b 32. K Coll Lon AKC56 BD57. **d** 57 **p** 58. Chapl Torgil Girls' Sch Aoba New Hebrides 57-59; Warden Catechist Coll Lolowai 59-63; Prin St Andr Coll Guadalcanal Solomon Is 63-66; C Hawley H Trin *Guildf* 66-68; V Shelf *Bradf* 68-73; R Checkendon *Ox* 73-81; RD Henley 78-84; TR Langtree 81-84; V Hungerford and Denford 84-89; Chapl Hungerford Hosp 84-89; P-in-c Harpsden *Ox* 89-95; Gen Sec Melanesian Miss 89-95; rtd 95; Perm to Offic *Guildf* and *Win* from 06. *31 Beech Drive, Blackwater, Camberley GU17 0NA* Tel (01276) 32145

✠**SALT, The Rt Revd John William.** b 41. Kelham Th Coll 61. **d** 66 **p** 67 **c** 99. C Barrow St Matt *Carl* 66-70; C Mohale's Hoek Lesotho 70-71; Asst Chapl St Agnes Sch Teyateyaneng 71-72; C Maseru Cathl 73-77; S Africa 77-99; OGS from 81; Superior 96-05; Dean Eshowe Cathl and Adn S Zululand 89-99; Bp St Helena from 99. *Bishopsholme, PO Box 62, St Helena, South Atlantic Ocean* Tel (00290) 4471 Fax 4728 E-mail bishop@cwimail.sh *or* jsalt@ogs.net

SALT, Leslie. b 29. Linc Th Coll 68. **d** 69 **p** 69. C Alford w Rigsby *Linc* 69-75; V Torksey 75-94; R Kettlethorpe 77-94; V Marton 77-94; V Newton-on-Trent 77-94; rtd 94; Perm to Offic *Linc* 94-97. *2 Holdenby Close, Lincoln LN2 4TQ*

SALT, Neil. b 64. Univ of Wales (Ban) BA85 New Coll Edin BD89 Man Metrop Univ BSc97. Edin Th Coll 86. **d** 89 **p** 90. C Stretford All SS *Man* 89-93; V Smallbridge and Wardle 93-94; Perm to Offic *Wakef* 94-01; Hon C Ripponden and Barkisland w W Scammonden 01-06; Chapl Rishworth Sch Ripponden 02-05; V Thornton-le-Fylde *Blackb* from 06. *The Vicarage, Meadows Avenue, Thornton-Cleveleys FY5 2TW* Tel (01253) 855099

SALTER, Arthur Thomas John. b 34. TD88. AKC60. **d** 61 **p** 62. C Ealing St Pet Mt Park *Lon* 61-65; C Shepherd's Bush St Steph w St Thos 65-66; C Holborn St Alb w Saffron Hill St Pet 66-70; P-in-c Barnsbury St Clem 70-77; P-in-c Islington St Mich 70-77; V Pentonville St Silas w All SS and St Jas 70-00; CF (TAVR) from 75; Gen Sec Angl and E Chs Assn from 76; Chmn from 90; P-in-c St Dunstan in the West *Lon* 79-99; rtd 00. *1 St James's Close, Bishop Street, London N1 8PH* Tel (020) 7359 0250

SALTER, Christopher. *See* SALTER, Nigel Christopher Murray

SALTER, David Whitton. b 69. Bris Univ BEng90. Trin Coll Bris 06. **d** 08 **p** 09. C Eynsham and Cassington *Ox* from 08. *Jovonne, Bell Lane, Cassington, Witney OX29 4DS* Tel (01865) 881434 Mobile 07768-582285 E-mail david.w.salter@btinternet.com

SALTER, George Alfred. b 25. TCD BA47 MA. CITC 49. **d** 49 **p** 50. C Rathdowney *C & O* 49-51; C Cork St Luke *C, C & R* 51-53; I Fermoy Union 53-55; I Cork St Luke w St Ann 55-73; Can Ross Cathl 69-88; Can Cork Cathl 69-88; Treas 88-94; I Cork St Luke Union 73-94; Preb Tymothan St Patr Cathl Dublin 88-94; rtd 94. *Mount Vernon House, 66 Wellington Road, Cork, Republic of Ireland* Tel (00353) (21) 450 6844

SALTER, Janet Elizabeth. b 48. Leeds Univ CertEd69. SWMTC 92. **d** 95 **p** 98. C Coleshill *Birm* 95-97; Hon C St Dennis *Truro* 97-00; TV Gillingham *Sarum* 00-04; V Stour Vale from 04. *The Vicarage, Kington Magna, Gillingham SP8 5EW* Tel (01747) 838494 E-mail kmvicarage@tiscali.co.uk

SALTER, John. *See* SALTER, Arthur Thomas John

SALTER, Canon John Frank. b 37. Dur Univ BA62. Cranmer Hall Dur 62. **d** 64 **p** 65. C Bridlington Priory *York* 64-67; Travelling Sec IVF 67-70; V Stoughton *Guildf* 70-02; RD Guildf 89-94; Hon Can Guildf Cathl 99-02; rtd 03. *7 Aldershot Road, Guildford GU2 8AE* Tel (01483) 511165 E-mail j.salter@btinternet.com

SALTER, Canon John Leslie. b 51. AKC76 Heythrop Coll Lon MA05. Coll of Resurr Mirfield 77. **d** 78 **p** 79. C Tottenham St Paul *Lon* 78-82; P-in-c Castle Vale *Birm* 82-83; TV Curdworth w Castle Vale 83-90; V Castle Vale St Cuth 90-92; V Wantage *Ox* from 93; AD Wantage 01-08; Hon Can Ch Ch from 06. *The Vicarage, The Cloisters, Wantage OX12 8AQ* Tel (01235) 762214

SALTER, Nigel Christopher Murray. b 46. Loughb Univ BTech. Ripon Coll Cuddesdon 79. **d** 81 **p** 82. C Glouc St Aldate 81-84; C Solihull *Birm* 84-88; V Highters Heath 88-97; Asst Chapl Greenwich Healthcare NHS Trust 97-01; Asst Chapl Qu Eliz Hosp NHS Trust 01-03; P-in-c Leaton and Albrighton w Battlefield *Lich* 03-06; rtd 06. *56 Chamberlain Crescent, Shirley, Solihull B90 2DQ* Tel 0121-745 9771 E-mail chris@princehal.freeserve.co.uk

SALTWELL, Ms Kathleen. b 48. Edin Univ BD00 Cam Univ MA02. Westcott Ho Cam 00. **d** 02 **p** 03. C Worc SE 02-06; Teacher Amity Foundn China from 07. *3 Chiserley Stile, Hebden Bridge HX7 8SB* Tel (01422) 842532 E-mail kathsaltwell@tiscali.co.uk

SALWAY, Canon Donald Macleay. b 31. St Pet Hall Ox BA54 MA59. Oak Hill Th Coll 54. **d** 56 **p** 57. C Holloway St Mary w

St Jas *Lon* 56-67; V Cambridge St Phil *Ely* 67-81; V Mile Cross *Nor* 81-96; RD Nor N 89-95; Hon Can Nor Cathl 91-96; rtd 96; Perm to Offic *B & W* from 96; C Langport Area 98-00. *Lype House, Long Load, Langport TA10 9LD* Tel (01458) 241623

SAMBROOK, Kenneth Henry. b 42. NOC 04. **d** 05 **p** 06. NSM Wistaston *Ches* from 05. *6 Westfield Drive, Wistaston, Crewe CW2 8ES* Tel (01270) 662455 E-mail kensambrook@beeb.net

SAMMÉ, Raymond Charles. b 50. Trent Poly MIBiol80 Anglia Poly Univ MA03 St Andr Univ MLitt08. Oak Hill Th Coll 85. **d** 87 **p** 88. C Holmer w Huntington *Heref* 87-90; C Derby St Alkmund and St Werburgh 90-93; V Romford Gd Shep *Chelmsf* 93-08; P-in-c Swanley St Paul *Roch* from 08. *2 Bower Road, Swanley BR8 7SE* E-mail ray.samme@btinternet.com

SAMMON, Helen Mary. b 57. Newnham Coll Cam MA79 Bris Univ MB, ChB82 MRCGP98. WEMTC 00. **d** 03 **p** 04. NSM Painswick, Sheepscombe, Cranham, The Edge etc *Glouc* 03-07; P-in-c Tuffley from 07. *St Barnabas' Vicarage, 200 Reservoir Road, Gloucester GL4 6SB* Tel (01452) 543738 E-mail helen.sammon@doctors.org.uk

SAMMONS, Elizabeth Mary. *See* SLATER, Mrs Elizabeth Mary

SAMPFORD, John Alfred. b 36. Lich Th Coll 58. **d** 61 **p** 62. C Lambeth St Phil *S'wark* 61-65; C Beddington 65-69; V Hampstead Ch Ch *Lon* 69-79; V Enfield Chase St Mary 79-02; rtd 02; Perm to Offic *Ches* from 02. *Ellisland, Bryn Gwyn Lane, Northop Hall, Mold CH7 6JT* Tel (01244) 810635

SAMPLE, Mrs Fiona Jean. b 55. **d** 08 **p** 09. OLM Bolam w Whalton and Hartburn w Meldon *Newc* from 08; OLM Netter Witton from 08. *South Middleton, Scots Gap, Middleton, Morpeth NE61 4EB* Tel (01670) 774245 Mobile 07905-207117

SAMPSON, Brian Andrew. b 39. **d** 94 **p** 95. C Glemsford, Hartest w Boxted, Somerton etc *St E* 94-96; C Pentlow, Foxearth, Liston and Borley *Chelmsf* 96-97; P-in-c 97-04; C N Hinckford 04-09; rtd 09. *4 Friars Court, Edgworth Road, Sudbury CO10 2TG* Tel (01787) 371529 E-mail captainbrianca@waitrose.co.uk

SAMPSON, Clive. b 38. St Jo Coll Cam BA61 MA64. Ridley Hall Cam 63. **d** 65 **p** 66. C Tunbridge Wells St Jo *Roch* 65-69; Travelling Sec Scripture Union 69-79; V Maidstone St Luke *Cant* 79-94; rtd 98. *108 Bure Homage Gardens, Christchurch BH23 4DR* Tel (01425) 279029

SAMPSON, Desmond William John. b 25. FRICS60. Roch Th Coll 63. **d** 65 **p** 66. C Hythe *Cant* 65-70; V Alkham w Capel le Ferne and Hougham 70-76; V Wingham w Elmstone and Preston w Stourmouth 76-86; RD E Bridge 81-86; C Hythe 86-91; rtd 91; Perm to Offic *Cant* from 91. *25 Albert Road, Hythe CT21 6BP* Tel (01303) 268457

SAMPSON, Jeremy John Egerton. b 23. Dur Univ BSc45. Wells Th Coll 46. **d** 48 **p** 49. C Longbenton St Bart *Newc* 48-51; V N Perak Singapore 51-52; P-in-c Johore Bahru 52-57; V Ipoh St Jo 57-62; V Killingworth *Newc* 62-76; V Consett *Dur* 76-90; RD Lanchester 80-85; rtd 90; Perm to Offic *Dur* and *York* 90-06. *3 Ferens House, Sherburn Hospital, Durham DH1 2SE*

SAMPSON, Julian Robin Anthony. b 78. St Jo Coll Cam BA00. St Steph Ho Ox 01. **d** 03. C Notting Hill All SS w St Columb *Lon* 03-04; C Staines and Asst Chapl HM Pris Bronzefield 04-07; Chapl HM Pris Birm from 07. *HM Prison, Winson Green Road, Birmingham B18 4AS* Tel 0121-345 2500 E-mail jrasampson@yahoo.co.uk

SAMPSON, Terence Harold Morris. b 41. ACA64 FCA75. Bps' Coll Cheshunt 64. **d** 67 **p** 68. C Penrith St Andr *Carl* 67-72; V Carl St Barn 72-80; TR Carl H Trin and St Barn 80-84; Chapl Cumberland Infirmary 83-84; R Workington St Mich *Carl* 84-01; Hon Can Carl Cathl 89-01; RD Solway 90-95; Perm to Offic *Carl* from 02 and *Eur* from 03. *Edificio Balcon de San Miguel, Avenida de Alicante 17/19, 03193 San Miguel de Salinas (Alicante) Spain* Tel 07775-683275 (mobile) E-mail terenceandmargaret@hotmail.co.uk

SAMS, Michael Charles. b 34. FCA62. Ox NSM Course 81. **d** 84 **p** 85. NSM Abingdon *Ox* 84-92 and 99-04; P-in-c Shippon 92-99; Perm to Offic from 04. *13 Hound Close, Abingdon OX14 2LU* Tel (01235) 529084

SAMS, Raymond Victor. b 51. Goldsmiths' Coll Lon TCert73. ERMC 03. **d** 06 **p** 07. NSM Colchester Ch Ch w St Mary V *Chelmsf* from 06. *18 Munnings Road, Colchester CO3 4QG* Tel (01206) 560691 E-mail ray@issachar.freeserve.co.uk

SAMSON, Hilary Lynn. b 50. SWMTC. **d** 03 **p** 04. NSM St Agnes and Mithian w Mount Hawke *Truro* 03-06; P-in-c St Enoder from 06; P-in-c Newlyn St Newlyn from 06. *The Rectory, Penhale View, My Lords Road, Fraddon, St Columb TR9 6LX* Tel (01726) 860514 E-mail hilarysamson@lineone.net

SAMSON, Mrs Susan Mary. b 52. Southn Univ BA73. **d** 09. OLM Sittingbourne H Trin w Bobbing *Cant* from 09. *60 Rock Road, Sittingbourne ME10 1JG* Tel (01795) 478635 E-mail suesamson@sky.com

SAMUEL, Adrian Frank Graham. b 68. Essex Univ BA94 PhD02 Warwick Univ MA95. NTMTC 04. **d** 07 **p** 08. C Twickenham St Mary *Lon* from 07. *27 Strafford Road, Twickenham TW1 3AD* Tel (020) 8891 4807 Mobile 07766-664345 E-mail adriansamuel@msn.com

SAMUEL, Alwin John. b 55. **d** 81 **p** 83. Pakistan 81-03; Interfaith Worker and Dioc Adv *Ox* 03-05; Inter Faith Adv Cowley Deanery from 05. *Flat 1, 14 Magdalen Road, Oxford OX4 1RW* Tel (01865) 723220

SAMUEL, Brother. *See* DOUBLE, Richard Sydney

SAMUEL, Canon James Louis. b 30. Birm Poly CQSW72 Open Univ BA77. Sarum Th Coll 59. **d** 61 **p** 62. C Dursley *Glouc* 61-63; C Matson 63-65; C Leckhampton SS Phil and Jas 65-66; C Blakenall Heath *Lich* 67-69; P-in-c Dudley St Aug Holly Hall *Worc* 81-86; V 86-94; RD Dudley 87-93; Hon Can Worc Cathl 88-94; rtd 94; Perm to Offic *Worc* 94-96 and from 98; C Kidderminster St Mary and All SS w Trimpley etc 96-98. *44 Broadwaters Drive, Kidderminster DY10 2RY* Tel (01562) 68533 E-mail jimsam@sagainternet.co.uk

SAMUEL, Kerry Jay. b 71. Nottm Univ BA92 Hughes Hall Cam PGCE93 K Coll Lon PhD07. NTMTC 05. **d** 07 **p** 08. C Twickenham St Mary *Lon* from 07. *27 Strafford Road, Twickenham TW1 3AD* Tel (020) 8891 4807 Mobile 07717-470403 E-mail kerrysamuel@hotmail.com

✠**SAMUEL, The Most Revd Kunnumpurathu Joseph.** b 42. Union Bibl Sem Yavatmal BRE68 Texas Chr Univ MDiv86. **d** 68 **c** 90. Ch of S India from 68; Bp E Kerala from 90; Moderator Ch of S India 99-04. *CSI Bishop's House, Melukavumattom PO, Kottayam 686 652, Kerala State, India* Tel (0091) (482) 291026 Fax 291044

SAMUEL, Luther Fiaz. b 47. Karachi Univ BA83. St Thos Th Coll Karachi BTh88. **d** 88 **p** 89. Pakistan 88-96; Oman 96-03; Perm to Offic *Lich* 03-04; NSM Walsall from 04; Minority Ethnic Angl Concerns Officer 04-05; Asian Missr from 05. *16 Bescot Drive, Walsall WS2 9DF* Tel (01543) 631814 Mobile 07901-718371 E-mail revlfs@hotmail.com

SAMUEL, Mrs Mary Rose. b 42. Newc Univ BA65 CQSW67. STETS 95. **d** 98 **p** 99. C Waltham on the Wolds, Stonesby, Saxby etc *Leic* 98-01; P-in-c Wymondham w Edmondthorpe, Buckminster etc 01-04; R S Framland 04-08; rtd 08; Hon C Barrow upon Soar w Walton le Wolds *Leic* from 08; Hon C Wymeswold and Prestwold w Hoton from 08. *The Vicarage, 5 The Stockwell, Wymeswold, Loughborough LE12 6UF* Tel (01509) 889568 E-mail mary.rosesamuel@tiscali.co.uk

SAMUEL, Oliver Harold. b 53. **d** 05 **p** 07. OLM Old Trafford St Bride *Man* from 05. *115 Northumberland Road, Old Trafford, Manchester M16 9PY* Tel 0161-876 5055

SAMUEL, Stuart. b 48. AKC70. St Aug Coll Cant 70. **d** 71 **p** 72. C Golcar *Wakef* 71-77; V Brampton St Mark *Derby* 77-79; P-in-c Hathern *Leic* 79-83; R Hathern, Long Whatton and Diseworth 83-90; R Hathern, Long Whatton and Diseworth w Belton etc 90-97; RD Akeley E 92-96; P-in-c Waltham on the Wolds, Stonesby, Saxby etc 97-02; P-in-c Wymondham w Edmondthorpe, Buckminster etc 97-01; P-in-c High Framland Par 97-01; P-in-c Helpringham w Hale *Linc* from 02. *The Vicarage, 2 Vicarage Lane, Helpringham, Sleaford NG34 0RP* Tel (01529) 421435 E-mail stuart@marymag.freeserve.co.uk

SAMUELS, Canon Ann Elizabeth. b 51. Birm Univ BA73 CertEd74. Trin Coll Bris 85. **d** 87 **p** 94. Par Dn Moreton *Ches* 87-91; Par Dn Halton 91-94; C 94-03; Bp's Adv for Women in Min 94-96; Asst Dir of Ords 96-03; RD Frodsham 99-03; Chapl Halton Gen Hosp NHS Trust 99-03; V Higher Bebington *Ches* from 03; Hon Can Ches Cathl from 01. *The Vicarage, King's Road, Bebington, Wirral CH63 8LX* Tel 0151-609 0943 E-mail vicar@higher.bebington.fsnet.co.uk

SAMUELS, Canon Christopher William John. b 42. AKC66. **d** 67 **p** 68. C Kirkholt *Man* 67-72; C-in-c Houghton Regis St Thos CD *St Alb* 72-76; R Tarporley *Ches* 76-83; R Ches St Mary 83-05; RD Ches 95-02; Hon Can Ches Cathl 97-05; Chapl to The Queen from 01; rtd 05; Perm to Offic *Ches* from 07. *Riverleigh House, Station Road, Rossett, Wrexham LL12 0HE* Tel (01244) 579097 E-mail cwjsamuels@tiscali.co.uk

SAMUELS, Raymond John. b 42. Ou Mary Coll Lon BSc73 Essex Univ CertEd74. Trin Coll Bris 85. **d** 87 **p** 88. C Moreton *Ches* 87-91; V Halton 91-02; Dioc Dir of Ords from 03. *The Vicarage, King's Road, Bebington, Wirral CH63 8LX* Tel 0151-609 0942 *or* (01244) 346945 E-mail ray.samuels@chester.anglican.org

SAMWAYS, Denis Robert. b 37. Leeds Univ BA62. Coll of Resurr Mirfield 62. **d** 64 **p** 65. C Clun w Chapel Lawn *Heref* 64-69; C Pocklington w Yapham-cum-Meltonby, Owsthorpe etc *York* 69-71; C Millington w Gt Givendale 69-71; R Hinderwell w Roxby 71-76; Hon C 80-91; Hon C Loftus 76-80; V Boosbeck w Moorsholm 91-95; R Kirby Misperton w Normanby, Edston and Salton 95-02; rtd 02. *7 High Street, Gatehouse of Fleet, Castle Douglas DG7 2HR* Tel (01557) 814095

SAMWAYS, John Feverel. b 44. BA. Trin Coll Bris 81. **d** 83 **p** 84. C Patcham *Chich* 83-86; C Ox St Aldate w St Matt 86-94; R Ox St Matt 95-97; TR Keynsham *B & W* from 97. *St John's Rectory, 1 The Park, Keynsham, Bristol BS31 2BL* Tel 0117-986 3354 E-mail john.samways@blueyonder.co.uk

✠**SAN SI HTAY, The Most Revd Samuel.** BA. **d** 67 **c** 89. Asst Pastor Indaw Burma 67-69; P-in-c Mawbi 70-76; Prin H Cross Coll 76-91; Asst Bp Yangon 91-93; Gen Sec Myanmar 93-01; Abp Myanmar and Bp Yangon from 01. *Bishopscourt, 140*

Pyidaungsu Yeiktha Road, Dagon, Yangon 11191, Myanmar Tel (0095) (1) 246813 Fax 251405 E-mail cpm.140@mptmail.net.mm

✠**SANANA, The Rt Revd Rhynold Ewaruba.** b 39. Newton Th Coll 60 St Barn Coll Adelaide 71 St Aug Coll Cant 75. **d** 67 **p** 67 **c** 76. Papua New Guinea 67-72, 73-90 and from 92; Asst P Dogura Cathl 67-69; Asst P Popondetta Resurr 69-70; St Barn Coll Adelaide Australia 72-73; Dean Dogura and Adn E Region 74-76; Asst Bp New Guinea 76-77; Bp Dogura 77-89; Asst P Lakenham St Mark *Nor* 90-92; rtd 99. *Diocesan Office, PO Box 26, Popondetta, Oro Province, Papua New Guinea*

SANDAY, Robert Ward. b 55. Sarum & Wells Th Coll 89. **d** 91 **p** 92. C Swindon Ch Ch *Bris* 91-94; V Lyddington and Wanborough and Bishopstone etc 94-00; Chapl to the Deaf *Win* from 00. *3 Wheat Close, Chandlers Ford, Eastleigh SO53 4HA* Tel (023) 8027 0551

SANDBERG, Canon Peter John. b 37. Lon Univ LLB59. Lon Coll of Div 67. **d** 69 **p** 70. C Hailsham *Chich* 69-72; C Billericay St Mary *Chelmsf* 72-77; TV Billericay and Lt Burstead 77-83; R Thundersley 83-02; RD Hadleigh 90-00; Hon Can Chelmsf Cathl 00-02; rtd 02; Perm to Offic *Chelmsf* from 02. *Hethersett, School Road, Pentlow, Sudbury CO10 7JR* Tel (01787) 281006 E-mail psandberg@talktalk.net

SANDELLS-REES, Kathy Louise. *See* JONES, Ms Kathy Louise

SANDERS, Mrs Alexandra Jane. b 58. Ex Univ BA80 Leeds Univ MA09. NOC 06. **d** 09. NSM Tarporley *Ches* from 09. *Woodstock, Hill Close, Bunbury, Tarporley CW6 9QJ* Tel and fax (01829) 262494 Mobile 07813-326313 E-mail alex@oftheriver.com

SANDERS, Colin Anthony Wakefield. b 26. Wadh Coll Ox MA55. Ox Univ Course 89. **d** 90 **p** 91. NSM Eynsham and Cassington *Ox* 90-95; NSM Bladon w Woodstock 95-05; NSM Blenheim from 05. *Little Firs, 41 Bladon Road, Woodstock OX20 1QD* Tel (01993) 813357

SANDERS, Diana Faye. b 46. Auckland Univ MA68 LSE PhD75. Westcott Ho Cam 02. **d** 04 **p** 05. NSM Cottenham *Ely* 04-08; P-in-c Farley Hill St Jo *St Alb* from 08. *The Vicarage, 47 Rotheram Avenue, Luton LU1 5PP* Tel (01582) 729466 E-mail revdsanders@googlemail.com

SANDERS, Diana Louise. b 59. Southn Univ BSc80 ACA83. STETS 95. **d** 98 **p** 99. NSM Alderbury Team *Sarum* 98-01; NSM Clarendon 01-08. *Address temp unknown* E-mail diana@ds1999.force9.co.uk

SANDERS, Graham Laughton. b 32. Kelham Th Coll 52. **d** 56 **p** 57. C Glouc St Paul 56-60; India 61-68; V Heaton St Martin *Bradf* 68-76; V Gt Waltham *Chelmsf* 76-79; V Gt Waltham w Ford End 79-87; Sec Dioc Liturg Cttee 78-87; TR Guiseley w Esholt *Bradf* 87-94; rtd 97. *77 Malletts Close, Stony Stratford, Milton Keynes MK11 1DG* Tel (01908) 265290 Mobile 07808-123165 E-mail sanders966@btinternet.com

SANDERS, Canon Hilary Clare. b 57. Hull Univ BA79 UEA CertEd81. EAMTC 83. **dss** 85 **d** 87 **p** 94. Haverhill w Withersfield, the Wrattings etc *St E* 85-87; Hon Par Dn Melton 87-94; Hon C 94-99; Dioc Dir Educn (Schools) 88-99; P-in-c Earl Soham w Cretingham and Ashfield 99-05; P-in-c Boulge w Burgh, Grundisburgh and Hasketon from 05; Hon Can St E Cathl from 04. *The Rectory, Woodbridge Road, Grundisburgh, Woodbridge IP13 6UF* Tel (01473) 735183 E-mail claresanders@suffolkonline.net

SANDERS, James Alexander. b 29. **d** 65 **p** 66. Australia 65-78 and from 81; C Enfield St Jas *Lon* 78-81; rtd 94. *Apt 8, 82 Sandy Bay Road, Battery Point Tas 7004, Australia*

SANDERS, Canon Mark. b 57. Hull Univ BA79 Cam Univ BA82. Westcott Ho Cam 83. **d** 83 **p** 84. C Haverhill w Withersfield, the Wrattings etc *St E* 83-87; P-in-c Melton 87-91; R 91-98; Dioc Dir Post-Ord Tr from 97; Asst Dioc Dir of Ords 98-99; Dioc Dir of Ords from 99; Dioc Dir of CME 99-01; Hon Can St E Cathl from 01. *The Rectory, Woodbridge Road, Grundisburgh, Woodbridge IP13 6UF* Tel and fax (01473) 735182 E-mail mark@stedmundsbury.anglican.org

SANDERS, Michael Barry. b 45. Fitzw Coll Cam BA67 MA71 Lon Univ BD71. St Jo Coll Nottm 68 Lon Coll of Div. **d** 71 **p** 72. C Ashtead *Guildf* 71-74; Chapl St Jo Coll Cam 75-79; V Dorridge *Birm* 79-89; TR Walsall *Lich* 89-01; Preb Lich Cathl 97-01; Chapl The Hague *Eur* 01-07; P-in-c Kemble, Poole Keynes, Somerford Keynes etc *Glouc* from 07. *The Vicarage, Kemble, Cirencester GL7 6AG* Tel (01285) 770049

SANDERS, Nigel Wilding. b 29. Mert Coll Ox MA55. Ox Min Course 91. **d** 92 **p** 93. NSM Maidenhead St Andr and St Mary *Ox* 92-97; NSM Furze Platt 97-04; rtd 04; Perm to Offic *B & W* from 05. *Fry's Barn, Home Farm, Barton, Winscombe BS25 1DX* Tel (01934) 843818 E-mail nigelisan@btinternet.com

SANDERS, Mrs Nora Irene. b 29. Lon Univ BA50 CertEd51. WMMTC 74. **dss** 78 **d** 87 **p** 94. Dorridge *Birm* 78-90; Par Dn 87-90; rtd 90; Hon C Tanworth *Birm* 94-96; Perm to Offic from 96. *10 Dove House Court, Warwick Grange, Solihull B91 1EW* Tel 0121-704 1765

SANDERS (née **SHAW), Mrs Pamela Joyce.** b 54. Liv Univ BA76. WEMTC 02. **d** 05 **p** 06. C Leominster *Heref* 05-09; P-in-c

Crathorne *York* from 09; P-in-c Kirklevington w Picton, and High and Low Worsall from 09; P-in-c Rudby in Cleveland w Middleton from 09. *2 Langbaurgh Road, Hutton Rudby, Yarm TS15 0HL* Tel (01568) 620539
E-mail pam.notsaunders@dsl.pipex.com

SANDERS, Roderick David Scott. b 58. Southn Univ BA80 CertEd81. Cranmer Hall Dur 85. **d** 88 **p** 89. C Luton St Mary *St Alb* 88-93; P-in-c Clovelly *Ex* 93-94; P-in-c Woolfardisworthy and Buck Mills 93-94; TV Parkham, Alwington, Buckland Brewer etc 94-98; NSM Cove St Jo *Guildf* 98-03; NSM Guildf Ch Ch w St Martha-on-the-Hill from 03. *Christ Church Vicarage, 25 Waterden Road, Guildford GU1 2AZ* Tel (01483) 568886 Mobile 07720-856460
E-mail rod.sanders@ntlworld.com

SANDERS (née COLLINGRIDGE), Mrs Susan Rachel. b 61. St Mary's Coll Dur BA83. Cranmer Hall Dur 85. **d** 88 **p** 94. Par Dn Luton St Mary *St Alb* 88-93; Perm to Offic *Ex* 93-94; NSM Parkham, Alwington, Buckland Brewer etc 94-98; TV Cove St Jo *Guildf* 98-03; V Guildf Ch Ch w St Martha-on-the-Hill from 03. *Christ Church Vicarage, 25 Waterden Road, Guildford GU1 2AZ* Tel (01483) 568886 Mobile 07913-840820
E-mail susie@christchurchguildford.com

SANDERS, Mrs Wendy Elizabeth. b 49. Carl Dioc Tr Course 87. **d** 90 **p** 94. NSM Bampton w Mardale *Carl* 90-92; C Walney Is 92-94; C Stanwix w 94-98; TV Chippenham St Paul w Hardenhuish etc *Bris* 98-03; TV Kington St Michael 98-03; RD Chippenham 99-03; TR Cockermouth Area *Carl* from 03. *The Rectory, Lorton Road, Cockermouth CA13 9DU* Tel and fax (01900) 823269 Mobile 07980-598892
E-mail wendy@parishofcockermouth.org.uk

SANDERS, William John. b 48. Liv Inst of Educn BA80. Wycliffe Hall Ox 81. **d** 83 **p** 84. C Netherton *Liv* 83-87; P-in-c Wavertree St Bridget 87-97; V Wavertree St Bridget and St Thos from 97. *The Vicarage, Ashfield, Wavertree, Liverpool L15 1EY* Tel 0151-733 1117

SANDERSON, Colin James. b 54. Univ of Wales MA95 SEN SRN. St Mich Coll Llan 85. **d** 87 **p** 88. C Merthyr Dyfan *Llan* 87-90; C Cadoxton-juxta-Barry 90-91; V Llangeinor 91-99; Lic to Offic from 04. *99 West Lee, Cowbridge Road East, Cardiff CF11 9DT* Tel (029) 2039 8771 Mobile 07713-742365

SANDERSON, Daniel. b 40. AKC66. **d** 67 **p** 68. C Upperby St Jo *Carl* 67-72; V Addingham 72-75; V Ireleth w Askam 75-02; C Dalton-in-Furness and Ireleth-with-Askam 02-05; Hon Can Carl Cathl 95-05; RD Furness 01-04; rtd 05. *52 Parklands Drive, Askam-in-Furness LA16 7JP* Tel (01229) 463018

SANDERSON, Canon Gillian. b 47. Cranmer Hall Dur 80. **dss** 82 **d** 87 **p** 94. Allesley *Cov* 82-86; Warwick 86-00; C 87-94; TV 94-00; Hon Can Cov Cathl 94-00; Perm to Offic from 00. *17 Marlborough Drive, Leamington Spa CV31 1XY* Tel (01926) 459749 Mobile 07714-193776
E-mail gillian-7_wine@tiscali.co.uk

SANDERSON, Paul. b 59. Univ of Wales (Abth) BSc80 Ches Coll of HE PGCE81 Man Univ MEd92. **d** 05 **p** 06. OLM Bury St Jo w St Mark *Man* from 05. *261 Walmersley Road, Bury BL9 6NX* Tel 0161-764 3452 E-mail paul261@fsmail.net

SANDERSON, Canon Peter Oliver. b 29. St Chad's Coll Dur BA52. **d** 54 **p** 55. C Houghton le Spring *Dur* 54-59; R Linstead Jamaica 59-63; Chapl RAF 63-67; P-in-c Winksley cum Grantley and Aldfield w Studley *Ripon* 67-68; V 68-74; V Leeds St Aid 74-84; Can and Provost St Paul's Cathl Dundee 84-91; R Dundee St Paul 84-91; USA from 91; rtd 94; Interim Dean Trin Cathl Iowa 05-06; Asst to the Dean 06-07. *410 Brentwood Drive, Alamogordo NM 88310-5439, USA*
E-mail frpeter.sanderson@gmail.com

SANDERSON, Peter Richard Fallowfield. b 18. St Cath Soc Ox BA41 MA46. Chich Th Coll 41. **d** 42 **p** 44. C Bishops Hull St Jo *B & W* 42-48; C Ox St Paul 48-49; Perm to Offic *Ex* 49-55; V Poundstock *Truro* 56-74; P-in-c Hove St Patr *Chich* 74-79; P-in-c Buxted St Mary 79-82; P-in-c Hadlow Down 79-82; P-in-c Buxted and Hadlow Down 82-83; rtd 83; Perm to Offic *Chich* 83-00. *Nova Scotia, 48 Parklands Road, Hassocks BN6 8JZ* Tel (01273) 843117

SANDERSON, Scott. b 42. Oak Hill Th Coll. **d** 82 **p** 83. C Galleywood Common *Chelmsf* 82-88; P-in-c Newport w Widdington 88-92; V Newport 92-98; V Walton le Soken 98-05; rtd 05; Perm to Offic *Chelmsf* from 07. *The Bungalow, 2 Captains Road, West Mersea, Colchester CO5 8QS* Tel (01206) 385571
E-mail scott.sanderson@lineone.net

SANDERSON, Timothy. b 68. York Univ BSc89 Glos Univ BA03 St Jo Coll Dur MA09. Cranmer Hall Dur 07. **d** 09. C Jesmond H Trin *Newc* from 09; C Newc St Barn and St Jude from 09. *52 Fern Avenue, Jesmond, Newcastle upon Tyne NE2 2QX* Tel 07724-136581 (mobile)

SANDES, Canon Denis Lindsay. b 46. CITC BTh86. **d** 89 **p** 90. C Bandon Union *C, C & R* 89-92; I Kells Gp *C & O* 92-07; Can Leighlin Cathl 03-07; I Omey w Ballynakill, Errislannan and Roundstone *T, K & A* from 07; Can Tuam Cathl from 08. *The Rectory, Clifden, Co Galway, Republic of Ireland* Tel (00353) (95) 21147 Mobile 86-647 5056 E-mail revdlsandes@gmail.com

SANDFORD, Nicholas Robert. b 63. Kent Univ BA84 Univ of Wales (Cardiff) BD87. St Mich Coll Llan 84. **d** 87 **p** 88. C Neath w Llantwit 87-90; C Cardiff St Jo 90-94; R Cilybebyll 94-97; Chapl HM Pris Swansea 95-97; Chapl HM Pris Parc (Bridgend) 97-04; Chapl HM Pris Usk and Prescoed from 04. *HM Prison Usk, 47 Maryport Street, Usk NP15 1XP* Tel (01291) 671600

SANDFORD, Paul Richard. b 47. Em Coll Cam BA69 MA73. Wycliffe Hall Ox 72. **d** 75 **p** 76. C Upper Holloway St Pet *Lon* 75-77; C Finchley St Paul Long Lane 77-81; Ind Chapl *Newc* 81-88; TV Dronfield *Derby* 88-90; TV Dronfield w Holmesfield 90-02; P-in-c Sinfin from 02; RD Derby S from 02. *St Stephen's Vicarage, 313 Sinfin Lane, Derby DE24 9GP* Tel (01332) 760135
E-mail prsandford@ntlworld.com

SANDHAM, Daniel Paul. b 82. St Chad's Coll Dur BA05. St Steph Ho Ox BA09. **d** 09. C Hendon St Mary and Ch Ch *Lon* from 09. *St Mary's Cottage, 48 Church End, London NW4 4JT* E-mail danielsandham@hotmail.com

SANDHAM, Shaun Graham. b 60. Cranmer Hall Dur 02. **d** 04 **p** 05. C Workington St Mich *Carl* 04-08; TV Sutton St Jas and Wawne *York* from 08. *11 Sovereign Way, Kingswood, Hull HU7 3JG* Tel (01482) 838486 Mobile 07778-334356
E-mail shaun@sandham121.wanadoo.co.uk

SANDHAM, Stephen McCourt. b 41. K Coll Lon BD65 AKC65. **d** 66 **p** 67. C Stockton St Pet *Dur* 66-69; C Bishopwearmouth Gd Shep 69-71; C Bishopwearmouth St Mich w St Hilda 71-75; C Darlington St Mark w St Paul 75-82; P-in-c Sunderland St Chad 82-87; R Shincliffe 87-98; P-in-c 98-06; rtd 06; Chapl Sherburn Hosp Dur 98-07. *21 Hill Meadows, High Shincliffe, Durham DH1 2PE* E-mail stephensandham@yahoo.co.uk

SANDOM, Miss Carolyn Elizabeth. b 63. Homerton Coll Cam BEd85. Wycliffe Hall Ox BTh93. **d** 94. C St Helen Bishopsgate w St Andr Undershaft etc *Lon* 94-96; C Cambridge H Sepulchre *Ely* 96-05. *12 Eden Street, Cambridge CB1 1EL* Tel (01223) 578016 E-mail carrie@sandom63.freeserve.co.uk

SANDS, Colin Robert. b 38. JP84. Ches Coll of HE CertEd64. NOC 82. **d** 85 **p** 86. Hd Master St Andr Magull Primary Sch 80-00; NSM Bootle Ch Ch *Liv* 85-94; NSM Maghull 94-01; rtd 01; Perm to Offic *Carl* 01-07 and *Liv* from 01. *16 Strafford Drive, Bootle L20 9JW* Tel 0151-525 8709 *or* (01768) 863968

SANDS, Frederick William. b 25. St Deiniol's Hawarden 86. **d** 87 **p** 88. Chapl Asst Leic Gen Hosp 87-89; Chapl 89-95; rtd 95; Perm to Offic *Leic* from 95. *Cobblestones, Laughton, Lutterworth LE17 6QD* Tel 0116-240 3163

SANDS, Nigel Colin. b 39. Dur Univ BA64 MA68. Oak Hill Th Coll 65. **d** 67 **p** 68. C Skelmersdale St Paul *Liv* 67-71; C Childwall All SS 71-72; V Wavertree St Bridget 72-78; P-in-c Welford w Wickham and Gt Shefford *Ox* 78-86; P-in-c Boxford w Stockcross and Speen 84-86; R Welford w Wickham and Gt Shefford, Boxford etc 86-09; rtd 09; Perm to Offic *Ox* from 09. *Applemead, Chilton Way, Hungerford RG17 0JR* Tel (01488) 680618

SANDS, William James. b 55. Nottm Univ LTh83 Birm Univ MA99. St Jo Coll Nottm 80. **d** 83 **p** 84. C St Mary-at-Latton *Chelmsf* 83-86; R Mvurwi Zimbabwe 86-87; C-in-c Barkingside St Cedd *Chelmsf* 87-89; C Woodford St Mary w St Phil and St Jas 87-89; P-in-c Elmsett w Aldham *St E* 89-92; P-in-c Kersey w Lindsey 89-92; R Esigodini Zimbabwe 92-96; Sub Dean Harare 97; Chapl Algarve *Eur* 98-00; V Castle Bromwich St Clem *Birm* from 00. *St Clement's Vicarage, Lanchester Way, Castle Bromwich, Birmingham B36 9JG* Tel and fax 0121-747 4460 E-mail w.j.sands@btinternet.com

SANER-HAIGH, Robert James. b 73. Birm Univ BA94 MPhil98. Wycliffe Hall Ox BA04 MA08. **d** 05 **p** 06. C Appleby *Carl* 05-07; Bp's Dom Chapl from 07; Officer for IME 4-7 07-08; C Dalston w Cumdivock, Raughton Head and Wreay from 07; Dir of Ords from 08. *The Vicarage, Wreay, Carlisle CA4 0RL* Tel (01697) 473883 *or* 476274
E-mail bishop.chaplain@carlislediocese.org.uk

SANGSTER, Andrew. b 45. K Coll Lon BD67 AKC67 BA71 MA84 Lon Inst of Educn MPhil93 LLB97 FCollP. St Boniface Warminster. **d** 69 **p** 70. C Aylesford *Roch* 69-72; C Shirley *Win* 73-76; V Woolston 76-79; Prov Youth Chapl Ch in Wales 79-82; Chapl Collegiate Sch New Zealand 82-89; Chapl Eton Coll 89-92; Hd Master St Edm Sch Hindhead 92-96; Hd Thos Day Schs Lon 96-99; V Ormesby St Marg w Scratby, Ormesby St Mich etc *Nor* 99-04; Chapl Bromley Coll from 04. *The Chaplain's House, Bromley College, London Road, Bromley BR1 1PE* Tel (020) 8464 3558 E-mail bromcoll@aol.com

SANKEY, Julian. b 52. Qu Coll Ox BA74 MA79. St Jo Coll Nottm 84. **d** 86 **p** 87. C New Barnet St Jas *St Alb* 86-89; C Mansfield SS Pet and Paul *S'well* 89-94; Chapl St Luke's Hospice Sheff from 94. *St Luke's Hospice, Little Common Lane, Sheffield S11 9NE* Tel 0114-236 9911 Fax 262 1242

SANKEY, Terence Arthur Melville. b 51. Trin Coll Bris 87. **d** 89 **p** 90. C Chalke Valley W *Sarum* 89-93; NSM Chalke from 93; Chapl HM Pris Dorchester from 99. *HM Prison Dorchester, 7 North Square, Dorchester DT1 1JD* Tel (01305) 266021
E-mail terry@rkhaye.globalnet.co.uk

SANSBURY, Canon Christopher John. b 34. Peterho Cam BA57 MA. Westcott Ho Cam 58. **d** 59 **p** 60. C Portsea N End St Mark *Portsm* 59-63; C Weeke *Win* 63-71; V N Eling St Mary 71-78; R Long Melford *St E* 78-00; P-in-c Shimpling and Alpheton 98-00; Hon Can St E Cathl 97-00; rtd 00; Perm to Offic *St E* from 00. *2 Deacon's Close, Lavenham, Sudbury CO10 9TT* Tel (01787) 248068

SANSOM, John Reginald. b 40. St Jo Coll Nottm 73. **d** 75 **p** 76. C Ipswich St Marg *St E* 75-79; P-in-c Emneth *Ely* 79-85; P-in-c Hartford 85-86; TV Huntingdon 86-91; R Sawtry 91-97; R Sawtry and Glatton 97-99; TV Ely 99-05; rtd 05; Perm to Offic *Ely* from 06. *77 St Ovins Green, Ely CB6 3AW* Tel (01353) 614913

SANSOM, Canon Michael Charles. b 44. Bris Univ BA66 St Jo Coll Dur PhD74. Cranmer Hall Dur 68. **d** 72 **p** 73. C Ecclesall *Sheff* 72-76; Lic to Offic *Ely* 76-88; Dir of Studies Ridley Hall Cam 76-88; Vice-Prin 79-88; Dir of Ords *St Alb* from 88; Can Res St Alb from 88. *4D Harpenden Road, St Albans AL3 5AB* Tel (01727) 833777 E-mail ddo@stalbans.anglican.org

SANSOM, Robert Arthur. b 29. St Aid Birkenhead 60. **d** 62 **p** 63. C Sutton in Ashfield St Mary *S'well* 62-65; V Holbrooke *Derby* 65-70; Canada from 70; R North Saanich St Andr and H Trin 70-80; R Oak Bay St Mary 80-84; R Saanichton St Mary 84-89; rtd 89. *1-9871 Resthaven Drive, Sidney BC V8L 3E9, Canada*

SANSOME, Geoffrey Hubert. b 29. Man Univ BA53. Qu Coll Birm. **d** 62 **p** 63. C Prenton *Ches* 62-68; P-in-c Liscard St Thos 68-72; V Kingsley 72-83; V Wybunbury w Doddington 83-91; V Marbury 91-99; rtd 99; Perm to Offic *Blackb* from 00 and *Ches* from 01. *21 Ash Drive, Warton, Preston PR4 1DD* Tel (01772) 633799

SANSUM, Canon David Henry. b 31. Bris Univ BA52 MA63. St Aid Birkenhead 54. **d** 56 **p** 57. C Henleaze *Bris* 56-59; C Stratton St Margaret 59-60; C Stoke Bishop 60-64; V Stechford *Birm* 64-76; V Ashbourne w Mapleton *Derby* 76-98; P-in-c Thorpe 77-83; V Ashbourne St Jo 81-98; RD Ashbourne 91-98; Hon Can Derby Cathl 95-98; rtd 98; Perm to Offic *Bris* and *Glouc* from 98. *Greenleaze, Main Road, Easter Compton, Bristol BS35 5SQ* Tel (01454) 632563

✠**SANTER, The Rt Revd Mark.** b 36. Qu Coll Cam BA60 MA64 Lambeth DD99. Westcott Ho Cam. **d** 63 **p** 64 **c** 81. Tutor Cuddesdon Coll 63-67; C Cuddesdon *Ox* 63-67; Fell and Dean Clare Coll Cam 67-72; Tutor 68-72; Prin Westcott Ho Cam 73-81; Hon Can Win Cathl 78-81; Area Bp Kensington *Lon* 81-87; Bp Birm 87-02; rtd 02; Hon Asst Bp *Worc* from 02 and *Birm* from 03. *81 Clarence Road, Kings Heath, Birmingham B13 9UH* Tel 0121-441 2194

SANTRA, Jagat Ranjan. b 54. Utkal Univ BA74 Serampore Univ BD81 MTh88. **d** 00 **p** 00. NSM Edin Old St Paul 00-06; Lect Union Bibl Sem Pune India from 06. *Union Biblical Seminary, PO Box 1425, Bibwewadi, Pune, India* Tel (0091) (20) 2421 1747, 2421 1203, or 2421 8670 Fax 2421 5471 E-mail jagat_s@hotmail.com

SANTRAM, Philip James. b 27. MA Delhi Univ BSc48 Serampore Univ BD53. Bp's Coll Calcutta 49. **d** 52 **p** 54. India 52-66; Lect Bp's Coll Calcutta 61-65; R Delhi St Martin w H Trin and Gurgaon Epiphany 65-66; Ethiopia 66-68; C Horton *Bradf* 68-71; C Whitley Ch Ch *Ox* 71-72; P Missr Tilehurst St Mary CD 72-76; V Tilehurst St Mary 76-78; R Lakefield Canada 78-82; R Chomedey-Bordeaux 82-97; rtd 97; Hon C Oakville Epiphany from 00. *2336 Adirondak Trail, Oakville ON L6M 0E9, Canada* Tel (001) (905) 827 6327 E-mail rpsantram@aol.com

SAPWELL, Mrs Lynette Lilian. b 51. Sussex Univ BEd73 Middx Univ BA03. NTMTC 00. **d** 03 **p** 04. NSM Rochford *Chelmsf* 03-07; P-in-c Appleton *Ox* from 07; P-in-c Besselsleigh from 07. *The Rectory, Oakesmere, Appleton, Abingdon OX13 5JS* Tel (01865) 862458 E-mail lynandphil@tiscali.co.uk

SARALIS, Preb Christopher Herbert. b 34. Univ of Wales BA54 St Cath Coll Ox BA56 MA60. Wycliffe Hall Ox. **d** 57 **p** 58. C Abergavenny St Mary w Llanwenarth Citra *Mon* 57-61; C Bridgwater St Mary w Chilton Trinity *B & W* 61-65; V Berrow 65-72; R Berrow and Breane 72-76; RD Burnham 72-76; V Minehead 76-92; RD Exmoor 80-86; Preb Wells Cathl 84-92; V Bovey Tracey SS Pet, Paul and Thos w Hennock *Ex* 92-99; rtd 99; Perm to Offic *B & W* from 99. *1 Broadway Road, Horton, Ilminster TA19 9RX* Tel (01460) 52416

SARAPUK, Susan. b 59. Lon Univ BA80 Univ of Wales PGCE81. St Mich Coll Llan. **d** 90 **p** 97. C Morriston *S & B* 90-94; C Swansea St Pet 94-97; P-in-c Llangyfelach 97-98; V 98-02; C Sketty 02-08. *13 Edison Crescent, Clydach, Swansea SA6 5JF* Tel (01792) 843521

SARGANT, John Raymond. b 38. CCC Cam BA61 MA70. Westcott Ho Cam 64 Harvard Div Sch 66. **d** 67 **p** 68. C Croydon St Jo *Cant* 67-72; Sec Zambia Angl Coun 72-75; P-in-c Bradford-on-Avon Ch Ch *Sarum* 76-81; V 81-90; TV Marlborough 90-03; Dioc Inter-Faith Adv 90-00; Can and Preb Sarum Cathl 92-01; rtd 03. *48 Summerhill Road, Lyme Regis DT7 3DT* Tel (01297) 445922

SARGEANT, Prof Anthony John. b 44. Goldsmiths' Coll Lon BEd70 Univ Coll Lon MSc73 LSHTM PhD76. Westcott Ho Cam 99. **d** 00 **p** 01. NSM Goostrey w Swettenham *Ches* 00-08; TV Rye *Chich* from 08. *The Vicarage, 21 Fair Meadow, Rye TN31 7NL* Tel (01797) 227621 E-mail a.j.sargeant@hotmail.com

✠**SARGEANT, The Rt Revd Frank Pilkington.** b 32. St Jo Coll Dur BA55. Cranmer Hall Dur 57. **d** 58 **p** 59 **c** 84. C Gainsborough All SS *Linc* 58-62; C Gt Grimsby St Jas 62-66; V Hykeham 66-73; Dir In-Service Tr and Adult Educn *Bradf* 73-84; Can Res Bradf Cathl 73-77; Adn Bradf 77-84; Suff Bp Stockport *Ches* 84-94; Bp at Lambeth (Hd of Staff) *Cant* 94-99; rtd 99; Hon Asst Bp Eur 99-07; Perm to Offic *Ches* from 99. *32 Brotherton Drive, Trinity Gardens, Salford M3 6BH* Tel 0161-839 7045 E-mail franksargeant68@hotmail.com

SARGEANTSON, Kenneth William. b 30. **d** 90 **p** 91. NSM The Marshland *Sheff* 90-93; NSM Goole 93-97; Perm to Offic 97-06; NSM The Marshland from 06; Hon Chapl Miss to Seafarers from 95. *97 High Street, Swinefleet, Goole DN14 8AH* Tel (01405) 704256 E-mail kensargeantson@yahoo.co.uk

SARGENT, Miss Ann. b 65. **d** 98 **p** 99. C Bris St Andr Hartcliffe 98-01; P-in-c Flax Bourton *B & W* 01-09; P-in-c Barrow Gurney 01-09; P-in-c Long Ashton 05-09; R Long Ashton w Barrow Gurney and Flax Bourton from 09. *The Vicarage, 7 Church Lane, Long Ashton, Bristol BS41 9LU* Tel (01275) 393109

SARGENT, Benjamin Charles. b 83. K Coll Lon BA05 MA07 AKC05. Wycliffe Hall Ox MTh09. **d** 09. C Warblington w Emsworth *Portsm* from 09. *1 Godwin Close, Emsworth PO10 7XT* Tel 07990-695830 (mobile) E-mail benjamin.sargent@wycliffe.ox.ac.uk

SARGENT, Charles Edward. b 68. K Coll Lon BD89 Leeds Univ MA96. Coll of Resurr Mirfield 94. **d** 96 **p** 97. C Notting Dale St Clem w St Mark and St Jas *Lon* 96-00; P-in-c S Kensington St Aug 00-04; Chapl Imp Coll 00-04; Chapl Brunel Univ from 04. *26 Church Road, Uxbridge UB8 3NA* Tel (01895) 203308 E-mail charles_sargent@priest.com

SARGENT, David Gareth. b 63. Sheff Univ BA85 St Jo Coll Dur BA96. Cranmer Hall Dur 93. **d** 96 **p** 97. C Norbury *Ches* 96-01; V Hooton 01-06; TR Penrith w Newton Reigny and Plumpton Wall *Carl* from 06. *The Rectory, 3 Lamley Gardens, Penrith CA11 9LR* Tel (01768) 863000 E-mail revdave.sargent@talk21.com

SARGENT, Derek Connor. b 66. TCD BTh99. CITC 96. **d** 99 **p** 00. C Waterford w Killea, Drumcannon and Dunhill *C & O* 99-01; V 01-03; I Dublin Clontarf *D & G* from 03. *The Rectory, 15 Seafield Road West, Clontarf, Dublin 3, Republic of Ireland* Tel (00353) (1) 833 1181 E-mail clontarf@dublin.anglican.org

SARGENT, Mrs Janet. b 54. **d** 07 **p** 08. OLM Birchencliffe *Wakef* 07-08; OLM Birkby and Birchencliffe from 08. *11 Kirkwood Drive, Huddersfield HD3 3WA* Tel (01484) 650390

SARGENT, Preb Richard Henry. b 24. Man Univ BA50. Ridley Hall Cam 50. **d** 52 **p** 53. C Rusholme H Trin *Man* 52-54; C Cheadle *Ches* 54-59; V Cheadle Hulme St Andr 59-67; V Bushbury *Lich* 67-73; V Castle Church 73-89; RD Stafford 81-88; Preb Lich Cathl 87-89; rtd 89; Perm to Offic *Lich* from 90. *57 Deanshill Close, Stafford ST16 1BW* Tel (01785) 605335

SARGISSON, Conrad Ralph. b 24. Keble Coll Ox BA46 MA50. Wells Th Coll 48. **d** 50 **p** 51. C Charlton Kings St Mary *Glouc* 50-53; C Prestbury 53-55; V St Briavels 55-58; V Lanteglos by Fowey *Truro* 58-62, V Penzance St Mary 62-73; RD Penwith 72-73; V Westbury-on-Trym H Trin *Bris* 73-79; P-in-c Blisland w St Breward *Truro* 79-83; V Mylor w Flushing 83-91; rtd 91; Perm to Offic *Heref* 91-93; P-in-c St Hilary *Truro* 93-96; Perm to Offic from 96. *Casacawn Farmhouse, Blisland, Bodmin PL30 4JU* Tel (01208) 850371

SARMEZEY, George Arpad. b 61. Qu Mary Coll Lon BA83 Goldsmiths' Coll Lon PGCE86. Westcott Ho Cam 89. **d** 92 **p** 93. C Eastville St Anne w St Mark and St Thos *Bris* 92-94; C Stratton St Margaret w S Marston etc 94-97; Asst Chapl Northn Gen Hosp NHS Trust 97-00; Sen Chapl from 00. *Northampton General Hospital, Billing Road, Northampton NN1 5BD* Tel (01604) 545773 Fax 544608 E-mail george.sarmezey@ngh.nhs.uk

SARUM, Archdeacon of. See JEANS, The Ven Alan Paul

SARVANANTHAN, Sudharshan. b 70. Trin Coll Bris 06. **d** 08 **p** 09. C Heart of Eden *Carl* from 08. *92 Rivington Park, Appleby-in-Westmorland CA16 6HU* Tel (01768) 354099 Mobile 07879-656492 E-mail sudharshan@sarva.info

SASADA, Benjamin John. b 33. EAMTC. **d** 82 **p** 83. NSM Dickleburgh, Langmere, Shimpling, Thelveton etc *Nor* 82-88; NSM Diss 88-95; P-in-c Dickleburgh, Langmere, Shimpling, Thelveton etc 95-99; rtd 99; Perm to Offic *St E* from 84 and *Nor* from 99 *The Grange, Walcott Green, Diss IP22 5SS* Tel (01379) 642174 E-mail benjamin@sasada2.freeserve.co.uk

SASSER, Col the Revd Canon Howell Crawford. b 37. Maryland Univ BA72 Geo Mason Univ Virginia MA74 Westmr Coll Ox MTh97. Washington Dioc Course 75. **d** 77 **p** 78. W Germany 77-80; Somalia 80-83; Cyprus 84-92; Chapl Montreux w Gstaad *Eur* 92-97; Chapl Oporto 97-05; Adn Gib 02-05; Bp's Chapl and

Research Asst 05-06; rtd 06. *11944 Artery Drive, Fairfax VA 22030-6710, USA* Tel (001) (703) 631 0466

SATTERLY, Gerald Albert. b 34. Lon Univ BA56 Ex Univ Hon BA. Wycliffe Hall Ox 58. **d** 60 **p** 61. C Southborough St Pet *Roch* 60-63; C S Lyncombe *B & W* 63-66; V Sheff St Barn 66-69; R Adwick-le-Street 69-73; V Awre and Blakeney *Glouc* 73-82; P-in-c Newnham 80-82; V Newnham w Awre and Blakeney 82-90; R Instow *Ex* 90-98; V Westleigh 90-98; rtd 98; Perm to Offic *Ex* from 98. *Tryst Lea, 2 Cameron Close, Maer Lane, Bude EX23 8SP* Tel (01288) 359256

✠**SATTERTHWAITE, The Rt Revd John Richard.** b 25. CMG91. Leeds Univ BA46. Coll of Resurr Mirfield 48. **d** 50 **p** 51 **c** 70. C Carl St Barn 50-53; C Carl St Aid and Ch 53-55; Asst Gen Sec C of E Coun on Foreign Relns 55-59; C St Mich Paternoster Royal *Lon* 55-59; P-in-c 59-65; Gen Sec C of E Coun on Foreign Relns 59-70; V St Dunstan in the West *Lon* 59-70; Hon Can Cant Cathl 63-70; Gen Sec Abp's Commn on RC Relns 65-70; Suff Bp Fulham *Lon* 70-80; Bp Gib 70-80; Bp Eur 80-93; Dean Malta 70-93; rtd 93; Hon Asst Bp Carl 94-01 and from 04; Perm to Offic 01-04. *25 Spencer House, St Paul's Square, Carlisle CA1 1DG* Tel (01228) 594055

SAUL, Norman Stanley. b 30. St Aid Birkenhead 51. **d** 54 **p** 55. C S Shore H Trin *Blackb* 54-57; C Poulton-le-Fylde 57-59; PC Freckleton 59-66; V Blackb St Luke 66-68; V Barton 68-72; V Foxdale *S & M* 72-77; V Maughold 77-90; CF (ACF) 80-86; rtd 90; Perm to Offic *Blackb* from 90. *15 Croft Meadow, Bamber Bridge, Preston PR5 8HX* Tel (01772) 314475

SAUNDERS, Andrew Vivian. b 44. Leeds Univ BA65. Coll of Resurr Mirfield 66. **d** 68 **p** 69. C Goodmayes St Paul *Chelmsf* 68-71; C Horfield H Trin *Bris* 71-75; C Oldland 75-77; Ind Chapl *B & W* 77-80; P-in-c Buckland Dinham w Elm, Orchardleigh etc 77-78; P-in-c Buckland Dinham 78-80; V Westfield 80-90; R Clutton w Cameley 90-99; C Christchurch *Win* 99-05; rtd 05; Perm to Offic *B & W* from 06. *8 Mill House Court, Willow Vale, Frome BA11 1BG* Tel (01373) 467683

SAUNDERS, Barry. *See* SAUNDERS, John Barry

SAUNDERS, Brian Gerald. b 28. Pemb Coll Cam BA49 MA53. Cuddesdon Coll 63. **d** 66 **p** 67. NSM Gt Berkhamsted *St Alb* 66-87; P-in-c Lt Gaddesden 87-92; rtd 92; Perm to Offic *Ox* 92-94; *St Alb* 92-02; *Linc* from 01; Hon C Newton Longville w Stoke Hammond and Whaddon 94-01. *2 Bruce Close, Lincoln LN2 1SL* Tel (01522) 523193

SAUNDERS, Canon Bruce Alexander. b 47. St Cath Coll Cam BA68 MA72. Cuddesdon Coll 68. **d** 71 **p** 72. C Westbury-on-Trym H Trin *Bris* 71-74; Hon C Clifton St Paul 74-78; Asst Chapl Bris Univ 74-78; TV Fareham H Trin *Portsm* 78-84; TR Mortlake w E Sheen *S'wark* 84-97; RD Richmond and Barnes 89-94; Can Missr for Ch in Soc 97-03; Can Res S'wark Cathl from 03; C-in-c Bermondsey St Hugh CD from 03. *7 Temple West Mews, West Square, London SE11 4TJ* Tel (020) 7735 0143 or 7367 6706 Fax 7367 6725
E-mail bruce.saunders@southwark.anglican.org

SAUNDERS, David. b 28. Keble Coll Ox BA50 MA59. Cuddesdon Coll 51. **d** 53 **p** 54. C Mexborough *Sheff* 53-56; C Sheff St Cuth 56-60; V New Bentley 60-67; V Grimsby All SS *Linc* 67-78; V Caistor w Clixby 78-88; P-in-c Grasby 78-94; Chapl Caistor Hosp 78-94; P-in-c Searby w Owmby *Linc* 79-94; V Dunholme 88-92; P-in-c Welton and Dunholme w Scothern 92-94; rtd 94; Perm to Offic *Linc* from 94. *2 Oundle Close, Washingborough, Lincoln LN4 1DR* Tel (01522) 793164

SAUNDERS, Gareth John McKeith. b 71. St Andr Univ BD93 Edin Univ MTh99. TISEC 99. **d** 99 **p** 00. C Inverness St Andr *Mor* 99-03; C Edin St Salvador and Edin Gd Shep 03-06. *45 Lindsay Berwick Place, Anstruther KY10 3YP* Tel (01333) 310140 Mobile 07732-356123
E-mail gareth@garethjmsaunders.co.uk

SAUNDERS, Geoffrey David. b 51. Bris Univ BSc73. **d** 01 **p** 02. OLM Rockland St Mary w Hellington, Bramerton etc *Nor* 01-07; NSM from 07. *13 The Street, Rockland St Mary, Norwich NR14 7ER* Tel (01508) 538550
E-mail geoffsaunders@waitrose.com

SAUNDERS, Graham Howard. b 53. Hatf Poly BSc77. Trin Coll Bris BA86. **d** 86 **p** 87. C Birm St Martin w Bordesley St Andr 86-89; C Olton 89-96; TV Bedminster *Bris* 96-02; P-in-c Farnham Royal w Hedgerley *Ox* 02-08; R from 08. *The Rectory, Victoria Road, Farnham Common, Slough SL2 3NJ* Tel (01753) 643233 Fax 644130

SAUNDERS, Ivor John. b 37. Wolv Poly CQSW81. **d** 04 **p** 05. OLM Wolverhampton St Jude *Lich* from 04. *34 Wrottesley Road, Wolverhampton WV6 8SF* Tel (01902) 751162
E-mail ivor.wendy@talktalk.net

SAUNDERS, James Benedict John. b 72. St Aid Coll Dur BA93 St Jo Coll Cam PhD97 St Jo Coll Dur BA00. Cranmer Hall Dur 98. **d** 01 **p** 02. C Sole Bay *St E* 01-04; P-in-c Teigh w Whissendine and Market Overton *Pet* 04-09; Asst Chapl HM Pris Ashwell 04-07; Chapl Uppingham Sch from 09. *48 High Street West, Uppingham, Oakham LE15 9QD* Tel (01572) 822144 Mobile 07952-498814 E-mail revjames@supanet.com

SAUNDERS, Mrs Joan Mary (Jo). b 44. Univ Coll Lon BA66 PGCE67. EAMTC 00. **d** 03 **p** 04. NSM Gt and Lt Casterton w Pickworth and Tickencote *Pet* 03-05; P-in-c from 09; P-in-c Castle Bytham w Creeton *Linc* 05-09. *Mellstock, Bourne Road, Essendine, Stamford PE9 4LH* Tel (01780) 480479
E-mail revjosaunders@aol.com

SAUNDERS, John Barry. b 40. Chich Th Coll. **d** 83 **p** 84. C St Breoke *Truro* 83-84; C St Breoke and Egloshayle 84-87; V Treverbyn 87-96; RD St Austell 91-96; V Perranzabuloe 96-03; rtd 03; Perm to Offic *Truro* from 04. *48 Cormorant Drive, St Austell PL25 3BA* Tel (01726) 71994

SAUNDERS, Canon John Michael. b 40. Brasted Th Coll 66 Clifton Th Coll 68. **d** 70 **p** 71. C Homerton St Luke *Lon* 70-74; SAMS Brazil 74-91; P-in-c Horsmonden *Roch* 91-97; Area Sec (SE England) SAMS 91-97; V Gillingham St Mark *Roch* 97-08; rtd 08; Hon C Newton Longville and Mursley w Swanbourne etc *Ox* from 08. *The Rectory, Drayton Road, Newton Longville, Milton Keynes MK17 0BH* Tel (01908) 647694
E-mail jandjsaunders@aol.com

SAUNDERS, Kenneth John. b 35. Linc Th Coll 73. **d** 75 **p** 76. C Boultham *Linc* 75-79; V Swinderby 79-87; V Cherry Willingham w Greetwell 87-95; P-in-c S Kelsey Gp 95-98; P-in-c N Kelsey 95-98; P-in-c Kelsey Gp 98-00; rtd 00; Perm to Offic *Linc* from 01. *Pew End, 17 Wentworth Drive, Dunholme, Lincoln LN2 3UH* Tel (01673) 862930

SAUNDERS, Malcolm Walter Mackenzie. b 34. Em Coll Cam BA58 MA62. Wycliffe Hall Ox 58. **d** 60 **p** 61. C Northampton St Giles *Pet* 60-63; C Northampton St Alb 63-66; V Corby St Columba 66-84; Nat Dir Evang Explosion 84-91; V Ketton *Pet* 91-92; R Ketton w Tinwell 92-01; rtd 01; Perm to Offic *Pet* from 01. *35 Main Street, Barrowden, Oakham LE15 8EQ* Tel (01572) 747036

SAUNDERS, Mrs Margaret Rose. b 49. Newnham Coll Cam BA71 St Jo Coll York PGCE72. St Alb Minl Tr Scheme 85. **d** 88 **p** 94. Hon Par Dn Gt Berkhamsted *St Alb* 88-90; Hon Chapl Asst Gt Ormond Street Hosp for Sick Children Lon 88-90; Asst Chapl Aylesbury Vale HA 90-92; Chapl Milton Keynes Gen NHS Trust 92-98; Chapl Milton Keynes Community NHS Trust 92-98; C Newport Pagnell w Lathbury and Moulsoe *Ox* 98-01; TV Grantham *Linc* 01-02; P-in-c Grantham, Manthorpe 02-04; Chapl United Lincs Hosps NHS Trust from 01. *2 Bruce Close, Lincoln LN2 1SL* Tel (01522) 523193 *or* 537403
E-mail margaret@saunderstd.fsnet.co.uk

SAUNDERS, Mark Richard. *See* VASEY-SAUNDERS, Mark Richard

SAUNDERS, Martin Paul. b 54. K Coll Lon BD76 AKC76 Univ of Northumbria at Newc DipSW96. Westcott Ho Cam 77. **d** 78 **p** 79. C Seaton Hirst *Newc* 78-81; Regional Chapl Hong Kong Miss to Seamen 81; C Egglescliffe *Dur* 81-82; Chapl to Arts and Recreation 81-84; C Jarrow 82-84; TV 84-88; V Southwick St Columba 88-94; Perm to Offic from 94. *55 The Meadows, Burnopfield, Newcastle upon Tyne NE16 6QW* Tel (01207) 271242 Mobile 07710-325197
E-mail martinsaunders@derwentheights.freeserve.co.uk

SAUNDERS, Martyn Leonard John. b 69. Magd Coll Cam MEng92. Wycliffe Hall Ox BA97. **d** 98 **p** 99. C Quinton Road W St Boniface *Birm* 98-02; TV Barnsbury *Lon* from 02. *5 Huntingdon Street, London N1 1BU* Tel (020) 7700 4097 *or* 7837 0720 E-mail martyn.saunders@london.anglican.org

SAUNDERS, Michael. b 38. Charing Cross Hosp Medical Sch MB, BS62 FRCPEd74 FRCP78 MSOSc84. NEOC 82. **d** 84 **p** 85. Lic to Offic *York* 84-92; Tutor NEOC 84-93; NSM Stokesley *York* 92-93; C Ripon Cathl 93-95; Perm to Offic *York* from 93; NSM Gt and Lt Ouseburn w Marton cum Grafton etc *Ripon* 95-02; NSM Masham and Healey from 02. *College Grove, 2 College Lane, Masham, Ripon HG4 4HE* Tel (01765) 688306 Mobile 07711-567160
E-mail michael.saunders@btinternet.com

SAUNDERS, Michael Walter. b 58. Grey Coll Dur BSc79 CChem MRSC84. Wycliffe Hall Ox 86. **d** 89 **p** 90. C Deane *Man* 89-93; TV Eccles 93-02; Chapl Eccles Sixth Form Coll 96-02; Dioc Adv on Evang *Man* 98-02; C Yateley and Eversley *Win* 02-06; P-in-c Darby Green 05-06; V Darby Green and Eversley from 06. *The Rectory, Glaston Hill Road, Eversley, Hook RG27 0LX* Tel 0118-973 6595
E-mail mikethevicar@thesaunders.plus.com

SAUNDERS, Moira Ruth Forbes. b 76. Birm Univ BA99. Ridley Hall Cam 02. **d** 04 **p** 05. C Welling *Roch* 04-08. *Address temp unknown*

SAUNDERS, Canon Reginald Frederick. b 15. St And NSM Tr Scheme 76. **d** 79 **p** 79. NSM Perth St Ninian *St And* from 79; NSM Stanley from 79; Hon Can St Ninian's Cathl Perth from 04. *31 Muirend Road, Perth PH1 1JU* Tel (01738) 626217

SAUNDERS, Canon Richard Charles Hebblethwaite. b 17. Qu Coll Ox BA40 MA42. Westcott Ho Cam 41. **d** 42 **p** 43. C Darnall *Sheff* 42-45; India 46-49; Asst Chapl HM Pris Ashwell 46-49; Asst Chapl HM Pris Wermwood-le-street w Thornton-le-Moor etc *York* 49-52; V Eastwood *Sheff* 52-62; V Bris St Ambrose Whitehall 62-75; P-in-c Easton All Hallows 65-68; TR E Bris 75-77; P-in-c Colerne 77-82; P-in-c N Wraxall 77-82;

RD Chippenham 80-82; Hon Can Bris Cathl 82; rtd 82; Hon C Honiton, Gittisham, Combe Raleigh, Monkton etc *Ex* from 85. *St Michael's Cottage, Gittisham, Honiton EX14 3AH* Tel (01404) 850634

SAUNDERS, Richard George. b 54. BNC Ox BA76 MA81. St Jo Coll Nottm 82. **d** 85 **p** 86. C Barrow St Mark *Carl* 85-89; C Cranham Park *Chelmsf* 89-97; TV Kinson *Sarum* 97-00; TR Kinson and W Howe from 00. *St Philip's Vicarage, 41 Moore Avenue, Kinson, Bournemouth BH11 8AT* Tel and fax (01202) 581135 *or* fax 581485 E-mail dick.saunders@ntlworld.com

SAUNDERS, Ronald. b 37. St Pet Coll Birm CertEd62 Memorial Univ Newfoundland CertEd80 Columbia Univ MA82 PhD87 ACP67. Sarum Th Coll 69. **d** 68 **p** 70. Lic to Offic Malawi 68-70; C Blantyre 71-72; C Kensington St Mary Abbots w St Geo *Lon* 72-73; C Bournemouth St Fran *Win* 73-75; I Twillingate Canada 76; Lic to Offic 77-81; C St Marlow *Ox* 81-82; Area Org Leprosy Miss 82-85; V Penycae *St As* 85-87; TV Wrexham 87-89; Lic to Offic *Ox* 90-91; Chapl Mowden Coll Blackheath 91-97; Master Wyggeston's Hosp Leic 97-03; P-in-c Nerja and Almuécar *Eur* 05-07. *Barrio San Isidro 92, 18830 Huescar (Granada), Spain* E-mail ron1937uk@hotmail.co.uk

SAUNDERS, Sheila Lilian. b 42. **d** 03 **p** 04. OLM Walworth St Pet *S'wark* 03-08; NSM Camberwell St Mich w All So w Em from 08. *9 Wooler Street, London SE17 2ED* Tel (020) 7252 5045 E-mail sheila.saunders3@btopenworld.com

SAUNDERS (née CORNWALL), Valerie Cecilia. b 40. Bedf Coll Lon BSc62 Lon Inst of Educn PGCE63. Scottish Chs Open Coll 96. **d** 03 **p** 04. NSM Dingwall *Mor* from 03; NSM Strathpeffer from 03. *Chessbury, 12 Firthview, Dingwall IV15 9PF* Tel (01349) 865445 Mobile 07747-066993 E-mail valeriestj@btopenworld.com

SAUNDERS, Ms Wendy Jennifer. b 49. S'wark Ord Course 86. **d** 95 **p** 96. Bp's Adv for Urban Min and Leadership *S'wark* 90-91; C Thamesmead 95-98; P-in-c Eltham St Sav from 98. *St Saviour's Vicarage, 98 Middle Park Avenue, London SE9 5JH* Tel (020) 8850 6829 Mobile 07802-603754 E-mail wendy.saunders@sunday.surfaid.org

SAUNT, James Peter Robert. b 56. Chich Th Coll 73. **d** 75 **p** 76. C Portland All SS w St Pet *Sarum* 75-78; P-in-c Bratton 78-81; V 81-94; Chapl HM Pris Erlestoke 80-94; P-in-c Oldbury *Sarum* 94-99; R 99-01; rtd 01; Perm to Offic *Sarum* from 02. *Elms, Waddon, Portesham, Weymouth DT3 4ER* Tel (01305) 871553

SAUSBY, John Michael. b 39. AKC. **d** 63 **p** 64. C Crosland Moor *Wakef* 63-65; C Halifax St Jo Bapt 65-67; V Birkby 67-77; V Holmfirth 77-89; TR Upper Holme Valley 89-01; rtd 01; Perm to Offic *Wakef* from 04. *15 River Holme View, Brockholes, Huddersfield HD9 7BP* Tel (01484) 667228

SAVAGE, Andrew Michael. b 67. Wye Coll Lon BSc89 Cranfield Inst of Tech MSc91. Wycliffe Hall Ox 93. **d** 96 **p** 97. C Ecclesall *Sheff* 96-99; TV Kirk Ella and Willerby *York* 99-06; Chapl Kingham Hill Sch from 06. *Kingham Hill School, Kingham, Chipping Norton OX7 6TH* Tel (01608) 658999

SAVAGE, Canon Christopher Marius. b 46. Hull Univ MA94 FRSA99. Bps' Coll Cheshunt 66 Qu Coll Birm 68. **d** 70 **p** 71. C Battersea St Luke *S'wark* 70-75; TV Newbury *Ox* 75-80; R Lich St Mary w St Mich 80-85; V Chessington *Guildf* 85-91; Ind Chapl *Win* 91-00; Chapl Basingstoke Coll of Tech 91-00; V Newc Ch Ch w St Ann 00-07; Team Ldr Chapl to People at Work in Cam *Ely* from 07. *31 Thornton Close, Girton, Cambridge CB3 0NF* Tel (01223) 279145 *or* 276657 Mobile 07788-741489 E-mail chris@csavage7.wanadoo.co.uk

SAVAGE, Graham John. b 47. Univ of Wales (Ban) BSc69 PhD78. CITC 89. **d** 92 **p** 94. Lic to Offic *D & D* from 92; NSM Down Cathl 94-97; NSM Lecale Gp from 97. *7 Cedar Grove, Ardglass, Downpatrick BT30 7UE* Tel (028) 4484 1501

SAVAGE, Helen. b 55. Birm Univ BA76 Dur Univ BA82 MA90 Newc Univ MLitt83. Cranmer Hall Dur 80. **d** 83 **p** 84. C Newc St Gabr 83-86; Adult Educn Adv 86-94; V Bedlington 94-04. *Address temp unknown*

SAVAGE, Mrs Hilary Linda. b 48. RGN71 RM86. WMMTC 89. **d** 92 **p** 94. C Quinton Road W St Boniface *Birm* 92-96; P-in-c Edgbaston SS Mary and Ambrose 96-01; V 01-02; TV Cramlington *Newc* from 02. *1 Cateran Way, Cramlington NE23 6EX* Tel (01670) 714271

SAVAGE, Mrs Jennifer Anne. b 52. CertEd73. NOC 96. **d** 99 **p** 00. C Haworth *Bradf* 99-02; R 02-09; P-in-c Cross Roads cum Lees 07-09; V Thornton in Lonsdale w Burton in Lonsdale from 09. *The Vicarage, Low Street, Burton in Lonsdale, Carnforth LA6 3LF* Tel (01524) 261579 E-mail jenny.savage@bradford.anglican.org *or* revdjenny@aol.com

SAVAGE, John. b 48. Bris Univ BEd76. SWMTC 94. **d** 97 **p** 98. C Falmouth K Chas *Truro* 97-00; P-in-c Mabe from 00; Chapl Miss to Seafarers 00-07. *1 Willow Close, Mylor Bridge, Falmouth TR11 5SG* Tel (01326) 259739

SAVAGE, Jonathan Mark. b 57. Kingston Poly BSc79 MSc89 Roehampton Inst PGCE80. Ridley Hall Cam 94. **d** 96 **p** 97. C Ely 96-99; TV Huntingdon 99-07; C Gt w Lt Stukeley 04-07; TV Huntingdon w the Stukeleys from 07. *The Vicarage, 3A*

Longstaff Way, Hartford, Huntingdon PE28 7XT Tel (01480) 434463 E-mail marksavage@onetel.com

SAVAGE, Michael Atkinson. b 33. St Pet Hall Ox BA57 MA61. Tyndale Hall Bris 57. **d** 59 **p** 60. C Rugby St Matt *Cov* 59-62; C Welling *Roch* 62-66; V Bowling St Steph *Bradf* 66-73; V Ben Rhydding 73-92; RD Otley 87-92; TR Quidenham *Nor* 92-97; R Quidenham Gp 97-99; rtd 99; Perm to Offic *Bradf* from 00. *42 Hollins Lane, Utley, Keighley BD20 6LT* Tel (01535) 606790

SAVAGE, Paul James. b 58. Liv Univ BA81. Wycliffe Hall Ox 88. **d** 91 **p** 92. C Litherland St Phil *Liv* 91-94; CMS from 94. *CMS, PO Box 1799, Oxford OX4 9BN* Tel 08456-201799

SAVEGE, Timothy. b 38. **d** 00 **p** 01. OLM Blyth Valley *St E* 00-05; OLM Bury St Edmunds St Mary from 05. *2 Chequer Square, Bury St Edmunds IP33 1QZ* E-mail tim.savege@btinternet.com

SAVIGEAR, Miss Elfrida Beatrice. b 49. Wye Coll Lon BSc71 Bath Univ MSc85 Lambeth STh94. Ridley Hall Cam 91. **d** 93 **p** 94. C Ross w Brampton Abbotts, Bridstow, Peterstow etc *Heref* 93-97; P-in-c Butlers Marston and the Pillertons w Ettington *Cov* 97-99; P-in-c Alderminster and Halford 97-99; P-in-c Bicknoller w Crowcombe and Sampford Brett *B & W* 99-00; P-in-c Stogumber w Nettlecombe and Monksilver 99-00; R Quantock Towers 00-08; C Darlington H Trin *Dur* from 08. *76 Merrybent, Darlington DL2 2LE*

SAVILE, Canon Ian Keith Wrey. b 26. Trin Hall Cam BA50 MA54. Ridley Hall Cam 51. **d** 53 **p** 54. C Bootle St Matt *Liv* 53-56; C Birkdale St Jo 56-57; V Barrow St Mark *Carl* 57-64; V Wandsworth All SS *S'wark* 64-74; RD Wandsworth 69-74; V S'well H Trin 74-80; Bp's Adv on Evang 74-80; V Canford Magna *Sarum* 80-88; TR 88; RD Wimborne 85-88; Can and Preb Sarum Cathl 86-88; Patr Sec CPAS 88-93; rtd 93; Perm to Offic *Cov* 88-93 and *Sarum* from 93. *23A Avenue Road, Wimborne BH21 1BS* Tel (01202) 880210

SAVILL, David. b 27. TD69 and Bar 75. Em Coll Cam BA49 MA52. Ridley Hall Cam 50. **d** 52 **p** 53. Chapl St E Cathl 52-54; C St Martin-in-the-Fields *Lon* 54-57; V Sunbury 57-67; V Heston 67-73; Hon C Mettingham w Ilketshall St John *St E* 73-79; Hon C Mettingham 79-80; Chapl Felixstowe Coll 80-90; rtd 90; Perm to Offic *B & W* from 90. *30 Victoria Court, 2 Victoria Avenue, Chard TA20 1GA* Tel (01460) 239835

SAVILLE, Andrew. b 66. Worc Coll Ox BA92 MA92 Cov Univ PhD00. Wycliffe Hall Ox. **d** 95 **p** 96. C Tonbridge SS Pet and Paul *Roch* 95-99; NSM Bromley Ch Ch 99-03; Dir Bromley Chr Tr Cen 99-03; C Fordham *Chelmsf* from 03. *The Rectory, Wood Lane, Fordham Heath, Colchester CO3 9TR* Tel (01206) 242112 E-mail andy@savilles.org.uk

SAVILLE, Preb David James. b 39. Ch Ch Ox BA60 MA64. Clifton Th Coll 61. **d** 63 **p** 64. C Darfield *Sheff* 63-66; C St Leonards St Leon *Chich* 66-68; Cand Sec CPAS 69-74; Hon C Bromley Ch Ch *Roch* 69-74; V Taunton St Jas *B & W* 74-80; RD Taunton N 78-80; V Chorleywood Ch Ch *St Alb* 80-90; RD Rickmansworth 86-90; Adv for Evang Edmonton *Lon* 91-96; Dioc Adv for Evang 96-01; TR Hackney Marsh 01-07; Preb St Paul's Cathl 97-07; rtd 07; Perm to Offic *Ox* from 08. *22 Latimer Road, Headington, Oxford OX3 7PF* Tel (01865) 766431 E-mail david.j.saville@tesco.net

SAVILLE, Edward Andrew. b 47. Leeds Univ CertEd70 Open Univ BA75. Carl Dioc Tr Inst. **d** 90 **p** 91. C Accrington St Jo w Huncoat *Blackb* 90-93; C Standish 93-95; V Brierfield 95-09; P-in-c from 09; AD Pendle 98-05; Lead Officer Dioc Bd for Soc Resp from 09. *The Vicarage, 5 Reedley Farm Close, Reedley, Burnley BB10 2RB* Tel and fax (01282) 613235 E-mail e.saville@btinternet.com

SAVILLE (née McCULLAGH), Mrs Elspeth Jane Alexandra. b 68. Man Univ BSc90. Wycliffe Hall Ox BTh95. **d** 95 **p** 96. C Huddersfield H Trin *Wakef* 95-98; NSM Tonbridge SS Pet and Paul *Roch* 98-99; NSM Bromley Ch Ch 99-03; NSM Fordham *Chelmsf* 03-07. *The Rectory, Wood Lane, Fordham Heath, Colchester CO3 9TR* Tel (01206) 242112

SAVILLE, Canon Jeremy David. b 35. Oriel Coll Ox BA59 MA62. Chich Th Coll 58. **d** 60 **p** 61. C Tynemouth Cullercoats St Paul *Newc* 60-63; C Hexham 63-65; Lic to Offic *Ox* 65-68; Chapl Cuddesdon Coll 65-68; R Holt *Nor* 68-73; P-in-c Kelling w Salthouse 68-71; R Edgefield 71-73; R Hoe 73-78; R E Dereham w Hoe 73-80; V E Dereham 80-81; R Scarning w Wendling 78-81; R Beckenham St Geo *Roch* 81-89; Hon Can Roch Cathl 86-89; R Ashdon w Hadstock *Chelmsf* 89-01; RD Saffron Walden 97-01; Hon Can Chelmsf Cathl 00-01; rtd 01; Perm to Offic *Nor* from 01. *8B Hillside, Sheringham NR26 8DB* Tel (01263) 820164

SAVILLE, Mrs Margaret. b 46. SW Minl Tr Course 93. **d** 94 **p** 95. C Over St Chad *Ches* 94-98; V Crewe All SS and St Paul 98-05; P-in-c Helsby and Dunham-on-the-Hill from 05. *St Paul's Vicarage, Vicarage Lane, Helsby, Frodsham WA6 9AB* Tel (01928) 722151 E-mail thesavilles@tiscali.co.uk

SAWARD, Canon Michael John. b 32. Bris Univ BA55. Tyndale Hall Bris. **d** 56 **p** 57. C Croydon Ch Ch Broad Green *Cant* 56-59; C Edgware *Lon* 59-64; Sec Liv Coun of Chs 64-67; Radio and TV Officer CIO 67-72; Hon C Beckenham St Jo *Roch* 70-72; V Fulham St Matt *Lon* 72-78; V Ealing St Mary 78-91; AD Ealing

E 79-84; P-in-c Ealing St Paul 86-89; Preb St Paul's Cathl 85-91; Can Res and Treas St Paul's Cathl 91-00; rtd 01; Perm to Offic *Lon* from 02. *6 Discovery Walk, London E1W 2JG* Tel (020) 7702 1130 E-mail michaelsaward@googlemail.com

SAWLE, Martin. b 49. Solicitor 74 Dundee Univ LLB70. NOC 87. **d** 90 **p** 91. NSM Longton *Blackb* 90-92; P-in-c Hoghton 92-04; Perm to Offic from 04. *38 Chepstow Gardens, Garstang, Preston PR3 1TJ* E-mail martin@sawleandco.com

SAWLE, Ralph Burford. b 14. Lich Th Coll 34. **d** 37 **p** 38. C Sawley *Derby* 37-40; C Walthamstow St Barn *Chelmsf* 40-43; P-in-c Hanley All SS *Lich* 43-46; V Hanford 46-52; V Malins Lee 52-57; V Ocker Hill 57-61; V Werrington *Truro* 61-72; RD Trigg Major 66-72; V St Giles on the Heath w Virginstow 68-72; V St Neot 72-79; rtd 79; Perm to Offic *Win* 79-08. *Peninney House, Lewannick, Launceston PL15 7QD*

SAWYER, Andrew William. b 49. AKC71 St Aug Coll Cant 71. **d** 72 **p** 73. C Farnham *Guildf* 72-75; C Dawlish *Ex* 75-78; R Colkirk w Oxwick, Whissonsett and Horningtoft *Nor* 78-82; R Colkirk w Oxwick w Pattesley, Whissonsett etc 82-90; V Hungerford and Denford *Ox* from 90. *The Vicarage, Parsonage Lane, Hungerford RG17 0JB* Tel (01488) 682844

SAWYER, Derek Claude. b 33. ALCD58. **d** 58 **p** 59. C Kirby Muxloe *Leic* 58-60; C Braunstone 60-65; R Vacoas St Paul Mauritius 65-68; V Knighton St Mich *Leic* 68-82; Chapl Kifissia *Eur* 82; Lic to Offic *Glouc* 85-87; V Glouc St Aldate 87-01; rtd 01; R Capisterre w Dieppe St Kitts 01-08; Lic to Offic from 09. *Old School House, Church Ghaut, St Paul's Village, PO Box 4031, Sandy Point, St Kitts and Nevis, WI* Tel (001) (869) 465 3711 Mobile 669 5697 E-mail derekcsawyer@gmail.com

SAX, Ms Katharine Margaret. b 50. Ripon Coll Cuddesdon. **d** 03 **p** 06. NSM Pokesdown All SS and Southbourne St Chris *Win* 04-05; C Swaythling 06-09; Ecum Officer (Wilts Area) *Sarum* from 09. *2A Little Court Lane, Edington, Westbury BA13 4PW* Tel (01380) 831239 E-mail kate@kinkiizi.fsnet.co.uk

✠**SAXBEE, The Rt Revd John Charles.** b 46. Bris Univ BA68 St Jo Coll Dur PhD74. Cranmer Hall Dur 68. **d** 72 **p** 73 **c** 94. C Compton Gifford *Ex* 72-77; P-in-c Weston Mill 77-80; V 80-81; TV Cen Ex 81-87; Jt Dir SW Minl Tr Course 81-92; Preb Ex Cathl 88-92; Adn Ludlow *Heref* 92-01; Preb Heref Cathl 92-01; P-in-c Wistanstow 92-94; P-in-c Acton Scott 92-94; Suff Bp Ludlow 94-01; Bp Linc from 01. *The Bishop's House, 13 Eastgate, Lincoln LN2 1QQ* Tel (01522) 534701 Fax 511095 E-mail bishop.lincoln@lincoln.anglican.org

SAXBY, Martin Peter. b 52. St Jo Coll Dur BA77. Cranmer Hall Dur 74. **d** 78 **p** 79. C Peckham St Mary Magd *S'wark* 78-81; C Ramsey *Ely* 81-84; P-in-c Mattishall w Mattishall Burgh *Nor* 84-89; P-in-c Welborne 84-89; P-in-c Yaxham 84-89; R Mattishall w Mattishall Burgh, Welborne etc 89-90; V Rugby St Matt *Cov* 90-07; V Rugby W from 08; RD Rugby from 06. *St Matthew's Vicarage, 7 Vicarage Road, Rugby CV22 7AJ* Tel (01788) 330442 *or* 330447 Fax 08701-391160 E-mail martinpa@stmatthews.org.uk

SAXBY, Steven Michael Paul. b 70. Fitzw Coll Cam BA98 MA02 Univ Coll Lon MA08. Aston Tr Scheme 92 Linc Th Coll 94 Westcott Ho Cam 95. **d** 98 **p** 01. C E Ham w Upton Park St Alb *Chelmsf* 98-00; C Barking St Marg w St Patr 00-02; Waltham Forest Deanery Development Worker 02-07; NSM Walthamstow 02-03; V Walthamstow St Pet 03-09; P-in-c Walthamstow St Barn and St Jas Gt from 09; RD Waltham Forest from 07. *St Barnabas' Vicarage, St Barnabas Road, London E17 8JZ* Tel (020) 8520 5323 E-mail stevensaxby@btinternet.com

SAXTON, James. b 54. Lanc Univ BEd77 Hull Univ MEd85. Linc Th Coll 84. **d** 86 **p** 87. C Moor Allerton *Ripon* 86-90; C Knaresborough 90-92; TV Seacroft 92-95; V Ireland Wood 95-00; TV Becontree S *Chelmsf* 02-09; C Camberwell St Geo *S'wark* from 09; Chapl S Lon and Maudsley NHS Foundn Trust from 09. *131 Coleman Road, London SE5 7TF* Tel (020) 7703 2704 E-mail james.saxton@talktalk.net

SAYER, Derek John. b 32. St Steph Ho Ox 55. **d** 58 **p** 58. C Tottenham All Hallows *Lon* 58-61; C Letchworth *St Alb* 61-63; Chapl RADD 63-64 and 66-82; C Leatherhead *Guildf* 64-66; C Leatherhead St Mich *Chich* 64-66; C Dorking w Ranmore *Guildf* 89-92; V Holmwood 92-95; Perm to Offic 95-04; rtd 97. *Richeldis, 24 Chalkpit Lane, Dorking RH4 1ER* Tel (01306) 882610

SAYER, Penelope Jane. b 59. Newc Univ BA80 Open Univ BA93. SEITE 04. **d** 07 **p** 08. NSM Upper St Leonards St Jo *Chich* from 07. *39 Brittany Road, St Leonards-on-Sea TN38 0RD* Tel (01424) 461776 *or* 774409 E-mail penny.st.john@btinternet.com *or* pennysayer@fsmail.net

SAYER, Canon William Anthony John. b 37. St Mich Coll Llan 60. **d** 64 **p** 65. C Gorleston St Andr *Nor* 64-67; P-in-c Witton w Ridlington 67-71; P-in-c Honing w Crostwight 67-71; V Bacton w Edingthorpe 67-71; CF 71-84; Miss to Seafarers from 84; V Holkham w Egmere w Warham, Wells and Wighton *Nor* 84-02; RD Burnham and Walsingham 87-92; Hon Can Nor Cathl 97-02; rtd 02; Perm to Offic *Nor* from 02. *Greenway Lodge, Mill Road, Wells-next-the-Sea NR23 1RF* Tel (01328) 711224

SAYERS, Karen Jane. See GARDINER, Mrs Karen Jane

SAYERS, Simon Philip. b 59. Cam Univ MA81. Oak Hill Th Coll 83. **d** 85 **p** 86. C Alperton *Lon* 85-89; C Hornsey Rise Whitehall Park Team 89-90; TV 90-96; Min Panshanger CD *St Alb* 96-02; R Warblington w Emsworth *Portsm* from 02. *The Rectory, 20 Church Path, Emsworth PO10 7DP* Tel (01243) 372428 E-mail simonsayers@hotmail.com

SAYERS, Susan. b 46. Bp Otter Coll Chich BEd69 Middx Univ BA02. NTMTC 99. **d** 02 **p** 03. NSM Southend *Chelmsf* from 02; TV from 05; Asst Chapl HM Pris Bullwood Hall 02-06. *17 Claremont Close, Westcliff-on-Sea SS0 7UA* Tel (010702) 431843 Mobile 07765-857320 E-mail susansayers@yahoo.com

SAYLE, Philip David. b 61. Nottm Univ BA98. St Jo Coll Nottm 92. **d** 94 **p** 95. C Helston and Wendron *Truro* 94-97; R St Stephen in Brannel 97-00; R Kenwyn w St Allen 00-06; V Upton Ascension *Ches* from 06. *49 Heath Road, Upton, Chester CH2 1HT* Tel (01244) 381181 E-mail pdsayle@btinternet.com

SAYWELL, Philip. b 33. Linc Th Coll 57. **d** 60 **p** 61. C Stepney St Dunstan and All SS *Lon* 60-63; C Calstock *Truro* 63-66; V Lanteglos by Fowey 66-73; Iran 73-77; R Cockley Cley w Gooderstone *Nor* 78-81; V Didlington 78-81; R Gt and Lt Cressingham w Threxton 78-81; R Hilborough w Bodney 78-81; R Oxborough w Foulden and Caldecote 78-81; UAE 81-84; Perm to Offic *Chich* 84-88; Nat Co-ord (UK) SOMA UK 85-88; rtd 93. *Riverside, Exford, Minehead TA24 7PX* Tel (01643) 831619 Fax 831416 E-mail philip.saywell@virgin.net

SCAIFE, Andrew. b 50. Ex Coll Ox BA73 MA76. Wycliffe Hall Ox 74. **d** 77 **p** 78. C Everton St Geo *Liv* 77-81; P-in-c Liv St Mich 81; TV St Luke in the City 81-86; V Litherland St Phil 86-96; Sen Chapl Cheshire and Wirral Partnerships NHS Trust from 96. *Arrowe Park Hospital, Upton, Wirral CH49 5PE* Tel 0151-678 5111 ext 2275 *or* 632 0646 E-mail andrew.scaife@whnt.nhs.uk

SCALES, Barbara Marion. b 24. S'wark Ord Course. dss 82 **d** 87 **p** 94. St Helier *S'wark* 82-87; Hon Par Dn 87-89; Chapl Asst St Helier Hosp Carshalton 82-88; NSM Cheam Common St Phil *S'wark* 89-95; rtd 95; Perm to Offic *S'wark* 95-04. *51 Tonfield Road, Sutton SM3 9JP* Tel (020) 8644 3712

SCAMMAN (née BEWES), Mrs Helen Catherine. b 71. Leeds Univ BA94 York Univ PGCE95 Cam Univ BA01. Ridley Hall Cam 99. **d** 02 **p** 03. C Win Ch Ch 02-06; NSM 06-07; Perm to Offic *Ely* from 07. *80 St Barnabas Road, Cambridge CB1 2DE* Tel (01223) 367578 E-mail scampersons@yahoo.com

SCAMMAN, Jonathan Leitch. b 73. St Andr Univ MA96 Ex Coll Ox MPhil98 Cam Univ BA01. Ridley Hall Cam 99. **d** 02 **p** 03. C Win Ch Ch 02-07; C Cambridge St Barn *Ely* from 07. *80 St Barnabas Road, Cambridge CB1 2DE* Tel (01223) 367578 E-mail scampersons@yahoo.com *or* jon.scamman@stbs.org.uk

SCAMMELL, Frank. b 56. Cam Univ MA. St Jo Coll Nottm BA83. **d** 82 **p** 83. C Stapenhill w Cauldwell *Derby* 82-86; TV Swanage and Studland *Sarum* 86-92; Min Southgate LEP *St E* 92-03; V Stoughton *Guildf* from 03. *Stoughton Vicarage, 3 Shepherds Lane, Guildford GU2 9SJ* Tel (01483) 561603

SCANLAN, Helen Tracy. b 66. Dioc OLM tr scheme 06. **d** 09. NSM Heaton Reddish *Man* from 09. *36 Cordova Avenue, Denton, Manchester M34 2WP* Tel 0161-223 1397 E-mail helen.scanlan@btinternet.com

SCANLON, Geoffrey Edward Leyshon. b 44. Coll of Resurr Mirfield. **d** 76 **p** 77. C Beamish *Dur* 76-79; C-in-c Bishopwearmouth St Mary V w St Pet CD 79-81; V Laurens Epiphany USA 81-85; V Columbia St Dav 85-87; R Danville H Trin from 87. *PO Box 1922, Danville IL 61832-1922, USA* Tel (001) (217) 442 3498 E-mail gelsus@insightbb.com

SCANTLEBURY, James Stanley. b 48. St Jo Coll Dur BA69 Heythrop Coll Lon MTh80. Westcott Ho Cam 70. **d** 72 **p** 73. C Upperby St Jo *Carl* 72-75; C Guildf H Trin w St Mary 75-77; Order of St Aug 77-86; Chapl Austin Friars Sch Carl 80-86; Chapl Mayfield Coll E Sussex 86-88; Chapl H Trin Sen Sch Halifax 88-90; NSM Ripponden *Wakef* 88-90; V Torpenhow *Carl* 91-94; V Allhallows 91-94; V Falmouth All SS *Truro* 94-98; V Harden and Wilsden *Bradf* 98-02; rtd 03. *5 Westhill Avenue, Cullingworth, Bradford BD13 5BB* Tel (01535) 272980

SCARBOROUGH, John Richard Derek. b 32. Lon Univ BA54. Cuddesdon Coll. **d** 69 **p** 70. C Fulbeck *Linc* 69-72; C Bassingham 73-74; Lic to Offic 74-76 and 78-93; R Boothby Graffoe 76-77; R Navenby 76-77; V Wellingore w Temple Bruer 76-77; V Graffoe 77-78; NSM Bassingham 93-97; NSM Aubourn w Haddington 93-97; NSM Carlton-le-Moorland w Stapleford 93-97; NSM Thurlby w Norton Disney 93-97; Perm to Offic from 97. *Hales Cottage, 47 High Street, Navenby, Lincoln LN5 0DZ* Tel (01522) 811031

SCARGILL, Christopher Morris. b 57. UEA BA79 York Univ MA81 Leeds Univ CertEd81 Nottm Univ BTh89. Linc Th Coll 86. **d** 89 **p** 90. C Desborough *Pet* 89-92; C Buxton w Burbage and King Sterndale *Derby* 92-93; TV 93-98; V Ipstones w Berkhamsytch and Onecote w Bradnop *Lich* 98-09; RD Alstonfield 08-09; Sen Chapl Torrevieja *Eur* from 09. *Apartado 3257, 03180 Torrevieja Suc 1 (Alicante), Spain* Tel and fax (0034) 966 925 205 E-mail revdcms@gmail.com

SCARISBRICK, Mrs Helen. b 60. Sheff Univ BA81 Sheff Poly PGCE82 Ches Coll of HE BTh99. NOC 97. **d** 99 **p** 00. C

Norbury *Ches* 99-03; P-in-c Cheadle Heath 03-07; C Edgeley and Cheadle Heath 07-09; V Broadheath from 09. *The Vicarage, Lindsell Road, West Timperley, Altrincham WA14 5NX* Tel 0161-928 4820 E-mail helenscarisbrick@btinternet.com

SCARR, Mrs Hazel Anne. b 44. SAOMC. **d** 00 **p** 01. NSM Adderbury w Milton *Ox* 00-04; NSM Chadlington and Spelsbury, Ascott under Wychwood 04-05; NSM Hardington Vale *B & W* 05-07; Perm to Offic *Ox* from 07. *Wooden Hill Farm, Barford Road, Bloxham, Banbury OX15 4LP* Tel (01295) 72022 E-mail hazel@jandhscarr.sagehost.co.uk

SCARTH, John Robert. b 34. Leeds Univ BSc55 CertEd. Cranmer Hall Dur 63. **d** 65 **p** 66. C Dewsbury All SS *Wakef* 65-68; V Shepley 68-72; Asst Master Kingston-upon-Hull Gr Sch 72-78; St Mary's C of E Sch Hendon 78-81; V Ossett cum Gawthorpe 81-88; R Tarrington w Stoke Edith, Aylton, Pixley etc *Heref* 88-96; rtd 96; Perm to Offic *Wakef* 96-97 and from 98. *44 Gagewell Drive, Horbury, Wakefield WF4 6BS* Tel (01924) 272055

SCARTH, Maurice John. b 31. MInstPS AMBIM. St Deiniol's Hawarden 81. **d** 83 **p** 84. C Llandrillo-yn-Rhos *St As* 83-87; V Rhosymedre 87-91; V Kerry and Llanmerewig and Dolfor 91-93; rtd 93. *Homelands, 11A Compton Way, Abergele LL22 7BL* Tel (01745) 833783

SCATTERGOOD, William Henry. b 26. **d** 56 **p** 57. C Gilgandra Australia 56-57; C Bourke 57-60; P-in-c Cobar 61-64; V Miriam Vale 64-67; R Balranald 67-74; R Hillston 74-76; 76-84; V Lonan and Laxey *S & M* 84-92; rtd 92; Perm to Offic *Chich* from 92. *18 Coldstream House, Bramber Lane, Seaford BN25 1AF* Tel (01323) 492203

SCEATS, Preb David Douglas. b 46. Ch Coll Cam BA68 MA72 Bris Univ MA71. Clifton Th Coll 68. **d** 71 **p** 72. C Cambridge St Paul *Ely* 71-74; Lect Trin Coll Bris 74-83; V Shenstone *Lich* 83-86; Dioc Tr Officer 86-91; P-in-c Colton 86-90; Dir Local Min Development 91-98; Warden of Readers 91-96; C Lich St Chad 94-98; Dioc Board of Min Team 94-98; Preb Lich Cathl 96-98; Prin NTMTC 99-07; Preb St Paul's Cathl 02-07; P-in-c Selkirk *Edin* from 07. *St John's Rectory, Viewfield Park, Selkirk TD7 4LH* Tel (01750) 21364 E-mail d-sceats@sky.com

SCHAEFER, Carl Richard. b 67. Coll of Resurr Mirfield 91. **d** 94 **p** 95. C Ribbleton *Blackb* 94-98; V Blackb St Thos w St Jude 98-08; P-in-c Blackb St Mich w St Jo and H Trin 03-08; V Goldthorpe w Hickleton *Sheff* from 08. *Goldthorpe Presbytery, Lockwood Road, Goldthorpe, Rotherham S63 9JY* Tel (01709) 898426 E-mail carl@schaeferc.freeserve.co.uk

SCHARF, Brian Howard. b 39. Alberta Univ BA60. Trin Coll Toronto 60 Coll of Resurr Mirfield 61. **d** 63 **p** 65. C Vancouver St Faith Canada 63-65; C Broadstairs *Cant* 65-68. *3236 Robinson Road, North Vancouver BC V7J 3E9, Canada* Tel (001) (604) 987 0219 E-mail brianscharf@shaw.ca

SCHARF, Ulrich Eduard Erich Julian. b 35. Melbourne Univ BA59 MA67 Linacre Coll Ox BA67 MA72 Lon Univ PhD81. Ripon Hall Ox 65. **d** 67 **p** 68. C Hackney St Jo *Lon* 68-71; Chapl to Bp Stepney 71-75; P-in-c Shadwell St Paul w Ratcliffe St Jas 75-90; R St Geo-in-the-East w St Paul 79-86; P-in-c W Ham *Chelmsf* 90-95; V 95-05; rtd 05; Perm to Offic *Chelmsf* from 06. *8 Horace Road, London E7 0JG* Tel (020) 8534 2141

SCHARIAH, Canon Zechariah. b 43. Zürich Univ BD87. Baptist Th Sem Rueschlikon 83. **d** 93 **p** 93. Chapl to Miss to Minorities from 93; Perm to Offic *Eur* from 95; Can Dar es Salaam from 00. *Schaubhus 7, 6020 Emmenbrücke, Switzerland* E-mail karibumade@hotmail.com

SCHATZ, Stefani. b 62. Mills Coll Oakland (USA) BA84. Episc Div Sch Cam Mass MDiv01. **d** 01 **p** 02. C Hermosa Beach USA 01-04; C Brookline All SS 04-06; Perm to Offic *Man* 06-07; TV Gorton and Abbey Hey 07-08; USA from 08. *Address temp unknown* E-mail sbcamb2001@aol.com

SCHEMANOFF, Ms Natasha Anne. b 50. CertEd71. **d** 96 **p** 97. C Freshford, Limpley Stoke and Hinton Charterhouse *B & W* 96-99; TV Worle 99-00; V Kewstoke w Wick St Lawrence 00-07; Bp's Adv for Racial Justice 00-07; rtd 07; Perm to Offic *Truro* from 97. *4 The Terrace, Lostwithiel PL22 0DT* Tel (01208) 871330

SCHIBILD, Nigel Edmund David. b 47. Oak Hill Th Coll BA81. **d** 81 **p** 82. C Eccleston Ch Ch *Liv* 81-85; P-in-c Sydenham H Trin *S'wark* 85-87; V 87-91; Chapl Mildmay Miss Hosp 91-98; Assoc V Beirut All SS Lebanon 99-04; C Westminster St Jas the Less *Lon* 05-07; Chapl John Taylor Hospice Birm from 07. *John Taylor Hospice, 76 Grange Road, Erdington, Birmingham B24 0DF* Tel 0121-465 2000 E-mail nigel.schibild@benpct.nhs.uk

SCHILD, John. b 38. ALCD64. **d** 64 **p** 65. C Cheltenham Ch Ch *Glouc* 64-67; Area Sec CMS *Sheff* and *S'well* 67-73; Area Sec CMS *Chelmsf* and *St Alb* 73-76; V Lt Heath *St Alb* 76-88; R Bedford St Pet w St Cuth 88-94; P-in-c King's Walden and Offley w Lilley 94-98; V 98-03; rtd 03. *Trenarren, St Cleer, Liskeard PL14 5DN* Tel (01579) 347047 E-mail john@schild.demon.co.uk

SCHLEGER, Ms Maria Francesca. b 57. LSE BA78 SS Coll Cam BA84 MA89. Westcott Ho Cam 82. **dss** 85 **d** 87 **p** 94. De Beauvoir Town St Pet *Lon* 85-90; Par Dn 87-90; TD Bow H Trin and All Hallows 90-94; Dean of Women's Min (Stepney Area) 90-94; Perm to Offic *Birm* 94-98; NSM Stepney St Dunstan and All SS *Lon* 99-03; Chapl Mildmay Miss Hosp from 03. *75 Lansdowne Drive, London E8 3EP* Tel (020) 7683 0051 *or* 7613 6300 ext 6170 E-mail schleger@waitrose.com *or* chaplain@mildmay.org

SCHLUTER, Nathaniel David. b 71. Pemb Coll Ox BA93 MA97 Green Coll Ox DPhil98. Wycliffe Hall Ox BA. **d** 00 **p** 01. C Gerrards Cross and Fulmer *Ox* 00-05; Prin Johannesburg Bible Coll S Africa from 05. *PO Box 374, Auckland Park, 2006 South Africa* E-mail info@johannesburgbiblecollege.org

SCHMIDT, Mrs Karen Rosemarie. b 48. Surrey Univ BSc70 Solicitor 76. STETS 96. **d** 99 **p** 00. NSM Lee-on-the-Solent *Portsm* 99-05; P-in-c Purbrook 05-06; V 06-09; rtd 09; Bp's Dom Chapl *Portsm* from 09. *43 Deal Close, Fareham PO14 2LZ* Tel (023) 9223 0143 Mobile 07990-518541 E-mail karenrschmidt@yahoo.co.uk

SCHNAAR, Howard William. b 71. Wilson Carlile Coll 95. **d** 08. C Worthing H Trin w Ch Ch *Chich* from 08. *5 Christchurch Road, Worthing BN11 1JH* Tel (01903) 202433

SCHOFIELD, Andrew Thomas. b 47. K Coll Lon BD70 AKC71 PGCE72. St Aug Coll Cant 70. **d** 81 **p** 82. C Whittlesey *Ely* 81-84; C Ramsey 84-87; P-in-c Ellington, Grafham, Easton and Spaldwick w Barham and Woolley 87-94; R March St Jo 94-05; P-in-c Duxford 05-09; P-in-c Hinxton 05-09; P-in-c Ickleton 05-09; rtd 09; P-in-c Beetham *Carl* from 09. *The Parsonage, Stanley Street, Beetham, Milnthorpe LA7 7AS* Tel (01539) 562216 E-mail atschofield@msn.com

SCHOFIELD, David. b 43. Linc Th Coll 74. **d** 75 **p** 76. C Gainsborough All SS *Linc* 75-78; R Bolingbroke w Hareby 78-79; P-in-c Hagnaby 78-79; P-in-c Hagworthingham w Asgarby and Lusby 78-79; P-in-c Mavis Enderby w Raithby 78-79; P-in-c E Kirkby w Miningsby 78-79; R Bolingbroke 79-81; C-in-c Stamford Ch Ch CD 81-90; V Crowle 90-97; V Crowle Gp 97-07; rtd 07. *19 Station Road, Hadfield, Glossop SK13 1BQ* Tel (01457) 857885 E-mail david@schofield1.freeserve.co.uk

SCHOFIELD, David Leslie. b 40. MISM89. EMMTC 98. **d** 01 **p** 02. NSM Derby St Mark 01-04; P-in-c Dukinfield St Luke *Ches* from 07. *72 Bromley Cross Road, Bromley Cross, Bolton BL7 9LT* Tel (01204) 303137

SCHOFIELD, Edward Denis. b 20. **d** 61 **p** 62. C Addiscombe St Mildred *Cant* 61-63; P-in-c Croydon St Jas 63-64; V 64-66; V Boughton under Blean 66-75; P-in-c Dunkirk 73-75; V Boughton under Blean w Dunkirk 75-76; V Sandgate St Paul 76-85; rtd 85; Perm to Offic *Ex* from 95. *c/o C H Schofield Esq, Copperbeech House, Tipton St John, Sidmouth EX10 0AL* Tel (01404) 814858

SCHOFIELD, Gary. b 64. Ripon Coll Cuddesdon 97. **d** 99 **p** 00. C Exhall *Cov* 99-02; V Wales *Sheff* from 02; P-in-c Harthill and Thorpe Salvin from 08. *The Vicarage, Manor Road, Wales, Sheffield S26 5PD* Tel (01909) 771111 E-mail g5rev@tiscali.co.uk

SCHOFIELD, John Martin. b 47. Selw Coll Cam BA69 MA73. St Steph Ho Ox 70. **d** 72 **p** 73. C Palmers Green St Jo *Lon* 72-75; C Friern Barnet St Jas 75-80; V Luton St Aug Limbury *St Alb* 80-89; V Biddenham 89-94; Dir CME 89-94; Dir Minl Tr *Guildf* 94-99; Can Res Guildf Cathl 95-99; Perm to Offic from 03; Dir Local Min Progr from 05. *1 Addley House, 72-78 Molesey Road, Walton-on-Thames KT12 4RG* Tel (01932) 227642 E-mail john.schofield@cofeguildford.org.uk

SCHOFIELD, John Verity. b 29. Jes Coll Ox BA52 MA56. Cuddesdon Coll 53. **d** 55 **p** 56. C Cirencester *Glouc* 55-59; R Stella *Dur* 59-67; Kenya 67-69; Asst Chapl St Paul's Sch Barnes 69-70; Chapl 71-80; Australia 81-83; Gen Sec Friends of Elderly & Gentlefolk's Help 83-94; Perm to Offic *Sarum* from 83; rtd 94. *Bishops Barn, Foots Hill, Cann, Shaftesbury SP7 0BW* Tel (01747) 853852

SCHOFIELD, Canon Nigel Timothy. b 54. Dur Univ BA76 Nottm Univ BCombStuds83 FRCO. Linc Th Coll 80. **d** 83 **p** 84. C Cheshunt *St Alb* 83-86; TV Colyton, Southleigh, Offwell, Widworthy etc *Ex* 86-94; V Seaton 94-03; P-in-c Beer and Branscombe 01-03; V Seaton and Beer 03-06; RD Honiton 99-03; Can Res Chich Cathl from 06. *4 Vicars Close, Chichester PO19 1PT* Tel (01243) 813589 E-mail precentor@chichestercathedral.org.uk

SCHOFIELD, Canon Rodney. b 44. St Jo Coll Cam BA64 MA67 St Pet Hall Ox BA70 MA73. St Steph Ho Ox 68. **d** 71 **p** 72. C Northampton St Mary *Pet* 71-76; V Irchester 76-84; Lesotho 84-86; R W Monkton *B & W* 86-00; Asst Dir of Ords 87-89; Dir of Ords 89-99; Preb Wells Cathl 90-00; Lect Zomba Th Coll Malawi 00-03; Can Upper Shire from 03; Perm to Offic *Sarum* from 04. *15 Johnson's Courtyard, South Street, Sherborne DT9 3TD* Tel (01935) 814932 E-mail rodney.schofield@gmail.com

SCHOFIELD, Ruth Elizabeth. b 65. Imp Coll Lon BEng87. STETS 06. **d** 09. NSM Botley *Portsm* from 09; NSM Curdridge from 09; NSM Durley from 09. *5 Myers Close, Swanmore, Southampton SO32 2RN* Tel (01489) 895824 E-mail rschofield@f2s.com

SCHOFIELD, Ms Sarah. b 70. Man Univ BA95. Qu Coll Birm 95. **d** 97 **p** 98. C Longsight St Luke *Man* 97-02; Tutor (Man Ho) Westcott Ho Cam 00-04; P-in-c Gorton St Phil *Man* 02-06; P-in-c Abbey Hey 04-06; TV Cen Wolverhampton *Lich* from 06. *All Saints Vicarage, 2A Vicarage Road, Wolverhampton WV2 1DT* Tel (01902) 452584 E-mail sarahschof@aol.com

SCHOFIELD, Timothy. *See* SCHOFIELD, Canon Nigel Timothy

SCHOFIELD, Mrs Victoria Louise. b 56. Liv Poly BSc88 Liv Univ PGCE91. Wycliffe Hall Ox BTh05. **d** 02 **p** 03. C Hattersley *Ches* 02-05; P-in-c Runcorn St Mich 05-06; V from 06. *145 Greenway Road, Runcorn WA7 4NR* Tel (01928) 500993

SCHOLEFIELD, John. b 27. Leeds Univ BSc50. Wells Th Coll 51. **d** 53 **p** 54. C Ossett cum Gawthorpe *Wakef* 53-56; C Hebden Bridge 56-58; V Sowerby St Geo 58-64; V Darton 64-70; V Stoke Gabriel *Ex* 70-84; P-in-c Collaton St Mary 82-84; V Stoke Gabriel and Collaton 84-92; rtd 92; Perm to Offic *Ex* from 92. *25 Droridge, Dartington, Totnes TQ9 6JQ* Tel (01803) 863192

SCHOLEFIELD, Mrs Judith Lenore. b 45. RN66 Open Univ BA97. WEMTC 99. **d** 04 **p** 05. OLM Ledbury *Heref* from 04. *Oakland Lodge, The Homend, Ledbury HR8 1AR* Tel (01531) 632279

SCHOLES, Ms Victoria Prichard. b 68. Man Univ BSc89. St Jo Coll Nottm 97. **d** 00 **p** 01. C Macclesfield St Jo *Ches* 00-02; NSM 02-03; Perm to Offic from 03. *87B Gawsorth Road, Macclesfield SK11 8UF* Tel (01625) 425049

SCHOLEY, Thomas. b 38. Leeds Univ CertEd60. Lich Th Coll 69. **d** 72 **p** 73. C Blaby *Leic* 72-75; TV Daventry w Norton *Pet* 75-78; R Wootton w Quinton and Preston Deanery 78-06; rtd 06. *14 Fields Close, Epworth, Doncaster DN9 1TL*

SCHOLFIELD, Peter. b 35. Sarum Th Coll 64. **d** 66 **p** 67. C S Kirkby *Wakef* 66-69; P-in-c Carlton 69-90; rtd 90; Perm to Offic *Wakef* from 90. *31 Springhill Avenue, Crofton, Wakefield WF1 1HA* Tel (01924) 863430

SCHOLLAR, Canon Pamela Mary. b 39. Southn Univ DipEd80. S Dios Minl Tr Scheme 89. **d** 92 **p** 94. NSM Bournemouth St Andr *Win* 92-94; NSM Pokesdown St Jas from 94; Hon Can Win Cathl from 02. *22 Bethia Road, Bournemouth BH8 9BD* Tel (01202) 397925 E-mail schollar@ukgateway.net

SCHOLZ, Terence Brinsley. b 44. St Martin's Coll Lanc MA98. CBDTI 94. **d** 97 **p** 98. NSM St Annes St Thos *Blackb* 97-01; NSM Broughton 01-02; Perm to Offic 02-04; NSM Freckleton from 04. *14 Further Ends Road, Freckleton, Preston PR4 1RL* Tel (01772) 632966 Fax 635779 Mobile 07768-441400

SCHOOLING, Bruce James. b 47. Rhodes Univ BA73. St Paul's Coll Grahamstown 76. **d** 76 **p** 77. C Rondebosch St Thos S Africa 76-79; C St Geo Cathl Cape Town 79-83; R Malmesbury 83-86; C Wanstead St Mary *Chelmsf* 87-90; V Leigh-on-Sea St Jas 90-04; Perm to Offic from 05; rtd 07. *249 Woodgrange Drive, Southend-on-Sea SS1 2SQ* Tel (01702) 613429 Mobile 07710-208476 E-mail b.schooling@btinternet.com

SCHRIMSHAW, Angela Anna Violet. b 51. SRN73 SCM76 Hull Univ BSc98. NEOC 01. **d** 04 **p** 05. NSM Welton w Melton *York* from 04. *22 Bricknell Avenue, Hull HU5 4JS* Tel (01482) 446609 E-mail schrim@schrim.karoo.co.uk

SCHRODER, Edward Amos. b 41. Cant Univ (NZ) BA64. Cranmer Hall Dur. **d** 67 **p** 68. C St Marylebone All So w SS Pet and Jo *Lon* 67-71; Dean Gordon Coll USA and C Hamilton Ch Ch 71-76; Can Missr and Asst to Bp Florida 76-79; R Orange Park Grace Ch 79-86; R San Antonio Coll Ch 86-00; Chapl Amelia Plantation Chpl 00-06; rtd 06. *15 Hickory Lane, Amelia Island FL 32034-5064, USA* Tel (001) (904) 277 6752 Fax 277 8323 E-mail tschroder@ameliachapel.com

SCHRYVER, Mrs Linda Jean. b 56. Ch Ch Coll Cant BSc00. SEITE 00. **d** 03 **p** 04. NSM Willesborough *Cant* from 03. *2 Church Cottages, Canterbury Road, Godmersham, Canterbury CT4 7DS* Tel (01227) 730750 Mobile 07768-566372 E-mail linda.schryver@mariecurie.org.uk

SCHULD DE VERNY, Dietrich Gustave. *See* DE VERNY, David Dietrich Schuld

SCHUMAN, Andrew William Edward. b 73. Birm Univ BA95 MSc96 Bris Univ PhD00 FRGS02. Trin Coll Bris BA03 MA04. **d** 04 **p** 05. C Shirehampton *Bris* 04-08; C Bris Ch the Servant Stockwood from 08; Partnership P Bris S from 08. *69 Bifield Road, Bristol BS14 8TT* Tel (01275) 830944 E-mail aschuman@waitrose.com

SCHUNEMANN, Bernhard George. b 61. K Coll Lon BD86 AKC86 LRAM83. Ripon Coll Cuddesdon 88. **d** 90 **p** 91. C Kirkby *Liv* 90-93; C St Martin-in-the-Fields *Lon* 93-97; Chapl Br Sch of Osteopathy 93-97; P-in-c Littlemore *Ox* 97-06; V S Dulwich St Steph *S'wark* from 06. *St Stephen's Vicarage, 111 College Road, London SE21 7HN* Tel (020) 8693 3797 *or* 8766 7281 Fax 8693 7194 E-mail bschunemann@compuserve.com

SCHUTTE, Ms Margaret Ann. b 50. Natal Univ BA71. SAOMC. **d** 04 **p** 05. C Overbury w Teddington, Alstone etc *Worc* 04-07; Chapl HM Pris Brockhill from 07; Chapl HM Pris Hewell

Grange from 07. *HM Prison Brockhill, Hewell Lane, Redditch B97 6RD* Tel (01527) 552650 E-mail schuttefamily@tesco.net

SCHWIER, Paul David. b 55. **d** 96 **p** 97. OLM Pulham Market, Pulham St Mary and Starston *Nor* 96-99; OLM Dickleburgh and The Pulhams from 99. *Street Farm, Pulham Market, Diss IP21 4SP* Tel (01379) 676240

SCHWIER, Peter Andrew. b 52. **d** 91 **p** 92. NSM Fressingfield, Mendham etc *St E* from 91. *Valley Farm, Metfield, Harleston IP20 0JZ* Tel (01379) 586517

SCLATER, Jennifer. b 44. TISEC. **d** 02 **p** 04. Par Dn Elgin w Lossiemouth *Mor* 02-04; NSM from 04. *82 Pluscarden Road, Elgin IV30 1SU* Tel (01343) 549442 E-mail jenny@sclater.com

SCLATER, John Edward. b 46. Nottm Univ BA68 St Edm Hall Ox CertEd71. Cuddesdon Coll 69. **d** 71 **p** 72. C Bris St Mary Redcliffe w Temple etc 71-75; Chapl Bede Ho Staplehurst 75-79; Chapl Warw Sch 79; P-in-c Offchurch *Cov* 79-80; Belgium 81-89; Willen Priory 89-91; C Linslade *Ox* 91-94; P-in-c Hedsor and Bourne End 94-02; rtd 02; Perm to Offic *B & W* from 03. *3 East Court, South Horrington Village, Wells BA5 3HL* Tel (01749) 671349 E-mail john@jes07.freeserve.co.uk

SCOBIE, Geoffrey Edward Winsor. b 39. Bris Univ BSc62 MSc68 Birm Univ MA70 Glas Univ PhD78 FRSA96 AFBPsS. Tyndale Hall Bris 62. **d** 65 **p** 66. C Summerfield *Birm* 65-66; C Moseley St Anne 66-67; Lect Psychology Glas Univ 67-04; Hon C Glas St Silas 70-83; P-in-c 83-84; Hon R 84-85; TR 85-86; Team Chapl 86-88; Hon Asst Team Chapl 88-99; Assoc P Bishopbriggs 99-08; P-in-c Lenzie from 06. *3 Norfolk Crescent, Bishopbriggs, Glasgow G64 3BA* Tel 0141-722 2907 *or* 330 4699 E-mail gscobie@ntlworld.com

SCOONES, Roger Philip. b 48. Trin Coll Bris. **d** 82 **p** 83. C Childwall All SS *Liv* 82-85; Bradf Cathl 85-90; V Congleton St Pet *Ches* 90-96; P-in-c Congleton St Steph 94-96; R Stockport St Mary from 96; Perm to Offic *Man* from 06. *St Mary's Rectory, 24 Gorsey Mount Street, Stockport SK1 4DU* Tel 0161-429 6564 *or* 480 1815 Fax 429 6564 E-mail roger@scoones9.freeserve.co.uk

SCORER, Canon John Robson. b 47. Westcott Ho Cam 73. **d** 75 **p** 76. C Silksworth *Dur* 75-78; C Newton Aycliffe 78-82; V Sherburn 82-83; V Sherburn w Pittington 83-89; P-in-c Croxdale 89-93; Chapl Dur Constabulary from 89; Chapl Dur Police Tr Cen 93-05; Hon Can Dur Cathl from 04. *1 Vicarage Close, Howden le Wear, Crook DL15 8RB* Tel and fax (01388) 764938

SCOTFORD, Bethan Lynne. b 44. Univ of Wales (Cardiff) BA67 PGCE68. St As Minl Tr Course 95. **d** 99 **p** 00. Fieldworker (Wales) USPG from 98; C Guilsfield w Pool Quay *St As* 99-02; R Corwen and Llangar w Gwyddelwern and Llawrybetws from 02. *The Rectory, Ffordd ty Cerrig, Corwen LL21 9RP* Tel (01490) 412278 Mobile 07802-656607 E-mail bscotford@toucansurf.com

SCOTLAND, Nigel Adrian Douglas. b 42. McGill Univ Montreal MA71 Aber Univ PhD75 CertEd75 Bris Univ MLitt85. Gordon-Conwell Th Sem MDiv70 Lon Coll of Div ALCD66 LTh74. **d** 66 **p** 67. C Harold Wood *Chelmsf* 66-69; USA 69-70; R Lakefield Canada 70-72; Lic to Offic *Ab* 72-75; Chapl and Lect St Mary's Coll Cheltenham 75-79; Sen Lect 77-79; Chapl and Sen Lect Coll of SS Paul and Mary Cheltenham 79-84; NSM Cheltenham St Mark *Glouc* 85-92; Field Chair RS Cheltenham and Glouc Coll of HE 89-01; Field Chair Glos Univ 01-05; Prin Lect 96-08; Research Fell from 08; Perm to Offic *Glouc* from 92; Tutor Trin Coll Bris from 06; Lic to Offic *Bris* from 07. *23 School Road, Charlton Kings, Cheltenham GL53 8BG* Tel (01242) 529167 E-mail nigel.scotland@btopenworld.com

SCOTLAND, Primus of the Episcopal Church in. *See* CHILLINGWORTH, The Rt Revd David Robert

SCOTT, Adam. b 47. OBE09 TD78. Ch Ch Ox BA68 MA72 City Univ MSc79 Barrister 72 FRSA95 CEng81 MIET81 FIEE94. S'wark Ord Course 73. **d** 75 **p** 76. MSE Blackheath Park St Mich S'wark from 75; Dean for MSE, Woolwich from 90; Prof Fell St Andr Univ 96-97 and from 98; Perm to Offic from 96. *19 Blackheath Park, London SE3 9RW, or The Gateway, North Haugh, St Andrews KY16 9SS* Tel (020) 8852 3286 *or* (01334) 462800 Fax (020) 8852 6247 *or* (01334) 426812 E-mail adam.scott@btinternet.com

SCOTT, Preb Allan George. b 28. Man Univ BA61. Coll of Resurr Mirfield 61. **d** 63 **p** 64. C Bradford cum Beswick *Man* 63-66; P-in-c 66-72; Hon C Bramhall *Ches* 72-74; Hon C Tottenham St Jo *Lon* 74-76; Hon C Bush Hill Park St Steph 76-79; R Stoke Newington St Mary 79-02; P-in-c Brownswood Park 95-97; Preb St Paul's Cathl 91-04; rtd 04. *8 West Hackney House, 15 Northwold Road, London N16 7HJ* Tel (020) 7923 0153

SCOTT, Andrew Charles Graham. b 28. Mert Coll Ox BA57 MA. Wells Th Coll 57. **d** 59 **p** 60. C Rugby St Andr *Cov* 59-64; Chapl RN 64-68; C Prenton *Ches* 68-71; V Tow Law *Dur* 71-81; RD Stanhope 77-81; V Bampton w Clanfield *Ox* 81-95; rtd 95; Perm to Offic *Ex* from 95. *99 Speedwell Crescent, Plymouth PL6 5SZ* Tel (01752) 773570

SCOTT, Barrie. b 63. Birm Univ BA85 Goldsmiths' Coll Lon PGCE86. St Steph Ho Ox 93. **d** 95 **p** 96. C Tilehurst St Mich *Ox*

95-98; Perm to Offic *Birm* from 98. *3 Old Langley Hall, Ox Leys Road, Sutton Coldfield B75 7HP* Tel 0121-351 2050
E-mail barrie@waitrose.com

SCOTT, Basil John Morley. b 34. Qu Coll Cam BA59 Banaras Hindu Univ MA65. Ridley Hall Cam 58. **d** 60 **p** 61. C Woking St Pet *Guildf* 60-63; India 63-83; TR Kirby Muxloe *Leic* 83-89; Asian Outreach Worker (Leic Martyrs) 89-95; Derby Asian Chr Min Project 95-00; rtd 00; Perm to Offic *Ely* from 00. *14 Scotsdowne Road, Trumpington, Cambridge CB2 9HU* Tel (01223) 476565

SCOTT, Mrs Beryl May. b 28. Lon Univ BD91 Westmr Coll Ox MTh00. **d** 02 **p** 04. NSM Dalbeattie *Glas* from 02. *Islecroft House, Mill Street, Dalbeattie DG5 4HE* Tel (01556) 610283
E-mail berylm.scott@virgin.net

SCOTT, Brian. b 35. CCC Ox BA58. Coll of Resurr Mirfield 59. **d** 61 **p** 65. C Carl St Aid and Ch Ch 61-62; Asst Master Hutton Gr Sch 63-65; Perm to Offic *Leic* 65-67; Lic to Offic 67-70; V Lubenham and P-in-c Theddingworth 71-78; Asst Chapl Oundle Sch 78-83; R Barrowden and Wakerley w S Luffenham *Pet* 83-98; rtd 98; Perm to Offic *Leic* and *Pet* from 98. *The Cedars, 3 Glaston Road, Preston, Oakham LE15 9NH* Tel (01572) 737242

SCOTT, Charles Geoffrey. b 32. St Jo Coll Cam BA54 MA58. Cuddesdon Coll 56. **d** 58 **p** 59. C Brighouse *Wakef* 58-61; C Bathwick w Woolley *B & W* 61-64; V Frome Ch Ch 64-78; R Winchelsea *Chich* 78-93; R Winchelsea and Icklesham 93-95; rtd 95; Perm to Offic *Chich* from 95. *Hickstead, Main Street, Iden, Rye TN31 7PT* Tel (01797) 280096

SCOTT, Christopher. *See* DAVIES, Christopher

SCOTT, Christopher John Fairfax. b 45. Magd Coll Cam BA67 MA71. Westcott Ho Cam 68. **d** 70 **p** 71. C Nor St Pet Mancroft 70-73; Chapl Magd Coll Cam 73-79; V Hampstead Ch Ch *Lon* 79-94; rtd 00. *49 St Barnabas Road, Cambridge CB1 2BX* Tel (01223) 359421

SCOTT, Canon Christopher Michael. b 44. SS Coll Cam BA66 MA70. Cuddesdon Coll 66. **d** 68 **p** 69. C New Addington *Cant* 68-73; C Westmr St Steph w St Jo *Lon* 73-78; V Enfield St Mich 78-81; V Effingham w Lt Bookham *Guildf* 81-87; R Esher 87-98; RD Emly 91-96; R Bude Haven and Marhamchurch *Truro* 98-08; Hon Can Truro Cathl 03-08; rtd 08. *Lantyan, Poughill, Bude EX23 9EU* Tel (01288) 350741
E-mail chriscott98@yahoo.co.uk

SCOTT, Christopher Stuart. b 48. Surrey Univ BA92 MBPsS92. Sarum & Wells Th Coll 79. **d** 81 **p** 82. C Enfield Chase St Mary *Lon* 81-82; C Coalbrookdale, Iron-Bridge and Lt Wenlock *Heref* 82-86; P-in-c Breinton 86-89; Chapl Hickey's Almshouses Richmond 89-01; Perm to Offic *S'wark* from 06. *164 Sheen Road, Richmond TW9 1XD* Tel (020) 8940 6560

SCOTT, Claude John. b 37. Qu Mary Coll Lon BSc60 PhD64 Lon Inst of Educn PGCE61 FRSA94. EAMTC 88. **d** 91 **p** 92. NSM Heigham H Trin *Nor* 91-98; Perm to Offic from 98. *17 Lime Tree Road, Norwich NR2 2NQ* Tel (01603) 455686
E-mail cjscott@talktalk.net

SCOTT, Colin. b 32. Dur Univ BA54. Coll of Resurr Mirfield 58. **d** 60 **p** 61. C Wallsend St Pet *Newc* 60-64; C Seaton Hirst 64-68; C Longbenton St Bart 68-70; V Benwell St Aid 70-77; V Sleekburn 77-89; P-in-c Cambois 77-89; V Longhoughton w Howick 89-96; rtd 96; Perm to Offic *Newc* from 96. *Pele Cottage, Hepple, Morpeth NE65 7LH* Tel (01669) 640258

✠**SCOTT, The Rt Revd Colin John Fraser.** b 33. Qu Coll Cam BA56 MA60. Ridley Hall Cam 56. **d** 58 **p** 59 **c** 84. C Clapham Common St Barn *S'wark* 58-61; C Hatcham St Jas 61-64; V Kennington St Mark 64-71; RD Lambeth 68-71; Vice-Chmn Dioc Past Cttee 71-77; Hon Can S'wark Cathl 73-84; TR Sanderstead All SS 77-84; Suff Bp Hulme *Man* 84-98; Chmn CCC 94-98; rtd 99; Hon Asst Bp Leic from 99; Perm to Offic *Derby* from 00. *The Priest House, Prior Park Road, Ashby-de-la-Zouch LE65 1BH* Tel (01530) 564403

SCOTT, David. b 40. Rhodes Univ BA63. St Paul's Coll Grahamstown. **d** 65 **p** 66. S Africa 65-91; TV Cheltenham St Mark *Glouc* 92-96; R Swanscombe *Roch* from 96. *The Rectory, Swanscombe Street, Swanscombe DA10 0JZ* Tel (01322) 383160 E-mail davidscott@stpeterandstpaul.org.uk

SCOTT, Canon David Victor. b 47. St Chad's Coll Dur BA69. Cuddesdon Coll 69. **d** 71 **p** 72. C St Mary-at-Latton *Chelmsf* 71-73; Chapl Haberdashers' Aske's Sch Elstree 73-80; V Torpenhow *Carl* 80-91; V Allhallows 80-91; R Win St Lawr and St Maurice w St Swithun from 91; Warden Sch of Spirituality Win from 91; Hon Can Win Cathl from 02. *The Rectory, Colebrook Street, Winchester SO23 9LH* Tel (01962) 868056

SCOTT, Mrs Erica Jane. b 58. Trin Coll Bris BA02. **d** 02 **p** 03. C Ilminster and Distr *B & W* 02-05; C Nailsea Ch Ch w Tickenham 05-07; P-in-c Portishead *Bris* 07-08. *Address temp unknown* E-mail reverica@btinternet.com

SCOTT, Francis Richard. b 63. St Jo Coll Dur BA85 Selw Coll Cam PGCE86. St Jo Coll Nottm MA02. **d** 00 **p** 01. C Huntington *York* 00-03; TV from 03. *402 Huntington Road, Huntington, York YO31 9HU* Tel (01904) 658659
E-mail fandfscott@aol.com

SCOTT, Gary James. b 61. Edin Univ BD87. Edin Th Coll 85. **d** 87 **p** 88. C Edin St Cuth 87-90; R Peebles 90-92; P-in-c Innerleithen 92-96; R Penicuik 96-98; R W Linton 96-98; Sen Chapl ACF 98-06; Lic to Offic *Edin* from 98. *3 Crossburn Farm Road, Peebles EH45 8EG* Tel (01721) 721886

SCOTT, Geoffrey. *See* SCOTT, Charles Geoffrey

SCOTT, Canon Gordon. b 30. Man Univ BA51. St Jo Coll Dur 51. **d** 53 **p** 54. C Monkwearmouth St Andr *Dur* 53-55; C Stranton 55-56; C Chester le Street 56-59; V Marley Hill 59-62; Chapl Forest Sch Snaresbrook 62-66; Chapl Dunrobin Sch Sutherland 66-72; Chapl Pocklington Sch York 72-74; V Barton w Pooley Bridge *Carl* 74-80; RD Penrith 79-82; P-in-c Lazonby 80; R Gt Salkeld w Lazonby 80-90; Hon Can Carl Cathl 83-94; P-in-c Patterdale 90-94; rtd 94; Perm to Offic *Carl* 94-97. *48 Lakeland Park, Keswick CA12 4AT* Tel (01768) 775862

SCOTT, Guy Charles. b 61. Coll of Resurr Mirfield. **d** 00 **p** 01. C Abington *Pet* 00-03; P-in-c Mullion *Truro* 03-07; C Cury and Gunwalloe 03-07; R Is of Scilly from 07. *The Chaplaincy, Church Road, St Mary's, Isles of Scilly TR21 0NA* Tel (01720) 423128

SCOTT, Mrs Helen Ruth. b 59. Surrey Univ BA97 K Coll Lon MA99 SRN81 RM85. S'wark Ord Course 89. **d** 92 **p** 94. NSM Richmond St Mary w St Matthias and St Jo *S'wark* 92-01; Chapl Hickey's Almshouses Richmond 01-08; Perm to Offic *S'wark* from 08; Chapl Ch Sch Richmond from 09. *164 Sheen Road, Richmond TW9 1XD* Tel (020) 8940 6560

SCOTT, Ian Michael. b 25. Bris Univ BA50 Leic Univ DipEd51 Open Univ MA99. Bps' Coll Cheshunt 52. **d** 53 **p** 54. C Rotherhithe St Mary w All SS *S'wark* 53-55; C Lavender Hill Ascension 55-59; C Camberwell St Mich w All So w Em 59-60; C Kettering St Mary *Pet* 60-63; V Haverstock Hill H Trin w Kentish Town St Barn *Lon* 63-93; rtd 93; Perm to Offic *Nor* 93-96. *Los Molinos 8, 03726 Benitachell (Alicante), Spain* Tel (0034) 965 741 342 E-mail ian_benitachell@yahoo.co.uk

SCOTT, Mrs Inez Margaret Gillette. b 26. St Alb Minl Tr Scheme 76. **dss** 79 **d** 87 **p** 94. Preston w Sutton Poyntz and Osmington w Poxwell *Sarum* 83-86; Dorchester 86-96; Par Dn 87-88; NSM 88-96; rtd 88; Perm to Offic *Sarum* 96-08. *14 Came View Road, Dorchester DT1 2AE* Tel (01305) 267547

SCOTT, James Alexander Gilchrist. b 32. Linc Coll Ox BA56 MA60. Wycliffe Hall Ox 56. **d** 58 **p** 59. C Shipley St Paul *Bradf* 58-61; Abp's Dom Chapl *York* 61-65; Brazil 65-68; V Grassendale *Liv* 68-77; V Thorp Arch w Walton *York* 77-89; RD Tadcaster 78-86; Chapl HM Pris Rudgate 77-82; Askham Grange 82-87; V Kirk Ella 89-92; TR 92-97; rtd 97; Perm to Offic *York* from 98. *2 Keld CLose, Pickering YO18 9NJ* Tel (01751) 476226

SCOTT, James William. b 39. S Dios Minl Tr Scheme 84. **d** 88 **p** 89. NSM Bremhill w Foxham and Hilmarton *Sarum* 88-94; NSM Derry Hill w Bremhill and Foxham 94-09. *14 Bremhill, Calne SN11 9LA* Tel (01249) 813114
E-mail james@bremhill.force9.co.uk

SCOTT, Canon Janice Beasant. b 44. MCSP66. EAMTC 89. **d** 92 **p** 94. NSM Fakenham w Alethorpe *Nor* 92-95; C Eaton 95-99; R Dickleburgh and The Pulhams 99-09; RD Redenhall 03-06; Hon Can Nor Cathl 08-09; rtd 09. *2 Reve Crescent, Blofield, Norwich NR13 4RX* Tel (01603) 712428 Mobile 07905-039243
E-mail janice@janice-scott.com

SCOTT, John. *See* SCOTT, The Ven William John

SCOTT, John. b 54. QUB BD79. CITC 80. **d** 81 **p** 82. C Willowfield *D & D* 81-83; C Newtownards 83-85; I Kilskeery w Trillick *Clogh* 85-90; Lic to Offic *D & D* 90-96; I Bright w Ballee and Killough 96-01; Perm to Offic from 01. *Ash Tree House, Moor Road, Ballyward, Castlewellan BT31 9TY* Tel (028) 4065 0908 E-mail john@ashtreehouse.net

SCOTT, John. b 54. Heriot-Watt Univ BA76 Leeds Univ BA97 Heythrop Coll Lon MA05. Coll of Resurr Mirfield 95. **d** 97 **p** 98. C Bethnal Green St Matt w St Jas the Gt *Lon* 97-00; Asst Chapl Qu Mary and Westf Coll 97-00; C Heston 00-04; Prison Health Adv 00-05; rtd 05; Perm to Offic *Win* from 07. *The Old Pottery, Baptist Hill, St Mary Bourne, Andover SP11 6BQ* Tel (01264) 738972 Mobile 07889-977593
E-mail absalom1662@yahoo.co.uk

SCOTT, John Eric. b 16. St Cath Coll Ox BA38 MA42 FSA. Ripon Hall Ox 39. **d** 40 **p** 41. C Heworth St Alb *Dur* 40-43; C Gateshead St Mary 43-45; Chapl and Sacr Ch Ch Ox 45-47; Ho Master Forest Sch Snaresbrook 55-81; P-in-c St Mich Cornhill w St Pet le Poer etc *Lon* 81-85; rtd 85. *17 Harman Avenue, Woodford Green IG8 9DS* Tel (020) 8505 7093

SCOTT, John Harold. b 46. Univ of Wales (Cardiff) BSc69. St Steph Ho Ox 69. **d** 72 **p** 73. C Skewen *Llan* 72-74; C Port Talbot St Theodore 74-77; P-in-c Bedlinog 77-78; V 78-85; R Penderyn w Ystradfellte and Pontneathvaughan *S & B* 85-04; R Penderyn Mellte from 04. *The Vicarage, Ystradfellte, Aberdare CF44 9JE* Tel (01639) 720405 Mobile 07711 961667
E-mail jhs46@tiscali.net

SCOTT, John Peter. b 47. Open Univ BA80. Lambeth STh81 K Coll Lon 69 St Aug Coll Cant 74. **d** 75 **p** 76. C Dartford St Alb *Roch* 75-78; C-in-c Goring-by-Sea *Chich* 78-81; Chapl Wells and

Meare Manor Hosps 81-86; CF (TAVR) 82-90; Chapl Pangbourne Coll 86-90; Min Reigate St Phil CD *S'wark* 90-92; P-in-c Reigate St Phil from 92; Chapl St Bede's Ecum Sch Reigate from 90. *The Parsonage, 102A Nutley Lane, Reigate RH2 9HA* Tel (01737) 244542

SCOTT, John Vickers. b 48. Open Univ BA88 MCIOB81. CBDTI 02. d 05 p 06. NSM Penwortham St Leon *Blackb* from 05. *10 Cuerden Rise, Lostock Hall, Preston PR5 5YD* Tel and fax (01772) 490225 Mobile 07977-049829
E-mail scottjv@blueyonder.co.uk

SCOTT (*née* GOLDIE), Katrina Ruth. b 76. Fitzw Coll Cam BA97 MPhil00 MA01. Westcott Ho Cam 98. d 00 p 01. C Cov E 00-04; V Willenhall from 04; Dioc Adv for Women's Min from 06. *Willenhall Vicarage, Robin Hood Road, Coventry CV3 3AY* Tel (024) 7630 3266 E-mail krgscott@hotmail.com

SCOTT, Keith Brounton de Salve. b 55. QUB BD. d 83 p 84. C Belfast St Matt *Conn* 83-87; I Ardclinis and Tickmacrevan w Layde and Cushendun 87-01. *20 Princess Gardens, Holywood, Belfast BT18 0PN* Tel (028) 9042 2266
E-mail keithbscott@msn.com

SCOTT, Kenneth James. b 46. Bris Univ BA68. Trin Coll Bris 71. d 73 p 74. C Illogan *Truro* '73-76; C Camberley St Paul *Guildf* 76-81; R Bradford Peverell, Stratton, Frampton etc *Sarum* 81-08; RD Dorchester 95-99; rtd 08; Perm to Offic *St E* from 09. *2 Fir Close, Wickham Market, Woodbridge IP13 0UB* Tel (01728) 747232 E-mail kenscott@surfaid.org

SCOTT, Kevin Francis. b 51. Peterho Cam MA Mert Coll Ox DPhil76 CChem MRSC. Wycliffe Hall Ox BA83. d 83 p 84. C Ox St Ebbe w H Trin and St Pet 83-86; P-in-c Prestonpans *Edin* 86-93; R Musselburgh 86-93; R Edin SS Phil and Jas 93-08. *Kirklands, Craigend Road, Stow, Galashiels TD1 2RJ* Tel 0131-208 0402 E-mail drkfs@aol.com

SCOTT, Kevin Peter. b 43. Coll of Resurr Mirfield 93. d 93 p 94. C Rushall *Lich* 93-97; P-in-c Goldenhill from 97. *St John's Vicarage, Drummond Street, Stoke-on-Trent ST6 5RF* Tel (01782) 782736

SCOTT, Kevin Willard. b 53. Open Univ BA96 Glos Univ MA03. Linc Th Coll 92. d 92 p 93. C Walton-on-Thames *Guildf* 92-97; R Matson *Glouc* 97-03; RD Glouc City 01-03; V Malden St Jo *S'wark* from 03; AD Kingston from 05. *5 Vicarage Close, Worcester Park KT4 7LZ* Tel (020) 8337 8830
E-mail kevinwscott@btinternet.com

SCOTT, Laurence Stanley. b 33. Open Univ BSc99. d 05 p 06. NSM Calstock *Truro* from 05. *88 Priory Close, Tavistock PL19 9DG* Tel (01822) 613227

SCOTT, Lester Desmond Donald. NUI BA89. CITC BTh92. d 92 p 93. C Killeshandra w Killegar and Derrylane *K, E & A* 92-95; C Kilmore w Ballintemple 92-95; I Fenagh w Myshall, Aghade and Ardoyne *C & O* from 95. *The Glebe House, Ballon, Co Carlow, Republic of Ireland* Tel (059) 915 9367 Mobile 87-250 4322 E-mail lesterscott@oceanfree.net

SCOTT (*née* CURRELL), Mrs Linda Anne. b 62. K Alfred's Coll Win BEd84. Trin Coll Bris BA92. d 92 p 94. Par Dn Tunbridge Wells St Mark *Roch* 92-94; C 94-97; TV Walthamstow *Chelmsf* 97-02; Perm to Offic *Chelmsf* 02-04 and *S'wark* from 05. *35 Oswin Street, London SE11 4TF* Tel (020) 7735 4077
E-mail scottlindatim@aol.com

SCOTT, Canon Malcolm Kenneth Merrett. b 30. ACA53 FCA64. Clifton Th Coll 56. d 58 p 59. C Highbury Ch Ch *Lon* 58-60; CMS 60-61; Uganda 61-74; V Sunnyside w Bourne End *St Alb* 74-90; V Clapham 90-95; rtd 95; Perm to Offic *Lich* from 96. *10 The Ring, Little Haywood, Stafford ST18 0TP* Tel (01889) 881464

SCOTT, Nicholas Charles Andrew. b 74. Univ of Wales (Ban) BD95. Westcott Ho Cam 97. d 99 p 00. C Ryde H Trin and Swanmore St Mich *Portsm* 99-01; C Burbage w Aston Flamville *Leic* 01-04; Perm to Offic *Cov* 04-08; NSM Willenhall from 08. *Willenhall Vicarage, Robin Hood Road, Coventry CV3 3AY* Tel (024) 7630 3266 E-mail ncascott@hotmail.com

SCOTT, Paul Malcolm. b 57. Sheff City Poly BA79 CPFA85. Ripon Coll Cuddesdon 98. d 00 p 01. C N Shields *Newc* 00-03; V Shiremoor from 03. *St Mark's Vicarage, Brenkley Avenue, Shiremoor, Newcastle upon Tyne NE27 0PP* Tel 0191-253 3291
E-mail paulmscott@scott2.freeserve.co.uk

SCOTT, Mrs Pauline Claire Michalak. b 55. St Anne's Coll Ox BA77 MA82 Dur Univ PGCE78. TISEC 98. d 01 p 02. NSM Papworth *Ely* 01-05; TV Ely 05-09; P-in-c Alresford *Chelmsf* from 09; P-in-c Frating w Thorrington from 09. *The Rectory, St Andrew's Close, Alresford, Colchester CO7 8BL* Tel (01206) 822088 Mobile 07855-395840
E-mail paulinecm.scott@tiscali.co.uk

SCOTT, Peter Crawford. b 35. Ch Ch Ox BA56 MA61. Cuddesdon Coll 60. d 62 p 63. C Broseley w Benthall *Heref* 62-66; P-in-c Hughenden *Ox* 66-71; C Hykeham *Linc* 71-73; P-in-c Stottesdon *Heref* 73-76; Australia from 76; rtd 97. *33 Church Street, Coleraine Vic 3315, Australia* Fax (0061) (3) 5575 2491

SCOTT, Peter James Douglas Sefton. b 59. OBE03. Edin Univ BD83. Edin Th Coll 81. d 83 p 84. C Helensburgh *Glas* 83-86;

C-in-c Glas St Oswald 86-89; R 89-91; Chapl RN from 91. *Royal Naval Chaplaincy Service, Mail Point 1-2, Leach Building, Whale Island, Portsmouth PO2 8BY* Tel (023) 9262 5055 Fax 9262 5134

SCOTT, Peter Lindsay. b 29. Keble Coll Ox BA54 MA58. Linc Th Coll 54. d 56 p 57. C Weston-super-Mare St Sav *B & W* 56-59; C Knowle H Nativity *Bris* 59-61; P-in-c Glas St Pet 61-63; V Heap Bridge *Man* 63-73; V Rochdale St Geo w St Alb 73-86; R Droylsden St Andr 86-94; rtd 94; Perm to Offic *Man* from 94. *2 Chancel Place, Rochdale OL16 1FB* Tel (01706) 523270

SCOTT, Ruth. *See* SCOTT, Mrs Helen Ruth

SCOTT, Sara Rosamund. b 49. Portsm Poly BSc70 Plymouth Poly MPhil74. SEITE 97. d 00 p 01. NSM Rotherhithe H Trin *S'wark* 00-04; NSM Sydenham H Trin and St Aug from 04. *147 Jerningham Road, London SE14 5NJ* Tel (020) 7639 6311 Fax 7639 1842 E-mail sarascott@btinternet.com

SCOTT, Simon James. b 65. Ch Ch Ox BA87 MA90. Wycliffe Hall Ox 87. d 91 p 92. C Cheadle All Hallows *Ches* 91-95; Scripture Union 95-98; C Cambridge H Sepulchre *Ely* 98-05; R Lt Shelford from 05. *The Rectory, 2 Manor Road, Little Shelford, Cambridge CB22 5HF* Tel (01223) 841998 Mobile 07739-984323 E-mail simonjscott1965@btinternet.com

SCOTT, Canon Terence. b 56. QUB BSc77. CITC 77. d 80 p 81. C Ballymena *Conn* 80-83; C Antrim All SS 83-85; P-in-c Connor w Antrim St Patr 85-88; I Magherafelt *Arm* from 88; Hon V Choral Arm Cathl 95-06; Can Arm Cathl from 06. *The Rectory, 1 Churchwell Lane, Magherafelt BT45 6AL* Tel (028) 7963 2365 Mobile 07590-894529 E-mail terryscott123@btinternet.com

SCOTT, Canon Theresa Anne. b 53. Bris Univ BSc75 Lon Univ PGCE76. Ox Min Course 89. d 92 p 94. NSM Wickham Bishops w Lt Braxted *Chelmsf* 92-93; NSM Drayton St Pet (Berks) *Ox* 94-01; NSM Convenor (Berks) 97-01; Bp's Officer for NSM 98-01; Bp's Adv for Women in Ord Min 01-05; P-in-c Hurley and Stubbings 01-02; V Burchetts Green 02-08; AD Maidenhead and Windsor 05-07; TR Bicester w Bucknell, Caversfield and Launton from 08; Hon Can Ch Ch from 05. *The Rectory, 6 Tinkers Lane, Bicester OX26 6ES* Tel (01869) 241361
E-mail theresa.scott@driftway.co.uk

SCOTT, Timothy Charles Nairne. b 61. Ex Univ BA83. Westcott Ho Cam 84. d 87 p 88. C Romford St Edw *Chelmsf* 87-89; Community Priest 89-94; P-in-c Leytonstone H Trin Harrow Green 94-97; V 97-02; Educn and Tr Adv (Bradwell Area) 02-04; R S'wark Ch Ch from 04. *35 Oswin Street, London SE11 4TF* Tel (020) 7735 4077 E-mail tim.scott@southwark.anglican.org

SCOTT, Trevor Ian. b 57. Culham Coll Ox CertEd79. EAMTC 97. d 98 p 99. NSM Waltham H Cross *Chelmsf* from 98. *Hartland Villas, 208 High Road, Broxbourne EN10 6QF* Tel (01992) 420376 *or* 450321 E-mail trevor.scott2@ntlworld.com

SCOTT, Vernon Malcolm. b 30. TCD BA57 MA60. TCD Div Sch Div Test56 Ridley Hall Cam 58. d 58 p 59. C Limehouse St Anne *Lon* 58-62; C St Pancras All Hallows 62-66; V Enfield St Mich 66-77; R Tansor w Cotterstock and Fotheringhay *Pet* 77-81; R Barby w Onley 81-83; V Kilsby 81-83; R Barby w Kilsby 83-90; R Coxford Gp *Nor* 90-94; P-in-c S Raynham, E w W Raynham, Helhoughton, etc 94-96; R E and W Rudham, Houghton-next-Harpley etc 95-96; rtd 96; Perm to Offic *Nor* from 96. *5 Wells Road, Walsingham NR22 6DL* Tel (01328) 820151

SCOTT, Walter David Craig. b 22. Selw Coll Cam BA49 MA53. Sarum Th Coll 49. d 51 p 52. C Shildon *Dur* 51-55; Min Cleadon Park St Cuth CD 55-67; V Cleadon Park 67-71; V Bulkington *Cov* 72-83; RD Bedworth 76-79; V Bulkington w Shilton and Ansty 83-87; rtd 87; Perm to Offic *Cov* from 87. *8 Osprey Close, Nuneaton CV11 6TF* Tel (024) 7634 5561

SCOTT, William. b 20. MBE97. St Chad's Coll Dur BA46 Leeds Univ DipEd53. d 60 p 61. CR 60-99; C Wolborough w Newton Abbot *Ex* 60-63; Chapl St Cath Sch Bramley 63-67; Chapl St Mary and St Anne's Sch Abbots Bromley 67-76; Perm to Offic *Cant* 77-90; Chapl Boulogne-sur-Mer w Calais and Lille *Eur* 87-90; Chapl Lille 90-97; rtd 97; Perm to Offic *Eur* from 97. *42 Westgate Court Avenue, Canterbury CT2 8JR* Tel (01227) 456277

SCOTT, William. b 44. Langham Towers Teacher Tr Coll TCert67 Sunderland Poly BEd78. NEOC 00. d 03 p 04. NSM Chester le Street *Dur* 03-04; P-in-c Byers Green from 04; C Spennymoor and Whitworth from 04. *St Peter's Rectory, Byers Green, Spennymoor DL16 7NL* Tel (01388) 664994 Mobile 07808-078532

SCOTT, The Ven William John. b 46. TCD BA70. CITC. d 71 p 72. C Bangor St Comgall *D & D* 71-74; C Holywood 74-80; Dioc Min of Healing Team from 75; I Carnalea 80-90; N Ireland Wing Chapl ATC from 80; I Seapatrick *D & D* from 90; Treas Dromore Cathl 02-08; Adn Dromore from 05. *The Rectory, 63 Lurgan Road, Banbridge BT32 4LY* Tel (028) 4062 2612 *or* 4062 2744 E-mail john@seapatrick.fsnet.co.uk

SCOTT, Preb William Sievwright. b 46. Edin Th Coll 67. d 70 p 71. C Glas St Ninian 70-73; C Bridgwater St Fran *B & W* 73-77; R Shepton Beauchamp w Barrington, Stocklinch etc 77-81; P-in-c Cossington and Woolavington 82-84; Chapl Community of All Hallows Ditchingham 84-91; V Pimlico St Mary Bourne Street *Lon* 91-02; P-in-c Pimlico St Barn 97-01;

V 01-02; AD Westmr St Marg 97-04; Preb St Paul's Cathl from 00; Chapl to RVO and Qu Chpl of the Savoy 02-07; Chapl to The Queen 03-07; Sub-Dean HM Chpls R and Dep Clerk of the Closet from 07; Sub-Almoner and Dom Chapl to The Queen from 07. *Marlborough Gate, St James's Palace, London SW1A 1BG* Tel (020) 7024 5576 *or* 7930 9996 Mobile 07941-470399 E-mail william.scott@_royal.gsx.gov.uk

SCOTT-BROMLEY, Mrs Deborah Joan. b 58. Surrey Univ BA01 Open Univ BA96. STETS 98. **d** 01 **p** 02. C Hale w Badshot Lea *Guildf* 01-05; V Bordon from 05. *St Mark's Vicarage, 58 Forest Road, Bordon GU35 0BP* Tel (01420) 477550 Mobile 07855-704849 E-mail d.scott.bromley@ntlworld.com

SCOTT-DEMPSTER, Canon Colin Thomas. b 37. Em Coll Cam BA65 MA68. Cuddesdon Coll 64. **d** 66 **p** 67. C Caversham *Ox* 66-69; Chapl Coll of SS Mark and Jo Chelsea 69-73; V Chieveley w Winterbourne and Oare *Ox* 73-02; RD Newbury 77-98; Hon Can Ch Ch 90-02; rtd 02. *Old Faskally House, Killiecrankie, Pitlochry PH16 5LG* Tel (01796) 473575
E-mail colin@faskally25.freeserve.co.uk

SCOTT-GARNETT, Linda. b 44. **d** 07 **p** 08. NSM Bermondsey St Hugh CD *S'wark* from 07. *1 Strood House, Manciple Street, London SE1 4LR* Tel (020) 7642 1367
E-mail lindag@bulldoghome.com

SCOTT-HAMBLEN, Shane. b 66. Webster Univ (USA) BMus89 St Thos Aquinas Univ Rome STB94 MA96 STL96. **d** 94 **p** 95. In RC Ch 94-97; C Staines St Mary and St Pet *Lon* 97-99; USA from 99; R Highlands St Mary from 02. *The Episcopal Church of St Mary, 1 Chestnut Street, Cold Spring NY 10516, USA* Tel (001) (845) 265 2539

✠**SCOTT-JOYNT, The Rt Revd Michael Charles.** b 43. K Coll Cam BA65 MA68. Cuddesdon Coll 65. **d** 67 **p** 68 **c** 87. C Cuddesdon *Ox* 67-70; Tutor Cuddesdon Coll 67-71; Chapl 71-72; TV Newbury St Nic *Ox* 72-75; P-in-c Bicester 75-79; P-in-c Caversfield 75-79; P-in-c Bucknell 76-79; TR Bicester w Bucknell, Caversfield and Launton 79-81; RD Bicester and Islip 76-81; Can Res St Alb 82-87; Dir of Ords and Post-Ord Tr 82-87; Suff Bp Stafford *Lich* 87-92; Area Bp Stafford 92-95; Bp Win from 95. *Wolvesey, Winchester SO23 9ND* Tel (01962) 854050 Fax 897088 E-mail michael.scott-joynt@dsl.pipex.com

SCOTT-THOMPSON, Ian Mackenzie. b 57. Ch Ch Ox BA78. St Jo Coll Nottm BA82. **d** 83 **p** 84. C Hartley Wintney, Elvetham, Winchfield etc 83-85; C Bitterne 85-89; V Iford 89-99; P-in-c Holdenhurst 95-99; TR Cove St Jo *Guildf* 99-06; RD Aldershot 03-06; V Wonersh w Blackheath from 06. *The Vicarage, The Street, Wonersh, Guildford GU5 0PG* Tel (01483) 893131 E-mail ian.scott-thompson@virgin.net

SCRACE, David Peter. b 46. Sarum & Wells Th Coll 79. **d** 81 **p** 82. C Abbots Langley *St Alb* 81-85; TV Chippenham St Paul w Hardenhuish etc *Bris* 85-91; P-in-c Harnham *Sarum* 91-99; V from 99; RD Salisbury 93-98. *The Vicarage, Old Blandford Road, Salisbury SP2 8DQ* Tel (01722) 333564
E-mail d.scrace@btopenworld.com

SCRAGG, Michael John. b 39. Griffith Univ Brisbane BA93 MA01 Jas Cook Univ Townsville BCommWelf97. ACT. **d** 74 **p** 75. C Camp Hill w Carina Australia 74-77; C Chesterton Gd Shep *Ely* 77-79; C Maryborough Australia 79-80; V Biggenden 80-85; Chapl Wolston Park Hosp 85-91; P-in-c Taroom 91-96; C Willunga w Seaford Ecum Miss 96-97; Lic to Offic 97-98; rtd 98; Perm to Offic Brisbane 98-05; Guardian Community of the Epiphany from 05. *Clarendon Spence, 18/79 Spence Street, PO Box 5143, Cairns Qld 4870, Australia* Tel (0061) (7) 4041 5707 Mobile 41-876 4567 E-mail hapy5859@yahoo.com.au

SCRASE-FIELD, Edward Fraser Austin Longmer. b 76. Aber Univ BSc98 Man Univ PhD04 Cam Univ BA07. Ridley Hall Cam 05. **d** 08 **p** 09. C Denton Holme *Carl* from 08. *118 Dalston Road, Carlisle CA2 5PJ* Tel (01228) 522938 Mobile 07730-514074

SCREECH, Prof Michael. b 26. Ordre national du Mérite 83 Chevalier Légion d'Honneur 92. Univ Coll Lon BA50 Birm Univ DLitt59 Univ Coll Lon DLitt82 All So Coll Ox MA84 DLitt90 Ex Univ Hon DLitt93 Geneva Univ Hon DD98 FBA81 FRSL87. Ox Min Course 92. **d** 93 **p** 94. NSM Ox St Giles and SS Phil and Jas w St Marg 93-02; Perm to Offic from 02; Extraordinary Fell Wolfs Coll Ox from 93; Chapl and Fell All So Coll Ox 01-03. *5 Swanston Field, Whitchurch on Thames, Reading RG8 7HP* Tel and fax 0118-984 2513

✠**SCREECH, The Rt Revd Royden.** b 53. K Coll Lon BD74 AKC74. St Aug Coll Cant 75. **d** 76 **p** 77 **c** 00. C Hatcham St Cath *S'wark* 76-80; V Nunhead St Antony 80-87; P-in-c Nunhead St Silas 82-87; RD Camberwell 83-87; V New Addington 87-94; Selection Sec ABM 94-97; Sen Selection Sec Min Division Abps' Coun 97-00; Suff Bp St Germans *Truro* from 00. *32 Falmouth Road, Truro TR1 2HX* Tel (01872) 273190 Fax 277883 E-mail bishop@stgermans.truro.anglican.org

SCRINE, Ralph. b 19. Bris Univ BA40 Fitzw Ho Cam BA46 MA60 Lon Univ MPhil81. Westcott Ho Cam 45. **d** 46 **p** 47. C Moorfields *Bris* 46-51; P-in-c Biddestone w Slaughterford 51-52; P-in-c Locklease CD 52-60; V St Jas Less 60-65; Chapl Eliz Coll Guernsey 60-65; Lect Div Ch Ch Coll Cant 65-68; Chapl Ch Ch

Coll of HE Cant 68-75; Sen Lect Ch Ch Coll Cant 68-84; rtd 84; Perm to Offic Cant 84-03. *14 Riverdale, Harbertonford, Totnes TQ9 7TJ* Tel (01803) 731046

✠**SCRIVEN, The Rt Revd Henry William.** b 51. Sheff Univ BA72. St Jo Coll Nottm 73. **d** 75 **p** 76 **c** 95. C Wealdstone H Trin *Lon* 75-79; SAMS Argentina 79-82; USA 82-83; SAMS Spain 84-90; Chapl Madrid w Bilbao *Eur* 90-95; Suff Bp Eur 95-02; Dean Brussels 95-97; Dir of Ords 97-02; Asst Bp Pittsburgh USA 02-08; Miss Dir for S America SAMS/CMS from 09; Hon Asst Bp Ox from 09. *16 East St Helen Street, Abingdon OX14 5EA* Tel (01235) 536607 *or* (01865) 787500
E-mail henry.scriven@cms-uk.org

SCRIVEN, Hugh Alexander. b 59. Trin Coll Cam BA80. Cranmer Hall Dur 81. **d** 84 **p** 85. C Pudsey St Lawr and St Paul *Bradf* 84-87; C Madeley *Heref* 87-91; TV 91-00; V Edgbaston St Germain *Birm* from 00. *St Germain's Vicarage, 180 Portland Road, Birmingham B16 9TD* Tel 0121-429 3431

SCRIVENER, John Glenfield (Glen). b 78. Ball Coll Ox BA96. Oak Hill Th Coll BTh07. **d** 07 **p** 08. C Eastbourne All So *Chich* from 07. *Wellesley House, Longstone Road, Eastbourne BN21 3SL* Tel 07876-031734 (mobile)
E-mail glen@christthetruth.org.uk

SCRIVENER, Robert Allan. b 54. Nottm Univ BEd78 Hull Univ BTh98 De Montfort Univ Leic MA99 Huddersfield Univ BA03. Linc Th Coll 79. **d** 80 **p** 81. C Sherwood *S'well* 80-83; C Burghclere w Newtown and Ecchinswell w Sydmonton *Win* 83-86; TV Hemel Hempstead *St Alb* 86-93; V Kingston upon Hull St Nic *York* 93-03; V Mansfield Woodhouse *S'well* from 03. *The Vicarage, 7 Butt Lane, Mansfield Woodhouse, Mansfield NG19 9JS* Tel (01623) 621875 E-mail allanbedbt@aol.com

SCRIVENS, Mrs Elaine. b 53. TCert74 Man Univ BEd75. NEOC. **d** 00 **p** 01. NSM E Coatham *York* 00-02; NSM Coatham and Dormanstown 02-04; Chapl Ven Bede Sch Ryhope from 04. *Ven Bede C of E Secondary School, Tunstall Bank, Sunderland SR2 0SX* Tel 0191-523 9745 Fax 523 9775

SCROGGIE, Mrs Felicity Marie-Louise. b 62. Pemb Coll Ox BA86 St Andr Univ MPhil87. STETS BTh99. **d** 99 **p** 00. C Brondesbury St Anne w Kilburn H Trin *Lon* 99-02; V Sudbury St Andr from 02. *St Andrew's Vicarage, 956 Harrow Road, Wembley HA0 2QA* Tel (020) 8904 4016
E-mail felicity.scroggie@london.anglican.org

SCRUBY, The Ven Ronald Victor. b 19. Trin Hall Cam BA48 MA52. Cuddesdon Coll 48. **d** 50 **p** 51. Chapl K Edw VII Hosp Midhurst 50-53; C Rogate *Chich* 50-53; Ind Chapl Saunders-Roe E Cowes 53-58; V Eastney *Portsm* 58-65; RD Portsm 60-65; Adn Is of Wight 65-77; Adn Portsm 77-85; rtd 85; Perm to Offic *Chich* 85-94 and *Portsm* from 85. *Church House, Rogate, Petersfield GU31 5EA* Tel (01730) 821784

SCUFFHAM, Canon Frank Leslie. b 30. AKC56. **d** 57 **p** 58. C Kettering SS Pet and Paul 57-59; Ind Chapl *Sheff* 60-61; Ind Chapl *Pet* 61-95; Can Pet Cathl 72-95; RD Corby 76-79; P-in-c Stoke Albany w Wilbarston 79; R 79-95; rtd 95; Perm to Offic *St E* from 95. *The Orchard, Earlsford Road, Mellis, Eye IP23 8EA* Tel (01379) 783378 E-mail fscuff@yahoo.co.uk

SCULLY, Hazel Mary. RGN SCM. **d** 01 **p** 02. Aux Min Portarlington w Cloneyhurke, Lea etc *M & K* 01-06; Chapl Wilson's Hosp Sch Multyfarnham from 06. *Wilson's Hospital School, Multyfarnham, Co Westmeath, Republic of Ireland* Tel (00353) (44) 937 1115 Mobile 87-281 3956

SCULLY, Kevin John. b 55. NIDA RDA96. St Steph Ho Ox 91. **d** 93 **p** 94. C Stoke Newington St Mary *Lon* 93-97; C Stepney St Dunstan and All SS 97-00; Dir of Ords from 97; Voc Adv from 97; P-in-c Bethnal Green St Matt w St Jas the Gt 00-02; R from 02. *The Rectory, Hereford Street, London E2 6EX* Tel and fax (020) 7739 7586 E-mail revkev@onetel.com

SCURR, David. b 54. Wilson Carlile Coll 98 SAOMC 05. **d** 05 **p** 06. C Thatcham *Ox* 05-08; P-in-c Farndon and Coddington *Ches* from 08. *The Vicarage, Church Lane, Farndon, Chester CH3 6QD* Tel and fax (01829) 270270
E-mail david.scurr@tinyworld.co.uk

SCUTTER, Canon James Edward. b 36. OBE91. AKC59 St Boniface Warminster 59. **d** 60 **p** 61. C Tilbury Docks *Chelmsf* 60-63; Bechuanaland 63-65; Rhodesia 65-70; New Zealand 70-79; Singapore 79-81; New Zealand from 81; Prin Chapl NZ Defence Force 84-91; QHC from 84; Hon Can Wellington from 87. *32 Waiatheke Road, RD1, Otaki 5581, New Zealand* Tel (0064) (4) 364 3260 E-mail jandhscutter@asiaonline.net.nz

SEABRIGHT, Mrs Elizabeth Nicola. b 52. SRN73. WEMTC 01. **d** 04 **p** 05. NSM Ledbury *Heref* from 04. *The Grove Cottage, Fromes Hill, Ledbury HR8 1HP* Tel (01531) 640252
E-mail nicky.seabright@tesco.net

SEABROOK, Alan Geoffrey. b 43. ALCD65. **d** 66 **p** 67. C Bethnal Green St Jas Less *Lon* 66-70; C Madeley *Heref* 70-73; V Girlington *Bradf* 74-80; P-in-c Abdon w Clee St Margaret *Heref* 80-83; R Bitterley 80-83; P-in-c Cold Weston 80-83; P-in-c Hopton Cangeford 80-83; P-in-c Stoke St Milburgh w Heath 80-83; R Bitterley w Middleton, Stoke St Milborough etc 83-08; RD Ludlow 01-05; rtd 08. *Penhope House, Ballhurst, Bromyard HR7 4EF* Tel (01885) 482184

SEABROOK, Alistair William. b 78. CCC Ox BA99 MA03. Oak Hill Th Coll MTh06. **d** 06 **p** 07. C The Ortons, Alwalton and Chesterton *Ely* 06-09; C Elton w Stibbington and Water Newton 06-09; C Gladesville Australia from 09. *Address temp unknown* E-mail alistair_seabrook@yahoo.co.uk

SEABROOK, Preb Geoffrey Barry. b 45. Open Univ BA77 DipEd Lon Univ MA(Ed)84. Chich Th Coll 66. **d** 69 **p** 70. C Tottenham All Hallows *Lon* 69-72; C Winchmore Hill H Trin 72-74; V Hornsey St Geo 74-82; P-in-c Hornsey St Mary 80-82; R Hornsey St Mary w St Geo from 82; P-in-c Hornsey H Innocents 84-92; AD W Haringey 95-00; Preb St Paul's Cathl from 01. *Hornsey Rectory, 140 Cranley Gardens, London N10 3AH* Tel (020) 8883 6846 Fax 8352 0879 E-mail gb.seabrook@virgin.net

SEABROOK, Paul. b 60. Univ of Wales (Cardiff) BA81 Nottm Univ PGCE82. Ridley Hall Cam 01. **d** 03 **p** 04. C Wimborne Minster *Sarum* 03-07; R Taverham *Nor* from 07. *The Rectory, 173 Taverham Road, Taverham, Norwich NR8 6SG* Tel (01603) 868217 E-mail seabrooktribe@telco4u.net

SEABROOK, Mrs Penelope Anne. b 56. Hertf Coll Ox BA77 K Coll Lon MA98. SEITE 00. **d** 03 **p** 04. C Southfields St Barn *S'wark* 03-08; NSM 03-07; C Fulham All SS *Lon* from 08. *8 Deodar Road, London SW15 2NN* Tel 07985-108541 (mobile) E-mail pennyseabrook@hotmail.com

SEABROOK, Richard Anthony. b 68. Southn Univ BTh92. Chich Th Coll 92. **d** 92 **p** 93. C Cottingham *York* 92-94; C Hawley H Trin *Guildf* 94-98; V Hockley *Chelmsf* 98-05; R Benalla Australia from 05. *Holy Trinity Rectory, 77 Arundel Street, Benalla Vic 3672, Australia* Tel (0061) (3) 5762 2061 Fax 5762 7009

SEACH, Gregory John. b 65. Sydney Univ BA88 DipEd88 Clare Coll Cam PhD09. Trin Coll Melbourne BD02. **d** 02 **p** 02. C Camberwell St Jo Australia 02-04; Perm to Offic *Ely* 05-08; Dean Clare Coll Cam from 08. *Clare College, Cambridge CB2 1TL* Tel (01223) 333240 E-mail gjs32@cam.ac.uk

SEAFORD, The Very Revd John Nicholas. b 39. Dur Univ BA67. St Chad's Coll Dur 68. **d** 68 **p** 69. C Bush Hill Park St Mark *Lon* 68-71; C Stanmore *Win* 71-73; V N Baddesley 73-76; V Chilworth w N Baddesley 76-78; V Highcliffe w Hinton Admiral 78-93; RD Christchurch 90-93; Hon Can Win Cathl 93-05; Dean Jersey and R Jersey St Helier 93-05; Angl Adv Channel TV 93-05; Chapl Jersey Airport 98-00; Chapl HM Pris La Moye 03-05; rtd 05; Perm to Offic *Sarum* and *Win* from 05. *Claremont, Buffetts Road, Sturminster Newton DT10 1DZ* Tel (01258) 471479

SEAGO, Timothy Paul. b 59. Ripon Coll Cuddesdon 06. **d** 08 **p** 09. C Marlborough *Sarum* from 08. *The Firs, Salisbury Road, Marlborough SN8 4AE* Tel 07772-809136 (mobile) E-mail timseago@btinternet.com

SEAGRAVE, Katherine Victoria. b 81. Wycliffe Hall Ox. **d** 09. C Balham Hill Ascension *S'wark* from 09. *107B Ramsden Road, London SW12 8RD* Tel 07905-342802 (mobile)

SEAL, Nicholas Peter. b 57. Ex Univ BA. Linc Th Coll 81. **d** 83 **p** 84. C Wareham *Sarum* 83-87; Chapl K Alfred Coll *Win* 87-91; V Stanmore 91-01; P-in-c Win St Matt from 01; RD Win 99-07; Chapl Peter Symonds Coll Win from 01. *The Rectory, 44 Cheriton Road, Winchester SO22 5AY* Tel and fax (01962) 854849 E-mail peter.seal@ntlworld.com

SEAL, Philip Trevor. b 32. AKC55. **d** 56 **p** 57. C Godalming *Guildf* 56-60; C Tamworth *Lich* 60-61; R Lich St Chad 61-73; Chapl HM Youth Cust Cen Swinfen Hall 66-73; R Shere *Guildf* 74-88; RD Cranleigh 76-81; V Abbotsbury, Portesham and Langton Herring *Sarum* 88-97; rtd 97; Perm to Offic *Ex* 01-08. *Llys Helyg, Llwyncoed Road, Blaenannerch, Cardigan SA43 2AN*

SEAL, Ronald Frederick. b 28. Ca Tr Coll Linc Th Coll 59. **d** 61 **p** 62. C Bedhampton *Portsm* 61-65; R N and S Kilworth *Leic* 65-71; R Barwell w Potters Marston and Stapleton 71-80; P-in-c Upper Stour *Sarum* 80-82; R Upper Stour 84-90; RD Heytesbury 87-89; Miss to Seamen Bermuda 90-92; rtd 92; Perm to Offic *Sarum* from 92. *26 Freame Way, Gillingham SP8 4RA* Tel (01747) 825462

SEAL (formerly MILLER), Mrs Rosamund Joy. b 56. R Holloway Coll Lon BSc77 Whitelands Coll Lon PGCE80. EMMTC 89. **d** 94 **p** 96. NSM Grantham *Linc* 94-96; C Stamford All SS w St Jo 96-00; C Spalding 00-05; P-in-c Moulton from 05. *The Vicarage, 34 Church Lane, Moulton, Spalding PE12 6NP* Tel (01406) 370791 E-mail rosamund@sealatmoulton.co.uk

SEAL, William Christopher Houston. b 50. Occidental Coll (USA) BA72. Ch Div Sch of the Pacific (USA) MDiv81. **d** 81 **p** 82. USA 81-88 and from 94; R Etton w Helpston *Pet* 88-94. *The Rectory, 171 Grove Street, Nevada City CA 95959-2601, USA* Tel (001) (530) 265 8836

SEALE, William Arthur. b 62. NUI BA84. CITC. **d** 87 **p** 88. C Drumragh w Mountfield *D & R* 87-90; I Drumgath w Drumgooland and Clonduff *D & D* 90-01. *The Rectory, 4 Mullaghmenagh Avenue, Omagh BT78 5QH* Tel and fax (028) 8224 2130 E-mail waseale@btinternet.com *or* drumragh@derry.anglican.org

SEALY, Daniel O'Neill. b 21. Oak Hill Th Coll 62. **d** 64 **p** 65. C Walcot *B & W* 64-67; Chapl RN 67-73; Nigeria 73-79; Libya

79-82; Tunisia 82-86; rtd 86; I Kilgariffe Union *C, C & R* 87-92. *Swanhill, Culver Crest, Newent GL18 1JA*

SEALY, Canon Gordon William Hugh. b 27. Leeds Univ BA53 MA64. Coll of Resurr Mirfield 53. **d** 55 **p** 56. C Greenford H Cross *Lon* 55-58; Br Honduras 58-68; R Tarrant Gunville, Tarrant Hinton etc *Sarum* 68-74; V Leic St Paul 74-96; Hon Can Leic Cathl 86-96; rtd 96. *12 Kingfisher Court, West Bay, Bridport DT6 4HQ* Tel (01308) 422045

SEALY, Stephen. b 52. K Coll Lon BD86 AKC86. Linc Th Coll 86. **d** 88 **p** 89. C Botley *Portsm* 88-91; Min Can and Prec Cant Cathl 91-96; V Pembury *Roch* 96-04; V Sidcup St Jo from 04; AD Sidcup from 08. *St John's Vicarage, 13 Church Avenue, Sidcup DA14 6BU* Tel and fax (020) 8300 0383 E-mail stephen.sealy@diocese-rochester.org

SEAMAN, Canon Arthur Roland Mostyn. b 32. TCD BA55 DipEd56 Div Test56 MA58. Westcott Ho Cam 58. **d** 58 **p** 59. C Blackley St Pet *Man* 58-61; C Sanderstead All SS *S'wark* 61-62; V Heywood St Luke *Man* 62-70; Dir of Educn 70-85; Hon Can Man Cathl 74-95; R Chorlton-cum-Hardy St Werburgh 85-95; rtd 95; Perm to Offic *Newc* from 95. *10 The Haven, Beadnell, Chathill NE67 5AW* Tel (01665) 720510

SEAMAN, Christopher Robert. b 34. St Jo Coll Ox BA58 MA74 Solicitor 62. Ox Min Course 92 SAOMC 94. **d** 95 **p** 96. NSM Watlington w Pyrton and Shirburn *Ox* 95-97; NSM Icknield 97-98; Perm to Offic 98-99 and from 05; NSM Shippon 99-04. *5 Curtyn Close, Abingdon OX14 1SE* Tel (01235) 520380

SEAMAN, John. See SEAMAN, Robert John

SEAMAN, Miss Miranda Kate. b 66. Univ Coll Lon BSc88 Solicitor 90. EAMTC 02. **d** 05 **p** 06. NSM S Weald *Chelmsf* 05-08; NSM Ingatestone w Fryerning from 08. *Hollyhock Cottage, 25 Common Lane, Stock, Ingatestone CM4 9LP* Tel (01277) 841921 *or* 210021 Mobile 07909-522763 E-mail seaman-young@tiscali.co.uk

SEAMAN, Paul Robert. b 61. Bp Grosseteste Coll BEd82. Chich Th Coll 83. **d** 86 **p** 87. C Tilehurst St Mich *Ox* 86-91; TV Moulsecoomb *Chich* 91-95; R Whyke w Rumboldswhyke and Portfield 95-06; V E Grinstead St Mary from 06. *St Mary's Vicarage, Windmill Lane, East Grinstead RH19 2DS* Tel (01342) 323439

SEAMAN (née HEWLINS), Mrs Pauline Elizabeth. b 47. Lon Univ BD68 AKC. Ox Min Course 93. **d** 96 **p** 97. NSM Radley and Sunningwell *Ox* 96-99; NSM Shippon 99-09; P-in-c 06-09; Chapl SS Helen and Kath Sch Abingdon 96-04; Chapl SW Oxon Primary Care Trust 05-07. *5 Curtyn Close, Abingdon OX14 1SE* Tel (01235) 520380

SEAMAN, Robert John. b 44. Glos Univ BA04 Newland Park Teacher Tr Coll DipEd69 ACP84. EAMTC 84. **d** 84 **p** 85. NSM Downham Market w Bexwell *Ely* 84-90; V Southea w Murrow and Parson Drove 90-97; V Guyhirn w Ring's End 90-97; V Newnham w Awre and Blakeney *Glouc* 97-08; AD Forest N 04-08; rtd 08; Hon C Whitwick St Jo the Bapt *Leic* from 08; Hon C Thringstone St Andr from 08; Hon C Swannington from 08. *The Vicarage, 37 North Street, Whitwick, Coalville LE67 5HB* Tel (01530) 813268 E-mail seaman437@btinternet.com

SEAMER, Stephen James George. b 50. AKC73. Ridley Hall Cam 74. **d** 75 **p** 76. C Rustington *Chich* 75-78; C Bulwell St Jo *S'well* 78-79; P-in-c Camber and E Guldeford *Chich* 79-80; TV Rye 80-83; V Knowle *Birm* 83-87; Assoc Chapl Brussels Cathl 87-88; P-in-c Tervuren 88-94; Chapl 94-98; P-in-c Liège 90-98; V Tonbridge SS Pet and Paul *Roch* 98-06; Chapl Düsseldorf *Eur* from 06. *Mulvany House, Rotterdamer Strasse 135, 40474 Düsseldorf, Germany* Tel (0049) (211) 452759 E-mail christchurch@online.de

SEAR, Peter Lionel. b 37. Ex Univ BA72. Linc Th Coll 72. **d** 74 **p** 75. C Sheldon *Birm* 74-77; C Caversham *Ox* 77-81; C Caversham St Pet and Mapledurham etc 81-85; TR Thatcham 85-98; V Castle Cary w Ansford *B & W* 98-00; rtd 00; Perm to Offic *B & W* from 03. *Knowle Cottage, Lamyatt, Shepton Mallet BA4 6NP* Tel (01749) 813226 E-mail peter@knowlecottage.wanadoo.co.uk

SEAR, Terence Frank. b 39. LDS62 Univ Coll Lon BDS63. Portsm Dioc Tr Course 88. **d** 89. NSM Ryde H Trin *Portsm* 89-98; NSM Swanmore St Mich w Havenstreet 89-92; NSM Swanmore St Mich 92-98; NSM Wroxall 99-00; NSM Godshill 99-01; Perm to Offic from 02. *34 Whitehead Crescent, Wootton Bridge, Ryde PO33 4JF* Tel (01983) 883560

SEARE, Mrs Janice Mae. b 48. SEN. STETS 99. **d** 02 **p** 03. NSM Holdenhurst and Iford *Win* from 02. *Wood Farm, Holdenhurst Village, Bournemouth BH8 0EE* Tel (01202) 302468 Fax 391281

SEARL, John. b 37. Southn Univ BSc58 Edin Univ PhD69. **d** 00 **p** 01. NSM Edin St Cuth 00-03; Asst P Poolewe and Kishorn *Mor* 05-08; Lic to Offic from 08. *Tulach Ard, Badachro, Gairloch IV21 2AA* Tel (01445) 741231 E-mail m.jsearl@tiscali.co.uk

SEARLE, Alan Mansfield. b 47. SEITE 04. **d** 07 **p** 08. NSM E Malling, Wateringbury and Teston *Roch* from 07. *6 Cobbs Close, Wateringbury, Maidstone ME18 5NJ* Tel (01622) 814443 E-mail alan.searle8@btinternet.com

SEARLE, Charles Peter. b 20. Selw Coll Cam BA48 MA53. Ridley Hall Cam. **d** 50 **p** 51. C Becontree St Mary *Chelmsf*

50-53; P-in-c Bedford St Jo *St Alb* 53-56; R 56-60; V Weston-super-Mare Ch Ch *B & W* 60-70; V Woking Ch Ch *Guildf* 70-85; rtd 85; Perm to Offic *Ex* 85-07. *17 Woodlands Court, The Mount, St Johns, Woking GU21 7FA* Tel (01483) 773577 E-mail asearle@dialstart.net

SEARLE, David William. b 37. MASI89 ACIOB98. **d** 99 **p** 00. OLM E Bergholt and Brantham *St E* 99-07; rtd 07; Perm to Offic *St E* from 07. *46 Chaplin Road, East Bergholt, Colchester CO7 6SR* Tel (01206) 298932

SEARLE, Canon Hugh Douglas. b 35. St Cath Coll Cam BA59 MA63 Cranfield Inst of Tech MSc85. Oak Hill Th Coll 59. **d** 61 **p** 62. C Islington H Trin Cloudesley Square *Lon* 61-64; Chapl HM Pris Lewes 64-65; Chapl HM Borstal Roch 65-69; Chapl HM Youth Cust Cen Hollesley Bay Colony 70-74; Chapl HM Pris Parkhurst 74-78; P-in-c Barton *Ely* 78-84; V 84-00; P-in-c Coton 78-84; R 84-00; RD Bourn 81-92; Hon Can Ely Cathl 97-00; rtd 00; Perm to Offic *Ely* from 00. *38 Field End, Witchford, Ely CB6 2XE* Tel (01353) 659749

SEARLE, Jacqueline Ann. b 60. Whitelands Coll Lon BEd82 Bris Univ MA01. Trin Coll Bris 90. **d** 92 **p** 94. Par Dn Roxeth *Lon* 92-94; C Ealing St Steph Castle Hill 94-96; Tutor and Dean of Women Trin Coll Bris 96-03; P-in-c Littleover *Derby* 03-04; V from 04. *The Vicarage, 35 Church Street, Littleover, Derby DE23 6GF* Tel (01332) 767802 E-mail j.searle80@ntlworld.com *or* jackie@stpeterlittleover.org.uk

SEARLE, John Francis. b 42. OBE98. FRCA70 FRSM84 Lon Univ MB, BS66. SW Minl Tr Course 92. **d** 95 **p** 96. NSM Ex St Leon w H Trin 95-03; Assoc Staff Member SWMTC from 03; Perm to Offic *Truro* from 03. *Belle Isle Lodge, Belle Isle Drive, Exeter EX2 4RY* Tel (01392) 432153 E-mail johnlizex@aol.com

SEARLE, Mark Robin. b 73. Cen Sch Speech & Drama BA94. Trin Coll Bris BA03. **d** 03 **p** 04. C Ashtead St Mary Bredin 03-07; C Ashtead *Guildf* from 07. *1 Oakfield Road, Ashtead KT21 2RE* Tel (01372) 813334 E-mail marksearle@btinternet.com

SEARLE, Michael Stanley. b 38. AMIQ63. NOC 93. **d** 95 **p** 96. NSM Hoole *Ches* 95-99; P-in-c Marbury 99-06; P-in-c Tushingham and Whitewell 02-06; R Marbury w Tushingham and Whitewell; rtd 06. *2 Meadow Close, Farndon, Chester CH3 6PP* Tel (01829) 271198 Mobile 07850-720120 E-mail mike.s.searle@btinternet.com

SEARLE, Michael Westran. b 47. Leeds Univ LLB68. Cuddesdon Coll 69. **d** 71 **p** 72. C Norton St Mary *Dur* 71-74; C Westbury-on-Trym H Trin *Bris* 74-77; V Bedminster Down 77-84; V Bris Ch the Servant Stockwood 84-88; Dir of Tr *York* 88-00; R Dunnington 00-07; rtd 07. *Lamorna Vean, Lamorna, Penzance TR19 6NY* Tel (01736) 810218 E-mail msearle@yorktrain.demon.co.uk

SEARLE, Peter. *See* SEARLE, Charles Peter

SEARLE, Philip Robert. b 67. Westcott Ho Cam. **d** 95 **p** 96. C Plymstock *Ex* 95-97; C Plymstock and Hooe 97-98; TV Stoke-upon-Trent *Lich* from 98. *All Saints' Vicarage, 540 Leek Road, Stoke-on-Trent ST1 3HH* Tel (01782) 205713 E-mail hairetic@surfaid.org

SEARLE, Ralph Alan. b 57. G&C Coll Cam BA79 MA83. Coll of Resurr Mirfield 81. **d** 83 **p** 84. C Cockerton *Dur* 83-86; C S Shields All SS 86-88; TV 88-96; Assoc P Worksop Priory *S'well* 96-97; Assoc P Paignton St Jo *Ex* 97-01; V Horfield St Greg *Bris* 01-03; Hon Min Can Bris Cathl 02-03. *2 Temple Gate, Temple End, High Wycombe HP13 5DY* Tel (01494) 437012 E-mail fr.ralph@tinyonline.co.uk

SEARLE-BARNES, Albert Victor. b 28. Sheff Univ BA48 Lon Univ BD53. ALCD53. **d** 53 **p** 54. C Iver *Ox* 53-55; C Attenborough w Bramcote *S'well* 55-59; C Bramcote 55-59; R Cratfield w Heveningham and Ubbeston *St E* 59-64; R Wick w Doynton *Bris* 64-70; Perm to Offic 70-72; V Downend 73-78; V Market Rasen *Linc* 78-86; R Linwood 79-86; V Legsby 79-86; R Green's Norton w Bradden *Pet* 86-88; V Hambledon *Portsm* 88-92; rtd 92; Perm to Offic *Glouc* 92-09. *30 Gracey Court, Woodland Road, Exeter EX5 3GA* Tel (01392) 462613

SEARLE-BARNES, Belinda Rosemary. b 51. Lon Univ MA93 ARCM72 GRSM73. Sarum Th Coll 93. **d** 96 **p** 97. NSM Pimperne, Stourpaine, Durweston and Bryanston *Sarum* 96-00; Asst Par Development Adv 98-00; Asst Chapl Bryanston Sch 98-00; TV Southampton (City Cen) *Win* 00-04; Chapl Godolphin Sch 04-07; P-in-c Winslow w Gt Horwood and Addington *Ox* 07-08; R from 08. *The Vicarage, 19 Vicarage Road, Winslow, Buckingham MK18 3BJ* Tel (01296) 712564 E-mail bsbwinslow@fsmail.net

SEARS, Helen. *See* THAKE, Ms Helen

SEARS, Jacqueline Isabella. SRN69. NTMTC 95. **d** 99 **p** 00. NSM Hanwell St Mellitus w St Mark *Lon* 99-03; Asst Chapl Essex Rivers Healthcare NHS Trust 03-04; Chapl Colchester Hosp Univ NHS Foundn Trust from 04; C Ipswich St Matt *St E* 04-06; C Triangle, St Matt and All SS from 06. *4 Woodward Close, Ipswich IP2 0EA* Tel (01473) 214125 Mobile 07984-077990 E-mail jackie@searsfamily.fsnet.co.uk

SEARS, Jeanette. b 59. Man Univ BA80 PhD84 Lon Univ PGCE85. Wycliffe Hall Ox 90. **d** 92 **p** 94. NSM Ox St Aldate

92-96; Perm to Offic *Lon* 98-01 and *Ox* 01-04; Tutor Trin Coll Bris from 04. *1 Little Stoke Road, Bristol BS9 1HQ* Tel 0117-968 6810 Mobile 07950-047476 E-mail jeanette.sears@trinity-bris.ac.uk

SEARS, Michael Antony. b 50. Birm Univ BSc71 PGCE72. Linc Th Coll 78. **d** 80 **p** 81. C Willenhall H Trin *Lich* 80-83; C Caldmore 83-84; P-in-c 84-86; V 86-89; Abp Ilsley RC Sch Birm 89-97; TV Solihull *Birm* 98-02; R Castle Bromwich SS Mary and Marg 02-07; R Wroxham w Hoveton and Belaugh *Nor* from 07. *The Vicarage, 11 Church Lane, Wroxham, Norwich NR12 8SH* Tel (01603) 784536 E-mail rectorwhb@googlemail.com

SEATON, Canon James Bradbury. b 29. Ch Coll Cam BA53 MA57. Westcott Ho Cam 53. **d** 55 **p** 56. C Derby St Werburgh 55-58; C Darlington St Cuth *Dur* 58-64; V Preston on Tees 64-72; TV Stockton H Trin 72-73; TV Cen Stockton 73-75; R Anstey *Leic* 75-89; RD Sparkenhoe III 81-89; Hon Can Leic Cathl 87-94; R Market Harborough Transfiguration 89-94; rtd 94; Perm to Offic *Glouc* from 94. *Wayside, Sheep Street, Chipping Campden GL55 6DW* Tel (01386) 841753

SEATON-BURN, Paul Simon. b 70. Ex Univ BA92. St Jo Coll Nottm MTh06. **d** 06 **p** 07. C Broughton w Loddington and Cransley etc *Pet* 06-09; P-in-c Desborough, Brampton Ash, Dingley and Braybrooke from 09. *The Vicarage, Lower Street, Desborough, Kettering NN14 2NP* E-mail seaton-burn@tiscali.co.uk

SEBER, Derek Morgan. b 43. Man Poly MA87 Man Metrop Univ MPhil96. Oak Hill Th Coll 71. **d** 73 **p** 74. C Collyhurst *Man* 73-76; C Radcliffe St Thos and St Jo 76-77; Ind Missr 77-89; P-in-c Hulme St Geo 77-83; Hon C Moss Side St Jas w St Clem 83-96; Project Officer Linking Up 89-96; Lic Preacher 90-96; P-in-c Cheetham St Jo 97; P-in-c Thornton Hough *Ches* 97-05; V 05-08; Ind Chapl 97-05; rtd 08. *8 Hillside, Hawarden, Deeside CH5 3HQ* Tel (01244) 535583 E-mail derek@morganseber.freeserve.co.uk

SECCOMBE, Marcus John. b 34. Oak Hill Th Coll 60. **d** 63 **p** 64. C Woodthorpe *S'well* 63-67; C Doncaster St Mary *Sheff* 67-72; V Owston 72-90; R Rossington 90-99; rtd 99; Perm to Offic *Sheff* from 99. *39 Marlborough Road, Doncaster DN2 5DF* Tel (01302) 321505 E-mail mark@secco9.freeserve.co.uk

SECOMBE, Preb Frederick Thomas. b 18. St D Coll Lamp BA40 St Mich Coll Llan 40. **d** 42 **p** 43. C Swansea St Mark *S & B* 42-44; C Knighton 44-46; C Machen *Mon* 46-49; C Newport St Woolos 49-52; Chapl St Woolos Hosp Newport 49-52; V Llanarth w Clytha, Llansantffraed and Bryngwyn *Mon* 52-54; R Machen and Rudry 54-59; V Swansea St Pet *S & B* 59-69; R Hanwell St Mary *Lon* 69-83; AD Ealing W 78-82; Preb St Paul's Cathl 81-83; rtd 83. *30 Westville Road, Penylan, Cardiff CF23 5AG* Tel (029) 2048 3978

SECRETAN, Ms Jenny Ruth. b 54. St Aid Coll Dur BA76 Ex Univ PGCE77 Dur Univ MA97. Linc Th Coll 81 Cranmer Hall Dur 83. **dss** 84 **d** 87 **p** 94. Asst Chapl Newc Poly 84-86; Sunderland St Chad *Dur* 84-86; Bordesley St Oswald *Birm* 86-91; Par Dn 87-91; Assoc Soc Resp Officer *Dur* 92-95; Perm to Offic *Dur* and *Newc* 95-99. *14 Southwood Gardens, Newcastle upon Tyne NE3 3BU*

SEDANO, Juan Antonio. b 55. Centro de Discipulado Lima 85. **d** 88 **p** 88. Peru 88-90; Crosslinks 91-94; SAMS from 95; NSM Ingrave St Steph CD *Chelmsf* from 95. *5 The Chase, Middle Road, Ingrave, Brentwood CM13 3QT* Tel (01277) 810907 E-mail esedano@btinternet.com

SEDDON, Mrs Carol Susan. b 44. ARCM63 GNSM66 Man Univ CertEd67. Ripon Coll Cuddesdon. **d** 05 **p** 06. NSM Alsager St Mary *Ches* 05-08; Asst Chapl HM YOI Stoke Heath 05-08; V Northwich St Luke and H Trin *Ches* from 08. *1 Tall Trees Close, Northwich CW8 4YA* Tel (01606) 74632 Mobile 07973-737038 E-mail carol_seddon@hotmail.com

SEDDON, Ernest Geoffrey. b 26. Man Univ MA85 ARIBA51. St Deiniol's Hawarden 80. **d** 80 **p** 81. C Dunham Massey St Marg *Ches* 80-83; P-in-c Warburton 82-87; P-in-c Dunham Massey St Mark 85-86; 86-92; rtd 92; Perm to Offic *Ches* from 92. *7 Colwyn Place, Llandudno LL30 3AW* Tel (01492) 547639 *or* 642107

SEDDON, Philip James. b 45. Jes Coll Cam BA68 MA71 Birm Univ MPhil01. Ridley Hall Cam 67. **d** 70 **p** 71. C Tonge w Alkrington *Man* 70-74; CMS Nigeria 74-78; Lect St Jo Coll Nottm 78-79; Lic to Offic *Ely* 79-85; Chapl Magd Coll Cam 79-85; Lect Bibl Studies Selly Oak Colls 86-00; Lic to Offic *Birm* 87-05; Lect Th Birm Univ 00-05; Dir Min STETS from 05. *Sarum College, 19 The Close, Salisbury SP1 2EE* Tel (01722) 424820 Fax 424811 E-mail pjseddon@stets.ac.uk

SEDEN, Martin Roy. b 47. Man Univ MSc Salford Univ PhD. EMMTC 79. **d** 82 **p** 83. NSM Knighton St Mary Magd *Leic* 82-07; NSM Rutland Deanery from 08. *60 Leicester Road, Uppingham, Oakham LE15 9SD* Tel (01572) 822244 Mobile 07806-940407 E-mail rseden@googlemail.com

SEDGEWICK, Clive Malcolm. b 56. Loughb Univ BSc78 UEA MA92 PGCE79. SAOMC 00. **d** 04 **p** 05. NSM High Harrogate

743

SEDGLEY

Ch Ch *Ripon* from 04. *11 Bogs Lane, Harrogate HG1 4DY* Tel (01423) 548548 *or* 817553 Mobile 07903-326053 E-mail clives@brleducationteam.org.uk

SEDGLEY, Mrs Jean. b 41. Whitelands Coll Lon CertEd63. S Dios Minl Tr Scheme 92. **d** 95 **p** 96. NSM Haywards Heath St Wilfrid *Chich* 95-01; NSM Cuckfield 01-09; rtd 09. *25 Pasture Hill Road, Haywards Heath RH16 1LY* Tel (01444) 413974

SEDGLEY, Canon Timothy John. b 42. St Jo Coll Ox BA63 MA68. Westcott Ho Cam 64. **d** 66 **p** 67. C Nor St Pet Mancroft 66-70; V Costessey 70-79; RD Nor N 75-79; V Walton-on-Thames *Guildf* 79-05; RD Emly 86-91; Hon Can Guildf Cathl 86-05; Dir OLMs and NSMs 93-05; rtd 05. *6 St Paul's Court, Moreton-in-Marsh, Gloucester GL56 0ET* E-mail timsedgley@hotmail.com

SEDGWICK, Jonathan Maurice William. b 63. BNC Ox BA85 MA89 Leeds Univ BA88. Coll of Resurr Mirfield 86. **d** 89 **p** 90. C Chich St Paul and St Pet 89-91; Dean of Div and Chapl Magd Coll Ox 91-94; Perm to Offic *S'wark* 97-00; Hon C E Dulwich St Jo from 00. *46 Wood Vale, London SE23 3EE* Tel (020) 8693 8129 E-mail jonathan@woodvale46.freeserve.co.uk

SEDGWICK, Peter Humphrey. b 48. Trin Hall Cam BA70 Dur Univ PhD83. Westcott Ho Cam *71.* **d** 74 **p** 75. C Stepney St Dunstan and All SS *Lon* 74-77; P-in-c Pittington *Dur* 77-79; Lect Th Birm Univ 79-82; Hon C The Lickey *Birm* 79-82; Th Consultant for NE Ecum Gp *Dur* 82-88; Lect Th Hull Univ 88-94; Abp's Adv on Ind Issues *York* 88-94; Vice-Prin Westcott Ho Cam 94-96; Asst Sec Abps' Coun Bd for Soc Resp 96-04; NSM Pet St Barn 96-98; Prin St Mich Coll Llan from 04; Can Llan Cathl from 06. *St Michael's College, 54 Cardiff Road, Llandaff, Cardiff CF5 2YJ* Tel (029) 2056 3379 E-mail revgould@virgin.net

SEDLMAYR, Peter. b 53. Univ Coll Chich BA01. **d** 04. NSM Littlehampton and Wick *Chich* from 04. *83 Joyce Close, Wick, Littlehampton BN17 7JG* Tel (01903) 714968 Mobile 07941-921263 E-mail peterpaul@sedlmayr83.freeserve.co.uk

SEED, Richard Edward. b 55. UNISA BTh86 Westmr Coll Ox MEd. Kalk Bay Bible Inst S Africa. **d** 80 **p** 81. S Africa 80-85 and 87-89; Zimbabwe 85-87; Asst Chapl Kingham Hill Sch Oxon 89-90; C Beckenham Ch Ch *Roch* 90-95; Chapl Düsseldorf *Eur* 96-00; CMS from 00. *CMS, PO Box 1799, Oxford OX4 9BN* Tel 08456-201799

SEED, The Ven Richard Murray Crosland. b 49. Leeds Univ MA91. Edin Th Coll 69. **d** 72 **p** 73. C Skipton Ch Ch *Bradf* 72-75; C Baildon 75-77; Chapl HM Det Cen Kidlington 77-80; TV Kidlington *Ox* 77-80; V Boston Spa *York* 80-99; P-in-c Newton Kyme 84-85; P-in-c Clifford 89-99; P-in-c Thorp Arch w Walton 98-99; Chapl Martin House Hospice for Children Boston Spa 85-99; RD New Ainsty *York* 97-99; Adn York from 99; R York H Trin Micklegate from 00. *Holy Trinity Rectory, Micklegate, York YO1 6JA* Tel (01904) 623798 Fax 628155 E-mail archdeacon.of.york@yorkdiocese.org

SEEL, Richard Malcolm. b 45. **d** 04 **p** 05. OLM Bacton w Edingthorpe w Witton and Ridlington *Nor* 04-07; OLM Happisburgh, Walcott, Hempstead w Eccles etc 04-07; NSM Loddon, Sisland, Chedgrave, Hardley and Langley from 07. *31 Hillside, Chedgrave, Norwich NR14 6HZ* Tel (01508) 521938 Mobile 07711-069680 E-mail richard@emerging-church.org

SEELEY, Jutta. *See* BRUECK, Ms Jutta

SEELEY, Canon Martin Alan. b 54. Jes Coll Cam BA76 MA79. Ripon Coll Cuddesdon 76 Union Th Sem (NY) STM78. **d** 78 **p** 79. C Bottesford w Ashby *Linc* 78-80; USA 80-90; Selection Sec ABM 90-96; Sec for Continuing Minl Educn 90-96; V Is of Dogs Ch Ch and St Jo w St Luke *Lon* 96-06; Prin Westcott Ho Cam from 06; Hon Can Ely Cathl from 08. *St James's Vicarage, 110 Wulfstan Way, Cambridge CB1 8QJ* Tel (01223) 241791 *or* 741010 E-mail mas209@cam.ac.uk

SEGAL, Mrs Marie. b 57. Leeds Univ BEd78. NTMTC BA07. **d** 07 **p** 08. NSM Gt Ilford St Andr *Chelmsf* from 07. *31 Dryden Close, Ilford IG6 3DZ* Tel (020) 8501 0262 Mobile 07787-188449 E-mail segal.marie@btinternet.com

SEGGAR, Jennifer Mary. b 63. Open Univ PGCE01. **d** 05 **p** 06. OLM Bildeston w Wattisham and Lindsey, Whatfield etc *St E* 05-09; C Sudbury and Chilton from 09. *Semer Cottage, Bildeston Road, Semer, Ipswich IP7 6JG* Tel (01473) 822739 E-mail jmseggar@aol.com

SEGRAVE-PRIDE, Mrs Philippa Louise. b 73. Westhill Coll Birm BTh96. Ripon Coll Cuddesdon 97. **d** 99 **p** 00. C Harborne St Pet *Birm* 99-02; TV Tring *St Alb* 02-04; TV Bp's Hatfield 04-05; TV Bp's Hatfield, Lemsford and N Mymms from 05. *St Michael's Vicarage, 31 Homestead Road, Hatfield AL10 0QJ* Tel (01707) 882276

SELBY, Miss Carole Janis. b 50. Chelsea Coll of Physical Educn CertEd71 Sussex Univ BEd72 K Coll Lon MA03. Westcott Ho Cam 93. **d** 95 **p** 96. C Worc St Barn w Ch Ch 95-99; Min Turnford St Clem CD *St Alb* 99-08; TV Cheshunt from 08; RD Cheshunt from 04. *St Clement's House, 4 Haddestoke Gate, Cheshunt, Waltham Cross EN8 0XJ* Tel (01992) 479882 E-mail c_selby@talk21.com

✠**SELBY, The Rt Revd Peter Stephen Maurice.** b 41. St Jo Coll Ox BA64 MA67 Episc Th Sch Cam Mass BD66 K Coll Lon PhD75 Birm Univ Hon DD07. Bps' Coll Cheshunt 66. **d** 66 **p** 67 **c** 84. C Queensbury All SS *Lon* 66-69; C Limpsfield and Titsey *S'wark* 69-77; Assoc Dir of Tr 69-73; Vice-Prin S'wark Ord Course 70-72; Asst Dioc Missr *S'wark* 73-77; Dioc Missr *Newc* 77-84; Can Res Newc Cathl 77-84; Suff Bp Kingston *S'wark* 84-91; Area Bp 91-92; Wm Leech Prof Fell Dur 92-97; Asst Bp Dur and Newc 92-97; Bp Worc 97-07; Hon Prof Univ Coll Worc from 98; Bp HM Pris 01-07; rtd 07; Pres Nat Coun Ind Monitoring Boards from 08; Hon Asst Bp Portsm from 08; Visiting Prof K Coll Lon from 08. *Afton Cottage, Afton Road, Freshwater PO40 9TP* Tel (01983) 759216 E-mail peterselby@onetel.com

SELBY-BOOTHROYD, Richard George. b 46. SWMTC. **d** 09. NSM Halsetown *Truro* from 09; NSM St Ives from 09. *4 Brunel Close, Angarrack, Hayle TR27 5LL* Tel (01736) 752789 E-mail selbyboothroyd@btinternet.com

SELBY, Suffragan Bishop of. *See* WALLACE, The Rt Revd Martin William

SELDON, Francis Peter. b 58. St Jo Coll Nottm 98. **d** 00 **p** 01. C Styvechale *Cov* 00-02; C Cheylesmore 02-04; V from 04. *Christ Church Vicarage, 11 Frankpledge Road, Coventry CV3 5GT* Tel (024) 7650 2770

SELF, Canon David Christopher. b 41. Toronto Univ BSc62 MA64 K Coll Lon BD68 AKC68. **d** 69 **p** 70. C Tupsley *Heref* 69-73; Chapl Dur Univ 73-78; TV Southampton (City Cen) *Win* 78-84; TR Dunstable *St Alb* 84-95; RD Dunstable 90-91; TR Bris St Paul's 95-06; RD Bris City 98-99; AD City 99-03; Hon Can Bris Cathl 99-06; rtd 06. *3 Shannon Court, Thornbury, Bristol BS35 2HN* Tel (01454) 418006 E-mail self@supanet.com

SELF, John Andrew. b 47. Trin Coll Bris 74 CMS Tr Coll Crowther Hall 76. **d** 81 **p** 83. CMS Pakistan 77-91; Assoc V Bath Weston All SS w N Stoke *B & W* 91-92; V Sparkhill St Jo *Birm* from 92. *St John's Vicarage, 15 Phipson Road, Birmingham B11 4JE* Tel and fax 0121-449 2760 *or* tel 753 1415 E-mail john.self@stjohnssparkhill.org.uk

SELF, Peter Allen. b 41. S Dios Minl Tr Scheme 84. **d** 87 **p** 98. NSM Wilton *B & W* 87-91; NSM Taunton Lyngford 91-96; Asst Chapl Taunton and Somerset NHS Trust 96-08; rtd 08. *20 Dyers Close, West Buckland, Wellington TA21 9JU* Tel (01823) 663408 Fax 663448

SELFE, John Ronald. b 41. EMMTC 85. **d** 95 **p** 96. OLM Mid Marsh Gp *Linc* from 95. *Bookend, 236 Eastgate, Louth LN11 8DA* Tel (01507) 603809 E-mail john.dorothyselfe@tiscali.co.uk

SELIM, Claes Eric. b 48. Uppsala Univ MA73 BD76. **p** 77. C Rasbo Sweden 77-80; P-in-c Hablingbo 81-85; P-in-c Öja and Huddunge 85-89; Dep Lect Uppsala Univ 81-89; Lect 89-95; V Öja 89-92; V Vänge 95-00; C Holbeach *Linc* 00-02; R Guernsey Ste Marie du Castel *Win* from 02; V Guernsey St Matt from 02. *Castel Rectory, La Rue de la Lande, Castel, Guernsey GY5 7EJ* Tel (01481) 256793

SELLER, Prof Mary Joan. b 40. Qu Mary Coll Lon BSc61 Lon Univ PhD64 DSc82. S'wark Ord Course 89. **d** 91 **p** 94. NSM Hurst Green *S'wark* from 91. *11 Home Park, Oxted RH8 0JS* Tel (01883) 715675

SELLER, Timothy John. b 46. Qu Mary Coll Lon BSc67 Lon Univ PhD71. **d** 08 **p** 09. OLM Ewhurst *Guildf* from 08. *Kerne Hus, Walliswood, Dorking RH5 5RD* Tel (01306) 627548 Mobile 07845-192041 E-mail t.seller@dsl.pipex.com

SELLERS, Anthony. b 48. Southn Univ BSc71 PhD76. Wycliffe Hall Ox 84. **d** 86 **p** 87. C Luton St Mary *St Alb* 86-90; V Luton St Paul from 90. *St Paul's Vicarage, 37A Arthur Street, Luton LU1 3SG* Tel (01582) 481796 E-mail tsellers@route56.co.uk

SELLERS, George William. b 35. NOC. **d** 89 **p** 90. NSM Rothwell *Ripon* 89-05; rtd 05. *16 Thornegrove, Rothwell, Leeds LS26 0HP* Tel 0113-282 3522

SELLERS, Robert. b 58. Coll of Resurr Mirfield 90. **d** 92 **p** 93. C Wotton St Mary *Glouc* 92-95; TV Redruth w Lanner and Treleigh *Truro* 95-98; P-in-c Devoran 98-03; Bp's Dom Chapl 98-03; R Fountains Gp *Ripon* from 03. *Fountains Rectory, Winksley, Ripon HG4 3NR* Tel (01765) 658260 E-mail robert.sellers@ukonline.co.uk

SELLERS, Mrs Rosalind April. b 48. Liv Univ MA77. SWMTC 06. **d** 09. NSM Cannington, Otterhampton, Combwich and Stockland *B & W* from 09. *1 St Mary's Crescent, North Petherton, Bridgwater TA6 6RA* Tel (01278) 661279 Mobile 07794-666247 E-mail rosalind.sellers@virgin.net

SELLERS, Warren John. b 43. Bp Otter Coll Chich TCert73 W Sussex Inst of HE DipAdEd88. K Coll Lon 63 Sarum Th Coll 65. **d** 68 **p** 69. C Guildf H Trin w St Mary 68-72; Hon C Chich St Paul and St Pet 72-73; C Epping St Jo *Chelmsf* 73-76; Hon C Pulborough *Chich* 76-90; Hon C Fleet *Guildf* 90-92; Teacher 73-89; Waltham Abbey St Lawr and H Cross Schs Essex 73-76; Pulborough St Mary, Easeboure & Bp Tuffnell Schs 76-89; Hd Teacher St Pet Jun Sch Farnborough 90-92; TV Upper Kennet

744

Sarum 92-95; TR 95-03; rtd 03. *71 Bay Crescent, Swanage BH19 1RD* E-mail wjandmjs27@btinternet.com

SELLEY, Paul Edward Henry. b 47. Bris Univ BEd70 ALCM67 LTCL87. Sarum Th Coll 93. **d** 96 **p** 97. C Swindon Dorcan *Bris* 96-00; V Ashton Keynes, Leigh and Minety 00-07; rtd 07. *577 Dorchester Road, Weymouth DT3 5BT* Tel (01305) 814948 E-mail paul.selley@which.net

SELLGREN, Eric Alfred. b 33. AKC61. **d** 62 **p** 63. C Ditton St Mich *Liv* 62-66; V Hindley Green 66-72; V Southport St Paul 72-80; Warden Barn Fellowship Winterborne Whitchurch 80-86; V The Iwernes, Sutton Waldron and Fontmell Magna *Sarum* 86-98; rtd 98; Perm to Offic *Sarum* from 98. *16 The Limes, Motcombe, Shaftesbury SP7 9QL* Tel (01747) 850747

SELLICK, Peter James. b 67. Wadh Coll Ox BA89. Edin Th Coll BD94. **d** 94 **p** 95. C Kippax w Allerton Bywater *Ripon* 94-97; C Stanningley St Thos 97-02; C W Bromwich All SS *Lich* from 02; Ind Chapl Black Country Urban Ind Miss from 02. *7 Hopkins Drive, West Bromwich B71 3RR* Tel 0121-588 3744

SELLIN, Deborah Mary. b 64. St Andr Univ MA86. STETS 04. **d** 07 **p** 08. NSM Guildf St Sav from 07. *206 Stoughton Road, Guildford GU2 9PN* Tel (01483) 870955
E-mail d.sellin@ntlworld.com *or* debbie@stsaviours.org.uk

SELLIX, Mrs Pamela Madge. b 47. Lon Univ BA68 PGCE68. SWMTC 00. **d** 04 **p** 05. NSM Saltash *Truro* from 04. *Farthings, Quarry Road, Pensilva, Liskeard PL14 5NT* Tel (01579) 363464

SELLORS, Glenys Margaret. b 43. NOC. **d** 07 **p** 08. NSM Offerton *Ches* from 07. *36 Brookside Avenue, Stockport SK2 5HR* E-mail glenys.sellors@virgin.net

SELLORS, Michael Harry. b 36. K Coll Lon 60 St Boniface Warminster 61. **d** 61 **p** 62. C Willesden St Mary *Lon* 61-64; C Aldershot St Mich *Guildf* 64-67; V Hale 67-84; P-in-c E w W Beckham *Nor* 84-85; P-in-c Bodham 84-85; V Weybourne w Upper Sheringham 84-85; R Kelling w Salthouse 84-85; R Weybourne Gp 85-91; V Hunstanton St Edm w Ringstead 91-97; Dean Jerusalem 97-02; rtd 02. *Cranford House, 56 Cromer Road, West Runton, Cromer NR27 9AD* Tel (01263) 837293

SELMAN, Michael Richard. b 47. Sussex Univ BA68 Bris Univ MA70. Coll of Resurr Mirfield 71. **d** 73 **p** 74. C Hove All SS *Chich* 73-74; C Horfield H Trin *Bris* 74-78; P-in-c Landkey *Ex* 78-79; C Barnstaple and Goodleigh 78-79; TV Barnstaple, Goodleigh and Landkey 79-82; TR 82-84; P-in-c Sticklepath 83-84; TR Barnstaple 85; RD Barnstaple 83-85; TR Cen Ex 85-00; Chapl Aquitaine *Eur* 00-08; Partnership P E Bris from 08. *St Aidan's Vicarage, 2 Jockey Lane, Bristol BS5 8NZ* Tel 0117-904 2830 Mobile 07735-499920

SELMES, Brian. b 48. Nottm Univ BTh74 Dur Univ MA97. Linc Th Coll 70. **d** 74 **p** 75. C Padgate *Liv* 74-77; C Sydenham St Bart *S'wark* 77-80; Chapl Darlington Memorial Hosp from 80; Chapl Darlington Memorial Hosp NHS Trust 94-98; Chapl S Durham Healthcare NHS Trust 98-02; Chapl Co Durham and Darlington NHS Foundn Trust from 02. *Darlington Memorial Hospital, Hollyhurst Road, Darlington DL3 6HX* Tel (01325) 743029 *or* 359688 E-mail brian.selmes@cddah.nhs.uk

SELVARATNAM, Christian Nathan. b 68. Warwick Univ BSc90. Cranmer Hall Dur 06. **d** 08 **p** 09. NSM York St Mich-le-Belfrey from 08. *11/12 Minster Yard, York YO1 7HH* Tel (01904) 624190 Mobile 07773-784728
E-mail christian.selvaratnam@gmail.com

SELVEY, Canon John Brian. b 33. Dur Univ BA54. Cuddesdon Coll 56. **d** 58 **p** 59. C Lancaster St Mary *Blackb* 58-61; C Blackb Cathl 61-65; Cathl Chapl 64-65; V Foulridge 65-69; V Walton-le-Dale 69-82; V Cleveleys 82-89; Hon Can Bloemfontein Cathl from 88; V Slyne w Hest *Blackb* 89-97; Hon Can Blackb Cathl 93-97; rtd 97; Perm to Offic *Carl* from 98. *Low Quietways, Borrowdale Road, Keswick CA12 5UP* Tel (01768) 773538

SELWOOD, Michael. b 40. Oak Hill Th Coll BA91. **d** 91 **p** 92. Canada 91-95; P-in-c Sherborne, Windrush, the Barringtons etc *Glouc* 95-07; rtd 07. *17 Croft Holm, Moreton-in-Marsh GL56 0JH* Tel (01608) 812384
E-mail 106631.11@compuserve.com

SELWOOD, Robin. b 37. ALCD61. **d** 61 **p** 62. C Lenton *S'well* 61-63; V Norbury *Ches* 63-66; V Newton Flowery Field 66-75; V Kelsall 75-89; V Sale St Paul 89-02; rtd 02; P-in-c Langtoft w Foxholes, Butterwick, Cottam etc *York* 02-06. *16 Harewood Avenue, Bridlington YO16 7PY* Tel (01262) 603078

SELWOOD, Timothy John. b 45. Lon Univ LLB66. Sarum Th Coll. **d** 83 **p** 84. NSM Colbury *Win* 83-85; NSM Copythorne and Minstead 85-90; Perm to Offic from 98. *Monks Barn, Knapp Lane, Ampfield, Romsey SO51 9BT*
E-mail tim_selwood@btinternet.com

SELWYN, David Gordon. b 38. MEHS Clare Coll Cam BA62 MA66 DD New Coll Ox MA66. Ripon Hall Ox 62. **d** 64 **p** 65. C Ecclesall *Sheff* 64-65; Asst Chapl New Coll Ox 65-68; Lect Univ of Wales (Lamp) 68-98; Reader 98-05; Perm to Offic 68-05. *62A Swiss Valley, Llanelli SA14 8BT* Tel (01554) 773983

SEMEONOFF, Canon Jean Mary Agnes. b 36. Leic Coll of Educn MEdSc56 PGCE57. EMMTC 84. **d** 87 **p** 94. Par Dn Leic H Spirit 87 and 89-94; Chapl for Deaf People *Derby* 87-89; Chapl for Deaf People *Leic* 89-94; Hon Can Leic Cathl 92-99; rtd

Bp's Adv for Women's Min *Leic* 93-97; Min for Special Past Duties 94-99; Perm to Offic from 99. *7 Sunnycroft Road, Leicester LE3 6FU* Tel 0116-285 8854
E-mail rjsem@tiscali.co.uk

SEMPER, The Very Revd Colin Douglas. b 38. Keble Coll Ox BA62. Westcott Ho Cam 61. **d** 63 **p** 64. C Guildf H Trin w St Mary 63-67; Sec ACCM 67-69; Producer Relig Broadcasting Dept BBC 69-75; Overseas Relig Broadcasting Org BBC 75-79; Hd Relig Progr BBC Radio 79-82; Hon Can Guildf Cathl 80-82; Provost Cov 82-87; Can and Treas Westmr Abbey 87-97; Steward 87-90; rtd 97; Perm to Offic *Sarum* 97-03; Hon C Rowledge and Frensham *Guildf* 03-06. *Beech House, 1 Twycross Road, Godalming GU7 2HH* Tel (01483) 422790
E-mail sempers@freezone.co.uk

SEMPLE, Henry Michael. b 40. K Coll Lon BSc62 Birkbeck Coll Lon PhD67 CMath FIMA FCMI FRSA. S Dios Minl Tr Scheme. **d** 87 **p** 88. NSM Steyning *Chich* 87-91; Perm to Offic *Guildf* 87-91 and *Linc* 92-93; NSM Linc Cathl 93-99; TR Headley All SS *Guildf* 99-02; R from 02. *All Saints' Rectory, High Street, Headley, Bordon GU35 8PP* Tel (01428) 717321
E-mail mandpsemple@waitrose.com

SEMPLE, Studdert Patrick. b 39. TCD BA66. CITC 66. **d** 67 **p** 68. C Orangefield *D & D* 67-70; USA 70-71; I Stradbally *C & O* 71-82; Ch of Ireland Adult Educn Officer 82-88; I Donoughmore and Donard w Dunlavin *D & G* 88-96; Bp's C Dublin St Geo and St Thos 96-99; Chapl Mountjoy Pris and Mater Hosps 96-99; rtd 99. *49 Richmond Park, Monkstown, Co Dublin, Republic of Ireland* Tel (00353) (1) 230 1712

SEN, Arani. b 61. R Holloway Coll Lon BA84 St Martin's Coll Lanc PGCE86 Open Univ MA94 Fitzw Coll Cam BA98 MA02. Ridley Hall Cam 96. **d** 99 **p** 00. C Mildmay Grove St Jude and St Paul *Lon* 99-02; C-in-c Southall Em CD 02-06; V Southall Em 06-08; V Upper Armley *Ripon* from 08. *22 Hill End Crescent, Leeds LS12 3PW* Tel 0113-263 8788 E-mail rev.sen@virgin.net

SENIOR, Brian Stephen. b 55. Brighton Coll of Educn CertEd76. Oak Hill Th Coll 91. **d** 93 **p** 94. C Hildenborough *Roch* 93-98; TV Tunbridge Wells St Jas w St Phil 98-04; V Tunbridge Wells St Phil from 04; RD Tunbridge Wells from 07. *St Philip's Vicarage, Birken Road, Tunbridge Wells TN2 3TE* Tel (01892) 512071 *or* 531031 E-mail brian.senior@diocese-rochester.org

SENIOR, David John. b 47. Oak Hill Th Coll. **d** 82 **p** 83. C Market Harborough *Leic* 82-85; TV Marfleet *York* 85-91; R Desford and Peckleton w Tooley *Leic* 91-96; P-in-c Hall Green Ascension *Birm* 96-99; V from 99; P-in-c Gospel Lane St Mich 97-03. *The Vicarage, 592 Fox Hollies Road, Birmingham B28 9DX* Tel 0121-777 3689
E-mail david@ascensionhallgreen.fsnet.co.uk

SENIOR, John Peter. b 23. Lon Univ BSc48. Edin Th Coll 63. **d** 65 **p** 66. C Marton *Blackb* 65-68; C Heysham 68-71; V Blackpool St Mich 71-79; V Heddon-on-the-Wall *Newc* 79-88; rtd 88; Perm to Offic *Wakef* from 88. *56 Thorpe Lane, Huddersfield HD5 8TA* Tel (01484) 530466

SENIOR, Mrs Lisa Elaine. b 65. Leeds Univ BA09. NOC 06. **d** 09. C Dewsbury *Wakef* from 09. *The Vicarage, 24 Intake Lane, Brownhill, Batley WF17 0BT* Tel (01924) 471999
E-mail lisasenior24@fsmail.net

SENIOR, Patrick Nicolas Adam. b 63. Univ of Wales (Ban) BA86. Trin Coll Bris BA94. **d** 94 **p** 95. C Derringham Bank *York* 94-98; V Brownhill *Wakef* from 98. *The Vicarage, 24 Intake Lane, Brownhill, Batley WF17 0BT* Tel and fax (01924) 471999
E-mail pals@thedogcollar.fsnet.co.uk

✠**SENTAMU, The Most Revd and Rt Hon John Tucker Mugabi.** b 49. Makerere Univ Kampala LLB71 Selw Coll Cam BA76 MA MPhil79 PhD84. Ridley Hall Cam. **d** 79 **p** 79. c 96. Chapl HM Rem Cen Latchmere Ho 79-82; C Ham St Andr *S'wark* 79-82; C Herne Hill St Paul 82-83; P-in-c Tulse Hill H Trin 83-84; V Upper Tulse Hill St Matthias 83-84; V Tulse Hill H Trin and St Matthias 85-96; P-in-c Brixton Hill St Sav 87-89; Hon Can S'wark Cathl 93-96; Area Bp Stepney *Lon* 96-02; Bp Birm 02-05; Abp York from 05. *Bishopthorpe Palace, Bishopthorpe, York YO23 2GE* Tel (01904) 707021 Fax 709204
E-mail office@archbishopofyork.org

SEPHTON, John. b 43. **d** 01 **p** 02. OLM Newburgh w Westhead *Liv* from 01; Asst Chapl HM Pris Risley 02-09. *c/o Crockford, Church House, Great Smith Street, London SW1P 3AZ* Tel (01695) 576774 *or* (01925) 733333
E-mail johnsephton@postmaster.co.uk

SEPPALA, Christopher James. b 59. St Jo Coll Dur BA82 Ch Ch Coll Cant CertEd92. Chich Th Coll 83. **d** 85 **p** 86. C Whitstable *Cant* 85-88; C S Ashford Ch Ch 88-91; Perm to Offic from 01. *2 The Briars, Long Reach Close, Whitstable CT5 4QF* Tel (01227) 282622 E-mail xpristopheros@netscapeonline.co.uk

SERBUTT, Rita Eileen. b 33. Man Univ BA54 Univ of Wales (Cardiff) DipEd56 FRSA94. Dioc OLM tr scheme 98. **d** 01 **p** 01. OLM Balham St Mary and St Jo *S'wark* from 01. *5 Veronica Road, London SW17 8QL* Tel (020) 8772 1031
E-mail eileen.serbutt@virgin.net

SERGEANT, John Richard Arthur. b 43. K Coll Dur BA65 Newc Univ DipEd66 DAES87. **d** 06 **p** 07. NSM Cullercoats St Geo

Newc from 06. *5 Jedburgh Close, North Shields NE29 9NU* Tel 0191-259 1752 E-mail serjeantjra@aol.com

SERJEANT, Frederick James. b 28. Lon Inst of Educn BEd77. AKC53 St Boniface Warminster 53. **d** 54 **p** 55. C Leytonstone St Marg w St Columba *Chelmsf* 54-58; C Parkstone St Pet w Branksea *Sarum* 58-59; V Reigate St Luke S Park *S'wark* 59-65; V Battersea St Pet 65-71; C-in-c Battersea St Paul 67-71; V W Mersea *Chelmsf* 71-73; P-in-c E Mersea 71-73; R W w E Mersea 73-75; rtd 93. *3 Church Hill View, Sydling, Dorchester DT2 9SY* Tel (01300) 341670

SERJEANT, Mrs Heather Faith. b 60. Stirling Univ BSc80 Ox Univ BTh04. Ripon Coll Cuddesdon 00. **d** 02 **p** 03. C Caversham St Pet and Mapledurham *Ox* 02-06. *4A The Mount, Caversham, Reading RG4 7RU* Tel 0118-947 2729
E-mail heatherserjeant@aol.com

SERJEANT, John Frederick. b 33. K Coll Lon 52. **d** 56 **p** 57. C Over St Chad *Ches* 56-59; C-in-c Brinnington St Luke CD 59-63; V Brinnington 63-69; V Gatley 69-79; TV Halesworth w Linstead and Chediston *St E* 79-80; TV Halesworth w Linstead, Chediston, Holton etc 80-82; C Chesterfield St Mary and All SS *Derby* 82-88; Chapl Chesterfield R Hosp 82-88; Chapl Chesterfield and N Derbyshire R Hosp 88-95; rtd 95. *188 Queen Victoria Road, New Tupton, Chesterfield S42 6DW* Tel (01246) 863395

SERJEANTSON, John Cecil Mylles. b 36. Bp's Univ Lennoxville BA63 McGill Univ Montreal BD66. Montreal Dioc Th Coll LTh66. **d** 66 **p** 67. C Westmount St Matthias Canada 66-68; R Huntingdon w Ormstown 68-72; C Gt and Lt Driffield *York* 72-76; V Bilton St Pet 76-79; R Brome Canada 79-01; rtd 01. *19 Mountain Road, Bolton Est QC J0E 1G0, Canada* Tel (001) (450) 292 0850

SERMON, Michael John. b 61. Univ of Cen England in Birm ACIB85. Qu Coll Birm BA98 MA99. **d** 99 **p** 00. C W Heath *Birm* 99-03; V Blackheath from 03. *St Paul's Vicarage, 83 Vicarage Road, Halesowen B62 8HX* Tel 0121-559 1000
E-mail mike@mikesermon.co.uk

SERTIN, John Francis. b 22. Fitzw Ho Cam BA50 MA54. Tyndale Hall Bris. **d** 45 **p** 46. C Sidcup Ch Ch *Roch* 45-47; Chapl Fitzw Ho Cam 47-50; C-in-c St Paul's Cray St Barn CD *Roch* 50-59; V Chitts Hill St Cuth *Lon* 59-62; Sec Ch Soc 62-67; P-in-c Woburn Square Ch Ch *Lon* 67-77; R Holborn St Geo w H Trin and St Bart 67-80; R Donyatt w Horton, Broadway and Ashill *B & W* 80-92; rtd 92; Perm to Offic *B & W* 92-02. *23 Birstan Gardens, Andover SP10 4NY* Tel (01264) 334544

SERVANT, Canon Alma Joan. b 51. Nottm Univ BA76. Westcott Ho Cam 83. **dss** 85 **d** 87 **p** 94. Ordsall *S'well* 85-88; Par Dn 87-88; Par Dn Man Whitworth 88-94; TV Man 94-96; Chapl Man Poly 88-92; Chapl Man Metrop Univ 92-96; P-in-c Heaton Norris St Thos 96-00; P-in-c Hulme Ascension 00-05; R from 05; Hon Can Man Cathl from 02. *The Rectory, Royce Road, Hulme, Manchester M15 5FQ* Tel 0161-226 5568

SERVANTE, Kenneth Edward. b 29. AKC55. **d** 56 **p** 57. C Chaddesden St Phil *Derby* 56-58; C Brampton St Thos 58-61; C Whitfield 61-63; V Derby St Paul 63-70; V Elmton 70-81; P-in-c Winster 81-82; P-in-c Elton 81-82; R S Darley, Elton and Winster 82-94; rtd 94; Perm to Offic *Derby* from 94. *13 Chestnut Avenue, Belper DE56 1LY* Tel (01773) 820513

SESSFORD, Canon Alan. b 34. Bps' Coll Cheshunt 65. **d** 66 **p** 67. C Highcliffe w Hinton Admiral *Win* 66-69; C Minehead *B & W* 70; C Chandler's Ford *Win* 70-73; V Burton and Sopley 73-00; RD Christchurch 93-98; Hon Can Win Cathl 98-00; rtd 00; Perm to Offic *Win* from 00; Chapl R Bournemouth and Christchurch Hosps NHS Trust from 01. *4 Benson Close, Bransgore, Christchurch BH23 8HX* Tel (01425) 673412

SETTERFIELD, Nicholas Manley. b 63. Colchester Inst of Educn BA89. St Steph Ho Ox 89. **d** 92 **p** 93. C Prestbury *Glouc* 92-96; R Letchworth *St Alb* 96-03; V Northampton St Matt *Pet* from 03. *St Matthew's Vicarage, 30 East Park Parade, Northampton NN1 4LB* Tel (01604) 604412
E-mail vicar@stmatthews-northampton.org

SETTIMBA, John Henry. b 52. Nairobi Univ BSc78 Leeds Univ MA91. Pan Africa Chr Coll BA78. **d** 78 **p** 80. Kenya 78-81; Uganda 81-85; C Allerton *Bradf* 86-87; C W Ham *Chelmsf* 87-91; C-in-c Forest Gate All SS 91-94; P-in-c 94-96; TV Hackney *Lon* 96-02; rtd 07. *63 Belvedere Court, Upper Richmond Road, London SW15 6HZ* Tel (020) 8789 8376

SEVILLE, Thomas Christopher John. b 57. Trin Hall Cam MA80. Coll of Resurr Mirfield 87. **d** 89 **p** 90. C Knowle *Bris* 89-93; CR from 93. *House of the Resurrection, Stocks Bank Road, Mirfield WF14 0BN* Tel (01924) 483315
E-mail tseville@mirfield.org.uk

SEWARD, Jolyon Frantom. b 57. Univ of Wales (Cardiff) BA81. Chich Th Coll 83. **d** 86 **p** 87. C Llanblethian w Cowbridge and Llandough etc 86-88; C Newton Nottage 88-93; Dioc Children's Officer 88-98; V Penyfai w Tondu 93-01; TV Heavitree and St Mary Steps *Ex* from 01. *St Lawrence's Vicarage, 36 Lower Hill Barton Road, Exeter EX1 3EH* Tel (01392) 466302 *or* 677152 E-mail frjolyon@eurobell.co.uk

SEWARD, Nicholas. b 70. Imp Coll Lon BEng91 St Jo Coll Dur BA96 MA98. Cranmer Hall Dur 94. **d** 98 **p** 99. C Bearsted w Thurnham *Cant* 98-02; Chapl and Hd RS Magd Coll Sch Ox 02-08; Hd Kingham Hill Sch from 08. *Kingham Hill School, Kingham, Chipping Norton OX7 6TH* Tel (01608) 658999
E-mail n.seward@kingham-hill.oxon.sch.uk

SEWELL, Andrew. *See* SEWELL, John Andrew Clarkson

SEWELL, Andrew William. b 61. Nottm Univ BSc83. St Jo Coll Nottm 93. **d** 93 **p** 94. C Adel *Ripon* 93-96; C Far Headingley St Chad 96-98; Asst Dioc Missr 96-98; P-in-c Otham w Langley *Cant* 98-01; R from 01. *The Rectory, Church Road, Otham, Maidstone ME15 8SB* Tel (01622) 861470
E-mail asewell@aol.com

SEWELL, Barry. *See* SEWELL, John Barratt

SEWELL, Miss Elizabeth Jill. b 56. Reading Univ BSc77. Trin Coll Bris BA97. **d** 97 **p** 98. C Rothley *Leic* 97-01; TV Market Harborough and The Transfiguration etc 01-07; RD Gartree I 06-07; TR Knaresborough *Ripon* from 07. *The Rectory, High Bond End, Knaresborough HG5 9BT* Tel (01423) 865273
E-mail ejsewell@leicester.anglican.org

SEWELL, John Andrew Clarkson. b 58. Aston Tr Scheme 93 Ripon Coll Cuddesdon 95. **d** 97 **p** 98. C Horsham *Chich* 97-99; C Cleobury Mortimer w Hopton Wafers etc *Heref* 99-01; R 01-03; TV Ludlow, Ludford, Ashford Carbonell etc 03-04; Chapl Shropshire's Community NHS Trust 03-04; Hon C Weston super Mare St Jo *B & W* 06-07; P-in-c Westbury sub Mendip w Easton from 07. *The Vicarage, Crow Lane, Westbury sub Mendip, Wells BA5 1HB* Tel (01749) 870293 E-mail jacsewell@aol.com

SEWELL, John Barratt (Barry). b 39. St Bart Hosp Medical Coll MB, BS63. Ridley Hall Cam. **d** 92 **p** 93. C Ulverston St Mary w H Trin *Carl* 92-94; Asst Chapl R Cornwall Hosps Trust 94-98; Chapl 98-99; P-in-c Gerrans w St Anthony-in-Roseland and Philleigh *Truro* 00-03; rtd 03; Perm to Offic *Truro* from 04. *Cleswyth, Creegbrawse, St Day, Redruth TR16 5QF* Tel (01209) 821696 E-mail barry@cleswyth.freeserve.co.uk

SEWELL, Jonathan William. b 60. Lanc Univ BA82 BTh86. Linc Th Coll 83. **d** 86 **p** 87. C Ilkeston St Mary *Derby* 86-89; C Enfield Chase St Mary *Lon* 89-92; Dioc Youth Officer *Win* 92-97; P-in-c Headington St Mary *Ox* from 98. *St Mary's Vicarage, Bayswater Road, Headington, Oxford OX3 9EY* Tel (01865) 761886 E-mail jonathan.sewell@ntlworld.com

SEWELL, Peter Alexis. b 35. Lon Univ BSc61 PhD67 FRSC86. Cyprus & Gulf Ord Course 92. **d** 94 **p** 95. Cyprus and the Gulf 94-97; NSM Ormskirk *Liv* 97-01; Perm to Offic from 01. *Shakelady Hey, Sandy Lane, Lathom, Ormskirk L40 5TU* Tel and fax (01695) 572095

SEWELL, Richard Michael. b 62. Birm Univ BA84. SEITE 99. **d** 02 **p** 03. C Putney St Mary *S'wark* 02-05; TV Wimbledon from 05. *55 Alwyne Road, London SW19 7AE* Tel (020) 8946 4175

SEWELL, Robin Warwick. b 42. Trin Coll Bris 80. **d** 82 **p** 83. C Hinckley H Trin *Leic* 82-85; C Broadwater St Mary *Chich* 85-89; Chapl Barcelona *Eur* 89-02; V Braintree St Paul *Chelmsf* from 02. *St Paul's Vicarage, Hay Lane, Braintree CM7 3DY* Tel (01376) 325095 E-mail robin@sewellgospel.fsnet.co.uk

SEWELL, Miss Sarah Frances. b 61. Wycliffe Hall Ox 87. **d** 91 **p** 94. C Binley *Cov* 91-94; Asst Chapl Derriford Hosp Plymouth 94-96; Chapl Stoke Mandeville Hosp NHS Trust 96-00; Chapl R Marsden NHS Foundn Trust 00-05; Chapl Team Ldr Epsom and St Helier Univ Hosps NHS Trust 05-07; Sen Co-ord Chapl from 07. *The Chaplains' Office, Epsom General Hospital, Dorking Road, Epsom KT18 7EG* Tel (01372) 735322
E-mail sarah.sewell@epsom-sthelier.nhs.uk

SEXTON, Canon Michael Bowers. b 28. SS Coll Cam BA52 MA56. Wells Th Coll 52. **d** 54 **p** 55. C Miles Platting St Luke *Man* 54-57; C Bradford cum Beswick 57-58; C-in-c Oldham St Chad Limeside CD 58-62; R Filby w Thrigby w Mautby *Nor* 62-72; P-in-c Runham 67-72; P-in-c Stokesby w Herringby 68-72; R Hethersett w Canteloff 72-85; V Ketteringham 73-84; RD Humbleyard 81-86; Hon Can Nor Cathl 85-93; R Hethersett w Canteloff w Lt and Gt Melton 85-86; V Hunstanton St Mary w Ringstead Parva, Holme etc 86-93; rtd 94; Perm to Offic *Nor* from 94. *3 Forge Close, Poringland, Norwich NR14 7SZ* Tel (01508) 493885

SEYMOUR, Dom Anthony Nicholas. b 39. QUB BA61. **d** 96 **p** 97. Community of Our Lady and St John 86-01; Perm to Offic *Win* from 01. *Alton Abbey, Abbey Road, Beech, Alton GU34 4AP* Tel (01420) 562145 *or* 563575 Fax 561691

SEYMOUR, Brian Anthony. b 45. **d** 07 **p** 08. OLM Ottershaw *Guildf* from 07. *50 Rowtown, Addlestone KT15 1HQ* Tel (01932) 705260 E-mail brianandchrisseymour@yahoo.co.uk

SEYMOUR, David. b 43. Kelham Th Coll 60. **d** 68 **p** 69. C Cowley St Jas *Ox* 68-73; TV Lynton, Brendon, Countisbury, Lynmouth etc *Ex* 73-77; C-in-c Luton (Princes Park) CD *Roch* 78-79; V Rosherville 79-90; rtd 90. *3 Fosbrooke House, 8 Clifton Drive, Lytham St Annes FY8 5RQ*
E-mail markbeech@boltblue.com

SEYMOUR, David Raymond Russell. b 56. Keble Coll Ox BA79 MA88. St Steph Ho Ox 79. **d** 81 **p** 82. C Tilehurst St Mich *Ox* 81-85; TV Parkstone St Pet w Branksea and St Osmund *Sarum*

85-91; V Bradford-on-Avon Ch Ch 91-01; P-in-c Sturminster Newton and Hinton St Mary 01-02; V Sturminster Newton, Hinton St Mary and Lydlinch from 02; C Hazelbury Bryan and the Hillside Par from 08; C Okeford from 08; RD Blackmore Vale from 08. *The Vicarage, Church Street, Sturminster Newton DT10 1DB* Tel (01258) 471276
E-mail drrseymour@hotmail.co.uk

SEYMOUR, John. b 73. Bris Univ BSc95 MB, ChB98 Heythrop Coll Lon MA03 Trin Coll Cam BA05. Westcott Ho Cam 03. **d** 06 **p** 07. C Poplar *Lon* 06-09; Chapl Twyford C of E High Sch Acton from 09. *St Edward's House, 12A Medway Drive, Greenford UB6 8LN* Tel (020) 8930 9305
E-mail john.seymour@london.anglican.org

SEYMOUR, John Anthony. b 46. SWMTC. **d** 08 **p** 09. NSM Carbis Bay w Lelant *Truro* from 08. *5 Station Hill, Lelant, St Ives TR26 3DJ* Tel (01736) 755622
E-mail tonysw@talktalk.net

SEYMOUR, Canon John Charles. b 30. Oak Hill Th Coll 51 and 55 Wycliffe Coll Toronto 54. **d** 57 **p** 58. C Islington St Andr w St Thos and St Matthias *Lon* 57-60; C Worthing St Geo *Chich* 60-63; V Thornton *Leic* 63-70; R Kirby Muxloe 70-81; TR 81-83; Hon Can Leic Cathl 82-93; RD Sparkenhoe I 83-88; R Market Bosworth w Shenton 83-87; TR Market Bosworth, Cadeby w Sutton Cheney etc 87-93; RD Sparkenhoe W 89-92; rtd 93. *7 Merton Close, Broughton Astley, Leicester LE9 6QP* Tel (01455) 282525

SEYMOUR, Nicholas. *See* SEYMOUR, Dom Anthony Nicholas
SEYMOUR, Paul Edward. b 62. Humberside Univ BA92. St Jo Coll Nottm 01. **d** 03 **p** 04. C Ingleby Barwick *York* 03-07; C Hatfield Hyde *St Alb* from 07. *All Saints' House, 7C Hall Grove, Welwyn Garden City AL7 4PJ* Tel (01707) 391425 Mobile 07815-729831 E-mail revdpaul@tiscali.co.uk

SEYMOUR-JONES, Michael D'Israeli. b 37. **d** 09. OLM Shiplake w Dunsden and Harpsden *Ox* from 09. *6 Heathfield Close, Binfield Heath, Henley-on-Thames RG9 4DS* Tel 0118-947 8632 E-mail m.seymour-jones@btinternet.com

SEYMOUR-WHITELEY, Ms Alison. b 51. City of Lon Poly MA90 Homerton Coll Cam PGCE95. CITC 04. **d** 07 **p** 08. Lic to Offic *Clogh* from 07. *The Rectory, 23 Drumcru Road, Newtownbutler, Enniskillen BT92 8GP* Tel (028) 6773 8245
E-mail alisonsw@hotmail.co.uk

SEYMOUR-WHITELEY, Richard Dudley. b 59. Leic Poly BSc80. Linc Th Coll 82. **d** 85 **p** 86. C Bushey *St Alb* 85-89; C Stevenage St Mary Shephall w Aston 89-93; P-in-c Blunham w Tempsford and Lt Barford 93-99; P-in-c The Stodden Churches 99-01; I Grey Abbey w Kircubbin *D & D* 01-06; I Galloon w Drummully and Sallaghy *Clogh* from 06. *The Rectory, 23 Drumcru Road, Newtownbutler, Enniskillen BT92 8GP* Tel (028) 6773 8245 Mobile 07789-550508
E-mail galloon@clogher.anglican.org

SHACKELL, Daniel William. b 42. **d** 95 **p** 96. Dir Spires Cen *S'wark* 93-06; OLM Streatham St Leon *S'wark* 95-99; Lic to Offic 99-06; rtd 07; Perm to Offic *Guildf* from 01. *83 Hillside, Banstead SM7 1EZ* Tel (01737) 361569
E-mail dan@shackell83.freeserve.co.uk

SHACKELL, Kenneth Norman. b 26. S'wark Ord Course 66. **d** 69 **p** 70. NSM Greenwich St Alfege w St Pet and St Paul *S'wark* 69-95; Perm to Offic *Sarum* 95-03. *17 Portman Drive, Child Okeford, Blandford Forum DT11 8HU* Tel and fax (01258) 861583

SHACKERLEY, Canon Albert Paul. b 56. K Coll Lon MA97 Sheff Univ PhD07. Chich Th Coll 91. **d** 93 **p** 94. C Harlesden All So *Lon* 93-96; P-in-c Chelmsf All SS 96-98; V 98-02; Can Res Sheff Cathl from 02; Vice Dean from 05. *9 Stumperlowe Hall Road, Sheffield S10 3QR* Tel 0114-230 4181 *or* 263 6066 Mobile 07786-927715
E-mail paul.shackerley@sheffield-cathedral.org.uk

SHACKLADY, Mrs Thelma. b 38. Liv Univ BA60. St Alb Minl Tr Scheme 89. **d** 92 **p** 94. NSM Luton St Andr *St Alb* 92-96; NSM Luton All SS w St Pet 96-03; Perm to Offic from 03. *45 Lilly Hill, Olney MK46 5EZ* Tel (01234) 712997
E-mail bill.shacklady@virgin.net

SHACKLEFORD, Richard Neal. b 40. Univ of Denver BA64 Univ of N Colorado MA74. St Steph Ho Ox 84. **d** 86 **p** 87. C Poulton-le-Fylde *Blackb* 86-88; USA from 88; Can St Jo Cathl Colorado 88-92; C Denver St Mich 92-96; R Lindenhurst St Boniface from 96. *100 46th Street, Lindenhurst NY 11747-2009, USA*

SHACKLETON, Canon Alan. b 31. Sheff Univ BA53. Wells Th Coll 54. **d** 56 **p** 57. C Ladybarn *Man* 56-58; C Bolton St Pet 58-61; V Middleton Junction 61-70; V Heywood St Luke 70-84; AD Rochdale 82-92; Hon Can Man Cathl 84-97; V Heywood St Luke w All So 85-86; TV Rochdale 86-91; TR 91-97; rtd 97; Perm to Offic *Man* from 97. *28 Taunton Avenue, Rochdale OL11 5LD* Tel (01706) 645335
E-mail alan@ashackleton.demon.co.uk

SHACKLETON, Anthea. b 42. **d** 07. OLM Ravensthorpe and Thornhill Lees w Savile Town *Wakef* from 07. *1 Fearnley Drive,*

Ossett WF5 9EU Tel (01924) 270830 Mobile 07815-445757
E-mail ant.shackleton@talktalk.net

SHACKLETON, Ian Roderick. b 40. St Fran Coll Brisbane 69. **d** 72 **p** 72. C Toowoomba Australia 72-74; P-in-c Milmerran 74-75; R 75-78; C Birch St Agnes *Man* 79-80; P-in-c Newton Heath St Wilfrid and St Anne 80-87; NSM W Derby St Jo *Liv* 87-90; C 90-94; P-in-c Southport St Luke 94-05; Asst Chapl HM Pris Liv 94-05; rtd 06; Perm to Offic *Cant* from 06. *31 The Shrubbery, Walmer, Deal CT14 7PZ* Tel (01304) 379773

SHACKLEY, Prof Myra Lesley. b 49. Southn Univ BA70 PhD75 Nottm Univ MA99 FRGS. EMMTC 96. **d** 99 **p** 00. NSM Ordsall *S'well* 99-02; Dioc Tourism Adv 02-08; PV S'well Minster 02-06; P-in-c N and S Muskham 06-08; P-in-c Averham w Kelham 06-08; Hon C Spofforth w Kirk Deighton *Ripon* from 08. *The Rectory, Church Lane, Spofforth, Harrogate HG3 1AF* Tel (01937) 590770 Mobile 07889-591504

SHAFTO, Robert James. b 38. FCA61. OLM course 96. **d** 99 **p** 00. NSM W Dulwich All SS *S'wark* 99-07; rtd 07; Perm to Offic *S'wark* from 08. *46 Cedar Close, London SE21 8HX* Tel (020) 8761 7395 E-mail bob@shafto46.wanadoo.co.uk

SHAHZAD, Sulaiman. b 60. BA. Oak Hill Th Coll BA93. **d** 96 **p** 97. C Winchmore Hill St Paul *Lon* 96-00; TV Digswell and Panshanger *St Alb* from 00. *71 Haldens, Welwyn Garden City AL7 1DH* Tel (01707) 335537
E-mail sulishahzad@tiscali.co.uk

SHAIL, Canon William Frederick. b 15. Kelham Th Coll. **d** 41 **p** 42. C Deptford St Paul *S'wark* 41-44; C Lewisham St Mary 44-47; C Christchurch *Win* 47-52; R N Stoneham 52-68; V Bournemouth St Alb 68-78; V Burley Ville 78-84; rtd 84; Perm to Offic *Win* 84-97. *19 Halton Close, Bransgore, Christchurch BH23 8HZ* Tel (01425) 673064

SHAKESPEARE, James Douglas Geoffrey. b 71. Fitzw Coll Cam BA93 MA97 Man Univ MA96. Westcott Ho Cam 97. **d** 99 **p** 00. C Cherry Hinton St Jo *Ely* 99-02; Bp's Chapl and Policy Adv *Leic* 02-05; P-in-c Birstall and Wanlip from 05; V from 09. *The Rectory, 251 Birstall Road, Birstall, Leicester LE4 4DJ* Tel 0116-267 4517 E-mail jshakespeare@btinternet.com

SHAKESPEARE, Steven. b 68. CCC Cam BA89 PhD94. Westcott Ho Cam 93. **d** 96 **p** 97. C Cambridge St Jas *Ely* 96-99; V Endcliffe and Chapl Sheff Hallam Univ 99-03; Chapl Liv Hope Univ from 03. *Anglican Chaplaincy, Hope Park, Taggart Avenue, Liverpool L16 9JD* Tel 0151-291 3545
E-mail shakess@hope.ac.uk

SHAMBROOK, Roger William. b 46. Sarum & Wells Th Coll 78. **d** 83 **p** 84. OSP 76-82; C Southbourne St Kath *Win* 83-86; TV Bridport *Sarum* 86-01; Chapl Bridport Community Hosp 86-94; Chapl Dorset Community NHS Trust 94-01; P-in-c Torre All SS *Ex* from 01. *All Saints' Vicarage, 45 Barton Road, Torquay TQ1 4DT* Tel (01803) 328865

SHAND, Brian Martin. b 53. Univ Coll Lon BA76 PhD82. St Steph Ho Ox 85. **d** 87 **p** 88. C Uxbridge St Marg *Lon* 87-88; C Uxbridge 88-90; C Worplesdon *Guildf* 90-94; Relig Affairs Producer BBC Radio Surrey 90-94; V Weston 94-01; V Witley from 01. *The Vicarage, Petworth Road, Witley, Godalming GU8 5LT* Tel and fax (01428) 681872
E-mail allsaints.witley@btinternet.com

SHANKS, Canon Robert Andrew Gulval. b 54. Ball Coll Ox BA75 G&C Coll Cam BA79 Leeds Univ PhD90. Westcott Ho Cam 77. **d** 80 **p** 81. C Potternewton *Ripon* 80-83; C Stanningley St Thos 84-87; Lect Leeds Univ 87-91; Teaching Fell Lanc Univ 91-95; Research Fell in Th Cheltenham and Glouc Coll of HE 95-96; NSM Leeds City *Ripon* 95-96; P-in-c Upper Ryedale and CME Officer Cleveland Adnry *York* 97-04; Can Res Man Cathl from 04. *3 Booth-Clibborn Court, Salford M7 4PJ* Tel 0161-792 8820
E-mail ragshanks@hotmail.com

SHANNON, Mrs Annette Denise. b 61. Hatf Poly BSc83 Anglia Poly Univ CertEd99. ERMC 05. **d** 08 **p** 09. C St Edm Way *St E* from 08. *53 Raynsford Road, Great Welnetham, Bury St Edmunds IP30 0TN* Tel (01284) 386115
E-mail revannettes@aol.com

SHANNON, Brian James. b 35. St Chad's Coll Dur BA59. **d** 61 **p** 62. C Palmers Green St Jo *Lon* 61-65; C Kenton 65-70; V Roxbourne St Andr 70-81; V Thorpe-le-Soken *Chelmsf* 81-91; V Gt Wakering w Foulness 91-99; rtd 99; Perm to Offic *Chelmsf* from 99. *154 Bournemouth Park Road, Southend-on-Sea SS2 5LT* Tel (01702) 464737

SHANNON, The Ven Malcolm James Douglas. b 49. TCD BA72 MA75. CITC 73. **d** 75 **p** 76. C Clooney *D & R* 75-78; I Kilcolman w Kiltallagh, Killorglin, Knockane etc *L & K* from 78; Adn Ardfert and Aghadoe 88-04; Adn Limerick from 04; Treas Limerick Cathl from 88; Dir of Ords from 91. *Kilcolman Rectory, Miltown, Killarney, Co Kerry, Republic of Ireland* Tel (00353) (66) 976 7302 Fax 976 7197 Mobile 88-539 906

SHANNON, Canon Trevor Haslam. b 33. Selw Coll Cam BA59 MA61 Lon Univ BD69. Westcott Ho Cam 57. **d** 59 **p** 60. C Moss Side Ch Ch *Man* 59-62; V Woolfold 62-66; Chapl Forest Sch Snaresbrook 66-80 and 87-88; V Gt Ilford St Marg *Chelmsf* 88-90; TR Gt Ilford St Clem and St Marg 90-96; V 96-99; RD Redbridge 90-95; Hon Can Chelmsf Cathl 93-99; rtd 99; Perm to

Offic *Nor* from 00. *Honeysuckle Cottage, Clubbs Lane, Wells-next-the-Sea NR23 1DP* Tel (01328) 711409

SHAPLAND, David Edward. b 26. Cuddesdon Coll 51. **d** 53 **p** 54. C Cranbrook *Cant* 53-55; Chapl St Cath Coll Cam 55-61; R Fittleworth *Chich* 62-65; Warden Bede Ho Staplehurst 65-69; Warden Llanerchwen Trust 70-91; Lic to Offic *S & B* 70-79; Perm to Offic *Chich* 79-91; rtd 91. *6 The Stables, Flete House, Ermington, Ivybridge PL21 9NZ* Tel (01752) 830308

SHARE, David James. b 30. Sarum Th Coll 56. **d** 58 **p** 59. C Whipton *Ex* 58-63; Min Tiverton St Andr Statutory Distr 63-69; RD Tiverton 67-74; V Tiverton St Andr 69-79; P-in-c Ex St Thos 79-80; TR Ex St Thos and Em 80-83; V Woodbury 83-95; rtd 95; Corps Chapl ATC 94-02; Perm to Offic *Ex* from 95. *57 Coombeshead Road, Newton Abbot TQ12 1PZ* Tel (01626) 362516

SHARKEY, Philip Michael. b 50. York Univ BA73 MA08 CQSW78. ERMC 06. **d** 08 **p** 09. NSM Shingay Gp *Ely* from 08. *23 Cherry Drive, Royston SG8 7DL* Tel (01763) 221284 Mobile 07917-619124 E-mail sharkey_phil@yahoo.co.uk

SHARLAND, Canon Marilyn. b 40. City of Birm Coll CertEd61. Oak Hill Th Coll 84. **dss** 86 **d** 87 **p** 94. Barkingside St Laur *Chelmsf* 86-88; Hon Par Dn Hucclecote *Glouc* 88-89; C Coney Hill 89-98; P-in-c Tuffley 98-99; V 99-06; Hon Can Glouc Cathl 02-06; rtd 06. *51 Lynmouth Road, Hucclecote, Gloucester GL3 3JD*

SHARMAN, Hilary John. b 32. Leeds Univ BA58. Coll of Resurr Mirfield 58. **d** 60 **p** 61. C Hertford St Andr *St Alb* 60-64; C Harpenden St Nic 64-72; V High Cross from 72; V Thundridge from 72. *7 Ducketts Wood, Thundridge, Ware SG12 0SR* Tel (01920) 465561

SHARP, Alfred James Frederick. b 30. Oak Hill Th Coll 62. **d** 64 **p** 65. C Hanley Road St Sav w St Paul *Lon* 64-68; P-in-c Leverton *Linc* 68-84; Chapl Pilgrim Hosp Boston 76-84; P-in-c Benington w Leverton *Linc* 84; V Ch Broughton w Boylestone amd Sutton on the Hill *Derby* 84-89; R Ch Broughton w Barton Blount, Boylestone etc 89-94; rtd 94. *14 Edgefield, Weston, Spalding PE12 6RQ* Tel (01406) 370376

SHARP, Andrew Timothy. b 58. K Alfred's Coll Win BA79. Wycliffe Hall Ox 82. **d** 85 **p** 86. C Scarborough St Mary w Ch Ch and H Apostles *York* 85-89; C Luton St Fran *St Alb* 89-90; V 90-98; P-in-c Guernsey St Jo *Win* 98-01; V from 01; Vice-Dean Guernsey from 01. *St John's Vicarage, Les Amballes, St Peter Port, Guernsey GY1 1WY* Tel and fax (01481) 720879

SHARP, Mrs Barbara Elaine. b 52. Open Univ BA84. Ripon Coll Cuddesdon 01. **d** 03. C Timperley *Ches* 03-06; P-in-c Lostock Gralam from 06. *The Vicarage, Station Road, Lostock Gralam, Northwich CW9 7PS* Tel (01606) 43477 E-mail barbara@sharp6152.fsnet.co.uk

SHARP, Brian Phillip. b 48. Cant Sch of Min 85. **d** 88 **p** 89. C S Ashford Ch Ch *Cant* 88-92; C St Laur in Thanet 92-96; V Margate St Jo from 96. *The Vicarage, 24 St Peter's Road, Margate CT9 1TH* Tel (01843) 230766 *or* 223144 E-mail vicarpstjohns@yahoo.co.uk

SHARP, Canon David Malcolm. b 33. Hertf Coll Ox BA56 MA59. Cuddesdon Coll 56. **d** 58 **p** 59. C Bris St Mary Redcliffe w Temple 58-65; V Henleaze 65-75; V Nor St Pet Mancroft 75-82; R Nor St Pet Mancroft w St Jo Maddermarket 82-98; Hon Can Nor Cathl 86-98; Dioc Eur Contact from 91; rtd 98; Perm to Offic *Nor* from 98. *The Pines, Field Lane, Fakenham NR21 9QX* Tel (01328) 864121 E-mail dmsharp.revcanon@ukonline.co.uk

SHARP, Harold. b 41. JP90. FCCA76. CITC 03. **d** 06 **p** 07. Aux Min Larne and Inver *Conn* from 06; Aux Min Glynn w Raloo from 06. *110 Dreen Road, Cullybackey, Ballymena BT42 1EE* Tel (028) 2588 0461 E-mail sharpharold@aol.com

SHARP, Mrs Hazel Patricia. b 39. Qu Eliz Coll Lon BSc61. SWMTC 05. **d** 06 **p** 07. NSM St Merryn and St Issey w St Petroc Minor *Truro* from 06. *The Coppice, Vicarage Gardens, St Issey, Wadebridge PL27 7QB* Tel (01841) 540334 E-mail hh.psharp@btinternet.com

SHARP, Mrs Heather Karin. b 48. **d** 04 **p** 05. OLM Blackrod *Man* from 04. *27 Hill Lane, Blackrod, Bolton BL6 5JW* Tel (01204) 693609 E-mail heatherksharp@hotmail.com

SHARP (née BROWN), Mrs Jane Madeline. b 54. **d** 97 **p** 98. C Aylestone St Andr w St Jas *Leic* 97-00; NSM Knighton St Mary Magd 00-08; NSM Leic St Jas from 08. *10 St Mary's Road, Leicester LE2 1XA* Tel 0116-270 6002 E-mail a.sharp53@ntlworld.com

SHARP, Mrs Janice Anne. b 54. Aston Tr Scheme 91 NOC 93. **d** 96 **p** 97. C Skipton H Trin *Bradf* 96-00; V Buttershaw St Paul 00-02; Chapl Hull and E Yorks Hosps NHS Trust from 02; Hon C Patrington w Hollym, Welwick and Winestead *York* from 07. *The Hull Royal Infirmary, Anlaby Road, Hull HU3 2JZ* Tel (01482) 328541

SHARP, Nicholas Leonard. b 64. Grey Coll Dur BA85. St Jo Coll Nottm MA95. **d** 95 **p** 96. C Oakwood St Thos *Lon* 95-99; TV N Farnborough *Guildf* 99-05; Chapl Farnborough Sixth Form Coll 01-05; P-in-c Lt Amwell *St Alb* 05-08; TV Hertford from 08. *The*

Vicarage, 17 Barclay Close, Hertford Heath, Hertford SG13 7RW Tel (01992) 589140 E-mail nick.sharp@xalt.co.uk

SHARP, Philip Paul Clayton. b 66. Open Univ BSc97. Trin Coll Bris 04. **d** 06 **p** 07. C Liskeard and St Keyne *Truro* from 06. *The New Vicarage, Maddever Crescent, Liskeard PL14 3PT* Tel (01579) 347145

SHARP, Preb Robert. b 36. FLCM58. St Aid Birkenhead 64. **d** 67 **p** 68. C Shipley St Paul *Bradf* 67-70; C-in-c Thwaites Brow CD 70-74; V Thwaites Brow 74-77; P-in-c Alberbury w Cardeston *Heref* 77-78; V 78-87; V Ford 77-87; V Claverley w Tuckhill 87-97; RD Bridgnorth 89-96; Preb Heref Cathl 91-97; rtd 97; Perm to Offic *Heref* 97-99 and from 01; C Stoke Lacy, Moreton Jeffries w Much Cowarne etc 99-00. *62 Biddulph Way, Ledbury HR8 2HN* Tel (01531) 631972

SHARP, Miss Sarah Elizabeth. b 67. Bp Otter Coll Chich BA89 Anglia Poly Univ MA00 Coll of Ripon & York St Jo PGCE90. Westcott Ho Cam 98. **d** 00 **p** 01. C Ross *Heref* 00-03; R Lower Windrush *Ox* from 03. *The Rectory, Main Road, Stanton Harcourt, Witney OX29 5RP* Tel (01865) 880249 E-mail s550sharp@btinternet.com

SHARPE, Canon Alan Brian. b 39. Lich Th Coll 64. **d** 67 **p** 68. C Croydon Woodside *Cant* 67-70; C Portsea St Mary *Portsm* 70-75; V Sheerness H Trin w St Paul *Cant* 75-83; V Hove St Patr w Ch Ch and St Andr *Chich* 83-90; V Hove St Patr 90-08; Can and Preb Chich Cathl 93-08; rtd 08; P-in-c Sedlescombe w Whatlington *Chich* from 08. *The Rectory, Church Hill, Sedlescombe, Battle TN33 0QP* Tel (01424) 870233 E-mail absharp@yahoo.co.uk

SHARPE, Anthony Mark. b 67. Leeds Univ BA01. Coll of Resurr Mirfield 99. **d** 01 **p** 02. C Acomb Moor *York* 01-02; C Norton juxta Malton 02-03; C W Buckrose 03-04; Chapl RN 04-05; R Teme Valley S *Worc* from 05. *The Rectory, Broadheath, Tenbury Wells WR15 8QW* Tel (01886) 853286

SHARPE, Canon Bruce Warrington. b 41. JP88. Ely Th Coll 62 St Steph Ho Ox 64. **d** 65 **p** 66. C Streatham St Pet *S'wark* 65-67; C Castries St Lucia 67-68; Hon C Leic St Matt and St Geo 68-69; Hon C Catford St Laur *S'wark* 69-70; Hon C Deptford St Paul 70-75; Hon C Lamorbey H Redeemer *Roch* 76-83; Hon C Sidcup St Andr 88-99; Locum Chapl Morden Coll Blackheath 98-08; Perm to Offic *Roch* 83-88 and 99-01; *Lon* 97-06; *S'wark* from 98; Hon C Bickley *Roch* from 01; Hon Can Windward Is from 01. *72 Faraday Avenue, Sidcup DA14 4JF* Tel (020) 8300 0695 E-mail bruce.sharpe@diocese-rochester.org *or* canonbruce1@aol.com

SHARPE, Cecil Frederick. b 23. Edin Th Coll 52. **d** 54 **p** 55. C Falkirk *Edin* 54-56; C Kings Norton *Birm* 56-58; V Withall 58-80; Perm to Offic from 80; rtd 88. *35 Shirley Park Road, Shirley, Solihull B90 2BZ* Tel 0121-745 6905

SHARPE, David Francis. b 23. Ex Coll Ox BA56 MA59. St Steph Ho Ox 57. **d** 60 **p** 61. C Hunslet St Mary and Stourton *Ripon* 60-63; C Notting Hill St Jo *Lon* 63-68; V Haggerston St Mary w St Chad 68-78; P-in-c Haggerston St Aug w St Steph 73-78; V Haggerston St Chad 78-83; V Mill Hill St Mich 83-98; rtd 98; Chapl St Raphaël *Eur* 98-02; Perm to Offic *Lon* 02-09. *10 Up The Quadrangle, Morden College, London SE3 0PW* Tel (020) 8853 5104 E-mail davidsharpe32@waitrose.com

SHARPE, Derek Martin Brereton (Pip). b 29. Birkbeck Coll Lon BA60. NEOC 90. **d** 90 **p** 91. NSM Scarborough St Luke *York* 90-92; Asst Chapl Scarborough Distr Hosp 90-92; P-in-c Sherburn and W and E Heslerton w Yedingham *York* 92-99; Hon C Buckrose Carrs 99; rtd 99; Perm to Offic *York* from 00. *Byland Lodge, 68A Low Moorgate, Rillington, Malton YO17 8JW* Tel (01723) 759063

SHARPE, Gerard John. b 23. Westcott Ho Cam. **d** 64 **p** 65. C Thetford St Cuth w H Trin *Nor* 64-70; V Holme *Ely* 70-76; R Conington 70-76; V Holme w Conington 76-93; R Glatton 74-93; RD Yaxley 82-88; rtd 93; Perm to Offic *Ely* 93-00. *24 St Margaret's Road, Girton, Cambridge CB3 0LT* Tel (01223) 574246

SHARPE, Miss Joan Valerie. b 33. EMMTC 73. **dss** 84 **d** 88 **p** 94. Hon Par Dn Warsop *S'well* 88-94; Hon C 94-98; rtd 98; Perm to Offic *S'well* from 04. *1 Forest Court, Eakring Road, Mansfield NG18 3DP* Tel (01623) 424051

SHARPE, John Edward. b 50. St Jo Coll Dur BSc72. Cranmer Hall Dur 73. **d** 76 **p** 77. C Woodford Wells *Chelmsf* 76-79; C Ealing St Mary *Lon* 79-83; Min Walsall St Martin *Lich* 83-87; TV Walsall 87-96; R Glenfield *Leic* from 96; RD Sparkenhoe E from 03. *The Rectory, Main Street, Glenfield, Leicester LE3 8DG* Tel 0116-287 1604 E-mail jesharpe@leicester.anglican.org

SHARPE, The Ven Kenneth William. b 40. Univ of Wales (Lamp) BA61. Sarum Th Coll 61. **d** 63 **p** 64. C Holywell *St D* 63-71; TV Cwmbran *Mon* 71-74; Dioc Children's Adv 72-82; Dioc Youth Chapl 74-82; V Dingestow and Llangovan w Penyclawdd and Tregaer 74-82; V Newport St Mark 82-97; Chapl Alltyryn Hosp Gwent 83-97; RD Newport *Mon* 93-97; Can St Woolos Cathl 94-08; Adn Newport 97-08; rtd 08. *27 Incline Way, Saundersfoot SA69 9LX* Tel (01834) 813674

SHARPE, Mrs Margaret Joy. b 43. Qu Coll Birm. **d** 09. OLM Bilton *Cov* from 09. *60 Cymbeline Way, Bilton, Rugby CV22 6LA* Tel (01788) 810794

SHARPE, Mrs Margaret Theresa. b 48. Man Univ BEd70. Cranmer Hall Dur 72 WMMTC 90. **d** 91 **p** 94. C W Bromwich H Trin *Lich* 91-96; Asst Chapl Glenfield Hosp NHS Trust Leic 96-99; Chapl 99-00; Chapl Univ Hosps Leic NHS Trust 00-04; Chapl Team Ldr from 04. *Chaplains' Department, Glenfield Hospital, Groby Road, Leicester LE3 9QP* Tel 0116-256 3413 *or* 287 1604 E-mail margaret.sharpe@uhl-tr.nhs.uk

SHARPE, Mark. *See* SHARPE, Anthony Mark

SHARPE, Miss Mary. b 31. CQSW71. Dalton Ho Bris 58. **dss** 78 **d** 87 **p** 94. Upton (Overchurch) *Ches* 78-83; Harlescott *Lich* 83-84; New Brighton All SS *Ches* 85-89; Par Dn 87-89; rtd 89; Perm to Offic *Ches* from 89. *20 Winstanley Road, Little Neston, Neston CH64 0UZ*

SHARPE, Mrs Mary Primrose. b 22. Coll of St Matthias Bris CertEd55. Gilmore Ho 51. **dss** 81 **d** 87. Coley *Wakef* 81-89; Hon Par Dn 87-89; rtd 89; Perm to Offic *Bradf* 89-99. *54 Bradford Road, Menston, Ilkley LS29 6BX* Tel (01943) 877710

SHARPE, Peter Richard. b 55. Salford Univ BSc76 ACIB81. STETS 98. **d** 01 **p** 02. C Ex St Jas 01-04; R S Hill w Callington *Truro* from 04; C St Ive and Pensilva w Quethiock from 09. *The Rectory, Liskeard Road, Callington PL17 7JD* Tel (01579) 383341 Mobile 07767-251136 E-mail prshome@clara.net

SHARPE, Pip. *See* SHARPE, Derek William Brereton

SHARPE, Richard Gordon. b 48. Birm Univ BA69. St Jo Coll Nottm BA74. **d** 75 **p** 76. C Hinckley H Trin *Leic* 75-78; C Kingston upon Hull H Trin *York* 78-85; Chapl Marston Green Hosp Birm 85-88; Chapl Chelmsley Hosp Birm 86-88; TV Chelmsley Wood *Birm* 85-88; P-in-c Dosthill 88-93; V 93-97; R Desford and Peckleton w Tooley *Leic* from 97. *The Rectory, 27 Church Lane, Desford, Leicester LE9 9GD* Tel (01455) 822276 E-mail sharpeblackhorse@aol.com

SHARPE, Canon Roger. b 35. TCD BA60 MA63. Qu Coll Birm 60. **d** 62 **p** 63. C Stockton H Trin *Dur* 62-64; C Oakdale St Geo *Sarum* 64-68; V Redlynch and Morgan's Vale 68-86; RD Alderbury 82-86; V Warminster St Denys 86-88; R Upton Scudamore 86-88; V Horningsham 86-88; R Warminster St Denys, Upton Scudamore etc 88-95; Can and Preb Sarum Cathl 89-00; RD Heytesbury 89-95; Chmn Dioc Assn for Deaf from 91; P-in-c Corsley 92-95; TR Cley Hill Warminster 95-00; rtd 00; Perm to Offic *Sarum* from 01. *Woodside, Bugmore Lane, East Grimstead SP5 3SA* Tel (01722) 712753

SHARPE, William Wilberforce. b 62. **d** 05 **p** 06. NSM Brixton St Matt w St Jude *S'wark* from 05; Chapl Guy's and St Thos' NHS Foundn Trust from 08. *1D Lovelace Road, London SE21 8JY* Tel and fax (020) 8761 8539 Mobile 07956-546394 E-mail sharpeww@aol.com

SHARPLES, Canon Alfred Cyril. b 09. Man Univ BA33. Linc Th Coll 33. **d** 35 **p** 36. C Rochdale *Man* 35-39; C Ashton St Mich 39-42; R Cheetham St Mark 42-46; V Tonge w Alkrington 46-51; V Hope St Jas 51-76; Hon Can Man Cathl 74-76; rtd 76; Perm to Offic *Ches* and *Man* from 77. *30 Greenbank Drive, Bollington, Macclesfield SK10 5LW* Tel 01061-207 5073

SHARPLES, Angela (Ella). b 65. **d** 07 **p** 08. C Timperley *Ches* 07-09; C Congleton from 09. *The Rectory, Astbury, Congleton CW12 4RQ* Tel (01260) 272625 E-mail ella_sharples@hotmail.com

SHARPLES, David. b 41. Linc Th Coll 71. **d** 73 **p** 74. C Reddish *Man* 73-75; C Prestwich St Mary 76-78; V Ashton St Jas 78-86; V Hope St Jas 86-06; rtd 06; Perm to Offic *Man* from 06. *18 Holly Avenue, Worsley, Manchester M28 3DW* Tel 0161-950 8675

SHARPLES, Canon David John. b 58. Lon Univ BD81 AKC81. Coll of Resurr Mirfield. **d** 82 **p** 83. C Prestwich St Mary *Man* 82-87; V Royton St Anne 87-02; AD Tandle 94-02; Dir of Ords from 02; Hon Can Man Cathl from 06. *St Thomas's New Vicarage, Church Street, Milnrow, Rochdale OL16 3QS* Tel (01706) 291539 *or* 0161-708 9366 Fax 0161-792 6826 E-mail ddo@bishopscourt.manchester.anglican.org

SHARPLES, Derek. b 35. SS Paul & Mary Coll Cheltenham CertEd57 Liv Univ DipEd63 Man Univ MEd66 Bath Univ PhD72 Open Univ BA79 FCollP86. WMMTC 83. **d** 86 **p** 87. NSM Malvern H Trin and St Jas *Worc* 86-90; C St Jo in Bedwardine 90-92; R Belbroughton w Fairfield and Clent 92-00; rtd 00; Perm to Offic *Worc* from 00. *Witton, 16 Moorlands Road, Malvern WR14 1VA* Tel (01684) 575742 E-mail witton@clara.co.uk

SHARPLES, Ella. *See* SHARPLES, Angela

SHARPLES, Jean. *See* ROLT, Mrs Jean

SHARPLES, Canon John Charles. b 29. St Jo Coll York TCert48 Lon Univ BSc55. St Deiniol's Hawarden 87. **d** 87 **p** 88. Hon C Wigan St Mich *Liv* 87-89; P-in-c New Springs 89-96; Hon Can Liv Cathl 97; rtd 97; Perm to Offic *Liv* from 97. *New Springs Vicarage, 7 Lealholme Avenue, Wigan WN2 1EH* Tel (01942) 243071

SHARPLES, Jonathan David. b 65. Lon Bible Coll BA95. Wycliffe Hall Ox 03. **d** 05 **p** 06. C Ashton-upon-Mersey St Mary

Magd *Ches* 05-09; R Astbury and Smallwood from 09. *The Rectory, Astbury, Congleton CW12 4RQ* Tel (01260) 272625 E-mail jonsharples@hotmail.com

SHARPLEY, The Ven Roger Ernest Dion. b 28. Ch Ch Ox BA52 MA56. St Steph Ho Ox 52. **d** 54 **p** 55. C Southwick St Columba *Dur* 54-60; V Middlesbrough All SS *York* 60-81; P-in-c Middlesbrough St Hilda w St Pet 64-72; P-in-c Middlesbrough St Aid 79; V 79-81; RD Middlesbrough 70-81; Can and Preb York Minster 74-81; V St Andr Holborn *Lon* 81-92; Adn Hackney 81-92; rtd 92; Perm to Offic *Dur* from 92; Chapl Grey Coll Dur 96-01. *2 Hill Meadows, High Shincliffe, Durham DH1 2PE* Tel 0191-386 1908

SHAVE, Norman Rossen. b 60. G&C Coll Cam BA82 MA95 Newc Univ MB, BS85 MRCGP90. Cranmer Hall Dur 98. **d** 00 **p** 01. C Preston on Tees *Dur* 00-03; C Preston-on-Tees and Longnewton 03-04; V Norton St Mary from 04; P-in-c Stockton St Chad from 04. *2 Brambling Close, Norton, Stockton-on-Tees TS20 1TX* Tel (01642) 558888

SHAW, Alan Taylor. b 52. Sarum & Wells Th Coll 88. **d** 90 **p** 91. C Beeston *Ripon* 90-93; C Stanningley St Thos 93-96; TV Seacroft 96-98; V Ryhill *Wakef* 98-02; rtd 03; Perm to Offic *Wakef* from 04. *65 Throstlehurst Avenue, Hall Green, Wakefield WF4 3NP* Tel (01924) 255210

SHAW, Alan Walter. b 41. TCD BA63 BAI63 Chu Coll Cam MSc66. **d** 94 **p** 95. NSM Drumcliffe w Kilnasoolagh *L & K* 94-97; NSM Kenmare w Sneem, Waterville etc 97-09; Can Limerick Cathl 07-09; rtd 09. *22 Ceann Mara Court, Pairc na Gloine, Kenmare, Co Kerry, Republic of Ireland* Tel (00353) 87-678 8700 (mobile) E-mail shawa@eircom.net

✠**SHAW, The Rt Revd Alexander Martin.** b 44. AKC67. **d** 68 **p** 69 c 04. C Glas St Oswald 68-70; C Edin Old St Paul 70-75; Chapl K Coll Cam 75-77; C St Marylebone All SS *Lon* 77-78; R Dunoon *Arg* 78-81; Succ Ex Cathl 81-83; Dioc Miss and Ecum Officer 83-89; TV Cen Ex 83-87; Can Res St E Cathl 89-04; Prec 96-04; Bp Arg from 04. *The Pines, Ardconnel Road, Oban, Argyll PA34 5DR* Tel and fax (01631) 566912 *or* tel 570870 Fax 570411 Mobile 07801-549615 E-mail bishop@argyll.anglican.org

SHAW, Mrs Alison Barbara. b 55. Open Univ BA92. SWMTC 98. **d** 01 **p** 02. NSM St Breoke and Egloshayle *Truro* 01-03; C Bodmin w Lanhydrock and Lanivet 03-05; TV from 05. *The Vicarage, Rectory Road, Lanivet, Bodmin PL30 5HG* Tel (01208) 831743 E-mail alishaw2001@yahoo.co.uk

SHAW, Andrew Jonathan. b 50. Wycliffe Hall Ox 85. **d** 87 **p** 88. C Witton w Brundall and Braydeston *Nor* 87-89; C Brundall w Braydeston and Postwick 89-90; C Grayswood *Guildf* 90-91; P-in-c 91-99; Chapl RN Sch Haslemere 90-96; V Hendon St Paul Mill Hill *Lon* from 99. *St Paul's Vicarage, Hammers Lane, London NW7 4EA* Tel (020) 8959 1856 *or* tel and fax 8906 3793 E-mail parishoffice@stpaulsmillhill.freeserve.co.uk

SHAW, Ms Anne Lesley. b 50. SRN SCM. Linc Th Coll 77. **dss** 80 **d** 87 **p** 94. Camberwell St Luke *S'wark* 80-85; Chapl Asst Lon Hosp (Whitechapel) 85-90; Chapl Lewisham Hosp 90-94; Chapl Hither Green Hosp 90-94; Chapl Sydenham Childrens' Hosp 90-94; Chapl Lewisham Hosp NHS Trust from 94. *The Chaplain's Office, University Hospital Lewisham, High Street, London SE13 6LH* Tel (020) 8333 3299 *or* 8333 3000 E-mail annk.shaw@uhl.nhs.uk

SHAW, Anne Patricia Leslie. b 39. MB, BS63 MRCS63 LRCP63. Qu Coll Birm 79. **dss** 81 **d** 87 **p** 94. Pinner *Lon* 81-84; Rickmansworth *St Alb* 84-09; NSM 87-09; rtd 09; Perm to Offic *St Alb* from 09. *37 Sandy Lodge Road, Moor Park, Rickmansworth WD3 1LP* Tel (01923) 827663 E-mail anneshaw@doctors.net.uk

SHAW, Anthony Keeble. b 36. K Alfred's Coll Win CertEd60 Birkbeck Coll Lon CPsychol98. SW Minl Tr Course 78. **d** 81 **p** 82. Hd Teacher Wolborough C of E Primary Sch 73-87; NSM E Teignmouth *Ex* 81-83; NSM Highweek and Teigngrace 83-87; Sub Chapl HM Pris Channings Wood 85-87; C Southbourne St Kath *Win* 87-89; Teaching 89-96; NSM Regent's Park St Mark *Lon* 93-96; P-in-c Winthorpe and Langford w Holme *S'well* 96-01; Dioc Chief Insp of Schs 96-01; rtd 01; Perm to Offic *Win* from 01. *Manlea Cottage, Centre Lane, Everton, Lymington SO41 0JP* Tel (01590) 645451

SHAW, Clive Ronald. b 54. UEA BA75 Hatf Coll Dur PGCE76. CBDTI 99. **d** 02 **p** 03. C Westfield St Mary *Carl* 02-06; V Aspatria w Hayton and Gilcrux from 06. *St Kentigern's Vicarage, King Street, Aspatria, Wigton CA7 3AL* Tel (01697) 320398 E-mail c.shaw@rowan1.fslife.co.uk

SHAW, Colin Clement Gordon. b 39. RMN60. Linc Th Coll 65. **d** 67 **p** 68. C Tettenhall Regis *Lich* 67-70; C Tile Cross *Birm* 70-72; V Edstaston *Lich* 72-75; V Whixall 72-75; Chapl Stoke Mandeville Hosp and St Jo Hosp 75-90; Manor Ho Hosp and Tindal Gen Hosp Aylesbury 75-90; R Bledlow w Saunderton and Horsenden *Ox* 90-96; rtd 96. *5 Wyre Close, Haddenham, Aylesbury HP17 8AU* Tel (01844) 292741 E-mail ccg.shaw@btinternet.com

SHAW, David George. b 40. Lon Univ BD64 MA03. Tyndale Hall Bris 58. **d** 65 **p** 66. C Kirkdale St Lawr *Liv* 65-68; C Bebington *Ches* 68-70; V Swadlincote *Derby* 70-75; R Eyam 75-04; rtd 04.

86 Higher Street, Okeford Fitzpaine, Blandford Forum DT11 0RQ Tel (01258) 860571

SHAW, David Michael. b 61. Univ Coll Dur BA83 Bris Univ BA97. Trin Coll Bris 91. **d** 93 **p** 94. C Wotton-under-Edge w Ozleworth and N Nibley *Glouc* 93-97; P-in-c Jersey St Clem *Win* 97-98; R from 98. *The Rectory, La rue du Presbytere, St Clement, Jersey JE2 6RB* Tel (01534) 851992 E-mail st.clement@jerseymail.co.uk

SHAW, David Parlane. b 32. CITC. **d** 69 **p** 70. Bp's C Lower w Upper Langfield *D & R* 69-75; R Chedburgh w Depden and Rede *St E* 75-78; R Chedburgh w Depden, Rede and Hawkedon 79-82; R Desford *Leic* 82-83; R Desford and Peckleton w Tooley 84-91; P-in-c Ramsden Crays w Ramsden Bellhouse *Chelmsf* 91-95; rtd 95; Perm to Offic *Leic* from 95. *9 Hambleton Close, Leicester Forest East, Leicester LE3 3NA* Tel 0116-224 6507 E-mail david.shaw15@ntlworld.com

SHAW, David Thomas. b 45. Open Univ BA78. WMMTC 87. **d** 90 **p** 91. C Sheldon *Birm* 90-93; R Chelmsley Wood 93-02; TR Broughton Astley and Croft w Stoney Stanton *Leic* from 02. *The Rectory, St Mary's Close, Broughton Astley, Leicester LE9 6ES* Tel (01455) 283150 E-mail rev.shaw@btopenworld.com

SHAW, Dennis Alfred Arthur. b 24. Wells Th Coll 64. **d** 65 **p** 66. C Redditch St Steph *Worc* 65-70; R Addingham *Bradf* 70-92; rtd 92; Perm to Offic *Bradf* from 92. *67 Crowther Avenue, Calverley, Pudsey LS28 5SA* Tel (01274) 611746

SHAW, Mrs Felicity Mary. b 46. UEA BSc67 MSc68. NOC 88. **d** 91 **p** 94. Par Dn Benchill *Man* 91-94; C 94-95; TV E Farnworth and Kearsley 95-98; TR 98-03; V Woodhall *Bradf* 03-07; rtd 07; Perm to Offic *Man* from 08. *99 Pennine Road, Horwich, Bolton BL6 7HW* Tel (01204) 696851 E-mail rev.fmshaw@tesco.net

SHAW, Frederick Hugh. b 16. CChem MRSC Dur Univ BSc49 MSc66. EMMTC 73. **d** 76 **p** 77. Hon C Wingerworth *Derby* 76-96; Perm to Offic from 96. *1 Frances Drive, Wingerworth, Chesterfield S42 6SJ* Tel (01246) 278321

SHAW, Canon Geoffrey Norman. b 26. Jes Coll Ox MA50. Wycliffe Hall Ox 49. **d** 51 **p** 52. C Rushden *Pet* 51-54; C Woking Ch Ch *Guildf* 54-59; V Woking St Paul 59-62; R St Leonards St Leon *Chich* 62-68; Lic to Offic *Sheff* 68-72; Vice-Prin and Lect Oak Hill Th Coll 72-79; Prin Wycliffe Hall Ox 79-88; Hon Can Ch Ch *Ox* 86-88; rtd 88; Lic to Offic *Nor* 88-91. *15A West Street, Kingham, Chipping Norton OX7 6YF* Tel (01608) 658006

SHAW, Gerald Oliver. b 32. K Coll Lon 56. **d** 60 **p** 61. C Burnley St Cuth *Blackb* 60-62; C Heysham 62-65; C-in-c Oswaldtwistle All SS CD 65-66; V Oswaldtwistle All SS 66-69; Chapl Leavesden Hosp Abbots Langley 69-75; Chapl Broadmoor Hosp Crowthorne 75-88; C Easthampstead *Ox* 88-92; P-in-c Beech Hill, Grazeley and Spencers Wood 92-97; rtd 97; Lic to Offic *Ox* from 99; Perm to Offic *Win* from 02. *1 Mortimer House Cottage, Mortimer Lane, Mortimer, Reading RG7 3PR* Tel 0118-933 3660

SHAW, Graham. b 44. Worc Coll Ox BA65. Cuddesdon Coll. **d** 69 **p** 70. C Esher *Guildf* 69-73; R Winford *B & W* 73-78; Chapl Ex Coll Ox 78-85; R Farnborough *Roch* 88-95; rtd 04. *21 Ulster Court, Albany Park Road, Kingston upon Thames KT2 5SS*

SHAW, Graham Lister. b 81. Fitzw Coll Cam BA04. Wycliffe Hall Ox 05. **d** 07 **p** 08. C Camberley St Paul *Guildf* from 07. *Cornerways, 3 Upper Gordon Road, Camberley GU15 2HJ* Tel (01276) 700210 E-mail glshaw@gmail.com

SHAW, Canon Grahame Donald. b 44. Lich Th Coll 65. **d** 68 **p** 69. C Grange St Andr *Ches* 68-73; TV E Runcorn w Halton 73-74; TV Thamesmead *S'wark* 74-79; V Newington St Paul from 79; S'wark Adnry Ecum Officer from 90; RD S'wark and Newington 96-02; Hon Can S'wark Cathl from 99. *The Vicarage, Lorrimore Square, London SE17 3QU* Tel (020) 7735 2947 *or* 7735 3506 E-mail grahame@leat.org.uk

SHAW, Mrs Irene. b 45. Gilmore Course 80 NEOC 82. **dss** 83 **d** 87 **p** 94. Elloughton and Brough w Brantingham *York* 83-86; Westborough *Guildf* 86-88; C 87-88; C Shottermill 88-91; C Lamorbey H Redeemer *Roch* 91-97; V Belvedere All SS 97-02; TV Em TM *Wakef* 02-05; rtd 05; Perm to Offic *York* from 07. *10 Rowan Avenue, Beverley HU17 9UN* Tel (01482) 871095

SHAW, Canon Jane Alison. b 63. Ox Univ BA85 MA91 Harvard Div Sch MDiv88 Univ of California Berkeley PhD94. SAOMC 96. **d** 97 **p** 98. Fell Regent's Park Coll Ox 94-01; Dean 98-01; Hon Cathl Chapl Ch Ch Ox from 00; Fell, Chapl and Dean of Div New Coll Ox from 01; NSM Ox St Mary V w St Cross and St Pet 97-01; Hon Can Ch Ch from 05; Can Th Sarum Cathl from 07. *New College, Oxford OX1 3BN* Tel (01865) 279541 E-mail jane.shaw@theology.oxford.ac.uk

SHAW, Miss Jane Elizabeth. b 47. New Hall Cam BA68 MA72 Brunel Univ MPhil79. NEOC 98. **d** 01 **p** 02. NSM Moor Allerton *Ripon* 01-05; Chapl Bp Rooke Chpl Raiwind Pakistan from 06. *Diocese of Raiwind, 17 Warris Road, Lahore, Pakistan* E-mail shawjane2005@yahoo.co.uk

SHAW, Mrs Jane Louise Claridge. b 66. Birm Poly BA87. WMMTC 00. **d** 03 **p** 04. C Longbridge *Birm* 03-07; V Dosthill from 07. *The Vicarage, 1 Church Road, Dosthill, Tamworth B77 1LU* Tel (01827) 281349 E-mail louiseshaw6@yahoo.co.uk

SHAW, Mrs Janet Elaine. b 53. EMMTC 94. **d** 97 **p** 98. C Cleveleys *Blackb* 97-01; P-in-c Blackpool St Paul 01-03; V from 03. *St Paul's Vicarage, 253 Warbreck Hill Road, Blackpool FY2 0SP* Tel (01253) 350007 E-mail mail@vicstp.fsnet.co.uk

SHAW, Mrs Jayne. St Mich Coll Llan. **d** 08 **p** 09. NSM Tonyrefail w Gilfach Goch *Llan* from 08. *11 Portreeve Close, Llantrisant, Pontyclun CF72 8DU* Tel (01443) 238356

SHAW, John Boyde. b 52. St Jo Coll Nottm BA00. **d** 00 **p** 01. C Gorleston St Andr *Nor* 00-04; P-in-c Rockland St Mary w Hellington, Bramerton etc 04-06; R from 06. *The Rectory, 2 Rectory Lane, Rockland St Mary, Norwich NR14 7EY* Tel (01508) 538619 E-mail revjohnshaw@gmail.com

SHAW, Jonathan. *See* SHAW, Andrew Jonathan

SHAW, Kenneth James. b 36. St Jo Coll Nottm 85 Edin Th Coll 88. **d** 87 **p** 89. NSM Troon *Glas* 87-89; C Glas St Mary 89-90; R Lenzie 90-01; Warden of Readers 96-01; rtd 01; Hon C Glas St Mary 02-06. *19 Mailerbeg Gardens, Moodiesburn, Glasgow G69 0JP* Tel (01236) 873987 E-mail ken@kjshaw.fsnet.co.uk

SHAW, Louise. *See* SHAW, Mrs Jane Louise Claridge

SHAW, Malcolm. b 46. Trin Coll Bris. **d** 01 **p** 02. C Bolsover *Derby* 01-05; R Brimington from 05. *The Rectory, Church, Brimington, Chesterfield S43 1JG* Tel (01246) 273103 Mobile 07713-624005 E-mail malshw@aol.com

SHAW, Malcolm Roy. b 47. Lon Univ BA69 CQSW76. NEOC 03. **d** 05 **p** 06. NSM Hunmanby w Muston *York* 05-08; NSM Rufforth w Moor Monkton and Hessay from 08; NSM Long Marston from 08; NSM Healaugh w Wighill, Bilbrough and Askham Richard from 08; NSM Tockwith and Bilton w Bickerton from 08. *32 Westfield Road, Tockwith, York YO26 7PY* Tel (01423) 359003

SHAW, Mrs Margaret Ann. b 58. Bp Otter Coll Chich BA80 SS Paul & Mary Coll Cheltenham PGCE81. EAMTC 00. **d** 03 **p** 04. C Langdon Hills *Chelmsf* 03-06; TV Basildon St Andr w H Cross from 06. *St Andrew's Vicarage, 3 The Fremnells, Basildon SS14 2QX* Tel (01268) 520516 E-mail sh.ma@btinternet.com

SHAW, Martin. *See* SHAW, The Rt Revd Alexander Martin

SHAW, Michael. *See* SHAW, Ralph Michael

SHAW, Michael Howard. b 38. Leeds Univ BSc61. Linc Th Coll 64. **d** 66 **p** 67. C W Hartlepool St Paul *Dur* 66-68; Asst Master Stockbridge Co Sec Sch 68; Totton Coll 69; Gravesend Boys' Gr Sch 70-72; Maidstone Gr Sch 72-94; Perm to Offic *Cant* and *Roch* from 70; rtd 03. *2 Bredgar Close, Maidstone ME14 5NG* Tel (01622) 673415

SHAW, Neil Graham. b 61. St Jo Coll Nottm 89. **d** 91 **p** 92. C Leamington Priors St Paul *Cov* 91-95; TV Bestwood *S'well* 95-99; Chapl HM YOI Thorn Cross 99-01; Chapl HM Pris Hindley 01-07; Chapl HM Pris Liv from 07. *HM Prison Liverpool, 68 Hornby Road, Liverpool L9 3DF* Tel 0151-530 4127

SHAW, Norman. b 33. Cranmer Hall Dur. **d** 82 **p** 83. C Beamish *Dur* 82-84; P-in-c Craghead 84-88; V Cleadon 88-98; rtd 98. *3 St Mary's Drive, Sherburn Village, Durham DH6 1RL* Tel 0191-372 2540 E-mail normandcon@aol.com

SHAW, Peter Haslewood. b 17. Pemb Coll Cam BA39 MA65. Worc Ord Coll 65. **d** 67 **p** 68. C S Kensington St Jude *Lon* 67-69; V Alderney *Win* 69-78; V Disley *Ches* 78-82; rtd 82; Chapl Athens w Kifissia, Patras and Corfu *Eur* 82-85; Hon C Las Palmas 84-85; Hon C Breamore *Win* 85-89; Perm to Offic *Pet* from 07. *Manor Cottage, Church Road, Greatworth, Banbury OX17 2DU* Tel (01295) 712102

SHAW, Ralph. b 38. Man Univ MEd70. Sarum & Wells Th Coll 78. **d** 80 **p** 81. C Consett *Dur* 80-84; P-in-c Tanfield 84-88; V 88-97; R S Shields St Aid and St Steph 97-05; rtd 05. *10 Shipley Court, Gateshead NE8 4EZ* Tel 0191-420 5137

SHAW, Ralph Michael. b 45. DipAdEd. Lich Th Coll 68. **d** 70 **p** 71. C Dewsbury All SS *Wakef* 70-75; TV Redcar w Kirkleatham *York* 75-76; Dioc Youth Officer *St Alb* 76-91; Lic to Offic from 91; Chief Exec Jo Grooms 91-08; Team Ldr Workplace Min *St Alb* from 08. *18 Wyton, Welwyn Garden City AL7 2PF* Tel (01707) 321813 E-mail revmshaw@gmail.com

SHAW, Richard. b 46. **d** 89 **p** 90. NSM Porchester *S'well* 89-91; NSM Daybrook 04-06; P-in-c Basford St Aid from 06; P-in-c Basford St Leodegarius from 09. *The Vicarage, 152 Perry Road, Nottingham NG5 1GL* Tel 0115-829 2369

SHAW, Preb Richard Tom. b 42. AKC69. St Aug Coll Cant 69. **d** 70 **p** 71. C Dunston St Nic *Dur* 70-72; C Maidstone All SS w St Phil and H Trin *Cant* 73-75; Chapl RN 75-79; V Barrow-on-Humber *Linc* 79-83; V Linc St Faith and St Martin w St Pet 83-91; V Clun w Bettws-y-Crwyn and Newcastle *Heref* from 91; RD Clun Forest 94-05 and from 08; P-in-c Hopesay from 98; Preb Heref Cathl from 02. *The Vicarage, Vicarage Road, Clun, Craven Arms SY7 8JG* Tel (01588) 640809

SHAW, Robert Christopher. b 34. Man Univ BA BD. Union Th Sem (NY) STM. **d** 82 **p** 83. C Sharlston *Wakef* 82-83; C Scissett St Aug 83-85; R Cumberworth w Denby Dale 85-90; P-in-c Denby 85-90; R Bolton w Ireby and Uldale *Carl* 90-95; rtd 95; Perm to Offic *York* from 95. *Stonecroft, Sproxton, York YO62 5EF* Tel (01439) 770178

SHAW, Canon Robert William. b 46. Lon Univ BD69. St Aug Coll Cant 69. **d** 70 **p** 71. C Hunslet St Mary and Stourton *Ripon*

70-71; C Hunslet St Mary 71-74; C Hawksworth Wood 74-76; R Stanningley St Thos 76-84; V Potternewton 84-94; V Manston 94-02; P-in-c Beeston Hill H Spirit 02-04; P-in-c Hunslet Moor St Pet and St Cuth 02-04; V Beeston Hill and Hunslet Moor from 04; Hon Can Ripon Cathl from 08. *St Peter's Vicarage, 139 Dewsbury Road, Leeds LS11 5NW* Tel 0113-277 2464
E-mail bob@anitashaw.freeserve.co.uk

SHAW, Roderick Kenneth. b 37. MBIM77. Moray Ord Course 88. **d** 92 **p** 95. Hon C Grantown-on-Spey *Mor* 92-96; Hon C Rothiemurchus 92-00; P Companion Missr from 00. *The Cottage, Balliefurth, Grantown-on-Spey PH26 3NH* Tel (01479) 821496

SHAW, Mrs Rosemary Alice. b 44. CertEd65 CQSW78 Heythrop Coll Lon MA96 MA04. S'wark Ord Course 87. **d** 89 **p** 94. Par Dn Walworth *S'wark* 89-92; Par Dn E Dulwich St Jo 92-95; NSM 95-96; Eileen Kerr Mental Health Fell Maudsley Hosp 95-96; Chapl King's Healthcare NHS Trust 96-01; Sen Chapl Guy's and St Thos' NHS Foundn Trust 02-07; Hon C E Dulwich St Jo *S'wark* from 96. *19 Scutari Road, London SE22 0NN* Tel (020) 8693 6325 E-mail stjohnsenq33@black1.org.uk

SHAW, Roy. *See* SHAW, Malcolm Roy

SHAW, Stewart James. b 64. Wilson Carlile Coll 97 NTMTC BA07. **d** 07 **p** 08. C Hounslow H Trin w St Paul *Lon* from 07; Chapl RAF from 09. *Chaplaincy Services, HQ Air Command, RAF High Wycombe HP14 4UE* Tel (01494) 496800 Fax 496343 E-mail stewchaplain82@blueyonder.co.uk

SHAW, Wendy Jane. b 54. Shenstone Coll of Educn CertEd75 Man Univ MEd90. EAMTC 01. **d** 05 **p** 06. C Thurton *Nor* 05-08; Bp's Officer for Visual Arts from 08. *The Rectory, 2 Rectory Lane, Rockland St Mary, Norwich NR14 7EY* Tel (01508) 537045 Mobile 07830-306384
E-mail wendyjane.shaw@virgin.net

SHAYLER-WEBB, Peter. b 57. Bath Univ BSc81 BArch83. Ripon Coll Cuddesdon 93. **d** 95 **p** 96. C Bedford St Paul *St Alb* 95-99; C Dorking w Ranmore *Guildf* 99-04; R Sherwood Australia from 04. *PO Box 107, Sherwood Qld 4075, Australia* Tel (0061) (7) 3278 2498 *or* 3379 3437 Fax 3278 2048
E-mail psw5957@bigpond.net.au

SHEA, Martyn Paul Leathley. b 66. City Univ BSc89. Wycliffe Hall Ox. **d** 00 **p** 01. C Ches Square St Mich w St Phil *Lon* 00-03; C Stamford St Geo w St Paul *Linc* 03-08; P-in-c Jersey St Mark *Win* from 08. *The Vicarage, St Mark's Road, St Helier, Jersey JE2 4LY* Tel (01534) 720595 Mobile 07976-869467
E-mail martyn.shea@stmarksjersey.org

SHEAD, John Frederick Henry. b 38. ACP74 FCP81. Westcott Ho Cam 72. **d** 74 **p** 75. Hd Master Thaxted Co Primary Sch 70-85; Hon C Thaxted *Chelmsf* 74-85; C Saffron Walden w Wendens Ambo and Littlebury 86-88; P-in-c Wethersfield w Shalford 88-96; P-in-c Finchingfield and Cornish Hall End 94-96; V Finchingfield and Cornish Hall End etc 96-04; RD Braintree 95-00; rtd 04. *57 Kenworthy Road, Braintree CM7 1JJ* Tel (01376) 321783 E-mail j.shead@tiscali.co.uk

SHEARCROFT, Sister Elizabeth Marion. b 57. SRN76. **d** 94 **p** 95. CA from 84; NSM Margate H Trin *Cant* 94-98; Chapl Thanet Healthcare NHS Trust 94-98; Chapl E Kent Hosps NHS Trust 99-02; C Kendal H Trin *Carl* 02-05; V Streatham Immanuel and St Andr *S'wark* from 05. *Immanuel Vicarage, 51A Guildersfield Road, London SW16 5LS* Tel (020) 8764 5103
E-mail liz@thekingfishery.co.uk

SHEARD, Andrew Frank. b 60. York Univ BA81. St Jo Coll Nottm 92. **d** 94 **p** 95. C Uxbridge *Lon* 94-96; TV 96-99; P-in-c 99-01; TR from 01. *St Margaret's Vicarage, 72 Harefield Road, Uxbridge UB8 1PL* Tel (01895) 237853 *or* 258766 Fax 812194
E-mail andrewf.sheard@btinternet.com

SHEARD, Ernest. b 29. Linc Th Coll 73. **d** 74 **p** 75. NSM Birstall *Leic* 74-82; NSM Birstall and Wanlip 82-84; Asst Chapl Loughb Univ and Colls 75-90; Lic to Offic *Leic* 90-94; Perm to Offic from 94. *21 Orchard Road, Birstall, Leicester LE4 4GD* Tel 0116-267 3901

SHEARD, Gillian Freda. *See* COOKE, Ms Gillian Freda

SHEARD, Preb Michael Rowland. b 42. K Coll Lon BA Man Univ PhD. **d** 95 **p** 95. World Miss Officer *Lich* 86-09; TV Willenhall H Trin *Lich* 95-09; Preb Lich Cathl 99-09; rtd 09. *9 Queen Street, Kirton Lindsay, Gainsborough DN21 4NS* Tel (01652) 648846 Mobile 07711-541983
E-mail michael.sheard@btinternet.com

SHEARER, John Frank. b 35. Ex Univ BSc60. Tyndale Hall Bris 62. **d** 63 **p** 64. C Blackheath St Jo *S'wark* 63-67; R Nuffield *Ox* 67-06; rtd 06. *Denbeigh Spring Gardens, Oak Street, Lechlade GL7 3AY* Tel (01367) 252806

SHEARING, Michael James. b 39. Lanc Univ BA71. Linc Th Coll. **d** 66 **p** 67. NSM Hartlepool St Paul *Dur* 66-76; Asst Master Dyke Ho Comp Sch Hartlepool 76-87; C Houghton le Spring 87; P-in-c Wheatley Hill 87-95; V Bishopwearmouth St Nic 95-97; R Cockfield and V Lynesack 97-04; rtd 04. *83 Welham Road, Norton, Malton YO17 9DS* Tel (01653) 694928

SHEARLOCK, The Very Revd David John. b 32. FRSA91 Birm Univ BA55. Westcott Ho Cam 56. **d** 57 **p** 58. C Guisborough *York* 57-60; C Christchurch *Win* 60-64; V Kingsclere 64-71; V

Romsey 71-82; Dioc Dir of Ords 77-82; Hon Can Win Cathl 78-82; Dean Truro 82-97; R Truro St Mary 82-97; Chapl Cornwall Fire Brigade 91-97; rtd 98; Perm to Offic *Sarum* from 98. *3 The Tanyard, Shadrack Street, Beaminster DT8 3BG* Tel (01308) 863170

SHEARMAN, Michael Alan. b 22. Down Coll Cam BA44 MA48. Coll of Resurr Mirfield 46. **d** 48 **p** 49. C Bounds Green *Lon* 48-53; C Wembley Park St Aug 53-58; V Enfield St Luke 58-87; rtd 87; Perm to Offic *Nor* 87-02. *18 Thompson Avenue, Holt NR25 6EN* Tel (01263) 713072

SHEARN, Andrew William. b 43. Ex Univ BA65. WMMTC 04. **d** 06 **p** 07. NSM Wellesbourne *Cov* from 06. *32 Birmingham Road, Alcester B49 5EP* Tel (01789) 763348
E-mail andy_shearn@hotmail.com

SHEARS, Canon Michael George Frederick. b 33. Pemb Coll Cam BA57 MA68. St Steph Ho Ox 57. **d** 59 **p** 60. C Grantham St Wulfram *Linc* 59-68; R Waltham 68-80; R Barnoldby le Beck 74-80; RD Haverstoe 78-80; V Soham *Ely* 80-99; RD Fordham 83-95; Hon Can Ely Cathl 94-99; rtd 99; Perm to Offic *Nor* from 00. *Woodcutter's Cottage, 19 High Street, Wicklewood, Wymondham NR18 9QE* Tel (01953) 605535

SHEATH, Allan Philip. b 48. SWMTC 95. **d** 98 **p** 99. NSM Tiverton St Pet and Chevithorne w Cove *Ex* 98-03; C Honiton, Gittisham, Combe Raleigh, Monkton etc 03-04; TV from 04. *The Vicarage, Awliscombe, Honiton EX14 3PJ* Tel (01404) 42983
E-mail allan.sheath@virgin.net

SHEDD, Mrs Christine Elizabeth. b 49. City of Birm Coll CertEd70 St Jo Coll York MA02. NOC 02. **d** 04 **p** 05. C Thornton St Jas *Bradf* 04-07; TV Oakenshaw, Wyke and Low Moor from 07; Warden of Readers from 09. *Holy Trinity Vicarage, Park House Road, Low Moor, Bradford BD12 0HR* Tel (01274) 678859 Mobile 07814-958919

SHEDDEN, Mrs Valerie. b 56. Ripon Coll of Educn CertEd77. Cranmer Hall Dur 81. **dss** 84 **d** 87 **p** 94. Tudhoe Grange *Dur* 84-85; Whitworth w Spennymoor 85-91; Par Dn 87-91; Par Dn E Darlington 91-94; P-in-c Bishop Middleham 94-00; Dioc RE Adv 94-00; V Heworth St Mary from 00; AD Gateshead from 06. *Heworth Vicarage, High Heworth Lane, Gateshead NE10 0PB* Tel 0191-469 2111 E-mail val.shedden@talk21.com

SHEEHAN, Patrick Edward Anthony. b 37. Campion Ho Middx 58 English Coll Lisbon 62. **d** 67 **p** 69. In RC Ch 67-73; C Clapham H Spirit *S'wark* 73-75; P-in-c Wimbledon 75-77; R Balga Good Shep Australia 77-80; R Melville H Cross 80-85; Chapl R Newcastle Hosp 85-91; Chapl Jo Hunter Hosp 91-97; R Terrigal 97-01; rtd 01. *22 Abby Crescent, Ashmore Qld 4214, Australia* Tel (0061) (7) 5564 7064

SHEEHY, Jeremy Patrick. b 56. Magd Coll Ox BA78 MA81 New Coll Ox DPhil90. St Steph Ho Ox 78. **d** 81 **p** 82. C Erdington St Barn *Birm* 81-83; C Small Heath St Greg 83-84; Dean Div, Fell and Chapl New Coll Ox 84-90; V Leytonstone St Marg w St Columba *Chelmsf* 90-96; P-in-c Leytonstone St Andr 93-96; Prin St Steph Ho Ox 96-06; TR Swinton and Pendlebury *Man* from 06. *St Peter's Rectory, Vicarage Road, Swinton, Manchester M27 0WA* Tel 0161-794 1578

SHEEKEY, Raymond Arthur. b 23. Chich Th Coll 51. **d** 53 **p** 54. C Ramsgate St Geo *Cant* 53-56; C Birchington w Acol 56-61; V Brabourne w Smeeth 61-79; RD N Lympne 75-78; R Lenham w Boughton Malherbe 79-88; Chapl Lenham Hosp 79-88; rtd 88; Perm to Offic *Bris* 88-97 and *Glouc* 98-99. *41 Barleycorn, Leybourne, West Malling ME19 5PS* Tel (01732) 847722

SHEEN, David Kenneth. b 70. Cov Univ BSc95 Univ of Wales (Cardiff) BA04. St Mich Coll Llan 01. **d** 04 **p** 05. C Cowbridge *Llan* 04-07; C Penarth and Llandough from 07. *Church House, 153 Windsor Road, Penarth CF64 1JF* Tel (01446) 773515
E-mail dk.sheen@btinternet.com

SHEEN, Canon John Harold. b 32. Qu Coll Cam BA54 MA58. Cuddesdon Coll 56. **d** 58 **p** 59. C Stepney St Dunstan and All SS *Lon* 58-62; V Tottenham St Jo 62-68; V Wood Green St Mich 68-78; P-in-c Southgate St Mich 77-78; R Kirkbride *S & M* 78-97; Chapl Ramsey Cottage Hosp 80-98; V Lezayre St Olave Ramsey 80-98; RD Ramsey 88-97; Can St German's Cathl 91-98; Dir of Ords 93-01; rtd 98; Perm to Offic *S & M* from 99. *Kentraugh Mill, Colby, Isle of Man IM9 4AU* Tel (01624) 832406

SHEEN, Canon Victor Alfred. b 17. Tyndale Hall Bris 47. **d** 49 **p** 50. Uganda 50-58; C Cheltenham St Mark *Glouc* 56-58; V W Streatham St Jas *S'wark* 58-65; V Clapham St Jas 65-86; RD Clapham and Brixton 75-82 and 85-86; Hon Can S'wark Cathl 80-86; rtd 86; Perm to Offic *Chich* from 86. *10 Porters Way, Polegate BN26 6AP* Tel (01323) 487487

SHEERAN, Antony. b 58. Birm Poly BA80. SEITE 02. **d** 05 **p** 06. NSM Mildmay Grove St Jude and St Paul *Lon* 05-09; NSM Dalston St Mark w St Bart from 09. *26 Harcombe Road, London N16 0SA* Tel (020) 7275 9190 Mobile 07881-811586
E-mail tony.sheeran@hotmail.com

SHEFFIELD, Julia. b 55. MCSP78 SRP78. NTMTC BA05 **d** 05 **p** 06. NSM Yiewsley *Lon* 05-09; Chapl Mid-Essex Hosp Services NHS Trust from 09. *Latton Vicarage, The Gowers, Harlow CM20 2JP* Tel (01279) 423609 E-mail julishef@hotmail.co.uk *or* julia.sheffield@meht.nhs.uk

SHEFFIELD, Michael Julian. b 53. Brentwood Coll of Educn CertEd. Sarum & Wells Th Coll 76. **d** 79 **p** 80. C Locks Heath *Portsm* 79-83; C Ryde All SS 83-86; P-in-c Ryde H Trin 86-92; V 92-96; P-in-c Swanmore St Mich w Havenstreet 86-92; V Swanmore St Mich 92-96; V W Leigh 96-04; V Waterlooville from 04. *The Vicarage, 5 Deanswood Drive, Waterlooville PO7 7RR* Tel (023) 9226 2145 Mobile 07818-031902 E-mail mikejs99@hotmail.com

SHEFFIELD AND ROTHERHAM, Archdeacon of. *See* BLACKBURN, The Ven Richard Finn

SHEFFIELD, Bishop of. *See* CROFT, The Rt Revd Steven John Lindsey

SHEFFIELD, Dean of. *See* BRADLEY, The Very Revd Peter Edward

SHEGOG, Preb Eric Marshall. b 37. City Univ MA88 FRSA92. Lich Th Coll 64. **d** 65 **p** 66. C Benhilton *S'wark* 65-68; Asst Youth Adv 68-70; V Abbey Wood 70-76; Chapl Sunderland Town Cen 76-83; C Bishopwearmouth St Mich w St Hilda *Dur* 76-83; Hd Relig Broadcasting IBA 84-90; Perm to Offic *Lon* 85-90 and *St Alb* 85-89; Hon C Harpenden St Nic *St Alb* 89-97; Dir Communications for C of E 90-97; Dir Communications *Lon* 97-00; Preb St Paul's Cathl 97-00; Acting Dioc Gen Sec 99; rtd 00; Perm to Offic *St Alb* from 00. *9 Colbron Close, Ashwell, Baldock SG7 5TH* Tel (01462) 743251

SHEHADI, Nabil Faouzi. b 58. Wycliffe Hall Ox 00. **d** 02 **p** 03. C Cobbold Road St Sav w St Mary *Lon* 02-05; V Internat Congregation Beirut All SS Lebanon from 05. *All Saints' Church, PO Box 11-2211, Riad El Solh, Beirut 1107 2100, Lebanon* Tel (00961) (4) 530551 E-mail nabilshehadi@hotmail.com

SHELDON, Jennifer Christine. b 43. K Coll Lon BA99. NTMTC 00. **d** 02 **p** 03. NSM Poplar *Lon* from 02. *23 Lancaster Drive, London E14 9PT* Tel (020) 7538 2375 *or* 7538 9198 Fax 7538 1551 E-mail jensheldon@aol.com

SHELDON, Jonathan Mark Robin. b 59. Cam Univ MA83. Ridley Hall Cam 81. **d** 83 **p** 84. C Dulwich St Barn *S'wark* 83-86; C Worle *B & W* 86-88; V Chesterton St Andr *Ely* 88-97. *21 Chancery Lane, Thrapston, Kettering NN14 4JL* Tel (01832) 731173 E-mail jsheldon@agnet.co.uk

SHELDON, Martin David. b 67. Sussex Univ BA89. St Jo Coll Nottm MTh01. **d** 01 **p** 02. C Milton *Win* 01-05; V Lightwater *Guildf* from 05. *The Vicarage, 28 Broadway Road, Lightwater GU18 5SJ* Tel (01276) 472270 E-mail vicar.lightwater@talktalk.net

SHELDRAKE, Mrs Varlie Ivy. b 39. SRN64 SCM65. **d** 03 **p** 04. OLM E w W Harling, Bridgham w Roudham, Larling etc *Nor* 03-09; rtd 09; Perm to Offic *Nor* from 09. *Springfield, Lopham Road, East Harling, Norwich NR16 2PX* Tel (01953) 717404 E-mail varlie@eastharling.com

SHELLEY, Derrick Sydney David. b 38. Lon Univ LLB60 AKC65. Linc Th Coll 66. **d** 68 **p** 69. C Weybridge *Guildf* 68-72; Chapl Red Bank Schs 71-76; Perm to Offic *Blackb* 76-96; rtd 96; Perm to Offic *Truro* 96-03 and *Lich* 04-09. *57 Kenilworth Road, Lytham St Annes FY8 1LB* Tel (01253) 780298 E-mail notatmyage@ntlworld.com

SHELLEY, Robin Arthur. b 34. CEng MIMechE. St Jo Coll Nottm 85. **d** 87 **p** 88. C Countesthorpe w Foston *Leic* 87-90; V Enderby w Lubbesthorpe and Thurlaston 90-00; rtd 00; Perm to Offic *Leic* 00-03; *York* from 02. *10 West Leys Park, Swanland, North Ferriby HU14 3LS* Tel (01482) 637063

SHELLS, Canon Charles Harry. b 15. St Chad's Coll Dur BA38 MA43. **d** 39 **p** 40. C Almondbury *Wakef* 39-42; C Camberwell St Geo *S'wark* 42-47; V Newington St Paul 47-54; V Wandsworth St Anne 54-65; RD Wandsworth 63-65; R Trunch w Swafield *Nor* 65-71; R Bradfield 65-71; P-in-c Gimingham 65-71; P-in-c Trimingham 65-71; P-in-c Antingham w Thorpe Market 65-71; P-in-c Felmingham 65-68; P-in-c Suffield 65-68; P-in-c Gunton St Pet 65-71; RD Tunstead 65-68; Can Res Bris Cathl 71-81; rtd 81; Lic to Offic *B & W* 81-96 and *Sarum* from 81; Perm to Offic *Bris* 81-02 and *B & W* 88-07. *29 Kenwith Castle, Abbotsham, Bideford EX39 5BE*

SHELTON, Canon Ian Robert. b 52. BEd74 Lon Univ MA79. Ripon Coll Cuddesdon BA81 MA90. **d** 82 **p** 83. C Wath-upon-Dearne w Adwick-upon-Dearne *Sheff* 82-86; TV Grantham *Linc* 86-93; P-in-c Waltham 93-97; R from 97; P-in-c Barnoldby le Beck 93-97; R from 97; RD Haverstoe from 01; Can and Preb Linc Cathl from 05. *The Rectory, 95 High Street, Waltham, Grimsby DN37 0PN* Tel (01472) 822172 E-mail robertshelton954@hotmail.com

SHELTON, Ms Pauline Mary. b 52. K Coll Lon BA73. NOC 96. **d** 99 **p** 00. C Baswich *Lich* 99-02; TV Stoke-upon-Trent 02-06; Dioc OLM Course Ldr from 06. *Dray Cottage, Cheadle Road, Draycott, Stoke-on-Trent ST11 9RQ* Tel (01782) 388834 E-mail rev.pauline@virgin.net

SHEMILT, Lisa. b 69. St Jo Coll Nottm 03. **d** 05 **p** 06. C Walton St Jo *Derby* from 05. *8 Birkdale Drive, Chesterfield S40 3JL* Tel (01246) 207939 E-mail lisa@shemilt.fslife.co.uk

SHENTON, Canon Brian. b 43. Chich Th Coll 73. **d** 75 **p** 76. C Mill Hill Jo Keble Ch *Lon* 75-78; C New Windsor *Ox* 78-81; TV

81-82; P-in-c Cherbury 82-83; V Calcot 83-89; R Reading St Mary w St Laur from 89; P-in-c Reading St Matt 96-00; RD Reading from 95; Hon Can Ch Ch from 98. *Hamelsham, Downshire Square, Reading RG1 6NJ* Tel 0118-956 8163 *or* 957 1057 Mobile 07710-490250 E-mail stmaryshouserdg@waitrose.com

SHEPHARD, Brian Edward. b 34. Magd Coll Cam BA56 MA60 Ox Univ CertEd71. Wycliffe Hall Ox 58. **d** 60 **p** 61. C Wigan St Cath *Liv* 60-62; C Kidderminster St Geo *Worc* 62-65; Lect CA Tr Coll Blackheath 65-70; Lect Hamilton Coll of Educn 70-77; Chapl Buchan Sch Castletown 77-88; Tutor Wilson Carlile Coll of Evang 88-89; C Andreas St Jude *S & M* 89-91; C Jurby 89-91; V Lezayre 91-02; rtd 02; Perm to Offic *S & M* from 02. *Keayn Ard, Queens Road, Port St Mary, Isle of Man IM9 5EP* Tel (01624) 833315 E-mail kyriosvoskos@manx.net

SHEPHEARD-WALWYN, John. b 16. Oriel Coll Ox BA38 MA44. Wells Th Coll 38. **d** 40 **p** 42. C Roch St Pet w St Marg 41-44; C Lamorbey H Redeemer 44-49; C Edenbridge 49-56; V Rosherville 56-61; R Horwood and V Westleigh *Ex* 61-78; P-in-c Harberton w Harbertonford 78-82; rtd 82; Perm to Offic *Bris* 82-05. *5 Holly Road, Bramhall, Stockport SK7 1HH* Tel 0161-439 9458

SHEPHERD, Canon Anthony Michael. b 50. Em Coll Cam BA72 MA76. Westcott Ho Cam 72. **d** 74 **p** 75. C Folkestone St Mary and St Eanswythe *Cant* 74-79; Bp's Dom Chapl *Ripon* 79-87; Dioc Communications Officer 79-87; V High Harrogate St Pet from 87; Hon Can Ripon Cathl from 99. *St Peter's Vicarage, 13 Beech Grove, Harrogate HG2 0ET* Tel (01423) 500901 E-mail ashepherd@onetel.net

SHEPHERD, Mrs Bridget. b 76. Open Univ BSc01 K Coll Lon MA04. Trin Coll Bris BA08. **d** 08 **p** 09. C S Croydon Em *S'wark* from 08. *12 Hurst View Road, South Croydon CR2 7AG* Tel (020) 8688 6676 Mobile 07977-555135 E-mail shoesnbags_addict@yahoo.co.uk

SHEPHERD, Christopher Francis Pleydell. b 44. St Steph Ho Ox 68. **d** 69 **p** 70. C Milber *Ex* 69-72; C Ex St Thos 72-74; TV Ilfracombe, Lee and W Down 74-78; TV Ilfracombe, Lee, W Down, Woolacombe and Bittadon 78-80; P-in-c Tregony w St Cuby and Cornelly *Truro* 80-83; R 83-96; rtd 04. *2 Cherry Meadow, Cheriton Fitzpaine, Crediton EX17 4JX* Tel (01363) 866896

SHEPHERD, David. b 42. St Jo Coll Dur BA65 MA68 MLitt76. Edin Th Coll 66. **d** 68 **p** 69. Chapl St Paul's Cathl Dundee 68-79; Chapl Dundee Univ 73-79; R Dundee St Mary Magd from 79; Hon Chapl Abertay Univ from 01. *14 Albany Terrace, Dundee DD3 6HR* Tel (01382) 223510

SHEPHERD, David Mark. b 59. Reading Univ BA81 Nottm Univ BTh86. Linc Th Coll 83. **d** 86 **p** 87. C Wilmslow *Ches* 86-89; C Bromborough 89-92; V Leasowe 92-97; V Oxhey St Matt *St Alb* from 97. *The Vicarage, St Matthew's Close, Eastbury Road, Watford WD19 4ST* Tel (01923) 241420 E-mail davidshepherd@matts52.fsnet.co.uk

SHEPHERD, Donald. *See* SHEPHERD, John Donald

SHEPHERD, Ernest John Heatley. b 27. TCD BA48 BD53. **d** 50 **p** 51. C Belfast St Mary Magd *Conn* 50-54; I Whitehouse 54-96; Can Conn Cathl 86-90; Co-ord Aux Min 87-96; Treas Conn Cathl 90-96; Prec Conn Cathl 90-96; rtd 96. *15 Downshire Gardens, Carrickfergus BT38 7LW* Tel (028) 9336 2243

SHEPHERD, Miss Jayne Elizabeth. b 57. Reading Univ BA78. Cranmer Hall Dur 79. **dss** 82 **d** 87 **p** 94. Wombourne *Lich* 82-85; Harlescott 85-90; Par Dn 87-90; Chapl Asst Qu Medical Cen Nottm Univ Hosp 90-97; Asst Chapl Cen Notts Healthcare NHS Trust 90-97; Chapl Pet Hosps NHS Trust 97-02; Chapl St Helens and Knowsley Hosps NHS Trust 02-08; V Knutsford St Cross *Ches* from 08. *The Vicarage, Mobberley Road, Knutsford WA16 8EL* Tel (01565) 640702 E-mail j.shepherd57@ntlworld.com

SHEPHERD, Joan Francis Fleming. *See* STENHOUSE, Joan Frances Fleming

SHEPHERD, John Donald. b 33. Cranmer Hall Dur BA59. **d** 61 **p** 62. C Dewsbury All SS *Wakef* 61-63; C Chapelthorpe 63-66; V Stainland 66-70; Dioc Youth Chapl *Truro* 70-74; V Newquay 74-84; RD Pydar 81-84; Chapl Borocourt Mental Handicap Hosp 84-95; TR Langtree *Ox* 84-95; rtd 98; Perm to Offic *Lich* from 99. *20 Grangefields, Shrewsbury SY3 9DE*

SHEPHERD, The Very Revd John Harley. b 42. Melbourne Univ BA64 Union Th Sem (NY) MSacMus73 St Cath Coll Cam PhD84. Trin Coll Melbourne ThL66. **d** 67 **p** 68. C W Footscray Australia 67-68; C Brunswick 69-70; C Stretford St Matt *Man* 71; Asst P Sayville Long Is USA 72-77; C Cherry Hinton St Andr *Ely* 78-80; Chapl Ch Ch Ox 80-88; Chapl Univ W Australia 88-90; Dean Perth from 90. *St George's Cathedral, 38 St George's Terrace, Perth WA 6000, Australia* Tel (0061) (8) 9325 5766 *or* 9322 7265 Fax 9325 5242 E-mail thedean@perthcathedral.org

SHEPHERD, John Martin. b 68. St Jo Coll Cam BA90. Oak Hill Th Coll BA96. **d** 96 **p** 97. C Rusholme H Trin *Man* 96-00; SAMS

Brazil 00-03; TV Gt Chesham *Ox* from 03. *14A Manor Way, Chesham HP5 3BG* Tel (01494) 771471
E-mail john@theshepherds.org.uk

SHEPHERD, Canon John Michael. b 42. BNC Ox BA63 MA72. Coll of Resurr Mirfield 64. **d** 66 **p** 67. C Clapham H Spirit *S'wark* 66-69; C Kingston All SS 69-72; V Upper Tooting H Trin 73-80; V Wandsworth St Paul 80-90; P-in-c Mitcham SS Pet and Paul 90-92; V 92-97; RD Merton 96-97; V Battersea St Luke 97-07; RD Battersea 01-04; Hon Can S'wark Cathl 01-07; rtd 07. *15 Whitehaven, Waterlooville PO8 0DN* Tel (023) 9259 8130
E-mail johnshepherd@waitrose.com

SHEPHERD, Mrs Julie Margaret. b 37. **d** 03 **p** 04. OLM Halliwell *Man* 03-08; Perm to Offic from 08. *Apple Cottage, 16 Grove Street, Bolton BL1 3PG* Tel (01204) 844508 Mobile 07742-667903 E-mail julie.shepherd@care4free.net

SHEPHERD, Keith Frederick. b 42. EMMTC 86. **d** 89 **p** 90. NSM Stocking Farm *Leic* 89-93; NSM Church Langton w Tur Langton, Thorpe Langton etc 93-99; TV Syston 99-07; rtd 07; Perm to Offic *Leic* from 07. *57 Fielding Road, Birstall, Leicester LE4 3AG* Tel 0116-267 4172
E-mail keithshepherd55@btinternet.com

SHEPHERD, Michael John. b 54. St Chad's Coll Dur BA75 St Paul Univ Ottawa LCL81 Ottawa Univ MCL81. Ushaw Coll Dur 73. **d** 77 **p** 78. In RC Ch 77-93; NSM Evesham *Worc* 95-97; NSM Evesham w Norton and Lenchwick 97-99; NSM Badsey w Aldington and Offenham and Bretforton 99-03; R Ab Kettleby and Holwell w Asfordby *Leic* 03-08; TV Beacon *Carl* from 08. *St George's Vicarage, 3 Firbank, Sedbergh Road, Kendal LA9 6EG* Tel (01539) 723039
E-mail rev.shepherd@btinternet.com

SHEPHERD, Mrs Pauline. b 53. Stockwell Coll of Educn TCert73. WMMTC 00. **d** 03 **p** 04. C Walsall Pleck and Bescot *Lich* 03-08; P-in-c Yoxall 08; rtd 09. *134 Birmingham Road, Aldridge, Walsall WS9 0AQ* Tel (01922) 452493 Mobile 07814-680304 E-mail p.shepherd140@btinternet.com

SHEPHERD, Canon Peter William. b 48. Reading Univ BA71 Lon Univ BD80 Brighton Poly MPhil87 Lanc Univ MA94 Open Univ PhD04. Chich Th Coll 77. **d** 80 **p** 81. NSM Eastbourne St Sav and St Pet *Chich* 80-82; NSM Clitheroe St Mary *Blackb* from 82; Hd Master Wm Temple Sch Preston 83-88; Hd Master Canon Slade Sch Bolton 89-06; rtd 06; Perm to Offic *Man* from 89; Hon Can Man Cathl from 06. *Homestead, Eastham Street, Clitheroe BB7 2HY* Tel and fax (01200) 425053
E-mail pws.canonslade@btconnect.com

✠**SHEPHERD, The Rt Revd Ronald Francis.** b 26. Univ of BC BA48. AKC52 St Jo Coll Winnipeg Hon DD89. **d** 52 **p** 53 **c** 85. C Westmr St Steph w St Jo *Lon* 52-57; Canada from 57; Dean Edmonton 65-70; Dean Montreal 70-82; Bp BC 85-92; rtd 92; Hon V St Barn Miss San Diego USA 95-00. *Easter Hill, 110 Ensilwood Road, Salt Spring Island BC V8K 1N1, Canada* Tel (001) (250) 537 1399

SHEPHERD, Thomas. b 52. Man Univ BA79 Didsbury Coll Man PGCE83 SRN74. NOC 92. **d** 95 **p** 96. C Baguley *Man* 95-99; C Timperley *Ches* 99-03; V Sale St Paul 03-08; V Sandbach from 08. *The Vicarage, 15 Offley Road, Sandbach CW11 1GY* E-mail revts@mac.com

SHEPHERD, Timothy Roy. b 34. Selw Coll Cam BA58. Linc Th Coll 62. **d** 64 **p** 65. C Selly Oak St Mary *Birm* 64-67; C Stockland Green 67-72; V Perry Common 72-76; V Holton-le-Clay *Linc* 76-84, V Habrough Gp 84-93; P in c Uffington 93-95; R Uffington Gp 95-99; rtd 99; Perm to Offic *Pet* 99-01 and *Linc* 00-01. *Chapelside, Chapel Hill, Wootton, Woodstock OX20 1DX* Tel (01993) 813319

SHEPHERDSON, Mrs Maria Thérèse. b 65. STETS. **d** 07 **p** 08. C Warmley, Syston and Bitton *Bris* from 07. *25 Poplar Road, Warmley, Bristol BS30 5JX*

SHEPPARD, Derrick Richard Adam. b 44. **d** 07 **p** 08. OLM Quidenham Gp *Nor* from 07; OLM Guiltcross from 07. *Orchard House, Back Street, Garboldisham, Diss IP22 2SD* Tel (01953) 681445 E-mail derrick.sheppard@btconnect.com

SHEPPARD, Evelyn Anne Frances. **d** 08 **p** 09. OLM Hanbury, Newborough, Rangemore and Tutbury *Lich* from 08. *Melbourne House, Knightsfield Road, Hanbury, Burton-on-Trent DE13 8TH* Tel (01283) 575551 E-mail frances@melbourne-house.com

SHEPPARD, Ian Arthur Lough. b 33. Sarum & Wells Th Coll 71. **d** 74 **p** 75. C Bishop's Cleeve *Glouc* 74-77; Chapl RAF 77-81; V Gosberton *Linc* 81-87; V Leven Valley *Carl* 87-90; Deputation and Gen Appeals Org Children's Soc 90-98; rtd 98. *57 Seymour Grove, Eaglescliffe, Stockton-on-Tees TS16 0LE* Tel (01642) 791612 E-mail ials@topenworld.com

SHEPPARD, Canon Martin. b 37. Hertf Coll Ox BA61 MA65. Chich Th Coll 63. **d** 65 **p** 66. C N Hull St Mich *York* 65-68; C Hove St Jo *Chich* 68-71; V Heathfield St Rich 71-77; V New Shoreham and Old Shoreham 77-94; TR Rye 94-03; RD Rye 95-02; Can and Preb Chich Cathl 02-03; rtd 03; Perm to Offic *Chich* from 03. *62 St Pancras Road, Lewes BN7 1JG* Tel (01273) 474999

SHEPPARD, Norman George. b 32. Wolv Teacher Tr Coll CertEd73. St D Coll Lamp 57. **d** 59 **p** 60. C Burry Port and Pwll

St D 59-64; SAMS Chile 64-68; C Madeley *Heref* 68-69; Asst Master Madeley Court Sch 73-75; Gilbert Inglefield Sch Leighton Buzzard 75-80; USPG 80-81; Argentina from 80; rtd 95. *Doering 528, Capilla del Monte 5184, Provincia de Cordoba, Argentina*

SHEPPARD, Roger Malcolm. b 47. Aston Univ MBA86 Wolv Poly PGCE81 Solicitor 74. WMMTC 98. **d** 01 **p** 02. NSM Castle Vale w Minworth *Birm* 01-07; NSM Four Oaks from 08; Chapl CF(V) from 07. *193 Dower Road, Sutton Coldfield B75 6SY* Tel 0121-682 3976 or 308 8850
E-mail roger_m_sheppard@hotmail.com

SHEPPARD, Stanley Gorton. b 18. St Jo Coll Dur 46. **d** 62 **p** 63. C Leic St Mark 62-65; R Cole Orton 65-75; V Ashby Folville and Twyford w Thorpe Satchville 75-88; rtd 88; Perm to Offic *Ex* from 89. *1 Peak Coach House, Cotmaton Road, Sidmouth EX10 8SY* Tel (01395) 516124

SHEPPARD, Mrs Susan. b 59. Ex Univ BA80 MA99 SS Hild & Bede Coll Dur PGCE81. SWMTC 95. **d** 98 **p** 99. NSM Stoke Canon, Poltimore w Huxham and Rewe etc *Ex* 98-01; Chapl St Pet High Sch *Ex* 99-06; Tutor SWMTC from 05; NSM Thorverton, Cadbury, Upton Pyne etc *Ex* from 08; NSM Stoke Canon, Poltimore w Huxham and Rewe etc from 08. *Autumn Haze, Rewe, Exeter EX5 4HA* Tel and fax (01392) 841284
E-mail sueshepppard@supanet.com

SHEPTON, Robert Leonard McIntyre. b 35. Jes Coll Cam BA58 MA61. Oak Hill Th Coll 59. **d** 61 **p** 62. C Weymouth St Jo *Sarum* 61-63; Boys' Ldr Cam Univ Miss Bermondsey 63-66; Warden Ox-Kilburn Club 66-69; Chapl St D Coll Llandudno 69-77; Chief Instructor Carnoch Outdoor Cen 77-80; Chapl Kingham Hill Sch Oxon 80-92; rtd 92. *Innisfree, Duror, Appin PA38 4DA* Tel (01631) 730437 Fax 730382
E-mail bob@innisfree.free-online.co.uk

SHER, Falak. b 65. Coll of Resurr Mirfield. **d** 07 **p** 08. C Radcliffe *Man* from 07. *6 Pool Field Close, Radcliffe, Manchester M26 3UE* Tel 0161-723 5276 Mobile 07930-573624
E-mail falakfalak@hotmail.com

SHERBORNE, Archdeacon of. See TAYLOR, The Ven Paul Stanley

SHERBORNE, Area Bishop of. See KINGS, The Rt Revd Graham Ralph

SHERCLIFF, Elizabeth Ann. b 56. Salford Univ BSc79 Open Univ MA96. St Jo Coll Nottm 08. **d** 09. Dir of Studies for Readers *Ches* from 09; NSM Marple All SS from 09. *56 Ernocroft Road, Marple Bridge, Stockport SK6 5DY* Tel 07515-633856 (mobile) E-mail lizshercliff@hotmail.com

SHERDLEY, Mrs Margaret Ann. b 46. Ches Coll of HE BTh03. NOC 00. **d** 03 **p** 04. NSM Fellside Team *Blackb* from 03; Chapl Myerscough Coll from 06. *The Granary, Moons Farm, Hollowforth Lane, Woodplumpton, Preston PR4 0BD* Tel (01772) 691101 Mobile 07931-592787
E-mail m.sherdley@sky.com

SHERIDAN, Andrew Robert (Drew). b 61. Edin Univ MA83 Jordanhill Coll Glas PGCE86. TISEC 95. **d** 98 **p** 99. C Glas St Mary 98-01; R Greenock from 01; P-in-c Gourock from 06. *The Rectory, 96 Finnart Street, Greenock PA16 8HL* Tel (01475) 732441 E-mail drew@frsheridan.fsnet.co.uk

SHERIDAN, Mrs Deborah Jane. b 47. Kent Univ BA69 ALA73. WMMTC 90. **d** 93 **p** 94. NSM Lich St Chad 93-03; NSM The Ridwares and Kings Bromley from 03; Voc Educn Officer from 06; Chapl St Giles Hospice Lich from 98. *45 High Grange, Lichfield WS13 7DU* Tel (01543) 264363 or 416595
E-mail d.sheridan@postman.org.uk

SHERIDAN, Peter. b 37. Saltley Tr Coll Birm CertEd59 Leic Poly BEd82. NOC 89. **d** 92 **p** 93. NSM Braunstone *Leic* 92-95; NSM Ratby cum Groby 95-98; NSM Newtown Linford 95-98; TV Bradgate Team 98-00; Perm to Offic 00-01 and from 06; NSM Woodhouse, Woodhouse Eaves and Swithland 01-06. *16 Turnpike Way, Markfield LE67 9QT* Tel (01530) 245166

SHERIDAN, Stephen Anthony. b 62. RMN87. SEITE 04. **d** 07 **p** 08. NSM Bexhill St Pet *Chich* 07-08; NSM Stone Cross St Luke w N Langney from 08. *14 Chailey Close, Hastings TN34 2RG* Tel 07871-727743 (mobile)
E-mail steveasheridan@btinternet.com

SHERIFF, (née WORRALL), Canon Suzanne. b 63. Trin Coll Bris BA86. **d** 87 **p** 94. Par Dn Kingston upon Hull St Nic *York* 87-91; Par Dn Kingston upon Hull St Aid Southcoates 91-94; C 94-96; TV Marfleet 96-00; TR 00-07; V Tadcaster w Newton Kyme from 07; Can and Preb York Minster from 01. *The Vicarage, 78 Station Road, Tadcaster LS24 9JR*
E-mail sue@sheriff256.freeserve.co.uk

SHERLOCK, Mrs Barbara Lee Kerney. b 48. Dur Univ PhD07. Westcott Ho Cam. **d** 05 **p** 06. C Norton St Mary and Stockton St Chad *Dur* 05-07; P-in-c Newport and Widdington *Chelmsf* from 07. *The Vicarage, 5 Meadowford, Newport, Saffron Walden CB11 3QL* Tel (01799) 540339 E-mail b.kerney@onetel.net

SHERLOCK, Charles Patrick. b 51. New Coll Ox BA73 MA76 Open Univ MBA00. Ripon Coll Cuddesdon 75. **d** 77 **p** 78. C Ashtead *Guildf* 77-81; Ethiopia 81-82; Chapl Belgrade w Zagreb *Eur* 82-84; USPG Ethiopia 84-91; R Dollar *St And* 91-97; Bursar

Fistula Hosp Ethiopia 97-00; P-in-c Crieff *St And* 01-04; R 04-07; P-in-c Comrie 01-04; R 04-07; P-in-c Lochearnhead 01-04; R 04-07; Perm to Offic from 07; Assoc Chapl Addis Ababa St Matt Ethiopia from 07. *The Ibert, Monzie, Crieff PH7 3LL* Tel (01764) 652619 *or* 656222 Mobile 07740-981951 E-mail cpsherlock@msn.com

SHERLOCK, Canon Thomas Alfred. b 40. Aux Course 87. **d** 90 **p** 91. NSM Kilmallock w Kilflynn, Kilfinane, Knockaney etc *L & K* 90-94; C Templemore w Thurles and Kilfithmone *C & O* 95-98; I 98-00; I Castlecomer w Colliery Ch, Mothel and Bilbo from 00; Preb Ossory Cathl from 05. *The Rectory, Castlecomer, Co Tipperary, Republic of Ireland* Tel and fax (00353) (56) 444 1677 E-mail castlecomer@ossory.anglican.org

SHERMAN, Cornelia. b 70. STETS 06. **d** 09. C Portchester *Portsm* from 09. *24 Jute Close, Fareham PO16 8EZ* Tel (01329) 510432 E-mail connie.27@hotmail.co.uk

SHERRATT, David Arthur. b 60. Univ of Wales (Lamp) BA82 Leeds Univ BA91. Coll of Resurr Mirfield 92. **d** 92 **p** 93. C St Jo on Bethnal Green *Lon* 92-95; C W Hampstead St Jas 95-98; V Abbey Wood *S'wark* from 98. *St Michael's Vicarage, 1 Conference Road, London SE2 0YH* Tel (020) 8311 0377

SHERRED, Peter William. b 47. Kent Univ BA69. SEITE 96. **d** 99 **p** 00. NSM Dover St Mary *Cant* 99-02; Perm to Offic from 02. *Copthorne, Canal Road, Guston, Dover CT15 5EN* Tel (01304) 203548 Fax 206950 E-mail copthorne@talk21.com

SHERRING, Patrick. b 55. Trent Park Coll of Educn BEd78 CertEd77. Ridley Hall Cam 95. **d** 97 **p** 98. C Leyton St Mary w St Edw and St Luke *Chelmsf* 97-01; P-in-c Ingatestone w Buttsbury 01-04; V Ingatestone w Fryerning from 04. *The Rectory, 1 Rectory Close, Fryerning Lane, Ingatestone CM4 0DB* Tel (01277) 352562 E-mail patrick.sherring@ingatestoneparishchurch.org.uk

SHERRING, Toby Bruce. b 76. Ex Univ BA97 St Luke's Coll Ex PGCE98. St Steph Ho Ox MTh04. **d** 02 **p** 03. C W Derby St Jo *Liv* 02-05; Chapl St Hilda's Sch for Girls Perth Australia from 06. *St Hilda's, Bay View Terrace, Mosman Park WA 6012, Australia* Tel (0061) (8) 9285 4100

SHERSBY, Brian Alfred. b 41. Clifton Th Coll 68. **d** 71 **p** 72. C Stoughton *Guildf* 71-74; C Heref St Pet w St Owen 75-79; V Earlham St Mary *Nor* 79-91; R Murston w Bapchild and Tonge *Cant* 91-07; rtd 07. *4 Blenheim Gardens, Chichester PO19 7XE*

SHERWIN, David Royston. b 56. St Jo Coll Nottm 84. **d** 89 **p** 90. C Conisbrough *Sheff* 89-95; V Wheatley Park and Dioc Adv for Evang 95-01; P-in-c Martley and Wichenford, Knightwick etc *Worc* 01-08; TR Worcs W from 09. *The Rectory, Martley, Worcester WR6 6QA* Tel and fax (01886) 888664 E-mail davidwin56@aol.com

SHERWIN, Mrs Jane. b 41. Sarum Th Coll 93. **d** 96 **p** 97. NSM Brightling, Dallington, Mountfield etc *Chich* 96-02; P-in-c Waldron from 02. *The Rectory, Sheepsetting Lane, Waldron, Heathfield TN21 0UY* Tel (01435) 862816 E-mail sherwinajsherwin@aol.com

SHERWIN, Canon Margaret Joyce. b 65. NOC BTh99. **d** 99 **p** 00. C Litherland St Phil *Liv* 99-03; V Hindley Green from 03; AD Wigan from 08; Hon Can Liv Cathl from 08. *3 Green Lane, Hindley Green, Wigan WN2 4HN* Tel (01942) 255833 E-mail revmarg@btopenworld.com

SHERWIN, Miss Margaret Miriam. b 32. dss 83 **d** 87 **p** 94. Holborn St Alb w Saffron Hill St Pet *Lon* 83-88; Par Dn 87-88; Par Dn Highgate St Mich 88-93; rtd 93; Hon C Purbrook *Portsm* 93-99; Perm to Offic from 99. *16 Lombard Court, Lombard Street, Portsmouth PO1 2HU* Tel (023) 9283 8429

SHERWIN, Mrs Philippa Margaret. b 46. Lon Univ BDS70 LDS70. **d** 99 **p** 00. OLM Queen Thorne *Sarum* 99-08; rtd 08; Perm to Offic *Sarum* from 08. *Woodford Lodge, Sandford Orcas, Sherborne DT9 4RP* Tel (01963) 220380 E-mail p.sherwin@virgin.net

SHERWOOD, David Charles. b 56. LRPS94. WEMTC 98. **d** 01 **p** 02. C Taunton Lyngford *B & W* 01-05; P-in-c Hemyock w Culm Davy, Clayhidon and Culmstock *Ex* from 05. *The Rectory, Hemyock, Cullompton EX15 3RQ* Tel (01823) 681589 E-mail revdcs@yahoo.co.uk

SHERWOOD, David James. b 45. Univ of Wales (Cardiff) LLM94 Solicitor 69. St Steph Ho Ox 81. **d** 83 **p** 84. C Westbury-on-Trym H Trin *Bris* 83-85; C Corringham *Chelmsf* 85-87; V Hullbridge 87-94; V Kenton *Lon* 94-06; rtd 06. *130 St Helens Road, Hastings TN34 2EJ* Tel (01424) 719768 Mobile 07891-783719 E-mail canddsherwood@aol.co.uk

SHERWOOD, Gordon Frederick. b 29. Sarum & Wells Th Coll 77. **d** 80 **p** 81. Hon C Weeke *Win* 80-82; C Kirk Ella *York* 82-85; P-in-c Burstwick w Thorngumbald 85-87; V 87-90; R Kirby Misperton w Normanby, Edston and Salton 90-94; rtd 94; Perm to Offic *Cant* from 95. *Sandycroft, Lewson Street, Norton, Faversham ME9 9JN* Tel (01795) 522696 E-mail g5sherwood@tiscali.co.uk

SHERWOOD, Canon Ian Walter Lawrence. b 57. TCD BA80. **d** 82 **p** 84. C Dublin St Patr Cathl Gp 82-83; Chapl Billinge Hosp Wigan 83-86; C Orrell *Liv* 83-86; Chapl Bucharest w Sofia *Eur* 86-89; Chapl Istanbul w Moda from 89; Can Malta Cathl from

97. *c/o FCO (Istanbul), King Charles Street, London SW1A 2AH* Tel (0090) (212) 251 5616 Fax 243 5702 E-mail parson@tnn.net

SHERWOOD, Mrs Jane. b 62. Ripon Coll Cuddesdon 05. **d** 07 **p** 08. NSM Ox St Matt from 07. *36 Canning Crescent, Oxford OX1 4XB* Tel (01865) 250672 E-mail jane@sherwoodz.plus.com

SHERWOOD, Kenneth Henry. b 37. CITC 90. **d** 93 **p** 94. NSM Malahide w Balgriffin *D & G* 93-96 and from 04; NSM Castleknock and Mulhuddart w Clonsilla 96-97; NSM Leighlin w Grange Sylvae, Shankill etc *C & O* 97-04. *6 Beverton Way, Donabate, Co Dublin, Republic of Ireland* Tel (00353) (1) 843 5287 E-mail kensherwood07@eircom.net

SHERWOOD, Nigel John Wesley. b 58. CITC 86. **d** 86 **p** 87. C Kilmore w Ballintemple, Kildallan etc *K, E & A* 86-89; I Tullow w Shillelagh, Aghold and Mullinacuff *C & O* 89-95; I Arklow w Inch and Kilbride *D & G* from 95; Sec SPCK Glendalough from 98. *The Rectory, Emoclew Road, Arklow, Co Wicklow, Republic of Ireland* Tel (00353) (402) 32439

SHERWOOD, Suffragan Bishop of. *See* PORTER, The Rt Revd Anthony

SHEWAN, Alistair Boyd. b 44. Open Univ BA83 BSc95. Edin Th Coll 63. **d** 67 **p** 68. Prec St Andr Cathl Inverness 67-69; C Shepherd's Bush St Steph w St Thos *Lon* 70-72; Hon C Edin St Mich and All SS 73-75; Perm to Offic 75-81; Hon C Edin Old St Paul 81-86; NSM Edin St Columba 87-91; Asst Dioc Supernumerary from 91; C Edin St Ninian 95-08. *Limegrove, High Street, Gifford, Haddington EH41 4QU* Tel (01620) 810402

SHEWAN, James William. b 36. Sarum Th Coll 61. **d** 63 **p** 64. C Rainbow Hill St Barn *Worc* 63-64; C Newton Aycliffe *Dur* 64-66; C Harton 66-69; V S Moor 69-72; CF 72-77; CF(V) from 81; P-in-c Benwell St Aid *Newc* 77-79; V Longhoughton w Howick 79-88; V Spittal and Scremerston 88-00; RD Norham 96-00; rtd 00; Perm to Offic *Newc* 00-04; Hon C Norham and Duddo 04-08; Hon C Cornhill w Carham 04-08; Hon C Branxton 04-08. *55 Marsden Road, South Shields NE34 6DF*

SHEWRING (*née* SMITH), **Mrs Susan Helen.** b 51. Univ of Cen England in Birm BEd87 Warwick Univ PGDE90. WMMTC 01. **d** 04 **p** 05. NSM Billesley Common *Birm* 04-07; Asst Chapl Univ Hosp Birm NHS Foundn Trust from 07. *48 St Helens Road, Solihull B91 2DA* Tel 0121-705 1845 E-mail sue_shewring@yahoo.co.uk

SHIELD, Barry Graham. b 39. Univ of Qld BA79 Univ of New England DipEd83 MLitt86 Kent Univ MA95 Washington Univ PhD00. **d** 83 **p** 84. Australia 83-00 and from 01; P-in-c Haselbury Plucknett, Misterton and N Perrott *B & W* 00-01. *107 Molesworth Street, Tenterfield NSW 2372, Australia* Tel (0061) (2) 6736 1405 E-mail barryshield1@bigpond.com

SHIELD, Graham Friend. b 63. Ripon Coll Cuddesdon. **d** 00 **p** 01. C Camborne *Truro* 00-03; P-in-c St Mawgan w St Ervan and St Eval from 03; C St Columb Major w St Wenn from 09. *The Rectory, West Street, St Columb TR9 6AE* Tel (01637) 880252 E-mail stcolumbrectory@btinternet.com

SHIELD, Ian Thomas. b 32. Hertf Coll Ox BA56 MA60 BLitt60. Westcott Ho Cam 59. **d** 61 **p** 62. C Shipley St Paul *Bradf* 61-64; Tutor Lich Th Coll 64-71; Chapl 67-71; V Dunston w Coppenhall *Lich* 71-79; TV Wolverhampton 79-86; rtd 87; Perm to Offic *Lich* from 87. *13 Duke Street, Penn Fields, Wolverhampton WV3 7DT* Tel (01902) 337037 E-mail ianshield@aol.com

SHIELDS, Dennis. Brighton Coll of Educn CertEd72 Brighton Poly DipEd84 Roehampton Inst MA87. **d** 05 **p** 06. NSM Meltham *Wakef* from 05. *11 The Hollow, Meltham, Holmfirth HD9 5LA* Tel (01484) 850074 Fax 326222 Mobile 07974-146120 E-mail dennis_shields@btinternet.com

SHIELDS, Mrs Jennifer Jill. b 39. Heref Coll of Educn CertEd74. SAOMC 99. **d** 02 **p** 03. OLM Lenborough *Ox* from 02. *8 West Furlong, Padbury, Buckingham MK18 2BP* Tel (01280) 814474

SHIELDS, Canon Michael Penton. b 30. Bps' Coll Cheshunt. **d** 64 **p** 65. C Kingsbury St Andr *Lon* 64-67; C Friern Barnet All SS 67-69; V Colindale St Matthias 69-76; V Sevenoaks St Jo *Roch* 76-95; RD Sevenoaks 84-95; Chapl Sevenoaks Hosp 78-94; Chapl St Mich Sch Otford 90-95; Hon Can Roch Cathl 94-95; rtd 95; CMP from 79; Hon PV Roch Cathl 96-05; Perm to Offic from 05. *16 Bromley College, London Road, Bromley BR1 1PE* Tel and fax (020) 8464 7906 E-mail pentonhook@tiscali.co.uk

SHILL, Kenneth Leslie. b 49. Leic Univ BA70 Lon Univ BD73. Ridley Hall Cam 75. **d** 77 **p** 78. C Harborne Heath *Birm* 77-83; V Mansfield St Jo *S'well* 83-93; Bp's Adv on Healing 89-93; Chapl Amsterdam w Heiloo *Eur* 93-95; TR Bath Twerton-on-Avon *B & W* 95-04; V Arnold *S'well* from 04. *St Mary's Vicarage, Church Lane, Arnold, Nottingham NG5 8HJ* Tel 0115-926 2946 E-mail shill1@tinyworld.co.uk

SHILLAKER, Mrs Christine Frances. b 39. Gilmore Ho 74. dss 86 **d** 87 **p** 94. Colchester St Leon, St Mary Magd and St Steph *Chelmsf* 86-89; Par Dn 87-89; Par Dn Colchester, New Town and The Hythe 89-94; C 94-96; P-in-c Ramsey w Lt Oakley 96-02; rtd 02; Perm to Offic *Chelmsf* from 02. *21 Nelson Road, Colchester CO3 9AP* Tel (01206) 570234

SHILLAKER, John. b 34. K Coll Lon BD60 AKC60. **d** 61 **p** 62. C Bush Hill Park St Mark *Lon* 61-65; C Milton *Win* 65-69; C-in-c Moulsham St Luke CD *Chelmsf* 69-78; V Moulsham St Luke 78-85; P-in-c Colchester St Leon, St Mary Magd and St Steph 85-86; R 86-89; R Colchester, New Town and The Hythe 89-96; rtd 96; Perm to Offic *Chelmsf* from 00. *21 Nelson Road, Colchester CO3 9AP* Tel (01206) 570234 Mobile 07889-816264

SHILLING, Ms Audrey Violet. b 26. Dur Univ BA69. CA Tr Coll 51 Cranmer Hall Dur 66. **d** 87 **p** 94. CA from 53; NSM Gillingham H Trin *Roch* 87-93; NSM Rainham 94-96; Perm to Offic from 96. *13 Guardian Court, London Road, Rainham, Gillingham ME8 7HQ* Tel (01634) 233654
E-mail audrey.shilling@diocese-rochester.org

SHILLINGFORD, Brian. b 39. Lich Th Coll 65. **d** 68 **p** 69. C Lewisham St Swithun *S'wark* 68-71; C Godstone 71-75; TV Croydon St Jo *Cant* 75-81; TV N Creedy *Ex* 81-93; TR 93-05; rtd 05. *Lyndbank, Albert Road, Crediton EX17 2BZ* Tel (01363) 877221 E-mail brianandkajshil@aol.com

SHILSON-THOMAS, Mrs Annabel Margaret. b 60. Jes Coll Ox BA82. Westcott Ho Cam 87. **d** 89 **p** 98. Par Dn Sydenham St Bart *S'wark* 89-93; Journalist CAFOD 95-03; Hon C Kingston All SS w St Jo *S'wark* 97-98; Perm to Offic *Ely* 00-03; Chapl Anglia Poly Univ 03-04; C Kingston All SS w St Jo *S'wark* 04-05; Spirituality Consultant CAFOD from 05; Hon C Cambridge Gt St Mary w St Mich *Ely* from 07. *28 Fulbrooke Road, Cambridge CB3 9EE*

SHILSON-THOMAS, Hugh David. b 64. Ex Coll Ox BA86 MA98 K Coll Lon MA99. Westcott Ho Cam 87. **d** 89 **p** 90. C Sydenham All SS *S'wark* 89-92; C Lower Sydenham St Mich 89-92; Ecum Chapl Kingston Univ 93-98; Chapl Rob Coll Cam 98-03; Nat Adv for HE/Chapl Abps' Coun 03-08; Chapl and Dean of Chpl Selw Coll Cam from 08; Chapl Newnham Coll Cam from 08. *28 Fulbrooke Road, Cambridge CB3 9EE*
E-mail hds21@cam.ac.uk

SHILVOCK, Geoffrey. b 47. Univ of Wales (Lamp) BA69. Sarum Th Coll 70. **d** 72 **p** 73. C Kidderminster St Mary *Worc* 72-78; P-in-c Gt Malvern Ch Ch 78-85; V Wolverley and Cookley from 85; RD Kidderminster 95-01. *The Vicarage, Wolverley, Kidderminster DY11 5XD* Tel (01562) 851133
E-mail geoffshilvock@hotmail.com

SHIMWELL, Robert John. b 46. ARCM65. Trin Coll Bris 75. **d** 78 **p** 79. C Richmond H Trin *S'wark* 78-79; C Cullompton and Kentisbeare w Blackborough *Ex* 79-81; V S Cave and Ellerker w Broomfleet *York* 81-87; Chapl Lee Abbey 87-88; R Glas St Silas 88-94; V Upton (Overchurch) *Ches* 94-05; RD Wirral N 97-98; Hon Can Ches Cathl 02-05; V Lee St Mildred *S'wark* from 05. *The Vicarage, 1A Helder Grove, London SE12 0RB* Tel (020) 8857 5205 E-mail rob@shimwell.org

SHIN, Allen Kunho. b 56. Seabury-Western Th Sem MDiv96 STM01. **d** 96 **p** 96. C Manhattan St Mary USA 94-05; Chapl Keble Coll Ox from 05. *Keble College, Parks Road, Oxford OX1 3PG* Tel (01865) 272727 *or* 272700 Fax 272705
E-mail allen.shin@keble.oxford.ac.uk

SHINE, Ann Aisling. RGN SCM. **d** 03 **p** 04. Aux Min Dublin Drumcondra w N Strand *D & G* 03-05; Aux Min Clondalkin w Rathcoole from 05. *1 Roselawn Grove, Castleknock, Dublin 15, Republic of Ireland* Tel (00353) (1) 820 1707 Mobile 87 220 7002
E-mail aislingshine@hotmail.com

SHINER, Michael Joseph. b 21. Chich Th Coll 51. **d** 53 **p** 54. C Weymouth H Trin *Sarum* 53-56; V Stanbridge w Tilsworth *St Alb* 56-63; V Powerstock w W Milton, Witherstone and N Poorton *Sarum* 63-73; V Knutsford St Cross *Ches* 73-75; Area Sec Age Concern Cornwall 75-86; Co Org W Sussex 80-86; rtd 86. *55 Tennyson Drive, Malvern WR14 2UL* Tel (01684) 563269

SHINKINS, Pamela Mhairi. b 41. Leeds Univ BSc62 Open Univ BA84. TISEC 05. **d** 07 **p** 08. Lic to Offic *Mor* from 08. *Homelea, 7 Blair, Poolewe, Achnasheen IV22 2LP* Tel (01445) 781346
E-mail pam.shinkins@btinternet.com

SHINN, William Raymond. b 22. Sarum & Wells Th Coll 71. **d** 73 **p** 74. C Letchworth St Paul *St Alb* 73-75; C Dunstable 76-78; TV 78-80; V Luton St Chris Round Green 80-88; rtd 88; Perm to Offic *St Alb* from 88. *31 Coleridge Close, Hitchin SG4 0QX* Tel (01462) 641883

SHINTON, Bertram David. b 41. WMMTC 95. **d** 98 **p** 99. NSM Broseley w Benthall, Jackfield, Linley etc *Heref* from 98. *Gestiana, Woodlands Road, Broseley TF12 5PU* Tel (01952) 882765 *or* 0121-311 2104

SHIPLEY, Christopher John. b 44. Leeds Univ BSc65 MSc70 BA72. Coll of Resurr Mirfield 70. **d** 73 **p** 74. C Preston St Jo *Blackb* 73-77; Chapl Lancs (Preston) Poly 75-77; V Blackb St Mich w St Jo 77-81; P-in-c Blackb H Trin 78-81; V Blackb St Mich w St Jo and H Trin 81-82; V Walthamstow St Pet *Chelmsf* 82-85; Gen Sec Mary Feilding Guild Lon 85-86; Org Waltham Forest Coun for Voluntary Service 86-89; Gen Sec Hull 89-91; Dir Grimsby and Cleethorpes 91; Teacher Upbury Manor High Sch Gillingham 92-94; Hd of Science 94-02; Teacher Whitstable Community Coll 02-03; Hd of Science Cheyne Middle Sch Sheerness 03-09; Team Ldr Science Isle of Sheppey Academy from 09; Hon C Minster-in-Sheppey *Cant* from 09.

Villa Rosa, Nelson Avenue, Minster-on-Sea, Sheerness ME12 3SF Tel (01795) 870575
E-mail chrisshply@googlemail.com

SHIPLEY, Canon Stephen Edwin Burnham. b 52. Univ Coll Dur BA74. Westcott Ho Cam 85. **d** 87 **p** 88. C Ipswich St Marg *St E* 87-90; P-in-c Stuntney *Ely* 90-95; Min Can, Prec and Sacr Ely Cathl 90-95; Producer Worship Progr BBC Relig Broadcasting from 95; Lic to Offic *Derby* from 96; Hon Can Derby Cathl from 09. *21 Devonshire Road, Buxton SK17 6RZ* Tel (01298) 78383 *or* 0161-244 3292 Mobile 07808-403812 Fax 0161-244 3290
E-mail stephen.shipley@bbc.co.uk

SHIPP, Miss Elizabeth Ann. b 81. Leic Univ BA02. Ripon Coll Cuddesdon BA06. **d** 07 **p** 08. C Wymondham *Nor* from 07. *118 Tuttles Lane West, Wymondham NR18 0JJ* Tel (01953) 604576 Mobile 07554-013547
E-mail lizzie.shipp@googlemail.com

SHIPP, Linda Mary. b 49. Cranmer Hall Dur 00. **d** 02 **p** 03. C Kirkleatham and Hon Chapl among Deaf People *York* 02-05; V Whorlton w Carlton and Faceby from 05. *Whorlton Vicarage, 18 Church Lane, Swainby, Northallerton DL6 3EA* Tel (01642) 701777 Fax 706131 Mobile 07970-908517
E-mail linda.shipp@btinternet.com

SHIPP, Susan. *See* HOLLINS, Patricia Susan

SHIPSIDES, Brian Kenneth. b 56. Reading Univ BA. Westcott Ho Cam 79. **d** 82 **p** 83. C Bramley *Ripon* 82-85; C Notting Dale St Clem w St Mark and St Jas *Lon* 85-90; Chapl N Lon Poly 90-92; Chapl Univ of N Lon 92-97; P-in-c Forest Gate All SS and St Edm *Chelmsf* from 97. *The Vicarage, 79 Claremont Road, London E7 0QA* Tel (020) 8534 7463 *or* 8472 8584

SHIPTON, Canon Andrew James. b 60. Leeds Univ BA82 Univ of Northumbria at Newc MEd99 Leeds Univ MPhil06. Cranmer Hall Dur 83. **d** 85 **p** 86. C Fishponds St Jo *Bris* 85-88; C Gosforth All SS *Newc* 88-91; V Long Benton St Mary 91-96; Chapl Univ of Northumbria at Newc 96-06; TV Ch the King 06-07; TR from 07; Dioc Development Officer for Youth Work from 06; Hon Can Newc Cathl from 07. *24 Chipchase Mews, Newcastle upon Tyne NE3 5RH* Tel 0191-236 3788
E-mail andrewshipton085@aol.com

SHIPTON, Linda Anne. *See* GREEN, Mrs Linda Anne

SHIPTON (née WILSON), Mrs Marjorie Jayne. b 59. Hull Univ BA80 Leeds Univ MA01 K Alfred's Coll Win PGCE81. Cranmer Hall Dur 85. **dss** 86 **d** 87 **p** 94. Ormesby *York* 86-89; Par Dn 87-89; Chapl Asst Newc Gen Hosp 89-91; Chapl 91-95; Dep Hd Chapl Newcastle upon Tyne Hosps NHS Foundn Trust from 95; NSM Whorlton *Newc* 94-97. *Royal Victoria Infirmary, Queen Victoria Road, Newcastle upon Tyne NE1 4LP* Tel 0191-232 5131 *or* 266 6172

SHIRE, William Stanley. b 17. TCD BA39 MA43. **d** 40 **p** 41. C Dundalk *Arm* 40-43; C Portadown St Mark 43-45; P-in-c Mullaglass 45-51; I 51-57; C Enniskillen w Bramcote and Chilwell *S'well* 57-58; V Lowdham 58-66; R Pilton w Wardenhoe and Stoke Doyle *Pet* 67-70; R Aldwincle w Thorpe Achurch, Pilton, Wadenhoe etc 70-82; rtd 82; Lic to Offic *Pet* 82-85; Perm to Offic from 85. *18 Victoria Road, Oundle, Peterborough PE8 4AY* Tel (01832) 272125

SHIRES, Alan William. b 36. Lon Univ BA60. Oak Hill Th Coll 57. **d** 61 **p** 62. C York St Paul 61-64; C Southgate Chich 64-67; V Doncaster St Mary *Sheff* 67-75; Perm to Offic *Portsm* 75-96; Student Counsellor Portsm Poly 75-88; Hd Student Services Portsm Poly 88-96; rtd 96. *15 Broomfield Road, Admaston, Wellington TF5 0AR*

SHIRESS, Canon David Henry Faithfull. b 27. St Cath Coll Cam BA49 MA53. Ridley Hall Cam 51. **d** 53 **p** 54. C Southport Ch Ch *Liv* 53-55; C St Helens St Mark 55-58; V Shrewsbury St Julian *Lich* 58-67; V Blackheath Park St Mich *S'wark* 67-93; Sub-Dean Greenwich 81-90; RD Greenwich 90-91; Hon Can S'wark Cathl 89-93; rtd 93; Perm to Offic *Sarum* from 93. *35 Rempstone Road, Wimborne BH21 1SS* Tel (01202) 887845

SHIRLEY, Gary Ronald. b 57. **d** 09. C Devonport St Budeaux *Ex* from 09. *The Vicarage, Bridwell Lane North, Weston Mill, Plymouth PL5 1AN* Tel (01752) 369489

SHIRLEY, Valerie Joy. b 42. **d** 96 **p** 97. OLM Sydenham H Trin *S'wark* 96-07; OLM Sydenham H Trin and St Aug from 07. *9 Faircroft, 5 Westwood Hill, London SE26 6BG* Tel (020) 8778 2551

SHIRRAS, The Ven Edward Scott. b 37. St Andr Univ BSc61. Clifton Th Coll 61. **d** 63 **p** 64. C Surbiton Hill Ch Ch *S'wark* 63-66; C Jesmond Clayton Memorial *Newc* 66-68; CPAS 68-75; Hon C Wallington *S'wark* 69-75; V Roxeth Ch Ch Lon 75-82; V Roxeth Ch Ch and Harrow St Pet 82-85; AD Harrow 82-85; Adn Northolt 85-92; V Win Ch Ch 92-01; rtd 01; Perm to Offic *Ox* 01-02 and from 09; P-in-c Marcham w Garford 02-09. *4 Culham Close, Abingdon OX14 2AS* Tel (01235) 553129
E-mail epshirras@aol.com

SHIRRAS, Mrs Pamela Susan. b 41. St Andr Univ BSc62 Brunel Univ PGCE80. Wycliffe Hall Ox 04. **d** 05 **p** 06. NSM Marcham w Garford *Ox* 05-09; Perm to Offic from 09. *4 Culham Close, Abingdon OX14 2AS* Tel (01235) 553129
E-mail epshirras@aol.com

SHIRRAS, Rachel Joan. *See* COLLINS, Rachel Joan

SHOCK, Rachel Alexandra. b 63. Nottm Trent Univ LLB94. EMMTC 95. **d** 98 **p** 00. NSM Radford All So w Ch Ch and St Mich *S'well* 98-99; NSM Lenton Abbey 99-02; NSM Wollaton 02-08; Chapl Development Worker from 06. *1 May Avenue, Wollaton, Nottingham NG8 2NE*

SHOESMITH (*née* HALL), Mrs Judith Frances. b 64. SS Coll Cam BA85 MEng86 MA89 BTh02 CEng97. Ridley Hall Cam 99. **d** 02 **p** 03. C Drayton in Hales *Lich* 02-05; Lic to Offic *Liv* from 05. *136 Southport Road, Bootle, Liverpool L20 9EH* Tel 0151-523 5774 E-mail frances@shoesmith.org.uk

SHOESMITH, Ms Kathia. b 64. Leeds Univ BA08 RN98. Coll of Resurr Mirfield 06. **d** 08 **p** 09. C Ripponden *Wakef* from 08; C Barkisland w W Scammonden from 08. *6 Long Meadow, Barkisland, Halifax HX4 0AR*

SHONE, The Very Revd John Terence. b 35. Selw Coll Cam BA58 MA64 Newc Univ MA92. Linc Th Coll 58. **d** 60 **p** 61. C St Pancras w St Jas and Ch Ch *Lon* 60-62; Chapl Aber Univ 62-68; Chapl St Andr Cathl 62-65; V Gt Grimsby St Andr and St Luke *Linc* 68-69; Chapl Stirling Univ 69-80; R Bridge of Allan 69-86; P-in-c Alloa 77-85; Can St Ninian's Cathl Perth 80-89; P-in-c Dollar 81-86; Dean St Andr 82-89; Research and Development Officer 86-89; Dioc Supernumerary 86-89; TV Cullercoats St Geo *Newc* 89-00; rtd 00. *33D Grange Road, Alloa FK10 1LR* Tel (01259) 721388 E-mail husnwif@aol.com

SHONE, Miss Ursula Ruth. b 34. Stirling Univ BA75 Open Univ BPhil88. **dss** 81 **d** 86 **p** 94. Bridge of Allan *St And* 81-85; Lochgelly 85-87; Chapl Cov Cathl 87-90; Ind Chapl 87-90; Par Dn Ainsdale *Liv* 90-94; Dioc Science Adv 90-99; C Ainsdale 94-96; C Childwall St Dav 96-99; rtd 99; NSM Brechin from 00. *4 Park Road, Brechin DD9 7AF* Tel (01356) 626087

SHOOTER, Philippa Margaret. b 49. Hull Univ BA70 Nottm Univ MA72 CQSW72. NOC 04. **d** 06 **p** 07. NSM Fence-in-Pendle and Higham *Blackb* from 06. *234 Briercliffe Road, Burnley BB10 2NZ* Tel (01282) 412404

SHOOTER, Robert David. b 44. Lon Univ BSc70 Lanc Univ MA94 CQSW72 LRAM92. NOC 99. **d** 02 **p** 03. NSM Brierfield *Blackb* 02-04; NSM Briercliffe 04-09; Perm to Offic from 09. *234 Briercliffe Road, Burnley BB10 2NZ* Tel (01282) 412404

SHOOTER, Ms Susan. b 58. Nottm Univ BA81 PGCE82. St Jo Coll Nottm MA96. **d** 96 **p** 98. C Dartford H Trin *Roch* 96-97; C Crayford 97-00; V Bostall Heath 00-09. *131 Pengelly, Delabole PL33 9AT* Tel (01840) 213645 Mobile 07929-496942 E-mail shooter160@btinternet.com

SHORROCK, John Musgrave. b 29. TCD BA54 MA58. Bps' Coll Cheshunt 54. **d** 56 **p** 57. C Fleetwood St Pet *Blackb* 56-59; C Lancaster St Mary 59-61; C-in-c Blackpool St Wilfrid CD 61-65; V Blackpool St Wilfrid 65-67; Min Can and Sacr Cant Cathl 67-70; V Chorley St Geo *Blackb* 71-78; P-in-c Bredgar w Bicknor and Huckinge *Cant* 78-82; P-in-c Frinsted w Wormshill and Milstead 78-82; R Bredgar w Bicknor and Frinsted w Wormshill etc 82-92; rtd 92; Perm to Offic *Cant* 92-06; Clergy Widows Officer Cant Adnry 97-06; Perm to Offic *Portsm* from 06. *55 Brook Gardens, Emsworth PO10 7JY* Tel (01243) 389430 E-mail jshorrock@talktalk.net

SHORT, Brian Frederick. b 29. St Jo Coll Nottm 70. **d** 72 **p** 73. C Walton *St E* 72-75; P-in-c Barking w Darmsden and Gt Bricett 75-78; P-in-c Ringshall w Battisford and Lt Finborough 75-78; TV Nor St Pet Parmentergate w St Jo 78-88; R Winfarthing w Shelfanger w Burston w Gissing etc 88-90; rtd 90; Perm to Offic *Nor* from 92. *31 Nursery Gardens, Blofield, Norwich NR13 4JE* Tel (01603) 712396

SHORT, Bryan Raymond. b 37. Bris Univ BSc59 CertEd60. Dioc OLM tr scheme 00. **d** 02 **p** 03. OLM Kirkheaton *Wakef* from 02. *12 Bankfield Lane, Kirkheaton, Huddersfield HD5 0JG* Tel (01484) 425832 E-mail bryan@b-s-short.fsnet.co.uk

SHORT, Ms Clare. b 50. Leic Univ BA72 St Mary's Coll Twickenham PGCE73. S Dios Minl Tr Scheme 89. **d** 92 **p** 94. NSM Horsham *Chich* 92-99; Perm to Offic *Newc* from 04. *Hedgelea, South Road, Lowick, Berwick-upon-Tweed TD15 2TX* Tel (01289) 389222

SHORT, Eileen. b 45. Ex Univ BA66. NOC 93. **d** 96 **p** 97. NSM Castleton Moor *Man* 96-98; NSM Chorlton-cum-Hardy St Clem 98-00; NSM Baguley from 00. *2 Netherwood Road, Northenden, Manchester M22 4RQ*

SHORT, Mrs Heather Mary. b 50. LWCMD71 Cardiff Coll of Educn CertEd72. WEMTC 98. **d** 01 **p** 02. C Heref S Wye 01-05; P-in-c Bodenham, Felton and Preston Wynne from 05; P-in-c Marden w Amberley and Wisteston from 05; P-in-c Sutton St Nicholas w Sutton St Michael from 05. *The Vicarage, Bodenham, Hereford HR1 3JX* Tel (01568) 797370

SHORT, Canon John Sinclair. b 33. Oak Hill Th Coll 64. **d** 66 **p** 67. C Islington St Mary *Lon* 66-70; V Becontree St Mary *Chelmsf* 70-76; V New Malden and Coombe *S'wark* 76-90; RD Kingston 79-84; Hon Can S'wark Cathl 83-90; P-in-c Peldon w Gt and Lt Wigborough *Chelmsf* 90-93; rtd 93; Perm to Offic *S'wark* 93-08. *22 Chart Lane, Reigate RH2 7BP* Tel (01737) 245244

SHORT, Canon John Timothy. b 43. Kelham Th Coll 63. **d** 68

p 69. C St Marylebone Ch Ch w St Barn *Lon* 68-93; C Southgate Ch Ch 70-72; P-in-c Mosser and Dioc Youth Officer *Carl* 72-78; R Heyford w Stowe Nine Churches *Pet* 78-87; V Northampton St Jas 87-96; RD Wootton 88-96; TR Kingsthorpe w Northampton St Dav 96-08; Can Pet Cathl 97-08; rtd 08; Perm to Offic *Pet* from 09. *11 Cytringan Close, Kettering NN15 6GW* Tel (01536) 310633 E-mail tim@johnshort.orangehome.co.uk

SHORT, Kenneth Arthur. b 33. Tyndale Hall Bris 64. **d** 67 **p** 68. C E Twickenham St Steph *Lon* 67-71; C Paddock Wood *Roch* 71-74; SE Area Sec BCMS 74-82; Hon C Sidcup Ch Ch *Roch* 74-82; V Tollington Park St Mark w St Anne *Lon* 82-86; V Holloway St Mark w Em 86-89; R Alfold and Loxwood *Guildf* 89-98; rtd 98; Perm to Offic *Roch* from 00 and *Lon* from 02. *10 Montague Graham Court, Kidbrooke Gardens, London SE3 0PD* Tel (020) 8858 8033 E-mail jukebox.short@btinternet.com

SHORT, Martin Peter. b 54. Peterho Cam BA77 MA81. Wycliffe Hall Ox 77. **d** 79 **p** 80. C Shipley St Pet *Bradf* 79-82; C Becontree St Mary *Chelmsf* 82-86; V Bolton St Jas w St Chrys *Bradf* 86-92; Dioc Communications Officer 92-98; C Otley 92-98; Hd Media Tr Communications Dept Abps' Coun 98-05; Hon C and Hon Chapl Bradf Cathl 98-05; Chapl to Bp Dover *Cant* from 06; Hon Min Can Cant Cathl from 06. *The Bishop's Office, The Old Palace, The Precincts, Canterbury CT1 2EE* Tel (01227) 459382 E-mail martin.short@bishcant.org

SHORT, Martin Ronald. b 57. Crewe & Alsager Coll CertEd78 Leic Univ BEd85. St Jo Coll Nottm 93. **d** 93 **p** 94. C Frankby w Greasby *Ches* 93-97; TV Horwich and Rivington *Man* 97-02; TV Turton Moorland Min 02-08; P-in-c Rawtenstall St Mary from 08; P-in-c Constable Lee from 08. *St Paul's Vicarage, Hollin Lane, Rawtenstall, Rossendale BB4 8HT* Tel (01706) 215585 E-mail martin.short1@btopenworld.com

SHORT, Canon Michael John. b 38. Univ of Wales (Lamp) BA59. Sarum Th Coll 59. **d** 61 **p** 62. C Swansea St Nic *S & B* 61-64; C Oystermouth 64-69; V Merthyr Vale w Aberfan *Llan* 69-82; RD Merthyr Tydfil 76-82; R Caerphilly 82-08; RD Caerphilly 83-04; Can Llan Cathl 89-08; Prec 02-08; rtd 08. *238 Abercynon Road, Abercynon, Mountain Ash CF45 4LU* Tel (01443) 742650 Mobile 07831-742515

SHORT, Neil Robert. b 58. Loughb Univ BSc81 St Jo Coll Dur BA86. Cranmer Hall Dur 83. **d** 86 **p** 87. C Whitfield *Derby* 86-90; C Bradf St Aug Undercliffe 90-96; V Burscough Bridge *Liv* 96-07; Pioneer Min Toxteth from 07. *8 Lady Chapel Close, Liverpool L1 7BZ* Tel 0151-708 8559 E-mail neil@theshorts.go-plus.net

SHORT, Mrs Patricia Ann (Pip). b 41. K Coll Lon BA62 AKC62. **d** 00 **p** 01. NSM Etwall w Egginton *Derby* from 00; Chapl Asst Derby Hosps NHS Foundation Trust from 00; Perm to Offic *Lich* from 05. *Ivy Cottage, 19 Monk Street, Tutbury, Burton-on-Trent DE13 9NA* Tel (01283) 813640 *or* (01332) 347141 Mobile 07711-823082 Fax (01283) 814373 E-mail pip.short@derbyhospitals.nhs.uk

SHORT, Robert Leslie. b 48. Em Coll Cam BA70 MA76. Wycliffe Hall Ox 87. **d** 92 **p** 92. Mexico 92-93; Chapl Repton Sch Derby 93-04; P-in-c Ibiza *Eur* from 04. *Capellania Anglicana de Ibiza, Apartado 547, 07820 San Antonio, Ibiza (Baleares), Spain* Tel and fax (0034) 971 343 383 E-mail chaplainibiza@netscape.net

SHORT, Stephen Timothy. b 71. Cheltenham & Glouc Coll of HE BA96. Ripon Coll Cuddesdon 05. **d** 07 **p** 08. C Tewkesbury w Walton Cardiff and Twyning *Glouc* from 07. *43 Cypress Road, Walton Cardiff, Tewkesbury GL20 7RB* Tel (01684) 292031 Mobile 07801-357612 E-mail theshorties@tiscali.co.uk

SHORT, Timothy. *See* SHORT, Canon John Timothy

SHORT, Vincent Charles. b 57. Oak Hill Th Coll 95. **d** 97 **p** 98. C Chatham St Phil and St Jas *Roch* 97-01; V Istead Rise from 01. *The Vicarage, Upper Avenue, Gravesend DA13 9DA* Tel and fax (01474) 832403 E-mail vince.short@diocese-rochester.org

SHORTER, Mrs Anne Roberta. b 56. Edin Univ BA77. Westcott Ho Cam 07. **d** 09. C Brackley St Pet w St Jas from 09. *36 Prices Way, Brackley NN13 6NR* E-mail anne.shorter@btinternet.com

SHORTER, Robert Edward. b 48. Ripon Coll Cuddesdon 89. **d** 91 **p** 92. C Braunton *Ex* 91-94; C Bishopsnympton, Rose Ash, Mariansleigh etc 94-96; TV 96-98; P-in-c E w W Harptree and Hinton Blewett *B & W* 98-03; Dioc Ecum Officer 98-03; rtd 03. *Fleur de la Passion, 61330 Torchamp, France* Tel (0033) (2) 33 38 56 53 E-mail outofit.shorter@wanadoo.fr

SHORTHOUSE, Raymond Trevor. b 34. DipAdEd Warwick Univ DPhil00. Ridley Hall Cam 68. **d** 70 **p** 71. C Gt Ilford St Andr *Chelmsf* 70-73; C Ludlow *Heref* 73-75; P-in-c Cressage w Sheinton 76-80; P-in-c Harley w Kenley 76-80; P-in-c Denby *Derby* 80-84; Adult Educn Officer 80-85; RD Heanor 83-84; V Chellaston 84-88; P-in-c Breadsall 88-98; Dioc Dir of Studies 88-96; rtd 98; P-in-c Symondsbury *Sarum* 99-04. *6 Heatherwood, Forden, Welshpool SY21 8LQ* E-mail justin@shorthouse.netlineuk.net

SHORTT, Canon Noel Christopher. b 36. Open Univ BA76 Ulster Univ MA DPhil91. Bps' Coll Cheshunt 63. **d** 63 **p** 64. C Belfast St Mary *Conn* 63-66; C Agherton 66-68; Chapl RAF 68-69; I

Duneane w Ballyscullion *Conn* 69-79; I Belfast St Steph w St Luke 79-89; I Ballyrashane w Kildollagh 89-99; Can Belfast St Anne 96-99; rtd 99. *2 Woodview Park, Ballymoney BT53 6DJ*

SHOTLANDER, Lionel George. b 27. Cant Univ (NZ) BA49 MA51. **d** 51 **p** 52. New Zealand 51-58 and 60-74; C Southsea St Pet *Portsm* 58-60; V Curdridge 74-85; R Durley 79-85; V Twyford and Owslebury and Morestead *Win* 85-91; rtd 91; Perm to Offic *Win* and *Portsm* from 91. *Cambria, High Street, Shirrell Heath, Southampton SO32 2JN* Tel (01329) 832353

SHOTTER, The Very Revd Edward Frank. b 33. Univ of Wales (Lamp) BA58 FRSM76 Hon FRCP07. St Steph Ho Ox 58. **d** 60 **p** 61. C Plymouth St Pet *Ex* 60-62; Inter-Colleg Sec SCM (Lon) 62-66; Perm to Offic *Lon* 62-69; Dir Lon Medical Gp 63-89; Chapl Lon Univ Medical Students 69-89; Dir Inst of Medical Ethics 74-89; Preb St Paul's Cathl 77-89; Dean Roch 89-03; rtd 03; Perm to Offic *St E* from 04. *Hill House, School Road, Westhall, Halesworth IP19 8QZ* Tel (01502) 575364

SHOULER, Mrs Margaret Fiona. b 55. Nottm Univ BEd78. St Jo Coll Nottm MTh03. **d** 01 **p** 02. C Sherwood *S'well* 01-06; P-in-c Selston from 06. *The Vicarage, 58 Church Lane, Selston, Nottingham NG16 6EW* Tel (01773) 813777
E-mail fionashouler@hotmail.com

SHOULER, Simon Frederic. b 54. Pemb Coll Cam MA79 FRICS89. EMMTC 82. **d** 85 **p** 86. NSM Asfordby *Leic* 85-89; Lic to Offic from 89. *1 West End, Long Clawson, Melton Mowbray LE14 4PE* Tel (01664) 822698
E-mail oldmanorhouse@shoulers.co.uk

SHREEVE, The Ven David Herbert. b 34. St Pet Hall Ox BA57 MA61. Ridley Hall Cam 57. **d** 59 **p** 60. C Plymouth St Andr *Ex* 59-64; V Bermondsey St Anne *S'wark* 64-71; V Eccleshill *Bradf* 71-84; RD Calverley 78-84; Hon Can Bradf Cathl 83-84; Adn Bradf 84-99; rtd 99; Perm to Offic *Bradf* from 99 and *Ripon* from 00. *26 Kingsley Drive, Harrogate HG1 4TJ* Tel (01423) 886479

SHREWSBURY, Preb Michael Buller. b 30. St Jo Coll Dur BA54. Linc Th Coll 54. **d** 56 **p** 57. C Salford St Phil w St Steph *Man* 56-60; Chapl RN 60-63; Chapl HM Pris Pentonville 64-67; Bermuda 67-70; V Dalston H Trin w St Phil *Lon* 70-86; AD Hackney 79-84; Preb St Paul's Cathl 86-92; R Stepney St Dunstan and All SS 86-92; rtd 92; Perm to Offic *Lon* from 92. *Flat 1, 150 Wapping High Street, London E1W 3PH* Tel (020) 7480 5479 E-mail mike.shrewsbury@btinternet.com

SHREWSBURY, Area Bishop of. See RYLANDS, The Rt Revd Mark James

SHRIMPTON, Mrs Sheila Nan. b 32. Qu Mary Coll Lon BA54 LSE CertSS55. St Chris Coll Blackheath 55. **dss** 83 **d** 87 **p** 94. Lic to Offic *B & W* 83-90; NSM Barkston and Hough Gp *Linc* 90-97; Asst Local Min Officer 90-97; C Brant Broughton and Beckingham 97-98; P-in-c Churchstanton, Buckland St Mary and Otterford *B & W* 98-02; rtd 02; Perm to Offic *B & W* from 03. *2 King William Mews, Church Street, Curry Rivel, Langport TA10 0HD* Tel (01458) 259293 E-mail nanshrimpton@aol.com

SHRINE, Robert Gerald. b 44. Birm Univ BA65 Univ of Zambia PGCE70 Lanc Univ MA74 Open Univ BA80. St Jo Coll Nottm MA97. **d** 97 **p** 98. C Blackpool St Thos *Blackb* 97-99; Dioc Chapl among Deaf People *Bradf* and *Wakef* from 99. *The Vicarage, 80 Carr House Road, Halifax HX3 7RJ* Tel (Typetalk) 18002 (01274) 671576 Fax 677693
E-mail bob.shrine@bradford.anglican.org

SHRINE, Mrs Susan Elaine Walmsley. b 56. NOC. **d** 02 **p** 03. C Bradshaw and Holmfield *Wakef* 02-04; TV Shelf w Buttershaw St Aid *Bradf* from 04. *The Vicarage, 80 Carr House Road, Halifax HX3 7RJ* Tel (01274) 671576 Fax 677693
E-mail sue.shrine@ukonline.co.uk

SHRISUNDER, David Shripat. b 29. Osmania Univ Hyderabad BA52 Serampore Univ BD59 Shivaji Univ Kolhapur MA69. Bp's Coll Calcutta 54. **d** 57 **p** 58. C Poona St Paul w Kirkee All SS India 57-58; P I Bombay Em 58-61; I Solapur Epiphany 61-71, 72-75 and 88-90; Lect Dayanand Coll Solapur 69-71, 72-75 and 78-79; C Batley All SS *Wakef* 71-72; C Skegness *Linc* 75-77; C Derringham Bank *York* 80-81; TV Grays Thurrock *Chelmsf* 81-85; R Uddingston *Glas* 85-88; R Cambuslang 85-88; P-in-c Sinfin Moor *Derby* 90-94; rtd 94; Perm to Offic *Wakef* 94-96 and from 98. *23 Foundry Street, Ravensthorpe, Dewsbury WF13 3HW* Tel (01924) 501336

SHRISUNDER, Romita Jones. b 78. Kolhapur Univ India BSc98 Leeds Univ BA03. St Steph Ho Ox 04. **d** 06 **p** 07. C Brighouse and Clifton *Wakef* from 06. *262A Halifax Road, Brighouse HD6 2PB* Tel (01484) 722012
E-mail romitashrisunder@yahoo.com

SHRIVES, Austen Geoffrey. b 28. Lon Univ BD68 MTh77. S'wark Ord Course. **d** 64 **p** 65. C Lower Sydenham St Mich *S'wark* 64-68; Miss to Seamen 68-74; V Epsom St Martin *Guildf* 74-84; V York Town St Mich 84-87; R Churchstanton, Buckland St Mary and Otterford *B & W* 87-93; rtd 93; Perm to Offic *Ex* 94-96 and *Heref* from 97. *16 Watling Street, Ross-on-Wye HR9 5UF* Tel (01989) 566237

SHUFFLEBOTHAM, Alastair Vincent. b 32. Nottm Univ CSocSc57. Lich Th Coll 63. **d** 65 **p** 66. C W Kirby St Bridget *Ches* 65-69; V Tranmere St Paul 69-71; V Tranmere St Paul w

St Luke 71-78; V Neston 78-97; rtd 97. *Y-Clystyrau, 5 Tan-y-Bryn, Llanbedr Dyffryn Clwyd, Ruthin LL15 1AQ* Tel (01824) 704619

SHUKER, Linda Kathleen. b 56. Imp Coll Lon BSc77 PhD81. St Jo Coll Nottm 05. **d** 07 **p** 08. C Rothley *Leic* from 07. *11 Oldfield Lane, Rothley, Leicester LE7 7QD* E-mail dlshuker@aol.com

SHUKMAN, Ann Margaret. b 31. Girton Coll Cam BA53 MA58 LMH Ox DPhil74. WMMTC 80. **dss** 84 **d** 92 **p** 94. Steeple Aston w N Aston and Tackley *Ox* 84-96; NSM 92-96; rtd 96; Perm to Offic *Ox* from 96; Hon C Dumfries *Glas* from 01. *Elshieshields Tower, Lockerbie DG11 1LY* Tel (01387) 810280 Fax 811777
E-mail ann.shukman@virgin.net

SHULER, Patricia Ann Margaret. b 52. Anglia Ruskin Univ MA08 Univ of Wales (Ban) BTh08. Ridley Hall Cam 02. **d** 05 **p** 06. C Ipswich St Aug *St E* 05-09; C Woodbridge St Jo and Bredfield from 09. *18 Fitzmaurice Road, Ipswich IP3 9AX* Tel (01473) 436938 E-mail tricia.shuler@gmail.com

SHUTT, Anthony John. b 57. Brunel Univ BSc79. Trin Coll Bris 87. **d** 89 **p** 90. C Epsom St Martin *Guildf* 89-95; P-in-c Send from 95. *St Mary's Vicarage, Vicarage Lane, Send, Woking GU23 7JN* Tel (01483) 222193

SHUTT, Laurence John. b 42. MPS64 MRPharmS88. St Steph Ho Ox 87 Llan Dioc Tr Scheme 80. **d** 84 **p** 85. NSM Whitchurch *Llan* 84-87; C Llanishen and Lisvane 88-90; V Middlestown *Wakef* 90-97; P-in-c Arnside *Carl* 97-04; Chapl RNR 89-04; rtd 04. *PO Box 59448, Pissouri, 4607 Limassol, Cyprus* Tel (00357) 2522 2507 Mobile 9913 8292 *or* 9913 9416
E-mail shasting@cytanet.com.cy

SHUTT, Nicholas Stephen. b 58. Qu Mary Coll Lon LLB80 Solicitor 83. SWMTC 91. **d** 94 **p** 95. NSM Yelverton, Meavy, Sheepstor and Walkhampton *Ex* from 94; P-in-c from 08. *12 Blackbrook Close, Walkhampton, Yelverton PL20 6JF* Tel (01822) 854653 E-mail nsshutt@aol.com

SIBANDA, Melusi Francis. b 72. Univ of Zimbabwe BSc96 BA99 St Martin's Coll Lanc MA06. Bp Gaul Th Coll Harare 97. **d** 98 **p** 99. C Bulawayo Cathl Zimbabwe 98-01; R Bulawayo St Marg 01-03; C Colne and Villages *Blackb* 03-06; P-in-c Rednal *Birm* from 06. *St Stephen's Vicarage, Edgewood Road, Rednal, Birmingham B45 8SG* Tel 0121-453 3347 Mobile 07887-745427 E-mail mfsibanda@tiscali.co.uk

SIBBALD, Olwyn. See MARLOW, Mrs Olwyn Eileen

SIBLEY, Jonathan Paul Eddolls. b 55. Newc Univ BA77. Westcott Ho Cam 78 Ripon Coll Cuddesdon 85. **d** 87 **p** 88. C Waltham Cross *St Alb* 87-90; C Chalfont St Peter *Ox* 90-96; P-in-c Sulhamstead Abbots and Bannister w Ufton Nervet 96-02; P-in-c Sutton St Mary *Linc* from 02. *The Vicarage, Market Place, Long Sutton, Spalding PE12 9JJ* Tel and fax (01406) 362033 E-mail jonathan.sibley3@btinternet.com

SIBLEY, Peter Linsey. b 40. Selw Coll Cam BA61 MA63. Oak Hill Th Coll 79. **d** 81 **p** 82. C Crofton *Portsm* 81-84; TV Cheltenham St Mark *Glouc* 84-93; P-in-c Tewkesbury H Trin 93-96; V 96-05; RD Tewkesbury and Winchcombe 97-02; rtd 05. *14 Griffiths Avenue, Cheltenham GL51 7BH* Tel (01242) 514640 E-mail sibglos@aol.com

SIBSON, Canon Edward John. b 39. Brasted Th Coll 61 St Aid Birkenhead 63. **d** 65 **p** 66. C Gt Parndon *Chelmsf* 65-69; C Saffron Walden 69-72; P-in-c Colchester St Leon 72-77; Ind Chapl 72-80; TV Colchester St Leon, St Mary Magd and St Steph 77-80; V Layer de la Haye 80-90; R Chipping Ongar w Shelley 90-98; RD Ongar 94-98; P-in-c High and Gd Easter w Margaret Roding 98-04; P-in-c Gt Canfield w High Roding and Aythorpe Roding 02-04; Hon Can Chelmsf Cathl 01-04; rtd 04; Perm to Offic *Chelmsf* from 04. *73 Thaxted Road, Saffron Walden CB11 3AG* Tel (01799) 520007
E-mail john@trsw73.wanadoo.co.uk

SIBSON, Canon Robert Francis. b 46. Leeds Univ CertEd68. Sarum & Wells Th Coll 78. **d** 80 **p** 81. C Watford St Mich *St Alb* 80-83; TV Digswell and Panshanger 83-90; V Biggleswade 90-02; Chapl Bedford and Shires Health and Care NHS Trust 94-02; RD Biggleswade *St Alb* 96-01; Hon Can St Alb from 98; V Sawbridgeworth from 02. *The Vicarage, 144 Sheering Mill Lane, Sawbridgeworth CM21 9ND* Tel (01279) 723305 Fax 721541 E-mail robert.sibson@btinternet.com

SICHEL, Stephen Mackenzie. b 59. UEA BA80 Birm Univ MA95. Ripon Coll Cuddesdon 87. **d** 90 **p** 91. C Tettenhall Regis *Lich* 90-95; C Camberwell St Giles w St Matt *S'wark* 95-01; P-in-c Brixton St Matt 01-02; V Brixton St Matt w St Jude from 02. *The Vicarage, 5 St Matthew's Road, London SW2 1ND* Tel and fax (020) 7733 9605 E-mail sichel@freenet.co.uk

SIDAWAY, The Ven Geoffrey Harold. b 42. Kelham Th Coll 61. **d** 66 **p** 67. C Beighton *Derby* 66-70; C Chesterfield St Mary and All SS 70-72; P-in-c Derby St Bart 72-74; V 74-77; V Maidstone St Martin *Cant* 77-86; V Bearsted w Thurnham 86-00; RD Sutton 92-99; Hon Can Cant Cathl 94-00; Adn Glouc from 00; Can Res Glouc Cathl from 07. *Glebe House, Church Road, Maisemore, Gloucester GL2 8EY* Tel (01452) 528500 Fax 381528 E-mail archdglos@star.co.uk

SIDDALL, The Ven Arthur. b 43. Lanc Univ MA81 Surrey Univ PGCE94 MCMI96. ALCD67. **d** 67 **p** 68. C Formby H Trin *Liv*

67-70; C Childwall All SS 70-72; CMS 72-77; Chapl Chittagong Ch Ch Bangladesh 74-77; V Clitheroe St Paul Low Moor *Blackb* 77-82; V Blackb St Gabr 82-90; Dep Gen Sec Miss to Seamen 90-93; Hon C Leatherhead *Guildf* 93-96; V Chipping and Whitewell *Blackb* 96-04; Rural Chapl 03-04; Chapl Naples w Sorrento, Capri and Bari *Eur* 04-07; Chapl Montreux w Gstaad 07-09; Adn Italy and Malta 05-09; Adn Switzerland 07-09; rtd 09. *24 Shaw Crescent, Liverpool L37 8DA*

SIDDLE, Michael Edward. b 33. Dur Univ BA54. St Aid Birkenhead 55. d 57 p 58. C Fazakerley Em *Liv* 57-59; C Farnworth 59-62; V Swadlincote *Derby* 62-70; Distr Sec (Northd and Dur) BFBS 70-72; Yorkshire 72-82; V Bamber Bridge St Aid *Blackb* 82-87; V Horsforth *Ripon* 87-00; rtd 00; Perm to Offic *Ripon* from 00. *28 Carr Bridge Drive, Cookridge, Leeds LS16 7JY* Tel 0113-261 0498 Mobile 07941-209069 E-mail mirisiddle@aol.com

SIDEBOTHAM, Canon Stephen Francis. b 35. Qu Coll Cam BA58 MA80. Linc Th Coll 58. d 60 p 61. C Bitterne Park *Win* 60-64; Hong Kong 64-83; Dean 76-83; Archdeacon 78-83; Chapl Gravesend and N Kent Hosp 83-94; R Gravesend St Geo *Roch* 83-94; RD Gravesend 91-94; P-in-c Rosherville 91-94; Acorn Chr Foundn from 94; rtd 97; Perm to Offic *Ox* 97-98. *87 Aston Abbotts Road, Weedon, Aylesbury HP22 4NH* Tel (01296) 640098

SIDEBOTTOM, Andrew John. See DAVIES, Andrew John
SIDEBOTTOM, Susan. Yorks Min Course. d 09. NSM Chesterton *Lich* from 09. *18 Leech Avenue, Newcastle ST5 7PN*
SIDES, James Robert. b 37. TCD BA66. CITC 68. d 67 p 68. C Belfast St Clem *D & D* 67-70; C Antrim All SS *Conn* 70-73; I Tomregan w Drumlane *K, E & A* 73-80; I Killesher 80-97; I Kildrumferton w Ballymachugh and Ballyjamesduff 97-06; Can Kilmore Cathl 89-06; rtd 06. *1 Goldsmith Meadow, Edgeworthstown, Co Longford, Republic of Ireland* Tel (00353) (43) 72676 Mobile 87-979 0080
SIEBERT, Mrs Rosemary Clare. b 48. Solicitor 03. SEITE 99. d 08 p 09. NSM Folkestone St Mary and St Eanswythe *Cant* from 08. *35 Warren Way, Folkestone CT19 6DT* Tel (01303) 244114 Mobile 07763-330113 E-mail rsiebert@btinternet.com
SIEJKOWSKI, Piotr Jan. See ASHWIN-SIEJKOWSKI, Piotr Jan
SIGRIST, Mrs Catherine Mary. b 55. Westcott Ho Cam. d 07 p 08. C Cheriton St Martin *Cant* from 07; C Cheriton All So w Newington from 07. *All Souls Vicarage, 1 Ashley Avenue, Folkestone CT19 4PX* Tel (01303) 270080 E-mail catherine.sigrist@btinternet.com
SIGRIST, Richard Martin. b 46. Bernard Gilpin Soc Dur 67 Sarum Th Coll 68. d 71 p 72. C Yeovil St Mich *B & W* 71-74; Chapl RN 74-84; TV Sidmouth, Woolbrook and Salcombe Regis *Ex* 84-86; TR 86-91; TR Sidmouth, Woolbrook, Salcombe Regis, Sidbury etc 91-94; RD Ottery 90-94; USA 94-99; P-in-c Devonport St Bart *Ex* 99-02; V 02-07; V Devonport St Bart and Ford St Mark from 08; RD Plymouth Devonport from 01. *St Bartholomew's Vicarage, 13 Outland Road, Plymouth PL2 3BZ* Tel (01752) 562623 E-mail rmsigrist@onetel.com
SILCOCK, Donald John. b 30. AKC59. d 60 p 61. C Hackney St Jo *Lon* 60-63; C-in-c Plumstead Wm Temple Ch Abbey Wood CD *S'wark* 63-68; C Felpham w Middleton *Chich* 68-74; R Ightham *Roch* 74-84; R Cliffe at Hoo w Cooling 84-92; RD Strood 85-91; rtd 92; Perm to Offic *Chich* from 92. *Puck's House, 26 Ancton Way, Bognor Regis PO22 6JN* Tel (01243) 582589
SILINS, Jacqueline. See JOHNSON, Ms Jacqueline
SILK, David. See SILK, The Rt Revd Robert David
SILK, Canon Ian Geoffrey. b 60. Pemb Coll Cam BA81 MA85. Trin Coll Bris BA89. d 89 p 90. C Linc St Giles 89-93; P-in-c Linc St Geo Swallowbeck 93-98; V from 98; PV Linc Cathl from 01; Can and Preb Linc Cathl from 07. *St George's Vicarage, 87 Eastbrook Road, Lincoln LN6 7EW* Tel (01522) 870881
SILK, John Arthur. b 52. Selw Coll Cam BA73 MA77 K Coll Lon MTh80. Westcott Ho Cam 75. d 77 p 78. C Banstead *Guildf* 77-80; C Dorking w Ranmore 80-84; R Ringwould w Kingsdown *Cant* 84-95; V Thames Ditton *Guildf* from 95. *The Vicarage, Summer Road, Thames Ditton KT7 0QQ* Tel (020) 8398 3446 E-mail johnsilk@tiscali.co.uk
SILK, Richard Trevor. b 67. St Steph Ho Ox 01. d 03 p 04. C St Marychurch *Ex* 03-06; P-in-c Bovey Tracey St Jo w Heathfield 06-09; V Hamilton Ch Ch Australia from 09. *The Rectory, 39 Griffin Street, Hamilton Vic 3300, Australia* Tel (0061) (3) 5571 1317 E-mail fr.richard@bigpond.com
✠**SILK, The Rt Revd Robert David.** b 36. Ex Univ BA58. St Steph Ho Ox 58. d 59 p 60 c 94. C Gillingham St Barn *Roch* 59-62; C Lamorbey H Redeemer 63-69; R Swanscombe SS Pet and Paul 69-71; P-in-c Swanscombe All SS 69-71; R Swanscombe 71-75; R Beckenham St Geo 75-80; Adn Leic 80-94; TR Leic H Spirit 82-88; Bp Ballarat 94-03; rtd 03; Perm to Offic *Chich* 03-04; Hon Asst Bp Ex from 04. *1 Centenary Way, Torquay TQ2 7SB* Tel (01803) 614456
SILK, Timothy James. b 73. Ox Brookes Univ BSc96. Oak Hill Th Coll BA99. d 99 p 00. C Stamford St Geo w St Paul *Linc* 99-02; C Arborfield w Barkham *Ox* 02-07; Ireland Team Ldr

Crosslinks from 07; C Kill *D & G* from 08. *17 Clonkeen Grove, Dun Laoghaire, Co Dublin, Republic of Ireland* Tel (00353) (1) 235 2821 *or* 497 6103 E-mail tsilk@crosslinks.org
SILKSTONE, Thomas William. b 27. St Edm Hall Ox BA51 MA55 BD67. Wycliffe Hall Ox 51. d 53 p 54. C Aston SS Pet and Paul *Birm* 53-56; Div Master Merchant Taylors' Sch Crosby 56-62; Lect K Alfred's Coll Win 62-65; Sen Lect 65-75; Prin Lect 75-85; Lic to Offic *Win* 62-85; Perm to Offic *Truro* from 82; rtd 92. *Trevalyon, Lansallos, Looe PL13 2PX* Tel (01503) 72110
SILLER, Canon James Robert William. b 44. Pemb Coll Ox BA65 MA70. Westcott Ho Cam 67. d 70 p 71. C Spring Grove St Mary *Lon* 70-73; C Leeds St Pet *Ripon* 73-77; P-in-c Quarry Hill 73-77; V Gilling and Kirkby Ravensworth 77-82; P-in-c Melsonby 77-82; R Farnley 82-94; V Potternewton 94-05; Hon Can Ripon Cathl 99-05; rtd 05; Perm to Offic *York* from 06. *1 Sandhill Oval, Leeds LS17 8EB* Tel 0113-268 0014
SILLETT, Angela Veronica Isabel. See BERNERS-WILSON, Preb Angela Veronica Isabel
SILLEY, Michael John. b 48. Ripon Coll Cuddesdon 82. d 84 p 85. C Frodingham *Linc* 84-87; V Ingham w Cammeringham w Fillingham 87-96; R Aisthorpe w Scampton w Thorpe le Fallows etc 87-96; RD Lawres 92-96; P-in-c N w S Carlton 93-96; P-in-c Brigg 96-97; V Brigg, Wrawby and Cadney cum Howsham 97-04; RD Yarborough 01-02; Bp's Dom Chapl from 05; Gen Preacher from 05. *Bishop's House, Eastgate, Lincoln LN2 1QQ* Tel (01522) 534701 E-mail michael.silley@lincoln.anglican.org
SILLIS, Andrew Keith. b 66. Wolv Poly BSc87. Aston Tr Scheme 91 Westcott Ho Cam 93. d 96 p 97. C Boyne Hill Ox 96-99; C Hayes St Nic CD *Lon* 99-00; C-in-c 00-05; V N Hayes St Nic 05-09; V Cuddington *Guildf* from 09. *St Mary's Vicarage, St Mary's Road, Worcester Park KT4 7JL* Tel (020) 8337 4704 E-mail asillis@aol.com
SILLIS, Eric Keith. b 41. NW Ord Course 75. d 78 p 79. C Blackpool St Steph *Blackb* 78-82; V Huncoat 82-86; V Blackpool St Wilfrid 86-95; V Fleetwood St Dav 95-06; Dioc Chapl MU 99-06; rtd 06; Perm to Offic *Blackb* from 06. *23 Fernwood Avenue, Thornton-Cleveleys FY5 5EU* Tel (01253) 865449 E-mail ksillis@stdavid.freeserve.co.uk *or* ksillis@fsnet.co.uk
SILLIS, Graham William. b 46. S'wark Ord Course 73. d 76 p 77. C Palmers Green St Jo *Lon* 76-79; C Dawlish *Ex* 79-81; V Ipswich St Thos *Et* 81-87; V Babbacombe *Ex* 87-95; C Tividale *Lich* 98-00; R Winchelsea and Icklesham *Chich* 00-03; V Derby St Luke from 03. *St Luke's Vicarage, 48 Peet Street, Derby DE22 3RF* Tel (01332) 345720 E-mail graham.sillis@freezone.co.uk
SILLITOE, William John. b 37. Lich Th Coll 67. d 69 p 70. C Ettingshall *Lich* 69-71; C March St Jo *Ely* 72-74; P-in-c Kennett 74-77; V Fordham St Pet 74-77; V Castle Bromwich St Clem *Birm* 77-00; rtd 00; Perm to Offic *Birm* 00-04. *St Clement's Croft, 11 Wood Green Road, Wednesbury WS10 9AX* Tel 0121-505 5954 E-mail mwm@fort34.freeserve.co.uk
SILLS, Canon Peter Michael. b 41. Nottm Univ BA63 LLM68 Kent Univ PhD00 Barrister 76. S'wark Ord Course 78. d 81 p 82. C W Wimbledon Ch Ch *S'wark* 81-85; P-in-c Barnes H Trin 85-93; Wandsworth Adnry Ecum Officer 90-93; V Purley St Mark 93-00; Can Res Ely Cathl 00-08; rtd 08; Perm to Offic *Chich* from 08. *The Coach House, Keymer Road, Hassocks BN6 8JR* Tel (01273) 842760
SILVA, Peter John. b 47. Rhodes Univ BA73 HDipEd77 BEd79. St Paul's Coll Grahamstown 68. d 74 p 74. S Africa 74-98; C Bloemfontein Cathl 74-75; Chapl Dioc Sch for Girls Grahamstown 75-79 and 89-95; Lect Rhodes Univ 79-81; Dir Academic Support Services Natal Univ 81-85; Regional Manager Performance and Educn Services 86; Dir Tape Aids for the Blind 87; R Overport Ch Ch 88-89; Dir Educn Projects Grahamstown Foundn 95-98; TV Abingdon *Ox* 99-02; Chief Exec Officer Peers Early Educn Partnership from 02. *Woodford Bridge Cottage, Drystone Hill, Enstone, Chipping Norton OX7 4AA* Tel (01608) 678627 *or* (01865) 395145 Mobile 07980-264472 E-mail peter.silva@virgin.net
SILVERMAN, Prof Bernard Walter. b 52. Jes Coll Cam BA73 MA76 PhD78 ScD89 Southn Univ BTh00 FRS97. STETS 97. d 99 p 00. Prof Statistics Bris Univ 93-03; Prof Statistics Ox Univ from 03; Master St Pet Coll Ox 03-09; Hon C Cotham St Saw w St Mary and Clifton St Paul *Bris* 99-05; Lic to Offic *Ox* 05-09; Hon C Ox St Giles and SS Phil and Jas w St Marg from 09. *St Margaret's Church, 19 St Margaret's Road, Oxford OX2 6RX* E-mail bernard.silverman@smithschool.ox.ac.uk
SILVERSIDES, Mark. b 51. Lon Univ BD73. St Jo Coll Nottm 74. d 76 p 77. C Hornchurch St Andr *Chelmsf* 76-80; P-in-c Becontree St Thos 80-85; TR Becontree W 85-86; CPAS Staff 86-92; New Media Producer from 92. *15 Glenhurst Drive, Whickham, Newcastle upon Tyne NE16 5SH* Tel 0191-488 1937 E-mail msilversides@ambitnewmedia.com
SILVERTHORN, Alan. b 37. St Mich Coll Llan 62. d 65 p 66. C Machen and Rudry *Mon* 65-71; V New Tredegar 71-83; V Llanfrechfa and Llanddewi Fach w Llandegfeth 83-04; rtd 04.

14 Davies Street, Ystrad Mynach, Hengoed CF82 8AD Tel (01443) 816649

SILVESTER, Christine. b 51. WMMTC 02. **d** 05 **p** 06. NSM Walsall Wood *Lich* 05-08; NSM Shelfield and High Heath from 08; Chapl R Wolv Hosps NHS Trust from 08. *31 Field Lane, Pelsall, Walsall WS4 1DN*
E-mail silvesterchristine@hotmail.com

SILVESTER, David. b 59. Qu Mary Coll Lon BSc80 Nottm Univ BCombStuds85. Linc Th Coll 82. **d** 85 **p** 86. C Walthamstow St Mary w St Steph *Chelmsf* 85-90; TV Barking St Marg w St Patr 90-96; V Mildmay Grove St Jude and St Paul *Lon* 96-08; AD Islington 03-07; TR Hackney Marsh from 08. *St Barnabas' Rectory, 111 Homerton High Street, London E9 6DL* Tel (020) 8533 1156 E-mail dsilve5737@aol.com

SILVESTER, Stephen David. b 59. Chu Coll Cam BA80 MA83 Man Univ PGCE82. St Jo Coll Nottm 88. **d** 91 **p** 92. C Nottingham St Jude *S'well* 91-96; V Gamston and Bridgford 96-08; AD W Bingham 04-07; P-in-c Nottingham St Nic from 08. *37 Lyme Park, West Bridgford, Nottingham NG2 7TR* Tel 0115-982 0407

SIM, David Hayward. b 29. Qu Coll Birm 57. **d** 59 **p** 60. C Foleshill St Laur *Cov* 59-62; C Kenilworth St Nic 62-64; V Devonport St Aubyn *Ex* 64-69; V Frampton *Linc* 69-74; V Gainsborough St Geo 74-82; V Sturminster Newton and Hinton St Mary *Sarum* 82-89; R Stock and Lydlinch 82-89; Dorchester 89-94; Chapl HM Pris Dorchester 89-94; rtd 95; Perm to Offic *Sarum* from 95. *12 Eldridge Close, Dorchester DT1 2JS* Tel (01305) 269262

SIMCOCK, Canon Michael Pennington. b 27. Qu Coll Cam BA50 MA52. Bps' Coll Cheshunt 50. **d** 52 **p** 53. C Andover w Foxcott *Win* 52-55; C Eastleigh 55-57; Min Tadley St Mary CD 57-67; V Altarnon and Bolventor *Truro* 67-70; V Treleigh 70-87; RD Carnmarth N 75-91; Hon Can Truro Cathl 82-92; R Redruth w Lanner 87-88; TR Redruth w Lanner and Treleigh 88-92; rtd 92; Perm to Offic *Truro* from 92. *1C Stratton Place, Falmouth TR11 2ST*

SIMCOX, Stephen Roy. b 59. Ridley Hall Cam 02. **d** 04 **p** 05. C The Ramseys and Upwood *Ely* 04-07; P-in-c Tyseley *Birm* from 07; P-in-c Sparkbrook Ch Ch from 07. *St Edmund's Vicarage, 277 Reddings Lane, Tyseley, Birmingham B11 3DD* Tel 0121-777 2433 E-mail stevesimcox@bigfoot.com

SIMESTER, Paul Stephen. b 57. Oak Hill Th Coll 97. **d** 99 **p** 00. C Branksome Park All SS *Sarum* 99-03; TV Wareham 03-07. *27 Weyman's Avenue, Bournemouth BH10 7JR* Tel (01202) 574995 E-mail psimester@hotmail.com
or paul@church2.freeserve.co.uk

SIMISTER, Charles Arnold. b 19. MM44. Edin Th Coll 49. **d** 52 **p** 53. C Glas Ch Ch 52-57; C Worsley *Man* 57-60; V Downton *Sarum* 60-63; CF 63-84; R Kirkcudbright *Glas* 63-84; R Gatehouse of Fleet 63-84; rtd 84; Perm to Offic *Glas* from 84. *98 High Street, Kirkcudbright DG6 4JQ* Tel (01557) 330747

SIMISTER, Norman Harold. b 39. Bris Univ BSc60. **d** 93 **p** 94. OLM Wainford *St E* from 93. *Romaine, 1 School Road, Ringsfield, Beccles NR34 8NZ* Tel (01502) 715549

SIMM, Michael Keith. b 63. Trin Coll Bris BA. **d** 00 **p** 01. C Ipswich St Matt *St E* 00-03; C Gorleston St Andr *Nor* from 03. *283 Lowestoft Road, Gorleston, Great Yarmouth NR31 6JW* Tel (01493) 667914 E-mail mike_simm@talk21.com

SIMMONDS, David Brian. b 38. Selw Coll Cam BA62 MA66 Heidelberg Univ 62. Ridley Hall Cam 63. **d** 65 **p** 66. C Newcastle w Butterton *Lich* 65-69; V Branston 69-97; RD Tutbury 95-97; rtd 97; Perm to Offic *Pet* 97-00 and from 04; P-in-c Easton on the Hill, Collyweston w Duddington etc 00-02; Hon C Ketton, Collyweston, Easton-on-the-Hill etc 03-04. *8 Plover Road, Essendine, Stamford PE9 4UR* Tel (01780) 751967
E-mail david.simmonds38@btopenworld.com

SIMMONDS, Edward Alan. b 32. St Edm Hall Ox MA60. Ripon Coll Cuddesdon 88. **d** 89 **p** 90. NSM Ox St Mich w St Martin and All SS 89-92; NSM Ox St Mary V w St Cross and St Pet 92-94; Chapl Lugano *Eur* 94-98; rtd 98; Perm to Offic *Ex* from 98. *Rokesdown, Higher Duryard, Pennsylvania Road, Exeter EX4 5BQ* Tel (01392) 270311
E-mail asimmonds@eclipse.co.uk

SIMMONDS, John. b 24. Sheff Univ BA50. Ridley Hall Cam 50. **d** 52 **p** 53. C Portsdown *Portsm* 52-55; C-in-c Fareham St Jo Ev CD 55-65; V W Streatham St Jas *S'wark* 65-73; V Congresbury *B & W* 73-75; P-in-c Puxton w Hewish St Ann and Wick St Lawrence 73-75; V Congresbury w Puxton and Hewish St Ann 75-84; Warden Home of Divine Healing Crowhurst 84-89; rtd 89. *Beach Villa, 14 The Beach, Clevedon BS21 7QU* Tel (01275) 342295

SIMMONDS, Paul Andrew Howard. b 50. Nottm Univ BSc73. Trin Coll Bris 75. **d** 78 **p** 79. C Luton St Mary w St Hugh *St Alb* 78-82; SW Regional Co-ord CPAS 83-86; Hd Adult Tr and Resources CPAS 86-95; Hon C Wolston and Church Lawford *Cov* from 89; Dioc Miss Adv 95-03; Research Dir Forward Vision 03-05; Team Ldr Foundations21 BRF from 05; Ind Chapl *Cov* from 08. *31 John Simpson Close, Wolston, Coventry CV8 3HX* Tel (024) 7654 3188 E-mail paul@workcare.org

SIMMONDS, Canon Paul Richard. b 38. AKC63. **d** 64 **p** 65. C Newington St Mary *S'wark* 64-67; C Cheam 68-73; P-in-c Stockwell Green St Andr 73-87; V 87-03; Hon Can S'wark Cathl 97-03; rtd 03. *Timbers, 37 Ocean Drive, Ferring, Worthing BN12 5QP* Tel (01903) 242679
E-mail paulangela@hotmail.com

SIMMONDS, Robert John. b 58. Aston Tr Scheme 92 Ripon Coll Cuddesdon 94. **d** 96 **p** 97. C Southampton Thornhill St Chris *Win* 96-00; TV Basingstoke 00-05; Chapl Co-ord HM Pris Peterborough 05-08; Chapl W Lon Mental Health NHS Trust from 08. *The Chaplaincy, Broadmoor Hospital, Crowthorne RG45 7EG* Tel (01344) 773111
E-mail bobsimmondsvic@aol.com

SIMMONDS, Robert William. b 52. Nottm Univ BTh77. Linc Th Coll 72. **d** 80 **p** 81. C Roehampton H Trin *S'wark* 80-83; TV Hemel Hempstead *St Alb* 83-90; V S Woodham Ferrers *Chelmsf* 90-94; rtd 94; Perm to Offic *Cant* from 03. *21 Copperfield Court, Rectory Road, Broadstairs CT10 1HE* Tel (01843) 863564
E-mail bobwsimmonds@tiscali.co.uk

SIMMONS, Mrs Ann. b 56. WMMTC 04. **d** 07 **p** 08. C Blackheath *Birm* from 07. *25 Garland Crescent, Halesowen B62 9NJ* Tel 0121-602 0590 *or* 421 1370

SIMMONS, Barry Jeremy. b 32. Leeds Univ BA54 MA62. Ridley Hall Cam 61. **d** 63 **p** 64. C Buttershaw St Aid *Bradf* 63-65; Jamaica 65-68; V Earby *Bradf* 68-73; Hong Kong 73-74; Bahrain 75-79; Chapl Luxembourg *Eur* 80-91; V Shoreham *Roch* 91-00; rtd 00; Perm to Offic *Glouc* and *Worc* from 01. *Touchdown, 57 Griffin Close, Stow on the Wold, Cheltenham GL54 1AY* Tel (01451) 831637

SIMMONS, Bernard Peter. b 26. CA Tr Coll 48 S'wark Ord Course 86. **d** 88 **p** 88. C Chatham St Wm *Roch* 88-91; rtd 91; P-in-c Underriver and Seal St Lawr *Roch* 91-95; Perm to Offic *Pet* from 95. *5 Sycamore Drive, Desborough, Kettering NN14 2YH* Tel (01536) 763302

SIMMONS, Canon Brian Dudley. b 35. Master Mariner. St Steph Ho Ox 62. **d** 64 **p** 65. C Bournemouth St Pet *Win* 64-67; Miss to Seamen 67-71; Hon C Milton next Gravesend w Denton *Roch* 67-70; Hon C Gravesend St Geo 70-71; V Larnorbey H Trin 71-90; R Hever w Mark Beech 90-93; P-in-c Four Elms 90-93; R Hever, Four Elms and Mark Beech 93-94; V Langton Green 94-01; Hon Can Roch Cathl 91-01; rtd 01; Perm to Offic *Roch* from 04. *17 Chancellor House, Mount Ephraim, Tunbridge Wells TN4 8BT* Tel (01892) 617262

SIMMONS, Canon Christopher John. b 49. Mert Coll Ox MA77. NEOC 88. **d** 90 **p** 91. C Kirkleatham *York* 90-93; P-in-c Barlby 93-95; V Barlby w Riccall 95-02; RD Derwent 98-01; R Pocklington and Owsthorpe and Kilnwick Percy etc 02-08; P-in-c Burnby 06-08; P-in-c Londesborough 06-08; P-in-c Nunburnholme and Warter and Huggate 06-08; P-in-c Shiptonthorpe and Hayton 06-08; P-in-c Skirlaugh w Long Riston, Rise and Swine from 08; RD N Holderness from 09; Can and Preb York Minster from 08. *105 Main Street, Brandesburton, Driffield YO25 8RG* Tel (01964) 541593

SIMMONS, Eric. b 30. Leeds Univ BA51. Coll of Resurr Mirfield 51. **d** 53 **p** 54. C Chesterton St Luke *Ely* 53-57; Chapl Keele Univ 57-61; CR from 63; Warden Hostel of the Resurr Leeds 66-67; Superior CR 74-87; R Foundn of St Kath in Ratcliffe 89-92; Prior St Mich Priory 93-97; rtd 98. *House of the Resurrection, Stocks Bank Road, Mirfield WF14 0BN* Tel (01924) 494318 Fax 490489

SIMMONS, Gary David. b 59. Trin Coll Bris BA86. **d** 87 **p** 88. C Ecclesfield *Sheff* 87-90; Min Stapenhill Immanuel CD *Derby* 90-96; V Stapenhill Immanuel 97-98; R Slaugham *Chich* from 98; P-in-c Staplefield Common from 08. *The Rectory, Brighton Road, Handcross, Haywards Heath RH17 6BU* Tel (01444) 400221

SIMMONS, Godfrey John. b 39. Open Univ BA81. St And NSM Tr Scheme 71 Edin Th Coll 77. **d** 74 **p** 74. Dioc Supernumerary *St And* 74-75 and 80-81; C Strathtay and Dunkeld 75-77; C Bridge of Allan and Alloa 77-80; Asst Chapl Stirling Univ 77-80; Chapl 80; Min Crieff, Muthill and Comrie 80-81; R 81-85; Chapl HM Pris Perth 80-85; R Kirkwall and Stromness *Ab* 85-91; R Strichen 91-94; R Longside, Old Deer and Peterhead 91-92; Chapl HM Pris Peterhead 91-94; Miss to Seafarers 85-02; Hon Chapl (Scotland) 85-90; Hon Area Chapl (Scotland) 90-94; Chapl Supt Mersey Miss to Seafarers 94-02; TV Ch the K *Dur* 02-06; rtd 06; Perm to Offic *Glas* from 07. *11/13 High Street, Lochmaben, Lockerbie DG11 1NG* Tel (01387) 810490
E-mail joandjohnsimmons@aol.com

SIMMONS, Miss Joan Yvonne. b 14. Gilmore Ho 57. **dss** 61 **d** 87. Harringay St Paul *Lon* 61-63; Belsize Park 63-69; Adult Educn Officer 69-78; rtd 78; Perm to Offic *Chich* 87-05. *Merlewood, Hollow Lane, Virginia Water GU25 4LR* Tel (01344) 845314

SIMMONS, John. b 53. Carl Dioc Tr Course 82. **d** 85 **p** 86. C Wotton St Mary *Glouc* 85-88; P-in-c Amberley 88-92; R Burton Latimer *Pet* 92-98; RD Kettering 94-98; R Paston 98-01; V Irchester from 01. *The Vicarage, 19 Station Road, Irchester, Wellingborough NN29 7EH* Tel (01933) 312674
E-mail john@simmons6.freeserve.co.uk

SIMMONS, John Graham. b 54. Westf Coll Lon BSc75 Man Univ PGCE76. NOC 89. **d** 92 **p** 93. C Thame w Towersey *Ox* 92-97; R Heydon, Gt and Lt Chishill, Chrishall etc *Chelmsf* 97-05; V Chadderton Ch Ch *Man* from 05. *The Vicarage, Block Lane, Chadderton, Oldham OL9 7QB* Tel 0161-652 2950
E-mail john@christchurchchadderton.co.uk

SIMMONS, John Harold. b 46. FCCA. Sarum & Wells Th Coll 86. **d** 89 **p** 90. NSM The Iwernes, Sutton Waldron and Fontmell Magna *Sarum* 89-01; NSM Iwerne Valley from 01. *Fourways, Frog Lane, Iwerne Courtney, Blandford Forum DT11 8QL* Tel (01258) 860515 E-mail john@fourways.plus.com

SIMMONS, Mrs Margaret Irene. Cov Univ BSc02 RGN RSCN. **d** 08 **p** 09. NSM Leam Valley *Cov* from 08. *76 Bilton Road, Rugby CV22 7AL* Tel (01788) 574497

SIMMONS, Ms Marion. b 45. NOC 95. **d** 98 **p** 99. NSM Stoneycroft All SS *Liv* 98-99; C 00-01; TV Fazakerley Em 01-08; TR from 08. *St Paul's Vicarage, Formosa Drive, Liverpool L10 7LB* Tel 0151-521 3344 E-mail marionstpauls@aol.com

SIMMONS, Canon Maurice Samuel. b 27. St Chad's Coll Dur BA50 Newc Univ MA99 MPhil02. **d** 52 **p** 53. C S Shields St Hilda *Dur* 52-58; Youth Chapl 56-60; R Croxdale 58-81; Soc and Ind Adv to Bp Dur 61-70; Gen Sec Soc Resp Gp 70-75; Hon Can Dur Cathl from 71; Sec Dioc Bd for Miss and Unity 75-82; V Norton St Mary 81-92; RD Stockton 85-92; rtd 92. *11 Roecliffe Grove, Stockton-on-Tees TS19 8JU* Tel (01642) 618880 E-mail m.simmons1@ntlworld.com

SIMMONS, Peter. *See* SIMMONS, Bernard Peter

SIMMONS, Richard Andrew Cartwright. b 46. Trin Coll Bris 73. **d** 75 **p** 76. C Worting *Win* 75-80; R Six Pilgrims *B & W* 80-92; R Bincombe w Broadwey, Upwey and Buckland Ripers *Sarum* from 92. *The Rectory, 526 Littlemoor Road, Weymouth DT3 5PA* Tel (01305) 812542 E-mail rac_simmons@lineone.net

SIMMS, Miss Melanie Laura. b 73. Trin Coll Bris 06. **d** 08. C Southway *Ex* from 08. *16 Southway Lane, Plymouth PL6 7DH* Tel 07984-316812 (mobile)
E-mail revmelaniesimms@hotmail.co.uk

SIMMS, William Michael. b 41. Open Univ BA87 BSc01 ACIS70 MCIPD75. NEOC 84. **d** 87 **p** 88. C Croft and Eryholme and Middleton Tyas and Melsonby *Ripon* 87-88; C Headingley 88-90; C Richmond w Hudswell and C-in-c Downholme and Marske 90-93; V Hawes and Hardraw 93-09; rtd 09. *56 Ronaldshay Drive, Richmond DL10 5BW* Tel (01748) 826702

SIMON, Brother. *See* BROOK, Peter Geoffrey

SIMON, David Sidney. b 49. Univ of Wales (Abth) BSc(Econ)70 Hull Univ MA83 Lanc Univ MA05. NEOC 84. **d** 87 **p** 88. NSM Beverley St Mary *York* 87-94; NSM Beverley Deanery 94-98; Lect Humberside Coll of HE 87-90; Humberside Poly 90-92; Humberside Univ 92-96; Lincs and Humberside Univ 96-98; Admin Rydal Hall *Carl* 98-01; Perm to Offic 01-02; NSM Cartmel Peninsula from 02; Dioc Officer for NSM from 08. *3 Kent's Bank House, Kentsford Road, Grange-over-Sands LA11 7BB* Tel (01539) 536762
E-mail davidsimon@ktdbroadband.com

SIMON, Fiona Elizabeth. b 64. Bradf Univ BEng86. STETS 06. **d** 09. C Stoke-next-Guildf from 09. *35 Woking Road, Guildford GU1 1QD* Tel (01483) 569862 E-mail fiona@stjohnstoke.com

SIMON, Frederick Fairbanks. b 42. Ripon Coll Cuddesdon 74. **d** 77 **p** 78. C Cheddleton *Lich* 77-79; C Woodley St Jo the Ev *Ox* 79-82; V Spencer's Wood 82-85; P-in-c Steventon w Milton 85-87; Chapl Grenville Coll Bideford 87-95; rtd 96; Perm to Offic *Ex* 96-04. *Fairview Cottage, Link Road, Pillowell, Lydney GL15 4QY* Tel (01594) 560308

SIMON, Haydn Henry England. *See* ENGLAND-SIMON, Haydn Henry

SIMON, Oliver. b 45. Dur Univ BA67 Sussex Univ MA68 Sheff Univ MMinTheol94. Cuddesdon Coll 69. **d** 71 **p** 72. C Kidlington *Ox* 71-74; C Bracknell 74-78; V Frodsham *Ches* 78-88; R Easthampstead *Ox* 88-00; Chapl Ripon Coll Cuddesdon 00-05; Chapl Pemb Coll Ox 03-04; TV Rugby *Cov* from 05; OLM Officer and Dir Studies from 06. *The Vicarage, St John's Avenue, Rugby CV22 5HR* Tel (01788) 577331
E-mail oliversimon@dunelm.org.uk

SIMONS, Miss Christine. b 40. RGN62 RM64 RHV69. St Jo Coll Nottm 82. **dss** 84 **d** 87 **p** 94. Claygate *Guildf* 84-87; C Camberley St Paul 87-93; NSM 93-99; C Woking Ch Ch 99-05; rtd 05. *25 Kingsway, Blackwater, Camberley GU17 0JW* Tel (01276) 503174 E-mail chris.simons2@ntlworld.com

SIMONS, Preb John Trevor. b 34. Lon Univ BD67. ALCD66. **d** 67 **p** 68. C Becontree St Mary *Chelmsf* 67-71; V Cranham Park 71-78; P-in-c Nailsea H Trin *B & W* 78-83; R 83-97; Sen Asst P 97-99; Preb Wells Cathl 90-99; Nat Dir Crosswinds Prayer Trust from 97; Perm to Offic *B & W* from 99. *11 Spring Hill, Weston-super-Mare BS22 9AP* Tel and fax (01934) 624302
E-mail crosswinds@btopenworld.com

SIMONS, Mark Anselm. b 38. ARCM60. Oak Hill Th Coll 62. **d** 65 **p** 66. C Nottingham St Ann *S'well* 65-68; C N Ferriby *York* 68-75; P-in-c Sherburn 75-78; V Gt and Lt Driffield 78-93; Perm

to Offic from 95; rtd 03. *7 Royal Crescent, Scarborough YO11 2RN* Tel (01723) 378056
E-mail m&f@bibleschool.go-plus.net

SIMONS, William Angus. b 18. Keble Coll Ox BA39 MA47. Cuddesdon Coll 40. **d** 41 **p** 42. C Poplar All SS w St Frideswide *Lon* 41-44 and 47-48; RAChD 44-47; C Is of Dogs Ch Ch and St Jo w St Luke *Lon* 48-54; V Fulham St Jas Moore Park 54-62; Ind Chapl *Worc* 62-63; Ind Missr R Foundn of St Kath in Ratcliffe 63-65; Chapl Hammersmith Hosp Lon 65-68; Chapl St Edm Hosp Northn 68-88; Chapl Northn Gen Hosp 68-72; P-in-c Northampton St Lawr *Pet* 72-76; C Northampton H Sepulchre w St Andr and St Lawr 76-81; rtd 81; Northants Past Coun Service from 76; Founder Dir *Pet* 76-84; Supervisor from 84; Perm to Offic *Pet* from 81. *54 Park Avenue North, Northampton NN3 2JE* Tel (01604) 713767

SIMONSON, Canon Juergen Werner Dietrich. b 24. Lon Univ BD52. ALCD52. **d** 52 **p** 53. C W Kilburn St Luke w St Simon and St Jude *Lon* 52-56; Nigeria 57-63; Chapl CMS Tr Coll Chislehurst 64-65; Vice-Prin 65-67; Prin CMS Tr Coll Chislehurst 67-69; V Putney St Marg *S'wark* 69-81; RD Wandsworth 74-81; Hon Can S'wark Cathl 75-90; R Barnes St Mary 81-90; rtd 90; Perm to Offic *Win* from 90. *Elm Cottage, Horseshoe Lane, Ibthorpe, Andover SP11 0BY* Tel (01264) 736381

SIMPER, Rachel Dawn. *See* WATTS, Mrs Rachel Dawn

SIMPKINS, Frank Charles. b 19. MCIT52 MILT99. Oak Hill Th Coll 72. **d** 75 **p** 76. C Harrow Weald St Mich *Lon* 75-78; Hon C 81-84; P-in-c Dollis Hill St Paul 78-80; Chapl Northwick Park Hosp Harrow 81-83; Hon C Harrow Trin St Mich *Lon* 84-94; Perm to Offic from 94. *7 Milne Feild, Pinner HA5 4DP* Tel (020) 8428 2477

SIMPKINS, Canon Lionel Frank. b 46. UEA BSc68 Lambeth STh77. St Jo Coll Nottm LTh74. **d** 73 **p** 74. C Leic H Apostles 73-77; C Bushbury *Lich* 77-80; V Sudbury w Ballingdon and Brundon *St E* 80-96; Chapl Sudbury Hosps 80-96; RD Sudbury 88-96; Hon Can St E Cathl from 94; V Ipswich St Aug from 96; Warden of Readers from 03. *St Augustine's Vicarage, 2 Bucklesham Road, Ipswich IP3 8TJ* Tel (01473) 728654
E-mail lionel.staug@btconnect.com

SIMPKINS, Susan Carol. b 58. St Steph Ho Ox 03. **d** 05. NSM Ruislip St Martin *Lon* from 05. *70 Park Avenue, Ruislip HA4 7UJ* Tel (01895) 630170
E-mail sue.simpkins@btopenworld.com

SIMPSON, Alan Eric. b 52. Ch Ch Ox BA73 MA77 Birm Univ PhD77 Dur Univ MA01 CPhys77 MInstP77. Cranmer Hall Dur 96. **d** 98 **p** 99. C Long Benton *Newc* 98-02; P-in-c Cresswell and Lynemouth 02-06; V from 06. *The Vicarage, 33 Till Grove, Ellington, Morpeth NE61 5ER* Tel (01670) 860242
E-mail fr.alan@talk21.com

SIMPSON, Alexander. b 31. Oak Hill Th Coll 74. **d** 76 **p** 77. Hon C Lower Homerton St Paul *Lon* 76-81; Hon C Homerton St Barn w St Paul 81-85; TV Hackney Marsh 85-87; V Kensington St Helen w H Trin 87-97; rtd 97; Perm to Offic *Derby* 01-07 and *Nor* from 08. *2 Ferndale Close, Norwich NR6 5SD* Tel (01603) 443412

SIMPSON, Alison Jane. b 60. St Andr Univ BSc83 BD86 Princeton Univ MTh87. **d** 99 **p** 99. C Ellon *Ab* 99-02; R Huntly *Mor* from 02; R Keith from 02; R Aberchirder from 02; P-in-c Fochabers from 04. *Holy Trinity Rectory, Seafield Avenue, Keith AB55 5BS* Tel (01542) 882782
E-mail alison.simpson2@tesco.net

SIMPSON, Andrew. b 48. Liv Univ BEng69. Sarum Th Coll 83. **d** 86 **p** 87. NSM Canford Magna *Sarum* from 86. *17 Sopwith Crescent, Wimborne BH21 1SH* Tel (01202) 883996
E-mail andrew.simpson6@virgin.net

SIMPSON, Andrew Charles. b 65. NEOC 06. **d** 09. C Hessle *York* from 09. *167 First Lane, Hessle HU13 9EY* Tel (01482) 645745
E-mail andy@allsaintshessle.karoo.co.uk

SIMPSON, Charles Michael. b 38. St Cath Coll Cam MA64 Campion Hall Ox MA65 Heythrop Coll Lon STL69 K Coll Lon PhD71. **d** 68 **p** 69. Lect Th Lon Univ 72-84; Chapl Prince of Peace Community Greenwich 85-87; Retreat Dir St Beuno's Clwyd 87-91; P-in-c Selkirk *Edin* 91-94; P-in-c Offchurch *Cov* 94-96; Warden Offa Retreat Ho and Dioc Spirituality Adv 94-00; P-in-c Stoke Canon, Poltimore w Huxham and Rewe etc *Ex* 00-04; Dioc Adv in Adult Tr 00-04; rtd 04; Perm to Offic *Cov* from 05. *15 Shepherds Way, Stow on the Wold, Cheltenham GL54 1EA* Tel (01451) 831028
E-mail michaelandsharon@shepherdsway.wanadoo.co.uk

SIMPSON, Christine. **d** 07 **p** 08. OLM Drayton in Hales *Lich* from 07. *18 Mortimer Road, Buntingsdale Park, Market Drayton TF9 2EP* Tel (01630) 638794
E-mail christine@simpson12.plus.com

SIMPSON, Colin George. b 63. Qu Coll Birm 06. **d** 08 **p** 09. C Astwell Gp *Pet* from 08. *6 Wappenham Road, Syresham, Brackley NN13 5HQ* Tel (01280) 850709
E-mail revcolinsimpson@btinternet.com

SIMPSON, David Charles Edward. b 51. NEOC 02. **d** 05 **p** 06. NSM York St Chad 05-09; Perm to Offic from 09. *98 Brunswick Street, York YO23 1ED* Tel (01904) 635085

SIMPSON, David John. b 61. Univ Coll Dur BA85. Sarum & Wells Th Coll 89. **d** 91 **p** 92. C Selby Abbey *York* 91-94; C Romsey *Win* 94-97; Chapl Southn Univ 97-05; Chapl RN from 05. *Royal Naval Chaplaincy Service, Mail Point 1-2, Leach Building, Whale Island, Portsmouth PO2 8BY* Tel (023) 9262 5055 Fax 9262 5134 E-mail dpersce@aidii.mod.uk

SIMPSON, Derek John. b 59. Oak Hill Th Coll BA89. **d** 89 **p** 90. C Alperton *Lon* 89-95; TR Brentford from 95; AD Hounslow from 02. *The Rectory, 3 The Butts, Brentford TW8 8BJ* Tel (020) 8568 6502 *or* 8568 7442 E-mail derek.simpson@btinternet.com

SIMPSON, Mrs Elizabeth Ann. b 59. Lon Bible Coll BA80 Trin Coll Bris 84. **dss** 86 **d** 97 **p** 98. Thornbury *Glouc* 86-87; Beckenham Ch Ch *Roch* 87-90; Heydon, Gt and Lt Chishill, Chrishall etc *Chelmsf* 90-93; Shirwell, Loxhore, Kentisbury, Arlington, etc *Ex* 93-97; NSM S Molton w Nymet St George, High Bray etc 97-99; C 99-03; P-in-c W Buckingham *Ox* from 03. *The Vicarage, Orchard Place, Westbury, Brackley NN13 5JT* Tel (01280) 704964

SIMPSON, Geoffrey Sedgwick. b 32. Hamilton Coll (NY) BA54 Wisconsin Univ MA Pemb Coll Cam PhD70. Gen Th Sem (NY) STB57. **d** 57 **p** 57. USA 57-77; Chapl Birm Univ 77-80; V Shoreham *Roch* 80-90; TR Street *York* 90-02; rtd 02; Perm to Offic *Sarum* from 03. *The Laurels, Queen Street, Yetminster, Sherborne DT9 6LL* Tel (01935) 872915

SIMPSON, Mrs Georgina. b 46. Westmr Coll Ox BTh93 Birm Univ MA95 DipEd98. SAOMC 95. **d** 97 **p** 98. NSM Littlemore *Ox* 97-98; C Ox St Giles and SS Phil and Jas w St Marg 98-09; Perm to Offic from 09. *85 Church Road, Sandford-on-Thames, Oxford OX4 4YA* Tel (01865) 512319

SIMPSON, Godfrey Lionel. b 42. Sarum Th Coll 63. **d** 66 **p** 67. C Leintwardine *Heref* 66-70; C Leominster 70-73; P-in-c Whitbourne 73-79; V Barlaston *Lich* 79-02; RD Trentham 85-00; P-in-c The Guitings, Cutsdean and Farmcote *Glouc* 02-03; R The Guitings, Cutsdean, Farmcote etc from 03. *The Rectory, Copse Hill Road, Lower Slaughter, Cheltenham GL54 2HY* Tel (01451) 810812

SIMPSON, Herbert. b 20. Carl Dioc Tr Course. **d** 82 **p** 83. NSM Barrow St Aid *Carl* 82; NSM Barrow St Jo 82-90; rtd 90; Perm to Offic *Carl* 90-07. *3 Glenridding Drive, Barrow-in-Furness LA14 4PE* Tel (01229) 823707

SIMPSON, Mrs Janet Mary. b 42. New Coll Edin LTh94. EAMTC 99. **d** 00 **p** 01. C Aldringham w Thorpe, Knodishall w Buxlow etc *St E* 00-03; R Elmsett w Aldham, Hintlesham, Chattisham etc 03-06; rtd 06. *8 Meadow Close, Wootton Basset, Swindon SN4 7JL* Tel (01793) 848006 E-mail revjanelmsett@tiscali.co.uk

SIMPSON, The Very Revd John Arthur. b 33. OBE01. Keble Coll Ox BA56 MA60. Clifton Th Coll 56. **d** 58 **p** 59. C Low Leyton *Chelmsf* 58-59; C Orpington Ch Ch *Roch* 59-62; Tutor Oak Hill Th Coll 62-72; V Ridge *St Alb* 72-79; P-in-c 79-81; Dir of Ords and Post-Ord Tr 75-81; Hon Can St Alb 77-79; Can Res St Alb 79-81; Adn Cant and Can Res Cant Cathl 81-86; Dean Cant 86-00; rtd 00; Perm to Offic *Cant* from 01. *Flat D, 9 Earls Avenue, Folkestone CT20 2HW* Tel (01303) 211868

SIMPSON, Canon John Bernard. b 40. St Paul's Cheltenham CertEd62 Ox Univ MTh95 ACP66. **d** 93 **p** 93. In URC 63 93; Asst to RD Lothingland *Nor* 93-94; RD from 99; C Hopton w Corton 93-94; P-in-c 94-99; TR Lowestoft St Marg from 99; Hon Can Nor Cathl from 01. *St Margaret's Rectory, 147 Hollingsworth Road, Lowestoft NR32 4BW* Tel (01502) 573046 Fax 538253 E-mail john.simpson5@tesco.net

SIMPSON, Canon John Lawrence. b 33. DL04. SS Coll Cam BA55 MA59 ARCM60 UWE Hon MMus. Wells Th Coll 63. **d** 65 **p** 66. Chapl Win Cathl 65-66; C Win St Bart 65-69; Chapl Repton Sch Derby 69-71; Hd of RE Helston Sch 71-78; P-in-c Curry Rivel *B & W* 79-80; R Curry Rivel w Fivehead and Swell 80-86; V Tunbridge Wells K Chas *Roch* 86-89; Can Res Bris Cathl 89-99; rtd 99; Perm to Offic *B & W* from 00. *Yardes Cottage, Windmill Hill, Ilminster TA19 9NT* Tel (01823) 480593

SIMPSON, John Peter. b 39. ALCD66. **d** 66 **p** 67. C Woodside *Ripon* 66-69; C Burnage St Marg *Man* 69-72; V Rochdale Deeplish St Luke 72-80; R Lamplugh w Ennerdale *Carl* 80-04; rtd 04. *8 Queens Avenue, Seaton, Workington CA14 1DN* Tel (01900) 604215 E-mail revpetersim@supanet.com

SIMPSON, John Raymond. b 41. Univ of S Aus DipEd92. Chich Th Coll 65. **d** 67 **p** 68. C Scarborough St Martin *York* 67-71; C Grangetown 71-72; Youth Chapl Bermuda 72-75; C Lewisham St Mary *S'wark* 76; C Albany Australia 76-78; R Carey Park 78-84; Chapl RAN 84-90; Chapl RAAF 90-99; Grace Cathl San Francisco USA 99-00; Chapl RANSR from 00. *44/19 Oakleigh Drive, Erskine Grove, Erskine WA 6210, Australia* Tel (0061) (8) 9586 4144 E-mail johnsimpson_94108@yahoo.com

SIMPSON, John Verrent. b 68. Univ of Wales (Cardiff) BScEcon93. Ripon Coll Cuddesdon BTh98. **d** 98 **p** 99. C Cardiff St Jo *Llan* 98-00; C Cen Cardiff 00-01; C Upper Chelsea H Trin

Lon 01-04; P-in-c Lt Missenden *Ox* from 05. *The Vicarage, Little Missenden, Amersham HP7 0RA* Tel (01494) 862008 Mobile 07779-136757 E-mail office@littlemissendenparish.org.uk

SIMPSON, Kevin Gordon. b 54. QPM02. Univ of Wales BEd96 MCIPD94. St Mich Coll Llan. **d** 02 **p** 03. NSM Llantwit Fardre from 02. *95 St Anne's Drive, Pontypridd CF38 2PB* Tel (01443) 207033 Mobile 07870-397494 E-mail k.g.simpson@btinternet.com

SIMPSON, Miss Margery Patricia. b 36. SRN57 SCM59. Oak Hill Th Coll BA86. **dss** 86 **d** 87 **p** 94. Rodbourne Cheney *Bris* 86-87; Par Dn 87-90; Par Dn Warmley 90-94; C Warmley, Syston and Bitton 94-95; TV Yate New Town 95-96; rtd 97; Perm to Offic *Sarum* from 97. *19 Wentworth Park, Stainburn, Workington CA14 1XP* Tel (01900) 61523

SIMPSON, Mark Lawrence. b 73. Oak Hill Th Coll BA03. **d** 03 **p** 04. C Leyland St Andr *Blackb* from 03. *45 Westgate, Leyland PR25 2LX* Tel (01772) 622446

SIMPSON, Michael. See SIMPSON, Charles Michael

SIMPSON, Peter. See SIMPSON, John Peter

SIMPSON, Canon Peter Wynn. b 32. Birm Univ BA53. Ripon Hall Ox 55. **d** 57 **p** 58. C Leamington Priors H Trin *Cov* 57-60; C Croydon St Jo *Cant* 60-63; V Foleshill St Laur *Cov* 63-70; V Radford 70-79; RD Cov N 76-79; V Finham 79-91; RD Cov S 82-88; Hon Can Cov Cathl 83-91; rtd 91; Perm to Offic *Cov* from 91. *Faith Cottage, 118 Main Street, Wolston, Coventry CV8 3HP* Tel (024) 7654 3965

SIMPSON, Philip Alexander. b 54. Keele Univ BA79 CQSW79 Sunderland Univ MSc03. CMS Tr Coll Selly Oak 85. **d** 89 **p** 07. CMS from 85; Pakistan 85-98; Regional Dir for Eurasia from 98; Perm to Offic *Guildf* 06-07; NSM Woking Ch Ch from 07. *CMS, PO Box 1799, Oxford OX4 9BN* Tel 08456-201799 E-mail phil.simpson@cms-uk.org

SIMPSON, Raymond James. b 40. Lon Coll of Div ALCD63 LTh74. **d** 63 **p** 64. C Longton St Jas *Lich* 64-68; C Upper Tooting H Trin *S'wark* 68-71; BFBS Distr Sec E Anglia 71-77; C-in-c Bowthorpe CD *Nor* 78-84; V Bowthorpe 84-96; Perm to Offic *Newc* from 96; Guardian Community of Aid and Hilda from 96. *Lindisfarne Retreat, Marygate, Holy Island, Berwick-upon-Tweed TD15 2SD* Tel and fax (01289) 389249 E-mail raysimpson@ndirect.co.uk

SIMPSON, Richard Lee. b 66. Keble Coll Ox BA88 MPhil91 Westmr Coll Ox PGCE89. Wycliffe Hall Ox 91. **d** 93 **p** 94. C Newc St Gabr 93-97; P-in-c Jesmond H Trin 97-06; P-in-c Newc St Barn and St Jude 97-06; P-in-c Brancepeth *Dur* from 06; Dir IME 4-7 *Dur* and *Newc* from 06. *The Rectory, Brancepeth, Durham DH7 8EL* Tel 0191-380 0440 Mobile 07867-802671 E-mail ricksimpson300@btinternet.com

SIMPSON, Robert Charles. b 46. Ridley Hall Cam. **d** 85 **p** 86. C Eastwood *S'well* 85-88; V Yardley St Cypr Hay Mill *Birm* 88-93; P-in-c Newent and Gorsley w Cliffords Mesne *Glouc* 93-95; R 95-05; Dioc Ecum Officer 04-05; P-in-c Glouc St Jas and All SS from 05; AD Glouc City from 08. *The Vicarage, 1 The Conifers, Gloucester GL1 4LP* Tel (01452) 422349 E-mail robertcsimpson@onetel.com

SIMPSON, Robert David. b 61. Fitzw Coll Cam BA83 MA87 Bris Univ MLitt94. Trin Coll Bris 85. **d** 87 **p** 88. C Beckenham Ch Ch *Roch* 87-90; C Heydon w Gt and Lt Chishill *Chelmsf* 90; C Chrishall 90; C Elmdon w Wendon Lofts and Strethall 90; C Heydon, Gt and Lt Chishill, Chrishall etc 91-93; TV Shirwell, Loxhore, Kentisbury, Arlington, etc *Ex* 93-97; TR S Molton w Nymet St George, High Bray etc 97-03. *The Vicarage, Orchard Place, Westbury, Brackley NN13 5JT* Tel (01280) 782893 E-mail revsimpson@supanet.com

SIMPSON, Robert John. NUU BA PGCE. **d** 03 **p** 04. NSM Ballymoney w Finvoy and Rasharkin *Conn* 03-08; NSM Ballywillan from 08. *28 Willowfield Park, Coleraine BT52 2NF* Tel (028) 7035 8552 E-mail robert@robertheather.fsnet.co.uk

SIMPSON, Robert Theodore. b 34. Linc Coll Ox BA58 MA61 K Coll Lon PhD71 UNISA MEd85. Chich Th Coll 58. **d** 60 **p** 61. C Ellesmere Port *Ches* 60-63; CR 63-66; S Africa 68-88; Prin St Pet Coll 72-75; Pres Federal Th Sem 73-75; Sen Lect Th Swaziland Univ 83-87; Assoc Prof Th 87-88; Chapl and Lect Coll of SS Mark and Jo Plymouth 88-90; Tutor Simon of Cyrene Th Inst 90-92; Perm to Offic *S'wark* 91-92; P-in-c Shadwell St Paul w Ratcliffe St Jas *Lon* 92-01; rtd 01. *36 Whitton Dene, Hounslow TW3 2JT* E-mail theo@cologon.org

SIMPSON, Roger Westgarth. b 51. Lon Univ BSc72. St Jo Coll Nottm 77. **d** 79 **p** 80. C St Marylebone All So w SS Pet and Jo *Lon* 79-85; R Edin St Paul and St Geo 85-95; R Vancouver H Trin Canada 95-99; V York St Mich-le-Belfrey from 99. *The Parish Centre, 11/12 Minster Yard, York YO1 7HH* Tel (01904) 624190 *or* 412470 Fax 622290 E-mail roger.simpson@stmichaelsyork.org

SIMPSON, The Ven Samuel. b 26. TCD BA55 MA69 Div Test 56 TCD Div Sch. **d** 56 **p** 57. C Coleraine *Conn* 56-60; I Donagh w Cloncha and Clonmany *D & R* 60-64; I Ballyscullion 64-81; Can Derry Cathl 78-96; I Errigal w Garvagh 81-96; Adn Derry 89-96; rtd 96. *53 Magheramenagh Drive, Atlantic Road, Portrush BT56 8SP* Tel (028) 7082 4292

SIMPSON (*née* **RALPHS**), **Mrs Sharon Ann.** b 55. St Mary's Coll Dur BA77. Cranmer Hall Dur 81. **dss** 83 **d** 87 **p** 94. Caverswall *Lich* 83-87; Par Dn 87-89; Asst Dioc Officer for Minl Tr *St As* 90-91; NSM Selkirk *Edin* 91-94; C Offchurch *Cov* 94-96; Warden Offa Retreat Ho and Dioc Spirituality Adv 94-00; C Stoke Canon, Poltimore w Huxham and Rewe etc *Ex* 00-04; Dioc Adv in Adult Tr 00-04; rtd 04; Perm to Offic *Cov* from 05. *15 Whately Way, Stow on the Wold, Cheltenham GL54 1EA* Tel (01451) 831028
E-mail michaelandsharon@shepherdsway.wanadoo.co.uk

SIMPSON, Mrs Susie Alexandra. b 58. Hertf Coll Ox BA81. St Steph Ho Ox BA98. **d** 99 **p** 00. C High Wycombe *Ox* 99-03; TV 03-08; Chapl HM YOI Roch from 09. *HM Young Offender Institution, 1 Fort Road, Rochester ME1 3QS* Tel (01634) 803100
E-mail susie.simpson@hmps.gsi.gov.uk

SIMPSON, Ursula Lucy. b 51. St Anne's Coll Ox MA73 Leeds Univ MA05. NOC 02. **d** 05 **p** 06. NSM York St Paul from 05. *St Barnabas' Vicarage, Jubilee Terrace, York YO26 4YZ* Tel and fax (01904) 654214 E-mail u.simpson@btopenworld.com

SIMS, Bernard David. b 40. Bath Univ BSc66. Ox Min Course 91. **d** 94 **p** 95. NSM Beedon and Peasemore w W Ilsley and Farnborough *Ox* 94-98; TV Blakenall Heath *Lich* from 98. *St Chad's Vicarage, Edison Road, Walsall WS2 7HT* Tel (01922) 612081 E-mail sims@beechdale.fsnet.co.uk

SIMS, Christopher Sidney. b 49. Wycliffe Hall Ox 74. **d** 77 **p** 78. C Walmley *Birm* 77-80; V Yardley St Cypr Hay Mill 80-88; V Stanwix *Carl* 88-96; RD Carl 89-95; Hon Can Carl Cathl 91-95; P-in-c Bassenthwaite, Isel and Setmurthy 96-00; P-in-c Bolton w Ireby and Uldale 96-00; P-in-c Allhallows 96-00; P-in-c Torpenhow 96-00; TR Binsey 00-03; V Shrewsbury H Cross *Lich* from 03; RD Shrewsbury from 08. *1 Underdale Court, Underdale Road, Shrewsbury SY2 5DD* Tel (01743) 248859

SIMS, Graeme. *See* SIMS, Michael Graeme

SIMS, James Henry. b 35. St Jo Coll Nottm 87. **d** 89 **p** 91. NSM Bangor Abbey *D & D* 89-93; C Holywood 93; Bp's C Kilbroney 93-01; Min Can Belf Cathl 99-09; P-in-c Clonallon w Warrenpoint *D & D* 01-09; Can Dromore Cathl 03-09; rtd 09. *7 Prior's Lea, Holywood BT18 9QW* Tel (028) 9042 4360 E-mail jim.sims321@tiscali.co.uk

SIMS, Mrs Julia Mary Heaton. b 56. STETS 04. **d** 07 **p** 08. NSM Winscombe and Sandford *B & W* from 07. *7 Round Oak Grove, Cheddar BS27 3BW* Tel (01934) 740120
E-mail jms125@hotmail.co.uk

SIMS, Keith George. b 29. **d** 95 **p** 96. OLM Forest Hill St Aug *S'wark* 95-04. *Address temp unknown*

SIMS, Michael Graeme. b 37. SWMTC 96. **d** 98 **p** 99. NSM Parkham, Alwington, Buckland Brewer etc *Ex* 98-00; NSM Blymhill w Weston-under-Lizard *Lich* 00-07; rtd 07. *Address temp unknown*

SIMS, Peter George Russell. b 36. Univ of Wales (Swansea) BA57. St Mich Coll Llan 63. **d** 65 **p** 66. C Brecon w Battle *S & B* 65-72; Min Can Brecon Cathl 65-72; V Llanfrynach and Cantref w Llanhamlach 72-05; rtd 05. *2 Buckingham Place, Brecon LD3 7DL* Tel (01874) 610371

SIMS, Ruth. b 40. **d** 06 **p** 07. NSM Alveley and Quatt *Heref* from 06. *Church Farm House, Alveley, Bridgnorth WV15 6ND*

SIMS, Sidney. b 20. Wycliffe Hall Ox. **d** 64 **p** 65. C Attenborough w Bramcote *S'well* 64-67; V Ramsey St Mary's w Ponds Bridge *Ely* 67-70; V Cambridge St Matt 70-85; Algeria 85-86; rtd 86; Perm to Offic *Nor* from 86. *Cockley Cottage, 66 Morston Road, Blakeney, Holt NR25 7BE* Tel (01263) 740184

SIMS, Vickie Lela. b 56. Iowa State Univ BA79. Ripon Coll Cuddesdon 00. **d** 02 **p** 03. C Grantham *Linc* 02-05; P-in-c Coulsdon St Andr *S'wark* from 05. *St Andrew's Vicarage, Julien Road, Coulsdon CR5 2DN* Tel (020) 8660 0398
E-mail simstabbat@hotmail.com

SINCLAIR, Andrew John McTaggart. b 58. Ex Univ BA80. Westcott Ho Cam 81. **d** 84 **p** 85. C Aston cum Aughton and Ulley *Sheff* 84-87; C Rotherham 87-88; TV Edin Old St Paul 88-93; Hon Angl Chapl Edin Univ and Moray Ho Coll 89-93; TV Dunstable *St Alb* 93-00; V Verwood *Sarum* from 00. *The Vicarage, 34 Dewlands Way, Verwood BH31 6JN* Tel (01202) 822298 *or* 813256 E-mail ansinclair@aol.com

SINCLAIR, Canon Arthur Alfred. b 46. **d** 87 **p** 89. Hon C St Andr Cathl Inverness 87-92; C 93-97; Chapl Asst Inverness Hosp 87-89; Dioc Chapl 87-89; NSM Culloden St Mary-in-the-Fields 89-92; P-in-c from 93; P-in-c Inverness St Jo from 93; Edin Th Coll 92-93; Chapl Raigmore Hosp NHS Trust Inverness from 93; Can St Andr Cathl Inverness from 05. *St John's Rectory, Southside Road, Inverness IV2 3BG* Tel (01463) 716288
E-mail sinclairstjohns@aol.com

SINCLAIR, Charles Horace. b 19. Keble Coll Ox BA40 MA44. Linc Th Coll 41. **d** 42 **p** 43. C Upper Norwood St Jo *Cant* 42-45; Chapl K Coll Auckland 46-50; Hd Master Prebendal Sch Chich 51-53; PV Chich Cathl 51-53; Chapl and Sen Tutor Brookland Hall Welshpool 53-57; Hd Master St Aid Sch Denby Dale 57-64; Perm to Offic *Wakef* 58-64; rtd 84; Perm to Offic *Cant* 84-09. *21 St Andrews, The Durlocks, Folkestone CT19 6AW* Tel (01303) 250882 Mobile 07974-294886

SINCLAIR, Colin. b 30. **d** 84 **p** 85. NSM Ramoan w Ballycastle and Culfeightrin *Conn* 84-92. *4 Bushfoot Cottages, Portballintrae, Bushmills BT57 8RN* Tel (028) 2073 1551

✠**SINCLAIR, The Rt Revd Gordon Keith.** b 52. Ch Ch Ox MA. Cranmer Hall Dur. **d** 84 **p** 85 **c** 08. C Summerfield *Birm* 84-88; V Aston SS Pet and Paul 88-01; AD Aston 00-01; Hon Can Birm Cathl 00-01; V Cov H Trin 01-07; Suff Bp Birkenhead *Ches* from 07. *Bishop's Lodge, 67 Bidston Road, Prenton CH43 6TR* Tel 0151-652 2741 Fax 651 2330
E-mail bpbirkenhead@chester.anglican.org

SINCLAIR, Horace. *See* SINCLAIR, Charles Horace

SINCLAIR, The Ven Jane Elizabeth Margaret. b 56. St Hugh's Coll Ox BA78 MA80. St Jo Coll Nottm BA82. **dss** 83 **d** 87 **p** 94. Herne Hill St Paul *S'wark* 83-86; Chapl and Lect St Jo Coll Nottm 86-93; Can Res Sheff Cathl 93-03; Hon Can 03-07; V Rotherham 03-07; Adn Stow *Linc* from 07; Adn Lindsey from 07. *Sanderlings, Willingham Road, Market Rasen LN8 3RE* Tel (01673) 849896
E-mail archdeacon.stowlindsey@lincoln.anglican.org

SINCLAIR, Canon John Robert. b 58. Oak Hill Th Coll 90. **d** 92 **p** 93. C Ponteland *Newc* 92-96; V Long Benton St Mary 96-01; V Newburn from 01; AD Newc W from 07; Hon Can Newc Cathl from 08. *The Vicarage, High Street, Newburn, Newcastle upon Tyne NE15 8LQ* Tel 0191-229 0522 Fax 267 0582
E-mail john.r.sinclair@lineone.net

SINCLAIR, Keith. *See* SINCLAIR, The Rt Revd Gordon Keith

✠**SINCLAIR, The Rt Revd Maurice Walter.** b 37. Nottm Univ BSc59 Leic Univ PGCE60. Tyndale Hall Bris 62 Nashotah Ho Hon DD01. **d** 64 **p** 65 **c** 90. C Boscombe St Jo *Win* 64-67; SAMS 67-02; Argentina 67-78; Personnel Sec 79-83; Asst Gen Sec 83-84; Prin Crowther Hall CMS Tr Coll Selly Oak 84-90; Bp N Argentina 90-02; Primate of S Cone 95-02; rtd 02; Hon Asst Bp Birm from 02. *55 Selly Wick Drive, Birmingham B29 7JQ* Tel 0121-471 2617 E-mail mandg@sinclair401.fsnet.co.uk

SINCLAIR, Michael David Bradley. b 42. NOC Coll of Resurr Mirfield. **d** 97 **p** 98. NSM Settrington w N Grimston, Birdsall w Langton *York* 97-99; R W Buckrose 99-08; rtd 08; NSM Helmsley *York* from 09; NSM Upper Ryedale from 09. *Witham Cottage, Langton, Malton YO17 9QP* Tel (01653) 658360

SINCLAIR, Nigel Craig. b 65. Teesside Poly BA87 Coll of Ripon & York St Jo MA00. St Jo Coll Dur BA93. **d** 94 **p** 95. C Marton-in-Cleveland *York* 94-97; TV Thirsk 97-02; V Pannal w Beckwithshaw *Ripon* from 02; AD Harrogate from 09. *St Robert's Vicarage, 21 Crimple Meadows, Pannal, Harrogate HG3 1EL* Tel (01423) 870202
E-mail nigelsinclair@btinternet.com

SINCLAIR, Peter. b 44. Oak Hill Th Coll. **d** 88 **p** 89. C Darlington H Trin *Dur* 88-91; C-in-c Bishop Auckland Woodhouse Close CD 91-98; P-in-c Consett from 98. *The Vicarage, 10 Aynsley Terrace, Consett DH8 5NF* Tel (01207) 502235

SINCLAIR, Peter Monteith. b 52. St Andr Univ BSc73. NEOC. **d** 01 **p** 02. NSM Darlington St Cuth *Dur* from 01. *Sundial Cottage, 7 Haughton Green, Darlington DL1 2DD* Tel (01325) 358424 Fax 361572 Mobile 07710-017625
E-mail peter@psld.co.uk

SINCLAIR, Reginald William. b 53. Wolv Poly BSc77 CEng MIMechE. **d** 07 **p** 08. OLM Atherton and Hindsford w Howe Bridge *Man* from 07. *Bumbles, 23 Millers Lane, Atherton, Manchester M46 9BW* Tel (01942) 892996 Mobile 07707-419642 E-mail reg.sinclair@tiscali.co.uk

SINCLAIR, Robert Charles. b 28. Liv Univ LLB49 QUB LLM69 PhD82. Ely Th Coll 58. **d** 60 **p** 61. C Glenavy *Conn* 60-63; Chapl RN 63-67; C Cregagh *D & D* 67-68; Perm to Offic *Conn* from 69. *Juniper Cottage, 11A Glen Road, Glenavy, Crumlin BT29 4LT* Tel (028) 9445 3126

SINCLAIR, Robert Michael. b 41. CQSW81. Edin Th Coll 63. **d** 66 **p** 67. C Dunfermline *St And* 66-68; C Edin Old St Paul 68-72; P-in-c Edin St Dav 72-77; Hon Dioc Supernumerary 77-96. *121/119 Comiston Drive, Edinburgh EH10 5QU* Tel 0131-447 5068

SINDALL, Canon Christine Ann. b 42. ALA69. EAMTC 84. **d** 87 **p** 94. NSM Sutton *Ely* 87-89; C Cambridge Ascension 89-94; TV 94-96; R Cheveley 96-07; R Ashley w Silverley 96-07; V Kirtling 96-07; V Wood Ditton w Saxon Street 96-07; RD Linton 01-07; Hon Can Ely Cathl 01-07; rtd 07. *9 East Moor, Longhoughton, Alnwick NE66 3JB* Tel (01665) 572287
E-mail csindall@btinternet.com

SINGAPORE, Bishop of. *See* CHEW, The Most Revd John Hiang Chea

SINGH, Balwant. b 32. BA60. Saharanpur Th Coll 50. **d** 53 **p** 58. India 53-67 and 71-73; Hon C Handsworth St Jas *Birm* 67-71; Hon C N Hinksey *Ox* 73-80; Lic to Offic 80-81; Hon C S Hinksey 82-05; Perm to Offic *Ox* from 05. *9 Jersey Road, Oxford OX4 4RT* Tel (01865) 717277

SINGH, Graham Andrew. b 77. Huron Coll Ontario BA00 LSE MSc01. Ridley Hall Cam 06. **d** 08 **p** 09. C W Hampstead Trin

Lon from 08. *The Church House, Ospringe Road, London NW5 2JB* Tel (020) 7435 0083 Mobile 07940-385688 E-mail graham@htsc.org

SINGH, Thomas Balwant. b 62. Westmr Coll Ox BTh98. Wycliffe Hall Ox 98. **d** 00 **p** 01. C Houghton Regis *St Alb* 00-04; V Biscot from 04. *The Vicarage, 161 Bishopscote Road, Luton LU3 1PD* Tel (01582) 579410 E-mail thomassingh@hotmail.com

SINGH, Timon Balwant. b 60. Ripon Coll Cuddesdon. **d** 08 **p** 09. C Waterlooville *Portsm* from 08. *5 Chilsdown Way, Waterlooville PO7 5DT* Tel (023) 9225 2315 E-mail timon_ox@hotmail.com

SINGH, Vivian Soorat. b 30. Trin Coll Cam BA MA53. Westcott Ho Cam 54. **d** 55 **p** 56. C Yardley Wood *Birm* 55-57; C Birm St Paul 57-59; Asst Master Framlingham Coll 59-72; Chapl 60-72; Chapl Wymondham Coll 72-75; Dep Hd Litcham High Sch 75-88; rtd 88; Perm to Offic *Nor* from 88. *Manor Cottage, Wendling Road, Longham, Dereham NR19 2RD* Tel (01362) 687382

SINGLETON, David Brinley. b 59. St Steph Ho Ox. **d** 00 **p** 01. C Soham *Ely* 00-01; C Soham and Wicken 02-04; P-in-c Capel St Mary w Lt and Gt Wenham *St E* 04-08; R from 08. *The Rectory, Days Road, Capel St Mary, Ipswich IP9 2LE* Tel (01473) 310759 E-mail brin.singleton@ukgateway.net

SINGLETON, Mrs Editha Mary. b 27. WMMTC 85. **dss** 84 **d** 87 **p** 94. Lich St Chad 84-90; Hon Par Dn 87-90; Hon Par Dn Beaulieu and Exbury and E Boldre *Win* 90-94; Hon C 94-97; Perm to Offic from 97. *The Peregrine, The Lane, Fawley, Southampton SO45 1EY* Tel (023) 8089 4364

SINGLETON, Ernest George (Paul). b 15. St Aug Coll Cant 38. **d** 41 **p** 42. C Portsea N End St Mark *Portsm* 41-46; C Hendon St Mary *Lon* 46-48; CR 48-68; Lic to Offic *Wakef* 49-51; Lic to Offic *Lon* 52-56; S Africa 56-60; Prior St Teilo's Priory Cardiff 61-68; Perm to Offic *Lon* 68-91 and 93-95; rtd 80; Hon C Twickenham St Mary *Lon* 91-93. *Suite 268, Postnet X31, Saxonwold, Johannesburg, 2132 South Africa* Tel (0027) (11) 880 2982 Fax 447 5144

SINGLETON, Kenneth Miller. b 58. Oak Hill Th Coll 89. **d** 91 **p** 92. C Grove *Ox* 91-95; P-in-c Ashbury, Compton Beauchamp and Longcot w Fernham 95-99; C Kirkheaton *Wakef* 99-04. *34 Arlington Way, Huddersfield HD5 9TF* Tel (01484) 319592 E-mail kensingleton@hotmail.com

SINGLETON, Mary. *See* SINGLETON, Mrs Editha Mary

SINNAMON, Canon William Desmond. b 43. TCD BA65 MA80 MPhil95. CITC 66. **d** 66 **p** 67. C Seapatrick *D & D* 66-70; C Arm St Mark 70-74; V Choral Arm Cathl 73-74; I Ballinderry 75-80; I Dublin St Patr Cathl Gp 80-83; Preb Tipperkevin St Patr Cathl Dublin 80-83; I Taney *D & G* from 83; Can St Patr Cathl Dublin from 91; Treas 91-96; Chan from 96. *Taney Rectory, 6 Stoney Road, Dundrum, Dublin 14, Republic of Ireland* Tel (00353) (1) 298 4497 *or* tel and fax 298 5491 E-mail taney@dublin.anglican.org *or* parishoftaney@eircom.net

SINTON, Bernard. b 43. Leic Univ BSc66. Sarum & Wells Th Coll 87. **d** 90 **p** 91. NSM Horsham *Chich* from 90. *The Vicarage, Red Lane, Shipley, Horsham RH13 8PH* Tel (01403) 741238

SINTON, Mrs Patricia Ann. b 41. RGN62 SCM64. STETS 95. **d** 98 **p** 99. NSM Horsham *Chich* 98-01; P-in-c Shipley from 01. *The Vicarage, Red Lane, Shipley, Horsham RH13 8PH* Tel (01403) 741238 E-mail pa.sinton@tesco.net

SINTON, Vera May. b 43. Somerville Coll Ox BA65 MA69 Bris Univ CertEd66. Trin Coll Bris 79. **dss** 81 **d** 87 **p** 94. Broxbourne w Wormley *St Alb* 81-87; Hon Par Dn 87; Tutor All Nations Chr Coll Ware 81-87; Chapl St Hilda's Coll Ox 87-90; Tutor Wycliffe Hall Ox 87-98; NSM Ox St Clem 99-09; Tutor Ox Cen for Youth Min 01-04; rtd 09. *Rookhurst, West End, Gayle, Hawes DL8 3RT*

SIRCAR, Deepak Debchandan. b 46. Lon Hosp BDS72 Leeds Univ BA06. NOC 03. **d** 06 **p** 07. NSM Doncaster St Geo *Sheff* from 06. *5 Barnsdale Mews, Campsall, Doncaster DN6 9RH* Tel and fax (01302) 707170 Mobile 07768-830393 E-mail deesircar@btinternet.com

SIRMAN, Allan George. b 34. Lon Univ BA58. Oak Hill Th Coll 55. **d** 59 **p** 60. C Uphill *B & W* 59-61; C Morden *S'wark* 61-65; R Chadwell *Chelmsf* 65-75; V Wandsworth All SS *S'wark* 75-95; rtd 95; Perm to Offic *Ripon* from 95. *Marydale, Kingsley Drive, Middleham, Leyburn DL8 4PZ* Tel (01969) 624582 E-mail sirmans@freeuk.com

SIRR, The Very Revd John Maurice Glover. b 42. TCD BA63. CITC 65. **d** 65 **p** 66. C Belfast St Mary *Conn* 65-68; C Finaghy 68-69; I Drumcliffe w Lissadell and Munninane *K, E & A* 69-87; Preb Elphin Cathl 81-87; Dean Limerick and Ardfert *L & K* from 87; I Limerick City from 87; Chapl Limerick Pris from 87. *The Deanery, 7 Kilbane, Castletroy, Limerick, Republic of Ireland* Tel and fax (00353) (61) 338697 *or* tel 310293 Fax 315721 Mobile 87-254 1121 E-mail dean@limerick.anglican.org

SISTIG, Andreas. b 75. St Geo Th Sem Frankfurt 96. **d** 04 **p** 05. C Hillcrest S Africa 04-08; C Fleet *Guildf* from 08. *38 Oasthouse Drive, Fleet GU51 2UL* Tel (01252) 621139 Mobile 07595-542143 E-mail andreas@parishoffleet.org.uk

SISTIG (née STEWART), Mrs Jennifer Jane. b 71. Urban Univ Rome STB00. St Jos Th Inst Cedara BTh00. **d** 99 **p** 00. C Kirby-

Hilton S Africa 99-00; C Scottsville 00-01; R Woodlands-Montclair-cum-Yellowwood Park 01-05; R Hillcrest 05-08; NSM Fleet *Guildf* from 08. *38 Oasthouse Drive, Fleet GU51 2UL* Tel (01252) 621139 Mobile 07546-120844 E-mail jennifer@parishoffleet.org.uk

SITCH, Keith Frank. b 40. Ex Univ BA63 Lon Univ MA95. S'wark Ord Course 72. **d** 75 **p** 76. NSM Romford St Edw *Chelmsf* 75-78; NSM Kidbrooke St Jas *S'wark* from 78. *92 Kidbrooke Park Road, London SE3 0DX* Tel (020) 8856 3843

SITWELL, Mrs Mary Elizabeth. b 49. Brighton Coll of Educn DipEd71 Sussex Univ BEd72. **d** 03. NSM Bishopstone *Chich* 03-06; NSM Alfriston w Lullington, Litlington and W Dean from 06; Chapl Roedean Sch Brighton from 03. *49 Fitzgerald Avenue, Seaford BN25 1AZ* Tel (01323) 892424 E-mail isla.sitwell@btinternet.com

SIXSMITH, David. b 39. Lon Univ BD66. **d** 97 **p** 98. OLM Narborough w Narford *Nor* 97-99; OLM Pentney St Mary Magd w W Bilney 97-99; OLM Westacre 97-99; OLM Castleacre w Newton and Southacre 97-99; C Hunstanton St Mary w Ringstead Parva etc 99-01; P-in-c Foulsham w Hindolveston and Guestwick 01-06; P-in-c N Elmham w Billingford and Worthing 02-05; rtd 06; Perm to Offic *Nor* from 06. *Old Mill Cottage, Broadmeadow Common, Castle Acre, King's Lynn PE32 2BU* Tel (01760) 755703 *or* 577253

SIXTUS, Bernd (Bernard). b 68. German Armed Forces Univ BA(Ed)93 Hamburg Univ PhD02 Leeds Univ MA03. Coll of Resurr Mirfield 01. **d** 03 **p** 04. C Paris St Geo *Eur* 03-07; C Abergavenny St Mary w Llanwenarth Citra *Mon* from 07; C Abergavenny H Trin from 07. *Holy Trinity Vicarage, Baker Street, Abergavenny NP7 5BH* Tel (01873) 851062 E-mail frbernard@gmx.com

SIZER, Stephen Robert. b 53. Sussex Univ BA Ox Univ MTh94. Trin Coll Bris 80. **d** 83 **p** 84. C St Leonards St Leon *Chich* 83-86; C Guildf St Sav w Stoke-next-Guildford 86-89; R Stoke-next-Guildf 89-97; V Virginia Water from 97. *Christ Church Vicarage, Callow Hill, Virginia Water GU25 4LD* Tel and fax (01344) 842374 Mobile 07970-789549 E-mail stephen.sizer@btinternet.com *or* stephen@sizers.org

SKELDING, Mrs Hazel Betty. b 25. LGSM66 CertEd45. Gilmore Course 80. **dss** 83 **d** 87 **p** 94. Hinstock and Sambrook *Lich* 83-84; Asst Children's Adv RE 86-91; Hon Par Dn Alderbury Team *Sarum* 91-94; C 94-96; rtd 96; Perm to Offic *Sarum* 96-01 and *Truro* 01-06. *308 Grafton Road, Thames 3500, New Zealand* Tel (0064) (7) 868 3231

SKELLEY, Mrs Janice Ann. b 66. St Jo Coll Nottm 04. **d** 06 **p** 07. C Barnard Castle w Whorlton *Dur* 06-08; C Hedworth from 09. *134 Wenlock Road, South Shields NE34 9AL* E-mail jas66@hotmail.com

SKELTON, Beresford. b 52. St Chad's Coll Dur BA74. Chich Th Coll 74. **d** 76 **p** 77. CMP from 77; C Byker St Ant *Newc* 76-80; C Newc St Jo 80-82; Chapl Asst Newc Gen Hosp 80-81; Chapl Asst Freeman Hosp Newc 81-82; V Cresswell and Lynemouth *Newc* 82-88; P-in-c Millfield St Mary *Dur* 88-93; V from 93; P-in-c Bishopwearmouth Gd Shep from 04. *St Mary Magdalene's Vicarage, Wilson Street, Sunderland SR4 6HJ* Tel and fax 0191-565 6318

SKELTON, Dennis Michael. b 33. K Coll Lon BSc55. NEOC 76. **d** 79 **p** 80. NSM Pennywell St Thos and Grindon St Oswald CD *Dur* 79-84; V Heathercleugh 84-99; V St John in Weardale 84-99; V Westgate 84-99; rtd 99; Perm to Offic *Dur* from 99. *52 Vicarage Close, New Silksworth, Sunderland SR3 1JF* Tel 0191-523 7135

SKELTON, Canon Henry John Nugent. b 13. Linc Th Coll 37. **d** 40 **p** 41. C Grantham St Wulfram *Linc* 40-43; Chapl RAFVR 43-47; V Heckington w Howell *Linc* 47-56; V Holbeach 56-73; RD Elloe E 68-73; Can and Preb Linc Cathl 70-73; rtd 78; Perm to Offic *St D* from 78. *Lisand, Cosheston, Pembroke Dock SA72 4SB* Tel (01646) 682435

SKELTON, Melvyn Nicholas. b 38. St Pet Coll Ox BA61 MA65 Selw Coll Cam BA63 MA68. Ridley Hall Cam 62. **d** 64 **p** 65. C St Marychurch *Ex* 64-66; C Bury St Edmunds St Mary *St E* 66-69; Hon C 69-78; Lic to Offic from 78; rtd 03. *Milburn House, The Street, Moulton, Newmarket CB8 8RZ* Tel (01638) 750563 *or* 712243

SKELTON, Canon Pamela Dora. b 38. Hull Coll of Educn DipEd60. Edin Th Coll 80. **dss** 78 **d** 86 **p** 94. Edin St Barn 78-86; Dn-in-c 86-90; Dioc Youth Chapl 83-90; Min Edin Ch Ch 91-97; Chapl Lothian Primary Healthcare NHS Trust 91-06; Lic to Offic *Edin* from 06; Hon Can St Mary's Cathl from 00. *112 St Alban's Road, Edinburgh EH9 2PG* Tel 0131-667 1280 E-mail pdskelton@yahoo.com *or* pdskelton@blueyonder.co.uk

SKEOCH, Canon David Windsor. b 37. Ch Ch Ox BA58 MA62. Westcott Ho Cam 73. **d** 74 **p** 75. NSM Pimlico St Mary Graham-street *Lon* 74-79; Bp's Dom Chapl *Truro* 79-81; Bp's Chapl *Lon* 81-83; V Pimlico St Gabr 83-07; rtd 07; Can The Murray from 92; Perm to Offic *St E* from 07. *La Canonica, 81 Wilkinson Drive, Kesgrave, Ipswich IP5 2DS* Tel (01473) 612178

SKEPPER, Mrs Suzanne. b 63. Trin Coll Bris BA09. **d** 09. C Wotton St Mary *Glouc* from 09. *30 Simon Road, Longlevens,*

Gloucester GL2 0TP Tel (01452) 528065   Mobile 07981-429259
E-mail troppusrekrow@hotmail.com
SKETCHLEY, Edward Sydney. b 20. Qu Coll Birm. **d** 49 **p** 50. C
Bakewell *Derby* 49-53; PC Ridgeway 53-57; PC Abbey Dale
57-65; V Walsgrave on Sowe *Cov* 65-73; V Hound *Win* 73-90; rtd
90; Perm to Offic *Win* 90-05 and *Portsm* 02-05. *107A Lenthay
Road, Sherborne DT9 6AQ*
SKEVINGTON, Michael James. b 56. Natal Univ BA79.
St Paul's Coll Grahamstown. **d** 82 **p** 83. S Africa 82-88 and from
90; C Slough *Ox* 88-90. *PO Box 38088, Point, 4069 South Africa*
Tel (0027) (31) 337 7521 *or* 337 5573
SKIDMORE (née **CANNINGS), Karen Rachel.** b 75. Nottm
Univ BA96. Ridley Hall Cam 04. **d** 06 **p** 07. C Pitsmoor Ch Ch
Sheff from 06. *85 Malton Street, Sheffield S4 7EA* Tel 0114-272
2662   E-mail karen.skidmore@yahoo.co.uk
SKIDMORE, Michael Anthony. b 38. **d** 98 **p** 99. NSM Rainworth
and Blidworth *S'well* 98-00; P-in-c Basford St Leodegarius
00-05; P-in-c Willoughby-on-the-Wolds w Wysall and
Widmerpool 05-07; NSM Carlton-in-the-Willows from 07;
NSM Porchester from 07; NSM Woodthorpe from 07.
11 Graveney Gardens, Arnold, Nottingham NG5 6QW Tel
0115-926 0773   E-mail mike.skidmore@breathemail.net
SKIDMORE, Mrs Sheila Ivy. b 36. **d** 87 **p** 94. Hon Par Dn Leic
Resurr 87-91; Par Dn Clarendon Park St Jo w Knighton St Mich
91-94; TV 94-01; rtd 01; Perm to Offic *Leic* from 01. *15 School
Lane, Birstall, Leicester LE4 4EA* Tel 0116-267 3318
E-mail revd.sheila@theskidmores.f9.co.uk
SKILLEN, John Clifford Tainish. b 50. NUU BA72 MA82 TCD
BTh89 QUB DipEd73. CITC 86. **d** 89 **p** 90. C Bangor Abbey
D & D 89-92; I Kilwarlin Upper w Kilwarlin Lower 92-96; I
Finaghy *Conn* 96-09; Asst Ed *The Church of Ireland Gazette* from
99; Bp's Sen Dom Chapl from 08. *Address temp unknown*
SKILLINGS, Martyn Paul. b 46. St Chad's Coll Dur BA68. Linc
Th Coll 68. **d** 70 **p** 71. C Stanley *Liv* 70-72; C Warrington
St Elphin 72-75; Ind Chapl 75-76; V Surfleet *Linc* 88-92; V
Burton St Chad *Lich* 92-08; R Calton, Cauldon, Grindon,
Waterfall etc from 08. *The Vicarage, Waterfall Lane,
Waterhouses, Stoke-on-Trent ST10 3HT* Tel (01538) 308506
Mobile 07887-854525   E-mail paul_skillings@talktalk.net
SKILTON, The Ven Christopher John. b 55. Magd Coll Cam
BA76 MA80. Wycliffe Hall Ox 77. **d** 80 **p** 81. C Ealing St Mary
Lon 80-84; C New Borough and Leigh *Sarum* 84-88; TV St
Baddow *Chelmsf* 88-95; TR Sanderstead All SS *S'wark* 95-04;
P-in-c Sanderstead St Mary 02-04; RD Croydon S 00-04; Adn
Lambeth from 04; P-in-c Kennington St Mark from 08.
7 Hoadly Road, London SW16 1AE Tel (020) 8769 4384 *or* 8545
2440 Fax 8677 2854 *or* 8545 2441
E-mail christopher.skilton@southwark.anglican.org
SKILTON, Joseph Laurence. b 41. Univ of Wales TCert64
Murdoch Univ Aus BA90 Aus Pacific Coll MA93. St Mich Coll
Llan. **d** 70 **p** 71. C Bicester *Ox* 71-73; C Shrewsbury St Chad
Lich 73-76; V W Bromwich St Phil 76-80; Australia from 80; rtd
06. *11 Tillbrook Street, Glen Forrest WA 6071, Australia* Tel
(0061) (8) 9298 9454   E-mail pax@isage.net.au
SKINGLEY, Christopher George. b 49. K Coll Lon MA98. Oak
Hill Th Coll BA90 Qu Coll Birm. **d** 00 **p** 01. C Enfield St Jas *Lon*
00-03; V Ramsgate St Mark *Cant* from 03. *St Mark's Vicarage,
198 Margate Road, Ramsgate CT12 6AQ* Tel (01843) 581042
E-mail chris.skingley@btinternet.com
SKINNER, Arthur. b 38. **d** 97 **p** 98. NSM Selling w Throwley,
Sheldwich w Badlesmere etc *Cant* 97-08; rtd 08; Perm to Offic
Cant from 08. *Brucklay Bungalow, Ashford Road, Badlesmere,
Faversham ME13 0NZ* Tel (01233) 740666
E-mail askinner@lineone.net
✠**SKINNER, The Rt Revd Brian Antony.** b 39. Reading Univ
BSc60. Tyndale Hall Bris 66. **d** 67 **p** 68 **c** 77. C Woking St Pet
Guildf 67-70; Chile 70-86; Adn Valparaiso 76-77; Suff Bp
Valparaiso 77-86; C Chorleywood St Andr *St Alb* 87-96; V Iver
Ox 96-06; rtd 06. *10 Benton Drive, Chinnor OX39 4DP* Tel
(01844) 353504   E-mail skinnerofiver@go-plus.net
SKINNER, David Malcolm. b 26. CCC Cam BA55 MA59. Wells
Th Coll 55. **d** 57 **p** 58. C Bris Lockleaze St Mary Magd w St Fran
57-60; Sec C of E Radio and TV Coun 60-64; Sec Abps' Radio
and TV Coun 64-67; V Ston Easton w Farrington Gurney
B & W 67-70; rtd 70. Glasha, *Cromane, Killorglin, Co Kerry,
Republic of Ireland* Tel (00353) (66) 69149
SKINNER, Mrs Elaine Teresa (Terri). b 55. Bath Univ BSc78.
EMMTC 99. **d** 02 **p** 03. NSM Whitwick St Jo the Bapt *Leic*
02-05; NSM Thorpe Acre w Dishley from 05. *2 Mount Grace
Road, Loughborough LE11 4ER* Tel (01509) 843790   Mobile
07810-241381   E-mail terri.skinner@btopenworld.com
SKINNER, Graeme John. b 57. Southn Univ BSc79. Trin Coll
Bris BA86. **d** 86 **p** 87. C Bebington Ches 86-90; V Ashton-upon-
Mersey St Mary Magd 90-96; V Upton (Overchurch) from 06.
The Vicarage, 20 Church Road, Upton, Wirral CH49 6JZ Tel
0151-677 4810   E-mail graeme@stm-upton.org.uk
SKINNER, Mrs Jane Mary. b 59. Leeds Univ BA81. Cranmer
Hall Dur 82. **dss** 84 **d** 87 **p** 94. Chatham St Phil and St Jas *Roch*
84-87; Hon Par Dn Church Coniston *Carl* 87-91; Hon Par Dn

Torver 87-91; NSM Dalton-in-Furness 91-97; Chapl HM Pris
Haverigg 92-97; Chapl Carl Hosps NHS Trust 97-01; Chapl N
Cumbria Acute Hosps NHS Trust 01-02; TV Carl H Trin and
St Barn 98-02; Hon C W Swindon and the Lydiards *Bris* 02-09;
Chapl Swindon and Marlborough NHS Trust 03-09; NSM
Golden Cap Team *Sarum* from 09. *The Rectory, 5 George's Close,
Charmouth, Bridport DT6 6RU* Tel (01297) 560409
SKINNER, Mrs Jean. b 47. Univ of Northumbria at Newc BA03
RN68 RM70. NEOC 93. **d** 96 **p** 97. NSM Ch the King *Newc*
96-03; NSM Newc St Thos Prop Chpl from 03; NSM City Cen
Chapl 03-06; Dioc Child Protection Adv from 07. *32 Easedale
Avenue, Melton Park, Newcastle upon Tyne NE3 5TB* Tel
0191-236 3474   E-mail revjeanskinner@yahoo.com
SKINNER, Preb John Cedric. b 30. Bris Univ BA55. Tyndale
Hall Bris 55. **d** 57 **p** 58. C St Leonard *Ex* 57-62; Univ Sec IVF
62-68; V Guildf St Sav 68-76; R Stoke next Guildf St Jo 74-76; R
Guildf St Sav w Stoke-next-Guildford 76-84; R Ex St Leon w H
Trin 84-98; Chapl R W of England Sch for the Deaf 84-98; Preb
Ex Cathl 92-98; rtd 98; Perm to Offic *Ex* from 00. *386 Topsham
Road, Exeter EX2 6HE* Tel (01392) 876540
SKINNER, John Richard. b 45. NOC 84. **d** 87 **p** 88. C Allerton *Liv*
87-90; C Huyton St Mich 90-97; P-in-c Fairfield 97-03; rtd 03.
30 Duke Street, Formby, Liverpool L37 4AT Tel (01704) 874899
SKINNER, John Timothy. b 55. Linc Th Coll 79. **d** 81 **p** 82. C
Newton Aycliffe *Dur* 81-82; Perm to Offic *Newc* 95-01; Bermuda
from 01. *St John's Church, PO Box HM 1856, Hamilton HM
HX, Bermuda* Tel (001441) 292 6802
SKINNER, Leonard Harold. b 36. K Coll Lon BD62 AKC62.
d 63 **p** 64. C Hackney Wick St Mary of Eton w St Aug *Lon*
63-66; C Palmers Green St Jo 66-70; V Grange Park St Pet 70-86;
TV Hanley H Ev *Lich* 80-86; Chapl Sunderland Poly *Dur* 86-92;
Chapl Sunderland Univ 92-93; P-in-c Hebburn St Oswald 93-01;
rtd 01; Perm to Offic *Newc* from 01. *28 Brighton Grove, Whitley
Bay NE26 1QH* Tel 0191-251 4891
SKINNER, Maurice Wainwright. b 30. St Jo Coll Ox BA53
MA59 FRSC70. Ox NSM Course. **d** 86 **p** 87. NSM Furze Platt
Ox 86-94; NSM Hurley and Stubbings 94-00; rtd 00; Perm to
Offic *Ox* from 00. *133 Beverley Gardens, Maidenhead SL6 6ST*
Tel (01628) 624875
SKINNER, Michael Thomas. b 39. Open Univ BA88 BA90.
S'wark Ord Course 73. **d** 78 **p** 79. NSM Orpington St Andr *Roch*
78-82; P-in-c from 99; NSM Orpington All SS 82-99; Assoc Bp's
Officer for NSMs 90-98; Bp's Officer for NSMs from 98; Perm to
Offic *S'wark* 02-05. *The Vicarage, Anglesea Road, Orpington
BR5 4AN* Tel and fax (01689) 823775
E-mail michael.skinner@rochester.anglican.org
SKINNER, Mrs Nicola Jayne. b 70. Birm Univ BA92.
Cuddesdon Coll MTh. **d** 98 **p** 99. C Bartley Green *Birm* 98-01;
Assoc Min Aurora Trin Ch Canada 01-06; P-in-c King City All
SS from 06. *All Saints Church, 12935 Keele Street, King City ON
L4G 1R3, Canada* Tel (001) (905) 833 5432 Fax 833 2597
SKINNER, Peter William. b 47. Sarum & Wells Th Coll 85. **d** 87
p 88. C Latchford St Jas *Ches* 87-89; C Weymouth St Paul *Sarum*
89; Perm to Offic *Lon* 97-99; C Leic St Aid 99-01; TV Staveley
and Barrow Hill *Derby* 01-04; V Middlesbrough St Thos *York*
04-06; rtd 06. *5 Oakwood Court, Marton-in-Cleveland,
Middlesbrough TS7 8TA*
SKINNER, Philip Harold. b 30. **d** 97 **p** 98. OLM Tisbury *Sarum*
97-01; rtd 01; Perm to Offic *Sarum* 02-08. *Ladydown House,
Vicarage Road, Tisbury, Salisbury SP3 6HY* Tel (01747) 870394
SKINNER, Raymond Frederick. b 45. St Jo Coll Dur BA67 Dur
Univ MA93. Cranmer Hall Dur. **d** 70 **p** 71. C High Elswick
St Paul *Newc* 70-76; V Newbottle *Dur* 76-87; Ind Chapl 81-87;
RD Houghton 84-87; Oman 87-90; TR Morden *S'wark* from 90;
Asst RD Merton from 91. *The Rectory, London Road, Morden
SM4 5QT* Tel (020) 8648 3920 *or* 8658 0012
E-mail skinhicks@aol.com
SKINNER, Stephen John. b 52. Bris Univ BSc St Jo Coll Dur BA
Dur Univ MLitt AIA. Cranmer Hall Dur. **d** 83 **p** 84. C Chatham
St Phil and St Jas *Roch* 83-87; P-in-c Torver *Carl* 87-90; V 90-91;
P-in-c Church Coniston 87-90; V 90-91; V Dalton-in-Furness
91-97; TR Carl H Trin and St Barn 97-02; TR W Swindon and
the Lydiards *Bris* 02-09; TR Golden Cap Team *Sarum* from 09.
The Rectory, 5 George's Close, Charmouth, Bridport DT6 6RU
Tel (01297) 560409   E-mail sjmskinners@btinternet.com
SKINNER, Terri. *See* SKINNER, Mrs Elaine Teresa
SKIPPER, Kenneth Graham. b 34. St Aid Birkenhead 65. **d** 68
p 69. C Newland St Aug *York* 68-71; C Newby 71-74; V
Dormanstown 74-78; V Aldbrough, Mappleton w Goxhill and
Withernwick 79-89; R Londesborough 89-96; R Burnby 90-96;
R Nunburnholme and Warter 90-96; V Shiptonthorpe w Hayton
90-96; rtd 96. *18 Elder Crescent, Bowmore, Isle of Islay
PA43 7HU* Tel (01496) 810321   Mobile 07776-373057
E-mail kgsbow@onetel.net
SKIPPON, Kevin John. b 54. St Steph Ho Ox 78. **d** 81 **p** 82. C Gt
Yarmouth *Nor* 81-84; C Kingstanding St Luke *Birm* 84-86; V
Smethwick SS Steph and Mich 86-92; Chapl Derbyshire R
Infirmary 92-94; Chapl Derbyshire R Infirmary NHS Trust
94-98; Chapl S Derbyshire Acute Hosps NHS Trust 98-04;

Chapl Derby Hosps NHS Foundation Trust 04-08. *Address temp unknown*

SKIPWORTH, Nicola Rachael. b 72. Southn Inst BA95. Trin Coll Bris BA01. **d** 01 **p** 02. C Bassaleg *Mon* 01-05; TV High Wycombe *Ox* from 05. *St James's Vicarage, Plomer Hill, High Wycombe HP13 5NB* Tel (01494) 526896 Mobile 07725-106529 E-mail nicky.skipworth@btinternet.com

SKIRROW, Paul Richard. b 52. Hull Univ BA82 Ches Coll of HE MTh00. NOC 97. **d** 00 **p** 01. C St Luke in the City *Liv* 00-03; V Ditton St Mich w St Thos 03-07; Asst Dir CME 03-07; rtd 07. *1 Cap Martin, The Serpentine, Crosby, Liverpool L23 6TD* Tel 0151-924 6181 E-mail paulskirrow@googlemail.com

SKLIROS, Michael Peter. b 33. Clare Coll Cam BA57 MA62. Ridley Hall Cam 57. **d** 59 **p** 60. C Hornchurch St Andr *Chelmsf* 59-61; Asst Chapl Denstone Coll Uttoxeter 61-65; Chapl RAF 65-77; P-in-c Stowmarket *St E* 77-78; Lic to Offic 78-85; C Gt Finborough w Onehouse and Harleston 85-91; P-in-c 91; R Gt and Lt Bealings w Playford and Culpho 91-96; rtd 96; Hon Asst to Bp Brandon Canada from 03. *49 Almond Crescent, Brandon MB R7B 1A2, Canada* Tel (001) (204) 726 9144 E-mail pifont@westman.wave.ca

SKOYLES, John Alan. b 32. Breakspear Coll 50 Christleton Hall 53. **d** 58 **p** 59. In RC Ch 59-80; Soc worker 80-99; NSM The Hydneye *Chich* 99-00; C Kenton, Mamhead, Powderham, Cofton and Starcross *Ex* 00-01. *6 Greencroft, Trinity Place, Eastbourne BN21 3DA*

SKRINE, Charles Walter Douglas. b 75. Qu Coll Ox BA98. Oak Hill Th Coll BA03. **d** 03 **p** 04. C St Helen Bishopsgate w St Andr Undershaft etc *Lon* from 03. *64 Arbery Road, London E3 5DD* Tel (020) 8980 8596 *or* 7283 2231 E-mail charles@cwdskrine.freeserve.co.uk

SKUBLICS, Ernest. b 36. Sant' Anselmo Univ Rome STB62 Ottawa Univ MTh64 STL64 Nijmegen Univ DrTheol67. **d** 73 **p** 73. R Whitewood Canada 73-76; Chapl Manitoba Univ 76-77; Soc Worker 77-86; Registrar and Asst Prof Manitoba Univ 86-90; Assoc Dir Inst for Th Studies Seattle Univ USA 90-93; Dean Graduate Sch Mt Angel Sem Oregon 93-00; C Hawley H Trin *Guildf* 04-07; rtd 07. *Broadfield House, Dent, Sedbergh LA10 5TG* Tel (015396) 25296 E-mail eskublics1@freeuk.com

SKUCE, David. b 56. NUU BSc79 QUB PGCE80 TCD BTh89. CITC 87. **d** 89 **p** 90. C Templemore *D & R* 89-92; I Kilbarron w Rossnowlagh and Drumholm 92-99; I Urney w Sion Mills 99-06; Bp's Dom Chapl 94-06; I Maguiresbridge w Derrybrusk *Clogh* from 06. *The Rectory, Maguiresbridge, Enniskillen BT94 4PJ* Tel (028) 6772 1250

SLACK, Michael. b 53. St Jo Coll Dur BA74 Lon Univ PGCE79 RGN83. St Steph Ho Ox 74. **d** 76 **p** 77. C Wolverhampton St Steph *Lich* 76-77; NSM Bywell *Newc* 89-93; TV Cullercoats St Geo 93-98; TR 98-05. *8 Kittiwake Drive, Washington NE38 0DW* Tel 0191-416 6257

SLACK, Mrs Moira Elizabeth. b 52. Brunel Univ BTech74 Leeds Univ BA06. NOC 03. **d** 06 **p** 07. C Heaton Ch Ch *Man* 06-09; P-in-c Stretford All SS from 09. *The Rectory, 233 Barton Road, Stretford, Manchester M32 9RB* Tel 0161-865 1350 E-mail moslack@btinternet.com

SLADDEN, David. *See* SLADDEN, John David

SLADDEN, Duncan Julius Edward. b 25. K Coll Cam BA50 MA51. Cuddesdon Coll 51. **d** 53 **p** 54. C Huddersfield St Pet *Wakef* 53-55; C Reading St Mary V *Ox* 55-61; R Largs *Glas* 61-65; P-in-c Stevenage *St Alb* 65-70; R Johnstone *Glas* 70-76; Prayer Gp Adv Scottish Chs Renewal 76-81; Sec Scottish Episc Renewal Fellowship 81-84; R E Kilbride 85-90; rtd 90. *17 Bruce Avenue, Dunblane FK15 9JB* Tel (01786) 825520

SLADDEN, Canon John Cyril. b 20. Mert Coll Ox BA42 MA46 BD66. Wycliffe Hall Ox 46. **d** 48 **p** 49. C Oswestry St Oswald *Lich* 48-51; Tutor St Aid Birkenhead 51-53; R Todwick *Sheff* 53-59; V Lower Peover *Ches* 59-86; RD Knutsford 80-85; Hon Can Ches Cathl 80-86; rtd 86. *Rossa, Penmon, Beaumaris LL58 8SN* Tel (01248) 490207

SLADDEN, John David. b 49. RN Eng Coll Plymouth BSc74 St Edm Coll Cam MA86. Ridley Hall Cam 80. **d** 83 **p** 84. C St Bees *Carl* 83-85; Perm to Offic *Lich* 85-87; Miss Co-ord Down to Earth Evangelistic Trust 85-87; V Doncaster St Jas *Sheff* 87-94; Perm to Offic *Ely* from 07. *9 Teal Close, Chatteris PE16 6PR* Tel (01354) 694097

SLADE, Canon Adrian Barrie. b 47. K Alfred's Coll Win DipEd68. St Jo Coll Nottm BTh73 ALCD72. **d** 73 **p** 74. C Streatham Immanuel w St Anselm *S'wark* 73-76; C Chipping Barnet *St Alb* 76-78; C Chipping Barnet w Arkley 78-80; V Sundon 80-85; Soc Resp Officer *Glouc* from 86; Hon Can Glouc Cathl from 91. *38 Sydenham Villas Road, Cheltenham GL52 6DZ* Tel (01242) 253162 Fax 242672 E mail glossr@star.co uk

SLADE, Alfred Laurence. b 12. ACII. Roch Th Coll 67. **d** 69 **p** 70. NSM Cliftonville *Cant* 69-71; NSM Westgate St Jas 71-75; Perm to Offic *Sarum* 75-81 and *Cant* 81-93. *21 McKinlay Court, The Parade, Birchington CT7 9QG* Tel (01843) 46882

SLADE, Michael John. b 55. Trin Coll Bris 94. **d** 96 **p** 97. C Blagdon w Compton Martin and Ubley *B & W* 96-99; V

Winscombe and Sandford from 99; RD Locking 05-08. *The Vicarage, Winscombe Hill, Winscombe BS25 1DE* Tel (01934) 843164 E-mail michaeljohnslade@aol.com

SLADE, Canon William Clifford. b 24. St Jo Coll Dur BA47 MA53. **d** 49 **p** 50. C Northallerton w Deighton and Romanby *York* 49-52; C Eston 52-54; V Anlaby Common St Mark 54-60; V Brompton w Snainton 60-67; R Stokesley 67-71; V Felixkirk w Boltby and Kirby Knowle 71-82; Abp's Adv for Spiritual Direction 82-86; C Topcliffe w Dalton and Dishforth 82-86; Can and Preb York Minster 79-86; Perm to Offic from 86; rtd 86. *Bede House, Beck Lane, South Kilvington, Thirsk YO7 2NL* Tel (01845) 522915

SLATER, Mrs Ann. b 46. Somerville Coll Ox BA67 MA71. WMMTC 92. **d** 95 **p** 96. C Northampton St Benedict *Pet* 95-99; TV Daventry, Ashby St Ledgers, Braunston etc 99-05; R Heyford w Stowe Nine Churches and Flore etc from 05; RD Daventry from 08. *The Rectory, Church Lane, Nether Heyford, Northampton NN7 3LQ* Tel (01327) 342201 E-mail ann.slater@btinternet.com

SLATER, Christopher Richard. b 69. Oak Hill Th Coll BA08. **d** 08. C Rock Ferry *Ches* from 08; C Tranmere St Cath from 08. *21 Alpha Drive, Birkenhead CH42 1PH* Tel 0151-644 1018 Mobile 07899-807507 E-mail slater.cr@btinternet.com

SLATER, David. *See* SLATER, Canon Philip David

SLATER (née SAMMONS), Mrs Elizabeth Mary. b 71. RN94 RHV98. Wycliffe Hall Ox 03. **d** 05 **p** 06. C Stoke Gifford *Bris* 05-09; Perm to Offic from 09. *20 Railton Jones Close, Stoke Gifford, Bristol BS34 8BF* E-mail wizsammons@hotmail.com

SLATER, Ian Stuart. St Jo Coll Nottm. **d** 04 **p** 05. NSM Gt Horton *Bradf* from 04. *Stable Cottage, 5 The Drive, Denholme, Bradford BD13 4DY* Tel (01274) 831437 E-mail ianandjoan@slateri.freeserve.co.uk

SLATER, James Richard David. b 61. New Univ of Ulster BA83 TCD BTh89 Univ of Ulster MA92. CITC 86. **d** 89 **p** 90. C Clooney w Strathfoyle *D & R* 89-93; I Aghadowey w Kilrea 93-05; I Cumber Upper w Learmount from 05; Bp's Dom Chapl from 07. *248B Glenshane Road, Killaloo, Londonderry BT47 3SN* Tel (028) 7130 1724

SLATER, John Albert. b 25. Lon Univ BA52. Oak Hill Th Coll 47. **d** 52 **p** 53. C Everton Em *Liv* 52-55; V Kirkdale St Paul N Shore 55-61; V Bacup St Sav *Man* 61-70; V Blackpool St Thos *Blackb* 70-84; rtd 84; Perm to Offic *Blackb* 84-08. *18 Church Road, Thornton-Cleveleys FY5 2TZ* Tel (01253) 853330

SLATER, John Ralph. b 38. Kent Univ BA90. Linc Th Coll 71. **d** 73 **p** 74. C S Hackney St Mich w Haggerston St Paul *Lon* 73-74; C Leytonstone St Marg w St Columba *Chelmsf* 74-77; C Whitstable All SS w St Pet *Cant* 77-80; V Gt Ilford St Alb *Chelmsf* 80-83; V Clipstone *S'well* 83-87; rtd 87. *117 Canterbury Road, Westgate-on-Sea CT8 8NW* Tel (01227) 831593

SLATER, Mark Andrew. b 56. ARCS79 Imp Coll Lon BSc79. Ridley Hall Cam 87. **d** 89 **p** 90. C Northampton St Giles *Pet* 89-92; C Stopsley *St Alb* 92-93; C-in-c Bushmead CD 93-99; V St Alb St Luke from 99. *St Luke's Vicarage, 46 Cell Barnes Lane, St Albans AL1 5QJ* Tel (01727) 865399 Fax 865399 E-mail mark.slater@saint-lukes.co.uk

SLATER, The Ven Paul John. b 58. CCC Ox MA83 St Jo Coll Dur BA83. Cranmer Hall Dur 81. **d** 84 **p** 85. C Keighley St Andr *Bradf* 84-88; P-in-c Cullingworth and Dir Dioc Foundn Course 88-93; Bp's Personal Exec Asst 93-95; Warden of Readers 92-96; R Haworth 95-01; Bp's Officer for Min and Miss from 01; Adn Craven from 05. *Woodlands, Nethergyll Lane, Cononley, Keighley BD20 8PB* Tel (01535) 635113 E-mail paulj.slater@dial.pipex.com

SLATER, Canon Philip David. b 27. K Coll Lon 58. **d** 60 **p** 61. C Havant *Portsm* 60-67; C Leigh Park 68-69; Hants Co RE Adv 69-74; Gosport and Fareham RE Adv 74-82; Hon C Bishop's Waltham 76-82; V Bulford, Figheldean and Milston *Sarum* 82-93; RD Avon 89-95; Can and Preb Sarum Cathl 91-95; V Avon Valley 93-95; rtd 95; V of Close Sarum Cathl 95-02; Chapl Godolphin Sch 95-04. *102 Coombe Road, Salisbury SP2 8BD* Tel (01722) 332529 E-mail voc@salcath.co.uk

SLATER, Robert Adrian. b 48. St Jo Coll Nottm 76. **d** 79 **p** 80. C Bedworth *Cov* 79-82; TV Billericay and Lt Burstead *Chelmsf* 82-88; V Rounds Green *Birm* 88-94; rtd 07. *11 Lewis Road, Birmingham B30 2SU* Tel 0121-689 2721 E-mail robslater@freeuk.com

SLATER, Thomas Ernest. b 37. Chelsea Coll Lon TCert60 Lon Univ BD71. ALCD66. **d** 67 **p** 68. C Bootle Ch Ch *Liv* 67-72; C Stapleford *S'well* 72-75; Supt Tower Hamlets Miss 75-77; Hon C Stepney St Pet w St Benet *Lon* 78-79; Asst Chapl The Lon Hosp (Whitechapel) 79-83; Chapl 83-89; NSM Poplar *Lon* 89-92 and 94-02; Perm to Offic 92-94; rtd 02. *11 Elgin House, Cordelia Street, London E14 6EG* Tel (020) 7987 4504

SLATER, Victoria Ruth. b 59. Hertf Coll Ox BA82 MA87 Selw Coll Cam BA89 MA94. Westcott Ho Cam 88. **d** 89 **p** 94. Chapl Asst Man R Infirmary 89-90; Chapl 90-94; Chapl St Mary's Hosp Man 90-94; Chapl Ox Radcliffe Hosp NHS Trust 94-97; Chapl Sir Michael Sobell Ho Palliative Care Unit 97-05; Asst

Soc Resp Adv *Ox* from 05. *Diocesan Church House, North Hinksey Lane, Botley, Oxford OX2 0NB* Tel (01865) 208214

SLATER, Preb William Edward. b 51. Aston Tr Scheme 85 Oak Hill Th Coll 87. **d** 89 **p** 90. C Balderstone *Man* 89-94; V Newchapel *Lich* from 94; RD Stoke N 99-08; Preb Lich Cathl from 08. *The Vicarage, 32 Pennyfield Road, Newchapel, Stoke-on-Trent ST7 4PN* Tel (01782) 782837
E-mail willslater@tinyworld.co.uk

SLATOR, Edward Douglas Humphreys. b 18. TCD BA41 MA47 Hull Univ BPhil75. **d** 43 **p** 44. C Taney *D & G* 43-46; Chapl St Columba's Coll Dub 46-60; I Killea *C & O* 60-73; C Taney *D & G* 74-80; P-in-c Rathmolyon w Castlerickard, Rathcore and Agher *M & K* 80-87; rtd 87; PV Ch Ch Cathl Dublin from 93. *31 St John's, Park Avenue, Dublin 4, Republic of Ireland* Tel (00353) (1) 283 9395

SLATTER, Barrie John. b 44. Nottm Univ BSc66 FRICS97. Dioc OLM tr scheme 97. **d** 00 **p** 01. OLM Hundred River *St E* 00-03; C Alde River 03-06; R from 06. *The Rectory, Stratford St Andrew, Saxmundham IP17 1LJ* Tel (01728) 603180 Mobile 07802-924738 E-mail rectory@barrieslatter.fsnet.co.uk

SLATTERY, Maurice Michael. b 43. Southlands Coll Lon TCert73 Lon Inst of Educn BEd74. S'wark Ord Course 91. **d** 94 **p** 95. NSM Malden St Jas *S'wark* 94-97; NSM Niton, Whitwell and St Lawrence *Portsm* 97-99; NSM Selsdon St Jo w St Fran *S'wark* 99-03; Perm to Offic *Portsm* 03-04 and 07-08; P-in-c St Lawrence 04-06; NSM Clayton w Keymer *Chich* from 08. *11 The Spinney, Hassocks BN6 8EJ* Tel (01273) 846529 *or* 843023
E-mail maurice@slattery6800.fsnet.com

SLAUGHTER, Clive Patrick. b 36. St Paul's Coll Grahamstown. **d** 77 **p** 78. S Africa 77-87; R Thorley w Bishop's Stortford H Trin *St Alb* 87-90; R Thorley 90-01; RD Bishop's Stortford 96-01; rtd 01; Perm to Offic *St Alb* 01-03; P-in-c Much Hadham 03-04; P-in-c Braughing w Furneux Pelham and Stocking Pelham 04-05. *53 High Street, Hunsdon, Ware SG12 8QB* Tel (01279) 844955 E-mail clive.slaughter@virgin.net

SLAUGHTER, Canon Maurice Basil. b 20. Leeds Univ BA42. Coll of Resurr Mirfield 42. **d** 44 **p** 45. C Kingswinford St Mary *Lich* 44-46; C Roch St Nic w St Clem 46-47; C Luton Ch Ch *St Alb* 47-50; V Birm St Marg Ladywood 50-52; V Newsome *Wakef* 52-60; V Queensbury *Bradf* 60-63; V Skipton Ch Ch 63-78; Hon Can Bradf Cathl 67-85; RD Skipton 73-82; P-in-c Bolton Abbey 78-85; P-in-c Rylstone 78-85; P-in-c Arncliffe w Halton Gill 79-82; rtd 85; Perm to Offic *Bradf* 85-99; *Wakef* 85-96; *Ely* 96-00. *Hawkhill House, 234 North Deeside Road, Milltimber AB13 0DQ* Tel (01224) 734609

SLEDGE, The Ven Richard Kitson. b 30. Peterho Cam BA52 MA57. Ridley Hall Cam 52. **d** 54 **p** 55. C Compton Gifford *Ex* 54-57; C Ex St Martin, St Steph, St Laur etc 57-63; V Dronfield *Derby* 63-76; TR 76-78; RD Chesterfield 72-78; Adn Huntingdon *Ely* 78-96; R Hemingford Abbots 78-89; Hon Can Ely Cathl 78-99; rtd 96; Bp's Dom Chapl *Ely* 96-99; Retired Clergy Officer 98-07; Asst (Huntingdon/Pet Area) from 07; Perm to Offic from 99. *7 Budge Close, Brampton, Huntingdon PE29 4PL* Tel (01480) 380284 *or* (01353) 662749 Fax (01480) 437789

SLEDGE, Timothy Charles Kitson. b 64. Coll of Ripon & York St Jo BA87 York Univ MA88. Trin Coll Bris. **d** 95 **p** 96. C Huddersfield St Thos *Wakef* 95-98; V Luddenden w Luddenden Foot 98-03; P-in-c Sowerby 02-03; Dioc Miss Enabler *Pet* 03-08; V Romsey *Win* from 08. *The Vicarage, Church Lane, Romsey SO51 8EP* Tel (01794) 513125
E-mail vicarofromsey@hotmail.co.uk

SLEE, The Very Revd Colin Bruce. b 45. OBE01. K Coll Lon BD69 AKC69 FKC01. St Aug Coll Cant 69. **d** 70 **p** 71. C Nor Heartsease St Fran 70-73; C Cambridge St Mary w St Mich *Ely* 73-76; Chapl Girton Coll Cam 73-76; Tutor and Chapl K Coll Lon 76-82; Can Res and Sub-Dean St Alb 82-94; Provost S'wark 94-00; Dean S'wark from 00; Hon Lect Harvard Div Sch from 01. *The Provost's Lodging, 51 Bankside, London SE1 9JE* Tel (020) 7928 6414 *or* 7367 6731 Fax 7367 6725
E-mail colin.slee@southwark.anglican.org

SLEE, John Graham. b 51. Brunel Univ BTech73. Oak Hill Th Coll 85. **d** 87 **p** 88. C St Columb Minor and St Colan *Truro* 87-91; R St Mawgan w St Ervan and St Eval 91-02; RD Pydar 93-95; P-in-c St Just-in-Roseland and St Mawes 02-07; rtd 07; Perm to Offic from 08. *Oaklea, Manor Road, Great Bourton, Banbury OX17 1QP* E-mail john@nbepiphany.co.uk

SLEEMAN, Matthew Timothy. b 68. St Cath Coll Cam BA90 MA95 PhD96 K Coll Lon PhD07. Wycliffe Hall Ox BA97 MA07. **d** 98 **p** 99. C Eynsham and Cassington *Ox* 98-02; Perm to Offic *Lon* 03-06 and *St Alb* from 03; Lect Oak Hill Th Coll from 06. *Oak Hill College, Chase Side, London N14 4PS* Tel (020) 8449 0467

SLEGG, John Edward. b 36. St Pet Coll Ox BA62 MA66. Ridley Hall Cam 62. **d** 64 **p** 65. C Perranzabuloe *Truro* 64-66; CF 66-86; V Lyminster and Poling *Chich* 86-05; rtd 06. *20 Tregarrick Close, Helston TR13 8YA* Tel (01326) 560272

SLEIGHT, Gordon Frederick. b 47. AKC69. St Aug Coll Cant 69. **d** 70 **p** 71. C Boston *Linc* 70-74; P-in-c Louth St Mich and

Stewton 74; TV Louth 74-81; V Crosby 81-95; P-in-c Nettleham 95-97; V 97-05; RD Lawres 04-05; rtd 05; Lic to Offic *Mor* from 05. *Elderbank, Stoer, Lochinver, Lairg IV27 4JE* Tel (01571) 855207 E-mail gordon@gsleight.freeserve.co.uk

SLENNETT, Mrs Jane Alison. b 57. St Mich Coll Llan. **d** 08. NSM Aberavon *Llan* from 08. *42 Carlton Place, Porthcawl CF36 3ET* Tel (01656) 784840
E-mail deacon@parishofaberavon.org

SLIM, David Albert. b 49. Westhill Coll Birm CertEd72. Linc Th Coll 90. **d** 90 **p** 91. C Walmley *Birm* 90-93; R Marchwiel and Isycoed *St As* 93-03; TV Wrexham 03-08; Chapl Ellesmere Coll from 08. *The Shippon, Ellesmere College, Ellesmere SY12 9BE* Tel (01691) 622380

SLIPPER, Charles Callan. b 55. Lanc Univ BA77 PhD84. S Dios Minl Tr Scheme 91. **d** 93 **p** 94. Focolare Movement from 77; NSM N Acton St Gabr *Lon* 93-96. *38 Audley Road, London W5 3ET* Tel (020) 8991 2022 *or* 8354 0763 Fax 8453 1621
E-mail callan@onetel.com

SLIPPER, Robert James. b 64. St Jo Coll Cam BA87 MA91. Wycliffe Hall Ox BA92. **d** 92 **p** 93. C Southgate *Chich* 92-95; C Stoughton *Guildf* 95-00; V Terrington St Clement *Ely* from 00. *The Vicarage, 27 Sutton Road, Terrington St Clement, King's Lynn PE34 4PQ* Tel (01553) 828430
E-mail robert@slipper.fsnet.co.uk

SLOAN, William. b 49. Lanc Univ CertEd78 BEd79. CBDTI 04. **d** 07 **p** 08. NSM Croston and Bretherton *Blackb* from 07. *5 Red House Lane, Eccleston, Chorley PR7 5RH* Tel (01257) 453665 Mobile 07721-923001 E-mail bill_sloan29@hotmail.com

SLOANE, Niall James. b 81. TCD BA03. CITC 03. **d** 05 **p** 06. C Agherton *Conn* 05-07; C Taney *D & G* from 07. *Church Lodge, 21 Taney Road, Dundrum, Dublin 14, Republic of Ireland* Tel (00353) (1) 295 1895 E-mail curate.taney@dublin.anglican.org

SLOGGETT, Donald George. b 49. Trin Coll Bris 81. **d** 83 **p** 84. C Horfield H Trin *Bris* 83-86; C Highworth w Sevenhampton and Inglesham etc 86-88; P-in-c Upavon w Rushall *Sarum* 88-90; R Upavon w Rushall and Charlton 90-01; R Stoulton w Drake's Broughton and Pirton etc *Worc* from 01. *The Rectory, Manor Farm, Stoulton, Worcester WR7 4RS* Tel (01905) 840528
E-mail donsloggett@zetnet.co.uk

SLOW, Leslie John. b 47. Liv Univ BSc68 MSc69. NOC 77. **d** 80 **p** 81. NSM Gt Horton *Bradf* 80-07; Perm to Offic *York* from 08. *21 Mile End Park, Pocklington, York YO42 2TH* Tel (01759) 303888

SLUMAN, Richard Geoffrey Davies. b 34. St Jo Coll Ox BA68 MA68. Sarum Th Coll 68. **d** 70 **p** 71. C Gt Yarmouth *Nor* 70-73; V Churchdown *Glouc* 73-82; P-in-c Blockley w Aston Magna 82-83; V Blockley w Aston Magna and Bourton on the Hill 83-94; rtd 94; Perm to Offic *Cov* from 94. *21 Manor Farm Road, Tredington, Shipston-on-Stour CV36 4NZ* Tel (01608) 662317

SLY, Canon Christopher John. b 34. Selw Coll Cam BA58 MA62. Wycliffe Hall Ox. **d** 60 **p** 61. C Buckhurst Hill *Chelmsf* 60-64; V Berechurch 64-75; V Southend St Sav Westcliff 75-87; R Wickham Bishops w Lt Braxted 87-99; RD Witham 87-96; Hon Can Chelmsf Cathl 93-99; rtd 99. *Ludlow Cottage, Church Lane, Little Leighs, Chelmsford CM3 1PQ* Tel (01245) 361489

SLYFIELD, John David. b 32. TD67. Roch Th Coll 66. **d** 68 **p** 69. C St Mary in the Marsh *Cant* 68-71; P-in-c Steeple Claydon *Ox* 71-76; P-in-c Middle w E Claydon 71-76; RD Claydon 73-78; R The Claydons 76-78; V S Westoe *Dur* 78-82; V Tideswell *Derby* 82-92; RD Buxton 84-91; rtd 92; Perm to Offic *Derby* 92-02 and from 06; P-in-c Beeley and Edensor 02-06. *Stile Close, Main Road, Taddington, Buxton SK17 9TR* Tel (01298) 85507

SMAIL, Richard Charles. b 57. CCC Ox BA80 MA83. Ox Min Course 90. **d** 93 **p** 95. NSM Keble Coll Ox 93-96; Chapl, Fell and Lect BNC Ox 97-02; Perm to Offic *Ox* 02-05; P-in-c Rousham from 05. *Address temp unknown*
E-mail richardsmail@supanet.com

SMAIL, Canon Thomas Allan. b 28. Glas Univ MA49 Edin Univ BD52. **d** 79 **p** 79. Vice-Prin St Jo Coll Nottm 80-85; TR Sanderstead All SS *S'wark* 85-94; Hon Can S'wark Cathl 91-94; rtd 94; Perm to Offic *S'wark* from 94. *The College of St Barnabas, Blackberry Lane, Lingfield RH7 6NJ* Tel (01342) 872879 E-mail tasmail@blueyonder.co.uk

SMAILES, Ian Collingwood. b 46. Brighton Poly BSc71. NTMTC BA07. **d** 07 **p** 08. NSM Laleham *Lon* from 07. *Gadebridge House, 211 Thames Side, Staines TW18 1UF* Tel (01784) 461195

SMALE, Frederick Ronald. b 37. K Coll Lon BD60 AKC60. **d** 61 **p** 62. C Bearsted *Cant* 61-64; C Fishponds St Mary *Bris* 64-69; V Hartlip *Cant* 69-71; P-in-c Stockbury w Bicknor and Huckinge 69-71; V Hartlip w Stockbury 71-75; R River 75-85; V Birchington w Acol and Minnis Bay 85-00; rtd 00; Perm to Offic *Cant* from 01. *28 Margate Road, Broomfield, Herne Bay CT6 7BL* Tel (01227) 283880

SMALE, Ian Keith. b 53. Wycliffe Hall Ox 98. **d** 00 **p** 01. C Overton w Laverstoke and Freefolk *Win* 00-04; P-in-c E Dean w Friston and Jevington *Chich* 04-06; R 06-08; P-in-c Overton w Laverstoke and Freefolk *Win* from 08. *The Rectory, 54 Lordshill*

Gardens, Overton, Basingstoke RG25 3EW Tel (01256) 770207
E-mail iansue.smale@btinternet.co.uk

SMALE, Ian Stuart. b 49. **d** 07. NSM Chich Cathl from 07.
65 Stockbridge Road, Chichester PO19 8QE Tel 07973-747694
(mobile)

SMALL, David Binney. b 39. Brasted Th Coll 61 Westcott Ho
Cam 63. **d** 65 **p** 66. C Milton *Portsm* 65-69; CF 69-92; R
Wickwar w Rangeworthy *Glouc* 92-97; RD Hawkesbury 94-97;
rtd 97; Perm to Offic *Glouc* from 97; Sub Chapl HM Pris Glouc
98-01. *16 Wotton Road, Charfield, Wotton-under-Edge
GL12 8TP* Tel and fax (01454) 261746

SMALL, Gordon Frederick. b 41. St Jo Coll Nottm 77. **d** 79 **p** 80.
C Belper *Derby* 79-84; NSM Matlock Bath 90-91; C Ripley
91-93; TV Bucknall and Bagnall *Lich* 93-98; Assoc P Deal St
Leon w St Rich and Sholden etc *Cant* 98-06; rtd 06. *10 Elmer
Close, Malmesbury SN16 9UE* Tel (01666) 823722
E-mail gordon.small1@btopenworld.com

SMALL, Marcus Jonathan. b 67. Univ of Wales (Ban) BD94.
Ripon Coll Cuddesdon 94. **d** 96 **p** 97. C Moseley St Mary *Birm*
96-99; TV Wenlock *Heref* 99-05; R Eardisley w Bollingham,
Willersley, Brilley etc from 05. *Church House, Church Road,
Eardisley, Hereford HR3 6NN* Tel (01544) 327440
E-mail marcus@flying-goose.freeserve.co.uk

SMALL, Mrs Shirley Maureen. b 45. WEMTC. **d** 09. NSM
Pontesbury I and II *Heref* from 09. *Nills Farm House, Habberley
Road, Pontesbury, Shrewsbury SY5 0TN* Tel (01743) 791885

SMALL, Simon William. b 57. Cuddesdon Coll. **d** 98 **p** 99. C
Kidderminster St Mary and All SS w Trimpley etc *Worc* 98-01;
Chapl to Bp Dudley 01-07; Perm to Offic from 08. *5 The
Armoury, Glastonbury BA6 9EN* Tel (01458) 835503
E-mail info@simonsmall.info

SMALLDON, Canon Keith. b 48. Open Univ BA76 Newc Univ
MA94. St Mich Coll Llan. **d** 71 **p** 72. C Cwmbran *Mon* 71-73; C
Chepstow 73-75; Dioc Youth Adv *Bradf* 75-79; P-in-c Woolfold
Man 82-85; Dioc Youth and Community Officer 82-90; P-in-c
Thursby *Carl* 90-94; Dir of Clergy Tr 90-94; TR Daventry,
Ashby St Ledgers, Braunston etc *Pet* 94-98; Chapl Danetre Hosp
94-98; TR Llantwit Major 98-03; Can Res Brecon Cathl from 03;
Dioc Dir of Min from 03; P-in-c Swansea St Barn from 08.
St Barnabas' Vicarage, 57 Sketty Road, Swansea SA2 0EN Tel
(01792) 299884 E-mail keithsmalldon@btinternet.com

SMALLEY, The Very Revd Stephen Stewart. b 31. Jes Coll Cam
BA55 MA58 PhD79. Eden Th Sem (USA) BD57 Ridley Hall
Cam. **d** 58 **p** 59. C Portman Square St Paul *Lon* 58-60; Chapl
Peterho Cam 60-63; Dean 62-63; Lect RS Ibadan Univ Nigeria
63-69; Lect Th Man Univ 70-77; Can Res and Prec Cov Cathl
77-87; Vice-Provost 86-87; Dean Ches 87-01; rtd 01; Perm to
Offic *Glouc* from 02. *The Old Hall, The Folly, Longborough,
Moreton-in-Marsh GL56 0QS* Tel (01451) 830238
E-mail stephen@sssss.fsworld.co.uk

SMALLMAN, Miss Margaret Anne. b 43. Hull Univ BSc64 Bris
Univ CertEd65. St Jo Coll Nottm. **dss** 83 **d** 87 **p** 94. Bromsgrove
St Jo *Worc* 83-88; Par Dn 87-88; Par Dn Stoke Prior, Wychbold
and Upton Warren 88-90; TD Tettenhall Wood *Lich* 91-94; TV
94-99; P-in-c W Bromwich H Trin 99-08; C W Bromwich Gd
Shep w St Jo 99-08; RD W Bromwich 04-08; rtd 08; Perm to
Offic *Lich* 08-09; Hon C Wellington All SS w Eyton from 09.
10 St Agatha's Close, Telford TF1 3QP Tel (01952) 253643
E-mail mas@msmallman.fsnet.co.uk

SMALLMAN, Mrs Wilhelmina Tokcumboh. b 56. Cen Sch
Speech & Drama BEd88 Middx Univ BA06. NTMTC 03. **d** 06
p 08. C S Harrow St Paul *Lon* 06-07; C Gt Stanmore from 07.
St John's House, 16 The Chase, Stanmore HA7 3RY Tel (020)
8954 0455 E-mail minaexp@hotmail.com

SMALLS, Peter Harry. b 34. FCCA. **d** 97 **p** 98. OLM
Narborough w Narford *Nor* 97-99; OLM Pentney St Mary
Magd w W Bilney 97-99; OLM Castle Acre w Newton and
Southacre 97-99; OLM Westacre 97-99; OLM Narborough w
Narford and Pentney 99-02; Perm to Offic *Nor* from 03 and *St E*
from 07. *Windward, Drapers Lane, Ditchingham, Bungay
NR35 2JW* Tel (01986) 894667
E-mail peter@smalls6740.freeserve.co.uk

SMALLWOOD, Simon Laurence. b 58. St Jo Coll Dur BSc80.
Cranmer Hall Dur 89. **d** 92 **p** 93. C Stapenhill w Cauldwell *Derby*
92-96; TV Dagenham *Chelmsf* 96-03; V Becontree St Geo from
03. *The Vicarage, 86 Rogers Road, Dagenham RM10 8JX* Tel
(020) 8593 2760 E-mail thesmallies@ntlworld.com

SMART, Barry Anthony Ignatius. b 57. Lanc Univ BEd79.
St Steph Ho Ox 85. **d** 88 **p** 89. C Wantage *Ox* 88-91; C Abingdon
91-93; TV 93-95; C Princes Risborough w Ilmer 95-97; C
Kingstanding St Luke *Birm* 97-00; V Small Heath 00-09; Chapl
Compton Hospice from 09. *Chaplain's Office, Compton Hospice,
4 Compton Road West, Wolverhampton WV3 9DH* Tel
08452-255497

SMART, Beryl. b 33. Sheff Univ BSc55 FCMI83. **d** 01 **p** 02. OLM
Newchurch w Croft *Liv* from 01. *41 Culcheth Hall Drive,
Culcheth, Warrington WA3 4PT* Tel (01925) 762655

SMART, Mrs Carol. b 45. SSF SRN67. S Dios Minl Tr Scheme
89. **d** 92 **p** 94. Chapl St Mary's Hosp NHS Trust 92-99; NSM

Shorwell w Kingston *Portsm* 99-02; NSM Gatcombe 92-02;
NSM Chale 92-02; Perm to Offic from 02. *20 Sydney Close,
Shide, Newport PO30 1YG* Tel (01983) 526242
E-mail revcarolsmart@tiscali.co.uk

SMART, Clifford Edward James. b 28. Kelham Th Coll 48. **d** 53
p 54. C Blackb St Pet 53-56; Korea 56-65 and 66-93; C Birm
St Aid Small Heath 65-66; rtd 93. *6045 Glennaire Drive, St Louis
MO 63129-4761, USA* Tel (001) (314) 846 5927

SMART, Harry Gavin. b 67. St D Coll Lamp BA90. Westcott Ho
Cam 90. **d** 94 **p** 95. C Thirsk *York* 94-97; C Sheff St Leon
Norwood 97-99; Mental Health Chapl Sheff Care Trust 99-06;
Chapl Team Ldr Lincs Partnership NHS Trust from 07.
*Lincolnshire Partnership NHS Trust, Cross O'Cliff, Bracebridge
Heath, Lincoln LN4 2HN* Tel (01522) 513355

SMART, Canon Haydn Christopher. b 38. Wells Th Coll 66. **d** 69
p 70. C Hillmorton *Cov* 69-72; C Duston *Pet* 72-75; V Woodford
Halse 75-79; V Woodford Halse w Eydon 79-82; V
Wellingborough All SS 82-92; RD Wellingborough 87-92; V
Longthorpe 92-03; Can Pet Cathl 92-03; RD Pet 96-01; rtd 03;
P-in-c Madeira *Eur* 03-06; Perm to Offic *Pet* from 06; Chapl to
Retired Clergy and Clergy Widows' Officer from 08. *4 Silvester
Road, Castor, Peterborough PE5 7BA* Tel (01733) 380460

SMART, Mrs Hilary Jean. b 42. SOAS Lon BA63. EMMTC 85.
d 88 **p** 94. Par Dn Walsall Pleck and Bescot *Lich* 88-94; TV Sheff
Manor 94-02; Bp's Ecum Officer 94-02; rtd 02; Chapl Compton
Hospice 02-06. *77 Denton Drive, West Bridgford, Nottingham
NG2 7FS* Tel 0115-923 1097

SMART, John Francis. b 36. Keble Coll Ox BA59 MA69.
Cuddesdon Coll 59. **d** 61 **p** 66. C Cannock *Lich* 61-63; Hon C Gt
Wyrley 63-66; C Wednesfield St Thos 66-70; V Brereton 70-85; R
E Clevedon and Walton w Weston w Clapton *B & W* 85-02;
Chapl Southmead Health Services NHS Trust 85-99; Chapl N
Bris NHS Trust 99-02; rtd 02. *Sunnymead, Ford Cross, South
Zeal, Okehampton EX20 2JL* Tel (01837) 840233
E-mail andrsmart@tiscali.co.uk

SMART, Neil Robert. b 61. Bris Univ BVSc84. Ridley Hall Cam
01. **d** 03 **p** 04. C Shirley *Win* 03-07; P-in-c Brockenhurst from 07;
P-in-c Boldre w S Baddesley from 09. *The Vicarage, Meerut
Road, Brockenhurst SO42 7TD* Tel (01590) 623309
E-mail somesmarts@btopenworld.com

SMART, Richard Henry. b 23. Lon Univ BA51. Oak Hill Th Coll.
d 53 **p** 54. C Bedworth *Cov* 53-56; C New Malden and Coombe
S'wark 56-59; V Hanley Road St Sav w St Paul *Lon* 59-71; V
Plumstead All SS *S'wark* 71-88; rtd 88; Perm to Offic *Chich* from
88. *2 Annington Road, Eastbourne BN22 8NG* Tel (01323)
726850

SMEATON, William Brian Alexander. b 37. CITC 69. **d** 71 **p** 72.
C Belfast St Luke *Conn* 71-81; I Tullyaughnish w Kilmacrennan
and Killygarvan *D & R* 81-02; Bp's Dom Chapl 87-02; Can
Raphoe Cathl 88-02; Dioc Radio Officer 90-02; rtd 02. *Bearna
Ghaoithe, Drumcavney, Trentagh, Letterkenny, Co Donegal,
Republic of Ireland* Tel (0353) 74-913 7917 (mobile)
E-mail smeaton@indigo.ie

SMEDLEY, Christopher John. b 62. Trent Poly BSc90. St Jo Coll
Nottm MA98. **d** 98 **p** 99. C Cotmanhay *Derby* 98-02; R Wilne
and Draycott w Breaston from 02. *The Rectory, 68 Risley Lane,
Breaston, Derby DE72 3AU* Tel (01332) 872242

SMEDLEY, Paul Mark. b 59. Bris Univ BA80 Lanc Univ MA81.
S Dios Minl Tr Scheme 89. **d** 92 **p** 93. NSM Acton St Mary *Lon*
92-08; Perm to Offic from 08. *12 Baldwyn Gardens, London
W3 6HH* Tel (020) 8993 5527 *or* 8932 8497 Fax 8932 8315
E-mail paul@planningforum.co.uk

SMEETON (née GRESHAM), Mrs Karen Louise. b 75. Hull
Univ LLB96. Ripon Coll Cuddesdon BA01. **d** 02 **p** 03. C
Leesfield *Man* 02-05; V Hamer from 05. *All Saints' Vicarage, 128
Foxholes Road, Rochdale OL12 0EF* Tel and fax (01706) 355591

SMEETON, Nicholas Guy. b 74. Trin Hall Cam MA99. Ripon
Coll Cuddesdon BA03. **d** 04 **p** 05. C Ashton Ch Ch *Man* 04-07;
P-in-c Oldham St Steph and All Martyrs from 07; TV Oldham
from 07. *All Saints' Vicarage, 128 Foxholes Road, Rochdale
OL12 0EF* Tel and fax (01706) 355591
E-mail nick@smeeton100.freeserve.co.uk

SMEJKAL, Yenda Marcel. b 68. Van Mildert Coll Dur BA97.
Coll of Resurr Mirfield 97. **d** 99 **p** 00. C S Shields All SS *Dur*
99-03; TV N Wearside 03-04; P-in-c Sundon *St Alb* from 04.
St Mary's Vicarage, 1 Selina Close, Luton LU3 3AW Tel (01582)
583076 E-mail yenda.smejkal@virgin.net

SMETHAM, Abigail Laura. b 75. K Coll Lon BMus97 Clare Coll
Cam BA05. Westcott Ho Cam 03. **d** 06 **p** 07. C Sheff Manor
from 06. *St Andrew's Vicarage, 225 Prince of Wales Road,
Sheffield S2 1FG* Tel 0114-239 9346 Mobile 07947-475073
E-mail abi_smetham@hotmail.com

SMETHURST, David Alan. b 36. Lon Univ BD60 Man Univ
MPhil84. Tyndale Hall Bris 57. **d** 61 **p** 62. C Burnage St Marg
Man 61-63; P-in-c Whalley Range St Marg 63-65; R Haughton
St Mary 65-74; R Ulverston St Mary w H Trin *Carl* 74-87; Dean
Hong Kong 87; Dir Acorn Chr Healing Trust Resource Cen
88-93; V Epsom St Martin *Guildf* 93-00; RD Epsom 97-00; rtd

01; Perm to Offic *Carl* from 01. *3 Friars Ground, Kirkby-in-Furness LA17 7YB* Tel and fax (01229) 889725
E-mail friarsground@yahoo.com

SMETHURST, Gordon McIntyre. b 40. Man Univ BA62 BD69. Wells Th Coll 70. **d** 70 **p** 71. C Sandal St Helen *Wakef* 70-73; P-in-c Whitwood and Smawthorpe St Mich 73-75; Hd RE Goole Gr Sch 75-79; S Hunsley Sch Melton 80-00; V Anlaby Common St Mark *York* 00-03; P-in-c Roos and Garton w Tunstall, Grimston and Hilston 03-07; rtd 07. *43 Ebor Manor, Keyingham, Hull HU12 9SN* Tel 07817-434209 (mobile)
E-mail revsmev@hotmail.com

SMETHURST, Leslie Beckett. b 22. CEng. NW Ord Course 72. **d** 75 **p** 76. C Baguley *Man* 75-78; TV Droylsden St Mary 78-81; V Droylsden St Martin 81-86; rtd 87; Perm to Offic *Blackb* from 87. *27 Calf Croft Place, Lytham St Annes FY8 4PU* Tel (01253) 733159

SMILLIE, Linda Barbara. b 46. Oak Hill Th Coll 85. **d** 87 **p** 94. Par Dn Holloway St Mary w St Jas *Lon* 87-88; Par Dn Holloway St Mary Magd 88-90; Chapl W End Stores 90-91; C Holloway St Mark w Em 90-91; Hon C Islington St Mary 92-94; C-in-c Southall Em CD 95-01; rtd 01; Perm to Offic *Ox* 01-04; Hon C Hanger Hill Ascension and W Twyford St Mary *Lon* 04-07. *20 Wyvern Place, Warnham, Horsham RH12 3QU* Tel (01403) 273788 E-mail rsmillie@freenetname.co.uk

SMITH, Adrian Paul. b 73. Ches Coll of HE BA94. Cranmer Hall Dur 07. **d** 09. C Mablethorpe w Trusthorpe *Linc* from 09. *30 Trusthorpe Road, Sutton-on-Sea, Mablethorpe LN12 2LT* Tel (01507) 440888 Mobile 07773-581065
E-mail aksmith96@btopenworld.com

SMITH, Aidan John. b 54. Leic Univ BA76 Man Univ MBA81. STETS 04. **d** 07 **p** 08. NSM St Martin Ludgate *Lon* from 07. *4 Terrilands, Pinner HA5 3AJ* Tel (020) 3226 0061

✠**SMITH, The Rt Revd Alan Gregory Clayton.** b 57. Birm Univ BA78 MA79 Univ of Wales (Ban) PhD02. Wycliffe Hall Ox 79. **d** 81 **p** 82 **c** 01. C Pudsey St Lawr *Bradf* 81-82; C Pudsey St Lawr and St Paul 82-84; Chapl Lee Abbey 84-90; TV Walsall *Lich* 90-97; Dioc Missr 90-97; Adn Stoke 97-01; Area Bp Shrewsbury 01-09; Bp St Alb from 09. *Abbey Gate House, 4 Abbey Mill Lane, St Albans AL3 4HD* Tel (01727) 853305 Fax 846715
E-mail bishop@stalbans.anglican.org

SMITH, Alan Leonard. b 51. Madeley Coll of Educn CertEd72. Trin Coll Bris 93. **d** 95 **p** 96. C Taunton St Mary *B & W* 95-98; V Taunton Lyngford 98-07; RD Taunton 04-06; V Chatham St Steph *Roch* from 07. *St Stephen's Vicarage, 55 Pattens Lane, Chatham ME4 6JR* Tel (01634) 849791
E-mail revdalansmith@talktalk.co.uk

SMITH, Alan Pearce Carlton. b 20. Trin Hall Cam BA40 MA45 LLB46. Westcott Ho Cam 76. **d** 78 **p** 79. NSM Cherry Hinton St Jo *Ely* 78-82; P-in-c Madingley and Dry Drayton 82-83; P-in-c Swaffham Bulbeck 84-88; rtd 88; Perm to Offic *Ely* 88-03 and from 07. *38 Alpha Road, Cambridge CB4 3DG* Tel (01223) 358124

SMITH, Alan Thomas. b 35. Open Univ BA78 Sussex Univ DipEd79. Ridley Hall Cam 82. **d** 84 **p** 85. C Bedworth *Cov* 84-89; R Carlton Colville w Mutford and Rushmere *Nor* 89-97; rtd 97; Perm to Offic *Nor* from 01. *17 St Martins Gardens, New Buckenham, Norwich NR16 2AX* Tel (01953) 860550 Mobile 07811-229493

SMITH, Alec John. b 29. AKC53. **d** 54 **p** 55. C Charlton Kings St Mary *Glouc* 54-56; C-in-c Findon Valley CD *Chich* 56-57; V Viney Hill *Glouc* 57-65; V Churchdown St Jo 65-66; V Bishop's Cannings *Sarum* 66-69; CF 69-88; V Douglas St Thos *S & M* 88-92; rtd 92; Perm to Offic *S & M* 92-05. *17 Saddle Mews, Douglas, Isle of Man IM2 1JA* Tel (01624) 670093

SMITH, Alexander Montgomery. b 36. TCD BA59 MA64 BD65. TCD Div Sch Div Test60. **d** 61 **p** 62. C Knock *D & D* 61-64; C Belfast St Thos *Conn* 64-66; Lect St Kath Coll Liv 66-69; Sen Lect 69-98; Asst Chapl St Kath Coll *Liv* 66-69; Chapl 69-80; NSM Allerton 80-98; NSM Christchurch *Win* from 98. *Priory Cottage, 4 Quay Road, Christchurch BH23 1BU* Tel (01202) 476103

SMITH, Andrew. b 84. Southn Univ BSc06. Wycliffe Hall Ox 06. **d** 09. C Lymington *Win* from 09. *20 Ramley Road, Lymington SO41 8HF* E-mail revandysmith@gmail.com

SMITH, Andrew Clifford. b 67. Ridley Coll Melbourne BMin00. **d** 01 **p** 01. C Clayton All SS Australia 01-03; C Gainsborough and Morton *Linc* 03-06; TV 06-08; P-in-c Woodhall Spa Gp from 08. *The Vicarage, Alverston Avenue, Woodhall Spa LN10 6SN* Tel (01526) 353973
E-mail smithbanda@hotmail.com

SMITH, Andrew John. b 37. Leeds Univ BA61. Coll of Resurr Mirfield 61. **d** 63 **p** 64. C W Hackney St Barn *Lon* 63-65; Dir and Chapl Northorpe Hall Trust Yorkshire 65-72; Warden Ox Ho Bethnal Green 72-78; Dir and Chapl The Target Trust 78-86; P-in-c Gt Staughton *Ely* 86-88; Norfolk DTI Educn Adv 89-91; Perm to Offic *Ex* 92-96 and from 98; C Widecombe-in-the-Moor, Leusdon, Princetown etc 96-97; rtd 97. *Mountjoy, Rilla Mill, Callington PL17 7NT*

SMITH, Andrew John. b 46. Lon Univ BScEng67 PhD71 Bath Univ MEd88 CEng96 MIET96. Coll of Resurr Mirfield 74. **d** 76 **p** 77. C Swindon New Town *Bris* 76-78; C Southmead 78-79; Perm to Offic 79-91. *15 Dyrham Close, Bristol BS9 4TF* Tel 0117-942 8594

SMITH, Andrew John. b 53. Loughb Univ BTech74. Lon Bible Coll 95 St Jo Coll Nottm MA98. **d** 99 **p** 00. C Hailsham *Chich* 99-02; P-in-c Worc St Mich 02-03; TV Almondbury w Farnley Tyas *Wakef* 03-07; V Woolston New Zealand from 07. *10 St John's Street, Woolston, Christchurch 8062, New Zealand* Tel (0064) (3) 981 6144 E-mail ajsinz@clear.net.nz
or woolstonvicar@clear.net.nz

SMITH, Andrew John. b 59. Birm Univ BSc80 PhD81. WMMTC 89. **d** 91 **p** 92. C Lower Mitton *Worc* 91-92; C Stourport and Wilden 92-95; TV Redditch, The Ridge 95-05; P-in-c Redditch St Steph 02-05; Ind Chapl 95-05; Chapl Redditch and Bromsgrove Primary Care Trust 01-05; V W Bromwich All SS *Lich* from 05; RD W Bromwich from 08. *All Saints' Vicarage, 90 Hall Green Road, West Bromwich B71 3LB* Tel 0121-588 3698

SMITH, Andrew Perry Langton. b 56. Sheff City Poly BSc79 Imp Coll Lon MSc80. Trin Coll Bris 89. **d** 91 **p** 92. C Littleover *Derby* 91-95; TV Walsall *Lich* from 95; Ind Chapl Black Country Urban Ind Miss from 95; Hon C Walsall St Paul from 05; Hon C Walsall Pleck and Bescot from 05. *21 Buchanan Road, Walsall WS4 2EW* Tel (01922) 634859 *or* 710407
E-mail aplsmith@o2.co.uk

SMITH, Angela Elisabeth. b 53. Southn Univ BA75 Bp Grosseteste Coll PGCE76. WEMTC 03. **d** 06 **p** 07. NSM Matson *Glouc* from 06. *St George's Vicarage, Grange Road, Gloucester GL4 0PE* Tel (01452) 520851
E-mail angela.draesmith@blueyonder.co.uk

SMITH, Mrs Anita Elisabeth. b 57. Westhill Coll Birm BEd79. Trin Coll Bris 85. **d** 88 **p** 94. Par Dn Bermondsey St Anne *S'wark* 88-92; Par Dn Brockley Hill St Sav 92-94; C 94-99; Miss Partner CMS Kenya from 99. *CMS, PO Box 40360, Nairobi, Kenya*

SMITH, Ann Veronica. b 38. Doncaster Coll of Educn DipEd. Edin Dioc NSM Course 88. **d** 95 **p** 96. NSM S Queensferry *Edin* 95-99; NSM Falkirk from 99. *16 Mannerston, Linlithgow EH49 7ND* Tel (01506) 834361

SMITH (née JENNINGS), Mrs Anne. b 41. CertEd63 STh. Gilmore Ho 65. **dss** 71 **d** 87 **p** 94. Barton w Peel Green *Man* 71-76; Wythenshawe Wm Temple Ch 76-79; Rochdale 79-83; Chapl Rochdale Colls of FE 79-83; Hillock *Man* 83-88; Dn-in-c 87-88; Chapl Wakef Cathl 88-96; P-in-c Whitwell *Derby* 96-00; V Mansfield Woodhouse *S'well* 00-01; rtd 01; Perm to Offic *Carl* 02-05; *Blackb* and *Bradf* from 05. *20 Bendwood Close, Padiham, Burnley BB12 8RT* Tel (01282) 680372

SMITH, Canon Anthony Charles. b 43. Sarum & Wells Th Coll 90. **d** 92 **p** 93. C Dartford H Trin *Roch* 92-95; V Northfleet 95-05; TR Northfleet and Rosherville 05-07; Bp's Dom Chapl from 07; Hon Can Roch Cathl from 05. *Bishopscourt, Rochester ME1 1TS* Tel (01634) 814439 Mobile 07958-739301
E-mail chaplain@rochester.anglican.org

SMITH, Anthony Cyril. b 40. K Coll Lon 65. **d** 69 **p** 70. C Crewkerne *B & W* 69-74; TV Hemel Hempstead *St Alb* 74-76; Asst Chapl K Coll Taunton 76-80; Chapl 80-02; rtd 02; Perm to Offic *B & W* from 03. *1 Castle Street, Stogursey, Bridgwater TA5 1TG* Tel (01278) 733577

SMITH, Anthony James. b 57. ACA Sheff Univ BA. Ridley Hall Cam 83. **d** 86 **p** 87. C Woking St Pet *Guildf* 86-90; C Reigate St Mary *S'wark* 90-94; CMS Kenya 94-00; Finance Team Ldr World Vision UK 00-05. *7 Shuttleworth Grove, Wavendon Gate, Milton Keynes MK7 7RX* Tel (01908) 586156
E-mail anthony.smith@summitskills.org.uk

SMITH, The Ven Anthony Michael Percival. b 24. G&C Coll Cam BA48 MA53. Westcott Ho Cam 48. **d** 50 **p** 51. C Leamington Priors H Trin *Cov* 50-53; Abp's Dom Chapl *Cant* 53-57; Chapl Norwood and Distr Hosp 57-66; V Norwood All SS 57-66; V Yeovil St Jo w Preston Plucknett *B & W* 66-72; RD Merston 68-72; Preb Wells Cathl 70-72; V Addiscombe St Mildred *Cant* 72-79; Adn Maidstone 79-89; Dir of Ords 80-89; Hon Can Cant Cathl 80-89; rtd 89; Perm to Offic *Cant* 90-06; Chich 89-91 and 93-06; RD Rye *Chich* 91-93. *Birchwood House Rest Home, Stockland Green Road, Tunbridge Wells TN3 0TU* Tel (01892) 860601

SMITH, Antoinette. b 47. NTMTC 95. **d** 98 **p** 99. NSM Chigwell and Chigwell Row *Chelmsf* 98-02; TV from 02. *St Winifred's Church House, 115 Manor Road, Chigwell IG7 5PS* Tel (020) 8500 4608 E-mail reverend@tonismith.freeserve.co.uk

SMITH, Miss Audrey. b 47. S'wark Ord Course 89. **d** 92 **p** 94. NSM Croydon St Aug *S'wark* 92-98; P-in-c Redmarley D'Abitot, Bromesberrow w Pauntley etc *Glouc* 98-00; Perm to Offic 05-06; NSM Newent and Gorsley w Cliffords Mesne 06-08; Chapl Hartpury Coll 06-08; NSM Brampton St Thos *Derby* from 08. *Rose Cottage, Cotton Mill Hill, Holymoorside, Chesterfield S42 7EJ* Tel (01246) 569632

SMITH, Mrs Audrey Isabel. b 20. Lon Univ. Qu Coll Birm IDC79. **dss** 84 **d** 87 **p** 94. NSM Kingston All SS w St Jo *S'wark*

87-95; Perm to Offic *Truro* 95-08. *31 Copes Gardens, Truro TR1 3SN* Tel (01872) 261813

SMITH, Austin John Denyer. b 40. Worc Coll Ox BA62. Cuddesdon Coll 64. **d** 66 **p** 67. C Shepherd's Bush St Steph w St Thos *Lon* 66-69; C W Drayton 69-72; Chapl Sussex Univ 72-79; V Caddington *St Alb* 79-06; rtd 06. *209 Bedford Road, Hitchin SG5 2UE* Tel (01462) 437433
E-mail ajdsmith@waitrose.com

SMITH, Mrs Barbara Jean. b 39. Bris Univ BA62 Surrey Univ PGCE93. S'wark Ord Course 83. **dss** 86 **d** 87 **p** 94. Hon Dss Chislehurst St Nic *Roch* 86; Hon Par Dn 87-90; Hon C Wrecclesham *Guildf* 90-94; Hon C Herriard w Winslade and Long Sutton etc 94-99; P-in-c 99-03; P-in-c Newnham w Nately Scures w Mapledurwell etc 99-03; rtd 03; Perm to Offic *Portsm* 06-07. *15 The Ridings, Paddock Wood, Tonbridge TN12 6YA* Tel (01892) 833564 E-mail barbarajsmith@btopenworld.com

SMITH, Mrs Barbara Mary. b 47. Doncaster Coll of Educn CertEd68. St Jo Coll Dur 82. **dss** 85 **d** 87 **p** 94. Beverley St Nic *York* 85-87; Par Dn 87; NSM S'wark H Trin w St Matt 89-90; Ind Chapl Teesside *York* 91-95; Hon C Middlesbrough St Chad 94-95; Perm to Offic *St Alb* 96-02; Locum Chapl Anglia Poly Univ 96-98; TV Linton 00-04; rtd 04. *Catref, Rookhope, Bishop Auckland DL13 2BG*

SMITH, Canon Barry. b 41. Univ of Wales (Lamp) BA62 Fitzw Ho Cam BA64 MA68 Man Univ MPhil91. Ridley Hall Cam. **d** 65 **p** 66. C Rhyl w St Ann *St As* 65-70; Chapl Scargill Ho 70-72; C Flint *St As* 72-74; V Broughton 74-86; Dioc Ecum Officer 82-86; RD Wrexham 82-86; TR Wrexham 86-95; Can Cursal St As Cathl 86-95; Chan 95; Perm to Offic S'wark 97-02. *1 Acorn Keep, Rowhills, Farnham GU9 9BL* Tel (01252) 322111

SMITH, Barry Roy. b 46. STETS. **d** 00 **p** 04. NSM Blendworth w Chalton w Idsworth *Portsm* 00-05; Asst Chapl Portsm Hosps NHS Trust 03-05; Team Chapl from 05; NSM Blendworth w Chalton w Idsworth *Portsm* from 07. *298 Milton Road, Cowplain, Waterlooville PO8 8JP* Tel (023) 9226 5620
E-mail barry.roy.smith@googlemail.com

SMITH, Beverley Anne. b 56. Univ of Wales Coll of Medicine MSc97 RN78 RM80 RHV87 Univ of Wales PGCE00. St Mich Coll Llan. **d** 05 **p** 06. NSM Whitchurch *Llan* from 05. *3 Solva Avenue, Cardiff CF14 0NP* Tel (029) 2076 1746 Mobile 07841-707525 E-mail beverley.anne@btinternet.com

SMITH, The Ven Brian. b 44. Westmr Coll Ox MTh95. Sarum & Wells Th Coll 71. **d** 74 **p** 75. C Pennywell St Thos and Grindon St Oswald CD *Dur* 74-77; Chapl RAF 77-95; P-in-c Keswick St Jo *Carl* 95-96; V 96-05; RD Derwent 98-05; Hon Can Carl Cathl 99-05; Adn Man *S & M* from 05; V Douglas St Geo from 05. *St George's Vicarage, 16 Devonshire Road, Douglas, Isle of Man IM2 3RB* Tel (01624) 675430 Fax 616136
E-mail archd-sodor@mcb.net

✠**SMITH, The Rt Revd Brian Arthur.** b 43. Edin Univ MA66 Fitzw Coll Cam BA68 MA72 Jes Coll Cam MLitt73. Westcott Ho Cam 66. **d** 72 **p** 73 **c** 93. Tutor and Lib Cuddesdon Coll 72-75; Dir of Studies 75-78; Sen Tutor Ripon Coll Cuddesdon 78-79; C Cuddesdon *Ox* 76-79; Dir Tr *Wakef* 79-87; P-in-c Halifax St Jo 79-85; Hon Can Wakef Cathl 81-87; Adn Craven *Bradf* 87-93; Suff Bp Tonbridge *Roch* 93-01; Hon Can Roch Cathl 93-01; Bp Edin from 01. *3 Eglinton Crescent, Edinburgh EH12 5DH,* or *Bishop's Office, 21A Grosvenor Crescent Edinburgh EH12 5EL* Tel 0131-226 5099 *or* 538 7044 Fax 538 7088 E-mail bishop@edinburgh.anglican.org

SMITH, Brian Godfrey. b 24. Chich Th Coll 63. **d** 65 **p** 66. C Newc H Cross 65-68; C Redcar *York* 68-72; C Kirkleatham 68-72; V Wortley de Leeds *Ripon* 72-76; Chapl Costa del Sol E *Eur* 76-82; Chapl Estoril 82-84; V Worfield *Heref* 84-89; rtd 89; Perm to Offic *Heref* from 92. *2 Pineway, Lodge Farm, Bridgnorth WV15 5DT* Tel (01746) 764088

SMITH, Brian Michael. b 42. Kelham Th Coll 69. **d** 69 **p** 70. C Somers Town *Lon* 70-74; C Stamford Hill St Jo 74-75; C Stamford Hill St Bart 75-84; P-in-c Edmonton St Pet w St Martin 84-92; V 92-07; rtd 07. *16 Hurst Rise, Matlock DE4 3EP* E-mail bms@sple.freeserve.co.uk

SMITH, Canon Bridget Mary. b 46. Bp Otter Coll CertEd67. S Dios Minl Tr Scheme 88. **d** 91 **p** 94. C Pet H Spirit Bretton 91-95; P-in-c Silverstone and Abthorpe w Slapton 95-03; R Silverstone and Abthorpe w Slapton etc 03-09; Warden of Past Assts 00-06; Can Pet Cathl 01-09; rtd 09. *2 Merryweather Close, Southwell NG25 0BN* Tel (01636) 812215 E-mail quickvic@lineone.net

SMITH, Mrs Carol. b 55. SEITE 01. **d** 04 **p** 05. C Epping Distr *Chelmsf* 04-07; Chapl Epping Forest Primary Care Trust 05-07; V Moulsham St Luke *Chelmsf* from 07. *St Luke's House, 26 Lewis Drive, Chelmsford CM2 9EF* Tel (01245) 354479
E-mail carolrev@gotadsl.co.uk

SMITH, Mrs Catherine Eleanor Louise. b 52. SAOMC 99. **d** 02 **p** 03. NSM Denham *Ox* 02 05; NSM Penn Street from 05; Chapl Heatherwood and Wexham Park Hosp NHS Trust from 05. *55 Penn Road, Beaconsfield HP9 2LW* Tel and fax (01494) 670389

SMITH, Charles Henry Neville. b 31. Nottm Univ BA52 MA65. Sarum Th Coll 55. **d** 57 **p** 58. C Thirsk w S Kilvington *York*

57-60; C Linthorpe 60-61; V Danby 61-66; Chapl United Cam Hosps 66-76; Chapl Lanc Moor Hosp 76-84; Hon Can Blackb Cathl 81-84; Asst Sec Gen Syn Hosp Chapl Coun 84-88; Hon C Lee St Marg *S'wark* 84-88; Chapl Guy's Hosp Lon 88-96; rtd 96; Hon Chapl S'wark Cathl from 96. *57 Belmont Park, London SE13 5BW* Tel (020) 8318 9993

SMITH, Charles Rycroft. b 46. Sarum & Wells Th Coll 76. **d** 78 **p** 79. C Heref St Martin 78-81; C Southampton Maybush St Pet *Win* 81-83; R The Candover Valley 83-99; RD Alresford 90-99; P-in-c Guernsey St Andr 99-01; R 01-07; Vice-Dean Guernsey 02-07; P-in-c Beaulieu and Exbury and E Boldre from 07. *The Rectory, Palace Lane, Beaulieu, Brockenhurst SO42 7YG* Tel (01590) 612242 E-mail ryc@beaulieu-rectory.org.uk

SMITH, Charles Septimus. b 23. Bris & Glouc Tr Course. **d** 79 **p** 80. NSM Bris St Agnes and St Simon w St Werburgh 79-86; C 86-87; C Bris St Paul's 87-89; rtd 89. *2432 Jarvis Street West, Mississauga ON L5C 2P6, Canada*

SMITH, Mrs Christine. b 46. NOC 94. **d** 97 **p** 98. C Salterhebble All SS *Wakef* 97-01; P-in-c Siddal 01-06; V Cornholme and Walsden from 06. *The Heights, 30 Cross Lee Road, Todmorden OL14 8EH* Tel (01706) 813604

SMITH, Christine Lydia. *See* CARTER, Mrs Christine Lydia

SMITH, The Ven Christopher Blake Walters. b 63. Univ of Wales (Cardiff) BMus84 BD88 LLM95. St Mich Coll Llan 85. **d** 88 **p** 89. C Aberdare *Llan* 88-93; V Tongwynlais 93-00; Dioc Dir Post-Ord Tr 95-05; Dom Chapl Bp Llan and Warden of Ords 01-07; Chapl to Abp Wales 03-07; Adn Morgannwg from 06; P-in-c Cwmbach from 07; Metrop Can from 04. *The Heights, Nant y Groes Drive, Tirfounder Road, Aberdare CF44 0BE* Tel (01685) 875845
E-mail archdeacon.morgannwg@churchinwales.org.uk

SMITH, Canon Christopher Francis. b 46. K Coll Lon BD68 AKC68. St Aug Coll Cant 69. **d** 70 **p** 71. C Norwood All SS *Cant* 70-72; Asst Chapl Marlborough Coll 72-76; C Deal St Leon w Sholden *Cant* 77-81; P-in-c Benenden 81-83; V 83-07; P-in-c Sandhurst w Newenden 04-07; Hon Can Cant Cathl 03-07; AD Tenterden 05-07; Chapl Benenden Sch 81-92; Chapl Benenden Hosp 91-07; rtd 07; Perm to Offic *Cant* from 07. *34 Richmond Road, Whitstable CT5 3PH* Tel (01227) 266569
E-mail christopherfrancissmith@yahoo.co.uk

SMITH, Christopher James. b 72. Newc Univ BSc94. Wycliffe Hall Ox BTh01. **d** 02 **p** 03. C Cambridge H Trin *Ely* 02-04; Assoc R Zion Ch USA 04-08. *Address temp unknown*
E-mail revsmith@ntlworld.com

SMITH, Christopher Matthew. b 67. New Coll Ox BA89 MA93 Homerton Coll Cam PGCE90 LLB07. St Steph Ho Ox BA94. **d** 95 **p** 96. C Wantage *Ox* 95-99; Dom Chapl to Bp Horsham *Chich* 99-01; V Beckenham St Mich w St Aug *Roch* from 01. *St Michael's Vicarage, 120 Birkbeck Road, Beckenham BR3 4SS* Tel (020) 8778 6569

SMITH, Canon Christopher Milne. b 44. Selw Coll Cam BA66. Cuddesdon Coll 67. **d** 69 **p** 70. C Liv Our Lady and St Nic 69-74; TV Kirkby 74-81; R Walton St Mary 81-91; Can Res Sheff Cathl 91-02; V Doncaster St Geo from 02; Bp's Adv on the Paranormal from 97; Hon Can Sheff Cathl from 03; Chapl to The Queen from 04. *The Vicarage, 98 Thorne Road, Doncaster DN2 5BJ* Tel (01302) 368796 *or* 323748

SMITH, Clarice Mary. b 25. St Mich Coll Llan 76. **dss** 77 **d** 80. Llangiwg *S & B* 77-80; C Llwynderw 80-84; C Newton St Pet 84-88; rtd 88. *33 Sherringham Drive, Newton, Swansea SA3 4UG* Tel (01792) 367984

SMITH, Clifford. b 31. St Aid Birkenhead 59. **d** 61 **p** 62. C Limehouse St Anne *Lon* 61-63; C Ashtead *Guildf* 63-66; R Bromley All Hallows *Lon* 66-76; V Hillsborough and Wadsley Bridge *Sheff* 76-89; V Stainforth 89-96; rtd 96; Hon C Hurst *Ox* from 97. *23 King Street Lane, Winnersh, Wokingham RG41 5AX* Tel 0118-978 9453

SMITH, Clive Leslie. b 50. Leeds Univ BA72 MA03 Ch Coll Liv PGCE73. Coll of Resurr Mirfield 75. **d** 77 **p** 78. C Goldington *St Alb* 77-81; C Cheshunt 81-84; V Watford St Pet 84-89; Chapl Leavesden Hosp Abbots Langley 89-94; Chapl St Alb and Hemel Hempstead NHS Trust 94-00; Chapl W Herts Hosps NHS Trust 00-01; Sen Chapl Doncaster and Bassetlaw Hosps NHS Trust from 01; Perm to Offic *S'well* from 02. *Chaplaincy Department, Doncaster Royal Infirmary, Armthorpe Road, Doncaster DN2 5LT* Tel (01302) 381484 *or* 881351
E-mail chaplaincy.department@dbh.nhs.uk

SMITH, Colin. b 39. MBE. Open Univ BA80 LRSC65 CChem88 FRSC88. NEOC 94. **d** 97 **p** 98. NSM Jesmond H Trin and Newc St Barn and St Jude 97-03; rtd 08. *1 Cayton Grove, Newcastle upon Tyne NE5 1HL* Tel 0191-267 9519
E-mail colinandevelyn@btopenworld.com

SMITH, Colin Graham. b 59. Hatf Poly BA82 CQSW82. Trin Coll Bris DA88. **d** 88 **p** 89. C Bermondsey St Jas w Ch Ch *S'wark* 88-92; V Brockley Hill St Sav 92 99; Miss Partner CMS Kenya from 99. *CMS, PO Box 40360, Nairobi, Kenya*

SMITH, Colin Richard. b 53. Liv Poly BA80 Liv Univ MTD83. Oak Hill Th Coll 84. **d** 86 **p** 87. C Ormskirk *Liv* 86-89; V Wigan St Cath 89-94; C St Helens St Helen 94-99; TV from 99; P-in-c

St Helens St Mark from 06. *14 Alpine Close, St Helens WA10 4EY* Tel (01744) 453681

SMITH, Mrs Corinne Anne. b 52. St Andr Univ MTheol91. SAOMC 95. **d** 97. C Abingdon *Ox* 97-02; Chapl Pemb Coll Ox 02-03; Chapl Ox Radcliffe Hosps NHS Trust 03-07; Chapl Portsm Hosps NHS Trust from 07. *Chaplaincy Office, De La Court House, Queen Alexandria Hospital, Portsmouth PO6 3LY* Tel (023) 9228 6000 E-mail corinne.smith@vizzavi.net

SMITH, Craig Philip. b 61. Sheff City Poly BA86. St Jo Coll Nottm 90. **d** 93 **p** 94. C Bramley and Ravenfield w Hooton Roberts etc *Sheff* 93-97; C Rainham w Wennington *Chelmsf* 97-00; TV Gainsborough and Morton *Linc* 00-03; V Catshill and Dodford *Worc* 03-07; New Zealand from 07. *PO Box 64, Culverden, North Canterbury 7345, New Zealand* Tel (0064) (3) 315 8210

SMITH, Daniel Bradley. b 69. Harris Man Coll Ox BTh05. St Steph Ho Ox 04. **d** 06 **p** 07. C Bexhill St Pet *Chich* from 06. *14 Barrack Road, Bexhill-on-Sea TN40 2AT* Tel (01424) 212453 E-mail db.smith@alumni.oxon.net

SMITH, Darren John Anthony. b 62. Nottm Univ BCombStuds84. Linc Th Coll 84. **d** 86 **p** 87. C Leic Ascension 86-90; C Curdworth w Castle Vale *Birm* 90; C Castle Vale St Cuth 90-91; C Kingstanding St Luke 91-92; P-in-c 92-93; V 93-08; P-in-c Kingstanding St Mark 01-02; Gen Sec ACS from 08. *Gordon Browning House, 8 Spitfire Road, Birmingham B24 9PB* Tel 0121-382 5533 Fax 382 6999

SMITH, David. See SMITH, Terence David

SMITH, David Charles Stuart. CertEd53 Wheaton Coll Illinois MA74. Oak Hill Th Coll 61. **d** 61 **p** 62. Australia 61-72, 75-89 and from 90; Wellington Coll Berks 72-75; C Luton Lewsey St Hugh *St Alb* 90; rtd 96. *Troon, 19-746 Orrong Road, Toorak Vic 3142, Australia* Tel (0061) (3) 9824 2652 E-mail davidcssmith@futureweb.com.au

SMITH, David Earling. b 35. AKC60. **d** 61 **p** 62. C Knebworth *St Alb* 61-63; C Chipping Barnet 64-66; C S Ormsby w Ketsby, Calceby and Driby *Linc* 66-69; R Claxby w Normanby-le-Wold 69-74; R Nettleton 69-74; R S Kelsey 69-74; R N Owersby w Thornton le Moor 69-74; R Stainton-le-Vale w Kirmond le Mire 69-74; V Ancaster 74-79; Warden and Chapl St Anne Bedehouses *Linc* 79-89; C Linc Minster Gp 79-89; rtd 89; Perm to Offic *Linc* 90-02. *17 Egerton Road, Lincoln LN2 4PJ* Tel (01522) 510336 E-mail david@limani17.fsnet.co.uk

✠**SMITH, The Rt Revd David James.** b 35. AKC58 FKC99. **d** 59 **p** 60 **c** 87. C Gosforth All SS *Newc* 59-62; C Newc St Fran 62-64; C Longbenton St Bart 64-68; V Longhirst 68-75; V Monkseaton St Mary 75-82; RD Tynemouth 80-82; Hon Can Newc Cathl 81-87; Adn Lindisfarne 81-87; V Felton 82-83; Suff Bp Maidstone *Cant* 87-92; Bp HM Forces 90-92; Bp Bradf 92-02; rtd 02; Hon Asst Bp York from 02; Hon Asst Bp Eur from 02. *34 Cedar Glade, Dunnington, York YO19 5QZ* Tel (01904) 481225 E-mail david@djmhs.force9.co.uk

SMITH, Canon David John. b 32. Goldsmiths' Coll Lon BA76 LSE MSc79. Lon Coll of Div 68. **d** 70 **p** 71. C Clerkenwell St Jas and St Jo w St Pet *Lon* 70-73; P-in-c Penge St Paul *Roch* 74-78; V 78-89; RD Beckenham 86-89; Chapl Bromley and Sheppard's Colls 90-97; Perm to Offic *S'wark* 90-97; Dioc Clergy Widows and Retirement Officer *Roch* 90-97; Hon Can Roch Cathl 95-97; rtd 98; Perm to Offic *St Alb* from 98 and *Lon* from 99. *13 Park Way, Rickmansworth WD3 7AU* Tel (01923) 775963

SMITH, David Leonard. b 37. St Alb Minl Tr Scheme 84. **d** 91 **p** 92. NSM Potton w Sutton and Cockayne Hatley *St Alb* 91-09. *2 Broom Road, Stanford, Biggleswade SG18 9JE* Tel (01462) 815071 E-mail davidlsmith@hotmail.com

SMITH, David Robert. b 54. Southn Univ BSc75 Loughb Univ MSc86 CEng84 MRAeS84. WEMTC 02. **d** 05 **p** 06. C Matson *Glouc* 05-09; P-in-c Glouc St Geo w Whaddon from 09. *St George's Vicarage, Grange Road, Gloucester GL4 0PE* Tel (01452) 520851 E-mail draesmith@blueyonder.co.uk

SMITH, David Roland Mark. b 46. Dur Univ BA68 ACP78 FRSA87. Edin Th Coll 68. **d** 70 **p** 71. C Southwick St Columba *Dur* 70-74 and 81-82; Asst Chapl Univ of Wales (Cardiff) *Llan* 74-76; Hon C E Bris 76-78; Hon C Filton 78-79; Min Leam Lane CD *Dur* 80-81; Co-ord Chapl Service Sunderland Poly 81-86; Chapl Birm Univ 86-95; Chapl Heathrow Airport *Lon* 95-00; rtd 00; Chapl Wolv Airport *Lich* 00-09. *5 The Keepings, 12 Priory Road, Dudley DY1 4AD* Tel (01384) 259540 Mobile 07778-876695 E-mail revdrmsmith@aol.com

SMITH, David Stanley. b 41. Ox NSM Course. **d** 84 **p** 85. NSM Burghfield *Ox* 84-86; NSM Stratfield Mortimer 86-88; NSM Mortimer W End w Padworth 86-88; C St Breoke and Egloshayle *Truro* 88-93; V Penwerris 93-07; rtd 07; Perm to Offic *Ox* 09-10. *51 Manchester Road, Reading RG1 3QL* Tel 0118-926 4104

SMITH, David Watson. b 31. Sarum Th Coll 63. **d** 65 **p** 66. C W Wimbledon Ch Ch *S'wark* 65-69; C Cheam 69-74; V Haslington *Ches* 74-83; V Haslington w Crewe Green 83-87; V Daresbury 87-98; rtd 98; Perm to Offic *Pet* from 98. *4 Wakefield Way, Nether Heyford, Northampton NN7 3LU* Tel (01327) 341561 E-mail rev.dw.smith@freeuk.com

SMITH, Canon David William. b 46. Sarum Th Coll 70. **d** 72 **p** 73. C Stokesley *York* 72-75; C Edin St Mich and All SS 75-77; R Galashiels 77-85; R Yarm *York* 85-00; TR Whitby w Ruswarp from 00; P-in-c Fylingdales and Hawsker cum Stainsacre 03-05; Can and Preb York Minster from 05. *The Rectory, Chubb Hill Road, Whitby YO21 1JP* Tel (01947) 602590

SMITH, Deborah Jane. b 62. Newc Poly BA83. STETS 00. **d** 03 **p** 04. C Dorchester *Sarum* 03-07; R Wyke Regis from 07. *The Rectory, 1 Portland Road, Weymouth DT4 9ES* Tel and fax (01305) 784649 Mobile 07870-560354 E-mail smithsmania@btopenworld.com

SMITH, Mrs Deborah Louise. b 56. WEMTC 02 NOC 03. **d** 05 **p** 06. C Honley *Wakef* 05-07; Chapl HM Pris and YOI New Hall 05-07; NSM Woolston New Zealand from 07. *10 St John's Street, Woolston, Christchurch 8062, New Zealand* Tel (0064) (3) 981 6144

SMITH, Mrs Decia Jane. b 47. ALAM66. WMMTC 92. **d** 95 **p** 96. C Edgbaston St Germain *Birm* 95-99; P-in-c Abbots Leigh w Leigh Woods *Bris* from 00. *The Vicarage, 51 Church Road, Abbots Leigh, Bristol BS8 3QU* Tel (01275) 373996 Fax 371799 E-mail revdavic@yahoo.co.uk

SMITH, Declan. See SMITH, Godfrey Declan Burfield

SMITH, Denis Richard. b 53. MA. St Jo Coll Nottm 83. **d** 85 **p** 86. C Hersham *Guildf* 85-88; C Thatcham *Ox* 89-91; V Shefford *St Alb* 91-02; P-in-c Tilehurst St Cath *Ox* 02-07; V Tilehurst St Cath and Calcot from 07. *The Vicarage, Wittenham Avenue, Tilehurst, Reading RG31 5LN* Tel 0118-942 7786 E-mail revdenissmith@hotmail.com

SMITH, Mrs Denise. b 46. Didsbury Coll of Educn CertEd67. **d** 08 **p** 09. OLM Goodshaw and Crawshawbooth *Man* from 08. *122 Goodshaw Lane, Rossendale BB4 8DD* Tel (01706) 830251 Mobile 07954-645212 E-mail mrsbucket122@btinternet.com

SMITH, Dennis Austin. b 50. Lanc Univ BA71 Liv Univ PGCE72. NW Ord Course 74. **d** 77 **p** 78. NSM Seaforth *Liv* 77-83; NSM St Crosby St Faith 77-83; Hon C 83-98; Hon C Gt Crosby St Faith and Waterloo Park St Mary from 98; Asst Chapl Merchant Taylors' Sch Crosby 79-83; Chapl from 83. *16 Fir Road, Liverpool L22 4QL* Tel 0151-928 5065

SMITH, Derek Arthur. b 38. Chich Th Coll 63. **d** 66 **p** 67. C Cheadle *Lich* 66-70; C Blakenall Heath 70-72; P-in-c 76-77; TR 77-86; V Knutton 72-76; R Lich St Mary w St Mich 86-96; P-in-c Wall 90-96; R Lich St Mich w St Mary and Wall 96-98; V W Bromwich St Andr w Ch Ch 98-02; rtd 02. *20 Tiverton Drive, West Bromwich B71 1DA* Tel 0121-525 0260

SMITH, Derek Arthur Byott. b 26. Hull Univ MA89. S Dios Minl Tr Scheme 78. **d** 81 **p** 82. NSM Wimborne Minster and Holt *Sarum* 81-83; C Northampton St Alb *Pet* 83-85; Ind Chapl *York* 85-89; P-in-c Kingston upon Hull St Mary 88-89; P-in-c Newington w Dairycoates 89-93; rtd 93; Perm to Offic *York* 93. *107 Cardigan Road, Bridlington YO15 3LP* Tel (01262) 678852

SMITH, Derek Arthur Douglas. b 26. Dur Univ BA51. Qu Coll Birm 58. **d** 60 **p** 61. C Evesham *Worc* 60-63; C Bollington St Jo *Ches* 63-68; V Thelwall 68-78; V Whitegate w Lt Budworth 78-92; rtd 92; Perm to Offic *Ches* from 92. *10 Newtons Crescent, Winterley, Sandbach CW11 9NS* Tel (01270) 589130

SMITH, Derek Graham. b 52. St Cath Coll Cam BA74 MA77. Westcott Ho Cam 74. **d** 76 **p** 77. C Weymouth H Trin *Sarum* 76-79; P-in-c Bradpole 79; TV Bridport 79-84; R Monkton Farleigh, S Wraxall and Winsley 84-98; TR Melksham from 98; C Atworth w Shaw and Whitley from 07; C Broughton Gifford, Gt Chalfield and Holt from 07; RD Bradford 01-08; Chapl Wilts and Swindon Healthcare NHS Trust 00-02; Can and Preb Sarum Cathl 03-09; Chapl Limassol St Barn from 09. *PO Box 51494, 3506 Limassol, Cyprus SN12 6LX* Tel (00357) (22) 671220 E-mail stbac@spidernet.com.cy

SMITH, Diana Linnet. b 47. Sheff Univ BSc69 Goldsmiths' Coll Lon MA83 Trin Coll Carmarthen PhD99. EAMTC 02. **d** 03 **p** 04. C Oundle w Ashton and Benefield w Glapthorn *Pet* 03-06; R Brundall w Braydeston and Postwick *Nor* from 06. *The Rectory, 73 The Street, Brundall, Norwich NR13 5LZ* Tel (01603) 715136

SMITH, Donald Edgar. b 56. Oak Hill Th Coll 89. **d** 91 **p** 92. C Holloway St Mark w Em *Lon* 91-92; C Tollington 92-95; TV W Ealing St Jo w St Jas 95-08; R Frinton *Chelmsf* from 08. *The Rectory, 22 Queens Road, Frinton-on-Sea CO13 9BL* Tel (01255) 674664 E-mail donthevic@btinternet.com

SMITH, The Ven Donald John. b 26. Univ of Wales (Cardiff) LLM96. Clifton Th Coll 50. **d** 53 **p** 54. C Edgware *Lon* 53-56; C Ipswich St Marg *St E* 56-58; V Hornsey Rise St Mary *Lon* 56-62; R Whitton and Thurleston w Akenham *St E* 62-75; Hon Can St E Cathl 73-91; Adn Suffolk 75-84; R The Rickinghalls 75-76; P-in-c Redgrave w Botesdale 75-76; R Redgrave cum Botesdale w Rickinghall 76-78; Adn Sudbury 84-91; rtd 91; Perm to Offic *Cov*, *Ox*, *St E* and *Worc* from 91; *Glouc* 91-96 and from 03. *1 Manor Lane, Shipston-on-Stour CV36 4EF*

✠**SMITH, The Rt Revd Donald Westwood.** b 28. Edin Th Coll 54 St D Coll Lamp 50. **d** 54 **p** 55 **c** 90. Asst Dioc Supernumerary *Ab* 54-55; Chapl St Andr Cathl 55-56; Canada 56-57; R Longside

Ab 57-65; Mauritius 65-85; P-in-c St Geo-in-the-East St Mary *Lon* 85-86; Seychelles 86-87; Madagascar 87-99; Bp Toamasina 90-99. *Avenue Cote d'Emeraude, Morcellement Raffray, Albion, Mauritius* Tel (00230) 238 5966
E-mail tighdhonuil@hotmail.com

SMITH, Edward George. b 61. Surrey Univ BSc82 Cov Univ MSc95. Ox Min Course 06. **d** 09. NSM Aynho and Croughton w Evenley etc *Pet* from 09. *7 Chacombe Road, Middleton Cheney, Banbury OX17 2QS* Tel (01295) 711915 Mobile 07740-909756
E-mail eddie.smith@talk21.com

SMITH, Elaine Joan. *See* GARRISH, Elaine Joan

SMITH, Ms Elizabeth. b 46. Liv Inst of Educn CertEd67 Heythrop Coll Lon BD76 Lon Univ MPhil84. Westcott Ho Cam 90. **d** 92 **p** 94. Par Dn Moulsham St Jo *Chelmsf* 92-94; C 94-96; V Westcliff St Andr 96-00; V Sedgley St Mary *Worc* 00-09; rtd 09. *2 Buckstone Close, Leeds LS17 5EU* E-mail revdeliz@aol.com

SMITH (*née* HOWSE), Mrs Elizabeth Ann. b 39. Bath Academy of Art CertEd60 Warwick Univ BEd85. WMMTC 91. **d** 94 **p** 95. C Fletchamstead *Cov* 94-97; P-in-c Leamington Hastings and Birdingbury 97-03; P-in-c Grandborough w Willoughby and Flecknoe 97-03; V Leam Valley 03-05; rtd 05; Perm to Offic *Cov* from 05. *35 Coniston Close, Rugby CV21 1LE* Tel (01788) 330931 E-mail beth@bethemail.co.uk

SMITH, Elizabeth Anne. *See* ETHERINGTON, Mrs Elizabeth Anne

SMITH, Miss Elizabeth Jane. b 50. Birm Univ BA72. Trin Coll Bris 88. **d** 90 **p** 95. C Lowestoft and Kirkley *Nor* 90-94; TV Rugby *Cov* 94-01; C Shepton Mallet w Doulting *B & W* 01-03; R from 03; Chapl Mendip Primary Care Trust 01-06; Chapl Somerset Primary Care Trust from 06. *23 Compton Road, Shepton Mallet BA4 5QR* Tel (01749) 346184
E-mail revdlizsmith@btinternet.com

SMITH, Canon Elizabeth Marion. b 52. ACA76 FCA82. Carl Dioc Tr Inst 91. **d** 94 **p** 95. C Appleby *Carl* 94-98; P-in-c Hesket-in-the-Forest and Armathwaite 98-04; P-in-c Skelton and Hutton-in-the-Forest w Ivegill 98-04; R Inglewood Gp from 04; RD Penrith 06-09; Hon Can Carl Cathl from 08. *St Mary's Vicarage, High Hesket, Carlisle CA4 0HU* Tel (01697) 473320 Fax 473167 E-mail revdesmith@hotmail.com

SMITH, Eric Frederick. b 19. Lon Univ BA40 BD42. ALCD42. **d** 42 **p** 43. C Talbot Village *Sarum* 42-44; C S'wark St Jude 44-48; P-in-c Mottingham St Edward LD 48-56; V Lee Gd Shep w St Pet 56-67; Sub-Dean Lewisham 61-67; R Long Ditton 67-81; V Deal St Geo *Cant* 81-85; RD Sandwich 82-85; rtd 85; Perm to Offic *Cant* 85-09; Chapl Cant Sch of Min 88-94. *2 Parkside Avenue, London SW19 5ES*

SMITH, Eustace. b 20. St Pet Hall Ox BA43 MA46. Wycliffe Hall Ox 43. **d** 46 **p** 46. C Tiverton St Pet *Ex* 46-47; C Lenton *S'well* 47-49; C Aston SS Pet and Paul *Birm* 49-53; V Bermondsey St Anne S'wark 53-59; V Buckminster w Sewstern *Leic* 59-74; V Buckminster w Sewstern, Sproxton and Coston 74-82; R Algarkirk *Linc* 82-88; V Fosdyke 82-88; rtd 89; Perm to Offic *Leic* 89-00. *32 Wordsworth Way, Measham, Swadlincote DE12 7ER* Tel (01530) 273765

SMITH (*née* DAVIS), Felicity Ann. b 40. Bris Univ MB, ChB63. Qu Coll Birm 83. **dss** 86 **d** 87 **p** 94. NSM Dioc Bd for Soc Resp *Cov* 86-96; NSM Leamington Spa H Trin and Old Milverton from 96. *14 Oakwood Grove, Warwick CV34 5TD* Tel (01926) 492452 E-mail felicity@fandi.me.uk

SMITH, Francis Christian Lynford. b 36. Padgate Coll of Educn TCert59. Cuddesdon Coll 72. **d** 74 **p** 75. C Catford St Laur *S'wark* 74-79; P-in-c Vacoas St Paul Mauritius 79-80; Chapl Dulwich Coll 81-91; Chapl St Mich Univ Sch Victoria Canada from 91; rtd 01. *Apartment 403, 2626 Blackwood Street, Victoria BC V8T 3W3, Canada* Tel (001) (250) 598 3459
E-mail smudge4147@hotmail.com

SMITH, Francis James Prall. b 22. Nor Ord Course 73. **d** 76 **p** 77. NSM Gunthorpe w Bale *Nor* 76-82; NSM Friston *St E* 82-86; NSM Knodishall w Buxlow 82-86; NSM Aldringham w Thorpe, Knodishall w Buxlow etc 86-89; rtd 89; Perm to Offic *St E* 90-08. *6 Bluebell Way, Worlingham, Beccles NR34 7BT* Tel (01502) 711528

SMITH, Francis Malcolm. b 44. Open Univ BA82 FCMI ACIB69. EAMTC 90. **d** 93 **p** 94. NSM Prittlewell *Chelmsf* 93-08; Perm to Offic from 08. *14 St James Avenue, Southend-on-Sea SS1 3LH* Tel (01702) 586680 Fax 291166
E-mail franksmith44@hotmail.com

SMITH, Canon Frank. b 39. Nottm Univ CertEd65 Open Univ BA76. Paton Congr Coll Nottm 61 Cuddesdon Coll 68. **d** 69 **p** 70. C Davyhulme St Mary *Man* 69-72; PC Peak Forest and Wormhill *Derby* 72-78; R W Hallam and Mapperley 78-85; V Henleaze *Bris* 85-91; R Old Clifton 93-99; Hon Can Bris Cathl 99-01; rtd 01; Perm to Offic *Derby* from 01. *4 Hall Court, The Village, West Hallam, Ilkeston DE7 6GS* Tel 0115-944 3474

SMITH, Mrs Gabrielle Lynette Claire. b 55. St Aid Coll Dur BA70 ARCM73. SAOMC 95. **d** 98 **p** 99. NSM Gt Marlow w Marlow Bottom, Lt Marlow and Bisham *Ox* from 98. *29 Bovingdon Heights, Marlow SL7 2JR* Tel (01628) 482923

SMITH (*née* SAMPSON), Ms Gail Sampson. b 49. Towson State Univ (USA) BA85. Virginia Th Sem MDiv93. **d** 93 **p** 94. Assoc R Ellicott City St Jo USA 93-99; Perm to Offic *S'wark* 00-01; Hon C Kew St Phil and All SS w St Luke 01-02 and 06-07; The Netherlands 02-06; USA from 07. *Address temp unknown*
E-mail ukrevgss@aol.com

SMITH, Gareth Hugh St John. b 46. FCA69. SEITE BA06. **d** 06 **p** 07. NSM Tunbridge Wells St Phil *Roch* 06-08. *Hill View, Willetts Lane, Blackham, Tunbridge Wells TN3 9TU* Tel 07780-907066 (mobile)
E-mail gareth.smith@diocese-rochester.org

SMITH, Gary Russell. b 56. Southn Univ BTh94 Ox Brookes Univ DipEd02. Cuddesdon Coll 94. **d** 96 **p** 97. C Southampton Maybush St Pet *Win* 96-00. *Soar Valley College, Gleneagles Avenue, Leicester LE4 7GY* Tel 0116-266 9625

SMITH, Gavin Craig. b 71. Ridley Hall Cam 02. **d** 04 **p** 05. C Heatons *Man* 04-07; CF from 07. *clo MOD Chaplains (Army)* Tel (01980) 615804 Fax 615800 Mobile 07919-354796
E-mail gavinsmith1971@hotmail.com

SMITH, Geoffrey. *See* SMITH, Richard Geoffrey

SMITH, Geoffrey. b 45. Bernard Gilpin Soc Dur 65 Sarum Th Coll 66. **d** 69 **p** 70. C Hatfield *Sheff* 69-71; C Bolton St Pet *Man* 71-74; V Lt Hulton 74-78; P-in-c Newc St Andr and Soc Resp Adv *Newc* 78-87; Hon Can Newc Cathl 84-87; Dir Cen for Applied Chr Studies 87-91; Team Ldr Home Office Birm Drug Prevention Unit 91-93; Public Preacher *Birm* 87-93; C Brampton and Farlam and Castle Carrock w Cumrew *Carl* 93-96; ACUPA Link Officer 94-96; Can Res Bradf Cathl 96-00; Nat Dir Toc H 00-07; Perm to Offic *Ox* 00-02; Hon C Biddenham *St Alb* 02-07; rtd 07; Perm to Offic *Carl* and *Eur* from 07. *30 Waters Meet, Warwick Bridge, Carlisle CA4 8RT* Tel (01228) 560981 *or* 05602-231702 E-mail geoffsmith1@btinternet.com

SMITH, Canon Geoffrey Cobley. b 30. Bps' Coll Cheshunt 63. **d** 65 **p** 66. C Hockerill *St Alb* 65-68; C Evesham *Worc* 68-72; V Walberswick w Blythburgh *St E* 72-85; RD Halesworth 81-85; R Newmarket St Mary w Exning St Agnes 85-00; RD Mildenhall 86-00; Hon Can St E Cathl 87-00; rtd 00; Perm to Offic *St E* from 00. *78 Eastgate Street, Bury St Edmunds IP33 1YR* Tel (01284) 731061

SMITH, Geoffrey Keith. b 37. Lon Coll of Div 57. **d** 60 **p** 61. C Leek St Luke *Lich* 60-63; C Trentham 63-66; V Lilleshall 66-84; P-in-c Sheriffhales w Woodcote 83-84; V Lilleshall and Sheriffhales 84-87; P-in-c Haughton 87-91; R Derrington, Haughton and Ranton 91-93; RD Stafford 95-03; rtd 03. *19 Meadow Drive, Haughton, Stafford ST18 9HU* Tel (01785) 259076

SMITH, Geoffrey Raymond. b 49. AKC71. St Aug Coll Cant 71. **d** 72 **p** 73. C Hendon St Alphage *Lon* 72-75; C Notting Hill St Mich and Ch Ch 75-78; P-in-c Isleworth St Fran 78-83; P-in-c Chipping Ongar *Chelmsf* 83-84; R 84-86; R Shelley 84-86; R Chipping Ongar w Shelley 86-89; RD Ongar 88-89; P-in-c Harlow St Mary Magd 89-90; V 90-98; R Woodford St Mary w St Phil and St Jas 98-08; TR Loughton St Jo from 08. *The Rectory, Church Lane, Loughton IG10 1PD* Tel (020) 8508 1224

SMITH, George Frederick. b 35. AKC59. **d** 60 **p** 61. C Radford *Cov* 60-64; C Kenilworth St Nic 64-67; V Burton Dassett 67-71; OCF 67-71; CF 71-74; V Lapley w Wheaton Aston *Lich* 74-80; V Gt Wyrley 80-90; V Shareshill 90-95; rtd 95. *Brantome, North Road, Lampeter SA48 7JA*

SMITH, Canon George Robert Henry. b 24. Chich Th Coll 49. **d** 52 **p** 53. C Glouc St Steph 52-56; V Parkend 56-65; P-in-c Clearwell 60-62; V Tuffley 65-82; Hon Can Glouc Cathl 81-95; R Leckhampton St Pet 82-94; rtd 94; NSM Westcote w Icomb and Bledington *Glouc* 95-98; Perm to Offic from 98. *1 The Paddocks, Church Lane, Bledington, Chipping Norton OX7 6XB* Tel (01608) 659194

SMITH, Gerald. b 36. Sarum Th Coll 61. **d** 63 **p** 64. C Menston w Woodhead *Bradf* 63-66; Chapl RAF 66-70; C Hoylake *Ches* 70-72; R Inverurie *Ab* 72-74; R Kemnay 72-74; TV Hucknall Torkard *S'well* 74-75; R Falkland Is 75-78; V Luddenden w Luddenden Foot *Wakef* 79-86; V Scopwick Gp *Linc* 86-94; P-in-c Leasingham 94-96; rtd 96; Perm to Offic *Ex* from 96 and *Truro* from 00. *Ivy Cottage, Woolsery, Bideford EX39 5QS* Tel and fax (01237) 431298

SMITH, Mrs Gillian. b 55. EAMTC 02. **d** 05 **p** 06. NSM Burwell w Reach *Ely* 05-09; P-in-c Potton w Sutton and Cockayne Hatley *St Alb* from 09. *The Rectory, Hatley Road, Potton, Sandy SG19 2RP* Tel (01767) 260782
E-mail gillsmith.pot@gmail.com

SMITH, Mrs Gillian Angela. b 39. RGN60 RM62. All Nations Chr Coll IDC65. **d** 94 **p** 95. NSM Haydock St Mark *Liv* 94-96; Perm to Offic *Ely* 96-02; rtd 99; Hon C Milton *Win* 02-03; Perm to Offic *Ely* from 03 and *Chelmsf* from 04. *15 The Sheltons, Frinton-on-Sea CO13 0LX* Tel (01255) 671041
E-mail gill.rev@gmail.com

SMITH, Godfrey Declan Burfield. b 42. TCD BA64 MA67 PGCE65. Sarum Th Coll. **d** 69 **p** 70. Zambia 70-75; Perm to Offic *D & G* 81-02; S Regional Sec (Ireland) CMS 81-99; Overseas Sec 87-93; Miss Personnel Sec 93-99; I Donoughmore and Donard w Dunlavin *D & G* from 02. *The Rectory, Donard, Co Wicklow, Republic of Ireland* Tel (00353) (45) 404631 Fax 404800 Mobile 87-298 7364 E-mail declansmith14@gmail.com *or* 3deesparish@gmail.com

SMITH, Graeme Richard. b 65. Leeds Univ BA87 MA91 Birm Univ PhD97. Qu Coll Birm 87. **d** 89 **p** 90. C Daventry *Pet* 89-92; Perm to Offic *Birm* 92-97; Lect Th Westmr Coll Ox 97-00; Co Ecum Officer *Ox* 97-00; Sen Lect Ox Brookes Univ 00-02; Dean Non-Res Tr St Mich Coll Llan 04-08; Sen Lect Chich Univ from 08. *37 Middleton Hall Road, Birmingham B30 1AB* Tel 0121-459 0565

SMITH, Graham. *See* SMITH, John Graham

SMITH, Graham. b 39. Univ of Wales (Ban) CertEd60 Lon Univ DipEd75. **d** 01 **p** 02. OLM Upper Holme Valley *Wakef* 01-05; NSM E Richmond *Ripon* 05-08; rtd 08. *15 Church Street, Denby Village, Ripley DE5 8PA* Tel (01332) 881324 Mobile 07918-025346 E-mail graham.smith50@btopenworld.com

SMITH, Graham Arthur James. b 43. MRICS68. STETS 98 Coll of Resurr Mirfield 01. **d** 01 **p** 02. NSM Broadstone *Sarum* 01-06; NSM Christchurch *Win* from 06. *The Priest's House, Magdalen Lane, Christchurch BH23 1PH* Tel 07710-328685 (mobile) E-mail fr.graham.smith@talk21.com

SMITH, The Very Revd Graham Charles Morell. b 47. St Chad's Coll Dur BA74. Westcott Ho Cam 74. **d** 76 **p** 77. C Tooting All SS *S'wark* 76-80; TV Thamesmead 80-87; TR Kidlington w Hampton Poyle *Ox* 87-97; RD Ox 89-95; TR Leeds City *Ripon* 97-04; Hon Can Ripon Cathl 97-04; Dean Nor from 04. *The Deanery, Cathedral Close, Norwich NR1 4EG* Tel (01603) 218308 Mobile 07798-916321

E-mail graham@gcmsmith.org.uk *or* dean@cathedral.org.uk

SMITH, Graham David Noel. b 37. Oak Hill Th Coll 72. **d** 73 **p** 74. C Southborough St Pet w Ch Ch and St Matt *Roch* 73-76; C Bedworth *Cov* 76-79; R Treeton *Sheff* 79-84; V Riddlesden *Bradf* 84-96; RD S Craven 91-96; rtd 96; Hon C Ilkley All SS *Bradf* 97-03; Perm to Offic from 03. *26 Hawthorne Grove, Burley in Wharfdale, Ilkley LS29 7RF* Tel (01943) 864754 E-mail grahams@26hawthorne.freeserve.co.uk

SMITH, Graham John. b 31. **d** 75 **p** 76. NSM Devonport St Mark Ford *Ex* 75-81; NSM Plympton St Maurice 81-90; V Ernesettle 90-03; P-in-c 03-08; rtd 08. *15 Abingdon Road, Plymouth PL4 6HZ* Tel (01752) 603812 Mobile 07974-815552 E-mail fathergrahamsmith@hotmail.com

SMITH, Graham John. b 60. RN Eng Coll Plymouth BScEng84. Trin Coll Bris BA90 St Jo Coll Nottm MA00. **d** 90 **p** 91. C Herne *Cant* 90-93; Chapl RN 93-96; C Henfield w Shermanbury and Woodmancote *Chich* 96-98; Chapl Sussex Police 96-98; Chapl Portsm Hosps NHS Trust 98-00; P-in-c Cosham and Chapl Highbury Coll of FE Portsm 00-05; CME Officer *Portsm* 03-05; rtd 05; Perm to Offic *Portsm* from 06. *18 Poynings Place, Portsmouth PO1 2PB* Tel (023) 9229 1239 Mobile 07970-826160 E-mail gjsmith@first-web.co.uk

SMITH, Graham Russell. b 60. New Coll Ox BA81 MA89 Lon Univ BD89. Qu Coll Birm 02. **d** 04 **p** 05. C Yardley St Edburgha *Birm* 04-08; TV Bushbury *Lich* from 08. *The Good Shepherd Vicarage, 17 Goodyear Avenue, Wolverhampton WV10 9JX* Tel (01902) 731713 Mobile 07746-994186 E-mail grakiew@talktalk.net

SMITH, Grahame Clarence. b 32. Lich Th Coll 58. **d** 60 **p** 61. C New Sleaford *Linc* 60-63; R Tydd 63-76; V Barholm w Stowe 76-81; V Tallington 76-81; R Uffington 76-81; P-in-c W Deeping 76-77; R 77-81; R Uffington 81-92; rtd 92; Perm to Offic *Linc* 92-95. *Keeper's Cottage, Careby Road, Aunby, Stamford PE9 4EG* Tel (01780) 66386

SMITH, Greg Peter. b 60. Warwick Univ BA86 Qu Coll Birm BA99. WMMTC 97. **d** 99 **p** 00. C Binley *Cov* 99-04; P-in-c E Green from 04. *St Andrew's Vicarage, Church Lane, Eastern Green, Coventry CV5 7BX* Tel (024) 7642 2856 E-mail gregsmith31760@aol.com

SMITH, Gregory James. *See* CLIFTON-SMITH, Gregory James

SMITH, Canon Guy Howard. b 33. Man Univ BA54. Coll of Resurr Mirfield 60. **d** 62 **p** 63. C Oswestry H Trin *Lich* 62-66; Chapl RNR 63-03; Prin St Aug Sch Betong Malaysia 66-69; V Willenhall St Anne *Lich* 69-79; P-in-c Willenhall St Steph 75-79; Tr Officer Dio Lake Malawi 79-82; Adn Lilongwe 80-82; V Tettenhall Wood *Lich* 82-89; TR 89-91; TR Kidderminster St Jo and H Innocents *Worc* 91-99; rtd 99; Perm to Offic *Worc* from 99; P-in-c St Petersburg *Eur* 05-06. *11 Church Walk, Stourport-on-Severn DY13 0AL* Tel (01299) 828120 E-mail mandgs36@tiscali.co.uk

SMITH, Mrs Gwendoline Anne. b 52. K Coll Lon BA97. SEITE 97. **d** 99 **p** 00. C Erith St Paul *Roch* 99-02; V Hadlow from 02. *The Vicarage, Maidstone Road, Hadlow, Tonbridge TN11 0DJ* Tel (01732) 850238 E-mail gwen@diocese-rochester.org

SMITH, Harold. *See* SMITH, Robert Harold

SMITH, Harold. b 20. Qu Coll Birm 77. **d** 80 **p** 81. NSM Gravelly Hill *Birm* 80-85; NSM Duddeston w Nechells 85-93; Perm to Offic from 93. *37 Dovey Tower, Duddeston Manor Road, Birmingham B7 4LE* Tel 0121-682 9417

SMITH, Harvey Jefferson. b 19. AMCT39 FIEE38 FIMechE52 FIPlantE67 ACIArb78. St Alb Minl Tr Scheme 81. **d** 88 **p** 97. NSM Hemel Hempstead *St Alb* 88-92 and 95-00; Perm to Offic 92-95 and from 00. *43 Garland Close, Hemel Hempstead HP2 5HU* Tel (01442) 266377

SMITH, Sister Hazel Ferguson Waide. b 33. Univ Coll Lon BA55. **dss** 64 **d** 87. CSA 58-77; St Etheldreda's Children's Home Bedf 64-85; Bedford St Paul *St Alb* 85-92; Par Dn 87-92; Perm to Offic *St Alb* from 92; *Ox* 93-00; Assoc Sister CSA from 03. *Paddock House, 6 Linford Lane, Willen, Milton Keynes MK15 9DL* Tel and fax (01908) 397267 Mobile 07789-654881 E-mail hazel.s35@ukonline.co.uk

SMITH, Henry Robert. b 41. Lancaster Poly Cov BSc66. Qu Coll Birm 75. **d** 78 **p** 79. Hon C Hillmorton *Cov* 78-81; Lic to Offic *S'well* 81-85; Hon C Radcliffe-on-Trent and Shelford etc 85-89; C Sutton in Ashfield St Mary 89-92; P-in-c Forest Town 92-98; P-in-c Babworth w Sutton-cum-Lound 98-02; P-in-c Scofton w Osberton 98-02; R Babworth w Sutton-cum-Lound and Scofton etc 02-06; rtd 06. *61 Eldon Street, Tuxford, Newark NG22 0LG* Tel (01777) 872819 E-mail bobsmith@dircon.co.uk

SMITH, Howard Alan. b 46. St Jo Coll Dur BA73. Cranmer Hall Dur. **d** 74 **p** 75. C Brighton St Matthias *Chich* 74-77; C Henfield w Shermanbury and Woodmancote 77-80; R Northiam 80-87; Chapl St Ebba's Hosp Epsom 87-94; Chapl Qu Mary's Hosp Carshalton 87-94; Chapl Merton and Sutton Community NHS Trust 94-99; Chapl Epsom and St Helier Univ Hosps NHS Trust 99-08; rtd 08; Perm to Offic *S'wark* from 08. *72 Park Lane, Wallington SM6 0TL* Tel (020) 8643 3300 E-mail howard_a_smith2003@yahoo.co.uk

SMITH, Howard Gilbert. b 48. Leeds Univ BA69. St Steph Ho Ox BA71 MA75 Ridley Hall Cam 73. **d** 73 **p** 74. C Wallsend St Luke *Newc* 73-76; C Farnworth and Kearsley *Man* 76-77; P-in-c Farnworth All SS 77-78; TV E Farnworth and Kearsley 78-82; V Belfield 82-93; V Leesfield 93-04; V Northallerton w Kirby Sigston *York* from 04. *27 Mowbray Road, Northallerton DL6 1QT* Tel (01609) 770082

SMITH, Ian. b 62. Hull Univ BA83. Oak Hill Th Coll BA88. **d** 88 **p** 89. C W Hampstead St Luke *Lon* 88-90; C Woking St Pet *Guildf* 90-95; V Leyland St Jo *Blackb* 95-02; C Goole *Sheff* 02-03; P-in-c Sheff St Paul from 03. *St Paul's Vicarage, Wheata Road, Sheffield S5 9FP* Tel 0114-246 8494 E-mail ian.smith@sheffield.anglican.org

SMITH, Canon Ian Walker. b 29. Leeds Univ BA52. Coll of Resurr Mirfield 52. **d** 54 **p** 55. C Moulsecoomb *Chich* 54-61; Chapl K Sch Cant 61-62; C Crawley *Chich* 62-79; TV 79-81; R Clenchwarton *Ely* 81-94; RD Lynn Marshland 84-94; Hon Can Ely Cathl 88-94; Perm to Offic *Nor* 88-94; rtd 94; Perm to Offic *Ely* from 94. *27 Jubilee Drive, Dersingham, King's Lynn PE31 6YA* Tel (01485) 540203

SMITH, Irene Lillian. b 47. **d** 99 **p** 00. OLM Moston St Chad *Man* from 99. *1 Walmersley Road, Manchester M40 3RS* Tel 0161-682 5927 E-mail irenel.smith@ukgateway.net

SMITH, Mrs Irene Mary. b 43. Shenstone Coll of Educn CertEd64 Lon Univ BD77. OLM course 96. **d** 99 **p** 00. OLM Uttoxeter Area *Lich* from 99. *16 Teanhurst Close, Tean, Stoke-on-Trent ST10 4NN* Tel (01538) 722975 E-mail irene.smith0@btinternet.com

SMITH, Miss Irene Victoria. b 45. SRN66 SCM69. **d** 03 **p** 04. OLM Lawton Moor *Man* from 03. *288 Wythenshawe Road, Manchester M23 9DA* Tel 0161-998 4100 Mobile 07889-116856

SMITH, James. *See* SMITH, Michael James

SMITH, James. *See* SMITH, Philip James

SMITH, James. b 26. NEOC 76. **d** 79 **p** 80. NSM Seaton Hirst *Newc* 79-82; NSM Cresswell and Lynemouth 82-88; NSM Cambois 88-93; rtd 93; Perm to Offic *Newc* from 93. *140 Pont Street, Ashington NE63 0PX* Tel (01670) 816557

SMITH, James Edward. b 30. Chich Th Coll 57. **d** 58 **p** 59. C Ellesmere Port *Ches* 58-61; C W Bromwich All SS *Lich* 61-63; Chapl RN 63-65; V Walton St Jo *Liv* 65-71; V Anfield St Columba 71-79; V Altcar 79-92; rtd 92; Perm to Offic *Linc* 93-02. *The Hollies, 43 Carlton Road, Bassingham, Lincoln LN5 9HB* Tel (01522) 788260

SMITH, James Harold. b 31. Ch Coll Tasmania ThL61. **d** 61 **p** 61. Australia 61-63, 66-85 and 92-94; Canada 64-65; Chapl St Chris Hospice Lon 86-87; Asst Chapl Brook Gen Hosp Lon 87-92; Asst Chapl Greenwich Distr Hosp Lon 87-92; Perm to Offic *S'wark* 94-07. *Poplar Cottage, 80 Charlton Road, London SE7 7EY* Tel (020) 8858 4692

SMITH, James Henry. b 32. St Aid Birkenhead. **d** 65 **p** 66. C Wigan St Cath *Liv* 65-68; V Parkfield in Middleton *Man* 68-77; V Bolton Breightmet St Jas 77-97; rtd 97; Perm to Offic *Liv* from 97. *Flat 4, 14A Cropton Road, Formby, Liverpool L37 4AD* Tel (01704) 833682

SMITH, Janet. *See* SMITH, Ms Patricia Janet

SMITH, Mrs Janice Lilian. b 51. Open Univ BSc98. NOC 98. **d** 01 **p** 02. NSM Yeadon St Jo *Bradf* 01-06; P-in-c Bramhope *Ripon* from 06; P-in-c Ireland Wood from 09. *The Vicarage, 26 Leeds Road, Bramhope, Leeds LS16 9BQ* Tel 0113-203 7523 E-mail revjanice.smith@tiscali.co.uk

SMITH, Jeffery Donald Morris. b 23. d 53 p 54. S Rhodesia 53-61; R Old Deer *Ab* 61-63; R Fraserburgh 63-68; S Africa 68-73; P-in-c Bintree w Themelthorpe *Nor* 73-76; V Twyford w Guist 73-76; R Twyford w Guist and Bintry w Themelthorpe 76-80; RD Sparham 79-81; R Twyford w Guist w Bintry w Themelthorpe etc 81; TR Hempnall 81-84; R Catfield 84-89; R Ingham w Sutton 84-89; rtd 89; Perm to Offic *Nor* from 89. *27 Dale Road, Dereham NR19 2DD* Tel (01362) 697022

SMITH, Canon Jeffry Bradford. b 56. BA82. Ch Div Sch of the Pacific (USA) MDiv85 Ripon Coll Cuddesdon. d 86 p 87. C Frimley *Guildf* 87-91; R E and W Clandon 91-03; Chapl HM Pris Send 94-96; Chapl HM Pris Channings Wood 03-04; Can Res and Sub-Dean Bermuda from 04. *Cathedral of the Most Holy Trinity, Church Street, Hamilton HM CX, Bermuda* Tel (001441) 292 4033

SMITH, Mrs Jennifer Pamela. b 63. Girton Coll Cam BA85 MA88. Oak Hill Th Coll BA91. d 91 p 94. C Rawdon *Bradf* 91-93; Chapl Bradf Cathl 93-96; P-in-c Kelbrook 96-00; Asst Chapl Airedale NHS Trust from 01. *24 Greenacres, Skipton BD23 1BX* Tel (01756) 790852
E-mail jenny.smith@bradford.anglican.org

SMITH, Jeremy John Hawthorn. b 52. Birm Univ BSc73 Lanc Univ MA97. CBDTI 94. d 97 p 98. NSM Long Marton w Dufton and w Milburn *Carl* 97-00; NSM Hesket-in-the-Forest and Armathwaite 00-04; NSM Skelton and Hutton-in-the-Forest w Ivegill 00-04; NSM Ainstable 00-04; NSM Inglewood Gp from 04. *St Mary's Vicarage, High Hesket, Carlisle CA4 0HU* Tel (01697) 473320

SMITH, Jeremy Victor. b 60. Keble Coll Ox BA82. Chich Th Coll 83. d 85 p 86. C Alton St Lawr *Win* 85-88; C W Hampstead St Jas *Lon* 88-93; V St Geo-in-the-East St Mary 93-97. *18 The Grange, Grange Road, London W4 4DE* Tel (020) 8742 7104

SMITH, Jesse Lee. b 70. Man Univ BA93 Nottm Univ MA96. Linc Th Coll 94 Westcott Ho Cam 95. d 96 p 97. C Gomersal *Wakef* 96-00; C Penarth All SS *Llan* 00-02; TV Cen Cardiff 02-03; V Hartlepool H Trin *Dur* 03-08; V Caerau w Ely *Llan* from 08. *The Vicarage, Cowbridge Road West, Cardiff CF5 5BQ* Tel (029) 2056 32564 E-mail jls4hart@yahoo.co.uk

SMITH, John. *See* SMITH, Stephen John

SMITH, John Alec. b 37. Lon Coll of Div ALCD62 BD63. d 63 p 64. C Cromer *Nor* 63-66; C Barking St Marg *Chelmsf* 66-69; V Attercliffe *Sheff* 69-75; P-in-c Sheff St Barn 76-78; V Sheff St Barn and St Mary 78-89; Ind Chapl 78-89; RD Ecclesall 80-85; TR Chippenham St Paul w Hardenhuish etc *Bris* 89-00; V Kington St Michael 89-00; rtd 00. *82 Victoria Road, Bidford-on-Avon, Alcester B50 4AR* Tel (01789) 772072

SMITH, John Bartlett. b 50. St Chad's Coll Dur BA73 ACIPD. Cuddesdon Coll 73. d 76 p 77. C Heref St Martin 76-86; NSM Isleworth St Mary *Lon* 86-89; NSM Millom *Carl* 89-92; NSM Balham St Mary and St Jo *S'wark* 92-04. *101 Gosberton Road, London SW12 8LG* Tel (020) 8675 1743

SMITH, John Denmead. b 44. Keble Coll Ox BA65 MA69 St Jo Coll Ox DPhil71. Coll of Resurr Mirfield 72. d 75 p 76. NSM Win St Lawr and St Maurice w St Swithun 75-80; Chapl Win Coll 75-04; Sen Chapl 04-06; rtd 06; Lect Uganda Chr Univ Mukono from 06. *56D North Bar Without, Beverley HU17 7AR* Tel (01482) 865513 E-mail jds1000@gmail.com

SMITH, John Ernest. b 52. St Andr Univ MTheol77. Wycliffe Hall Ox 78. d 79 p 80. C Bermondsey St Mary w St Olave, St Jo etc *S'wark* 79-87; P-in-c Whyteleafe 8/-9/; RD Caterham 96-98; P-in-c Merstham and Gatton from 98. *The Rectory, Gatton Bottom, Merstham, Redhill RH1 3BH* Tel (01737) 643755 Fax 642954 E-mail revjohn.e.smith@btinternet.com

SMITH, John Graham. b 32. d 78 p 79. NSM Hordle *Win* 78-00; rtd 00; Perm to Offic *Win* from 00. *3 Marryat Road, New Milton BH25 5LW* Tel (01425) 615701

SMITH, John Lawrence. b 43. Birm Univ BSc65. Linc Th Coll 67. d 70 p 71. C Frodingham *Linc* 70-75; TV Gt Grimsby St Mary and St Jas 75-83; V Wolverhampton St Andr *Lich* from 83. *St Andrew's Vicarage, 66 Albert Road, Wolverhampton WV6 0AF* Tel (01902) 712935

SMITH, Canon John Leslie. b 44. Trin Coll Cam BA65 MA71. Ripon Coll Cuddesdon 79. d 81 p 82. C Ollerton *S'well* 81-84; P-in-c Farndon and Thorpe 84-88; P-in-c Winthorpe and Langford w Holme 88-95; Dioc Chief Insp Ch Schs 88-95; Dir of Educn *Pet* 95-99; P-in-c Cottingham w E Carlton 97-99; Dir of Educn *Roch* from 99; Hon Can Roch Cathl from 04; P-in-c Bredgar w Bicknor and Frinsted w Wormshill etc *Cant* from 05. *The Vicarage, Parsonage Lane, Bredgar, Sittingbourne ME9 8HA* Tel (01622) 884387 *or* (01634) 843667 Fax (01634) 843674 E-mail john.smith@rochester.anglican.org

SMITH, John Macdonald. b 29. Ch Coll Cam BA52 MA56. Wells Th Coll 56. d 58 p 59. C Westbury on-Trym H Trin *Bris* 58-60, C Reading St Giles *Ox* 60-63; V Kidmore End 63 82; rtd 82. *38 Main Road, Evesham WR11 4TL* Tel (01386) 870918

SMITH, John Malcolm. b 36. ACIB60. NOC 81. d 84 p 85. NSM Bury St Pet *Man* from 84. *46 Ajax Drive, Bury BL9 8EF* Tel 0161-766 8378

SMITH, John Roger. b 36. Dur Univ BA59. Tyndale Hall Bris 59. d 61 p 62. C Chaddesden St Mary *Derby* 61-63; C Gresley 63-66; V Burton Ch Ch *Lich* 66-76; V Doncaster St Mary *Sheff* 76-92; R Barnburgh w Melton on the Hill etc 92-01; rtd 01; Perm to Offic *Bradf* from 03. *2 Fieldhead Drive, Cross Hills, Keighley BD20 7RJ* Tel (01535) 634062

SMITH, John Simon. b 46. Middx Hosp MB, BS70 FRCGP91. Ripon Coll Cuddesdon 05. d 06 p 07. NSM Kettering SS Pet and Paul from 06. *34 Poplars Farm Road, Barton Seagrave, Kettering NN15 5AG* Tel (01536) 513786 E-mail john@poplarsfarm.org

SMITH, John Sydney. b 36. Lanc Univ MA97 ALA59 FLA68 FISM82. CBDTI 94. d 97 p 98. NSM Arthuret, Nicholforest and Kirkandrews on Esk *Carl* 97-02; rtd 02; Perm to Offic *Carl* from 01. *The Jays, 3 White House, Walton, Brampton CA8 2DJ* Tel (01697) 741114 E-mail johnandjill.thejays@btinternet.com

SMITH, John Thomas. b 29. Keele Univ DASE72 Wolv Poly MPhil81 PhD87. WMMTC 87. d 91 p 92. NSM Drayton in Hales *Lich* 91-96; NSM Cheswardine, Childs Ercall, Hales, Hinstock etc 96-98; rtd 98; Perm to Offic *Lich* from 98. *Red Bank House, Market Drayton TF9 1AY* Tel (01630) 652302

SMITH, John Thompson. b 30. Wycliffe Hall Ox 64. d 66 p 67. C Walsall *Lich* 66-69; V Stoke Prior *Worc* 69-75; Asst Gen Sec Red Triangle Club 75-85; R Tendring and Lt Bentley w Beaumont cum Moze *Chelmsf* 85-89; R Fairstead w Terling and White Notley etc 89-92; Chapl Heath Hosp Tendring 85-92; rtd 92; Perm to Offic *B & W* from 92. *1 Harvey Close, Weston-super-Mare BS22 7DW* Tel (01934) 514256

SMITH, John Trevor. b 47. GGSM. Coll of Resurr Mirfield 74. d 77 p 78. C Loughton St Jo *Chelmsf* 77-80; C Ruislip St Martin *Lon* 80-84; P-in-c Southall Ch Redeemer 84-91; V Kingsbury St Andr from 91. *St Andrew's Vicarage, 28 Old Church Lane, London NW9 8RZ* Tel (020) 8205 7447 Fax 8205 7652 E-mail standrews.kingsbury@london.anglican.org

SMITH, John William. b 51. EAMTC 00. d 03 p 04. NSM Erpingham w Calthorpe, Ingworth, Aldborough etc *Nor* 03-06; P-in-c Roughton and Felbrigg, Metton, Sustead etc from 06. *18 Pound Lane, Aylsham, Norwich NR11 6DR* Tel (01263) 734761 E-mail ajksmith@btinternet.com

SMITH, Jonathan Paul. b 60. Univ of Wales (Lamp) BA81. Wycliffe Hall Ox 82. d 84 p 85. C Baglan *Llan* 84-88; C Gabalfa 88-90; R Llangammarch w Llanganten and Llanlleonfel etc *S & B* 90-01; Dioc Missr 95-01; R Denbigh *St As* from 01. *The Rectory, 5 St David's Court, Denbigh LL16 3EJ* Tel (01745) 812284 E-mail plwyfdinbych@googlemail.com

SMITH, The Ven Jonathan Peter. b 55. K Coll Lon BD77 AKC77 Cam Univ PGCE78. Westcott Ho Cam 79. d 80 p 81. C Gosforth All SS *Newc* 80-82; C Waltham Abbey *Chelmsf* 82-85; Chapl City Univ 85-88; R Harrold and Carlton w Chellington *St Alb* 88-97; Chapl Beds Police 90-97; V Harpenden St Jo 97-08; RD Wheathampstead 99-04; adn Bart from 08. *6 Sopwell Lane, St Albans AL1 1RR* Tel (01727) 818121 E-mail archdstalbans@stalbans.anglican.org

SMITH, Joseph Paul Tobias George. b 73. Ox Univ BTh95 Ex Univ MA97. d 08 p 09. OLM Talbot Village *Sarum* from 08. *16 Southlea Avenue, Bournemouth BH6 3AB* Tel (01202) 424148 E-mail sudibb1@aol.com

SMITH, Joyce Mary. b 52. Lon Hosp BDS74 Nottm Univ MMedSc77 Lon Univ PhD84 MCCDRCS89. EAMTC. d 00 p 01. C Harlow St Mary and St Hugh w St Jo the Bapt *Chelmsf* 00-02; C Waltham H Cross 02-03; TV from 03. *St Lawrence House, 46 Mallion Court, Waltham Abbey EN9 3EQ* Tel (01992) 767916 E-mail joyce@smith2767.fsnet.co.uk

SMITH, Miss Judith. b 74. SS Coll Cam BA95 MA98 PGCE97. Trin Coll Bris BA09. d 09. C Beeston *Ripon* from 09. *38 Beechcroft View, Leeds LS11 0LN* Tel 0113-270 0631 Mobile 07974-248841 E-mail jude@judesmith.me.uk

SMITH, Preb Julian. b 48. K Coll Lon 67 Linc Th Coll 71. d 73 p 74. C Taunton Lyngford *B & W* 73-76; TV Wellington and Distr 76-81; R Axbridge w Shipham and Rowberrow 81-96; Chapl St Jo Hosp Axbridge 84-93; V Taunton St Andr *B & W* 96-07; P-in-c Wells St Thos w Horrington from 07; P-in-c Chewton Mendip w Ston Easton, Litton etc from 08; Preb Wells Cathl from 07; Sub-Dean from 09. *The Vicarage, 94 St Thomas's Street, Wells BA5 2UZ* Tel (01749) 672193 E-mail picstthomas@btconnect.com

SMITH, Julian William. b 64. Liv Univ BSc85. Trin Coll Bris BA93. d 93 p 94. C Henfynyw w Aberaeron and Llanddewi Aberarth *St D* 93-97; V Llansantffraed and Llanbadarn Trefeglwys etc 97-05; V Llansantffraed w Llanrhystud and Llanddeiniol from 05. *The Vicarage, 11 Maes Wyre, Llanrhystud SY23 5AH* Tel (01974) 202336

SMITH, Mrs Katherine. b 42. Sussex Univ BA65. d 07 p 08. NSM Battersea St Luke *S'wark* from 07. *74 Alfriston Road, London SW11 6NW* Tel (020) 7228 3079 E-mail katherine.smith42@btopenworld.com

SMITH, Keith. b 46. ACIB. S Dios Minl Tr Scheme 85. d 87 p 88. NSM W Worthing St Jo *Chich* 87-94; NSM Maybridge 94-96; C Durrington 96-01; V Pagham from 01. *The Vicarage, Church Lane, Pagham, Bognor Regis PO21 4NX* Tel (01243) 262713

SMITH, Kenneth Robert. b 48. K Coll Lon BD75 AKC75. St Aug Coll Cant 75. **d** 76 **p** 77. C Birtley *Dur* 76-80; V Lamesley 80-90; R Whitburn from 90. *The Rectory, 51 Front Street, Whitburn, Sunderland SR6 7JD* Tel 0191-529 2232

SMITH, Kenneth Victor George. b 37. ALCD61 Lon Univ BD62. **d** 62 **p** 63. Hon C Bromley Common St Aug *Roch* 62-66; Hon C Streatham Immanuel w St Anselm *S'wark* 66-68; Perm to Offic 68-78; Chapl Whitgift Sch and Ho Croydon 78-97; Hon C Sanderstead All SS 78-91; Hon C Croydon St Jo 91-97; rtd 02. *Bridle Ways, Haling Grove, South Croydon CR2 6DQ* Tel (020) 8680 4460

SMITH, Kevin. b 66. Westmr Coll Ox BA89. Chich Th Coll 90. **d** 92 **p** 93. C Worksop Priory *S'well* 92-96; V New Cantley *Sheff* 96-03; P-in-c Horden *Dur* 03-06; V from 06. *The Vicarage, 4 Stapylton Drive, Peterlee SR8 4HY*

SMITH, Laurence Sidney. b 37. Sarum & Wells Th Coll 70. **d** 73 **p** 74. C Surbiton St Matt *S'wark* 73-76; C Horley 76-81; V W Ewell *Guildf* 81-90; V W Byfleet 90-02; rtd 02; Perm to Offic *Glouc* from 03. *Candlemill Cottage, Millbank, George Street, Nailsworth, Stroud GL6 0AG* Tel (01453) 836432

SMITH, Lawrence Paul. b 51. Ch Ch Coll Cant CertEd72 Southn Univ BTh81. Chich Th Coll 76. **d** 79 **p** 80. C Margate St Jo *Cant* 79-84; R Eythorne and Elvington w Waldershare etc 84-97; Par Min Development Adv Kensington Area *Lon* from 97; NSM Isleworth St Fran from 00; P-in-c from 05. *St Francis Vicarage, 865 Great West Road, Isleworth TW7 5PD* Tel (020) 8568 9098 *or* 8580 2142 Fax 8560 8113
E-mail lawrence.smith@london.anglican.org

SMITH, Lewis Shand. b 52. Aber Univ MA74 Edin Univ BD78 FRSA00. Edin Th Coll 74. **d** 77 **p** 78. C Wishaw *Glas* 77-79; P-in-c 79-80; C Motherwell 77-79; P-in-c 79-80; R Lerwick and Burravoe *Ab* 80-00; Can St Andr Cathl 93-00; R Dumfries *Glas* 00-05; Miss to Seamen 80-00; Lic to Offic *Edin* from 08. *27 Abbotsford Court, Colinton Road, Edinburgh EH10 5EH* Tel 0131-447 2595 E-mail shand.smith@talk21.com

SMITH, Mrs Linda Jean. b 61. Ripon Coll Cuddesdon 97. **d** 99 **p** 00. C St Martin w Looe *Truro* 99-03; P-in-c Talland from 03; C Lanreath, Pelynt and Bradoc from 03. *Trelawne Glebe, Trelawne Cross, Pelynt, Looe PL13 2NA* Tel (01503) 272640
E-mail trelawnevicarage@ukonline.co.uk

SMITH, Linnet. *See* SMITH, Diana Linnet

SMITH, Miss Lorna Cassandra. b 43. Open Univ BA76. Cant Sch of Min 82. **dss** 86 **d** 87 **p** 94. Birchington w Acol and Minnis Bay *Cant* 86-92; Par Dn 87-92; C Addlestone *Guildf* 92-97; V Englefield Green 97-05; rtd 05; Perm to Offic *Guildf* from 05 and *Lon* from 08. *39 Simons Walk, Englefield Green, Egham TW20 9SJ* Tel (01784) 470800 E-mail revlcs@aol.com

SMITH, Mrs Lorna Rosalind. b 53. Oak Hill NSM Course 89. **d** 92 **p** 94. NSM Squirrels Heath *Chelmsf* 92-94; NSM Stanford-le-Hope w Mucking 94-97; P-in-c Fobbing 97-04; P-in-c Tillingham from 04. *The Vicarage, 6 Bakery Close, Tillingham, Southminster CM0 7TT* Tel (01621) 778017
E-mail lornads24@aol.com

SMITH, Lynford. *See* SMITH, Francis Christian Lynford

SMITH (née THORNTON), Magdalen Mary. b 69. Warwick Univ BA90. Qu Coll Birm BD95. **d** 96 **p** 97. C Kirkby *Liv* 96-98; C Birm St Martin w Bordesley St Andr 00-03; NSM Tilston and Shocklach *Ches* 03-08; C Wilmslow from 08. *15 Parkway, Wilmslow SK9 1LS* Tel (01625) 524717
E-mail revmagssmith@btinternet.com

SMITH, Margaret Elizabeth. b 46. Bretton Hall Coll CertEd67. NOC 85. **d** 88 **p** 94. Hon Par Dn Battyeford *Wakef* 88-89; Hon C Mirfield 89-91; Chapl HM Pris and YOI New Hall 90-95; Dn-in-c Flockton cum Denby Grange *Wakef* 91-94; P-in-c 94-96; V Scholes 96-01; P-in-c Buckden *Ely* 01-05; P-in-c Offord D'Arcy w Offord Cluny 01-05; R Buckden w the Offords 05-06; rtd 06. *9 Bobbin Mill Court, Steeton, Keighley BD20 6PU* Tel (01535) 654721 E-mail memagsmith@tesco.net

SMITH, Mrs Marion Elizabeth. b 51. Bris Univ CertEd73 Middx Univ BA99. NTMTC. **d** 98 **p** 99. NSM Cowley *Lon* 98-00; P-in-c Harlington 00-08; R from 08. *The Rectory, St Peter's Way, Hayes UB3 5AB* Tel (020) 8759 9569 Mobile 07803-617509
E-mail marion.smith@tiscali.co.uk

SMITH, Mark Andrew. b 59. UNISA BA86. St Paul's Coll Grahamstown. **d** 85 **p** 86. P Port Elizabeth St Mary Magd S Africa 88-89; R Cradock St Pet 89-92; R Alexandra Plurality 92; Chapl St Andr Coll Grahamstown 94-01; Chapl Denstone Coll Uttoxeter 02-07; NSM Alton w Bradley-le-Moors and Oakamoor w Cotton *Lich* 06-07; NSM Mayfield 06-07; Chapl K Coll Taunton from 07. *King's College, South Road, Taunton TA1 3LA* Tel (01823) 328211 *or* 328137
E-mail masmith@kings-taunton.co.uk

SMITH, Mark David. *See* LAYNESMITH, Mark David

SMITH, Mark Gordon Robert Davenport. b 56. St Jo Coll Dur BA77. Ridley Hall Cam 78. **d** 80 **p** 81. C Sheff St Jo 80-83; C Brightside w Wincobank 83-86; V Kimberworth Park 86-91; Consultant NE England CPAS 91-98; Nat Co-ord Cert in Evang Studies (CA) 98-04; Chapl for Deaf People *Derby* from 04. *6 Old*

Chester Road, Derby DE1 3SA Tel (01332) 370905 Mobile 07702-269608 E-mail mark@deafchurch.co.uk

SMITH, Mark Graham. b 63. Ex Univ BA86 Lanc Univ PhD03. Westcott Ho Cam 87. **d** 90 **p** 91. C Cottingham *York* 90-92; C Guisborough 92-94; Sen Chapl St Martin's Coll *Blackb* 94-98; V Ashton-on-Ribble St Mich w Preston St Mark 98-03; V Scotforth from 03; Dioc World Development Adv from 00. *St Paul's Vicarage, 24 Scotforth Road, Lancaster LA1 4ST* Tel (01524) 32106 E-mail marklisasmith@aol.com

SMITH, Mark Peter. b 61. Reading Univ BA Open Univ BA93 MA97 Liv Univ MTh02 Keele Univ PGCE84. NOC 99. **d** 02 **p** 03. C Wingerworth *Derby* 02-06; TV Ex St Thos and Em from 06. *St Andrew's Vicarage, 78 Queens Road, Exeter EX2 9EW* Tel (01392) 423707 E-mail mark@mpsosb1.demon.co.uk

SMITH, Mark Winton. b 60. St Jo Coll Dur BA81 Barrister-at-Law (Middle Temple) 82. SEITE 01. **d** 04 **p** 05. NSM E Wickham *S'wark* 04-07. *16 Watersmeet Way, London SE28 8PU* Tel and fax (020) 8310 5063 E-mail revdmarksmith@aol.com

SMITH, Martin David. b 52. Hull Univ BA75 LTCL. Cuddesdon Coll 75. **d** 78 **p** 79. C Brentwood St Thos *Chelmsf* 78-80; C Reading St Giles *Ox* 80-91; R Colkirk w Oxwick w Pattesley, Whissonsett etc *Nor* 91-95; P-in-c Gt and Lt Ryburgh w Gateley and Testerton 94-95; P-in-c Hempton and Pudding Norton 94-95; P-in-c Nor St Pet Parmentergate w St Jo 95-03; R Nor St Jo w St Julian from 03. *The Rectory, 8 Kilderkin Way, Norwich NR1 1RD* Tel (01603) 622509 Fax 628417
E-mail frmartinsmith@clara.net

SMITH, Martin Lee. b 47. Worc Coll Ox BA68 MA72. Cuddesdon Coll 68. **d** 70 **p** 71. C Digswell *St Alb* 70-71; C Cheshunt 71-73; Perm to Offic *Ox* 74-80; SSJE 76-02; USA from 81. *1245 4th Street SW E208, Washington DC 20024, USA* E-mail martin.l.smith@worldnet.att.net

SMITH, Martin Stanley. b 53. Univ of Wales (Abth) BScEcon75. STETS. **d** 99 **p** 00. NSM Woking Ch Ch *Guildf* from 99. *Brackenlea, Heather Close, Horsell, Woking GU21 4JR* Tel (01483) 714307 E-mail martin.wokingsmiffs@ntlworld.com

SMITH, Canon Martin William. b 40. K Coll Lon BD63 AKC63. **d** 64 **p** 65. C Ashford St Hilda CD *Lon* 64-67; R Labuan Sabah Malaysia 67-69; R Likas Sabah 69-71; V Lakenham St Mark *Nor* 72-85; V N Walsham w Antingham 85-01; P-in-c Neatishead, Barton Turf and Irstead 94-95; RD Tunstead 91-96; RD St Benet 96-99; Hon Can Nor Cathl 93-05; V Wymondham 01-05; rtd 06; Perm to Offic *Nor* from 06. *Dragon House, 72 Besthorpe Road, Attleborough NR17 2NQ* Tel (01953) 456003
E-mail martinsmith@nwvicarage.freeserve.co.uk

SMITH, Martyn. b 52. CertEd73. Oak Hill Th Coll BA81. **d** 81 **p** 82. C Halliwell St Pet *Man* 81-86; V Cambridge St Martin *Ely* 86-89; Vineyard Chr Fellowship from 89. *M V Centre, 1 Belmont House, Deakins Park, Blackburn Road, Egerton, Bolton BL7 9RP* Tel 08452-303321 E-mail smithm@manchestervineyard.co.uk

SMITH, Megan Rachel. b 70. Man Univ MB, ChB94 Liv Univ MTh00 Univ of Wales Coll of Medicine MSc04 MRCP97 FRCPCH05. EMMTC 06. **d** 07 **p** 08. NSM Wilford *S'well* from 07. *112 Ruddington Lane, Nottingham NG11 7BZ* Tel 0115-981 2370 Mobile 07843-051960
E-mail megansmith@doctors.net.uk

SMITH, Melvyn. *See* SMITH, Canon William Melvyn

SMITH, Merrick Thomas Jack. b 37. CEng65 MCIBSE65. Oak Hill NSM Course 90. **d** 92 **p** 93. NSM Isleworth St Mary *Lon* 92-94; Perm to Offic *Birm* 94-96; NSM Warfield *Ox* 96-98; TV Wallingford 98-01; P-in-c Tredington and Darlingscott w Newbold on Stour *Cov* 01-03; rtd 03; Perm to Offic *Sarum* from 03; P-in-c Ilsington *Ex* from 06. *The Vicarage, Ilsington, Newton Abbot TQ13 9RW* Tel (01364) 661193
E-mail smith.merrick@virgin.net

SMITH, Michael. *See* SMITH, The Ven Anthony Michael Percival

SMITH, Michael David. b 57. BA80. St Steph Ho Ox 81. **d** 83 **p** 84. C Beaconsfield *Ox* 83-87; V Wing w Grove 87-92; R Farnham Royal w Hedgerley 92-01; P-in-c Cookham 01-03; V The Cookhams from 03. *The Vicarage, Church Gate, Cookham, Maidenhead SL6 9SP* Tel (01628) 810345

SMITH, Michael Ian Antony. b 69. Warwick Univ BSc91. Oak Hill Th Coll BA95. **d** 95 **p** 96. C Cheadle *Ches* 95-98; C Hollington St Leon *Chich* 98-01; C Hartford *Ches* 01-04; V from 04. *The Vicarage, 7 The Green, Hartford, Northwich CW8 1QA* Tel (01606) 77557 *or* 783063 Fax 786758
E-mail mike@stjohnshartford.org

SMITH, Michael James. b 47. AKC69. St Aug Coll Cant 70. **d** 71 **p** 72. C Corby St Columba *Pet* 71-78; V Collierley *Dur* 78-80; CPAS Evang 83-90. *56 Kingsmere, Chester le Street DH3 4DE* Tel 0191-209 2985

SMITH, Michael John. b 47. Kelham Th Coll 65. **d** 71 **p** 72. C Cov St Mary 71-75; Chapl RN 75-90; CF 90-95; R Lynch w Iping Marsh and Milland *Chich* 95-03; RD Midhurst 98-03; Community Chapl Bielefeld Station Germany from 03. *Community Chaplain's Office, 7 Regt RLC, Catterick Barracks, Bielefeld, BFPO 39* Tel (0049) (521) 9254 3118
E-mail revmjsmith@hotmail.com

SMITH, Michael Keith John. b 66. Thames Poly BSc88. Linc Th Coll BTh95. **d** 95 **p** 96. C Birch St Agnes w Longsight St Jo w St Cypr *Man* 95-99; TV Pendleton 99-06; P-in-c Lower Kersal 03-06; Bp's Chapl and Policy Adv *Leic* from 06. *Bishop's Lodge, 10 Springfield Road, Leicester LE2 3BD* Tel 0116-270 3390
E-mail bpchap@leicester.anglican.org

SMITH, Michael Raymond. b 36. Qu Coll Cam BA59 MA63 ARCM56 ARCO56. Cuddesdon Coll 64. **d** 65 **p** 66. C Redcar *York* 65-70; V Dormanstown 70-73; Prec Worc Cathl 73-77; TR Worc St Barn w Ch Ch 77-83; RD Worc E 79-83; V Eskdale, Irton, Muncaster and Waberthwaite *Carl* 83-87; Chapl Uppingham Sch 87-93; P-in-c Stoke Lacy, Moreton Jeffries w Much Cowarne etc *Heref* 93-01; Dioc Schs Officer 93-03; rtd 01; Perm to Offic *Heref* from 04. *Plough House, Wellington, Hereford HR4 8AT* Tel (01432) 839087
E-mail theploughhouse@btinternet.com

SMITH, Michael Richard Guy. b 55. Man Univ BA77. Ripon Coll Cuddesdon 88. **d** 90 **p** 91. C Wallasey St Hilary *Ches* 90-93; C Howden *York* 93-94; TV 94-97; V Gt and Lt Driffield from 04; RD Harthill from 08. *The Vicarage, Downe Street, Driffield YO25 6DX* Tel (01377) 253394

SMITH, Neville. *See* SMITH, Charles Henry Neville

SMITH, Norman George. b 27. K Coll Lon BD52 AKC52. **d** 53 **p** 54. C Pennington *Man* 53-56; C Chorlton-cum-Hardy St Clem 56-57; V Heywood St Jas 57-63; R Bedhampton *Portsm* 63-81; V Win St Bart 81-92; RD Win 84-89; rtd 92; Perm to Offic *Win* from 92. *89 Priors Dean Road, Winchester SO22 6JY* Tel (01962) 883015

SMITH, Norman Jordan. b 30. Sarum Th Coll 57. **d** 60 **p** 61. C Parkend *Glouc* 60-61; C Clearwell 60-61; C W Tarring *Chich* 61-65; Australia 65-68; V Chidham *Chich* 68-94; rtd 95. *Potters Paradise, 82 Church Road, Hayling Island PO11 0NX*

SMITH, Peter Olwen. b 44. Birm Univ BA66. Selly Oak Coll 67. **d** 87 **p** 94. Ind Chapl Black Country Urban Ind Miss *Lich* 84-98; TV Cen Wolverhampton from 94; Preb Lich Cathl from 99. *66 Albert Road, Wolverhampton WV6 0AF* Tel (01902) 712935 *or* 710407 Fax 685222 E-mail bcuim3@nascr.net

SMITH, Mrs Pamela Christina. b 46. SAOMC 97. **d** 00 **p** 01. NSM Ironstone *Ox* from 00; Chapl Kath Ho Hospice from 00. *The Vicarage, Horley, Banbury OX15 6BJ* Tel (01295) 730951
E-mail pamela@banx.fsnet.co.uk

SMITH, Miss Pamela Frances. b 44. St Mary's Coll Chelt TCert65. WEMTC 91. **d** 94 **p** 95. NSM Badgeworth, Shurdington and Witcombe w Bentham *Glouc* 94-02; NSM The Lavingtons, Cheverells, and Easterton *Sarum* 02-05; C E Clevedon w Clapton in Gordano etc *B & W* 05-08; rtd 08. *15 Lambert Gardens, Shurdington, Cheltenham GL51 4SW* Tel (01242) 863916 E-mail pfsmith@freeuk.com

SMITH, Ms Pamela Jane Holden. b 56. Warwick Univ BA78 Lon Inst of Educn PGCE82. Qu Coll Birm BA04. **d** 04 **p** 05. C Coventry Caludon 04-08; NSM 04-06; Perm to Offic from 08; Web Pastor i-church *Ox* from 08. *34 Styvechale Avenue, Coventry CV5 6DX* Tel (024) 7667 2893
E-mail rev.pam.smith@gmail.com *or* webpastor@i-church.org

SMITH, Ms Patricia Janet. b 45. Oak Hill Th Coll 87. **d** 89 **p** 90. Canada 89-02; V Charminster and Stinsford *Sarum* from 02; RD Dorchester from 09. *The Vicarage, Mill Lane, Charminster, Dorchester DT2 9QP* Tel (01305) 262477
E-mail plumsmith@tiscali.co.uk

SMITH, Paul. b 48. STETS 99. **d** 02 **p** 03. NSM Copthorne *Chich* from 02. *7 Heather Close, Copthorne, Crawley RH10 3PZ* Tel (01342) 714308 E-mail heatherclose@freenet.co.uk

SMITH, Paul. b 52. **d** 98 **p** 99. OLM Leominster *Heref* from 98. *32 The Meadows, Leominster HR6 8RF* Tel (01568) 615862 *or* 612124

SMITH, Paul Aidan. b 59. Birm Univ BA82. Wycliffe Hall Ox 82. **d** 85 **p** 86. C Selly Park St Steph and St Wulstan *Birm* 85-88; C Kensal Rise St Mark and St Martin *Lon* 88-91; V Water Eaton *Ox* 91-00; TR Hale w Badshot Lea *Guildf* 00-02; TV Stantonbury and Willen *Ox* 02-09; TR from 09. *2 Hooper Gate, Willen, Milton Keynes MK15 9JR* Tel (01908) 606689 Mobile 07930-308644 E-mail paul_a_smith@bigfoot.com

SMITH, Paul Allan. b 66. Ch Coll Cam BA88 MA00 PhD94. WMMTC 98 Ripon Coll Cuddesdon 99. **d** 00 **p** 01. C Moseley St Mary *Birm* 00-03; P-in-c Tilston and Shocklach *Ches* 03-08; Officer for Initial Min Tr 03-08; R Wilmslow from 08. *15 Parkway, Wilmslow SK9 1LS* Tel (01625) 524717
E-mail revpaulsmith@btinternet.com

SMITH, Paul Andrew. b 55. St Chad's Coll Dur BA76. Chich Th Coll 78. **d** 80 **p** 81. C Habergham Eaves St Matt *Blackb* 80-83; C Ribbleton 83-86; V Rishton 86-05; RD Whalley 95-01; R Cottingham *York* from 05. *The Rectory, Hallgate, Cottingham HU16 4DD* Tel (01482) 847668
E-mail dreadnoughtfam@aol.com

SMITH, Paul Anthony. b 66. Ripon Coll Cuddesdon. **d** 00 **p** 01. C Prestwood and Gt Hampden *Ox* 00-05; P-in-c W Leigh *Portsm* 05-06; V from 06. *St Alban's Vicarage, Martin Road, Havant PO9 5TE* Tel (023) 9245 1751

SMITH, Preb Paul Gregory. b 39. Ex Univ BA61. St Steph Ho Ox 61. **d** 63 **p** 64. C Walthamstow St Mich *Chelmsf* 63-66; C Devonport St Mark Ford *Ex* 66-69; C Hemel Hempstead *St Alb* 69-71; TV 71-83; R Bideford *Ex* 83-96; TR Bideford, Northam, Westward Ho!, Appledore etc 96; Chapl Bideford and Torridge Hosps 83-96; P-in-c Ex St Jas 96-98; R 98-03; rtd 03; Preb Ex Cathl from 95. *Valrose, Broad Lane, Appledore, Bideford EX39 1ND* Tel (01237) 423513
E-mail fatherpaulsmith@aol.com

SMITH, Mrs Paula Mary. b 57. Sheff Poly BA79 Qu Coll Birm BA06. WMMTC 03. **d** 06 **p** 07. C Walsall *Lich* from 06. *21 Buchanan Road, Walsall WS4 2EW* Tel (01922) 634859
E-mail revdpaula@tiscali.co.uk

SMITH, Mrs Pauline Frances. b 37. Bris Univ BA58 Lon Univ CertEd59. Sarum & Wells Th Coll 87. **d** 90 **p** 94. C Cobham *Guildf* 90-96; P-in-c Lower Wylye and Till Valley *Sarum* 96-97; TV Wylye and Till Valley 97-03; RD Stonehenge 01-03; rtd 03; Perm to Offic *Glouc* from 04. *267B London Road, Charlton Kings, Cheltenham GL52 6YG* Tel (01242) 222810
E-mail panda.smith@talktalk.net

SMITH, Peter. b 36. Keele Univ BA60. Cuddesdon Coll 73. **d** 75 **p** 76. C Shrewsbury St Chad *Lich* 75-80; V Burton St Chad 80-90; P-in-c Berwick w Selmeston and Alciston *Chich* 90-91; R 91-02; rtd 02; Perm to Offic *Sarum* from 03. *40 Homefield, Child Okeford, Blandford Forum DT11 8EN* Tel (01258) 861833

SMITH, Peter. b 49. Ex Univ BSc69 PGCE73. Carl Dioc Tr Course. **d** 82 **p** 83. NSM Kendal H Trin *Carl* from 82. *55 Empson Road, Kendal LA9 5PR* Tel (01539) 721467
E-mail rev.p.smith@btinternet.com

SMITH, Peter Alexander. *See* GRAYSMITH, Peter Alexander

SMITH, Peter Denis Frank. b 52. Local Minl Tr Course. **d** 81 **p** 83. OLM Camberwell St Mich w All So w Em *S'wark* 81-95; OLM Croydon St Jo 95-04. *57 Alton Road, Croydon CR0 4LZ* Tel (020) 8760 9656

SMITH, Peter Francis Chasen. b 28. Leeds Univ BA54. Coll of Resurr Mirfield 54. **d** 56 **p** 57. C E Dulwich St Clem *S'wark* 56-59; C Sutton St Nic 59-62; C-in-c Wrangbrook w N Elmsall CD *Wakef* 62-68; Chapl St Aid Sch Harrogate 68-85; P-in-c Lower Nidderdale *Ripon* 85-93; rtd 93; Perm to Offic *Ripon* from 93 and *York* from 95. *Clematis Cottage, Main Street, Kilburn, York YO61 4AH* Tel (01347) 868394
E-mail peter.f.c.smith@btinternet.com

SMITH, Peter Henry. b 62. Bris Univ BA83. SEITE 96. **d** 99 **p** 00. C Romford St Edw *Chelmsf* 99-02; V Aldersbrook from 02. *St Gabriel's Vicarage, 12 Aldersbrook Road, London E12 5HH* Tel (020) 8989 0315 E-mail peterhxsmith@aol.com

SMITH, Peter Howard. b 55. St Andr Univ MTheol78. Trin Coll Bris 78. **d** 79 **p** 80. C Handforth *Ches* 79-82; C Eccleston St Luke *Liv* 82-85; V Leyton St Paul *Chelmsf* 85-91; V Darwen St Barn *Blackb* 91-99; TR Bushbury *Lich* 99-06; R Hawkwell *Chelmsf* from 06. *The Rectory, Ironwell Lane, Hawkwell, Hockley SS5 4JY* Tel (01702) 200620 E-mail peterhsmith@talktalk.net

SMITH, Peter Howard. b 57. St Jo Coll Dur BSc78 Selw Coll Cam BA82 MA85. Ridley Hall Cam 80. **d** 83 **p** 84. C Welling *Roch* 83-87; C Hubberston w Herbrandston and Hasguard etc *St D* 87-89; C Hubberston 89-91; V Canley *Cov* 91-00; V Burney Lane *Birm* 00-06; P-in-c 06-07; P-in-c Ward End 06-07; P-in-c Bordesley Green 06-07; V Ward End w Bordesley Green from 07; AD Yardley and Bordesley from 05. *Christ Church Vicarage, Burney Lane, Birmingham B8 2AS* Tel 0121-783 7455
E-mail peter@ccbl.org.uk

SMITH, Peter James. b 23. K Coll Lon 49. **d** 53 **p** 54. C Atherton *Man* 53-57; C Wokingham All SS *Ox* 55-56; C Doncaster St Geo *Sheff* 56-59; V Whitgift w Adlingfleet 59-62; Chapl Highcroft Hosp Birm 62-71; C Wolborough w Newton Abbot *Ex* 71-74; C Furze Platt *Ox* 74-78; Travelling Sec Ch Coun for Health and Healing 78-81; P-in-c Bisham *Ox* 82-90; rtd 90; NSM Hindhead *Guildf* 90-96; Perm to Offic *Guildf* 96-97 and *Portsm* 97-07. *37 St Mary's Square, Gloucester GL1 2QT*

SMITH, Peter Michael. b 28. Open Univ BA75. K Coll Lon 52. **d** 56 **p** 57. C Pokesdown St Jas *Win* 56-59; C Weeke 59-63; V Hutton Roof *Carl* 63-69; V Barrow St Aid 69-72; V Preston Patrick 72-93; rtd 93; Chapl to the Deaf and Hard of Hearing *Carl* from 93; Perm to Offic from 93. *7 Green Road, Kendal LA9 4QR* Tel (01539) 726741 Mobile 07973-224289
E-mail peter@smith687.freeserve.co.uk

SMITH, Peter William. b 31. Glouc Th Course 74. **d** 77 **p** 77. C Coleford w Staunton *Glouc* 77; Hon C 77-87; P-in-c Alderton w Gt Washbourne 87-94; R Alderton, Gt Washbourne, Dumbleton etc 94-97; rtd 97; Perm to Offic *Ex* from 97. *5 Western Drive, Starcross, Exeter EX6 8EH* Tel (01626) 890115

SMITH, Philip David. b 55. Shoreditch Coll Lon BEd78. Oak Hill Th Coll BA98. **d** 98 **p** 99. C Cheltenham St Mary, St Matt, St Paul and H Trin *Glouc* 98-03; TV Cheltenham St Mark from 03. *3 Deacon Close, Cheltenham GL51 3NY* Tel (01242) 528567

SMITH, Philip Hathway. b 66. St Andr Univ MTheol88. Coll of Resurr Mirfield 90. **d** 92 **p** 93. C Shrewsbury St Giles w Sutton and Atcham *Lich* 92-94; C Clayton 94-97; TV Hanley H Ev 97-02; C Croydon St Mich w St Jas *S'wark* 02-04; P-in-c

Sydenham All SS from 04. *All Saints' Vicarage, 41 Trewsbury Road, London SE26 5DP* Tel (020) 8778 3065

SMITH, Philip James. b 32. St Alb Minl Tr Scheme. **d** 82 **p** 83. NSM Radlett *St Alb* 82-85; C 85-89; V Codicote 89-99; RD Hatfield 95-01; rtd 99; Perm to Offic *St Alb* from 00. *34 Cherry Tree Rise, Walkern, Stevenage SG2 7JL* Tel (01438) 861951

SMITH, Philip James. b 60. Imp Coll Lon BScEng82 Fitzw Coll Cam BA94. Ridley Hall Cam 92. **d** 95 **p** 96. C Aldborough w Boroughbridge and Roecliffe *Ripon* 95-99; V from 99. *The Vicarage, Church Lane, Boroughbridge, York YO51 9BA* Tel (01423) 322433 Mobile 07958-024689
E-mail vicar@aldwithbb.freeserve.co.uk

SMITH, Philip Lloyd Cyril. b 22. Ch Coll Cam BA47 MA49. Wycliffe Hall Ox 47. **d** 49 **p** 50. C St Helens St Helen *Liv* 49-52; C Woking St Jo *Guildf* 52-56; R Burslem St Jo *Lich* 56-83; P-in-c Burslem St Paul 82-83; R Burslem 83-86; rtd 86; Perm to Offic *Sheff* 86-01. *Upper Treasurer's House, 42 Bromley College, London Road, Bromley BR1 1PE* Tel (020) 8290 1566

SMITH, Ralston Antonio. b 28. St Pet Coll Jamaica 53. **d** 56 **p** 57. Jamaica 56-60 and from 72; C Ex St Thos 60-62; C Withycombe Raleigh 62-68; V Exwick 68-72; rtd 93. *PO Box 136, Anglican House, United Theological College, Kingston 7, Jamaica* Tel (001) (876) 977 6263

SMITH, Raymond Charles William. b 56. K Coll Lon BD78 AKC78. Coll of Resurr Mirfield 79. **d** 80 **p** 81. C Iffley *Ox* 80-83; C Wallingford w Crowmarsh Gifford etc 83-86; V Tilehurst St Mary 86-96; TR Haywards Heath St Wilfrid *Chich* 96-08; V from 08. *The Rectory, St Wilfrid's Way, Haywards Heath RH16 3QH* Tel (01444) 413300

SMITH, Canon Raymond Douglas. b 31. TCD BA53 MA56 BD56. **d** 54 **p** 55. C Belfast St Mich *Conn* 54-56; C Ballymacarrett St Patr *D & D* 56-58; CMS Tr Coll Chislehurst 58-60; Kenya (CMS) 60-71; Asst Gen Sec (Hibernian) CMS 71-74; Gen Sec CMS 74-86; CMS Ireland 76-86; Hon Can N Maseno from 78; I Powerscourt w Kilbride and Annacrevy *D & G* 86-96; Can Ch Ch Cathl Dublin 94-96; rtd 96. *Glencarrig Lodge, Kindlestown Upper, Delgany, Co Wicklow, Republic of Ireland* Tel (00353) (1) 287 3229

SMITH, Raymond Frederick. b 28. Lon Univ BSc51 Leeds Univ MA65. Oak Hill Th Coll 51. **d** 53 **p** 54. C Toxteth Park St Philemon *Liv* 53-56; C Halliwell St Pet *Man* 56-58; V Denton and Weston *Bradf* 58-66; V Normanton *Wakef* 66-81; RD Chevet 73-81; R Moreton *Ches* 81-90; rtd 90; Perm to Offic *Lich* from 03. *Cornerways, Station Road, Llanymynech SY22 6EG* Tel (01691) 839294

SMITH, Raymond George Richard. b 38. Univ of Wales (Ban) BSc61 MSc65. WMMTC 91. **d** 94 **p** 95. NSM Edgmond w Kynnersley and Preston Wealdmoors *Lich* 94-97; Chapl Princess R Hosp NHS Trust Telford 95-03; V Llandegfan w Llandysilio *Ban* 03-08; rtd 09. *41 Cae Mair, Beaumaris LL58 8YN* Tel (01248) 810032

SMITH, Raymond Horace David. b 30. Sir John Cass Coll Lon FIBMS61. Lon Coll of Div 64. **d** 67 **p** 68. C Shoreditch St Leon *Lon* 67-70; SAMS 71-73; Chile 71-80; P-in-c Castle Hedingham *Chelmsf* 80-83; P-in-c Cambridge St Phil *Ely* 83-86; V 86-91; Chapl Ibiza *Eur* 91-94; C Lowton St Mary *Liv* 94-96; rtd 96; Perm to Offic *Ely* 96-02 and from 03; *Win* 02-03; *Chelmsf from 04. 15 The Sheltons, Frinton-on-Sea CO13 0LX* Tel (01255) 671041 E-mail rev.raysmith@gmail.com

SMITH, Canon Richard. b 47. Westmr Coll Ox MTh99. St D Coll Lamp. **d** 75 **p** 76. C Aberavon *Llan* 75-78; Ind Chapl *St Alb* 78-81; TV Bournemouth St Pet w St Swithun, H Trin etc *Win* 81-85; Chapl Colchester Gen Hosp 85-94; Chapl Severalls Hosp Colchester 85-94; Sen Chapl Colchester Hosp Univ NHS Foundn Trust from 94; Sen Chapl NE Essex Mental Health NHS Trust 94-01; Sen Chapl N Essex Mental Health Partnership NHS Trust from 01; Bp's Adv for Hosp Chapl *Chelmsf* from 99; Hon Can Chelmsf Cathl from 01. *The Chaplain's Office, Colchester General Hospital, Turner Road, Colchester CO4 5JL* Tel (01206) 742513 E-mail richard.smith@colchesterhospital.nhs.uk

SMITH, Richard Geoffrey. b 46. St Jo Coll Dur BA68 MA69. St Steph Ho Ox BA74 MA78. **d** 75 **p** 76. C Brentwood St Thos *Chelmsf* 75-78; C Corringham 78-81; R Shepton Beauchamp w Barrington, Stocklinch etc *B & W* 81-83; TV Redditch, The Ridge *Worc* 85-89; R Teme Valley N 89-98; Perm to Offic *Heref* 02-05; Hon C Cleobury Mortimer w Hopton Wafers etc from 05. *Churchbridge, Nash, Ludlow SY8 3AX* Tel (01584) 891329 E-mail churchbridge@tinyworld.co.uk

SMITH, Richard Harwood. b 34. Sarum Th Coll 57. **d** 59 **p** 60. C Kington w Huntington *Heref* 59-62; Br Guiana 62-66; Guyana 66-69; C Broseley w Benthall *Heref* 69-70; Lic to Offic 70-76; USPG Area Sec (Dios Heref and Worc) 70-76; R Wigmore Abbey 76-84; V Eye w Braiseworth and Yaxley *St E* 84-96; P-in-c Bedingfield 84-96; P-in-c Occold 84-96; rtd 96. *33 Broad Street, Leominster HR6 8DD* Tel (01568) 610676

SMITH, Canon Richard Ian. b 46. Jes Coll Ox BA69 MA80. Ripon Hall Ox 69. **d** 70 **p** 71. C Eston *York* 70-76; TV E Ham w Upton Park St Alb *Chelmsf* 76-80; R Crook *Dur* 80-86; V Stanley 80-86; V Billingham St Cuth from 86; AD Stockton

92-01; Hon Can Dur Cathl from 98. *St Cuthbert's Vicarage, Church Road, Billingham TS23 1BW* Tel (01642) 659538 Fax 553236

SMITH, Richard Keith. b 44. St Jo Coll Nottm. **d** 84 **p** 85. C Wirksworth w Alderwasley, Carsington etc *Derby* 84-87; R Hulland, Atlow, Bradley and Hognaston 87-96; P-in-c Long Compton, Whichford and Barton-on-the-Heath *Cov* 96-08; P-in-c Wolford w Burmington 97-08; P-in-c Cherington w Stourton 97-08; P-in-c Barcheston 97-08; R S Warks Seven Gp from 08; RD Shipston 05-09. *The Vicarage, Broad Street, Long Compton, Shipston-on-Stour CV36 5JH* Tel (01608) 684207

SMITH, Richard Michael. b 52. Lon Univ BA74. EAMTC 79. **d** 82 **p** 83. NSM Cambridge Ascension *Ely* 82-84; C Rainham *Roch* 84-88; V Southborough St Thos 88-96; P-in-c Lake *Portsm* 96-99; V 99-06; P-in-c Shanklin St Sav 96-99; V 99-06; V Eastney from 06. *St Margaret's Vicarage, 13 Cousins Grove, Southsea PO4 9RP* Tel (023) 9273 1316

SMITH, Robert Alfred William. b 53. **d** 08 **p** 09. OLM Withington St Paul *Man* from 08. *61 Burnside Drive, Burnage, Manchester M19 2NA* Tel 0161-225 2509
E-mail bob.smith@sumojo.co.uk

SMITH, Robert Harold. b 23. Lon Univ BA49. Oak Hill Th Coll 46. **d** 50 **p** 51. C Nottingham St Ann *S'well* 50-52; C-in-c Elburton CD *Ex* 52-57; V Lowestoft Ch Ch *Nor* 57-67; R Upton *Ex* 67-80; R Bressingham *Nor* 80-81; P-in-c N w S Lopham 80-81; P-in-c Fersfield 80-81; R Bressingham w N and S Lopham and Fersfield 81-87; rtd 87; Perm to Offic *Nor* from 87. *22 St Walstan's Road, Taverham, Norwich NR8 6NG* Tel (01603) 861285

✠**SMITH, The Rt Revd Robin Jonathan Norman.** b 36. Worc Coll Ox BA60 MA64. Ridley Hall Cam 60. **d** 62 **p** 63 **c** 90. C Barking St Marg *Chelmsf* 62-67; Chapl Lee Abbey 67-72; V Chesham St Mary *Ox* 72-80; RD Amersham 79-82; TR Gt Chesham 80-90; Hon Can Ch Ch 88-90; Suff Bp Hertford *St Alb* 90-01; rtd 01; Hon Asst Bp St Alb from 02. *7 Aysgarth Road, Redbourn, St Albans AL3 7PJ* Tel and fax (01582) 791964
E-mail bprobin@no7.me.uk

SMITH, Rodney Frederic Brittain. b 37. Jes Coll Cam BA61 MA64. St Steph Ho Ox 87. **d** 88 **p** 89. NSM Rainworth *S'well* 88-89; C Basford St Aid 89-91; C Sneinton St Cypr 91-94; P-in-c Sneinton St Matthias 94-96; V 96-02; P-in-c Sneinton St Steph w St Alb 01-02; rtd 02. *43 Cyprus Road, Nottingham NG3 5EB* Tel 0115-962 0378

SMITH, Roger. *See* SMITH, Canon Thomas Roger

SMITH, Roger. *See* SMITH, John Roger

SMITH, Roger Owen. b 50. Univ of Wales (Abth) BA72 St Chad's Coll Dur CertEd73 FRGS. S'wark Ord Course 84. **d** 87 **p** 88. NSM Nunhead St Antony w St Silas *S'wark* 87-91; NSM Forest Hill St Aug 91-98; NSM Crofton Park St Hilda w St Cypr 91-98; NSM Brockley Hill St Sav 91-98; NSM Camberwell St Giles w St Matt 98-00; Perm to Offic *Cant* 01-07; NSM Folkestone Trin from 07. *22 Wear Bay Road, Folkestone CT19 6BN* Tel (01303) 259896

SMITH, Canon Roger Stuart. b 41. Chich Th Coll 65. **d** 66 **p** 67. C Garforth *Ripon* 66-70; C Hilborough Gp *Nor* 70-73; TV 73-78; V Mendham w Metfield and Withersdale *St E* 78-89; P-in-c Fressingfield w Weybread 86-89; R Fressingfield, Mendham etc 90-91; RD Hoxne 86-91; R Kelsale-cum-Carlton, Middleton, Theberton etc 91-01; C Yoxmere Conf 01-04; RD Saxmundham 96-03; Hon Can St E Cathl 97-04; rtd 04; Perm to Offic *St E* from 04. *Rookery Nook, The Green, St Margaret South Elmham, Harleston IP20 0PN* Tel (01986) 782465
E-mail canonroger@middleton3112.freeserve.co.uk

SMITH, Roger William. b 48. Imp Coll Lon BSc70. EAMTC. **d** 00 **p** 01. NSM Rothwell w Orton, Rushton w Glendon and Pipewell *Pet* from 00. *6A Kipton Close, Rothwell, Kettering NN14 6DR* Tel (01536) 710981 E-mail kipton@ntlworld.com

SMITH, Ronald Deric. b 21. Lon Univ BA46. Bps' Coll Cheshunt 59. **d** 61 **p** 62. C Crayford *Roch* 61-67; USA 67-68; C W Malling w Offham *Roch* 68-71; V Slade Green 71-78; V Bromley Common St Luke 78-91; rtd 91; Perm to Offic *S'wark* and *Roch* from 91. *5 Bromley College, London Road, Bromley BR1 1PE* Tel (020) 8464 0212

SMITH, Ronald Eric. b 43. EMMTC 93. **d** 93 **p** 94. NSM Wingerworth *Derby* 93-99; NSM Newbold w Dunston 99-01; NSM Loundsley Green 01-05; rtd 05; Perm to Offic *Derby* from 05 and from 06. *20 Oak Tree Lane, Haxby, York YO32 2YH* Tel (01904) 767691 E-mail revron@btinternet.com

SMITH, Canon Ronald James. b 36. Linc Th Coll 73. **d** 75 **p** 76. C Bilborough St Jo *S'well* 75-78; P-in-c Colwick 78-81; R 81-85; P-in-c Netherfield 78-81; V 81-85; C Worksop Priory 85-90; TV Langley and Parkfield *Man* 90-95; P-in-c Barton w Peel Green 95-01; Hon Can Tamale from 01; rtd 01; Perm to Offic *Man* from 01 and *Ches* from 03. *12 Bramhall Drive, Holmes Chapel, Crewe CW4 7EJ* Tel (01477) 544072
E-mail anne@vicarage01.freeserve.co.uk

SMITH, Ronald William. b 45. St Jo Coll York CertEd67. Chich Th Coll 70. **d** 73 **p** 74. C Scarborough St Martin *York* 73-76; C Stainton-in-Cleveland 76-80; V E Coatham 80-89; V Brookfield

from 89. *Brookfield Vicarage, 89 Low Lane, Brookfield, Middlesbrough TS5 8EF* Tel (01642) 282241
E-mail ronald.smith180@ntlworld.com

SMITH, The Very Revd Rowan Quentin. b 43. AKC66. **d** 67 **p** 68. C Matroosfontein S Africa 67-69; C Bonteheuwel 70; C Plumstead All SS 71-72; P-in-c Grassy Park 72-77; CR 77-88; Chapl Cape Town Univ 88-90; Prov Exec Officer 90-95; Dean Cape Town from 96. *St George's Cathedral, 5 Wale Street, Cape Town, 8001 South Africa* Tel (0027) (21) 424 7360
E-mail dean@sgcathedral.co.za

SMITH, Preb Roy Leonard. b 36. Clifton Th Coll 63. **d** 66 **p** 67. C Clapham St Jas *S'wark* 66-70; C Kennington St Mark 70-74; C-in-c Southall Em CD *Lon* 74-83; V Stonebridge St Mich 83-06; Preb St Paul's Cathl 96-06; rtd 06; Hon C Kensal Rise St Mark and St Martin *Lon* from 06. *82 Herbert Gardens, London NW10 3BU* Tel (020) 8969 2875
E-mail prebroy@yahoo.co.uk

SMITH, Royston. b 55. EMMTC 87. **d** 90 **p** 91. NSM Shirland *Derby* 90-94; NSM Ashover and Brackenfield 95-00; Lic to Offic from 00. *Kirkdale Cottage, Oakstedge Lane, Milltown, Ashover, Chesterfield S45 0HA* Tel (01246) 590975
E-mail royston@kirkdalecottage.freeserve.co.uk

SMITH, Royston Burleigh. b 26. St Deiniol's Hawarden 76. **d** 79 **p** 80. C Prestatyn *St As* 79-83; V Kerry and Llanmerewig 83-90; C Rhyl w St Ann 90-91; rtd 91. *45 Clwyd Park, Kinmel Bay, Rhyl LL18 5EJ* Tel (01745) 337684

SMITH, Ruth. *See* SMITH, Ms Vivienne Ruth

SMITH, Rycroft. *See* SMITH, Charles Rycroft

SMITH, Mrs Sally Anne. b 63. RN85. St Jo Coll Nottm 07. **d** 09. C Stone St Mich and St Wulfad w Aston St Saviour *Lich* from 09. *Covenant Cottage, Cotes Heath, Stafford ST21 6QU* Tel (01782) 791043 Mobile 07962-025659 E-mail silsmth@aol.com

SMITH, Sarah Anne Louise. *See* PIX, Mrs Sarah Anne Louise

SMITH, Mrs Shirley Ann. b 46. RSCN68 RM82 RGN84 RHV86. Sarum & Wells Th Coll 89. **d** 93 **p** 94. C Totton *Win* 93-96; Chapl Portsm Hosps NHS Trust 96-98; V Lord's Hill *Win* 98-01; TV Beaminster Area *Sarum* 01-05; rtd 05; Perm to Offic *Sarum* 05-08; P-in-c Hazelbury Bryan and the Hillside Par from 08; P-in-c Okeford from 08. *The Rectory, Church Road, Shillingstone, Blandford Forum DT11 0SL* Tel (01258) 860261
E-mail shirleywinch@aol.com

SMITH, Stephen. b 53. CQSW78. Sarum & Wells Th Coll 87. **d** 89 **p** 90. C Redcar *York* 89-92; C Leeds St Aid *Ripon* 92-96; R Lanteglos by Camelford w Advent *Truro* 96-99; Chapl Hull and E Yorks Hosps NHS Trust 99-01; V Leeds St Marg and All Hallows *Ripon* from 08; AD Headingley from 09. *All Hallows Vicarage, 24 Regent Terrace, Leeds LS6 1NP* Tel 0113-242 2205
E-mail simeve@ntlworld.com

SMITH, Stephen. b 60. Coll of Resurr Mirfield 02. **d** 04 **p** 05. C Burnley St Cath w St Alb and St Paul *Blackb* 04-07; C St Annes St Anne from 07. *66 Leach Lane, Lytham St Annes FY8 3AN*

SMITH, Stephen John. b 46. Kelham Th Coll 65. **d** 69 **p** 70. C Warsop *S'well* 69-73; C Heaton Ch Ch *Man* 73-75; V Bolton St Bede 75-78; R Bilborough w Strelley *S'well* 78-84; R E Leake 84-92; P-in-c Costock 84-92; P-in-c Rempstone 84-92; P-in-c Stanford on Soar 84-92; R E and W Leake, Stanford-on-Soar, Rempstone etc 92-97; RD W Bingham 92-97; V Swaffham *Nor* from 97; C Gt and Lt Dunham w Gt and Lt Fransham and Sporle from 03; RD Breckland 02-06; Chapl NW Anglia Healthcare NHS Trust from 99. *The Vicarage, White Cross Road, Swaffham PE37 7QY* Tel and fax (01760) 721373
E-mail s-smith102@sky.com

SMITH, Stephen John. b 55. Lon Univ BD80. Trin Coll Bris 77. **d** 81 **p** 82. C Fulham St Matt *Lon* 81-86; C Stoke Gifford *Bris* 86-90; TV 90-01; rtd 01; Perm to Offic *Bris* from 01. *47 Saxon Way, Bradley Stoke, Bristol BS32 9AR* Tel (01454) 616429
E-mail steve@revsmith.freeserve.co.uk

SMITH, Canon Stephen John Stanyon. b 49. Sussex Univ BA81 Birm Univ MSocSc83. Westcott Ho Cam 83. **d** 85 **p** 86. C Four Oaks *Birm* 85-89; Asst P Cheyenne River Reservation USA 89-91; Miss P Rosebud Reservation 91-94; Assoc R Ivoryton and Essex 94-98; Can St Paul's Cathl Buffalo 98-04; Asst P Buffalo St Andr from 04. *3105 Main Street, Buffalo NY 14214, USA* Tel (001) (716) 834 9337 Fax 836 0558 E-mail sjsmith@buffalo.edu

SMITH, Stephen Thomas. b 55. Westcott Ho Cam 95. **d** 97 **p** 98. C Kempston Transfiguration *St Alb* 97-01; C Bromham w Oakley and Stagsden 01-05; TV Elstow from 05. *St Michael's Vicarage, Faldo Road, Bedford MK42 0EH* Tel (01234) 266920

SMITH, Steven Barnes. b 60. Cov Poly BA83 Leeds Univ BA86 MSc02. Coll of Resurr Mirfield 84. **d** 87 **p** 88. C Darlington St Mark w St Paul *Dur* 87-89; C Prescot *Liv* 89-91; V Hindley Green 91-96; Asst Chapl Havering Hosps NHS Trust 96-98; Hd Multi-Faith Chapl Chelsea and Westmr Hosp NHS Foundn Trust 98-07; Perm to Offic *Lon* from 07 *Address temp unknown*

SMITH, Steven Gerald Crosland. b 48. Linc Th Coll 82. **d** 84 **p** 85. Chapl St Jo Sch Tiffield 84-87; C Towcester w Easton Neston *Pet* 84-87; P-in-c Kings Heath 87-89; V 89-93; TV N Creedy *Ex* 93-06; TR from 06; RD Cadbury from 02. *The Vicarage,*

Cheriton Fitzpaine, Crediton EX17 4JB Tel (01363) 866352
E-mail stevengcsmith@aol.com

SMITH, Susan. b 48. FInstD87. Ox Min Course 93. **d** 96 **p** 97. C Burnham w Dropmore, Hitcham and Taplow *Ox* 96-00; TV Whitton *Sarum* 00-02; TV W Slough *Ox* 02-08; V Cippenham from 08. *St Andrew's House, Washington Drive, Slough SL1 5RE* Tel (01628) 661994

SMITH, Miss Susan Ann. b 50. Bris Univ BA72 St Jo Coll York PGCE73. Ripon Coll Cuddesdon 97. **d** 99 **p** 00. C Swaffham *Nor* 99-02; R King's Beck from 02. *The Rectory, Aylsham Road, Felmingham, North Walsham NR28 0LD* Tel (01692) 402382

SMITH, Mrs Susan Elizabeth. b 53. Man Univ BSc94 Brunel Univ MSc98. SEITE 05. **d** 08. NSM Reigate St Mark *S'wark* from 08. *The Rectory, Gatton Bottom, Merstham, Redhill RH1 3BH* Tel (01737) 643755

SMITH, Mrs Susan Jennifer. b 52. MCIPD90. SAOMC 94. **d** 97 **p** 98. C Ascot Heath *Ox* 97-01; P-in-c Flixton St Mich *Man* from 01. *The Rectory, 348 Church Road, Urmston, Manchester M41 6HR* Tel and fax 0161-748 2884
E-mail saxoncross@talk21.com

SMITH, Terence. b 38. Brunel Univ BSc79 Cranfield Inst of Tech MSc80. Tyndale Hall Bris 67. **d** 69 **p** 70. C Cheylesmore *Cov* 69-71; C Leamington Priors St Paul 71-74; V Halliwell St Paul *Man* 74-75; Lect Uxbridge Coll 80-86; R Medstead w Wield *Win* 86-99; P-in-c Kennington *Ox* 99-03; V 03-08; rtd 08. *15 Grove Road, Seaford BN25 1TP* E-mail ter.s@btinternet.com

SMITH, Terence David. b 59. **d** 02. NSM Myddle *Lich* 02-08; NSM Broughton 02-08; NSM Loppington w Newtown 02-08; NSM Wem from 08; NSM Lee Brockhurst from 08. *Lamorna, Scholars' Lane, Loppington, Shrewsbury SY4 5RE* Tel 07703-183034 (mobile)

SMITH, Terrence Gordon. b 34. TD83. MCSP58 SRN60. St Mich Coll Llan 68. **d** 70 **p** 71. C Gelligaer *Llan* 70-73; CF (TA) 72-99; C Aberavon *Llan* 73-75; V Pontlottyn w Fochriw 75-77; V Kenfig Hill 77-84; V Dyffryn 84-99; rtd 99. *1 Gnoll Crescent, Neath SA11 3TF*

SMITH, Canon Thomas Roger. b 48. Cant Sch of Min 77. **d** 80 **p** 81. NSM Folkestone St Sav *Cant* 80-82; NSM Lyminge w Paddlesworth, Stanford w Postling etc 82-85; Chapl Cant Sch of Min 82-91; R Biddenden and Smarden *Cant* 86-91; TR Totnes, Bridgetown and Berry Pomeroy etc *Ex* 91-96; P-in-c Haslingden w Grane and Stonefold *Blackb* 96-98; V from 98; P-in-c Musbury from 07; AD Accrington from 03; Hon Can Blackb Cathl from 08. *St James's Vicarage, Church Street, Haslingden, Rossendale BB4 5QU* Tel (01706) 215533
E-mail rsmith9456@aol.com

SMITH, Timothy. b 58. Trin Coll Bris 00. **d** 02 **p** 03. C Warminster Ch Ch *Sarum* 02-06; P-in-c Plymouth St Jude *Ex* from 06. *St Jude's Vicarage, Knighton Road, Plymouth PL4 9BU* Tel (01752) 224178 E-mail timmy.smith@virgin.net

SMITH, Timothy Brian. b 62. Brisbane Coll BA(Theol)92. **d** 92 **p** 92. C Australia 92-94 and from 96; C Grafton St Jo Ev 92-94; C Heald Green St Cath *Ches* 94-96; R Mid Richmond 96-01; I Belmont St Steph from 01. *42 Regent Street, Belmont Vic 3216, Australia* Tel (0061) (3) 5243 2557 Mobile 412-673152
E-mail timsandy@turboweb.net.au

SMITH, Toni. *See* SMITH, Antoinette

SMITH, Trevor Andrew. b 60. St Jo Coll Dur BA86. Cranmer Hall Dur 83. **d** 87 **p** 88. C Guisborough *York* 87-90; C Northallerton w Kirby Sigston 90-95; R Middleton, Newton and Sinnington 95-01; Chapl St Luke's Hospice Plymouth from 01. *St Luke's Hospice, Stamford Road, Plymouth PL9 9XA* Tel (01752) 401172 *or* 316868 Fax 481878

SMITH, Trevor Bernard. b 33. Culham Coll of Educn CertEd70 Ox Poly BEd82. Oak Hill Th Coll 61. **d** 64 **p** 65. C Bispham *Blackb* 64-66; C Chesham St Mary *Ox* 66-68; Perm to Offic 90-94; rtd 96. *126 The Broadway, Herne Bay CT6 8HA* Tel (01227) 362665

SMITH (née WOOD), Mrs Valerie Rosemary. b 53. Warwick Univ BA74. WEMTC 06. **d** 09. NSM Highley w Billingsley, Glazeley etc *Heref* from 09. *20 Yew Tree Grove, Highley, Bridgnorth WV16 6DG* Tel (01746) 861966
E-mail keithandvals@aol.com

SMITH, Vernon Hemingway. b 33. St Alb Minl Tr Scheme 83. **d** 86 **p** 87. NSM Leighton Buzzard w Eggington, Hockliffe etc *St Alb* 86-98; NSM Newbury *Ox* 98-03; rtd 03. *41 Orion Way, Leighton Buzzard LU7 8XJ* Tel (01525) 370304

SMITH, Mrs Virginia Jane. b 41. Nottm Univ BSc63. Guildf Dioc Min Course 04. **d** 09. NSM Surrey Weald *Guildf* from 09. *Dove Cottage, 14 The Paddock, Westcott, Dorking RH4 3NT* Tel (01306) 885349 E-mail virginia.smith@smartemail.co.uk

SMITH, Ms Vivienne Ruth. b 57. St Jo Coll Dur BA79. NOC 95. **d** 00 **p** 01. C Heckmondwike *Wakef* 00-03; TV Dewsbury 03-06. *Address temp unknown*

SMITH, Walter. b 37. Westcott Ho Cam 67. **d** 69 **p** 70. C N Hull St Mich *York* 69-72; C Whitby 72-74; V Newington w Dairycoates 74-77; P-in-c Skipton Bridge 77-78; P-in-c Baldersby 77-78; TV Thirsk 77-88; P-in-c Topcliffe w Dalton and Dishforth 82-87; V Lythe w Ugthorpe 88-97; rtd 97; Perm to

Offic *York* from 98. *102 Upgang Lane, Whitby YO21 3JW* Tel (01947) 605456

SMITH, Miss Wendy Hamlyn. b 41. ALA70 Open Univ BA85. Ridley Hall Cam 85. **d** 87 **p** 94. C Stroud H Trin *Glouc* 87-90 and 91-92; Australia 90-91; TD Stoke-upon-Trent *Lich* 92-94; TV 94-97; V Pheasey 97-02; P-in-c Barlaston 02-06; Chapl Douglas Macmillan Hospice Blurton 04-06; rtd 07; Perm to Offic *Lich* from 07. *38 St Paul's Court, Congreve Road, Stoke-on-Trent ST3 2HJ* Tel (01782) 311924

SMITH, William Joseph Thomas. b 20. Chich Th Coll 54. **d** 55 **p** 56. C Laindon w Basildon *Chelmsf* 56-61; R Stifford 61-65; V Boreham 65-90; rtd 90; Perm to Offic *Chelmsf* from 90. *7 Trelawn, Church Road, Boreham, Chelmsford CM3 3EF* Tel (01245) 466930

SMITH, William Manton. b 64. Univ of Wales (Abth) LLB85 St Jo Coll Dur PGCE90. United Th Coll BD89 St Jo Coll Nottm 91. **d** 93 **p** 94. C Coventry Caludon 93-97; V Exhall 97-09; TR Coventry Caludon from 09. *Stoke Rectory, 365A Walsgrave Road, Coventry CV2 4BG* Tel (024) 7663 5731 *or* 7644 3691 E-mail wms.smith@btinternet.com

SMITH, Canon William Melvyn. b 47. K Coll Lon BD69 AKC69 PGCE70. St Aug Coll Cant 71. **d** 71 **p** 72. C Kingswinford H Trin *Lich* 71-73; Hon C Coseley Ch Ch 73-74; C Wednesbury St Paul Wood Green 75-78; V Coseley St Chad 78-91; TR Wordsley 91-93; RD Himley 83-93; TR Wordsley *Worc* 93-96; RD Himley 93-96; Stewardship and Resources Officer from 97; Hon Can Worc Cathl from 03. *14 Beech Tree Close, Kingswinford DY6 7DR* Tel (01384) 357062 *or* (01905) 20537 E-mail melvynsm@aol.com *or* msmith@cofe-worcester.org.uk

SMITH-CAMERON, Canon Ivor Gill. b 29. Madras Univ BA50 MA52. Coll of Resurr Mirfield. **d** 54 **p** 55. C Rumboldswyke *Chich* 54-58; Chapl Imp Coll *Lon* 58-72; Dioc Missr *S'wark* 72-92; Can Res S'wark Cathl 72-94; C Battersea Park All SS 92-94; Hon C 94-96; Hon C Battersea Fields 96-05; Co-ord All Asian Chr Consultation 92-93; rtd 94; Chapl to The Queen 95-99; Perm to Offic *S'wark* from 05. *24 Holmewood Gardens, London SW2 3RS* Tel (020) 8678 8977

SMITHAM, Ann. *See* HOWELLS, Mrs Elizabeth Ann

✠**SMITHSON, The Rt Revd Alan.** b 36. Qu Coll Ox BA62 MA68. Qu Coll Birm 62. **d** 64 **p** 65 **c** 90. C Skipton Ch Ch *Bradf* 64-68; C Ox St Mary V w St Cross and St Pet 68-72; Chapl Qu Coll Ox 69-72; Chapl Reading Univ 72-77; V Bracknell 77-83; TR 83-84; Can Res Carl Cathl and Dir Dioc Tr Inst *Carl* 84-90; Dioc Dir of Tr 85-90; Suff Bp Jarrow *Dur* 90-01; rtd 02; Hon Asst Bp Glas 02-08; Hon C Challoch 02-08. *4 Eskside East, Musselburgh EH21 7RS* Tel 0131-665 0383

SMITHSON, Michael John. b 47. Newc Univ BA68 Lon Univ BD79 Dur Univ PGCE FRGS. Trin Coll Bris 76. **d** 79 **p** 80. C S Mimms Ch Ch *Lon* 79-81; Support and Public Relations Sec UCCF 82-84; R Frating w Thorrington *Chelmsf* 84-88; V Portsea St Luke *Portsm* 88-04. *52 Walmer Road, Portsmouth PO1 5AS* Tel 07802-482584 (mobile)

SMITHSON, Philip George Allan. b 55. Bede Coll Dur TCert72 Open Univ BA82. **d** 07 **p** 08. OLM Monkwearmouth *Dur* from 07. *2 Sea View Gardens, Sunderland SR6 9PN* E-mail philipsmithson@talktalk.net

SMITHURST, Jonathan Peter. b 54. FInstLEx81. EMMTC 91. **d** 94 **p** 95. NSM Bramcote *S'well* 94-03; NSM Attenborough 03-06; AD Beeston 99-06; P-in-c Everton, Mattersey, Clayworth and Gringley from 06. *The Rectory, Abbey Road, Mattersey, Doncaster DN10 5DX* Tel (01777) 817364

SMITS, Eric. b 29. **d** 61 **p** 62. C Thornaby on Tees St Paul *York* 61-66; R Brotton Parva 66-98; rtd 98. *7 Pikes Nurseries, Ludham, Great Yarmouth NR29 5NW* Tel (01692) 678156

SMOUT, Francis David James. b 36. TD. **d** 03 **p** 04. NSM Eyemouth *Edin* from 03. *Benedict House, Coldingham, Eyemouth TD14 5NE* Tel (01890) 771220 E-mail mail@davidsmout.free-online.co.uk

SMOUT, Canon Michael John. b 37. St Pet Coll Ox BA61 MA75 Lon Univ BD64. Lon Coll of Div 62. **d** 64 **p** 65. C Toxteth Park St Philemon w St Silas *Liv* 64-69; C Everton St Sav 69-70; Missr E Everton Gp of Chs 70-74; V Everton St Sav w St Cuth 74-79; R Aughton St Mich 79-02; RD Ormskirk 82-89; AD 89-02; Hon Can Liv Cathl 92-02; rtd 02. *4 Victoria Road, Aughton, Ormskirk L39 5AU* Tel (01695) 423054

SMYTH, Anthony Irwin. b 40. TCD BA63 MA66. Clifton Th Coll 64. **d** 66 **p** 67. C Worthing St Geo *Chich* 66-69; SAMS Chile 70-75; Dir Th Educn Valparaiso 72-75; C Woodley St Jo the Ev *Ox* 75-80; V St Leonards St Ethelburga *Chich* 80-93; R Stopham and Fittleworth 93-05; rtd 05; Perm to Offic *Portsm* and *Chich* from 05. *20 Grenehurst Way, Petersfield GU31 4AZ* Tel (01730) 260370 E-mail anthony.smyth@btinternet.com

SMYTH, Francis George. b 20. Ridley Hall Cam 64. **d** 65 **p** 66. C Ormskirk *Liv* 65-70; V Bicton *Lich* 70-90; Chapl HM Pris Shrewsbury 71-90; rtd 90; Perm to Offic *Lich* from 90. *41 Sutton Road, Shrewsbury SY8 6DL* Tel (01743) 360030

SMYTH, Canon Gordon William. b 47. Open Univ BA. St Jo Coll Nottm 81. **d** 83 **p** 84. C St Keverne *Truro* 83-86; V Landrake w St Erney and Botus Fleming 86-95; RD E Wivelshire 94-95; V

Highertown and Baldhu from 95; Hon Can Truro Cathl from 06. *All Saints' Vicarage, Highertown, Truro TR1 3LD* Tel (01872) 261944 E-mail gordon@asht.org.uk

SMYTH, Canon Kenneth James. b 44. TCD BA67 MA72. **d** 68 **p** 69. C Bangor Abbey *D & D* 68-71; C Holywood 71-74; I Gilnahirk 74-82; I Newtownards w Movilla Abbey 82-89; I Newtownards from 89; Preb Wicklow St Patr Cathl Dublin from 93. *The Rectory, 36 Belfast Road, Newtownards BT23 4TT* Tel and fax (028) 9181 2527 *or* 9181 3193 E-mail kennethjsmyth@aol.com

SMYTH, Peter Charles Gordon. b 72. Univ of Wales (Ban) BA94 TCD BTh98. CITC. **d** 98 **p** 99. C Stillorgan w Blackrock *D & G* 98-01; R Thunder Bay St Mich Canada from 01. *2 Sydney Street, Thunder Bay ON P7B 1P7, Canada* Tel (001) (807) 767 4711 Fax 768 0382 E-mail stmichaelsch@tbaytel.net

SMYTH, Robert Andrew Laine (Brother Anselm). b 30. Trin Coll Cam BA53 MA59 Lon Univ PGCE60 DipEd65. **d** 79 **p** 80. SSF from 53; Min Prov Eur Prov SSF 79-91; Lic to Offic *Linc* 84-92; P-in-c Cambridge St Benedict *Ely* 92-93; V 93-00; rtd 00. *Glasshampton Monastery, Shrawley, Worcester WR6 6TQ* Tel (01299) 896345

SMYTH, Trevor Cecil. b 45. Chich Th Coll 66. **d** 69 **p** 70. C Cookridge H Trin *Ripon* 69-73; C Middleton St Mary 73-75; C Felpham w Middleton *Chich* 75-78; P-in-c Wellington Ch Ch *Lich* 78-80; V 80-86; P-in-c W Wittering *Chich* 86; R W Wittering and Birdham w Itchenor 86-94; Perm to Offic 00; TV Withycombe Raleigh *Ex* from 01. *All Saints' Vicarage, Church Road, Exmouth EX8 1RZ* Tel (01395) 278534

SMYTH, William Richard Stephen. b 56. Cape Town Univ BA77. **d** 90 **p** 92. S Africa 90-07; C Ballyholme *D & D* from 09. *34 Beverley Gardens, Bangor BT20 4NQ* Tel (028) 9127 1922 *or* 9127 4912 E-mail stephensmyth17@gmail.com

SMYTHE, Mrs Angela Mary. b 53. St Jo Coll Nottm 85. **d** 87 **p** 94. Par Dn Forest Town *S'well* 87-90; Dn-in-c Pleasley Hill 90-94; V 94-03; AD Mansfield 98-03; P-in-c Sneinton St Chris w St Phil 03-08; Chapl Qu Eliz Sch and Samworth Ch Academy from 08. *67 Bagshaw Street, Pleasley, Mansfield NG19 7SA* E-mail angiesmythe@aol.com

SMYTHE, Peter John Francis. b 32. Lon Univ LLB56 Barrister-at-Law (Middle Temple) 76. Wells Th Coll 56. **d** 58 **p** 59. C Maidstone All SS *Cant* 58-62; V Barrow St Jo *Carl* 62-65; V Billesdon w Goadby and Rolleston *Leic* 65-71; rtd 97. *The Gables, 16 Geraldine Road, Malvern WR14 3PA* Tel (01684) 573266

SNAITH, Bryan Charles. b 33. Univ of Wales BSc55. St Mich Coll Llan 61. **d** 61 **p** 62. C Bargoed w Brithdir *Llan* 61-62; C Llanishen and Lisvane 62-71; Ind Chapl *Dur* 71-76; Ind Chapl *Worc* 76-81; P-in-c Stone 76-81; C Chaddesley Corbett 77-81; Ind Chapl *Chelmsf* 81-03; TV Colchester St Leon, St Mary Magd and St Steph 81-86; rtd 03; Perm to Offic *Chelmsf* from 04. *4 Wren Close, Stanway, Colchester CO3 8ZB* Tel (01206) 767793 E-mail bryansnaith-colchester@msn.com

SNAPE, Gary John Stanley. b 50. STETS. **d** 05 **p** 06. NSM Fareham H Trin *Portsm* 05-09; NSM Whiteley CD from 09. *20 Sheridan Gardens, Whiteley, Fareham PO15 7DY* Tel (01489) 589205 E-mail gary.snape1@ntlworld.com

SNAPE, Harry. b 21. Qu Coll Birm 76. **d** 78 **p** 79. NSM Highters Heath *Birm* 78-82; NSM Stirchley 82-84; TV Corby SS Pet and Andr w Gt and Lt Oakley 84-89; rtd 89; Perm to Offic *Chich* 89-05. *16 Capel Court, The Burgage, Prestbury, Cheltenham GL52 3EL* Tel (01242) 513289

SNAPE, Mrs Lorraine Elizabeth. b 52. STETS. **d** 02 **p** 07. NSM Titchfield *Portsm* 02-06; C-in-c Whiteley CD from 06. *20 Sheridan Gardens, Whiteley, Fareham PO15 7DY* Tel (01489) 589205

SNAPE, Paul Anthony Piper. b 44. **d** 98 **p** 99. OLM Tettenhall Wood and Perton *Lich* from 98. *24 Windsor Gardens, Castlecroft, Wolverhampton WV3 8LY* Tel (01902) 763577 E-mail p-snape44@tiscali.co.uk

SNARE, Peter Brian. b 39. Cape Town Univ BSc63. SEITE 99. **d** 02 **p** 03. NSM Dymchurch w Burmarsh and Newchurch *Cant* 02-09; NSM New Romney w Old Romney and Midley 07-09; NSM St Mary's Bay w St Mary-in-the-Marsh etc 07-09; Perm to Offic from 09. *35 Shepherds Walk, Hythe CT21 6PW* Tel (01303) 269242 *or* (020) 7320 1701 E-mail peter.snare@btinternet.com

SNASDELL, Canon Antony John. b 39. St Chad's Coll Dur BA63. **d** 65 **p** 66. C Boston *Linc* 65-70; Hon C Worksop Priory *S'well* 71-82; P-in-c Gt Massingham *Nor* 82-84; P-in-c Lt Massingham 82-84; P-in-c Harpley 82-84; R Gt and Lt Massingham and Harpley 84-91; R Thorpe St Andr 91-04; Hon Can Nor Cathl 03-04; rtd 04; Perm to Offic *Nor* from 05. *1 Speedwell Road, Wymondham NR18 0XQ* Tel (01953) 857509

SNEARY, Michael William. b 38. Brentwood Coll of Educn CertEd71 Open Univ BA79. Ely Th Coll 61. **d** 64 **p** 65. C Loughton St Jo *Chelmsf* 64-67; Youth Chapl 67-70; Hon C Ingrave 70-71; Teacher Harold Hill Gr Sch Essex 71-74; Ivybridge Sch 74-76; Coombe Dean Sch Plymouth 76-03; rtd 03. *The Lodge, 1 Lower Port View, Saltash PL12 4BY*

SNEATH, Canon Sidney <u>Dennis</u>. b 23. Leeds Univ BA50. Bps' Coll Cheshunt 50. **d** 52 **p** 53. C Nuneaton St Mary *Cov* 52-59; C-in-c Galley Common Stockingford CD 59-68; V Camp Hill from 68; Hon Can Cov Cathl from 80. *The Vicarage, Cedar Road, Nuneaton CV10 9DL* Tel (024) 7639 2523

✠**SNELGROVE, The Rt Revd Donald George.** b 25. TD72. Qu Coll Cam BA48 MA53 Hull Univ Hon DD97. Ridley Hall Cam. **d** 50 **p** 51 **c** 81. C Oakwood St Thos *Lon* 50-53; C Hatch End St Anselm 53-56; V Dronfield *Derby* 56-62; CF (TA) 60-73; V Hessle *York* 63-70; RD Hull 67-70 and 81-90; Can and Preb York Minster 69-81; Adn E Riding 70-81; R Cherry Burton 70-78; Suff Bp Hull 81-94; rtd 94; Hon Asst Bp Linc from 95. *Kingston House, 8 Park View, Barton-upon-Humber DN18 6AX* Tel (01652) 634484 E-mail donaldsnelgrove@aol.com

SNELL, Mrs Brigitte. b 43. BA85. EAMTC 86. **d** 89 **p** 94. NSM Cambridge Gt St Mary w St Mich *Ely* 89-91; Par Dn Cambridge St Jas 91-94; C 94-95; V Sutton 95-03; R Witcham w Mepal 95-03; rtd 03; Perm to Offic *Ely* from 05. *45 London Road, Harston, Cambridge CB22 7QQ* Tel (01223) 872839 E-mail brigittesnell@aol.com

SNELL, Colin. b 53. Trin Coll Bris 94. **d** 96 **p** 97. C Martock w Ash *B & W* 96-00; TV Wilton 00-08; V Galmington from 08. *St Michael's House, 1 Comeytrowe Lane, Taunton TA1 5PA* Tel (01823) 326525

SNELLGROVE, Martin Kenneth. b 54. City Univ BSc77 CEng80 MICE84. Aston Tr Scheme 85 Ridley Hall Cam 87. **d** 89 **p** 90. C Four Oaks *Birm* 89-92; TV Wrexham *St As* 92-01; R Hope from 01; AD Hawarden from 03. *The Rectory, Kiln Lane, Hope, Wrexham LL12 9PH* Tel (01978) 762127

SNELLING, Brian. b 40. **d** 69 **p** 70. C Slough *Ox* 69-72; C Hoole *Ches* 72-76; V Millbrook 76-80; V Homerton St Luke *Lon* 80-90; R Marks Tey w Aldham and Lt Tey *Chelmsf* 90-98; V Stebbing w Lindsell 98-04; V Stebbing and Lindsell w Gt and Lt Saling 04-05; rtd 05; Perm to Offic *Chelmsf* from 06. *69 Reymead Close, West Mersea, Colchester CO5 8DN* Tel (01206) 383717 E-mail revbrians@aol.com

SNELSON, William Thomas. b 45. Ex Coll Ox BA67 Fitzw Coll Cam BA69 MA75. Westcott Ho Cam 67. **d** 69 **p** 70. C Godalming *Guildf* 69-72; C Leeds St Pet *Ripon* 72-75; V Chapel Allerton 75-81; V Bardsey 81-93; Dioc Ecum Officer 86-93; W Yorkshire Ecum Officer *Bradf* 93-97; Gen Sec Chs Together in England 97-08; rtd 08; Perm to Offic *St Alb* from 97 and *Ely* from 03; Development Officer Angl Cen Rome from 08. *6 Abbey Crags Way, Knaresborough HG5 8EF* Tel (01423) 862660 Mobile 07917-663250 E-mail developmentUK@anglicancentre.it

SNOOK, Hywel Geraint. b 77. Aston Univ BSc99 Leeds Univ BA04. Coll of Resurr Mirfield 02. **d** 05 **p** 06. C Marton *Blackb* 05-06; C Chorley St Laur 06-09; P-in-c Lt Drayton *Lich* from 09. *The Vicarage, 1 Christ Church Copse, Christ Church Lane, Market Drayton TF9 1DY* Tel (01630) 652801 E-mail hywel.snook@tiscali.co.uk

SNOOK, Mrs Margaret Ann. b 41. S Dios Minl Tr Scheme. **d** 91 **p** 94. NSM Keynsham *B & W* 91-04; Chapl Univ Hosps Bris NHS Foundn Trust from 91; Perm to Offic *B & W* from 04. *32 Hurn Lane, Keynsham, Bristol BS31 1RS* Tel 0117-986 3439

SNOOK, Walter Currie. *See* CURRIE, Walter

SNOW, Campbell Martin Spencer. b 35. JP75. Roch Th Coll 65. **d** 67 **p** 68. C Dover St Mary *Cant* 67-72; C Birchington w Acol 72-74; V Reculver 74-80; P-in-c New Addington 80-81; V 81-84; V New Addington *S'wark* 85-87; P-in-c Caterham Valley 87-99; CF (ACF) 84-87; CF (TA) 87-92; OCF 92-95; rtd 99; Perm to Offic *S'wark* from 99; Widows' Officer 99-04. *28 The Crossways, Merstham, Redhill RH1 3NA* Tel (01737) 643388 E-mail csnow@talktalk.net

SNOW, Frank. b 31. Lon Univ BD57. **d** 83 **p** 84. Hon C Tweedmouth *Newc* 83-86; Hon C Berwick H Trin 86-89; Hon C Berwick St Mary 86-89; Hon C Berwick H Trin and St Mary 89-90; R Gt Smeaton w Appleton Wiske and Birkby etc *Ripon* 90-97; rtd 97; Perm to Offic *Ripon* from 97 and *Sheff* from 02. *11 The Green, Sheffield S17 4AT* Tel 0114-235 0024 E-mail frank@fcrsnow.freeserve.co.uk

SNOW, Martyn James. b 68. Sheff Univ BSc89. Wycliffe Hall Ox BTh95. **d** 95 **p** 96. C Brinsworth w Catcliffe and Treeton *Sheff* 95-97; CMS Guinea 98-01; V Pitsmoor Ch Ch *Sheff* from 01; P-in-c Stocksbridge 07-08; AD Ecclesfield from 07. *The Vicarage, 257 Pitsmoor Road, Sheffield S3 9AQ* Tel 0114-272 7756 E-mail martyn.snow@sheffield.anglican.org

SNOW, Miss Patricia Margaret. b 21. Dub Bible Coll 45 St Mich Ho Ox 51. **dss** 72 **d** 87 **p** 96. W Ham *Chelmsf* 72-78; Acomb St Steph *York* 78-83; rtd 83; NSM Northfleet *Roch* 96-01; Perm to Offic from 01. *29 Huggens' College, College Road, Northfleet, Gravesend DA11 9DL* Tel (01474) 369463

SNOW, Peter David. b 37. St Jo Coll Cam BA61 MA67. Ridley Hall Cam 62. **d** 64 **p** 65. C Kingshurst *Birm* 64-66; C Santa Barbara All SS USA 67-71; Can Missr for Youth Los Angeles 71-75; R Jackson St Jo 75-81; Asst R Bellevue Resurr 81-85; R Redmond H Cross 89-01; rtd 01; P-in-c Edmonds SS Hilda and

Patr 02-03. *927 36th Avenue, Seattle WA 98122-5216, USA* Tel (001) (206) 329 3784 E-mail peterorlisa@cs.com

SNOW, Richard John. b 57. Bris Univ BSc80. **d** 90 **p** 91. C Preston Plucknett *B & W* 90-95; TV Stratton St Margaret w S Marston etc *Bris* 95-02; R Box w Hazlebury and Ditteridge 02-07; TR Kirkby Lonsdale *Carl* from 07. *The Rectory, Vicarage Lane, Kirkby Lonsdale, Carnforth LA6 2BA* Tel (01524) 272044

SNOWBALL, Miss Deborah Jane. b 67. Middx Poly BEd90. Ripon Coll Cuddesdon 02. **d** 04 **p** 05. C Sawbridgeworth *St Alb* 04-07; P-in-c Rickmansworth from 07. *The Vicarage, Bury Lane, Rickmansworth WD3 1ED* Tel (01923) 772627 E-mail vicar@stmarysrickmansworth.org.uk

SNOWBALL, Dorothy Margaret. b 52. Sunderland Univ BA98. NEOC 98. **d** 01 **p** 02. NSM Heworth St Mary *Dur* 01-07; P-in-c Eighton Banks from 07. *2 Oval Park View, Felling, Gateshead NE10 9DS* Tel 0191-469 5059 E-mail dsnowball@talk21.com

SNOWBALL, Michael Sydney. b 44. Dur Univ MA MA72. Cranmer Hall Dur. **d** 72 **p** 73. C Stockton St Pet *Dur* 72-75; C Dunston St Nic 75-77; C Dunston 77-78; C Darlington St Jo 78-81; V Chilton 81-91; V Brompton w Deighton *York* from 91. *The Vicarage, Brompton, Northallerton DL6 2QA* Tel (01609) 772436 E-mail mickthevic@aol.com

SNOWDEN, Miss Alice Isabel Glass. b 55. Lanc Univ BA77 Humberside Coll of Educn PGCE84. Ripon Coll Cuddesdon 91. **d** 94 **p** 95. C Mirfield *Wakef* 94-97; TV Guiseley w Esholt *Bradf* 97-02; V Bankfoot 02-09; P-in-c Leeds All So *Ripon* from 09. *All Souls' Vicarage, Blackman Lane, Leeds LS2 9EY* Tel 0113-212 0035 E-mail sobak@blueyonder.co.uk

SNOWDEN (née **HALL), Mrs Elizabeth.** b 58. Plymouth Poly BSc79 Birm Univ BA01 Lon Inst of Educn PGCE80. Qu Coll Birm 98. **d** 01 **p** 02. C Burntwood *Lich* 01-04; C and Youth Work Co-ord Ogley Hay from 04. *25 Snowdrop Close, Walsall WS8 7RN* Tel (01543) 454816

SNUGGS, David Sidney. b 49. Keble Coll Ox BA71 PGCE72 MA75. S Dios Minl Tr Scheme 89. **d** 92 **p** 93. C Bitterne *Win* 92-96; V Fair Oak from 96. *The Vicarage, Fair Oak Court, Fair Oak, Eastleigh SO50 7BG* Tel (023) 8069 2238

SNYDER, Miss Susanna Jane. b 78. Em Coll Cam BA00 MA05. Qu Coll Birm BA04. **d** 05 **p** 06. C Brownswood Park and Stoke Newington St Mary *Lon* 05-08; Perm to Offic *Ox* from 08. *103 High Street, Wheatley, Oxford OX33 1XP* Tel 07862-289315 (mobile) E-mail susanna.snyder@btinternet.com

SNYDER GIBSON, Catherine. *See* GIBSON, Catherine Snyder

SOADY, Mark. b 60. RMN84 Univ of Wales BTh. St Mich Coll Llan 96. **d** 96 **p** 97. C Tenby *St D* 96-99; TV 99-03; Min Can St Woolos Cathl 03-08; P-in-c Newport All SS from 08; Chapl Univ of Wales (Newport) from 08; CF(V) from 98. *The Vicarage, Brynglas Road, Newport NP20 5QY* Tel (01633) 854657 Mobile 07968-753978 E-mail marksoady@btinternet.com

SOAR, Martin William. b 54. Wye Coll Lon BSc78. Wycliffe Hall Ox 86. **d** 88 **p** 89. C Henfynyw w Aberaeron and Llanddewi Aberarth *St D* 88-91; C Hubberston 91-93; P-in-c Low Harrogate St Mary *Ripon* 93-95; V 95-06; Chapl Old Swinford Hosp Sch Stourbridge from 06. *Old Swinford Hospital, Heath Lane, Stourbridge DY8 1QX* Tel (01384) 817300 Fax 441686 E-mail soars@blueyonder.co.uk

✠**SOARES, The Rt Revd Fernando da Luz.** b 43. Univ of Porto. **d** 71 **p** 72 **c** 80. Bp Lusitanian Ch from 80; Hon Asst Bp Eur from 95. *Rua Elias Garcia 107-1 Dto, 4430-091 Vila Nova de Gaia, Portugal* Tel (00351) (22) 375 4646 Fax 375 2016 E-mail fernandols@netc.pt *or* ilcae@mail.telepac.pt

SOCHON, David Lomas Philipe. b 40. Univ Coll Lon BA62. **d** 07 **p** 08. OLM Newton Flotman, Swainsthorpe, Tasburgh, etc *Nor* from 07; RD Depwade from 09. *The Bungalow, Chapel Lane, Shotesham All Saints, Norwich NR15 1YP* Tel (01508) 558495 E-mail davids@tasvalley.org

SODADASI, David Anand Raj. b 63. Osmania Univ Hyderabad BCom85 MA99 Union Bibl Sem Pune BD95. United Th Coll Bangalore MTh00. **d** 01 **p** 02. C Jabalpur Cathl India 01-04; Lect Leonard Th Coll 00-04; Perm to Offic *Ox* 04-05; NSM Ray Valley from 05. *St Mary's House, High Street, Charlton-on-Otmoor, Kidlington OX5 2UQ* Tel (01865) 331124 Mobile 07906-924883 E-mail sdanandraj@hotmail.com

SODOR AND MAN, Bishop of. *See* PATERSON, The Rt Revd Robert Mar Erskine

SOER, Patricia Kathleen Mary. b 40. Hull Coll of Educn CertEd61. OLM Deptford St Jo w H Trin *S'wark* **d** 99 **p** 00. OLM Deptford St Jo w H Trin and Ascension from 06. *350 Wood Vale, London SE23 3DY* Tel (020) 8699 4616 E-mail pat@sjht.org.uk

SOFIELD, Martin. b 60. **d** 02 **p** 03. OLM Clifton *Man* from 02. *16 Ross Drive, Clifton, Swinton, Manchester M27 6PS* Tel 0161-959 6517 E-mail martin.sofield@ntlworld.com

SOGA, Hector Ian. b 47. Glas Univ MA70 BMus78 PhD90 Selw Coll Cam BA72 MA76. St And NSM Tr Scheme 87. **d** 88 **p** 89. NSM Dollar *St And* from 88. *2 Harviestoun Road, Dollar FK14 7HF* Tel (01259) 743169

SOKANOVIC (née **HARRIS), Mrs Mary Noreen Cecily.** b 58. Suffolk Coll BA97 RGN79 RN96. EAMTC 02. **d** 05 **p** 06. NSM

Whitton and Thurleston w Akenham *St E* from 05. *Sideview, School Road, Coddenham, Ipswich IP6 9PS* Tel (01449) 760527 E-mail marysok@tiscali.co.uk

SOKOLOWSKI (*née* **MAHON**), **Mrs Stephanie Mary.** b 56. Liv Univ BSc80 SRN80 K Coll Lon BA00. S'wark Ord Course 91. **d** 94 **p** 95. C Warlingham w Chelsham and Farleigh *S'wark* 94-97; C Godstone and Blindley Heath 97-04; C Shere, Albury and Chilworth *Guildf* from 07. *The Vicarage, Brook Road, Chilworth, Guildford GU4 8ND* Tel (01483) 534293 Mobile 07731-783924 E-mail ssokolowski@btinternet.com

✠**SOLIBA, The Most Revd Ignacio Capuyan.** b 44. Univ of Philippines AB72. St Andr Th Sem Manila BTh73 MDiv88. **d** 73 **p** 74 **c** 91. Chapl St Paul's Memorial Sch Philippines 73-75; Officer-in-charge 75-76; P-in-c Balbalasang 74-76; V Balantoy 77-78 and 82-91; V Mt Data 79-81; Bp N Luzon 91-97; Prime Bp Philippines 97-08; rtd 09. *Address temp unknown* E-mail soliba@edsamail.com.ph *or* soliba@hotmail.com

SOLMAN, Mrs Fiona Barbara. b 53. SRN75 RSCN75 RHV80. STETS 03. **d** 06 **p** 07. C Cottesmore and Barrow w Ashwell and Burley *Pet* from 06; C Empingham and Exton w Horn w Whitwell from 06; C Greetham and Thistleton w Stretton and Clipsham from 06. *The Vicarage, 40 Church Lane, Greetham, Oakham LE15 7NF* Tel (01572) 812260 E-mail fionasolman@aol.com

SOLOMON, Arthur Creagh. b 33. ACT LTh Ch Coll Hobart. **d** 62 **p** 63. Australia 62-67; C Addiscombe St Mildred *Cant* 67-68; Chapl Pierrepont Sch Frensham 69-72; R Clifton Campville w Chilcote *Lich* 72-95; P-in-c Thorpe Constantine 83-95; R Clifton Campville w Edingale 95; Perm to Offic *Derby* 96-98; rtd 98; Perm to Offic *S & M* from 98. *Poppy Cottage, Ballacannell, Laxey, Isle of Man IM4 7HD* Tel (01624) 861235

SOMERS-EDGAR, Carl John. b 46. Otago Univ BA69. St Steph Ho Ox 72. **d** 75 **p** 76. C Northwood H Trin *Lon* 75-79; C St Marylebone All SS 79-82; V Liscard St Mary w St Columba *Ches* 82-85; V Caversham St Pet New Zealand from 85. *The Vicarage, 57 Baker Street, Caversham, Dunedin 9012, New Zealand* Tel (0064) (3) 455 3961

SOMERS HESLAM, Peter. *See* HESLAM, Peter Somers

SOMERVELL, Mrs Katherine Mary. b 30. Edin Univ CQSW51. WMMTC 86. **d** 88 **p** 94. Par Dn Caldmore *Lich* 88-92; Par Dn Wilnecote 92-94; C 94-95; rtd 95; NSM Loppington w Newtown *Lich* 95-99. *3 Orchard Close, Cressage, Shrewsbury SY5 6BZ* Tel (01952) 510755

SOMERVILLE, David. b 58. QUB BEd. **d** 00 **p** 01. C Lisburn Ch Ch *Conn* 00-03; I Drumgath w Drumgooland and Clonduff *D & D* from 03. *The Rectory, 29 Cross Road, Hilltown, Newry BT34 5TF* Tel (028) 4063 1171 Mobile 07811-916825 E-mail revds@btinternet.com

SOMERVILLE, John William Kenneth. b 38. St D Coll Lamp 60. **d** 63 **p** 64. C Rhosllannerchrugog *St As* 63-67; C Llangystennin 67-70; V Gorsedd 70-77; V Gorsedd w Brynford and Ysgeifiog 77-02; RD Holywell 96-02; rtd 02. *15 Bryn Marl Road, Mochdre, Colwyn Bay LL28 5DT*

SOMMERVILLE, Prof Robert Gardner. b 27. Glas Univ MB50 ChB50 MD60 FRCPGlas67 Lon Univ FRCPath68. **d** 96 **p** 96. NSM Blairgowrie *St And* 96-97; NSM Coupar Angus 96-97; NSM Alyth 96-97; P-in-c Killin 97-99; Perm to Offic 99-01; P-in-c Tayport from 01. *Monkmyre, Myreriggs Road, Coupar Angus, Blairgowrie PH13 9HS* Tel and fax (01828) 627131 E-mail rsommerville120@btinternet.com

SONG, James. b 32. Lon Coll of Div 57. **d** 60 **p** 61. C Virginia Water *Guildf* 60-63; C Portman Square St Paul *Lon* 63-66; V Matlock Bath *Derby* 66-76; V Woking St Jo *Guildf* 76-94; RD Woking 87-92; rtd 94; Perm to Offic *Guildf* from 94. *Ash House, Churt, Farnham GU10 2NU* Tel and fax (01428) 714493

SONG, Leonardo. b 60. Angl Th Coll Seoul BA. Angl Th Sem Seoul MDiv. **d** 91 **p** 93. Korea 91-03; Fell Crowther Hall CMS Tr Coll Selly Oak 03-04; Consultant CMS 05-06; Chapl Angl Korean Community from 07. *268C New Cross Road, London SE14 5PL* Tel (020) 7732 2377 Mobile 07834-831022 E-mail leonardosong@hotmail.com

SOOSAINAYAGAM, Xavier. b 50. Sri Lanka Nat Sem BPh73 St Paul's Sem Trichy BTh77 S'wark Ord Course 89. **d** 76 **p** 77. In RC Ch 76-89; C Streatham St Leon *S'wark* 89-94; C Merton St Jas 94-97; V Croydon H Sav from 97. *The Vicarage, 115 St Saviour's Road, Croydon CR0 2XF* Tel (020) 8684 1345 Mobile 07789-567842

SOPER, Jonathan Alexander James. b 64. Univ Coll Dur BA85. Wycliffe Hall Ox 94. **d** 96 **p** 97. C Bath Weston All SS w N Stoke and Langridge *B & W* 96-00; C Bryanston Square St Mary w St Marylebone St Mark *Lon* 00-07; Lic to Offic *Ex* from 07. *22 Mont le Grand, Exeter EX1 2PA* Tel (01392) 274728 E-mail enccontact@enc.eclipse.co.uk

SOPHIANOU, Neofitos Anthony. b 47. Sarum & Wells Th Coll 86. **d** 88 **p** 89. C St Peter-in-Thanet *Cant* 88-91; Perm to Offic *St Alb* 97-99; C Stevenage St Nic and Graveley 99-03; Perm to Offic 03-04; V Wheatley Park *Sheff* 04-07; V Goole from 07; Bp's

Urban Adv from 05. *7 Salisbury Avenue, Goole DN14 5JW* E-mail tonysophianou@blueyonder.co.uk

SORENSEN, Ms Anna Katrine Elizabeth. b 58. Man Univ BA82 MPhil94 Open Univ PGCE95. Ripon Coll Cuddesdon 83. **d** 87 **p** 94. Par Dn Ashton H Trin *Man* 87-88; Asst Chapl St Felix Sch Southwold 89-90; Chapl 90-99; Hon Par Dn Reydon *St E* 89-92; Hon Par Dn Blythburgh w Reydon 92-94; Hon C 94-99; C Gislingham and Thorndon 99-03; P-in-c Billingborough Gp *Linc* from 03. *The Vicarage, 13 High Street, Billingborough, Sleaford NG34 0QG* Tel (01529) 240750 Mobile 07932-031479 E-mail anna_sor@yahoo.com

SOTONWA, Canon Oladapo Oyegbola. b 56. Ibadan Univ Nigeria BEd79 MEd81 PhD86. Immanuel Coll Ibadan 91. **d** 94 **p** 95. C Italupe Em Nigeria 94-95; V Egbeba All SS 95-03; V Simeon Adeyemi Ashiru Mem Ch 03-04; V Odogbondu St Pet 04-05; Hon Can Ijebu from 05; Perm to Offic *S'wark* 06-07; Hon C W Dulwich Em from 07. *Emmanuel Church, 94 Clive Road, London SE21 8BU* Tel (020) 8764 2133 Mobile 07904-866635 E-mail oladaposotonwa@yahoo.co.uk

SOULSBY, Canon Michael. b 36. Dur Univ BSc57. Westcott Ho Cam 61. **d** 62 **p** 63. C Selly Oak St Mary *Birm* 62-66; C Kings Norton 66-72; TV 73-76; TR Sutton *Liv* 76-88; RD Prescot 84-88; P-in-c Orton Longueville *Ely* 88-96; RD Yaxley 92-02; TR The Ortons, Alwalton and Chesterton 96-04; Hon Can Ely Cathl 94-04; rtd 04; Perm to Offic *Ely* from 05. *8 Leiston Court, Eye, Peterborough PE6 7WL* Tel (01733) 221124 E-mail m.soulsby@talk21.com

SOULT, Mrs Pamela Elizabeth. b 46. SNWTP. **d** 09. NSM Goostrey w Swettenham *Ches* from 09. *The Tower House, The Courtyard, Swettenham, Congleton CW12 2JZ* Tel (01477) 571844

SOUPER, Patrick Charles. b 28. K Coll Lon BD55 AKC55. **d** 57 **p** 58. Chapl Derby City Hosp 57-62; Chapl Derby Cathl 57-62; Asst Chapl Lon Univ 62-64; C St Marylebone w H Trin 64-65; Chapl St Paul's Sch Barnes 65-70; Lect in Educn Southn Univ 70-87; rtd 87. *PO Box 11, 741 00 Rethymnon, Crete, Greece* Tel (0030) (831) 31521 Fax 31903 E-mail pigiaki@phl.uoc.gr

SOUPPOURIS, Ms Gail Camilla. b 52. Essex Univ BA75. SEITE 02. **d** 05 **p** 06. C W Wickham St Fran and St Mary *S'wark* 05-08; P-in-c Shoreham Beach *Chich* from 08. *The Vicarage, 1 West Beach, Shoreham-by-Sea BN43 5LF* Tel (01273) 453768 Mobile 07950-665051 E-mail gail.souppouris@ntlworld.com

SOURBUT, Catherine Ann. b 67. Bath Univ BA91 MSc93 PhD97. STETS MA07. **d** 07 **p** 08. C Saltford w Corston and Newton St Loe *B & W* from 07. *2 Fenton Close, Saltford, Bristol BS31 3AT* Tel (01225) 874459 E-mail catherine.sourbut@tiscali.co.uk

SOURBUT, Philip John. b 57. Cam Univ BA MA. Cranmer Hall Dur BA. **d** 85 **p** 86. C Springfield All SS *Chelmsf* 85-88; C Roxeth Ch Ch and Harrow St Pet *Lon* 88-91; P-in-c Bath St Sav *B & W* 91-93; R Bath St Sav w Swainswick and Woolley 93-98; V Cullompton and R Kentisbeare w Blackborough *Ex* 98-01; TR Cullompton, Willand, Uffculme, Kentisbeare etc 01-09; Dioc Voc Development Officer from 09; Tutor SWMTC from 09; C Ex St Mark, St Sidwell and St Matt from 09. *45 Spicer Road, Exeter EX1 1TA* Tel (01392) 817296 E-mail psourbut@lineone.net

SOUTER, Ruth Rosemary. b 55. Dur Univ BEd77. EMMTC 00. **d** 03 **p** 04. C Braunstone Park CD *Leic* 03-07; V Erdington Ch the K *Birm* from 07. *St Margaret's Vicarage, Somerset Road, Erdington, Birmingham B23 6NQ* Tel 0121-373 9209 E-mail ruthsouter@yahoo.com

SOUTER, William Ewen Logan. b 66. Em Coll Cam BA88 Univ Coll Lon PhD93. Trin Coll Bris BA94 MA97. **d** 97 **p** 98. C Harborne Heath *Birm* 97-01; TV Horsham *Chich* from 01. *St John's House, Church Road, Broadbridge Heath, Horsham RH12 3ND* Tel (01403) 265238 Mobile 07889-612861 E-mail ewen@souter.me.uk

SOUTH, Gillian. *See* HARWOOD, Mrs Gillian

SOUTH EAST ASIA, Archbishop of. *See* CHEW, The Most Revd John Hiang Chea

SOUTHALL, Colin Edward. b 36. Lich Th Coll 63. **d** 65 **p** 82. C Wylde Green 65-67; Perm to Offic *Birm* 68-73 and *Pet* 73-81; Hon C Linc St Faith and St Martin w St Pet 82-85; Hon C Gt Glen, Stretton Magna and Wistow etc *Leic* 85-93; Chapl Asst Leic R Infirmary 93-96; Hon C Fleckney and Kilby *Leic* 96-98; Perm to Offic from 99. *1 Spinney View, Great Glen, Leicester LE8 9EP* Tel 0116-259 2959

SOUTHAMPTON, Suffragan Bishop of. *Vacant*

SOUTHEE, Mrs Sandra Margaret. b 43. EAMTC 97. **d** 00 **p** 01. NSM Galleywood Common *Chelmsf* 00-02; NSM Moulsham St Jo 02-06; Perm to Offic 06-07; NSM Gt Baddow from 07; Asst Chapl Mid-Essex Hosp Services NHS Trust from 02. *6 Hampton Road, Chelmsford CM2 8ES* Tel (01245) 475456 E-mail sandysouthee@hotmail.co.uk

SOUTHEND, Archdeacon of. *See* LOWMAN, The Ven David Walter

✠SOUTHERN, The Rt Revd Humphrey Ivo John. b 60. Ch Ch Ox BA82 MA86. Ripon Coll Cuddesdon 83. **d** 86 **p** 87 **c** 07. C Rainham *Roch* 86-90; C Walton St Mary *Liv* 90-92; C Walton-on-the-Hill 92; V Hale *Guildf* 92-96; TR 96-97; TR Hale w Badshot Lea 97-99; Dioc Ecum Officer 92-99; TR Tisbury *Sarum* 99-01; TR Nadder Valley 01-07; RD Chalke 00-07; Can and Preb Sarum Cathl 06-07; Suff Bp Repton *Derby* from 07; Warden of Readers from 09. *Repton House, Church Street, Lea, Matlock DE4 5JP* Tel (01629) 534644 Fax 534003 E-mail bishop@repton.free-online.co.uk

SOUTHERN, John Abbott. b 27. Leeds Univ BA47. Coll of Resurr Mirfield. **d** 51 **p** 52. C Leigh St Mary *Man* 51-55; C Gt Grimsby St Jas *Linc* 55-58; V Oldham St Jas *Man* 58-60; V Haigh *Liv* 60-75; V Pemberton St Jo 75-98; rtd 98; Perm to Offic *Liv* from 00. *145 Moor Road, Orrell, Wigan WN5 8SJ* Tel (01942) 732132

SOUTHERN, Mrs Lindsay Margaret. b 70. Univ of Wales (Abth) BA01 Reading Univ PGCE04 St Jo Coll Dur BA08. Cranmer Hall Dur 06. **d** 08 **p** 09. C Kirklington w Burneston and Wath and Pickhill *Ripon* from 08. *21 Melltowns Green, Pickhill, Thirsk YO7 4LL* Tel (01845) 567961 E-mail lindsay.southern@talk21.com

SOUTHERN, Paul Ralph. b 48. Oak Hill Th Coll 85. **d** 87 **p** 88. C Chadwell Heath *Chelmsf* 87-91; P-in-c Tolleshunt D'Arcy and Tolleshunt Major 91-01; V 01-08; rtd 08; Perm to Offic *Chelmsf* from 08. *12 Guisnes Court, Back Road, Tolleshunt D'Arcy, Maldon CM9 8TW* Tel (01621) 860381

SOUTHERN CONE OF AMERICA, Primate of. *See* VENABLES, The Most Revd Gregory James

SOUTHERTON, Kathryn Ruth. *See* TRIMBY, Mrs Kathryn Ruth

SOUTHERTON, Canon Peter Clive. b 38. MBE01. Univ of Wales (Lamp) BA59. Qu Coll Birm. **d** 61 **p** 62. C Llandrillo-yn-Rhos *St As* 61-68; Bermuda 68-71; V Esclusham *St As* 72-82; V Prestatyn 82-04; Hon Can St As Cathl 96-04; rtd 04. *6 Llwyn Mesen, Prestatyn LL19 8NS* Tel (01745) 853176

SOUTHEY, George Maurice. b 34. St Mich Coll Llan 84. **d** 86 **p** 87. C Hessle *York* 86-89; P-in-c Scarborough St Columba 89-92; V 92-99; rtd 99; Perm to Offic *Glouc* 00-06. *9 Smokey Glade, Doreen Vic 3754, Australia* Tel (0061) (3) 9717 5717 Mobile 43-833 9877 E-mail george.southey@bigpond.com

SOUTHGATE, Graham. b 63. GIBiol85 NE Surrey Coll of Tech PhD89. Ripon Coll Cuddesdon BTh93. **d** 93 **p** 94. C Tisbury *Sarum* 93-97; TV Chalke Valley 97-03; R Bratton, Edington and Imber, Erlestoke etc from 03. *The Vicarage, Upper Garston Lane, Bratton, Westbury BA13 4SN* Tel (01380) 830374 E-mail grahamsouthgate63@hotmail.com

SOUTHGATE, Patricia. **d** 03 **p** 04. OLM Parkstone St Pet and St Osmund w Branksea *Sarum* from 03. *60 Orchard Avenue, Poole BH14 8AJ* Tel (01202) 745081 E-mail pat.southgate@virgin.net

SOUTHGATE, Stephen Martin. b 61. Lanc Univ BA83 St Martin's Coll Lanc PGCE84. Cranmer Hall Dur 96. **d** 98 **p** 99. C Witton *Ches* 98-01; R Backford and Capenhurst from 01. *The Vicarage, Grove Road, Mollington, Chester CH1 6LG* Tel (01244) 851071 E-mail mollingtonvicarage@tiscali.co.uk

SOUTHWARD, Douglas Ambrose. b 32. St Jo Coll Nottm LTh74 FBS02. ALCD57. **d** 57 **p** 58. C Otley *Bradf* 57-61; C Sedbergh 61-63; C Cautley w Dowhiggin 61-63; C Garsdale 61-63; PV Lich Cathl 63-65; V Hope *Derby* 65-72; V Crosby Ravensworth *Carl* 72-82; V Bolton 74-82; Sec Dioc Past and Redundant Chs Uses Cttees 78-82; RD Appleby 78-82; Hon Can Carl Cathl 81-95; R Asby 81-82; V Hawkshead and Low Wray w Sawrey 82-98; P-in-c Windermere St Jo 84-89; RD Windermere 84-89; P-in-c Satterthwaite 94-95; rtd 98; Perm to Offic *Carl* from 98. *Hawthorn House, Town End, Witherslack, Grange-over-Sands LA11 6RL* Tel (01539) 552078

SOUTHWARD, James Fisher. b 57. St Martin's Coll Lanc BEd80. Chich Th Coll 83. **d** 86 **p** 87. C Woodford St Barn *Chelmsf* 86-89; TV Crawley *Chich* 89-95; V Higham and Merston *Roch* from 95; RD Strood from 02. *The Vicarage, Hermitage Road, Higham, Rochester ME3 7NE* Tel and fax (01634) 717360 E-mail james.southward@diocese-rochester.org

SOUTHWARK, Archdeacon of. *See* IPGRAVE, The Ven Michael Geoffrey

SOUTHWARK, Bishop of. *See* BUTLER, The Rt Revd Thomas Frederick

SOUTHWARK, Dean of. *See* SLEE, The Very Revd Colin Bruce

SOUTHWELL, Peter John Mackenzie. b 43. New Coll Ox BA64 MA68. Wycliffe Hall Ox 66. **d** 67 **p** 68. C Crookes St Thos *Sheff* 67-70; Lect Sheff Univ 67-70; Sen Tutor Wycliffe Hall Ox 70-08; Chapl and Lect Qu Coll Ox from 82. *The Queen's College, Oxford OX1 4AW* Tel (01865) 279120 E-mail peter.southwell@queens.ox.ac.uk

SOUTHWELL, The Ven Roy. b 14. AKC42. **d** 42 **p** 43. C Wigan St Mich *Liv* 42-44; C Kennington St Jo *S'wark* 44-48; V Ixworth *St E* 48-51; P-in-c Ixworth Thorpe 48-51; V Bury St Edmunds St Jo 51-56; R Bucklesham w Brightwell and Foxhall 56-59; Dir

RE 59-68; Hon Can St E Cathl 59-68; V Hendon St Mary *Lon* 68-71; Adn Northolt 70-80; rtd 80; Warden Community of All Hallows Ditchingham 83-89; Lic to Offic *Nor* 83-89; Perm to Offic from 89. *397 Sprowton Road, Norwich NR3 4HY* Tel (01603) 405977

SOUTHWELL AND NOTTINGHAM, Bishop of. *See* BUTLER, The Rt Revd Paul Roger

SOUTHWELL, Dean of. *See* GUILLE, The Very Revd John Arthur

SOWDEN, Charles William Bartholomew. b 47. **d** 97 **p** 98. OLM Saxonwell *Linc* 97-06; NSM Metheringham w Blankney and Dunston 06-09; P-in-c Wyberton from 09; P-in-c Frampton from 09. *The Rectory, Church Lane, Wyberton, Boston PE21 7AF* Tel (01205) 353593 E-mail charles.sowden1@btinternet.com

SOWDEN, Geoffrey David. b 57. Kingston Poly BA79. Wycliffe Hall Ox 95. **d** 97 **p** 98. C Ware Ch Ch *St Alb* 97-02; V Highworth w Sevenhampton and Inglesham etc *Bris* from 02; P-in-c Broad Blunsdon from 05. *The Vicarage, 10 Stonefield Drive, Highworth, Swindon SN6 7DA* Tel (01793) 765554 E-mail the.sowdens@btinternet.com

SOWDON, Henry Lewis Malcolm. b 37. TCD BA. Bps' Coll Cheshunt. **d** 64 **p** 65. C Newport w Longford *Lich* 64-66; C Caverswall 66-69; Chapl Clayesmore Sch Blandford 69-72; Hon C Hornsey Ch Ch *Lon* 72-80; Chapl Gordon's Sch Woking 80-86; TV Hodge Hill *Birm* 86-91; Perm to Offic from 91 rtd 02. *157 Heathfield Road, Birmingham B19 1JD* Tel 0121-240 3557

SOWERBUTTS, Alan. b 49. Sheff Univ BSc70 PhD73 Qu Coll Cam BA75 MA79. Westcott Ho Cam 74. **d** 76 **p** 77. C Salesbury *Blackb* 76-80; V Lower Darwen St Jas 80-84; V Musbury 84-93; P-in-c Brindle 93-98; Sec Dioc Adv Cttee for the Care of Chs 93-98; V Read in Whalley from 98. *The Vicarage, George Lane, Read, Burnley BB12 7RQ* Tel (01282) 771361 E-mail anseres@ukonline.co.uk

SOWERBUTTS, Philip John. b 67. Ches Coll of HE BEd89 Edge Hill Coll of HE PGCE99. Oak Hill Th Coll BA03. **d** 03 **p** 04. C Kirk Ella and Willerby *York* 03-07; V Castle Church *Lich* from 07. *Castle Church Vicarage, 18 Castle Bank, Stafford ST16 1DJ* Tel (01785) 223673 Mobile 07957-122836 E-mail philip-claire@hotmail.com

SOWERBY, Geoffrey Nigel Rake. b 35. St Aid Birkenhead 56. **d** 60 **p** 61. C Armley St Bart *Ripon* 60-63; Min Can Ripon Cathl 63-65; V Thornthwaite w Thruscross and Darley 65-69; V Leeds All SS 69-73; V Leyburn w Bellerby 73-81; R Edin Old St Paul 81-86; V Hawes and Hardraw *Ripon* 86-92; Dioc Adv in Deliverance Min 91-92; rtd 92; Perm to Offic *Dur* and *Ripon* from 92. *6 Wycar Terrace, Bedale DL8 2AG* Tel (01677) 425860 Mobile 07749-229189 E-mail geoffreysowerby@onetel.com

✠SOWERBY, The Rt Revd Mark Crispin Rake. b 63. K Coll Lon BD85 AKC85 Lanc Univ MA94. Coll of Resurr Mirfield 85. **d** 87 **p** 88 **c** 09. C Knaresborough *Ripon* 87-90; C Darwen St Cuth w Tockholes St Steph *Blackb* 90-92; V Accrington St Mary 92-97; Chapl St Chris High Sch Accrington 92-97; Chapl Victoria Hosp Accrington 92-97; Asst Dir of Ords *Blackb* 93-96; Voc Officer and Selection Sec Min Division 97-01; V Harrogate St Wilfrid *Ripon* 01-04; TR 04-09; Asst Dir of Ords 05-09; Area Bp Horsham *Chich* from 09. *Bishop's House, 21 Guildford Road, Horsham RH12 1LU* Tel (01403) 211139 Fax 217349 E-mail bishop.horsham@diochi.org

SOWTER, Colin Victor. b 35. Ball Coll Ox BA56 MA59 DPhil60. Oak Hill NSM Course 88. **d** 91 **p** 92. NSM Cranleigh *Guildf* 91-93; NSM Wonersh 93-98; NSM Wonersh w Blackheath 98-05; rtd 05; Perm to Offic *Guildf* from 05. *Hollycroft, Grantley Avenue, Wonersh Park, Guildford GU5 0QN* Tel (01483) 892094 Fax 892894 E-mail sowter@lineone.net

SOWTON, Mrs Alison. b 62. Qu Coll Birm. **d** 09. C Oxhey All SS *St Alb* from 09. *14 The Hoe, Watford WD19 5AY* Tel 07739-712548 (mobile) E-mail alisonsowton@live.com

SOX, Harold David. b 36. N Carolina Univ BA58. Union Th Sem (NY) MDiv61. **d** 61 **p** 61. USA 61-74; Hon C Richmond St Mary *S'wark* 74-79; Hon C Richmond St Mary w St Matthias and St Jo 79-82; Hon C Kensington St Mary Abbots w St Geo *Lon* 82-84 and 89-93; Perm to Offic 84-89; Hon C Beedon and Peasemore w W Ilsley and Farnborough *Ox* 93-94; Perm to Offic *Ox* 93-97 and *S'wark* 97-04. *20 The Vineyard, Richmond TW10 6AN* Tel (020) 8940 0094

SPACKMAN (*née* MORRISON), Mrs Ailsa. b 40. Qu Univ Kingston Ontario BA82. Montreal Dioc Th Coll. **d** 83 **p** 85. Canada 83-95; Dn Caspe 83-85; I Malbay Miss Par 85-92; Chapl Drummondville Penitentiary 92-93; rtd 93; Perm to Offic *Ex* from 99. *Cofton Lodge, Cofton Hill, Cockwood, Exeter EX6 8RB* Tel (01626) 891584

SPACKMAN, Canon Peter John. b 37. Southn Univ BSc60. Westcott Ho Cam 65. **d** 66 **p** 67. C Boxmoor St Jo *St Alb* 66-69; C Alnwick St Paul *Newc* 69-72; C-in-c Stewart Town Jamaica 72-74; Canada 74-95; I Sept-Iles 74-77; R Baie Comeau 77-80; R Gaspe 80-92; Adn Gaspe 88-92; R Richmond 92-94; Hon Can Quebec 92-94; Perm to Offic *Ex* 95-97; Hon C Kenton, Mamhead, Powderham, Cofton and Starcross 97-02; Perm to

Offic from 02. *Cofton Lodge, Cofton Hill, Cockwood, Exeter EX6 8RB* Tel (01626) 891584
E-mail spackman1@btinternet.com

SPAFFORD, The Very Revd Christopher Garnett Howsin. b 24. St Jo Coll Ox BA48 MA54. Wells Th Coll 48. **d** 50 **p** 51. C Brighouse *Wakef* 50-53; C Huddersfield St Pet 53-55; V Hebden Bridge 55-61; R Thornhill 61-69; V Shrewsbury St Chad *Lich* 69-76; V Newc St Nic 76-89; Provost Newc 76-89; rtd 89; Perm to Offic *Heref* from 93. *Low Moor, Elm Close, Leominster HR6 8JX* Tel (01568) 614395

SPAIGHT, Robert George. b 45. Ridley Hall Cam. **d** 84 **p** 85. C St Columb Minor and St Colan *Truro* 84-87; C Worksop St Jo *S'well* 87-89; V Barlings *Linc* from 89. *The Vicarage, Station Road, Langworth, Lincoln LN3 5BB* Tel (01522) 754233

SPANISH REFORMED CHURCH, Bishop of. *See* LÓPEZ-LOZANO, The Rt Revd Carlos

SPANNER, Handley James. b 51. Lanchester Poly Cov BSc73 BA. Oak Hill Th Coll 82. **d** 85 **p** 86. C Cov H Trin 85-89; V Rye Park St Cuth *St Alb* 89-01; V Colney Heath St Mark from 01. *St Mark's Vicarage, St Mark's Close, Colney Heath, St Albans AL4 0NQ* Tel (01727) 822040 E-mail jamesspanner@aol.com

SPARGO, Anne Elizabeth. b 51. Newnham Coll Cam MA76 MB, BChir76. WEMTC 03. **d** 06 **p** 07. NSM Frampton on Severn, Arlingham, Saul etc *Glouc* from 06. *Ashleigh House, The Street, Frampton on Severn, Gloucester GL2 7ED* Tel (01452) 741147 Fax 740989 E-mail anne.spargo@btinternet.com

SPARHAM, Canon Anthony George. b 41. St Jo Coll Dur BA69. Cranmer Hall Dur 66. **d** 71 **p** 72. C Bourne *Linc* 71-74; TV Tong *Bradf* 74-76; V Windhill 76-81; Dioc Dir of Educn *St E* 82-85; V Goostrey *Ches* 85-99; R Wilmslow 99-08; Dir Lay Tr 85-90; Jt Dir Lay Tr 90-97; Hon Can Ches Cathl 94-08; rtd 08; Perm to Offic *Lich* from 08. *8 Sycamore Close, St Martins, Oswestry SY11 3EL* Tel (01691) 770320
E-mail tony.sparham@virgin.net

SPARKES, Donald James Henry. b 33. Oak Hill Th Coll. **d** 59 **p** 60. C Southall Green St Jo *Lon* 59-63; P-in-c Pitsmoor *Sheff* 63-70; V 70-73; P-in-c Wicker w Neepsend 70-73; V Pitsmoor w Wicker 73-79; V Pitsmoor w Ellesmere 79-86; V Pitsmoor Ch Ch 86-96; rtd 96; Perm to Offic *Derby* and *Sheff* from 96. *8 Grosvenor Mansions, Broad Walk, Buxton SK17 6JH* Tel (01298) 25134

SPARKES, Mrs Lynne. b 55. Chelt & Glouc Coll of HE BEd96. WEMTC 06. **d** 09. NSM Barnwood *Glouc* from 09. *25 The Plantation, Abbeymead, Gloucester GL4 5TR*

SPARKS, Christopher Thomas. b 29. Lanc Univ PGCE69 Birm Univ 81. St D Coll Lamp BA53 Lich Th Coll 53. **d** 55 **p** 56. C Macclesfield St Mich *Ches* 55-59; C W Kirby St Bridget 59-61; V Altrincham St Jo 61-68; Lic to Offic *Blackb* 68-79; C Lancaster St Mary 79-83; Chapl HM Pris Lanc 83-84; Perm to Offic *Blackb* from 84; rtd 94. *1 Yealand Drive, Scotforth, Lancaster LA1 4EW* Tel (01524) 67507

SPARKS, Ian. b 59. Lanc Univ BSc(Econ)81. Cranmer Hall Dur 94. **d** 96 **p** 97. C Bowdon *Ches* 96-00; V Chelford w Lower Withington 00-06; P-in-c Macclesfield St Jo from 06. *St John's Vicarage, 25 Wilwick Lane, Macclesfield SK11 8RS* Tel (01625) 424185 E-mail sparks.family@ntlworld.com

SPARROW, Michael Kenneth. St Jo Coll Dur BA74. Coll of Resurr Mirfield 74. **d** 75 **p** 76. C N Hinksey *Ox* 75-78; C Portsea St Mary *Portsm* 78-85; V Midsomer Norton w Clandown *B & W* 85-93; Chapl Schiedam Miss to Seafarers *Eur* 93-03; Chapl Mombasa Seamen from 04. *Missions to Seamen, PO Box 80424, Mombasa, Kenya* Tel (00254) (41) 223 0027 Fax 223 0001 E-mail missions@wananchi.com

SPEAKMAN, Anthony Ernest. b 43. **d** 71 **p** 72. C Newtown *St As* 71-72; C Holywell 72-75; C St Marylebone w H Trin *Lon* 75-77; V Camberwell St Phil and St Mark *S'wark* 77-80; Lic to Offic *Lon* 94-96; NSM Kensington St Jo 96-05; rtd 99. *24 McAuley Close, Kennington Road, London SE1 7BX* Tel (020) 7928 8721 *or* 7602 3898

SPEAKMAN, Joseph Frederick. b 26. NW Ord Course 75. **d** 78 **p** 79. NSM Wallasey St Hilary *Ches* 78; C 79-82; V Marthall w Over Peover 82-91; rtd 91; Perm to Offic *Ches* from 91. *1 Kinnaird Court, Cliff Road, Wallasey CH44 3AX* Tel 0151-637 0109 E-mail revjoe@talktalk.net

SPEAR, Andrew James Michael. b 60. Dur Univ BA81. Ridley Hall Cam 83. **d** 86 **p** 87. C Haughton le Skerne *Dur* 86-90; C Eastbourne H Trin *Chich* 90-95; C Patcham 95-02; V Oldland *Bris* from 02. *Oldland Vicarage, Grangeville Close, Longwell Green, Bristol BS30 9YJ* Tel 0117-932 7178 *or* 932 3291 E-mail andrewjmspear@hotmail.com

SPEAR, Miss Jennifer Jane. b 53. Westhill Coll Birm BEd76. Trin Coll Bris 82. **dss** 84 **d** 87 **p** 95. Reading St Jo *Ox* 84-90; Par Dn 87-90; Hon Par Dn Devonport St Barn *Ex* 90-91; Hon Par Dn Devonport St Mich 90-91; Par Dn Plymstock 91-94; C 94-97; TV Plymstock and Hooe from 97. *63 Plymstock Road, Plymstock, Plymouth PL9 7NX* Tel (01752) 405202

SPEAR, John Cory. b 33. Open Univ BA87. Ridley Hall Cam 68. **d** 70 **p** 71. C Gerrards Cross *Ox* 70-73; TV Washfield, Stoodleigh, Withleigh etc *Ex* 73-79; R Instow 79-90; V Westleigh

79-90; RD Hartland 82-89; V Pilton w Ashford 90-97; TR Barnstaple 97-99; rtd 99; Perm to Offic *Ex* from 00. *Abbots Lodge, Abbotsham Court, Abbotsham, Bideford EX39 5BH* Tel (01237) 476607

SPEAR, Sylvia Grace. b 36. St Chris Coll Blackheath 60. **dss** 76 **d** 87 **p** 94. S Wimbledon H Trin and St Pet *S'wark* 76-80; Lee Gd Shep w St Pet 80-95; Par Dn 87-94; C 94-95; rtd 95; Perm to Offic *Nor* from 95. *19 Grovelands, Ingoldisthorpe, King's Lynn PE31 6PG* Tel (01485) 543469

SPEARS, Reginald Robert Derek. b 48. Trin Coll Ox BA72 MA75. Cuddesdon Coll 72. **d** 75 **p** 76. C Hampton All SS *Lon* 75-79; C Caversham *Ox* 79-81; C Caversham St Pet and Mapledurham etc 81-84; V Reading St Matt 84-94; V Earley St Pet from 94. *St Peter's Vicarage, 129 Whiteknights Road, Reading RG6 7BB* Tel and fax 0118-926 2009
E-mail derekspears@compuserve.com

SPECK, Ms Jane Elisabeth. b 72. Univ of Cen England in Birm BA94 St Jo Coll Dur BA01 MA02. Cranmer Hall Dur 98. **d** 02 **p** 03. C Stourport and Wilden *Worc* 02-05; C N Lambeth *S'wark* from 05; Chapl K Coll Lon from 05. *1 Havilland House, 13 Sancroft Street, London SE11 5UG* Tel (020) 7582 4915
E-mail janespeck@hotmail.com

SPECK, Preb Peter William. b 42. Univ of Wales (Ban) BSc64 Birm Univ BA66 MA71. Qu Coll Birm 64. **d** 67 **p** 68. C Rhosddu *St As* 67-71; C Wrexham 71-72; Asst Chapl United Sheff Hosps 72-73; Chapl N Gen Hosp Sheff 73-79; Chapl R Free Hosp Lon 79-95; Hon Sen Lect Sch of Med 87-95; Preb St Paul's Cathl 92-95; Chapl Southn Univ Hosps NHS Trust 95-02; rtd 02; Public Preacher *Win* from 02; Visiting Fell Southn Univ from 02; Hon Sen Research Fell K Coll Lon from 02. *22 The Harrage, Romsey SO51 8AE* Tel (01794) 516937

SPECK, Raymond George. b 39. Oak Hill Th Coll 64. **d** 67 **p** 68. C Stretford St Bride *Man* 67-70; C Roxeth Ch Ch *Lon* 70-74; V Woodbridge St Jo *St E* 74-85; R Jersey St Ouen w St Geo *Win* 85-98; rtd 98; Perm to Offic *Win* from 98. *Rosevale Lodge, rue du Craslin, St Peter, Jersey JE3 7BU* Tel (01534) 634987

SPEDDING, Clare. *See* FRYER-SPEDDING, Mrs Clare Caroline

SPEDDING, Geoffrey Osmond. b 46. Hull Univ BA67 Fitzw Coll Cam BA69 MA BD. **d** 70 **p** 71. C Bradf Cathl 70-73; C Sutton St Jas and Wawne *York* 73-76; TV Preston St Jo *Blackb* 76-82; TV Yate New Town *Bris* 82-87; TR Bestwood *S'well* 87-94; V Ravenshead 94-04; rtd 04; Estate Manager Scargill Ho 06-08; P-in-c Cullingworth *Bradf* 08-09; Hon C E Richmond *Ripon* from 09. *The Vicarage, St Paul's Drive, Brompton on Swale, Richmond DL10 7HQ*

SPEDDING, William Granville. b 39. Tyndale Hall Bris BD60. **d** 62 **p** 63. C Man Albert Memorial Ch 62-65; Hd RE Whitecroft Sch Bolton 65-71; Co-ord Humanities Hayward Sch Bolton 71-93; Perm to Offic 65-67 and from 02; NSM New Bury 67-79; NSM Bolton St Paul w Em 79-86; NSM Pennington 86-02. *26 Milverton Close, Lostock, Bolton BL6 4RR* Tel (01204) 841248 E-mail granvillespedding@ntlworld.com

SPEEDY (née BRINDLEY), Mrs Angela Mary. b 44. Oak Hill Th Coll 93 NOC 99. **d** 00 **p** 01. C Handforth *Ches* 00-03; R Whaley Bridge 03-05; rtd 05; Hon C Barthomley *Ches* from 07. *The Rectory, Rushy Lane, Barthomley, Crewe CW2 5PE* Tel (01270) 877112

SPEEDY, Canon Darrel Craven. b 35. St Chad's Coll Dur BA57. Wells Th Coll 57. **d** 59 **p** 60. C Frodingham *Linc* 59-63; V Heckington w Howell 63-71; V Barton upon Humber 71-79; R Tain *Mor* 79-85; Dioc Sec 82-85; Can St Andr Cathl Inverness 83-85; Syn Clerk 83-85; R Whaley Bridge *Ches* 85-01; RD Chadkirk 88-95; Hon Can Ches Cathl from 96; rtd 01; P-in-c Barthomley *Ches* from 01. *The Rectory, Rushy Lane, Barthomley, Crewe CW2 5PE* Tel (01270) 877112
E-mail darrel.speedy@btopenworld.com

SPEEKS, Mark William. b 62. Ex Univ BA82 Ex Coll Ox MSt83 Yale Univ MDiv02. **d** 02 **p** 02. C Los Angeles St Alban USA 02-03; NSM Kilburn St Mary w All So and W Hampstead St Jas *Lon* 04-08; NSM St Botolph Aldgate w H Trin Minories from 08. *Flat 9, 23 Bunhill Row, London EC1Y 8LP* Tel 07966-768127 (mobile) E-mail mspeeks@hotmail.com
or m.speeks@stbotolphs.org.uk

SPEERS, Canon Samuel Hall. b 46. TCD BA70 MA75. Cuddesdon Coll 70. **d** 73 **p** 74. C Boreham Wood All SS *St Alb* 73-76; Madagascar 76-88; Hon Can Antananarivo from 85; R S Lafford *Linc* 88-02; RD Lafford 96-02; TR Chipping Barnet *St Alb* from 02. *The Rectory, 38 Manor Road, Barnet EN5 2JJ* Tel (020) 8449 3894 E-mail hall.speers@talk21.com

SPENCE, Beth Ann. b 65. Smith Coll (USA) BA87 St Hilda's Coll Ox MA90. SAOMC 02. **d** 05 **p** 06. C Cowley St Jas *Ox* 05-08; Australia from 08. *Address temp unknown*
E-mail beth.spence@ntlworld.com

SPENCE, Brian Robin. b 39. St Chad's Coll Dur BA61. **d** 63 **p** 64. C Weston *Guildf* 63-67; Lesotho 67-68; C Chobham w Valley End *Guildf* 68-71; C Gt Yarmouth *Nor* 71-74; V Warnham *Chich* 74-81; V E Grinstead St Mary 81-86; V Crowthorne *Ox* 86-05;

rtd 05; Hon C Theale and Englefield *Ox* from 05. *St Mark's House, Englefield, Reading RG7 5EP* Tel 0118-930 2227
E-mail brian@stmarkshouse.f9.co.uk

SPENCE, James Knox. b 30. Worc Coll Ox BA55 MA58. Ridley Hall Cam. **d** 57 **p** 58. C W Hampstead Trin *Lon* 57-60; C Ox St Ebbe w St Pet 61-64; Cand Sec CPAS 64-68; V Reading Greyfriars *Ox* 68-78; C St Helen Bishopsgate w St Andr Undershaft etc *Lon* 78-82; P-in-c Gt Baddow *Chelmsf* 82-86; V 86-88; TR 88-95; rtd 95; Hon C Wallingford *Ox* from 96. *15 High Street, Wallingford OX10 0BP* Tel (01491) 826814
E-mail jim@spence341.fsnet.co.uk

SPENCE, Canon John Edis. b 24. St Edm Hall Ox BA46 MA48. Westcott Ho Cam 47. **d** 48 **p** 49. C Newland St Jo *York* 48-50; Australia 50-54; C Uckfield *Chich* 54-55; Chapl RN 55-59 and 60-65; V Thornton-le-Street w Thornton-le-Moor etc *York* 59-60; Chapl RNR 65-94; V St Germans *Truro* 65-73; V Tideford 65-73; P-in-c Sheviock 69-70; Perm to Offic 73-76; Dioc Chapl to Bp 76-78; C Newlyn St Newlyn 76-78; Chapl for Maintenance of the Min 78-87; Stewardship Adv 80-87; Hon Can Truro Cathl 84-89; Bp's Dom Chapl 87-89; P-in-c St Allen 87-89; rtd 89; Lic to Offic *Truro* 89-95; Perm to Offic *Ex* 91-98; Hon C Diptford, N Huish, Harberton, Harbertonford etc from 98. *26 Kerries Road, South Brent TQ10 9DA* Tel (01364) 72578

SPENCE, Michael James. b 62. Sydney Univ BA85 LLB87 St Cath Coll Ox DPhil96. St Steph Ho Ox. **d** 06 **p** 07. NSM Cowley St Jas *Ox* 06-08; Australia from 08. *Address temp unknown*

SPENCE, Mrs Moira Joan. b 44. SAOMC 96. **d** 01 **p** 02. OLM Risborough *Ox* 01-06; NSM Ewenny w St Brides Major *Llan* from 07. *Ty Bara, 33 Main Road, Ogmore-by-Sea, Bridgend CF32 0PD*

SPENCE, Canon Philip Arthur. b 39. Lon Univ BD71 Open Univ BA76. Westcott Ho Cam 78. **d** 78 **p** 79. In Methodist Ch 67-78; C Walthamstow St Pet *Chelmsf* 78-80; Dioc Adv on Evang 80-87; Dep Dir Dept of Miss (Evang Division) 80-85; P-in-c Greensted 80-86; Bp's Adv on Tourism 81-87; Asst Dir of Miss and Unity 85-87; R Greensted-juxta-Ongar w Stanford Rivers 86-87; V Cambridge St Mark *Ely* 87-95; Chapl Wolfs Coll Cam 87-95; Relig Adv Anglia TV 91-95; V Pet St Jo 95-01; Can Res and Warden Pet Cathl 97-01; Can 01-06; P-in-c Preston and Ridlington w Wing and Pilton 01-06; Adult Educn Officer 01-05; rtd 06; Perm to Offic *Pet* from 06. *20 Bayley Close, Uppingham, Oakham LE15 9TG* Tel (01572) 820199

SPENCE, The Very Revd Walter Cyril. b 19. TCD BA40 MA43 BD43. **d** 42 **p** 43. C Maghera *D & R* 43-48; C Roscommon *K, E & A* 48-50; I Ballysumaghan w Killery 50-55; I Tubbercurry w Kilmactigue *T, K & A* 55-60; I Achonry w Tubbercurry and Killoran 60-66; Can Achonry Cathl 62-66; Dean Tuam 66-81; I Tuam 66-81; Dioc Registrar 66-85; Preb Kilmactalway St Patr Cathl Dublin 67-85; I Kilmoremoy w Castleconnor, Easkey, Kilglass etc *T, K & A* 81-85; rtd 85. *Beth Shalom, 1 Gracefield Avenue, Dublin 5, Republic of Ireland*

SPENCELEY, Douglas. b 49. Edin Univ MA70 SS Mark & Jo Univ Coll Plymouth PGCE71. ERMC 07. **d** 09. NSM Arthingworth, Harrington w Oxendon and E Farndon *Pet* from 09; NSM Maidwell w Draughton, Lamport w Faxton from 09. *50 Orchard Hill, Little Billing, Northampton NN3 9AG* Tel (01604) 407977 E-mail dspenceley@lineone.net

SPENCELEY, Malcolm. b 40. Open Univ BA92 Dur Inst of Educn CertEd72. Cranmer Hall Dur 78. **d** 80 **p** 81. C Redcar *York* 80-85; V Middlesbrough Ascension 85-93; V Newby 93-05; rtd 05; Perm to Offic *York* from 06. *6 Tameside, Stokesley, Middlesbrough TS9 5PE* Tel (01642) 710443

SPENCER, Andrew. b 47. St Matthias Coll Bris BEd70 Univ of Wales (Ban) BTh05. **d** 04 **p** 05. Moderator for Reader Tr *Guildf* 01-06; OLM Busbridge and Hambledon from 04; Tutor Local Min Progr from 07. *24 Park Road, Godalming GU7 1SH* Tel (01483) 416333 E-mail andy.spencer@busbridgechurch.org

SPENCER, Antony Wade. b 50. Ridley Hall Cam 92. **d** 94 **p** 95. C Bury St Edmunds St Geo *St E* 94-96; Perm to Offic 96-97; C Rougham, Beyton w Hessett and Rushbrooke 97-99; TV Mildenhall 99-07; Dir Past Development Harborne Heath *Birm* from 07. *74 Croftdown Road, Birmingham B17 8RD* Tel 0121-426 6228 Mobile 07704-324444
E-mail antonyspencer@stjohns-church.co.uk

SPENCER, Christopher Graham. b 61. Magd Coll Cam BA83 MA87 Bath Univ MSc84. St Jo Coll Nottm 93. **d** 93 **p** 94. C Ore St Helen and St Barn *Chich* 93-97; V Deal St Geo *Cant* from 97. *The Vicarage, 8 St George's Road, Deal CT14 6BA* Tel (01304) 372587 E-mail vicar@stgeorgesdeal.org.uk
or vicar.chris@macunlimited.net

SPENCER, David William. b 43. EAMTC 80. **d** 81 **p** 82. NSM Wisbech St Aug *Ely* 81-84; C Whittlesey 84-86; R Upwell Christchurch 86-90; R March St Pet and March St Mary 90-98; TV Stanground and Farcet 98-01; V Farcet 01-04; V Farcet Hampton 04-08; rtd 08; Perm to Offic *Ely* from 08. *10 Hemingford Crescent, Peterborough PE2 8LL*
E-mail davidspencer@freezone.co.uk

SPENCER, Derek Kenneth. b 67. St Jo Coll Nottm BA98. **d** 03 **p** 05. Storrington Deanery Youth Missr *Chich* 01-06; C Steyning

05-06; P-in-c Sullington and Thakeham w Warminghurst from 07. *The Rectory, The Street, Thakeham, Pulborough RH20 3EP* Tel (01798) 813121 Mobile 07734-330678
E-mail noba@btinternet.com

SPENCER, Mrs Gail. b 57. STETS. **d** 03 **p** 04. NSM Wilton w Netherhampton and Fugglestone *Sarum* 03-06; NSM Radcliffe-on-Trent and Shelford *S'well* 06-07; Chapl Qu Medical Cen Nottm Univ Hosp NHS Trust from 07. *2 Gatcombe Close, Radcliffe-on-Trent, Nottingham NG12 2GG* Tel 0115-933 6068
E-mail gailespencer@yahoo.co.uk

SPENCER, Geoffrey. b 50. Nottm Univ CertEd78 Open Univ BA84 ALCM76 ACertCM79. Linc Th Coll 85. **d** 87 **p** 88. C Skegness and Winthorpe *Linc* 87-90; V Heckington 90-93; P-in-c Bottesford and Muston *Leic* 93-98; P-in-c Harby, Long Clawson and Hose 94-98; P-in-c Barkestone w Plungar, Redmile and Stathern 94-98; RD Framland 97-98; Perm to Offic *Linc* 03-05; Lic Preacher 05-06; P-in-c Church Langton cum Tur Langton etc *Leic* from 07. *The Vicarage, Gaulby Road, Billesdon, Leicester LE7 9AG* Tel 0116-259 6321

SPENCER, Canon Gilbert Hugh. b 43. Lon Univ BD67. ALCD66. **d** 67 **p** 68. C Bexleyheath Ch Ch *Roch* 67-73; C Bexley St Jo 73-76; P-in-c Bromley St Jo 76-78; V R Chatham St Mary w St Jo 81-91; V Minster-in-Sheppey *Cant* from 91; P-in-c Queenborough 99-05; AD Sittingbourne 94-00, 03-04 and 06-09; Hon Can Cant Cathl from 99; Chapl Sheppey Community Hosp 91-98; Chapl Thames Gateway NHS Trust from 98. *The Vicarage, Vicarage Road, Minster-on-Sea, Sheerness ME12 2HE* Tel and fax (01795) 873185 Mobile 07961-545934 E-mail gilbert_spencer@hotmail.com

SPENCER, Gordon Thomas. b 45. ACA68. STETS 03. **d** 06 **p** 07. NSM W Tarring *Chich* from 06. *3 Haysham Close, Goring-by-Sea, Worthing BN12 5BA* Tel (01903) 243998
E-mail gordon.spencer8@btinternet.com

SPENCER, Graham Lewis. b 48. St Jo Coll Nottm 80. **d** 82 **p** 83. C Leic St Anne 82-85; P-in-c Frisby-on-the-Wreake w Kirby Bellars 85-86; TV Melton Gt Framland 86-93; V Upper Wreake 93-99; V Glen Magna cum Stretton Magna etc 99-05; rtd 05; Perm to Offic *Leic* from 05. *18 Chetwynd Drive, Melton Mowbray LE13 0HU* Tel (01664) 564266
E-mail grahamandtrish@talktalk.net

SPENCER, Ian John. b 61. Qu Coll Birm 03. **d** 05 **p** 06. C Gt Malvern St Mary *Worc* 05-08; Warden Dioc Retreat Ho (Holland Ho) Cropthorne from 08. *Holland House, Main Street, Cropthorne, Pershore WR10 3NB* Tel (01386) 860330
E-mail ian.spencer@talktalk.net

SPENCER, Joan. b 50. **d** 98 **p** 99. OLM Norwich St Mary Magd w St Jas from 98. *94 Mousehold Avenue, Norwich NR3 4RS* Tel (01603) 404471 E-mail joanspencer@talktalk.net

SPENCER, John Edward. b 36. Bris Univ BA60. Tyndale Hall Bris 60. **d** 61 **p** 62. C St Helens St Mark *Liv* 61-64; Japan 65-70; Area Sec CMS *Leic* and *Pet* 70-71; Warden and Chapl Rikkyo Japanese Sch Rudgwick 71-73; Hd Master and Chapl Pennthorpe Sch Rudgwick 74-96; NSM Rudgwick *Chich* 95-96; rtd 96; Perm to Offic *Chich* and *Guildf* 96-98; Hd Master Ardingly Coll Jun Sch Haywards Heath 97-98; Chapl Rowcroft Hospice Torquay 99-01; Hon C Bovey Tracey SS Pet, Paul and Thos w Hennock *Ex* from 99. *5 Anthony Cottages, Alfington Road, Alfington, Ottery St Mary EX11 1FE* Tel (01404) 850430

SPENCER, Mrs Margot Patricia Winifred. b 48. Coll of St Matthias Bris CertEd69. STETS 98. **d** 01 **p** 02. NSM Wonersh w Blackheath *Guildf* 01-05; NSM Busbridge and Hambledon from 05. *24 Park Road, Godalming GU7 1SH* Tel (01483) 416333 E-mail margotspencer@btinternet.com

SPENCER, Neil Richard. b 49. Leeds Univ BA70 ALA72. WEMTC 96. **d** 99 **p** 00. NSM Ludlow, Ludford, Ashford Carbonell etc *Heref* 99-02; C Letton w Staunton, Byford, Mansel Gamage etc 02-05; P-in-c Ormesby St Marg w Scratby, Ormesby St Mich etc *Nor* 05-07; V *The Rectory, 11 Church View, Ormesby, Great Yarmouth NR29 3PZ* Tel (01493) 730234 E-mail nspencer@revd.freeserve.co.uk

SPENCER, Peter Cecil. b 30. Lich Th Coll 58. **d** 61 **p** 62. C Alton St Lawr *Win* 61-63; C Bournemouth St Luke 63-66; C W End 67-70; C Reading St Mary V *Ox* 70-72; C-in-c Reading St Matt CD 72-76; V Reading St Matt 76-78; TV Sidmouth, Woolbrook and Salcombe Regis *Ex* 78-86; R Birch w Layer Breton and Layer Marney *Chelmsf* 86-96; rtd 96; Perm to Offic *Chelmsf* from 99. *11 Dray Court, Colchester Road, West Bergholt, Colchester CO6 3TD* Tel (01206) 243453

SPENCER, Peter Roy. b 40. CertEd. Sarum & Wells Th Coll 72. **d** 74 **p** 75. C Northampton St Alb *Pet* 74-77; TV Cov E 77-90; V Erdington St Barn *Birm* 90-02; TR Erdington 02-07; Chapl John Taylor Hospice Birm 90-07; rtd 07. *15 Poplar Road, Smethwick B66 4AW* Tel 0121-429 4514

SPENCER, Richard Dennis. b 50. Imp Coll Lon BSc71. NTMTC 93. **d** 96 **p** 97. C Leek and Meerbrook *Lich* 96-00; P-in-c Shrewsbury H Trin w St Julian from 00. *Holy Trinity Vicarage, Greyfriars Road, Shrewsbury SY3 7EP* Tel (01743) 244891
E-mail rds@htbv.org.uk

SPENCER, Richard Hugh. b 62. Univ of Wales (Cardiff) LLB84 BD88 Bris Univ MA92. St Mich Coll Llan 85. **d** 88 **p** 89. C Barry All SS *Llan* 88-90; Asst Chapl Univ of Wales (Cardiff) 90-92; Lect NT Studies 92-98; Tutor St Mich Coll Llan 92-98; R Llangenni and Llanbedr Ystrad Yw w Patricio *S & B* 98-00; Dir Post-Ord Tr 00; TV Cowbridge *Llan* 02-03; NSM 03-04; Hd of Th Trin Coll Carmarthen 03-04; P-in-c Kenfig Hill *Llan* from 04. *5 Redman Close, Kenfig Hill, Bridgend CF33 6BF* Tel (01656) 670058 E-mail r.spencer@trinity-cm.ac.uk

SPENCER, Richard William Edward. b 33. FSCA66. WMMTC 78. **d** 81 **p** 82. NSM The Lickey *Birm* 81-83; Area Sec (Warks and W Midl) Chr Aid 83-93; Perm to Offic *Worc* from 95 and *Heref* from 98. *Honey Hedge, 165 Godiva Road, Leominster HR6 8TB* Tel (01568) 620097

SPENCER, Robert. b 48. St Jo Coll Nottm. **d** 93 **p** 94. NSM Ellon *Ab* 93-95 and 99-09; NSM Cruden Bay 93-95; NSM Fraserburgh w New Pitsligo 95-99; P-in-c Oldmeldrum from 09. *12 Riverview Place, Ellon AB41 9NW* Tel (01358) 723193 Fax (01224) 248515 E-mail revbob.spencer@btinternet.com

SPENCER, Roy Primett. b 26. Oak Hill Th Coll 50. **d** 53 **p** 54. C Bedford St Pet *St Alb* 53-55; C Luton Ch Ch 55-58; C Nottingham St Mary *S'well* 58-60; V Middlestown *Wakef* 60-61; Chapl Crumpsall Hosp Man 61-66; R Fleet *Linc* 66-69; V Accrington St Paul *Blackb* 69-78; V Woodplumpton 78-83; P-in-c Preston St Luke 83-89; P-in-c Preston St Luke and St Oswald 89-90; Chapl Preston Hosp N Shields 83-91; rtd 91; Perm to Offic *Blackb* from 91. *5 Hollywood Avenue, Penwortham, Preston PR1 9AS* Tel (01772) 743783

SPENCER, Stephen Christopher. b 60. Ball Coll Ox BA82 DPhil90. Edin Th Coll 88. **d** 90 **p** 91. C Harlesden All So *Lon* 90-93; P-in-c Nyamandhlovu Zimbabwe 93-99; R Bulawayo All SS 96-99; V Caton w Littledale *Blackb* 99-03; Dep Prin CBDTI 99-03; Tutor NOC 03-08; Tutor Yorks Min Course from 08; Co-ord Yorks Regional Tr Partnership from 08. *The Mirfield Centre, Stocks Bank Road, Mirfield WF14 0BW* Tel (01484) 715889 *or* (01924) 481906 E-mail stephen@ymc.org.uk

SPENCER, Stephen Nigel Howard. b 53. Pemb Coll Ox BA75 MA03 Jes Coll Cam PGCE76. Trin Coll Bris 80. **d** 82 **p** 83. C Partington and Carrington *Ches* 82-85; C Brunswick *Man* 85-88; Chapl UEA *Nor* 88-92; rtd 92; Perm to Offic *Nor* 92-95. *43 College Lane, Norwich NR4 6TW* Tel (01603) 506815 E-mail howard.spencer@btinternet.com

SPENCER, Stephen Robert. b 61. NTMTC BA08. **d** 08 **p** 09. C Langdon Hills *Chelmsf* from 08. *5 Kilowan Close, Langdon Hills, Basildon SS16 6UT* Tel (01268) 490869 Mobile 07736-415857

SPENCER, Steven Christopher. b 47. RGN69. NTMTC 98. **d** 98 **p** 99. NSM Chatham St Phil and St Jas *Roch* from 98; Asst Chapl Medway NHS Foundn Trust from 04. *278 Churchill Avenue, Chatham ME5 0LH* Tel (01634) 302581 E-mail steve.spencer@diocese-rochester.org

SPENCER, Canon Susan. b 47. EMMTC 87. **d** 90 **p** 94. Par Dn Cotgrave *S'well* 90-94; C 94-98; P-in-c Rolleston w Fiskerton, Morton and Upton from 98; Asst Warden of Readers 98-07; AD S'well from 07; Jt AD S'well and Newark 08-09; Hon Can S'well Minster from 08. *The Vicarage, 29 Marlock Close, Fiskerton, Southwell NG25 0UB* Tel (01636) 830331 E-mail suespencer@fiskertonvcb.net

SPENCER, Mrs Susan Lesley. b 55. **d** 00 **p** 01. OLM Middleton w Thornham *Man* from 00. *1 Westbrook Close, Rochdale OL11 2XY* Tel (01706) 350668 E-mail suespencer@bigfoot.com

SPENCER, Sylvia. b 48. Chapl Grampian Univ Hosp NHS Trust from 98. *Aberdeen Royal Infirmary, Foresterhill, Aberdeen AB9 2ZB* Tel (01224) 681818

SPENCER-THOMAS, Canon Owen Robert. b 40. MBE08. Lon Univ BSc(Soc)70 LGSM96 MRTvS76. Westcott Ho Cam 70. **d** 72 **p** 73. C S Kensington St Luke *Lon* 72-76; Lect RS S Kensington Inst 74-76; Dir Lon Chs Radio Workshop & Relig Producer BBC 76-78; Relig Producer Anglia TV 78-95; Lic to Offic *Lon* 76-87; NSM Cambridge Ascension *Ely* 87-07; Chapl St Jo Coll Sch Cam 93-98; Chapl St Bede's Sch Cam 96-97; Chapl Ch Coll Cam 97-01; Dioc Dir of Communications *Ely* 02-07; Bp's Press Officer from 07; Hon Can Ely Cathl from 04. *52 Windsor Road, Cambridge CB4 3JN* Tel and fax (01223) 358448 Mobile 07801-492151 E-mail owenst@btinternet.com

SPENDLOVE, Mrs Lindsay Kate. b 55. Man Univ LLB77 Essex Univ BA88. EAMTC 89. **d** 92 **p** 94. NSM Lexden *Chelmsf* 92-94; NSM Colchester Ch Ch w St Mary V 94-96; NSM Pleshey 97-02; Perm to Offic *St E* from 02 and *Chelmsf* from 04. *Green Blade, The Street, Wenhaston, Halesworth IP19 9EF* Tel (01502) 478301 E-mail ikspendlove@supanet.com

SPERRING, Clive Michael. b 43. Oak Hill Th Coll 71. **d** 75 **p** 76. C Hawkwell *Chelmsf* 75-78; C-in-c St Basildon 78-82; Asst P Kohimarama New Zealand 82-85; V Orakei St Jas from 86. *132 Gowing Drive, Meadowbank, Auckland 1072, New Zealand* Tel (0064) (9) 528 4400 E-mail cmsperring@vodafone.co.nz

SPICER, David John. b 52. Sussex Univ BA76 Lon Univ MTh78. Westcott Ho Cam 77. **d** 79 **p** 80. C E Dulwich St Jo *S'wark* 79-82; C Richmond St Mary w St Matthias and St Jo 82-87; V

Lewisham St Swithun 87-91; Chapl Community of All Hallows Ditchingham from 91. *St Edmund's House, All Hallows Convent, Ditchingham, Bungay NR35 2DZ* Tel (01986) 892139

SPICER (formerly RIMMER), Dorothy Janet Rosalind. b 49. Cen Sch of Art Lon BA72 Middx Poly ATD74 E Lon Univ MA98. Westcott Ho Cam. **d** 00 **p** 01. C Notting Hill St Jo and St Pet *Lon* 00-02; V Totternhoe, Stanbridge and Tilsworth *St Alb* from 02. *The Vicarage, Mill Road, Stanbridge, Leighton Buzzard LU7 9HX* Tel (01525) 210253 E-mail revjanetspicer@btinternet.com

SPICER, Leigh Edwin. b 56. Sarum & Wells Th Coll 78. **d** 81 **p** 82. C Harborne St Pet *Birm* 81-83; C Bloxwich *Lich* 83-87; Chapl RAF from 87. *Chaplaincy Services, Valiant Block, HQ Air Command, RAF High Wycombe HP14 4UE* Tel (01494) 496800 Fax 496343

SPICER, Nicolas. b 61. Univ of Wales (Lamp) BA84. Coll of Resurr Mirfield 84. **d** 86 **p** 87. C Westbury-on-Trym H Trin *Bris* 86-89; C Willesden Green St Andr and St Fran *Lon* 89-93; Chapl Asst Charing Cross Hosp Lon 93-94; Asst Chapl Hammersmith Hosps NHS Trust 94-97; R Ardleigh and The Bromleys *Chelmsf* 97-07; P-in-c Worksop Priory *S'well* from 07. *The Vicarage, Cheapside, Worksop S80 2HX* Tel (01909) 472180 E-mail nspicer@lineone.net

SPICER, Robert Patrick. b 39. FCA68. SAOMC 94. **d** 97 **p** 98. NSM Riverside *Ox* 97-01; NSM Beaconsfield 01-07. *16 Hayse Hill, Windsor SL4 5SZ* Tel (01753) 864697 E-mail spicerrevrob@aol.com

SPIERS, Canon Peter Hendry. b 61. St Jo Coll Dur BA82. Ridley Hall Cam 83. **d** 86 **p** 87. C W Derby St Luke *Liv* 86-90; TV Everton St Pet 90-95; V Everton St Geo 95-05; P-in-c Gt Crosby St Luke from 05; Hon Can Liv Cathl from 06. *St Luke's Vicarage, Liverpool Road, Crosby, Liverpool L23 5SE* Tel 0151-924 1737 E-mail pete@spiersfamily.eclipse.co.uk

SPIKIN, Simon John Overington. b 48. Nottm Univ BTh74. Linc Th Coll 70. **d** 75 **p** 76. C Sawbridgeworth *St Alb* 75-79; C Odiham w S Warnborough and Long Sutton *Win* 79-81; R Dickleburgh w Thelveton w Frenze and Shimpling *Nor* 81-82; P-in-c Rushall 81-82; R Dickleburgh, Langmere, Shimpling, Thelveton etc 82-96; rtd 96; Perm to Offic *Cant* from 01. *Marley Court, Kingston, Canterbury CT4 6JH* Tel (01227) 832405

SPILLER, Canon David Roger. b 44. St Jo Coll Dur BA70 Fitzw Coll Cam BA72 MA76 Nottm Univ DipAdEd80. Ridley Hall Cam 70. **d** 73 **p** 74. C Bradf Cathl 73-77; C Stratford-on-Avon w Bishopton *Cov* 77-80; Chapl Geo Eliot Hosp Nuneaton 80-90; V Chilvers Coton w Astley *Cov* 80-90; RD Nuneaton 84-90; Prin Aston Tr Scheme 90-97; C Kings Norton *Birm* 98-99; C Shirley 99-00; Dir of Min and Dioc Dir of Ords *Cov* from 00; Hon Can Cov Cathl from 04. *The Parsonage, Sambourne Lane, Sambourne, Redditch B96 6PA* Tel (01527) 892372 *or* (024) 7671 0504 Fax (024) 7671 0550 E-mail rogerspiller@btinternet.com

SPILLER, Edward William. b 32. Cranmer Hall Dur 80. **d** 82 **p** 83. C Kirkleatham *York* 82-85; R The Thorntons and The Otteringtons 85-00; rtd 01; Perm to Offic *York* from 01. *Carlton House, Topcliffe Road, Thirsk YO7 1RL* Tel (01845) 522811 E-mail rev.ted@skypilot.flyer.co.uk

SPILMAN, Derrick Geoffrey. b 27. Roch Th Coll 61. **d** 63 **p** 64. C Dover St Mary *Cant* 63-67; CF 67-71; Canada from 71; rtd 92. *5398 Walter Place, Burnaby BC V5G 4K2, Canada* Tel (001) (604) 294 6816

SPILSBURY, Stephen Ronald Paul. b 39. Nottm Univ BSc69 MPhil72 Bris Univ PhD99. Linc Th Coll 71. **d** 64 **p** 65. In RC Ch 64-71; C Cricklade w Latton *Bris* 72-75; P-in-c Swindon All SS 76-81; V Lawrence Weston 81-95; RD Westbury and Severnside 89-91; rtd 99; Perm to Offic *Bris* from 03. *10 Woodside Grove, Bristol BS10 7RF* Tel 0117-959 1079 E-mail paul.spilsbury@btinternet.com

SPINDLER, Miss Jane Diana. b 54. Southn Univ BA75 CertEd76. Wycliffe Hall Ox 87. **d** 89 **p** 94. C Bishopsworth *Bris* 89-93; C Brislington St Luke 93-94; rtd 95; Perm to Offic *Bris* from 95. *143 Highridge Road, Bishopsworth, Bristol BS13 8HT* Tel 0117-935 8137

SPINK, Mrs Diana. b 40. Ex Univ BA63 PGCE64. SAOMC 97. **d** 00 **p** 01. NSM Hemel Hempstead *St Alb* from 00. *39 Garland Close, Hemel Hempstead HP2 5HU* Tel (01442) 262133 Mobile 07808-184321 E-mail diana2spink@hotmail.com

SPINK, Canon George Arthur Peter. b 26. Oak Hill Th Coll 54. **d** 56 **p** 57. C Thurnby w Stoughton *Leic* 56-58; C-in-c Thurnby Lodge CD 58-59; Chapl Bonn w Cologne *Eur* 59-62; Chapl Vienna w Budapest and Prague 62-68; Chapl Cov Cathl 68-70; Can Res Cov Cathl 70-77; Warden The Dorothy Kerin Trust Burrswood 77-81; Prior Omega Order from 80; Lic to Offic *Roch* 80-86; Lic to Offic *B & W* 86-95; rtd 89. *The Priory, Winford Manor, Winford, Bristol BS40 8DW* Tel (01275) 472262 Fax 472065

SPINKS, Prof Bryan Douglas. b 48. St Chad's Coll Dur BA70 BD79 K Coll Lon MTh72 Dur Univ DD88 Yale Univ Hon MA98 FRHistS85. **d** 75 **p** 76. C Witham *Chelmsf* 75-78; C Clacton St Jas 78-79; Chapl Chu Coll Cam 80-97; Affiliated Lect Div Cam Univ 82-97; Prof Liturg Studies Yale Univ and Fell

Morse Coll 98-07; Prof Past Th Yale Univ from 07; Perm to Offic *Ely* from 02. *Institute of Sacred Music, 409 Prospect Street, New Haven, CT 06511, USA* Tel (001) (203) 432 5186
E-mail bryan.spinks@yale.edu *or* bryspinkus@aol.com

SPINKS, Christopher George. b 53. Oak Hill Th Coll BA88. **d** 88 **p** 89. C Hove Bp Hannington Memorial Ch *Chich* 88-92; Travelling Sec UCCF 92-95; Itinerant Min 95-98; Chapl Martlets Hospice Hove from 98; TV Hove *Chich* from 99. *35 St Heliers Avenue, Hove BN3 5RE* Tel (01273) 730027
E-mail chrisgspinks@hotmail.com

SPINKS, John Frederick. b 40. Westmr Coll Ox MTh97. Oak Hill Th Coll 79. **d** 82 **p** 83. NSM Roxbourne St Andr *Lon* 82-89; C Northwood H Trin 89-93; P-in-c Greenhill St Jo 93-96; V 96-04; rtd 04; Perm to Offic *Lon, Ox* and *St Alb* from 04. *Woodpecker Cottage, 232 Northwood Road, Harefield, Uxbridge UB9 6PT* Tel (01895) 822477 Mobile 07711-635199
E-mail woodpecker232@tiscali.co.uk

SPITTLE, Christopher Bamford. b 74. St Jo Coll Dur BA95. Ridley Hall Cam 97. **d** 99 **p** 00. C Netherton *Liv* 99-03; TR Sutton from 03. *St Michael's Vicarage, Gartons Lane, Clock Face, St Helens WA9 4RB* Tel (01744) 813738

SPITTLE, Robin. b 57. St Jo Coll Nottm 84. **d** 86 **p** 87. C Ipswich St Fran *St E* 86-91; Min Shotley St Mary CD 91-92; R Shotley 92-99; P-in-c Copdock w Washbrook and Belstead 93-99; V Kesgrave from 99. *The Vicarage, 18 Bell Lane, Kesgrave, Ipswich IP5 1JQ* Tel (01473) 622181 E-mail robin.spittle@lineone.net

SPIVEY, Colin. b 35. ACII61. Oak Hill Th Coll 74. **d** 76 **p** 77. C Egham *Guildf* 76-79; C Edgware *Lon* 79-83; R Haworth *Bradf* 83-95; Sub Chapl HM Pris Leeds 94-99; V Thorpe Edge *Bradf* 95-00; rtd 01; Perm to Offic *Ripon* from 01. *2 Woodhill View, Wetherby LS22 6PP* Tel (01937) 581508
E-mail ca.spivey@virgin.net

SPIVEY, Canon Peter. b 19. Edin Th Coll 46. **d** 48 **p** 49. C Dewsbury Moor *Wakef* 48-50; C Mirfield 50-53; R Whitwood Mere 53-61; Chapl Castleford, Normanton and Distr Hosp 53-61; V Meltham *Wakef* 61-85; RD Blackmoorfoot 79-85; Hon Can Wakef Cathl 81-85; Chapl Moorview Hosp 61-68; Chapl St Luke's Hosp Huddersfield NHS Trust 80-00; rtd 85; Perm to Offic *Wakef* from 85. *3 Follett Avenue, Huddersfield HD4 5LW* Tel (01484) 654674

SPOKES, David Lawrence. b 57. Nottm Univ BCombStuds85. Linc Th Coll 82. **d** 85 **p** 86. C Rushall *Lich* 85-89; TV Thornaby on Tees *York* 89-93; R Yardley Hastings, Denton and Grendon etc *Pet* from 02; Rural Adv Northn Adnry from 05. *The Rectory, 14 The Leys, Denton, Northampton NN7 1DH* Tel (01604) 891294 E-mail mail@davidspokes.com

SPOKES, Keith John. b 29. EAMTC. **d** 84 **p** 85. NSM Bury St Edmunds St Mary *St E* 84-89; P-in-c Helmingham w Framsden and Pettaugh w Winston 89-92; rtd 93; Perm to Offic *St E* from 93. *34 Southgate House, Rougham Road, Bury St Edmunds IP33 2RN* Tel (01284) 706742

SPONG, Bennett Jarod. b 49. Coll of Charleston (USA) BA74 Thames Poly PGCE87. **d** 05 **p** 06. OLM Charlton *S'wark* from 05. *10 Mayhill Road, London SE7 7JQ* Tel (020) 8853 4457
E-mail bjspong@hotmail.com

SPONG, Mrs Hilary Vida. b 44. Ex Univ BTh09. SWMTC 06. **d** 09. NSM St Stythians w Perranarworthal and Gwennap *Truro* from 09. *Nansough Manor, Ladock, Truro TR2 4PB* Tel (01726) 883315 Mobile 07855-781134 E-mail hilaryspong@sent.com

SPONG, Terence John. *See* MESLEY-SPONG, Terence John

SPOONER, Anthony Patrick David. b 45. Univ Coll of Rhodesia Univ Coll of Nyasaland BA68. Linc Th Coll 71. **d** 74 **p** 75. C Glynde, W Firle and Beddingham *Chich* 74-77; Rhodesia 77-80; Zimbabwe 80-86; P-in-c Clacton St Jas *Chelmsf* 86-90; V from 90. *St James's Vicarage, 44 Wash Lane, Clacton-on-Sea CO15 1DA* Tel (01255) 422007
E-mail revapdspooner@aol.com

SPOTTISWOODE, Anthony Derek. b 25. Solicitor 50 Pemb Coll Cam BA47 MA86. Sarum & Wells Th Coll 85. **d** 86 **p** 87. C Hampstead St Jo *Lon* 86-94; rtd 95; Perm to Offic *Lon* from 95. *Flat 6, 38-40 Eton Avenue, London NW3 3HL* Tel (020) 7435 6756

SPRAGGETT, Miss Agnes Louise. b 29. Bp Otter Coll Chich TCert55. CBDTI 06. **d** 06 **p** 07. NSM Embsay w Eastby *Bradf* from 06. *16 Millholme Rise, Embsay, Skipton BD23 6NU* Tel (01756) 793575 E-mail loutin@tesco.net

SPRATLEY, Deryck Edward. b 30. BSc. Oak Hill Th Coll 62. **d** 64 **p** 65. C Ramsgate St Luke *Cant* 64-67; C W Holloway St Dav *Lon* 67-73; V Upper Holloway St Pet 73-79; V Upper Holloway St Pet w St Jo 79-82; P-in-c Dagenham *Chelmsf* 82-88; P-in-c Becontree St Geo 84-88; TR Dagenham 88-93; rtd 93; Perm to Offic *Chelmsf* 93-01. *35 Upper Second Avenue, Frinton-on-Sea CO13 9LP* Tel (01255) 851216

SPRATT, Laurence Herbert. b 28. Linc Th Coll 76. **d** 78 **p** 79. C Mexborough *Sheff* 78-80; R Wrentham w Benacre, Covehithe, Frostenden etc *St E* 80-88; Perm to Offic *Arg* 89-90 and 91-98; P-in-c Inveraray 90-91; rtd 93. *19 Church Street, Ellesmere SY12 0HD*

SPRATT, Robert Percival. b 31. MBE08. FCIOB MRSH ABEng. Carl Dioc Tr Inst 84. **d** 87 **p** 88. NSM Kendal St Thos *Carl* 87-89; Chapl HM Pris Preston 89-96; Dir Miss to Pris from 96; Perm to Offic *Blackb* from 96 and *Carl* from 97; Asst Chapl HM Pris Haverigg from 06. *Missions to Prisons, PO Box 37, Kendal LA9 6GF* Tel and fax (01539) 720475

SPRAY, Canon Charles Alan Francis Thomas. b 27. Lon Univ BScEng51 ARSM51. Ridley Hall Cam 57. **d** 59 **p** 60. C Chich St Pancras and St Jo 59-63; V Shipley 63-69; R Ore St Helen and St Barn 70-85; V Burgess Hill St Andr 85-93; Can and Preb Chich Cathl 88-93; rtd 93; Perm to Offic *Chich* from 93. *6 Silverdale Road, Burgess Hill RH15 0EF* Tel (01444) 232149

SPRAY, John William. b 29. Sarum & Wells Th Coll 71. **d** 73 **p** 74. C Clayton *Lich* 73-77; V Hartshill 77-82; P-in-c Aston 82-83; P-in-c Stone St Mich 82-83; P-in-c Stone St Mich w Aston St Sav 83-84; R 84-90; rtd 90; Perm to Offic *Lich* from 90. *2 Belvoir Avenue, Trentham, Stoke-on-Trent ST4 8SY* Tel (01782) 644959

SPRAY, Mrs Josephine Ann. b 44. Nottm Coll of Educn TCert65. SAOMC 95. **d** 98 **p** 99. NSM Watford St Mich *St Alb* 98-02; P-in-c Turvey from 02. *The Rectory, Bamfords Lane, Turvey, Bedford MK43 8DS* Tel (01234) 881312 Fax 881817
E-mail jas@watfordgb.freeserve.co.uk

SPRAY, Mrs Karen. b 55. **d** 06 **p** 07. NSM Littleham w Exmouth 06-07; C Honiton, Gittisham, Combe Raleigh, Monkton etc from 07. *5 Glen Farm Crescent, Honiton EX14 2GX* Tel (01404) 42327

SPRAY, Richard Alan. b 43. EMMTC 85. **d** 88 **p** 89. NSM Cotgrave *S'well* 88-96; P-in-c Barton in Fabis 96-01; P-in-c Thrumpton 96-01; P-in-c Kingston and Ratcliffe-on-Soar 96-01; P-in-c Blyth 01-02; P-in-c Scrooby 01-02; V Blyth and Scrooby w Ranskill from 02; AD Bawtry from 06. *The Vicarage, St Martin's Close, Blyth, Worksop S81 8DW* Tel (01909) 591229
E-mail revrich@talktalk.net

SPREADBRIDGE, Alison Margaret. b 50. Open Univ BSc96. SEITE 04. **d** 07 **p** 08. C Dartford St Edm *Roch* from 07. *12 Keyes Road, Dartford DA1 5EQ* Tel (01322) 292335 Mobile 07940-121267 E-mail allyspreadbridge@aol.com

SPREADBRIDGE, Paul Andrew. b 49. Greenwich Univ CertEd02 Kent Univ BA05. SEITE 99. **d** 98 **p** 03. In RC Ch 98-01; NSM Chatham St Steph *Roch* 02-04; C Orpington All SS 04-07; V Bexley St Mary from 07. *The Vicarage, 29 Hill Crescent, Bexley DA5 2DA* Tel (01322) 523457
E-mail paul.spreadbridge@btopenworld.com

SPREADBURY, Joanna Mary Magdalen. b 65. Magd Coll Ox BA90 MA93 K Coll Lon PhD99. Westcott Ho Cam MA99. **d** 99 **p** 00. C Watford St Mich *St Alb* 99-03; C Leavesden 03-06; V Abbots Langley from 06. *The Vicarage, 6 High Street, Abbots Langley WD5 0AS* Tel (01923) 263013

SPREADBURY, John Graham. b 59. **d** 99 **p** 00. OLM Billingborough Gp *Linc* from 99. *Osbourne House, 3-5 Low Street, Billingborough, Sleaford NG34 0QJ* Tel (01529) 240440

SPREDBURY, Mary Jane. b 59. Open Univ BA99. STETS 03. **d** 06 **p** 07. NSM Acton St Mary *Lon* from 06. *6 St Catherine's Court, Bedford Road, London W4 1UH* Tel (020) 8723 1035 Mobile 07803-759886 E-mail spredbury@btinternet.com

SPRENT, Michael Francis (Brother Giles). b 34. Ex Coll Ox BA58 MA62. Kelham Th Coll 58. **d** 61 **p** 62. C Plaistow St Andr *Chelmsf* 61-63; SSF from 61; Papua New Guinea 65-69; Hilfield Friary 69-74, 77-78, 97-02 and 03-04; Alnmouth Friary 74-76; Sweden 76-77; TV High Stoy *Sarum* 77 78; Harbledown Friary 78-82; Solomon Is 83-97; Zimbabwe 02-03; Stepney Friary 05-08; Canning Town Friary from 08. *St Matthias' Vicarage, 45 Mafeking Road, London E16 4NS* Tel (020) 7511 7848
E-mail gilesssf@franciscans.org.uk

SPRIGGS, John David Robert. b 36. BNC Ox BA58 MA63. S'wark Ord Course 73. **d** 75 **p** 76. Lic to Offic *Ox* 75-97; Chapl Pangbourne Coll 95-97; Perm to Offic *Linc* from 97. *Glen House, Great Ponton Road, Boothby Pagnell, Grantham NG33 4DH* Tel (01476) 585756

SPRINGATE, Paul Albert Edward. b 48. Oak Hill Th Coll 81. **d** 83 **p** 84. C Pennycross *Ex* 83-87; TV Sileby, Cossington and Seagrave *Leic* 87-96; Chapl and Warden Harnhill Healing Cen from 96; Bp's Adv on Healing *Glouc* from 03. *Centre of Christian Healing, Harnhill Centre, Harnhill, Cirencester GL7 5PX* Tel (01285) 850283 Fax 850519
E-mail office@harnhillcentre.org.uk

SPRINGBETT, John Howard. b 47. Pemb Coll Cam BA70 MA74. Ridley Hall Cam 70. **d** 72 **p** 73. C Ulverston St Mary w H Trin *Carl* 72-76; V Dewsbury Moor *Wakef* 76-84; V Hoddesdon *St Alb* 84-00; RD Cheshunt 94-00; TR Shelf w Buttershaw St Aid *Bradf* 00-03; V Woodford Bridge *Chelmsf* from 03. *St Paul's Vicarage, 4 Cross Road, Woodford Green IG8 8BS* Tel (020) 8504 3815
E-mail springbett25@hotmail.com

SPRINGETT, Canon Robert Wilfred. b 62. Nottm Univ BTh89 Lon Univ MA92. Linc Th Coll 86. **d** 89 **p** 90. C Colchester St Jas, All SS, St Nic and St Runwald *Chelmsf* 89-92; C Basildon St Martin w Nevendon 92-94; P-in-c Belhus Park and S Ockendon 94-01; RD Thurrock 98-01; R Wanstead St Mary w

Ch Ch from 01; AD Redbridge from 08; Hon Can Chelmsf Cathl from 08. *The Rectory, 37 Wanstead Place, London E11 2SW* Tel (020) 8989 9101
E-mail robertspringett@tiscali.co.uk

SPRINGETT, Simon Paul. b 56. Warwick Univ LLB78. Wycliffe Hall Ox 78. d 81 p 82. C Harlow St Mary and St Hugh w St Jo the Bapt *Chelmsf* 81-84; C Gt Clacton 84-86; R Rayne 86-91; Chapl RN from 91. *Royal Naval Chaplaincy Service, Mail Point 1-2, Leach Building, Whale Island, Portsmouth PO2 8BY* Tel (023) 9262 5055 Fax 9262 5134

SPRINGFORD, Patrick Francis Alexander. b 45. Wycliffe Hall Ox 71. d 74 p 75. C Finchley Ch Ch *Lon* 74-79; CF 79-06; Rtd Officer Chapl RAChD from 06. *c/o MOD Chaplains (Army)* Tel (01980) 615804 Fax 615800

SPRINGHAM, Desmond John. b 32. Bris Univ BA56. Oak Hill Th Coll 56. d 58 p 59. C St Alb St Paul *St Alb* 58-61; C Reading St Jo *Ox* 61-66; R Worting *Win* 66-80; V Jersey St Andr 80-97; rtd 97; Perm to Offic *Sarum* from 97. *19 Balmoral Crescent, Dorchester DT1 2BN* Tel (01305) 268022

SPRINGTHORPE, Canon David Frederick. b 47. Open Univ BA. AKC72. d 73 p 74. C Dartford St Alb *Roch* 73-77; C Biggin Hill 77-80; R Ash 80-89; R Ridley 80-89; R Eynsford w Farningham and Lullingstone 89-94; V Barnehurst 94-04; RD Erith 98-04; R Keston from 04; Hon Can Roch Cathl from 02. *The Rectory, 24 Commonside, Keston BR2 6BP* Tel (01689) 853186 E-mail david.springthorpe@btopenworld.com

SPROSTON, Bernard Melvin. b 37. St Jo Coll Dur 77. d 79 p 80. C Westlands St Andr *Lich* 79-82; P-in-c Heage *Derby* 82-87; V Heath 87-02; rtd 02; Perm to Offic *Derby* from 02. *2 Upwood Close, Holmehall, Chesterfield S40 4UP* Tel (01246) 207401

SPROULE, Gerald Norman. b 26. TCD Div Sch. d 60 p 61. C Monaghan *Clogh* 60-62; I Cleenish 62-68; I Magheracross 68-73; Admin Sec (Ireland) BCMS 73-79; I Belfast St Aid *Conn* 79-86; I Magherally w Annaclone *D & D* 86-94; rtd 94. *4 Hilden Park, Lisburn BT27 4UG* Tel (028) 9260 1528

SPRY, Miss Elisabeth Roselie. b 47. Open Univ BA82. d 06 p 07. OLM Stratton St Mary w Stratton St Michael etc *Nor* from 06. *13 Whitehouse Drive, Long Stratton, Norwich NR15 2TD* Tel (01508) 530478 E-mail erspry@yahoo.co.uk

SPURGEON, Michael Paul. b 53. MIEx. Linc Th Coll 83. d 85 p 86. C Lillington *Cov* 85-89; C Min Can Ripon Cathl 89-95; R Lower Nidderdale from 95. *Lower Nidderdale Rectory, 6 Old Church Green, Kirk Hammerton, York YO26 8DL* Tel (01423) 331142 E-mail lowernidderdale@aol.com

SPURIN, Canon Richard Mark. b 28. Peterho Cam BA52 MA60. Wycliffe Hall Ox 54. d 55 p 56. C Foleshill St Laur *Cov* 55-58; C Atherstone 58-60; CMS 60-61; Kenya 61-73; C-in-c Ewell St Paul Howell Hill CD *Guildf* 73-82; V Netherton *Liv* 82-86; V Brandwood *Birm* 86-91; C Padiham *Blackb* 91-93; Hon Can Nambale Cathl Kenya from 92; rtd 93; Perm to Offic *Blackb* from 93. *11 Rosemount Avenue, Burnley BB11 2JU* Tel (01282) 421402

SPURR, Andrew. b 58. St Jo Coll Dur BA80. Qu Coll Birm 92. d 93 p 94. C Rainham *Roch* 93-96; C Stansted Mountfitchet *Chelmsf* 96; C Stansted Mountfitchet w Birchanger and Farnham 97; R 97-06; V Evesham w Norton and Lenchwick *Worc* from 06. *Church House, Market Place, Evesham WR11 4RW* Tel (01386) 446219
E-mail vicar@eves.hamparish.com

SPURRELL, John Mark. b 34. CCC Ox BA57 MA61 FSA87. Linc Th Coll 58. d 60 p 61. C Tilbury Docks *Chelmsf* 60-65; C Boston *Linc* 65-76; R Stow in Lindsey 76-85; P-in-c Willingham 76-85; P-in-c Coates 76-85; P-in-c Brightwell w Sotwell *Ox* 85-97; rtd 97; Perm to Offic *B & W* from 97. *10 The Liberty, Wells BA5 2SU* Tel (01749) 678966

SPURRIER, Richard Patrick Montague. b 25. Bris Univ BA59. Wycliffe Hall Ox 59. d 61 p 62. C S Lyncombe *B & W* 61-63; C Weston St Jo 63-64; rtd 90. *48 Longford Road, Melksham SN12 6AU* Tel (01225) 707419

SPURWAY, Christine Frances. b 54. Cuddesdon Coll 96. d 98 p 99. C Coulsdon St Andr *S'wark* 98-02; P-in-c Riddlesdown 02-05; V from 05; RD Croydon S from 04. *St James's Vicarage, 1B St James's Road, Purley CR8 2DL* Tel (020) 8660 5436

SQUIRE, Clenyg. b 31. TCert53. Cuddesdon Coll 89. d 90 p 91. NSM Hale and Ashley *Ches* 90-93; P-in-c Kingsley 93-95; Perm to Offic *Ches* and *Man* 95-03; Newc 00-03; *Lon* from 04. *19 Priory Road, Hampton TW12 2NR* Tel (020) 8979 3579
E-mail clenyg@blueyonder.co.uk

SQUIRE, Geoffrey Frank. b 36. Ex & Truro NSM Scheme. d 83 p 84. NSM Barnstaple *Ex* 83-98; NSM Swimbridge w W Buckland and Landkey from 98. *Little Cross, Northleigh Hill, Goodleigh, Barnstaple EX32 7NR* Tel (01271) 344935

SQUIRE, Humphrey Edward. b 29. St Chad's Coll Dur BA55. Coll of Resurr Mirfield. d 57 p 58. C Newbold w Dunston *Derby* 57-59; C Thorpe St Andr *Nor* 59-61; Zanzibar 61-63; C Whittington *Derby* 63-64; R Drayton *Nor* 64-75; Chapl Dover Coll 75-83; TV Wareham *Sarum* 83-94; rtd 94; Perm to Offic *Sarum* from 94. *La Retraite, Burbidge Close, Lytchett Matravers, Poole BH16 6EG* Tel (01202) 623204

SQUIRES, John Anthony. b 50. CPFA78. LCTP. d 08 p 09. OLM Waterside Par *Blackb* from 08. *11 Carr Lane, Hambleton, Poulton-le-Fylde FY6 9BA* Tel (01253) 701895 Mobile 07704-659556 E-mail squiresja@aol.com

SQUIRES, John Wallace Howden. b 45. Sydney Univ BA67 DipEd68 MTh97 PhD05 Lon Univ BD75. Moore Th Coll Sydney ThL74. d 76 p 76. C Normanhurst Australia 76-78; C Luton St Mary *St Alb* 78-79; Chapl Home of Divine Healing Crowhurst 79-80; C-in-c Putney Australia 80-82; R Longueville 83-97; Dir Inst for Values Univ of NSW 97-02; Dir Aus Human Rights Cen Univ of NSW 03-05. *22 Moorehead Street, Redfern NSW 2016, Australia* Tel (0061) (2) 9690 0206 or 9385 3637 Fax 9385 1778 Mobile 41-822 6976 E-mail j.squires@unsw.edu.au

SQUIRES, The Ven Malcolm. b 46. St Chad's Coll Dur BA72. Cuddesdon Coll 72. d 74 p 75. C Headingley *Ripon* 74-77; C Stanningley St Thos 77-80; V Bradshaw *Wakef* 80-85; V Ripponden 85-89; V Barkisland w W Scammonden 85-89; V Mirfield 89-96; TR Wrexham *St As* 96-02; Hon Can St As Cathl 00-01; Adn Wrexham from 01; R Llandegla from 02. *The Rectory, Llandegla, Wrexham LL11 3AW* Tel (01978) 790362 Fax 790574 E-mail squiresmalcolm@aol.com

SQUIRES, Miss Rachel Louise. b 79. Coll of Ripon & York St Jo BA00. Ripon Coll Cuddesdon MA07. d 07 p 08. C Alnwick *Newc* from 07. *2 Northumberland Street, Alnwick NE66 1LT* E-mail rachelsquires@googlemail.com

SSERUNKUMA, Michael Wilberforce. b 54. Trin Coll Bris BA90. Bp Tucker Coll Mukono. d 77 p 78. Uganda 77-87; C Gabalfa *Llan* 90-94; TV Cyncoed *Mon* 94-95; R Canton St Jo *Llan* 95-01; Asst Chapl R Berks and Battle Hosps NHS Trust 01-02; Chapl Team Ldr R Berks NHS Foundn Trust from 02. *The Chaplaincy, Royal Berkshire Hospital, London Road, Reading RG1 5AN* Tel 0118-987 7105

STABLES, Courtley Greenwood. b 13. Keble Coll Ox BA49 MA54. St Steph Ho Ox 48. d 50 p 51. C Watlington *Ox* 50-51; C Bracknell 51-55; Br Honduras 55-57; C Guildf H Trin w St Mary 57-61; Chapl Bedford Modern Sch 61-63; Sen Lect Coll of All SS Tottenham 63-72; Chmn Coun of Ch Schs Co 68-87; C St Andr Undershaft w St Mary Axe *Lon* 64-72; Hon C Uckfield *Chich* 72-94; rtd 78; Perm to Offic *Chich* from 94. *Abotslare, Pound Green, Buxted, Uckfield TN22 4JZ* Tel (01825) 732467

STABLES, Miss Katharine Ruth. b 45. R Holloway Coll Lon BA67. WMMTC 90. d 93 p 94. NSM Knutton *Lich* 93-05; NSM Silverdale and Alsagers Bank 93-96; Soc Resp Officer 96-99; Officer for NSMs 03-05; NSM Startforth and Bowes and Rokeby w Brignall *Ripon* 05-09; rtd 09. *15 Greenbank, Eggleston, Barnard Castle DL12 0BQ* Tel (01833) 650006
E-mail kruth@btopenworld.com

STACE, Michael John. b 44. Open Univ BA80. SEITE 94. d 97 p 98. NSM Cant St Dunstan w H Cross 97-01; NSM Cant All SS 01-06; P-in-c from 06. *124 St Stephen's Road, Canterbury CT2 7JS* Tel (01227) 451169 Fax 455627 Mobile 07831-174900 E-mail michaelstace@btconnect.com

STACEY, Graham John. b 68. Lon Bible Coll BA97. Ripon Coll Cuddesdon 05. d 08 p 09. C Brightwalton w Catmore, Leckhampstead etc *Ox* from 08; C Beedon and Peasemore w W Ilsley and Farnborough from 08. *3 Drakes Farm, Peasemore, Newbury RG20 7DF* Tel (01635) 247817 Mobile 07753-687389 E-mail graham@thestaceys.tv

STACEY, Helen Norman. Edin Univ MB, ChB45 PhD49. S'wark Ord Course 82. dss 83 d 87 p 94. Notting Hill St Jo and St Pet *Lon* 83-85; Upper Kennet *Sarum* 85-93; Hon Par Dn 87-93; Perm to Offic 93-04. *Greystones House, Green Street, Avebury, Marlborough SN8 1RE* Tel (01672) 539289

STACEY, Mrs Kate Elizabeth. b 73. Lon Bible Coll BTh97. Ripon Coll Cuddesdon 05. d 08 p 09. C Brightwalton w Catmore, Leckhampstead etc *Ox* from 08; C Beedon and Peasemore w W Ilsley and Farnborough from 08. *3 Drakes Farm, Peasemore, Newbury RG20 7DF* Tel (01635) 247817 E-mail kate@thestaceys.tv

STACEY, Nicolas David. b 27. St Edm Hall Ox BA51 MA55. Cuddesdon Coll 51. d 53 p 54. C Portsea N End St Mark *Portsm* 53-58; Bp's Dom Chapl *Birm* 58-59; R Woolwich St Mary w H Trin *S'wark* 59-68; Borough Dean Greenwich 65-68; Dep Dir Oxfam 68-70; Perm to Offic *Ox* 68-71; P-in-c Selling *Cant* 76-78; Perm to Offic 79-84 and from 90; Six Preacher Cant Cathl 84-89; rtd 92. *The Old Vicarage, Selling, Faversham ME13 9RD* Tel (01227) 752833 Fax 752889 E-mail nicolas@nstacey.fsnet.co.uk

STACEY (née O'BRIEN), Mrs Shelagh Ann. b 55. RGN83 Bedf Coll Lon BSc77. NOC 89. d 92 p 94. Par Dn S Elmsall *Wakef* 92-94; C 94-95; C Carleton 95-97; P-in-c 97-99; C E Hardwick 95-97; P-in-c 97-99; V Carleton and E Hardwick from 99. *The Vicarage, 10 East Close, Pontefract WF8 3NS* Tel (01977) 702478

STACEY, Timothy Andrew. b 58. Imp Coll Lon BSc79 York Univ PGCE83. St Jo Coll Nottm 94. d 94 p 95. C Chorleywood Ch Ch *St Alb* 94-99; P-in-c Chalfont St Giles *Ox* 99-08; R from 08; Chapl Bucks New Univ from 99. *The Rectory, 2 Deanway, Chalfont St Giles HP8 4DX* Tel (01494) 872097
E-mail tands.stacey@virgin.net or tstace01@bcuc.ac.uk

STACEY, Canon Victor George. b 44. NUI BA69 QUB MTh. CITC 72. **d** 72 **p** 73. C Derriaghy *Conn* 72-76; C Knock *D & D* 76-79; I Ballymacarrett St Martin 79-86; I Dublin Santry w Glasnevin *D & G* 86-95; Bp's Dom Chapl from 90; I Dun Laoghaire from 95; Prov and Dioc Registrar from 95; Preb Maynooth St Patr Cathl Dublin from 97. *Christ Church Vicarage, 2 Park Road, Dun Laoghaire, Co Dublin, Republic of Ireland* Tel (00353) (1) 280 9537

STAFF, Mrs Jean. b 44. CertEd64. EMMTC 81. **dss** 84 **d** 87 **p** 94. Old Brumby *Linc* 84-88; C 87-88; C Gainsborough St Geo 88-91; Dn-in-c 91-94; P-in-c 94-96; P-in-c Haxey 96-97; P-in-c Owston 96-97; V Haxey 97-04; V Owston 97-04; rtd 04. *5 South Furlong Croft, Epworth, Doncaster DN9 1GB* Tel (01427) 871422

STAFF, Susan. *See* JACKSON, Mrs Susan

STAFFORD, Christopher James. b 67. Birm Univ BSc88 PhD92. St Jo Coll Nottm MA98. **d** 99 **p** 00. C Westbrook St Phil *Liv* 99-03; R Newchurch w Croft from 03. *Newchurch Rectory, 17 Jackson Avenue, Culcheth, Warrington WA3 4ED* Tel (01925) 766300 E-mail cjstaff@surfaid.org

STAFFORD, David George. b 45. Qu Coll Birm 75. **d** 77 **p** 78. C Chesterfield St Aug *Derby* 77-80; C Ranmoor *Sheff* 80-83; V Bolton-upon-Dearne from 83. *The Vicarage, 41 Station Road, Bolton-upon-Dearne, Rotherham S63 8AA* Tel (01709) 893163

STAFFORD, Canon John Ingham Henry. b 31. TCD BA52 MA58. **d** 53 **p** 55. C Clonallon *D & D* 53-56; C Belfast Malone St Jo *Conn* 56-59; Australia 59-64; Min Can Down Cathl 64-68; Hd of S Ch Miss Ballymacarrett 68-73; I Bright w Killough 73-83; C Bangor Primacy 83-92; Can Down Cathl 90-92; I Urney w Sion Mills *D & R* 92-98; rtd 98. *14 Cleland Park North, Bangor BT20 3EN* Tel (028) 9145 6311 Mobile 07709-978874 E-mail jihstafford@btinternet.com

STAFFORD, Mark Anthony. b 64. Huddersfield Univ BSc92. St Jo Coll Nottm MA98. **d** 98 **p** 99. C Stafford St Jo and Tixall w Ingestre *Lich* 98-01; C W Retford *S'well* 01; TV Retford 02-09; P-in-c Babworth w Sutton-cum-Lound and Scofton etc 08-09. *Address temp unknown*

STAFFORD, Matthew Charles. b 73. Wilson Carlile Coll 94 Ripon Coll Cuddesdon 99. **d** 99 **p** 00. C High Wycombe *Ox* 99-02; P-in-c Wrockwardine Wood *Lich* 02-04; R Oakengates and Wrockwardine Wood from 04. *The New Rectory, Church Road, Wrockwardine Wood, Telford TF2 7AH* Tel (01952) 613865 Mobile 07981-380226 E-mail oranconall@aol.com

STAFFORD, Canon Richard William. b 46. Ringsent Tech Inst TCert69. CITC 96. **d** 99 **p** 00. NSM Annagh w Drumgoon, Ashfield etc *K, E & A* 99-07; P-in-c Drumgoon from 07; Can Kilmore Cathl from 08. *12 Cherrymount, Keadue Lane, Cavan, Co Cavan, Republic of Ireland* Tel (00353) (49) 437 1173 Mobile 87-240 4630 E-mail rwstafford@yahoo.com

STAFFORD, Area Bishop of. *See* MURSELL, The Rt Revd Alfred Gordon

STAFFORD-WHITTAKER, William Paul. b 69. Chich Th Coll 91. **d** 94 **p** 95. C Brighton Resurr *Chich* 94-97; C Holborn St Alb w Saffron Hill St Pet *Lon* 97-02; V Stanwell from 02. *Stanwell Vicarage, 1 Lord Knyvett Close, Stanwell, Staines TW19 7PF* Tel (01784) 252044 E-mail vicar.stanwell@btinternet.com

STAGG, Jeremy Michael. b 47. Leeds Univ BSc69 Fontainebleau MBA77. Sarum & Wells Th Coll 90. **d** 92 **p** 93. C Basing *Win* 92-96; P-in-c Barton, Pooley Bridge and Martindale *Carl* 96-99; Hon CMS Rep 96-99; C Burgh-by-Sands and Kirkbampton w Kirkandrews etc *Carl* 99-00; C Barony of Burgh 00-01; P-in-c Distington 01-05; Dioc Past Sec 00-05; TR Cheswardine, Childs Ercall, Hales, Hinstock etc *Lich* from 05; RD Hodnet from 06. *The Vicarage, Childs Ercall, Market Drayton TF9 2DA* Tel (01952) 840229

STAGG, Canon Michael Hubert. b 39. St Chad's Coll Dur 58. **d** 63 **p** 64. C Weston-super-Mare St Sav *B & W* 63-66; P-in-c Fosdyke *Linc* 66-71; R Brompton Regis w Upton and Skilgate *B & W* 71-78; P-in-c Kidderminster St Jo *Worc* 78-80; P-in-c Cannington *B & W* 80-84; R Cannington, Otterhampton, Combwich and Stockland 84-87; Dioc Communications Officer *Nor* 88-93; Bp's Chapl 88-93; R Sprowston w Beeston 93-01; P-in-c Nor St Andr 01-04; P-in-c Nor St Geo Colegate 01-04; RD Nor N 95-04; Hon Can Nor Cathl 98-04; rtd 05; Perm to Offic *Nor* from 05. *31 Ash Grove, Norwich NR3 4BE* Tel (01603) 444549 E-mail michaelstagg@waitrose.com

STAGG, Roy Ernest. b 48. **d** 01 **p** 02. OLM Birchington w Acol and Minnis Bay *Cant* 01-04; OLM St Laur in Thanet 04-05. *7 Minster Road, Acol, Birchington CT7 0JB* Tel (01843) 841551 Mobile 07802-406066 E-mail roystagg@hotmail.co.uk

STAINER, Helene Lindsay. b 59. SWMTC 01. **d** 04 **p** 05. NSM Ivybridge w Harford *Ex* 04-09; P-in-c Milverton w Halse and Fitzhead *B & W* from 09. *The Vicarage, Parsonage Lane, Milverton, Taunton TA4 1LR* Tel (01823) 400305 E-mail helenestainer@aol.com

STAINER, Richard Bruce. b 62. Anglia Ruskin Univ MA09. Linc Th Coll 92. **d** 94 **p** 95. C N Walsham w Antingham *Nor* 94-97; R Cogenhoe and Gt and Lt Houghton w Brafield *Pet* from 97; RD

Wootton 01-07. *The Rectory, Church Street, Cogenhoe, Northampton NN7 1LS* Tel and fax (01604) 891166 E-mail richard@stbenedict.fsnet.co.uk

STAINES, Edward Noel. b 26. Trin Coll Ox BA48 BSc49 MA52 MSc85. Chich Th Coll 51 57. **d** 57 **p** 58. C Eastbourne St Mary *Chich* 57-61; V Amberley w N Stoke 61-70; V Forest Row 70-75; V Bexhill St Aug 75-79; TR Ovingdean w Rottingdean and Woodingdean 79-85; V Rottingdean 85-86; Chapl Gtr Lisbon *Eur* 88; Chapl Marseille 90; rtd 90; Perm to Offic *Worc* 86-09. *16 Conningsby Drive, Pershore WR10 1QX* Tel (01386) 554382

STAINES, Michael John. b 28. Trin Coll Ox BA52 MA56. Wells Th Coll 62. **d** 64 **p** 65. C Southwick St Mich *Chich* 64-67; TV Harling Gp *Nor* 67-73; P Missr S Chilterns Gp *Ox* 74-75; R W Wycombe w Bledlow Ridge, Bradenham and Radnage 76-93; RD Wycombe 83-87; rtd 93; Perm to Offic *Heref* from 93 and *Worc* 93-06. *The Old Forge, Lyonshall, Kington HR5 3JW, or PO Box 28077, Kitwe, Zambia* Tel (01544) 340013

STAINSBY, Alan. b 48. NEOC 01. **d** 04 **p** 05. NSM Hart w Elwick Hall *Dur* 04-06; NSM Haswell, Shotton and Thornley from 06. *6 Church View, Shotton Colliery, Durham DH6 2YD* Tel 0191-526 5200 E-mail astainsbyshotton@aol.com

STALEY, Andrew. b 50. Rhode Is Univ BA83. Westcott Ho Cam 01. **d** 04 **p** 05. C Bridport *Sarum* 04-08; TV Nadder Valley from 08. *The Rectory, Park Road, Tisbury, Salisbury SP3 6LF* Tel (01747) 870312 E-mail rev.staley@googlemail.com

STALEY, John Colin George. b 44. Hull Univ MA83. Wycliffe Hall Ox 68. **d** 71 **p** 72. C Tinsley *Sheff* 71-73; C Slaithwaite w E Scammonden *Wakef* 73-75; V Wakef St Andr and St Mary 75-80; Warden Scargill Ho 80-82; P-in-c Macclesfield St Pet *Ches* 82-85; TV Macclesfield Team 85-99; Sen Ind Chapl 86-99; Hon Ind Chapl 99-02. *Greenhills, Swanscoe, Rainow, Macclesfield SK10 5SZ* Tel (01625) 421296 Mobile 07824-736383 E-mail jjstaley@hotmail.co.uk

STALKER, Harry. b 47. **d** 04 **p** 05. OLM Felixstowe SS Pet and Paul *St E* from 04. *2 Ascot Drive, Felixstowe IP11 9DW* Tel (01394) 210826 Fax 210663 Mobile 07710-221275 E-mail aitchess@clara.net

STALKER, William John. b 49. NOC 89. **d** 91 **p** 92. C Formby H Trin *Liv* 91-94; V Stoneycroft All SS 94-03; Chapl R Liv Univ Hosp NHS Trust 94-03; P-in-c Lowton St Mary *Liv* from 03. *The Vicarage, 1 Barford Drive, Lowton, Warrington WA3 1DD* Tel (01942) 607705

STALLARD, John Charles. b 34. Selw Coll Cam BA58 MA62. Ripon Hall Ox 62. **d** 64 **p** 65. C Hall Green Ascension *Birm* 64-66; C Sutton Coldfield H Trin 66-68; C-in-c Brandwood CD 68-71; Chapl Dame Allan's Schs Newc 71-74; V Warley Woods *Birm* 75-84; TR Droitwich *Worc* 84-87; P-in-c Dodderhill 84-87; TR Droitwich Spa 87-94; V Pennsett 94-00; rtd 00; Perm to Offic *St D* 00-07. *Craigievar, Abbey Road, Llangollen LL20 8SN* Tel (01978) 860654 E-mail greengates@breathemail.net

STALLARD, Canon Mary Kathleen Rose. b 67. Selw Coll Cam BA88 Lon Inst of Educn PGCE90. Qu Coll Birm 91. **d** 93 **p** 97. C Newport St Matt *Mon* 93-96; P-in-c Ysbyty Cynfyn w Llantrisant and Eglwys Newydd *St D* 96-97; V 97-02; Min Can and Chapl St As Cathl 02-03; Can Res from 03; Dir of Ords from 09. *The Vicarage, Abbey Road, Llangollen LL20 8SN* Tel (01978) 860231

STALLEY, Brian Anthony. b 38. Oak Hill Th Coll 60. **d** 63 **p** 64. C Summerstown *S'wark* 63-70; Surrey BFBS Sec 70-73; Manager Action Cen BFBS 73-76; R Branston *Linc* 76-91; rtd 91; Perm to Offic *Linc* from 91. *6 Sunningdale Grove, Washingborough, Lincoln LN4 1SP* Tel (01522) 794164 Fax 794663 Mobile 07941-508445 E-mail brian@bstalley.freeserve.co.uk

STAMFORD, Brian. b 37. **d** 91 **p** 92. CMS Uganda 88-95; P-in-c North Hill and Lewannick *Truro* 95-03; P-in-c Altarnon w Bolventor, Laneast and St Clether 03-07; rtd 07. *2 William Dalby House, South Street, Oakham LE15 6HY* Tel (01572) 723493 E-mail brianstamford@btopenworld.com

STAMFORD, Dean of. *Vacant*

STAMP, Andrew Nicholas. b 44. Ex Univ BA67. Sarum Th Coll 67. **d** 69 **p** 70. C S Beddington St Mich *S'wark* 69-73; Tutor Sarum & Wells Th Coll 73-76; Chapl RN 76-81; C-in-c W Leigh CD *Portsm* 81-82; V W Leigh 82-87; R Botley 87-95; V Curdridge and R Durley 94-95; P-in-c Compton, the Mardens, Stoughton and Racton *Chich* 95-08; P-in-c Stansted 95-08; Tutor Bp Otter Coll Chich 99-08; Dioc Rural Officer *Chich* 00-08; rtd 08. *10 rue du Duc d'Aquitaine, 85120 Vouvant, France* E-mail revastamp@aol.com

STAMP, Ian Jack. b 47. Aston Tr Scheme 82 NOC 83. **d** 86 **p** 87. C Tonge w Alkrington *Man* 86-89; V Heywood St Marg 89-98; P-in-c Heywood St Luke w All So 96-98; TR Heywood 98-01; V Bury St Jo w St Mark from 01. *St John's Vicarage, 270 Walmersley Road, Bury BL9 6NH* Tel and fax 0161-764 3412 E-mail revistamp@aol.com

STAMP, Philip Andrew. b 53. Linc Th Coll 86. **d** 88 **p** 89. C Barton w Peel Green *Man* 88-91; R Blackley H Trin from 91; P-in-c Lightbowne from 04. *Holy Trinity Rectory, Goodman Street, Manchester M9 4BW* Tel 0161-205 2879

STAMP, Richard Mark. b 36. St Chad's Coll Dur BA60. **d** 62 **p** 63. Australia 62-69 and from 72; C Greenhill St Jo *Lon* 69-72; rtd 01. *127 Hilda Drive, RMB Ravenswood, Harcourt Vic 3453, Australia* Tel and fax (0061) (3) 5435 3576
E-mail stamp@netcon.net.au

STAMPS, Canon Dennis Lee. b 55. Biola Univ (USA) BA78 Trin Evang Div Sch (USA) MDiv83 MA87 Dur Univ PhD95. Westcott Ho Cam 90. **d** 92 **p** 93. C Moseley St Mary *Birm* 92-96; Dir WMMTC 96-01; Dean Qu Coll Birm 01-02; Minl Development Officer *St Alb* from 02; Can Res St Alb from 02. *7 Corder Close, St Albans AL3 4NH* Tel (01727) 841116
E-mail dstampsuk@aol.com

✠**STANAGE, The Rt Revd Thomas Shaun.** b 32. Pemb Coll Ox BA56 MA60 Nashotah Ho Wisconsin Hon DD86. Cuddesdon Coll 56. **d** 58 **p** 59 **c** 78. C Gt Crosby St Faith *Liv* 58-61; Min Orford St Andr CD 61-63; V Orford St Andr 63-70; S Africa from 70; Dean Kimberley 75-78; Suff Bp Johannesburg 78-82; Bp Bloemfontein 82-97; rtd 97; Acting Lect Th Univ of the Free State from 97. *PO Box 13598, Noordstad, Bloemfontein, 9301 South Africa* Tel (0027) (51) 436 7282

STANBRIDGE, The Ven Leslie Cyril. b 20. St Jo Coll Dur BA47 MA54. **d** 49 **p** 50. C Erith St Jo *Roch* 49-51; Tutor St Jo Coll Dur 51-55; Chapl 52-55; V Kingston upon Hull St Martin *York* 55-64; R Cottingham 64-72; Can and Preb York Minster 68-00; Succ Canonicorum from 88; RD Hull 70-72; Adn York 72-88; rtd 88; Perm to Offic *York* from 00. *39 Lucombe Way, New Earswick, York YO32 4DS* Tel (01904) 750812

✠**STANCLIFFE, The Rt Revd David Staffurth.** b 42. Trin Coll Ox BA65 MA68 Lambeth DD04. Cuddesdon Coll 65. **d** 67 **p** 68 **c** 93. C Armley St Bart *Ripon* 67-70; Chapl Clifton Coll Bris 70-77; Dir of Ords *Portsm* 77-82; Can Res Portsm Cathl 77-82; Provost Portsm 82-93; Bp Sarum from 93. *South Canonry, 71 The Close, Salisbury SP1 2ER* Tel (01722) 334031 Fax 413112
E-mail dsarum@salisbury.anglican.org

STAND, Andrew George. b 68. St Jo Coll Dur BA06. Cranmer Hall Dur 04. **d** 06 **p** 07. C Bromsgrove St Jo *Worc* from 06. *74 Carol Avenue, Bromsgrove B61 8RW* Tel (01527) 559447

STANDEN, David Charles. b 68. K Coll Lon BA91 AKC91 PGCE92 Lon Univ PhD00. Westcott Ho Cam 01. **d** 03 **p** 04. C Prittlewell *Chelmsf* 03-07; P-in-c Stratton and Launcells *Truro* from 07; P-in-c Bude Haven and Marhamchurch from 09. *The Vicarage, Diddies Road, Stratton, Bude EX23 9DW* Tel (01288) 352254 E-mail davidstanden@onetel.com

STANDEN, Mark Jonathan. b 63. LMH Ox BA85 Cam Univ BA94 Barrister 86. Ridley Hall Cam 92. **d** 95 **p** 96. C Sevenoaks St Nic *Roch* 95-99; R Angmering *Chich* from 99; RD Arundel and Bognor from 08. *The Rectory, Rectory Lane, Angmering, Littlehampton BN16 4JU* Tel (01903) 784979

STANDEN McDOUGAL, Canon John Anthony Phelps. b 33. AKC58. **d** 59 **p** 60. C Ipswich St Marg *St E* 59-63; C Bury St Edmunds St Mary 63-65; C Wadhurst *Chich* 65-70; C Tidebrook 65-70; R Tollard Royal w Farnham *Sarum* 70-81; P-in-c Gussage St Michael and Gussage All Saints 71-76; R 76-81; RD Milton and Blandford 81-86; R Tollard Royal w Farnham, Gussage St Michael etc 82-86; Can and Preb Sarum Cathl 86-94; TR Bride Valley 86-94; rtd 94; Perm to Offic *Sarum* from 94. *Silverbridge Cottage, North Chideock, Bridport DT6 6LG* Tel (01297) 489408

STANDING, Victor. b 44. Lon Univ BMus66 FRCO67 Clare Coll Cam CertEd68. Ripon Coll Cuddesdon 75. **d** 78 **p** 79. C Wimborne Minster *Sarum* 78-80; TV Wimborne Minster and Holt 80-83; R Ex St Sidwell and St Matt 83-94; Dep PV Ex Cathl 83-01; Chapl R Devon and Ex Hosp 83-94; Chapl W of England Eye Infirmary Ex 83-94; P-in-c Tedburn St Mary, Whitestone, Oldridge etc *Ex* 94-96; P-in-c Dunsford and Doddiscombsleigh 95-96; P-in-c Cheriton Bishop 95-96; R Tedburn St Mary, Whitestone, Oldridge etc 96-01; RD Kenn 97-01; V New Shoreham *Chich* from 01; V Old Shoreham from 01. *The Vicarage, Church Street, Shoreham-by-Sea BN43 5DQ* Tel (01273) 452109 E-mail victorstanding@tiscali.co.uk

STANDISH, Derrick Edgar. b 41. Univ of Wales (Lamp) BA67. Wycliffe Hall Ox 68. **d** 68 **p** 69. C Brynmawr *S & B* 68-69; C Morriston 69-74; V Merthyr Cynog and Dyffryn Honddu 74-76; R Llanwenarth Ultra *Mon* 76-83; V Abersychan and Garndiffaith 83-91. *7 Intermediate Road, Brynmawr, Ebbw Vale NP23 4SF* Tel (01495) 312183

STANDRING, Rupert Benjamin Charles. b 68. Pemb Coll Ox BA90 MA99 Cam Univ BA94. Ridley Hall Cam 92. **d** 95 **p** 96. C Bromley Ch Ch *Roch* 95-99; Tutor Cornhill Tr Course 99-04; Hon C W Hampstead St Luke *Lon* 99-04; Perm to Offic 04-05; Min Mayfair Ch Ch 05-09; Lic Preacher from 09. *56 Langthorne Street, London SW6 6JY* Tel (020) 7385 4950
E-mail rupert@emmanuelfulham.org

STANES, The Ven Ian Thomas. b 39. Sheff Univ BSc62 Linacre Coll Ox BA65 MA69. Wycliffe Hall Ox 63. **d** 65 **p** 66. C Leic H Apostles 65-69; V Broom Leys 69-76; Warden Marrick Priory *Ripon* 76-82; Officer Miss, Min and Evang Willesden Area *Lon* 82-92; CME Officer 82-92; Preb St Paul's Cathl 89-92; Adn

Loughborough *Leic* 92-05; rtd 05. *192 Bath Road, Bradford-on-Avon BA15 1SP* Tel (01225) 309036

STANESBY, Derek Malcolm. b 31. Leeds Univ BA56 Man Univ MEd75 PhD84 SOSc. Coll of Resurr Mirfield 56. **d** 58 **p** 59. C Lakenham St Jo *Nor* 58-61; C Welling *S'wark* 61-63; V Bury St Mark *Man* 63-67; R Ladybarn 67-85; Can and Steward Windsor 85-97; rtd 97; Perm to Office *Leic* and *Pet* from 00. *32 Elizabeth Way, Uppingham, Oakham LE15 9PQ* Tel (01572) 821298

STANFORD, Canon Mark Roger. b 59. Cranmer Hall Dur 96. **d** 98 **p** 99. C Aughton Ch Ch *Liv* 98-02; TV Toxteth St Philemon w St Gabr and St Cleopas from 02; AD Toxteth and Wavertree from 06; Hon Can Liv Cathl from 06; Chapl St Hilda's Priory and Sch Whitby from 03. *St Philemon's Vicarage, 40 Devonshire Road, Princes Park, Liverpool L8 3TZ* Tel 0151-727 1248
E-mail mark@stphilemons.co.uk

STANGHAN, Eileen. b 40. Whitelands Coll Lon CertEd75. **d** 98 **p** 99. OLM Reigate St Phil *S'wark* from 98. *20 Saxon Way, Reigate RH2 9DH* Tel (01737) 240920 *or* (01293) 430043

STANIER, Robert Sebastian. b 75. Magd Coll Ox BA98 Selw Coll Cam BA05. Westcott Ho Cam 03. **d** 06 **p** 07. C Perry Hill St Geo w Ch Ch and St Paul *S'wark* from 06. *20 Gaynesford Road, London SE23 2UQ* Tel (020) 8699 3466
E-mail robertstanier@btinternet.com

STANIFORD, Mrs Doris Gwendoline. b 43. Gilmore Course IDC79. **dss** 80 **d** 87 **p** 94. Hangleton *Chich* 80-82; Durrington 82-89; Par Dn 87-89; Chich Th Coll 83-89; C Crawley and Chapl Crawley Gen Hosp 89-97; Dioc Voc Adv and Chapl St Cath Hospice 92-97; Asst Dir of Ords *Chich* from 97; C Southwick St Mich 97-99; TV Ifield from 99. *St Alban's Vicarage, Gossops Drive, Crawley RH11 8LD* Tel (01293) 529848

STANLEY, Arthur Patrick. b 32. TCD BA54 Div Test55 MA64. **d** 55 **p** 56. C Waterford H Trin *C & O* 55-57; CF 58-74; Dep Asst Chapl Gen 74-83; USA 84-04; rtd 94; Perm to Offic *B & W* from 05. *10 Knights Court, Keyford, Frome BA11 1JD* Tel (01373) 301694 E-mail patnpaddy@hotmail.com

STANLEY, Baden Thomas. b 68. TCD BA91. CITC BTh94. **d** 94 **p** 95. C Seapatrick *D & D* 94-98; I Bray *D & G* from 98. *The Rectory, Church Road, Bray, Co Wicklow, Republic of Ireland* Tel and fax (00353) (1) 286 2968 Mobile 87-948 4407
E-mail bray@dublin.anglican.org

STANLEY, Canon John Alexander. b 31. OBE99. Tyndale Hall Bris. **d** 56 **p** 57. C Preston All SS *Blackb* 56-60; C St Helens St Mark *Liv* 60-63; V Everton St Cuth 63-70; P-in-c Everton St Sav 69-70; V Everton St Sav w St Cuth 70-74; V Huyton St Mich from 74; Hon Can Liv Cathl from 87; AD Huyton 89-02; Chapl to The Queen 93-01. *The Vicarage, Bluebell Lane, Liverpool L36 7SA* Tel 0151-449 3900 Fax 480 6002 Mobile 07740-621833 E-mail huytonchurch@btconnect.com

STANLEY, Mrs Nicola Vere. b 56. Surrey Univ BA07 MCIPD83. STETS 99. **d** 02 **p** 03. C Bedford Park *Lon* 02-06; V Twickenham All Hallows from 06; Asst Dir of Ords Kensington Area from 04. *All Hallows' Vicarage, 138 Chertsey Road, Twickenham TW1 1EW* Tel (020) 8892 1322
E-mail nvs@mosaicpublishing.co.uk

STANLEY, Patrick. *See* STANLEY, Arthur Patrick

STANLEY, Canon Simon Richard. b 44. Wells Th Coll 66. **d** 69 **p** 70. C Foleshill St Laur *Cov* 69-71; C Hessle *York* 71-75; P-in-c Flamborough 75-80; R Dunnington 80-92; P-in-c York St Barn 92-99; P-in-c York St Chad 99-09; P-in-c York All SS Pavement w St Crux and St Mich 03-09; P-in-c York St Denys 04-09; Can and Preb York Minster from 05; Relig Progr Producer BBC Radio York 94-03; rtd 09; NSM York St Chad from 09. *St Chad's Vicarage, 36 Campleshon Road, York YO23 1EY* Tel (01904) 674524 Mobile 07946-466364
E-mail simonstanley@clara.net

STANLEY-SMITH, James. b 29. Hatf Coll Dur BA54 DipEd55. S Dios Minl Tr Scheme 81. **d** 84 **p** 85. C Bournemouth St Jo w St Mich *Win* 84-87; R Hale w S Charford 87-94; rtd 94; Perm to Offic *Win* from 94. *10 Rownhams Way, Rownhams, Southampton SO16 8AE* Tel (023) 8073 2529
E-mail jstanley-smith@cwcom.net

STANNARD, Miss Beryl Elizabeth. b 36. SRN62 SCM64. Oak Hill Th Coll BA92. **d** 92 **p** 94. Par Dn Streatham Park St Alb *S'wark* 92-94; C 94-96; C Gerrards Cross and Fulmer *Ox* 96-01; rtd 01; Perm to Offic *Ox* from 02. *20 Wey Lane, Chesham HP5 1JH* Tel (01494) 774715

STANNARD, Brian. b 46. MICE71 MIStructE71. Cranmer Hall Dur 86. **d** 88 **p** 89. C Burnage St Marg *Man* 88-91; V Walmersley 91-03; TV Westhoughton and Wingates 03-04; rtd 04. *63 Portland Street, Southport PR8 5AF* Tel (01704) 534632
E-mail brian@stannardrev.fsnet.co.uk

STANNARD, The Ven Colin Percy. b 24. TD66. Selw Coll Cam BA47 MA49. Linc Th Coll 47. **d** 49 **p** 50. C St E Cathl 49-52; C-in-c Nunsthorpe CD *Linc* 52-55; CF (TA) 53-67; V Barrow St Jas *Carl* 55-64; V Upperby St Jo 64-70; R Gosforth 70-75; RD Calder 70-75; P-in-c Natland 75-76; V 76-84; RD Kendal 75-84; Hon Can Carl Cathl 75-84; Can Res Carl Cathl 84-93; Adn Carl

84-93; rtd 93; Perm to Offic *Carl* from 93. *51 Longlands Road, Carlisle CA3 9AE* Tel (01228) 538584

STANNARD, Canon Peter Graville. b 59. Univ of Wales (Abth) BSc(Econ)81. St Steph Ho Ox BA85 MA86. d 86 p 87. C Worksop Priory *S'well* 86-89; Prin St Nic Th Coll Ghana 89-96; Hon Can Koforidua from 93; TR Shelf w Buttershaw St Aid *Bradf* 96-99; P-in-c Heaton Norris St Thos *Man* 00-02; TV Heatons 02-08; P-in-c S Shields St Hilda w St Thos *Dur* from 08; P-in-c S Shields St Aid and St Steph from 08. *40 Lawe Road, South Shields NE33 2EU* Tel 0191-454 1414

STANTON, Ms Angela. b 59. Loughb Univ BSc80 Ch Coll Liv PGCE81. Westcott Ho Cam 03. d 05 p 06. C Atherton and Hindsford w Howe Bridge *Man* 05-08; P-in-c Reddish from 08. *St Elisabeth's Rectory, 28 Bedford Street, Stockport SK5 6DJ* Tel 0161-432 3033 E-mail angiestanton27@yahoo.co.uk

STANTON, Miss Barbara. b 51. Whitelands Coll Lon TCert72 Lon Univ BD86. WMMTC 89. d 92 p 94. NSM Hinckley St Mary *Leic* 92-97; P-in-c Husbands Bosworth w Mowsley and Knaptoft etc 97-06; P-in-c Arnesby w Shearsby and Bruntingthorpe 02-06; Bp's Ecum Adv 97-03; Dioc Rural Officer 03-06; R Bildeston w Wattisham and Lindsey, Whatfield etc *St E* from 06. *7 Chamberlin Close, Bildeston, Ipswich IP7 7EZ* Tel (01449) 744190 E-mail barbarastanton@supanet.com

STANTON, Canon David John. b 60. St Andr Univ MTheol82 Ex Univ MA00 FSAScot89 FRSA98. Ripon Coll Cuddesdon 83. d 85 p 86. C Beckenham St Geo *Roch* 85-88; Asst Chapl Shrewsbury Sch 88-90; Hon C Shrewsbury All SS w St Mich *Lich* 88-90; P-in-c Abbotskerswell *Ex* 90-94; Chapl Plymouth Univ 92-97; P-in-c Bovey Tracey St Jo, Chudleigh Knighton etc 94-99; V Bovey Tracey St Jo w Heathfield 99-05; Dioc Voc Adv 95-05; Warden of Readers 96-03; Acting Dioc Dir of Ords 03-05; RD Moreton 98-05; Can Prec and Can Past Worc Cathl from 05. *15A College Green, Worcester WR1 2LH* Tel (01905) 732940 Fax 29119 E-mail davidstanton@worcestercathedral.co.uk

STANTON, Gregory John. b 47. Sarum & Wells Th Coll 84. d 86 p 87. C Willenhall H Trin *Lich* 86-89; C Plympton St Mary *Ex* 89-91; V Milton Abbot, Dunterton, Lamerton etc from 91. *The Vicarage, The Parade, Milton Abbot, Tavistock PL19 0NZ* Tel (01822) 612732 E-mail gjstanton31@hotmail.com

STANTON, John Maurice. b 18. Univ Coll Ox BA45 MA45. Wycliffe Hall Ox 51. d 52 p 53. C Tonbridge SS Pet and Paul *Roch* 52-54; Hd Master Blundell's Sch Tiverton 59-71; Public Preacher *Ex* 71-72; C Ex St Matt 72-73; R Chesham Bois *Ox* 73-83; rtd 83; Perm to Offic *Ox* from 83. *16 Emden House, Barton Lane, Headington OX3 9JU* Tel (01865) 765206

STANTON, Miss Julie Elizabeth. b 59. Matlock Coll of Educn CertEd80. EMMTC 00. d 03 p 04. NSM Matlock Bath and Cromford *Derby* from 03. *35 Intake Lane, Cromford, Matlock DE4 3RH* Tel (01629) 822653 Fax 760903 Mobile 07769-748276 E-mail revjs@hotmail.com

STANTON, Ms Karen Janis. b 55. NOC 00. d 03 p 04. C Withington St Paul *Man* 03-04; C Urmston 04-07; TV Wythenshawe from 07. *St Luke's Vicarage, Brownley Road, Manchester M22 4PT* Tel 0161-998 2071 Mobile 07814-254744 E-mail kaz@thestantons.me.uk

STANTON, Thomas Hugh (Timothy). b 17. Trin Coll Cam BA38 MA45. Coll of Resurr Mirfield 46. d 47 p 48. C Camberwell St Geo *S'wark* 47-49; CR from 52; S Africa 54-87; rtd 87. *House of the Resurrection, Stocks Bank Road, Mirfield WF14 0BN* Tel (01924) 494318

STANTON-HYDE, Mrs Marjorie Elizabeth. b 37. TCert58. Cranmer Hall Dur 86. d 88 p 94. Par Dn Elmley Lovett w Hampton Lovett and Elmbridge etc *Worc* 88-91; Par Dn Wilden 88-91; Par Dn Hartlebury 88-91; Dn-in-c 91-94; P-in-c 94-97; R 97-98; rtd 98; Hon C Gt Malvern St Mary *Worc* 99-02; Warden Jes Hosp Cant 02-05; Chapl Worcs Community and Mental Health Trust from 05. *4 Severn Drive, Malvern WR14 2SZ* Tel (01684) 569589

STANTON-SARINGER, Maurice Charles. b 49. Bris Univ BSc71 PGCE72 Fitzw Coll Cam BA77 MA81. Ridley Hall Cam 75. d 78 p 79. C Gerrards Cross *Ox* 78-80; C Bletchley 80-83; Chapl Stowe Sch 83-91; R Sherington w Chicheley, N Crawley, Astwood etc *Ox* 91-06; RD Newport 95-04; TR Loddon Reach from 06. *The Vicarage, 12 The Manor, Shinfield, Reading RG2 9DP* Tel and fax 0118-988 3363 E-mail saringer@onetel.com

STANWAY, Peter David. b 48. K Coll Lon BD71. St Aug Coll Cant 72. d 73 p 74. C Maidstone All SS w St Phil and H Trin *Cant* 73-77; Canada 77-84; C Waterlooville *Portsm* 84-87; R Laughton w Ripe and Chalvington *Chich* 87-90; Chapl Witney Community Hosp 90-91; C Wheatley w Forest Hill and Stanton St John *Ox* 91-92; C Cowley St Jas 93-02; rtd 02. *22 Colleywood, Kennington, Oxford OX1 5NF* Tel (01865) 739342

STAPLE, Miss Patricia Ann. b 54. Birm Univ BA75. St Steph Ho Ox 00. d 02 p 05. C Dartmouth and Dittisham *Ex* 02-04; C Colyton, Musbury, Southleigh and Branscombe 04-07; V Athelney *B & W* from 07. *Athelney Rectory, Stoke Road, North Curry, Taunton TA3 6HN* Tel (01823) 490255 Mobile 07719-129008 E-mail tricia_staple@hotmail.com

STAPLEFORD, Robin Duncan. b 62. Aston Tr Scheme 92 St Jo Coll Nottm 94. d 96 p 97. C Evington *Leic* 96-99; TV Vale of Belvoir Par 00-08; R Upper Wensum Village Gp *Nor* from 08. *The Rectory, Market Hill, Colkirk, Fakenham NR21 7NU* Tel (01328) 864128 E-mail stapleford@tiscali.co.uk

STAPLES, David. b 35. Jes Coll Ox BA59 MA63 BD75. Linc Th Coll 59. d 61 p 62. C Kettering St Andr *Pet* 61-64; C Doncaster St Geo *Sheff* 64-66; Dioc Youth Chapl 66-71; V Mexborough 71-83; Chapl Montagu Hosp Mexborough 71-83; RD Wath *Sheff* 77-83; Hon Can Sheff Cathl 80-83; V W Haddon w Winwick *Pet* 83-88; RD Brixworth 83-89; V W Haddon w Winwick and Ravensthorpe 88-00; ACUPA Link Officer 90-00; rtd 00; Perm to Offic *Linc* from 00. *1 Sycamore Close, Bourne PE10 9RS* Tel (01778) 423121

STAPLES, Jeffrey Joseph. b 61. St Jo Coll Nottm 97. d 99 p 00. C Prenton *Ches* 99-03; P-in-c Wallasey St Nic 03-04; P-in-c New Brighton All SS 03-04; V Wallasey St Nic w All SS from 04. *St Nicholas' Vicarage, 22 Groveland Road, Wallasey CH45 8JY* Tel 0151-639 3589 E-mail jeffstaples4@hotmail.com

STAPLES, John Michael. b 45. STETS 94. d 97 p 98. C Tisbury *Sarum* 97-01; P-in-c Barford St Martin, Dinton, Baverstock etc 00-01; TV Nadder Valley 01-08; C Fovant, Sutton Mandeville and Teffont Evias etc 06-08; rtd 08. *Crabstone Cottage, Locarno Road, Swanage BH19 1HY* Tel (01929) 421421 E-mail john_staples@btinternet.com

STAPLES, John Wedgwood. b 42. Hertf Coll Ox BA64 MA. Wycliffe Hall Ox 64. d 66 p 67. C Yardley St Edburgha *Birm* 66-69; C Knowle 69-74; R Barcombe *Chich* 74-81; V Old Windsor *Ox* 81-96; P-in-c Pangbourne w Tidmarsh and Sulham 96-99; R 99-07; rtd 07. *6 Douglas Road, Bournemouth BH6 3ER* Tel (01202) 425269 E-mail revd_john@staplesj.fsnet.co.uk

STAPLES, Peter. b 35. Jes Coll Ox BA59. Ripon Hall Ox 59. d 62 p 63. C Fairfield *Derby* 62-63; C Dore 63-66; C Wilne and Draycott w Breaston 66-71; The Netherlands from 72; Asst Chapl Utrecht w Zwolle *Eur* 94-08. *Doldersweg 39C, 3712 BN Huis Ter Heide, Utrecht, The Netherlands* Tel (0031) (30) 693 1928 Fax 253 3241

STAPLES, Canon Peter Brian. b 38. Bps' Coll Cheshunt 66. d 68 p 69. C Birkdale St Jas *Liv* 68-71; C Sevenoaks St Jo *Roch* 71-74; V Treslothan *Truro* 74-80; V Truro St Paul and St Clem 80-02; Hon Can Truro Cathl 98-02; rtd 02; Perm to Offic *St E* from 03. *25 Osmund Walk, Bury St Edmunds IP33 3UU* Tel (01284) 760620

STAPLES, Terence Malcolm. b 43. Trin Coll Bris MA01. BA95. d 95 p 96. C Bath St Sav w Swainswick and Woolley *B & W* 95-99; R Exton and Winsford and Cutcombe w Luxborough from 99. *The Rectory, Winsford, Minehead TA24 7JE* Tel (01643) 851301 E-mail staplest@freenet.co.uk

STAPLETON, The Very Revd Henry Edward Champneys. b 32. MBE09. FSA74 Pemb Coll Cam BA54 MA58. Ely Th Coll 54. d 56 p 57. C York St Olave w St Giles 56-59; C Pocklington w Yapham-cum-Meltonby, Owsthorpe etc 59-61; R Seaton Ross w Everingham and Bielby and Harswell 61-67; RD Weighton 66-67; R Skelton by York 67-75; V Wroxham w Hoveton *Nor* 75-81; P-in-c Belaugh 76-81; Can Res and Prec Roch Cathl 81-88; Dean Carl 88-98; rtd 98; Perm to Offic *Wakef* from 98 and *York* from 03. *Rockland House, 20 Marsh Gardens, Honley, Huddersfield HD9 6AF* Tel (01484) 666629

STAPLETON, Leonard Charles. b 37. Chich Th Coll 75. d 77 p 78. C Crayford *Roch* 77-81; C Lamorbey H Redeemer 81-83; V Belvedere St Aug 83-89; V Beckenham St Jas 89-02; rtd 02; Perm to Offic *Roch* 03-04 and *Win* from 04. *14 Howlett Close, Lymington SO41 9LA* Tel (01590) 679414

STAPLETON, Robert Michael Vorley. b 25. ALCD51. d 51 p 52. C Plymouth St Andr *Ex* 51-56; Chapl RN 56-60; C Surbiton St Matt *S'wark* 60-64; R Chenies and Lt Chalfont *Ox* 64-87; P-in-c Latimer w Flaunden 86-87; R Chenies and Lt Chalfont, Latimer and Flaunden 87-92; rtd 92. *Woodside, Swannaton Road, Dartmouth TQ6 9RL* Tel (01803) 832972

STAPLETON, Robert Vauvelle. b 47. St Jo Coll Dur BA70. Cranmer Hall Dur. d 71 p 72. C Moreton *Ches* 71-73; C Monkwearmouth All SS *Dur* 73-76; C Stranton 76-79; P-in-c Kelloe 79-86; V New Shildon 86-96; R Stoke Albany w Wilbarston and Ashley etc *Pet* 96-04; P-in-c Somborne w Ashley *Win* from 04; Dioc Rural Officer from 04. *The New Vicarage, Romsey Road, Kings Somborne, Stockbridge SO20 6PR* Tel (01794) 388223 E-mail robertstapleton@hotmail.com

STARBUCK, Francis Tony. b 36. Kelham Th Coll 57. d 61 p 62. C Mansfield St Mark *S'well* 61-63; C Clifton H Trin CD 63-64; C Didcot *Ox* 67-71; P Missr California CD 71-75; R Barkham 74-75; V Hagbourne 75-82; V Maidenhead St Luke 82-87; V Te Puke St Jo New Zealand 87-96; Can Waiapu 90-94; V Clevedon All So 96-01; rtd 01; Chapl Selwyn Oaks Papakura from 01. *16 Selwyn Oaks, 21 Youngs Road, Papakura 2110, New Zealand*

STARES, Canon Brian Maurice William. b 44. St Deiniol's Hawarden 74. d 74 p 75. C Risca *Mon* 74-77; V Newport St Steph and H Trin 77-87; V Fleur-de-Lis 87-92; Chapl HM Pris Belmarsh 92-93; Chapl HM YOI Dover 93-98; Feltham 98-99; V

Bishton *Mon* 99-09; Hon Can St Woolos Cathl 07-09; rtd 09. *37 St Mary's Court, Baneswell, Newport NP20 4DP*

STARES, Mrs Olive Beryl. b 33. Sarum Th Coll 83. **dss** 86 **d** 87 **p** 94. Crofton *Portsm* 86-87; Hon C 87-01; rtd 01. *62 Mancroft Avenue, Hill Head, Fareham PO14 2DD* Tel (01329) 668540

STARK, Mrs Beverley Ann. b 52. Bp Otter Coll CertEd73 EMMTC 92. **d** 92 **p** 94. Par Dn Bulwell St Jo *S'well* 92-94; C 94-97; TV Bestwood 97-03; V Bestwood Em w St Mark 03-04; R Ironstone Villages *Leic* from 04; RD Framland from 06. *The Rectory, 23 Melton Road, Waltham on the Wolds, Melton Mowbray LE14 4AJ* Tel (01664) 464600
E-mail beverley.stark@ntlworld.com

STARK, John Jordan. b 40. Hull Univ BA62. St Chad's Coll Dur. **d** 64 **p** 65. C Buxton *Derby* 64-67; C Wolborough w Newton Abbot *Ex* 67-74; R Belstone 74-79; P-in-c Plymouth St Gabr 79-80; V from 80. *The Vicarage, 1 Peverell Terrace, Plymouth PL3 4JJ* Tel (01752) 663938

STARK, Margaret Alison. b 46. Univ of Wales BA70 BA71. St Mich Coll Llan. **d** 90 **p** 97. C Llanishen and Lisvane 90-93; C Llanishen 93-94; C Aberavon 94-98; R Llanfabon 98-01; rtd 01. *6 Alexandra House, Beach Road, Penarth CF64 1FN* Tel (029) 2070 1303

STARK, Michael. b 35. Dur Univ BSc56 SEN58. Chich Th Coll 58. **d** 60 **p** 61. C Middlesbrough St Paul *York* 60-64; C S Bank 64-66; R Skelton in Cleveland 66-74; P-in-c Upleatham 66-67; R 67-74; Asst Chapl HM Pris Wormwood Scrubs 74-76; Liv 75-76; Chapl HM Pris Featherstone 76-83; Zx 83-89; Leic 89-97; rtd 97; Perm to Offic *Leic* and *S'well* from 99; P-in-c Rotterdam *Eur* 04-06. *28 St Peter's Road, Leicester LE2 1DA*

STARKEY, Gerald Dennis. b 34. Qu Coll Birm 79. **d** 82 **p** 83. C Wilnecote *Lich* 82-86; Min Stoke-upon-Trent 86-90; P-in-c W Bromwich St Pet 90-00; rtd 00; Perm to Offic *Lich* from 01. *6 Hazelwood Drive, Wednesfield, Wolverhampton WV11 1SH* Tel (01902) 726252

STARKEY, John Douglas. b 23. St Chad's Coll Dur BA47. **d** 48 **p** 49. C Horninglow *Lich* 48-52; C Lower Gornal 52-55; C-in-c W Bromwich Ascension CD 55-57; V Coseley Ch Ch 57-66; V Freehay 66-84; P-in-c Oakamoor w Cotton 78-84; R Dunstall w Rangemore and Tatenhill 84-88; rtd 88; Perm to Offic *Lich* and *Derby* from 88. *34 Park Crescent, Doveridge, Ashbourne DE6 5NE* Tel (01889) 566384

STARKEY, Michael Stuart. b 63. LMH Ox BA85 Nottm Univ BTh92 MA93. St Jo Coll Nottm 90. **d** 93 **p** 94. C Ealing St Mary *Lon* 93-95; C Brownswood Park 95-97; P-in-c 97-01; V Twickenham Common H Trin 01-09; V Kennington St Mark *S'wark* from 09. *St Mark's Vicarage, 56 Kennington Oval, London SE11 5SW* Tel (020) 7582 5613 Mobile 07870-281055
E-mail revstarkey@yahoo.co.uk

STARKEY, Naomi Faith Ezitt (Ness). b 61. Lanc Univ BSc97 MA02 Leeds Univ MA07 RGN83 RM85. NOC 04. **d** 07 **p** 08. C Broughton *Blackb* from 07. *25 Northway, Fulwood, Preston PR2 9TP* Tel (01772) 713880 *or* (01995) 61719
E-mail ness.starkey@ic24.net

STARKEY, Patrick Robin. b 37. **d** 64 **p** 65. C Tonbridge SS Pet and Paul *Roch* 64-68; Asst Chapl Sherborne Sch 68-72; Scripture Union 73-85; rtd 99. *14 Heol Twrch, Lower Cwmtwrch, Swansea SA9 2TD*

STARKEY, Simon Mark. b 36. Liv Univ BA78 MA96. Clifton Th Coll 63. **d** 66 **p** 67. C Ox St Ebbe w St Pet 66-72; Community Chapl CPAS Kirkdale 72-75; TV Toxteth Park St Bede *Liv* 75-78; P-in-c 78-80; V 80-90; RD Toxteth 81-89; Chapl Ches Coll of HE 90-96; TV St Luke in the City *Liv* 96-03; rtd 03; Perm to Offic *Liv* from 03. *23 Merlin Street, Liverpool L8 8HY* Tel 0151-709 0208

STARKEY, Susan Anne. b 52. St Jo Coll Nottm. **d** 97 **p** 98. C Watford St Luke *St Alb* 97-02; C Oxhey All SS 02-04; V Findern *Derby* from 04; V Willington from 04. *The Vicarage, 66 Castle Way, Willington, Derby DE65 6BU* Tel (01283) 703928
E-mail susan.starkey@btopenworld.com

STARKIE, Andrew Edward. b 70. Regent's Park Coll Ox BA91 MA95 Selw Coll Cam MPhil03 PhD03. Ridley Hall Cam 97. **d** 02 **p** 03. C Long Benton *Newc* 02-06; C Seaton Hirst 06-09; V Middleton Junction *Man* from 09. *The Vicarage, Greenhill Road, Middleton Junction, Manchester M24 2BD* Tel 0161-643 5064
E-mail a.e.starkie@googlemail.com

STARNES, Peter Henry. b 19. St Jo Coll Cam BA42 MA47 Ch Ch Coll Cant PGCE72 LTCL74. Linc Th Coll 42. **d** 44 **p** 45. C Gillingham *Sarum* 44-50; C St Peter-in-Thanet *Cant* 50-52; CF 52-55; Hon CF from 55; R Hothfield *Cant* 56-60; V Westwell 56-65; R Eastwell w Boughton Aluph 60-65; rtd 84. *Whitebeams, High Halden, Ashford TN26 3LY* Tel (01233) 850245

STARNS, Helen Edna. *See* PATTEN, Mrs Helen Edna

STARR, Michael Richard. b 43. Sarum Th Coll 65. **d** 68 **p** 69. C Plymouth St Pet *Ex* 68-72; C Blackpool St Paul *Blackb* 72-74; V Burnley St Cuth 74-79; C Eastbourne St Mary *Chich* 79-84; P-in-c Eastbourne Ch Ch 84-87; V 87-88; R Guernsey Ste Marie du Castel *Win* 88-01; V Guernsey St Matt 94-01; Vice-Dean Guernsey 99-01; P-in-c Win St Bart 01-08; rtd 09. *62 Beresford Road, Chandler's Ford, Eastleigh SO53 2LY*

STARRS, Lindsey Carolyn. b 49. Alsager Coll of Educn CertEd70 Liv Inst of HE BEd85. Ripon Coll Cuddesdon 00. **d** 02 **p** 03. C Penkridge *Lich* 02-06; TV N Creedy *Ex* from 06. *The Rectory, Church Street, Morchard Bishop, Crediton EX17 6PJ* Tel (01363) 877221 E-mail starrs@lstarrs.fsnet.com

STARTIN, Nicola Gail. b 57. K Coll Lon LLB79. St Steph Ho Ox 88. **d** 90 **p** 96. C Wellingborough All SS *Pet* 90-92; NSM Pyle w Kenfig *Llan* 94-95; Asst Chapl Mid Kent Healthcare NHS Trust 95-97; Chapl HM Pris E Sutton Park 97-00; Chapl HM Pris Haslar 00-02; Chapl Haslar Immigration Removal Cen from 02. *Haslar Immigration Removal Centre, 2 Dolphin Way, Gosport PO12 2AW* Tel (023) 9260 4047
E-mail nicola.startin@hmps.gsi.gov.uk

STATHAM, Brian Edward. b 55. K Coll Lon MA AKC76. St Steph Ho Ox 77. **d** 78 **p** 79. C Ches H Trin 78-81; C Birkenhead Priory 81-82; TV 82-86; V Newton 86-91; SSF 91-94; TV Horsham *Chich* 95-99; Chapl Horsham Gen Hosp 95-99; TV Ches 99-03; P-in-c Stockport St Matt 03-07; C Edgeley and Cheadle Heath from 07. *St Matthew's Vicarage, 99 Chatham Street, Stockport SK3 9EG* Tel 0161-480 5515
E-mail brianstatham@aol.com

STATHAM, John Francis. b 31. Kelham Th Coll 51. **d** 56 **p** 57. C Ilkeston St Mary *Derby* 56-58; C New Mills 58-59; V 69-81; C Newbold w Dunston 59-62; PC Ridgeway 62-69; RD Glossop 78-81; R Matlock 81-89; R Killamarsh 89-93; rtd 93; Perm to Offic *Derby* and *S'well* from 93. *33 Ackford Drive, The Meadows, Worksop S80 1YG* Tel (01909) 476031

STATHER, Thomas William John. b 79. Van Mildert Coll Dur BSc00. St Steph Ho Ox BTh04. **d** 04 **p** 05. C Colchester St Jas and St Paul w All SS etc *Chelmsf* 04-08; P-in-c Tunstall *Lich* from 08. *Christ Church Vicarage, 26 Stanley Street, Tunstall, Stoke-on-Trent ST6 6BW* E-mail john_stather@hotmail.com

STATON, Preb Geoffrey. b 40. Wells Th Coll 64. **d** 66 **p** 67. C Wednesfield St Thos *Lich* 66-69; C Cannock 69-72; V Cheddleton 72-82; RD Leek 77-82; V Harlescott 82-90; TR Penkridge 90-05; Preb Lich Cathl 87-05; rtd 05; C Colton, Colwich and Gt Haywood *Lich* from 05. *The Vicarage, Main Road, Little Haywood, Stafford ST18 0TS* Tel (01889) 881262
E-mail geoffrey.staton@virgin.net

STATTER, Ms Deborah Hilary. b 55. **d** 00 **p** 01. OLM Everton St Pet *Liv* 00-02; OLM Everton St Pet w St Chrys 02-04; C 04-08; P-in-c Netherton from 08. *St Oswald's Vicarage, 183 St Oswald's Lane, Bootle L30 5SR* Tel 0151-525 1882 Mobile 07952-105466

STAUNTON, Mrs Mary Provis. b 52. Leic Univ BSc74. EMMTC 05. **d** 07 **p** 08. NSM Mickleover All SS *Derby* from 07; NSM Mickleover St Jo from 07. *165A Pastures Hill, Littleover, Derby DE23 4AZ* Tel (01332) 510264

STAUNTON, Richard Steedman. b 25. Wadh Coll Ox BA49 MA50 BSc45. Cuddesdon Coll 63. **d** 64 **p** 65. C Wyken *Cov* 64-68; V Tile Hill 68-76; V Hillmorton 76-90; rtd 90; Perm to Offic *Ban* from 90. *2 Tan-y-fron, Corris Uchaf, Machynlleth SY20 9BN* Tel (01654) 761466

STAVELEY-WADHAM, Robert Andrew. b 43. ACII. Ridley Hall Cam 79. **d** 81 **p** 82. C Saffron Walden w Wendens Ambo and Littlebury *Chelmsf* 81-84; P-in-c Austrey and Warton *Birm* 84-87; Perm to Offic *Chich* 87-02; Ely 88-96; P-in-c Tillington 02-07; P-in-c Duncton 02-07; P-in-c Up Waltham 02-07; rtd 07. *2 Little Bognor Cottage, Little Bognor, Fittleworth, Pulborough RH20 1JT* Tel (01798) 865668 E-mail bobswpic@aol.com

STAVROU, Stephen Francis. b 83. Westcott Ho Cam. **d** 09. C Bedford Park *Lon* from 09. *33 Quick Road, London W4 2BU* Tel 07528-930966 (mobile)
E-mail stephenfrancisstavrou@yahoo.co.uk

STEACY, William Leslie. b 59. UCD BAgrSc82 MAgrSc88 TCD BTh06. CITC 03. **d** 06 **p** 07. C Dunboyne Union *M & K* from 06. *5 Newcastle Woods Crescent, Enfield, Co Meath, Republic of Ireland* Tel (00353) (46) 954 2301
E-mail williamsteacy@eircom.net

STEAD, Andrew Michael. b 63. BA84. Coll of Resurr Mirfield 84. **d** 87 **p** 88. C Wellingborough All Hallows *Pet* 87-90; Chapl St Alb Abbey 90-94; Chapl Aldenham Sch Herts 94-04; Ho Master 01-08; Teacher from 08; Perm to Offic *St Alb* from 04; Assoc Min St Alb Abbey from 05. *7 Wallingford Walk, St Albans AL1 2JL* Tel (01727) 764666
E-mail andrew.stead700@ntlworld.com

STEAD, Philip John. b 60. Sheff Univ LLB82 City of Lon Poly ACII85. Linc Th Coll 95. **d** 95 **p** 96. C Warsop *S'well* 95-99; P-in-c Forest Town from 99; P-in-c Mansfield Oak Tree Lane from 07. *The Vicarage, Old Mill Lane, Forest Town, Mansfield NG19 0EP* Tel (01623) 622177

STEAD, Timothy James. b 60. Ex Univ BSc82. St Steph Ho Ox 93. **d** 95 **p** 97. C Broseley w Benthall, Jackfield, Linley etc *Heref* 95-99; TV Haywards Heath St Wilfrid *Chich* 99-07; P-in-c Headington Quarry *Ox* from 07. *The Vicarage, 46 Quarry Road, Headington, Oxford OX3 8NU* Tel (01865) 307939 *or* 762931
E-mail susieandtim@lycos.co.uk

STEADMAN, Mrs Gloria Ann. b 44. STETS BA04. **d** 04 **p** 05. NSM Farlington *Portsm* 04-08; NSM W Leigh from 08. *Lane*

End House, 63 Glamorgan Road, Waterlooville PO8 0TS Tel (023) 9259 5561 E-mail gloria_nembles@yahoo.co.uk

STEADMAN, Mark John. b 74. Southn Univ LLB95 Ch Coll Cam BA01 MA05 Barrister-at-Law (Inner Temple) 96. Westcott Ho Cam 99. **d** 02 **p** 03. C Portsea St Mary *Portsm* 02-05; P-in-c Camberwell St Phil and St Mark *S'wark* from 05; AD Bermondsey from 08. *St Philip's Vicarage, Avondale Square, London SE1 5PD* Tel (020) 7237 3239
E-mail gonetorome@yahoo.co.uk

STEADMAN, Mrs Wendy Anne Eleanor. b 35. Somerville Coll Ox BA56 MA61. **d** 06 **p** 09. NSM Lache cum Saltney *Ches* from 06. *32 Curzon Park South, Chester CH4 8AB* Tel (01244) 682989
E-mail wsteadman@tiscali.co.uk

STEADMAN-ALLEN, Miss Barbara. b 53. Trent Park Coll of Educn CertEd74 Birm Univ BMus77 ARCM83. Cranmer Hall Dur 88. **d** 90 **p** 94. C Chessington *Guildf* 90-94; C Chertsey 94-99; P-in-c Mickleham 99-01; C Leatherhead and Mickleham 01-04; Chapl Box Hill Sch 99-04; TV Surrey Weald *Guildf* from 04. *The Vicarage, Horsham Road, Holmwood, Dorking RH5 4JX* Tel (01306) 889118 Mobile 07817-006254
E-mail bsa311@freenet.co.uk

STEADY, Miss Vilda May. b 51. Linc Th Coll 87. **d** 89 **p** 94. Par Dn Cannock *Lich* 89-91; Par Dn Hammerwich 91-94; C 94-95; Asst Chapl Eastbourne Hosps NHS Trust 95-97; Chapl Luton and Dunstable Hosp NHS Trust 97-01; Sen Chapl Jas Paget Healthcare NHS Trust from 01. *James Paget Hospital, Lowestoft Road, Gorleston, Great Yarmouth NR31 6LA* Tel (01493) 452452 *or* 452408 E-mail vilda.steady@jpaget.nhs.uk

STEAR, Michael Peter Hutchinson. b 47. Goldsmiths' Coll Lon TCert68. Wycliffe Hall Ox 71. **d** 74 **p** 75. C Streatham Vale H Redeemer *S'wark* 74-77; C-in-c Ramsgate St Mark *Cant* 77-82; V 82-83; Min Jersey St Paul Prop Chpl *Win* 83-94; TR Radipole and Melcombe Regis *Sarum* 94-00; Chapl Weymouth Coll 94-97; rtd 00; Perm to Offic *Sarum* from 01. *132 Preston Road, Weymouth DT3 6BH*

STEAR, Mrs Patricia Ann. b 38. Birm Univ BSc60. **d** 97 **p** 98. OLM Bradford Peverell, Stratton, Frampton etc *Sarum* 97-09; rtd 09; Perm to Offic *Sarum* from 09. *Westwood House, Bradford Peverell, Dorchester DT2 9SE* Tel (01305) 889227 Fax 889718
E-mail patstear@saqnet.co.uk

STEBBING, Christopher Henry. b 64. G&C Coll Cam MEng87 MA90. Cranmer Hall Dur 98. **d** 00 **p** 01. C Malin Bridge *Sheff* 00-04; V Sheff St Jo from 04. *St John's Vicarage, 91 Manor Oaks Road, Sheffield S2 5EA* Tel 0114-272 7423 *or* 272 8678
E-mail chris@stebbingfamily.go-plus.net

STEBBING, Michael Langdale (Nicolas). b 46. Univ of Zimbabwe BA68 UNISA MTh86. Coll of Resurr Mirfield. **d** 74 **p** 75. C Borrowdale *Carl* 74-75; P-in-c Chikwaka Rhodesia 76-77; S Africa 79-86; CR from 80. *House of the Resurrection, Stocks Bank Road, Mirfield WF14 0BN* Tel (01924) 494318

STEDDON, Peter James Raymond. b 46. St Edm Hall Ox BA67 MA71 FCIPD. STETS 96. **d** 99 **p** 00. NSM Goring w S Stoke *Ox* 99-03; Team Missr Langtree from 03; Dir Ind Chapl from 06. *Oxford Industrial Chaplaincy, New Road Baptist Church, Bonn Square, Oxford OX1 1LQ* Tel (01865) 245349 Mobile 07766-514874 E-mail oicdirector@btinternet.com
or petersteddon@hotmail.com

STEDMAN, Barrie John. b 49. **d** 00 **p** 01. OLM Mildenhall *St E* 00-07. *The Cottage, Tudor Grange, Poy Street Green, Rattlesden, Bury St Edmunds IP30 0RX* Tel (01638) 750505 Mobile 07864-0/6896 E-mail barriestedman@aol.com

STEDMAN, Preb Michael Sydney. b 34. MRICS58. Clifton Th Coll 62. **d** 65 **p** 66. C Lindfield *Chich* 65-68; C gt Baddow *Chelmsf* 68-73; TV Ashby w Thurton, Claxton and Carleton *Nor* 73-75; P-in-c 75-85; TV Rockland St Mary w Hellington 73-75; P-in-c 75-85; TV Framingham Pigot 73-75; P-in-c 75-85; TV Bramerton w Surlingham 73-75; P-in-c 75-85; TV Bergh Apton w Yelverton 73-75; P-in-c 75-85; RD Loddon 78-85; R Church Stretton *Heref* 85-99; RD Condover 88-96; Preb Heref Cathl 94-99; rtd 99; Perm to Offic *St E* from 00. *44 The Mowbrays, Framlingham, Woodbridge IP13 9DL* Tel (01728) 724479
E-mail michael@stedmanm.freeserve.co.uk

STEDMAN, Robert Alfred. b 24. Qu Coll Birm 50. **d** 52 **p** 53. C Portchester *Portsm* 52-55; V Brighton St Anne *Chich* 55-61; V Salehurst 61-76; R Newhaven 76-90; rtd 90; Perm to Offic *Chich* 90-99. *12 Lady Wootton's Green, Canterbury CT1 1NG*

STEED, Christopher Denis. b 55. Lon Univ BD92 Ex Univ PGCE01 Bris Univ MSc03 Ex Univ EdD05. Sarum Th Coll 05. **d** 06 **p** 07. C Yatton Moor *B & W* from 06. *227 Mendip Road, Yatton, Bristol BS49 4RZ* Tel (01934) 835258 Mobile 07704-138433 E-mail chrissteed@uwclub.net

STEED, Mrs Helene. b 70. Uppsala Univ MDiv95. Past Inst Uppsala 95. **p** 96. C Stora Melby Sweden 96-97; TV Essunga 97-04; Dean's V Cork Cathl 04-08; I Clones w Killeevan *Clogh* from 08. *The Rectory, Scotshouse, Clones, Co Monaghan, Republic of Ireland* Tel (00353) (47) 56962
E-mail helenesteed@yahoo.com

STEEL, Coralie Mary. b 47. Bedf Coll Lon BA69 Solicitor 73. St Mich Coll Llan 98. **d** 01 **p** 02. NSM Llangunnor w Cwmffrwd

St D from 01. *Llwyn Celyn, 24 Picton Terrace, Carmarthen SA31 3BX* Tel (01267) 236369

STEEL, Graham Reginald. b 51. Cam Univ MA. Trin Coll Bris 80. **d** 83 **p** 84. C Gt Parndon *Chelmsf* 83-86; C Barking St Marg w St Patr 86-89; P-in-c Westcliff St Cedd 89-96; P-in-c Prittlewell St Pet 92-96; Chapl Southend Gen Hosp 89-92; V Prittlewell St Pet w Westcliff St Cedd *Chelmsf* 96-07; P-in-c S Trin Broads *Nor* 07-08; R from 08. *The Rectory, Main Road, Fleggburgh, Great Yarmouth NR29 3AG* Tel (01493) 368210
E-mail grahamsteel@tiscali.co.uk

STEEL, Leslie Frederick. b 34. Webster Univ Geneva MA88. St Jo Coll Auckland 57 LTh65. **d** 59 **p** 60. C Roslyn New Zealand 59-62; V Waimea Plains 62-69; CF 70-73; Singapore 72-73; V Dunstan New Zealand 74-81; Adn Otago 77-82; V Anderson's Bay and Chapl Police Force 82-86; Can Dunedin Cathl 82-85; Adn Dunedin 85-86; Hon C Geneva *Eur* 87-90; Chapl Lausanne 90-97; Perm to Offic *Pet* 98-99; P-in-c Potterspury, Furtho, Yardley Gobion and Cosgrove 99-02; R Potterspury w Furtho and Yardley Gobion etc 02-04; rtd 04. *43 Fidelis Avenue, Snells Beach, Warkworth 0920, New Zealand* Tel (0064) (9) 425 4520
E-mail ehsteel@xtra.co.nz

STEEL, Norman William. b 53. Sarum & Wells Th Coll 85. **d** 87 **p** 88. C S Woodham Ferrers *Chelmsf* 87-91; V Woolavington w Cossington and Bawdrip *B & W* 91-99; P-in-c Pitminster w Corfe 99-02; Chapl Huish Coll Taunton from 99; Perm to Offic *B & W* 02-05. *28 Wilton Street, Taunton TA1 3JR* Tel (01823) 368098 E-mail norman.steel@btinternet.com

STEEL, Richard John. b 57. Dur Univ BA79 Cam Univ MA86 Edin Univ MTh97. Ridley Hall Cam 81. **d** 84 **p** 85. C Hull St Jo Newland *York* 84-87; Relig Broadcasting Officer *Derby* 88-92; Dioc Communications Officer *Blackb* 92-97; Communication Dir CMS 97-05; NSM Stoke-next-Guildf 00-05; R Kirkheaton *Wakef* from 05; RD Almondbury from 06. *The New Rectory, Church Lane, Kirkheaton, Huddersfield HD5 0BH* Tel (01484) 532410 E-mail richard.steel@ntlworld.com

STEEL, Thomas Molyneux. b 39. Man Univ BA61. Ripon Hall Ox 61. **d** 63 **p** 64. C Newc H Cross 63-66; P-in-c Man St Aid 66-71; R Failsworth St Jo 71-79; P-in-c Farnham Royal *Ox* 79-81; P-in-c Hedgerley 80-81; R Farnham Royal w Hedgerley 81-91; V Prescot *Liv* 91-03; rtd 03; Perm to Offic *Lon* from 04. *20 Barnet Way, London NW7 3BH* Tel (020) 8906 0271

STEELE, Alan Christopher. b 63. Cape Town Univ BA85 Univ of Zimbabwe BA91. Gaul Ho Harare 89. **d** 91 **p** 93. C Harare St Mary Magd 91-93; C Harare St Luke 93-95; Chapl Ruzawi Sch 96-99; CF from 99. *c/o MOD Chaplains (Army)* Tel (01980) 615804 Fax 615800

STEELE, Charles Edward Ernest. b 24. Cuddesdon Coll 72. **d** 74 **p** 75. C Rubery *Birm* 74-77; P-in-c Shaw Hill 77-79; V 79-82; C Curdworth 82-83; C Curdworth w Castle Vale 83-85; rtd 85; Perm to Offic *Birm* from 85. *3 Dominic Drive, Middleton Hall Road, Birmingham B30 1DW* Tel 0121-451 3372

STEELE, Derek James. b 53. St Jo Coll Nottm. **d** 97 **p** 98. Aux Min Ballywillan *Conn* from 97. *106 Mountsandel Road, Coleraine BT52 1TA* Tel (028) 7035 1633

STEELE, Edwin Harry. b 80. Mattersey Hall BA05. Ridley Hall Cam 06. **d** 08 **p** 09. C Ecclesall *Sheff* from 08. *30 Montrose Road, Sheffield S7 2EE* Tel 0114-258 5895
E-mail harry@uncutproject.com

STEELE, Canon Gordon John. b 55. Kent Univ BA76 Worc Coll Ox BA82 MA87. Coll of Resurr Mirfield 82. **d** 84 **p** 85. C Greenhill St Jo *Lon* 84-88; C Uxbridge St Andr w St Jo 88; TV Uxbridge 88-94; V Northampton St Alb *Pet* 94-01; V Pet St Jo from 01; RD Pet from 04; Can Pet Cathl from 04. *26 Minster Precincts, Peterborough PE1 1XZ* Tel (01733) 566265
E-mail gordon@gsteele.entadsl.com

STEELE, Keith Atkinson. b 28. CEng MIMechE FInstMC. Qu Coll Birm Oak Hill Th Coll 80. **d** 81 **p** 82. NSM Westoning w Tingrith *St Alb* 81-87; NSM Chalgrave 87-88; P-in-c 88-96; RD Dunstable 91-96; Perm to Offic from 96. *Mariner's Lodge, Church Road, Westoning, Bedford MK45 5JW* Tel (01525) 714111

STEELE, Peter Gerald. b 44. Bournemouth Tech Coll BSc67 Essex Univ MSc69. Sarum & Wells Th Coll 91. **d** 93 **p** 94. C Beaminster Area *Sarum* 93-97; P-in-c Aldermaston w Wasing and Brimpton *Ox* 97-08; P-in-c Woolhampton w Midgham and Beenham Valance 05-08; R Aldermaston and Woolhampton from 08; AD Bradfield from 07. *The Vicarage, Wasing Lane, Aldermaston, Reading RG7 4LX* Tel 0118-971 2281
E-mail petesteele@btinternet.com

STEELE, Canon Terence. b 54. Linc Th Coll 85. **d** 87 **p** 88. C New Sleaford *Linc* 87-90; V Cowbit 90-95; P-in-c Burgh le Marsh 95-97; V 97-06; P-in-c Orby 95-97; V 97-06; P-in-c Bratoft w Irby-in-the-Marsh 95-97; R 97-06; P-in-c Welton-le-Marsh w Gunby 95-97; R 97-06, R Burgh Gp from 06; RD Calcewaithe and Candleshoe from 05; Can and Preb Linc Cathl from 07. *The Vicarage, Glebe Rise, Burgh le Marsh, Skegness PE24 5BL* Tel (01754) 810216 E-mail father.terry@btclick.com

STEELE-PERKINS, Mrs Barbara Anita. b 46. Whitelands Coll Lon CertEd68 Spurgeon's Coll MTh98. STETS 99. **d** 01 **p** 02.

Tutor Local Min Progr *Guildf* from 95; NSM Wisley w Pyrford 01-04; NSM Haslemere and Grayswood from 04. *Church House, Church Close, Grayswood, Haslemere GU27 2DB* Tel (01428) 656504 E-mail barbarasteeleperkins@tiscali.co.uk

STEELE-PERKINS, Richard De Courcy. b 36. Clifton Th Coll 61. **d** 64 **p** 65. C Stoke Damerel *Ex* 64-65; C Washfield 65-68; P-in-c Wimbledon *S'wark* 68-70; Chapl Lambeth Hosp 70-74; Asst Chapl St Thos Hosp Lon 70-74; P-in-c Tawstock *Ex* 74-75; R 75-81; P-in-c Sticklepath 74-75; R 75-81; V Buckfastleigh w Dean Prior 81-91; TR Camelot Par *B & W* 91-94; Asst Chapl R Surrey Co and St Luke's Hosps NHS Trust 94-99; Asst Chapl Heathlands Mental Health Trust Surrey 94-99; P-in-c Ockham w Hatchford *Guildf* 99-01; rtd 02; Hon C E Horsley and Ockham w Hatchford and Downside *Guildf* 02-04; Perm to Offic from 04. *Church House, Church Close, Grayswood, Haslemere GU27 2DB* Tel (01428) 656504 E-mail richard@steele-perkins.fsnet.co.uk

STEEN, Canon Jane Elizabeth. b 64. Newnham Coll Cam BA88 MA90 PhD92. Westcott Ho Cam 93. **d** 96 **p** 97. C Chipping Barnet w Arkley *St Alb* 96-99; Chapl and Personal Asst to Bp S'wark 99-05; Hon Chapl S'wark Cathl 00-05; Chan and Can Th and Dir Min Tr from 05. *2 Harmsworth Mews, London SE11 4SQ* Tel (020) 7820 8079 *or* 7939 9449 Fax 7939 9466 E-mail jane.steen@southwark.anglican.org

STEER, Norman William. b 35. MBE00. SRN57. EAMTC 01. **d** 03 **p** 04. NSM Dickleburgh and The Pulhams *Nor* from 03. *Brook Cottage, Harleston Road, Starston, Harleston IP20 9NL* Tel (01379) 854245 Mobile 07941-473255 E-mail norman@nandrsteer.com

STEIN, Ms Ann Elizabeth. b 57. Loughb Univ BSc78 Liv Hope MA01. NOC 05. **d** 07 **p** 08. C Ormskirk *Liv* from 07. *5 Hillcrest Road, Ormskirk L39 1NH*

STEINBERG, Eric Reed (Joseph). b 65. Trin Coll Bris BA94. **d** 94 **p** 95. C Chigwell and Chigwell Row *Chelmsf* 94-99; Dir Y2000 99-00; Dir Jews for Jesus UK 00-05; Dir CMS from 05. *CMS, PO Box 1799, Oxford OX4 9BN* Tel 08456-201799 E-mail kosherjoe@mac.com

STEINER, Eduard Samuel. b 52. Liv Univ MB, ChB74. EMMTC 93. **d** 96 **p** 97. NSM Ravenshead *S'well* 96-03; Lic to Offic from 03. *La Corbière, Cauldwell Drive, Mansfield NG18 4SL* Tel (01623) 653615 Mobile 07971-546470

STELL, Peter Donald. b 50. Leeds Univ 74 Southn Univ BA81 Man Univ 93 MInstM. Sarum & Wells Th Coll 78. **d** 81 **p** 82. C Rothwell w Lofthouse *Ripon* 81-85; TV Brayton *York* 85-87; Chapl Asst Leybourne Grange Hosp W Malling 87-88; Chapl Asst Kent, Sussex and Pembury Hosps Tunbridge Wells 87-88; C Spalding St Jo w Deeping St Nicholas *Linc* 87-93; Chapl S Lincs HA Mental Handicap Unit 88-93; Chapl HM Pris Liv 93-94; Chapl HM Pris Wayland 94-99; Chapl HM Pris Grendon and Spring Hill 99-02; Chapl HM Pris Rye Hill 02-05; Chapl HM Pris N Sea Camp from 05. *HM Prison North Sea Camp, Croppers Lane, Freiston, Boston PE22 0QX* Tel (01205) 769300 Fax 769301

STENHOUSE, Joan Frances Fleming. b 45. RGN66. Ab Dioc Tr Course 82. **dss** 84 **d** 86 **p** 94. Ellon and Cruden Bay *Ab* 84-97; NSM 86-97; Bp's Chapl for Tr and Educn 95-97; Asst P Cuminestown 97-00; C Nova Scotia St Martin Canada from 00. *27 Birch Grove, Upper Tantallon NS B3Z 1L1, Canada* E-mail jstenhouse@bwr.eastlink.ca

STENTIFORD, Canon Pauline Cecilia Elizabeth. b 48. EAMTC 98. **d** 00 **p** 01. NSM Gt and Lt Bealings w Playford and Culpho *St E* 00-03; P-in-c from 03; RD Woodbridge from 05; Hon Can St E Cathl from 08. *Sheepstor, Boyton, Woodbridge IP12 3LH* Tel (01394) 411469 E-mail pauline.stentiford@btopenworld.com

STEPHEN, Canon Kenneth George. b 47. Strathclyde Univ BA69 Edin Univ BD72. Edin Th Coll 69. **d** 72 **p** 73. C Ayr *Glas* 72-75; R Renfrew 75-80; R Motherwell 80-93; R Wishaw 80-93; R Kilmarnock 93-06; R Dalbeattie from 06; Can St Mary's Cathl from 87; Syn Clerk from 87. *The Rectory, 1 Alpine Terrace, Dalbeattie DG5 4HJ* Tel (01556) 610671 E-mail ken.stephen@tiscali.co.uk

STEPHEN, Robert. b 63. Lon Bible Coll BA85 Westmr Coll Ox MTh96 FSAScot01. EMMTC. **d** 04 **p** 05. In Bapt Min 85-97; NSM Burbage w Aston Flamville *Leic* from 04; Perm to Offic *Cov* from 05; Chapl K Henry VIII Sch Cov from 07. *Small Change, 4 Woodland Road, Hinckley LE10 1JG* Tel (01455) 615503 Mobile 07957-312892 E-mail revrstephen@ntlworld.com

STEPHENI, Frederick William. b 28. TD73. FSAScot81 FRSA82 Cranfield Inst of Tech MSc82. Lambeth STh83 Qu Coll Birm 54. **d** 55 **p** 56. C Arnold *S'well* 55-57; P-in-c 57-58; P-in-c Hucknall Torkard 58-59; Chapl Stoke-on-Trent City Gen Hosp 59-62; Chapl N Staffs R Infirmary Stoke-on-Trent 59-62; CF (TA) 60-88; Chapl K Coll Hosp Lon 62-63; R Cotgrave *S'well* 63-76; V Owthorpe 63-76; Chapl Addenbrooke's Hosp Cam 76-88; Lic to Offic *Ely* 76-99; rtd 88; Perm to Offic *York* from 00. *64A Scarborough Road, Norton, Malton YO17 8AE* Tel (01653) 694995

STEPHENS, Anthony Wayne. b 54. Surrey Univ BSc80. St Jo Coll Nottm 02. **d** 04 **p** 05. C Preston w Sutton Poyntz and Osmington w Poxwell *Sarum* 04-08; C Pioneer Min Weymouth Town Cen from 08. *16 Lynmoor Road, Weymouth DT4 7TW* Tel (01305) 780844

STEPHENS, Canon Archibald John. b 15. Selw Coll Cam BA37 MA44. Wells Th Coll 46. **d** 47 **p** 48. C Gt Malvern St Mary *Worc* 47-50; Nigeria 50-68 and 70-71; Hon Can Ondo 57-71; Hon Can Owerri from 71; C Swindon Ch Ch *Bris* 68-70; C-in-c Ash Vale CD *Guildf* 71-72; V Ash Vale 72-77; P-in-c Thursley 77-82; rtd 82; Perm to Offic *Guildf* 85-06. *26 Cruse Close, Sway, Lymington SO41 6AY* Tel (01590) 682097 E-mail resfernhill@aol.com

STEPHENS, Grahame Frank Henry. b 33. **d** 02 **p** 03. OLM Woolwich St Mary w St Mich *S'wark* 02-05; Perm to Offic from 05. *121 The Drive, Bexley DA5 3BY* Tel (020) 8303 3546 Fax 8306 2155 Mobile 07775-796896

STEPHENS, Canon Harold William Barrow. b 47. Lon Univ BEd71. S Dios Minl Tr Scheme 80. **d** 82 **p** 83. NSM Heytesbury and Sutton Veny *Sarum* 82-83; NSM Bishopstrow and Boreham 83-91; Dep Hd Master Westwood St Thos Sch Salisbury 91-99; P-in-c Market Lavington and Easterton 99-03; P-in-c W Lavington and the Cheverells 02-03; R The Lavingtons, Cheverells, and Easterton 03-07; TR Dorchester from 07; P-in-c The Winterbournes and Compton Valence from 09; Can and Preb Sarum Cathl from 09. *The Rectory, 17A Edward Road, Dorchester DT1 2HL* Tel and fax (01305) 268434 E-mail harold.stephens@ukonline.co.uk

STEPHENS, James Charles. b 62. **d** 91 **p** 92. C Kilcolman w Kiltallagh, Killorglin, Knockane etc *L & K* from 91. *Kilderry, Miltown, Co Kerry, Republic of Ireland* Tel (00353) (66) 976 7735 E-mail jstephens@klinge.ie

STEPHENS, Mrs Jean. b 46. St As Minl Tr Course. **d** 89 **p** 97. NSM Gwernaffield and Llanferres *St As* 89-02; NSM Hawarden from 02. *Noddfa, Pen-y-Fron Road, Pantymwyn, Mold CH7 5EF* Tel (01352) 740037

STEPHENS, Jill. *See* STEPHENS, Mrs Rosemary Jill

STEPHENS, Mrs Joan. b 38. Dioc OLM tr scheme 97. **d** 00 **p** 01. OLM Irlam *Man* from 00; OLM Cadishead from 09. *77 Baines Avenue, Irlam, Manchester M44 6AS* Tel 0161-775 7538

STEPHENS, Mrs Joanna Louise. b 69. St Jo Coll Nottm BA08. **d** 08 **p** 09. C Bramcote *S'well* from 08. *22 Church Street, Bramcote, Nottingham NG9 3HD* Tel 0115-943 0177 Mobile 07890-385133 E-mail joke.stephens@talktalk.net

STEPHENS, John. *See* STEPHENS, Canon Archibald John

STEPHENS, John Michael. b 29. MRICS52. Lich Th Coll 62. **d** 64 **p** 65. C Birchington w Acol *Cant* 64-70; V Tovil 70-79; V Brabourne w Smeeth 79-94; Rtd N Lympne 87-94; rtd 94; Perm to Offic *York* from 94. *Southacre, Kirby Mills, Kirkbymoorside, York YO62 6NR* Tel (01751) 432766

STEPHENS (née FLIPPANCE), Mrs Kim Sheelagh May. b 64. RGN85 RM88. Trin Coll Bris 97. **d** 99 **p** 00. C Alderbury Team *Sarum* 99-01; C Clarendon 01-02; Asst Chapl Salisbury Health Care NHS Trust from 02. *The Chaplain's Office, Salisbury District Hospital, Salisbury SP2 8BJ* Tel (01722) 336262 E-mail chaplains.department@salisbury.nhs.uk

STEPHENS, Martin Nicholas. b 64. Brunel Univ BSc88 Nottm Univ MTh01. St Jo Coll Nottm 99. **d** 01 **p** 02. C Newchapel *Lich* 01-04; TV Stoke Bucknall from 04. *St John's Parsonage, 28 Greasley Road, Stoke-on-Trent ST2 8JE* Tel (01782) 542861

STEPHENS, Michael. *See* STEPHENS, John Michael

STEPHENS, Paul. b 53. AGSM73 Newton Park Coll Bath PGCE74. Trin Coll Bris 91. **d** 93 **p** 94. C S Molton w Nymet St George, High Bray etc *Ex* 93-97; R Norton Fitzwarren *B & W* 97-99; Chapl St Aug Sch Taunton 97-99; Chapl Monkton Combe Sch Bath 99-08; P-in-c Winford w Felton Common Hill *B & W* from 08. *The Rectory, 4 Parsonage Lane, Winford, Bristol BS40 8DG* Tel (01275) 474636

STEPHENS, Mrs Penny Clare. b 60. St Anne's Coll Ox BA83 Lon Inst of Educn PGCE85. Oak Hill Th Coll. **d** 99 **p** 00. C Turnham Green Ch Ch *Lon* 99-03; P-in-c Brasted *Roch* from 03. *The Rectory, Coles Lane, Brasted, Westerham TN16 1NR* Tel (01959) 565829

STEPHENS, Canon Peter John. b 42. Oriel Coll Ox BA64 MA67. Clifton Th Coll 63. **d** 68 **p** 68. C Lenton *S'well* 68-71; C Brixton Hill St Sav *S'wark* 71-73; P-in-c 73-82; TV Barnham Broom *Nor* 82-89; V Gorleston St Mary 89-94; RD Flegg (Gt Yarmouth) 92-94; P-in-c High Oak 94-97; RD Humbleyard 95-98; C Hingham w Wood Rising w Scoulton 96-97; TR High Oak, Hingham and Scoulton w Wood Rising 97-05; Hon Can Nor Cathl 99-05; rtd 05. *15 Church Row, Wootton, Bedford MK43 9HQ* Tel (01234) 765403 Mobile 07768-425349 *or* 07973-322513 E-mail peterstephens@aol.com

STEPHENS, Preb Peter Stanley. b 33. **d** 59 **p** 60. C Paignton St Paul Preston *Ex* 59-64; V Buckland Monachorum 64-74; RD Tavistock 70-74; V Compton Gifford 74-85; RD Plymouth Sutton 83-86; Preb Ex Cathl 84-05; TR Plymouth Em w Efford 85-86; R Thurlestone w S Milton 86-98; rtd 98. *Headland View, 14 Court Park, Thurlestone, Kingsbridge TQ7 3LX* Tel and fax (01548) 560891

STEPHENS, Richard William. b 37. Dur Univ BSc62. Cranmer Hall Dur 62. **d** 64 **p** 65. C Hensingham *Carl* 64-67; C Norbury *Ches* 67-71; R Elworth and Warmingham 71-79; V Bootle St Matt *Liv* 79-89; P-in-c Litherland St Andr 79-83; P-in-c Failsworth H Trin *Man* 89-93; R 93-02; P-in-c Oldham St Barn 01-02; AD Oldham 99-02; rtd 02; Hon C Dalbeattie *Glas* from 02. *Cloverstone, 3 Craignair Street, Dalbeattie DG5 4AX* Tel (01556) 610627 E-mail revrstephens@btinternet.com

STEPHENS, Mrs Rosemary Jill. b 46. SRN68. WEMTC 96. **d** 08. NSM Walford and St John, Howle Hill etc *Heref* 08; NSM Llangarron w Llangrove, Whitchurch and Ganarew 08; NSM Goodrich, Marstow, Welsh Bicknor, Llangarron etc from 08. *Sunnyside Cottage, Coppett Hill, Goodrich, Ross-on-Wye HR9 6JG* Tel (01600) 890975 E-mail jill.stephens1@btinternet.com

STEPHENS, Canon Simon Edward. b 41. OBE97. Qu Coll Birm PhD80. Bps' Coll Cheshunt 63. **d** 67 **p** 68. C Cov St Mark 67-71; C Lillington 71-76; C-in-c Canley CD 76-79; V Canley 79-80; Chapl RN 80-97; Asst Chapl Menorca *Eur* 97-98; Chapl 98-99; Chapl Moscow from 99; Hon Can Malta Cathl from 01. *British Embassy - Moscow, FCO, King Charles Street, London SW1A 2AH* Tel and fax (007) (495) 629 0990 E-mail chaplain@standrewsmoscow.org

STEPHENS, Mrs Susanne Hilary. b 44. St Jo Coll Nottm. Guildf Dioc Min Course. **d** 00 **p** 01. OLM Camberley St Paul *Guildf* from 00. *St Paul's Church, Crawley Ridge, Camberley GU15 2AD* Tel (01276) 700210 E-mail suestephens@onetel.com

STEPHENSON, David John. b 65. Bris Univ BSc(Soc)87 Dur Univ BA91. Cranmer Hall Dur 92. **d** 92 **p** 93. C Whickham *Dur* 92-94; C Sunderland Pennywell St Thos 94-97; V Stockton St Jo and Stockton St Jas 99-06; V W Dulwich All SS *S'wark* from 06. *The Vicarage, 165 Rosendale Road, London SE21 8LN* Tel (020) 8670 0826 E-mail david.stephenson2@ntlworld.com

STEPHENSON, Canon Eric George. b 41. Bede Coll Dur CertEd63. Qu Coll Birm. **d** 66 **p** 67. C Wakef St Jo 66-69; C Seaham w Seaham Harbour *Dur* 69-73; C Cockerton 73-75; Lic to Offic 75-85; V E Boldon 85-08; AD Jarrow 92-01; Hon Can Dur Cathl 93-08; rtd 08; Chapl to The Queen from 02. *39 Haversham Park, Sunderland SR5 1HW* Tel 0191-549 5278 E-mail ericgstephenson@googlemail.com

STEPHENSON, Ian Clarke. b 24. Tyndale Hall Bris 52. **d** 56 **p** 57. C Bedworth *Cov* 56-58; C Edgware *Lon* 58-65; R Biddulph Moor *Lich* 65-70; Hon C Biddulph 70-88; Hon C Burslem 85-88; New Zealand from 87; rtd 89. *5 Arthur Terrace, Balclutha 9230, New Zealand* Tel (0064) (3) 418 2657 E-mail clarkeia@es.co.nz

STEPHENSON, Mrs Jane Eleanor. b 50. Leeds Univ BA72 PGCE73. **d** 05 **p** 06. NSM Bunbury and Tilstone Fearnall *Ches* 05-09; Educn and Tr Officer 07-09; P-in-c Tilston and Shocklach from 09; Past Worker Tr Officer from 06. *The Mount, Hobb Hill, Tilston, Malpas SY14 7DU* Tel (01829) 250249 *or* 250628 E-mail stephenson256@btinternet.com

STEPHENSON, John Joseph. b 35. St Jo Coll Dur BA74. Qu Coll Birm 75. **d** 76 **p** 77. C Whitworth w Spennymoor *Dur* 76-79; V Eppleton 79-96; rtd 96; Perm to Offic *Dur* from 96. *29 Launceston Drive, Sunderland SR3 3QB* Tel 0191-528 2144

STEPHENSON (née BRYAN), Judith Claire. b 57. Aston Univ BSc79 PhD82 Trent Poly PGCE83. St Jo Coll Nottm BTh94 LTh95. **d** 95 **p** 96. C Wolverhampton St Matt *Lich* 95-99; Chapl Hull Univ 99-08; Chapl W Lon YMCA from 08. *Flat B, Edenhall, Montpelier Road, London W5 2QT* Tel (020) 8991 9134 Mobile 07880-602577

STEPHENSON, Juliet. b 69. St Jo Coll Dur BA05. Cranmer Hall Dur 03. **d** 05 **p** 06. C Retford *S'well* 05-08; V Newnham w Awre and Blakeney *Glouc* from 08. *The Vicarage, 1 Whetstones, Unlawater Lane, Newnham GL14 1BT* Tel (01594) 516690 E-mail juliet_stephenson@hotmail.com

STEPHENSON, Martin Woodard. b 55. St Cath Coll Cam BA77 MA82. Westcott Ho Cam 78. **d** 81 **p** 82. C Eastleigh *Win* 81-85; C Ferryhill *Dur* 85-87; Asst Dir of Ords 87-89; Chapl St Chad's Coll 87-89; TR Clarendon Park St Jo w Knighton St Mich *Leic* 89-98; P-in-c Hall Green St Pet *Birm* 98-99; V from 99. *St Peter's Vicarage, 33 Paradise Lane, Birmingham B28 0DY* Tel 0121-777 1935 E-mail martinw.stephenson@virgin.net

STEPHENSON, Nicolas William. b 22. Ely Th Coll 60. **d** 62 **p** 63. C S Westoe *Dur* 62-65; CR 68-74; Hon C Westgate Common *Wakef* 74-75; Lic to Offic 75-87; Asst Chapl HM Pris Wakef 84-87; rtd 87; Perm to Offic *Ripon* 87-02. *24 Nicholson Court, 25 Fitzroy Drive, Leeds LS8 4AP* Tel 0113-248 5166

STEPHENSON, Norman Keith. b 62. St Jo Coll Cam MA88 Strathclyde Univ MBA91. NEOC 04. **d** 07 **p** 08. NSM Kingston upon Hull H Trin *York* 07-08; NSM Ealing St Pet Mt Park *Lon* from 08. *Flat B, Edenhall, Montpelier Road, London W5 2QT* Tel (020) 8991 9134 Mobile 07880-602577 E-mail n.k.stephenson@btinternet.com

STEPHENSON, Canon Robert. b 36. St Chad's Coll Dur BA58. **d** 60 **p** 61. C Whickham *Dur* 60-63; C Gateshead St Mary 63-65; PC Low Team 65-67; R Stella 67-74; V Comberton *Ely* 74-04; RD Bourn 94-97; P-in-c Dry Drayton 97-01; Hon Can Ely Cathl 01-04; rtd 04; Perm to Offic *Ely* from 04. *1 Porthmore*

Close, Highfields, Caldecote, Cambridge CB23 7ZR Tel (01954) 210638

STEPHENSON, Simon George. b 44. St Jo Coll Dur BA67. Trin Coll Bris 74. **d** 76 **p** 77. C Hildenborough *Roch* 76-82; C Bishopsworth *Bris* 82-85; C-in-c Withywood CD 85-90; TV Wreningham *Nor* 90-97; P-in-c Tasburgh w Tharston, Forncett and Flordon 94-97; TV High Oak, Hingham and Scoulton w Wood Rising 98-05; Asst Chapl HM Pris Wayland from 98. *The Chaplain's Office, HM Prison Wayland, Griston, Thetford IP25 6RL* Tel (01953) 804080 *or* 804100

STEPNEY, Area Bishop of. *See* OLIVER, The Rt Revd Stephen John

STERLING, Anne. *See* HASELHURST, Mrs Anne

STERLING, John Haddon. b 40. Pemb Coll Cam BA62 MA66. Cuddesdon Coll 63. **d** 65 **p** 66. C Pretoria Cathl 65-69; Lic to Offic Natal 69-70; Chapl Bris Cathl 71-74; Member Dioc Soc and Ind Team 71-74; Ind Chapl *Linc* 74-87; Ind Chapl *Ripon* 87-92; TV Hanley H Ev and Min in Ind *Lich* 92-97; P-in-c Hixon w Stowe-by-Chartley 97-02; P-in-c Fradswell, Gayton, Milwich and Weston 97-02; TR Mid Trent 02-06; rtd 06; Perm to Offic *Lich* from 07. *10 Newquay Avenue, Stafford ST17 0EB* Tel (01785) 662870

STERRY, Christopher. b 54. K Coll Lon BD77 AKC77. Episc Sem Austin Texas 78 St Jo Coll Nottm 79. **d** 80 **p** 81. C Huddersfield St Jo *Wakef* 80-84; V Middlestown 84-89; Chapl and Tutor NOC 89-94; Lect Ches Coll of HE 93-94; NSM Padgate *Liv* 92-94; Bp's Dom Chapl *Blackb* 94-97; Chapl Whalley Abbey 94-97; Warden 97-04; V Whalley 97-09; P-in-c Sabden and Pendleton 07-09; C Colne and Villages from 09. *Christ Church Vicarage, Keighley Road, Colne BB8 7HF* Tel 07010-717992 (mobile)

STERRY, Timothy John. b 34. Oriel Coll Ox BA58 MA62. Wycliffe Hall Ox 58. **d** 60 **p** 61. C Cromer *Nor* 60-64; Chapl Oundle Sch 64-72; Teacher Cheam Prep Sch 72-75; Hd Master Temple Grove Sch E Sussex 75-80; Team Ldr Scripture Union Independent Schs 81-99; rtd 00; Perm to Offic *Sarum* from 02. *60 Amberwood, Ferndown BH22 9JT* Tel (01202) 873053 E-mail tim@sterry.org

STEVEN, Canon David Bowring. b 38. AKC64. **d** 64 **p** 65. C Grantham St Wulfram *Linc* 64-68; S Africa 68-75; C Bramley *Ripon* 76-77; V Sutton Valence w E Sutton and Chart Sutton *Cant* 77-82; P-in-c Littlebourne 82-86; V Mansfield Woodhouse *S'well* 86-98; P-in-c Mullion *Truro* 98-03; RD Kerrier 01-03; Hon Can Truro Cathl 03 and from 04; rtd 03; Perm to Offic *Truro* from 03. *5 Guinea Port Parc, Wadebridge PL27 7BY* Tel (01208) 815393

STEVEN, James Henry Stevenson. b 62. CCC Cam MA84 St Jo Coll Dur BA87 K Coll Lon PhD99. Cranmer Hall Dur 84. **d** 87 **p** 88. C Welling *Roch* 87-91; C Bournemouth St Jo w St Mich *Win* 91-94; TV Bournemouth St Pet w St Swithun, H Trin etc 94-00; Chapl Bournemouth and Poole Coll of FE 94-00; Tutor Trin Coll Bris from 00. *Trinity College, Stoke Hill, Bristol BS9 1JP* Tel 0117-968 2803 E-mail james.steven@trinity-bris.ac.uk

STEVEN, Richard John. b 54. Oak Hill Th Coll BA99. **d** 99 **p** 01. Asst P Bluff Pt Australia 00-03; P-in-c Horsmonden *Roch* from 04. *The Rectory, Goudhurst Road, Horsmonden, Tonbridge TN12 8JU* Tel (01892) 722521 E-mail richard.steven@diocese-rochester.org

STEVENETTE, John Maclachlan. b 30. St Pet Coll Ox MA60. Ripon Hall Ox 60. **d** 61 **p** 62. C Newhaven *Chich* 61-66; R Lynch w Iping Marsh 66-74; R Birdham w W Itchenor 74-78; R Byfleet *Guildf* 78-86; V Whittlesey *Ely* 86-90; TR Whittlesey and Pondersbridge 91; R Itchen Valley *Win* 91-99; rtd 99; Perm to Offic *Bris* from 00. *35 Ballard Chase, Abingdon OX14 1XQ* Tel (01235) 526706

STEVENETTE, Simon Melville. b 62. Hull Univ BA83. Wycliffe Hall Ox 84. **d** 87 **p** 88. C Carterton *Ox* 87-90; C Keynsham *B & W* 90-91; TV 91-98; Chapl Keynsham Hosp Bris 92-98; V Swindon Ch Ch *Bris* from 98. *Christ Church Vicarage, 26 Cricklade Street, Swindon SN1 3HG* Tel and fax (01793) 529166 *or* tel 522832 Mobile 07880-710117 E-mail simon@stevenette.freeserve.co.uk

STEVENS, Andrew. *See* STEVENS, John David Andrew

STEVENS, Andrew Graham. b 54. BEd MA. Coll of Resurr Mirfield. **d** 83 **p** 84. C Leigh Park *Portsm* 83-87; TV Brighton Resurr *Chich* 87-94; V Plumstead St Nic *S'wark* from 94. *St Nicholas's Vicarage, 64 Purrett Road, London SE18 1JP* Tel (020) 8854 0461 Fax 8265 5065 E-mail frandrew@dircon.co.uk

STEVENS, Canon Anne Helen. b 61. Warwick Univ BA82 Fitzw Coll Cam BA90 MA94 Heythrop Coll Lon MTh99. Ridley Hall Cam 88. **d** 91 **p** 94. Par Dn E Greenwich Ch Ch w St Andr and St Mich *S'wark* 91-94; Chapl Trin Coll Cam 94-99; P-in-c Battersea St Mich *S'wark* 99-07; V from 07; Dir Readers' Tr from 99; Hon Can S'wark Cathl from 05. *93 Bolingbroke Grove, London SW11 6HA* Tel (020) 7228 1990 E-mail anne.stevens@southwark.anglican.org

STEVENS, Anthony Harold. b 46. CEng71 MIStructE71 FIStructE87 MICE75 FICE92. St Mich Coll Llan 94. **d** 95 **p** 96.

C Cardiff St Jo *Llan* 95-98; TV Cowbridge 98-01; R Eglwysilan 01-08; R Gelligaer from 08; AD Caerphilly from 04. *The Rectory, Church Road, Gelligaer, Hengoed CF82 8FW* Tel (01443) 830300 E-mail revtonystevens@sky.com

STEVENS, Brian Henry. b 28. Oak Hill Th Coll. **d** 69 **p** 70. C Chadwell *Chelmsf* 69-75; V Penge Ch Ch w H Trin *Roch* 75-85; V St Mary Cray and St Paul's Cray 85-93; rtd 93; Perm to Offic *Cant* from 93. *53 Middle Deal Road, Deal CT14 9RG*

STEVENS, Brian Henry. b 45. Open Univ BA80. S Dios Minl Tr Scheme 81. **d** 84 **p** 85. NSM S Malling *Chich* 84-86; C Langney 86-87; TV Wolverton *Ox* 87-88; V Welford w Sibbertoft and Marston Trussell *Pet* 88-91; V Hardingstone and Horton and Piddington from 91. *The Vicarage, 29 Back Lane, Hardingstone, Northampton NN4 6BY* Tel (01604) 760110 Fax 702547 Mobile 07710-207201 E-mail fr.brian@tesco.net

STEVENS, Cyril David Richard. b 25. NZ Bd of Th Studies. **d** 59 **p** 60. New Zealand 59-65 and 67-68; V Playford w Culpho and Tuddenham St Martin *St E* 65-67; R Rendham w Sweffling and Cransford 69-73; RD Saxmundham 72-74; R Rendham w Sweffling 73-95; rtd 95; Perm to Offic *St E* from 95. *Meadow Cottage, Low Road, Marlesford, Woodbridge IP13 0AW* Tel (01728) 746013

STEVENS, David Charles. b 31. Keble Coll Ox BA55 MA59. Wycliffe Hall Ox 55. **d** 57 **p** 58. C Plymouth St Andr *Ex* 57-60; S Rhodesia 61-65; Rhodesia 65-66; Asst Chapl Bryanston Sch 66-70; Chapl 70-73; P-in-c Shilling Okeford *Sarum* 73-76; Chapl Chigwell Sch Essex 76-86; R Tarrant Valley *Sarum* 86-94; rtd 94; Perm to Offic *Sarum* from 94. *Bumble Cottage, 3 Yondover, Loders, Bridport DT6 4NW* Tel (01308) 421025

STEVENS, David John. b 45. Bris Univ BA67. Clifton Th Coll. **d** 70 **p** 71. C Ex St Leon w H Trin 70-75; P-in-c Lt Burstead *Chelmsf* 75-77; TV Billericay and Lt Burstead 77-81; P-in-c Illogan *Truro* 81-83; R St Illogan 83-96; RD Carnmarth N 96; V Highworth w Sevenhampton and Inglesham etc *Bris* 96-01; P-in-c Constantine *Truro* from 01; RD Kerrier from 03. *The Vicarage, Chalbury Heights Brill, Constantine, Falmouth TR11 5UR* Tel (01326) 340259

STEVENS, Pauline Lynne. b 59. Poly of Wales BA81 York St Jo Coll MA06. NOC 99. **d** 02 **p** 03. C Horsforth *Ripon* 02-06; P-in-c Potternewton from 06; Chapl Abbey Grange High Sch Leeds from 04. *St Martin's Vicarage, 2A St Martin's View, Leeds LS7 3LB* Tel 0113-262 4271 Mobile 07963-060911 E-mail davidstev1@aol.com

STEVENS, David Norman. b 44. QPM91. EAMTC 01. **d** 03 **p** 04. NSM Necton, Holme Hale w N and S Pickenham *Nor* 03-05; Asst Chapl HM Pris Wayland 04-06; New Zealand from 06. *Address temp unknown* E-mail david.sue.stevens@hotmail.co.uk

STEVENS, Douglas George. b 47. Lon Univ BA69. Westcott Ho Cam 69. **d** 72 **p** 73. C Portsea St Geo CD *Portsm* 72-75; C Portsea N End St Mark 75-79; Chapl NE Lon Poly *Chelmsf* 79-83; C-in-c Orton Goldhay CD *Ely* 83-87; V Elm 87-91; V Coldham 87-91; V Friday Bridge 87-91; R Woodston 91-98; P-in-c Fletton 94-98; rtd 98. *28 Francis Gardens, Peterborough PE1 3XX* Tel (01733) 755430

STEVENS, Frederick Crichton. b 42. K Coll Lon BD78 AKC78. St Steph Ho Ox 78. **d** 79 **p** 80. C Newquay *Truro* 79-81; C St Martin-in-the-Fields *Lon* 81-85; P-in-c Soho St Anne w St Thos and St Pet 85-96; R 96-98; R Lostwithiel, St Winnow w St Nectan's Chpl etc *Truro* 98-07; C Lanreath, Pelynt and Bradoc 03-07; rtd 07. *12 Penmare Court, Hayle TR27 4RD* Tel (01736) 757516 E-mail stevens.fred@tiscali.co.uk

STEVENS, Miss Gillian. b 51. K Alfred's Coll Win CertEd72. EAMTC 98. **d** 01 **p** 02. C March St Mary and March St Pet *Ely* 01-03; C Whittlesey, Pondersbridge and Coates 03-05; TV from 05. *8 The Grove, Whittlesey, Peterborough PE7 2RF* Tel and fax (01733) 202563 E-mail gill@stevens.net

STEVENS, James Anthony. b 47. Worc Coll Ox MA69. Trin Coll Bris 78. **d** 80 **p** 81. C Heref St Pet w St Owen and St Jas 80-84; C Lowestoft and Kirkley *Nor* 84-85; TV 85-89; V Dorridge *Birm* 89-05; AD Shirley 02-05; R Sarratt and Chipperfield *St Alb* from 05. *The Vicarage, The Street, Chipperfield, Kings Langley WD4 9BJ* Tel (01923) 265848 E-mail jimandjudy@6manor.fsnet.co.uk

STEVENS, Jane. *See* KRAFT, Mrs Jane

STEVENS, Janice Hazel. b 42. **d** 00 **p** 01. Hon C Warlingham w Chelsham and Farleigh *S'wark* from 00; Chapl S Lon and Maudsley NHS Foundn Trust 00-07. *7 Harrow Road, Warlingham CR6 9EY* Tel (01883) 626308 *or* (020) 8776 4361

STEVENS, John David Andrew. b 44. Wycliffe Hall Ox. **d** 68 **p** 69. C Standish *Blackb* 68-71; C Stonehouse *Glouc* 71-75; P-in-c Closworth *B & W* 76-77; P-in-c Barwick 76-77; TV Yeovil 77-80; R Chewton Mendip w Ston Easton, Litton etc 80-94; R Quantoxhead 94-07; RD Quantock 95-01; rtd 07. *Amberwell, Holywell Road, Edington, Bridgwater TA7 9LE* E-mail andrewstevens@zetnet.co.uk

STEVENS, Martin Leonard. b 35. St Jo Coll Dur BA60 MA72. Oak Hill Th Coll 60. **d** 62 **p** 63. C Low Elswick *Newc* 62-65; C S Croydon Em *Cant* 65-69; Hon C 69-74; S England Deputation Sec ICM 69-74; V Felling *Dur* 74-86; NSM Ches Square St Mich

w St Phil *Lon* 92-96; rtd 95; Hon C Cullompton and Kentisbeare w Blackborough *Ex* 96-01; Perm to Offic *Cov* from 03. *11 Foxes Way, Warwick CV34 6AX* Tel (01926) 490864

STEVENS, Matthew. b 80. Cam Univ BTh07. Ridley Hall Cam 04. **d** 07 **p** 08. C Reading St Mary w St Laur *Ox* from 07. *88 Connaught Road, Reading RG30 2UF* E-mail rev.mattstevens@googlemail.com

STEVENS, Michael John. b 37. St Cath Coll Cam BA63. Coll of Resurr Mirfield 63. **d** 65 **p** 66. C Poplar All SS w St Frideswide *Lon* 65-71; Asst Chapl The Lon Hosp (Whitechapel) 71-74; Chapl St Thos Hosp Lon 75-96; Hospitaller St Bart Hosp Lon 96-05; P-in-c St Bart Less *Lon* 96-99; V 99-05; rtd 05; Perm to Offic *Chelmsf* from 05. *3 Stable Court, Charterhouse, Charterhouse Square, London EC1M 6AU* Tel (020) 7608 0072

STEVENS, Norman William. b 38. St Chad's Coll Dur BA61. **d** 63 **p** 99. C Wingate Grange *Dur* 63-64; NSM Ansty and Shilton *Cov* from 99. *60 Clinton Lane, Kenilworth CV8 1AT* Tel (01926) 858090 *or* (024) 7622 7597

STEVENS, Olive. b 48. Ex Univ BA04. SWMTC 01. **d** 04 **p** 05. C Camborne *Truro* from 04; RD Carnmarth N from 08. *Hideaway, The Square, Portreath, Redruth TR16 4LA* Tel (01209) 842372 E-mail oste621439@aol.com

STEVENS, Penelope Ann. *See* PRINCE, Penelope Ann

STEVENS, Peter David. b 36. MRICS. Oak Hill Th Coll 79. **d** 81 **p** 82. C Branksome St Clem *Sarum* 81-87; R Moreton and Woodsford w Tincleton 87-98; rtd 98; Hon C Hordle *Win* 98-02; Perm to Offic from 02. *34 Wisbech Way, Hordle, Lymington SO41 0YQ* Tel (01425) 628922

STEVENS, Philip Terence. b 55. Man Univ BSc76 Lon Univ BD81 St Jo Coll Dur MA86 MCMI MIED. Cranmer Hall Dur 81. **d** 83 **p** 84. C Withington St Paul *Man* 83-86; C Middleton 86-88; V Saddleworth 88-92; V Sheff St Paul 93-96; TR Sheff Manor 96-00; Perm to Offic 00-02; Soc Inclusion Manager Sheff City Coun from 00. *238 Carter Knowle Road, Sheffield S7 2EB* Tel 0114-250 8044

STEVENS, Richard William. b 36. AKC59. St Boniface Warminster 59. **d** 60 **p** 61. C Greenhill St Jo *Lon* 60-63; Chapl RAF 63-79; CF 79-01; rtd 01; Perm to Offic *Cant* from 02. *The Old Vicarage, Stockbury, Sittingbourne ME9 7UN* Tel (01795) 844891

STEVENS, Robin George. b 43. Leic Univ BA65. Cuddesdon Coll 74. **d** 74 **p** 75. C Hemel Hempstead *St Alb* 74-77; Chapl K Coll Sch Wimbledon 77-03; TV Wimbledon *S'wark* 98-08; rtd 09. *9 Thornton Road, London SW19 4NE* Tel (020) 8946 4464

STEVENS, Simon Mark. b 72. Lon Univ BD Cam Univ MPhil. STETS 00. **d** 01 **p** 02. C Sholing *Win* 01-05; Chapl Southn Univ from 05. *Chaplain's Lodge, St Mary's Church Close, Southampton SO18 2ST* Tel (023) 8055 8126 E-mail simon.m.stevens@btinternet.com

STEVENS, Mrs Susan Ann. b 46. Lon Univ BEd85. St Mich Coll Llan. **d** 07 **p** 08. NSM Bargoed and Deri w Brithdir *Llan* from 07. *The Rectory, Church Road, Gelligaer, Hengoed CF82 8FW* Tel (01443) 830300 E-mail salutsue@aol.com

STEVENS, Mrs Susan Marjorie Earlam. b 52. RGN74. WMMTC 97. **d** 00 **p** 01. NSM Harborne St Faith and St Laur *Birm* 00-02; NSM Publow w Pensford, Compton Dando and Chelwood *B & W* from 03; Chapl R United Hosp Bath NHS Trust from 06. *Woollard Place, Woollard, Pensford, Bristol BS39 4HU* Tel (01761) 490898 E-mail smestevens@hotmail.co.uk

STEVENS, Miss Sylvia Joyce. b 41. Qu Mary Coll Lon BA63 Bris Univ CertEd64 St Jo Coll Dur BA77. Cranmer Hall Dur 75. dss 78 **d** 87 **p** 94. Chapl Trent (Nottm) Poly *S'well* 78-92; Chapl Nottm Trent Univ 92-93; CME Officer *Bris* 93-95; Tutor Trin Coll Bris 93-95; Hon C Chippenham St Pet *Bris* 93-95; C 95-97; R Everton and Mattersey w Clayworth *S'well* 97-03; rtd 03; Perm to Offic *S'well* from 04. *3 Claricoates Drive, Coddington, Newark NG24 2TF* Tel (01636) 611322

STEVENS, Thomas Walter. b 33. Bps' Coll Cheshunt. **d** 65 **p** 66. C Newc St Matt w St Mary 65-69; C Wallsend St Luke 69-70; C Cranford *Lon* 70-87; C Fulwell St Mich and St Geo 87-90; C Teddington SS Pet and Paul and Fulwell 90-91; rtd 92; Perm to Offic *S'wark* from 92. *23A Samos Road, London SE20 7UQ* Tel (020) 8776 7960

✠**STEVENS, The Rt Revd Timothy John.** b 46. Selw Coll Cam BA68 MA72. Ripon Coll Cuddesdon 75. **d** 76 **p** 77 **c** 95. C E Ham w Upton Park St Alb *Chelmsf* 76-80; TR Canvey Is 80-88; Dep Dir Cathl Cen for Research and Tr 82-84; Bp's Urban Officer 87-91; Hon Can Chelmsf Cathl 87-91; Adn W Ham 91-95; Suff Bp Dunwich *St E* 95-99; Bp Leic from 99. *Bishop's Lodge, 10 Springfield Road, Leicester LE2 3BD* Tel 0116-270 8985 Fax 270 3288 E-mail bptim@leicester.anglican.org

STEVENSON, Canon Alastair Rice. b 42. Open Univ BA78. Ripon Coll Cuddesdon 78. **d** 80 **p** 81. C Bexhill St Pet *Chich* 80-82; C Brighton St Matthias 82-84; C Swindon Ch Ch *Bris* 84-87; Bp's Soc and Ind Adv 87-97; P-in-c Swindon All SS w St Barn 97-01; V from 01; Hon Can Bris Cathl from 02. *The Vicarage, Southbrook Street, Swindon SN2 1HF* Tel and fax (01793) 612385 E-mail alastair@asteve.fsbusiness.co.uk

STEVENSON, Andrew James. b 63. IEng AMICE MIAT. SWMTC 94. **d** 97 **p** 98. NSM Highertown and Baldhu *Truro* 97-08; NSM Mylor w Flushing from 08. *31 Nansavallon Close, Truro TR1 3JU* Tel (01872) 241880
E-mail theblackstuff@sky.com

STEVENSON, Beaumont. *See* STEVENSON, Canon Frank Beaumont

STEVENSON, Bernard Norman. b 57. Kent Univ BA78 Fitzw Coll Cam BA81 MA86. Ridley Hall Cam. **d** 82 **p** 83. C Mortlake w E Sheen *S'wark* 82-84; C Kensal Rise St Martin *Lon* 84-88; C Headstone St Geo 88-90; V Worfield *Heref* 90-95; R Hutton *B & W* 95-07; RD Locking 04-05. *55 Smyth Road, Bristol BS3 2DS* E-mail bstevenson@clara.net

STEVENSON, Brian. *See* STEVENSON, Canon Robert Brian

STEVENSON, Brian. b 34. JP66. NW Ord Course 76. **d** 79 **p** 80. C Padiham *Blackb* 79-82; V Clitheroe St Paul Low Moor 82-89; V Blackb St Silas 89-01; rtd 01; Perm to Offic *Blackb* from 01. *1 Chatburn Close, Great Harwood, Blackburn BB6 7TL* Tel (01254) 885051

STEVENSON, Christopher James. b 43. TCD BA65 MA73 Em Coll Cam BA69 MA73. Westcott Ho Cam 68. **d** 70 **p** 71. C Newc H Cross 70-72; C Arm St Mark 72-73; C Dublin Crumlin *D & G* 73-76; Hon Clerical V Ch Ch Cathl Dublin 75-76; C-in-c Appley Bridge All SS CD *Blackb* 76-82; P-in-c Appley Bridge 82-91; Bp's C Cloonclare w Killasnett, Lurganboy and Drumlease *K, E & A* from 91. *The Rectory, Manorhamilton, Co Leitrim, Republic of Ireland* Tel (00353) (71) 985 5041 Mobile 07982-262862

STEVENSON, David Andrew. b 60. Trin Coll Bris BA92. **d** 92 **p** 93. C Nottingham St Sav *S'well* 92-96; P-in-c Darlaston All SS *Lich* 96-00; Ind Chapl Black Country Urban Ind Miss 96-00; C Darlaston St Lawr 99-00; TV Broadwater *Chich* 00-08; P-in-c Eastwood *S'well* from 08. *The Rectory, 5A Woodland Way, Eastwood, Nottingham NG16 3BU* Tel (01773) 710770

STEVENSON, David Eugene. b 66. Luton Univ BA02. St Steph Ho Ox 06. **d** 08 **p** 09. C Nor St Jo w St Julian from 08. *18 Kilderkin Way, Norwich NR1 1RD* Tel (01603) 661401 Mobile 07860-315534
E-mail rev.davidstevenson@googlemail.com

STEVENSON, Donald Macdonald. b 48. Lon Univ BSc(Econ)70 Leeds Univ MA72 Univ of Wales (Abth) PGCE73 Warwick Univ MEd78. Oak Hill Th Coll BA88. **d** 88 **p** 89. C Gt Malvern St Mary *Worc* 88-92; Chapl Bedford Sch 92-98; Sen Chapl 96-98; Perm to Offic *St Alb* 99-02. *94 Curlew Crescent, Bedford MK41 7HZ* Tel (01234) 217013
E-mail donstevenson100@hotmail.com

STEVENSON, Canon Frank Beaumont. b 39. Duke Univ (USA) BA61 MInstGA. Episc Th Sch Harvard MDiv64. **d** 64 **p** 64. USA 64-66; Zambia 66-68; Lect Th Ox Univ from 68; Bp's Tr Officer *Ox* 69-70; Chapl Keble Coll Ox 71-72; Chapl Oxon Mental Healthcare NHS Trust 75-07; Officer for CME from 90; Dioc Adv Past Care from 90; Hon Can Ch Ch *Ox* from 98. *The School House, Wheatley Road, Stanton St John, Oxford OX33 1ET* Tel (01865) 351635 *or* 778911
E-mail 101531.3264@compuserve.com

STEVENSON, Gerald Ernest. b 35. S'wark Ord Course 80. **d** 83 **p** 84. NSM Eltham Park St Luke *S'wark* 83-88; Asst Chapl HM Pris Wormwood Scrubs 88-98; Perm to Offic *S'wark* 88-99; rtd 99; Hon C Eltham St Barn *S'wark* from 99. *7 Moira Road, London SE9 1SJ* Tel (020) 8850 2748

STEVENSON, James Christian William. b 79. New Coll Ox BA00. Trin Coll Bris 05. **d** 07 **p** 08. C Henbury *Bris* from 07. *2 Applegate, Brentry, Bristol BS10 6QJ* Tel 0117-373 6708
E-mail thestevensons2002@yahoo.co.uk

STEVENSON, John. b 39. Glas Univ MA64 Jordan Hill Coll Glas TCert65. St Jo Coll Nottm Edin Th Coll. **d** 87 **p** 88. NSM Moffat *Glas* 87-92; P-in-c Eastriggs 92-95; P-in-c Gretna 92-95; P-in-c Langholm 92-95; Israel 95-01; P-in-c Thurso and Wick *Mor* 01-06; rtd 06. *Hoppertitty, Beattock, Moffat DG10 9PJ* Tel (01683) 300164 Mobile 07958-307390
E-mail hoppertitty@msn.com

STEVENSON, John William. b 44. Salford Univ BSc66 UNISA BTh89. St Paul's Coll Grahamstown 84. **d** 87 **p** 87. S Africa 87-93; V Broom Leys *Leic* from 93. *St David's Vicarage, 7 Greenhill Road, Coalville LE67 4RL* Tel (01530) 836262
E-mail johnandrene@btinternet.com

✠**STEVENSON, The Rt Revd Kenneth William.** b 49. Edin Univ MA70 Southn Univ PhD75 Man Univ DD87 FRHistS90. Sarum & Wells Th Coll 72. **d** 73 **p** 74 **c** 95. C Grantham w Manthorpe *Linc* 73-76; Lect Boston 76-80; Chapl and Lect Man Univ 80-86; TV Man Whitworth 80-82; TR 82-86; R Guildf H Trin w St Mary 86-95; Bp Portsm 95-09. *18 Melbourne Road, Chichester PO19 7NE* E-mail bossyports@aol.com

STEVENSON, The Ven Leslie Thomas Clayton. b 59. TCD BA MPhil. **d** 83 **p** 84. C Dundela St Mark *D & D* 83-87; I Kilmore and Inch 87-92; R Donaghadee 92-99; I Portarlington w Cloneyhurke, Lea etc *M & K* from 99; Can Meath from 08; Can Kildare Cathl from 08; Adn Meath from 09; Adn Kildare from

09. *The Rectory, Portarlington, Co Laois, Republic of Ireland* Tel and fax (00353) (57) 864 0117
E-mail lesliestevenson@eircom.net

STEVENSON, Michael Richard Nevin. b 52. Univ Coll Lon MA77. CITC. **d** 86 **p** 87. C Clooney w Strathfoyle *D & R* 86-89; CF from 89. *c/o MOD Chaplains (Army)* Tel (01980) 615804 Fax 615800

STEVENSON, Miss Pamela Mary. b 35. CQSW74. **d** 97 **p** 98. OLM Mitcham Ascension *S'wark* 97-05; Perm to Offic from 05; Retirement Officer Kingston Area from 08. *7 Robin Hood Close, Mitcham CR4 1JN* Tel (020) 8764 8331 Mobile 07702-928204

STEVENSON, Peter John. b 70. Southn Univ BSc91 MSc93. Wycliffe Hall Ox 00. **d** 02 **p** 03. C Watford St Luke *St Alb* 02-06; TV Hemel Hempstead from 06. *The Vicarage, 436 Warners End Road, Hemel Hempstead HP1 3QF* Tel (01442) 251897

STEVENSON, Richard Clayton. b 22. TCD BA48 MA56. CITC 48. **d** 48 **p** 49. C Belfast St Mary Magd *Conn* 48-51; C Bangor St Comgall *D & D* 51-54; I Comber 54-60; I Belfast St Barn *Conn* 60-70; I Belfast St Nic 70-88; Adn Conn 79-88; rtd 88. *42 Malone Heights, Belfast BT9 5PG* Tel (028) 9061 5006

STEVENSON, Robert. b 52. UWIST BSc73 MRTPI78 MCIM89. SEITE 03. **d** 05 **p** 06. NSM Woodnesborough w Worth and Staple *Cant* from 05. *The Old Rectory, 5 Cowper Road, Deal CT14 9TW* Tel (01304) 366003
E-mail robert@robstevenson.fsnet.co.uk

STEVENSON, Canon Robert Brian. b 40. QUB BA61 Qu Coll Cam BA67 MA71 Pemb Coll Ox BA69 BD76 MA76 Birm Univ PhD70. Cuddesdon Coll 69. **d** 70 **p** 71. C Lewisham St Jo Southend *S'wark* 70-73; C Catford (Southend) and Downham 73-74; Lect and Dir Past Studies Chich Th Coll 74-81; Acting Vice-Prin 80-81; V W Malling w Offham *Roch* from 81; RD Malling 93-02; Hon Can Roch Cathl from 98. *The Vicarage, 138 High Street, West Malling ME19 6NE* Tel (01732) 842245

STEVENSON, Sheila Reinhardt. *See* SWARBRICK, Mrs Sheila Reinhardt

STEVENSON, Trevor Donald. b 59. TCD Div Sch BTh. **d** 91 **p** 92. C Magheralin w Dollingstown *D & D* 91-95; CMS Uganda 95-98; Dir Fields of Life from 98. *Tree Tops, Brides Glen Road, Shankill, Dublin 18, Republic of Ireland* Tel and fax (00353) (1) 282 0150 E-mail fieldsoflife@oceanfree.net

STEVENTON, Canon June Lesley. b 61. Aston Tr Scheme 86 Sarum & Wells Th Coll BTh91. **d** 91 **p** 94. Par Dn Chatham St Steph *Roch* 91-94; C 94-96; Perm to Offic *York* 96-97 and *Liv* 97-00; V Abram *Liv* from 00; V Bickershaw from 00; Hon Can Liv Cathl from 06. *The Vicarage, 9 Lee Lane, Abram, Wigan WN2 5QU* Tel and fax (01942) 866396
E-mail abram.vicarage@btinternet.com

STEVENTON, Kenneth. b 59. Cuddesdon Coll 94. **d** 96 **p** 97. C Spalding *Linc* 96-99; R Sutterton, Fosdyke, Algarkirk and Wigtoft 99-05; P-in-c Staindrop *Dur* from 05; P-in-c Ingleton from 05; P-in-c Evenwood from 05. *St Mary's Vicarage, 7 Beechisle, Staindrop, Darlington DL2 3PE* Tel (01833) 660237
E-mail revken2@freeuk.co.uk

STEVINSON, Harold John Hardy. b 34. Selw Coll Cam BA57 MA61. Qu Coll Birm. **d** 59 **p** 60. C Bris St Mary Redcliffe w Temple 59-63; C Caversham *Ox* 63-73; Soc Resp Officer *Dur* 74-82; Sec Dioc Bd for Miss and Unity 82-88; P-in-c Croxdale 82-88; P-in-c Leamington Hastings and Birdingbury *Cov* 88-96; rtd 96; Perm to Offic *Cov* and *Glouc* from 96. *8 Greenways, Winchcombe, Cheltenham GL54 5LG* Tel (01242) 602195

STEVINSON, Mrs Josephine Mary. b 25. STh56. Cranmer Hall Dur 86. dss 86 **d** 87 **p** 94. Croxdale *Dur* 86-87; Lic to Offic 87-88; Lic to Offic *Cov* 88-96; NSM Leamington Hastings and Birdingbury 94-96; rtd 96; Perm to Offic *Glouc* from 96. *8 Greenways, Winchcombe, Cheltenham GL54 5LG* Tel (01242) 602195

STEWARD, Mrs Linda Christine. b 46. NE Lon Poly CQSW82. S'wark Ord Course 85. **d** 88 **p** 94. NSM E Ham w Upton Park St Alb *Chelmsf* 88-91; Chapl Newham Healthcare NHS Trust Lon 91-98; NSM Plaistow *Chelmsf* 91-96; NSM Plaistow and N Canning Town 96-98; P-in-c Rawreth w Rettendon 98-06; rtd 06. *2 Belfairs Park Close, Leigh-on-Sea SS9 4TR* Tel (01702) 525638
E-mail steward_linda@hotmail.com

STEWART, Alan. *See* STEWART, Hugh Alan

STEWART, Alan Valentine. b 47. Univ Coll Galway BA98. **d** 97 **p** 98. NSM Mullingar, Portnashangan, Moyliscar, Kilbixy etc *M & K* 97-00; NSM Clane w Donadea and Coolcarrigan 00-05; NSM Dunboyne Union from 05; NSM Rathmolyon w Castlerickard, Rathcore and Agher from 05. *Casteway, Baltrasna, Ashbourne, Co Meath, Republic of Ireland* Tel (00353) (1) 835 0997 *or* 814 0297 Mobile 87-179 3197
E-mail casteway@hotmail.com *or* alan.stewart@fas.ie

STEWART, Alice Elizabeth. b 42. **d** 00 **p** 01. C Cloughfern *Conn* from 00. *3 Fergus Court, Carrickfergus BT38 8HT* Tel (028) 9336 5721

STEWART (née BARBER), Mrs Anne Louise. b 71. QUB BA93 PGCE94. CITC 97. **d** 00 **p** 01. C Belfast Malone St Jo *Conn* from

00. *St George's Rectory, 28 Myrtlefield Park, Belfast BT9 6NF*
Tel (028) 9066 7134   Mobile 07833-116512
E-mail stewartrevslb@yahoo.com

STEWART, Miss Betty. b 25. S'wark Ord Course 91. **d** 93 **p** 94.
NSM Wandsworth Common St Mary *S'wark* 93-95; NSM
Hampton Hill *Lon* 95-05. *71 Ormond Drive, Hampton
TW12 2TL*   Tel (020) 8979 2069

STEWART, Ms Brenda Alice. b 60. ERMC. **d** 09. C Abbots
Ripton w Wood Walton *Ely* from 09; C Kings Ripton from 09; C
Houghton w Wyton from 09. *The Rectory, 3 Rectory Lane,
Wyton, Huntingdon PE28 2AQ*

STEWART, Brian. b 59. TCD BTh91. CITC 88. **d** 91 **p** 92. C
Ballywillan *Conn* 91-94; I Belfast St Geo from 94. *St George's
Rectory, 6 Royal Lodge Park, Belfast BT8 7YP*   Tel (028) 9070
1350   Mobile 07902-792080

STEWART, Charles. b 55. St Jo Coll Cam BA77 MA81
CertEd79. Wycliffe Hall Ox 85. **d** 87 **p** 88. C Bowdon *Ches* 87-90;
C Bath Abbey w St Jas *B & W* 90-94; Can Res, Prec and Sacr
Win Cathl 94-06; V Walton-on-Thames *Guildf* from 06. *The
Vicarage, 53 Ashley Park Avenue, Walton-on-Thames KT12 1EU*
Tel (01932) 227184   E-mail vicar@waltonparish.org.uk

STEWART, Charles Michael. b 50. Ball Coll Ox MA82 K Coll
Lon BA05 AKC05 MA07 FCA82. Ripon Coll Cuddesdon 06.
d 07 **p** 08. NSM Leatherhead and Mickleham *Guildf* from 07.
Rickstones, Punchbowl Lane, Dorking RH5 4BN   Tel (01306)
884153   Mobile 07936-524152
E-mail mikestewart999@btinternet.com

STEWART, Hugh Alan. b 67. Lon Inst BA91 Middx Univ BA03.
NTMTC 00. **d** 03 **p** 04. C Gt Stanmore *Lon* 03-06; P-in-c
Hertford St Andr *St Alb* 06-08; P-in-c Hertingfordbury 06-08;
TV Hertford from 08. *St Andrew's Rectory, 7 Elizabeth Close,
Hertford SG14 2DB*   Tel (01992) 582726
E-mail _h.alanstewart@tiscali.co.uk

STEWART, Ian Guild. b 43. Edin Th Coll 89. **d** 84 **p** 85. NSM
Dundee St Mary Magd *Bre* 84-87; NSM Dundee St Jo 87-90; C
90-92; NSM Dundee St Martin 87-90; C 90-92; R Montrose
92-08; P-in-c Inverbervie 92-08; Can St Paul's Cathl Dundee
01-08; Dean Bre 07-08; rtd 08. *36 Forbes Road, Edinburgh
EH10 4ED*

STEWART, James. *See* STEWART, Malcolm James

STEWART, James. b 32. Div Hostel Dub. **d** 69 **p** 70. C Belfast St
Donard *D & D* 69-72; C Dundonald 72-74; I Rathmullan w
Tyrella 74-80; I Belfast St Clem 80-97; I Moy w Charlemont *Arm*
97-04; rtd 04. *25 Barnish Road, Kells, Ballymena BT42 3PA*   Tel
(028) 2589 8787   Mobile 07833-791790

STEWART, Canon James Patrick. b 55. Keele Univ BA77 Birm
Univ MA78. Ridley Hall Cam 86. **d** 88 **p** 89. C Boulton *Derby*
88-91; C Cove St Jo *Guildf* 91-92; TV 92-97; TR Tunbridge Wells
St Jas w St Phil *Roch* 97-04; V Tunbridge Wells St Jas from 04;
RD Tunbridge Wells 99-07; Hon Can Roch Cathl from 05. *The
Vicarage, 12 Shandon Close, Tunbridge Wells TN2 3RE*   Tel
(01892) 530687 *or* 521703   E-mail jpstewart4@googlemail.com

STEWART, Mrs Janet Margaret. b 41. Roehampton Inst
CertEd62. Cranmer Hall Dur 67. **d** 87 **p** 94. Hon Par Dn Oulton
Broad *Nor* 87-94; Hon C 94-97; Chapl Lowestoft Hosp 94-97;
Perm to Offic *B & W* 97-98; C Quidenham Gp *Nor* 98-01; Asst
Chapl Norfolk and Nor Univ Hosp NHS Trust from 00.
30 St Joseph's Road, Sheringham NR26 8JA   Tel (01263) 824497

STEWART, Jennifer Jane. *See* SISTIG, Mrs Jennifer Jane

STEWART, John. b 39. Oak Hill Th Coll 75. **d** 77 **p** 78. C
Accrington Ch Ch *Blackb* 77-79; TV Darwen St Pet w
Hoddlesden 79-86; R Coppull St Jo 86-04; rtd 04; Perm to Offic
Blackb from 05. *55 Bolton Road, Chorley PR7 3AU*

✠**STEWART, The Rt Revd John Craig.** b 40. Ridley Coll
Melbourne LTh64. **d** 65 **p** 66 **c** 84. Australia 65-68 and from 70;
C Prospect 65-67; C Mt Gambier 67-68; C Crawley *Chich* 68-70;
I Frankston E 74-79; Gen Sec CMS Vic 79-84; Asst Bp
Melbourne 84-01; W Region 84-91; N Region 91-94; E Region
94-01; V Gen 88-01; R Woodend 01-04; rtd 04. *PO Box 928,
Bacchus Marsh Vic 3440, Australia*   Tel (0061) (3) 5367 0081
E-mail bishopjcstewart@bigpond.com

STEWART, Canon John Roberton. b 29. Sarum Th Coll 63. **d** 65
p 66. C Gillingham *Sarum* 65-70; R Langton Matravers 70-84;
RD Purbeck 82-89; Can and Preb Sarum Cathl 83-90; R
Kingston, Langton Matravers and Worth Matravers 84-90; Can
Res Sarum Cathl 90-95; Treas 90-95; rtd 95; Perm to Offic *Sarum*
from 95. *Hillrise, 26 Durlston Road, Swanage BH19 2HX*   Tel
(01929) 422802

STEWART, Canon John Wesley. b 52. QUB BD76 TCD 76. **d** 77
p 78. C Seagoe *D & D* 77-79; C Lisburn Ch Ch *Conn* 79-85; I
Ballybay w Mucknoe and Clontibret *Clogh* 85-90; I Derryvullen
S w Garvary from 90; Bp Dom Chapl 95-00; Glebes Sec from 95;
Dioc Registrar from 98; Exam Can Clogh Cathl 98-00; Preb
from 00. *The Rectory, 2 Ballylucas Road, Tullyharney, Enniskillen
BT74 4PR*   Tel and fax (028) 6638 7236
E-mail jva.stewart@freenet.co.uk

STEWART, Keith Malcolm Morris. b 45. **d** 08 **p** 09. OLM
Stalybridge *Man* from 08. *10 Ladysmith Road, Stalybridge
SK15 1HB*   Tel 0161-303 7483

STEWART, Louise. *See* STEWART, Mrs Anne Louise

STEWART, Malcolm James. b 44. TD78. York Univ BA66 K
Coll Lon MA68 Lon Inst of Educn PGCE69 Solicitor 79.
NEOC 89. **d** 93 **p** 94. NSM Upper Nidderdale *Ripon* 93-95; C
Fountains Gp 95-98; V Catterick 98-03; P-in-c Culmington w
Onibury, Bromfield etc *Heref* 03-06; TV Ludlow from 06; RD
Ludlow from 07. *The Vicarage, Bromfield, Ludlow SY8 2JP*   Tel
(01584) 856625

STEWART, Marcus Patrick Michael. b 66. Ox Univ BA89
MSc93 Cam Univ BA92. Ven English Coll Rome 89 Westcott
Ho Cam 96. **d** 98 **p** 99. C Headington *Ox* 98-00; Hon C S
Hinksey 00-01; CF 01-04; Chapl RN 04-07; Perm to Offic *Cant*
08-09; Chapl HM Pris Elmley from 09; Hon C St Peter-in-
Thanet *Cant* from 09; Chapl Kent Police from 09. *The
Chaplaincy, HM Prison Elmley, Church Road, Eastchurch,
Sheerness ME12 4DZ*   Tel (01795) 880900 Fax 882001   Mobile
07948-218521   E-mail frmarcus@rncom.mod.uk

STEWART, Maxwell Neville Gabriel. b 33. Essex Univ MA68
Hertf Coll Ox BA58 MA59. Wycliffe Hall Ox 58. **d** 60 **p** 61. C
Perry Beeches *Birm* 60-62; Chapl Rosenberg Coll St Gallen
62-64; Perm to Offic *Chelmsf* 64-70; Warden Leics Poly 70-92; De
Montfort Univ Leic 92-93; Hon C Leic St Mary 74-79; rtd 93;
Perm to Offic *Leic* from 79. *25 Sidney Court, Norwich Road,
Leicester LE4 0LR*

STEWART, Michael. b 65. St Jo Coll Nottm LTh89. **d** 89 **p** 90. C
Ealing St Paul *Lon* 89-93; P-in-c N Wembley St Cuth 93-98; V
98-02; Assoc P Abbotsford Canada from 02. *St Matthew's
Anglican Church, 2010 Guilford Drive, Abbotsford BC, Canada,
V2S 5R2*   Tel (001) (604) 853 2416
E-mail mikes@stmatthewsanglicanchurch.com

STEWART, Ms Monica Frances Ethel. b 35. RGN57 RM59.
d 08. NSM Stamford Hill St Thos *Lon* from 08. *2 The Heights,
165 Mountview Road, London N4 4JU*   Tel (020) 8340 4746
Mobile 07947-026297
E-mail monica.f.stewart@googlemail.com

STEWART, Canon Raymond John. b 55. TCD BA79 MA82.
CITC Div Test77. **d** 79 **p** 80. C Clooney *D & R* 79-82; I
Dunfanaghy 82-87; I Gweedore Union 85-87; Dioc Youth Adv
83-87; Bp's Dom Chapl 85-87; I Castledawson 87-03; I Tamlaght
O'Crilly Upper w Lower from 03; Ed *D & R Dioc News* 89-93;
Dioc Glebes Sec from 93; Stewardship Adv from 98; Can Derry
Cathl from 99. *Hervey Hill Rectory, 16 Hervey Hill, Kilrea,
Coleraine BT51 5TT*   Tel and fax (028) 2954 0296   Mobile
07761-585412
E-mail raymondandpatricia@herveyhill.wanadoo.co.uk

STEWART, Stephen John. b 62. Oak Hill Th Coll. **d** 99 **p** 00. C
Mile Cross *Nor* 99-04; TV Cove St Jo *Guildf* from 04. *Southwood
Vicarage, 15 The Copse, Farnborough GU14 0QD*   Tel (01252)
513422   E-mail stevestewartc@hotmail.com

STEWART, Susan Theresa. b 58. NOC 01. **d** 04 **p** 05. C Lodge
Moor St Luke *Sheff* 04-08; V Mosbrough from 08. *The Vicarage,
25 Kelgate, Mosborough, Sheffield S20 5EJ*   Tel 0114-248 6518
Mobile 07966-695095

STEWART, William. **d** 01 **p** 02. NSM Kilroot and Templecorran
Conn from 01. *63 Victoria Road, Carrickfergus BT38 7JJ*   Tel
(028) 9336 2145

STEWART, William Jones. b 32. Trin Hall Cam BA55 MA59
Cam Univ CertEd56. Edin Th Coll 67. **d** 69 **p** 69. Chapl
St Ninian's Cathl Perth 69-71; Bp's Dom Chapl *Ox* 71-75; V
Lambourn 75-03; P-in-c Lambourne Woodlands 83-90; P-in-c
Eastbury and E Garston 83-03; rtd 04. *9 Ascott Way, Newbury
RG14 2FH*   Tel (01635) 580244
E-mail stewart.clan4@btopenworld.com

STEWART-DARLING, Fiona Lesley. b 58. Kingston Poly
GRSC79 Lon Univ PhD82 K Coll Lon MA99. Trin Coll Bris
BA91. **d** 91 **p** 94. C Cirencester *Glouc* 91-94; Chapl Cheltenham
and Glouc Coll of HE 94-97; Chapl Portsm Univ 97-04; Hon
Chapl Portsm Cathl 97-04; Bp's Chapl in Docklands *Lon* from
04. *143 New Atlas Wharf, 3 Arnhem Place, London E14 3ST*   Tel
(020) 7537 7753   Mobile 07739-461090
E-mail fiona.stewart-darling@port.ac.uk

STEWART ELLENS, Gordon Frederick. *See* ELLENS, Gordon
Frederick Stewart

STEWART-SYKES, Alistair Charles. b 60. St Andr Univ MA83
Birm Univ PhD92. Qu Coll Birm 86. **d** 89 **p** 90. C Stevenage
St Andr and St Geo *St Alb* 89-92; C Castle Vale St Cuth *Birm*
92-93; Barbados 93-96; Assoc Min Hanley H Ev *Lich* 97-98;
USA 98-01; V Bridge Par *Sarum* from 01. *The Vicarage, Newton
Road, Sturminster Marshall, Wimborne BH21 4BT*   Tel (01258)
857255 Fax 08701-358049

STEWART-SYKES, Teresa Melanie. b 64. Bris Univ BA85. Qu
Coll Birm 87. **d** 89. Par Dn Stevenage St Andr and St Geo *St Alb*
89-92; Perm to Offic *Birm* 92-93; Barbados 93-97; C Meir Heath
Lich 97-98; USA 98-01. *The Vicarage, Newton Road, Sturminster
Marshall, Wimborne BH21 4BT*   Tel (01258) 857255

STIBBE, Mrs Hazel Mary. **d** 99 **p** 00. NSM Wolverhampton
St Andr *Lich* 99-02; Lic to Offic *St As* 03-08; rtd 08. *Braemar,
Kerry Street, Montgomery SY15 6PG*   Tel (01686) 668912

STIBBE, Mark William Godfrey. b 60. Trin Coll Cam BA83 MA86 Nottm Univ PhD88. St Jo Coll Nottm 83. **d** 86 **p** 87. C Stapleford *S'well* 86-90; C Crookes St Thos *Sheff* 90-93; Lect Sheff Univ 90-97; V Grenoside 93-97; V Chorleywood St Andr *St Alb* 97-09; Ldr Father's Ho Trust from 09. *3rd Floor, 26 The Parade, Watford WD17 1AA* Tel (01923) 256352
E-mail markstibbe@aol.com

STICKLAND, David Clifford. b 44. Surrey Univ BA01 CPFA68 MAAT77 FCCA80. STETS 98. **d** 01 **p** 02. NSM Greatham w Empshott and Hawkley w Prior's Dean *Portsm* 01-05; NSM Petersfield and Buriton from 05. *St Mary's House, 41 North Lane, Buriton, Petersfield GU31 5RS* Tel (01730) 269390 Mobile 07836-282561
E-mail david_stickland.t21@btinternet.com

STICKLAND, Geoffrey John Brett. b 42. Open Univ BSc96. St D Coll Lamp. **d** 66 **p** 67. C Aberavon H Trin *Llan* 66-69; C-in-c Llanrumney CD *Mon* 69-72; C Tetbury w Beverston *Glouc* 72-75; V Hardwicke 75-82; R Hardwicke, Quedgeley and Elmore w Longney 82-98; V Quedgeley from 98. *The Rectory, School Lane, Quedgeley, Gloucester GL2 6PN* Tel (01452) 720411
E-mail geoffstickland@hotmail.com

STICKLEY, Mrs Annette Frances. b 44. Bp Otter Coll Chich 67. **d** 00. NSM Worth *Chich* 00-06; Perm to Offic from 06. *19 Locksash Close, West Wittering, Chichester PO20 8QP* Tel (01243) 512616

STIDOLPH, Canon Robert Anthony. b 54. GBSM76 ARCM75 FRSA92. St Steph Ho Ox 77. **d** 80 **p** 80. C Hove All SS *Chich* 80-84; TV Brighton Resurr 84-87; Chapl Cheltenham Coll 87-94; Sen Chapl and Hd RS Wellington Coll Berks 94-01; Chapl and Asst Master Radley Coll 01-05; Hon Can Ch Ch *Ox* 00-04; P-in-c Worth, Pound Hill and Maidenbower *Chich* from 05. *The Rectory, Church Road, Worth, Crawley RH10 7RT* Tel (01293) 882229

STIFF, Canon Derrick Malcolm. b 40. Lich Th Coll 69. **d** 72 **p** 73. C Cov St Geo 72-75; R Benhall w Sternfield *St E* 75-79; P-in-c Snape w Friston 75-79; V Cartmel *Carl* 79-87; R Sudbury and Chilton *St E* 87-94; P-in-c Lavenham 94-95; P-in-c Preston 94-95; R Lavenham w Preston 95-03; Min Can St E Cathl 90-00; Hon Can 00-03; RD Lavenham 95-03; rtd 03; Perm to Offic *St E* and *Sarum* from 03. *9 Fisherton Island, Salisbury SP2 7TG* Tel (01722) 320177 E-mail canonstiff@hotmail.com

STILEMAN, William Mark Charles. b 63. Selw Coll Cam BA85 MA89 PGCE86. Wycliffe Hall Ox. **d** 91 **p** 92. C Ox St Andr 91-95; TV Gt Chesham 95-03; P-in-c Maidenhead St Andr and St Mary 03-04; V from 04. *St Mary's Vicarage, 14 Juniper Drive, Maidenhead SL6 8RE* Tel (01628) 624908

STILL, Colin Charles. b 35. Selw Coll Cam BA67 MA71 United Th Sem Dayton STM69. Cranmer Hall Dur 67. **d** 69 **p** 70. C Drypool St Columba w St Andr and St Pet *York* 69-72; Abp's Dom Chapl 72-75; Recruitment Sec ACCM 76-80; P-in-c Ockham w Hatchford *Guildf* 76-80; R 80-90; Can Missr and Ecum Officer 80-90; Perm to Offic *Chich* from 92; rtd 96. *Flat 9, 16 Lewes Crescent, Brighton BN2 1GB* Tel (01273) 686014

STILL (*née* STACEY), Mrs Gillian. b 53. SWMTC 94. **d** 97 **p** 98. NSM Peter Tavy, Mary Tavy, Lydford and Brent Tor *Ex* 97-06; C Abbotskerswell from 06; Chapl Rowcroft Hospice Torquay from 01. *The Vicarage, Church Path, Abbotskerswell, Newton Abbot TQ12 5NY* Tel (01626) 334445 *or* (01803) 210829 Mobile 07971-412511 E-mail gillstill@yahoo.co.uk

STILL, Jonathan Trevor Lloyd. b 59. Ex Univ BA81 Qu Coll Cam BA84 MA88. Westcott Ho Cam 82. **d** 85 **p** 86. C Weymouth H Trin *Sarum* 85-88; Chapl for Agric *Heref* 88-93; V N Petherton w Northmoor Green *B & W* 93-00; V The Bourne and Tilford *Guildf* from 00; RD Farnham from 05. *The Vicarage, 2 Middle Avenue, Farnham GU9 8JL* Tel and fax (01252) 715505
E-mail thevicar@thebourne.org.uk

STILL, Kenneth Donald. b 37. St Aid Birkenhead 64. **d** 67 **p** 95. C Ainsdale *Liv* 67-68; C Kirkby 68-69; C Sutton 96-98; TV 98-03; rtd 03. *The Cottage, Wash Road, Kirton, Boston PE20 1QG* Tel (01205) 724043

STILLWELL, Wayne Anthony. b 68. Univ of Greenwich BA91. Oak Hill Th Coll 94. **d** 96 **p** 97. C Necton, Holme Hale w N and S Pickenham *Nor* 96-98; C Eastbourne H Trin *Chich* 98-03; V Chaddesden St Mary *Derby* from 03. *The Vicarage, 133 Chaddesden Lane, Chaddesden, Derby DE21 6LL* Tel (01332) 280924 E-mail chaddesden.church@ntlworld.com

STILWELL, Malcolm Thomas. b 54. Coll of Resurr Mirfield 83. **d** 86 **p** 87. C Workington St Mich *Carl* 86-90; P-in-c Flimby 90-93; Perm to Offic 93-95; NSM Westfield St Mary from 95. *18 Moorfield Avenue, Workington CA14 4HJ* Tel (01900) 66757 E-mail stilwellstudio@supanet.com

STILWELL, Timothy James. b 65. Birm Univ BA87. Wycliffe Hall Ox 96. **d** 98 **p** 99. C Clifton Ch Ch w Em *Bris* 98-02; C Hammersmith St Paul *Lon* 02-05; V Fulham St Dionis Parson's Green from 05. *St Dionis' Vicarage, 18 Parson's Green, London SW6 4UH* Tel (020) 7731 1376 E-mail tim@stdionis.org.uk

STIMPSON, Nigel Leslie. b 60. St Martin's Coll Lanc BA92 Lanc Univ MA99. Coll of Resurr Mirfield 94. **d** 94 **p** 95. C Heyhouses on Sea *Blackb* 94-96; C Torrisholme 96-99; V

Ravensthorpe and Thornhill Lees w Savile Town *Wakef* 99-05; TR Ribbleton *Blackb* from 05. *The Rectory, 238 Ribbleton Avenue, Ribbleton, Preston PR2 6QP* Tel (01772) 791747
E-mail nls@dircon.co.uk

STINSON, William Gordon. b 29. Lon Univ BSc50. Ely Th Coll 51. **d** 52 **p** 53. C Kingston upon Hull St Alb *York* 52-56; Br Guiana 56-61; V E and W Ravendale w Hatcliffe *Linc* 61-67; R Beelsby 61-67; P-in-c Ashby w Fenby and Brigsley 62-66; R 66-67; V New Cleethorpes 67-76; RD Grimsby and Cleethorpes 73-76; P-in-c Dovercourt *Chelmsf* 76-83; TR Dovercourt and Parkeston 83-91; V Gosfield 91-95; rtd 95; Perm to Offic *Chelmsf* and *St E* from 95. *14 The Columbines, Melford Road, Cavendish, Sudbury CO10 8AB* Tel (01787) 281381

STIRLING, Canon Christina Dorita (Tina). b 48. Lon Univ BEd73. Wycliffe Hall Ox 87. **d** 89 **p** 94. Par Dn Thame w Towersey *Ox* 89-94; C 94-98; P-in-c Brill, Boarstall, Chilton and Dorton 98; R Bernwode from 98; AD Aylesbury from 05; Hon Can Ch Ch from 09. *The Vicarage, 7 High Street, Brill, Aylesbury HP18 9ST* Tel and fax (01844) 238325

STIRZAKER, Maureen Ann. b 51. **d** 08 **p** 09. NSM Chadderton St Matt w St Luke *Man* from 08. *4 Turfton Road, Royton, Oldham OL2 6EW* Tel 0161-665 1415
E-mail stirzaker776@btinternet.com

STOBART, Stuart Malcolm. b 64. Glos Univ BA07. Yorks Min Course 07. **d** 09. C Clayton *Bradf* from 09. *Claverings, Chrisharben Park, Clayton, Bradford BD14 6AE* Tel (01274) 881502 Mobile 07545-631387
E-mail stuart.stobart@yahoo.co.uk

STOBER, Brenda Jacqueline. b 57. Liv Univ BSc79 Leeds Univ BA08 Lanc Univ PGCE80. NOC 04. **d** 07 **p** 08. C Southport Em *Liv* from 07. *28 Elswick Green, Southport PR9 9XT* Tel (01704) 227294 Mobile 07812-471269 E-mail ukjacquel@yahoo.co.uk

STOCK, Lionel Crispian. b 58. ACMA85 ACIS94. Linc Th Coll BTh94. **d** 94 **p** 95. C Preston w Sutton Poyntz and Osmington w Poxwell *Sarum* 94-97; P-in-c Stalbridge 97-00; Hon C Hillingdon All SS *Lon* 01-04; NSM Kendal H Trin *Carl* from 04. *29 Kendal Green, Kendal LA9 5PN* E-mail revlstock@hotmail.com

STOCK, Nigel. See STOCK, The Rt Revd William Nigel

STOCK, Miss Ruth Vaughan. b 51. Birkbeck Coll Lon BA79 MA85. Wycliffe Hall Ox 91. **d** 93 **p** 94. Par Dn Toxteth St Philemon w St Gabr and St Cleopas *Liv* 93-94; C 94-97; TV from 97. *St Gabriel's Vicarage, 2 Steble Street, Liverpool L8 6QH* Tel 0151-708 7751

STOCK, The Very Revd Victor Andrew. b 44. OAM02. AKC68 FRSA95. **d** 69 **p** 70. C Pinner *Lon* 69-73; Chapl Lon Univ 73-79; R Friern Barnet St Jas 79-86; R St Mary le Bow w St Pancras Soper Lane etc 86-02; P-in-c St Mary Aldermary 87-98; Dean Guildf from 02. *The Deanery, 1 Cathedral Close, Guildford GU2 7TL* Tel (01483) 560328 *or* 547861 Fax 303350
E-mail dean@guildford-cathedral.org

✠STOCK, The Rt Revd William Nigel. b 50. St Cuth Soc Dur BA72. Ripon Coll Cuddesdon. **d** 76 **p** 77 **c** 00. C Stockton St Pet *Dur* 76-79; Papua New Guinea 79-84; V Shiremoor *Newc* 85-91; TR N Shields 91-98; RD Tynemouth 92-98; Hon Can Newc Cathl 97-98; Can Res Dur Cathl 98-00; Chapl Grey Coll Dur 99-00; Suff Bp Stockport *Ches* 00-07; Bp St E from 07. *The Bishop's House, 4 Park Road, Ipswich IP1 3ST* Tel (01473) 252829 Fax 232552

STOCKBRIDGE, Alan Carmichael. b 33. MBE89. Keble Coll Ox BA55 MA62. Wycliffe Hall Ox 66. **d** 68 **p** 69. CF 68-78 and 82-92; Chapl Reading Sch 78-82; R Harrietsham w Ulcombe *Cant* 92-98; rtd 98; Perm to Offic *Eur* from 00. *Albrecht Dürerstrasse 4, 96106 Ebern, Germany* Tel and fax (0049) (9531) 942799 E-mail erikastockbridge@aol.com

STOCKBRIDGE, Nelson William. b 35. Trin Th Coll Auckland 61. **d** 84 **p** 85. C Ohinemutu New Zealand 85-86; C Shildon w Eldon *Dur* 87; C Norton St Mary 87-88; C Cottingham *York* 88-91; V Aldbrough, Mappleton w Goxhill and Withernwick 91-96; C Baildon *Bradf* 96-01; rtd 01; New Zealand from 02. *3 Alison Street, Mangakakahi, Rotorua 3015, New Zealand* Tel (0064) (7) 348 7327 E-mail nelsonandruth@xtra.co.nz

STOCKER, David William George. b 37. Bris Univ BA58 CertEd. Qu Coll Birm 59. **d** 60 **p** 61. C Sparkhill St Jo *Birm* 60-64; C Keighley *Bradf* 64-66; V Grenoside *Sheff* 66-83; V Sandbach *Ches* 83-01; rtd 01; Perm to Offic *Ches* from 01. *18 Mill Bridge Close, Crewe CW1 5DZ* Tel (01270) 212865

STOCKER, John Henry. b 48. Cov Univ BSc71 Sheff Univ BEd81 ACP88. St Mich Coll Llan 01. **d** 04 **p** 05. NSM Knighton, Norton, Whitton, Pilleth and Cascob *S & B* 04-06; NSM Irfon Valley 06-09; rtd 09. *1 Tai Cae Mawr, Llanwrtyd Wells LD5 4RJ* Tel (01592) 610231 Mobile 07891-086631

STOCKER, Rachael Ann. See KNAPP, Mrs Rachael Ann

STOCKITT, Robin Philip. b 56. Liv Univ BA77 Crewe & Alsager Coll PGCE78. Ridley Hall Cam 95. **d** 97 **p** 98. C Billing *Pet* 97-01; P-in-c Freiburg-im-Breisgau *Eur* from 01; Asst Chapl Basle from 01. *Talvogteistrasse 16, 79199 Kirchzarten Burg-Hofen, Freiburg, Germany* Tel (0049) (7661) 904693 Fax 967726
E-mail stockitt@t-online.de

STOCKLEY, Mrs Alexandra Madeleine Reuss. b 43. Cranmer Hall Dur 80 Carl Dioc Tr Inst. **dss** 84 **d** 87 **p** 94. Upperby St Jo *Carl* 84-89; Par Dn 87-89; Dn-in-c Grayrigg, Old Hutton and New Hutton 90-94; P-in-c 94-95; P-in-c Levens 95-03; rtd 03; Perm to Offic *Carl* from 03. *Crowberry, Ulpha, Broughton-in-Furness LA20 6DZ* Tel (01229) 716875

STOCKPORT, Suffragan Bishop of. *See* ATWELL, The Rt Revd Robert Ronald

STOCKS, Simon Paul. b 68. Rob Coll Cam BA89 MA93. Trin Coll Bris BA03 MPhil06. **d** 04 **p** 05. C Coulsdon St Jo *S'wark* from 04; Hon C from 07. *316 Coulsdon Road, Coulsdon CR5 1EB* Tel (01737) 553190
E-mail simon@spstocks.freeserve.co.uk

STOCKTON, Ian George. b 49. Selw Coll Cam BA72 MA76 Hull Univ PhD90. St Jo Coll Nottm PGCE74. **d** 75 **p** 76. C Chell *Lich* 75-78; C Trentham 78-80; R Dalbeattie *Glas* 80-84; P-in-c Scotton w Northorpe *Linc* 84-88; Asst Local Min Officer 84-88; Local Min Officer and LNSM Course Prin 88-97; TR Monkwearmouth *Dur* from 97. *The Rectory, 2A Park Avenue, Sunderland SR6 9PU* Tel 0191-548 6607 *or* 516 0135
E-mail ian.stockton@durham.anglican.org

STODDART, David Easton. b 36. K Coll Dur BSc60 PhD66 CEng66 MIMechE66 FCMI72 FIQA76. WEMTC 92. **d** 95 **p** 96. OLM Stroud H Trin *Glouc* 95-99; OLM Woodchester and Brimscombe 99-00; NSM from 00; Jt Angl Chapl Severn NHS Trust from 99. *Woodstock, Hampton Green, Box, Stroud GL6 9AD* Tel (01453) 885338
E-mail stoddart@david-isabel.co.uk

STOKE-ON-TRENT, Archdeacon of. *See* STONE, The Ven Godfrey Owen

STOKER, Andrew. b 64. Coll of Ripon & York St Jo BA86. Coll of Resurr Mirfield 87. **d** 90 **p** 91. C Horton *Newc* 90-92; C Clifford *York* 92-96; P-in-c Cawood 96-98; P-in-c Ryther 96-98; P-in-c Wistow 96-98; R Cawood w Ryther and Wistow 98-04; P-in-c York St Clem w St Mary Bishophill Senior 04-05; R York St Clem w St Mary Bishophill from 05. *13 Nunthorpe Avenue, York YO23 1PF* Tel (01904) 624425

STOKER, Howard Charles. b 62. Linc Th Coll BTh93. **d** 93 **p** 94. C Hessle *York* 93-96; C Richmond w Hudswell *Ripon* 96-99; C Downholme and Marske 96-99; R Holt w High Kelling *Nor* from 99; RD Holt from 05. *The Rectory, 11 Church Street, Holt NR25 6BB* Tel (01263) 712048 Fax 711397
E-mail holtrectory@dialstart.com

STOKER, Canon Joanna Mary. b 57. Leic Univ BA79 Nottm Univ BCombStuds83. Linc Th Coll 80. **dss** 83 **d** 87 **p** 94. Greenford H Cross *Lon* 83-87; Par Dn 87-89; Par Dn Farnham Royal w Hedgerley *Ox* 89-92; Dn-in-c Seer Green and Jordans 92-94; P-in-c 94-97; TV Stantonbury and Willen 97-03; TR Basingstoke *Win* from 03; Hon Can Win Cathl from 08. *The Rectory, Church Street, Basingstoke RG21 7QT* Tel (01256) 326654 E-mail jostoker@dsl.pipex.com

STOKES, Canon Andrew John. b 38. G&C Coll Cam BA60 MA64. Ripon Hall Ox 60. **d** 62 **p** 63. C Northampton All SS w St Kath *Pet* 62-65; C Endcliffe *Sheff* 65-68; Ind Missr 65-68; Sen Ind Chapl 69-74; P-in-c Bridport *Sarum* 75-79; TR 79-80; V Holbeach Marsh *Linc* 82-88; Bp's Dom Chapl 88-92; Can Res and Prec Linc Cathl 92-03; rtd 03; Perm to Offic *Linc* from 03. *2 Lupin Road, Lincoln LN2 4GD* Tel (01522) 537595
E-mail andrew.stokes@ntlworld.com

STOKES, Colin Arthur (Ted). b 59. Birm Univ BDS82. WEMTC 00. **d** 03 **p** 04. NSM Bromyard *Heref* 03-08; NSM Bromyard and Stoke Lacy from 09. *Solmor Paddocks, Linley Green Road, Whitbourne, Worcester WR6 5RE* Tel (01886) 821625

STOKES, David Francis Robert. b 53. Lon Inst of Educn PGCE76 Peterho Cam MA81 Trin Coll Bris BA87. Cranmer Hall Dur 01. **d** 03 **p** 04. C Salisbury St Mark *Sarum* 03-08; Perm to Offic from 08. *Address temp unknown*
E-mail dsjs_stokes@lineone.net

STOKES (née VASTENHOUT), Mrs Jeannetta Hermina. b 62. St Jo Coll Nottm BA07. **d** 07 **p** 08. C Newport w Longford, Chetwynd and Forton *Lich* from 07. *4 Sandy Croft, Newport TF10 7NG* Tel (01952) 820420 Mobile 07985-923202
E-mail jeannetta.stokes@btopenworld.com

STOKES, Miss Mary Patricia. b 39. St Hilda's Coll Ox BA62 MA66 Lanc Univ MA80 Bris Univ CertEd63. EMMTC 78. **d** 87 **p** 94. Par Dn Pheasey *Lich* 87-93; C Walton-on-Thames *Guildf* 93-05; rtd 05. *21 Brittain Road, Walton-on-Thames KT12 4LR* Tel (01932) 248945 E-mail marystokes1@excite.co.uk

STOKES, Michael John. b 34. Lich Th Coll 63. **d** 65 **p** 66. C Worplesdon *Guildf* 65-68; Chapl RAF 68-84; Asst Chapl-in-Chief RAF 84-89; QHC 87-95; V Chesterton w Middleton Stoney and Wendlebury *Ox* 89-95; Chapl Bicester and Islip 90-95; Chapl Kyrenia St Andr Cyprus 95-00; rtd 00; Perm to Offic *Ox* from 00. *Keeper's Cottage, Manor Farm Lane, Chesterton, Bicester OX25 1UD* Tel and fax (01869) 248744

STOKES, Roger Sidney. b 47. Clare Coll Cam BA68 MA72. Sarum & Wells Th Coll 69. **d** 72 **p** 73. C Keighley *Bradf* 72-74; C Bolton St Jas w St Chrys 74-78; V Hightown *Wakef* 78-85; Dep

Chapl HM Pris Wakef 85-87; Chapl HM Pris Full Sutton 87-89; Perm to Offic *Wakef* 92-95; P-in-c Carlinghow 95-99; P-in-c Bedford St Martin *St Alb* from 99. *St Martin's Vicarage, 76 Clapham Road, Bedford MK41 7PN* Tel (01234) 357862
E-mail r.s.stokes.65@cantab.net

STOKES, Canon Simon Colin. b 62. Nene Coll Northn BSc83. Ridley Hall Cam 89. **d** 92 **p** 93. C New Catton Ch Ch *Nor* 92-96; P-in-c King's Lynn St Jo the Ev 96-06; P-in-c Bowthorpe from 06; Chapl Coll of W Anglia 01-06; Hon Can Nor Cathl from 06. *Church House, Bowthorpe Hall Road, Norwich NR5 9AA* Tel (01603) 747871 E-mail simon@simonstokes.co.uk

STOKES, Simon Jeremy. b 63. St Anne's Coll Ox BA86 MA90 Mass Inst of Tech SM88 Univ of Wales (Cardiff) LLM97 Solicitor 92. NTMTC BA08. **d** 08 **p** 09. NSM Clerkenwell H Redeemer *Lon* from 08. *Blake Lapthorn, Watchmaker Court, 33 St John's Lane, London EC1M 4DB* Tel (020) 7814 5482
E-mail frsstokes@googlemail.com

STOKES, Ted. *See* STOKES, Colin Arthur

STOKES, Terence Harold. b 46. Open Univ BA89. Sarum & Wells Th Coll 71. **d** 73 **p** 74. C Blakenall Heath *Lich* 73-75; C Walsall Wood 75-78; C Northampton St Alb *Pet* 78-81; TV Swinton St Pet *Man* 81-85; V Daisy Hill 85-92. *8 Westbury Close, Westhoughton, Bolton BL5 3UL* Tel (01942) 819057

STOKES, Terence Ronald. b 35. Linc Th Coll. **d** 69 **p** 70. C Bramley *Ripon* 69-72; C Osbournby w Scott Willoughby *Linc* 72-74; C Hykeham 74-77; V Birchwood 77-94; P-in-c Scopwick Gp 94-00; rtd 01; Perm to Offic *Linc* from 01. *47 Paddock Lane, Metheringham, Lincoln LN4 3YG* Tel (01526) 321753

STOKES, Preb Terence Walter. b 34. Bps' Coll Cheshunt 62. **d** 64 **p** 65. C Wanstead St Mary *Chelmsf* 64-67; C St Alb Abbey 67-70; Asst Dir RE *B & W* 70-75; Youth Chapl 70-75; P-in-c Yeovil 75-77; TV 77-82; TR Wellington and Distr 82-99; RD Tone 89-96; Preb Wells Cathl 90-99; rtd 99; Perm to Offic *B & W* from 99. *57 Mountfields Avenue, Taunton TA1 3BW* Tel (01823) 351424

STOKES-HARRISON, David Neville Hurford. b 41. FCA65 FCCA67 FInstM68. Qu Coll Birm 97. **d** 00 **p** 01. NSM Walsall *Lich* 00-07; NSM Edgmond w Kynnersley and Preston Wealdmoors from 07; NSM Tibberton w Bolas Magna and Waters Upton from 07. *The Rectory, Mill Lane, Tibberton, Newport TF10 8NL* Tel (01952) 551063
E-mail stokesharrison@btinternet.com

STOKOE, Prof Rodney James Robert. b 20. Dur Univ BSc46 BA48. Crozer Th Sem Pennsylvania ThM67 Atlantic Sch of Th Halifax (NS) Hon DD87. **d** 49 **p** 50. C W Hartlepool St Paul *Dur* 49-53; R Edin Ch Ch 53-57; P-in-c Bishopwearmouth St Gabr *Dur* 57-60; Canada from 60; Prof Div K Coll NS 60-71; Prof Past Th Atlantic Sch Th NS 71-85; rtd 85. *Fergus Hall C61, 378 Young Street, Truro NS B2N 7H2, Canada* Tel (001) (902) 843 8076 E-mail rodstokoe20@yahoo.ca

STOKOE, Wayne Jeffrey. b 56. Coll of Resurr Mirfield 94. **d** 96 **p** 97. C Sheff St Cath Richmond Road 96-99; V Edlington from 99. *The Vicarage, 17 Heaton Gardens, Edlington, Doncaster DN12 1SY* Tel (01709) 858358
E-mail wjs@stokoej.freeserve.co.uk

STOLTZ, Christopher Barry. b 76. St Olaf Coll Minnesota BA99. Concordia Th Sem Indiana MDiv03. **d** 06 **p** 07. C Highgate St Mich *Lon* from 06. *10B The Grove, London N6 6LB* Tel (020) 8341 7589 E-mail cbstoltz@yahoo.com

STONE, Adrian Gordon. b 68. Trent Poly BSc89 Nottm Univ PGCE92. St Jo Coll Nottm 01. **d** 03 **p** 04. C Bayston Hill *Lich* 03-06; V Stafford St Jo and Tixall w Ingestre from 06. *St John's Vicarage, Westhead Avenue, Stafford ST16 3RP* Tel (01785) 253493 Mobile 07739-043709
E-mail adrian@the-stone-family.net

STONE, Albert John. b 44. Loughb Univ BTech67 BSc. Sarum & Wells Th Coll 83. **d** 85 **p** 86. C Plymstock *Ex* 85-88; P-in-c Whitestone 88-92; P-in-c Oldridge 88-92; P-in-c Holcombe Burnell 88-92; R Tedburn St Mary, Whitestone, Oldridge etc 93-94; P-in-c Yarcombe w Membury and Upottery 94; P-in-c Cotleigh 94; V Yarcombe, Membury, Upottery and Cotleigh 95-99; P-in-c Bampton, Morebath, Clayhanger and Petton from 99. *The Vicarage, Station Road, Bampton, Tiverton EX16 9NG* Tel and fax (01398) 331466 E-mail ajstone@argonet.co.uk

STONE, Miss Carol Ann. b 54. TD04. Leic Univ BA75 Qu Coll Cam BA77 MA81. Westcott Ho Cam 76. **d** 79 **p** 79. C Bradford-on-Avon *Sarum* 78-81; R Corsley 81-83; Chapl Dauntsey's Sch Devizes 83-88; V Studley *Sarum* 89-94; Chapl Cheltenham Coll 94-95; Venezuela 95-96; V Upper Stratton *Bris* from 96; P-in-c Penhill from 06; CF (ACF) 84-89; CF(V) 90-04. *The Vicarage, 67 Beechcroft Road, Swindon SN2 7RE* Tel (01793) 723095 Mobile 07702-342848 E-mail revcarolstone@btopenworld.com

STONE, Christopher. *See* STONE, Canon John Christopher

STONE, Christopher John. b 49. Lanc Univ MA89 Keele Univ MA92. Lambeth STh84 Linc Th Coll 78. **d** 81 **p** 82. C Bromley St Mark *Roch* 81-84; R Burgh-by-Sands and Kirkbampton w Kirkandrews etc *Carl* 84-89; Chapl N Staffs R Infirmary Stoke-on-Trent 89-93; Co-ord Staff Support Services N Staffs Hosp

93-09; rtd 09. *28 Apedale Road, Wood Lane, Stoke-on-Trent ST7 8PH* Tel (01782) 720332
E-mail christopherstn550@googlemail.com

STONE, Christopher Martyn Luke. b 78. Glam Univ BA99. St Steph Ho Ox 99. **d** 02 **p** 03. C Merthyr Tydfil Ch Ch *Llan* 02-07; TV Bassaleg *Mon* from 07. *St John's Vicarage, Wern Terrace, Rogerstone, Newport NP10 9FG* Tel (01633) 893357
E-mail vicchris@waitrose.com

STONE, David Adrian. b 56. Oriel Coll Ox BA78 MA83 BM, BCh83. Wycliffe Hall Ox 85. **d** 88 **p** 89. C Holborn St Geo w H Trin and St Bart *Lon* 88-91; C S Kensington St Jude 91-93; V 93-02; AD Chelsea 96-02; TR Newbury *Ox* from 02. *The Rectory, 64 Northcroft Lane, Newbury RG14 1BN* Tel (01635) 40326 *or* 47018 Fax 30725 Mobile 07973-215927
E-mail david@dandb.org.uk *or* rector@st-nicolas-newbury.org

STONE, Dominic Charles. b 63. Ridley Hall Cam 97. **d** 99 **p** 00. C Ashbourne w Mapleton *Derby* 99-02; TV Uttoxeter Area *Lich* from 02. *13 Moisty Lane, Marchington, Uttoxeter ST14 8JY* Tel (01283) 820030

STONE, Elizabeth Karen Forbes. *See* FORBES STONE, Elizabeth Karen

STONE, Geoffrey. *See* STONE, John Geoffrey Elliot

STONE, The Ven Godfrey Owen. b 49. Ex Coll Ox BA71 MA75 W Midl Coll of Educn PGCE72. Wycliffe Hall Ox BA78. **d** 81 **p** 82. C Rushden w Newton Bromswold *Pet* 81-87; Dir Past Studies Wycliffe Hall Ox 87-92; TR Bucknall and Bagnall *Lich* 92-02; RD Stoke 98-02; Adn Stoke from 02; P-in-c Edensor 04-07. *Archdeacon's House, 39 The Brackens, Newcastle ST5 4JL* Tel (01782) 663066 Fax 711165
E-mail archdeacon.stoke@lichfield.anglican.org

STONE, Ian Matthew. b 72. Ox Univ BTh08. Ripon Coll Cuddesdon 03. **d** 05 **p** 06. C Hammersmith St Pet *Lon* 05-08; V Queensbury All SS from 08. *The Vicarage, 24 Waltham Drive, Edgware HA8 5PQ* Tel (020) 8952 4536
E-mail matthew.stone1@virgin.net

STONE, Jeffrey Peter. b 34. Nottm Univ TCert72 BEd73. Lich Th Coll 58. **d** 61 **p** 62. C Newark St Mary *S'well* 61-65; C Sutton in Ashfield St Mich 65-69; Robert Smyth Sch Market Harborough 72-89; R Waltham on the Wolds, Stonesby, Saxby etc *Leic* 90-96; rtd 96; Perm to Offic *Leic* from 99. *71 Redland Road, Oakham LE15 6PH* Tel (01572) 756842

STONE, John. *See* STONE, Albert John

STONE, John Anthony. b 46. St Chad's Coll Dur BA68 Univ of Wales (Lamp) MA05. **d** 69 **p** 70. C New Addington *Cant* 69-72; C Tewkesbury w Walton Cardiff *Glouc* 72-76; C-in-c Dedworth CD *Ox* 76-82; V Dedworth 82-86; TV Chipping Barnet w Arkley *St Alb* 86-95; R Baldock w Bygrave 95-03; R Ches H Trin from 03. *The Rectory, 50 Norris Road, Chester CH1 5DZ* Tel (01244) 372721 E-mail jastone@dunelm.org.uk

STONE, Canon John Christopher. b 53. Newc Univ BA74 Birkbeck Coll Lon MA77 MSTSD74 LGSM73 MIPR FRSA. Oak Hill Nm Course 89. **d** 92 **p** 93. NSM Southfleet *Roch* 92-07; Dioc Communications Officer 96-03; Chapl Univ of Greenwich 98-99; Hon Can Roch Cathl from 02; Bp's Dom Chapl 03-07; Bp's Media Adv 03-07; Bp's Communications Consultant from 07; R Gravesend St Geo from 07. *St George's Rectory, 54 The Avenue, Gravesend DA11 0LX* Tel (01474) 534965 E-mail chris.stone@rochester.anglican.org

STONE, John Geoffrey Elliot. b 20. Ch Coll Cam BA41 MA45. Ridley Hall Cam 47. **d** 49 **p** 50. C Wellingborough St Barn *Pet* 49-51; C Bexhill St Pet *Chich* 51-56; C Field St Pet 56-59; V Southwater 59-70; V Thornham w Titchwell *Nor* 70-74; R Copdock w Washbrook and Belstead *St E* 74-77; P-in-c Therfield *St Alb* 77-82; P-in-c Kelshall 77-82; C Littlehampton St Jas *Chich* 82-85; C Littlehampton St Mary 82-85; C Wick 82-85; TV Littlehampton and Wick 86; rtd 86; C Compton, the Mardens, Stoughton and Racton *Chich* 86-92; Perm to Offic *Nor* 92-96 and *Chich* from 96. *11 Ramsay Hall, Byron Road, Worthing BN11 3HN* Tel (01903) 212947

STONE, Martyn. *See* STONE, Christopher Martyn Luke

STONE, Matthew. *See* STONE, Ian Matthew

STONE, Michael Graham. b 33. FBCS. S Dios Minl Tr Scheme. **d** 83 **p** 84. NSM Chich St Paul and St Pet 83-95; NSM Chich 95-98; rtd 98; Perm to Offic *Chich* from 98. *125 Cedar Drive, Chichester PO19 3EL* Tel (01243) 784484

STONE, Michael John. b 33. Trin Hall Cam MA56 LLB58. EAMTC 78. **d** 80 **p** 81. NSM Whitton and Thurleston w Akenham *St E* 80-84; NSM Westerfield and Tuddenham w Witnesham 84-95; Dioc Chr Stewardship Adv 93-95; P-in-c Coddenham w Gosbeck and Hemingstone w Henley 95-98; Asst P 98-02; Asst P Crowfield w Stonham Aspal and Mickfield 98-02; Dioc Voc Adv 95-99; rtd 02; Perm to Offic *St E* from 02. *10 Coppice Close, Melton, Woodbridge IP12 1RX* Tel (01394) 385810 E-mail mjaystone@aol.com

STONE, Nigel John. b 57. Bedf Coll Lon BSc82 Lon Bible Coll MA95. St Jo Coll Nottm 82. **d** 85 **p** 86. C Battersea Park St Sav *S'wark* 85-87; C Battersea St Sav and St Geo w St Andr 87-89; P-in-c Brixton St Paul 89-92; V 92-97; Adult Education and Tr Officer from 97; Hon Chapl S'wark Cathl from 97. *11 Wilkinson*

Street, London SW8 1DD Tel (020) 7582 6424 *or* 8545 2440 Fax 8545 2441 E-mail nigel.stone@southwark.anglican.org

STONE, Philip William. b 58. Ridley Hall Cam 85. **d** 88 **p** 89. C Hackney Marsh *Lon* 88-97; V Kensal Rise St Mark and St Martin 97-04; TR from 04; AD Brent from 03. *Kensal Rise Vicarage, 93 College Road, London NW10 5EU* Tel (020) 8969 4598 E-mail philstone@freenet.co.uk
or phil.stone@london.anglican.org

STONEBANKS, David Arthur. b 34. Louvain Univ Belgium MA70. Coll of Resurr Mirfield 64. **d** 66 **p** 67. C Burgess Hill St Jo *Chich* 66-68; Chapl City Univ 70-73; Chapl Strasbourg w Stuttgart and Heidelberg *Eur* 73-80; Chapl Geneva 80-86; Chapl Zürich w St Gallen and Winterthur 86-89; R Horsted Keynes *Chich* 89-99; rtd 99; Perm to Offic *S'wark* from 01. *42 Home Park, Oxted RH8 0JU* Tel (01883) 732339

STONEHOLD, Wilfred Leslie. b 33. St Luke's Coll Ex TCert71. **d** 99 **p** 00. OLM Harlescott *Lich* 99-06; Perm to Offic from 06. *19 Wendsley Road, Harlescott Grange, Shrewsbury SY1 3PE* Tel (01743) 369237

STONES, John Graham. b 49. Southn Univ BSc72. SWMTC 91. **d** 94 **p** 95. C Okehampton w Inwardleigh, Bratton Clovelly etc *Ex* 94-97; TV Sidmouth, Woolbrook, Salcombe Regis, Sidbury etc 97-04; R Church Stretton *Heref* 04-07; TR Teignmouth, Ideford w Luton, Ashcombe etc *Ex* from 07. *The Rectory, 30 Dawlish Road, Teignmouth TQ14 8TG* Tel (01626) 774445

STONESTREET, George Malcolm. b 38. MBE05. AKC61. **d** 62 **p** 63. C Leeds St Pet *Ripon* 62-64; C Far Headingley St Chad 64-67; V Askrigg w Stallingbusk 67-82; V Bramley 82-85; TR 85-94; V Eskdale, Irton, Muncaster and Waberthwaite *Carl* 94-03; rtd 03. *Northside, Grange, Keswick CA12 5UQ* Tel (01768) 777671 E-mail malcolm@dip.edi.co.uk

STOODLEY, Peter Bindon. b 47. Linc Th Coll 89. **d** 91 **p** 92. C Holbeck *Ripon* 91-94; P-in-c Osmondthorpe St Phil 94-99; V Sowerby Bridge *Wakef* 99-09; rtd 09; Perm to Offic *Wakef* from 09. *24 Benomley Drive, Huddersfield HD5 8LX* Tel (01484) 420613 E-mail maverick.stoodley@tiscali.co.uk

STORDY, Richard Andrew. b 64. St Jo Coll Ox BA86 Barrister 86. Cranmer Hall Dur BA97. **d** 98 **p** 99. C Gt Horton *Bradf* 98-02; V Chapeltown *Sheff* from 02. *St John's Vicarage, 23 Housley Park, Chapeltown, Sheffield S35 2UE* Tel 0114-257 0966

STOREY, Earl. *See* STOREY, William Earl Cosbey

STOREY, Gerard Charles Alfred. b 57. Thames Poly BSc80 Lon Univ PhD84 GRSC80. Wycliffe Hall Ox 84. **d** 87 **p** 88. C Broadwater *Chich* 87-92; TV 92-95; Chapl Northbrook Coll of Design and Tech 90-95; Oman 95-99; P-in-c Guernsey H Trin *Win* 99-01; V 01-07; P-in-c Bream *Glouc* from 07. *The Vicarage, Coleford Road, Bream, Lydney GL15 6ES* Tel (01594) 563579 E-mail gerardstorey@yahoo.co.uk

STOREY, Canon Michael. b 36. Chich Th Coll 73. **d** 75 **p** 76. C Illingworth *Wakef* 75-78; V Rastrick St Jo 78-87; V Crosland Moor 87-06; Hon Can Wakef Cathl 00-06; rtd 06; Perm to Offic *Wakef* from 07. *198 Healey Wood Road, Brighouse HD6 3RW* Tel (01484) 713663 E-mail mickthevic@googlemail.com

STOREY, Mrs Patricia Louise. b 60. TCD MA83. CITC BTh94. **d** 97 **p** 98. C Ballymena w Ballyclug *Conn* 97-00; C Glenavy w Tunny and Crumlin 00-04; I Londonderry St Aug *D & R* from 04. *St Augustine's Rectory, 4 Bridgewater, Londonderry BT47 6YA* Tel (028) 7134 7532
E-mail patriciastorey56@yahoo.co.uk

STOREY, Timothy. b 60. Trin Coll Bris 92. **d** 94 **p** 95. C Bath Weston St Jo w Kelston *B & W* 94-98; C Shirley *Win* 98-03; R Blandford Forum and Langton Long *Sarum* from 03. *The Rectory, 2 Portman Place, Blandford Forum DT11 7DG* Tel (01258) 480092 E-mail t.storey@btopenworld.com

STOREY, William Earl Cosbey. b 58. Kent Univ BA MPhil. CITC. **d** 82 **p** 83. C Drumglass w Moygashel *Arm* 82-86; I Crinken *D & G* 86-96; I Glenavy w Tunny and Crumlin *Conn* 98-04. *St Augustine's Rectory, 4 Bridgewater, Londonderry BT47 6YA* Tel (028) 7134 7532
E-mail es@cofire.freeserve.co.uk

STOREY, William Leslie Maurice. b 31. Oak Hill Th Coll 67. **d** 69 **p** 70. C Wembley St Jo *Lon* 69-71; C Ealing Dean St Jo 71-75; V W Derby St Luke *Liv* 75-80; Hon C Brixton Hill St Sav 83-86; P-in-c 87-88; P-in-c Brixton Hill St Sav 83-86; rtd 88; Perm to Offic *S'wark* 88-02. *124 Surbiton Hill Park, Surbiton KT5 8EP* Tel (020) 8390 2821

STORY, Victor Leonard. b 45. St Mark & St Jo Coll Lon TCert66 Brighton Poly BSc74 LIMA74. Ripon Coll Cuddesdon 80. **d** 81 **p** 82. C Evesham *Worc* 81-85; P-in-c Ilmington w Stretton on Fosse and Ditchford *Cov* 85-90; P-in-c Ilmington w Stretton-on-Fosse etc 90-96; Chapl Vlissingen (Flushing) Miss to Seamen *Eur* 96-97; Chapl Rotterdam Miss to Seamen 97-99; R Gt w Lt Milton and Gt Haseley *Ox* from 99. *The Rectory, Great Milton, Oxford OX44 7PN* Tel (01844) 279498

STOTE, Mrs Judith Ann. b 50. Qu Coll Birm 07. **d** 09. OLM Studley *Cov* from 09. *The Paddocks, Birmingham Road, Mappleborough Green, Studley B80 7DJ* Tel (01527) 852515 E-mail judy@ardenmarches.com

STOTE, Mrs Pamela Anne. b 49. Dudley Coll of Educn TCert70 Open Univ BA83. WMMTC 97. **d** 00 **p** 01. NSM Cov St Geo 00-03; NSM Whitley from 03. *St James's Church, 171 Abbey Road, Coventry CV3 4BG* Tel and fax (024) 7630 1617 Mobile 07905-230924 E-mail st.james@stote.force9.co.uk

STOTER, David John. b 43. MBE02. K Coll Lon AKC66. **d** 67 **p** 68. C Reading St Giles *Ox* 67-71; C Luton Lewsey St Hugh *St Alb* 71-73; Chapl Westmr Hosp Lon 73-79; Convenor of Chapls Notts Distr HA 79-94; Chapl Univ Hosp Nottm 79-94; Chapl Nottm Gen Hosp 79-02; Sen Chapl Qu Medical Cen Nottm Univ Hosp NHS Trust 94-02; Sen Chapl Notts Healthcare NHS Trust 94-02; Manager Chapl and Bereavement Services 94-02; R Gedling *S'well* 02-06; rtd 06; Hon C Nettlebed w Bix, Highmoor, Pishill etc *Ox* from 08. *203 Greys Road, Henley-on-Thames RG9 1SP* Tel (01491) 579773 E-mail david-stoter@yahoo.co.uk

STOTESBURY, Robert John. d 06 **p** 07. Aux Min Ferns w Kilbride, Toombe, Kilcormack etc *C & O* from 06. *Croneyhorn, Carnew, Arklow, Co Wicklow, Republic of Ireland* Tel (00353) (53) 942 6300 E-mail robertstotesbury2002@eircom.net

STOTT, Andrew David. b 61. NOC 03. **d** 05 **p** 06. C Walton Breck *Liv* 05-09; P-in-c W Derby St Luke from 09. *St Luke's Vicarage, Princess Drive, West Derby, Liverpool L14 8XG* Tel 0151-259 8125 Mobile 07510-222374 E-mail andrew@stott401.fsnet.co.uk

STOTT, Antony. b 21. Bps' Coll Cheshunt 53. **d** 55 **p** 56. Australia 55-62; V Longbridge Deverill w Hill Deverill *Sarum* 62-66; V Bratton 66-74; R Marnhull 74-81; P-in-c Broad Chalke and Bower Chalke 81; P-in-c Ebbesbourne Wake w Fifield Bavant and Alvediston 81; P-in-c Berwick St John 81; V Chalke Valley W 81-87; rtd 87; Perm to Offic *Ex* from 87. *11 Luscombe Close, Ivybridge PL21 9TT* Tel (01752) 896142 E-mail revtony1@aol.com

STOTT, Christopher John. b 45. Lon Univ BD68. Tyndale Hall Bris. **d** 69 **p** 70. C Croydon Ch Ch Broad Green *Cant* 69-72; Ethiopia 73-76; Area Sec (SW) BCMS 76-78; Tanzania 78-85; R Harwell w Chilton *Ox* from 85; RD Wallingford 91-95. *The Rectory, Harwell, Didcot OX11 0EW* Tel (01235) 835365

STOTT, Eric. b 36. ALCD62. **d** 62 **p** 63. C Penn Fields *Lich* 62-65; C Normanton *Derby* 65-71; R Lower Broughton St Clem w St Matthias *Man* 71-79; V Chadderton Em 79-01; rtd 01; Perm to Offic *Glouc* from 01. *21 Laynes Road, Hucclecote, Gloucester GL3 3PU* Tel (01452) 534492

STOTT, Frederick. b 23. Portsm Univ MA05 CQSW71. Sarum & Wells Th Coll 83. **d** 85 **p** 86. NSM Sholing *Win* 85-90; Perm to Offic *Portsm* 89-06; *Win* 90-06; *Sarum* 93-06; rtd 06. *35 Broadwater Road, Southampton SO18 2DW* Tel (023) 8055 7193

STOTT, Gary. b 69. Leeds Univ BA92 St Jo Coll Dur MA99. Cranmer Hall Dur 97. **d** 99 **p** 00. C Farnley *Ripon* 99-03; V Manston 03-06; Care Cen Manager St Geo Crypt Leeds 06-07; Dir from 07. *St George's Crypt, Great George Street, Leeds LS1 3BR* Tel 0113-245 9061 Fax 244 3646 E-mail gary.stott@stgeorgescrypt.org.uk

STOTT, John Robert Walmsley. b 21. CBE06. Trin Coll Cam BA45 MA50 Lambeth DD83. Ridley Hall Cam 44. **d** 45 **p** 46. C St Marylebone All So w SS Pet and Jo *Lon* 45-50; R 50-75; Hon C 75-88; Hon C Langham Place All So from 88; Chapl to The Queen 59-91; Extra Chapl to The Queen from 91; Dir Lon Inst of Contemporary Christianity 82-86; Pres from 86; rtd 91. *12 Weymouth Street, London W1W 5BY* Tel (020) 7580 1867

STOTT, Jonathan. d 07 **p** 07. NSM Cheltenham H Trin and St Paul *Glouc* from 07. *29 Brizen Lane, Cheltenham GL53 0NG* Tel (01242) 228894 E-mail jonathan@glenfall.org.uk

STOTT, Jonathan Robert. b 67. Ripon Coll Cuddesdon. **d** 01 **p** 02. C Anfield St Columba *Liv* 01-05; V Dovecot from 05. *Holy Spirit Vicarage, Dovecot Avenue, Liverpool L14 7QJ* Tel 0151-220 6611 Mobile 07971-876517 E-mail jonathan_r_stott@hotmail.com

STOTT, Miss Teresa. b 57. Linc Th Coll 94. **d** 94 **p** 95. C Lee-on-the-Solent *Portsm* 94-97; C Spalding St Jo w Deeping St Nicholas *Linc* 97-98; P-in-c Freiston w Butterwick 98-99; R Freiston w Butterwick and Benington 99-03; R Freiston, Butterwick w Bennington, and Leverton 03-04; C-in-c Cleethorpes St Fran CD from 04; Chapl Matthew Humberston Sch from 04; Chapl St Andr Hospice Grimsby from 04. *St Francis House, 19B Sandringham Road, Cleethorpes DN35 9HA* Tel (01472) 691215

STOW, John Mark. b 51. Selw Coll Cam BA73 MA77. Linc Th Coll 76. **d** 78 **p** 79. C Harpenden St Jo *St Alb* 78-82; TV Beaminster Area *Sarum* 82-87; P-in-c Hawkchurch 87-90; P-in-c Marshwood Vale 87-88; TR Marshwood Vale 88-91; Past Co-ord Millfield Jun Sch from 93. *Chestnut House, Edgarley, Glastonbury BA6 8LL* Tel (01458) 832245

STOW, Peter John. b 50. Oak Hill Th Coll. **d** 89 **p** 90. C Forest Gate St Mark *Chelmsf* 89-94; V from 94. *St Mark's Vicarage, Tylney Road, London E7 0LS* Tel (020) 8555 2988 E-mail saintmarks@clara.co.uk

STOW, Archdeacon of. *See* SINCLAIR, The Ven Jane Elizabeth Margaret

STOWE, Brian. b 32. Trin Coll Cam BA55 BA56 MA59. Ridley Hall Cam 55. **d** 57 **p** 58. C New Catton St Luke *Nor* 57-59; Chapl R Masonic Sch Bushey 59-70; Tutor Rickmansworth Sch Herts 70-71; Chapl Alleyn's Foundn Dulwich 71-75; Hon C Dulwich St Barn *S'wark* 71-75; Chapl Ellerslie Sch Malvern 75-92; Chapl Malvern Coll 92-93; TV Malvern Link w Cowleigh *Worc* 93-94; rtd 95; P-in-c Malvern St Andr *Worc* 95-96; Perm to Offic from 96. *31 Park View, Grange Road, Malvern WR14 3HG* Tel 07792-515307 (mobile) E-mail bandmstowe@onetel.com

STOWE, Mrs Katharine Elizabeth. b 78. Birm Univ BA01 PGCE02 Trin Coll Cam BA06. Westcott Ho Cam 04. **d** 07 **p** 08. C Salter Street and Shirley *Birm* from 07. *93 Baxters Road, Shirley, Solihull B90 2RS* Tel 0121-745 8896 E-mail katestowe@yahoo.com

STOWE, Nigel James. b 36. Bris Univ BSc57. Clifton Th Coll 59. **d** 61 **p** 62. C Ware Ch Ch *St Alb* 61-64; C Reigate St Mary *S'wark* 64-67; V Islington St Jude Mildmay Park *Lon* 67-75; V Penn Street *Ox* 75-01; rtd 01. *27 Snowdrop Way, Widmer End, High Wycombe HP15 6BL* Tel (01494) 717496

STOWE, Canon Rachel Lilian. b 33. Qu Coll Birm 79. **dss** 83 **d** 87 **p** 94. Dean w Yelden, Melchbourne and Shelton *St Alb* 82-87; Pertenhall w Swineshead 82-87; Bp's Officer for NSMs and Asst Dir of Ords 87-93; NSM The Stodden Churches *St Alb* 87-96; Hon Can St Alb 92-96; Convenor Dioc Adv Gp for Chr Healing *Ripon* 98-03; Perm to Offic *Ripon* from 97 and *York* from 98. *Preston Cottage, East Cowton, Northallerton DL7 0BD* Tel and fax (01325) 378173 Mobile 07860-618600 E-mail rachel@stowe2106.freeserve.co.uk

STRACHAN, Donald Philip Michael. b 37. St D Coll Lamp 60. **d** 62 **p** 63. C Aberdeen St Mary 62-64; P-in-c Aberdeen St Paul 64-66; Chapl St Andr Cathl 65-68; Itinerant Priest *Mor* 68-73; R Coatbridge *Glas* 73-85; Chapl HM Pris Glas (Barlinnie) 84-87; Dioc Supernumerary *Glas* 85-94; rtd 94; Perm to Offic *Arg* 87-06; Lic to Offic from 06. *Reul na Mara, Claddach Kirkibost, Isle of North Uist HS6 5EP* Tel (01876) 580392

STRACHAN, Mrs Gillian Lesley. b 44. Furzedown Coll of Educn TCert65 Open Univ BA77 Hatf Poly MA87. EAMTC 03. **d** 06 **p** 07. C Aquitaine *Eur* from 06. *La Gravette, 24150 Bayac, France* Tel and fax (0033) (5) 53 58 12 58 Mobile (6) 76 39 25 15 E-mail gillstrachan@wanadoo.fr

STRAFFORD, Mrs Elizabeth. d 09. NSM Dur N from 09. *41 The Orchard, Pity Me, Durham DH1 5DA* Tel 0191-384 9802

STRAFFORD, Nigel Thomas Bevan. b 53. Univ of Wales (Lamp) BA80. Sarum & Wells Th Coll 80. **d** 82 **p** 94. C Kidderminster St Mary *Worc* 82; C Kidderminster St Mary and All SS, Trimpley etc 82-83; Hon C Stockton St Mark *Dur* 84-86; Asst P Longwood *Wakef* 86-94; V Athersley 94-97; P-in-c Ferrybridge 97-03; P-in-c Holme and Seaton Ross Gp *York* 03-04; R from 04. *The Vicarage, Market Weighton Road, Holme-on-Spalding-Moor, York YO43 4AG* Tel (01430) 860248

STRAIN, Christopher Malcolm. b 56. Solicitor Southn Univ LLB77. Wycliffe Hall Ox 83. **d** 86 **p** 87. C Werrington *Pet* 86-89; C Broadwater *Chich* 89-94; TV Hampreston *Sarum* 94-00; P-in-c Parkstone St Luke 00-03; V from 03. *The Vicarage, 2 Birchwood Road, Parkstone, Poole BH14 9NP* Tel (01202) 741030

STRAIN, John Damian. b 49. Keele Univ BA72 Birkbeck Coll Lon MSc83 PhD89 AFBPsS89. STETS BTh00. **d** 00 **p** 01. NSM Hindhead *Guildf* 00-03; NSM Churt and Hindhead from 03. *Pinewoods, Church Lane, Grayshott, Hindhead GU26 6LY* Tel (01428) 607115 E-mail j.strain@surrey.ac.uk

STRAINE, Gillian Kathleen. b 79. Imp Coll Lon BSc00 PhD05. Ripon Coll Cuddesdon BA08. **d** 09. C Kidlington w Hampton Poyle *Ox* from 09. *29 Andersons Close, Kidlington, Oxford OX5 1ST* Tel 07747-010249 (mobile) E-mail gstraine@yahoo.co.uk

STRANACK, The Very Revd David Arthur Claude. b 43. Chich Th Coll 65. **d** 68 **p** 69. C Forest Gate St Edm *Chelmsf* 68-69; C Colchester St Jas, All SS, St Nic and St Runwald 69-74; V Brentwood St Geo 74-82; V Nayland w Wiston *St E* 82-99; R Hadleigh 99-02; V Hadleigh, Layham and Shelley 02-08; Dean Bocking 99-08; RD Hadleigh 99-07; Hon Can St E Cathl 94-08; rtd 08; Perm to Offic *St E* from 08. *12 Sandy Lane, Sudbury CO10 7HG* Tel (01787) 881657

STRANACK, Canon Richard Nevill. b 40. Leeds Univ BA63. Coll of Resurr Mirfield 63. **d** 65 **p** 66. C Bush Hill Park St Mark *Lon* 65-68; C Brighton St Martin *Chich* 68-72; P-in-c Toftrees w Shereford *Nor* 72-74; V 74-81; P-in-c Pensthorpe 72-74; R 74-81; V Hempton and Pudding Norton 72-81; RD Burnham and Walsingham 78-81; V Par *Truro* 81-94; P-in-c St Blazey 87-91; Hon Chapl Miss to Seafarers from 81; V Stratton and Launcells *Truro* 94-06; RD Stratton 02-05; Chapl Cornwall Healthcare NHS Trust 97-02; Chapl N and E Cornwall Primary Care Trust 02-06; rtd 06; P-in-c Duloe, Herodsfoot, Morval and St Pinnock *Truro* 06-08; Hon Can Truro Cathl 98-08. *8 Sunwine Place, Exmouth EX8 2SE* Tel (01395) 225638 E-mail rnstranack@yahoo.co.uk

STRANG, Martin Guthrie. b 55. Bris Univ BSc76 Paisley Coll of Tech MSc83 MIMechE85. St Jo Coll Nottm 07. **d** 09. C Trowell, Awsworth and Cossall *S'well* from 09. *The Vicarage, The Lane, Awsworth, Nottingham NG16 2QP* Tel 0115-932 8143 Mobile 07908-995450

STRANGE, Alan Michael. b 57. Pemb Coll Ox BA79 MA89. Wycliffe Hall Ox BA84. **d** 84 **p** 85. C York St Paul 84-87; Asst Chapl Brussels Cathl 87-91; Assoc Chapl 91-95; P-in-c Heigham H Trin *Nor* 95-99; R from 99. *The Rectory, 17 Essex Street, Norwich NR2 2BL* Tel (01603) 622225
E-mail rector@trinitynorwich.org *or* big1al@ntlworld.com

STRANGE, Brian. b 47. QUB BA69. SWMTC 98. **d** 01 **p** 02. NSM Georgeham *Ex* 01-03; P-in-c from 03. *Southcombe, Putsborough Road, Georgeham, Braunton EX33 1JU* Tel (01271) 890961 E-mail brian@croyde.org

STRANGE, Bryan. b 26. Sarum & Wells Th Coll 73. **d** 75 **p** 76. C King's Worthy *Win* 75-78; C Wilton *B & W* 78-80; V Kewstoke w Wick St Lawrence 80-89; rtd 89; Perm to Offic *Ex* from 90. *29 Bluebell Avenue, Tiverton EX16 6SX*

STRANGE, Malcolm. b 58. Westmr Coll Ox MTh95. Sarum & Wells Th Coll 82. **d** 85 **p** 86. C Seaton Hirst *Newc* 85-88; C Ridgeway *Sarum* 88-89; TV 89-91; TV Newbury *Ox* 91-98; TR Bideford, Northam, Westward Ho!, Appledore etc *Ex* 98-01; RD Hartland 99-01. *Address withheld by request*

✠**STRANGE, The Rt Revd Mark Jeremy.** b 61. Aber Univ LTh82. Linc Th Coll 83. **d** 89 **p** 90 **c** 07. C Worc St Barn w Ch Ch 89-92; V Worc St Wulstan 92-98; R Edinburgh w Lossiemouth *Mor* 98-07; P-in-c Dufftown 04-07; P-in-c Aberlour 04-07; Can St Andr Cathl Inverness 00-07; Syn Clerk 03-07; Bp Mor from 07. *Bishop's House, St John's, Arpafeelie, North Kessock, Inverness IV1 3XD* Tel (01463) 811333
E-mail bishop@moray.anglican.org

STRANGE, Canon Peter Robert. b 48. Univ Coll Lon BA69 Ex Coll Ox BA71 MA76. Cuddesdon Coll 71. **d** 72 **p** 73. C Denton *Newc* 72-74; C Newc St Jo 74-79; Chapl for Arts and Recreation 79-90; R Wallsend St Pet 79-86; Can Res Newc Cathl from 86; Angl Adv Tyne Tees TV from 90; Asst Dioc Dir of Ords *Newc* 94-98. *55 Queen's Terrace, Jesmond, Newcastle upon Tyne NE2 2PL* Tel 0191-281 0181 *or* 232 1939 Fax 230 0735
E-mail peterstrange@stnicnewcastle.co.uk

STRANGE, Preb Robert Lewis. b 45. Sarum & Wells Th Coll 72. **d** 74 **p** 75. C Walthamstow St Barn and St Jas Git *Chelmsf* 74-77; C Wickford 77-80; P-in-c Treverbyn *Truro* 80-83; V 83-86; Asst Stewardship Adv 82-96; V Newlyn St Pet from 86; Preb Trehaverock from 94; Hon Chapl Miss to Seafarers from 86. *St Peter's Vicarage, Newlyn, Penzance TR18 5HT* Tel (01736) 362678 Fax 351174 E-mail robert.sarov@tiscali.co.uk

STRANGE, The Ven William Anthony. b 53. Qu Coll Cam BA76 MA80 K Alfred's Coll Win CertEd77 Ox Univ DPhil89. Wycliffe Hall Ox 79. **d** 82 **p** 83. Tutor Wycliffe Hall Ox 82-87; C Aberystwyth *St D* 87; TV 87-91; V Llandeilo Fawr and Taliaris 91-96; Hd of Th and RS Trin Coll Carmarthen 96-01; V Carmarthen St Pet *St D* 03-09; AD Carmarthen 06-09; V Pencarreg and Llanycrwys from 09; Adn Cardigan from 09. *The Vicarage, Cwmann, Lampeter SA48 8DU* Tel (01570) 422385
E-mail archdeacon.cardigan@churchinwales.org.uk

STRANRAER-MULL, The Very Revd Gerald Hugh. b 42. AKC69. St Aug Coll Cant 69. **d** 70 **p** 71. C Hexham *Newc* 70-72; C Corbridge w Halton 72; R Ellon *Ab* 72-08; R Cruden Bay 72-08; Can St Andr Cathl 81-08; Dean Ab 88-08; P-in-c Peterhead 02-04; rtd 08. *75 The Cairns, Muir of Ord IV6 7AT* Tel (01463) 870986 E-mail stranraermull@btinternet.com

STRAPPS, Canon Robert David. b 28. St Edm Hall Ox BA52 MA56. Wycliffe Hall Ox 52. **d** 54 **p** 55. C Low Leyton *Chelmsf* 54-57; C Ox St Aldate w H Trin 57-60; V Sandal St Helen *Wakef* 60-94; RD Chevet 81-93; Hon Can Wakef Cathl 92-94; rtd 94; Perm to Offic *Wakef* 94-98; *Glouc* and *Worc* from 94. *Brookside, Hill Road, Kemerton, Tewkesbury GL20 7JN* Tel (01386) 725515

STRASZAK, Edmund Norman. b 57. Coll of Resurr Mirfield 88. **d** 90 **p** 91. C Adlington *Blackb* 90-93; C Harrogate St Wilfrid and St Luke *Ripon* 93-95; V Chorley All SS *Blackb* from 95. *All Saints' Vicarage, Moor Road, Chorley PR7 2LR* Tel (01257) 265665 E-mail edmund@straszak.freeserve.co.uk

STRATFORD, Mrs Anne Barbara. Southn Univ CertEd58 Ox Univ MTh99. Qu Coll Birm 88. **d** 91 **p** 94. Officer Dioc Bd of Soc Resp (Family Care) *Lich* 85-97; NSM Kinnerley w Melverley and Knockin w Maesbrook 91-95; Chapl Robert Jones and Agnes Hunt Orthopaedic Hosp 95-97; NSM Maesbury *Lich* 95-96; P-in-c 96-97; Chapl Moreton Hall Sch from 96; P-in-c Ford *Heref* 97-02; V 02-05; P-in-c Alberbury w Cardeston 97-02; V 02-05; rtd 05; Perm to Offic *Lich* and *St As* from 05. *Pentre Cleddar, Hengoed, Oswestry SY10 7AB* Tel (01691) 650469

STRATFORD, David. b 46. **d** 98 **p** 99. OLM Ditton St Mich w St Thos *Liv* from 98. *96 Clincton View, Widnes WA8 8RW* Tel 0151-423 4912

STRATFORD, Niall. CITC. **d** 09. NSM Killiney Ballybrack *D & G* from 09. *Address temp unknown*

STRATFORD, Ralph Montgomery. b 30. TCD BA53 MA67. CITC 53. **d** 54 **p** 54. Dioc C *C & O* 54-55; C Waterford Ch Ch 55-56; I Ballisodare w Collooney 56-00; Adn Killala and Achonry *T, K & A* 69-00; Can Killala Cathl 69-00; Preb Kilmactalway St Patr Cathl Dublin 85-00; rtd 00. *Knoxpark House, Robinstown, Mullingar, Co Westmeath, Republic of Ireland* Tel (00353) (44) 933 5292

STRATFORD, Terence Stephen. b 45. Chich Th Coll 67. **d** 69 **p** 70. C Old Shoreham *Chich* 69-73; C New Shoreham 69-73; C Uckfield 73-75; C Lt Horsted 73-75; C Isfield 73-75; P-in-c Waldron 76-80; R 80-82; V Blacklands Hastings Ch Ch and St Andr 82-89; P-in-c Ovingdean 89-95; Dioc Ecum Officer 89-95; P-in-c Staplefield Common 95-00; Sussex Ecum Officer 95-01; V Ferring 00-08; C New Shoreham from 08; C Old Shoreham from 08. *The Vicarage, 19 Grange Park, Ferring, Worthing BN12 5LS* Tel (01903) 241645

STRATFORD, Timothy Richard. b 61. York Univ BSc82 Sheff Univ PhD08. Wycliffe Hall Ox 83. **d** 86 **p** 87. C Mossley Hill St Matt and St Jas *Liv* 86-89; C St Helens St Helen 89-91; Bp's Dom Chapl 91-94; V W Derby Gd Shep 94-03; TR Kirkby from 03. *The Rectory, Old Hall Lane, Liverpool L32 5TH* Tel 0151-547 2155 Fax 08701-673589
E-mail tim.stratford@btinternet.com

STRATHIE, Duncan John. b 58. Heythrop Coll Lon MA02. Cranmer Hall Dur BA95. **d** 97 **p** 98. C Yateley *Win* 97-01; V Kempshott 01-07; Min Tr Officer from 07; Dioc Convener of Voc Adv from 03. *10 Pigeonhouse Field, Sutton Scotney, Winchester SO21 3NJ* Tel (01962) 760339
E-mail duncan@strathie.net

STRATON, Christopher James. b 46. **d** 93 **p** 94. Chapl Miss to Seamen S Africa 93-96; Asst P Gingindlovu All SS 97-99; R 99-00; P-in-c Tyldesley w Shakerley *Man* 00-06; TV Astley, Tyldesley and Mosley Common from 06. *11 Peel Hall Avenue, Tyldesley, Manchester M29 8TA* Tel (01942) 882914

STRATTA, Antony Charles. b 36. ACIS. S'wark Ord Course 82. **d** 85 **p** 86. C Southborough St Pet w Ch Ch and St Matt *Roch* 85-88; R Gt Mongeham w Ripple and Sutton by Dover *Cant* 88-96; rtd 96; Perm to Offic *St E* from 96. *Well House, The Great Yard, Rougham Green, Bury St Edmunds IP30 9JP* Tel (01284) 386140 E-mail antonystratta@btinternet.com

STRATTON, Mrs Anne Margaret. b 58. JP98. Nottm Univ BEng79. EMMTC 03. **d** 06 **p** 07. NSM Bradgate Team *Leic* from 06. *41 Rosslyn Road, Whitwick, Coalville LE67 5PU* Tel (01530) 458796 Mobile 07773-076555
E-mail anne.stratton@ntlworld.com

STRATTON, Henry William. b 39. Bris Univ CertEd74 BEd75. Glouc Sch of Min 80. **d** 83 **p** 84. NSM Cainscross w Selsley *Glouc* 83-87; C Odd Rode *Ches* 87-92; V Runcorn H Trin 92-96; V Lostock Gralam 96-05; rtd 05; Perm to Offic *Ches* from 05. *10 The Beeches, Great Sutton, Ellesmere Port CH66 4UJ* Tel 0151-339 3715 E-mail harry@hstratton.fsnet.co.uk

STRATTON, John Jefferies. b 27. Bps' Coll Cheshunt 53. **d** 55 **p** 56. C Watford St Mich *St Alb* 55-60; C Stevenage 60-65; R Cottered w Broadfield and Throcking 65-82; RD Buntingford 75-82; V S Mimms St Mary and Potters Bar *Lon* 82-84; V Potters Bar *St Alb* 85-94; P-in-c Flamstead 94-96; rtd 94; Hon C Taunton H Trin *B & W* from 97. *17 The Fairways, Sherford, Taunton TA1 3PA* Tel (01823) 330564
E-mail jj.stratton@btinternet.com

STRAUGHAN, Keith. b 60. Imp Coll Lon BSc81 Lon Univ PhD87 Imp Coll Lon ARCS81 CPhys87 MInstP87 Trin Coll Cam BA94. Westcott Ho Cam 94. **d** 97 **p** 98. C Abbots Langley *St Alb* 97-00; Fell SS Coll Cam from 00; Chapl 00-03; Dean 03-05; Perm to Offic *Ely* from 05. *Sidney Sussex College, Cambridge CB2 3HU* Tel (01223) 338800 *or* 338870 Fax 338884 E-mail senior.tutor@sid.cam.ac.uk *or* ks10019@cam.ac.uk

STRAW (*née* CAUDWELL), Mrs Juliet Lesley. b 49. Univ of Wales (Ban) BA70 Leeds Univ PGCE71. SAOMC 00. **d** 03 **p** 04. NSM Stratfield Mortimer and Mortimer W End etc *Ox* from 03. *Centre Lodge, Leighton Park School, Pepper Lane, Reading RG2 7EB* Tel 0118-986 3111
E-mail juliet.straw@btinternet.com

STREATER, David Arthur. b 33. Oak Hill Th Coll 67. **d** 68 **p** 69. C Lindfield *Chich* 68-71; S Africa 71-86; R Kingham w Churchill, Daylesford and Sarsden *Ox* 86-91; Dir Ch Soc 91-98; Sec Ch Soc Trust 91-96; rtd 98; Perm to Offic *St Alb* 98-03. *16 Linden Avenue, West Cross, Swansea SA3 5LE* Tel (01792) 406849 E-mail monty@ukgateway.net

STREATFEILD, Peter Michael Fremlyn. b 53. Newc Univ BSc77 St Jo Coll Dur BA03. Cranmer Hall Dur 00. **d** 03 **p** 04. C Solway Plain *Carl* 03-08; TV Binsey from 08. *The Vicarage, Bassenthwaite, Keswick CA12 4QH* Tel (017687) 76198
E-mail petermfa@hotmail.com

STREET, Anthony James. b 57. Trin Coll Bris 79. **d** 85 **p** 87. SAMS 85-95; C Temuco H Trin Chile 85-87; V Temuco St Matt 87-95; P-in-c Warley *Wakef* 96-99; V from 99. *The Vicarage, 466 Burnley Road, Warley, Halifax HX2 7LW* Tel (01422) 363623 E-mail familiastreet@btinternet.com

STREET, Matthew Graham. b 61. Regent's Park Coll Ox BA83. Wycliffe Hall Ox 99. **d** 01 **p** 02. C Combe Down w Monkton Combe and S Stoke *B & W* 01-05; P-in-c Peasedown St John w Wellow from 05. *The Vicarage, 18 Church Road, Peasedown St John, Bath BA2 8AA* Tel (01761) 432293 Mobile 07762-794371 Fax 08701-307814
E-mail mgstreet@hotmail.com

STREET, Peter Jarman. b 29. K Coll Lon BD59 AKC59. **d** 59 **p** 60. C Highters Heath *Birm* 59-60; C Shirley 60-62; Lect Cheshire Coll of Educn 62-66; St Pet Coll of Educn Birm 66-70; RE Adv Essex Co Coun 70-92; Hon C Gt Dunmow *Chelmsf* 71-85; Sen Insp RE and Humanities 74-92; R Gt w Lt Yeldham 85-92; RD Belchamp 90-92; rtd 92; Perm to Offic *Chelmsf* from 92. *18 Jubilee Court, Great Dunmow CM6 1DY* Tel (01371) 876871

STREET, Philip. b 47. Lon Univ BPharm68. NW Ord Course 75. **d** 78 **p** 79. C Heaton St Barn *Bradf* 78-81; C Evington *Leic* 82-84; R Wymondham w Edmondthorpe, Buckminster etc 84-88; V Gosberton Clough and Quadring *Linc* 88-95; Asst Local Min Officer 88-95; V Buttershaw St Paul *Bradf* 95-99; P-in-c Gt and Lt Casterton w Pickworth and Tickencote *Pet* 99-04; R 04-09; P-in-c Exton w Horn 02-06; rtd 09. *23 Foundry Walk, Thrapston, Kettering NN14 4LS* Tel (01832) 731661
E-mail p.street08@btinternet.com

STREETER, Brian Thomas. b 68. Reading Univ BSc89. Ridley Hall Cam 05. **d** 08 **p** 09. C Windermere St Mary and Troutbeck *Carl* from 08. *4 St Mary's Park, Windermere LA23 1AY* Tel 07981-951882 (mobile) E-mail bts@rapport.ltd.uk

STREETER, Christine Mary. *See* HADDON-REECE, Mrs Christine Mary

STREETER, David James. b 42. Pemb Coll Cam BA64 MA68. Qu Coll Birm 65. **d** 67 **p** 68. C Saffron Walden *Chelmsf* 67-71; C Shrub End 71-73; R Rayne 73-79; V Highams Park All SS 79-82; P-in-c Stradbroke w Horham and Athelington *St E* 82-87; R Stradbroke, Horham, Athelington and Redlingfield from 87; RD Hoxne 91-00. *The Rectory, Doctors Lane, Stradbroke, Eye IP21 5HU* Tel (01379) 384363 Mobile 07798-784179
E-mail david.streeter@stedmundsbury.anglican.org

STREETING, John William. b 52. ACertCM89 Cam Inst of Educn CertEd74 Birm Univ BEd77 FGMS98 FRSA98 Anglia Poly Univ MA99. St Steph Ho Ox 90. **d** 92 **p** 93. C Upminster *Chelmsf* 92-95; C Chingford SS Pet and Paul 95-97; Assoc V Chelsea St Luke and Ch Ch *Lon* 97-03; V Sheerness H Trin w St Paul *Cant* from 03; P-in-c Queenborough from 05; AD Sittingbourne 04-06; PV Westmr Abbey from 05. *The Vicarage, 241 High Street, Sheerness ME12 1UR* Tel (01795) 662589 Fax 581336 E-mail john@htsheerness.fsnet.co.uk

STREETING, Laurence Storey. b 14. VRD65. St Jo Coll Dur BA39 MA42. **d** 40 **p** 41. C Bishopwearmouth St Gabr *Dur* 40-46; Chapl RNVR 42-46; S Africa 46-49; Chapl Garden City Woodford Bridge 49-51; Chapl Village Home Barkingside 49-51; Chapl RAF 51-56; Chapl RNR 56-90; Asst Chapl Eliz Coll Guernsey 56-60; Chapl Eshton Hall Sch Gargrave 60-64; Perm to Offic *Cant* 64-65; R Guernsey St Sampson *Win* 65-71; St Vincent 72-76; Chapl Madeira *Eur* 76-80; rtd 80; Perm to Offic *Win* from 79. *Apartment 8, de Hubie Court, Les Cotils Christian Centre, St Peter Port, Guernsey GY1 1VV*

STRETCH, Richard Mark. b 53. **d** 93 **p** 94. OLM Stowmarket *St E* from 93. *91 Kipling Way, Stowmarket IP14 1TS* Tel (01449) 676219

STRETTON, Reginald John. b 37. MRPharmS63 CBiol70 MIBiol70 Man Univ BSc62 Nottm Univ PhD65. EMMTC 88. **d** 91 **p** 92. NSM Loughb Gd Shep *Leic* 91-94; P-in-c Burrough Hill Pars 94-02; rtd 02; Perm to Offic *Leic* and *S'well* from 02; *Derby* from 05. *19 Paddock Close, Quorn, Loughborough LE12 8BJ* Tel (01509) 412935
E-mail rstretton@leicester.anglican.org

STRETTON, Robert John. b 45. Kelham Th Coll. **d** 69 **p** 70. C Hendon St Ignatius *Dur* 69-73; C Middlesbrough St Thos *York* 73-77; OSB 77-78; V Brandon *Dur* 78-85; SSM from 85; Lic to Offic *Dur* 85-91; Tr in Evang Ch in Wales 91-94; Perm to Offic *S'wark* 94-01; Lesotho from 01. *Society of the Sacred Mission Priory, PO Box 1579, Maseru, Lesotho* Tel (00266) 315979
E-mail priorssm@ilesotho.com

STREVENS, Brian Lloyd. b 49. St Jo Coll Dur BA70. Ripon Hall Ox 70. **d** 73 **p** 74. C Old Trafford St Jo *Man* 73-76; C Bolton St Pet 76-78; Org Sec Southn Coun of Community Service 78-92; Perm to Offic *Win* 82-86, 92-95 and from 01; Hon C Bitterne Park *Win* 86-92; Hon C N Stoneham 95-01. *186 Hill Lane, Southampton SO15 5DB* Tel (023) 8033 3301
E-mail hq@scaccs.org.uk

STREVENS, Richard Ernest Noel. b 34. Nottm Univ BA60. Linc Th Coll 60. **d** 62 **p** 63. C St Botolph Aldgate w H Trin Minories *Lon* 62-66; C Ealing St Steph Castle Hill 66-68; Hon C St Botolph without Bishopgate 68-76; V Clent *Worc* 76-86; V Pirbright *Guildf* 86-00; Perm to Offic *Ex* 69-98 and from 00; rtd 00. *83 Head Weir Road, Cullompton EX15 1NN* Tel (01884) 35823

STRIBLEY, William Charles Harold. b 29. SW Minl Tr Course 84. **d** 87 **p** 88. NSM Kenwyn St Geo *Truro* 87-92; NSM Truro St Paul and St Clem 92-98; Perm to Offic from 99. *54 Chirgwin Road, Truro TR1 1TT* Tel (01872) 272958

STRICKLAND (née CUTTS), Mrs Elizabeth Joan Gabrielle. b 61. St Jo Coll Dur BA83. Westcott Ho Cam 87. **d** 90 **p** 94. C Cayton w Eastfield *York* 90-92; NSM Biggin Hill *Roch* 93-96; Perm to Offic *Ox* 96-00 and *Ely* 00-02; P-in-c Holywell w Needingworth *Ely* 02-07. *Windswept, Holywell, St Ives PE27 4TQ* Tel (01480) 495275 or 460107
E-mail epstrickland@ukonline.co.uk

STRICKLAND, Jonathan Edward Tully. b 56. Westf Coll Lon BSc78. Ridley Hall Cam 00. **d** 02 **p** 03. C Margate H Trin *Cant* 02-06; P-in-c Bawtry w Austerfield and Misson *S'well* from 07. *The Vicarage, Martin Lane, Bawtry, Doncaster DN10 6NJ* Tel (01302) 710298 E-mail strickers@tesco.net

STRIDE, Clifford Stephen. b 21. Ex & Truro NSM Scheme. **d** 81 **p** 82. NSM Chulmleigh *Ex* 81-83; NSM Hardham *Chich* 87-93; NSM Coldwaltham and Hardham 93-97; NSM Bury w Houghton and Coldwaltham and Hardham 97-05. *Ambleside, Sandy Lane, Watersfield, Pulborough RH20 1NF* Tel (01798) 831851

STRIDE, John David. b 46. Ex Univ BSc68. Oak Hill Th Coll 86. **d** 88 **p** 89. C Ashtead *Guildf* 88-96; V Lodge Moor St Luke *Sheff* from 96. *St Luke's House, 18 Blackbrook Road, Sheffield S10 4LP* Tel 0114-230 5271
E-mail vicar@stlukeslodgemoor.org.uk

STRIDE, John Michael. b 48. Oak Hill Th Coll BA77. **d** 80 **p** 81. C Edmonton All SS *Lon* 80-82; C Edmonton All SS w St Mich 82-83; C Wembley St Jo 83-85; P-in-c Hockering *Nor* 85-89; R Hockering, Honingham, E and N Tuddenham 89-91; V Tuckswood 91-93; Chapl HM Pris Leeds 93-94; Chapl HM Pris Littlehey 94-96; V Heeley *Sheff* 96-99; TR Heeley and Gleadless Valley 99-04; AD Attercliffe 02-04; V Goole 04-06; Chapl Combined Courts from 06; Hon C Darfield from 07. *54 George Street, Thurnscoe, Rotherham S63 0DF* Tel (01709) 898744
E-mail mojnst@aol.com

STRIKE, Maurice Arthur. b 44. FRSA66. Sarum & Wells Th Coll 85. **d** 87 **p** 88. C Chippenham St Andr w Tytherton Lucas *Bris* 87-91; R Corfe Castle, Church Knowle, Kimmeridge etc *Sarum* 91-04; R Guernsey St Philippe de Torteval *Win* from 04; R Guernsey St Pierre du Bois from 04. *The Rectory, St Pierre du Bois, Guernsey GY7 9SB* Tel (01481) 263544
E-mail mauricestrike@stpeters.ndo.co.uk

STRINGER, Adrian Nigel. b 60. Univ of Wales (Cardiff) BD82 Lanc Univ PGCE83. Sarum & Wells Th Coll 86. **d** 88 **p** 89. C Barrow St Matt *Carl* 88-92; TV Westhoughton *Man* 92-94; I Inver w Mountcharles, Killaghtee and Killybegs *D & R* 94-96; V Tuckingmill *Truro* 96-01; Chapl R Alexandra and Albert Sch Reigate 01-03; I Desertlyn w Ballyeglish *Arm* from 03. *The Rectory, 24 Cookstown Road, Moneymore, Magherafelt BT45 7QF* Tel (028) 8674 8200
E-mail adrianstringer@gatton-park.org.uk

STRINGER, Harold John. b 36. Peterho Cam BA58. Ripon Hall Ox 62. **d** 64 **p** 65. C Hackney St Jo *Lon* 64-68; C Roehampton H Trin *S'wark* 68-71; P-in-c Southampton St Mich w H Rood, St Lawr etc *Win* 71-73; TV Southampton (City Cen) 73-82; Ind Chapl 77-82; V Notting Hill St Jo *Lon* 82-87; V Notting Hill St Pet 82-87; V Notting Hill St Jo and St Pet 87-01; AD Kensington 98-01; rtd 02; Perm to Offic *Lon* from 03. *56 Mountfield Road, London W5 2NQ* Tel (020) 8998 8049
E-mail mail@haroldandchristina.co.uk

STRINGER, Canon John Roden. b 33. AKC61. **d** 62 **p** 63. C Auckland St Helen *Dur* 62-63; C Hebburn St Cuth 63-67; V Cassop cum Quarrington 67-88; RD Sedgefield 84-88; V Lumley 88-98; Hon Can Dur Cathl 88-98; rtd 98; Perm to Offic *Dur* 98-03. *4 Darwin Road, Walsall WS2 7EW* Tel (01922) 649243

STROEBEL, Mrs Stephanie Suzanne. b 47. Middx Univ BA06. NTMTC 03. **d** 06 **p** 07. NSM Ashingdon w S Fambridge *Chelmsf* 06-08; NSM S Woodham Ferrers from 08. *27 Orchard Avenue, Hockley SS5 5BA* Tel and fax (01702) 204513 Mobile 07930-105163 E-mail s.stroebel@virgin.net

STRØMMEN, Mrs Mary Natasha. b 52. Kent Univ BA73 Bp Otter Coll Chich PGCE74. EAMTC 00. **d** 03 **p** 04. NSM Oslo w Bergen, Trondheim and Stavanger *Eur* from 03. *Lykkestien 4, 7053 Ranheim, Norway* Tel (0047) 7391 3281
E-mail mary.strommen@c2i.net

STRONG, Christopher Patterson. b 43. Ridley Hall Cam. **d** 83 **p** 84. C Dalton-in-Furness *Carl* 83-87; V Wootton *St Alb* 87-02; RD Elstow 94-02; R Fowlmere, Foxton, Shepreth and Thriplow *Ely* 02-08; rtd 08. *Kiln Farm, Priory Road, Campton, Shefford SG17 5PG* Tel (01462) 819274
E-mail christopherpstrong@hotmail.com

STRONG, Jack. b 16. St Aid Birkenhead 52. **d** 54 **p** 55. C Radcliffe St Thos *Man* 54-58; V Chadderton St Mark 58-66; V Burgh-by-Sands w Kirkbampton *Carl* 66-83; R Burgh-by-Sands and Kirkbampton w Kirkandrews etc 83; rtd 83; Perm to Offic *Glouc* 84-99. *Aballava, 18 Wincel Road, Winchcombe, Cheltenham GL54 5YE* Tel (01242) 603347

STRONG, John. *See* STRONG, Capt William John Leonard

STRONG, Canon John David. b 34. Cuddesdon Coll 59. **d** 61 **p** 62. C Gosforth All SS *Newc* 61-65; Chapl Malvern Coll 65-71; R Welford w Weston on Avon *Glouc* 72-79; V Nailsworth 79-01; RD Tetbury 83-00; Hon Can Glouc Cathl 91-01; rtd 01. *Glebe House, The Meads, Leighterton, Tetbury GL8 8UW* Tel (01666) 890236 E-mail canondavid@penshouse.freeserve.co.uk

STRONG *(formerly* **BULMAN), Ms Madeline Judith.** b 61. K Coll Lon BD AKC. **dss** 86 **d** 87 **p** 94. Shepperton *Lon* 86-88; Par Dn 87-88; Par Dn Brentford 88-94; C 94-96; V Cobbold Road St Sav w St Mary 96-04; Dean of Women's Min 99-02; Chapl Stamford Ho Secure Unit 02-04; Spiritual Cllr PROMIS from 04. *27 Winchelsea Street, Dover CT17 9ST* Tel 07973-954802 (mobile)

STRONG, Matthew John. b 60. Lon Univ BA81 Cam Univ BA84 MA89. Ridley Hall Cam 82. **d** 85 **p** 86. C Houghton *Carl* 85-89; C Hirwaun *Llan* 89-91; V Troedyrhiw w Merthyr Vale 91-95; Tutor Llan Ord Course 91-95. *22 Birch Lane, Oldbury B68 0NZ* Tel 0121-421 5978

STRONG, Rowan Gordon William. b 53. Victoria Univ Wellington BA76 Edin Univ PhD92 Melbourne Univ of Div ThM88. St Jo Coll (NZ) LTh80. **d** 77 **p** 78. C Kapiti New Zealand 77-79; C Palmerston N St Pet 79-81; V Shannon 81-83; Assoc P E Hill Australia 83-89; NSM Edin Old St Paul 89-92; Tutor Edin Univ 91-92; Lect Murdoch Univ Australia from 92; Sen Lect from 02. *150 George Street, East Fremantle WA 6158, Australia* Tel (0061) (8) 9339 0643 *or* 9360 6470 Fax 9360 6480 Mobile 439-988896 E-mail r.strong@murdoch.edu.au

STRONG, Capt William John Leonard. b 44. CA Tr Coll 64 Chich Th Coll 87. **d** 89 **p** 90. CA from 66; C Mayfield *Chich* 89-92; C Seaford w Sutton 92-94; V Crawley Down All SS 94-97; rtd 01. *21 Carroll Close, Poole BH12 1PL* Tel (01202) 733940 Mobile 07944-670125

STROUD, David Alan. b 74. Kent Univ BA96 Ch Ch Coll Cant PGCE95. Westcott Ho Cam 02. **d** 04 **p** 05. C Liss *Portsm* 04-08; Asst Chapl Cant Ch Ch Univ from 08. *Canterbury Christ Church University, North Holmes Road, Canterbury CT1 1QU* Tel (01227) 767700 E-mail david.stroud@canterbury.ac.uk

STROUD, The Ven Ernest Charles Frederick. b 31. St Chad's Coll Dur BA59. **d** 60 **p** 61. C S Kirkby *Wakef* 60-63; C Whitby *York* 63-66; C-in-c Chelmsf All SS CD 66-69; V Chelmsf All SS 69-75; V Leigh-on-Sea St Marg 75-83; Asst RD Southend 76-79; RD Hadleigh 79-83; Hon Can Chelmsf Cathl 82-83; Adn Colchester 83-97; rtd 97; Perm to Offic *Chelmsf* from 97. *54 London Road, Hadleigh, Benfleet SS7 2QL* Tel (01702) 554941 Fax 500789

STROUD, Canon Robert Owen. b 29. AKC56. **d** 57 **p** 58. C Aylesbury *Ox* 57-60; C Bexhill St Pet *Chich* 60-64; C Gosforth All SS *Newc* 64-66; V High Elswick St Phil 66-72; V Tynemouth Cullercoats St Paul 72-77; R Orlestone w Ruckinge w Warehorne *Cant* 77-81; RD N Lympne 79-81; V Folkestone H Trin w Ch Ch 81-83; TR Folkestone H Trin and St Geo w Ch Ch 83-90; V Folkestone H Trin w Ch Ch 90-93; RD Elham 90-93; Hon Can Cant Cathl 92-93; rtd 93; Perm to Offic *Ex* 94-02; *Cant* 02-06 and from 08. *27 Rochester Avenue, Canterbury CT1 3YE* Tel (01227) 767312

STROWGER, Mrs Patricia. b 04 **p** 05. NSM The Lavingtons, Cheverells, and Easterton *Sarum* from 04. *60 High Street, Littleton Panell, Devizes SN10 4ES* Tel (01380) 812840 E-mail pstrowger@waitrose.com

✠**STROYAN, The Rt Revd John Ronald Angus.** b 55. St Andr Univ MTheol76. Qu Coll Birm 81 Bossey Ecum Inst Geneva 82. **d** 83 **p** 84 **c** 05. C Cov E 83-87; V Smethwick St Matt w St Chad *Birm* 87-94; V Bloxham w Milcombe and S Newington *Ox* 94-05; AD Deddington 02-05; Suff Bp Warw *Cov* from 05. *Warwick House, 139 Kenilworth Road, Coventry CV4 7AF* Tel (024) 7641 2627 Fax 7641 5254 E-mail bishop.warwick@covcofe.org

STRUDWICK, Canon Vincent Noel Harold. b 32. Nottm Univ BA59 DipEd. Kelham Th Coll 52. **d** 59 **p** 60. Tutor Kelham Th Coll 59-63; Sub-Warden 63-70; C Crawley *Chich* 70-73; Adult Educn Adv 73-77; R Fittleworth 73-77; Planning Officer for Educn Milton Keynes 77-80; Dir of Educn *Ox* 80-89; Hon Can Ch Ch from 82; Continuing Minl Educn Adv 85-89; Dir Dioc Inst for Th Educn 89-97; Prin Ox Min Course 89-94; Prin SAOMC 94-96; Fell and Tutor Kellogg Coll Ox 94-00; C Aylesbury w Bierton and Hulcott *Ox* 97-98. *31 The Square, Brill, Aylesbury HP18 9RP* Tel (01865) 280354 Fax 270309 E-mail vincent.strudwick@conted.ox.ac.uk

STRUGNELL, John Richard. b 30. Lon Univ BA52 Leeds Univ MA61 Univ of Qld PhD77. Wells Th Coll 54. **d** 56 **p** 57. C Leeds Halton St Wilfrid *Ripon* 56-59; C Moor Allerton 59-62; Australia from 65; rtd 95. *231 Grandview Road, Pullenvale Qld 4069, Australia* Tel (0061) (7) 3374 1776

STRUTT, Peter Edward. b 40. SAOMC 94. **d** 97 **p** 98. NSM Penn Street *Ox* 97-02; Perm to Offic from 02. *59 King's Ride, Penn, High Wycombe HP10 8BP* Tel (01494) 812418

STRUTT, Preb Susan. b 45. Glouc Sch of Min 87. **d** 90 **p** 94. NSM Eye, Croft w Yarpole and Lucton *Heref* 90-94; C

Leominster 94-96; Hon Chapl RAF 94-96; P-in-c Bosbury w Wellington Heath etc *Heref* 96-98; TV Ledbury from 98; Dioc Adv on Women in Min 99-03; Preb Heref Cathl from 07. *The Vicarage, Bosbury, Ledbury HR8 1QA* Tel (01531) 640225 E-mail suestrutt@strutts.fsnet.co.uk

STUART, Angus Fraser. b 61. Bedf Coll Lon BA83 K Coll Lon PhD91 St Jo Coll Dur BA92. Cranmer Hall Dur 90. **d** 93 **p** 94. C Twickenham St Mary *Lon* 93-96; Sen Chapl Bris Univ 96-05; Hon C Bris St Mich and St Paul 96-98; P-in-c 98-00; Hon C Cotham St Sav w St Mary and Clifton St Paul 00-05; I W Vancouver St Fran in the Wood Canada from 05. *4773 South Piccadilly, West Vancouver BC V7W 1J8, Canada* Tel (001) (604) 922 3531

STUART, Sister Ann-Marie Lindsay. b 41. Westmr Coll Lon CertEd69 Kent Univ BA80 Univ of Wales (Lamp) MA03. Franciscan Study Cen 76. **d** 99 **p** 00. NSM Sherborne w Castleton and Lillington *Sarum* 99-01; TV Golden Cap Team 01-08; rtd 08; Hon C Crosslacon *Carl* from 08; Dioc Adv for Spirituality from 09. *The Vicarage, Arlecdon, Frizington CA26 3UB* Tel (01946) 861353 E-mail annmarie.isabel@zen.co.uk

STUART, Brother. *See* BURNS, The Rt Revd Stuart Maitland

STUART, Christopher John. b 74. Keble Coll Ox BA95 MA04 Loughb Univ MSc98 St Jo Coll Dur BA05 MA06. Cranmer Hall Dur 03. **d** 06 **p** 07. C Pershore w Pinvin, Wick and Birlingham *Worc* from 06. *16 Acorn Grove, Pershore WR10 1PQ* Tel (01386) 556696 Mobile 07906-721060 E-mail chris.j.stuart@connectfree.co.uk

STUART, Francis David. b 32. Barrister-at-Law Lon Univ BA54 AKC57. Ridley Hall Cam 62. **d** 64 **p** 65. C Addiscombe St Mildred *Cant* 64-67; Chapl RN 67-71; Lic to Offic *Liv* 76-80; TV Oldham *Man* 84-89; Chapl Oldham and Distr Gen Hosp 84-89; Chapl Oldham R Infirmary 86-89; Chapl Oldham Hosp 89-94; Chapl Oldham NHS Trust 94-98; rtd 97; Perm to Offic *Man* 00-03. *17 rue de la Villeneuve, 56150 Baud, France* Tel (0033) (2) 97 51 11 38 E-mail davidetpam@orange.fr

STUART, Canon Herbert James. b 26. CB83. TCD BA48 MA55. **d** 49 **p** 50. C Sligo Cathl 49-53; C Dublin Rathmines *D & G* 53-55; Chapl RAF 55-73; Asst Chapl-in-Chief RAF 73-80; Chapl-in-Chief and Archdeacon for the RAF 80-83; Can and Preb Linc Cathl 81-83; R Cherbury *Ox* 83-87; Perm to Offic *Glouc* 87-97 and *Ox* 87-96; rtd 91. *1 Abbot's Walk, Lechlade GL7 3DB* Tel (01367) 253299

✠**STUART, The Rt Revd Ian Campbell.** b 42. New England Univ (NSW) BA70 CertEd70 Melbourne Univ DipEd77 MA92 MACE72 FAIM91. St Barn Coll Adelaide 84. **d** 85 **p** 85 **c** 92. Australia 85-99; Asst Bp N Queensland 96-99; Chapl Liv Hope Univ from 99; Hon Asst Bp Liv from 99. *The Chaplaincy, Liverpool Hope, Hope Park, Taggart Avenue, Liverpool L16 9JD* Tel 0151-291 3547 Fax 291 3873 E-mail stuarti@hope.ac.uk

STUART-LEE, Nicholas Richard. b 54. Wycliffe Hall Ox. **d** 83 **p** 84. C Costessey *Nor* 83-85; TV Dewsbury *Wakef* 85-90; R Rowlands Castle *Portsm* 90-00; V Nottingham St Jude *S'well* 00-03; TR Thame *Ox* 03-07. *69 Harefields, Oxford OX2 8NR* Tel (01865) 511454 E-mail nrsl@ciloros.fsnet.co.uk

STUART-SMITH, David. b 36. St Pet Coll Ox BA61 MA65. Tyndale Hall Bris. **d** 63 **p** 64. C Tooting Graveney St Nic *S'wark* 63-67; C Richmond H Trin 67-70; Lic to Offic 70-74; NSM Canonbury St Steph *Lon* 70-74; Travelling Sec IVF 70-74; Bangladesh 74-79; V Clapham Park St Steph *S'wark* 79-95; RD Streatham 83-87; Chapl Wye Coll Kent 95-01; P-in-c Wye w Brook *Cant* 95-01; P-in-c Hastingleigh 00-01; rtd 01; Perm to Offic *Cant* 01-07 and *Lon* from 07. *42 Rennie Court, 11 Upper Ground, London SE1 9LP* Tel (020) 7261 1866

STUART-WHITE, Canon William Robert. b 59. Ox Univ BA. Trin Coll Bris BA. **d** 86 **p** 87. C Upper Armley *Ripon* 86-91; P-in-c Austrey *Birm* 91-92; P-in-c Warton 91-92; V Austrey and Warton 92-98; R Camborne *Truro* 98-06; P-in-c Stoke Climsland from 06; P-in-c Linkinhorne from 06; Hon Can Truro Cathl from 09. *The Rectory, Stoke Climsland, Callington PL17 8NZ* Tel (01579) 370501 E-mail wstuartwhi@aol.com

STUBBINGS, Frank Edward. b 20. Fitzw Coll Cam BA48 MA53. Worc Ord Coll 60. **d** 61 **p** 62. C Rowbarton *B & W* 61-64; V Catcott 64-74; V Burtle 64-74; Chapl St Cath Sch Bramley 74-83; R Barkestone w Plungar, Redmile and Stathern *Leic* 83-87; rtd 87; Perm to Offic *B & W* 88-91; Hon C Lostwithiel, St Winnow w St Nectan's Chpl etc *Truro* from 91. *Gooseydown, Park Road, Lostwithiel PL22 0BU* Tel (01208) 872762

STUBBS, Ian Kirtley. b 47. Man Univ DipAE90. Kelham Th Coll 66. **d** 70 **p** 71. C Chandler's Ford *Win* 70-75; C Farnham Royal *Ox* 75-80; Ind Chapl 75-80; Ind Chapl *Man* 81-86; TV Oldham 81-86; TR Langley and Parkfield 86-88; Community Work Officer Dioc Bd of Soc Resp 88-90; Dir Laity Development 90-96; Nat Adv in Adult Learning C of E Bd of Educn 97-02; V Stalybridge *Man* from 02. *The Vicarage, 2 Tintagel Court, Astley Road, Stalybridge SK15 1RA* Tel and fax 0161-338 2368 Mobile 07712-451710 E-mail iks47@o2.co.uk

STUBBS, Stanley Peter Handley. b 23. Lon Univ BD52 Lille 3 Univ MèsL82. Ely Th Coll 55. **d** 55 **p** 56. C Fletton *Ely* 55-58;

Hon Min Can Pet Cathl 56-58; C Hounslow Heath St Paul *Lon* 58-63; CF (TA) 59-78; V Northampton St Alb *Pet* 63-76; R Brondesbury Ch Ch and St Laur *Lon* 76-93; rtd 93; Perm to Offic *Lon* from 93. *3 Westbury Lodge Close, Pinner HA5 3FG* Tel (020) 8868 8296

STUBBS, Canon Trevor Noel. b 48. AKC70. St Aug Coll Cant 73. **d** 74 **p** 75. C Heckmondwike *Wakef* 74-77; Australia 77-80; V Middleton St Cross *Ripon* 80-89; R Wool and E Stoke *Sarum* 89-95; TR Bridport 95-09; RD Lyme Bay 06-09; Admin Bp Gwynne Th Coll Sudan from 09; Lic to Offic *Sarum* from 09; Can and Preb Sarum Cathl from 03. *Address temp unknown* E-mail trevor.stubbs@uk.com

STUBENBORD, Jess William. b 48. BA72. Trin Coll Bris 75. **d** 78 **p** 79. C Cromer *Nor* 78-82; C Gorleston St Mary 82-85; P-in-c Saxthorpe and Corpusty 85-89; P-in-c Blickling 86-89; R Saxthorpe w Corpusty, Blickling, Oulton etc 89-93; P-in-c Mulbarton w Kenningham 93-97; P-in-c Flordon 94-97; P-in-c Wreningham 95-97; R Mulbarton w Bracon Ash, Hethel and Flordon from 98. *The Rectory, The Common, Mulbarton, Norwich NR14 8JS* Tel (01508) 570296
E-mail jess.stubenbord@btinternet.com

STUCKES, Stephen. b 62. Trin Coll Bris. **d** 96 **p** 97. C Dunster, Carhampton and Withycombe w Rodhuish *B & W* 96-00; V Alcombe from 00. *The Vicarage, 34 Manor Road, Minehead TA24 6EJ* Tel (01643) 703285 E-mail sjstuckes@hotmail.com

STUDD, John Eric. b 34. Clare Coll Cam BA58 MA62. Coll of Resurr Mirfield 58. **d** 60 **p** 61. C Westmr St Steph w St Jo *Lon* 60-65; Australia 65-69; Hon C Kensington St Mary Abbots w St Geo *Lon* 70-71; P-in-c Monks Risborough *Ox* 72-77; P-in-c Gt and Lt Kimble 72-77; C Aylesbury 78; Chapl to the Deaf 78-82; Chapl Hants, Is of Wight and Channel Is Assn for Deaf 82-91; Chapl to the Deaf *Win* 91-99; rtd 99; Perm to Offic *Guildf* 82-96 and *Portsm* 82-99. *28 Elgin Way, Flagstaff Hill SA 5159, Australia* Tel (0061) (8) 8370 4707 Fax 8370 6517
E-mail jonea@senet.com.au

STUDDERT, Michael John de Clare. b 39. Trin Coll Cam BA64 MA67 K Alfred's Coll Win PGCE74. Cuddesdon Coll 64. **d** 66 **p** 67. C Langley All SS and Martyrs *Man* 66-69; C Fleet *Guildf* 69-73; Teacher Guildf C of E Secondary Sch 73-77; Chapl Eagle Ho Sch Sandhurst 77-88; rtd 04. *14 Lilac Court, Cambridge CB1 7AY*

STUDDERT-KENNEDY, Andrew Geoffrey. b 59. Ch Ch Ox BA80 MA86. Ripon Coll Cuddesdon BA88. **d** 89 **p** 90. C Wimbledon *S'wark* 89-94; V Norbury St Oswald 94-02; RD Croydon N 99-02; TR Marlborough *Sarum* from 02; RD Marlborough from 09. *The Rectory, 1 Rawlingswell Lane, Marlborough SN8 1AU* Tel (01672) 514357 or 512357
E-mail andrew@studdert-kennedy.wanadoo.co.uk

STUDDERT-KENNEDY, Canon Christopher John. b 22. BNC Ox BA49 MA53. Wells Th Coll 49. **d** 51 **p** 52. C Bermondsey St Mary w St Olave and St Jo *S'wark* 51-54; C Clapham H Trin 54-56; V Putney St Marg 56-66; R Godstone 66-91; RD Godstone 76-88; Hon Can S'wark Cathl 80-91; rtd 91; Perm to Offic *Chich* from 91. *Orchard House, The Street, Washington, Pulborough RH20 4AS* Tel (01903) 892774

STUDHOLME, Muriel Isabel. b 25. **d** 96. NSM Bromfield w Waverton *Carl* 96-02; NSM Solway Plain from 02. *Yew Tree Cottage, Dundraw, Wigton CA7 0DP* Tel (01697) 342506

STURCH, Richard Lyman. b 36. Ch Ch Ox BA58 MA61 DPhil70 Open Univ BSc06. Ely Th Coll. **d** 62 **p** 63. C Hove All SS *Chich* 62-65; C Burgess Hill St Jo 65-66; C Ox St Mich w St Martin and All SS 67-68; Tutor Ripon Hall Ox 67-71; Lect Univ of Nigeria 71-74; Lect Lon Bible Coll 75-80; TV Wolverton 80-86; R Islip w Charlton on Otmoor, Oddington, Noke etc 86-01; rtd 01. *35 Broomfield, Stacey Bushes, Milton Keynes MK12 6HA* Tel (01908) 316779 E-mail rsturch@fsmail.net

STURMAN, Robert George. b 50. Nottm Univ BTh79. Linc Th Coll 75. **d** 79 **p** 80. C Cainscross w Selsley *Glouc* 79-83; TV Bottesford w Ashby *Linc* 83-88; V Prescot *Liv* 88-91; P-in-c Abenhall w Mitcheldean *Glouc* 93-97; R from 97; AD Forest N 99-04 and from 08. *St Michael's Rectory, Hawker Hill, Mitcheldean GL17 0BS* Tel (01594) 542774

STURROCK, Marian Elizabeth. b 46. Westmr Coll Ox BTh97. St Mich Coll Llan 97. **d** 99 **p** 00. C Swansea St Pet *S & B* 99-03; Chapl Swansea NHS Trust 00-03; R Thundersley *Chelmsf* from 03. *St Peter's Rectory, Church Road, Thundersley, Benfleet SS7 3HG* Tel (01268) 566206 E-mail mariansturrock@sky.com

STURT, Rock André Daniel. b 56. Liv Univ BSc79 Lon Univ CertEd80. Oak Hill Th Coll BA88. **d** 88 **p** 89. Chapl St Bede's Sch Cam 88-90; Par Dn Cambridge St Martin *Ely* 88-90; C 90-91; P-in-c Alwalton and Chesterton 91-96; TV The Ortons, Alwalton and Chesterton 96-03; R Gravesend St Geo *Roch* 03-06. *51G Lower Higham Road, Gravesend DA12 2NQ*

STUTZ, Clifford Peter. b 25. **d** 83 **p** 84. OLM Cusop w Blakemere, Bredwardine w Brobury etc *Heref* 83-08. *Burnt House, Dorstone, Hereford HR3 5SX* Tel (01497) 831472

STUTZ, Ms Sally Ann. b 64. Univ of Wales BSc88 Leeds Metrop Univ MSc93 Birm Univ BD95 SRD90. Qu Coll Birm 93. **d** 96 **p** 97. C Middleton St Mary *Ripon* 96-00; C Wilmslow *Ches*

00-03; Dioc Adv in Chr Worship 00-03; Perm to Offic from 03. *1 Arundel Close, Knutsford WA16 9BZ* Tel (01565) 650919 E-mail sally.stutz@stutzsanyal.fsnet.co.uk

STYLER, Jamie Cuming. b 36. Sarum & Wells Th Coll 70. **d** 72 **p** 73. C Whipton *Ex* 72-75; C Paignton St Jo 76-78; V Topsham 78-88; V Plymouth St Simon 88-01; Chapl Plymouth Community Services NHS Trust 94-01; rtd 01; Perm to Offic *Ex* from 01. *Drey House, 27 Langham Way, Ivybridge PL21 9BX* Tel (01752) 691592

STYLES, Charles Adam Mark. b 81. Oak Hill Th Coll. **d** 09. C Britwell *Ox* from 09. *19 Goodwin Road, Slough SL2 2ET* Tel 07725-264991 (mobile) E-mail charliestyles@dunelm.org.uk

STYLES, Clive William John. b 48. WMMTC 87. **d** 90 **p** 91. C Burslem *Lich* 90-94; TV Wednesfield 94-99; V Ashwellthorpe, Forncett, Fundenhall, Hapton etc *Nor* from 99. *The Vicarage, 16 The Fields, Tacolneston, Norwich NR16 1DG* Tel (01953) 788227

STYLES, Canon Lawrence Edgar. b 19. AM88. Pemb Coll Cam BA48 MA52. Ridley Hall Cam. **d** 50 **p** 51. C Bishop's Stortford St Mich *St Alb* 50-53; V Tyldesley w Shakerley *Man* 53-60; Australia from 60; Can Melbourne 82-86; rtd 86. *25 Carson Street, Kew Vic 3101, Australia* Tel and fax (0061) (3) 9853 9749 E-mail lstyles@co31.aone.net.au

SUART, Geoffrey Hugh. b 49. Man Univ BSc70 Nottm Univ PGCE71. Oak Hill Th Coll. **d** 83 **p** 84. C Ogley Hay *Lich* 83-86; TV Wenlock *Heref* 86-90; TR Kirby Muxloe *Leic* 90-04; RD Sparkenhoe E 99-03; R Snettisham w Ingoldisthorpe and Fring *Nor* from 04. *The Vicarage, 18 Park Lane, Snettisham, King's Lynn PE31 7NW* Tel (01485) 541301
E-mail geoffsuart@talk21.com

SUCH, Colin Royston. b 62. UEA LLB83. Ripon Coll Cuddesdon 94. **d** 97 **p** 98. C Streetly *Lich* 97-00; P-in-c Wednesfield St Greg 00-04; V Rushall from 04; P-in-c Walsall St Pet from 08. *Rushall Vicarage, 10 Tetley Avenue, Walsall WS4 2HE* Tel (01922) 624677

SUCH, Howard Ingram James. b 52. Southn Univ BTh81 Lon Univ MA97. Sarum & Wells Th Coll 77. **d** 81 **p** 82. C Cheam *S'wark* 81-84; Prec Cant Cathl 84-91; V Borden 91-03; Hon Min Can Cant Cathl 84-03; AD Sittingbourne 00-03; Can Res and Prec Sheff Cathl 03-07; Warden St Barn Coll Lingfield *S'wark* from 07; Superior Soc of Retreat Conductors from 05. *The Lodge, The College of St Barnabas, Blackberry Lane, Lingfield RH7 6NJ* Tel (01342) 872805

SUCH, Paul Nigel. b 52. FGA72 BTh84. Chich Th Coll 79. **d** 84 **p** 85. C Handsworth St Andr *Birm* 84-87; C Rugeley *Lich* 87-88; TV 88-91; R Longton 91-02; R Cov St Jo from 02. *St John's Rectory, 9 Davenport Road, Coventry CV5 6QA* Tel and fax (024) 7667 3203

SUCH, Royston Jeffery. b 46. Solicitor Univ Coll Lon LLB67. Sarum & Wells Th Coll 83. **d** 83 **p** 84. NSM Ringwood *Win* 83-90; R Bishop's Sutton and Ropley and W Tisted from 90. *The Vicarage, Lyeway Lane, Ropley, Alresford SO24 0DW* Tel (01962) 772205

SUCKLING, Keith Edward. b 47. CChem FRSC Darw Coll Cam PhD71 Liv Univ BSc87 DSc89. Oak Hill NSM Course 91. **d** 94 **p** 95. NSM Digswell and Panshanger *St Alb* from 94. *291 Knightsfield, Welwyn Garden City AL8 7NH* Tel (01707) 330022 E-mail keith@suckling291.freeserve.co.uk

SUDAN, Archbishop of the Episcopal Church of the. *See* MARONA, The Most Revd Joseph Biringi Hassan

SUDBURY, Archdeacon of. *Vacant*

SUDDABY, Susan Eveline. b 43. Bedf Coll of Educn CertEd64. S'wark Ord Course 93. **d** 96 **p** 97. NSM Rusthall *Roch* 96-00; C Northfleet 00-02; Perm to Offic 03-06; P-in-c N Chapel w Ebernoe *Chich* 06-08; rtd 08. *54 Garden Wood Road, East Grinstead RH19 1JX* Tel (01342) 313042

SUDDARDS, John Martin. b 52. Trin Hall Cam BA74 MA77 Barrister-at-Law 75. Qu Coll Birm 86. **d** 89 **p** 90. C Halstead St Andr w H Trin and Greenstead Green *Chelmsf* 89-93; P-in-c Gt w Lt Yeldham 93-97; P-in-c Toppesfield and Stambourne 93-97; R Upper Colne 97-01; RD Hinckford 98-01; TR Witham from 01; AD Witham from 07. *The Vicarage, 7 Chipping Dell, Witham CM8 2JX* Tel (01376) 513509
E-mail rector@suddards.plus.com

SUDELL, Philip Henry. b 61. Thames Poly BScEng84 Lon Univ PGCE85. Wycliffe Hall Ox 89. **d** 92 **p** 93. C Worthing Ch the King *Chich* 92-96; C Muswell Hill St Jas w St Matt *Lon* 96-05; Lic to Offic from 05. *163 Colney Hatch Lane, London N10 1HA* Tel (020) 8883 7417 E-mail philip.sudell@gracech.org.uk

SUDRON, David Jeffrey. b 78. Univ Coll Dur BA99 MA00. St Steph Ho Ox 01. **d** 03 **p** 04. C Gt Grimsby St Mary and St Jas *Linc* 03-08; Min Can Dur Cathl from 08. *3 The College, Durham DH1 3EQ* Tel 0191-384 2481
E-mail david.sudron@dunelm.org.uk

SUDWORTH, Frank. b 43. Open Univ BA92. Oak Hill Th Coll. **d** 78 **p** 79. C Deane *Man* 78-81; C Worksop St Jo *S'well* 82-85; V Wollaton Park 85-90; P-in-c Lenton Abbey 85-86; V 86-90; V Upper Armley *Ripon* 90-97; RD Armley 92-95; Dep Chapl HM Pris Liv 97-98; P-in-c Low Moor H Trin *Bradf* 98-03; V Low Moor 03; P-in-c Wyke 03-05; TR Oakenshaw, Wyke and Low

Moor 06-07; rtd 07; Perm to Offic *Blackb* from 07. *12 Brampton Avenue, Thornton-Cleveleys FY5 2JY* Tel (01253) 858377

SUDWORTH, Timothy Mark. b 70. St Martin's Coll Lanc BA93 K Coll Lon MA03. St Paul's Th Cen Lon 06. **d** 08 **p** 09. NSM Egham *Guildf* from 08; Chapl Strode's Coll from 08. *25 Mead Close, Egham TW20 8JA* Tel (01784) 437935
E-mail timsudworth@btinternet.com

SUFFERN, Richard William Sefton. b 57. Reading Univ BSc79. Trin Coll Bris 88. **d** 90 **p** 91. C Radipole and Melcombe Regis *Sarum* 90-94; TV Cheltenham St Mark *Glouc* 94-99; R Whitnash Cov from 99. *St Margaret's Rectory, 2 Church Close, Whitnash, Leamington Spa CV31 2HJ* Tel (01926) 425070
E-mail rwss@talktalk.net

SUFFOLK, Archdeacon of. *See* HUNT, The Ven Judith Mary

SUGDEN, Charles Edward. b 59. Magd Coll Cam PGCE82 MA83. Trin Coll Bris 89. **d** 91 **p** 92. C Gidea Park *Chelmsf* 91-94; TV Melksham *Sarum* 94-01; NSM Poole 02-08; V Locks Heath *Portsm* from 08. *The Vicarage, 125 Locks Heath Park Road, Locks Heath, Southampton SO31 6LY*
E-mail cesthevicar28@hotmail.com

SUGDEN, Canon Christopher Michael Neville. b 48. St Pet Coll Ox BA70 MA74 Nottm Univ MPhil74 Westmr Coll Ox PhD88. St Jo Coll Nottm 72. **d** 74 **p** 75. C Leeds St Geo *Ripon* 74-77; Assoc P Bangalore St Jo India 77-83; Lic to Offic *Ox* from 83; Can St Luke's Cathl Jos Nigeria from 00; Exec Dir Ox Cen for Miss Studies 01-04; Exec Sec Angl Mainstream Internat from 04. *Anglican Mainstream International, 21 High Street, Eynsham, Oxford OX29 4HE* Tel (01865) 883388
E-mail csugden@anglican-mainstream.net

SUGDEN, Kara Kerstin. b 58. Man Univ BSc81 W Midl Coll of Educn PGCE82. Trin Coll Bris BA91. **d** 91 **p** 96. NSM Gidea Park *Chelmsf* 91-94; NSM Melksham *Sarum* 95-01; Chapl Canford Sch Wimborne from 01. *Canford School, Canford Magna, Wimborne BH21 3AD* Tel (01202) 847586
E-mail kks@canford.com

SULLIVAN, Adrian Michael. b 55. Sarum & Wells Th Coll 85. **d** 87 **p** 88. C Louth *Linc* 87-90; P-in-c E and W Keal 90; P-in-c Marden Hill Gp 90-92; R from 92; P-in-c Stickney Gp from 07; RD Bolingbroke 97-00. *The Rectory, Hall Lane, West Keal, Spilsby PE23 4BJ* Tel (01790) 753534 E-mail rev.sully@ic24.net

SULLIVAN, Canon Julian Charles. b 49. Lon Univ BSc74 CertEd75. Wycliffe Hall Ox 80. **d** 83 **p** 84. C Southall Green St Jo *Lon* 83-87; C Wells St Cuth w Wookey Hole *B & W* 87-90; V Sheff St Barn and St Mary 90-91; V Sheff St Mary w Highfield Trin 91-95; V Sheff St Mary Bramall Lane from 95; P-in-c Endcliffe 04-07; Hon Can Sheff Cathl from 01; AD Ecclesall 01-06; Bp's Urban Adv from 05. *St Mary's Vicarage, 42 Charlotte Road, Sheffield S1 4TL* Tel 0114-272 4987
E-mail jandvsullivan@blueyonder.co.uk

SULLIVAN, The Ven Nicola Ann. b 58. SRN81 RM84. Wycliffe Hall Ox BTh95. **d** 95 **p** 96. C Earlham St Anne *Nor* 95-99; Assoc V Bath Abbey w St Jas *B & W* 99-02; Chapl R Nat Hosp for Rheumatic Diseases NHS Trust 99-02; Bp's Chapl and Past Asst *B & W* 02-07; Sub-Dean and Preb Wells Cathl 03-07; Adn Wells and Can Res Wells Cathl from 07. *6 The Liberty, Wells BA5 2SU* Tel (01749) 685147 E-mail adwells@bathwells.anglican.org

SULLIVAN, Trevor Arnold. b 40. CITC 69. **d** 70 **p** 71. C Lurgan Ch the Redeemer *D & D* 71-72; C Tralee *L & K* 72-75; Irish Sch of Ecum 75-77; Ind Chapl *D & G* 77-80; I Ematris *Clogh* 80-84; I Aughrim w Ballinasloe etc *L & K* 84-07; Can Limerick and Killaloe Cathls 89-07; rtd 07. *4 Woodview, Ballinasloe, Co Galway, Republic of Ireland* Tel (00353) 87-241 2194 (mobile)

SULLY, Andrew Charles. b 67. Southn Univ BA88 Birm Univ MPhil95. Qu Coll Birm 90. **d** 93 **p** 94. C Maindee Newport *Mon* 93-96; V Llanfihangel w Llanafan and Llanwnnws etc *St D* 96-02; TV St As 03-06; PV St As Cathl 02-06; V Llangollen w Trevor and Llantysilio from 06. *The Vicarage, Abbey Road, Llangollen LL20 8SN* Tel (01978) 860231

SULLY, Martin John. b 44. AIAS. St Jo Coll Nottm 80. **d** 82 **p** 83. C Lindfield *Chich* 82-86; V Walberton w Binsted 86-01; R Lewes St Jo sub Castro from 01. *St John's Rectory, 1 The Avenue, Lewes BN7 1BA* Tel (01273) 473080 E-mail msully@stjohnlewes.com

SUMARES, Manuel. b 43. Stonehill Coll USA BA66 Dominican Coll of Philosophy and Th Ottawa BPh74 Catholic Univ of Portugal PhD84 Roehampton Inst MPh99. **d** 97 **p** 99. Hon Asst Chapl Oporto *Eur* 97-05; P-in-c from 05. *Casa do Brrio-Monsul, P-Pvoa de Lanhoso 4830, Portugal* Tel (00351) (253) 993067
E-mail op14089@mail.telepac.pt

SUMMERS, Alexander William. b 75. Leic Univ BA98 MA00 Fitzw Coll Cam BTh09 Open Univ PGCE01. Westcott Ho Cam 07. **d** 09. C Chingford SS Pet and Paul *Chelmsf* from 09. *50 Mayfield Road, London E4 7JA* Tel (020) 8529 3963 Mobile 07717-575772 E-mail lex.summers@yahoo.co.uk

SUMMERS, Jeanne. *See* SUMMERS, Preb Ursula Jeanne

SUMMERS, John Ewart. b 35. MIMechE66 Ex Univ MA95. ALCD69. **d** 69 **p** 70. C Fulham St Matt *Lon* 69-72; Chapl RN 72-81; V Devonport St Barn *Ex* 81-98; V Devonport St Mich and St Barn 98-00; rtd 00; Perm to Offic *Ex* from 00. *Box Cottage, Aish, South Brent TQ10 9JH* Tel (01364) 72976

SUMMERS (née PASCOE), Mrs Lorraine Eve. b 51. SAOMC 98. **d** 01 **p** 02. NSM Sandon, Wallington and Rushden w Clothall *St Alb* 01-06; P-in-c Kimpton w Ayot St Lawrence from 06; Asst Chapl E and N Herts NHS Trust from 06. *The Vicarage, 11 High Street, Kimpton, Hitchin SG4 8RA* Tel (01438) 833419

SUMMERS, Neil Thomas. b 58. Roehampton Inst BA93 K Coll Lon MA94 St Mary's Coll Strawberry Hill PGCE95. SEITE 97. **d** 00 **p** 01. NSM Richmond St Mary w St Matthias and St Jo *S'wark* from 00. *2 Ravensbourne Road, Twickenham TW1 2DH* Tel (020) 8892 8313 E-mail ntsummers@aol.com

SUMMERS, Paul Anthony. b 53. St Jo Coll York CertEd75. Coll of Resurr Mirfield 77. **d** 80 **p** 81. C Manston *Ripon* 80-83; Min Can and Prec Ripon Cathl 83-88; Chapl Univ Coll of Ripon and York St Jo 84-88; V Whitkirk *Ripon* 88-95; R Lower Wharfedale 95-00; AD Harrogate 98-00; rtd 04; Perm to Offic *Bradf* from 05. *16 Beacon Street, Addingham, Ilkley LS29 0QX* Tel (01943) 839552 Mobile 07747-131731
E-mail paulsummers65@hotmail.com

SUMMERS, Canon Raymond John. b 41. Univ of Wales TCert63 Open Univ BA75. St Mich Coll Llan 77. **d** 77 **p** 78. NSM Mynyddislwyn *Mon* 77-81; NSM Abercarn 81-82; P-in-c 82-89; V 89-91; V Mynyddislwyn 91-95; TR 95-08; RD Bedwellty 93-04; Can St Woolos Cathl 01-08; rtd 08. *12A Maple Gardens, Risca, Newport NP11 6AR* Tel (01633) 613676

SUMMERS, Stephen Bruce. b 63. St Andr Univ MTheol95 Chich Univ PhD08. STETS 98. **d** 00 **p** 01. C Bishop's Waltham *Portsm* 00-02; R Farlington from 02. *The Rectory, 27 Farlington Avenue, Cosham, Portsmouth PO6 1DF* Tel (023) 9237 5145
E-mail steve@farlingtonparish.co.uk

SUMMERS, Preb Ursula Jeanne. b 35. Birm Univ BA56 Liv Univ CertEd57. Glouc Sch of Min. **dss** 85 **d** 87 **p** 94. Fownhope *Heref* 85-87; Hon C 87; Brockhampton w Fawley 85-87; Hon C 87; C Marden w Amberley and Wisteston 88-94; P-in-c 94-02; RD Heref Rural 93-99; P-in-c Moreton-on-Lugg 96-02; Preb Heref Cathl 96-02; rtd 02; Perm to Offic *Heref* from 02. *33 St Botolph's Green, Leominster HR6 8ER* Tel (01568) 617456
E-mail rolandandjeanne@yahoo.co.uk

SUMNER, Preb Gillian Mansell. b 39. St Anne's Coll Ox BA61 MA65 MLitt76. Wycliffe Hall Ox BA85. **dss** 86 **d** 87 **p** 94. Ox St Andr 86-91; Hon C 87-91; Tutor Wycliffe Hall Ox 86-89; Prin Ox Area Chr Tr Scheme 89-91; Vice-Prin Ox Min Course 89-91; Assoc Prin 91-94; Hon C Kirtlington w Bletchingdon, Weston etc 91-94; Hon Can Ch Ch 94; Local Min Officer *Heref* 95-02; P-in-c Wistanstow 95-98; Preb Heref Cathl from 97; Adv for NSM 02-05; rtd 05. *Black Venn, Reeves Lane, Stanage, Knighton LD7 1NA* Tel (01547) 530281
E-mail gandmsumner@compuserve.com

SUMNER, John Gordon. b 46. CCC Cam BA68 MA72. Ridley Hall Cam 69. **d** 72 **p** 73. C Liskeard w St Keyne *Truro* 72-75; C Caversham *Ox* 75-81; V Swallowfield 81-93; Asst Chapl Reading Univ 81-93; C Glastonbury w Meare *B & W* 93-04; Ldr Quest Community 93-08; Chapl Laslett's *Worc* 04-08; Hon C Worcs W from 08; Bp's Adv on New Relig Movements from 08. *The Rectory, Church Road, Clifton-on-Teme, Worcester WR6 6DJ* E-mail johngordonsumner@tiscali.co.uk

SUMNERS, Ms Cristina Jordan. b 47. Vassar Coll (NY) BA73 BNC Ox MPhil85. Princeton Th Sem 73 Gen Th Sem (NY) MDiv76. **d** 78 **p** 82. USA 79-91 and from 02; Asst to R San Antonio St Dav 80-90; P-in-c Rockport Trin by Sea 90-91; Asst Chapl K Edw Sch Witley 93-95; Perm to Offic *Guildf* 93-96; NSM Guildf H Trin w St Mary 97-02; Educn Officer 98-00. *NDCBU 5798, Taos NM 87571, USA*

SUMSION, Paul Henry. b 74. UMIST BSc97. Trin Coll Bris BA03. **d** 04 **p** 05. C Hawkshaw Lane *Man* 04-08; P-in-c 08; C Holcombe 04-08; P-in-c 08; R Holcombe and Hawkshaw from 09; Chapl Bury Coll of FE from 05. *St Mary's Vicarage, Bolton Road, Hawkshaw, Bury BL8 4JN* Tel (01204) 888064
E-mail paul@sumsion.org.uk

SUNDERLAND, Christopher Allen. b 52. BA75 St Pet Coll Ox MA80 DPhil80. Trin Coll Bris 84. **d** 86 **p** 87. C Stratton St Margaret w S Marston etc *Bris* 86-90; V Barton Hill St Luke w Ch Ch 90-98; RD Bris City 94-98; Perm to Offic from 98; Research Assoc Churches' Coun for Ind & Soc Resp from 98. *50 Guest Avenue, Emersons Green, Bristol BS16 7GA* Tel and fax 0117-957 4652 E-mail csunderland@pavilion.co.uk

SUNDERLAND, Preb Geoffrey. b 21. St Edm Hall Ox BA43 MA47. St Steph Ho Ox 46. **d** 48 **p** 49. C Clifton All SS *Bris* 48-51; C Elland *Wakef* 52-54; C Devonport St Mark Ford *Ex* 55-56; C-in-c Plymouth St Jas Ham CD 56-59; V Plymouth St Jas Ham 59-63; Chapl K Coll Taunton 63-65; C Clifton All SS *Bris* 65-68; V Plymstock *Ex* 68-86; RD Plympton 76-81; Preb Ex Cathl 82-89; rtd 86; Perm to Offic *B & W* and *Ex* 86-08. *30 Capel Court, The Burgage, Prestbury, Cheltenham GL52 3EL*
E-mail geoffrey.sunderland@tiscali.co.uk

SUNDERLAND, Wendy Jillian. b 47. **d** 99 **p** 00. OLM Bury St Edmunds St Mary St E 99-08; rtd 08. *9 Crown Street, Bury St Edmunds IP33 1QU* Tel (01284) 766883
E-mail wendy.sunderland@btinternet.com

SUNDERLAND, Archdeacon of. *See* BAIN, The Ven John Stuart

SUNLEY, Denis John. b 50. **d** 02. OLM Cannock *Lich* from 02. *22 Huntsman's Rise, Huntington, Cannock WS12 4PH* Tel (01543) 570572 E-mail dsunley@bigfoot.com

SURMAN, Malcolm Colin. b 48. Birm Univ CertEd72 Southn Univ BTh88. Sarum & Wells Th Coll 76. **d** 78 **p** 79. C Basingstoke *Win* 78-81; P-in-c Alton All SS 81-85; V 85-01; Chapl N Hants Loddon Community NHS Trust 84-01; P-in-c Burton and Sopley *Win* from 01. *The Vicarage, Preston Lane, Burton, Christchurch BH23 7JU* Tel (01202) 489807 Fax 475793 E-mail malcolm.surman@dsl.pipex.com

SURREY, Mrs Maureen. b 53. Man OLM Scheme 98. **d** 01 **p** 03. OLM Davyhulme Ch Ch *Man* 01-02; OLM Walkden and Lt Hulton from 03. *56 Abingdon Road, Urmston, Manchester M41 0GN* Tel 0161-748 3961 E-mail sidandmo@hotmail.com

SURREY, Archdeacon of. *See* BEAKE, The Ven Stuart Alexander

SURRIDGE, Mrs Faith Thomas. b 45. Open Univ BA75 Lon Univ PGCE76 BPhil(Ed)96. SWMTC 83. **dss** 85 **d** 87 **p** 94. St Breoke and Egloshayle *Truro* 85-87; NSM St Mawgan w St Ervan and St Eval 91-95; NSM St Columb Major w St Wenn 95-03; P-in-c 03-08. *The Gables, Union Hill, St Columb TR9 6AR* Tel (01637) 881197 E-mail faith@ftsurridge.wanadoo.co.uk

SURTEES, Brian Lawrence. b 44. NTMTC. **d** 01 **p** 02. NSM Hatfield Heath and Sheering *Chelmsf* 01-05; NSM Tye Green w Netteswell from 05; NSM Chipping Ongar w Shelley from 08. *13 Bowes Drive, Ongar CM5 9AU* Tel (01277) 363607 E-mail bsurtees@ntlworld.com

SURTEES, Timothy John de Leybourne. b 31. G&C Coll Cam BA54 MA58. Westcott Ho Cam 54. **d** 56 **p** 57. C Guisborough *York* 56-59; C Grantham St Wulfram *Linc* 59-61; V Cayton w Eastfield *York* 61-72; R Cheam *S'wark* 72-96; rtd 96; Perm to Offic *Heref* from 96. *Dove Cottage, Leysters, Leominster HR6 0HW* Tel (01568) 750203

SUTCH, The Ven Christopher David. b 47. TD92. AKC69. St Aug Coll Cant 69. **d** 70 **p** 71. C Bris St Andr Hartcliffe 70-75; C Swindon Dorcan 75-78; TV 78-79; P-in-c Alveston 79-83; V 83-89; RD Westbury and Severnside 86-89; CF (TA) 80-03; TR Yate New Town *Bris* 89-99; RD Stapleton 95-99; V Cainscross w Selsley *Glouc* 99-07; AD Stonehouse 04-07; Chapl Costa del Sol E *Eur* from 07; Adn Gib from 08. *Edificio Jupiter 1, Avenida Nuestro Padre Jesus Cautivo, 74 Los Boliches, 29640 Fuengirola (Málaga), Spain* Tel and fax (0034) (95) 258 0600 E-mail frdavid@standrews-cofe-spain.com

SUTCH, Canon Christopher Lang. b 21. Oriel Coll Ox BA47 MA47. Cuddesdon Coll 47. **d** 49 **p** 50. C Westbury-on-Trym H Trin *Bris* 49-53; V Bedminster Down 53-58; V Hanham 58-74; R Brinkworth w Dauntsey 74-86; RD Malmesbury 79-85; Hon Can Bris Cathl 82-86; rtd 86; Perm to Offic *Bris* 91-08 and *Glouc* 01-08. *36 Arrowsmith Drive, Stonehouse GL10 2QR* Tel (01453) 791896

SUTCLIFFE, Crispin Francis Henry. b 48. Keble Coll Ox BA69. Sarum & Wells Th Coll 73. **d** 74 **p** 75. C Truro St Paul 74-77; S Africa 77-80; P-in-c Treslothan *Truro* 80-85; R Ilchester w Northover, Limington, Yeovilton etc *B & W* from 91. *The Rectory, Ilchester, Yeovil BA22 8LJ* Tel (01935) 840296

SUTCLIFFE, Howard Guest. b 44. Fitzw Coll Cam BA66 MA70 Birm Univ MA75. Westcott Ho Cam 73. **d** 74 **p** 75. C Chorlton-cum-Hardy St Clem *Man* 74-77; Chapl Chetham's Sch of Music 77-80; V Oldham St Paul *Man* 80-94; Co-ord Werneth and Freehold Community Development Project 94-06; Perm to Offic 94-09; rtd 09; Hon C Saddleworth *Man* from 09. *The Vicarage, Station Road, Uppermill, Oldham OL3 6HQ* Tel (01457) 872412 E-mail howardguestsutcliffe@yahoo.co.uk

SUTCLIFFE, Ian. b 31. Surrey Univ BSc69. Qu Coll Birm 61. **d** 63 **p** 65. C W Wimbledon Ch Ch *S'wark* 61-65; C Battersea St Phil 65-66; C Kingston Hill St Paul 71-73; Lic to Offic *Carl* 75-96; rtd 96. *42 Hill Street, Arbroath DD11 1AB*

SUTCLIFFE, John Leslie. b 35. Liv Univ BA56. Sarum Th Coll 58. **d** 60 **p** 61. C Lytham St Cuth *Blackb* 60-62; C Altham w Clayton le Moors 62-65; C-in-c Penwortham St Leon CD 65-71; Ind Chapl *Liv* 71-74; V Orford St Andr 74-79; V Burnley St Cuth *Blackb* 79-88; Bp's Adv on UPA *Ripon* 88-94; Hon C Leeds Gipton Epiphany 88-94; I Carrickmacross w Magheracloone *Clogh* 94-01; rtd 01; Perm to Offic *Blackb* from 02. *1 Beckside, Barley, Burnley BB12 9JZ* Tel (01282) 449687

SUTCLIFFE, Peter John. b 58. BA. Linc Th Coll. **d** 82 **p** 83. C Skipton Ch Ch *Bradf* 82-85; C Tettenhall Regis *Lich* 85-86; TV 86-89; TV Warwick *Cov* 89-93; Relig Producer BBC Radio Cov and Warks 89-93; V Burley in Wharfedale *Bradf* 93-03; RD Otley 97-02; P-in-c Yeadon St Andr 03-06; V Lightcliffe *Wakef* 06-09; V Lesbury w Alnmouth *Newc* from 09; V Longhoughton w Howick from 09. *The Vicarage, Lesbury, Alnwick NE66 3AU* Tel (01665) 830281 E-mail peter.sutcliffe@btinternet.com

SUTER, Richard Alan. b 48. Rhodes Univ BA72 St Jo Coll Dur BA74. Cranmer Hall Dur 72. **d** 75 **p** 76. C Darlington H Trin *Dur* 75-77; C Wrexham *St As* 77-82; R Llansantffraid Glan Conwy and Eglwysbach 82-87; V Broughton 87-92; RD Wrexham 90-97; V Rossett 92-04; V Holt, Rossett and Isycoed

from 04. *The Vicarage, Rossett, Wrexham LL12 0HE* Tel (01244) 570498 E-mail etsuterral@aol.com

SUTHERLAND, Alistair Campbell. b 31. Lon Univ BSc50 Ex Univ BA77 CEng MIET. Wycliffe Hall Ox 77. **d** 78 **p** 79. C Nottingham St Jude *S'well* 78-81; R Barton in Fabis 81-96; P-in-c Thrumpton 81; V 81-96; RD W Bingham 87-92; Dioc Adv on Ind Society 92-96; NSM Gotham 93-96; NSM Kingston and Ratcliffe-on-Soar 93-96; rtd 96; Perm to Offic *S'wark* 88-01 and *Ex* 99-05. *36 Pyrton Lane, Watlington OX49 5LX* Tel (01491) 612705

SUTHERLAND, Mark Robert. b 55. Univ of NZ LLB77 Lon Inst of Educn MA95. Ripon Coll Cuddesdon 82. **d** 85 **p** 86. C Pinner *Lon* 85-88; C Sudbury St Andr 88-91; Perm to Offic *S'wark* 91-92; Chapl Maudsley Hosp Lon 91-94; Chapl Bethlem R Hosp Beckenham 91-94; Chapl Bethlem and Maudsley NHS Trust Lon 94-99; Presiding Chapl S Lon and Maudsley NHS Foundn Trust from 99. *The Maudsley Hospital, London SE5 8AZ* Tel (020) 7919 2815 E-mail mark.sutherland@slam.nhs.uk

SUTHERLAND, Robert. b 78. Newc Univ BA00 St Jo Coll Dur MA09 SS Hild & Bede Coll Dur PGCE01. Cranmer Hall Dur 05 Coll of Resurr Mirfield 08. **d** 09. C Morley *Wakef* from 09. *2 Bridge Court, Morley, Leeds LS27 0BD* Tel 0113-238 1984 Mobile 07751-306568 E-mail robb@priest.com

SUTTIE, Miss Jillian. b 53. ERMC. **d** 08 **p** 09. NSM Colney Heath St Mark *St Alb* from 08. *51 West Riding, Bricket Wood, St Albans AL2 3QE* Tel (01923) 662772

SUTTLE, Neville Frank. b 38. Reading Univ BSc61 Aber Univ PhD64. **d** 76 **p** 77. NSM Penicuik *Edin* from 76. *44 St James's Gardens, Penicuik EH26 9DU* Tel and fax (01968) 673819

SUTTON, Charles Edwin. b 53. Bris Univ BEd77 Ox Univ. Ripon Coll Cuddesdon 77. **d** 80 **p** 81. C Stanwix *Carl* 80-84; Warden Marrick Priory *Ripon* 84-88. *7 Beech Close, Baldersby, Thirsk YO7 4QB* Tel (01765) 640616

SUTTON, Colin Phillip. b 51. Birm Univ BA73. Chich Th Coll 73. **d** 75 **p** 76. C Penarth All SS *Llan* 75-77; C Roath 77-80; C Caerau w Ely 80-84; V Rhydyfelin 84-04; V Fairwater from 04. *St Peter's Parsonage, 211 St Fagans Road, Cardiff CF5 3DW* Tel (029) 2056 2551

SUTTON, David John. b 49. St Mich Coll Llan 97. **d** 99 **p** 00. C Maesglas and Duffryn *Mon* 99-05; Chapl Paphos Cyprus 05; R Luton Ch Ch *Roch* from 06. *Luton Rectory, Capstone Road, Chatham ME5 7PN* Tel (01634) 843780

SUTTON, David Robert. b 49. Birm Univ BA69 Ox Univ CertEd72. St Steph Ho Ox 70. **d** 72 **p** 73. C Clitheroe St Mary *Blackb* 72-75; C Fleetwood St Pet 75-78; V Calderbrook *Man* 78-88; V Winton 80-88; Chapl Salford Mental Health Services NHS Trust 92-08; Chapl Gtr Man W Mental Health NHS Foundn Trust from 08. *The Chaplaincy, Knowsley Building, Bury New Road, Prestwich, Manchester M25 3BL* Tel 0161-772 3833 Mobile 07770-737887 E-mail david.sutton@gmw.nhs.uk

SUTTON, Eves. *See* SUTTON, The Rt Revd Peter Eves

SUTTON, James William. b 41. Oak Hill Th Coll 81. **d** 84 **p** 85. NSM Chorleywood St Andr *St Alb* 84-06; Perm to Offic *Eur* from 06. *1A Mediterranean Terrace, Library Ramp, Gibraltar* Tel (00350) 200 46796 E-mail sutton@gibtelecom.net

SUTTON, Jeremy John Ernest. b 60. Ridley Hall Cam 83. **d** 86 **p** 87. C Seacombe *Ches* 86-88; C Northwich St Luke and H Trin 88-90; TV Birkenhead Priory 90-94; V Over St Chad 94-01; V Dunham Massey St Marg and St Mark from 01. *St Margaret's Vicarage, Dunham Road, Altrincham WA14 4AQ* Tel and fax 0161-928 1609 E-mail jerrysutton@dunhamvicarage.fsnet.co.uk

SUTTON, Canon John. b 47. St Jo Coll Dur BA70. Ridley Hall Cam 70. **d** 72 **p** 73. C Denton St Lawr *Man* 72-77; R 77-82; V High Lane *Ches* 82-88; V Sale St Anne 88-96; V Timperley from 96; Hon Can Ches Cathl from 01; RD Bowdon from 03. *The Vicarage, 12 Thorley Lane, Timperley, Altrincham WA15 7AZ* Tel 0161-980 4330 E-mail jfsuttontimp@aol.com

SUTTON, John Stephen. b 33. Em Coll Cam BA57 MA61. Wycliffe Hall Ox 57. **d** 59 **p** 60. C Dagenham *Chelmsf* 59-62; C Bishopwearmouth St Gabr *Dur* 62-63; V Over Kellet *Blackb* 63-67; V Darwen St Barn 67-74; V Walthamstow St Jo *Chelmsf* 74-84; V Stebbing w Lindsell 84-98; RD Dunmow 94-98; rtd 98; Perm to Offic *Chich* from 98. *20 Firwood Close, Eastbourne BN22 9QL* Tel (01323) 504654

SUTTON, Canon John Wesley. b 48. Rolle Coll CertEd71. All Nations Chr Coll. **d** 76 **p** 77. Chile 76-77; Peru 79-84; Area Sec SAMS 84-88; Youth Sec 88-91; Personnel Sec and Asst Gen Sec 91-03; Gen Sec 03-09; Dir Strategic Partnerships and Miss Nationwide Chr Trust from 09; Hon Can Peru from 93. *88 Horn Lane, Woodford Green IG8 9AH* Tel (020) 8505 7888 Fax (01892) 525797 E-mail johnsutton.woodford99@ntlworld.com

✠**SUTTON, The Rt Revd Keith Norman.** b 34. Jes Coll Cam BA58 MA62. Ridley Hall Cam. **d** 59 **p** 60 **c** 78. C Plymouth St Andr *Ex* 59-62; Chapl St Jo Coll Cam 62-67; Chapl Bp Tucker Coll Uganda 68-72; Prin Ridley Hall Cam 73-78; Suff Bp Kingston *S'wark* 78-84; Bp Lich 84-03; rtd 03. *Afton Farmhouse, Newport Road, Freshwater PO40 9UE* Tel (01983) 756487

SUTTON, Kingsley Edwin. b 70. TCD BTh94. **d** 97 **p** 98. C Belfast St Matt *Conn* 97-99; C Willowfield *D & D* 99-02; I Newry from 02. *Glebe House, Windsor Avenue, Newry BT34 1EQ* Tel (028) 3026 2621 E-mail revsutton@gmail.com

SUTTON, Canon Malcolm David. b 26. Selw Coll Cam BA47 MA52. Ridley Hall Cam 48. **d** 50 **p** 51. C Owlerton *Sheff* 50-52; C Kew *S'wark* 52-54; C Hornchurch St Andr *Chelmsf* 54-56; V Roxeth Ch Ch *Lon* 56-63; R Beccles St Mich *St E* 63-82; TR 82-94; RD Beccles 65-73; Hon Can St E Cathl 70-94; rtd 94; Perm to Offic *St E* from 94 and *Nor* from 95. *10 Merville, Carlton Colville, Lowestoft NR33 8UF*

SUTTON, Mrs Monica Rosalind. b 48. Sheff Hallam Univ MSc99 Leeds Univ BA09. Yorks Min Course. **d** 09. NSM Sheff St Cuth from 09. *4 Cyprus Terrace, Sheffield S6 3QH* Tel 0114-232 3559 E-mail monica_r_sutton@yahoo.com

SUTTON, Canon Peter Allerton. b 59. Ex Univ BA85. Linc Th Coll 85. **d** 87 **p** 88. C Fareham H Trin *Portsm* 87-90; C Alverstoke 90-93; Chapl HM Pris Haslar 90-93; V Lee-on-the-Solent *Portsm* from 93; Warden of Readers 96-00; RD Gosport from 06; Hon Can Portsm Cathl from 09. *St Faith's Vicarage, Victoria Square, Lee-on-the-Solent PO13 9NF* Tel and fax (023) 9255 0269

✠**SUTTON, The Rt Revd Peter Eves.** b 23. CBE90. Wellington Univ (NZ) BA45 MA47. NZ Bd of Th Studies LTh48. **d** 47 **p** 48 **c** 65. C Wanganui New Zealand 47-50; C Bethnal Green St Jo *Lon* 50-51; C Bp's Hatfield *St Alb* 51-52; V Berhampore New Zealand 52-58; V Whangarei 58-64; Adn Waimate 62-64; Dean St Paul's Cathl Dunedin 64-65; Bp Nelson 65-90; Acting Primate of New Zealand 85-86; rtd 90. *3 Ngatiawa Street, Nelson 7010, New Zealand* Tel and fax (0064) (3) 546 6591 E-mail bishop.sutton@xtra.co.nz

SUTTON, Philip Frank. b 55. SAOMC 92. **d** 95 **p** 96. NSM Akeman *Ox* 95-00; Chapl Ox Radcliffe Hosps NHS Trust 96-00; Sen Chapl R United Hosp Bath NHS Trust 00-07; Dioc Adv Hosp Chapl 04-07; Chapl Team Ldr Ox Radcliffe Hosps NHS Trust from 07. *The John Radcliffe, Headley Way, Headington, Oxford OX3 9DU* Tel (01865) 741166

SUTTON, Richard Alan. b 39. Reading Univ BSc61. Wycliffe Hall Ox 70. **d** 72 **p** 73. C Galleywood Common *Chelmsf* 72-76; Pakistan 76-79; C Walsall St Martin *Lich* 79-83; V Barton Hill St Luke w Ch Ch *Bris* 83-89; V Sidcup Ch Ch *Roch* 89-95; rtd 95; Perm to Offic *Roch* 95-98. *30 Mill Road Avenue, Angmering, Littlehampton BN16 4HS* Tel (01903) 856721

SUTTON, Richard John. b 45. Lon Inst of Educn CertEd68. St Alb Minl Tr Scheme 77 Linc Th Coll 81. **d** 82 **p** 83. C Royston *St Alb* 82-87; C Bp's Hatfield 87-95; P-in-c Kempston and Biddenham 95-05; P-in-c Rackheath and Salhouse *Nor* 05-08; rtd 08; Perm to Offic *Nor* from 08. *Augusta Cottage, 1 Old School Court, Upper Sheringham, Sheringham NR26 8UA* Tel (01263) 821918 E-mail suttonsea@greenbee.net

SUTTON, Ronald. b 27. FSCA. NW Ord Course 76. **d** 79 **p** 80. C Helsby and Dunham-on-the-Hill *Ches* 79-81; R Church Lawton 81-92; RD Congleton 91-92; rtd 92; Perm to Offic *Ches* from 92. *79 Thornton Avenue, Macclesfield SK11 7XL* Tel (01625) 430212

SWABEY, Brian Frank. b 44. BA. Oak Hill Th Coll 79. **d** 82 **p** 83. C Clapham St Jas *S'wark* 82-84; C Wallington 84-88; Chapl Mt Gould Hosp Plymouth 88-89; V Plymouth St Jude *Ex* 88-92; Chapl RN 92-99; V Penn Fields *Lich* 99-01; rtd 01; Perm to Offic *Ex* from 01. *2 Drax Gardens, Crownhill, Plymouth PL6 5BJ* Tel (01752) 210643 E-mail brianswabey@eurobell.co.uk

SWABY, Anthony. *See* SWABY, Leward Anthony Woodrow

SWABY, Desrene. SEITE 00. **d** 03 **p** 04. NSM S'wark St Geo w St Alphege and St Jude from 03. *36 Gabriel House, 10 Odessa Street, London SE16 7HQ* Tel (020) 7231 9834

SWABY, Keith Graham. b 48. Southn Univ BA75. St Steph Ho Ox 75. **d** 77 **p** 78. C Lt Stanmore St Lawr *Lon* 77-80; C Hove All SS *Chich* 80-83; TV Haywards Heath St Wilfrid 83-95; C Clayton w Keymer 95-02; rtd 02. *The Old String of Horses, 2 and 4 Stephenson's Lane, Brampton CA8 1RU* Tel (016977) 3803

SWABY, Leward Anthony Woodrow. b 60. Trin Coll Bris 86 Ripon Coll Cuddesdon 89. **d** 92 **p** 93. C Wembley St Jo *Lon* 92-95; C Northampton St Matt *Pet* 95-97; TV Kingsthorpe w Northampton St Dav 97-01; Asst Chapl Worcs Acute Hosps NHS Trust 01-05; P-in-c Willenhall St Anne *Lich* from 05; Asst Chapl HM Pris Brinsford from 06. *St Anne's Vicarage, Ann Street, Willenhall WV13 1EN* Tel (01902) 606516

SWAIN, Allan. *See* SWAIN, Canon William Allan

SWAIN, David Noel. b 36. Wellington Univ (NZ) BA63 MA66. Coll of Resurr Mirfield 65. **d** 67 **p** 68. C Clapham H Trin *S'wark* 67-70; New Zealand 70-75; P-in-c Hermitage *Ox* 75-76; P-in-c Hampstead Norris 75-76; V Hermitage w Hampstead Norreys 76-80; TR Hermitage and Hampstead Norreys, Cold Ash etc 80-82; R Bingham *S'well* 82-94; rtd 94; Perm to Offic *S'well* 94-07 and *Ox* from 08. *9 Stephen Court, 3 Stephen Road, Headington, Oxford OX3 9AY* Tel (01865) 767068 E-mail swain936@btinternet.com

SWAIN, John Edgar. b 44. Lich Th Coll 67. **d** 69 **p** 70. C E Dereham w Hoe *Nor* 69-73; V Haugh *Linc* 73-74; R S Ormsby w Ketsby, Calceby and Driby 73-74; R Harrington w Brinkhill 73-74; R Oxcombe 73-74; R Ruckland w Farforth and Maidenwell 73-74; R Somersby w Bag Enderby 73-74; R Tetford and Salmonby 73-74; R Belchford 73-74; V W Ashby 73-74; C Attleborough *Nor* 74-78; Canada 78-90; P-in-c Oxford Cen w Eastwood and Princeton 78-84; P-in-c Oldcastle w Colchester N 84-90; P-in-c Kirton w Falkenham *St E* 90-95; Chapl Suffolk Constabulary 90-01; P-in-c Gt and Lt Whelnetham w Bradfield St George 95-01; P-in-c Lawshall 98-01; R Wawa w White River and Hawk Junction Canada 01-09; rtd 09. *93 Princeton Drive, Sault Ste Marie ON P6B 5T4, Canada* Tel (001) (705) 942 4370 E-mail j_eswain@hotmail.com

SWAIN, Canon John Roger. b 29. Fitzw Ho Cam BA55 MA59. Bps' Coll Cheshunt 55. **d** 57 **p** 58. C Headingley *Ripon* 57-60; C Moor Allerton 60-65; V Wyther 65-75; V Horsforth 75-86; P-in-c Roundhay St Edm 86-88; V 88-95; RD Allerton 89-94; Hon Can Ripon Cathl 89-95; rtd 95; Perm to Offic *Ripon* from 05. *3 Harlow Court, Park Avenue, Leeds LS8 2JH* Tel 0113-246 1274

SWAIN, Preb Peter John. b 44. Sarum & Wells Th Coll 86. **d** 88 **p** 89. C Beaminster Area *Sarum* 88-92; P-in-c W Newton and Bromfield w Waverton *Carl* 92-98; Member Rural Life and Agric Team 93-96; Ldr 96-98; RD Solway 95-98; Hon Can Carl Cathl 96-98; TR Leominster *Heref* 98-05; RD Leominster 98-05; Preb Heref Cathl 03-05; rtd 05. *10 Market Hall Street, Kington HR5 3DP* Tel (01544) 230999

SWAIN, Ronald Charles Herbert. b 08. Dur Univ BA42 MA50. St Aug Coll Cant 29. **d** 32 **p** 33. C S Wimbledon H Trin *S'wark* 32-34; SPG China 34-40; Perm to Offic *Dur* and *Newc* 41-42; P-in-c Padgate Ch Ch *Liv* 42-46; Perm to Offic *S'wark* 46-47; Chapl RAF 47-54; CF 54-62; V Walsham le Willows *St E* 62-70; V Shipley *Chich* 70-74; rtd 74; Perm to Offic *St E* 74-02. *81 Westley Road, Bury St Edmunds IP33 3RU* Tel (01284) 761655

SWAIN, Mrs Sharon Juanita. b 46. Sussex Univ BA75 CertEd76 Heythrop Coll Lon MA04. Glouc Sch of Min 81. **dss** 84 **d** 87 **p** 94. Upton St Leonards *Glouc* 84-88; C 87-88; Children's Officer *Worc* 88-95; Min Can Worc Cathl 94-95; V Hanley Castle, Hanley Swan and Welland 95-01; R E Bergholt and Brantham *St E* 01-06; RD Samford 01-06; TR Solway Plain *Carl* from 06. *The Vicarage, Langrigg, Wigton CA7 3NA* Tel (01697) 322014 E-mail s.swain@freeuk.com

SWAIN, Canon William Allan. b 38. Kelham Th Coll 63. **d** 68 **p** 69. C Welwyn Garden City *St Alb* 68-72; C Romsey *Win* 72-74; C Weeke 74-78; V Bournemouth H Epiphany 78-91; P-in-c Moordown 91-94; V 94-08; Hon Can Win Cathl 04-08; rtd 08. *20 Elizabeth Road, Wimborne BH21 1AX* E-mail canon.swain@talktalk.net

SWAINE, Judith Ann. b 55. STETS. **d** 09. C Portsea All SS *Portsm* from 09. *102 Copnor Road, Portsmouth PO3 5AL* Tel (023) 9266 0259

SWAINSON, Norman. b 38. Salford Univ MSc75. St Jo Coll Nottm 77. **d** 79 **p** 80. C Levenshulme St Pet *Man* 79-84; R Jarrow Grange *Dur* 84-97; rtd 97; Perm to Offic *Ches* from 98. *176 George Street, Compstall, Stockport SK6 5JD* Tel 0161-449 0551

SWALES, David James. b 58. Warwick Univ BA79. Cranmer Hall Dur 81. **d** 84 **p** 85. C Eccleshill *Bradf* 84-88; C Prenton *Ches* 88-92; V Oakworth *Bradf* 92-00; V Bolton St Jas w St Chrys 00-09; V Haughley w Wetherden and Stowupland *St E* from 09. *The Vicarage, The Folly, Haughley, Stowmarket IP14 3NS* Tel (01449) 675503 Mobile 07806-785714 E-mail david.swales@blueyonder.co.uk

SWALES, Peter. b 52. ACIB78 Open Univ BA99. Ridley Hall Cam 85. **d** 87 **p** 88. C Allestree *Derby* 87-91; P-in-c Horsley 91-99; RD Heanor 97-99; V Heckmondwike *Wakef* 99-03; V Chellaston *Derby* from 03. *The Vicarage, St Peter's Road, Chellaston, Derby DE73 6UT* Tel (01332) 704835 E-mail revpeterswales@btinternet.com

SWALLOW, Mrs Alice Gillian. b 51. Birm Univ BA72 CertEd73. NEOC 82. **dss** 84 **d** 87 **p** 94. Morpeth *Newc* 84-86; Uttoxeter w Bramshall *Lich* 86-88; Par Dn 87-88; Par Dn Rocester 88; Chapl to the Deaf *Man* 88-90; Par Dn Goodshaw and Crawshawbooth 88-93; C Barkisland w W Scammonden *Wakef* 93-95; V Ripponden 95-97; rtd 97; Perm to Offic *Wakef* from 02. *22 Scholes Lane, Scholes, Cleckheaton BD19 6NR* Tel (01274) 875529 E-mail jill_swallow@yahoo.co.uk

SWALLOW, John Allen George. b 28. St Jo Coll Dur BA53. **d** 54 **p** 55. C Billericay St Mary *Chelmsf* 54-57; C Bishop's Stortford St Mich *St Alb* 57-59; V Roxwell *Chelmsf* 59-64; V S Weald 64-81; R W w E Mersea 81-93; rtd 93; Perm to Offic *Chelmsf* from 93 and *St E* from 95. *72 Rembrandt Way, Bury St Edmunds IP33 2LT* Tel (01284) 725136

SWALLOW, John Brian. b 36. Trent Poly 78. **d** 84 **p** 85. C Cleveleys *Blackb* 84-87; V Blackpool St Mich 87-93; P-in-c Burnley St Steph 93-98; V 98-01; RD Burnley 97-00; rtd 01; Perm to Offic *Dur* from 02. *6 Chichester Walk, Haughton-le-Skerne, Darlington DL1 2SG*

SWAN, Duncan James. b 65. Imp Coll Lon BSc88 SS Coll Cam

BA91 MA95 K Coll Lon MA04. Ridley Hall Cam 89. **d** 92 **p** 93. C Stevenage St Andr and St Geo *St Alb* 92-95; C Harpenden St Nic 95-99; V Redbourn 99-06; TR Caterham *S'wark* from 06. *The Rectory, 5 Whyteleafe Road, Caterham CR3 5EG* Tel (01883) 373083 E-mail duncpen@hotmail.com

SWAN, Owen. b 28. ACP71. Edin Th Coll 56. **d** 59 **p** 60. C Lewisham St Jo Southend *S'wark* 59-64; CF (TA) from 60; V Richmond St Luke *S'wark* 64-82; C-in-c Darlington St Hilda and St Columba CD *Dur* 82-84; R Feltwell *Ely* 84-87; R Holywell w Needingworth 87-97; rtd 97; P-in-c Gt Staughton *Ely* 97-02; P-in-c Hail Weston and Southoe 00-02; Perm to Offic *Ely* and *St E* from 02. *Primrose Cottage, Hawes Lane, Norton, Bury St Edmunds IP31 3LS* Tel (01359) 231108

SWAN, Philip Douglas. b 56. Wye Coll Lon BSc78 Qu Coll Cam MA81 CertEd81. St Jo Coll Nottm 86. **d** 88 **p** 89. C Birm St Martin w Bordesley St Andr 88-92; C Selly Park St Steph and St Wulstan 92-96; P-in-c The Lickey 96-98; V from 98. *The Vicarage, 30 Lickey Square, Rednal, Birmingham B45 8HB* Tel 0121-445 1262 E-mail swan@lickey30.freeserve.co.uk

SWAN, Preb Ronald Frederick. b 35. St Cath Coll Cam BA59 MA. Coll of Resurr Mirfield. **d** 61 **p** 62. C Staveley *Derby* 61-65; Chapl Lon Univ 65-72; C St Martin-in-the-Fields *72-77*; V Ealing St Barn 77-88; V Ealing St Steph Castle Hill 81-88; AD Ealing E 84-88; V Harrow St Mary 88-97; AD Harrow 89-94; Preb St Paul's Cathl 91-06; Master R Foundn of St Kath in Ratcliffe 97-06; rtd 06. *8 Moat Lodge, London Road, Harrow HA1 3LU* Tel (020) 8864 4625

SWANBOROUGH, Alan William. b 38. Southn Univ BEd75. Sarum & Wells Th Coll 77. **d** 80 **p** 81. NSM Ventnor H Trin *Portsm* 80-85; NSM Ventnor St Cath 80-85; Chapl Upper Chine Sch Shanklin 85-99; Chapl Ryde Sch w Upper Chine from 99; NSM Shanklin St Blasius *Portsm* 91-93; P-in-c from 93. *The Rectory, Rectory Road, Shanklin PO37 6NX* Tel (01983) 862407 E-mail awsstblasiusiow@fsmail.net

SWANEPOEL, David John. b 41. Rhodes Univ BA62 UNISA BA64 BTh84. **d** 75 **p** 76. S Africa 75-94; Dean George 85-89; NSM Hellingly and Upper Dicker *Chich* 94-99. *Providence House, Coldharbour Road, Upper Dicker, Hailsham BN27 3QE* Tel (01323) 843887

SWANN, Ms Anne Barbara. b 49. St Mich Coll Llan BTh07 MTh08. **d** 08 **p** 09. Hon C Peterston-super-Ely w St Brides-super-Ely *Llan* from 08. *19 Fairways Crescent, Cardiff CF5 3DZ* Tel (029) 2056 2641 Mobile 07810-798465 E-mail revdanne@live.co.uk

SWANN, Antony Keith. b 34. St Aid Birkenhead 58. **d** 61 **p** 62. C Bilston St Leon *Lich* 61-66; Sierra Leone 66-70; V W Bromwich St Phil *Lich* 70-75; Nigeria 76-78; R Church Lench w Rous Lench and Abbots Morton *Worc* 78-88; Chapl HM Pris Coldingley 88-90; Chapl HM Pris Leyhill 91-97; rtd 97; P-in-c Kemble, Poole Keynes, Somerford Keynes etc *Glouc* 97-02; Perm to Offic from 03. *30 Perry Orchard, Upton St Leonards, Gloucester GL4 8DQ*

SWANN, The Ven Edgar John. b 42. TCD BA66 MA70 BD77 HDipEd80. CITC 68. **d** 68 **p** 69. C Crumlin *Conn* 68-70; C Howth *D & G* 70-73; I Greystones 73-08; Can Ch Ch Cathl Dublin 90-08; Adn Glendalough 93-08; rtd 08. *Noah's Ark, 4 Mount Haven, New Road, Greystones, Co Wicklow, Republic of Ireland* Tel (00353) (1) 255 7572 Mobile 87-255 7032 E-mail edgarjswann@eircom.net

SWANN, Frederick David. b 38. **d** 69 **p** 70. C Lurgan Ch the Redeemer *D & D* 69-77; I Ardmore w Craigavon 77-79; I Comber 79-85; I Drumglass w Moygashel *Arm* 85-06; Can Arm Cathl 96-06; Preb 98-01; Treas 01-06; rtd 06. *Branchfield, Ballymote, Co Sligo, Republic of Ireland* Tel (00353) (71) 919 7097 E-mail derickswann@eircom.net

SWANN, Paul David James. b 59. Ch Ch Ox BA81 MA88. St Jo Coll Nottm 87. **d** 90 **p** 91. C Old Hill H Trin *Worc* 90-94; V 94-02; C Worc City St Paul and Old St Martin etc 02-06; C Worc City 06-09; Chapl Worc Tech Coll 02-09. *21 Tower Road, Worcester WR3 7AF* Tel (01905) 731135 E-mail paul@swannfamily.co.uk

SWANSEA AND BRECON, Bishop of. See DAVIES, The Rt Revd John David Edward

SWANTON, John Joseph. b 61. Bradf and Ilkley Coll BA84 MCIH89 MRSH95. S Dios Minl Tr Scheme 92. **d** 95 **p** 96. NSM Shalford *Guildf* 95-99; NSM Compton w Shackleford and Peper Harow from 99. *90 Busbridge Lane, Godalming GU7 1QH* Tel (01483) 427160

SWARBRICK (née PITE), Mrs Sheila Reinhardt. b 60. St Jo Coll Dur BA82 Nottm Univ MA98. Oak Hill Th Coll BA88. **d** 88 **p** 94. Par Dn Derby St Aug 88-92; C Brampton St Thos 92-95; Perm to Offic *St Alb* 95-96; P-in-c The Stodden Churches 96-98; Chapl Papworth Hosp NHS Trust 98-99; TV Braunstone *Leic* 99-02; P-in-c 02-07; Perm to Offic *Ex* 07-08; Hon C Cen Ex from 08. *7 Lower Kings Avenue, Exeter EX4 6JT* Tel (01392) 438866 E-mail sheila.pite@cooptel.net

SWARBRIGG, David Cecil. b 42. TCD BA64 MA67. **d** 65 **p** 66. C Lisburn Ch Ch *Conn* 65-67; C Thames Ditton *Guildf* 72-76;

Chapl Hampton Sch Middx 76-97; rtd 97. *39 Harefield, Hinchley Wood, Esher KT10 9TY* Tel and fax (020) 8398 3950

SWART-RUSSELL, Phoebe. b 58. Cape Town Univ BA79 MA82 DPhil88. Ox NSM Course 89. **d** 90 **p** 94. C Riverside *Ox* 90-95; Hon C Chenies and Lt Chalfont, Latimer and Flaunden 96-00. *The Rectory, Latimer, Chesham HP5 1UA* Tel (01494) 762281

SWARTZ, Clifford Robert. b 71. Trin Coll Connecticut BA92 Trin Coll Cam BA99. Ridley Hall Cam 97. **d** 00 **p** 01. C Kirk Ella *York* 00-03; Regional Dir FOCUS USA from 03; Hon C Tariffville Trin Ch from 03. *242 Steele Road, West Hartford CT 06117, USA* E-mail clifford@swartz.karoo.co.uk

SWARTZ, The Very Revd Oswald Peter Patrick. b 53. St Paul's Coll Grahamstown 76. **d** 80 **p** 80. C Welkom St Matthias S Africa 80-81; R Heidedal 81-87; R Mafikeng 87-92; Adn Mafikeng 89-92; Bp's Exec Officer Kimberley and Kuruman 93-94; Sub-Dean Kimberley 94-96; Dioc Sec and Bp's Exec Officer 96-00; Can Kimberley from 93; Regional Desk Officer USPG 01-06; Hon Chapl S'wark Cathl 01-06; Dean Pretoria from 06. *St Alban's Cathedral, PO Box 3053, Pretoria, 0001 South Africa* Tel and fax (0027) (12) 322 7670 or tel 348 4955 E-mail cathedral@mail.ngo.za

SWAYNE, Jeremy Michael Deneys. b 41. Worc Coll Ox BA63 BM, BCh67 MRCGP71 FFHom91. **d** 00 **p** 01. NSM Fosse Trinity *B & W* 00-04; P-in-c 04-05; rtd 05. *Tanzy Cottage, Rimpton, Yeovil BA22 8AQ* E-mail jem.swayne@btinternet.com

SWEATMAN, John. b 44. Open Univ BA89. Bernard Gilpin Soc Dur 67 Oak Hill Th Coll 68. **d** 71 **p** 72. C Rayleigh *Chelmsf* 71-73; C Seaford w Sutton *Chich* 73-77; Chapl RN 77-82; CF 82-85; V Hellingly and Upper Dicker *Chich* 85-90; Hon C Mayfield 95-96; P-in-c Malborough w S Huish, W Alvington and Churchstow *Ex* 96-02; V Ash w Westmarsh *Cant* from 02; C Nonington w Wymynswold and Goodnestone etc from 07; AD E Bridge from 08. *The Vicarage, Queen's Road, Ash, Canterbury CT3 2BG* Tel (01304) 812296 E-mail thevicar@s8nicholas.org.uk

SWEED, John William. b 35. Bernard Gilpin Soc Dur 58 Clifton Th Coll 59. **d** 62 **p** 63. C Shrewsbury St Julian *Lich* 62-64; C Sheff St Jo 64-70; V Doncaster St Jas 70-79; V Hatfield 79-00; RD Snaith and Hatfield 84-93; rtd 00; Perm to Offic *Sheff* from 00. *21 The Oval, Tickhill, Doncaster DN11 9HF* Tel (01302) 743293

SWEENEY, Andrew James. b 61. Wycliffe Hall Ox 96. **d** 96 **p** 97. C Bladon w Woodstock *Ox* 96-99; C Coleraine *Conn* 99-02; V Cogges and S Leigh *Ox* from 02; V N Leigh from 09; AD Witney 07-08. *Cogges Priory, Church Lane, Witney OX28 3LA* Tel (01993) 702155 Mobile 07720-472556 E-mail sweeney@coggespriory.freeserve.co.uk

SWEENEY, Robert Maxwell. b 38. Ch Ch Ox BA63 MA66 Birm Univ MA78. Cuddesdon Coll 63. **d** 65 **p** 66. C Prestbury *Glouc* 65-68; C Handsworth St Andr *Birm* 68-70; Asst Chapl Lancing Coll 70-73; V Wotton St Mary *Glouc* 74-79; V Ox St Thos w St Frideswide and Binsey 79-03; Chapl Magd Coll Ox 82-88; rtd 03. *22 Park House, 39 Park Place, Cheltenham GL50 2RF* Tel (01242) 254028

SWEET, Miss Lynette Jessica. b 59. Kent Univ BA80. Westcott Ho Cam 03. **d** 05 **p** 06. C Wilton w Netherhampton and Fugglestone *Sarum* from 05. *25 Riverside, Wilton, Salisbury SP2 0HW* Tel (01722) 744974 Mobile 07941-477727 E-mail lynette@sweet96.fsnet.co.uk

SWEET, Mrs Margaret Adelaide. b 33. Open Univ BA75 UEA MA83 FCollP83 FRSA89. St Steph Ho Ox BTh05. **d** 06 **p** 07. NSM Stratford-upon-Avon, Luddington etc *Cov* from 06. *5 Broad Street, Stratford-upon-Avon CV37 6HN* Tel (01789) 297395 E-mail sweetmargaret@btinternet.com

SWEET, Reginald Charles. b 36. Open Univ BA74. Ripon Hall Ox 61. **d** 62 **p** 63. C Styvechale *Cov* 62-65; Chapl RN 65-69 and 74-93; R Riddlesworth w Gasthorpe and Knettishall *Nor* 69-74; R Brettenham w Rushford 69-74; Perm to Offic 93-96; Chapl Miss to Seamen 96-99; rtd 99; Chapl Win St Cross w St Faith from 99. *The Chaplain's Lodge, The Hospital of St Cross, St Cross Road, Winchester SO23 9SD* Tel (01962) 853525 Mobile 07889-375085

SWEET, Preb Vaughan Carroll. b 46. Aston Univ BSc69 MSc70. Linc Th Coll 89. **d** 91 **p** 92. C Uttoxeter w Bramshall *Lich* 91-95; P-in-c Hadley 95-98; V 98-07; P-in-c Wellington Ch Ch 03-07; V Hadley and Wellington Ch Ch from 07; RD Telford from 00; RD Telford Severn Gorge *Heref* 00-03; Preb Lich Cathl from 05. *The Vicarage, 180 Holyhead Road, Wellington, Telford TF1 2DW* Tel and fax (01952) 254251 E-mail vaughan.sweet@virgin.net

SWEETING, David Charles. b 67. Nottm Univ BSc89. STETS 04. **d** 08. C Holbeach *Linc* from 08. *15 Greenwich Avenue, Holbeach, Spalding PE12 7JF* Tel (01406) 423963 Mobile 07973-841799 E-mail david@davidsweeting.orangehome.co.uk

SWEETING, Paul Lee. b 68. Lanc Univ BSc90 St Martin's Coll Lanc PGCE92. Cranmer Hall Dur BA99. **d** 99 **p** 00. C Blackb St Gabr 99-03; R Falkland Is 03-06; Chapl Sedbergh Sch from

06. *4 The Leyes, Station Road, Sedbergh LA10 5DJ* Tel (015396) 21968 Mobile 07736-672016
E-mail paulsweeting1968@hotmail.com

SWEETMAN (*née* BURNIE), **Ms Judith.** b 57. Leic Univ BA79 Anglia Ruskin Univ BA07. Westcott Ho Cam 05. **d** 07 **p** 08. C Coggeshall w Markshall *Chelmsf* from 07. *Hopgrounds, Church Street, Great Maplestead, Halstead CO9 2RH* Tel (01376) 563861 E-mail judithsweetman@st-peter-ad-vincula.org.uk

SWENSSON, Sister Gerd Inger. b 51. Lon Univ MPhil85 Uppsala Univ 70. **dss** 74 **d** 87. In Ch of Sweden 74-75; Notting Hill *Lon* 75-77; CSA from 75; Abbey Ho Malmesbury 77-79; R Foundn of St Kath 79-81; Notting Hill All SS w St Columb *Lon* 81-84; Kensington St Mary Abbots w St Geo 85-89; C Bedford Park 91-95; Sweden from 95. *Christens Gård, Pl 8, St Slågarp, S-231 95 Trelleborg, Sweden* Tel and fax (0046) (40) 487059 Mobile 708-743994 E-mail tedeum@mail.bip.net

SWIFT, Ainsley Laird. b 56. Liv Univ BEd80. Ripon Coll Cuddesdon. **d** 94 **p** 95. C Prescot *Liv* 94-98; TV New Windsor *Ox* 98-01; P-in-c from 01. *The Vicarage, Hermitage Lane, Windsor SL4 4AZ* Tel (01753) 858720 *or* 855447 Fax 860839 E-mail ainsley@swift9485.fsnet.co.uk

SWIFT, Andrew Christopher. b 68. Edin Univ BEng90 Aber Univ MSc97 Ox Univ BTh08. Ripon Coll Cuddesdon 05. **d** 07 **p** 08. C Glouc St Cath from 07. *29 Windfall Way, Gloucester GL2 0RP* Tel (01452) 383177 E-mail rev.andrew@familyswift.org.uk

SWIFT, Christopher James. b 65. Hull Univ BA86 Man Univ MA95 Sheff Univ PhD06. Westcott Ho Cam 89. **d** 91 **p** 92. C Longton *Blackb* 91-94; TV Chipping Barnet w Arkley *St Alb* 94-97; Chapl Wellhouse NHS Trust 97-98; Chapl Dewsbury Health Care NHS Trust 98-01; Hd Chapl Services Leeds Teaching Hosps NHS Trust from 01. *The Chaplaincy, St James's University Hospital, Beckett Street, Leeds LS9 7TF* Tel 0113-206 4658 Mobile 07866-563640 E-mail chris.swift@leedsth.nhs.uk

SWIFT, Christopher John. b 54. Linc Coll Ox BA76 MA Selw Coll Cam BA80. Westcott Ho Cam 79. **d** 81 **p** 82. C Portsea N End St Mark *Portsm* 81-84; C Alverstoke 84-87; V Whitton SS Phil and Jas *Lon* 87-94; R Shepperton 94-08; R Shepperton and Littleton from 08; AD Spelthorne 98-04. *The Rectory, Church Square, Shepperton TW17 9JY* Tel and fax (01932) 220511 E-mail christopher.swift@london.anglican.org

SWIFT (*formerly* LAKER), **Mrs Grace.** b 39. RN63. Sarum & Wells Th Coll BTh91. **d** 91 **p** 94. C Helston and Wendron *Truro* 91-95; Chapl Havering Hosps NHS Trust 95-02; NSM Rush Green *Chelmsf* 98-02; Bp Barking's Adv for Hosp Chapl 99-02; NSM Gt Burstead 06-08; NSM Purleigh, Cold Norton and Stow Maries from 08. *The Rectory, Church Hill, Purleigh, Chelmsford CM3 6QH* Tel (01621) 826905
E-mail graceswift@hotmail.com

SWIFT, Ian John Edward. b 46. NTMTC 99. **d** 02 **p** 03. NSM Basildon St Martin *Chelmsf* 02-06; C Vange from 06; Ind Chapl from 06. *79 Bull Lane, Rayleigh SS6 8LD* Tel (01268) 775593 Mobile 07725-037680 E-mail ijeswift@googlemail.com

SWIFT, Jessica Suzanne. b 75. Univ of New Brunswick BSc99. Wycliffe Hall Ox 99. **d** 02 **p** 03. C Islington St Mary *Lon* 02-05; C Mildmay Grove St Jude and St Paul 05-09; C Barnsbury from 09. *306B Amhurst Road, London N16 7UE* Tel (020) 7923 0114 Mobile 07812-676240 E-mail swift_jessica@hotmail.com

SWIFT, Ms Pamela Joan. b 47. Liv Univ BSc68. NEOC 85. **d** 88 **p** 94. Par Dn Bermondsey St Jas w Ch Ch *S'wark* 88-91; Par Dn Middleton St Cross *Ripon* 91-92; C Leeds All So and Dioc Stewardship Adv 92-95; TR Bramley 95-99; Miss Adv USPG *Blackb, Bradf, Carl* and *Wakef* 99-01; Hon C Kildwick *Bradf* 99-01; R and Community P Glas St Matt 01-05; rtd 05; Hon C Lanercost, Walton, Gilsland and Nether Denton *Carl* from 06; Chapl N Cumbria Acute Hosps NHS Trust 06-08. *6 Irthing Park, Gilsland, Brampton CA8 7DL* Tel (01697) 747652 Mobile 07833-938843 E-mail pam.swift@tiscali.co.uk

SWIFT, Richard Barrie. b 33. Selw Coll Cam BA58 MA64. Ripon Hall Ox. **d** 60 **p** 61. C Stepney St Dunstan and All SS *Lon* 60-64; C Sidmouth St Nic *Ex* 64-72; P-in-c W Hyde St Thos *St Alb* 72-77; V Mill End 72-77; V Mill End and Heronsgate w W Hyde 77-82; V Axminster *Ex* 82-83; P-in-c Chardstock 82-83; P-in-c Combe Pyne w Rousdon 82-83; TR Axminster, Chardstock, Combe Pyne and Rousdon 83-94; rtd 94; Perm to Offic *Ex* from 94. *15 Paternoster Row, Ottery St Mary EX11 1DP* Tel (01404) 813102

SWIFT, Sarah Jane. b 65. St Aid Coll Dur BSc88. St Jo Coll Nottm 05. **d** 06 **p** 07. C Wealdstone H Trin *Lon* from 06. *414 Northolt Road, Harrow HA2 8EZ* Tel (020) 8864 9007 E-mail sarah@sarahswift.org.uk

SWIFT, Selwyn. b 41. Trin Coll Bris 73. **d** 76 **p** 77. C Melksham *Sarum* 76-79; TV 79-81; TV Whitton 81-84; V Derry Hill 84-89; R Bunwell, Carleton Rode, Tibenham, Gt Moulton etc *Nor* 89-01; RD Depwade 97-01; rtd 01. *2 Kembold Close, Bury St Edmunds IP32 7EF* Tel (01284) 701258

SWIFT, Stanley. b 47. Open Univ BA86 ACIS71. Linc Th Coll 71. **d** 74 **p** 75. C Heaton St Barn *Bradf* 74-77; C Bexhill St Pet *Chich* 77-81; R Crowland *Linc* 81-86; RD Elloe W 82-86; R Upminster

Chelmsf 86-95; P-in-c N Ockendon 94-95; V Rush Green 95-02; V Gt Burstead from 02. *The Vicarage, 111 Church Street, Billericay CM11 2TR* Tel (01277) 625947
E-mail stanswift@hotmail.com

SWINBANK, Mrs Anne Jennifer. b 52. SS Paul & Mary Coll Cheltenham BA90. St Steph Ho Ox 08. **d** 09. NSM N Cheltenham *Glouc* from 09. *5 Priory Mews, Sidney Street, Cheltenham GL52 6DJ* Tel (01242) 700128
E-mail jennifer.swinbank@northchelt.org.uk

SWINBURNE, Harold Noel. b 27. Univ Coll Lon BA49. St Chad's Coll Dur. **d** 53 **p** 54. C Cockerton *Dur* 53-57; C Wisbech St Aug *Ely* 57-59; V Chilton Moor *Dur* 59-71; Lect RS New Coll Dur 71-93; Lic to Offic *Dur* 71-85; V Bishopwearmouth St Nic 85-93; rtd 93. *39 Durham Moor Crescent, Durham DH1 5AS* Tel 0191-386 2603

SWINDELL, Anthony Charles. b 50. Selw Coll Cam BA73 MA77 Leeds Univ MPhil77 PhD07. Ripon Hall Ox 73. **d** 75 **p** 76. C Hessle *York* 75-78; P-in-c Litlington w W Dean *Chich* 78-80; Adult Educn Adv E Sussex 78-80; TV Heslington *York* 80-81; Chapl York Univ 80-81; R Harlaxton *Linc* 81-91; RD Grantham 85-90; R Jersey St Sav *Win* from 91; Perm to Offic *Nor* 93-96. *The Rectory, Rectory Lane, St Saviour's Hill, St Saviour, Jersey JE2 7NP* Tel (01534) 736679
E-mail anthonyswindell@aol.co.uk

SWINDELL, Brian. b 35. St Jo Coll Nottm 86. **d** 88 **p** 89. C Wombwell *Sheff* 88-91; V Brinsworth w Catcliffe 91-93; TR Brinsworth w Catcliffe and Treeton 93-99; rtd 99; Perm to Offic *S'well* from 04. *36 Wasdale Close, West Bridgford, Nottingham NG2 6RG* Tel 0115-914 1125

SWINDELL, Richard Carl. b 45. Didsbury Coll Man CertEd70 Open Univ BA73 Leeds Univ MEd86. NOC 79 Qu Coll Birm 77. **d** 82 **p** 83. Hd Teacher Moorside Jun Sch 78-96; NSM Halifax St Aug *Wakef* 82-92; NSM Huddersfield H Trin from 92; Family Life and Marriage Officer 96-02; Bp's Adv for Child Protection from 02. *13 Moor Hill Court, Laund Road, Salendine Nook, Huddersfield HD3 3GQ* Tel (01484) 640473 Mobile 07946-761364 E-mail rswin25004@aol.com

SWINDELLS, Jonathan Reid. b 66. Bp Otter Coll Chich BA90 Cam Univ PGCE93 Leeds Univ BA02. Coll of Resurr Mirfield 00. **d** 02 **p** 03. C Sherborne w Castleton and Lillington *Sarum* 02-05; TV Hove *Chich* from 05. *The Vicarage, 17 Vallance Gardens, Hove BN3 2DB* Tel (01273) 734859 Mobile 07790-430070 E-mail jonathan@swindellsj.fsworld.co.uk

SWINDELLS, Philip John. b 34. St Edm Hall Ox BA56 MA60. Ely Th Coll 56. **d** 58 **p** 59. C Upton cum Chalvey *Ox* 58-62; C Bishops Hull St Jo *B & W* 62-66; C Stevenage St Geo *St Alb* 66-71; V Stevenage All SS Pin Green 71-78; R Clophill 78-00; P-in-c Upper w Lower Gravenhurst 83-93; P-in-c Shillington 96-99; rtd 00; Perm to Offic *Ely* from 00. *21 Wertheim Way, Huntingdon PE29 6UH* Tel (01480) 436886 Mobile 07980-093219 E-mail philip.swindells@btinternet.com

SWINDLEHURST, Canon Michael Robert Carol. b 29. Worc Coll Ox BA52 MA56. Cuddesdon Coll 61. **d** 63 **p** 64. C Havant *Portsm* 63-66; C Hellesdon *Nor* 66-69; V Brightlingsea *Chelmsf* 69-95; Miss to Seamen 69-95; RD St Osyth *Chelmsf* 84-94; Hon Can Chelmsf Cathl 89-95; rtd 95; Perm to Offic *Chelmsf* from 95 and *St Alb* 95-98. *9 Radwinter Road, Saffron Walden CB11 3HU* Tel (01799) 513788

SWINDON, Suffragan Bishop of. See RAYFIELD, The Rt Revd Lee Stephen

SWINGLER, Preb Jack Howell. b 19. St Jo Coll Cam BA41 MA47. Ridley Hall Cam 46. **d** 48 **p** 49. C Yeovil St Jo w Preston Plucknett *B & W* 48-53; V Henstridge 53-79; P-in-c Charlton Horethorne w Stowell 78-79; R Henstridge and Charlton Horethorne w Stowell 79-85; RD Merston 74-84; Preb Wells Cathl 79-05; rtd 85; Perm to Offic *B & W* from 85. *St Andrew's, March Lane, Galhampton, Yeovil BA22 7AN* Tel (01963) 440842

SWINHOE, Terence Leslie. b 49. Man Univ BA71 PGCE72 Lon Univ BD95. NOC. **d** 84 **p** 85. C Harborne St Pet *Birm* 84-87; V Warley *Wakef* 87-96; V Rastrick St Matt 96-06; P-in-c Greetland and W Vale from 06. *The Vicarage, 2 Goldfields Way, Greetland, Halifax HX4 8LA* Tel (01422) 372802
E-mail swinfam@aol.com

SWINN, Gerald Robert. b 40. Leeds Univ BSc60 Lon Univ BD70. Oak Hill Th Coll 63. **d** 66 **p** 67. C Weston-super-Mare Ch Ch *B & W* 66-69; C Harefield *Lon* 70-72; Lic to Offic *Sarum* from 72. *7 Witchampton Road, Broadstone BH18 8HY* Tel (01202) 249782 E-mail geraldswinn@ntlworld.com

SWINN, Philip Daniel. b 65. Oak Hill Th Coll BA01. **d** 01 **p** 02. C Harpenden St Nic *St Alb* 01-04; TV Bp's Hatfield 04-05; TV Bp's Hatfield, Lemsford and N Mymms from 05. *St John's Vicarage, Hill View, Bishops Rise, Hatfield AL10 9BZ* Tel (01707) 262689 E-mail pd_swinn@smims.com

SWINNERTON, Ernest George Francis. b 33. Clare Coll Cam BA54 MA57. Linc Th Coll 56. **d** 58 **p** 59. C Kirkholt *Man* 58-61; C Swindon Ch Ch *Bris* 61-67; C-in-c Walcot St Andr CD 67-75; P-in-c Chilton Foliat *Sarum* 76; TV Whitton 76-85; V Bolton St Matt w St Barn *Man* 85-95; rtd 95; Perm to Offic *Man* from 95. *15 Orchard Close, Chelmsford CM2 9SL* Tel (01245) 491366

SWINNEY, Shawn Douglas. b 76. Oak Hill Th Coll BA01 Regent Coll Vancouver MA04. Ox Min Course 07. **d** 09. *7 Layters Avenue, Chalfont St Peter, Gerrards Cross SL9 9HW* Tel (01753) 890741 Mobile 07507-304902
E-mail shawnswinney@hotmail.com

SWINTON, Garry Dunlop. b 59. SS Mark & Jo Univ Coll Plymouth BA81 CertEd82. Ripon Coll Cuddesdon 85. **d** 88 **p** 89. C Surbiton St Andr and St Mark *S'wark* 88-92; Succ S'wark Cathl 92-97; P-in-c Wandsworth St Faith 97-01; Chapl YMCA Wimbledon 97-01; Chapl Greycoat Hosp Sch from 01; Chapl Westmr City Sch from 01; PV Westmr Abbey from 06. *4 Greenham Close, London SE1 7RP* Tel (020) 7261 9321 Mobile 07961-422303 E-mail garry.swinton1@btinternet.com

SWIRES-HENNESSY, Matthew. b 81. Lon Sch of Th BA06. Wycliffe Hall Ox 06. **d** 09. C Luton St Fran *St Alb* from 09. *15 Lancing Road, Luton LU2 8JN* Tel 07803-928006 (mobile) E-mail revd.msh@googlemail.com

SWITHINBANK, Kim Stafford. b 53. SS Coll Cam BA77 MA79. Cranmer Hall Dur 78. **d** 82 **p** 81. C Heigham H Trin *Nor* 80-83; Chapl Monkton Combe Sch Bath 83-85; C Langham Place All So *Lon* 85-89; R Stamford St Geo w St Paul *Linc* 90-02; Chapl NW Anglia Healthcare NHS Trust 90-02; V Falls Ch Virginia USA 02-05; Dir Alpha Network 05-07; V Muswell Hill St Jas w St Matt *Lon* from 08. *St James's Vicarage, 2 St James's Lane, London N10 3DB* Tel (020) 8883 6277 Fax 8883 4459 Mobile 07891-615984 E-mail kim.swithinbank@st-james.org.uk

SWITHINBANK, Mrs Penelope Jane. b 53. St Andr Univ MTheol74 Hughes Hall Cam PGCE75. Ridley Hall Cam 00. **d** 02 **p** 03. Dir Connections Falls Ch Virginia USA 02-07; R Johns Island Ch of Our Sav 07-08; Chapl St Mellitus Coll *Lon* from 08. *St James's Vicarage, 2 St James's Lane, London N10 3DB* Tel (020) 8442 2821 *or* 7481 9477 Mobile 07870-497365 E-mail penelope.swithinbank@st-james.org.uk

SWITZERLAND, Archdeacon of. *See* POTTER, The Ven Peter Maxwell

SWORD, Bernard James. b 46. **d** 04 **p** 05. NSM Millbrook *Ches* 04-07; P-in-c Bredbury St Barn from 07. *St Barnabas' Vicarage, Osborne Street, Lower Bredbury, Stockport SK6 2DA* Tel 0161-406 6569 Mobile 07866-446681
E-mail bernardsword1@aol.com

SWYER, David Martin. b 64. Univ of Wales (Abth) BA87 PGCE89. St Mich Coll Llan 89. **d** 91 **p** 92. C Killay *S & B* 91-93; C Newton St Pet 93-95; R Albourne w Sayers Common and Twineham *Chich* from 95. *The Rectory, 5 The Twitten, Albourne, Hassocks BN6 9DF* Tel (01273) 832129

SWYER (née HARRIS), Mrs Rebecca Jane. b 67. Univ of Wales (Lamp) BA88 Univ of Wales (Cardiff) MPhil93. St Mich Coll Llan 89. **d** 91. C Sketty *S & B* 91-95; Perm to Offic *Chich* 95-02; Lic to Offic from 02; Lect Th Chich Univ 97-09; Min Development Officer *Chich* from 09. *The Rectory, 5 The Twitten, Albourne, Hassocks BN6 9DF* Tel (01273) 832129

SWYNNERTON, Brian Thomas. b 31. JP77. Ox Univ Inst of Educn 56 NY Univ BA74 PhD75 FRGS42 LCP62. Lich Th Coll 67. **d** 69 **p** 70. C Swynnerton *Lich* 69-71; CF (TAVR) 70-80; C Eccleshall *Lich* 71-74; C Croxton w Broughton 74-80; Chapl and Lect Stafford Coll 80-84; Chapl Naples w Sorrento, Capri and Bari *Eur* 84-85; Perm to Offic *Lich* from 85; Chapl Rishworth Sch Ripponden 85-88; Chapl Acton Reynald Sch Shrewsbury 88-96; Chapl Telford City Tech Coll from 96. *Hales Farm, Market Drayton TF9 2PF* Tel (01630) 657156

SYDNEY, Archbishop of. *See* JENSEN, The Most Revd Peter Frederick

SYER, Mrs Angela. b 48. ARCM69 Philippa Fawcett Coll CertEd71. Qu Coll Birm. **d** 00 **p** 01. C Oakdale *Sarum* 00-04; P-in-c Coxley w Godney, Henton and Wookey *B & W* from 04. *The Vicarage, Vicarage Lane, Wookey, Wells BA5 1JT* Tel (01749) 676710 E-mail angelasyer@hotmail.com

SYKES, Alan Roy. b 53. Sheff Univ BA75. Dioc OLM tr scheme 05. **d** 08. NSM Richmond St Mary w St Matthias and St Jo *S'wark* from 08. *251 King's Road, Kingston upon Thames KT2 5JH* Tel (020) 8549 3887
E-mail alan.sykes10@btinternet.com

SYKES, Christine Virginia. **d** 07 **p** 08. NSM Castle Church *Lich* from 07. *18 Delamere Lane, Stafford ST17 9TL* Tel (01785) 240529 E-mail curate@castlechurch.co.uk

SYKES, Mrs Clare Mary. b 61. WMMTC 93. **d** 96 **p** 97. C Tupsley w Hampton Bishop *Heref* 96-01; NSM Bromyard 01-08; NSM Stanford Bishop, Stoke Lacy, Moreton Jeffries w Much Cowarne etc 01-08; NSM Bromyard and Stoke Lacy from 09; NSM Frome Valley from 09; RD Bromyard from 05. *The Vicarage, 28 Church Lane, Bromyard HR7 4DZ* Tel (01885) 482438 E-mail clare@thesykes.plus.com

SYKES, Cynthia Ann. b 41. **d** 05 **p** 06. OLM Em TM *Wakef* from 05. *The Old Dairy, Parkhead Farm, Birdsedge, Huddersfield HD8 8XW* Tel (01484) 603894

SYKES, Mrs Emma Caroline Mary. b 75. Warwick Univ BA96. St Jo Coll Nottm 06. **d** 08 **p** 09. C Birm St Martin w Bordesley

St Andr from 08. *159 Boldmere Road, Sutton Coldfield B73 5UL* Tel 0121-354 3130 Mobile 07859-066510
E-mail emmarsykes@hotmail.com

SYKES, Gerald Alfred. b 58. Univ of Wales (Abth) BSc79 PhD83 Univ of Wales (Cardiff) BD98. St Mich Coll Llan 95. **d** 98 **p** 99. C Cardigan w Mwnt and Y Ferwig w Llangoedmor *St D* 98-01; P-in-c Brechfa w Abergorlech etc 01-08; P-in-c Alverthorpe *Wakef* from 08; P-in-c Westgate Common from 08. *The Vicarage, St Paul's Drive, Wakefield WF2 0BT* Tel (01924) 383724 E-mail sykesga@bigfoot.com

SYKES, Graham Timothy Gordon. b 59. ACIB89. St Jo Coll Nottm BTh92. **d** 92 **p** 93. C Kington w Huntington, Old Radnor, Kinnerton etc *Heref* 92-95; C Breinton 95-97; TV W Heref 97-98; Dioc Co-ord for Evang 95-01; V Bromyard 01-08; P-in-c Stanford Bishop, Stoke Lacy, Moreton Jeffries w Much Cowarne etc 01-08; V Bromyard and Stoke Lacy from 09. *The Vicarage, 28 Church Lane, Bromyard HR7 4DZ* Tel (01885) 482438 E-mail vicar@stpetersbromyard.plus.com

SYKES, Ian. b 44. Leic Univ DipEd. Bris Bapt Coll 64 Ripon Coll Cuddesdon 84. **d** 85 **p** 86. In Bapt Min 64-84; C Headington *Ox* 85-88; TV Bourne Valley *Sarum* 88-97; R Peter Tavy, Mary Tavy, Lydford and Brent Tor *Ex* 97-07; Hon C from 07. *The Rectory, Lydford, Okehampton EX20 4BH* Tel (01822) 820542

SYKES, James Clement. b 42. Keble Coll Ox BA64 MA71. Westcott Ho Cam 65. **d** 67 **p** 68. C Bishop's Stortford St Mich *St Alb* 67-71; Chapl St Jo Sch Leatherhead 71-73; Bermuda 74-79; V Northaw *St Alb* 79-87; Chapl St Marg Sch Bushey 87-98; R Guernsey St Sampson *Win* 99-07; rtd 07. *Petit Robinet, Rue de Bouverie, Castel, Guernsey GY5 7UA* Tel (01481) 256381 Mobile 07781-111459 E-mail jimandsue@cwgsy.net

SYKES, Miss Jean. b 45. Leeds Univ BA66 Bris Univ CertEd67. Ripon Coll Cuddesdon 86. **d** 88 **p** 94. C N Huddersfield *Wakef* 88-91; TD 91-93; TV Kippax w Allerton Bywater *Ripon* from 93; AD Whitkirk from 05. *The Vicarage, 134 Leeds Road, Allerton Bywater, Castleford WF10 2HB* Tel 0113-286 9415
E-mail vicar@stmarykippax.org.uk

SYKES, Jeremy Gordon. b 63. Hull Univ BA85. St Alb Minl Tr Scheme 92 Ripon Coll Cuddesdon 97. **d** 99 **p** 00. C Ipswich St Mary-le-Tower *St E* 99-02; P-in-c Briston w Burgh Parva and Melton Constable *Nor* 02-06; P-in-c Briston, Burgh Parva, Hindolveston etc from 06. *The Vicarage, 1 Grange Close, Briston, Melton Constable NR24 2LY* Tel (01263) 860280
E-mail jeremy@sykes-uk.com

SYKES, Jeremy Jonathan Nicholas. b 61. Girton Coll Cam BA83 MA86. Wycliffe Hall Ox BA88. **d** 89 **p** 90. C Knowle *Birm* 89-92; Asst Chapl Oakham Sch 92-98; Chapl Giggleswick Sch 98-06; Hd Master Gt Walstead Sch from 06. *Great Walstead School, East Mascalls Lane, Lindfield, Haywards Heath RH16 2QL* Tel (01444) 483528 Fax 482122
E-mail admin@greatwalstead.co.uk

SYKES, Canon John. b 39. Man Univ BA62. Ripon Hall Ox 61. **d** 63 **p** 64. C Heywood St Luke *Man* 63-67; C Bolton H Trin 67-71; Chapl Bolton Colls of H&FE 67-71; R Reddish *Man* 71-78; V Saddleworth 78-87; TR Oldham 87-04; Hon Can Man Cathl 91-04; rtd 04; Chapl to The Queen from 95. *53 Ivy Green Drive, Springhead, Oldham OL4 4PR* Tel 0161-678 6767
E-mail j.sykes@rdplus.net

SYKES, John Harold. b 50. Van Mildert Coll Dur BA71 K Coll Lon BD73 AKC74 MTh75 Linc Coll Ox MSc89 ALAM71 FRSA92. S'wark Ord Course 75. **d** 09 **p** 09. NSM Ashburnham w Penhurst *Chich* from 09. *Woodlands, Dorothy Avenue, Cranbrook TN17 3AL* Tel (01580) 712793

SYKES, Margaret. b 48. CITC 03. **d** 06 **p** 07. Aux Min Ardamine w Kilnenor, Glascarrig etc *C & O* from 06. *Friedland, Holdine, Gorey, Co Wexford, Republic of Ireland* Tel (00353) (53) 942 1958 Mobile 87-640 7627 E-mail margaretsykes@eircom.net

✠**SYKES, The Rt Revd Prof Stephen Whitefield.** b 39. St Jo Coll Cam BA61 MA65. Ripon Hall Ox 63. **d** 64 **p** 65 **c** 90. Fell and Dean St Jo Coll Cam 64-74; Asst Lect Div Cam Univ 64-68; Lect 68-74; Van Mildert Prof Div Dur Univ 74-85; Can Res Dur Cathl 74-85; Regius Prof Div Cam Univ 85-90; Hon Can Ely Cathl 85-90; Bp Ely 90-99; Prin St Jo Coll Dur 99-06; Hon Asst Bp Dur from 99. *Ingleside, Whinney Hill, Durham DH1 3BE* Tel 0191-384 6465

SYKES, William George David. b 39. Ball Coll Ox BA63 MA68. Wycliffe Hall Ox 63. **d** 65 **p** 66. Chapl Bradf Cathl 65-69; Chapl Univ Coll *Lon* 69-78; Chapl Univ Coll Ox 78-05; rtd 05. *Yew Tree Cottage, 6 Glebe Road, Cumnor, Oxford OX2 9QJ* Tel (01865) 861810

SYLVESTER, Jeremy Carl Edmund. b 56. Cape Town Univ BA78 HDipEd79. Coll of Resurr Mirfield 84. **d** 87 **p** 88. C St Cypr Cathl Kimberley S Africa 87-89; C Ganyesa 89-92; Chapl Informal Settlements Johannesburg 92-96; P-in-c Stoke Newington St Olave *Lon* 96-98; TV Maypstan Em, St Paul Efford and St Aug *Ex* 98-01; CMS 01-06; V Nether w Upper Poppleton *York* from 06. *The Vicarage, 15 Nether Way, Upper Poppleton, York YO26 6JQ* Tel (01904) 789522

SYLVIA, Keith Lawrence Wilfred. b 63. Chich Th Coll 85. **d** 88

T

p 89. C Newbold w Dunston *Derby* 88-91; C Heston *Lon* 91-95; V Brighton St Matthias *Chich* 95-00; C Hove St Patr 00-04; P-in-c Croydon St Andr *S'wark* from 04. *St Andrew's Vicarage, 6 St Peter's Road, Croydon CR0 1HD* Tel (020) 8688 6011
E-mail frkeithsylvia@hotmail.com

SYMES, Andrew John Barrington. b 66. Magd Coll Cam BA88 MA92. All Nations Chr Coll 90. **d** 00 **p** 00. C Walmer St Jo S Africa 00-02; Dir Ext Progr Bible Inst E Cape 02-06; P-in-c Kings Heath *Pet* from 07; C Northampton St Giles from 07. *95 Harlestone Road, Northampton NN5 7AB* Tel (01604) 453598 Mobile 07726-796306
E-mail andrew.symes1@ntlworld.com

SYMES, Percy Peter. b 24. Leeds Univ BA50. Coll of Resurr Mirfield 50. **d** 52 **p** 53. C Ox St Barn 52-54; C Headington 54-56; C Abingdon w Shippon 56-61; V Reading St Luke 61-81; V Drayton St Pet (Berks) 81-89; rtd 89; Perm to Offic *Ox* 94-02. *Merrileas, 23 Hollesley Road, Alderton, Woodbridge IP12 3BX* Tel (01394) 410452

SYMES-THOMPSON, Hugh Kynard. b 54. Peterho Cam BA76 MA81. Cranmer Hall Dur. **d** 79 **p** 80. C Summerfield *Birm* 79-82; C Harlow New Town w Lt Parndon *Chelmsf* 82-83; Australia 84-89; TV Dagenham *Chelmsf* 89-95; R Cranfield and Hulcote w Salford *St Alb* from 95; Chapl Cranfield Univ from 02. *The Rectory, Court Road, Cranfield, Bedford MK43 0DR* Tel (01234) 750214
E-mail revhugh@symes-thom.freeserve.co.uk

SYMMONS, Roderic Paul. b 56. Chu Coll Cam BA77 MA81 Oak Hill Th Coll BA83 Fuller Th Sem California DMin90. **d** 83 **p** 84. C Ox St Aldate w St Matt 83-88; Lic to Offic *LA* USA 89-90; R Ardingly *Chich* 90-99; RD Cuckfield 95-99; P-in-c Redland *Bris* from 99; Tutor Trin Coll Bris from 99. *Redland Vicarage, 151 Redland Road, Bristol BS6 6YE* Tel 0117-946 4691 Fax 946 6862 E-mail rod@redland.org.uk

SYMON, Canon John Francis Walker. b 26. Edin Univ MA50. Edin Th Coll 50. **d** 52 **p** 53. C Edin St Cuth 52-56; CF 56-59; R Forfar *St And* 59-68; R Dunblane 68-85; Can St Ninian's Cathl Perth 74-91; Can Emer St Andr from 00; Chapl Trin Coll Glenalmond 85-91; rtd 91; P-in-c Killin *St And* 95-98. *20 Cromlix Crescent, Dunblane FK15 9JQ* Tel (01786) 822449
E-mail johnsymon@freeola.net

SYMON, Canon Roger Hugh Crispin. b 34. St Jo Coll Cam BA59. Coll of Resurr Mirfield 59. **d** 61 **p** 62. C Westmr St Steph w St Jo *Lon* 61-66; P-in-c Hascombe *Guildf* 66-68; Chapl Surrey Univ 66-74; V Paddington Ch Ch *Lon* 74-78; V Paddington St Jas 78-79; USPG 80-87; Abp Cant's Acting Sec for Angl Communion Affairs 87-94; Can Res Cant Cathl 94-02; rtd 02; Perm to Offic *Glouc* from 02. *5 Bath Parade, Cheltenham GL53 7HL* Tel (01242) 700645
E-mail rogersymon@blueyonder.co.uk

SYMONDS, Alan Jeffrey. b 56. Ridley Hall Cam 93. **d** 95 **p** 96. C Bath St Luke *B & W* 95-99; R Abbas and Templecombe w Horsington 99-06; P-in-c Somerton w Compton Dundon, the Charltons etc from 06. *Rosemount, Sutton Road, Somerton TA11 6QP* Tel (01458) 272029

SYMONDS, James Henry. b 31. Ripon Hall Ox 67. **d** 69 **p** 70. C Southampton (City Cen) *Win* 69-71; CF 71-78; CF 79-90; P-in-c Arrington *Ely* 78-79; P-in-c Orwell 78-79; P-in-c Wimpole 78-79; P-in-c Croydon w Clopton 78-79; CF (R of O) 90-96; rtd 96; P-in-c Coughton, Spernall, Morton Bagot and Oldberrow *Cov* 99-02; Perm to Offic *Lich* from 00 and *Cov* from 02. *Thimble Cottage, Kings Coughton, Alcester B49 5QD* Tel (01789) 400814

SYMONS, Stewart Burlace. b 33. Keble Coll Ox BA55 MA59. Clifton Th Coll 55. **d** 57 **p** 58. C Hornsey Rise St Mary *Lon* 57-60; C Gateshead St Geo *Dur* 60-61; C Patcham *Chich* 61-64; R Stretford St Bride *Man* 64-71; V Waterloo St Jo *Liv* 71-83; R Ardrossan *Glas* 83-96; C-in-c Irvine St Andr LEP 83-96; Miss to Seamen 83-96; rtd 96; Perm to Offic *Carl* from 96. *8 Carlingdale, Burneside, Kendal LA9 6PW* Tel (01539) 728750

SYMONS (née BARKER), Mrs Susannah Mary. b 59. LMH Ox BA81 La Sainte Union Coll PGCE94. STETS 02. **d** 05 **p** 06. C Nadder Valley *Sarum* 05-09; TV Beaminster Area from 09. *The Vicarage, Orchard Mead, Broadwindsor, Beaminster DT8 3RA* Tel (01308) 867472
E-mail sue@symons.ctlconnect.co.uk

SYMS, Richard Arthur. b 43. Ch Coll Cam BA66 MA71. Wycliffe Hall Ox 66. **d** 68 **p** 69. C New Eltham All SS *S'wark* 68-72; Chapl to Arts and Recreation *Dur* 72-73; C Hitchin St Mary *St Alb* 73-76; TV Hitchin 77-78; Perm to Offic 78-97; P-in-c Datchworth 97-03; rtd 03; Perm to Offic *Lon* and *St Alb* from 03. *8 Lytton Fields, Knebworth SG3 6AZ* Tel (01438) 811933 Mobile 07900-241470 E-mail richard.syms@sky.com

SYNNOTT, Alan Patrick Sutherland. b 59. **d** 85 **p** 86. C Lisburn Ch Ch *Conn* 85-88; CF 88-95; I Galloon w Drummully *Clogh* 95-01; I Monkstown *Conn* 01-04; Perm to Offic *Conn* 04-09; I Skreen w Kilmacshalgan and Dromard *T, K & A* from 09. *The Rectory, Skreen, Co Sligo, Republic of Ireland* Tel (00353) (71) 916 6941 E-mail alan.synnott@yahoo.ie or skreen@killala.anglican.org

TABER-HAMILTON, Nigel John. b 53. Univ of Wales (Ban) BA75. Qu Coll Birm Ch Div Sch of Pacific 77. **d** 78 **p** 81. C W Wimbledon Ch Ch *S'wark* 78-79; USA from 79; C Berkeley St Mark 79-81; C Bloomington H Trin 81-90 and 92-94; Interim R Crawfordsville St Jo 90-91; Interim R New Harmony St Steph 91-92; V Seymour All SS 94-00; R St Aug in-the-Woods from 00. *PO Box 11, Freeland WA 98249, USA* Tel (001) (360) 331 4887 Fax 331 4822 E-mail rector@whidbey.com

TABERN, James. b 23. St Aid Birkenhead 57. **d** 59 **p** 60. C Garston *Liv* 59-61; V Litherland St Paul Hatton Hill 61-72; V Gillingham St Mark *Roch* 72-79; V Lindow *Ches* 79-85; rtd 85; Perm to Offic *Liv* 86-91 and from 98; *Ches* from 97. *12 Dickinson Road, Formby, Liverpool L37 4BX* Tel (01704) 831131

TABERNOR, Brian Douglas. **d** 07 **p** 08. OLM Brereton and Rugeley *Lich* from 07. *31 Ashtree Bank, Rugeley WS15 1HN* Tel (01889) 804587 E-mail brian.tabernor@ntlworld.com

TABOR, James Hugh. b 63. Univ of W Aus BA85. Ripon Coll Cuddesdon BTh06. **d** 04 **p** 05. C Alverstoke *Portsm* 04-07; Chapl RN from 07. *Royal Naval Chaplaincy Service, Mail Point 1-2, Leach Building, Whale Island, Portsmouth PO2 8BY* Tel (023) 9262 5055 Fax 9262 5134

TABOR, John Tranham. b 30. Ball Coll Ox BA56 MA58. Ridley Hall Cam 55. **d** 58 **p** 59. C Lindfield *Chich* 58-62; Tutor Ridley Hall Cam 62-63; Chapl 63-68; Warden Scargill Ho 68-75; R Berkhamsted St Mary *St Alb* 75-96; rtd 96; Perm to Offic *St Alb* from 96 and *Ox* 99-00. *2 Warwick Close, Aston Clinton, Aylesbury HP22 5JF* Tel and fax (01296) 631562
E-mail johnttabor@yahoo.co.uk

TAFT, Mrs Janet. b 59. Sheff Univ BA80 Wolv Univ PGCE82. Wycliffe Hall Ox 06. **d** 08 **p** 09. NSM Abingdon *Ox* from 08. *9 The Chestnuts, Abingdon OX14 3YN* Tel (01235) 200593 Mobile 07929-543626 E-mail janet.taft@ntlworld.com

TAGGART, William Joseph. b 54. **d** 85 **p** 86. C Belfast St Mich *Conn* 85-90; I Belfast St Kath from 90; Dioc Registrar from 06. *St Katharine's Rectory, 24 Lansdowne Road, Belfast BT15 4DB* Tel (028) 9077 7647
E-mail belfast.stkatharine@connor.anglican.org

TAGUE, Russell. b 59. Aston Tr Scheme 90 Linc Th Coll 92. **d** 94 **p** 95. C Astley *Man* 94-97; Chapl HM YOI Swinfen Hall 97-00; Chapl HM Pris Risley 00-05; TV Kirkby *Liv* 05-08; R Arthuret w Kirkandrews-on-Esk and Nicholforest *Carl* from 08. *Arthuret Rectory, 1 Arthuret Drive, Longtown, Carlisle CA6 5SG* Tel (01228) 791338 E-mail taguejosh@yahoo.co.uk

TAILBY, Ms Jane Dorothy. b 56. Culham Coll of Educn BEd79. WEMTC 01. **d** 04 **p** 05. NSM Frampton Cotterell and Iron Acton *Bris* 04-09; NSM Winterbourne and Frenchay and Winterbourne Down 08-09; TV Nadder Valley *Sarum* from 09. *The Vicarage, 11A Tyndale's Meadow, Dinton, Salisbury SP3 5HU* Tel (01722) 717883 E-mail jdtailby@aol.com

TAILBY, Mark Kevan. b 36. K Coll Lon 60. **d** 64 **p** 65. C Newbold on Avon *Cov* 64-67; C Stratford-on-Avon w Bishopton 67-70; CF 70-76; P-in-c S Shoebury *Chelmsf* 76-79; P-in-c Stambridge 79-89; Chapl Rochford Gen Hosp 79-89; TV Dovercourt and Parkeston *Chelmsf* 89-93; P-in-c Colchester St Botolph w H Trin and St Giles 93-97; V 97-01; rtd 01; Perm to Offic *Worc* from 01; OCF from 93. *53 Jamaica Road, Malvern WR14 1TX* Tel (01684) 573869

TAILBY, Peter Alan. b 49. Chich Th Coll 83. **d** 85 **p** 86. C Stocking Farm *Leic* 85-88; C Knighton St Mary Magd 88-90; P-in-c Thurnby Lodge 90-98; P-in-c W Molesey *Guildf* 98-05; V from 05. *The Vicarage, 518 Walton Road, West Molesey KT8 2QF* Tel (020) 8979 3846 E-mail ptailby@supanet.com

TAINTON, Mrs Carol Anne. b 50. EMMTC 96. **d** 99 **p** 00. NSM Gamston and Bridgford *S'well* 99-03; P-in-c Lowdham w Caythorpe, and Gunthorpe 03-04; V from 04. *4 Hazelas Drive, Gunthorpe, Nottingham NG14 7FZ* Tel 0115-966 5922 E-mail revcaroltainton@ukonline.co.uk

TAIT, James Laurence Jamieson. b 47. St Jo Coll Dur 78. **d** 80 **p** 81. C Heyside *Man* 80-81; C Westhoughton 81-84; R Aldingham and Dendron and Rampside *Carl* 84-88; V Flookburgh 88-92; V Hunterville New Zealand 92-94; V Palmerston N from 94. *PO Box 5134, Terrace End, Palmerston North 4441, New Zealand* Tel (0064) (6) 358 9134 or tel and fax 358 5403 E-mail stpeters@inspire.net.nz

TAIT, Philip Leslie. b 52. Ex Univ BA73 Hull Univ PGCE74. NEOC 87. **d** 90 **p** 91. NSM Osbaldwick w Murton *York* 90-92; Chapl and Hd RS Berkhamsted Sch Herts 93-97; P-in-c Woodhorn w Newbiggin *Newc* 98; Chapl HM Pris Wolds 98-00; Chapl R Russell Sch Croydon 00-05; Chapl Hurstpierpoint Coll 05-07; TV Upper Skerne *Dur* from 07. *The Vicarage, Trimdon Grange, Trimdon Station TS29 6EX* Tel (01429) 883470 E-mail philip.tait@hppc.co.uk

TAIT (née DAVIS), Canon Ruth Elizabeth. b 39. St Andr Univ MA62 Moray Ho Coll of Educn DipEd63. Moray Ord Course

89. **dss** 90 **d** 94 **p** 95. Elgin w Lossiemouth *Mor* 90-96; C 94-96; NSM Dufftown *Ab* 96-03; C Forres *Mor* 96-98; NSM Aberlour 98-03; Dioc Dir of Ords from 02; NSM Elgin w Lossiemouth from 04; Hon Can St Andr Cathl Inverness from 03. *Benmore, Burnbank, Birnie, Elgin IV30 8RW* Tel (01343) 862808
E-mail ruth.e.tait@btinternet.com

TAIT, Ms Valerie Joan. b 60. Open Univ BA96 SRN82 RSCN82. Trin Coll Bris 99. **d** 01 **p** 02. C W Heref 01-06; P-in-c Ford from 06; P-in-c Alberbury w Cardeston from 06; P-in-c Gt Wollaston from 08. *The Vicarage, Ford, Shrewsbury SY5 9LZ* Tel (01743) 850254

TALBOT, Alan John. b 23. BNC Ox BA49 MA55. Coll of Resurr Mirfield 49. **d** 51 **p** 52. C Hackney Wick St Mary of Eton w St Aug *Lon* 51-54; C Portsea St Sav *Portsm* 54-63; Chapl St Jo Coll Chidya Tanzania 63-65; P-in-c Namakambale 65-68; V Stepney St Aug w St Phil *Lon* 69-78; V Twickenham All Hallows 78-86; rtd 88; Perm to Offic *S'wark* from 88. *46 Brandon Street, London SE17 1NL* Tel (020) 7703 0719

TALBOT, Derek Michael (Mike). b 55. St Jo Coll Dur BSc77. St Jo Coll Nottm 84. **d** 87 **p** 88. C Rushden w Newton Bromswold *Pet* 87-90; C Barton Seagrave w Warkton 90-95; V Kettering Ch the King 95-02; V Northwood Em *Lon* from 02; AD Harrow 02-07. *Emmanuel Vicarage, 3 Gatehill Road, Northwood HA6 3QB* Tel (01923) 828914 *or* 845203 Fax 845209 Mobile 07767-763715 E-mail mike.talbot@lineone.net *or* mike.talbot@ecn.org.uk

TALBOT (*née* THOMSON), Mrs Elizabeth Lucy. b 74. Lanc Univ BA96 Bris Univ BA00 MA01. Trin Coll Bris 98. **d** 01 **p** 02. C Bitterne *Win* 01-05; Chapl Dean Close Sch Cheltenham from 05. *Dean Close School, Shelburne Road, Cheltenham GL51 6HE* Tel (01242) 258000 Mobile 07977-115923
E-mail libby@thomson74.fslife.co.uk

TALBOT, George Brian. b 37. Qu Coll Birm 78. **d** 80 **p** 81. C Heref St Martin 80-83; R Bishop's Frome w Castle Frome and Fromes Hill 83-90; P-in-c Acton Beauchamp and Evesbatch w Stanford Bishop 83-90; R Burstow *S'wark* 90-02; rtd 02. *Box No 237, Bellaluz 10.03, La Manga Club, 30389 Los Belones (Murcia), Spain* Tel (0034) 968 138 103

TALBOT, John Herbert Boyle. b 30. TCD BA51 MA57. CITC 52. **d** 53 **p** 54. C Dublin St Pet *D & G* 53-57; Chan Vicar St Patrick's Cathl Dub 56-61; C Dublin Zion Ch 57-61; Chapl Asst St Thos Hosp Lon 61-64; Min Can and Sacr Cant Cathl 64-67; R Brasted *Roch* 67-84; R Ightham 84-95; P-in-c Shipbourne 87-91; RD Shoreham 89-95; rtd 95; Perm to Offic *Roch* from 01. *12 Waterlakes, Edenbridge TN8 5BX* Tel (01732) 865729

TALBOT, John Michael. b 23. Lon Univ MD52 FRSM FRCPath68. S'wark Ord Course 75. **d** 78 **p** 79. NSM S Croydon Em *Cant* 78-81; Perm to Offic *Nor* 82-85 and from 96; NSM Hethersett w Canteloff w Lt and Gt Melton 85-96. *3 White Gates Close, Hethersett, Norwich NR9 3JG* Tel (01603) 811709
E-mail johnmtalbot@waitrose.com

TALBOT, Mrs June Phyllis. b 46. Ripon Coll of Educn CertEd67. NEOC 88. **d** 91 **p** 94. NSM Cleadon *Dur* 91-97; Dioc Voc Adv from 94; NSM Bishopwearmouth St Gabr from 97. *66 Wheatall Drive, Whitburn, Sunderland SR6 7HQ* Tel 0191-529 2265

TALBOT (*née* KINGHAM), Canon Mair Josephine. b 59. Univ Coll Lon BA84. Ridley Hall Cam 85. **d** 88 **p** 94. C Gt Yarmouth *Nor* 88-94; Sen Asst P Raveningham Gp 94-99; Chapl Norfolk Mental Health Care NHS Trust 94-02; Bp's Adv for Women's Min *Nor* 01-04; P-in-c Watton w Carbrooke and Ovington 02-06; Project Manager Magd Gp from 06; Hon Can Nor Cathl from 02. *The Magdalene Group, 61 King Street, Norwich NR1 1PH* Tel (01603) 610256
E-mail mair@mairtalbot.fsnet.co.uk

TALBOT, Mrs Margaret Eileen Coxon. b 52. Whitelands Coll Lon TCert73. STETS 01. **d** 04 **p** 05. NSM Herstmonceux and Wartling *Chich* 04-06; C Seaford w Sutton from 06. *3 Shortlands Close, Eastbourne BN22 0JE* Tel (01323) 504645 Mobile 07792-140076 E-mail mtalbot3@toucansurf.com

TALBOT, Mrs Marian. b 25. Qu Coll Birm 86. **dss** 78 **d** 87 **p** 94. Droitwich *Worc* 78-87; Par Dn Droitwich Spa 87-88; Chapl Droitwich Hosps 83-88; Asst Chapl Alexandra Hosp Redditch 88-98; Perm to Offic 88-98; rtd 98; Perm to Offic *Truro* from 00. *Number Ten The Fairway, Mawnan Smith, Falmouth TR11 5LR* Tel (01326) 250035

TALBOT, Mike. See TALBOT, Derek Michael

TALBOT, Simon George Guy. b 79. Reading Univ BSc01. Oak Hill Th Coll BA07. **d** 07 **p** 08. C Ipswich St Marg *St E* from 07. *44 Corder Road, Ipswich IP4 2XD* Tel (01473) 211072
E-mail simon@thetalbots.org.uk

TALBOT, Stephen Richard. b 52. BSc. Trin Coll Bris. **d** 84 **p** 85. C Tonbridge SS Pet and Paul *Roch* 84-89; P-in-c Hemingford Abbots *Ely* 89-96; P-in-c Hemingford Grey 89-01; P-in-c Ashburnham w Penhurst *Chich* 01-06; Perm to Offic from 06. *3 Shortlands Close, Eastbourne BN22 0JE* Tel (01323) 504645

TALBOT, Sister Susan Gabriel. b 46. Leeds Univ BA69 Man Poly CertEd70 Man Univ PhD00. NOC 91. **d** 94 **p** 95. C

Wythenshawe St Martin *Man* 94-98; P-in-c Cheetham St Jo 98-02; Lic Preacher 02-04; C Wilmslow *Ches* 04-05; Dioc Adv Healing 06-08; NSM Bowdon from 06. *34 Eaton Road, Bowdon, Altrincham WA14 3EH* Tel 0161-233 0630
E-mail susangabriel@btinternet.com

TALBOT-PONSONBY, Preb Andrew. b 44. Coll of Resurr Mirfield 66. **d** 68 **p** 70. C Radlett *St Alb* 68-70; C Salisbury St Martin *Sarum* 70-73; P-in-c Acton Burnell w Pitchford *Heref* 73-80; P-in-c Frodesley 73-80; P-in-c Cound 73-80; Asst Dioc Youth Officer 73-80; P-in-c Bockleton w Leysters 80-81; V 81-92; P-in-c Kimbolton w Middleton-on-the-Hill 80-81; V Kimbolton w Hamnish and Middleton-on-the-Hill 81-92; P-in-c Wigmore Abbey 92-96; R 97-98; RD Leominster 97-98; Public Preacher from 98; Warden of Readers from 02; Preb Heref Cathl from 87; rtd 09. *The Old Barn, Cleeve Lane, Ross-on-Wye HR9 7TB* Tel (01989) 565003 E-mail andrew@talbot-ponsonby.org

TALBOT-PONSONBY, Mrs Gillian. b 50. Sarum & Wells Th Coll 89. **d** 91 **p** 94. C Leominster *Heref* 91-92; NSM Wigmore Abbey 92-98; Public Preacher from 98; Asst Dioc Adv on Women in Min 99-03; Dioc Adv from 03. *The Old Barn, Cleeve Lane, Ross-on-Wye HR9 7TB* Tel (01989) 565003
E-mail jill@talbot-ponsonby.org

TALBOT, Brian Hugh. b 34. RD78. St Pet Hall Ox BA57 MA64. Westcott Ho Cam. **d** 59 **p** 60. C Newc H Cross 59-61; C Newc St Jo 61-64; Chapl RNR 63-91; Chapl Barnard Castle Sch 64-71; Chapl Bishop's Stortford Coll 71-96; Hon C Bishop's Stortford St Mich *St Alb* 71-96; rtd 96; Perm to Offic *B & W* from 96; Acting Chapl Wells Cathl Sch 97-98. *Four Seasons, Milton Lane, Wookey Hole, Wells BA5 1DG* Tel (01749) 679678

TALBOTT, Scott Malcolm. b 55. SAOMC 00. **d** 03 **p** 04. NSM Watford St Andr *St Alb* from 03. *Elmhurst, 40 Berks Hill, Chorleywood, Rickmansworth WD3 5AH* Tel (01923) 282370 Mobile 07802-244877 E-mail scott.talbott@talk21.com

TALBOTT, Simon John. b 57. Pontifical Univ Maynooth BD81. **d** 81 **p** 82. In RC Ch 81-87; C Headingley *Ripon* 88-91; V Gt and Lt Ouseburn w Marton cum Grafton 91-97; Chapl Qu Ethelburga's Coll York 91-97; P-in-c Markington w S Stainley and Bishop Thornton *Ripon* 97-01; AD Ripon 97-01; P-in-c Epsom St Martin *Guildf* 01-02; V from 02; Chapl Univ for the Creative Arts from 06. *35 Burgh Heath Road, Epsom KT17 4LP* Tel (01372) 743336 Fax 749193 E-mail s.talbott@virgin.net

TALING, Johannes Albert (Hans). b 59. St Jo Coll Nottm 93. EAMTC 02. **d** 02 **p** 03. C Littleborough *Man* 02-05; P-in-c N Buckingham *Ox* 05-08; R from 08. *The Rectory, South Hall, Maids Moreton, Buckingham MK18 1QD* Tel (01280) 813246
E-mail family@taling.fsnet.co.uk

TALKS, David. b 57. Trin Hall Cam BA78 MA81. Trin Coll Bris BA06. **d** 06 **p** 07. C Colchester St Jo *Chelmsf* from 06. *11 Broad Oaks Park, Colchester CO4 0JX* Tel (01206) 864114 Mobile 07867-808207 E-mail dave.talks@btinternet.com

TALLANT, John. b 45. Edin Th Coll 86. **d** 88 **p** 89. C Cayton w Eastfield *York* 88-90; C N Hull St Mich 90-91; V Scarborough St Sav w All SS 91-93; V Fleetwood St Nic *Blackb* 93-99; P-in-c Sculcoates St Paul w Ch Ch and St Silas *York* 99-03; P-in-c Hull St Mary Sculcoates 99-03; P-in-c Hull St Steph Sculcoates 99-03; R Woldsburn from 03. *The New Rectory, West End, Bainton, Driffield YO25 9NR* Tel (01377) 217622

TALLINN, Dean of. See PIIR, The Very Revd Gustav Peeter

TALLON, Jonathan Robert Roe. b 66. Rob Coll Cam BA88 MA92. St Jo Coll Nottm BTh94. **d** 97 **p** 98. C Bury St Jo w St Mark *Man* 97-01; P-in-c Cadishead 01-08; V from 08. *St Mary's Vicarage, Penry Avenue, Cadishead, Manchester M44 5ZE* Tel 0161-775 2171

TAMPLIN, Peter Harry. b 44. Sarum & Wells Th Coll 71. **d** 73 **p** 74. C Digswell *St Alb* 73-76; C Chesterton St Luke *Ely* 76-82; V Chesterton St Geo 82-95; R Durrington *Sarum* 95-07; rtd 07. *2 The Lynch, Mere, Warminster BA12 6DQ*
E-mail phtamplin@yahoo.co.uk

TAMPLIN, Roger Ian. b 41. K Coll Lon BD63 AKC63. St Boniface Warminster 60. **d** 64 **p** 65. C St Helier *S'wark* 64-68; C Camberwell St Giles 68-72; C Tanga St Aug Tanzania 72-73; P-in-c Brent Pelham w Meesden *St Alb* 74-78; P-in-c Anstey 75-78; rtd 01. *31 Shackleton Spring, Stevenage SG2 9DF* Tel (01438) 316031 E-mail roger.tamplin@ic24.net

TAMS, Gordon Thomas Carl. b 37. Leeds Univ BA60 Newc Univ MLitt84 Reading Univ CertEd61 LLCM76. Edin Dioc NSM Course 83. **d** 90 **p** 91. NSM Kelso *Edin* 90-92; P-in-c Coldstream 92-02; rtd 02; Lic to Offic *Edin* from 06. *47 Lennel Mount, Coldstream TD12 4NS* Tel (01890) 882479
E-mail tamsga@btinternet.com

TAMS, Paul William. b 56. Huddersfield Poly CertEd77. EAMTC 87. **d** 90 **p** 91. NSM Mildenhall *St E* 90-93; NSM Brandon and Santon Downham w Elveden etc from 93. *38 Raven Close, Mildenhall, Bury St Edmunds IP28 7LF* Tel (01638) 715475 E-mail paultams@lineone.net

TAN (*née* MITCHELL), Mrs Sarah Rachel. b 79. Birm Univ BA00 Fitzw Coll Cam BA04. Westcott Ho Cam 02. **d** 05 **p** 06. C Reddal Hill St Luke *Worc* 05-08; Chapl HM Pris Wayland from 08. *HM Prison Wayland, Griston, Thetford IP25 6RL* Tel (01953) 804100 E-mail sarah.tan@hmps.gsi.gov.uk

TANCOCK, Steven John. b 73. Westmr Coll Ox BTh01. St Steph Ho Ox 02. **d** 04 **p** 05. C Wincanton and Pen Selwood *B & W* 04-09; C Warren Park *Portsm* from 09; C Leigh Park from 09. *St Clare's House, Strouden Court, Havant PO9 4JX*
E-mail rev.steve@btinternet.com

TANN, Canon David John. b 31. K Coll Lon BD57 AKC57. **d** 58 **p** 59. C Wandsworth St Anne *S'wark* 58-60; C Sholing *Win* 60-64; Asst Chapl Lon Univ 64-65; C Fulham All SS 65-68; Hon C 72-82; Lic to Offic 68-72; Teacher Godolphin and Latymer Sch Hammersmith 68-73; Ealing Boys Gr Sch 69-73; Hd of RE Green Sch Isleworth 73-82; V Dudley St Jas *Worc* 82-95; Chapl Burton Road Hosp Dudley 83-95; Hon Can Worc Cathl 90-95; RD Dudley 93-95; rtd 95; Perm to Offic *Lon* from 97. *75 Parkview Court, Fulham High Street, London SW6 3LL* Tel (020) 7736 6018

TANNER, Preb Alan John. b 25. OBE97. SS Coll Cam 43 Linc Coll Ox BA52 MA65. Coll of Resurr Mirfield 52. **d** 54 **p** 55. C Hendon St Mary *Lon* 54-58; V S Harrow St Paul 58-60; Dir Coun for Chr Stewardship 60-65; Dir Lay Tr 65-71; Sec Coun for Miss and Unity 65-80; V St Nic Cole Abbey 66-78; Sec Gtr Lon Chs' Coun 76-83; P-in-c St Ethelburga Bishopgate 78-85; R St Botolph without Bishopgate 78-97; P-in-c All Hallows Lon Wall 80-97; Bp's Ecum Officer 81-97; AD The City 90-97; Preb St Paul's Cathl 91-97; P-in-c St Clem Eastcheap w St Martin Orgar 93-97; P-in-c St Sepulchre w Ch Ch Greyfriars etc 93-97; P-in-c St Kath Cree 93-97; P-in-c Smithfield St Bart Gt 94-95; rtd 97; Preacher Charterhouse 73-00; Perm to Offic *Lon* from 00; *B & W* 01-02; *Cant* from 03. *The White House, Derringstone Hill, Barham, Canterbury CT4 6QD* Tel (01227) 830356

TANNER, Canon Frank Hubert. b 38. St Aid Birkenhead 63. **d** 66 **p** 67. C Ipswich St Marg *St E* 66-69; C Mansfield SS Pet and Paul *S'well* 69-72; V Huthwaite 72-79; Chapl to the Deaf 79-92; Hon Can S'well Minster 90-92; Chapl Northn and Rutland Miss to the Deaf 92-01; rtd 01; Perm to Offic *Truro* from 03. *The Tamarisks, Trenow Lane, Perranuthnoe, Penzance TR20 9NY* Tel (01736) 719426 E-mail franktanner@lineone.net

TANNER, Leonard John. **d** 03 **p** 04. C Taney *D & G* 03-07; I Tullow from 07; Dioc Dir Lay Min from 09. *Tullow Rectory, Brighton Road, Carrickmines, Dublin 18, Republic of Ireland* Tel (00353) (1) 289 3154 Mobile 86-302 1376
E-mail tanner1@eircom.net

TANNER, Mark Simon Austin. b 70. Ch Ch Ox BA92 MA96 St Jo Coll Dur BA98 Liv Univ MTh05. Cranmer Hall Dur 95. **d** 98 **p** 99. C Upton (Overchurch) *Ches* 98-01; V Doncaster St Mary *Sheff* 01-07; V Ripon H Trin from 07. *Holy Trinity Vicarage, 3 College Road, Ripon HG4 2AE* Tel (01765) 690930 *or* 605865
E-mail mark.tanner@holytrinityripon.org.uk

TANNER, Canon Mark Stuart. b 59. Nottm Univ BA81. Sarum & Wells Th Coll. **d** 85 **p** 86. C Radcliffe-on-Trent *S'well* 85; C Radcliffe-on-Trent and Shelford etc 85-88; C Bestwood 88-89; TV 89-93; Bp's Research Officer 93-97; P-in-c S'well H Trin 93-98; V from 98; AD S'well 01-06; Hon Can S'well Minster from 07. *Holy Trinity Vicarage, Westhorpe, Southwell NG25 0NB* Tel (01636) 813243 E-mail mark.tanner@tesco.net

TANNER, Martin Philip. b 54. Univ Coll Lon BSc(Econ)75. Ridley Hall Cam 79. **d** 82 **p** 83. C Bitterne *Win* 82-85; C Weeke 85-88; V Long Buckby w Watford *Pet* 88-96; P-in-c Desborough 96-97; R Desborough, Brampton Ash, Dingley and Braybrooke 97-08; P-in-c Drayton in Hales *Lich* from 08. *The Vicarage, Mount Lane, Market Drayton TF9 1AQ* Tel (01630) 652527
E-mail mp.tanner@btinternet.com

TANSILL, Canon Derek Ernest Edward. b 36. Univ of Wales (Lamp) BA61. Ripon Hall Ox 61. **d** 63 **p** 64. C Chelsea St Luke *Lon* 63-67; C-in-c Saltdean CD *Chich* 67-69; V Saltdean 69-73; V Billingshurst 73-82; R Bexhill St Pet 82-85; RD Battle and Bexhill 84-86; V Horsham 85-86; TR 86-06; RD Horsham 77-82 and 85-93; Can and Preb Chich Cathl from 81; Chapl Chich Cathl from 06. *Drew House, 17 Westgate, Chichester PO19 3ET* Tel (01243) 775596 E-mail derek@tansill.plus.com

TANSWELL, Stuart Keith. b 79. Reading Univ BSc01. Ripon Coll Cuddesdon BTh08. **d** 08 **p** 09. C St Blazey *Truro* from 08; C Luxulyan from 08; C Tywardreath w Tregaminion from 08. *4 Churchfield Place, St Blazey, Par PL24 2NT* Tel (01726) 813824 E-mail stuart@tanswell.net

TANZANIA, Archbishop of. *See* MOKIWA, The Most Revd Valentino

TAPHOUSE, Bryan George. b 50. STETS 95. **d** 98 **p** 99. NSM Romsey *Win* from 98. *2 Campion Drive, Romsey SO51 7RD* Tel (01794) 516022

TAPLIN, John. b 35. St Alb Minl Tr Scheme 78. **d** 81 **p** 82. NSM Knebworth *St Alb* 81-88; R Lt Hadham w Albury 88-00; rtd 00; Perm to Offic *St E* from 00. *77 Hepworth Road, Stanton, Bury St Edmunds IP31 2UA* Tel (01359) 250212
E-mail johntaplin@supanet.com

TAPLIN, Kim. b 58. Lon Bible Coll DA79 Homerton Coll Cam PGCE84. S Dios Minl Tr Scheme 94. **d** 94 **p** 95. C Sholing *Win* 94-97; P-in-c Rendcomb *Glouc* 97-00; Chapl Rendcomb Coll Cirencester 97-00; Chapl Clifton Coll Bris from 01. *The Chaplaincy, Clifton College, 83B Pembroke Road, Clifton BS8 3EA* Tel 0117-315 7257 *or* 315 7258

TAPLIN, Stewart Tennent Eaton. b 46. Melbourne Univ BEd92 MEd97. ACT ThL69. **d** 72 **p** 73. C Reservoir Australia 72-74; C Stocking Farm *Leic* 74-76; Lic to Offic *Carl* 76-77; Chapl Yarra Valley Sch Australia 78-82; Perm to Offic Melbourne 83-85; Asst Chapl St Mich Gr Sch 86-91; C Mornington 91-93; Chapl Tintern Girls' Gr Sch from 94. *2 Boston Street, Ashwood Vic 3147, Australia* Tel (0061) (3) 9888 3328 *or* 9845 7777 Fax 9845 7710 Mobile 40-208 0366 E-mail staplin@tintern.vic.edu.au

TAPPER, Canon John A'Court. b 42. FCA64. Sarum & Wells Th Coll 89. **d** 91 **p** 92. C Ashford *Cant* 91-94; P-in-c Folkestone H Trin w Ch Ch 94-96; V 96-06; P-in-c Sandgate St Paul w Folkestone St Geo 01-06; V Folkestone Trin 06-07; AD Elham 00-05; Hon Can Cant Cathl 06-07; rtd 07; Perm to Offic *Cant* 07-08; Hon C Cranbrook from 08; Retirement Officer (Maidstone Adnry) 07-08. *Mill Cottage, Mill Lane, Sissinghurst, Cranbrook TN17 2HX* Tel (01580) 713836
E-mail johnliztapper@tesco.net

TARGETT, Kenneth. b 28. Qu Coll Birm 54. **d** 57 **p** 58. C Mansfield Woodhouse *S'well* 57-59; C Skipton Ch Ch *Bradf* 59-62; V Bradf St Jo 62-65; Perm to Offic 65-82; Australia 82-87; V Old Leake w Wrangle *Linc* 87-94; rtd 94; Perm to Offic *Linc* from 00. *The Sloop, Sea Lane, Old Leake, Boston PE22 9JA* Tel (01205) 871991 E-mail ken@thesloop.fsnet.co.uk

TARLETON, Peter. b 46. TCD BA72 MA80 HDipEd77. TCD Div Sch Div Test 73. **d** 73 **p** 74. C Cork St Luke w St Ann *C, C & R* 73-75; C Dublin Drumcondra *D & G* 75-77; I Limerick City *L & K* 77-82; I Drumgoon w Dernakesh, Ashfield etc *K, E & A* 82-85; Chapl HM YOI Hindley 85-89; Chapl HM Pris Lindholme 89-99; Hon Can Sheff Cathl 98-99; Chapl HM Pris Leeds 99-06; Chapl Lancs Teaching Hosps NHS Trust from 08. *Royal Preston Hospital, Sharoe Green Lane, Fulwood, Preston PR2 9HT* Tel (01772) 523552
E-mail peter.tarleton@lthtr.nhs.uk

TARLING, Matthew Paul. b 79. Nottm Univ MEng03. Oak Hill Th Coll BA09. **d** 09. C Blaydon and Swalwell *Dur* from 09. *21 Park Terrace, Dunston, Gateshead NE11 9PA* Tel 0191-460 6706 Mobile 07714-212374
E-mail mattandkatetarling@blueyonder.co.uk

TARLING, Preb Paul. b 53. Oak Hill Th Coll BA. **d** 85 **p** 86. C Old Hill H Trin *Worc* 85-89; V Walford w Bishopswood *Heref* 89-90; P-in-c Goodrich w Welsh Bicknor and Marstow 89-90; R Walford and St John w Bishopswood, Goodrich etc 90-96; RD Ross and Archenfield 95-96; P-in-c Kington w Huntington, Old Radnor, Kinnerton etc 96-00; R 00-08; RD Kington and Weobley 02-07; Preb Heref Cathl 07-08; rtd 08. *1 Alexandra Road, Llandrindod Wells LD1 5LT* E-mail ptarling@yahoo.com

TARPER, Miss Ann Jennifer. b 47. SRN71 Nottm Univ BCombStuds82. Linc Th Coll 79. **dss** 83 **d** 87 **p** 96. Stamford All SS w St Jo *Linc* 82-85; Witham *Chelmsf* 85-90; Par Dn 87-90; Min and Educn Adv to Newmarch Gp Min *Heref* 93-95; Perm to Offic 93-95; Dep Chapl HM Pris Dur 95-97; Chapl HM Pris Foston Hall 97-00; Perm to Offic *Lich* 97-02; C W End *Win* 02-05; V Slade Green *Roch* from 05. *St Augustine's Vicarage, Slade Green Road, Erith DA8 2HX* Tel (01322) 332669 *or* 346258

TARR, James Robert. b 39. Bps' Coll Cheshunt 64. **d** 67 **p** 68. C Wortley de Leeds *Ripon* 67-69; C Hunslet St Mary and Stourton St Andr 70-73; V Moorends *Sheff* 73-77; V Cross Stone *Wakef* 77-83; V Chilworth w N Baddesley *Win* 83-90; V Andover St Mich 90-93; V W Andover 93-00; Chapl Mojcar *Eur* 00-02; rtd 02. *Les Courades, 16350 Le Vieux-Cerier, France* Tel (0033) (5) 45 30 00 39

TARRANT, Canon Ian Denis. b 57. G&C Coll Cam BA MA. St Jo Coll Nottm 81. **d** 84 **p** 85. C Ealing St Mary *Lon* 84-87; CMS Republic of Congo 88-98; Can Boga from 97; Sen Angl Chapl Nottm Univ 98-09; R Woodford St Mary w St Phil and St Jas *Chelmsf* from 09. *The Rectory, 8 Chelmsford Road, London E18 2PL* Tel (020) 8504 3472

TARRANT, John Michael. b 38. St Jo Coll Cam BA59 MA63 Ball Coll Ox BA62 MA76. Ripon Hall Ox 60. **d** 62 **p** 63. C Chelsea All SS *Lon* 62-65; Chapl and Lect St Pet Coll Saltley 66-70; Belize 70-74; V Forest Row *Chich* 75-87; Perm to Offic *Heref* 93-99; NSM Ross 99-00; P-in-c Guilsborough w Hollowell and Cold Ashby *Pet* 00-08; Jt P-in-c Cottesbrooke w Gt Creaton and Thornby 00-08; P-in-c Ravensthorpe 03-08; P-in-c Spratton 07-08; rtd 08. *16 Windsor Road, Salisbury SP2 7DX* Tel (01722) 340058 E-mail madjohn@revtarrant.freeserve.co.uk

TARREN, Eileen. b 46. Cranmer Hall Dur. **d** 02 **p** 03. NSM Shadforth and Sherburn *Dur* from 02. *St Mary's Vicarage, 89 Front Street, Sherburn Village, Durham DH6 1HD*

TARRIS, Canon Geoffrey John. b 27. Em Coll Cam BA50 MA55. Westcott Ho Cam 51. **d** 53 **p** 54. C Abbots Langley *St Alb* 53-55; Prec St E Cathl 55-59; V Bungay H Trin w St Mary 59-72; RD S Elmham 65-72; V Ipswich St Mary le Tower 72-78; V Ipswich St Mary le Tower w St Lawr and St Steph 78-82; Hon Can St E Cathl 74-82; Can Res 82-93; Dioc Dir of Lay Min and Warden of Readers 82-87; Dioc Dir of Ords 87-93; rtd 93; Perm to Offic *Nor* and *St E* from 93; Hon PV Nor Cathl from 94. *53 The Close, Norwich NR1 4EG* Tel (01603) 622136

TARRY, Canon Gordon Malcolm. b 54. Leeds Univ BSc75 Lon Bible Coll BA83. Ridley Hall Cam. **d** 85 **p** 86. C Gt Ilford

St Andr *Chelmsf* 85-89; C Rainham 89-92; C Rainham w
Wennington 92-93; V Gt Ilford St Jo 93-06; RD Redbridge
01-06; TR Barking St Marg w St Patr from 06; Hon Can
Chelmsf Cathl from 05. *20 Sandringham Road, Barking
IG11 9AB* Tel (020) 8594 4513
E-mail gordontarry@yahoo.co.uk

TASH, Stephen Ronald. b 56. Warw Univ BEd79. WMMTC 88.
d 91 **p** 92. C Studley *Cov* 91-95; P-in-c Salford Priors 95-09; Dioc
Youth Officer 95-00; P-in-c Temple Grafton w Binton 00-09;
P-in-c Exhall w Wixford 03-09; V Fulford *York* from 09. *The
Vicarage, 1 Fulford Park, Fulford, York YO10 4QE* Tel (01904)
633261 E-mail stevetash@aol.com

TASKER, Harry Beverley. b 41. BA76. Wycliffe Hall Ox 64. **d** 67
p 68. C Withington St Paul *Man* 67-71; C Bingley All SS *Bradf*
71-72; Chapl RAF 72-76; R Publow w Pensford, Compton
Dando and Chelwood *B & W* 76-84; V Long Ashton 84-04; RD
Portishead 86-91; rtd 04. *The Malthouse, Manor Court, Manor
Lane, Ettington, Stratford-upon-Avon CV37 7TW* Tel (01789)
748290

TASSELL, Canon Dudley Arnold. b 16. K Coll Lon BD49
AKC49. **d** 49 **p** 50. C New Eltham All SS *S'wark* 49-55; V
Catford St Andr 55-63; R Rotherhithe St Mary w All SS 63-77;
RD Bermondsey 69-76; Hon Can S'wark Cathl 72-76; V Spring
Park *Cant* 76-84; RD Croydon Addington 81-84; V Spring Park
All SS *S'wark* 85-86; rtd 86; Perm to Offic *Guildf* from 86.
72 Sandy Lane, Woking GU22 8BH Tel (01483) 762944

TASSELL, Mrs Stella Venetia. b 39. RGN60 RNT63 RMN66
RHV72. Guildf Dioc Min Course 97. **d** 01 **p** 02. OLM
Woodham *Guildf* from 01. *72 Sandy Lane, Woking GU22 8BH*
Tel (01483) 762944 Mobile 07790-521567
E-mail stella.tassell@btinternet.com

TATE, David. b 44. Open Univ BA78 CIPFA70. **d** 02 **p** 03. OLM
N w S Wootton *Nor* from 02. *36 The Birches, South Wootton,
King's Lynn PE30 3JG* Tel (01553) 672474
E-mail revdavidtate@talktalk.net

TATE, Mrs Harriet Jane. b 62. Hull Univ BA84. **d** 02 **p** 03. OLM
Heatons *Man* from 02. *70 Winchester Drive, Stockport SK4 2NU*
Tel 0161-431 7051 E-mail harriettate@supanet.com

TATE, James. b 56. Oak Hill Th Coll 93. **d** 95 **p** 96. C
Hammersmith St Simon *Lon* 95-98; C N Hammersmith St Kath
98-99; P-in-c from 99. *St Katherine's Vicarage, Primula Street,
London W12 0RF* Tel (020) 8746 2213 *or* 8743 3951
E-mail jim@stkats.wanadoo.co.uk

TATE, John Robert. b 44. Dur Univ BA61 MA71. Cranmer Hall
Dur. **d** 70 **p** 71. C Bare *Blackb* 70-73; V Over Darwen St Jas
73-81; V Caton w Littledale 81-98; rtd 98; Perm to Offic *Blackb*
from 98. *19 Clifton Drive, Morecambe LA4 6SR* Tel (01524)
832840

TATE, Pauline Marilyn. b 42. Westcott Ho Cam 05. **d** 07 **p** 08.
NSM Gt w Lt Addington and Woodford *Pet* from 07. *2 Manor
Close, Great Addington, Kettering NN14 4BU* Tel (01536)
330740 Mobile 07803-455700 E-mail pmtate@tiscali.co.uk

TATE, Robert John Ward. b 24. St Jo Coll Morpeth ThL48. **d** 49
p 50. Australia from 49; Chapl RN 53-79; QHC 76-79; rtd 79.
58 Skye Point Road, Carey Bay NSW 2283, Australia Tel (0061)
(2) 4959 2921

TATHAM, Andrew Francis. b 49. Grey Coll Dur BA71 K Coll
Lon PhD84 AKC88 FBCartS96. S'wark Ord Course 89. **d** 92
p 93. NSM Headley w Box Hill *Guildf* 92-02; TV Ilminster and
Distr *B & W* from 02; RD Crewkerne and Ilminster from 07. *The
Rectory, Broadway, Ilminster TA19 9RE* Tel (01460) 52559
E-mail aftatham@ukonline.co.uk

TATTERSALL, John Hartley. b 52. Ch Coll Cam BA73 MA76
FCA89. SEITE 04. **d** 07 **p** 08. NSM Wykeham *Ox* from 07.
Abingdon House, Park Lane, Swalcliffe, Banbury OX15 5EU Tel
(01295) 780283 Mobile 07711-733978
E-mail jhtatters@aol.com

TATTON-BROWN, Simon Charles. b 48. Qu Coll Cam BA70
MA78 Man Univ CQSW72. Coll of Resurr Mirfield 78. **d** 79
p 80. C Ashton St Mich *Man* 79-82; P-in-c Prestwich St Gabr
82-87; V 87-88; Bp's Dom Chapl 82-88; TR Westhoughton
88-96; TR Westhoughton and Wingates 97-00; V Chippenham
St Andr w Tytherton Lucas *Bris* from 00; RD Chippenham
03-06. *The Vicarage, 54A St Mary Street, Chippenham
SN15 3JW* Tel (01249) 656834 E-mail stbrown@aol.com

TATTUM, Ian Stuart. b 58. N Lon Poly BA79 Fitzw Coll Cam
BA89. Westcott Ho Cam 87. **d** 90 **p** 91. C Beaconsfield *Ox* 90-94;
C Bushey *St Alb* 94-96; P-in-c Pirton 96-01; P-in-c St Ippolyts
00-06; P-in-c Gt and Lt Wymondley 01-06; P-in-c Southfields
St Barn *S'wark* from 06. *144 Elsenham Street, London
SW18 5NP* Tel (020) 8874 7768 *or* 8480 2290
E-mail office@stbarnabas-online.org

TATTUM, Ruth Margaret. *See* LAMPARD, Ms Ruth Margaret

TAULTY, Mrs Eileen. b 45. **d** 03. OLM Pemberton St Mark
Newtown *Liv* 03-07; OLM Marsh Green w Newtown from 08.
38 Alexandra Crescent, Wigan WN5 9JP Tel (01942) 208021

TAUNTON, Archdeacon of. *See* REED, The Ven John Peter Cyril

TAUNTON, Suffragan Bishop of. *See* MAURICE, The Rt Revd
Peter David

TAVERNER, Lorraine Dawn. *See* COLAM, Mrs Lorraine Dawn

TAVERNOR (née LLOYD), Mrs Eileen. b 50. FIBMS74. NOC
88. **d** 91 **p** 94. C Heref St Martin w St Fran 91-95; P-in-c
Bucknell w Chapel Lawn, Llanfair Waterdine etc 95-01; V 01-09;
rtd 09. *Froglands, Rosemary Lane, Leintwardine, Craven Arms
SY7 0LP* Tel (01547) 540365

TAVERNOR, James Edward. b 23. Lich Th Coll 41 St D Coll
Lamp BA49. **d** 50 **p** 51. C Monmouth 50-52; C Prestbury *Glouc*
52-53; C Newbold w Dunston *Derby* 53-55; C Buxton 67-69;
Perm to Offic *Derby* 70-75; *Heref* 75-83; *St D* 83-91; rtd 88. *c/o
Mrs E M Akers, 101 Stourport Road, Bewdley DY12 1BJ* Tel
(01299) 404104

TAVERNOR, William Noel. b 16. Lich Th Coll 37. **d** 40 **p** 41. C
Ledbury *Heref* 40-43; C Kidderminster St Mary *Worc* 43-46; V
Bettws-y-Crwyn w Newcastle *Heref* 46-50; V Upton Bishop
50-57; V Aymestrey and Leinthall Earles 57-65; P-in-c Shobdon
58-65; V Canon Pyon w Kings Pyon and Birley 65-88; rtd 88;
Perm to Offic *Heref* from 97. *Vine Cottage, Kingsland,
Leominster HR6 9QS* Tel (01568) 708711

TAVINOR, The Very Revd Michael Edward. b 53. Univ Coll Dur
BA75 Em Coll Cam CertEd76 K Coll Lon MMus77 AKC77
ARCO77. Ripon Coll Cuddesdon BA81 MA86. **d** 82 **p** 83. C
Ealing St Pet Mt Park *Lon* 82-85; Min Can, Prec and Sacr Ely
Cathl 85-90; P-in-c Stuntney *Ely* 87-90; V Tewkesbury w Walton
Cardiff *Glouc* 90-99; P-in-c Twyning 98-99; V Tewkesbury w
Walton Cardiff and Twyning 99-02; Hon Can Glouc Cathl
97-02; Dean Heref from 02. *The Deanery, Cathedral Close,
Hereford HR1 2NG* Tel (01432) 374203 Fax 374220
E-mail dean@herefordcathedral.org

TAWN, Andrew Richard. b 61. Trin Coll Cam BA83 Ox Univ
BA88. Ripon Coll Cuddesdon 86. **d** 89 **p** 90. C Dovecot *Liv*
89-93; TV Dorchester *Ox* 93-98; Student Supervisor Cuddesdon
Coll 93-98; R Addingham *Bradf* from 98. *The Rectory, Low Mill
Lane, Addingham, Ilkley LS29 0QP* Tel (01943) 830276
E-mail saintpeter@addinghamrectory.fsnet.co.uk

TAYLER, Raymond James. b 38. K Alfred's Coll Win TCert74.
SWMTC 98. **d** 01 **p** 02. NSM Mlaga *Eur* 01-07. *Casa Palomero,
Oficina de Correos, 29714 Salares (Málaga), Spain* Tel (0034) 952
030 461 E-mail rjtayler@yahoo.co.uk

TAYLEUR, Mrs Gillian Sarah. b 61. Bedf Coll Lon BSc82. OLM
course 05. **d** 08. NSM Herne Hill *S'wark* from 08. *27 Finsen
Road, London SE5 9AX* Tel (020) 7737 1991
E-mail gill@hernehillparish.org

TAYLOR, Alan Clive. b 48. Southn Univ BTh79. Sarum Th Coll
69. **d** 74 **p** 75. C Watford St Pet *St Alb* 74-78; C Broxbourne w
Wormley 78-83; Chapl to the Deaf 83-91; V Shefford 83-91; R
Portishead *B & W* 91-02; TR 02-08; rtd 08. *Larkhill, The Green,
Dauntsey, Chippenham SN15 4HY*
E-mail padreact@yahoo.co.uk

TAYLOR, Alan Gerald. b 33. Roch Th Coll 61 St Aid Birkenhead
61. **d** 63 **p** 64. C W Bridgford *S'well* 63-66; C E w W Barkwith
Linc 66-69; V E Stockwith 69-76; V Morton 69-76; Countryside
Officer 69-88; R Ulceby w Fordington 76-88; R Willoughby w
Sloothby w Claxby 76-88; R Woolpit w Drinkstone *St E* 88-98;
Rural Min Adv from 88; rtd 98; Perm to Offic *St E* from 01.
5 Finch Close, Stowmarket IP14 5BQ Tel (01449) 614078

TAYLOR, Canon Alan Leonard. b 43. Chich Th Coll 67. **d** 69
p 70. C Walton St Mary *Liv* 69-73; C Toxteth St Marg 73-75; V
Stanley 75-83; V Leeds St Aid *Ripon* from 84; V Leeds
Richmond Hill from 06; Hon Can Ripon Cathl from 97; AD
Allerton from 08. *The Vicarage, Elford Place West, Leeds
LS8 5QD* Tel and fax 0113-248 6992
E-mail alan.taylor@leeds.gov.uk

TAYLOR, Andrew David. b 58. Regent's Park Coll Ox BA81
MA86 Toronto Univ MDiv92 K Coll Lon MTh95. Westcott Ho
Cam 85. **d** 87 **p** 89. C Leckhampton SS Phil and Jas w
Cheltenham St Jas *Glouc* 87-91; P-in-c Swindon w Uckington
and Elmstone Hardwicke 92-93; C Highgate St Mich *Lon* 94-97;
Chapl R Holloway and Bedf New Coll *Guildf* 97-03; Public
Preacher 04; Perm to Offic from 05. *8 Stable Mews, Coworth
Park, London Road, Sunninghill, Ascot SL5 7SE* Tel (01344)
870319

TAYLOR, Ann. *See* TAYLOR, Margaret Ann

TAYLOR, Ms Anne Elizabeth. b 68. Ulster Univ BSc91 MA99.
CITC BTh94. **d** 94 **p** 95. C Dublin Rathfarnham *D & G* from 94;
Chapl Adelaide and Meath Hosp Dublin 01-03; Abp's Dom
Chapl *D & G* from 03; Children's Min Officer Sunday Sch Soc of
Ireland from 05. *The Rectory, 41 Rathfarnham Road, Terenure,
Dublin 6W, Republic of Ireland* Tel and fax (00353) (1) 490 5543
E-mail sundayschoolsociety@ireland.anglican.org

TAYLOR, Arthur Alfred. b 32. Univ Coll Ox MA56. Ox NSM
Course 80. **d** 83 **p** 84. NSM Monks Risborough *Ox* 83-96; NSM
Aylesbury Deanery from 96. *3 Place Farm Way, Monks
Risborough, Princes Risborough HP27 9JJ* Tel (01844) 347197

TAYLOR, Miss Averil Mary. b 36. Sarum Dioc Tr Coll TCert56
Westmr Coll Ox TCert (Mus) 66. WEMTC 99. **d** 00 **p** 01. OLM
Longden and Annscroft w Pulverbatch *Heref* 00-08. *Sheaves,
Lyth Bank, Lyth Hill, Shrewsbury SY3 0BE* Tel and fax (01743)
872071

TAYLOR, Avril Fiona. b 58. NEOC 02. **d** 05 **p** 06. NSM Byker St Silas *Newc* from 05. *125 Rawling Road, Gateshead NE8 4QS* E-mail avriltaylor@blueyonder.co.uk

TAYLOR, Bernard Richmond Hartley. b 30. Reading Univ MEd. S Dios Minl Tr Scheme 82. **d** 85 **p** 86. NSM Englefield Green *Guildf* 85-90; NSM Lyddington w Stoke Dry and Seaton *Pet* 90-95; rtd 95; Perm to Offic *Guildf* from 96. *Middleton House, 40 Bond Street, Egham TW20 0PY* Tel (01784) 435886

TAYLOR, Brian. b 38. Bris Univ BA60 Liv Univ BA70 Southn Univ MA90. Ridley Hall Cam 60. **d** 66 **p** 66. Chapl Victoria Coll Ondo Nigeria 66-72; Perm to Offic *Derby* 74-78; Chapl Newbury Coll 76-94; P-in-c Shaw cum Donnington *Ox* 89-90; R 90-08; rtd 08; Perm to Offic *Ox* from 08. *39 Chaucer Crescent, Speen, Newbury RG14 1TP* Tel 07925-126761 (mobile) E-mail brian_harker_taylor@yahoo.co.uk

TAYLOR, Brian. b 42. St Deiniol's Hawarden 78. **d** 80 **p** 81. C Mold *St As* 80-84; V Bagillt 84-08; rtd 08. *13 Bryn Awel, Pentre Halkyn, Holywell CH8 8JB* Tel (01352) 780744 Mobile 07803-305956 E-mail brian@prayers.freeserve.co.uk

TAYLOR, Brian. b 61. St Mich Coll Llan 91. **d** 94 **p** 95. C Aberdare *Llan* 94-97; V Cwmparc 97-07; V Pen Rhondda Fawr from 07. *The Vicarage, Vicarage Terrace, Cwmparc, Treorchy CF42 6NA* Tel (01443) 773303

TAYLOR, Brian John Chatterton. b 30. Trin Hall Cam BA53 Kent Univ MA57 Melbourne Univ BEd66 Lon Univ MA78. Westcott Ho Cam 53. **d** 55 **p** 56. C Leigh St Jo *Man* 55-57; C Ashton Ch 57-58; Australia from 58; Miss to Seamen 58-60; Vic State High Schs 60-71; Sen Lect Toorak Teachers' Coll 72-80; Prin Lect Inst of Cath Educn 80-88; Co-ord RE Tintern Angl Girls' Gr Sch 89-93; Supernumerary Asst Redhill St Geo from 90. *RMB 6047, Merricks North Vic 3926, Australia* Tel and fax (0061) (3) 5989 7564 Mobile 408-250630 E-mail sumptonv@surf.net

TAYLOR, Brian Valentine. b 34. St Deiniol's Hawarden 69. **d** 71 **p** 72. C Workington St Mich *Carl* 71-72; C Carl St Aid and Ch Ch 73-74; Chapl Rotterdam Miss to Seamen *Eur* 74-75; Asst Chapl Madrid 75-76; Chapl Marseille w St Raphaël, Aix-en-Provence etc 77-78; Chapl Alassio w Genoa and Rapallo 78-81; C Higher Broughton *Man* 82-83; P-in-c Cheetwood St Alb 83-84; Lic to Offic 84-85; rtd 85; Perm to Offic *Man* 85-97. *36A Station Road, Thornton-Cleveleys FY5 5HZ* Tel (01253) 827704

TAYLOR, Charles Derek. b 36. Trin Hall Cam BA59 MA62. Ripon Hall Ox 59. **d** 61 **p** 62. C Nottingham All SS *S'well* 61-64; C Binley *Cov* 64-67; C Stoke 67-70; R Purley *Ox* 70-74; V Milton *B & W* 74-93; RD Locking 86-87 and 90-93; V Wells St Cuth w Wookey Hole 93-98; rtd 98; Perm to Offic *Roch* from 00. *5 Banner Farm Road, Tunbridge Wells TN2 5EA* Tel (01892) 526825

TAYLOR, The Very Revd Charles William. b 53. Selw Coll Cam BA74 MA78. Cuddesdon Coll 74. **d** 76 **p** 77. C Wolverhampton *Lich* 76-79; Chapl Westmr Abbey 79-84; V Stanmore *Win* 84-90; R N Stoneham 90-95; Can Res and Prec Lich Cathl 95-07; Dean *Pet* from 07. *The Deanery, Minster Precincts, Peterborough PE1 1XS* Tel (01733) 562780 E-mail deanpetoffice@aol.com

TAYLOR, Christopher Drewett. b 58. Qu Coll Birm 06. **d** 09. C Shepshed and Oaks in Charnwood *Leic* from 09. *12 Smithy Way, Shepshed, Loughborough LE12 9TQ* Tel (01509) 556014 Mobile 07946-765137 E-mail christaylor.50beacon@nish.com

TAYLOR, Christopher Vincent. b 47. Cranmer Hall Dur 94. **d** 96 **p** 97. C Kendal St Geo *Carl* 96-99; TV Wheatley *Ox* 99-03; TV Leeds City *Ripon* 03-06; rtd 06; Hon C Beacon *Carl* from 08. *78 Windermere Road, Kendal LA9 5EZ* Tel (01539) 727424

TAYLOR, Preb Clive Cavanagh. b 28. MBE91. Cranmer Hall Dur 61. **d** 63 **p** 64. C Wembley St Jo *Lon* 63-66; C Edmonton All SS 66-69; V Tottenham St Jo 69-76; RD E Haringey 73-76; Dir of Ords 76-85; Chapl Metrop Police Coll Hendon 76-93; Sen Chapl Metrop Police 78-93; V Temple Fortune St Barn 76-93; Preb St Paul's Cathl 78-93; AD W Barnet 79-85; rtd 93; Perm to Offic *Chich* from 93. *26 Wenthill Close, East Dean, Eastbourne BN20 0HT* Tel (01323) 422346

TAYLOR, Colin John. b 66. Witwatersrand Univ BCom87 BTh94. Wycliffe Hall Ox MTh97. **d** 97 **p** 98. C Denton Holme *Carl* 97-01; Bp's Dom Chapl 01-06; Dir CME 1-4 00-06; V Felsted and Lt Dunmow *Chelmsf* from 06. *The Vicarage, Bury Chase, Felsted, Dunmow CM6 3DQ* Tel (01371) 820242 E-mail vicar.felsted@btinternet.com

TAYLOR, Canon David. b 53. St Jo Coll Dur BA74 PGCE75 Liv Univ MTh04. Sarum & Wells Th Coll 91. **d** 93 **p** 94. C Cheadle Hulme All SS *Ches* 93-97; V Macclesfield St Jo 97-05; RD Macclesfield 03-05; TR Congleton from 05; RD Congleton from 08; Hon Can Ches Cathl from 09. *2 Hartley Gardens, Congleton CW12 3WA* Tel (01260) 273182 E-mail revddtaylor@hotmail.com

TAYLOR, David Christopher Morgan. b 56. Leeds Univ BSc77 Univ Coll Lon PhD80 Univ Coll Ches MEd96 3OSc MIBiol. NOC 91. **d** 94 **p** 95. Tutor Liv Univ from 86; NSM Waterloo Ch Ch and St Mary 94-99; P-in-c Altcar 98-00; NSM Altcar and Hightown from 03. *20 Liverpool Road, Formby, Liverpool L37 4BW* Tel (01704) 873304 Fax 0151-794 5337 E-mail dcmt@liverpool.ac.uk *or* taylordcm@aol.com

TAYLOR, Dennis James. b 31. ACIS62. Ripon Hall Ox 63. **d** 68 **p** 69. C Baswich *Lich* 68-77; P-in-c Hastings H Trin *Chich* 77-81; V 81-86; R Catsfield and Crowhurst 86-01; rtd 01; Perm to Offic *B & W* 01-05. *24 Larkhill, Bexhill-on-Sea TN40 1QZ* Tel (01424) 211751

TAYLOR, Derek. *See* TAYLOR, Charles Derek

TAYLOR, The Very Revd Derek John. b 31. Univ of Wales (Lamp) BA52 Fitzw Ho Cam BA54 MA58 Ex Univ CertEd70. St Mich Coll Llan 54. **d** 55 **p** 56. C Newport St Paul *Mon* 55-59; CF (TA) 57-59 and 62-64; CF 59-62; V Bettws *Mon* 62-64; V Exminster 64-70; Hd of RE Heathcote Sch Tiverton 70-71; W Germany 71-75; Chapl R Russell Sch Croydon 75-79; Chapl St Andr Sch Croydon 79-84; P-in-c Croydon St Andr *Cant* 79-81; V 81-84; Chapl Bromsgrove Sch 84-89; Provost St Chris Cathl Bahrain 90-97; Hon Chapl Miss to Seamen 90-97; NSM Droitwich Spa *Worc* 97-99; Asst P Finstall 99-00; P-in-c Milngavie *Glas* 00-03; Perm to Offic *Worc* from 04. *19 Warwick Hall Gardens, Bromsgrove B60 2AU* Tel and fax (01527) 872144 Mobile 07904-205669 E-mail dervaltaylor@talktalk.net

TAYLOR, Donald Alastair. b 26. Lon Univ BD Linc Coll Ox DPhil77. St Paul's Coll Mauritius. **d** 65 **p** 65. C Ware St Mary *St Alb* 65-66; Seychelles 66-78; SSJE from 68; Lect RS Middx Poly *Lon* 78-92. *74 Woodcote Road, Caversham, Reading RG4 7EX* Tel and fax 0118-946 3965 E-mail da.taylor3@ntlworld.com

TAYLOR, Edward Frank. b 23. Lon Univ BSc44. Chich Th Coll 50. **d** 52 **p** 53. C Manston *Ripon* 52-55; Chapl Chich Th Coll 55-59; PV Chich Cathl 57-59; C Ifield 59-63; V Hangleton 63-73; V Wivelsfield 73-88; rtd 88; Perm to Offic *Bradf* 88-00. *8 Linkway, Westham, Pevensey BN24 5JB*

TAYLOR, Elizabeth. *See* TAYLOR, Mrs Mary Elizabeth

TAYLOR, Garry Kenneth. b 53. Edin Univ BMus75 Southn Univ BTh81 Ch Ch Coll Cant PGCE95. Sarum & Wells Th Coll 76. **d** 79 **p** 80. C Southsea H Spirit *Portsm* 79-82; C Croydon St Jo *Cant* 82-84; C Croydon St Jo *S'wark* 85-86; V Choral S'well Minster 86-90; V Portsea St Alb *Portsm* 90-94; NSM Hamble le Rice *Win* 96-97; P-in-c Southampton St Jude 97-04; V Highcliffe w Hinton Admiral 04-09; V Highcliffe from 09. *The Vicarage, 33 Nea Road, Christchurch BH23 4NB* Tel (01425) 272761 E-mail garrykt@aol.com

TAYLOR, George James Trueman. b 36. Ripon Hall Ox 66. **d** 69 **p** 70. C Wavertree H Trin *Liv* 69-73; V Newton-le-Willows 73-79; V Stoneycroft All SS 79-83; V Haigh 83-04; Jt P-in-c Aspull and New Springs 02-03; rtd 04. *228 Wigan Road, Aspull, Wigan WN2 1DU* Tel (01942) 830430

TAYLOR, Canon Godfrey Alan. b 36. Oak Hill Th Coll. **d** 61 **p** 62. C Herne Bay Ch Ch *Cant* 61-64; C Tunbridge Wells St Jas *Roch* 64-68; V Guernsey H Trin *Win* 68-81; V Boscombe St Jo 81-03; Hon Can Win Cathl 96-03; AD Bournemouth 99-03; rtd 03; Perm to Offic *Truro* from 05. *Bosnoweth Vean, 21 Cullen View, Probus, Truro TR2 4NY* Tel (01726) 884493 E-mail canongmrsdt@btinternet.com

TAYLOR, Canon Gordon. b 46. AKC68. St Aug Coll Cant 69. **d** 70 **p** 71. C Rotherham *Sheff* 70-74; P-in-c Brightside St Thos 74-79; P-in-c Brightside St Marg 77-79; V Brightside St Thos and St Marg 79-82; R Kirk Sandall and Edenthorpe 82-91; V Beighton 91-96; V Goole 96-03; AD Snaith and Hatfield 98-03; V Tickhill w Stainton from 03; Hon Can Sheff Cathl from 95. *The Vicarage, 2 Sunderland Street, Tickhill, Doncaster DN11 9QJ* Tel (01302) 742224

TAYLOR, Graham Peter. b 58. NEOC 92. **d** 95 **p** 96. NSM Pickering w Lockton and Levisham *York* 95-96; C Whitby 96-98; C Whitby w Aislaby and Ruswarp 98-99; V Cloughton and Burniston w Ravenscar etc 99-04; rtd 04; Perm to Offic *York* from 04. *Address withheld by request*

TAYLOR, Canon Graham Smith. b 70. TISEC 98. **d** 01 **p** 02. C Ellon, Cruden Bay and Peterhead *Ab* 01-04; P-in-c 04-06; R Aberdeen St Mary from 06; Dioc Dir Ords from 06; Can St Andr Cathl from 08. *St Mary's Rectory, 28 Stanley Street, Aberdeen AB10 6UR* Tel (01224) 584123 Mobile 07773-482174 E-mail revgraham@tiscali.co.uk

TAYLOR, Hugh Nigel James. b 43. MCMI FInstD. NTMTC 04. **d** 06 **p** 07. NSM Loughton St Mary *Chelmsf* from 06. *4 Twentyman Close, Woodford Green IG8 0EW* Tel and fax (020) 8504 8901 Mobile 07770-365255 E-mail hughnj@btinternet.com

✠**TAYLOR, The Rt Revd Humphrey Vincent.** b 38. Pemb Coll Cam BA61 MA66 Lon Univ MA70. Coll of Resurr Mirfield 61. **d** 63 **p** 64 **c** 91. C N Hammersmith St Kath *Lon* 63-64; C Notting Hill St Mark 64-66; USPG 67-71; Malawi 67-71; Chapl Bp Grosseteste Coll Linc 72-74; Sec Chapls in HE Gen Syn Bd of Educn 75-80; Gen Sec USPG 80-91; Sec Miss Progr 80-84; Hon Can Bris Cathl 86-91; Lic to Offic *S'wark* 89-91; Suff Bp Selby *York* 91-03; rtd 03; Hon Asst Bp *Glouc* and *Worc* from 03. *10 High Street, Honeybourne, Evesham WR11 7PQ* Tel (01386) 834846 E-mail humane.taylor@virgin.net

TAYLOR, Iain William James. b 41. **d** 03 **p** 04. OLM Cant St Pet w St Alphege and St Marg etc from 03. *11 Keyworth Mews, Canterbury CT1 1XQ* Tel (01227) 766585

TAYLOR, Ian. b 53. Saltley Tr Coll Birm CertEd75. **d** 95 **p** 96.

OLM Heywood *Man* from 95. *818A Edenfield Road, Rochdale OL12 7RB* Tel (01706) 355738

TAYLOR, Mrs Jacqueline Margaret. b 56. Trin Coll Bris 02. **d** 04 **p** 05. C Bath St Luke *B & W* 04-08; Chapl Univ Hosps Bris NHS Foundn Trust from 08. *United Bristol Healthcare NHS Trust, Trust Headquarters, Marlborough Street, Bristol BS1 3NU* Tel 0117-923 0000 E-mail wookeyjackie@hotmail.com

TAYLOR, Jamie Alexander Franklyn. b 73. Kent Univ BA95. Westcott Ho Cam. **d** 98 **p** 99. C Walton-on-Thames *Guildf* 98-02; C St Peter-in-Thanet *Cant* 02-08; Chapl E Kent NHS and Soc Care Partnership Trust 03-06; Chapl Kent & Medway NHS and Soc Care Partnership Trust 06-08; V Sonning *Ox* from 08. *The Vicarage, Thames Street, Sonning, Reading RG4 6UR* Tel 0118-969 3298 E-mail revjaft@yahoo.co.uk

TAYLOR, Jan William Karel. b 59. QUB BD82 MSocSc89. CITC. **d** 84 **p** 85. C Belfast St Simon w St Phil *Conn* 84-87; I Belfast St Paul 87-92; Chapl RAF from 92; Perm to Offic *Ban* from 97. *Chaplaincy Services, Valiant Block, HQ Air Command, RAF High Wycombe HP14 4UE* Tel (01494) 496800 Fax 496343

TAYLOR, Jane Suzanne. b 54. Ex Univ BA73. SEITE 96. **d** 99 **p** 00. NSM Knaphill w Brookwood *Guildf* 99-00; C Frimley Green and Mytchett 00-04. *Rocknell Manor Farm, Westleigh, Tiverton EX16 7ES* Tel (01884) 829000

TAYLOR, Jason Victor. b 71. Lon Bible Coll BTh01 St Jo Coll Dur MA03. Cranmer Hall Dur 01. **d** 03 **p** 04. C Ripley *Derby* 03-07; TV Drypool *York* 07-09; Chapl Abp Sentamu Academy Hull from 09. *Archbishop Sentamu Academy, Hopewell Road, Kingston-upon-Hull HU9 4HD* Tel (01482) 781912 Mobile 07825-408351 E-mail revjasontaylor@gmail.com

TAYLOR, Miss Jean. b 37. Nottm Univ TCert58. St Andr Coll Pampisford 62. **dss** 68 **d** 00 **p** 01. CSA 62-79; E Crompton *Man* 79-97; Chadderton St Luke 97-04; OLM 00-04; OLM Chadderton St Matt w St Luke 04-05; Warden Jes Hosp Cant 05-08; Perm to Offic *Cant* from 05. *7 Chantry Court, St Radigund's Street, Canterbury CT1 2AD* Tel (01227) 761652

TAYLOR, Mrs Jennifer Anne. b 53. Sussex Univ BEd75 Surrey Univ BA01. STETS 98. **d** 01 **p** 02. Chapl Salisbury Cathl Sch from 01; NSM Salisbury St Thos and St Edm *Sarum* 01-09; TV Chalke Valley from 09. *27 Viking Way, Salisbury SP2 8TA* Tel and fax (01722) 503081 E-mail geoffrey.taylor5@ntlworld.com

TAYLOR, Sister Jennifer Mary. b 41. CA Tr Coll IDC65. **dss** 77 **d** 87 **p** 07. CA from 65; Chapl Asst HM Pris Holloway 75-79; Ho Mistress Ch Hosp Sch Hertf 78-79; Chapl Asst RAChD 80-90; Germany 90-96; rtd 96; Perm to Offic *Eur* from 96 and *Nor* 06-07; Hon C Dereham and Distr *Nor* from 07. *4 Eckling Grange, Norwich Road, Dereham NR20 3BB* Tel (01362) 692547

TAYLOR, Jeremy Christopher. b 75. Birm Univ BA97. Oak Hill Th Coll BA07. **d** 07 **p** 08. C Chell *Lich* from 07. *The Vicarage, 110 Sprinkbank Road, Stoke-on-Trent ST6 6HZ* Tel (01782) 826577 Mobile 07787-514058 E-mail juneandjerry@btinternet.com

TAYLOR, Joanna Beatrice. *See* NEARY, Mrs Joanna Beatrice

TAYLOR, John. b 58. Aston Tr Scheme 94 Ripon Coll Cuddesdon 96. **d** 98 **p** 99. C Southport Em *Liv* 98-03; V Hindley All SS from 03. *The Vicarage, 192 Atherton Road, Hindley, Wigan WN2 3XA* Tel and fax (01942) 255175 E-mail johntaylor@supanet.com

TAYLOR, John Alexander. b 54. S Dios Minl Tr Scheme 89. **d** 92 **p** 93. NSM Abbotts Ann and Upper and Goodworth Clatford *Win* 92-99; Perm to Offic 99-00; NSM Hatherden w Tangley, Weyhill and Penton Mewsey 00-02; NSM W Andover 02-09; NSM Portway and Danebury from 09. *256 Weyhill Road, Andover SP10 3LR* Tel (01264) 359160 E-mail john@w256.fsnet.co.uk

TAYLOR, Canon John Andrew. b 53. Linc Th Coll 86. **d** 88 **p** 89. C Stanley *Liv* 88-91; V Wigan St Jas w St Thos 91-04; AD Wigan W 99-04; Hon Can Liv Cathl 03-04; V Prescot from 04; AD Huyton from 06; Hon Can Liv Cathl from 07. *The Vicarage, Vicarage Place, Prescot L34 5LA* Tel 0151-426 6119 or 426 6719

✠**TAYLOR, The Rt Revd John Bernard.** b 29. KCVO97. Jes Coll Cam BA50 MA54 Jes Coll Cam 52 Hebrew Univ Jerusalem 54. Ridley Hall Cam 55. **d** 56 **p** 57 **c** 80. C Morden *S'wark* 56-59; V Henham *Chelmsf* 59-64; V Elsenham 59-64; Sen Tutor Oak Hill Th Coll 64-65; Vice-Prin 65-72; V Woodford Wells *Chelmsf* 72-75; Dioc Dir of Ords 72-80; Adn W Ham 75-80; Bp St Alb 80-95; High Almoner 88-97; rtd 95; Hon Asst Bp Ely from 95; Hon Asst Bp Eur from 98. *22 Conduit Head Road, Cambridge CB3 0EY* Tel (01223) 313783 E-mail john.taylor6529@ntlworld.com

TAYLOR, Canon John Michael. b 30. St Aid Birkenhead 56. **d** 59 **p** 60. C Chorley St Jas *Blackb* 59-62; C Broughton 62-64; Chapl St Boniface Coll Warminster 64-68; V Altham w Clayton le Moors *Blackb* 68-76; RD Accrington 71-76; Can Res Blackb Cathl 76-96; Tutor CBDTI 88-96; rtd 96; Perm to Offic *Blackb* from 96. *Edenholme, 25 Gorse Road, Blackburn BB2 6LZ* Tel (01254) 693772

✠**TAYLOR, The Rt Revd John Mitchell.** b 32. Aber Univ MA54. Edin Th Coll 54. **d** 56 **p** 57 **c** 91. C Aberdeen St Marg 56-58; R Glas H Cross 58-64; R Glas St Ninian 64-73; R Dumfries and Chapl Dumfries and Galloway R Infirmary 73-91; Can St Mary's Cathl 79-91; Bp Glas 91-98; rtd 98; Hon Asst Bp Glas from 99. *10 St Georges, Castle Douglas DG7 1LN* Tel and fax (01556) 502593

TAYLOR, John Porter. b 48. Ex Univ BA71 MA76. Cranmer Hall Dur 93. **d** 93 **p** 94. C Ossett cum Gawthorpe *Wakef* 93-96; R Crofton 96-02; Chapl Mid Yorks Hosps NHS Trust 03-06; Chapl Oakham Sch from 06. *Oakham School, Market Place, Oakham LE15 6DT* Tel (01572) 758695 E-mail jpt@oakham.rutland.sch.uk

TAYLOR, John Ralph. b 48. St Jo Coll Nottm BTh74. **d** 74 **p** 75. C Clitheroe St Jas *Blackb* 74-77; C Kidsgrove *Lich* 77-79; C Hawkwell *Chelmsf* 79-82; V Linc St Geo Swallowbeck 82-92; rtd 92. *The Vicarage, Vicarage Lane, Sibsey, Boston PE22 0RT* Tel (01205) 750305

TAYLOR, Canon John Rowland. b 29. OBE74. St Mich Coll Llan 57. **d** 58 **p** 59. C Caerau St Cynfelin *Llan* 58-59; C Aberdare 59-61; Chapl Miss to Seamen 61-88; Dar-es-Salaam Tanzania 61-73; Adn Dar-es-Salaam 65-73; V-Gen 67-73; Hon Can Dar-es-Salaam from 73; V Bangkok Ch Ch Thailand 73-84; Chapl Rotterdam w Schiedam *Eur* 84-88; V Warnham *Chich* 88-98; rtd 98; Perm to Offic *Chich* 98-00; P-in-c Streat w Westmeston 00-07. *The Rectory, Streat Lane, Streat, Hassocks BN6 8RX* Tel (01273) 890607

TAYLOR, Joseph Robin Christopher. b 34. St Aid Birkenhead 58. **d** 61 **p** 62. C Aldershot St Mich *Guildf* 61-64; C Fleet 64-68; R Manaton *Ex* 69-74; R N Bovey 69-74; V Dawlish 74-87; P-in-c Christow, Ashton, Trusham and Bridford 87-88; R 88-95; Perm to Offic *Ex* 95-98; *St E* from 98; rtd 99. *24 Edwin Panks Road, Hadleigh, Ipswich IP7 5JL* Tel (01473) 824262

TAYLOR, Julia Mary. b 73. Reading Univ LLB94. Ridley Hall Cam 06. **d** 08 **p** 09. C Penkridge *Lich* from 08. *31 Nursery Drive, Penkridge ST19 5SJ* Tel 07990-976859 (mobile) E-mail jules.m.taylor@googlemail.com

TAYLOR, Kelvin John. b 53. Portsm Univ CertEd94 BA96. Trin Coll Bris 02. **d** 04 **p** 05. C Overton w Laverstoke and Freefolk *Win* 04-08; V Kempshott from 08. *The Vicarage, 171 Kempshott Lane, Kempshott, Basingstoke RG22 5LF* Tel (01256) 356400

TAYLOR, Kingsley Graham. b 55. Univ of Wales (Cardiff) BD93. St Mich Coll Llan 90. **d** 93 **p** 94. C Llanelli *St D* 93-97; V Whitland w Cyffig and Henllan Amgoed etc from 97. *The Vicarage, North Road, Whitland SA34 0BH* Tel (01994) 240494 E-mail ktaylor559@aol.com

TAYLOR, Luke Alastare John. b 68. Brunel Univ BA97. Oak Hill Th Coll BA00. **d** 00 **p** 01. C Hanworth St Rich *Lon* 00-04; C E Twickenham St Steph from 04. *11 Brantwood Avenue, Isleworth TW7 7EX* Tel (020) 8847 3979 E-mail lukeandgissy@talk21.com

TAYLOR, Lyndon John. b 49. St Mich Coll Llan 92. **d** 95 **p** 96. NSM Swansea St Nic *S & B* 95-99; C Llwynderw 99-01; V Waunarllwydd 01-06; V Clydach from 08. *The Vicarage, Woodland Park, Ynystawe, Swansea SA6 5AR* Tel (01792) 843203

TAYLOR, Lynne. b 51. Sheff Univ BMet73 Salford Univ PhD80. Man OLM Scheme 98. **d** 01 **p** 02. OLM Turton Moorland Min *Man* from 01. *56 Station Road, Turton, Bolton BL7 0HA* Tel (01204) 852551

TAYLOR, Margaret Ann. b 46. **d** 98 **p** 99. OLM Newcastle w Butterton *Lich* from 98. *12 Silverton Close, Bradwell, Newcastle ST5 8LU* Tel (01782) 660174 E-mail revanntaylor@yahoo.co.uk

TAYLOR, Marian Alexandra. b 62. Newc Univ BA85. Qu Coll Birm 89. **d** 91 **p** 96. C Earls Barton *Pet* 91-93; NSM Wellingborough St Barn 95-96; NSM Beaumont Leys *Leic* 96-97; Perm to Offic *Pet* 99-00; NSM Kingsthorpe w Northampton St Dav 00-04; TV from 04. *75 Kentstone Close, Northampton NN2 8UH* Tel (01604) 843471 Mobile 07749-047933 E-mail marian.taylor62@ntlworld.com

TAYLOR, Mark Frederick. b 62. N Ireland Poly BA84. CITC. **d** 87 **p** 88. C Ballymacarrett St Patr *D & D* 87-90; C Dundela St Mark 90-93; I Kilmore and Inch 93-02; I Whitehead and Islandmagee *Conn* from 02. *St Patrick's Rectory, 74 Cable Road, Whitehead, Carrickfergus BT38 9SJ* Tel and fax (028) 9337 3300

TAYLOR, Mark John. b 73. St Andr Univ MTheol99. Coll of Resurr Mirfield 01. **d** 03 **p** 04. C N Meols *Liv* 03-07; TV Sutton from 07. *40 Eaves Lane, St Helens WA9 3UB* E-mail mtaylor@mirfield.org.uk

TAYLOR, Martyn Andrew Nicholas. b 66. **d** 96 **p** 97. C Stamford St Geo w St Paul *Linc* 96-03; R from 03. *St George's Rectory, 16 St George's Square, Stamford PE9 2BN* Tel (01780) 757343 or 481800 E-mail rector@stgeorgeschurch.net

TAYLOR, Mrs Mary Elizabeth. b 39. **d** 01 **p** 02. OLM Parr *Liv* from 01. *16 Hignett Avenue, St Helens WA9 2PJ* Tel (01744) 21086

TAYLOR, Mrs Maureen. b 36. Lon Bible Coll BTh90 MA94. **d** 97 **p** 98. NSM Borehamwood *St Alb* 97-00; NSM Radlett 00-05; Perm to Offic from 06. *57A Loom Lane, Radlett WD7 8NX* Tel (01923) 855197

TAYLOR, Michael. *See* TAYLOR, Canon John Michael

TAYLOR, Michael Alan. b 47. Bris Univ CertEd70 Lon Univ BD85. Trin Coll Bris 72. **d** 76 **p** 77. C Chilwell *S'well* 76-79; Chapl RAF 79-87; New Zealand from 87. *31 Kiteroa Place, Cashmere, Christchurch 8022, New Zealand* Tel (0064) (3) 352 331 8440 E-mail strategic@chch.planet.org.nz

TAYLOR, Michael Allan. b 50. Nottm Univ BTh80. St Jo Coll Nottm 76. **d** 80 **p** 81. C Bowling St Jo *Bradf* 80-82; C Otley 82-85; P-in-c Low Moor St Mark 85-92; P-in-c Bris St Andr w St Bart 92-96. *25 Cornfield Close, Bradley Stoke, Bristol BS32 9DN* Tel (01454) 618677

TAYLOR, Michael Andrew James. b 40. Univ Coll Ches BTh96. **d** 99 **p** 00. NSM Halliwell *Man* from 99; TV from 03. *123 Smithills Dean Road, Bolton BL1 6JZ* Tel (01204) 491503

TAYLOR, Michael Barry. b 38. Bps' Coll Cheshunt 63. **d** 65 **p** 66. C Leeds St Cypr Harehills *Ripon* 65-68; C Stanningley St Thos 68-70; V Hunslet Moor St Pet and St Cuth 70-78; V Starbeck 78-00; rtd 00; Perm to Offic *Leic* from 00. *11 Aulton Crescent, Hinckley LE10 0XA* Tel (01455) 442218

TAYLOR, Michael Frank Chatterton. b 30. St Aid Birkenhead 59. **d** 61 **p** 62. C Knighton St Jo *Leic* 61-65; V Briningham *Nor* 65-86; R Melton Constable w Swanton Novers 65-86; P-in-c Thornage w Brinton w Hunworth and Stody 85-86; R Lyng w Sparham 86-90; R Elsing w Bylaugh 86-90; R Lyng, Sparham, Elsing and Bylaugh 90-95; RD Sparham 92-95; rtd 95; Perm to Offic *Portsm* from 95. *The Rhond, 33 Station Road, St Helens, Ryde PO33 1YF* Tel and fax (01983) 873531 Mobile 07989-274848 E-mail mfct@tesco.net

TAYLOR, Michael John. b 50. **d** 07 **p** 08. OLM Went Valley *Wakef* from 07. *19 Windsor Rise, Pontefract WF8 4PZ* Tel (01977) 702824 Mobile 07968-932135 E-mail mjtaylor0@hotmail.co.uk

TAYLOR, Canon Michael Joseph. b 49. Gregorian Univ Rome STB72 PhL74 Birm Univ MA81 Nottm Univ PhD05. English Coll Rome 67. **d** 72 **p** 73. In RC Ch 72-83; Hon C Newport Pagnell w Lathbury *Ox* 83-86; TV Langley Marish 86-90; Vice Prin EMMTC *S'well* 90-97; Prin 97-06; R Gedling from 06; Hon Can S'well Minster from 00. *The Rectory, Rectory Drive, Gedling, Nottingham NG4 4BG* Tel 0115-961 3214

TAYLOR, Michael Laurence. b 43. Ch Coll Cam BA66 MA70 CertEd72 MPhil90 ARCM68. Cuddesdon Coll 66. **d** 68 **p** 69. C Westbury-on-Trym H Trin *Bris* 68-72; Asst Chapl Wellington Coll Berks 72-76; C St Helier *S'wark* 76-78; TV Bedminster *Bris* 78-82; P-in-c Chippenham St Andr w Tytherton Lucas 82-88; V 88-89; Dioc Ecum Officer *B & W* 89-90; P-in-c Rodney Stoke w Draycott 89-90. *The Paddock, Wells Road, Rodney Stoke, Cheddar BS27 3UU* Tel (01749) 870684 E-mail mendipadvolacy@btinternet.com

TAYLOR, Michael Noel. b 40. Leeds Univ BSc62 PGCE63. EMMTC 95. **d** 98 **p** 99. NSM Woodthorpe *S'well* 98-02; NSM Gedling Deanery 02-03; NSM Epperstone from 03; NSM Gonalston from 03; NSM Oxton from 03; NSM Calverton from 03; NSM Woodborough from 03. *16 Church Meadow, Calverton, Nottingham NG14 6HG* Tel 0115-847 3718 Fax 912 7671 Mobile 07713-125771 E-mail michael.taylor21@ntlworld.com

TAYLOR, Michael Stewart. b 58. St Mich Coll Llan BTh91. **d** 91 **p** 92. C Llangunnor w Cwmffrwd *St D* 91-94; V Llansantffraed and Llanbadarn Trefeglwys etc 94-97; P-in-c Jersey St Andr *Win* 97-99; V from 99. *The Vicarage, St Andrew's Road, First Tower, St Helier, Jersey JE2 3JG* Tel and fax (01534) 734975 E-mail vicarmike@aol.com

TAYLOR, Mrs Monica. b 39. **d** 06 **p** 07. OLM Wyke *Guildf* from 06. *Glifada, Guildford Road, Normandy, Guildford GU23 2AR* Tel (01483) 234427 E-mail mrsmonicataylor@hotmail.com

TAYLOR, Nancy. b 49. SRN70 SCM72. Ox Min Course 88. **d** 91 **p** 94. Chapl Asst Stoke Mandeville Hosp Aylesbury 91-94; Asst Chapl Aylesbury Vale Community Healthcare NHS Trust 94-97; NSM Weston Turville *Ox* 91-99; Chapl Kneesworth Ho Hosp from 98. *Kneesworth House Hospital, Old North Road, Bassingbourn, Royston SG8 5JP* Tel (01763) 255700

TAYLOR, Neil Hamish. b 48. Open Univ BA87. Linc Th Coll 72. **d** 75 **p** 76. C Rotherham *Sheff* 75-78; C Doncaster St Geo 78-82; V Alston cum Garrigill w Nenthead and Kirkhaugh *Newc* 82-87; P-in-c Lambley w Knaresdale 82-87; TR Alston Team 87-88; V Maidstone St Paul *Cant* 88-98; OCF 89-94; Sen Chapl Mid Kent Healthcare NHS Trust 98-00; Sen Chapl Maidstone and Tunbridge Wells NHS Trust 00-01; R Eynsford w Farningham and Lullingstone *Roch* 02-09; rtd 09; Chapl Pilgrims Hospice Thanet from 09. *Pilgrims Hospice, Ramsgate Road, Margate CT9 4AD* Tel (01843) 233923 E-mail neil_taylor@pilgrimshospice.org

TAYLOR, Canon Nicholas Hugh. b 63. Cape Town Univ BA83 MA87 Dur Univ PhD91 Ox Univ MTh07. **d** 96 **p** 97. Lect and Chapl Univ of Swaziland 95-98; Chapl St Mich Sch Manzini 96-98; Sen Lect Africa Univ Zimbabwe 98-01; Can Th Mutare Cathl from 99; Dioc Dir Th Educn Manicaland 99-01; R Penhalonga 00-01; Assoc Prof Pretoria Univ S Africa 02-04; R Pretoria St Hilda 02-03; R Pretoria N St Mary 03; Hon C Smithfield St Bart Gt *Lon* 04; Research Fell Univ of Zululand from 04; Hon Tutor Ripon Coll Cuddesdon 04-05; Lect K Coll

Lon 06; Perm to Offic *Nor* from 04 and *Ox* 05-07; R Clarkston *Glas* from 09. *St Aidan's Rectory, 8 Golf Road, Clarkston, Glasgow G76 7LZ* Tel 0141-638 3080 Mobile 07944-091132 E-mail nhtaylor@dunelm.org.uk

TAYLOR, Preb Nicholas James. b 46. St Chad's Coll Dur BA67. **d** 69 **p** 70. C Beamish *Dur* 69-74; C Styvechale *Cov* 74-77; P-in-c Wilmcote w Billesley 77-79; P-in-c Aston Cantlow 77-79; V Aston Cantlow and Wilmcote w Billesley 79-87; V Cov St Fran N Radford 87-97; RD Cov N 93-97; V Wilton *B & W* from 97; Preb Wells Cathl from 08. *The Vicarage, Fons George, Wilton, Taunton TA1 3JT* Tel (01823) 284253 E-mail church@ta13jt.freeserve.co.uk

TAYLOR, Nicholas John. b 48. Leeds Univ BSc69. St Mich Coll Llan BTh09. **d** 09. NSM Griffithstown *Mon* from 09. *82 Greenhill Road, Sebastopol, Pontypool NP4 5BQ* Tel (01495) 740189 Mobile 07860-507258 E-mail njt.littlebarton@btinternet.com

TAYLOR, Nigel Thomas Wentworth. b 60. Bris Univ BA82 Ox Univ BA86. Wycliffe Hall Ox 84. **d** 87 **p** 88. C Ches Square St Mich w St Phil *Lon* 87-91; C Roxeth Ch Ch and Harrow St Pet 91-93; TV Roxeth 93-97; V S Mimms Ch Ch from 97; AD Cen Barnet from 04. *Christ Church Vicarage, St Albans Road, Barnet EN5 4LA* Tel (020) 8449 0942 *or* 8449 0832 E-mail nigel.taylor@london.anglican.org

TAYLOR, Mrs Noelle Rosemary. b 58. NTMTC 02. **d** 05 **p** 06. C St Mary-at-Latton *Chelmsf* 05-08; TV Gt Parndon from 08. *80 Deer Park, Harlow CM19 4LF* E-mail noelletaylor@hotmail.com

TAYLOR, Norman. b 26. CCC Cam BA49 MA52. Cuddesdon Coll 49. **d** 51 **p** 52. C Clitheroe St Mary *Blackb* 51-54; C Pontesbury I and II *Heref* 54-55; R Lt Wilbraham *Ely* 55-71; Chapl St Faith's Sch Cam 71-86; Hon C Chesterton St Andr *Ely* 87-91; rtd 91; Perm to Offic *Sarum* from 91. *Shire End West, Cobb Road, Lyme Regis DT7 3JP* Tel (01297) 442922

TAYLOR, Norman Adrian. b 48. St D Coll Lamp. **d** 73 **p** 74. C Fleur-de-Lis *Mon* 73-75; C W Drayton *Lon* 75-79; C-in-c Hayes St Edm CD 79-85; V Hayes St Edm 85-87; V Pilton w Ashford *Ex* 87-89; V Sidley *Chich* 89-02; Chapl Hastings and Rother NHS Trust 00-02; V Durrington *Chich* from 02. *Durrington Vicarage, Bramble Lane, Worthing BN13 3JE* Tel (01903) 693499 E-mail frnorman@nataylor.freeserve.co.uk

TAYLOR, Norman Wyatt. b 23. Wells Th Coll 58. **d** 60 **p** 61. C Lawrence Weston *Bris* 60-63; V 63-69; V Bishop's Cannings *Sarum* 69-77; V Bishop's Cannings, All Cannings etc 77-80; V W Moors 80-87; rtd 88; Perm to Offic *Ex* 89-98. *3 Kits Close, Chudleigh, Newton Abbot TQ13 0LG* Tel (01626) 852733

TAYLOR, Mrs Patricia Anne. Glos Univ BA. BTh. **d** 05 **p** 06. C Wicklow w Killiskey *D & G* from 05. *22 Church Gate, Station Road, Wicklow, Republic of Ireland* Tel (00353) (404) 20653 E-mail patricia.taylor@gmail.com

TAYLOR, Patricia Mary. b 52. Goldsmiths' Coll Lon BEd80. Wycliffe Hall Ox 06. **d** 08 **p** 09. NSM Upper Holloway *Lon* from 09. *4 Anatola Road, London N19 5HN* Tel (020) 7272 8990 E-mail p.taylor2410@btinternet.com

TAYLOR, Patrick James. b 72. Magd Coll Cam BA96 MA99 MEng96. Ripon Coll Cuddesdon BA00. **d** 01 **p** 02. C Kenilworth St Nic *Cov* 01-05; TV Solihull *Birm* from 05. *45 Park Avenue, Solihull B91 3EJ* Tel 0121-705 4927 *or* 705 5350 E-mail patrick@solihullparish.org.uk

TAYLOR, Paul. b 63. RGN85 Sarum & Wells Th Coll 92 Linc Th Coll BTh95. **d** 95 **p** 96. C Boultham *Linc* 95-98; C Ditton St Mich w St Thos *Liv* 98-00; V Bickerstaffe and Melling 00-06; TV N Meols 06-08; rtd 08. *139 Sussex Road, Southport PR8 6AF* Tel (01704) 500617 E-mail joandpaultaylor@talktalk.net

TAYLOR, Paul Frank David. b 60. Leic Poly BSc84 MRICS87. Trin Coll Bris BA91. **d** 91 **p** 92. C Edin St Thos 91-94; C Kempshott *Win* 94-98; C-in-c Hatch Warren CD 98-01; V Salisbury St Fran and Stratford sub Castle *Sarum* from 01; C Bourne Valley from 09. *The Vicarage, 52 Park Lane, Salisbury SP1 3NP* Tel (01722) 333762 E-mail paul@pfdt.freeserve.co.uk

TAYLOR, Paul Jeremy. b 72. Brunel Univ BSc96. Ridley Hall Cam 02. **d** 04 **p** 05. C Longfleet *Sarum* 04-08; V Hordle *Win* from 08. *The Vicarage, Stopples Lane, Hordle, Lymington SO41 0HX* Tel (01425) 614428 Mobile 07776-425621 E-mail pjtaylorsurfing@hotmail.com

TAYLOR, Paul Michael. b 66. EMMTC 03. **d** 05 **p** 05. C Derby St Pet and Ch Ch w H Trin 05-07; P-in-c Brailsford w Shirley, Osmaston w Edlaston etc from 07. *The Rectory, Church Lane, Brailsford, Derby DE6 3BX* Tel (01335) 361221

TAYLOR, The Ven Paul Stanley. b 53. Dur Univ BEd75 MTh98. Westcott Ho Cam. **d** 84 **p** 85. C Bush Hill Park St Steph *Lon* 84-88; Asst Dir Post Ord Tr Edmonton Episc Area 87-94; Dir Post Ord Tr 94-00 and 02-04; V Southgate St Andr 88-97; V Hendon St Mary 97-01; V Hendon St Mary and Ch Ch 01-04; AD W Barnet 00-04; Adn Sherborne *Sarum* from 04; Can and Preb Sarum Cathl from 04. *Aldhelm House, West Stafford, Dorchester DT2 8AB* Tel and fax (01305) 269074 *or* tel (01258) 859110 E-mail adsherborne@salisbury.anglican.org *or* ptatstmarys@aol.com

TAYLOR, Peter. b 35. Sussex Univ MA72. Wells Th Coll 58. **d** 60 **p** 61. C Godalming *Guildf* 60-62; C Epsom St Martin 62-65; R E Clandon and W Clandon 65-75; rtd 96; P-in-c Burpham *Chich* 96-04; Perm to Offic from 04. *Jordan's Bank, 20 Penfold Place, Arundel BN18 9SA* Tel (01903) 885706
E-mail pburpham@globalnet.co.uk

TAYLOR, Peter. b 51. St Jo Coll Cam BA72 MA76. Ridley Hall Cam 73. **d** 76 **p** 77. C Roch 76-79; Perm to Offic *Ely* 79-99 and 05-06; NSM Downham 99-05; P-in-c Coveney from 06; RD Ely from 09. *Gravel Head Farm, Downham Common, Little Downham, Ely CB6 2TY* Tel (01353) 698714 Fax 699107
E-mail peter@taylormonroe.co.uk

TAYLOR, Peter David. b 38. FCA. NOC 77. **d** 80 **p** 81. C Penwortham St Mary *Blackb* 80-84; V Farington 84-92; V Euxton 92-04; rtd 04; Perm to Offic *Blackb* from 04. *33 Aspendale Close, Longton, Preston PR4 5LJ* Tel (01772) 614795

TAYLOR, Canon Peter David. b 47. Liv Univ BEd74 Man Univ MEd78 Lanc Univ MA88. NOC 78. **d** 81 **p** 82. C Formby H Trin *Liv* 81-84; V Stoneycroft All SS 84-91; Chapl St Kath Coll 91-96; Dioc RE Field Officer 91-96; Dioc Dir of Educn *Leic* 96-09; Hon Can Leic Cathl 98-09; Dir Operations Ch Academy Services Ltd *Pet* from 09; Perm to Offic *Leic* from 09. *87 Main Street, Humberstone, Leicester LE5 1AE* Tel 0116-220 1461 *or* (01733) 566575 E-mail peter.taylor@leccofe.org *or* peter@churchacademies.org.uk

TAYLOR, The Ven Peter Flint. b 44. Qu Coll Cam BA65 MA69. Lon Coll of Div BD70. **d** 70 **p** 71. C Highbury New Park St Aug *Lon* 70-73; C Plymouth St Andr w St Paul and St Geo *Ex* 73-77; V Ironville *Derby* 77-83; P-in-c Riddings 82-83; R Rayleigh *Chelmsf* 83-96; Chapl HM YOI Bullwood Hall 85-90; RD Rochford *Chelmsf* 89-96; Adn Harlow 96-09; rtd 09. *Palstone Park, Palstone Lane, South Brent TQ10 9JR* Tel (01364) 734427
E-mail peterftaylor@lineone.net

TAYLOR, Peter John. b 40. Oak Hill Th Coll 62. **d** 65 **p** 66. C St Paul's Cray St Barn *Roch* 65-69; C Woking St Jo *Guildf* 69-77; R Necton w Holme Hale *Nor* 77-94; R Necton, Holme Hale w N and S Pickenham 95-05; RD Breckland 86-94; Hon Can Nor Cathl 98-03; rtd 05; Perm to Offic *Nor* from 05. *5 Starling Close, Aylsham, Norwich NR11 6XG* Tel (01263) 731964

TAYLOR, Peter John. b 46. Tyndale Hall Bris 70. **d** 73 **p** 74. C Walshaw Ch Ch *Man* 73-75; C Rodbourne Cheney *Bris* 75-78; Asst Chapl HM Pris Pentonville 78-79; Chapl HM Borstal Roch 79-84; Chapl HM Pris Highpoint 84-90; Asst Chapl Gen of Pris 90-01; rtd 01. *Address temp unknown*

TAYLOR, Peter John. b 60. New Coll Edin LTh87. Edin Th Coll 83. **d** 87 **p** 88. C Edin SS Phil and Jas 87-90; USA 90-92; R Glas St Oswald 92-97; R Kirkcudbright and Gatehouse of Fleet 97-07. *Address temp unknown* E-mail ptktb@aol.com

TAYLOR, Peter John. b 71. St Andr Univ MA94 Sussex Univ PGCE99. Oak Hill Th Coll BA05. **d** 05 **p** 06. C Boscombe St Jo *Win* from 05. *1 High Trees, 2 Beach Road, Branksome Park, Poole BH13 7BT* Tel (01202) 700222

TAYLOR, Peter Joseph. b 41. Bps' Coll Cheshunt 66. **d** 68 **p** 69. C Wollaton *S'well* 68-71; C Cockington *Ex* 71-74; V Broadhembury 74-79; V Broadhembury w Payhembury 79-81; V Gt Staughton *Ely* 81-86; V Gt Paxton and R Offord D'Arcy w Offord Cluny 86-01; Chapl HM YOI Gaynes Hall 81-91; rtd 01; Perm to Offic *Ely* from 01. *9 Park Way, Offord Cluny, St Neots PE19 5RW* Tel (01480) 811662

TAYLOR, Mrs Rachel Sara. b 60. Univ Coll Lon BA81. SEITE 98. **d** 01 **p** 02. C Wimbledon *S'wark* 01-05; V Motspur Park from 05. *The Vicarage, 2 Douglas Avenue, New Malden KT3 6HT* Tel (020) 8942 3117 E-mail rachel@taylortalk.fsnet.co.uk

TAYLOR (or URMSON-TAYLOR), Ralph Urmson. Tulsa Univ MA72 Man Coll of Educn DipEd74 TCert82. Kelham Th Coll. **d** 56 **p** 57. C Redcar *York* 57-59; C Bridlington Quay H Trin 59-62; C Sewerby w Marton 60-62; USA 62-02; Asst P Tulsa H Trin 62-65; Sacr 93-02; Chapl Holland Hall Sch 65-93; rtd 93. *Via Porta Perlici 47A, 06081 Assisi PG, Italy*

TAYLOR, Raymond. b 34. Lon Coll of Div 62. **d** 65 **p** 66. C Pennington *Man* 65-70; P-in-c Wombridge *Lich* 70-80; R S Normanton *Derby* 80-88; RD Alfreton 86-88; V Youlgreave, Middleton, Stanton-in-Peak etc 88-98; rtd 99; Perm to Offic *Derby* from 99. *4 Jeffries Avenue, Crich, Matlock DE4 5DU* Tel (01773) 856845

TAYLOR, Raymond George. b 39. Bucknell Univ BS59 Univ of Penn MS65 EdD66 Penn State Univ MPA77 Maine Univ MBA85. Episc Th Sch Cam Mass BD62. **d** 62 **p** 63. C Chestnut Hill St Martin USA 62-66; V Warwick St Mary 70-77; Assoc P Smithfield St Paul 87-90; Assoc P Oriental St Thos 90-00; Superintendent of Schs Maine 77-86; Prof N Carolina State Univ 86-01; P-in-c Mlaga *Eur* 04-06. *Cortijo Moya, 29710 Periana (Málaga), Spain* Tel and fax (0034) 609 885 479 Mobile 650 780 087 E-mail cortijomoya@terra.es

TAYLOR, Raymond Montgomery. b 43. Oak Hill Th Coll 77. **d** 80 **p** 81. Hon C Cricklewood St Pet *Lon* 80-85; Hon C Golders Green 85-87; V New Southgate St Paul 87-00; AD Cen Barnet 96-00; V Thaxted *Chelmsf* from 00. *The Vicarage, Watling Lane,*

Thaxted, Dunmow CM6 2QY Tel and fax (01371) 830221
E-mail furor@scribendi.freeserve.co.uk

TAYLOR, Richard David. b 44. Worc Coll Ox BA67 MA70. Coll of Resurr Mirfield 67. **d** 69 **p** 70. C Barrow St Geo w St Luke *Carl* 69-73; C Gosforth All SS *Newc* 73-80; TR Newc Epiphany 80-83; V Tynemouth Priory 83-91; TR Benwell 91-98; P-in-c Blyth St Cuth 98-01; V from 01. *The Vicarage, 29 Ridley Avenue, Blyth NE24 3BA* Tel (01670) 352410
E-mail rdtaylor@metronet.co.uk

TAYLOR, Richard Godfrey. b 73. Pemb Coll Cam MA99. Oak Hill Th Coll BA00. **d** 00 **p** 01. C Brunswick *Man* 00-04; C Aldridge *Lich* 04-09; V Clapham Common St Barn *S'wark* from 09. *The Vicarage, 8 Lavender Gardens, London SW11 1DL* Tel (020) 7738 2111 E-mail fatboytaylor@hotmail.com

TAYLOR, Preb Richard John. b 21. Kelham Th Coll 38. **d** 45 **p** 46. C Tunstall Ch Ch *Lich* 45-48; C Uttoxeter w Bramshall 48-52; V Croxden 52-57; V Willenhall H Trin 57-68; R Edgmond 68-77; V Streetly 77-87; Preb Lich Cathl 78-87; rtd 87; Perm to Offic *Lich* from 87. *15 Covey Close, Lichfield WS13 6BS* Tel (01543) 268558

TAYLOR, Richard John. b 46. Ripon Coll Cuddesdon 85. **d** 85 **p** 86. C Moseley St Mary *Birm* 85-87; V Kingsbury 87-91; TR Hodge Hill 91-03; P-in-c 03-05; R Weston super Mare St Jo *B & W* from 05; RD Locking from 08. *The Rectory, Cecil Road, Weston-super-Mare BS23 2NF* Tel (01934) 623399

TAYLOR, Robert Ian. b 68. St Jo Coll Nottm. **d** 08 **p** 09. C Buttershaw St Paul *Bradf* from 08; Chapl Bradf Academy from 08. *1 Bowling Hall Road, East Bowling, Bradford BD4 7LE* Tel (01274) 734600 E-mail robtlr@aol.com

TAYLOR, Robert Stirling. b 62. Ball Coll Ox BA83 Leeds Univ PhD88 Nottm Trent Univ PGCE93. Cranmer Hall Dur 00. **d** 02 **p** 03. C Mansfield St Jo *S'well* 02-04; C Eastwood 04-06; Chapl Loughb Univ from 06. *Loughborough University, Loughborough LE11 3TU* Tel (01509) 268203

TAYLOR, Robin. *See* TAYLOR, Joseph Robin Christopher

TAYLOR, Roger James Benedict. b 42. Glouc Sch of Min 89 WMMTC 95. **d** 96 **p** 97. NSM Cromhall w Tortworth and Tytherington *Glouc* 96-99; P-in-c Wistanstow *Heref* 99-01; Min Can Brecon Cathl 01-07; rtd 07. *The Chaplain's House, St Oswald's Hospital, Upper Tything, Worcester WR1 1HR* Tel (01905) 294380

TAYLOR, Canon Roland Haydn. b 29. St Chad's Coll Dur BA53. **d** 55 **p** 56. C N Gosforth *Newc* 55-58; C Barnsley St Mary *Wakef* 58-61; V Brotherton 61-68; V Purston cum S Featherstone 68-74; RD Pontefract 74-94; R Badsworth 76-97; Hon Can Wakef Cathl 81-97; rtd 97. *57 Fairview, Carleton, Pontefract WF8 3NU* Tel (01977) 796564

TAYLOR, Rosemary Edith. b 47. Nottm Univ MA04 RGN68 RHV71. EMMTC 01. **d** 04 **p** 05. NSM Bassingham Gp *Linc* 04-08; P-in-c Sibsey w Frithville from 08. *The Vicarage, Vicarage Lane, Sibsey, Boston PE22 0RT* Tel (01205) 750305
E-mail natuna@btopenworld.com

TAYLOR, Roy. b 63. Ex Coll Ox BA86 Ox Univ MA89 York Univ PGCE87 Univ of Wales (Cardiff) BD97. St Mich Coll Llan 95. **d** 97 **p** 98. C Guisborough *York* 97-99; Chapl Rossall Sch Fleetwood 99-02; V Dolphinholme w Quernmore and Over Wyresdale *Blackb* 02-08; Chapl Geneva *Eur* from 08. *Rue de Montbrillant 84, #72, 1202 Geneva, Switzerland*

TAYLOR, Roy Partington. b 33. Birm Univ BA54 PGCE55 Bulmershe Coll of HE MPhil87. SAOMC 96. **d** 98 **p** 99. NSM Hurley and Stubbings *Ox* 98-02; NSM Burchetts Green 02-03; rtd 03; Perm to Offic *Ox* 03-04; Hon C Maidenhead St Andr and St Mary from 04; Lect Bp Hannington Inst Kenya 01-02; Prin from 04. *16 Highfield Road, Maidenhead SL6 5DF* Tel (01628) 625454 E-mail roy.taylor@telco4u.net

TAYLOR, Roy William. b 37. Ch Coll Cam BA61 MA64. Clifton Th Coll 61. **d** 63 **p** 64. C Blackb Sav 63-66; C Hensingham *Carl* 66-68; CMS Taiwan 69-79; TV Bushbury *Lich* 79-85; OMF 85-93; Hon C Wolverhampton St Jude *Lich* 93-94; P-in-c Torquay St Jo and Ellacombe *Ex* 94-99; R Instow and V Westleigh 99-03; RD Hartland 01-03; rtd 03. *31 Shore Road, Millisle, Newtownards BT22 2BT* Tel (028) 9186 2749

TAYLOR, Simon Dominic Kent. b 69. Surrey Univ BSc90 W Sussex Inst of HE PGCE91 Sussex Univ MA(Ed)99. Trin Coll Bris BA01. **d** 01 **p** 02. C Southgate *Chich* 01-04; TV from 04. *21 Anglesey Close, Crawley RH11 9HG* Tel (01293) 552287

TAYLOR, Simon John. b 72. Worc Coll Ox BA94 MPhil96 MA99 DPhil00. St Mich Coll Llan 00 Ven English Coll Rome 01. **d** 02 **p** 03. C Cotham St Sav w St Mary and Clifton St Paul *Bris* 02-06; P-in-c Bris St Mary Redcliffe w Temple etc from 06. *The Vicarage, 10 Redcliffe Parade West, Bristol BS1 6SP* Tel 0117-929 1962 E-mail simon.taylor@stmaryredcliffe.co.uk

TAYLOR, Mrs Stella Isabelle. b 46. S Dios Minl Tr Scheme 86. **d** 89 **p** 94. NSM Haworth *Bradf* 89-91; Par Dn Keighley St Andr 92-94; C 94-96; rtd 97; Perm to Offic *Bradf* 97-00. *8 The Linkway, Westham, Pevensey BN24 5JB*

TAYLOR, Stephen. b 53. St Edm Hall Ox BA75 Ex Univ PGCE78. WEMTC 05. **d** 08 **p** 09. NSM Highnam, Lassington, Rudford, Tibberton etc *Glouc* from 08. *Perrick's Farmhouse,*

Northwood Green, Westbury-on-Severn GL14 1NB Tel (01452) 760568 E-mail sct@churchdown.gloucs.sch.uk

TAYLOR, Stephen. b 65. City Univ BSc87 Lon Univ PGCE90. NTMTC 95. **d** 98 **p** 99. Chapl Bp Stopford's Sch Enfield 98-02 and 03-06; NSM Enfield Chase St Mary *Lon* 98-02; Perm to Offic *Eur* 02-03; C Hornsey St Mary w St Geo *Lon* 03-06; P-in-c March St Jo 06-08; Hon Asst Dir of Ords 07-08; P-in-c Enfield St Mich *Lon* from 08. *The Vicarage, 2 Gordon Hill, Enfield EN2 0QP* Tel (020) 8363 1063 Mobile 07711-559107 E-mail stephen.taylor@london.anglican.org

TAYLOR, Stephen Gordon. b 35. Bris Univ BA60. Ridley Hall Cam 60. **d** 62 **p** 63. C Gt Baddow *Chelmsf* 62-65; C Portsdown *Portsm* 65-69; P-in-c Elvedon *St E* 69-70; R 70-75; P-in-c Eriswell 69-70; R 70-75; P-in-c Icklingham 69-70; R 70-75; Chapl St Felix Sch Southwold 75-77; R Lt Shelford w Newton *Ely* 77-96; rtd 96; Perm to Offic *Ely* from 96. *15 Church Close, Whittlesford, Cambridge CB22 4NY* Tel (01223) 830461

TAYLOR, Stephen Graham. b 77. St Jo Coll Nottm. **d** 08. C Sparkhill St Jo *Birm* from 08. *132 Oakwood Road, Sparkhill, Birmingham B11 4HD* Tel 0121-247 9428

TAYLOR, Stephen James. b 48. Chich Th Coll 70. **d** 73 **p** 74. C Tottenham St Paul *Lon* 73-76; St Vincent 78-85; Grenada 85-88; C-in-c Hammersmith SS Mich and Geo White City Estate CD *Lon* 88-96; AD Hammersmith 92-96; P-in-c Hammersmith St Luke 94-96; USPG Brazil 96-08. *Rua Dr Boureau 127/203, Costa Azul, Salvador, BA 41 760-050, Brazil* Tel (0055) (71) 3341 6797 E-mail stephentaylor2001@hotmail.com

TAYLOR, Canon Stephen Ronald. b 55. MBE09. Dur Univ MA99. Cranmer Hall Dur 80. **d** 83 **p** 84. C Chester le Street *Dur* 83-87; V Newbottle 87-92; V Stranton 92-00; TR Sunderland 00-07; Provost Sunderland Minster from 07; Hon Can Rift Valley Tanzania from 00; Hon Can Dur Cathl from 06. *10 Beresford Park, Sunderland SR2 7JU* Tel 0191-514 0447 *or* 565 4066 Fax 567 1002
E-mail stephen.taylor@durham.anglican.org

TAYLOR, Stewart. b 51. St Jo Coll Dur 74. **d** 77 **p** 78. C Norwood St Luke *S'wark* 77-81; C Surbiton Hill Ch Ch 81-91; V Cambridge St Phil *Ely* from 91. *St Philip's Vicarage, 252 Mill Road, Cambridge CB1 3NF* Tel (01223) 247652 *or* 414775 E-mail vicar@stphilipschurch.org.uk

TAYLOR, Canon Stuart Bryan. b 40. St Chad's Coll Dur BA64. **d** 66 **p** 67. C Portsea N End St Mark *Portsm* 66-70; C Epsom St Martin *Guildf* 70-76; Chapl Clifton Coll Bris 76-88; Dir Bloxham Project 88-93; Chapl Giggleswick Sch 93-95; Bp's Officer for Miss and Evang *Bris* 96-01; Bp's Adv for Past Care for Clergy and Families from 01; Hon Min Can Bris Cathl from 02; Chapl Bris Cathl Sch from 01; Hon Can Bris Cathl from 04. *62 Providence Lane, Long Ashton, Bristol BS41 9DN* Tel (01275) 393625 *or* 0117-906 0100
E-mail stuart.taylor@bristoldiocese.org

TAYLOR, Mrs Susan Mary. b 51. Ex Univ LLB73 St Anne's Coll Ox BCL75 Solicitor 76. SEITE 03. **d** 06 **p** 07. NSM Barkingside St Laur *Chelmsf* from 06. *Norwood, North End, Buckhurst Hill IG9 5RA* Tel (020) 8504 9867
E-mail suetaylorathome@aol.com

TAYLOR, Mrs Teresa Mary. b 53. SRN76 SCM78. WEMTC 98. **d** 02 **p** 03. NSM Kingswood *Bris* from 02; Chapl Freeways Trust from 07. *15 Hampton Street, Bristol BS15 1TP* Tel 0117-373 2410 E-mail revtmt@blueyonder.co.uk

TAYLOR, Thomas. b 33. Sarum & Wells Th Coll 77. **d** 80 **p** 81. NSM Heatherlands St Jo *Sarum* 80-82; TV Kinson 82-88; TV Shaston 88-98; Chapl Westmr Memorial Hosp Shaftesbury 88-98; rtd 98; Perm to Offic *Sarum* from 98. *10 Hanover Lane, Gillingham SP8 4TA* Tel (01747) 826569

TAYLOR, Thomas. b 42. St Jo Coll Dur BA64 Leeds Univ MA02. Linc Th Coll 64. **d** 66 **p** 67. C Clitheroe St Mary *Blackb* 66-69; C Skerton St Luke 69-71; C-in-c Penwortham St Leon CD 71-72; V Penwortham St Leon 72-78; R Poulton-le-Sands 78-81; P-in-c Morecambe St Lawr 78-81; R Poulton-le-Sands w Morecambe St Laur 81-85; Chapl Ld Wandsworth Coll Hants 85-92; V Walton-le-Dale *Blackb* 92-94; P-in-c Samlesbury 92-94; V Walton-le-Dale St Leon w Samlesbury St Leon 95-96; RD Leyland 94-96; Hon C Tarleton from 03. *52 Hesketh Lane, Tarleton, Preston PR4 6AQ* Tel (01772) 813871
E-mail rustichouse@bigfoot.com

TAYLOR, Thomas Ronald Bennett. b 23. TCD BA46 MA54. Div Test. **d** 47 **p** 48. C Larne and Inver *Conn* 47-49; Chapl RAF 49-65; I Narraghmore w Fontstown and Timolin *D & G* 65-68; I Tynan w Middletown *Arm* 68-85; rtd 85. *34 Kernan Park, Portadown, Craigavon BT63 5QY* Tel (028) 3833 7230

TAYLOR, Willam Goodacre Campbell. *See* CAMPBELL-TAYLOR, William Goodacre

TAYLOR, William Austin. b 36. Linc Th Coll 65. **d** 67 **p** 68. C Tyldesley w Shakerley *Man* 67-71; R Cheetham St Mark 71-79; TR Peel 79-90; AD Farnworth 83-90; V Pelton *Dur* 90-96; rtd 96; Perm to Offic *Man* from 96. *36 Tynesbank, Worsley, Manchester M28 8SL* Tel 0161-790 5327

TAYLOR, William Henry. b 56. Kent Univ BA79 Lon Univ

MTh81 Lanc Univ MPhil87 FRAS80. Westcott Ho Cam. **d** 83 **p** 84. C Maidstone All SS and St Phil w Tovil *Cant* 83-86; Abp's Adv on Orthodox Affairs 86-88; C St Marylebone All SS *Lon* 86-88; Chapl Guy's Hosp Lon 88; CMS Jordan 88-91; V Ealing St Pet Mt Park *Lon* 91-00; AD Ealing 93-98; Dean Portsm 00-02; P-in-c Notting Hill St Jo and St Pet *Lon* 02; V Notting Hill St Jo from 03. *St John's Vicarage, 25 Ladbroke Road, London W11 3PD* Tel (020) 7727 3439 *or* tel and fax 7727 4262 E-mail vicar@stjohnsnottinghill.com

TAYLOR, William Richard de Carteret Martin. b 33. CCC Cam MA57. Westcott Ho Cam 58. **d** 59 **p** 60. C Eastney *Portsm* 59-63; Chapl RN 63-67 and 70-87; V Childe Okeford *Sarum* 67-70; V Manston w Hamoon 67-70; QHC from 83; TR Tisbury *Sarum* 87-89; Chapl Hatf Poly *St Alb* 89-92; Chapl Herts Univ 92-98; rtd 98; Perm to Offic *Ely* from 00. *Lark Rise, 47A New Street, St Neots, Huntingdon PE19 1AJ* Tel (01480) 473598

TAYLOR, Capt William Thomas. b 61. Rob Coll Cam BA83 BA90. Ridley Hall Cam 88. **d** 91 **p** 92. C Bromley Ch Ch *Roch* 91-95; C St Helen Bishopsgate w St Andr Undershaft etc *Lon* 95-98; R from 98; R St Pet Cornhill from 01. *The Old Rectory, Merrick Square, London SE1 4JB* Tel (020) 7378 8186

TAYLOR-COOK, Andrew. b 62. ERMC. **d** 08 **p** 09. C Wirksworth *Derby* from 08. *57 Yokecliffe Drive, Wirksworth, Matlock DE4 4PF* Tel (01629) 820049
E-mail captainandrewtc@btinternet.com

TAYLOR-KENYON (née WATSON), Louise Margaret. b 61. Clare Coll Cam BA83 MA07 Homerton Coll Cam PGCE84 Leeds Univ MA07. NOC 04. **d** 07 **p** 08. C Skipton H Trin *Bradf* from 07; C Skipton Ch Ch w Carleton from 07. *10 Carleton Avenue, Skipton BD23 2TE* Tel 07703-538961 (mobile) E-mail toft@blueyonder.co.uk

TEAGUE, Gaythorne Derrick. b 24. MBE05. Bris Univ MB, ChB49 MRCGP53. **d** 74 **p** 75. NSM Bris St Andr Hartcliffe 74-86; Perm to Offic *B & W* from 86. *Innisfree, Bell Square, Blagdon, Bristol BS40 7UB* Tel (01761) 462671

TEAL, Andrew Robert. b 64. Birm Univ BA85 PhD06 Ox Brookes Univ PGCE05 Pemb Coll Ox MA08. Ripon Coll Cuddesdon 86. **d** 88 **p** 89. C Wednesbury St Paul Wood Green *Lich* 88-92; TV Sheff Manor 92-97; Asst Dioc Post Ord Tr Officer 93-98; Tutor Ripon Coll Cuddesdon 92-97; V Tickhill w Stainton *Sheff* 97-02; Warden of Readers 98-02; Hd of Th Plater Coll 02-03; Hd of Th and Past Studies 03-05; Lect Ripon Coll Cuddesdon from 05; Chapl Pemb Coll Ox from 05; Fell from 08; Lect Th Ox Univ from 07. *Pembroke College, Oxford OX1 1DW* Tel (01865) 286276 Fax 276418 E-mail andrew.teal@theology.ox.ac.uk

TEALE, Adrian. b 53. Univ of Wales (Abth) BA74 CertEd77 MA80 Univ of Wales (Cardiff) MTh89. Wycliffe Hall Ox 78. **d** 80 **p** 81. C Betws w Ammanford *St D* 80-84; V Brynaman w Cwmllynfell from 84; RD Dyffryn Aman 95-01. *Y Dalar Deg, 10 Bryn Road, Upper Brynamman, Ammanford SA18 1AU* Tel (01269) 822275

TEAR, Jeremy Charles. b 67. Westmr Coll Ox BA89 Birm Univ MA99 MCIPD94. Aston Tr Scheme 95 Qu Coll Birm 97. **d** 99 **p** 00. C Timperley *Ches* 99-03; V Macclesfield St Paul from 03. *St Paul's Vicarage, Swallow Close, Macclesfield SK10 1QN* Tel (01625) 422910 *or* 501773 E-mail revjtear@btinternet.com

TEARE, Mrs Marie. b 46. Open Univ BA81 RSCN67. NOC 95. **d** 98 **p** 99. C Brighouse and Clifton *Wakef* 98-01; V Waggoners *York* 01-08; RD Harthill 02-08, rtd 08, Perm to Offic *York* from 08. *Mayfield Bungalow, Easingwold Road, Huby, York YO61 1HN* Tel (01347) 811565
E-mail marie.teare@btinternet.com

TEARE, Canon Robert John Hugh. b 39. Bris Univ BSc62. Coll of Resurr Mirfield 67. **d** 70 **p** 71. C Fareham SS Pet and Paul *Portsm* 70-73; Chapl K Alfred Coll *Win* 73-78; V Pokesdown St Jas 78-82; R Winnall 82-06; RD Win 99-99; Hon Can Win Cathl 92-06; rtd 06; Chapl CSMV 06-09. *29 Elizabeth Drive, Wantage OX12 9YA* Tel (01235) 770966 *or* 763141
E-mail robertteare@googlemail.com

TEARNAN, John Herman Janson. b 37. Bris Univ BSc59. Kelham Th Coll 62. **d** 66 **p** 67. C Kettering SS Pet and Paul 66-71; Lic to Offic 71-85; Perm to Offic *St Alb* 82-85 and *Pet* 85-94; Chapl HM YOI Wellingborough 89-90; Chapl HM YOI Glen Parva 90-94; Guyana 94-03; rtd 03; Perm to Offic *Pet* from 05. *14 Rectory Walk, Barton Seagrave, Kettering NN15 6SP* Tel (01536) 510629

TEASDALE, Keith. b 56. Cranmer Hall Dur 86. **d** 88 **p** 89. C Crook *Dur* 88-92; V Dunston from 92; AD Gateshead W from 00. *St Nicholas' Vicarage, Willow Avenue, Dunston, Gateshead NE11 9UN* Tel 0191-460 0509 *or* fax and tel 460 9327 Mobile 07718-907660 E-mail stn@ukonline.co.uk

TEASDEL, David Charles. b 77. Coll of Resurr Mirfield 05. **d** 08 **p** 09. C Ouzel Valley *St Alb* from 08. *All Saints' House, 138 Brooklands Drive, Leighton Buzzard LU7 3PG* Tel (01525) 850204 E-mail fatherdavidteasdel@gmail.com

TEATHER, Andrew James. b 75. Leeds Univ BA09. Yorks Min Course 07. **d** 09. C Preston St Jo and St Geo *Blackb* from 09. *The*

Glebe House, 33 Bairstow Street, Preston PR1 3TN
E-mail andrewteather@fsmail.net

TEBBS, Richard Henry. b 52. Southn Univ BTh. Sarum & Wells Th Coll 75. **d** 78 **p** 79. C Cinderhill *S'well* 78-82; C Nor St Pet Mancroft w St Jo Maddermarket 82-85; TV Bridport *Sarum* 85-94; TR Yelverton, Meavy, Sheepstor and Walkhampton *Ex* 94-08; P-in-c Frankley *Birm* from 08. *The Rectory, Frankley Green, Birmingham B32 4AS* Tel 0121-475 3724
E-mail tebbsfamily@tiscali.co.uk

TEBBUTT, Christopher Michael. b 55. St Jo Coll Nottm BA94. **d** 96 **p** 97. C Catherington and Clanfield *Portsm* 96-00; P-in-c Southbroom *Sarum* 00-07; V from 07. *The Vicarage, 31 Fruitfields Close, Devizes SN10 5JY* Tel and fax (01380) 721441 *or* tel 723891 E-mail thetebbutts@southbroom.fslife.co.uk

TEBBUTT, Sandra Eileen. b 56. FBDO78. STETS 96. **d** 99 **p** 00. NSM Blendworth w Chalton w Idsworth *Portsm* 99-00; Chapl Wilts and Swindon Healthcare NHS Trust 00-05; Regional Manager Bible Soc from 05; NSM Southbroom *Sarum* from 04. *The Vicarage, 31 Fruitfields Close, Devizes SN10 5JY* Tel and fax (01380) 721441 *or* tel 723891
E-mail sandratebbutt@biblesociety.org.uk

TEBBUTT, Simon Albert. b 27. Westmr Coll Ox BTh04. Qu Coll Birm 88. **d** 89 **p** 90. NSM Northampton St Matt *Pet* 89-92; TV Duston Team 92-94; rtd 94; NSM Gt and Lt Houghton w Brafield on the Green *Pet* 94-96; NSM Cogenhoe and Gt and Lt Houghton w Brafield 96-97; Dioc Sec St Luke's Hosp for the Clergy from 00; Perm to Offic from 01. *9 St Martins Court, St Christophers, Abington Parc Crescent, Northampton NN3 3AD* Tel (01604) 628520 E-mail tebbutt@gotadsl.co.uk

TEBBY, Ms Janet Elizabeth. b 52. Lady Spencer Chu Coll of Educn CertEd73 Open Univ BA88. ERMC 05. **d** 08 **p** 09. NSM Wootton w Quinton and Preston Deanery *Pet* from 08. *1 New Cottages, Whiston, Northampton NN7 1NN* Tel (01604) 891989 E-mail jantebby@aol.com

TEDD, Christopher Jonathan Richard. *See* HOWITZ, Christopher Jonathan Richard

TEDMAN, Alfred. b 33. AKC59. **d** 60 **p** 61. C Newington St Mary *S'wark* 60-64; C Milton *Portsm* 64-68; V Bonchurch 68-98; RD E Wight 78-83; P-in-c Whitwell 79-82; P-in-c St Lawrence 82-84; V Wroxall 84-98; rtd 98. *Winfrith House, Blackgang Road, Niton, Ventnor PO38 2BW*

TEECE, David. b 54. MIET. **d** 06 **p** 07. OLM Normanton *Wakef* from 06. *61 Fairway, Normanton WF6 1SE* Tel (01924) 891326 Mobile 07757-263627 E-mail david.teece@hotmail.co.uk

TEED, John Michael. b 44. Middx Univ BA04. NTMTC 01. **d** 04 **p** 05. NSM Hanworth All SS *Lon* 04-07; NSM Staines from 07. *5 Island Close, Staines TW18 4YZ* Tel (01784) 458583 Mobile 07702-244078 E-mail johnteed@sky.com

TEGALLY, Narinder Jit Kaur. b 57. RGN93. SAOMC 99. **d** 02 **p** 03. NSM Welwyn Garden City *St Alb* 02-05; Asst Chapl R Free Hampstead NHS Trust 05-07; Sen Chapl Guy's and St Thos' NHS Foundn Trust from 07; Perm to Offic *St Alb* from 05. *Guy's and St Thomas' NHS Foundation Trust, St Thomas Street, London SE1 9RT* Tel (020) 7188 7188 E-mail narinder@grove-house.org.uk

TEGGARTY, Samuel James Karl. b 53. Dundee Univ BSc77. CITC 98. **d** 01 **p** 02. NSM Newry *D & D* 01-03; NSM Kilkeel from 03. *79 Knockchree Avenue, Kilkeel, Newry BT34 4BP* Tel (028) 4176 9076 E-mail karl@teggarty.fsnet.co.uk

TEGGIN, John. b 26. **d** 83 **p** 84. NSM Dublin Sandford w Milltown *D & G* 84-93; Dir Leprosy Miss 86-96. *Apartment 4, 69 Strand Road, Sandymount, Dublin 4, Republic of Ireland* Tel (00353) (1) 261 1792

TELFER, Andrew Julian. b 68. Essex Univ BA94. Wycliffe Hall Ox BTh97. **d** 97 **p** 98. C Skelmersdale St Paul *Liv* 97-01; C Ashton-in-Makerfield St Thos 01-03; V Whiston from 03. *The Vicarage, 90 Windy Arbor Road, Prescot L35 3SG* Tel 0151-426 6329

TELFER, Canon Frank Somerville. b 30. Trin Hall Cam BA53 MA58. Ely Th Coll 53. **d** 55 **p** 56. C Liv Our Lady and St Nic 55-58; Chapl Down Coll Cam 58-62; Bp's Chapl *Nor* 62-65; Chapl Kent Univ 65-73; Can Res Guildf Cathl 73-95; rtd 96; Perm to Offic *Nor* from 96. *Holbrook, Glandford, Holt NR25 7JP* Tel (01263) 740586

TELFORD, Alan. b 46. St Jo Coll Nottm. **d** 83 **p** 84. C Normanton *Derby* 83-86; TV N Wingfield, Pilsley and Tupton 86-90; TV N Wingfield, Clay Cross and Pilsley 90-92; P-in-c Oakwood 92-94; V Leic St Chris 94-05; P-in-c Leic St Theodore 05-09; rtd 09. *2 Springfield Cottage, Newmarket Lane, Clay Cross, Chesterfield S45 9AR* Tel (01246) 866988 Mobile 07854-937449 E-mail atelford@talktalk.net

TELFORD, Ms Carolin Judith. b 57. Victoria Univ Wellington BA78. SEITE 02. **d** 05 **p** 06. NSM Lee St Aug *S'wark* 05-07; Chapl St Cuth Coll Epsom New Zealand from 07. *St Cuthbert's College, PO Box 26020, Epsom, Auckland 1344, New Zealand*

TELFORD, Richard Francis. b 46. K Coll Lon 65. **d** 69 **p** 70. C Barkingside H Trin *Chelmsf* 69-72; C Wickford 72-77; P-in-c Romford St Jo 77-80; V 80-82; Perm to Offic 93-96; rtd 08. *Juglans, The Street, Wattisfield, Diss IP22 1NS* E-mail richard_telford@hotmail.com

TELLINI, Canon Gianfranco. b 36. Gregorian Univ Rome DTh65. Franciscan Sem Trent 57. **d** 61 **p** 61. In RC Ch 61-66; C Mill Hill Jo Keble Ch *Lon* 66; C Roxbourne St Andr 66-67; Lect Sarum Th Coll 67-69; Sen Tutor 69-74; Vice-Prin Edin Th Coll 74-82; Lect Th Edin Univ 74-95; R Pittenweem *St And* 82-85; R Elie and Earlsferry 82-85; R Dunblane 85-98; Can St Ninian's Cathl Perth from 90; rtd 99. *53 Buchan Drive, Dunblane FK15 9HW* Tel (01786) 823281 E-mail giantellini@mac.com

TEMBEY, David. b 51. **d** 96 **p** 97. NSM Whitehaven *Carl* 96-00; NSM Holme Cultram St Cuth 00-02; NSM Holme Cultram St Mary 00-02; NSM Bromfield w Waverton 00-02; TV Solway Plain from 02. *The Vicarage, Abbeytown, Wigton CA7 4SP* Tel (01697) 361246 Fax 361506 E-mail tembey6@aol.com

TEMPERLEY, Robert Noble. b 29. JP. St Jo Coll York CertEd50 ACP52 Dur Univ DAES62. NEOC 85. **d** 88 **p** 88. NSM Ryhope *Dur* 88-97; rtd 98; Perm to Offic *Dur* from 98. *18 Withernsea Grove, Ryhope, Sunderland SR2 0BU* Tel 0191-521 1813

TEMPLE, Mrs Sylvia Mary. b 48. Ex Univ BA70 Univ of Wales (Abth) PGCE71. St D Dioc Tr Course 93. **d** 94 **p** 97. NSM Tenby *St D* 94-99; C 99-00; V Martletwy w Lawrenny and Minwear etc 00-05. *Llwyn Onn, Trafalgar Road, Tenby SA70 7DW*

TEMPLE-WILLIAMS, Alexander. **d** 04 **p** 05. C Pontypool *Mon* from 04. *St Matthew's House, Victoria Road, Pontymoile, Pontypool NP44 5JU* Tel (01495) 752233

TEMPLEMAN (née WILLIAMS), Mrs Ann Joyce. b 50. St Hugh's Coll Ox BA72 MA75 PGCE73. Cranmer Hall Dur 03. **d** 05 **p** 06. NSM Peterlee Dur High Sch for Girls from 98; NSM Peterlee *Dur* from 05. *The Vicarage, Manor Way, Peterlee SR8 5QW* Tel 0191-586 2630 Mobile 07919-620259 E-mail ann@templeman99.freeserve.co.uk

TEMPLEMAN, Peter Morton. b 49. Ch Ch Ox BA71 MA75. Wycliffe Hall Ox MA75. **d** 76 **p** 77. C Cheltenham St Mary, St Matt, St Paul and H Trin *Glouc* 76-79; Chapl St Jo Coll Cam 79-84; P-in-c Finchley St Paul Long Lane 84-85; P-in-c Finchley St Luke 84-85; V Finchley St Paul and St Luke 85-99; V Peterlee *Dur* from 99. *The Vicarage, Manor Way, Peterlee SR8 5QW* Tel 0191-586 2630

TEMPLETON, Iain McAllister. b 57. St Andr Coll Drygrange 80. **d** 85 **p** 86. In RC Ch 85-92; NSM Dornoch *Mor* 95; P-in-c Kirriemuir *St And* 95-99; R Eccleston *Blackb* 99-09; V Walsall St Andr *Lich* from 09. *St Andrew's Vicarage, 119 Hollyhedge Lane, Walsall WS2 8PZ* Tel (01922) 722565 E-mail fatheriain@aol.com *or* fatheriain@priest.com

TEN WOLDE, Christine Caroline. b 57. **d** 99 **p** 00. NSM Llanegryn w Aberdyfi w Tywyn *Ban* from 99. *Aber-groes, Abertafol, Aberdovey LL35 0RE* Tel (01654) 767047 Fax 767572 Mobile 07977-108438 E-mail curate@stpeterschurch.org.uk

TENNANT, Cyril Edwin George. b 37. Keble Coll Ox BA59 MA63 Lon Univ BD61 Ex Univ MA03. Clifton Th Coll 59. **d** 62 **p** 63. C Stapleford *S'well* 62-65; C Felixstowe SS Pet and Paul *St E* 65-69; V Gipsy Hill Ch Ch *S'wark* 69-84; V Lee St Mildred 84-90; P-in-c Lundy Is *Ex* 90-92; V Ilfracombe SS Phil and Jas w W Down 90-01; rtd 01; Perm to Offic *Ex* 01-06. *27 Harvest Way, Witney OX28 1BX* Tel (01993) 778977 E-mail candc.tennant@virgin.net

TER BLANCHE, Harold Daniel. b 35. St Paul's Coll Grahamstown LTh85. **d** 63 **p** 64. C Pietermaritzburg St Pet S Africa 63-65; C Durban St Thos 65-72; R Gingindlovu 73-78; Dioc Missr Zululand 78-82; Chapl Miss to Seamen 82-84; Chapl Grimsby Distr Gen Hosp 84-94; Chapl NE Lincs NHS Trust 94-00; rtd 00; Perm to Offic *Linc* from 00. *25 Collingwood Crescent, Grimsby DN34 5RG* Tel (01472) 276624 E-mail harold.terblanche@virgin.net

TER HAAR, Roger Edward Lound. b 52. QC92. Magd Coll Ox BA73. **d** 06 **p** 07. OLM Bramley and Grafham *Guildf* from 06. *Howicks, Hurlands Lane, Dunsfold, Godalming GU8 4NT* Tel (020) 7797 8100 E-mail terhaar@crownofficechambers.com

TERESA, Sister. *See* WHITE, Sister Teresa Joan

✠TEROM, The Rt Revd Zechariah James. b 41. St Columba's Coll Hazaribagh BA Ranchi Univ MA66. Bp's Coll Calcutta BD71. **d** 71 **c** 86. C Hazaribagh India 71-73; Par P Manoharpur 73-76; Bp Chotanagpur 86-09; Moderator Ch of N India 01-09; rtd 09. *Address temp unknown*

TERRANOVA, Jonathan Rossano (Ross). b 62. Sheff Poly BA85. Oak Hill Th Coll BA88. **d** 88 **p** 89. C Carl St Jo 88-91; C Stoughton *Guildf* 91-94; R Ditton *Roch* from 94; RD Malling 02-07. *The Rectory, 2 The Stream, Ditton, Maidstone ME20 6AG* Tel (01732) 842027

TERRELL, Richard Charles Patridge. b 43. Wells Th Coll 69. **d** 71 **p** 72. C Shepton Mallet *B & W* 71-76; P-in-c Drayton 76-78; P-in-c Muchelney 76-78; TV Langport Area 78-82; P-in-c Tatworth 82-89; V 89-96; R W Coker w Hardington Mandeville, E Chinnock etc 96-09; rtd 09. *2 Hamdon View, Norton sub Hamdon, Stoke-sub-Hamdon TA14 6SE* Tel (01935) 881330

TERRETT, Mervyn Douglas. b 43. AKC65. **d** 66 **p** 67. C Pet St Mary Boongate 66-69; C Sawbridgeworth *St Alb* 69-74; V Stevenage H Trin 74-85; Perm to Offic from 86; rtd 08. *Red*

Roofs, 20 Woodfield Road, Stevenage SG1 4BP   Tel (01438) 720152 E-mail a-top@tiscali.co.uk

TERRY, Christopher Laurence. b 51. FCA80. St Alb Minl Tr Scheme. **d** 83 **p** 84. Hon C Dunstable St Alb 83-89; C Abbots Langley 89-92; TV Chambersbury 92-99; Chapl Abbot's Hill Sch Herts 96-99; R Southwick St Mich Chich 99-03; RD Hove 00-03; Finance and Admin Sec Min Division Abps' Coun from 04; Perm to Offic St Alb from 04. Ministry Division, Church House, Great Smith Street, London SW1P 3AZ   Tel (020) 7898 1393 or (01525) 633529 E-mail chris.terry@c-of-e.org.uk or tecrry@aol.com

TERRY, Colin Alfred. b 49. Trin Coll Bris. **d** 00 **p** 01. C Bexleyheath Ch Ch Roch 00-03; V Belvedere All SS from 03. All Saints' Vicarage, Nuxley Road, Belvedere DA17 5JE   Tel (01322) 432169 E-mail colin.terry@diocese-rochester.org

TERRY, Ms Helen Barbara. b 58. Keele Univ BA80 ATCL98. Ripon Coll Cuddesdon 01. **d** 03 **p** 04. C Cainscross w Selsley Glouc 03-07; C Minchinhampton 07-08. 48 Cashes Green Road, Stroud GL5 4LN   Tel (01453) 752792

TERRY, Ian Andrew. b 53. St Jo Coll Dur BA74 St Jo Coll York PGCE75 St Mary's Coll Twickenham MA99 Surrey Univ PhD05. Coll of Resurr Mirfield 78. **d** 80 **p** 81. C Beaconsfield Ox 80-83; C N Lynn w St Marg and St Nic Nor 83-84; Chapl and Hd RE Eliz Coll Guernsey 84-89; Chapl St Jo Sch Leatherhead 89-92; R Bisley and W End Guildf 92-02; Asst Chapl HM Pris Coldingley 99-02; Dioc Dir of Educn Heref 02-08; Hon TV W Heref 03-08; Chapl St Edm Sch Cant 08-09; TR Bournemouth Town Cen Win from 09. St Peter's Rectory, 18 Wimborne Road, Bournemouth BH2 6NT   Tel and fax (01202) 554058 E-mail ianterry@live.co.uk

TERRY, James Richard. b 74. Linc Coll Ox BA95 ACA98. Oak Hill Th Coll BA03. **d** 03 **p** 04. C Harold Wood Chelmsf 03-07; C Blackb Ch Ch w St Matt from 07. 5 Faroes Close, Blackburn BB2 3EL   Tel (01254) 670480 E-mail james_terry1@hotmail.com

TERRY, John Arthur. b 32. S'wark Ord Course. **d** 66 **p** 67. C Plumstead All SS S'wark 66-69; C Peckham St Mary Magd 69-72; V Streatham Vale H Redeemer 72-80; R Sternfield w Benhall and Snape St E 80-84; V Stevenage St Mary Shephall St Alb 84-86; V Stevenage St Mary Shephall w Aston 86-90; V Cople w Willington 90-97; Chapl Shuttleworth Agric Coll 90-97; rtd 97; Perm to Offic St E from 98; Nor 98-04; Ely from 03. 2 Kestrel Drive, Brandon IP27 0UA   Tel (01842) 812055

TERRY, John Michael. b 56. Ex Univ BSc78 Southn Univ MSc88 Anglia Ruskin Univ BA09 CEng93 MIMarEST93. Ridley Hall Cam 06. **d** 09. NSM Fareham St Jo Portsm from 09. 112 Abbeyfield Drive, Fareham PO15 5PQ   Tel (01329) 845193 Mobile 07979-815026 E-mail mike@terry-home.co.uk

TERRY, Justyn Charles. b 65. Keble Coll Ox BA86 St Jo Coll Dur BA95 K Coll Lon PhD03. Cranmer Hall Dur 92. **d** 95 **p** 96. C Paddington St Jo w St Mich Lon 95-99; V Kensington St Helen w H Trin 99-05; Assoc Prof Trin Episc Sch for Min USA 05-08; Dean and Pres from 08. Trinity Episcopal School for Min, 311 Eleventh Street, Ambridge PA 15003-2302, USA   Tel (001) (800) 874 8754 E-mail jterry@tesm.edu

TERRY, Lydia Patricia Maud. b 44. Open Univ BSc00. **d** 08 **p** 09. OLM Lydd Cant from 08. 5 Eastern Road, Lydd, Romney Marsh TN29 9EE   Tel (01797) 320218

TERRY (née LEONARD), Mrs Nicola Susan. b 61. Keele Univ BA85. Ridley Hall Cam 07. **d** 09. NSM Alverstoke Portsm from 09. 112 Abbeyfield Drive, Fareham PO15 5PQ   Tel (01329) 845193 E-mail revnsterry@googlemail.com

TERRY, Stephen John. b 49. K Coll Lon BD72 AKC74. **d** 75 **p** 76. C Tokyngton St Mich Lon 75-78; C Hampstead St Steph w All Hallows 78-81; V Whetstone St Jo 81-89; TR Aldrington Chich 89-07; R from 07. The Rectory, 77 New Church Road, Hove BN3 4BB   Tel (01273) 737915 Fax 206348 E-mail stephenterry@aldrington.wanadoo.co.uk

TESTA, Luigi Richard Frederick. b 30. EMMTC. **d** 85 **p** 86. NSM Castle Donington and Lockington cum Hemington Leic 85-95; Perm to Offic from 95. 50 Huntingdon Drive, Castle Donington, Derby DE74 2SR   Tel (01332) 814671

TESTER, Clarence Albert. b 20. Qu Coll Birm 47. **d** 50 **p** 51. C Southmead Bris 50-53; C Knowle St Barn 53-55; Chapl Ham Green Hosp Bris 55-70; V Halberton Ex 70-85; rtd 85; Perm to Offic B & W 86-98. Elmside, Elmside Walk, Hitchin SG5 1HB

TETLEY, Brian. b 38. St Jo Coll Dur BA82 ACA62 FCA72. Cranmer Hall Dur 80. **d** 83 **p** 84. C Chipping Sodbury and Old Sodbury Glouc 83-86; Chapl and Succ Roch Cath 86-89; R Gravesend H Family w Ifield 89-93; Tutor Westcott Ho Cam 93-94 and 95-96; Tutor Ridley Hall and Prec Ely Cathl 95; C Duxford, Hinxton and Ickleton 97; Perm to Offic 98-99; NSM Worc Cathl 00-03; rtd 03; Perm to Offic Worc 03-08 and Ox from 08. 23 Cripley Road, Oxford OX2 0AH   Tel (01865) 250209

TETLEY, Miss Carol Ruth. b 61. Ches Coll of HE BA84. NEOC 06. **d** 09. NSM Anlaby St Pet York from 09. 27 Cranberry Way, Hull HU4 7AQ   Tel (01482) 351644 E-mail carol_betley@lineone.net

TETLEY, The Ven Joy Dawn. b 46. St Mary's Coll Dur BA68 Leeds Univ CertEd69 St Hugh's Coll Ox BA75 MA80 Dur Univ PhD88. NW Ord Course 77. **dss** 77 **d** 87 **p** 94. Bentley Sheff 77-79; Buttershaw St Aid Bradf 79-80; Dur Cathl 80-83; Lect Trin Coll Bris 83-86; Chipping Sodbury and Old Sodbury Glouc 83-86; Dn Roch Cathl 87-89; Hon Can 90-93; Assoc Dir of Post Ord Tr 87-88; Dir Post Ord Tr 88-93; Hon Par Dn Gravesend H Family w Ifield 89-93; Prin EAMTC Ely 93-99; Adn Worc and Can Res Worc Cathl 99-08; rtd 08; Perm to Offic Ox from 08. 23 Cripley Road, Oxford OX2 0AH   Tel (01865) 250209

TETLEY, Matthew David. b 61. Bucks Coll of Educn BSc83. Sarum & Wells Th Coll BTh89. **d** 87 **p** 88. C Kirkby Liv 87-90; C Hindley St Pet 90-93; TV Whorlton Newc 93-96; V Newbiggin Hall 96-01; P-in-c Longhorsley and Hebron 01-06; Chapl HM Pris Acklington 01-06 and from 08; Chapl HM Pris Frankland 06-08. HM Prison Acklington, Morpeth NE65 9XF   Tel (01670) 762300 E-mail matthew.tetley@hmps.gsi.gov.uk

TETLOW, John. b 46. St Steph Ho Ox 73. **d** 76 **p** 77. C Stanwell Lon 76-77; C Hanworth All SS 77-80; C Somers Town 80-83; TV Wickford and Runwell Chelmsf 83-90; P-in-c Walthamstow St Mich 90-96. 6A Bushwood, London E11 3AY   Tel (020) 8989 9076 E-mail johntetlow@tiscali.co.uk

TETLOW, Richard Jeremy. b 42. Trin Coll Cam MA66 Goldsmiths' Coll Lon CQSW74. Qu Coll Birm 81. **d** 83 **p** 84. C Birm St Martin 83-85; C Birm St Martin w Bordesley St Andr 85-88; V Birm St Jo Ladywood 89-01; V Ladywood St Jo and St Pet 01-08; rtd 08; Perm to Offic Birm from 08. 26 Sovereign Way, Moseley, Birmingham B13 8AT   Tel 0121-449 4892

TETZLAFF, Silke. b 67. Friedrich Schiller Univ 87 K Coll Lon BA97 AKC97 Anglia Poly Univ MA01. Westcott Ho Cam 99. **d** 01 **p** 02. C Leagrave St Alb 01-05; TV Baldock w Bygrave and Weston from 05. The Vicarage, 14 Munts Meadow, Weston, Hitchin SG4 7AE   Tel (01462) 790330 E-mail silke.tetzlaff@ntlworld.com

TEVERSON, Ms Nicola Jane. b 65. SEITE. **d** 05 **p** 06. C Bromley St Mark Roch 05-09; Perm to Offic from 09. The Farm House, Blackness Lane, Keston BR2 6HR   Tel (01689) 851174 E-mail nicky.teverson@btinternet.com

TEWKESBURY, Suffragan Bishop of. See WENT, The Rt Revd John Stewart

THACKER, Christine Mary. b 44. Simon Fraser Univ BC BA90. Vancouver Sch of Th MDiv93. **d** 92 **p** 93. R Kitimat Ch Ch Canada 93-00; C Boultham Linc from 00. 13 Earls Drive, Lincoln LN6 7TY   Tel (01522) 805183 E-mail christine.thacker1@ntlworld.com

THACKER, Ian David. b 59. Oak Hill Th Coll BA91. **d** 91 **p** 92. C Illogan Truro 91-94; C Eglwysilan Llan 94-96; TV Hornsey Rise Whitehall Park Team Lon 96-97; TV Upper Holloway 97-01; Chapl HM YOI Huntercombe and Finnamore from 01. HM Young Offender Institution, Huntercombe Place, Nuffield, Henley-on-Thames RG9 5SB   Tel (01491) 641711 or 641715 Fax 641902 E-mail ithacker@talk21.com

THACKER, Jonathan William. b 53. Lon Univ BA74. Linc Th Coll 76. **d** 79 **p** 80. C Bromyard Heref 79-82; C Penkridge w Stretton Lich 82-87; V Brothertoft Gp Linc 87-96; RD Holland W 92-95, P-in-c Crosby 96-01, V from 01; Chapl Scunthorpe and Goole Hosps NHS Trust 99-01; Chapl N Lincs and Goole Hosps NHS Trust 01. St George's Vicarage, 87 Ferry Road, Scunthorpe DN15 8LY   Tel and fax (01724) 843328 or tel 843336 E-mail johan195.freeserve.co.uk

THACKER, Roger Ailwyn Mackintosh. b 46. CCC Cam BA68 MA73. Westcott Ho Cam 68. **d** 70 **p** 71. C St John's Wood Lon 70-74; P-in-c Hammersmith St Paul 74-79; TV 79-99; rtd 00; Perm to Offic St Alb from 01. 24A Petersham Mews, London SW7 5NR

THACKRAY, John Adrian. b 55. Southn Univ BSc76 ACIB84. Coll of Resurr Mirfield 81. **d** 84 **p** 85. C Loughton St Jo Chelmsf 84-87; Chapl Bancroft's Sch Woodford Green 87-92; Sen Chapl K Sch Cant 92-01; Chapl Abp's Sch Cant 01-02; Hon Min Can Cant Cathl from 93; Sen Chapl K Sch Roch from 02; Hon PV Roch Cathl from 02. King's School, Satis House, Boley Hill, Rochester ME1 1TE   Tel (01634) 888555 E-mail thereverendfather@hotmail.com

THACKRAY, William Harry. b 44. Leeds Univ CertEd66. Chich Th Coll 70. **d** 73 **p** 74. C Sheff St Cuth 73-76; C Stocksbridge 76-78; P-in-c Newark St Leon S'well 79-80; TV Newark w Hawton, Cotham and Shelton 80-82; V Choral S'well Minster 82-85; V Bawtry w Austerfield 85; P-in-c Misson 85; V Bawtry w Austerfield and Misson 86-93; RD Bawtry 90-93; P-in-c Balderton 93-03; P-in-c Coddington w Barnby in the Willows 98-03; V Biggleswade St Alb 03-09; RD Biggleswade 07-09; rtd 09; Hon C Lower Swale Ripon from 09. The Vicarage, 11 Meadow Drive, Scruton, Northallerton DL7 0QW   Tel (01609) 748245 E-mail vicar@the-thackrays.eclipse.co.uk

THAKE (née SEARS), Ms Helen. b 50. Birm Coll of Educn CertEd71. Qu Coll Birm 96. **d** 98 **p** 99. C Hadley Lich 98-01; C Cannock 01-06; Chapl HM Pris Swinfen Hall 06-07; Chapl HM

Pris Foston Hall from 07. *HM Prison Foston Hall, Foston, Derby DE65 5EN* Tel (01283) 584300

THAKE, Preb Terence. b 41. ALCD65. **d** 66 **p** 67. C Gt Faringdon w Lt Coxwell *Ox* 66-70; C Aldridge *Lich* 70-73; V Werrington 73-82; Chapl HM Det Cen Werrington Ho 73-82; TR Chell *Lich* 82-94; Chapl Westcliffe Hosp 82-94; RD Stoke N 91-94; V Colwich w Gt Haywood 94-00; P-in-c Colton 95-00; R Colton, Colwich and Gt Haywood 00-04; RD Rugeley 98-06; Preb Lich Cathl from 94; rtd 04. *4 St Catherine's Road, Lichfield WS13 7RD* Tel (01543) 264614 E-mail tthake@tiscali.co.uk

THAME, Miss Margaret Eve. b 31. SRN54 SCM55. Glouc Sch of Min 85. **d** 88 **p** 94. NSM Pittville All SS *Glouc* 88-94; NSM Cheltenham St Mich 94-02; Perm to Offic from 02. *13 Brighton Road, Cheltenham GL52 6BA* Tel (01242) 241228

THATCHER, Barbara Mary. b 25. Lon Univ BCom. **d** 90 **p** 94. NSM Helensburgh *Glas* 90-01. *228 West Princes Street, Helensburgh G84 8HA* Tel (01436) 672003

THATCHER, Stephen Bert. b 58. Greenwich Univ PGCE03. St Jo Coll Nottm LTh87 ALCD87. **d** 87 **p** 88. C Bargoed and Deri w Brithdir *Llan* 87-89; C Llanishen and Lisvane 89-91; V Llanwnda, Goodwick w Manorowen and Llanstinan *St D* 91-95; P-in-c Coberley, Cowley, Colesbourne and Elkstone *Glouc* 95-96; Dioc Rural Adv 95-96; R New Radnor and Llanfihangel Nantmelan etc *S & B* 96-00; Dioc Tourism Officer 96-99; Dioc Chs and Tourism Rep 97-00; CF from 00. *c/o MOD Chaplains (Army)* Tel (01980) 615804 Fax 615800 E-mail stephen.thatcher2@btopenworld.com

THAWLEY, The Very Revd David Laurie. b 24. St Edm Hall Ox BA47 MA49. Cuddesdon Coll 49. **d** 51 **p** 52. C Bitterne Park *Win* 51-56; C-in-c Andover St Mich CD 56-60; Australia from 60; Can Res Brisbane 64-72; Dean Wangaratta 72-89; rtd 89. *Lavender Cottage, 2 Bond Street, North Caulfield Vic 3161, Australia* Tel (0061) (3) 9571 0513 Mobile 407-811870 E-mail dthawley@bigpond.com

THAYER, Michael David. b 52. Sarum & Wells Th Coll 77. **d** 80 **p** 81. C Minehead *B & W* 80-85; Chapl RN 85-89; TV Lowestoft and Kirkley *Nor* 89-92; Chapl St Helena Hospice Colchester 92-97; Chapl HM Pris Acklington 99-01; Chapl HM Pris Erlestoke 01-03; R S Tawton and Belstone *Ex* 03-07; P-in-c Highweek from 07. *The Rectory, 15 Stoneleigh Close, Newton Abbot TQ12 1PX* Tel (01626) 201436 E-mail michael.thayer@btopenworld.com

THEAKER, David Michael. b 41. **d** 68 **p** 69. C Folkingham w Laughton *Linc* 68-71; C New Cleethorpes 71-74; P-in-c Gt Grimsby St Andr and St Luke 74-77; P-in-c Thurlby 77-79; Perm to Offic *Ely* from 00. *11 Willow Way, Hauxton, Cambridge CB22 5JB* Tel (01223) 873132 E-mail the-theakers@issue-forth.com

THEAKER, John Henry. b 42. MBE01. WEMTC 05. **d** 08. NSM Leominster *Heref* from 08. *Monkland House, Monkland, Leominster HR6 9DE* Tel (01568) 720472 Mobile 07796-595664 E-mail theaker958@btinternet.com

THEAKSTON, Ms Sally Margaret. b 62. UEA BSc84 Ox Univ BA89 K Coll Lon MA94. Ripon Coll Cuddesdon 86. **d** 89 **p** 94. Par Dn Hackney *Lon* 89-93; Par Dn Putney St Mary *S'wark* 93-94; C 94-96; Chapl RN 96-02; TR Gaywood *Nor* 02-09; TR Dereham and Distr from 09. *The Rectory, Vicarage Meadows, Dereham NR19 1TW* Tel (01362) 693680 Mobile 07904-070654 E-mail stheakston@aol.com

THELWELL, The Ven John Berry. b 49. Univ of Wales (Ban) BD72. Qu Coll Birm 73. **d** 73 **p** 74. C Minera *St As* 73-80; Dioc Youth Chapl 78-86; V Gwernaffield and Llanferres 80-93; Chapl Clwyd Fire Service 88-94; RD Mold 91-95; TR Hawarden 93-02; Can Cursal St As Cathl 95-02; Prec 98-02; Adn Montgomery from 02; V Berriew from 03. *The Vicarage, Berriew, Welshpool SY21 8PL* Tel and fax (01686) 640223

THEOBALD, Graham Fitzroy. b 43. ALCD67. **d** 67 **p** 68. C Crookham *Guildf* 67-71; C York Town St Mich 71-74; V Wrecclesham 74-83; Chapl Green Lane Hosp 74-81; R Frimley 83-85; Chapl Frimley Park Hosp 83-85; Perm to Offic *Ox* 90-92; C Easthampstead 92-97; Chapl E Berks NHS Trust 92-03; rtd 03; Perm to Offic *Ox* from 03. *50 Viking, Bracknell RG12 8UL* Tel (01344) 823279 Mobile 07721-408740

THEOBALD, Henry Charles. b 32. S'wark Ord Course 60. **d** 63 **p** 64. C Battersea St Phil *S'wark* 63-65; C Caterham 65-68; C Reigate St Luke S Park 68-73; Chapl S Lon Hosp for Women & St Jas Hosp Balham 73-83; Chapl St Mary's Hosp Preston 83-95; rtd 93; Perm to Offic *Portsm* from 93; Chapl SSB 93-02. *141 Warren Avenue, Southsea PO4 8PP* Tel (023) 9281 7443

THEOBALD, John Walter. b 33. St Aid Birkenhead 62. **d** 65 **p** 66. C Hindley All SS *Liv* 65-68; C Beverley Minster *York* 68-71; R Loftus 71-86; P-in-c Carlin How w Skinningrove 73-86; Dep Chapl HM Pris Leeds 86-89; Chapl HM Pris Rudgate 89-93; Thorp Arch 89-93; Leeds 93-97; V Leeds St Cypr Harehills *Ripon* 97-01; rtd 01; Perm to Offic *Ripon* 01-05. *8 Inverness Road, Garforth, Leeds LS25 2LS*

THEODOSIUS, Hugh John. b 32. Trin Coll Cam BA56 MA60. Cuddesdon Coll 56. **d** 58 **p** 59. C Milton *Win* 58-62; C Romsey

62-64; C Southampton Maybush St Pet 64-70; V Malden St Jo *S'wark* 70-81; V Billingborough *Linc* 81-94; V Horbling 81-94; V Sempringham w Pointon and Birthorpe 81-94; RD Aveland and Ness w Stamford 87-93; rtd 97; Perm to Offic *Linc* from 00 and *Ely* from 01. *Sempringham House, East Bank, Sutton Bridge, Spalding PE12 9YN* Tel (01406) 351977

THEODOSIUS, James William Fletcher. b 73. Univ of Wales (Cardiff) BA94 Selw Coll Cam BA04 MA08 Cant Ch Ch Univ Coll PGCE96 Sussex Univ DPhil09. Westcott Ho Cam 02. **d** 05 **p** 06. C Chich St Paul and Westhampnett 05-09; Chapl Ex Univ from 09; Dir Reader Tr SWMTC from 09. *The Chaplaincy, University of Exeter, St Luke's Campus, Heavitree Road, Exeter EX1 2LU* E-mail j.w.f.theodosius@ex.ac.uk

THEODOSIUS, Richard Francis. b 35. Fitzw Coll Cam BA59. Lich Th Coll 69. **d** 71 **p** 72. C Bloxwich *Lich* 71-73; Chapl Blue Coat Comp Sch Walsall 71-73; Chapl Ranby Ho Sch Retford 73-96; P-in-c Norton Cuckney *S'well* 96-02; rtd 02. *Downlea, 51 Town Street, Lound, Retford DN22 8RT* Tel (01777) 818744

THETFORD, Suffragan Bishop of. *See* WINTON, The Rt Revd Alan Peter

THEWLIS, Andrew James. b 64. Man Univ BSc86. Cranmer Hall Dur 87. **d** 90 **p** 91. C Walshaw Ch Ch *Man* 90-95; P-in-c Jersey St Jo *Win* 95-98; R from 98. *The Rectory, La rue des Landes, St John, Jersey JE3 4AF* Tel (01534) 861677 Mobile 07797-723828 E-mail athewlis@jerseymail.co.uk

THEWLIS, Brian Jacob. b 24. Melbourne Univ BA49. Coll of Resurr Mirfield 52. **d** 53 **p** 54. C Wednesbury St Jas *Lich* 53-57; Chapl K Coll Auckland New Zealand 57-61; C Sidley *Chich* 59-60; Australia from 61; I Reservoir St Geo 61-68; I Malvern St Paul 68-82; I Beaumaris St Mich 82-87; I Frankston St Paul 87-94; rtd 94. *41 Sixth Street, Parkdale Vic 3194, Australia* Tel (0061) (3) 9587 3095

THEWLIS, John Charles. b 49. Van Mildert Coll Dur BA70 PhD75. NOC 78. **d** 81 **p** 82. NSM Hull St Mary Sculcoates *York* 81-83; C Spring Park *Cant* 83-84; C Spring Park All SS *S'wark* 85-86; V Eltham Park St Luke 86-01; R Carshalton from 01. *The Rectory, 2 Talbot Road, Carshalton SM5 3BS* Tel (020) 8647 2366 E-mail rector@jctclerk.demon.co.uk

THEWSEY, Robert Sydney. b 65. Ripon Coll Cuddesdon 99. **d** 01 **p** 02. C Chorlton-cum-Hardy St Clem *Man* 01-04; P-in-c Stretford All SS 04-08; P-in-c Boscastle w Davidstow *Truro* from 08. *The Rectory, Forrabury, Boscastle PL35 0DJ* Tel (01840) 250359 E-mail robert.thewsey@btinternet.com

THICKE, James Balliston. b 43. Sarum & Wells Th Coll 74. **d** 77 **p** 78. C Wareham *Sarum* 77-80; TV 80-83; Dioc Youth Adv *Dur* 83-87; C Portishead *B & W* 87-90; V Westfield 90-08; RD Midsomer Norton 98-04; Chapl Norton Radstock Coll of FE 00-08; rtd 08. *11 Welton Grove, Midsomer Norton, Radstock BA3 2TS* Tel (01761) 411905 E-mail james@balliston.demon.co.uk

✠**THIRD, The Rt Revd Richard Henry McPhail.** b 27. Em Coll Cam BA50 MA55 Kent Univ Hon DCL90. Linc Th Coll 50. **d** 52 **p** 53 **c** 76. C Mottingham St Andr *S'wark* 52-55; C Sanderstead All SS 55-59; V Sheerness H Trin w St Paul *Cant* 59-67; V Orpington All SS *Roch* 67-76; RD Orpington 73-76; Hon Can Roch Cathl 74-76; Suff Bp Maidstone *Cant* 76-80; Suff Bp Dover 80-92; rtd 92; Hon Asst Bp B & W from 92. *25 Church Close, Martock TA12 6DS* Tel (01935) 825519

THIRLWELL, Miss Margaret. b 36. Bris Univ BA59 St Aid Coll Dur DipEd61. **d** 03 **p** 04. OLM Binfield *Ox* 03-09; Perm to Offic from 09. *70 Red Rose, Binfield, Bracknell RG42 5LD* Tel (01344) 423920 E-mail margaret@mthirlwell.fsnet.co.uk

THIRTLE, Ms Lucy Rachel. b 62. Ex Univ BA85. Cranmer Hall Dur 97. **d** 99 **p** 00. C Basingstoke *Win* 99-04; P-in-c Kingsclere 04-06; P-in-c Ashford Hill w Headley 06; V Kingsclere and Ashford Hill w Headley from 06. *The Vicarage, Fox's Lane, Kingsclere, Newbury RG20 5SL* Tel (01635) 299489 E-mail lucythirtle@btinternet.com

THISELTON, Prof Anthony Charles. b 37. Lon Univ BD59 K Coll Lon MTh64 Sheff Univ PhD77 Dur Univ DD93 Lambeth DD02. Oak Hill Th Coll 58. **d** 60 **p** 61. C Sydenham H Trin *S'wark* 60-63; Tutor Tyndale Hall Bris 63-67; Sen Tutor 67-70; Lect Bibl Studies Sheff Univ 70-79; Sen Lect 79-85; Prof Calvin Coll Grand Rapids 82-83; Special Lect Th Nottm Univ 86-88; Prin St Jo Coll Nottm 86-88; Prin St Jo Coll w Cranmer Hall Dur 88-92; Prof Chr Th Nottm Univ from 92; Can Th Leic Cathl from 94 and S'well Minster from 00. *Department of Theology, Nottingham University, University Park, Nottingham NG7 2RD* Tel 0115-951 5852 Fax 951 5887 E-mail thiselton@ntlworld.com

THISTLETHWAITE, Canon Nicholas John. b 51. Selw Coll Cam BA73 MA77 PhD80. Ripon Coll Cuddesdon BA78 MA83. **d** 79 **p** 80. C Newc St Gabr 79-82; Chapl G&C Coll Cam 82-90; Lic to Offic *Ely* 82-90; V Trumpington 90-99; Can Res and Prec Guildf Cathl from 99; Sub-Dean from 06. *3 Cathedral Close, Guildford GU2 7TL* Tel and fax (01483) 569682 *or* tel 565287 E-mail precentor@guildford-cathedral.org

THISTLEWOOD, Michael John. b 31. Ch Coll Cam BA53

MA57. Linc Th Coll 54. **d** 56 **p** 57. C N Hull St Mich *York* 56-59; C Scarborough St Mary 59-61; V Kingston upon Hull St Jude w St Steph 61-67; V Newland St Aug 67-72; Asst Master Bemrose Sch Derby 72-80; V Derby St Andr w St Osmund 80-82; Lic to Offic *Ox* 84-95; rtd 88; Perm to Offic *Carl* 88-98 and *Derby* 98-05. *Fosbrooke House, 8 Clifton Drive, Lytham St Annes FY8 5RQ*

THODAY, Margaret Frances. b 38. **d** 03 **p** 04. OLM Roughton and Felbrigg, Metton, Sustead etc *Nor* 03-08; Perm to Offic from 08. *Flat 3, 4 Norwich Road, Cromer NR27 0AX* Tel (01263) 510945

THODY, Charles Michael Jackson. b 62. Linc Th Coll BTh94. **d** 94 **p** 95. C Immingham *Linc* 94-97; P-in-c Leasingham and Cranwell 97-01; P-in-c Bishop Norton, Wadingham and Snitterby 01-03; Chapl Doncaster and S Humber Healthcare NHS Trust 01-03; Chapl Notts Healthcare NHS Trust from 03. *Rampton Hospital, Retford DN22 0PD* Tel (01777) 247524 E-mail charles.thody@nottshc.nhs.uk

THOM, Alastair George. b 60. G&C Coll Cam BA81 MA84 ACA86. Ridley Hall Cam 88. **d** 91 **p** 92. C Lindfield *Chich* 91-94; C Finchley St Paul and St Luke *Lon* 94-98; P-in-c Paddington Em Harrow Road from 98; P-in-c W Kilburn St Luke w St Simon and St Jude from 98; AD Westmr Paddington from 06. *The Vicarage, 19 Macroom Road, London W9 3HY* Tel (020) 8962 0294 E-mail alastairthom@yahoo.co.uk

THOM, Christopher Henry. **d** 03 **p** 04. NSM Loose *Cant* from 03. *Old Hill House, Old Loose Hill, Loose, Maidstone ME15 0BN* Tel (01622) 744833 E-mail chthom@ukonline.co.uk

THOM, James. b 31. St Chad's Coll Dur BA53. **d** 57 **p** 58. C Middlesbrough St Thos *York* 57-60; C Hornsea and Goxhill 60-62; C S Bank 62-63; V Copmanthorpe 63-75; V Coxwold 75-77; RD Easingwold 77-82; V Coxwold and Husthwaite 77-87; Abp's Adv for Spiritual Direction 86-93; P-in-c Topcliffe 87-93; rtd 93; Perm to Offic *Ripon* and *York* from 93. *34 Hell Wath Grove, Ripon HG4 2JT* Tel (01765) 605083

THOMAS, Adrian Leighton. b 37. Univ of Wales (Lamp) BA62 Univ of Wales (Cardiff) PGCE73. St D Coll Lamp. **d** 63 **p** 64. C Port Talbot St Theodore *Llan* 63-70; V Troedrhiwgarth 70-73; C Sandhurst *Ox* 73-77; V Streatley 77-84; P-in-c Moulsford 81-84; V Streatley w Moulsford 84-90; P-in-c Sutton Courtenay w Appleford 90-00; V 00-02; AD Abingdon 96-02; rtd 02; P-in-c Lugano *Eur* 02-06. *13 The Birches, Goring, Reading RG8 9BW* Tel (01491) 872696 E-mail adrianleighton.thomas@virgin.net

THOMAS, Alan. See THOMAS, Thomas Alan

THOMAS, Aled Huw. b 59. Univ of Wales (Abth) BD81. St Mich Coll Llan 84. **d** 85 **p** 86. C Llandeilo Fawr and Taliaris *St D* 85-86; P-in-c Llangrannog and Llandysiliogogo 86-88; Chapl RAF 88-92; R Ystradgynlais *S & B* 92-94; CF from 94. *c/o MOD Chaplains (Army)* Tel (01980) 615804 Fax 615800

THOMAS, The Ven Alfred James Randolph. b 48. St D Coll Lamp. **d** 71 **p** 72. C Cydweli and Llandyfaelog *St D* 71-74; C Carmarthen St Dav 74-76; TV Aberystwyth 76-81; V Betws w Ammanford 81-93; RD Dyffryn Aman 90-93; V Carmarthen St Pet and Chapl Carmarthenshire NHS Trust 93-02; Can St D Cathl 96-02; V Bronllys w Llanfilo *S & B* 02-06; P-in-c Llanfrynach and Cantref w Llanhamlach from 06; Adn Brecon from 03. *The Rectory, Llanfrynach, Brecon LD3 7AJ* Tel (01874) 665667

THOMAS, Andrew Herbert Redding. b 41. Lon Coll of Div 66. **d** 69 **p** 70. C Cromer *Nor* 69-72; Holiday Chapl 72-76; R Grimston w Congham 76 83; R Roydon All SS 76-83; C-in-c Ewell St Paul Howell Hill CD *Guildf* 83-89; V Howell Hill 89-95; RD Epsom 93-95; TR Beccles St Mich *St E* 95-04; P-in-c Worlingham w Barnby and N Cove 98-01; rtd 04; Perm to Offic *Nor* and *St E* from 04. *9A Corner Street, Cromer NR27 9HW* Tel (01263) 515091 E-mail ahrthomas@waitrose.com

THOMAS, Andrew John. b 62. Univ of Wales (Abth) BSc84 ACA87. ERMC 04. **d** 07 **p** 08. NSM Stevenage H Trin *St Alb* from 07. *1 Ash Drive, St Ippolyts, Hitchin SG4 7SJ* Tel (01462) 421647 E-mail ajt250762@aol.com

THOMAS, Andrew Peter. **d** 08. C Llanishen *Llan* from 08. *100 Templeton Avenue, Llanishen, Cardiff CF14 5JH* Tel (029) 2075 7507

THOMAS, Andrew Robert. b 80. G&C Coll Cam BA03. Oak Hill Th Coll BA09. **d** 09. C Angmering *Chich* from 09. *34 Arundel Road, Angmering, Littlehampton BN16 4LL* Tel 07786-376615 (mobile) E-mail andythomas196@yahoo.co.uk

THOMAS, Anne. See THOMAS, Miss Eileen Anne Harwood

THOMAS, Anne Valerie. See NOBLE, Anne Valerie

THOMAS, Arun. See THOMAS, John Arun

THOMAS, Austin George. b 23. Open Univ BA75. Wells Th Coll 65. **d** 67 **p** 68. C Brislington St Luke 67-73; P-in-c Bris St Geo 73-74; P-in-c Bris St Leon Redfield 74-75; TV E Bris 75-80; R Lyddington w Wanborough 80-88; rtd 88; Perm to Offic *Bris* from 88. *36 Purdy Court, New Station Road, Bristol BS16 3RT* Tel 0117-958 3511

THOMAS, Canon Barry Wilfred. b 41. Univ of Wales (Cardiff) BD75. St Mich Coll Llan 72. **d** 75 **p** 76. C Porthmadog *Ban* 75-78; V Llanegryn and Llanfihangel-y-Pennant etc 78-82; TR Llanbeblig w Caernarfon and Betws Garmon etc 82-94; Sec

Dioc Coun for Miss and Unity 81-94; Can Ban Cathl 89-94; Chapl Monte Carlo *Eur* 95-00; V Llanfihangel Ystrad and Cilcennin w Trefilan etc *St D* 00-06; rtd 06. *6 Diana Road, Llandeilo SA19 6RR* Tel (01558) 824230

THOMAS, Bernard. See THOMAS, The Ven Elwyn Bernard

THOMAS, Bryan. b 36. Univ of Wales (Abth) BA59. St Deiniol's Hawarden 68. **d** 70 **p** 71. C Llangynwyd w Maesteg 70-72; V Cwmllynfell *St D* 72-76; V Gors-las 76-82; R Yarnbury *Sarum* 82-97; TR Wylye and Till Valley 97-02; RD Wylye and Wilton 94-98; rtd 02; Perm to Offic *Sarum* from 03 and *B & W* from 05. *11 Ebble Crescent, Warminster BA12 9PF* Tel (01985) 300519

THOMAS, The Ven Charles Edward (Ted). b 27. Univ of Wales (Lamp) BA51. Coll of Resurr Mirfield 51. **d** 53 **p** 54. C Ilminster w Whitelackington *B & W* 53-56; Chapl St Mich Coll Tenbury 56-57; C St Alb St Steph *St Alb* 57-58; V Boreham Wood St Mich 58-66; R Monksilver w Brompton Ralph and Nettlecombe *B & W* 66-74; P-in-c Nettlecombe 68-69; R S Petherton w the Seavingtons 74-83; RD Crewkerne 77-83; Adn Wells, Can Res and Preb Wells Cathl 83-93; rtd 93; Perm to Offic *St D* from 93. *Geryfelin, Pentre, Tregaron SY25 6JG* Tel (01974) 298102

THOMAS, Charles Moray Stewart Reid. b 53. BNC Ox BA74 MA79. Wycliffe Hall Ox 75. **d** 78 **p** 79. C Bradf Cathl 78-81; C Barnsbury St Andr and H Trin w All SS *Lon* 81-90; TV Barnsbury 90-99; Chapl Lon Goodenough Trust 99-08; V Grayshott *Guildf* from 08. *The Vicarage, 10 Vicarage Gardens, Grayshott, Hindhead GU26 6NH* Tel (01428) 606703 E-mail moray@thethomases.org.uk

THOMAS, Cheeramattathu John. b 25. Travancore Univ BA46 BT49 Serampore Coll BD55 United Th Coll Bangalore MA66. Andover Newton Th Coll. **d** 55 **p** 57. Singapore 55-60; Sarawak 60-65; C Eastham *Ches* 66-74; V Gt Sutton 75-83; USA from 83; rtd 91. *4622 Pin Oak Lane, Bellaire TX 77401-2504, USA*

THOMAS, Chloe Ann Mary. b 60. GMusRNCM83. Ripon Coll Cuddesdon 07. **d** 09. C Knighton St Mary Magd *Leic* from 09. *62 Elms Road, Leicester LE2 3JB* Tel 0116-270 0228 Mobile 07801-886736 E-mail chloe.thomas5@btinternet.com

THOMAS, Clive Alexander. b 49. St Luke's Coll Ex CertEd71 Open Univ BA77. STETS 94. **d** 97 **p** 99. NSM Southwick St Mich *Chich* 97-01; C Bridport *Sarum* 01-04; TV Shaston from 04. *The Rectory, 10 Heathfields Way, Shaftesbury SP7 9JZ* Tel (01747) 852547 E-mail rev.cathomas@lineone.net

THOMAS, Preb Colin Norman. b 41. Open Univ BA78. Trin Coll Bris 72. **d** 74 **p** 75. C Handforth *Ches* 74-77; C Bucknall and Bagnall *Lich* 77-80; TV 80-86; V Ogley Hay 86-06; RD Lich 99-04; Preb Lich Cathl 04-06; rtd 06; Perm to Offic *Derby* from 07. *96 Church Street, Church Gresley, Swadlincote DE11 9NR* Tel (01283) 221033 E-mail thomas@vicars.co.uk

✠**THOMAS, The Rt Revd David.** b 42. Keble Coll Ox BA64 BA66 MA67. St Steph Ho Ox 64. **d** 67 **p** 68 **c** 96. C Hawarden *St As* 67-69; Tutor St Mich Coll Llan 69-70; Chapl 70-75; Sec Ch in Wales Liturg Commn 70-75; Vice-Prin St Steph Ho Ox 75-79; Prin 82-87; V Chepstow *Mon* 79-82; Lic to Offic *Ox* 82-87; V Newton St Pet *S & B* 87-96; Can Brecon Cathl 94-96; RD Clyne 96; Prov Asst Bp 96-08; rtd 08. *65 Westland Avenue, West Cross, Swansea SA3 5NR*

THOMAS, David Brian. b 45. MIEEE. St D Dioc Tr Course 82. **d** 85 **p** 86. NSM Llandysul *St D* 85-87; NSM Lampeter Pont Steffan w Silian 88-92; NSM Lampeter and Ultra-Aeron 92-96; P-in-c Llanfihangel Genau'r-glyn and Llangorwen 96-97; V from 97; AD Llanbadarn Fawr from 00. *The Vicarage, Maes y Garn, Bow Street SY24 5DS* Tel (01970) 828638

THOMAS, David Edward. b 60. Univ of Wales (Lamp) BA83. St Mich Coll Llan 85. **d** 86 **p** 87. C Killay *S & B* 86-89; P-in-c Newbridge-on-Wye and Llanfihangel Brynpabuan 89-90; V 90-91; V Brecon St David w Llanspyddid and Llanilltyd 91-09; V Glasbury and Llowes w Clyro and Betws from 09. *The Vicarage, 4 The Birches, Glasbury, Hereford HR3 5NW* Tel (01497) 847156

THOMAS, Canon David Geoffrey. b 24. AKC48. **d** 49 **p** 50. C Milford Haven *St D* 49-52; Miss to Seamen 52-53 and 68-81; C Pembroke St Mary w St Mich 53-54; R Rhoscrowther and Pwllcrochan 54-68; V Milford Haven 68-89; Can St D Cathl 77-89; Treas 85-89; rtd 89. *49 Pill Lane, Milford Haven SA73 2LD* Tel (01646) 695792

THOMAS, David Geoffrey. b 37. Univ of Wales (Cardiff) BA58. Launde Abbey 70 Qu Coll Birm 71. **d** 71 **p** 72. Hon C Fenny Drayton *Leic* 71-75; Chapl Community of the H Family Baldslow *Chich* 75-77; Perm to Offic *Chich* 77-79; P-in-c Mill End and Heronsgate w W Hyde *St Alb* 79-81; Sen Lect Watford Coll 82-91; R Walgrave w Hannington and Wold and Scaldwell *Pet* 91-01; rtd 01; Perm to Offic *Pet* 01-06. *1 Cypress Close, Desborough, Kettering NN14 2XU* Tel and fax (01536) 763749

THOMAS, The Very Revd David Glynne. b 41. Dur Univ BSc63. Westcott Ho Cam 64. **d** 67 **p** 68. C St John's Wood *Lon* 67-70; Min Can St Alb 70-72; Chapl Wadh Coll Ox 72-75; C Ox St Mary V w St Cross and St Pet 72-75; Bp's Dom Chapl 75-78; P-in-c Burnham 78-82; TR Burnham w Dropmore, Hitcham and Taplow 82-83; R Coolangatta Australia 83-86; R Toowoomba 86-87; Can Res Worc Cathl 87-99; Dean Brisbane 99-03; Chapl to Abp Brisbane 03-06; rtd 06. *173 Edgewater Village, David Low Way, Bli Bli Qld 4560, Australia* Tel (0061) (7) 5450 8224 E-mail davidthomas@westnet.com.au

THOMAS, David Godfrey. b 50. St Chad's Coll Dur BA71 Fitzw Coll Cam BA74 MA78. Westcott Ho Cam 72. **d** 75 **p** 76. C Kirkby *Liv* 75-78; TV Cov E 78-88; TR Canvey Is *Chelmsf* 88-92; R Wivenhoe 92-09; R Shenfield from 09. *The Rectory, 41 Worrin Road, Shenfield, Brentwood CM15 8DH* Tel (01277) 220360 E-mail davidthomas50@tiscali.co.uk

THOMAS, David John. b 34. Univ of Wales (Swansea) St D Coll Lamp. St D Dioc Tr Course 85. **d** 88 **p** 89. NSM Cwmaman *St D* 88-96; Public Preacher from 96. *9 New School Road, Garnant, Ammanford SA18 1LL* Tel (01269) 823936

THOMAS, David Richard. b 48. BNC Ox BA71 MA74 Fitzw Coll Cam BA75 MA80 Lanc Univ PhD83. Ridley Hall Cam 73 Qu Coll Birm 79. **d** 80 **p** 81. C Anfield St Columba *Liv* 80-83; C Liv Our Lady and St Nic w St Anne 83-85; Chapl CCC Cam 85-90; V Witton *Blackb* 90-93; Bp's Adv on Inter-Faith Relns 90-93; Dir Cen for Study of Islam and Chr-Muslim Relns Selly Oak 93-04; Sen Lect Birm Univ 99-04; Perm to Offic *Derby* from 05. *The Vicarage, Church Square, Melbourne, Derby DE73 8JH* Tel (01332) 864121

THOMAS, David Ronald Holt. b 28. Lich Th Coll 55. **d** 58 **p** 59. C Uttoxeter w Bramshall *Lich* 58-61; C Hednesford 61-66; R Armitage from 66; RD Rugeley 80-84. *The Rectory, Hood Lane, Armitage, Rugeley WS15 4AG* Tel (01543) 490278 E-mail davidthomas015@btinternet.com

THOMAS, Canon David Thomas. b 44. St Cath Coll Cam BA66 MA70. Cranmer Hall Dur. **d** 71 **p** 72. C Chorlton-cum-Hardy St Clem *Man* 71-74; Chapl Salford Tech Coll 74-79; P-in-c Pendleton St Thos *Man* 75-77; V 77-80; TR Gleadless *Sheff* 80-90; RD Attercliffe 86-90; V Benchill *Man* 90-99; TV Wythenshawe 99-00; AD Withington 99-00; P-in-c Stretford St Matt from 00; Hon Can Man Cathl from 09. *St Matthew's Rectory, 39 Sandy Lane, Stretford, Manchester M32 9DB* Tel 0161-865 2535 E-mail tom-hil@talk21.com

THOMAS, Canon David William. b 17. Univ of Wales BA63 MA67. St D Coll Lamp BA38 St Mich Coll Llan 39. **d** 41 **p** 43. C Cynwyl Gaeo w Llansawel *St D* 41-46; C Llandysul 46-48; V Clydau and Penrhydd w Castellan 48-55; V Llanfihangel Genau'r Glyn 55-67; V Llangynfelyn 58-62; V Pontyberem 67-76; V Llanilar w Rhostie and Llangwyryfon etc 76-83; Hon Can St D Cathl 78-83; rtd 83. *Nantyddorwen, 138 Marged Street, Ammanford SA18 2NN* Tel (01269) 594986

THOMAS, David William Wallace. b 51. St Chad's Coll Dur BA72. St Mich Coll Llan 72. **d** 75 **p** 76. C Bargoed and Deri w Brithdir *Llan* 75-79; Hon C 79-81; V Nantymoel w Wyndham 81-84; Chapl RN 84-07. *Address temp unknown*

THOMAS, David Wynford. b 48. Univ of Wales (Abth) LLB70. Qu Coll Birm 76. **d** 79 **p** 80. C Swansea St Mary w H Trin and St Mark *S & B* 79-83; P-in-c Swansea St Mark 83-89; Lic to Offic 90. *74 Terrace Road, Swansea SA1 6HU*

THOMAS, Canon Dillwyn Morgan. b 26. Univ of Wales (Lamp) BA50. Qu Coll Birm 50. **d** 52 **p** 53. C Dowlais *Llan* 52-59; C Pontypridd St Cath 59-63; V Llanwynno 63-68; V Bargoed w Brithdir 68-74; V Bargoed and Deri w Brithdir 74-75; V Penarth All SS 75-88; Can Llan Cathl 86-88; rtd 88; Perm to Offic *Llan* from 88. *11 Baroness Place, Penarth CF64 3UL* Tel (029) 2025 1698

THOMAS, Dorothy Judith. b 47. Univ of Wales (Cardiff) BA68. Princeton Th Sem MDiv94 MTh96 San Francisco Th Sem DMin01. **d** 03 **p** 04. NSM Wargrave w Knowl Hill *Ox* 03-07; Perm to Offic from 09. *Spreydon, Lutmans Haven, Knowl Hill, Reading RG10 9YN* Tel (01628) 825347 E-mail djudthomas@hotmail.com

THOMAS (née THOMSON), Mrs Dorothy Lucille. b 39. Univ of Wales (Lamp). **d** 00. OLM Pontnewydd *Mon* from 00. *Raldoro, Mount Pleasant Road, Pontnewydd, Cwmbran NP44 1BD* Tel (01633) 771353

THOMAS, Edward. *See* THOMAS, The Ven Charles Edward

THOMAS, Edward Bernard Meredith. b 21. Leeds Univ BA44 Univ of Qld BEd68 BD72. Coll of Resurr Mirfield 47. **d** 49 **p** 50. C St Mary-at-Lambeth *S'wark* 49-54; C Portsea North St Mark *Portsm* 54-56; V Portsea All SS 56-64; Australia from 64; rtd 92. *33 Highfield Street, Durack Qld 4077, Australia* Tel (0061) (7) 3372 3517

THOMAS, Edward Walter Dennis. b 32. St Mich Coll Llan 61. **d** 63 **p** 64. C Loughor *S & B* 63-69; V Ystradfellte 69-74; V Dukinfield St Mark and St Luke *Ches* 74-04; Chapl Gtr Man Police from 77; OCF 88-00; rtd 04; Perm to Offic *Ches* from 04. *16 Boyd's Walk, Dukinfield SK16 4TW* Tel 0161-330 1324 E-mail revewdt@aol.com

THOMAS, Miss Eileen Anne Harwood. b 35. Univ of Wales (Swansea) BA59 Kent Univ MA80. Cant Sch of Min 80. **dss** 83 **d** 87 **p** 94. Mill Hill Jo Keble Ch Lon 83-86; The Lydiards *Bris* 86-92; Par Dn 87-92; C-in-c Woodgate Valley CD *Birm* 92-96; rtd 96; Perm to Offic *Truro* from 96. *2 Trelinnoe Gardens, South Petherwin, Launceston PL15 7TH* Tel (01566) 773380

THOMAS, Canon Eirwyn Wheldon. b 35. St Mich Coll Llan 58. **d** 61 **p** 62. C Glanadda *Ban* 61-67; R Llantrisant and Llandeusant 67-75; V Nefyn w Tudweiliog w Llandudwen w Edern 75-01; Can Ban Cathl 97-01; rtd 01. *11 Wenfro Road, Abergele LL22 7LE* Tel (01745) 823587

THOMAS (née REEVES), Mrs Elizabeth Anne. b 45. Sheff Univ BA67 PGCE75. SW Minl Tr Course 87. **d** 90 **p** 94. Par Dn Stoke Damerel *Ex* 90-93; Dioc Children's Adv *Bradf* 93-01; Par Dn Baildon 93-94; C 94-96; P-in-c Denholme Gate 96-01; P-in-c Tuxford w Weston and Markham Clinton *S'well* 01-08; rtd 08. *The Lyrics, 113 The Oval, Retford DN22 7SD* Tel (01777) 700047 E-mail l.a.thomas@btinternet.com

THOMAS, The Ven Elwyn Bernard. b 45. Univ of Wales (Swansea) BSc68. St Mich Coll Llan BD71. **d** 71 **p** 72. C Aberdare St Fagan *Llan* 71-74; C Merthyr Dyfan 74-76; R Dowlais 76-86; V Llangynwyd w Maesteg 86-00; Can Llan Cathl 98-00; Adn St As from 00; R Llandyrnog and Llangwyfan from 00. *The Rectory, Ffordd Las, Llandyrnog, Denbigh LL16 4LT* Tel (01824) 790777 Fax 790877 E-mail bernardthomas@bun.com

THOMAS, Canon Ernest Keith. b 49. St Mich Coll Llan 73. **d** 76 **p** 77. C Swansea St Gabr *S & B* 76-79; C Killay 79-81; S Africa 81-92 and from 96; Prec Kimberley Cathl 81-84; R Kimberley St Aug 84-92; R Kimberley St Alb 89-92; Can Kimberley Cathl 86-92; V Aberdare *Llan* 93-96; Sub-Dean Bloemfontein Cathl from 96. *PO Box 1523, Bloemfontein, 9300 South Africa* Tel (0027) (51) 447 5951

THOMAS, Canon Euros Lloyd. b 53. Bris Poly LLB75. St Mich Coll Llan 77. **d** 79 **p** 80. C Llanelli *St D* 79-84; R Cilgerran w Bridell and Llantwyd 84-07; R Cilgerran w Bridell and Llantwyd and Eglwyswrw from 07; P-in-c Clydau 00-04; AD Cemais and Sub-Aeron 93-08; Can St D Cathl from 03. *The Rectory, Penllyn, Cilgerran, Cardigan SA43 2RZ* Tel (01239) 614500

THOMAS, Frank Lowth. b 22. Lon Coll of Div 64. **d** 66 **p** 67. C Walthamstow St Mary *Chelmsf* 66-68; C Bickenhill w Elmdon *Birm* 68-71; R Carlton Colville *Nor* 71-81; R Smallburgh w Dilham w Honing and Crostwight 81-85; rtd 85; Perm to Offic *Nor* from 86. *7 Mill Close, Salhouse, Norwich NR13 6QB* Tel (01603) 720376

THOMAS, Geoffrey. *See* THOMAS, David Geoffrey

THOMAS, Geoffrey Brynmor. b 34. K Coll Lon BA56 AKC56. Ridley Hall Cam 58. **d** 60 **p** 61. C Harlow New Town w Lt Parndon *Chelmsf* 60-65; V Leyton All SS 65-74; V Haley Hill *Wakef* 74-82; R The Winterbournes and Compton Valence *Sarum* 82-89; TV Cheltenham St Mark *Glouc* 89-92; P-in-c Dowdeswell and Andoversford w the Shiptons etc 92-95; RD Northleach 92-95; rtd 95; Perm to Offic *B & W* from 96. *48 Riverside Walk, Midsomer Norton, Bath BA3 2PD* Tel (01761) 414146 E-mail gbt34@btinternet.com

THOMAS, Geoffrey Charles. b 37. St Jo Coll Nottm LTh ALCD64. **d** 64 **p** 65. C York St Paul 64-67; C Cheltenham Ch Ch *Glouc* 67-70; V Whitgift w Adlingfleet *Sheff* 70-74; P-in-c Eastoft 72-74; V Mortomley St Sav 74-88; R Middleton Cheney w Chacombe *Pet* 88-93; rtd 94; Perm to Offic *York* from 94. *55 Oakland Avenue, York YO31 1DF* Tel (01904) 414082

THOMAS, Canon Geoffrey Heale. b 29. St Mich Coll Llan 58. **d** 60 **p** 61. C Llansamlet *S & B* 60-63; Nigeria 63-67; V Swansea St Nic *S & B* 67-80; CF (TA) 72; V Oystermouth *S & B* 80-98; Hon Can Brecon Cathl 92-96; Can 97-98; rtd 98. *19 Ffordd Dryden, Killay, Swansea SA2 7PA* Tel (01792) 206308

THOMAS, George. b 46. Leeds Univ BEd69. Cranmer Hall Dur 75. **d** 78 **p** 79. C Highfield *Liv* 78-83; V Chorley St Jas *Blackb* 83-02; P-in-c Blackb St Gabr 02-08; rtd 08; Perm to Offic *Blackb* from 08. *80 Severn Drive, Walton-le-Dale, Preston PR5 4TE* Tel (01772) 330152

THOMAS, Glyn. b 36. Lon Univ BPharm61. St Deiniol's Hawarden 80. **d** 82 **p** 83. C Rhyl w St Ann *St As* 83-85; R Llanycil w Bala and Frongoch and Llangower etc 85-03; RD Penllyn 96-03; rtd 03. *Blaen-y-Coed, 7 Lon Helyg, Abergele LL22 7JQ*

THOMAS, Gordon Herbert. b 43. Guildf Dioc Min Course 00. **d** 00 **p** 01. OLM Cove St Jo *Guildf* from 00. *13 Tay Close, Farnborough GU14 9NB* Tel (01252) 512347 E-mail rev.gordon@tiscali.co.uk

THOMAS, Greville Stephen. b 64. Qu Coll Birm 94. **d** 96 **p** 97. C Hillingdon All SS *Lon* 96-99; C Acton Green 99-04; P-in-c Northolt St Mary 04-06; R from 06. *St Mary's Rectory, Ealing Road, Northolt UB5 6AA* Tel (020) 8841 5691 E-mail greville.thomas@london.anglican.org *or* stmary@northolt.org

THOMAS, Harald Daniel. b 34. FInstTT. **d** 97 **p** 05. Par Dn Pontnewydd *Mon* from 97. *Raldoro, Mount Pleasant Road, Pontnewydd, Cwmbran NP44 1BD* Tel (01633) 771353

THOMAS, Miss Hilary Faith. b 43. Ex Univ BA65 Southn Univ PGCE66. Trin Coll Bris 90. **d** 94 **p** 95. C Yeovil w Kingston Pitney *B & W* 94-98; V Brislington St Luke 98-07; rtd 07. *Brierley, Lower North Street, Cheddar BS27 3HH* Tel (01934) 742207

THOMAS, Hugh. b 25. St D Coll Lamp BA50. **d** 51 **p** 52. C Penbre *St D* 51-55; P-in-c Moelgrove and Monington 55-63; V

Llanfynydd 63-74; V Pontyates 74-80; V Pontyates and Llangyndeyrn 80-90; rtd 91. *90 Priory Street, Kidwelly SA17 4TY* Tel (01554) 890114

THOMAS, Hugh Vivian. b 57. Kingston Poly LLB80 Barrister-at-Law (Lincoln's Inn) 86. SEITE 02. **d** 05 **p** 06. NSM Knockholt w Halstead *Roch* from 05. *5 The Meadows, Halstead, Sevenoaks TN14 7HD* Tel (01959) 532664
E-mail hughvthomas@btopenworld.com

THOMAS, Canon Huw Glyn. b 42. MBE07. St D Coll Lamp BA62 Linacre Coll Ox BA65 MA69. Wycliffe Hall Ox 62. **d** 65 **p** 66. C Oystermouth *S & B* 65-68; Asst Chapl Solihull Sch 68-69; Chapl and Hd Div 69-73; Selection Sec ACCM 73-78; C Loughton St Jo *Chelmsf* 73-77; V Bury St Jo *Man* 78-83; V Bury St Jo w St Mark 83-86; Dir of Ords 82-87; Can Res and Treas Liv Cathl 87-95; USPG 95-06; Chapl Addis Ababa Ethiopia 95-97; Provost All St Cathl Cairo 97-01; Can from 01; Prin Edwardes Coll Peshawar Pakistan 01-06; rtd 06; Hon Sen Fell Liv Hope Univ from 07; Perm to Offic *Lon* from 07. *2 Bella Best House, 5B Westmoreland Terrace, London SW1V 4AW* Tel (020) 7630 5654 Mobile 07981-114255
E-mail huwapglyn@yahoo.com

THOMAS, Ian Melville. b 50. Jes Coll Ox BA71 MA75. St Steph Ho Ox 71. **d** 73 **p** 74. PV St D Cathl 73-77; Chapl RAF 77-95; Command Chapl RAF 95-00; V Llanelli *St D* 01-02; TR 02-06; R Eccleston and Pulford *Ches* from 06. *The Rectory, Church Road, Eccleston, Chester CH4 9HT* Tel (01244) 659205
E-mail imt50@hotmail.com

THOMAS, Ian William. b 53. Bedf Coll of Educn CertEd74. Ox Min Course 89. **d** 92 **p** 93. NSM Fenny Stratford *Ox* from 92. *5 Laburnum Grove, Bletchley, Milton Keynes MK2 2JW* Tel (01908) 644457

THOMAS, Canon Idris. b 48. St D Coll Lamp. **d** 71 **p** 72. C Llanbeblig w Caernarfon and Betws Garmon etc *Ban* 71-75; P-in-c Llanaelhaiarn 75-77; R Llanaelhaearn w Clynnog Fawr from 77; RD Arfon 93-00; AD 02-04; Hon Can Ban Cathl from 99. *Y Rheithordy, Trefor, Caernarfon LL54 5HN* Tel (01286) 660547

THOMAS, Irene Jean. b 42. **d** 04 **p** 05. OLM E Wickham *S'wark* from 04. *35 Bowford Avenue, Bexleyheath DA7 4ST* Tel and fax (020) 8303 1855 E-mail irene.thomas@lineone.net

THOMAS, Mrs Iris. b 18. Univ of Wales (Abth) BA39 DipEd40. Llan Ord Course. **d** 80 **p** 97. Hon C Tylorstown *Llan* 80-84; Hon C Ferndale w Maerdy 84-85; rtd 85; Perm to Offic *Llan* from 86. *1 Maesy Court, Maerdy Road, Ferndale CF3 4BT* Tel (01443) 755235

THOMAS, Jennifer Monica. b 58. Wilson Carlile Coll 79 Sarum & Wells Th Coll 91. **d** 93 **p** 94. Par Dn Wandsworth St Paul *S'wark* 93-94; C 94-97; V Forest Hill 97-02; V Mitcham Ascension from 02. *The Vicarage, Sherwood Park Road, Mitcham CR4 1NE* Tel (020) 8764 1258

THOMAS, Jeremy Paul. b 63. Lanc Univ BSc87. Trin Coll Bris 04. **d** 06 **p** 07. C Aughton Ch *Liv* from 06. *25 Peet Avenue, Ormskirk L39 4SH* Tel (01695) 577958

THOMAS, John. *See* THOMAS, Cheeramattathu John

THOMAS, John Arun. b 47. Bombay Univ BA69 MA72 Nottm Univ CertEd80. Oak Hill Th Coll 84. **d** 88 **p** 89. C Liv Ch Ch Norris Green 88-89; C Wavertree St Mary 89-93; V St Mary Cray and St Paul's Cray *Roch* 93-96; India 96-99 and from 04; V Malabar Hill All SS 96-97; Hon Min Scotskirk 97-99; Prin Bombay Scottish Sch 97-99; Australia 99-04. *Address temp unknown* w karann51@hotmail.com

THOMAS, Canon John Herbert Samuel. b 34. Pemb Coll Cam BA57 MA64. St Mich Coll Llan 57. **d** 58 **p** 59. C Port Talbot St Theodore *Llan* 58-60; C Llantwit Major and St Donat's 60-67; P-in-c Barry All SS 67-74; V Dinas w Penygraig 74-85; V Pontypridd St Cath 85-90; V Pontypridd St Cath w St Matt 90-99; RD Pontypridd 90-99; Can Llan Cathl from 95; rtd 99. *Ty Canon, Salisbury Road, Abercynon, Mountain Ash CF45 4NU* Tel (01443) 742577

THOMAS, John Roger. Trin Coll Carmarthen BA. St Mich Coll Llan. **d** 03 **p** 04. C Cardigan w Mwnt and Y Ferwig w Llangoedmor *St D* 03-06; P-in-c Crymych Gp 06-07; V from 07. *The Vicarage, Newport Road, Crymych SA41 3RJ* Tel (01239) 831811

THOMAS, John Thurston. b 28. Univ of Wales (Swansea) BSc48 DipEd49 Leeds Univ PhD58 CChem FRSC65. Glouc Sch of Min 88. **d** 90 **p** 91. NSM S Cerney w Cerney Wick and Down Ampney *Glouc* 90-96; Perm to Offic *Glouc* 96-01; *S & B* from 01. *4 Nicholl Court, Mumbles, Swansea SA3 4LZ* Tel (01792) 360098

THOMAS, Judith. *See* THOMAS, Dorothy Judith

THOMAS, Julian Mark. b 48. Ex Univ BA05. SWMTC 00. **d** 03 **p** 04. C Okehampton w Inwardleigh, Bratton Clovelly etc *Ex* 03-07; C Essington *Lich* from 07. *The Vicarage, 21 Wolverhampton Road, Essington, Wolverhampton WV11 2BX* Tel (01922) 447540 E-mail mark.thomas108@o2.co.uk

THOMAS, Mrs June Marion. b 31. Univ of Wales BA53 DipEd54. NEOC 83. **dss** 86 **d** 87 **p** 94. Stockton St Pet *Dur* 86-87; Hon Par Dn 87-89; NSM Stockton St Mark 89-94; P-in-c

94-01; rtd 01. *50 Brisbane Grove, Stockton-on-Tees TS18 5BP* Tel (01642) 582408

THOMAS, Mrs Karen Rosemary. b 53. Qu Coll Birm 04. **d** 06 **p** 07. C Glenfield *Leic* from 06. *8 Lynmouth Close, Glenfield, Leicester LE3 8RW* Tel 0116-287 8224
E-mail karen@fish5.fsnet.co.uk

THOMAS, Keith. b 55. Southlands Coll Lon TCert80. NOC 92. **d** 95 **p** 96. NSM Knuzden *Blackb* 95-98; NSM Darwen St Pet w Hoddlesden 98-04; Tullyallan Sch Darwen 99-04; NSM Turton Moorland Min *Man* from 04. *20 Duxbury Street, Darwen BB3 2LA* Tel (01254) 776484

THOMAS, Kenneth. *See* THOMAS, Canon William Kenneth

THOMAS, Kimberley Ann. b 59. Cranmer Hall Dur 02. **d** 04 **p** 05. C Chesterton *Lich* 04-07; V Stretton w Claymills from 07. *The Vicarage, Church Road, Stretton, Burton-on-Trent DE13 0HD* Tel (01283) 565141 E-mail kimberley.thomas@btinternet.com

THOMAS, Leighton. *See* THOMAS, Adrian Leighton

THOMAS, Canon Leslie Richard. b 45. Lon Coll of Div 65. **d** 69 **p** 70. C Knotty Ash St Jo *Liv* 69-72; C Sutton 72-74; TV 74-77; V Banks 77-82; V Gt Crosby All SS 82-92; P-in-c Marthall and Chapl David Lewis Cen for Epilepsy *Ches* 92-02; V Bickerton, Bickley, Harthill and Burwardsley from 02; RD Malpas from 04; Hon Can Ches Cathl from 07. *The Vicarage, Harthill Road, Burwardsley, Chester CH3 9NU* Tel (01829) 771225
E-mail sandstone@tesco.net

THOMAS, Mark. *See* THOMAS, Julian Mark

THOMAS, Mark Wilson. b 51. Dur Univ BA72 Hull Univ MA89. Ripon Coll Cuddesdon 76. **d** 78 **p** 79. C Chapelthorpe *Wakef* 78-81; C Seaford w Sutton *Chich* 81-84; V Gomersal *Wakef* 84-92; TR Almondbury w Farnley Tyas 92-01; RD Almondbury 93-01; Hon Can Wakef Cathl 99-01; P-in-c Shrewsbury St Chad w St Mary *Lich* 01-07; V Shrewsbury St Chad, St Mary and St Alkmund from 07. *The Crescent, Town Walls, Shrewsbury SY1 1TH* Tel and fax (01743) 343761
E-mail saint.chads@ukonline.co.uk

THOMAS, Sister Mary Josephine. b 30. Ripon Dioc Tr Coll TCert50 Carl Dioc Tr Course 88. **d** 90 **p** 94. NSM Hawes Side *Blackb* 90-93; NSM St Annes St Marg 93-00; Perm to Offic from 00. *112 St Andrew's Road North, Lytham St Annes FY8 2JQ* Tel (01253) 728016

THOMAS, Michael Longdon Sanby. b 34. Trin Hall Cam BA55 MA60. Wells Th Coll 56. **d** 58 **p** 59. C Sandal St Helen *Wakef* 58-60; Chapl Portsm Cathl 60-64; V Shedfield 64-69; V Portchester 69-98; rtd 98. *188 Castle Street, Portchester, Fareham PO16 9QH* Tel and fax (023) 9242 0416
E-mail thomasfamily73@cwtv.net

THOMAS, Michael Rosser David. b 74. Kent Univ BA96. St Steph Ho Ox BTh02. **d** 02 **p** 03. C Aberavon *Llan* 02-05; Min Can Brecon Cathl 05-08; Succ from 08; P-in-c Brecon St Mary w Llanddew from 08. *The Almonry, Cathedral Close, Brecon LD3 9DP* Tel (01874) 622972
E-mail fr.michael@ntlworld.co.uk

THOMAS, Moray. *See* THOMAS, Charles Moray Stewart Reid

THOMAS, Nigel Bruce. b 63. Univ of Wales BD91. St Jo Coll Nottm MA98. **d** 97 **p** 98. C Millom *Carl* 97-02; R Bentham *Bradf* 02-07; P-in-c St Breoke and Egloshayle *Truro* 07-08; TR Carew *St D* from 08. *The Vicarage, Church Street, Pembroke Dock SA72 6AR* Tel (01646) 682943
E-mail thomas-tribe@hotmail.com

THOMAS, Owen James. b 17. Univ of Wales BA38 Tyndale Hall Bris 38. **d** 40 **p** 41. C Wandsworth St Steph *S'wark* 40-43; C Dagenham *Chelmsf* 43-46; R Glas St Silas 46-51; Tutor Lon Bible Coll 51-62; Chapl and Lect 62-76; P-in-c Woburn Square Ch Ch *Lon* 51-52; Aux Chapl US Airforce 66-68; Hon C Northwood Em *Lon* 70-76; V Canonbury St Steph 76-85; rtd 85; Perm to Offic *Chich* from 85. *27 Fairlight Gardens, Fairlight, Hastings TN35 4AY* Tel (01424) 813613
E-mail oth83ogt@aol.com

THOMAS, Ms Pamela Sybil. b 38. Ripon Coll Cuddesdon 88. **d** 90 **p** 94. Par Dn Preston w Sutton Poyntz and Osmington w Poxwell *Sarum* 90-94; C 94-96; P-in-c Weymouth St Edm 96-05; P-in-c Abbotsbury, Portesham and Langton Herring 97-08; Chapl Westhaven Hosp Weymouth 96-08; rtd 08; Hon C Cullompton, Willand, Uffculme, Kentisbeare etc *Ex* from 08. *5 Cotters Close, Kentesbeare, Cullompton EX15 2DJ* Tel (01884) 266741 E-mail rev.thomas@btinternet.com

THOMAS, Canon Patrick Hungerford Bryan. b 52. St Cath Coll Cam BA73 MA77 Leeds Univ BA78 Univ of Wales PhD82. Coll of Resurr Mirfield 76. **d** 79 **p** 80. C Aberystwyth *St D* 79-81; C Carmarthen St Pet 81-82; R Llangeitho and Blaenpennal w Betws Leucu etc 82-84; Warden of Ords 83-86; R Brechfa w Abergorlech 84-01; V Carmarthen St Dav from 01; Can St D Cathl from 00. *St David's Vicarage, 4 Penllwyn Park, Carmarthen SA31 3BU* Tel (01267) 234183
E-mail canon.patrick@yahoo.co.uk

THOMAS, Paul Richard. b 75. Univ of Wales (Cardiff) BA96 MA99. Ripon Coll Cuddesdon BA01 MA06. **d** 02 **p** 03. C Wanstead St Mary w Ch Ch *Chelmsf* 02-06; C St Marylebone w H Trin *Lon* from 06; Chapl R Academy of Music from 08; Chapl

St Marylebone C of E Sch from 08. *16 Clarence Gate Gardens, Glentworth Street, London NW1 6AY* Tel (020) 7563 1388 E-mail pthomas@stmarylebone.com

THOMAS, Canon Paul Robert. b 42. OBE02. NOC. **d** 82 **p** 83. C Hull St Jo Newland *York* 82-84; P-in-c Rowley 84-87; Soc Resp Officer Hull 84-87; R Rowley w Skidby 87-88; TR Barking St Marg w St Patr *Chelmsf* 88-93; Gen Sec and Admin St Luke's Hosp for Clergy 93-03; Can and Preb Chich Cathl from 98; P in O from 99; rtd 03; Perm to Offic *Nor* from 03. *St Anne's Cottage, 37 Scarborough Road, Walsingham NR22 6AB* Tel (01328) 820571

THOMAS, Paul Wyndham. b 55. Oriel Coll Ox BA76 BTh78 MA80. Wycliffe Hall Ox 77. **d** 79 **p** 80. C Llangynwyd w Maesteg 79-85; TV Langport Area *B & W* 85-90; P-in-c Thorp Arch w Walton *York* 90-93; Clergy Tr Officer 90-04; V Nether w Upper Poppleton 93-04; P-in-c Castle Town *Lich* from 04; RD Stafford from 05. *St Thomas's Vicarage, Doxey, Stafford ST16 1EQ* Tel (01785) 258796

THOMAS, Peter James. b 53. Lon Univ BSc75. Trin Coll Bris 77. **d** 80 **p** 81. C Hucclecote *Glouc* 80-84; C Loughborough Em *Leic* 84-85; TV Parr *Liv* 85-92; V Eckington and Defford w Besford *Worc* 92-05; RD Pershore 00-05; P-in-c Norton sub Hamdon, W Chinnock, Chiselborough etc *B & W* from 05; RD Ivelchester from 07. *The Rectory, Cat Street, Chiselborough, Stoke-sub-Hamdon TA14 6TT* Tel (01935) 881202 E-mail pthomas5@aol.com

THOMAS, Peter Rhys. b 37. TCD BA59 MA72 MInstPkg MCIPD. **d** 72 **p** 73. C Cong *T, K & A* 73-75; I 75-77; C Bingley All SS *Bradf* 77-79; V Shelf 79-81; Producer Relig Broadcasting Viking Radio 81-84; P-in-c Croxton *Linc* 81-82; P-in-c Ulceby 81-82; P-in-c Wootton 81-82; P-in-c Ulceby Gp 82; V 82-84; R E and W Tilbury and Linford *Chelmsf* 84-89; I Celbridge w Straffan and Newcastle-Lyons *D & G* 89-93; I Youghal Union *C, C & R* 93-99; Dioc Communications Officer (Cork) 95-99; Can Cork Cathl 97-99; Preb Cloyne Cathl 97-99; rtd 99; Rep Leprosy Miss Munster from 00. *Abina Cottage, Ballykenneally, Ballymacoda, Co Cork, Republic of Ireland* Tel and fax (00353) (24) 98082 E-mail prthomas@iol.ie

THOMAS, Peter Wilson. b 58. K Coll Lon BD80 AKC80. Ripon Coll Cuddesdon 80. **d** 82 **p** 83. C Stockton St Pet *Dur* 82-85; TV Solihull *Birm* 85-90; V Rednal 90-05; Chapl MG Rover 95-05; P-in-c Balsall Common from 05. *St Peter's House, Holly Lane, Balsall Common, Coventry CV7 7EA* Tel and fax (01676) 532721 E-mail frpeter@ukonline.co.uk

THOMAS, Philip Harold Emlyn. b 41. Cant Univ (NZ) BA64 MA77 Dur Univ PhD82. Melbourne Coll of Div BD68. **d** 68 **p** 69. Australia 68-71; New Zealand 71-77; Fell and Chapl Univ Coll Dur 77-83; V Heighington *Dur* from 84; AD Darlington 94-00. *The Vicarage, 15 East Green, Heighington, Newton Aycliffe DL5 6PP* Tel and fax (01325) 312134 E-mail philip.thomas@durham.anglican.org

THOMAS, Philip John. b 52. Liv Poly BSc74 Leeds Poly 77. Trin Coll Bris 94. **d** 96 **p** 97. C Skelton w Upleatham *York* 96-97; C Acomb St Steph 97-01; V Woodthorpe *S'well* from 01; Chapl MU from 03. *St Mark's Vicarage, 37A Melbury Road, Nottingham NG5 4PG* Tel 0115-926 7859 E-mail stmarks.woodthorpe@ntlworld.com

THOMAS, Ramon Lorenzo. b 44. Victoria Univ Wellington BCA73 Mass Inst of Tech MSc80 CA73. Oak Hill Th Coll 89. **d** 97 **p** 98. NSM Yateley *Win* 97-99; Chairman Judah Trust from 99. *1 Dickens Way, Yateley GU46 6XX* Tel (01252) 682224 E-mail judahtrust@aol.com

THOMAS, Rhys. *See* THOMAS, Peter Rhys

THOMAS, Richard Frederick. b 24. Qu Coll Cam BA45 MA49. Ridley Hall Cam 47. **d** 49 **p** 50. C S Croydon Em *Cant* 49-51; Chapl and Ho Master Haileybury Coll 51-67; Hd Master Angl Ch Sch Jerusalem 67-73; Ho Master Bp Luffa Sch Chich 74-80; Hon C Chich St Pancras and St Jo 78-80; R N Mundham w Hunston and Merston 80-89; Perm to Offic *Portsm* from 89; C Stansted and Compton, the Mardens, Stoughton and Racton *Chich* 96-00; rtd 00; Perm to Offic *Chich* from 00. *16 Brent Court, Emsworth PO10 7JA* Tel (01243) 430613 Mobile 07947-518314 E-mail thomasrb@ntlworld.com

THOMAS, Richard Paul. b 50. MIPR. Wycliffe Hall Ox 74. **d** 76 **p** 77. C Abingdon w Shippon *Ox* 76-80; R Win All SS w Chilcomb and Chesil 80-88; Dioc Communications Officer *Win* 83-89; *Ox* 89-07. *71B St Thomas Street, Wells BA5 2UY* Tel (01749) 671478

THOMAS, Robert Graham. b 53. G&C Coll Cam BA75 MA79 Imp Coll Lon PhD78 CEng82 FIMechE93. SAOMC 04. **d** 06 **p** 07. C Bathampton w Claverton *B & W* from 06. *28 Hantone Hill, Bathampton, Bath BA2 6XD* Tel (01225) 428618 E-mail rob.thomas@cantab.net

THOMAS, Robin. b 27. St Steph Ho Ox 89. **d** 89 **p** 90. NSM Clifton All SS w St Jo *Bris* 89-94; P-in-c Tintagel *Truro* 94-97; rtd 97; Perm to Offic *Truro* from 97. *22 Hendra Vean, Truro TR1 3TU* Tel (01872) 271276

THOMAS, Roderick Charles Howell. b 54. LSE BSc75. Wycliffe Hall Ox 91. **d** 93 **p** 94. C Plymouth St Andr w St Paul and

St Geo *Ex* 93-95; C Plymouth St Andr and Stonehouse 95-99; P-in-c Elburton 99-05; V from 05. *St Matthew's Vicarage, 3 Sherford Road, Plymouth PL9 8DQ* Tel (01752) 402771 E-mail roderick.t@virgin.net

THOMAS, Roger. *See* THOMAS, John Roger

THOMAS, Roy. *See* LUTHER THOMAS, The Ven Ilar Roy

THOMAS, Russen William. b 30. Univ of Wales (Lamp) BA55. St Mich Coll Llan 55. **d** 57 **p** 58. C Newport St Jo Bapt *Mon* 57-59; C Pembroke Dock *St D* 59-62; R St Florence and Redberth 62-69; V Newport St Julian *Mon* 69-79; V Stratton *Truro* 79-88; RD Stratton 83-88; V Lanteglos by Fowey 88-91; Hon Chapl Miss to Seafarers from 88; rtd 92; Chapl Playa de Las Americas Tenerife *Eur* 93-97; Perm to Offic *Cov* 97-06 and *B & W* from 06. *St Peter's Cottage, Langford Budville, Wellington TA21 0QZ* Tel (01823) 400525 E-mail wen.rus@virgin.net

THOMAS, Mrs Ruth Alison Mary. b 57. York Univ BA79 Dur Univ PGCE80 MA96. NEOC 07. **d** 09. NSM Dur St Giles from 09. *68 Gilesgate, Durham DH1 1HY* Tel 0191-386 0402 Mobile 07966-387146 E-mail ruththomas@fsmail.net

THOMAS, Mrs Sheila Mary Witton. b 49. STETS 06. **d** 09. NSM Marnhull *Sarum* from 09. *5 Burtonhayes, Burton Street, Marnhull, Sturminster Newton DT10 1PR* Tel (01258) 820469 Mobile 07748-974806 E-mail sheila2is@yahoo.co.uk

THOMAS, Simon Jonathan Francklin. b 51. Sheff Univ BA72 Nottm Univ BA78 Open Univ MA02. St Jo Coll Nottm 76. **d** 80 **p** 80. SAMS 80-82 and 83-95; Peru 80-82; Bolivia 83-95; C Camberwell All SS *S'wark* 82; C Ashtead *Guildf* 96-06; rtd 06. *4 Masefield Road, Harpenden AL5 4JN* Tel (01582) 462227 E-mail simonjfthomas@aol.com

THOMAS, Preb Stephen Blayney. b 35. St D Coll Lamp BA62. Bp Burgess Hall Lamp. **d** 63 **p** 64. C Ledbury *Heref* 63-67; C Bridgnorth w Tasley 67-68; C Clun w Chapel Lawn, Bettws-y-Crwyn and Newcastle 68-73; C Clungunford w Clunbury and Clunton, Bedstone etc 68-73; V Worfield 73-84; RD Bridgnorth 81-83; R Kingsland 84-96; P-in-c Eardisland 84-96; P-in-c Aymestrey and Leinthall Earles w Wigmore etc 84-96; R Kingsland w Eardisland, Aymestrey etc 97-99; Preb Heref Cathl 85-01; rtd 99; Perm to Offic *Heref* and *Worc* from 00. *28 Castle Close, Burford, Tenbury Wells WR15 8AY* Tel (01584) 819642

THOMAS, Stuart Grahame. b 54. Pemb Coll Cam BA77 MA81 ATCL97. Ridley Hall Cam 85. **d** 87 **p** 88. C Guildf H Trin w St Mary 87-91; V Churt 91-94; V Ewell St Fran from 94; Dioc Ecum Officer 99-07; RD Epsom from 07. *The Minister's House, 71 Ruxley Lane, Epsom KT19 9FF* Tel (020) 8391 1127 E-mail revstuart.thomas@btinternet.com

THOMAS, Canon Sydney Robert. b 44. Univ of Wales (Swansea) BA65 MA83. St D Coll Lamp LTh67. **d** 67 **p** 68. C Llanelli *St D* 67-77; V Pontyberem 77-01; TR Cwm Gwendraeth 01-08; RD Cydweli 94-05; Can St D Cathl 94-08; Chan 01-03; Treas 03-08; rtd 09. *40 Waungoch, Upper Tumble, Llanelli SA14 6BX* Tel (01269) 841677 E-mail sydvic@sydvic.plus.com

THOMAS, Theodore Eilir. b 36. Univ of Wales (Lamp) BA58. Sarum Th Coll 58. **d** 60 **p** 61. C Fenton *Lich* 60-63; C Stourport All SS and St Mich CD *Worc* 63-67; V Worc H Trin 67-74; P-in-c Dudley St Fran 74-79; V 79-83; R Plympton St Maurice *Ex* 83-03; rtd 03; P-in-c St John w Millbrook *Truro* from 04. *The Vicarage, Millbrook, Torpoint PL10 1BW* Tel (01752) 822264

THOMAS, Thomas. b 68. Selw Coll Cam BA90. Wycliffe Hall Ox 91. **d** 93 **p** 94. C Much Woolton *Liv* 93-97; V Carr Mill from 97. *St David's Vicarage, 27 Eskdale Avenue, St Helens WA11 7EN* Tel (01744) 732330

THOMAS, Thomas Alan. b 37. K Coll Lon BD60 AKC60. St Boniface Warminster 60. **d** 61 **p** 62. C Washington *Dur* 61-65; C Bishopwearmouth St Mary V w St Pet CD 65-70; V Ruishton w Thornfalcon *B & W* 70-82; R Hutton 82-94; V Frome Ch Ch 94-96; Chapl Victoria Hosp Frome 94-96; R Camerton w Dunkerton, Foxcote and Shoscombe *B & W* 96-00; rtd 00; Perm to Offic *B & W* from 00. *12 Farrington Way, Farrington Gurney, Bristol BS39 6US* Tel (01761) 453434

THOMAS, Thomas John Samuel. b 21. St D Coll Lamp BA48. **d** 49 **p** 50. C Dafen and Llwynhendy *St D* 49-50; Chapl RAF 52-77; QHC 73-85; V Horsham *Chich* 77-85; rtd 85; Perm to Offic *St D* from 85. *1 Glynhir Road, Llandybie, Ammanford SA18 2TA* Tel (01269) 850726

THOMAS, Virginia Jacqueline. b 48. UEA BA70. Yale Div Sch MDiv97. **d** 00 **p** 01. NSM Chelsea St Luke and Ch Ch *Lon* 00-04; NSM W Brompton St Mary w St Pet 04-06; P-in-c 05-06; NSM W Brompton St Mary w St Peter and St Jude from 06. *The Vicarage, 24 Fawcett Street, London SW10 9EZ* Tel (020) 7352 5880 or 7835 1440 Fax 7370 6562 E-mail ginny@stmarytheboltons.demon.co.uk

THOMAS, Vivian Ivor. b 52. S Bank Univ MSc95 Regent Coll Vancouver MCS97 K Coll Lon PhD02. **d** 08 **p** 09. NSM Hammersmith St Paul *Lon* from 08. *76 Rannoch Road, London W6 9SP* Tel (020) 7384 5954 Mobile 07767-777891 E-mail vivian.thomas@btinternet.com

THOMAS, William George. b 29. JP. FRSA Birm Univ BA50 CertEd51. EAMTC 82. **d** 85 **p** 86. NSM Brampton *Ely* 85-87; NSM Bluntisham w Earith 87-89; P-in-c Foxton 89-95; rtd 95;

Perm to Offic *Ely* from 95. *3 The Paddock, Bluntisham, Huntingdon PE28 3NR* Tel (01487) 842057

THOMAS, The Ven William Jordison. b 27. K Coll Cam BA50 MA55. Cuddesdon Coll 51. **d** 53 **p** 54. C Byker St Ant *Newc* 53-56; C Berwick H Trin 56-59; V Alwinton w Holystone and Alnham 59-70; V Alston cum Garrigill w Nenthead and Kirkhaugh 70-80; P-in-c Lambley w Knaresdale 72-80; RD Bamburgh and Glendale 81-83; TR Glendale Gp 80-83; Adn Northd and Can Res Newc Cathl 83-92; rtd 92; Perm to Offic *Newc* from 92. *6 New Barns Court, Warkworth, Morpeth NE65 0XW* Tel (01665) 713901

THOMAS, Canon William Kenneth. b 19. Mert Coll Ox BA40 MA44. Westcott Ho Cam 40. **d** 42 **p** 43. C Brislington St Luke *Bris* 42-47; C Westbury-on-Trym St Alb 47-52; CF 49-51; V Oldland and Longwell Green *Bris* 52-71; V Minety w Oaksey 71-82; P-in-c 82-84; RD Malmesbury 73-79; Hon Can Bris Cathl 77-84; P-in-c Crudwell w Ashley 82-84; rtd 84; Perm to Offic *Bris* 84-03. *48 Main Street, Cosgrove, Milton Keynes MK19 7JL*

THOMAS, Wilson Hugo. d 01 **p** 05. Barbados 01-05; NSM Frimley *Guildf* from 05. *3B Ansell Road, Frimley GU16 8BS* Tel (01276) 681652 E-mail wilsonthomas56@googlemail.com

THOMAS ANTHONY, Brother. *See* DEHOOP, Brother Thomas Anthony

THOMASSON, Keith Duncan. b 69. St Pet Coll Ox BA91 MA97 Lon Inst of Educn PGCE92. Ripon Coll Cuddesdon BA01 Bossey Ecum Inst Geneva. **d** 02 **p** 03. C Lancaster St Mary w St John and St Anne *Blackb* 02-04; C Longridge 04-06; Partnership P E Bris from 06. *11 Vicars Close, Bristol BS16 3TH* Tel 0117-965 7740 E-mail keiththomasson@hotmail.com

THOMPSON, Adrian David. b 68. Univ of Wales (Abth) BSc93 PhD97 Bris Univ PGCE98. Wycliffe Hall Ox 93. **d** 05 **p** 06. C Blackb St Gabr 05-08; Chapl Abp Temple Sch Preston from 09. *4 St Annes Close, Brookhouse, Lancaster LA2 9PQ*

THOMPSON, Alan. b 61. Qu Coll Birm 04. **d** 07 **p** 08. NSM Saltley and Washwood Heath *Birm* from 07. *9 Old Oscott Hill, Birmingham B44 9SR* Tel 0121-350 8847 E-mail alant@whstools.co.uk

THOMPSON, Andrew David. b 68. Poly of Wales BSc90 Nottm Univ MA03. Wycliffe Hall Ox 98. **d** 00 **p** 01. C Oakwood *Derby* 00-04; Asst Chapl UAE 05-06; Chapl Kuwait from 06. *PO Box 9999, Ahmadi, Kuwait* Tel (00965) 398 5929 E-mail andythompson1968@swissmail.org

THOMPSON, Mrs Angela Lorena Jennifer. b 44. SAOMC 96. **d** 99 **p** 00. NSM Chalfont St Giles *Ox* from 99. *3 The Leys, Chesham Bois, Amersham HP6 5NP* Tel (01494) 726654 E-mail angelalj70@hotmail.com

THOMPSON, Canon Anthony Edward. b 38. Bris Univ BA61. Ridley Hall Cam 61. **d** 63 **p** 64. C Peckham St Mary Magd *S'wark* 63-66; SAMS Paraguay 67-72; C Otley *Bradf* 72-75; TV Woughton *Ox* 75-82; P-in-c Lower Nutfield *S'wark* 82-02; V S Nutfield w Outwood 02-03; RD Reigate 91-93; Local Min Adv Croydon Episc Area 93-03; Hon Can S'wark Cathl 03; rtd 03; Perm to Offic *Chich* from 04. *3 The Curlews, Shoreham-by-Sea BN43 5UQ* Tel (01273) 440182 E-mail tonythompsonsbs@hotmail.com

THOMPSON, Athol James Patrick. b 34. St Paul's Coll Grahamstown 72. **d** 74 **p** 75. S Africa 74-83; P-in-c Dewsbury St Matt and St Jo *Wakef* 84; TV Dewsbury 84-93; Chapl Staincliffe and Dewsbury Gen Hosps Wakef 84-90; Chapl Dewsbury and Distr Hosp 90-93; V Shiregreen St Jas and St Chris *Sheff* 93-99; rtd 99; Perm to Offic *Sheff* from 99. *109 Park Avenue, Chapeltown, Sheffield S35 1WH* Tel 0114-245 1028

THOMPSON, Canon Barry Pearce. b 40. St Andr Univ BSc63 Ball Coll Ox PhD66 Hull Univ MA82. NW Ord Course 76. **d** 79 **p** 80. C Cottingham *York* 79-82; V Swine 82-83; Lect Th Hull Univ 83-88; Ind Chapl *York* 83-85; Abp's Adv on Ind Issues 85-88; Can Res Chelmsf Cathl 88-98; Treas and Can Windsor 98-02; rtd 02; Perm to Offic *York* from 03. *44 Topcliffe Road, Sowerby, Thirsk YO7 1RB* Tel (01845) 525170 Mobile 07768-515790 E-mail barry.thompson10@btopenworld.com

THOMPSON, Brian. b 34. MRICS65 FRICS75. St Jo Coll Nottm 81. **d** 84 **p** 85. C Bletchley *Ox* 84-87; V Sneyd Green *Lich* 87-99; rtd 99; Perm to Offic *Lich* from 99. *85 Harrington Croft, West Bromwich B71 3RJ* Tel 0121-588 6120 E-mail brian.thompson40@btinternet.com

THOMPSON, Carrie Julia Lucy Jadwiga. b 77. Keble Coll Ox BA99 MA04. St Steph Ho Ox MA06. **d** 04 **p** 05. C Camberwell St Giles w St Matt *S'wark* 04-08; V Forton *Portsm* from 08; Chapl St Vincent Sixth Form Coll from 08. *The Vicarage, 10 Spring Garden Lane, Gosport PO12 1HY* Tel (023) 9250 3140 E-mail mother.carrie@btinternet.com

THOMPSON, David. *See* THOMPSON, John David

THOMPSON, David Arthur. b 37. Clifton Th Coll. **d** 69 **p** 70. C Finchley Ch Ch *Lon* 69-72; C Barking St Marg w St Patr *Chelmsf* 72-75; TV 75-81; V Toxteth Park St Clem *Liv* 81-91; TR Parr 91-03; rtd 03; Perm to Offic *Sarum* from 03. *Charis, 72 Harkwood Drive, Hamworthy, Poole BH15 4PE* Tel (01202) 668904

THOMPSON, David John. b 64. Cranmer Hall Dur 92. **d** 95 **p** 96. C Poulton-le-Sands w Morecambe St Laur *Blackb* 95-99; V Farington Moss 99-02; V Lea 02-09; Warden Past Assts 06-09; P-in-c Ringley w Prestolee *Man* from 09. *The Vicarage, 9 Stoneleigh Drive, Radcliffe, Manchester M26 1FZ* Tel (01204) 570992

THOMPSON, David Simon. b 57. Aston Univ BSc82 MRPharmS83. STETS 01. **d** 04 **p** 05. NSM Bournemouth H Epiphany *Win* from 04. *15 Cheriton Avenue, Bournemouth BH7 6SD* Tel (01202) 426764 Mobile 07763-052009 E-mail david_iford@hotmail.com

THOMPSON, Canon Donald Frazer. b 20. St Cath Coll Cam BA46 MA49. Coll of Resurr Mirfield 46. **d** 48 **p** 49. C Cheshunt *St Alb* 48-52; C Norton 52-56; V Wigan St Anne *Liv* 56-62; V Leeds St Aid *Ripon* 62-73; RD Allerton 70-73; R Adel 73-87; Hon Can Ripon Cathl 75-87; RD Headingley 85-87; rtd 87; Perm to Offic *Cov* from 87. *75 Cubbington Road, Leamington Spa CV32 7AQ* Tel (01926) 773298

THOMPSON, Edward Ronald Charles. b 25. AKC51. **d** 52 **p** 53. C Hinckley St Mary *Leic* 52-54; Asst Master St Geo Upper Sch Jerusalem 54-55; Chapl St Boniface Coll Warminster 56-59; R Hawkchurch w Fishpond *Sarum* 59-63; V Camberwell St Mich w All So w Em *S'wark* 63-67; P-in-c St Mary le Strand w St Clem Danes *Lon* 67-74; R 74-93; rtd 93; Perm to Offic *S'wark* from 95. *3 Woodsyre, Sydenham Hill, London SE26 6SS* Tel (020) 8670 8289

THOMPSON, Ms Eileen Carol. b 46. Lon Univ BA69. New Coll Edin MTh92. **d** 96 **p** 97. Par Dn Dhaka St Thos Bangladesh 96-97; Presbyter Madras H Cross w St Mich India 97-99; Presbyter in charge Madras St Mary 99-02; V Pallikunu St Geo and Palla Ch 02-04; Min Livingston LEP *Edin* from 04. *53 Garry Walk, Livingston EH54 5AS* Tel (01506) 433451 E-mail eileencthompson@gmail.com

THOMPSON, Elizabeth Gray McManus. d 06 **p** 07. NSM Garrison w Slavin and Belleek *Clogh* 06-07; NSM Rossorry from 07. *The Deanery, 10 Augher Road, Clogher BT76 0AD* Tel (028) 8554 9797 E-mail thompson.clogher@ntlworld.com

THOMPSON, Frederick Robert. b 15. Dur Univ LTh40. St Aug Coll Cant 37. **d** 40 **p** 41. C Northampton Ch Ch *Pet* 40-44; C Maidstone All SS *Cant* 44-46; India 46-57; Area Sec (Dios Birm and Lich) SPG 57-64; V Tutbury *Lich* 64-80; rtd 80; Perm to Offic *Sarum* from 80. *1 Panorama Road, Poole BH13 7RA* Tel (01202) 700735

THOMPSON, Garry John. b 49. Qu Coll Birm. **d** 96 **p** 97. C Wilnecote *Lich* 96-99; V Lapley w Wheaton Aston from 99; P-in-c Blymhill w Weston-under-Lizard from 99. *The Vicarage, Pinfold Lane, Wheaton Aston, Stafford ST19 9PD* Tel (01785) 840395 E-mail garry@garrythompson2.wanadoo.co.uk

✠**THOMPSON, The Rt Revd Geoffrey Hewlett.** b 29. Trin Hall Cam BA52 MA56. Cuddesdon Coll 52. **d** 54 **p** 55 **c** 74. C Northampton St Matt *Pet* 54-59; V Wisbech St Aug *Ely* 59-66; V Folkestone St Sav *Cant* 66-74; Suff Bp Willesden *Lon* 74-79; Area Bp Willesden 79-85; Bp Ex 85-99; rtd 99; Hon Asst Bp Carl from 99. *Low Broomrigg, Warcop, Appleby-in-Westmorland CA16 6PT* Tel (01768) 341281

THOMPSON, Geoffrey Peter. b 58. St Pet Coll Ox BA80 MA82. SEITE 99. **d** 02 **p** 03. C Cheam *S'wark* 02-06; C Croydon St Jo from 06. *8 The Ridgeway, Croydon CR0 4AB* Tel (020) 8680 1370 E-mail gtchurch@waitrose.com

THOMPSON, Giles. d 06 **p** 07. NSM Kirkby Stephen w Mallerstang etc *Carl* from 06. *Cairn Cottage, 13 High Street, Kirkby Stephen CA17 4SG*

THOMPSON, Preb Gordon Henry Moorhouse. b 41. Univ of Wales LLM95. K Coll Lon 63 St Boniface Warminster 66. **d** 67 **p** 68. C Leominster *Heref* 67-70; C Burford II w Greete and Hope Bagot 70-74; TV 74-89; C Burford III w Lt Heref 70-74; TV 74-89; C Tenbury 70-74; TV 74-89; TV Burford I 74-89; RD Ludlow 83-89; Preb Heref Cathl 85-97; rtd 89; Perm to Offic *Heref* from 89. *The Poplars, Bitterley Village, Ludlow SY8 3HQ* Tel (01584) 891093

THOMPSON, Harold Anthony. b 41. NOC 84. **d** 87 **p** 88. C Leeds Belle Is St Jo and St Barn *Ripon* 87-90; V Leeds St Cypr Harehills 90-96; V Shadwell 96-06; rtd 06. *551 Shadwell Lane, Leeds LS17 8AP* Tel 0113-266 5913 E-mail haroldthompson41@hotmail.com

THOMPSON, Hewlett. *See* THOMPSON, The Rt Revd Geoffrey Hewlett

THOMPSON, Ian David. b 51. Hull Univ BSc72. NOC 94. **d** 97 **p** 98. C Blackley St Andr *Man* 97-00; P-in-c 00-06; R Burnage St Marg from 06. *St Margaret's Rectory, 250 Burnage Lane, Manchester M19 1FL* Tel 0161-432 1844 E-mail ian@thompsonrev.freeserve.co.uk

THOMPSON, Ian George. b 60. SEITE 99. d 02 p 03. NSM Walworth St Pet *S'wark* 02-05; NSM Dulwich St Clem w St Pet 05-07; Chapl HM Pris Pentonville from 07. *HM Prison Pentonville, Caledonian Road, London N7 8TT* Tel (020) 7023 7000 Mobile 07985-582257
E-mail ian.thompson@hmps.gsi.gov.uk

THOMPSON, Ian Malcolm. b 59. Wm Booth Memorial Coll CertEd79 Aber Univ BTh98 Selw Coll Cam MA02. Edin Th Coll 91. d 94 p 95. C Longside, Old Deer and Strichen *Ab* 94-96; R Aberdeen St Mary 96-99; Chapl and Dean of Chpl Selw Coll Cam 99-05; Chapl Newnham Coll Cam 99-05; Dean K Coll Cam from 05; Hon C Cambridge St Mary Less *Ely* 03-07. *King's College, Cambridge CB2 1ST* Tel (01223) 331419
E-mail dean@kings.cam.ac.uk

THOMPSON, James. b 30. Nottm Univ DipEd65. Wycliffe Hall Ox 66. d 66 p 67. C Woodlands *Sheff* 66-69; R Firbeck w Letwell 69-71; V Milnsbridge *Wakef* 71-80; Chapl St Luke's Hosp Huddersfield 71-80; NSM Dewsbury 80-84; Lect Huddersfield Coll FE 80-84; Dioc Chapl Aber Hosps 84-89; Dioc Supernumerary *Ab* 84-89; R Buckie and Portsoy 89-94; rtd 95. *Peace Haven, Fron Park Road, Holywell CH8 7UY* Tel (01352) 712368

THOMPSON, James. b 37. Coll of Resurr Mirfield 64. d 67 p 68. C Shieldfield Ch Ch *Newc* 67-69; C Hendon *Dur* 69-74; V Gateshead St Chad Bensham 74-85; R Easington 85-90; Chapl Thorpe Hosp Easington 85-90; V Cassop cum Quarrington *Dur* 90-06; rtd 06. *43 Heathfield, Sunderland SR2 9EW* Tel 0191-522 9490

THOMPSON, Jeremy James Thomas. b 58. Sunderland Univ BEd92. Cranmer Hall Dur 94. d 96 p 97. C Bedlington *Newc* 96-00; P-in-c Choppington 00-02; V 02-08; R St John Lee from 08; V Warden w Newbrough from 08. *St John Lee Rectory, Acomb, Hexham NE46 4PE* Tel (01434) 600268
E-mail jeremyjtthompson@operamail.com

THOMPSON, John David. b 40. Lon Univ BD65 Ch Ch Ox DPhil69. St Steph Ho Ox 65. d 67 p 68. C Solihull *Birm* 67-71; C Biddestone w Slaughterford *Bris* 71-73; Lect Wells Th Coll 71-72; C Yatton Keynell *Bris* 71-73; C Castle Combe 71-73; V Braughing *St Alb* 74-77; R Digswell 77-82; TR Digswell and Panshanger 82-98; rtd 00. *11 Russell Street, Boddam, Peterhead AB42 3NG* Tel (01779) 472680

THOMPSON, John Michael. b 47. Nottm Univ BTh77. Linc Th Coll 73. d 77 p 78. C Old Brumby *Linc* 77-80; C Grantham 80-81; TV 81-84; V Holton-le-Clay and Tetney 84-94; V Holton-le-Clay and Tetney 94-97; R Humshaugh w Simonburn and Wark *Newc* from 97. *The Vicarage, Humshaugh, Hexham NE46 4AA* Tel (01434) 681304

THOMPSON, John Turrell. b 57. Sheff Univ BA(Econ)79 Southn Univ BTh88. Sarum & Wells Th Coll 83. d 86 p 87. C Tavistock and Gulworthy *Ex* 86-90; TV Pinhoe and Broadclyst 90-95; P-in-c Northam w Westward Ho! and Appledore 95-96; TV Bideford, Northam, Westward Ho!, Appledore etc 96-00; rtd 00; Perm to Offic *Ex* from 00. *Brambles Patch, 39 Westermore Drive, Roundswell, Barnstaple EX31 3XU*

THOMPSON, John Wilfred. b 44. CA Tr Coll 66 St Deiniol's Hawarden 84. d 85 p 86. C Rhyl w St Ann *St As* 85-87; R Fritwell w Souldern and Ardley w Fewcott *Ox* 87-97; rtd 09. *19 Tangmere Close, Bicester OX26 4YZ* Tel (01869) 601082

THOMPSON (née LILLIE), Mrs Judith Virginia. b 44. LMH Ox BA66 Essex Univ MA73 Univ of E Africa DipEd67. Gilmore Course IDC82. dss 82 d 87 p 94. Lawrence Weston *Bris* 82-85; E Bris 85-95; Hon Par Dn 87-95; Chapl HM Rem Cen Pucklechurch 87-91; Chapl Asst Southmead Hosp Bris 91-95; C Knowle St Barn Bris 95-02; Bp's Adv for Past Care for Clergy and Families 97-00; Community Th St Mich Coll Llan 00-05; Dir In-House Tr 02-05; Chapl Worcs Acute Hosps NHS Trust 05-09; rtd 09. *Grove Cottage, Barton Lane, Mere, Warminster BA12 6JA* Tel (01747) 860553
E-mail judithvthompson@aol.com

THOMPSON, Kenneth. b 31. St Deiniol's Hawarden 84. d 87 p 88. Hon Par Dn Upton (Overchurch) *Ches* 87-90; NSM Tranmere St Cath 90-95; rtd 96; Perm to Offic *Ches* from 96. *33 Meadway, Upton, Wirral CH49 6JQ* Tel 0151-677 6433

THOMPSON, Kenneth (Brother Nathanael). b 29. St Deiniol's Hawarden 76. d 78 p 79. SSF from 62; C Llanbeblig w Caernarfon *Ban* 78-80; C Swansea St Gabr *S & B* 84-87; C Dolgellau w Llanfachreth and Brithdir etc *Ban* 95-09; rtd 98. *The Vicarage, 3A High Street, Bentley, Doncaster DN5 0AA* Tel (01302) 876272

THOMPSON, Kevin. b 55. Sheff Univ BEd77. Oak Hill Th Coll. d 89 p 90. C Brinsworth w Catcliffe *Sheff* 89-92; V Kimberworth Park 92-97; V Grenoside 97-98; Perm to Offic from 98. *30 Arnold Avenue, Charnock, Sheffield S12 3JB* Tel 0114-239 6986
E-mail kevin.thompson10@virgin.net

THOMPSON, Livingstone Anthony. b 59. Univ of W Indies BA82 Irish Sch of Ecum MPhil00 TCD PhD03. McCormick Th Sem Chicago MA(TS)89. d 83 p 90. Jamaica 83-05; CITC 05-06. *83 Hermitage Glen, Kells, Co Meath, Republic of Ireland* Tel (00353) (46) 929 3861 Mobile 86-373 7135

THOMPSON, Mark William. b 52. St Jo Coll Nottm 77. d 81 p 82. C Barnsbury St Andr and H Trin w All SS *Lon* 81-84; C Addiscombe St Mary *Cant* 84; C Addiscombe St Mary *S'wark* 85-87; V Thorpe Edge *Bradf* 87-94; Chapl Colchester Hosp Univ NHS Foundn Trust from 94. *Colchester General Hospital, Turner Road, Colchester CO4 5JL* Tel (01206) 747474 or 742513
E-mail mark.thompson@essexrivers.nhs.uk

THOMPSON, Martin Eric. b 52. FCCA. Trin Coll Bris 95. d 97 p 98. C Heref St Pet w St Owen and St Jas 97-01; P-in-c Huntley and Longhope *Glouc* 01-02; R Huntley and Longhope, Churcham and Bulley 03-05; V Worfield *Heref* from 05. *The Vicarage, Hallon, Worfield, Bridgnorth WV15 5JZ* Tel (01746) 716698 E-mail revmartin@lineone.net

THOMPSON, Matthew. b 68. CCC Cam BA90 MA94 MPhil94. Ridley Hall Cam 91. d 94 p 95. C Hulme Ascension *Man* 94-97; C Langley and Parkfield 97-98; TV 98-00; P-in-c Man Clayton St Cross w St Paul 00-08; AD Ardwick 03-08; P-in-c Bolton St Pet from 08; P-in-c Bolton St Phil from 08. *35 Sherbourne Road, Bolton BL1 5NN*
E-mail vicar@boltonparishchurch.co.uk

THOMPSON, Mervyn Patrick. b 59. Wilson Carlile Coll 84 Coll of Resurr Mirfield 90. d 92 p 93. C Sheff St Cath Richmond Road 92-95; V Thurnscoe St Hilda 95-06; P-in-c Thurnscoe St Helen 99-06; R Thurnscoe from 06. *The Vicarage, Hanover Street, Thurnscoe, Rotherham S63 0HJ* Tel (01709) 893259

THOMPSON, Michael. b 49. NEOC 83. d 86 p 87. C Ashington *Newc* 86-88; C Ponteland 88-91; TV Newc Epiphany 91-98; P-in-c Choppington 98-99; P-in-c Woldingham *S'wark* 99-02; TV Caterham 02-03; TV Saffron Walden w Wendens Ambo, Littlebury etc *Chelmsf* 03-08; R N Hartismere *St E* from 08. *The Rectory, Oakley, Diss IP21 4AN* Tel (01379) 742708
E-mail frmichael.thompson@btinternet.com

THOMPSON, Michael Bruce. b 53. N Carolina Univ BA75 Dallas Th Sem ThM79 Virginia Th Sem 79 Ch Coll Cam PhD88. d 80 p 81. Asst Min New Bern N Carolina 80-83; Chair Youth and Evang and Renewal in E Carolina 81-83; Lect Greek Cam Univ 87-88; Lect St Jo Coll Nottm 88-95; Lect NT and Dir of Studies Ridley Hall Cam from 95; Vice-Prin from 00. *Dashwood House, Sidgwick Avenue, Cambridge CB3 9DA* Tel (01223) 741077 or 741066 Fax 741081 E-mail mbt2@cam.ac.uk

THOMPSON, Michael James. b 55. St Andr Univ MTheol78 Dur Univ MA93. St Mich Coll Llan 78. d 79 p 80. C Aberavon *Llan* 79-81; C Kensington St Mary Abbots w St Geo *Lon* 81-85; Chapl and Sacr Westmr Abbey 85-87; R Lowick w Sudborough and Slipton *Pet* 87-94; P-in-c Islip 87-94; V Sneinton St Steph w St Alb *S'well* 96-98; R Stamford St Mary and St Martin *Linc* 98-04; I Dublin St Bart w Leeson Park *D & G* 04-07; Min Can St Patr Cathl Dublin 04-07; I Youghal Union *C, C & R* from 08. *The Rectory, Knockacally, Youghal, Co Cork, Republic of Ireland* Tel (00353) (24) 92350 E-mail ecccolldeyoughal@eircom.net

THOMPSON, Michael John. b 39. Cam Univ MA. d 00 p 01. OLM Badgeworth, Shurdington and Witcombe w Bentham *Glouc* 00-06. *Cornerways, 1 Church Lane, Shurdington, Gloucester GL51 4TJ* Tel (01242) 862467
E-mail mthompson123@aol.com

THOMPSON, Mrs Michelle. b 68. Man Univ BA89. Ripon Coll Cuddesdon 90. d 92 p 94. Par Dn Leigh St Mary *Man* 92-94; Asst Chapl HM Pris Full Sutton 95-97; V York St Nikla 97-00; Dir Reader Tr and Local Min Development *Man* 00-03; Chapl HM Pris Styal from 04. *HM Prison Styal, Styal Road, Styal, Wilmslow SK9 4HR* Tel (01625) 553000

THOMPSON, Canon Neil Hamilton. b 48. SS Hild & Bede Coll Dur BEd72 Leic Univ MA75. S'wark Ord Course 77 Ven English Coll Rome. d 80 p 81. C Merton St Mary *S'wark* 80-82; C Dulwich St Barn 82-84; V Shooters Hill Ch Ch 84-87; V S Dulwich St Steph 87-96; Ldr Post Ord Tr Woolwich Area 94-96; R Limpsfield and Titsey 96-08; Can Res and Prec Roch Cathl from 08. *Easter Garth, The Precinct, Rochester ME1 1SX* Tel (01634) 405265 or 810063 Fax 401410
E-mail precentor@rochestercathedral.org

THOMPSON, Patricia. b 60. SRN. NEOC 94. d 97 p 98. NSM Sunderland St Chad *Dur* from 97; Voc Adv from 99. *11 Friarsfield Close, Chapelgarth, Sunderland SR3 2RZ* Tel 0191-522 7911

THOMPSON, Patrick Arthur. b 36. Dur Univ BA59. Qu Coll Birm. d 61 p 62. C W Wickham St Fran *Cant* 61-65; C Portchester *Portsm* 65-68; C Birchington w Acol *Cant* 68-71; V S Norwood St Mark 71-77; P-in-c Norbury St Oswald 77-81; V Norbury St Oswald *S'wark* 81-93; V Sutton New Town St Barn 93-00; rtd 00; Resident P Grantown-on-Spey *Mor* from 04. *Rose Cottage, 2 Market Street, Forres IV36 1EF* Tel (01309) 675917

THOMPSON, Paul. b 58. Ox Univ BA. Ripon Coll Cuddesdon 80. d 83 p 84. Chapl Fazakerley Hosp 83-86; C Kirkby *Liv* 83-86; TV 86-89; Ind Chapl 86-89; Chapl Kirkby Coll of FE 86-89; CF 89-01; Chapl Epsom Coll from 01. *Epsom College, Epsom KT17 4JQ* Tel (01372) 821288
E-mail s-chaplain@epsomcollege.org.uk

THOMPSON, Paul. b 65. TCD BA87. CITC 87. d 89 p 90. C Orangefield w Moneyreagh *D & D* 89-92; I Dromara w

Garvaghy 92-97; I Ramoan w Ballycastle and Culfeightrin *Conn* 97-00; Dep Chapl HM Pris Liv 00-01; Chapl HM YOI Portland from 01. *HM Young Offender Institution, The Grove, Portland DT5 1DL* Tel (01305) 820301 Fax 823718

THOMPSON, Paul Noble. b 54. Univ of Wales (Cardiff) BMus77 Univ of Wales (Ban) MPhil04. Coll of Resurr Mirfield. **d** 80 **p** 81. C Bargoed and Deri w Brithdir *Llan* 80-83; C Whitchurch 83-84; V Porth w Trealaw 84-90; V Llanharan w Peterston-super-Montem 90-97; Hon C Barry All SS 97-01; Dioc Youth Chapl 90-01; V Lisvane 01-09; Chapl Univ Coll of SS Mark and Jo Plymouth *Ex* from 09. *The College of St Mark and St John, Derriford Road, Plymouth PL6 8BH* Tel (01752) 636847 ext 2047

THOMPSON, Pauline. See WILLCOX, Mrs Pauline

THOMPSON, Peter Alrick. b 79. QUB BA01 TCD MPhil04 ARIAM99 ACertCM. CITC 01. **d** 03 **p** 04. C Clooney w Strathfoyle *D & R* 03-06; I Donaghmore w Upper Donaghmore *Arm* from 06. *St Michael's Rectory, 66 Main Street, Castlecaulfield, Dungannon BT70 3NP* Tel (028) 8776 1214 Mobile 07732-856306
E-mail donaghmore@armagh.anglican.org

THOMPSON, Peter Kerr. b 32. Kelham Th Coll. **d** 56 **p** 57. Solomon Is 56-76; Adn Malaita and Outer E Solomon 62-76; Adn N Melanesia 68-70; Australia from 76; R S Gulf 76-78; R Port Hedland 78-82; R Melville 85-88; R Childers 89-91; R Bundaberg W 91-92. *28 Saunders Street, Point Vernon Qld 4655, Australia* Tel (0061) (7) 4124 3645

THOMPSON, Canon Peter Ross. b 26. St Jo Coll Cam BA47 MB, BChir50. Tyndale Hall Bris. **d** 60 **p** 61. C New Malden and Coombe *S'wark* 60-61; BCMS Burma 61-66; R Slaugham *Chich* 66-72; V Polegate 72-92; Can and Preb Chich Cathl 91-92; rtd 92; Perm to Offic *Guildf* from 92. *Tregenna, Barley Mow Lane, Knaphill, Woking GU21 2HX* Tel (01483) 480595

THOMPSON, Mrs Rachel Mary. b 65. Roehampton Inst BA87 Rolle Coll PGCE88 Nottm Univ MA07. EMMTC 04. **d** 07 **p** 08. NSM Wilne and Draycott w Breaston *Derby* from 07. *16 Edge Hill Court, Long Eaton, Nottingham NG10 1PQ* Tel 0115-972 7275 E-mail rev.rachel@googlemail.com

THOMPSON, Randolph. b 25. Lich Th Coll 63. **d** 65 **p** 66. C Boultham *Linc* 65-68; V Paddock *Wakef* 68-69; P-in-c Cornholme 69-71; V 71-72; Chapl Barnsley Hall and Lea Hosps Bromsgrove 72-84; V Hanley Castle, Hanley Swan and Welland *Worc* 84-89; rtd 89; Perm to Offic *Lich* from 90. *37 Hampton Fields, Oswestry SY11 1TL* Tel (01691) 658484

THOMPSON, Raymond Craigmile. b 42. Man Univ BTh. **d** 84 **p** 85. C Clooney *D & R* 84-86; I Urney w Sion Mills 86-92; I Derryvullen N w Castlearchdale *Clogh* 92-05; Chapl to Bp Clogh 02-05; Can Clogh Cathl 03-05; Dean Clogh 05-09; I Clogh w Errigal Portclare 05-09; rtd 09. *Address temp unknown*

THOMPSON, Richard Brian. b 60. Sheff Poly BSc83. Ripon Coll Cuddesdon 86. **d** 89 **p** 90. C Thorpe Bay *Chelmsf* 89-92; V Rushmere *St E* 92-97; Dep Chapl HM Pris Nor 97-98; Chapl HM Pris Wayland 98-01; Chapl HM Pris Hollesley Bay 01-06; Chapl HM Pris Whitemoor from 06. *The Chaplain's Office, HM Prison Whitemoor, Longhill Road, March PE15 0PR* Tel (01354) 602350 Fax 602351

THOMPSON, Robert Craig. b 72. Univ Coll Dur BA92. Westcott Ho Cam 94. **d** 96 **p** 97. C Wigan All SS *Liv* 96-00; P-in-c Ladybrook *S'well* 00-05; P-in-c Bengeo *St Alb* 05-08; TV Hertford from 08. *The Rectory, Byde Street, Hertford SG14 3BS* Tel (01992) 413691 E-mail revrobert@tiscali.co.uk

THOMPSON, Robert George. b 71. K Coll Cam BA93 MA97. Ripon Coll Cuddesdon MTh95. **d** 97 **p** 98. C Ruislip St Martin *Lon* 97-01; Chapl Parkside Community NHS Trust Lon 01-09; Chapl R Brompton and Harefield NHS Trust from 09; Hon C Holland Park *Lon* from 09. *Chaplain's Office, Royal Brompton Hospital, Sydney Street, London SW3 6NP* Tel (020) 7352 8121 ext 4740 E-mail r.thompson2@rbht.nhs.uk

THOMPSON, Roger Quintin. b 63. K Coll Lon BA85 AKC85 Nottm Univ PGCE86 MA96. Aston Tr Scheme 92 St Jo Coll Nottm 94. **d** 96. C Easton H Trin w St Gabr and St Lawr and St Jude *Bris* 96-00; C Lisburn Ch Ch Cathl 00-04; I Kilwaughter w Cairncastle and Craigy Hill from 04. *Cairncastle Rectory, 15 Cairncastle Road, Ballygally, Larne BT40 2RB* Tel (028) 2858 3220 *or* 2826 9552 E-mail rqtfi@btinternet.com

THOMPSON, Ross Keith Arnold. b 53. Sussex Univ BA75 Bris Univ PhD82. Coll of Resurr Mirfield 80. **d** 82 **p** 83. C Knowle *Bris* 82-85; TV E Bris 85-94; V Bristol St Aid w St Geo 94-95; V Knowle St Barn and H Cross Inns Court 95-02; Tutor St Mich Coll Llan 02-05. *Grove Cottage, Barton Lane, Mere, Warminster BA12 6JA* Tel (01747) 860553

THOMPSON, Ruth Jean. See GOSTELOW, Mrs Ruth Jean

THOMPSON, Mrs Shanthi Hazel Peiris. b 67. Cranmer Hall Dur 07. **d** 09. C Kirkby Lonsdale *Carl* from 09. *4 Abbotsgate, Kirkby Lonsdale, Carnforth LA6 2JS* Tel 07931-446043 (mobile) E-mail shpt@btinternet.com

THOMPSON, Stephen Peter. b 45. Lon Univ BSc67 Lon Inst of Educn PGCE71 K Coll Lon BD77 AKC77 SOAS Lon BA82 Poona Univ MPhil85 PhD87 FRAS91. Ripon Coll Cuddesdon.

d 00. NSM Bedford Park *Lon* 00-01; NSM Isleworth St Fran 01-08; Perm to Offic from 08. *12 Minsterley Avenue, Shepperton TW17 8QT* Tel (01932) 781805
E-mail revdocstephen@gmail.com

THOMPSON, Thomas Oliver. b 27. TCD 61. **d** 63 **p** 64. C Lisburn Ch Ch *Conn* 63-68; Chapl to Ch of Ireland Miss to Deaf and Dumb 68-76; I Glenavy w Tunny and Crumlin 77-92; rtd 92. *34 Strandview Avenue, Portstewart BT55 7LL* Tel (028) 7083 3267

THOMPSON, Canon Timothy. b 34. Fitzw Ho Cam BA59 MA64. Cuddesdon Coll 59. **d** 61 **p** 62. C Noel Park St Mark *Lon* 61-64; C Shrub End *Chelmsf* 64-67; New Zealand 67-70; R Tolleshunt Knights w Tiptree *Chelmsf* 70-81; R Colchester St Jas, All SS, St Nic and St Runwald 81-88; RD Colchester 84-88; Hon Can Chelmsf Cathl 85-88; Can Res Chelmsf Cathl 88-01; Vice-Provost 88-00; Vice-Dean 00-01; rtd 01. *44 Sixth Avenue, Chelmsford CM1 4ED* Tel (01245) 260382

THOMPSON, Timothy Charles. b 51. Lon Univ BSc73 AKC. Westcott Ho Cam 75. **d** 78 **p** 79. C Ipswich St Mary at Stoke w St Pet etc *St E* 78-81; Ind Chapl *Nor* 81-88; C Lowestoft and Kirkley 81-83; TV 83-88; V Coney Hill *Glouc* 88-94; P-in-c Caister *Nor* 94-00; R from 00. *The Rectory, Rectory Close, Caister-on-Sea, Great Yarmouth NR30 5EG* Tel (01493) 720287 E-mail tim.thompson@ukonline.co.uk

THOMPSON, Canon Timothy William. b 47. Bris Univ CertEd70 Open Univ BA78. EMMTC. **d** 88 **p** 89. C Scartho *Linc* 88-91; V Haxey 91-95; P-in-c Surfleet 95-00; Asst Local Min Officer 95-00; RD Elloe W 98-00; P-in-c Linc St Pet-at-Gowts and St Andr 00-09; P-in-c Linc St Botolph 00-09; RD Christianity 02-08; rtd 09; Can and Preb Linc Cathl from 02. *16 Nocton Park Road, Nocton, Lincoln LN4 2BE* Tel (01526) 320171 Mobile 07885-238813
E-mail timwthompson@btinternet.com

THOMPSON, Canon Tom Malcolm. b 38. Dur Univ BA60 Man Univ MPhil93. Bps' Coll Cheshunt 60. **d** 62 **p** 63. C Standish *Blackb* 62-65; C Lancaster St Mary 65-67; V Chorley All SS 67-72; V Barrowford 72-78; RD Pendle 75-78; R Northfield *Birm* 78-82; RD Kings Norton 79-82; V Longton *Blackb* 82-94; RD Leyland 89-94; V Nunthorpe *York* 94-03; Can and Preb York Minster 98-03; RD Stokesley 00-03; rtd 03; Perm to Offic *Carl* from 03 and *Blackb* from 08. *Wainstones, 6 Greengate Crescent, Levens, Kendal LA8 8QB* Tel (015395) 61409

THOMPSON-McCAUSLAND, Marcus Perronet. b 31. Trin Coll Cam BA54 MA60. Coll of Resurr Mirfield 57. **d** 59 **p** 60. C Perry Barr *Birm* 59-65; V Rubery 65-72; R Cradley *Heref* 72-82; P-in-c Storridge 72-82; P-in-c Mathon 72-82; P-in-c Castle Frome 72-82; Hon C Camberwell St Giles *S'wark* 82-87; Hon C Lydbury N *Heref* 88-89; Hon C Lydbury N w Hopesay and Edgton 89-94; Hon C Wigmore Abbey 95-01; Perm to Offic from 01. *18 Watling Street, Leintwardine, Craven Arms SY7 0LW* Tel (01547) 540228

THOMPSON-VEAR, John Arthur. b 76. Sunderland Univ BA98. St Steph Ho Ox BA02 MA06. **d** 03 **p** 04. C Plymouth Crownhill Ascension *Ex* 03-06; Chapl RN 06-08; TV Harrogate St Wilfrid from 08. *St Wilfrid's House, 23 Azerley Grove, Harrogate HG3 2SY* Tel (01423) 709432 Mobile 07799-215148
E-mail frjohn@btinternet.com

THOMPSTONE, Canon John Deaville. b 39. BNC Ox BA63 MA67. Ridley Hall Cam 63. **d** 65 **p** 66. C Hoole *Ches* 65-68; C Fulwood *Sheff* 68-71; V Skirbeck H Trin *Linc* 71-77; V Shipley St Pet *Bradf* 77-91; RD Airedale 82-88; V Poynton *Ches* 91-04; Hon Can Ches Cathl 02-04; rtd 04. *Greyfriars, Broadway Road, Childswickham, Broadway WR12 7HP* Tel (01386) 852930
E-mail greyfriars@homecall.co.uk

THOMSETT, Murray Richard. b 32. MBKSTS. Oak Hill Th Coll 91. **d** 92 **p** 93. NSM Whitton SS Phil and Jas *Lon* 92-96; NSM Hampton All SS 96-02; Chapl Terminal 4 Heathrow Airport from 96. *27 Coombe Road, Hampton TW12 3PB* Tel (020) 8979 7549 *or* 8745 2700 E-mail murrayt@nildram.co.uk

THOMSON, Alexander Keith. b 38. Cranmer Hall Dur BA63. **d** 64 **p** 65. C Middleton *Man* 64-68; Chapl Rannoch Sch Perthshire 68-72; P-in-c Kinloch Rannoch *St And* 68-72; Asst Chapl Oundle Sch 72-94; Chapl Laxton Sch 88-94; Lic to Offic *Pet* 73-94; Perm to Offic from 94; rtd 98. *Holly Lodge, Achurch Road, Thorpe Waterville, Kettering NN14 3ED* Tel (01832) 720083

THOMSON, Andrew Maitland. b 43. CA(Z)67. Westcott Ho Cam 78. **d** 80 **p** 81. C Harare Cathl Zimbabwe 80-82; R Kadoma and P-in-c Chegutu 82-87; R Marlborough St Paul Harare 87-92; P-in-c E w N and W Barsham *Nor* 92-95; P-in-c N and S Creake w Waterden 92-94; P-in-c Sculthorpe w Dunton and Doughton 92-94; R N and S Creake w Waterden, Syderstone etc from 95. *The Rectory, 18 Front Street, South Creake, Fakenham NR21 9PE* Tel (01328) 823433
E-mail pandathomson@btinternet.com

THOMSON, Bruce. See THOMSON, Sydney Bruce

THOMSON, Canon Celia Stephana Margaret. b 55. LMH Ox MA83 Birkbeck Coll Lon MA87 K Coll Lon MA94. Sarum & Wells Th Coll 89. **d** 91 **p** 94. Par Dn Southfields St Barn *S'wark*

91-94; C 94-95; V W Wimbledon Ch Ch 95-03; Tutor SEITE 95-00; Voc Adv Lambeth Adnry 96-00; Can Res Glouc Cathl from 03. *3 Miller's Green, Gloucester GL1 2BN* Tel (01452) 415824 E-mail cthomson@gloucestercathedral.org.uk

THOMSON, Christopher Grant. b 71. Cam Univ BTh07. Westcott Ho Cam 05. **d** 07 **p** 08. C Bletchingley and Nutfield *S'wark* from 07. *The Clerk's House, 48 High Street, Bletchingley, Redhill RH1 4PA* Tel (01883) 743252

THOMSON, Preb Clarke Edward Leighton. b 19. TD65. Pemb Coll Ox BA41 MA45. Wycliffe Hall Ox 44. **d** 45 **p** 46. C Penge Lane H Trin *Roch* 45-47; Egypt 47-50; C Chelsea All SS *Lon* 50-51; V 51-92; CF (TA) 52-69; Preb St Paul's Cathl 86-92; rtd 92; Perm to Offic *Lon* from 93. *15 Redburn Street, London SW3 4DA* Tel (020) 7351 5371

✠**THOMSON, The Rt Revd David.** b 52. Keble Coll Ox MA78 DPhil78 Selw Coll Cam BA80 MA84 FRSA06 FSA08 FRHistS08. Westcott Ho Cam 78. **d** 81 **p** 82 **c** 08. C Maltby *Sheff* 81-84; TV Banbury *Ox* 84-94; Sec Par and People 84-93; TR Cockermouth w Embleton and Wythop *Carl* 94-02; Adn Carl and Can Res Carl Cathl 02-08; Suff Bp Huntingdon *Ely* from 08. *14 Lynn Road, Ely CB6 1DA* Tel (01353) 662137 Fax 669357 Mobile 07771-864550

THOMSON, David Francis. b 54. Salford Univ BA81 CPFA84. NOC 05. **d** 07 **p** 08. NSM New Bury w Gt Lever *Man* from 07. *30 Appledore Drive, Bolton BL2 4HH* Tel (01204) 418731 Mobile 07970-461907 E-mail thomsondf@hotmail.com

THOMSON, Elizabeth Jane. b 64. Univ Coll Ox MA85 DPhil89 Trin Coll Cam BA02 Moray Ho Coll of Educn PGCE90. Westcott Ho Cam 00. **d** 03 **p** 04. C Pilton w Croscombe, N Wootton and Dinder *B & W* 03-07; TV Witney *Ox* from 07. *Holy Trinity Vicarage, 4 Maidley Close, Witney OX28 1ER* Tel (01993) 834875 E-mail ejt@jinkaboot.net

THOMSON, Elizabeth Lucy. *See* TALBOT, Mrs Elizabeth Lucy

THOMSON, James. b 39. St Andr Coll Melrose 58 Episc Sem Austin Texas 88. **d** 62 **p** 63. In RC Ch 62-83; C Oklahoma City All So USA 89-90; R Oklahoma St Matt 90-95; Assoc P Oklahoma H Trin 95-05; P-in-c Pittenweem *St And* 06-09; P-in-c Elie and Earlsferry 06-09; rtd 09. *41A South Street, St Andrews KY16 9QR* Tel (01334) 479645 E-mail revjthomson@btinternet.com

THOMSON, James Maclaren. b 69. Grey Coll Dur BA91 Univ Coll Lon MA93. Wycliffe Hall Ox BA99. **d** 00 **p** 01. C Oulton Broad *Nor* 00-04; V Chatteris *Ely* from 04. *The Vicarage, Church Lane, Chatteris PE16 6JY* Tel (01354) 692173 E-mail james@chatteris.org

THOMSON, Canon John Bromilow. b 59. York Univ BA81 Wycliffe Hall Ox BA84 MA91 Nottm Univ PhD01. **d** 85 **p** 86. C Ecclesall *Sheff* 85-89; S Africa 89-92; Tutor St Paul's Coll Grahamstown 89-92; Asst P Grahamstown St Bart 90-92; Asst Lect Rhodes Univ 91-92; V Doncaster St Mary *Sheff* 93-01; Dir Min from 01; Hon Can Sheff Cathl from 01. *15 Grange View, Balby, Doncaster DN4 0XL* Tel (01302) 570205 *or* (01709) 309143 Fax (01709) 309108 E-mail john.thomson@sheffield.anglican.org

THOMSON, Julian Harley. b 43. AKC70. St Aug Coll Cant 70. **d** 71 **p** 72. C Wellingborough All Hallows *Pet* 71-74; Min Can, Prec and Sacr Ely Cathl 74-80; P-in-c Stuntney 76-80; V Arrington 80-91; R Croydon w Clopton 80-91; R Orwell 80-91; R Wimpole 80-91; V Linton 91-96; R Bartlow 91-96; P-in-c Castle Camps 91-96; TR Linton 96-01; RD Linton 99-01; rtd 01; Perm to Offic *Nor* from 01. *Lavender Cottage, 7 Abbey Road, Great Massingham, King's Lynn PE32 2HN* Tel (01485) 520721 E-mail thomson5816@btinternet.com

THOMSON, Keith. *See* THOMSON, Alexander Keith

THOMSON, Matthew James. b 63. Nottm Univ BA92. St Jo Coll Nottm 92. **d** 95 **p** 96. C Cosham *Portsm* 95-98; C Nailsea Ch Ch w Tickenham *B & W* 98-01; V Congresbury w Puxton and Hewish St Ann from 01; Bp's Healing Adv from 01. *The Vicarage, Station Road, Congresbury, Bristol BS49 5DX* Tel (01934) 833126 E-mail revmatthomson@hotmail.com

THOMSON, Monica Anne. b 38. **d** 06 **p** 07. NSM Stockton Heath *Ches* from 06. *9 Broomfields Road, Appleton, Warrington WA4 3AE* Tel (01925) 604235 E-mail jomo.tomsky@ntlworld.com

THOMSON, Peter Ashley. b 36. Ox Univ BA74 MA78 MACE77. Ridley Coll Melbourne ThL57. **d** 59 **p** 60. Australia 59-62, 64-96 and from 01; C Fen Ditton *Ely* 62-63; V Upwood w Gt and Lt Raveley 63-64; C W Holloway St Luke *Lon* 96-97; 2000 by 2000 (Millennium Projects) Officer 97-01; rtd 02. *PO Box 498, Mansfield Vic 3722, Australia* Tel (0061) (3) 5777 5635

THOMSON, Peter Malcolm. b 44. Trin Coll Bris 75. **d** 78 **p** 79. C Tonbridge St Steph *Roch* 78-82; R Cobham w Luddesdowne and Dode 82-90; V Wythall *Birm* 90-02; rtd 02; Perm to Offic *Birm* from 02. *37 Northbrook Road, Shirley, Solihull B90 3NR* Tel 0121-745 9042 E-mail peter@petcar.me.uk

THOMSON, Canon Richard Irving. b 32. Oak Hill Th Coll 57. **d** 60 **p** 61. C Kingston upon Hull H Trin *York* 60-63; C S Croydon Em *Cant* 63-66; V Shoreditch St Leon *Lon* 66-73; Chapl Vevey w Château d'Oex and Villars *Eur* 73-78; V Reigate

St Mary *S'wark* 78-97; Hon Can S'wark Cathl 90-97; rtd 97; Perm to Offic *Win* from 97. *Little Heathfield, Forest Front, Dibden Purlieu, Southampton SO45 3RG* Tel (023) 8084 9613 E-mail richardithomson@compuserve.com

THOMSON, Richard William Byars. b 60. Birm Univ BA86. Ripon Coll Cuddesdon 86. **d** 88 **p** 89. C Moulsecoomb *Chich* 88-90; P-in-c Kirriemuir *St And* 90-94; P-in-c Piddletrenthide w Plush, Alton Pancras etc *Sarum* 94-02; P-in-c Milborne St Andrew w Dewlish 94-02; Chapl Milton Abbey Sch Dorset from 02. *Nether Fen, Milton Abbey, Blandford Forum DT11 0DA* Tel (01258) 881513 E-mail byars22@aol.com

THOMSON, Robert Douglass. b 37. Lon Univ TCert61 Newc Univ DAES70 Dur Univ BEd75. NEOC 76. **d** 79 **p** 80. NSM Shincliffe *Dur* 79-98; Chapl St Aid Coll Dur 93-99. *11 Hill Meadows, High Shincliffe, Durham DH1 2PE* Tel 0191-386 3358

THOMSON, Robin Alexander Stewart. b 43. Ch Coll Cam MA69 K Coll Lon MTh72. SEITE 94. **d** 96 **p** 97. NSM Wimbledon Em Ridgway Prop Chpl *S'wark* 96-02; NSM Tooting Graveney St Nic from 02. *2 Coppice Close, London SW20 9AS* Tel (020) 8540 7748 *or* 8770 9717 Fax 8770 9747 E-mail 100126.3641@compuserve.com

THOMSON, Canon Ronald. b 24. Leeds Univ BA49. Coll of Resurr Mirfield 49. **d** 51 **p** 52. C Sunderland *Dur* 51-54; C Attercliffe w Carbrook *Sheff* 54-57; V Shiregreen St Hilda 57-73; RD Ecclesfield 72-73; V Worsbrough St Mary 73-88; RD Tankersley 75-85; Hon Can Sheff Cathl 77-88; rtd 88; Perm to Offic *Sheff* from 88. *4 St Mary's Garden, Worsbrough, Barnsley S70 5LU* Tel (01226) 203553

THOMSON, Ronald Arthur. b 29. G&C Coll Cam BA53 MA57. Ripon Hall Ox. **d** 57 **p** 58. C Sanderstead All SS *S'wark* 57-60; C Kidbrooke St Jas 60-62; Chapl RAF 62-68; C Amersham *Ox* 68; R Watton at Stone *St Alb* 68-94; rtd 94. *Ashby, 65 Edmonds Drive, Aston Brook, Stevenage SG2 9TJ* Tel (01438) 362192

THOMSON, Russell. b 39. AKC62. **d** 63 **p** 64. C Hackney *Lon* 63-66; C Plumstead Wm Temple Ch Abbey Wood CD *S'wark* 66-69; TV Strood *Roch* 69-75; V Gillingham St Mary 75-89; V Roch 89-04; Chapl St Bart Hosp Roch 89-94; Chapl Medway NHS Trust 94-04; Chapl Wisdom Hospice 89-04; rtd 04. *Little Heath, Shepherds Way, Fairlight, Hastings TN35 4BD* Tel and fax (01424) 812526

THOMSON, Sydney Bruce. b 49. Fuller Th Sem California MA91 ThM92 Stirling Univ MLitt98. Ox Min Course 05. **d** 07 **p** 08. C Worcs W from 07. *Wichenford Oak, Wichenford, Worcester WR6 6YY* Tel (01886) 888098 E-mail beagle67@btinternet.com

THOMSON, Wendy Leigh. b 64. Trin W Univ Vancouver BA87. Wycliffe Hall Ox BTh99. **d** 00 **p** 01. C Oulton Broad *Nor* 00-04; C Chatteris *Ely* from 04. *The Vicarage, Church Lane, Chatteris PE16 6JA* Tel (01354) 692173 E-mail wendy@chatteris.org

THOMSON, Mrs Winifred Mary. b 33. St Mary's Coll Dur BA57 MA58. Qu Coll Birm 79. **dss** 82 **d** 87 **p** 94. Leic H Spirit 82-86; Oadby 86-92; Par Dn 87-92; rtd 93; Perm to Offic *Leic* from 94. *140 Knighton Church Road, Leicester LE2 3JJ* Tel 0116-270 5863

THOMSON GIBSON, Thomas. *See* GIBSON, Thomas Thomson

THOMSON-GLOVER, Canon William Hugh. b 28. Trin Hall Cam BA52 MA56. Cuddesdon Coll 52. **d** 54 **p** 55. C Stepney St Dunstan and All SS *Lon* 54-58; C Tiverton St Andr *Ex* 58-60; P-in-c 60-63; Chapl Clifton Coll Bris 63-69; V Bris Lockleaze St Mary Magd w St Fran 70-76; P-in-c Sherston Magna w Easton Grey 76-81; P-in-c Luckington w Alderton 76-81; V Sherston Magna, Easton Grey, Luckington etc 81-93; P-in-c Foxley w Bremilham 84-86; RD Malmesbury 88-93; Hon Can Bris Cathl 91-93; rtd 93; Perm to Offic *Ex* from 93. *Woodgate Farm House, Woodgate, Culmstock, Cullompton EX15 3HW* Tel (01884) 841465

THORBURN, Guy Douglas Anderson. b 50. Ridley Hall Cam. **d** 83 **p** 84. C Putney St Marg *S'wark* 83-87; R Moresby *Carl* 87-97; V Gt Clacton *Chelmsf* from 97; RD St Osyth from 07. *St John's Vicarage, Valley Road, Clacton-on-Sea CO15 4AR* Tel (01255) 423435 E-mail revguy.thorburn@virgin.net

THORBURN, Peter Hugh. b 32. Worc Coll Ox BA41 MA43. Wells Th Coll 46. **d** 47 **p** 48. C Mill Hill Jo Keble Ch *Lon* 47-51; Lon Dioc Home Missr Colindale St Matthias 51; V 51-54; V Wigan St Mich *Liv* 54-65; USA 65-68; V Chipping Sodbury and Old Sodbury *Glouc* 68-72; Chapl Withington Hosp Man 72-82; rtd 82; Perm to Offic *B & W* from 83; *Bris* from 85; *Lon* 95-97; Warden Servants of Ch the K from 89. *8 Stoberry Crescent, Wells BA5 2TG* Tel (01749) 672919

THORBURN, Simon Godfrey. b 51. Newc Univ BSc73 Fitzw Coll Cam BA77 MA81 Sheff Univ MMinTheol97. Westcott Ho Cam 75. **d** 78 **p** 79. C Stafford *Lich* 78-82; C Tettenhall Regis 82-83; TV 83-90; Soc Resp Officer *S'wark* 90-97; V Edgbaston St Geo *Birm* 97-09; AD Edgbaston 03-08; Chapl St Geo Sch Edgbaston 99-08; V Oswestry *Lich* from 09; R Rhydycroesau from 09. *The Vicarage, Penylan Lane, Oswestry SY11 2AJ* Tel (01691) 653467 E-mail simon@thorburns.plus.com

THORESEN, Ms Alveen Fern. b 46. Avondale Coll NSW BA(Ed)69 Newc Univ Aus BA76 New England Univ NSW MA82. SAOMC 96. **d** 01 **p** 02. NSM Caversham St Pet and Mapledurham *Ox* from 01. *25 Ilkley Road, Caversham, Reading RG4 7BD* Tel 0118-946 4786
E-mail alveen.thoresen@mon.bbc.co.uk

THORLEY, Canon Barry. b 44. Westcott Ho Cam 70. **d** 73 **p** 74. C Camberwell St Giles *S'wark* 73-76; C Moseley St Mary *Birm* 76-78; V Birchfield 78-83; V Brixton St Matt *S'wark* 84-89; C Greenwich St Alfege 96-00; C Thamesmead 00-01; TR 01-06; rtd 06; Hon Can Zanzibar from 04. *St Benet's Chapel, PO Box 104, Nkawie-Toase, Ghana* E-mail thorleybarry@yahoo.co.uk

THORLEY, Mrs Mary Kathleen. b 53. OBE00. Univ of Wales (Swansea) BA74 Glos Coll of Educn PGCE75. St Mich Coll Llan 99. **d** 02 **p** 03. NSM Carmarthen St Pet *St D* 02-05; NSM Carmarthen St Dav from 05. *Bryn Heulog, Heol Penllanffos, Carmarthen SA31 2HL* Tel (01267) 235927

THORLEY-PAICE, Alan. *See* PAICE, Alan

THORN (*formerly* KINGS)**, Mrs Jean Alison.** b 63. RGN85 Heythrop Coll Lon MTh. Cranmer Hall Dur BA90. **d** 91 **p** 93. Chapl Bris Poly 91-92; Chapl UWE 92-95; Hon C Bris Lockleaze St Mary Magd w St Fran 91-95; C Fishponds All SS 95-96; Hon C 96-97; V Bris Ch the Servant Stockwood 97-01; Hon C Whitchurch 01-04. *The Rectory, Church Street, Burton Bradstock, Bridport DT6 4QS* Tel (01308) 898799

THORN, Kevan. b 67. CBDTI 03. **d** 06 **p** 07. NSM Blackpool H Cross *Blackb* from 06. *16 Bannistre Close, Lytham St Annes FY8 3HS* Tel (01253) 713088 Fax 08707-621548
E-mail kevanthorn@btopenworld.com

THORN, Mrs Pamela Mary. b 46. Brentwood Coll of Educn BEd78. EAMTC 01. **d** 04 **p** 05. NSM Waterbeach *Ely* from 04. *31 Lode Avenue, Waterbeach, Cambridge CB25 9PX* Tel (01223) 864262 Mobile 07989-491557
E-mail pamandtrevorthorn@btinternet.com

THORN, Peter. b 50. Man Poly BEd79. Ridley Hall Cam 82. **d** 84 **p** 85. C Aughton Ch Ch *Liv* 84-87; C Skelmersdale St Paul 87-90; Dioc Children's Officer 87-92; P-in-c Croft w Southworth 90-92; C Streatley *St Alb* 92-95; R Blofield w Hemblington *Nor* 95-96; P-in-c 96-99; Assoc Dioc Dir of Tr 97-99; V Sheff St Bart 99-01; P-in-c Shotley *St E* 01-07; P-in-c Tweedmouth *Newc* 07-09; P-in-c Claydon and Barham *St E* from 09; C Gt and Lt Blakenham w Baylham and Nettlestead from 09. *The Rectory, 7 Back Lane, Claydon, Ipswich IP6 0EB* Tel (01473) 830362 Mobile 07810-363291 E-mail peterthorn15@hotmail.com

THORN, Robert Anthony D'Venning. b 54. AKC76. Chich Th Coll 75. **d** 77 **p** 78. C Bodmin *Truro* 77-80; TV N Hill w Altarnon, Bolventor and Lewannick 80-83; V Feock and Dioc Ecum Officer 83-90; Broadcasting Officer *Linc* 90-93; V Whitchurch *Bris* 93-04; TR Bride Valley *Sarum* 04-07; R from 07; RD Lyme Bay from 09. *The Rectory, Church Street, Burton Bradstock, Bridport DT6 4QS* Tel (01308) 898799
E-mail jeanandbob@jeanabdbob.demon.co.uk

THORN, Simon Alexander. b 66. Bris Univ BSc89 PhD92 FLS98 FCollP96. Ox Min Course 06. **d** 09. *8 Upper Shrubbery, Radley College, Radley, Abingdon OX14 2JG* Tel (01235) 543195 Mobile 07714-194591 E-mail sat@radley.org.uk

THORNALLEY, Graham Paul. b 70. Coll of Resurr Mirfield 05. **d** 07 **p** 08. C Brumby *Linc* 07-09; C Frodingham from 09. *11 Kingsway, Scunthorpe DN17 1BL* Tel (01724) 856401
E-mail gthornalley@tiscali.co.uk

THORNBOROUGH (*née* O'MEARA)**, Ms Colette Margaret Mary.** b 63. Univ of Wales (Abth) BA85. Moorlands Bible Coll. **d** 98 **p** 99. C Much Woolton *Liv* 02-08; V Blundellsands St Nic from 02; AD Sefton 08-09; Hon Can Liv Cathl 08-09. *St Nicholas' Vicarage, Nicholas Road, Blundellsands, Liverpool L23 6TS* Tel 0151-924 3551 E-mail revcolette@aol.com

THORNBURGH, Richard Hugh Perceval. b 52. Sarum & Wells Th Coll. **d** 84 **p** 85. C Broadstone *Sarum* 84-87; TV Beaminster Area 87-95; TV Hanley H Ev *Lich* 96-01; R S Elmham and Ilketshall *St E* from 01. *Parsonage House, Low Street, Ilketshall St Margaret, Bungay NR35 1QZ* Tel and fax (01986) 781345
E-mail richard.thornburgh@btinternet.com

THORNBURY, Peter Dawson. b 43. Open Univ BA84 TCD BTh93. CITC 90. **d** 93 **p** 94. C Annagh w Drumgoon, Ashfield etc *K, E & A* 93-96; I Clondehorkey w Cashel *D & R* 96-98; I Mevagh w Glenalla 96-98; Bp's C Kilsaran w Drumcar, Dunleer and Dunany *Arm* 98-06; I Aghaderg w Donaghmore and Scarva *D & D* from 06. *Aghaderg Rectory, 32 Banbridge Road, Loughbrickland, Banbridge BT32 3YB* Tel (028) 4062 4073
E-mail wildthorn@btinternet.com

THORNBY, Mrs Janet. b 40. **d** 06 **p** 07. OLM Cheriton All So w Newington *Cant* from 06. *11 Peene Cottages, Peene, Folkestone CT18 8BB* Tel (01303) 271767 E-mail thornbyrobjan@aol.com

THORNE, Mrs Anita Dawn. b 46. Trin Coll Bris 84. **dss** 86 **d** 87 **p** 94. Asst Chapl Bris Poly 86-88; Par Dn Olveston 88-94; P-in-c 94-96; P-in-c Portland All SS w St Pet *Sarum* 96-05; P-in-c Clutton w Cameley *B & W* from 05. *The Rectory, Main Road, Temple Cloud, Bristol BS39 5DA* Tel (01761) 451248 or 451315 E-mail anita.thorne@btinternet.com

THORNE, Mrs Anne. b 55. SWMTC 95. **d** 98 **p** 99. C Crediton and Shobrooke *Ex* 98-01; C Beer and Branscombe 01-03; C Seaton and Beer 03-06; P-in-c Braunton from 06. *The Vicarage, Church Street, Braunton EX33 2EL* Tel (01271) 815330
E-mail vicarthorne@aol.com

THORNE, Mrs Margaret. b 58. Kingston Poly BA79 Heythrop Coll Lon MA02 LGSM78. Ox Min Course 05. **d** 08. C Earley St Pet *Ox* from 08. *33 Clevedon Drive, Earley, Reading RG6 5XF* Tel 0118-987 4118 E-mail maggie.thorne@googlemail.com

THORNE, Mrs Marie Elizabeth. b 47. EMMTC 83. **dss** 86 **d** 87 **p** 94. Cleethorpes *Linc* 86-90; C 87-90; C Brigg 90-96; P-in-c New Waltham 96-00; V 00-07; R Gt w Lt Massingham, Harpley, Rougham etc *Nor* from 07. *The Rectory, 68 Station Road, Great Massingham, King's Lynn PE32 2HW* Tel (01485) 520211

THORNETT, Frederick Charles. b 34. Harris Coll CQSW68. **d** 85 **p** 86. OLM Skegness and Winthorpe *Linc* 85-90; C New Sleaford 90-92; P-in-c Harlaxton 92-95; R Harlaxton Gp 95-99; rtd 99; Perm to Offic *Linc* 99-02. *93 Boston Road, Spilsby PE23 5HH* Tel (01790) 754151

THORNETT, Joan. b 38. **d** 07 **p** 09. OLM Stickney Gp *Linc* from 07. *93 Boston Road, Spilsby PE23 5HH* Tel (01790) 754151

THORNEWILL, Canon Mark Lyon. b 25. ALCD56. **d** 56 **p** 58. C-in-c Bradf Cathl 56-59; C-in-c Otley 59-62; R Lifton *Ex* 62-66; R Kelly w Bradstone 62-66; Dir Past Care Norton Hosps Louisville USA 69-84; Hon Can Louisville Cathl from 70; rtd 90. *Soma House, 116 East Campbell Street, Frankfort KY 40601-3508, USA* Tel (001) (502) 696 9274
E-mail mthornewill@aol.com

THORNEYCROFT, Preb Pippa Hazel Jeanetta. b 44. Ex Univ BA65. WMMTC 85. **d** 88 **p** 94. NSM Albrighton *Lich* 88-90; NSM Beckbury, Badger, Kemberton, Ryton, Stockton etc 90-96; P-in-c Shareshill 96-09; P-in-c Essington 07-09; Dioc Adv for Women in Min 93-00; Preb Lich Cathl 99-09; RD Penkridge 01-05; rtd 09; Chapl to The Queen from 01. *Poole's Yard, Kemberton, Shifnal TF11 9LL* Tel (01952) 580588 Mobile 07970-869011 E-mail pippa@thorneycroft.plus.com

THORNILEY, Richard James Gordon. b 56. Portsm Poly BA78. St Jo Coll Nottm MTh95. **d** 97 **p** 98. C Bowbrook S *Worc* 97-01; R Church Lench w Rous Lench and Abbots Morton etc from 01. *The Rectory, Station Road, Harvington, Evesham WR11 8NJ* Tel (01386) 870527 E-mail richardgill@rthorniley.fsnet.co.uk

THORNLEY, David Howe. b 43. Wycliffe Hall Ox 77. **d** 79 **p** 80. C Burgess Hill St Andr *Chich* 79-83; P-in-c Amberley w N Stoke 83-84; P-in-c Parham and Wiggonholt w Greatham 83-84; V Amberley w N Stoke and Parham, Wiggonholt etc 84-92; P-in-c S w N Bersted 92-99; V 99-08; rtd 08. *Spinnaway Cottage, Church Hill, Slindon, Arundel BN18 0RD* Tel 07941-834920 (mobile)

THORNLEY, Geoffrey Pearson. b 23. Pemb Coll Cam BA47 MA52. Cuddesdon Coll. **d** 50 **p** 51. C Stepney St Dunstan and All SS *Lon* 50-53; Chapl RN 53-73; Bp's Dom Chapl *Linc* 73-75; P-in-c Riseholme 73-78; P-in-c Scothern w Sudbrooke 77-78; V Dunholme 75-85; Hon PV Linc Cathl 75-85; rtd 85; Chapl Allnutt's Hosp Goring Heath 85-96. *c/o E Hylton, Messrs Humphrey & Co, 8-9 The Avenue, Eastbourne BN21 3YA* Tel (01323) 730631 Fax 738355

THORNLEY, Canon Nicholas Andrew. b 56. St Jo Coll Nottm BTh81. **d** 81 **p** 84. C Frodingham *Linc* 81-84; P-in-c Belton 84-85; V 85-90; V Horncastle w Low Toynton 90-98; V High Toynton 98; R Greetham w Ashby Puerorum 98; RD Horncastle 94-98; TR Gainsborough and Morton from 98; Can and Preb Linc Cathl from 98. *Gainsborough Rectory, 32 Morton Terrace, Gainsborough DN21 1RQ* Tel (01427) 612965
E-mail nick@gains98.fsnet.co.uk

THORNS, Mrs Joanne. b 64. Sunderland Univ BSc86 MRPharmS. Cranmer Hall Dur 97. **d** 99 **p** 00. C Norton St Mary *Dur* 99-04; C Stockton St Chad 02-04; TV Dur N from 04. *25 Barnard Close, Durham DH1 5XN* Tel 0191-386 8049
E-mail joanne.thorns@durham.anglican.org

THORNTON, Darren Thomas. b 68. Wilson Carlile Coll 90 EAMTC 00. **d** 02 **p** 03. C E Dereham and Scarning *Nor* 02-05; Chapl UEA from 05; P-in-c Nor St Giles from 05. *St Giles's Vicarage, 44 Heigham Road, Norwich NR2 3AU* Tel (01603) 623724 E-mail d.thornton@uea.ac.uk

THORNTON, David John Dennis. b 32. Kelham Th Coll 52. **d** 56 **p** 57. C New Eltham All SS *S'wark* 56-58; C Stockwell Green St Andr 58-62; V Tollesbury *Chelmsf* 62-74; P-in-c Salcot Virley 72-74; V Kelvedon 74-00; rtd 00; Perm to Offic *Nor* 01-07. *The Old Stable, 24 Pauls Lane, Overstrand, Cromer NR27 0PE* Tel (01263) 579279

THORNTON, Mrs Diana Rachel. b 64. Mert Coll Ox MA86. SEITE 03. **d** 06 **p** 07. C S Wimbledon H Trin and St Pet *S'wark* 06-09; C Cobham and Stoke D'Abernon *Guildf* from 09. *The Rectory, Blundel Lane, Stoke D'Abernon, Cobham KT11 2SE*
E-mail thethorntons@waitrose.com

THORNTON, Howard Deyes. b 52. Canadian Th Sem MA99. **d** 01 **p** 03. NSM Hanborough and Freeland *Ox* 01-02; C Luton St Mary *St Alb* 02-04; Chapl Luton Univ 02-07; TR Cowley

St Jas *Ox* from 07. *Cowley Rectory, 11 Beauchamp Lane, Oxford OX4 3LF* Tel (01865) 747680
E-mail oxfordpilgrims@hotmail.com

THORNTON, John. b 26. St Edm Hall Ox BA53 MA57. Westcott Ho Cam 53. **d** 55 **p** 56. C Woodhall Spa *Linc* 55-58; C Glouc St Steph 58-60; C Wotton St Mary 60-62; P-in-c Gt Witcombe 62-63; R 63-91; Chapl HM Pris Glouc 82-91; rtd 91; Perm to Offic *Glouc* from 91. *24 Spencer Close, Hucclecote, Gloucester GL3 3EA* Tel (01452) 619775

THORNTON, Magdalen Mary. *See* SMITH, Magdalen Mary

THORNTON, Timothy Charles Gordon. b 35. Ch Ch Ox BA58 MA61. Linc Th Coll 60. **d** 62 **p** 63. C Kirkholt CD *Man* 62-64; Tutor Linc Th Coll 64-68; Chapl 66-68; Fiji 69-73; Chapl Brasted Place Coll Westerham 73-74; Can Missr *Guildf* 74-79; P-in-c Hascombe 74-79; V Chobham w Valley End 79-84; V Spelsbury and Chadlington *Ox* 84-87; V Chadlington and Spelsbury, Ascott under Wychwood 87-00; rtd 00; Perm to Offic *Carl* from 01. *The Old Cottage, Warcop, Appleby-in-Westmorland CA16 6NX* Tel (01768) 341239

✠**THORNTON, The Rt Revd Timothy Martin.** b 57. Southn Univ BA78 K Coll Lon MA97. St Steph Ho Ox 78. **d** 80 **p** 81 **c** 01. C Todmorden *Wakef* 80-82; P-in-c Walsden 82-85; Lect Univ of Wales (Cardiff) *Llan* 85-87; Chapl 85-86; Sen Chapl 86-87; Bp's Chapl *Wakef* 87-91; Dir of Ords 88-91; Bp's Chapl *Lon* 91-94; Dep P in O 92-01; Prin NTMTC 94-98; V Kensington St Mary Abbots w St Geo *Lon* 98-01; AD Kensington 00-01; Area Bp Sherborne *Sarum* 01-08; Bp Truro from 08. *Lis Escop, Feock, Truro TR3 6QQ* Tel (01872) 862657 Fax 862037
E-mail bishop@truro.anglican.org

THOROGOOD, Preb John Martin. b 45. Birm Univ BA68 PGCE69. Ox NSM Course 82. **d** 85 **p** 86. NSM Sunningdale *Ox* 85-90; Chapl St Geo Sch Ascot 88-90; TV Camelot Par *B & W* 90-97; V Evercreech w Chesterblade and Milton Clevedon 97-03; RD Cary and Bruton 96-03; R Dulverton and Brushford from 03; P-in-c Brompton Regis w Upton and Skilgate from 08; RD Exmoor from 05; Preb Wells Cathl from 07. *The Vicarage, High Street, Dulverton TA22 9DW* Tel (01398) 323425
E-mail johnthevicar@toucansurf.com

THOROLD, Alison Susan Joy. *See* HEALY, Mrs Alison Susan Joy

THOROLD, Jeremy Stephen. b 59. **d** 04 **p** 05. OLM Gainsborough and Morton *Linc* 04-07; Hon C Lanteglos by Camelford w Advent Truro from 07; Hon C St Teath from 07. *The Vicarage, St Teath, Bodmin PL30 3LH* Tel (01208) 850841
E-mail jem33wheel@aol.com

THOROLD, John Robert Hayford. b 16. K Coll Cam BA43 MA45. Cuddesdon Coll 42. **d** 42 **p** 43. C Cheltenham St Mary *Glouc* 42-44; C Limehouse St Anne *Lon* 44-45; Tutor Ripon Hall Ox 47-52; V Mitcham SS Pet and Paul *S'wark* 52-86; OGS from 53; rtd 87; Perm to Offic *Blackb* 87-06; Hon Fell St Deiniol's Lib Hawarden from 00. *St Mary's Convent, Burlington Lane, London W4 2QE* Tel (020) 8747 1892

THOROLD, Canon John Stephen. b 35. Bps' Coll Cheshunt 61. **d** 63 **p** 64. C Cleethorpes *Linc* 63-70; V Cherry Willingham w Greetwell 70-77; P-in-c Firsby w Gt Steeping 77-79; R 79-86; R Aswardby w Sausthorpe 77-86; R Halton Holgate 77-86; R Langton w Sutterby 77-86; V Spilsby w Hundleby 77-86; R Lt Steeping 79-86; R Raithby 79-86; V New Sleaford 86-01; RD Lafford 87-96; Can and Preb Linc Cathl 98-01; rtd 01; Perm to Offic *Linc* from 01. *8 Ashwood Close, Horncastle LN9 5HA* Tel (01507) 526562

THOROLD, Trevor Neil. b 63. Hull Univ BA87. Ripon Coll Cuddesdon 87. **d** 89 **p** 90. C W Bromwich St Andr w Ch Ch *Lich* 89-93; Res Min Oswestry 93-97; P-in-c Petton w Cockshutt, Welshampton and Lyneal etc 97-05; Local Min Adv (Shrewsbury) 97-05; RD Ellesmere 98-02. *66B High Street, Wem, Shrewsbury SY4 5DR*

THORP, Adrian. b 55. Clare Coll Cam BA77 MA80 Lon Univ BD80. Trin Coll Bris 77. **d** 80 **p** 81. C Kendal St Thos *Carl* 80-83; C Handforth *Ches* 83-86; V Siddal *Wakef* 86-91; V Bishopwearmouth St Gabr *Dur* 91-05; C Upper Skerne 05-07; R Blaydon and Swalwell from 07. *St Cuthbert's Rectory, Shibdon Road, Blaydon-on-Tyne NE21 5AE* Tel 0191-414 2720
E-mail ahthorp@btinternet.com

THORP, Mrs Alison Claire. b 63. Kingston Poly BSc85. EMMTC 06. **d** 09. NSM Bosworth and Sheepy Gp *Leic* from 09. *Culloden Farm, Gopsall, Atherstone CV9 3QJ* Tel (01530) 270350 E-mail alisonthorp@btconnect.com

THORP, Catherine. b 57. St Luke's Coll Ex BEd79. Oak Hill Th Coll 93. **d** 96 **p** 02. NSM Watford Ch *St Alb* 96-99; NSM Kings Langley 99-05; Perm to Offic from 05. *111 Barton Way, Croxley Green, Rickmansworth WD3 3PB* Tel and fax (01923) 442713 E-mail cthorp5@hotmail.com

THORP, Mrs Helen Mary. b 54. Bris Univ BA75 MA(Theol)77 Dur Univ MA98. Trin Coll Bris 78. **d** 87 **p** 94. NSM Siddal *Wakef* 87-91; NSM Bishopwearmouth St Gabr *Dur* 91-05; NSM Upper Skerne 05-07; NSM Blaydon and Swalwell from 07; Voc Adv 93-05; Tutor Cranmer Hall Dur from 98. *St Cuthbert's*

Rectory, Shibdon Road, Blaydon-on-Tyne NE21 5AE Tel 0191-414 2720 E-mail ahthorp@btinternet.com
or h.m.thorp@durham.ac.uk

THORP, Mrs Maureen Sandra. b 47. Man OLM Scheme 92. **d** 95 **p** 96. OLM Heywood *Man* 95-01; P-in-c Shore and Calderbrook 01-06; V Tonge w Alkrington from 06. *St Michael's Vicarage, 184 Kirkway, Middleton, Manchester M24 1LN* Tel 0161-643 2891 E-mail thorpmaureen@aol.com

THORP, Norman Arthur. b 29. Tyndale Hall Bris 63. **d** 65 **p** 66. C Southsea St Jude *Portsm* 65-68; C Braintree *Chelmsf* 68-73; P-in-c Tolleshunt D'Arcy w Tolleshunt Major 73-75; V 75-83; R N Buckingham *Ox* 83-95; RD Buckingham 90-95; rtd 95; Perm to Offic *Ox* 97-00. *27 Baisley Gardens, Napier Street, Bletchley, Milton Keynes MK2 2NE* Tel (01908) 370221

THORP, Roderick Cheyne. b 44. Ch Ch Ox BA65 MA69. Ridley Hall Cam 66. **d** 69 **p** 70. C Reading Greyfriars *Ox* 69-73; C Kingston upon Hull St Martin *York* 73-76; C Heworth H Trin 76-79; C-in-c N Bletchley CD *Ox* 79-86; TV Washfield, Stoodleigh, Withleigh etc *Ex* 86-96; RD Tiverton 91-96; P-in-c Dolton 96-00; P-in-c Iddesleigh w Dowland 96-00; P-in-c Monkokehampton 96-00; rtd 00; P-in-c Etton w Dalton Holme *York* 00-08; Perm to Offic from 08. *4 Stonegate Court, Stonegate, Hunmanby, Filey YO14 0NZ* E-mail aranjay@freeuk.com

THORP, Stephen Linton. b 62. Trin Coll Bris BA92. **d** 92 **p** 93. C Knutsford St Jo and Toft *Ches* 92-96; TV Newton Tracey, Horwood, Alverdiscott etc *Ex* 96-06; R Necton, Holme Hale w N and S Pickenham *Nor* from 06. *The Rectory, School Road, Necton, Swaffham PE37 8HT* Tel (01760) 722021
E-mail slthorp@homecall.co.uk

THORP, Timothy. b 65. St Steph Ho Ox BTh93. **d** 96 **p** 97. C Jarrow *Dur* 96-99; P-in-c N Hylton St Marg Castletown 99-02; C Felpham and Missr Arundel and Bognor *Chich* 02-07; C Arundel w Tortington and S Stoke 07-08; P-in-c Ernesettle *Ex* from 08; P-in-c Whitleigh from 08; C Honicknowle from 08. *St Aidan's Vicarage, 122 Rochford Crescent, Plymouth PL5 2QD* Tel (01752) 350580 E-mail fathertimt@bigfoot.com

THORPE, Preb Christopher David Charles. b 60. Cov Poly BA83. Ripon Coll Cuddesdon 85. **d** 88 **p** 89. C Norton *St Alb* 88-92; TV Blakenall Heath *Lich* 92-99; TR Bilston 99-08; V Shifnal and Sheriffhales from 08; Preb Lich Cathl from 07. *The Vicarage, Manor Close, Shifnal TF11 9AJ* Tel (01952) 463694
E-mail chris@christhorpe.org

THORPE, Donald Henry. b 34. St Aid Birkenhead 57. **d** 60 **p** 61. C Mexborough *Sheff* 60-64; C Doncaster St Leon and St Jude 64-67; V Doncaster Intake 67-74; V Millhouses H Trin 74-85; Prec Leic Cathl 85-89; TR Melton Gt Framland 89-93; rtd 93; Perm to Offic *Sheff* and *S'well* from 93. *18 All Hallows Drive, Tickhill, Doncaster DN11 9PP* Tel (01302) 743129
E-mail dsthorpe1@tiscali.co.uk

THORPE, Canon Kerry Michael. b 51. Oak Hill Th Coll BD78. **d** 78 **p** 79. C Upton (Overchurch) *Ches* 78-81; C Chester le Street *Dur* 81-84; V Fatfield 84-93; V Margate H Trin *Cant* 93-98; C from 98; Dioc Missr from 06; Hon Can Cant Cathl from 08. *1 Wealdhurst Park, St Peter's, Broadstairs CT10 2LD* Tel (01843) 871183 E-mail kerrythorpe@harvestnac.freeserve.co.uk

THORPE, Lynne Gail. b 62. Dioc OLM tr scheme 99. **d** 02 **p** 03. OLM Ipswich St Jo *St E* 02-06. *31 King Edward Road, Ipswich IP3 9AN* Tel (01473) 717833

THORPE, Martin Xavier. b 66. Collingwood Coll Dur BSc87 Bris Univ MPhil00 GRSC87. Trin Coll Bris BA94. **d** 94 **p** 95. C Ravenhead *Liv* 94-98; TV Sutton 98-02; Asst Dir CME from 01; V Westbrook St Phil from 02. *St Philip's Vicarage, 89 Westbrook Crescent, Warrington WA5 8TN* Tel and fax (01925) 654400
E-mail martinpol.thorpe@talk21.com
or martin.cme1-4@talk21.com

THORPE, Michael William. b 42. Lich Th Coll 67. **d** 70 **p** 71. C Walthamstow St Mich *Chelmsf* 70-71; C Plaistow St Andr 71; P-in-c Plaistow St Mary 72-74; TV Gt Grimsby St Mary and St Jas *Linc* 74-78; Chapl Grimsby Distr Hosps 78-83; Chapl Roxbourne, Northwick Park and Harrow Hosps 83-87; Chapl St Geo Linc and Linc Co Hosps 87-92; Chapl Ipswich Hosp NHS Trust 92-00; rtd 00. *Moselle Cottage, 68 Lacey Street, Ipswich IP4 2PH* Tel (01473) 421850

THORPE, Richard Charles. b 65. Birm Univ BSc87. Wycliffe Hall Ox 93. **d** 96 **p** 97. C Brompton H Trin w Onslow Square St Paul *Lon* 96-05; P-in-c Shadwell St Paul w Ratcliffe St Jas from 05. *St Paul's Rectory, 298 The Highway, London E1W 3DH* Tel (020) 7481 2883 *or* 7680 2772
E-mail ric.thorpe@stpaulsshadwell.org

THORPE, Trevor Cecil. b 21. Em Coll Cam BA47 MA52. Ridley Hall Cam 48. **d** 50 **p** 51. C Farnborough *Guildf* 50-53; C W Ham All SS *Chelmsf* 53-57; V N Weald Bassett from 57. *The Vicarage, Vicarage Lane, North Weald, Epping CM16 6AL* Tel (01992) 522246

THRALL, Canon Margaret Eleanor. b 28. Girton Coll Cam BA50 MA54 PhD60 Cam Univ BA52. Ban Ord Course 81. **d** 82 **p** 97. Asst Chapl Univ of Wales (Ban) 82-88; Lect Th Univ of Wales (Ban) 83-96; Hon Can Ban Cathl 94-98; rtd 98; Perm to

Offic *Ban* from 98. *Bryn Mel Nursing Home, Allt Bryn Mel, Glyngarth, Menai Bridge LL59 5PF* Tel (01248) 712999

THREADGILL, Steven Alan. b 59. Cant Univ (NZ) BA84 MA88 Christchurch Teachers' Coll Dip Teaching88. STETS MA08. **d** 08 **p** 09. C Lee-on-the-Solent *Portsm* from 08. *3 Martlet Close, Lee-on-the-Solent PO13 8FP*
E-mail steventhreadgill@yahoo.co.uk

THRELFALL-HOLMES, Miranda. b 73. Ch Coll Cam BA95 MA99 Univ Coll Dur MA97 PhD00 St Jo Coll Dur BA02. Cranmer Hall Dur 00. **d** 03 **p** 04. C Newc St Gabr 03-06; Chapl and Fell Univ Coll Dur from 06. *University College, The Castle, Palace Green, Durham DH1 3RW* Tel 0191-334 4116
E-mail rev.miranda@dsl.pipex.com

THROSSELL, John Julian. b 30. Nottm Univ BSc53 Syracuse Univ PhD56. Oak Hill Th Coll 72. **d** 75 **p** 76. NSM Wheathampstead *St Alb* 75-82; V Codicote 82-88; NSM Halesworth w Linstead, Chediston, Holton etc *St E* 89-95; rtd 91. *1A Sharpe's Hill, Barrow, Bury St Edmunds IP29 5BY* Tel (01284) 810314

THROWER, Clive Alan. b 41. Sheff Univ BSc62 CEng70. EMMTC 76. **d** 79 **p** 80. C Derby Cathl 79-86; C Spondon 86-91; Soc Resp Officer 86-91; Faith in the City Link Officer 88-91; Dioc Rural Officer 91; P-in-c Ashford w Sheldon 91; V Ashford w Sheldon and Longstone 92-07; Dioc Rural and Tourism Officer 96-07; RD Bakewell and Eyam 04-07; rtd 07; Perm to Offic *Derby* from 07. *Longstone House, 5 Vernon Green, Bakewell DE45 1DT* Tel (01629) 814863 E-mail clive@thrower.org.uk

THROWER, The Very Revd Martin Charles. b 61. EAMTC 95. **d** 98 **p** 99. NSM Ipswich St Bart *St E* 98-01; NSM Bury St Edmunds All SS w St Jo and St Geo 01-03; P-in-c Gt and Lt Whelnetham w Bradfield St George 03-04; P-in-c Lawshall 03-04; P-in-c Hawstead and Nowton w Stanningfield etc 03-04; R St Edm Way 04-09; RD Lavenham 05-09; V Hadleigh, Layham and Shelley from 09; Dean Bocking from 09. *The Deanery, Church Street, Hadleigh, Ipswich IP7 5DT* Tel (01473) 822218 E-mail martin.thrower@btinternet.com

THROWER, Philip Edward. b 41. Kelham Th Coll 61. **d** 66 **p** 67. C Hayes St Mary *Lon* 66-69; C Yeovil *B & W* 69-71; C Shirley St Jo *Cant* 71-77; P-in-c S Norwood St Mark 77-81; V 81-84; V S Norwood St Mark *S'wark* 85-97; V Malden St Jas 97-07; rtd 07; Perm to Offic *S'wark* from 07. *243 Chipstead Way, Banstead SM7 3JN* Tel (01737) 218306

THRUSH, Margaret. b 37. St Mary's Coll Dur BA60. Cranmer Hall Dur BA96. **d** 97 **p** 98. NSM Houghton le Spring *Dur* 97-03; NSM Shadforth and Sherburn from 03. *45 Highgate, Durham DH1 4GA* Tel 0191-386 1958

THUBRON, Thomas William. b 33. Edin Th Coll 62. **d** 65 **p** 66. C Gateshead St Mary *Dur* 65-66; C Shildon 66-67; E Pakistan 68-71; Bangladesh 71-80; V Wheatley Hill *Dur* 80-87; V Dur St Giles 87-98; rtd 98. *The Old Vicarage, Gable Terrace, Wheatley Hill, Durham DH6 3RA* Tel (01429) 823940

THURBURN-HUELIN, David Richard. b 47. St Chad's Coll Dur BA69 Ex Univ MA98. Westcott Ho Cam 69. **d** 71 **p** 72. C Poplar *Lon* 71-76; Chapl Liddon Ho Lon 76-80; R Harrold and Carlton w Chellington *St Alb* 81-88; V Godalming 88-95; Dir OLM *Truro* 95-00; P-in-c Shipston-on-Stour w Honington and Idlicote *Cov* 01-05; R from 05. *Shipston Rectory, 8 Glen Close, Shipston-on-Stour CV36 4ED* Tel (01608) 661724
E-mail d.r.thurburnhuelin@homecall.co.uk

THURGILL, Sally Elizabeth. b 60. **d** 02 **p** 03. OLM Mattishall and the Tudd Valley *Nor* from 02. *3 Dereham Road, Yaxham, Dereham NR19 1RF* Tel (01362) 692745
E-mail csmsthurgill@ukonline.co.uk

THURLOW, Ms Judith Mary Buller. b 44. Ch Ch Coll Cant CertEd63 Natal Univ DipEd78 BTh94 MTh00. **d** 95 **p** 96. S Africa 95-00; C Port Shepstone St Kath 95-98; C Durban St Paul 99-00; C Orpington All SS *Roch* 00-02; R Kingsdown from 02. *The Rectory, School Lane, West Kingsdown, Sevenoaks TN15 6JL* Tel and fax (01474) 852265 Mobile 07949-272106 E-mail judiththurlow@ukgateway.net

THURMER, Canon John Alfred. b 25. Oriel Coll Ox BA50 MA55 Ex Univ Hon DD91. Linc Th Coll 50. **d** 52 **p** 53. C Lt Ilford St Mich *Chelmsf* 52-55; Chapl and Lect Sarum Th Coll 55-64; Chapl Ex Univ 64-73; Lect 64-85; Can Res and Chan Ex Cathl 73-91; rtd 91; Perm to Offic *Ex* from 91. *38 Velwell Road, Exeter EX4 4LD* Tel (01392) 272277

THURSTON, Ian Charles. b 54. SS Hild & Bede Coll Dur CertEd78. S Dios Minl Tr Scheme 87. **d** 89 **p** 90. C St Chris Cathl Bahrain 89-91; C All Hallows by the Tower etc *Lon* 91-97; V Tottenham H Trin 97-00; R Cheadle w Freehay *Lich* from 00. *The Rectory, Church Street, Cheadle, Stoke-on-Trent ST10 1HU* Tel (01538) 753337

THURSTON-SMITH, Trevor. b 59. Chich Th Coll 83. **d** 86 **p** 87. C Rawmarsh w Parkgate *Sheff* 86-87; C Horninglow *Lich* 87-91; Chapl for People affected by HIV *Leic* from 05. *The Lodge, Margaret Road, Leicester LE5 5FW* Tel 0116-283 4159 *or* 273 3377 E-mail trevor@faithinpeople.org.uk

THURTELL, Victoria Ann. b 59. St Jo Coll Dur BSc82 PGCE96. STETS 02. **d** 05 **p** 06. C Chickerell w Fleet *Sarum* 05-08; TV

Dorchester from 08. *The Vicarage, 38 Herringston Road, Dorchester DT1 2BS* Tel (01305) 268767
E-mail vickythurtell@gmail.com

THORNQVIST, Miss Karin Elisabet. b 41. Uppsala Univ 64 BD83. **p** 84. Sweden 84-97 and 98-07; C Skegness and Winthorpe *Linc* 97-98; Gen Preacher from 07. *22 Jarvis Gate, Sutton St James, Spalding PE12 0EP*

TIBBO, George Kenneth. b 29. Reading Univ BA50 MA54. Coll of Resurr Mirfield 55. **d** 57 **p** 58. C W Hartlepool St Aid *Dur* 57-61; V Darlington St Mark 61-74; V Darlington St Mark w St Paul 74-75; R Crook 75-80; V Stanley 76-80; V Oldham St Chad Limeside *Man* 80-87; V Hipswell *Ripon* 87-95; OCF 90-95; rtd 95; P-in-c Nidd *Ripon* 95-01; Perm to Offic 02-04; Hon C Saddleworth *Man* from 04. *The Vicarage, Woods Lane, Dobcross, Oldham OL3 5AN* Tel (01457) 829702

TIBBOTT, (née VINE), Mrs Carolyn Ann. b 63. Anglia Poly Univ BSc04. NTMTC BA07. **d** 07 **p** 08. C Gidea Park *Chelmsf* from 07. *113 Mashiters Walk, Romford RM1 4BS* Tel (01708) 730608 E-mail ctibbott@hotmail.com

TIBBS, Canon John Andrew. b 29. AKC53. **d** 54 **p** 55. C Eastbourne St Mary *Chich* 54-57; S Africa 57-62; C Bourne *Guildf* 62-64; Swaziland 64-68; V Sompting *Chich* 69-73; R Ifield 73-78; TR 78-83; V Elstow *St Alb* 83-89; rtd 90; Chapl Bedf Gen Hosp 90-95; Hon Can St Alb 91-95; Perm to Offic from 00. *19 Adelaide Square, Bedford MK40 2RN* Tel (01234) 308737

TIBBS, Simon John. b 71. **d** 08. C Edin Old St Paul from 08. *41 Jeffrey Street, Edinburgh EH1 1DH*
E-mail tibbs.simon@googlemail.com

TICE, Richard Ian. b 66. Bris Univ BA88. Wycliffe Hall Ox BTh94. **d** 94 **p** 95. C Langham Place All So *Lon* from 94. *Basement Flat, 141 Cleveland Street, London W1T 6QG* Tel (020) 7388 3280 *or* 7580 3522 E-mail ricospa-grace@allsouls.org

TICKLE, Robert Peter. b 54. St Chad's Coll Dur BA74. St Steph Ho Ox 74. **d** 76 **p** 77. *5 Bramley Court, Orchard Lane, Harrold, Bedford MK43 7BG* Tel (01234) 721417

TICKNER, Canon Colin de Fraine. b 37. Chich Th Coll. **d** 66 **p** 67. C Huddersfield SS Pet and Paul *Wakef* 66-68; C Dorking w Ranmore *Guildf* 68-74; V Shottermill 74-91; RD Godalming 89-91; R Ockley, Okewood and Forest Green 91-97; Hon Can Guildf Cathl 96-97; rtd 97; Adv for Past Care *Guildf* from 97; Chapl St Cath Sch Bramley from 97. *11 Linersh Drive, Bramley, Guildford GU5 0EJ* Tel (01483) 898161
E-mail colin.tickner@sky.com

TICKNER, David Arthur. b 44. MBE89. AKC67. **d** 69 **p** 70. C Thornhill Lees *Wakef* 69-71; C Billingham St Aid *Dur* 71-74; TV 74-78; CF 78-98; Perm to Offic *Guildf* 96-98; R Heysham *Blackb* from 98. *The Rectory, Main Street, Heysham, Morecambe LA3 2RN* Tel and fax (01524) 851422
E-mail david.tickner@tesco.net

TICKNER, Geoffrey John. b 55. Univ of Wales BD82. St Mich Coll Llan 79. **d** 82 **p** 83. C Bourne *Guildf* 82-85; C Grayswood 85-90; V New Haw 90-02; RD Runnymede 98-02; P-in-c Stevenage H Trin *St Alb* from 02; RD Stevenage from 06. *Holy Trinity Vicarage, 18 Letchmore Road, Stevenage SG1 3JD* Tel (01438) 353229 E-mail vicar@holytrinity-stevenage.info

TIDESWELL, Mrs Lynne Maureen Ann. b 49. NOC 02. **d** 05 **p** 06. NSM Stoke-upon-Trent *Lich* from 05. *14 High Lane, Cheddleton Heath Road, Leek ST13 7DY* Tel (01538) 361134 E-mail vicarsrest@talktalk.net

TIDSWELL, David Alan. b 42. CEng73 FIEE84 Univ Coll Chich BA03. St Steph Ho Ox 99. **d** 00 **p** 01. NSM Forest Row *Chich* 00-07; P-in-c Fairwarp from 07; P-in-c High Hurstwood from 07. *Manapouri, Hammerwood Road, Ashurst Wood, East Grinstead RH19 3SA* Tel (01342) 822808
E-mail datidswell@btinternet.com

TIDY, John Hylton. b 48. AKC72 St Aug Coll Cant 72. **d** 73 **p** 74. C Newton Aycliffe *Dur* 73-78; V Auckland St Pet 78-84; V Burley in Wharfedale *Bradf* 84-92; Dean Jerusalem 92-97; V Surbiton St Andr and St Mark *S'wark* 97-05; RD Kingston 00-05; Israel 05-06; P-in-c Miami Beach All So USA from 06. *4025 Pine Tree Drive, Miami Beach FL 33140-3601, USA* Tel (001) (305) 538 2244
E-mail parishoffice@allsoulsmiamibeach.org

TIERNAN, Paul Wilson. b 54. Man Univ BA76. Coll of Resurr Mirfield 77. **d** 79 **p** 80. C Lewisham St Mary *S'wark* 79-83; V Sydenham St Phil from 83. *St Philip's Vicarage, 122 Wells Park Road, London SE26 6AS* Tel (020) 8699 4930

TIGHE, Derek James. b 58. ACertCM87. Ripon Coll Cuddesdon 05. **d** 07 **p** 08. C Wimborne Minster *Sarum* from 07. *29 Venator Place, Wimborne BH21 1DQ* Tel (01202) 849466
E-mail derek.tighe@btinternet.com

TIGWELL, Brian Arthur. b 36. S'wark Ord Course 74. **d** 77 **p** 78. C Purley St Mark *S'wark* 77-80; V Upper Kennet *Sarum* 80-85; V Devizes St Pet 85-99; Wilts Adnry Ecum Officer 88-99; RD Devizes 92-98; rtd 99; Perm to Offic *Sarum* from 01 and *B & W* from 04. *7 Valentines, Dulverton TA22 9ED* Tel (01398) 324051

TILBY, Miss Angela Clare Wyatt. b 50. Girton Coll Cam BA72 MA76. Cranmer Hall Dur 77. **d** 97 **p** 98. Tutor Westcott Ho Cam from 97; Vice-Prin 01-06; Hon C Cherry Hinton St Jo *Ely*

97-06; V Cambridge St Benedict from 07. *47 New Square, Cambridge CB1 1EZ* Tel (01223) 355146 Mobile 07966-132045 E-mail angela.tilby@ntlworld.com

TILDESLEY, Edward William David. b 56. SS Hild & Bede Coll Dur BEd79. SAOMC 93. **d** 96 **p** 97. Chapl Shiplake Coll Henley 96-99; NSM Emmer Green *Ox* 96-99; Chapl Oakham Sch 99-00; TV Dorchester *Ox* 00-05; C Aldershot St Mich *Guildf* 05-08; rtd 08. *Address withheld by request* E-mail etildesley@home.gb.com

TILL, Barry Dorn. b 23. Jes Coll Cam BA49 MA49. Westcott Ho Cam 48. **d** 50 **p** 51. C Bury St Mary *Man* 50-53; Fell Jes Coll Cam 53-60; Chapl 53-56; Dean 56-60; Dean Hong Kong 60-64; Attached Ch Assembly 64-65; Prin Morley Coll Lon 66-87; Dir Baring Foundn 87-92; rtd 92. *44 Canonbury Square, London N1 2AW* Tel (020) 7359 0708

TILL, The Very Revd Michael Stanley. b 35. Linc Coll Ox BA60 MA67. Westcott Ho Cam 64. **d** 64 **p** 65. C St John's Wood *Lon* 64-67; Chapl K Coll Cam 67-70; Dean 70-80; V Fulham All SS and AD Hammersmith *Lon* 81-86; Adn Cant and Can Res Cant Cathl 86-96; Dean Win 96-05; rtd 05; Perm to Offic *Chich* 06-07; P-in-c Petworth and Egdean 07-09. *Ryde House, Angel Street, Petworth GU28 0BG* Tel (01798) 342734

TILLBROOK, Richard Ernest. b 50. St Mark & St Jo Coll Lon CertEd71 ACP76. NTMTC 96. **d** 99 **p** 00. Hd RE Davenant Foundn Sch Loughton 71-03; NSM High Laver w Magdalen Laver and Lt Laver etc *Chelmsf* 99-03; V Colchester St Barn from 03. *St Barnabas' Vicarage, 13 Abbot's Road, Colchester CO2 8BE* Tel (01206) 797481 Mobile 07818-440530 E-mail fathercap@hotmail.com

TILLER, Edgar Henry. b 22. Ex Univ CertEd69 Open Univ BA78 ACP71. Wells Th Coll 57. **d** 59 **p** 60. C Weston-super-Mare St Jo *B & W* 59-62; V Stoke Lane and Leigh upon Mendip 62-67; Asst Master Chaddiford Sch Barnstaple 69-81; Perm to Offic *Ex* 67-05 and *Llan* from 06; rtd 91. *42 Llys Pegasus, Ty Glas Road, Llanishen, Cardiff CF14 5ER*

TILLER, The Ven John. b 38. Ch Ch Ox BA60 MA64 Bris Univ MLitt72. Tyndale Hall Bris 60. **d** 62 **p** 63. C Bedford St Cuth *St Alb* 62-65; C Widcombe *B & W* 65-67; Tutor Tyndale Hall Bris 67-71; Chapl 67-71; Lect Trin Coll Bris 71-73; P-in-c Bedford Ch Ch *St Alb* 73-78; Chief Sec ACCM 78-84; Hon Can St Alb 79-84; Can Res Heref Cathl 84-04; Chan 84-02; Dioc Dir of Tr 91-00; Adn Heref 02-04; rtd 05; Local Miss and Min Adv (Shrewsbury Area) *Lich* from 05; Hon C Meole Brace from 09. *2 Pulley Lane, Bayston Hill, Shrewsbury SY3 0JH* Tel (01743) 873595 E-mail canjtiller@aol.com

TILLETT, Leslie Selwyn. b 54. Peterho Cam BA75 MA79 Leeds Univ BA80. Coll of Resurr Mirfield 78. **d** 81 **p** 82. C W Dulwich All SS and Em *S'wark* 81-85; R Purleigh, Cold Norton and Stow Maries *Chelmsf* 85-93; R Beddington *S'wark* 93-05; R Wensum Benefice *Nor* from 05; RD Sparham from 08. *The Rectory, Weston Longville, Norwich NR9 5JU* Tel (01603) 880563 E-mail selwyn@tillett.org.uk

TILLETT, Michael John Arthur. b 57. Ridley Hall Cam 96. **d** 98 **p** 99. C Framlingham w Saxtead *St E* 98-01; P-in-c Stoke by Nayland w Leavenheath and Polstead 01-03; R from 03; RD Hadleigh from 07. *Oak Tree House, Straight Road, Polstead Heath, Colchester CO6 5BB* Tel 07703-794548 (mobile) E-mail revtillett@aol.com

TILLETT, Miss Sarah Louise. b 59. Regent Coll Vancouver MCS00. Wycliffe Hall Ox 01. **d** 03 **p** 03. C Knowle *Birm* 03-07; P-in-c Bloxham w Milcombe and S Newington *Ox* from 07. *St Mary's Vicarage, Church Street, Bloxham, Banbury OX15 4ET* Tel (01295) 867685 Mobile 07764-608796 E-mail sarahtillett@tiscali.co.uk

TILLETT, Selwyn. *See* TILLETT, Leslie Selwyn

TILLEY, Canon David Robert. b 38. Selwan Th Coll 58. **d** 63 **p** 64. C Bournemouth St Fran *Win* 63-67; C Moulsecoomb *Chich* 67-70; C Ifield 70-75; TV Warwick *Cov* 76-85; P-in-c Alderminster and Halford 85-96; Dioc Min Tr Adv 85-90; CME Adv 90-04; Assoc Min Willenhall 96-04; Hon Can Cov Cathl 03-04; rtd 04; Perm to Offic *Cov* from 04. *17 Coventry Road, Baginton, Coventry CV8 3AD* Tel and fax (024) 7630 2508 E-mail david.tilley@sagainternet.co.uk

TILLEY, Elizabeth Anne. b 45. Bris Univ BA62 PGCE68. All Nations Chr Coll 72 Lon Bible Coll MA89. **d** 07 **p** 08. OLM Wonersh w Blackheath *Guildf* from 07. *Shop Flat, The Street, Wonersh, Guildford GU5 0PF* Tel (01483) 891730 E-mail etilley@waitrose.com

TILLEY, James Stephen. b 55. St Jo Coll Nottm BTh84. **d** 84 **p** 85. C Nottingham St Jude *S'well* 84-88; C Chesterle Street *Dur* 88-92; Tr and Ed CYFA (CPAS) 92-94; Hd W92-02; Perm to Offic *Cov* 92-06 and *Bris* from 06; C Nailsea H Trin *B & W* from 06. *29 Vynes Way, Nailsea, Bristol BS48 2UG* Tel (01275) 543332 Fax 545803 Mobile 07971-563229 E-mail steve.tilley@htnailsea.org.uk

TILLEY, Peter Robert. b 41. Bris Univ BA62. Sarum & Wells Th Coll 77. **d** 79 **p** 80. C Wandsworth St Paul *S'wark* 79-82; V Mitcham St Mark 82-91; RD Merton 89-91; R Walton St Mary *Liv* 91-92; TR Walton-on-the-Hill 92-98; rtd 98; P-in-c Ghent

Eur from 98; P-in-c Knokke from 08. *Begijnhoflaan 29, 9000 Gent, Belgium* Tel (0032) (9) 223 7691 Fax 330 7691 E-mail peter.tilley@telenet.be

TILLIER, Jane Yvonne. b 59. New Hall Cam BA81 PhD85. Ripon Coll Cuddesdon BA90. **d** 91 **p** 94. Par Dn Sheff St Mark Broomhill 91-94; C 94-95; Chapl Glouc Cathl 95-97; P-in-c Madeley *Lich* 97-03; P-in-c Betley 02-03; Perm to Offic 03-04; Chapl and Team Ldr Douglas Macmillan Hospice Blurton from 04; P-in-c Barlaston *Lich* from 08. *8 Plantation Park, University of Keele, Keele, Newcastle ST5 5NA* Tel (01782) 639720 E-mail jane@atherton-tillier.co.uk

TILLMAN, Miss Mary Elizabeth. b 43. S Dios Minl Tr Scheme 86. **d** 89 **p** 95. NSM Bridgemary *Portsm* 89-93; NSM Portsea All SS from 93; Adv in Min to People w Disabilities from 93. *391 Fareham Road, Gosport PO13 0AD* Tel (01329) 232589

TILLOTSON, Simon Christopher. b 67. Lon Univ BA90 Trin Coll Cam BA93 MA96. Ridley Hall Cam 91. **d** 94 **p** 95. C Paddock Wood *Roch* 94-98; C Ormskirk *Liv* 98-00; V Aylesford *Roch* 00-07; TV Whitstable *Cant* from 07. *The Vicarage, Church Street, Whitstable CT5 1PG* Tel (01227) 272308 Mobile 07946-527471 E-mail sct@tillotsons.freeserve.co.uk

TILLYER, Preb Desmond Benjamin. b 40. Ch Coll Cam BA63 MA67. Coll of Resurr Mirfield 64. **d** 66 **p** 67. C Hanworth All SS *Lon* 66-70; Chapl Liddon Ho Lon 70-74; V Pimlico St Pet w Westmr Ch Ch *Lon* 74-06; AD Westmr St Marg 85-92; Preb St Paul's Cathl 01-06; rtd 06; Perm to Offic *Nor* from 06. *The Croft House, The Croft, Costessey, Norwich NR8 5DT* Tel (01603) 745654

TILSON, Alan Ernest. b 46. TCD. **d** 70 **p** 71. C Londonderry Ch Ch *D & R* 70-73; I Inver, Mountcharles and Killaghtee 73-79; I Leckpatrick w Dunnalong 79-89; Bermuda 89-05; Hon Can Bermuda Cathl 96-05; I Tullyaughnish w Kilmacrennan and Killygarvan *D & R* from 05. *The Rectory, Ramelton, Letterkenny, Co Donegal, Republic of Ireland* Tel (00353) (74) 915 1013 E-mail canonalan@eircom.net

TILSTON, Derek Reginald. b 27. NW Ord Course. **d** 73 **p** 74. NSM Bury St Mark *Man* 73-77; NSM Holcombe 77-82; NSM Bury St Jo 82-83; NSM Bury St Jo w St Mark 83-84; C Bramley *Ripon* 85-87; TV 87-90; R Tendring and Lt Bentley w Beaumont cum Moze *Chelmsf* 90-92; rtd 93; Perm to Offic *St E* from 93. *Cobbler's Cottage, 19 The Street, Wissett, Halesworth IP19 0JE* Tel (01986) 874693

TILT, Dawn Caroline. b 59. Llan Ord Course. **d** 99 **p** 00. NSM Pyle w Kenfig *Llan* 99-00; NSM Ewenny w St Brides Major 00-04; Chapl HM Pris Parc (Bridgend) 04-06. *Address temp unknown* E-mail thetilts@hotmail.com

TILTMAN, Alan Michael. b 48. Selw Coll Cam BA70 MA74. Cuddesdon Coll 71. **d** 73 **p** 74. C Chesterton Gd Shep *Ely* 73-77; C Preston St Jo *Blackb* 77-79; Chapl Lancs (Preston) Poly 77-79; TV Man Whitworth 79-86; Chapl Man Univ (UMIST) 79-86; V Urmston 86-99; Dir CME 99-03; C Salford Sacred Trin and St Phil 99-02; V Buckley *St As* from 03. *St Matthew's Vicarage, 114 Church Road, Buckley CH7 3JN* Tel (01244) 550645 E-mail a.tiltman@zoo.co.uk

TIMBERLAKE, Neil Christopher. b 26. Kelham Th Coll 47. **d** 51 **p** 52. C Ardwick St Benedict *Man* 51-54; C Moss Side Ch Ch 54-55; C Stockport St Alb Hall Street *Ches* 55-57; C Cov St Jo 57-60; V Heath *Derby* 60-68; R Bridgetown Australia 68-70; C Leyland St Ambrose *Blackb* 70-72; C Bilborough w Strelley *S'well* 72-74; V Langold 74-86; rtd 86. *7 Thirlmere Avenue, Colne BB8 7DD* Tel (01282) 863879

TIMBRELL, Keith Stewart. b 48. Edin Th Coll 72. **d** 74 **p** 75. C Chorley St Pet *Blackb* 74-77; C Altham w Clayton le Moors 77-79; Chapl Whittingham Hosp Preston 79-95; Trust Chapl Dorset Health Care NHS Trust 95-08; rtd 08. *9 Whitecross Close, Poole BH17 9HN* Tel (01202) 604985 Mobile 07788-907965 E-mail clerigo@btinternet.com

TIMBRELL, Maxwell Keith. b 28. St Jo Coll Morpeth ThL51. **d** 51 **p** 52. Australia 51-58 and 64-82; C Hanworth All SS *Lon* 59-63; V Ingleby Greenhow w Bilsdale Priory *York* 83-85; P-in-c Kildale 83-85; V Ingleby Greenhow w Bilsdale Priory, Kildale etc 85-96; rtd 96; Perm to Offic *York* from 96. *Jasmine House, Nunnington, York YO62 5US* Tel (01439) 748319

TIMMINS, Susan Katherine. b 64. Leic Univ BScEng85 MICE91. St Jo Coll Nottm MTh94. **d** 96 **p** 97. C Iver *Ox* 96-00; P-in-c Pendlebury St Jo *Man* 00-06; V from 06. *St John's Vicarage, 91 Broomhall Road, Pendlebury, Manchester M27 8XR* Tel 0161-925 0171 E-mail susanktimmins@aol.com

TIMMIS (née PITT), Mrs Karen Lesley Finella. b 62. Lon Univ BA84. Chich Th Coll BTh94. **d** 94 **p** 95. C Walton-on-the-Hill *Liv* 94-98; P-in-c Warrington St Barn 98-00; V from 00. *The Vicarage, 73 Lovely Lane, Warrington WA5 1TY* Tel (01925) 633556

TIMOTHY, Miss Bronwen Doris (Bonnie). b 57. Sheff City Poly BSc81 Univ of Wales (Cardiff) PGCE82. St Mich Coll Llan 99. **d** 02 **p** 03. C Tenby *St D* 02-04; C Lampeter and Llanddewibrefi Gp 04-06; V Llanfihangel-ar-arth w Capel Dewi from 06. *Y Ficerdy, Llanfihangel-ar-Arth, Pencader SA39 9HU* Tel (01559) 384858 Mobile 07773-645694

TIMS, Brian Anthony. b 43. Solicitor 64. STETS 95. **d** 98 **p** 99. NSM Whitchurch w Tufton and Litchfield *Win* 98-02; NSM Shipton Bellinger 02-06. *7 Hillside, Whitchurch RG28 7SN* Tel (01256) 895181 E-mail brian@timsfamily.com

TINGAY, Kevin Gilbert Xavier. b 43. Sussex Univ BA79. Chich Th Coll 79. **d** 80 **p** 81. C W Tarring *Chich* 80-83; TV Worth 83-90; R Burnham w Oake, Hillfarrance and Heathfield *B & W* 90-01; RD Tone 96-01; P-in-c Camerton w Dunkerton, Foxcote and Shoscombe from 01; Bp's Inter Faith Officer from 01; Bp's Adv for Regional Affairs from 01. *The Rectory, Skinners Hill, Camerton, Bath BA2 0PU* Tel and fax (01761) 470249 E-mail kgxt@btinternet.com

TINGLE, Michael Barton. b 31. Bps' Coll Cheshunt 65. **d** 67 **p** 68. C Totteridge *St Alb* 67-70; C Hitchin St Mary 70-73; V Gt Gaddesden 73-78; V Belmont *Lon* 78-86; V Burford w Fulbrook, Taynton, Asthall etc *Ox* 86-97; Perm to Offic *St Alb* 97-05. *The College of St Barnabas, Blackberry Lane, Lingfield RH7 6NJ* Tel (01342) 872836

TINKER, Christopher Graham. b 78. Collingwood Coll Dur BA00. Wycliffe Hall Ox 02. **d** 04 **p** 05. C Houghton *Carl* 04-08; NSM Terrington St Clement *Ely* from 08. *8 Sutton Road, Terrington St Clement, King's Lynn PE34 4PQ* Tel (01553) 827372 E-mail christinker04@aol.com

TINKER, Preb Eric Franklin. b 20. OBE89. Ex Coll Ox BA42 MA46 City Univ Hon DD87 Lon Univ Hon DD89 Middx Univ DUniv93. Linc Th Coll 42. **d** 44 **p** 45. C Gt Berkhamsted *St Alb* 44-46; C Rugby St Andr *Cov* 46-48; CF 48-49; Lon Sec SCM 49-51; Chapl Lon Univ 51-55; V Handsworth St Jas *Birm* 55-65; V Enfield St Andr *Lon* 65-69; Preb St Paul's Cathl 69-90; Sen Chapl Lon Univs and Polys 69-90; Dir of Educn *Lon* and *S'wark* 72-80; Gen Sec Lon Dioc Bd of Educn 80-82; rtd 90; Perm to Offic *Lon* from 90. *35 Theberton Street, London N1 0QY* Tel and fax (020) 7359 4750

TINKER, Melvin. b 55. Hull Univ BSc Ox Univ MA. Wycliffe Hall Ox 80. **d** 83 **p** 84. C Wetherby *Ripon* 83-85; Chapl Keele Univ 85-90; V Cheadle All Hallows *Ches* 90-94; V Hull St Jo Newland *York* from 94. *St John's Vicarage, Clough Road, Hull HU6 7PA* Tel (01482) 343658 E-mail melvin@tink.karoo.co.uk

TINNISWOOD, Robin Jeffries. b 41. K Coll Lon BSc Eng64. Wells Th Coll 67. **d** 70 **p** 71. C Yeovil St Mich *B & W* 70-72; C Gt Marlow *Ox* 72-74; C Christow, Ashton, Trusham and Bridford *Ex* 74-77; P-in-c Ex St Paul 77; TV Heavitree w Ex St Paul 78-79; TV Ifield *Chich* 79-85; Perm to Offic *S'wark* 98-01; P-in-c Cury and Gunwalloe w Mawgan *Truro* 01-03. *The College of St Barnabas, Blackberry Lane, Lingfield RH7 6NJ* Tel (01342) 872826

TINSLEY, Bernard Murray. b 26. Nottm Univ BA51. Westcott Ho Cam 51. **d** 53 **p** 54. C Rotherham *Sheff* 53-56; C Goole 56-58; V Thorpe Hesley 58-61; R Alverdiscott w Huntshaw *Ex* 61-78; R Newton Tracey 61-78; R Beaford and Roborough 67-78; V St Giles in the Wood 67-78; V Yarnscombe 67-78; R Newton Tracey, Alverdiscott, Huntshaw etc 78-88; RD Torrington 81-86; rtd 88; Perm to Offic *Ex* from 88. *The Grange, Grange Road, Bideford EX39 4AS* Tel (01237) 471414

TINSLEY, Derek. b 31. ALCM65 BTh93 PhD97. NW Ord Course 73. **d** 76 **p** 77. C Gt Crosby St Faith *Liv* 76-80; V Wigan St Anne 80-85; V Colton w Satterthwaite and Rusland *Carl* 85-93; rtd 93; Perm to Offic *Liv* from 93. *Lyndale, 43 Renacres Lane, Ormskirk L39 8SG*

TINSLEY, Preb Derek Michael. b 35. Lon Coll of Div ALCD66 LTh. **d** 66 **p** 67. C Rainhill *Liv* 66-68; C Chalfont St Peter *Ox* 68-73; P-in-c Maids Moreton w Foxcote 73-74; P-in-c Akeley w Leckhampstead 73-74; P-in-c Lillingstone Dayrell w Lillingstone Lovell 73-74; R N Buckingham 74-82; RD Buckingham 78-82; P-in-c Alstonfield *Lich* 82-84; P-in-c Butterton 82-84; P-in-c Warslow and Elkstones 82-84; P-in-c Wetton 82-84; V Alstonfield, Butterton, Warslow w Elkstone etc 85-95; RD Alstonfield 82-95; Preb Lich Cathl 91-98; V Cheddleton 95-98; Chapl St Edw Hosp Cheddleton 96-98; rtd 98; Perm to Offic *Lich* and *Derby* from 98. *3 Windsor Close, Manor Green, Ashbourne DE6 1RJ* Tel (01335) 346226

TIPLADY, Peter. b 42. Dur Univ MB, BS65 MRCGP72 FFPHM86. Carl Dioc Tr Course 86. **d** 89 **p** 90. NSM Wetheral w Warwick *Carl* 89-05; NSM Holme Eden and Wetheral w Warwick from 05. *Meadow Croft, Wetheral, Carlisle CA4 8JG* Tel (01228) 561611 *or* 603608 E-mail peter.tiplady@mac.com

TIPP, Canon James Edward. b 45. Heythrop Coll Lon MA93. Oak Hill Th Coll 73. **d** 75 **p** 76. C St Mary Cray and St Paul's Cray *Roch* 75-78; C Southborough St Pet w Ch Ch and St Matt 78-82; R Snodland All SS w Ch Ch 82-08; RD Cobham 96-08; Hon Can Roch Cathl 01-08; rtd 08. *14 Church Road, Murston, Sittingbourne ME10 3RU* Tel (01795) 472574 E-mail ?xp@talktalk.net

TIPPER, Michael William. b 38. Hull Univ BSc59 MSc61. Em Coll Saskatoon 72. **d** 73 **p** 74. Canada 73-77, 79-80, 83-88 and from 91; R Amcotts *Linc* 77-79; V Aycliffe *Dur* 80-83; V Kneesall w Laxton and Wellow *S'well* 88-91; rtd 98. *106 Purdue Court West, Lethbridge AB T1K 4R8, Canada*

TIPPING, Mrs Brenda Margaret. b 44. N Lon Univ CQSW85 Dur Univ MA96. SAOMC 96. **d** 99 **p** 00. NSM Stevenage St Andr and St Geo *St Alb* 99-05; P-in-c S Mymms and Ridge from 05; Chapl among Deaf People from 05; NSM Officer Hertford Adnry from 06. *The Vicarage, 6 Hamilton Close, South Mimms, Potters Bar EN6 3PG* Tel (01707) 643142 E-mail ken@tipping1941.freeserve.co.uk

TIPPING, Canon John Woodman. b 42. AKC65. **d** 66 **p** 67. C Croydon St Sav *Cant* 66-70; C Plaistow St Mary *Roch* 70-72; V Brockley Hill St Sav *S'wark* 72-83; P-in-c Sittingbourne St Mary *Cant* 83-86; V 86-94; P-in-c Mersham w Hinxhill 94-03; P-in-c Mersham w Hinxhill and Sellindge 03-07; P-in-c Sevington 94-07; P-in-c Brabourne w Smeeth 95-06; AD N Lympne 95-02; Hon Can Cant Cathl 03-07; rtd 07; Perm to Offic *St E* from 08. *5 Peace Place, Thorpeness, Leiston IP16 4NA* Tel (01728) 454165 E-mail jwtipping@talk21.com

TIPPLE, Neil. b 58. Loughb Univ BTech81 Aston Univ MSc86. WMMTC 01. **d** 04 **p** 05. C Cov E 04-08; V Haywards Heath Ascension *Chich* from 08. *Ascension Vicarage, 1 Redwood Drive, Haywards Heath RH16 4ER* Tel (01444) 416262 Mobile 07792-198451 E-mail ginandwhisky@aol.com

TIRWOMWE, Stephen Warren. b 46. TCert73 Bp Tucker Coll Mukono BD88 Open Univ MA94 Leeds Univ MA01. **d** 81 **p** 82. Uganda 87-97 and from 02; C Osmondthorpe St Phil *Ripon* 97-02; Dioc Miss Co-ord Kigezi from 02. *Abaho Ahurira, PO Box 1091, Kabale, Uganda* Tel (00256) (77) 870467 E-mail swtirwomwe@hotmail.com

TISSINGTON, Irene Frances. b 50. EMMTC 03. **d** 06 **p** 07. NSM Harworth *S'well* from 06. *14 Station Avenue, Ranskill, Retford DN22 8LF* Tel (01777) 818923 Mobile 07856-892759 E-mail irene@itissington.freeserve.co.uk

TITCOMB, Mrs Claire. b 35. SAOMC 95. **d** 98 **p** 99. OLM Witney *Ox* from 98; Assoc P for Min Development from 01. *30 Beech Road, Witney OX28 6LW* Tel (01993) 771234 E-mail claireroyt@clara.net

TITCOMBE, Peter Charles. See JONES, Peter Charles

TITFORD, Richard Kimber. b 45. UEA BA67. Ripon Coll Cuddesdon 78. **d** 80 **p** 80. C Middleton *Man* 80-83; P-in-c Edwardstone w Groton and Lt Waldingfield *St E* 83-90 and 95-02; R 90-94; P-in-c Boxford 00-02; C Assington w Newton Green and Lt Cornard 00-02; R Boxford, Edwardstone, Groton etc 02-03; rtd 03; Perm to Offic *St E* from 03. *2 Chestnut Mews, Friars Street, Sudbury CO10 2AH* Tel and fax (01787) 880303 E-mail titford@keme.co.uk

TITLEY, David Joseph. b 47. Ex Univ BSc Surrey Univ PhD. Wycliffe Hall Ox. **d** 82 **p** 83. C Stowmarket *St E* 82-85; C Bloxwich *Lich* 85-90; TV 90-95; V Prees and Fauls 95-00; V Clacton St Paul *Chelmsf* from 00. *The Vicarage, 7 St Alban's Road, Clacton-on-Sea CO15 6BA* Tel (01255) 424760 E-mail titleys@supanet.com

TITLEY, Canon Robert John. b 56. Ch Coll Cam BA78 MA82 K Coll Lon PhD95. Westcott Ho Cam. **d** 85 **p** 86. C Lower Sydenham St Mich *S'wark* 85-88; C Sydenham All SS 85-88; Chapl Whitelands Coll of HE 88-94; V W Dulwich All SS 94-06; RD Streatham 04-05; Dioc Dir of Ords from 06; Can Res and Treas S'wark Cathl from 06. *483C Southwark Park Road, London SE16 2JP* Tel (020) 7237 3865 E-mail robert.titley@southwark.anglican.org

TIVEY, Nicholas. b 65. Liv Poly BSc89. Ridley Hall Cam 91. **d** 94 **p** 95. C Bromborough *Ches* 94-97; TV Walton H Trin *Ox* 97-01; Chapl HM Pris Wayland 01-08; Chapl Nor Sch from 08. *The Chaplain's Office, Norwich School, 70 The Close, Norwich NR1 4DD* Tel (01603) 728450 E-mail ntivey@norwich-school.org.uk

TIZZARD, Peter Francis. b 53. Oak Hill Th Coll 88. **d** 90 **p** 91. C Letchworth St Paul w Willian *St Alb* 90-95; I Drumkeeran w Templecarne and Muckross *Clogh* 95-00; P-in-c Ramsgate Ch Ch *Cant* 00-02; V from 02. *24 St Mildred's Avenue, Ramsgate CT11 0HT* Tel (01843) 853732

TOAN, Robert Charles. b 50. Oak Hill Th Coll. **d** 84 **p** 85. C Upton (Overchurch) *Ches* 84-87; V Rock Ferry 87-99; RD Birkenhead 97-99; V Plas Newton 99-06; P-in-c Ches Ch Ch 03-06; V Plas Newton w Ches Ch Ch 07-09; RD Ches 02-08; Cambodia from 09. *c/o Ben Toan Esq, 123 Hope Farm Road, Great Sutton, Ellesmere Port CH66 2TJ* Tel 0151-347 9220 E-mail bob.toan@xaltmail.com

TOBIN, Richard Francis. b 44. CertEd. Chich Th Coll 76. **d** 78 **p** 79. C W Leigh CD *Portsm* 78-79; C Halstead St Andr w H Trin and Greenstead Green *Chelmsf* 79-87; Youth Chapl 82-87; V S Shields St Simon *Dur* 87-04; V Ipswich All Hallows *St E* from 04. *All Hallows' Vicarage, Reynolds Road, Ipswich IP3 0JH* Tel (01473) 727467 E-mail ricktobin@btinternet.com

TOBIN, Robert Benjamin. b 70. Harvard Univ AB93 TCD MPhil98 Mert Coll Ox DPhil04 Em Coll Cam BA07. Westcott Ho Cam 04. **d** 07 **p** 08. C Beaconsfield *Ox* from 07; Chapl Harvard Univ USA from 09. *The Episcopal Chaplaincy, 2 Garden Street, Cambridge MA 02138, USA* Tel (001) (617) 495 4340

TODD, Alastair. b 20. CMG71. CCC Ox BA45. Sarum & Wells Th Coll 71. **d** 73 **p** 74. C Willingdon *Chich* 73-77; P-in-c Brighton

St Aug 77-78; V Brighton St Aug and St Sav 78-86; rtd 86; Perm to Offic *Chich* from 86. *59 Park Avenue, Eastbourne BN21 2XH* Tel (01323) 505843

TODD, Canon Andrew John. b 61. Univ Coll Dur BA84 K Coll Lon MPhil98. Coll of Resurr Mirfield 85. **d** 87 **p** 88. C Thorpe St Andr *Nor* 87-91; Chapl K Alfred Coll *Win* 91-94; Sen Asst P E Dereham and Scarning *Nor* 94-97; Dir Studies EAMTC *Ely* 94-01 and 97-01; CME Officer *St E* 01-06; Can Res St E Cathl 01-06; Sub Dean 04-06; Dean Chapl Studies St Mich Coll Llan from 06; Hon Research Fell Cardiff Univ from 07. *St Michael's College, 54 Cardiff Road, Llandaff, Cardiff CF5 2YJ* Tel (029) 2083 8001 *or* 2056 3379 Fax 2083 8008 Mobile 07785-560558 E-mail ajt@stmichaels.ac.uk

TODD, Catherine Frances. b 61. Surrey Univ BSc84 Westmr Coll Ox BTh99 RGN84 RM86. EAMTC 96. **d** 99 **p** 00. NSM Sutton and Witcham w Mepal *Ely* 99-01; C Horringer *St E* 01-03; R 03-07; Chapl HM Pris Erlestoke from 07. *HM Prison, Erlestoke, Devizes SN10 5TU* Tel (01380) 814250 Fax 814272

TODD, Clive. b 57. Linc Th Coll 89. **d** 91 **p** 92. C Consett *Dur* 91-93; C Bensham 93-95; P-in-c S Hetton w Haswell 95-98; R Ebchester and V Medomsley 98-04; P-in-c S Lawres Gp *Linc* 04-09; RD Lawres 06-07; P-in-c Thanington *Cant* from 09; Dir of Ords from 09. *The Vicarage, 70 Thanington Road, Canterbury CT1 3XE* Tel (01227) 464516 E-mail clive.todd1@btinternet.com

TODD, Edward Peter. b 44. Cranmer Hall Dur 86. **d** 88 **p** 89. C Hindley All SS *Liv* 88-91; P-in-c Wigan St Steph 91-96; V 96-98; P-in-c N Meols 98-03; TR 03-05; rtd 05. *1B Nixons Lane, Southport PR8 3ES* Tel (01704) 572422 E-mail revtodd@btopenworld.com

TODD, George Robert. b 21. Sarum & Wells Th Coll 74. **d** 76 **p** 77. Hon C Wellington and Distr *B & W* 76-86; Perm to Offic 86-06. *15 John Grinter Way, Wellington TA21 9AR* Tel (01823) 662828

TODD, Ian Campbell. b 68. Westcott Ho Cam. **d** 04 **p** 05. C Scotforth *Blackb* 04-08; TV Hitchin *St Alb* from 09. *Holy Saviour Vicarage, St Anne's Road, Hitchin SG5 1QB* Tel (01462) 456140 E-mail iancamtodd@googlemail.com

TODD, Jeremy Stephen Bevan. b 69. Trin Coll Bris BA92. **d** 97 **p** 98. C Tufnell Park St Geo and All SS *Lon* 97-99; Perm to Offic *Lon* 03-07 and *S'wark* from 07. *St Augustine's Vicarage, 336 Baring Road, London SE12 0DX* Tel (020) 8857 4941 E-mail jeremytodd@me.com

TODD, Joy Gertrude. b 28. Ox Univ MTh99. **d** 90 **p** 94. OLM Guildf H Trin w St Mary 90-99; Perm to Offic from 99. *165 Stoke Road, Guildford GU1 1EY* Tel (01483) 567500

TODD, Michael Edward. b 62. Brighton Poly BA84 Surrey Univ PGCE85. SEITE 96 Ven English Coll Rome 98. **d** 99 **p** 05. C Farnham *Guildf* 99-00; Chapl Surrey Inst Art and Design 99-00; Development Officer Surrey Univ 00-02; Progr Manager and Lect Croydon Coll 02-05; Dep Dir City and Islington Coll 05-07; Hon C Camberwell St Giles w St Matt *S'wark* 04-05; Hon C Newington St Mary from 05; Hd of Sch S Thames Coll from 07. *St Mary's Vicarage, 35 Elmfield Road, London SW17 8AG* Tel (020) 8675 9619 Mobile 07946-701279 E-mail mikeytodd@hotmail.com

TODD, Nicholas Stewart. b 61. Open Univ BA03 MA08. Wycliffe Hall Ox 94. **d** 96 **p** 97. C Gt Wyrley *Lich* 96-99; V Leaton and Albrighton w Battlefield 99-02; R Holbrook, Stutton, Freston, Woolverstone etc *St E* 02-06; CF from 06. *c/o MOD Chaplains (Army)* Tel (01980) 615804 Fax 615800 E-mail nick@toddsrus.org

TODD, Canon Norman Henry. b 19. PhC Lon Univ BPharm42 Fitzw Ho Cam BA50 MA55 Nottm Univ PhD78. Westcott Ho Cam 50. **d** 52 **p** 53. C Aspley *S'well* 52-54; Chapl Westcott Ho Cam 55-58; V Arnold *S'well* 58-65; V Rollaston w Morton 65-69; Can Res S'well Minster 65-69; R Elston w Elston Chapelry 71-76; R E Stoke w Syerston 72-76; V Sibthorpe 72-76; Bp's Adv on Tr 76-83; C Averham w Kelham 76-80; V Rollaston w Morton 80-83; P-in-c Upton 80-83; V Rollaston w Fiskerton, Morton and Upton 83-88; Hon Can S'well Minster 82-88; rtd 88; Perm to Offic *S'well* from 88; Bp's Adv for Bps' Min 88-94. *39 Beacon Hill Road, Newark NG24 2JH* Tel (01636) 671857 E-mail n.todd1@ntlworld.com

TODD, Canon William Moorhouse. b 26. Lich Th Coll 54. **d** 57 **p** 58. C W Derby St Mary *Liv* 57-61; V Liv St Chris Norris Green 61-97; Hon Can Liv Cathl 92-97; rtd 97; Perm to Offic *Liv* from 97. *3 Haymans Grove, West Derby, Liverpool L12 7LD* Tel 0151-256 1712

TOFTS, Jack. b 31. Roch Th Coll 66. **d** 68 **p** 69. C Richmond *Ripon* 68-71; C Croydon St Jo *Cant* 71-74; P-in-c Welney *Ely* 74-78; P-in-c Upwell Christchurch 74-79; V Gorefield 78-94; R Newton 78-94; R Tydd St Giles 78-94; Perm to Offic *Ely* from 96. *The Birches, Church Road, Walpole St Peter, Wisbech PE14 7NU* Tel (01945) 780455

TOLHURST, David. b 72. Cranmer Hall Dur 07. **d** 09. C Middleton St George *Dur* from 09. *8 Westacres, Middleton St George, Darlington DL2 1LJ* Tel (01325) 401850 E-mail david.tolhurst@gmail.com

TOLL, Brian Arthur. b 35. Ely Th Coll 62 Linc Th Coll 64. **d** 65 **p** 66. C Cleethorpes *Linc* 65-68; C Hadleigh w Layham and Shelley *St E* 69-72; R Claydon and Barham 72-86; P-in-c Capel w Lt Wenham 86-94; P-in-c Holton St Mary w Gt Wenham 87-91; R Capel St Mary w Lt and Gt Wenham 94-96; P-in-c Ipswich St Mary at the Elms 96-01; Bp's Adv on Deliverance and Exorcism 89-97; rtd 01; Perm to Offic *St E* from 01. *39 Derwent Road, Ipswich IP3 0QR* Tel (01473) 424305 E-mail batoll@ntlworld.com

TOLLER, Elizabeth Margery. b 53. Leeds Univ BA75. Ripon Coll Cuddesdon 84. **d** 87 **p** 00. Asst Chapl Leeds Gen Infirmary 87-90; Perm to Offic *Nor* 90-91; Chapl Lt Plumstead Hosp 92-93; Chapl Co-ord HM Pris Nor 93-95; Chapl Gt Yarmouth Coll 96-99; Perm to Offic *S'wark* 99-00; Hon C Wandsworth St Paul from 00; Hon Asst Chapl St Chris Hospice Lon from 03. *116 Augustus Road, London SW19 6EW* Tel (020) 8788 2024 E-mail mtoller@gmx.de

TOLLER, Heinz Dieter. b 52. NEOC 86. **d** 87 **p** 88. C Leeds Gipton Epiphany *Ripon* 87-90; R Coltishall w Gt Hautbois and Horstead *Nor* 90-99; V Wandsworth St Paul *S'wark* from 99; AD Wandsworth from 05. *116 Augustus Road, London SW19 6EW* Tel (020) 8788 2024 Fax 08702-843237 Mobile 07941-291120 E-mail htoller@gmail.com

TOLLERSON, Peter Joseph Moncrieff. b 65. Oak Hill Th Coll 99. **d** 01 **p** 02. C Ulverston St Mary w H Trin *Carl* 01-04; Chapl RAF from 04. *Chaplaincy Services, Valiant Block, HQ Air Command, RAF High Wycombe HP14 4UE* Tel (01494) 496800 Fax 496343 E-mail pedroandcarmen@yahoo.com

TOLLEY, Canon George. b 25. Lon Univ BSc45 MSc48 PhD52 Sheff Univ Hon DSc83 Open Univ Hon DUniv84 Hon DSc86 FRSC CBIM. Linc Th Coll 65. **d** 67 **p** 68. C Sharrow St Andr *Sheff* 67-90; Hon Can Sheff Cathl 76-98. *74 Furniss Avenue, Sheffield S17 3QP* Tel 0114-236 0538

TOLWORTHY, Canon Colin. b 37. Chich Th Coll 64. **d** 67 **p** 68. C Hulme St Phil *Man* 67-70; C Lawton Moor 70-71; C Hangleton *Chich* 72-76; V Eastbourne St Phil 76-87; V Hastings H Trin from 87; Can and Preb Chich Cathl from 03. *Holy Trinity Vicarage, 72 Priory Avenue, Hastings TN34 1UG* Tel (01424) 441766 E-mail colintolworthy@hotmail.com

TOMALIN, Stanley Joseph Edward. b 66. Oak Hill Th Coll BA93. **d** 96 **p** 97. C Bitterne *Win* 96-00; C Hailsham *Chich* 00; P-in-c Hawkswood CD 01-05; V Hawkswood from 05; RD Dallington from 07. *Harmers Hay House, 1 Barn Close, Hailsham BN27 1TL* Tel (01323) 846680 E-mail tomalinstan@aol.com

TOMBS, Kenneth Roberts. b 42. Open Univ BA84. S Dios Minl Tr Scheme 92. **d** 95 **p** 96. Dep Hd Twyford C of E High Sch Acton 86-97; Chapl 98-02; rtd 02; NSM Ickenham *Lon* from 95. *91 Burns Avenue, Southall UB1 2LT* Tel (020) 8574 3738 E-mail ken.tombs@btinternet.com

TOME DA SILVA, Carlos Alberto. d 01 **p** 01. Brazil 01-04; C Risca *Mon* 04-05; C Bassaleg 05-06; CF from 06. *c/o MOD Chaplains (Army)* Tel (01980) 615804 Fax 615800 E-mail betotome@hotmail.com

TOMKINS, Ian James. b 60. Univ of Wales (Cardiff) LLB81 Aston Business Sch MBA90. Ridley Hall Cam. **d** 00 **p** 01. C Bourton-on-the-Water w Clapton *Glouc* 00-04; P-in-c Broxbourne w Wormley *St Alb* 04-07; R from 07. *The Vicarage, Churchfields, Broxbourne EN10 7AU* Tel (01992) 462382 E-mail ian-tomkins@lineone.net

TOMKINS, James Andrew. b 66. R Holloway & Bedf New Coll Lon BA88. SAOMC 01. **d** 04 **p** 06. C Lavendon w Cold Brayfield, Clifton Reynes etc *Ox* 04-05; C Risborough 05-08; TV from 08. *The Rectory, Mill Lane, Monks Risborough, Princes Risborough HP27 9JE* Tel (01844) 275944 E-mail jamestomkins@btinternet.com

TOMKINS, Jocelyn Rachel. *See* WALKER, Jocelyn Rachel

TOMKINSON, Raymond David. b 47. EAMTC 86. **d** 89 **p** 90. NSM Chesterton St Geo *Ely* 89-91; C Sawston 91-93; C Babraham 91-93; P-in-c Wimbotsham w Stow Bardolph and Stow Bridge etc 93-94; R 94-00; RD Fincham 94-97; Dir Old Alresford Place *Win* 00-06; P-in-c Old Alresford and Bighton 00-06; rtd 06; Perm to Offic *Pet* from 07. *8 Uppingham Road, Oakham LE15 6JD* Tel (01572) 756844 E-mail raymond@tomkinson54.fsnet.co.uk

TOMLIN, Graham Stuart. b 58. Linc Coll Ox BA80 MA83 Ex Univ PhD96. Wycliffe Hall Ox BA85. **d** 86 **p** 87. C Ex St Leon w H Trin 86-89; Chapl Jes Coll Ox 89-94; Tutor Wycliffe Hall Ox 89-98; Vice-Prin 98-05; Prin St Paul's Th Cen *Lon* from 05; Dean St Mellitus Coll from 07. *33 Foskett Road, London SW6 3LY* Tel (020) 7731 2732 Mobile 07929-048720 E-mail graham.tomlin@htb.org.uk

TOMLIN, Keith Michael. b 53. Imp Coll Lon BSc75. Ridley Hall Cam 77. **d** 80 **p** 81. C Heywood St Jas *Man* 80-83; C Rochdale 83-84; TV 84-85; Chapl Rochdale Tech Coll 83-85; R Benington w Leverton *Linc* 85-99; R Leverton 99-01; Chapl HM Pris N Sea Camp 97-01; P-in-c Fotherby *Linc* 01-06; Louthesk Deanery Chapl from 06. *Parish Office, 6 Upgate, Louth LN11 9ET* Tel (01507) 610247

TOMLINE, Stephen Harrald. b 35. Dur Univ BA57. Cranmer Hall Dur. **d** 61 **p** 62. C Blackley St Pet *Man* 61-66; V Audenshaw St Steph 66-90; V Newhey 90-01; rtd 01; Perm to Offic *Carl* from 01. *3 Humphrey Cottages, Stainton, Kendal LA8 0AD* Tel (01539) 560988

TOMLINSON, Anne Lovat. b 56. Edin Univ MA78 PhD85 MTh98. St Jo Coll Nottm 84. **d** 93. Tutor TISEC 93-02; Dir Past Studies 98-00; Perm to Offic *Edin* from 93. *3 Bright's Crescent, Edinburgh EH9 2DB* Tel and fax 0131-668 1322
E-mail anne.tomlinson1@btinternet.com

TOMLINSON, Barry William. b 47. Clifton Th Coll 72. **d** 72 **p** 73. C Pennington *Man* 72-76; SAMS 76-80; Chile 77-80; C-in-c Gorleston St Mary CD *Nor* 80; V Gorleston St Mary 80-88; Chapl Jas Paget Hosp Gorleston 81-87; P-in-c Gt w Lt Plumstead *Nor* 88-89; R Gt w Lt Plumstead and Witton 89-93; R Gt and Lt Plumstead w Thorpe End and Witton 93-98; Chapl Lt Plumstead Hosp 88-94; Chapl Norwich Community Health Partnership NHS Trust 94-95; RD Blofield *Nor* 96-98; R Roughton and Felbrigg, Metton, Sustead etc 99-02; V Margate H Trin *Cant* 98-99; rtd 02; Perm to Offic *Nor* from 02. *12 Heath Road, Sheringham NR26 8JH* Tel (01263) 820266
E-mail bwtomlinson@btinternet.com

TOMLINSON, David Robert. b 60. Kent Univ BSc82 Chelsea Coll Lon PGCE83 Jes Coll Cam BA92 MA96. Ridley Hall Cam 90. **d** 93 **p** 94. C Godalming *Guildf* 93-98; V Grays North *Chelmsf* 98-08; RD Thurrock 03-08; TR Saffron Walden w Wendens Ambo, Littlebury etc from 08; RD Saffron Walden from 09. *The Rectory, 17 Borough Lane, Saffron Walden CB11 4AG* Tel (01799) 500947
E-mail rector@stmaryssaffronwalden.org

TOMLINSON, David Robert. b 63. Open Univ BA07 St Jo Coll Dur BA09. Cranmer Hall Dur 07. **d** 09. C Shildon *Dur* from 09. *St Francis Vicarage, Burnhope, Newton Aycliffe DL5 7ER* Tel (01325) 310804 Mobile 07546-596079
E-mail smileydavid63@gmail.com

TOMLINSON, David William. b 48. Lon Bible Coll MA95 Westcott Ho Cam 97. **d** 97 **p** 98. NSM W Holloway St Luke *Lon* 97-00; P-in-c 00-01; V from 01. *St Luke's Vicarage, Penn Road, London N7 9RE* Tel and fax (020) 7607 1504
E-mail revdavetomlinson@hotmail.com

TOMLINSON, Edward James. b 74. Homerton Coll Cam BEd96. Westcott Ho Cam 99. **d** 02 **p** 03. C Brentwood St Thos *Chelmsf* 02-06; V Tunbridge Wells St Barn *Roch* from 06. *St Barnabas' Vicarage, 114 Upper Grosvenor Road, Tunbridge Wells TN1 2EX* Tel (01892) 533826 Mobile 07788-855646
E-mail frtomlinson@yahoo.co.uk

TOMLINSON, Eric Joseph. b 45. Lich Th Coll 70 Qu Coll Birm 72. **d** 73 **p** 74. C Cheadle *Lich* 73-76; C Sedgley All SS 77-79; V Ettingshall 79-94; V Horton, Lonsdon and Rushton Spencer from 94. *The Vicarage, Longsdon, Stoke-on-Trent ST9 9QF* Tel (01538) 385318

TOMLINSON, Frederick William. b 58. Glas Univ MA80 Edin Univ BD83. Edin Th Coll 80. **d** 83 **p** 84. C Cumbernauld *Glas* 83-86; C Glas St Mary 86-88; R Edin St Hilda 88-01; R Edin St Fillan 88-01; R Edin St Pet from 01. *3 Bright's Crescent, Edinburgh EH9 2DB* Tel and fax 0131-667 6224
E-mail fred.tomlinson@talk21.com

TOMLINSON, Helen. b 53. **d** 07 **p** 08. OLM Stretford All SS *Man* from 07. *23 Gairloch Avenue, Stretford, Manchester M32 9LL* Tel 0161-865 2723

TOMLINSON, Canon Ian James. b 50. K Coll Lon AKC72 Hull Univ MA90 Ox Univ MTh01. St Aug Coll Cant 72. **d** 73 **p** 74. C Thirsk w S Kilvington and Carlton Miniott etc *York* 73-76; C Harrogate St Wilfrid *Ripon* 76-79; R Appleshaw, Kimpton, Thruxton, Fyfield etc *Win* from 79; Dioc Adv in Past care and Counselling from 01; Hon Can Win Cathl from 04. *The Rectory, Ragged Appleshaw, Andover SP11 9HX* Tel (01264) 772414 Fax 771302 E-mail ian@raggedappleshaw.freeserve.co.uk

TOMLINSON, Mrs Jean Mary. b 32. K Coll Lon BEd75. S Dios Minl Tr Scheme 84. **d** 87 **p** 94. Hon Par Dn Spring Park All SS *S'wark* 87-92; Chapl HM YOI Hatfield 92-98; Perm to Offic *S'well* from 92. *6 Cheyne Walk, Bawtry, Doncaster DN10 6RS* Tel (01302) 711281

TOMLINSON (née MILLS), Mrs Jennifer Clare. b 61. Trin Hall Cam BA82 MA86. Ridley Hall Cam 88. **d** 91 **p** 94. C Busbridge *Guildf* 91-95; C Godalming 95-98; NSM Grays North *Chelmsf* from 98; NSM Saffron Walden w Wendens Ambo, Littlebury etc from 08; Chapl Thurrock Primary Care Trust 99-08. *The Rectory, 17 Borough Lane, Saffron Walden CB11 4AG* Tel (01799) 500757 E-mail tomlinson.jenny@ntlworld.com

TOMLINSON, John Howard. b 54. New Univ BSc76 MICE83. Chich Th Coll 91. **d** 93 **p** 94. C Blewbury, Hagbourne and Upton *Ox* 93-96; C Cowley St Jas 96-97; TV 97-04; TR Upper Wylye Valley *Sarum* from 04; RD Heytesbury from 07. *The Rectory, 1 Bests Lane, Sutton Veny, Warminster BA12 7AU* Tel (01985) 840014 E-mail johnandclare-atuwvt@tiscali.co.uk

TOMLINSON, John William Bruce. b 60. Univ of Wales (Abth) BA82 Man Univ MA90 Birm Univ PhD08. Hartley Victoria Coll 87 Mar Thoma Th Sem Kottayam 90 Linc Th Coll 91. **d** 92

p 93. In Methodist Ch 90-91; C Sawley *Derby* 92-95; P-in-c Man Victoria Park 95-98; Dioc CUF Officer 95-98; Chapl St Anselm Hall Man Univ 96-98; V Shelton and Oxon *Lich* 98-04; Ecum Co-ord for Miss and Chief Exec Officer Lincs Chapl Services 04-06; Perm to Offic from 08. *31 Rivehall Avenue, Welton, Lincoln LN2 3LH* Tel (01673) 866159
E-mail dr.pelican@hotmail.com

TOMLINSON, Matthew Robert Edward. b 61. St Chad's Coll Dur BA83 Univ of Wales (Cardiff) BD94. St Mich Coll Llan 92. **d** 94 **p** 95. C Abergavenny St Mary w Llanwenarth Citra *Mon* 94-96; PV Llan Cathl and Chapl Llan Cathl Sch 96-00; V Edgbaston St Aug *Birm* from 00. *St Augustine's Vicarage, 44 Vernon Road, Birmingham B16 9SH* Tel and fax 0121-454 0127 Mobile 07989-915499 E-mail jm.tomlinson@blueyonder.co.uk

TOMPKINS, April. b 51. Man Univ BEd75. EMMTC 05. **d** 07 **p** 08. NSM Belper *Derby* from 07. *8 Derwent Grove, Alfreton DE55 7PB* Tel (01773) 835122
E-mail april_tompkins@hotmail.com

TOMPKINS, David John. b 32. Oak Hill Th Coll 55. **d** 58 **p** 59. C Northampton St Giles *Pet* 58-61; C Heatherlands St Jo *Sarum* 61-63; V Selby St Jas and Wistow *York* 63-73; V Retford St Sav *S'well* 73-87; P-in-c Clarborough w Hayton 84-87; V Kidsgrove *Lich* 87-90; V Tockwith and Bilton w Bickerton *York* 90-97; rtd 97; Perm to Offic *Pet* from 00. *49 Wentworth Drive, Oundle, Peterborough PE8 4QF* Tel (01832) 275176

TOMPKINS, Michael John Gordon. b 35. JP76. Man Univ BSc58 MPS59. NOC 82. **d** 85 **p** 86. C Abington *Pet* 85-87; TV Daventry 87-92; P-in-c Braunston 87-92; TV Daventry, Ashby St Ledgers, Braunston etc 92-93; R Paston 93-98; Perm to Offic *Ches* from 98; rtd 00. *19 Clarendon Close, Chester CH4 7BL* Tel (01244) 659147 E-mail michaeltompkins@onetel.com

TOMPKINS, Peter Michael. b 58. Open Univ BA92 SS Hild & Bede Coll Dur CertEd79. St Jo Coll Nottm MA96. **d** 96 **p** 97. C Bromfield w Waverton *Carl* 96-99; R Woldsburn *York* 99-01; TV E Farnworth and Kearsley *Man* 01-05; P-in-c Laceby and Ravendale Gp *Linc* from 05. *The Rectory, 4 Cooper Lane, Laceby, Grimsby DN37 7AX* Tel (01472) 870884

TOMS, Sheila Patricia. b 33. Cam Univ TCert54 Univ of Wales (Cardiff) BEd77. Llan Ord Course 90. **dss** 91 **d** 94 **p** 97. Canton St Luke *Llan* 91-94; NSM Peterston-super-Ely w St Brides-super-Ely 94-00; P-in-c Newport St Paul *Mon* 00-06; Perm to Offic from 07. *East Wing, Dingestow Court, Dingestow, Monmouth NP25 4DY* Tel (01600) 740262

TONBRIDGE, Archdeacon of. See MANSELL, The Ven Clive Neville Ross

TONBRIDGE, Suffragan Bishop of. See CASTLE, The Rt Revd Brian Colin

TONES, Kevin Edward. b 64. Hertf Coll Ox BA85. Ridley Hall Cam 88. **d** 91 **p** 92. C Warmsworth *Sheff* 91-92; C Thorne 92-96; V Greasbrough from 96. *The Vicarage, 16 Church Street, Greasbrough, Rotherham S61 4DX* Tel (01709) 551288
E-mail kevt@worshiptrax.co.uk

TONG, Canon Peter Laurence. b 29. Lon Univ BA50. Oak Hill Th Coll 52. **d** 54 **p** 55. C Everton St Chrys *Liv* 54-56; P-in-c Liv St Sav 56-59; V Blackb Sav 59-65; Chapl Blackb R Infirmary 63-65; V Islington St Andr w St Thos and St Matthias *Lon* 65-75; V Welling *Roch* 75-82; TR Bedworth *Cov* 82-94; Hon Can Cov Cathl 88-94; Hon Can Chile from 89; rtd 94; Perm to Offic *Roch* from 94. *46 Bladindon Drive, Bexley DA5 3BP* Tel (020) 8303 0085

TONGE, Brian. b 36. St Chad's Coll Dur BA58. Ely Th Coll 59. **d** 61 **p** 62. C Fleetwood St Pet *Blackb* 61-65; Chapl Ranby Ho Sch Retford 65-69; Hon C Burnley St Andr w St Marg *Blackb* 69-97; rtd 97; Perm to Offic *Blackb* from 97. *50 Fountains Avenue, Simonstone, Burnley BB12 7PY* Tel (01282) 776518

TONGE, Lister. b 51. K Coll Lon AKC74 Loyola Univ Chicago MPS95. St Aug Coll Cant 74. **d** 75 **p** 76. C Liv Our Lady and St Nic w St Anne 75-78; C Johannesburg Cathl S Africa 78-79; CR 79-91; Lic to Offic *Wakef* 83-91; Perm to Offic *Man* 89-94; USA 93-95; Perm to Offic *Liv* 95-96; Chapl Community of St Jo Bapt from 96; Chapl Ripon Coll Cuddesdon from 05; Lic to Offic Newark USA from 08. *38 Empress Court, Woodin's Way, Oxford OX1 1HF* Tel (01865) 247966
E-mail listertonge@talktalk.net

TONGE, Malcolm. b 53. Lancs Poly BA74 FCA77. NEOC 00. **d** 03 **p** 04. NSM Brookfield *York* 03-07; NSM Ingleby Barwick 07-08; NSM Lower Swale *Ripon* from 08. *65 Belmont Avenue, Middlesbrough TS5 8EW* Tel (01642) 599209
E-mail malcolm.tonge@huntsman.com

TONGUE, Charles Garth. b 32. **d** 01 **p** 01. P-in-c Strontian *Arg* from 01; P-in-c Kinlochmoidart from 01. *The Old Smiddy, Anaheilt, Strontian, Acharacle, Argyll PH36 4JA* Tel (01967) 402467 Fax 402269 Mobile 07713-955204

TONGUE, Canon Paul. b 41. St Chad's Coll Dur BA63. **d** 64 **p** 65 C Dudley St Edm *Worc* 64-69; C Sedgley All SS *Lich* 69-70; V Amblecote *Worc* 70-07; Chapl Dudley Gp of Hosps NHS Trust 93-07; Hon Can Worc Cathl 93-07; RD Stourbridge 96-01; rtd 07. *99 Woolhope Road, Worcester WR5 2AP* Tel (01905) 352052
E-mail fatherpaul@freeuk.com

TONKIN, The Ven David Graeme. b 31. Univ of NZ LLB56 LLM57 Barrister-at-Law. Coll of Resurr Mirfield 57. **d** 59 **p** 60. C Hackney Wick St Mary of Eton w St Aug *Lon* 59-62; Chapl Worksop Coll Notts 62-68; Lic to Offic *S'well* 63-68; Jordan 68-74; New Zealand from 74; Can St Pet Cathl Waikato 88-89; Adn Waitomo 89-98; rtd 93. *Box 91, Owhango, New Zealand* Tel and fax (0064) (7) 895 4738

TONKIN, Canon Richard John. b 28. Lon Coll of Div ALCD59 BD60. **d** 60 **p** 61. C Leic Martyrs 60-63; C Keynsham *B & W* 63-66; V Hinckley H Trin *Leic* 66-74; RD Sparkenhoe II 71-74; R Oadby 74-84; V Leic H Apostles 84-93; Hon Can Leic Cathl 83-93; rtd 93; Perm to Offic *Leic* from 93. *39 Shackerdale Road, Wigston, Leicester LE8 1BQ* Tel 0116-281 2517

TONKINSON, Canon David Boyes. b 47. K Coll Lon BD71 AKC71. St Aug Coll Cant 71. **d** 72 **p** 73. C Surbiton St Andr *S'wark* 72-74; C Selsdon St Jo w St Fran *Cant* 75-81; V Croydon St Aug *Cant* 81-84; V Croydon St Aug *S'wark* 85-89; C Easthampstead and Ind Chapl *Ox* 89-96; Chapl Bracknell Coll 93-96; Soc Resp Adv *Portsm* 96-02; Hon Can Portsm Cathl 96-02; Ind Chapl *Win* 02-08; Hon C Heckfield w Mattingley and Rotherwick 06-08; Soc Resp Partnership Development Officer *Guildf* from 08. *Diocesan House, Quarry Street, Guildford GU1 3XG* Tel (01483) 571826
E-mail david.tonkinson@cofeguildford.org.uk

TOOBY, Anthony Albert. b 58. Sarum & Wells Th Coll 89. **d** 91 **p** 92. C Warsop *S'well* 91-95; C Ollerton w Boughton 95-98; V Girlington *Bradf* from 98. *The Vicarage, 27 Baslow Grove, Bradford BD9 5JA* Tel (01274) 544987
E-mail anthony.tooby@bradford.anglican.org

TOOGOOD, John Peter. b 73. Leeds Univ BA95. Ripon Coll Cuddesdon 98. **d** 00 **p** 01. C Sherborne w Castleton and Lillington *Sarum* 00-03; P-in-c Chieveley w Winterbourne and Oare *Ox* from 03. *The Vicarage, Church Lane, Chieveley, Newbury RG20 8UT* Tel (01635) 247566 Fax 812206 Mobile 07748-822336 E-mail john@cwando.orangehome.co.uk

TOOGOOD, Ms Melanie Lorraine. b 57. K Coll Lon BD78 AKC78. Ripon Coll Cuddesdon 94. **d** 96 **p** 97. C Shepperton *Lon* 96-99; C Greenford H Cross 99-04; P-in-c Tufnell Park St Geo and All SS 04-06; V from 06. *St George's Vicarage, 72 Crayford Road, London N7 0ND* Tel (020) 7700 0383
E-mail melanietoogood@tesco.net or melanie@toogood.info

TOOGOOD, Noel Hare. b 32. Birm Univ BSc54. Wells Th Coll 59. **d** 61 **p** 62. C Rotherham *Sheff* 61-65; C Darlington St Jo *Dur* 65-70; V Burnopfield 70-81; P-in-c Roche *Truro* 81-84; P-in-c Withiel 81-84; R Roche and Withiel 84-91; RD St Austell 88-91; V Madron 91-96; rtd 96; Perm to Offic *Portsm* from 97. *Acorn Cottage, Oakhill Road, Seaview PO34 5AP*

TOOGOOD, Robert Charles. b 45. AKC70. St Aug Coll Cant 70. **d** 71 **p** 72. C Shepperton *Lon* 71-74; C Kirk Ella *York* 74-76; P-in-c Levisham w Lockton 76-81; P-in-c Ebberston w Allerston 76-81; R Kempsey and Severn Stoke w Croome d'Abitot *Worc* 81-92; V Bramley *Win* from 92. *The Vicarage, Silchester Road, Bramley, Basingstoke RG26 5DQ* Tel (01256) 881373

TOOGOOD, Robert Frederick. b 43. St Paul's Cheltenham CertEd65 Open Univ BA74. Trin Coll Bris 93. **d** 95 **p** 96. C Southbroom *Sarum* 95-99; TV Langport Area *B & W* 99-04; rtd 04; Perm to Offic *Ox* and *Sarum* from 05. *49 Barrow Close, Marlborough SN8 2BE* Tel (01672) 511468
E-mail bob@toogood12.wanadoo.co.uk

TOOKE, Mrs Sheila. b 44. EAMTC 89. **d** 91 **p** 94. NSM March St Wendreda 91-95; P-in-c Upwell Christchurch 95-97; P-in-c Welney 95-97; P-in-c Manea 95-97; R Christchurch and Manea and Welney 97-03; rtd 03; Perm to Offic *Ely* from 03. *The Haven, 21 Wisbech Road, March PE15 8ED* Tel (01354) 652844
E-mail stooke@c-m-w.fsnet.co.uk

TOOKEY, Preb Christopher Tom. b 41. AKC67. **d** 68 **p** 69. C Stockton St Pet *Dur* 68-71; C Burnham *B & W* 71-77; R Clutton w Cameley 77-81; V Wells St Thos w Horrington 81-06; RD Shepton Mallet 86-95; Chapl Bath and West Community NHS Trust 95-06; Preb Wells Cathl from 90; rtd 06; Perm to Offic *B & W* from 06. *47 Drake Road, Wells BA5 3LE* Tel (01749) 676006 E-mail christophertookey@hotmail.com

TOOLEY, Geoffrey Arnold. b 27. Lon Coll of Div 55. **d** 58 **p** 59. C Chalk *Roch* 58-60; C Meopham 60-62; P-in-c Snodland and Paddlesworth 62-68; P-in-c Burham 68-76; C Riverhead w Dunton Green 76-79; C S w N Bersted *Chich* 79-83; C-in-c N Bersted CD 83-96; rtd 97. *Hawksworth, Charnwood Road, Bognor Regis PO22 9DN*

TOOLEY, Norman Oliver. b 27. Roch Th Coll. **d** 65 **p** 66. C Gravesend St Mary *Roch* 65-68; C Ormskirk *Liv* 68-73; Chapl Merseyside Cen for the Deaf 73-78; C Bootle Ch Ch 78-80; C W Ham *Chelmsf* 80-86; Chapl RAD 86-92; rtd 92; Perm to Offic *Roch* 92-98. *30 Blackbrook Lane, Bromley BR2 8AY*

TOOMBS, Ian Melvyn. b 39. Hull Univ BA64 MSc90 FCIPD93. Ripon Coll Cuddesdon 07. **d** 07 **p** 08. NSM Alton St Lawr *Win* from 07. *31 Princess Drive, Alton GU34 1QE* Tel (01420) 88130

TOON, John Samuel. b 30. Man Univ BA. Bps' Coll Cheshunt 64. **d** 65 **p** 66. C Newark St Mary *S'well* 65-67; C Clewer St Andr *Ox* 67-69; Canada 70, 73-76 and from 78; R Osgathorpe *Leic* 70-72;

C Maidstone All SS w St Phil and H Trin *Cant* 76-78; rtd 95; Hon C Portage la Prairie St Mary 95-02; P-in-c N Peace Par 02-05; R Oshawa Gd Shep from 05. *St George's Residence, Unit 104, 505 Simcoe Street South, Oshawa ON L1H 4J9, Canada* Tel (001) (905) 571 5976 E-mail fathertoon@rogers.com

TOOP, Preb Allan Neil. b 49. St Alb Minl Tr Scheme 79 Linc Th Coll 82. **d** 83 **p** 84. C Kempston Transfiguration *St Alb* 83-87; C Ludlow *Heref* 87-92; P-in-c Stokesay and Sibdon Carwood w Halford 92-01; P-in-c Acton Scott 96-01; RD Condover 96-00; V Minsterley from 01; R Habberley from 01; P-in-c Hope w Shelve from 07; Preb Heref Cathl from 06. *The Vicarage, Minsterley, Shrewsbury SY5 0AA* Tel (01743) 791213

TOOP, Mrs Mary-Louise. b 55. Glouc Sch of Min 90. **d** 04 **p** 05. Dir of Ords *Heref* from 00; NSM Minsterley from 04; NSM Habberley from 04; NSM Hope w Shelve from 04. *The Vicarage, Minsterley, Shrewsbury SY5 0AA* Tel (01743) 790399
E-mail maryloutoop@lineone.net

TOOTH, Nigel David. b 47. RMN69. Sarum & Wells Th Coll 71. **d** 74 **p** 75. C S Beddington St Mich *S'wark* 74-77; C Whitchurch *Bris* 77-83; TV Bedminster 83-87; Chapl Dorchester Hosps 87-94; Chapl Herrison Hosp Dorchester 87-94; Chapl W Dorset Gen Hosps NHS Trust from 94. *Dorset County Hospital, Williams's Avenue, Dorchester DT1 2JY* Tel (01305) 255198 or 889576 E-mail nigel.tooth@dchft.nhs.uk

TOOVEY, Preb Kenneth Frank. b 26. K Coll Lon BD51 AKC51. **d** 52 **p** 53. C Munster Square St Mary Magd *Lon* 52-60; V Upper Teddington SS Pet and Paul 60-70; V Ruislip St Martin 70-81; RD Hillingdon 75-81; V Greenhill St Jo 81-91; Preb St Paul's Cathl 83-91; rtd 91; Perm to Offic *Lon* from 91. *10 Fort Road, Northolt UB5 5HH* Tel (020) 8842 2812

TOOZE, Margaret Elizabeth. b 27. St Mich Ho Ox 54. dss 83 **d** 89 **p** 94. Kenya 61-88; C Bath Walcot *B & W* 89-95; Perm to Offic from 95. *33 Walcot Court, Walcot Gate, Bath BA1 5UB* Tel (01225) 465642

TOPALIAN, Berj. b 51. Sheff Univ BA72 PhD77. Sarum Th Coll 95. **d** 97 **p** 98. NSM Clifton Ch Ch w Em *Bris* 97-98; C Bris St Mich and St Paul 98-99; C Cotham St Sav w St Mary and Clifton St Paul 99-01; V Pilning w Compton Greenfield 01-08; Chapl St Monica Home Westbury-on-Trym from 08; Hon Min Can Bris Cathl from 04. *Gate Lodge, St Monica Home, Cote Lane, Bristol BS9 3UN* Tel 0117-949 4020
E-mail berj.topalian@st.monicatrust.org.uk

TOPHAM, Paul Rabey. b 31. Columbia Pacific Univ MA81 DipEd58 MIL66. **d** 85 **p** 86. Chapl St Paul's Prep Sch Barnes 85-91; Chapl Toulouse w Biarritz, Cahors and Pau *Eur* 91-94; Perm to Offic *Eur* from 94 and *Lon* 94-97; P-in-c St Margaret's-on-Thames *Lon* 97-00; Hon C Hounslow W Gd Shep 00-05; Hon C Teddington SS Pet and Paul and Fulwell from 00. *5 Marlingdene Close, Hampton TW12 3BJ* Tel (020) 8979 4277 Mobile 07714-650980 E-mail prt418topham@btinternet.com

TOPLEY (née BRANCHE), Caren Teresa. b 59. Avery Hill Coll BEd81. SEITE 94. **d** 97 **p** 98. NSM Arlesey w Astwick *St Alb* 97-99; NSM Clifton and Southill from 99. *7 Fairfax Close, Clifton, Shefford SG17 5RH* Tel (01462) 615499
E-mail topley@ntlworld.com

TOPPING, Kenneth Bryan Baldwin. b 27. Bps' Coll Cheshunt 58. **d** 59 **p** 60. C Fleetwood St Pet *Blackb* 59-63; V Ringley *Man* 63-70; V Cleator Moor w Cleator *Carl* 70-91; rtd 92; Perm to Offic *Blackb* 92-07. *9 Brunton Park, Bowden, Melrose TD6 0SZ* Tel (01835) 824754

TOPPING, Roy William. b 37. MBE92. S Dios Minl Tr Scheme 91. **d** 92 **p** 93. Bahrain 89-94; Chapl Miss to Seamen Milford Haven 94-99; rtd 99; Perm to Offic *Sarum* from 00. *1 Lady Down View, Tisbury, Salisbury SP3 6LL* Tel (01747) 871909

TORDOFF, Donald William. b 45. Nottm Univ BA69. Qu Coll Birm 69. **d** 71 **p** 72. C High Harrogate Ch Ch *Ripon* 71-75; C Moor Allerton 75-80; V Bilton 80-92; R Spennithorne w Finghall and Hauxwell 92-01; rtd 01; Perm to Offic *Ripon* from 02. *4 Weavers Green, Northallerton DL7 8FJ* Tel (01609) 760155
E-mail don@tordoffs.eclipse.co.uk

TORDOFF (née PARKER), Mrs Margaret Grace. b 40. SRN65 SCM67. Cranmer Hall Dur 81. dss 83 **d** 87 **p** 94. Bilton *Ripon* 83-87; C 87-92; Chapl Spennithorne Hall 92; NSM Spennithorne w Finghall and Hauxwell 92-00; rtd 00; Perm to Offic *M & K* and *Ripon* from 00. *4 Weavers Green, Northallerton DL7 8FJ* Tel (01609) 760155
E-mail margaret@tordoffs.eclipse.co.uk

TORODE, Brian Edward. b 41. FCollP93 St Paul's Cheltenham TCert63. WEMTC 90. **d** 93 **p** 94. Hd Master Elmfield Sch Cheltenham from 82; NSM Up Hatherley *Glouc* 93-94; NSM Cheltenham St Steph 93-95; NSM Cheltenham Em 94-95; NSM Cheltenham Em w St Steph from 95. *23 Arden Road, Leckhampton, Cheltenham GL53 0HG* Tel (01242) 231212
E-mail btsarnia@aol.com

TORRENS, Marianne Rose. See ATKINSON, Marianne Rose

TORRENS, Robert Harrington. b 33. Trin Coll Cam BA56 MA61. Ridley Hall Cam 56. **d** 58 **p** 59. C Bromley SS Pet and Paul *Roch* 58-60; C Aylesbury *Ox* 60-63; V Eaton Socon *St Alb* 63-73; Lic to Offic 73-75; V Pittville All SS *Glouc* 75-84; Chapl

Frenchay Hosp Bris 84-94; Chapl Manor Park Hosp Bris 84-94; Chapl St Pet Hospice Bris 94-98; P-in-c Chippenham *Ely* 98-01; P-in-c Snailwell 98-01; Perm to Offic *Ely* and *St E* from 01. *68 Barons Road, Bury St Edmunds IP33 2LW* Tel (01284) 752075 E-mail torrensatkinson@aol.com

TORRY, Malcolm Norman Alfred. b 55. St Jo Coll Cam BA76 MA80 K Coll Lon MTh79 LSE MSc96 Lon Univ BD78 PhD90 BA01. Cranmer Hall Dur 79. **d** 80 **p** 81. C S'wark H Trin w St Matt 80-83; C S'wark Ch Ch 83-88; Ind Chapl 83-88; V Hatcham St Cath 88-96; V E Greenwich Ch Ch w St Andr and St Mich 96-97; TR E Greenwich from 97; RD Greenwich Thameside 98-01. *37 Becquerel Court, West Parkside, London SE10 0QQ* Tel (020) 8858 3006 E-mail malcolm@torry.org.uk

TOSTEVIN, Alan Edwin John. b 41. Trin Coll Bris BA86. **d** 86 **p** 87. C Hildenborough *Roch* 86-89; TV Ipsley *Worc* 89-06; rtd 06. *Bowling Green Cottage, Hanley Road, Malvern WR14 4HZ* Tel (01684) 561468 E-mail alan@tostevin41.freeserve.co.uk

TOTNES, Archdeacon of. *See* RAWLINGS, The Ven John Edmund Frank

TOTNEY (*née* YATES), **Mrs Jennifer Clare.** b 83. Dur Univ BA04 MA05 Selw Coll Cam BA08. Westcott Ho Cam 06. **d** 09. C White Horse *Sarum* from 09. *20 The Knoll, Westbury BA13 3UB*

TOTTEN, Andrew James. b 64. MBE01. QUB BA87 TCD BTh90 Univ of Wales (Cardiff) MTh07. CITC. **d** 90 **p** 91. C Newtownards *D & D* 90-94; CF from 94. *c/o MOD Chaplains (Army)* Tel (01980) 615804 Fax 615800 E-mail andrewjtotten@hotmail.com

TOTTERDELL, Mrs Rebecca Helen. b 57. Lon Bible Coll BA80 MA99. Oak Hill Th Coll 88. **d** 91 **p** 94. Par Dn Broxbourne w Wormley *St Alb* 91-94; C 94-95; C Stevenage St Nic and Graveley 95-99; P-in-c Benington w Walkern 99-08; Asst Dir of Ords 03-08; Bp's Officer for Women 03-07; Asst Dioc Dir of Ords *Ex* from 09; Hon C Bovey Tracey SS Pet, Paul and Thos w Hennock from 09. *9 Crokers Meadow, Bovey Tracey, Newton Abbot TQ13 9HL* Tel (01626) 833084 E-mail becky.totterdell@mypostoffice.co.uk

TOTTLE, Nicola Rachael. *See* SKIPWORTH, Nicola Rachael

✠**TOUCHÉ-PORTER, The Most Revd Carlos.** Bp Mexico; Presiding Bp Mexico from 04. *San Jeronimo #117, Angel CP 01000, Del Alvaro Obregón, DF, Mexico* Tel (0052) (55) 5616 3193 Fax 5616 2205 E-mail diomex@avantel.net

TOUCHSTONE, Grady Russell. b 32. Univ of S California 61. Wells Th Coll 63. **d** 65 **p** 66. C Maidstone St Mich *Cant* 65-70; USA from 70; rtd 95. *1069 South Gramercy Place, Los Angeles CA 90019-3634, USA* Tel (001) (323) 731 5822 Fax 731 5880

TOULMIN, Miles Roger. b 74. BNC Ox BA95. Wycliffe Hall Ox BA06. **d** 07 **p** 08. C Brompton H Trin w Onslow Square St Paul *Lon* from 07. *90 Abercrombie Street, London SW11 2JD* Tel (020) 7052 0263 E-mail miles.toulmin@htb.org.uk

TOURNAY, Ms Corinne Marie Eliane Ghislaine. b 57. Louvain Univ Belgium Lic82 STB90 MA90. Cuddesdon Coll 92. **d** 94 **p** 95. C Redhill St Jo *S'wark* 94-98; V Brockley St Pet from 98. *St Peter's Vicarage, Wickham Way, London SE4 1LT* Tel (020) 8469 0013

TOVAR, Miss Gillian Elaine. b 48. Sussex Univ CertEd69. Trin Coll Bris BA86. dss 86 **d** 87 **p** 94. Tonbridge SS Pet and Paul *Roch* 86-00; Par Dn 87-94; C 94-00; V Gillingham H Trin from 00. *Holy Trinity Vicarage, 2 Waltham Road, Gillingham ME8 6XQ* Tel (01634) 231690 E-mail gill.tovar@diocese-rochester.org *or* gilltovar@supanet.com

TOVEY, John Hamilton. b 50. Cant Univ (NZ) BA72. St Jo Coll Nottm 78. **d** 80 **p** 81. C Hyson Green *S'well* 80-83; C Cashmere New Zealand 83-85; Chapl Christchurch Cathl 85-89; P-in-c Amuri 89-90; V 90-94; C Johnsonville and Churton Park 94-96; P-in-c Churton Park 96-00; V Wainuiomata from 00. *117 Main Road, Wainuiomata, Lower Hutt 5014, New Zealand* Tel (0064) (4) 478 4099 Fax 478 4087 E-mail john.tovey@xtra.co.nz

TOVEY, Phillip Noel. b 56. Lon Univ BA77 Lon Bible Coll BA83 Nottm Univ MPhil88 Lambeth STh95 Ox Brookes Univ PhD06. St Jo Coll Nottm 85. **d** 87 **p** 88. C Beaconsfield *Ox* 87-90; C Banbury 90-91; TV 91-95; Chapl Ox Brookes Univ 95-98; P-in-c Holton and Waterperry w Albury and Waterstock 95-97; TV Wheatley 97-98; Dioc Tr Officer from 98; Dir Reader Tr from 04; NSM Wootton and Dry Sandford from 05; Lect Ripon Coll Cuddesdon from 04. *20 Palmer Place, Abingdon OX14 5LZ* Tel (01235) 527077 E-mail phillip.tovey@oxford.anglican.org

TOVEY, Canon Ronald. b 27. AKC51. **d** 52 **p** 53. C Glossop *Derby* 52-55; C Chorlton upon Medlock *Man* 55-57; C Hulme St Phil 55-57; C Hulme St Jo 55-57; C Hulme H Trin 55-57; Malawi 57-69; Lesotho 69-85; Adn S Lesotho 77-85; Hon Can Lesotho 85-92; R Reddish *Man* 85-92; rtd 92; Perm to Offic *Pet* from 92; Lic 99-02. *86 Kings Road, Oundle LE15 6PD* Tel (01572) 770628 E-mail ronshir@tovey2.fsnet.co.uk

TOWELL, Alan. b 37. Sarum & Wells Th Coll 86 WMMTC 87. **d** 89 **p** 90. C Boultham *Linc* 89-93; P-in-c Scunthorpe Resurr 93-97; rtd 97. *154 Upper Eastern Green Lane, Coventry CV5 7DN* Tel (024) 7646 1881

TOWELL, Geoffrey Leonard. b 37. K Coll Lon BA59. Linc Th Coll 59. **d** 61 **p** 62. C Ashbourne w Mapleton *Derby* 61-65; C Claxby w Normanby-le-Wold *Linc* 65-67; V Alkborough w Whitton 67-80; R W Halton 68-80; P-in-c Winteringham 75-80; V Alkborough 81-85; Dioc Ecum Officer 85-91; rtd 91. *40 Lady Frances Drive, Market Rasen, Lincoln LN8 3JJ* Tel (01673) 843983

TOWERS, Canon David Francis. b 32. G&C Coll Cam BA56 MA60. Clifton Th Coll 56. **d** 58 **p** 59. C Gresley *Derby* 58-63; V Brixton St Paul *S'wark* 63-75; V Chatteris *Ely* 75-87; RD March 82-87; Hon Can Ely Cathl 85-87; R Burnley St Pet *Blackb* 87-97; rtd 97; Perm to Offic *Bradf* from 99. *9 West View, Langcliffe, Settle BD24 9LZ* Tel (01729) 825803

TOWERS, John Keble. b 19. Keble Coll Ox BA41 MA57. Edin Th Coll 41. **d** 43 **p** 44. Chapl Dundee St Paul *Bre* 43-47; India 47-62; R Edin Ch Ch-St Jas 62-71; V Bradf St Oswald Chapel Green 71-78; P-in-c Holme Cultram St Mary *Carl* 78-80; V 80-85; rtd 85; Perm to Offic *Glas* 85-92; Hon C *Moffat* 92-00. *Flat 22/20, Croft-an-Righ, Edinburgh EH8 8ED* Tel (0131) 557 1385

TOWERS, Patrick Leo. b 43. AKC68 Hull Univ CertEd69. **d** 74 **p** 75. Japan 74-81; TV Bourne Valley *Sarum* 81-83; Dioc Youth Officer 81-83; Chapl Oundle Sch 83-86; I Rathkeale w Askeaton and Kilcornan *L & K* 86-89; I Nenagh 89-00; Can Limerick, Killaloe and Clonfert Cathls 97-00; Provost Tuam *T, K & A* 00-09; Can 00-09; I Galway w Kilcummin 00-09; rtd 09. *Doonwood, Mountbellew, Co Galway, Republic of Ireland* Tel (00353) (90) 968 4547 Mobile 86-814 0458 E-mail towers@iol.ie

TOWERS, Terence John. b 33. AKC60. **d** 61 **p** 62. C Bishopwearmouth Gd Shep *Dur* 61-65; V Runham *Nor* 65-67; R Stokesby w Herringby 65-67; V Ushaw Moor *Dur* 67-93; rtd 93. *8 Beech Court, Langley Park, Durham DH7 9XL* Tel 0191-373 0210

TOWLER, Canon David George. b 42. Cranmer Hall Dur 73. **d** 76 **p** 77. C Newbarns w Hawcoat *Carl* 76-80; V Huyton St Geo *Liv* 80-98; V Newburgh w Westhead 98-07; AD Ormskirk 01-06; Hon Can Liv Cathl 03-07; rtd 07. *7 Padstow Close, Southport PR9 9RX* E-mail davidtowler@postmaster.co.uk

TOWLER, John Frederick. b 42. Surrey Univ PhD05. Bps' Coll Cheshunt 62. **d** 66 **p** 67. C Lowestoft St Marg *Nor* 66-71; R Horstead 71-77; Warden Dioc Conf Ho Horstead 71-77; Prec and Min Can Worc Cathl 77-81; rtd 02; Hon C Fordingbridge and Breamore and Hale etc *Win* from 06. *24 Oak Road, Alderholt, Fordingbridge SP6 3BL* Tel (01425) 656595 Mobile 07940-855952 E-mail cjtptners@talktalk.net

TOWLSON, George Eric. b 40. NOC 80. **d** 83 **p** 84. NSM Wakef St Andr and St Mary 83-84; NSM Ox St Mich w St Martin and All SS 84-86; Perm to Offic 86-87; NSM Hoar Cross w Newchurch *Lich* 87-93; C Wednesbury St Paul Wood Green 93-01; rtd 01; Perm to Offic *Lich* from 01. *58 Church Lane, Barton under Needwood, Burton-on-Trent DE13 8HX* Tel (01283) 713673

TOWNEND, John Philip. b 52. Southn Univ BTh95. Sarum & Wells Th Coll 89. **d** 91 **p** 92. C Sherborne w Castleton and Lillington *Sarum* 91-95; P-in-c Wool and E Stoke 95-98; Sacr and Chapl Westmr Abbey 98-01; P-in-c Brightwalton w Catmore, Leckhampstead etc *Ox* from 01; P-in-c Beedon and Peasemore w W Ilsley and Farnborough from 05. *The Rectory, Main Street, Chaddleworth, Newbury RG20 7EW* Tel (01488) 638566 E-mail john@jptownend.freeserve.co.uk

TOWNEND, Lee Stuart. b 65. St Jo Coll Dur MA08. Cranmer Hall Dur 96. **d** 98 **p** 99. C Buxton w Burbage and King Sterndale *Derby* 98-01; V Loose *Cant* 01-08; P-in-c Ilkley All SS *Bradf* from 08. *The Vicarage, 58 Curly Hill, Ilkley LS29 0BA* Tel (01943) 816035 E-mail leenliz@ukonline.co.uk

TOWNER, Andrew Paul John. b 76. Bris Univ BSc98 Surrey Univ Roehampton PGCE02. Oak Hill Th Coll MTh07. **d** 07. C St Helen Bishopsgate w St Andr Undershaft etc *Lon* from 07. *Address temp unknown* Tel 07956-569983 (mobile) E-mail andy@christchurchmayfair.org *or* andrewpjtowner@yahoo.co.uk

TOWNER, Colin David. b 39. St Pet Coll Ox BA61 MA65 Lon Univ BD63 ARCM72 LRAM73. Tyndale Hall Bris 61. **d** 64 **p** 65. C Southsea St Simon *Portsm* 64-67; C Penge St Jo *Roch* 67-70; V Leic St Chris 70-74; Hon C Southsea St Jude *Portsm* 75-82; Perm to Offic 86-90 and 00-01; C Southsea St Pet 01-03; P-in-c 03-07; P-in-c Portsea St Luke 05-07; rtd 07; Perm to Offic *Ely* from 08. *24 Fenland Road, Wisbech PE13 3QD* Tel (01945) 584556 E-mail sctowner@btinternet.com

TOWNER, Preb Paul. b 51. Bris Univ BSc72 BTh81. Oak Hill Th Coll 78. **d** 81 **p** 82. C Aspley *S'well* 81-84; R Gt Hanwood *Heref* 84-99; RD Pontesbury 93-99; Preb Heref Cathl from 96; P-in-c Heref St Pet w St Owen and St Jas from 99; RD Heref City from 07; RD Heref Rural from 07. *The Vicarage, 102 Green Street, Hereford HR1 2QW* Tel (01432) 273676 E-mail preb.paul@btinternet.com

TOWNLEY, The Ven Peter Kenneth. b 55. Sheff Univ BA78. Ridley Hall Cam 78. **d** 80 **p** 81. C Ashton Ch Ch *Man* 80-83; C-in-c Holts CD 83-88; R Stretford All SS 88-96; V Ipswich St Mary-le-Tower *St E* 96-08; RD Ipswich 01-08; Hon Can St E Cathl 03-08; Adn Pontefract *Wakef* from 08. *The Vicarage,*

Kirkthorpe Lane, Kirkthorpe, Wakefield WF1 5SZ Tel and fax (01924) 896327 *or* Tel 434459 Fax 364834
E-mail archdeacon.pontefract@wakefield.anglican.org

TOWNLEY, Robert Keith. b 44. TCD MPhil04. St Jo Coll Auckland LTh67. **d** 67 **p** 68. C Devonport H Trin New Zealand 67-70; C Lisburn Ch Ch *Conn* 71-74; C Portman Square St Paul *Lon* 75-80; Dean Ross and I Ross Union *C, C & R* 82-94; Chan Cork Cathl 82-94; Dean Kildare and I Kildare w Kilmeague and Curragh *M & K* 95-06; Chapl Defence Forces 95-06; rtd 06; Lic to Offic *Arm* from 06. *10 Beresford Row, Armagh BT61 9AU* Tel (028) 3752 5667

TOWNLEY, Roger. b 46. Man Univ BSc York Univ MSc. St Deiniol's Hawarden 82. **d** 84 **p** 85. C Longton *Blackb* 84-88; V Penwortham St Leon 88-92; V Wrightington from 92; Chapl Wrightington Hosp NHS Trust 92-01; Chapl Wrightington Wigan and Leigh NHS Trust from 01. *The Vicarage, Church Lane, Wrightington, Wigan WN6 9SL* Tel (01257) 451332
E-mail r.townley@talk21.com

TOWNROE, Canon Edward John. b 20. St Jo Coll Ox BA42 MA48 FKC59. Linc Th Coll 42. **d** 43 **p** 44. C Sunderland *Dur* 43-48; Chapl St Boniface Coll Warminster 48-56; Warden 56-69; Lic to Offic *Sarum* 48-93; Perm to Offic from 93; Can and Preb Sarum Cathl 69-93; rtd 85. *St Boniface Lodge, Church Street, Warminster BA12 8PG* Tel (01985) 212355

TOWNS, Ms Claire Louise. b 69. Portsm Poly BA90 Univ of Wales (Cardiff) MSc93 St Jo Coll Nottm MA01. EMMTC 06. **d** 07 **p** 08. C Beeston *S'well* from 07. *3 Muriel Road, Beeston, Nottingham NG9 2HH* Tel 07766-541152 (mobile)
E-mail clairetowns@googlemail.com

TOWNSEND, Allan Harvey. b 43. WMMTC 89. **d** 92 **p** 93. NSM Fenton *Lich* 92-96; C Tividale 96-98; P-in-c Saltley and Shaw Hill *Birm* 98-06; P-in-c Washwood Heath 01-06; V Saltley and Washwood Heath 06-09; rtd 09. *5 The Croft, Stoke-on-Trent ST4 5HT* Tel (01782) 416333

TOWNSEND, Anne Jennifer. b 38. Lon Univ MB, BS60 MRCS60 LRCP60. S'wark Ord Course 88. **d** 91 **p** 94. NSM Wandsworth St Paul *S'wark* 91-08; Chapl Asst St Geo Hosp Tooting 91-92; Dean MSE 93-99; Perm to Offic from 08. *89E Victoria Drive, London SW19 6PT* Tel (020) 8785 7675
E-mail revdrannetow@yahoo.co.uk

TOWNSEND, Christopher Robin. b 47. St Jo Coll Nottm. **d** 74 **p** 75. C Gt Horton *Bradf* 74-77; C Heaton St Barn 77-78; C Wollaton *S'well* 78-80; V Slaithwaite w E Scammonden *Wakef* from 80. *The Vicarage, Station Road, Slaithwaite, Huddersfield HD7 5AW* Tel and fax (01484) 842748
E-mail robin.townsend@homecall.co.uk

TOWNSEND, Mrs Diane Rosalind. b 45. Stockwell Coll of Educn CertEd66 K Alfred's Coll Win BEd88. Sarum Th Coll 93. **d** 96 **p** 97. NSM Botley, Durley and Curdridge *Portsm* 96-00; NSM Buriton 00-05; NSM Portsea N End St Mark from 05; TV from 06. *186 Northern Parade, Portsmouth PO2 9LU* Tel (023) 9266 2467 E-mail dirobdaisy@aol.com

TOWNSEND, Gary. b 65. Trin Coll Bris. **d** 00 **p** 01. C Minster-in-Sheppey *Cant* 00-04; C Tonbridge SS Pet and Paul *Roch* from 04. *12 Salisbury Road, Tonbridge TN10 4PB* Tel (01732) 357205 Mobile 07719-876452
E-mail gary@tonbridgeparishchurch.org.uk

TOWNSEND, Canon John Clifford. b 24. St Edm Hall Ox BA48 MA49. Wells Th Coll. **d** 50 **p** 51. C Machen *Mon* 50-51; C Usk and Monkswood w Glascoed Chpl and Gwehelog 51-55; R Melbury Osmond w Melbury Sampford *Sarum* 55-60; Chapl RNVR 57-58; Chapl RNR 58-75; V Branksome St Aldhelm *Sarum* 60-70; R Melksham 70-73; TR 73-80; Can and Preb Sarum Cathl 72-90; RD Bradford 73-80; P-in-c Harnham 80-81; V 81-90; RD Salisbury 80-85; rtd 90; Perm to Offic *Sarum* from 90. *19 Wyke Oliver Close, Preston, Weymouth DT3 6DR* Tel (01305) 833641

TOWNSEND, John Elliott. b 39. ALCD63. **d** 64 **p** 65. C Harold Wood *Chelmsf* 64-68; C Walton *St E* 68-72; V Kensal Rise St Martin *Lon* 72-83; V Hornsey Ch Ch 83-98; V Forty Hill Jes Ch 98-06; rtd 06; Perm to Offic *Chelmsf* from 06. *4 Harper Way, Rayleigh SS6 9NA* Tel (01268) 780938
E-mail johnetbar@internet.com

TOWNSEND, Mark Timothy. b 67. Aston Tr Scheme 93 Cuddesdon Coll 93. **d** 96 **p** 97. C Ludlow, Ludford, Ashford Carbonell etc *Heref* 96-99; TV Leominster 99-07. *Address temp unknown*

TOWNSEND, Peter. b 35. AKC63. **d** 64 **p** 65. C Norbury St Oswald *Cant* 64-67; C New Romney w Hope 67-69; C Westborough *Guildf* 69-74; P-in-c Wicken *Pet* 74-87; R Paulerspury 74-84; P-in-c Whittlebury w Silverstone 82-84; V Whittlebury w Paulerspury 84-87; V Greatham and Thistleton w Stretton and Clipsham 87-01; rtd 01; Perm to Offic *Pet* from 01 and *Leic* from 04. *26 King's Road, Oakham LE15 6PD* Tel (01572) 759286

TOWNSEND, Peter. b 37. Open Univ BA87. Wells Th Coll 67. **d** 69 **p** 70. C Desborough *Pet* 69-72; C Bramley *Ripon* 72-75; C-in-c Newton Hall LEP *Dur* 75-80; P-in-c Newton Hall 80-81;

V Hartlepool St Luke 81-03; rtd 03. *348 Stockton Road, Hartlepool TS25 2PW* Tel (01429) 291651
E-mail townsendfamgo@ntlworld.com

TOWNSEND, Philip Roger. b 51. Sheff Univ BA78. Trin Coll Bris 78. **d** 80 **p** 81. C W Streatham St Jas *S'wark* 80-85; C Ardsley *Sheff* 85-88; V Crookes St Tim from 88; AD Hallam from 05. *St Timothy's Vicarage, 152 Slinn Street, Sheffield S10 1NZ* Tel 0114-266 1745 E-mail vicar@sttims.org.uk

TOWNSEND, Robert William. b 68. Univ of Wales (Ban) BA90. St Mich Coll Llan BTh93. **d** 93 **p** 95. C Dolgellau w Llanfachreth and Brithdir etc *Ban* 93-94; Min Can Ban Cathl 94-96; P-in-c Amlwch 96-97; R 97-99; R Llanfair-pwll and Llanddaniel-fab etc 99-03; P-in-c Llanilar w Rhostie and Llangwyryfon etc *St D* 03-06; Dioc Schools Officer 03-06; R Llanberis, Llanrug and Llandinorwig *Ban* from 06. *The Rectory, Church Road, Llanberis, Caernarfon LL55 4TF* Tel (01286) 873678 Mobile 07855-492006 E-mail robert@rectory.net

TOWNSEND, Robin. *See* TOWNSEND, Christopher Robin

TOWNSHEND, Charles Hume. b 41. St Pet Coll Ox BA64 MA69. Westcott Ho Cam 64. **d** 66 **p** 67. C Warlingham w Chelsham and Farleigh *S'wark* 66-75; R Old Cleeve, Leighland and Treborough *B & W* 75-85; R Bishops Lydeard w Bagborough and Cothelstone 85-95; V N Curry 95-06; rtd 06. *Mutterings, Church Road, Colaton Raleigh, Sidmouth EX10 0LW* Tel (01395) 567460

TOWNSHEND, David William. b 57. Lon Univ PGCE80 Ox Univ MA85. Cranmer Hall Dur 81. **d** 84 **p** 85. C Barking St Marg w St Patr *Chelmsf* 84-87; Canada from 87. *225 Colonel Douglas Crescent, Brockville ON K6V 6W1, Canada*

TOWNSHEND, Edward George Hume. b 42. Pemb Coll Cam BA66 MA70. Westcott Ho Cam 68. **d** 70 **p** 71. C Hellesdon *Nor* 70-74; Ind Chapl 74-81; TV Lowestoft St Marg 74-79; TV Lowestoft and Kirkley 79-81; V Stafford St Jo 81-85; P-in-c Tixall w Ingestre 81-85; V Stafford St Jo and Tixall w Ingestre 85-87; R Lich St Chad 87-99; RD Lich 94-99; P-in-c Hammerwich 94-96; C Hamstead St Paul *Birm* 99-02; Chapl Birm Airport 00-05; Sen Ind Chapl 02-05; rtd 05; Perm to Offic *Birm* 05-06. *4 Cathedral Close, Guildford GU2 7TL* Tel (01483) 207831 Mobile 07931-928114 E-mail dryfly57@hotmail.com

TOY, Elizabeth Margaret. b 37. CQSW77. Oak Hill NSM Course 85. **d** 88 **p** 94. NSM Hildenborough *Roch* 88-07. *2 Francis Cottages, London Road, Hildenborough, Tonbridge TN11 8NQ* Tel (01732) 833886 E-mail liz.toy@diocese-rochester.org

TOY, Canon John. b 30. Hatf Coll Dur BA53 MA62 Leeds Univ PhD82. Wells Th Coll 53. **d** 55 **p** 56. C Newington St Paul *S'wark* 55-58; S Sec SCM 58-60; Chapl Ely Th Coll 60-64; Chapl Gothenburg w Halmstad and Jönköping *Eur* 65-69; Asst Chapl St Jo Coll York 69-72; Sen Lect 72-79; Prin Lect 79-83; Can Res and Chan York Minster 83-99; rtd 99; Perm to Offic *Eur* from 99 and *S'well* from 03. *11 Westhorpe, Southwell NG25 0ND* Tel and fax (01636) 812609

TOZE, Lissa Melanie. *See* GIBBONS, Mrs Lissa Melanie

TOZE, Stephen James. b 51. Birm Univ BA79. Qu Coll Birm 76 Westcott Ho Cam 93. **d** 93 **p** 94. C Leominster *Heref* 93-94; R Gt Brickhill w Bow Brickhill and Lt Brickhill *Ox* 94-02; Rural Officer Buckm Adnry 95-02; V Wilshamstead and Houghton Conquest *St Alb* from 02. *The Vicarage, 15 Vicarage Lane, Wilstead, Bedford MK45 3EU* Tel (01234) 740423

TOZER, Frank William. b 21. Open Univ BSc94. Wells Th Coll 61. **d** 63 **p** 64. C Kemp Town St Mark *Chich* 63-65; C Crawley 65-73; V Heathfield 73-87; rtd 87; Perm to Offic from 87. *Ashley Gardens, Willoughby Crescent, Eastbourne BN22 8RA*

TOZER, Reginald Ernest. b 25. St Aid Birkenhead 57. **d** 59 **p** 60. C Plaistow St Andr *Chelmsf* 59-62; P-in-c Clayton *Lich* 62-69; V E Ham w Upton Park *Chelmsf* 69-75; V Hatfield Peverel w Ulting 75-91; rtd 91; Perm to Offic *St E* from 91. *Basil's Place, 4 Church Road, Snape, Saxmundham IP17 1SZ* Tel (01728) 688895

TRACEY, Gareth Paul. b 81. K Alfred's Coll Win BA03. St Jo Coll Nottm 06. **d** 09. C Roby *Liv* from 09. *42 Buttermere Road, Liverpool L16 2NN* Tel 07880-928644 (mobile)
E-mail gaz@traceytalk.me.uk

TRAFFORD, Mrs Joyce. b 35. NOC 84. **d** 87 **p** 94. Par Dn Chapelthorpe *Wakef* 87-94; C 94-98; rtd 98; Perm to Offic *Wakef* from 98. *1 Gillion Crescent, Durkar, Wakefield WF4 6PP* Tel (01924) 252033

TRAFFORD, Peter. b 39. Chich Th Coll. **d** 83 **p** 84. C Bath Bathwick *B & W* 83-86; Chapl RN 86-90; P-in-c Donnington *Chich* 90-99; V Jarvis Brook 99-04; rtd 04. *26 Bourne Way, Midhurst GU29 9HZ* Tel (01730) 815710

TRAFFORD-ROBERTS, Rosamond Jane. b 40. Qu Coll Birm BA. **d** 95 **p** 96. C Ledbury *Heref* 95-00; Lect St Botolph Aldgate w H Trin Minories *Lon* 00-05; Chapl Ho of St Barn-in-Soho 03-05; rtd 05; Perm to Offic *Lon* from 05. *47C St George's Square, London SW1V 3QN* Tel (020) 7828 1122 Mobile 07736-335959 E-mail revdros@hotmail.com

TRAILL, Geoffrey Conway. b 58. Ridley Coll Melbourne BA82 BTh87. **d** 85 **p** 85. Australia 85-87 and from 88; C Shrub End *Chelmsf* 87-88. *1 Albert Street, Point Lonsdale Vic 3225,*

Australia Tel (0061) (3) 5258 4624 Mobile 412-381225 Fax 5258 4623 E-mail gtraill@optusnet.com.au

TRAIN, Paul Michael. b 57. Stellenbosch Univ BChD82. SEITE 03. **d** 06 **p** 07. NSM Loughton St Jo *Chelmsf* from 06. *5 Monkchester Close, Loughton IG10 2SN* Tel (020) 8508 2937 E-mail ungaa3@aol.com

TRAINOR, Mrs Lynn Joanna. b 65. Bris Univ BSc87 Ex Univ PGCE89. SAOMC 99. **d** 02 **p** 03. C Ascot Heath *Ox* 02-06. *5 Lavender Row, King Edward's Rise, Ascot SL5 8QR* Tel (01344) 890577 E-mail lynn@lynnie.co.uk

TRANTER, John. b 51. St Jo Coll Nottm. **d** 00 **p** 01. C Gt Wyrley *Lich* 00-04; V Altham w Clayton le Moors *Blackb* from 04. *The Vicarage, Church Street, Clayton le Moors, Accrington BB5 5HT* Tel (01254) 384321

TRANTER, Stephen. b 61. Lanc Univ BA81 RGN87 RM89. Trin Coll Bris BA99. **d** 99 **p** 00. C Blackpool St Thos *Blackb* 99-03; P-in-c Blackb St Jas from 03; P-in-c Blackb St Steph from 04. *St James's Vicarage, Cromer Place, Blackburn BB1 8EL* Tel (01254) 56465

TRAPNELL, Miss Sandra. b 51. SEN73 SRN79 RGN87. **d** 08. OLM W Derby Gd Shep *Liv* from 08. *70 Ince Avenue, Anfield, Liverpool L4 7UX* Tel 07999-715201 (mobile)

TRAPNELL, Canon Stephen Hallam. b 30. G&C Coll Cam BA53 MA57 Virginia Th Sem BD56 MDiv70 Hon DD02. Ridley Hall Cam 53. **d** 56 **p** 57. C Upper Tulse Hill St Matthias *S'wark* 56-59; C Reigate St Mary 59-61; V Richmond Ch Ch 61-72; P-in-c Sydenham H Trin 72-80; V Worting *Win* 80-92; Field Officer Decade of Evang 92-96; Can Shyogwe (Rwanda) from 93; rtd 96; Perm to Offic *Sarum* from 93 and *Win* from 96. *Downs Cottage, River Road, Shalbourne, Marlborough SN8 3QE* Tel and fax (01672) 870514
E-mail stephen.trapnell@tiscali.co.uk

TRASK, Mrs Marion Elizabeth. b 54. Leic Univ BSc75 Brunel Univ PGCE76. Moorlands Bible Coll 82 Oak Hill Th Coll 93. **d** 96 **p** 97. C Bermondsey St Mary w St Olave, St Jo etc *S'wark* 96-00; C Peckham St Mary Magd 00-04. *14 The Peacheries, Chichester PO19 7TP* Tel (01243) 778843

TRASLER, Canon Graham Charles George. b 44. Ch Ch Ox BA65 MA69. Cuddesdon Coll 66. **d** 68 **p** 69. C Gateshead St Mary *Dur* 68-71; P-in-c Monkwearmouth St Pet 71-79; R Bentley and Binsted *Win* 79-84; R New Alresford w Ovington and Itchen Stoke 84-01; RD Alresford 99-01; P-in-c Stockbridge and Longstock and Leckford 01-03; R 03-09; Hon Can Win Cathl 05-09; rtd 09. *30 Cole Close, Andover SP10 4NL* Tel (01264) 359843 Mobile 07810-693910
E-mail grahamtrasler@tiscali.co.uk

TRATHEN, Paul Kevin. b 69. York Univ BA91 MA93 Jordanhill Coll Glas PGCE94 Middx Univ BA03. NTMTC 00. **d** 03 **p** 04. C Wickford and Runwell *Chelmsf* 03-07; P-in-c Rawreth w Rettendon from 07. *The Rectory, Church Road, Rawreth, Wickford SS11 8SH* Tel (01268) 766766 Mobile 07742-422175 E-mail paul.trathen@btopenworld.com

TRAVERS, Canon Colin James. b 49. St Pet Coll Ox BA70 MA74. Ridley Hall Cam 70. **d** 72 **p** 73. C Hornchurch St Andr *Chelmsf* 72-75; Youth Chapl 75-77; C Aldersbrook 75-77; V Barkingside St Laur 77-82; V Waltham Abbey 82-88; VS Weald 88-95; Co-ord NTMTC and Hon C Gt Warley and Ingrave St Nic 95-98; P-in-c Gt Canfield w High Roding and Aythorpe Roding 98-02; V Theydon Bois 02-09; Hon Can Chelmsf Cathl 01-09; rtd 09. *7 Springhead Lane, Ely CB7 4QY* Tel (01353) 659732 E-mail colin@travers.name

TRAVERS, John William. b 48. Open Univ BA84 Hull Univ MA86. Linc Th Coll 75. **d** 78 **p** 79. C Headingley *Ripon* 78-81; TV Louth *Linc* 81-89; P-in-c Shingay Gp *Ely* 89; R 90-95; V Hamble le Rice *Win* from 95. *The Vicarage, High Street, Hamble, Southampton SO31 4JF* Tel and fax (023) 8045 2148
E-mail johntravers@tiscali.co.uk

TRAVES, Stephen Charles. b 44. Sheff City Coll of Educn CertEd66 Open Univ BA79. NOC 96. **d** 99 **p** 00. NSM Barnsley St Pet and St Jo *Wakef* 99-02; NSM Cudworth 02-07; NSM Lundwood 02-04; Perm to Offic *Wakef* from 07 and *Eur* from 08. *La Barrière, 24230 Vélines, France* Tel (0033) (5) 53 57 53 72
E-mail stephen.traves@orange.fr

TRAVIS, Mrs Jean Kathleen. b 42. **d** 03 **p** 04. OLM Benson *Ox* from 03. *25 Old London Road, Benson, Wallingford OX10 6RR* Tel (01491) 838713 E-mail jeantravis@tesco.net

TRAYNOR, Nigel Martin Arthur. b 58. St Jo Coll Nottm 94. **d** 96 **p** 97. C Wellington All SS w Eyton *Lich* 96-00; P-in-c Pype Hayes *Birm* 00-02; TV Erdington from 02. *St Mary's Vicarage, 1162 Tyburn Road, Birmingham B24 0TB* Tel 0121-373 3534
E-mail nigelt6@msn.com *or* revnigel@yahoo.co.uk

TREACY, Richard James. b 74. Aber Univ BD Univ of Wales (Cardiff) MTh99. **d** 98 **p** 99. C Hillsborough *D & D* 98-02. *14 Downshire Crescent, Hillsborough BT26 6DD* Tel (028) 9268 3098 Mobile 07917-854222
E-mail richard.treacy@btinternet.com

TREADGOLD, The Very Revd John David. b 31. LVO90. Nottm Univ BA58 FRSA91. Wells Th Coll 58. **d** 59 **p** 60. V Choral S'well Minster 59-64; R Wollaton 64-74; V Darlington St Cuth w

St Hilda *Dur* 74-81; Can Windsor and Chapl in Windsor Gt Park 81-89; Dean Chich 89-01; CF (TA) 62-67; CF (TAVR) 74-78; Chapl to The Queen 81-89; rtd 01; Perm to Offic *Chich* from 04. *43 Priors Acre, Boxgrove, Chichester PO18 0ER* Tel (01243) 782385 E-mail treadgold@connectfree.co.uk

TREANOR, Canon Desmond Victor. b 28. St Jo Coll Dur BA53 MA59. **d** 54 **p** 55. C Oakwood St Thos *Lon* 54-57; C Sudbury St Andr 57-59; V Lansdown *B & W* 59-66; V Derby St Werburgh 66-68; V Leic St Anne 68-75; V Humberstone 75-86; Hon Can Leic Cathl 78-93; P-in-c Leic St Eliz Nether Hall 81-86; RD Christianity N 82-86; R Gt Bowden w Welham, Glooston and Cranoe 86-93; RD Gartree I 88-93; rtd 93; Perm to Offic *Leic* from 93. *5 Brookfield Way, Kibworth, Leicester LE8 0SA* Tel 0116-279 2750

TREANOR, Terence Gerald. b 29. St Jo Coll Ox BA52 MA56. Wycliffe Hall Ox 52. **d** 54 **p** 55. C Hornsey Ch Ch *Lon* 54-57; C Cambridge H Trin *Ely* 57-60; V Doncaster St Mary *Sheff* 60-66; Chapl Oakham Sch 66-94; rtd 94; Perm to Offic *Leic* and *Pet* from 94. *Linc* 94-99. *35 Glebe Way, Oakham LE15 6LX* Tel (01572) 757495

TREANOR, Timothy Lyons Victor. b 62. St Jo Coll Dur BA83 MA87 K Coll Lon MA95 Cranfield Univ MSc01. Ripon Coll Cuddesdon BTh08. **d** 08. C Tavistock and Gulworthy *Ex* from 08. *8 Greensway Road, Tavistock PL19 8HB* Tel (01822) 610510 E-mail tlvtreanor@btinternet.com

TREASURE, Canon Andrew Stephen. b 51. Oriel Coll Ox BA73 MA77. St Jo Coll Nottm BA76. **d** 77 **p** 78. C Beverley Minster *York* 77-81; C Cambridge H Trin *Ely* 81-84; C Cambridge H Trin w St Andr Gt 84-85; V Eccleshill *Bradf* 85-98; P-in-c Bradf St Oswald Chapel Green 98-04; P-in-c Horton 98-04; V Lt Horton from 04; C Bowling St Steph from 05; Hon Can Bradf Cathl from 04. *St Oswald's Vicarage, Christopher Street, Bradford BD5 9DH* Tel (01274) 522717
E-mail stephen.treasure@bradford.anglican.org

TREASURE, Geoffrey. b 39. Hatf Coll Dur BA61 Univ of Wales (Cardiff) DipEd62. Oak Hill NSM Course 90. **d** 93 **p** 94. NSM Forty Hill Jes Ch *Lon* 93-95; Consultant SW England CPAS 95-02; Perm to Offic *B & W* 95-04; P-in-c Stoke St Gregory w Burrowbridge and Lyng 04-07; rtd 07; Perm to Offic *B & W* from 07. *Gable Cottage, West Lyng, Taunton TA3 5AP* Tel (01823) 490458 E-mail gtreasure@onetel.com

TREASURE, Mrs Joy Elvira. b 23. St Anne's Coll Ox MA50 CertEd. S Dios Minl Tr Scheme 80. **dss** 82 **d** 87 **p** 94. Tisbury *Sarum* 82-91; Hon Par Dn 87-91; rtd 92; Perm to Offic *Sarum* 92-06. *Address temp unknown*

TREASURE, Ronald Charles. b 24. Oriel Coll Ox BA48 MA52. Cuddesdon Coll. **d** 50 **p** 51. C Whitby *York* 50-54; C-in-c N Hull St Mich 54-58; V 58-62; V New Malton 62-89; RD Malton 63-75; rtd 89; Perm to Offic *York* from 89. *Castle Walls, Castlegate, Kirkbymoorside, York YO62 6BW* Tel (01751) 432916

TREASURE, Stephen. *See* TREASURE, Canon Andrew Stephen

TREBY, David Alan. b 47. FIBMS72 Bris Poly MSc90. St Jo Coll Nottm MA95. **d** 95 **p** 96. C Camborne *Truro* 95-00; V Stoke Gabriel and Collaton *Ex* from 00. *The Vicarage, Stoke Gabriel, Totnes TQ9 6QX* Tel (01803) 782358
E-mail dave@treby.freeserve.co.uk

TREDENNICK, Canon Angela Nicolette. b 38. SRN62 SCM63. S'wark Ord Course 87. **d** 90 **p** 94. NSM Charlwood *S'wark* 90-92; Par Dn Roehampton H Trin 92-94; C 94-97; RD Wandsworth 95-97; V Redhill St Matt 97-06; RD Reigate 00-03; Hon Can S'wark Cathl 05-06; rtd 06; Hon C Godstone and Blindley Heath *S'wark* 06-09; Perm to Offic from 09. *The Old Curiosity Shop, Chapel Road, Smallfield, Horley RH6 9NW* Tel (01342) 843570 E-mail rev.nicky.hello@amserve.com

TREDWELL, Mrs Samantha Jane. b 69. Nottm Trent Univ BEd92. EMMTC 00. **d** 03 **p** 04. C Skegby w Teversal *S'well* 03-07; TV Newark from 07. *Christ Church Vicarage, Boundary Road, Newark NG24 4AJ* Tel (01636) 704969

TREE, Robin Leslie. b 46. Brunel Univ MSc00. S Dios Minl Tr Scheme 89. **d** 92 **p** 93. NSM St Leonards Ch Ch and St Mary *Chich* 92-95; NSM Hastings H Trin 95-98; TV Bexhill St Pet 98-01; V Hampden Park from 01; P-in-c The Hydneye from 08. *St Mary's Vicarage, 60 Brassey Avenue, Eastbourne BN22 9QH* Tel (01323) 503166 Mobile 07967-954411
E-mail frrobin.tree@btinternet.com

TREEBY, Stephen Frank. b 46. Man Univ LLB67 Lambeth STh01. Cuddesdon Coll 69. **d** 71 **p** 72. C Ashbourne w Mapleton *Derby* 71-74; C Boulton 74-76; Chapl Trowbridge Coll *Sarum* 76-79; TV Melksham 79-87; V Dilton's-Marsh 87-01; Chapl Westbury Hosp 87-01; R Spetisbury w Charlton Marshall etc *Sarum* from 01. *The Rectory, Spetisbury, Blandford Forum DT11 9DF* Tel (01258) 453153

TREEN, Preb Robert Hayes Mortlock. b 19. New Coll Ox BA46 MA46. Westcott Ho Cam 45. **d** 47 **p** 48. C Bath Abbey w St Jas *B & W* 47-52; PC Pill 52-61; R Bath St Sav 61-76; Preb Wells Cathl from 74; V Bishops Hull 76-84; RD Taunton S 77-81; RD Taunton 81-84; rtd 84; Perm to Offic *B & W* from 84. *20 Dunkirk*

Memorial House, Bishops Lydeard, Taunton TA4 3BT Tel (01823) 431220

TREETOPS, Ms Jacqueline. b 47. NEOC 83. **dss** 86 **d** 87 **p** 94. Low Harrogate St Mary *Ripon* 86-87; C Roundhay St Edm 87-95; C Potternewton 95-97; rtd 97; Perm to Offic *Ripon* from 01. *43 Lincombe Bank, Leeds LS8 1QG* Tel 0113-237 0474

TREFUSIS, Charles Rodolph. b 61. Hull Univ BA83. Wycliffe Hall Ox 85. **d** 90 **p** 91. C Blackheath St Jo *S'wark* 90-94; V Purley Ch Ch from 94. *The Vicarage, 38 Woodcote Valley Road, Purley CR8 3AJ* Tel (020) 8660 1790 E-mail ctrefusis@aol.com

TREGALE, Diane Ruth. b 68. Spurgeon's Coll MTh05. St Jo Coll Nottm 07. **d** 08 **p** 09. C Wilford *S'well* from 08. *7 Chancery Court, Wilford, Nottingham NG11 7EQ* E-mail diane@tregale.co.uk

TREGALE, John Ernest. b 69. Ex Univ BSc90 Sheff Univ MA01. St Jo Coll Nottm 05. **d** 08 **p** 09. C Wilford *S'well* from 08. *7 Chancery Court, Wilford, Nottingham NG11 7EQ* E-mail jono@tregale.co.uk

TREGENZA, Matthew John. b 69. Univ of Wales (Lamp) BA92 BA(Theol)08 SS Coll Cam PGCE93 Lon Univ MA01 FRGS96. Westcott Ho Cam 01. **d** 03 **p** 04. C Marnhull *Sarum* 03-06; TV Mynyddislwyn *Mon* 06-08; P-in-c Blackwood from 08. *The Vicarage, Central Avenue, Oakdale, Blackwood NP12 0JS* Tel (01495) 223043 E-mail matthew@tregenza.clara.co.uk

TREGUNNO, Timothy Frederick. b 79. St Andr Univ MTheol02. St Steph Ho Ox 04. **d** 06 **p** 07. C St Leonards Ch Ch and St Mary *Chich* from 06. *17 Alfred Street, St Leonards-on-Sea TN38 0HD* Tel (01424) 433614 E-mail frtimt@yahoo.co.uk

TREHARNE, David Owen. b 73. Univ of Wales (Cardiff) BMus94 MPhil06 Bris Univ MEd04 Bris Coll PGCE00. Trin Coll Bris 94. **d** 99 **p** 04. NSM Bassaleg *Mon* 99-00; C Caerphilly *Llan* 04-08; P-in-c Porthkerry and Rhoose from 08; Dioc Voc Adv from 08. *The Vicarage, 6 Milburn Close, Rhoose, Barry CF62 3EJ* Tel (01446) 711713 E-mail dtrevd@aol.com

TREHERNE, Canon Alan Thomas Evans. b 30. Univ of Wales (Lamp) BA53. Wycliffe Hall Ox. **d** 55 **p** 56. C Heref St Pet w St Owen 55-57; India 57-72; C-in-c Netherley Ch Ch CD *Liv* 72-74; R Gateacre 74-75; TR 75-96; RD Farnworth 81-89; Hon Can Liv Cathl 94-96; rtd 96; Perm to Offic *Lich* 96-00 and from 03; RD Oswestry 01-02. *19 Smale Rise, Oswestry SY11 2YL* Tel (01691) 671569 E-mail a.treherne@tiscali.co.uk

TRELENBERG, Olaf. b 72. Ridley Hall Cam 06. **d** 08 **p** 09. C Scotforth *Blackb* from 08. *97 Barton Road, Lancaster LA1 4EN* Tel 07877-357332 (mobile)

TRELLIS, The Very Revd Oswald Fitz-Burnell. b 35. Chich Th Coll 73. **d** 74 **p** 75. C Chelmsf All SS 74-79; C-in-c N Springfield CD 79-85; V Heybridge w Langford 85-94; Dean Georgetown Guyana 94-02; P-in-c Doddinghurst and Mountnessing *Chelmsf* 02-04; P-in-c Doddinghurst 04-05; rtd 06; Perm to Offic *Chelmsf* from 06. *31 Douglas Matthew House, White Lyons Road, Brentwood CM14 4YT* Tel (01277) 215954

TREMBATH, Canon Martyn Anthony. b 65. Leeds Univ BA86. Ripon Coll Cuddesdon. **d** 90 **p** 91. C Bodmin w Lanhydrock and Lanivet *Truro* 90-91; C St Erth 92-96; C Phillack w Gwithian and Gwinear 94-96; C Hayle 94-96; Asst Chapl R Free Hampstead NHS Trust 96-98; Sen Chapl R Cornwall Hosps Trust from 98; NSM Godrevy *Truro* from 08; Hon Can Truro Cathl from 09. *Royal Cornwall Hospitals NHS Trust, Treliske, Truro TR1 3LJ* Tel (01872) 252899 *or* 250000 E-mail martin.trembath@rcht.cornwall.nhs.uk

TREMELLING, Peter Ian. b 53. Ex & Truro NSM Scheme 94. **d** 96 **p** 98. NSM St Illogan *Truro* from 96. *38 Rosewarne Park, Higher Enys Road, Camborne TR14 0AG* Tel (01209) 710518 E-mail reverendpeter@tesco.net

TREMLETT, Canon Andrew. b 64. Pemb Coll Cam BA86 MA90 Qu Coll Ox BA88 MA95 Ex Univ MPhil96 Liv Univ PGCE03. Wycliffe Hall Ox 86. **d** 89 **p** 90. C Torquay St Matthias, St Mark and H Trin *Ex* 89-92; Miss to Seamen 92-94; Asst Chapl Rotterdam *Eur* 92-94; Chapl 94-95; TV Fareham H Trin *Portsm* 95-98; Bp's Dom Chapl 98-03; V Goring-by-Sea *Chich* 03-08; Can Res Bris Cathl from 08. *41 Salisbury Road, Redland, Bristol BS6 7AR* Tel 0117-909 9479 E-mail andrew.tremlett@blueyonder.co.uk

TREMLETT, The Ven Anthony Frank. b 37. Ex & Truro NSM Scheme 78. **d** 81 **p** 82. C Southway *Ex* 81-82; P-in-c 82-84; V 84-88; RD Plymouth Moorside 86-88; Adn Totnes 88-94; Adn Ex 94-02; rtd 02. *57 Great Berry Road, Crownhill, Plymouth PL6 5AY* Tel (01752) 240052 E-mail tremlettaf@aol.com

TREMTHTHANMOR, Chrys. b 66. Univ of California BA88. St Mich Coll Llan BA05. **d** 06 **p** 07. C Coity, Nolton and Brackla *Llan* from 06. *2 Fenwick Drive, Brackla, Bridgend CF31 2LD* Tel (01656) 659749 E-mail chrysandxander@tesco.net

TRENCHARD, Hubert John. b 56. **d** 83 **p** 84. NSM Sturminster Marshall *Sarum* 83-87; NSM Blandford Forum and Langton Long 87-96. *20 Chapel Gardens, Blandford Forum DT11 7UY* Tel (01258) 459576

TRENCHARD, Paul Charles Herbert Anstiss. b 53. Liv Univ LLB76. St Steph Ho Ox 77. **d** 80 **p** 81. C Torquay St Martin Barton *Ex* 80-84; R Ashprington, Cornworthy and Dittisham

84-92; R Barnwell w Tichmarsh, Thurning and Clapton *Pet* 92-04. *Place de la Courtille, 71460 Saint-Gengoux-le-National, France* Tel (0033) (3) 85 92 64 47 E-mail trenchard@aliceadsl.fr

TRENDALL, Peter John. b 43. Oak Hill Th Coll 66. **d** 69 **p** 70. C Beckenham Ch Ch *Roch* 69-73; C Bedworth *Cov* 73-76; V Hornsey Rise St Mary *Lon* 76-82; P-in-c Upper Holloway St Steph 80-82; V Hornsey Rise St Mary w St Steph 82-84; V Walthamstow St Mary w St Steph *Chelmsf* 84-85; TR 85-93; P-in-c Chigwell 93-94; TR Chigwell and Chigwell Row 94-08; rtd 08; Perm to Offic *St E* from 08. *11 Harrison Green, Reydon, Southwold IP18 6XA* Tel (01502) 722962

TRENDER, Lawrence. b 37. Bps' Coll Cheshunt 64. **d** 66 **p** 67. C Petersham *S'wark* 66-71; C Malden St Jo 71-73; R Thornham Magna w Thornham Parva *St E* 73-81; R Thornhams Magna and Parva, Gislingham and Mellis 81-87; P-in-c Mellis 73-81; P-in-c Gislingham 73-81; RD Hartismere 85-87; R Skipsea w Ulrome and Barmston w Fraisthorpe *York* 92-01; rtd 01; Perm to Offic *York* from 01. *Stone Cottage, 5 Far Lane, Bewholme, Driffield YO25 8EA* Tel (01964) 533020

TRENHOLME (née ROBERTSON), Mrs Jane Lesley. b 54. Man Univ BSc76 Leeds Univ BA06. NOC 03. **d** 06 **p** 07. NSM Northowram *Wakef* 06-08; C Tong *Bradf* from 08; C Laisterdyke from 08. *Stretchgate, Rookes Lane, Halifax HX3 8PU* Tel (01274) 693392 *or* 402873 Fax 693356 E-mail jltrenholme@hotmail.co.uk

TRESIDDER, Alistair Charles. b 65. Qu Coll Ox BA88. Cranmer Hall Dur 93. **d** 93 **p** 94. C Limehouse *Lon* 93-98; V W Hampstead St Luke from 98. *St Luke's Vicarage, 12 Kidderpore Avenue, London NW3 7SU* Tel (020) 7794 2634 *or* 7431 6317 E-mail alistair@alistairtresidder.wanadoo.co.uk

TRETHEWEY, The Ven Frederick Martyn. b 49. Lon Univ BA70 Lambeth STh79. Oak Hill Th Coll 75. **d** 78 **p** 79. C Tollington Park St Mark w St Anne *Lon* 78-82; C Whitehall Park St Andr Hornsey Lane 82-87; TV Hornsey Rise Whitehall Park Team 87-88; V Brockmoor *Lich* 88-93; V Brockmoor *Worc* 93-01; Chapl Russells Hall Hosp Dudley 88-94; Chapl Dudley Gp of Hosps NHS Trust 94-01; RD Himley *Worc* 96-01; Hon Can Worc Cathl 99-01; Adn Dudley from 01. *15 Worcester Road, Droitwich WR9 8AA* Tel and fax (01905) 773301 E-mail fred.trethewey@ntlworld.com

TRETHEWEY, Richard John. b 74. Jes Coll Ox MA02. Wycliffe Hall Ox BA02. **d** 02 **p** 03. C Biddulph *Lich* 02-06; C Knowle *Birm* from 06. *46 Crabmill Close, Knowle, Solihull B93 0NP* Tel (01564) 201010 Mobile 07759-650572 E-mail richard@trethewey.org.uk

TRETT, Peter John. b 44. **d** 97 **p** 98. OLM High Oak, Hingham and Scoulton w Wood Rising *Nor* from 97. *Holly House, 35 Plough Lane, Hardingham, Norwich NR9 4AE* Tel (01953) 850369 E-mail trett@nnbus.co.uk

TREVELYAN, Preb James William Irvine. b 37. Selw Coll Cam BA64 MA67. Cuddesdon Coll 62. **d** 65 **p** 66. C Heston *Lon* 65-68; C Folkestone St Sav *Cant* 68-72; R Lenham w Boughton Malherbe 72-78; P-in-c Honiton, Gittisham, Combe Raleigh, Monkton etc *Ex* 78-79; R 79-83; TR 83-00; Chapl Ex and Distr Community Health Service NHS Trust 78-00; P-in-c Farway w Northleigh and Southleigh *Ex* 84-86; Preb Ex Cathl 95-00; rtd 00; Perm to Offic *Carl* from 02. *Bridge End, Barbon, Carnforth LA6 2LT* Tel (01524) 276530 E-mail jwitrevelyan@onetel.com

TREVOR, Canon Charles Frederic. b 27. Sarum Th Coll 54. **d** 56 **p** 57. C Sutton in Ashfield St Mich *S'well* 56-58; C Birstall *Leic* 58-61; V Prestwold w Hoton 61-66; V Thornton in Lonsdale w Burton in Lonsdale *Bradf* 66-74; V Kirkby Malham 74-85; P-in-c Coniston Cold 81-85; Hon Can Bradf Cathl 85-92; V Sutton 85-92; RD S Craven 86-91; rtd 92; Perm to Offic *Bradf* from 92. *5 Brooklyn, Threshfield, Skipton BD23 5ER* Tel (01756) 752640

TREVOR-MORGAN, Canon Basil Henry. b 27. Univ of Wales (Lamp) BA51. Wells Th Coll 51. **d** 53 **p** 54. C Chepstow *Mon* 53-56; C Halesowen *Worc* 56-59; CF (TA) 59-92; V Stourbridge St Thos *Worc* 59-76; Chapl Christchurch Hosp 76-92; V Christchurch *Win* 76-92; Hon Can Win Cathl 84-92; rtd 93; Perm to Offic *Sarum* 96-04. *2 Avon House, 112 Graham Road, Malvern WR14 2HX* Tel (01684) 561672

TREW, Mrs Ann Patricia. b 58. Ripon Coll Cuddesdon. **d** 00 **p** 01. C Hambleden Valley *Ox* 00-03; P-in-c Hedsor and Bourne End 03-08; R from 08. *34 Fieldhead Gardens, Bourne End SL8 5RN* Tel (01628) 523046 E-mail ann@aptrew.purplecloud.net

TREW, Jeremy Charles. b 66. Univ of Wales (Abth) BSc89 Leeds Univ MSc92. St Jo Coll Nottm MA94. **d** 97 **p** 98. C Roundhay St Edm *Ripon* 97-01; P-in-c Spofforth w Kirk Deighton 01-07; V Seaton and Beer *Ex* from 07. *The Vicarage, Colyford Road, Seaton EX12 2DF* Tel (01297) 20391 E-mail jctrew@tiscali.co.uk

TREW, Robin Nicholas. b 52. UWIST BSc74. St Jo Coll Nottm 87. **d** 89 **p** 90. C Cov H Trin 89-93; V Snitterfield w Bearley 93-02; R Allesley from 02. *The Rectory, Rectory Lane, Allesley, Coventry CV5 9EQ* Tel (024) 7640 2006 E-mail robtrew@lineone.net

TREWEEK, Guy Matthew. b 65. LSE BSc(Econ)86 Peterho Cam BA07. Westcott Ho Cam 05. **d** 08 **p** 09. C Hammersmith St Pet *Lon* from 08. *16 Baldwyn Gardens, London W3 6HL* Tel (020) 8896 1804 E-mail guy.treweek@london.anglican.org

TREWEEK (née MONTGOMERY), The Ven Rachel. b 63. Reading Univ BA85. Wycliffe Hall Ox BTh94. **d** 94 **p** 95. C Tufnell Park St Geo and All SS *Lon* 94-99; V Bethnal Green St Jas Less 99-06; CME Officer 99-06; Adn Northolt from 06. *16 Baldwyn Gardens, London W3 6HL* Tel and fax (020) 8993 6415 E-mail archdeacon.northolt@london.anglican.org

TREWEEKS, Mrs Angela Elizabeth. b 35. Gilmore Ho IDC59. **dss** 59 **d** 87 **p** 94. Chapl Asst St Nic Hosp Newc 85-87; Chapl 87; Hon C Newc St Geo 87-89; Chapl St Mary's Hosp Stannington 92-95; Hon C Rothbury *Newc* 94-96; rtd 95; Perm to Offic *Newc* from 96. *The Nook, Pondicherry, Rothbury, Morpeth NE65 7YS* Tel (01669) 620393

TRICK, Matthew John Harvey. Univ of Wales (Abth) BSc02. St Mich Coll Llan BTh08. **d** 08 **p** 09. C Cowbridge *Llan* from 08. *3 Leoline Close, Cowbridge CF71 7BU* Tel (01446) 773515 Mobile 07793-823406 Fax matthewtrick@btinternet.com

TRICKETT, Canon Judith. b 50. Open Univ BA00. St Jo Coll Nottm 89. **d** 91 **p** 94. Par Dn Kimberworth *Sheff* 91-93; Dn-in-c Worsbrough Common 93-94; V 94-01; V Herringthorpe from 01; Hon Can Sheff Cathl from 08. *The Vicarage, 493 Herringthorpe Valley Road, Rotherham S60 4LB* Tel (01709) 836052 Mobile 07974-404831
E-mail judith.trickett@blueyonder.co.uk

TRICKETT, Stanley Mervyn Wood. b 27. Lich Th Coll 64. **d** 66 **p** 67. C Kington w Huntington *Heref* 66-70; P-in-c Old Radnor 70-81; P-in-c Knill 70-81; V Shrewton *Sarum* 81-97; P-in-c Winterbourne Stoke 81-92; RD Wylye and Wilton 85-89; rtd 97; Perm to Offic *Sarum* from 97. *3 Oakwood Grove, Alderbury, Salisbury SP5 3BN* Tel (01722) 710275

TRICKETT, Preb Susan. b 42. JP89. S Dios Minl Tr Scheme 91. **d** 94 **p** 95. NSM Combe Down w Monkton Combe and S Stoke *B & W* 94-99; Dean Women Clergy and V High Littleton 99-05; Preb Wells Cathl from 00; rtd 05; Perm to Offic *B & W* from 05. *Granville House, Tyning Road, Combe Down, Bath BA2 5ER* Tel (01225) 833007 E-mail susitrickett@mbzonline.net

TRICKEY, Christopher Jolyon. b 57. Barrister-at-Law 80 Jes Coll Cam BA79 MA83. Trin Coll Bris BA90. **d** 90 **p** 91. C Chesham Bois *Ox* 90-94; R Busbridge *Guildf* 94-98; P-in-c Hambledon 97-98; R Busbridge and Hambledon from 98; Chapl Godalming Coll from 01. *Busbridge Rectory, Brighton Road, Godalming GU7 1XA* Tel (01483) 418820 Fax 421267
E-mail jolyon.trickey@busbridgechurch.org

TRICKEY, The Very Revd Frederick Marc. b 35. Dur Univ BA62. Cranmer Hall Dur. **d** 64 **p** 65. C Alton St Lawr *Win* 64-68; V Win St Jo cum Winnall 68-77; Angl Adv Channel TV from 77; R Guernsey St Martin *Win* 77-02; P-in-c Sark 02-03; Dean Guernsey 95-03; Hon Can Win Cathl 95-03; rtd 03. *L'Esperance, La Route des Camps, St Martin, Guernsey GY4 6AD* Tel (01481) 238441

TRICKLEBANK, Steven. b 56. Nottm Univ BTh88. Linc Th Coll 85. **d** 88 **p** 89. C Ditton St Mich *Liv* 88-91; C Wigan All SS 91-93; Chapl Aintree Hosps NHS Trust Liv 93-97; C-in-c St Edm Anchorage Lane CD *Sheff* 97-00; Chapl Doncaster R Infirmary and Montagu Hosp NHS Trust 97-00; V Stocksbridge *Sheff* 00-04; P-in-c Streatham Ch Ch *S'wark* 04-05; P-in-c Streatham Hill St Marg 04-05; V Streatham Ch w St Marg from 05. *Christ Church Vicarage, 3 Christchurch Road, London SW2 3ET* Tel (020) 8674 5723 E-mail steventricklebank@hotmail.com

TRIFFITT, Jonathan Paul. b 74. St Jo Coll Nottm BA03. **d** 03 **p** 04. C W Kilburn St Luke w St Simon and St Jude *Lon* 03-06; C Paddington Em Harrow Road 03-06; C Sherborne w Castleton, Lillington and Longburton *Sarum* from 06; Chapl Gryphon Sch Sherborne from 06. *St Aldhelm's House, 69 Granville Way, Sherborne DT9 4AT* Tel (01935) 389333
E-mail j.triffitt@btinternet.com

TRIGG, Jeremy Michael. b 51. Open Univ BA88. Ripon Coll Cuddesdon 80. **d** 81 **p** 82. C Roundhay St Edm *Ripon* 81-84; C Harrogate St Wilfrid and St Luke 84-87; TV Pocklington Team *York* 87-90; R Rowley w Skidby 90-97; TV Wolverton *Ox* 97-98; R from 98. *28 Harvester Close, Greenleys, Milton Keynes MK12 6LE* Tel (01908) 222802
E-mail jeremy.trigg@btinternet.com

TRIGG, Jonathan David. b 49. Ex Coll Ox BA71 MA75 Dur Univ PhD92. Cranmer Hall Dur BA82. **d** 83 **p** 84. C Enfield St Andr *Lon* 83-87; V Oakwood St Thos 87-96; AD Enfield 92-96; V Highgate St Mich from 96; P-in-c Highgate All SS from 09; AD W Haringey 00-06; Dir of Ords Edmonton Area from 08. *The Vicarage, 10 The Grove, London N6 6LB* Tel (020) 8347 5124 *or* 8340 7279 Fax 8348 4635
E-mail jonathan.trigg@ukonline.co.uk

TRILL, Barry. b 42. Chich Th Coll 65. **d** 68 **p** 69. C W Hackney St Barn *Lon* 68-73; TV Is of Dogs Ch Ch and St Jo w St Luke 73-78; P-in-c Hastings All So *Chich* 78-79; V 79-99; rtd 99; Perm to Offic *Chich* from 01. *12 Heathlands, Westfield, Hastings TN35 4QZ* Tel (01424) 753595

TRILL, Victor Alfred Mansfield. b 21. St Deiniol's Hawarden. **d** 81 **p** 82. Hon C Prestbury *Ches* 81-83; Hon C Church Hulme 83-85; V Marbury 85-90; rtd 90; Perm to Offic *Ches* from 90. *5 Maisterson Court, Nantwich CW5 5TZ* Tel (01270) 628948

TRIMBLE, Eleanor Louise. b 69. Yorks Min Course. **d** 09. C Old Trafford St Jo *Man* from 09. *29 Old Crofts Bank, Urmston, Manchester M41 7AA* Tel 0161-747 3073
E-mail eleanor.trimble@btinternet.com

TRIMBLE, Canon John Alexander. b 33. Lon Univ BD65. Edin Th Coll 55. **d** 58 **p** 59. C Glas St Mary 58-60; C Edin St Jo 60-61; R Baillieston *Glas* 65-69; R Falkirk *Edin* 69-86; R Troon *Glas* 86-98; Can St Mary's Cathl 91-98; rtd 98; Perm to Offic *Newc* from 98. *4 Hencotes Mews, Hexham NE46 2DZ* Tel (01434) 603032

TRIMBLE, Thomas Henry. b 36. TCD BTh90. CITC 79. **d** 82 **p** 83. C Seapatrick *D & D* 82-85; I Magheracross 85-90; Bp's Appeal Sec 89-90; I Donegal w Killymard, Lough Eske and Laghey *D & R* 90-01; Can Raphoe Cathl 93-01; rtd 01. *Tyrone House, Tullycullion, Donegal, Republic of Ireland* Tel (00353) (74) 974 0706

TRIMBY, George Henry. b 44. Trin Coll Bris 84. **d** 86 **p** 87. C Newtown w Llanllwchaiarn w Aberhafesp *St As* 86-88; P-in-c Llanfair DC, Derwen, Llanelidan and Efenechtyd 88-90; V 90-95; V Llanasa 95-09; P-in-c Whitford 98-02; P-in-c Ffynnongroew 99-09; AD Holywell 03-08; rtd 09. *The Rectory, Charlestown Road, Tubbercurry, Co Sligo, Republic of Ireland* Tel (00353) (71) 918 6909

TRIMBY (née SOUTHERTON), Mrs Kathryn Ruth. b 66. Univ of Wales (Lamp) BA88. Sarum & Wells Th Coll 90. **d** 92 **p** 97. C Connah's Quay *St As* 92-97; R Halkyn w Caerfallwch w Rhesycae 97-04; I Tubbercurry w Killoran *T, K & A* from 04. *The Rectory, Charlestown Road, Tubbercurry, Co Sligo, Republic of Ireland* Tel (00353) (71) 918 6909
E-mail kathsoutherton@iol.ie

TRIMMER, Miss Penelope Marynice. b 65. STETS 01. **d** 04 **p** 05. C Talbot Village *Sarum* 04-08; TV Dunstable *St Alb* from 08. *St Augustine's Vicarage, 83 Halfmoon Lane, Dunstable LU5 4AE* Tel (01582) 668019 Mobile 07733-172460
E-mail p.trimmer1@ntlworld.com

TRIPLOW, Keith John. b 44. Selw Coll Cam BA66 MA70. Chich Th Coll 70. **d** 72 **p** 73. C Ipswich All Hallows *St E* 72-76; C Dartford H Trin *Roch* 76-78; V Fyfield w Tubney and Kingston Bagpuize *Ox* 78-08; rtd 08. *5 Hyde Road, Denchworth, Wantage OX12 0DR* Tel (01235) 868915

TRIST, Richard McLeod. b 55. Univ of NSW BSEd76. Ridley Coll Melbourne BTh86. **d** 87 **p** 87. C Camberwell St Jo Australia 87-88; P-in-c Cranbourne 88-91; I 91-92; Sen Assoc Min Kew St Hilary 93-96; C Langham Place All So *Lon* 97-01; V Camberwell St Mark Australia from 01; AD Camberwell 03-05. *1 Canterbury Road, Camberwell Vic 3124, Australia* Tel (0061) (3) 9897 1532 *or* 9882 3776 Fax 9882 6514
E-mail richard.trist@bigpond.com *or* stmarksc@bigpond.com

TRISTRAM, Canon Catherine Elizabeth. b 31. Somerville Coll Ox BA53 MA57. **dss** 83 **d** 87 **p** 94. Holy Is *Newc* 84-87; Hon C 87-01; Hon Can Newc Cathl 94-01; Perm to Offic from 01. *4 Lewins Lane, Holy Island, Berwick-upon-Tweed TD15 2SB* Tel (01289) 389306

TRISTRAM, Geoffrey Robert. b 53. K Coll Lon BA76 Pemb Coll Cam BA78 MA80. Westcott Ho Cam 77. **d** 79 **p** 80. C Weymouth H Trin *Sarum* 79-82; C Gt Berkhamsted *St Alb* 83-85; OSB 85-99; Asst Chapl Oundle Sch 86-88; Sen Chapl 88-91; R Welwyn w Ayot St Peter *St Alb* 91-99; Chapl Qu Victoria Hosp and Danesbury Home 91-99; SSJE USA from 99. *SSJE, 980 Memorial Drive, Cambridge MA 02138, USA* Tel (001) (617) 876 3037

TRISTRAM, Canon Michael Anthony. b 50. Solicitor 76 Ch Coll Cam BA72 MA76. Ripon Coll Cuddesdon 79. **d** 82 **p** 83. C Stanmore *Win* 82-85; R Abbotts Ann and Upper and Goodworth Clatford 85-92; V Pershore w Pinvin, Wick and Birlingham *Worc* 92-03; Hon Can Worc Cathl 00-03; Can Res Portsm Cathl from 03. *51 High Street, Portsmouth PO1 2LU* Tel (023) 9273 1282 *or* 9234 7605 Fax 9229 5480
E-mail michael.tristram@ntlworld.com

TRIVASSE, Keith Malcolm. b 59. Man Univ BA81 CertEd82 MPhil90 Dur Univ MA98. Qu Coll Birm 84. **d** 86 **p** 87. C Prestwich St Marg *Man* 86-88; C Orford St Marg *Liv* 88-90; TV Sunderland Dur 90-91; P-in-c N Hylton St Marg Castletown 91-95; R Bothal and Pegswood w Longhirst *Newc* 95-97; P-in-c Bury Ch King *Man* from 01; P-in-c Bury St Paul 01-03. *St Paul's Vicarage, Fir Street, Bury BL9 7QG* Tel 0161-761 6991
E-mail keith.trivasse@care4free.net

TRIVASSE, Ms Margaret. b 59. Dur Univ BA80 MA97 New Coll Dur PGCE01 Liv Univ MTh05. NOC 01. **d** 04 **p** 05. NSM Radcliffe *Man* 04-08; NSM Prestwich St Gabr from 08. *St Paul's Vicarage, Fir Street, Bury BL9 7QG* Tel 0161-761 6991
E-mail margtriv@yahoo.co.uk

TRODDEN, Michael John. b 54. K Coll Lon BD77 AKC77 CertEd. Wycliffe Hall Ox 79. **d** 80 **p** 81. C Woodford St Mary w St Phil and St Jas *Chelmsf* 80-87; V Aldborough Hatch 87-96; R

Ampthill w Millbrook and Steppingley *St Alb* from 96. *The Rectory, Rectory Lane, Ampthill, Bedford MK45 2EL* Tel (01525) 402320

TROLLOPE, David Harvey. b 41. BSc63. Lon Coll of Div 66. **d** 68 **p** 69. C Bermondsey St Jas w Ch Ch *S'wark* 68-71; CMS Namibia 71-72; Uganda 72-77; Kenya 77-82; V Gt Crosby St Luke *Liv* 82-04; rtd 04; Perm to Offic *Ches* from 04. *26 White House Lane, Heswall, Wirral CH60 1UQ* Tel 0151-342 2648

TROMANS, Kevin Stanley. b 57. St Martin's Coll Lanc BEd79. Aston Tr Scheme 90 Coll of Resurr Mirfield 92. **d** 94 **p** 95. C Rawdon *Bradf* 94-96; C Woodhall 96-98; V Liversedge w Hightown *Wakef* 98-02; V Bierley *Bradf* 02-07; Chapl Co Durham and Darlington NHS Foundn Trust from 07. *University Hospital Durham, North Road, Durham DH1 5TW* Tel 0191-333 2333

TROMBETTI, Lynda Joan. b 52. **d** 03 **p** 04. OLM Dorking w Ranmore *Guildf* from 03. *Mead Cottage, Pilgrims Way, Westhumble, Dorking RH5 6AP* Tel and fax (01306) 884360 Mobile 07968-629364 E-mail theflyingtrombettis@talktalk.net

TROOD, James William. b 68. Cov Poly BSc90 St Jo Coll Dur PGCE91. St Jo Coll Nottm MTh02. **d** 02 **p** 03. C Anchorsholme *Blackb* 02-06; TV Glascote and Stonydelph *Lich* from 06; RD Tamworth from 09. *The Vicarage, 86 Bamford Street, Tamworth B77 2AS* Tel (01827) 305313 Mobile 07713-139571 E-mail jimtrood@btinternet.com

TROTT, Stephen. b 57. Hull Univ BA79 Fitzw Coll Cam BA83 MA87 Univ of Wales (Cardiff) LLM03 FRSA86. Westcott Ho Cam 81. **d** 84 **p** 85. C Hessle *York* 84-87; C Kingston upon Hull St Alb 87-88; R Pitsford w Boughton *Pet* from 88; Sec CME 88-93; Chapl Northants Gr Sch from 91. *The Rectory, Humfrey Lane, Boughton, Northampton NN2 8RQ* Tel (01604) 845655 Mobile 07712-863000 E-mail revstrott@btinternet.com

TROTTER, Harold Barrington (Barry). b 33. Sarum Th Coll 64. **d** 66 **p** 67. C Salisbury St Fran *Sarum* 66-69; Dioc Youth Officer 69-72; V Horton and Chalbury 69-73; R Frenchay *Bris* 73-81; V Henbury 81-99; rtd 99; Perm to Offic *Ex* 00-02; *Glouc* from 02. *14 Butlers Mead, Blakeney GL15 4EH* Tel (01594) 510176

TROUT, Keith. b 49. Trin Coll Bris 90. **d** 92 **p** 93. C Pudsey St Lawr and St Paul *Bradf* 92-97; V Burley *Ripon* from 97. *St Matthias Vicarage, 271 Burley Road, Leeds LS4 2EL* Tel 0113-278 5872 *or* 230 4408 E-mail keithtrout03@stmatthias.co.uk

TRUBY, Canon David Charles. b 57. BA79. Linc Th Coll 79. **d** 82 **p** 83. C Stanley *Liv* 82-85; C Hindley St Pet 85-90; R Brimington *Derby* 90-98; Can Res Derby Cathl 98-03; TR Wirksworth from 03; RD Wirksworth from 08; Hon Can Derby Cathl from 04. *The Rectory, Coldwell Street, Wirksworth, Matlock DE4 4FB* Tel (01629) 824707 E-mail david.truby@btinternet.com

TRUDGETT, Raymond John. b 46. Wilson Carlile Coll 86. **d** 04 **p** 05. Port Chapl and C Aqaba SS Pet and Paul Jordan 04-06; Chapl Medway and Thames Ports *Roch* from 07; Perm to Offic *Cant* and *Chelmsf* from 07. *12 Grizedale Close, Rochester ME1 2UX* Tel (01634) 402720 E-mail trudgett831@btinternet.com

TRUDGILL, Harry Keith. b 25. LCP54 Leeds Univ DipEd49 Lon Univ BD61. St Deiniol's Hawarden 76. **d** 76 **p** 76. In Methodist Ch 58-75; C Glas St Marg 76-78; R Lenzie 78-86; rtd 86; Perm to Offic *Bradf* from 86. *10 Wharfe View, Grassington, Skipton BD23 5NL* Tel (01756) 752114

TRUMAN, Miss Catherine Jane. b 64. Coll of Ripon & York St Jo BEd88. St Jo Coll Nottm 01. **d** 03 **p** 04. C Owlerton *Sheff* 03-06; Hd Academic Progr Wilson Carlile Coll of Evang from 06. *Wilson Carlile College of Evangelism, 50 Cavendish Street, Sheffield S3 7RZ* Tel 0114-278 7020 E-mail j.truman@churcharmy.org.uk

TRUMAN, Miss Charlotte Jane. b 71. Birm Univ BPhil96. Westcott Ho Cam 96. **d** 99 **p** 00. C High Harrogate Ch Ch *Ripon* 99-03; P-in-c Oulton w Woodlesford 03-06; Chapl HM YOI Northallerton from 06. *HM Young Offender Institution, 15A East Road, Northallerton DL6 1NW* Tel (01609) 780078 Fax 779664 E-mail charlottetruman@yahoo.co.uk

TRUMPER, Roger David. b 52. Ex Univ BSc74 K Coll Lon MSc75 Ox Univ BA80 MA85. Wycliffe Hall Ox 78. **d** 81 **p** 82. C Tunbridge Wells St Jo *Roch* 81-84; C Slough *Ox* 84-87; TV Shenley and Loughton 87-88; TV Watling Valley 88-93; R Byfleet *Guildf* 93-05; TV Sidmouth, Woolbrook, Salcombe Regis, Sidbury etc *Ex* from 05. *All Saints' Vicarage, All Saints' Road, Sidmouth EX10 8ES* Tel (01395) 515963 E-mail roger.thetrumpers@virgin.net

TRURO, Bishop of. *See* THORNTON, The Rt Revd Timothy Martin

TRURO, Dean of. *See* HARDWICK, The Very Revd Christopher George

TRUSS, Canon Charles Richard. b 42. Reading Univ BA63 Linacre Coll Ox BA66 MA69 K Coll Lon MPhil79. Wycliffe Hall Ox 64. **d** 66 **p** 67. C Leic H Apostles 66-69; C Hampstead St Jo *Lon* 69-72; V Belsize Park 72-79; V Wood Green St Mich 79-82; TR Wood Green St Mich w Bounds Green St Gabr etc 82-85; V Shepperton 85-94; V Waterloo St Jo w St Andr *S'wark* 94-08; RD Lambeth 95-05; Hon Can S'wark Cathl 01-08; Sen

Chapl Actors' Ch Union 04-08; rtd 08; Perm to Offic *S'wark* from 08. *12 Camden Cottages, Church Walk, Weybridge KT13 8JT* E-mail richard.truss@btinternet.com

TRUSTRAM, Canon David Geoffrey. b 49. Pemb Coll Ox BA71 MA76 Qu Coll Cam BA73 MA77. Westcott Ho Cam 74. **d** 75 **p** 76. C Surbiton St Mark *S'wark* 75-77; C Surbiton St Andr and St Mark 77-78; C Richmond St Mary 78-79; C Richmond St Mary w St Matthias and St Jo 79-82; P-in-c Eastry *Cant* 82-88; R Eastry and Northbourne w Tilmanstone etc 88-90; Chapl Eastry Hosp 82-90; V Tenterden St Mildred w Smallhythe *Cant* from 90; P-in-c Tenterden St Mich from 07; Hon Can Cant Cathl from 96; AD Tenterden 99-05. *The Vicarage, Church Road, Tenterden TN30 6AT* Tel (01580) 763118 Fax 761173 Mobile 07811-874806 E-mail trustram@btinternet.com

TSANG, Wing Man. b 52. Lon Univ BSc74 MPhil84 MCB88 MRCPath88 FRCPath96. STETS 99. **d** 02 **p** 03. C Merthyr Tydfil Ch Ch *Llan* 02-05; TV Broadwater *Chich* from 05. *67 Normandy Road, Worthing BN14 7EA* Tel 07961-839018 (mobile) E-mail wing2699@hotmail.com

TSIPOURAS, John George. b 38. Trin Coll Bris 76. **d** 78 **p** 79. C Cheadle Hulme St Andr *Ches* 78-82; V Hurdsfield 82-03; rtd 03; P-in-c W Heath *Birm* from 04; Perm to Offic *Cov* from 04. *5 Ashfurlong Close, Balsall Common, Coventry CV7 7QA* Tel (01676) 534048 E-mail john@tsipouras.org.uk

TUAM, Archdeacon of. *See* HASTINGS, The Ven Gary Lea

TUAM, Dean of. *See* GRIMASON, The Very Revd Alistair John

TUAM, KILLALA and ACHONRY, Bishop of. *See* HENDERSON, The Rt Revd Richard Crosbie Aitken

TUAM, Provost of. *Vacant*

TUBBS, Preb Brian Ralph. b 44. AKC66. **d** 67 **p** 68. C Ex St Thos 67-72; TV Sidmouth, Woolbrook and Salcombe Regis 72-77; R Ex St Jas 77-96; RD Christianity 89-95; Preb Ex Cathl from 95; V Paignton St Jo from 96; Chapl S Devon Healthcare NHS Foundn Trust from 96. *The Vicarage, Palace Place, Paignton TQ3 3AQ* Tel (01803) 559059 E-mail fathertubbs@aol.com

TUBBS, Canon Christopher Norman. b 25. G&C Coll Cam BA51 MA54. Wycliffe Hall Ox. **d** 52 **p** 53. C Neston *Ches* 52-55; C Nor St Pet Mancroft 55-59; V Scalby *York* 59-68; V Scalby w Ravenscar and Staintondale 68-95; RD Scarborough 76-82; Can and Preb York Minster 85-96; rtd 95; Perm to Offic *York* from 96. *9 Mill Lane, West Ayton, Scarborough YO13 9JT* Tel (01723) 863211

TUBBS, Gary Andrew. b 59. Univ of Wales (Swansea) BA82 Bris Univ MSc84 Bris Poly PGCE84. Oak Hill Th Coll. **d** 00 **p** 01. C Stanwix *Carl* 00-02; C Carl H Trin and St Barn 02-08; P-in-c Pennington and Lindal w Marton and Bardsea from 08. *Trinkeld Vicarage, Main Road, Swarthmoor, Ulverston LA12 0RZ* Tel (01229) 583174 E-mail garytubbs@bigfoot.com

TUBBS, Mrs Margaret Amy. b 39. SWMTC. **d** 01. OLM St Martin w Looe *Truro* 01-05; Warden Epiphany Ho 04-08; C Liskeard and St Keyne from 06. *An Gwella House, Brentfields, Looe PL13 2JJ* Tel (01503) 272425 E-mail stablesretreat@onetel.com

TUBBS, Peter Alfred. b 22. G&C Coll Cam BA48 MA53. Linc Th Coll 55. **d** 57 **p** 58. C Tettenhall Regis *Lich* 57-60; C Wellington Ch Ch 60-64; Asst Chapl Keele Univ 65-69; V Cardington *St Alb* 69-85; RD Elstow 77-82; C Sandy 85-89; rtd 89; Perm to Offic *St Alb* from 89. *1 Foster Grove, Sandy SG19 1HP* Tel (01767) 682803

TUCK, Canon Andrew Kenneth. b 42. Kelham Th Coll 63. **d** 68 **p** 69. C Poplar *Lon* 68-74; TV 74-76; V Walsgrave on Sowe *Cov* 76-90; R Farnham *Guildf* from 90; Chapl Surrey Hants Borders NHS Trust 90-05; Chapl Surrey and Borders Partnership NHS Trust from 05; RD Farnham *Guildf* 00-05; Hon Can Guildf Cathl from 09. *The Rectory, Upper Church Lane, Farnham GU9 7PW* Tel (01252) 715412 E-mail office@standrewsfarnham.org

TUCK, David John. b 36. St Cath Coll Cam BA61 MA65. Cuddesdon Coll 61. **d** 63 **p** 64. C Holt and Kelling w Salthouse *Nor* 63-68; Zambia 68-73; V Sprowston *Nor* 73-84; R Beeston St Andr 73-84; RD Nor N 81-84; V Pinner *Lon* 84-01; rtd 01; Perm to Offic *Lon* 01-04 and *St Alb* from 04; Hon C N Harrow St Alb *Lon* from 04. *119 High Street, Northwood HA6 1ED* Tel (01923) 825806 E-mail dandtuck@freeuk.com

TUCK, Gillian. b 40. SRN64 SCM66. Llan Dioc Tr Scheme 93. **d** 97 **p** 98. NSM Pontypridd St Cath w St Matt *Llan* 97-01; P-in-c Pontypridd St Matt and Cilfynydd 01-05; NSM Pontypridd St Matt and Cilfynydd w Llanwynno 05-08; rtd 08. *4 Maes Glas, Coed y Cwm, Pontypridd CF37 3EJ* Tel (01443) 791049

TUCK, Nigel Graham. b 57. Chich Th Coll 82. **d** 85 **p** 86. C Port Talbot St Theodore *Llan* 85-87; C Llantrisant 87-90; TV Duston Team 90-95; C Aldwick *Chich* 95-98; C-in-c N Bersted CD 98-00; V N Bersted 01-02; rtd 02. *102 Wallace Avenue, Worthing BN11 5QA*

TUCK, Ralph Thomas. b 42. Worc Coll Ox BA64 Bris Univ CertEd66. NOC 87. **d** 90 **p** 91. NSM S Crosland *Wakef* 90-93; NSM Helme 90-93; Perm to Offic 93-05. *48 Kirkwood Drive, Huddersfield HD3 3WJ*

TUCK, Ronald James. b 47. S'wark Ord Course 75. d 78 p 79. C Upper Holloway St Pet w St Jo *Lon* 78-81; P-in-c Scottow and Swanton Abbott w Skeyton *Nor* 81-88; R Bradwell from 88. *The Rectory, Church Walk, Bradwell, Great Yarmouth NR31 8QQ* Tel (01493) 663219 E-mail revtuck@evemail.net

TUCKER, Andrew Michael. b 64. K Coll Lon BD87. Wycliffe Hall Ox 93. d 95 p 96. C Moreton *Ches* 95-96; C Poynton 96-99; C Polegate *Chich* 99-02; C-in-c Lower Willingdon St Wilfrid CD from 03. *St Wilfrid's House, 90 Broad Road, Lower Willingdon, Eastbourne BN20 9RA* Tel (01323) 482088 E-mail tucker.a@btconnect.com

TUCKER, Canon Anthony Ian. b 50. CA Tr Coll 73 S'wark Ord Course 81. d 85 p 86. NSM E Ham w Upton Park St Alb *Chelmsf* 85-86; NSM S'well Minster 86-90; C Rolleston w Fiskerton, Morton and Upton 90-93; P-in-c Teversal 93-96; Chapl Sutton Cen 93-96; P-in-c Norwell w Ossington, Cromwell and Caunton 96-04; Dioc Tourism Adv 96-04; V Balderton and Barnby-in-the-Willows from 04; AD Newark from 00; Jt AD Newark and S'well from 08; Hon Can S'well Minster from 08. *The Vicarage, Main Street, Balderton, Newark NG24 3NN* Tel (01636) 704811 E-mail tony@cloud9-online.com

TUCKER, Desmond Robert. b 29. Bris Sch of Min 83. d 86 p 87. C Bris St Mich 86-88; P-in-c 88-94; rtd 94; Perm to Offic *Bris* from 94. *94 Fremantle House, Dove Street, Bristol BS2 8LH* Tel 0117-924 6803

TUCKER, Douglas Greening. b 17. St Aid Birkenhead 49. d 52 p 53. C Jesmond Clayton Memorial *Newc* 52-56; C Fenham St Jas and St Basil 56-58; V Cowgate 58-62; V Elsham *Linc* 62-85; V Worlaby 62-85; V Bonby 73-85; rtd 85; Perm to Offic *Newc* 85-02. *Balintore, 4 Kilrymont Place, St Andrews KY16 8DH* Tel (01334) 476738

TUCKER, Mrs Gillian Mary. b 57. Bris Poly BEd79. WEMTC 04. d 07 p 08. NSM Sharpness, Purton, Brookend and Slimbridge *Glouc* from 07. *Hinton Cottage, Hinton, Berkeley GL13 9HZ* Tel (01453) 811105

TUCKER, Harold George. b 21. St Aug Coll Cant 48 Sarum Th Coll 50. d 51 p 52. C S Molton w Nymet St George *Ex* 51-56; V Mariansleigh and Romansleigh w Meshaw 56-64; R Bratton Fleming 64-73; P-in-c Goodleigh 67-73; P-in-c Stoke Rivers 67-73; P-in-c Parracombe 69-73; P-in-c Martinhoe 69-73; R Whimple 73-86; rtd 86; Perm to Offic *Ex* and *Truro* from 86. *St Anne's Residential Home, Whitstone, Holsworthy EX22 6UA* Tel (01288) 341800

TUCKER, Ian Malcolm. b 46. S Dios Minl Tr Scheme 86. d 89 p 90. NSM Pill w Easton in Gordano and Portbury *B & W* 89-95; C Frome St Jo and St Mary 95-99; TV Redruth w Lanner and Treleigh *Truro* 99-04; P-in-c Par from 04; Hon Chapl Miss to Seafarers from 04. *The Vicarage, 42 Vicarage Road, Tywardreath, Par PL24 2PH* Tel (01726) 812775 E-mail iandm@parpenworld.com

TUCKER, Jill. b 47. UMIST BSc68 MSc69 PhD77. Qu Coll Birm 05. d 06 p 07. NSM Ilmington w Stretton-on-Fosse etc *Cov* 06-09; NSM Shipston-on-Stour w Honington and Idlicote from 09; RD Shipston from 09. *The Old House, Back Lane, Oxhill, Warwick CV35 0QN* Tel (01295) 680663 Fax 688193 Mobile 07973-994800 E-mail revjill.tucker@tiscali.co.uk

TUCKER, John Yorke Raffles. b 24. Magd Coll Cam BA49 MA56. Westcott Ho Cam 49. d 51 p 52. C Shadwell St Paul w Ratcliffe St Jas *Lon* 51-54; C Preston Ascension 54-58; V S Hackney St Mich 58-67; V Belmont 67-78; V Sunbury 78-89; rtd 89; Perm to Offic *Ex* 89-93 and *B & W* from 93. *Tudor Cottage, Fivehead, Taunton TA3 6PJ* Tel (01460) 281330

TUCKER, Michael. b 33. d 84 p 85. NSM Sawston *Ely* 84-87; C Ely 87-90; P-in-c Barton Bendish w Beachamwell and Shingham 90-98; P-in-c Wereham 90-98; rtd 98; Perm to Offic *Nor* 99-04 and *Ely* from 00. *20 Priory Lane, King's Lynn PE30 5DU* Tel (01553) 774707

TUCKER, Canon Michael Owen. b 42. Lon Univ BSc66 Surrey Univ PhD69. Glouc Sch of Min 81. d 84 p 85. NSM Uley w Owlpen and Nympsfield *Glouc* 84-92; P-in-c Amberley 92-09; Dioc NSM Officer 94-09; Hon Can Glouc Cathl 98-09; RD Stonehouse 99-04; rtd 09. *18 Bownham Mead, Rodborough Common, Stroud GL5 5DZ* E-mail mike@tuckers.org.uk

TUCKER, Nicholas Harold. b 41. Reading Univ BSc66. NOC 90. d 93 p 94. NSM Ilkley All SS *Bradf* 93-98; P-in-c Uley w Owlpen and Nympsfield *Glouc* 98-06; rtd 06; NSM Nailsworth w Shortwood, Horsley etc *Glouc* 07-08. *29 The Chipping, Tetbury GL8 8EU* Tel (01666) 503188 E-mail nick@tucker141.fsnet.co.uk

TUCKER, Nicholas John Cuthbert. b 74. Birm Univ BSc. Oak Hill Th Coll MTh04. d 04 p 05. C Bebington *Ches* 04-07; Research Fell Oak Hill Th Coll from 07. *Oak Hill Theological College, Chase Side, London N14 4PS* Tel 0795/-566/14 (mobile) E-mail njctucker@hotmail.com

TUCKER, Richard Parish. b 51. Cam Univ BA72 MA76 Lon Univ BD83. Wycliffe Hall Ox 80. d 83 p 84. C Wellington w Eyton *Lich* 83-84; C Walsall 84-88; TV Dronfield *Derby* 88-96; TV Dronfield w Holmesfield 96-98; V Sutton Coldfield

St Columba *Birm* from 98. *St Columba's Vicarage, 280 Chester Road North, Sutton Coldfield B73 6RR* Tel 0121-354 5873 E-mail richardtucker@tiscali.co.uk

TUCKER, Stephen Reid. b 51. New Coll Ox BA72 MA76. Ripon Coll Cuddesdon. d 77 p 78. C Hove All SS *Chich* 77-80; Lect Chich Th Coll 80-86; V Portsea St Alb *Portsm* 86-90; Chapl and Dean of Div New Coll Ox 90-95; P-in-c Ovingdean *Chich* 96-01; Bp's Adv on CME 96-01; V Hampstead St Jo *Lon* from 01. *The Vicarage, 14 Church Row, London NW3 6UU* Tel (020) 7435 0553 *or* 7794 5808 E-mail stucker957@btinternet.com

TUCKER, Mrs Susan. b 53. Stockwell Coll of Educn CertEd74. d 97 p 98. C Taunton St Andr *B & W* 97-01; V Bishops Hull from 01; RD Taunton from 06; Chapl St Marg Hospice Taunton 01-07. *The Vicarage, Bishops Hull Hill, Bishops Hull, Taunton TA1 5EB* Tel (01823) 333032 E-mail suetucker99@btinternet.com

TUCKER, Vivian Clive Temple. b 39. Univ of Wales (Swansea) BSc60 Univ of Wales DipEd61. St As Minl Tr Course 93. d 96 p 97. NSM Gresford w Holt *St As* 96-04; NSM Holt, Rossett and Isycoed from 04. *8 Snowdon Drive, Ty Gwyn, Wrexham LL11 2UY* Tel (01978) 359226

TUCKETT, Prof Christopher Mark. b 48. Qu Coll Cam MA71 Lanc Univ PhD79. Westcott Ho Cam 71. d 75 p 76. C Lancaster St Mary *Blackb* 75-77; Chapl and Fell Qu Coll Cam 77-79; Lect NT Man Univ 79-89; Sen Lect 89-91; Prof Bibl Studies 91-96; Lect NT Ox Univ 96-06; Prof NT Studies from 06. *Pembroke College, Oxford OX1 1DW* Tel (01865) 276426 E-mail christopher.tuckett@theology.ox.ac.uk

TUCKWELL, Richard Graham. b 46. SS Mark & Jo Univ Coll Plymouth TCert67 Open Univ BA. d 07 p 08. NSM Tarvin *Ches* from 07. *5 Walkers Lane, Tarporley CW6 0BX* Tel (01829) 732732 Mobile 07713-485318 E-mail richardtuckwell@tiscali.co.uk

TUDBALL, Arthur James. b 28. AKC54. d 54 p 55. C Munster Square St Mary Magd *Lon* 54-56; Lic to Offic Borneo 56-59; P-in-c Beaufort 59-61; R Labuan 61-65; C All SS Cathl Kota Kinabalu 65-67; R Kudat 67-68; C St Thos Cathl Kuching 70-73; V Seria St Marg Brunei 73-75; Chapl Angl Community Cen Kuching Malaysia 75-79; Warden St Pet Hall Singapore 79-81; V Singapore St Pet 81-86; V Singapore St Paul 86-88; rtd 89. *61 Farleigh Avenue, Singapore 557835, Republic of Singapore* Tel (0065) 3422258 Fax 3422259

TUDGE, Paul Quartus. b 55. Leeds Univ BEd78. Cranmer Hall Dur 84. d 87 p 88. C Roundhay St Edm *Ripon* 87-90; C Leeds City 91; V Woodside 91-99; Warden of Readers 96-99; V Ilkley All SS *Bradf* 99-08; RD Otley 02-08; P-in-c Farsley from 08. *The Vicarage, 9 St John's Avenue, Farsley, Pudsey LS28 5DN* Tel 0113-257 0059 E-mail paul.tudge@bradford.anglican.org

TUDGEY, Stephen John. b 51. Nottm Univ BTh81 Westmr Coll Ox MTh00. St Jo Coll Nottm LTh81. d 81 p 82. C Grays Thurrock *Chelmsf* 81-84; C Madeley *Heref* 84-87; R Chilcompton w Downside and Stratton on the Fosse *B & W* 87-03; P-in-c Falmouth K Chas *Truro* from 03; Hon Chapl Miss to Seafarers from 04. *The Rectory, 19 Trescobeas Road, Falmouth TR11 2JB* Tel (01326) 319141 E-mail steve.tudgey@tiscali.co.uk

TUDOR, David Charles Frederick. b 42. Sarum Th Coll 70. d 73 p 74. C Plymouth St Pet *Ex* 73-75; C Reddish *Man* 75-78; P-in-c Hamer 78-80; V Goldenhill *Lich* 80-87; V Meir 87-91; Chapl Asst Nottm City Hosp 91-94; Chapl Cen Sheff Univ Hosps NHS Trust 94-96; V Nottingham St Geo w St Jo S'well 96-04; rtd 05; Perm to Offic *Derby* and *S'well* from 05. *102 St Albans Road, Nottingham NG6 9HG* Tel 0115-975 0184 Mobile 07811-866348

TUDOR, David St Clair. b 55. K Coll Lon BD77 AKC77 K Coll Lon MTh89. Ripon Coll Cuddesdon 77. d 78 p 79. C Plumstead St Nic S'wark 78-80; C Redhill St Matt 80-83; C-in-c Reigate St Phil CD 83-87; Asst Sec Gen Syn Bd for Miss and Unity 87-88; Perm to Offic S'wark 94-97; TV Canvey Is *Chelmsf* 97-00; TR from 00; AD Hadleigh from 08. *St Nicholas House, 210 Long Road, Canvey Island SS8 0JR* Tel (01268) 682586 E-mail dstudor@tinyworld.co.uk

TUFFEL, Kennedy Joseph. b 20. Worc Ord Coll 64. d 66 p 67. C Belmont *Lon* 66-68; C Goring-by-Sea *Chich* 68-72 and 81-89; NSM 89-96; V Barnham 72-78; Hon C W Worthing St Jo 78-81; rtd 89; Perm to Offic *Chich* from 96. *c/o Messrs Thomas Eggar, Arundel House, 1 Liverpool Gardens, Worthing BN11 1SL*

TUFFIN, Mrs Gillian Patricia. b 43. S Dios Minl Tr Scheme 91. d 94 p 95. C Gidea Park *Chelmsf* 94-98; TV Stoke-upon-Trent *Lich* 98-01; Admin and Prayer Co-ord Shalom Chr Healing Cen from 02; NSM Northolt Park St Barn *Lon* 02-08; Perm to Offic from 08. *76 Stowe Crescent, Ruislip HA4 7SS* Tel (020) 8864 5394 E-mail g.tuffin@btopenworld.com

TUFFNELL, Nigel Owen. b 65. Teesside Poly BSc90. St Jo Coll Nottm 91. d 94 p 95. C Guisborough *York* 94-97; P-in-c Northwold *Ely* 97-98; P-in-c Stoke Ferry w Wretton 97-98; P-in-c Whittington 97-98; R Northwold and Wretton w Stoke Ferry etc 98-03; Bp's Adv on Environmental issues 02-03; TR

Kegworth, Hathern, Long Whatton, Diseworth etc *Leic* 04-06. *17 Blyford Road, Lowestoft NR32 4PZ* Tel (01502) 583389

TUFNELL, Edward Nicholas Pember. b 45. Chu Coll Cam MA68. St Jo Coll Nottm BA73. **d** 73 **p** 74. C Ealing St Mary *Lon* 73-76; BCMS Tanzania 76-88; P-in-c Lt Thurrock St Jo *Chelmsf* 89-91; V Grays North 91-98; Chapl Thurrock Community Hosp Grays 89-98; P-in-c Bourton-on-the-Water w Clapton *Glouc* 98-05; R Bourton-on-the-Water w Clapton etc from 05. *The Rectory, School Hill, Bourton-on-the-Water, Cheltenham GL54 2AW* Tel (01451) 820386 E-mail edward@stlawbourton.freeserve.co.uk

TUFT, Preb Patrick Anthony. b 31. Selw Coll Cam BA56 MA60. Edin Th Coll 56. **d** 58 **p** 59. C Keighley *Bradf* 58-63; PV Chich Cathl 63-68; Min Can St Paul's Cathl 68-74; Hon Min Can St Paul's Cathl 74-94; V Chiswick St Nic w St Mary 74-06; PV Westmr Abbey 74-79; AD Hounslow *Lon* 87-93; P-in-c Chiswick St Paul Grove Park 88-90; Preb St Paul's Cathl 95-06; rtd 07. *68 Worple Road, Isleworth TW7 7HU* Tel (020) 8581 3014 Mobile 07768-892099 E-mail patrick@tuft.tv

TUGWELL, Elizabeth Ann. b 36. SWMTC. **d** 94 **p** 95. NSM Ludgvan *Truro* 94-97; NSM St Hilary w Perranuthnoe 94-97; Perm to Offic 99-05; P-in-c Stranraer *Glas* from 05; P-in-c Portpatrick from 05. *Dally Farmhouse, Kirkcolm, Stranraer DG9 0QD* Tel (01776) 853582

TULK, Giles David. b 65. Leeds Univ BA86. ERMC 06. **d** 09. C Stansted Mountfitchet w Birchanger and Farnham *Chelmsf* from 09. *43 Gilbey Crescent, Stansted CM24 8DT* Tel (01279) 817155 E-mail gtulk@waitrose.com

TULL, Preb Christopher Stuart. b 36. Hertf Coll Ox BA60 MA64. Oak Hill Th Coll 60. **d** 62 **p** 63. C Stoodleigh *Ex* 62-71; C Washfield 62-71; TV Washfield, Stoodleigh, Withleigh etc 71-74; RD Tiverton 74-75; R Bishops Nympton w Rose Ash 75-77; V Mariansleigh 75-77; TR Bishopsnympton, Rose Ash, Mariansleigh etc 77-99; RD S Molton 80-87 and 95-99; Preb Ex Cathl 84-99; rtd 99; Perm to Offic *B & W* from 04. *The Old Smithy, Challacombe, Barnstaple EX31 4TU* Tel (01598) 763201

TULLETT, Paul Budworth. b 71. Lanc Univ BSc92 Birm Univ MBA00 Anglia Ruskin Univ BA09. Ridley Hall Cam 07. **d** 09. C Taunton St Mary *B & W* from 09. *The Glebe House, Whirligig Lane, Taunton TA1 1SQ* Tel 07738-042217 (mobile) E-mail paulof3decades@hotmail.com

TULLETT, Peter Watts. b 46. Qu Coll Birm 92. **d** 94 **p** 95. C Worle *B & W* 94-96; Chapl HM YOI Portland 96-01; Perm to Offic *B & W* 02-04; Hon C Uphill 04-06; Perm to Offic from 07. *2 Ferry Lane, Lympsham, Weston-super-Mare BS24 0BT* Tel (01934) 814284 E-mail peter@tullett73.fsnet.co.uk

TULLOCH, Richard James Anthony. b 52. Wadh Coll Ox BA74 Selw Coll Cam BA79. Ridley Hall Cam 76. **d** 79 **p** 80. C Morden *S'wark* 79-83; C Jesmond Clayton Memorial *Newc* 83-94; V New Borough and Leigh *Sarum* from 94. *The Vicarage, 15 St John's Hill, Wimborne BH21 1BX* Tel (01202) 883490 E-mail stjohns-wimborne@tiscali.co.uk

TULLY, David John. b 56. St Jo Coll Dur BA77 Nottm Univ PGCE78. Ridley Hall Cam 81. **d** 84 **p** 85. C Gosforth St Nic *Newc* 84-86; C Newburn 86-90; TV Whorlton 90-96; V 96-00; R Gateshead Fell *Dur* 00-09; R Chester le Street from 09. *The Rectory, Lindisfarne Avenue, Chester le Street DH3 3PT* Tel 0191-388 4027 E-mail david.tully@tesco.net

TULLY, Janet Florence. b 43. **d** 03 **p** 04. OLM Margate St Jo *Cant* 03-08; Perm to Offic *Nor* from 09. *4 Westgate Court, Wymondham NR18 0PX* Tel 07866-839275 (mobile)

TUNBRIDGE, Genny Louise. b 64. Clare Coll Cam BA85 St Cross Coll Ox DPhil93. Qu Coll Birm BD95. **d** 96 **p** 97. C Boston *Linc* 96-00; Lect 00-01; Prec Chelmsf Cathl 01-06; Can Res 02-06; V Gosforth All SS *Newc* from 06. *All Saints' Vicarage, 33 Brackenfield Road, Newcastle upon Tyne NE3 4DX* Tel 0191-246 1155 *or* 213 0450 E-mail g.tunbridge@allsaints-gosforth.org.uk

TUNBRIDGE, John Stephen. b 31. Keble Coll Ox BA54 MA59. Ely Th Coll 54. **d** 56 **p** 57. C Upper Norwood All SS w St Marg *Cant* 56-57; C Ramsgate St Geo 57-60; P-in-c 76-84; C Folkestone St Mary and St Eanswythe 60-62; R Gt Chart 62-67; V Womenswold 67-76; C-in-c Aylesham CD 67-76; R Harbledown 84-94; Perm to Offic *St D* from 94; rtd 96. *Ashdown, 11 Castle Road, St Ishmaels, Haverfordwest SA62 3SF* Tel (01646) 636584

TUNLEY, Timothy Mark. b 61. Ridley Hall Cam 89. **d** 92 **p** 93. C Aldborough w Boroughbridge and Roecliffe *Ripon* 92-95; C Knaresborough 95-98; V Swaledale 98-05; TV Seacroft from 05; Dioc Adv for NSM 03-08. *51 St James Approach, Leeds LS14 6JJ* Tel 0113-273 0693 E-mail timtunley@hotmail.com

TUNNICLIFFE, Mrs Jean Sarah. b 36. RGN69. Glouc Sch of Min 89. **d** 92 **p** 94. NSM Dixton *Heref* 92-05; rtd 05. *Bryn Awelon, 21 Ridgeway, Wyesham, Monmouth NP25 3JX* Tel (01600) 714115

TUNNICLIFFE, Canon Martin Wyndham. b 31. Keele Univ BA56. Qu Coll Birm 59. **d** 60 **p** 61. C Castle Bromwich SS Mary and Marg *Birm* 60-65; V Shard End 65-73; R Over Whitacre w Shustoke 73-78; V Tanworth 78-98; RD Solihull 89-96; Hon Can

Birm Cathl 91-98; rtd 98; Perm to Offic *Birm* from 98. *202 Ralph Road, Shirley, Solihull B90 3LE* Tel and fax 0121-745 6522 E-mail martin@ralph202.wanadoo.co.uk

TUNNICLIFFE, Mrs Siv. b 33. Stockholm Univ MPhil58. SAOMC 94. **d** 97 **p** 98. OLM Wingrave w Rowsham, Aston Abbotts and Cublington *Ox* from 97; OLM Wing w Grove from 04. *Baldway House, Wingrave, Aylesbury HP22 4PA* Tel and fax (01296) 681374

TUNSTALL, Barry Anthony. b 29. Sarum Th Coll 53. **d** 55 **p** 56. C Croxley Green All SS *St Alb* 55-58; C Apsley End 58-63; V N Mymms 63-81; R Kirkby Overblow *Ripon* 81-94; rtd 94; Perm to Offic *B & W* from 01. *23 Mondyes Court, Wells BA5 2QX* Tel (01749) 677004

TUPLING, Mrs Catherine Louise. b 74. Westhill Coll Birm BTh96. Wycliffe Hall Ox 01. **d** 03 **p** 04. C Belper *Derby* 03-07; P-in-c Hathersage w Bamford and Derwent 07-08; P-in-c Hathersage w Bamford and Derwent and Grindleford from 08. *The Vicarage, Church Bank, Hathersage, Hope Valley S32 1AJ* Tel (01433) 650215 E-mail revtup@tup-house.freeserve.co.uk

TUPPER, Michael Heathfield. b 20. St Edm Hall Ox BA41 MA46. Ridley Hall Cam 41. **d** 43 **p** 44. C Win Ch Ch 43-45; Chapl Monkton Combe Sch Bath 45-48; Asst Chapl Shrewsbury Sch 48-59 and 60-79; Kenya 59-60; Hon C Bayston Hill *Lich* 80-98; rtd 98; Perm to Offic *Lich* 99-08. *9 Eric Lock Road, Bayston Hill, Shrewsbury SY3 0HQ* Tel (01743) 722674

✠**TUREI, The Most Revd William Brown.** b 24. BTS76. **d** 49 **p** 50 **c** 92. C Tauranga New Zealand 49-52; V Whangaro Pastorate 52-59; V Te Puke Tauranga Miss Distr 59-64; V Ruatoki Whakatane Pastorate 64-70; V Turanga Pastorate 70-74; V Phillipstown and Maori Missr 74-81; V Waipatu-Moteo Pastorate 81-84; Chapl Napier Febs 84-88; Taonga Whakamana Mahi Minita 89-92; Adn Tairawhiti 82-92; Bp in Tairawhiti 92-05; Bp Aotearoa from 05; Abp New Zealand from 06. *PO Box 568, Gisborne, New Zealand* Tel (0064) (6) 867 8856 Fax 867 8859

✠**TURNBULL, The Rt Revd Anthony Michael Arnold.** b 35. CBE03 DL05. Keble Coll Ox BA58 MA62 Dur Univ Hon DD03. Cranmer Hall Dur. **d** 60 **p** 61 **c** 88. C Middleton *Man* 60-61; C Luton w E Hyde *St Alb* 61-65; Dir of Ords *York* 65-69; Abp's Dom Chapl 65-69; Chapl York Univ 69-76; V Heslington 69-76; Chief Sec CA 76-84; Can Res Roch Cathl 84-88; Adn Roch 84-88; Bp Roch 88-94; Bp Dur 94-03; rtd 03; Hon Asst Bp *Cant* and *Eur* from 03. *67 Strand Street, Sandwich CT13 9HN* Tel (01304) 611389 E-mail bstmt@btopenworld.com

TURNBULL, Brian Robert. b 43. Chich Th Coll 71. **d** 74 **p** 75. C Norbury St Phil *Cant* 74-76; C Folkestone St Sav 76-77; Hon C Tong *Lich* 83-88; C Jarrow *Dur* 88-89; TV 89-94; P-in-c Hartlepool St Oswald 94-96; V 96-04; rtd 04. *50 The Chare, Leazes Square, Newcastle upon Tyne NE1 4DD* Tel 0191-221 2312 E-mail frbrian@turnball23.freeserve.co.uk

TURNBULL, James Awty. b 28. Solicitor Bradf Univ HonDLaws97. Cranmer Hall Dur 89. **d** 89 **p** 90. NSM Bolton Abbey *Bradf* 89-98; Perm to Offic from 98. *Deerstones Cottage, Deerstones, Skipton BD23 6JB*

TURNBULL, Michael. *See* TURNBULL, The Rt Revd Anthony Michael Arnold

TURNBULL, Michael Francis. b 62. Liv Univ BTh99. NOC 95. **d** 98 **p** 99. C Birkenhead Ch Ch *Ches* 98-02; P-in-c Leasowe 02-08; R Wistaston from 08; Asst Warden of Readers from 08. *The Rectory, 44 Church Lane, Wistaston, Crewe CW2 8HA* Tel (01270) 665742 *or* 567119 Mobile 07817-498260 E-mail mfturnbull@gmail.com

TURNBULL, Peter Frederick. b 64. SS Mark & Jo Univ Coll Plymouth BA85. Sarum & Wells Th Coll BTh91. **d** 91 **p** 92. C Upper Norwood All SS *S'wark* 91-95; Chapl HM Pris Dorchester 95-98; C Dorchester *Sarum* 95-98; NSM Melbury 98-99; C Maltby *Sheff* 99-02; TV 02-08; TV Crosslacon *Carl* from 08. *The Vicarage, Trumpet Road, Cleator CA23 3EF* Tel (01946) 810510 E-mail p.turnbull@dogcollar.org.uk

TURNBULL, Richard Duncan. b 60. Reading Univ BA82 St Jo Coll Dur BA92 Dur Univ PhD97 Ox Univ MA05 MICAS85. Cranmer Hall Dur 90. **d** 94 **p** 95. C Portswood Ch Ch *Win* 94-98; V Chineham 98-05; Prin Wycliffe Hall Ox from 05. *Wycliffe Hall, 54 Banbury Road, Oxford OX2 6PW* Tel (01865) 274200 Fax 274215 E-mail richard.turnbull@wycliffe.ox.ac.uk

TURNBULL, William George. b 25. Lich Th Coll BA81. **d** 81 **p** 82. C Nunhead St Silas *S'wark* 65-69; C Portishead *B & W* 69-73; C Holsworthy w Cookbury *Ex* 73-76; P-in-c Bridgerule 76-79; P-in-c Pyworthy w Pancraswyke 77-79; P-in-c Pyworthy, Pancrasweek and Bridgerule 79-80; R 80-81; V Otterton and Colaton Raleigh 81-90; rtd 90; Chapl Convent Companions Jes Gd Shep W Ogwell 90-94; Perm to Offic *Chich* from 94 and *S'wark* 00-07. *The College of St Barnabas, Blackberry Lane, Lingfield RH7 6NJ* Tel (01342) 872871

TURNER, Alan James. b 40. Oak Hill Th Coll BA81. **d** 81 **p** 82. C Bradley *Wakef* 81-84; C Sandal St Helen 84-86; P-in-c Sileby *Leic* 86-87; TR Sileby, Cossington and Seagrave 87-94; R Hollington St Leon *Chich* 94-01; R Frant w Eridge 01-08; rtd 08.

Charters Garth, Hutton-le-Hole, York YO62 6UD Tel (01751) 411949 E-mail alan@ajturner.wanadoo.co.uk

TURNER, Alan Roy. b 51. Sheff Univ BA96 MA99. EMMTC. **d** 00 **p** 01. C Bladon w Woodstock *Ox* 00-03; Chapl Cokethorpe Sch Witney 01-03; TV Brize Norton and Carterton *Ox* 03-09; P-in-c Stonesfield w Combe Longa from 09. *The Rectory, Brook Lane, Stonesfield, Witney OX29 8PR* Tel (01993) 898552 Mobile 07777-670006 E-mail r.turner131@btinternet.com

TURNER, Albert Edward. b 41. Glouc Sch of Min 83. **d** 89 **p** 90. C Woodford St Mary w St Phil and St Jas *Chelmsf* 89-91; R Greatworth and Marston St Lawrence etc *Pet* 91-99; R Somersham w Pidley and Oldhurst *Ely* 99-02; rtd 02; Perm to Offic *St Alb* from 04. *83 Horslow Street, Potton, Sandy SG19 2NX* Tel (01767) 260546 Mobile 07950-097525 E-mail aet546@hotmail.com *or* eddie.turner@bedfordhospital.nhs.uk

TURNER, Alison Joan. b 66. EAMTC. **d** 97 **p** 98. Perm to Offic *Chelmsf* 97-01; PV Ex Cathl from 04. *6 Cathedral Close, Exeter EX1 1EZ* Tel (01392) 272498 Mobile 07958-276651

TURNER, Andrew John. b 52. St Jo Coll Nottm. **d** 83 **p** 84. C Framlingham w Saxtead *St E* 83-86; P-in-c Badingham w Bruisyard and Cransford 86-88; P-in-c Dennington 86-88; R Badingham w Bruisyard, Cransford and Dennington 88-91; Chapl RAF from 91. *Chaplaincy Services, Valiant Block, HQ Air Command, RAF High Wycombe HP14 4UE* Tel (01494) 496800 Fax 496343 E-mail andrewandliz@turner211274.fsnet.co.uk

TURNER, Ann. *See* TURNER, Canon Patricia Ann

TURNER, Mrs Ann Elizabeth Hamer. b 38. Ex Univ BA59 PGCE60. Trin Coll Bris 84. **dss** 86 **d** 87 **p** 94. Bath St Luke *B & W* 86-91; Hon C 87-91; Chapl Dorothy Ho Foundn 89-91; C Bath Twerton-on-Avon 91-94; TV 94-96; rtd 98; Perm to Offic *Ex* 00-06; Hon C Ottery St Mary, Alfington, W Hill, Tipton etc from 06. *4 Beech Park, West Hill, Ottery St Mary EX11 1UH* Tel (01404) 813476

TURNER, Anthony John. b 49. St Mich Coll Llan 89. **d** 91 **p** 92. C Coity w Nolton *Llan* 91-95; R Castlemartin w Warren and Angle etc *St D* 95-04; TV Monkton 04-07; TV Cwmbran *Mon* from 07; OCF 95-01. *The Vicarage, Llantarnam, Cwmbran NP44 3BW* Tel (01633) 489280

TURNER, The Ven Antony Hubert Michael. b 30. FCA63. Tyndale Hall Bris 54. **d** 56 **p** 57. C Nottingham St Ann *S'well* 56-58; C Cheadle *Ches* 58-62; PC Macclesfield Ch Ch 62-68; Lic to Offic *S'wark* 68-74; Home Sec BCMS 68-74; V Southsea St Jude *Portsm* 74-86; P-in-c Portsea St Luke 75-80; RD Portsm 79-84; Hon Can Portsm Cathl 85-86; Adn Is of Wight 86-96; rtd 96; Perm to Offic *Portsm* from 96. *15 Avenue Road, Hayling Island PO11 0LX* Tel (023) 9246 5881

TURNER, Benjamin John. b 45. CEng MICE. NOC 82. **d** 85 **p** 86. C Worsley *Man* 85-88; V Elton St Steph 88-95; Asst P Greystoke, Matterdale, Mungrisdale etc *Carl* 95-98; TV Gd Shep TM 98-01; Asst Chapl Leeds Teaching Hosps NHS Trust 01-02; Chapl 02-07; rtd 07. *40 Nightingale Walk, Bingley BD16 3QB* Tel (01274) 568035

TURNER, Mrs Beryl Rose. b 31. Nottm Univ CertEd75 BEd76. **dss** 84 **d** 87 **p** 94. Mortomley St Sav *Sheff* 84-86; Whitgift w Adlingfleet and Eastoft 86; The Marshland 86-87; Par Dn Goole 87-94; C 94; rtd 95; Perm to Offic *Sheff* 95-08. *17 Grizedale Court, 50 Forest Gate, Blackpool FY3 9AP* Tel (01253) 393277

TURNER, Canon Carl Francis. b 60. St Chad's Coll Dur BA81. St Steph Ho Ox 83. **d** 85 **p** 86. C Leigh-on-Sea St Marg *Chelmsf* 85-88; C Brentwood St Thos 88-92; V Plaistow 90-95; P-in-c 95-96; TR Plaistow and N Canning Town 96-01; Prec and Can Res Ex Cathl from 01. *6 Cathedral Close, Exeter EX1 1EZ* Tel (01392) 272498 E-mail precentor@exeter-cathedral.org.uk

TURNER, Charles Maurice Joseph. b 13. **d** 79 **p** 80. NSM Brislington St Luke 79-83; NSM Bris Ch Ch w St Ewen and All SS 83-84; NSM Bris St Steph w St Nic and St Leon 83-84; NSM City of Bris 84-89; Perm to Offic 89-98. *31 Eagle Road, Bristol BS4 3LQ* Tel 0117-977 6329

TURNER, Mrs Christina Caroline. b 64. **d** 99 **p** 00. C Castle Church *Lich* 99-02; C Rugby *Cov* 02-03; TV 03-05; Perm to Offic *Sheff* 06-07; NSM Arbourthorne and Norfolk Park from 07. *St Paul and St Leonard's Vicarage, 458 East Bank Road, Sheffield S2 2AD* Tel 0114-265 3145 E-mail tina.turner@tinyworld.co.uk

TURNER, Mrs Christine. b 42. EMMTC. **d** 94 **p** 95. Asst Chapl Qu Medical Cen Nottm Univ Hosp NHS Trust 94-97; NSM Hickling w Kinoulton and Broughton Sulney *S'well* 94-97; NSM Cotgrave 97-99; P-in-c Willoughby-on-the-Wolds w Wysall and Widmerpool 99-04; rtd 04. *The Rosarie, Milcombe, Banbury OX15 4RS* Tel (01295) 722330 E-mail revd.christine@care4free.net

TURNER, Christopher Gilbert. b 29. New Coll Ox BA52 MA55. Ox Min Course 91. **d** 92 **p** 93. NSM Hook Norton w Gt Rollright, Swerford etc *Ox* from 92. *Rosemullion, High Street, Great Rollright, Chipping Norton OX7 5RQ* Tel (01608) 737359

TURNER, Christopher James Shepherd. b 48. Uflc Ox BA70 MA74. Wycliffe Hall Ox 71. **d** 74 **p** 75. C Rusholme H Trin *Man* 74-78; C Chadderton Ch Ch 78-80; V 80-89; V Selly Park

St Steph and St Wulstan *Birm* 89-99; P-in-c Locking *B & W* 99-05; Chapl Weston Hospice 99-05; P-in-c The Quinton *Birm* from 05; AD Edgbaston from 08. *The Rectory, 773 Hagley Road West, Birmingham B32 1AJ* Tel 0121-422 2031 E-mail chris@turner2075.fslife.co.uk

TURNER, Christopher Matthew. b 68. Brunel Univ BSc90. Cranmer Hall Dur 01. **d** 03 **p** 04. C Hykeham *Linc* 03-06; P-in-c Mid Marsh Gp from 06; P-in-c Saltfleetby from 06; P-in-c Theddlethorpe from 06. *Mid Marsh Rectory, 37 Tinkle Street, Grimoldby, Louth LN11 8SW* Tel (01507) 327735 E-mail c.turner@which.net

TURNER, Colin Peter John. b 42. Clifton Th Coll 63. **d** 66 **p** 67. C Kinson *Sarum* 66-68; C York St Paul 68-72; Org Sec (SE Area) CPAS 73-78; TV Radipole and Melcombe Regis *Sarum* 78-87; R Radstock w Writhlington *B & W* 90-07; R Kilmersdon w Babington 90-07; RD Midsomer Norton 04-07; rtd 07; Perm to Offic *B & W* from 07. *12 Gainsborough Rise, Trowbridge BA14 9HX*

TURNER, Canon David Stanley. b 35. Westmr Coll Ox BA84 MISM69 MISE69. WMMTC 86. **d** 87 **p** 88. NSM Worc St Mich 87-90; Min Shelfield St Mark CD *Lich* 90-95; C Walsall Wood 90-95; Min Can and Chapl St Woolos Cathl 95-97; V Tredegar St Jas 97-05; Hon Can St Bart's Cathl Barrackpore from 96; rtd 05. *30 Wolsey Close, Worcester WR4 9ES* Tel (01905) 350859

TURNER, Derek John. b 54. Univ of Wales (Ban) BSc81 PhD86. St Jo Coll Nottm. **d** 87 **p** 88. C Pelsall *Lich* 87-91; C Stratford-on-Avon w Bishopton *Cov* 91-99; R Leire w Ashby Parva and Dunton Bassett *Leic* 00-06; rtd 06. *The Parsonage, La Rue du Crocquet, St Brelade, Jersey JE3 8BZ* Tel 07713-832676 (mobile) E-mail frderek@cesmail.net

TURNER, Donald. b 29. S'wark Ord Course. **d** 71 **p** 72. C Hounslow St Steph *Lon* 71-76; Hon C Isleworth St Jo 76-78; C Brighton St Pet w Chpl Royal *Chich* 78-80; C Brighton St Pet w Chpl Royal and St Jo 80-85; P-in-c St Leonards SS Pet and Paul 85-87; V 87-91; rtd 91; Hon C Malborough w S Huish, W Alvington and Churchstow *Ex* 93-98; Chapl Las Palmas *Eur* 98-01; Perm to Offic *Ex* from 02. *15 Coombe Meadows, Chillington, Kingsbridge TQ7 2JL* Tel (01548) 531440

TURNER, Dylan Lawrence. b 72. Goldsmiths' Coll Lon BMus96 SS Coll Cam BTh08. Westcott Ho Cam 06. **d** 08 **p** 09. C Strood St Nic w St Mary *Roch* from 08. *12 Cadnam Close, Strood, Rochester ME2 3TS* Tel 07779-225810 (mobile) E-mail dylan.turner@diocese-rochester.org

TURNER, Edgar. *See* TURNER, Canon Robert Edgar

TURNER, Edward. *See* TURNER, Albert Edward

TURNER, Edward. b 80. Birm Univ BA01 Anglia Ruskin Univ MA08. Westcott Ho Cam 06. **d** 08 **p** 09. C Winchmore Hill St Paul *Lon* from 08. *St Paul's Lodge, 58 Church Hill, London N21 1JA* Tel (020) 8882 3298 Mobile 07788-782646 E-mail edd.turner@expertit.net

TURNER, Canon Edward Robert. b 37. Em Coll Cam BA62 BTh66 MA67. Westcott Ho Cam 64. **d** 66 **p** 67. C Salford St Phil w St Steph *Man* 66-69; Chapl Tonbridge Sch 69-81; Adv for In-Service Tr *Roch* 81-89; Dir of Educn 81-96; Can Res Roch Cathl 81-00; Vice-Dean Roch Cathl 88-00; Dioc Adv on Community Affairs 96-00; Consultant Rochester 2000 Trust and Bp's Consultant on Public Affairs 00-02; Perm to Offic *Nor* from 01; rtd 02. *Glebe House, Church Road, Neatishead, Norwich NR12 8BT* Tel (01692) 631295 E-mail aandeturner@broadlandnet.co.uk

TURNER, Mrs Eileen Margaret. b 45. Goldsmiths' Coll Lon TCert66 Ches Coll of HE MTh02. NOC 90. **d** 93 **p** 94. Par Dn Sandal St Cath *Wakef* 93-94; C 94-96; P-in-c Hammerwich *Lich* 96-02; Dir OLM Course 96-02; Dir Ext Studies St Jo Coll Nottm from 02. *St John's College, Chilwell Lane, Bramcote, Beeston, Nottingham NG9 3DS* Tel 0115-925 1114 Mobile 07774-623769 E-mail e.turner@stjohns-nottm.ac.uk

TURNER, Mrs Elaine. b 58. Birm Univ BSc79 CEng84 MICE84 MIStructE85. **d** 04 **p** 05. OLM Walesby *Linc* from 04. *Rose Cottage, Normanby-le-Wold, Market Rasen LN7 6SS* Tel (01673) 828142 E-mail elaine-turner58@supanex.com

TURNER, Miss Elizabeth Jane. b 67. Leeds Univ BEng88. Trin Coll Bris 93. **d** 96 **p** 97. C Eccles *Man* 96-00; P-in-c Barrow *Ches* 00-08; Dioc Ecum Officer 00-08; R Thurstaston from 08; Dioc Ecum Officer from 08. *Thurstaston Rectory, 77 Thingwall Road, Wirral CH61 3UB* Tel 0151-648 1816 E-mail jane@turner267.plus.com

TURNER, Canon Francis Edwin. b 29. Sarum Th Coll 54. **d** 57 **p** 58. C Cheriton Street *Cant* 57-61; C Willesborough w Hinxhill 61-64; P-in-c Betteshanger w Ham 64-65; R Northbourne w Betteshanger and Ham 64-70; R Northbourne, Tilmanstone w Betteshanger and Ham 70-74; V Sittingbourne St Mich 74-94; RD Sittingbourne 78-84; Hon Can Cant Cathl 84-94; rtd 94. *6 Cherry Grove, Hungerford RG17 0HP* Tel (01488) 682683

TURNER, Canon Frederick Glynne. b 30. Univ of Wales (Lamp) BA52. St Mich Coll Llan 52. **d** 54 **p** 55. C Aberaman *Llan* 54-60; C Oystermouth *S & B* 60-64; V Abercynon *Llan* 64-71; V Ton Pentre 71-73; TR Ystradyfodwg 73-77; R Caerphilly 77-82; V Whitchurch 82-96; Can Llan Cathl 84-96; Prec 95-96; rtd 96;

Perm to Offic *Llan* from 96. *83 Newborough Avenue, Llanishen, Cardiff CF14 5DA* Tel (029) 2075 4443

TURNER, Miss Gaynor. b 44. LNSM course 93. **d** 96 **p** 97. NSM Salford Sacred Trin *Man* 96-99; Asst Chapl among Deaf People from 96. *19 Ellesmere Avenue, Worsley, Manchester M28 0AL*

TURNER, Geoffrey. b 51. Selw Coll Cam BA75 MA78 PGCE75. NOC 90. **d** 93 **p** 94. C E Crompton *Man* 93-96; C Heywood St Luke w All So 96-98; TV Heywood 98-01; TR 01-08; TR Worsley from 08. *8 Landrace Drive, Worsley, Manchester M28 1UY* Tel 0161-799 6082 E-mail gt1951@btinternet.com

TURNER, Geoffrey Edwin. b 45. Aston Univ BSc68 Newc Univ MSc69 PhD72. Cranmer Hall Dur BA74. **d** 75 **p** 76. C Wood End *Cov* 75-79; V Huyton Quarry *Liv* 79-86; Press and Communications Officer *Ely* 86-94; P-in-c Gt w Lt Abington 86-94; P-in-c Hildersham 86-94; V Letchworth St Paul w Willian *St Alb* 94-01; P-in-c Willingham *Ely* 01-02; R 02-08; P-in-c Rampton 01-02; R 02-08; rtd 08; Perm to Offic *Ripon* from 09. *8 Wayside Crescent, Harrogate HG2 8NJ* Tel (01423) 885668 E-mail geoffrey168@btinternet.com

TURNER, Geoffrey James. b 46. St Deiniol's Hawarden 85. **d** 87 **p** 88. C Loughor *S & B* 87-89; C Swansea St Pet 89-90; R New Radnor and Llanfihangel Nantmelan etc 90-96; V Ystalyfera 96-07; RD Cwmtawe 00-06; V Loughor from 07. *The Rectory, 109 Glebe Road, Loughor, Swansea SA4 6SR* Tel (01792) 891958

✠**TURNER, The Rt Revd Geoffrey Martin.** b 34. Oak Hill Th Coll 60. **d** 63 **p** 64 **c** 94. C Tonbridge St Steph *Roch* 63-66; C Heatherlands St Jo *Sarum* 66-69; V Derby St Pet 69-73; V Chadderton Ch Ch *Man* 73-79; R Bebington *Ches* 79-93; Hon Can Ches Cathl 89-93; RD Wirral N 89-93; Adn Ches 93-94; Suff Bp Stockport 94-00; rtd 00; Perm to Offic *Ches* from 00. *23 Lang Lane, West Kirby, Wirral CH48 5HG* Tel 0151-625 8504

TURNER, Gerald Garth. b 38. Univ of Wales (Lamp) BA61 St Edm Hall Ox BA63 MA67. St Steph Ho Ox 63. **d** 65 **p** 66. C Drayton in Hales *Lich* 65-68; Chapl Prebendal Sch Chich 68-70; PV Chich Cathl 68-70; C Forest Row 70-72; V Hope *Derby* 72-78; Prec Man Cathl 78-86; Can Res 78-86; R Tattenhall and Handley *Ches* 86-04; rtd 04; Perm to Offic *S'well* from 04. *3 Westgate, Southwell NG25 0JN* Tel (01636) 815233 E-mail ggarthturner@hotmail.com

TURNER, Graham Colin. b 55. Bradf Univ BTech. Oak Hill Th Coll BA81. **d** 81 **p** 82. C Upper Armley *Ripon* 81-86; V Bordesley Green *Birm* 86-05; AD Yardley and Bordesley 00-05; TR Macclesfield Team *Ches* from 05. *The Rectory, 85 Beech Lane, Macclesfield SK10 2DY* Tel (01625) 426110 or 421984 E-mail grahamcturner@hotmail.com

TURNER, Mrs Heather Winifred. b 43. Open Univ BA08 SRN65. Cant Sch of Min 89. **d** 90 **p** 94. Par Dn Orpington All SS *Roch* 90-93; Chapl to the Deaf 93-00; P-in-c Wrotham 95-01; TV E Dereham and Scarning *Nor* 01-02; rtd 02; Perm to Offic *Nor* 02-04; C Darsham *St E* 04-06; C Middleton cum Fordley and Theberton w Eastbridge 04-06; C Westleton w Dunwich 04-06; C Yoxford, Peasenhall and Sibton 04-06; C Blyth Valley 06-07; TV 07; Perm to Offic *St E* from 07 and *Cov* from 08. *Nightingale House, 3 Heathlands, St George's Lane, Reydon, Southwold IP18 6RW* Tel (01502) 723386 E-mail revheatherturner@btinternet.com

TURNER, Henry John Mansfield. b 24. Magd Coll Cam BA45 MA48 Man Univ PhD85. Westcott Ho Cam 48. **d** 50 **p** 51. C Crosby *Linc* 50-52; C Chorlton upon Medlock *Man* 52-55; Inter-Colleg Sec SCM (Man) 52-55; C Leigh St Mary *Man* 55-57; V Rochdale Spotland 57-62; India 63-67; V Becontree St Geo *Chelmsf* 67-71; R Weeley 71-79; Chapl St Deiniol's Lib Hawarden 79-80; Sub-Warden 80-86; Perm to Offic *Chelmsf* from 86; Hon C St Botolph without Bishopgate *Lon* from 87. *Merrywood, 25 Fourth Avenue, Frinton-on-Sea CO13 9DU* Tel (01255) 677554

TURNER, James Alfred. b 34. MCIPS76. Ox Min Course 91. **d** 94 **p** 95. NSM Kidlington w Hampton Poyle *Ox* 94-06; Perm to Offic from 06. *11 St Mary's Close, Kidlington, Oxford OX5 2AY* Tel (01865) 375562

TURNER, James Henry. b 51. NOC 99. **d** 02 **p** 03. NSM Middleton St Cross *Ripon* from 02. *38 Acre Crescent, Middleton, Leeds LS10 4DJ* Tel 0113-277 2681 E-mail jameshpturner@aol.com

TURNER, Jane. *See* TURNER, Miss Elizabeth Jane

TURNER, Jessica Mary. b 60. SS Coll Cam BA81 PGCE82. Trin Coll Bris 88. **d** 91 **p** 94. Par Dn Preston Em *Blackb* 91-94; C Bamber Bridge St Aid 94-95; Chapl Preston Acute Hosps NHS Trust 95-98; Chapl Blackpool Victoria Hosp NHS Trust 98-03; Chapl Blackpool, Fylde and Wyre Hosps NHS Trust 03-05; Hon Can Blackb Cathl 02-05; Chapl Ox Radcliffe Hosps NHS Trust from 06. *Chaplain's Office, The Churchill Hospital, Old Road, Headington, Oxford OX3 7LJ* Tel (01865) 226090 E-mail jessica.turner@orh.nhs.uk

TURNER, John. *See* TURNER, Henry John Mansfield

TURNER, John David Maurice. b 22. Keble Coll Ox BA45 MA48. Ripon Hall Ox 69. **d** 70 **p** 71. C Crowthorne *Ox* 70-73; V Cropredy w Gt Bourton 73-79; V Cropredy w Gt Bourton and Wardington 80-83; Perm to Offic *Ox* and *Pet* 83-03; rtd 87.

16 Stuart Court, High Street, Kibworth, Leicester LE8 0LR Tel (01858) 881378

TURNER, John William. b 43. Sheff Univ BSc73. Wycliffe Hall Ox 86. **d** 88 **p** 89. C Clayton *Bradf* 88-91; C Horton 91-92; V Bankfoot 92-01; V Holland-on-Sea *Chelmsf* 01-05; rtd 05. *20 Grantley Drive, Harrogate HG3 2ST* Tel (01423) 504998 E-mail john.turner15@virgin.net

TURNER, Mrs Karen Lesley. b 48. ERMC. **d** 08 **p** 09. NSM Chambersbury *St Alb* from 08. *139 Marlins Turn, Hemel Hempstead HP1 3LW* Tel (01442) 250809

TURNER, Canon Keith Howard. b 50. Southn Univ BA71. Wycliffe Hall Ox 72. **d** 75 **p** 76. C Enfield Ch Ch Trent Park *Lon* 75-79; C Chilwell *S'well* 79-83; P-in-c Linby w Papplewick 83-90; R from 90; Hon Can S'well Minster from 02. *The Rectory, Main Street, Linby, Nottingham NG15 8AE* Tel 0115-963 2346 E-mail k.h.turner@btopenworld.com

TURNER, Keith Stanley. b 51. ACIB80. NTMTC 96. **d** 99 **p** 00. C S Hornchurch St Jo and St Matt *Chelmsf* from 99. *16 Wells Gardens, Rainham RM13 7LU* Tel (01708) 554274

TURNER, Kevin Louis Sinclair. b 60. St Jo Coll Nottm BA00. **d** 00 **p** 01. C Mount Pellon *Wakef* 00-03; P-in-c Sowerby 03-05; Evang Adv Croydon Area Miss Team *S'wark* 05-08. *26 Calder, Barkisland Mill, Beestonley Lane, Barkisland, Halifax HX4 0HG* Tel (01422) 377099 Mobile 07702-661527

TURNER, Lawrence John. b 43. Kelham Th Coll 65. **d** 70 **p** 71. C Lower Gornal *Lich* 70-73; C Wednesbury St Paul Wood Green 73-74; C Porthill 75-77; C Wilton *York* 77-80; P-in-c 80-82; R Jersey St Martin *Win* from 82; Chmn Jersey Miss to Seamen from 82. *The Rectory, La rue de la Croix au Maitre, St Martin, Jersey JE3 6HW* Tel (01534) 854294 E-mail ljturner@jerseymail.co.uk

TURNER, Leslie. b 29. NE Lon Poly BSc87. St Jo Coll Dur 50 St Aid Birkenhead 51. **d** 54 **p** 55. C Darwen St Cuth *Blackb* 54-56; C Haslingden w Grane and Stonefold 56-59; V Oswaldtwistle St Paul 59-65; Chapl Belmont and Henderson Hosps Sutton 65-71; St Ebba's Hosp Epsom 65-71; Qu Mary's Carshalton 67-71; Chapl Princess Marina and St Crispin's Hosps 71-87; Chapl Northn Gen Hosp 87-94; Chapl Manfield Hosp Northn 87-94; Chapl St Edm Hosp Northn 87-94; rtd 94; Perm to Offic *Pet* from 94. *20 Banbury Close, Northampton NN4 9UA* Tel (01604) 769233

TURNER, Mrs Lorraine Elizabeth. b 67. Brunel Univ BSc90 Open Univ MA96. Cranmer Hall Dur 01. **d** 03 **p** 04. C Birchwood *Linc* 03-06; TV Louth from 06; C Legbourne and Wold Marsh from 06; Chapl United Lincs Hosps NHS Trust from 07. *Mid Marsh Rectory, 37 Tinkle Street, Grimoldby, Louth LN11 8SW* Tel (01507) 327735 or 327667 E-mail lorraine.t@which.net

TURNER, Mark. b 60. Aston Tr Scheme 87 Sarum & Wells Th Coll BTh92. **d** 92 **p** 93. C New Sleaford *Linc* 92-94; C Bottesford and Muston *Leic* 94-98; C Harby, Long Clawson and Hose 94-98; C Barkestone w Plungar, Redmile and Stathern 94-98; P-in-c Thurnby Lodge 98-00; C Aylestone Park CD 00-03; P-in-c Areley Kings *Worc* 03-05; R from 05; RD Stourport 06-08. *14 Dunley Road, Stourport-on-Severn DY13 0AX* Tel (01299) 829557 E-mail revturner@tinyworld.co.uk

TURNER, Mark Richard Haythornthwaite. b 41. TCD MA67 Linc Coll Ox BA68. Wycliffe Hall Ox 65. **d** 68 **p** 69. C Birtley *Newc* 68-71; C Cambridge Gt St Mary w St Mich *Ely* 71-74; Chapl Loughb Univ 74-79; P-in-c Keele *Lich* 80-85; Chapl Keele Univ 80-85; P-in-c Ashley 85-95; P-in-c Mucklestone 86-95; R Farnborough *Roch* 95-00; P-in-c Upper Tean *Lich* 00-06; Local Min Adv (Stafford) 00-06; rtd 06; Perm to Offic *Lich* from 06; Local Miss and Min Adv (Shrewsbury Area) from 09. *Craignant Isa, Selattyn, Oswestry SY10 7NS* Tel (01691) 718315 E-mail markrhturner@hotmail.com

TURNER, Martin John. b 34. Trin Hall Cam BA55 MA59. Cuddesdon Coll 58. **d** 60 **p** 61. C Rugby St Andr *Cov* 60-65; C Cov Cathl 65-68; USA 68-70; V Rushmere *St E* 70-82; V Monkwearmouth St Pet *Dur* 82-90; V Bathford *B & W* 90-99; rtd 99; Perm to Offic *B & W* 00-07 and *Truro* from 97. *4 The Terrace, Lostwithiel PL22 0DT* Tel (01208) 871330 Mobile 07932-143345 E-mail turnerschemanoff@aol.com

TURNER, Mrs Maureen. b 55. Leeds Univ BA78 MA01. St Jo Coll Nottm 84. **d** 87 **p** 94. Par Dn Darlaston St Lawr *Lich* 87-91; C Stratford-on-Avon w Bishopton *Cov* 91-98; Chapl Myton Hamlet Hospice 91-98; NSM Leire w Ashby Parva and Dunton Bassett *Leic* 00-06; Chapl Team Ldr Univ Hosps Leic NHS Trust 01-07; Chapl Team Ldr Jersey Gp of Hosps from 07. *Chaplain's Office, General Hospital, Gloucester Street, St Helier, Jersey JE1 3QS* Tel (01534) 622000

TURNER, Maurice. *See* TURNER, Charles Maurice Joseph

TURNER, Maurice William. b 29. Cant Coll Th 53. **d** 56 **p** 57. C Thornhill *Wakef* 56-60; V Gawber 60-71; V Alverthorpe 71-74; V Shelton and Oxon *Lich* 74-81; V Leaton 81-82; P-in-c Battlefield w Albrighton 81-82; V Leaton and Albrighton w Battlefield 82-92; rtd 92; Perm to Offic *Lich* from 93 and *Heref* from 96. *10 Melbourne Rise, Bicton Heath, Shrewsbury SY3 5DA* Tel (01743) 352667

TURNER, Michael Andrew. b 34. K Coll Cam BA59 MA62. Cuddesdon Coll 59. **d** 61 **p** 62. C Luton St Andr *St Alb* 61-64; V 70-77; C-in-c Northolt St Mary *Lon* 64-70; Perm to Offic *St Alb* 77-93; Dep Hd and Chapl Greycoat Hosp Sch 86-93; P-in-c Shilling Okeford *Sarum* 93-99; Chapl Croft Ho Sch Shillingstone 93-99; rtd 99; V of Close Sarum Cathl 02-07. *12 Berkshire Road, Harnham, Salisbury SP2 8NY* Tel (01722) 504000 E-mail voc@salcath.co.uk

TURNER, Michael John Royce. b 43. St Jo Coll Dur BA65. Chich Th Coll 65. **d** 67 **p** 68. C Hodge Hill *Birm* 67-71; C Eling, Testwood and Marchwood *Win* 71-72; TV 72-77; R Kirkwall *Ab* 77-85; R Drumlithie *Bre* from 85; R Drumtochty from 85; R Fasque from 85; R Laurencekirk from 85. *Beattie Lodge, Laurencekirk AB30 1HJ* Tel and fax (01561) 377380 E-mail mjrturner@zoo.co.uk

TURNER, Canon Nicholas Anthony. b 51. Clare Coll Cam BA73 MA77 Keble Coll Ox BA77 MA81. Ripon Coll Cuddesdon 76. **d** 78 **p** 79. C Stretford St Matt *Man* 78-80; Tutor St Steph Ho Ox 80-84; V Leeds Richmond Hill *Ripon* 84-91; Offg Chapl RAF and V Ascension Is 91-96; Can Th St Helena Cathl from 94; V Raynes Park St Sav *S'wark* 96-01; P-in-c Broughton, Marton and Thornton *Bradf* 01-02; R from 02. *The Rectory, Broughton, Skipton BD23 3AN* Tel (01282) 842332 E-mail nicholas.turner@bradford.anglican.org

TURNER (*née* SYMINGTON), Canon Patricia **Ann.** b 46. SRN68 RMN71 SCM72. St Steph Ho Ox 82. **dss** 84 **d** 87. Buttershaw St Aid *Bradf* 84-87; TM Manningham 87-91; Ascension Is 91-96; Par Dn Raynes Park St Sav *S'wark* 96-01; Par Dn Broughton, Marton and Thornton *Bradf* from 01; RD Skipton from 05; Assoc Dioc Dir of Ords 04-07; Dir of Ords from 07; Hon Can Bradf Cathl from 09. *The Rectory, Broughton, Skipton BD23 3AN* Tel (01282) 842332 E-mail ann.turner@bradford.anglican.org

TURNER, Peter Carpenter. b 39. Oak Hill Th Coll 63. **d** 66 **p** 67. C Chadwell *Chelmsf* 66-69; C Braintree 69-73; R Fyfield 73-87; P-in-c Moreton 77-87; C-in-c Bobbingworth 82-87; P-in-c Willingale w Shellow and Berners Roding 84-87; V E Ham St Geo 87-04; rtd 04; Perm to Offic *Lon* from 05. *9 Llandovery House, Chipka Street, London E14 3LE* Tel (020) 7987 5902 E-mail detox.uk@btinternet.com *or* petercturner@btinternet.com

TURNER, The Ven Peter **Robin.** b 42. CB98. St Luke's Coll Ex PGCE70 Open Univ BA79 Westmr Coll Ox MTh96 AKC65. St Boniface Warminster 65. **d** 66 **p** 67. C Crediton *Ex* 66-69; Perm to Offic 69-70; Chapl RAF 70-88; Asst Chapl-in-Chief RAF 88-95; Chapl-in-Chief RAF 95-98; QHC 92-98; Can and Preb Linc Cathl 95-98; Chapl Dulwich Coll 98-02; Bp's Dom Chapl *S'well* 02-07; Hon Can S'well Minster 02-07; rtd 07; Chapl for Sector Min *S'well* from 07. *12 Chimes Meadow, Southwell NG25 0GB* Tel (01636) 812250 Mobile 07860-583475 E-mail pr.turner@lineone.net

TURNER, Ms Philippa Anne. b 64. Trevelyan Coll Dur BA86 Yale Univ MDiv88. **d** 94 **p** 95. Chapl New York Hosp USA 91-95; Assoc P New York Ch of Heavenly Rest 95-08; Chapl R Veterinary Coll *Lon* from 08; Chapl R Free and Univ Coll Medical Sch from 08. *15 Ormonde Mansions, 106A Southampton Row, London WC1B 4BP* Tel (020) 7242 2574 *or* 7408 3143 Mobile 07525-2343 E-mail pturner@rvc.ac.uk

TURNER, Canon Robert **Edgar.** b 20. TCD BA42 MA51. Linc Th Coll 44. **d** 45 **p** 46. C Kings Heath *Birm* 45-51; Min Can Belf Cathl 51-63; Dean of Res QUB 51-58; Bp's Dom Chapl *D & D* 56-67; I Belfast St Geo *Conn* 58-90; Can Belf Cathl 71-76; Preb Clonmethan St Patr Cathl Dublin 76-90; Dioc Registrar *Conn* 82-06; Prin Registrar from 90; rtd 90. *19 Cricklewood Park, Belfast BT9 5GU* Tel (028) 9066 3214 Fax 9058 6843 E-mail returner@ntlworld.com *or* registrar@connor.anglican.org

TURNER, Robin Edward. b 35. Selw Coll Cam BA57 MA63. Qu Coll Birm 57. **d** 63 **p** 64. C Aveley *Chelmsf* 63-67; C Upminster 67-71; R Goldhanger w Lt Totham 71-80; R Lt Baddow 80-00; Hon Chapl New Hall Sch Essex 80-00; rtd 00; Perm to Offic *Nor* from 00. *29 Swann Grove, Holt NR25 6DP* Tel (01263) 711330

TURNER, Canon Roger Dyke. b 39. Trin Coll Bris 79. **d** 81 **p** 82. C Clevedon St Andr and Ch Ch *B & W* 81-85; R Freshford, Limpley Stoke and Hinton Charterhouse 85-88; V Kenilworth St Jo *Cov* 88-04; RD Kenilworth 90-98; Hon Can Cov Cathl 00-04; rtd 04; Perm to Offic *Birm* 04-05 and *Cov* from 04; P-in-c Barston *Birm* from 05. *8 Priors Close, Balsall Common, Coventry CV7 7FJ* Tel (01676) 533847

TURNER, Roy. *See* TURNER, Alan Roy

TURNER, Ms Ruth Carpenter. b 63. Anglia Ruskin Univ BA09 LLCM83 GLCM84. Ridley Hall Cam 07. **d** 09. C Brampton St Thos *Derby* from 09. *6 Westfield Close, Chesterfield S40 3RS* Tel (01246) 569810 Mobile 07855-714538 E-mail curate@st-thomas-brampton.org

TURNER, St John Alwin. b 31. Dur Univ BA57 MA61. Cranmer Hall Dur. **d** 59 **p** 60. C W Hartlepool St Paul *Dur* 59-62; C S Shore H Trin *Blackb* 62-65; V Huncoat 65-67; Org Sec CMS *Ripon* and *York* 67-72; V Harrogate St Mark *Ripon* 72-94; rtd 96;

Perm to Offic *Linc* from 01. *2 The Tilney, Whaplode, Spalding PE12 6UW* Tel (01406) 371390

TURNER, Stewart Gordon. b 54. Ex Univ BTh06. SWMTC 03. **d** 06 **p** 07. NSM Falmouth All SS *Truro* from 06. *3 Parc Briwer, Penryn TR10 8LF* Tel (01326) 373834 E-mail stewart.turner@tiscali.co.uk

TURNER, Susan. b 58. Man Univ BA89. NOC 89. **d** 92 **p** 94. NSM Balderstone *Man* 92-93; NSM E Crompton 93-94; Hon C 94-96; Chapl Man Coll of Arts and Tech 92-96; Asst Chapl S Man Univ Hosps NHS Trust 96-97; Chapl Burnley Health Care NHS Trust 97-03; Chapl Cen Man/Man Children's Univ Hosp NHS Trust from 02. *Chaplaincy Office, Manchester Royal Infirmary, Oxford Road, Manchester M13 9WL* Tel 0161-276 45824

TURNER, Sylvia Jean. b 46. Lon Univ 72 Open Univ BA77. Westcott Ho Cam 93. **d** 95 **p** 96. C Whitstable *Cant* 95-99; R Wigmore Abbey *Heref* 99-09; P-in-c Pontesbury I and II from 09. *Wheelwrights, Witton, Ludlow SY8 3DB* Tel (01584) 890586 E-mail sylvia.turner@virgin.net

TURNER, Tina. b 60. St Jo Coll Nottm BA02. **d** 02 **p** 03. C Halifax All So and St Aug *Wakef* 02-05; C S Beddington and Roundshaw *S'wark* 05-06; TV Warlingham w Chelsham and Farleigh 06-08. *26 Calder, Barkisland Mill, Beestonley Lane, Barkisland, Halifax HX4 0HG* E-mail tina@revturner.fsnet.co.uk

TURNER, Valerie Kay. b 50. SS Paul & Mary Coll Cheltenham BEd72. WMMTC 97 Wycliffe Hall Ox 99. **d** 00 **p** 01. C Cheltenham St Luke and St Jo *Glouc* 00-04; P-in-c Forest of Dean Ch Ch w English Bicknor from 04; P-in-c Lydbrook 04-05. *Christ Church Vicarage, Ross Road, Christchurch, Coleford GL16 7NS* Tel (01594) 836830 E-mail valmark@freenetname.co.uk

TURNER, Canon Walter John. b 29. Bris Univ BA53. Clifton Th Coll 49. **d** 54 **p** 55. C W Bromwich All SS *Lich* 54-58; C-in-c Oxley 58-60; V 60-65; V Wednesfield St Thos 65-74; RD Shifnal 75-83; V Boningale 75-83; V Shifnal 75-83; Preb Lich Cathl 80-83; Can Res and Prec Lich Cathl 83-94; rtd 94; Perm to Offic *Lich* from 94. *9 Kestrel Close, Newport TF10 8QE* Tel (01952) 820758

TURNER, William Edward. b 41. Keble Coll Ox BA63 MA73. Linc Th Coll 76. **d** 78 **p** 79. C Lich St Chad 78-80; Chapl Trent (Nottm) Poly *S'well* 80-89; Chapl Lancs (Preston) Poly *Blackb* 89-92; Chapl Cen Lancs Univ 92-04; rtd 04. *Lunesdale, Rowgate, Kirkby Stephen CA17 4SP* Tel (017683) 72554

TURNER-CALLIS, Mrs Gillian Ruth. b 79. Aber Univ BD03. Wycliffe Hall Ox MTh05. **d** 05 **p** 06. C Shepshed and Oaks in Charnwood *Leic* 05-08; TR Kegworth, Hathern, Long Whatton, Diseworth etc from 08. *The Rectory, 24 Nottingham Road, Kegworth, Derby DE74 2FH* Tel (01509) 673146 Mobile 07974-139881 E-mail gill@thets.demon.co.uk

TURNER-LOISEL, Mrs Elizabeth Anne. b 57. Lanc Univ BA79 MA80 York Univ PGCE81. EMMTC 96. **d** 99 **p** 00. C Eastwood *S'well* and Chapl Nat Sch Hucknall 99-04; P-in-c Annesley w Newstead *S'well* from 04. *The Vicarage, Annesley Cutting, Annesley, Nottingham NG15 0AJ* Tel (01623) 759666 E-mail revd.liz@virgin.net

TURNOCK, Geoffrey. b 38. Leeds Univ BSc61 PhD64 MIBiol. EMMTC 84. **d** 87 **p** 88. NSM Oadby *Leic* 87-00; NSM Okeford *Sarum* 00-04; NSM Dorchester from 05. *10 Billingsmoor Lane, Poundbury, Dorchester DT1 3WT* Tel (01305) 757177 E-mail gt@woodplace.u-net.com

TURP, Paul Robert. b 48. Oak Hill Th Coll BA79. **d** 79 **p** 80. C Southall Green St Jo *Lon* 79-83; V Shoreditch St Leon w St Mich 83-88 and from 00; TR Shoreditch St Leon and Hoxton St Jo 88-00. *The Vicarage, 36 Hoxton Square, London N1 6NN* Tel (020) 7739 2063 E-mail paul@shoreditch0.demon.co.uk

TURPIN, Christine Lesley. b 63. Westcott Ho Cam. **d** 09. C Bredon w Bredon's Norton *Worc* from 09. *20 Cornfield Way, Ashton-under-Hill, Evesham WR11 7TA* Tel (01386) 882263

TURPIN, Canon John Richard. b 41. St D Coll Lamp BA63 Magd Coll Cam BA65 MA70. Cuddesdon Coll 65. **d** 66 **p** 67. C Tadley St Pet *Win* 66-71; V Southampton Thornhill St Chris 71-85; V Ringwood from 85; Hon Can Win Cathl from 99. *The Vicarage, 65 Southampton Road, Ringwood BH24 1HE* Tel (01425) 473219 E-mail johnturpin@ringwoodparish.org.uk

TURPIN, Raymond Gerald. b 35. **d** 97 **p** 98. OLM Brockley Hill St Sav *S'wark* 97-05; Perm to Offic from 05; Retirement Officer Woolwich Area from 08. *60 Bankhurst Road, London SE6 4XN* Tel (020) 8690 6877 *or* 8311 2000

TURRELL, Peter Charles Morphett. b 47. **d** 01 **p** 02. OLM Carshalton Beeches *S'wark* from 01. *62 Stanley Park Road, Carshalton SM5 3HW* Tel (020) 8669 0318

TURRELL, Stephen John. b 35. S'wark Ord Course. **d** 83 **p** 84. NSM W Wickham St Jo *Cant* 83-84; NSM Addington *S'wark* 85-92; NSM Blendworth w Chalton w Idsworth *Portsm* 92-97; Perm to Offic 97-01; NSM Storrington *Chich* 01-06; rtd 06. *29 Timberlands, Storrington, Pulborough RH20 3NF* Tel (01903) 741272

TURTON, Arthur Bickerstaffe. b 19. Oak Hill Th Coll 46. **d** 48 **p** 49. C Rawtenstall St Mary *Man* 48-51; C Islington St Mary *Lon* 51-52; V Lozells St Silas *Birm* 52-56; V Streatham Park St Alb *S'wark* 56-60; Org Sec CPAS Metrop Area 60-64; V Southborough St Pet *Roch* 64-68; P-in-c Southborough St Matt 67-68; V Southborough St Pet w Ch Ch and St Matt 68-76; V Histon *Ely* 76-82; rtd 84; Perm to Offic *Chich* 82-88; *Ely* 88-99. *1172 Greenwood Avenue, Victoria BC V9A 5M1, Canada* Tel (001) (250) 385 0062

TURTON, Douglas Walter. b 38. Kent Univ BA77 Surrey Univ MSc90 Univ of Wales (Ban) DPhil04. Oak Hill Th Coll 77. **d** 78 **p** 79. C Cant St Mary Bredin 78-80; P-in-c Thornton Heath St Paul 80-81; V 81-84; V Thornton Heath St Paul *S'wark* 85-91; R Eastling w Ospringe and Stalisfield w Otterden *Cant* 91-00; rtd 00. *16 Weatherall Close, Dunkirk, Faversham ME13 9UL* Tel (01227) 752244

TURTON, Neil Christopher. b 45. Wycliffe Hall Ox 77. **d** 79 **p** 80. C Guildf Ch Ch 79-83; C Godalming 83-89; V Wyke 86-92; R Frimley 92-02; RD Surrey Heath 97-02; V All SS Bay Head NJ USA from 02. *All Saints Rectory, 509 Lake Avenue, Bay Head NJ 08742, USA* E-mail neil.turton@virgin.net

TURTON, Paul Edward. b 26. St Pet Hall Ox BA50 MA55. Qu Coll Birm 50. **d** 52 **p** 53. C Selly Oak St Mary *Birm* 52-55; C Ward End 55-57; I Netherton CD *Liv* 57-64; V Brockley Hill St Sav *S'wark* 64-68; Perm to Offic 68-70; Dir of Educn *Nor* 70-75; Dep Dir Nat Soc Cen Camberwell 75-77; Dir Nat Soc RE Cen Kensington 78-84; C Eastbourne St Mary *Chich* 84-86; rtd 86; Perm to Offic *Chich* from 87. *32 Churchill Close, Eastbourne BN20 8AJ* Tel (01323) 638089

TUSCHLING, Ruth Mary Magdalen. b 65. Freiburg Univ MA94 CCC Cam PhD04. Westcott Ho Cam BA97. **d** 98 **p** 99. C Hampstead St Jo *Lon* 98-01; Perm to Offic *Ely* 02-04; OSB 04-08; Warden Offa Retreat Ho and Dioc Spirituality Adv *Cov* from 08. *The Vicarage, School Hill, Offchurch, Leamington Spa CV33 9AL* Tel (01926) 334990 E-mail florinequals@googlemail.com

✠**TUSTIN, The Rt Revd David.** b 35. Magd Coll Cam BA57 MA61 Lambeth DD98. Cuddesdon Coll 58. **d** 60 **p** 61 **c** 79. C Stafford St Mary *Lich* 60-63; C St Dunstan in the West *Lon* 63-67; Asst Gen Sec C of E Coun on Foreign Relns 63-67; V Wednesbury St Paul Wood Green *Lich* 67-71; V Tettenhall Regis 71-79; RD Trysull 76-79; Suff Bp Grimsby *Linc* 79-00; Can and Preb Linc Cathl 79-00; rtd 00; Hon Asst Bp Linc from 01. *The Ashes, Tunnel Road, Wrawby, Brigg DN20 8SF* Tel and fax (01652) 655584 E-mail tustindavid@hotmail.com

TUTTON, Canon John Knight. b 30. Man Univ BSc51. Ripon Hall Ox 53. **d** 55 **p** 56. C Tonge w Alkrington *Man* 55-57; C Bushbury *Lich* 57-59; R Blackley St Andr *Man* 59-67; R Denton Ch Ch 67-95; Hon Can Man Cathl 90-95; rtd 95; Hon C Exminster and Kenn 96-01; Perm to Offic from 01. *2 Hescane Park, Cheriton Bishop, Exeter EX6 6JP* Tel (01647) 24651 E-mail johnktutton@onetel.com

✠**TUTU, The Most Revd Desmond Mpilo.** b 31. UNISA BA K Coll Lon BD MTh FKC78. St Pet Rosettenville LTh. **d** 60 **p** 61 **c** 76. S Africa 60-62; C Golders Green St Alb *Lon* 62-65; C Bletchingley *S'wark* 65-66; S Africa 67-70; Lesotho 70-72; Assoc Dir Th Educn Fund WCC 72-75; C Lee St Aug *S'wark* 72-75; Dean Johannesburg 75-76; Bp Lesotho 76-78; Asst Bp Johannesburg 78-85; Bp Johannesburg 85-86; Abp Cape Town 86-96; rtd 96. *PO Box 1092, Milnerton, 7435 South Africa* Tel (0027) (21) 552 7524 Fax 552 7529 E-mail mpilo@iafrica.com

TWADDELL, William Reginald. b 33. TCD 61. **d** 62 **p** 63. C Belfast Whiterock *Conn* 62-65; I Loughgilly w Clare *Arm* 65-71; I Milltown 71-84; I Portadown St Mark 84-01; Preb Arm Cathl 88-96; Treas 96-98; Perm 98-01; rtd 01. *Tea Cottage, 19 Birches Road, Portadown BT62 1LS* Tel (028) 3885 2520 E-mail reggie.twaddell@hotmail.co.uk

TWEDDELL, Christopher Noel. b 66. Auckland Univ BA93. St Jo Coll Auckland. **d** 92 **p** 93. New Zealand 92-97; C Maindee Newport *Mon* 97-98; P-in-c Discovery Bay Hong Kong 98-00; V New Lynn New Zealand 00-05; Chapl St Pet Sch Cambridge from 06. *St Peter's School, Private Bag 884, Cambridge, New Zealand* Tel (0064) (7) 827 9888 Mobile 27-454 1306 E-mail chaplain@stpeters.school.nz

TWEDDLE, David William Joseph. b 28. Dur Univ BSc50 Open Univ BA97 ATCL56. Wycliffe Hall Ox 54. **d** 56 **p** 57. C Darlington H Trin *Dur* 56-60; P-in-c Prestonpans *Edin* 60-63; PV Linc Cathl 63-65; C Pet St Jo 65-71; Hon Min Can Pet Cathl 68-93; V Southwick w Glapthorn 71-83; P-in-c Benefield 80-83; R Benefield and Southwick w Glapthorn 83-93; RD Oundle 84-89; rtd 94; Perm to Offic *Ely* 94-07. *6 Barton Square, Ely CB7 4DF* Tel (01353) 614393

TWEED, Andrew. b 48. Univ of Wales (Cardiff) BA69 Trin Coll Carmarthen MA97. St Deiniol's Hawarden. **d** 81 **p** 84. NSM Llandrindod w Cefnllys *S & B* 81-87; NSM Llandrindod w Cefnllys and Disserth from 87. *Gwenallt, Wellington Road, Llandrindod Wells LD1 5NB* Tel (01597) 823671 E-mail andrewtweed1@aol.com

TWEEDIE-SMITH, Ian David. b 60. Newc Univ BA83. Wycliffe Hall Ox 83. **d** 85 **p** 86. C Hatcham St Jas *S'wark* 85-89; C Bury St Edmunds St Mary *St E* 89-02; TV Woking St Pet *Guildf* from 02. *The Vicarage, 66 Westfield Road, Woking GU22 9NG* Tel (01483) 770779 Fax 770786 E-mail iantweediesmith@waitrose.com

TWEEDY, Andrew Cyril Mark. b 61. Man Univ BA(Econ)81. SAOMC 98. **d** 01 **p** 02. C Carterton *Ox* 01-03; C Brize Norton and Carterton 03-04; V Bromham w Oakley and Stagsden *St Alb* 04-08; Chapl Barcelona *Eur* from 08. *St George's Church, calle Horacio 38, 08022 Barcelona, Spain* Tel (0034) 934 178 867 Fax 932 128 433 E-mail revdrew61@yahoo.es

TWIDELL, Canon William James. b 30. St Mich Coll Llan 58. **d** 60 **p** 61. C Tonge w Alkrington *Man* 60-63; C High Wycombe All SS *Ox* 63-65; P-in-c Elkesley w Bothamsall *S'well* 65-66; V Bury St Thos *Man* 66-72; V Daisy Hill 72-84; R Flixton St Mich 84-00; AD Stretford 88-98; Hon Can Man Cathl 97-00; rtd 00; Perm to Offic *Man* and *Ches* from 00. *11 Mercer Way, Nantwich CW5 5YD* Tel (01270) 620328

TWINING, Kathryn. b 60. Westcott Ho Cam. **d** 07 **p** 08. C Greenwich St Alfege *S'wark* from 07. *88 Ashburnham Grove, London SE10 8UL* Tel 07810-542007 (mobile) E-mail revdmk.twining@btinternet.com

TWINLEY, David Alan. b 66. Ox Univ BTh00. St Steph Ho Ox 97. **d** 00 **p** 01. C Saffron Walden w Wendens Ambo, Littlebury etc *Chelmsf* 00-03; V Bury w Houghton and Coldwaltham and Hardham *Chich* from 03. *The Vicarage, Church Lane, Bury, Pulborough RH20 1PB* Tel (01798) 839057 E-mail frdavid@twinley.me.uk

TWISLETON, John Fiennes. b 48. St Jo Coll Ox BA69 MA73 DPhil73. Coll of Resurr Mirfield 73. **d** 76 **p** 77. C New Bentley *Sheff* 76-79; P-in-c Moorends 79-80; V 80-86; USPG 86-90; Prin Alan Knight Tr Cen Guyana 87-90; V Holbrooks *Cov* 90-96; Edmonton Area Missr *Lon* 96-01; Dioc Adv for Miss and Renewal *Chich* 01-09; C Haywards Heath St Rich 01-09; R Horsted Keynes from 09. *The Rectory, Station Road, Horsted Keynes, Haywards Heath RH17 7ED* Tel (01825) 790317 E-mail john@twisleton.co.uk

TWISLETON, Peter. b 50. Linc Th Coll. **d** 84 **p** 85. C Bodmin w Lanhydrock and Lanivet *Truro* 84-87; C Par 87-90; R St Breoke and Egloshayle 90-93; R Bude Haven and Marhamchurch 93-97; V Horbury w Horbury Bridge *Wakef* 98-07; P-in-c Seaham Harbour and Dawdon *Dur* 07; V from 08. *The Vicarage, Maureen Terrace, Seaham SR7 7SN* Tel 0191-581 3385

TWISLETON-WYKEHAM-FIENNES, Oliver William. *See* FIENNES, The Very Revd the Hon Oliver William

TWISS, Dorothy Elizabeth. Gilmore Ho 68 Linc Th Coll 70. **d** 87 **p** 94. Chapl Asst RAF 78-91; TV Pewsey *Sarum* 91-95; Chapl HM Pris Drake Hall 95-01; Chapl HM Pris Ford 01-03; rtd 03; Perm to Offic *Portsm* from 05. *41 Rosecott, Havant Road, Horndean, Waterlooville PO8 0XA* Tel 07929-650284 (mobile) E-mail dorothy@dtwiss.freeserve.co.uk

TWITTY, Miss Rosamond Jane. b 54. Univ of Wales (Ban) BSc75 CertEd76. Trin Coll Bris BA89. **d** 90 **p** 94. Par Dn Lt Thurrock St Jo *Chelmsf* 90-94; C 94-95; C Upper Armley *Ripon* 95-08; TV Langport Area *B & W* from 08. *The Vicarage, 1 New Street, Long Sutton, Langport TA10 9JW* Tel (01458) 241260 E-mail janetwitty@supanet.com

TWOHIG, Brian Robert. b 48. La Trobe Univ Vic BA77 PhD86. St Mich Th Coll Crafers 70. **d** 72 **p** 73. Australia 72-78 and 80-82; C Leatherhead *Guildf* 78-80; TV New Windsor *Ox* 82-92; V Sheff St Cuth 92-97; rtd 97; Perm to Offic *Chich* from 08. *26A Bloomsbury Street, Brighton BN2 1HQ* Tel (01273) 270481

TWOMEY, Jeremiah Francis (Derry). b 50. Man Poly BA83 Univ of Wales (Ban) PGCE85. NEOC 92. **d** 94 **p** 95. C Beverley St Nic *York* 94-96; V Anlaby Common St Mark 96-99; Ind Chapl *Newc* 99-05; V Bedlington from 05. *The Vicarage, 21 Church Lane, Bedlington NE22 5EL* Tel (01670) 829220 E-mail derrytwomey@aol.com

TWOMEY, Jeremiah Thomas Paul. b 46. CITC 87. **d** 87 **p** 88. C Derryloran *Arm* 87-90; I Brackaville w Donaghendry and Ballyclog 90-97; I Mohill w Farnaught, Aughavas, Oughteragh etc *K, E & A* 97-00; Bp's C Belfast Whiterock *Conn* 00-08; C Belfast St Anne from 08. *Address temp unknown* E-mail ptwomey@esatclear.ie

TWYFORD, Canon Arthur Russell. b 36. ALCD60. **d** 60 **p** 61. C Speke All SS *Liv* 60-64; R Maids Moreton w Foxcote *Ox* 64-72; Asst Dioc Youth Officer 64-70; P-in-c Lillingstone Dayrell w Lillingstone Lovell 70-72; V Desborough *Pet* 72-88; P-in-c Brampton Ash w Dingley 73-77; P-in-c Braybrooke 73-77; R Brampton Ash w Dingley and Braybrooke 77-88; RD Kettering 79-87; Can Pet Cathl 81-95; R Stanwick w Hargrave 88-95; rtd 95; Perm to Offic *Pet* 95-07. *Chemin des Fées, 46250 Cazals, France* Tel (0033) (5) 65 21 66 93 E-mail artwyford@aol.com

TWYNAM, Mrs Susan Elizabeth. b 59. Bath Coll of HE BEd81. SEITE 09. **d** 09. NSM Sidcup St Jo *Roch* from 09. *6 Williams Way, Dartford DA2 7WF* Tel (01322) 559501 E-mail susantwynam@btconnect.com

TYDEMAN, Canon Richard. b 16. St Jo Coll Ox BA39 MA43. Ripon Hall Ox 38. **d** 39 **p** 40. C Langley St Mich *Birm* 39-41; C Ipswich All SS *St E* 41-45; P-in-c Ipswich St Helen 45-46; V Woodbridge St Jo 46-53; V Newmarket All SS 53-63; RD

Newmarket 54-63; Hon Can St E Cathl 59-63; R St Sepulchre w Ch Ch Greyfriars etc *Lon* 63-81; Dep Min Can St Paul's Cathl 63-81; Preacher Lincoln's Inn 72-81; rtd 81; Perm to Offic *St E* from 82. *Cornwallis Court, Hospital Road, Bury St Edmunds IP33 3NH* Tel (01284) 769114

TYDEMAN, Rosemary. *See* WILLIAMS, Mrs Rosemary

TYE, Dominic Geoffrey Bernard. b 43. Lanc Univ BA70 PhD75. Kelham Th Coll 62. **d** 67 **p** 68. SSM 66-78; C Lancaster St Mary *Blackb* 67-70; Lect Kelham Th Coll 70-73; Chapl Woden Hosp Australia 75-76; Teacher Lancaster 83-84; Hd Sixth Form Fleetwood Sch 84-87; Dep Hd Lancaster Girls Gr Sch 87-90; Hd Thorncliffe Sch Barrow-in-Furness 90-97; Co-ord Cen Educn Leadership Man Univ 98-02; rtd 08. *9 Sea View Drive, Hest Bank, Lancaster LA2 6BY* Tel (01524) 823462 E-mail member@dtye.freeserve.co.uk

TYE, Eric John. b 37. St Alb Minl Tr Scheme 78. **d** 81 **p** 82. NSM Rushden St Mary w Newton Bromswold *Pet* 81-07; Perm to Offic from 07. *29 Kingsmead Park, Bedford Road, Rushden NN10 0NF* Tel (01933) 353274

TYE, John Raymond. b 31. Lambeth STh64 Linc Th Coll 66. **d** 68 **p** 69. C Crewe St Mich *Ches* 68-71; C Wednesfield St Thos *Lich* 71-76; P-in-c Petton w Cockshutt 76-79; P-in-c Hordley 79; P-in-c Weston Lullingfield 79; R Petton w Cockshutt and Weston Lullingfield etc 79-81; V Hadley 81-84; R Ightfield w Calverhall 84-89; V Ash 84-89; R Calton, Cauldon, Grindon and Waterfall 89-96; RD Alstonfield 95-96; rtd 96. *38 Aston Street, Wem, Shrewsbury SY4 5AU*

TYERS, Canon John Haydn. b 31. Lon Univ BSc51 Open Univ BA00. Ridley Hall Cam 53. **d** 55 **p** 56. C Nuneaton St Nic *Cov* 55-58; C Rugby St Andr 58-62; V Cov St Anne 62-71; V Keresley and Coundon 71-78; V Atherstone 78-85; P-in-c Pleshey *Chelmsf* 85-91; Warden Pleshey Retreat Ho 85-91; Hon Can Chelmsf Cathl 86-91; P-in-c Ash *Lich* 91-96; P-in-c Ightfield w Calverhall 91-96; rtd 96; Perm to Offic *Heref* 97-08. *30 Stuart Court, High Street, Kibworth, Leicester LE8 0LR* Tel 0116-279 3093

TYERS, Philip Nicolas. b 56. St Jo Coll Nottm BTh84. **d** 84 **p** 85. C Rugby St Matt *Cov* 84-88; TV Cov E 88-95; P-in-c Preston St Matt *Blackb* 95-96; TR Preston Risen Lord 96-06; Co-ord Chapl HM Pris Leeds 06-07; Co-ord Chapl HM Pris Wymott from 07. *HM Prison Wymott, Ulnes Walton Lane, Leyland PR26 8LW* Tel (01772) 442000

TYLDESLEY, Mrs Vera. b 47. Man Coll of Educn BEd80. **d** 98 **p** 99. OLM Pendlebury St Jo *Man* from 98. *7 Kingsway, Swinton, Manchester M27 4JU* Tel 0161-736 3845

TYLER, Canon Alan William. b 60. Ridley Hall Cam 84. **d** 86 **p** 87. C Bedwellty *Mon* 86-89; C St Mellons and Michaelston-y-Fedw 89-92; V Abersychan and Garndiffaith 92-97; Chapl Glan Hafren NHS Trust 97-99; Sen Chapl Gwent Healthcare NHS Trust from 99; Can St Woolos Cathl from 08. *The Royal Gwent Hospital, Cardiff Road, Newport NP20 2UB* Tel (01633) 234263 *or* 871457 E-mail alan.tyler@gwent.wales.nhs.uk

TYLER, Alison Ruth. b 51. Keele Univ BA74 CQSW78. S'wark Ord Course 93. **d** 95 **p** 96. NSM Hatcham St Cath *S'wark* 95-99; Dep Chapl HM Pris Brixton 99-02; Chapl HM Pris Wormwood Scrubs 02-07; Learning and Development Manager HM Pris Service Chapl from 07; Hon Chapl S'wark Cathl from 06. *Chaplaincy HQ, Room 410 Abell House, John Islip Street, London SW1P 4LH* Tel (020) 7217 8443 *or* 7207 0756 E mail alison.tyler01@hmps.gsi.gov.uk *or* ar.tyler@ntlworld.com

TYLER, Andrew. b 57. Univ of Wales (Lamp) BA79 Warw Univ MA80 Man Univ BD86. Coll of Resurr Mirfield 83. **d** 87 **p** 88. C Glen Parva and S Wigston *Leic* 87-90; C Didcot All SS *Ox* 90-92; Asst Chapl Chu Hosp Ox 92-93; NSM Caversham St Andr *Ox* 93-97; Co-ord Tr Portfolio (Berks) 96-97; P-in-c Nor St Giles 97-99; P-in-c Norwich St Mary Magd w St Jas 99-00; V 00-08; rtd 08; Hon C Eaton Ch Ch *Nor* from 09. *32 Brian Avenue, Norwich NR1 2PH* Tel (01603) 622158 E-mail xatyler@aol.com

TYLER, Brian Sidney. b 32. MIPI79. Chich Th Coll 62. **d** 64 **p** 65. C Brighton St Mich *Chich* 64-69; C-in-c Southwick St Pet 69-75; Perm to Offic 80; NSM Brighton Resurr 93-94; Chapl St Dunstan's Hosp Brighton 93-95; C Brighton St Matthias *Chich* 95-02; Hon C 02-05; rtd 02; Perm to Offic *Chich* from 05. *318 Ditchling Road, Brighton BN1 6JG* Tel (01273) 559292

TYLER, David Stuart. b 69. Hull Univ BSc91 ACA94. Wycliffe Hall Ox 01. **d** 03 **p** 04. C Ashby-de-la-Zouch St Helen w Coleorton *Leic* 03-05; C Ashby-de-la-Zouch and Breedon on the Hill 05-07; P-in-c Hanborough and Freeland *Ox* from 07. *The Rectory, Swan Lane, Long Hanborough, Witney OX29 8BT* Tel (01993) 881270 E-mail revdavidtyler@googlemail.com

TYLER (née FOSTER), Mrs Frances Elizabeth. b 55. Linc Th Coll 84. **dss** 84 **d** 87 **p** 94. Hampton All SS *Lon* 84-87; Par Dn Brentford 87-91; NSM Walsgrave on Sowe *Cov* from 91; Dioc Adv for Women's Min 97-05; Chapl S Warks Gen Hosps NHS Trust from 08. *The Vicarage, 4 Farber Road, Coventry CV2 2BG* Tel (024) 7661 5152 E-mail revtyler@aol.com

TYLER, Mrs Gaynor. b 46. Univ of Wales (Abth) BA68. S'wark Ord Course 87. **d** 90 **p** 94. NSM Reigate St Luke S Park *S'wark*

90-97; Deanery NSM Maelienydd *S & B* 97-04; NSM Cwmdauddwr w St Harmon and Llanwrthwl 04-05; NSM Llanwrthwl w St Harmon, Rhayader, Nantmel etc 05-06; Perm to Offic from 06. *Dyffryn Farm, Llanwrthwl, Llandrindod Wells LD1 6NU* Tel (01597) 811017

TYLER, John Thorne. b 46. Selw Coll Cam BA68 MA71. Sarum & Wells Th Coll 70. **d** 72 **p** 73. C Frome St Jo *B & W* 72-74; Chapl Huish Coll Taunton 74-93; Hon C Stoke St Gregory w Burrowbridge and Lyng *B & W* 77-93; P-in-c Shepton Beauchamp w Barrington, Stocklinch etc 93-94; TV Ilminster and Distr 94-98; rtd 99; Hon C Quantock Towers *B & W* 99-01; P-in-c Stogursey w Fiddington 01-06; Perm to Offic 06-09; C Chard St Mary from 09; C Combe St Nicholas w Wambrook from 09; C Whitestaunton from 09. *24 Ganges Close, Fivehead, Taunton TA3 6PG* Tel (01460) 281574 E-mail tyleruk@hotmail.com

TYLER, The Ven Leonard George. b 20. Liv Univ BA41 Ch Coll Cam BA46 MA50. Westcott Ho Cam. **d** 43 **p** 44. C Toxteth Park Ch Ch *Liv* 43-44; Ceylon 46-50; R Bradford cum Beswick *Man* 50-55; V Leigh St Mary 55-66; RD Leigh 57-62; Adn Rochdale 62-66; Prin Wm Temple Coll 66-73; R Easthampstead *Ox* 73-85; rtd 85; Perm to Offic *Ox* from 85. *11 Ashton Place, Kintbury, Hungerford RG17 9XS* Tel (01488) 658510

TYLER, Malcolm. b 56. Kent Univ BSc77 Cam Univ BA84. Ridley Hall Cam 82. **d** 85 **p** 86. C Twickenham St Mary *Lon* 85-88; C Acton St Mary 88-91; V Walsgrave on Sowe *Cov* from 91; AD Cov E from 07. *The Vicarage, 4 Farber Road, Coventry CV2 2BG* Tel (024) 7661 5152 *or* 7661 8845 E-mail stmaryssowe@aol.com

TYLER, Samuel John. b 32. Lon Univ BD57. Oak Hill Th Coll 57. **d** 58 **p** 59. C W Ham All SS *Chelmsf* 58-61; V Berechurch 61-64; R Aythorpe w High and Leaden Roding 64-72; Perm to Offic 73-74; P-in-c Gt Ilford St Jo 74-76; V 76-92; rtd 92. *21 Ash Green, Canewdon, Rochford SS4 3QN* Tel (01702) 258526

TYLER (née WAITE), Mrs Sheila Margaret. b 25. SRN47. Trin Coll Bris 71. **dss** 79 **d** 87 **p** 94. Eastcn H Trin w St Gabr and St Lawr *Bris* 79-80; Westbury-on-Trym St Alb 81-85; rtd 85; Hon Par Dn Henleaze *Bris* 87-94; Hon C 94-95; Chapl Stoke Park and Purdown Hosps Stapleton 88-90; Perm to Offic *Bris* 95-08; *B & W* 95-00; *Chich* 01-02. *6 Gracey Court, Woodland Road, Broadclyst, Exeter EX5 3GA* Tel (01392) 462872

TYNDALL, Daniel Frank. b 61. Aston Tr Scheme 90 Sarum & Wells Th Coll BTh93. **d** 93 **p** 94. C Wolverhampton *Lich* 93-96; C Bris St Mary Redcliffe w Temple etc 96-01; V Earley St Nic *Ox* 01-08; P-in-c Caversham St Pet and Mapledurham from 08. *St John's Vicarage, St John's Road, Caversham, Reading RG4 5AN* Tel 0118-947 1814 E-mail dftyndall@googlemail.com

TYNDALL, Mrs Elizabeth Mary. b 30. St Andr Univ MA51 Hughes Hall Cam CertEd52. Qu Coll Birm 81. **dss** 83 **d** 87 **p** 94. Rugby *Cov* 83-87; Par Dn Feltham *Lon* 87-91; rtd 92; NSM Vale of White Horse Deanery *Ox* 93-03. *clo The Revd D F Tyndall, St John's Vicarage, St John's Road, Caversham, Reading RG4 5AN* Tel 0118-947 1814

TYNDALL, Jeremy Hamilton. b 55. Birm Univ MPhil01. St Jo Coll Nottm BTh81 LTh81. **d** 81 **p** 82. C Oakwood St Thos *Lon* 81-84; C Upper Holloway St Pet w St Jo 84-87; TV Halewood *Liv* 87-96; P-in-c Yardley St Edburgha *Birm* 96-99; V 99-01; R Eugene St Thos USA 01-08; Dean Cen Convocation 06-08; TR Cove St Jo *Guildf* from 08. *The Rectory, 55 Cove Road, Farnborough GU14 0EX* Tel (01252) 544544 E-mail rector@parishofcove.org.uk

TYNDALL, Simon James. b 54. LSE BSc(Econ)77 Lon Univ PGCE82 Open Univ MA98. St Jo Coll Nottm 88. **d** 90 **p** 91. C Yeovil w Kingston Pitney *B & W* 90-94; V Rastrick St Jo *Wakef* 94-01; TR Chippenham St Paul w Hardenhuish etc *Bris* from 01; V Kington St Michael from 01; AD Chippenham from 08. *The Rectory, 9 Greenway Park, Chippenham SN15 1QG* Tel (01249) 657216 E-mail simon@tyndall.plus.com

TYNDALL, Canon Timothy Gardner. b 25. Jes Coll Cam BA50. Wells Th Coll 50. **d** 51 **p** 52. C Warsop *S'well* 51-55; R Newark St Leon 55-60; V Sherwood 60-75; P-in-c Bishopwearmouth St Mich w St Hilda *Dur* 75-85; RD Wearmouth 75-85; Hon Can Dur Cathl 83-90; Chief Sec ACCM 85-90; rtd 90; Perm to Offic *Lon* and *S'wark* from 90. *29 Kingswood Road, London W4 5EU* Tel (020) 8994 4516

TYNEY, Canon James Derrick. b 33. TCD. **d** 62 **p** 63. C Ballynafeigh St Jude *D & D* 62-64; C Bangor St Comgall 64-69; I Clonallon w Warrenpoint 69-75; I Groomsport 75-00; Can Belf Cathl 93-00; Dioc Registrar *D & D* 95-00; rtd 00. *27 Sandringham Drive, Bangor BT20 5NA* Tel (028) 9145 5670

TYRER, Ms Jayne Linda. b 59. Goldsmiths' Coll Lon BA81 CertEd82. Sarum & Wells Th Coll 85. **d** 87 **p** 95. C Rochdale *Man* 87-88; Par Dn Heywood St Luke w All So 88-91; Hon Par Dn Burneside *Carl* 91-07; Hon Par Dn Beacon from 07; Chapl Kendal Hosps 91-94; Chapl Westmorland Hosps NHS Trust 94-98; Chapl Morecambe Bay Hosps NHS Trust from 98. *St Oswald's Vicarage, Burneside, Kendal LA9 6QX* Tel (01539) 722015 E-mail jayne.tyrer@wgh.mbht.nhs.uk

TYREUS, Per Jonas Waldemar (Peter). b 45. Uppsala Univ 66. p 71. Sweden 71-00; C Pelton *Dur* 00-03; C Chester le Street from 03. *16 Park Road North, Chester le Street DH3 3SD* Tel 0191-388 6801 E-mail peter@petertyreus.plus.com

TYRREL, John Cockett. b 16. Qu Coll Cam BA38 MA42. Ridley Hall Cam 38. **d** 40 **p** 41. C Southall H Trin *Lon* 40-43; Chapl RNVR 43-46; S Africa 46-50; Australia from 50; rtd 81; Perm to Offic Canberra and Goulburn from 81. *20/58 Shackleton Circuit, Mawson ACT 2607, Australia* Tel (0061) (2) 6286 1317

TYRRELL, The Very Revd Charles Robert. b 51. SRN73 Open Univ BA80. Oak Hill Th Coll 74. **d** 77 **p** 78. C Halewood *Liv* 77-80; C St Helens St Helen 80-83; V Banks 83-88; New Zealand from 88; Can Wellington 88-94; Dean Nelson from 94. *The Deanery, 365 Trafalgar Street, Nelson 7010, New Zealand* Tel (0064) (3) 548 8574 *or* 548 1008 E-mail charles.tyrell@clear.net.nz

TYRRELL, John Patrick Hammond. b 42. Cranmer Hall Dur 62. **d** 65 **p** 66. C Edin St Jo 65-68; Chapl RN 68-72; Chapl St John's Cathl Hong Kong 72-74 and 78-82; Area Sec SE Asia SOMA UK 78-82; V Westborough *Guildf* 74-78; C Yateley *Win* 82-83; C-in-c Darby Green CD 83-88; V Darby Green 88-96; V Chineham 96-97; rtd 02; Perm to Offic *Linc* from 06. *5 Blacksmith's Court, Metheringham, Lincoln LN4 3YQ* Tel (01526) 322147 E-mail john_tyrrell42@hotmail.com

TYRRELL, Stephen Jonathan. b 39. Sheff Univ BA62. Clifton Th Coll. **d** 65 **p** 66. C Rodbourne Cheney *Bris* 65-68; C Lillington *Cov* 68-72; P-in-c Bishop's Itchington 73-78; V 78-86; V Kingston upon Hull St Nic *York* 86-92; TV Cheltenham St Mary, St Matt, St Paul and H Trin *Glouc* 92-04; rtd 04; Perm to Offic *Glouc* from 05. *96A Fosseway Avenue, Moreton-in-Marsh GL56 0EA* Tel (01608) 812350

TYSOE, James Raymond. b 19. Qu Coll Birm 70. **d** 75 **p** 76. NSM Cov E 75-85; NSM Cov Cathl 85-87; Perm to Offic *Glouc* from 87. *Wisma Mulia, Bridge Road, Frampton on Severn, Gloucester GL2 7HE* Tel (01452) 740890

TYSON, Mrs Frances Mary. b 44. Reading Univ BScAgr68 Wolv Univ PGCE91. St Jo Coll Nottm 01. **d** 02 **p** 03. NSM Walsall *Lich* 02-07; NSM Portswood Ch Ch *Win* from 07. *26 Reynolds Road, Southampton SO15 5GS*

TYSON, Mrs Nigella Jane. b 44. RGN66 Kent Univ BA95. SEITE 96. **d** 97 **p** 98. NSM Aylesham w Adisham, Nonington w Wymynswold and Goodnestone etc *Cant* 97-00; P-in-c Kingsland w Eardisland, Aymestrey etc *Heref* 00-04; R from 04. *The Rectory, Kingsland, Leominster HR6 9QW* Tel (01568) 708255 Fax 08701-324310 E-mail nigella@kingslandgroup.org.uk

TYSON, Canon William Edward Porter. b 25. St Cath Coll Cam BA49 MA52. Ridley Hall Cam 49. **d** 51 **p** 52. C Wilmslow *Ches* 51-54; C Astbury 54-57; V Macclesfield St Pet 57-62; V Over Tabley 62-70; V High Legh 62-70; CF (TA) 64-91; V Church Hulme *Ches* 70-91; Chapl Cranage Hall Hosp 70-91; Hon Can Ches Cathl 82-91; RD Congleton 85-90; rtd 91; Perm to Offic *Ches* and *Carl* from 91. *59 Kirkhead Road, Allithwaite, Grange-over-Sands LA11 7DD* Tel (01539) 535291

TÄRNEBERG, Helene. *See* STEED, Mrs Helene

U

UDAL, Canon Joanna Elizabeth Margaret. b 64. SS Hild & Bede Coll Dur BSc86. Ripon Coll Cuddesdon BTh94. **d** 97 **p** 98. C Whitton St Aug *Lon* 97-00; Asst to Abp Sudan 00-09; Abp's Sec for Angl Communion Affairs *Cant* from 09. *Lambeth Palace, London SE1 7JU* Tel (020) 7898 1400 E-mail joanna.udal@c-of-e.org.uk

UDDIN, Mohan. b 52. Sussex Univ BA74 PGCE75 Lon Bible Coll MA87 Brunel Univ PhD98 Anglia Poly Univ MA02. Ridley Hall Cam 99. **d** 03 **p** 04. C Hornchurch St Andr *Chelmsf* 03-07; Perm to Offic from 08. *55A Chelmsford Drive, Upminster RM14 2PH* Tel (01708) 452705 E-mail mohan.uddin@btopenworld.com

UFFINDELL, David Wilfred George. b 37. Qu Coll Birm 72. **d** 75 **p** 76. NSM Harlescott *Lich* 75-07; Perm to Offic from 08. *13 Kenley Avenue, Heath Farm, Shrewsbury SY1 3HA* Tel and fax (01743) 352029 E-mail revuffindell@talktalk.net

UFFINDELL, Harold David. b 61. Down Coll Cam MA87. Wycliffe Hall Ox BA86 MA91 Oak Hill Th Coll 86. **d** 87 **p** 88. C Kingston Hill St Paul *S'wark* 87-91; C Surbiton St Matt 91-98; V Sunningdale *Ox* from 98. *The Vicarage, Sidbury Close, Sunningdale, Ascot SL5 0PD* Tel (01344) 620061 E-mail david@htpcsunn.freeserve.co.uk

UGANDA, Archbishop of. *See* OROMBI, The Most Revd Henry Luke

UGWUNNA, Sydney Chukwunma. b 45. Nebraska Wesleyan Univ BSc67 Univ of Nebraska, Linc MSc70 Wayne State Univ PhD79. Virginia Th Sem MDiv96. **d** 96 **p** 97. USA 96-98; C Knaresborough *Ripon* 98-02; Nigeria from 02. *St Stephen's Cathedral, Umuahia, Nigeria*

ULLMANN, Clair. *See* FILBERT-ULLMANN, Mrs Clair

ULOGWARA, Canon Obinna Chiadikobi. b 68. Univ of Nigeria BA(Ed)98 Lagos Univ MEd03. Trin Coll Umuahia 87. **d** 90 **p** 91. V Ahiara H Trin Nigeria 90-93; Chapl Secondary Schs Dio Mbaise 90-93; V Irete St Pet 93-95; Chapl Secondary Schs Dio Owerri 94-99; V Egbeada Em 99; V Sari Iganmu St Phil 00-01; V Igbobi St Steph and Hon Chapl to Abp Lagos 01-05; C Dublin Whitechurch *D & G* from 05. *1 Woodstown Heath, Ballycullen Road, Dublin 16, Republic of Ireland* Tel and fax (00353) (1) 495 8710 Mobile 87-247 6339 E-mail binagwara@yahoo.com

UMPLEBY, Mark Raymond. b 70. Trin Coll Bris BA99. **d** 99 **p** 00. C Birstall *Wakef* 99-02; TV N Huddersfield 02-06; Dioc Voc Adv 04-06; Chapl David Young Community Academy Leeds from 06. *David Young Community Academy, North Parkway, Leeds LS14 6RF* E-mail markumpleby@hotmail.com

UNDERDOWN, Margaret Jean (Meg). b 49. Univ of Wales (Abth) BSc70. St Mich Coll Llan 06. **d** 08 **p** 09. Chapl HM Pris Cardiff from 03. *HM Prison Cardiff, 1 Knox Road, Cardiff CF24 0UG* Tel (029) 2092 3100

UNDERDOWN, Steven. Hull Univ BSc75 CertEd76 K Coll Lon PhD02. **d** 88 **p** 04. CSWG 82-02; NSM Hove *Chich* from 03; Chapl Brighton and Sussex Univ Hosps NHS Trust from 03. *29 Brunswick Place, Hove BN3 1ND* Tel (01273) 747889 *or* (01243) 696955 Mobile 07981-423973 E-mail steven.underdown@hotmail.com *or* steven.underdown@bsuh.nhs.uk

UNDERHILL, Edward Mark Thomas. b 24. Univ Coll Dur BA50. St Aid Birkenhead 50. **d** 52 **p** 53. C Meopham *Roch* 52-54; Prin Kigari Coll Kenya 55-57; PC Gateshead St Geo *Dur* 57-68; V from 68. *St George's Vicarage, 327 Durham Road, Gateshead NE9 5AJ* Tel 0191-487 5587

UNDERHILL, Robin. b 31. Marymount Coll California BA89 Woodbury Univ California BSc90. Claremont Sch of Th MA92. **d** 93 **p** 94. Asst P Beverly Hills All SS USA 93-00; Pastor San Fernando St Simon 00-01; rtd 01; P-in-c Stranraer and Portpatrick *Glas* 01-04; Sec for Scotland Miss to Seafarers from 04. *Tigh Ban, Hightae, Lockerbie DG11 1JN* Tel (01387) 811112 Mobile 07800-798483 E-mail mts_scotland@onetel.com

UNDERHILL, Stanley Robert. b 27. Cant Sch of Min. **d** 82 **p** 83. C New Addington *Cant* 82-84; C Cannock *Lich* 84-86; TV 86-88; R Dymchurch w Burmarsh and Newchurch *Cant* 88-92; rtd 92; Chapl Menorca *Eur* 92-94; Perm to Offic *Cant* 94-04 and *Lon* 05-08. *Charterhouse, Charterhouse Square, London EC1M 6AN* Tel (020) 7490 5059 Mobile 07970-954958 E-mail stanunder@aol.com

UNDERWOOD, Adrian Anthony. b 67. **d** 02 **p** 03. C Sparkhill w Greet and Sparkbrook *Birm* 02-06; C Selly Park St Steph and St Wulstan from 06. *119 Selly Park Road, Selly Park, Birmingham B29 7HY* Tel 0121-777 6093 Mobile 07752-001698

UNDERWOOD, Brian. b 35. Dur Univ BA57 Keble Coll Ox PGCE76 Dur Univ MA72. Clifton Th Coll 57. **d** 59 **p** 60. C Blackpool Ch Ch *Blackb* 59-61; C New Malden and Coombe *S'wark* 61-64; Travel Sec Pathfinders 64-68; Chapl Chantilly *Eur* 68-69; Home Sec CCCS 69-71; P-in-c Gatten St Paul *Portsm* 71-72; Chapl Lyon w Grenoble and Aix-les-Bains *Eur* 72-75; Asst Chapl Trent Coll Nottm 76-80; Chapl Qu Eliz Gr Sch Blackb 80-85; R Bentham St Jo *Bradf* 85-92; V St Alb Ch Ch *St Alb* 92-00; rtd 00; Perm to Offic *St Alb* from 00. *16 Mitford Close, Bedford MK41 8RF* Tel (01234) 407856

UNDERWOOD, Charles Brian. b 23. Leeds Univ BA48 CertEd. Coll of Resurr Mirfield 48. **d** 50 **p** 51. C Tilehurst St Mich *Ox* 50-53; C Leic St Paul 53-54; Youth Chapl 54-61; V Leic St Geo 57-59; R Harby 59-61; New Zealand 61-62; Dioc Youth Chapl *Bradf* 63-72; R Carleton-in-Craven 63-76; V Twyning *Glouc* 76-88; RD Tewkesbury 81-88; rtd 88; Perm to Offic *Glouc* from 00. *Chavender, 9 Ellendene Drive, Pamington, Tewkesbury GL20 8LU* Tel (01684) 772504 E-mail brian@chavender.fsnet.co.uk

UNDERWOOD, David Richard. b 47. AKC69 St Osyth Coll of Educn PGCE72. St Aug Coll Cant 69. **d** 70 **p** 92. C Witham *Chelmsf* 70-71; Teacher 71-82; Hd Teacher Gt Heath Sch Mildenhall 82-91; NSM Chevington w Hargrave and Whepstead w Brockley *St E* 82-91; Par Dn Haverhill w Withersfield, the Wrattings etc 91-92; TV 92-94; P-in-c Bury St Edmunds St Jo 94-99; RD Thingoe 95-99; P-in-c Bury St Edmunds St Geo 98-99; Dioc Dir of Educn 99-04; Hon Can St E Cathl 03-04; rtd 07. *1 Green Farm Close, Lilbourne, Rugby CV23 0TE* Tel (01788) 860833 E-mail davidunderwood2@aol.com

UNDERWOOD, John Alan. b 40. Glos Coll of Arts & Tech BSc88 Ox Poly CertEd84 MBCS74. SAOMC 96. **d** 99 **p** 00. OLM Eynsham and Cassington *Ox* from 99. *17 Witney Road,*

Eynsham, Oxford OX29 4PH Tel (01865) 881254 *or* 301305 Fax 301301 E-mail junderw549@aol.com

UNDERWOOD, Mrs Susannah Lucy. b 72. Westmr Coll Ox BTh98. ERMC 05. **d** 08 **p** 09. C Stevenage H Trin *St Alb* from 08. *3 Glebe Road, Welwyn AL6 9PB* Tel (01438) 367246 E-mail curate@holytrinity-stevenage.info

UNGOED-THOMAS, Peter. b 27. Pemb Coll Ox BA51 MA67. St Mich Coll Llan. **d** 60 **p** 61. C Llangeinor *Llan* 60-64; I Dublin Donnybrook *D & G* 64-67; RAChD 67-70; Chapl Leigh C of E Schs 70-74; C Leigh St Mary *Man* 70-74; Lect Warley Coll 74-86; Perm to Offic *Birm* 75-00 and *St D* from 75; Lect Sandwell Coll of F&HE from 86; rtd 94. *93 Heol Felin-Foel, Llanelli SA15 3JQ*

UNITED STATES OF AMERICA, Presiding Bishop of. *See* JEFFERTS SCHORI, The Most Revd Katharine

UNSWORTH, Philip James. b 41. UEA BEd82 Nottm Coll of Educn CertEd63 Nottm Univ DipEd72. EAMTC 94. **d** 97 **p** 98. NSM Hethersett w Canteloff w Lt and Gt Melton *Nor* 97-00; P-in-c Blofield w Hemblington 00-06; rtd 06; Perm to Offic *Nor* from 06. *55 Campbell Close, Hunstanton PE36 5PJ* Tel (01485) 532436

UNSWORTH, Thomas Foster. b 28. Lon Univ BA56. Lich Th Coll 60. **d** 62 **p** 63. C Northfield *Birm* 62-64; C The Lickey 64-66; V Forcett *Ripon* 66-68; V Bellerby and Leyburn 68-73; Chapl Whittingham Hosp Preston 73-79; V Freckleton *Blackb* 79-83; V S Yardley St Mich *Birm* 83-86; V Sutton w Carlton and Normanton upon Trent etc *S'well* 86-90; rtd 90; Chapl St Raphaël *Eur* 90-97; Perm to Offic *Cant* from 99. *31 Broadlands Avenue, New Romney TN28 8JE* Tel (01797) 361922

UNWIN, Barry. b 70. Sheff Univ BA91. Oak Hill Th Coll BA05. **d** 05 **p** 06. C Hebburn St Jo *Dur* 05-09; C Jarrow Grange 05-09; P-in-c New Barnet St Jas *St Alb* from 09. *St James' Vicarage, 11 Park Road, Barnet EN4 9QA* Tel (020) 8449 4043 E-mail barryunwin@gmail.com

UNWIN, Christopher Michael Fairclough. b 31. Dur Univ BA57. Linc Th Coll 65. **d** 67 **p** 68. C S Shields St Hilda w St Thos *Dur* 67-73; R Tatsfield *S'wark* 73-81; RE Adv to Ch Secondary Schs 73-81; V Newc St Gabr 81-96; RD Newc E 96; rtd 96; Perm to Offic *Dur* and *Newc* from 96. *2 The Cottage, West Row, Greatham, Hartlepool TS25 2HW* Tel (01429) 872781

UNWIN, The Ven Kenneth. b 26. St Edm Hall Ox BA48 MA52. Ely Th Coll 49. **d** 51 **p** 52. C Leeds All SS *Ripon* 51-55; C Dur St Marg 55-59; V Dodworth *Wakef* 59-69; V Royston 69-73; V Wakef St Jo 73-82; Hon Can Wakef Cathl 80-82; RD Wakef 80-81; Adn Pontefract 82-92; rtd 92; Perm to Offic *Bradf* and *Wakef* from 92. *2 Rockwood Close, Skipton BD23 1UG* Tel (01756) 791323

UNWIN, Michael. *See* UNWIN, Christopher Michael Fairclough

UPCOTT, Derek Jarvis. b 26. CEng FIMechE FBIM. S'wark Ord Course 81. **d** 84 **p** 85. NSM Gt Chesham *Ox* 84-99; Perm to Offic *St Alb* 90-99 and *Ox* from 99. *Bluff Cottage, Blackthorne Lane, Ballinger, Great Missenden HP16 9LN* Tel (01494) 837505 E-mail derek.upcott@activelives.co.uk

UPHILL, Ms Ann Carol. b 54. Westcott Ho Cam 95. **d** 97 **p** 98. C Strood St Nic w St Mary *Roch* 97-01; R Footscray w N Cray from 01. *The Rectory, Rectory Lane, Sidcup DA14 5BP* Tel and fax (020) 8300 7096 Mobile 07802-883121 E-mail ann.uphill@diocese-rochester.org *or* annuphill@lineone.net

UPHILL, Keith Ivan. b 35. Keble Coll Ox BA70 MA74. Wycliffe Hall Ox 67. **d** 70 **p** 71. C Wroxall *Liv* 70-73; V Wroxall *Portsm* 73-77; TV Fareham H Trin 77-82; C Havant 82-84; P-in-c Merton St Jo *S'wark* 84-85; V 85-95; rtd 95; Perm to Offic *Portsm* from 95. *20 Wiley Lane, Anchorage Park, Portsmouth PO3 5UF* Tel (023) 9266 6998

UPPER SHIRE, Bishop of. *See* MALANGO, The Most Revd Bernard Amos

UPTON, Anthony Arthur. b 30. Leic Univ MA97 PhD03. Wells Th Coll 61. **d** 63 **p** 64. C Milton *Portsm* 63-67; Chapl RN 67-83; V Foleshill St Laur *Cov* 83-91; rtd 91; Perm to Offic *Cov* from 91. *Redlands Bungalow, Banbury Road, Lighthorne CV35 0AH*

UPTON, Ms Caroline Tracey. b 67. Lon Univ BMus90 Edin Univ BD94. Edin Th Coll 91. **d** 94 **p** 95. C Edin St Martin 94-96; Hon C Edin St Pet 97-99; C 99-01; Chapl Lothian Univ Hosps NHS Trust from 01. *10 (3F1) Montagu Terrace, Edinburgh EH3 5QX* Tel 0131-552 0731 *or* 536 0144 E-mail carrie.upton@luht.scot.nhs.uk

UPTON, Mrs Christina Phoebe. b 61. Man Univ MB, ChB85 Ches Univ MTh04 MRCPsych93. NOC 06. **d** 08 **p** 09. C W Kirby St Bridget *Ches* from 08. *Priory Lodge, Ford Road, Wirral CH49 0TD* Tel 0151-488 5290 E-mail tina.upton@tesco.net

UPTON, Christopher Martin. b 53. Bp Grosseteste Coll CertEd74. EAMTC 94. **d** 97 **p** 98. NSM Gorleston St Andr *Nor* 97-05; NSM Bradwell from 05. *27 Curlew Way, Bradwell, Great Yarmouth NR31 8QX* Tel (01493) 668184 E-mail rev.martin.upton@talk21.com

UPTON, Clement Maurice. b 49. Linc Th Coll 88. **d** 90 **p** 91. C

Northampton St Alb *Pet* 90-93; V Laxey and Lonan *S & M* 93-96; V Hipswell *Ripon* 96-01; V Wellingborough St Andr *Pet* from 01; Chapl Northants Police from 05. *St Andrew's Vicarage, Berrymoor Road, Wellingborough NN8 2HU* Tel (01933) 222692 E-mail clem7@btopenworld.com

UPTON, Ms Julie. b 61. Ripon Coll Cuddesdon 87. **d** 88 **p** 94. C Kirkstall *Ripon* 88-91; Par Dn E Greenwich Ch w St Andr and St Mich *S'wark* 91-94; C 94; Perm to Offic *S'wark* 01-03 and *St E* 02-03; NSM Manningham *Bradf* 03-04; TV Bramley *Ripon* from 04. *St Margaret's Vicarage, Newlay Lane, Leeds LS13 2AJ* Tel 0113-257 4811

UPTON, Martin. *See* UPTON, Christopher Martin

UPTON, Michael Gawthorne. b 29. AKC53. **d** 54 **p** 55. C Middleton *Man* 54-57; C Plymouth St Andr *Ex* 57-59; Dep Dir of Educn *Cant* 59-63; Hon C Riverhead *Roch* 63-70; Youth Chapl 63-70; Lic to Offic *Ex* 70-94; Chr Aid Area Sec (Devon and Cornwall) 70-94; Chr Aid SW Region Co-ord 73-89; rtd 94; Perm to Offic *Ex* from 94. *Otter Dell, Harpford, Sidmouth EX10 0NH* Tel (01395) 568448

UPTON, Mrs Susan Dorothy. b 53. Bp Grosseteste Coll CertEd74 Nottm Univ BEd75. EAMTC 99. **d** 02 **p** 03. NSM Bradwell *Nor* from 02. *27 Curlew Way, Bradwell, Great Yarmouth NR31 8QX* Tel (01493) 668184 E-mail sue-upton@talk21.com

UPTON-JONES, Peter John. b 38. Selw Coll Cam BA63 MA67 Liv Univ CertEd64. NOC 90. **d** 92 **p** 93. NSM Formby H Trin *Liv* 92-00; P-in-c Lezayre St Olave Ramsey *S & M* 00-03; V 03-08; P-in-c Kirkbride 00-03; R 03-08; rtd 08. *Clock Cottage, Glen Road, Colby, Isle of Man IM9 4NT* Tel (01624) 830216 E-mail peteru_j@hotmail.com

URMSON-TAYLOR, Ralph. *See* TAYLOR, Ralph Urmson

✠**URQUHART, The Rt Revd David Andrew.** b 52. Ealing Business Sch BA77. Wycliffe Hall Ox 82. **d** 84 **p** 85 **c** 00. C Kingston upon Hull St Nic *York* 84-87; TV Drypool 87-92; V Cov H Trin 92-00; Hon Can Cov Cathl 99-00; Suff Bp Birkenhead *Ches* 00-06; Bp Birm from 06. *Bishop's Croft, Old Church Road, Birmingham B17 0BG* Tel 0121-427 1163 Fax 426 1322 E-mail bishop@birmingham.anglican.org

URQUHART, Canon Edmund Ross. b 39. Univ Coll Ox BA62 MA68. St Steph Ho Ox 62. **d** 64 **p** 65. C Milton *Win* 64-69; C Norton *Derby* 69-73; V Bakewell 73-05; RD Bakewell and Eyam 95-04; Hon Can Derby Cathl 02-05; rtd 05; Perm to Offic *Derby* from 05 and *Lich* from 08. *1 Hambleton Close, Ashbourne DE6 1NG* Tel (01335) 346454

URQUHART, Ian Garnham. b 46. Univ Coll Lon LLB71. Wycliffe Hall Ox 98. **d** 99 **p** 00. C Barnston *Ches* from 99. *8 Antons Road, Wirral CH61 9PT* Tel 0151-648 1512 Fax 648 2402 Mobile 07770-823373 E-mail ian@papintalo.co.uk

URSELL, David John. b 45. MRAC70. SWMTC 92. **d** 95 **p** 96. NSM Dolton *Ex* from 95; Rural Convenor from 95. *Aller Farm, Dolton, Winkleigh EX19 8PP* Tel (01805) 804414 *or* 804737 E-mail ursell@farmersweekly.net

URSELL, Canon Philip Elliott. b 42. Univ of Wales BA66 Ox Univ MA82 Nashotah Ho Wisconsin DD08. St Steph Ho Ox 66. **d** 68 **p** 69. C Newton Nottage *Llan* 68-71; Asst Chapl Univ of Wales (Cardiff) 71-77; Chapl Wales Poly 74-77; Lic to Offic *Llan* 77-97; Chapl Em Coll Cam 77-82; Prin Pusey Ho 82-03; Warden Ascot Priory from 85; Lic to Offic *Ox* from 82; Can Rio Grande from 05. *St Edward's, Ascot Priory, Priory Road, Ascot SL5 8RT* Tel (01344) 885157 E-mail peu@cantab.net

✠**URWIN, The Rt Revd Lindsay Goodall.** b 56. Heythrop Coll Lon MA03. Ripon Coll Cuddesdon 77. **d** 80 **p** 81 **c** 93. C Walworth *S'wark* 80-83; V N Dulwich St Faith 83-88; Dioc Missr *Chich* 88-93; Area Bp Horsham 93-09; Can and Preb Chich Cathl 93-09; P Admin Shrine of Our Lady of Walsingham from 09; Hon Asst Bp Nor from 09; Hon Asst Bp Chich from 09; OGS from 91; Provost Woodard Corp (S Division) from 06. *The College, Knight Street, Walsingham NR22 6EF* Tel (01328) 824204 E-mail pr.adm@olw-shrine.org.uk

URWIN, Preb Roger Talbot. b 22. Ex Coll Ox BA43 MA47. Sarum Th Coll 48. **d** 50 **p** 50. C Weymouth H Trin *Sarum* 50-53; V Netheravon w Fittleton 53-57; CF (R of O) 56-77; V Townstall w Dartmouth *Ex* 57-66; V Dartmouth St Petrox 58-66; RD Ipplepen 61-66; V Littleham w Exmouth 66-72; TR 72-87; RD Aylesbeare 69-73; P-in-c Withycombe Raleigh 72-74; Preb Ex Cathl 82-87; rtd 87; Perm to Offic *Truro* from 87. *Bishop's Lodge, Kelly Park, St Mabyn, Bodmin PL30 3RL* Tel (01208) 841606

USHER, George. b 30. Univ of Wales (Swansea) BSc51. St Deiniol's Hawarden 73. **d** 75 **p** 76. NSM Clun w Chapel Lawn *Heref* 75-78; NSM Clun w Chapel Lawn, Bettws-y-Crwyn and Newcastle 79-80; C Shrewsbury St Giles *Lich* 80-83; C Shrewsbury St Giles w Sutton and Atcham 83-84; R Credenhill w Brinsop and Wormsley etc *Heref* 84-89; rtd 98; Perm to Offic *Ex* from 02. *1 Trinity Court, The Esplanade, Sidmouth EX10 8BE* Tel (01395) 513889 E-mail georgeusher@clara.net

USHER, Canon Graham Barham. b 70. Edin Univ BSc93 CCC Cam BA95 MA00. Westcott Ho Cam 93 St Nic Th Coll Ghana 96. **d** 96 **p** 97. C Nunthorpe *York* 96-99; V N Ormesby 99-04; R Hexham *Newc* from 04; AD Hexham from 06; Hon Can Kumasi

Ghana from 07. *The Rectory, Eilansgate, Hexham NE46 3EW*
Tel (01434) 603121 *or* 602031
E-mail rector@hexhamabbey.org.uk

USHER, Robin Reginald. b 50. AKC74. St Aug Coll Cant 75. **d** 76
p 77. C Hulme Ascension *Man* 76-80; P-in-c Newall Green
St Fran 80-85; C Atherton 85-87; TV 87-90; V Leigh St Jo 90-99;
Chapl Wigan and Leigh Health Services NHS Trust 93-99; V
Milnrow *Man* from 99. *The Vicarage, 40 Eafield Avenue,
Milnrow, Rochdale OL16 3 UN* Tel (01706) 642988
E-mail milnrow.parishchurch@zen.co.uk

USHER-WILSON, Lucian Neville. b 36. Linc Coll Ox MA63 St
Andr Univ DipEd64 Open Univ BA75. St Steph Ho Ox 91. **d** 94
p 96. NSM Compton and Otterbourne *Win* 94-96; NSM Shill
Valley and Broadshire *Ox* from 96. *The Tallat, Westwell, Burford
OX18 4JT* Tel (01993) 822464 E-mail neville.uw@virgin.net

UTLEY, Canon Edward Jacob. b 24. AKC52. **d** 53 **p** 54. C
Pontefract St Giles *Wakef* 53-56; C Bexhill St Pet *Chich* 56-60;
Chapl Asst Bexhill Hosp 56-60; Chapl Dudley Road Hosp *Birm*
60-89; RD Birm City 75-82; Hon Can Birm Cathl 80-89; rtd 89;
Perm to Offic *Birm* from 89. *36 Silverthorne Road, Tamworth B79 8BA* Tel (01827) 59647

UTTLEY, Mrs Valerie Gail. b 43. Man Univ BA64. NOC 80.
dss 83 **d** 87 **p** 94. Otley *Bradf* 83-87; Hon Par Dn 87-89; Par Dn
Calverley 89-92; Ind Chapl *Ripon* 92-97; C Kirkstall 95-97; V
Lofthouse from 97. *The Vicarage, 8 Church Farm Close,
Lofthouse, Wakefield WF3 3SA* Tel (01924) 823286
E-mail gailuttley@yahoo.co.uk

V

VAIL, David William. b 30. Dur Univ BA56 Sheff Univ DipEd71.
Oak Hill Th Coll 56. **d** 58 **p** 59. C Toxteth Park St Bede *Liv*
58-61; Kenya 61-77; Chapl Versailles *Eur* 77-82; Gen Sec
Rwanda Miss 82-88; V Virginia Water *Guildf* 88-96; rtd 96; Perm
to Offic *Ox* from 98. *36 Silverthorne Drive, Caversham, Reading
RG4 7NS* Tel 0118-954 6667

VAIZEY, Martin John. b 37. AKC64. **d** 65 **p** 66. C
Bishopwearmouth Gd Shep *Dur* 65-69; C Darlington H Trin
69-72; V Easington Colliery 72-80; C-in-c Bishopwearmouth
St Mary V w St Pet CD 80-85; V Sunderland Springwell w
Thorney Close 85-88; R Witton Gilbert 88-96; P-in-c Wingate
Grange 96-99; V Wheatley Hill and Wingate w Hutton Henry
99-07; rtd 07. *2 Etherley Lane, Bishop Auckland DL14 7QR*

VALE, Thomas Stanley George. b 52. Chich Th Coll 85. **d** 87 **p** 88.
C Leic St Phil 87-90; C Knighton St Mary Magd 90-93; P-in-c
Leic St Chad 93-97; V 97-01; V Blackfordby and Woodville from
01. *The Vicarage, 11 Vicarage Close, Blackfordby, Swadlincote
DE11 8AZ* Tel (01283) 211310
E-mail tvale@webleicester.co.uk

VALENTINE, Derek William. b 24. S'wark Ord Course 65. **d** 68
p 69. NSM Battersea St Luke *S'wark* 68-77; NSM Fenstanton
Ely 77-88; Perm to Offic *Bradf* 88-96. *Address withheld by request*

VALENTINE, Hugh William James. b 56. Bradf Univ BA83
CQSW. S'wark Ord Course 86. **d** 89 **p** 90. NSM Stoke
Newington Common St Mich *Lon* 89-92; NSM Westmr St Jas
from 92; Bps' Adv in Child Protection Stepney and Two Cities
Areas from 96; Bp's Adv in Child Protection *Ox* 96-05. *The
Clerk's House, 127 Kennington Road, London SE11 6SF* Tel
(020) 7735 3138 Mobile 07760-176704
E-mail mail@hughvalentine.net

VALENTINE, Jeremy Wilfred. b 38. NW Ord Course 76. **d** 79
p 80. C Cundall *Ripon* 79-82; TV Huntington *York* 82-87; V
Sand Hutton 87-08; P-in-c Whitwell w Crambe, Flaxton and
Foston 01-08; RD Buckrose and Bulmer and Malton 98-02; rtd
08; Perm to Offic *York* from 08. *5 Sand Hutton Court, Sand
Hutton, York YO41 1LU* Tel (01904) 468443
E-mail jeremyvalentine@tinyworld.co.uk

VALENTINE, John Harvey. b 63. Ch Ch Ox BA85 MA85. Ridley
Hall Cam BA92. **d** 93 **p** 94. C Heigham H Trin *Nor* 93-97; C
Ches Square St Mich w St Phil *Lon* 97-00; C Brompton H Trin w
Onslow Square St Paul 00-02; P-in-c Holborn St Geo w H Trin
and St Bart 02-09; R from 09. *13 Doughty Street, London
WC1N 2PL* Tel (020) 7404 9606 *or* 7404 4407 Fax 7831 0588
Mobile 07736-066091 E-mail john.valentine@sgtm.org

VALENTINE, Mrs Katherine Anne. b 58. Newc Poly BA80.
ERMC 03. **d** 06 **p** 07. C Haughley w Wetherden and Stowupland
St E from 06. *1 Church View, Haughley, Stowmarket IP14 3NU*
Tel (01449) 673687

VALIANT, Mrs Lesley Jean. b 51. Whitelands Coll Lon CertEd74
Univ Coll Chich BA99. STETS 99. **d** 01 **p** 02. NSM

Bedhampton *Portsm* 01-04; C Southsea St Jude 04-06; Asst to
RD Portsm 04-06; TV Pewsey and Swanborough *Sarum* from
06. *The Vicarage, Wilcot, Pewsey SN9 5NS* Tel (01672) 564867
Mobile 07751-168228 E-mail ljvaliant@tiscali.co.uk

VALLINS, Canon Christopher. b 43. Hon FRSocMed06. Lich Th
Coll 63. **d** 66 **p** 67. C Cuddington *Guildf* 66-70; C Aldershot
St Mich 70-73; V W Ewell 73-81; R Worplesdon and Chapl
Merrist Wood Coll of Agric and Horticulture 81-89; RD Guildf
86-89; Chapl Epsom Health Care NHS Trust 89-99; Hd Past
Care Epsom and St Helier Univ Hosps NHS Trust 99-07; Bp's
Adv on Healing *Guildf* 97-07; Bp's Adv for Hosp Chapl from 07;
Hon Can Guildf Cathl from 01; Perm to Offic *S'wark* from 07.
Little Watermead, Reigate Road, Hookwood, Horley RH6 0HD
Tel (01293) 824188 Fax 823282 Mobile 07917-337920
E-mail chrisvallins@yahoo.com

VALLIS, Brett Paul Stanley. b 72. G&C Coll Cam BA93 St Jo
Coll Dur BA01. Cranmer Hall Dur 99. **d** 02 **p** 03. C Monkseaton
St Mary *Newc* 02-05; P-in-c Fatfield *Dur* from 05. *14 Ewesley,
Washington NE38 9JG* E-mail vallisbrett@yahoo.co.uk

VAN BEVEREN (née FORBES), Mrs Susan Margaret. b 64. St
Hugh's Coll Ox BA85 MA89. Trin Th Sch Melbourne 95. **d** 96
p 96. Ind Chapl Inter-Ch Trade and Ind Miss Australia 96-99;
NSM Amsterdam w Den Helder and Heiloo *Eur* 00-03; Officer
for Miss in Work and Economic Life *Ox* 03-07; Dioc Adv from
08; NSM S Ascot 07-09; NSM Sunninghill and S Ascot from 09.
5 Vicarage Gardens, Ascot SL5 9DX Tel (01344) 622045
E-mail svan.beveren@well-centre.org

VAN BLERK, Etienne. b 68. Pretoria Univ BA88 Stellenbosch
Univ BTh92 Lebanese American Univ BA96. Ox Min Course
07. **d** 09. C Bicester w Bucknell, Caversfield and Launton *Ox*
from 09. *75 Ravencroft, Bicester OX26 6 YE* Tel 07795-985942
(mobile) E-mail etiennevanblerk@btinternet.com

VAN CARRAPIETT, Timothy Michael James. b 39. Chich Th
Coll 60. **d** 63 **p** 64. C Sugley *Newc* 63-65; C Newc St Fran 65-69;
P-in-c Wrangbrook w N Elmsall CD *Wakef* 69-74; P-in-c
Flushing *Truro* 74-75; P-in-c Mylor w Flushing 75-76; P-in-c
St Day 76-82; R Aldrington *Chich* 82-87; V Bexhill St Barn
87-01; rtd 01; Perm to Offic *St E* from 01 and *Chelmsf* from 08.
Bear-Wuff Cottage, 9 Tacon Road, Felixstowe IP11 2DT Tel
(01394) 271338

VAN CULIN, Canon Samuel. b 30. OBE. Princeton Univ AB52.
Virginia Th Sem DB55 Hon DD77 Gen Th Sem NY Hon
DD83. **d** 55 **p** 56. USA 55-83; Sec Gen ACC 83-94; Hon C All
Hallows by the Tower etc *Lon* 89-04; Hon Can Cant Cathl 83-94;
Hon Can Ibadan from 83; Hon Can Jerusalem from 84; Hon
Can S Africa from 89; Hon Can Honolulu from 91; rtd 94; Hon
Can Nat Cathl USA from 04. *3900 Watson Place, NW B-5D,
Washington DC 20016, USA* Tel (001) (202) 537 6200

VAN D'ARQUE, Christopher Simon Wayne. b 62. St Jo Coll Dur
BA99. **d** 99 **p** 00. C Letchworth St Paul w Willian *St Alb* 99-02; C
Westminster St Jas the Less *Lon* 02-03; V W Bessacarr *Sheff*
from 03. *The Vicarage, 39 Sturton Close, Doncaster DN4 7JG*
Tel (01302) 534864 E-mail wordsmith.twentyone@talktalk.net

VAN DE KASTEELE, Peter John. b 39. Magd Coll Cam BA61
MA65. Clifton Th Coll 61. **d** 63 **p** 64. C Eastbourne H Trin *Chich*
63-66; C N Pickenham w S Pickenham etc *Nor* 66-70; R Mursley
w Swanbourne and Lt Horwood *Ox* 70-80; Admin Sec Clinical
Th Assn from 83; Gen Dir 88-99; Perm to Offic *Glouc* from 83;
Hon C Westcote w Icomb and Bledington 88-89; rtd 99.
St Mary's House, Church Westcote, Chipping Norton OX7 6SF
Tel (01993) 830193

van de WEYER, Robert William Bates. b 50. Lanc Univ BA76.
S'wark Ord Course 78. **d** 81 **p** 82. Warden Lt Gidding
Community 77-98; Hon C Gt w Lt Gidding and Steeple Gidding
Ely 81-83; P-in-c 83-93; P-in-c Winwick 83-93; P-in-c Hamerton
83-93; P-in-c Upton and Copmanford 83-93; Perm to Offic from
93. *1 Church Cottages, Green Lane, Upton, Huntingdon
PE28 5 YE* Tel (01480) 890333

VAN DEN BERG, Jan Jacob. b 56. Sarum & Wells Th Coll 86.
d 88 **p** 89. C Glouc St Aldate 88-91; C Ollerton w Boughton
S'well 91-95; P-in-c Scrooby 95-00; P-in-c Blyth 97-00; C
Brampton and Farlam and Castle Carrock w Cumrew *Carl*
00-02; TV Eden, Gelt and Irthing 02-05; P-in-c Rockcliffe and
Blackford from 05. *The Vicarage, Rockcliffe, Carlisle CA6 4AA*
Tel (01228) 674209 E-mail jan@vandenberg.fsnet.co.uk

VAN DEN BERGH, Victor Michael Cornelius. b 53. ALBC92.
Ridley Hall Cam 02. **d** 03 **p** 04. C Tamworth *Lich* from 03.
St Francis's Vicarage, Masefield Drive, Tamworth B79 8JB Tel
(01827) 65926 Mobile 07770-900712
E-mail vic.vdb@btinternet.com

VAN DEN BOS (née MUMFORD), Mrs Clare. b 74. Man Univ
BA00. Ripon Coll Cuddesdon 04. **d** 07 **p** 09. C Monkseaton
St Mary *Newc* 07-08; C N Shields from 08. *St Augustine's
Vicarage, 51 Drummond Terrace, North Shields NE30 2AW* Tel
0191-259 6202 Mobile 07780-612760
E-mail pestokids@aol.com

van den HOF, Ariadne Rolanda Magdalena. b 71. Univ of Wales
(Cardiff) MTh96 Leiden Univ MA05. Old Cath Sem
Amersfoort 90 St Mich Coll Llan 98. **d** 99 **p** 00. C Dolgellau w

Llanfachreth and Brithdir etc *Ban* 99-01; Min Can Ban Cathl 01-02; P-in-c Trefdraeth w Aberffraw, Llangadwaladr etc 02-03; R 03-06; R Llanffestiniog w Blaenau Ffestiniog etc from 06; Rural Life Co-ord from 04. *The Rectory, The Square, Blaenau Ffestiniog LL41 3UW* Tel (01766) 831536
E-mail rheithorstiniog@gmail.com

VAN DER HART, William Richard. b 76. Homerton Coll Cam BEd99. Wycliffe Hall Ox BTh04. **d** 04 **p** 05. C Bryanston Square St Mary w St Marylebone St Mark *Lon* 04-08; TV Roxeth from 08. *65 Butler Road, Harrow HA1 4DS* Tel (020) 8537 7332 Mobile 07968-132129 E-mail vanders@tinyworld.co.uk

VAN DER LELY, Janice Kay. b 55. Sheff Univ BA76 Dur Univ PhD79 Webster Univ (USA) MA05. Ripon Coll Cuddesdon 08. **d** 09. C Cirencester *Glouc* from 09. *54 Alexander Drive, Cirencester GL7 1UH* Tel 07595-270438 (mobile)
E-mail janderlely@hotmail.com

van der LINDE, Herbert John. b 43. Rhodes Univ BA66. Coll of Resurr Mirfield. **d** 68 **p** 69. C Kingston St Luke *S'wark* 68-75; C Chipping Campden w Ebrington *Glouc* 75-78; V Cheltenham St Pet 78-84; V Bussage from 84. *St Michael's Vicarage, Bussage, Stroud GL6 8BB* Tel (01453) 883556

VAN DER PUMP, Charles Lyndon. b 25. FRCM. S'wark Ord Course 86. **d** 88 **p** 89. NSM Primrose Hill St Mary w Avenue Road St Paul *Lon* 88-02; Perm to Offic from 02. *48 Canfield Gardens, London NW6 3EB* Tel and fax (020) 7624 4512
E-mail office@smvph.freeserve.co.uk

VAN DER TOORN, Mrs Stephne. b 53. Natal Univ BA73 Stellenbosch Univ HDipEd75. Th Ext Educn Coll. **d** 93 **p** 95. NSM Pretoria St Mary S Africa 93-01; C Fawley *Win* 01-07; R E Bergholt and Brantham *St E* from 07. *The Rectory, Rectory Lane, Brantham, Manningtree CO11 1PZ* Tel (01206) 392646
E-mail revsteph3@vodafoneemail.co.uk

van der VALK, Jesse. b 59. Nottm Univ BTh84 Birm Univ MPhil88 Avery Hill Coll PGCE85. St Jo Coll Nottm 81. **d** 88 **p** 89. C Droitwich Spa *Worc* 88-92; V Hartshead and Hightown *Wakef* 92-96; R Woolwich St Mary w St Mich *S'wark* from 96; USPG (Lon Volunteers and Co-workers Team) from 97. *The Rectory, 43 Rectory Place, London SE18 5DA* Tel (020) 8854 2302 E-mail jessevdvalk@aol.com

VAN KOEVERING, Mrs Helen Elizabeth Parsons. b 60. SS Hild & Bede Coll Dur BA82 Trin Coll Bris MPhil99. S Wales Ord Course 01. **d** 02 **p** 03. C Bettws *Mon* 02-03; Bp's Sec Niassa Mozambique from 03. *CP 264, Lichinga, Niassa, Mozambique* Tel and fax (00258) 712 0735 E-mail mark@koev.freeserve.co.uk *or* diocese.niassa@teledata.mz

✠**VAN KOEVERING, The Rt Revd Mark Allan.** b 57. Michigan State Univ BSc79 MSc85. Trin Coll Bris BA99. **d** 99 **p** 00 **c** 03. C Bettws *Mon* 99-01; P-in-c 01-03; Bp Niassa Mozambique from 03. *Diocese do Niassa, CP 264, Lichinga, Niassa, Mozambique* Tel and fax (00258) 712 0735 E-mail mark@koev.freeserve.co.uk *or* diocese.niassa@teledata.mz

VAN KRIEKEN VANNERLEY, David. *See* VANNERLEY, David van Krieken

VAN LEER, Samuel Wall. b 67. Virginia Univ BA90 California Univ MA91 St Jo Coll Dur BA01. Cranmer Hall Dur 99. **d** 02 **p** 03. C Berne w Neuchâtel *Eur* 02-05; Chapl E Netherlands from 05. *Marijkestraat 1, 6991 XJ Rheden, The Netherlands* Tel (0031) (26) 495 0620

VAN LEEUWEN, Canon Dirk Willem. b 45. Utrecht Univ LLD71. Th Faculty Brussels 71 S'wark Ord Course 80. **d** 82 **p** 83. Asst Chapl Brussels Cathl 82-84; Chapl Haarlem 84-93; Chapl Antwerp St Boniface 94-06; Assoc Chapl 06-07; Chapl Charleroi 94-00; P-in-c Ypres 97-99; P-in-c Leuven 98-99; Can Brussels Cathl 96-07; Chapl Knokke 01-07; P-in-c Ostend 01-06; P-in-c Bruges 01-03; V Gen to Bp Eur 02-07; Adn NW Eur 05-07; rtd 08. *Koningin Elisabethlei 6, Box 22, 2018 Antwerp, Belgium* Tel (0032) (3) 238 3162
E-mail dirk.vanleeuwen@scarlet.be

VAN STRAATEN, Christopher Jan. b 55. Bris Univ BA77 Natal Univ HDipEd78. Oak Hill Th Coll 90. **d** 92 **p** 93. C Woodley *Ox* 92-96; V Gillingham St Aug *Roch* 96-07; V Aylesford from 07. *The Vicarage, Vicarage Close, Aylesford ME20 7BB* Tel (01622) 717434 E-mail chris.vanstraaten@diocese-rochester.org

van WENGEN, Rosemary Margaret. b 38. Westf Coll Lon BA60 Univ of Leiden MA77 PhD81. SEITE 98. **d** 01 **p** 02. NSM Benenden *Cant* from 01; NSM Sandhurst w Newenden from 04. *Beach House, Grange Road, St Michaels, Tenterden TN30 6EF* Tel (01580) 764857 Fax 761405
E-mail r.vanwengen@tiscali.co.uk

VAN ZANDBERGEN, Karen. *See* BURNETT-HALL, Mrs Karen

VANDERSTOCK, Alan. b 31. St Jo Coll Dur BA57, Cranmer Hall Dur. **d** 59 **p** 60. C Kersal Moor *Man* 59-62; C-in-c Lower Kersal CD 63-67; Lic Preacher *Cant* from 67; Sen Tutor Heath Clark High Sch Croydon 73-83; Dep Hd Teacher Norbury Manor High Sch Croydon 83-86; Sen Master Shirley High Sch Croydon 86-92; rtd 92. *17 Snowbell Road, Kingsnorth, Ashford TN23 3NF* Tel (01233) 503889

VANDYCK, Mrs Salli Diane Seymour. b 39. SEITE 93. **d** 96 **p** 97. NSM Chertsey *Guildf* 96-98; NSM Ross *Heref* 98-03; rtd 03; Perm to Offic *Heref* from 03. *Mickleden, Linton, Ross-on-Wye HR9 7RY* Tel (01989) 720197

VANN, The Ven Cherry Elizabeth. b 58. ARCM78 GRSM80. Westcott Ho Cam 86. **d** 89 **p** 94. Par Dn Flixton St Mich *Man* 89-92; Chapl Bolton Inst of F&HE 92-98; Par Dn Bolton St Pet 92-94; C 94-98; TV E Farnworth and Kearsley 98-04; TR 04-08; Chapl among Deaf People 98-04; AD Farnworth 05-08; Adn Rochdale from 08. *57 Melling Road, Oldham OL4 1PN* Tel 0161-678 1454 Fax 678 1455 E-mail vann.cherry@yahoo.co.uk

VANN, Canon Paul. b 41. Univ of Wales (Cardiff) BTh01. St D Coll Lamp 62. **d** 65 **p** 66. C Griffithstown *Mon* 65-67; C Llanfrechfa All SS 67-71; Dioc Youth Chapl 69-74; Chapl St Woolos Cathl 71-72; P-in-c Llanrumney 72-76; V 76-97; Asst Chapl HM Pris Cardiff 75-78; RD Bassaleg *Mon* 90-99; R Machen 97-07; Can St Woolos Cathl 01-07; rtd 07. *2 Mawdlam Way, North Cornelly, Bridgend CF33 4PJ* Tel (01656) 741543 E-mail vann651@btinternet.com

VANNERLEY, David van Krieken. b 50. Ch Ch Coll Cant CertEd71 Kent Univ BA78 MPhil07. SEITE 00. **d** 05 **p** 06. NSM St Laur in Thanet *Cant* from 05. *34 Cherry Gardens, Herne Bay CT6 5QE* Tel (01227) 369096 E-mail vannerley@aol.com

VANNOZZI, Peter. b 62. Lon Univ BA83 Heythrop Coll Lon MA06. Ripon Coll Cuddesdon BA86 MA91. **d** 87 **p** 88. C Kenton *Lon* 87-90; C Fleet *Guildf* 90-93; V Northwood Hills St Edm *Lon* 93-97; AD Harrow 95-97; V S Dulwich St Steph *S'wark* 97-05; RD Dulwich 02-05; Can Res Wakef Cathl 05-07; V Hampton Hill *Lon* from 07. *The Vicarage, 46 St James's Road, Hampton TW12 1DQ* Tel and fax (020) 8979 2069
E-mail vicar@stjames-hamptonhill.org.uk

VANSTON, The Ven William Francis Harley. b 24. TCD BA48 MA52. **d** 48 **p** 49. C Belfast St Mary *Conn* 48-51; C Dublin Rathfarnham *D & G* 51-58; I Narraghmore w Fontstown and Timolin 58-65; I Arklow 65-67; I Arklow w Inch 67-73; I Arklow w Inch and Kilbride 73-89; RD Rathdrum 77-89; Adn Glendalough 83-89; rtd 89. *Apt 9, 65 Strand Road, Sandymount, Dublin 4, Republic of Ireland* Tel (00353) (1) 260 8882

VANSTONE, Preb Walford David Frederick. b 38. Open Univ BA81. AKC69. **d** 70 **p** 71. C Feltham *Lon* 70-75; TV E Runcorn w Halton *Ches* 75-80; V Grange St Andr 80-82; V Hampton All SS *Lon* 82-05; P-in-c Teddington SS Pet and Paul and Fulwell 99-00; AD Hampton 95-03; Preb St Paul's Cathl 99-05; Chapl Richmond Coll 02-05; rtd 05; Perm to Offic *Lon* from 05. *13 Lammas Close, Staines TW18 4XT*
E-mail wvanstone@aol.com

VARAH, Canon Paul Hugh. b 46. St Deiniol's Hawarden 83. **d** 85 **p** 86. C Prestatyn *St As* 85-87; P-in-c Hawarden 87-88; TV 88-89; V Esclusham 89-96; V Connah's Quay from 96; Can Cursal St As Cathl from 08. *The Vicarage, Church Hill, Connah's Quay, Deeside CH5 4AD* Tel and fax (01244) 830224

VARGAS, Eric Arthur Dudley. b 27. BD. S Dios Minl Tr Scheme 81. **d** 83 **p** 84. C Farncombe *Guildf* 83-86; R Ockley, Okewood and Forest Green 86-90; V Kirdford *Chich* 90-93; rtd 93; Perm to Offic *Chich* and *Portsm* from 93. *33 Park Crescent, Emsworth PO10 7NT* Tel (01243) 430611

VARGESON, Canon Peter Andrew. b 53. Wycliffe Hall Ox 85. **d** 87 **p** 88. C Yateley *Win* 87-92; V Bursledon from 92; AD Eastleigh 99-06; P-in-c Hound from 07; Hon Can Tororo Uganda from 99. *The Vicarage, School Road, Bursledon, Southampton SO31 8BW* Tel (023) 8040 2821 *or* 8040 6021 E-mail peter.vargeson@ukgateway.net

VARLEY (née TRIM), Elizabeth Ann. b 52. Homerton Coll Cam BEd75 Van Mildert Coll Dur PhD85 St Jo Coll Dur BA96. NEOC 94. **d** 96 **p** 97. C Sedgefield *Dur* 96-99; Dir Post-Ord Tr Stepney Area *Lon* 99-02; V Hipswell *Ripon* 02-07; Hon Can Ripon Cathl 05-07; R Bacton w Wyverstone, Cotton and Old Newton etc *St E* from 07. *The Rectory, Church Road, Bacton, Stowmarket IP14 4LJ* Tel (01449) 781245
E-mail liz.varley@csbb.co.uk

VARLEY, Robert. b 36. St Jo Coll Cam BA57 MA64 Man Poly PGCE92. NW Ord Course 71. **d** 74 **p** 75. C Wallasey St Hilary *Ches* 74-77; V Rock Ferry 77-81; Perm to Offic *Man* 82-83; Hon C E Farnworth and Kearsley 83-86; Hon C Walkden Moor 86-87; C 87-89; V Lt Hulton 89-90; Perm to Offic from 97. *66 Normanby Road, Worsley, Manchester M28 7TS* Tel 0161-790 8420

VARNEY, Donald James. b 35. Chich Th Coll 84. **d** 86. NSM Liss *Portsm* 86-05; rtd 05; Perm to Offic *Portsm* from 05. *12 Birch Close, Liss, Petersfield GU33 7HS* Tel (01730) 893945

VARNEY, Peter David. b 38. Univ Coll Dur BA61 MA64. Qu Coll Birm 61. **d** 64 **p** 65. C Newington St Paul *S'wark* 64-66; C Camberwell St Mich w All So w Em 66-67; Perm to Offic Kuching Malaysia 67-68, Hon C Croxley Green All SS *St Alb* 69; Perm to Offic *Roch* 69-72 and 74-84; Asst Chapl CSJB 72-73; Asst Sec Chrs Abroad 74-79; Dir Bloxham Project 84-86; Perm to Offic *Cant* 84-85 and *S'wark* 85-86; P-in-c Thornage w Brinton w Hunworth and Stody *Nor* 87-88; P-in-c Briningham 87-88; P-in-c Melton Constable w Swanton Novers 87-88; Perm to Offic from 88; Chapl Yare and Norvic Clinics and St Andr Hosp Nor 90-95; rtd 03. *1 Thomas Wyatt Close, Norwich NR2 2TB* Tel (01603) 760838 E-mail varney@waitrose.com

VARNEY, Stephen Clive. b 59. Qu Mary Coll Lon BSc80 Sussex Univ MSc82 Southn Univ BTh88. Sarum & Wells Th Coll 83. **d** 86 **p** 87. C Riverhead w Dunton Green *Roch* 86-91; V Bostall Heath 91-99; V Bromley St Mark from 99. *St Mark's Vicarage, 51 Hayes Road, Bromley BR2 9AE* Tel (020) 8460 6220 Mobile 07961-117578

VARNHAM, Gerald Stanley. b 29. Sarum & Wells Th Coll 74. **d** 77 **p** 78. Hon C Portchester *Portsm* 77-86; Perm to Offic 88-99. *15 Southampton Road, Fareham PO16 7DZ* Tel (01329) 234182

VARNON, Nicholas Charles Harbord. b 45. St Luke's Coll Ex CertEd71 Open Univ BA83 BPhil91 MA94 Univ of Wales MPhil00. St Mich Coll Llan 91. **d** 93 **p** 94. C Pontypridd St Cath w St Matt *Llan* 93-97; P-in-c Sutton St Nicholas w Sutton St Michael *Heref* 97-04; P-in-c Withington w Westhide 97-04; P-in-c Weybourne Gp *Nor* 04-06; R N Elmham, Billingford, Bintree, Guist etc from 06; CF (ACF) from 00. *The Rectory, 48 Holt Road, North Elmham, Dereham NR20 5JQ* Tel (01362) 668030 E-mail nchv@btinternet.com

VARQUEZ, Leo Bacleon. b 61. St Andr Th Sem Manila 82. **d** 86 **p** 86. P St Andr Philippines 86-91; P St Isidore 92-94; SSF 95-99; NSM Edin St Jo 98-99; NSM Mill End and Heronsgate w W Hyde *St Alb* 99-00; Asst Chapl HM Pris Featherstone 00-02; C Hednesford *Lich* 00-04; C Kingstanding St Luke *Birm* 04-06; Asst Chapl Univ Coll Lon Hosps NHS Foundn Trust 06-08; Chapl N Staffs Hosp NHS Trust from 08. *North Staffordshire Royal Infirmary, Princes Road, Stoke-on-Trent ST4 7LN* Tel (01782) 715444 E-mail leovarquez@yahoo.co.uk

VARTY, John Eric. b 44. Tyndale Hall Bris 68. **d** 71 **p** 72. C Barrow St Mark *Carl* 71-74; C Cheadle *Ches* 74-82; V Cheadle All Hallows 82-89; V Alsager Ch Ch 89-06; rtd 06; Chapl to Bp Stockport *Ches* from 07. *14 Gowy Close, Alsager, Stoke-on-Trent ST7 2HX* Tel (01270) 877360 E-mail vartyj1j2@clara.co.uk

VARTY, Robert. b 46. LRAM. Sarum & Wells Th Coll 84. **d** 86 **p** 87. C Plympton St Mary *Ex* 86-89; TV Northam w Westward Ho! and Appledore 89-95; P-in-c Wigginton *St Alb* 95-00; TV Tring 95-00; rtd 00; Clergy Widow(er)s Officer *Ex* 02-04; Perm to Offic *Ex* 01-04 and *Eur* from 05. *La Butte, 61110 Bellou-sur-Huisne, France* Tel (0033) (2) 33 25 55 64 E-mail varty.robert@wanadoo.fr

VASBY-BURNIE, Timothy Roy. b 79. Trin Coll Cam MA00. Wycliffe Hall Ox BTh07. **d** 07 **p** 08. C Stone Ch Ch and Oulton *Lich* from 07. *1 Navigation Loop, Stone ST15 8YU* Tel (01785) 814244 E-mail tim@timvb.plus.com

VASEY, Arthur Stuart. b 37. Qu Coll Birm 68. **d** 71 **p** 72. C Shelf *Bradf* 71-73; Australia 74-76; Chapl St Jo Hosp Linc 76-79; P-in-c Tanfield *Dur* 79-84; C Birtley 84-85; C Middlesbrough St Thos *York* 85-86; rtd 02. *Glen Esk, 3 Quarry Bank, Malton YO17 7HA*

VASEY-SAUNDERS, Mrs Leah Beverley. b 77. Huddersfield Univ BMus98 St Jo Coll Dur BA03. Cranmer Hall Dur 00. **d** 03 **p** 04. C Whorlton *Newc* 03-04; Hon C Newc St Geo 05-08; TV Cannock *Lich* from 08; C Hednesford from 08. *St John's Vicarage, 226 Hednesford Road, Heath Hayes, Cannock WS12 3DZ* Tel (01543) 450361 E-mail leah@vasey-saunders.co.uk

VASEY-SAUNDERS, Mark Richard. b 74. Coll of Ripon & York St Jo BA95 St Jo Coll Dur BA00. Cranmer Hall Dur 98. **d** 01 **p** 02. C Ponteland *Newc* 01-04; Chapl Newc Univ 04-08. *St John's Vicarage, 226 Hednesford Road, Heath Hayes, Cannock WS12 3DZ*

VASTENHOUT, Jeannetta Hermina. See STOKES, Mrs Jeannetta Hermina

VAUGHAN, Canon Andrew Christopher James. b 61. Univ of Wales (Lamp) BA82. Linc Th Coll 84. **d** 84 **p** 85. C Caerleon *Mon* 84-86; C Magor w Redwick and Undy 86-88; Ind Chapl 84-94; Linc Ind Miss from 94; Can and Preb Linc Cathl from 05. *4 Grange Close, Canwick, Lincoln LN4 2RH* Tel and fax (01522) 528266 Mobile 07702-468549 E-mail vaughanlim@tesco.net

VAUGHAN, Andrew Kenneth. b 64. MCIOB01. Ridley Hall Cam 04. **d** 07 **p** 08. C Chislehurst Ch Ch *Roch* from 07. *56 Walden Road, Chislehurst BR7 5DL* Tel (020) 8467 4610 Mobile 07977-154809 E-mail andrewvaughan@akv64s.com

VAUGHAN, Brian John. b 38. Lich Th Coll 65. **d** 68 **p** 69. C Fisherton Anger *Sarum* 68-70; C Wareham w Arne 70-73; Australia from 73; Asst P Mt Lawley 73; R Dalwallinu 73-76; R Morawa 75-78; Field Officer Bible Soc of W Australia 78-81; Assoc P Mt Lawley 82-86; R Pinjarra 86-96; R Manjimup 96-00; rtd 00. *Milborne, 6 Steeple Retreat, Busselton WA 6280, Australia* Tel (0061) (8) 9751 1225 E-mail sherton@optusnet.com.au

VAUGHAN, Carole Ann. b 47. Leeds Univ CertEd68. STETS 95. **d** 98 **p** 99. NSM Oakley w Wootton St Lawrence *Win* from 98. *The Rectory, Glebe Lane, Worting, Basingstoke RG23 8QA* Tel (01256) 331531 Fax and E-mail carole@venco.fsnet.co.uk

VAUGHAN, Charles Jeremy Marshall. b 52. Man Univ BSc75. St Jo Coll Nottm 83. **d** 85 **p** 86. C Epsom Common Ch Ch *Guildf* 85-88; C Woking Ch Ch 88-93; R Worting *Win* 93-07; R

Winklebury and Worting from 07. *The Rectory, Glebe Lane, Worting, Basingstoke RG23 8QA* Tel (01256) 331531 E-mail jeremy@cjvaughan.co.uk

VAUGHAN, Edward Michael. b 59. Univ of NSW BA80 Sydney Univ DipEd81. Moore Th Coll Sydney BTh87. **d** 89 **p** 89. C Jannali Australia 89-91; C Rozelle 92-94; R Darling Street 95-05; I Crinken *D & G* from 05. *15 Shrewsbury Hall, Shankill, Co Dublin, Republic of Ireland* Tel (00353) (1) 282 4391 Mobile 87-904 2092 E-mail ed@crinken.com

VAUGHAN, Idris Samuel. b 46. Sarum Th Coll 70. **d** 72 **p** 73. C Workington St Jo *Carl* 72-76; C Foley Park *Worc* 76-79; V Hayton St Mary *Carl* 79-85; Chapl Asst Univ Hosp Nottm 85-90; Chapl Asst Nottm Gen Hosp 85-90; Chapl Stafford Distr Gen Hosp 90-94; Chapl Chase Hosp Cannock 90-94; Chapl Mid Staffs Gen Hosps NHS Trust 94-06; P-in-c Lanzarote *Eur* from 06. *Calle Sabendos 37, 35510 Puerto del Carmen (Las Palmas), Canary Islands* Tel and fax (0034) 928 514 241

VAUGHAN, Jeffrey Charles. b 45. S'wark Ord Course 85. **d** 88 **p** 89. NSM Tottenham St Paul *Lon* 88-91; C Hendon St Alphage 91-95; V Enfield SS Pet and Paul from 95. *The Vicarage, 177 Ordnance Road, Enfield EN3 6AB* Tel (01992) 719770 Fax (020) 8292 8456

VAUGHAN, Jeremy. See VAUGHAN, Charles Jeremy Marshall

VAUGHAN, Jeremy. b 30. Sarum Th Coll 53. **d** 56 **p** 57. C Wigan St Andr *Liv* 56-59; Australia 59-64; P-in-c Riddings *Derby* 64-71; R Hasland 71-80; V Temple Normanton 71-80; TV Dronfield 80-86; V Bradwell 86-95; rtd 95; Perm to Offic *Derby* from 95. *11 Millstone Close, Dronfield Woodhouse, Dronfield S18 8ZL* Tel (01246) 415647

VAUGHAN, Patrick Handley. b 38. TCD BA60 BD65 Selw Coll Cam BA62 MA66 Nottm Univ PhD88. Ridley Hall Cam 61. **d** 63 **p** 64. Min Can Bradf Cathl 63-66; Uganda 67-73; P-in-c Slingsby *York* 74-77; Tutor NW Ord Course 74-77; P-in-c Hovingham *York* 74-77; Prin EMMTC *S'well* 77-90; Hon Can Leic Cathl 87-90; Assoc Lect Open Univ from 94. *113 Upperthorpe Road, Sheffield S6 3EA* Tel 0114-272 2675

✠**VAUGHAN, The Rt Revd Peter St George.** b 30. Selw Coll Cam BA55 MA59 BNC Ox MA63. Ridley Hall Cam. **d** 57 **p** 58 **c** 89. C Birm St Martin 57-63; Chapl Ox Pastorate 63-67; Asst Chapl BNC Ox 63-67; Ceylon 67-72; New Zealand 72-75; Prin Crowther Hall CMS Tr Coll Selly Oak 75-83; Adn Westmorland and Furness *Carl* 83-89; Hon Can Carl Cathl 83-89; Area Bp Ramsbury *Sarum* 89-98; Can and Preb Sarum Cathl 89-98; rtd 98; Hon Asst Bp Bradf 98-01; Hon Can Bradf Cathl from 98; Perm to Offic *Glouc* 01-06; Hon Asst Bp Glouc from 06; Hon Asst Bp Bris from 02. *Willowbrook, Downington, Lechlade GL7 3DL* Tel (01367) 252216

VAUGHAN, Preb Roger Maxwell. b 39. AKC62. **d** 63 **p** 64. C W Bromwich All SS *Lich* 63-65; C Wolverhampton 65-70; V Tunstall Ch Ch 70-79; V Abbots Bromley 79-86; P-in-c Blithfield 85-86; V Abbots Bromley w Blithfield 86-93; V Stafford St Jo and Tixall w Ingestre 93-04; Preb Lich Cathl 99-04; rtd 04; Perm to Offic *Lich* from 04. *51 Crestwood Drive, Stone ST15 0LW* Tel (01785) 812192 E-mail salrog.vaughan@btinternet.com

VAUGHAN, Trevor. b 41. TD91. Cen Lancs Univ BA91. Linc Th Coll 66. **d** 69 **p** 70. C Wyken *Cov* 69-72; C Stratford-on-Avon w Bishopton 72-73; P-in-c Monks Kirby w Withybrook and Copston Magna 73-75; P-in-c Wolvey, Burton Hastings and Stretton Baskerville 73-77; P-in-c Withybrook w Copston Magna 73-77; V Heyhouses *Blackb* 77-80; CF (TA) from 79; V Chorley St Geo *Blackb* 80-83; R Bolton by Bowland w Grindleton *Bradf* 83-89; V Settle 89-91; R Broughton, Marton and Thornton 91-00; V Morecambe St Barn *Blackb* 00-03; P-in-c Sabden and Pendleton 03-06; rtd 06. *3 Westmount Close, Ripon HG4 2HU* Tel (01765) 605591

VAUGHAN-JONES, Canon John Paschal. b 18. Keble Coll Ox BA39 MA43. St Steph Ho Ox 39. **d** 41 **p** 42. C Laindon w Basildon *Chelmsf* 41-43 and 47-49; CF 43-47; R Chipping Ongar *Chelmsf* 49-83; R Shelley 49-83; RD Ongar 72-82; Hon Can Chelmsf Cathl 78-83; rtd 83; Perm to Offic *Chelmsf* from 03. *Armadale, 3 Great Lane, Malborough, Kingsbridge TQ7 3AS* Tel (01548) 562138

VAUGHAN-WILSON, Jane Elizabeth. b 61. Magd Coll Ox MA87. Cranmer Hall Dur. **d** 89 **p** 94. Par Dn Ormesby *York* 89-93; Dn-in-c Middlesbrough St Agnes 93-94; P-in-c 94-95; TV Basingstoke *Win* 95-03; Perm to Offic *Truro* from 03. *4 Tolver Road, Penzance TR18 2AG* Tel (01736) 351825

VAYRO, Mark Shaun. b 66. Aston Tr Scheme 88 Linc Th Coll BTh93. **d** 93 **p** 94. C Northampton St Mich w St Edm *Pet* 93-96; TV Duston Team 96-98; V Elm and Friday Bridge w Coldham *Ely* 98-01. *125 Spalding Road, Pinchbeck, Spalding LN11 3UE*

VEEN, Keith Henry. b 46. **d** 01 **p** 02. OLM Croydon St Pet *S'wark* 01-02; OLM Croydon Ch Ch from 02. *91 The Ridgeway, Croydon CR0 4AH* Tel (020) 8688 3565 E-mail keithveen@veenco.fsnet.co.uk

VELLACOTT, John Patrick Millner. b 29. Ox NSM Course 86. **d** 89 **p** 90. NSM Cholsey *Ox* 89-93; Chapl Nerja *Eur* 93-97; rtd 97; Perm to Offic *Truro* 97-00; *Glouc* 00-02 and *Carl* from 03.

5 Stonycroft Drive, Arnside, Carnforth LA5 0EE Tel (01524) 762800

VELLACOTT, Peter Graham. b 38. EAMTC 90. **d** 93 **p** 94. NSM Framlingham w Saxtead *St E* 93-95; NSM Brandeston w Kettleburgh 95-99; NSM Easton 95-99; P-in-c Brandeston w Kettleburgh and Easton 99-07; rtd 07; Perm to Offic *St E* from 07. *Soham House, Brandeston, Woodbridge IP13 7AX* Tel (01728) 685423

✠**VENABLES, The Most Revd Gregory James.** b 49. Lon Univ CertEd74. **d** 84 **p** 84 **c** 93. SAMS from 77; Paraguay 78-90; C Rainham *Chelmsf* 90-92; C Rainham w Wennington 92-93; Aux Bp Peru and Bolivia 93-95; Bp Bolivia 95-00; Asst Primate of S Cone 95-02; Bp Coadjutor Argentina 00-02; Dioc Bp from 02; Presiding Bp of S Cone from 01. *Rioja 2995, B1636DMG - Olivos, Provincia de Buenos Aires, Argentina* Tel (0054) (11) 4799 7124 E-mail bpgreg@ciudad.com.ar

VENABLES, Canon Margaret Joy. b 37. Bp Otter Coll CertEd57. S Dios Minl Tr Scheme 86. **d** 89 **p** 94. NSM Wilton *B & W* 89-91; C Taunton St Andr 91-97; P-in-c Haynes *St Alb* 97-03; P-in-c Clophill 00-03; R Campton, Clophill and Haynes 03-06; RD Shefford 01-06; Hon Can St Alb 05-06; rtd 06; P-in-c Barnack w Ufford and Bainton *Pet* from 06. *The Rectory, Millstone Lane, Barnack, Stamford PE9 3ET* Tel (01780) 740234 E-mail margsv@waitrose.com

VENABLES, Philip Richard Meredith. b 58. Magd Coll Ox BA79 CertEd80. Wycliffe Hall Ox 85. **d** 88 **p** 89. C Gillingham St Mark *Roch* 88-93; V Penge St Jo 93-07; R Bebington *Ches* from 07. *The Rectory, Church Road, Bebington, Wirral CH63 3EX* Tel 0151-645 6478 E-mail philip.venables@ntlworld.com

VENESS, Allan Barry. b 39. Lon Inst of Educn TCert60 Sussex Univ BEd81. Bp Otter Coll 94. **d** 97. NSM Felpham *Chich* 97-01; NSM Aldwick 01-06. *1 rue du Tertre Gicquel, 22430 Erquy, France* E-mail veness.allan@orange.fr

VENEZUELA, Bishop of. *See* GUERRERO, The Rt Revd Orlando

VENN, Prof Richard Frank. b 49. Leeds Univ BSc72 Strathclyde Univ PhD77 CChem FRSC97. Ridley Hall Cam 04. **d** 05 **p** 06. C Margate H Trin *Cant* 05-08; P-in-c Len Valley from 08. *The Vicarage, Old Ashford Road, Lenham, Maidstone ME17 2PX* Tel (01622) 853919 Mobile 07967-146842 E-mail dickvenn@gmail.com

VENNELLS, Ms Paula Anne. b 59. Bradf Univ BA81 FRSA88. SAOMC 02. **d** 05 **p** 06. NSM Bromham w Oakley and Stagsden *St Alb* from 05. *Rushey Ford House, West End Road, Kempston, Bedford MK43 8RU* Tel (01234) 851594 Mobile 07786-174638 E-mail paula@rusheyford.freeserve.co.uk

✠**VENNER, The Rt Revd Stephen Squires.** b 44. Birm Univ BA65 Linacre Coll Ox BA67 MA71 Lon Univ PGCE72 Birm Univ Hon DD08. St Steph Ho Ox 65. **d** 68 **p** 69 **c** 94. C Streatham St Pet *S'wark* 68-71; C Streatham Hill St Marg 71-72; C Balham Hill Ascension 72-74; V Clapham St Pet 74-76; Bp's Chapl to Overseas Students 74-76; P-in-c Studley *Sarum* 76; V 76-82; V Weymouth H Trin 82-94; RD Weymouth 88-93; Can and Preb Sarum Cathl 89-94; Suff Bp Middleton *Man* 94-99; Suff Bp Dover *Cant* from 99; Bp HM Forces from 09. *The Bishop's Office, Old Palace, Canterbury CT1 2EE* Tel (01227) 459382 Fax 784985 E-mail bishop@bishcant.org

VENNING, Nigel Christopher. b 50. K Coll Lon BD75 AKC75. St Aug Coll Cant /5. **d** 76 **p** 77. C Minchead *B & W* 76-80; C Fawley *Win* 80-83; P-in-c Whitestaunton and Combe St Nicholas w Wambrook *B & W* 83-89; R Staplegrove 89-01; P-in-c Norton Fitzwarren 00-01; R Staplegrove w Norton Fitzwarren 01-03; R Blackdown 03-05; RD Taunton 96-01; rtd 05; Perm to Offic *B & W* from 05. *Crispin House, 5 Mendip Edge, Weston-super-Mare BS24 9JF* E-mail nigelvenning@lycos.co.uk

VERE HODGE, Preb Francis. b 19. MC43. Worc Coll Ox BA46 MA46. Cuddesdon Coll 46. **d** 48 **p** 49. C Battle *Chich* 48-54; R Iping 54-58; R Linch 54-58; V Kingswood *S'wark* 58-65; V Moorlinch w Stawell and Sutton Mallet *B & W* 65-79; R Greinton 68-79; RD Glastonbury 75-79; P-in-c Lydeard St Lawrence w Combe Florey and Tolland 79-84; Preb Wells Cathl 79-98; rtd 84; Perm to Offic *B & W* 84-99 and *Ex* from 99. *1 Gracey Court, Woodland Road, Broadclyst, Exeter EX5 3GA* Tel (01392) 469005

VERE NICOLL, Charles Fiennes. b 55. Solicitor 79. SAOMC 96. **d** 99 **p** 00. NSM Basildon w Aldworth and Ashampstead *Ox* 99-08; Perm to Offic from 08. *Ashvine, Westridge, Highclere, Newbury RG20 9RY* Tel 07768-238128 (mobile) E-mail cvn@cvnsbh.com

VEREKER, Jennifer Lesley. b 45. Totley Hall Coll CertEd66. WMMTC 96. **d** 99 **p** 00. NSM Rugby *Cov* 99-03; TV Gt and Lt Coates w Bradley *Linc* 03-08; rtd 08; Perm to Offic *St E* from 08. *Laurelwood, Thurston Road, Great Barton, Bury St Edmunds IP31 2PW* Tel (01359) 234413 E-mail j.vereker@btinternet.com

VEREY, Christopher Douglas. b 46. St Chad's Coll Dur BA68 MA70. Ripon Coll Cuddesdon 02. **d** 04 **p** 05. NSM Yate New

Town *Bris* from 04. *2 The Green, Heathend, Wotton-under-Edge GL12 8AR* E-mail chrisverey@tiscali.com.uk

VERHEY, Shawn Gordon. b 59. Ottawa Univ BA88 Liv Univ BTh03. NOC 00. **d** 04 **p** 05. NSM Southport SS Simon and Jude w All So *Liv* 04-07; Asst Chapl HM Pris Garth 04-07; Chapl HM YOI Thorn Cross from 07. *HM Young Offender Institution, Arley Road, Appleton, Warrington WA4 4RL* Tel (01925) 605085 E-mail vrhshawn@aol.com

✠**VERNEY, The Rt Revd Stephen Edmund.** b 19. MBE45. Ball Coll Ox BA48 MA48. **d** 50 **p** 51 **c** 77. C Gedling *S'well* 50-52; C-in-c Clifton CD 52-57; V Clifton St Fran 57-58; Dioc Missr *Cov* 58-64; V Leamington Hastings 58-64; Can Res Cov Cathl 64-70; Can Windsor 70-77; Suff Bp Repton *Derby* 77-85; Hon Can Derby Cathl 77-85; Dioc Dir of Post-Ord Tr 83-85; rtd 86; Perm to Offic *Ox* 86-91; Hon Asst Bp Ox from 91. *Cherry Patch, Church Road, Blewbury, Didcot OX11 9PY* Tel (01235) 850004

VERNON, Bryan Graham. b 50. Qu Coll Cam BA72 MA76. Qu Coll Birm 73. **d** 75 **p** 76. C Newc St Gabr 75-79; Chapl Newc Univ 79-91; Lect Health Care Ethics from 91; Chmn Newc Mental Health Trust 91-94; Perm to Offic from 94. *34 Queens Road, Jesmond, Newcastle upon Tyne NE2 2PQ* Tel 0191-281 3861 E-mail b.g.vernon@ncl.ac.uk

VERNON, John Christie. b 40. Imp Coll Lon BScEng62. Linc Th Coll 63. **d** 65 **p** 66. C Barnard Castle *Dur* 65-69; CF 69-90; Asst Chapl Gen 90-92; Chapl Ellesmere Coll 92-99; Perm to Offic *Lich* 99-01; NSM Ellesmere Deanery 01-05 and 06-08; P-in-c Petton w Cockshutt, Welshampton and Lyneal etc 05-06; RD Ellesmere 02-08; Perm to Offic from 08. *The Drift House, Lake House Mews, Grange Road, Ellesmere SY12 9DE* Tel (01691) 623765 Mobile 07778-312226 E-mail john@jvernon.go-plus.net

VERNON, Canon Matthew James. b 71. Collingwood Coll Dur BSc93 Fitzw Coll Cam BA96 MA98. Westcott Ho Cam 94. **d** 97 **p** 98. C Guildf H Trin w St Mary 97-01; Chapl St Jo Cathl and P-in-c Pokfulam Em Hong Kong 01-09; Can Res St E Cathl from 09. *2 Abbey Precincts, Bury St Edmunds IP33 1RS* Tel (01284) 701472 E-mail canon.pastor@stedscathedral.org.uk

VERNON, Robert Leslie. b 47. Sarum & Wells Th Coll 73. **d** 76 **p** 77. C Hartlepool St Luke *Dur* 76-79; C Birm St Geo 79-82; V Bordesley Green 82-86; Dioc Youth Officer *Carl* 86-89; P-in-c Holme 86-89; Dioc Youth Adv *Newc* 89-95; V Ulgham and Widdrington 95-01; P-in-c Pokesdown St Jas *Win* from 01. *St James's Vicarage, 12 Harewood Avenue, Bournemouth BH7 6NQ* Tel (01202) 425918

VERWEY, Mrs Eileen Susan **Vivien.** b 41. Open Univ BA78 BA93 Goldsmiths' Coll Lon PGCE82. WEMTC 03. **d** 05 **p** 06. NSM Burghill *Heref* from 05; NSM Stretton Sugwas from 05; NSM Pipe-cum-Lyde and Moreton-on-Lugg from 05. *Mill Croft House, Staunton-on-Wye, Hereford HR4 7LW* Tel (01981) 500626

VESEY, Nicholas Ivo. b 54. Bris Univ BSc73. Cranmer Hall Dur 95. **d** 97 **p** 98. C Tunbridge Wells St Mark *Roch* 97-01; V New Catton St Luke w St Aug *Nor* from 01. *St Luke's Vicarage, 61 Aylsham Road, Norwich NR3 2HF* Tel (01603) 416973 E-mail nicholas.vesey@btopenworld.com

VESSEY, Andrew John. b 45. Bp Otter Coll CertEd67. Sarum & Wells Th Coll 84. **d** 86 **p** 87. C Framlingham w Saxtead *St E* 86-89; V Catshill and Dodford *Worc* 89-94; P-in-c Areley Kings 94-95; R 95-02; RD Stourport 00-02; TV Kidderminster St Jo and H Innocents 02-05; TR Cen Swansea *S & B* from 05. *The Rectory, 7 Eden Avenue, Uplands, Swansea SA2 0PS* Tel (01792) 298616 E-mail andrew.vessey@homecall.co.uk

VESSEY, Peter Allan Beaumont. b 36. ALCD65. **d** 64 **p** 65. C Rayleigh *Chelmsf* 64-67; C Cambridge H Trin *Ely* 67-71; V Kingston upon Hull St Aid Southcoates *York* 71-80; V Swanwick and Pentrich *Derby* 80-94; Perm to Offic from 94; rtd 96. *32 Scarthin Terrace, Scarthin, Cromford, Matlock DE4 3QF* Tel (01629) 825572

VESTERGAARD, David Andrew. b 64. Reading Univ BSc86. Wycliffe Hall Ox 97. **d** 99 **p** 00. C Chadderton Ch Ch *Man* 99-02; V Wednesfield Heath *Lich* from 02; AD Wolverhampton from 07. *Holy Trinity Vicarage, Bushbury Road, Wolverhampton WV10 0LY* Tel (01902) 738313 E-mail david@vestergaard.co.uk

VETTERS, Miss Shirley Jacqueline Margaret. b 34. S'wark Ord Course 85. **d** 88 **p** 94. NSM E Ham w Upton Park St Alb *Chelmsf* 88-91; C Birm St Martin w Bordesley St Andr 91-04; Chapl to the Markets 91-04; rtd 04; Perm to Offic *Chelmsf* from 05. *62 South Street, Manningtree CO11 1BQ* Tel (01206) 393691

VEVERS, Canon Geoffrey Martin. b 51. Oak Hill Th Coll. **d** 82 **p** 83. C Wealdstone H Trin *Lon* 82-84; C Harrow Trin St Mich 84-88; V Wandsworth St Steph *S'wark* 88-96; V Battersea Fields from 96; RD Battersea from 04; Hon Can S'wark Cathl from 06. *St Saviour's Vicarage, 351A Battersea Park Road, London SW11 4LH* Tel (020) 7498 1662

VIBERT (*née* GREEN), Imogen Elizabeth.** b 73. Birm Univ BA96 Cam Univ BTh02. Westcott Ho Cam 99. **d** 02 **p** 03. C Poplar *Lon* 02-06; Hon C Upper Clapton St Matt from 06; Hon C Stamford

Hill St Thos from 06. *20 Moresby Road, London E5 9LF* Tel (020) 8880 0696 E-mail imogen@vibert.wannadoo.co.uk

VIBERT, Simon David Newman. b 63. Oak Hill Th Coll BA89. **d** 89 **p** 90. C Houghton *Carl* 89-92; C-in-c Buxton Trin Prop Chpl *Derby* 92-99; V Wimbledon Park St Luke *S'wark* 99-07; Vice Prin Wycliffe Hall Ox from 07; Dir Sch of Preaching from 08. *Wycliffe Hall, 54 Banbury Road, Oxford OX2 6PW* Tel (01865) 274200 E-mail simon.vibert@wycliffe.ox.ac.uk

VICARS, David. b 22. Leeds Univ BA48. Coll of Resurr Mirfield 48. **d** 50 **p** 51. C Newington St Paul *S'wark* 50-54; C Kingston St Luke 54-56; C Cirencester *Glouc* 56-59; Malaysia 59-66; Area Sec USPG *Llan, Mon, St D* and *S & B* 67-77; R Coychurch w Llangan and St Mary Hill 77-90; rtd 90; Perm to Offic *Llan* from 90. *43 Bryn Rhedyn, Pencoed, Bridgend CF35 6TL* Tel (01656) 860920

VICK, Samuel Kenneth Lloyd. b 31. Univ of Wales (Lamp) BA53. Linc Th Coll. **d** 55 **p** 56. C Shotton *St As* 55-56; C Wrexham 56-61; C Knowle H Nativity *Bris* 61-67; V Mirfield Eastthorpe St Paul *Wakef* 67-78; V Altofts 73-98; rtd 98; Master Abp Holgate Hosp Hemsworth 98-09. *12 St Peter's Court, Horbury, Wakefield WF4 6AP* Tel (01924) 280136

VICKERMAN, Canon John. b 42. Chich Th Coll 69. **d** 72 **p** 73. C Horbury *Wakef* 72-76; C Elland 76-78; V Glass Houghton 78-89; V Bruntcliffe 89-96; V King Cross from 96; RD Halifax 00-06; Hon Can Wakef Cathl from 02. *The Vicarage, West Royd Avenue, Halifax HX1 3NU* Tel (01422) 352933

VICKERS (née CONWAY), Mrs Catherine Mary. b 61. Newc Univ BA82 Leeds Univ PGCE83. NEOC 03. **d** 06 **p** 07. C Bedale and Leeming *Ripon* 06-08; C Bedale and Leeming and Thornton Watlass from 08. *23 Kingfisher Drive, Aiskew, Bedale DL8 1XG* Tel (01677) 422834 E-mail cathvickers@hotmail.com

VICKERS, Dennis William George. b 30. RIBA72 York Univ MA91 IHBC99. Glouc Th Course 83. **d** 86 **p** 87. NSM Stokesay *Heref* 86-88; NSM Bucknell w Chapel Lawn, Llanfair Waterdine etc 88-92; NSM Wigmore Abbey 93-01; Perm to Offic from 01. *Reeves Holding, Reeves Lane, Stanage, Knighton LD7 1NA* Tel (01547) 530577 Fax 530773

VICKERS, Donald. b 48. Edge Hill Coll of HE DASE80 Univ of Wales (Ban) MEd87. NOC 97. **d** 00 **p** 01. NSM Leigh St Mary *Man* 00-05; NSM Westleigh St Pet from 05; Asst Chapl HM Pris *Man* from 00. *21 Broom Way, Westhoughton, Bolton BL5 3TZ* Tel (01942) 815193 Mobile 07768-492581 E-mail don@dvickers20.freeserve.co.uk

VICKERS, Mrs Janice Audrey Maureen. b 56. **d** 96 **p** 97. OLM Woking Ch Ch *Guildf* 96-06; OLM Ottershaw from 06. *7 Langdale Close, Woking GU21 4RS* Tel (01483) 720873 E-mail bobjan@bjvickers.eclipse.co.uk

VICKERS, Mrs Mary Janet. b 57. Westmr Coll Ox MTh97. St Jo Coll Nottm BTh85. **dss** 85 **d** 87 **p** 99. Worc City St Paul and Old St Martin etc 85-89; Par Dn 87-89; World Miss Officer *Worc* 89-92; USPG 92-00; Lic to Offic *Eur* 95-99; Perm to Offic from 99; Perm to Offic Adnry of the Army from 97; NSM Cheswardine, Childs Ercall, Hales, Hinstock etc *Lich* 99-01; NSM Wrecclesham *Guildf* 01-02; NSM Pimperne, Stourpaine, Durweston and Bryanston *Sarum* 03-05; NSM Hipswell *Ripon* 05-06; NSM W Andover *Win* 07-09; NSM Portway and Danebury from 09. *3 Millers Lane, Middle Wallop, Stockbridge SO20 8GD* E-mail revsvickers@tiscali.co.uk

VICKERS, Michael. b 60. Cranmer Hall Dur BA98. **d** 98 **p** 99. C Monkwearmouth *Dur* 98-00; C Kowloon St Andr Hong Kong 00-07; V Cranham Park *Chelmsf* from 07. *St Luke's Vicarage, 201 Front Lane, Upminster RM14 1LD* Tel (01708) 222562 Fax 223253 E-mail revmichaelvickers@gmail.com

✠**VICKERS, The Rt Revd Michael Edwin.** b 29. Worc Coll Ox BA56 MA56. Cranmer Hall Dur. **d** 59 **p** 60 **c** 88. C Bexleyheath Ch Ch *Roch* 59-62; Chapl Lee Abbey 62-67; V Hull St Jo Newland *York* 67-81; AD Cen and N Hull 72-81; Can and Preb York Minster 81-88; Adn E Riding 81-88; Area Bp Colchester *Chelmsf* 88-94; rtd 94; Asst Bp Blackb from 94. *2 Collingham Park, Lancaster LA1 4PD* Tel (01524) 848492 E-mail micjan@tiscali.co.uk

VICKERS, Peter. b 56. St Jo Coll Nottm LTh85. **d** 85 **p** 86. C Worc St Barn w Ch Ch 85-88; TV Kidderminster St Mary and All SS w Trimpley etc 88-92; Ind Chapl 88-92; CF from 92. *c/o MOD Chaplains (Army)* Tel (01980) 615804 Fax 615800 E-mail revsvickers@msn.com

VICKERS, Peter George. b 41. Local Minl Tr Course 90. **d** 93 **p** 94. OLM Cobham *Guildf* 93-04; OLM Cobham and Stoke D'Abernon from 04. *24 Station Road, Stoke D'Abernon, Cobham KT11 3BN* Tel (01932) 862497 E-mail revpgv@googlemail.com

VICKERS, Randolph. b 36. Newc Univ MA93 FCIM FInstD. St Alb Minl Tr Scheme 77. **d** 80 **p** 82. NSM Hitchin *St Alb* 80-87; NSM Luton Lewsey St Hugh 87-89; NSM Shotley *Newc* 89-01; rtd 01; Perm to Offic *Newc* from 01. *Beggar's Roost, 26 Painshawfield Road, Stocksfield NE43 7PF* Tel and fax (01661) 842364 E-mail rvickers@christian-healing.com

VICKERSTAFF, John Joseph. b 60. Dur Univ BEd82 Teesside

Univ BA84 MA86 MPhil88 ARCO92. Westcott Ho Cam 97. **d** 97 **p** 98. C Halesworth w Linstead, Chediston, Holton etc *St E* 97-99; C Blyth Valley 99-00; TV Ch the King *Newc* 00-05; P-in-c Doveridge, Scropton, Sudbury etc *Derby* from 05; C Alkmonton, Cubley and Marston Montgomery from 07. *The Rectory, Main Road, Sudbury, Ashbourne DE6 5HS* Tel (01283) 585098 E-mail grumpy.revs@tiscali.co.uk

VICKERY, Charles William Bryan. b 38. Lich Th Coll 63. **d** 65 **p** 66. C Hove St Barn *Chich* 65-73; Chapl Hostel of God Clapham 73-76; P-in-c Kingston St Luke *S'wark* 76-82; V 82-94; rtd 94. *4 The Coach House, 194 High Road, Byfleet, West Byfleet KT14 7BT* Tel (01932) 354119

VICKERY, Jonathan Laurie. b 58. Bretton Hall Coll BEd80. Wycliffe Hall Ox 81. **d** 84 **p** 85. C Gorseinon *S & B* 84-86; P-in-c Whitton and Pilleth and Cascob etc 86-87; R 87-91; V Crickhowell w Cwmdu and Tretower 91-02; P-in-c Downend *Bris* 02-07; V from 07. *Christ Church Vicarage, Shrubbery Road, Bristol BS16 5TB* Tel 0117-908 9868 E-mail vicar@christchurchdownend.com

VICKERY, Robin Francis. b 48. K Coll Lon BD73 AKC73. **d** 74 **p** 75. C Clapham St Jo *S'wark* 74-77; C Clapham Ch Ch and St Jo 75-77; C Reigate St Luke S Park 77-79; Hon C Clapham H Spirit 80-87 and from 02; Hon C Clapham Team 87-01. *13 Chelsham Road, London SW4 6NR* Tel (020) 7622 4792

VIDAL-HALL, Roderic Mark. b 37. Sheff Univ BSc60. Lich Th Coll 62. **d** 64 **p** 65. C Ilkeston St Mary *Derby* 64-67; C Nether and Over Seale 67-70; V Chellaston 70-84; C Marchington w Marchington Woodlands *Lich* 85-97; TV Uttoxeter Area 97-01; rtd 01. *Le Perhou, 22630 Saint-Juvat, France* Tel (0033) (2) 96 88 16 34 E-mail mark@vidalhall.co.uk

VIGARS, Anthony Roy. b 54. St Jo Coll Dur BA75. Trin Coll Bris 77. **d** 78 **p** 79. C Barking St Marg w St Patr *Chelmsf* 78-81; C Littleover *Derby* 81-84; C-in-c Stapenhill Immanuel CD 84-90; V Meltham *Wakef* 90-97; V Reading St Jo *Ox* 97-06; rtd 07; Perm to Offic *Ox* 07-08 and *Ex* from 09. *15 Edgcumbe Drive, Tavistock PL19 0ET* Tel (01822) 610539 E-mail vigars@lineone.net

VIGEON, Canon Owen George. b 28. Peterho Cam BA52 MA57. Ely Th Coll 52. **d** 54 **p** 55. C Barrow St Luke *Carl* 54-58; Chapl St Jo Coll York 58-61; V Burnley St Steph *Blackb* 61-69; V Bilsborrow and Asst Dir RE 69-73; V St Annes St Thos 74-85; RD Fylde 80-85; R Halton w Aughton 85-93; Hon Can Blackb Cathl 92-93; rtd 93; Perm to Offic *Worc* 93-04 and *Cov* from 04. *10 Hall Lane, Coventry CV2 2AW* Tel (024) 7661 1712 E-mail owenvig@talktalk.net

VIGERS, Neil Simon. b 62. K Coll Lon BD84 MTh87. Linc Th Coll 88. **d** 90 **p** 91. C Chelsea St Luke and Ch Ch *Lon* 90-93; C Staines St Mary and St Pet 93-96; P-in-c Hook *Win* 96-02; R 02-07. *Address temp unknown*

VIGERS, Patricia Anne. b 31. Lon Inst of Educn TCert53. **d** 99 **p** 00. OLM Betchworth and Buckland *S'wark* 99-06; Perm to Offic from 06. *5 Normanton, Buckland Road, Reigate RH2 9RQ* Tel (01737) 243698

VIGOR, Ms Margaret Ann. b 45. Ripon Coll Cuddesdon 85. **d** 87 **p** 96. Chapl Asst All SS Convent Ox 87-89; Par Dn Basildon St Martin w Nevendon *Chelmsf* 89-91; NSM Billingham St Cuth *Dur* from 96. *15 Mitchell Street, Hartlepool TS26 9EZ* Tel (01429) 867458

VILLAGE, Andrew. b 54. Collingwood Coll Dur BSc75 Edin Univ PhD80 Bris Univ PhD03. Trin Coll Bris BA92. **d** 92 **p** 93. C Northampton St Giles *Pet* 92-95; R Middleton Cheney w Chacombe 95-04; Dir Cen for Min Studies Univ of Wales (Ban) 04-07; Lect Relig Studies Univ York from 07; Perm to Offic *York* from 08. *York St John University, Lord Mayor's Walk, York YO31 7EX* Tel (01904) 876723 Mobile 07749-484425 E-mail a.village@yorksj.ac.uk

VILLER, Canon Allan George Frederick. b 38. EAMTC 78. **d** 81 **p** 82. NSM Ely 81-85; V Emneth 85-92; V Littleport 92-03; RD Ely 98-03; rtd 03; Hon Can Ely Cathl 01-06; Hon C Barton Bendish w Beachamwell etc 03-06; Perm to Offic *Ely* from 06 and *Nor* from 07. *41 Westfields, Narborough, King's Lynn PE32 1SX* Tel and fax (01760) 337633 E-mail allan@viller.net

VINCE, Mrs Barbara Mary Tudor. b 29. St Alb Minl Tr Scheme 79. **dss** 82 **d** 87 **p** 94. Northwood H Trin *Lon* 82-86; Belmont 86-89; Par Dn 87-89; rtd 90. *10 Risinghill Close, Northwood HA6 3PH*

VINCE, David Eric. b 59. Birm Univ BA81 Nottm Univ BCombStuds83 Goldsmiths' Coll Lon PGCE90. Linc Th Coll 82. **d** 85 **p** 86. C Gt Malvern St Mary *Worc* 85-88; C All Hallows by the Tower etc *Lon* 88-90; Min St Giles Cripplegate w St Bart Moor Lane etc 90-92; R Salwarpe and Hindlip w Martin Hussingtree *Worc* 92-97; R Willersey, Saintbury, Weston-sub-Edge etc *Glouc* 97-03; P-in-c Quinton 02-03; R Mickleton, Willersey, Saintbury etc 03-06; RD Campden 01-06; Perm to Offic *Glouc* and *Worc* from 06; CF from 07. *40 Elmside, Evesham WR11 3DZ* Tel 07890-304399 (mobile) E-mail david@devince.freeserve.co.uk

VINCENT, Preb Alfred James. b 30. Bris Univ BA54 Lon Univ BD56. Tyndale Hall Bris 50. **d** 54 **p** 55. C Shrewsbury St Julian *Lich* 54-56; C Camborne *Truro* 56-59; V Kenwyn 59-68; Lic to Offic *St Alb* 68; Lect Qu Coll Birm 68-70; Lic to Offic *Birm* 68-70; V Bordesley St Oswald 70-76; V S Shields St Hilda w St Thos *Dur* 76-84; Hon Chapl Miss to Seafarers from 79; V Bude Haven *Truro* 84-89; R Bude Haven and Marhamchurch 89-92; RD Stratton 88-92; Preb St Endellion 90-95; rtd 92; P-in-c Chacewater *Truro* 92-95; Perm to Offic from 95. *5 Raymond Road, Redruth TR15 2HD* Tel (01209) 219263

VINCENT, Bruce Matthews. b 24. Open Univ BA76 Surrey Univ MPhil83. **d** 88 **p** 88. NSM Sidcup St Jo *Roch* 88-94; Perm to Offic from 94. *17 Glenrose Court, 55 Sidcup Hill, Sidcup DA14 6HG* Tel (020) 8302 1869

VINCENT, Christopher Robin. b 30. Sarum Th Coll 57. **d** 60 **p** 61. C Frome St Jo *B & W* 60-64; V Puxton w Hewish St Ann and Wick St Lawrence 64-70; V Buckland Dinham w Elm 70-71; V Buckland Dinham w Elm, Orchardleigh etc 71-77; P-in-c Frome H Trin 77-90; Chapl St Adhelm's Hosp Frome 77-88; RD Frome *B & W* 85-89; V Kewstoke w Wick St Lawrence 90-94; rtd 94; Perm to Offic *B & W* from 94. *Willows Edge, 2 Westwood Close, Weston-super-Mare BS22 6JU* Tel (01934) 517425

VINCENT, David Cyril. b 37. Selw Coll Cam BA60 MA64. Coll of Resurr Mirfield 60. **d** 62 **p** 63. C Cheetwood St Alb *Man* 62-65; C Lawton Moor 65-67; V Wandsworth Common St Mary *S'wark* 67-84; RD Tooting 75-80; R Stoke D'Abernon *Guildf* 84-02; rtd 02; Perm to Offic *B & W* from 04. *29 North Street, Stoke-sub-Hamdon TA14 6QS* Tel (01935) 825438

VINCENT, George William Walter. b 13. ALCD40. **d** 40 **p** 41. C Hammersmith St Simon *Lon* 40-44; C Stowmarket *St E* 44-47; R Earl Stonham 47-55; R Alderton w Ramsholt and Bawdsey 55-86; rtd 86; Perm to Offic *St E* from 86. *c/o B Vincent Esq, Rectory House, Alderton, Woodbridge IP12 3BL* Tel (01394) 411306

VINCENT, Henry William Gordon. b 16. Leeds Univ BA42. Coll of Resurr Mirfield 42. **d** 44 **p** 45. C Bridgwater St Jo *B & W* 44-46; C Greenford H Cross *Lon* 46-52; C Teddington St Alb 52-55; V N Hammersmith St Kath 55-64; V Whitton St Aug 64-81; rtd 81; Perm to Offic *Sarum* from 81. *Legh House, 117 Rylands Lane, Weymouth DT4 9QB* Tel (01305) 779509

VINCENT, James. *See* VINCENT, Preb Alfred James

VINCENT, John Leonard. b 61. Univ of Wales (Lamp) BA83 Southn Univ BTh87. Chich Th Coll 84. **d** 87 **p** 88. C Hampton All SS *Lon* 87-90; C Shepperton 90-95; V Whitton SS Phil and Jas 95-03; CF from 03. *c/o MOD Chaplains (Army)* Tel (01980) 615804 Fax 615800 E-mail pipnjim@aol.com

VINCENT, Michael Francis. b 48. CertEd70 Open Univ BA83. Sarum & Wells Th Coll 85. **d** 87 **p** 88. C Nuneaton St Mary *Cov* 87-90; C Stockingford 90-91; P-in-c 91-99; V from 99. *Stockingford Vicarage, 90 Church Road, Nuneaton CV10 8LG* Tel and fax (024) 7637 2089
E-mail mick@vincent4850.freeserve.co.uk

VINCENT, Robin. *See* VINCENT, Christopher Robin

VINCENT, Roy David. b 37. Chich Th Coll 81. **d** 83 **p** 84. C Atherton *Man* 83-86; V E Crompton 86-95; P-in-c Burwash *Chich* 95-00; R 00-04; rtd 04. *1 Kelton Croft, Kirkland, Frizington CA26 3YE* Tel (01946) 861300

VINCER, Ms Louise Claire. b 69. Roehampton Inst BA90 Edin Univ MTh93. Westcott Ho Cam 97. **d** 00 **p** 01. C Waltham H Cross *Chelmsf* 00-04; C Perry Hill St Geo w Ch Ch and St Paul *S'wark* 04-06; C Bermondsey St Anne and St Aug from 06; C Bermondsey St Jas w Ch Ch and St Crispin from 06. *The Rectory, 57 Kennington Park Road, London SE11 4JQ* Tel (020) 7735 2807 E-mail lcvincer@ukonline.co.uk

VINCER, Canon Michael. b 41. S Dios Minl Tr Scheme 77. **d** 80 **p** 81. Hon C Littleham w Exmouth 80-92; Area Sec USPG *Ex* and *Truro* 86-92; Ind Chapl Gtr Man Ind Miss 92-05; Chapl Man Airport 92-05; Hon Can Man Cathl 02-05; rtd 06; Perm to Offic *Man* 06-07 and *York* from 08. *28 Farmanby Close, Thornton Dale, Pickering YO18 7TD* Tel (01751) 467136 E-mail mike.vincer@gmail.com

VINCE, Carolyn Ann. *See* TIBBOTT, Mrs Carolyn Ann

VINE, James David. b 67. Brighton Univ BSc95. St Steph Ho Ox. **d** 00 **p** 01. C Eastbourne St Mary *Chich* 00-03; V Stone Cross St Luke w N Langney from 03. *The Vicarage, 8 Culver Close, Eastbourne BN23 8EA* Tel (01323) 764473

VINE, John. b 24. Keble Coll Ox BA45 MA50. St Steph Ho Ox 45. **d** 48 **p** 49. C Hackney Wick St Mary of Eton w St Aug *Lon* 48-50; C Holborn St Alb w Saffron Hill St Pet 50-53; Chapl Ely Th Coll 53-56; Vice-Prin Ely Th Coll 56-60; Hon C St Leonards Ch Ch *Chich* 60-62; Chapl Lich Th Coll 62-67; R Wrington *B & W* 67-69; V Earl's Court St Cuth w St Matthias *Lon* from 69. *St Cuthbert's Clergy House, 50 Philbeach Gardens, London SW5 9EB* Tel (020) 7370 3263

VINE, Michael Charles. b 51. Worc Coll Ox BA73 MA80. Cuddesdon Coll 73. **d** 76 **p** 77. C Wallsend St Luke *Newc* 76-79; C Denton 79-81; V Sugley 81-91; V Shiremoor 91-02; R

Wallsend St Pet and St Luke from 02. *148 Park Road, Wallsend NE28 7QS* Tel 0191-262 3723
E-mail vinemichael@freeuk.co.uk

VINE, Michael Derek. b 35. Ch Ch Ox BA58 MA63 Reading Univ PGCE. Ely Th Coll 58. **d** 60 **p** 61. C Syston *Leic* 60-63; C S Ascot *Ox* 63-66; Chapl RN 66-70; Perm to Offic *Portsm* 71-74 and *Lon* 74-91; C Chepstow *Mon* 91-94; V Llantilio Pertholey w Bettws Chpl etc 94-00; rtd 00. *2 The Tythe Barn, Chapel Lane, Abergavenny NP7 7BT* Tel (01873) 856250

VINE, Canon Neville Peter. b 54. K Coll Lon BD80 AKC80. Linc Th Coll 80. **d** 81 **p** 82. C Peterlee *Dur* 81-86; Chapl Peterlee Coll 84-86; V Auckland St Pet *Dur* 86-89; Perm to Offic 89-91; R Easington 91-99; R Easington, Easington Colliery and S Hetton 99-03; AD Easington 98-03; V Auckland St Andr and St Anne from 03; AD Auckland from 03; Hon Can Dur Cathl from 03. *4 Conway Grove, Bishop Auckland DL14 6AF* Tel (01388) 604397 E-mail neville.vine@btinternet.com

VINER, Canon Leonard Edwin. b 20. Univ Coll Dur BA43. St Aug Coll Cant 38. **d** 43 **p** 44. C W Molesey *Guildf* 43-45; Miss Likoma Nyasaland 46-52; Warden St Andr Th Coll Likoma 52-56 and 58-60; C Roxbourne St Andr *Lon* 56-58; Chapl St Mich Teacher Tr Coll Malindi 60-64; Warden St Andr Th Coll Mponda's 64-67; P-in-c Malindi 67-69; R Zomba 69-71; Hon Can S Malawi from 71; R Honing w Crostwight *Nor* 71-75; P-in-c E Ruston 71-73; V 73-75; P-in-c Witton w Ridlington 71-73; V 73-75; C Corby Epiphany w St Jo *Pet* 75-79; V Brigstock w Stanion 79-86; rtd 86; Asst Chapl Lisbon *Eur* 86-87; Chapl Tangier 87-89; Perm to Offic *Pet* from 90. *38 High Street, Brigstock, Kettering NN14 3HA* Tel (01536) 373104

VINEY, Arthur William. b 32. BEd. S Dios Minl Tr Scheme. **d** 82 **p** 83. NSM Clayton w Keymer *Chich* 82-86; NSM Streat w Westmeston 86-94; rtd 94; Perm to Offic *Chich* from 94. *3 The Almshouses of the Holy Name, Brighton Road, Hurstpierpoint, Hassocks BN6 9EF* Tel (01273) 832570
E-mail a.viney@btopenworld.com

VINEY, Peter. b 43. Ox NSM Course. **d** 76 **p** 77. NSM High Wycombe *Ox* from 76. *76 Westmead, Princes Risborough HP27 9HS* Tel (01844) 275461

VIPOND, Canon John. b 17. Lon Univ BD48. ALCD48. **d** 48 **p** 49. C Roxeth Ch Ch *Lon* 48-51; V 51-56; V Pudsey St Lawr *Bradf* 56-73; Hon Can Bradf Cathl 67-73; V St Austell *Truro* 73-83; rtd 83; Perm to Offic *Truro* from 83. *Wisteria, 15 Coffeelake Meadow, Lostwithiel PL22 0LT* Tel (01208) 873141

VIRDEN, Richard. b 40. K Coll Lon BSc61 Univ Coll Lon MSc62 PhD66. **d** 04 **p** 05. OLM N Tyne and Redesdale *Newc* from 04. *Ingram Cottage, West Woodburn, Hexham NE48 2SB* Tel (01434) 270334 E-mail richard.virden@ncl.ac.uk

VIRGO, Canon Leslie Gordon. b 25. Linc Th Coll 56. **d** 58 **p** 59. C Hatcham Park All SS *S'wark* 58-61; C Selsdon *Cant* 61-65; Chapl Warlingham Park Hosp Croydon 65-73; Dioc Adv on Past Care and Counselling from 74; R Chelsfield *Roch* from 74; Hon Can Roch Cathl from 83. *Chelsfield Rectory, Skibbs Lane, Orpington BR6 7RH* Tel (01689) 825749 Mobile 07792-085809 E-mail leslie.virgo@diocese-rochester.org

VIRTUE, Thomas James. b 32. QUB BA56 TCD58. **d** 58 **p** 59. C Belfast St Mich *Conn* 58-61; C Belfast St Bart 61-63; I Tempo *Clogh* 63-66; P-in-c Glynn w Raloo and Templecorran *Conn* 66-70; TV Ellesmere Port *Ches* 70-74; TV Ches 74-83; V Gt Sutton 83-97; rtd 97; Perm to Offic *Ches* from 97. *48 Saughall Road, Blacon, Chester CH1 5EY* Tel (01244) 399531

VIVASH, Peter Henry. b 57. Hockerill Coll of Educn CertEd78 CQSW85. Cranmer Hall Dur 90. **d** 92 **p** 93. C Malpas *Mon* 92-95; R Bettws 95-01; P-in-c Upper Derwent *Carl* from 01; Dioc Rep CMS from 01; Warden of Readers *Carl* from 05. *Thornthwaite Vicarage, Braithwaite, Keswick CA12 5RY* Tel (01768) 778243 E-mail peter.vivash@dsl.pipex.com

VIVIAN, Adrian John. b 42. K Coll Lon BD65 AKC66. St Denys Warminster 62. **d** 66 **p** 67. C Bromley St Andr *Roch* 66-69; C Egg Buckland *Ex* 69-73; Perm to Offic 73-84; P-in-c Newton Ferrers w Revelstoke 84-87. *9 Munro Avenue, Yealmpton, Plymouth PL8 2NQ*

VIVIAN, Thomas Keith. b 27. St Jo Coll Cam BA48 MA52. St Deiniol's Hawarden 76. **d** 80 **p** 81. Hd Master Lucton Sch Leominster 62-85; Lic to Offic *Heref* 80-85; P-in-c Chew Stoke w Nempnett Thrubwell *B & W* 85-88; R 88-97; P-in-c Norton Malreward 85-88; R 88-97; RD Chew Magna 92-97; rtd 97; Perm to Offic *B & W* and *Sarum* from 97. *Timberley, Sidmouth Road, Lyme Regis DT7 3ES* Tel (01297) 443547

VIVIAN, Victor Ivan. b 38. Nottm Poly LLB87. EMMTC 91. **d** 94 **p** 95. NSM Bestwood *S'well* 94-99; Korea 99-03; rtd 03; Perm to Offic *S'well* from 03. *12 Deepdale Road, Wollaton, Nottingham NG8 2FU* Tel 0115-928 3954 E-mail vicvivian@yahoo.com

VOAKE, Andrew James Frederick. b 28. Dur Univ BA55. Oak Hill Th Coll 51. **d** 55 **p** 56. C Uxbridge St Marg *Lon* 55; C Fulham St Matt 55-58; C Hove Bp Hannington Memorial Ch *Chich* 58-61; V Kirkdale St Lawr *Liv* 61-63; Chapl Millfield Sch Somerset 63-71; R Bp Latimer Memorial Ch *Birm* 71-73; R Birm Bp Latimer w All SS 73-80; V Crondall and Ewshot *Guildf* 80-90;

rtd 90; Perm to Offic *B & W* from 90. *1 St Aubyns Avenue, Weston-super-Mare BS23 4UJ* Tel (01934) 620587

✠VOBBE, The Rt Revd Joachim Gerhard. b 47. p 72 c 95. Chapl Cologne (Old Catholic Ch) 72-74; Chapl Düsseldorf 74-77; R Blumberg 77-82; R Offenbach 82-95; Bp Bonn from 95; Hon Asst Bp Eur from 99. *Gregor-Mendel-Strasse 28, D-53115 Bonn, Germany* Tel (0049) (228) 232285 Fax 238314
E-mail ordinariat@alt-katholisch.de

VOCKINS, Preb Michael David. b 44. OBE96. Univ of Wales (Abth) BSc69. Glouc Sch of Min 85. d 88 p 89. NSM Cradley w Mathon and Storridge *Heref* from 88; RD Ledbury from 02; Perm to Offic *Worc* from 88; Preb Heref Cathl from 09. *Birchwood Lodge, Birchwood, Storridge, Malvern WR13 5EZ* Tel (01886) 884366 *or* (01905) 748474
E-mail michaelvockins@birchwoodlodge.fsnet.co.uk

VODEN, Capt Raymond William Lang. b 35. CQSW74. SW Minl Tr Course 85. d 88 p 89. CA from 60; NSM Bideford *Ex* 88-94; C Northlew w Ashbury 94; C Bratton Clovelly w Germansweek 94; TV Okehampton w Inwardleigh, Bratton Clovelly etc 94-01; Chapl Ex and Distr Community Health Service NHS Trust 94-01; Bp's Adv for Child Protection *Ex* 96-01; rtd 01; Hon C Calstock *Truro* 01, Perm to Offic *Ex* from 99 and *Truro* from 01. *1 School Lane, Harrowbarrow, Callington PL17 8BS* Tel (01579) 350135 E-mail ray.voden@btinternet.com

VOGT, Charles William Derek. b 36. Ex Univ BA07. EMMTC 83. d 86 p 87. NSM Ilkeston H Trin *Derby* 86-87; C Derby St Anne and St Jo 87-90; TV Staveley and Barrow Hill 90-95; P-in-c Hasland 95-96; R 97-01; P-in-c Temple Normanton 95-96; V 97-01; rtd 01; Perm to Offic *Ex* from 01. *54 Old Bakery Close, Exeter EX4 2UZ* Tel (01392) 271943

VOGT, Robert Anthony. b 25. Jes Coll Cam BA50 MA54. S'wark Ord Course 60. d 63 p 64. C Sutton New Town St Barn *S'wark* 63-67; C Kidbrooke St Jas 67-72; V Wood End *Cov* 72-80; RD Cov E 77-80; R Kidbrooke St Jas *S'wark* 80-85; TR 85-90; rtd 90; Perm to Offic *S'wark* from 90. *15 Serica Court, 154 Greenwich High Road, London SE10 8NZ* Tel (020) 8853 3430

VOLLAND, Michael John. b 74. Northumbria Univ BA96 K Coll Lon MA04. Ridley Hall Cam 04. d 06 p 07. Pioneer Min Glouc City from 06; C Glouc Cathl from 07. *35 St Mary's Square, Gloucester GL1 2QT* Tel (01452) 525762
E-mail michaelvolland@btinternet.com

VOLTZENLOGEL, Timothy John. b 60. St Jo Coll Dur BA81. Wycliffe Hall Ox BTh00. d 00 p 01. C Eastbourne All SS *Chich* 00-04; V Church Langley *Chelmsf* from 04. *7 Ashworth Place, Harlow CM17 9PU* Tel (01279) 629950
E-mail tim@timv.freeserve.co.uk

VON MALAISE, Nicolas Axel Christoph. b 62. Univ Coll Ox BA84 MA. Ripon Coll Cuddesdon BA87. d 87 p 88. C Oxhey St Matt *St Alb* 87-90; C Northfield *Birm* 90-92; Asst Chapl Win Coll 92-05; Perm to Offic *Win* from 06; V Bordesley St Benedict *Birm* from 06. *St Benedict's Vicarage, 55 Hob Moor Road, Small Heath, Birmingham B10 9AY* Tel 0121-772 2726
E-mail utunumsint7@aol.com

VOOGHT, Canon Michael George Peter. b 38. St Pet Hall Ox BA61 MA65. Chich Th Coll 61. d 63 p 64. C E Dulwich St Jo *S'wark* 63-66; C Prestbury *Glouc* 66-72; R Minchinhampton 72-85; RD Stonehouse 79-85; V Thornbury 85-02; Hon Can Glouc Cathl 86-02; rtd 02; Perm to Offic *Glouc* from 03. *62 High Street, Thornbury, Bristol BS35 2AN* Tel (01454) 414915

VORLEY, Kenneth Arthur. b 27. Sarum Th Coll 65. d 67 p 68. C Ashbourne w Mapleton and Clifton *Derby* 67-71; R W Hallam and Mapperley 71-77; V Hemingford Grey *Ely* 78-88; rtd 88; Perm to Offic *Carl* 88-01 and from 03. *2 Glen Cottage, Braithwaite, Keswick CA12 5SX* Tel (01768) 778535

VOSS, Mrs Philomena Ann. b 35. Edge Hill Coll of HE CertEd55. St Alb Minl Tr Scheme 87 EAMTC 95. d 96 p 97. NSM Tye Green w Netteswell *Chelmsf* 96-03; NSM Ware St Mary *St Alb* 03-06; Perm to Offic from 06. *21 Queen's Road, Hertford SG13 8AZ* Tel (01992) 554676 E-mail annvoss@tesco.net

VOST, Mrs Jane. b 62. d 04 p 06. OLM Radcliffe St Andr *Man* from 04. *16 Edgworth Avenue, Ainsworth, Bolton BL2 5RL* Tel 0161-762 0614 E-mail j.beswick@tiscali.co.uk

VOUSDEN, Canon Alan Thomas. b 48. K Coll Lon BSc69. Qu Coll Birm. d 72 p 73. C Orpington All SS *Roch* 72-76; C Belvedere All SS 76-80; R Cuxton and Halling 80-86; V Bromley St Mark 86-98; Chapl Bromley Hosp 86-94; Chapl Bromley Hosps NHS Trust 94-98; V Rainham *Roch* from 98; Hon Can Roch Cathl from 99; RD Gillingham from 00. *The Vicarage, 80 Broadview Avenue, Gillingham ME8 9DE* Tel (01634) 231538 *or* tel and fax 362023 E-mail vicar@rainhamchurch.co.uk *or* alanvousden@btinternet.com

VOWLES, Miss Patricia. b 50. S'wark Ord Course 84. d 87 p 94. USPG 70-91; NSM Nunhead St Antony w St Silas *S'wark* 87-91; Par Dn Newington St Mary 91; Dn-in-c Camberwell St Mich w All So w Em 91; Par Dn 91-94; V 94-06; Chapl Cautley Ho from 06. *Cautley House, 95 Seabrook Road, Hythe CT21 5QY* Tel (01303) 230762 Fax 237447
E-mail p.vowles@btinternet.com
or cautleyhouse@compuserve.com

VOWLES, Canon Peter John Henry. b 25. Magd Coll Ox BA50 MA55. Westcott Ho Cam 50. d 52 p 53. C Kings Heath *Birm* 52-56; C Huddersfield St Pet *Wakef* 56-57; PC Perry Beeches *Birm* 57-64; V 64-72; R Cottingham *York* 72-83; R Man St Ann 83-91; Hon Can Man Cathl 83-91; rtd 91; Perm to Offic *Man* from 91. *10 Redshaw Close, Manchester M14 6JB* Tel 0161-257 2065

VROLIJK, Paul Dick. b 64. Delft Univ of Tech MSc88. Trin Coll Bris BA03 PhD08. d 04 p 05. NSM Stoke Gifford *Bris* 04-08; Chapl Aquitaine *Eur* from 09. *8 chemin du Garonna, 24240 Sigoules, France* Tel (0033) (5) 53 23 40 73
E-mail paul.vrolijk@orange.fr
or aquitainechaplain@gmail.com

✠VUNAGI, The Most Revd David. Univ of Papua New Guinea BEd82 St Jo Coll Auckland BTh90 Vancouver Sch of Th MTh98. c 00. Lect Bp Patteson Th Coll Kohimarama Solomon Is 92-96; C Vancouver St Anselm Canada 96-98; Solomon Is from 98; Prin Selwyn Coll 99-00; Bp Temotu 00-09; Abp Melanesia and Bp Cen Melanesia from 09. *Church of Melanesia, PO Box 19, Honiara, Solomon Islands* Tel (00677) 21137 Fax 21098 E-mail dvunagi@comphq.org.sb

VYE, Mrs Georgina Ann. b 57. SWMTC 06. d 09. C Littleham w Exmouth from 09. *The Rectory, Burgmanns Hill, Lympstone, Exmouth EX8 5HP* Tel (01395) 273343

W

✠WABUKALA, The Most Revd Eliud. b 51. St Paul's Coll Limuru 85. d 88 c 96. Canada 91-94; Lect St Paul's Th Coll Limuru 94-96; Bp Bungoma 96-09; Abp Kenya from 09. *PO Box 40502, Nairobi 00100, Kenya* Tel (00254) (2) 714753 Fax 718442 E-mail archoffice@swiftkenya.com

WADDELL, James William Boece. b 74. Trin Coll Bris 06. d 08 p 09. C Slaugham *Chich* from 08. *13 Warren Cottages, Horsham Road, Handcross, Haywards Heath RH17 6BU* Tel 07813-872871 (mobile)

WADDELL, Peter Matthew. b 75. Keble Coll Ox BA96 Fitzw Coll Cam MPhil98 PhD02. Westcott Ho Cam 98. d 02 p 03. C Oxton *Ches* 02-04; Chapl SS Coll Cam from 05. *Sidney Sussex College, Cambridge CB2 3HU* Tel (01223) 338872
E-mail chaplain@sid.cam.ac.uk *or* peterwad@hotmail.com

WADDINGTON, Gary Richard. b 69. St Chad's Coll Dur BSc91 Heythrop Coll Lon MA05. St Steph Ho Ox BTh96. d 96 p 97. C Southsea H Spirit *Portsm* 96-00; V Paulsgrove from 00. *St Michael's Vicarage, Hempsted Road, Portsmouth PO6 4AS* Tel (023) 9237 8808 Mobile 07778-402490
E-mail frgaryw@btinternet.com

WADDINGTON-FEATHER, John Joseph. b 33. Leeds Univ BA54 Keele Univ PGCE74 FRSA87. St Deiniol's Hawarden 75. d 77 p 78. NSM Longden and Annscroft w Pulverbatch *Heref* 77-03; Chapl Asst HM Pris Shrewsbury from 77; Sudan 84-85; Chapl Prestfelde Sch Shrewsbury 86-96; Ed *The Poetry Church* 95-08; Perm to Offic *Lich* from 99 and *Heref* from 03. *Fair View, Old Coppice, Lyth Bank, Shrewsbury SY3 0BW* Tel and fax (01743) 872177 E-mail john@feather-books.com

WADDLE, Simon. b 60. Wellington Univ (NZ) BA81. St Jo Coll Auckland 86. d 88 p 89. New Zealand 88-97; Perm to Offic *Roch* 97-00; Hon C Roch St Marg from 00. *19 Honeypot Close, Rochester ME2 3DU* Tel (020) 7898 1610 Fax 7898 1769

WADDY, Canon Lawrence Heber. b 14. Ball Coll Ox BA37 MA45. Westcott Ho Cam 39. d 40 p 41. Asst Master Win Coll 38-42 and 46-49; Chapl RNVR 42-46; Hd Master Tonbridge Sch 49-62; Lic Preacher *Roch* 50-63; Hon Can Roch Cathl 61-63; Hon Bp's Chapl 63; USA from 63; Chapl Bps' Sch 63-67; Hd Master and Chapl Santa Maria Internat Academy Chula Vista 67-69; Assoc Min Coronado Ch Ch 68-70; Lect California Univ San Diego 69-80; V San Diego Gd Samaritan 70-74; rtd 75; Hon Asst Min La Jolla St Jas-by-the-Sea from 75; Hon Can San Diego from 98. *5910 Camino de la Costa, La Jolla CA 92037, USA* Tel (001) (858) 459 5221

WADE, Canon Andrew John. b 50. Trin Coll Bris. d 86 p 87. C St Keverne *Truro* 86-89; TV Probus, Ladock and Grampound w Creed and St Erme 89-92; V Constantine 92-00; P-in-c Ludgvan 00-01; P-in-c Marazion 00-01; P-in-c St Hilary w Perranuthnoe 00-01; R Ludgvan, Marazion, St Hilary and Perranuthnoe 01-08; RD Penwith 03-08; TR Probus, Ladock and Grampound w Creed and St Erme from 08; Hon Can Truro Cathl from 08. *The Sanctuary, Wagg Lane, Probus, Truro TR2 4JX* Tel (01726) 882746 E-mail andrewsanctuary@aol.com

WADE, Christopher John. b 54. Trent Poly BSc81 MRICS82 ACIArb88. Aston Tr Scheme 88 Trin Coll Bris. **d** 92 **p** 93. C Barnsley St Geo *Wakef* 92-95; C Whittle-le-Woods *Blackb* 95-99; P-in-c Bulwell St Jo *S'well* 99-03; Dir Heavenfire Min from 03. *46 Hastings Avenue, Whitley Bay NE26 4AG* Tel 084516-65277 E-mail chris@heavenfire.org

WADE, Canon David Peter. b 65. St Jo Coll Nottm LTh92. **d** 92 **p** 93. C Victoria Docks Ascension *Chelmsf* 92-95; P-in-c Victoria Docks St Luke 95-97; V from 97; AD Newham from 07; Hon Can Chelmsf Cathl from 08. *The Vicarage, 16A Ruscoe Road, London E16 1JB* Tel (020) 7476 2076 E-mail davenicky@hotmail.com

WADE, Geoffrey Adrian. b 61. Ripon Coll Cuddesdon. **d** 01 **p** 02. C Worc City St Paul and Old St Martin etc 01-02; C Wordsley 02-04; TV Ilminster and Distr *B & W* from 04. *The Rectory, Shepton Beauchamp, Ilminster TA19 0LP* Tel (01460) 240228 E-mail wadesinsomerset@waitrose.com

WADE, Walter. b 29. Oak Hill Th Coll 64. **d** 66 **p** 67. C Denton Holme *Carl* 66-69; V Jesmond H Trin *Newc* 69-78; R Moresby *Carl* 78-87; P-in-c Langdale 87-94; Member Rural Life and Agric Team 93-94; rtd 94; Perm to Offic *Carl* from 94. *Manor Cottage, Fellside, Caldbeck, Wigton CA7 8HA* Tel (01697) 478214

WADEY, Ms Rachel Susan. b 71. Lanc Univ BA94 Ox Univ BA98. St Steph Ho Ox 95. **d** 98 **p** 99. C Poulton-le-Fylde *Blackb* 98-01; C Blackpool H Cross 01-03; V Skerton St Chad 03-09; Chapl Prospect Park Hosp Reading from 09. *Prospect Park Hospital, Honey End Lane, Tilehurst, Reading RG30 4EJ* Tel 0118-960 5000 E-mail rachel.wadey@talktalk.net

WADGE, Alan. b 46. Grey Coll Dur BA68 MA72. St Chad's Coll Dur. **d** 70 **p** 71. C Cockerton *Dur* 70-74; C Whitworth w Spennymoor 74-75; P-in-c Shipton Moyne w Westonbirt and Lasborough *Glouc* 75-80; Chapl Westonbirt Sch 75-80; V Dean Forest H Trin *Glouc* 80-83; Chapl Gresham's Sch Holt 83-91; R Ridgeway *Ox* from 91; RD Wantage 95-01. *The Rectory, Letcombe Regis, Wantage OX12 9LD* Tel (01235) 763805

WADHAM, Canon Philip Andrew. b 41. Saltley Tr Coll Birm CertEd70 Bradf Univ MA92. Vancouver Sch of Th BTh80. **d** 79 **p** 80. Canada 80-82; Ecuador 82-85; Canada 85-88; Area Sec USPG *Wakef* and *Bradf* 88-92; Canada from 93. *4544 Rocky Point Road, Victoria BC V9C 4E4, Canada* Tel (001) (250) 391 7436 E-mail pwadham@telus.net

WADLAND, Douglas Bryan. b 33. K Coll Dur BA61 CQSW62. Oak Hill Th Coll 90. **d** 91 **p** 92. NSM Cowley *Lon* 91-93; Asst Chapl Hillingdon Hosp NHS Trust 91-93; P-in-c Wembley St Jo *Lon* 93-00; Chapl Cen Middx Hosp NHS Trust 93-00; rtd 00; Kenya 01-03; Hon C Alperton *Lon* from 03. *55 Copthall Road East, Uxbridge UB10 8SE* Tel (01895) 613904 E-mail wadland@lizbryan.freeserve.co.uk

WADMAN, Vera Margaret. b 51. EAMTC 97. **d** 00 **p** 01. NSM Burnham *Chelmsf* 00-02; NSM Creeksea w Althorne, Latchingdon and N Fambridge from 02. *Fernlea Cottage, 8 Fernlea Road, Burnham-on-Crouch CM0 8EJ* Tel (01621) 783963 E-mail verawadman@onetel.net.uk

WADSWORTH (née REID), Mrs Alison Margaret. b 36. Bris Univ CertEd57. **d** 97 **p** 98. OLM Cley Hill Warminster *Sarum* 97-06. *2 Saxon's Acre, Warminster BA12 8HT* Tel (01985) 212510 E-mail awap@blueyonder.co.uk

WADSWORTH, Andrew James. b 56. St Jo Coll Dur BA79 Cam Univ CertEd80 Lambeth STh95 FRSA93. Sarum & Wells Th Coll 84 Chich Th Coll 86. **d** 87 **p** 88. NSM Forest Road and E Grinstead St Swithun *Chich* 87-89; C Shrewsbury St Chad w St Mary *Lich* 89-91; TV Honiton, Gittisham, Combe Raleigh, Monkton etc *Ex* 91-97; P-in-c Bulkington w Shilton and Ansty *Cov* 97-06; P-in-c Bognor *Chich* 06-07; V from 07. *St Wilfrid's Vicarage, 17 Victoria Drive, Bognor Regis PO21 2RH* Tel (01243) 821965 E-mail rev.andrew@wadswortha.fsnet.co.uk

WADSWORTH, Andrew John. b 67. Reading Univ BSc88 MRICS90. Wycliffe Hall Ox 99. **d** 01 **p** 02. C Plymouth St Andr and Stonehouse *Ex* 01-05; C Enfield Ch Ch Trent Park *Lon* from 05. *2 Firs Lane, London N21 2HU* Tel (020) 8441 6444 E-mail awadsworth@waddy20.freeserve.co.uk

WADSWORTH, Jean. b 44. St Jo Coll Dur BA71. Cranmer Hall Dur 85. **d** 87 **p** 94. Par Dn Thamesmead *S'wark* 87-92; Par Dn Rotherhithe H Trin 92-94; C 94-98; V New Eltham All SS 98-08; RD Eltham and Mottingham 01-05; rtd 08. *2 Peak Coach House, Cotmaton Road, Sidmouth EX10 8SY*

WADSWORTH, Mrs Mary. b 44. **d** 08 **p** 09. NSM Ashton *Man* from 08. *99 Cranbourne Road, Ashton-under-Lyne OL7 9BW* Tel 0161-330 0713 Mobile 07712-527981 E-mail thewadsat99@aol.com

WADSWORTH, Canon Michael Philip. b 43. Qu Coll Ox BA65 MA68 DPhil75 Cam Univ PhD78. Ripon Coll Cuddesdon. **d** 70 **p** 71. C Sutton St Mich *York* 70-73; Lect Sussex Univ 73-78; Hon C Hove St Jo 75-78; Fell and Chapl SS Coll Cam 78-81; Dir Th Studies 79-81; CF (TA) from 80; C Ditton St Mich *Liv* 81; TV 82-84; Dioc Lay Tr Officer 83-89; V Orford St Marg 84-89; V Haddenham *Ely* 89-98; V Wilburton 89-98; RD Ely 94-98; P-in-c Gt Shelford 98-01; Hon Can Ely Cathl 96-01; rtd 01; Perm to

Offic *Ely* and *Linc* from 01. *9 Eastgate, Sleaford NG34 7DL* Tel (01529) 304251

WADSWORTH, Peter Richard. b 52. Qu Coll Ox BA73 MA77. Cuddesdon Coll 74 English Coll Rome 76. **d** 77 **p** 78. C High Wycombe *Ox* 77-81; C Farnham Royal w Hedgerley 81-84; Dioc Ecum Officer *Portsm* 84-90; V E Meon 84-96; V Langrish 84-96; V Elson 96-04; RD Gosport 96-02; V St Alb St Sav *St Alb* from 04. *St Saviour's Vicarage, 25 Sandpit Lane, St Albans AL1 4DF* Tel (01727) 851526 E-mail peter.wadsworth52@ntlworld.com

WADSWORTH, Roy. b 37. NEOC 89. **d** 89 **p** 90. NSM Alne *York* from 89; Ind Chapl 94-03; rtd 02. *The Rosery, Tollerton, York YO61 1PX* Tel (01347) 838212

WAGGETT, Geoffrey James. b 49. Sarum & Wells Th Coll 83. **d** 85 **p** 86. C Newton Nottage *Llan* 85-88; TV Glyncorrwg w Afan Vale and Cymmer Afan 88-89; R 89-99; V Glyncorrwg and Upper Afan Valley 99-00; TR Ebbw Vale from 00. *The Rectory, Eureka Place, Ebbw Vale NP23 6PN* Tel (01495) 301723

WAGSTAFF (née JONES), Ms Alison. b 40. K Coll Dur BA63 Man Univ CertEd64. TISEC 95. **d** 98 **p** 99. C Edin St Cuth 98-00; Assoc P Edin St Columba from 00; Chapl St Columba's Hospice 01-05. *27 Cambridge Gardens, Edinburgh EH6 5DH* Tel 0131-554 6702

WAGSTAFF, Andrew Robert. b 56. K Coll Lon BD79 AKC79. Coll of Resurr Mirfield 81. **d** 83 **p** 84. C Newark w Hawton, Cotham and Shelton *S'well* 83-86; C Dublin St Bart w Leeson Park *D & G* 86-89; V Nottingham St Geo w St Jo *S'well* 89-95; V Worksop Priory 95-06; Chapl Antwerp St Boniface *Eur* from 06. *Grétrystraat 39, 2018 Antwerp, Belgium* Tel (0032) (3) 239 3339 E-mail chaplain@boniface.be

WAGSTAFF, The Ven Christopher John Harold. b 36. St D Coll Lamp BA62. **d** 63 **p** 64. C Queensbury All SS *Lon* 63-68; V Tokyngton St Mich 68-73; V Coleford w Staunton *Glouc* 73-83; RD Forest S 76-82; Adn Glouc 83-00; Hon Can Glouc Cathl 83-00; Hon Can St Andr Cathl Njombe (Tanzania) from 93; rtd 00; Perm to Offic *Glouc* from 00. *Karibuni, Collafield, Littledean, Cinderford GL14 3LG* Tel (01594) 825282

WAGSTAFF, Miss Joan. b 33. Gilmore Ho. **dss** 75 **d** 87 **p** 94. Ellesmere Port *Ches* 86-87; Par Dn 87-93; rtd 93; Perm to Offic *Ches* from 93. *41 Heywood Road, Great Sutton, South Wirral CH66 3PS* Tel 0151-348 0884

WAGSTAFF, Michael. b 59. R Holloway Coll Lon BA81. Coll of Resurr Mirfield 86. **d** 89 **p** 90. C Worksop Priory *S'well* 89-92; C Ab Kettleby Gp *Leic* 92-94; TV Leic Resurr 94-00; Dioc Soc Resp Officer *Sheff* 00-08; Chapl RN from 08. *Royal Naval Chaplaincy Service, Mail Point 1-2, Leach Building, Whale Island, Portsmouth PO2 8BY* Tel (023) 9262 5055 Fax 9262 5134

WAGSTAFF, Robert William. b 36. Edin Th Coll 61. **d** 63 **p** 64. C Harringay St Paul *Lon* 63-64; C Mill Hill Jo Keble Ch 64-69; NSM N Lambeth *S'wark* 70-80; NSM Wilden, Hartlebury and Ombersley w Doverdale 80-97; C Shrawley, Witley, Astley and Abberley *Worc* 90-02; rtd 02; Perm to Offic *Worc* from 02. *The Red House, Quarry Bank, Hartlebury, Kidderminster DY11 7TE* Tel (01299) 250883

WAGSTAFFE, Eric Herbert. b 25. St Aid Birkenhead 55. **d** 57 **p** 58. C Harpurhey Ch Ch *Man* 57-60; R 60-69; V Pendlebury St Jo 69-84; V Hoghton *Blackb* 84-91; rtd 91; Perm to Offic *Blackb* 91-02 and *Man* from 95. *3 Chelwood Close, Bolton BL1 7LN* Tel (01204) 596048

WAIN, Phillip. b 54. Aston Tr Scheme 89 Linc Th Coll 93. **d** 93 **p** 94. C Witton *Ches* 93-97; R Lea Gp *Linc* from 97. *The Rectory, 18 Gainsborough Road, Lea, Gainsborough DN21 5HZ* Tel (01427) 613188

WAINAINA, Francis Samson Kamoko. b 51. St Jo Coll Dur MA89. Oak Hill Th Coll BA84. **d** 84 **p** 85. Kenya 84-88; C Upton (Overchurch) *Ches* 89-92; V Ellesmere St Pet *Sheff* 92-95; C York St Mich-le-Belfrey 95-01; V Starbeck *Ripon* from 01. *The Vicarage, 78 High Street, Harrogate HG2 7LW* Tel (01423) 546477 or 889162 E-mail francis.wainaina@ntlworld.com

✠**WAINE, The Rt Revd John.** b 30. KCVO96. Man Univ BA51. Ridley Hall Cam 53. **d** 55 **p** 56 **c** 75. C W Derby St Mary *Liv* 55-58; C Sutton 58-60; V Ditton St Mich 60-64; V Southport H Trin 64-69; V Kirkby 69-71; TR 71-75; Suff Bp Stafford *Lich* 75-78; Preb Lich Cathl 75-78; Bp St E 78-86; Bp Chelmsf 86-96; Clerk of the Closet 89-96; rtd 96; Perm to Offic *St E* from 96; Hon Asst Bp St E from 08. *Broadmere, Ipswich Road, Grundisburgh, Woodbridge IP13 6TJ* Tel (01473) 738296 E-mail bpjohn@jwaine.mail1.co.uk

WAINE, Stephen John. b 59. Westcott Ho Cam 81. **d** 84 **p** 85. C Wolverhampton *Lich* 84-88; Min Can and Succ St Paul's Cathl 88-93; V Romford St Edw *Chelmsf* from 93; P-in-c Romford St Jo from 02. *St Edward's Vicarage, 15 Oaklands Avenue, Romford RM1 4DB* Tel (01708) 740385 E-mail stephen.waine01@ntlworld.com

WAINWRIGHT, John Pounsberry. b 42. St Steph Ho Ox 64. **d** 66 **p** 67. C Palmers Green St Jo *Lon* 66-70; C Primrose Hill St Mary w Avenue Road St Paul 70-71; P-in-c St John's Wood All SS 71-73; V Hendon All SS Childs Hill from 73. *All Saints' Vicarage, Church Walk, London NW2 2TJ* Tel (020) 7435 3182

WAINWRIGHT, Joseph Allan. b 21. K Coll Lon BD50 AKC50 Columbia Pacific Univ PhD82 Sussex Univ DPhil85. **d** 50 **p** 51. C Boston *Linc* 50-53; Chapl St Paul's Coll Cheltenham 53-62; Educn Sec BCC 62-66; Lect Moray Ho Coll of Educn Edin 66-78; Perm to Offic *Chich* 79-88; rtd 86. *Beggar's Roost, Lewes BN7 1LX* Tel (01273) 477453

WAINWRIGHT, Kevin Frank. b 46. Linc Th Coll 73. **d** 75 **p** 76. C Stand *Man* 75-78; C Radcliffe St Thos and St Jo 78-80; V Kearsley Moor from 80. *St Stephen's Vicarage, Blair Street, Kearsley, Bolton BL4 8QP* Tel (01204) 572535

WAINWRIGHT, Malcolm Hugh. b 47. Man Univ BA68 Nottm Univ MA89. St Jo Coll Nottm MA98. **d** 98 **p** 99. NSM Cotgrave and Owthorpe *S'well* 98-02; P-in-c Plumtree 02-09; P-in-c Tollerton 02-09; Hon C Burton Fleming w Fordon, Grindale etc *York* from 09. *The Vicarage, Back Street, Burton Fleming, Driffield YO25 3PD* Tel (01262) 470873
E-mail malcolm@mhwainright.eclipse.co.uk

WAINWRIGHT, Mrs Margaret Gillian. b 45. Qu Mary Coll Lon BA68. EAMTC 00. **d** 03 **p** 04. NSM Combs and Lt Finborough *St E* 03-05; NSM Creeting St Mary, Creeting St Peter etc from 05. *The Cottage, Elmswell Road, Wetherden, Stowmarket IP14 3LN* Tel (01359) 242653
E-mail margwain@btopenworld.com

WAINWRIGHT, Martin John. b 69. Loughb Univ BEng92. Trin Coll Bris BA98. **d** 98 **p** 99. C Chislehurst Ch Ch *Roch* 98-02; V Camberley St Mary *Guildf* from 02. *St Mary's House, 37 Park Road, Camberley GU15 2SP* Tel and fax (01276) 22085 *or* 685167 E-mail martin.wainwright@ntlworld.com

WAINWRIGHT, Pauline Barbara. *See* FLORANCE, Mrs Pauline Barbara

WAINWRIGHT, Peter Anthony. b 45. K Coll Lon BD73 MRICS67. Ridley Hall Cam 73. **d** 75 **p** 76. C Ashtead *Guildf* 76-79; V Woking St Paul 79-84; Perm to Offic *Ox* 87-92 and 03-05; P-in-c Harston w Hauxton and Newton *Ely* from 05. *The Vicarage, Church Street, Harston, Cambridge CB22 7NP* Tel (01223) 874231 Mobile 07814-835528
E-mail revpeterwainwright@tiscali.co.uk

WAINWRIGHT, Robert Neil. b 52. NEOC 99. **d** 02 **p** 03. NSM Barlby w Riccall *York* 02-05; NSM Selby Abbey from 05. *33 Hillfield, Selby YO8 3ND* Tel (01757) 706216 Mobile 07768-390060 E-mail robbwain@yahoo.com

WAIT, Canon Alan Clifford. b 33. St Cath Soc Ox BA58 MA70. Coll of Resurr Mirfield. **d** 60 **p** 61. C Charlton St Luke w St Paul *S'wark* 60-67; C Caterham 67-72; V N Dulwich St Faith 72-83; RD Dulwich 78-83; V Purley St Barn 83-01; RD Croydon S 93-01; Hon Can S'wark Cathl 01; rtd 01; Perm to Offic *Cant* from 01. *Forgefield Oast, Church Hill, Bethersden, Ashford TN26 3AQ* Tel (01233) 820529

WAITE, Daniel Alfred Norman. b 42. **d** 04 **p** 05. OLM Gorleston St Andr *Nor* from 04. *15 Laburnum Close, Bradwell, Great Yarmouth NR31 8JB* Tel (01493) 664591
E-mail djwaite@btinternet.com

WAITE, John Langton (Tony). b 10. Solicitor 34 ACP37 Man Univ 30. Wycliffe Hall Ox 37. **d** 39 **p** 40. C Hove Bp Hannington Memorial *Chich* 39-41; C Walcot *B & W* 41-42; V Blackheath St Jo *S'wark* 42-48; V Leeds St Geo *Ripon* 48-58; V Woking St Jo *Guildf* 58-76; rtd 76; Perm to Offic *Portsm* from 82. *11 The Crescent, Alverstoke, Gosport PO12 2DH* Tel and fax (023) 9252 1458 E-mail tonywaite@cwcom.net

WAITE, Julian Henry. b 47. Open Univ BA98. Brasted Th Coll 68 Ridley Hall Cam 70. **d** 72 **p** 73. C Wollaton *S'well* 72-76; C Herne Bay Ch Ch *Cant* 76-79; P-in-c Mersham 79-87; Chapl Wm Harvey Hosp Ashford 79-87; V Marden *Cant* 87-93; Chapl HM Pris Blantyre Ho 90-93; Chapl HM Pris Swaleside from 01. *HM Prison Swaleside, Eastchurch, Sheerness ME12 4AX* Tel (01795) 804042 Fax 804200

WAITE, Robin Derek. **d** 05 **p** 06. NSM Derringham Bank *York* 05-06; NSM Woldsburn from 06. *Mulberry Cottage, Parklands Drive, North Ferriby HU14 3EU* Tel (01482) 631162
E-mail rojaw@freezone.co.uk

WAITE, Sheila Margaret. *See* TYLER, Mrs Sheila Margaret

WAIYAKI, Canon Jennie. b 34. MBE88. ALA64. NEOC 89. **d** 92 **p** 94. NSM Ulgham and Widdrington *Newc* 92-97; Chapl MU 96-02; Chapl Northumbria Healthcare NHS Trust from 97; NSM Longhorsley and Hebron *Newc* 97-04; Hon Can Newc Cathl from 02. *6 Woodburn Street, Stobswood, Morpeth NE61 5QD* Tel (01670) 791066

WAIZENEKER, Ms Ann Elizabeth. b 56. Southn Univ BSc78. SEITE 05. **d** 08 **p** 09. C Chich St Paul and Westhampnett from 08. *37 Somerstown, Chichester PO19 6AL* Tel (01243) 539849

WAKE, Colin Walter. b 50. Oriel Coll Ox BA72 MA. Cuddesdon Coll 74. **d** 75 **p** 76. C Sandhurst *Ox* 75-78; C Faversham *Cant* 79-80; TV High Wycombe *Ox* 80-89; R Weston Favell *Pet* 89-06; Chapl St Jo Hosp Weston Favell 89-06; rtd 06. *35 Greenhill, Wootton Bassett, Swindon SN4 8EH*
E-mail c.w.wake@talk21.com

WAKEFIELD, Allan. b 31. Qu Coll Birm 72. **d** 74 **p** 75. C Kingsthorpe w Northampton St Dav *Pet* 74-77; TV Clifton *S'well* 77-81; V Bilborough St Jo 81-85; R Bere Ferrers *Ex* 85-91;

R Mevagissey and St Ewe *Truro* 91-96; rtd 96; Perm to Offic *Truro* 96-98; Hon C Malborough w S Huish, W Alvington and Churchstow *Ex* 98-02; Perm to Offic from 01. *4 Eden Cottages, Exeter Road, Ivybridge PL21 0BL* Tel (01752) 698724

WAKEFIELD, Andrew Desmond. b 55. K Coll Lon BD77 AKC77. Coll of Resurr Mirfield 77. **d** 78 **p** 79. C Mitcham Ascension *S'wark* 78-81; C Putney St Mary 81-86; TV Wimbledon 86-91; Ind Chapl from 90; Dioc Urban Missr 91-97; P-in-c S Wimbledon St Andr 91-97; V from 97. *105 Hartfield Road, London SW19 3TJ* Tel (020) 8542 6566
E-mail andrew.d.wakefield@btopenworld.com

WAKEFIELD, Anne Frances. b 58. St Aid Coll Dur BSc79 Sheff Univ PGCE80. NTMTC 94. **d** 97 **p** 98. NSM Sherburn w Pittington *Dur* 98-01; Asst Chapl HM Pris Dur 01-03; Chapl HM YOI Northallerton 03-05; Chapl HM Pris Low Newton 05-08; P-in-c Stamford Bridge Gp *York* from 09. *The Rectory, 8 Viking Road, Stamford Bridge, York YO41 1BR* Tel (01759) 371264
E-mail fran.wakefield@btopenworld.com

WAKEFIELD, David Geoffrey. b 43. AMIC90. S'wark Ord Course 84. **d** 87 **p** 88. C Addiscombe St Mildred *S'wark* 87-89; C Reigate St Luke S Park 89-93; Chapl HM Pris Bullingdon 93-96; Chapl HM Pris Ranby 96-99; P-in-c Flintham *S'well* 99-08; P-in-c Car Colston w Screveton 99-08; Chapl HM Pris Whatton 99-03; rtd 08; Perm to Offic *York* from 08. *5 Manor Gardens, Hunmanby, Filey YO14 0PT* Tel (01723) 891212 Mobile 07754-219741 E-mail david.wakefield@mypostoffice.co.uk

WAKEFIELD, David Kenneth. b 64. Ridley Hall Cam 02. **d** 04 **p** 05. C Bures w Assington and Lt Cornard *St E* 04-07; P-in-c Burlingham St Edmund w Lingwood, Strumpshaw etc *Nor* 07-09; R from 09. *The Rectory, Barn Close, Lingwood, Norwich NR13 4TS* Tel (01603) 713880
E-mail rev.wake@btinternet.com

WAKEFIELD, Frances. *See* WAKEFIELD, Anne Frances

WAKEFIELD, Gavin Tracy. b 57. Van Mildert Coll Dur BSc78 Sheff Univ CertEd80 Kent Univ PhD98. St Jo Coll Nottm 83. **d** 86 **p** 87. C Anston *Sheff* 86-89; C Aston cum Aughton and Ulley 89-91; TV Billericay and Lt Burstead *Chelmsf* 91-98; Dir Miss & Past Studies Cranmer Hall Dur 98-08; Dir Tr, Miss and Min *York* from 09. *The Rectory, 8 Viking Road, Stamford Bridge, York YO41 1BR* Tel (01759) 371264
E-mail gavin.wakefield@yorkdiocese.org

WAKEFIELD, Kenneth. b 54. St Jo Coll Dur BA95. **d** 95 **p** 96. C E and W Leake, Stanford-on-Soar, Rempstone etc *S'well* 95-98; TV Launceston *Truro* 98-03; P-in-c Boyton, N Tamerton, Werrington etc 03-08; R from 08. *The Rectory, Werrington, Launceston PL15 8TP* Tel (01566) 773932

WAKEFIELD, Mark Jeremy. b 55. York Univ BA77. NTMTC BA07. **d** 07 **p** 08. NSM Primrose Hill St Mary w Avenue Road St Paul *Lon* from 07. *15 Evangelist Road, London NW5 1UA* Tel (020) 7267 8202 Mobile 07899-668493
E-mail mark.wakefield@blueyonder.co.uk

WAKEFIELD, Peter. b 48. St Jo Coll Nottm BTh72 ALCD72. **d** 72 **p** 73. C Hinckley H Trin *Leic* 72-75; C Kirby Muxloe 75-78; V Barlestone 78-85; TV Padgate *Liv* 85-88; V Quinton w Marston Sicca *Glouc* 91-97; rtd 97. *7 Le Petit Murat, Benevent L'Abbaye, 23210 Creuse, France* Tel (0033) (5) 55 62 29 68
E-mail pete.wakefield@orange.fr

WAKEFIELD, Bishop of. *See* PLATTEN, The Rt Revd Stephen George

WAKEFIELD, Dean of. *See* GREENER, The Very Revd Jonathan Desmond Francis

WAKEHAM, Miss Ellen Liesel. b 82. York Univ BA04 CCC Cam BA08. Westcott Ho Cam 06 Yale Div Sch 08. **d** 09. C Frodingham *Linc* from 09. *102 Bushfield Road, Scunthorpe DN16 1NA* Tel (01724) 271737 E-mail ellenwakeham@me.com

WAKEHAM, Geoffrey. b 96 **p** 97. P-in-c Torrevieja *Eur* 96-00; Asst Chapl 00-01; rtd 01. *6 Juniper Court, Roundswell, Barnstaple EX31 3RL* Tel (01271) 325170

WAKEHAM-DAWSON, Andrew Whistler. b 65. Wye Coll Lon BSc87 Open Univ PhD94. STETS 98. **d** 01 **p** 02. NSM Paddington St Sav *Lon* 01-04; Chapl RAF from 04. *Chaplaincy Services, Valiant Block, HQ Air Command, RAF High Wycombe HP14 4UE* Tel (01494) 496800 Fax 496343

WAKELIN, Brian Roy. b 53. Westf Coll Lon BSc74. STETS 96. **d** 99 **p** 00. NSM Win Ch Ch from 99. *11 Elm Court, Elm Road, Winchester SO22 5BA* Tel (01962) 868659

WAKELING, Bruce. b 50. Lon Univ BA74. Westcott Ho Cam 74. **d** 77 **p** 78. C Weymouth H Trin *Sarum* 77-82; TV Oakdale 82-89; R Clopton w Otley, Swilland and Ashbocking *St E* 89-98; V Rushmere from 98. *The Vicarage, 253 Colchester Road, Rushmere, Ipswich IP4 4SH* Tel (01473) 270976

WAKELING, Hugh Michael. b 42. Cape Town Univ BSc63 CEng82 FIChemE94. Wycliffe Hall Ox 71. **d** 74 **p** 75. C Kennington St Mark *S'wark* 74-78; C Surbiton Hill Ch Ch 78-80; NSM Richmond H Trin and Ch Ch 80-84; NSM California *Ox* 85-89 and 00-07; NSM Arborfield w Barkham 89-00; Lic to Offic from 07. *61 Roycroft Lane, Finchampstead, Wokingham RG40 4HN* Tel 0118-973 4078

WAKELING, Mrs Joan. b 44. Hockerill Coll Cam CertEd65. S'wark Ord Course 76. **dss** 79 **d** 90 **p** 94. Surbiton Hill Ch Ch S'wark 79-80; Richmond H Trin and Ch Ch 80-84; California Ox 84-89; Arborfield w Barkham 89-00; NSM 90-00; Chapl Luckley-Oakfield Sch Wokingham 90-05; NSM Finchampstead Ox 00-05; P-in-c Raglan w Llandenny and Bryngwyn Mon from 05. The Vicarage, Primrose Green, Raglan, Usk NP15 2DU Tel (01291) 690330

WAKELING, Rayner Alan. b 58. Portsm Poly BSc79 Bris Univ PGCE80. St Steph Ho Ox. **d** 01 **p** 02. C Willesden Green St Andr and St Fran Lon 01-05; V Greenhill St Jo from 05. St John's Vicarage, 11 Flambard Road, Harrow HA1 2NB Tel (020) 8907 7956 E-mail raynerwakeling@hotmail.com

WAKELY, Marcus. b 40. Solicitor 62 FRSA88. EMMTC 84. **d** 87 **p** 88. NSM Carrington S'well 87-91; C Worksop Priory 91-95; V Sheff St Matt 95-01; rtd 01. 16 Park House Gates, Nottingham NG3 5LX Tel 0115-960 9038

WAKELY, Roger. b 42. St Paul's Cheltenham CertEd. S'wark Ord Course 67. **d** 70 **p** 71. C Ealing St Mary Lon 70-76; Chapl Bp Wand Sch Sunbury-on-Thames 76-82; R Gaulby Leic 82-87; V Galleywood Common Chelmsf 87-95; Warden of Ords 89-95; rtd 95; Perm to Offic Chelmsf 95-99 and Ex from 99. Linford, Broadway, Sidmouth EX10 8XH

WAKELY, Simon Nicolas. b 66. K Alfred's Coll Win BA88. St Jo Coll Nottm 89. **d** 92 **p** 93. C Wymondham Nor 92-95; P-in-c Babbacombe Ex 95-08; rtd 08. 67 Lutyens Drive, Paignton TQ3 3LA Tel 01803 536181 (mobile) E-mail finbar@tesco.net

WAKEMAN, Canon Hilary Margaret. b 38. EAMTC. **dss** 85 **d** 87 **p** 94. Heigham St Thos Nor 85-90; C 87-90; C Nor St Mary Magd w St Jas 90-91; Dn-in-c Norwich-over-the-Water Colegate St Geo 90-91; TD Norwich Over-the-Water 91-94; TV 94-96; Hon Can Nor Cathl 94-96; I Kilmoe Union C, C & R 96-01; Dir of Ords 99-01; rtd 01. Skeagh, Schull, Co Cork, Republic of Ireland Tel (00353) (28) 28263
E-mail hilary.wakeman@gmail.com

WAKERELL, Richard Hinton. b 55. Qu Coll Birm 81. **d** 84 **p** 85. C Gillingham St Mary Roch 84-87; C Kingswinford St Mary Lich 87-93; V Rickerscote 93. 70 Truro Drive, Plymouth PL5 4PB

WALDEN, Alan Howard. b 64. Bris Univ BSc86 Lon Business Sch MBA93. Trin Coll Bris BA09. **d** 09. C Frimley Guildf from 09. 4 Warren Rise, Frimley, Camberley GU16 8SH Tel 07957-773043 (mobile) E-mail alan.walden@ukgateway.net

✠**WALDEN, The Rt Revd Graham Howard.** b 31. Univ of Qld BA52 MA54 Ch Ch Ox BLitt60 MLitt80. St Fran Coll Brisbane ThL54. **d** 54 **p** 55 **c** 81. C W Hackney St Barn Lon 54-56; C Poplar St Sav w St Gabr and St Steph 57-58; Perm to Offic Ox 55-59; Australia from 59; Adn Ballarat 70-89; Bp in Hamilton 81-84; Asst Bp Ballarat 84-89; Bp The Murray 89-01; rtd 01. 13 O'Connor Place, Dubbo NSW 2380, Australia Tel (0061) (2) 6884 0883

WALDEN, Mrs Jane. b 55. Cartrefle Coll of Educn CertEd76 Chelt & Glouc Coll of HE BA01. WEMTC 02. **d** 05 **p** 06. NSM Minchinhampton Glouc from 05. Rose Acre, London Road, Brimscombe, Stroud GL5 2TL Tel (01453) 882314
E-mail jane_walden@hotmail.com

WALDEN, John Edward Frank. b 38. Oak Hill Th Coll 67. **d** 69 **p** 70. C Rainham Chelmsf 69-73; P-in-c Bris H Cross Inns Court 73-78; Conf and Publicity Sec SAMS 78-81; Hon C Southborough St Pet w Ch Ch and St Matt Roch 78-81; Exec Sec Spanish and Portuguese Ch Aid Soc 80-81; Hon C Tonbridge St Steph 81-84; R Earsham w Alburgh and Denton Nor 84-89; Perm to Offic from 01; rtd 03. 11 Hemmings Close, Norwich NR5 9EH Tel (01603) 746062
E-mail reverendjohn@fsmail.net

WALDSAX, Mrs Heather. b 58. Bris Univ BA79 PGCE80. STETS 06. **d** 08 **p** 09. NSM Canford Magna Sarum from 08. 60 Floral Farm, Canford Magna, Wimborne BH21 3AU Tel (01202) 889289 E-mail heather@waldsax.net

WALES, David Neville. b 55. Rhodes Univ BA78 Open Univ BSc01. Coll of Resurr Mirfield 80. **d** 82 **p** 83. Zimbabwe 82-88; C Linslade Ox 89-91; P-in-c Weston Turville 91-07; R from 07; Voc Adv from 99. The Rectory, Church Walk, Weston Turville, Aylesbury HP22 5SH Tel (01296) 613212
E-mail davidnwales@tiscali.co.uk

WALES, Stephen Francis. b 70. Leic Univ BSc93 Leeds Univ BA07. Coll of Resurr Mirfield 05. **d** 07 **p** 08. C Carrington S'well from 07. 65 Osborne Grove, Nottingham NG5 2HE Tel 0115-969 1913 E-mail walesstephen@aol.com

WALES, Archbishop of. See MORGAN, The Most Revd Barry Cennydd

WALFORD, Mrs Angela. b 44. Whitelands Coll Lon CertEd76. S Dios Minl Tr Scheme 85. **d** 92 **p** 94. NSM Boyatt Wood Win 92-99; Asst Chapl Epsom and St Helier Univ Hosps NHS Trust 99-07; Perm to Offic S'wark from 07. 58 Wolseley Road, Mitcham Junction, Mitcham CR4 4JQ Tel (020) 8646 2841

WALFORD, David. b 45. S'wark Ord Course 75. **d** 78 **p** 79. NSM Hackbridge and N Beddington S'wark 78-83; C Fawley Win 83-87; C-in-c Boyatt Wood CD 87-90; V Boyatt Wood 90-97; rtd 97; Perm to Offic S'wark 98-02; Assoc P S Beddington and Roundshaw 00-07; Hon Chapl Epsom and St Helier NHS Trust 00-03; Asst Chapl Epsom and St Helier Univ Hosps NHS Trust from 03. 58 Wolseley Road, Mitcham Junction, Mitcham CR4 4JQ Tel (020) 8646 2841 E-mail wols@tinyworld.co.uk

WALFORD, David John. b 47. St Luke's Coll Ex CertEd68 AKC71. St Aug Coll Cant 71. **d** 72 **p** 73. C Oxton Ches 72-77; C Neston 77-80; V Backford and Youth Chapl 80-81; C Woodchurch 81; Chapl Fulbourn Hosp 82; Chapl N Man Gen Hosp 82-85; Distr Chapl in Mental Health Ex HA 85-87; Chapl Manager R Devon and Ex Hosp (Wonford) 87-94; Chapl Manager R Devon and Ex NHS Foundn Trust 94-07; rtd 07; Chapl Ex Hospiscare from 08. Barnhayes Farm, Whimple, Exeter EX5 2UD Tel (01404) 822863

WALFORD, David Sanderson. b 23. BEM49. Chich Th Coll 78. **d** 79 **p** 80. Hon C Chich St Pet 79-81; C Chich St Paul and St Pet 81-83; P-in-c Wisbech St Aug Ely 83-86; rtd 88. Sibford, Church Hill, Marnhull, Sturminster Newton DT10 1PU Tel (01258) 820201

WALFORD, Frank Roy. b 35. Birm Univ MB, ChB58. Qu Coll Birm 78. **d** 80 **p** 81. Hon C Walsall Pleck and Bescot Lich 80-85; Chr Healing Cen Bordon 85-88; Dep Medical Dir St Wilfrid's Hospice Chich from 88; Perm to Offic Chich from 88. 15 Grove Road, Chichester PO19 8AR Tel (01243) 533947
E-mail ronowal@aol.com

WALFORD, Mrs Marion Gladys. b 54. NTMTC BA08. **d** 08 **p** 09. C Canvey Is Chelmsf from 08. 37 Ruskoi Road, Canvey Island SS8 9QN Tel (01268) 698991
E-mail revmarion@google.com

WALFORD, Robin Peter. b 46. Qu Coll Birm 75. **d** 78 **p** 79. C Radcliffe-on-Trent S'well 78-81; TV Newark w Hawton, Cotham and Shelton 81-84; P-in-c Forest Town 84-92; Co-ord Chapl Leeds Community and Mental Health Services 92-97; Perm to Offic Ripon from 97. 2A Weetwood Lane, Leeds LS16 5LS Tel 0113-2789 9953 E-mail robin.walford@lpti.org.uk

WALKER, Alan Robert Glaister. b 52. K Coll Cam BA76 MA79 New Coll Ox MA84 Poly Cen Lon LLB91 Heythrop Coll Lon MTh93 Univ of Wales LLM96. St Steph Ho Ox 82. **d** 84 **p** 85. C St John's Wood Lon 84-86; Chapl Poly Cen Lon 87-92; Chapl Univ of Westmr 92-94; Chapl Univ Ch Ch the K 87-94; V Hampstead Garden Suburb from 94. The Vicarage, 1 Central Square, London NW11 7AH Tel and fax (020) 8455 7206 Mobile 07956-491037 E-mail fatherwalker@aol.com

WALKER, Albert William John. b 14. Linc Th Coll 43. **d** 45 **p** 46. C Ches St Mary 45-48; C Hoylake 48-51; V Lower Tranmere 51-56; V Plumstead St Nic S'wark 56-66; V Merton St Jas 66-67; V Kingston St Luke 67-74; V Mickleton Glouc 74-79; rtd 79; Chapl Convent of St Mary at the Cross Edgware 79-87; Lic to Offic Lon 79-87; Perm to Offic Carl 87-95 and Truro from 95. 1 Sunley Orford House, St Austell Street, Truro TR1 1UB Tel (01872) 241988

WALKER, Canon Allen Ross. b 46. Portsm Univ BA94 MA98. Chich Th Coll 86. **d** 88. C Cosham Portsm 88-91; Chapl Portsm Mental Health Community 91-97; Dn Portsm Deanery 91-97; Community Chapl Burnham and Slough Deanery Ox from 97; AD Burnham and Slough from 05; Hon Can Ch Ch from 08. The Vicarage, Mill Street, Colnbrook, Slough SL3 0JJ Tel and fax (01753) 684181 E-mail mrarwalker@aol.com

WALKER, Mrs Amanda Frances. b 62. Cen Sch Speech & Drama BSc85 Univ Coll Lon MSc94 Qu Coll Birm BA09. WMMTC 06. **d** 09. C Stafford Lich from 09. The Vicarage, Victoria Terrace, Stafford ST16 3HA Tel 07811-326204 (mobile)
E-mail mandywalker@talktalk.net

WALKER, Andrew Stephen. b 58. St Chad's Coll Dur BA80 Heythrop Coll Lon MA99. St Steph Ho Ox 83. **d** 85 **p** 86. C Fareham SS Pet and Paul Portsm 85-87; C St John's Wood Lon 87-93; V Streatham St Pet S'wark 93-98; Perm to Offic Bris 98-00 and S'wark from 98; R St Edm the King and St Mary Woolnoth etc Lon from 00. St Mary Woolnoth Vestry, Lombard Street, London EC3V 9AN Tel and fax (020) 7626 9701 Mobile 07931-745853 E-mail rector@marywoolnoth.org

WALKER, Ms Angela Jean. b 55. St Jo Coll Nottm 03. **d** 05 **p** 06. C Kempshott Win 05-09; Hon C Chilworth w N Baddesley from 09. 188 Rownhams Lane, North Baddesley, Southampton SO52 9LQ E-mail ahiangel@aol.com

WALKER, Canon Anthony Charles St John. b 55. Trin Coll Ox MA80. Wycliffe Hall Ox 78. **d** 81 **p** 82. C Bradf Cathl 81-84; C Nottingham St Ann w Em S'well 84-88; V Retford St Sav 88-01; TR Retford from 02; AD Retford 00-09; Hon Can S'well Minster from 04. St Saviour's Vicarage, 31 Richmond Road, Retford DN22 6SJ Tel and fax (01777) 703800
E-mail tony@tonywalker.f9.co.uk

WALKER, Canon Arthur Keith. b 33. Dur Univ BSc57 Fitzw Ho Cam BA60 MA64 Leeds Univ PhD68 FRSA94. Lich Th Coll 62. **d** 63 **p** 64. C Slaithwaite w E Scammonden Wakef 63-66; V N Wootton B & W 66-71; Lect Wells Th Coll 66-71; Can Res and Prec Chich Cathl 71-80; TV Basingstoke Win 81-87; Can Res Win Cathl 87-03; rtd 03. 29 Sussex Street, Winchester SO23 8TG Tel (01962) 864751 E-mail jwalker@prettel.nl

WALKER, Brian Cecil. b 28. FCA62. Cranmer Hall Dur 68. **d** 70 **p** 71. C Heworth w Peasholme St Cuth *York* 70-73; C Attenborough w Chilwell *S'well* 73-75; C Chilwell 75-78; R Trowell 78-89; rtd 89; Perm to Offic *Worc* 89-05 and *Birm* 98-05. *1 Chaucer Road, Bromsgrove B60 2EE* Tel (01527) 579382

WALKER, Cameron. *See* WALKER, Canon John Cameron

WALKER, Christina. d 08 **p** 09. NSM Birkenshaw w Hunsworth *Wakef* from 08. *Upper Chatts Farm, Cliff Hollins Lane, East Brierley, Bradford BD4 6RH* Tel (01274) 670551 E-mail tinalet@hotmail.com

WALKER, Christopher James Anthony. b 43. Sarum & Wells Th Coll 85. **d** 87 **p** 88. Hon C Durrington *Sarum* 87-89; CF 87-98. *Horseshoe Meadow Farm, Cholderton, Salisbury SP4 0ED* Tel (01980) 629234 E-mail horseshoewalkers@supanet.com

WALKER, Christopher John. b 52. ALA74. Chich Th Coll 75. **d** 78 **p** 79. C Reading All SS *Ox* 78-82; C Stony Stratford 82-84; C Wokingham All SS 84-90; V Headington St Mary 90-98; R S w N Moreton, Aston Tirrold and Aston Upthorpe 98-05; C Abingdon 05-07; rtd 07. *11 Boston Avenue, Reading RG1 6JU* Tel 0118-959 0127 E-mail rwalker1202@aol.com

WALKER, Christopher John Deville. b 42. St Jo Coll Dur BA69. Westcott Ho Cam 69. **d** 71 **p** 72. C Portsea St Mary *Portsm* 71-75; C Saffron Walden w Wendens Ambo and Littlebury *Chelmsf* 75-77; C St Martin-in-the-Fields *Lon* 77-80; V Riverhead w Dunton Green *Roch* 80-89; V Chatham St Steph 89-97; R Chislehurst St Nic 97-05; rtd 05; Perm to Offic *Heref* from 05 and *Lich* 06-07; Hon C Shrewsbury St Chad, St Mary and St Alkmund *Lich* from 07. *2 Springbank, Shrewsbury Road, Church Stretton SY6 6HA* Tel (01694) 723444 E-mail chris@riberac.force9.co.uk

WALKER, Canon David. b 48. Linc Th Coll 71. **d** 74 **p** 75. C Arnold *S'well* 74-77; C Crosby *Linc* 77-79; V Scrooby *S'well* 79-86; V Sutton in Ashfield St Mary 86-94; P-in-c Sutton in Ashfield St Mich 89-94; TR Birkenhead Priory *Ches* 94-05; RD Birkenhead 99-05; R Bromborough from 05; Hon Can Ches Cathl from 03. *The Rectory, Mark Rake, Wirral CH62 2DH* Tel 0151-201 5026 E-mail dave.walker48@ntlworld.com

WALKER, Canon David Andrew. b 52. St Andr Univ MTheol75 MA Hull Univ MPhil00. Linc Th Coll 79. **d** 81 **p** 82. C Hessle *York* 81-84; C N Hull St Mich 84-86; V from 86; AD Cen and N Hull from 99; RD Hull from 00; Can and Preb York Minster from 01. *St Michael's Vicarage, 214 Orchard Park Road, Hull HU6 9BX* Tel (01482) 803375 E-mail david@stmichaelsnorthhull.org.uk

WALKER, David Andrew. b 76. Van Mildert Coll Dur BSc97. Oak Hill Th Coll MTh07. **d** 07 **p** 08. C Cheadle All Hallows *Ches* from 07. *26 Kelsall Road, Cheadle SK8 2NE* Tel 0161-491 0322 Mobile 07980-360408 E-mail davasarahwava@yahoo.co.uk

WALKER, David Gilmour. b 73. Plymouth Univ BA96. Wycliffe Hall Ox 07. **d** 09. C Brompton H Trin w Onslow Square St Paul *Lon* from 09. *69 Revelstoke Road, London SW18 5NL* Tel 07807-876525 (mobile) E-mail davidgwalker@hotmail.co.uk

WALKER, Canon David Grant. b 23. Bris Univ BA49 Ball Coll Ox DPhil54 FSA60 FRHistS62. **d** 62 **p** 62. NSM Swansea St Mary w H Trin *S & B* 62-86; Chapl and Lect Univ of Wales (Swansea) 62; Sen Lect 63-82; Dir Post-Ord Tr 65-93; Can Brecon Cathl from 72; Prec 79-90; Chan 90-93; Chapl Univ of Wales (Swansea) 75-76; Dir of In-Service Tr from 77; P-in-c Caereithin 86-87. *52 Eaton Crescent, Swansea SA1 4QN* Tel (01792) 472624

WALKER, David Ian. b 41. Bernard Gilpin Soc Dur 64 Bps' Coll Cheshunt 65. **d** 68 **p** 69. C Todmorden *Wakef* 68-72; V Rastrick St Jo 72-77; V Crossland Moor 77-86; R Kirton in Lindsey w Manton *Linc* 86-99; R Grayingham 86-99; V Clee 99-06; OCF 88-06; rtd 07; Perm to Offic *Linc* from 07. *48 Pretymen Crescent, New Waltham, Grimsby DN36 4PB* Tel (01472) 826958 E-mail davidian8@btinternet.com

WALKER, David John. b 47. St Jo Coll Nottm 88. **d** 90 **p** 91. C Strood St Fran *Roch* 90-94; V Larkfield from 94. *The Vicarage, 206 New Hythe Lane, Larkfield, Maidstone ME20 6PT* Tel and fax (01732) 843349 E-mail david.walker@diocese-rochester.org

WALKER, David Meuryn. b 44. Bris Univ BSc66 Nottm Univ PGCE67. NOC 97. **d** 00 **p** 01. NSM Wakef St Jo 00-02; NSM Horbury Junction from 02. *188 Stanley Road, Wakefield WF1 4AE* Tel (01924) 210797 Mobile 07775-583764 E-mail meuryn@blueyonder.co.uk

✠**WALKER, The Rt Revd David Stuart.** b 57. K Coll Cam MA81. Qu Coll Birm. **d** 83 **p** 84 **c** 00. C Handsworth *Sheff* 83-86; TV Maltby 86-91; Ind Chapl 86-91; V Bramley and Ravenfield 91-95; R Bramley and Ravenfield w Hooton Roberts etc 95-00; Hon Can Sheff Cathl 00; Suff Bp Dudley *Worc* from 00. *Bishop's House, Bishop's Walk, Cradley Heath B64 7RH* Tel 0121-550 3407 Fax 550 7340 E-mail bishop.dudley@cofe-worcester.org.uk

WALKER, Derek Fred. b 46. Trin Coll Bris 71. **d** 74 **p** 75. C St Paul's Cray St Barn *Roch* 74-78; C Rushden w Newton Bromswold *Pet* 78-80; R Kirkby Thore w Temple Sowerby and Newbiggin *Carl* 80-83; V Coppull *Blackb* 83-87; V New Ferry *Ches* 87-96; R Akeman *Ox* from 96. *The Rectory, Alchester*

Road, Chesterton, Bicester OX26 1UW Tel and fax (01869) 369815 E-mail akemanbenefice@yahoo.com

WALKER, Duncan Andrew. b 59. **d** 90 **p** 91. C Gorseinon *S & B* 90-91; C Morriston 92-94; V Llanelli Ch Ch *St D* 94-98; V Swansea St Jas *S & B* from 98. *St James's Vicarage, 1 Ffynone Drive, Swansea SA1 6DB* Tel (01792) 470532

✠**WALKER, The Rt Revd Edward William Murray (Dominic).** b 48. AKC73 Heythrop Coll Lon MA97 Brighton Univ Hon DLitt98 Univ of Wales LLM05. **d** 72 **p** 72 **c** 97. CGA 67-83; C Wandsworth St Faith *S'wark* 72-73; Bp's Dom Chapl 73-76; R Newington St Mary 76-85; RD S'wark and Newington 80-85; OGS from 83; Superior 90-96; V Brighton St Pet w Chpl Royal and St Jo *Chich* 85-86; P-in-c Brighton St Nic 85-86; TR Brighton St Pet and St Nic w Chpl Royal 86-97; RD Brighton 85-97; Can and Preb Chich Cathl 85-97; Area Bp Reading *Ox* 97-03; Bp Mon from 03. *Bishop's House, Stow Hill, Newport NP20 4EA* Tel (01633) 263510 Fax 259946 E-mail bishop.monmouth@churchinwales.org.uk

WALKER, Mrs Elizabeth. b 42. CQSW85. NEOC 91. **d** 94 **p** 00. NSM Stockton St Chad *Dur* from 94. *29 Bramble Road, Stockton-on-Tees TS19 0NQ* Tel (01642) 615332

WALKER, Canon Elizabeth Margaret Rea. b 49. Ch Ch Coll Cant CertEd70. S'wark Ord Course 89. **d** 92 **p** 94. NSM Ash and Ridley *Roch* 92-97; Chapl St Geo Sch Gravesend 92-97; P-in-c Burham and Wouldham *Roch* 97-05; P-in-c Platt from 05; Assoc Dir of Ords from 97; Hon Can Roch Cathl from 09. *The Vicarage, Comp Lane, Platt, Sevenoaks TN15 8NR* Tel and fax (01732) 885482 Mobile 07931-356502 E-mail liz.walker@diocese-rochester.org

WALKER, Gavin Russell. b 43. FCA78. Coll of Resurr Mirfield 76. **d** 78 **p** 79. C Wakef St Jo 78-81; C Northallerton w Kirby Sigston *York* 81-83; V Whorlton w Carlton and Faceby 83-85; P-in-c Brotherton *Wakef* 85-89; Chapl Pontefract Gen Infirmary 85-89; V Earl's Heaton *Wakef* 89-97; TV Dewsbury 97-99; TV Egremont and Haile *Carl* 99-04; rtd 04. *4 South Parade, Seascale CA20 1PZ* Tel (019467) 29463 Mobile 07986-505886 E-mail staffa@lineone.net

WALKER, Geoffrey. *See* WALKER, Canon Philip Geoffrey

WALKER, Gerald Roger. b 41. K Coll Lon BD67 AKC67. **d** 68 **p** 69. C High Elswick St Phil *Newc* 68-70; C Goring-by-Sea *Chich* 70-75; R Selsey 75-81; V Hove St Andr Old Ch 81-91; V Copthorne 91-95; rtd 95; NSM Streat w Westmeston *Chich* 95-99; Perm to Offic *S'wark* from 00. *1 Glebe Cottages, Newdigate, Dorking RH5 5AA* Tel (01306) 631587

WALKER, Canon Harvey William. b 26. Edin Univ MA52. St Steph Ho Ox 58. **d** 60 **p** 61. C Newc St Matt w St Mary 60-64; V 64-94; Hon Can Newc Cathl 80-94; rtd 95; Perm to Offic *Newc* from 95. *21 Grosvenor Drive, Whitley Bay NE26 2JP* Tel 0191-252 1858

WALKER, Mrs Hazel. b 47. Coll of Ripon & York St Jo MA01. NOC 97. **d** 00 **p** 01. NSM Crofton *Wakef* 00-04; Asst Chapl SW Yorks Mental Health NHS Trust from 04. *30 Heron Drive, Sandal, Wakefield WF2 6SW* Tel (01924) 259687 *or* 327319 E-mail hazelw@heron55.freeserve.co.uk

WALKER, Hugh. *See* WALKER, John Hugh

WALKER, Ian Richard Stevenson. b 51. Univ of Wales (Lamp) BA73. Qu Coll Birm. **d** 76 **p** 77. C Stainton-in-Cleveland *York* 76-79; C Fulford 79-81; C Kidderminster St Mary *Worc* 81-82; TV Kidderminster St Mary and All SS, Trimpley etc 82-86; R Keyingham w Ottringham, Halsham and Sunk Is *York* 86-98; RD S Holderness 94-98; R Scartho *Linc* 98-08; P-in-c Epworth Gp from 08. *St Andrew's Rectory, Belton Road, Epworth, Doncaster DN9 1JL* Tel (01427) 873790

WALKER, Mrs Jane Louise. b 64. STETS 03. **d** 06 **p** 07. NSM Alton All SS *Win* from 06. *101 Salisbury Close, Alton GU34 2TP* Tel (01420) 88730 E-mail walker101@btconnect.com

WALKER, Mrs Jillian Francesca. b 41. **d** 99 **p** 00. OLM Blackbourne *St E* from 99. *The Woolpack, Bury Road, Ixworth, Bury St Edmunds IP31 2HX* Tel (01359) 230776 E-mail digger.walker@tiscali.co.uk

WALKER (*formerly* TOMKINS), **Jocelyn Rachel.** b 64. Univ of Wales (Ban) BA85 Man Univ PGCE86. NOC 98. **d** 01 **p** 02. C Chadderton St Matt *Man* 01-04; Chapl Asst Salford R Hosps NHS Trust 04-07; P-in-c Maidstone St Martin *Cant* from 07. *St Martin's Vicarage, Northumberland Road, Maidstone ME15 7LP* Tel (01622) 676282 E-mail joss.walker@tiscali.co.uk

WALKER, John. *See* WALKER, Albert William John

WALKER, Canon John. b 51. Aber Univ MA74 Edin Univ BD78. Edin Th Coll 75. **d** 78 **p** 79. C Broughty Ferry *Bre* 78-81; P-in-c Dundee St Jo 81-85; Ind Chapl 83-88; R Dundee St Luke 85-95; R Alyth *Ab* 95-02; R Inverurie from 95; R Auchindoir from 95; P-in-c Kemnay from 95; Syn Clerk from 08; Can St Andr Cathl from 01. *The Rectory, St Mary's Place, Inverurie AB51 3NW* Tel (01467) 620470 E-mail jwcan@tiscali.co.uk

WALKER, John Anthony Patrick. b 58. Man Metrop Univ PGCE97. Trin Coll Bris BA86. **d** 86 **p** 87. C Canford Magna *Sarum* 86-90; TV Glyncorrwg w Afan Vale and Cymmer Afan

Llan 90-96; Hd of RE Wentworth High Sch Eccles 97-99; Community Chapl and C Gorton St Phil *Man* 00-03; P-in-c Oldham St Paul 03-04; Perm to Offic *Man* 04-07 and *Cant* from 07. *St Martin's Vicarage, Northumberland Road, Maidstone ME15 7LP* Tel (01622) 676282
E-mail johnwalker-uk@btinternet.com

WALKER, Canon John Cameron. b 31. St Andr Univ MA52. Edin Th Coll 63. **d** 65 **p** 66. C Edin H Cross 65-67; C Perth St Jo *St And* 67-70; Chapl Angl Students Glas 70-74; Youth Chapl Warks Educn Cttee 75-77; Officer Gen Syn Bd of Educn 78-82; C W Hendon St Jo *Lon* 79-82; PV Westmr Abbey 82-84; Chapl Ghent w Ypres *Eur* 84-92; Chapl Ghent 92-98; Miss to Seamen 84-98; Can Brussels Cathl 93-98; rtd 98. *Le Petit Clos, rue des Lilas, 11300 Bouriège, France* Tel and fax (0033) (4) 68 31 17 04

WALKER, John David. b 44. St Jo Coll Dur BA76. Cranmer Hall Dur 77. **d** 77 **p** 78. C Heworth H Trin *York* 77-81; P-in-c Allerthorpe and Barmby on the Moor w Fangfoss 81-83; TV Pocklington Team 84-89; P-in-c Hovingham 89; TV Street 89-92; R Dunnington 92-99; V Thorne *Sheff* 99-03; rtd 03; Perm to Offic *York* from 03. *9 Bishop Blunt Close, Hessle HU13 9NJ*
E-mail john.d.walker@btinternet.com

WALKER, John Frank. b 53. Leeds Univ BEd76 Ripon Coll of Educn CertEd75. NW Ord Course 78. **d** 81 **p** 82. NSM Whitkirk *Ripon* 81-82; C 82-85; V Sutton Courtenay w Appleford *Ox* 85-90; Dioc Children's Adv *S'wark* 90-94; V Walworth St Jo from 94; Youth and Children's Officer Woolwich Episc Area 95-99. *St John's Vicarage, 18 Larcom Street, London SE17 1NQ* Tel (020) 7703 4375

WALKER, John Howard. b 47. Brasted Th Coll 67 Clifton Th Coll 69. **d** 72 **p** 73. C Upton (Overchurch) *Ches* 72-76; Asst Chapl Liv Univ 76-79; V Everton St Chrys 79-82; C Parr Mt 83-86; SAMS 86-94; Area Sec (NE and E Midl) SAMS 86-89; Paraguay 89-94; V Calverley *Bradf* from 95. *Calverley Vicarage, Town Gate, Calverley, Pudsey LS28 5NF* Tel 0113-257 7968 Mobile 07903-836806
E-mail john.walker@bradford.anglican.org

WALKER, John Hugh. b 34. K Coll Lon BD57 AKC57 K Coll Lon MTh75 MA85 Lon Inst of Educn PGCE68. St Boniface Warminster 57. **d** 58 **p** 59. C Southend St Alb *Chelmsf* 58-61; V Gt Ilford St Alb 61-67; Perm to Offic 67-68; Hon C Forest Gate St Edm 68-74; Perm to Offic *Cant* 75-82 and from 87; R Dymchurch w Burmarsh and Newchurch 82-87; rtd 94. *14 Danes Court, Dover CT16 2QE* Tel (01304) 202233

WALKER, Canon John Percival. b 45. CITC 68. **d** 71 **p** 72. C Belfast St Clem *D & D* 71-74; C Magheraculmoney *Clogh* 74-78; C Lisburn St Paul *Conn* 78-81; I Belfast St Ninian 81-88; I Belfast St Mary 88-89; I Belfast St Mary w H Redeemer from 89; Preb Conn Cathl from 98; Treas Conn Cathl from 04. *St Mary's Rectory, 558 Crumlin Road, Belfast BT14 7GL* Tel and fax (028) 9058 4540 *or* tel 9074 8423
E-mail walkerjohnpercival@googlemail.com

WALKER, Judith Anne. See WALKER-HUTCHINSON, Mrs Judith Anne

WALKER, Keith. See WALKER, Canon Arthur Keith

WALKER, Keith. b 48. Linc Th Coll 82. **d** 84 **p** 85. C Whickham *Dur* 84-87; C Trimdon Station 87; P-in-c 87-89; V 89-90; R Penshaw 90-98; P-in-c Shiney Row 92-95; P-in-c Herrington 93-95; rtd 98; Hon C Jersey St Brelade *Win* 01-03. *Hallgarth Heights, Kirk Merrington, Spennymoor DL16 7HY* Tel (01388) 827319

WALKER, Mrs Lesley Ann. b 53. Westmr Coll Ox MTh00. S Dios Minl Tr Scheme 85. **d** 88 **p** 94. Par Dn Oakdale *Sarum* 88-92; TD Bridgnorth, Tasley, Astley Abbotts, etc *Heref* 92-94; TV 94-03; Vice-Prin OLM Tr Scheme *Cant* 03-04; Perm to Offic 06-07; R Meneage *Truro* from 07. *The Rectory, St Martin, Helston TR12 6BU* Tel (01326) 231971

WALKER, Mrs Linda Joan. b 47. **d** 04 **p** 05. OLM Blurton *Lich* from 04. *6 Thackeray Drive, Blurton, Stoke-on-Trent ST3 2HE* Tel (01782) 324895 E-mail linda.walker910@ntlworld.com

WALKER, Marcus Dian Dennison. b 59. WEMTC 04. **d** 07 **p** 08. NSM Churchdown St Jo and Innsworth *Glouc* from 07. *16 Meadowleaze, Gloucester GL2 0PN* Tel (01452) 531621 Mobile 07732-966174
E-mail marcus-walker@blueyonder.co.uk

WALKER, Mrs Margaret Joy. b 44. Westhill Coll Birm TCert66 Newc Univ MA93. CA Tr Coll 80. **dss** 86 **d** 87 **p** 94. Scargill Ho 86-87; Hon Par Dn Monkwearmouth St Andr *Dur* 87; Hon Par Dn Chester le Street 87-93; Hon Chapl Wells Cathl 93-01; Perm to Offic *Cant* 02-05; NSM Stone Street App from 05; AD W Bridge from 09. *The Rectory, Curtis Lane, Stelling Minnis, Canterbury CT4 6BT* Tel (01227) 709318
E-mail margiwalker@uwclub.net

WALKER, Margaret (Mother Lucy Clare). b 37. Guildf Dioc Min Course 99. **d** 01 **p** 02. CSP from 88; Mother Superior from 06; NSM Aldershot St Mich *Guildf* 01-04; NSM Chertsey, Lyne and Longcross 04-07; Lic to Offic from 07. *27 Northcliffe Close, Worcester Park KT4 7DS*

WALKER, Mrs Marion Joyce. b 52. **d** 08 **p** 09. NSM Triangle, St Matt and All SS *St E* from 08. *43 Newbury Road, Ipswich IP4 5EY* Tel (01473) 423753
E-mail mjwalker7653@btinternet.com

WALKER, Preb Martin Frank. b 39. St Jo Coll Nottm 71. **d** 73 **p** 74. C Penn *Lich* 73-78; V Bentley 78-82; V Kinver 82-88; R Kinver and Enville 88-91; V Harlescott 91-02; R Broughton w Croxton and Cotes Heath w Standon 02-04; P-in-c 04-07; Preb Lich Cathl from 00; rtd 04; Hon C Hadley and Wellington Ch Ch *Lich* from 08. *4 Berberis Road, Leegomery, Telford TF1 6XF*
E-mail martin.walker7@btinternet.com

WALKER, Martin John. b 52. Linc Coll Ox BA73 PGCE74 St Jo Coll Dur BA78. Cranmer Hall Dur. **d** 79 **p** 80. C Harlow New Town w Lt Parndon *Chelmsf* 79-81; C Dorchester *Ox* 81-83; Chapl Bath Coll of HE 83-89; TV Southampton (City Cen) *Win* 89-91; Adv in RE and Resources *Sarum* 91-92; Hon C Northolt St Mary *Lon* 92-00; Chapl Bancroft's Sch Woodford Green 92-99; Chapl St Helen's Sch Northwood 99-00; Chapl Wellingborough Sch from 00. *Marsh House, Wellingborough School, Irthlingborough Road, Wellingborough NN8 2BX* Tel (01933) 277271 E-mail revmjwalker@yahoo.com

WALKER, Meuryn. See WALKER, David Meuryn

WALKER, Michael John. b 39. St D Coll Lamp BA61. St Aid Birkenhead 61. **d** 63 **p** 64. C Clifton *York* 63-66; C Marfleet 66-69; V Saltehebble St Jude *Wakef* 69-83; V Llangollen w Trevor and Llantysilio *St As* 83-93; RD Llangollen 87-93; V Kerry and Llanmerewig and Dolfor 93-01; RD Cedewain 97-01; rtd 01; Perm to Offic *Ban* from 01. *Sylfaen-y-Graig, 21 Garth Terrace, Porthmadog LL49 9BE* Tel (01766) 515192

WALKER, Canon Nigel Maynard. b 39. ALCD66. **d** 67 **p** 68. C Southsea St Jude *Portsm* 67-70; C Addington S Africa 70-73; R 73-76; C Abingdon w Shippon *Ox* 76-80; V Upton (Overchurch) *Ches* 80-94; Chapl Brussels and Chan Brussels Cathl 94-04; P-in-c Leuven 02-04; rtd 05; Perm to Offic *Cant* from 05. *25 Viking Court, Dumpton Park Drive, Broadstairs CT10 1RF* Tel (01843) 867535 E-mail nigelmwalker@gmail.com

WALKER, Mrs Pamela Sarah. b 52. Somerville Coll Ox BA73 MA77 St Jo Coll Dur BA78. Cranmer Hall Dur 76. **dss** 79 **d** 87 **p** 94. Harlow New Town w Lt Parndon *Chelmsf* 79-81; Dorchester *Sarum* 82-83; Bath St Bart *B & W* 85-88; Hon Par Dn 87-88; Par Dn Warmley *Bris* 88-89; Par Dn Bitton 88-89; Par Dn Southampton (City Cen) *Win* 89-92; Par Dn Northolt St Mary *Lon* 92-94; R 94-04; R Corfe Mullen *Sarum* from 04. *The Rectory, 32 Wareham Road, Corfe Mullen, Wimborne BH21 3LE* Tel (01202) 692129 E-mail pswlkr@btinternet.com

WALKER, Paul Gary. b 59. Lon Univ BD. St Jo Coll Nottm 82. **d** 84 **p** 85. C Bowling St Steph *Bradf* 84-87; C Tong 87-90; P-in-c Oakenshaw cum Woodlands 90-97; V Wrose from 97; RD Calverley from 01. *St Cuthbert's Vicarage, 71 Wrose Road, Bradford BD2 1LN* Tel (01274) 611631
E-mail paul.walker@bradford.anglican.org

WALKER, Paul Laurence. b 63. St Chad's Coll Dur BA84. Chich Th Coll BTh90. **d** 88 **p** 89. C Shildon w Eldon *Dur* 88-91; C Barnard Castle w Whorlton 91-93; C Silksworth 93-96; C-in-c Moorside St Wilfrid CD 96-99; V Norton St Mary 99-04; Chapl Manager Tees and NE Yorks NHS Trust from 04. *St Luke's Hospital, Marton Road, Middlesbrough TS4 3AF* Tel (01642) 516068 E-mail paul.walker@tney.northy.nhs.uk

WALKER, Pauline Ann. b 51. Open Univ BA87. St As Minl Tr Course 88. **d** 93 **p** 97. NSM Bistre *St As* 93-99; C Bistre 99-04, V Llay from 04. *The Vicarage, First Avenue, Llay, Wrexham LL12 0TN* Tel (01978) 852262

WALKER, Pauline Jean. b 49. St Hild Coll Dur BSc72 Homerton Coll Cam PGCE73 Nottm Univ MA96. All Nations Chr Coll 89 St Jo Coll Nottm 94. **d** 96 **p** 97. C Bitterne *Win* 96-01; CMS from 01. *CMS, PO Box 1799, Oxford OX4 9BN* Tel 08456-201799

WALKER, Mrs Pepita. **d** 07 **p** 08. OLM Kemble, Poole Keynes, Somerford Keynes etc *Glouc* from 07. *Woodstock, Frampton Mansell, Stroud GL6 8JE* Tel (01285) 760211
E-mail pepitawalker1@hotmail.co.uk

WALKER, Percival. See WALKER, Canon John Percival

WALKER, Peter Anthony. b 57. Pemb Coll Cam BA79 MA83 St Jo Coll Dur BA86. Cranmer Hall Dur 84. **d** 87 **p** 88. C Chesham Bois *Ox* 87-90; Chapl Bradf Cathl 90-93; TV W Swindon and the Lydiards *Bris* 93-99; V Keresley and Coundon Cov from 99. *Keresley Vicarage, 34 Tamworth Road, Coventry CV6 2EL* Tel and fax (024) 7633 2717
E-mail peter@st-thomas-keresley.org.uk

WALKER, Canon Peter Anthony Ashley. b 46. Chich Th Coll 67. **d** 70 **p** 71. C Stamford Hill St Thos *Lon* 70-74; C Bethnal Green St Matt 74-77; V Hackney Wick St Mary of Eton w St Aug 77-84; Warden Rydal Hall *Carl* 84-95; P-in-c Rydal 84-95; P-in-c Porthleven w Sithney *Truro* 95-01; RD Kerrier 96-01; Can Res Truro Cathl from 01; P-in-c Feock from 01. *The Vicarage, Feock, Truro TR3 6SD* Tel (01872) 862534
E-mail feockvic@btinternet.com

WALKER, Peter Jeffrey. b 46. Kelham Th Coll 65. **d** 70 **p** 71. C Middlesbrough All SS *York* 70-75 and 77-78; SSF 75-77; C-in-c

Wrangbrook w N Elmsall CD *Wakef* 78-82; V Athersley 82-86; SSM 86-88; Perm to Offic *Dur* 88-89; V Hartlepool H Trin 89-95; Dep Chapl HM Pris Birm 95-96; Chapl HM Pris Moorland 96-01; Full Sutton 01-04; Co-ord Chapl HM Pris Ford 04-05 and from 06; P-in-c Ferrybridge and Brotherton *Wakef* 05-06; OGS from 01. *The Chaplains' Office, HM Prison Ford, Arundel BN18 0BX* Tel (01903) 663085 Fax 663001

✠**WALKER, The Rt Revd Peter Knight.** b 19. Qu Coll Ox BA47 MA47 Cam Univ Hon DD78. Westcott Ho Cam 53. **d** 54 **p** 55 **c** 72. Asst Master Merchant Taylors' Sch Lon 50-56; C Hemel Hempstead St Mary *St Alb* 56-58; Fell Dean and Lect Th CCC Cam 58-62; Asst Tutor 59-62; Prin Westcott Ho Cam 62-72; Hon Can Ely Cathl 66-72; Suff Bp Dorchester *Ox* 72-77; Can Res Ch 72-77; Bp Ely 77-89; rtd 89; Hon Asst Bp Ox 89-95; Perm to Offic *Ely* from 95. *24 Lammas Court, 14 Grantchester Street, Cambridge CB3 9HY* Tel (01223) 363481

WALKER, Peter Ronald. b 50. Southn Univ BA72 K Alfred's Coll Win PGCE73. WMMTC 02. **d** 05 **p** 06. NSM Hadley and Wellington Ch Ch *Lich* from 05. *4 Harvington Close, Wellington TF1 3EX* Tel (01952) 256927

WALKER, Peter Sidney Caleb. b 50. St Mich Th Coll Crafers 76. **d** 80 **p** 81. Australia 80-88; C Devonport 80-81; P-in-c Fingal Valley 81-84; R E Devonport and Spreyton 84-88; R Swallow *Linc* 88-94; R Selworthy, Timberscombe, Wootton Courtenay etc *B & W* 94-01; Chapl Costa del Sol W *Eur* 01-04; R Coxheath, E Farleigh, Hunton, Linton etc *Roch* from 05. *The Rectory, 144 Heath Road, Coxheath, Maidstone ME17 4PL* Tel and fax (01622) 747570 E-mail peterdiana@talktalk.net

WALKER, Canon Peter Stanley. b 56. SRN RMN Nottm Univ BCombStuds. Linc Th Coll 80. **d** 83 **p** 84. C Woodford St Barn *Chelmsf* 83-86; C Brentwood St Thos 86-88; V Colchester St Barn 88-94; P-in-c Colchester St Jas, All SS, St Nic and St Runwald 94-96; R Colchester St Jas and St Paul w All SS etc from 96; Hon Can Chelmsf Cathl from 09. *The Rectory, 76 East Hill, Colchester CO1 2QW* Tel (01206) 866802 Fax 799444 E-mail fatherpeter@walkerssc.freeserve.co.uk

WALKER, Peter William Leyland. b 61. CCC Cam BA82 MA86 PhD87 Ox Univ DPhil96. Wycliffe Hall Ox 87. **d** 89 **p** 90. C Tonbridge SS Pet and Paul *Roch* 89-93; Fell Tyndale Ho Cam 93-96; Tutor Wycliffe Hall Ox from 96; Hon C Abingdon *Ox* 97-06. *Wycliffe Hall, 54 Banbury Road, Oxford OX2 6PW* Tel (01865) 274214 E-mail peter.walker@wycliffe.ox.ac.uk

WALKER, Canon Philip Geoffrey. b 47. St Jo Coll Dur BA70 Oriel Coll Ox BA72 MA76 Newc Univ MA93 Bris Univ PhD01. Ripon Hall Ox 70. **d** 74 **p** 75. C Sheff St Geo 74-77; C Cambridge Gt St Mary w St Mich *Ely* 77-81; V Monkwearmouth St Andr *Dur* 81-87; R Chester le Street 87-93; RD Chester-le-Street 89-93; Dioc Missr *B & W* 93-01; Can Res Wells Cathl 94-01; Prin OLM Tr Scheme *Cant* 02-05; Prin Whitelands Coll Roehampton Inst from 05. *The Principal's Office, Whitelands College, Holybourne Avenue, London SW15 4JD* Tel (020) 8392 3511 Fax 8392 3531 E-mail drgeoffrey.walker@virgin.net

WALKER, Philip Kingsley. b 47. Ox Univ BA70. St Mich Coll Llan. **d** 90 **p** 91. C Maindee Newport *Mon* 90-92; C Llanmartin 92-94; V Bishton 94-98; R Panteg 98-03; R Panteg w Llanfihangel Pontymoile 03-07; rtd 07. *Glan Aber, Lon Isallt, Trearddur Bay, Holyhead LL65 2UP*

WALKER, Raymond. b 28. Carl Dioc Tr Inst 83. **d** 86 **p** 87. NSM Gt Salkeld w Lazonby *Carl* 86-91; C Greystoke, Matterdale, Mungrisdale etc 91-92; TV 92-95; rtd 95. *Brackenrigg, Town Head, Lazonby, Penrith CA10 1AT* Tel (01768) 898314

WALKER, Richard David. b 45. Hull Univ BSc68. S Dios Minl Tr Scheme 92. **d** 95 **p** 96. NSM Horfield St Greg *Bris* 95-98; NSM Lawrence Weston and Avonmouth 98-00; Chapl HM Pris Leic 00-01; Chapl HM Pris Usk and Prescoed 01-03; Hon C Cromhall, Tortworth, Tytherington, Falfield etc *Glouc* 04-07. *Address temp unknown* E-mail j.walker16@btinternet.com

WALKER, Richard John. b 67. Humberside Coll of Educn BSc88 Leeds Univ MSc(Eng)97 St Jo Coll Dur BA04. Cranmer Hall Dur 02. **d** 04 **p** 05. C Scarborough St Mary w Ch Ch and H Apostles *York* 04-08; V Elloughton and Brough w Brantingham from 08. *The Vicarage, Church Lane, Elloughton, Brough HU15 1SP* Tel (01482) 667431

WALKER, Richard Mainprize. b 43. Keele Univ BA DipEd. Wycliffe Hall Ox 84. **d** 86 **p** 87. C Guildf Ch Ch 86-90; V Bradley St Martin *Lich* 90-05; rtd 05. *10 Rockland Park, Largs KA30 8HB*

WALKER, Richard Mark. b 63. York Univ BSc84. St Jo Coll Nottm MA00. **d** 00 **p** 01. C Ben Rhydding *Bradf* 00-04; P-in-c Yeadon St Jo 04-08; V Yeadon from 08. *St John's Vicarage, Barcroft Grove, Yeadon, Leeds LS19 7XZ* Tel 0113-250 2272 E-mail richard.walker@bradford.anglican.org

WALKER, Roger. *See* WALKER, Gerald Roger

WALKER, Mrs Ruth. b 51. MAAT95. **d** 03 **p** 04. OLM Camberley St Mary *Guildf* from 03. *73 Verran Road, Camberley GU15 2ND* Tel (01276) 503551 E-mail tandr.walker@ntlworld.com

WALKER (née APPLETON), Mrs Ruth Elizabeth. b 58. St Jo Coll Dur BA79 Hughes Hall Cam PGCE80. St Jo Coll Nottm 86. **d** 88 **p** 94. Par Dn Princes Risborough w Ilmer *Ox* 88-90; C and Congr Chapl Bradf Cathl 90-93; C The Lydiards *Bris* 93-94; NSM W Swindon and the Lydiards 94-96; C Swindon St Jo and St Andr 96-98; Perm to Offic 98-99; C Keresley and Coundon *Cov* from 99; AD Cov N from 04. *Keresley Vicarage, 34 Tamworth Road, Coventry CV6 2EL* Tel and fax (024) 7633 2717 E-mail ruth@st-thomas-keresley.org.uk

WALKER, Sharon Anne. b 60. Derby Univ BA99. St Jo Coll Nottm. **d** 02 **p** 03. C Greetham and Thistleton w Stretton and Clipsham *Pet* 02-05; C Cottesmore and Barrow w Ashwell and Burley 02-05; P-in-c Pet St Mary Boongate from 05. *St Mary's Vicarage, 214 Eastfield Road, Peterborough PE1 4BD* Tel (01733) 343418 E-mail sharonannewalker@hotmail.com

WALKER, Simon Patrick. b 71. Ch Ch Ox BA93. Wycliffe Hall Ox BTh94. **d** 97 **p** 98. C Abingdon *Ox* 97-01; Perm to Offic *Ches* 01-04 and *Ox* from 04. *3 Gladstone Road, Headington, Oxford OX3 8LL* Tel (01865) 766356 or 08701-417077 E-mail simon@humanecogroup.com

WALKER, Stanley Frederick. b 48. St Jo Coll Nottm. **d** 84 **p** 85. C Ellesmere Port *Ches* 84-89; V Seacombe 89-97; C Lache cum Saltney 97-03; TV Wrexham *St As* from 03. *St Mark's Vicarage, Menai Road, Wrexham LL13 9LB* Tel (01978) 356647 Mobile 07802-960430 E-mail stanwalker@02.co.uk

WALKER, Stephen Michael Maynard. b 62. St Jo Coll Dur BA84. Trin Coll Bris 86. **d** 88 **p** 89. C Eastwood *S'well* 88-92; CF 92-02; C Marple All SS *Ches* 02-06; P-in-c Tewkesbury H Trin *Glouc* from 06. *Holy Trinity Vicarage, 49 Barton Street, Tewkesbury GL20 5PU* Tel (01684) 293233

WALKER, Stephen Patrick. b 62. York Univ BSc83 PGCE84. St Jo Coll Nottm 87. **d** 90 **p** 91. C Hull St Jo Newland *York* 90-94; Min Grove Green LEP *Cant* 94-98; Children's Min Adv 96-98; TV Drypool *York* 98-99; TR 99-04; TR Binsey *Carl* from 04. *The Vicarage, Torpenhow, Wigton CA7 1HT* Tel (016973) 71541 E-mail rector@binsey.org.uk

WALKER, Mrs Susan Joy. b 52. Univ of Wales (Lamp) BA73 Hull Univ MA91. Qu Coll Birm 75. **dss** 83 **d** 87 **p** 94. Kidderminster St Mary and All SS, Trimpley etc *Worc* 83-86; Keyingham w Ottringham, Halsham and Sunk Is *York* 86-87; Hon Par Dn 87-94; Hon C 94-98; Chapl Hull Coll of FE 89-98; Chapl N Lindsey Coll *Linc* from 98. *St Andrew's Rectory, Belton Road, Epworth, Doncaster DN9 1JL* Tel (01427) 873790 E-mail susanwalker@leggott.ac.uk

WALKER, The Ven Thomas Overington. b 33. Keble Coll Ox BA58 MA61. Oak Hill Th Coll 58. **d** 60 **p** 61. C Woking St Paul *Guildf* 60-62; C St Leonards St Leon *Chich* 62-64; Travelling Sec IVF 64-67; Succ Birm Cathl 67-70; V Harborne Heath 70-91; P-in-c Edgbaston St Germain 83-91; Hon Can Birm Cathl 80-91; RD Edgbaston 89-91; Adn Nottingham *S'well* 91-96; rtd 96; Perm to Offic *Heref* 97-08. *6 Cornbrook, Clee Hill, Ludlow SY8 3QQ* Tel (01584) 890176

WALKER, Trevor John. b 51. Southn Univ BTh80. Sarum & Wells Th Coll 75. **d** 78 **p** 79. C Standish *Blackb* 78-81; P-in-c N Somercotes *Linc* 81-82; P-in-c S Somercotes 81-82; V Somercotes 82-85; R Binbrook Gp from 85. *The Rectory, Louth Road, Binbrook, Lincoln LN8 6BJ* Tel (01472) 398227 Fax 399547 E-mail priest1@compuserve.com

WALKER, Canon Walter Stanley. b 21. AKC42. Cuddesdon Coll 42. **d** 44 **p** 45. C Southport All SS *Liv* 44-47; Miss to Seamen 47-48; C-in-c Kelsall CD *Ches* 48-53; V Birkenhead St Mary w St Paul 53-61; Chapl Barony Hosp Nantwich 61-66; R Wistaston 61-66; R Bromborough 66-77; R Wallasey St Hilary 77-86; RD Wallasey 77-86; Hon Can Ches Cathl 80-86; rtd 86; Perm to Offic *Ches* from 86. *2 Mill Croft, Neston CH64 3TN* Tel 0151-336 5009

WALKER-HILL, Richard John. b 51. WMMTC 06. **d** 09. NSM Oakengates and Wrockwardine Wood *Lich* from 09. *65 Trench Road, Trench, Telford TF2 6PF* Tel (01952) 608086 Mobile 07970-379448 E-mail richard@synnexuk.com

WALKER-HUTCHINSON, Mrs Judith Anne. b 58. St Jo Coll Dur BA07. Cranmer Hall Dur 05. **d** 07 **p** 08. C Penhill *Ripon* from 07. *New Cottage, Swinithwaite, Leyburn DL8 4UH* Tel (01969) 663171 Mobile 07777-507038 E-mail walker.hutchinson@virgin.net

WALKEY, Malcolm Gregory Taylor. b 44. Lon Univ. Kelham Th Coll 63. **d** 68 **p** 69. C Oadby *Leic* 68-72; TV Corby SS Pet and Andr w Gt and Lt Oakley 72-79; R Ashton w Hartwell 79-86; TR Halesworth w Linstead, Chediston, Holton etc *St E* 86-91; P-in-c Laxfield 93-01; rtd 01; Perm to Offic *St E* from 02. *4 Church View, Holton, Halesworth IP19 8PB* Tel (01986) 872594

WALL, Colin. b 52. Hull Univ BEd74 Humberside Coll of Educn BA80. NEOC 02. **d** 05 **p** 06. NSM Hedon w Paull *York* 05-08; P-in-c Tuxford w Weston and Markham Clinton *S'well* from 08. *The Vicarage, 30 Lincoln Road, Tuxford, Newark NG22 0HP* Tel (01777) 872917

WALL, Canon David Oliver. b 39. TD JP. Bps' Coll Cheshunt 62. **d** 65 **p** 66. C Lt Ilford St Mich *Chelmsf* 65-68; CF 68-73; R

Sudbourne w Orford *St E* 73-76; R Orford w Sudbourne and Chillesford w Butley 76-79; P-in-c Iken 76-79; R Drinkstone 79-82; R Rattlesden 79-82; R Chedburgh w Depden, Rede and Hawkedon 82-99; Sen Chapl ACF from 88; Chapl to Suffolk Fire Service *St E* 91-03; Hon Can St E Cathl 96-00; rtd 00; Perm to Offic *Ely* from 01. *Orford House, 43 Corsbie Close, Bury St Edmunds IP33 3ST* Tel (01284) 723232

WALL, Miss Elizabeth Anne. b 51. Birm Univ BDS73. WMMTC 97. d 00 p 01. NSM Lich St Chad from 00. *Gaia Cottage, 15 Gaia Lane, Lichfield WS13 7LW* Tel (01543) 254891 Mobile 07711-557770 E-mail elizabeth@gaiacottage.wanadoo.co.uk

✠**WALL, The Rt Revd Eric St Quintin.** b 15. BNC Ox BA37 MA46. Wells Th Coll 37. d 38 p 39 c 72. C Boston *Linc* 38-41; Chapl RAFVR 41-45; V Sherston Magna w Easton Grey *Bris* 44-53; RD Malmesbury 51-53; V Cricklade w Latton 53-60; Bp's Chapl and Dioc Adv in Chr Stewardship 60-66; Hon Can Bris Cathl 60-72; V Westbury-on-Trym St Alb 66-72; RD Clifton 67-72; Suff Bp Huntingdon and Can Res Ely Cathl 72-80; rtd 80; Perm to Offic *Nor* from 80; *St E* from 81; *Ely* 86-00; Hon Asst Bp Glouc from 00. *Forest House, Cinderhill, Coleford GL16 8HQ* Tel (01594) 832424

WALL, John Caswallen. b 60. York Univ BA83 MA85. St Steph Ho Ox BA89. d 89 p 90. C Ifield *Chich* 89-94; C Brighton St Pet and St Nic w Chpl Royal 94-97; C Brighton St Pet w Chpl Royal 97-98; TV Newbury *Ox* 98-05; TR Moulsecoomb *Chich* from 05. *St Andrew's Rectory, Hillside, Brighton BN2 4TA* Tel (01273) 680680 E-mail jocaswall@hotmail.com

WALL, Mrcia Zélia. b 59. NOC 04. d 07 p 08. C Oakenrod and Bamford *Man* from 07. *35 Hawthorn Road, Rochdale OL11 5JQ* Tel (01706) 860518 Mobile 07981-146558 E-mail mzwall@hotmail.com

WALL, Nicholas John. b 46. MBE02 TD01. Brasted Th Coll 69 Trin Coll Bris 71. d 73 p 74. C Morden *S'wark* 73-78; R Dunkeswell and Dunkeswell Abbey *Ex* 78-83; V Sheldon 78-83; P-in-c Luppitt 81-83; V Dunkeswell, Sheldon and Luppitt 83-03; V Dunkeswell, Luppitt, Sheldon and Upottery from 03; CF(V) from 87. *The Rectory, Dunkeswell, Honiton EX14 4RE* Tel (01404) 891243 E-mail nickandgrete@hotmail.com

WALL, Mrs Pauline Ann. b 39. Bris Sch of Min 87. dss 85 d 87 p 94. Bris Ch the Servant Stockwood 85-99; Hon Par Dn 87-94; Hon C 94-99; Chapl St Brendan's Sixth Form Coll 90-99; rtd 99; Perm to Offic *Bris* from 99. *41 Ladman Road, Bristol BS14 8QD* Tel (01275) 833083

WALL, Richard David. b 78. Ch Ch Ox BA99. St Steph Ho Ox 00. d 02 p 03. C Bocking St Mary *Chelmsf* 02-05; C Philadelphia St Clem USA from 05. *2013 Appletree Street, Philadelphia PA 19103-1409, USA* Tel (001) (215) 563 1876 Fax 563 7627 E-mail frrichardwall@s-clements.org *or* frrichardwall@yahoo.com

WALL, Robert William. b 52. Ex Coll Ox MA Ex Univ BPhil77. Trin Coll Bris 80. d 83 p 84. C Blackb Sav 83-86; C Edgware *Lon* 86-89; C Barnsbury 89-90; TV 90-99; V Dalston St Mark w St Bart 99-07; Chapl St Geo Healthcare NHS Trust Lon from 07. *St George's Hospital, Blackshaw Road, London SW17 0QT* Tel (020) 8725 3285 E-mail rob.wall@care4free.net

WALLACE, Preb Alastair Robert. b 50. St Cath Coll Cam BA71 MA75 Lon Univ BD75. Trin Coll Bris 72. d 75 p 76. C Ex St Leon w H Trin 75-79; Chapl Ridley Hall Cam 79-80; R Bath St Mich w St Paul *B & W* 83-96; RD Bath 90-96; Sub-Dean Wells 96-99; Hon Asst Dioc Missr from 96; Preb Wells Cathl from 96; TR Ilminster and Distr from 99. *The Rectory, Court Barton, Ilminster TA19 0DU* Tel (01460) 52610 E-mail alastair.wallace@btinternet.com

WALLACE, Mrs Ann. b 29. CITC 92. d 95 p 96. Aux Min Abbeyleix w Ballyroan etc *C & O* from 95. *Knapton, Abbeyleix, Portlaoise, Co Laois, Republic of Ireland* Tel (00353) (57) 873 1010

WALLACE, Mrs Brenda Claire. b 52. Linc Th Coll 73 S'wark Ord Course 78. dss 80 d 87 p 94. Sutton at Hone *Roch* 80-83; Borstal 83-89; Hon Par Dn 87-89; HM Pris Cookham Wood 83-89; Asst Chapl 87-89; NSM Stansted Mountfitchet *Chelmsf* 89-96; NSM Stansted Mountfitchet w Birchanger and Farnham 97; C Hutton from 97. *The Rectory, 175 Rayleigh Road, Hutton, Brentwood CM13 1LX* Tel (01277) 215115 Fax 263407 E-mail huttonchurch@zetnet.co.uk

WALLACE, David Alexander Rippon. b 39. CEng MIET. Ox Min Course 94. d 96 p 97. NSM Haddenham w Cuddington, Kingsey etc *Ox* 96-97; NSM Worminghall w Ickford, Oakley and Shabbington 97-02; NSM Aylesbury Deanery from 02. *11 Station Road, Haddenham, Aylesbury HP17 8AN* Tel and fax (01844) 290670 E-mail revd@wallaces.org

WALLACE, Mrs Edwina Margaret. b 49. EMMTC 00. d 03 p 04. C Broughton Astley and Croft w Stoney Stanton *Leic* 03-07; C Sutton Coldfield St Chad *Birm* from 07. *The Vicarage, 41 Hollyfield Road, Sutton Coldfield B75 7SN* Tel 07766-714261 (mobile) E-mail edwina.wallace@onetel.net

WALLACE, Godfrey Everingham. *See* EVERINGHAM, Georgina Wendy

WALLACE, Ian Malcolm. b 57. Southn Univ LLB78 Solicitor 79. STETS 06. d 09. C Wisley w Pyrford *Guildf* from 09. *Church House, Coldharbour Road, Woking GU22 8SP* Tel (01483) 857592 Mobile 07799-076697 E-mail ian.m.wallace@ntlworld.com

WALLACE, James Stephen. b 60. Plymouth Poly BSc81 St Martin's Coll Lanc 90. Westcott Ho Cam 96. d 98 p 99. C Newport Pagnell w Lathbury and Moulsoe *Ox* 98-02; USPG Sri Lanka 02-08. *21 Walpole Terrace, Brighton BN2 0ED* Tel (01273) 689289

WALLACE, Julie Michele. b 58. Ox Univ MTh93 Univ Coll Lon MSc02. CA Tr Coll 77. d 88 p 94. Chapl Middx Poly *Lon* 86-90; Voc Adv CA 90-92; Member CA Counselling Service 92-96; Hon C Bellingham St Dunstan *S'wark* 91-96; TV Kidbrooke St Jas 96-99; Perm to Offic 99-01; Hon C Croydon Woodside 01-03. *6 Pantanas, Treharris CF46 5BN*

WALLACE, Mark David. b 76. Worc Coll Ox BA98 MA01. Oak Hill Th Coll 05. d 08 p 09. C Trull w Angersleigh *B & W* from 08. *5 Barton Green, Trull, Taunton TA3 7NA* Tel (01823) 350991 Mobile 07772-615378 E-mail lizandmark.wallace@btinternet.com

WALLACE, Mark George. b 72. Qu Coll Cam BA94. Oak Hill Th Coll BA08. d 08. C Guildf Ch Ch w St Martha-on-the-Hill from 08. *2 Ivor Close, Guildford GU1 2ET* Tel (01483) 567072 E-mail mark@christchurchguildford.com

✠**WALLACE, The Rt Revd Martin William.** b 48. K Coll Lon BD70 AKC70. St Aug Coll Cant 70. d 71 p 72 c 03. C Attercliffe *Sheff* 71-74; C New Malden and Coombe *S'wark* 74-77; V Forest Gate St Mark *Chelmsf* 77-93; RD Newham 82-91; P-in-c Forest Gate Em w Upton Cross 85-89; Hon Can Chelmsf Cathl 89-03; P-in-c Forest Gate All SS 91-93; Dioc ACUPA Link Officer 91-97; P-in-c Bradwell on Sea 93-97; P-in-c St Lawrence 93-97; Ind Chapl Maldon and Dengie Deanery 93-97; Adn Colchester 97-03; Bp's Adv for Hosp Chapl 97-03; Suff Bp Selby *York* from 03. *Bishop's House, Barton-le-Street, Malton YO17 6PL* Tel (01653) 627191 Fax 627193 E-mail bishselby@clara.net

WALLACE (née ALEXANDER), Mrs Nancy Joan. b 42. Roehampton Inst TCert64 Ox Brookes Univ BA97 PQCSW97. SAOMC 95. d 98 p 99. NSM Worminghall w Ickford, Oakley and Shabbington *Ox* 98-02; NSM Aylesbury Deanery from 02. *11 Station Road, Haddenham, Aylesbury HP17 8AN* Tel and fax (01844) 290670 E-mail revn@wallaces.org

WALLACE, Nicholas Robert. b 56. Trin Coll Bris 93. d 95 p 96. C Fishponds St Jo *Bris* 95-98; P-in-c Barton Hill St Luke w Ch Ch 98-99; P-in-c Barton Hill St Luke w Ch Ch and Moorfields 99-00; R Binstead *Portsm* from 00; V Havenstreet St Pet from 00. *The Rectory, Pitts Lane, Ryde PO33 3SU* Tel (01983) 562890

WALLACE, Raymond Sherwood. b 28. Selw Coll Dunedin (NZ). d 52 p 54. C Roslyn New Zealand 52-54; C Invercargill 54-55; P-in-c Waitaki 55-58; C St Pancras H Cross w St Jude and St Pet *Lon* 58-64; C N Harrow St Alb 64-67; V Stroud Green H Trin 67-79; V Penwerris *Truro* 79-84; R Wymington w Podington *St Alb* 84-87; rtd 87; Perm to Offic *St Alb* from 87. *141 Dunsmore Road, Luton LU1 5JX* Tel (01582) 455882

WALLACE, Richard Colin. b 39. Mert Coll Ox BA61 MA64. St Chad's Coll Dur 69. d 71 p 72. Tutor St Chad's Coll Dur 71-72; P-in-c Kimblesworth *Dur* 72-74; Chapl Bradf Univ 74-79; C Bingley All SS 79-80; TV 80-89; V Earby 89-96; P-in-c Kelbrook 01-06; RD Skipton 00-05; rtd 06. *15 Holme Park, Bentham, Lancaster LA2 7ND* Tel (015242) 63136 E-mail richard@drwallace.co.uk

WALLACE, Richard Ernest. b 35. Ridley Coll Melbourne ThL61 ACT 61. d 61 p 62. C Balwyn St Barn Australia 61-62; C S Yarra 62-64; C Bentleigh St Jo 64-65; I Northcote 65-66; C Ipswich St Fran *St E* 67-69; I Belgrave Australia 69-79; Dir Angl Renewal Min 79-82; I Blackburn St Jo 83-92; I Syndal St Jas 92-95; Sen Assoc P Glen Waverley 95-97; I Ringwood E H Trin 97-03; rtd 03. *3 Panorama Road, Kalorama Vic 3766, Australia* Tel (0061) (3) 9728 4595 Mobile 408-596535 E-mail rwallace@melbpc.org.au

WALLACE, Richard John. b 56. Coll of Resurr Mirfield. d 82 p 83. C Catford St Laur *S'wark* 82-85; C Bellingham St Dunstan 85-87; V 87-95; TR Stanley *Dur* 95-99; V Cockerton from 99. *St Mary's Vicarage, Newton Lane, Cockerton, Darlington DL3 9EX* Tel (01325) 367892

WALLACE, Richard Samuel. b 17. TCD BA39 MA53. d 41 p 42. C Belfast St Steph *Conn* 41-43; C Hammersmith St Pet *Lon* 43-44; India 44-51; Perivale *Lon* 51-54; V Notting Hill St Mark 54-60; V Teddington St Mark 60-83; rtd 83; Perm to Offic *Ex* from 83. *St Christopher, 17 Hartley Road, Exmouth EX8 2SG* Tel (01395) 279595

WALLACE, Robert. b 52. Sussex Univ BSc73. Linc Th Coll 73. d 76 p 77. C Plaistow St Mary *Roch* 76-79; C Dartford H Trin 79-83; V Borstal 83-89; Chapl The Foord Almshouses 83-89; Chapl HM Pris Cookham Wood 83-89; P-in-c Farnham *Chelmsf* 89-96; V Stansted Mountfitchet 89-96; R Stansted Mountfitchet w Birchanger and Farnham from 97; R Hutton from 97. *The Rectory, 175 Rayleigh Road, Hutton, Brentwood CM13 1LX* Tel (01277) 215115 Fax 263407 E-mail huttonchurch@zetnet.co.uk

WALLACE

WALLACE, Mrs Susan Marilyn. b 67. Ch Ch Coll Cant
BA(Ed)90 Leeds Univ MA06. NOC 03. **d** 06 **p** 07. NSM Acomb
St Steph *York* from 06. *40 Milton Street, York YO10 3EP* Tel
(01904) 411867 Mobile 07962-071621
E-mail sue@visions-york.org

WALLBANK, Alison Patricia. b 59. **d** 09. OLM Whitworth w
Facit *Man* from 09. *1 Waingap View, Whitworth, Rochdale
OL12 8QD* Tel (01706) 353616 Mobile 07800-955799
E-mail alison@awallbank.fslife.co.uk

WALLER, Annalu. b 63. Cape Town Univ BSc83 MSc88 Dundee
Univ PhD92. TISEC 01. **d** 04 **p** 05. Hon C Dundee St Marg *Bre*
from 04; Hon Chapl Dundee Univ from 07. *9 Invergowrie Drive,
Dundee DD2 1RD* Tel (01382) 644570

WALLER, David Arthur. b 61. Leeds Univ BA83. Chich Th Coll
89. **d** 91 **p** 92. C Aldwick *Chich* 91-95; TV Crawley 95-00; V
Walthamstow St Sav *Chelmsf* from 00. *St Saviour's Vicarage, 210
Markhouse Road, London E17 8EP* Tel (020) 8520 2036
E-mail d.a.waller@btinternet.com

WALLER, David James. b 58. Whitelands Coll Lon BA85 K Coll
Lon MA95. Ripon Coll Cuddesdon 85. **d** 88 **p** 89. C Tettenhall
Regis *Lich* 88-91; Chapl Greenwich Univ 92-97; P-in-c Yiewsley
Lon 97-01; TR Plymstock and Hooe *Ex* from 01. *The Rectory, 5
Cobb Lane, Plymstock, Plymouth PL9 9BQ* Tel (01752) 403126
E-mail david@waller2000.freeserve.co.uk

WALLER, Derek James Keith. b 54. Em Coll Cam BA75
PGCE76. Trin Coll Bris 88. **d** 91 **p** 92. C Church Stretton *Heref*
91-95; R Appleby Gp *Leic* 95-04; P-in-c Rushden St Pet 04-07; V
from 08. *St Peter's Vicarage, 12 Kensington Close, Rushden
NN10 6RR* Tel (01933) 356398
E-mail derekwaller@btinternet.com

WALLER, Mrs Elizabeth Alison. b 49. Open Univ BA89 Univ of
Cen England in Birm MA99 Wolfs Coll Cam PGCE91.
EAMTC 02. **d** 05 **p** 06. NSM Oundle w Ashton and Benefield w
Glapthorn *Pet* 05-08; NSM Aldwincle, Clopton, Pilton, Stoke
Doyle etc from 08. *Priory Cottage, 40 Church Street, Stilton,
Peterborough PE7 3RF* Tel (01733) 242412
E-mail lizwaller@waitrose.com

WALLER, Ms Elizabeth Jean. b 58. Keswick Hall Coll BEd BTh.
Linc Th Coll 84. **d** 87 **p** 94. Par Dn Mile End Old Town H Trin
Lon 87-90; Manna Chr Cen 90-91; Chapl LSE *Lon* 91-96; Hon C
Soho St Anne w St Thos and St Pet 91-96; Community Pastor
CARA 96-00; NSM Notting Dale St Clem w St Mark and St Jas
Lon 96-99; Chapl Ealing Hosp NHS Trust from 07. *55 Browning
Avenue, London W7 1AX* Tel (020) 8578 3827
E-mail lizawaller@hotmail.com

WALLER, Gordon Robert. b 50. Jes Coll Cam BA72 MA75. **d** 03
p 05. OLM Tooting All SS *S'wark* from 03. *131 Ribblesdale
Road, London SW16 6SP* Tel (020) 8769 6733
E-mail baldypevsner@yahoo.co.uk

WALLER, John. b 60. Man Univ BA84 Liv Univ MA07. St Jo
Coll Nottm 85. **d** 87 **p** 88. C Chorlton-cum-Hardy St Clem *Man*
87-90; R Openshaw 90-95; Chapl Ancoats Hosp Man 93-95; TV
Watling Valley *Ox* 95-96; TR 96-03; R Brickhills and Stoke
Hammond from 03; AD Mursley from 06. *The Rectory, 10
Pound Hill, Great Brickhill, Milton Keynes MK17 9AS* Tel
(01525) 261062 E-mail john.waller1@virgin.net

WALLER, John Pretyman. b 41. Sarum Th Coll 68. **d** 71 **p** 72. C
Ipswich St Jo *St E* 71-74; R Waldringfield w Hemley 74-78;
P-in-c Newbourn 74-78; R Waldringfield w Hemley and
Newbourn from 78. *The Rectory, Mill Road, Waldringfield,
Woodbridge IP12 4PY* Tel (01473) 736247

✠**WALLER, The Rt Revd John Stevens.** b 24. Peterho Cam BA48
MA53. Wells Th Coll 48. **d** 50 **p** 51 **c** 79. C Hillingdon St Jo *Lon*
50-52; C Twerton *B & W* 52-55; C-in-c Weston-super-Mare
St Andr Bournville CD 55-59; V Weston-super-Mare St Andr
Bournville 59-60; R Yarlington 60-63; Youth Chapl 60-63; Tr
Officer C of E Youth Coun 63-67; V Frindsbury w Upnor *Roch*
67-72; P-in-c Strood St Fran 67-72; P-in-c Strood St Mary 67-72;
P-in-c Strood St Nic 67-72; TR Strood 72-73; RD Strood 67-73;
R Harpenden St Nic *St Alb* 73-79; Suff Bp Stafford *Lich* 79-87;
Asst Bp B & W 87-04; P-in-c Long Sutton w Long Load 87-88;
TV Langport Area 88-89; rtd 89. *102 Harnham Road, Salisbury
SP2 8JW* Tel (01722) 329739 Fax 411492
E-mail jwaller@talk21.com

WALLER, Canon John Watson. b 35. Qu Mary Coll Lon BSc57.
Wycliffe Hall Ox 58. **d** 61 **p** 62. C Pudsey St Lawr *Bradf* 61-65; V
74-82; V Mortomley St Sav *Sheff* 65-74; V Pudsey St Lawr and
St Paul *Bradf* 82-88; Hon Can Bradf Cathl 84-88; RD Calverley
84-88; V Kingston upon Hull H Trin *York* 88-01; AD Cen and N
Hull 94-99; Can and Preb York Minster 95-04; RD Hull 96-00;
rtd 01; Perm to Offic *York* from 04. *7 Seven Wells, Amotherby,
Malton YO17 6TT* Tel (01653) 691388
E-mail johnandmarywaller@hotmail.com

WALLER, Orlando Alfred. b 12. St Aid Birkenhead 39. **d** 41 **p** 42.
C Birkenhead St Pet *Ches* 41-42; C Crewe St Barn 42-45; C
Gatley 45-49; Min Heald Green St Cath CD 49-51; V
Haslington w Crewe Green 51-54; Australia 54-59; V Runcorn
St Jo Weston *Ches* 59-63; V Merrington *Dur* 63-70; P-in-c

Bearpark 70-71; V 71-76; rtd 77. *22 Thornley Close, Broom Park,
Durham DH7 7NN*

WALLER, Philip Thomas. b 56. Ex Coll Ox BA78 MA88 St Jo
Coll Dur BA87. Cranmer Hall Dur 85. **d** 88 **p** 89. C Enfield
St Andr *Lon* 88-91; C Belper *Derby* 91-95; P-in-c Oakwood
95-05; P-in-c Long Eaton St Jo from 05. *St John's Vicarage, 59
Trowell Grove, Long Eaton, Nottingham NG10 4AY* Tel 0115-973
4819 E-mail waller.family59@tiscali.co.uk

WALLES, Bruce Andrew. b 54. Coll of Resurr Mirfield 90. **d** 92
p 93. C Maidstone St Martin *Cant* 92-96; TV Banbury *Ox* 96-98;
V Banbury St Leon 98-04; V Aintree St Giles w St Pet *Liv* from
04. *St Giles's Vicarage, 132 Aintree Lane, Liverpool L10 8LE* Tel
0151-476 5554 E-mail wallba@ntlworld.com

WALLET, Barend Theodoor Bernd. b 71. Hull Univ BA03 MA05.
Old Cath Sem Amersfoort 04. **d** 06 **p** 07. C Northallerton w
Kirby Sigston *York* from 06. *26 Helmsley Way, Northallerton
DL7 8SX* Tel (01609) 780071
E-mail berndwallet@hotmail.com

WALLEY, Peter Francis. b 60. Bris Univ BSc82 CEng89
MICE89. Trin Coll Bris 96. **d** 98 **p** 99. C Ex St Jas 98-01; Asst
Chapl Brussels *Eur* 01-05; Bp's Dom Chapl *Lich* from 05.
Bishop's House, 22 The Close, Lichfield WS13 7LG Tel (01543)
306000 Fax 306009 E-mail peter.walley@lichfield.anglican.org

WALLING, Mrs Carolyn. b 47. Rolle Coll CertEd69. Episc Div
Sch Cam Mass MDiv87. **d** 86 **p** 87. Saudi Arabia 89; Par Dn
Battersea St Mary *S'wark* 91-94; USA 94-96; C Lee Gd Shep w
St Pet *S'wark* 96; rtd 07. *PO Box 947, General Post Office,
Georgetown, 10820 Penang, Malaysia*

WALLINGTON, Martin John. b 59. SAOMC 95. **d** 98 **p** 99. NSM
Chorleywood St Andr *St Alb* 98-03; P-in-c Wooburn *Ox* 03-08;
V from 08. *Wooburn Vicarage, Windsor Hill, Wooburn Green,
High Wycombe HP10 0EH* Tel (01628) 521209

WALLINGTON, Paul. b 62. Birm Univ BCom83 ACA86. Trin
Coll Bris BA94. **d** 94 **p** 95. C Chorley St Laur *Blackb* 94-97; C
Darwen St Pet w Hoddlesden 97-98; TV 98-00; R from 00.
551 Darwen Road, Dunscar, Bolton BL7 9RT Tel (01204) 308637
E-mail thewallingtons@hotmail.com

WALLIS, Anna Louise. b 73. Leic Univ BSc95 PhD99 Selw Coll
Cam BA05. Westcott Ho Cam 03. **d** 06 **p** 07. C Huddersfield
St Pet *Wakef* from 06. *85 New North Road, Huddersfield
HD1 5ND* Tel (01484) 538381
E-mail anna.wallis@hotmail.co.uk

WALLIS, Benjamin John. b 55. Wimbledon Sch of Art BA79.
Chich Th Coll 92. **d** 94 **p** 95. C Battersea Ch Ch and St Steph
S'wark 94-98; C Wood Green St Mich w Bounds Green St Gabr
etc *Lon* 98-03; V Barkingside St Geo *Chelmsf* from 03.
St George's Vicarage, Woodford Avenue, Ilford IG2 6XQ Tel
(020) 8550 4149

WALLIS, David Peter. b 72. Ripon Coll Cuddesdon BTh03. **d** 03
p 04. C Eastbourne St Mary *Chich* 03-07; P-in-c Ditchling,
Streat and Westmeston 07-08; R from 08. *St Margaret's
Vicarage, 2 Charlton Gardens, Lewes Road, Ditchling, Hassocks
BN6 8WA* Tel (01273) 843165

WALLIS, Ian George. b 57. Sheff Univ BA79 PhD92 St Edm Ho
Cam MLitt87. Ridley Hall Cam 88. **d** 90 **p** 91. C Armthorpe
Sheff 90-92; Chapl and Fell SS Coll Cam 92-95; Hon C
Chesterton Gd Shep *Ely* 93-95; R Houghton le Spring *Dur*
95-07; AD Houghton 04-07; Tutor Aston Tr Scheme 93-97; Prin
NOC 07-08; V Sheff St Mark Broomhill from 09. *St Mark's
Vicarage, 4 St Mark's Crescent, Sheffield S10 2SG* Tel 0114-267
0362 Mobile 07717-417760 E-mail ian.wallis@sero.co.uk

WALLIS, John Anthony. b 36. St Pet Coll Ox BA60 MA65.
Clifton Th Coll 60. **d** 62 **p** 63. C Blackpool St Mark *Blackb*
62-65; C Leeds St Geo *Ripon* 65-69; Korea 69-74; Nat Sec
(Scotland) OMF 75-78; Home Dir OMF 78-89; Hon C
Sevenoaks St Nic *Roch* 78-89; Chapl The Hague *Eur* 89-95; V
Northwood Em *Lon* 95-01; rtd 01; Perm to Offic *Nor* from 03.
*Church Cottage, 61 Gayton Road, Grimston, King's Lynn
PE32 1BG* Tel (01485) 600336 E-mail john.wallis@virgin.net

WALLIS, Peter. b 42. K Coll Lon MB, BS68 MRCS AKC68.
STETS 98. **d** 01. NSM Clymping and Yapton w Ford *Chich* from
01. *Chanters, 3 Second Avenue, Felpham, Bognor Regis PO22 7LJ*
Tel (01243) 584080 Mobile 07885-542651
E-mail revdocpw@gotadsl.co.uk

WALLIS, Raymond Christopher. b 38. Moor Park Coll Farnham
62 Sarum Th Coll 63. **d** 66 **p** 67. C Allerton *Bradf* 66-68; C
Langley Marish *Ox* 68-69; C Caister *Nor* 69-73; P-in-c E w W
Bradenham 73-80; R Upwell St Pet and Outwell *Ely* 80-84; V
Bishopstone *Chich* 84-97; rtd 97; Perm to Offic *Chich* from 97.
15 Llewellyn Lodge, Cooden Drive, Bexhill-on-Sea TN39 3DB Tel
(01424) 220245

WALLMAN-GIRDLESTONE, Jane Elizabeth. b 61. Homerton
Coll Cam BEd83. St Steph Ho Ox 89 Sarum & Wells Th Coll
BTh92. **d** 93 **p** 94. C Woodbridge St Mary *St E* 93-96; V Ipswich
St Thos 96-00; Dir Past Studies and Adv for Women's Min
St Mich Coll Llandaff 00-02; Lect TISEC from 03; Lect Qu
Foundn Birm 04-05. *Isle View, The Clattach, Alturlie Point,
Allanfearn, Inverness IV2 7HZ* Tel (01463) 230708
E-mail wallmanj@isleview.claranet.co.uk

WALLS, Michael Peter. b 38. Cape Town Univ BA57. Wells Th Coll 59. **d** 61 **p** 62. C Morecambe St Barn *Blackb* 61-64; C Birm St Paul 64-66; Ind Chapl 64-74; V Temple Balsall 66-74; Chapl Wroxall Abbey Sch 72-74; V Kings Heath *Birm* 74-76; Hon C Bordesley St Benedict 76-78; Sen Chapl Oakham Sch 78-83; P-in-c Leic St Sav 83-85; P-in-c Knossington and Cold Overton 85-87; P-in-c Owston and Withcote 85-87; V Tilton w Lowesby 85-87; P-in-c 87; V Whatborough Gp 87-90; Bp's Adv Relns w People of Other Faiths 89-93; Hon Can Leic Cathl 89-93; V Leic St Mary 90-93; rtd 93; Perm to Offic *Ban* from 02. *Gwynt y Mor, 1A Bro Cymerau, Pwllheli LL53 5PY* Tel (01758) 613495 E-mail michael.w@tinyworld.co.uk

WALMISLEY, Andrew John. b 55. Ex Univ BA75 San Francisco State Univ MA90. Ridley Hall Cam 76. **d** 78 **p** 79. C W Brompton St Mary w St Pet *Lon* 78-81; C Portola Valley Ch Ch USA 81-83; C San Francisco St Mary V 83-86; Chapl San Mateo St Matt 86-90; Chapl New York Trin Ch 90-93; R Redwood City St Pet 93-97; R Berkely All So 97-07; Chapl Seabury Hall Coll Prep Sch Makawao from 07. *65 North Holokai Road, Haiku HI 96708, USA* Tel (001) (808) 573 6848 E-mail frandreww@aol.com

WALMISLEY, Derek. b 57. Oak Hill Th Coll 89. **d** 91 **p** 92. C Bletchley *Ox* 91-95; C Utley *Bradf* 95-00; V from 00. *St Mark's Vicarage, Green Head Road, Keighley BD20 6ED* Tel (01535) 607003 E-mail derek.walmsley@bradford.anglican.org *or* dwalmsley9@aol.com

WALMISLEY, Jane. *See* LLOYD, Patricia Jane

WALMSLEY, John William. b 37. Hull Univ BA71 MA73 PhD81. Wycliffe Hall Ox 71. **d** 72 **p** 73. C Clifton *York* 72-74; C Acomb St Steph 74-76; P-in-c Newton upon Ouse 76-81; P-in-c Shipton w Overton 76-81; V York St Thos w St Maurice 81-89; V Barkingside St Laur *Chelmsf* 89-92; Dir Children in Distress 92-01; rtd 01. *51 Nursery Gardens, Yarm TS15 9UY*

WALMSLEY-McLEOD, Paul Albert. b 56. St Cuth Soc Dur BA82 Cam Univ CertEd83. Westcott Ho Cam 85. **d** 87 **p** 88. C Gt Bookham *Guildf* 87-90; Asst Chapl St Chris Hospice Lon 90-93; Soc Care Team Member Phoenix Ho Fountain Project 93-95; C Catford (Southend) and Downham *S'wark* 95-96; TV 96-99; P-in-c Downham St Barn 00-02; R Friern Barnet St Jas *Lon* from 02. *The Rectory, 147 Friern Barnet Lane, London N20 0NP* Tel (020) 8445 7844 E-mail pawm_friernbarnet@hotmail.com

WALROND-SKINNER, Susan Mary. *See* PARFITT, Susan Mary

WALSALL, Archdeacon of. *Vacant*

WALSER (*née* SHIELS), Mrs Rosalinde Cameron. b 47. Edin Univ MA68 Moray Ho Coll of Educn PGCE69. NOC 92. **d** 95 **p** 97. NSM Scarborough St Mary w Ch Ch and H Apostles *York* 95-97; Chapl St Cath Hospice Scarborough 95-97; Chapl Scarborough Coll 95-97; P-in-c E Ayton *York* 97-06; rtd 06; Perm to Offic *York* from 07. *29 Sea Cliff Road, Scarborough YO11 2XU* Tel (01723) 372382

WALSH, Mrs Alexandra (Gussie). b 50. Wycliffe Hall Ox 06. **d** 08 **p** 09. C Penrith w Newton Reigny and Plumpton Wall *Carl* from 08. *18 Skirsgill Close, Penrith CA11 8QF* Tel (01768) 899957

WALSH, David Christopher. b 59. Warwick Univ BA81 St Jo Coll Nottm BA83. Ripon Coll Cuddesdon 00. **d** 02 **p** 03. C Greenwich St Alfege *S'wark* 02-06; C Kensington St Mary Abbots w Ch Ch and St Phil *Lon* from 06. *2 Pembroke Road, London W8 6NT* Tel 07957-656643 (mobile) E-mail david@walsh.name

✠**WALSH, The Rt Revd Geoffrey David Jeremy.** b 29. Pemb Coll Cam BA53 MA58. Linc Th Coll 53. **d** 55 **p** 56 **c** 86. C Southgate Ch Ch *Lon* 55-58; SCM Sec Cam 58-61; C Cambridge Gt St Mary w St Mich *Ely* 58-61; V Marlborough *Bris* 61-66; R Marlborough *Sarum* 66-76; Can and Preb Sarum Cathl 73-76; Adn Ipswich *St E* 76-86; R Elmsett w Aldham 76-80; Suff Bp Tewkesbury *Glouc* 86-95; rtd 95; Perm to Offic *St E* from 95; Hon Asst Bp St E from 08. *6 Warren Lane, Martlesham Heath, Ipswich IP5 3SH* Tel (01473) 620797

WALSH, Geoffrey Malcolm. b 46. Sarum & Wells Th Coll 82. **d** 84 **p** 85. C Wellington and Distr *B & W* 84-87; TV Axminster, Chardstock, Combe Pyne and Rousdon *Ex* 87-90; Chapl RN 90-94; R Huntspill *B & W* from 94. *The Rectory, Church Road, West Huntspill, Highbridge TA9 3RN* Tel and fax (01278) 793950 E-mail g.walsh1@ntlworld.co.uk

WALSH, Gussie. *See* WALSH, Mrs Alexandra

WALSH, John Alan. b 37. Chich Th Coll 63. **d** 66 **p** 67. C Wigan St Anne *Liv* 66-69; C Newport w Longford *Lich* 69-73; V Dunstall 73-83; V Rangemore 73-83; P-in-c Tatenhill 77-83; R Dunstall w Rangemore and Tatenhill 83; V Hartshill 83-03; rtd 03; Perm to Offic *Ches* from 04. *49 Plumley Close, Vicars Cross, Chester CH3 5PD* Tel (01244) 310936

WALSH, Neil-Allan. b 72. Cant Ch Ch Univ BA03 Cape Town Univ DipEd97. Westcott Ho Cam 06. **d** 08 **p** 09. C L tt Ilford St Mich *Chelmsf* from 08. *3 Toronto Avenue, London E12 5JF* Tel (020) 8478 8552 Mobile 07903-652874 E-mail neilallanwalsh@yahoo.com

WALSH, Peter. b 64. Liv Univ BA86 Nottm Univ BTh90. Linc Th Coll 87. **d** 90 **p** 91. C Cantley *Sheff* 90-93; C Poulton-le-Fylde *Blackb* 93-95; V Blackpool St Steph 95-03; TR Ches 03-05; V Ches St Oswald and St Thos from 05; Min Can Ches Cathl 04-05. *The Vicarage, 33 Abbots Grange, Chester CH2 1AJ* Tel (01244) 399990 E-mail vicar@peterwalsh.plus.com

WALSH, Sarah Elaine. b 60. LLCM(TD)90 CTABRSM95. NEOC 04. **d** 07. NSM Waggoners *York* 07-08; NSM Crookes St Tim *Sheff* from 09. *211 Heavygate Road, Sheffield S10 1PH* Tel 0114-268 2824 Fax 297 2995 E-mail sewalsh@sewalsh.karoo.co.uk

WALSHE, Marie Sylvia. b 54. RGN RCNT. **d** 99 **p** 00. NSM Kilkeel *D & D* 99-00; NSM Down H Trin w Hollymount 00-08; NSM Rathmullan w Tyrella 00-08; NSM Newcastle from 08. *8 Castle View, Dundrum, Newcastle BT33 0SA* Tel (028) 4375 1757 E-mail walshemarie@hotmail.com

WALT, Canon Trevor William. b 52. MBE03. RMN74 RNT79. Ox NSM Course 83. **d** 86 **p** 87. NSM Crowthorne *Ox* 86-89; Chapl Asst Broadmoor Hosp Crowthorne 86-89; Chapl from 89; Hon Can Ch Ch *Ox* 00-07. *Broadmoor Hospital, Crowthorne RG45 7EG* Tel (01344) 773111 ext 4450

WALTER, Donald Alex. b 34. Ripon Hall Ox 57. **d** 60 **p** 61. C Ealing St Steph Castle Hill *Lon* 60-63; Jamaica 63-80; V Twickenham Common H Trin *Lon* 81-00; rtd 00; Perm to Offic *Lon* from 03. *Ebenezer, 23 Hawley Close, Hampton TW12 3XX* Tel (020) 8941 5193 E-mail daw@maperche.co.uk

WALTER, Giles Robert. b 54. Cam Univ MA76. Cranmer Hall Dur 78. **d** 82 **p** 83. C Finchley Ch Ch *Lon* 82-86; C Cambridge H Sepulchre w All SS *Ely* 86-92; C Cambridge H Sepulchre 92-93; P-in-c Tunbridge Wells St Jo *Roch* 93-95; V from 95. *St John's Vicarage, 1 Amherst Road, Tunbridge Wells TN4 9LG* Tel (01892) 521183 *or* 540897

WALTER, Ian Edward. b 47. Edin Univ MA69 Keble Coll Ox BA71 MA78. Cuddesdon Coll 71. **d** 73 **p** 74. C Greenock *Glas* 73-76; C Glas St Mary and Chapl Angl Students Glas 76-79; R Paisley St Barn 79-84; P-in-c Bolton St Phil *Man* 84-86; V 86-91; Dioc Ecum Officer 88-94; V Elton All SS 91-98; V Stalybridge 98-01; R Hawick *Edin* 01-08; rtd 08. *Balaclava, 56 Dalriach Road, Oban PA34 5JE* Tel (01631) 564855 E-mail ian_walter@btinternet.com

WALTER, Michael. b 36. AKC62. **d** 63 **p** 64. C Middlesbrough St Jo the Ev *York* 63-65; C Sherborne *Win* 65-68; C Bournemouth St Fran 68-69; Prec Newc Cathl 69-71; C Dur St Marg 72-74; P-in-c Deaf Hill cum Langdale 74-77; V Newington w Dairycoates *York* 77-88; Perm to Offic 88-92; C Feltham *Lon* 92-96; Perm to Offic 96-03; rtd 01. *15 Glanville Road, Bromley BR2 9LN* Tel (020) 8313 3390

WALTER, Noël. b 41. St D Coll Lamp. **d** 66 **p** 67. C Mitcham Ascension *S'wark* 66-71; C Caterham 71-74; OCF 71-74; V Welling *S'wark* 74-82; C Warlingham w Chelsham and Farleigh 82-88; Chapl Warlingham Park Hosp Croydon 82-88; Chapl R Earlswood Hosp Redhill 88-90; Chapl Redhill Gen Hosp 88-91; Chapl E Surrey Hosp Redhill 88-96; Sen Chapl Gt Ormond Street Hosp for Children NHS Trust 96-06; rtd 06; Perm to Offic *Ex* 97-07; C Chagford, Drewsteignton, Hittisleigh etc from 07. *Whiddon View, 13 Bretteville Close, Chagford, Newton Abbot TQ13 8DW* Tel (01647) 432610

WALTER, Peter John. b 44. CEng MIGasE. Chich Th Coll 80. **d** 82 **p** 83. C Leominster *Heref* 82-85; P-in-c Brimfield 85-90; P-in-c Orleton 85-90; R Orleton w Brimfield 91-95; rtd 04. *Mews Cottage, 39 West Street, Leominster HR6 8EP*

WALTER, Robin. b 37. Univ Coll Dur BA63 MA90 Linacre Coll Ox BA69 MA69. St Steph Ho Ox 63. **d** 66 **p** 68. C Peckham St Jo *S'wark* 66-69; Chapl Lon Univ 69-70; C Dur St Marg 70-74; R Burnmoor 74-79; Asst Master Barnard Castle Sch 79-97; NSM Barnard Castle Deanery 88-97; Hon C Whorlton *Dur* 82-88; P-in-c Redmarshall 97-01; R 01-03; P-in-c Bishopton w Gt Stainton 97-01; V 01-03; rtd 03; Perm to Offic *York* from 03 and *Worc* from 04. *The Laurels, Worcester Road, Great Witley, Worcester WR6 6HR* Tel (01299) 890190

WALTERS, Andrew Farrar. b 42. ACP67 St Luke's Coll Ex CertEd71. **d** 81 **p** 82. Hd Master and Warden St Mich Coll Tenbury 77-85; Chapl Ex Cathl Sch 85-87; Hd Master Homefield Sch Sutton 87-92; Hd Master Lich Cathl Sch 92-02; Hon C Sutton St Nic *S'wark* 87-92; Chan's V Lich Cathl 93-02; rtd 02. *The Drey, Trallong, Brecon LD3 8HP* Tel and fax (01874) 636374 E-mail thedrey@tiscali.co.uk

WALTERS, Christopher Rowland. b 47. Open Univ BA78 Univ of Wales PGCE94. **d** 02. Hd Master Mayflower Chr Sch Pontypool from 90; OLM Abergavenny H Trin *Mon* from 02. *3 Whites Close, Belmont Road, Abergavenny NP7 5HZ* Tel 07967-945320 (mobile) E-mail church@chriswalters.co.uk

WALTERS, David Michael Trenham. b 46. Open Univ BA86. St D Coll Lamp. **d** 69 **p** 70. C Killay *S & B* 69-72; CF 72-89 and 91-01; Chapl Eagle Ho Prep Sch Crowthorne 89-91; Chapl R Memorial Chpl Sandhurst 97-01; P-in-c Llanrhidian *S & B* 01-05; V Llanrhidian w Llanyrnewydd from 05. *Westwood*

Cottage, 65 Pennard Road, Pennard, Swansea SA3 2AD Tel (01792) 234307

WALTERS, David Trevor. b 37. Ex Coll Ox BA58 MA62. St Steph Ho Ox 62. **d** 64 **p** 65. C Cardiff St Mary *Llan* 64-69; C Brecon w Battle *S & B* 69-73; Min Can Brecon Cathl 69-73; V Llanddew and Talachddu 73-78; V Cefncoed and Capel Nantddu 78-80; V Cefn Coed and Capel Nantddu w Vaynor etc 80-87; V Talgarth and Llanelieu 87-04; rtd 04. *16 Dan-y-Bryn, Glasbury, Hereford HR3 5NH* Tel (01497) 842966

WALTERS, Mrs Felicity Ann. b 56. WEMTC. **d** 01 **p** 02. C Glouc St Geo w Whaddon 01-05; C Matson 05-06; P-in-c Huntley and Longhope, Churcham and Bulley from 06. *The Rectory, 56 Byfords Road, Huntley, Gloucester GL19 3EL* Tel (01452) 831735

WALTERS, Canon Francis Raymond. b 24. Ball Coll Ox BA49 MA54. Wycliffe Hall Ox 51. **d** 53 **p** 54. C Boulton *Derby* 53-56; Lect Qu Coll Birm 56-64; Succ Birm Cathl 56-58; C Harborne St Pet 58-64; V Leic St Nic 64-74; Chapl Leic Univ 64-74; R Appleby 74-77; Dioc Dir of Educn 77-89; Hon Can Leic Cathl 77-91; P-in-c Swithland 77-91; rtd 91; Perm to Offic *Nor* from 91. *2 Beeston Common, Sheringham NR26 8ES* Tel (01263) 824414

WALTERS, Ian Robert. b 51. ACA74 FCA81. **d** 85 **p** 86. OLM Ingoldsby *Linc* 85-92; NSM Grantham St Anne New Somerby and Spitalgate 92-94; NSM N Beltisloe Gp 94-06; P-in-c Gosberton, Gosberton Clough and Quadring from 06. *The Vicarage, 6 Wargate Way, Gosberton, Spalding PE11 4NH* Tel and fax (01775) 840694 Mobile 07831-645683 E-mail ian@businessdevelopmentassociation.net

WALTERS, James Arthur. b 78. Selw Coll Cam BA00. Westcott Ho Cam 03. **d** 07 **p** 08. C Hampstead St Jo *Lon* from 07. *3 Holly Bush Vale, London NW3 6TX* Tel (020) 7433 1115 E-mail j.a.walters.97@cantab.net

WALTERS, Ms Jennifer Betty. b 56. Birm Univ BA77. STETS. **d** 00 **p** 01. NSM Freemantle *Win* 00-07; NSM Southampton Thornhill St Chris from 07. *41A Waterloo Road, Southampton SO15 3BD* Tel (023) 8033 2613

WALTERS, John Philip Hewitt. b 50. Coll of Resurr Mirfield 72. **d** 73 **p** 74. C Llangiwg *S & B* 73-76; Min Can Brecon Cathl 76-79; C Brecon w Battle 76-79; V Merthyr Cynog and Dyffryn Honddu etc 79-83; V Llandeilo Tal-y-bont from 83. *The Vicarage, 28 Bolgoed Road, Pontardulais, Swansea SA4 8JE* Tel (01792) 882468

WALTERS, Leslie Ernest Ward. b 27. Wadh Coll Ox BA51 MA55. Ridley Hall Cam 55. **d** 57 **p** 58. C Heref St Pet w St Owen 57-59; C Morden *S'wark* 59-61; V Felbridge 61-68; V Streatham Immanuel w St Anselm 68-81; V Cotmanhay *Derby* 81-92; Chapl Ilkeston Gen Hosp 81-88; Chapl Ilkeston Community Hosp 88-92; rtd 92; Perm to Offic *Nor* from 93. *Rokeby, 18 Taverham Road, Felthorpe, Norwich NR10 4DR* Tel (01603) 755134

WALTERS, Canon Michael William. b 39. Dur Univ BSc61. Clifton Th Coll 61. **d** 63 **p** 64. C Aldershot H Trin *Guildf* 63-66; C Upper Armley *Ripon* 66-69; NE Area Sec CPAS 69-75; V Hyde St Geo *Ches* 75-82; V Knutsford St Jo and Toft 82-97; P-in-c Congleton St Pet 97-98; TR Congleton 98-05; Hon Can Ches Cathl from 94; rtd 05; Hon C Davenham *Ches* from 05. *27 Alvanley Rise, Northwich CW9 8AY* Tel (01606) 333126 E-mail michael@alvanleyrise.co.uk

WALTERS, Nicholas Humphrey. b 45. K Coll Lon BD67 AKC67. **d** 68 **p** 69. C Weston *Guildf* 68-71; Chapl and Lect NE Surrey Coll of Tech Ewell 71-77; Hon C Ewell 71-77; Warden Moor Park Coll Farnham 77-80; Tutor Surrey Univ from 80; Dir of Studies Guildf Inst from 82; Lic to Offic from 84. *9 Valley View, Godalming GU7 1RD* Tel (01483) 415106 *or* 562142 E-mail n.walters@surrey.ac.uk

WALTERS, Peter. b 27. Leeds Univ BSc48 Univ of Wales (Abth) MSc52. Ripon Coll Cuddesdon 78. **d** 79 **p** 80. C Kingswood *Bris* 79-82; R Stanton St Quintin, Hullavington, Grittleton etc 82-88; rtd 88; Perm to Offic *Glouc* 88-97. *Holly Tree House, 12 Bethany Lane, West Cross, Swansea SA3 5TL* Tel (01792) 405197

WALTERS, Raymond. *See* WALTERS, Canon Francis Raymond

WALTERS, Mrs Sheila Ann Beatrice. b 37. Bris Univ DipEd58. EMMTC 85. **d** 89 **p** 94. NSM Ashby-la-Zouch St Helen w Coleorton *Leic* 89-98; Perm to Offic 99-02; NSM Packington w Normanton-le-Heath 02-05; rtd 05; Perm to Offic *Sheff* from 06. *8 Kensington Park, Sheffield S10 4NJ* Tel 0114-229 5497 E-mail churchmatters@sabwalters.co.uk

WALTERS, William Ivan. b 49. CBDTI 04. **d** 07 **p** 08. NSM Lea *Blackb* from 07. *9 Thornpark Drive, Lea, Preston PR2 1RE* Tel (01772) 732573 E-mail ivanwalters@btinternet.com

WALTHEW, Mrs Nancy Jennifer. b 39. Leeds Inst of Educn CertEd59. NOC 92. **d** 95 **p** 96. NSM Wilmslow *Ches* 95-02; Perm to Offic from 04. *44 Upper Culver Road, St Albans AL1 4EE*

WALTON, Mrs Alison Claire. b 59. Homerton Coll Cam BEd82. Lon Bible Coll Oak Hill Th Coll BA90 MPhil92. **d** 92 **p** 98. C Bedford Ch Ch *St Alb* 92-94; Perm to Offic *St Alb* 94-95 and *S'well* 95-98; NSM Lenton Abbey *S'well* 98-99; Assoc Lect St Jo

Coll Nottm 97-99; C Thorley *St Alb* 00-03; V Croxley Green St Oswald 03-07; Dir Ch Study and Practice Ridley Hall Cam from 07. *Ridley Hall, Ridley Hall Road, Cambridge CB3 9HG* Tel (01223) 741080 E-mail aw438@cam.ac.uk *or* walton.ali@ntlworld.com

WALTON, Ann Beverley. b 56. Huddersfield Poly BSc78 Sheff Poly MPhil84 Coll of Ripon & York St Jo MA97. NOC 00. **d** 03 **p** 04. C Ecclesfield *Sheff* 03-06; R Adwick-le-Street w Skelbrooke from 06. *The Rectory, Village Street, Adwick-le-Street, Doncaster DN6 7AD* Tel (01302) 723224

WALTON, Brian. b 53. Sarum & Wells Th Coll 83. **d** 85 **p** 86. C Silksworth *Dur* 85-86; C Bishopwearmouth St Mich w St Hilda 86-88; Chapl RN 88-92; V Sugley *Newc* 92-95; Chapl Lemington Hosp 92-95; CF from 95. *c/o MOD Chaplains (Army)* Tel (01980) 615804 Fax 615800

WALTON, Mrs Camilla Iris. b 56. STETS 97. **d** 00 **p** 01. C Lyndhurst and Emery Down and Minstead *Win* 00-04; V Boldre w S Baddesley 04-08; TV Beaconsfield *Ox* from 08. *The Parsonage, St Michael's Green, Beaconsfield HP9 2BN* Tel (01494) 673464 Fax 676694 E-mail camillawalton@aol.com

WALTON, David William. b 52. Open Univ BA84 Leeds Univ BA06 Alsager Coll of Educn CertEd74. NOC 03. **d** 06 **p** 07. C Prenton *Ches* 06-08; V Baddiley and Wrenbury w Burleydam from 08. *The Vicarage, The Green, Wrenbury, Nantwich CW5 8EY* Tel (01270) 780398 E-mail rev.david.walton@btinternet.com

WALTON, Frank. b 39. **d** 04 **p** 05. OLM Woodhorn w Newbiggin *Newc* from 04. *6 New Queen Street, Newbiggin-by-the-Sea NE64 6AZ* Tel (01670) 817568 E-mail notlaw@btopenworld.com

WALTON, The Ven Geoffrey Elmer. b 34. Dur Univ BA59. Qu Coll Birm. **d** 61 **p** 62. C Warsop *S'well* 61-65; Dioc Youth Chapl 65-69; V Norwell 65-69; Recruitment Sec ACCM 69-75; V Weymouth H Trin *Sarum* 75-82; RD Weymouth 79-82; Can and Preb *Sarum* Cathl 81-00; Adn Dorset 82-00; P-in-c Witchampton and Hinton Parva, Long Crichel etc 92-96; V Witchampton, Stanbridge and Long Crichel etc 96-00; rtd 00; Perm to Offic *Sarum* from 01. *Priory Cottage, 6 Hibberds Field, Cranborne, Wimborne BH21 5QL* Tel (01725) 517167

WALTON, John Victor. b 45. Lon Univ BSc67. Linc Th Coll 79. **d** 81 **p** 82. C Stevenage St Mary Shephall *St Alb* 81-85; TV Bourne Valley *Sarum* 85-95; P-in-c Puddletown and Tolpuddle 95-02; R Puddletown, Tolpuddle and Milborne w Dewlish 02-04; rtd 04. *Serenity, Wootton Grove, Sherborne DT9 4DL* Tel (01935) 814435 E-mail life@clara.co.uk

WALTON, Canon Kevin Anthony. b 64. St Chad's Coll Dur BA87 Dur Univ PhD99. Trin Coll Bris BA91. **d** 92 **p** 93. C Stranton *Dur* 92-95; C Hartlepool H Trin 95-96; V Sunderland St Mary and St Pet 96-08; AD Wearmouth 05-08; Can and Chan St Alb from 08. *2 Sumpter Yard, St Albans AL1 1BY* Tel (01727) 890242 E-mail canon@stalbanscathedral.org.uk

WALTON, Luke. b 64. Leeds Univ LLB87. Cranmer Hall Dur BA94. **d** 97 **p** 98. C Didsbury St Jas and Em *Man* 97-02; C Clifton Ch Ch w Em *Bris* 02-06; Arts Development Officer Bible Soc from 06. *Bible Society, Stonehill Green, Westlea, Swindon SN5 7DG* Tel (01793) 418100 Mobile 07799-414199 Fax 418118

WALTON, Mrs Marjorie Sandra. b 46. WMMTC 97. **d** 00 **p** 01. NSM The Whitacres and Shustoke *Birm* 00-04; NSM Water Orton 04-06; NSM Lea Hall from 06. *51 Station Road, Nether Whitacre, Coleshill, Birmingham B46 2JB* Tel (01675) 464641

WALTON, Maurice James. b 31. Liv Univ BArch53 MCD54 RIBA54 MRTPI55. Wycliffe Hall Ox 93. **d** 94 **p** 95. NSM Billing *Pet* 94-97; NSM Brington w Whilton and Norton etc 97-02; rtd 02; Perm to Offic *Pet* from 02. *10A Sutton Street, Flore, Northampton NN7 4LE* Tel (01327) 340254 E-mail wal.gill@virgin.net

WALTON, Michael Roy. b 74. St Cuth Soc Dur BA95. Oak Hill Th Coll BA09. **d** 09. C W Kilburn St Luke w St Simon and St Jude *Lon* from 09. *2 Church Flats, Fernhead Road, London W9 3EH* Tel 07949-637377 (mobile) E-mail mikewalton@gmail.com

WALTON, Reginald Arthur. b 45. St Jo Coll Nottm 80. **d** 81 **p** 82. C Woodthorpe *S'well* 81-84; P-in-c Nottingham St Andr 84-85; V 85-91; R Moreton *Ches* 91-01; P-in-c Whatton w Aslockton, Hawksworth, Scarrington etc *S'well* 01-05; V 05-07; rtd 07. *19 The Maltsters, Newark NG24 4RU* Tel (01949) 850523 E-mail regwalton@talktalk.net

WALTON, Richard James. b 55. UMIST BSc77 Sheff Univ MEd84 Leeds Univ PhD98 CPhys MInstP. NOC 07. **d** 09. NSM Warmsworth *Sheff* from 09. *The Rectory, Village Street, Adwick-le-Street, Doncaster DN6 7AD* Tel (01302) 723224 Mobile 07931-526333 E-mail r.j.walton@shu.ac.uk

WALTON, Stephen James. b 71. Mert Coll Ox BA92 MA97. Oak Hill Th Coll BA01. **d** 02 **p** 03. C Thurnby w Stoughton *Leic* 02-07; R Marbury w Tushingham and Whitewell *Ches* from 07. *The Vicarage, Marbury, Whitchurch SY13 4LN* Tel (01948) 663758 E-mail walton_stephen@hotmail.com

WALTON, Stephen John. b 55. Birm Univ BSc76 Fitzw Coll Cam BA79 MA82 Sheff Univ PhD97. Ridley Hall Cam 77. **d** 83 **p** 84. C Bebington *Ches* 83-86; Voc and Min Adv CPAS 86-92; Lic to Offic *St Alb* 86-94; Public Preacher 00-04; Bp's Dom Chapl 94-95; Lect St Jo Coll Nottm 95-99; Lect Lon Bible Coll 99-03; Sen Lect Lon Sch of Th from 03. *London School of Theology, Green Lane, Northwood HA6 2UW* Tel (01923) 456326 Fax 456327 E-mail steve.walton@lst.ac.uk

WAMBUNYA, Timothy Livingstone (Amboko). b 66. Simon of Cyrene Th Inst 93 Oak Hill Th Coll BA94. **d** 97 **p** 98. C Southall Green St Jo *Lon* 97-00; TV Tollington 00-07; Prin Carlile Coll Nairobi from 07. *Carlile College, Jogoo Road, PO Box 72584, Nairobi 00200, Kenya* Tel (00254) (20) 550490 Fax 554970 E-mail t.wamb@virgin.net *or* tim.wambunya@carlilecollege.org

WANDREY, Bryce. b 77. St Olaf Coll Minnesota BA99. Concordia Th Sem Indiana MDiv03 St Steph Ho Ox 07. **d** 08 **p** 09. C Highgate St Mich *Lon* from 08. *17 Bisham Gardens, London N6 6DJ* Tel (020) 8348 0264 E-mail wandreyb@yahoo.com

WANDSWORTH, Archdeacon of. *See* ROBERTS, The Ven Stephen John

WANJIE, Lukas Macharia. b 50. Fitzw Coll Cam BA79 MA83 Birkbeck Coll Lon MSc98. St Paul's Coll Limuru 72 Ridley Hall Cam 76. **d** 75 **p** 76. C Uthiru St Pet Kenya 75-76; C Mill End and Heronsgate w W Hyde *St Alb* 79; V Westlands St Mark Nairobi 80-84; Prin Trin Bible Coll Nairobi 85-91; C St Alb St Steph 91-94; Perm to Offic 94-95; Race Relations Adv Croydon *S'wark* 95-01; V Bermondsey St Kath w St Bart from 01. *St Katharine's Vicarage, 90 Eugenia Road, London SE16 2RA* Tel (020) 7237 3679 E-mail lukas.wanjie@southwark.anglican.org

WANLISS, Hector. b 62. St Paul's Coll Grahamstown 85. **d** 88 **p** 90. S Africa 88-97; P-in-c Aylesham w Adisham *Cant* 97-99; CF from 99. *c/o MOD Chaplains (Army)* Tel (01980) 615804 Fax 615800

WANN, Canon Denis Francis. b 27. TCD BA55 MA77 Div Test 56. **d** 56 **p** 57. C Belfast St Donard *D & D* 56-58; BCMS Tanzania 58-72; Hon Can Moro from 72; C Lurgan Ch the Redeemer *D & D* 72-73; Australia 73-91 and from 95; R Port Kembla 73-78; R Albion Park 78-84; RD Shoalhaven 79-82; Adn Wollongong and Camden 82-84; R Turramurra 84-91; I Bailieborough w Knockbride, Shercock and Mullagh *K, E & A* 91-95; rtd 95; Assoc Min Wollongong from 96. *4/28 Robertson Street, Coniston NSW 2500, Australia* Tel (0061) (2) 4227 6906 Fax 4229 2144 E-mail dwann@telstra.easymail.com.au

WANSTALL, Noelle Margaret. *See* HALL, Canon Noelle Margaret

WANT, Mrs Angela Patricia. b 47. Kent Univ BA68. EAMTC 02. **d** 05 **p** 06. NSM Newport and Widdington *Chelmsf* from 05. *3 Orchard Close, Newport, Saffron Walden CB11 3QT* Tel (01799) 540051 E-mail angelawant@f2s.com

WANYOIKE, Julius Njuguna. b 70. Catholic Univ of E Africa BA99. Bp Kariuki Bible Coll 91. **d** 93 **p** 93. Kenya 93-03; Provost Thika 02-03; Perm to Offic *Birm* 04-05; NSM Erdington from 05. *1 Abbotts Road, Birmingham B24 8HE* Tel 0121-351 1245 E-mail wanyoikejrev@yahoo.com

WARBRICK, Quentin David. b 66. Jes Coll Ox BA88. Cranmer Hall Dur 89. **d** 92 **p** 93. C Birm St Martin w Bordesley St Andr 92-96; C Handsworth St Jas 96-00; V Packwood w Hockley Heath from 00; AD Shirley from 05. *The Vicarage, Nuthurst Lane, Hockley Heath, Solihull B94 5RP* Tel (01564) 783121 E-mail qd@dwarbrick.fsnet.co.uk

WARBURTON, Andrew James. b 44. Oak Hill Th Coll 64. **d** 69 **p** 70. C New Milverton *Cov* 69-72; C Fulham St Matt *Lon* 72-76; C Chesham St Mary *Ox* 76-80; TV Gt Chesham 80-94; Chapl Paris St Mich *Eur* 94-97; Asst Chapl Amsterdam w Heiloo 97-99; rtd 99. *Burnbrae, Riccarton, Newcastleton TD9 0SN* Tel (01387) 376293 Mobile 07962-622740 E-mail borderwarburton@yahoo.co.uk

WARBURTON, John Bryce. b 33. St Aid Birkenhead 64. **d** 66 **p** 67. C Padiham *Blackb* 66-69; C Burnley St Pet 69-70; V Tideswell *Derby* 70-81; V Bollington St Jo *Ches* 81-91; V Capesthorne w Siddington and Marton 91-98; rtd 98; Perm to Offic *St E* from 98. *64 Friars Street, Sudbury CO10 2AG* Tel (01787) 371132

WARBURTON, Piers Eliot de Dutton. b 30. Cranmer Hall Dur BA65. **d** 65 **p** 66. C Grassendale *Liv* 65-68; Bermuda 68-71; R Sherborne *Win* 71-76; V Yateley 76-82; R Guernsey St Andr 82-89; V Hartley Wintney, Elvetham, Winchfield etc 89-98; rtd 98; Perm to Offic *Win* from 98; Clergy Widows Officer (Win Adnry) from 04. *Rowan Cottage, Station Road, Chilbolton, Stockbridge SO20 6AL* Tel (01264) 860275 E-mail b.warburton@rowan51.fsnet.co.uk

WARBURTON, Walter George. b 16. Bede Coll Dur BA40 MA43. **d** 41 **p** 42. C Witton *Blackb* 41-45; C Accrington Ch Ch 45-46; V Bolton St Barn 46-52; V Haslingden St Jo Stonefold *Blackb* 52-60; V Gt Marsden 60-81; rtd 81; Perm to Offic *Blackb* 81-02. *145 Halifax Road, Nelson BB9 0EL* Tel (01282) 697589

WARCHUS, Michael Edward George. b 37. Roch Th Coll 65. **d** 68 **p** 69. C Buckhurst Hill *Chelmsf* 68-71; C Stainton-in-Cleveland *York* 71-76; V Carlton and Drax 76-86; V Acomb St Steph 86-98; rtd 98; Perm to Offic *York* 98-08 and *Ripon* 00-08; Hon C By Brook *Bris* from 08. *The Vicarage, 2 Coopers Meadow, Yatton Keynell, Chippenham SN14 7PZ* Tel (01249) 782279

WARD, Alan William. b 56. Trin Coll Bris 80. **d** 81 **p** 82. C New Ferry *Ches* 81-86; Dioc Youth Officer 86-91; C Charlesworth and Dinting Vale *Derby* 91-96; V Mickleover All SS from 96; C Mickleover St Jo from 06. *All Saints' Vicarage, Etwall Road, Mickleover, Derby DE3 0DL* Tel (01332) 513793 E-mail alanward3@tiscali.co.uk

WARD, Alfred John. b 37. Coll of Resurr Mirfield 93. **d** 93 **p** 94. C Hendon St Mary *Lon* 93-00; Chapl Convent of St Mary at the Cross Edgware 00-04; rtd 04; Perm to Offic *Cant* from 05. *60 Valley Road, Dover CT17 0QW* Tel (01304) 824767

WARD, Mrs Alisoun Mary. b 52. Univ of Wales BA74. Ridley Hall Cam 94. **d** 96 **p** 97. C S Woodham Ferrers *Chelmsf* 96-00; TV Southend 00-02. *160 Upper Fant Road, Maidstone ME16 8DJ* Tel (01622) 728202 E-mail rev_soun@hotmail.com

WARD, Andrew John. b 65. Cliff Th Coll 85 Trin Coll Bris BA99. **d** 99 **p** 00. C Belper *Derby* 99-03; TV Walbrook Epiphany from 03. *81 Palmerston Street, Derby DE23 6PF* Tel (01332) 760846 E-mail andyward.parish@tiscali.co.uk

WARD, Canon Anthony Peter. b 46. Bris Univ BSc67 Ox Univ DipEd68. St Jo Coll Nottm. **d** 82 **p** 83. C Hellesdon *Nor* 82-85; P-in-c Nor St Aug w St Mary 85-91; P-in-c Norwich-over-the-Water Colegate St Geo 85-90; Norfolk Churches' Radio Officer 85-95; TV Norwich Over-the-Water 91-95; V Gorleston St Andr from 95; RD Gt Yarmouth 98-02; Hon Can Nor Cathl from 03. *St Andrew's Vicarage, 16 Duke Road, Gorleston, Great Yarmouth NR31 6LL* Tel (01493) 663477

WARD, Arthur John. b 32. Lon Univ BD57. St Aid Birkenhead 57. **d** 57 **p** 58. C Ecclesfield *Sheff* 57-60; C Fulwood 60-63; Tutor St Aid Birkenhead 63-66; R Denton St Lawr *Man* 66-74; CMS 74-82; TV Wolverhampton *Lich* 82-90; V Edgbaston SS Mary and Ambrose *Birm* 90-96; rtd 96; Perm to Offic *Heref* from 97. *Bramble Cottage, 6 Lower Forge, Eardington, Bridgnorth WV16 5LQ* Tel (01746) 764758

WARD, Miss Beverley Jayne. b 61. Bolton Inst of Educn CertEd97. St Steph Ho Ox 00. **d** 02 **p** 01. C Standish *Blackb* 02-07; C Thornton-le-Fylde 07-09; P-in-c Eccleston from 09. *64 The Hawthorns, Eccleston, Chorley PR7 5QW* Tel 07811-907274 (mobile)

WARD, Brett Ernest. b 62. Univ of Wales MTh06. ACT 86. **d** 89 **p** 89. C E Maitland Australia 89; Asst P 89-91; Asst P Singleton 91-92; P-in-c Weston 92-97; C Forton *Portsm* 97-99; P-in-c 99-05; V 05-07; P-in-c Eltham H Trin *S'wark* from 07. *Holy Trinity Vicarage, 59 Southend Crescent, London SE9 2SD* Tel (020) 8859 6274 *or* 8850 1246 E-mail fr.brett@holytrinityeltham.co.uk

WARD, Canon Calvin. b 34. Univ of Wales BA57 DipEd60 Fitzw Ho Cam BA63 MA67. Westcott Ho Cam 61. **d** 64 **p** 65. C Handsworth St Mich *Birm* 64-66; C Shaw Hill 66-69; V Windhill *Bradf* 69-76; V Esholt 76-81; V Oakworth 81-91; V Allerton 91-99; Hon Can Bradf Cathl 94-99; rtd 99; Perm to Offic *Bradf* from 99. *47 Wheatlands Drive, Heaton, Bradford BD9 5JN*

WARD, Christopher John William. b 36. Bps' Coll Cheshunt 66 Qu Coll Birm 68. **d** 69 **p** 70. C Wednesbury St Bart *Lich* 69-73; CF 73-93; rtd 93; Perm to Offic *Sarum* from 93. *6 Meadow View, Blandford Forum DT11 7JB* Tel (01258) 455140

WARD, Daran. b 65. Brunel Univ BSc88. St Jo Coll Nottm 07. **d** 09. C Hartley Wintney, Elvetham, Winchfield etc from 09. *40 Pool Road, Hartley Wintney, Hook RG27 8RD* Tel (01252) 849572 E-mail daran.ward@gmail.com

WARD, David. b 40. St Jo Coll Nottm 83. **d** 85 **p** 86. C Aspley *S'well* 89-94; rtd 04; Perm to Offic *S'well* from 06. *150 Robins Wood Road, Nottingham NG8 3LD* Tel 0115-929 3231 Mobile 07971-092089

WARD, David Conisbee. b 33. St Jo Coll Cam BA54 MA59. S'wark Ord Course 77. **d** 80 **p** 81. NSM Surbiton St Matt *S'wark* 80-83; C Streatham Immanuel w St Anselm 83-84; P-in-c 84-87; V Hook 87-93; rtd 93; Perm to Offic *Chich* and *S'wark* from 94. *50 Elgar Avenue, Surbiton KT9 9JN* Tel (020) 8399 9679

WARD, David Graham. b 51. CBDTI 03. **d** 06 **p** 07. OLM Higher Walton *Blackb* 06-07; NSM from 07. *Trillick, 119 Hoghton Lane, Higher Walton, Preston PR5 4EH* Tel (01254) 852995 Fax 851101

WARD, Canon David Robert. b 51. Oak Hill Th Coll 74. **d** 77 **p** 78. C Kirkheaton *Wakef* 77-81; V Earl's Heaton 81-88; V Bradley from 88; Hon Can Wakef Cathl from 02. *The Vicarage, 3 St Thomas Gardens, Huddersfield HD2 1SL* Tel (01484) 427838

WARD, Edward. *See* WARD, William Edward

WARD, Mrs Elizabeth Joyce. b 42. Open Univ BA. WEMTC 04. **d** 06 **p** 07. OLM Painswick, Sheepscombe, Cranham, The Edge etc *Glouc* from 06. *The Gate House, Back Edge Lane, Edge, Stroud GL6 6PE* Tel (01452) 812188

WARD, Canon Frances Elizabeth Fearn. b 59. St Andr Univ MTheol83 Man Univ PhD00 Bradf Univ MA06 RGN87. Westcott Ho Cam 87. **d** 89 **p** 94. Par Dn Westhoughton *Man*

89-93; Tutor Practical Th N Coll Man 93-98; Hon C Bury St Pet 93-98; C Unsworth 98-99; V Bury St Pet 99-05; C Leverhulme 05-06; Bp's Adv on Women in Min 02-04; Hon Can Man Cathl 04-06; Can Res Bradf Cathl from 06. *3 Cathedral Close, Bradford BD1 4EG* Tel (01274) 307021 *or* 777733 Mobile 07791-165774 E-mail fefward@btinternet.com

WARD, Frank Neal. b 16. EAMTC 78. **d** 80 **p** 81. NSM Weybourne w Upper Sheringham *Nor* 80-84; NSM Kelling w Salthouse 80-84; NSM Briningham 84-92; NSM Brinton, Briningham, Hunworth, Stody etc 92-97; Perm to Offic from 97. *Newlands, The Street, Sharrington, Melton Constable NR24 2AB* Tel (01263) 860337

WARD, Frank Wyatt. b 30. Oak Hill NSM Course 84. **d** 92 **p** 94. NSM Paddington St Pet *Lon* 92-09; NSM Paddington St Mary Magd and St Pet from 09. *82 Hill Rise, Greenford UB6 8PE* Tel (020) 8575 5515

WARD, Garry William. b 67. RGN90 RM92. Qu Coll Birm 01. **d** 03 **p** 04. C Wednesfield *Lich* 03-06; TV Wordsley *Worc* from 06. *1 Denleigh Road, Kingswinford DY6 8QB* Tel (01384) 357703 E-mail garry@pundle.co.uk

WARD, Geoffrey Edward. b 30. Linc Th Coll 62. **d** 64 **p** 65. C Oundle *Pet* 64-68; C Weston Favell 68-70; TV 70-72; R Cottingham w E Carlton 72-95; rtd 95; Perm to Offic *Pet* from 95. *4 Sovereigns Court, Saxonfields, Kettering NN16 9SS* Tel (01536) 520498

WARD, Prof Graham John. b 55. Fitzw Coll Cam BA80 Selw Coll Cam MA83. Westcott Ho Cam 87. **d** 90 **p** 91. C Bris St Mary Redcliffe w Temple etc 90-92; Chapl Ex Coll Ox 92-94; Dean Peterho Cam 95-99; Prof Contextual Th Man Univ from 99. *Room WG8, University of Manchester, Oxford Road, Manchester M13 9PL* Tel 0161-275 3151 Fax 275 3256 E-mail graham.ward@manchester.ac.uk

WARD, Helen Frances. b 48. EAMTC 02. **d** 04 **p** 05. NSM Gorleston St Andr *Nor* from 04. *St Andrew's Vicarage, 16 Duke Road, Gorleston, Great Yarmouth NR31 6LL* Tel (01493) 664700 E-mail revhw@btinternet.com

WARD, Ian Stanley. b 62. K Coll Lon BD83. Cranmer Hall Dur 84. **d** 86 **p** 87. C Moreton *Ches* 86-89; Chapl RAF from 89. *Chaplaincy Services, Valiant Block, HQ Air Command, RAF High Wycombe HP14 4UE* Tel (01494) 496800 Fax 496343

WARD, Mrs Janice Ann. b 65. Univ of Wales (Lamp) BA86. ERMC 05. **d** 08 **p** 09. C Haverhill w Withersfield *St E* from 08. *St Mary's House, 44 Falklands Road, Haverhill CB9 0EA* Tel (01440) 766894 E-mail jawgransden@aol.com

WARD, Jason David. b 71. Glas Univ BSc93 PhD98. Oak Hill Th Coll BA06. **d** 06 **p** 07. C Cheadle Hulme St Andr *Ches* from 06. *33 Kingsley Drive, Cheadle Hulme, Cheadle SK8 5LZ* Tel 0161-486 9956 Mobile 07866-361054 E-mail jasethebass@gmail.com

WARD, Jayne. *See* WARD, Miss Beverley Jayne

WARD, John. *See* WARD, Arthur John

WARD, John Frederick. b 55. St Mich Coll Llan 81. **d** 84 **p** 85. C Pembroke Dock *St D* 84-86; PV Llan Cathl 86-89; R St Brides Minor w Bettws 89-97; V Shard End *Birm* 97-04; V Twigworth, Down Hatherley, Norton, The Leigh etc *Glouc* from 04. *The Rectory, Tewkesbury Road, Twigworth, Gloucester GL2 9PQ* Tel (01452) 731483 E-mail wardjohn23@aol.com

WARD, John Raymond. b 31. St Jo Coll Dur BA54. **d** 56 **p** 57. C Leeds St Pet *Ripon* 56-60; C Seacroft 60-63; V Kirkstall 63-75; V Bramhope 75-95; rtd 96; Perm to Offic *Ripon* from 01. *95A Gilling Road, Richmond DL10 5AW*

WARD, Prof John Stephen Keith. b 38. Univ of Wales (Cardiff) BA62 Linacre Coll Ox BLitt68 DD97 Trin Hall Cam MA72 DD97. Westcott Ho Cam 72. **d** 72 **p** 73. Lect Philosophy of Relig Lon Univ 71-75; Hon C Hampstead St Jo 72-75; Dean Trin Hall Cam 75-82; Prof Moral and Soc Th K Coll Lon 82-85; Prof Hist and Philosophy of Relig 85-91; Regius Prof Div Ox Univ from 91; Can Res Ch Ch *Ox* from 91. *Christ Church, Oxford OX1 1DP* Tel (01865) 276246 E-mail keith.ward@chch.ox.ac.uk

WARD, Canon John Stewart. b 43. St Jo Coll Dur BA66. Ripon Coll Cuddesdon 77. **d** 79 **p** 80. C High Harrogate Ch Ch *Ripon* 79-82; V Ireland Wood 82-86; Chapl Wells Cathl Sch 86-88; V Menston w Woodhead *Bradf* 88-95; R Bolton Abbey 95-06; RD Skipton 98-00; Hon Can Bradf Cathl 05-06; rtd 06. *41 Lennel Mount, Coldstream TD12 4NS* Tel (01890) 882306

WARD, Jonathan James Hanslip. b 75. Southn Univ LLB98 Anglia Ruskin Univ BA07 Solicitor 02. Ridley Hall Cam 05. **d** 07 **p** 08. C Cheltenham St Mark *Glouc* from 07. *50 Robert Burns Avenue, Cheltenham GL51 6NT* Tel 07812-026072 (mobile)

WARD, Keith Raymond. b 37. Dur Univ BSc60. Chich Th Coll 63. **d** 65 **p** 66. C Wallsend St Luke *Newc* 65-68; C Wooler 68-74; V Dinnington 74-81; V Bedlington 81-93; V Stannington 93-99; rtd 99; Perm to Offic *Newc* from 00. *2 Ethel's Close, Gloster Meadows, Amble, Morpeth NE65 0GD* Tel (01665) 714357

WARD, Kenneth Arthur. b 22. St D Coll Lamp BA53. Chich Th Coll 53. **d** 52 **p** 53. C Wellingborough St Barn *Pet* 52-55; C Stevenage *St Alb* 55-58; R Daventry *Pet* 58-72; RD Daventry 68-76; V Daventry w Norton 73-79; R Daventry 79-82; V

Pattishall w Cold Higham 82-88; rtd 88; Perm to Offic *Pet* from 89. *43 Inlands Rise, Daventry NN11 4DQ*

WARD, Kevin. b 47. Edin Univ MA69 Trin Coll Cam PhD76. **d** 78 **p** 79. CMS 75-92; Uganda 76-90; Qu Coll Birm 91; Perm to Offic *Birm* 91; C Halifax *Wakef* 91-92; P-in-c Charlestown 92-95; NSM Headingley *Ripon* from 95; Lect Leeds Univ from 95. *8 North Grange Mews, Leeds LS6 2EW* Tel 0113-278 7801 E-mail trskw@leeds.ac.uk

WARD, Lionel Owen. b 37. Univ of Wales (Cardiff) BA58 Univ of Wales (Swansea) DipEd59 MA65 Lon Univ PhD70. St Mich Coll Llan 83. **d** 85 **p** 86. NSM Swansea St Mary w H Trin *S & B* 85-89; P-in-c Swansea St Matt w Greenhill 89-00; TV Cen Swansea 00-01; Dioc Dir of Educn 97-01; RD Swansea 98-01; rtd 02. *17 Gresham Court, 11 Pampisford Road, Purley CR8 2UU*

WARD, Mrs Marjorie. b 38. Univ of Wales (Abth) BA59 DipEd60. NOC 83. **dss** 86 **d** 87 **p** 94. Keighley St Andr *Bradf* 86-88; Hon Par Dn 87-88; Hon Par Dn Oakworth 88-90; C Allerton 91-99; rtd 99; Perm to Offic *Bradf* from 00. *47 Wheatlands Drive, Heaton, Bradford BD9 5JN*

WARD, Mark. b 62. Imp Coll Lon BScEng84. Wycliffe Hall Ox BTh93. **d** 93 **p** 94. C Parkham, Alwington, Buckland Brewer etc *Ex* 93-96; C S Molton w Nymet St George, High Bray etc 96-97; TV 97-05; TV Ottery St Mary, Alfington, W Hill, Tipton etc from 05. *The Vicarage, Newton Poppleford, Sidmouth EX10 0HB* Tel (01395) 568390 E-mail revmarkward@btinternet.com

WARD, Matthew Alan James. b 69. Nottm Poly BSc91. Ridley Hall Cam 94. **d** 97 **p** 98. C Birchwood *Linc* 97-00; Chapl Cov Univ 00-05; Chapl Leeds Univ from 05. *96 Becketts Park Drive, Leeds LS6 3PL* Tel 0113-275 5692

WARD, Canon Michael Anthony. b 42. Sarum Th Coll 67. **d** 70 **p** 71. C Bridport *Sarum* 70-74; TV Swanborough 74-77; P-in-c Chute w Chute Forest 77-79; P-in-c Shalbourne w Ham 77-79; TR Wexcombe 79-86; V Southbroom 86-99; TR Alderbury Team 99-01; TR Clarendon 01-07; Can and Preb Sarum Cathl 95-07; rtd 07. *Victoria Cottage, 11 Pennys Lane, Fordingbridge SP6 1HQ* Tel (01425) 655635

WARD, Michael Henry. b 42. St Martin's Coll Lanc BA02. **d** 03 **p** 04. NSM S Shore H Trin *Blackb* 03-06; NSM S Shore St Pet from 06. *509A Lytham Road, Blackpool FY4 1TE* Tel (01253) 404204

WARD, Michael Paul. b 68. Regent's Park Coll Ox BA90 MA95 Peterho Cam BA01 MA05 St Andr Univ PhD06. Ridley Hall Cam 99. **d** 04 **p** 05. Chapl Peterho Cam and NSM Gt Shelford *Ely* 04-07; Chapl St Pet Coll Ox from 09. *7A Mortimer Road, Oxford OX4 4UQ* Tel (01865) 771299 Mobile 07941-998072 E-mail mpw27@cam.ac.uk

WARD, Michael Reginald. b 31. BNC Ox BA54 MA58. Tyndale Hall Bris 54. **d** 56 **p** 57. C Ealing St Mary *Lon* 56-59; C Morden *S'wark* 59-61; Area Sec (Midl and E Anglia) CCCS 61-66; V Chelsea St Jo *Lon* 66-73; P-in-c Chelsea St Andr 72-73; V Chelsea St Jo w St Andr 73-76; P-in-c Hawkesbury *Glouc* 76-80; P-in-c Alderley w Hillesley 79-80; P-in-c Bibury w Winson and Barnsley 80-85; V Barkby and Queniborough *Leic* 85-90; R Gunthorpe w Bale w Field Dalling, Saxlingham etc *Nor* 90-98; rtd 98; Perm to Offic *Heref* 98-08 and *Glouc* 00-08. *4 Framland Drive, Melton Mowbray LE13 1HY* Tel (01664) 500039

WARD, Nigel Andrew. b 50. Peterho Cam BA72 MA76. Oak Hill NSM Course 89. **d** 92 **p** 93. NSM Frogmore *St Alb* from 92. *15 Park Street, St Albans AL2 2PE* Tel (01727) 872667

WARD, Patricia. b 43. QUB BA65. St Mich Coll Llan 89. **d** 91 **p** 97. NSM Swansea St Mary w H Trin *S & B* 91-98; C Glantawe 98-99; NSM 99-02; rtd 02. *17 Gresham Court, 11 Pampisford Road, Purley CR8 2UU*

WARD, Peter Macdonald. b 41. **d** 09. NSM Harrow Weald All SS *Lon* from 09. *129 Sylvia Avenue, Pinner HA5 4QL* Tel (020) 8428 7887 Mobile 07733-001777 E-mail wardhatchend@hotmail.com

WARD, Peter Nicholas. b 59. Ban Ord Course 03. **d** 08 **p** 09. NSM Llanwnnog and Caersws w Carno *Ban* from 08. *Coed Cae, Clatter, Caersws SY17 5NW* Tel (01686) 688034 E-mail peteandsand@btopenworld.com

WARD, Robert. b 60. Em Coll Cam BA81 MA85. Chich Th Coll. **d** 86 **p** 87. C Horfield H Trin *Bris* 86-90; C Stantonbury and Willen *Ox* 90; TV 90-96; V Knowle St Martin *Bris* 96-07; R Cradley w Mathon and Storridge *Heref* from 07. *The Rectory, Cradley, Malvern WR13 5LQ* Tel (01886) 880438 E-mail frrob@wardmail.fslife.co.uk

WARD, Robert Arthur Philip. b 53. Lon Univ BD82 Open Univ BA88. Qu Coll Birm 77. **d** 79 **p** 80. C Balsall Heath St Paul *Birm* 79-82; Chapl RAF 82-98; TR Blakenall Heath *Lich* 98-07; Perm to Offic 05-07; V Ravensthorpe and Thornhill Lees w Savile Town *Wakef* from 07. *The Vicarage, Church Street, Ravensthorpe, Dewsbury WF13 3LA* Tel (01924) 465959

WARD, Robert Charles Irwin. b 48. Leic Univ LLB70 Madras Bible Sem DD01 Called to the Bar (Inner Temple) 72. St Jo Coll Dur 78. **d** 80 **p** 81. C Byker St Mich w St Lawr *Newc* 80-85; Perm to Offic 86-07; NSM Newc St Andr and St Luke from 07; Dir Clarence Trust and NE Area Revival Min from 86; Asst Chapl HM Pris Frankland 91-95. *1 Hawthorn Villas, The Green,*

Wallsend NE28 7NT Tel and fax 0191-234 3969 Mobile 07768-528181 E-mail rwarduk@mac.com

WARD, Canon Robin. b 66. Magd Coll Ox BA87 MA91 K Coll Lon PhD03. St Steph Ho Ox 88. **d** 91 **p** 92. C Romford St Andr *Chelmsf* 91-94; C Willesden Green St Andr and St Fran *Lon* 94-96; V Sevenoaks St Jo *Roch* 96-06; Chapl Invicta Community Care NHS Trust 97-06; Can Roch Cathl 04-06; Prin St Steph Ho Ox from 06. *St Stephen's House, 16 Marston Street, Oxford OX4 1JX* Tel (01865) 247874

WARD, Ronald Albert. b 29. Shoreditch Coll Lon TCert54. Spurgeon's Coll 85. **d** 03 **p** 04. NSM E Blatchington *Chich* 03-06; rtd 07. *4 Albany Road, Seaford BN25 2QB* Tel (01323) 890977 Mobile 07962-120975 E-mail revroncurate@aol.com

WARD (*née* NIXSON), **Mrs Rosemary Clare.** b 57. Westf Coll Lon BA79 Liv Univ MA80 MPhil92. Aston Tr Scheme 89 Trin Coll Bris BA94. **d** 94 **p** 95. C Bris St Andr Hartcliffe 94-98; C Downend 98-02; P-in-c Broad Blunsdon 02-05; C Highworth w Sevenhampton and Inglesham etc 02-05; Dioc Lay Tr Adv 02-05; Leadership Development Adv CPAS from 05. *25 Leam Road, Leamington Spa CV31 3PA* Tel (01926) 420193 E-mail rward@cpas.org.uk

WARD, Mrs Sheena Mary. b 55. Newc Univ BA76 PGCE77. **d** 00 **p** 01. OLM Cramlington *Newc* from 00. *17 Yarmouth Drive, Cramlington NE23 1TL* Tel (01670) 732211 E-mail sheena.ward@dsl.pipex.com

WARD, Simon William James. b 71. Dur Univ BA94 Westmr Coll Ox PGCE96. Ripon Coll Cuddesdon 98. **d** 00 **p** 01. C Aldershot St Mich *Guildf* 00-03; TV Sole Bay *St E* 03-09; Bp's Chapl *Nor* from 09. *The Bishop's House, Norwich NR3 1SB* Tel (01603) 614172 Fax 761613 E-mail bishopschaplain@bishopofnorwich.org *or* revdsimon@msn.com

WARD, Stanley. b 34. NEOC. **d** 84 **p** 85. NSM Jarrow *Dur* 84-90; P-in-c Thornley 90-99; rtd 99; Perm to Offic *Ex* from 00. *4 Church Walk, Thornley, Durham DH6 3EN* Tel and fax (01429) 821766

WARD, Stephen Philip. b 49. Sheff Univ BA72. St Steph Ho Ox 77. **d** 79 **p** 80. C Narborough *Leic* 79-80; C Brentwood St Thos *Chelmsf* 81-82; Perm to Offic *Leic* 03-05; NSM Leic St Mary from 05. *56 Moor Lane, Loughborough LE11 1BA* Tel (01509) 216945 E-mail casula@tiscali.co.uk

WARD, Mrs Susan Elizabeth. b 50. NOC 92. **d** 95 **p** 96. NSM Heyside *Man* from 95. *45 Fold Green, Chadderton, Oldham OL9 9DX* Tel 0161-620 2839

WARD, Timothy James. b 67. CCC Ox BA90 MA95 Edin Univ PhD99. Oak Hill Th Coll BA95. **d** 99 **p** 00. C Crowborough *Chich* 99-04; TV Hinckley H Trin *Leic* from 04. *Holy Trinity Vicarage, 1 Cleveland Road, Hinckley LE10 0AJ* Tel (01455) 635711 *or* 442750 E-mail wardtmthy@aol.com

WARD, Timothy John Conisbee. b 62. New Coll Ox BA85 MA02 PGCE86. Wycliffe Hall Ox BA91. **d** 92 **p** 93. C Dorking St Paul *Guildf* 92-96; C Herne Hill *S'wark* 96-02; V Walberton w Binsted *Chich* from 02. *St Mary's Vicarage, The Street, Walberton, Arundel BN18 0PQ* Tel (01243) 551488 E-mail tjcward@uwclub.net

WARD, Timothy William. b 49. Open Univ BA74 Birm Univ BPhil(Ed)93. St Deiniol's Hawarden 78. **d** 79 **p** 80. NSM Handsworth St Mary *Birm* 79-95; Perm to Offic 95-05; NSM Gt Barr *Lich* from 95. *3 Dale Close, Birmingham B43 6AS* Tel 0121-358 1880 *or* 358 2807 E-mail curate.greatbarr@btinternet.com

WARD, William Edward. b 48. FSAScot71. AKC71. **d** 72 **p** 73. C Heref St Martin 72-77; C Blakenall Heath *Lich* 77-78; TV 78-82; V Astley, Clive, Grinshill and Hadnall 82-91; P-in-c Tibberton w Bolas Magna and Waters Upton from 91; Chapl Harper Adams Agric Coll from 96. *The Rectory, 37 High Street, Edgmond, Newport TF10 8JW* Tel (01952) 820217

WARD, William Francis. b 35. Ely Th Coll 61 Coll of Resurr Mirfield 64. **d** 64 **p** 65. C Byker St Ant *Newc* 64-67; C Glas St Marg 67-69; R Glas Ascension 69-74; Chapl RNR 72-74; Chapl RN 74-78; R Arbroath *Bre* 78-90; Hon Chapl Miss to Seafarers from 78; P-in-c Auchmithie *Bre* 79-90; rtd 99. *1 Denholm Gardens, Letham, Angus DD8 2XT* Tel (01307) 818032 Fax 818924 E-mail bykerbill@btinternet.com

WARD-SMITH, Richard. b 46. Ch Ch Coll Cant TCert87 Ex Univ BTh08. SWMTC 05. **d** 08 **p** 09. NSM Week St Mary Circle of Par *Truro* from 08. *5 Southernhaye, Launceston PL15 9DH* Tel (01566) 776840 E-mail r.wardsmith@btinternet.com

WARDALE, Harold William. b 40. BSc PhD. Wycliffe Hall Ox 83. **d** 85 **p** 86. C Bedminster St Mich *Bris* 85-89; TV Bishopston 89-96; V Lawrence Weston 96-98; V Lawrence Weston and Avonmouth 99; rtd 05. *3 Cleeve Rise, Newent GL18 1BZ* Tel (01531) 822390

WARDALE, Robert Christopher. b 46. Newc Univ BA69. Coll of Resurr Mirfield 77. **d** 79 **p** 80. C Cockerton *Dur* 79-84; P-in-c Hedworth 84-87; V 87-92; V Darlington H Trin 92-06; rtd 06. *24 Beechcroft, Kenton Road, Newcastle upon Tyne NE3 4NB* Tel 0191-285 5284 E-mail wardalerc@aol.com

WARDELL, Gareth Kevin. b 59. York Univ BA81 MA01. Ridley Hall Cam 03. **d** 05 **p** 06. C Selby Abbey *York* 05-08; C Kensington St Mary Abbots w Ch Ch and St Phil *Lon* from 08. *Cottage 1, St Mary Abbot's Vicarage, Vicarage Gate, London W8 4HW* Tel (020) 7937 2364 E-mail wardellgareth@hotmail.com

WARDELL, Stewart Francis. b 68. Chu Coll Cam BA89 Bris Univ MA95. Cuddesdon Coll BA98. **d** 98 **p** 99. C Brentwood St Thos *Chelmsf* 98-02; R Hawkinge w Acrise and Swingfield *Cant* 02-07; C Hound *Win* from 07. *The Vicarage, Grange Road, Netley Abbey, Southampton SO31 5FF* Tel (023) 8045 6866 E-mail sfwardell@onetel.com

WARDEN, John Michael. b 41. Univ Coll Lon BA63 Trin Coll Ox BA65 MA. NEOC 80. **d** 82 **p** 83. NSM Osmotherley w E Harlsey and Ingleby Arncliffe *York* 82-86; V Kirkdale 86-97; V Kirkdale w Harome, Nunnington and Pockley 98-07; rtd 07; Perm to Offic *York* from 07. *Laithwaite Cottage, Appleton Lane, Appleton-le-Street, Malton YO17 6TP* Tel (01653) 699795

WARDEN, Richard James. b 57. Kent Univ BA79 K Coll Lon MTh86. Wycliffe Hall Ox 81. **d** 83 **p** 84. C Fulham St Mary N End *Lon* 83-85; CF 85-89; Chapl Wycombe Abbey Sch 89-01; Sen Chapl and Hd RS Wellington Coll Berks 01-04; P-in-c Finchampstead *Ox* from 04. *The Rectory, The Village, Finchampstead, Wokingham RG40 4JX* Tel 0118-973 2102 E-mail revrjw@hotmail.com

WARDLE, John Argyle. b 47. St Jo Coll Dur BA71 ARCM67 CertEd73. **d** 73 **p** 74. C Mansfield SS Pet and Paul *S'well* 73-77; Chapl St Felix Sch Southwold 77-87; TV Haverhill w Withersfield, the Wrattings etc *St E* 87-90; V Choral S'well Minster 90-99; Bp's Adv on Healing 94-99; R Bridlington Priory *York* 99-08; RD Bridlington 03-08; rtd 08. *27 First Avenue, Bridlington YO15 2JW* Tel (01262) 400127 E-mail g4cva@talktalk.net

WARDLE-HARPUR, Canon James. b 31. St Jo Coll Dur BA55. Wells Th Coll 55. **d** 56 **p** 57. C Sheff St Cecilia Parson Cross 56-59; C Maltby 59-61; V Doncaster St Jude 61-64; Pakistan 64-68; R Man Victoria Park 68-75; V Foxton w Gumley and Laughton *Leic* 75-79; V Foxton w Gumley and Laughton and Lubenham 79-82; TR Leic Resurr 82-88; V Burrough Hill Pars 88-94; Hon Can Leic Cathl 88-94; rtd 96. *Laburnum Cottage, 1 Coates Lane, Starbotton, Skipton BD23 5HZ* Tel (01756) 760401

WARDMAN, Carol Joy. b 56. Lon Univ BA79. NOC 91. **d** 94 **p** 95. NSM Hebden Bridge *Wakef* 94-97; NSM Sowerby from 97; Dioc Adv for Older People's Issues from 08. *25 Scarr Head Road, Sowerby Bridge HX6 3PU* Tel (01422) 316723 E-mail carol-joy@tiscali.co.uk

WARE, Canon John Lawrence. b 37. Nottm Univ BA59. Ridley Hall Cam 62. **d** 62 **p** 63. C Attercliffe *Sheff* 62-66; C Ranmoor 66-68; R Liddington and Soc and Ind Chapl *Bris* 68-74; P-in-c Eastville St Thos *Bris* 74-79; Bp's Soc and Ind Adv 74-79; V Kingswood 79-88; RD Bitton 85-87; P-in-c Broad Blunsdon 88-94; P-in-c Blunsdon St Andrew 88-94; V The Blunsdons 94-01; RD Cricklade 88-94; Hon Can Bris Cathl 76-01; rtd 01; Perm to Offic *Bris* from 01. *26 Dongola Road, Bishopston, Bristol BS7 9HP* Tel 0117-924 1304

WARE, Ms Judith Marian. b 52. St Hugh's Coll Ox BA74 MA78 PGCE75. CBDTI 00. **d** 02 **p** 03. NSM Windermere St Mary and Troutbeck *Carl* 02-05; C Thornes St Jas w Ch Ch *Wakef* from 05; C Lupset from 05; Chapl Wakef Cathl Sch from 05. *The Vicarage, St James Court, Wakefield WF2 8DW* Tel (01924) 299889 E-mail jmware@ecosse.net

WARE, Stephen John. b 55. Univ of Wales (Lamp) BA76. Ripon Coll Cuddesdon 77. **d** 79 **p** 80. C Lighthorne *Cov* 79-82; Chapl RAF 82-00; Command Chapl RAF 00-05; Selection Sec Min Division 05; V Bloxham w Milcombe and S Newington *Ox* 05-06; Warden of Readers *Glouc* from 06. *Department of Ministry, 4 College Green, Gloucester GL1 2LR* Tel (01452) 410022 ext 261 E-mail sware@glosdioc.org.uk

WAREHAM, Mrs Caroline. b 32. Lightfoot Ho Dur 55. **dss** 80 **d** 87 **p** 94. Stanwell *Lon* 80-88; Par Dn 87-88; C Epsom St Barn *Guildf* 88-95; C Aldershot St Mich 95-98; rtd 98; Perm to Offic *Sarum* from 00. *17 Homefield, Mere, Warminster BA12 6LT* Tel (01747) 861716

WAREHAM, Mrs Sheila. b 36. CertEd56. NOC 85. **d** 88 **p** 94. NSM Lostock Hall *Blackb* 88-90; NSM Allithwaite *Carl* 90-91; NSM Windermere RD 91-94; P-in-c Colton 94-96; Perm to Offic 97-07. *Lyng Nook, Church Road, Allithwaite, Grange-over-Sands LA11 7RD* Tel (01539) 535237

WARHAM, Mrs Jean. b 55. **d** 00 **p** 01. OLM Newcastle w Butterton *Lich* from 00. *166 High Street, Alsagers Bank, Stoke-on-Trent ST7 8BA* Tel (01782) 721505

WARHURST, (née HART), Mrs Jane Elizabeth. b 56. Sheff Univ BA77. NOC 98. **d** 01 **p** 02. C Edge Hill St Cypr w St Mary *Liv* 01-06; V Toxteth St Bede w St Clem from 06. *The Vicarage, 76 Beaumont Street, Liverpool L8 0XA* Tel 0151-709 9880

WARHURST, Richard. b 76. Univ Coll Chich BA99. St Steph Ho Ox 00. **d** 02 **p** 03. C New and Old Shoreham *Chich* 02-06; R

Chailey from 06. *Chailey Rectory, Chailey Green, Lewes BN8 4DA* Tel (01825) 722286

WARING, Graham George Albert. b 37. ACII62. Portsm Dioc Tr Course 86. **d** 87 **p** 02. Chapl Asst Qu Alexandra Hosp Portsm 87-92; NSM Portsea All SS *Portsm* 92-94; NSM Widley w Wymering 94-95; NSM Wisbech St Aug *Ely* 95-98; Chapl King's Lynn and Wisbech Hosps NHS Trust 96-00; NSM Leverington *Ely* 98-00; NSM Southea w Murrow and Parson Drove 98-00; Perm to Offic *York* 00-02; NSM Scarborough St Sav w All SS 02-09; Perm to Offic from 09. *28 Newby Farm Road, Newby, Scarborough YO12 6UN*
E-mail grachel.waring2@btinternet.com

WARING, Jeffery Edwin. b 53. Trin Coll Bris 80. **d** 83 **p** 84. C Harpurhey Ch Ch *Man* 83-86; TV Eccles 86-92; P-in-c Hamworthy *Sarum* 92-04; P-in-c Red Post from 04. *The Vicarage, East Morden, Wareham BH20 7DW* Tel (01929) 459244

WARING, John Valentine. b 29. St Deiniol's Hawarden 65. **d** 67 **p** 68. C Bistre *St As* 67-71; C Blackpool St Thos *Blackb* 71-72; R Levenshulme St Pet *Man* 72-87; R Caerwys and Bodfari *St As* 87-94; rtd 94. *13 St Mellors Road, Southdown Park, Buckley CH7 2ND* Tel (01244) 547290

WARING, Mrs Margaret Ruth. b 44. Keele Univ CertEd65. SW Minl Tr Course 86. **d** 90 **p** 94. Par Dn Tavistock and Gulworthy *Ex* 90-94; C 94-96; TV Axminster, Chardstock, All Saints etc 96-04; rtd 04; Perm to Offic *Ex* from 04. *5 The Battens, Stockland, Honiton EX14 9DS* Tel (01404) 881516

WARING, Roger. b 32. ACP66 CertEd56 Open Univ BA74. SW Minl Tr Course 83. **d** 86 **p** 87. NSM Ex St Sidwell and St Matt 86-90; NSM Tavistock and Gulworthy 90-96; NSM Axminster, Chardstock, All Saints etc 96-99; Perm to Offic from 99. *5 The Battens, Stockland, Honiton EX14 9DS* Tel (01404) 881516

WARING, Mrs Sheila May. b 29. SS Paul & Mary Coll Cheltenham CertEd49. Oak Hill Th Coll 85. **dss** 86 **d** 87 **p** 94. Eastwood *Chelmsf* 86-92; NSM 87-92; Chapl Rochford Hosp 87-92; Chapl Southend Community Care Services NHS Trust 92-99; NSM Prittlewell St Pet *Chelmsf* 92-96; NSM Prittlewell St Pet w Westcliff St Cedd 96-99; Perm to Offic from 99. *42 Manchester Drive, Leigh-on-Sea SS9 3HR* Tel (01702) 711046

✠WARKE, The Rt Revd Robert Alexander. b 30. TCD BA52 BD60. **d** 53 **p** 54 c 88. C Newtownards *D & D* 53-56; C Dublin St Cath w St Victor *D & G* 56-58; C Dublin Rathfarnham 58-64; Min Can St Patr Cathl Dublin 59-64; I Dunlavin w Ballymore Eustace and Hollywood *D & G* 64-67; I Dublin Drumcondra w N Strand 67-71; I Dublin St Barn 67-71; I Dublin Zion Ch 71-88; Adn Dublin 80-88; Bp C, C & R 88-98; rtd 98. *6 Kerdiff Park, Monread Road, Naas, Co Kildare, Republic of Ireland* Tel (00353) (45) 898144 E-mail rawarke@eircom.net

WARLAND, Peter William. b 35. K Coll Lon 56. **d** 60 **p** 61. C Pemberton St Jo *Liv* 60-64; C Warrington St Elphin 64-66; V Farnworth All SS *Man* 66-71; Chapl RN 71-92; QHC 88-92; Chapl Greenbank and Freedom Fields Hosps Ex 92-00; Chapl St Luke's Hospice Plymouth 94-00; rtd 00; Perm to Offic *Ex* from 00. *122 Wingfield Road, Stoke, Plymouth PL3 4ER* Tel (01752) 561381

WARMAN, Canon John Richard. b 37. Pemb Coll Ox BA61 MA. Ridley Hall Cam 61. **d** 63 **p** 64. C Huyton St Mich *Liv* 63-67; Asst Chapl Liv Univ 67-68; Chapl 68-74; P-in-c Holbrooke *Derby* 74-80; P-in-c Lt Eaton 74-80; R Sawley 80-96; RD Ilkeston 82-92; Hon Can Derby Cathl 91-02; V Allestree 96-02; rtd 02; Perm to Offic *Derby* from 02. *27 Swanmore Road, Littleover, Derby DE23 3SD* Tel (01332) 510089

WARMAN, Miss Marion Alice. b 20. Newnham Coll Cam BA43 MA50. S'wark Ord Course 76. **dss** 79 **d** 87 **p** 94. Spring Grove St Mary *Lon* 79-87; Hon Par Dn 87-94; Hon C from 94; Chapl Asst W Middx Hosp Isleworth 80-93; Chapl Volunteer Hounslow and Spelthorne NHS Trust 93-04; Perm to Offic *Lon* from 93. *43 Thornbury Road, Isleworth TW7 4LE* Tel (020) 8560 5905

WARMAN, Philip Noel. b 64. Roehampton Inst BSc85 PGCE86. Ridley Hall Cam 99. **d** 01 **p** 02. C Burney Lane *Birm* 01-06; C Luton St Mary *St Alb* 06-09; V Brightside w Wincobank *Sheff* from 09. *The Vicarage, 24 Beacon Road, Sheffield S9 1AD* Tel 0114-281 9360

WARNE, Miss Susan Annette. b 39. Man Univ BSc61 Nottm Univ DipEd62. **d** 00 **p** 01. OLM Kelsale-cum-Carlton, Middleton, Theberton etc *St E* 00-04; OLM Middleton cum Fordley and Theberton w Eastbridge 04-08; OLM Darsham 04-08; OLM Westleton w Dunwich 04-08; OLM Yoxford, Peasenhall and Sibton 01-08; OLM Yoxmere from 08. *Wynkyns, 22 Oakwood Park, Yoxford, Saxmundham IP17 3JU* Tel (01728) 668410

WARNER, Alan Winston. b 51. Lon Univ BSc73. Coll of Resurr Mirfield 73. **d** 76 **p** 77. C Willenhall St Anne *Lich* 76-78; C Baswich 78-81; V Wednesfield St Greg 81-87; Chapl Frimley Park Hosp 87-94; Chapl Frimley Park Hosp NHS Trust 94-04; Team Ldr Shrewsbury and Telford NHS Trust from 04; Bp's Adv on Hosp Chapl *Lich* from 06; OCF from 95. *The Princess Royal Hospital, Apley Castle, Telford TF1 6TF* Tel (01952) 641222 E-mail alanwarner@igclick.net

WARNER, Alison Mary. b 44. Pace Univ USA BA. SAOMC 01. **d** 04 **p** 05. NSM Waterloo St Jo w St Andr *S'wark* from 04. *5 Mace Close, London E1W 2JX* Tel (020) 7481 9197 Mobile 07900-552665 E-mail ali@aliwarner.freeserve.co.uk

WARNER, Canon Andrew Compton. b 35. Fitzw Ho Cam BA58 MA62. Westcott Ho Cam 59. **d** 60 **p** 61. C Addlestone *Guildf* 60-64; C-in-c Ash Vale CD 64-71; V Hinchley Wood 71-80; R Gt Bookham 80-00; RD Leatherhead 88-93; Hon Can Guildf Cathl 99-00; rtd 00; Perm to Offic *Win* from 00. *5 Pearman Drive, Andover SP10 2SB* Tel (01264) 391325
E-mail dandawarner@yahoo.co.uk

WARNER, Clifford Chorley. b 38. Hull Univ MA88. EMMTC 76. **d** 79 **p** 80. NSM Swanwick and Pentrich *Derby* 79-88; NSM Allestree 88-98; Perm to Offic from 98. *17 Amber Heights, Ripley DE5 3SP* Tel (01773) 745089

WARNER, David. b 40. AKC63. **d** 64 **p** 65. C Castleford All SS *Wakef* 64-68; Warden Hollowford Tr and Conf Cen Sheff 68-72; R Wombwell *Sheff* 72-83; V Wortley w Thurgoland 83-95; RD Tankersley 88-93; V Worsbrough St Mary 95-00; P-in-c Bildeston w Wattisham *St E* 00-02; P-in-c Whatfield w Semer, Nedging and Naughton 00-02; R Bildeston w Wattisham and Lindsey, Whatfield etc 02-05; rtd 05; Perm to Offic *St E* from 05. *10 Magdalen Street, Eye IP23 7AJ* Tel (01379) 870459 Mobile 07050-111478

WARNER, David Leonard John. b 24. Kelham Th Coll 47. **d** 51 **p** 52. C Mill Hill St Mich *Lon* 51-54; C Pimlico St Sav 54-56; S Africa 56-68; V Bournemouth H Epiphany *Win* 68-78; V Whitchurch w Tufton and Litchfield 78-89; RD Whitchurch 79-89; rtd 89; Perm to Offic *Win* from 89; Hon Chapl Win Cathl from 97. *9 Sparkford Close, Winchester SO22 4NH* Tel (01962) 867343 E-mail david.warner@btinternet.com

WARNER, Dennis Vernon. b 46. Lon Univ BA68 K Coll Lon BD71. **d** 72 **p** 73. C W Bromwich All SS *Lich* 72-75; C Uttoxeter w Bramshall 75-79; NSM Stretton w Claymills from 79. *90 Beech Lane, Stretton, Burton-on-Trent DE13 0DU* Tel (01283) 548058 or (01543) 306080 E-mail dennis.warner@lichfield.anglican.org

WARNER, Canon George Francis. b 36. Trin Coll Ox BA60 MA64 Qu Coll Cam BA63. Westcott Ho Cam 61. **d** 63 **p** 64. C Birm St Geo 63-66; C Maidstone All SS w St Phil and H Trin *Cant* 66-69; Chapl Wellington Coll Berks 69-78; TR Coventry Caludon 78-95; Hon Can Cov Cathl 85-02; RD Cov E 89-95; P-in-c Leamington Priors All SS 95-02; P-in-c Leamington Spa H Trin and Old Milverton 95-02; rtd 02; Perm to Offic *Cov* from 02. *Coll Leys Edge, Fant Hill, Upper Brailes, Banbury OX15 5AY* Tel (01608) 685550

WARNER, James Morley. b 32. S'wark Ord Course 66. **d** 69 **p** 70. C S Mymms K Chas *Lon* 69-72; C Bush Hill Park St Steph 72-75; V W Hendon St Jo 75-98; rtd 98; Perm to Offic *Lon* 98-00; Hon C Wembley Park from 00. *46 Churchill Avenue, Harrow HA3 0AY* Tel (020) 8907 8505
E-mail jim@warner8322.freeserve.co.uk

WARNER, John Philip. b 59. Keble Coll Ox BA80 MA84. St Steph Ho Ox 83. **d** 83 **p** 84. C Brighton Resurr *Chich* 83-87; C Paddington St Mary *Lon* 87-90; V Teddington St Mark and Hampton Wick 90-00; P-in-c Belgrade *Eur* 00-03; P-in-c St Magnus the Martyr w St Marg New Fish Street *Lon* from 03; P-in-c St Mary Abchurch from 04; P-in-c St Clem Eastcheap w St Martin Orgar from 08. *St Magnus the Martyr, Lower Thames Street, London EC3R 6DN* Tel (020) 7626 4481
E-mail saintmagnus@bulldoghome.com

WARNER, Mrs Marjorie Anne. b 53. York Univ BA74 York St Jo Univ MA04. NEOC 06. **d** 09. NSM Masham and Healey *Ripon* from 09. *26 Larkhill Crescent, Ripon HG4 2HN* Tel (01765) 606961 E-mail marjorie@26lhc.freeserve.co.uk

WARNER, Canon Martin Clive. b 58. St Chad's Coll Dur BA80 MA85 PhD03. St Steph Ho Ox 82. **d** 84 **p** 85. C Plymouth St Pet *Ex* 84-88; TV Leic Resurr 88-93; Admin Shrine of Our Lady of Walsingham 93-02; P-in-c Hempton and Pudding Norton 98-00; Hon Can Nor Cathl 00-02; Can Res St Paul's Cathl from 03. *3 Amen Court, London EC4M 7BU* Tel and fax (020) 7248 2559 E-mail treasurer@stpaulscathedral.org.uk

WARNER, Mary. b 52. Univ of Wales (Swansea) BSc73 Aber Univ PhD77. NEOC 90. **d** 93 **p** 94. C Bensham *Dur* 93-96; Asst Chapl Newcastle upon Tyne Hosps NHS Trust 96-98; Chapl Hartlepool and E Durham NHS Trust 98-99; Chapl N Tees and Hartlepool NHS Trust 99-04; Chapl City Hosps Sunderland NHS Trust from 04. *The Chaplain's Office, Sunderland Royal Hospital, Kayll Road, Sunderland SR4 7TP* Tel 0191-569 9180 or 522 6444

WARNER, Canon Michael John William. b 41. Ex Univ MPhil06. Sarum Th Coll 68. **d** 71 **p** 72. C Plympton St Mary *Ex* 71-75; V St Goran w Caerhays *Truro* 75-78; V Bishops Tawton *Ex* 78-79; V Newport 78-79; Perm to Offic *Truro* 79-83; V St Stythians w Perranarworthal and Gwennap 83-93; Sec Dioc Adv Cttee 93-01; P-in-c Budock 93-97; P-in-c Tregony w St Cuby and Cornelly 97-03; C Probus, Ladock and Grampound w Creed and St Erme 02-03; Hon Can Truro Cathl 98-03; rtd 03; Perm to

Offic *Truro* from 03. *98 Porthpean Road, St Austell PL25 4PN* Tel (01726) 64130 E-mail m.j.w.w@btinternet.com

WARNER, Nigel Bruce. b 51. St Jo Coll Cam BA72 MA76 ALCM67. Wycliffe Hall Ox 75. **d** 77 **p** 78. C Luton St Mary *St Alb* 77-80; Prec Dur Cathl 80-84; R St John Lee *Newc* 84-91; V Lamesley *Dur* 91-98; V Bishopwearmouth St Nic from 98; AD Wearmouth 99-05. *St Nicholas' Vicarage, 200 Queen Alexandra Road, Sunderland SR3 1XQ* Tel 0191-522 6444 *or* 520 2127 E-mail nigel.warner@durham.anglican.org

WARNER, Philip. *See* WARNER, John Philip

WARNER, Canon Robert William. b 32. TCD BA54 MA65 BD65. TCD Div Sch Div Test56. **d** 56 **p** 57. C Wythenshawe St Martin CD *Man* 56-60; R Hulme St Steph w St Mark 60-66; R Droylsden St Mary 66-76; R Stand 76-97; AD Radcliffe and Prestwich 85-96; Hon Can Man Cathl 87-97; rtd 97; Perm to Offic *Man* from 99. *28 Cow Lees, Westhoughton, Bolton BL5 3EG* Tel (01942) 818821

WARNER, Mrs Stephanie Patricia. b 49. Lon Inst BA96. SEITE 05. **d** 07 **p** 08. NSM Mottingham St Andr *S'wark* from 07. *54 Stanley Close, London SE9 2BA* Tel (020) 8859 0489

WARNER, Terence. b 36. **d** 92 **p** 93. NSM Leek and Meerbrook *Lich* 92-98; NSM Odd Rode *Ches* 98-03; Perm to Offic *Lich* from 03. *36 Haig Road, Leek ST13 6BZ* Tel (01538) 371988

WARNES, Brian Leslie Stephen. b 37. Natal Univ BSocSc76. Kelham Th Coll 59. **d** 67 **p** 68. C Tonge Moor *Man* 67-71; S Africa 71-87; V Blean *Cant* 87-94; V Te Awamutu St Jo New Zealand 94-98; Chapl to Bp Christchurch 98-04; rtd 05. *13 Velma Crescent, Nawton, Hamilton 3200, New Zealand* Tel (0064) (7) 846 3866 *or* 839 4683 E-mail swarnes.cathedral@xtra.co.nz

WARNES, David John. b 50. Jes Coll Cam BA72 MA76 PGCE73. EAMTC 01. **d** 04 **p** 05. NSM Ipswich St Mary-le-Tower *St E* from 04; Chapl Ipswich Sch from 04. *Ipswich School, 25 Henley Road, Ipswich IP1 3SG* Tel (01473) 408300 Fax 400058 Mobile 07732-654603 E-mail warnesdavid@googlemail.com

WARNES, Miss Marjorie. b 32. Leeds Inst of Educn CertEd53. St Jo Coll Nottm 85. **d** 87 **p** 94. C Leamington Priors St Mary *Cov* 87-97; rtd 97; Perm to Offic *Cov* 97-05. *38 Ruston Avenue, Rustington, Littlehampton BN16 2AN* Tel (01903) 778859

WARNES, Warren Hugh. b 23. St Barn Coll Adelaide. **d** 50 **p** 50. C N Adelaide Ch Ch Australia 50-51; Miss Chapl Pinnaroo 51-55; C Narracoorte 55-57; P-in-c Tailem Bend Miss 57-58; C Northolt St Mary *Lon* 58-60 and 62-64; R Tatiara Australia 60-62; V Kings Heath *Pet* 64-71; V Rockingham w Caldecote 71-73; V Gretton w Rockingham and Caldecote 73-83; V Marston St Lawrence w Warkworth and Thenford 83-89; rtd 89; Perm to Offic *Pet* from 89; Officer for Clergy Widows (Northampton) from 90. *17 Thorpe Road, Earls Barton, Northampton NN6 0PJ* Tel (01604) 812935

WARR, Timothy Gerald. b 59. Trin Coll Bris BA86. **d** 88 **p** 89. C Yateley *Win* 88-91; C Chapel Allerton *Ripon* 91-93; V Wortley de Leeds 93-01; TR Borehamwood *St Alb* 01-05; TR Elstree and Borehamwood from 05. *The Rectory, 94 Shenley Road, Borehamwood WD6 1EB* Tel and fax (020) 8207 6603 *or* tel 8905 1365 E-mail tim.warr@btinternet.com

WARREN, The Very Revd Alan Christopher. b 32. CCC Cam BA56 MA60. Ridley Hall Cam 56. **d** 57 **p** 58. C Cliftonville *Cant* 57-59; C Plymouth St Andr *Ex* 59-62; Chapl Kelly Coll Tavistock 62-64; V Leic H Apostles 64-72; Hon Can Cov Cathl 72-78; Dioc Missr 72-78; Provost Leic /8-92; rtd 92, Perm to Offic *Nor* from 92. *9 Queen's Drive, Hunstanton PE36 6EY* Tel (01485) 534533

WARREN, Mrs Barbara. b 46. **d** 08 **p** 09. NSM Rocester and Croxden w Hollington *Lich* from 08; NSM Uttoxeter Area from 08. *The Cottage, Common End, Hollington, Stoke-on-Trent ST10 4HS* Tel (01889) 507316 E-mail barbara.warren@tiscali.co.uk

WARREN, Bunny. *See* WARREN, Gordon Lenham

✠**WARREN, The Rt Revd Cecil Allan.** b 24. Sydney Univ BA51 Qu Coll Ox BA56 MA56. ACT ThL52. **d** 50 **p** 51 **c** 65. Australia 50-83; Can Canberra and Goulburn 63-65; Asst Bp 65-72; Bp 72-83; Asst Bp Derby 83-89; TR Old Brampton and Loundsley Green 83-89; Hon Can Derby Cathl 83-89; rtd 89. *2/19 Sidney Street, Toowoomba Qld 4350, Australia* Tel (0061) (7) 4638 4487

WARREN, Christopher Pelham. b 55. Middx Univ BA05. NTMTC 02. **d** 05 **p** 06. NSM Saffron Walden w Wendens Ambo, Littlebury etc *Chelmsf* 05-08; P-in-c Gt w Lt Chesterford from 08. *The Vicarage, Church Street, Great Chesterford, Saffron Walden CB10 1NP* Tel (01799) 530317 E-mail revchriswarren@googlemail.com

WARREN, David. b 39. S'wark Ord Course. **d** 87 **p** 88. NSM Mottingham St Andr *S'wark* 87-05; rtd 05; Perm to Offic *S'wark* from 07. *26 Longcroft, London SE9 1RQ* Tel (020) 8851 4824

WARREN, Eric Anthony. b 28. MBE. Ex & Truro NSM Scheme. **d** 83 **p** 84. NSM Chudleigh *Ex* 83-88; Perm to Offic from 88. *Lower Radway House, Bishopsteignton, Teignmouth TQ14 9SS* Tel (01626) 772135 *or* 779277

WARREN, Frederick Noel. b 30. TCD BA52 MA58 BD66 QUB PhD72. **d** 53 **p** 54. C Belfast St Matt *Conn* 53-56; C Belfast St

Geo 56-59; I Castlewellan *D & D* 59-65; I Clonallon w Warrenpoint 65-69; I Newcastle 69-87; Can Belf Cathl 73-76; Preb Wicklow St Patr Cathl Dublin 76-88; I Dunfanaghy, Raymunterdoney and Tullaghbegley *D & R* 87-97; Preb Swords St Patr Cathl Dublin 89-97; rtd 97. *Runclevin, Dufanaghy, Letterkenny, Co Donegal, Republic of Ireland* Tel (00353) (74) 913 6635

WARREN, Geoffrey. *See* WARREN, Robert Geoffrey

WARREN, Geoffrey Richard. b 44. Middx Poly MA91 Middx Univ PhD02. Bps' Coll Cheshunt 66 Qu Coll Birm 68. **d** 69 **p** 70. C Waltham Cross *St Alb* 69-73; C Radlett 73-78; C Tring 78-80; TV Tring 80-95; V Watford St Andr from 95; RD Watford from 05. *St Andrew's Vicarage, 18 Park Road, Watford WD17 4QN* Tel (01923) 239265 E-mail geoffwarren@btinternet.com

WARREN, Mrs Gillian. b 53. Sheff Univ BA74 PGCE75. WMMTC 89. **d** 92 **p** 94. Par Dn Tettenhall Regis *Lich* 92-94; C 94-95; TV Bilston 95-00; R Lich St Chad 00-02; V Wednesbury St Paul Wood Green from 02. *St Paul's Vicarage, 68 Wood Green Road, Wednesbury WS10 9QT* Tel 0121-556 0687

WARREN, Gordon Lenham (Bunny). b 45. Wycliffe Hall Ox 91. **d** 93 **p** 94. C Sunbury *Lon* 93-96; C Laleham 96-98; R Limehouse from 98; Hon Chapl RN from 08. *Limehouse Rectory, 5 Newell Street, London E14 7HP* Tel (020) 7987 1502 E-mail cpsalm9@aol.com

WARREN, Preb Henry Fiennes. b 21. Keble Coll Ox BA42 MA47. Cuddesdon Coll 42. **d** 48 **p** 49. C Weston-super-Mare St Jo *B & W* 48-53; R Exford 53-75; RD Wiveliscombe 65-73; Preb Wells Cathl from 73; R W Monkton 75-86; rtd 86; Perm to Offic *B & W* from 86. *6 Brookside, Broadway, Ilminster TA19 9RT* Tel (01460) 57922

WARREN, James Randolph. b 54. St Paul's Cheltenham CertEd75 Bris Univ BEd76 Birm Univ MEd84. Ridley Hall Cam 90. **d** 92 **p** 93. C Boldmere *Birm* 92-95; V Torpoint *Truro* 95-01; Hon Chapl RN 98-01; V Shottery St Andr *Cov* from 01. *The Vicarage, Church Lane, Shottery, Stratford-upon-Avon CV37 9HQ* Tel (01789) 293381 Fax 296648

WARREN, Malcolm Clive. b 46. St D Coll Lamp. **d** 74 **p** 75. C Newport St Andr *Mon* 74-78; C Risca 78-79; V St Hilary Greenway 79-84; TV Grantham *Linc* 84-90; Ind Chapl *Linc* 87-90 and *Worc* 90-05; P-in-c Dudley St Aug Holly Hall *Worc* 95-96; Perm to Offic 96-97; TV Kidderminster St Mary and All SS w Trimpley etc 97-05; Ind Chapl *Bris* from 05. *The Glebe House, 1 McLaren Road, Avonmouth, Bristol BS11 9FE* Tel 0117-373 2546 Mobile 07971-222739 E-mail malcolm_warren@hotmail.com *or* malcolmwarren9@aol.com

WARREN, Martin John. b 59. Ch Coll Cam BA81 MA85. St Jo Coll Nottm LTh85. **d** 86 **p** 87. C Littleover *Derby* 86-90; C Hermitage and Hampstead Norreys, Cold Ash etc *Ox* 90-91; TV 91-97; TV Hermitage 97-02; P-in-c Shebbear, Buckland Filleigh, Sheepwash etc *Ex* from 02. *The Rectory, Shebbear, Beaworthy EX21 5RU* Tel (01409) 281424

WARREN, Michael John. b 40. Kelham Th Coll 59. **d** 64 **p** 65. C Withington St Chris *Man* 64-67; C Worsley 67-69; C Witney *Ox* 69-72; V S Hinksey 72-80; Canada 80-99 and from 02; C Verwood *Sarum* 99-00; rtd 00. *1005-5th Avenue North, Lethbridge AB T1H 0MB, Canada*

WARREN, Michael Philip. b 62. Oak Hill Th Coll BA91 MA04. **d** 94 **p** 95. C Tunbridge Wells St Jo *Roch* 94-98; Assoc Min Heydon, Gt and Lt Chishill, Chrishall etc *Chelmsf* 98-04; TV Tunbridge Wells St Pet *Roch* from 04. *St Peter's Vicarage, Bayhall Road, Tunbridge Wells TN2 4TP* Tel (01892) 530384 E-mail elmdonvic@aol.com

WARREN, The Ven Norman Leonard. b 34. CCC Cam BA58 MA62. Ridley Hall Cam 58. **d** 60 **p** 61. C Bedworth *Cov* 60-63; V Leamington Priors St Paul 63-77; R Morden *S'wark* 77-88; TR 88-89; RD Merton 86-89; Adn Roch and Can Res Roch Cathl 89-00; rtd 00; Perm to Offic *Roch* from 00. *Cornerstone, 6 Hill View, Stratford-upon-Avon CV37 9AY* Tel (01789) 414255

WARREN, Canon Paul Kenneth. b 41. Selw Coll Cam BA63 MA67. Cuddesdon Coll 64. **d** 67 **p** 68. C Lancaster St Mary *Blackb* 67-70; Chapl Lanc Univ 70-78; V Langho Billington 78-83; Bp's Dom Chapl and Chapl Whalley Abbey 83-88; R Standish 88-01; P-in-c Silverdale from 01; Hon Can Blackb Cathl from 91; RD Chorley 92-98; AD Tunstall from 08. *The Vicarage, St John's Grove, Silverdale, Carnforth LA5 0RH* Tel (01524) 701268

WARREN, Peter. b 40. FCA64. Oak Hill Th Coll 77. **d** 79 **p** 80. C Newcastle w Butterton *Lich* 79-82; TV Sutton St Jas and Wawne *York* 82-87; V Ledsham w Fairburn 87-95; R Ainderby Steeple w Yafforth and Kirby Wiske etc *Ripon* 95-03; rtd 03. *5 Bridge Farm, Pollington, Goole DN14 0BF* Tel (01405) 862925 E-mail peter@warren303.orangehome.co.uk

WARREN, Peter John. b 55. Worc Coll of Educn CertEd76. Trin Coll Bris BA86. **d** 86 **p** 87. C W Streatham St Jas *S'wark* 86-91; P-in-c Edin Clermiston Em 91-98; P-in-c Blackpool Ch Ch w All SS *Blackb* 98-03; V 03-09; Co-Pastor Internat Chr Fellowship Phnom Penh from 09. *International Christian Fellowship, PO*

Box 98, Phnom Penh, Cambodia Tel (00855) (12) 235182
E-mail revpwarren@blueyonder.co.uk

WARREN, Philip James. b 65. SS Paul & Mary Coll Cheltenham BA87 Hughes Hall Cam PGCE88 Kingston Univ MA93. St Jo Coll Nottm MA99. **d** 00 **p** 01. C Reigate St Mary *S'wark* 00-03; P-in-c Jersey Millbrook St Matt *Win* 03-06; V from 06; P-in-c Jersey St Lawr 03-06; R from 06. *The Rectory, La Route de l'Eglise, St Lawrence, Jersey JE3 1FF* Tel (01534) 869013
E-mail philwarren@jerseymail.co.uk

WARREN, Canon Robert. b 54. TCD BA78 MA81. CITC 76. **d** 78 **p** 79. C Limerick City *L & K* 78-81; Dioc Youth Adv (Limerick) 79-86; I Adare w Kilpeacon and Croom 81-88; Bp's Dom Chapl 81-95; Dioc Registrar (Limerick etc) from 81; Dioc Registrar (Killaloe etc) from 86; I Tralee w Kilmoyley, Ballymacelligott etc from 88; Can Limerick, Killaloe and Clonfert Cathls 95-96; Chan from 97; Asst Dioc Sec *L & K* from 90; Preb Taney St Patr Cathl Dublin from 04. *St John's Rectory, Ashe Street, Tralee, Co Kerry, Republic of Ireland* Tel (00353) (66) 712 2245 *or* 712 4152 Fax 712 9004 Mobile 87-252 1133
E-mail rwarren@indigo.ie

WARREN, Robert Geoffrey. b 51. Trin Coll Bris 79. **d** 82 **p** 83. C Felixstowe SS Pet and Paul *St E* 82-86; V Gazeley w Dalham, Moulton and Kentford 86-90; P-in-c Ipswich St Clem w St Luke and H Trin 90-98; C Gt Finborough w Onehouse and Harleston 98-00; rtd 01; Perm to Offic *B & W* from 02. *11 Homefield, Locking, Weston-super-Mare BS24 8ED* Tel (01934) 824408

WARREN, Robert Irving. b 38. Univ of BC BA58 Ox Univ MA73. Angl Th Coll (BC). **d** 61 **p** 63. C Lakes Miss Canada 61-66; R Hazelton 69-75; R New Westmr St Barn 75-89; R Northfield *Birm* 89-08; rtd 08; Perm to Offic *Birm* from 08. *300 Lickey Road, Rednal, Birmingham B45 8RY* Tel 0121-453 1572 E-mail riwarren@hotmail.com

WARREN, Robert James. b 58. McGill Univ Montreal BTh82. Montreal Dioc Th Coll. **d** 84 **p** 85. C Victoria St Phil Canada 84-87; R Chibougamau Ch Ch 87-90; R Mascouche and P-in-c Montreal St Ignatius 90-92; R Westmount Ch of the Advent 92-99; Exec Dir Old Brewery Miss 99-03; Chapl Canadian Grenadier Guards 91-96; Chapl Miss to Seafarers 93-99; R Penicuik *Edin* from 03; P-in-c W Linton from 03. *The Rectory, 23 Broomhill Road, Penicuik EH26 9EE* Tel (01968) 672862 Mobile 07963-910865 E-mail padre@btinternet.com

WARREN, Canon Robert Peter Resker. b 39. Jes Coll Cam BA63 MA. ALCD65. **d** 65 **p** 66. C Rusholme H Trin *Man* 65-68; C Bushbury *Lich* 68-71; V Crookes St Thos *Sheff* 71-90; TR 90-93; RD Hallam 78-83; Hon Can Sheff Cathl 82-93; Can Th Sheff Cathl 93-04; Nat Officer for Evang 93-04; Springboard Missr 98-04; rtd 04; Perm to Offic *Ripon* from 03. *Willow Bank House, Borrage Lane, Ripon HG4 2PZ* Tel (01765) 602996
E-mail robert.warren@ukgateway.net

WARREN, William Frederick. b 55. Sarum & Wells Th Coll 83. **d** 86 **p** 87. C E Greenwich Ch Ch w St Andr and St Mich *S'wark* 86-91; C Richmond St Mary w St Matthias and St Jo 91-95; TV 96-97; V Putney St Marg 97-08; V S Croydon St Pet and St Aug from 08. *St Peter's Vicarage, 20 Haling Park Road, South Croydon CR2 6NE* Tel (020) 8688 4715
E-mail wfwarren2003@yahoo.co.uk

WARRICK, Mark. b 54. Aston Univ BSc76 Nottm Univ BCombStuds83. Linc Th Coll 80. **d** 83 **p** 84. C Grantham *Linc* 83-87; C Cirencester *Glouc* 87-91; V Over *Ely* 91-97; V Deeping St James *Linc* 97-09; RD Aveland and Ness w Stamford 06-09; P-in-c Stamford All SS w St Jo from 09. *All Saints' Vicarage, Casterton Road, Stamford PE9 2YL* Tel (01780) 756942
E-mail mark.warrick@stamfordallsaints.org.uk

WARRILLOW, Brian Ellis. b 39. Linc Th Coll 81. **d** 83 **p** 84. C Tunstall *Lich* 83-85; C Shrewsbury H Cross 86-87; P-in-c Tilstock 88; P-in-c Whixall 88; V Tilstock and Whixall 89-92; TV Hanley H Ev 92-94; rtd 94; Perm to Offic *Lich* 01-02; P-in-c Menton *Eur* 02-05; Hon C Wolstanton *Lich* from 07. *14 Dorrington Grove, Newcastle ST5 0HY* Tel (01782) 253465
E-mail thewarrillows@netscapeonline.co.uk

WARRILOW, Mrs Christine. b 42. Lanc Univ BA86. NOC 86. **d** 89 **p** 94. C Netherton *Liv* 89-92; C Cantril Farm 92-94; V 94-96; V Hindley Green 96-02; rtd 02; Perm to Offic *Liv* 03-08; Hon C Stanley w Stoneycroft St Paul from 08. *10 Beacon View Drive, Upholland, Skelmersdale WN8 0HL*

WARRINGTON, Katherine Irene (Kay). b 44. Univ of Wales (Swansea) BSc67 King/Edw St. St Mich Coll Llan 93. **d** 95. NSM Knighton and Norton *S & B* 95-98; NSM Llywel and Traeanglas w Llanulid 98-00; NSM Trallwng w Bettws Penpont w Aberyskir etc 00-04; Dioc Children's Officer from 96. *17 Ffordd Emlyn, Ystalyfera, Swansea SA9 2EW* Tel (01639) 842874

WARRINGTON, Archdeacon of. See BRADLEY, The Ven Peter David Douglas

WARRINGTON, Suffragan Bishop of. See BLACKBURN, The Rt Revd Richard Finn

WARWICK, Gordon Melvin. b 31. NOC 79. **d** 80 **p** 81. NSM Darrington *Wakef* 80-87; TV Almondbury w Farnley Tyas 87-95; rtd 95; Perm to Offic *Newc* from 95. *Andante, Christon Bank, Alnwick NE66 3ES* Tel (01665) 576742

WARWICK, Hugh Johnston. b 39. ARCM63. SAOMC 97. **d** 00 **p** 01. NSM Rotherfield Peppard *Ox* 00-02; NSM Rotherfield Peppard and Kidmore End etc 02-08; rtd 08; Perm to Offic *Ox* and *Pet* from 08. *Witan House, 38 Wheeler's Rise, Croughton, Brackley NN13 5ND* Tel (01869) 819577

WARWICK, Canon John Michael. b 37. Fitzw Ho Cam BA58 MA62. Ely Th Coll 58. **d** 60 **p** 61. C Towcester w Easton Neston *Pet* 60-63; C Leighton Buzzard *St Alb* 63-64; C Boston *Linc* 64-66; P-in-c Sutterton 66-72; V 72-74; V Sutton St Mary 74-84; V Bourne 84-02; Can and Preb Linc Cathl 89-02; RD Aveland and Ness w Stamford 93-00; Chapl Bourne Hosps Lincs 84-93; Chapl NW Anglia Healthcare NHS Trust 93-98; rtd 02. *24 Hurst Park Road, Twyford, Reading RG10 0EY* Tel 0118-932 0649

WARWICK, Neil Michael. b 64. Nottm Univ BA86. Ridley Hall Cam 03. **d** 05 **p** 06. C Towcester w Caldecote and Easton Neston etc *Pet* 05-09; V Earley St Nic *Ox* from 09. *St Nicolas' Vicarage, 53 Sutcliffe Avenue, Reading RG6 7JN* Tel 0118-966 5060
E-mail revwarwick@btinternet.com

WARWICK, Archdeacon of. *Vacant*

WARWICK, Suffragan Bishop of. *See* STROYAN, The Rt Revd John Ronald Angus

WASEY, Kim Alexandra Clare. b 77. Man Univ BA99 Birm Univ MPhil03. Qu Coll Birm 00. **d** 02 **p** 03. C Rochdale *Man* 02-04; Chapl Man Univ 04-06; Chapl Man Metrop Univ 04-06; Chapl Salford Univ 06-09; Hon C Man Victoria Park from 09. *St Chrysostom's Rectory, 38 Park Range, Manchester M14 5HQ* Tel 0161-224 6971 Mobile 07944-155772
E-mail kim.wasey@gmail.com

WASH, John Henry. b 46. CEng MIStructE70. OLM Newington St Mary *S'wark* 81-04; Perm to Offic Cyprus and the Gulf from 05. *PO Box 60187, Paphos 8101, Cyprus SE17 3AD* Tel (00357) (26) 923860 E-mail wash@emailkissonerga.com

WASHFORD, Mrs Rhonwen Richarde Foster. b 50. RGN99. ERMC 05. **d** 08 **p** 09. NSM Stalham, E Ruston, Brunstead, Sutton and Ingham *Nor* from 08. *Homeleigh, Town Road, Ingham, Norwich NR12 9TA* Tel (01692) 580423
E-mail rhonwenwashford@hotmail.com

WASHINGTON, Linda Jennifer. b 56. BA PGCE. **d** 07 **p** 08. NSM Woburn w Eversholt, Milton Bryan, Battlesden etc *St Alb* from 07. *3 Avenue Mews, Flitwick, Bedford MK45 1BF* Tel (01525) 714442

WASHINGTON, Nigel Leslie. b 50. St Paul's Cheltenham BEd73 Lon Univ MA83. SAOMC 97. **d** 00 **p** 01. NSM Westoning w Tingrith *St Alb* 00-07; P-in-c from 07. *Bracken, 3 Avenue Mews, Flitwick, Bedford MK45 1BF* Tel (01525) 714442 Mobile 07794-754986 E-mail nigelwash@hotmail.com

WASHINGTON, Canon Patrick Leonard. b 44. Nottm Univ BSc66. St Steph Ho Ox 65. **d** 68 **p** 69. C Fleet *Guildf* 68-71; C Farnham 71-74; TV Staveley and Barrow Hill *Derby* 74-83; V Norbury St Phil *Cant* 83-84; V Norbury St Phil *S'wark* from 85; RD Croydon N 90-99; Hon Can S'wark Cathl from 01. *St Philip's Vicarage, 66 Pollards Hill North, London SW16 4NY* Tel (020) 8764 1812 E-mail stphil-norbury@supanet.com

WASSALL, Canon Keith Leonard. b 45. Bede Coll Dur TCert67. Chich Th Coll 68. **d** 71 **p** 72. C Upper Gornal *Lich* 71-74; C Codsall 74-75; TV Hanley All SS 75-79; Asst P Pembroke Bermuda 79-81; V Rickerscote *Lich* 81-92; P-in-c Coven 92-99; Asst Chapl HM Pris Featherstone 92-99; Can Res Bermuda 99-04; C Houghton le Spring *Dur* 04-06; C Eppleton and Hetton le Hole 04-06; C Lyons 04-06; C Millfield St Mark and Pallion St Luke from 06. *28 Montaigne Drive, Bowburn, Durham DH6 5QB* Tel 0191-377 8709 E-mail klwassall@tiscali.co.uk

WASTELL, Canon Eric Morse. b 33. St Mich Coll Llan. **d** 62 **p** 63. C Oystermouth *S & B* 62-65; C St Jo Cathl Antigua 65-66; R St Mary 66-73; R St Paul 73-74; Dioc Registrar 69-74; Hon Can Antigua 71-74; V Swansea St Gabr *S & B* 74-98; RD Clyne 88-96; Can Brecon Cathl from 90; rtd 98. *18 Belgrave Court, Walter Road, Uplands, Swansea SA1 4PY* Tel (01792) 466709

WASTIE, Canon David Vernon. b 37. Open Univ BA84. Chich Th Coll 79. **d** 81 **p** 82. C Bitterne Park *Win* 81-83; TV Chambersbury *St Alb* 83-87; V Jersey St Luke *Win* 87-95; P-in-c Jersey St Jas 87-93; V 93-95; V Southbourne St Kath 95-99; Hon Can Bukavu from 94; rtd 02; Perm to Offic *Derby* 05-08 and *Win* from 09. *60 High Street, Milford on Sea, Lymington SO41 0QD* Tel (01590) 641375 E-mail canonwastie@hotmail.com

WATCHORN, Canon Brian. b 39. Em Coll Cam BA61 MA65 Ex Coll Ox BA62. Ripon Hall Ox 61. **d** 63 **p** 64. C Bolton St Pet *Man* 63-66; Chapl G&C Coll Cam 66-74; V Chesterton St Geo *Ely* 75-82; Fell Dean and Chapl Pemb Coll Cam 82-06; Hon Can Ely Cathl from 94; Chapter Can from 00. *34 Petersfield Mansions, Petersfield, Cambridge CB1 1BB* Tel (01223) 322378

WATERFIELD, Janet Lyn. b 60. Birm Univ BA06. WMMTC 99. **d** 02 **p** 03. C Bilston *Lich* 02-07; TV from 07. *8 Cumberland Road, Bilston WV14 6LT* Tel (01902) 497794 Mobile 07905-539111
E-mail janwaterfield@blueyonder.co.uk

WATERFORD, Dean of. *See* LESTER, The Very Revd Trevor Rashleigh

WATERHOUSE, Eric Thomas Benjamin. b 24. Lon Univ 60. Kelham Th Coll 47 Qu Coll Birm 50. **d** 51 **p** 52. C Wolverhampton St Pet *Lich* 51-56; C Lower Gornal 56-57; V Walsall St Mark 57-60; R Kington w Dormston *Worc* 60-64; R Worc St Clem 64-77; P-in-c Abberton, Naunton Beauchamp and Bishampton etc 77-80; R 80-92; rtd 92; Perm to Offic *Worc* from 92. *7 Hazel Avenue, Evesham WR11 1XT* Tel (01386) 421312

WATERHOUSE, Canon Peter. b 46. Linc Th Coll 68. **d** 70 **p** 71. C Consett *Dur* 70-73; C Heworth St Mary 73-76; V Stockton St Chad 76-83; V Lanchester from 83; P-in-c Holmside from 03; AD Lanchester 90-99; Hon Can Dur Cathl from 03. *The Vicarage, 1 Lee Hill Court, Lanchester, Durham DH7 0QE* Tel (01207) 521170

WATERMAN, Canon Albert Thomas. b 33. Roch Th Coll 61. **d** 64 **p** 65. C Dartford St Alb *Roch* 64-67; V Ilkeston St Jo *Derby* 67-75; V Mackworth St Fran 75-79; V Dartford St Alb *Roch* 79-98; RD Dartford 84-97; Hon Can Roch Cathl 96-98; rtd 98. *19 Beachfield Road, Bembridge PO35 5TN* Tel (01983) 874286

WATERMAN, Mrs Jacqueline Mahalah. b 45. ALCM71. Cant Sch of Min 82. **dss** 85 **d** 87 **p** 94. Wavertree H Trin *Liv* 85-90; Par Dn 87-90; Par Dn Anfield St Columba 90-94; C 94; TV Speke St Aid 94-97; P-in-c Walton St Jo 97-99; V 99-01; C Baildon *Bradf* 01-05; rtd 05. *5 Lansdowne Close, Baildon, Shipley BD17 7LA* Tel (01274) 468556

WATERS (née MUNRO-SMITH), Alison Jean. b 73. Regent's Park Coll Ox MA94. Wycliffe Hall Ox 02. **d** 04 **p** 05. C Lostwithiel, St Winnow w St Nectan's Chpl etc *Truro* 04-08; C Shepperton and Littleton *Lon* from 08. *Littleton Rectory, Squires Bridge Road, Shepperton TW17 0QE* Tel (01932) 562249
E-mail alisonmunrosmith@hotmail.com

WATERS, Arthur Brian. b 34. St Deiniol's Hawarden 71. **d** 73 **p** 74. C Bedwellty *Mon* 73-76; P-in-c Newport All SS 76-81; V Mynyddislwyn 81-91; C-in-c Maesglas Newport CD 91-95; V Maesglas and Duffryn 95-99; rtd 99. *3B Blaen-y-Pant Crescent, Blaen-y-Pant, Newport NP20 5QB* Tel (01633) 855805

WATERS, Brenda Mary. b 51. Bp Otter Coll. **d** 99. NSM Whyke w Rumboldswhyke and Portfield *Chich* 99-04; NSM Chich Cathl from 05; Chapl St Wilfrid's Hospice Chich from 01. *69 Chatsworth Road, Chichester PO19 7YA* Tel (01243) 839415
E-mail brenda.waters@stwh.co.uk

WATERS, Mrs Carolyn Anne. b 52. St Jo Coll Nottm BA02. **d** 00 **p** 01. NSM Frodsham *Ches* 00-02; C Penhill *Bris* 02-06; P-in-c Stopham and Fittleworth *Chich* from 06. *The Rectory, Church Lane, Fittleworth, Pulborough RH20 1HL* Tel (01798) 865455 Mobile 07789-430317 E-mail caswaters@dsl.pipex.com

WATERS, Geoffrey. b 44. UMIST BSc85 St Hild Coll Dur PGCE86 Trin Coll Bris BA99. WMMTC 06. **d** 08 **p** 09. NSM Northampton St Giles *Pet* from 08. *26 The Vale, Northampton NN1 4ST* Tel (01604) 792289 E-mail geoffreyjwaters@aol.com

WATERS, Miss Jill Christine. b 43. CertEd64. Cranmer Hall Dur 82. **dss** 82 **d** 87 **p** 94. New Milverton *Cov* 82-86; Draycott-le-Moors w Forsbrook *Lich* 86-96; Par Dn 87-94; C 94-96; P-in-c Mow Cop from 96. *The Vicarage, 5 Congleton Road, Mow Cop, Stoke-on-Trent ST7 3PJ* Tel (01782) 515077

WATERS, John Michael. b 30. Qu Coll Cam BA53 MA58. Ridley Hall Cam 53. **d** 55 **p** 56. C Southport Ch Ch *Liv* 55-57; C Farnworth 57-62; V Blackb H Trin 63-70; Sec Birm Coun Chr Chs 70-77; Chapl Birm Cathl 70-74; Dioc Ecum Officer 74-77; V Hednesford *Lich* 77-93; RD Rugeley 78-88; rtd 93; P-in-c Etton w Dalton Holme *York* 93-99; Perm to Offic from 99. *Blacksmith's Cottage, Middlewood Lane, Fylingthorpe, Whitby YO22 4UB* Tel (01947) 880422

WATERS, Mark. b 52. Southn Univ BTh85. Sarum & Wells Th Coll 79. **d** 82 **p** 83. C Clifton All SS w St Jo *Bris* 82-85; P-in-c Brislington St Anne 85-91; Dioc Soc Resp Officer *Sheff* 91-94; Community Org Citizen Organisation Foundn 94-00; NSM Rotherham 94-97; Hon C Gt Crosby St Faith and Waterloo Park St Mary *Liv* 97-00; NSM 05-09; TV Kirkby 00-04; Project Development Manager Ch Action on Poverty 04-05; Progr Manager Participation for Change from 05; NSM Toxteth Park Ch Ch and St Mich w St Andr *Liv* from 09. *30 Victoria Road West, Crosby, Liverpool L23 8UQ* Tel 0151-931 1031
E-mail markwaters@blueyonder.co.uk

WATERS, Stephen. b 49. Chich Th Coll 83. **d** 85 **p** 86. C Baildon *Bradf* 85-87; C Altrincham St Geo *Ches* 87-89; TV Ellesmere Port 89-91; P-in-c Crewe St Jo 91-93; V Mossley 93-98; TV Congleton 98-99; P-in-c Alvanley 99-02; V Penhill *Bris* 02-05; rtd 05. *The Rectory, Church Lane, Fittleworth, Pulborough RH20 1HL* Tel (01798) 865455 Mobile 07796-694139
E-mail stephen@soulfriend.org.uk

WATERS, William Paul. b 52. Aston Tr Scheme 84 Chich Th Coll 86. **d** 88 **p** 89. C Tottenham St Paul *Lon* 88-91; C Stroud Green H Trin 91-95; TV Wickford and Runwell *Chelmsf* 95-98; Chapl Runwell Hosp Wickford 95-98; Chapl Qu Medical Cen Nottm Univ Hosp NHS Trust from 98. *Queen's Medical Centre University Hospital, Derby Road, Nottingham NG7 2UH* Tel 0115-924 9924 ext 43799 *or* 917 4412 Mobile 07711-721483
E-mail paul.waters@nottshc.nhs.uk

WATERSON, Graham Peter. b 50. **d** 07 **p** 08. OLM Astley Bridge *Man* from 07. *702 Crompton Way, Bolton BL1 8TJ* Tel (01204) 419160 Mobile 07747-757657
E-mail peter.waterson@ntlworld.com

WATERSTONE, Albert Thomas. b 23. TCD BA45 BD67. CITC 46. **d** 46 **p** 47. C Kilkenny St Canice Cathl 46-50; P-in-c Borris-in-Ossory w Aghavoe 50-51; I 52-54; I Fiddown w Kilmacow 54-64; I Tullamore w Lynally and Rahan *M & K* 64-73; I Tullamore w Durrow, Newtownfertullagh, Rahan etc 73-90; Can Meath 81-90; rtd 90. *Lynally House, Mocklagh, Blue Ball, Tullamore, Co Offaly, Republic of Ireland* Tel and fax (00353) (57) 932 1367

WATERSTREET, Canon John Donald. b 34. Trin Hall Cam BA58 MA62. Lich Th Coll 58. **d** 60 **p** 61. C Blackheath *Birm* 60-64; C Aston SS Pet and Paul 64-67; R Sheldon 67-77; RD Coleshill 75-77; V Selly Oak St Mary 77-89; RD Edgbaston 84-89; Hon Can Birm Cathl 86-00; R The Whitacres and Shustoke 89-97; C Acocks Green 97-00; rtd 00; Perm to Offic *Birm* from 00. *547 Fox Hollies Road, Hall Green, Birmingham B28 8RL* Tel 0121-702 2080

WATERTON, Dawn. b 46. WMMTC 95. **d** 98 **p** 99. NSM Nuneaton St Nic *Cov* 98-07; NSM Chilvers Coton w Astley from 07. *65 Main Street, Higham on the Hill, Nuneaton CV13 6AH* Tel (01455) 212861

WATES, John Norman. b 43. JP82. BNC Ox MA65 Solicitor 72 FRSA00. **d** 02 **p** 03. OLM Chipstead *S'wark* from 02. *Elmore, High Road, Chipstead, Coulsdon CR5 3SB* Tel (01737) 557550 Fax 552918 E-mail john.wates@btinternet.com

WATHAN, Geraint David. b 75. Univ of Wales (Abth) BTh01. St Mich Coll Llan. **d** 07 **p** 08. C Oystermouth *S & B* 07-09; C Sketty from 09. *19 Coedsaeson Crescent, Sketty, Swansea SA2 9DG* Tel (01792) 298342 Mobile 07789-254165
E-mail g_wathan@hotmail.com

WATHEN, Mark William Gerard. b 12. TD45. ACIB. K Coll Lon 31. **d** 82 **p** 82. Hon C Broadford *Arg* 82-91; Hon C Fort William 82-91; Hon C Portree 82-96; rtd 96. *Tollgate Cottage, Norwich Road, Marsham, Norwich NR10 5PX* Tel (01263) 732673

WATHERSTON, Peter David. b 42. Lon Univ BSc69 FCA76. Ridley Hall Cam 75. **d** 77 **p** 78. C Barnsbury St Andr *Lon* 77-81; Chapl Mayflower Family Cen Canning Town *Chelmsf* 81-96; Perm to Offic from 96; Dir First Fruit Charity from 97. *264 Plashet Grove, London E6 1DQ* Tel (020) 8548 4676 Fax 8548 4110 Mobile 07913-694678 E-mail pwatherston@aol.com

WATKIN, David Glynne. b 52. Univ of Wales (Lamp) BA74 PhD78 Wolv Univ PGCE87 MTS FRGS. **d** 02 **p** 03. OLM Wolverhampton St Matt *Lich* from 02; Dioc OLM Officer from 06. *3 Alder Dale, Wolverhampton WV3 9JF* Tel (01902) 710842
E-mail d.g.watkin@wlv.ac.uk

WATKIN, David William. b 42. FCA70. Qu Coll Birm 84. **d** 86 **p** 87. C Tunstall *Lich* 86-89; Camberwell Deanery Missr *S'wark* 89-95; V Trent Vale *Lich* 95-01; V Milton from 01. *The Vicarage, Baddeley Green Lane, Stoke-on-Trent ST2 7EY* Tel (01782) 534062

WATKIN, Deborah Gail. b 58. Wolv Univ BEd82. **d** 08 **p** 09. OLM Wolverhampton St Matt *Lich* from 08. *3 Alder Dale, Wolverhampton WV3 9JF* Tel (01902) 710842
E-mail debbie_in_the_classroom@hotmail.co.uk

WATKIN, Paul Stephen George. b 75. Anglia Ruskin Univ BA08. Westcott Ho Cam 06. **d** 08 **p** 09. C Harwich Peninsula *Chelmsf* from 08. *19 Beacon Hill Avenue, Harwich CO12 3NR* Tel (01255) 504322 E-mail psgw100@aol.com

WATKIN, Prof Thomas Glyn. b 52. Pemb Coll Ox BA74 MA77 BCL75 Barrister-at-Law (Middle Temple) 76. Llan Dioc Tr Scheme 89. **d** 92 **p** 94. NSM Roath St Martin *Llan* from 92. *49 Cyncoed Road, Penylan, Cardiff CF23 5SB* Tel (029) 2049 5662

WATKINS, Adrian Raymond. b 57. St Andr Univ MA80. Lon Bible Coll 82. **d** 07 **p** 08. Regional Manager (Asia) CMS from 00; Lic to Offic Amritsar India from 07; Perm to Offic *St E* from 08. *13 Churchill Avenue, Ipswich IP4 5DR* Tel (01473) 434024 Mobile 07958-617665 E-mail adrianrwatkins@aol.com

WATKINS, Mrs Andrea. b 71. ERMC. **d** 08 **p** 09. C Heyford w Stowe Nine Churches and Flore etc *Pet* from 08. *2 Bricketts Lane, Flore, Northampton NN7 4LU* Tel (01327) 340441
E-mail andrealwatkins@hotmail.co.uk

WATKINS, Anthony John. b 42. St D Coll Lamp BA64. St Steph Ho Ox 64. **d** 66 **p** 67. C E Dulwich St Jo *S'wark* 66-71; C Tewkesbury w Walton Cardiff *Glouc* 71-75; Prec and Chapl Choral Ches Cathl 75-81; V Brixworth w Holcot *Pet* from 81. *The Vicarage, Station Road, Brixworth, Northampton NN6 9DF* Tel (01604) 880286

WATKINS, Charles Mark. b 57. Bradf Univ BTech79. Westcott Ho Cam 06. **d** 08 **p** 09. C Almondbury w Farnley Tyas *Wakef* from 08. *61 Longcroft, Huddersfield HD5 8XW* Tel (01484) 541083 Mobile 07751-930968 E-mail waltycm@mac.com

WATKINS, Mrs Christine Dorothy (Sue). b 29. **d** 89 **p** 00. Deacon Port Macquarie Australia 89-95; Chapl Port Macquarie Gen Hosp 89-95; Perm to Offic *Chich* 97-00; NSM Crawley 00-05;

NSM Edin Gd Shep 05-06; Lic to Offic Grafton Australia from 06. *Garden Village, 132 Findlay Avenue, Port Macquarie NSW 2444, Australia*

WATKINS, Christopher. b 43. Sarum & Wells Th Coll 88. **d** 90 **p** 91. C Abergavenny St Mary w Llanwenarth Citra *Mon* 90-94; TV Cwmbran 94-96; TV Wordsley *Worc* 00-09; rtd 09. *287 Malpas Road, Newport NP20 6WA* E-mail chriswat@blueyonder.co.uk

WATKINS, David James Hier. b 39. Trin Coll Carmarthen CertEd60 Univ of Wales DipEd67 BEd76. St Mich Coll Llan. **d** 90 **p** 91. NSM Oysterbmouth *S & B* from 90; Dioc Youth Chapl from 91; Lect Gorseinon Coll from 92. *10 Lambswell Close, Langland, Swansea SA3 4HJ* Tel (01792) 369742

WATKINS (née ROBERTS), Mrs Gwyneth. b 35. Univ of Wales (Swansea) BA MEd. St Mich Coll Llan 90. **d** 91 **p** 97. C Llanbadarn Fawr w Capel Bangor and Goginan *St D* 91-94; P-in-c Maenordeifi and Capel Colman w Llanfihangel etc 94-97; R 97-98; rtd 98. *17 Carlinford, Boscombe Cliff Road, Bournemouth BH5 1JW* Tel (02102) 391076 E-mail gwynethwatkins1@hotmail.com

WATKINS, Mrs Hilary Odette. b 47. New Hall Cam MA73. SAOMC 98. **d** 01 **p** 02. NSM Appleton and Besselsleigh *Ox* 01-04; C Aisholt, Enmore, Goathurst, Nether Stowey etc *B & W* from 04. *The Rectory, Church Road, Spaxton, Bridgwater TA5 1DA* Tel (01278) 671265 E-mail hilary.watkins1@tesco.net

WATKINS, John Graham. b 48. N Lon Poly CQSW74. WEMTC 04. **d** 07 **p** 08. NSM Ledbury *Heref* from 07. *18 Pound Close, Tarrington, Hereford HR1 4AZ* Tel (01432) 890595 E-mail john.watkins@cafcass.gov.uk

WATKINS, Jonathan. b 58. Padgate Coll of Educn BEd79. Trin Coll Bris 90. **d** 92 **p** 93. C Wallington *S'wark* 92-97; C Hartley Wintney, Elvetham, Winchfield etc 97-99; Chapl Win Univ 99-08. *Address temp unknown*

WATKINS, Michael John. b 61. RGN90. Trin Coll Bris 03. **d** 05 **p** 06. C Bath Weston All SS w N Stoke and Langridge *B & W* 05-09; TV Chippenham St Paul w Hardenhuish etc *Bris* from 09; TV Kington St Michael from 09. *1 Hardenhuish Avenue, Chippenham SN15 1NL* Tel (01249) 463402 Mobile 07814-430782 E-mail mikeandsarah@xalt.co.uk

WATKINS, Michael Morris. b 32. MRCS65 LRCP60. St Jo Coll Nottm 77. **d** 81 **p** 81. C Hornchurch St Andr *Chelmsf* 81-84; P-in-c Snitterfield w Bearley *Cov* 84-90; V 90-92; rtd 93; Perm to Offic *Cov* from 93. *Glaslyn, Riverside, Tiddington Road, Stratford-upon-Avon CV37 7BD* Tel (01789) 298085 E-mail michaelwatkins@talktalk.net

WATKINS, Ms Betty Anne. See MOCKFORD, Mrs Betty Anne

WATKINS, Canon Peter. b 51. Oak Hill Th Coll BA. **d** 82 **p** 83. C Whitnash *Cov* 82-86; V Wolston and Church Lawford 86-99; RD Rugby 94-99; V Finham from 99; Hon Can Cov Cathl from 04. *St Martin's Vicarage, 136 Green Lane South, Coventry CV3 6EA* Tel and fax (024) 7641 8330 E-mail st-martins@freeuk.com

WATKINS, Peter Gordon. b 34. St Pet Coll Ox BA57 MA61. Wycliffe Hall Ox 58. **d** 59 **p** 60. C Wolverhampton St Geo *Lich* 59-60; C Burton St Chad 60-61; C Westmr St Jas *Lon* 61-63; USA 63-65; V Ealing Common St Matt *Lon* from 67. *St Matthew's Vicarage, 7 North Common Road, London W5 2QA* Tel (020) 8567 3820 E-mail peterwatkins@amserve.com

WATKINS, Robert Henry. b 30. New Coll Ox BA54 MA60. Westcott Ho Cam 59. **d** 60 **p** 61. C Newc H Cross 60-63; C Morpeth 63-67; V Delaval 67-80; V Lanercost w Kirkcambeck and Walton 80-90; rtd 90; Perm to Offic *Carl* from 90. *Lowpark, Loweswater, Cockermouth CA13 0RU* Tel (01900) 85242

WATKINS, Sue. See WATKINS, Mrs Christine Dorothy

WATKINS, Susan Jane. See HEIGHT, Susan Jane

WATKINS, Canon William Hywel. b 36. St D Coll Lamp BA58. Wycliffe Hall Ox 58. **d** 61 **p** 62. C Llanelli *St D* 61-68; V Llwynhendy 68-78; V Slebech and Uzmaston w Boulston 78-01; RD Daugleddau 87-01; Hon Can St D Cathl 91-93; Can St D Cathl 93-01; rtd 01. *Nant-yr-Arian, Llanbadarn Fawr, Aberystwyth SY23 3SZ* Tel and fax (01970) 623359

WATKINS-JONES, Arthur Basil. b 24. Sarum Th Coll 67. **d** 69 **p** 70. C Broadstone *Sarum* 69-73; P-in-c Winterbourne Stickland and Turnworth etc 73-76; R 76-78; P-in-c Lilliput 78-82; V 82-89; rtd 89; Perm to Offic *Sarum* from 89. *Oak Cottage, 31 Danecourt Road, Poole BH14 0PG* Tel (01202) 746074

WATKINSON, Adam John McNicol. b 68. Keble Coll Ox BA89 MA93 St Martin's Coll Lanc PGCE90. NOC 01. **d** 03 **p** 04. NSM Croston and Bretherton *Blackb* 03-05; Chapl Ormskirk Sch 02-03; Chapl Liv Coll 03-06; Chapl Repton Sch Derby from 06. *4 Boot Hill, Repton, Derby DE65 6FT* Tel (01283) 559284 E-mail ajw@repton.org.uk

WATKINSON, Neil. b 64. Univ Coll Lon BSc86. Oak Hill Th Coll BA04. **d** 04 **p** 05. C Maidenhead St Andr and St Mary *Ox* 04-08; C Singapore St Geo from 08. *St George's Church, Minden Road, Singapore 248816, Republic of Singapore* Tel (0065) 6473 2877 E-mail info@stgeorges.org.sg

WATKINSON, Ronald Frank. b 48. BA. EAMTC. **d** 04 **p** 05. NSM Paston *Pet* from 04. *20 Welbourne, Peterborough PE4 6NH* Tel (01733) 751733 E-mail ronwatkinson@kingdomyouth.freeserve.co.uk

WATKINSON, Stephen Philip. b 75. York Univ BSc96 DPhil03 Edin Univ MSc97. Oak Hill Th Coll BTh09. **d** 09. C Blackb Redeemer from 09. *17 Douglas Close, Blackburn BB2 4FF* Tel 07793-143393 (mobile) E-mail spwatkinson@talktalk.net

WATLING, His Honour Brian. b 35. QC79. K Coll Lon LLB56 Barrister 57. **d** 87 **p** 88. NSM Lavenham *St E* 87-90; NSM Nayland w Wiston 90-03; NSM Boxford, Edwardstone, Groton etc 03-07; Perm to Offic from 07. *5 High Street, Nayland, Colchester CO6 4JE*

WATLING, Sister Rosemary Dawn. b 32. Newnham Coll Cam BA70 MA73. Gilmore Course 70. **dss** 85 **d** 87 **p** 94. CSA 79-90; Paddington St Mary *Lon* 85-86; E Bris 86-87; Hon Par Dn 87; Par Dn Clifton H Trin, St Andr and St Pet 87-94; C 94-95; rtd 95; NSM Wraxall *B & W* 96-02; Perm to Offic 02-08. *20 Gracey Court, Woodland Road, Broadclyst, Exeter EX5 3GA* Tel (01392) 460319

WATSON, Canon Alan. b 34. Lon Univ LLB58. Linc Th Coll 58. **d** 60 **p** 61. C Spring Park *Cant* 60-63; C Sheerness H Trin w St Paul 63-68; R Allington 68-73; P-in-c Maidstone St Pet 73; R Allington and Maidstone St Pet 73-79; Hon Can Cant Cathl 85-99; RD Sutton 86-92; rtd 99; Perm to Offic *B & W* and *Sarum* from 00. *68 Southgate Drive, Wincanton BA9 9ET* Tel (01963) 34368 E-mail alan@watson.orbitalnet.co.uk

WATSON, Alan. b 41. AKC64. St Boniface Warminster. **d** 65 **p** 66. C Hendon St Ignatius *Dur* 65-68; C Sheff St Cecilia Parson Cross 68-70; C Harton Colliery *Dur* 70-72; TV 72-74; R Gorton Our Lady and St Thos *Man* 74-82; TR Swinton St Pet 82-87; TR Swinton and Pendlebury 87-89; R Rawmarsh w Parkgate *Sheff* 89-94; P-in-c Dunscroft St Edwin 96-99; V from 99; CMP from 98. *The Vicarage, 162 Station Road, Dunscroft, Doncaster DN7 4JR* Tel (01302) 841328 E-mail a.watsondunscroft@whsmithnet.co.uk

WATSON, Albert Victor. b 44. Ridley Hall Cam 85. **d** 87 **p** 88. C Hornchurch St Andr *Chelmsf* 87-94; P-in-c Tye Green w Netteswell 94-95; R from 95; RD Harlow 99-04. *The Rectory, Tawneys Road, Harlow CM18 6QR* Tel (01279) 425138 E-mail albert@watson2119.fsworld.co.uk

WATSON, Alfred Keith. b 39. Birm Univ BSc61. Ox Min Course 93. **d** 96 **p** 97. NSM Aylesbury w Bierton and Hulcott *Ox* 96-01; NSM Ludgvan, Marazion, St Hilary and Perranuthnoe *Truro* 01-06; rtd 06. *Studio Cottage, Wesley Square, Mousehole, Penzance TR19 6RU* Tel (01736) 732906 Mobile 07963-434697

✠**WATSON, The Rt Revd Andrew John.** b 61. CCC Cam BA82 MA90. Ridley Hall Cam 84. **d** 87 **p** 88 **c** 08. C Ipsley *Worc* 87-91; C Notting Hill St Jo and St Pet *Lon* 91-96; V E Twickenham St Steph 96-08; AD Hampton 03-08; Suff Bp Aston *Birm* from 08. *Bishop's Lodge, 16 Coleshill Street, Sutton Coldfield B72 1SH* Tel 0121-427 5141 *or* 354 6632 Fax 428 1114 E-mail bishopofaston@birmingham.anglican.org

WATSON, Andrew Murray. b 57. St Jo Coll Nottm BA07. **d** 07 **p** 09. C Kennington St Jo w St Jas *S'wark* 07-09; C Sanderstead from 09. *285 Limpsfield Road, South Croydon CR2 9DG* Tel (020) 3252 2045 Mobile 07970-677241 E-mail andrew.email@btopenworld.com

WATSON, Anne-Marie Louise. See RENSHAW, Mrs Anne-Marie Louise

WATSON, Beverly Anne. b 64. K Coll Cam BA86 MA90 Surrey Univ MA08 ALCM83. STETS 05. **d** 08 **p** 09. C Spring Grove St Mary *Lon* 08; C Aston and Nechells *Birm* from 08. *Bishop's Lodge, 16 Coleshill Street, Sutton Coldfield B72 1SH* Tel 0121-355 3365 Mobile 07895-197940 E-mail beverly@watsons.myzen.co.uk

WATSON, Craig. b 60. Bath Univ BSc82 CertEd82 York St Jo Coll MA04. NOC 00. **d** 03 **p** 04. NSM Thorpe Edge *Bradf* 03-04; NSM Halliwell St Pet *Man* from 04. *39 New Church Road, Bolton BL1 5QQ* Tel (01204) 457559 E-mail craig@stpetersparish.info

WATSON, David. See WATSON, Canon Leonard Alexander David

WATSON, The Very Revd Derek Richard. b 38. Selw Coll Cam BA61 MA65. Cuddesdon Coll 62. **d** 64 **p** 65. C New Eltham All SS *S'wark* 64-66; Chapl Ch Coll Cam 66-70; Bp's Dom Chapl *S'wark* 70-73; V Surbiton St Mark 73-77; V Surbiton St Andr and St Mark 77-78; Can Res and Treas S'wark Cathl 78-82; Dioc Dir of Ords 78-82; P-in-c Chelsea St Luke *Lon* 82-85; R 85-87; P-in-c Chelsea Ch Ch 86-87; R Chelsea St Luke and Ch Ch 87-96; AD Chelsea 94-96; Dean Sarum 96-02; rtd 02. *29 The Precincts, Canterbury CT1 2EP* Tel (01227) 865238

WATSON, Derek Stanley. b 54. NEOC 92. **d** 95 **p** 96. C W Acklam *York* 95-98; C-in-c Ingleby Barwick CD 98-00; V Ingleby Barwick 00-06; V Middlesbrough St Martin w St Cuth from 06. *St Martin's Vicarage, Kirby Avenue, Middlesbrough TS5 4LA* Tel (01642) 814999 E-mail derek@watson1954.freeserve.co.uk

WATSON, Mrs Diane Elsie. b 44. NOC 92. **d** 95 **p** 96. C Grange St Andr *Ches* 95-00; C Runcorn H Trin 96-00; R Thurstaston 00-07; rtd 07; C Oxton *Ches* from 08. *32 School Lane, Prenton CH43 7RQ* Tel 0151-652 4288
E-mail de.watson@btinternet.com

WATSON, Mrs Elsada Beatrice (Elsie). b 30. WMMTC. **d** 89 **p** 94. NSM Birm St Pet 89-90; NSM Lozells St Paul and St Silas 90-93; Par Dn 93-94; C 94-96; Perm to Offic from 96; rtd 96. *4 Maidstone Road, Birmingham B20 3EH* Tel 0121-356 0626

WATSON, Geoffrey. b 48. Liv Univ BEd71. Linc Th Coll 81. **d** 83 **p** 84. C Hartlepool St Luke *Dur* 83-87; P-in-c Shadforth 87-94; Soc Resp Officer 87-94; Dioc Rural Development Adv 90-94; V Staveley, Ings and Kentmere *Carl* from 94. *The Vicarage, Kentmere Road, Staveley, Kendal LA8 9PA* Tel (01539) 821267
E-mail geof_watson@lineone.net

WATSON, Mrs Gillian Edith. b 49. Cov Coll of Educn CertEd70. LCTP 06. **d** 09. NSM Standish *Blackb* from 09. *89 Whitehall Avenue, Appley Bridge, Wigan WN6 9JY* Tel (01257) 251326
E-mail gillian.e.watson@gmail.com

WATSON, Gordon Mark Stewart. b 67. Wolv Poly BA90 DipEd. CITC BTh95. **d** 95 **p** 96. C Ballymoney w Finvoy and Rasharkin *Conn* 95-98; I Brackaville w Donaghendry and Ballyclog *Arm* 98-01; I Killesher *K, E & A* 01-06; I Trory w Killadeas *Clogh* from 06. *Trory Rectory, Rossfad, Ballinamallard, Enniskillen BT94 2LS* Tel and fax (028) 6638 8477 Mobile 07710-924460
E-mail trory@clogher.anglican.org

WATSON, Graeme Campbell Hubert. b 35. Ch Ch Ox BA58 BA59 MA61. Coll of Resurr Mirfield 59. **d** 61 **p** 62. C Edin St Mary 61-63; C Carrington *S'well* 63-67; Tanzania 67-77; Tutor St Cyprian's Coll Ngala 67-69; Vice-Prin St Mark's Th Coll Dar es Salaam 69-73; P-in-c Dar es Salaam St Alb 74-77; P-in-c Kingston St Mary w Broomfield *B & W* 77-80; V 80-81; R Kingston St Mary w Broomfield etc 81-95; P-in-c Feock *Truro* 95-00; Tutor SWMTC 95-00; rtd 00; Perm to Offic *Truro* 00-02 and *Lon* from 02. *75 Winston Road, London N16 9LN* Tel (020) 7249 8701 E-mail gchwatson@blueyonder.co.uk

WATSON, Hartley Roger. b 40. Lon Univ BD91 MTh94. K Coll Lon. **d** 64 **p** 65. C Noel Park St Mark *Lon* 64-67; C Munster Square St Mary Magd 67-68; C Stamford Hill St Jo 68-70; Chapl RAF 70-76; R St Breoke *Truro* 76-84; P-in-c Egloshayle 82-84; R Wittering w Thornhaugh and Wansford *Pet* 84-00; RD Barnack 98-00; R Brigstock w Stanion and Lowick and Sudborough 00-07; rtd 07; Chapl Beauchamp Community from 07. *The Chaplain's House, Newland, Malvern WR13 5AX* Tel (01684) 891529 *or* 562100

WATSON, Henry Stanley. b 36. **d** 72 **p** 74. NSM Bethnal Green St Jas Less *Lon* 72-83 and 89-93; NSM Old Ford St Paul w St Steph and St Mark 83-88; NSM Scarborough St Mary w Ch Ch and H Apostles *York* 93-97; P-in-c Seamer 97-03; rtd 03; Hon C Fauls *Lich* 03-08. *14 Oakfield Park, Much Wenlock TF13 6HJ* Tel (01952) 728794

WATSON, The Ven Ian Leslie Stewart. b 50. Wycliffe Hall Ox 79. **d** 81 **p** 82. C Plymouth St Andr w St Paul and St Geo *Ex* 81-85; TV Ipsley *Worc* 85-90; V Woodley St Jo the Ev *Ox* 90-92; TR Woodley 92-95; Chapl Amsterdam w Den Helder and Heiloo *Eur* 95-01; Chief Exec ICS 01-07; Can Gib Cathl 02-07; Adn Cov from 07. *9 Armorial Road, Coventry CV3 6GH* Tel (024) 7641 7750 *or* 7652 1337 Mobile 07714-214790
E-mail ian.watson@covcofe.org *or* bootsandden@hotmail.com

WATSON, James Valentine John Giles. b 65. Newc Univ BA87 Ox Univ BA91 MA97. Ripon Coll Cuddesdon 89. **d** 92 **p** 93. C Newc St Geo 92-95; TV Daventry, Ashby St Ledgers, Braunston etc *Pet* 95-00; V Woodplumpton *Blackb* 00-03; TR Wheatley *Ox* from 03. *The Vicarage, 18 London Road, Wheatley, Oxford OX33 1YA* Tel (01865) 872224
E-mail james@jvrswatson.freeserve.co.uk

WATSON, The Ven Jeffrey John Seagrief. b 39. Em Coll Cam BA61 MA65. Clifton Th Coll 62. **d** 65 **p** 66. C Beckenham Ch Ch *Roch* 65-69; C Southsea St Jude *Portsm* 69-71; V Win Ch Ch 71-81; V Bitterne 81-93; RD Southampton 83-93; Hon Can Win Cathl 91-93; Adn Ely 93-04; Hon Can Ely Cathl 93-04; rtd 04; Perm to Offic *Win* from 04. *7 Ferry Road, Hythe, Southampton SO45 5GB* Tel (023) 8084 1189

WATSON, John. b 34. AKC59. **d** 60 **p** 61. C Stockton St Pet *Dur* 60-64; C Darlington H Trin 64-66; V Swalwell 66-68; Perm to Offic *Dur* 68-69; *Leic* 69-74; *Man* 74-76; rtd 96. *The Flat, 194 Abington Avenue, Northampton NN1 4QA* Tel (01604) 624300
E-mail john.moirawatson@btopenworld.com

WATSON, John Calum. b 69. Spurgeon's Coll BD96. Trin Coll Bris MA03. **d** 03 **p** 04. C Richmond H Trin and Ch Ch *S'wark* 03-06; TV Deptford St Jo w H Trin and Ascension 06-08; V Tupsley w Hampton Bishop *Heref* from 08. *The Vicarage, 107 Church Road, Hereford HR1 1RT* Tel (01432) 379110
E-mail john@allyu.org.uk

WATSON, Preb John Francis Wentworth. b 28. St Jo Coll Nottm LTh59. **d** 59 **p** 60. C Egham *Guildf* 59-62; C-in-c Ewell St Paul Howell Hill CD 62-66; R Ashtead 66-72; V Plymouth St Andr w St Paul and St Geo *Ex* 72-94; Angl Adv TV SW 83-93; Westcountry TV 93-94; Preb Ex Cathl 84-94; rtd 94; Perm to

Offic *Ex* from 97. *Woodland House, Western Road, Ivybridge PL21 9AL* Tel (01752) 893735

WATSON, John Lionel. b 39. G&C Coll Cam BA61 MA65. Ridley Hall Cam 62. **d** 64 **p** 65. C Toxteth Park St Philemon w St Silas *Liv* 64-69; C Morden *S'wark* 69-73; C Cambridge St Phil *Ely* 73-74; Chapl Elstree Sch Woolhampton 74-77; R Woolhampton w Midgham *Ox* 77-81; R Woolhampton w Midgham and Beenham Valance 81-95; Perm to Offic *Win* from 97; rtd 00. *Westfield House, Littleton Road, Crawley, Winchester SO21 2QD* Tel (01962) 776892

WATSON, John Robertson Thomas. b 27. CITC 68. **d** 70 **p** 71. C Belfast St Steph *Conn* 71-73; Bp's C Swanlinbar w Templeport *K, E & A* 73-82; I Arvagh w Carrigallen, Gowna and Columbkille 82-97; Preb Kilmore Cathl 88-97; rtd 97. *75 Church Road, Dundonald, Belfast BT16 2LW* Tel (028) 9048 2520

WATSON, Jonathan Ramsay George. b 38. Oriel Coll Ox BA61 MA65 DipEd62. Ridley Hall Cam 88. **d** 90 **p** 91. C Locks Heath *Portsm* 90-94; V Erith St Paul *Roch* 94-01; rtd 01; Perm to Offic *Chich* from 01. *14 Park Crescent, Midhurst GU29 9ED* Tel (01730) 816145 E-mail jrgwatson@netscapeonline.co.uk

WATSON, Julie Sandra. b 59. Liv Poly BSc81 Teesside Poly PhD86. NEOC 99. **d** 02 **p** 03. NSM Redcar *York* from 02; Dean Self-Supporting Min from 09. *20 Talisker Gardens, Redcar TS10 2TG* Tel (01642) 478147 E-mail j.s.watson@tees.ac.uk

WATSON, Keith. *See* WATSON, Alfred Keith

WATSON, Kenneth Roy. b 27. CEng68 MIMechE68. EMMTC 83. **d** 86 **p** 87. NSM Ashby-de-la-Zouch St Helen w Coleorton *Leic* 86-90; R Breedon cum Isley Walton and Worthington 90-93; rtd 93; Perm to Offic *Leic* and *Derby* from 93. *9 Thornley Place, Ashbourne DE6 1PQ* Tel (01335) 343929

WATSON, Laurence Leslie. b 31. Keble Coll Ox BA55 MA59. Ely Th Coll. **d** 57 **p** 58. C Solihull *Birm* 57-60; C Digswell *St Alb* 60-62; V Smethwick St Steph *Birm* 62-67; V Billesley Common 67-95; rtd 95; Perm to Offic *Cov* and *Birm* from 95. *10 Redwing Close, Bishopton, Stratford-upon-Avon CV37 9EX* Tel (01789) 294569

WATSON, Canon Leonard Alexander David. b 37. Man Univ BSc59. Coll of Resurr Mirfield 62. **d** 64 **p** 65. C Rawmarsh w Parkgate *Sheff* 64-68; C Empangeni S Africa 69-74; TV E Runcorn w Halton *Ches* 74-79; TV Sanderstead All SS *S'wark* 79-86; TR Selsdon St Jo w St Fran 86-98; RD Croydon Addington 90-95; P-in-c Horne and Outwood 98-02; Hon Can S'wark Cathl 02-03; rtd 02; Perm to Offic *Win* from 03. *White Gables, Station Road, East Tisted, Alton GU34 3QX* Tel (01420) 588317 E-mail dadiwatson@hotmail.com

WATSON, Louise Margaret. *See* TAYLOR-KENYON, Louise Margaret

WATSON, Mark. *See* WATSON, Gordon Mark Stewart

WATSON, Mark Edward. b 68. St Jo Coll Nottm. **d** 09. C Higher Bebington *Ches* from 09. *3 Beech Road, Bebington, Wirral CH63 8PE*

WATSON, Michael Paul. b 58. Trin Coll Bris 91. **d** 93 **p** 94. C Derby St Alkmund and St Werburgh 93-99; USA from 00; Lt Rock St Andr 00-01; R Bridge Community Austin from 01. *10636 Floral Park Drive, Austin TX 78759-5104, USA* Tel (001) (512) 527 8823 E-mail mike.bridgepoint@worldnet.att.net

WATSON, Nicholas Edgar. b 67. St Cath Coll Cam BA88 MA92. Wycliffe Hall Ox BA91. **d** 92 **p** 93. C Benfieldside *Dur* 92-95; C-in-c Stockton Green Vale H Trin CD 95-96; P-in-c Stockton H Trin 96-00; Chapl Ian Ramsey Sch Stockton 95-00; P-in-c Breadsall and Warden of Readers *Derby* 00-09; TR Wednesfield *Lich* from 09. *The Rectory, 9 Vicarage Road, Wednesfield, Wolverhampton WV11 1SB* Tel (01902) 731462
E-mail newatson@btopenworld.com

WATSON, Prof Paul Frederick. b 44. MRCVS69 RVC(Lon) BSc66 BVetMed69 Sydney Univ PhD73 Lon Univ DSc95. Oak Hill NSM Course 86. **d** 88 **p** 89. NSM Muswell Hill St Jas w St Matt *Lon* 88-96; NSM Edmonton St Aldhelm 96-01; Perm to Offic *Lon* and *St Alb* from 01. *50 New Road, Ware SG12 7BY* Tel (01920) 466941 E-mail pwatson@rvc.ac.uk

WATSON, Paul Robert. b 66. St Andr Univ MA89 Glas Univ BD95 MTh00. **d** 00 **p** 01. C Glas St Ninian 00-04; R Bieldside *Ab* from 09. *The Rectory, Baillieswells Road, Bieldside, Aberdeen AB15 9AP*

WATSON, Paul William. b 55. Huddersfield Poly BA. St Jo Coll Nottm. **d** 86 **p** 87. C Meltham Mills *Wakef* 86-89; C Meltham 89-90; TV Borehamwood *St Alb* 90-96; V Oswaldtwistle Immanuel and All SS *Blackb* 96-08; rtd 08. *214 Union Road, Oswaldtwistle, Accrington BB5 3EG* Tel (01254) 381441

WATSON, Peter David. b 69. St Andr Univ MA92 Westmr Coll Ox PGCE93. Cranmer Hall Dur 04. **d** 06 **p** 07. C Boston Spa *York* from 06; C Thorp Arch w Walton from 06. *The Vicarage, Church Causeway, Thorp Arch, Wetherby LS23 7AE* Tel (01937) 842430 E-mail petercharlotte@pwatson14.freeserve.co.uk

WATSON, Philip. b 60. RGN83. Qu Coll Birm 86. **d** 89 **p** 90. C Ordsall *S'well* 89-93; TV Benwell *Newc* 93-99; V Stocking Farm *Leic* from 99. *St Luke's Vicarage, 97 Halifax Drive, Leicester LE4 2DR* Tel 0116-235 3206 E-mail frpwatson@aol.com

WATSON, Richard Francis. b 40. Yorks Min Course 08. **d** 09. NSM Ilkley All SS *Bradf* from 09. *23 St Helen's Way, Ilkley LS29 8NP* Tel (01943) 430108

WATSON, Richard Frederick. b 66. Avery Hill Coll BA87. Trin Coll Bris 91. **d** 93 **p** 94. C Kempston Transfiguration *St Alb* 93-97; TV Dunstable 97-03; R E Barnet from 03; RD Barnet from 05. *The Rectory, 136 Church Hill Road, Barnet EN4 8XD* Tel (020) 8368 3840 *or* 8361 7524
E-mail rf.watson@btopenworld.com

WATSON, Richard Rydill. b 47. Sarum & Wells Th Coll 74. **d** 77 **p** 78. C Cayton w Eastfield *York* 77-80; C Howden 80-82; P-in-c Burton Pidsea and Humbleton w Elsternwick 82-83; V Dormanstown 83-87; V Cotehill and Cumwhinton *Carl* 87-89; Chapl Harrogate Distr and Gen Hosp 89-94; Chapl Harrogate Health Care NHS Trust 94-99; Asst Chapl Oldham NHS Trust 99-02; Asst Chapl Pennine Acute Hosps NHS Trust 02-07; Chapl from 07; P-in-c Shaw *Man* 99-07. *North Manchester General Hospital, Delaunays Road, Manchester M8 6RB* Tel 0161-795 4567

WATSON, Robert Bewley. b 34. Bris Univ BA59. Clifton Th Coll 56. **d** 61 **p** 62. C Bebington *Ches* 61-65; C Woking St Jo *Guildf* 65-68; V Knaphill 68-98; rtd 98; Perm to Offic *Guildf* from 98. *Endrise, 1 Wychelm Road, Lightwater GU18 5RT* Tel (01276) 453822

WATSON, Roger. *See* WATSON, Hartley Roger

WATSON, The Ven Sheila Anne. b 53. St Andr Univ MA75 MPhil80. Edin Th Coll 79. **dss** 79 **d** 87 **p** 94. Bridge of Allan *St And* 79-80; Alloa 79-80; Monkseaton St Mary *Newc* 80-84; Adult Educn Officer *Lon* 84-87; Hon C Chelsea St Luke and Ch Ch 87-96; Selection Sec ABM 92-93; Sen Selection Sec 93-96; Adv on CME *Sarum* 97-02; Dir of Min 98-02; Can and Preb Sarum Cathl 00-02; Adn Buckingham *Ox* 02-07; Adn Cant and Can Res Cant Cathl from 07. *29 The Precincts, Canterbury CT1 2EP* Tel (01227) 865238
E-mail archdeacon@canterbury-cathedral.org

WATSON, Stephanie Abigail. *See* MOYES, Mrs Stephanie Abigail

WATSON, Canon Timothy Patrick. b 38. ALCD66. **d** 66 **p** 67. C Northwood Em *Lon* 66-70; TV High Wycombe *Ox* 70-76; Gen Sec ICS 76-82; R Bath Weston All SS w N Stoke *B & W* 82-93; R Bath Weston All SS w N Stoke and Langridge 93-94; TR Cheltenham St Mary, St Matt, St Paul and H Trin *Glouc* 94-03; rtd 03; Perm to Offic *Glouc* from 04; Can Kitgum from 05. *The Gateways, Farm Lane, Leckhampton, Cheltenham GL53 0NN* Tel (01242) 514298 E-mail suejwatson@chelters.fsnet.co.uk

WATSON, William. b 36. Ripon Hall Ox 64. **d** 66 **p** 67. C Leamington Priors H Trin *Cov* 66-69; V Salford Priors 69-74; V Malin Bridge *Sheff* 74-79; Chapl Shrewsbury R Hosps 79-89; Chapl R Hallamshire Hosp Sheff 89-92; Chapl Cen Sheff Univ Hosps NHS Trust 92-93; P-in-c Alveley and Quatt *Heref* 93-96; Chapl N Gen Hosp NHS Trust Sheff 96-01; Chapl Weston Park Hosp Sheff 96-99; Chapl Cen Sheff Univ Hosps NHS Trust 99-01; rtd 96; Perm to Offic *Sheff* 01-07. *101 Larkfield Lane, Southport PR9 8NP* Tel (01704) 226055

WATSON, William Henry Dunbar. b 31. Univ of W Ontario BA60. **d** 58 **p** 60. C Westmr St Jas *Lon* 58-60; Canada 60-04; Asst Chapl and Prec Gibraltar Cathl 04-04. *The Port Chaplain's Flat, Mission to Seafarers, North Mole, Gibraltar* Tel (00350) 200 41799 E-mail anglicangib@gibtelecom.net

WATSON, Lysander Rowan. b 26. TCD BA47 MA50 Clare Coll Cam MA52 St Pet Hall Ox MA57. **d** 49 **p** 50. C Chapelizod and Kilmainham *D & G* 49-51; Tutor Ridley Hall Cam 51-55; Chapl 55-57; Chapl St Pet Coll Ox 57-93; Fell and Tutor 59-93; Sen Tutor 77-81; Vice Master 83-85; Lect Th Ox Univ 60-93; rtd 93. *Llandaff Barn, 11 Thames Street, Eynsham, Witney OX29 4HF* Tel (01865) 464198 E-mail lysander.watson@spc.ox.ac.uk

WATSON WILLIAMS, Richard Hamilton Patrick. b 31. SS Coll Cam BA57 MA62. St Aug Coll Cant. **d** 59 **p** 60. C Dorking St Paul *Guildf* 59-63; C Portsea St Mary *Portsm* 63-66; V Culgaith *Carl* 66-71; V Kirkland 66-71; V Wigton 72-79; Warden Dioc Conf Ho Crawshawbooth *Man* 79-82; P-in-c Crawshawbooth 79-82; Master Lady Kath Leveson Hosp 82-98; P-in-c Temple Balsall *Birm* 82-84; V Temple Balsall 84-98; rtd 98; Perm to Offic *Glouc* from 98. *16 Barton Mews, Barton Road, Tewkesbury GL20 5RP* Tel (01684) 290509

WATT, The Very Revd Alfred Ian. b 34. FRSA95. Edin Th Coll 57. **d** 60 **p** 61. Chapl St Paul's Cathl Dundee 60-63; Prec 63-66; P-in-c Dundee H Cross 64-66; R Arbroath 66-69; R Perth St Ninian *St And* 69-82; Provost St Ninian's Cathl Perth 69-82; Can St Ninian's Cathl Perth 82-98; R Kinross 82-95; Dean St Andr 89-98; rtd 98. *33 Stirling Road, Milnathort, Kinross KY13 9XS* Tel and fax (01577) 865711
E-mail alfred@alfredwatt4.orangehome.co.uk

WATT-WYNESS, Gordon. b 25. St Jo Coll Dur 70. **d** 72 **p** 73. C Scarborough St Mary w Ch Ch, St Paul and St Thos *York* 72-76; R Rossington *Sheff* 76-90; rtd 90; Perm to Offic *York* from 90. *15 Newton Court, Crescent Road, Filey YO14 9LL* Tel (01723) 516608

WATTERS, Mrs Kay. b 44. SAOMC 98. **d** 01 **p** 02. OLM Prestwood and Gt Hampden *Ox* 01-07; Chapl to Bp Buckingham 04-07; rtd 07; Perm to Offic *Ox* and Cyprus and the Gulf from 07. *44 Akamantos, 8700 Drouseia, Paphos, Cyprus* Tel (00357) (26) 332128 E-mail kay_watters@hotmail.com

WATTERSON, Mrs Susan Mary. b 50. S & M Dioc Inst 84. **d** 87 **p** 94. NSM Rushen *S & M* 87-89; Hon Par Dn Castletown 89-94; C 94-96; Dioc Youth Officer 87-91; Bp's Adv for Healing Min 91-94; Asst Chapl Bris Univ 96-99; Hon C Bris St Mich and St Paul 96-99; Project Leader Galway Chr Tr Inst 99-00; I Youghal Union *C, C & R* 00-03; Dir Ch's Min of Healing 03-07; P-in-c Killarney w Aghadoe and Muckross *L & K* from 07. *The Rectory, Rookery Road, Ballycasheen, Killarney, Co Kerry, Republic of Ireland* Tel (00353) (64) 31832

WATTLEY, Jeffery Richard. b 57. Univ of Wales (Abth) BSc(Econ)79. Trin Coll Bris BA92. **d** 92 **p** 93. C Reading Greyfriars *Ox* 92-96; V Wonersh *Guildf* 96-98; V Wonersh w Blackheath 98-06; V Egham from 06. *Mauley Cottage, 13 Manorcrofts Road, Egham TW20 9LU* Tel (01784) 432066 E-mail jeff@stjohnsegham.com

WATTS, Mrs Aline Patricia. b 57. St Jo Coll Nottm 02. **d** 04 **p** 05. C Lache cum Saltney *Ches* 04-08; P-in-c Leasowe from 08. *St Chad's Vicarage, 70 Castleway North, Wirral CH46 1RW* Tel 0151-677 6889 E-mail alinewatts@tiscali.co.uk

WATTS, Canon Anthony George. b 46. K Coll Lon BD69 AKC69 Lon Univ CertEd70. Sarum & Wells Th Coll 82. **d** 84 **p** 85. C Wimborne Minster and Holt *Sarum* 84-87; P-in-c Shilling Okeford 87-92; Chapl Croft Ho Sch Shillingstone 87-92; R W Parley *Sarum* 92-00; RD Wimborne 98-00; TR Cley Hill Warminster 00-06; Can and Preb Sarum Cathl 00-06; rtd 06; Chapl Warminster Sch from 07. *12 Freesia Close, Warminster BA12 7RL* Tel (01985) 847302 E-mail tandgwatts@aol.com

WATTS, Anthony John. b 30. AKC59. **d** 60 **p** 61. C Whitburn *Dur* 60-63; C Croxdale 63-65; V Warrington St Pet *Liv* 65-70; V Peel *Man* 70-78; P-in-c Bury St Mark 78-81; V Davyhulme Ch Ch 81-99; Chapl Trafford Gen Hosp 89-94; Chapl Trafford Healthcare NHS Trust 94-98; rtd 99; Perm to Offic *Ches* from 00. *11 Brackenfield Way, Winsford CW7 2UX* Tel (01606) 590803

WATTS, Daniel John. b 70. Wycliffe Hall Ox 04. **d** 06 **p** 07. C Paddock Wood *Roch* 06-09; C Harrogate St Mark *Ripon* from 09. *20 Stone Rings Lane, Harrogate HG2 9HY* Tel 07977-126438 (mobile) E-mail daniel.watts11@btinternet.com

WATTS, David Henry. b 27. Ex Coll Ox BA50 MA55. Wells Th Coll 51. **d** 53 **p** 54. C Haslemere *Guildf* 53-55; C Chelmsf Cathl 55-58; Succ Chelmsf Cathl 55-58; V Chessington *Guildf* 58-62; Educn Officer Essex Educn Cttee 62-70; HMI of Schs 70-87; Hon C Wetherby *Ripon* 79-87; P-in-c Healaugh w Wighill, Bilbrough and Askham Richard *York* 87-89; Chapl HM Pris Askham Grange 87-96; rtd 89; Perm to Offic *York* from 98. *24 Grove Road, Boston Spa, Wetherby LS23 6AP* Tel (01937) 842317

WATTS, Canon Frank Walter. b 30. St Boniface Warminster 53 K Coll Lon AKC54. **d** 54 **p** 55. C Llandough w Leckwith 54-56; C Llanishen and Lisvane 56-59; C Gt Marlow *Ox* 59-60; R Black Bourton 60-63; V Carterton 60-63; C-in-c Brize Norton 61-63; V Brize Norton and Carterton 63-69; Australia from 69; Hon Can Perth from 78; rtd 95. *Villa 5, 178-180 Fern Road, Wilson WA 6107, Australia* Tel and fax (0061) (8) 9258 4532 Mobile 408-094991 E-mail frawawa@southwest.com.au

WATTS, Canon Fraser Norman. b 46. Magd Coll Ox BA68 MA74 K Coll Lon MSc70 PhD75 CPsychol89 FBPsS80. Westcott Ho Cam 88. **d** 90 **p** 91. NSM Harston w Hauxton *Ely* 90-95; P-in-c 95-97; Fell Qu Coll Cam from 94; Lect Cam Univ from 94; Chapl Cam St Edw *Ely* from 95; Hon Can Ely Cathl from 08. *19 Grantchester Road, Cambridge CB3 9ED* Tel (01223) 359223 Fax 763003
E-mail fnw1001@hermes.cam.ac.uk

WATTS, Gordon Sidney Stewart. b 40. CITC 63. **d** 66 **p** 67. C Belfast St Steph *Conn* 66-69; CF 69-94; V Boldre w S Baddesley *Win* 94-96; P-in-c Warmfield *Wakef* 96-02; Sub Chapl HM Pris Wakef 97-02; Chapl Huggens Coll Northfleet 02-07; rtd 07. *8 Bramwell Avenue, Prenton CH43 0RH* Tel 0151-200 0861 Mobile 07967-134101 E-mail gss.watts@ntlworld.com

WATTS, Graham Hadley Lundie. b 74. Man Metrop Univ BA95. Ridley Hall Cam 98. **d** 02 **p** 03. C Camberley St Paul *Guildf* 02-06; C Northwood Em *Lon* from 06. *10 Northwood Way, Northwood HA6 1AT* Tel (01923) 823718
E-mail graham.watts7@ntlworld.com

WATTS, Ian Charles. b 63. Hull Univ BA85. Linc Th Coll 86. **d** 88 **p** 89. C W Kirby St Bridget *Ches* 88-93; V High Lane 93-00; P-in-c Newton in Mottram 00-04; P-in-c Burnley St Cuth *Blackb* from 04. *St James's Vicarage, Church Street, Briercliffe, Burnley BB10 2HU* Tel (01282) 423700 *or* 424978

WATTS, John Michael. **d** 04. OLM Ashtead *Guildf* from 04; Asst Chapl Guy's and St Thos' NHS Foundn Trust from 04. *31 Broadhurst, Ashtead KT21 1QB* Tel (01372) 275134 E-mail jmwatts@waitrose.com

WATTS, John Robert. b 39. Leeds Univ BSc60 MSc63 DipEd63. Oak Hill Th Coll 88. **d** 90 **p** 91. C Partington and Carrington

Ches 90-93; P-in-c Tintwistle 93-98; V Hollingworth w Tintwistle 98-04; RD Mottram 99-03; rtd 04; Perm to Offic *Ches* from 04. *16 Norley Drive, Vicars Cross, Chester CH3 5PG* Tel (01244) 350439 E-mail revrobwatts@hotmail.co.uk

WATTS, John Stanley. b 28. LCP62 Birm Univ DipEd65 MEd72 Nottm Univ MPhil83. Qu Coll Birm 83. **d** 86 **p** 87. Lect Wolverhampton Poly 77-90; Hon C Dudley St Fran *Worc* 86-91; Lect Wolverhampton Univ 90-93; Hon C Sedgley St Mary 91-98; Perm to Offic from 98. *5 Warren Drive, Sedgley, Dudley DY3 3RQ* Tel (01902) 661265

WATTS, Jonathan Peter (Jonah). b 52. Lon Univ BA74. Ripon Coll Cuddesdon 07. **d** 08 **p** 09. C Crayford *Roch* from 08. *1A Iron Mill Place, Dartford DA1 4RT* Tel (01322) 552884
E-mail jonah.watts1@btinternet.com

WATTS, Mrs Mary Kathleen. b 31. Lon Univ BA86. Gilmore Ho 73. **dss** 77 **d** 87 **p** 94. Lower Streatham St Andr *S'wark* 77-88; C 87-88; C Streatham Immanuel w St Anselm 87-88; C Streatham Immanuel and St Andr 90-91; rtd 91; Perm to Offic *S'wark* 91-94 and from 05; Hon C Norbury St Oswald 94-05. *15 Bromley College, London Road, Bromley BR1 1PE* Tel (020) 8290 6615

WATTS, Matthew David. b 79. Clare Coll Cam BA01 MA04 MSci01 St Jo Coll Dur BA05. Cranmer Hall Dur 03. **d** 06 **p** 07. C Comberton *Ely* from 06; C Toft w Caldecote and Childerley from 06. *18 Fox's Way, Comberton, Cambridge CB23 7DL* Tel (01223) 264089 E-mail mattdwatts@hotmail.com

WATTS, Paul George. b 43. Nottm Univ BA67. Wells Th Coll 67. **d** 69 **p** 70. C Sherwood *S'well* 69-74; Chapl Trent (Nottm) Poly 74-80; V Nottingham All SS 80-84; Public Preacher 84-06; rtd 06. *14 Chestnut Grove, Nottingham NG3 5AD* Tel 0115-960 9964 Mobile 07952-369066 E-mail wattses@yahoo.co.uk

WATTS, (née SIMPER), Mrs Rachel Dawn. b 67. K Coll Lon BD89. Westcott Ho Cam 90. **d** 92 **p** 94. Par Dn Clitheroe St Mary *Blackb* 92-94; C 94-95; C Nor St Pet Mancroft w St Jo Maddermarket 95-97; V Slyne w Hest *Blackb* 97-04; V Briercliffe from 04; Women's Min Adv from 00. *St James's Vicarage, Church Street, Briercliffe, Burnley BB10 2HU* Tel (01282) 423700

WATTS, Ms Rebecca Harriet. b 61. St Cath Coll Cam BA83 MA Welsh Coll of Music & Drama 84. Wycliffe Hall Ox 87. **d** 90 **p** 94. C Goldsworth Park *Guildf* 90-94; Chapl Wadh Coll Ox 94-97; C Ox St Mary V w St Cross and St Pet 94-97; Chapl Somerville Coll Ox 97-98; Perm to Offic *Newc* 98-99 and from 02. *15 Woodbine Avenue, Gosforth, Newcastle upon Tyne NE3 4EU* Tel 0191-285 9840

WATTS, Robert. *See* WATTS, John Robert

WATTS, Roger Edward. b 39. S'wark Ord Course 85. **d** 88 **p** 89. C Belmont *S'wark* 88-92; R Godstone 92-97; R Godstone and Blindley Heath from 97. *The Rectory, 17 Ivy Mill Lane, Godstone RH9 8NK* Tel (01883) 742354

WATTS, Roger Mansfield. b 41. Univ of Wales (Cardiff) BSc63 CEng76 MIET76. Chich Th Coll 89. **d** 91 **p** 92. C Chippenham St Andr w Tytherton Lucas *Bris* 91-93; C Henfield w Shermanbury and Woodmancote *Chich* 93-96; R Jedburgh *Edin* 96-99; R Wingerworth *Derby* 99-06; rtd 06. *Chez Watts, Vedelle, 24610 Villefranche-de-Lonchat, France* Tel (0033) (5) 53 81 82 16

WATTS, Ms Samantha Alison Lundie. b 70. Birm Univ BA92 Cam Univ BA01. Ridley Hall Cam 99. **d** 02 **p** 03. C Camberley St Paul *Guildf* 02-06; NSM Northwood Em *Lon* from 06. *10 Northwood Way, Northwood HA6 1AT* Tel (01923) 823718 E-mail sami.watts@ntlworld.com

WATTS, Scott Antony. b 67. JP08. FRMetS99 MCMI00. EAMTC 00. **d** 03 **p** 04. NSM Brampton *Ely* 03-07; Chapl St Jo Hospice Moggerhanger from 07. *St John's Hospice, St John's Road, Moggerhanger, Bedford MK44 3RJ* Tel (01767) 640622 Fax 641262 Mobile 07733-307679
E-mail scott.watts@suerydercare.org

WATTS, Thomas Annesley. b 79. K Coll Cam BA01 MA05. Oak Hill Th Coll MTh08. **d** 08. C Wharton *Ches* from 08. *27 Leven Avenue, Winsford CW7 3TA* Tel 07764-679210 (mobile)
E-mail tom@tomandsue.net

WATTS, Mrs Valerie Anne. b 44. UEA BEd79. EAMTC 90. **d** 93 **p** 94. NSM N Walsham and Edingthorpe *Nor* from 93. *15 Millfield Road, North Walsham NR28 0EB* Tel (01692) 405119 E-mail topcatjohn@talktalk.net

WATTS, William Henry Norbury. b 51. CertEd. St Jo Coll Nottm 87. **d** 89 **p** 90. C S Molton w Nymet St George, High Bray etc *Ex* 89-93; TV Swanage and Studland *Sarum* from 93. *The Vicarage, School Lane, Studland, Swanage BH19 3AJ* Tel (01929) 450441 E-mail will.watts@tesco.net

WAUD, John David. b 31. NOC 82. **d** 85 **p** 86. C Cayton w Eastfield *York* 85-88; R Brandesburton 88-93; R Beeford w Frodingham and Foston 93-99; rtd 99; Perm to Offic *York* from 00. *21 Lowfield Road, Beverley HU17 9RF* Tel (01482) 864726 E-mail jdw2@jdw2.karoo.co.uk

WAUDBY, Miss Christine. b 45. TCert66. Trin Coll Bris. **d** 90 **p** 94. C Weston-super-Mare Ch Ch *B & W* 90-94; C Blackheath *Birm* 94-99; Perm to Offic 99-03; NSM Ipsley *Worc* from 03. *The Rectory, Icknield Street, Redditch B98 0AN* Tel (01527) 521082

WAUDE, Andrew Leslie. b 74. Leeds Univ BA02. Coll of Resurr Mirfield 99. **d** 02 **p** 03. C Swinton and Pendlebury *Man* 02-05; C Lower Broughton Ascension 05-07; P-in-c Nottingham St Geo w St Jo *S'well* from 07; P-in-c Sneinton St Cypr from 07. *The Vicarage, 19 Marston Road, Nottingham NG3 7AN* Tel 0115-940 2868 Mobile 07708-004478
E-mail father.waude@googlemail.com

WAUGH, Ian William. b 52. Bede Coll Dur DipEd74 BEd75. NEOC 99. **d** 02 **p** 03. NSM Benfieldside *Dur* from 02. *36 Muirfield Close, Shotley Bridge, Consett DH8 5XE* Tel (01207) 591923 Mobile 07808-412953
E-mail ian-barbara-waugh@lineone.net

WAUGH, Mrs Jane Leitch. b 38. CertEd61 Toronto Univ MDiv83. Trin Coll Toronto 80. **d** 84 **p** 94. Canada 84-87; Par Dn Dunnington *York* 88-90; Perm to Offic 90-93 and from 96; NSM York St Olave w St Giles 93-96; rtd 98. *Moonrakers, Rectory Corner, Brandsby, York YO61 4RJ* Tel (01347) 888637

WAUGH, Nigel John William. b 56. TCD BA78 MA81. CITC 76. **d** 79 **p** 80. C Ballymena *Conn* 79-82; C Ballyholme *D & D* 82-84; I Bunclody w Kildavin *C & O* 84-86; I Bunclody w Kildavin and Clonegal 86-91; I Bunclody w Kildavin, Clonegal and Kilrush 91-98; Preb Ferns Cathl 88-91; Treas 91-96; Radio Officer (Cashel) 90-91; (Ferns) 92-98; Dioc Info Officer (Ferns) 91-98; Prec Ferns Cathl 96-98; I Delgany *D & G* from 98. *The Rectory, 8 Elsinore, Delgany, Greystones, Co Wicklow, Republic of Ireland* Tel (00353) (1) 287 4515 Fax 287 7578
E-mail delgany@glendalough.anglican.org

WAXHAM, Derek Frank. b 33. Oak Hill Th Coll 76. **d** 79 **p** 80. NSM Old Ford St Paul w St Steph and St Mark *Lon* 79-89; NSM Bow w Bromley St Leon 89-06; NSM Bow w Bromley St Leon from 06. *39 Hewlett Road, London E3 5NA* Tel (020) 8980 1748

WAY, Miss Alison Janet. b 61. York Univ BSc83 FIBMS86. St Mich Coll Llan 02. **d** 04 **p** 05. C Basingstoke *Win* 04-08; P-in-c Broad Town, Clyffe Pypard, Hilmarton etc *Sarum* from 08. *The Vicarage, Clyffe Pypard, Swindon SN4 7PY* Tel (01793) 739044 E-mail alisonway@tiscali.co.uk

WAY, Andrew Lindsay. b 43. Linc Th Coll 76. **d** 78 **p** 79. C Shenfield *Chelmsf* 78-82; C Waltham *Linc* 82-84; V New Waltham 84-89; R Duxford *Ely* 89-94; V Hinxton 89-94; V Ickleton 89-94; P-in-c Doddington w Benwick 94-97; P-in-c Wimblington 94-97; R Doddington w Benwick and Wimblington 97-98; R Eythorne and Elvington w Waldershare etc *Cant* from 98; AD Dover 00-03. *The Rectory, Barfrestone Road, Eythorne, Dover CT15 4AH* Tel (01304) 830241 Fax 08701-255866 E-mail albeway@clara.co.uk

WAY, Mrs Barbara Elizabeth. b 47. Open Univ BA82 Hull Univ PGCE86. Linc Th Coll IDC78. **dss** 78 **d** 87 **p** 94. Shenfield *Chelmsf* 78-82; Adult Educn Adv *Linc* 82-85; Dioc Lay Min Adv 85; New Waltham 82-89; Min 87-89; Tetney 86-89; Min 87-89; NSM Duxford *Ely* 89-94; NSM Ickleton 89-94; NSM Hinxton 89-94; Dir Past Studies EAMTC 91-94; Min Pampisford 92-94; P-in-c Coates 94-95; TV Whittlesey, Pondersbridge and Coates 95-98; Local Min Adv *Cant* 98-02; Dioc Dir of Reader Selection and Tr 00-02; Dioc Adv in Women's Min 02-04; P-in-c Whitfield w Guston from 02; Chapl E Kent Hosps NHS Trust 06-08. *The Rectory, Barfrestone Road, Eythorne, Dover CT15 4AH* Tel (01304) 830241 Fax 08701-255866 E-mail belway@clara.co.uk

WAY, Colin George. b 31. St Cath Coll Cam BA55 MA59 Lon Inst of Educn PGCE58. EAMTC. **d** 84 **p** 85. NSM Hempnall *Nor* 84-87; C Gaywood, Bawsey and Mintlyn 87 90; R Acle w Fishley and N Burlingham 90-96; RD Blofield 95-96; rtd 96; Perm to Offic *Nor* 96-97 and from 02; P-in-c Pulham Market, Pulham St Mary and Starston 97-99; Hon C Eaton 99-02. *347 Unthank Road, Norwich NR4 7QG* Tel (01603) 458363 E-mail cw@eatonparish.com

WAY, David. b 54. Pemb Coll Ox MA DPhil St Jo Coll Dur BA. Cuddesdon Coll 83. **d** 85 **p** 86. C Chenies and Lt Chalfont *Ox* 85-87; C Chenies and Lt Chalfont, Latimer and Flaunden 87-88; Tutor and Dir Studies Sarum & Wells Th Coll 88-93; Selection Sec Min Division from 94; Sec Minl Educn Cttee from 94; Th Educn Sec Min Division from 99. *Ministry Division, Church House, Great Smith Street, London SW1P 3AZ* Tel (020) 7898 1405 Fax 7898 1421 E-mail david.way@c-of-e.org.uk

WAY, David Charles. b 61. St Mich Coll Llan BTh94. **d** 97 **p** 98. C Cardiff St Mary and St Steph w St Dyfrig etc *Llan* 97-02; V Aberaman and Abercwmboi w Cwmaman from 02. *St Margaret's Vicarage, Gladstone Street, Aberaman, Aberdare CF44 6SA* Tel (01685) 872871 E-mail david.way@dtn.ntl.com

WAY, Lawrence William. b 32. St Mich Coll Llan 77. **d** 79 **p** 80. C Merthyr Dyfan *Llan* 79-82; V Abercynon 82-84; TV Cwmbran *Mon* 84-86; V Caerwent w Dinham and Llanfair Discoed etc 86-90; V Pontnewydd 90-93; rtd 93. *8 Ceredig Court, Llanyravon, Cwmbran NP44 8S4* Tel (01633) 865309 Fax 876830 E-mail frway.angelus@virgin.net

WAY, Michael David. b 57. K Coll Lon BD78 AKC78. St Steph Ho Ox 79. **d** 80 **p** 83. C Bideford *Ex* 80-81; Hon C Wembley Park St Aug *Lon* 81-84; C Kilburn St Aug w St Jo 84-89; V Earlsfield St Jo *S'wark* 89-92; Project Co-ord CARA 92-99; Consultant

Cen Sch for Counselling and Therapy 99-00; Dir RADICLE *Lon* from 00. *14 St Peter's Gardens, London SE27 0PN* Tel (020) 8670 3439 *or* 7932 1129

WAYNE, Kenneth Hammond. b 31. Bps' Coll Cheshunt 58. **d** 61 **p** 62. C Eyres Monsell CD *Leic* 61-62; C Loughborough Em 62-65; C-in-c Staunton Harold 65-73; V Breedon w Isley Walton 65-73; V Leic St Phil 73-85; V Ault Hucknall *Derby* 85-95; rtd 95; Perm to Offic *S'well* from 96. *The Haven, 3 Burton Walk, East Leake, Loughborough LE12 6LB* Tel (01509) 852848

WAYTE, Christopher John. b 28. Lon Univ BSc54. Wells Th Coll 54. **d** 56 **p** 57. C Maidstone St Martin *Cant* 56-60; C W Wickham St Jo 60-61; C Birchington w Acol 61-64; C-in-c Buckland Valley CD 64-68; R Biddenden 68-80; Chapl ATC 71-86; P-in-c Boughton Monchelsea *Cant* 80-85; V St Margarets-at-Cliffe w Westcliffe etc 85-91; rtd 92; Perm to Offic *Cant* from 92. *9 St John's Road, Hythe CT21 4BE* Tel (01303) 263060 E-mail audrey@wayte93.freeserve.co.uk

WEAKLEY, Susan Margaret. b 52. SEITE 05. **d** 08. NSM Merstham and Gatton *S'wark* from 08. *81 Parkhurst Road, Horley RH6 8EX* Tel (01293) 786693 Mobile 07834-368509

WEALE, Colin Alexander. b 26. Univ of Wales (Lamp) BA49 Open Univ MPhil87 Middx Univ PhD96 Lambeth STh81. Sarum Th Coll 49. **d** 51 **p** 52. C Swansea St Mary and H Trin *S & B* 51-55; Min Can Brecon Cathl 55-59; C Brecon w Battle 55-59; V Llanbister and Llanbadarn Fynydd w Llannano 59-61; R Bengeo H Trin *St Alb* 61-69; R Bengeo 69-93; rtd 93; Perm to Offic *Nor* from 93. *1 Diana Way, Caister-on-Sea, Great Yarmouth NR30 5TP* Tel (01493) 377946

WEARMOUTH, Alan Wilfred. b 54. St Paul's Cheltenham CertEd75 Bris Univ BEd76. Glouc Sch of Min 85. **d** 88 **p** 89. NSM Coleford w Staunton *Glouc* 88-06; NSM Coleford, Staunton, Newland, Redbrook etc from 06. *Windhover, Broadwell Bridge, Coleford GL16 7GA* Tel (01594) 832660 E-mail alanw22uk@yahoo.co.uk

WEARN, Simon Joseph. b 76. Pemb Coll Cam BA00 MEng00. Oak Hill Th Coll BA09. **d** 09. C Gt Faringdon w Lt Coxwell *Ox* from 09. *42 Tuckers Road, Faringdon SN7 7YG* Tel (01367) 243553 Mobile 07980-910104 E-mail simon@wearn.org.uk

WEATHERHEAD, The Very Revd Thomas Leslie. b 13. Hatf Coll Dur BA37 LTh37. St Aug Coll Cant 32. **d** 37 **p** 38. C Beeston Hill H Spirit *Ripon* 37-40; C Wensley 40-42; Chapl RAFVR 42-47; C Leeds Halton St Wilfrid *Ripon* 47-48; V New Mills *Derby* 48-59; R Staveley 59-65; Dean and V-Gen Nassau 65-72; R Felmingham *Nor* 72-79; P-in-c Suffield 72-74; R 74-79; P-in-c Colby w Banningham and Tuttington 72-74; R 74-79; RD Tunstead 76-79; rtd 79; Perm to Offic *Ripon* from 79. *St Nicholas' Lodge, 25 Bishopton Lane, Ripon HG4 2QN* Tel (01765) 600413

WEATHERILL, Stephen Robert. b 70. Roehampton Inst BA98 Nottm Univ MA00. St Jo Coll Nottm 98. **d** 00 **p** 02. C Bridlington Priory *York* 00-01; NSM Kendal St Thos *Carl* from 02. *31 Hallgarth Circle, Kendal LA9 5NW* E-mail stephen@stkmail.org.uk

WEATHERLEY, Miss Mary Kathleen. b 36. SRN57 SCM59. SWMTC 78. **dss** 82 **d** 87 **p** 94. Littleham w Exmouth 82-84; Heavitree w Ex St Paul 85-87; Hon Par Dn 87-88; Chapl Asst R Devon and Ex Hosp 85-93; Lic to Offic *Ex* 88-94; NSM Littleham w Exmouth 94-98; Perm to Offic from 98. *11 The Hollows, Exmouth EX8 1QT* Tel (01395) 265528

WEATHERSTONE, Timothy Andrew Patrick. b 59. Bedf Coll Lon BSc81 UEA MSc82. ERMC 05. **d** 08 **p** 09. C Bowthorpe *Nor* from 08. *39 Tizzick Close, Norwich NR5 9HB* Tel 07967-190976 (mobile) E-mail timweatherstone@mac.com

WEATHRALL, Ian Charles. b 22. OBE75. AKC47. **d** 47 **p** 48. C Southampton St Mary w H Trin *Win* 47-51; India from 51; Brotherhood of Ascension from 51; Hd 70-88; rtd 92. *7 Court Lane, Delhi 110 054, India* Tel (0091) (11) 396 8515

WEAVER, Alan William. b 63. Linc Th Coll 95. **d** 95 **p** 96. C Seaford w Sutton *Chich* 95-98; C Langney 98-01; P-in-c The Haven CD 02-05; P-in-c Jarvis Brook 05-07; V from 07. *St Michael's Vicarage, Crowborough Hill, Crowborough TN6 2HJ* Tel (01892) 661565 E-mail angyalanweaver@waitrose.com

WEAVER, Canon Angela Mary. b 48. WMMTC 92. **d** 95 **p** 96. C Hill *Birm* 95-99; V Hamstead St Paul 99-06; AD Handsworth 05-06; Hon Can Birm Cathl 05-06; Can Res Guildf Cathl from 06. *4 Cathedral Close, Guildford GU2 7TL* Tel (01483) 547863 Mobile 07813-807853 E-mail angela@guildford-cathedral.org

WEAVER, Prof Arthur Kenneth (Ken). b 17. Trin Coll Cam BA30 MA44 MRAeS50. Ox NSM Course 81 Wycliffe Hall Ox 81. **d** 81 **p** 82. NSM Ashbury, Compton Beauchamp and Longcot w Fernham *Ox* 81-87; Perm to Offic from 87. *White Lodge, King's Lane, Longcot, Faringdon SN7 7SS* Tel (01793) 782364

WEAVER, Brian John. b 34. Oak Hill Th Coll 82. **d** 84 **p** 85. C Nailsea H Trin *B & W* 84-87; R Nettlebed w Bix and Highmore *Ox* 88-98; rtd 98; Hon C Warfield *Ox* 99-05; Perm to Offic *Lich* from 06. *11A Leslie Road, Sutton Coldfield B74 3BS* Tel 0121-580 8086 E-mail bri_jac@onetel.com

WEAVER, David Anthony. b 43. Hatf Coll Dur BSc65. Lich Th Coll 68. **d** 71 **p** 72. C Walsall Wood *Lich* 71-75; C Much Wenlock w Bourton *Heref* 75-76; Canada 76-79 and 82; V Mow Cop *Lich* 79-82; P-in-c Burntwood 82-00; V 00-08; Chapl St Matt Hosp Burntwood 83-95; rtd 08. *Stone Gables, Ampney Crucis, Cirencester GL7 5RS* Tel (01285) 851674

WEAVER, David Sidney George. b 46. Univ of Wales (Cardiff) BA67 MA71 Goldsmiths' Coll Lon MA01 Lon Univ CertEd76. SEITE 07. **d** 09. NSM Hove *Chich* from 09. *17 Lauriston Road, Brighton BN1 6SN* Tel (01273) 566551 Mobile 07811-145656 E-mail david@synapticslearning.co.uk

WEAVER, Mrs Diane Beverley. b 57. LCTP 06. **d** 09. C Steeton *Bradf* from 09. *1 Westview Way, Keighley BD20 6JD* Tel (01535) 664566

WEAVER, Duncan Charles. b 60. Open Univ BA99. St Jo Coll Nottm 92. **d** 94 **p** 95. C Watford *St Alb* 94-98; TV Bourne Valley *Sarum* 98-01; CF from 01. *c/o MOD Chaplains (Army)* Tel (01980) 615804 Fax 615800 E-mail dweaver385@aol.com

WEAVER, Fiona Margaret. b 61. Westcott Ho Cam 99. **d** 00 **p** 01. C Islington St Jas w St Pet *Lon* 00-03; Asst Chapl Univ of N Lon 00-02; Asst Chapl Lon Metrop Univ 01-03; Chapl 03-05; Lead Chapl from 05. *123 Calabria Road, London N5 1HS* Tel (020) 7359 5808 *or* 7133 2030 Fax 7133 2813 E-mail f.weaver@londonmet.ac.uk

WEAVER, Ian Douglas. b 65. Ridley Coll Melbourne BMin96. **d** 96 **p** 96. C Essendon St Thos Australia 96; C E Frankston 97-98; TV Rushden St Mary w Newton Bromswold *Pet* 98-02; Dioc Youth Min Facilitator Melbourne Australia 03-05; P-in-c E Geelong from 05. *230 McKillop Street, East Geelong Vic 3219, Australia* Tel (0061) (3) 5241 6895 *or* 5221 5353 Fax 5222 5400 Mobile 409-604006 E-mail ianweaver@optusnet.com.au

WEAVER, Canon John. b 28. Ex Coll Ox BA51 MA55. St Steph Ho Ox 52. **d** 55 **p** 56. C Ex St Dav 55-58; S Africa from 58; Hon Can Mthatha from 81; Adn Midl 84-95; Hon Can Pietermaritzburg from 95. *PO Box 56, Underberg, 3257 South Africa* Tel (0027) (33) 701 1124

WEAVER, Mrs Joyce Margaret. b 43. **d** 00 **p** 01. OLM Warrington St Ann *Liv* from 00. *71 Orford Avenue, Warrington WA2 8PQ* Tel (01925) 634993 E-mail joycearniew@aol.com

WEAVER, Ken. *See* WEAVER, Prof Arthur Kenneth

WEAVER, Canon Michael Howard. b 39. Southn Univ MPhil95. Chich Th Coll 63. **d** 66 **p** 67. C Kidderminster St Jo *Worc* 66-69; Br Honduras 69-71; TV Droitwich *Worc* 71-76; V Arundel w Tortington and S Stoke *Chich* 76-96; P-in-c Clymping 84-87; RD Arundel and Bognor 88-93; Sub-Chapl HM Pris Ford 77-96; Hon Can Enugu from 94; V Lymington *Win* 96-04; Chapl Southn Community Services NHS Trust 96-04; rtd 04; Perm to Offic *Win* from 04 and *Portsm* from 05. *Dolphin Cottage, High Street, Freshwater PO40 9JU* Tel and fax (01983) 753786 E-mail junovicarage@hotmail.com

WEAVER, Canon William. b 40. Man Univ BA63 BD65. **d** 74 **p** 75. Lect Th Leeds Univ 67-91; Hon C Clifford *York* 82-86; Chapl K Edw Sch Birm 91-94; Provost Woodard Schs (Midl Division) 94-03; Hon Can Derby Cathl from 96; Perm to Offic from 96. *20 St Peter's Garth, Thorner, Leeds LS14 3EE* Tel 0113-289 3689

WEBB, Anthony John. b 24. Sarum & Wells Th Coll 79. **d** 81 **p** 82. C Yeovil *B & W* 81-84; P-in-c Cossington 84-87; P-in-c Woolavington 87; P-in-c Bawdrip 87; V Woolavington w Cossington and Bawdrip 87-91; rtd 91; Perm to Offic *B & W* from 91. *4 Brue Crescent, Burnham-on-Sea TA8 1LR* Tel (01278) 787483

WEBB, Arthur Robert. b 33. Lanc Univ MA82 FRSA LCP67. Wells Th Coll 69. **d** 70 **p** 70. C W Drayton *Lon* 70-72; Hd Master St Jas Cathl Sch Bury St Edmunds 72-86; Min Can St E Cathl 72-87; Succ St E Cathl 81-87; P-in-c Seend and Bulkington *Sarum* 87-88; V 88-91; R Heytesbury and Sutton Veny 91-96; rtd 96; Perm to Offic *B & W* from 96; *Sarum* from 98; *Bris* from 00; P-in-c Las Palmas *Eur* 04-08. *27 Marlborough Buildings, Bath BA1 2LY* Tel (01225) 484042

WEBB, Mrs Barbara Mary. b 39. Bedf Coll Lon BA60 Cam Univ PGCE61. Wycliffe Hall Ox 00. **d** 02 **p** 03. NSM Cumnor *Ox* 02-05; NSM Stanford in the Vale w Goosey and Hatford 05-09; rtd 09. *50 West St Helen Street, Abingdon OX14 5BP* Tel (01235) 202873 E-mail derry_barbara@msn.com

WEBB, Mrs Brenda Lynn. b 45. Stockwell Coll of Educn CertEd66. EAMTC 97. **d** 00 **p** 01. NSM Saxmundham w Kelsale cum Carlton *St E* from 00; Teacher Beacon Hill Sch from 00. *The Rectory, Manor Gardens, Saxmundham IP17 1ET* Tel (01728) 604234 E-mail richard@saxrectory.freeserve.co.uk

WEBB, Catharine Rosemary Wheatley. b 39. **d** 05 **p** 06. OLM Redhill St Matt *S'wark* from 05. *6 Hurstleigh Drive, Redhill RH1 2AA* Tel and fax (01737) 769763 Mobile 07709-700602 E-mail webbcrw@aol.com

WEBB, Christopher Scott. b 70. Univ of Wales (Abth) BSc. Trin Coll Bris BA96. **d** 96 **p** 97. C Dafen *St D* 96-98; C Cowbridge *Llan* 98-01; Officer for Renewal, Par Development and Local Ecum 01-04; V Llanfair Caereinion, Llanllugan and Manafon

St As 04-07; President of Renovaré USA from 07. *8 Inverness Drive East, Suite 102, Englewood CO 80112-5609, USA*

WEBB, Cyril George. b 19. Roch Th Coll 64. **d** 66 **p** 67. C Bournemouth St Andr *Win* 66-71; V Micheldever 71-72; V Micheldever and E Stratton, Woodmancote etc 72-79; V Bubwith w Ellerton and Aughton *York* 79-83; I Tomregan w Drumlane *K, E & A* 83-86; rtd 86; Perm to Offic *Cant* 90-98. *62 Columbia Avenue, Whitstable CT5 4EH* Tel (01227) 264687

WEBB, David William. b 30. MRINA. Cant Sch of Min 86. **d** 89 **p** 90. NSM Sittingbourne St Mary *Cant* 89-95; Hon C Iwade 95-02; Perm to Offic from 02. *16 School Lane, Iwade, Sittingbourne ME9 8SE* Tel (01795) 424502

WEBB, Mrs Diane. b 45. **d** 93 **p** 94. OLM Stowmarket *St E* 93-05; OLM Haughley w Wetherden and Stowupland from 05. *36 Wordsworth Road, Stowmarket IP14 1TT* Tel (01449) 677880

WEBB, Diane Silvia. Birm Univ BA66 Dur Univ MA93. NOC 82. **dss** 85 **d** 03 **p** 04. Wyther *Ripon* 85-86; Perm to Offic *York* 95-99; rtd 03; NSM Bow Common *Lon* 03-08; NSM Selling w Throwley, Sheldwich w Badlesmere etc from 09. *The Rectory, Vicarage Lane, Selling, Faversham ME13 9RD* Tel (01227) 750144
E-mail diane@webb.lcbroadband.co.uk

WEBB, Dominic Mark. b 68. Oriel Coll Ox BA91. Wycliffe Hall Ox BA93. **d** 96 **p** 97. C Cradley *Worc* 96-99; C Leyton Ch Ch *Chelmsf* 99-02; P-in-c St Helier *S'wark* 02-06; Hon C Stratford New Town St Paul *Chelmsf* from 07. *32A Lister Road, London E11 3DS* Tel (020) 8558 6354
E-mail webbdom@googlemail.com

WEBB, Mrs Eileen Marion. b 46. Bingley Coll of Educn CertEd. **d** 08 **p** 09. OLM Cheriton St Martin *Cant* from 08; OLM Cheriton All So w Newington from 08. *4 Westfield Lane, Etchinghill, Folkestone CT18 8BZ* Tel (01303) 864272 Fax 864272 Mobile 07867-546929 E-mail bryleen@aol.com

WEBB, Frances Mary. *See* BATTIN, Mrs Frances Mary

WEBB, Mrs Gillian Anne. b 49. Whitelands Coll Lon CertEd71 Heythrop Coll Lon MA04. St Alb Minl Tr Scheme 83. **dss** 86 **d** 87 **p** 94. Kempston Transfiguration *St Alb* 86-96; NSM 87-96; NSM Kempston All SS 96-08; P-in-c Marston Morteyne w Lidlington from 08. *2 Hillson Close, Marston Moreteyne, Bedford MK43 0QN* Tel (01234) 767256
E-mail webbg@marston2.freeserve.co.uk

WEBB, Canon Gregory John. b 55. Man Univ LLB77. Oak Hill Th Coll 89. **d** 91 **p** 92. C Bury St Edmunds St Geo *St E* 91-94; P-in-c Bury St Edmunds All SS 94-02; TR Bury St Edmunds All SS w St Jo and St Geo 02-08; RD Thingoe 01-08; P-in-c Sudbury and Chilton from 08; Hon Can St E Cathl from 07. *The Rectory, Christopher Lane, Sudbury CO10 2AS* Tel (01787) 372611
E-mail gregorywebb@btinternet.com

WEBB, Harold William. b 37. St Chad's Coll Dur BA59. St Steph Ho Ox 59. **d** 61 **p** 62. C Plumstead St Nic *S'wark* 61-65; C De Aar S Africa 65; R Prieska 65-68; R Vryburg 68-70; Sacr Wakef Cathl 71-72; P-in-c Lane End *Ox* 72-76; V Lane End w Cadmore End 76-84; Chapl to the Deaf *Guildf* 84-96; V Roade and Ashton w Hartwell *Pet* 96-02; rtd 02; Perm to Offic *Chich* from 02. *16 Harrow Drive, West Wittering, Chichester PO20 8EJ* Tel (01243) 673460

WEBB (*née* EDWARDS), **Mrs Helen Glynne.** b 57. SRN79 RMN81 Birkbeck Coll Lon MSc94. Wycliffe Hall Ox 88. **d** 90 **p** 94. Par Dn Clapham St Jas *S'wark* 94-97; Chapl Asst Southmead Health Services NHS Trust 94-97; Perm to Offic *Bris* from 97. *13 The Green, Olveston, Bristol BS35 4DN* Tel and fax (01454) 615827

WEBB, Mrs Janice Beryl. b 49. Dioc OLM tr scheme 05. **d** 08 **p** 09. NSM Stour Vale *Sarum* from 08. *The Old Bakery, Kington Magna, Gillingham SP8 5EW* Tel (01747) 838196

WEBB, Jennifer Rose. b 48. Leeds Univ BA70 Bedf Coll Lon CQSW72. **d** 96 **p** 97. OLM Ham St Rich *S'wark* 96-05; NSM March St Mary *Ely* from 05; NSM March St Pet from 05. *3 Wherry Close, March PE15 9BX* Tel (01354) 650855
E-mail revdjennywebb@btinternet.com

WEBB, John. *See* WEBB, William John

WEBB, John Christopher Richard. b 38. ACA63 FCA74. Wycliffe Hall Ox 64. **d** 67 **p** 68. C Hendon St Paul Mill Hill *Lon* 67-71; CF 71-93; R Bentworth and Shalden and Lasham *Win* 93-03; RD Alton 98-02; rtd 03; Perm to Offic *B & W* from 04. *Lower Farm Cottage, Church Street, Podimore, Yeovil BA22 8JE* Tel (01935) 841465 E-mail john.c.r.webb@ukgateway.net

WEBB, Jonathan Paul. b 62. Bapt Th Coll Johannesburg BTh98. **d** 02 **p** 03. NSM Linden S Africa 02-04; Asst P Bryanston 04-06; TV Bury St Edmunds All SS w St Jo and St Geo *St E* from 07. *2 Fen Way, Bury St Edmunds IP33 3ZA* Tel and fax (01284) 752906 E-mail jp.webb@btinternet.com

WEBB, Kenneth Gordon. b 47. Lon Univ MB, BS71. Trin Coll Bris BA92. **d** 93 **p** 94. C Cheltenham St Mark *Glouc* 93-97; Banchang Ch Ch Thailand 97-02; P-in-c Duns *Edin* from 02. *The Rectory, Wellfield, Duns TD11 3EH* Tel (01361) 884658 *or* 882209 Mobile 07990-866918
E-mail ken.webb@homecall.co.uk

WEBB, Marjorie Valentine (Sister Elizabeth). b 31. Bedf Coll Lon Westmr Coll Ox MTh98. **d** 88 **p** 94. CSF from 55; Revd Mother 71-86; Lic to Bp Heref 86-90; Perm to Offic *Lon* 88-90; Lic to Offic *Lich* 90-91; *B & W* from 95; *Cant* 95-00; *Birm* 97-00; *Lich* from 00; *Lon* from 02; *Chelmsf* from 09. *The Vicarage, 11 St Mary's Road, London E13 9AE* Tel (020) 8852 4019
E-mail elizabethcsf@franciscans.org.uk

WEBB, Martin George. b 46. SS Mark & Jo Coll Chelsea CertEd68 Leeds Univ MEd95. NOC 82. **d** 85 **p** 86. NSM Brotherton *Wakef* 85-87; Perm to Offic *York* 95-98; NSM Bethnal Green St Barn *Lon* 98-03; NSM Bromley by Bow All Hallows 03-08; P-in-c Selling w Throwley, Sheldwich w Badlesmere etc *Cant* from 08. *The Rectory, Vicarage Lane, Selling, Faversham ME13 9RD* Tel (01227) 750144
E-mail martin@webb.lcbroadband.co.uk

WEBB, Michael David. b 59. K Coll Lon BD82 PGCE83. Ripon Coll Cuddesdon 88. **d** 90 **p** 91. C Broughton Astley *Leic* 90-93; C Hugglescote w Donington, Ellistown and Snibston 93-94; TV 94-98; R Castleford All SS and Whitwood *Wakef* 98-01; P-in-c Glass Houghton 98-01; TR Castleford 02; rtd 02; Perm to Offic *S'well* from 06. *7 St Peter's Close, Farndon, Newark NG24 3SN* Tel (01636) 702548 E-mail michael@webbs-web.co.uk

WEBB, Canon Michael John. b 49. Linc Coll Ox BA70 MA74. Linc Th Coll 70. **d** 72 **p** 73. C Tring *St Alb* 72-75; C Chipping Barnet 75-78; C Chipping Barnet w Arkley 78-82; TV Cullercoats St Geo *Newc* 82-89; V Newc H Cross 89-97; Chapl MU 96-02; V Newc St Gabr 97-06; AD Newc E 97-04; V Alnwick from 06; Hon Can Newc Cathl from 02. *St Michael's Vicarage, Howling Lane, Alnwick NE66 1DH* Tel (01665) 602184
E-mail michaeljwebb@tiscali.co.uk

WEBB, Nikola. *See* MARSHALL, Pauline Nikola

WEBB, Norma Fay. b 39. K Coll Dur BDS62. **d** 04 **p** 05. OLM Thornhill and Whitley Lower *Wakef* from 04. *24 High Street, Thornhill, Dewsbury WF12 0PS* Tel (01924) 463574
E-mail normafwebb@aol.com

WEBB, Paul. *See* WEBB, Jonathan Paul

WEBB, Peter Henry. b 55. Nottm Univ BA77. St Steph Ho Ox 77. **d** 79 **p** 80. C Lancing w Coombes *Chich* 79-82; C The Hydneye CD 82-84; C-in-c 84-86; Chapl Sunderland Distr Gen Hosp 86-94; Chapl City Hosps Sunderland NHS Trust from 94. *The Chaplain's Office, Sunderland Royal General Hospital, Kayll Road, Sunderland SR4 7TP* Tel 0191-565 6256 *or* 569 9180

WEBB, Rex Alexander Francis. b 32. Ely Th Coll 56. **d** 58 **p** 59. C Millbrook *Win* 58-60; Australia from 60; rtd 97. *54 Annaburoo Crescent, Tiwi, Darwin NT 0810, Australia* Tel (0061) (8) 8927 6084

WEBB, Richard. b 38. Oak Hill NSM Course 91. **d** 94 **p** 95. NSM Hanwell St Mary w St Chris *Lon* 94-04; rtd 04; Perm to Offic *Cant* from 05. *1 Haffenden Meadow, Charing, Ashford TN27 0JR* Tel (01233) 714663

WEBB, Canon Richard Frederick. b 42. Cant Sch of Min. **d** 84 **p** 85. C Ipswich St Clem w H Trin *St E* 84-87; R Rougham and Beyton w Hessett 87-91; R Rougham, Beyton w Hessett and Rushbrooke 91-92; P-in-c Woodbridge St Jo 92-98; P-in-c Saxmundham 98-04; P-in-c Kelsale-cum-Carlton, Middleton, Theberton etc 02-04; R Saxmundham w Kelsale cum Carlton from 04; RD Saxmundham 03-05; Hon Can St E Cathl from 06. *The Rectory, Manor Gardens, Saxmundham IP17 1ET* Tel (01778) 604234 E-mail richard@saxrectory.freeserve.co.uk

WEBB, Robert. *See* WEBB, Arthur Robert

WEBB, Rosemary. *See* WEBB, Catharine Rosemary Wheatley

WEBB, Rowland James. b 33. Roch Th Coll 64. **d** 67 **p** 68. C Tavistock and Gulworthy *Ex* 67-70; Chapl RN 70-86; R Mundford w Lynford *Nor* 86-90; V Burnham *Chelmsf* 90-98; rtd 98; Perm to Offic *Chelmsf* from 98. *4 Pine Drive, Ingatestone CM4 9EF*

WEBB, Timothy Robert. b 57. Univ of Wales (Abth) BA79 Univ of Wales (Ban) BTh03 CQSW89. **d** 02 **p** 03. C Machynlleth w Llanwrin and Penegoes *Ban* 03-06. *Ty'n yr Ardd, Lon Gerddi, Edern, Pwllheli LL53 8YS* Tel (01758) 720416 Mobile 07765-298575

WEBB, William John. b 43. Cuddesdon Coll 68. **d** 71 **p** 72. C Weston Favell *Pet* 71-73; C Newport w Longford *Lich* 74-77; C Baswich 77-79; P-in-c Stonnall and Wall 79-83; V Prees and Fauls 83-95; V St Martin's 95-06; rtd 06; Perm to Offic *Lich* from 09. *29 Newington Way, Craven Arms SY7 9PS* Tel (01588) 673442

WEBBER, David Price. b 39. Chich Th Coll 90. **d** 91 **p** 92. NSM Shoreham Beach *Chich* 91-93; NSM Hove St Patr 93-96; Turks and Caicos Is from 96. *PO Box 24, Grand Turk, Turks and Caicos Islands*

WEBBER, The Very Revd Eric Michael. b 16. Lon Univ BD54 Univ of Tasmania MEd77 MHums85 AKC43. **d** 43 **p** 44. C Clapham H Spirit *S'wark* 43-47; C Wimbledon 47-50; R Eshowe S Africa 56-58; R Lapworth and Baddesley-Clinton 56-58; Dean Hobart 59-71; Sen Lect RS Tasmanian Coll Adv Educn 71-81; rtd 94. *5B Kendrick Court, Dynnyrne Tas 7005, Australia* Tel (0061) (3) 6223 6413

WEBBER, John Arthur. b 45. Keble Coll Ox BA67 MA71 Gen Th Sem NY STM85. Cuddesdon Coll 70. **d** 71 **p** 72. C Penarth All SS *Llan* 71-74; USPG Bangladesh 75-84 and 85-91; USA 84-85; Asst P Stepney St Dunstan and All SS *Lon* 91-97; Bp's Adv on Inter-Faith Relns 91-04; P-in-c Bethnal Green St Barn 97-00; Dir of Ords 00-04; TR Llantwit Major from 04. *The Rectory, High Street, Llantwit Major CF61 1SS* Tel (01446) 792324

WEBBER, Lionel Frank. b 35. Kelham Th Coll St Mich Coll Llan. **d** 60 **p** 61. C Bolton Sav *Man* 60-63; C Aberavon *Llan* 63-65; R Salford Stowell Memorial *Man* 65-69; V Aberavon H Trin *Llan* 69-74; TV Stantonbury *Ox* 74-76; TR Basildon St Martin w H Cross and Laindon *Chelmsf* 76-79; P-in-c Nevendon 77-79; RD Basildon 79-89; R Basildon St Martin w Nevendon 79-95; R Basildon St Martin 95-01; Hon Can Chelmsf Cathl 84-01; Chapl to The Queen 94-01; rtd 01. *12 Ramblers Way, Burnham-on-Crouch CM0 8LR* Tel (01621) 785152

WEBBER, Lorna Violet. b 40. **d** 06 **p** 07. OLM Woodbridge St Jo and Bredfield *St E* from 06. *Deo Gratias, 43 Through Duncans, Woodbridge IP12 4EA* Tel (01394) 384634
E-mail lorna@stjohnswoodbridge.org.uk

WEBBER, Canon Michael Champneys Wilfred. b 48. Man Univ BA71 MA(Theol)78. Cuddesdon Coll 73. **d** 75 **p** 76. C Caterham S'wark 75-79; P-in-c Kidbrooke St Jas 79-84; TV 84-85; V Earls Barton *Pet* 87-09; RD Wellingborough 00-06; P-in-c Daventry, Ashby St Ledgers, Braunston etc from 09; Can Pet Cathl from 04. *The Rectory, Golding Close, Daventry NN11 4FB* Tel (01327) 876893 E-mail michaelc.webber@btinternet.com

WEBBER, Raymond John. b 40. Linc Th Coll 84. **d** 85 **p** 86. C Helston *Truro* 85; C Helston and Wendron 85-90; TV 90-93; R Kenton, Mamhead, Powderham, Cofton and Starcross *Ex* 93-03; rtd 03; Perm to Offic *Truro* from 03. *1 Seton Gardens, Camborne TR14 7JS* Tel (01209) 711360

WEBBER, Thomas George Edward. b 63. LSE BSc84. Trin Coll Bris. **d** 98 **p** 99. C Churchdown *Glouc* 98-02; TV Stoke Gifford *Bris* from 02. *The Vicarage, Mautravers Close, Bradley Stoke, Bristol BS32 8ED* Tel 0117-931 2222
E-mail tomandchriswebber@tiscali.co.uk

WEBBER, Toby Roderic. b 75. St Jo Coll Dur BA96. Wycliffe Hall Ox BA01. **d** 02 **p** 03. C Chorley St Laur *Blackb* 02-06; P-in-c Bamber Bridge St Aid from 06. *St Aidan's Vicarage, Longworth Street, Bamber Bridge, Preston PR5 6GN* Tel (01772) 335310

WEBBLEY, Ms Rachel Catharine. b 75. Hatf Coll Dur BA98. Qu Coll Birm BA03. **d** 04 **p** 05. C Bicester w Bucknell, Caversfield and Launton *Ox* 04-07; TV Whitstable *Cant* from 07. *28A West Cliff, Whitstable CT5 1DN* Tel (01227) 273329
E-mail rcwebbley@hotmail.com

WEBER, Douglas John Craig. b 20. Ex Coll Ox BA46 MA46. Sarum Th Coll. **d** 49 **p** 50. C Portsea N End St Mark *Portsm* 49-52; C Alverstoke 52-55; V Hook w Warsash 55-88; rtd 88; Perm to Offic *Portsm* from 88. *1 Trevose Way, Titchfield, Fareham PO14 4NG* Tel (01489) 583065

WEBLEY, Robin Bowen. b 32. St Mich Coll Llan 87. **d** 89 **p** 90. C St D Cathl 89-91; Min Can St D Cathl 89-91; R Castlemartin w Warren and Angle etc 91-94; Succ St D Cathl 94-00; rtd 00. *Whiteleys, Stepaside, Narberth SA67 8YN* Tel (01834) 813603

WEBSTER, David Edward. b 39. K Coll Lon 60 Edin Th Coll 62. **d** 64 **p** 65. C Maghull *Liv* 64-69; R Wavertree St Mary 69-76; TV Greystoke, Matterdale and Mungrisdale *Carl* 76-81; R Lowton St Luke *Liv* 81-88; R Stoneleigh w Ashow and Baginton *Cov* 88-01; Chapl Nat Agric Cen 88-01; P-in-c Pennington and Lindal w Marton and Bardsea *Carl* 01-02; V 02-06; rtd 06. *4 Chelsea Court, Milnthorpe LA7 7DJ* Tel (015395) 63369 *or* 564731 E-mail d.webster@ruralnet.org.uk

WEBSTER, David Leslie Holbarow. b 37. SAOMC 00. **d** 02 **p** 03. NSM Hurst *Ox* 02-04; NSM Earley St Nic 04-07; Perm to Offic from 07. *515 Reading Road, Winnersh, Wokingham RG41 5HL* Tel 0118-979 4568 Fax 961 9575
E-mail dlhwebster@supanet.com

WEBSTER, David Robert. b 32. Selw Coll Cam BA56 MA60. Linc Th Coll 56. **d** 58 **p** 59. C Billingham St Cuth *Dur* 58-61; C Doncaster St Geo *Sheff* 61-64; Chapl Doncaster R Infirmary 61-64; V Lumley *Dur* 64-76; V Belmont 76-93; rtd 93. *25 Eldon Grove, Hartlepool TS26 9LY* Tel (01429) 425915
E-mail david.webster50@ntlworld.com

WEBSTER, Dennis Eric. b 39. Fitzw Ho Cam BA60 MA64 Linacre Coll Ox MA70 Lon Univ CertEd61. Wycliffe Hall Ox 62. **d** 65 **p** 66. C Herne Bay Ch Ch *Cant* 65-68; C Tulse Hill H Trin *S'wark* 68-69; Missr Kenya 70-75; Chapl Pierrepont Sch Frensham 75-91; R Chiddingfold *Guildf* 91-02; rtd 02; Perm to Offic *Guildf* from 02. *Sylvan Cottage, 24 Longdown Road, Lower Bourne, Farnham GU10 3JL* Tel (01252) 713919

WEBSTER, Derek Herbert. b 34. FRSA82 Hull Univ BA55 Lon Univ BD55 Leic Univ MEd68 PhD73. Lambeth STh67 Linc Th Coll 76. **d** 76 **p** 77. Lect Hull Univ from 72; Reader from 97; NSM Cleethorpes *Linc* from 76. *60 Queen's Parade, Cleethorpes DN35 0DG* Tel (01472) 693786
E-mail dwebster@edrev.demon.co.uk

WEBSTER, Canon Diane Margaret. b 43. Oak Hill NSM Course 91. **d** 94 **p** 95. NSM Welwyn Garden City *St Alb* 94-99; P-in-c Burley Ville *Win* from 99; RD Christchurch from 03; Hon Can Win Cathl from 08. *The Vicarage, Church Corner, Burley, Ringwood BH24 4AP* Tel (01425) 402303
E-mail diane.mwebster@tiscali.co.uk

WEBSTER, Geoffrey William. b 36. St Alb Minl Tr Scheme 77. **d** 80 **p** 81. NSM Harlington *St Alb* 80-82; C Belmont *Dur* 82-86; R Gateshead Fell 86-94; P-in-c Hamsterley 94-95; V Hamsterley and Witton-le-Wear 95-02; rtd 02. *38A Owton Manor Lane, Hartlepool TS25 3AE* Tel (01429) 265798

WEBSTER, Canon Glyn Hamilton. b 51. SRN73. Cranmer Hall Dur 74. **d** 77 **p** 78. C Huntington *York* 77-81; V York St Luke 81-92; Chapl York Distr Hosp 81-92; Sen Chapl York Health Services NHS Trust 92-99; Can and Preb York Minster 94-99; Can Res York Minster from 99; RD City of York 97-04; Assoc Dioc Dir of Ords from 05. *4 Minster Yard, York YO1 7JD* Tel (01904) 620877 Fax 557201 E-mail chancellor@yorkminster.org

WEBSTER, Prof John Bainbridge. b 55. Clare Coll Cam MA81 PhD82. **d** 83 **p** 84. Chapl and Dep Sen Tutor St Jo Coll Dur 83-86; Hon C Bearpark *Dur* 83-86; Assoc Prof Systematic Th Wycliffe Coll Toronto 86-93; Prof Systematic Th 93-95; Ramsay Armitage Prof Systematic Th 95-96; Lady Marg Prof Div and Can Res Ch Ch *Ox* 96-03; Prof Systematic Th Aber Univ from 03. *King's College, University of Aberdeen, Aberdeen AB24 3FX* Tel (01224) 272890

WEBSTER, John Kelsey. b 62. SAOMC 00. **d** 03 **p** 04. NSM Woolhampton w Midgham and Beenham Valance *Ox* 03-06; P-in-c Tallangatta Australia from 06. *61 Queen Elizabeth Drive, Tallangatta Vic 3700, Australia* Tel and fax (0061) (2) 6071 2545 Mobile 44-849 9093 E-mail frjohnw@bigpond.com

WEBSTER, The Ven Martin Duncan. b 52. Nottm Univ BSc74. Linc Th Coll 75. **d** 78 **p** 79. C Thundersley *Chelmsf* 78-81; C Canvey Is 81-82; TV 82-86; V Nazeing 86-99; RD Harlow 88-99; TR Waltham H Cross 99-09; Hon Can Chelmsf Cathl 00-09; Adn Harlow from 09. *Glebe House, Church Lane, Sheering, Bishop's Stortford CM22 7NR* Tel (01279) 734524 Fax 734426
E-mail a.harlow@chelmsford.anglican.org

WEBSTER, Mrs Monica. b 39. DipCOT60. WMMTC 94. **d** 97 **p** 98. NSM Wolverton w Norton Lindsey and Langley *Cov* 97-01; Asst Chapl to the Deaf 97-01; NSM Stoneleigh w Ashow and Baginton 98-01; Chapl to the Deaf and Hard of Hearing *Carl* from 01; NSM Aldingham, Dendron, Rampside and Urswick 02-06; NSM Pennington and Lindal w Marton and Bardsea 02-06; rtd 06. *4 Chelsea Court, Milnthorpe LA7 7DJ* Tel (01539) 564731

WEBSTER, Mrs Patricia Eileen. b 34. St Gabr Coll Lon TCert54. Gilmore Ho 56. **d** 87 **p** 94. Par Dn Belmont *Dur* 87-93; rtd 93. *25 Eldon Grove, Hartlepool TS26 9LY* Tel (01429) 425915
E-mail david.webster50@ntlworld.com

WEBSTER, Rosamond Mary. *See* LATHAM, Mrs Rosamond Mary

WEBSTER, Sarah Vernoy. b 38. Univ of Georgia BSc61. S'wark Ord Course 87. **d** 90 **p** 94. NSM Primrose Hill St Mary w Avenue Road St Paul *Lon* 90-01; Hon C Ann Arbor St Andr USA from 02. *4179 Eastgate Drive, Ann Arbor MI 48103, USA* Tel (001) (734) 424 2750 E-mail revsallyweb@comcast.net

WEBSTER, Mrs Sheila Mary. b 22. Bedf Coll Lon CertSS43. Gilmore Ho **dss** 81 **d** 87. Patcham *Chich* 77-83; Hove All SS 84-90; Hon Par Dn 87-90; rtd 90; Perm to Offic *Chich* from 90. *30 New Larchwood, Waldron Avenue, Brighton BN1 9EZ* Tel (01273) 607574

WEBSTER, Stephen Jeremy. b 71. Leic Univ BA92 PGCE93. Wycliffe Hall Ox 05. **d** 07 **p** 08. C Oundle w Ashton and Benefield w Glapthorn *Pet* from 07. *41 Hillfield Road, Oundle, Peterborough PE8 4QR* Tel (01832) 275631

WEDDERSPOON, The Very Revd Alexander Gillan. b 31. Jes Coll Ox BA54 MA61 Lon Univ BD62. Cuddesdon Coll. **d** 61 **p** 62. C Kingston All SS *S'wark* 61-63; Lect RE Lon Univ 63-66; Educn Adv C of E Sch Coun 66-70; Can Res Win Cathl 70-87; Treas 80-85; Vice-Dean 80-87; Dean Guildf 87-01; rtd 01; Perm to Offic *Guildf* from 01. *1 Ellery Close, Cranleigh GU6 8DF* Tel (01483) 548586 E-mail alex@wedderspoon.fsnet.co.uk

WEDGBURY, John William. b 53. RMCS BSc78. St Jo Coll Nottm 84. **d** 87 **p** 88. C Foord St Jo *Cant* 87-91; V Mangotsfield *Bris* 91-92; NSM Manselton *S & B* 00-02; P-in-c Caereithin 02-05; NSM Swansea St Thos and Kilvey from 05. *4 Ffynone Drive, Swansea SA1 6DD* Tel (01792) 464194

WEDGE, Christopher Graham. b 67. LSE BSc(Econ)89 Huddersfield Univ PGCE94. NOC 99. **d** 06 **p** 07. C Castleford *Wakef* 06-09; Asst Chapl Leeds Teaching Hosps NHS Trust from 09. *Trust Headquarters, St James University Hospital, Beckett Street, Leeds LS9 7TF* Tel 0113-206 5859
E-mail christopher.wedge@leedsth.nhs.uk

WEDGEWORTH, Canon Michael John. b 40. Nottm Univ BSc62. Wesley Ho Cam MA66. **d** 93 **p** 94. In Methodist Ch 66-93; NSM Feniscowles *Blackb* 93-96; Sec DBF 95-05; Hon P Blackb Cathl from 95; Lic to Offic from 96; Hon Can Blackb

Cathl from 03. *Abbott House, 74 King Street, Whalley, Clitheroe BB7 9SN* Tel (01254) 825694
E-mail mike.wedgeworth@blackburn.anglican.org.uk

WEDGWOOD, George Peter. b 26. St Jo Coll Dur BA51 MA56. **d** 52 **p** 53. C Barrow St Mark *Carl* 52-54; Chapl Sedbergh Sch 54-57; P-in-c Dur St Cuth 57-63; Chapl Dur High Sch 58-63; Chapl, Hd of Div and Sen Lect St Kath Coll *Liv* 63-69; Prin Lect 69-83; Hd of Div Liv Coll of HE 84-86; P-in-c Kirkoswald, Renwick and Ainstable *Carl* 86-88; rtd 88; Perm to Offic *Carl* 88-92 and *Liv* 92-97; Hon C Hawick *Edin* 02-05. *Lakeside View, Auchry, Turriff AB53 5TP* Tel (01888) 544619

WEDGWOOD GREENHOW, Stephen John Francis. b 57. Man Univ BA82. Edin Th Coll MTh84. **d** 84 **p** 85. C Wythenshawe Wm Temple Ch *Man* 84-87; USA from 87. *556 North George Washington Blvd, Yuba City CA 95993, USA* Tel (001) (530) 822 0691

WEEDEN, Simon Andrew. b 55. York Univ BA79. Wycliffe Hall Ox 88. **d** 90 **p** 91. C Gt Chesham *Ox* 90-94; P-in-c Haversham w Lt Linford, Tyringham w Filgrave 94-97; R Lamp 97-99; P-in-c Bramshott and Liphook *Portsm* 99-00; R from 00; RD Petersfield 04-09. *The Rectory, 22 Portsmouth Road, Liphook GU30 7DJ* Tel (01428) 723119 Fax 725390
E-mail simon@weeden.plus.com

WEEDING, Paul Stephen. b 62. Leic Poly BSc. Ripon Coll Cuddesdon 88. **d** 90 **p** 91. C Llanishen and Lisvane 90-93; C Merthyr Tydfil Ch Ch 93-97; V Abercynon 97-03; Asst Chapl Qu Medical Cen Nottm Univ Hosp NHS Trust from 03. *Trust Headquarters, Derby Road, Nottingham NG7 2UH* Tel 0115-924 9924

✠**WEEKES, The Rt Revd Ambrose Walter Marcus.** b 19. CB70. AKC41 Linc Th Coll 41. **d** 42 **p** 43 **c** 77. C New Brompton St Luke *Roch* 42-44; Chapl RNVR 44-46; Chapl RN 46-69; Chapl of the Fleet and Adn for the RN 69-72; QHC from 69; Can Gib Cathl 71-73; Chapl Tangier 72-73; Dean Gib 73-77; Aux Bp Eur 77-80; Suff Bp Eur 80-86; Bp Brussels 81-86; rtd 86; Hon Asst Bp Roch 86-88; Hon Asst Bp Eur from 89; Chapl Montreux w Gstaad 89-92; Perm to Offic *Lon* from 03. *Charterhouse, Charterhouse Square, London EC1M 6AN* Tel (020) 7251 4201

WEEKES, Cecil William. b 31. CITC. **d** 78 **p** 79. NSM Glenageary *D & G* 78-80; Bp's V Kilkenny Cathl 80-83; I Carlow w Urglin and Staplestown 83-90; Can Leighlin Cathl 88-96; Can Ossory Cathl 88-96; I Lismore w Cappoquin, Kilwatermoy, Dungarvan etc 90-96; Dean Lismore 90-96; Chan Cashel Cathl 90-96; Prec Waterford Cathl 90-96; rtd 96. *The Cottage, Danesfort Road, Bennettsbridge, Co Kilkenny, Republic of Ireland* Tel and fax (00353) (56) 772 7711 E-mail cwweekes@eircom.net

WEEKES, David John. b 34. Magd Coll Cam BA59 MA68 Lon Univ PGCE68 Aber Univ MTh79. Clifton Th Coll 62. **d** 64 **p** 65. C Cheadle *Ches* 64-68; Uganda 69-73; Perm to Offic *St And* 73-74; Chapl and Hd of RE Fettes Coll Edin 74-94; Warden and Chapl Lee Abbey Internat Students' Club Kensington 94-01; rtd 01; Perm to Offic *Lon* 94-03. *Loaning Hill, Kilmany, Cupar KY15 4PT* Tel (01382) 330137 Mobile 07855-761970
E-mail davidweekes@hotmail.com

WEEKES, Robin Alasdair Rutley. b 73. Peterho Cam MA94. Wycliffe Hall Ox BA98 MA98. **d** 99 **p** 00. C Wimbledon Em Ridgway Prop Chpl *S'wark* 99-05. *Address temp unknown*

WEEKS, Ms Jane Anne. b 61. UEA BA00. Aston Tr Scheme 95 EAMTC 97. **d** 00 **p** 01. C Hadleigh *St E* 00-02; C Hadleigh, Layham and Shelley 02-03; Chapl HM Pris Bullwood Hall 03-06; Chapl HM Pris Cookham Wood 06-08; Perm to Offic *Cant* from 09. *4 St Eanswythes Mews, Folkestone CT20 1SR* Tel (01303) 227154 E-mail revweeks@hotmail.com

WEEKS, Timothy Robert. b 47. SAOMC 03. **d** 08. NSM Royston *St Alb* from 08; Chapl Princess Alexandra Hosp NHS Trust from 08. *6 Chantry Road, Bishop's Stortford CM23 2SF* Tel (01279) 831404 *or* (01763) 243265 Mobile 07974-866016
E-mail angela.mweeks@ntlworld.com

WEETMAN, Mrs Dorothy. b 41. **d** 03 **p** 04. OLM Prudhoe *Newc* 03-09; rtd 09. *Station Gate East, Eltringham Road, Prudhoe NE42 6LA* Tel (01661) 834538

WEETMAN, Canon John Charles. b 66. Qu Coll Ox BA87 MA92. Trin Coll Bris BA91. **d** 91 **p** 92. C Hull St Jo Newland *York* 91-95; V Boosbeck w Moorsholm 95-02; V Redcar from 02; RD Guisborough from 99; Can and Preb York Minster from 05. *St Peter's Vicarage, 66 Aske Road, Redcar TS10 2BP* Tel (01642) 490700

WEIGHTMAN, Miss Andrea Frances. b 66. Sheff Univ BA87. Ridley Hall Cam 00. **d** 03 **p** 04. C Handforth *Ches* 03-07; V Blendon *Roch* from 07. *The Vicarage, 37 Bladindon Drive, Bexley DA5 3BS* Tel (020) 8301 5387 Mobile 07983-851105
E-mail andrea.weightman@tesco.net

WEIGHTMAN, David Courtenay. b 47. FRICS88. **d** 04 **p** 05. OLM Oxted and Tandridge *S'wark* from 04. *13 Silkham Road, Oxted RH8 0NP* Tel (01883) 715420 Fax 717336 Mobile 07739-456947 E-mail david@survez.co.uk

WEIL, Thomas James. b 53. K Coll Lon BSc74 PhD79 AKC74. S Tr Scheme 95. **d** 97 **p** 99. NSM Stoughton *Guildf* 97-03; Perm to

Offic *Lon* from 03. *17 Lyons Drive, Guildford GU2 9YP* Tel (01483) 234535

WEIR, David Alexander. b 69. City Univ BSc91 Fitzw Coll Cam BA94 Chich Univ BA08. Westcott Ho Cam 92. **d** 95 **p** 97. C Locks Heath *Portsm* 95-96; C W Leigh 96-00; C Leigh Park and Warren Park 00-01; Perm to Offic 03-05; NSM Portsea St Mary 05-08; Perm to Offic *Truro* from 08. *The Rectory, Priory Road, Bodmin PL31 2AB* Tel (01208) 73867

WEIR, Graham Francis. b 52. GSM LASI. NOC 88. **d** 91 **p** 92. NSM High Crompton *Man* 91-92; NSM Heyside 92-94; Asst Chapl Bolton Hosps NHS Trust 94-96; Chapl from 96; Dep Hd of Chapl from 04. *The Chaplain's Office, Royal Bolton Hospital, Minerva Road, Farnworth, Bolton BL4 0JR* Tel (01204) 390770 *or* 390390 E-mail graham.weir@boltonh-tr.nwest.nhs.uk

WEIR, John Michael Vavasour. b 48. K Coll Lon BD72 AKC72 MA00. **d** 73 **p** 74. C Hatfield Hyde *St Alb* 73-76; C Watford St Mich 76-79; Asst Chapl Oslo St Edm *Eur* 80-81; V Bethnal Green St Pet w St Thos *Lon* 81-04; Chapl Qu Eliz Hosp for Children Lon 81-98; Chapl Team Ldr Toc H from 01; Sen Chapl Dubai and Sharjah w N Emirates from 04. *Holy Trinity Dubai, PO Box 7415, Dubai, United Arab Emirates* Tel (00971) (4) 337 0247 E-mail chap7415@emirates.net.ae

WEIR, John William Moon. b 36. St Luke's Coll Ex CertEd69 Ex Univ BEd76. SW Minl Tr Course 82. **d** 85 **p** 86. NSM Meavy, Sheepstor and Walkhampton *Ex* 85-87; NSM Yelverton, Meavy, Sheepstor and Walkhampton from 87; Hd Master Princetown Primary Sch 86-94; Sub-Chapl HM Pris Dartmoor 86-94. *Goblin's Green, Dousland, Yelverton PL20 6ND* Tel (01822) 852671

WEIR, Ms Rachel Sian Shapland. b 66. Newnham Coll Cam BA88 MA91 Barrister 91. Ripon Coll Cuddesdon 04. **d** 07 **p** 08. NSM Wolvercote *Ox* 07-09; NSM Headington Quarry from 09; Asst Nat Adv for Inter Faith Relns from 07. *Blackhall Farm, Garford Road, Oxford OX2 6UY* Tel 07815-729565 (mobile) E-mail rachelssweir@yahoo.co.uk

WEIR, William Daniel Niall. b 57. UEA BA79. Ripon Coll Cuddesdon 80. **d** 83 **p** 84. C Chelsea St Luke *Lon* 83-87; PV Westmr Abbey 85-89; C Poplar *Lon* 87-88; TV 88-93; P-in-c Forest Gate Em w Upton Cross *Chelmsf* 93-97; V 97-99; Asst Chapl Southn Univ Hosps NHS Trust 99-00; Trust Chapl 00-03; R W Hackney St Barn *Lon* from 03. *The Rectory, 306 Amhurst Road, London N16 7UE* Tel (020) 7254 3235
E-mail niall.weir@mac.com

WEISSERHORN, Julian Timothy David Moritz. *See* GADSBY, Julian Timothy David Moritz

WELANDER, Canon David Charles St Vincent. b 25. FSA. Lon Coll of Div BD47 ALCD47. **d** 48 **p** 49. C Heigham H Trin *Nor* 48-51; Tutor Oak Hill Th Coll 51-52; Chapl and Tutor Lon Coll of Div 52-56; V Iver *Ox* 56-63; V Cheltenham Ch Ch *Glouc* 63-75; RD Cheltenham 73-75; Can Res Glouc Cathl 75-91; rtd 91; Perm to Offic *Glouc* 91-98 and *Bris* from 91. *Willow Cottage, 1 Sandpits Lane, Sherston Magna, Malmesbury SN16 0NN* Tel (01666) 840180

WELBOURN, David Anthony. b 41. K Coll Lon BD63 AKC63. St Boniface Warminster 63. **d** 64 **p** 65. C Stockton St Chad *Dur* 64-67; C S Westoe 69-74; Ind Chapl 69-80; Ind Chapl *Nor* 80-90; Ind and Commerce Officer *Guildf* 90-06; rtd 06. *3 Windgates, Guildford GU4 7DJ* Tel and fax (01483) 825541
E-mail david@dwelbourn.freeserve.co.uk

WELBY, Alexander. *See* WELBY, Richard Alexander Lyon

WELBY, The Very Revd Justin Portal. b 56. Trin Coll Cam BA78 MA90 St Jo Coll Dur BA91. Cranmer Hall Dur 89. **d** 92 **p** 93. C Chilvers Coton w Astley *Cov* 92-95; R Southam 95-02; V Ufton 96-02; Can Res Cov Cathl 02-07; Co-Dir Internat Min 02-05; Sub-Dean 05-07; P-in-c Cov H Trin 07; Dean Liv from 07. *1 Cathedral Close, Liverpool L1 7BR* Tel 0151-702 7202 Fax 702 7292 Mobile 07940-594953
E-mail dean@liverpoolcathedral.org.uk

WELBY, Peter Edlin Brown. b 34. Open Univ BA75. St Jo Coll Dur 75. **d** 77 **p** 78. C Auckland St Andr and St Anne *Dur* 77-79; C S Westoe 79-81; V Tudhoe 81-93; R Croxdale and Tudhoe 93-99; rtd 99. *Blyth House, 9 Rhodes Terrace, Nevilles Cross, Durham DH1 4JW* Tel 0191-384 8295

WELBY, Richard Alexander Lyon. b 58. St Jo Coll Nottm BTh81 Leeds Univ MA93. Ridley Hall Cam 83. **d** 84 **p** 85. C Stoke Bishop *Bris* 84-88; V Bowling St Steph *Bradf* 88-95; P-in-c Hatherleigh, Meeth, Exbourne and Jacobstowe 95-05. *Address temp unknown* Tel 07966-409788 (mobile)
E-mail alex.welby@virgin.net

WELCH, Amanda Jane. b 58. **d** 04 **p** 05. OLM Worplesdon *Guildf* from 04. *Glenlea, Liddington New Road, Guildford GU3 3AH* Tel (01483) 233091 E-mail curate@worplesdonparish.com
or welchfam@tiscali.co.uk

WELCH, David John. b 52. NTMTC 98. **d** 01 **p** 02. C Walthamstow *Chelmsf* 01-05; V Harlow St Mary and St Hugh w St Jo the Bapt from 05. *St Mary's Vicarage, 5 Staffords, Harlow CM17 0JR* Tel and fax (01279) 450633
E-mail davewelch@talktalkbusiness.net

WELCH, Derek. b 27. Keble Coll Ox BA51 MA57. Coll of Resurr Mirfield 51. **d** 53 **p** 54. C Middlesbrough St Jo the Ev *York* 53-58; C Oswaldtwistle Immanuel *Blackb* 58-59; V Accrington St Andr 59-65; V Salesbury 66-72; V Heyhouses on Sea 73-92; rtd 92; Perm to Offic *Blackb* from 92. *76 St Thomas's Road, Lytham St Annes FY8 1JR* Tel (01253) 781469

WELCH, Gordon Joseph. b 47. Man Univ BSc68 MSc69 PhD72. NOC 84. **d** 87 **p** 88. NSM Upton Ascension *Ches* 87-98; Lic to Offic 99-00; NSM Backford and Capenhurst 00-02; NSM Ellesmere Port from 02; RD Wirral S from 06. *6 St James's Avenue, Upton, Chester CH2 1NA* Tel (01244) 382196 Mobile 07890-993948

WELCH, Canon Grant Keith. b 40. AKC63. **d** 64 **p** 65. C Nottingham St Mary *S'well* 64-68; V Cinderhill 68-73; R Weston Favell *Pet* 73-88; Master St Jo Hosp Weston Favell 73-88; Can Pet Cathl 83-88; P-in-c Gt Houghton 84-85; C Loughton St Jo *Chelmsf* 89-92; TR 92-05; AD Epping Forest 00-04; rtd 05; Perm to Offic *B & W* from 05. *7 Hayes Lane, Compton Dundon, Somerton TA11 6PB* Tel (01458) 272526
E-mail juliawelch@waitrose.com

WELCH, Harold Gerald. b 16. St Cath Soc Ox BA48 MA53. Wycliffe Hall Ox 48. **d** 50 **p** 51. C Ipswich St Jo *St E* 50-53; V Offton, Nettlestead and Willisham 53-58; V Lozells St Paul *Birm* 58-66; V Austrey 66-83; V Warton 66-83; rtd 83; Perm to Offic *Lich* from 88 and *Birm* 88-00. *2 Clifford Close, Tamworth B77 2DD* Tel (01827) 53678

WELCH, Ian Michael. b 59. Warwick Univ BA81 Connecticut Univ MA84. Ripon Coll Cuddesdon 00. **d** 02 **p** 03. C Lee St Aug *S'wark* 02-05; P-in-c Mottingham St Andr from 05. *The Rectory, 233 Court Road, London SE9 4TQ* Tel (020) 8851 1909
E-mail office@standrewschurch.freeserve.co.uk

WELCH, John Harry. b 52. Oak Hill Th Coll 85. **d** 87 **p** 88. C Parr *Liv* 87-90; V W Derby St Luke 90-00; V Eccleston Park 00-07; P-in-c St Helens St Matt Thatto Heath 06-07; TR Eccleston from 07. *St James's Vicarage, 159A St Helen's Road, Prescot L34 2QB* Tel 0151-426 6421

WELCH, Pamela Jean. b 47. Girton Coll Cam MA76 K Coll Lon BD79 AKC79 PhD05. Qu Coll Birm 79. **dss** 80 **d** 87. Tottenham H Trin *Lon* 80-84; Asst Chapl Bryanston Sch 84-87; Perm to Offic *Chich* 87-94; C Mornington St Mary New Zealand from 02; rtd 07. *23 Byron Street, Mornington, Dunedin 9011, New Zealand* Tel and fax (0064) (3) 453 0052
E-mail welchfam@xtra.co.nz

WELCH, Paul Baxter. b 47. Lanc Univ BEd74 MA75. St Alb Minl Tr Scheme 80. **d** 83 **p** 84. NSM Heath and Reach *St Alb* 83-84; Bp's Sch Adv *Win* 84-89; P-in-c Clungunford w Clunbury and Clunton, Bedstone etc *Heref* 89-93; V Wellingborough All SS *Pet* 93-01; R Pulborough *Chich* from 01; RD Storrington from 04. *The Rectory, 2 London Road, Pulborough RH20 1AP* Tel (01798) 875773 E-mail paul.welch@virgin.net

WELCH, Rebecca Jane. b 79. Leic Univ BSc00. Wycliffe Hall Ox 06. **d** 09. C Cov Cathl from 09. *65 Cotswold Drive, Coventry CV3 6EZ* Tel (024) 7652 1200
E-mail becky.welch@coventrycathedral.org.uk

WELCH, Mrs Sally Ann. b 62. Pemb Coll Ox MA88. SAOMC 96. **d** 99 **p** 00. NSM Abingdon *Ox* 99-01; P-in-c Kintbury w Avington 01-05; R Cherbury w Gainfield 05-09; C Ox St Giles and SS Phil and Jas w St Marg from 09. *St Margaret's Vicarage, St Margaret's Road, Oxford OX2 6RX* Tel (01865) 512319 Mobile 07974-439630 E-mail sally.welch@19a.org.uk

WELCH, The Ven Stephan John. b 50. Hull Univ BA74 Lon Univ MTh98. Qu Coll Birm 74. **d** 77 **p** 78. C Waltham Cross *St Alb* 77-80; P-in-c Reculver Canterbury 80-86; P-in-c Herne Bay St Bart 82-86; V Reculver and Herne Bay St Bart 86-92; V Hurley and Stubbings *Ox* 92-00; P-in-c Hammersmith St Pet *Lon* 00-06; AD Hammersmith and Fulham 01-06; Adn Middx from 06. *98 Dukes Avenue, London W4 2AF* Tel (020) 8742 8308
E-mail stephanjwelch@dsl.pipex.com

WELDON, Nicholas Patrick. b 77. UWE BSc99. Oak Hill Th Coll BA07. **d** 07 **p** 08. C Moreton-in-Marsh w Batsford, Todenham etc *Glouc* from 07. *32 Croft Holm, Moreton-in-Marsh GL56 0JH* Tel (01608) 652199 Mobile 07970-984190
E-mail nickweldon70@hotmail.com

WELDON, Robert Price. b 57. SEITE 06. **d** 09. NSM Caterham *S'wark* from 09. *Arran Lodge, 45 Boxwood Way, Warlingham CR6 9SB* Tel (01883) 624646 Mobile 07929-866879
E-mail bob.weldon@tiscali.co.uk

WELDON, William Ernest. b 41. TCD BA62 MA66. **d** 64 **p** 65. C Belfast Trin Coll Miss *Conn* 64-67; C Carnmoney 67-71; Chapl RN 71-96; QHC 93-96; Hon C Holberton *Ex* 96-01; Perm to

Offic from 01. *3 Garden Close, Holbeton, Plymouth PL8 1NQ* Tel (01752) 830139
E-mail billanddinahweldon@btopenworld.com

WELFORD, Gillian Margaret. Westf Coll Lon BA65. **d** 04 **p** 05. OLM Chiddingfold *Guildf* from 04. *15 Woodberry Close, Chiddingfold, Godalming GU8 4SF* Tel (01428) 683620

WELHAM, Clive Richard. b 54. **d** 80 **p** 81. C Bellingham St Dunstan *S'wark* 80-84; Chapl Goldsmiths' Coll Lon 84-95; V Plumstead Ascension from 95; P-in-c Plumstead St Mark and St Marg from 07. *The Ascension Vicarage, Thornhill Avenue, London SE18 2HS* Tel (020) 8854 3395

WELLER, David Christopher. b 60. UWIST BSc83. St Jo Coll Nottm MA94. **d** 96 **p** 97. C Wednesfield Heath *Lich* 96-99; TV Glascote and Stonydelph 99-05; Chapl Rio de Janeiro Ch Ch Brazil from 05. *Rua Real Grandeza 99, Botafogo, Rio de Janeiro, RJ 22281-030, Brazil* Tel (0055) (21) 2539 9488

WELLER, Richard Morton. b 33. Selw Coll Cam BA57 MA61. Wells Th Coll 61. **d** 63 **p** 64. C Stockingford *Cov* 63-66; C Pontefract St Giles *Wakef* 66-68; C-in-c Stockton St Jas CD *Dur* 68-74; V E Ardsley *Wakef* 74-83; V Heckmondwike 83-91; V Birstall 91-96; RD Birstall 92-96; V Gawber 96-01; rtd 01; Perm to Offic *Wakef* from 02. *14 Callis Way, Penistone, Sheffield S36 6UH* Tel (01226) 379760

WELLER (née SPENCE), Susan Karen. b 65. Leeds Univ BSc86 Liv Univ PhD89. Wycliffe Hall Ox BA95. **d** 96 **p** 97. C Caverswall and Weston Coyney w Dilhorne *Lich* 96-00; C Wilnecote 00-05; Dioc Adv for Women in Min 00-04; Brazil from 05. *Rua Real Grandeza 99, Botafogo, Rio de Janeiro, RJ 22281-030, Brazil* Tel (0055) (21) 2539 9488

WELLING, Anthony Wyndham. b 29. Ely Th Coll 55. **d** 58 **p** 83. C Coppenhall St Paul *Ches* 58-60; Lic to Offic *Ox* 82; Hon C Cookham 83-03; Hon C The Cookhams from 03. *Broadway Barn, High Street, Ripley, Woking GU23 6AQ* Tel (01483) 225384

WELLINGTON, Bishop of. See BROWN, The Rt Revd Thomas John

WELLINGTON, James Frederick. b 51. Leic Univ LLB72 Fitzw Coll Cam BA76. Ridley Hall Cam 74. **d** 77 **p** 78. C Mill Hill Jo Keble Ch *Lon* 77-80; C Wood Green St Mich w Bounds Green St Gabr etc 80-83; V Stocking Farm *Leic* 83-90; V Gt Glen, Stretton Magna and Wistow etc 90-98; Warden of Readers 91-97; RD Gartree II 96-98; TR Syston 98-07; RD Goscote 00-06; Hon Can Leic Cathl 94-07; R Keyworth and Stanton-on-the-Wolds and Bunny etc *S'well* from 07; AD E Bingham from 08. *The Rectory, Nottingham Road, Keyworth, Nottingham NG12 5FD* Tel 0115-937 2017 E-mail jhcwelli@btinternet.com

WELLS, Adrian Mosedale. b 61. SWMTC 96. **d** 99 **p** 00. NSM Kingskerswell w Coffinswell *Ex* 99-02; NSM Wolborough and Ogwell 02-07; C from 07. *St Bartholomew's House, 1 St Bartholomew Way, Ogwell, Newton Abbot TQ12 6YW* Tel (01626) 331147 E-mail amwells@talktalk.net

WELLS, Andrew Stuart. b 48. St Jo Coll Dur BA71 Man Metrop Univ PGCE04. Cranmer Hall Dur. **d** 74 **p** 75. C Walmsley *Man* 74-77; C Failsworth H Family 77-79; R Openshaw 79-90; V Hindsford 90-98. *1 Henry Street, Haslington, Crewe CW1 5PS* Tel (01270) 585303 E-mail andrewwells@hotmail.com

WELLS, Canon Anthony Martin Giffard. b 42. Open Univ BA02. St Jo Coll Nottm 72. **d** 74 **p** 75. C Orpington Ch Ch *Roch* 74-78; P-in-c Odell *St Alb* 78-82; R 82-86; P-in-c Pavenham 78-82; V 82-86; RD Sharnbrook 81-86; R Angmering *Chich* 86-98; RD Arundel and Bognor 93-98; Chapl Paris St Mich *Eur* 98-06; Adn France 02-06; Can Gib Cathl 02-06; rtd 06; Perm to Offic *Eur* from 06. *Shaunbrook House, Clark's Lane, Long Compton, Shipston-on-Stour CV36 5LB* Tel (01608) 684337
E-mail anthonymgwells@btinternet.com

WELLS, Antony Ernest. b 36. Oak Hill Th Coll 58. **d** 61 **p** 62. C Bethnal Green St Jas Less *Lon* 61-64; SAMS Paraguay 64-69; V Kirkdale St Athanasius *Liv* 69-73; SAMS Argentina 73-75; V Warfield *Ox* 75-81; V Fairfield *Liv* 81-83; C Rainhill 83-85; TV Cheltenham St Mark *Glouc* 85-89; P-in-c Forest of Dean Ch Ch w English Bicknor 89-95; rtd 97; C Pinhoe and Broadclyst *Ex* 02-04. *4 Case Gardens, Seaton EX12 2AP* Tel (01297) 20482

WELLS, Miss Cecilia Isabel. b 24. Bedf Coll Lon BA45. St Mich Ho Ox 56. **dss** 62 **d** 87. Chester le Street *Dur* 74-84; rtd 84; Perm to Offic *Ches* from 84. *12 Rectory Close, Nantwich CW5 5SW* Tel (01270) 627258

WELLS, Charles Francis. b 39. Oak Hill Th Coll. **d** 85 **p** 86. C Southend St Sav Westcliff *Chelmsf* 85-89; P-in-c E and W Horndon w Lt Warley 89-96; V E and W Horndon w Lt Warley and Childerditch 96-97; P-in-c Tillingham 97-04; rtd 04; Perm to Offic *Chelmsf* from 04. *14 Irvington Close, Leigh-on-Sea SS9 4NJ* Tel (01702) 512041

WELLS, Daniel Michael. b 74. Trin Coll Cam MA95 Cam Inst of Educn PGCE97. Wycliffe Hall Ox BTh05. **d** 06 **p** 07. C Plymouth St Andr and Stonehouse *Ex* from 06. *18 Glenhurst Road, Plymouth PL3 5LT* Tel (01752) 267025
E-mail dan@wellsweb.org.uk

WELLS, David. See WELLS, Canon William David Sandford

WELLS, David. b 63. Imp Coll Lon BSc85 ARCS85. EAMTC 97. **d** 00 **p** 01. C Sprowston w Beeston *Nor* 00-03; P-in-c Drayton w Felthorpe 03-05; R Drayton from 05. *The Rectory, 46 School Road, Drayton, Norwich NR8 6EF* Tel (01603) 864749
E-mail david.wells@btinternet.com

WELLS, Canon Edward Arthur. b 23. MBE97. SRN. Oak Hill Th Coll. **d** 57 **p** 58. C Wednesfield Heath *Lich* 57-60; R Mettingham w Ilketshall St John *St E* 60-62; R Sproughton w Burstall 62-74; V Ipswich St Nic 74-80; Hon Can St E Cathl 80-90; Chapl Ipswich Hosp 66-90; rtd 90; Perm to Offic *St E* from 90. *74 Christchurch Street, Ipswich IP4 2DH* Tel (01473) 254046

WELLS, Isabel. *See* WELLS, Miss Cecilia Isabel

WELLS, Jeremy Stephen. b 47. Nottm Univ BA69 UWE MSc97. Chich Th Coll 72. **d** 73 **p** 74. C S Yardley St Mich *Birm* 73-76; C St Marychurch *Ex* 76-78; P-in-c Bridgwater H Trin *B & W* 78-82; P-in-c Brent Knoll 82-84; P-in-c E Brent w Lympsham 82-84; R Brent Knoll, E Brent and Lympsham 84-99; Perm to Offic *Chich* 99-07; rtd 07. *15A Victoria Close, Burgess Hill RH15 8QS* Tel (01444) 244275

WELLS, Jo Bailey. b 65. CCC Cam BA87 MA90 Minnesota Univ MA90 St Jo Coll Dur BA92 PhD97. Cranmer Hall Dur. **d** 95 **p** 96. Chapl Clare Coll Cam 95-98; Dean 98-01; Perm to Offic *Nor* 99-04; Tutor Ridley Hall Cam 01-05; Dir Angl Studies Duke Div Sch N Carolina USA from 05. *Duke University Divinity School, Durham NC 27708-0967, USA* Tel (001) (919) 660 3576 Fax 660 3473 E-mail jwells@div.duke.edu

WELLS, John Michael. b 35. Mert Coll Ox BA58 MA61. Westcott Ho Cam 60. **d** 62 **p** 63. C Hornchurch St Andr *Chelmsf* 62-64; C Barking St Marg 64-66; C Wanstead H Trin Hermon Hill 66-69; V Elm Park St Nic Hornchurch 69-76; Offg Chapl RAF 69-76; R Wakes Colne w Chappel *Chelmsf* 76-79; Project Officer Cathl Cen for Research and Tr 79-81; Hon Chapl Chelmsf Cathl 79-81; Area Sec CMS *Chelmsf* and *Ely* 81-88; E Cen Co-ord 85-91; Area Sec *Chelmsf* and *St E* 88-91; Public Preacher *Chelmsf* 82-91; V Hanging Heaton *Wakef* 92-96; rtd 00; Perm to Offic *Chelmsf* from 00. *2 Clarkesmead, Tiptree, Colchester CO5 0BX* Tel (01621) 819899

WELLS, John Rowse David. b 27. Kelham Th Coll 53. **d** 57 **p** 58. SSM from 57; Lic to Offic *S'well* 57-59; Australia 59-65 and from 97; Tutor St Mich Th Coll 61-65; Lesotho 65-96; R Mantsonyane St Jas 67-77; Can SS Mary and Jas Cathl Maseru 77-96; Adn Cen Lesotho 85-95. *St Michael's Priory, 75 Watsons Road, Diggers Rest Vic 3427, Australia* Tel (0061) (3) 9740 1618 Fax 9740 0007 E-mail ssm.melbourne@bigpond.com

WELLS, Leslie John. b 61. Univ of Wales (Ban) BTh06. **d** 04 **p** 05. OLM St Helier *S'wark* 04-08; C Morden from 08. *23 Cedars Road, Morden SM4 5AB* Tel (020) 8715 1084
E-mail leswells80@hotmail.com

WELLS, Lydia Margaret. b 50. St Aid Coll Dur BA72 Sheff Univ MPhil92 Leeds Univ MA00. NOC 97. **d** 00 **p** 01. C Adwick-le-Street w Skelbrooke *Sheff* 00-03; V Doncaster Intake from 03. *The Vicarage, Kingston Road, Intake, Doncaster DN2 6LS* Tel (01302) 343119 Mobile 07977-740813
E-mail lydwells@tesco.net

WELLS, Mark Wynne-Eyton. b 20. Peterho Cam BA48 MA54. Westcott Ho Cam 48. **d** 50 **p** 51. C Heene *Chich* 50-53; C Sullington 53-57; R Slinfold 57-59; S Rhodesia 59-62; V Stoke by Nayland w Leavenheath *St E* 62-88; RD Hadleigh 71-76 and 85-86; rtd 88; Perm to Offic *Nor* from 88. *Stable Cottage, Church Lane, South Raynham, Fakenham NR21 7HE* Tel (01328) 838386

WELLS, Michael John. b 46. Univ Coll Ox BA68 MA73 Solicitor 74. S Dios Minl Tr Scheme 92. **d** 95 **p** 96. NSM Brighton St Pet w Chpl Royal *Chich* 95-98; Sen C 99-04; NSM Brighton St Bart 98-99; rtd 04; Perm to Offic *Chich* from 04. *35 Park Crescent, Brighton BN2 3HB* Tel (01273) 600735

WELLS, Canon Nicholas Anthony. b 60. Cranmer Hall Dur 88. **d** 91 **p** 92. C Accrington St Jo w Huncoat *Blackb* 91-94; C Douglas St Geo and St Barn *S & M* 94-95; C Douglas All SS and St Thos 95-97; V Onchan 97-03; V Netherton *Liv* 03-07; AD Bootle 05-07; P-in-c Maghull 07-09; TR Maghull and Melling from 09; Hon Can Liv Cathl from 05. *The Rectory, 20 Damfield Lane, Liverpool L31 6DD* Tel 0151-286 2310
E-mail nick.the-vic@virgin.net

WELLS, Peter Robert. b 59. Wilson Carlile Coll 78 Sarum & Wells Th Coll 87. **d** 89 **p** 90. CA from 81; C Mortlake w E Sheen *S'wark* 89-93; Dir St Marylebone Healing and Counselling Cen 93-97; TV N Lambeth *S'wark* 97-00; Chapl Trin Hospice Lon 97-03; Chapl Brighton and Sussex Univ Hosps NHS Trust from 03. *Royal Sussex County Hospital, Eastern Road, Brighton BN2 5BE* Tel (01273) 696955 ext 7495
E-mail peter.wells@bsuh.nhs.uk

WELLS, Philip Anthony. b 57. BA MPhil. Coll of Resurr Mirfield. **d** 84 **p** 85. C Wylde Green *Birm* 84-87; Chapl and Succ Birm Cathl 87-91; Bp's Dom Chapl 91-97; V Polesworth from 97. *The Vicarage, High Street, Polesworth, Tamworth B78 1DU* Tel (01827) 892340 E-mail polesworthabbey@aol.com

WELLS, Philip Anthony. b 83. UEA BA04 Leeds Univ BA07 MA08. Coll of Resurr Mirfield 05. **d** 08 **p** 09. C Holt w High

Kelling *Nor* from 08. *Lodge Farm Bungalow, Norwich Road, Holt NR25 6SW* Tel (01263) 710005 Mobile 07813-929549

WELLS, Richard John. b 46. St Mich Coll Llan 68 Cuddesdon Coll 70. **d** 71 **p** 72. C Kingston upon Hull St Alb *York* 71-75; C Addlestone *Guildf* 75-80; V Weston 80-88; V Milford and Chapl Milford Hosp Godalming 88-96; R Westbourne *Chich* 96-08; rtd 08. *39 Merryfield Crescent, Angmering, Littlehampton BN16 4DA* Tel (01903) 776607

WELLS, Robert Crosby. b 28. St Jo Coll Dur BA52. **d** 54 **p** 55. C S Shore H Trin *Blackb* 54-59; C-in-c Lea CD 59-69; V Ribby w Wrea 69-93; rtd 93; Perm to Offic *Blackb* from 93. *4 Myra Road, Fairhaven, Lytham St Annes FY8 1EB* Tel (01253) 739851

WELLS, The Ven Roderick John. b 36. Dur Univ BA63 Hull Univ MA85. Cuddesdon Coll 63. **d** 65 **p** 66. C Lambeth St Mary the Less *S'wark* 65-68; P-in-c 68-71; R Skegness *Linc* 71-77; P-in-c Winthorpe 77; R Skegness and Winthorpe 77-78; TR Gt and Lt Coates w Bradley 78-89; RD Grimsby and Cleethorpes 83-89; Can and Preb Linc Cathl 86-01; Adn Stow 89-01; V Hackthorn w Cold Hanworth 89-93; P-in-c N w S Carlton 89-93; rtd 01; Perm to Offic *Linc* and *Pet* from 01. *9 Hardwick Close, Oakham LE15 6FF* Tel (01572) 756532
E-mail wells1@wells1.netlineuk.net

WELLS, Mrs Sally Ursula. b 40. St Mark's Coll Canberra BTh93 Ripon Coll Cuddesdon 96. **d** 97 **p** 98. Asst Chapl Vienna *Eur* 97-02; Perm to Offic 02-06; rtd 06. *Chemin des Huguenots, 84360 Puget-sur-Durance, France* Tel (0033) (4) 90 08 40 46
E-mail wellsfrance@gmail.com

WELLS, Canon Samuel Martin Bailey. b 65. Mert Coll Ox BA87 MA95 Edin Univ BD91 Dur Univ PhD96. Edin Th Coll 88. **d** 91 **p** 92. C Wallsend St Luke *Newc* 91-95; C Cherry Hinton St Andr *Ely* 95-97; C Teversham 95-97; P-in-c Earlham St Eliz *Nor* 97-03; RD Nor S 99-03; P-in-c Cambridge St Mark *Ely* 03-05; Can Th and Wiccamical Preb Chich Cathl from 04; Dean Duke Chpl Duke Univ N Carolina USA from 05. *Duke University, Durham NC 27708-0967, USA* Tel (001) (919) 684 2177 Fax 681 8660
E-mail samwells@bigfoot.com

WELLS, Terry Roy John. b 45. EAMTC 89. **d** 92 **p** 93. C Martlesham w Brightwell *St E* 92-95; R Higham, Holton St Mary, Raydon and Stratford 95-00; TV Walton and Trimley 00-07; rtd 07; Perm to Offic *Chelmsf* from 07. *Apartment 2, 1 The Maltings, The Quayside Maltings, High Street, Mistley, Manningtree CO11 1AL* Tel (01206) 392957
E-mail terry.wells@tesco.net

WELLS, Canon William David Sandford. b 41. JP. Oriel Coll Ox BA64 MA66. Ridley Hall Cam 63. **d** 65 **p** 66. C Gt Malvern St Mary *Worc* 65-70; V Crowle 70-84; P-in-c Himbleton w Huddington 78-84; V E Bowbrook 84-89; Hon Can Worc Cathl 84-07; RD Droitwich 84-96; R Bowbrook S 89-07; rtd 07. *25 Greenmead Avenue, Everton, Lymington SO41 0UF* Tel (01590) 642499 E-mail david.wells25@tiscali.co.uk

WELLS, Archdeacon of. *See* SULLIVAN, The Ven Nicola Ann

WELLS, Dean of. *See* CLARKE, The Very Revd John Martin

WELSBY, George Andrew. b 61. St Martin's Coll Lanc BA82 Leeds Univ BA98. Coll of Resurr Mirfield 96. **d** 98 **p** 99. C W Derby St Jo *Liv* 98-02; V Nuneaton St Mary *Cov* 02-07; Perm to Offic *Lich* from 08; CMP from 06. *1 Hollies Drive, Wednesbury WS10 9EQ* Tel 0121-505 1568

WELSH, Angus Alexander. b 30. Trin Coll Cam BA54 MA59. St Jo Coll Dur. **d** 56 **p** 57. C Jesmond Clayton Memorial *Newc* 56-60; C Fenham St Jas and St Basil 60-62; V Bacup St Jo *Man* 62-68; Tristan da Cunha 68-71; St Vincent 72-78; R Heysham *Blackb* 78-88; V Blackb St Steph 88-96; rtd 96; Perm to Offic *Newc* from 96. *23 Low Stobhill, Morpeth NE61 2SF* Tel (01670) 513261

WELSH, Colin. CITC. **d** 09. C Jordanstown *Conn* from 09. *4 Regent Street, Carrickfergus BT38 7TZ*
E-mail colin.welsh@talktalk.net

WELSH, Jennifer Ann. b 48. Univ Coll Lon BA. **d** 81 **p** 98. NSM Newport St Matt *Mon* 81-85; NSM Risca 85-04; NSM Maindee Newport from 04. *470 Caerleon Road, Newport NP19 7LW* Tel (01633) 258287

WELSH, Mrs Jennifer Lee. b 59. Calgary Univ BSc81. Cam Episc Div Sch (USA) MDiv87. **d** 87 **p** 88. C Calgary H Nativity Canada 87-89; Asst Chapl HM Pris Linc 89-94; Asst Chapl HM Pris Win 95-02; Chapl to Lutheran Students 03-08; Perm to Offic *Win* 95-02 and *Lon* 03-08; Chapl Univ Coll *Lon* from 08; C St Pancras w St Jas and Ch Ch from 08. *21 Vincent Square, London SW1P 2NA* Tel (020) 7834 1300
E-mail jenniferwelsh@yahoo.co.uk

WELSH, Maxwell Wilfred. b 29. Bp's Coll Calcutta 55. **d** 58 **p** 59. India 58-72; C Cannock *Lich* 73-76; C Wednesfield 76-79; V Milton 79-86; V Croxton w Broughton and Adbaston 86-00; rtd 00; Perm to Offic *Lich* from 01. *24 Churchfield Road, Eccleshall, Stafford ST21 6AG* Tel (01785) 850330

WELSH, Philip Peter. b 48. Keble Coll Ox BA69 MA73 Selw Coll Cam BA72 MA76. Westcott Ho Cam 71. **d** 73 **p** 74. C W Dulwich All SS and Em *S'wark* 73-76; C Surbiton St Andr and St Mark 76-79; Lect St Steph Coll Delhi India 79-81; V Malden St Jo *S'wark* 81-87; Min Officer *Linc* 87-94; TR Basingstoke *Win*

94-02; V Westmr St Steph w St Jo *Lon* from 02. *21 Vincent Square, London SW1P 2NA* Tel (020) 7834 1300
E-mail parishoffice@sswsj.org

WELSH, Robert Leslie. b 32. Sheff Univ BA54. St Jo Coll Dur. **d** 58 **p** 59. C S Westoe *Dur* 58-62; C Darlington St Cuth 62-66; CF (TA) 64-67; V E Rainton *Dur* 66-85; R W Rainton 66-85; R Wolsingham and Thornley 85-97; rtd 97. *12 Lea Green, Wolsingham, Bishop Auckland DL13 3DU* Tel (01388) 528529

WELSMAN, Derek Brian. b 65. Trin Coll Bris. **d** 99 **p** 00. C Ash *Guildf* 99-02; V Easebourne *Chich* from 02; P-in-c Lurgashall, Lodsworth and Selham from 08; Chapl K Edw VII Hosp Midhurst from 02. *The Priory, Easebourne, Midhurst GU29 0AJ* Tel (01730) 812655 *or* 813341
E-mail derekwelsman@btinternet.com

WELTERS, Mrs Elizabeth Ann. b 49. Bris Univ BSc70 Reading Univ PGCE71. SAOMC 94. **d** 97 **p** 98. NSM Aylesbury w Bierton and Hulcott *Ox* 97-03; NSM Schorne from 03. *The Rectory, Rectory Drive, Waddesdon, Aylesbury HP18 0JQ* Tel (01296) 655069 *or* 651312 Mobile 07986-733645
E-mail lizwelters@waitrose.com

WEMYSS, Canon Gary. b 52. Cranmer Hall Dur 79. **d** 80 **p** 81. C Blackb St Jas 80-83; C Padiham 83-86; V Stalmine 86-90; P-in-c Egton-cum-Newland and Lowick *Carl* 90-03; V Egton-cum-Newland and Lowick and Colton from 03; RD Furness from 04; Hon Can Carl Cathl from 08. *The Vicarage, Penny Bridge, Ulverston LA12 7RQ* Tel (01229) 861285
E-mail gwemyss@clara.co.uk

WENHAM, David. b 45. Pemb Coll Cam BA67 MA Man Univ PhD70. Ridley Hall Cam 81. **d** 84 **p** 85. Tutor Wycliffe Hall Ox 84-07; Dean 02-05; Vice-Prin 05-06; NSM Shelswell *Ox* 96-02; NSM Cumnor 03-07; Sen Tutor Trin Coll Bris from 07. *Trinity College, Stoke Hill, Bristol BS9 1JP* Tel 0117-968 0244 Fax 968 7470

WENHAM, Michael Timothy. b 49. Pemb Coll Cam MA75. Wycliffe Hall Ox. **d** 86 **p** 87. C Norbury *Ches* 86-89; V Stanford in the Vale w Goosey and Hatford *Ox* 89-09; rtd 09; Perm to Offic *Ox* from 09. *19 Churchward Close, Grove, Wantage OX12 0QZ* Tel (01235) 760094 Mobile 07719-715640
E-mail michaeltwenham@googlemail.com

WENHAM, Peter William. b 47. Pemb Coll Cam MA73 MD85 FRCS76. St Jo Coll Nottm 98. **d** 01 **p** 02. NSM Wollaton Park *S'well* 01-06; NSM Nottingham W Deanery 06-07; P-in-c Edwalton from 07. *The Vicarage, Village Street, Edwalton, Nottingham NG12 4AB* Tel 0115-923 2034

✠**WENT, The Rt Revd John Stewart.** b 44. CCC Cam BA66 MA70. Oak Hill Th Coll 67. **d** 69 **p** 70 **c** 96. C Northwood Em *Lon* 69-75; V Margate H Trin *Cant* 75-83; Vice-Prin Wycliffe Hall Ox 83-89; Adn Surrey *Guildf* 89-96; Chmn Dioc Coun for Unity and Miss 90-96; Suff Bp Tewkesbury *Glouc* from 96; Hon Can Glouc Cathl from 96. *Bishop's House, Church Road, Staverton, Cheltenham GL51 0TW* Tel (01242) 680188 Fax 680233 E-mail bshptewk@star.co.uk

WENZEL, Peggy Sylvia. STh. Gilmore Ho. **d** 88 **p** 94. Perm to Offic *Sarum* 88-08. *Church Cottage, Church Street, Pewsey SN9 5DL* Tel (01672) 563834

WERNER, David Robert Edmund. b 33. Clifton Th Coll 61. **d** 63 **p** 64. C Holywell *St As* 63-68; C Llanrhos 68-70; R Tedburn St Mary *Ex* 71-91; RD Kenn 80-83; Perm to Offic from 92; rtd 98. *The Old Rectory, Church Lane, Tedburn St Mary, Exeter EX6 6EN* Tel (01647) 61253

WERNER, Canon Donald Kilgour. b 39. Univ of Wales BA61 Linacre Coll Ox BA64 MA67. Wycliffe Hall Ox 61. **d** 64 **p** 65. C Wrexham *St As* 64-69; Chapl Brasted Place Coll Westerham 69-73; Chapl Bris Univ 73-76; Hon C Clifton St Paul 73-76; Chapl Keele Univ 77-79; P-in-c Keele 77-79; C York St Mich-le-Belfrey 79-83; Dir of Evang 79-83; R Holbeton St Geo w H Trin and St Bart *Lon* 83-92; Hon Can Bujumbura from 99; Prof and Dean Th Light Univ Burundi from 03; Lic Preacher *Lon* 02-04; rtd 05. *7 Minstrel Close, Hucknall NG15 7NZ* Tel 0115-963 1504 Mobile 07837-181565 E-mail donaldinburundi@hotmail.com

WERRELL, Ralph Sidney. b 29. Hull Univ PhD02. Tyndale Hall Bris 54. **d** 56 **p** 57. C Penn Fields *Lich* 56-60; C Champion Hill St Sav *S'wark* 60-61; R Danby Wiske w Yafforth *Ripon* 61-65; P-in-c Hutton Bonville *York* 61-65; R Combs *St E* 65-75; V Bootle Ch Ch *Liv* 75-80; R Scole, Brockdish, Billingford, Thorpe Abbots etc *Nor* 80-83; R Southam w Stockton *Cov* 83-89; R Southam 89-94; rtd 95; Perm to Offic *Birm* and *Cov* from 95; *Lich* from 01. *Sameach, 2A Queens Road, Kenilworth CV8 1JQ* Tel and fax (01926) 858677

WERRETT, Olivia Margaret. b 50. Bp Otter Coll 00. **d** 03. NSM Bexhill St Pet *Chich* from 03. *127 Pebsham Lane, Bexhill-on-Sea TN40 2RP* Tel (01424) 214144
E-mail olivia@werrett.freeserve.co.uk

WERWATH, Wolfgang Albert Richard Kurt. b 22. Ripon Hall Ox 54. **d** 56 **p** 57. C Hamer *Man* 56-58; C N Reddish 58-59; V Chadderton St Luke 59-67; V Whitfield *Derby* 67-75; V Bretby w Newton Solney 75-88; rtd 88; Perm to Offic *Derby* from 88 and *S'well* from 90. *28 D'Ayncourt Walk, Farnsfield, Newark NG22 8DP* Tel (01623) 882635

WESSON, Preb John Graham. b 38. St Pet Coll Ox BA62 MA68. Clifton Th Coll 63. **d** 65 **p** 66. C Southport Ch Ch w St Andr *Liv* 65-68; C Ox St Ebbe w St Pet 68-71; Chapl Poly Cen Lon 71-76; C-in-c Edin St Thos 76-82; Dir Past Studies Trin Coll Bris 82-86; R Birm St Martin w Bordesley St Andr 86-96; RD Birm City 88-95; Hon Can Birm Cathl 91-96; Dir Local Min Development *Lich* 96-98; Team Ldr Min Division 99-03; Team Ldr Bd of Min 99-03; C Lich St Mich w St Mary and Wall 96-03; Preb Lich Cathl 99-03; rtd 03. *11 Gordon Drive, Abingdon OX14 3SW* Tel (01235) 526088

WESSON, William James. b 60. Lon Univ BA82 Leeds Univ BA07. Coll of Resurr Mirfield 05. **d** 07 **p** 08. C Moulsecoomb *Chich* from 07. *St Andrew's Rectory, Hillside, Brighton BN2 4TA*

WEST, Alan David. b 61. Southn Univ BTh92 Thames Valley Univ MA97. Aston Tr Scheme 87 Sarum & Wells Th Coll 89. **d** 92 **p** 93. C S'wark St Geo the Martyr w St Jude 92-94; C S'wark St Geo w St Alphege and St Jude 95-96; V Boscoppa *Truro* 96-02; Chapl Mt Edgcumbe Hospice 02-05; Chapl R Cornwall Hosps Trust from 05. *Royal Cornwall Hospital, Treliske, Truro TR1 3LJ* Tel (01872) 252883
E-mail alan.west@rcht.cornwall.nhs.uk

WEST, Andrew Victor. b 59. Wycliffe Hall Ox 87. **d** 90 **p** 91. C Leyland St Andr *Blackb* 90-94; C Blackpool St Jo 94-96; TV Bedworth *Cov* 96-98; Chapl Cheltenham and Glouc Coll of HE 98-01; Chapl Glos Univ 01-03; Chapl St Martin's Coll *Carl* 03-07; Chapl Cumbria Univ from 07; C Carl St Jo from 03. *Crocus Hill, Heads Nook, Brampton CA8 9AF* Tel (01228) 564037

WEST, Bernard Kenneth. b 31. Linc Th Coll. **d** 67 **p** 68. C E Ham St Geo *Chelmsf* 67-71; C Gt Bookham *Guildf* 71-73; R Esperance Australia 73-76; C Dalkeith 76-79; P-in-c Carine 80-82; R Carine w Duncraig 82-84; C Ravensthorpe 85-87; rtd 87. *9 Beaufort Street, Katanning WA 6317, Australia* Tel (0061) (8) 9821 4571

WEST, Bryan Edward. b 39. Avery Hill Coll CertEd69 BEd80 Kent Univ MA86. Cant Sch of Min 85. **d** 88 **p** 89. NSM Gravesend H Family w Ifield *Roch* 88-92; C Gravesend St Geo 92-95; NSM Hatcham Park All SS *S'wark* 95-98; NSM Stambridge and Ashingdon w S Fambridge *Chelmsf* 98-01; NSM Canvey Is 01-06; Chapl Southend Health Care NHS Trust 99-06; Perm to Offic *Chelmsf* from 06. *The Rectory, 7 Merlin End, Colchester CO4 3FW* Tel (01206) 866145
E-mail bryanwest@tiscali.co.uk

WEST, Miss Caroline Elisabeth. b 61. RGN84. Wycliffe Hall Ox 93. **d** 95. NSM Eastrop *Win* from 95. *19 Beaulieu Court, Riverdene, Basingstoke RG21 4DQ* Tel (01256) 350389 *or* 464249
E-mail caroline.west@stmarys-basingstoke.org.uk

WEST, Mrs Christine Cecily. TCD BA60 MA63 HDipEd61. CITC 91. **d** 94 **p** 95. NSM Bray *D & G* 94-96; NSM Kilternan 96-99; Lic to Offic from 99. *55 Beech Park Road, Foxrock, Dublin 18, Republic of Ireland* Tel (00353) (1) 289 6374

WEST, Clive. b 35. QUB BD75 Stranmillis Coll TCert57. CITC 62. **d** 64 **p** 65. C Lisburn Ch Ch Cathl 64-68; Asst Master Lisnagarvey Sec Sch Lisburn 68-70; C Belfast All SS 70-75; I 84-00; Can Belf Cathl 95-00; I Mullabrack w Kilcluney *Arm* 76-84; rtd 00. *16 Stormont Park, Belfast BT4 3GX* Tel (028) 9041 9317 E-mail clivewest@tiscali.co.uk

WEST, David Marshall. b 48. St Jo Coll Dur BA70. **d** 73 **p** 74. C Wylde Green *Birm* 73-76; C Wokingham St Paul *Ox* 76-79; V Hurst 79-88; V Maidenhead St Luke 88-95; C Whitley Ch Ch 95-99; P-in-c Reading Ch Ch 99-05; V from 05. *Christ Church Vicarage, 4 Vicarage Road, Reading RG2 7AJ* Tel 0118-987 1250
E-mail revdmwest@hotmail.com

WEST, Derek Elvin. b 47. Hull Univ BA69. Westcott Ho Cam 71. **d** 73 **p** 74. C Walthamstow St Pet *Chelmsf* 73-77; C Chingford SS Pet and Paul 77-80; TV W Slough *Ox* 80-88; Slough Community Chapl 88-95; TV Upton cum Chalvey from 95. *St Peter's Vicarage, 52 Montem Lane, Slough SL1 2QJ* Tel (01753) 520725

WEST, Mrs Elizabeth Maxine. b 47. Liv Univ BA69 Lon Inst of Educn PGCE70 K Coll Lon BA95 AKC. NTMTC. **d** 99 **p** 00. NSM Hornsey H Innocents *Lon* 99-00; NSM Highgate St Mich 00-03; C from 03. *West Villa, Inderwick Road, London N8 9JU* Tel (020) 8348 3042

WEST, Eric Edward. b 32. Leeds Univ BA60. Bps' Coll Cheshunt 63. **d** 64 **p** 65. C Biscot *St Alb* 64-71; V 71-02; rtd 03; Perm to Offic *St Alb* from 03. *134 Brompton Close, Luton LU3 3QU* Tel (01582) 581417

WEST, Eric Robert Glenn. b 55. QUB BA79 Man Univ DipEd80. CITC BTh92. **d** 92 **p** 93. C Enniskillen *Clogh* 92-95; I Lisbellaw 95-00; CF 00-03; I Annagh w Drumgoon, Ashfield etc *K, E & A* 03-06; I Derryvullen N w Castlearchdale *Clogh* from 06. *6 The Everglades, Enniskillen BT74 6FE* Tel (028) 6634 6870 Mobile 07969-332530

WEST, Harold Reginald. b 15. Dur Univ BA43 MA46. Coll of Resurr Mirfield 43. **d** 45 **p** 46. C Tynemouth H Trin W Town *Newc* 45-48; C Sugley 48-55; V Cresswell 55-61; V Newc St Luke 61-82; rtd 82; Perm to Offic *Newc* from 82. *42 Linden Road, Gosforth, Newcastle upon Tyne NE3 4HB* Tel 0191-284 4291

WEST, Henry Cyrano. b 28. K Coll Lon. **d** 51 **p** 52. C Braunstone *Leic* 51-53; C Wandsworth St Anne *S'wark* 53-55; C Raynes Park St Sav 55-58; CF 58-63; V Sculcoates *York* 63-71; P-in-c Kingston upon Hull St Jude w St Steph 67-71; Lic to Offic *Cov* 71-75 and *Man* 75-87; Hon C Hulme Ascension *Man* 87-94; rtd 91; Perm to Offic *Man* from 91. *6 King's Drive, Middleton, Manchester M24 4FB* Tel 0161-643 4410

WEST, Jeffrey James. b 50. OBE06. Worc Coll Ox BA72 BPhil74 MA76 FRSA01. Ripon Coll Cuddesdon 05. **d** 07 **p** 08. NSM Banbury *Ox* from 07. *St Mary's Centre, Horse Fair, Banbury OX16 0AA* Tel 07766-198484 (mobile)
E-mail curate@stmaryschurch-banbury.org.uk

WEST, Keith. *See* RYDER-WEST, Keith

WEST (formerly WINDIATE), Mrs Mary Elizabeth. b 49. Linc Th Coll 94. **d** 94 **p** 95. C Loughton St Jo *Chelmsf* 94-98; P-in-c Ashingdon w S Fambridge 98-01; P-in-c Stambridge 98-01; TV Canvey Is 01-07; P-in-c Greenstead w Colchester St Anne 07-08; TR from 08. *The Rectory, 7 Merlin End, Colchester CO4 3FW* Tel (01206) 866145 E-mail mothermary2@tiscali.co.uk

WEST, Maxine. *See* WEST, Mrs Elizabeth Maxine

WEST, Canon Michael Brian. b 39. Bris Univ BSc60. Linc Th Coll 64. **d** 66 **p** 67. C Bp's Hatfield *St Alb* 66-69; Ind Chapl 69-81; Sen Ind Chapl 71-81; Hon Can St Alb 78-81; Sen Ind Chapl and Hon Can Sheff Cathl 81-01; Dir Open Forum for Economic Regeneration 02-04; rtd 04; Perm to Offic *Sheff* from 02. *23 Walton Road, Sheffield S11 8RE* Tel 0114-266 2188
E-mail mikepamwest@tinyworld.co.uk

WEST, Michael Frederick. b 50. Trin Coll Ox BA72 MA76 UEA PhD96. Westcott Ho Cam 72. **d** 74 **p** 75. C Wolverhampton *Lich* 74-78; C Hanley H Ev 78-79; TV 79-82; Dioc Youth Officer *St E* 83-88; V Ipswich St Thos 88-95; Prin OLM Scheme 96-03; Hon Can St E Cathl 96-03; Can Res and Chan Linc Cathl 03-08; Dioc Dir Formation in Discipleship and Min 03-06; TR Wrexham *St As* from 08; AD Wrexham from 08. *The Rectory, 7 Westminster Drive, Wrexham LL12 7AT* Tel (01978) 263905
E-mail rector@wrexhamparish.org.uk

WEST, Michael John. b 33. Imp Coll Lon BScEng54 ARSM52 CEng60 FIMMM68 FREng89 Hon FIMMM96. S'wark Ord Course 85. **d** 88 **p** 89. NSM Caterham *S'wark* 88-98; Perm to Offic *Chich* from 97. *Minstrels, The Causeway, Horsham RH12 1HE* Tel (01403) 263437 Fax 249604
E-mail mwest.viabt@btinternet.com

WEST, Michael Oakley. b 31. Open Univ BA97. Bris Bapt Coll 53 Wells Th Coll 62. **d** 63 **p** 64. C Swindon Ch Ch *Bris* 63-66; Surg 66-68; R Lydiard Millicent w Lydiard Tregoz *Bris* 68-75; V Breage w Germoe *Truro* 75-82; CMS 82-91; Chapl Tel Aviv 82-89; Chapl Shiplake Coll Henley 91-94; Asst Chapl Bryanston Sch 94-95; Perm to Offic *Eur* 95-97; rtd 96; Perm to Offic *Lon* 96-97; Lic to Offic Spokane USA from 97. *1932 East 25th Avenue, Spokane WA 99203, USA*

WEST, Paul Leslie. b 57. OLM course 96. **d** 99 **p** 00. OLM Kinnerley w Melverley and Knockin w Maesbrook *Lich* from 99. *Braddan, Farm Hall, Kinnerley, Oswestry SY10 8EG* Tel (01691) 682600

WEST, Peter Harcourt. b 29. **d** 59 **p** 60. C Histon *Ely* 59-60; C Hampreston *Sarum* 60-61; C Braintree *Chelmsf* 61-63; Perm to Offic from 72; rtd 94. *Westgates, 139 Witham Road, Black Notley, Braintree CM7 8LR* Tel (01376) 323048

WEST, Canon Philip William. b 48. Magd Coll Ox BA70 MA78. St Jo Coll Nottm BA74. **d** 75 **p** 76. C Rushden w Newton Bromswold *Pet* 75-79; C Pitsmoor w Ellesmere *Sheff* 79-83; V Attercliffe 83-89; Ind Chapl 85-90; P-in-c Darnall 86-89; V Stannington from 89; P-in-c Sheff St Barn 02-07; AD Hallam 96-02; Hon Can Sheff Cathl from 01. *The Vicarage, 214 Oldfield Road, Stannington, Sheffield S6 6DY* Tel 0114-232 4490 *or* 234 5586

WEST, Reginald Roy. b 28. St Deiniol's Hawarden 74. **d** 74 **p** 75. C Abergavenny St Mary w Llanwenarth Citra *Mon* 74-77; V Tredegar St Jas 77-96; rtd 96; Lic to Offic *Mon* from 96. *2 Croesonen Park, Abergavenny NP7 6PD* Tel (01873) 857043

WEST, Ruth. d 09. C Waterford w Killea, Drumcannon and Dunhill *C & O* from 09. *8 Cathedral Close, Henrietta Street, Waterford, Republic of Ireland* Tel (00353) (51) 843648
E-mail ruthjwest@hotmail.com

WEST, Stephen Peter. b 52. Liv Univ CertEd74. Oak Hill Th Coll 87. **d** 89 **p** 90. C Gateacre *Liv* 89-92; V Liv All So Springwood 92-02; TV Teignmouth, Ideford w Luton, Ashcombe etc *Ex* from 02. *The Vicarage, 3 Moors Park, Bishopsteignton, Teignmouth TQ14 9RH* Tel and fax (01626) 775247
E-mail spmwest@btinternet.com

WEST, Mrs Suzanne Elizabeth. b 46. STETS 04. **d** 07 **p** 08. NSM Portsea St Geo *Portsm* from 07. *64 Melville Road, Gosport PO12 4QX* Tel (023) 9278 8782
E-mail melville64@ntlworld.com

WEST, Canon Thomas Roderic. b 55. BTh90. TCD Div Sch. **d** 86 **p** 87. C Dromore Cathl 86-89; I Carrowdore w Millisle 89-95; I Moira from 95; Can Dromore Cathl from 05; Chan from 08. *The Rectory, 1 Main Street, Moira, Craigavon BT67 0LE* Tel (028) 9261 1268 *or* 9261 7333 E-mail roderic@moiraparish.org.uk

WEST, Timothy Ralph. b 53. Bath Univ BSc75. Ridley Hall Cam 82. **d** 85 **p** 86. C Mildenhall *St E* 85-88; TV Melbury *Sarum* 88-92; TR 92-98; TR Preston w Sutton Poyntz and Osmington w Poxwell from 98. *The Rectory, Sutton Road, Preston, Weymouth DT3 6BX* Tel (01305) 833142 Mobile 07000-785720
E-mail t.r.west@psion.net

WEST AFRICA, Archbishop of. *See* AKROFI, The Most Revd Justice Ofei

WEST CUMBERLAND, Archdeacon of. *See* PRATT, The Ven Richard David

WEST HAM, Archdeacon of. *See* COCKETT, The Ven Elwin Wesley

WEST INDIES, Archbishop of. *Vacant*

WEST-LINDELL, Stein Erik. b 54. BA. Linc Th Coll 82. **d** 84 **p** 85. C Allington and Maidstone St Pet *Cant* 84-87; R Orlestone w Snave and Ruckinge w Warehorne 87-93; R Byfield w Boddington and Aston le Walls *Pet* 93-99; V Nor Lakenham St Alb and St Mark from 99. *St Alban's Vicarage, Eleanor Road, Norwich NR1 2RE* Tel (01603) 621843

WESTALL, Jonathan Mark. b 67. Nottm Univ BSc88 K Coll Lon PGCE93 St Jo Coll Dur BA98. Cranmer Hall Dur 96. **d** 99 **p** 00. C St Helier *S'wark* 99-02; C Reading Greyfriars *Ox* 02-06; V E Acton St Dunstan w St Thos *Lon* from 06. *The Vicarage, 54 Perryn Road, London W3 7NA* Tel (020) 8743 4117
E-mail jonwestall@btinternet.com

✠**WESTALL, The Rt Revd Michael Robert.** b 39. Qu Coll Cam BA62 MA66. Cuddesdon Coll 63 Harvard Div Sch 65. **d** 66 **p** 67 **c** 01. C Heref St Martin 66-70; India 70-83; Vice Prin Bp's Coll Calcutta 76-79; Prin 79-83; Prin St Mark's Th Coll Dar-es-Salaam Tanzania 84-92; R Alfrick, Lulsley, Suckley, Leigh and Bransford *Worc* 93-00; Bp SW Tanganyika 01-06; rtd 06; P-in-c Torquay St Luke *Ex* from 07; Hon Asst Bp Ex from 07. *St Luke's Vicarage, 1 Mead Road, Torquay TQ2 6TE* Tel (01803) 605437

WESTBROOK, Canon Colin David. b 36. Oriel Coll Ox BA59. St Steph Ho Ox MA63. **d** 61 **p** 62. C Roath St Martin *Llan* 61-66; C Roath 66-74; V Llantarnam *Mon* 74-79; V Newport St Jo Bapt 79-07; P-in-c from 07; Hon Can St Woolos Cathl 88-91; Can from 91; Warden of Ords 91-99. *St John's Vicarage, 62 Oakfield Road, Newport NP20 4LP* Tel (01633) 265581

WESTBROOK (née REED), Mrs Ethel Patricia Ivy. b 42. Bris Univ CertEd63. Cant Sch of Min 82. **dss** 84 **d** 87 **p** 94. Fawkham and Hartley *Roch* 84-85; Asst Dir of Educn 84-86; Cliffe at Hoo w Cooling 85-86; Corby SS Pet and Andr w Gt and Lt Oakley 86-90; Par Dn 87-90; Par Dn Roch 90-94; C Rainham 94-99; V Joydens Wood St Barn 99-05; Dioc Chapl MU 01-05; rtd 05; Hon C Banstead *Guildf* from 05; Perm to Offic *Roch* from 05. *14 Glenfield Road, Banstead SM7 2DG* Tel (01737) 353938
E-mail patwestbrook@wipe.fsnet.co.uk

WESTBY, Martyn John. b 61. Leeds Univ BA83. Trin Coll Bris 96. **d** 98 **p** 99. C Drypool *York* 98-01; P-in-c Cherry Burton from 01; Chapl Bp Burton Coll York from 01; Assoc Dioc Dir of Ords *York* from 05. *The Rectory, Main Street, Cherry Burton, Beverley HU17 7RF* Tel (01964) 503036

WESTCOTT, James John. b 55. St Jo RC Sem Surrey 76. **d** 81 **p** 82. In RC Ch 81-93; C Westmr St Steph w St Jo *Lon* 93-96; P-in-c Haggerston St Chad 96-01; V from 01. *St Chad's Vicarage, Dunloe Street, London E2 8JR* Tel (020) 7613 2229
E-mail chad@jameswestcott.co.uk

WESTERMANN-CHILDS, Miss Emma Jane. b 71. Univ of Wales (Ban) BA93 Ox Univ MTh99. Ripon Coll Cuddesdon 96. **d** 98 **p** 99. C Launceston *Truro* 98-01; P-in-c St Stephen in Brannel from 01. *The Rectory, 70 Rectory Road, St Stephen, St Austell PL26 7RL* Tel (01726) 822236
E-mail emma.childs@btinternet.com

WESTERN, Canon Robert Geoffrey. b 37. Man Univ BSc60. Qu Coll Birm. **d** 62 **p** 63. C Sedbergh *Bradf* 62-65; PV Linc Cathl 65-73; Hd Master Linc Cathl Sch 74-96; Can and Preb Linc Cathl 74-96; rtd 97. *2 Guldrey House, Guldrey Lane, Sedbergh LA10 5DS* Tel (01539) 621426

WESTHAVER, George Derrick. b 68. St Mary's Univ Halifax NS BA92. Wycliffe Coll Toronto MDiv98. **d** 97 **p** 98. C Teversham and Cherry Hinton St Andr *Ely* 97-00; TV The Ramseys and Upwood 00-03; Chapl Linc Coll Ox 03-06; C Ox St Mich w St Martin and All SS 03-06; R Halifax St Geo Canada from 07. *2222 Brunswick Avenue, Halifax NS B3K 2Z3, Canada* Tel (001) (902) 423 1059 Fax 423 0897 E-mail gwesthaver@gmail.com

WESTLAKE, Michael Paul. b 34. Ex Coll Ox BA56 MA64. Wells Th Coll 59. **d** 61 **p** 62. C Southmead *Bris* 61-67; V Eastville St Thos 67-74; V Eastville St Thos w St Anne 74-83; P-in-c Easton St Mark 79-83; V Marshfield w Cold Ashton and Tormarton etc 83-01; rtd 01; Perm to Offic *Birm* from 03. *65 Duxford Road, Great Barr, Birmingham B42 2JD* Tel 0121-358 7030

WESTLAND, Richard Theodore. b 27. **d** 87 **p** 88. OLM Freiston w Butterwick *Linc* 87-97; rtd 97; Perm to Offic *Linc* from 97. *76 Brand End Road, Butterwick, Boston PE22 0JD* Tel (01205) 760572

WESTLEY, Stuart. b 24. Em Coll Cam BA48 MA52 Man Univ DASE84. Wells Th Coll 49. **d** 50 **p** 51. C Prestwich St Marg *Man* 50-53; C Tonge w Alkrington 53-55; C-in-c Oldham St Ambrose 55-58; Lic to Offic *Blackb* 58-70; Chapl Arnold Sch Blackpool 58-66; Asst Chapl Denstone Coll Uttoxeter 70-73; Chapl Ermysted's Gr Sch Skipton 73-85; Hon C Blackpool St Mich *Blackb* 75-77; Perm to Offic *Bradf* 77-78; Lic to Offic 78-85; C Padiham *Blackb* 85-89; rtd 89; Perm to Offic *Blackb* from 89. *20 Crichton Place, Blackpool FY4 1NS* Tel (01253) 347962 E-mail s.westley@amserve.net

WESTMINSTER, Archdeacon of. *Vacant*

WESTMINSTER, Dean of. *See* HALL, The Very Revd John Robert

WESTMORELAND, Mrs Diane Ruth. b 57. Man Univ BA78. NEOC 95. **d** 98 **p** 99. NSM Tadcaster w Newton Kyme *York* 98-99; C 99-02; P-in-c Stamford Bridge Gp 02-08; P-in-c Amble *Newc* from 08. *The Vicarage, Straffen Court, Amble, Morpeth NE65 0HA* Tel (01665) 714560 E-mail diane@dianewestmoreland.com

WESTMORLAND AND FURNESS, Archdeacon of. *See* HOWE, The Ven George Alexander

WESTNEY, Michael Edward William. b 29. Lich Th Coll 64. **d** 65 **p** 66. C Hughenden *Ox* 65-68; C Banbury 68-71; TV Trunch *Nor* 71-78; V Reading St Matt *Ox* 78-83; TV W Slough 83-88; TR 88-94; rtd 94; Perm to Offic *Ox* 97-00. *59 Portland Close, Burnham, Slough SL2 2LT* Tel (01628) 660052

WESTON, Canon David Wilfrid Valentine. b 37. Lanc Univ PhD93. **d** 67 **p** 68. OSB 60-84; Lic to Offic *Ox* 67-84; Prior Nashdom Abbey 71-74; Abbot 74-84; C Chorley St Pet *Blackb* 84-85; V Pilling 85-89; Bp's Dom Chapl *Carl* 89-94; Can Res Carl Cathl 94-05; Lib 95-05; Vice-Dean 00; rtd 05. *40 St James Road, Carlisle CA2 5PD* Tel (01228) 550331

WESTON, Gary James. b 72. Westmr Coll Ox BTh95. Wycliffe Hall Ox 02. **d** 04 **p** 05. C Barrow St Paul *Carl* 04-08; C S Barrow 08-09; P-in-c Hinckley H Trin *Leic* from 09. *7 Rosemary Way, Hinckley LE10 0LN* Tel (01455) 233552 E-mail gary.weston@ukonline.co.uk

WESTON, Ivan John. b 45. MBE88. Chich Th Coll 71. **d** 74 **p** 75. C Harlow St Mary Magd *Chelmsf* 74-77; Chapl RAF 77-00; Perm to Offic *Nor* 93-95 and *Ely* from 00. *2 The Furlongs, Needingworth, St Ives PE27 4TX* Tel (01480) 462107

WESTON, John Oglivy. b 30. St Pet Coll Ox BA66 MA70. Linc Th Coll 71. **d** 71 **p** 72. Lect Trent (Nottm) Poly 66-82; Hon C Long Clawson and Hose *Leic* 71-82; Hon C Bingham *S'well* 82-85; Lic to Offic 85-91; rtd 91; Perm to Offic *Heref* from 91. *Mowbray Lodge, Marshbrook, Church Stretton SY6 6QE* Tel (01694) 781288

WESTON, Mrs Judith. b 36. Open Univ BA75 MSR56. St Jo Coll Nottm 84. dss 85 **d** 87 **p** 94. Huddersfield H Trin *Wakef* 85-87; Par Dn 87-91; Par Dn Wakef St Andr and St Mary 91-94; C 94-95; Chapl Huddersfield NHS Trust 95-98; rtd 96; Perm to Offic *Wakef* from 98. *Overcroft, 8A Newland Road, Huddersfield HD5 0QT* Tel (01484) 453591

WESTON, Canon Keith Aitken Astley. b 26. Trin Hall Cam BA51 MA55. Ridley Hall Cam 51. **d** 53 **p** 54. C Weston-super-Mare Ch Ch *B & W* 53-56; C Cheltenham St Mark *Glouc* 56-59; PC Clevedon Ch Ch *B & W* 59-64; R Ox St Ebbe w H Trin and St Pet 64-85; RD Ox 71-76; Hon Can Ch Ch 81-85; Dir Post-Ord Tr *Nor* 85-90; Dioc Dir of Ords 85-91; P-in-c Nor St Steph 85-91; Hon Brigade Chapl Norfolk Co Fire Service 90-91; rtd 91; Hon C Thame *Ox* from 91. *18 Moor End Lane, Thame OX9 3BQ* Tel (01844) 215441

WESTON, Neil. b 51. Jes Coll Ox BA73 MA78. Ridley Hall Cam 74. **d** 76 **p** 77. C Ealing St Mary *Lon* 76-80; P-in-c Pertenhall w Swineshead *St Alb* 80-89; P-in-c Dean w Yelden, Melchbourne and Shelton 80-89; R The Stodden Churches 89-91; R Newhaven *Chich* 91-98; P-in-c Radcliffe-on-Trent and Shelford etc *S'well* 98-04; R 04-05; V Radcliffe-on-Trent and Shelford 06-09; R Kington w Huntington, Old Radnor, Kinnerton etc *Heref* from 09. *The Vicarage, Church Road, Kington HR5 3AG* Tel (01544) 230525 E-mail neilweston@ntlworld.com

WESTON, Paul David Astley. b 57. Trin Hall Cam BA80 MA83 Westmr Coll Ox MPhil92 K Coll Lon PhD02. Wycliffe Hall Ox 83. **d** 85 **p** 86. C New Malden and Coombe *S'wark* 85-89; Lect Oak Hill Th Coll 89-97; Vice-Prin 97-00; Gen Sec UCCF 00-01; Assoc Lect Ridley Hall Cam 02-03; Tutor from 03; Perm to Offic *Ely* from 01. *Ridley Hall, Ridley Hall Road, Cambridge CB3 9HG* Tel (01223) 741080 E-mail pdaw2@cam.ac.uk

WESTON, Ralph Edward Norman. b 30. Worc Ord Coll 67. **d** 69 **p** 70. C Harborne St Pet *Birm* 69-71; CF 71-75; Chapl Oswestry Sch 75-85; Chapl Rotherham Distr Gen Hosp 85-95; CF (ACF) 87-95; TV Thorverton, Cadbury, Upton Pyne etc *Ex* 95-99; rtd 95; Perm to Offic *Ex* from 99. *10 Rogers Close, Tiverton EX16 6UW* Tel and fax (01884) 259622

WESTON, Canon Stephen John Astley. b 55. Aston Univ BSc77. Ridley Hall Cam 78. **d** 81 **p** 82. C Gt Chesham Ox 81-85; C Southport Ch Ch *Liv* 85-87; P-in-c Gayhurst w Ravenstone, Stoke Goldington etc *Ox* 87-91; R 91-96; RD Newport 92-95; V Chipping Norton 96-01; TR from 01; AD Chipping Norton

02-07; Hon Can Ch Ch from 06. *The Vicarage, Church Street, Chipping Norton OX7 5NT* Tel (01608) 642688 E-mail revsweston@lineone.net

WESTON, Timothy Bernard Charles. b 48. **d** 03 **p** 04. OLM Watton w Carbrooke and Ovington *Nor* 03-07; OLM Ashill, Carbrooke, Ovington and Saham Toney from 07. *The Oaks, Shipdham Road, Carbrooke, Thetford IP25 6SX* Tel (01362) 820292 E-mail rev.weston@dsl.pipex.com

WESTON, Mrs Virginia Anne. b 58. UEA BSc79. Wycliffe Hall Ox 84. **d** 87 **p** 02. Par Dn New Malden and Coombe *S'wark* 87-89; Lic to Offic *Lon* 89-01; Chapl to People at Work in Cam *Ely* 02-06. *65 Manor Place, Cambridge CB1 1LJ* Tel (01223) 462279 E-mail virginiaweston@yahoo.co.uk

WESTWOOD, Canon John Richard. b 55. Clare Coll Cam BA77 MA81 Lambeth MA98. Ripon Coll Cuddesdon 77. **d** 79 **p** 80. C Oakham w Hambleton and Egleton *Pet* 79-81; C Oakham, Hambleton, Egleton, Braunston and Brooke 81-83; V Gt w Lt Harrowden and Orlingbury 83-90; V Wellingborough St Andr 90-99; RD Wellingborough 92-97; R Irthlingborough from 99; Warden of Readers 95-05; Can Pet Cathl from 97. *The Rectory, 79 Finedon Road, Irthlingborough, Wellingborough NN9 5TY* Tel (01933) 650278 E-mail john@johnwestwood.fsnet.co.uk

WESTWOOD, Peter. b 38. Open Univ BA76. AKC65. **d** 65 **p** 66. C Acomb St Steph *York* 65-68; Chapl HM Youth Cust Cen Onley 69-73; Chapl HM Pris Leic 73-77; Maidstone 77-81; Dur 81-87; Brixton 87-93; Wormwood Scrubs 93-98; Perm to Offic *S'wark* from 98; rtd 99. *St Stephen's Church, College Road, London SE21 7HN* Tel (020) 8693 0082

WESTWOOD, Richard Andrew. b 64. Nottm Univ BSc85 PGCE86. St Jo Coll Nottm 02. **d** 04 **p** 05. C Gt Wyrley *Lich* from 04. *46 Gorsey Lane, Great Wyrley, Walsall WS6 6EX* Tel (01922) 419161 E-mail rrejas@ic24.net

WESTWOOD, Timothy. b 61. Wolv Poly MBA91. WMMTC 95. **d** 98 **p** 99. NSM Sedgley St Mary *Worc* from 98. *5 Deborah Close, Wolverhampton WV2 3HS* Tel (01902) 831078 E-mail twestwood@blueyonder.co.uk

WETHERALL, Canon Cecil Edward (Ted). b 29. St Jo Coll Dur 49. **d** 56 **p** 57. C Ipswich St Aug *St E* 56-59; R Hitcham 59-79; P-in-c Brettenham 61-63; P-in-c Kettlebaston 71-91; R Hitcham w Lt Finborough 79-91; P-in-c Preston 85-91; Hon Can St E Cathl 83-91; rtd 92; Perm to Offic *St E* 92-97; Asst Chapl Patras w Kifissia, Patras, Thessaloniki etc *Eur* 92-96. *Kastraki, Tolo, Nafplio, 210 56 Argolis, Greece*

WETHERALL, Mrs Joanne Elizabeth Julia. b 62. STETS 02. **d** 05 **p** 06. NSM Godalming *Guildf* 05-09; TV Tring *St Alb* from 09. *The Vicarage, Station Road, Aldbury, Tring HP23 5RS* Tel (01442) 851200 E-mail simon.wetherall@which.net

WETHERALL, Nicholas Guy. b 52. Lon Univ BMus73 Ox Univ CertEd75. Chich Th Coll 82. **d** 84 **p** 85. C Cleobury Mortimer w Hopton Wafers *Heref* 84-87; TV Leominster 87-92; V Cuckfield *Chich* from 92; RD Cuckfield 99-03. *The Vicarage, Broad Street, Cuckfield, Haywards Heath RH17 5LL* Tel (01444) 454007

WETHERELL, Ms Eileen Joyce. b 44. Westf Coll Lon BSc66. S Dios Minl Tr Scheme 89. **d** 92 **p** 94. Par Dn Southampton Maybush St Pet *Win* 92-94; C 94-96; TV Totton 96-04; V Hythe from 04; Dioc Adv for Women's Min from 02. *The Vicarage, 14 Atheling Road, Hythe, Southampton SO45 6BR* Tel (023) 8084 2461 E-mail eileenwetherell@btinternet.com

WETHERELL, Philip Anthony. b 45. Leic Univ MPhil87. AKC72. **d** 73 **p** 74. C Walthamstow St Sav *Chelmsf* 73-75; Chapl and Tutor Namibia Internat Peace Cen 75-76; C Knighton St Mary Magd *Leic* 76-80; TV Southampton (City Cen) *Win* 80-84; Miss Personnel Sec USPG 84-96; Admin Coun for Educn in World Citizenship 97-98; Development Officer Kaloko Trust UK 98-00; Dir Chrs Abroad 00-07; rtd 07. *3 Champford Mews, Wellington TA21 8JW* Tel (01823) 665951

WETHERELL, Philippa Clare. b 80. Univ of Wales (Cardiff) BSc02. Trin Coll Bris BA08. **d** 09. C W Derby St Mary and St Jas *Liv* from 09. *4 The Armoury, West Derby, Liverpool L12 5EL* Tel 07770-892639 (mobile) E-mail phillyfrog@yahoo.com

WEYMAN, Canon Richard Darrell George. b 46. Lon Univ BA Bris Univ PhD. Sarum & Wells Th Coll. **d** 84 **p** 85. C Sherborne w Castleton and Lillington *Sarum* 84-88; V Malden St Jo *S'wark* 88-92; P-in-c Marnhull *Sarum* from 92; Dir Post Ord Tr from 92; Can and Preb Sarum Cathl from 99; Dioc Adv in Spiritual Direction from 06; C Hazelbury Bryan and the Hillside Par from 08; C Okeford from 08. *The Rectory, New Street, Marnhull, Sturminster Newton DT10 1PY* Tel (01258) 821130 E-mail dweyman@weyman.fsnet.co.uk

WEYMAN PACK-BERESFORD, John Derek Henry. b 31. Wells Th Coll 69. **d** 70 **p** 71. C Headley All SS *Guildf* 70-76; V Westcott 76-97; RD Dorking 84-89; rtd 97; Perm to Offic *Truro* from 99. *Kittiwake, Polurrian Cliff, Mullion, Helston TR12 7EW* Tel (01326) 240457

WEYMONT, Martin Eric. b 48. St Jo Coll Dur BA69 MA74 Fitzw Coll Cam PGCE73 Lon Inst of Educn PhD89 Open Univ BSc96. Westcott Ho Cam 71. **d** 73 **p** 74. C Blackheath *Birm* 73-76; Hon C Willesden St Matt *Lon* 76-77; Hon C Belmont

77-79; P-in-c W Twyford 79-85; NSM Cricklewood St Mich 85-88; Chapl St Pet Colleg Sch Wolv 88-91; Hon C Wolverhampton *Lich* 88-91; NSM Bickershaw *Liv* 91-97; P-in-c Mells w Buckland Dinham, Elm, Whatley etc *B & W* from 97. *The Rectory, Gay Street, Mells, Frome BA11 3PT* Tel (01373) 812320 Fax 813778

WHALE, Desmond Victor. b 35. Bris Sch of Min 81. **d** 84 **p** 85. Lic to Offic *Bris* 84-88; C Parr *Liv* 88-91; R Winfarthing w Shelfanger w Burston w Gissing etc *Nor* 91-00; RD Redenhall 97-99; rtd 00; Perm to Offic *Nor* from 00 and *Sarum* from 01. *47 Cornbrash Rise, Hilperton, Trowbridge BA14 7TS* Tel (01225) 768537 Mobile 07887-717052 E-mail deswhale@talktalk.net

WHALE, Noel Raymond. b 41. Ox Univ 67. **d** 70 **p** 71. C Amersham *Ox* 70-73; Australia from 73; C Geelong 73-76; P-in-c Altona 76-79; I 79-85; I Ivanhoe 86-97; Prec/Min Can St Paul's Cathl 97-01; P-in-c Bundoora St Pet from 01. *12 Alma Road, PO Box 1225, Bundoora Vic 3083, Australia* Tel (0061) (3) 9467 4442 *or* 9467 3769 Fax 9467 6642 Mobile 412-196127
E-mail jonahnoel@hotmail.com

WHALE, Peter Richard. b 49. Auckland Univ MA72 BSc73 Down Coll Cam BA74 MA79 Otago Univ BD78 Ex Univ PhD90. St Jo Coll Auckland 75. **d** 77 **p** 78. C Takapuna New Zealand 77-80; Chapl K Coll Auckland 81-85; TV Saltash *Truro* 85-90; Jt Dir SW Minl Tr Course 86-90; Preb St Endellion 89-90; Prin WMMTC 90-92; rtd 04. *6 Bluebell Walk, Coventry CV4 9XR* Tel (024) 7646 4894 E-mail petegray@btinternet.com

WHALES, Jeremy Michael. b 31. Bris Univ MA82. Lambeth STh72 Wycliffe Hall Ox 59. **d** 61 **p** 62. C W Wimbledon Ch Ch *S'wark* 61-64; Lect St Paul's Coll Cheltenham 64-67; Asst Chapl and Sen Lect 67-74; Chapl 74-78; Assoc Chapl and Sen Lect Coll of SS Paul and Mary Cheltenham 78-84; V Cheltenham St Luke and St Jo *Glouc* 85-92; rtd 92; Perm to Offic *Glouc* from 92; Clergy Widows Officer (Cheltenham Adnry) 96-99. *5 Robert Burns Avenue, Cheltenham GL51 6NU* Tel (01242) 527583

WHALEY, Stephen John. b 57. York Univ BA79. Cranmer Hall Dur BA85. **d** 86 **p** 87. C Selby Abbey *York* 86-90; V Derringham Bank from 90; AD W Hull 98-00. *110 Calvert Road, Hull HU5 5DH* Tel (01482) 352175

WHALLEY, Anthony Allen. b 41. Linc Th Coll 77. **d** 79 **p** 80. C Upton cum Chalvey *Ox* 79-83; R Newton Longville w Stoke Hammond and Whaddon 83-96; R Winslow w Gt Horwood and Addington 99-06; rtd 06. *2 Charlock Road, Malvern WR14 3SR* Tel (01684) 562897 E-mail tony.rosemary@btinternet.com

WHALLEY, Mrs Constance Mary. b 55. CBDTI 99. **d** 02 **p** 03. NSM Garstang St Helen and St Michaels-on-Wyre *Blackb* from 02. *Brierfield, Stoney Lane, Goosnargh, Preston PR3 2WH* Tel (01995) 640652

WHALLEY, Edward Ryder Watson. b 31. G&C Coll Cam BA54 MA59. Westcott Ho Cam 55. **d** 57 **p** 58. C Ashton-on-Ribble St Andr *Blackb* 57-60; Chapl Magd Coll Cam 60-63; C Arnold *S'well* 63-67; rtd 96; Perm to Offic *Lon* from 03. *6 Cranleigh, 137-139 Ladbroke Road, London W11 3PX* Tel (020) 7727 1985

WHALLEY, George Peter. b 40. **d** 86 **p** 86. NSM Ellon *Ab* from 86; NSM Cruden Bay from 86. *128 Braehead Drive, Cruden Bay, Peterhead AB42 0NW* Tel (01779) 812511
E-mail peter_whalley@btinternet.com

WHALLEY, Jonathan Peter Lambert. b 60. Wm Booth Memorial Coll 87. St Jo Coll Nottm BA97. **d** 97 **p** 98. C Hattersley *Ches* 97-01; V The Marshland *Sheff* 01-09; P-in-c Wolsingham and Thornley *Dur* from 09; P-in-c Satley, Stanley and Tow Law from 09; CF(V) from 02. *The Rectory, 14 Rectory Lane, Wolsingham, Bishop Auckland DL13 3AJ* Tel (01388) 527340

WHALLEY, Michael Thomas. b 30. AKC55. **d** 56 **p** 57. C Nottingham All SS *S'well* 56-58; C Clifton St Fran 58-60; C Mansfield SS Pet and Paul 60-67; V N Wilford St Faith 60-66; Asst Chapl HM Pris Man 66-67; Chapl HM Youth Cust Cen Dover 67-69; Lic to Offic *Linc* 70-75; Chapl HM Pris Aylesbury 75-79; C Aylesbury *Ox* 79-83; P-in-c Bierton w Hulcott 83-89; TV Aylesbury w Bierton and Hulcott 89-95; rtd 95; Perm to Offic *Linc* from 97. *17 Willowfield Avenue, Nettleham, Lincoln LN2 2TH* Tel (01522) 595372

WHALLEY, Peter. *See* WHALLEY, George Peter

✠**WHALON, The Rt Revd Pierre Welté.** b 52. Boston Univ BMus74 Duquesne Univ MMus81. Virginia Th Sem MDiv85. **d** 85 **p** 85 **c** 01. USA 85-01; R N Versailles All So 85-91; R Philadelphia St Paul 91-93; R Fort Pierce St Andr 93-01; Bp in Charge Convocation of American Chs in Eur from 01; Hon Asst Bp Eur from 02. *23 Avenue George V, 75008 Paris, France* Tel (0033) (1) 53 23 84 04 *or* tel and fax 47 20 02 23
E-mail bppwhalon@aol.com
or cathedral@american.cathedral.com

WHARTON, Christopher Joseph. b 33. Keble Coll Ox BA57 MA61. **d** 79 **p** 80. NSM Harpenden St Nic *St Alb* 79-93; R Kimpton w Ayot St Lawrence 93-00; Perm to Offic from 00. *97 Overstone Road, Harpenden AL5 5PL* Tel (01582) 761164

WHARTON, Ms Gillian Vera. b 66. TCD BTh93 MPhil99 HDipEd02. CITC 90. **d** 93 **p** 94. C Glenageary *D & G* 93-96; PV Ch Ch Cathl Dublin from 96; Dioc Youth Officer 96-00; C

Lucan w Leixlip 96-00; Chapl Rathdown Sch 00-04; I Dublin Booterstown *D & G* from 04; I Dublin Mt Merrion from 04. *The Rectory, 10 Cross Avenue, Blackrock, Co Dublin, Republic of Ireland* Tel (00353) (1) 288 7118 *or* 283 5873 Mobile 87-230 0767
E-mail gillwharton@hotmail.com
or booterstown@dublin.anglican.org

✠**WHARTON, The Rt Revd John Martin.** b 44. Van Mildert Coll Dur BA69 Linacre Coll Ox BTh71 MA76. Ripon Hall Ox 69. **d** 72 **p** 73 **c** 92. C Birm St Pet 72-75; C Croydon St Jo *Cant* 76-77; Dir Past Studies Ripon Coll Cuddesdon 77-83; C Cuddesdon *Ox* 79-83; Sec to Bd of Min and Tr *Bradf* 83-92; Dir Post-Ord Tr 84-92; Hon Can Bradf Cathl 84-92; Can Res Bradf Cathl 92; Bp's Officer for Min and Tr 92; Area Bp Kingston *S'wark* 92-97; Bp Newc from 97. *The Bishop's House, 29 Moor Road South, Newcastle upon Tyne NE3 1PA* Tel 0191-285 2220 Fax 284 6933
E-mail bishop@newcastle.anglican.org

WHARTON, Miss Kate Elizabeth. b 78. Leeds Metrop Univ BSc00. Wycliffe Hall Ox BTh05. **d** 05 **p** 06. C W Derby St Luke *Liv* 05-09; P-in-c Everton St Geo from 09. *St George's Vicarage, 40 Northumberland Terrace, Liverpool L5 3QG* Tel 0151-263 6005

WHARTON, Richard Malcolm. b 69. Univ of Cen England in Birm BA91 PGCE92. Ripon Coll Cuddesdon BTh98. **d** 98 **p** 99. C Weoley Castle *Birm* 98-01; C Hall Green Ascension 01-04; P-in-c Hall Green St Mich 03-08; Chapl Univ Hosp Birm NHS Foundn Trust from 08. *15 Raglan Road, Birmingham B5 7RA* Tel 0121-440 2196

WHARTON, Susan Jane. b 58. Leeds Univ BSc79 Coll of Ripon & York St Jo MA00. NOC 96. **d** 99 **p** 00. C Bingley All SS *Bradf* 99-03; P-in-c Weston w Denton 03-08; P-in-c Leathley w Farnley, Fewston and Blubberhouses 03-08; C Washburn and Mid-Wharfe 08-09; P-in-c from 09. *The Vicarage, Askwith, Otley LS21 2HX* Tel (01943) 461139
E-mail sue.wharton@bradford.anglican.org
or sue@whartons.org.uk

WHARTON, Thomas Anthony. b 21. Bps' Coll Cheshunt 49. **d** 52 **p** 53. C Beeston *S'well* 52-55; C Ambleside w Rydal *Carl* 55-58; V Northowram *Wakef* 58-65; V Chipping Norton *Ox* 65-86; Chapl Berne *Eur* 86-89; rtd 89; Perm to Offic *Glouc* from 89. *7 Capel Court, The Burgage, Prestbury, Cheltenham GL52 3EL*

WHARTON, Thomas Geoffrey. b 72. Glas Univ BA93. Westcott Ho Cam 03. **d** 05 **p** 06. C Linton in Craven and Burnsall w Rylstone *Bradf* 05-09; TV Knight's Enham and Smannell w Enham Alamein *Win* from 09. *The Rectory, Dunhills Lane, Enham Alamein, Andover SP11 6HU* Tel (01264) 352827
E-mail thomas@wharton15.plus.com

WHATELEY, Stuart David. b 44. Ripon Hall Ox 71. **d** 73 **p** 74. C Chilvers Coton w Astley *Cov* 73-76; Chapl Miss to Seafarers from 76. *10 Merryman Garth, Hedon, Hull HU12 8NJ* Tel (01405) 764730 E-mail padre@marinersclub.org

WHATELEY, Thomas Roderick (Rod). b 52. St Jo Coll Nottm 94. **d** 96 **p** 97. C Willesborough *Cant* 96-99; P-in-c Cliftonville 99-03; R Orlestone w Snave and Ruckinge w Warehorne etc from 03. *The Rectory, Cock Lane, Ham Street, Ashford TN26 2HU* Tel (01233) 732274 E-mail rod.whateley@tiscali.co.uk

WHATLEY, Lionel Frederick. b 50. St Paul's Coll Grahamstown 77. **d** 79 **p** 80. C Uitenhage E Africa 79-80; R Newton Park 80-83; R Alexandria Plurality 83-84; R Waterberg 84-90; R Letaba 90-99; Adn NE 95-99; V Gen 97-99; R Ashington, Washington and Wiston w Buncton *Chich* 99-05; TV Langport Area *B & W* 05-07; P-in-c Worthing Ch the King *Chich* 07-08; V Worthing H Trin w Ch Ch from 08. *The Rectory, 4 Shakespeare Road, Worthing BN11 4AL* Tel (01903) 205185
E-mail whatley@onetel.com *or* whatley@telco4u.net

WHATLEY, Roger James. b 49. Chich Th Coll 94. **d** 96 **p** 04. NSM Newport St Jo *Portsm* from 96. *Beechcroft, 46 Trafalgar Road, Newport PO30 1QG* Tel (01983) 825938
E-mail whatleys138@btinternet.com

WHATMORE, Michael John. b 30. Bris Univ BA51 St Cath Soc Ox BA53 MA54. Wycliffe Hall Ox 56. **d** 56 **p** 58. C Bexley St Mary *Roch* 56-57; C Keston 57-59; C Bromley St Mark 59-61; Distr Sec (GB) Bible Soc 61-64; R Stanningley St Thos *Ripon* 64-67; V Speke St SS *Liv* 67-70; Teacher & Sen Tutor Barton Peveril Coll 70-92; rtd 92; Perm to Offic *Win* from 92. *26 Grebe Close, Milford on Sea, Lymington SO41 0XA* Tel (01590) 644892

WHATMOUGH, Michael Anthony. b 50. ARCO71 Ex Univ BA72. Edin Th Coll BD81. **d** 81 **p** 82. C Edin St Hilda and Edin St Fillan 81-84; C Salisbury St Thos and St Edm *Sarum* 84-86; R 86-93; RD Salisbury 90-93; V Bris St Mary Redcliffe w Temple etc 93-04; Perm to Offic *Lich* from 08. *30 Gaia Lane, Lichfield WS13 7LW* Tel (01543) 257019 Mobile 07711-335050
E-mail tony@whatmough.org.uk

WHATSON, Mark Edwin Chadwick. b 57. Southn Univ BSc79 CEng83 MIMechE83. NOC 86. **d** 88 **p** 91. NSM Church Hulme *Ches* 88-91; NSM Goostrey 91-95; NSM Hardwicke, Quedgeley and Elmore w Longney *Glouc* 95-98; C Thornbury 98-01; Ind Chapl 99-01; R Freshwater *Portsm* from 01; R Yarmouth from 01. *1 The Nurseries, Freshwater PO40 9FG* Tel and fax (01983) 752010 E-mail mark.whatson@bigfoot.com

WHATTON, Miss Joanna Nicola. b 72. Liv Univ BA93 Bris Univ BA00 Homerton Coll Cam PGCE95. Trin Coll Bris 98. **d** 01 **p** 02. C Chislehurst St Nic *Roch* 01-06. *Address temp unknown*

WHAWELL, Arthur <u>Michael</u>. b 38. SRN59. Sarum & Wells Th Coll 74. **d** 76 **p** 77. C Cottingham *York* 76-79; P-in-c Bessingby and Carnaby 79-84; V Birchencliffe *Wakef* 84-87; Chapl Huddersfield R Infirmary 84-87; V St Bart Less and Chapl St Bart Hosp Lon 87-95; P-in-c Wormingford, Mt Bures and Lt Horkesley *Chelmsf* 95-00; V 00-03; rtd 03; Perm to Offic *Pet* from 05. *Cherry Trees, Benefield Road, Upper Glapthorn, Peterborough PE8 5BQ* Tel (01832) 272500
E-mail michael@whawell.freeserve.co.uk

WHEALE, Alan Leon. b 43. Hull Univ MA92 AKC69. St Aug Coll Cant 69. **d** 70 **p** 71. C Tamworth *Lich* 70-73; C Cheddleton 73-75; V Garretts Green *Birm* 75-78; V Perry Beeches 78-83; V Winshill *Derby* 83-84; Deputation Appeals Org (E Midl) CECS 84-86; C Arnold *S'well* 86-88; V Daybrook 88-96; R Clifton Campville w Edingale and Harlaston *Lich* 96-06; P-in-c Thorpe Constantine 96-06; P-in-c Elford 97-06; rtd 06; Perm to Offic *Lich* 06-08; Hon C Tamworth from 08. *33 Churchward Drive, Stretton, Burton-on-Trent DE13 0AU* Tel (01283) 542309
E-mail alan-wheale@supanet.com

WHEALE, Sarah Ruth. *See* BULLOCK, Canon Sarah Ruth

WHEAT, Charles Donald <u>Edmund</u>. b 37. Nottm Univ BA70 Sheff Univ MA76. Kelham Th Coll 57. **d** 62 **p** 63. C Sheff Arbourthorne 62-67; Lic to Offic *S'well* 67-70; SSM from 69; Chapl St Martin's Coll Lanc 70-73; Prior SSM Priory Sheff 73-75; Lic to Offic *Sheff* 73-97; C Ranmoor 75-77; Asst Chapl Sheff Univ 75-77; Chapl 77-80; Prov SSM in England 81-91; Dir 82-89; Lic to Offic *Blackb* 81-88; V Middlesbrough All SS *York* 88-95; Roehampton Inst *S'wark* 96-97; Chapl OHP 97-98; Prior St Antony's Priory Dur 98-01; V Middlesbrough St Thos *York* 01-03; rtd 03; Hon C S Bank *York* 03-07; Perm to Offic from 07. *St Clare's Bungalow, Sneaton Castle, Whitby YO21 3QN* Tel (01947) 820361 E-mail ssmmbro@aol.com

WHEATLEY, David. b 44. **d** 02 **p** 03. OLM Castleford *Wakef* 02-09; Master Abp Holgate Hosp Hemsworth from 09. *The Master's Lodge, Robin Lane, Hemsworth, Pontefract WF9 4PP* Tel (01977) 610434

WHEATLEY, David Maurice. b 69. Man Poly BA91. Wycliffe Hall Ox 02. **d** 05 **p** 06. C Cheltenham St Mary, St Matt, St Paul and H Trin *Glouc* 05-07; C Cheltenham H Trin and St Paul 07-08. *Address temp unknown*

WHEATLEY (née GRAHAM), Mrs Fiona Karen. b 57. Hull Univ BA84 De Montfort Univ PGCE94. SAOMC 03. **d** 06 **p** 07. C Stevenage St Hugh and St Jo *St Alb* from 06. *90 Ferrier Road, Stevenage SG2 0NZ* Tel (01438) 745971
E-mail fiona.wheatley@ntlworld.com

WHEATLEY, Gordon Howard. b 29. Trin Coll Cam MA52. Lon Bible Coll. **d** 90 **p** 91. C Cockley Cley w Gooderstone *Nor* 90-94; C Didlington 90-94; C Gt and Lt Cressingham w Threxton 90-94; C Hilborough w Bodney 90-94; C Oxborough w Foulden and Caldecote 90-94; P-in-c Mundford w Lynford 94-98; P-in-c Ickburgh w Langford 94-98; P-in-c Cranwich 94-98; rtd 98; Perm to Offic *Nor* from 98. *6 Mount Close, Swaffham PE37 7NQ* Tel (01760) 722450 E-mail revgordon@tiscali.co.uk

WHEATLEY, Ian James. b 62. Chich Th Coll BTh94. **d** 94 **p** 95. C Braunton *Ex* 94-97; Chapl RN from 97. *Royal Naval Chaplaincy Service, Mail Point 1-2, Leach Building, Whale Island, Portsmouth PO2 8BY* Tel (023) 9262 5055 Fax 9262 5134

WHEATLEY, Jane. *See* WHEATLEY, Miss Sarah Jane

WHEATLEY, John. b 14. **d** 77 **p** 78. NSM Cambois *Newc* 77-87; rtd 87; Perm to Offic *Newc* from 87. *20 Cypress Gardens, Blyth NE24 2LP* Tel (01670) 353353

WHEATLEY, The Ven Paul Charles. b 38. St Jo Coll Dur BA61. Linc Th Coll 61. **d** 63 **p** 64. C Bishopston *Bris* 63-68; Youth Chapl 68-73; V Swindon St Paul 73-77; TR Swindon Dorcan 77-79; R Ross *Heref* 79-81; P-in-c Brampton Abbotts 79-81; RD Ross and Archenfield 79-91; TR Ross w Brampton Abbotts, Bridstow and Peterstow 81-91; Preb Heref Cathl 87-91; Adn Sherborne *Sarum* 91-03; P-in-c W Stafford w Frome Billet 91-03; rtd 03; Perm to Offic *Heref* from 04. *The Farthings, Bridstow, Ross-on-Wye HR9 6QF* Tel (01989) 566965
E-mail paulwheatley@buckcastle.plus.com

✠**WHEATLEY, The Rt Revd Peter William.** b 47. Qu Coll Ox BA69 MA73 Pemb Coll Cam BA76. Ripon Hall Ox 72. **d** 73 **p** 74 **c** 99. C Fulham All SS *Lon* 73-78; V St Pancras H Cross w St Jude and St Pet 78-82; P-in-c Hampstead All So 82-90; P-in-c Kilburn St Mary 82-90; P-in-c Kilburn St Mary w All So 90-95; V W Hampstead St Jas 82-95; Dir Post-Ord Tr 85-95; AD N Camden 88-93; Adn Hampstead 95-99; Area Bp Edmonton from 99. *27 Thurlow Road, London NW3 5PP* Tel (020) 7435 5890 Fax 7435 6049
E-mail bishop.edmonton@london.anglican.org

WHEATLEY, Miss Sarah <u>Jane</u>. b 45. St Gabr Coll Lon Dip Teaching67. St Alb Minl Tr Scheme 77. **d** 96 **p** 97. NSM Meppershall w Campton and Stondon *St Alb* 96-99; P-in-c Shillington 99-03; V Gravenhurst, Shillington and Stondon from

03. *All Saints' Vicarage, Vicarage Close, Shillington, Hitchin SG5 3LS* Tel (01462) 713797 *or* 731170
E-mail jane.wheatley5@btinternet.com

WHEATLEY PRICE, Canon John. b 31. Em Coll Cam BA54 MA58. Ridley Hall Cam 54. **d** 56 **p** 57. C Drypool St Andr and St Pet *York* 56-59; CMS 59-76; Uganda 60-74; Adn Soroti 72-74; Hon Can Soroti 78-97; Adn N Maseno Kenya 74-76; V Clevedon St Andr *B & W* 76-82; V Clevedon St Andr and Ch Ch 82-87; Chapl Amsterdam *Eur* 87-92; P-in-c Cromford *Derby* 92-95; P-in-c Matlock Bath 92-95; V Matlock Bath and Cromford 95-96; rtd 96; Perm to Offic *Sarum* 96-01 and *Birm* from 01. *2 Beausale Drive, Knowle, Solihull B93 0NS* Tel (01564) 730067 E-mail johnwheatleyprice@lineone.net

WHEATON, Canon Christopher. b 49. St Jo Coll Nottm BTh80. **d** 80 **p** 81. C Hatcham St Jas *S'wark* 80-83; C Warlingham w Chelsham and Farleigh 83-87; V Carshalton Beeches from 87; RD Sutton from 03; Hon Can S'wark Cathl from 07. *The Vicarage, 38 Beeches Avenue, Carshalton SM5 3LW* Tel (020) 8647 6056 E-mail good.shepherd@btinternet.com

WHEATON, Canon David Harry. b 30. St Jo Coll Ox BA53 MA56 Lon Univ BD55. Oak Hill Th Coll 58. **d** 59 **p** 60. Tutor Oak Hill Th Coll 59-62; Prin 71-86; C Enfield Ch Ch Trent Park *Lon* 59-62; R Ludgershall *Ox* 62-66; V Onslow Square St Paul *Lon* 66-71; Chapl Brompton Hosp 69-71; Hon Can St Alb 76-96; V Ware Ch Ch 86-96; RD Hertford 88-91; Chapl to The Queen 90-00; rtd 96. *17 Riverside Road, Blandford Forum DT11 7ES* Tel (01258) 489996

WHEATON, Patrick Edward. b 78. Ex Coll Ox BA00. Trin Coll Bris BA08. **d** 09. C Shill Valley and Broadshire *Ox* from 09. *The Vicarage, Filkins, Lechlade GL7 3JQ* Tel 07974-986608 (mobile) E-mail paddywheaton@gmx.net

WHEATON, Canon Ralph Ernest. b 32. St Jo Coll Dur BA54. Cranmer Hall Dur. **d** 58 **p** 59. C Evington *Leic* 58-63; V Bardon Hill 63-71; V Whitwick St Jo the Bapt 71-81; RD Akeley S 79-81; V Blyth *S'well* 81-96; P-in-c Scofton w Osberton 83-86; V 86-96; RD Worksop 83-93; Hon Can S'well Minster 86-96; P-in-c Langold 86-91; rtd 96; Perm to Offic *Linc* 99-02 and *S'well* from 02. *Petriburg, Main Street, Hayton, Retford DN22 9LL* Tel (01777) 705910

WHEBLE, Eric Clement. b 23. S'wark Ord Course 68. **d** 71 **p** 72. C Croydon H Trin *Cant* 71-78; Hon C Croydon St Sav 78-80; Hon C Norbury St Oswald 80-81; TV Selsdon St Jo w St Fran 81-84; TV Selsdon St Jo w St Fran *S'wark* 85-88; rtd 88; Perm to Offic *Portsm* and *Win* from 88. *23 Holmesland Drive, Botley, Southampton SO30 2SH* Tel (01489) 798050

WHEELDON, William Dennis. b 25. Leeds Univ BA51. Coll of Resurr Mirfield 52. **d** 54 **p** 56. CR 55-76; Barbados 59-66; Prin Coll of Resurr Mirfield 66-75; P-in-c New Whittington *Derby* 83-87; P-in-c Belper Ch Ch and Milford 87-90; rtd 90; Perm to Offic *Bradf* 90-04. *10 Brooklyn, Threshfield, Skipton BD23 5ER* Tel (01756) 753187

WHEELER, Preb Alexander Quintin Henry (Alastair). b 51. Lon Univ BA73 MBACP07. St Jo Coll Nottm 74. **d** 77 **p** 78. C Kenilworth St Jo *Cov* 77-80; C Madeley *Heref* 80-83; P-in-c Draycott-le-Moors *Lich* 83-84; P-in-c Forsbrook 83-84; R Draycott-le-Moors w Forsbrook 84-91; V Nailsea Ch Ch *B & W* 91-96; R Nailsea Ch Ch w Tickenham from 96; RD Portishead 95-01; Preb Wells Cathl from 03. *The Rectory, 1 Christ Church Close, Nailsea, Bristol BS48 1RT* Tel (01275) 853187
E-mail aqhw@aol.com

WHEELER, Canon Andrew Charles. b 48. CCC Cam BA69 MA72 Makerere Univ Kampala MA72 Leeds Univ PGCE72. Trin Coll Bris BA88. **d** 88 **p** 88. CMS from 76; C Whitton *Sarum* 88-89; C All SS Cathl Cairo Egypt 89-92; Co-ord for Th Educn Sudan 92-00; C All SS Cathl Nairobi Kenya 92-00; Abp's Sec for Angl Communion Affairs *Cant* 00-01; C Guildf St Sav from 02; Dioc World Miss Adv from 06. *8 Selbourne Road, Guildford GU4 7JP* Tel (01483) 455333
E-mail andrew.wheeler@st-saviours.org.uk

WHEELER, Anthony. *See* WHEELER, Richard Anthony

WHEELER, Anthony William. b 28. **d** 76 **p** 77. NSM Shirehampton *Bris* 76-98; Chmn Avonmouth Miss to Seamen from 76; rtd 98; Perm to Offic *Bris* from 98. *3 The Priory, Priory Gardens, Bristol BS11 0BZ* Tel 0117-982 2261

WHEELER (née MILLAR), Mrs Christine. b 55. City of Lon Poly BSc76 DipCOT81. S Dios Minl Tr Scheme 84. **d** 87 **p** 88. NSM Kingston Buci *Chich* 87-89; Par Dn Merstham and Gatton *S'wark* 89-94; C 94-96; R Rockland St Mary w Hellington, Bramerton etc *Nor* 96-04; Perm to Offic from 04. *Mayland, Low Road, Strumpshaw, Norwich NR13 4HU* Tel (01603) 713583
E-mail emailcw@btinternet.com

WHEELER, David Ian. b 49. Southn Univ BSc70 PhD78. NOC 87. **d** 90 **p** 91. C Blackpool St Jo *Blackb* 90-94; R Old Trafford St Jo *Man* 94-05; P-in-c Irlam 05-08; V from 08. *The Vicarage, Vicarage Road, Irlam, Manchester M44 6WA* Tel 0161-775 2461

WHEELER, David James. b 49. Leeds Univ MA95 CQSW74. S Dios Minl Tr Scheme 87. **d** 90 **p** 91. C Hythe *Cant* 90-92; C Knaresborough *Ripon* 92-97; Asst Soc Resp Officer 94-97; P-in-c Gt and Lt Ouseburn w Marton cum Grafton etc 97-01; V 01-05;

Jt AD Ripon 01-05; V Cobbold Road St Sav w St Mary *Lon* from 05. *St Saviour's Vicarage, Cobbold Road, London W12 9LN* Tel (020) 8743 4769 E-mail sacerdote@btopenworld.com

WHEELER, Sister Eileen Violet. b 28. TCert48 Newnham Coll Cam MA52. Chich Th Coll 85. **dss** 86 **d** 87 **p** 95. Bexhill St Pet *Chich* 86-95; Hon Par Dn 87-90; Par Dn 90-94; Hon C 94-95; rtd 94; Hon C Bexhill St Mark *Chich* 95-00; Perm to Offic 00-02; Hon C Horsham 02-08; Hon C St Leonards St Ethelburga from 08; Hon C St Leonards St Leon from 08. *17 Glebe Close, Bexhill-on-Sea TN39 3UY*

WHEELER, Graham John. b 39. St Mich Coll Llan BD78. **d** 66 **p** 67. C Roath St Martin *Llan* 66-71; C Cadoxton-juxta-Barry 71-75; Perm to Offic 75-79; C Highcliffe w Hinton Admiral *Win* 79-83; C Milton 83-90; P-in-c Bournemouth St Ambrose 90-06; rtd 06. *10 Durley Chine Court, 36 West Cliff Road, Bournemouth BH2 5HJ* Tel (01202) 764957

WHEELER, Mrs Helen Mary. b 38. Qu Coll Birm 04. **d** 06 **p** 07. NSM Smethwick Resurr *Birm* from 06. *99 Brookfield Road, Birmingham B18 7JA* Tel 0121-554 4721 Mobile 07804-450099 E-mail helen.wheeler@mail.com

WHEELER, James Albert. b 49. Sarum & Wells Th Coll 74. **d** 76 **p** 77. C Orpington All SS *Roch* 76-79; C Roch 79-81; C Bexley St Jo 81-84; V Penge Lane H Trin 84-93; P-in-c Tunbridge Wells St Luke 93-99; V 99-09; P-in-c Southborough St Thos from 09. *The Vicarage, 28 Pennington Road, Southborough, Tunbridge Wells TN4 0SL* Tel (01892) 529624 E-mail james.wheeler@diocese-rochester.org

WHEELER, John David. b 31. Selw Coll Cam BA54 MA58. Ely Th Coll 54. **d** 56 **p** 57. C Charlton St Luke w St Paul *S'wark* 56-60; C Northolt St Mary *Lon* 61-63; V Bush Hill Park St Mark 64-71; V Ealing St Pet Mt Park 71-74; V Truro St Paul 74-79; V Truro St Paul and St Clem 79-80; P-in-c Hammersmith St Sav *Lon* 80-83; V Cobbold Road St Sav w St Mary 83-96; rtd 96; Perm to Offic *Heref* 96-01 and *Chich* 01-09. *63 Nelson Road, Twickenham TW2 7AR*

WHEELER, Julian Aldous. b 48. Nottm Univ BTh74. Kelham Th Coll 70. **d** 75 **p** 76. C Bideford *Ex* 75-79; Lic to Offic 79-86; Hon C Parkham, Alwington, Buckland Brewer etc 86-03. *Manorfield, Mount Raleigh Avenue, Bideford EX39 3NX* Tel (01237) 477271 E-mail jwheeler@connectfree.co.uk

WHEELER, Leonie Marjorie. b 50. Univ of W Aus BA75 St Ant Coll Ox DPhil81. Qu Coll Birm 04. **d** 06 **p** 07. C Hadley and Wellington Ch Ch *Lich* 06-09; P-in-c Church Aston from 09; Chapl to the Deaf from 09. *St Andrew's Rectory, 7 Wallshead Way, Church Aston, Newport TF10 9JG*

WHEELER, Preb Madeleine. b 42. Gilmore Course 76. **dss** 78 **d** 87 **p** 94. Ruislip Manor St Paul *Lon* 78-92; Par Dn 87-91; TD 91-92; Chapl for Women's Min (Willesden Episc Area) 86-95; P-in-c N Greenford All Hallows 94-00; Preb St Paul's Cathl 95-00; rtd 00; Perm to Offic *St Alb* from 00 and *Lon* from 02. *178A Harefield Road, Uxbridge UB8 1PP* Tel (01895) 257274

WHEELER, Nicholas Charles. b 50. LVO09. Aix Univ BA72. SEITE 00. **d** 03 **p** 04. NSM Blackheath St Jo *S'wark* 03-08; Perm to Offic from 08. *52 Oakways, London SE9 2PD* Tel (020) 8859 7819

WHEELER, Nicholas Gordon Timothy. b 59. BCombStuds84. Linc Th Coll. **d** 84 **p** 85. C Hendon St Alphage *Lon* 84-87; C Wood Green St Mich w Bounds Green St Gabr etc 87-89; TV 89-93; R Cranford 93-02; V Ruislip St Mary from 02. *St Mary's Vicarage, 9 The Fairway, Ruislip HA4 0SP* Tel (020) 8845 3485 Mobile 07946-111968 E-mail nicholasgwheeler@aol.com

WHEELER, Nicholas Paul. b 60. Ox Univ BA86 MA91. Wycliffe Hall Ox 83. **d** 87 **p** 88. C Wood Green St Mich w Bounds Green St Gabr etc *Lon* 87-91; Chapl to Bp Edmonton 91-96; P-in-c Somers Town 96-03; P-in-c Old St Pancras w Bedford New Town St Matt 96-03; P-in-c Camden Town St Mich w All SS and St Thos 96-03; P-in-c Camden Square St Paul 96-03; TR Old St Pancras 03-08; Brazil from 08. *Address temp unknown*

WHEELER, Richard Anthony (Tony). b 23. St Chad's Coll Dur BA46 MA48. **d** 48 **p** 49. C Kingswinford St Mary *Lich* 48-52; C Toxteth Park St Agnes *Liv* 52-54; V Upholland 54-64; R Dorchester H Trin w Frome Whitfield *Sarum* 64-73; TV Dorchester 73-87; rtd 87; Perm to Offic *Sarum* from 87. *30 Mountain Ash Road, Dorchester DT1 2PB* Tel (01305) 264811 E-mail peewheet@cix.compulink.co.uk

WHEELER, Canon Richard Roy. b 44. K Coll Lon BD72. St Aug Coll Cant. **d** 74 **p** 74. C Brixton St Matt *S'wark* 74-78; Dir St Matt Meeting Place Brixton 78-79; Sec BCC Community Work Resource Unit 79-82; TV Southampton (City Cen) *Win* 83-88; TR 88-98; Hon Can Win Cathl 94-98; Soc Resp Adv *St Alb* from 98; Can Res St Alb from 01. *Holywell Close, 43 Holywell Hill, St Albans AL1 1HE* Tel (01727) 856753 or 851748 Fax 830368 E-mail sro@stalbans.anglican.org

WHEELER, Mrs Sally Ann Violet. b 59. Westmr Coll Ox BEd81. SAOMC 94. **d** 97 **p** 98. NSM Chippenham St Paul w Hardenhuish etc *Bris* 97-01; C Gtr Corsham and Lacock 01-04; TV from 04. *The Vicarage, Folly Lane, Lacock, Chippenham SN15 2LL* Tel (01249) 730272 E-mail wheelers.7@btinternet.com

WHEELER-KILEY, Mrs Susan Elizabeth. b 47. **d** 06 **p** 07. NSM S Norwood St Mark *S'wark* from 06. *35 St Luke's Close, London SE25 4SX* Tel (020) 8656 9923 Mobile 07890-780572 E-mail fs.kiley@btinternet.com

WHEELHOUSE, Brian Clifford Dunstan. b 69. St Steph Ho Ox BTh93. **d** 96 **p** 97. C Brighton Resurr *Chich* 96-99; C Hangleton 99-00; Perm to Offic 00-01; C Kingstanding St Luke *Birm* 01-03; V Houghton Regis *St Alb* from 03. *The Vicarage, Bedford Road, Houghton Regis, Dunstable LU5 5DJ* Tel and fax (01582) 867593

WHEELWRIGHT, Michael Harvey. b 39. Bps' Coll Cheshunt 64. **d** 67 **p** 68. C Glen Parva and S Wigston *Leic* 67-70; C Evington 70-74; V Leic St Eliz Nether Hall 74-79; Chapl Prudhoe Hosp Northd 79-99; Perm to Offic *Dur* from 95 and *Newc* from 99; rtd 04. *6 Nunnykirk Close, Ovingham, Prudhoe NE42 6BP* Tel (01661) 835749

WHELAN, Miss Patricia Jean. b 33. ACA55 FCA82. Dalton Ho Bris 58. **dss** 64 **d** 87 **p** 94. Stapleford *S'well* 62-69; Aylesbury *Ox* 69-75; Bushbury *Lich* 75-77; Patchway *Bris* 77-81; Trin Coll Bris 81-82; W Swindon LEP 82-86; High Wycombe *Ox* 86-87; Par Dn 87-91; Par Dn Ox St Ebbe w H Trin and St Pet 91-93; rtd 93. *81 Cogges Hill Road, Witney OX28 3XU* Tel (01993) 779099

WHELAN, Peter Warwick Armstrong. b 34. Southn Univ BTh80 Open Univ BA80. Sarum Th Coll 69. **d** 71 **p** 72. C Salisbury St Mark *Sarum* 71-73; C Solihull *Birm* 73-77; TR Shirley 77-86; Chapl Whittington Hosp NHS Trust 86-99; Chapl Camden and Islington Community Health NHS Trust 86-98; Perm to Offic *Ex* from 98; rtd 99. *Olde Court Coach House, Higher Lincombe Road, Torquay TQ1 2EX* Tel (01803) 212483

WHELAN, Raymond Keith. b 40. Cant Sch of Min 85. **d** 88 **p** 91. C Eastbourne St Andr *Chich* 88-93; C-in-c Parklands St Wilfrid CD 93-95; TV Chich 95-00; V Chich St Wilfrid 00-01; rtd 04; Perm to Offic *Chich* from 04. *9 Ruislip Gardens, Aldwick, Bognor Regis PO21 4LB* Tel (01243) 264865 E-mail wdiosc@aol.com

WHERLOCK, Mrs Evalene Prudence. b 50. WEMTC 98. **d** 01 **p** 02. NSM Bishopsworth and Bedminster Down *Bris* from 01. *63 Bridgwater Road, Bedminster Down, Bristol BS13 7AX* Tel 0117-964 1035 Mobile 07899-932763 E-mail evawherlock@ukonline.co.uk

WHERRY, Anthony Michael. b 44. Nottm Univ BA65. WMMTC 88. **d** 91 **p** 92. NSM Worc City St Paul and Old St Martin etc 91-95; NSM Worc E Deanery 95-02; NSM Worc SE from 02. *2 Redfern Avenue, Worcester WR5 1PZ* Tel (01905) 358532 Mobile 07780-677942 E-mail tony@wherry222.fsnet.co.uk

WHETTEM, Canon John Curtiss. b 27. Peterho Cam BA50 MA55. Wycliffe Hall Ox 50. **d** 52 **p** 53. C Clifton Ch Ch *Bris* 52-55; C Wandsworth All SS *S'wark* 55-58; V Soundwell *Bris* 58-63; Youth Chapl 63-68; Chapl Bris Cathl 64-68; R N Mundham w Hunston *Chich* 68-80; P-in-c Oving w Merston 75-80; TR Swanborough *Sarum* 80-92; RD Pewsey 84-89; rtd 92; Perm to Offic *Sarum* from 92. *32 Hogshill Street, Beaminster DT8 3AA* Tel (01308) 863050

WHETTER, Michael Arnold. b 30. Bris Univ BA51. Wells Th Coll 53. **d** 55 **p** 56. C Dursley *Glouc* 55-58; C Coppenhall *Ches* 58-61; R Ches H Trin 61-71; V Stockport St Alb Hall Street 72-90; V Offerton 90-91; Chapl Cherry Tree Hosp Stockport 72-91; Chapl Offerton Hosp Stockport 72-91; V Bollington St Jo *Ches* 91-00; rtd 00; Perm to Offic *Glouc* from 00. *Knapp Cottage, Selsley West, Stroud GL5 5LJ* Tel (01453) 822920

WHETTINGSTEEL, Raymond Edward. b 44. S Dios Minl Tr Scheme 79. **d** 82 **p** 83. NSM Sholing *Win* 82-84; C Southampton Maybush St Pet 84-89; R Hatherden w Tangley, Weyhill and Penton Mewsey 89-09; rtd 09. *20 Clover Way, Hedge End, Southampton SO30 4RP* Tel (01489) 787033 E-mail ray_whettingsteel@hotmail.com

WHETTLETON, Timothy John. b 53. Univ of Wales (Swansea) BA74. St Mich Coll Llan 97. **d** 99 **p** 00. C Llansamlet *S & B* 99-01; P-in-c Gowerton 01-05. *18 The Orchard, Newton, Swansea SA3 4UQ*

WHETTON, Nicholas John. b 56. Open Univ BA94. St Jo Coll Nottm 83. **d** 86 **p** 87. C Hatfield *Sheff* 86-90; V Cornholme *Wakef* 90-96; P-in-c Livesey *Blackb* 96-99; V 99-03; P-in-c Ewood 96-97; Chapl HM Pris Hull from 03. *The Chaplain's Office, HM Prison, Hedon Road, Hull HU9 5LS* Tel (01482) 282200

WHIFFEN, Canon William Timothy. b 25. SS Coll Cam BA50 MA54 FRSA94. Linc Th Coll. **d** 52 **p** 53. C Wigan St Mich *Liv* 52-56; India 57-69; V Clay Cross *Derby* 69-74; Sec (Overseas Division) USPG 74-79; TR Woughton *Ox* 79-85; P-in-c Seer Green and Jordans 85-91; Hon Can Ch Ch 91-92; rtd 91. *337 Lovat Fields Village, Japonica Lane, Willen Park, Milton Keynes MK15 9EG* Tel (01908) 677466

✠**WHINNEY, The Rt Revd Michael Humphrey Dickens.** b 30. Pemb Coll Cam BA55 MA59. Gen Th Sem (NY) STM90 Ridley Hall Cam 55. **d** 57 **p** 58 **c** 82. C Rainham *Chelmsf* 57-60; Hd Cam Univ Miss Bermondsey 60-67; Chapl 61-73; V Bermondsey St Jas w Ch Ch *S'wark* 67-73; Adn S'wark 73-82; Suff Bp Aston *Birm* 82-85; Bp S'well 85-88; Asst Bp Birm 88-95; Can Res Birm Cathl 92-95; rtd 96; Hon Asst Bp Birm from 96. *3 Moor Green*

Lane, Moseley, Birmingham B13 8NE Tel and fax 0121-249 2856
E-mail michael.whinney@btinternet.com

WHINNEY, Nigel Patrick Maurice. b 43. Open Univ BA91. SWMTC 95. **d** 97 **p** 98. NSM Ilminster and Distr *B & W* 97-08; Bp's Officer for Ord NSM (Taunton Adnry) 99-06; RD Crewkerne and Ilminster 01-07; rtd 08. *The Monks Dairy, Isle Brewers, Taunton TA3 6QL* Tel (01460) 281975
E-mail n.whinney@virgin.net

WHINTON, William Francis Ivan. b 35. NOC 77. **d** 80 **p** 81. NSM Stockport St Mary *Ches* 80-82; NSM Disley 82-87; V Birtles 87-00; Dioc Officer for Disabled 89-00; rtd 00; Chapl for Deaf People *Ches* 00-04; Perm to Offic *Ches* from 05 and *Lich* from 09. *Allmeadows Cottage, Wincle, Macclesfield SK11 0QJ* Tel (01260) 227278

WHIPP, Antony Douglas. b 46. Leeds Univ BSc68 Lanc Univ PhD04. Ripon Coll Cuddesdon 84. **d** 86 **p** 87. C Dalston *Carl* 86-89; V Holme Cultram St Mary 89-96; V Holme Cultram St Cuth 89-96; V Kells 96-00; V Hartlepool St Aid *Dur* 00-05; R Ebchester from 05; V Medomsley from 05. *The Rectory, Shaw Lane, Consett DH8 0PY* Tel (01207) 563348
E-mail tony.whipp@durham.anglican.org

WHIPP, Margaret Jane. b 55. LMH Ox BA76 Sheff Univ MB, ChB79 MRCP82 FRCR86 Hull Univ MA99 Glas Univ PhD08. NOC 87. **d** 90 **p** 94. NSM Wickersley *Sheff* 90-98; Tutor Cranmer Hall Dur 98-99; Dir Practical Th NEOC 00-04; Ecum Chapl Ox Brookes Univ 04-08; Lect Past Studies Ox Min Course 06-08; Dean of Studies Ripon Coll Cuddesdon from 08. *The Mullings, 71 Sandfield Road, Headington, Oxford OX3 6RW* Tel (01865) 765409
E-mail margaret.whipp@ripon-cuddesdon.ac.uk

WHITAKER, Anthony. b 50. SS Mark & Jo Coll Chelsea CertEd72 Middx Univ BA02. NTMTC 99. **d** 02 **p** 03. C Blackmore and Stondon Massey *Chelmsf* 02-06; P-in-c St Keverne *Truro* from 06. *The Vicarage, Lemon Street, St Keverne, Helston TR12 6NG* Tel (01326) 280227 Mobile 07905-013017 E-mail whitaker_tony@hotmail.com

WHITAKER, Benjamin. *See* WHITAKER, Michael Benjamin

WHITAKER, David Arthur Edward. b 27. New Coll Ox BA50 MA55. Wells Th Coll 51. **d** 53 **p** 54. C W Bridgford *S'well* 53-56; CF 56-58; V Clifton St Fran *S'well* 58-63; Basutoland 63-66; Lesotho 66-69; R Buckerell *Ex* 69-76; R Feniton 69-76; P-in-c Tiverton St Pet 76-79; R 79-92; rtd 92; Perm to Offic *Heref* from 92. *Wits End, Hereford Road, Weobley, Hereford HR4 8SW* Tel (01544) 318669

WHITAKER, Irene Anne. b 57. **d** 01 **p** 02. OLM Parr *Liv* 01-06; TV Bootle from 06. *The Vicarage, Elm Road, Seaforth, Liverpool L21 1BH* Tel 0151-920 2205 Mobile 07771-581886
E-mail irene369@blueyonder.co.uk

WHITAKER, Margaret Scott. b 45. Dioc OLM tr scheme 00 EAMTC 04. **d** 03 **p** 04. OLM Eaton *Nor* 03-05; C Sprowston w Beeston 05-07; C New Catton Ch Ch from 07. *St Paul's Vicarage, 1 Mill Lane, Norwich NR3 4LD* Tel (01603) 621217 Mobile 07717-317900 E-mail mwhitaker1@btinternet.com

WHITAKER, Michael Benjamin. b 60. Nottm Univ BA83. Sarum & Wells Th Coll 85. **d** 87 **p** 88. C Gt Grimsby St Mary and St Jas *Linc* 87-91; C Abingdon *Ox* 91-95; Chapl to the Deaf *Sarum* 95-00; Perm to Offic *Win* 97-00; Asst Chapl to the Deaf *Ox* from 00; Chapl HM Pris Grendon and Spring Hill from 07. *HM Prison Grendon, Grendon Underwood, Aylesbury HP18 0TL* Tel (01865) 736100
E-mail whitaker@tribeandclan.freeserve.co.uk

WHITBY, Suffragan Bishop of. *Vacant*

WHITCOMBE, William Ashley. b 78. UEA BA01. St Steph Ho Ox BTh04. **d** 04 **p** 05. C W Hendon St Jo *Lon* 04-08; Chapl HM Pris Wormwood Scrubs from 08. *HM Prison Wormwood Scrubs, Du Cane Road, London W12 0TU* Tel (020) 8588 3227
E-mail williama.whitcombe@hmps.gsi.gov.uk

WHITCROFT, Graham Frederick. b 42. Oak Hill Th Coll 64. **d** 66 **p** 67. C Cromer *Nor* 66-69; C Attercliffe *Sheff* 69-72; V Kimberworth Park 72-85; V Lepton *Wakef* 85-07; RD Kirkburton 98-05; rtd 07. *18 Far Croft, Lepton, Huddersfield HD8 0LS* Tel (01484) 609868
E-mail whitcroft@btopenworld.com

WHITE, Alan. b 18. Man Univ BSc39 MSc40 St Cath Soc Ox BA42 MA46 Leeds Univ MEd52. Ripon Hall Ox 40. **d** 42 **p** 43. C Leic St Marg 42-45; Chapl and Asst Master Leeds Gr Sch 45-56; Lic to Offic *Worc* 56-89; Asst Master Bromsgrove Sch 56-72; Chapl 72-83; rtd 83; P-in-c Tardebigge *Worc* 89-00; Perm to Offic from 00. *25 Leadbetter Drive, Bromsgrove B61 7JG* Tel (01527) 877955

WHITE, Preb Alan. b 43. Ex Univ BA65. Chich Th Coll 65. **d** 68 **p** 69. C Upper Clapton St Matt *Lon* 68-72; C Southgate Ch Ch 72-76; P-in-c Friern Barnet St Pet le Poer 76-79; V 79-85; TR Ex St Thos and Em 85-08; RD Christianity 99-03; Preb Ex Cathl 03-08; rtd 08. *Flat 3, 7 Courtenay Road, Newton Abbot TQ12 1HP* Tel (01626) 332451
E-mail revalan.white@btopenworld.com

WHITE, Canon Alison Mary. b 56. St Aid Coll Dur BA78 Leeds Univ MA94. Cranmer Hall Dur 83. **dss** 86 **d** 87 **p** 94. NSM

Chester le Street *Dur* 86-89; Dioc Adv in Local Miss 89-93; Hon Par Dn Birtley 89-93; Dir Past Studies Cranmer Hall Dur 93-98; Dir of Ords *Dur* 98-00; Springboard Missr 00-04; Adult Educn Officer *Pet* from 05; Can Pet Cathl from 09. *4 The Avenue, Dallington, Northampton NN5 7AN* Tel (01604) 581400 Fax 750925 E-mail alisonmarywhite@btinternet.com

WHITE, Canon Andrew Paul Bartholomew. b 64. MIOT85 ABIST85. Ridley Hall Cam 86. **d** 90 **p** 91. C Battersea Rise St Mark *S'wark* 90-93; P-in-c Balham Hill Ascension 93-97; V 97-98; Dir Internat Min and Can Res Cov Cathl 98-05; Iraq from 05; President Foundn for Reconciliation from 05; Perm to Offic *Portsm* from 05. *The Croft, 66 Shepherds Way, Liphook GU30 7HH* Tel (01428) 723939 *or* (00964) (7901) 265723
E-mail apbw2@cam.ac.uk

WHITE, Andrew Peter. b 65. Lon Univ BA87. Sarum & Wells Th Coll BTh94. **d** 94 **p** 95. C Croydon St Matt *S'wark* 94-96; C S Wimbledon H Trin and St Pet 96-98; TV Droitwich Spa *Worc* 98-05; RD Droitwich 02-04; P-in-c Hartlebury 05-07; Bps' Chapl from 05. *Hartlebury Vicarage, Quarry Bank, Hartlebury, Kidderminster DY11 7TE* Tel (01299) 251738 *or* (01905) 731603
E-mail andrew.white@cofe-worcester.org.uk

WHITE, Antony. *See* FELTHAM-WHITE, Antony James

WHITE, Camilla Elizabeth Zoë. b 56. Somerville Coll Ox BA78 MA83 Heythrop Coll Lon MA06. Ripon Coll Cuddesdon 05. **d** 07 **p** 08. NSM Bramley and Grafham *Guildf* from 07. *28 Wolseley Road, Godalming GU7 3DX* Tel (01483) 417145
E-mail camillawhite@waitrose.com

WHITE, Mrs Christine Margaret. b 46. Cov Coll of Educn CertEd68 Kingston Univ BA96. **d** 07 **p** 08. OLM Cuddington *Guildf* from 07. *5 Lady Hay, Worcester Park KT4 7LT* Tel (020) 8337 1665

WHITE, Canon Christopher Norman Hessler. b 32. TD76. St Cath Coll Cam BA56 MA60. Cuddesdon Coll 57. **d** 59 **p** 60. C Solihull *Birm* 59-62; C Leeds St Aid *Ripon* 62-65; CF (TA) 64-85; V Aysgarth *Ripon* 65-74; R Richmond 74-76; P-in-c Hudswell w Downholme and Marske 75-76; R Richmond w Hudswell 76-97; RD Richmond 75-80 and 93-97; Hon Can Ripon Cathl 89-97; Chapl St Fran Xavier Sch Richmond 89-97; rtd 97; Perm to Offic *Ripon* from 97. *Orchard House, Aske, Richmond DL10 5HN* Tel (01748) 850968

WHITE, Colin Davidson. b 44. St And Dioc Tr Course 86. **d** 88 **p** 89. NSM Glenrothes *St And* 88-89; P-in-c 89-90; P-in-c Leven 90-92; R 92-95; V Grimethorpe *Wakef* 95-01; P-in-c Kellington w Whitley 01-02; TV Knottingley and Kellington w Whitley from 02. *The Vicarage, 1 Manor Farm Close, Kellington, Goole DN14 0PF* Tel (01977) 663728 Fax 663671 Mobile 07973-795560 E-mail cicol@whitefam67.fsnet.co.uk

WHITE, Crispin Michael. b 42. Southn Univ MA98 PhD06 FRSA94. Bps' Coll Cheshunt 62. **d** 65 **p** 66. C S Harrow St Paul *Lon* 65-67; C Mill Hill St Mich 67-68; I Labrador St Clem Canada 68-71; Toc H Padre (W Region) 71-75; (E Midl Region) 75-82; Ind Chapl *Portsm* 82-98; P-in-c Hatfield Broad Oak and Bush End *Chelmsf* 98-04; Ind Chapl 98-07; Harlow 98-04; Lon Thames Gateway 04-07; rtd 07. *6 Downlands, Firsdown Close, Worthing BN13 3BQ* Tel and fax (01903) 830785 Mobile 07962-057436 E-mail postmaster@crispinwhite.plus.com

WHITE, David Christopher. b 51. Lon Univ LLB73. St Jo Coll Nottm 86. **d** 88 **p** 89. C Bulwell St Mary *S'well* 88-92; V Nottingham All SS 92-98; TR Clarendon Park St Jo w Knighton St Mich *Leic* 98-05; R Emmaus Par Team 05-07; TR Syston from 07; Bp's NSM Officer from 02. *The Rectory, Upper Church Street, Syston, Leicester LE7 1HR* Tel 0116-260 8276
E-mail davidwhite264@btinternet.com

WHITE, David John. b 26. Leeds Univ BA53. Coll of Resurr Mirfield 53. **d** 55 **p** 56. C Brighton St Pet *Chich* 55-58; C Wednesbury St Jas *Lich* 58-60; C Bishops Hull St Jo *B & W* 60-61; R Morton *Derby* 61-62; In RC Ch 62-73; Lect Whitelands Coll Lon 73-75; R Tregony w St Cuby and Cornelly *Truro* 75-79; R Castle Bromwich SS Mary and Marg *Birm* 79-83; V Plymouth St Simon *Ex* 83-88; R Lapford, Nymet Rowland and Coldridge 88-93; RD Chulmleigh 93; rtd 93; Perm to Offic *Ex* 94-99. *The Belvedere, Peak Hill Road, Sidmouth EX10 0NW* Tel (01395) 513365

WHITE, Canon David Paul. b 58. Oak Hill Th Coll. **d** 84 **p** 85. C Toxteth Park St Clem *Liv* 84-87; C Woodford Wells *Chelmsf* 87-89; C Woodside Park St Barn *Lon* 89-90; TV Canford Magna *Sarum* 90-93; V York St Mich-le-Belfrey 93-99; V St Austell *Truro* from 99; Dioc Dir Miss from 05; Hon Can Truro Cathl from 05. *The Vicarage, 1 Carnsmerry Crescent, St Austell PL25 4NA* Tel (01726) 73839

WHITE, Derek. b 35. MBE97. **d** 84 **p** 85. C St Marylebone St Cypr *Lon* 84-96; Bp's Chapl for the Homeless 87-01; P-in-c St Mary le Strand w St Clem Danes 96-01; rtd 01; Perm to Offic *S'wark* from 04. *80 Coleraine Road, London SE3 7PE* Tel (020) 8858 3622

WHITE, Mrs Doreen. b 51. RCN BSc95. **d** 05 **p** 06. OLM Shelswell *Ox* 05-07; NSM Fawley *Win* from 07. *86 Rollestone Road, Holbury, Southampton SO45 2GZ* Tel (023) 8089 7062
E-mail revdoreen@yahoo.co.uk

WHITE, Douglas Richard Leon. b 49. Linc Th Coll 81. **d** 83 **p** 84. C Warsop *S'well* 83-88; V Kirkby in Ashfield St Thos 88-93; Asst Chapl Qu Medical Cen Nottm Univ Hosp NHS Trust 93-98; Chapl Cen Notts Healthcare NHS Trust 98-01; Chapl Mansfield Distr Primary Care Trust 01-02; Chapl Geo Eliot Hosp NHS Trust Nuneaton 02-06; Chapl Mary Ann Evans Hospice 02-06; Chapl Compton Hospice 06-08; Chapl Marie Curie Hospice Solihull from 08; Chapl Primrose Hospice Bromsgrove from 08. *1 Glebe Avenue, Bedworth CV12 0DP* Tel (024) 7636 0417 *or* 0121-254 7800 E-mail rickwhite29@btinternet.com

WHITE, Eric James. b 46. **d** 01 **p** 02. OLM Pennington *Man* from 01. *18 Clifton Road, Leigh WN7 3LS* Tel (01942) 678758

✠**WHITE, The Rt Revd Francis.** b 49. Univ of Wales (Cardiff) BSc(Econ)70. St Jo Coll Nottm. **d** 80 **p** 81 **c** 02. C Dur St Nic 80-84; C Chester le Street 84-87; Chapl Dur and Ches le Street Hosps 87-89; V Birtley *Dur* 89-97; RD Chester-le-Street 93-97; Adn Sunderland and Hon Can Dur Cathl 97-02; Can Pet Cathl from 02; Suff Bp Brixworth from 02. *4 The Avenue, Dallington, Northampton NN5 7AN* Tel (01604) 759423 Fax 750925 E-mail bishop.brixworth@btinternet.com

WHITE, Frederick William Hartland. b 22. MBE62. Kelham Th Coll 39. **d** 45 **p** 46. C Newc St Jo 45-50; CF 50-70; Asst Chapl Gen 70-74; Chapl Guards Chpl Lon 70-74; QHC from 73; V Harrow St Mary *Lon* 74-87; rtd 87; Perm to Offic *Sarum* from 87. *Whitesfield House, 5 Seend Cleeve, Melksham SN12 6PS* Tel (01380) 828525

WHITE, Canon Gavin Donald. b 27. Toronto Univ BA49 Trin Coll Toronto BD61 Gen Th Sem NY STM68 Lon Univ PhD70. St Steph Ho Ox 51. **d** 53 **p** 54. C Quebec St Matt 53-55; Chapl Dew Line 56-57; Miss Knob Lake 57-58; Miss Kideleko Zanzibar 59-62; Lect St Paul's Th Coll Limuru Kenya 62-66; C Hampstead St Steph *Lon* 68-70; Lect Glas Univ 71-92; Lic to Offic *Glas* 71-90; rtd 92; Hon Can St Mary's Cathl from 92; Hon C St Andrews All SS *St And* from 94. *85D Market Street, St Andrews KY16 9NX* Tel (01334) 477338 E-mail gavin.d.white@ukgateway.net

WHITE, Geoffrey Brian. b 54. Jes Coll Ox BA76 MA80. St Steph Ho Ox 76. **d** 79 **p** 80. C Huddersfield St Pet *Wakef* 79-82; C Flixton St Mich *Man* 82-84; TV Westhoughton 84-91; V Stevenage St Mary Shephall w Aston *St Alb* 91-06; RD Stevenage 01-06; R Norton *Sheff* from 06. *Norton Rectory, Norton Church Road, Norton, Sheffield S8 8JQ* Tel 0114-274 5066 E-mail geoffreywhite_333@hotmail.com

WHITE, Canon Geoffrey Gordon. b 28. Selw Coll Cam BA50 MA54. Cuddesdon Coll 51. **d** 53 **p** 54. C Bradford-on-Avon *Sarum* 53-56; C Kennington St Jo *S'wark* 56-61; V Leeds St Wilfrid *Ripon* 61-63; Chapl K Coll Hosp Lon 63-66; V Aldwick *Chich* 66-76; V Brighton Gd Shep Preston 76-93; Can and Preb Chich Cathl 90-93; rtd 93; Hon C Stepney St Dunstan and All SS *Lon* from 94. *Flat 65, Telfords Yard, London E1W 2BQ* Tel (020) 7480 6585 E-mail jwhite.telford@virgin.net

WHITE, Gillian Margaret. b 57. Qu Eliz Coll Lon BSc79 Sheff Univ MEd96 PhD02 Nottm Univ MA07. EMMTC 05. **d** 07 **p** 08. NSM Derby St Paul from 07. *The Rectory, The Village, West Hallam, Ilkeston DE7 6GR* Tel 0115-932 4695 Mobile 07973-866848 E-mail g.m.white@tesco.net

WHITE, Miss Hazel Susan. b 65. Nottm Univ BA88. Qu Coll Birm 05. **d** 07 **p** 08. C Woodfield Team *Leic* from 07. *The Vicarage, Mill Street, Packington, Ashby de la-Zouch LE65 1WL* Tel (01530) 564333

WHITE, Hugh Richard Bevis. b 55. New Coll Ox BA78 Ox Univ DPhil85. S'wark Ord Course 93. **d** 96 **p** 97. NSM Westcote Barton w Steeple Barton, Duns Tew etc Ox 96-99; NSM Ox St Mary V w St Cross and St Pet 99-01; V Deddington w Barford, Clifton and Hempton from 01. *28 Duns Tew, Bicester OX25 6JR* Tel (01869) 347889

WHITE, Ian Jeffrey. b 57. Leeds Univ BSc80 PhD86 BA05 CChem83 MRSC83. Coll of Resurr Mirfield 03. **d** 05 **p** 06. C Stanningley St Thos *Ripon* 05-09; P-in-c Adel from 09; Dioc Environment Officer from 06. *The Rectory, 25 Church Lane, Adel, Leeds LS16 8DQ* Tel 0113-267 3676 E-mail rev.ianwhite@tesco.net

WHITE, Ian Terence. b 56. CertEd. Ripon Coll Cuddesdon 83. **d** 86 **p** 87. C Maidstone St Martin *Cant* 86-89; C Earley St Pet *Ox* 89-91; TV Schorne 91-96; V St Osyth *Chelmsf* 96-00; V The Suttons w Tydd *Linc* 00-04; rtd 04; Perm to Offic *Nor* from 06. *9 Haling Way, Thetford IP24 1EY* Tel (01842) 820180 E-mail revianwhite@aol.com

WHITE, Jack Chapman. b 27. St Louis Univ BSc49 Univ of Cincinnati PhD82. St Louis *Eur* 54-62 and 65-94; C St Louis H Trin 54-55; C St Louis Ascension 54-56; P-in-c 56-57; P-in-c St Louis St Andr 57; Chapl Utica Coll Syracuse Univ NY 57-58; Adv and Asst Chapl Barnard Coll Columbia Univ 58-62; Can Res American Cathl Paris 62-65; Chapl American Coll France 62-65; Chapl Howard Univ Washington DC 65-66; Dir Youth Services Piedmont 66-67; Chapl Whittle Par on the Plains VA 66-67; Assoc Min Washington DC St Thos 68-74; Tutor Gestalt Inst Gt Duck Is 75; Dir Speakers Bureau Nat Cathls Assn

(NYC) from 78; Izmir (Smyrna) w Bornova *Eur* 95-96; rtd 96. *Address temp unknown*

WHITE, Miss Janice. b 49. Trin Coll Bris IDC76. **d** 91 **p** 94. C Claygate *Guildf* 91-98; Assoc Min Stanford-le-Hope w Mucking *Chelmsf* from 98. *Glebe House, Wharf Road, Stanford-le-Hope SS17 0BY* Tel (01375) 645542 E-mail wheeze4god@aol.com

WHITE, Jeremy Spencer. b 54. St Luke's Coll Ex BEd78. Wycliffe Hall Ox 81. **d** 84 **p** 85. C S Molton w Nymet St George, High Bray etc *Ex* 84-87; TV 87-95; V Sway *Win* 95-00; P-in-c Uplyme w Axmouth *Ex* 00-03; R 03-09; RD Honiton 06-07; rtd 09. *Oakleigh, Woodbury Lane, Axminster EX13 5TL* E-mail jeremy.white@onetel.net

WHITE, Jo. *See* WHITE, Julia Mary

WHITE, Canon John Austin. b 42. LVO04. Hull Univ BA64. Coll of Resurr Mirfield 64. **d** 66 **p** 67. C Leeds St Aid *Ripon* 66-69; Asst Chapl Leeds Univ 69-73; Chapl NOC 73-82; Can and Prec Windsor from 82. *4 The Cloisters, Windsor Castle, Windsor SL4 1NJ* Tel (01753) 848787 E-mail john.white@stgeorges-windsor.org

WHITE, John Christopher. b 62. Keble Coll Ox BA84. Wycliffe Hall Ox 86. **d** 89 **p** 90. C Southway *Ex* 89-93; TV Plymouth Em, St Paul Efford and St Aug 93-99; Hon C Abbotskerswell 99-05; Perm to Offic *Birm* from 05. *The Vicarage, 115 Balden Road, Harborne, Birmingham B32 2EL* Tel 0121-427 2410

WHITE, John Cooper. b 58. LTCL79 K Alfred's Coll Win BEd82 Lon Univ MA92 FRSA94. St Steph Ho Ox 86. **d** 89 **p** 90. C Christchurch *Win* 89-93; P-in-c Bournemouth St Alb 93-94; V 94-00; P-in-c Southbourne St Kath 00-04; V from 04. *St Katharine's Vicarage, 7 Wollaston Road, Bournemouth BH6 4AR* Tel (01202) 423986 E-mail jcoopw@btconnect.com

WHITE, Canon John Francis. b 47. Qu Coll Cam BA69 MA73. Cuddesdon Coll 72. **d** 72 **p** 73. Sacr Wakef Cathl 72-73; Prec 73-76; V Thurlstone 76-82; P-in-c Hoyland Swaine 81-82; V Chapelthorpe 82-06; RD Chevet 96-05; V Lindley from 06; Hon Can Wakef Cathl from 00. *The Vicarage, 2 The Clock Tower, Lidget Street, Huddersfield HD3 3JB* Tel (01484) 650996 E-mail johnfwhite@ntlworld.com

WHITE, John Malcolm. b 54. Aston Univ BSc77. Trin Coll Bris BA87. **d** 87 **p** 88. C Harborne Heath *Birm* 87-91; C S Harrow St Paul *Lon* 91-93; TV Roxeth 93-96; V Derby St Alkmund and St Werburgh from 96. *The Vicarage, 200 Duffield Road, Derby DE22 1BL* Tel and fax (01332) 348339

WHITE, John McKelvey. b 57. QUB BA. **d** 82 **p** 83. C Clooney *D & R* 82-84; C Belfast H Trin *Conn* 84-86; I Kilcronaghan w Draperstown and Sixtowns *D & R* 86-94; I Ballybeen *D & D* 94-04; I Lurgan St Jo from 04. *St John's Rectory, Sloan Street, Lurgan, Craigavon BT66 8NT* Tel (028) 3832 2770

WHITE, Canon John Neville. b 41. Edin Univ MA63. Cranmer Hall Dur. **d** 65 **p** 66. C Sedgefield *Dur* 65-68; C Stoke *Cov* 68-72; V Wrose *Bradf* 72-90; V Farsley 90-06; RD Calverley 93-98; Hon Can Bradf Cathl 96-06; rtd 06. *34 Fourlands Drive, Bradford BD10 9SJ* Tel (01274) 415875

WHITE, John William. b 37. CEng71 MIMechE71. SAOMC 98. **d** 01 **p** 02. NSM Sandhurst *Ox* from 01. *21 Broom Acres, Sandhurst GU47 8PN* Tel (01344) 774349

WHITE (née REDMAN), Mrs Julia Elizabeth Hithersay. b 43. St Alb Minl Tr Scheme 87 SAOMC 99. **d** 99 **p** 00. NSM Harpenden St Jo *St Alb* from 99. *The Folly, 71 Station Road, Harpenden AL5 4RL* Tel (01582) 763869

WHITE, Julia Mary (Jo). b 52. Harris Coll CertEd73 Man Univ BEd85 MEd87 PhD92. NOC 00. **d** 03 **p** 04. C Ashbourne w Mapleton *Derby* 03-07; R Wingerworth from 07. *The Rectory, Longedge Lane, Wingerworth, Chesterfield S42 6PU* Tel (01246) 234242 E-mail jo@whiteshouse.plus.net

WHITE, Julian Edward Llewellyn. b 53. St D Coll Lamp BA79 Bp Burgess Hall Lamp 73 Chich Th Coll 79. **d** 79 **p** 80. C Newport St Mark *Mon* 79-83; TV Llanmartin 83-86; R Llandogo and Tintern 86-90 and 91-98; P-in-c St Paul and St Thos St Kitts-Nevis 90-91; V Mathern and Mounton w St Pierre from 98; AD Netherwent from 05. *St Tewdric's Vicarage, Mathern, Chepstow NP16 6JA* Tel (01291) 622317

WHITE, Justin Michael. b 70. Keble Coll Ox MEng93 Warwick Univ MA94 Trin Coll Cam BA00. Westcott Ho Cam 98. **d** 01 **p** 02. C Chippenham St Andr w Tytherton Lucas *Bris* 01-04; Chapl SS Helen and Kath Sch Abingdon 04-06; Jun Chapl Win Coll from 06. *Winchester College, Winchester SO2 9NA* Tel (01962) 621100 Mobile 07866-073023 E-mail justin_white@mac.com

WHITE, Keith. b 54. Liv Poly BA78 Lon Univ BD82. Wycliffe Hall Ox 78. **d** 81 **p** 82. C Edin St Thos 81-84; C Fulwood *Sheff* 84-87; R Heigham H Trin *Nor* 87-95; Zimbabwe 95-97; V Ipswich St Jo *St E* 97-06. *Address temp unknown* E-mail keith@whites10.freeserve.co.uk

WHITE, Kenneth Charles. b 26. Tyndale Hall Bris 48. **d** 54 **p** 56. Chapl Lotome Sch Karamoja Uganda 54-55; Lic to Offic Mombasa Kenya 55-57; C Morden *S'wark* 57-60; V Ramsey St Mary's w Ponds Bridge *Ely* 60-66; V Leyton Ch Ch *Chelmsf* 66-81; V Totland Bay *Portsm* 81-91; rtd 91; Perm to Offic *Llan* 91-07 and *Lon* from 08. *286A Torbay Road, Harrow HA2 9QW*

WHITE, Malcolm Robert. b 46. Man Univ BSc68. Cranmer Hall Dur 74. **d** 77 **p** 78. C Linthorpe *York* 77-81; C Sutton St Jas and Wawne 81-83; V Upper Holloway St Pet w St Jo *Lon* 83-95; TV Burnham w Dropmore, Hitcham and Taplow *Ox* 95-00; CMS Jordan 00-07; rtd 07; Perm to Offic *Ox* from 08. *Cherry Cottage, 1 Wymers Wood Road, Burnham, Slough SL1 8JQ* Tel (01628) 669085 E-mail whitesmv@gmail.com

WHITE, Marilyn Jeanne. b 32. Avery Hill Coll CertEd69. WMMTC 85. **d** 88 **p** 94. NSM Westbury-on-Severn w Flaxley and Blaisdon *Glouc* 88-98; Perm to Offic *B & W* from 98. *4 Minster Way, Bath BA2 6RQ* Tel (01225) 464450

WHITE (née DUNCOMBE), Mrs Maureen Barbara. b 42. Bris Univ BA63 Ox Univ DipEd64. Oak Hill Th Coll 87. **d** 89 **p** 00. NSM Wallington *S'wark* 89-91; Perm to Offic *Win* 99-00; NSM Totton 00-07; rtd 07. *Meadowsweet, 132 Woodlands Road, Ashurst, Southampton SO40 7AP* Tel (023) 8029 2309 Mobile 07712-418224 E-mail derek@dhandmbwhite.plus.com

WHITE, Michael Godfrey. b 46. SAOMC 98. **d** 02 **p** 03. OLM Shelswell *Ox* 02-07; NSM Fawley *Win* from 07. *86 Rollestone Road, Holbury, Southampton SO45 2GZ* Tel (023) 8089 7062 E-mail revmikewhite@yahoo.co.uk

WHITE, Nancy Kathleen. b 71. Roehampton Inst BA96 PGCE97 Leeds Univ MA07. NOC 05. **d** 07 **p** 08. NSM Erringden *Wakef* from 07. *774 Rochdale Road, Todmorden OL14 7UA* Tel (01706) 812007 E-mail nancy.white3@tiscali.co.uk

✠**WHITE, The Rt Revd Patrick George Hilliard.** Toronto Univ BA67 DMin93. Wycliffe Coll Toronto MDiv77. **d** 77 **p** 78 **c** 09. Canada 77-97; Bermuda from 97; Bp Bermuda from 09. *Diocesan Office, PO Box HM 769, Hamilton HM CX, Bermuda* Tel (001) (441) 292 6987 Fax 292 5421

WHITE, Paul John. b 68. Middx Univ LLB90 Bris Univ LLM92. NTMTC BA08. **d** 08 **p** 09. C Appledore w Brookland, Fairfield, Brenzett etc *Cant* from 08; C Woodchurch from 08. *The Rectory, 6 Rectory Close, Woodchurch, Ashford TN26 3QJ* Tel (01233) 860686 Mobile 07970-072757 E-mail pauljohnwhite@gmail.com

WHITE, Paul Matthew. b 73. Ulster Univ Coll Lon BSc94 K Coll Lon PGCE95. Oak Hill Th Coll BA07. **d** 07 **p** 08. C Southborough St Pet w Ch Ch and St Matt etc *Roch* from 07. *54 Holden Park Road, Tunbridge Wells TN4 0EP* Tel (01892) 529153 Mobile 07790-697354 E-mail ppwhites@hotmail.com

✠**WHITE, The Rt Revd Paul Raymond.** b 49. Canberra Coll BTh86 Heythrop Coll Lon MTh89. St Mark's Coll Canberra 85. **d** 85 **p** 86 **c** 01. Australia 85-87, 89-92 and from 97; C N Goulburn 85-87; P-in-c Reigate St Phil *S'wark* 87-89; R Queanbeyan 89-92; V Redhill St Matt 92-97; V E Ivanhoe St Geo 97-00; Dir Th Educn from 00; Asst Bp Melbourne (W Region) from 01. *28, 43-51 Jeffcott Street, West Melbourne Vic 3003, Australia* Tel (0061) (3) 9640 0163 or 9653 4220 Fax 9650 2184 E-mail pwhite@melbourne.anglican.com.au

WHITE, Peter Francis. b 27. St Edm Hall Ox BA51 MA55. Ridley Hall Cam 51. **d** 53 **p** 54. C Drypool St Columba *York* 53-56; V Dartford St Edm *Roch* 56-62; CF 62-78; R Barming *Roch* 78-89; rtd 89; Perm to Offic *Wakef* 89-98. *Middleton House Cottage, Middleton on the Hill, Ludlow SY8 4BE* Tel (01568) 750454

WHITE, Peter John. b 26. St Aid Birkenhead 57. **d** 60 **p** 61. C Toxteth Park St Gabr *Liv* 60-62; C Huyton St Mich 62-63; V Thornham w Gravel Hole *Man* 63-68; C Keighley *Bradf* 68-71; C Newington w Dairycoates *York* 71-75; C Frodingham *Linc* 75-80; R Mareham-le-Fen and Revesby 80-86; V Wrawby 86-91; V Melton Ross w New Barnetby 86-91; rtd 91; Perm to Offic *Linc* 91-96, and *Wakef* from 96. *3 Park Avenue, Wakefield WF2 8DS* Tel (01924) 201438

WHITE, Philip Craston. b 59. York Univ BA81 Nottm Univ PGCE84. Trin Coll Bris. **d** 99 **p** 00. C Countesthorpe w Foston *Leic* 99-03; C-in-c Hamilton CD from 03. *2 Cransley Close, Hamilton, Leicester LE5 1QQ* Tel 0116-274 2088

WHITE, Philip William. b 53. Bede Coll Dur CertEd75 Coll of Ripon & York St Jo MA01. St Jo Coll Nottm 89. **d** 91 **p** 92. C Clifton *York* 91-95; TV Heworth H Trin 95-01; P-in-c Scarborough St Jas w H Trin from 01; Tr Officer E Riding from 01. *St James's Vicarage, 24 Seamer Road, Scarborough YO12 4DT* Tel (01723) 361469 Mobile 07720-010066 E-mail phil@vicarage.netkonect.co.uk

WHITE, Canon Phillip George. b 33. Univ of Wales (Lamp) BA54. St Mich Coll Llan 54. **d** 56 **p** 57. C Tongwynlais *Llan* 56-58; C Mountain Ash 58-60; C Aberavon 60-62; Area Sec (Middx) CMS 62-64; V Treherbert *Llan* 64-76; P-in-c Treorchy 75-76; V Treherbert w Treorchy 76-77; V Pyle w Kenfig 77-99; RD Margam 86-99; Can Llan Cathl from 91; rtd 99. *8 Heol Fair, Porthcawl CF36 5LA* Tel (01656) 786297

WHITE, Mrs Priscilla Audrey. b 62. St Hugh's Coll Ox BA84 MA88. Wycliffe Hall Ox 87. **d** 89 **p** 94. Par Dn Southway *Ex* 89-93; NSM Plymouth Em, St Paul Efford and St Aug 93-99; P-in-c Abbotskerswell 99-05; P-in-c Harborne St Faith and St Laur *Birm* from 05. *The Vicarage, 115 Balden Road,* *Harborne, Birmingham B32 2EL* Tel 0121-427 2410 E-mail priscillawhite.harborne@btinternet.com

WHITE, Richard. *See* WHITE, Douglas Richard Leon

WHITE, Richard Alfred. b 49. CQSW. St Jo Coll Nottm. **d** 90 **p** 91. C Leic St Phil 90-95; C Old Dalby and Nether Broughton 95-98; R Ibstock w Heather from 98. *The Rectory, 2 Hinckley Road, Ibstock LE67 6PB* Tel (01530) 260246 E-mail rev49white@aol.com

WHITE, Richard Allen. b 25. Open Univ BA78 Southn Univ MPhil88 MTh95. Sarum & Wells Th Coll 78. **d** 81 **p** 82. NSM Bursledon *Win* 81-85; C W End 85-90; C Fareham SS Pet and Paul *Portsm* 90-95; Chapl St Chris Hosp Fareham 92-98; rtd 96; Perm to Offic *Portsm* and *Win* from 96. *11 Quay Haven, Swanwick, Southampton SO31 7DE* Tel (01489) 576529

WHITE, Canon Richard Stanley. b 70. Trin Coll Bris BA02. **d** 03 **p** 04. C Haydock St Mark *Liv* 03-06; Pioneer Min Dream Network from 06; Can for Miss and Evang from 09. *3 Cathedral Close, Liverpool L1 7BR* Tel 0151-708 0934 E-mail richard@dream.uk.net

WHITE, Canon Robert Bruce. b 42. Sarum & Wells Th Coll 71. **d** 73 **p** 74. C Woodford St Barn *Chelmsf* 73-75; Youth Chapl 75-79; C-in-c Sutton 75-78; P-in-c 78-79; C-in-c Shopland 75-78; P-in-c 78-79; TR Southend St Jo w St Mark, All SS w St Fran etc 79-82; P-in-c Southend St Alb 80-82; TR Southend 82-89; V Brentwood St Thos 89-08; RD Brentwood 93-08; Chapl NE Lon Mental Health Tr 97-06; Hon Can Chelmsf Cathl 97-08; rtd 08; Perm to Offic *Chelmsf* from 09. *2 Yew Close, Laindon, Basildon SS15 4EU* Tel (01268) 543910 E-mail pilgrimclub@waitrose.com

WHITE, Canon Robert Charles. b 61. Mansf Coll Ox BA83. St Steph Ho Ox 83. **d** 85 **p** 86. C Forton *Portsm* 85-88; C Portsea N End St Mark 88-92; V Warren Park 92-00; P-in-c Leigh Park 94-96; V 96-00; Hon Can Portsm Cathl from 97; RD Havant 98-00; V Portsea St Mary from 00. *St Mary's Vicarage, Fratton Road, Portsmouth PO1 5PA* Tel (023) 9282 2687 or 9282 2990 Fax 9235 9320 E-mail revrcwhite@aol.com

WHITE, The Ven Robin Edward Bantry. b 47. TCD BA70 BD79. CITC 72. **d** 72 **p** 73. C Dublin Zion Ch *D & R* 73-76; Min Can St Patr Cathl Dublin 76-79; C Taney Ch Ch *D & G* 76-79; I Abbeystrewry Union *C, C & R* 79-89; I Douglas Union w Frankfield 89-02; I Moviddy Union from 02; Can Cork Cathl from 89; Can Ross Cathl 89-93; Adn Cork, Cloyne and Ross from 93; Preb Castleknock St Patr Cathl Dublin from 09. *Moviddy Rectory, Aherla, Co Cork, Republic of Ireland* Tel (00353) (21) 733 1511 Mobile 87-286 2178 E-mail archdeacon@cork.anglican.org or robinbw@ccrd.ie

WHITE, Roderick Harry. b 55. Trin Coll Bris BA86. **d** 86 **p** 87. C Northampton St Giles *Pet* 86-89; C Godley cum Newton Green *Ches* 89-93; P-in-c 93-99; R Northiam *Chich* from 99. *The Rectory, 24 High Meadow, Northiam, Rye TN31 6GA* Tel (01797) 253118 E-mail rod@rodwhite.freeuk.com

WHITE, Roger David. b 37. Univ of Wales (Cardiff) BTh91. St Mich Coll Llan. **d** 66 **p** 67. C Mountain Ash *Llan* 66-71; C Port Talbot St Theodore 71-74; V Caerhun w Llangelynin *Ban* 74-85; R Llanbedrog w Llannor w Llanfihangel etc 85-88; V Llangeinor 88-90; V Spittal w Trefgarn and Ambleston w St Dogwells *St D* 90-98; V Abergwili w Llanfihangel-uwch-Gwili etc 98-00; rtd 00. *Tir Na Nog, 18 Bryn Cir, Llanerchymedd LL71 8EG* Tel (01248) 470159

WHITE, Roger Ian Scott. b 41. Leeds Univ BA62 Culham Coll Ox PGCE70. Coll of Resurr Mirfield 62. **d** 64 **p** 65. C Wotton-under-Edge *Glouc* 64-69; NSM Rugby St Andr *Cov* 71-80; W Germany 80-82; P-in-c Brinklow *Cov* 82-86; R 86-90; P-in-c Harborough Magna 82-86; R 86-90; P-in-c Monks Kirby w Pailton and Stretton-under-Fosse 82-86; V 86-90; Germany 90-92; V Lydgate w Friezland *Man* 92-01; Chapl Hamburg *Eur* from 01. *Englische Planke 1A, 20459 Hamburg, Germany* Tel (0049) (40) 439 2334 Fax 4018 6735 E-mail st.thomas.becket@t-online.de

✠**WHITE, The Rt Revd Roger John.** b 41. Eden Th Sem (USA) BA65 Seabury-Western Th Sem Hon DCL86 Kelham Th Coll. **d** 66 **p** 67 **c** 84. C Manston *Ripon* 66-69; V Olney St Alb USA 69-81; R Alton St Paul 71-80; R Indianapolis Trin Ch 80-84; Bp Milwaukee 84-03; rtd 03. *700 Waters Edge Road, #25, Racine WI 53402-1557, USA* Tel (001) (262) 752 1415 Fax 752 1514 Mobile 414-630 2883 E-mail rjwhite787@aol.com

WHITE, Ronald Henry. b 36. Bris Univ BSc58. SW Minl Tr Course 82. **d** 85 **p** 86. C Ivybridge *Ex* 85-87; C Ivybridge w Harford 87-88; V Blackawton and Stoke Fleming 88-95; V Stoke Fleming, Blackawton and Strete 95-00; RD Woodleigh 95-99; rtd 00; Perm to Offic *Ex* from 02. *10 Hollingarth Way, Hemyock, Cullompton EX15 3XB* Tel (01823) 681020

WHITE, Canon Roy Sidney. b 34. Sarum Th Coll 62. **d** 65 **p** 66. C Selsdon *Cant* 65-68; C Ranmoor *Sheff* 68-72; V Croydon St Andr *Cant* 72-78; Dir Abp Coggan Tr Cen 78-85; Dir of Chr Stewardship *S'wark* 85-91; Hon Can S'wark Cathl 85-91; Can Res S'wark Cathl 91-99; Vice Provost S'wark 91-99; rtd 99; Perm to Offic *Cant* 00-09. *52 Manton Court, Kings Road, Horsham RH13 5AE* Tel (01403) 248036

WHITE, Mrs Ruth Anna. b 45. Aoyama Gakuin Tokyo BA68 Grenoble Univ. Westmr Coll Cam 83 EAMTC 98. **d** 99 **p** 00. NSM Leyton St Mary w St Edw and St Luke *Chelmsf* 99-03; NSM Leytonstone St Jo from 03; Asst Chapl among deaf and deaf-blind people from 99. *18A Barclay Road, London E11 3DG* Tel and fax (020) 8558 5692 Mobile 07960-580837
E-mail revrwhite@btinternet.com

WHITE, Mrs Sally Margaret. b 59. Univ of Wales (Cardiff) BTh01. St Mich Coll Llan 99. **d** 01 **p** 02. C Berkeley w Wick, Breadstone, Newport, Stone etc *Glouc* 01-05; Co-ord Chapl HM Pris Bedf from 05. *HM Prison, St Loyes Street, Bedford MK40 1HG* Tel (01234) 358671 *or* 373000 ext 3053

WHITE, Sandy Dulcie. b 44. **d** 98 **p** 99. OLM W Streatham St Jas *S'wark* 98-05; rtd 05; Perm to Offic *Wakef* from 05. *774 Rochdale Road, Todmorden OL14 7UA* Tel (01706) 812007

WHITE, Mrs Sheelagh Mary. NEOC 02. **d** 05 **p** 06. C Heworth St Alb *Dur* from 05. *28 Rectory Road East, Gateshead NE10 9DN* Tel 0191-438 5607

WHITE, Simon Inigo Dexter. b 58. York Univ BA80 Nottm Univ PGCE81. St Jo Coll Nottm 87. **d** 90 **p** 91. C Chadkirk *Ches* 90-94; C Stockport St Geo 94; TV Stockport SW 94-99; Chapl Stockport Gr Sch 94-99; P-in-c W Hallam and Mapperley *Derby* 99-02; P-in-c Stanley 99-02; R W Hallam and Mapperley w Stanley from 02. *The Rectory, The Village, West Hallam, Ilkeston DE7 6GR* Tel 0115-932 4695 E-mail s.i.d.white@tesco.net

WHITE, Simon James Hithersay. b 65. St Jo Coll Nottm 01. **d** 03 **p** 04. C Alnwick *Newc* 03-06; P-in-c Felton from 06; P-in-c Longframlington w Brinkburn from 06. *The Vicarage, 1 Benlaw Grove, Felton, Morpeth NE65 9NG* Tel (01670) 787263
E-mail simonjhwhite@breathemail.net

WHITE, The Very Revd Stephen Ross. b 58. Hull Univ BA79 QUB DPhil93. Ripon Coll Cuddesdon BA84. **d** 85 **p** 86. C Redcar *York* 85-88; P-in-c Gweedore, Carrickfinn and Templecrone *D & R* 88-92; Bp's Dom Chapl 91-92; Dean Raphoe 92-02; I Raphoe w Raymochy and Clonleigh 93-01; Dean Killaloe and Clonfert *L & K* from 02. *The Deanery, Killaloe, Co Clare, Republic of Ireland* Tel (00353) (61) 376687
E-mail dean@killaloe.anglican.org

WHITE, Mrs Susan Margaret. b 48. Univ of E Lon BA84 Brunel Univ MBA94 Anglia Poly Univ MA04. EAMTC 01. **d** 04 **p** 05. C Harwich Peninsula *Chelmsf* 04-08; P-in-c Alkham w Capel le Ferne and Hougham Cant from 08. *The Vicarage, 20 Alexandra Road, Capel le Ferne, Folkestone CT18 7LD* Tel (01303) 240539
E-mail suewhite712@hotmail.com

WHITE, Sister Teresa Joan. b 36. Wellesley Coll (USA) BA58 Harvard Univ STB61 Lon Univ CertEd74 Hon DD86. **dss** 75 **d** 87 **p** 94. CSA from 72; Teacher Burlington-Danes Sch 74-76; Lect Inst of Chr Studies *Lon* 76-78; Gen Sec World Congress of Faiths 77-81; Lect Dioc Readers' Course *S'wark* 81-89; Asst Abp's Sec for Ecum Affairs 81-82; Ed *Distinctive Diaconate News* from 81; Ed *DIAKONIA News* 87-03; Ed *Distinctive News of Women in Ministry* from 94; Lic to Offic *Lon* 94-06; Perm to Offic from 06; Chapl Angl Communion Office from 04. *St Andrew's House, 16 Tavistock Crescent, London W11 1AP* Tel (020) 7221 4604 E-mail teresajoan@btinternet.com

WHITE, Canon Vernon Philip. b 53. Clare Coll Cam BA75 MA79 Oriel Coll Ox MLitt80. Wycliffe Hall Ox. **d** 77 **p** 78. Tutor Wycliffe Hall Ox 77-83; Chapl and Lect Ex Univ 83-87; R Wotton and Holmbury St Mary *Guildf* 87 93; Dir of Ords 87-93; Can Res and Chan Linc Cathl 93-01; Prin STETS from 01; Can Th Win Cathl from 06. *19 The Close, Salisbury SP1 2EE* Tel (01722) 424804 *or* 424820 E-mail vpwhite@stets.ac.uk

WHITE, William Frederick. b 30. St Jo Coll Nottm. **d** 02. NSM Hillingdon St Jo *Lon* 02-06; NSM Cowley 06-08; Asst Chapl Hillingdon Hosp NHS Trust 02-08; Perm to Offic *Lon* from 08. *31A Copperfield Avenue, Hillingdon, Uxbridge UB8 3NU* Tel (01895) 236746 Mobile 07754-234233
E-mail billwhite2001@hotmail.com

WHITE, William John. b 54. BSc. Wycliffe Hall Ox. **d** 84 **p** 85. C Bowdon *Ches* 84-87; C Chadkirk 87-90; R Wistaston 90-07; RD Nantwich 98-01; TR Gd Shep TM *Carl* from 07. *The Rectory, Greystoke, Penrith CA11 0TJ* Tel (01768) 483293

WHITE SPUNNER, Mrs Jessie Janet. b 37. SRN59 SCM61. CITC 91. **d** 94 **p** 95. NSM Shinrone w Aghancon etc *L & K* from 94. *St Albans, Church Street, Birr, Co Offaly, Republic of Ireland* Tel (00353) (57) 912 5637 Mobile 86-814 0213
E-mail janwspun@iol.ie

WHITEHALL, Adrian Leslie. b 53. Leeds Univ MB, ChB76 Sheff Univ MMedSc93 MRCGP80. Ridley Hall Cam 04. **d** 06 **p** 07. C Todwick *Sheff* 06-09. *Bankside Cottage, Duffield Bank, Duffield, Belper DE56 4BG* Tel (01332) 842495 Mobile 07866-454148 E-mail adrian@awhitehall.freeserve.co.uk

WHITEHEAD, Alexander. *See* WHITEHEAD, Canon Matthew Alexander

WHITEHEAD, Barry. b 30. Oriel Coll Ox BA53 MA62. St Steph Ho Ox 53. **d** 55 **p** 56. C Edgehill St Dunstan *Liv* 55-58; C Upholland 58-61; Ind Chapl 61-90; CF (TA) 64-78; V Aspull *Liv* 77-96; rtd 96; Perm to Offic *Blackb* and *Liv* from 96; Nor

from 01. *5 Sedgely, Standish, Wigan WN6 0BZ* Tel (01257) 427160

WHITEHEAD, Brian. b 36. SRN58. S'wark Ord Course 72. **d** 75 **p** 77. C Croydon St Aug *Cant* 75-78; C St Marychurch *Ex* 78-80; V Devonport St Mark Ford 80-87; V Castle Donington and Lockington cum Hemington *Leic* 87-98; Chapl Asmara St Geo Eritrea 98-99; Vice Provost All SS Cathl Cairo 99-00; Assoc P Abu Dhabi 00-01; rtd 01; Perm to Offic *Nor* 01-07. *1 Sarisbury Close, Bognor Regis PO22 8JN* Tel (01243) 866549
E-mail britone@uk.packardbell.org

WHITEHEAD, Christopher Martin Field. b 36. ALCD62. **d** 62 **p** 63. C Higher Openshaw *Man* 62-63; C Halliwell St Pet 64-66; V Owlerton *Sheff* 66-75; V Hunmanby w Muston *York* 75-95; RD Scarborough 91-94; R Lockington and Lund and Scorborough w Leconfield 95-01; rtd 01; Perm to Offic *York* from 01. *59 Cornelian Drive, Scarborough YO11 3AL* Tel (01723) 377837

WHITEHEAD, David. b 62. Newc Univ BSc83 MSc85 PhD89. St Jo Coll Nottm 04. **d** 07 **p** 08. C Ambleside w Brathay *Carl* from 07. *Brandle Howe, Helm Road, Bowness-on-Windermere, Windermere LA23 3AA* Tel (015394) 45972
E-mail davidcwhitehead@btopenworld.com

WHITEHEAD, Canon Derek. b 27. St Jo Coll Cam BA50 MA55 Lon Univ BD60 Lanc Univ PhD73. Wells Th Coll 55. **d** 56 **p** 57. C Lower Broughton Ascension *Man* 56-59; Chapl Highgate Sch Lon 63-65; Lect Div Lancs (Preston) Poly *Blackb* 65-79; Dir of Educn *Chich* 79-94; rtd 94; P-in-c Fletching *Chich* 93-03; Can and Preb Chich Cathl 82-98; Perm to Offic from 05. *2 Sheffield Park House, Uckfield TN22 3QY* Tel (01825) 790734

WHITEHEAD, Frederick Keith. b 35. K Coll Lon BD46 AKC58. St Boniface Warminster 58. **d** 59 **p** 60. C S Shore H Trin *Blackb* 59-63; C Whitfield *Derby* 63-66; Lic to Offic 66-93; V Glossop 93-98; Chapl Shire Hill Hosp Glossop 93-99; rtd 99; Perm to Offic *Derby* from 98. *7 Badgers Way, Glossop SK13 6PP* Tel (01457) 852717

WHITEHEAD, Gordon James. b 42. Culham Coll of Educn DipEd64. Clifton Th Coll 66. **d** 73 **p** 74. C Romford Gd Shep *Chelmsf* 73; SAMS Santiago Chile 74-87; C Coleraine *Conn* 87-94; I Errigle Keerogue w Ballygawley and Killeshil *Arm* 94-02; I Bright w Ballee and Killough *D & D* 02-07; rtd 07. *75 Kensington Manor, Dollingstown, Craigavon BT66 7HR* Tel (028) 3831 7989 E-mail whitehead105@btinternet.com

WHITEHEAD, Canon Hazel. b 54. K Coll Lon BD76 AKC76 Lambeth MA97. Oak Hill Th Coll 93. **d** 94 **p** 95. Tutor Dioc Min Course *Guildf* 94-96; Prin 96-05; C Oatlands 95-04; Dioc Dir Minl Tr from 05; Hon Can Guildf Cathl from 03. *The Vicarage, 5 Burwood Road, Walton-on-Thames KT12 4AA* Tel (01932) 269343 Fax 230274
E-mail hazel.whitehead@cofeguildford.org.uk

WHITEHEAD, Ian Richard. b 63. St Jo Coll Nottm BA95. **d** 95 **p** 96. C Hillmorton *Cov* 95-97; C Whitnash 97-99; R Rolleston *Lich* from 99; V Anslow from 99. *The Rectory, Church Road, Rolleston-on-Dove, Burton-on-Trent DE13 9BE* Tel (01283) 810132 *or* 810151 E-mail revrwhite@aol.com

WHITEHEAD, Mrs Jennifer Jane. b 45. St Jo Coll York CertEd67. **d** 98 **p** 99. OLM Winterton Gp *Linc* from 98. *11 Queen Street, Winterton, Scunthorpe DN15 9TR* Tel (01724) 734027

WHITEHEAD, Mrs Joanne Louise. b 71. Hull Univ BA92 PGCE93 Nottm Univ MA08. EMMTC 05. **d** 08 **p** 09. NSM Oakwood *Derby* from 08. *4 Baverstock Close, Chellaston, Derby DE73 6ST* Tel (01332) 703464
E-mail jo.whitehead@tiscali.co.uk

WHITEHEAD, John Stanley. b 38. Jes Coll Cam BA63 MA67 MPhil. Westcott Ho Cam 63. **d** 64 **p** 65. C Batley All SS *Wakef* 64-67; C Mitcham St Mark *S'wark* 67-70; C Frindsbury w Upnor *Roch* 70-72; TV Strood 72-75; R Halstead 75-82; V Betley *Lich* 82-01; V Betley and Keele 85-01; Asst Chapl Keele Univ 82-01; rtd 01; Perm to Offic *Ches* from 02. *Paddock House, Longhill Lane, Hankelow, Crewe CW3 0JG* Tel (01270) 812607
E-mail john@whitehead400.freeserve.co.uk

WHITEHEAD, Canon Matthew Alexander. b 44. Leeds Univ BA65 Birm Univ MA75 St Chad's Coll Dur DipEd66 Newc Univ MPhil03. Qu Coll Birm. **d** 69 **p** 70. C Bingley All SS *Bradf* 69-72; C Keele and Asst Chapl Keele Univ 72-74; Bp's Dom Chapl *Dur* 74-80; V Escomb and Witton Park 74-80; V Birtley 80-89; RD Chester-le-Street 84-89; V Stockton St Pet 89-00; V The Trimdons 00-03; Dioc Warden of Readers 94-03; Hon Can Dur Cathl 96-03; P-in-c Stow Gp *Linc* 03-09; rtd 09; Dioc Warden of Readers *Linc* from 03; Can and Preb Linc Cathl from 04. *77 Yarborough Crescent, Lincoln LN1 3NE* Tel 07518-746643 (mobile)
E-mail alex.whitehead@lincoln.anglican.org

WHITEHEAD, Canon Michael Hutton. b 33. St Chad's Coll Dur 54. **d** 58 **p** 59. CMP from 59; C Southwick St Columba *Dur* 58-64; V Hendon St Ignatius 64-70; P-in-c Sunderland 67-80; V Hendon 70-80; V Hendon and Sunderland 80-87; Hon Can Dur Cathl from 84; V Hartlepool St Aid 87-98; RD Hartlepool

91-95; rtd 98. *4 West Row, Greatham, Hartlepool TS25 2HW* Tel (01429) 872922

WHITEHEAD, Nicholas James. b 53. ACIB. Ridley Hall Cam 86. **d** 88 **p** 89. C Bourne *Guildf* 88-92; V Hersham from 92; RD Emly from 06. *The Vicarage, 5 Burwood Road, Walton-on-Thames KT12 4AA* Tel (01932) 227445 Fax 230274

WHITEHEAD, Paul Conrad. b 60. St Jo Coll Nottm LTh92. **d** 92 **p** 93. C Mansfield Woodhouse *S'well* 92-96; C Carlton-in-the-Willows 96-02; C Colwick 96-02; CF (TA) from 96; NSM Trowell, Awsworth and Cossall *S'well* from 04. *84 Hillside Road, Beeston, Nottingham NG9 3AT* Tel 0115-919 7030 Mobile 07973-727221 E-mail paulkirsten@ntlworld.com

WHITEHEAD, Philip. b 34. Kelham Th Coll 55. **d** 59 **p** 60. C Sugley *Newc* 59-62; C Alnwick St Paul 62-63; C Newc St Gabr 63-66; C Gosforth All SS 66-67; V Kenton Ascension 67-75; V Spittal 75-88; P-in-c Scremerston 81-88; V Cresswell and Lynemouth 88-96; Perm to Offic from 96; rtd 96. *13 Abbey Gate, Morpeth NE61 2XL* Tel (01670) 514953

WHITEHEAD, Robin Lawson. b 53. Bris Univ BA76 Lon Univ MA96. St Steph Ho Ox 77. **d** 80 **p** 81. C Cheshunt *St Alb* 80-83; C E Grinstead St Swithun *Chich* 83-85; V Friern Barnet St Pet le Poer *Lon* 85-92; R Friern Barnet St Jas 92-95; C Wood Green St Mich w Bounds Green St Gabr etc 96-97; TR Leic Resurr 97-04; V Boston *Linc* 04-05; TR from 05. *The Vicarage, Wormgate, Boston PE21 6NP* Tel (01205) 362992 E-mail robin.whitehead@virgin.net

WHITEHORN, Arthur Basil. b 24. Ox Univ MA50. WMMTC 81. **d** 84 **p** 85. NSM Bromsgrove St Jo *Worc* 84-94; Asst Chapl Bromsgrove and Redditch HA 84-89; Perm to Offic from 94. *15 Perry Lane, Bromsgrove B61 7JL* Tel (01527) 874857

WHITEHOUSE, Alan Edward. b 35. CEng66. Glouc Sch of Min 89. **d** 92 **p** 93. NSM Evesham *Worc* 92-96; NSM Evesham w Norton and Lenchwick 96-02; rtd 02; Perm to Offic *Worc* from 03. *The Coppice, 56 Elm Road, Evesham WR11 3DW* Tel (01386) 442427 E-mail alan.coppice@btopenworld.com

WHITEHOUSE, David Garner. b 70. Sheff Univ BEng91. EAMTC 03. **d** 05 **p** 06. C Cheadle *Ches* from 05. *1 Warren Avenue, Cheadle SK8 1NB* Tel 0161-428 3001 E-mail david.youth@cheadle.org

WHITEHOUSE, Nigel Andrew. b 57. St Mary's RC Sem Birm 75 Westcott Ho Cam 91. **d** 80 **p** 81. In RC Ch 81-87; C Whittlesey and Pondersbridge *Ely* 92-94; P-in-c Newton 94-98; R 98-03; P-in-c Gorefield 94-98; V 98-03; P-in-c Tydd St Giles 94-98; R 98-03; TR Whittlesey, Pondersbridge and Coates from 03; Hon Asst Dir of Ords from 09. *The Rectory, 9A St Mary's Street, Whittlesey, Peterborough PE7 1BG* Tel (01733) 203676 E-mail nigel.whitehouse@talktalk.net

WHITEHOUSE, Canon Susan Clara. b 48. R Holloway Coll Lon BA70. Westcott Ho Cam 87. **d** 89 **p** 94. Par Dn Farnley *Ripon* 89-93; Dioc Development Rep 92-03; C Bedale and Thornton Watlass w Thornton Steward 93-96; V Aysgarth and Bolton cum Redmire 96-06; R Penhill from 06; Hon Can Ripon Cathl from 02; AD Wensley 03-05. *The Vicarage, Carperby, Leyburn DL8 4DQ* Tel (01969) 663235 E-mail suewhitehouse@carperby.fsnet.co.uk

WHITELEY, Canon Robert Louis. b 28. Leeds Univ BA48. Coll of Resurr Mirfield 50. **d** 52 **p** 53. C Hollinwood *Man* 52-55; Br Honduras 56-61; V Illingworth *Wakef* 61-68; V Westgate Common 68-75; Can Res Wakef Cathl 75-80; Hon Can Wakef Cathl 80-93; V Almondbury 80-82; TR Almondbury w Farnley Tyas 82-92; RD Almondbury 81-93; rtd 93; Perm to Offic *Wakef* from 93 and *Ox* from 98. *2 Woodclyffe Almshouses, Wargrave Hill, Wargrave, Reading RG10 8JH* Tel 0118-940 3877

WHITELOCK, Mrs Susan Karen. b 62. STETS 98. **d** 01 **p** 06. NSM Portsea N End St Mark *Portsm* 01-06; NSM Portsea St Mary from 06. *404 Copnor Road, Portsmouth PO3 5EW* Tel 07903-414029 (mobile) E-mail sue.whitelock@ntlworld.com

WHITEMAN, Canon Cedric Henry. b 28. Lich Th Coll 59. **d** 61 **p** 62. C Abington *Pet* 61-64; V Kettering St Andr 64-79; RD Kettering 73-79; Can Pet Cathl 77-79; V Rotherham *Sheff* 79-87; RD Rotherham 79-86; Hon Can Sheff Cathl 85-98; Bp's Dom Chapl 86-99; V Wentworth 87-91; rtd 91; Perm to Offic *Sheff* from 99. *11 Thornbrook Close, Chapeltown, Sheffield S35 2BB* Tel 0114-245 7479 E-mail cedric.whiteman@btinternet.com

WHITEMAN, Christopher Henry Raymond. b 51. Portsm Poly BA73 Worc Coll of Educn PGCE74 Open Univ BSc97. St Jo Coll Nottm MA99. **d** 90 **p** 91. C Rockland St Mary w Hellington, Bramerton etc *Nor* 90-93; P-in-c Gillingham w Geldeston, Stockton, Ellingham etc 93-94; R 94-04; R Culworth w Sulgrave and Thorpe Mandeville etc *Pet* from 04. *The Rectory, Queens Street, Culworth, Banbury OX17 2AT* Tel (01295) 760383

WHITEMAN, The Ven Rodney David Carter. b 40. Ely Th Coll 61. **d** 64 **p** 65. C Kings Heath *Birm* 64-70; V Rednal 70-79; V Erdington St Barn 79-89; RD Aston 81-86 and 88-89; Hon Can Birm Cathl 85-89; Adn Bodmin *Truro* 89-00; Adn Cornwall 00-05; P-in-c Cardynham and Helland 89-94; Hon Can Truro Cathl 89-05; rtd 06. *22 Treverbyn Gardens, Sandy Hill, St Austell PL25 3AW* Tel (01726) 879043

WHITESIDE, Canon Peter George. b 30. St Cath Coll Cam BA55 MA61. Cuddesdon Coll 55. **d** 57 **p** 58. C Westmr St Steph w St Jo *Lon* 57-61; Chapl Clifton Coll Bris 61-70; Hd Master Linc Cathl Sch 71-73; Can and Preb Linc Cathl 72-73; Australia 74-92; Prin and Chapl Wadhurst C of E Gr Sch 74-89; TV Brentford *Lon* 92-97; C Frankston E St Luke Australia 98-00; C Ormond 00-05; rtd 05. *52 Cove Road, Rustington, Littlehampton BN16 2QN* Tel (01903) 786566 E-mail linda655@btinternet.com

WHITFIELD, Charles. b 25. St Pet Hall Ox BA49 MA53. Ridley Hall Cam 49. **d** 51 **p** 52. C Ecclesfield *Sheff* 51-54; C Grassendale *Liv* 54-56; C Neasden cum Kingsbury St Cath *Lon* 56-58; C St Martin-in-the-Fields 58-59; V Bromley H Trin *Roch* 59-68; V Egg Buckland *Ex* 68-90; rtd 90; Perm to Offic *Ex* from 99. *23 Chapel Meadow, Buckland Monachorum, Yelverton PL20 7LR*

WHITFIELD, Joy Verity. See CHAPMAN, Mrs Joy Verity

WHITFIELD, Leslie Turnbull. b 43. CEng72 MIET72 MCMI74. St Jo Coll Nottm MA00. **d** 00 **p** 01. C Bottesford w Ashby *Linc* 00-03; P-in-c Mablethorpe w Trusthorpe 03-07; Ind Chapl 07-08; rtd 08. *3 Burland Court, Washingborough, Lincoln LN4 1HL* Tel (01522) 791195 Mobile 07913-247783 E-mail rev.les@tiscali.co.uk

WHITFIELD, Trevor. b 48. Bedf Coll Lon BSc71 Bris Univ PGCE73 Fitzw Coll Cam BA78 MA88. Ridley Hall Cam 76. **d** 79 **p** 80. C Battersea St Pet and St Paul *S'wark* 79-82; Chapl Stockholm w Uppsala *Eur* 82-83; C-in-c Roundshaw St Paul CD *S'wark* 83-89; Asst Chapl R Victoria Infirmary Newc 89-92; Asst Chapl Berne w Neuchâtel *Eur* 92-95; Chapl Utrecht w Amersfoort, Harderwijk and Zwolle 95-02; Chapl Maisons-Laffitte from 02. *15 avenue Carnot, 78600 Maisons-Laffitte, France* Tel (0033) (1) 39 62 34 97 E-mail htcml@aol.com

WHITFIELD, William. b 47. Open Univ BA80 Univ of Wales (Cardiff) LLM95 FRSH81. STETS 01. **d** 04 **p** 05. NSM Marchwood *Win* 04-08; NSM Millbrook from 08. *35 The Rowans, Marchwood, Southampton SO40 4YW* Tel (023) 8086 0399 E-mail william.whitfield@btinternet.com

WHITFORD, Judith. See POLLINGER, Mrs Judith

WHITFORD (née FAULKNER), Mrs Margaret Evelyn. b 54. Goldsmiths' Coll Lon BEd77. EAMTC 98. **d** 01 **p** 02. C Grays Thurrock *Chelmsf* 01-05; C Bradwell on Sea 05-08; C Bradwell on Sea and St Lawrence from 08. *The Rectory, East End Road, Bradwell-on-Sea, Southminster CM0 7PX* Tel (01621) 776203 E-mail margaretfaulkner@aol.com

WHITFORD, William Laurence. b 56. Open Univ BA92. NOC 92. **d** 95 **p** 96. C Hindley All SS *Liv* 95-99; P-in-c E and W Tilbury and Linford *Chelmsf* 99-04; R 04-05; P-in-c Bradwell on Sea 05-08; R Bradwell on Sea and St Lawrence from 08. *The Rectory, East End Road, Bradwell-on-Sea, Southminster CM0 7PX* Tel (01621) 776203 E-mail laurence@whitfordw.freeserve.co.uk

WHITHAM, Ian Scott. b 66. Oak Hill Th Coll. **d** 01 **p** 02. C Yateley *Win* 01-03; C Yateley and Eversley 03-05; V W Ewell *Guildf* from 05. *All Saints' Vicarage, 7 Church Road, West Ewell, Epsom KT19 9QY* Tel (020) 8393 4357 Mobile 07946-394467 E-mail ian.witham@ntlworld.com

WHITING, Graham James. b 58. Bris Univ BSc81. Chich Th Coll 83. **d** 86 **p** 88. C Portslade St Nic and St Andr *Chich* 86-87; C W Tarring 87-91; C Seaford w Sutton 91-94; P-in-c Bournemouth St Clem *Win* 94-02; V Findon Valley *Chich* from 02. *The Vicarage, 29 Central Avenue, Worthing BN14 0DS* Tel (01903) 872900 E-mail graham.whiting@lineone.net

WHITING, Joseph Alfred. b 41. Oak Hill Th Coll 82. **d** 85 **p** 86. Hon C Sidcup St Andr *Roch* 85-88; C Southborough St Pet w Ch Ch and St Matt 88-92; C Aldridge *Lich* 92-97; TV Rye *Chich* 97-02; rtd 02; Perm to Offic *Roch* from 02. *71 Ash Tree Drive, West Kingsdown, Sevenoaks TN15 6LW* Tel (01474) 853202 E-mail whitings71@tiscali.co.uk

WHITING, Mark Justin Robert. b 70. St Steph Ho Ox 99. **d** 01 **p** 02. C Sevenoaks St Jo *Roch* 01-04; P-in-c Derby St Bart 04-07; Chapl RN 07-08; Perm to Offic *Portsm* from 09. *Downlea, 59 Finchdean Road, Rowland's Castle PO9 6DA* Tel 07951-589024 (mobile) E-mail frmarkwhiting@aol.com

WHITING, Stephen. b 60. Cranmer Hall Dur 06. **d** 08 **p** 09. C Scarborough St Mary w Ch Ch and H Apostles *York* from 08. *13 Woodall Avenue, Scarborough YO12 7TH* Tel (01723) 350016 Mobile 07789-950881 E-mail stevewhiting.1@btinternet.com

WHITLEY, Brian. b 58. Dundee Univ BA97 Portsm Univ MA(Ed)00 RMN84 RGN84. STETS BA07. **d** 07 **p** 08. C Easthampstead *Ox* from 07. *Magdalene House, Crowthorne Road, Bracknell RG12 7ER* Tel (01344) 426905 Mobile 07851-859296 E-mail bwhitley2@ntlworld.com

WHITLEY, Eric Keir. b 47. Salford Univ BSc68. Trin Coll Bris 77. **d** 79 **p** 80. C Nottingham St Ann w Em *S'well* 79-83; V Donisthorpe and Moira w Stretton-en-le-Field *Leic* 83-91; V Thorpe Acre w Dishley 91-00; V Loughb Gd Shep from 00. *21 Parklands Drive, Loughborough LE11 2SZ* Tel (01509) 211005

WHITLEY, John Duncan Rooke. b 29. Trin Coll Cam BA51 MA55 Jordan Hill Coll Glas CertEd82. Coll of Resurr Mirfield 52. **d** 54 **p** 55. C Ashington *Newc* 54-59; C Chiswick St Nic w St Mary *Lon* 59-61; V Ware St Mary *St Alb* 61-71; Can Missr Edin 71-74; Chapl R Edin Hosp 71-74; Dioc Educn Officer *Edin* 71-74; Hon Asst Dioc Supernumerary from 74; Asst Chapl Lothian Primary Healthcare NHS Trust 95-04; TV Edin St Columba from 99. *114 Viewforth, Edinburgh EH10 4LN* Tel and fax 0131-229 0130 Mobile 07774-402551
E-mail john.whitley@blueyonder.co.uk

WHITLEY, John William. b 46. TCD BA68. Cranmer Hall Dur BA71. **d** 71 **p** 72. C Belfast St Mary Magd *Conn* 71-73; C Toxteth St Philemon w St Gabr *Liv* 73-78; P-in-c Toxteth Park St Cleopas 78-88; TV Toxteth St Philemon w St Gabr and St Cleopas 89-95; P-in-c Litherland St Paul Hatton Hill 95-02; V from 02. *St Paul's Vicarage, Watling Avenue, Liverpool L21 9NU* Tel 0151-928 2705 E-mail anthea.whitley@virgin.net

WHITLEY (née ALLISON), Rosemary Jean. b 45. LTCL67. Trin Coll Bris 75 St Jo Coll Nottm 94. **d** 95 **p** 99. NSM Loughb Gd Shep *Leic* 95-98 and from 00; NSM Thorpe Acre w Dishley 98-00. *21 Parklands Drive, Loughborough LE11 2SZ* Tel (01501) 211005

WHITLOCK, Canon James Frederick. b 44. Ch Coll Cam BA75 MA78. Westcott Ho Cam 73. **d** 76 **p** 77. C Newquay *Truro* 76-79; P-in-c St Mawgan w St Ervan and St Eval 79-81; R 81; Bp's Dom Chapl 82-85; Dioc Dir of Ords 82-85; V Leagrave *St Alb* 85-89; TR Probus, Ladock and Grampound w Creed and St Erme *Truro* 89-95; V Penzance St Mary w St Paul 95-00; P-in-c Penzance St Jo 97-00; Hon Can Truro Cathl 98-00; rtd 00; Perm to Offic *Truro* from 00. *10 Barlandhu, Newlyn, Penzance TR18 5QT* Tel (01736) 330474

WHITMARSH, Mrs Pauline. **d** 04 **p** 05. OLM Bramshaw and Landford w Plaitford *Sarum* 04-06; OLM Forest and Avon from 06. *Dovera, North Lane, Nomansland, Salisbury SP5 2BU* Tel (01794) 390534 E-mail plwhitmarsh@tiscali.co.uk

WHITMORE, Benjamin Nicholas. b 66. Imp Coll Lon BEng88. Cranmer Hall Dur 89. **d** 92 **p** 93. C Gt Wyrley *Lich* 92-95; C Hednesford 95-00; V Walsall Pleck and Bescot 00-07; Hon C Wallsall and Walsall St Paul 05-07; V Penn from 07. *St Bartholomew's Vicarage, 68 Church Hill, Penn, Wolverhampton WV4 5JD* Tel (01902) 341399
E-mail bennyjo@vicres.fsnet.co.uk

WHITMORE, Edward James. b 36. Lon Univ BD66. Tyndale Hall Bris. **d** 68 **p** 69. Tanzania 68-76; Lic to Offic *Blackb* from 77. *74 Greencroft, Penwortham, Preston PR1 9LB* Tel (01772) 746522

WHITMORE, Miss Jane Frances. b 30. dss 79 **d** 87 **p** 94. Elloughton and Brough w Brantingham *York* 79-83; Foley Park *Worc* 83-87; C Frimley *Guildf* 87-96; rtd 96; Perm to Offic *Worc* from 96. *The Grange, 26 Middleton Road, Marlpool, Kidderminster DY11 5EY*

WHITMORE, Stephen Andrew. b 53. Sheff Univ BSc74. St Jo Coll Nottm 89. **d** 91 **p** 92. C Newbury *Ox* 91-95; TV High Wycombe from 95. *70 Marlow Road, High Wycombe HP11 1TH* Tel (01494) 438722 E-mail steve@stjohnschurch.freeserve.co.uk

WHITNALL, Robert Edward (Dominic). b 14. Magd Coll Ox BA37. Cuddesdon Coll 37. **d** 38 **p** 39. C Staveley *Derby* 38-44; CR from 47; S Africa 47-66; Hon C Battyeford *Wakef* from 68; rtd 84. *House of the Resurrection, Stocks Bank Road, Mirfield WF14 0BN* Tel (01924) 483335

WHITNEY, Charles Edward. b 46. Goldsmiths' Coll Lon BA71 TCert72 ACP75. WEMTC 01. **d** 04 **p** 05. NSM Tewkesbury w Walton Cardiff and Twyning *Glouc* from 04. *Sarn Hill Lodge, Bushley Green, Bushley, Tewkesbury GL20 6AD* Tel (01684) 296764

WHITTA, Rex Alfred Rought. b 28. Leeds Inst of Educn CertEd52 Open Univ BA88. Qu Coll Birm. **d** 63 **p** 64. C Newland St Aug *York* 63-66; V Elloughton 66-68; P-in-c Brantingham 66-68; V Elloughton and Brough w Brantingham 68-74; TR Redcar w Kirkleatham 74-78; V Redcar 78-84; V Bassenthwaite, Isel and Setmurthy *Carl* 84-86; P-in-c Cloughton and Hackness w Harwood Dale *York* 86-88; rtd 89; Perm to Offic *York* 89-03 and *Ches* from 03. *1 The Orchards, Connah's Quay, Deeside CH5 4QZ* Tel (01244) 846347 Mobile 07941-461823 E-mail whitta@dsl.pipex.com

WHITTAKER, Mrs Angela. b 68. Birm Univ BA89 St Martin's Coll Lanc PGCE91. NEOC 98. **d** 00 **p** 01. C Houghton le Spring *Dur* 00-04; TV Kirkby Lonsdale *Carl* from 04. *The Vicarage, Vicarage Lane, Kirkby Lonsdale, Carnforth LA6 2BA* Tel (01524) 272078

WHITTAKER, Brian Lawrence. b 39. Univ of Wales MTh06. Clifton Th Coll 63. **d** 66 **p** 67. C Whitton and Thurleston w Akenham *St E* 66-69; C Normanton *Wakef* 69-74; P-in-c Castle Hall, Stalybridge and Dukinfield Ch Ch *Ches* 74-77; V Stalybridge H Trin and Ch Ch 77-83; TR Bucknall and Bagnall *Lich* 83-91; R Draycott-le-Moors w Forsbrook 91-05; rtd 05; Perm to Offic *Lich* from 05. *6 Rubens Way, Stoke-on-Trent ST3 7GQ* Tel (01782) 397765
E-mail brianlesley.whittaker@tesco.net

WHITTAKER, Bryan. b 58. Southn Univ BTh82. Chich Th Coll 82. **d** 84 **p** 85. C Whitleigh *Ex* 84-88; C Corringham *Chelmsf* 88-92; V Rush Green 92-94. *361 Dagenham Road, Romford RM7 0XX*

WHITTAKER, Derek. b 30. OBE85. Liv Univ BEng51 PhD58 CEng65. **d** 93 **p** 95. Zambia 93-96; NSM Broom Leys *Leic* 97-00; rtd 00; Perm to Offic *Leic* from 00. *44 St David's Crescent, Coalville LE67 4ST* Tel (01530) 831071

WHITTAKER, Mrs Diane Claire. b 57. Newc Poly BA79 Thames Poly BSc87 Univ of Wales (Abth) MA92. ERMC 06. **d** 08. C Welwyn *St Alb* from 08. *St Michael's House, 3 London Road, Woolmer Green, Knebworth SG3 6JU* Tel (01438) 811815

WHITTAKER, Edward Geoffrey. b 59. Birm Univ BSc82 Avery Hill Coll PGCE85 Dur Univ MA95. Westcott Ho Cam 97. **d** 99 **p** 00. C Neston *Ches* 99-02; V Rocester and Croxden w Hollington *Lich* from 02; P-in-c Uttoxeter Area from 07; RD Uttoxeter from 04. *The Rectory, 12 Orchard Close, Uttoxeter ST14 7DZ* Tel (01889) 563644

WHITTAKER, Garry. b 59. St Jo Coll Nottm 89. **d** 91 **p** 92. C Denton Ch Ch *Man* 91-95; P-in-c Waterhead 95-05; TR Bacup and Stacksteads from 05. *10 Park Crescent, Bacup OL13 9RL* Tel (01706) 873362

WHITTAKER, James Rawstron. b 14. Worc Coll Ox BA38 MA46. Wells Th Coll 38. **d** 40 **p** 41. C St Mary Bishophill Senior 40-43; Hornsea w Bewholme 43-47; R Neen Sollars w Milson *Heref* 47-55; V Annscroft 55-70; R Pontesbury III 55-70; V Longden 55-70; V Almeley 70-80; P-in-c Kinnersley w Norton Canon 74-80; rtd 81. *Eign Gate House, 142 Eign Street, Hereford HR4 0AP* Tel (01432) 268961

WHITTAKER, Mrs Jennifer Margaret. b 43. Glas Univ MA64. SAOMC 00. **d** 03 **p** 04. NSM Martley and Wichenford, Knightwick etc *Worc* 03-08; NSM Worcs W from 09. *The Key Barn, Half Key, Malvern WR14 1UP* Tel (01886) 833897
E-mail jen.whittaker@tiscali.co.uk

WHITTAKER, Jeremy Paul. b 59. Ox Univ MA. Ripon Coll Cuddesdon 82. **d** 84 **p** 85. C Crowthorne *Ox* 84-87; C Westborough *Guildf* 87-88; TV 88-91; Chapl Pierrepont Sch Frensham 91-95; Perm to Offic *Guildf* from 95. *6 Springhaven Close, Guildford GU1 2JP*

WHITTAKER, John. b 69. Leic Univ BA90 ACA93. Ripon Coll Cuddesdon BTh00. **d** 00 **p** 01. C Melton Mowbray *Leic* 00-03; P-in-c Barrow upon Soar w Walton le Wolds from 03; P-in-c Wymeswold and Prestwold w Hoton from 05. *The Rectory, 27 Cotes Road, Barrow upon Soar, Loughborough LE12 8JP* Tel (01509) 621834 E-mail johnhelena@tiscali.co.uk

WHITTAKER, Karl Paul. b 55. ATL. CITC BTh95. **d** 95 **p** 96. C Killowen *D & R* 95-99; I Annaghmore *Arm* 99-04; P-in-c Sunbury St Mary Australia 04-05; I Errigal w Garvagh *D & R* from 05. *St Paul's Rectory, 58 Station Road, Garvagh, Coleraine BT51 5LA* Tel (028) 2955 8226

WHITTAKER, Canon Peter Harold. b 39. AKC62. **d** 63 **p** 64. C Walton St Mary *Liv* 63-67; C Ross *Heref* 67-70; R Bridgnorth St Mary 70-78; P-in-c Oldbury 70-78; TR Bridgnorth, Tasley, Astley Abbotts and Oldbury 78-81; RD Bridgnorth 78-81; Preb Heref Cathl 80-81; V Leighton Buzzard w Eggington, Hockliffe etc *St Alb* 81-92; RD Dunstable 84-85; R Barton-le-Cley w Higham Gobion and Hexton 92-04; Hon Can St Alb from 92; rtd 04; Perm to Offic *Lich* from 06. *12 Aldersley Way, Ruyton XI Towns, Shrewsbury SY4 1NE* Tel (01939) 260059

WHITTAKER, William Paul. See STAFFORD-WHITTAKER, William Paul

WHITTAM, Canon Kenneth Michael. b 26. Ball Coll Ox BA50 MA54. Cuddesdon Coll 50. **d** 52 **p** 53. C Adlington *Blackb* 52-55; C St Annes St Thos 55-58; R Halton w Aughton 58-62; R Colne St Bart 62-66; Chapl Highgate Sch Lon 66-75; V Shotwick *Ches* 75-89; Can Res Ches Cathl and Dioc Missr 75-85; Hon Can Ches Cathl 85-90; Clergy Study Officer 85-91; rtd 91; Perm to Offic *Ches* from 91. *22 Warwick Close, Little Neston, Neston CH64 0SR* Tel 0151-336 8541

WHITTINGHAM, Mrs Janet Irene. b 49. **d** 03 **p** 04. OLM Pendleton *Man* 03-09; OLM Salford All SS from 09. *24 Aylesbury Close, Salford M5 4FQ* Tel 0161-736 5878

WHITTINGHAM, Peter. b 58. Sheff Univ BA79 PGCE. St Jo Coll Nottm 88. **d** 90 **p** 91. C Northowram *Wakef* 90-93; C Airedale w Fryston 93-96; V Wrenthorpe 96-06; P-in-c Alverthorpe 02-06; V Attercliffe and Darnall *Sheff* from 06. *25 Industry Road, Sheffield S9 5FP* Tel 0114-244 8543

WHITTINGHAM, Ronald Norman. b 43. Linc Coll Ox BA65 MA68. Coll of Resurr Mirfield 65. **d** 67 **p** 68. C Horninglow *Lich* 67-69; C Drayton in Hales 69-70; C Uttoxeter w Bramshall 71-75; P-in-c Burton St Paul 75-80; V Shareshill 80-83; V Silverdale and Knutton Heath 83-89; P-in-c Alsagers Bank 83-89; V Silverdale and Alsagers Bank 89-92; V Honley *Wakef* 92-99; TV Hugglescote w Donington, Ellistown and Snibston *Leic* 99-02, TV Leic Presentation 02-07; C Leic St Chad 03-07; rtd 07; Perm to Offic *Lich* from 08. *848 High Lane, Stoke-on-Trent ST6 6HG*

WHITTINGTON, David John. b 45. OBE01. Qu Coll Ox BA67 MA71. Coll of Resurr Mirfield 69. **d** 71 **p** 72. Chapl St Woolos

Cathl 71-72; Chapl Qu Coll and C Ox St Mary V w St Cross and St Pet 72-76; V Stockton *Dur* 77-98; Hon Can Dur Cathl 93-98; Can Res and Dioc Dir Educn 98-03; Nat Sch Development Officer Abps' Coun 03-08; rtd 08. *The Gatehouse Flat, Brancepeth Castle, Brancepeth, Durham DH7 8DE* Tel 07702-036344 (mobile) E-mail dj.whittington@btinternet.com
WHITTINGTON, Peter Graham. b 68. Ox Poly BA90. Trin Coll Bris BA95. d 95 p 96. C Gateacre *Liv* 95-99; V Huyton St Geo 99-05; V Orrell from 05. *St Luke's Vicarage, 10 Lodge Road, Orrell, Wigan WN5 7AT* Tel (01695) 623410 E-mail whitts01@surfaid.org
WHITTINGTON, Richard Hugh. b 47. MBE74. Sarum & Wells Th Coll. d 93 p 94. C Enfield St Jas *Lon* 93-96; P-in-c Ightham *Roch* 96-97; R 97-01; Chapl R Hosp Chelsea from 01. *The Chaplaincy, The Royal Hospital Chelsea, Royal Hospital Road, London SW3 4SL* Tel (020) 7881 5234 *or* 7881 5260 Fax 7881 5463 Mobile 07979-360633 E-mail chaplain@chelsea-pensioners.org.uk
WHITTINGTON, Mrs Sharon Ann. b 56. Leeds Univ BA79 PGCE80. NEOC. d 00 p 01. NSM The Street Par *York* 00-03; P-in-c York St Thos w St Maurice 03-05; NSM York St Olave w St Giles from 03; NSM York St Helen w St Martin from 04. *30 Marygate, York YO30 7BH* Tel (01904) 627401
WHITTLE, Alan. b 29. K Coll Lon BD52 AKC52. d 53 p 54. C Combe Down *B & W* 53-55; C Bath Twerton-on-Avon 55-57; Australia 57-66; R Aston Rowant w Crowell *Ox* 66-68; Lic to Offic *S'wark* 69-72; V Mitcham Ch Ch 72-92; rtd 92; Perm to Offic *S'wark* 92-07. *117 May Cross Avenue, Morden SM4 4DF* Tel (020) 8540 0201
WHITTLE, Ian Christopher. b 60. Univ Coll Dur BA81 Fitzw Coll Cam BA88 MA91. Ridley Hall Cam 85. d 88 p 89. C S Petherton w the Seavingtons *B & W* 88-91; Asst Chapl The Hague *Eur* 91-97; P-in-c Gayton Gp of Par *Nor* 97-99; R Gayton, Gayton Thorpe, E Walton, E Winch etc from 99; RD Lynn 02-08. *The Rectory, Grimston Road, Gayton, King's Lynn PE32 1QA* Tel (01553) 636227
WHITTLE, John William. b 46. Qu Mary Coll Lon BA68. Sarum & Wells Th Coll 84. d 86 p 87. C Blandford Forum and Langton Long etc *Sarum* 86-88; NSM Pimperne, Stourpaine, Durweston and Bryanston from 02. *The Cottage, Queens Road, Blandford Forum DT11 7JZ* Tel (01258) 454789 E-mail johnwwhittle@hotmail.com
WHITTLE, Naomi Clare. b 54. Colchester Inst of Educn BA75 Lon Univ PGCE76 Middx Univ MA(Theol)99 LGSM77. SEITE 95. d 98 p 99. C Catford (Southend) and Downham *S'wark* 98-02; P-in-c Shooters Hill Ch Ch 02; V from 02; Chapl Oxleas NHS Foundn Trust from 06. *The Vicarage, 1 Craigholm, Shooters Hill, London SE18 3RR* Tel (020) 8856 5858 E-mail naomiwhittle@tiscali.co.uk
WHITTLE, Robin Jeffrey. b 51. Bris Univ BA72 Leic Univ CQSW75. Sarum & Wells Th Coll 85. d 87 p 88. C Henbury *Bris* 87-91; V Capel *Guildf* 91-96; Chapl among Deaf People from 96; Perm to Offic *Roch* and *S'wark* 97-99; P-in-c Walton-on-the-Hill 99-04; V Tattenham Corner from 04. *St Mark's Vicarage, St Mark's Road, Epsom KT18 5RD* Tel (01737) 353011 E-mail bobwhittle@btinternet.com
WHITTLE, Mrs Sheila Margaret. b 36. Glouc Th Course 83 NY Th Sem MA88 Vancouver Sch of Th. d 90 p 90. R Bulkley Valley Canada 90-93; C Dunbar St Phil 93; P-in-c Maple Ridge St Jo the Divine 93-95; Lethbridge St Mary the Virgin 95-97; NSM Portsea N End St Mark *Portsm* 97-98; P-in-c Lezant w Lawhitton and S Petherwin w Trewen *Truro* 98-02; rtd 02; Perm to Offic *Glouc* from 03. *71 Graylag Crescent, Walton Cardiff, Tewkesbury GL20 7RR* Tel (01684) 299981 E-mail sheila_whittle@onetel.com
WHITTLESEA, Grahame Stanley Jack Hammond. b 37. Kent Univ LLM95. d 05 p 06. OLM Blean *Cant* 05-09; rtd 09; Perm to Offic *Cant* from 09. *4 Eastbridge Hospital, High Street, Canterbury CT1 2BD* Tel (01227) 472536 Mobile 07866-037774 E-mail gandawhittlesea@tiscali.co.uk
WHITTOCK (*née* MARBUS), Alida Janny. b 52. RGN78. STETS 00. d 03 p 07. NSM Weymouth H Trin *Sarum* 03-09; NSM Abbotsbury, Portesham and Langton Herring from 09. *The Rectory, Church Lane, Portesham, Weymouth DT3 4HB* Tel (01305) 871217 E-mail adamarbus@aol.com
WHITTOCK, Michael Graham. b 47. Hull Univ BA69 Fitzw Coll Cam BA71 MA76. Westcott Ho Cam 69 Union Th Sem Virginia 71. d 72 p 73. C Kirkby *Liv* 72-76; C Prescot 76-79; R Methley w Mickletown *Ripon* 79-92; RD Whitkirk 88-92; V Morley St Pet w Churwell *Wakef* 92-01; R Gt Hanwood *Heref* from 01; R Longden and Annscroft w Pulverbatch from 01; RD Pontesbury from 08. *The Rectory, Plealey Lane, Longden, Shrewsbury SY5 8ET* Tel (01743) 861003 Fax 861237
WHITTOME, David Marshall. b 26. Cam Univ BA50 MA53. S Dios Minl Tr Scheme. d 84 p 85. NSM Henfield w Shermanbury and Woodmancote *Chich* 84-93; P-in-c Poynings w Edburton, Newtimber and Pyecombe 93-97; rtd 97; Perm to Offic *Chich*

from 97. *Quaker's Rest, 7 Dean Court Road, Rottingdean, Brighton BN2 7DE* Tel (01273) 705508 Fax 271475 E-mail donaldwhitome@hotmail.com
WHITTY, Gordon William. b 35. WMMTC. d 82 p 83. NSM Willenhall St Giles *Lich* 82-84; NSM Coseley Ch Ch 84-85; C 85-87; TV Hanley H Ev 87-91; P-in-c Meir 91-98; P-in-c Hanbury w Newborough and Rangemore 98-99; V 99-03; rtd 03; Perm to Offic *Derby* from 04. *14 Cardrona Close, Oakwood, Derby DE21 2JN* Tel (01332) 726320 E-mail gordonwhitty@vinweb.co.uk
WHITTY, Harold George. b 41. TCD BA64 MA67. CITC Div Test65. d 65 p 66. C Willowfield *D & D* 65-68; C Lisburn Ch Ch *Conn* 68-71; Bp's Dom Chapl 70-71; Asst Dir Exhibitions CMJ 71-72; C Enfield Ch Ch Trent Park *Lon* 72-75; TV Washfield, Stoodleigh, Withleigh etc *Ex* 75-83; R 83-84; TR 84-93; P-in-c Aylesbeare, Rockbeare, Farringdon etc 02-04; RD Tiverton 82-84; P-in-c Allithwaite *Carl* 93-97; TV Cartmel Peninsula 97-02; Local Min Officer 99-02; rtd 04. *Wagon Works, Jericho Street, Thorverton, Exeter EX5 5PA* Tel (01392) 860397 E-mail harold.whitty@btinternet.com
WHITWAM, Miss Diana Morgan. b 28. MCSP54. d 93 p 94. OLM Stoke-next-Guildf 93-01; Perm to Offic from 02. *13 Abbots Hospital, High Street, Guildford GU1 3AJ* Tel (01483) 565977 E-mail dwhitwam@onetel.com
WHITWELL, Canon John Peter. b 36. Open Univ BA07. Qu Coll Birm 62. d 65 p 66. C Stepney St Dunstan and All SS *Lon* 65-68; C Chingford SS Pet and Paul *Chelmsf* 68-71; V Walthamstow St Sav 71-78; P-in-c Lt Ilford St Mich 78-88; R 88-98; RD Newham 91-97; Hon Can Chelmsf Cathl 96-98; rtd 98; Perm to Offic *Ox* from 99. *152 Bath Road, Banbury OX16 0TT* Tel (01295) 266243 E-mail jandawhitwell@aol.com
WHITWELL, Martin Corbett. b 32. Pemb Coll Ox BA55 MA59. Clifton Th Coll 55. d 57 p 58. C Wolverhampton St Jude *Lich* 57-60; C Aldridge 60-66; Chapl Sandbach Co Secondary Sch 68-74; C Chipping Campden *Glouc* 70-71; Perm to Offic *Chich* 74-75 and *Bris* 75-76; C Tranmere St Cath *Ches* 76-80; V Lt Leigh and Lower Whitley 80-90; rtd 90; Perm to Offic *Ches* from 90; *Heref* and *Lich* from 93. *11 Hollins Drive, Bayston Hill, Shrewsbury SY3 0NN* Tel (01743) 874241
WHITWELL, Timothy John. b 72. Westmr Coll Ox BTh97 Leeds Univ MA00. Coll of Resurr Mirfield 97. d 99 p 00. C Middlesbrough Ascension *York* 99-02; R Loftus and Carlin How w Skinningrove 02-08; Chapl Lich Cathl Sch from 08; Prec's V Lich Cathl from 08. *141 Walsall Road, Lichfield WS13 8AD* Tel (01543) 414248 Mobile 07715-137470 E-mail timothy.whitwell@talk21.com
WHITWORTH, Benjamin Charles Battams. b 49. CCC Ox BA71 MA85. Linc Th Coll 83. d 85 p 86. C Swanborough *Sarum* 85-88; C Sherborne w Castleton and Lillington 88-91; V Milborne Port w Goathill *B & W* from 91; Perm to Offic *B & W* from 00. *13 The Avenue, Taunton TA1 1EA* Tel (01823) 272442
WHITWORTH, Canon Duncan. b 47. K Coll Lon BD69 AKC69. St Aug Coll Cant 69. d 70 p 71. C Tonge Moor *Man* 70-73; C Upper Norwood St Jo *Cant* 73-78; Asst Chapl Madrid *Eur* 78-82; Chapl Br Embassy Ankara 82-83; V Douglas St Matt *S & M* from 84; RD Douglas from 91; Can St German's Cathl from 96. *St Matthew's Vicarage, Alexander Drive, Douglas, Isle of Man IM2 3QN* Tel (01624) 676310
WHITWORTH, Canon Patrick John. b 51. Ch Ch Ox BA72 MA76 St Jo Coll Dur MA78. d 76 p 77. C York St Mich-le-Belfrey 76-79; C Brompton H Trin w Onslow Square St Paul *Lon* 79-84; V Gipsy Hill Ch Ch *S'wark* 84-95; Hon Can Bauchi from 95; R Bath Weston All SS w N Stoke and Langridge *B & W* from 95; RD Bath from 03. *The Vicarage, Weston, Bath BA1 4BU* Tel (01225) 421159 E-mail pwhitworth@metronet.co.uk
WHITWORTH, Vincent Craig. b 80. Nottm Univ BA01. St Jo Coll Nottm MTh06. d 07 p 08. C Parr *Liv* from 07. *80 Waterdale Crescent, St Helens WA9 3PD* Tel (01744) 832793 Mobile 07759-920922 E-mail vincentwhitworth@hotmail.com
WHYBORN, Robert. b 42. NOC 87. d 90 p 91. NSM Milnrow *Man* 90-97; NSM Greenfield 97-03; NSM Saddleworth 03-05; rtd 05; Perm to Offic *Man* from 05. *4 Jackman Avenue, Heywood OL10 2NS* E-mail revrob8@aol.com
WHYBROW, Paul Andrew. b 59. St Paul's Cheltenham BEd80 Oak Hill Th Coll BA90. Wycliffe Hall Ox 95. d 97 p 98. C Magor *Mon* 97-00; V Poughill *Truro* from 00. *The Vicarage, Poughill, Bude EX23 9ER* Tel (01288) 355183 E-mail pa.whybrow@btinternet.com
WHYMAN, Oliver. b 27. ALCM52 LCP57. S'wark Ord Course 60. d 63 p 64. C Streatham Ch Ch *S'wark* 63-68; Lic to Offic 68-87; NSM Sutton New Town St Barn 87-92; rtd 92; Perm to Offic *S'wark* 92-00. *37 Jubilee Court, London Road, Thornton Heath CR7 6JL* Tel (020) 8684 5320
WHYSALL, Mrs Joan. b 42. Lady Mabel Coll CertEd64 Nottm Univ MA01. EMMTC 98. d 01 p 02. NSM Trowell, Awsworth and Cossall *S'well* 01-06; P-in-c Cinderhill from 06. *The Vicarage, 587 Nuthall Road, Nottingham NG8 6AD* Tel 0115-970 8151 Fax 08701-371114 E-mail joan.whysall@btinternet.com

WHYTE, Duncan Macmillan. b 25. St Jo Coll Dur BA49 St Cath Soc Ox BA51 MA57. Wycliffe Hall Ox 49. **d** 51 **p** 53. C Garston *Liv* 51-56; C St Leonards St Leon *Chich* 56-59; V Southsea St Simon *Portsm* 59-66; Gen Sec Lon City Miss 66-92; Hon C Blackheath St Jo *S'wark* 66-92; rtd 92; Perm to Offic *Sarum* from 92. *1 The Meadows, Salisbury SP1 2SS* Tel (01722) 330528

WHYTE, Mrs Elizabeth. b 48. SWMTC 04. **d** 07 **p** 08. NSM Ludgvan, Marazion, St Hilary and Perranuthnoe *Truro* from 07. *1 Cranfield, Alexandra Road, Penzance TR18 4LZ* Tel (01736) 362595 E-mail whytes8@aol.com

WHYTE, Henry Lewis. b 38. ALCD70 LTh74. **d** 70 **p** 71. C Crawley *Chich* 70-74; V Bermondsey St Jas w Ch Ch *S'wark* 74-82; V Kingston Hill St Paul 82-94; V Blackheath Park St Mich 94-02; rtd 02. Perm to Offic *S'wark* from 03. *6 Horn Park Lane, London SE12 8UU* Tel (020) 8318 9837

WHYTE, Canon Robert Euan. b 44. St Pet Coll Ox BA67. Cuddesdon Coll 67. **d** 69 **p** 70. C Blackheath Ascension *S'wark* 69-73; BCC 73-87; NSM Lewisham St Swithun *S'wark* 73-76; NSM Heston *Lon* 76-77; C Rusthall *Roch* 77-88; V 88-08; RD Tunbridge Wells 91-96; Hon Can Roch Cathl 00-08; rtd 08. *12B Maughan Terrace, Penarth CF64 1DT*
E-mail whyterobert@hotmail.com

WHYTE, William Hadden. b 75. Wadh Coll Ox BA97 MA03 MSt98 DPhil02. SAOMC 03. **d** 06 **p** 07. NSM Kidlington w Hampton Poyle *Ox* from 06. *St John's College, Oxford OX1 3JP* Tel (01865) 277338 Fax 277435
E-mail william.whyte@sjc.ox.ac.uk

WIBBERLEY, Anthony Norman. b 36. K Coll Lon BSc58 AKC58. Sarum & Wells Th Coll 76. **d** 79 **p** 80. Hon C Tavistock and Gulworthy *Ex* 79-86; R Hoby cum Rotherby w Brooksby, Ragdale & Thru'ton *Leic* 86-90; V Ingol *Blackb* 90-96; Perm to Offic *Ely* 97-05; rtd 00. *13 Missleton Court, Cherry Hinton Road, Cambridge CB1 8BL*

WIBROE, Andrew Peter. b 56. K Coll Lon BD83 AKC83 Thames Poly PGCE91. Ripon Coll Cuddesdon 83. **d** 86 **p** 87. C Purley St Mark *S'wark* 86-88; C Bowne Hill *Ox* 89-90; Hon C Milton next Gravesend Ch Ch *Roch* from 90. *32 Ayelands, New Ash Green, Longfield DA3 8JN* Tel (01474) 879014
E-mail peter.wibroe@diocese-rochester.org
or peterwibroe@aol.com

WICK, Canon Patricia Anne. b 54. Lon Bible Coll BA80. Oak Hill Th Coll 84. **dss** 86 **d** 87 **p** 94. Halliwell St Luke *Man* 86-87; Par Dn 87-91; Par Dn Drypool *York* 91-94; C 94-95; TV 95-97; Perm to Offic 98-99; CMS Sudan from 98; Can Maridi from 09. *PO Box 845, Arua, Uganda* E-mail t.wick@bushnet.net
or patricia@rcs-communication.com

WICKENS, Andrew Peter. b 63. St Jo Coll Dur BA85 Magd Coll Cam MEd97 PGCE95 ARCM84. Westcott Ho Cam 98. **d** 00 **p** 01. C Louth *Linc* 00-03; TV 03-07; C Boston from 07; PV Linc Cathl from 01. *5 Irby Street, Boston PE21 8SA* Tel (01205) 369266 E-mail andrew.wickens08@btinternet.com

WICKENS, Andrew St Lawrence John. b 63. Mert Coll Ox BA85 Birm Univ MPhil94 Dur Univ PGCE86. Qu Coll Birm 89. **d** 92 **p** 93. C Birchfield *Birm* 92-96; Perm to Offic 96-97 and 00-01; Zambia 97-00; P-in-c Mish Cathl Kitwe 99-00; Lect St Paul's United Th Coll Limuru Kenya 01-05; P-in-c Dudley St Jas *Worc* 05-09; TV Dudley TM from 09; Educn Chapl from 05. *St James's Vicarage, The Parade, Dudley DY1 3JA* Tel (01384) 214487 E-mail awickens@cofe-worcester.org.uk

WICKENS, John Philip. b 33. Open Univ BA76. K Coll Lon 57. **d** 61 **p** 62. C Hatcham Park All SS *S'wark* 61-64; USA 64-66; Tutor Richmond Fellowship Coll 66-95; Hon C Sutton Ch Ch *S'wark* 68-83; Hon C Benhilton 83-95; rtd 95; Perm to Offic *Worc* from 95. *West Villa, 196 West Malvern Road, Malvern WR14 4AZ* Tel (01684) 574043

WICKENS, Laurence Paul. b 52. Selw Coll Cam BA74 MA78 Leeds Univ PhD90 CEng80 MIET80 MIMechE81 EurIng90. EAMTC 02. **d** 06 **p** 07. NSM Cambridge St Barn *Ely* 06-08; NSM Meole Brace *Lich* from 08. *2 Perivale Close, Shrewsbury SY3 6DH* Tel (01743) 367707 Mobile 07811-551583
E-mail laurence.wickens@gmail.com

WICKENS, Mrs Moira. b 56. S Dios Minl Tr Scheme 91. **d** 94 **p** 08. NSM Ifield *Chich* 94-96; C Saltdean 96-03; C Ovingdean and Schs Liaison Officer 03-06; C Kingston Buci 06-08; P-in-c from 08; Dioc Voc Adv from 06. *The Rectory, Rectory Road, Shoreham-by-Sea BN43 6EB* Tel (01273) 592591

WICKHAM, Mrs Jennifer Ruth. b 68. Univ of W Ontario BA91. Cranmer Hall Dur BA98. **d** 98 **p** 99. C Ponteland *Newc* 98-00; Assoc P Ottawa St Geo Canada from 01. *57A Tauvette Street, Ottawa ON K1B 3A2, Canada* Tel (001) (613) 590 7921 *or* 235 1636 E-mail ajwickham@yahoo.com
or revjw.stgeorge@cyberus.ca

WICKHAM, Lionel Ralph. b 32. St Cath Coll Cam BA57 MA61 PhD LRAM. Westcott Ho Cam 57. **d** 59 **p** 60. C Boston *Linc* 59-61; Tutor Cuddesdon Coll 61-63; V Cross Stone *Wakef* 63-67; Lect Th Southn Univ 67-78; Sen Lect 78-81; V Honley 81-87; Lect Cam Univ 87-00; NSM W Wratting *Ely* 89-00; NSM Weston Colville 89-00; rtd 00; Perm to Offic *Wakef* from 99.

19 Barrowstead, Skelmanthorpe, Huddersfield HD8 9UW Tel (01484) 864185 E-mail lpatristic@aol.com

WICKHAM, Robert James. b 72. Grey Coll Dur BA94. Ridley Hall Cam 95. **d** 98 **p** 99. C Willesden St Mary *Lon* 98-01; C Somers Town 01-03; TV Old St Pancras 03-07; R St John-at-Hackney from 07. *The Rectory, 11 Clapton Square, London E5 8HP* Tel (020) 8985 5374 E-mail fr.rob@posp.co.uk
or rectorofhackney@aol.com

WICKINGS, Luke Iden. b 59. Sheff Poly BA81. Oak Hill Th Coll BA90. **d** 90 **p** 91. C Fulham St Mary N End *Lon* 90-94; C Bletchley *Ox* 94-00; V W Norwood St Luke *S'wark* 00-07. *12 Osborne Gardens, Thornton Heath CR7 8PA* Tel (020) 8653 7767

WICKREMASINGHE, Rosemary Ethel. b 32. Reading Univ ATD52 K Coll Lon BD85 AKC85. SAOMC 93. **d** 96 **p** 97. NSM Godrevy *Truro* 96-05; rtd 05; Perm to Offic *Truro* from 05. *10 Glebe Row, Phillack, Hayle TR27 5AJ* Tel (01736) 757850

WICKS, Christopher Blair. b 59. Oak Hill Th Coll BA88. **d** 88 **p** 89. C Edmonton All SS w St Mich *Lon* 88-92; C Southborough St Pet w Ch Ch and St Matt etc *Roch* 92-96; TV from 96. *72 Powder Mill Lane, Southborough, Tunbridge Wells TN4 9EJ* Tel (01892) 529098
E-mail chris.wicks@diocese-rochester.org

WICKS, Mrs Susan Joyce. b 51. SEN80 CSS89. EMMTC 97. **d** 00 **p** 01. C Birstall and Wanlip *Leic* 00-04; R Fenn Lanes Gp 04-07. *Address temp unknown* Tel 07808-917164 (mobile) E-mail sueterry.wicks@virgin.net

WICKS, Susan Lynn. b 66. Trin Coll Bris 96. **d** 98 **p** 99. C Whitburn *Dur* 98-03; TV S Carl from 03. *St Elisabeth's Vicarage, Arnside Road, Carlisle CA1 3QA* Tel (01228) 596427

WICKSTEAD, Canon Gavin John. b 46. St Chad's Coll Dur BA67. Linc Th Coll 82. **d** 84 **p** 85. C Louth *Linc* 84-87; P-in-c E Markham and Askham *S'well* 87-89; P-in-c Headon w Upton 87-89; P-in-c Grove 87-89; R E Markham w Askham, Headon w Upton and Grove 90-92; P-in-c Skegness and Winthorpe *Linc* 92-97; R 97-01; V Holbeach from 01; RD Elloe E 05-07; Can and Preb Linc Cathl from 05. *The Vicarage, 2 Church Walk, Holbeach, Spalding PE12 7DT* Tel (01406) 422185
E-mail wickstead@btopenworld.com

WIDDECOMBE, Canon Malcolm Murray. b 37. Tyndale Hall Bris 57. **d** 62 **p** 63. C Bris H Trin 62-65; C Barton Hill St Luke w Ch Ch 65-67; P-in-c Bris St Phil and St Jacob w Em 67-74; V 74-09; RD Bris City 79-85; Hon Can Bris Cathl 86-09; rtd 09. *10 Downend Road, Horfield, Bristol BS7 9PF*
E-mail merylwid@lineone.net

WIDDECOMBE, Roger James. b 70. Wycliffe Hall Ox 01. **d** 03 **p** 04. C Downend *Bris* 03-06; C Cheltenham St Mary, St Matt, St Paul and H Trin *Glouc* 06-07; TV Cheltenham H Trin and St Paul from 07. *85 Brunswick Street, Cheltenham GL50 4HA* Tel and fax (01242) 519520 E-mail roger@widde.com

WIDDESS, Jonathan Mark. b 73. Univ of Wales (Abth) BScEcon95. Wycliffe Hall Ox 07. **d** 09. C Gabalfa *Llan* from 09. *27 Pen-y-Bryn Road, Gabalfa, Cardiff CF14 3LG* Tel 07595-996534 (mobile) E-mail jwiddess@gmail.com

WIDDESS, Mrs Margaret Jennifer. b 48. Bedf Coll Lon BA70 Clare Hall Cam PGCE75 Lambeth MA03. EAMTC 94. **d** 97 **p** 98. NSM Cambridge St Botolph *Ely* from 97. *69 Gwydir Street, Cambridge CB1 2LG* Tel (01223) 313908
E-mail mjwiddess@btinternet.com

WIDDICOMBE, Peter John. b 52. Univ of Manitoba BA74 St Cath Coll Ox MPhil77 St Cross Coll Ox DPhil90. Wycliffe Coll Toronto MDiv81. **d** 81 **p** 82. Canada 81-84 and from 93; C Ox St Andr 84-86; Acting Chapl Trin Coll Ox 88; Linc Coll Ox 89; P-in-c Penn 90-93. *1204-36 James Street South, Hamilton ON L8P 4W4, Canada*

WIDDOWS, David Charles Roland. b 52. Hertf Coll Ox BA75 MA79. St Jo Coll Nottm BA77. **d** 79 **p** 80. C Blackley St Andr *Man* 79-83; P-in-c Rochdale Deeplish St Luke 83-84; V 84-92; TR Stoke Gifford *Bris* 92-06; Chapl Lee Abbey from 06. *Lee Abbey Fellowship, Lee Abbey, Lynton EX35 6JJ* Tel (01598) 754255 E-mail widdows@leeabbey.org.uk

WIDDOWS, Edward John. b 45. ACertCM00. Lon Coll of Div 66. **d** 70 **p** 71. C Formby St Pet *Liv* 70-72; C Uckfield, Isfield and Lt Horsted *Chich* 72-73; C Babbacombe *Ex* 73-76; V Sithney *Truro* 76-78; RD Kerrier 77-78; V Bude Haven 78-84; P-in-c Laneast w St Clether and Tresmere 84-85; P-in-c N Hill w Altarnon, Bolventor and Lewannick 84-85; P-in-c Boyton w N Tamerton 84-85; P-in-c N Petherwin 84-85; R Collingham w S Scarle and Besthorpe and Girton *S'well* 85-92; R Guernsey St Michel du Valle *Win* 92-99; R Compton and Otterbourne 99-02; rtd 02; Perm to Offic *Pet* from 02 and *Leic* from 08. *Glebe Cottage, 4 Spring Back Way, Uppingham, Oakham LE15 9TT* Tel (01572) 821980 E-mail ewiddows01@aol.com

WIDDOWS, Heather Susan. b 45. Open Univ BA76 Moray Ord Course 91. **d** 96 **p** 97. NSM Kishorn *Mor* from 96; NSM Poolewe from 96. *2 Fasaich, Strath, Gairloch IV21 2DB* Tel (01445) 712176 E-mail heather_widdows@yahoo.co.uk

WIDDOWSON, Charles Leonard. b 28. ALCD62. **d** 62 **p** 63. C Radcliffe-on-Trent *S'well* 62-66; R Newark Ch Ch 66-69;

Australia from 69; rtd 93. *5 Sharrock Avenue, Cheltenham Vic 3192, Australia* Tel (0061) (03) 9584 9004

WIDDOWSON, Robert William. b 47. Linc Th Coll 83. **d** 85 **p** 86. C Syston *Leic* 85-88; R Husbands Bosworth w Mowsley and Knaptoft etc 88-93; R Asfordby 93-98; P-in-c Ab Kettleby Gp 93-98; P-in-c Old Dalby and Nether Broughton 95-98; P-in-c Charlton Musgrove, Cucklington and Stoke Trister *B & W* 98-03; P-in-c Ashwick w Oakhill and Binegar from 03; Adv in Rural Affairs from 98. *The Rectory, Fosse Road, Oakhill, Bath BA3 5HU* Tel and fax (01749) 841688
E-mail ruralrobert@fsmail.net

WIECK, Malcolm Rayment. b 44. Solicitor 70. **d** 08 **p** 09. OLM Bratton, Edington and Imber, Erlestoke etc *Sarum* from 08. *Sandy Lane Cottage, 12 Westbury Road, Edington, Westbury BA13 4QD* Tel (01380) 830256 Mobile 07623-483986
E-mail malcolm.wieck@btinternet.com

WIFFEN, Richard Austin. b 58. St Pet Coll Ox BA80. Trin Coll Bris BA90. **d** 90 **p** 91. C Bowdon *Ches* 90-93; C Ellesmere Port 93-94; TV 94-02; Hon C 02-07. *Lime Tree Farm, Stanney Lane, Little Stanney, Chester CH2 4HT* Tel 0151-355 1654

WIFFEN, Ronald. b 38. Open Th Coll BA99. SEITE 99. **d** 01 **p** 02. NSM Canvey Is *Chelmsf* 01-04; NSM Bowers Gifford w N Benfleet 04-06; NSM SW Gower *S & B* 06-08; P-in-c Southport St Luke *Liv* 08-09; rtd 09. *40 Gladwyns, Basildon SS15 5JA* Tel (01268) 410682

WIFFIN, Susan Elizabeth. *See* MACDONALD, Susan Elizabeth

WIGFIELD, Thomas Henry Paul. b 26. Edin Th Coll 46. **d** 49 **p** 50. C Seaham w Seaham Harbour *Dur* 49-52; C Dur St Marg 52-54; V Fatfield 54-63; Asst Dir Chs' TV Cen 63-79; Perm to Offic *Lon* 63-91; Perm to Offic *St Alb* 66-91; Hd of Services Foundn for Chr Communication 79-84; Chs' Liaison Officer 84-91; rtd 91; Perm to Offic *Ox* from 91. *16 Fishers Field, Buckingham MK18 1SF* Tel (01280) 817893

WIGGEN, Richard Martin. b 42. Open Univ BA78 Hull Univ MA86. Qu Coll Birm 64. **d** 67 **p** 68. C Penistone w Midhope *Wakef* 67-70; C Leeds St Pet *Ripon* 70-73; Asst Youth Chapl *Glouc* 73-76; Youth Officer *Liv* 76-80; V Kirkstall *Ripon* 80-90; V Meanwood 90-07; rtd 07. *19 Shadwell Lane, Leeds LS17 6DP* Tel 0113-266 5421 E-mail wiggen@btopenworld.com

WIGGINS, Gillian Holt. b 33. Birm Univ MB, ChB56. **d** 03 **p** 04. NSM Ascot Heath *Ox* 03-08; Perm to Offic from 09. *Keren, 2 Kiln Lane, Winkfield, Windsor SL4 2DU* Tel (01344) 884008
E-mail gilliwig@aol.com

WIGGINS, Karl Patrick. b 38. MRICS64 FRICS87. Trin Coll Bris BD72. **d** 72 **p** 73. C Hildenborough *Roch* 72-76; Hon C Reading St Barn *Ox* 76-78; Hon C Chieveley w Winterbourne and Oare 78-80; Hon C Earley St Nic 80-83; Hon C Reading St Jo 83-88; Hon C Beech Hill, Grazeley and Spencers Wood 88-98; rtd 98; Perm to Offic *Ox* 99. *Willow Cottage, 37 New Road, Bradford-on-Avon BA15 1AP* Tel (01225) 867007
E-mail kk-wiggins@msn.com

WIGGINTON, Canon Peter Walpole. b 26. Edin Th Coll 40. **d** 43 **p** 44. C Derby St Jas 43-46; C Brimington 46; C Gedling *S'well* 46-49; PV S'well Minster 49-52; V Rolleston w Morton 52-56; R W Keal *Linc* 56-83; R E Keal 57-83; R and W Keal 83-88; RD Bolingbroke 66-88; Can and Preb Linc Cathl 77-88; R Bolingbroke 83-88; R Toynton All Saints w Toynton St Peter 83-88; rtd 88; Chapl Trin Hosp Retford 88-05; Perm to Offic *S'well* from 91. *Trinity Cottage, River Lane, Retford DN22 7DZ* Tel (01777) 860352

WIGGLESWORTH, Mark. b 60. Clare Coll Cam BA82. St Jo Coll Nottm 89. **d** 92 **p** 93. C Brinsworth w Catcliffe *Sheff* 92-93; C Brinsworth w Catcliffe and Treeton 93-95; C Goole 95-96; V Askern from 96; AD Adwick from 06. *The Vicarage, Church Street, Askern, Doncaster DN6 0PH* Tel (01302) 700404
E-mail markandbethwig@yahoo.co.uk

WIGGS, Robert James. b 50. Pemb Coll Cam BA72 MA CertEd. Qu Coll Birm 78. **d** 80 **p** 81. C Stratford St Jo and Ch Ch w Forest Gate St Jas *Chelmsf* 80-83; C E Ham w Upton Park St Alb 83-86; TV 86-91; TR Grays Thurrock 91-99; Perm to Offic from 99. *113 Moulsham Street, Chelmsford CM2 0JN* Tel (01245) 359138 E-mail robwiggs@live.com

WIGHT, Dennis Marley. b 53. Southn Univ BTh87. Sarum & Wells Th Coll 82. **d** 85 **p** 86. C Gillingham *Sarum* 85-87; Appeals Org CECS from 87; Perm to Offic *Birm* 89-90; V Coseley Ch Ch *Lich* 90-93; V Coseley Ch Ch *Worc* 93-94; R Stoke Prior, Wychbold and Upton Warren 94-02; RD Droitwich 96-99; V Dale and St Brides w Marloes *St D* from 02; AD Roose from 05; Dioc Warden Ords from 09. *The Vicarage, Dale, Haverfordwest SA62 3RN* Tel (01646) 636255
E-mail denniswight@btinternet.com

WIGHT (née JONES), Mrs Sian Hilary. b 54. CertEd75 Birm Univ BEd76 Southn Univ BTh87. Sarum & Wells Th Coll 82. **dss** 85 **d** 87 **p** 94. Ex St Sidwell and St Matt 85-88; Par Dn 87-88; Perm to Offic *Lich* 89-90 and 93-96; Hon Par Dn Coseley Ch Ch 90-93; Hon Par Dn Coseley Ch Ch *Worc* 93-94; NSM Stoke Prior, Wychbold and Upton Warren 94-02; NSM Dale and St Brides w Marloes *St D* 02-05; P-in-c Herbrandston and Hasguard w St Ishmael's from 05; P-in-c Walwyn's Castle w

Robeston W from 08. *The Vicarage, Dale, Haverfordwest SA62 3RN* Tel (01646) 636255

WIGHTMAN, David William Lyle. b 44. SNWTP. **d** 08 **p** 09. NSM Macclesfield Team *Ches* from 08. *The Old Vicarage, 12 Ryles Park Road, Macclesfield SK11 8AH* Tel (01625) 266283 *or* 428443 E-mail david.wightman1@ntlworld.com

WIGHTMAN, Canon David. b 39. Birm Univ BA61. Wells Th Coll 61. **d** 63 **p** 64. C Rotherham *Sheff* 63-67; C Castle Church *Lich* 67-70; V Buttershaw St Aid *Bradf* 70-76; V Cullingworth 76-83; R Peterhead *Ab* 83-91; R Strichen, Old Deer and Longside 90-91; Provost St Andr Cathl 91-02; R Aberdeen St Andr 91-02; P-in-c Aberdeen St Ninian 91-02; Hon Can Ch Ch Cathl Connecticut from 91; rtd 02; Perm to Offic *York* from 04. *66 Wold Road, Pocklington, York YO42 2QG* Tel (01759) 301369
E-mail davidwightman@ntlworld.com

WIGLEY, Brian Arthur. b 31. Qu Coll Birm. **d** 82 **p** 83. C Houghton le Spring *Dur* 82-85; C Louth *Linc* 85-86; TV 86-89; Chapl City Hosp NHS Trust Birm 89-95; rtd 95. *3 Willows Close, Frogmore, Kingsbridge TQ7 2NY* Tel (01548) 531374

WIGLEY, Canon Harry Maxwell (Max). b 38. Oak Hill Th Coll 61. **d** 64 **p** 65. C Upton (Overchurch) *Ches* 64-67; C Gateacre *Liv* 67-69; C Chadderton Ch Ch *Man* 67; V Gt Horton *Bradf* 69-88; Hon Can Bradf Cathl 85-03; V Pudsey St Lawr and St Paul 88-96; V Yeadon St Jo 96-03; rtd 03; Hon Dioc Ev *Bradf* from 04. *20 Collier Lane, Baildon, Shipley BD17 5LN* Tel (01274) 581988 E-mail max.wigley@bradford.anglican.org
or maxwigley@aol.com

WIGLEY, Ms Jennifer. b 53. Bris Univ BA74 Birm Univ MA75 Ox Univ CertEd76. Qu Coll Birm 86. **d** 87 **p** 97. C Llangollen w Trevor and Llantysilio *St As* 87-89; C Swansea St Jas *S & B* 89-94; NSM Aberystwyth *St D* 95-98; Tutor St Mich Coll Llan 98-00; C Sketty *S & B* 98-00; Chapl Univ of Wales (Swansea) 00-02; Dep Dir S Wales Ord Course from 02; TV Cen Cardiff *Llan* 03-06; R Radyr from 06. *The Rectory, 52 Heol Isaf, Radyr, Cardiff CF15 8DY* Tel (029) 2084 2417
E-mail jennifer.wigley@ntlworld.com

WIGMORE, John Anthony Kingsland. b 62. Oak Hill Th Coll 05. **d** 07 **p** 08. C Braintree *Chelmsf* from 07. *46 Lodge Road, Braintree CM7 1JA* Tel (01376) 552925
E-mail jakwigmore@ntlworld.com

WIGNALL, Daniel Robert Phillip. b 65. Ox Poly BEd88. St Jo Coll Nottm MA98. **d** 98 **p** 99. C Fletchamstead *Cov* 98-01; C Abingdon *Ox* 01-07; V Shottermill *Guildf* from 07. *The Vicarage, Vicarage Lane, Haslemere GU27 1LQ* Tel (01428) 645878
E-mail vicar@shottermillparish.org.uk

WIGNALL, Canon Paul Graham. b 49. Lanc Univ BA72 Qu Coll Cam BA74 MA78. Westcott Ho Cam 72. **d** 74 **p** 75. C Chesterton Gd Shep *Ely* 74-76; Min Can Dur Cathl 76-79; Tutor Ripon Coll Cuddesdon 80-84; P-in-c Aston Rowant w Crowell *Ox* 81-83; C Shepherd's Bush St Steph w St Thos *Lon* 84-85; P-in-c St Just-in-Roseland and St Mawes *Truro* 99-01; C St Agnes and Mithian w Mount Hawke 01-06; Dir Tr and Development 01-05; Dir Min and Miss Resources 05-06; Hon Can Truro Cathl 05-06; rtd 06; Hon C Aston Cantlow and Wilmcote w Billesley *Cov* from 08; IME Adv from 08. *Wilmcote Vicarage, Church Road, Wilmcote, Stratford-upon-Avon CV37 9XD* E-mail paul@paulwignall.wanadoo.co.uk

WIGRAM, Andrew Oswald. b 39. Lon Univ BD64. Bps' Coll Cheshunt 61. **d** 64 **p** 65. C Marton-in-Cleveland *York* 64-69; Kenya 69-82; Warden Trin Coll Nairobi 77-82; V Westcliff St Mich *Chelmsf* 82-95; RD Southend-on-Sea 89-94; R Cropwell Bishop w Colston Bassett, Granby etc *S'well* 95-05; rtd 05. *38 Pierremont Crescent, Darlington DL3 9PB* Tel (01325) 371473 E-mail andrew.wigram@ntlworld.com

WIGRAM, John Michael. b 67. Ex Univ BSc88. St Jo Coll Nottm MTh04. **d** 05 **p** 06. C Hazlemere *Ox* 05-08; R Hambleden Valley from 08. *The Rectory, Hambledon, Henley-on-Thames RG9 6RP* Tel (01491) 571231 Mobile 07986-732452
E-mail wigram@ntlworld.com

WIGRAM (née CHAPMAN), Mrs Rachel Grace. b 67. Ex Univ BA88. St Jo Coll Nottm 03. **d** 05 **p** 06. C Hazlemere *Ox* 05-08; Perm to Offic from 08. *The Rectory, Hambledon, Henley-on-Thames RG9 6RP* Tel (01494) 571231 Mobile 07986-732452
E-mail wigram@ntlworld.com

WIGRAM, Miss Ruth Margaret. b 41. CertEd63. Cranmer Hall Dur 83. **dss** 84 **d** 87 **p** 94. Shipley St Paul and Frizinghall *Bradf* 84-90; Par Dn 87-90; Asst Dioc Dir of Ords 90-96; C Skipton H Trin 90-96; V Easby w Skeeby and Brompton on Swale etc *Ripon* 96-06; rtd 07; Perm to Offic *York* from 07. *Maythorn, 30 Ainderby Road, Northallerton DL7 8HD* Tel (01609) 761852
E-mail ruthwigram@hotmail.co.uk

WIKELEY, Canon John Roger Ian. b 41. AKC64. **d** 65 **p** 66. C Southport H Trin *Liv* 65-69; C Padgate Ch Ch 69-71; TV Padgate 71-73; R 73-74; TR 74-85; TR W Derby St Mary 85-98; V 98-06; P-in-c W Derby St Jas 04-06; AD W Derby 89-06; Hon Can Liv Cathl 94-06; rtd 06. *72 Carisbrooke Drive, Southport PR9 7JD* Tel (01704) 225412 E-mail jviw@blueyonder.co.uk

WIKNER, Richard Hugh. b 46. MSI. St Alb Minl Tr Scheme 79. **d** 94 **p** 95. NSM Lt Heath *St Alb* from 94. *Koinonia, 5 The Avenue, Potters Bar EN6 1EG* Tel (01707) 650437
E-mail hughwikner@lineone.net

✠**WILBOURNE, The Rt Revd David Jeffrey.** b 55. Jes Coll Cam BA78 MA82. Westcott Ho Cam 79. **d** 81 **p** 82 **c** 09. C Stainton-in-Cleveland *York* 81-85; Chapl Asst Hemlington Hosp 81-85; R Monk Fryston and S Milford *York* 85-91; Abp's Dom Chapl 91-97; Dir of Ords 91-97; V Helmsley 97-09; P-in-c Upper Ryedale 09; Can and Preb York Minster 08-09; Asst Bp Llan from 09. *Llys Esgob, The Cathedral Green, Cardiff CF5 2YE* Tel (029) 2056 2400 Fax 2057 7129
E-mail asstbishop@churchinwales.org.uk

WILBOURNE, Geoffrey Owen. b 29. Lich Th Coll 60. **d** 62 **p** 63. C Marfleet *York* 62-65; V Ellerton Priory w Aughton and E Cottingwith 65-70; TV Scalby w Ravenscar and Staintondale 70-73; V Kingston upon Hull St Nic 73-76; V Keyingham 76-85; V Hemingbrough 85-91; rtd 91; Perm to Offic *Derby* 91-00 and *York* from 00. *40 Knipe Point Drive, Scarborough YO11 3JT* Tel (01723) 355255

WILBRAHAM, David. b 59. Oak Hill Th Coll BA88. **d** 88 **p** 89. C Ince Ch Ch *Liv* 88-91; Min St Helens St Helen 91-93; Perm to Offic *Guildf* 96-99; NSM Hindhead 99-00; V 00-03; V Churt and Hindhead 03-07; Chapl Thames Valley Police Force *Ox* from 07. *292 Thorney Leys, Witney OX28 5PB* Tel (01993) 706656 Mobile 07779-262302 E-mail davidwilbraham@lineone.net

WILBY, Mrs Janet (Sister Davina). b 38. Open Univ BA82. Wycliffe Hall Ox 83. **dss** 85 **d** 87 **p** 94. Maidenhead St Andr and St Mary *Ox* 85-87; C 87; TD Hermitage and Hampstead Norreys, Cold Ash etc 87-91; Lic to Offic 92-95; All SS Convent Ox 91-95; NSM Iffley *Ox* 94-95; C Denham 95-98; rtd 98; P-in-c Woolstone w Gotherington and Oxenton etc *Glouc* 98-06. *2 Somerset House, Knapp Road, Cheltenham GL50 3QQ* Tel (01242) 584096

WILBY, Timothy David. b 59. Univ Coll Dur BA80 MA87. Ripon Coll Cuddesdon 81. **d** 83 **p** 84. C Standish *Blackb* 83-86; CF 86-89; V Chorley All SS *Blackb* 89-95; V Penwortham St Leon 95-00; TR Fellside Team 00-07; P-in-c Chorley St Geo from 07. *St George's Vicarage, Letchworth Place, Chorley PR7 2HJ* Tel (01772) 263064
E-mail stgeorgeschorley@aol.com

WILBY, Canon Wendy Ann. b 49. St Hugh's Coll Ox BA71 MA93 Leeds Univ MA01 ARCM69 LRAM72. NEOC. **d** 90 **p** 94. Par Dn Barwick in Elmet *Ripon* 90-93; V High Harrogate St Pet 93-94; P-in-c Birstwith 94-01; AD Harrogate 00-01; Chapl St Aid Sch Harrogate 94-01; V Halifax *Wakef* 01-07; RD Halifax 06-07; Can Res Bris Cathl from 07. *55 Salisbury Road, Redland, Bristol BS6 7AS* Tel 0117-904 6903 *or* 926 4879
E-mail wwilby@blueyonder.co.uk

WILCOCK, Michael Jarvis. b 32. Dur Univ BA54. Tyndale Hall Bris 60. **d** 62 **p** 63. C Southport Ch Ch *Liv* 62-65; C St Marylebone All So w SS Pet and Jo *Lon* 65-69; V Maidstone St Faith *Cant* 69-77; Dir Past Studies Trin Coll Bris 77-82; V St Nic 82-98; rtd 98; Perm to Offic *Chich* from 98. *1 Tudor Court, 51 Carlisle Road, Eastbourne BN21 4JR* Tel (01323) 417170

WILCOX, Paul Trevor. b 59. Bris Univ BA Leeds Univ MA93. Trin Coll Bris 83. **d** 87 **p** 88. C Kirkheaton *Wakef* 87-90; Chapl Huddersfield Poly 90-92; Chapl Huddersfield Univ 92-93; Dir Student Services from 93; NSM Huddersfield H Trin from 92; Chapl W Yorkshire Police from 02. *25 Mendip Avenue, Huddersfield HD3 3QG* Tel (01484) 472675 Fax 473120
E-mail p.t.wilcock@hud.ac.uk

WILCOCK, Terence Granville. b 50. Open Univ BA82. EAMTC. **d** 02 **p** 03. NSM Oundle w Ashton and Benefield w Glapthorn *Pet* 02-04; NSM Crosscrake *Carl* from 04; P-in-c from 06; NSM Old Hutton and New Hutton from 06. *The Vicarage, Shyreakes Lane, Crosscrake, Kendal LA8 0AB* Tel (01539) 560333
E-mail terryatash@aol.com

WILCOCKSON, Stephen Anthony. b 51. Nottm Univ BA73 Ox Univ BA75 MA81. Wycliffe Hall Ox 73. **d** 76 **p** 77. C Pudsey St Lawr *Bradf* 76-78; C Wandsworth All SS *S'wark* 78-81; V Rock Ferry *Ches* 81-86; V Lache cum Saltney 86-95; V Howell Hill w Burgh Heath *Guildf* 95-09; RD Epsom 00-07; Par Miss Development Officer *Ches* from 09. *11 Lytham Drive, Winsford CW7 2GH* Tel (01606) 860322
E-mail stevewilcockson@yahoo.com

WILCOX, Anthony Gordon. b 41. ALCD67. **d** 67 **p** 68. C Cheltenham Ch Ch *Glouc* 67-72; C Beccles St Mich *St E* 72-74; TV 74-81; V Ipswich All SS 81-06; rtd 06; Perm to Offic *St E* from 08. *58 Sproughton Court Mews, Sproughton, Ipswich IP8 3AJ* Tel (01473) 461561

WILCOX, Brian Howard. b 46. Westcott Ho Cam 71. **d** 73 **p** 74. C Kettering SS Pet and Paul 73-78; V Eye 78-82; R Clipston w Naseby and Haselbech w Kelmarsh 82-90; V Hornsea w Atwick *York* 90-97; RD N Holderness 95-97; R Uckfield *Chich* from 97; R Isfield from 97; R Lt Horsted from 97. *The Rectory, Belmont Road, Uckfield TN22 1BP* Tel (01825) 762761
E-mail howab@aol.com

WILCOX, Canon Colin John. b 43. St Mich Coll Llan 84. **d** 86 **p** 87. C Newport St Andr *Mon* 86-88; C Llanmartin 88-90; TV 90-92; V Griffithstown 92-08; Hon Can St Woolos Cathl 07-08; rtd 08; Perm to Offic *Mon* from 08 and *Llan* from 09. *2 Davies Place, Cardiff CF5 3AQ, or The Bungalow, Dingestow, Monmouth NP25 4DZ* Tel (029) 2025 4294 *or* (01600) 740680

✠**WILCOX, The Rt Revd David Peter.** b 30. St Jo Coll Ox BA52 MA56. Linc Th Coll 52. **d** 54 **p** 55 **c** 86. C St Helier *S'wark* 54-56; C Ox St Mary V 56-59; Tutor Linc Th Coll 59-60; Chapl 60-61; Sub-Warden 61-63; India 64-70; R Gt w Lt Gransden *Ely* 70-72; Can Res Derby Cathl 72-77; Warden EMMTC 73-77; Prin Ripon Coll Cuddesdon 77-85; V Cuddesdon *Ox* 77-85; Suff Bp Dorking *Guildf* 86-95; rtd 95; Hon Asst Bp Chich from 95. *4 The Court, Hoo Gardens, Willingdon, Eastbourne BN20 9AX* Tel (01323) 506108

WILCOX, David Thomas Richard. b 42. Down Coll Cam BA63 Regent's Park Coll Ox BA66. **d** 95 **p** 96. C Bris St Mary Redcliffe w Temple etc 95-97; TV Yate New Town 97-02; Hon C 02-06; rtd 02; Perm to Offic *B & W* from 06. *26 Lethbridge Road, Wells BA5 2FN* Tel (01749) 673689

WILCOX, Graham James. b 43. Qu Coll Ox BA64 MA75 Lon Univ BD97 MTh02. Ridley Hall Cam 64. **d** 66 **p** 67. C Edgbaston St Aug *Birm* 66-69; C Sheldon 69-72; Asst Chapl Wrekin Coll Telford 72-74; C Asterby w Goulceby *Linc* 74-77; R 77-81; R Benniworth w Market Stainton and Ranby 77-81; R Donington on Bain 77-81; R Stenigot 77-81; R Gayton le Wold w Biscathorpe 77-81; V Scamblesby w Cawkwell 77-81; R Asterby Gp 81-88; V Sutton le Marsh 88-90; R Sutton, Huttoft and Anderby 90-98; R Fyfield, Moreton w Bobbingworth etc *Chelmsf* 98-07; rtd 07; Perm to Offic *Cov* from 07. *7 Swallow Close, Stratford-upon-Avon CV37 6TT* Tel (01789) 551759
E-mail g.wilcox4@ntlworld.com

WILCOX, Haydon Howard. b 56. Sarum & Wells Th Coll. **d** 82 **p** 83. C Fishponds St Jo *Bris* 82-85; TV Hucknall Torkard *S'well* 85-91; R Bilsthorpe 91-99; R Eakring 91-99; P-in-c Maplebeck 91-99; P-in-c Winkburn 91-99; P-in-c Aldershot St Mich *Guildf* 99-03; V 03; Perm to Offic from 03; Chapl CSP from 07. *46 Barn Meadow Close, Church Crookham, Aldershot GU52 0YB* Tel and fax (01252) 621639 E-mail haydonwilcox@mac.com

WILCOX, Heather Yvonne. b 72. ERMC 05. **d** 08 **p** 09. C Pakefield *Nor* from 08. *9 Ryedale, Carlton Colville, Lowestoft NR33 8TB* Tel (01502) 512864 Mobile 07932-416233
E-mail hwackywilcox@uwclub.net

WILCOX, Canon Hugh Edwin. b 37. St Edm Hall Ox BA62 MA66. St Steph Ho Ox 62. **d** 64 **p** 65. C Colchester St Jas, All SS, St Nic and St Runwald *Chelmsf* 64-66; Hon C Clifton St Paul *Bris* 66-68; SCM 66-68; Sec Internat Dept BCC 68-76; Asst Gen Sec 74-76; V Ware St Mary *St Alb* 76-03; Hon Can St Alb 96-03; rtd 03; Perm to Offic *St Alb* from 03. *The Briars, 1 Briary Lane, Royston SG8 9BX* Tel (01763) 244212
E-mail hugh.wilcox@btinternet.com

WILCOX, Canon Jeffry Reed. b 40. MBE05. K Coll Lon AKC65 BA78 Westmr Coll Ox MTh97. **d** 66 **p** 67. C Ryhope *Dur* 66-69; C Cockerton 69-71; P-in-c Pallion 71-82; R Streatham St Leon *S'wark* 82-06; RD Streatham 92-00; Hon Can S'wark Cathl 05-06; rtd 06. *4 Lower Broad Street, Ludlow SY8 1PQ* Tel (01584) 877199 E-mail jeffrywilcox@yahoo.co.uk

WILCOX, John Bower. b 28. AKC55. **d** 58 **p** 59. C Orford St Marg *Liv* 58-60; C W Derby St Mary 60-63; Ind Chapl *Linc* 63-74; R Aisthorpe w W Thorpe and Scampton 63-74; R Brattleby 64-74; Ind Chapl *York* 74-89; P-in-c Middlesbrough St Cuth 89-93; Urban Development Officer 89-93; rtd 93; Perm to Offic *York* from 93. *5 Duncan Avenue, Redcar TS10 5BX* Tel (01642) 489683

WILCOX, Canon Peter Jonathan. b 61. St Jo Coll Dur BA84 MA91 St Jo Coll Ox DPhil93. Ridley Hall Cam BA86. **d** 87 **p** 88. C Preston on Tees *Dur* 87-90; NSM Ox St Giles and SS Phil and Jas w St Marg 90-93; TV Gateshead *Dur* 93-98; Dir Urban Miss Cen Cranmer Hall 93-98; P-in-c Walsall St Paul *Lich* 98-06; Hon C Walsall and Walsall Pleck and Bescot 05-06; Can Res Lich Cathl from 06. *13 The Close, Lichfield WS13 7LD* Tel (01543) 306241 *or* 306240 E-mail pete.wilcox@lichfield-cathedral.org

WILCOX, Stephen Charles. b 75. Qu Coll Ox BA97 ACA00. Oak Hill Th Coll 04. **d** 07 **p** 08. C Kirk Ella and Willerby *York* from 07. *24 Redland Drive, Kirk Ella, Hull HU10 7UZ* Tel (01482) 653251 Mobile 07905-122239 E-mail scfwilcox@yahoo.co.uk

WILD, Alan James. b 46. **d** 97 **p** 98. OLM Walworth St Pet *S'wark* from 97. *67 Liverpool Grove, London SE17 2HP* Tel (020) 7708 1216

WILD, Hilda Jean. b 48. Linc Th Coll 95. **d** 95 **p** 96. C Newark *S'well* 95-99; V Earlsdon *Cov* from 99. *St Barbara's Vicarage, 24 Rochester Road, Coventry CV5 6AG* Tel (024) 7667 4057

WILD, Roger Bedingham Barratt. b 40. Hull Univ MA93. ALCD64. **d** 65 **p** 65. C Shipley St Pet *Bradf* 65-68; C Pudsey St Lawr 68-71; P-in-c Rawthorpe *Wakef* 71-73; V 73-78; V Ripon H Trin 78-93; RD Ripon 86-93; OCF 80-91; R Barwick in Elmet *Ripon* 93-01; Asst Chapl Trin Th Coll Singapore 02-05; rtd 05;

Perm to Offic *York* from 06. *Saddlers Cottage, 15 Chapel Street, Thirsk YO7 1LU* Tel (01845) 524985
E-mail rbbwild@hotmail.com

WILDE, David Wilson. b 37. Lon Coll of Div ALCD61 BD62. **d** 62 **p** 63. C Kirkheaton *Wakef* 62-66; C Attenborough w Chilwell *S'well* 66-72; P-in-c Bestwood Park 72-83; R Kimberley 83-07; rtd 07. *2 Main Street, Kimberley, Nottingham NG16 2LL* Tel 0115-938 5315 E-mail christwl@aol.co.uk

WILDEY, Canon Ian Edward. b 51. St Chad's Coll Dur BA72. Coll of Resurr Mirfield 72. **d** 74 **p** 75. C Westgate Common *Wakef* 74-77; C Barnsley St Mary 77-81; V Ravensthorpe 81-95; R Barnsley St Mary 95-07; Dir Educn 96-98 and from 07; Hon Can Wakef Cathl from 00. *29 Intake Lane, Barnsley S75 2HX* Tel (01226) 321109 E-mail ian@ewildey.freeserve.co.uk

WILDING, Canon Anita Pamela. b 38. MBE01. Blackpool and Fylde Coll of Further Tech TCert61. CMS Tr Coll Chislehurst 65. **dss** 89 **d** 92 **p** 93. CMS Kenya 87-04; Chapl Kabare Girls' High Sch 92-04; Chapl St Andr Primary Boarding Sch Kabare 92-04; rtd 04; Perm to Offic *Blackb* from 04. *5 The Fairways, 35 The Esplanade, Knott End-on-Sea, Poulton-le-Fylde FY6 0AD* Tel (01253) 810642 E-mail wildingp@tiscali.co.uk

WILDING, David. b 43. K Coll Lon BD67 AKC67. **d** 68 **p** 69. C Thornhill *Wakef* 68-70; C Halifax St Jo Bapt 70-72; V Scholes 72-79; V Lightcliffe 79-97; rtd 97; Perm to Offic *Wakef* from 97. *10 Stratton Park, Rastrick, Brighouse HD6 3SN* Tel (01484) 387651

WILDING, Michael Paul. b 57. Chich Th Coll 82. **d** 85 **p** 86. C Treboeth *S & B* 85-87; C Llangiwg 87-88; V Defynnog w Rhydybriw and Llandeilo'r-fan 88-00; V Defynnog, Llandilo'r Fan, Llanulid, Llywel etc from 00. *The Vicarage, Sennybank, Sennybridge, Brecon LD3 8PP* Tel (01874) 638927

WILDING, Pamela. See WILDING, Canon Anita Pamela

WILDS, The Ven Anthony Ronald. b 43. Dur Univ BA64. Bps' Coll Cheshunt 64. **d** 66 **p** 67. C Newport Pagnell *Ox* 66-72; Zambia 72-75; V Chandler's Ford *Win* 75-85; V Andover w Foxcott 85-97; RD Andover 89-94; Hon Can Win Cathl 91-97; TR Solihull *Birm* 97-01; Hon Can Birm Cathl 00-01; Adn Plymouth *Ex* from 01. *St Mark's Vicarage, 46A Cambridge Road, Plymouth PL2 1PU* Tel (01752) 793397 Fax 774618
E-mail archdeacon.of.plymouth@exeter.anglican.org

WILES, Mrs Cathryn. b 51. BEd. **d** 04 **p** 05. NSM Wandsworth Common St Mary *S'wark* from 04. *10 Waldeck Grove, London SE27 0BE* Tel (020) 8761 4017 *or* 8682 6627
E-mail cathy.mail@virgin.net

WILES, Roger Kenneth. b 58. Witwatersrand Univ BA80. St Paul's Coll Grahamstown 81. **d** 83 **p** 84. C Johannesburg St Gabr S Africa 83-84; C Belgravia St Jo 84-85; Chapl Jeppe Boys' High Sch 85-86; Chapl Witwatersrand Univ 86-93; R Edenvale Em 94-99; P-in-c Edin Clermiston Em 99-05; V Poulton Lancelyn H Trin *Ches* from 05. *6 Chorley Way, Wirral CH63 9LS* Tel 0151-334 6780

WILESMITH, Miss Mary Adelaide. b 50. WEMTC 03. **d** 05 **p** 06. NSM Badgeworth, Shurdington and Witcombe w Bentham *Glouc* from 05. *32 Leyson Road, The Reddings, Cheltenham GL51 6RX* Tel (01452) 712635 Mobile 07947-254509

WILFORD (formerly GIBSON), Laura Mary. b 50. NOC 85. **d** 88 **p** 94. Par Dn Foley Park *Worc* 88-90; Par Dn Kidderminster St Jo and H Innocents 90-94; TV 94-96; P-in-c Mamble w Bayton, Rock w Heightington etc 96-99; TV Cartmel Peninsula *Carl* 99-01; Jt Dir of Ords 00-01; P-in-c Worminghall w Ickford, Oakley and Shabbington *Ox* 01-06; rtd 06. *5 Cookson Way, Brough with St Giles, Catterick Garrison DL9 4XG* Tel (01748) 830017 E-mail lauramwilford@hotmail.co.uk

WILKERSON, Ms Valerie Anne. b 40. Leeds Univ BA62 RGN77 RM78. St Jo Coll Nottm 03. **d** 04 **p** 05. NSM Alrewas *Lich* from 04; NSM Wychnor from 04. *22 Chaseview Road, Alrewas, Burton-on-Trent DE13 7EL* Tel (01283) 790612
E-mail valwilkerson@aol.com

WILKES, Jonathan Peter. b 66. Leic Poly BA88 K Coll Lon MA00. Ripon Coll Cuddesdon BTh96. **d** 96 **p** 97. C Hackney *Lon* 96-00; P-in-c Paddington St Pet 00-06; P-in-c Paddington St Mary Magd 04-06; P-in-c Kingston All SS w St Jo *S'wark* 06-07; TR from 07. *All Saints' Vicarage, 15 Woodbines Avenue, Kingston upon Thames KT1 2AZ* Tel (020) 3132 8717

WILKES, The Very Revd Robert Anthony. b 48. Trin Coll Ox BA70 MA73. Wycliffe Hall Ox 71. **d** 74 **p** 75. C Netherton *Liv* 74-77; V 77-81; Bp's Dom Chapl 81-85; CMS Pakistan 85-86; Regional Sec Middle E and Pakistan 87-98; P-in-c Mossley Hill St Matt and St Jas *Liv* 98-05; TR Mossley Hill 05-06; Hon Can Liv Cathl 03-06; Dean Birm from 06. *120 Oakfield Road, Selly Park, Birmingham B29 7ED* Tel 0121-262 1840 Fax 262 1860 E-mail dean@birminghamcathedral.com
or revwilkes@btinternet.com

WILKIE, Michael John David. b 65. Oak Hill Th Coll BA90 Ex Univ PGCE94. SWMTC 98. **d** 00 **p** 01. NSM Combe Martin, Berrynarbor, Lynton, Brendon etc *Ex* 00-05. *Address temp unknown*

WILKIN, Kenneth. b 54. Open Univ BA97. S'wark Ord Course 86 Wilson Carlile Coll. **d** 88 **p** 89. C Wolverhampton *Lich* 88-92; V W Bromwich St Andr w Ch Ch 92-98; Dep Chapl HM Pris Pentonville 98-00; Chapl HM Pris Holloway from 00. *HM Prison Holloway, 1 Parkhurst Road, London N7 0NU* Tel (020) 7979 4561 E-mail kenneth.wilkin@hmps.gsi.gov.uk
or kwilkin@aol.com

WILKIN, Paul John. b 56. Linc Th Coll 88. **d** 90 **p** 91. C Leavesden *St Alb* 90-93; C Jersey St Brelade *Win* 93-97; V Squirrels Heath *Chelmsf* 97-07; R Stansted Mountfitchet w Birchanger and Farnham from 07. *The Rectory, 5 St John's Road, Stansted CM24 8JP* Tel (01279) 812203
E-mail paulwilkin@iname.com

WILKIN, Rose Josephine. See HUDSON-WILKIN, Mrs Rose Josephine

WILKINS, Mrs Janice Joy. b 49. St D Coll Lamp 90. **d** 93 **p** 97. NSM Tredegar St Jas *Mon* 93-96; NSM Newbridge 96-97; C Mynyddislwyn 97-01; V Abercarn and Cwmcarn 01-06; AD Bedwellty 05-06; rtd 06. *10 Overdene, Pontllanfraith, Blackwood NP12 2JS* Tel (01495) 225720

WILKINS, Michael Richard. b 71. W Sussex Inst of HE BA92. Trin Coll Bris 07. **d** 09. C Bath Walcot *B & W* from 09. *5 The Linleys, Bath BA1 2XE* Tel (01225) 789168 Mobile 07825-789168 E-mail mike@walcotchurch.org.uk

WILKINS, Nicki Anne. b 68. Indiana Univ BA91 Yale Univ MDiv03. **d** 05 **p** 07. NSM St Andrews St Andr *St And* from 05. *Address temp unknown* E-mail nwilkins@btinternet.com

WILKINS, Ralph Herbert. b 29. Lon Univ BD61. St Aug Coll Cant 72. **d** 73 **p** 74. C Epsom Common Ch Ch *Guildf* 73-76; C Haslemere 77-79; P-in-c Market Lavington and Easterton *Sarum* 79-82; V 82-90; P-in-c Puddletown and Tolpuddle 90-94; P-in-c Milborne St Andrew w Dewlish 92-94; P-in-c Piddletrenthide w Plush, Alton Pancras etc 92-94; rtd 94; Perm to Offic *Ab* 94-01 and *Heref* from 02. *The Mill, Marton, Welshpool SY21 8JY* Tel (01938) 580566

WILKINS, Miss Susan Stafford. b 47. Dur Univ BA. Sarum Th Coll. **dss** 82 **d** 87 **p** 94. Redlynch and Morgan's Vale *Sarum* 82-88; Hon Par Dn 87-88; Hon Par Dn Bemerton 88-90; Par Dn Hilperton w Whaddon and Staverton etc 90-94; TV Worle *B & W* 94-99; P-in-c Hallwood *Ches* 99-04; V Hallwood Ecum Par from 04; RD Frodsham from 06. *The Vicarage, 6 Kirkstone Crescent, Runcorn WA7 3JQ* Tel (01928) 713101
E-mail suewilkins@hallwoodlep.fsnet.co.uk

WILKINS, Vernon Gregory. b 53. Trin Coll Cam MA74 Ox Univ BA88. Wycliffe Hall Ox 86. **d** 89 **p** 90. C Boscombe St Jo *Win* 89-91; C Bursledon 91-94; V Ramsgate St Luke *Cant* 94-03; Dir Tr Bromley Chr Tr Cen Trust from 03; Hon C Bromley Ch Ch *Roch* from 03. *29 Heathfield Road, Bromley BR1 3RN* Tel (020) 8464 5135 E-mail vernon@vgwilkins.freeserve.co.uk

WILKINSON, Adrian Mark. b 68. TCD BA90 MA94 BTh94 NUI MA00 HDipEd91. CITC 91. **d** 94 **p** 95. C Douglas Union w Frankfield, *C, C & R* 94-97; I Dunboyne Union *M & K* 97-02; Chapl NUI 97-02; Min Can St Patr Cathl Dublin 97-02; I Rathmolyon w Castlerickard, Rathcore and Agher *M & K* 01-02; I Douglas Union w Frankfield *C, C & R* from 02. *The Rectory, Carrigaline Road, Douglas, Cork, Republic of Ireland* Tel (00353) (21) 489 1539 E-mail amwilkinson@eircom.net

WILKINSON, Canon Alan Bassindale. b 31. St Cath Coll Cam BA54 MA58 PhD59 DD97. Coll of Resurr Mirfield 57. **d** 59 **p** 60. C Kilburn St Aug Lon 59-61; Chapl St Cath Coll Cam 61-67; V Barrow Gurney *B & W* 67-70; Asst Chapl and Lect St Matthias's Coll Bris 67-70; Prin Chich Th Coll 70-74; Can and Preb Chich Cathl 70-74; Warden Verulam Ho 74-75; Dir of Aux Min Tr *St Alb* 74-75; Sen Lect Crewe and Alsager Coll of HE 75-78; Hon C Alsager St Mary *Ches* 76-78; Dioc Dir of Tr *Ripon* 78-84; P-in-c Thornthwaite w Thruscross and Darley 84-88; Hon Can Ripon Cathl 84-88; Perm to Offic *Portsm* from 88; Hon P Portsm Cathl from 88; Hon Dioc Th 93-01; Hon Chapl Portsm Cathl 94-01; rtd 96; Visiting Lect Portsm Univ 98-05. *17A High Street, Portsmouth PO1 2LP* Tel (023) 9273 6270

WILKINSON, Alice Margaret Marion. See BISHOP, Mrs Alice Margaret Marion

WILKINSON, Andrew Wilfrid. b 66. Nottm Univ BTh96 Lanc Univ MA99. Linc Th Coll 93. **d** 96 **p** 97. C Longridge *Blackb* 96-99; V Garstang St Helen and St Michaels-on-Wyre from 99; AD Garstang from 02; CF (TA) from 02. *The Vicarage, 6 Vicarage Lane, Churchtown, Preston PR3 0HW* Tel and fax (01995) 602294 E-mail areadean@tiscali.co.uk

WILKINSON (née PHILPOTT), Canon Barbara May. b 48. Leeds Univ BA69 CertEd70 MA90. NOC 90. **d** 93 **p** 94. NSM Carleton and Lothersdale *Bradf* 93-96; C Steeton 96-00; Asst Chapl Airedale NHS Trust 96-01; Hd Chapl Services from 01; Hon Can Bradf Cathl from 04; RD S Craven 04-07. *37 Aire Valley Drive, Bradley, Keighley BD20 9HY* Tel (01535) 636339 E-mail barbara.wilkinson@bradford.anglican.org

WILKINSON, Carol Ann. b 54. Lon Univ BD88 Man Univ PhD95. CBDTI 04. **d** 06 **p** 07. NSM Poulton Carleton and

Singleton *Blackb* 06-09; Lic to Offic from 09. *52 Lowick Drive, Poulton-le-Fylde FY6 8HB* Tel (01253) 350700
E-mail cwilkinson@swilkinson.direct.co.uk

WILKINSON, Mrs Christine Margaret. b 52. Man Univ BA74 Neville's Cross Coll of Educn Dur PGCE75 Birm Univ MEd78. **d** 04 **p** 05. OLM Eythorne and Elvington w Waldershare etc *Cant* from 04. *4 The Glen, Shepherdswell, Dover CT15 7PF* Tel (01304) 831025 E-mail chriswilk.shep@virgin.net

WILKINSON, David Andrew. b 62. BA83. Oak Hill Th Coll BA85. **d** 88 **p** 89. C Upton (Overchurch) *Ches* 88-91; C Fulham St Matt *Lon* 91-94; V Duffield *Derby* 94-99; V Finchley St Paul and St Luke *Lon* 99-03. *Honeysuckle Cottage, 19 Church Street, Windermere LA23 1AQ* Tel (015394) 43069

WILKINSON, David Edward Paul. b 36. Univ of Wales (Swansea) BSc57. St Mich Coll Llan 57. **d** 59 **p** 60. C Brecon w Battle *S & B* 59-60; Min Can Brecon Cathl 60-66; R Llanelwedd w Llanfaredd, Cwmbach Llechryd etc 66-72; V Tycoch 72-74; Asst Master Churchmead Sch Datchet 75-82; TV Seacroft *Ripon* 82-01; rtd 01; Hon Min Can Ripon Cathl 01-07; Hon C Bishop Monkton and Burton Leonard 01-07; Perm to Offic *St As* from 07. *Lyngrove, New High Street, Ruabon, Wrexham LL14 6PW* Tel (01978) 822725 Mobile 07909-961197
E-mail paulwilkinson36@googlemail.com

WILKINSON, Canon David James. b 45. St D Coll Lamp 65 Wycliffe Hall Ox 68. **d** 69 **p** 70. C Swansea St Thos and Kilvey *S & B* 69-73; C Clydach 73-76; R Llanbadarn Fawr, Llandegley and Llanfihangel etc 76-81; V Swansea St Nic 81-88; V Killay 88-94; V Ilston w Pennard from 94; AD Gower from 99; Can Brecon Cathl 99-04; Prec from 04. *The Vicarage, 88 Pennard Road, Pennard, Swansea SA3 2AD* Tel and fax (01792) 232928

WILKINSON, Edward. b 55. Cranmer Hall Dur 86. **d** 88 **p** 89. C Bishopwearmouth St Nic *Dur* 88-92; P-in-c Newbottle 92-96; V from 96. *The Vicarage, Newbottle, Houghton le Spring DH4 4EP* Tel 0191-584 3244

WILKINSON, Edwin. b 29. Oak Hill Th Coll 53. **d** 56 **p** 57. C Blackb Ch Ch 56-58; C Cheltenham St Mark *Glouc* 58-61; V Tiverton St Geo *Ex* 61-66; V Rye Harbour *Chich* 66-73; V Camber and E Guldeford 73-79; V Westfield 79-87; V Bexhill St Steph 87-93; rtd 93; Perm to Offic *Chich* from 93. *51 Anderida Road, Eastbourne BN22 0PZ* Tel (01323) 503083

WILKINSON, Mrs Elizabeth Mary. b 65. St Edm Hall Ox MA91. NEOC 02. **d** 05 **p** 06. C Harlow Green and Lamesley *Dur* 05-09; P-in-c Burnmoor from 09. *The Rectory, 91 Old Durham Road, Gateshead NE8 4BS* Tel 0191-477 3990

WILKINSON, Geoffrey. *See* WILKINSON, Roy Geoffrey

WILKINSON, Canon Guy Alexander. b 48. Magd Coll Cam BA69. Ripon Coll Cuddesdon 85. **d** 87 **p** 88. C Coventry Caludon 87-90; P-in-c Ockham w Hatchford *Guildf* 90-91; R 91-94; Bp's Dom Chapl 90-94; V Small Heath *Birm* 94-99; Adn Bradf 99-04; Abp's Sec for Inter Faith Relns from 05; Nat Adv for Inter Faith Relns from 05. *Lambeth Palace, London SE1 7JU,* or *Church House, Great Smith Street, London SW1P 3AZ* Tel (020) 7898 1477 *or* 7898 1247 Mobile 07932-652315
E-mail guy.wilkinson@c-of-e.org.uk

WILKINSON, Miss Helen Mary. b 53. Homerton Coll Cam BEd76. Trin Coll Bris 02. **d** 04 **p** 05. C Newbury *Ox* 04-08; C Northwood Em *Lon* from 08. *54 Rofant Road, Northwood HA6 3BE* Tel (01923) 829163 Mobile 07790-262631

WILKINSON, James Daniel. b 73. Westmr Coll Ox BTh95 Reading Univ MA07 MBACP04. St Steph Ho Ox 97. **d** 99 **p** 00. C Wantage *Ox* 99-02; P-in-c S Hinksey from 02; Sec to Bp Ebbsfleet 02-04. *The Vicarage, 33 Vicarage Road, Oxford OX1 4RD* Tel (01865) 245879
E-mail frwilkinson@ukonline.co.uk

WILKINSON, John Andrew. b 59. Pemb Coll Ox BA83 MA87 St Jo Coll Dur BA86. Cranmer Hall Dur 84. **d** 87 **p** 88. C Broadheath *Ches* 87-91; TV Worthing Ch the King *Chich* 91-97; Chapl Chantilly *Eur* 97-06; Asst Chapl Fontainebleau from 06. *9 rue des Provenceaux, 77300 Fontainebleau, France* Tel (0033) (1) 60 71 86 55 E-mail chaplain@fontainebleauchurch.org

WILKINSON, John David. b 36. AKC59. **d** 60 **p** 61. C Wythenshawe Wm Temple Ch CD *Man* 60-63; C Morley St Pet w Churwell *Wakef* 63-65; V Robert Town 65-75; V Battyeford 75-88; V Airedale w Fryston 88-98; P-in-c Cawthorne 98-04; rtd 04; Perm to Offic *Wakef* from 05; Retirement Officer (Pontefract Adnry) from 06. *29 Pontefract Road, Ferry Bridge, Knottingley WF11 8PN* Tel (01977) 607250

WILKINSON, Canon John Donald. b 29. Mert Coll Ox BA54 MA56 Louvain Univ Belgium LTh59 Lon Univ PhD82 FSA80. Gen Th Sem (NY) Hon STD63 Cuddesdon Coll 54. **d** 56 **p** 57. C Stepney St Dunstan and All SS *Lon* 56-59; Jerusalem 61-63; Gen Ed USPG 63-69; Dean St Geo Coll Jerusalem 69 75; Can Jerusalem 73-75; P-in-c S Kensington H Trin w All SS *Lon* 75-78; Bp's Dir of Clergy Tr 75-79; Dir Br Sch of Archaeology Jerusalem 79-83; USA 83-91; NSM Kensington St Mary Abbots w St Geo *Lon* 91-94; rtd 94; Hon C St Marylebone St Cypr *Lon* 94-98; Perm to Offic 98-08. *7 Tenniel Close, London W2 3LE* Tel and fax (020) 7229 9205

WILKINSON, John Lawrence. b 43. Ch Coll Cam BA65 MA69 Birm Univ MLitt91. Qu Coll Birm 67 Gen Th Sem (NY) STB69. **d** 69 **p** 70. C Braunstone *Leic* 69-71; C Hodge Hill *Birm* 71-74; P-in-c Aston St Jas 75-84; Tutor Qu Coll Birm 85-95; Hon C Birm St Geo 86-95; V Kings Heath 95-08; Hon Can Birm Cathl 99-08; rtd 09; Perm to Offic *Birm* from 09. *203 Barclay Road, Smethwick B67 5LA* Tel 0121-434 3526
E-mail jrwilkinson@dsl.pipex.com

WILKINSON, John Stoddart. b 47. CQSW83. St D Coll Lamp. **d** 70 **p** 71. C Kells *Carl* 70-72; C Barrow St Geo w St Luke 72-74; Perm to Offic *Mon* 74-89; Sub-Chapl HM YOI Hewell Grange 89-90; Sub-Chapl HM Rem Cen Brockhill 89-90; rtd 02. *10 Fern Drive, Neyland, Milford Haven SA73 1RA*

WILKINSON, Jonathan Charles. b 61. Leeds Univ BA83. Wycliffe Hall Ox 85. **d** 87 **p** 88. C Plymouth St Andr w St Paul and St Geo *Ex* 87-90; C Oulton Broad *Nor* 90-93; V Hallwood *Ches* 93-99; TR Gateshead *Dur* from 99. *The Rectory, 91 Old Durham Road, Gateshead NE8 4BS* Tel 0191-477 3990
E-mail wilkinson@clara.net

WILKINSON, Mrs Joyce Aileen. b 29. BSc(Econ) MA. **d** 99 **p** 00. NSM Bredon w Bredon's Norton *Worc* 99-04; rtd 04; Perm to Offic *Worc* from 04. *Foxgloves, Back Lane, Bredon, Tewkesbury GL20 7LH* Tel (01684) 773389

WILKINSON, Canon Julia Mary. b 52. Cam Inst of Educn CertEd73 Open Univ BA85 Univ of Wales (Ban) BD89. Linc Th Coll 92. **d** 92 **p** 94. Par Dn High Wycombe *Ox* 92-94; C 94-96; TV 96-01; Bp's Adv for Women in Ord Min 97-01; P-in-c St Merryn *Truro* 01-05; P-in-c St Issey w St Petroc Minor 01-05; R St Merryn and St Issey w St Petroc Minor from 06; Co Dioc Dir of Ords from 01; Hon Can Truro Cathl from 06. *The Rectory, Glebe Crescent, St Issey, Wadebridge PL27 7HJ* Tel and fax (01841) 540314 E-mail revjulia@stpetroc.fsnet.co.uk

WILKINSON, Canon Keith Howard. b 48. Hull Univ BA70 FRSA94 MCT99. Westcott Ho Cam 74. **d** 76 **p** 77. C Pet St Jude 76-79; Chapl Eton Coll 79-84; Perm to Offic *Pet* 82-94; Chapl Malvern Coll 84-89; Hd Master Berkhamsted Sch Herts 89-96; Lic to Offic *St Alb* 89-96; Hd Master K Sch Cant 96-07; Hon Can Cant Cathl 96-07; Sen Chapl Eton Coll from 08. *3 Savile House, Eton College, Windsor SL4 0TD*

WILKINSON, The Ven Kenneth Samuel. b 31. TCD BA60 MA69. CITC 60. **d** 60 **p** 61. C Dublin St Michan w St Paul *D & G* 60-63; Min Can St Patr Cathl Dublin 62-67; C Dublin Ch Ch Leeson Park *D & G* 63-67; I Killegney *C & O* 67-70; I Enniscorthy w Clone, Clonmore, Monart etc 70-02; Preb Ferns Cathl 83-88; Adn Ferns 88-02; Dioc Dir of Ords 94-02; rtd 02. *149 Hazelwood, Old Coach Road, Gorey, Co Wexford, Republic of Ireland* Tel (00353) (53) 942 0784

WILKINSON, Margaret Anne. b 46. Lon Univ MB, BS70 MSc74 MRCPsych77. SAOMC 95. **d** 99 **p** 99. NSM Hanwell *Lon* 98-06; Chapl HM YOI Feltham 01-06; NSM Penge Lane H Trin *Roch* from 07. *27 River Grove Park, Beckenham BR3 1HX* Tel (020) 8650 2312 E-mail revdrwilkinson@doctors.org.uk

WILKINSON, Miss Marlene Sandra. b 45. SRN71. Trin Coll Bris IDC78. **dss** 78 **d** 93 **p** 94. Wrose *Bradf* 78-82; Chapl St Luke's Hosp Bradf 78-82; Past Tutor Aston Tr Scheme 79-81; W Yorkshire CECS 82-84; Westgate Common *Wakef* 94 86. F Ardsley 86-92; Wakef St Jo 92-94; NSM 93-94; TV Barrow St Geo w St Luke *Carl* 94-00; TV Darwen St Pet w Hoddlesden *Blackb* 00-02; rtd 03. *4 Hopefield Court, East Ardsley, Wakefield WF3 2LL* Tel (01924) 872825

WILKINSON, Mrs Mary Frances. b 52. St As Minl Tr Course 99. **d** 03 **p** 04. NSM Shotton *St As* 03-05; NSM Llandrillo and Llandderfel from 05. *8 Felin Goed, Llandrillo, Corwen LL21 0SJ* Tel (01490) 440522

WILKINSON, Matthew John George. b 81. St Cuth Soc Dur BSc02. St Mich Coll Llan BA06. **d** 06 **p** 07. C Wrexham *St As* from 06. *St James's House, 16 Foster Road, Wrexham LL11 2LT* Tel (01978) 313401 E-mail mjgwilkinson@hotmail.com

WILKINSON, Michael Alan. b 27. Selw Coll Cam BA51. Westcott Ho Cam 52. **d** 53 **p** 54. C Swindon Ch Ch *Bris* 53-57; C Knowle St Barn 57-59; C Eltham St Jo *S'wark* 59-65; C Sydenham St Bart 65-77; Perm to Offic *Ex* 77-84; P-in-c Yealmpton 84-91; P-in-c Brixton 87-91; V Yealmpton and Brixton 91-97; RD Ivybridge 91-93; rtd 97; Perm to Offic *Ex* from 97. *The Old Forge, Kingston, Kingsbridge TQ7 4PT* Tel (01548) 810424

WILKINSON, Paul. *See* WILKINSON, David Edward Paul

WILKINSON, Paul. b 51. Sarum & Wells Th Coll 75. **d** 78 **p** 79. C Allerton *Bradf* 78-80; C Baildon 80-83; V Hengoed w Gobowen *Lich* 83-90; V Potterne w Worton and Marston *Sarum* 90-03; Chapl Roundway Hosp Devizes 92-03; P-in-c Leckhampton St Pet *Glouc* from 03, P-in-c Cheltenham Em w St Steph from 08. *The Rectory, Church Road, Leckhampton, Cheltenham GL53 0QJ* Tel (01242) 513647
E-mail pwilkinson@vicarage79.fsnet.co.uk

WILKINSON, Paul Martin. b 56. Brunel Univ BSc. Wycliffe Hall Ox 83. **d** 86 **p** 87. C Hinckley H Trin *Leic* 86-90; V Newbold on

Avon *Cov* from 90. *The Vicarage, Main Street, Newbold, Rugby CV21 1HH* Tel (01788) 543055 Fax 542458 E-mail paulwilkinson54@btinternet.com

WILKINSON, Peter David Lloyd. b 67. Trin Coll Ox BA89 MA93. Ridley Hall Cam BA94. **d** 95 **p** 96. C Brampton St Thos *Derby* 95-98; C Tunbridge Wells St Jo *Roch* 98-02; C Ox St Ebbe w H Trin and St Pet from 02. *10 Lincoln Road, Oxford OX1 4TB* Tel (01865) 728885 E-mail pete@peteandjules.freeserve.co.uk

WILKINSON, Robert. See WILKINSON, Walter Edward Robert

WILKINSON, Robert Ian. b 43. MIMunE73 MICE84 CEng73. Oak Hill NSM Course. **d** 88 **p** 89. NSM Hawkwell *Chelmsf* 88-89; NSM Thundersley 89-91; C New Thundersley 91-94; V Berechurch St Marg w St Mich 94-06; rtd 06. *140 Keighley Road, Skipton BD23 2QT* Tel (01756) 799748

WILKINSON, Robert John. b 66. Birkbeck Coll Lon BA98 Fitzw Coll Cam BA00 ACIB90. Westcott Ho Cam 98. **d** 01 **p** 02. C Southgate Ch Ch *Lon* 01-04; TV Wood Green St Mich w Bounds Green St Gabr etc from 04. *27 Collings Close, London N22 8RL* Tel (020) 8881 9836 E-mail robert.wilkinson@london.anglican.org

WILKINSON, Robert Matthew. b 21. TCD BA46. TCD Div Sch 47. **d** 47 **p** 48. C Limerick St Lawr w H Trin and St Jo *L & K* 47-49; C Arm St Mark 49-51; I Mullavilly 51-55; I Derryloran 55-73; Can Arm Cathl 67-73; I Ballymore 73-87; Treas Arm Cathl 73-75; Chan 75-83; Prec 83-87; rtd 87. *60 Coleraine Road, Portrush BT56 8HN* Tel (028) 7082 2758

WILKINSON, Robert Samuel. b 52. Wycliffe Hall Ox 92. **d** 94 **p** 95. C Boughton Monchelsea *Cant* 94-96; C Parkwood CD 95-96; C Plymouth St Andr and Stonehouse *Ex* 96-01; P-in-c Whimple, Talaton and Clyst St Lawr from 01. *The Rectory, Grove Road, Whimple, Exeter EX5 2TP* Tel (01404) 822521 E-mail rectory@whimplechurch.org

WILKINSON, Roger. b 46. K Coll Lon BA68 AKC68 AKC72. St Aug Coll Cant 72. **d** 73 **p** 74. C Lt Stanmore St Lawr *Lon* 73-76; Asst Chapl St Geo Hosp Lon 76-78; Chapl Hounslow and Spelthorne HA 78-88; TV Langley and Parkfield *Man* 88-89; C Shelf and Buttershaw St Aid *Bradf* 89-90; Chapl Asst Ipswich Hosp NHS Trust 90-94; C Fingringhoe w E Donyland and Abberton etc *Chelmsf* 94-01; P-in-c Greensted-juxta-Ongar w Stanford Rivers 01-04; P-in-c Stapleford Tawney w Theydon Mt 01-04; R Greensted-juxta-Ongar w Stanford Rivers etc 04-07; rtd 07; Perm to Offic *Chelmsf* from 07. *9 Iona Walk, Rowhedge, Colchester CO5 7JD* Tel (01206) 728882 E-mail roger606wilkinson@btinternet.com

WILKINSON, Roy Geoffrey. b 42. Open Univ BSc93 Linc Univ MSc99. Sarum Th Coll 67. **d** 70 **p** 71. C Belsize Park *Lon* 70-73; C Heston 73-75; C Hythe *Cant* 75-79; V Croydon Woodside 79-86; NSM Skegness and Winthorpe *Linc* 96-97; Asst Mental Health Chapl Linc Distr Healthcare NHS Trust 96-97; Chapl Lincs Partnership NHS Trust 97-05; rtd 05; Hon C Linc All SS from 06. *287 Monks Road, Lincoln LN2 5JZ* Tel (01522) 522671 Mobile 07745-755614 E-mail sarah@comfort123.freeserve.co.uk

WILKINSON, Canon Simon Evelyn. b 49. Nottm Univ BA74. Cuddesdon Coll 74. **d** 76 **p** 77. C Cheam *S'wark* 76-78; P-in-c Warlingham w Chelsham and Farleigh 78-83; Hd RS Radley Coll 83-89; R Bishop's Waltham and Upham *Portsm* 89-97; TR Shaston *Sarum* 97-03; P-in-c Amesbury from 03; RD Stonehenge from 03; Can and Preb Sarum Cathl from 05. *The Vicarage, Church Street, Amesbury, Salisbury SP4 7EU* Tel (01980) 623145 E-mail s-wilkinson@sky.com

WILKINSON, Stephen Graham. b 64. Leeds Univ BA08. NOC 05. **d** 08 **p** 09. NSM Pennington *Man* from 08. *Glen Thorne, 205 St Helens Road, Leigh WN7 3UB* Tel (01942) 606598 Mobile 07748-988091 E-mail steve.wilkinson@penningtonchurch

WILKINSON, Walter Edward Robert. b 38. St Andr Univ MA60. Lon Coll of Div BD63 ALCD63. **d** 63 **p** 64. C High Wycombe *Ox* 63-70; PV, Succ and Sacr Roch Cathl 70-73; P-in-c Asby w Ormside *Carl* 73-80; R Cherry Burton *York* 80-95; RD Beverley 88-94; P-in-c Grasmere *Carl* 95-03; rtd 03; Perm to Offic *Carl* from 03. *4 Heversham Gardens, Heversham, Milnthorpe LA7 7RA* Tel (01539) 564044 E-mail bob@carliol.clara.co.uk

WILKINSON, Canon Wilfred Badger. b 21. K Coll Lon BD50 AKC50. **d** 50 **p** 51. C Luton St Mary *St Alb* 50-53; C Gt Berkhamsted 53-57; C-in-c Wythenshawe Wm Temple Ch CD *Man* 57-65; R Clifton w Glapton *S'well* 65-71; TR Clifton 71-86; Hon Can S'well Minster 83-86; rtd 86; Perm to Offic *S'well* 86-04. *clo Dr Mark Wilkinson, The Granary, Yew Tree Lane, Spratton, Northampton NN6 8HL* Tel (01604) 845868

WILKS, Eric Percival. b 32. Wells Th Coll 67. **d** 68 **p** 69. C Fladbury w Throckmorton, Wyre Piddle and Moor *Worc* 68-70; Perm to Offic from 70. *4 Catherine Cottages, Droitwich Road, Hartlebury, Kidderminster DY10 4EL* Tel (01299) 251580

WILKS, Ernest Howard. b 26. Oak Hill Th Coll 64. **d** 66 **p** 67. C Slough *Ox* 66-69; R Gressenhall w Longham and Bittering Parva *Nor* 69-77; Area Sec CMS *St E* and *Nor* 77-83; P-in-c Deopham w Hackford *Nor* 83-84; P-in-c Morley 83-84; P-in-c Wicklewood and Crownthorpe 83-84; R Morley w Deopham,

Hackford, Wicklewood etc 84-88; CMS Nigeria 89-91; rtd 91; Perm to Offic *Nor* from 91. *Corner Cottage, Carbrooke Road, Griston, Thetford IP25 6QE* Tel (01953) 881413

WILL, Nicholas James. b 53. Birm Univ LLB75. Qu Coll Birm 93. **d** 95 **p** 96. C Bridgnorth, Tasley, Astley Abbotts, etc *Heref* 95-00; R Raveningham Gp *Nor* from 00. *The Rectory, Church Road, Thurlton, Norwich NR14 6RN* Tel (01508) 548648

WILLANS, Jonathan Michael Arthur. b 60. QUB BD. CITC 83. **d** 85 **p** 86. C Larne and Inver *Conn* 85-88; R Hawick *Edin* 88-91; P-in-c Brockham Green *S'wark* from 91; P-in-c Leigh from 91. *The Vicarage, Clayhill Road, Leigh, Reigate RH2 8PD* Tel and fax (01306) 611224

WILLANS, William Richard Gore. b 48. Qu Coll Ox BA70 MA74 Ox Univ PGCE71. CITC 77. **d** 79 **p** 80. Canada 79-98; C Bonne Bay 79-80; P-in-c Bonne Bay N 80-82; R 82-87; R Thunder Bay St Thos 87-98; RD Thunder Bay 89-93 and 95-97; I Craigs w Dunaghy and Killagan *Conn* from 98. *Craigs Rectory, 95 Hillmount Road, Cullybackey, Ballymena BT42 1NZ* Tel (028) 2588 0248 *or* 2588 2225 E-mail willans@btinternet.com

WILLARD, John Fordham. b 38. K Coll Lon BD62 AKC62. **d** 63 **p** 64. C Balham Hill Ascension *S'wark* 63-67; C Leigh Park *Portsm* 67-73; C-in-c Leigh Park St Clare CD 73-75; R Bishop's Waltham 75-87; P-in-c Upham 78-79; R 79-87; V Dalston H Trin w St Phil *Lon* 87-97; P-in-c Haggerston All SS 90-97; P-in-c Fairford *Glouc* 97-98; V Fairford and Kempsford w Whelford 98-04; rtd 04; Perm to Offic *Glouc* from 05. *15 Highwood Avenue, Cheltenham GL53 0JJ* Tel (01242) 530051

WILLCOCK, Canon Richard William. b 39. Hertf Coll Ox BA62 MA66. Ripon Hall Ox 62. **d** 64 **p** 65. C Ashton St Mich *Man* 64-68; Bp's Dom Chapl 68-72; V Charlestown 72-75; Chapl Casterton Sch Lancs 75-80; V Bamford *Man* 80-92; R Framlingham w Saxtead *St E* 92-04; RD Loes 95-97; Warden of Readers 98-03; Hon Can St E Cathl 00-04; rtd 04. *High Green Cottage, Sandford, Appleby-in-Westmorland CA16 6NR* Tel (017683) 51021

WILLCOX, Canon Frederick John. b 29. Kelham Th Coll 49. **d** 54 **p** 55. C Tranmere St Paul *Ches* 54-56; Lic to Offic *S'well* 57-61; S Africa 62-70; P-in-c Derby St Andr w St Osmund 70-74; V 74-80; V Netherton St Andr *Worc* 80-94; Hon Can Worc Cathl 91-94; rtd 94; Perm to Offic *Worc* from 94. *48 Meadow Croft, West Hagley, Stourbridge DY9 0LJ* Tel (01562) 887255

WILLCOX (née THOMPSON), Mrs Pauline. b 44. EMMTC 81. dss 84 **d** 87 **p** 94. Derby St Aug 84-88; Par Dn 87-88; Par Dn Boulton 88-90; Par Dn Allestree 91-94; C 94-97; Sub-Chapl HM Pris Sudbury 92-94; P-in-c Hartington, Biggin and Earl Sterndale *Derby* 97-01; rtd 01; Perm to Offic *Derby* 01-06; Chapl HM Pris Jersey from 06. *9 Clos du Roncherez, Le Pont du Val, St Brelade, Jersey JE3 8FG* Tel (01534) 745160 E-mail paulinewillcox@jerseymail.co.uk

WILLCOX, Ralph Arthur. b 32. Cranfield Inst of Tech MSc80. St Alb Minl Tr Scheme 86. **d** 89 **p** 90. NSM Aspley Guise w Husborne Crawley and Ridgmont *St Alb* 89-92; Chapl HM Pris Bedf 92-99; Asst Chapl 99-02; Lic to Offic *St Alb* 92-03; rtd 02; Perm to Offic *St Alb* from 03. *5 Church Road, Woburn Sands, Milton Keynes MK17 8TE* Tel (01908) 582510

WILLCOX, Richard John Michael. b 39. Birm Univ BSc62 PhD67. Qu Coll Birm 78. **d** 80 **p** 81. C Boldmere *Birm* 80-83; V Edgbaston SS Mary and Ambrose 83-89; V Evercreech w Chesterblade and Milton Clevedon *B & W* 89-97; Dioc Development Rep 90-01; V Bridgwater H Trin 97-01; rtd 01; Perm to Offic *Heref* from 05. *The Briars, Ledbury Road, Wellington Heath, Ledbury HR8 1NB* Tel (01531) 636191 E-mail rswillcox@aol.com

WILLCOX, Canon Sydney Harold. b 36. Univ of Wales (Lamp) BA58. St Mich Coll Llan. **d** 60 **p** 61. C Pwllheli *Ban* 60-62; C Llandegfan w Beaumaris and Llanfaes 62-65; R Llanenddwyn 65-70; R Dolgellau, Llanfachreth, Brithdir etc 70-76; TR Ridgeway *Sarum* 76-86; RD Marlborough 81-86; TR Cockermouth w Embleton and Wythop *Carl* 86-94; RD Derwent 89-94; Hon Can Carl Cathl 91-94; TR Chalke Valley *Sarum* 94-01; rtd 02. *7 Hillingdon, Bridport DT6 3DH* Tel (01308) 459139

WILLESDEN, Area Bishop of. See BROADBENT, The Rt Revd Peter Alan

WILLETT, Canon Allen Gardiner. b 20. Bris Univ BA51 Lon Univ BD54. Clifton Th Coll 47. **d** 54 **p** 55. C Rawtenstall St Mary *Man* 54-57; Nigeria 57-58; Tutor Clifton Th Coll 58-60; C Wallington *S'wark* 60-62; Tutor All Nations Miss Coll Taplow 62-63; V Bedminster St Luke w St Silas *Bris* 63-68; V Galleywood Common *Chelmsf* 68-87; RD Chelmsf 81-86; Hon Can Chelmsf Cathl 85-87; rtd 87; Perm to Offic *Pet* 87-00; *Ely* 90-97; *Linc* 90-99; *Chelmsf* and *St E* from 01. *61 Ashdown Way, Ipswich IP3 8DJ* Tel (01473) 423751 E-mail allenmary@willett61.freeserve.co.uk

WILLETT, Frank Edwin. b 45. Kelham Th Coll 64. **d** 68 **p** 69. C Oswestry H Trin *Lich* 68-71; C Bilston St Leon 71-74; USPG Coll of the Ascension Selly Oak 74-75; USPG 74-80; Zambia 75-80; V Curbar and Stoney Middleton *Derby* 80-88; Area Sec USPG *Derby* and *Leic* 88-91; V Chesterfield St Aug *Derby* 91-98;

Chapl Walton Hosp 91-98; Ind Chapl *Derby* 98-03; P-in-c Brampton St Mark from 03; P-in-c Loundsley Green from 03. *The Vicarage, 15 St Mark's Road, Chesterfield S40 1DH* Tel (01246) 234015 E-mail f@willett85.freeserve.co.uk

WILLETT, Canon Geoffrey Thomas. b 38. Dur Univ BA59 MA82. Cranmer Hall Dur. **d** 62 **p** 63. C Widnes St Paul *Liv* 62-65; C Harborne Heath *Birm* 65-68; V Wakef St Andr and St Mary 68-75; V Hinckley H Trin *Leic* 75-89; TR 89; RD Sparkenhoe II 84-87; RD Sparkenhoe W 87-89; P-in-c Markfield 89-90; R 90-99; P-in-c Thornton, Bagworth and Stanton 96-99; R Markfield, Thornton, Bagworth and Stanton etc 99-04; RD Sparkenhoe E 91-99; Hon Can Leic Cathl 87-04; rtd 04; Perm to Offic *Derby* and *Leic* from 04. *22 Clifton Way, Burton-on-Trent DE15 9DW* Tel (01283) 548868

WILLETT, Canon John Ivon. b 40. Ch Ch Ox BA63 MA65. Chich Th Coll 61. **d** 63 **p** 64. C Leic St Andr 63-66; C Bordesley St Alb *Birm* 66-72; Min Can, Prec and Sacr Pet Cathl 72-82; R Uppingham w Ayston and Wardley w Belton 82-99; Can Pet Cathl 97-99; V Cantley *Sheff* from 99; AD Doncaster from 04. *St Wilfrid's Vicarage, 200 Cantley Lane, Doncaster DN4 6PA* Tel (01302) 535133

WILLETT, Stephen John. b 54. Ridley Hall Cam 88. **d** 90 **p** 91. C Chapeltown *Sheff* 90-94; V Hackenthorpe from 94; AD Attercliffe from 07. *The Vicarage, 63 Sheffield Road, Sheffield S12 4LR* Tel 0114-248 4486 E-mail stephen.willet@tesco.net

WILLETTS, Alfred. b 15. **d** 62 **p** 63. C Canton St Jo *Llan* 62-65; V Afan Vale 65-67; R Man St Phil w St Mark 67-75; R Man Apostles 75-84; rtd 85; Perm to Offic *Ches* 85-91 and *Man* 85-97. *c/o Dr P Willetts, 10 Long Down, Petersfield GU31 4PD* Tel (01730) 262116

WILLETTS, Ms Mary Elizabeth Willetts. b 33. St Hild Coll Dur BA54 Hughes Hall Cam CertEd55. Cranmer Hall Dur 02. **d** 02 **p** 03. NSM Stockton-on-the-Forest w Holtby and Warthill *York* from 02. *Walnut Cottage, Warthill, York YO19 5XL* Tel (01904) 489874

WILLETTS, Mrs Susan. b 60. EMMTC 05. **d** 08 **p** 09. C Burton All SS w Ch Ch *Lich* from 08. *1A Moor Street, Burton-on-Trent DE14 3SU* Tel (01283) 538149

WILLEY, David Geoffrey. b 53. Imp Coll Lon BSc74. Oak Hill Th Coll BA86. **d** 86 **p** 87. C Cromer *Nor* 86-90; R High Halstow w All Hallows and Hoo St Mary *Roch* 90-94; R Gravesend St Geo 94-02; TR N Farnborough *Guildf* from 02; RD Aldershot from 06. *The Rectory, 66 Church Avenue, Farnborough GU14 7AP* Tel (01252) 544754 E-mail rector@stpetersfarnborough.org.uk

WILLEY, Graham John. b 38. Moray Ord Course 91. **d** 93 **p** 94. NSM W Coast Jt Congregations *Mor* 93-99; NSM Stirling *St And* 99-03; rtd 03; Perm to Offic *St And* from 03. *The Cedars, Main Street, Killin FK21 8TN* Tel (01567) 820366

WILLIAMS, Alan Ronald Norman. b 60. RMN85. Linc Th Coll 95. **d** 95 **p** 96. C Malvern Link w Cowleigh *Worc* 95-99; TV 03-08; V Risca *Mon* 99-03; P-in-c Amblecote *Worc* from 09. *The Vicarage, 4 The Holloway, Amblecote, Stourbridge DY8 4DL* E-mail alan.r.williams@btinternet.com

WILLIAMS, Aled Jones. b 56. Univ of Wales (Ban) BA77. St Mich Coll Llan 77. **d** 79 **p** 80. C Conwy w Gyffin *Ban* 79-82; R Llanrug 82-86; R Machynlleth and Llanwrin 86-87; Member L'Arche Community 88-95; V Ynyscynhaearn w Penmorfa and Porthmadog 95-01; V Porthmadog and Ynyscynhaearn and Dolbenmaen from 01. *The Vicarage, Ffordd Penamser, Porthmadog LL49 9PA* Tel (01766) 514951

WILLIAMS, Canon Aled Wyn. b 47. Univ of Wales (Abth) BA69. St Mich Coll Llan 69. **d** 71 **p** 72. C Llanelli *St D* 71-73; P-in-c Capel Colman w Llanfihangel Penbedw etc 73-74; V 74-81; V Llanddewi Brefi w Llanbadarn Odwyn 81-84; V Llanddewi Brefi w Llanbadarn Odwyn, Cellan etc 84-01; V Lampeter and Llanddewibrefi Gp 01-06; TR Bro Teifi Sarn Helen from 06; AD Lampeter and Ultra-Aeron 96-09; Can St D Cathl from 97. *Y Ficerdy Newydd, Maes y Llan, Lampeter SA48 7EN* Tel (01570) 422460

WILLIAMS, Alfred Donald. b 26. St Aid Birkenhead 57. **d** 59 **p** 60. C Ordsall *S'well* 59-62; V Ladybrook 62-70; P-in-c Newark Ch Ch 70-71; R Gotham 72-88; P-in-c W Leake w Kingston-on-Soar and Ratcliffe-on-Soar 72-81; rtd 88; Perm to Offic *Bradf* from 88. *20 Grassington Road, Skipton BD23 1LL* Tel (01756) 794496

WILLIAMS, Miss Alison Lindsay. b 47. Univ of Wales (Abth) BA69 PGCE70. Wycliffe Hall Ox 00. **d** 00 **p** 01. C Stratton St Margaret w S Marston etc *Bris* 00-04; TV Chalke Valley *Sarum* from 04. *The Vicarage, Nunton, Salisbury SP5 4HP* Tel (01722) 330628 E-mail alisonwilliams@fish.co.uk

WILLIAMS, Amanda Clare. See WILLIAMS-POTTER, Mrs Amanda Clare

WILLIAMS, Mrs Andrea Caroll. b 46. Brighton Univ BA05. Trin Coll Bris 06. **d** 07 **p** 08. NSM Ore St Helen and St Barn *Chich* from 07. *Flat 1, 17 Dane Road, St Leonards-on-Sea TN38 0QN* Tel (01424) 438394 Mobile 07806-463558 E-mail hastingsgang@onetel.com

WILLIAMS, Andrew Barrington. b 62. Ripon Coll Cuddesdon 96. **d** 98 **p** 99. C Oswaldtwistle Immanuel and All SS *Blackb* 98-01; C Whittle-le-Woods 01-02; P-in-c Hillock *Man* 02-08; P-in-c Unsworth 07-08; P-in-c Radcliffe St Andr from 08. *St Andrew's Vicarage, St Andrew's View, Radcliffe, Manchester M26 4HE* Tel 0161-723 2427 E-mail revandywilliams@yahoo.co.uk

WILLIAMS, Andrew David. b 67. Univ of Wales (Lamp) BA91. Linc Th Coll 93. **d** 93 **p** 94. C Perry Street *Roch* 93-96; C Ealing St Pet Mt Park *Lon* 96-00; R Finchley St Mary 00-08; Warden of Readers Edmonton Area 05-08; R Applecross Australia from 08. *2 Mitchell Street, Ardross WA 6153, Australia* Tel (0061) (8) 9417 4330 or 9364 1718 E-mail perth08@googlemail.com

WILLIAMS, Andrew Gibson. b 31. Edin Univ MA57. Edin Th Coll 56. **d** 59 **p** 60. C Todmorden *Wakef* 59-61; C Clitheroe St Mary *Blackb* 61-63; V Burnley St Jas 63-65; CF (TA) 64-65; CF 65-71; R Winterslow *Sarum* 71-84; P-in-c Condover *Heref* 84-88; P-in-c Acton Burnell w Pitchford 84-88; P-in-c Frodesley 84-88; R Condover w Frodesley, Acton Burnell etc 88-90; R Whimple, Talaton and Clyst St Lawr *Ex* 90-94; rtd 94; Perm to Offic *Ex* 94-08. *4 Lygon Lodge, Beauchamp Community, Newland, Malvern WR13 5AX* Tel (01684) 568061

WILLIAMS, Canon Andrew Joseph. b 55. St Jo Coll Nottm BTh81. **d** 81 **p** 82. C Hollington St Leon *Chich* 81-84; C Sutton Coldfield H Trin *Birm* 84-87; Perm to Offic 87-01; Chapl Blue Coat Comp Sch Walsall 91-01; Chapl St Elphin's Sch Matlock 01-04; Lic to Offic *Derby* 01-06; Can Res Bradf Cathl from 06. *2 Cathedral Close, Bradford BD1 4EG* Tel (01274) 777728 E-mail revandyw@aol.com

WILLIAMS, Andrew Thomas. b 66. Ex Univ LLB88 Solicitor 90. Trin Coll Bris BA00. **d** 00 **p** 01. C Whitchurch *Ex* 00-03; C Chorleywood St Andr *St Alb* from 03. *Wick Cottage, Quickley Lane, Chorleywood, Rickmansworth WD3 5AF* E-mail elena.w@virgin.net

WILLIAMS, Mrs Angela. b 50. Univ of Wales (Ban) BTh05. **d** 05 **p** 06. Min Can Ban Cathl 05-09; V Llandegfan w Llandysilio from 09; Dioc Children's Officer from 05. *The Vicarage, Mona Road, Menai Bridge LL59 5EA* Tel (01248) 717265

WILLIAMS, Mrs Anthea Elizabeth. b 50. Trevelyan Coll Dur BA71 Kent Univ MA97 Middx Univ MSc00. Linc Th Coll 72. **dss** 79 **d** 87 **p** 94. St Marylebone Ch Ch *Lon* 79-84; Maidstone St Martin *Cant* 84-91; Par Dn 87-91; Dn-in-c Rolvenden 91-94; P-in-c 94-04; P-in-c Newenden 01-04; Chapl E Kent NHS and Soc Care Partnership Trust 91-04; Hon Chapl Kent Police from 95; Perm to Offic *Cant* and *Roch* from 04. *2 Redwater Cottages, Cranbrook TN17 2LX* Tel (01580) 892191 E-mail willtyd@aol.com

WILLIAMS, Anthony. b 39. **d** 03 **p** 04. NSM Iver *Ox* from 03. *4 Syke Ings, Iver SL0 9ET* Tel (01753) 653849

WILLIAMS, Anthony David. b 38. LRCP62 MRCS62 MRCGP68. S Dios Minl Tr Scheme 87. **d** 90 **p** 91. NSM Jersey St Pet *Win* 90-92; NSM Jersey St Helier from 92. *Beau Vallon Ouest, Mont de la Rosier, St Saviour, Jersey JE2 7HF* Tel (01534) 863859 E-mail tonyw@jerseymail.co.uk

WILLIAMS, Anthony Francis. b 21. Trin Coll Ox BA49 MA53. Coll of Resurr Mirfield 49. **d** 51 **p** 52. C Paignton St Jo *Ex* 51-54; C Cov H Trin 54-60; V Cov All SS 60-67; V Lindridge *Worc* 67-77; P-in-c Bluntisham w Earith *Ely* 77-79; R 79-88; rtd 88; Perm to Offic *Ely* from 88. *21 King's Hedges, St Ives PE27 3XU* Tel (01480) 467686

WILLIAMS, Anthony James. b 57. **d** 08 **p** 09. NSM Bream *Glouc* from 08. *Sunnyside, Bailey Hill, Yorkley, Lydney GL15 4RT* Tel (01594) 516162 E-mail info@vineyhilladventure.org

WILLIAMS, The Very Revd Arfon. b 58. Univ of Wales (Abth) BD83 Univ of Wales (Ban) MA84. Wycliffe Hall Ox 83. **d** 84 **p** 85. C Carmarthen St Dav *St D* 84-86; TV Aberystwyth 86-88; V Glanogwen *Ban* 88-94; C Ewhurst and Dir Oast Ho Retreat Cen *Chich* 95-98; Asst to RD Rye 95-98; Co-ord for Adult Educn (E Sussex Area) 97-98; I Jordanstown *Conn* 98-02; Adn Meirionnydd *Ban* 02-04; R Dolgellau w Llanfachreth and Brithdir etc 02-04; Dean Elphin and Ardagh *K, E & A* from 04; I Sligo w Knocknarea and Rosses Pt from 04. *The Deanery, Strandhill Road, Sligo, Republic of Ireland* Tel (00353) (71) 915 7993 E-mail arvonwilliams@eircom.net

WILLIAMS, Preb Arthur Edwin. b 33. Leeds Univ BA57. Coll of Resurr Mirfield 57. **d** 59 **p** 60. C Wednesfield St Thos *Lich* 59-62; C Codsall 62-65; V 83-98; V Coseley St Chad 65-73; R Kingswinford H Trin 73-81; TR Wordsley 81-83; RD Himley 77-83; Preb Lich Cathl 82-98; RD Penkridge 89-94; rtd 98; Perm to Offic *Heref* from 99 and *Lich* from 01. *2 Campbell Close, Bridgnorth WV16 5PD* Tel (01746) 761344

WILLIAMS, Barrie. b 33. Em Coll Cam BA54 MA58 Bris Univ MLitt71. Lambeth STh75 Ripon Hall Ox 62. **d** 63 **p** 64. C Penwortham St Mary *Blackb* 63-65; Hon C Salisbury St Martin *Sarum* 65-77; Chapl St Edw K and Martyr Cam *Ely* 77-84; Asst Chapl Trin Hall Cam 77-84; R Ashley w Weston by Welland and Sutton Bassett *Pet* 84-85; Asst Chapl St Hilda's Priory and Sch Whitby 85-97; rtd 98; Perm to Offic *York* from 98. *Flat 5, Grinkle*

Court, 9 Chubb Hill Road, Whitby YO21 1JU Tel (01947) 600766

WILLIAMS, Benjamin Clive. b 24. Lon Univ BD59. Westcott Ho Cam 59. **d** 61 **p** 62. C Bury St Mark *Man* 61-63; C Christchurch *Win* 63-66; R Denton w S Heighton and Tarring Neville *Chich* 66-74; Dioc Stewardship Adv 74-81; P-in-c Clapham w Patching 76-81; V Ticehurst and Flimwell 81-89; rtd 89; Perm to Offic *Chich* from 89. *Victoria Royal Beach, 12 Grand Avenue, Worthing BN11 5AW*

WILLIAMS, Brian. *See* WILLIAMS, Herbert Brian

WILLIAMS, Brian. b 48. WMMTC. **d** 83 **p** 84. NSM Lich St Chad 83-03; Asst Chapl Sandwell Health Care NHS Trust 98; Angl Chapl 98-99; Chapl Burton Hosps NHS Trust 99-03; Chapl R Bournemouth and Christchurch Hosps NHS Trust from 03. *Royal Bournemouth Hospital, Castle Lane East, Bournemouth BH7 7DW* Tel (01202) 704221 *or* 303626

WILLIAMS, Brian Frederick. b 55. Philippa Fawcett Coll CertEd77 BEd78. SEITE 98. **d** 01 **p** 02. NSM Folkestone St Mary and St Eanswythe *Cant* from 01; NSM Folkestone St Sav from 09. *79 Surrenden Road, Folkestone CT19 4EB* Tel (01303) 276242 E-mail brianwilliams@cheritonfolk.fsnet.co.uk

WILLIAMS, Brian Luke. b 54. AKC75. St Steph Ho Ox 76. **d** 77 **p** 78. C Kettering St Mary *Pet* 77-80; C Walsall St Gabr Fulbrook 80-83; P-in-c Sneyd 83-85; V from 85; RD Stoke N 94-99. *Sneyd Vicarage, Hamil Road, Stoke-on-Trent ST6 1AP* Tel and fax (01782) 825841

WILLIAMS, Brian Thomas. b 48. Linc Th Coll 89. **d** 91 **p** 92. C Liss *Portsm* 91-95; C Portsea N End St Mark 95-98; Perm to Offic 98; NSM Wymering 05-07; NSM Lee-on-the-Solent from 07. *56 Old Road, Gosport PO12 1RE*

WILLIAMS, Bryan George. b 37. **d** 01 **p** 02. OLM Fazeley *Lich* 01-05; rtd 05. *Address temp unknown*

WILLIAMS, Ms Carol Jean Picknell. b 45. FCIPD89. Ox NSM Course 86. **d** 89 **p** 94. NSM High Wycombe *Ox* 89-97; P-in-c Penn 97-01; rtd 01; Perm to Offic *Heref* from 02. *Châtelaine House, Kinsham, Presteigne LD8 2HP* Tel (01544) 267067 E-mail caroljpwilliams@compuserve.com

WILLIAMS, Mrs Carole. b 61. LCTP 05. **d** 08 **p** 09. NSM Oswaldtwistle St Paul *Blackb* from 08. *20 Abbot Clough Avenue, Blackburn BB1 3LP* Tel (01254) 677708 E-mail carole.williams@blackburn.anglican.org

WILLIAMS, Mrs Catherine Anne. b 65. Selw Coll Cam BA87 MA91. SEITE 98. **d** 00 **p** 01. C Chatham St Steph *Roch* 00-02; C Bishop's Cleeve *Glouc* 03-06; Dioc Voc Officer from 06. *Abbey House, Church Street, Tewkesbury GL20 5SR* Tel (01684) 293333 Mobile 07966-709577 E-mail rev.catherine@virgin.net

WILLIAMS, Ms Catherine Lois. b 51. Swansea Coll of Educn CertEd74 Univ of Wales (Swansea) BEd80. St Mich Coll Llan. **d** 00 **p** 01. C Gorseinon *S & B* 00-02; C Cen Swansea 03; TV from 03. *Christ Church Vicarage, 226 Oystermouth Road, Swansea SA1 3UH* Tel (01792) 652606

WILLIAMS, (née BRERETON), Mrs Catherine Louise. b 69. St Aid Coll Dur BSc90 Cranfield Univ MSc92 Fitzw Coll Cam BTh00. Ridley Hall Cam 97. **d** 00 **p** 01. C S Bank *York* 00-03; V Middlesbrough St Chad 03-09; TV Woughton *Ox* from 09. *10 Forest Rise, Eaglestone, Milton Keynes MK6 5EU* Tel (01908) 674742 E-mail cathi@woughton.org

✠**WILLIAMS, The Rt Revd Cecil Javed.** b 42. Punjab Univ MA(Ed)67 Peshawar Univ MA72. **d** 87 **p** 88 **c** 02. C Tarnab and St Jo Cathl Peshawar Pakistan 87-90; V St Jo Cathl Peshawar 90-01; Asst Bp Peshawar 01-02; C Potternewton *Ripon* 02-06; rtd 07. *48 Potternewton Lane, Leeds LS7 3DA* Tel 0113-262 1408 Mobile 07882-171040 E-mail cecilwilliams42@hotmail.com

WILLIAMS, Canon Cecil Peter. b 41. TCD BA63 MA67 Lon Univ BD67 PhD86 Bris Univ MLitt77. Clifton Th Coll 64. **d** 67 **p** 68. C Maghull *Liv* 67-70; Lic to Offic *Bris* 70-91; Tutor Clifton Th Coll 70-72; Tutor Trin Coll Bris 72-91; Lib 73-81; Course Ldr 81-85; Vice-Prin 85-91; V Ecclesall *Sheff* 91-06; Hon Can Sheff Cathl 01-06; rtd 06; Hon C Jersey Gouray St Martin *Win* from 06. *Gouray Vicarage, La Grande Route de Faldouet, St Martin, Jersey JE3 6UA* Tel (01534) 853255 Mobile 07801-353786 E-mail peter.williams@gouraychurch.co.uk

WILLIAMS, Mrs Christine Mary. b 51. City Univ BSc72 Middx Univ BA05. NTMTC 02. **d** 05 **p** 06. NSM Pitsea w Nevendon *Chelmsf* 05-08; TV Grays Thurrock from 08. *2 Foxleigh, Billericay CM12 9NS* Tel (01277) 654370 E-mail christine.mwilliams@btopenworld.com

WILLIAMS, Christopher David. b 62. Spurgeon's Coll BD99. St Jo Coll Nottm MA06. **d** 06 **p** 07. C Haslemere and Grayswood *Guildf* 06-08; C Godalming from 08. *2 South Hill, Godalming GU7 1JT* Tel (01483) 410007 Mobile 07803-135739 E-mail chris.williams@godalming.org.uk *or* revchris@talktalk.net

WILLIAMS, Preb Clive Gregory. b 45. Trin Coll Bris 83. **d** 85 **p** 86. C Bedhampton *Portsm* 85-88; V Highley w Billingsley, Glazeley etc *Heref* from 88; P-in-c Stottesdon w Farlow, Cleeton St Mary etc from 98; RD Bridgnorth 96-05; Preb Heref Cathl from 99. *The Vicarage, Church Street, Highley, Bridgnorth WV16 6NA* Tel (01746) 861612 E-mail highleyrectory@aol.com

WILLIAMS, The Ven Colin Henry. b 52. Pemb Coll Ox BA73 MA78. St Steph Ho Ox BA80. **d** 81 **p** 82. C Liv St Paul Stoneycroft 81-84; TV Walton St Mary 84-89; Chapl Walton Hosp Liv 86-89; Bp's Dom Chapl *Blackb* 89-94; Chapl Whalley Abbey 89-94; V Poulton-le-Fylde 94-99; Adn Lancaster 99-05; Gen Sec Conf of Eur Chs from 05; Can Gib Cathl from 07. *PO Box 2100, 150 route de Ferney, CH-1211 Geneva 2, Switzerland* Tel (0041) (22) 791 6226 Fax 791 6227 E-mail cec@cec-kek.org *or* colin_w@bluewin.ch

WILLIAMS, David. b 19. **d** 66 **p** 67. Hon C Parkend *Glouc* 66-78; Hon C Coleford w Staunton 78-83; Perm to Offic from 83. *The Nook, 62 Parkend Road, Bream, Lydney GL15 6JZ* Tel (01594) 564449

WILLIAMS, David. b 43. ACA65 FCA. K Coll Lon AKC69 BD69. **d** 70 **p** 71. C Walkden Moor *Man* 70-72; C Deane 72-75; V Horwich St Cath 75-81; Hon C Chorley All SS *Blackb* 84-86; P-in-c Weeton 86-87; V Singleton w Weeton 87-97; C Lancaster St Mary w St John and St Anne 98-00; Chapl HM Pris Lanc Castle 98-00; rtd 00; Perm to Offic *Man* from 02. *153 Crompton Way, Bolton BL2 2SQ* Tel (01524) 382362 E-mail goodfornowt@aol.com

WILLIAMS, Canon David. b 49. BTh. **d** 88 **p** 89. C Lurgan etc w Ballymachugh, Kildrumferton etc *K, E & A* 88-91; I Kinsale Union *C, C & R* from 91; Miss to Seafarers from 91; Can Cork and Cloyne Cathls 95-97; Treas Cork Cathl from 97; Preb Tymothan St Patr Cathl Dublin from 97. *St Multose Rectory, Abbey Court, Kinsale, Co Cork, Republic of Ireland* Tel (00353) (21) 477 2220

WILLIAMS, David Alun. b 65. St Thos Hosp Lon MB, BS88 All Nations Chr Coll MA98. Wycliffe Hall Ox BTh94. **d** 94 **p** 95. C Ware Ch Ch *St Alb* 94-97; Crosslinks Kenya from 98; Perm to Offic *St Alb* 98-00. *PO Box 72584, Carlile College, Nairobi, Kenya* Tel (00254) (2) 715561

WILLIAMS, David Frank. b 48. S Dios Minl Tr Scheme 91. **d** 94 **p** 95. NSM Romsey *Win* from 94. *24 Feltham Close, Romsey SO51 8PB* Tel (01794) 524050 E-mail revdfw@talk21.com

WILLIAMS, David Gareth. b 58. Lon Univ BD81. Ripon Coll Cuddesdon 82. **d** 84 **p** 85. C Chandler's Ford *Win* 84-88; C Alton St Lawr 88-90; R Crawley and Littleton and Sparsholt w Lainston 90-97; P-in-c Andover from 97. *St Mary's Vicarage, Church Close, Andover SP10 1DP* Tel (01264) 350344 *or* 352729 E-mail david@twmpa.freeserve.co.uk

WILLIAMS, David Gerald Powell. b 35. St Mich Coll Llan. **d** 62 **p** 63. C Canton St Jo *Llan* 62-64; Field Tr Officer Ch in Wales Prov Youth Coun 63-70; Prov Youth Chapl 65-70; V Treharris *Llan* 70-75; R Flemingston w Gileston and St Hilary 75-78; Warden of Ords 77-80; Dir Past Studies and Chapl St Mich Coll Llan 78-80; Sub-Warden 79-80; Dir Ch in Wales Publications and Communications 80-85; Prov Dir of Educn Ch in Wales 80-85; Dir of Miss Ch in Wales 85-87; Hon Can Llan Cathl 84-93; V Pendoylan w Welsh St Donats 87-93; R Llandudno *Ban* 93-95; Prov Officer to Abp of Wales 93-00; rtd 00. *7 The Manor House, St Hilary, Cowbridge CF71 7DP*

WILLIAMS, Canon David Gordon. b 43. Selw Coll Cam BA65 MA69. Oak Hill Th Coll 66. **d** 68 **p** 69. C Maidstone St Luke *Cant* 68-71; C Rugby St Matt *Cov* 71-73; P-in-c Budbrooke 73-74; V 74-81; V Lenton *S'well* 81-87; TR Cheltenham St Mark *Glouc* 87-03; Hon Can Glouc Cathl 96-03; R Toodyay w Goomalling Australia 03-08; rtd 08; Miss Development P Avon Deanery 08-09; Perm to Offic Perth from 08 and *Derby* from 09. *Address temp unknown* E-mail revdrwilliams@westnet.com.au

WILLIAMS, David Grant. b 61. Bris Univ BSocSc83. Wycliffe Hall Ox 86. **d** 89 **p** 90. C Ecclesall *Sheff* 89-92; V Shore 92-02; RD Ecclesall 97-02; V Win Ch Ch from 02. *Christ Church Vicarage, Sleepers Hill, Winchester SO22 4ND* Tel (01962) 862414 Mobile 07889-547095 E-mail vicarccwinch@aol.com

WILLIAMS, David Henry. b 33. Trin Coll Cam BA56 MA60 PhD77. St D Coll Lamp 67. **d** 69 **p** 70. C Monmouth 69-70; Chapl St Woolos Cathl 70-71; P-in-c Six Bells 71-76; Libya 76-79; P-in-c Crumlin *Mon* 79-80; R Llanddewi Skirrid w Llanvetherine etc 80-83; Perm to Offic 83-87; Guest Master Caldey Abbey 83-87; V Buttington and Pool Quay *St As* 87-95; Chapl Warsaw *Eur* 95-97; rtd 97. *4 Clos-y-Drindod, Buarth Road, Aberystwyth SY23 1LR* Tel (01970) 612736 E-mail dhw.1933@ukonline.co.uk

WILLIAMS, Canon David Humphrey. b 23. Em Coll Cam BA49 MA54. St Steph Ho Ox 49. **d** 51 **p** 52. C Daybrook *S'well* 51-55; C-in-c Bilborough St Jo Bapt CD 55-62; V Bilborough St Jo 62-63; RD Bulwell 70-88; P-in-c Bestwood Park 71-78; P Hucknall Torkard 63-71; TR 71-88; Hon Can S'well Minster 75-88; rtd 88; Perm to Offic *S'well* from 88. *12 Wollaton Paddocks, Nottingham NG8 2ED* Tel 0115-928 0639

WILLIAMS, Canon David Ivan Ross. b 47. Imp Coll Lon BSc70 Leic Univ MSc72 ARCS70 FBIS. STETS 00. **d** 03 **p** 04. NSM Havant *Portsm* from 03. *9 St George's Road, Hayling Island PO11 0BS* Tel (023) 9246 7597 Mobile 07866-772025 E-mail david@dirw.demon.co.uk

WILLIAMS, David James. b 42. Chich Th Coll 67. **d** 70 **p** 71. C Charlton-by-Dover St Bart *Cant* 70-74; C Dorking w Ranmore

Guildf 74-77; C Guildf H Trin w St Mary 77-78; P-in-c E Molesey St Paul 78-88; V Burpham 88-94; rtd 95. *1 Taleworth Close, Ashtead KT21 2PU* Tel (01372) 278056

WILLIAMS, David John. b 30. Open Univ BA79. St D Coll Lamp 64. **d** 66 **p** 67. C Mold *St As* 66-69; C Llanrhos 69-71; R Llangynhafal and Llanbedr Dyffryn Clwyd 71-86; P-in-c Llanychan 77-86; RD Dyffryn Clwyd 86-95; R Ruthin w Llanrhydd 86-95; rtd 95. *16 The Park, Ruthin LL15 1PW* Tel (01824) 705746

WILLIAMS, Canon David John. b 38. AKC62. **d** 63 **p** 64. C Benchill *Man* 63-66; C Heywood St Jas 66-69; V Leesfield 69-73; Chapl TS Arethusa 73-74; TV Southend St Jo w St Mark, All SS w St Fran etc *Chelmsf* 74-80; V Horndon on the Hill 80-93; RD Thurrock 83-92; P-in-c Rochford 93-02; RD Rochford 96-02; P-in-c Sutton w Shopland 98-02; Hon Can Chelmsf Cathl 99-02; rtd 02; Perm to Offic *Ripon* from 02. *29 Stonebeck Avenue, Harrogate HG1 2BN* Tel (01423) 522828

WILLIAMS, David John. b 43. Wadh Coll Ox BA64. St Jo Coll Nottm 73. **d** 75 **p** 76. C Newcastle w Butterton *Lich* 75-79; P-in-c Oulton 79-89; P-in-c Stone Ch Ch 84-89; V Stone Ch Ch and Oulton 89-96; P-in-c Ashley 96-04; P-in-c Mucklestone 96-04; R Ashley and Mucklestone 04-07; rtd 07. *23 Gravel Hill, Ludlow SY8 1QR* Tel (01630) 672210
E-mail williamsjandm@btinternet.com

WILLIAMS, David John. b 52. NOC 92. **d** 95 **p** 96. C Gt Crosby St Luke *Liv* 95-99; V W Derby St Jas 99-04; Chapl R Liverpool Children's NHS Trust from 99. *Alder Hey Children's Hospital, Eaton Road, Liverpool L12 2AP* Tel 0151-228 4811

WILLIAMS, Canon David Leslie. b 35. ALCD63. **d** 63 **p** 64. C Bexleyheath Ch Ch *Roch* 63-64; C Gt Faringdon w L Coxwell *Ox* 64-66; CMS Uganda 67-73; C Shortlands *Roch* 73-74; Fiji 74-77; V Bromley H Trin *Roch* 77-86; R Meopham w Nurstead 86-96; RD Cobham 86-96; Chapl Thames Gateway NHS Trust 96-01; Hon Can Roch Cathl 98-01; Perm to Offic from 02. *107 Ploughmans Way, Gillingham ME8 8LT* Tel (01634) 372545

WILLIAMS, David Michael. b 50. JP86. Ex Univ BA71 Lon Univ MA77 FSA81 FRSA82. SEITE 05. **d** 08. NSM Redhill St Jo *S'wark* from 08. *Pine Cottage, Harrow Road West, Dorking RH4 3BE* Tel (01306) 885048
E-mail davidwilliams24@btinternet.com

WILLIAMS, David Michael Rochfort. b 40. St Mich Coll Llan 62. **d** 65 **p** 66. C Pembroke Dock *St D* 65-68; Chapl Miss to Seamen and Ind Chapl 68-71; P-in-c Walwyn's Castle w Robeston W 68-70; R 70-71; Ind Chapl *Mon* 71-74; Hon Chapl St Woolos Cathl 71-74; V Blaenavon w Capel Newydd 74-77; Ind Chapl *St As* 77-88; V Whitford 81-87; V Ruabon 87-92; TR Cen Telford *Lich* 92-00; R Burton and Rosemarket *St D* 00-02; Chapl Miss to Seafarers Milford Haven 00-02; Southampton 02-05; rtd 05; Perm to Offic *Ox* from 05. *13 Sturt Road, Charlbury, Chipping Norton OX7 3SX* Tel (01608) 811284

WILLIAMS, David Norman. b 54. Lanc Univ BSc76 Leeds Univ BA83. Coll of Resurr Mirfield 81. **d** 84 **p** 85. C Ireland Wood *Ripon* 84-87; C Beeston 87-91; V Cross Roads cum Lees *Bradf* 91-99; V Skipton Ch Ch 99-07; P-in-c Carleton and Lothersdale 03-07; V Skipton Ch Ch w Carleton from 07. *Christ Church Vicarage, Carleton Road, Skipton BD23 2BE* Tel (01756) 793612
E-mail dngc@hotmail.co.uk

WILLIAMS, David Paul. *See* HOWELL, David Paul

WILLIAMS, Canon David Roger. b 49. Open Univ BA. St D Coll Lamp. **d** 73 **p** 74. C Llansamlet *S & B* 73-76; C Oystermouth 76-79; V Aberedw w Llandeilo Graban and Llanbadarn etc 79-81; V Brynmawr 81-89; V Newport St Julian *Mon* 89-09; R Penarth and Llandough from 09; Hon Can St Woolos Cathl from 09. *The Rectory, 13 Hickman Road, Penarth CF64 2AJ* Tel (029) 2070 9897 E-mail fr.rogerwilliams@uwclub.net

WILLIAMS *(formerly* WRIGHT)*,* **Denise Ann.** b 42. **d** 98. Par Dn Machen *Mon* 98-07; Par Dn Bedwas w Machen w Rudry from 07. *16 Tollgate Close, Caerphilly CF83 3AY* Tel (029) 2086 9792

WILLIAMS, Denise Laraine. b 50. Liv Univ TCert71. NOC 00. **d** 03 **p** 04. C Padgate *Liv* 03-08; P-in-c Cinnamon Brow from 08. *The Rectory, 35 Station Road South, Padgate, Warrington WA2 0PD* Tel (01925) 831297

WILLIAMS, Derek. b 27. Man Univ BSc49. St Deiniol's Hawarden 76. **d** 78 **p** 79. NSM Abergele *St As* 78-97; rtd 97; Perm to Offic *St As* from 97. *48 Eldon Drive, Abergele LL22 7DA* Tel (01745) 833479

WILLIAMS, Derek Ivor. b 37. ACA61 FCA71. **d** 05 **p** 06. OLM Chollerton w Birtley and Thockrington *Newc* from 05. *Buteland House, Bellingham, Hexham NE48 2EX* Tel (01434) 220389

WILLIAMS, Derek Lawrence. b 45. Tyndale Hall Bris 65. **d** 69 **p** 70. C Cant St Mary Bredin 69-71; Sec Inter-Coll Chr Fellowship 71-75; Lic to Offic *St Alb* 78-84 and *Bris* 85-92; Par and Miss Co-ord Northampton St Giles *Pet* 93-97; Dioc Millennium Officer 98-00; Communications Officer *Pet* 00-05 and *Eur* 02-05; Bp's Admin and Press Officer from 05; Hon C Brington w Whilton and Norton etc 02-08. *The Rectory, Harlestone Road, Church Brampton, Northampton NN6 8AU* Tel

(01604) 843881 *or* (01733) 887014   Mobile 07770-981172 Fax (01604) 843894 *or* (01733) 890077
E-mail derek.williams@peterborough-diocese.org.uk

WILLIAMS, Derwyn Gavin. b 69. Trin Coll Cam BA89 MA93. Ripon Coll Cuddesdon. **d** 94 **p** 95. C Harpenden St Nic *St Alb* 94-97; Bp's Dom Chapl 97-00; R Sandy from 00; RD Biggleswade from 09. *The Rectory, High Street, Sandy SG19 1AQ* Tel (01767) 680512
E-mail rector@sandyparishchurch.org.uk

WILLIAMS, Diana Mary. b 53. Bris Univ CertEd56 Leeds Univ BSc57. Oak Hill Th Coll 86. **d** 87 **p** 94. C S Mymms K Chas *St Alb* 87-95; V 95-98; R Sandon, Wallington and Rushden w Clothall 98-04; RD Buntingford 01-06; rtd 04; Perm to Offic *Ely* from 05. *7 Cockhall Close, Litlington, Royston SG8 0RB* Tel (01763) 853079 E-mail di.williams@btinternet.com

WILLIAMS, Diane Patricia. b 53. Dur Univ CertEd74 Lanc Univ MA84. Cranmer Hall Dur 84. **dss** 86 **d** 87 **p** 94. Clubmoor *Liv* 86-90; Par Dn 87-90; Dioc Lay Tr Officer 90-96; Par Dn Everton St Geo 90-94; Assoc P 94-96; Chapl Lanc Univ 96-00; Chapl Edin Univ from 00. *Chaplaincy Centre, The University of Edinburgh, 1 Bristo Square, Edinburgh EH8 9AL* Tel 0131-650 2596 Fax 650 9111 E-mail chaplain@ed.ac.uk

WILLIAMS, Diane Ruth. b 52. Hull Univ BA80 Nottm Univ MA94. Linc Th Coll 92. **d** 94 **p** 95. C Stokesley *York* 94-98; TV Louth *Linc* 98-06; Chapl Linc and Louth NHS Trust 98-01; Chapl United Lincs Hosps NHS Trust 01-06; P-in-c Needham Market w Badley *St E* from 06; RD Bosmere from 09. *10 Meadow View, Needham Market, Ipswich IP6 8RH* Tel (01449) 720316 E-mail dnwil2@aol.com

WILLIAMS, Donald. *See* WILLIAMS, Alfred Donald

WILLIAMS, Mrs Donna Ann. b 64. St Jo Coll Nottm BA00. **d** 00 **p** 01. C Denton St Lawr *Man* 00-03; C Ashton Ch Ch 02-03; P-in-c Droylsden St Martin from 03. *St Martin's Vicarage, Greenside Lane, Droylsden, Manchester M43 7QS* Tel 0161-370 9833 E-mail sweetpea@dwilliams11.freeserve.co.uk

WILLIAMS, Dorian George. b 26. Barrister-at-Law (Gray's Inn) 52. WMMTC 91. **d** 93 **p** 94. NSM Edvin Loach w Tedstone Delamere etc *Heref* 93-98; Perm to Offic from 98. *Howberry, Whitbourne, Worcester WR6 5RZ* Tel (01886) 821189

WILLIAMS, Dylan John. b 72. Univ of Wales (Ban) BTh97. Ripon Coll Cuddesdon 97. **d** 99 **p** 00. C Holyhead *Ban* 99-01; C Dolgellau w Llanfachreth and Brithdir etc 01-02; P-in-c Amlwch 02-03; R from 03. *The Rectory, Bull Bay Road, Amlwch LL68 9EA* Tel (01407) 830740 E-mail dyljwilliams@lineone.net

WILLIAMS, Edward Ffoulkes (Peter). b 34. ALA65. Chich Th Coll 71. **d** 73 **p** 74. C Kidderminster St Geo *Worc* 73-78; TV Worc St Barn w Ch 78-82; R Exhall w Wixford and V Temple Grafton w Binton *Cov* 82-00; rtd 00; Perm to Offic *Truro* from 00. *Penpons Cottage, Treviskey, Lanner, Redruth TR16 6AU* Tel (01209) 820230

WILLIAMS, Edward Heaton. b 18. St Aid Birkenhead 56. **d** 58 **p** 59. C Timperley *Ches* 58-62; V Macclesfield St Pet 62-66; Sec Dioc Miss Bd 63-67; R Wistaston 66-81; Dioc Bd for Miss and Unity 67-69; V Burton 81-85; rtd 85; Perm to Offic *Ox* 85-94 and *Pet* from 85. *4 Bowmens Lea, Aynho, Banbury OX17 3AG* Tel (01869) 810533

WILLIAMS, Prof Edward Sydney. b 23. FRCP FRCR K Coll Lon BSc PhD MB, BS MD AKC. Sarum & Wells Th Coll 84. **d** 87 **p** 88. NSM Bramley and Grafham *Guildf* 87-89; Hon C Shamley Green 89-94; Perm to Offic from 94. *Little Hollies, The Close, Wonersh, Guildford GU5 0PA* Tel (01483) 892591

WILLIAMS *(née* WITHERS)*,* **Mrs Eleanor Jane.** b 61. Univ of Wales Coll of Medicine MB, BCh85 Anglia Ruskin Univ MA07 MRCGP89. ERMC 04. **d** 07 **p** 08. NSM Milton *Ely* from 07. *Holy Cross Vicarage, 192 Peverel Road, Cambridge CB5 8RL* Tel (01223) 413343 E-mail eleanorjw99@hotmail.com

WILLIAMS, Elfed Owain. b 24. Newc Univ DipAdEd74. St Deiniol's Hawarden 79. **d** 81 **p** 82. Hon C Whorlton *Newc* 81-82; Hon C Elham w Denton and Wootton *Cant* 82-86; R Barham w Bishopsbourne and Kingston 86-91; rtd 91; Perm to Offic *Newc* from 91. *Chusan, 31 Ryecroft Way, Wooler NE71 6DY* Tel (01668) 281253

WILLIAMS, Emlyn Cadwaladr. b 64. St Jo Coll Nottm 02. **d** 04 **p** 05. C Glanogwen w St Ann's w Llanllechid *Ban* 04-07; R Llanfihangel Ysgeifiog w Llangristiolus etc from 07. *The Rectory, Holyhead Road, Gaerwen LL60 6HP* Tel (01248) 421275 E-mail ecsaer@aol.com

WILLIAMS, Eric Rees. b 30. Roch Th Coll 60 St Deiniol's Hawarden 71. **d** 72 **p** 73. C Llanelli *St D* 72-75; P-in-c Tregaron 75-76; V 76-82; RD Lampeter and Ultra-Aeron 82-87; V Tregarron w Ystrad Meurig and Strata Florida 82-87; V St Dogmael's w Moylgrove and Monington 87-98; rtd 98. *Ty Elli, 1 Heol Derw, Cardigan SA43 1NH* Tel (01239) 612178

WILLIAMS, Evelyn Joyce. b 37. Cant Sch of Min 86. **d** 89 **p** 94. NSM Sittingbourne H Trin w Bobbing *Cant* 89-09; rtd 09; Perm to Offic *Cant* from 09. *32 Rock Road, Sittingbourne ME10 1JF* Tel (01795) 470372

WILLIAMS, Frederick Errol. b 41. MBIM80. Sarum & Wells Th Coll 86. **d** 88 **p** 89. C Milton *Win* 88-91; P-in-c Chilbolton cum

Wherwell 91-94; R 94-06; RD Andover 99-06; rtd 06. *1A Central Street, Ludgershall, Andover SP11 9RA* Tel (01264) 790135 E-mail errolsue69@btinternet.com

WILLIAMS, Gareth Wynn. b 67. St D Coll Lamp BA88 Hull Univ MA89 Trin Coll Carmarthen PGCE06. Westcott Ho Cam 89. **d** 91 **p** 92. C Mold *St As* 91-93; TV Hawarden 93-95; Ecum Chapl Glam Univ 95-99; Lect Cardiff Univ from 99; Dir Academic Studies St Mich Coll Llan 99-04; Vice-Prin 02-04; V Roath *Llan* 04-05; Perm to Offic from 05; Hd RS Hawthorn Comp Sch Pontypridd 06-08; Chapl Bp of Llan High Sch from 08. *12 Fairwater Grove West, Llandaff, Cardiff CF5 2JQ* Tel (029) 2056 9581 E-mail mail@gwwilliams.net

WILLIAMS, Gavin John. b 61. Down Coll Cam BA84 Wycliffe Hall Ox BA88 Barrister-at-Law 85. **d** 89 **p** 90. C Muswell Hill St Jas w St Matt *Lon* 89-92; Asst Chapl Shrewsbury Sch 92-95; Chapl 95-02; Chapl Westmr Sch from 02; PV Westmr Abbey from 05. *Westminster School, Little Dean's Yard, London SW1P 3PF* Tel (020) 7963 1128 E-mail gavin.williams@westminster.org.uk

WILLIAMS, Geoffrey Thomas. b 35. Ox NSM Course 77. **d** 80 **p** 81. NSM Earley St Bart *Ox* 80-82; NSM Reading St Luke 82-85; C Wembley Park St Aug *Lon* 85-86; C-in-c S Kenton Annunciation CD 86-90; V Streatham Hill St Marg *S'wark* 90-03; rtd 03; Perm to Offic *S'wark* from 04. *78 Park Court, Battersea Park Road, London SW11 4LE* Tel (020) 7498 8272

WILLIAMS, Preb George Maxwell Frazer. b 42. TCD BA65 MA69. Cuddesdon Coll 65. **d** 67 **p** 68. C Bolton St Jas w St Chrys *Bradf* 67-70; C Lich St Chad 70-73; V Shawbury 73-79; P-in-c Moreton Corbet 73-79; V Willenhall H Trin 79-86; TR 86-88; V Penn 88-07; Preb Lich Cathl 96-07; RD Trysull 02-06; rtd 07. *2 Highbury Close, Shrewsbury SY2 6SN* Tel (01743) 362315

WILLIAMS, George Ola. b 55. Bradf Univ PhD90 Waterloo Lutheran Univ MA83. St Jo Coll Nottm MTh95. **d** 96 **p** 97. C Enfield St Jas *Lon* 96-00; V Allerton *Bradf* from 00. *The Vicarage, Ley Top Lane, Allerton, Bradford BD15 7LT* Tel (01274) 541948 E-mail george.williams@bradford.anglican.org

WILLIAMS, Canon Giles Peter. b 54. Lon Univ BA77 Man MA78. Trin Coll Bris 80. **d** 82 **p** 83. C Reading Greyfriars *Ox* 82-85; Rwanda Miss 85-90; Mid-Africa Min (CMS) 90-94; Can Kigali Cathl Rwanda from 90; V Woking St Jo *Guildf* from 95; RD Woking from 08. *The Vicarage, St John's Hill Road, Woking GU21 7RQ* Tel (01483) 761253 E-mail g@gilespw.plus.com

WILLIAMS, Glyn. b 54. K Coll Lon BD77 AKC77. Ripon Coll Cuddesdon 77. **d** 78 **p** 79. C Coppenhall *Ches* 78-81; C Northampton St Alb *Pet* 81-82; TV Birkenhead Priory *Ches* 82-85; Chapl RAF 85-90 and from 96; Dep Chapl HM Pris Wandsworth 90-91; Chapl HM Pris Elmley 91-95. *Chaplaincy Services, Valiant Block, HQ Air Command, RAF High Wycombe HP14 4UE* Tel (01494) 496800 Fax 496343

WILLIAMS, Graham Parry. b 46. Bp Burgess Hall Lamp 67. **d** 70 **p** 71. C Ebbw Vale *Mon* 70-73; C Trevethin 73-74; V Nantyglo 74-76; Chapl RN 76-85; R Northlew w Ashbury *Ex* 85-87; R Bratton Clovelly w Germansweek 85-87; TV Pontypool *Mon* 88-90; C Skegness and Winthorpe *Linc* 90-91; V Sutton Bridge 91-94; P-in-c Witham Gp 94-97; P-in-c Ruskington 97-01; R 01-03; RD Lafford 02-03; P-in-c Ringstone in Aveland Gp from 03. *The Vicarage, 46A High Street, Morton, Bourne PE10 0NR* Tel (01778) 571474

WILLIAMS, Gwenllian. See GILES, Mrs Gwenllian

WILLIAMS, Gwilym Elfed. b 33. Univ of Wales (Lamp) BA53. St Mich Coll Llan 53. **d** 56 **p** 57. C Llandudno *Ban* 56-59; C Aberdare *Llan* 59-63; C Penarth All SS 63-65; R Eglwysilan 65-70; V Mountain Ash 70-81; V Llanblethian w Cowbridge and Llandough etc 81-93; P-in-c St Hilary 87-91; V Lisvane 93-00; rtd 00; Perm to Offic *Llan* from 02. *55 Heol Llanishen Fach, Cardiff CF14 6LB* Tel (029) 2062 3855

WILLIAMS, Preb Heather Marilyn. b 42. Oak Hill Th Coll 82. **dss** 85 **d** 87 **p** 94. Taunton Lyngford *B & W* 85-89; Hon C 87-89; C Worle 89-94; V Weston-super-Mare St Andr Bournville 94-03; Preb Wells Cathl 02-03; rtd 04; Perm to Offic *B & W* from 04. *2 Cliff Road, Worlebury, Weston-super-Mare BS22 9SF* Tel (01934) 420711 E-mail williams.heather@btinternet.com

WILLIAMS, Helena Maria Alija. See CERMAKOVA, Ms Helena Maria Alija

WILLIAMS, Henry Gordon. b 33. JP83. St Aid Birkenhead 57. **d** 60 **p** 61. C Radcliffe St Mary *Man* 60-63; Australia from 63; rtd 99. *36 Onslow Street, PO Box 259, Northampton WA 6535, Australia* Tel (0061) (8) 9934 1259 Fax 9934 1507 E-mail hgw@on.com.au

WILLIAMS, The Ven Henry Leslie. b 19. Univ of Wales (Lamp) BA41. St Mich Coll Llan 41. **d** 43 **p** 44. C Aberdovey *Ban* 43-45; C Ban Cathl 45-48; Chapl RN 48-49; C Ches St Mary 49-53; V Barnston 53-84; CF (TA) 54-62; RD Wirral N *Ches* 67-75; Hon Can Ches Cathl 72-75; Adn Ches 75-88; rtd 88; Perm to Offic *Ches* from 88. *1 Bartholomew Way, Chester CH4 7RJ* Tel (01244) 675296

WILLIAMS, Herbert Brian. b 18. BNC Ox BA39 MA48. Linc Th Coll 80. **d** 81 **p** 82. NSM Asterby Gp *Linc* 81-94; rtd 88; Perm to

Offic *Linc* 94-97. *55 Upgate, Louth LN11 9HD* Tel (01507) 608093

WILLIAMS, Hilary Susan. See PETTMAN, Mrs Hilary Susan

WILLIAMS, Howell Mark. b 56. Univ of Wales (Cardiff) BD87. St Mich Coll Llan 84. **d** 87 **p** 88. C Swansea St Thos and Kilvey *S & B* 87-89; TV Aberystwyth *St D* 89-93; V Hirwaun *Llan* 93-99; V Swansea St Pet *S & B* from 99; AD Penderi from 05. *St Peter's Vicarage, 59 Station Road, Fforestfach, Swansea SA5 5AU* Tel (01792) 581514 E-mail stpeters@googlemail.com

WILLIAMS, Hugh Marshall. b 38. Lon Univ MB, BS62 Liv Univ MChOrth71 FRCS70. SAOMC 95. **d** 97 **p** 98. NSM Lt Compton w Chastleton, Cornwell etc *Ox* 97-01; NSM Chipping Norton 01-08; rtd 08; Perm to Offic *Ox* from 08; *Cov* and *Glouc* from 09. *Wayside, Worcester Road, Salford, Chipping Norton OX7 5YJ* Tel (01608) 646933 Mobile 07889-343456 E-mail hmwwayside@yahoo.co.uk

WILLIAMS, Canon Hugh Martin. b 45. AKC73. St Aug Coll Cant 73. **d** 74 **p** 75. C Heston *Lon* 74-78; Chapl City Univ 78-84; PV Westmr Abbey 82-84; V Newquay *Truro* 84-93; V Christchurch *Win* from 93; Hon Can Win Cathl from 04. *The Priory Vicarage, Quay Road, Christchurch BH23 1BU* Tel (01202) 483102 E-mail hugh.m.williams@ukgateway.net

WILLIAMS, Ian Withers. b 43. Linc Th Coll 68. **d** 69 **p** 70. C Burney Lane *Birm* 69-72; C Cleobury Mortimer w Hopton Wafers *Heref* 72-75; V Knowbury 75-79; P-in-c Coreley and Doddington 75-79; V Lich Ch Ch 79-06; rtd 06; Perm to Offic *Heref* from 07. *23 The Oaklands, Tenbury Wells WR15 8FB* Tel (01584) 810528 Mobile 07711-260521

WILLIAMS, Ifan. b 24. St D Coll Lamp 54. **d** 56 **p** 57. C Llangefni w Tregaean *Ban* 56-60; R Llanfachreth 60-67; Dioc Youth Officer 62-65; Area Sec (Merioneth) USPG 63-89; P-in-c Brithdir and Bryncoedifor *Ban* 65-67; R Ffestiniog w Blaenau Ffestiniog 67-89; RD Ardudwy 80-89; rtd 89; Perm to Offic *Ban* from 89. *Cil-y-Coed, 6 Stad Penrallt, Llanystumdwy, Criccieth LL52 0SR* Tel (01766) 522974

WILLIAMS, Mrs Ikuko. b 58. Internat Chr Univ Tokyo BA82 W Michigan Univ MA83 Leeds Univ BA07. NOC 04. **d** 07 **p** 08. NSM Burmantofts St Steph and St Agnes *Ripon* from 07; NSM Leeds St Cypr Harehills from 07. *97 Gledhow Lane, Leeds LS8 1NE* Tel 0113-266 2385 E-mail ikuko.williams@ntlworld.com

WILLIAMS, James Llanfair Warren. b 48. St Mich Coll Llan 92. **d** 92 **p** 93. C Pembroke Dock *St D* 92-93; C Pembroke Dock w Cosheston w Nash and Upton 93-95; V Cwmaman 95-98; Chapl Costa Blanca *Eur* 98-00; V Meifod w Llangynyw w Pont Robert w Pont Dolanog *St As* from 01. *The Vicarage, Meifod SY22 6DH* Tel (01938) 500231

WILLIAMS, James Nicholas Owen. b 39. MBE. CEng. S'wark Ord Course. **d** 82 **p** 83. C Petersfield w Sheet *Portsm* 82-86; TV Droitwich Spa *Worc* 86-88; R Church Lench w Rous Lench and Abbots Morton 88-94; V Milton *B & W* 94-04; RD Locking 99-04; rtd 04; Dioc Ecum Officer *B & W* 04-08; Hon C Pill, Portbury and Easton-in-Gordano from 04. *151 Charlton Mead Drive, Brentry, Bristol BS10 6LP* Tel 0117-950 4152 E-mail nick.williams@bathwells.anglican.org

WILLIAMS, Janet Patricia. See FFRENCH, Mrs Janet Patricia

WILLIAMS, Janet Patricia. b 61. Univ Coll Ox BA83 MSt85 K Alfred's Coll Win PhD98. WEMTC 06. **d** 09. NSM Cirencester *Glouc* from 09. *April Cottage, Elkstone, Gloucester GL53 9PB* Tel (01242) 870148 Mobile 07989-707257 E-mail jpw@cirencester.ac.uk

WILLIAMS, Jeff. b 62. Southn Univ BA MA MPhil Univ of Wales PGCE Surrey Univ BA. STETS 04. **d** 07 **p** 08. NSM Hedge End St Luke *Win* from 07. *32 Goodlands Vale, Hedge End, Southampton SO30 4SL* Tel (01489) 781448 E-mail jeff.w@ntlworld.com

WILLIAMS, Jeffrey. See WILLIAMS, Robert Jeffrey Hopkin

WILLIAMS, Jeffrey. b 52. Llan Ord Course. **d** 03 **p** 04. NSM Cardiff St Mary and St Steph w St Dyfrig etc *Llan* 03-07; Chapl Malta and Gozo *Eur* from 07. *Bishop's House, 75 Rudolphe Street, Sliema SLM14, Malta GC* Tel (00356) 2133 0575 Fax 2133 3677 E-mail jeffreywilliams@ntlworld.com

WILLIAMS, Ms Jennifer Ruth. b 66. St Hugh's Coll Ox BA88 PGCE89 Man Univ MA00. Wycliffe Hall Ox 98 NOC 00. **d** 00 **p** 01. C Heatons *Man* 00-04; Hon C Burnage St Marg 04-05; Lect Wycliffe Hall Ox from 05. *Wycliffe Hall, 54 Banbury Road, Oxford OX2 6PW* Tel (01865) 274200 or 201821 E-mail jenniwilliams@wycliffe.ox.ac.uk

WILLIAMS, John. See WILLIAMS, David John

WILLIAMS, Canon John. b 31. AKC56. **d** 57 **p** 58. C Cockerton *Dur* 57-60; C Camberwell St Geo *S'wark* 60-62; C Stockton St Chad *Dur* 62-65; V 65-68; R Longnewton 68-75; Soc Resp Officer 68-83; Hon Can Dur Cathl 80-83; Bp's Officer for Min *Lich* 83-96; Preb Lich Cathl 83-96; V Lich St Mary w St Mich 95-96; rtd 96; NSM Edin Ch Ch from 97. *2 Fox Spring Rise, Edinburgh EH10 6NE* Tel and fax 0131-445 2983 E-mail jwilliams@foxsprings.plus.com

WILLIAMS, John. b 82. St Chad's Coll Dur BA04. Coll of Resurr Mirfield 05. **d** 07 **p** 08. C Upper Skerne *Dur* from 07. *19 Wallington Drive, Sedgefield, Stockton-on-Tees TS21 2HZ* Tel (01740) 621186 E-mail curate.upperskerne@yahoo.co.uk

WILLIAMS, John Anthony. b 53. G&C Coll Cam BA75 MA79 St Jo Coll Dur BA83 PhD86. Cranmer Hall Dur 81. **d** 86 **p** 87. C Beverley Minster *York* 86-89; C Cloughton 89-90; P-in-c 90-93; Clergy Tr Officer E Riding 89-93; P-in-c Emley and Dioc Minl Tr Officer *Wakef* 93-98; Min Scheme Officer 98-06; Co-ord for Local Min 02-06; Dean Wakef Min Scheme 06-08; Hon Can Wakef Cathl 08; Sen Lect York St Jo Univ from 08. *23 Walmer Carr, Wigginton, York YO32 2SX* Tel (01904) 750643

WILLIAMS, John Barrie. b 38. Univ of Wales (Cardiff) MSc77 DipEd80 PhD91. St Mich Coll Llan 89. **d** 87 **p** 88. NSM Newcastle *Llan* 87-89; C Port Talbot St Theodore 89; Perm to Offic from 89. *Shorncliffe, 11 Priory Oak, Bridgend CF31 2HY* Tel (01656) 660369

WILLIAMS, John Beattie. b 42. Univ of Wales BA66. Cuddesdon Coll 67. **d** 69 **p** 69. C St Helier *S'wark* 69-70; C Yeovil H Trin *B & W* 70-76; Chapl to the Deaf *Sarum* 76-78; P-in-c Ebbesbourne Wake w Fifield Bavant and Alvediston 76-78; Chapl to the Deaf *B & W* 78-83; TV Fareham H Trin *Portsm* 83-94; R W Wittering and Birdham w Itchenor *Chich* from 94. *The Rectory, Pound Road, West Wittering, Chichester PO20 8AJ* Tel (01243) 514057 E-mail info@stpeterandstpaul.plus.com

WILLIAMS, John David Anthony. b 55. Open Univ BA98. St Steph Ho Ox 85. **d** 87 **p** 88. C Paignton St Jo *Ex* 87-90; C Heavitree w Ex St Paul 90-91; TV 91-01; P-in-c Exminster and Kenn from 01. *The Rectory, Milbury Lane, Exminster, Exeter EX6 8AD* Tel (01392) 824283 E-mail john_williams55@btinternet.com

WILLIAMS, John Francis Meyler. b 34. St Jo Coll Cam BA56 MA60. Sarum & Wells Th Coll 79. **d** 81 **p** 82. C Hadleigh w Layham and Shelley *St E* 81-84; P-in-c Parham w Hacheston 84-87; P-in-c Campsey Ashe and Marlesford 84-87; R Campsea Ashe w Marlesford, Parham and Hacheston 87-95; P-in-c Kedington 95-97; rtd 97; Chapl St Kath Convent Parmoor 97-98; Perm to Offic *Ox* 01-05. *Ashgrove, Smyth Street, Fishguard SA65 9LG* Tel (01348) 871971 E-mail john.llwynonn@waitrose.com

WILLIAMS, John Frederick Arthur. b 26. Lon Univ BSc50 Southn Univ PhD53. Ridley Hall Cam 63. **d** 65 **p** 66. C Cambridge H Sepulchre w All SS *Ely* 65-66; P-in-c Cambridge St Mark 66-67; V Portswood Ch Ch *Win* 67-90; Assoc V 90-93; C Win Ch Ch 93-96; rtd 96; Perm to Offic *Win* from 96. *120 Bellemoor Road, Southampton SO5 7QY* Tel (023) 8077 1482

WILLIAMS, John Gilbert. b 36. St Aid Birkenhead 64. **d** 67 **p** 68. C Bollington St Jo *Ches* 67-69; C Oxton 69-72; P-in-c Acton Beauchamp and Evesbatch 72-76; P-in-c Castle Frome *Heref* 72-76; P-in-c Bishop's Frome 72-76; R Kingsland 76-83; P-in-c Eardisland 77-83; P-in-c Aymestry and Leinthall Earles 82-83; R Cradley w Mathon and Storridge 83-94; R Norton St Philip w Hemington, Hardington etc *B & W* 94-01; rtd 01; Perm to Offic *St D* from 02. *Bronydd, Parc y Plas, Aberporth, Cardigan SA43 2BZ* Tel (01239) 810268 E-mail j.s@johngwilliams.fsnet.co.uk

WILLIAMS, Canon John Ilcard. b 35. Bris Univ BA58. Clifton Th Coll 59. **d** 59 **p** 60. C Tunbridge Wells Ch Ch *Roch* 59-65; V Forest Gate St Sav *Chelmsf* 65-75; P-in-c W Ham St Matt 72-75; TR Forest Gate St Sav w W Ham St Matt from 75; Hon Can Chelmsf Cathl 82-05. *St Saviour's Rectory, Sidney Road, London E7 0EF* Tel (020) 8534 6109

WILLIAMS, Canon John James. b 20. TD61. Linc Coll Ox BA42 MA46. St Mich Coll Llan 42. **d** 44 **p** 45. C Rhosymedre *St As* 44-47; C Flint 47-50; CF 49-62; C Llanrhos *St As* 50-53; V Whixall *Lich* 53-57; V Prees 57-64; Sen CF (TA) 62-67; CF (TA) 67-68; V Powick *Worc* 64-85; Hon Can Worc Cathl 77-85; rtd 85; Perm to Offic *Worc* from 85. *1 Abbotts Road, Pershore WR10 1LL* Tel (01386) 553518

WILLIAMS, John Keith. b 63. Ridley Hall Cam 95. **d** 97 **p** 98. C Potters Bar *St Alb* 97-99; C Bishop's Stortford St Mich 99-01; P-in-c Bishop's Stortford 01-08; TR Cheshunt from 08. *The Vicarage, Churchgate, Cheshunt, Waltham Cross EN8 9DY* Tel (01992) 623121

WILLIAMS, Prof John Mark Gruffydd. b 52. St Pet Coll Ox BA73 MSc76 MA77 DPhil79 Ox Univ DSc FBPsS84. EAMTC 86. **d** 89 **p** 90. NSM Girton *Ely* 89-91; Perm to Offic *Ban* 91-03; NSM Wheatley *Ox* 03-09; Perm to Offic from 09. *Hollyfield Cottage, 17 Bell Lane, Wheatley, Oxford OX33 1XY* Tel (01865) 422037 E-mail mark.williams@psychiatry.oxford.ac.uk

WILLIAMS, John Michael. b 44. CQSW74 MBASW. St Deiniol's Hawarden 80. **d** 83 **p** 84. NSM Llanrhos *St As* 83-94; P-in-c Brynymaen w Trofarth 94-95; V 95-99; V Llanrhaeadr-yng-Nghinmeirch w Prion and Nantglyn from 99. *The Vicarage, Llanrhaeadr, Denbigh LL16 4NN* Tel (01745) 890250 E-mail vicar@stdyfnog.org.uk

WILLIAMS, Canon John Peter Philip. b 49. Open Univ BA84. Chich Th Coll 71. **d** 72 **p** 73. C Abergele *St As* 72-77; R Henllan and Llannefydd 77-82; R Henllan and Llannefydd and Bylchau from 82; AD Denbigh from 98; Hon Can St As Cathl from 01. *The Rectory, Henllan, Denbigh LL16 5BB* Tel (01745) 812628

WILLIAMS, John Roger. b 31. Bris Univ BA55 Lon Univ BD57. Tyndale Hall Bris 57. **d** 57 **p** 58. C Islington H Trin Cloudesley Square *Lon* 57-60; Travelling Sec IVF 60-64; V Selly Hill St Steph *Birm* 64-74; P-in-c Chilwell *S'well* 74-75; V 75-90; Dioc Tourism Officer 90-95; P-in-c Perlethorpe 90-95; P-in-c Norton Cuckney 90-95; rtd 95; Perm to Offic *Derby* from 95. *Derwent Lights, 4 Wyntor Avenue, Winster, Matlock DE4 2DU* Tel (01629) 650142

WILLIAMS, Canon John Roger. b 37. Westmr Coll Ox MTh97. Lich Th Coll 60. **d** 63 **p** 64. C Wem *Lich* 63-66; C Wolverhampton St Pet 66-69; R Pudleston w Hatf *Heref* 69-74; P-in-c Stoke Prior and Ford w Humber 69-74; P-in-c Docklow 69-74; V Fenton *Lich* 74-81; R Shipston-on-Stour w Honington and Idlicote *Cov* 81-92; RD Shipston 83-90; Hon Can Cov Cathl 90-00; R Lighthorne 92-00; V Chesterton 92-00; V Newbold Pacey w Moreton Morrell 92-00; P-in-c Denstone w Ellastone and Stanton *Lich* 00-05; Master St Jo Hosp Lich from 05. *The Master's House, St John's Hospital, St John Street, Lichfield WS13 6PB* Tel (01543) 251884 Fax 418062

WILLIAMS, John Strettle. b 44. MBE00. DipEd73 BA84. NOC 77. **d** 80 **p** 81. Chapl Cen Liv Coll of FE 80-85; Chapl City Coll Liv 85-09; NSM Liv St Paul Stoneycroft 80-83; NSM Liv Our Lady and St Nic 83-09; Chapl RNR 84-90; CF (TA) from 95; rtd 09. *28 Brook Street, Whiston, Prescot L35 5AP* Tel 0151-426 9598

WILLIAMS, John Trefor. b 23. Worc Ord Coll 65. **d** 67 **p** 68. C Paignton St Jo *Ex* 67-72; V Winkleigh 72-80; P-in-c Ashreigney 73-79; R 79-80; P-in-c Brushford 75-79; V 79-80; R Broadwoodkelly 79-80; P-in-c Berrynarbor 80-81; P-in-c Combe Martin 80-81; R Combe Martin and Berrynarbor 81-92; rtd 92; Perm to Offic *Ex* from 92. *97 Littleham Road, Exmouth EX8 2RA* Tel (01395) 264460

WILLIAMS, Jonathan Anthony. b 65. Wycliffe Hall Ox BTh95. **d** 98 **p** 99. C Denton Ch Ch *Man* 98-02; R Burnage St Marg 02-05; Hon C Ox St Matt from 09. *15 Wytham Street, Oxford OX1 4SU* Tel (01865) 201821

WILLIAMS, Jonathan Lane. b 59. Dorset Inst of HE 85. STETS 96. **d** 99 **p** 00. NSM Moordown *Win* from 99. *28 Queen Mary Avenue, Moordown, Bournemouth BH9 1TS* Tel and fax (01202) 531630 Mobile 07977-444186 E-mail jonathan.williams7@ntlworld.com

WILLIAMS, Canon Jonathan Simon. b 60. Univ of Wales (Cardiff) BSc81. Coll of Resurr Mirfield 83. **d** 86 **p** 87. C Gelligaer *Llan* 86-89; C Cwmbran *Mon* 89-90; TV 90-97; V Marshfield and Peterstone Wentloog etc 97-00; TR Bassaleg from 00; AD Bassaleg from 99; Can St Woolos Cathl from 07. *The Vicarage, 1 Church View, Bassaleg, Newport NP10 8ND* Tel (01633) 893258 E-mail jonathanwilliams770@btinternet.com

WILLIAMS, Mrs Josephine. b 42. NOC 05. **d** 07 **p** 08. NSM Bootle Ch Ch *Liv* from 07. *179 Worcester Road, Bootle L20 9AE* Tel 0151 933 7779 Fax 525 1995 E-mail josiewilliams1@aol.com

WILLIAMS, Ms Josephine Mary. b 47. Reading Univ BEd78 Hatf Poly MEd87. SAOMC 96. **d** 99 **p** 00. NSM Terriers *Ox* 99-02; Chapl HM YOI Aylesbury 02-09; rtd 09. *5 Abbotts Vale, Chesham HP5 3HN* Tel (01494) 791089

WILLIAMS, Joyce. *See* WILLIAMS, Mrs Kathleen Joyce

WILLIAMS, Julian Thomas. b 65. Clare Coll Cam BA87. Wycliffe Hall Ox BA90. **d** 91 **p** 92. Min Can St D Cathl 91-94; C St D Cathl 91-94; V Cil-y-Cwm and Ystrad-ffin w Rhandir-mwyn etc 94-00; R Nursling and Rownhams *Win* from 00. *The Vicarage, 27 Horns Drove, Rownhams, Southampton SO16 8AH* Tel (023) 8073 8293

WILLIAMS, Mrs Kathleen Joyce. b 47. Dur Univ TCert71. St Jo Coll Nottm 03. **d** 05 **p** 06. C Exning St Martin w Landwade *St E* 05-08; V from 08. *The Vicarage, 1 New River Green, Exning, Newmarket CB8 7HS* Tel (01638) 577825 E-mail joyfulwilliams2004@yahoo.co.uk

WILLIAMS, Keith. b 37. St Jo Coll Nottm 83. **d** 85 **p** 86. C Holbeck *Ripon* 85-88; R Swillington 88-95; V Batley All SS *Wakef* 95-01; P-in-c Purlwell 95-00; rtd 01; Perm to Offic *Ripon* from 01. *17 Kirkfield Drive, Colton, Leeds LS15 9DR* Tel 0113-260 5852 Mobile 07709-027328 E-mail kwilliams000@btclick.com

WILLIAMS, Keith Douglas. b 41. EMMTC 86. **d** 89 **p** 90. NSM Netherfield w Colwick *S'well* from 89; NSM Gedling from 95; Chapl Notts Healthcare NHS Trust 93-03. *19 Eastholme Croft, Nottingham NG2 4DZ* Tel 0115 961 4850 E-mail keiwil@ntlworld.com

WILLIAMS, Keith Graham. b 38. Reading Univ MSc70 MRICS62. Cranmer Hall Dur. **d** 77 **p** 78. C Almondbury *Wakef* 77-81; C Chapelthorpe 81-82; V Ryhill 82-88; V E Ardsley 88-99; RD Wakef 96-99; rtd 03; Perm to Offic *Chich* from 03. *The*

Granary, 52-54 Belle Hill, Bexhill-on-Sea TN40 2AP Tel (01424) 734093

WILLIAMS, Kelvin George John. b 36. ALCD62. **d** 62 **p** 63. C Bath Abbey w St Jas *B & W* 62-65; CF (TA) 64-65 and 70-79; Chapl R Nat Hosp for Rheumatic Diseases Bath 64-65; CF 65-68; C Clevedon St Andr *B & W* 68-70; V Ston Easton w Farrington Gurney 70-74; P-in-c Bradford 74-75; R Bradford w Oake, Hillfarrance and Heathfield 75-76; NSM Puriton and Pawlett 89-91; V 92-02; NSM Bridgwater Deanery 91-92; rtd 02; Perm to Offic *B & W* 03-04 and from 07; P-in-c Weston Zoyland w Chedzoy 04-07. *Highlands, Knowleyards Road, Middlezoy, Bridgwater TA7 0NY* Tel (01823) 698413
E-mail kelvin@revwilliams.freeserve.co.uk

WILLIAMS (*née* HANNAH), **Mrs Kimberley Victoria.** b 75. Bp Grosseteste Coll BSc98. Ripon Coll Cuddesdon BTh01. **d** 01 **p** 02. C Machynlleth w Llanwrin and Penegoes *Ban* 01-02; C Twrcelyn Deanery from 02. *The Rectory, Bull Bay Road, Amlwch LL68 9EA* Tel and fax (01407) 831670
E-mail kimwilliams@lineone.net

WILLIAMS, Lee Lawrence. b 75. St Steph Ho Ox 98. **d** 01 **p** 02. C Cowbridge *Llan* 01-04. *34 Queens Drive, Llantwit Fadre, Pontypridd CF83 2NT*

WILLIAMS, Mrs Linda Leonie Paula. b 56. UEA BA79. SEITE 04. **d** 07 **p** 08. NSM Kenley *S'wark* from 07. *63 The Vale, Coulsdon CR5 2AU* Tel (020) 8660 9240
E-mail lnv@williams8919.fsnet.co.uk

WILLIAMS, Lloyd. b 43. Oak Hill Th Coll 71. **d** 74 **p** 75. C Laisterdyke *Bradf* 74-77; C Hoole *Ches* 77-80; V Rawthorpe *Wakef* 80-84; HM Pris Leeds 84-85; Chapl HM Pris Cardiff 85-88; Chapl HM Pris Aldington 88-95; R Aldington w Bonnington and Bilsington *Cant* 88-95; RD N Lympne 94-95; P-in-c Tuen Mun Hong Kong 95-99; V Clayton *Bradf* 99-03; rtd 03; Perm to Offic *York* 04-07. *46 Royd Court, Mirfield WF14 9DJ* Tel (01924) 480898 Mobile 07866-604345

WILLIAMS, Lois. *See* WILLIAMS, Ms Catherine Lois

WILLIAMS, Mrs Louise Margaret. b 66. Lanc Univ BA87. St Jo Coll Nottm 88. **d** 91 **p** 94. Par Dn W Ham *Chelmsf* 91-94; C Harold Hill St Geo 94-95; Perm to Offic 95-96; C Southend St Sav Westcliff from 95; Chapl Asst Southend Health Care NHS Trust from 97. *St Saviour's Vicarage, 33 King's Road, Westcliff-on-Sea SS0 8LL* Tel (01702) 342920
E-mail stsasaviour@aol.com

WILLIAMS, Malcolm Clive. b 50. Univ Coll Worc BA(Ed)04. Trin Coll Bris 74. **d** 04 **p** 05. NSM Amesbury *Sarum* 04-08; P-in-c Brighstone and Brooke w Mottistone *Portsm* from 08; P-in-c Shorwell w Kingston from 08; P-in-c Chale from 08. *The Rectory, Rectory Lane, Brighstone, Newport PO30 4QH* Tel (01983) 740267 E-mail williamsmc@btinternet.com

WILLIAMS, Marion. **d** 08 **p** 09. NSM Glouc St Cath from 08. *6 Kingsholm Square, Gloucester GL1 2QJ* Tel (01452) 538440
E-mail marion-williams@hotmail.co.uk

WILLIAMS, Mark. b 64. St Mich Coll Llan BTh94. **d** 97 **p** 98. C Mountain Ash *Llan* 97; C Mountain Ash and Miskin 97-99; C Neath w Llantwit 99-01; C Neath 01-02; V Skewen from 02. *New Skewen Vicarage, 39 Hill Road, Neath Abbey, Neath SA10 7NP* Tel (01792) 814116

WILLIAMS, Mark. b 73. Pemb Coll Cam BA94 MA98 Ox Univ BA98 MA02. Ripon Coll Cuddesdon 95 Ven English Coll Rome 97. **d** 98 **p** 99. C Caerphilly *Llan* 98-00; V Walworth St Chris *S'wark* from 00; Warden Pemb Coll (Cam) Miss from 00; Dioc Voc Adv from 02. *45 Aldbridge Street, London SE17 2RG* Tel (020) 7701 4162 *or* 7703 3803 E-mail fr_mark@yahoo.com

WILLIAMS, Mark John. b 66. St Martin's Coll Lanc BA88 PGCE93 Heythrop Coll Lon MA07. Cranmer Hall Dur 98. **d** 00 **p** 01. C Hockerill *St Alb* 00-03; TV Chipping Barnet from 03; Chapl RAF from 09. *Chaplaincy Services, Valiant Block, HQ Air Command, RAF High Wycombe HP14 4UE* Tel (01494) 496800 Fax 496343 E-mail mark.john.williams@lineone.net

WILLIAMS, Mark Robert. b 62. Spurgeon's Coll Lon BA83 Univ Coll of Swansea PGCE84. Ripon Coll Cuddesdon 99. **d** 01 **p** 02. C Wellington and Distr *B & W* 01-05; V Belmont *S'wark* from 05. *St John's Vicarage, Belmont Rise, Sutton SM2 6EA* Tel (020) 8642 2363 E-mail blots@lineone.net

WILLIAMS, The Ven Martin Infeld. b 37. SS Coll Cam BA62 MA92. Chich Th Coll 62. **d** 64 **p** 65. C Greenford H Cross *Lon* 64-70; Tutor Chich Th Coll 70-75; Vice-Prin 75-77; V Roath St German *Llan* 77-92; Adn Margam 92-01; Adn Morgannwg 02-04; Treas Llan Cathl 92-04; V Penydarren 92-04; rtd 04. *29 Blackfriars Court, Brecon LD3 8LJ* Tel (01874) 622351

WILLIAMS, Martin Jonathan. b 63. Birm Univ BA84. Trin Coll Bris 96. **d** 98 **p** 99. C Bisley and W End *Guildf* 98-01; C Gerrards Cross and Fulmer Ox from 01; R from 06. *Willowbrook, 54 The Uplands, Gerrards Cross SL9 7JG* Tel (01753) 892571 Mobile 07974-010703 E-mail williamsmartinj@cs.com

WILLIAMS, Mary Edith. b 50. Darlington Tr Coll BEd73. Cranmer Hall Dur 00. **d** 02 **p** 03. C Filey *York* 02-06; V from 06. *The Vicarage, 5 Belle Vue Crescent, Filey YO14 9AD* Tel (01723) 512745 E-mail brmewilliams@supanet.com

WILLIAMS, Mary Elizabeth. b 72. Huddersfield Univ BMus96. Qu Coll Birm BA06. **d** 06 **p** 07. C Birstall and Wanlip *Leic* 06-09. *Address temp unknown* E-mail mary@eclectic.myzen.co.uk

WILLIAMS, Mervyn Gwynne. b 66. WEMTC 97. **d** 06 **p** 07. NSM Stokesay *Heref* from 06; NSM Halford w Sibdon Carwood from 06; NSM Acton Scott from 06; Perm to Offic *Lich* from 08. *Synolds Farm, All Stretton, Church Stretton SY6 6JP* Tel (01694) 722093

WILLIAMS, Mervyn Rees. b 28. Univ of Wales (Swansea) BA49 Lon Univ PGCE54. St Deiniol's Hawarden 68. **d** 72 **p** 73. NSM Llangollen w Trevor and Llantysilio *St As* 72-94; rtd 94. *12 Wern Road, Llangollen LL20 8DU* Tel (01978) 860369

WILLIAMS, The Ven Meurig Llwyd. b 61. Univ of Wales (Abth) BA83 PGCE84 Univ of Wales (Cardiff) BD90. Westcott Ho Cam 90. **d** 92 **p** 93. C Holyhead w Rhoscolyn w Llanfair-yn-Neubwll *Ban* 92-95; P-in-c Denio w Abererch 95-96; V 96-99; V Cardiff Dewi Sant *Llan* 99-05; Adn Ban from 05; TR Bangor from 06. *The Archdeaconry, 1 Belmont Road, Bangor LL57 2LL* Tel (01248) 354360 E-mail mllwyd@aol.com

WILLIAMS, Michael. *See* WILLIAMS, David Michael Rochfort

WILLIAMS, Michael. b 70. St Jo Coll Nottm BA98. **d** 98 **p** 99. C Shifnal *Lich* 98-01; TV Stafford 01-06; TR Penkridge from 06. *The Rectory, New Road, Penkridge, Stafford ST19 5DN* Tel (01785) 712378

WILLIAMS, Michael Dermot Andrew. b 57. Ex Univ BA86 Lon Univ MA02. Ripon Coll Cuddesdon 90. **d** 92 **p** 93. NSM Christow, Ashton, Trusham and Bridford *Ex* 92-97; NSM Marston w Elsfield Ox 97-99; Chief Exec Radcliffe Infirmary NHS Trust 97-99; V Shipton-under-Wychwood w Milton, Fifield etc Ox 99-02; RD Chipping Norton 01-02; Exec Dir Thames Valley HA 02-05; NSM Kennington 04-05; Chief Exec Taunton and Somerset NHS Trust from 05; Hon C Topsham *Ex* from 07. *3 Perriams, Old Ebford Lane, Ebford, Exeter EX3 0QB* Tel (01392) 874087 E-mail williamsmda@btinternet.com

WILLIAMS, Michael John. b 31. St Edm Hall Ox BA53 MA57. Wells Th Coll 53. **d** 55 **p** 56. C Wood Green St Mich *Lon* 55-59; C Bedminster St Aldhelm *Bris* 59-62; C Witney *Ox* 62-65; C Thatcham 66-70; Perm to Offic *Ex* 70-81; C Rainhill *Liv* 81-86; Chapl Whiston Hosp 83-86; rtd 86; Perm to Offic *Ex* from 86. *1 Bramble Lane, Crediton EX17 1DA* Tel (01363) 774005

WILLIAMS, Canon Michael Joseph. b 42. St Jo Coll Dur BA68. Bernard Gilpin Soc Dur 63 Cranmer Hall Dur 64. **d** 70 **p** 71. C Toxteth Park St Philemon *Liv* 70-75; TV Toxteth St Philemon w St Gabr 75-78; Dir Past Studies St Jo Coll Dur 78-88; Prin NOC 89-99; Hon Can Liv Cathl 92-99; P-in-c Bolton St Pet *Man* 99-04; V 04-07; P-in-c Bolton St Phil 04-07; Hon Can Man Cathl 00-07; AD Bolton 02-05; rtd 07; Perm to Offic *Man* from 08. *51 Cotswold Drive, Horwich, Bolton BL6 7DE* Tel (01204) 667162

WILLIAMS, Michael Robert John. b 41. Cranmer Hall Dur 67. **d** 70 **p** 71. C Middleton *Man* 70-73; C-in-c Blackley White Moss St Mark CD 73-79; R Blackley St Mark White Moss 79-86; R Gorton Em 86-96; R Gorton Em w St Jas 96-06; rtd 06; Perm to Offic *Man* from 06. *26 Hawthorn Avenue, Bury BL8 1DU* Tel 0161-761 4712

WILLIAMS, Mrs Nia Catrin. b 69. Univ of Wales (Cardiff) BTh96. St As Minl Tr Course 97. **d** 98 **p** 99. C Llanrhos *St As* 98-02; C Colwyn Bay 02-06; P-in-c Towyn and St George 06-08; V Glanogwen and Llanllechid w St Ann's and Pentir *Ban* from 08. *Y Ficardy, 5 Rhos y Nant, Bethesda, Bangor LL57 3PP* Tel (01248) 605149 E-mail niacatrinwilliams@btopenworld.com

WILLIAMS, Nicholas Jolyon. b 68. Univ of Wales (Swansea) BA89. Wycliffe Hall Ox BTh96. **d** 96 **p** 97. C Ditton *Roch* 96-99; C N Farnborough *Guildf* 99-05; P-in-c Tongham from 05. *The Vicarage, Poyle Road, Tongham, Farnham GU10 1DU* Tel (01252) 782224 E-mail nickthevic@stpaulstongham.org.uk

WILLIAMS, Nicholas Lindsey. b 62. Birkbeck Coll Lon BA02. SEITE 06. **d** 09. NSM Dartford H Trin *Roch* from 09. *36 Hawthorn Road, Bexleyheath DA6 7AE* Tel (020) 8301 0629 Mobile 07747-617262 E-mail nicholaslwilliams@tiscali.co.uk

WILLIAMS, Nick. *See* WILLIAMS, James Nicholas Owen

WILLIAMS, Nigel Howard. b 63. St Mich Coll Llan 93. **d** 95 **p** 96. C Denbigh and Nantglyn *St As* 95-97; P-in-c Llanrwst and Llanddoget and Capel Garmon 97-98; R 98-04; V Colwyn Bay 04-08; V Colwyn Bay w Brynymaen from 08; AD Rhos 04-09. *The Vicarage, 27 Walshaw Avenue, Colwyn Bay LL29 7UY* Tel (01492) 539522

WILLIAMS, Norman Ernest. b 23. IEng FIEEE MIET. Llan Dioc Tr Scheme 78. **d** 82 **p** 83. NSM Llanblethian w Cowbridge and Llandough etc *Llan* 82-93; rtd 93; Perm to Offic *Llan* from 93. *The Poplars, Southgate, Cowbridge CF71 7BD* Tel (01446) 772107 E-mail normanewilliams@compuserve.com

WILLIAMS, Norman Leigh. b 50. Univ BA86 Trin Coll Carmarthen 83. **d** 85 **p** 86. NSM Loughor *S & B* 85-96; NSM Adnry Gower 87-96; rtd 96. *Gorwydd Villa, 13 The Woodlands, Gowerton, Swansea SA4 3DP* Tel (01792) 874853

WILLIAMS, Olivia Hazel. b 55. Dun Laoghaire Inst CertEd98 TCD BTh01. CITC 98. **d** 01 **p** 02. C Greystones *D & G* 01-05; Abp's Dom Chapl 03-05; I Carlow w Urglin and Staplestown

C & O from 05. *The Rectory, Green Road, Carlow, Republic of Ireland* Tel (00353) (59) 913 2565
E-mail carlow@leighlin.anglican.org

WILLIAMS, Owen David. b 38. S'wark Ord Course 72. **d** 75 **p** 76. NSM Tatsfield *S'wark* 75-80; C Maidstone All SS w St Phil and H Trin *Cant* 80-81; C Maidstone All SS and St Phil w Tovil 81-82; V St Nicholas at Wade w Sarre and Chislet w Hoath 82-92; TV Bruton and Distr *B & W* 92-98; R Kirkby Fleetham w Langton on Swale and Scruton *Ripon* 98-03; rtd 03; P-in-c Walford and St John, Howle Hill etc *Heref* 03-08. *The Vicarage, Walford, Ross-on-Wye HR9 5QP* Tel (01989) 562703

WILLIAMS, Paul Andrew. b 62. Oak Hill Th Coll BA91. **d** 91 **p** 92. C Ware Ch Ch *St Alb* 91-94; C Harold Wood *Chelmsf* 94-99; C Langham Place All So *Lon* 99-06; V Fulwood *Sheff* from 06. *The Vicarage, 2 Chorley Drive, Sheffield S10 3RR* Tel 0114-230 1911 E-mail paul@fulwoodchurch.co.uk

✠**WILLIAMS, The Rt Revd Paul Gavin.** b 68. Grey Coll Dur BA89. Wycliffe Hall Ox 90. **d** 92 **p** 93 **c** 09. C Muswell Hill St Jas w St Matt *Lon* 92-96; C Clifton Ch Ch w Em *Bris* 96-99; R Gerrards Cross and Fulmer *Ox* 99-09; Hon Can Ch Ch 07-09; Area Bp Kensington *Lon* from 09. *Dial House, Riverside, Twickenham TW1 3DT* Tel 020-8892 7781 Fax 8891 3969
E-mail bishop.kensington@dlondon.org.uk

WILLIAMS, Canon Paul Rhys. b 58. St Andr Univ MTheol82. Westcott Ho Cam 83. **d** 86 **p** 87. Asst Chapl Selw Coll Cam 86-87; C Chatham St Steph *Roch* 87-90; V Gillingham St Aug 90-95; Bp's Dom Chapl 95-03; Hon Can Roch Cathl 01-03; V Tewkesbury w Walton Cardiff and Twyning *Glouc* from 03; Hon Can Glouc Cathl from 06. *Abbey House, Church Street, Tewkesbury GL20 5SR* Tel (01684) 293333 *or* 850959 Fax 273113 E-mail vicar@tewkesburyabbey.org.uk

WILLIAMS, Paul Robert. b 66. Huddersfield Poly BA88. Wycliffe Hall Ox. **d** 99 **p** 00. C Roxeth *Lon* 99-03; C Harlow St Mary and St Hugh w St Jo the Bapt *Chelmsf* 03-08; Eurasia Network Developer Radstock Min Mongolia from 09. *Address temp unknown* E-mail paul@radstock.org

WILLIAMS, Mrs Pauline Mary. b 52. Univ of Wales (Cardiff) BD96 Trin Coll Carmarthen PGCE97. St Mich Coll Llan 00. **d** 02 **p** 03. C Coity w Nolton *Llan* 02-06; P-in-c Abercynon from 06; Dioc Children's Officer from 06. *67 Grovers Field, Abercynon, Mountain Ash CF45 4PQ* Tel (01443) 740207 Mobile 07974-652211 E-mail williamspm89@hotmail.com

WILLIAMS, Penny. See ANDREWS, Ms Penny

WILLIAMS, Canon Peris Llewelyn. b 39. Univ of Wales (Lamp) BA59. Qu Coll Birm 59. **d** 62 **p** 63. C Upton Ascension *Ches* 62-65; C Davenham 65-68; C Grange St Andr 68-73; TV E Runcorn w Halton 73-74; V Backford 74-80; Youth Chapl 74-80; V Witton 80-86; V Hoylake 86-93; R Ches H Trin 93-02; Hon Can Ches Cathl 98-02; rtd 02; Perm to Offic *Ches* and *Lon* from 02. *Padarn, 65 Long Lane, Chester CH2 2PG* Tel (01244) 341305

WILLIAMS, Peter. See WILLIAMS, Canon Cecil Peter

WILLIAMS, Peter. See WILLIAMS, Edward Ffoulkes

WILLIAMS, Peter. b 67. Westcott Ho Cam 05. **d** 07 **p** 08. C Cant St Mary Bredin from 07. *38 Nunnery Road, Canterbury CT1 3LS* Tel (01227) 786185 Mobile 07765-920079
E-mail pete.williams@smb.org.uk

WILLIAMS, Peter Charles. b 50. SWMTC 98. **d** 01 **p** 02. OLM Landrake w St Erney and Botus Fleming *Truro* from 01. *5 North Road, Landrake, Saltash PL12 5EL* Tel (01752) 851260
E-mail peterfreda@5northroad.fsnet.co.uk

WILLIAMS, Peter Hurrell. b 34. Keble Coll Ox BA58 MA61. Tyndale Hall Bris 62. **d** 64 **p** 65. C Sparkbrook Ch Ch *Birm* 64-67; C Rushden St Pet 67-70; P-in-c Clapham Park All SS *S'wark* 70-78; R Stanford-le-Hope w Mucking *Chelmsf* 78-92; P-in-c Gt Oakley w Wix 92-96; R Gt Oakley w Wix and Wrabness 96-97; rtd 97; Perm to Offic *Chelmsf* from 01. *3 Hillcrest Close, Horndon-on-the-Hill, Stanford-le-Hope SS17 8LS* Tel (01375) 643697

WILLIAMS, Canon Peter John. b 55. Southn Univ BTh80. Chich Th Coll 76. **d** 80 **p** 81. C Chepstow *Mon* 80-84; C Morriston *S & B* 84-85; V Glantawe 85-88; R Reynoldston w Penrice and Llangennith 88-05; R Llangennith w Llanmadoc and Cheriton from 05; Hon Can Brecon Cathl from 04; Dioc Soc Resp Officer from 88. *The Vicarage, Llangennith, Swansea SA3 1HU* Tel (01792) 386391

WILLIAMS, Philip Allan. b 48. Bris Univ BSc69 CertEd74. Trin Coll Bris 86. **d** 88 **p** 89. C Heref St Pet w St Owen and St Jas 88-93; R Peterchurch w Vowchurch, Turnastone and Dorstone 93-96; P-in-c Holmer w Huntington 96-01; V from 01. *The Vicarage, Holmer, Hereford HR4 9RG* Tel (01432) 273200
E-mail revphil@holmer.supanet.com

WILLIAMS, Philip Andrew. b 64. Sheff Univ BA86. St Jo Coll Dur 88. **d** 90 **p** 91. C Hillsborough and Wadsley Bridge *Sheff* 90-94; V Lenton Abbey *S'well* 94-96; P-in-c 96-02; V Wollaton Park 94-96; V Porchester from 02; AD Gedling from 05. *St James's Vicarage, Marshall Hill Drive, Nottingham NG3 6FY* Tel 0115-960 6185 E-mail phil.stjames@virgin.net

WILLIAMS, Philip James. b 52. St Chad's Coll Dur BA73. Coll of Resurr Mirfield 74. **d** 76 **p** 77. C Stoke upon Trent *Lich* 76-80;

TV 80; Chapl N Staffs Poly 80-84; TV Stoke-upon-Trent 80-84; R Shrewsbury St Giles w Sutton and Atcham from 84. *St Giles's Rectory, 127 Abbey Foregate, Shrewsbury SY2 6LY* Tel (01743) 356426 E-mail flyingvic@btinternet.com

WILLIAMS, Ray. b 23. Lon Univ DipEd46. St Aid Birkenhead 56. **d** 58 **p** 59. C Sparkhill St Jo *Birm* 58-60; Area Sec CMS *Chelmsf* and *St Alb* 60-65; V Shenstone *Lich* 65-73; Asst P Blenheim New Zealand 73-78; V Wakefield and Tapawera 78-83; P-in-c Murchison 79-82; Asst P Nelson All SS 83-85; Asst P Havelock and the Sounds 92-96. *8 Kivell Street, Ranui Heights, Porirua 6006, New Zealand* Tel (0064) (4) 238 8911

WILLIAMS, Raymond Howel. b 27. St Jo Coll Cam BA49 MA51 Ball Coll Ox BLitt63. St Jo Coll Nottm 72 NW Ord Course 73. **d** 73 **p** 74. C Derby St Pet 73-76; C Enfield Ch Ch Trent Park *Lon* 75-81; V S Mymms K Chas *St Alb* 81-94; NSM 94-95; rtd 94; Perm to Offic *St Alb* from 95 and *Ely* from 05. *7 Cockhall Close, Litlington, Royston SG8 0RB* Tel (01763) 853079

WILLIAMS, Rhys. See WILLIAMS, Thomas Rhys

WILLIAMS, Richard Dennis. b 57. LTCL79. Coll of Resurr Mirfield 79. **d** 82 **p** 83. C Roath *Llan* 82-85; C Penarth w Lavernock 85-88; V Abertillery *Mon* 88-95; V Tredunnoc and Llantrisant w Llanhennock etc 95-01; V Hay w Llanigon and Capel-y-Ffin *S & B* from 01. *19 Gypsy Castle Lane, Hay-on-Wye, Hereford HR3 1XX* Tel (01497) 820448

WILLIAMS, Canon Richard Elwyn. b 57. Hull Univ BA79. Coll of Resurr Mirfield 79. **d** 81 **p** 82. C Altrincham St Geo *Ches* 81-84; C Stockport St Thos 84-86; C Stockport St Thos w St Pet 86; R Withington St Crispin *Man* 86-95; V Alveston *Cov* from 95; RD Fosse 99-07; Hon Can Cov Cathl from 06. *The Vicarage, Wellesbourne Road, Alveston, Stratford-upon-Avon CV37 7QB* Tel (01789) 292777 E-mail rickvic@fsmail.net

WILLIAMS, Canon Richard Henry Lowe. b 31. Liv Univ BA52. K Coll (NS) BD64 Ridley Hall Cam 54. **d** 56 **p** 57. C Drypool St Andr and St Pet *York* 56-59; Canada 59-64; V Kirkdale St Athanasius *Liv* 64-68; R Much Woolton 68-79; R Croft w Southworth 79-89; Dioc Communications Officer 79-97; Hon Can Liv Cathl 88-97; R Wavertree St Mary 89-97; rtd 97; Perm to Offic *Liv* from 97. *16 Childwall Crescent, Liverpool L16 7PQ* Tel 0151-722 7962

WILLIAMS, Richard Huw. b 63. Bradf and Ilkley Coll BA85. St Jo Coll Nottm 86. **d** 89 **p** 90. C Forest Gate St Edm *Chelmsf* 89-90; C Plaistow 90-92; C Canning Town St Matthias 92-96; V Southend St Sav Westcliff from 96; AD Southend-on-Sea from 05. *St Saviour's Vicarage, 33 King's Road, Westcliff-on-Sea SS0 8LL* Tel (01702) 342920 E-mail stsaviourwest@aol.com

WILLIAMS, Richard Lawrence. b 62. Warw Univ BSc83 ACA87. Wycliffe Hall Ox 95. **d** 97 **p** 98. C Wallington *S'wark* 97-00; V Addiscombe St Mary Magd w St Martin from 00. *The Vicarage, Canning Road, Addiscombe CR0 6QD* Tel and fax (020) 8654 3459 *or* 8656 3457 E-mail richard@rlwilliams.fsnet.co.uk

WILLIAMS, Robert. b 49. **d** 97 **p** 98. C W Derby St Mary *Liv* 97-01; R Golborne 01-07; V Childwall St Dav from 07; V Stoneycroft All SS from 07. *St David's Vicarage, Rocky Lane, Childwall, Liverpool L16 1JA* Tel 0151-722 4549

WILLIAMS, Robert Edward. b 42. Ex Univ BA63. Lich Th Coll. **d** 65 **p** 66. C Wednesbury St Paul Wood Green *Lich* 65-67; C Whitchurch 67-69; P-in-c Whixall 69-72; P-in-c Edstaston 69-72; CF 72-91; R Cheriton w Tichborne and Beauworth *Win* 91-01; R Upper Itchen 01-02; rtd 02. *84 Portway, Warminster BA12 8QF*

WILLIAMS, Robert Edward. b 50. St Mich Coll Llan BD74 CertEd79. **d** 74 **p** 75. C Flint *St As* 74-77; Asst Chapl Sandbach Sch 79-80; Chapl and Hd RE 80-88; CF 88-05; Chapl Ellesmere Coll 05-08. *Address temp unknown*

WILLIAMS, Robert Jeffrey Hopkin. b 62. Univ of Wales (Abth) BA84 ALAM. Chich Th Coll BTh90. **d** 90 **p** 91. C Eastbourne St Mary *Chich* 90-94; R Upper St Leonards St Jo 94-02; V Twickenham St Mary *Lon* from 02. *37 Arragon Road, Twickenham TW1 3NG* Tel (020) 8892 2318

WILLIAMS, The Ven Robert John. b 51. Cartrefle Coll of Educn CertEd72 Univ of Wales (Ban) BEd73 MA92. St Mich Coll Llan BD76. **d** 76 **p** 77. C Swansea St Mary and H Trin *S & B* 76-78; Chapl Univ of Wales (Swansea) 78-84; Children's Adv 81-88; Asst Dir of Educn 81-88; Bp's Chapl for Th Educn 83-88; R Reynoldston w Penrice and Llangennith 84-88; R Denbigh and Nantglyn *St As* 88-94; V Sketty *S & B* 94-99; Dir of Ords 94-99; P-in-c Port Eynon w Rhosili and Llanddewi and Knelston 99-03; Can Brecon Cathl 95-00; Adn Gower from 00. *56 Pinewood Road, Uplands, Swansea SA2 0LT* Tel (01792) 297817

WILLIAMS, Roger. See WILLIAMS, Canon David Roger

WILLIAMS, Roger. See WILLIAMS, Canon John Roger

WILLIAMS, Roger Anthony. b 54. Univ of Wales (Lamp) BA76. Bp Burgess Hall Lamp 72 Qu Coll Birm 76. **d** 78 **p** 79. C Llanelli St D 78-82; V Monkton 82-86; Chapl to the Deaf *B & W* 86-90; Chapl to the Deaf *Ox* from 90. *Denchworth House, Denchworth, Wantage OX12 0DX* Tel and Minicom (01235) 868442 Fax 867402 E-mail roger@williams24.freeserve.co.uk

WILLIAMS, Roger Stewart. b 54. Qu Coll Cam BA75 MA79. Wycliffe Hall Ox BA78 MA82. **d** 79 **p** 80. C Hamstead St Paul

Birm 79-82; C Barking St Marg w St Patr *Chelmsf* 82-85; V Mildmay Grove St Jude and St Paul *Lon* 85-95; P-in-c Charles w Plymouth St Matthias *Ex* 95-09; Chapl Plymouth Univ 95-09; TR Bloxwich *Lich* from 09. *Bloxwich Rectory, 3 Elmore Row, Walsall WS3 2HR* E-mail rswilliams@supanet.com

WILLIAMS, Roger Thomas. b 54. Man Univ BSc76 Birm Univ MSc78 PhD83 Pemb Coll Cam PGCE92. Ridley Hall Cam 00. **d** 02 **p** 03. C Cambridge St Martin *Ely* 02-05; V Cambridge H Cross from 05. *Holy Cross Vicarage, 192 Peverel Road, Cambridge CB5 8RL* Tel (01223) 413343 Mobile 07751-601066 E-mail rogertw1@hotmail.com

WILLIAMS, Ronald Ernest Nathan. b 66. Univ of Sierra Leone BSc95. St Jo Coll Nottm MTh05. **d** 05 **p** 06. C Cowplain *Portsm* from 05. *24 Wincanton Way, Waterlooville PO7 8NW* Tel (023) 9225 9129 Mobile 07796-655225
E-mail ronnierenw@hotmail.com

WILLIAMS, Ronald Hywel. b 35. St D Coll Lamp BA62. **d** 63 **p** 64. C Machynlleth and Llanwrin *Ban* 63-66; C Llanaber 66-69; C Hawarden *St As* 69-73; R Llansantffraid Glan Conwy and Eglwysbach 73-77; V Rhosllannerchrugog 77-88; R Cilcain and Nannerch and Rhydymwyn 88-92; V Llanbadarn Fawr w Capel Bangor and Goginan *St D* 92-95; V Llanbadarn Fawr 95-00; RD Llanbadarn Fawr 94-00; rtd 00. *15 Maes y Garn, Bow Street SY24 5DS* Tel (01970) 820247

WILLIAMS (née TYDEMAN), Mrs Rosemary (Rose). b 47. Roehampton Inst TCert69. SAOMC 97. **d** 00 **p** 01. NSM Walton H Trin *Ox* 00-03; NSM E and W Horndon w Lt Warley and Childerditch *Chelmsf* from 03. *The Rectory, 147 Thorndon Avenue, West Horndon, Brentwood CM13 3TR* Tel (01277) 811223 E-mail stevecgs@ukonline.co.uk

WILLIAMS, Ms Rowan Clare. b 67. K Coll Cam BA90 MA93 Jes Coll Cam BA05. Westcott Ho Cam 02. **d** 05 **p** 06. C Leic Resurr 05-08; Chapl Univ Hosps Leic NHS Trust from 08. *Chaplaincy Department, Leicester Royal Infirmary, Infirmary Square, Leicester LE1 5WW* Tel 0116-258 5487 Mobile 07919-861912 E-mail rowan.williams@uhl-tr.nhs.uk
or rcw40@cantabgold.net

✠**WILLIAMS, The Most Revd and Rt Hon Rowan Douglas.** b 50. PC02. Ch Coll Cam BA71 MA75 Wadh Coll Ox DPhil75 DD89 Erlangen Hon DrTheol99 FBA90 Hon FGCM00. Coll of Resurr Mirfield 75. **d** 77 **p** 78 **c** 92. Tutor Westcott Ho Cam 77-80; Hon C Chesterton St Geo *Ely* 80-83; Lect Div Cam Univ 80-86; Dean Clare Coll Cam 84-86; Can Th Leic Cathl 81-92; Lady Marg Prof Div Ox Univ 86-92; Can Res Ch Ch *Ox* 86-92; Bp Mon 92-02; Abp Wales 99-02; Abp Cant from 02. *Lambeth Palace, London SE1 7JU, or The Old Palace, Canterbury CT1 2EE* Tel (020) 7898 1200 *or* (01227) 459401 Fax (020) 7261 9836

WILLIAMS, Canon Roy. b 28. Ely Th Coll 58. **d** 60 **p** 61. C Daybrook *S'well* 60-63; V Bilborough St Jo 63-73; V Arnold 73-92; Hon Can S'well Minster 85-92; rtd 92; Perm to Offic *S'well* from 92. *10 Maris Drive, Burton Joyce, Nottingham NG14 5AJ* Tel 0115-931 2030

WILLIAMS, Mrs Sandra Elizabeth. b 60. STETS 06. **d** 09. C Wrockwardine Deanery *Lich* from 09. *The Parsonage, Upton Magna, Shrewsbury SY4 4TZ*
E-mail sandra.williams3@btinternet.com

WILLIAMS (née CROSLAND), Mrs Sarah Rosita. b 50. St Mary's Coll Chelt CertEd71 BEd72. EAMTC 01. **d** 03 **p** 04. C Warmley, Syston and Bitton *Bris* 03-06; Asst Chapl Tervuren *Eur* 06-09; P-in-c Lydd *Cant* from 09. *All Saints' Rectory, Park Street, Lydd, Romney Marsh TN29 9AY* Tel (01797) 320345 E-mail revsarahwilliams@porfalas.plus.com

WILLIAMS, Canon Shamus Frank Charles. b 57. St Cath Coll Cam BA79 MA83. Ripon Coll Cuddesdon 81. **d** 84 **p** 85. C Swanage and Studland *Sarum* 84-87; C St Alb St Pet *St Alb* 87-90; TV Saffron Walden w Wendens Ambo and Littlebury *Chelmsf* 90-95; R Shingay Gp *Ely* from 95; RD Shingay from 97; Hon Can Ely Cathl from 05. *The Vicarage, Church Street, Guilden Morden, Royston SG8 0JD* Tel (01763) 853067 E-mail shamuswilliams@waitrose.com

WILLIAMS, Stephen Clark. b 47. Univ of Wales (Cardiff) BSc(Econ)69 Warw Univ MSc70. Wycliffe Hall Ox 91. **d** 93 **p** 94. C High Wycombe *Ox* 93-96; C Walton H Trin 96-97; TV 97-03; Acting TR 01-03; P-in-c E and W Horndon w Lt Warley and Childerditch *Chelmsf* from 03; Ind Chapl from 05. *The Rectory, 147 Thorndon Avenue, West Horndon, Brentwood CM13 3TR* Tel (01277) 811223 E-mail stevecgs@ukonline.co.uk

WILLIAMS, Stephen Grant. b 51. K Coll Lon BD73 AKC73. **d** 75 **p** 76. C Paddington Ch Ch *Lon* 75-78; C Paddington St Jas 78-80; Chapl LSE 80-91; Chapl (Sen) Lon Univs from 91. *15 Wilmington Square, London WC1X 0ER* Tel (020) 7837 1782 *or* 7580 9812 Fax 7631 3210 E-mail chaplaincy@lon.ac.uk

WILLIAMS, Stephen James. b 52. Lon Univ BSc73. Ridley Hall Cam 73. **d** 78 **p** 79. C Waltham Abbey *Chelmsf* 78-82; C Bedford St Paul *St Alb* 82-86; P-in-c Clayhange 86-88; V Harlington from 86. *The Vicarage, Church Road, Harlington, Dunstable LU5 6LE* Tel (01525) 872413 E-mail sjw@harlingtonchurch.org.uk
or sjw@lutonsfc.ac.uk

WILLIAMS, The Very Revd Stephen John. b 49. Univ of NSW BA73 DipEd73 Cam Univ BA77 MA81 Macquarie Univ (NSW) MA92. Ridley Hall Cam 75. **d** 78 **p** 79. Lect Th Bp Tucker Coll Uganda 78; C Brompton H Trin w Onslow Square St Paul *Lon* 79-82; Australia from 82; C Shenton Park St Matt 82-83; Chapl Blue Mountains Gr Sch 84-90; R W Lindfield 91-01; Dean Armidale from 02. *PO Box 749, Armidale NSW 2350, Australia* Tel (0061) (2) 6772 2269 Fax 6772 0188

WILLIAMS, Stephen Lionel. b 48. St Kath Coll Liv CertEd73 Open Univ BA77. NOC 93. **d** 96 **p** 97. NSM Hough Green St Basil and All SS *Liv* 96-99; C Padgate 99-02; V Walton St Jo from 02. *St John's Vicarage, 66 Roseworth Avenue, Liverpool L9 8HF* Tel and fax 0151-525 3458
E-mail frstephen320@hotmail.com

WILLIAMS, Stephen Stuart. b 60. Magd Coll Ox BA82 Dur Univ BA88. Cranmer Hall Dur 86. **d** 89 **p** 90. C W Derby Gd Shep *Liv* 89-93; Relig Affairs Producer BBC Radio Merseyside 92-00; TV Liv Our Lady and St Nic w St Anne 93-01; P-in-c Prestwich St Gabr *Man* from 01; Bp's Dom Chapl 01-05; Interfaith Adv from 05. *St Gabriel's Vicarage, 8 Bishops Road, Prestwich, Manchester M25 0HT* Tel 0161-773 8839 *or* 792 2096 Mobile 07813-436170 E-mail saintgabriel@talktalk.net

WILLIAMS, Susan. b 50. Swansea Coll of Educn CertEd72. Ban Ord Course 94. **d** 97 **p** 98. NSM Criccieth w Treflys *Ban* 97-00; P-in-c 00-01; P-in-c Criccieth and Treflys w Llanystumdwy etc 01-02; R from 02. *Taleifion, High Street, Criccieth LL52 0RN* Tel (01766) 523222 *or* (01248) 354999 Fax 523183 E-mail rev.sue-williams@btopenworld.com

WILLIAMS, Mrs Susan Glynnis. b 41. Nottm Univ MA00. EMMTC 05. **d** 06 **p** 07. NSM Graffoe Gp *Linc* from 06. *69 High Street, Navenby, Lincoln LN5 0ET* Tel (01522) 810445

WILLIAMS, Ms Susan Jean. b 54. Ches Coll of HE MTh00 Lanc Univ MA02. NOC 95. **d** 98 **p** 99. C Prescot *Liv* 98-01; Perm to Offic *Blackb* 01-02; C Scotforth 02-05; P-in-c Chipping and Whitewell 05-09; Warden of Readers and Past Assts from 09; Vice-Prin LCTP from 05. *St Leonard's House, Potter Lane, Samlesbury, Preston PR5 0UE* Tel (01772) 877930 Mobile 07904-076864 E-mail williams.ammasue@googlemail.com

WILLIAMS, Mrs Susan Merrilyn Marsh. b 62. Univ of Wales (Ban) BTh05. Ban Ord Course 00. **d** 03 **p** 04. C Botwnnog w Bryncroes *Ban* 03-08; P-in-c Nefyn w Tudweiliog w Llandudwen w Edern from 08. *The Vicarage, Lon Isaf, Morfa Nefyn, Pwllheli LL53 6BS* Tel (01758) 720494 E-mail susannefyn@aol.com

WILLIAMS, Terence. b 36. Univ of Wales (Abth) BSc57 Univ of Wales (Cardiff) MA67 Aston Univ PhD71. Glouc Sch of Min 78. **d** 81 **p** 81. NSM Deerhurst, Apperley w Forthampton and Chaceley *Glouc* 81-87; NSM Tarrington w Stoke Edith, Aylton, Pixley etc *Heref* 87-88; P-in-c Upper and Lower Slaughter w Eyford and Naunton *Glouc* 88-91; P-in-c Redmarley D'Abitot, Bromesberrow w Pauntley etc 91-95; R 95-99; RD Forest N 95-99; rtd 99; Perm to Offic *Glouc* 99-02; P-in-c Hasfield w Tirley and Ashleworth 02-05. *Meadowside, Gloucester Road, Hartpury, Gloucester GL19 3BT* Tel (01452) 700644

WILLIAMS, Terence James. b 76. St Jo Coll Dur BA05. Cranmer Hall Dur 02. **d** 05 **p** 06. C Bolsover *Derby* 05-09; P-in-c Codnor from 09. *The Vicarage, 20 Codnor Denby Lane, Codnor, Ripley DE5 9SN* Tel (01773) 742516 E-mail wterry774@aol.com

WILLIAMS, Terence John. b 36. Univ of Wales BSc62. St Deiniol's Hawarden 85. **d** 86 **p** 87. C Llangyfelach *S & B* 86-88; C Morriston 88-89; V Llanwrtyd w Llanddulas in Tir Abad etc 89-91; V Llanedi w Tycroes and Saron *St D* 91-00; rtd 01. *Coedmawr, 50 Swansea Road, Penllergaer, Swansea SA4 9AQ* Tel (01792) 892110

WILLIAMS, Thomas Bruce. b 41. Oak Hill Th Coll 74. **d** 76 **p** 77. C Liskeard w St Keyne and St Pinnock *Truro* 76-79; Min Bush Ch Aid Soc Paraburdoo Australia 79-80; C W Pilbara 79-81; R Wyndham and Kununurra 81-83; R Wyalkatchem w Dowerin and Koorda 83-87; R Tennan Creek 93-99; rtd 99; Perm to Offic Bendigo from 99. *1 Thomas Street, Bendigo Vic 3550, Australia* Tel (0061) (3) 5444 0485

WILLIAMS, Thomas Rhys. **d** 04 **p** 05. NSM Llandygai and Maes y Groes *Ban* 04-05; NSM Bangor 05-07; Perm to Offic from 07. *Groeslon, Talybont, Bangor LL57 3YG* Tel (01248) 372934

WILLIAMS, Timothy John. b 54. BEd83. Trin Coll Carmarthen. **d** 89 **p** 90. NSM Llansamlet *S & B* 89-97; P-in-c Bryngwyn and Newchurch and Llanbedr etc 97-01; V Aberedw w Llandeilo Graban and Llanbadarn etc from 01. *The Vicarage, Aberedw, Builth Wells LD2 3UW* Tel (01982) 560359

WILLIAMS, Timothy John. b 64. Kent Univ BA86. St Mich Coll Llan BD89. **d** 89 **p** 90. C Killay *S & B* 89-91; C Llwynderw 91-94; V Knighton and Norton 94-00; P-in-c Whitton w Pilleth w Cascob 99-00; V Killay from 00. *The Vicarage, 30 Goetre Fach Road, Killay, Swansea SA2 7SG* Tel (01792) 204233 E-mail fr_tim_williams@ntlworld.com

✠**WILLIAMS, The Rt Revd Trevor Russell.** b 48. TCD BA71. St Jo Coll Nottm BA73. **d** 74 **p** 75 **c** 08. C Maidenhead St Andr and St Mary *Ox* 74-77; Asst Chapl QUB 78-80; Relig Broadcasting Producer BBC 81-88; I Newcastle *D & D* 88-93; Ldr Corrymeela Community 93-03; I Belfast H Trin and St Silas

Conn 03-08; Preb Rathmichael St Patr Cathl Dublin 02-08; Bp
L & K from 08. *Rien Roe, Adare, Co Limerick, Republic of
Ireland* Tel (00353) (61) 396244
E-mail bishop@limerick.anglican.org

WILLIAMS, Canon Trevor Stanley Morlais. b 38. Jes Coll Ox
BA63 Univ of E Africa MA67. Westcott Ho Cam BA67. **d** 67
p 68. C Clifton St Paul *Bris* 67-70; Asst Chapl Bris Univ 67-70;
Chapl and Fell Trin Coll Ox 70-05; Hon Can Ch Ch *Ox* 95-05;
rtd 05. *13 Southmoore End, Oxford OX2 6RF* Tel (01865)
553975 E-mail trevor.williams@trinity.ox.ac.uk

WILLIAMS, Valerie Jane. b 53. **d** 03 **p** 04. OLM Merstham and
Gatton *S'wark* from 03. *Merstham Lodge, Harps Oak Lane,
Merstham, Redhill RH1 3AN* Tel (01737) 644850
E-mail valwilliams@vwilliams99.freeserve.co.uk

WILLIAMS, Vincent Handley. b 24. LRAM LLCM ARCM
CertEd. St Deiniol's Hawarden 76. **d** 78 **p** 79. Hon C Barrow
Ches 78-81; C Dodleston 81-83; V Lostock Gralam 83-90; rtd 90;
Perm to Offic *Ches* from 90. *2 Springfield Close, Higher
Kinnerton, Chester CH4 9BU* Tel (01244) 660983

WILLIAMS, Walter Haydn. b 31. Univ of Wales (Lamp) BA53
Selw Coll Cam BA55 MA60. St Mich Coll Llan 55. **d** 56 **p** 57. C
Denbigh *St As* 56-58; V Choral St As Cathl 58-61; C St As 58-61;
R Llanfyllin 61-68; V Northop 68-73; V Mold 73-86; RD Mold
79-86; Can St As Cathl 77-82; Prec 81-82; Preb and Chan 82-86;
R Overton and Erbistock and Penley 86-94; Chmn Ch of Wales
Liturg Cttee 86-94; rtd 94. *2 Park Lane, Craig y Don, Llandudno
LL30 1PQ* Tel (01492) 877294

WILLIAMS, William David Brynmor. b 48. Open Univ BA89. St
D Coll Lamp 71. **d** 72 **p** 73. C Killay *S & B* 72-74; C Wokingham
All SS *Ox* 74-75; CF 75-77; C Spilsby w Hundleby *Linc* 83-87; R
Meppershall w Campton and Stondon *St Alb* 87-90; V Hemsby
Nor 90-96; P-in-c Winterton w E and W Somerton and Horsey
94-96; rtd 96. *The Old School, 14 Weekley, Kettering NN16 9UW*
Tel (01536) 417612

WILLIAMS-HUNTER, Ian Roy. b 44. Trin Coll Bris 71. **d** 73
p 74. C Redhill H Trin *S'wark* 73-75; C Deane *Man* 76-80; R
Hartshorne *Derby* 80-02; P-in-c Bretby w Newton Solney 01-02;
R Hartshorne and Bretby from 02. *The Rectory, 74 Woodville
Road, Hartshorne, Swadlincote DE11 7ET* Tel (01283) 217866
E-mail ianrwhunter@aol.com

WILLIAMS-POTTER, Mrs Amanda Clare. b 69. Univ of Wales
(Ban) BD90. Westcott Ho Cam 90. **d** 92 **p** 97. C Carmarthen
St Dav *St D* 92-94; Chapl Trin Coll Carmarthen 94-99; V Llan-
non *St D* 99-01; TV Cwm Gwendraeth 01-05; Bp's Chapl 05-08;
C Cynwil Elfed and Newchurch 05-07; Communications Officer
05-08. *Address temp unknown*

WILLIAMSON, Alfred Michael. b 28. Kelham Th Coll 53. **d** 58
p 59. C Nottingham St Geo w St Jo *S'well* 58-64; SSM 60-64; V
Kenwyn St Geo *Truro* 64-73; V St Agnes 73-87; R Beverley w
Brookton Australia 87-93; rtd 93. *19 Lakeview Crescent, Forster
NSW 2428, Australia* Tel and fax (0061) (2) 6555 8844
E-mail coomba@tin.cc

WILLIAMSON, Alister. *See* WILLIAMSON, Ivan Alister

WILLIAMSON, Andrew John. b 39. MRPharmS62. St Alb Minl
Tr Scheme 82. **d** 85 **p** 86. NSM Oxhey All SS *St Alb* 85-88; NSM
Bricket Wood 88-97; NSM Campbeltown *Arg* 97-08; Lic to Offic
from 08. *Pier View, Low Askomil, Campbeltown PA28 6EP* Tel
(01586) 551478 Mobile 0970-708191
E-mail aj.gsw@tiscali.co.uk

WILLIAMSON, Mrs Anne. b 57. **d** 04 **p** 05. NSM Blackheath
St Jo *S'wark* 04-08; Co-ord Chapl Greenwich and Bexley
Cottage Hospice from 08. *160 Langton Way, London SE3 7JR*
Tel (020) 8853 5309 E-mail annecwilliamson@lineone.net

WILLIAMSON, Canon Anthony William. b 33. OBE77 DL98.
Trin Coll Ox BA56 MA60. Cuddesdon Coll 56. **d** 60 **p** 61. Hon C
Cowley St Jas *Ox* 60-79; TV Iffley 79-82; Dir of Educn (Schs) 89-00;
Hon Can Ch Ch 94-00; rtd 00. *9 The Goggs, Watlington
OX49 5JX* Tel (01491) 612143
E-mail tony_williamson@lineone.net

WILLIAMSON, Brian. *See* WILLIAMSON, John Brian Peter

WILLIAMSON, David Barry. b 56. St Jo Coll Nottm 80. **d** 83
p 84. C N Mymms *St Alb* 83-86; C Burnley *Ripon* 86-92; Project
Worker CECS 92-96; Youth and Children's Adv *B & W* 96-04;
Dir Time For God from 04. *Time For God, 2 Chester House,
Pages Lane, London N10 1PR* Tel (020) 8883 1504 Fax 8365
2471

WILLIAMSON, Desmond Carl. b 63. QUB BSc84 Westmr Coll
Ox MTh03. Trin Coll Bris 03. **d** 05 **p** 06. C Portishead *B & W*
from 05. *110 Brampton Way, Portishead, Bristol BS20 6YT* Tel
(01275) 840596 E-mail des.williamson1@ntlworld.com

WILLIAMSON, Edward McDonald. b 42. CITC 67. **d** 69 **p** 70. C
Limerick St Mary *L & K* 69-70; CF 70-73; C Penzance St Mary
w St Paul *Truro* 73-76; V Mullion 76-81; rtd 81; Perm to Offic
Truro from 81. *Hazelmere, The Commons, Mullion, Helston
TR12 7HZ* Tel (01326) 240865

WILLIAMSON, Henry Lyttle (Ray). b 47. Lon Bible Coll BA02.
d 95 **p** 96. P-in-c Edin St Marg 96-02; P-in-c Edin St Salvador
02-04; NSM Edin St Ninian 04-07. *6/5 St Triduana's Rest,
Edinburgh EH7 6LN* Tel 0131-652 0111 Mobile 07718-971914

WILLIAMSON, Ivan Alister. b 63. TCD BTh90. CITC 87. **d** 90
p 91. C Lisburn St Paul *Conn* 90-95; C Roxbourne St Andr *Lon*
95-99; Lect QUB from 95; Bp's C Ematris w Rockcorry,
Aghabog and Aughnamullan *Clogh* 99-01; I Errigle Keerogue w
Ballygawley and Killeshil *Arm* from 05. *Richmond Rectory, 24
Old Omagh Road, Ballygawley, Dungannon BT70 2AA* Tel (028)
8556 7857 Mobile 07814-983746
E-mail revdalisterwilliamson@yahoo.co.uk

WILLIAMSON, Mrs Jennifer Irene. b 44. Glas Univ MA66
Sunderland Poly Dip Teaching79. NEOC 89. **d** 92 **p** 94. NSM
Easby w Brompton on Swale and Bolton on Swale *Ripon* 92-95;
P-in-c Gilling and Kirkby Ravensworth 95-05; rtd 05.
65 Whitefields Drive, Richmond DL10 7DL Tel (01748) 824365

WILLIAMSON, John Brian Peter. b 30. Selw Coll Cam PhD55
CEng EurIng FIMechE FIEE FInstP FWeldI. WMMTC. **d** 84
p 87. NSM Malvern H Trin and St Jas *Worc* 84-94; Perm to Offic
from 94. *Monkfield House, Newland, Malvern WR13 5BB* Tel
(01905) 830522

WILLIAMSON, Kathleen Lindsay. b 50. Leeds Univ Medical Sch
MB, ChB74 Liv Univ BSc87. NOC 00. **d** 03 **p** 04. NSM Stretton
and Appleton Thorn *Ches* 03-06; NSM Frodsham from 06.
37 Waterside Drive, Frodsham WA6 7NF Tel 07899-664068
(mobile)

WILLIAMSON, Mrs Mary Christine. b 46. Bulmershe Coll of
HE BEd79. SWMTC 05. **d** 09. NSM Launceston *Truro* from 09.
73 St John's Road, Launceston PL15 7DE Tel (01566) 778902
Mobile 07900-477181 E-mail marywilliamson73@tiscali.co.uk

WILLIAMSON, Michael. *See* WILLIAMSON, Alfred Michael

WILLIAMSON, Canon Michael John. b 39. ALCD63. **d** 64 **p** 65.
C Pennington *Man* 64-67; C Higher Openshaw 67-69; P-in-c
Man St Jerome w Ardwick St Silas 69-72; C-in-c Holts CD
72-77; R Droylsden St Mary 77-04; Hon Can Man Cathl 97-04;
rtd 04; Perm to Offic *Man* from 04. *49 Ennerdale Road, Astley,
Tyldesley, Manchester M29 7AR* Tel (01942) 870274

WILLIAMSON, Olwen Joan. b 43. **d** 03 **p** 04. OLM Mortlake w
E Sheen *S'wark* from 03. *25 Christchurch Road, London
SW14 7AB* Tel and fax (020) 8876 7183
E-mail olwenontour@hotmail.com

WILLIAMSON, Paul Nicholas. b 55. Univ of Otago BTh79
Nottm Univ MPhil93. St Jo Coll Auckland 80. **d** 80 **p** 81. C
Andersons Bay New Zealand 80-82; V Winton-Otautau 82-86; C
Selston *S'well* 86-88; V St Kilda New Zealand 88-90; Min
Educator 88-92; V Milton-Tuapeka and Taieri 92-96; V Hataitai-
Kilbirnie from 96; Nat Co-ord Angl Renewal Min 99-03; Ldr
New Wine from 03. *94 Hamilton Road, Hataitai, Wellington
6021, New Zealand* Tel (0064) (4) 971 2140 or 386 3042 Fax 386
3041 E-mail leader@new-wine.net.nz

WILLIAMSON, Paul Stewart. b 48. K Coll Lon BD71 AKC71.
d 72 **p** 73. C Deptford St Paul *S'wark* 72-75; Hon C Kennington
St Jo 76-77; C Hoxton H Trin w St Mary *Lon* 78-83; C
St Marylebone All SS 83-84; C Willesden St Mary 84-85; Perm
to Offic 86-89; C Hanworth St Geo 89-92; P-in-c from 92. *The
Rectory, 7 Blakewood Close, Feltham TW13 7NL* Tel (020) 8844
0457

WILLIAMSON, Ralph James. b 62. LSE BSc(Econ)84. Ripon
Coll Cuddesdon BA89 MA97. **d** 90 **p** 91. C Southgate St Andr
Lon 90-93; TV Ross w Brampton Abbotts, Bridstow, Peterstow
etc *Heref* 93-97; Chapl Ch Ch Ox from 97. *Christ Church, Oxford
OX1 1DP* Tel (01865) 276236

WILLIAMSON, Ray. *See* WILLIAMSON, Henry Lyttle

WILLIAMSON, Robert Harvey (Robin). b 45. **d** 02 **p** 03. OLM
Maidstone St Luke *Cant* from 02. *Holly Bank, Bower Mount
Road, Maidstone ME16 8AU* Tel (01622) 682959
E-mail robin.helen@tesco.net

WILLIAMSON, Robert John. b 55. K Coll Lon BA77. Coll of
Resurr Mirfield 78. **d** 79 **p** 80. C Kirkby *Liv* 79-82; C Warrington
St Elphin 82-84; P-in-c Burneside *Carl* 84-90; V Walney Is 90-00;
V Darlington St Cuth *Dur* from 00. *The Vicarage, 26 Upsall
Drive, Darlington DL3 8RB* Tel (01325) 358911

✠**WILLIAMSON, The Rt Revd Robert Kerr (Roy).** b 32.
Kingston Univ DEd98. Oak Hill Th Coll 61. **d** 63 **p** 64 **c** 84. C
Crowborough *Chich* 63-66; V Hyson Green *S'well* 66-72; V
Nottingham St Ann w Em 72-76; V Bramcote 76-79; Adn
Nottingham 78-84; Bp Bradf 84-91; Bp S'wark 91-98; rtd 98;
Hon Asst Bp S'well and Nottm from 98. *30 Sidney Road,
Beeston, Nottingham NG9 1AN* Tel and fax 0115-925 4901
E-mail roywilliamson@waitrose.com

WILLIAMSON, Robin. *See* WILLIAMSON, Robert Harvey

WILLIAMSON, Roger Brian. b 38. Imp Coll Lon BSc59
MIET61. St Steph Ho Ox 01. **d** 02 **p** 03. NSM Harting w Elsted
and Treyford cum Didling *Chich* 02-05; P-in-c Stedham w Iping
from 05. *The Rectory, The Street, Stedham, Midhurst GU29 0NQ*
Tel (01730) 817570 Mobile 07767-266031
E-mail rogerwilliamson1@btinternet.com

WILLIAMSON, Mrs Sheilagh Catherine. b 54. Dur Inst of
Educn CertEd76 St Martin's Coll Lanc MA00. CBDTI 97. **d** 00
p 01. C Darlington St Hilda and St Columba *Dur* 00-03; P-in-c
from 03. *The Vicarage, 26 Upsall Drive, Darlington DL3 8RB* Tel
(01325) 358911

WILLIAMSON, Canon Thomas George. b 33. AKC57. **d** 58 **p** 59. C Winshill *Derby* 58-61; C Hykeham *Linc* 61-64; V Brauncewell w Dunsby 64-78; R S w N Leasingham 64-78; RD Lafford 78-87; V Cranwell 78-80; R Leasingham 78-80; V Billinghay 80-87; V Gosberton 87-97; V Gosberton, Gosberton Clough and Quadring 97-98; Can and Preb Linc Cathl 94-98; rtd 98; Perm to Offic *Linc* 98-01. *10 Newton Way, Woolsthorpe, Grantham NG33 5NR* Tel (01476) 861749 E-mail thomas.williamson1@btinternet.com

WILLIE, Canon Andrew Robert. b 43. Bris Univ BA65 Fitzw Coll Cam BA73 MA77. Ridley Hall Cam 71. **d** 74 **p** 75. Chapl St Woolos Cathl 74-79; Chapl St Woolos Hosp Newport 75-79; V Newbridge *Mon* 79-85; V Mathern and Mounton w St Pierre 85-98; Post-Ord Tr Officer 85-98; Warden of Readers from 91; V Newport St Mark from 98; Can St Woolos Cathl from 02. *The Vicarage, 7 Gold Tops, Newport NP20 4PH* Tel (01633) 263321

WILLINK, Simon Wakefield. b 29. Magd Coll Cam BA52 MA55. Cuddesdon Coll 52. **d** 54 **p** 55. C Thornbury *Glouc* 54-57; C Tetbury w Beverston 57-60; R Siddington w Preston 60-64; New Zealand 65-71; C Kelburn St Mich 65; V Takapau 65-70; Lic to Offic Waiapu 70-80; Perm to Offic *Ex* 90-92; Perm to Offic *Ex* 01-08. *7 Court Road, Newent GL18 1SL* Tel (01531) 821159

WILLIS, Andrew Lyn. b 48. Univ of Wales (Lamp) BA73. **d** 74 **p** 75. C Swansea St Mary w H Trin and St Mark *S & B* 74-81; V Glasbury and Llowes 81-83; Chapl RAF 83-03; Chapl Moray Hosps from 04. *Deanshaugh Croft, Mulben, Keith AB55 6YJ* Tel (01542) 860240

WILLIS, Anthony Charles Sabine. b 53. Ex Coll Ox MA82. ERMC 05. **d** 07 **p** 08. NSM Hatfield Hyde *St Alb* from 07; Perm to Offic *Newc* from 08. *94 Park Meadow, Hatfield AL9 5HE* Tel (01707) 267565 E-mail anthony.willis4@ntlworld.com

WILLIS, Anthony David. b 40. Sarum & Wells Th Coll 87. **d** 89 **p** 90. C Ivybridge w Harford *Ex* 89-92; C Catherington and Clanfield *Portsm* 92-94; R Ellesborough, The Kimbles and Stoke Mandeville *Ox* 94-08; rtd 09; C Aylesbury w Bierton and Hulcott *Ox* from 09. *12 Fairford Leys Way, Aylesbury HP19 7FQ* Tel (01296) 431934 E-mail revwillis@btinternet.com

WILLIS, Canon Anthony John. b 38. MBE00. Univ of Wales (Lamp) BA62. Qu Coll Birm. **d** 64 **p** 65. C Kidderminster St Jo *Worc* 64-68; C Dunstable *St Alb* 68-72; V Rubery *Birm* 72-80; R Salwarpe and Hindlip w Martin Hussingtree *Worc* 80-92; Chapl to Agric and Rural Life 85-03; Hon Can Worc Cathl 99-03; rtd 03; Perm to Offic *Worc* from 04. *1 Snowberry Avenue, Home Meadow, Worcester WR4 0JA* Tel (01905) 723509 E-mail jwillis@cofe-worcester.org.uk

WILLIS, Christopher Charles Billopp. b 32. MCIPD. Bps' Coll Cheshunt 57. **d** 59 **p** 60. C Golders Green St Alb *Lon* 59-61; C N Harrow St Alb 61-64; V Shaw and Whitley *Sarum* 64-69; Ind Chapl *Ex* 69-77; C Swimbridge 70-77; Lic to Offic 77-92; Chapl W Buckland Sch Barnstaple 77-92; rtd 97; Perm to Offic *Ex* from 97. *Rose Cottage, Chittlehampton, Umberleigh EX37 9PU* Tel (01769) 540289

WILLIS, David George. b 45. Oak Hill Th Coll BA79. **d** 79 **p** 80. C Wallington *S'wark* 79-84; V Ramsgate St Mark *Cant* 84-89; Hon C Woodnesborough w Worth and Staple 94-02; Hon C Eastry and Northbourne w Tilmanstone etc 02-06; Perm to Offic from 06. *33 Boystown Place, Eastry, Sandwich CT13 0DS* Tel (01304) 611959 E-mail davidandjane@f2s.com

WILLIS, Geoffrey Stephen Murrell. b 58. Sussex Univ BA80. Wycliffe Hall Ox 83. **d** 86 **p** 87. C Ashtead *Guildf* 86-89; Chapl Lee Abbey 89-94; R Dunsfold *Guildf* 94-01; R Dunsfold and Hascombe 01-06. *Address temp unknown* E-mail geoffrey@rod.demon.co.uk

WILLIS, Hugh. b 39. Bris Univ BDS63 MGDSRCSEng82 FRSH87. **d** 98 **p** 99. OLM Charminster and Stinsford *Sarum* 98-08; Perm to Offic from 09. *Glebe Farmhouse, West Hill, Charminster, Dorchester DT2 9RD* Tel and fax (01305) 262940 E-mail tournai@aol.com

WILLIS, Mrs Jane Elizabeth. b 59. Wycliffe Hall Ox 06. **d** 08 **p** 09. C Shrewsbury H Cross *Lich* from 08. *14 Langholm Drive, Shrewsbury SY2 5UN* Tel (01743) 357404 E-mail willis5family@btinternet.com

WILLIS, John. See WILLIS, Canon Anthony John

WILLIS, Joyce Muriel. b 42. Open Univ BA86 CQSW73. EAMTC 86. **d** 89 **p** 94. NSM Hadleigh *St E* 89-02; NSM Hadleigh, Layham and Shelley 02-07; rtd 07; Perm to Offic *St E* from 07. *26 Ramsey Road, Hadleigh, Ipswich IP7 6AN* Tel (01473) 823165 E-mail willisjm@lineone.net

WILLIS, Mrs Patricia. b 50. RGN85 Brunel Univ BSc95 Ox Brookes Univ PGDE98. SAOMC 96. **d** 99 **p** 00. C Warmley, Syston and Bitton *Bris* 99-03; V Hanham from 03. *The Vicarage, 30 Church Road, Bristol BS15 3AE* Tel and fax 0117-967 3580 Mobile 07932-654833 E-mail rev.pat.willis@btinternet.com

WILLIS, Paul. b 54. SAOMC. **d** 06 **p** 07. C High Wycombe *Ox* from 06. *21 The Haystacks, High Wycombe HP13 6PY* Tel (01494) 523966 Mobile 07857-309018 E-mail paulwillis54@hotmail.com

WILLIS, Peter Ambrose Duncan. b 34. Kelham Th Coll 55 Lich Th Coll 58. **d** 59 **p** 60. C Sevenoaks St Jo *Roch* 59-63; Trinidad and Tobago 63-68; P-in-c Diptford *Ex* 68-69; R 69-85; P-in-c N Huish 68-69; R 69-85; R Diptford, N Huish, Harberton and Harbertonford 85-96; rtd 99. *Sun Cottage, Church Street, Modbury, Ivybridge PL21 0QR* Tel (01548) 830541

WILLIS, The Very Revd Robert Andrew. b 47. Warw Univ BA68. Cuddesdon Coll 70. **d** 72 **p** 73. C Shrewsbury St Chad *Lich* 72-75; V Choral Sarum Cathl 75-78; TR Tisbury 78-87; RD Chalke 82-87; V Sherborne w Castleton and Lillington 87-92; Can and Preb Sarum Cathl 88-92; RD Sherborne 91-92; Chapl Cranborne Chase Sch 78-92; Dean Heref 92-01; P-in-c Heref St Jo 92-01; Dean Cant from 01. *The Deanery, The Precincts, Canterbury CT1 2EP* Tel (01227) 865264 *or* 762862 E-mail dean@canterbury-cathedral.org

WILLIS, Mrs Rosemary Ann. b 39. **d** 93 **p** 96. OLM Fressingfield, Mendham etc *St E* from 93. *Priory House, Fressingfield, Eye IP21 5PH* Tel (01379) 586254

WILLIS, Thomas Charles. b 30. Bps' Coll Cheshunt 55. **d** 58 **p** 59. C Anlaby Common St Mark *York* 58-61; C Middlesbrough St Martin 61-63; V Kingston upon Hull St Paul w Sculcoates Ch Ch 63-69, P-in-c Sculcoates St Silas 67-69; V Sculcoates St Paul w Ch Ch and St Silas 69-80; V Bridlington H Trin and Sewerby w Marton 80-96; rtd 96; Perm to Offic *York* from 96. *23 Hillcrest Drive, Beverley HU17 7JL* Tel (01482) 888511

WILLMINGTON, John Martin Vanderlure. b 45. St D Coll Lamp BA69. St Steph Ho Ox 69. **d** 71 **p** 72. C Upper Teddington SS Pet and Paul *Lon* 71-75; C Kensington St Mary Abbots w St Geo 75-83; R Perivale 83-91; V Acton Green from 91. *206 St Alban's Avenue, London W4 5JU* Tel (020) 8994 5735 E-mail willmington@actongreen.demon.co.uk

WILLMONT, Anthony Vernon. b 35. Lich Th Coll 62. **d** 63 **p** 64. C Yardley St Edburgha *Birm* 63-65; C Smethwick H Trin w St Alb 65-68; V Ropley w W Tisted *Win* 68-77; V Ipswich St Aug *St E* 77-84; R King's Worthy *Win* 84-90; R Headbourne Worthy 84-90; R Lapworth *Birm* 90-99; R Baddesley Clinton 90-99; P-in-c Thornton in Lonsdale w Burton in Lonsdale *Bradf* 99-02; rtd 02; Perm to Offic *Bradf* from 02. *9 Lowcroft, Butts Lane, Bentham, Lancaster LA2 2FD* Tel (01524) 261655

WILLMOTT, Robert Owen Noel. b 41. Lich Th Coll 65. **d** 68 **p** 69. C Perry Hill St Geo *S'wark* 68-71; C Denham *Ox* 71-76; P-in-c Tingewick w Water Stratford 76-77; P-in-c Radclive 76-77; R Tingewick w Water Stratford, Radclive etc 77-89; R Wingrave w Rowsham, Aston Abbotts and Cublington 89-06; P-in-c Wing w Grove 04-06; rtd 06. *34 Portfield Way, Buckingham MK18 1BB* Tel (01280) 813057

✠**WILLMOTT, The Rt Revd Trevor.** b 50. St Pet Coll Ox BA71 MA74. Westcott Ho Cam. **d** 74 **p** 75 **c** 02. C Norton *St Alb* 74-77; Asst Chapl Oslo w Bergen, Trondheim and Stavanger *Eur* 78-79; Chapl Naples w Sorrento, Capri and Bari 79-83; R Ecton *Pet* 83-89; Warden Ecton Ho 83-89; Dioc Dir of Ords and Dir Post-Ord Tr *Pet* 86-97; Can Res, Prec and Sacr Pet Cathl 89-97; Adn Dur and Can Res Dur Cathl 97-02; Suff Bp Basingstoke *Win* from 02. *Bishopswood End, Kingswood Rise, Four Marks, Alton GU34 5BD* Tel (01420) 562925 Fax 561251 E-mail trevor.willmott@dial.pipex.com

WILLOUGHBY, Francis Edward John. b 38. St Jo Coll Nottm. **d** 83 **p** 84. C Tonbridge SS Pet and Paul *Roch* 83-87; V Sutton at Hone 87-02; P-in-c Horton Kirby 00-02; rtd 03; Perm to Offic *Chich* from 03. *23 Mountjoy, Battle TN33 0EQ* Tel (01424) 775234

WILLOUGHBY, The Ven George Charles. b 20. TCD BA43 MA46. CITC Div Test 44. **d** 44 **p** 45. C Conwall *D & R* 44-47; C Derry Cathl 47-51; I Clooney 59-85; Dioc Dir of Ords 62-72; Adn Derry 79-85; rtd 85. *21 Tyler Avenue, Limavady BT49 0DT* Tel (028) 7776 5382

WILLOUGHBY, Canon Paul Moore. b 60. BA. **d** 86 **p** 87. C Dublin St Patr Cathl Gp 86-90; C Glenageary 90-92; I Dublin Booterstown 92-94; I Kilmocomogue Union *C, C & R* from 94; Can Cork and Ross Cathls from 00. *The Rectory, Durrus, Bantry, Co Cork, Republic of Ireland* Tel (00353) (27) 61011 Fax 61608 E-mail canonpmw@iol.ie

WILLOUGHBY, Mrs Serena Louise. b 72. Oak Hill Th Coll BA96. **d** 96 **p** 97. C St Paul's Cray St Barn *Roch* 96-99; C Hildenborough 99-00; Perm to Offic 03-06; P-in-c Sevenoaks Weald from 06. *The Vicarage, Church Road, Weald, Sevenoaks TN14 6LT* Tel (01732) 463291 Mobile 07786-076382 E-mail johnser@20judd.fsnet.co.uk

WILLOWS, David Keith. b 70. St Jo Coll Dur BA90 K Coll Lon MA94 PhD99. Wycliffe Hall Ox. **d** 95 **p** 96. C Ox St Mary V w St Cross and St Pet 95-97; Asst Chapl Oxon Mental Healthcare NHS Trust 97-00; P-in-c St Martin Ludgate *Lon* 00-01; Research Dir Paternoster Cen from 00. *104C Camden Street, London NW1 0HY* Tel (020) 7248 6233 E-mail david.willows@paternostercentre.com

WILLOWS, Michael John. b 35. Sarum & Wells Th Coll 70. **d** 72 **p** 73. C Pershore w Wick *Worc* 72-75; Ind Chapl 75-88; P-in-c Astley 75-81; P-in-c Hallow 81-85; V 85-88; V Wollaston 88-05;

rtd 05. *39 Hyperion Road, Stourton, Stourbridge DY7 6SD* Tel (01384) 379794

WILLOX, Peter. b 63. Sunderland Poly BSc85. Cranmer Hall Dur 86. **d** 89 **p** 90. C Bradley *Wakef* 89-92; C Utley *Bradf* 92-95; TV Bingley All SS 95-02; Chapl St Martin's Coll and C Ambleside w Brathay *Carl* 02-07; P-in-c Ben Rhydding *Bradf* from 07. *St John's Vicarage, 28 Wheatley Avenue, Ben Rhydding, Ilkley LS29 8PT* Tel (01943) 607363 *or* 601430
E-mail peterwillox@yahoo.co.uk

WILLS, David. b 58. Oak Hill Th Coll 92. **d** 94 **p** 95. C Chadwell *Chelmsf* 94-99; P-in-c Darlaston St Lawr *Lich* 99-09; R from 09; C Darlaston All SS from 99. *The Rectory, 1 Victoria Road, Darlaston, Wednesbury WS10 8AA* Tel 0121-526 2240

WILLS, Preb David Stuart Ralph. b 36. Chich Th Coll 64. **d** 66 **p** 67. C Bodmin *Truro* 66-70; V Bude Haven 70-78; TV Banbury *Ox* 78-83; Accredited Cllr from 81; V Launceston St Steph w St Thos *Truro* 83-88; P-in-c Kenwyn St Geo 88-93; V Truro St Geo and St Jo 93-96; Preb St Endellion 95-01; rtd 96. *Garden Cottage, Penwinnick Road, St Agnes TR5 0LA* Tel (01872) 553020 Fax 553121 Mobile 07773-402109
E-mail david.wills@cpt.cornwall.nhs.uk

WILLS, Canon Ian Leslie. b 49. Wycliffe Hall Ox 77. **d** 80 **p** 81. C Henbury *Bris* 80; C Gtr Corsham 80-83; C Whitchurch 83-86; Chapl HM Rem Cen Pucklechurch 86-96; P-in-c Pucklechurch and Abson w Dyrham *Bris* 86-87; V Pucklechurch and Abson 87-99; V Soundwell from 99; Hon Can Bris Cathl from 06. *Soundwell Vicarage, 46 Sweets Road, Bristol BS15 1XQ* Tel 0117-967 1511 E-mail ian.wills@bristoldiocese.org

WILLS, Morley. b 35. Ex & Truro NSM Scheme. **d** 80 **p** 81. NSM St Enoder *Truro* 80-82; NSM Kenwyn St Geo 82-85; NSM Truro St Paul and St Clem 85-88; P-in-c Crantock 89-05; rtd 05. *81 Vyvyan Drive, Quintrell Downs, Newquay TR8 4NF* Tel (01637) 872648

WILLS, Nicholas Richard. b 71. Birm Univ BA93. Cranmer Hall Dur. **d** 99 **p** 00. C Boldmere *Birm* 99-03; P-in-c Kettering St Andr *Pet* from 03. *St Andrew's Vicarage, Lindsay Street, Kettering NN16 8RG* Tel and fax (01536) 513858
E-mail nickandbecky@nbwills.freeserve.co.uk

WILLSON, Andrew William. b 64. Oriel Coll Ox BA85 Nottm Univ BTh90 MA98. Linc Th Coll 87. **d** 90 **p** 91. C Northampton St Mary *Pet* 90-93; C Cov E 93-96; Perm to Offic 96-01; Chapl Solihull Sixth Form Coll 98-01; Assoc Chapl Imp Coll *Lon* 01-03; Co-ord Chapl from 03; Assoc Chapl R Coll of Art 01-03; Co-ord Chapl from 03. *1 Porchester Gardens, London W2 3LA* Tel (020) 7229 6359
E-mail mary-andrew@clarkewillson.fsnet.co.uk

WILLSON, Stephen Geoffrey. b 63. St Jo Coll Nottm BTh90. **d** 90 **p** 91. C Newport St Andr *Mon* 90-92; C Risca 92-94; TV Cyncoed 94-96; Dioc Youth Chapl 96-99; Lay Past Asst 96-98; TV Cyncoed 98-01; TR from 01. *The Rectory, 256 Cyncoed Road, Cardiff CF23 6RU* Tel (029) 2075 2138
E-mail swillson@talktalk.net

WILLSON, Stuart Leslie. b 61. Nottm Univ BA83. Sarum & Wells Th Coll 83. **d** 84 **p** 85. C Llandrindod w Cefnllys *S & B* 84-85; Chapl Angl Students Univ of Wales (Swansea) 85-88; C Llwynderw 85-88; Ind Chapl Gatwick Airport *Chich* 88-95; Nene Coll of HE Northn 95-98; Dir Fundraising and Communication CUF from 98. *1D Northstead Cottage, Northstead Road, London SW2 3JN* Tel (020) 8674 3146
E-mail stuart@willson.freeserve.co.uk

WILLSON-THOMAS, Chloe Ann Mary. *See* THOMAS, Chloe Ann Mary

WILMAN, Arthur Garth. b 37. EAMTC 84. **d** 87 **p** 88. NSM Swavesey *Ely* 87-90; NSM Fen Drayton w Conington 87-90; NSM Hardwick 90-98; NSM Toft w Caldecote and Childerley 90-98; Perm to Offic from 98. *37 Prentice Close, Longstanton, Cambridge CB24 3DY* Tel (01954) 781400

WILMAN, Mrs Dorothy Ann Jane. b 38. Reading Univ BSc60. Westcott Ho Cam 89. **d** 90 **p** 94. NSM Toft w Caldecote and Childerley *Ely* 90-93; Dean's Asst Trin Hall Cam 92-98; Asst Chapl Cam St Edw *Ely* 93-98; P-in-c Hemingford Abbots 98-02; P-in-c Houghton w Wyton 98-02; rtd 02; Perm to Offic *Ely* from 02. *37 Prentice Close, Longstanton, Cambridge CB24 3DY* Tel (01954) 781400 E-mail dorothywilman@ukonline.co.uk

WILMAN, Leslie Alan. b 38. Selw Coll Cam BA61 MA65. Ridley Hall Cam 61. **d** 63 **p** 64. C Skipton H Trin *Bradf* 63-67; C Guiseley 67-69; V Morton St Luke 69-79; R Swanton Morley w Worthing *Nor* 79-82; P-in-c E Bilney w Beetley 79-82; P-in-c Hoe 80-82; R Swanton Morley w Worthing, E Bilney, Beetley etc 82-89; R Swanton Morley w Beetley w E Bilney and Hoe 89-00; RD Brisley and Elmham 87-93; rtd 00; Perm to Offic *Nor* from 00. *Last House, Chapel Lane, Foulsham, Dereham NR20 5RA* Tel (01362) 684109

WILMER, John Watts. b 26. Lich Th Coll 56. **d** 58 **p** 59. C Wolverhampton Ch Ch *Lich* 58-60; C Fenton 60-63; V Dresden 63-76; TV Sutton St Jas and Wawne *York* 76-80; R Bishop Wilton w Full Sutton 80; P-in-c Kirby Underdale w Bugthorpe 80; R Bishop Wilton w Full Sutton, Kirby Underdale etc 80-87; V York St Hilda 87-91; rtd 92; Perm to Offic *York* from 92.

27 Hunters Way, Dringhouses, York YO24 1JL Tel (01904) 709591

WILMOT, David Mark Baty. b 60. Liv Univ BA82. Sarum & Wells Th Coll 84. **d** 87 **p** 88. C Penrith w Newton Reigny and Plumpton Wall *Carl* 87-91; C St Alb St Pet *St Alb* 91-93; Chapl City Coll St Alb 92-93; V Milton *Lich* 93-01; RD Leek 96-01; V Windermere St Mary and Troutbeck *Carl* from 01. *St Mary's Vicarage, Ambleside Road, Windermere LA23 1BA* Tel (01539) 443032

WILMOT, Canon Jonathan Anthony de Burgh. b 48. St Jo Coll Nottm BTh74. **d** 74 **p** 75. C Cambridge St Martin *Ely* 74-77; Chapl Chantilly *Eur* 77-82; Asst Chapl Paris St Mich 80-82; Chapl Versailles 82-87; V Blackheath St Jo *S'wark* 89-95; V Reading Greyfriars *Ox* from 95; Hon Can Ch Ch from 08. *Greyfriars Vicarage, 28 Westcote Road, Reading RG30 2DE* Tel 0118-959 6015 *or* 956 9688
E-mail jonathan.wilmot@greyfriars.org.uk

WILMOT, Stuart Leslie. b 42. Oak Hill Th Coll 64. **d** 68 **p** 69. C Spitalfields Ch Ch w All SS *Lon* 68-71; C Islington St Mary 71-74; P-in-c Brixton St Paul *S'wark* 75-81; R Mursley w Swanbourne and Lt Horwood *Ox* 81-91; P-in-c Bermondsey St Jas w Ch Ch *S'wark* 91-96; V 96-99; V Bermondsey St Jas w Ch Ch and St Crispin 99-02; P-in-c Bermondsey St Anne 91-93; P-in-c Bermondsey St Anne and St Aug 93-96; V 96-02; RD Bermondsey 96-00; rtd 02. *Amberlea, College, East Chinnock, Yeovil BA22 9DY*

WILSHERE, Daile Marie. b 70. STETS 06. **d** 09. C Preston w Sutton Poyntz and Osmington w Poxwell *Sarum* from 09. *8 Buddleia Close, Weymouth DT3 6SG* Tel (01305) 835096
E-mail team.curate@live.co.uk

✠**WILSON, The Rt Revd Alan Thomas Lawrence.** b 55. St Jo Coll Cam BA77 MA81 Ball Coll Ox DPhil89. Wycliffe Hall Ox 77. **d** 79 **p** 80 **c** 03. Hon C Eynsham *Ox* 79-81; C 81-82; C Caversham St Pet and Mapledurham 82-89; V Caversham St Jo 89-92; R Sandhurst 92-03; RD Sonning 98-03; Hon Can Ch Ch from 02; Area Bp Buckm from 03. *Sheridan, Grimms Hill, Great Missenden HP16 9BG* Tel (01494) 862173 Fax 890508
E-mail atwilson@macline.co.uk
or bishopbucks@oxford.anglican.org

WILSON, Canon Alfred Michael Sykes. b 32. Jes Coll Cam BA56 MA61. Ridley Hall Cam 56. **d** 58 **p** 59. C Fulwood *Sheff* 58-63; V Gt Horton *Bradf* 63-69; R Rushden w Newton Bromswold *Pet* 69-76; RD Higham 75-83; P-in-c Rushden St Pet 75-77; R Rushden w Newton Bromswold 77-83; Can Pet Cathl 77-97; R Preston and Ridlington w Wing and Pilton 83-97; RD Rutland 85-95; rtd 97; Perm to Offic *Nor* from 98. *Swallow Cottage, 2 Little Lane, Blakeney, Holt NR25 7NH* Tel (01263) 740975

WILSON, Andrew. *See* WILSON, Canon James Andrew Christopher

WILSON, Canon Andrew Alan. b 47. Nottm Univ BA68. St Steph Ho Ox 68. **d** 71 **p** 72. C Streatham St Paul *S'wark* 71-75; TV Catford (Southend) and Downham 75-80; V Malden St Jas 80-89; Chapl Croydon Community Mental Health Unit 89-94; Chapl Bethlem and Maudsley NHS Trust Lon 94-99; Chapl S Lon and Maudsley NHS Foundn Trust from 99; Mental Health Chapl (Croydon) from 00; Hon Can S'wark Cathl from 05. *Chaplaincy, Bethlem Royal Hospital, Monks Orchard Road, Beckenham BR3 3BX* Tel (020) 8776 4361
E-mail andrew.wilson@slam.nhs.uk

WILSON, Andrew Kenneth. b 62. Oak Hill Th Coll BA91. **d** 91 **p** 92. C Springfield H Trin *Chelmsf* 91-96; V Sidcup Ch Ch *Roch* from 96. *The Vicarage, 16 Christchurch Road, Sidcup DA15 7HE* Tel (020) 8308 0835
E-mail andrew.wilson@diocese-rochester.org

WILSON, Andrew Marcus William. b 69. Ex Coll Ox BA91 CCC Cam BA93 K Coll Lon MA99. Westcott Ho Cam 91. **d** 94 **p** 95. C Forest Gate Em w Upton Cross *Chelmsf* 94-99; TV Poplar *Lon* 99-09; R S Hackney St Jo w Ch Ch from 09. *The Rectory, 9 Church Crescent, London E9 7DH* Tel (020) 8985 5149
E-mail andrewwilson@bigfoot.com

WILSON, Andrew Martin. b 60. Bris Univ BSc82 Univ Coll Chich BA04. Trin Coll Bris 97. **d** 99 **p** 00. C Broadwater *Chich* 99-07; V Portsdown *Portsm* from 07. *Portsdown Vicarage, 1A London Road, Widley, Waterlooville PO7 5AT* Tel (023) 9237 5360 E-mail andrew.wilson@ntlworld.com

WILSON, Antony Charles. b 69. Em Coll Cam MA92 PGCE92. Wycliffe Hall Ox 01. **d** 03 **p** 04. C Bath Walcot *B & W* 03-08; V Ipswich St Jo *St E* from 08. *St John's Vicarage, Cauldwell Hall Road, Ipswich IP4 4QE* Tel (01473) 721070
E-mail antony@stjohnsipswich.org.uk

WILSON, Arthur Guy Ross. b 28. St Aid Birkenhead 58. **d** 59 **p** 60. C Bexley St Mary *Roch* 59-63; C Gravesend St Geo 63-66; C Belvedere All SS 66-70; V Brighton St Matthias *Chich* 70-77; V Bradf St Clem 77-84; Lic to Offic 84-87; C Baildon 87-88; V Skirwith, Ousby and Melmerby w Kirkland *Carl* 88-93; C Menston w Woodhead *Bradf* 93-96; Chapl High Royds Hosp Menston 93-96; rtd 96; Perm to Offic *Derby* 96-98; Hon C Tamworth *Lich* 98-03; Perm to Offic from 04. *43 Borough Road, Tamworth B79 8AW* Tel (01827) 310224

WILSON, Ashley Peter. b 58. Edin Univ BSc81 BVM&S83 St Jo Coll Dur BA99. Cranmer Hall Dur 97. **p** 01. C Nunthorpe *York* 00-03; P-in-c Rounton w Welbury 03-08; Chapl St Chad's Coll *Dur* from 08. *St Chad's College, 18 North Bailey, Durham DH1 3RH* Tel 0191-334 3362 *or* 334 3358
E-mail ashley.wilson@dur.ac.uk

WILSON, Mrs Barbara Anne. b 38. Brighton Poly BEd79. **d** 04. NSM Southwick *Chich* from 04. *10 Phoenix Crescent, Southwick, Brighton BN42 4HR* Tel (01273) 269771 Mobile 07814-655121 E-mail barbara.a.wilson@btinternet.com

WILSON, Mrs Barbara Joyce. b 51. CBDTI 98. **d** 01 **p** 02. OLM Leyland St Jo *Blackb* 01-07; NSM from 07. *43 Hall Lane, Leyland PR25 3YD* Tel (01772) 435340
E-mail barbara.j.wilson@btinternet.com

WILSON, Barry Frank. b 58. Man Metrop Univ BA89 MPhil94 MTh99 Keele Univ PGCE90. NOC 94. **d** 97 **p** 98. C Stone St Mich w Aston St Sav *Lich* 97-99; Chapl St Mary and St Anne's Sch Abbots Bromley 00-04; V Betley *Lich* from 04; V Madeley from 04. *The Vicarage, Vicarage Lane, Madeley, Crewe CW3 9PQ* Tel (01782) 750205

WILSON, Barry Richard. b 46. WMMTC 88. **d** 91 **p** 92. NSM Leek and Meerbrook *Lich* 91-93; C Styvechale *Cov* 93-98; V Chesterton *Lich* from 98. *The Vicarage, Church Street, Chesterton, Newcastle ST5 7HJ* Tel (01782) 562479
E-mail barry-hazel@breathemail.net

WILSON, Bernard Martin. b 40. St Jo Coll Cam BA63 MA68 Lon Univ CertEd67. Ripon Hall Ox 72. **d** 73 **p** 74. C Bilton *Cov* 73-77; Dioc Development Officer *Birm* 78-83; Soc Resp Officer *Derby* 83-90; V Darley Abbey 83-90; Chapl Derbyshire R Infirmary 88-90; Educn Unit Dir Traidcraft Exchange 91; V Mickleover St Jo *Derby* 92-98; Adv to Bd of Miss and Soc Resp *Leic* 98-03; rtd 03; Perm to Offic *Leic* 03-06 and *Lich* from 06. *2 Dargate Close, Shrewsbury SY3 9QE* Tel (01743) 236300

WILSON (née HESLOP), Mrs Caroline Susan. b 62. St Cath Coll Cam BA83 MA87 ALCM79. Ox Min Course 06. **d** 09. NSM Caversham St Andr *Ox* from 09. *Chilterns, 9 Beech Road, Purley on Thames, Reading RG8 8DR* Tel 0118-984 1523
E-mail caroline.s.wilson@btinternet.com

WILSON, Canon Cecil Henry. b 40. CITC 67. **d** 69 **p** 70. C Lurgan St Jo *D & D* 69-72; Min Can Dromore Cathl 72-75; Youth Sec CMS Ireland 75-80; N Regional Sec 80-87; Gen Sec 87-07; Can Belf Cathl 00-07; rtd 07. *42A Magheraknock Road, Ballynahinch BT24 8TJ* Tel (028) 9756 4300

WILSON, Charles Roy. b 30. Brasted Place Coll 56. St Aid Birkenhead 57. **d** 59 **p** 60. C Kirkdale St Paul N Shore *Liv* 59-62; C St Helens St Mark 62-66; V Wolverhampton St Matt *Lich* 66-74; V Ripley *Derby* 74-88; V Willington 88-95; V Findern 88-95; rtd 95; Perm to Offic *Derby* from 95. *Jubilate, 12 Oak Tree Close, Swanwick, Alfreton DE55 1FG* Tel (01773) 541822

WILSON (née BRAVERY), Mrs Christine Louise. b 58. STETS 94. **d** 97 **p** 98. C Henfield w Shermanbury and Woodmancote *Chich* 97-02; TV Hove 02-08; P-in-c Goring-by-Sea from 08. *The Vicarage, 12 Compton Avenue, Goring-by-Sea, Worthing BN12 4UJ* Tel (01903) 242525 E-mail revchristine@talk21.com

WILSON, Christopher Harry. b 59. Man Univ MusB80 Ox Univ MTh01. Wycliffe Hall Ox 88. **d** 91 **p** 92. C S Lafford *Linc* 91-95; P-in-c Billingborough 95-96; P-in-c Sempringham w Pointon and Birthorpe 95-96; P-in-c Horbling 95-96; P-in-c Aslackby and Dowsby 95-96; V Billingborough Gp 96-03; P-in-c Leamington Priors All SS *Cov* from 03; Jt P-in-c Leamington Spa H Trin and Old Milverton from 03. *Clive House, Kenilworth Road, Leamington Spa CV32 5TL* Tel (01926) 424016 Fax 337422
E-mail holy.trinity@btopenworld.com

WILSON, Mrs Claire Frances. b 43. Hull Univ BA65. SWMTC 85. **d** 87 **p** 94. Par Dn Belsize Park *Lon* 87-94; C 94-97; C Chingford SS Pet and Paul *Chelmsf* from 97; rtd 09. *Ground Floor Flat, 25 Frognal Lane, London NW3 7DT* Tel (020) 7794 3801 E-mail revclairewilson@btinternet.com

WILSON, Colin Edward. b 63. Oak Hill Coll Cuddesdon BTh94. **d** 94 **p** 95. C High Wycombe *Ox* 94-98; P-in-c Broadwell, Evenlode, Oddington and Adlestrop *Glouc* 98-00; P-in-c Westcote w Icomb and Bledington 98-00; R Broadwell, Evenlode, Oddington, Adlestrop etc 00-03; Perm to Offic *Eur* 03-05; P-in-c Finchingfield and Cornish Hall End etc *Chelmsf* from 05. *The Vicarage, Bardfield Road, Finchingfield, Braintree CM7 4JR* Tel (01371) 810309

WILSON, David. b 67. BSc94 St Jo Coll Dur BA00. Cranmer Hall Dur 97. **d** 00 **p** 01. C Nantwich *Ches* 00-03; P-in-c Waverton 03-05; R Waverton w Aldford and Bruera 05-08; R St Andrews St *And* from 08. *The Rectory, Queen's Terrace, St Andrews KY16 9QF* Tel 07760-378085 (mobile)

WILSON, David Brian. b 47. QUB BA68. CITC 71. **d** 71 **p** 72. C Ballyholme *D & D* 71-74; C Guildf Ch Ch 74-78; I Arvagh w Carrigallen, Gowna and Columbkille *K, E & A* 78-81; R Clogherny w Seskinore and Drumnakilly *Arm* 81-95; I Caledon w Brantry from 95. *The Rectory, 36 Church Hill Road, Caledon BT68 4UY* Tel (028) 3756 8205

WILSON, Preb David Gordon. b 40. Man Univ BSc61 Clare Coll Cam BA63 MA68. Ridley Hall Cam 63. **d** 65 **p** 66. C Clapham

Common St Barn *S'wark* 65-69; C Onslow Square St Paul *Lon* 69-73; V Leic H Apostles 73-84; V Spring Grove St Mary *Lon* 84-05; P-in-c Isleworth St Fran 00-05; Chapl Brunel Univ 90-02; AD Hounslow 97-02; Preb St Paul's Cathl 02-05; rtd 05; Perm to Offic *Portsm* from 05. *8 Clover Close, Locks Heath, Southampton SO31 6SQ* Tel and fax (01489) 571426
E-mail david.gwilson20@ntlworld.com

WILSON, David Mark. b 53. Lon Univ BSc75. Wycliffe Hall Ox BA77 MA82. **d** 78 **p** 79. C Romford Gd Shep *Chelmsf* 78-81; C Cheadle Hulme St Andr *Ches* 81-85; V Huntington and Chapl Bp's Blue Coat C of E High Sch 85-95; V Birkenhead Ch Ch *Ches* 95-04; V Over St Jo from 04. *St John's Vicarage, Delamere Street, Winsford CW7 2LY* Tel (01606) 594651
E-mail thevicar@fastmail.co.uk

WILSON, Deborah May. b 61. Man Univ BA84 PhD95 Lanc Univ PGCE88. Cranmer Hall Dur 03. **d** 06 **p** 07. NSM Hartlepool St Luke *Dur* from 06. *10 Lindisfarne Close, Hartlepool TS27 3JN* Tel (01429) 265938
E-mail deborah.wilson3@ntlworld.com

WILSON, Derrick. b 33. Oak Hill Th Coll 69. **d** 71 **p** 72. C Lurgan Ch the Redeemer *D & D* 71-74; C Willowfield 74-75; I 83-88; I Knocknamuckley 75-83; I Tullylish 88-98; rtd 98. *Hollycroft, 6 Thornhill Crescent, Tandragee, Craigavon BT62 2NZ* Tel (028) 3884 9900

WILSON, Mrs Dorothy Jean. b 35. St Mary's Coll Dur BA57 DipEd58 Newc Poly LLB78. NEOC 86. **d** 88 **p** 96. NSM Dur St Giles 88-03; Perm to Offic *Newc* 88-96; Chapl Univ of Northumbria at Newc 94-96; Chapl N Dur Healthcare NHS Trust 97-02; NSM Shadforth and Sherburn *Dur* from 03. *86 Gilesgate, Durham DH1 1HY* Tel 0191-386 5016

WILSON, Edith Yvonne. b 43. St Martin's Coll Lanc MA98. CBDTI 97. **d** 97 **p** 98. NSM Skerton St Chad *Blackb* 97-05; Perm to Offic from 05. *28 Roedean Avenue, Morecambe LA4 6SB* Tel (01524) 417097 E-mail yvonne@ywilson7.freeserve.co.uk

WILSON, Canon Erik. b 51. Lanc Univ BA72. Trin Coll Bris 83. **d** 85 **p** 86. C Linthorpe *York* 85-89; V Hull St Martin w Transfiguration 89-98; AD W Hull 96-98; V Linthorpe from 98; Can and Preb York Minster from 05; RD Middlesbrough from 05. *St Barnabas' Vicarage, 8 The Crescent, Middlesbrough TS5 6SQ* Tel (01642) 817306
E-mail erik.wilson@ntlworld.com

WILSON, Frances Mary. b 61. Leeds Univ BA98. Westcott Ho Cam. **d** 00 **p** 01. C Rothwell *Ripon* 00-04; V Catterick from 04; Initial Reader Tr Officer from 04. *The Vicarage, High Green, Catterick, Richmond DL10 7LN* Tel (01748) 811462
E-mail mo.frances@tiscali.co.uk

WILSON, Francis. b 34. ACP67. Cuddesdon Coll 71. **d** 73 **p** 74. C Newc St Fran 73-79; V Wallsend St Jo 79-99; rtd 99; Perm to Offic *Newc* from 99. *65 Bede Close, Holystone, Newcastle upon Tyne NE12 9SP* Tel 0191-270 0848

WILSON, Frederick John. b 25. Lon Univ BScEng45. Oak Hill Th Coll 68. **d** 70 **p** 71. C Wandsworth All SS *S'wark* 70-75; P-in-c Garsdon w Lea and Cleverton *Bris* 75-84; P-in-c Charlton w Brokenborough and Hankerton 80-84; Chapl Barn Fellowship Whatcombe Ho 84-87; C Corby Epiphany w St Jo *Pet* 87-92; rtd 92; Perm to Offic *Linc* 93-02; *Pet* from 93; *Ely* from 05. *2 Thorseby Close, Peterborough PE3 9QS* Tel (01733) 263386

WILSON, Geoffrey. *See* WILSON, Samuel Geoffrey

WILSON, Geoffrey. b 42. **d** 97 **p** 98. OLM Gunton St Pet *Nor* 97-08; NSM Lowestoft St Marg from 08. *7 Monet Square, Gunton, Lowestoft NR32 4LZ* Tel (01502) 564064

WILSON, Geoffrey Samuel Alan. b 46. TCD BA69 QUB DipEd70 TCD MA72. CITC BTh93. **d** 96 **p** 97. C Glendermott *D & R* 96-99; I Camus-juxta-Mourne from 99. *The Rectory, Newtown Street, Strabane BT82 8DW* Tel (028) 7188 2314 Mobile 07889-877790 E-mail recwil27@yahoo.co.uk

WILSON, George Thomas. b 47. CBDTI 97. **d** 00 **p** 01. NSM Barrow St Paul *Carl* 00-06; P-in-c Bootle, Corney, Whicham and Whitbeck from 06. *The Rectory, Bootle, Millom LA19 5TH* Tel (01229) 718223 E-mail george860@btinternet.com

✠**WILSON, The Rt Revd Godfrey Edward Armstrong.** b 26. Linc Th Coll. **d** 54 **p** 55 **c** 80. C Sheff St Geo and St Steph 54-57; New Zealand from 58; C Masterton 58-59; V Aramoho 59-62; V St Pet Wellington 62-78; Min Tr Officer Waiapu Dio 78-80; Asst Bp Auckland 80-91; rtd 91. *30 Maryland Street, Point Chevalier, Auckland 1022, New Zealand* Tel (0064) (9) 846 4669

WILSON, Graham Whitelaw. b 46. Leeds Univ CertEd77 Birm Univ MPhil90 Derby Univ DMin03. EMMTC. **d** 95 **p** 96. NSM Burbage w Aston Flamville *Leic* 95-97; C 97-01; C Fenn Lanes Gp 01-04; Perm to Offic from 04. *10 The Courtyard, Higham Lane, Stoke Golding, Nuneaton CV13 6EX* Tel (01455) 213598
E-mail gwwilson@btinternet.com

WILSON, Canon Harold. b 29. St Jo Coll Ox BA53 MA57. Ridley Hall Cam 57. **d** 59 **p** 60. C Leamington Priors St Mary *Cov* 59-61; C Walsgrave on Sowe 61-64; V Potters Green 64-67; Chapl Barcelona *Eur* 67-73; V Bursledon *Win* 73-83; RD Eastleigh 75-83; V Yateley 83-94; RD Odiham 85-88; Hon Can Win Cathl 87-94; rtd 94; Perm to Offic *Win* from 94. *11 Hill Meadow, Overton, Basingstoke RG25 3JD* Tel (01256) 771825

WILSON, Mrs Heather Clarissa. b 49. Hull Univ BA71 Leic Univ PGCE72 Anglia Poly Univ MA05. EAMTC 01. **d** 03 **p** 04. NSM Duston Team *Pet* from 03; TV from 06. *St Francis House, Eastfield Road, Duston, Northampton NN5 6TQ* Tel (01604) 753679 Mobile 07702-033727
E-mail heather@wilson1214.freeserve.co.uk

WILSON, Mrs Hilary Anne. b 47. **d** 05 **p** 06. OLM Gt Chesham *Ox* 05-09; NSM from 09. *6 Greenway, Chesham HP5 2BL* Tel and fax (01494) 775564 E-mail hilaryaw6@aol.com

WILSON, Ian Andrew. b 57. Nottm Univ BTh89. Linc Th Coll 86. **d** 89 **p** 90. C Whitton and Thurleston w Akenham *St E* 89-93; P-in-c Elmsett w Aldham 93-02; R Elmsett w Aldham, Hintlesham, Chattisham etc 02; Chapl Woodbridge Sch from 03. *12 Moorfield Road, Woodbridge IP12 4JN* Tel (01394) 384573

WILSON, James. b 65. St Steph Ho Ox. **d** 01 **p** 02. C Whitchurch *Bris* 01-03; C Horfield St Greg 03-05; P-in-c from 05. *St Gregory's Vicarage, Filton Road, Horfield, Bristol BS7 0PD* Tel 0117-969 2839 E-mail revjameswilson@aol.com

WILSON, Canon James Andrew Christopher. b 48. Ex & Truro NSM Scheme. **d** 82 **p** 83. NSM Plymouth Crownhill Ascension *Ex* 82-83; NSM Yelverton 83-85; C Plymstock 85-87; R Lifton 87-92; R Kelly w Bradstone 87-92; V Broadwoodwidger 87-92; R Calstock *Truro* from 92; RD E Wivelshire from 00; Hon Can Truro Cathl from 04. *The Rectory, Sand Lane, Calstock PL18 9QX* Tel (01822) 832518
E-mail andrew.wilson@virgin.net

WILSON, James Kenneth. b 47. **d** 88 **p** 89. C Holyhead w Rhoscolyn w Llanfair-yn-Neubwll *Ban* 88-91; Chapl RAF 91-07; Mental Health Chapl Lincs Partnership NHS Trust from 07. *Lincolnshire Partnership NHS Trust, Cross O'Cliff, Bracebridge Heath, Lincoln LN4 2HN* Tel (01522) 513355
E-mail ken.wilson@lpt.nhs.uk

WILSON, James Lewis. b 39. TCD BA62 HDipEd63 MA65 BD71. TCD Div Sch Div Test74. **d** 74 **p** 75. C Enniskillen *Clogh* 74-76; C Belfast St Matt *Conn* 76-79; I Killeshandra w Killegar *K, E & A* 79-81; I Derrylane 79-81; I Loughgilly w Clare *Arm* from 81. *The Rectory, 124 Gosford Road, Loughgilly, Armagh BT60 2DE* Tel (028) 3750 7265

WILSON, Lt Col James Phillip Maclean. b 31. MBIM75. Glouc Sch of Min 89. **d** 91 **p** 92. NSM Quinton w Marston Sicca *Glouc* 91-97; P-in-c 97-01. *The Old Bakery, Upper Quinton, Stratford-upon-Avon CV37 8SX* Tel (01789) 720224

WILSON, James Robert. b 36. CITC. **d** 66 **p** 67. C Ballywillan *Conn* 67-73; I Drummaul 73-79; I Drummaul w Duneane and Ballyscullion 79-01; Preb Conn Cathl 96; Treas 96-98; Chan 98-01; rtd 01. *90 Killycowan Road, Glarryford, Ballymena BT44 9HJ* Tel (028) 2568 5737

WILSON, Jane Jennifer. b 43. Ch Ch Coll Cant TCert65 Open Univ BA84. Wycliffe Hall Ox 89. **d** 91 **p** 94. Par Dn Northwood Em *Lon* 91-94; C 94-98; TV Blythburgh w Reydon *St E* 98; TV Sole Bay 98-02; TR 02-07; RD Halesworth 01-07; Hon Can St E Cathl 05-07; P-in-c Offwell, Northleigh, Farway, Cotleigh etc *Ex* from 07. *The Rectory, Offwell, Honiton EX14 9SB* Tel (01404) 831636 E-mail janeoffwell@aol.com

WILSON, Mrs Janet Mary. b 44. Bedf Coll of Educn TCert66 SRN74. **d** 03 **p** 04. OLM S Croydon Em *S'wark* from 03. *Elmwood, 2 Weybourne Place, Sanderstead CR2 0RZ* Tel (020) 8657 2195 E-mail revjanwilson@blueyonder.co.uk

WILSON, Janet Mary. b 54. SAOMC 02. **d** 05 **p** 06. C Oxhey All SS *St Alb* from 05. *14 The Hoe, Watford WD19 5AY* Tel (020) 8420 1047 E-mail janwilson@waitrose.com

WILSON, Jayaker. **d** 92 **p** 93. India 92-05; Perm to Offic *Chelmsf* from 05. *153 Northbrooks, Harlow CM19 4DQ* Tel (01279) 412240

WILSON, Jeffery. **d** 06 **p** 07. OLM Kirton in Lindsey w Manton *Linc* from 06; OLM Grayingham from 06. *34 Richdale Avenue, Kirton Lindsey, Gainsborough DN21 4BL* Tel (01652) 648687 E-mail jeff-wilson13@yahoo.co.uk

WILSON, John Anthony. b 34. Linc Th Coll. **d** 83 **p** 84. C Nunthorpe *York* 83-85; V Whorlton w Carlton and Faceby 85-94; V E Coatham 94-99; rtd 99; Perm to Offic *York* 00-08 and *Ripon* 00-03; P-in-c Lower Swale *Ripon* 03-08. *29 Letch Hill Drive, Bourton-on-the-Water, Cheltenham GL54 2DQ* Tel (01451) 820571 E-mail johnjean.wilson@virgin.net

WILSON, John Clifford. b 32. AKC56. **d** 57 **p** 58. C Bordesley St Andr *Birm* 57-59; C Kings Norton 59-61; Somalia and Aden 61-63; V Lydbrook *Glouc* 64-67; TV Bow w Bromley St Leon *Lon* 69-73; P-in-c Stepney St Pet w St Benet 73-80; P-in-c Long Marton w Dufton and w Milburn *Carl* 80-81; R 81-87; V Annesley Our Lady and All SS *S'well* 87-95; V Annesley w Newstead 95-97; rtd 97; Perm to Offic *Heref* from 98. *Cwm Well Cottage, Upper Cwm, Little Dewchurch, Hereford HR2 6PS* Tel (01432) 840559

WILSON, John Frederick. b 33. Qu Coll Birm 58. **d** 61 **p** 62. C Jarrow St Paul *Dur* 61-65; C Monkwearmouth All SS 65-68, Bi Honduras 68-71; V Scunthorpe Resurr *Linc* 71-90; Chapl Divine Healing Miss Crowhurst 90-91; V Terrington St Clement *Ely* 91-99; rtd 99; Perm to Offic *Ely* from 99. *7 Oakleigh Crescent, Godmanchester, Huntingdon PE29 2JJ* Tel (01480) 392791

WILSON, Canon John Hamilton. b 29. St Chad's Coll Dur BA53. Sarum Th Coll 53. **d** 55 **p** 56. C W Ford *Win* 55-59; C Fishponds St Mary *Bris* 59-64; V Bedminster St Fran 64-73; RD Bedminster 68-73; R Horfield H Trin 73-96; Hon Can Bris Cathl 77-96; rtd 96; Perm to Offic *Bris* from 96. *2 West Croft, Bristol BS9 4PQ* Tel and fax 0117-962 9204

WILSON, John Lake. b 34. Linc Th Coll 74. **d** 76 **p** 77. C N Lynn w St Marg and St Nic *Nor* 76-80; V Narborough w Narford 80-85; R Pentney St Mary Magd w W Bilney 80-85; V Lakenham St Mark 85-93; P-in-c Trowse 92-93; V Lakenham St Mark w Trowse 93-98; Chapl Whitlingham Hosp 93-98; rtd 98; Perm to Offic *Nor* from 98. *Slinmoor, Warham Road, Wells-next-the-Sea NR23 1NE* Tel (01328) 711035

WILSON, Canon Judith Anne. b 48. Keele Univ BA71 Leic Univ PGCE72. S Dios Minl Tr Scheme 92. **d** 95 **p** 96. NSM Slaugham *Chich* 95-96; Sub Chapl HM Pris Wandsworth 95-96; Chapl HM Pris and YOI Hollesley Bay 96-01; Chapl HM Pris Nor from 01; Bp's Adv for Women's Min *Nor* from 04; Hon Can Nor Cathl from 07. *HM Prison, Knox Road, Norwich NR1 4LU* Tel (01603) 437531 E-mail judith.wilson@virgin.net

WILSON, Julian John. b 64. Collingwood Coll Dur BSc85 Liv Univ BTh. NOC 01. **d** 04 **p** 05. C Uttoxeter Area *Lich* 04-07; Chapl Denstone Coll Uttoxeter 07-09; R Baschurch and Weston Lullingfield w Hordley *Lich* from 09. *The Rectory, Baschurch, Shrewsbury SY4 2EB* Tel (01939) 260305

WILSON, Mrs Kathleen. b 47. Bucks Coll of Educn BSc90 Ox Brookes Univ MBA93 RGN69. **d** 03 **p** 04. OLM Iver *Ox* from 03. *111 High Street, Iver SL0 9PW* Tel (01753) 652105 Fax 654105 Mobile 07770-944054 E-mail kate@iver-centre.co.uk

WILSON, Kenneth. b 59. Selw Coll Cam BA82 MA82 Birm Univ MPhil95 MRICS84. S'wark Ord Course 86. **d** 89 **p** 90. C Walthamstow St Pet *Chelmsf* 89-92; TV Wolverhampton *Lich* 92-97; Perm to Offic 00-08. *6 Westland Road, Wolverhampton WV3 9NY* Tel and fax (01902) 561485
E-mail kw@soulofindia.com

WILSON, Ms Lauretta Joy. b 64. Bath Univ BSc87 CertEd87. SAOMC 02. **d** 05 **p** 06. C Boxmoor St Jo *St Alb* 05-08; TV Chambersbury from 08. *St Benedict's Vicarage, Peascroft Road, Hemel Hempstead HP3 8EP* Tel (01442) 243934
E-mail ljwilson33@btinternet.com

WILSON, Louis. b 68. Bris Univ LLB91. Oak Hill Th Coll BA09. **d** 09. NSM Broadwell, Evenlode, Oddington, Adlestrop etc *Glouc* from 09. *The Vicarage, Chapel Lane, Bledington, Chipping Norton OX7 6UZ* E-mail louisandjennywilson@hotmail.com

WILSON, Maree Elizabeth. **d** 06 **p** 07. C Geneva *Eur* from 06. *Holy Trinity, 14 bis Rue du Mont Blanc, CH-1201 Geneva, Switzerland* Tel and fax (0041) (22) 731 5155
E-mail geneva-htc@anglican.ch

WILSON, Marjorie Jayne. *See* SHIPTON, Mrs Marjorie Jayne

WILSON, Mark Anthony John. b 56. TCD BA80. CITC 75. **d** 80 **p** 81. C Dublin Rathfarnham *D & G* 80-83; Bp's C Dublin Finglas 83-85; I Celbridge w Straffan and Newcastle-Lyons 85-88; CF 88-93; I Dundalk w Heynestown *Arm* 93-03; Chapl Adelaide and Meath Hosp Dublin from 04. *7 Newlands Park, Clondalkin, Dublin 22, Republic of Ireland* Tel (00353) 87-669 3215 (mobile)

WILSON, Canon Mark John Crichton. b 46. Clare Coll Cam BA67 MA70. Ridley Hall Cam 67. **d** 69 **p** 70. C Luton w E Hyde *St Alb* 69-72; C Ashtead *Guildf* 72-77; Chapl Epsom Coll 77-81; V Epsom Common Ch Ch *Guildf* 81-96; RD Epsom 87-91; Adn Dorking 96-05; Hon Can Guildf Cathl from 96; Warden Community of St Pet Woking 03-07; Public Preacher *Guildf* from 05. *The Rectory, 3 Parsonage Way, Frimley, Camberley GU16 8HZ* Tel (01276) 62820
E-mail markw.ptherapist@ntlworld.com

WILSON, Martin. *See* WILSON, Bernard Martin

WILSON, Canon Mavis Kirby. b 42. Ex Univ BA64 Cam Univ CertEd71. S Dios Minl Tr Scheme 82. **dss** 84 **d** 87 **p** 94. Chessington *Guildf* 84-85; Epsom St Martin 85-86; Epsom Common Ch Ch 86-87; C 87-96; Dioc Adv in Miss, Evang, and Par Development 90-02; R Frimley from 02; Hon Can Guildf Cathl from 94. *The Rectory, 3 Parsonage Way, Frimley, Camberley GU16 8HZ* Tel (01276) 23309
E-mail mwilson2@toucansurf.com

WILSON, Mervyn Raynold Alwyn. b 33. Qu Coll Cam BA57 MA61. Ripon Hall Ox 57. **d** 59 **p** 60. C Rubery *Birm* 59-62; C Kings Norton 62-63; V Hamstead St Bernard 63-69; R Bermondsey St Mary w St Olave, St Jo etc *S'wark* 69-78; R Bulwick, Blatherwycke w Harringworth and Laxton *Pet* 78-03; rtd 03; Perm to Offic *B & W* from 04. *The Red Post House, Fivehead, Taunton TA3 6PX* Tel (01460) 281555
E-mail mervyn@ratilova.freeserve.co.uk

WILSON, The Very Revd Mervyn Robert. b 22. Bris Univ BA51 Lon Univ BD58. Tyndale Hall Bris 52. **d** 52 **p** 53. C Ballymacarrett St Patr *D & D* 52 56; C Donaghcloney 56-59; C Newtownards 59-61; I Ballyphilip w Ardquin 61-70; I Newry St Patr 70-92; Preb Dromore Cathl 83-85; Can Belf Cathl 85-89; Dean Dromore *D & D* 90-92; rtd 92. *31 Manor Drive, Lisburn BT28 1JH* Tel (028) 9266 6361

WILSON, Michael. *See* WILSON, Canon Alfred Michael Sykes

WILSON, Canon Michael. b 44. Liv Univ BA66 Fitzw Coll Cam BA68 MA73 De Montfort Univ MBA94. Westcott Ho Cam. **d** 69 **p** 70. C Worksop Priory *S'well* 69-71; C Gt Malvern St Mary *Worc* 71-75; V Leic St Anne 75-85; TR Leic Ascension 85-88; Hon Can Leic Cathl 85-88; Can Res and Treas 88-09; rtd 09. *39 Meadowcroft Road, Leicester LE2 2PD* Tel 0116-272 0041 E-mail mwilson@keme.co.uk

WILSON, Neil. b 61. Newc Univ BA83. Ripon Coll Cuddesdon 85. **d** 88 **p** 89. C Wallsend St Luke *Newc* 88-91; C Monkseaton St Pet 91-93; V Earsdon and Backworth 93-04; P-in-c Newc St Jo from 04. *3 Crossway, Jesmond, Newcastle upon Tyne NE2 3QH* Tel 0191-212 0181 E-mail frneilwilson@aol.com

WILSON, Paul David. b 64. Cranmer Hall Dur 96. **d** 98 **p** 99. C Bramley and Ravenfield w Hooton Roberts etc *Sheff* 98-01; V Hatfield from 01. *The Vicarage, 2 Vicarage Close, Hatfield, Doncaster DN7 6HN* Tel (01302) 840280

WILSON, Paul Edward. b 43. Ridley Hall Cam 81. **d** 83 **p** 84. C Brighstone and Brooke w Mottistone *Portsm* 83-86; C Shorwell w Kingston 83-86; TV Tring *St Alb* 86-90; P-in-c Renhold 90-91; Chapl HM Pris Bedf 90-91; V Buckfastleigh w Dean Prior *Ex* 91-96; P-in-c Stockland, Dalwood, Kilmington and Shute 96-00; TR Melbury *Sarum* 00-03; rtd 03; P-in-c Ashford Hill w Headley *Win* 04-05; Perm to Offic *Portsm* from 05. *Palm Trees, 42 Whitecross Avenue, Shanklin PO37 7ER* Tel (01983) 864654 E-mail paul.elizabeth@btinternet.com

WILSON, Paul Thomas Wardley. b 43. AKC67. St Aug Coll Cant. **d** 70 **p** 71. C Tokyngton St Mich *Lon* 70-74; Soc Community Worker *Roch* 74-81; Perm to Offic 81-90; Lic to Offic *Cant* 83-88; Sen Adv Coun for Soc Resp from 83; Chief Exec Carr Gomm Soc from 88. *Carr Gomm Society, 6-12 Tabard Street, London SE1 4JU* Tel (020) 7397 5300

WILSON, Peter Dennis. b 51. **d** 03 **p** 04. OLM Benwell *Newc* from 03. *34 Benwell Lane, Benwell, Newcastle upon Tyne NE15 6RR* Tel 0191-273 2856

WILSON, Peter John. b 43. CertEd76 BEd84. Linc Th Coll. **d** 71 **p** 72. C Stretford St Matt *Man* 71-73; C Rugby St Andr *Cov* 73-76; TV Rugby 86-92; Hon C Bilton 76-79; Asst Dir of Educn *Blackb* 79-81; P-in-c Accrington St Paul 79-81; Dioc Officer for Stewardship *Carl* 92-02; P-in-c Dacre 95-02; Hon Can Carl Cathl 98-02; R Stone St Mich and St Wulfad w Aston St Sav *Lich* 02-05; rtd 05. *83 Salisbury Road, Stafford ST16 3SE* E-mail ptr@wln1.fsnet.co.uk

WILSON, Peter Sheppard. b 39. TCD BA61. CITC Div Test 62. **d** 62 **p** 63. C Killowen *D & R* 62-68; C Portadown St Columba *Arm* 68-70; I Convoy w Monellan and Donaghmore *D & R* 70-78; V Castletown *S & M* 78-83; R Kilmacolm and Bridge of Weir *Glas* 83-85; I Camus-juxta-Bann *D & R* 85-92; Bp's Dom Chapl 90-92; I Maguiresbridge w Derrybrusk *Clogh* 92-05; Chapl to Bp Clogh 98-00; Can Clogh Cathl 03-05; rtd 05. *25 Grogey Road, Fivemiletown BT75 0SQ* Tel (028) 8952 1883

WILSON, Peter Stuart. b 45. Yorks Min Course 08. **d** 09. NSM Haworth *Bradf* from 09; NSM Cross Roads cum Lees from 09. *25 Branshaw Grove, Keighley BD22 6NH* Tel (01535) 674972 Mobile 07870-134272 E-mail peter@peterwilson25.wanadoo.co.uk

WILSON, Quentin Harcourt. b 45. K Coll Lon AKC68 BD76 Cen Lancs Univ MA97 York Univ PhD07 FTCL75. St Aug Coll Cant 69. **d** 70 **p** 71. C Is of Dogs Ch Ch and St Jo w St Luke *Lon* 70-72; C Muswell Hill St Jas 72-77; Succ and Sacr Ex Cathl 77-81; Min Can Windsor 81-84; V Langho Billington *Blackb* 84-97; Chapl Brockhall Hosp Blackb 85-97; RD Whalley *Blackb* 89-95; P-in-c Burnley St Pet 97-98; R 98-02; rtd 02; Perm to Offic *York* from 03; Chapl Castle Howard 03-05; RD S Ryedale *York* from 06. *The Coach House, East Heslerton, Malton YO17 8RN* Tel (01944) 728060 E-mail qhwilson@btinternet.com

WILSON, Mrs Rachel Elizabeth. b 56. Keswick Hall Coll BEd79. NOC 00. **d** 03 **p** 04. NSM Slaidburn *Bradf* from 03; NSM Long Preston w Tosside from 03; Min in Deaf Community from 09. *The Vicarage, 7 Station Road, Long Preston, Skipton BD23 4NH* Tel (01729) 840513 E-mail revrachel.wilson@dsl.pipex.com

WILSON, Richard Graham. b 67. Bris Univ BSc91 DipSW93. Trin Coll Bris BA01. **d** 01 **p** 02. C Wandsworth St Mich *S'wark* 01-05; TR Bath Twerton-on-Avon *B & W* from 05. *The Rectory, Watery Lane, Bath BA2 1RL* Tel (01225) 421438 E-mail richardwilson@tiscali.co.uk

WILSON, Robert Brian. b 29. AKC55. **d** 56 **p** 57. C Wortley de Leeds *Ripon* 56-60; C Chapel Allerton 60-63; V Hunslet Moor St Pet and St Cuth 63-70; V Bilton 70-80; V Gt and Lt Ouseburn w Marton cum Grafton 80-90; rtd 90; Perm to Offic *Ripon* 01-04. *56 Church Avenue, Harrogate HG1 4HG* Tel (01423) 504398 E-mail branddyharrogate@aol.com

WILSON, Canon Robert Malcolm (Robin). b 35. St Andr Univ MA59. ALCD62. **d** 62 **p** 63. C Wallington *S'wark* 62-66; C Dur St Nic 66-70; V Colchester St Pet *Chelmsf* 70-01; RD Colchester 93-98; Hon Can Chelmsf Cathl 94-01; rtd 01; Perm to Offic *St E* and *Chelmsf* from 01. *Hawthorns, Melton Road, Melton, Woodbridge IP12 1NH* Tel (01394) 383514

WILSON, Robert Stoker. b 39. Dur Univ BSc62. Oak Hill Th Coll 62. **d** 64 **p** 65. C High Elswick St Paul *Newc* 64-68; C Kirkheaton 68-70; Youth Chapl *Liv* 70-73; P-in-c S Shields St Steph *Dur* 73-78; R 78-83; Youth Chapl 73-77; P-in-c S Shields St Aid 81-83; V Greenside 83-94; P-in-c Fatfield 94-98; P-in-c Coniscliffe 98-04; Dioc Adv for IT 98-04; rtd 04. *9 Augusta Close, Darlington DL1 3HT* Tel 07808-911928 (mobile) E-mail stoker.wilson@durham.anglican.org

WILSON, Canon Ronald. b 11. St Aid Birkenhead. **d** 51 **p** 52. C Lenton *S'well* 51-53; C Worksop St Anne 53-55; V Lenton Abbey 55-63; V Pinchbeck *Linc* 63-78; Can and Preb Linc Cathl 72-78; rtd 78; Perm to Offic *Ox* 01-07. *143 Vandyke Road, Leighton Buzzard LU7 3HQ*

WILSON, Mrs Rosamund Cynthia. b 54. Univ of Wales MSc94 MCSP75. Trin Coll Bris. **d** 01 **p** 02. NSM Stoke Bishop *Bris* 01-05; C Frenchay and Winterbourne Down 05-06; NSM Abbots Leigh w Leigh Woods from 07. *10 Druid Stoke Avenue, Bristol BS9 1DD* Tel 0117-968 7554 E-mail rosw@another.com

WILSON, Samuel Geoffrey. b 52. CITC BTh04. **d** 04 **p** 05. C Swanlinbar w Tomregan, Kinawley, Drumlane etc *K, E & A* 04-07; I Kildallon and Swanlinbar 07-09; I Lurgan Ch the Redeemer *D & D* from 09. *Shankill Rectory, 62 Bainbridge Road, Lurgan, Craigavon BT6 7HG* Tel (028) 3832 5673 E-mail geoffwilson@utvinternet.com

WILSON, Simon Anthony. b 67. Portsm Poly BA88. Cranmer Hall Dur 96. **d** 99 **p** 00. NSM Barnham Broom *Nor* 99-00; NSM Barnham Broom and Upper Yare 00-02; NSM Hellesdon 02-03; Public Preacher from 03; Chapl Norfolk Constabulary (Cen Area) from 05; Chapl Norfolk Fire Service from 05; Co-ord Dioc Forum for Soc and Community Concerns from 06. *The Rectory, 1 Guist Road, Foulsham, Dereham NR20 5RZ* Tel (01362) 683275 E-mail simon.wilson@norwich.anglican.org

WILSON, Stephen Charles. b 51. Newc Univ BA73 Cam Univ MA82. Westcott Ho Cam BA78. **d** 79 **p** 80. C Fulham All SS *Lon* 79-82; C W Hampstead St Jas 82-85; P-in-c Alexandra Park St Sav 85-93; V Preston next Faversham, Goodnestone and Graveney *Cant* from 93; Hon Min Can Cant Cathl from 98; Asst Dir of Ords from 07. *The Vicarage, Preston Lane, Faversham ME13 8LG* Tel (01795) 536801 E-mail scwilson@coolblue.eclipse.co.uk

WILSON, Canon Stephen John. b 45. Bradf Univ BTech69. Trin Coll Bris 90. **d** 92 **p** 93. C Marple All SS *Ches* 92-96; P-in-c Moulton 96-01; Chapl Mid Cheshire Hosps Trust 96-99; V Hyde St Geo *Ches* from 01; RD Mottram 03-08; Hon Can Ches Cathl from 06. *The Vicarage, 85 Edna Street, Hyde SK14 1DR* Tel 0161-367 8787 E-mail stephenjwilson@talktalk.net

WILSON, Stoker. *See* WILSON, Robert Stoker

WILSON, Stuart Arnold. b 47. SWMTC 94. **d** 97 **p** 98. NSM Okehampton w Inwardleigh, Bratton Clovelly etc *Ex* 97-02; TV from 02. *The Vicarage, Northlew, Okehampton EX20 3NJ* Tel (01409) 221714 E-mail s.wilson45@btinternet.com

WILSON, Susan Annette. b 60. Bath Univ BPharm81 PhD86 MRPharmS82. Westcott Ho Cam 98. **d** 00 **p** 01. C Newc St Geo 00-03; Chapl Dame Allan's Schs Newc 02-03; TV Willington *Newc* 03-07; V Newc St Gabr from 07. *St Gabriel's Vicarage, 9 Holderness Road, Newcastle upon Tyne NE6 5RH* Tel 0191-276 3957 E-mail susan.wilson@tinyworld.co.uk

WILSON, Miss Susan Elizabeth. b 52. Lady Spencer Chu Coll of Educn BEd75. WEMTC 94. **d** 99 **p** 00. NSM Saltford w Corston and Newton St Loe *B & W* 99-06; P-in-c Heversham and Milnthorpe *Carl* from 06. *The Vicarage, Woodhouse Lane, Heversham, Milnthorpe LA7 7EW* Tel (01539) 563125 E-mail revsuewilson@tiscali.co.uk

WILSON, Mrs Sylvia. b 57. Teesside Univ BA96 Newc Univ MA99. **d** 08 **p** 09. OLM Preston-on-Tees and Longnewton *Dur* from 08. *7 Daltry Close, Yarm TS15 9XQ* Tel (01642) 892254 Mobile 07886-852154 E-mail sylvianwilson@allsaints-church.co.uk

WILSON, Thomas Irven. b 30. TCD BA51 Div Test 52 MA58. **d** 53 **p** 54. C Ballymena *Conn* 53-56; Chapl RAF 56-85; Asst Chapl-in-Chief 73-85; QHC from 80; rtd 85. *Rathclaren House, Kilbrittain, Co Cork, Republic of Ireland* Tel (00353) (23) 49689

WILSON, Canon Thomas Roderick. b 26. St Pet Hall Ox BA50 MA55. Sarum Th Coll 50. **d** 52 **p** 53. C Poulton-le-Sands *Blackb* 52-56; C Altham w Clayton le Moors 56-58; V Habergham Eaves H Trin 58-78; RD Burnley 70-78; Hon Can Blackb Cathl 75-89; V Bare 78-81; P-in-c Accrington St Jas 81-82; P-in-c Accrington St Paul 81-82; V Accrington St Jas w St Paul 82-89; rtd 89; Perm to Offic *Blackb* from 89. *33 Nook Terrace, Blackburn BB2 4SW* Tel (01254) 209390

WILSON, Timothy Charles. b 62. Oak Hill Th Coll BA90. **d** 90 **p** 91. C Highley *Heref* 90-94; C Margate H Trin *Cant* 94-98; P-in-c Margate St Phil 98-02; V 02-03; P-in-c Gt Chart from 03. *The Rectory, The Street, Great Chart, Ashford TN23 3AY* Tel (01233) 620371 E-mail tandcwilson@lineone.net

WILSON, Timothy John. b 58. St Pet Coll Ox MA80. Trin Coll Bris 81. **d** 83 **p** 84. C Gt Horton *Bradf* 83-86; C Handforth *Ches* 86-90; V Halifax All SS *Wakef* 90-07; TR Southgate *Chich* from

07. *The Rectory, Forester Road, Crawley RH10 6EH* Tel (01293) 523463 E-mail wilsons@domini.org

WILSON, Tom. b 78. Ox Univ BA01. Wycliffe Hall Ox BA00. **d** 07 **p** 08. C Toxteth St Marg *Liv* from 07. *4 Caryl Grove, Liverpool L8 6RN* Tel 07759-823104 (mobile) E-mail tom@stphilemons.org.uk

WILSON (*née* **NICHOLSON**), **Mrs Veronica Mary.** b 66. Nene Coll Northn BSc88 Ches Coll of HE PGCE90. Cranmer Hall Dur 96. **d** 99 **p** 00. C Barnham Broom *Nor* 99-00; C Barnham Broom and Upper Yare 00-02; C Hellesdon 02-06; V Foulsham, Guestwick, Stibbard, Themelthorpe etc from 06. *The Rectory, Guist Road, Foulsham, Dereham NR20 5RZ* Tel (01362) 683275

WILSON, Walter. b 33. Wm Temple Coll Rugby 55. **d** 59 **p** 60. C Sheff St Swithun 59-63; Ind Chapl 63-66; C Attercliffe 63-66; R Swallow w Cabourn *Linc* 66-72; Dioc Youth Officer *Heref* 72-77; Chapl Ipswich Sch 77-94; rtd 94; Perm to Offic *St E* 94-02. *Riverside Cottage, Mendlesham Green, Stowmarket IP14 5RF* Tel (01449) 766198

WILSON, William Adam. b 53. Sheff Univ BA74 St Jo Coll Dur BA84. Cranmer Hall Dur 82. **d** 85 **p** 86. C S Croydon Em *S'wark* 85-89; C Wandsworth All SS 89-93; Chapl Fontainebleau *Eur* 93-00; V S Lambeth St Steph *S'wark* from 00. *The Vicarage, St Stephen's Terrace, London SW8 1DH* Tel (020) 7564 1930 *or* 7735 8461 Fax 7735 7171 E-mail vicar@ststephenssouthlambeth.org.uk

WILSON, William Gerard. b 42. St Chad's Coll Dur BA65. **d** 67 **p** 68. C Hollinwood *Man* 67-71; V Oldham St Jas 71-79; R Birch w Fallowfield 79-93; V Paddington St Jas *Lon* from 93; AD Westmr Paddington 97-06. *St James's Vicarage Maisonette, 6 Gloucester Terrace, London W2 3DD* Tel (020) 7262 2410 *or* 7262 9976 Mobile 07976-363480 E-mail synaxis52@hotmail.com

WILSON, William John. b 25. CEng MIET MRTvS. S Dios Minl Tr Scheme 79. **d** 82 **p** 83. NSM Weeke *Win* 82-88; NSM Win St Barn 89-95; Hon Chapl R Hants Co Hosp Win 89-95; rtd 95; Perm to Offic *Win* 95-04. *23 Buriton Road, Winchester SO22 6JE* Tel (01962) 881904

WILSON, Yvonne. *See* WILSON, Edith Yvonne

WILSON-BARKER, Mrs Carol Amanda. b 64. Ex Univ BA08. SWMTC 00. **d** 03 **p** 05. C Godrevy *Truro* 03-07; TV Hale w Badshot Lea *Guildf* from 07. *The Vicarage, 12 Badshot Lea Road, Badshot Lea, Farnham GU9 9LD* Tel (01252) 327044 E-mail carolw953@aol.com

WILSON-BROWN, Nigel Hugh. b 55. Goldsmiths' Coll Lon BSc87. Wycliffe Hall Ox 95. **d** 97 **p** 98. C Wimbledon Em Ridgway Prop Chpl *S'wark* 97-00; Chapl K Sch Bruton from 00. *King's School, Plox, Bruton BA10 0ED* Tel (01749) 814200 *or* 813326 E-mail chaplain@kingsbruton.somerset.sch.uk

WILTON, Mrs Carlyn Zena. b 54. R Holloway Coll Lon BA75 Southn Univ PGCE76. SWMTC 99. **d** 02 **p** 03. NSM Carbis Bay w Lelant *Truro* from 02. *Venton Elwyn, 61 Queensway, Hayle TR27 4NL* Tel (01736) 752863 E-mail ventonelwyn@aol.com

WILTON, Christopher. b 52. Lon Univ LLB75 Solicitor 79. NEOC 97. **d** 00 **p** 01. NSM Sherburn in Elmet w Saxton *York* from 00; P-in-c 03-09; V from 09; RD Selby from 06. *The Vicarage, 2 Sir John's Lane, Sherburn in Elmet, Leeds LS25 6BJ* Tel (01977) 682122 Mobile 07968-268622 E-mail frwilton@aol.com

WILTON, Canon Gary Ian. b 60. Bath Univ BSc83 Trin Coll Bris MA93 Nottm Univ EdD05. Wycliffe Hall Ox 85. **d** 88 **p** 89. C Clevedon St Andr and Ch Ch *B & W* 88-92; Lect UWE Bris 92-93; TV Bath Twerton-on-Avon *B & W* 93-97; Dir Studies and Lect Wilson Carlile Coll of Evang 94-04; Assoc Prin 04-05; Sen Lect York St Jo Univ 05-08; Hd Postgraduate Progr 06-08; C of E Rep Eur Union and Can Brussels Cathl from 08. *Pro-Cathedral of the Holy Trinity, 29 rue Capitaine Crespel, B-1050 Brussels, Belgium* Tel (0032) (2) 511 7183 E-mail gary.wilton@htbrussels.com

WILTON (*née* **ADAMS**), **Mrs Gillian Linda.** b 57. SRN79 SCM81. Trin Coll Bris 82. **dss** 85 **d** 87 **p** 94. Easton H Trin w St Gabr and St Lawr and St Jude *Bris* 85-91; Par Dn 87-91; Regional Adv (SW) CMJ 91-97; Perm to Offic *B & W* 92-93; NSM Bath Twerton-on-Avon 93-97; Chapl Sheff Children's Hosp NHS Trust 98-06; Chapl Team Ldr Sheff Children's NHS Foundn Trust from 06; Perm to Offic *Eur* from 08. *The Sheffield Children's NHS Trust, Western Bank, Sheffield S10 2TH* Tel 0114-236 9397 *or* 271 7000 E-mail gillian.wilton@sheffch-tr-trent.nhs.uk

WILTON, Glenn Warner Paul. b 33. Miami Univ Ohio BSc55 Catholic Univ of America 69 Univ of Washington Seattle MSW76. Pontifical Beda Coll Rome 66 Ch Div Sch of the Pacific (USA) 77. **d** 65 **p** 66. In RC Ch 65-72; NSM Seattle USA 77-81; Chapl Pasture Hosp Derby 82-88; Chapl St Martin's Hosp Cant 89-93; Chapl St Aug Hosp Cant 89-93; Chapl E Kent NHS and Soc Care Partnership Trust 93-03; rtd 03; Perm to Offic *Cant* from 03. *10 Lichfield Avenue, Canterbury CT1 3YA* Tel (01227) 454230 E-mail gwpaulwilton@yahoo.co.uk

WILTS, Archdeacon of. *See* WRAW, The Ven John Michael

WILTSE, Joseph August Jean Paul. b 41. Leeds Univ BA64. Coll of Resurr Mirfield 64. **d** 66 **p** 67. C Airedale w Fryston *Wakef* 66-70; Canada from 70. *6983 Richmond Street, Powell River BC V8A 1H7, Canada*

WILTSHIRE, John Herbert Arthur. b 27. S'wark Ord Course 63. **d** 66 **p** 67. C Lee Gd Shep w St Pet *S'wark* 66-69; Min W Dulwich Em CD 69-79; R Coulsdon St Jo 79-93; rtd 93; Perm to Offic *Ches* from 93. *66 Meadow Lane, Willaston, Neston CH64 2TZ* Tel 0151-327 6668

WILTSHIRE, Robert Michael. b 50. WMMTC. **d** 89 **p** 90. NSM Droitwich Spa *Worc* 89-93; Asst Chapl HM Pris Wormwood Scrubs 93-94; Chapl HM Pris Standford Hill 94-97; Chapl HM Pris Whitemoor 97-99; Asst Chapl Gen of Pris 99-06; Chapl HM Pris Shrewsbury from 06. *HM Prison, The Dana, Shrewsbury SY1 2HR* Tel (01743) 273000 Fax 273001 E-mail robert.wiltshire@hmps.gsi.gov.uk

WIMBUSH, Canon Timothy. b 44. JP. St Steph Ho Ox. **d** 68 **p** 69. C Hobs Moat *Birm* 68-71; C W Wycombe *Ox* 71-76; R Wykeham from 76; RD Deddington 86-00; Hon Can Ch Ch from 95. *The Rectory, Sibford Gower, Banbury OX15 5RW* Tel (01295) 780555

WIMSETT, Paul. b 58. Univ of Wales (Abth) BSc(Econ)79 Hull Univ MA86. St Jo Coll Nottm 82. **d** 85 **p** 86. C Nuneaton St Nic *Cov* 85-89; C Loughborough Em *Leic* 89-92; TV Totnes, Bridgetown and Berry Pomeroy etc *Ex* 92-99; V Chudleigh w Chudleigh Knighton and Trusham from 99; RD Moreton from 05. *The Vicarage, Parade, Chudleigh, Newton Abbot TQ13 0JF* Tel (01626) 853241 E-mail wimsett@tesco.net

WIMSHURST, Michael Alexander. b 33. St Jo Coll Ox BA58. Westcott Ho Cam 59. **d** 60 **p** 61. C Lewisham St Mary *S'wark* 60-65; India 66-70; V Battersea St Pet *S'wark* 71-73; V Battersea St Pet and St Paul 73-97; rtd 97; Perm to Offic *Cant* from 98. *50 Broad Street, Canterbury CT1 2LS* Tel (01227) 457889

WINBOLT-LEWIS, Martin John. b 46. Fitzw Coll Cam BA69 MA72. St Jo Coll Nottm. **d** 75 **p** 76. C Highbury Ch Ch *Lon* 75-78; C Nottingham St Nic *S'well* 79-82; R Carlton Colville *Nor* 82-83; R Carlton Colville w Mutford and Rushmere 83-88; V Burley *Ripon* 88-96; Asst Chapl Pinderfields and Pontefract Hosps NHS Trust 96-99; Chapl 99-00; Lead Chapl 00-02; Lead Chapl Mid Yorks Hosps NHS Trust 02-05; Hd Chapl Services from 05. *Owl Pen, 2 Old Manor Farm, Bramhope, Leeds LS16 9BA* Tel 0113-284 2274 *or* (01924) 814677 E-mail winboltlewis@btinternet.com

WINCHESTER, Gordon Law. b 50. Trin Coll Bris. **d** 82 **p** 83. C Cheadle *Ches* 82-84; Asst Chapl Amsterdam *Eur* 84-88; C Hove Bp Hannington Memorial Ch *Chich* 88-96; V Wandsworth All SS *S'wark* 96-04; P-in-c Ewhurst *Chich* 04-05; R from 05; P-in-c Bodiam 04-05; V from 05. *The Rectory, Ewhurst Green, Robertsbridge TN32 5TB* Tel (01580) 830268 E-mail gordon.winchester@btinternet.com

WINCHESTER, Paul. b 44. St Pet Coll Ox BA66 MA70 Weymouth Coll of Educn PGCE73. Ridley Hall Cam 67. **d** 69 **p** 70. C Wednesfield Heath *Lich* 69-72; Perm to Offic *Sarum* 73-84; R Tushingham and Whitewell *Ches* 84-02; Perm to Offic *Ox* from 02. *12 The Pines, Faringdon SN7 8AU* Tel (01367) 240725 E-mail paulwinchester@tiscali.co.uk

WINCHESTER, Paul Marc. b 53. Univ of Wales (Lamp) BA80. St Mich Coll Llan 82. **d** 84 **p** 85. C Bedwellty *Mon* 84-86; C Chepstow 86-89; V Cwmcarn 89-93; V Fleur-de-Lis 93-98; R Bedwas and Rudry 98-05; P-in-c Llantilio Pertholey w Bettws Chpl etc from 05. *The New Vicarage, 10 The Pines, Mardy, Abergavenny NP7 6HQ* Tel (01873) 854323

WINCHESTER, Archdeacon of. *See* HARLEY, The Ven Michael

WINCHESTER, Bishop of. *See* SCOTT-JOYNT, The Rt Revd Michael Charles

WINCHESTER, Dean of. *See* ATWELL, The Very Revd James Edgar

WINDEBANK, Clive Leonard. b 41. New Coll Ox BA62 MA85. Ox NSM Course 75. **d** 78 **p** 79. Asst Chapl Ahmadi Kuwait 78-83; NSM Brompton H Trin w Onslow Square St Paul *Lon* 83-84; NSM Basildon w Aldworth and Ashampstead *Ox* 85-88; NSM Streatley w Moulsford 88-00; NSM Wallingford 00-03; Chapl Abu Dhabi St Andr UAE from 03. *The Coombe House, The Coombe, Streatley, Reading RG8 9QL* Tel (01491) 872174

WINDER, John William. b 15. SS Coll Cam BA37 MA41. Ridley Hall Cam 37. **d** 39 **p** 40. C Huddersfield H Trin *Wakef* 39-43; C Sowerby Bridge w Norland 43-48; V Stainland 48-53; V Manningham St Paul *Bradf* 53-66; R Bolton by Bowland 66-81; rtd 81; Perm to Offic *Bradf* from 81. *26 Burley Hall, Cornmill Lane, Burley in Wharfedale, Ilkley LS29 7DP* Tel (01943) 863631

WINDIATE, Mary Elizabeth. *See* WEST, Mrs Mary Elizabeth

WINDLE, Mrs Catharine Elizabeth. b 72. Hatf Coll Dur BA95 Homerton Coll Cam PGCE96. St Jo Coll Nottm MTh02. **d** 03 **p** 04. C Hucknall Torkard *S'well* 03-05; Hon C Hullavington, Norton and Stanton St Quintin *Bris* 05-06; P-in-c Bath Widcombe *B & W* 06-08; Hon C Malmesbury w Westport and Brokenborough *Bris* from 09. *Selwyn House, Pool Gastons Road, Malmesbury SN16 0DE* Tel (01666) 826369 E-mail royandkatie@googlemail.com

WINDLE, Christopher Rodney. b 45. Univ of Wales (Lamp) BA66. Qu Coll Birm. **d** 70 **p** 71. C Lache cum Saltney *Ches* 70-73; C Stockton Heath 73-76; P-in-c Bredbury St Barn 76-83; V 83-07; rtd 07; Perm to Offic *Ches* from 07. *6 Norbury Avenue, Marple, Stockport SK6 6NB* Tel 0161-427 0375

WINDLEY, Caroline Judith. b 62. Trent Poly BA84 Nottm Univ MA97 CQSW84. St Jo Coll Nottm MA96. **d** 97 **p** 98. C Kidderminster St Geo *Worc* 97-01; P-in-c Quarry Bank 01-07; TV Brierley Hill 07-08; RD Kingswinford 04-08; Area Dir of Ord and Adv in Voc Development *Ox* from 08. *1 Cavalry Path, Aylesbury HP19 9RP* Tel (01296) 424251 E-mail cwindley@wfcsmail.com

WINDMILL, Roy Stanley. b 17. Sarum Th Coll. **d** 54 **p** 55. C Wells St Cuth w Coxley and Wookey Hole *B & W* 54-58; R Honiley *Cov* 58-64; PC Wroxall 58-64; V Meriden 64-66; C Cov H Trin 66-70; P-in-c Kineton 70-75; P-in-c Combroke w Compton Verney 70-75; C Wraxall *B & W* 76-78; P-in-c Holton 78-82; rtd 82; Perm to Offic *B & W* 82-97; Perm to Offic *Ex* 82-98. *21 Rectory Drive, Burnham-on-Sea TA8 2DT* Tel (01278) 782715

WINDON, Gary. b 62. N Staffs Poly BSc85. Qu Coll Birm 98. **d** 00 **p** 01. C Penn *Lich* 00-04; TV Radcliffe *Man* 04-08; P-in-c Wrexham *St As* from 08; Chapl Nightingale Ho Hospice from 08. *The Vicarage, Vicarage Hill, Rhostyllen, Wrexham LL14 4AR* Tel (01978) 311179 E-mail gary@windon.co.uk *or* minister@rhostyllenchurches.org.uk

WINDRIDGE, Michael Harry. b 47. Sarum & Wells Th Coll 91. **d** 93 **p** 94. C Hempnall *Nor* 93-96; NSM Twickenham St Mary *Lon* 96-97; Perm to Offic *Nor* from 98. *Fritton Cottage, The Common, Fritton, Norwich NR15 2QS* Tel (01508) 498577

WINDROSS, Preb Andrew. b 49. Univ of Wales (Ban) BA71. Cuddesdon Coll 71. **d** 74 **p** 75. C Wakef St Jo 74-78; C Bromley All Hallows *Lon* 78-83; V De Beauvoir Town St Pet 83-02; AD Hackney 89-94; Bp's Officer for Ordained Min Stepney Area from 02; Hon C S Hackney St Mich w Haggerston St Paul from 02; Preb St Paul's Cathl from 02. *31 Lavender Grove, London E8 3LU* Tel and fax (020) 7254 7440 E-mail andy.windross@london.anglican.org

WINDROSS, Anthony Michael. b 50. CCC Cam BA72 MA75 Birm Univ PGCE73. S Dios Minl Tr Scheme 90. **d** 93 **p** 94. NSM Eastbourne St Mary *Chich* 93-97; C E Grinstead St Swithun 97-99; V Sheringham *Nor* 99-08; V Hythe *Cant* from 08. *St Leonard's Vicarage, Oak Walk, Hythe CT21 5DN* Tel (01227) 266217 E-mail amw@windross.fsnet.co.uk

WINDSLOW, Miss Kathryn Alison. b 62. Southn Univ BTh83 K Coll Lon MPhil01. Linc Th Coll 84. **dss** 86 **d** 87 **p** 94. Littlehampton and Wick *Chich* 86-89; Par Dn 87-89; Dn-in-c Scotton w Northorpe *Linc* 89-94; P-in-c 94-97; Asst Local Min Officer 89-97; Local Min Officer and Prin OLM Course 97-02; V Graffoe Gp from 02. *The Rectory, Vicarage Lane, Wellingore, Lincoln LN5 0JF* Tel (01522) 810246 E-mail kathryn.windslow@btinternet.com

WINDSOR, Graham. b 35. G&C Coll Cam BA57 MA64 PhD67 Lon Univ BD60. Clifton Th Coll 58 Trin Coll Bris 79. **d** 79 **p** 80. C Rainham *Chelmsf* 79-82; rtd 00. *Yanbian University, College of Science and Technology, Yanji, Jilin, China 133000* Tel (0086) (43) 3291 2500 Fax 3291 2510 E-mail graham_windsor@hotmail.com

WINDSOR, Julie Fiona. b 59. Ridley Hall Cam 98. **d** 00 **p** 01. C Chertsey *Guildf* 00-04; TV Papworth *Ely* 04-08; TR from 08. *Elsworth Rectory, The Drift, Elsworth, Cambridge CB23 8JN* Tel (01954) 267535 E-mail fiona.windsor@ely.anglican.org

WINDSOR, Mark James. b 75. Bath Univ BSc98. Wycliffe Hall Ox BTh08. **d** 08 **p** 09. C Felsted and Lt Dunmow *Chelmsf* from 08. *7 Tanton Road, Little Dunmow, Dunmow CM6 3GS* Tel (01371) 821996 E-mail markwindsor923@btinternet.com

WINDSOR, Dean of. *See* CONNER, The Rt Revd David John

WINFIELD, Canon Flora Jane Louise. b 64. Univ of Wales (Lamp) BA85 FRSA98. Ripon Coll Cuddesdon 87. **d** 89 **p** 94. Par Dn Stantonbury and Willen *Ox* 89-92; Co Ecum Officer *Glouc* 92-94; Chapl Mansf Coll Ox 94-97; Local Unity Sec Coun for Chr Unity 97-02; CF (TA) from 97; Can Res Win Cathl 02-05; Asst Sec Gen World Conf of Relig for Peace 05-06; Special Adv from 06; Sec Internat Affairs CTBI 06-09; Abp's Sec for Angl Relns *Cant* from 07; P-in-c St Mary at Hill w St Andr Hubbard etc *Lon* from 08. *Lambeth Palace, London SE1 7JU* E-mail flora.winfield@lambethpalace.org.uk

WINFIELD, Miss June Mary. b 29. Gilmore Ho 57. **dss** 66 **d** 87 **p** 94. Is of Dogs Ch Ch and St Jo w St Luke *Lon* 66-68; Bracknell *Ox* 68-74; Dean of Women's Min 74-80; St Marylebone w H Trin *Lon* 80-82; rtd 89; NSM Ealing St Steph Castle Hill *Lon* 89-97; Asst Dioc Dir Ords Willesden Area 94-97; Perm to Offic 97-02. *25 Trinity Road, Marlow SL7 3AN* Tel (01628) 484317

WING, Mrs Julie. b 62. Teesside Univ BSc99. NEOC 02. **d** 05 **p** 06. C Sunderland St Chad *Dur* 05-09; TV St Aycliffe from 09. *20 Haslewood Road, Newton Aycliffe DL5 4XF* Tel (01325) 320278 Mobile 07910-293936 E-mail julie_wing_1@hotmail.com

WING, Miss Myra Susan. b 45. Cranmer Hall Dur 92. **d** 94 **p** 95. C Appledore w Brookland, Fairfield, Brenzett etc *Cant* 94-98; Hon C Wittersham w Stone-in-Oxney and Ebony 95-98; V Grayshott *Guildf* 98-08; rtd 08; Perm to Offic *Cant* from 09. *142 Minster Road, Westgate-on-Sea CT8 8DQ* Tel (01843) 836430 E-mail susan@wing63.fsnet.co.uk

WINGATE, Canon Andrew David Carlile. b 44. Worc Coll Ox BA66 MA71 MPhil68 Birm Univ PhD95. Linc Th Coll 70. **d** 72 **p** 73. C Halesowen *Worc* 72-75; Lect Tamilnadu Th Sem India 76-82; Prin WMMTC 82-90; Prin United Coll of Ascension Selly Oak 90-00; Hon Can Birm Cathl 97-00; Dir Min and Tr *Leic* 00-03; Dir Interfaith Relns and Co-ord Lay Tr from 03; Can Th Leic Cathl from 00; Chapl to The Queen from 07. *23 Roundhill Road, Leicester LE5 5RJ* Tel 0116-221 6146 *or* 248 7418 Fax 253 2889 Mobile 07808-586259 E-mail andrew.wingate@leccofe.org

WINGATE, Canon David Hugh. b 22. Qu Coll Cam BA48 MA53. Qu Coll Birm 47. **d** 49 **p** 50. C Cov St Mary 49-52; V Wolston 52-56; V Cov All SS 56-60; R Patterdale *Carl* 60-66; Chapl United Leeds Hosp 66-71; Chapl Garlands Cumberland and Westmoreland Hosps 71-86; V Cotehill and Cumwhinton *Carl* 72-86; Hon Can Carl Cathl 85-86; rtd 87; Perm to Offic *Carl* from 87-01 and *Bradf* from 02. *c/o Mrs T Grisdale, 3 Northolme Crescent, Leeds LS16 5HU*

WINGFIELD, Christoper Laurence. b 57. Westmr Coll Ox BTh99. Ripon Coll Cuddesdon 93. **d** 95 **p** 96. C Hadleigh w Layham and Shelley *St E* 95-98; C Hadleigh 98-99; P-in-c Melton 99-00; R 00-01; R Sproughton w Burstall, Copdock w Washbrook etc from 01; RD Samford from 06. *The Rectory, Glebe Close, Sproughton, Ipswich IP8 3BQ* Tel (01473) 241078 Mobile 07703-814022 E-mail chris.wingfield@stedmundsbury.anglican.org

WINGFIELD DIGBY, Andrew Richard. b 50. Keble Coll Ox BA72. Wycliffe Hall Ox 74. **d** 77 **p** 78. C Cockfosters Ch Ch CD *Lon* 77-80; C Hadley Wood St Paul Prop Chpl 80-84; Dir Chrs in Sport 84-02; V Ox St Andr from 02; Six Preacher Cant Cathl from 97. *St Andrew's Vicarage, 46 Charlbury Road, Oxford OX2 6UX* Tel (01865) 310370 *or* tel and fax 311212 Mobile 07768-611232 E-mail andrew.wingfield.digby@standrewsoxford.org

WINKETT, Canon Lucy Clare. b 68. Selw Coll Cam BA90 MA94 ARCM92. Qu Coll Birm BD94. **d** 95 **p** 96. C Lt Ilford St Mich *Chelmsf* 95-97; Min Can and Chapl St Paul's Cathl 97-03; Can Res and Prec from 03. *1 Amen Court, London EC4M 7BU* Tel (020) 7248 1817 E-mail precentor@stpaulscathedral.org.uk

WINKS, Paul David. b 45. Ex Univ BA67. Cuddesdon Coll 68. **d** 70 **p** 71. C Rickerscote *Lich* 70-73; Chapl RAF 73-75; C Yate *Bris* 76-77; TV Yate New Town 77-83; P-in-c Leigh upon Mendip w Stoke St Michael *B & W* 83-84; V from 84. *The Vicarage, Leigh Street, Leigh upon Mendip, Radstock BA3 5QP* Tel (01373) 812559

WINN, Alan John. b 42. FRSA73. **d** 01 **p** 02. OLM Ringwould w Kingsdown *Cant* 01-04; OLM Ringwould w Kingsdown and Ripple etc from 05. *Chilterns, Back Street, Ringwould, Deal CT14 8HL* Tel (01304) 361030 E-mail revjohnwinn@aol.com

WINN, Mrs Jean Elizabeth. b 58. Man Univ BSc80. Wycliffe Hall Ox 85. **d** 88 **p** 98. C W Derby St Luke *Liv* 88-89; Perm to Offic 89-98; NSM Seaforth 98-02; NSM Anfield St Marg from 02. *St Margaret's Vicarage, Rocky Lane, Liverpool L6 4BA* Tel 0151-263 3118

WINN, Paul William James. b 44. Liv Univ BSc66. EMMTC 86. **d** 89 **p** 90. NSM Spalding St Paul *Linc* 89-98; Perm to Offic 98-00; P-in-c Cowbit 00-01; V 01-07; rtd 07. *6 Hawthorn Chase, Moulton, Spalding PE12 6GA* Tel (01406) 373662 E-mail paulwinn80@hotmail.com

WINN, Peter Anthony. b 60. Worc Coll Ox BA82 MA86. Wycliffe Hall Ox 83. **d** 86 **p** 87. C W Derby Gd Shep *Liv* 86-89; V Seaforth 89-02; P-in-c Anfield St Marg from 02. *St Margaret's Vicarage, Rocky Lane, Liverpool L6 4BA* Tel 0151-263 3118

WINN, Simon Reynolds. b 66. Bris Univ BA88. Trin Coll Bris 96. **d** 98 **p** 99. C Portswood Ch Ch *Win* 98-02; V Northolt St Jos *Lon* from 02; Dir of Ords Willesden Area from 07. *St Joseph's Vicarage, 430 Yeading Lane, Northolt UB5 6JS* Tel (020) 8845 6161 *or* 8842 4766 E-mail simon.winn@tiscali.co.uk

WINNARD, Jack. b 30. Oak Hill Th Coll 79. **d** 81 **p** 82. C Skelmersdale St Paul *Liv* 81-84; C Goose Green 84-85; V Wigan St Barn Marsh Green 85-98; rtd 99; Perm to Offic *Liv* from 00. *Maranatha, 11 Beech Walk, Winstanley, Wigan WN3 6DH* Tel (01942) 222339

WINNINGTON-INGRAM, David Robert. b 59. Hertf Coll Ox BA82 MA85 K Coll Cam BA89. Westcott Ho Cam 87. **d** 90 **p** 91. C Bishop's Cleeve *Glouc* 90-94; TV Colyton, Southleigh, Offwell, Widworthy etc *Ex* 94-00; V S Brent and Rattery from 00. *The Vicarage, Firswood, South Brent TQ10 9AN* Tel (01364) 649070 *or* 72774 E-mail wis100acre.wood@virgin.net

WINSLADE, Richard Clive. b 69. Aston Tr Scheme 91 Linc Th Coll BTh93. **d** 96 **p** 97. C Waltham Cross *St Alb* 96-99; C Leavesden 99-03; R Maulden from 03. *The Rectory, Clophill*

Road, Maulden, Bedford MK45 2AA Tel and fax (01525) 403139
E-mail member@rwinslade.fsnet.co.uk

WINSPER, Arthur William (Brother Benedict). b 46. Glas NSM Course 89. **d** 91 **p** 92. SSF from 70; NSM Barrowfield Glas 91-96; P-in-c St Aug Miss Penhalonga Zimbabwe 96-98; Perm to Offic Worc from 98. Society of St Francis, Glasshampton, Shrawley, Worcester WR6 6TQ Tel (01299) 896345

✠**WINSTANLEY, The Rt Revd Alan Leslie.** b 49. Nottm Univ BTh72. St Jo Coll Nottm 68 ALCD72. **d** 72 **p** 73 **c** 88. C Livesey Blackb 72-75; C Gt Sankey Liv 75-77; P-in-c Penketh 75-77; V 78-81; SAMS 81-93; Bp Bolivia and Peru 88-93; V Eastham Ches 94-03; Hon Asst Bp Ches 94-03; V Whittle-le-Woods Blackb from 03; Hon Asst Bp Blackb from 03. The Vicarage, Preston Road, Whittle-le-Woods, Chorley PR6 7PS Tel and fax (01257) 263306 E-mail bpalan.winstanley@ic24.net

WINSTANLEY, John Graham. b 47. K Coll Lon 67. **d** 71 **p** 72. C Wandsworth St Paul S'wark 71-74; Chapl Salford Univ 75-79; R Kersal Moor 79-87. 14 Lyndhurst Avenue, Prestwich, Manchester M25 0GF Tel 0161-740 2715 Fax 720 6916
E-mail john@blots.co.uk

WINSTON, Canon Jeremy Hugh. b 54. Trin Coll Carmarthen BEd76 BA CertEd. St Steph Ho Ox 78. **d** 79 **p** 80. C Bassaleg Mon 79-83; Dioc Children's Adv 79-89; V Itton and St Arvans w Penterry and Kilgwrrwg etc 83-93; V Abergavenny St Mary w Llanwenarth Citra from 93; RD Abergavenny from 02; Can St Woolos Cathl from 02. St Mary's Vicarage, Monk Street, Abergavenny NP7 5ND Tel (01873) 853168
E-mail jeremy.winston@virgin.net

WINSTONE, Canon Peter John. b 30. Jes Coll Ox BA52 MA56. Ridley Hall Cam 53. **d** 55 **p** 56. C Bitterne Win 55-58; C Keighley Bradf 58-60; PC Fairweather Green 60-67; V Clapham 67-84; R Leathley w Farnley, Fewston and Blubberhouses 84-95; Hon Can Bradf Cathl 89-95; rtd 95; Perm to Offic Worc from 95. 7 Kingfisher Close, Worcester WR5 3RY Tel (01905) 763114

WINTER, Andrew Christopher. b 73. Dur Univ BSc95 PGCE96. **d** 03 **p** 04. C Mosman St Clem Australia 03-05; NSM Hinckley H Trin Leic from 06. 14 Priesthills Road, Hinckley LE10 1AJ Tel (01455) 488741

WINTER, Anthony Cathcart. b 28. FCA. Ridley Hall Cam 54. **d** 56 **p** 57. C Childwall St Dav Liv 56-58; C Hackney St Jo Lon 58-63; V Newmarket All SS St E 63-73; Lic to Offic 74-81; Perm to Offic Lon 78-81 and 97-99; Hon C St Andr-by-the-Wardrobe w St Ann, Blackfriars 81-86; Hon C Smithfield St Bart Gt 86-95; Chapl S'wark Cathl from 99. 25 Bowater House, Golden Lane Estate, London EC1Y 0RJ Tel (020) 7490 5765 Fax 7490 1064

WINTER, Dagmar. b 63. Heidelberg Univ DrTheol96. Herborn Th Sem 93. **d** 96 **p** 97. C Bromley St Mark Roch 96-99; C Hexham Newc 99-06; P-in-c Kirkwhelpington, Kirkharle, Kirkheaton and Cambo from 06; Dioc Officer for Rural Affairs from 06. The Vicarage, Kirkwhelpington, Newcastle upon Tyne NE19 2RT Tel (01830) 540260
E-mail dagmar@winternet.freeserve.co.uk

WINTER, Canon David Brian. b 29. K Coll Lon BA53 CertEd54. Oak Hill NSM Course. **d** 87 **p** 88. NSM Finchley St Paul and St Luke Lon 87-89; Hd Relig Broadcasting BBC 87-89; Bp's Officer for Evang Ox 89-95; P-in-c Ducklington 89-95; Hon Can Ch Ch 95; rtd 95; Hon C Hermitage Ox 95-00; Hon C Dorchester 02-05; Perm to Offic 00-02 and from 06. 51 Nideggen Close, Thatcham RG19 4HS Tel (01635) 873639
E-mail david_winter1@btinternet.com

WINTER, Canon Dennis Graham St Leger. b 33. K Coll Lon BSc54 AKC54. Tyndale Hall Bris BD62. **d** 61 **p** 62. C Pennycross Ex 61-64; C Maidstone St Faith Cant 64-66; V Paddock Wood Roch 66-99; RD Tonbridge 89-95; RD Paddock Wood 95-99; Hon Can Roch Cathl 90-99; rtd 99; Perm to Offic Newc from 00. 4 Oaky Balks, Alnwick NE66 2QE Tel (01665) 602623

WINTER, Mrs Fiona Helen. b 60. Sheff Univ BSc87. NEOC 97. **d** 00. NSM Gt Ayton w Easby and Newton-in-Cleveland York 00-02. 9 The Acres, Stokesley, Middlesbrough TS9 5QA Tel (01642) 713146

WINTER, Jonathan Gay. b 37. Lon Inst of Educn DipEd84. AKC64. **d** 65 **p** 66. C W Dulwich All SS and Em S'wark 65-69; Asst Master Kidbrooke Sch 69-77; Norwood Sch 77-80; Dep Hd Lewisham Sch 80-89; Hon C Dulwich St Barn 90-08; Chapl Dulwich Coll 95-98; Cllr from 98; Dean of MSE (Woolwich) 00-04; Perm to Offic S'wark from 08. 160 Turney Road, London SE21 7JJ Tel and fax (020) 7274 3060 Mobile 07811-529503
E-mail jonathanwinter@btinternet.com

WINTER, Nichola Jane. b 58. Trevelyan Coll Dur BA79. Dioc OLM tr scheme 99. **d** 02 **p** 03. OLM Aldeburgh w Hazlewood St E from 02; Chapl Suffolk Coastal Primary Care Trust from 06. Threeways, Donkey Lane, Friston, Saxmundham IP17 1PL Tel (01728) 688979 E-mail njwinter@clara.co.uk

WINTER, Raymond McMahon. b 23. Selw Coll Cam BA52 MA60 FSA73. Wycliffe Hall Ox 59. **d** 61 **p** 62. C Gaywood, Bawsey and Mintlyn Nor 61-64; P-in-c Horstead w Frettenham w Stanninghall 64-71; Youth Chapl and Warden Dioc Conf Ho 64-71; Chapl Loretto Sch Musselburgh 71-74; P-in-c Latchingdon w Mundon and N Fambridge Chelmsf 74-75;

P-in-c Brettenham w Rushford Nor 75-83; P-in-c Riddlesworth w Gasthorpe and Knettishall 76-83; P-in-c Garboldisham w Blo' Norton 77-83; Chapl Bedgebury Sch Kent 83-88; Hon C Kilndown Cant 83-87; Hon C Goudhurst w Kilndown 87-91; Warden Coll of St Barn Lingfield 88-94; rtd 91; Perm to Offic Nor 94-04. 27 Breydon Road, Norwich NR7 8EF Tel (01602) 484889

WINTER, Rebecca Anne. See BEVAN, Mrs Rebecca Anne

WINTER, Stephen Christopher. b 55. Southn Univ BA76. Trin Coll Bris 85. **d** 88 **p** 89. C Birm St Luke 88-92; TV Kings Norton 92-98; Ind Chapl Worc 98-04; Asst Dir Development (Discipleship) from 04; C Finstall from 04. 1 Marlborough Avenue, Bromsgrove B60 2PG Tel (01527) 575737 or (01905) 732813 E-mail swinter@cofe-worcester.co.uk

WINTER, Thomas Andrew. b 24. Wadh Coll Ox BA51 MA63. Ely Th Coll 51. **d** 53 **p** 54. C Horninglow Lich 53-56; S Africa 56-83; R Woodston Ely 83-90; rtd 90; Perm to Offic Ely 90-97 and Chich from 90. 6 The Close, Shoreham-by-Sea BN43 5AH Tel (01273) 452606

WINTERBOTTOM, Canon Ian Edmund. b 42. St Andr Univ MA66. Linc Th Coll 66. **d** 68 **p** 69. C Blackb St Steph 68-71; C Wingerworth Derby 71-73; P-in-c Brimington 73-77; R 77-89; RD Bolsover and Staveley 86-93; R Pleasley 89-94; P-in-c Shirebrook 92-94; TR E Scarsdale 94-00; Hon Can Derby Cathl 95-08; Prin Ind Chapl 00-08; rtd 08. 17 Coach Way, Willington, Derby DE65 6ES Tel (01283) 704322
E-mail ianwinterbottom@aol.com

WINTERBURN, Derek Neil. b 60. Bris Univ BSc82 Ox Univ BA85. Wycliffe Hall Ox 83. **d** 86 **p** 87. C Mildmay Grove St Jude and St Paul Lon 86-89; C Hackney Marsh 89-91; TV 91-96; V Hampton St Mary from 96; AD Hampton from 08. St Mary's Vicarage, Church Street, Hampton TW12 2EB Tel (020) 8979 3071 Fax 8941 7221 E-mail stmary@bigfoot.com or vicar@winterburn.me.uk

WINTGENS, Peter Brendon. b 47. Surrey Univ BSc70. SEITE 06. **d** 09. NSM Battersea St Mary S'wark from 09. 5 Beechmore Road, London SW11 4ET Tel (020) 7720 9708
E-mail wintgens@btinternet.com

WINTLE, Anthony Robert. b 44. K Coll Lon 64. St Mich Coll Llan. **d** 68 **p** 69. C Llandaff N 68-70; C Baglan 70-75; V Treharris 75-86; V Treharris w Bedlinog 86-90; R St Fagans w Michaelston-super-Ely from 90. The Rectory, Greenwood Lane, St Fagans, Cardiff CF5 6EL Tel (029) 2056 5869

WINTLE, David Robert. b 46. Open Univ BA84. Qu Coll Birm 93. **d** 95 **p** 96. C Cov St Mary 95-00; P-in-c Ryton-on-Dunsmore w Bubbenhall 00-05; P-in-c Baginton 02-05; V Baginton w Bubbenhall and Ryton-on-Dunsmore from 05. The Vicarage, Church Road, Ryton on Dunsmore, Coventry CV8 3ET Tel (024) 7630 1283 E-mail david@wintled.fsnet.co.uk

WINTLE, Graham. b 52. Bris Univ BSc73. Oak Hill Th Coll BA86. **d** 86 **p** 87. C Southgate Chich 86-89; C New Malden and Coombe S'wark 89-92; V Surbiton Hill Ch 92-06; R Willoughby Australia from 06. 211 Mowbray Road, Willoughby NSW 2068, Australia Tel (0061) (2) 9411 2172
E-mail graham.wintle@optusnet.com.au

WINTLE, Canon Ruth Elizabeth. b 31. Westf Coll Lon BA53 St Hugh's Coll Ox BA67 MA74. St Mich Ho Ox 63. **dss** 72 **d** 87 **p** 94. Tutor St Jo Coll Dur 72-74; Selection Sec ACCM 74-83; St Jo in Bedwardine Worc 83-87; Par Dn 87-94; Dir of Ords 84-92; Hon Can Worc Cathl 87-97; rtd 95; Bp's Adv on Women's Min Worc 95-00; Perm to Offic from 98. 6 Kenswick Manor, Lower Broadheath, Worcester WR2 6QB Tel (01905) 641470

✠**WINTON, The Rt Revd Alan Peter.** b 58. Sheff Univ BA83 PhD87. Linc Th Coll 91. **d** 91 **p** 92 **c** 09. C Southgate Ch Ch Lon 91-95; P-in-c St Paul's Walden and Dioc CME Officer St Alb 95-99; R Welwyn w Ayot St Peter 99-05; TR Welwyn from 05; Hon Can St Alb 07-09; Suff Bp Thetford Nor from 09. The Red House, 53 Norwich Road, Stoke Holy Cross, Norwich NR14 8AB Tel (01508) 491014 Fax 492015
E-mail bishop.thetford@norwich.anglican.org

WINTON, Ms Philippa Mary. b 56. Nottm Univ BA78. Trin Coll Bris 79. **dss** 83 **d** 87 **p** 94. Sheff St Jo 83-86; Sheff Gillcar St Silas 86-87; Chapl Asst R Hallamshire Hosp Sheff 87; Hon Par Dn Linc St Faith and St Martin w St Pet 90-92; Chapl Asst W Middx Univ Hosp Isleworth 92-93; Perm to Offic Lon 93-95 and St Alb 95-09. The Red House, 53 Norwich Road, Stoke Holy Cross, Norwich NR14 8AB

WINTON, Stanley Wootton. b 30. Sarum & Wells Th Coll 70. **d** 72 **p** 73. C Birkenhead St Jas w St Bede Ches 72-75; V 75-79; TR Ellesmere Port 79-88; Chapl Ellesmere Port and Manor Hosps 79-95; R Delamere Ches 88-95; rtd 95; Perm to Offic Ches from 95. 26 Wimborne Avenue, Thingwall, Wirral CH61 7UL Tel 0151-648 0176

WINTOUR, Mrs Anne Elizabeth. b 52. **d** 03 **p** 04. OLM Melksham Sarum from 03; OLM Atworth w Shaw and Whitley from 07; OLM Broughton Gifford, Gt Chalfield and Holt from 07. Weavers House, 264 Sandridge Lane, Bromham, Chippenham SN15 2JW Tel (01380) 850880
E-mail anniewintour@btinternet.com

WINWARD, Stuart James. b 36. Open Univ BA85. Lich Th Coll 65. d 68 p 69. C Lytham St Cuth *Blackb* 68-71; C Padiham 71-73; V Musbury 73-84; R Old Trafford St Hilda *Man* 84-89; V Davyhulme St Mary 89-98; rtd 98; Perm to Offic *Ches* from 99. *1 Walnut Grove, Sale M33 6AJ* Tel 0161-905 1039

WIPPELL, David Stanley. b 46. Univ of Qld BSc67 Selw Coll Cam BA77 MA. Westcott Ho Cam 76. d 78 p 79. C Wolvercote w Summertown *Ox* 78-80; Asst Chapl St Edw Sch Ox 78-00; Chapl 00-06; Housemaster 85-97; Chapl St Hugh's Coll Ox 80-85; NSM Ray Valley *Ox* from 06. *3 The Rise, Islip, Kidlington OX5 2TG* Tel (01865) 849497 Fax 319202 Mobile 07790-021032 E-mail wippelld@stedwards.oxon.sch.uk

WISE, David Reginald. b 46. Glas Univ BSc68 QUB PhD74 LRAM67. Edin Th Coll 72. d 74 p 75. Chapl St Andr Cathl 74-75; C Ayr *Glas* 75-78; R Airdrie 78-81; P-in-c Gartcosh 78-81; P-in-c Leic St Nic 81-82; Chapl Leic Univ 81-89; TV Leic H Spirit 82-89; Chapl St Hilda's Priory and Sch Whitby 89-96; TV Louth *Linc* 96-98; V Mexborough *Sheff* from 98. *The Vicarage, Church Street, Mexborough S64 0ER* Tel (01709) 582321

WISE, Jacqueline Joy. b 65. Yorks Min Course. d 09. C Crewe All SS and St Paul w St Pet *Ches* from 09. *41 South Crofts, Nantwich CW5 5SG*

WISE, Ms Pamela Margaret. b 51. CertEd73 BA79. Ripon Coll Cuddesdon 89. d 91 p 94. Par Dn Tokyngton St Mich *Lon* 91-94; C N Greenford All Hallows 94; C Bedford All SS *St Alb* 94-97; TV Hitchin 97-03; V Oxhey All SS from 03. *All Saints' Vicarage, Gosforth Lane, Watford WD19 7AX* Tel (020) 8421 5949 E-mail pamela.wise@gmail.com

WISE, Richard Edmund. b 67. Clare Coll Cam BA88 MusB89 LRAM91. Cranmer Hall Dur 01. d 03 p 04. C Stanmore *Win* 03-07; P-in-c Bishopstoke from 07. *The Rectory, 10 Stoke Park Road, Eastleigh SO50 6DA* Tel (023) 8061 2192

WISEMAN, Canon David John. b 51. Lon Univ BD80 Derby Univ MA99. Cranmer Hall Dur 77. d 80 p 81. C Bilston *Lich* 80-84; P-in-c W Bromwich St Phil 84-86; V 86-89; P-in-c Cheetham St Mark *Man* 89-94; Dioc Community Relns Officer 89-96; P-in-c Ashton H Trin 94-99; TR Ashton 00-03; Chapl Tameside Coll 94-03; Soc Resp Adv *Pet* 03-07; P-in-c Northampton Ch Ch from 07; AD Gtr Northn from 07; Can Pet Cathl from 09. *Christ Church Vicarage, 3 Christ Church Road, Northampton NN1 5LL* Tel (01604) 633254 E-mail david@wiseman50.freeserve.co.uk

WISEMAN, John. b 56. Sarum & Wells Th Coll 80. d 83 p 84. C Swinton St Pet *Man* 83-87; C Swinton and Pendlebury 87-88; TV Atherton 88-93; V Bedford Leigh 93-02; V Lt Lever from 02. *The Vicarage, Market Street, Little Lever, Bolton BL3 1HH* Tel (01204) 700936

WISEMAN, Sister Julie. b 53. ERMC 05. d 08 p 09. NSM Roughton and Felbrigg, Metton, Sustead etc *Nor* from 08. *32B Beeston Common, Sheringham NR26 8ES* Tel (01263) 825623 E-mail juliessl@btinternet.com

WISHART, Michael Leslie. b 45. St Mich Coll Llan 70. d 73 p 74. C Llangyfelach *S & B* 73-76; Chapl RN 76-80 and 85-96; V Beguildy and Heyope *S & B* 80-84; V Gowerton 84-85; Chapl RNR 80-85; R Dowlais *Llan* 97-04; R Bishops Lydeard w Bagborough and Cothelstone *B & W* from 04. *The Rectory, Church Street, Bishops Lydeard, Taunton TA4 3AT* Tel (01823) 432414 E-mail michael.wishart@btopenworld.com

WISKEN, Canon Brian Leonard. b 34. Dur Univ BA58. Linc Th Coll 58. d 60 p 61. C Lobley Hill *Dur* 60-63; C Ipswich All Hallows *St E* 63-65; P-in-c Scunthorpe All SS *Linc* 65-69; V 69-71; Dioc Stewardship Adv 70-75; R Panton w Wragby 71-75; V Langton by Wragby 71-75; R Cleethorpes 75-77; TR 77-89; V Linc St Nic w St Jo Newport 89-99; Can and Preb Linc Cathl 88-00; rtd 99; Perm to Offic *Nor* and *St E* from 99. *49 Gainsborough Drive, Lowestoft NR32 4NJ* Tel (01502) 512378 E-mail b.wisken@btinternet.com

WISKEN, Robert Daniel. b 30. ACT. d 60 p 60. C N Rockhampton St Barn Australia 60; V N Rockhampton St Matt 61-63; V Winton *Man* 63-65; R Luddington w Hemington and Thurning *Pet* 65-69; P-in-c Clopton *St E* 66-69; V Ipswich All SS 69-73; V Sompting *Chich* 74-78; Org Sec (SW England) CECS 78-80; R Edmundbyers w Muggleswick *Dur* 80-83; R Wexham *Ox* 83-86; Australia from 86; rtd 95. *Spiritus, PO Box 307, Nundah Qld 4012, Australia* Tel (0061) (7) 3266 3150 E-mail anglicareqld@bigpond.com

WITCHELL, David William. b 47. St Jo Coll Nottm BTh75. d 75 p 76. C Northampton St Mary *Pet* 75-78; C Oakham w Hambleton and Egleton 78-81; C Oakham, Hambleton, Egleton, Braunston and Brooke 81-82; V Weedon Bec w Everdon 82-90; V Wellingborough St Barn 90-00; RD Wellingborough 98-00; P-in-c Paignton St Paul Preston *Ex* 00-02; V Paignton Ch Ch and Preston St Paul from 03; RD Torbay 03-09. *St Paul's Vicarage, Locarno Avenue, Paignton TQ3 2DH* Tel (01803) 522872

WITCHELL, Derek William Frederick. b 49. SAOMC 00. d 03 p 04. C Bloxham w Milcombe and S Newington *Ox* 03-06; P-in-c Wing w Grove from 06; P-in-c Wingrave w Rowsham, Aston Abbotts and Cublington from 06; P-in-c Cheddington w Mentmore from 08. *The Vicarage, 27B Aylesbury Road, Wing,* Leighton Buzzard LU7 0PD Tel (01296) 682320 Mobile 07847-167507 E-mail witchell@psaconnect.net

WITCHER, Ian. b 49. CertEd93 Lon Inst of Educn Lic97. d 97 p 98. OLM Shaston *Sarum* 97-08. *7 Old Boundary Road, Shaftesbury SP7 8ND* Tel (01747) 854878

WITCOMBE, Canon John Julian. b 59. Cam Univ MA84 Nottm Univ MPhil91. St Jo Coll Nottm BA83. d 84 p 85. C Birtley *Dur* 84-87; C Chilwell *S'well* 87-91; V Lodge Moor St Luke *Sheff* 91-95; TR Uxbridge *Lon* 95-98; Dean St Jo Coll Nottm 98-05; Officer for Min *Glouc* from 05; Hon Can Glouc Cathl from 09. *St Paul's Vicarage, 2 King Edward's Avenue, Gloucester GL1 5DA* Tel (01452) 500443 E-mail jwitcombe@glosdioc.org.uk

WITCOMBE, Michael David. b 53. Univ of Wales (Lamp) BA76. Qu Coll Birm 76. d 78 p 79. C Neath w Llantwit *Llan* 78-80; C Whitchurch 80-83; V Newcastle 83-02; P-in-c Ewenny 84-86; V Llanishen from 02. *The Vicarage, 2 The Rise, Llanishen, Cardiff CF14 0RA* Tel (029) 2075 2545

WITCOMBE, Ricarda Jane. b 64. Ch Coll Cam BA86 MA90. St Jo Coll Nottm MA(TS)99. d 01 p 02. C Wilford *S'well* 01-05; P-in-c Glouc St Paul from 05. *St Paul's Vicarage, 2 King Edward's Avenue, Gloucester GL1 5DA* Tel (01452) 500443 E-mail ricarda@ricarda.fsnet.co.uk

WITCOMBE, Simon Christopher. b 61. Dundee Univ MA83 PGCE84 Dur Univ BA90. St Jo Coll Dur 88. d 91 p 92. C Earlham St Anne *Nor* 91-95; Assoc P Skegness and Winthorpe *Linc* 95-98; Gen Preacher 95-98; R Woodhall Spa Gp 98-07; V Codsall *Lich* from 07. *The Vicarage, 52 Church Road, Codsall, Wolverhampton WV8 1EH* Tel (01902) 842168 E-mail switcombe@tinyonline.co.uk

WITHERIDGE, John Stephen. b 53. Kent Univ BA76 Ch Coll Cam BA78 MA82 FRSA98. Ridley Hall Cam 78. d 79 p 80. C Luton St Mary *St Alb* 79-82; Asst Chapl Marlborough Coll 82-84; Abp's Chapl *Cant* 84-87; Conduct Eton Coll 87-96; Hd Charterhouse Sch Godalming from 96; Perm to Offic *Guildf* from 96. *Charterhouse, Godalming GU7 2DJ* Tel (01483) 291600 Fax 291647

WITHERS, Mrs Christine Mary. b 37. ALA60. Gilmore Ho. dss 81 d 87 p 94. Chorleywood Ch Ch *St Alb* 81-86; Darley *Derby* 86-92; C 87-92; Chapl HM Pris Drake Hall 92-95; P-in-c Standon and Cotes Heath *Lich* 96-98; Perm to Offic *Heref* from 98. *St Mary's Close, Westbury, Shrewsbury SY5 9QX* Tel (01743) 885038

WITHERS, Eleanor. See WILLIAMS, Mrs Eleanor Jane

WITHERS, Geoffrey Edward. b 68. QUB BSc90 TCD BTh93. CITC 90. d 93 p 94. C Ballymena w Ballyclug *Conn* 93-97; I Monkstown 97-01; Chapl RAF from 01. *Chaplaincy Services, Valiant Block, HQ Air Command, RAF High Wycombe HP14 4UE* Tel (01494) 496800 Fax 496343 E-mail stchap.dgcs@ptc.raf.mod.uk or gwithers@vodafone.net

WITHERS, Miss Gillian. b 58. Stranmillis Coll BEd80. St Jo Coll Nottm 94. d 97 p 98. NSM Mossley *Conn* 97-03; C Bangor St Comgall *D & D* 03-05; V Knock 05-08; I Grey Abbey w Kircubbin from 08. *4 Rectory Wood, Portaferry, Newtownards BT22 1LJ* Tel (028) 4272 9307 E-mail vicarofdibley@hotmail.com

WITHERS, John Geoffrey. b 39. St Jo Coll Dur BA61 Birm Univ CertEd63 CQSW72. SWMTC 84. d 87 p 88. NSM Drewsteignton *Ex* 87-01; P-in-c 99-01; P-in-c Hittisleigh and Spreyton 99-01; P-in-c Chagford, Drewsteignton, Hittisleigh etc 01; C 01-07; Sub Chapl HM Pris Ex 96-07; Perm to Offic *Ex* from 07. *Lane's End, Broadwoodwidger, Lifton PL16 0JH* Tel (01566) 780544

WITHERS, Michael. b 41. TCD BA66 Edin Univ BD70 QUB MTh83 Birm Univ PGCE67. Union Th Sem (NY) STM71. d 71 p 73. C Seagoe *D & D* 71-77; C Seapatrick 77-80; I Belfast St Chris 80-89; I Movilla 89-96; rtd 96. *11 Earlswood Road, Belfast BT4 3DY* Tel (028) 9047 1037

WITHERS, Michael Selby. b 36. Sheff Univ BA61 PGCE62. SAOMC 93. d 96 p 97. NSM Bletchley *Ox* 96-97; NSM Ellesborough, The Kimbles and Stoke Mandeville 97-01; NSM Risborough 01-05; Perm to Offic from 05. *The Welcome (rear house), Town Lane, Wooburn Green, High Wycombe HP10 0PL* Tel (01628) 526304 E-mail mandhwithers@waitrose.com

WITHEY, Michael John. b 45. Open Univ BA30 Ox Univ MTh98. Oak Hill Th Coll 71. d 74 p 75. C St Alb St Paul *St Alb* 74-76; C Luton St Mary 77; C Luton St Fran 77-80; V Woodside w E Hyde 80-87; CF (TA) 83-87; Dioc Stewardship Adv *Ox* 87-89; Chapl HM YOI Onley 89-91; V Hengoed w Gobowen *Lich* 91-95; Chapl Robert Jones and Agnes Hunt Orthopaedic Hosp 91-95; P-in-c Chasetown *Lich* 95-00; V 00-02; V Stroud H Trin *Glouc* from 02; Chapl Cotswold and Vale Primary Care Trust 02-06; Chapl Glos Primary Care Trust from 06; Chapl Glos Partnership Trust from 09. *Holy Trinity Vicarage, 10 Bowbridge Lane, Stroud GL5 2JW* Tel (01453) 764551

WITHINGTON, Brian James. b 54. Leic Univ MSc01 CQSW76. EAMTC 94. d 97 p 98. NSM Pet St Jo 97-04; P-in-c Broughton w Loddington and Cransley etc from 04; RD Kettering from 07. *The Rectory, Gate Lane, Broughton, Kettering NN14 1ND* Tel and fax (01536) 791373 E-mail brian.andco@virgin.net

WITHINGTON, George Kenneth. b 37. Birm Univ BA59. Wells Th Coll 59. **d** 61 **p** 62. C Hartcliffe St Andr CD *Bris* 61-65; V Swindon St Jo 65-73; V Cricklade w Latton 73-97; RD Cricklade 94-97; rtd 97; Perm to Offic *Heref* and *Worc* from 97. *19 Oak Drive, Colwall, Malvern WR13 6RA* Tel (01684) 540590

WITHINGTON, Canon Keith. b 32. Univ of Wales (Lamp) BA55. Qu Coll Birm 55. **d** 57 **p** 58. C Bournville *Birm* 57-61; V 61-00; RD Moseley 81-91; Hon Can Birm Cathl 83-00; rtd 00; Perm to Offic *Birm* and *Worc* from 00. *44 Dugard Way, Droitwich WR9 8UX* Tel (01905) 795847
E-mail kw1000@bushinternet.com

WITHINGTON, Paul Martin. b 60. Kent Univ BSc86. Trin Coll Bris 01. **d** 03 **p** 04. C Elworth and Warmingham *Ches* 03-06; TV Congleton from 06. *The Vicarage, 14 Chapel Street, Congleton CW12 4AB* Tel (01260) 278288

WITHNELL, Roderick David. b 55. EMMTC 86 Ridley Hall Cam 89. **d** 90 **p** 91. C Shenfield *Chelmsf* 90-94; C Woodleigh and Loddiswell *Ex* 94-95; TV Modbury, Bigbury, Ringmore w Kingston etc 95-00; Canada 00-01; TR Burrington, Chawleigh, Cheldon, Chulmleigh etc *Ex* from 01. *The Rectory, Church Lane, Chulmleigh EX18 7BY* Tel (01769) 580537

WITHY, John Daniel Forster. b 38. ALCD64. **d** 64 **p** 65. C Belfast St Aid *Conn* 64-68; Dir Chr Conf Cen Sion Mills from 68. *Zion House, 120 Melmont Road, Strabane BT82 9ET* Tel (028) 8165 8672

WITT, Bryan Douglas. b 52. St Mich Coll Llan BD84. **d** 84 **p** 85. C Betws w Ammanford *St D* 84-87; V Llanllwni 87-91; V Llangennech and Hendy 91-94; V St Clears w Llangynin and Llanddowror etc from 04. *The Vicarage, Bridge Street, St Clears, Carmarthen SA33 4EE* Tel (01994) 230266

WITTER, Mrs Tania Judy Ingram. b 37. Girton Coll Cam BA58 MA63. Oak Hill Th Coll 94. **d** 95 **p** 96. NSM Highbury Ch-the-w St Jo and St Sav *Lon* 95-03; Perm to Offic *Lon* and *Eur* from 03. *26 Viewpoint Apartments, 30-32 Highbury Grove, London N5 2DL* Tel (020) 7226 6908
E-mail tania.witter@btinternet.com

WITTS, Donald Roger. b 47. Cranmer Hall Dur 86. **d** 88 **p** 89. C Leyland St Andr *Blackb* 88-90; C Staines St Mary and St Pet *Lon* 90-93; Ind Missr *Man* 93-95; Dioc Communications Officer *Cant* 95-00; P-in-c Blean 95-01; P-in-c Birchington w Acol and Minnis Bay 01-03; V from 03. *All Saints' Vicarage, 15 Minnis Road, Birchington CT7 9SE* Tel (01843) 841117
E-mail don.witts@btopenworld.com

WITTS, Graham Robert. b 53. Newc Univ BEd Bris Univ MA01. Linc Th Coll 79. **d** 82 **p** 83. C Horncastle w Low Toynton *Linc* 82-85; TV Gt Grimsby St Mary and St Jas 85-89; TR Yelverton, Meavy, Sheepstor and Walkhampton *Ex* 89-93; C Glastonbury w Meare *B & W* 93-03; RD Glastonbury 00-03; V Burnham from 03. *The Vicarage, Rectory Road, Burnham-on-Sea TA8 2BZ* Tel (01278) 782991 E-mail thewittsonweb@hotmail.com

WOADDEN, Christopher Martyn. b 56. St Jo Coll Nottm LTh. **d** 87 **p** 88. C Mickleover All SS *Derby* 87-90; C Wirksworth w Alderwasley, Carsington etc 90-92; C Wirksworth 92; TV Gt and Lt Coates w Bradley *Linc* 92-98; V Holton-le-Clay and Tetney 98-07; V Holton-le-Clay, Tetney and N Cotes from 07. *The Vicarage, Church Walk, Holton-le-Clay, Grimsby DN36 5AN* Tel (01472) 824082

WOAN, Miss Susan Ann. b 52. Univ of Wales (Abth) BSc72 Lon Univ PGCE73 Ch Ch Coll Cant MA91 Rob Coll Cam BA95. Ridley Hall Cam 93. **d** 96 **p** 97. C Histon *Ely* 96-97; C Radipole and Melcombe Regis *Sarum* 97-00; Chapl Bournemouth and Poole Coll of FE *Win* 00-04; Hon C Bournemouth St Jo w St Mich 00-04; Vice-Prin Dioc Min Course *Nor* 04-06; Prin Dioc Min Course from 07; Vice-Prin ERMC from 07. *2 Conesford Drive, Norwich NR1 2BB* Tel (01603) 622579 *or* 729812
E-mail sue.woan@dial.pipex.com
or suewoan@norwich.anglican.org

WODEHOUSE, Armine Boyle. b 24. Oak Hill Th Coll 83. **d** 86 **p** 86. NSM Gt Parndon *Chelmsf* 86-92; Perm to Offic *Eur* 89-92; Chapl Menton 92-99; rtd 99; Perm to Offic *Lon* from 02. *Flat 12, 105 Onslow Square, London SW7 3LU* Tel (020) 7584 4845

WODEHOUSE, Carol Lylie. See KIMBERLEY, Countess of

WODEMAN, Cyril Peter Guy. b 28. Qu Coll Cam BA50 MA55 ARCO54 LRAM58 ARCM58. Cranmer Hall Dur 72. **d** 73 **p** 74. C Penwortham St Mary *Blackb* 73-77; V Burnley St Steph 77-85; V Hornby w Claughton 85-93; rtd 93; Perm to Offic *Blackb* and *Carl* from 93. *5 Harling Bank, Kirkby Lonsdale, Carnforth LA6 2DJ* Tel (01524) 272474

WOFFENDEN (née HANCOCK), Mrs Dorothy Myfanwy. b 41. NOC 01. **d** 03 **p** 04. NSM Brinnington w Portwood *Ches* 03-05; C Waverton w Aldford and Bruera 05-09. *8 Churchill Crescent, Marple, Stockport SK6 6HJ* Tel 0161-427 6839
E-mail dwoffenden@smartone.co.uk

WOLFE, Canon Michael Matheson. b 29. Pemb Coll Ox BA49 MA53. Cuddesdon Coll 51. **d** 53 **p** 54. C Moorfields *Bris* 53-57; P-in-c Fochabers *Mor* 57-58; Sub-Warden Aberlour Orphanage 58-59; V Southport St Paul *Liv* 59-65; V Upholland 65-73; TR 73-82; RD Ormskirk 78-82; RD Ormskirk and Hon Can Liv Cathl 78-82; Can Res Liv Cathl 82-96; Merseyside Ecum Officer

82-89; AD Toxteth and Wavertree 89-96; rtd 96; Perm to Offic *Liv* from 97; Hon Chapl Liv Cathl from 97. *23 Hunters Lane, Liverpool L15 8HL* Tel 0151-733 1541

WOLFENDEN, Peter Graham. b 40. St Pet Coll Ox BA63 MA66. Linc Th Coll 62. **d** 64 **p** 65. C Adlington *Blackb* 64-66; Asst Master Barton Peveril Gr Sch 66-69; Chapl Bp Wordsworth Sch Salisbury 69-72; Hon C Bishopstoke *Win* 66-72; Hon C Ponteland *Newc* 72-02; Hd Master Richard Coates Middle Sch Ponteland 78-01; Chapl Malta and Gozo *Eur* 02-07; Chapl Málaga from 07. *Paseo de Reding 21-2D, Málaga 29016 (Málaga), Spain* E-mail anglican@onvol.net

WOLLASTON, Canon Barbara Kathleen. b 30. LSE BSc(Soc)64. Gilmore Ho 51. **d** 87 **p** 94. Dir Past Studies Qu Coll Birm 80-89; Dioc Dir of Ords *S'wark* 89-94; rtd 94; Perm to Offic *Lich* from 94. *21 Chapel Street, Wem, Shrewsbury SY4 5ER* Tel (01939) 232229

WOLLEY, John. BSc. **d** 85 **p** 86. Hon C Croydon St Aug *S'wark* 85-89; Perm to Offic *Linc* 89-01. *7 Royal Oak Court, Upgate, Louth LN11 9JA* Tel (01507) 601614

WOLLEY, Richard. b 33. CCC Ox BA56 MA58. S Dios Minl Tr Scheme 82. **d** 85 **p** 86. NSM Brighton Resurr *Chich* 85-88; C 88-89; C Brighton St Geo w St Anne and St Mark 89-91; R Buxted and Hadlow Down 91-98; rtd 98; Perm to Offic *Chich* from 98; RD Uckfield 04-06. *18 Millington Court, Mill Lane, Uckfield TN22 5AZ* Tel (01825) 761042
E-mail elwandrw@tiscali.co.uk

WOLSTENCROFT, The Ven Alan. b 37. Cuddesdon Coll. **d** 69 **p** 70. C Halliwell St Thos *Man* 69-71; C Stand 71-73; V Wythenshawe St Martin 73-80; AD Withington 78-91; Chapl Wythenshawe Hosp Man 80-89; V Baguley *Man* 80-91; V Bolton St Pet 91-98; Hon Can Man Cathl 86-98; Can Res 98-04; Adn Man 98-04; rtd 04; Perm to Offic *Man* from 04; Rtd Clergy and Widows Officer from 04. *The Bakehouse, 1 Latham Row, Horwich, Bolton BL6 6QZ* Tel (01204) 469985
E-mail alanchrisw@tiscali.co.uk

WOLTON, Andrew John. b 54. Cranfield Univ MDA00. St Jo Coll Nottm BA08. **d** 08 **p** 09. C Bures w Assington and Lt Cornard *St E* from 08. *19 Normandie Way, Bures CO8 5BE* Tel (01787) 227283 Mobile 07769-946364
E-mail andywolton@btinternet.com

WOLVERHAMPTON, Area Bishop of. See GREGORY, The Rt Revd Clive Malcolm

WOLVERSON, Marc Ali Morad. b 68. Univ of Kansas BA91. Ripon Coll Cuddesdon 93. **d** 96 **p** 97. C Nantwich *Ches* 96-99; C Baton Rouge St Luke USA 99-00; C Bramhall *Ches* 00-04; V High Lane 04-09; P-in-c Douglas All SS and St Thos *S & M* from 09. *All Saints' Vicarage, 62 Ballabrooie Way, Douglas, Isle of Man IM1 4HB* Tel (01624) 621547
E-mail frmarcw@yahoo.co.uk

WOMERSLEY, Sally Ann. b 61. Westcott Ho Cam 06. **d** 08 **p** 09. C Charing w Charing Heath and Lt Chart *Cant* from 08. *The Vicarage, 8 Glebeland, Egerton, Ashford TN27 9DH* Tel (01233) 756224 E-mail sallywomersley@yahoo.co.uk

WONG (née RUNDLE), Hilary. b 65. St Hugh's Coll Ox BA88 Cheltenham & Glouc Coll of HE PGCE90. Trin Coll Bris 01. **d** 03 **p** 04. C Chipping Sodbury and Old Sodbury *Glouc* 03-07; P-in-c St Helier *S'wark* 07. *St Peter's Vicarage, 193 Bishopsford Road, Morden SM4 6BH* Tel (020) 8685 9878
E-mail hilary193wong@hotmail.co.uk

WOO, Arthur Cheumin. b 66. Qu Univ Kingston Ontario BSc89 MEng92. St Jo Coll Nottm MTh08. **d** 08 **p** 09. C Highworth w Sevenhampton and Inglesham etc *Bris* from 08. *14 Brookfield, Highworth, Swindon SN6 7HY* Tel (01793) 763197

WOOD, Alastair Paul. b 59. Ox Min Course 06. **d** 09. *35 Stapleton Road Headington, Oxford OX3 7LX* Tel 07948-989153 (mobile)
E-mail narniacurate09@btinternet.com

WOOD, Mrs Ann Rene. b 49. St Deiniol's Hawarden 87. **d** 90 **p** 94. Par Dn Bamber Bridge St Aid *Blackb* 90-93; C W Burnley All SS 93-95; V Marton Moss 95-00; Hon Can Blackb Cathl 98-00; R Whiston *Sheff* 00-07; V Kimberworth from 07; AD Rotherham 04-08. *49 Admirals Crest, Scholes, Rotherham S61 2SW* Tel (01709) 564422 E-mail ann.wood@ukonline.co.uk

WOOD (née BLACKBURN), Mrs Anne Dorothy. b 54. Keele Univ BA76 Bradf Univ MSc90. NOC 95. **d** 98 **p** 99. NSM Batley St Thos *Wakef* 98-00; St P in-c Morley St Paul 01-02; C Bruntcliffe 01-02; C Morley 02-03; TV 03-07; TV Oakenshaw, Wyke and Low Moor *Bradf* from 07. *15 Chats Wood Fold, Oakenshaw, Bradford BD12 7HG* Tel (01274) 693449 Mobile 07769-503147 E-mail anne.d.wood@talk21.com

WOOD, Preb Anthony James. b 38. Kelham Th Coll 58. **d** 63 **p** 64. C Shrewsbury St Alkmund *Lich* 63; C Harlescott 63-66; C Porthill 66-70; P-in-c Priorslee 70-76; Chapl Telford Town Cen 73-76; V Barton-under-Needwood 76-97; V Barton under Needwood w Dunstall 97-09; V Barton under Needwood w Dunstall and Tatenhill from 09; RD Tutbury from 02; Preb Lich Cathl from 08. *The Vicarage, 3 Church Lane, Barton under Needwood, Burton-on-Trent DE13 8HU* Tel (01283) 712359
E-mail tonywood@preb.co.uk

WOOD, Barbara Ann. b 49. St Mich Coll Llan 00. **d** 02 **p** 03. C

Glan Ely *Llan* 02-05; P-in-c Llanharan w Peterston-super-Montem from 05. *The Vicarage, Brynna Road, Brynna, Pontyclun CF72 9QE* Tel (01443) 226307
E-mail babswood01@hotmail.com

WOOD, Barry. b 56. Open Univ BA87 Sheff Univ MMin01 CQSW81. St Steph Ho Ox 87. **d** 89 **p** 90. C Tranmere St Paul w St Luke *Ches* 89-92; TV Ches 92-94; P-in-c S Tawton and Belstone *Ex* 94-00; R 00-02; RD Okehampton 98-02; TR Wylye and Till Valley *Sarum* 02-03; rtd 03; Perm to Offic *Ex* 03-05 and *Truro* 05-07; Hon C Chaffcombe, Cricket Malherbie etc *B & W* from 07. *34 Tansee Hill, Thorncombe, Chard TA20 4LQ*

WOOD, Beresford Donald Richard. b 32. Leeds Univ BA58. Cant Sch of Min 91. **d** 94 **p** 95. Chapl St Mary's Sch Westbrook from 94; NSM Folkestone St Mary and St Eanswythe *Cant* 94-02; Perm to Offic from 02. *St Katherine's Cottage, Pound Lane, Elham, Canterbury CT4 6TS* Tel (01303) 840817

WOOD, Canon Beryl Jean. b 54. Linc Th Coll 85. **d** 87 **p** 94. C Gaywood, Bawsey and Mintlyn *Nor* 87-92; C Gaywood 92-93; Asst Chapl Univ Hosp Nottm 93-95; R Shipdham w E and W Bradenham *Nor* 95-06; RD Dereham in Mitford 00-03; Hon Can Nor Cathl 05-06; Dep Warden Launde Abbey *Leic* from 06. *South Cottage, Launde Abbey, Launde Road, Launde, Leicester LE7 9XB* Tel (01572) 717853 E-mail brylwood@tiscali.co.uk

WOOD, Mrs Brenda. b 46. Eliz Gaskell Coll Man TCert67 Leeds Metrop Univ BEd94 Leeds Univ MA04. NOC 00. **d** 03 **p** 04. NSM Kirkstall *Ripon* from 03. *18 Wentworth Crescent, Leeds LS17 7TW* Tel 0113-226 7991 E-mail brenda.wood@ntlworld.com

WOOD, Canon Brian Frederick. b 31. Leeds Univ BA52. Coll of Resurr Mirfield 55. **d** 57 **p** 58. C Wigan St Anne *Liv* 57-60; C Elland *Wakef* 60-63; V Carlinghow 63-73; V Drighlington 73-94; RD Birstall 83-92; Hon Can Wakef Cathl 89-94; rtd 94; Perm to Offic *Bradf* and *Wakef* from 94. *10 Grove Road, Menston, Ilkley LS29 6JD* Tel (01943) 872820

WOOD, Brian Richard. b 49. Sheff Univ BA70 MCMI78 RIBA85 MRICS00 FCIOB00. Ox Min Course 04. **d** 07 **p** 08. NSM Blenheim *Ox* from 07. *Glebe Cottage, Shipton Bottom, Shipton-on-Cherwell, Kidlington OX5 1JJ* Tel (01865) 379203 E-mail brwood@brookes.ac.uk

WOOD, Ms Carolyn Marie Therese. b 57. Sussex Univ BA91. St Mich Coll Llan 02. **d** 04 **p** 05. C Monkton *St D* 04-07. *38 Trem y Mynydd, Burry Port SA16 0FZ* E-mail tuppywood@hotmail.com

WOOD, Catherine Rosemary. b 54. Melbourne Coll of Div 82 St Jo Coll Auckland 83. **d** 83 **p** 84. New Zealand 83-01; C Howick 83-87; C Auckland St Paul 88; P-in-c Mangere E 89-90; Co-ord Environmental Educn 90-95; N Fieldworker Chr World Service 96-01; Hon C Glen Eden 90-97; NSM Auckland Cathl 98-01; Perm to Offic *S'wark* 01-02; P-in-c Tatsfield 02-08; C Limpsfield and Titsey 02-03; Min Limpsfield Chart St Andr CD 03-08; Perm to Offic from 08; Chapl HM Pris Latchmere Ho from 09. *St Michael's Convent, 56 Ham Common, Richmond TW10 7JH* Tel (020) 8940 8711 Mobile 07960-088873 E-mail catswhiskers@ukonline.co.uk

WOOD, Christine Denise. b 48. EMMTC. **d** 05 **p** 06. NSM Clifton *S'well* 05-07; Asst Chapl Notts Healthcare NHS Trust from 07. *Rampton Hospital, Retford, Nottingham DN22 0PD* Tel (01777) 248321

WOOD, Christopher David. b 60. Worc Coll Ox BA83 Leeds Univ MA06. Coll of Resurr Mirfield 04. **d** 06 **p** 07. C King's Lynn St Marg w St Nic *Nor* 06-09; R Hunstanton St Mary w Ringstead Parva etc from 09. *10 Pilot Street, King's Lynn PE30 1QL* Tel (01553) 760157 E-mail christopherd1760@hotmail.co.uk

WOOD, Christopher William. b 44. Rhodes Univ BA66 UNISA BTh82. St Bede's Coll Umtata 79. **d** 80 **p** 82. S Africa 80-87; C Houghton Regis *St Alb* 87-00; C Milton *Portsm* 00-03; Perm to Offic *Lich* from 04. *27 Penton Walk, Stoke-on-Trent ST3 3DG* Tel (01782) 311779

WOOD, Mrs Claire. b 63. SAOMC 03. **d** 06 **p** 07. C Buckingham *Ox* 06-09; R Olney from 09. *Olney Rectory, 9 Orchard Rise, Olney MK46 5HB* Tel (01280) 821509 Mobile 07896-696842 E-mail revclairewood@gmail.com

WOOD, Canon Colin Arthur. b 41. S'wark Ord Course 86. **d** 89 **p** 90. C Tadworth *S'wark* 89-93; TV Morden 93-06; Hon Can S'wark Cathl 05-06; rtd 06. *4 Palm Close, 130 Barrack Lane, Bognor Regis PO21 4EF* Tel (01243) 264192

WOOD, David Arthur. b 30. Man Univ BA51. Lich Th Coll 59. **d** 61 **p** 62. C Ashton Ch Ch Man 61-64; C Elton All SS 64-68; Dioc Youth Adv *Newc* 68-72; R Cramlington 72-73; TR 73-83; V Wylam 83-86; TV Egremont and Haile *Carl* 86-94; rtd 94; Perm to Offic *Carl* from 94. *6 John Street, Maryport CA15 6JT* Tel (01900) 816706

WOOD, David Christopher. b 52. Oak Hill Th Coll 89. **d** 91 **p** 92. C Kendal St Thos *Carl* 91-95; P-in-c Asby, Bolton and Crosby Ravensworth 95-05; P-in-c Barton, Pooley Bridge and Martindale from 05. *The Vicarage, Pooley Bridge, Penrith CA10 2LT* Tel (01768) 486220 E-mail revdavidcwood@hotmail.com

WOOD, David John. b 48. Newc Univ BSc70 PGCE71 Open Univ MA91. **d** 01 **p** 02. OLM Bedlington *Newc* 01-07; NSM

Shotley from 07. *St John's Vicarage, Snod's Edge, Shotley Bridge, Consett DH8 9TL* Tel (01207) 255665
E-mail davwd50@hotmail.com

WOOD, David Michael. b 39. Chich Th Coll. **d** 82 **p** 83. C Epping St Jo *Chelmsf* 82-85; C Totton *Win* 85-88; V Southway *Ex* 88-97; P-in-c Black Torrington, Bradford w Cookbury etc 97-01; R 01-04; rtd 04; Perm to Offic *Portsm* from 04. *47 Queens Crescent, Stubbington, Fareham PO14 2QG*

WOOD, Dennis William. b 28. Qu Mary Coll Lon BSc53 Glas Univ PhD57. NEOC 82. **d** 85 **p** 85. NSM Stanhope *Dur* 85-86; NSM Stanhope w Frosterley 86-94; NSM Eastgate w Rookhope 86-94; NSM Melrose *Edin* from 94. *Gordonlee, Ormiston Terrace, Melrose TD6 9SP* Tel (01896) 823835

WOOD, Donald. b 40. **d** 95 **p** 96. NSM Caldicot *Mon* 95-99; P-in-c Llangwm Uchaf and Llangwm Isaf w Gwernesney etc 99-06; Lic to Offic from 06. *13 Deepweir, Caldicot NP26 5JG* Tel (01291) 672518 *or* 425214

WOOD, Edward Berryman. b 33. Ely Th Coll 54. **d** 57 **p** 58. C Aldershot St Mich *Guildf* 57-60; C Worplesdon 60-62; V Littleport St Matt *Ely* 62-64; V Balham St Jo Bedf Hill *S'wark* 64-71; V New Eltham All SS 71-84; RD Eltham (Sub-Deanery) 79-82; P-in-c Woldingham 84-98; rtd 98; Perm to Offic *Chich* 99-07. *The College of St Barnabas, Blackberry Lane, Lingfield RH7 6NJ* Tel (01342) 872844
E-mail tandem@collegeofstbarnabas.com

WOOD, Edward Francis. b 28. Chich Th Coll 56. **d** 58 **p** 59. C Newc St Fran 58-62; C High Elswick St Phil 62-64; C Delaval 64-67; C-in-c Shiremoor CD 67-68; V Shiremoor and Dioc Broadcasting Adv 68-78; C Newc St Geo 78-82; C Newc Epiphany 82-93; rtd 93; Perm to Offic *Newc* from 93. *52 Albemarle Avenue, Newcastle upon Tyne NE2 3NQ* Tel 0191-284 5338 E-mail franciswood@waitrose.com

WOOD, Elaine Mary. See RICHARDSON, Elaine Mary

WOOD, Mrs Elizabeth Jane. b 51. Ch Ch Coll Cant DipEd73. NEOC 98. **d** 01 **p** 02. C Denton *Newc* 01-04; V N Sunderland from 04; V Beadnell from 04. *The Vicarage, South Lane, North Sunderland, Seahouses NE68 7TU* Tel (01665) 720202
E-mail jane.wood3@btopenworld.com

WOOD, Elizabeth Lucy. b 35. WMMTC 89. **d** 92 **p** 94. NSM Wellingborough St Mark *Pet* 92-95; P-in-c Stanwick w Hargrave 95-00; Perm to Offic from 00; Chapl to Retired Clergy and Clergy Widows' Officer from 08. *21 Meadow Way, Irthlingborough, Wellingborough NN9 5RS* Tel (01933) 652319 E-mail elizwood@tiscali.co.uk

WOOD, Francis. See WOOD, Edward Francis

WOOD, Frederick Leonard. b 19. BEM59. Worc Ord Coll. **d** 64 **p** 65. C Paignton St Paul Preston *Ex* 64-68; V Charles w Plymouth St Matthias 68-81; rtd 82; Perm to Offic *B & W* 85-92 and *Ox* from 93. *Oaklands, 1 Windrush Heights, Sandhurst GU47 8ET* Tel (01344) 762368

WOOD, Geoffrey. b 33. Tyndale Hall Bris 56. **d** 61 **p** 62. C Tranmere St Cath *Ches* 61-64; C Newburn *Newc* 64-68; R Gt Smeaton w Appleton upon Wiske *Ripon* 69-79; P-in-c Cowton w Birkby 73-79; P-in-c Danby Wiske w Yafforth and Hutton Bonville 76-79; R Gt Smeaton w Appleton Wiske and Birkby etc 79-89; R Fressingfield, Mendham etc *St E* 92-98; rtd 98; Perm to Offic *Dur* 98-04; Lic to Offic *Edin* from 08. *Clova, 16 Main Street, Longniddry EH32 0NF* Tel (01875) 852323

WOOD, Geoffrey James. b 47. NOC 88. **d** 91 **p** 92. C Stainton-in-Cleveland *York* 91-94; V Middlesbrough St Oswald 94-99; V Eskdaleside w Ugglebarnby and Sneaton 99-06; rtd 06; Perm to Offic *York* from 06. *22 Hedley Street, Guisborough TS14 6EG* Tel (01287) 619286 E-mail frgeoff@btinternet.com

WOOD, George Albert. b 22. St Paul's Coll Grahamstown. **d** 54 **p** 55. C Hillcrest S Africa 54-57; C W Suburbs Pretoria 57-60; C Cheam *S'wark* 60-63; R Eshowe S Africa 63-69; Can Zululand 68-73; Dean Eshowe 70-73; R Port Elizabeth Ch the K 74-77; Area Sec USPG *Chich* from 78; TV Littlehampton and Wick *Chich* 86-88; rtd 88; Perm to Offic *Chich* from 88. *3 Orchard Gardens, Rustington, Littlehampton BN16 3HN* Tel (01903) 787746

WOOD, Heather Dawn. See ATKINSON, Mrs Heather Dawn

WOOD, Miss Helen Ruth. b 54. Bedf Coll Lon BA75. Glouc Sch of Min 87. **d** 91 **p** 94. NSM Up Hatherley *Glouc* 91-94; NSM Cheltenham Em w St Steph from 94; Asst Chapl Cheltenham Ladies' Coll from 91. *9 Southfield Manor Park, Sandy Lane, Charlton Kings, Cheltenham GL53 9DJ* Tel (01242) 242793 E-mail woodh@cheltladiescollege.org

WOOD, Jane. See WOOD, Mrs Elizabeth Jane

WOOD, Jane. b 52. Ripon Coll Cuddesdon. **d** 08 **p** 09. C Kirby Muxloe *Leic* from 08. *106 Hinckley Road, Leicester Forest East, Leicester LE3 3JS* Tel 0116-238 6344

WOOD, Mrs Jennifer Sarah. b 40. Sarum Dioc Tr Coll CertEd60. Oak Hill Th Coll 92. **d** 94 **p** 95. C St Illogan *Truro* 94-98; R Heanton Punchardon w Marwood *Ex* from 98. *The Rectory, Heanton, Barnstaple EX31 4DG* Tel and fax (01271) 812249

WOOD, John. b 37. LNSM course 75. **d** 77 **p** 79. NSM Haddington *Edin* from 77. *7 Herdmanflatt, Haddington EH41 3LN* Tel (01620) 822838

WOOD, John Anthony Scriven. b 48. Leeds Univ BSc70. St Jo Coll Nottm 76. **d** 79 **p** 80. C Colwich *Lich* 79-82; C W Bridgford *S'well* 82-90; V Gamston and Bridgford 90-95; Chapl Kings Mill Cen NHS Trust 95-01; Chapl Sherwood Forest Hosps NHS Trust from 01. *The King's Mill Centre, Mansfield Road, Sutton in Ashfield NG17 4JL* Tel (01623) 622515 ext 4137 *or* 0115-982 0969

WOOD, John Arthur. b 23. Roch Th Coll 68. **d** 70 **p** 71. C Wetherby *Ripon* 70-71; P-in-c Sheff Arbourthorne 71-75; TV Sheff Manor 75-81; R Rodney Stoke w Draycott *B & W* 81-88; rtd 88; Perm to Offic *Sheff* from 88. *36 The Glen, Sheffield S10 3FN* Tel 0114-266 5173

WOOD, John Maurice. b 58. Qu Coll Cam BA80 MA83. Wycliffe Hall Ox BA87. **d** 87 **p** 88. C Northwood Em *Lon* 87-91; C Muswell Hill St Jas w St Matt 91-94; P-in-c S Tottenham St Ann 94-01; V from 01. *St Ann's Vicarage, South Grove, London N15 5QG* Tel and fax (020) 8800 3506 Mobile 07771-867359 E-mail john.wood@st-anns.fsnet.co.uk

WOOD, John Samuel. b 47. Lanchester Poly Cov BSc69 Sheff Univ DipEd. Westcott Ho Cam 72. **d** 81 **p** 82. NSM Haverhill *St E* 81-83; C Whitton and Thurleston w Akenham 83-86; P-in-c Walsham le Willows 86-88; P-in-c Finningham w Westhorpe 86-88; R Walsham le Willows and Finningham w Westhorpe 88-94; Min Can St E Cathl 89-94; TR Whitstable *Cant* 94-02; Chapl E Kent Community NHS Trust 94-02; Hon Min Can Cant Cathl 96-02; TR Swanage and Studland *Sarum* from 02; RD Purbeck from 07. *The Rectory, 12 Church Hill, Swanage BH19 1HU* Tel (01929) 422916 Fax 422291 E-mail john.s.wood@btinternet.com

WOOD, Kathleen. b 46. EMMTC 04. **d** 06 **p** 07. NSM Newhall *Derby* 06-09; NSM Etwall w Egginton from 09. *28 Eastfield Road, Midway, Swadlincote DE11 0DG* Tel (01283) 212490 E-mail rgw140@aol.com

WOOD, Keith. b 49. St Steph Ho Ox 76. **d** 78 **p** 79. C Bognor *Chich* 78-81; C Hangleton 81-83; R W Blatchington 83-87; V W Worthing St Jo 87-96; R Winchelsea and Icklesham 96-00; rtd 00. *The Bungalow, Lower Locrenton, St Keyne, Liskeard PL14 4RN*

WOOD, Canon Keith Ernest. b 33. Qu Coll Ox BA55 BCL56 MA70. Wycliffe Hall Ox 56. **d** 58 **p** 59. C Barking St Marg *Chelmsf* 58-61; Min Basildon St Andr ED 61-70; V Brampton Bierlow *Sheff* 70-82; R Grasmere *Carl* 82-94; RD Windermere 89-94; Hon Can Carl Cathl 91-94 and 98-01; Bp's Dom Chapl 94-01; rtd 01; Perm to Offic *Carl* from 01. *The Old Tower, Brackenburgh, Calthwaite CA11 9PW* Tel (01768) 894273 Fax 894019

WOOD, Laurence Henry. b 27. Kelham Th Coll 47. **d** 52 **p** 53. C Ravensthorpe *Wakef* 52-55; C Almondbury 55-58; V Linthwaite 58-64; R Bonsall and V Cromford *Derby* 64-70; V Longwood *Wakef* 70-76; V Liversedge 76-92; rtd 92; Perm to Offic *Wakef* from 92. *203 The Rock, Gillroyd Lane, Linthwaite, Huddersfield HD7 5SR* Tel (01484) 843499

WOOD, Mrs Lorna. b 43. EAMTC 85. **d** 88 **p** 94. NSM Sprowston *Nor* 88-90; NSM Sprowston w Beeston 90-95; P-in-c Nor St Helen 95-01; Chapl Gt Hosp Nor 95-99; NSM Coltishall w Gt Hautbois and Horstead *Nor* 01-04; Perm to Offic 04-07; NSM Thorpe St Andr from 07. *39 Inman Road, Sprowston, Norwich NR7 8JT* Tel (01603) 400150 E-mail robert.wood68@btinternet.com

WOOD, Mark. *See* WOOD, The Rt Revd Stanley Mark

WOOD, Mark Robert. b 68. Trin Coll Ox BA89 ALCM83 ARCO89. STETS 02. **d** 05 **p** 06. C Mere w W Knoyle and Maiden Bradley *Sarum* 05-08; P-in-c Wilton w Netherhampton and Fugglestone from 08. *The Rectory, 27A West Street, Wilton, Salisbury SP2 0DL* Tel (01722) 742393 Mobile 07770-305990 E-mail mands@thewoods2006.orangehome.co.uk

WOOD, Martin. *See* WOOD, Canon Alban Martin

WOOD, Martin Robert. b 65. Birm Univ BSc86. Trin Coll Bris 98. **d** 00 **p** 01. C Wells St Cuth w Wookey Hole *B & W* 00-03; C Shepton Mallet w Doulting 03-07; P-in-c Tedburn St Mary, Whitestone, Oldridge etc *Ex* from 07. *The Rectory, Church Lane, Cheriton Bishop, Exeter EX6 6HY* Tel (01647) 24119 E-mail mrwood@tesco.net

WOOD, Michael Edmund. b 46. Dur Univ BA67 PGCE68. Coll of Resurr Mirfield 94. **d** 96 **p** 97. NSM Battyeford *Wakef* from 96; Asst Chapl Kirkwood Hospice Huddersfield 96-97; Chapl from 97. *9 Dorchester Road, Huddersfield HD2 2JZ* Tel (01484) 536496 E-mail revmike@kirkwoodhospice.co.uk

WOOD, Michael Frank. b 55. Nottm Univ BCombStuds. Linc Th Coll. **d** 84 **p** 85. C Marton *Blackb* 84-88; TV Ribbleton 88-93; V Blackpool St Mary 93-00; P-in-c S Shore St Pet 98-00; RD Blackpool 96-00; TR Brighouse and Clifton *Wakef* 00-08; RD Brighouse and Elland 06-08; TR Castleford from 08. *The Rectory, 15 Barnes Road, Castleford WF10 5AA* Tel (01977) 733796 E-mail frmw@hotmail.co.uk

WOOD, Mrs Michaela. b 67. **d** 01 **p** 02. NSM Sunbury *Lon* 01-04; NSM Whitton St Aug 04-06; NSM Aylesbury w Bierton and Hulcott *Ox* from 06. *The Rectory, 1 Parson's Fee, Aylesbury HP20 2QZ* Tel (01296) 424276 E-mail michaelawood@aol.com

WOOD, Canon Nicholas Martin. b 51. AKC74. **d** 75 **p** 76. C E Ham w Upton Park St Alb *Chelmsf* 75-78; C Leyton St Luke 78-81; V Rush Green 81-91; Chapl Barking Tech Coll 81-91; TR Elland *Wakef* 91-05; RD Brighouse and Elland 96-05; Hon Can Wakef Cathl 00-05; Par Development Adv (Bradwell Area) *Chelmsf* from 05; Hon Can Chelmsf Cathl from 08. *101 London Road, Bowers Gifford, Basildon SS13 2DU* Tel (01268) 552219 E-mail mwood@chelmsford.anglican.org

WOOD, Paul Dominic. b 52. Tas Coll of Ad Educn DipEd80. Ridley Coll Melbourne BTh87. **d** 87 **p** 88. C Newtown St Jas Australia 87-89; C Launceston St Jo 89-91; TV Ifield *Chich* 92-95; P-in-c Lancefield w Romsey Australia 96-97; I 97-00; R Mansfield 01-05. *38 Pine Street, Reservoir Vic 3073, Australia* Tel and fax (0061) (3) 9478 0841 E-mail qwoodies@bigpond.com

WOOD, Philip James. b 48. Bris Univ BSc69 Westmr Coll Ox MTh93. Oak Hill Th Coll 71. **d** 74 **p** 75. C Islington St Mary *Lon* 74-77; C Stapenhill w Cauldwell *Derby* 77-80; V Walthamstow St Luke *Chelmsf* 80-94; AD Waltham Forest 89-94; Can Chelmsf Cathl 93-94; NSM Hackney Wick St Mary of Eton w St Aug *Lon* 01-02; TV Becontree W *Chelmsf* 02-07; V Becontree St Thos from 07. *St Thomas's Vicarage, 187 Burnside Road, Dagenham RM8 2JN* Tel (020) 8590 6190 E-mail phillip.wood@tiscali.co.uk

WOOD, Philip Norman. b 52. EMMTC 97. **d** 00 **p** 01. NSM Pleasley Hill *S'well* 00-04; NSM Mansfield St Aug 00-04; NSM Ladybrook 00-04; TV Newton Flotman, Swainsthorpe, Tasburgh, etc *Nor* 04-08; R Bacton, Happisburgh, Hempstead w Eccles etc from 08. *The Rectory, The Hill, Happisburgh, Norwich NR12 0PW* Tel (01692) 650313 Mobile 07961-524495 E-mail philyvonne@hotmail.com

WOOD, Ms Rachel Astrid. b 71. Birm Univ BA92 MA99. Qu Coll Birm BD98. **d** 99 **p** 00. C Attercliffe, Darnall and Tinsley *Sheff* 99-01; C Roundhay St Edm *Ripon* 01-04. *The Vicarage, Dunblane Crescent, Newcastle upon Tyne NE5 2BE*

WOOD, Raymond John Lee. b 28. ACII55 ACIArb. Linc Th Coll 66. **d** 68 **p** 69. C Beaconsfield *Ox* 68-72; CF 70-72; V Wath-upon-Dearne w Adwick-upon-Dearne *Sheff* 72-77; R St Tudy w Michaelstow *Truro* 77-86; P-in-c St Mabyn 82-86; R St Tudy w St Mabyn and Michaelstow 86-95; Chapl Bodmin Fire Brigade from 91; rtd 95; Perm to Offic *Truro* from 96. *1 Wesley Chapel, Harewood Road, Calstock PL18 9QN* Tel (01822) 835918 E-mail rlwood@tesco.net

WOOD, Richard. *See* WOOD, Beresford Donald Richard

WOOD, Richard James. b 71. Oak Hill Th Coll BA07. **d** 08 **p** 09. C Dagenham *Chelmsf* from 08. *8 Church Lane, Dagenham RM10 9UL* Tel (020) 8517 2664 E-mail woodyis@mac.com

WOOD, Richard Stanton. b 79. Univ of Wales (Abth) BSc02 Univ of Wales (Cardiff) BA08. **d** 08 **p** 09. C Henfynyw w Aberaeron and Llanddewi Aberarth etc *St D* from 08. *Dyffryn, Lampter Road, Aberaeron SA46 0ED* Tel (01545) 571579 Mobile 07855-817740 E-mail r.s.wood@btopenworld.com *or* curate@aberaeronparish.org.uk

WOOD, Roger Graham. b 49. K Coll Lon BD. Chich Th Coll 74. **d** 76 **p** 77. C Skipton H Trin *Bradf* 76-79; Dioc Youth Chapl 79-87; V Queensbury 87-96; P-in-c Langcliffe w Stainforth and Horton 96-01; V from 01; RD Bowland from 08. *The Vicarage, Stainforth, Settle BD24 9PG* Tel (01729) 823010 E-mail roger.wood@bradford.anglican.org *or* rgwood@lineone.net

WOOD, Roger William. b 43. Leeds Univ BA65 MA67 Fitzw Coll Cam BA69 MA75. Westcott Ho Cam 67. **d** 70 **p** 71. C Bishop's Stortford St Mich *St Alb* 70-74; C Sundon w Streatley 75-79; V Streatley from 80. *17 Sundon Road, Streatley, Luton LU3 3PL* Tel (01582) 882780

WOOD, Ronald Ernest. b 49. Sarum & Wells Th Coll 79. **d** 81 **p** 82. C Weston-super-Mare Cen Par *B & W* 81-84; C Forest of Dean Ch Ch w English Bicknor *Glouc* 84-88; R Sixpenny Handley w Gussage St Andrew etc *Sarum* 88-05; P-in-c Seale, Puttenham and Wanborough *Guildf* from 05. *The Rectory, Elstead Road, Seale, Farnham GU10 1JA* Tel (01252) 783057 E-mail office@spw.org.uk

WOOD, Sarah. *See* WOOD, Mrs Jennifer Sarah

WOOD, Shane Grant Lindsay. b 60. Southn Univ BTh91. St Steph Ho Ox 95. **d** 97 **p** 98. C Parkstone St Pet w Branksea and St Osmund *Sarum* 97-00; V Teddington SS Pet and Paul and Fulwell *Lon* 00-06; TR Aylesbury w Bierton and Hulcott *Ox* from 06. *The Rectory, Parson's Fee, Aylesbury HP20 2QZ* Tel (01296) 424276 E-mail shaneglwood@aol.com

WOOD, Stanley Charles. b 26. Glouc Th Course 80. **d** 83 **p** 84. NSM Lower Cam w Coaley *Glouc* 83-87; P-in-c Shipton Moyne w Westonbirt and Lasborough 87-91; rtd 92; Perm to Offic *Glouc* 92-05. *Henlow Court, Henlow Drive, Dursley GL11 4BE* Tel (01453) 542850

▶WOOD, The Rt Revd Stanley Mark. b 19. Univ of Wales (Cardiff) BA40. Coll of Resurr Mirfield 40. **d** 42 **p** 43 **c** 71. C Cardiff St Mary *Llan* 42-45; C Sophiatown Miss S Africa 45-47; R Bloemhof 47-50; P-in-c St Cypr Miss Johannesburg 50-55; R Marandellas S Rhodesia 55-65; Can Mashonaland 61-65; Dean Salisbury 65-70; Bp Matabeleland 71-77; Asst Bp Heref 77-81;

Suff Bp Ludlow 81-87; Adn Ludlow 82-83; Preb Heref Cathl 77-87; rtd 87. *The College of St Barnabas, Blackberry Lane, Lingfield RH7 6NJ* Tel (01342) 872857
E-mail markwood@collegeofstbarnabas.com

WOOD, Stella Margaret. b 70. Trin Coll Ox BA91 MA DPhil95. STETS 95. **d** 97 **p** 98. NSM Mere w W Knoyle and Maiden Bradley *Sarum* 97-08; Chapl Sherborne Sch for Girls 00-08; Teacher from 08; Lic to RD Sarum from 08. *The Rectory, 27A West Street, Wilton, Salisbury SP2 0DL* Tel (01722) 744755
E-mail mands@thewoods2006.orangehome.co.uk

WOOD, Steven Paul. b 54. Fitzw Coll Cam MA75. ERMC. **d** 07 **p** 08. NSM Hitchin *St Alb* from 07. *Tythe Farmhouse, Streatley Road, Sundon, Luton LU3 3PH* Tel (01525) 876197 Mobile 07704-922984 E-mail francie@ukgateway.net

WOOD, Stuart Hughes. b 32. ACIB64. Guildf Dioc Min Course 93. **d** 95 **p** 96. OLM Camberley St Martin Old Dean *Guildf* 95-02; OLM Camberley St Paul 99-02; OLM Camberley St Mich Yorktown 99-02; rtd 02; Perm to Offic *Guildf* from 02. *42 Roundway, Camberley GU15 1NS* Tel (01276) 22115
E-mail stuart.wood1@tesco.net

WOOD, Susan Joyce. b 52. Sheff City Coll of Educn CertEd74. **d** 09. OLM Ramsbottom and Edenfield *Man* from 09. *243 Whittingham Drive, Ramsbottom, Bury BL0 9NY* Tel (01706) 825464 E-mail woodsuej@btinternet.com

WOOD, Sylvia Marian. *See* CHAPMAN, Canon Sylvia Marian

WOOD, Timothy Robert. b 55. **d** 02 **p** 03. OLM Maidstone St Paul *Cant* 02-06; NSM Hayling Is St Andr *Portsm* from 08; NSM N Hayling St Pet from 08. *9 Ward Court, 65 Seafront, Hayling Island PO11 0AL* Tel (023) 9246 1575
E-mail jane_wood@lineone.net

✠**WOOD, The Rt Revd Wilfred Denniston.** b 36. KA00. Gen Th Sem NY Hon DD86 Open Univ Hon DUniv00 Univ of W Indies Hon LLD02 FRSA93. Codrington Coll Barbados 57. **d** 61 **p** 62 **c** 85. C Hammersmith St Steph *Lon* 62-63; C Shepherd's Bush St Steph w St Thos 63-74; Bp's Chapl for Community Relns 67-74; V Catford St Laur *S'wark* 74-82; Hon Can S'wark Cathl 77-82; RD E Lewisham 77-82; Borough Dean S'wark 82-85; Adn S'wark 82-85; Suff Bp Croydon 85-91; Area Bp Croydon 91-02; rtd 02. *69 Pegwell Gardens, Christ Church, Barbados* Tel (001) (246) 420 1822 Fax 420 3426
E-mail wilfredwoodbarbados@caribsurf.com

WOOD-ROBINSON, David Michael. b 28. Glas Univ BSc50 Lon Univ BD54. **d** 57 **p** 57. C Erith St Jo *Roch* 57-58; CMS Japan 58-71; R Holton and Waterperry *Ox* 71-88; RD Aston and Cuddesdon 88-92; R Holton and Waterperry w Albury and Waterstock 88-94; Chapl Ox Brookes Univ 90-94; rtd 94. *16 Pound Meadow, Ledbury HR8 2EU* Tel (01531) 632347

WOODALL, David Paul. b 59. Ches Coll of HE BTh03. NOC 00. **d** 03 **p** 04. C Darwen St Pet w Hoddlesden *Blackb* 03-06; TV Bacup and Stacksteads *Man* from 06. *Christ Church Vicarage, Greensnook Lane, Bacup OL13 9DQ* Tel and fax (01706) 878293

WOODALL, Johanna Karin (Hanna). b 62. Leic Univ BA84 PGCE86. Trin Coll Bris BA06. **d** 06 **p** 07. C Winchcombe *Glouc* from 06. *38 Riverside, Winchcombe, Cheltenham GL54 5JP* E-mail hanna_woodall@yahoo.co.uk

WOODALL, Mrs Lynda Edith Maria. b 53. Leeds Univ BA07. NOC 04. **d** 07 **p** 08. C Goodshaw and Crawshawbooth *Man* from 07. *Christ Church Vicarage, Greensnook Lane, Bacup OL13 9DQ* Tel and fax (01706) 878293
E-mail lyn_53@hotmail.co.uk

WOODALL, Reginald Homer. b 38. St Mich Coll Llan 59. **d** 61 **p** 62. C Newtown w Llanllwchaiarn w Aberhafesp *St As* 61-65; C Rhosddu 65-66; C Hawarden 66-70; CF 70-74; C Thornton Heath St Jude *Cant* 74-77; TV Cannock *Lich* 77-79; TV Basildon St Martin w H Cross and Laindon etc *Chelmsf* 79-84; P-in-c Canning Town St Cedd 84-93; rtd 93. *64 Stephens Road, London E15 3JL*

WOODASON, Antony Norman. b 37. MCIPD96. SWMTC 02. **d** 04 **p** 05. NSM Bovey Tracey St Jo w Heathfield *Ex* 04-06; C Shaldon, Stokeinteignhead, Combeinteignhead etc from 06. *The Rectory, Stokeinteignhead, Newton Abbot TQ12 4QB* Tel (01626) 871013 E-mail woodason@nosadoow.fsnet.co.uk

WOODBRIDGE, Trevor Geoffrey. b 31. Lon Univ BSc52. ALCD57. **d** 58 **p** 59. C Bitterne Win 58-61; C Ilkeston St Mary *Derby* 61-65; Area Sec CMS *Ex* and *Truro* 65-81; SW Regional Sec 70-81; TV Clyst St George, Aylesbeare, Clyst Honiton etc *Ex* 82-84; V Aylesbeare, Rockbeare, Farringdon etc 85-95; rtd 95; Perm to Offic *Ex* 95-09. *17 Lowfield Crescent, Silsden, Keighley BD20 0QE* Tel (01535) 658216

WOODCOCK, Canon Carolyn. b 47. NOC BTh98. **d** 98 **p** 99. NSM Laneside *Blackb* 98-00; Chapl HM Pris Lanc Castle from 00; Hon Can Blackb Cathl from 08. *HM Prison Lancaster, The Castle, Lancaster LA1 1YL* Tel (01524) 385100

WOODCOCK, Edward Marsden. b 47. Hull Univ MSc01 Leeds Univ BA03. Coll of Resurr Mirfield 01. **d** 03 **p** 04. C Wrenthorpe *Wakef* 03-06; C Alverthorpe 03-06; P-in-c Ferrybridge from 06; P-in-c Brotherton from 06. *St Andrew's Vicarage, 5 Pontefract Road, Ferrybridge, Knottingley WF11 8PN* Tel (01977) 672772
E-mail edward@thewoodcocks.plus.com

WOODCOCK, John Charles Gerard. b 31. Kelham Th Coll 52. **d** 56 **p** 57. SSM 56-88; S Africa 56-62 and 76-83; Lesotho 62-76; Chapl Bede Ho Staplehurst 83-87; C Auckland St Andr and St Anne *Dur* 87-88. *3 Helena Terrace, Cockton Hill, Bishop Auckland DL14 6BP* Tel (01388) 604956

WOODCOCK, Michael David. b 67. Avery Hill Coll BEd91. Wycliffe Hall Ox BTh96. **d** 96 **p** 97. C Orpington Ch Ch *Roch* 96-99; R Knockholt w Halstead 99-06; P-in-c Crosthwaite Kendal *Carl* from 06; P-in-c Cartmel Fell from 06; P-in-c Winster from 06; P-in-c Witherslack from 06. *The Vicarage, Crosthwaite, Kendal LA8 8HT* Tel (01539) 568276

WOODCOCK, Michael Paul. b 71. Univ of Greenwich BA93. St Jo Coll Nottm MA98. **d** 99 **p** 00. C Brinsley w Underwood *S'well* 99-02; C New Malden and Coombe *S'wark* 02-07; C Ambleside w Brathay *Carl* from 07; Chapl Cumbria Univ from 07. *3 Ashley Green, Clappersgate, Ambleside LA22 9NQ* Tel (015394) 33177
E-mail paul-woodcock@sky.com

WOODCOCK, Nicholas Ethelbert. b 46. ACertCM74 FRSA90. Cant Sch of Min 80. **d** 90 **p** 91. Chief Exec and Co Sec Keston Coll Kent 89-92; NSM Clerkenwell H Redeemer w St Phil *Lon* 90-92; NSM Clerkenwell H Redeemer and St Mark 92-93; Chapl RN 93-01; Min Can, Prec and Sacr Ely Cathl 01-03; R Lavenham w Preston *St E* 03-09; Min Can St E Cathl 03-09; Chapl Morden Coll Blackheath from 09. *Morden College, 19 St Germans Place, London SE3 0PW* Tel (020) 8858 3365
E-mail chaplain@mordencollege.org

WOODE, Mrs Elizabeth. b 43. **d** 06 **p** 07. NSM Middlewich w Byley *Ches* from 06. *6 The Grange, Hartford, Northwich CW8 1QH* Tel (01606) 75030
E-mail tonylizwoode@hotmail.com

WOODERSON, Mrs Marguerite Ann. b 44. RGN SCM. Qu Coll Birm 86. **d** 89 **p** 94. Par Dn Stoneydelph St Martin CD *Lich* 89-90; Par Dn Glascote and Stonydelph 90-91; Par Dn Chasetown 91-94; C 94; C-in-c Chase Terrace St Jo Distr Ch 92-94; Chapl Naas Gen Hosp 94-98; I Celbridge w Straffan and Newcastle-Lyons *D & G* 98-06. *15 rue des Ecoles, Trélissac, 24750 Périgueux, France* Tel (0033) (5) 53 06 39 76 Mobile (8) 68 51 25 57 E-mail annwooderson@mac.com

WOODERSON, Michael George. b 39. Southn Univ BA61. Lon Coll of Div BD69. **d** 69 **p** 70. C Morden *S'wark* 69-73; C Aldridge *Lich* 73-81; V Chasetown and P-in-c Hammerwich 91-94; RD Lich 86-94; Preb Lich Cathl 89-94; I Naas w Kill and Rathmore *M & K* 94-06; rtd 06. *15 rue des Ecoles, Trélissac, 24750 Périgueux, France* Tel (0033) (5) 53 06 39 76
E-mail mgwooderson@eircom.net

WOODGATE, Mrs Elizabeth Mary. b 66. W Sussex Inst of HE BEd87. St Jo Coll Nottm MTh02. **d** 02 **p** 04. C Crofton *Portsm* 02-03; C Lee-on-the-Solent 03-05; C Rowner 05-07; C Bridgemary 05-07; Kuwait from 07. *Address temp unknown*
E-mail bethpoppy@hotmail.com

WOODGATES, Mrs Margaret. b 47. St D Coll Lamp BA67. WMMTC 00. **d** 03 **p** 04. NSM Redditch, The Ridge *Worc* 03-05; NSM Redditch Ch the K 05-06; NSM Finstall from 06. *18 Warwick Hall Gardens, Bromsgrove B60 2AU* Tel (01527) 577785 E-mail margaret.woody@tesco.net

WOODGER, John McRae. b 36. Univ of Wales MTh08. Tyndale Hall Bris 60. **d** 63 **p** 64. C Heref St Pet w St Owen 63-66; C Macclesfield St Mich *Ches* 66-69; V Llangarron w Llangrove *Heref* 69-74; P-in-c Garway 70-74; R Church Stretton 74-84; Preb Heref Cathl 82-84; V Watford *St Alb* 84-01; rtd 01; Perm to Offic *Heref* from 01. *39 Bronte Drive, Ledbury HR8 2FZ* Tel (01531) 636745 E-mail woodger@talktalk.net

WOODGER, John Page. b 30. Master Mariner 56. St Aid Birkenhead 56. **d** 59 **p** 60. C Kimberworth *Sheff* 59-62; Chapl HM Borstal Pollington 62-70; C Goole *Sheff* 62-63; V Balne 63-70; C Halesowen *Worc* 70-74; V Cookley 74-81; TV Droitwich 81-85; TV Bedminster *Bris* 85-93; rtd 93; Perm to Offic *Bris* 93-97 and *Worc* from 98. *1 Barbel Crescent, Worcester WR5 3QU* Tel (01905) 769065

WOODGER, Richard William. b 50. Sarum & Wells Th Coll 76. **d** 79 **p** 80. C Chessington *Guildf* 79-82; C Frimley and Frimley Green 82-85; V N Holmwood 85-90; TR Headley All SS 90-98; TR Penrith w Newton Reigny and Plumpton Wall *Carl* 98-05; P-in-c Northleach w Hampnett and Farmington etc *Glouc* from 05; C Sherborne, Windrush, the Barringtons etc from 08. *The Vicarage, Mill End, Northleach, Cheltenham GL54 3HL* Tel (01451) 860293 E-mail dickwoodger@yahoo.co.uk

WOODHALL, Peter. b 32. Edin Th Coll 57. **d** 60 **p** 61. C Carl St Barn 60-63; Hon Chapl Estoril *Eur* 63-65; Chapl RN 66-82; TR Is of Scilly *Truro* 82-90; V Mithian w Mount Hawke 90-95; rtd 97. *Tregarth, 4 Peverell Road, Porthleven, Helston TR13 9DH*

WOODHAM, Richard Medley Swift. b 43. Master Mariner 70. S'wark Ord Course 71. **d** 73 **p** 74. C Gravesend St Aid *Roch* 73-75; C Chessington *Guildf* 75-78; R Horstead and Newton Dioc Conf Ho *Nor* 78-87; Youth Chapl *Nor* 78-88; V Nor St Mary Magd w St Jas 87-91; TR Norwich Over-the-Water 91-98; P-in-c Lakenham St Jo 98-99; V Nor Lakenham St Jo and All SS and Tuckswood 99-06; RD Nor E 02-06; rtd 06; Perm to

Offic *Nor* from 06. *40 Anchor Street, Coltishall, Norwich NR12 7AQ* Tel (01603) 736411
E-mail richard.woodham@virgin.net

WOODHAMS, Raymond John. b 40. Garnett Coll Lon CertEd68 IEng. STETS 98. **d** 01 **p** 02. NSM E Blatchington *Chich* 01-08; NSM E Blatchington and Bishopstone from 08. *The Long House, West Dean, Seaford BN25 4AL* Tel and fax (01323) 870432 E-mail raymondj.woodhams@virgin.net

WOODHAMS, Roy Owen. b 57. ARCM76 GRSM78 Lon Inst of Educn TCert79. Ripon Coll Cuddesdon 91. **d** 93 **p** 94. C Deal St Leon and St Rich and Sholden *Cant* 93-97; P-in-c Cherbury *Ox* 97-02; P-in-c Gainfield 99-02; R Cherbury w Gainfield 02-04; AD Vale of White Horse 01-04; V Fleet *Guildf* from 04. *The Vicarage, Branksomewood Road, Fleet GU51 4JU* Tel (01252) 616361 E-mail vicar@parishoffleet.org.uk

WOODHAMS, Mrs Sophie Harriet. b 27. Cranmer Hall Dur 66. **dss** 80 **d** 87. Raveningham *Nor* 80-81; Henleaze *Bris* 81-87; rtd 87. *22 Manormead, Tilford, Hindhead GU26 6RA* Tel (01428) 602500

WOODHEAD, Mrs Bernice. b 45. **d** 01 **p** 02. OLM Shore *Man* from 01; OLM Calderbrook from 01. *2 Mount Avenue, Littleborough OL15 9JP* Tel (01706) 379517

WOODHEAD, Christopher Godfrey. b 26. Pemb Coll Cam BA50 MA55. Ely Th Coll 50. **d** 52 **p** 53. C Barnsley St Edw *Wakef* 52-54; C Mill Hill St Mich *Lon* 54-58; C Sandridge *St Alb* 58-66; R Earl Stonham *St E* 66-72; V Hoo St Werburgh *Roch* 72-88; C Cheam *S'wark* 88-91; rtd 91; Perm to Offic *Cant* from 91. *4 Eastgate Close, Herne Bay CT6 7ER* Tel (01227) 374137

WOODHEAD, Miss Helen Mary. b 35. Bedf Coll Lon BA57. Westcott Ho Cam 86. **d** 87 **p** 94. Par Dn Daventry *Pet* 87-90; Asst Dioc Dir of Ords *Guildf* 90-00; C Godalming 90-95; C Worplesdon 95-00; rtd 00; Perm to Offic *Lich* from 00. *12 Barley Croft, Whittington, Lichfield WS14 9LY* Tel (01543) 432345

WOODHEAD, Michael. b 51. St Jo Coll Nottm 88. **d** 90 **p** 91. C Stannington *Sheff* 90-93; V Deepcar 93-01; TV Crookes St Thos 01-05; TR from 05. *St Thomas Church, Nairn Street, Sheffield S10 1UL* Tel 0114-267 1090

WOODHEAD, Mrs Sandra Buchanan. b 42. Man Poly BA82 Man Univ BD85. St Deiniol's Hawarden. **dss** 86 **d** 87 **p** 94. High Lane *Ches* 86-90; Hon Par Dn 87-90; C Brinnington w Portwood 91-94; V 94-00; R Withington St Paul *Man* 00-09; rtd 09. *Woodbank, Light Alders Lane, Disley, Stockport SK12 2LW* Tel (01663) 765708 E-mail deniswoodhead@btinternet.com

WOODHEAD-KEITH-DIXON, James Addison. b 25. St Aid Birkenhead 44. **d** 48 **p** 49. C Upperby St Jo *Carl* 48-50; C Dalton-in-Furness 50-52; V Blawith w Lowick 52-59; V Lorton 59-80; Chapl Puerto de la Cruz Tenerife *Eur* 80-82; TV Bellingham/Otterburn Gp *Newc* 82-83; TR 83-91; TR N Tyne and Redesdale 91-92; rtd 92. *Culpee House, Creebridge, Newton Stewart DG8 6NR*

WOODHOUSE, Canon Alison Ruth. b 43. Bedf Coll of Educn CertEd64. Dalton Ho Bris 68. **dss** 79 **d** 87 **p** 94. Bayston Hill *Lich* 79-81; W Derby St Luke *Liv* 81-86; Burscough Bridge 86-95; Par Dn 87-94; C 94-95; V Formby St Luke 95-07; AD Sefton 00-05; Hon Can Liv Cathl 02-07; rtd 07; Chapl to The Queen from 06. *16 Fountains Way, Liverpool L37 4HE* Tel (01704) 877423

WOODHOUSE, The Ven Andrew Henry. b 23. DSC45. Qu Coll Ox BA48 MA49. Linc Th Coll 48. **d** 50 **p** 51. C Poplar All SS w St Frideswide *Lon* 50-56; V W Drayton 56-70; RD Hillingdon 67-70; Adn Ludlow *Heref* 82-91; R Wistanstow 70-82; P-in-c Acton Scott 70-73; Can Res Heref Cathl 82-91; Treas 82-91; Adn Heref 82-91; rtd 91; Perm to Offic *Guildf* from 91. *Orchard Cottage, Bracken Close, Woking GU22 7HD* Tel (01483) 760671

WOODHOUSE, Andrew Laurence. b 40. Nottm Univ DipEd72 ATCL64. NW Ord Course. **d** 82 **p** 83. NSM Bedale *Ripon* 82-02; NSM Bedale and Leeming 03-07; P-in-c Thornton Watlass 99-07; rtd 07. *Address temp unknown* Tel 07720-670163 (mobile) E-mail wdhandr@aol.com

WOODHOUSE, The Ven Charles David Stewart. b 34. Kelham Th Coll 55. **d** 59 **p** 60. C Leeds Halton St Wilfrid *Ripon* 59-63; Youth Chapl *Liv* 63-66; Bermuda 66-69; Asst Gen Sec CEMS 69-70; Gen Sec 70-76; Bp's Dom Chapl *Ex* 76-81; R Ideford, Luton and Ashcombe 76-81; V Hindley St Pet *Liv* 81-92; Adn Warrington 81-01; Hon Can Liv Cathl 83-01; rtd 01; Perm to Offic *Liv* from 03. *9 Rob Lane, Newton-le-Willows WA12 0DR*

WOODHOUSE, David Edwin. b 45. Lon Univ BSc68. Cuddesdon Coll 68. **d** 71 **p** 72. C E Dulwich St Jo *S'wark* 71-74; Lic to Offic 74-77; Perm to Offic *Bris* 77-79; Lic to Offic 79-98. *Kingsbury Hall, The Green, Calne SN11 8DG* Tel (01249) 821521 Fax 817246 E-mail kingsburyhallcd@aol.com

WOODHOUSE, David Maurice. b 40. Lon Univ BA62. Clifton Th Coll 63. **d** 65 **p** 66. C Wellington w Eyton *Lich* 65-68; C Meole Brace 68-71; V Colwich 71-82; P-in-c Gt Haywood 78-82; R Clitheroe St Jas *Blackb* 82-88; Ellel Grange Chr Healing Cen 88-91; V The Lye and Stambermill *Worc* 91-99; Chapl Acorn Chr Foundn 99-02; Dioc Healing Adv *Guildf* 00-02; rtd 02; Perm to Offic *Blackb* from 04. *1 Lilac Avenue, Penwortham, Preston PR1 9PB* Tel (01772) 742088
E-mail david.woodhouse@classicfm.net

WOODHOUSE, Hugh Frederic. b 12. TCD BA34 BD37 DD52. **d** 37 **p** 38. C Belfast St Donard *D & D* 37-39; C Bangor St Comgall 40-44; I Aghalee 44-46; I Newtownards 46-51; Prof Wycliffe Coll Toronto 51-54; Prin and Prof Angl Th Coll Vancouver 54-59; Prof Univ of K Coll Halifax 59-63; Regius Prof Div TCD 63-82; rtd 82. *4591 West 16th Avenue, Vancouver BC V6R 3E8, Canada* Tel (001) (604) 224 4812

WOODHOUSE, Canon Keith Ian. b 33. K Coll Lon 54. **d** 58 **p** 59. C Stockton St Chad CD *Dur* 58-61; C Man St Aid 61-64; V Peterlee *Dur* 64-99; AD Easington 72-98; Hon Can Dur Cathl 79-99; rtd 99; Dioc Pensions and Widows Officer *Dur* from 00. *85 Baulkham Hills, Penshaw, Houghton le Spring DH4 7RZ* Tel and fax 0191-584 3977 E-mail keithianwoodhouse@excite.com

WOODHOUSE, Canon Patrick Henry Forbes. b 47. Ch Ch Ox BA69 MA81. St Jo Coll Nottm 69 Lon Coll of Div ALCD71 LTh71. **d** 72 **p** 73. C Birm St Martin 72-74; C Whitchurch *Bris* 75-76; C Harpenden St Nic *St Alb* 76-80; Tanzania 80-81; Soc Resp Officer *Carl* 81-85; P-in-c Dean 81-85; Dir Soc Resp *Win* 85-90; V Chippenham St Andr w Tytherton Lucas *Bris* 90-00; Can Res and Prec Wells Cathl from 00. *4 The Liberty, Wells BA5 2SU* Tel and fax (01749) 673188
E-mail pwoodhouse@liberty4.fsnet.co.uk

WOODHOUSE, Thomas Mark Bews. b 66. Cheltenham & Glouc Coll of HE BA98 Glos Univ MA05 FRSA05. Aston Tr Scheme 90 Westcott Ho Cam 92. **d** 95 **p** 96. C Cainscross w Selsley *Glouc* 95-98; V Hardwicke and Elmore w Longney 98-05; P-in-c Wootton Bassett *Sarum* from 05; RD Calne from 06. *The Vicarage, Glebe Road, Wootton Bassett, Swindon SN4 7DU* Tel (01793) 854302

WOODING JONES, Andrew David. b 61. Oak Hill Th Coll BA91. **d** 91 **p** 92. C Welling *Roch* 91-95; TV Crookes St Thos *Sheff* 95-00; Resident Dir Ashburnham Trust from 00; NSM Ashburnham w Penhurst *Chich* from 01. *Ashburnham Christian Trust, Ashburnham Place, Battle TN33 9NF* Tel (01424) 892244 Fax 892243 E-mail andrewwj@ashburnham.org.uk

WOODLEY, David James. b 38. K Coll Lon BD61 AKC61 Open Univ BA98. **d** 62 **p** 63. C Lancing St Jas *Chich* 62-64; C St Alb St Pet *St Alb* 64-67; Malaysia 67-70; Lic to Offic *Linc* 71-72; V Westoning w Tingrith *St Alb* 72-77; Asst Chapl HM Pris Wormwood Scrubs 77-78; Chapl HM Pris Cardiff 78-84; Chapl HM Rem Cen Risley 84-92; Chapl HM Pris Styal 92-98; rtd 98; Perm to Offic *Ches* 98-07. *18 Longcroft Road, Yeovil BA21 4RR*

WOODLEY, Canon John Francis Chapman. b 33. Univ of Wales (Lamp) BA58. Edin Th Coll 58. **d** 60 **p** 61. C Edin All SS 60-65; Chapl St Andr Cathl 65-67; Prec 67-71; R Glas St Oswald 71-77; P-in-c Cumbernauld 77-93; Can St Mary's Cathl 82-99; CSG from 82; R Dalbeattie *Glas* 93-99; rtd 99; Hon Can St Mary's Cathl from 99; Dioc Supernumerary 99-03; Lic to Offic from 03. *3 Highburgh Drive, Rutherglen, Glasgow G73 3RR* Tel 0141-647 3118 E-mail jfcwoodley@talk21.com

WOODLEY, The Ven Ronald John. b 25. Bps' Coll Cheshunt 50. **d** 53 **p** 54. C Middlesbrough St Martin *York* 53-58; C Whitby 58-61; C-in-c Middlesbrough Berwick Hills CD 61-66; V Middlesbrough Ascension 66-71; R Stokesley 71-85; RD Stokesley 77-85; Can and Preb York Minster 82-00; Adn Cleveland 85-91; rtd 91; Perm to Offic *Ripon* from 91 and *York* from 00. *2A Minster Court, York YO1 7JJ* Tel (01904) 679675

WOODLEY, Simon Andrew. b 66. Liv Univ BA88 Univ of Cen England in Birm 96. Ridley Hall Cam BTh00. **d** 00 **p** 01. C Birm St Martin w Bordesley St Andr 00-04; TR Bemerton *Sarum* from 04. *St Michael's Rectory, St Michael's Road, Salisbury SP2 9EQ* Tel (01722) 333750

WOODMAN, Brian Baldwin. b 35. Leeds Univ BA57 PhD73. NOC 84. **d** 87 **p** 88. C Guiseley w Esholt *Bradf* 87-90; TV Bingley All SS 90-94; P-in-c St Merryn *Truro* 94-00; rtd 00; Perm to Offic *Truro* from 00. *Penty an Garth, Trevance, St Issey, Wadebridge PL27 7QF* Tel (01841) 541387

WOODMAN, Christopher James. b 65. Chich Th Coll BTh93. **d** 93 **p** 94. C Leigh-on-Sea St Marg *Chelmsf* 93-97; TV Canvey Is 97-00; TV Moulsecoomb *Chich* 00-03; C Brighton St Matthias 03-06; TV Brighton Resurr 06-09; V Brighton St Luke Queen's Park from 09. *St Luke's Vicarage, Queen's Park Terrace, Brighton BN2 9YA* Tel (01273) 688147 E-mail cjw@btinternet.com

WOODMAN, Oliver Nigel. b 47. FCIPD. Sarum Th Coll 67. **d** 70 **p** 82. C Stepney St Dunstan and All SS *Lon* 70-71; NSM Ovingdean w Rottingdean and Woodingdean *Chich* 81-87; NSM Eastbourne St Sav and St Pet 88-93; Asst to RD Eastbourne 93-98; NSM Eastbourne St Sav and St Pet 98-01; Perm to Offic *Win* from 02. *48 Old Kennels Lane, Winchester SO22 4JS* Tel (01962) 878937 E-mail oliver@seemp.co.uk
or ojwoodman@ntlworld.com

WOODMAN, The Ven Peter Wilfred. b 36. Univ of Wales (Lamp) BA58. Wycliffe Hall Ox 58. **d** 60 **p** 61. C New Tredegar *Mon* 60-61; C Newport St Paul 61-64; C Llanfrechfa All SS 64-66; Abp of Wales's Messenger 66-67; V Llantilio Pertholey w Bettws Chpl etc *Mon* 67-74; V Bassaleg 74-90; Can St Woolos Cathl 84-01; V Caerwent w Dinham and Llanfair Discoed etc 90-96; Adn Mon 93-01; R Mamhilad and Llanfihangel

Pontymoile 96-01; rtd 01. *Glaslyn, 40 Longhouse Barn, Penperlleni, Pontypool NP4 0BD* Tel (01873) 881322

WOODMANSEY, Michael Balfour. b 55. Leic Univ BSc. Ridley Hall Cam. **d** 83 **p** 84. C St Paul's Cray St Barn *Roch* 83-89; C S Shoebury *Chelmsf* 89-93; R Stifford 93-01; TR Heworth H Trin *York* 01-07; R Heworth H Trin and St Wulstan from 07. *Heworth Rectory, Melrosegate, York YO31 0RP* Tel (01904) 422958 E-mail michael@mwoodmansey.freeserve.co.uk

WOODMORE, Mrs Dilys Mary. b 44. SAOMC 98. **d** 01 **p** 02. NSM Dedworth *Ox* 01-04; NSM Burchetts Green from 04. *59 Terrington Hill, Marlow SL7 2RE* Tel (01628) 486274

WOODROFFE, Ian Gordon. b 46. Edin Th Coll 69. **d** 72 **p** 73. C Soham *Ely* 72-75; P-in-c Swaffham Bulbeck 75-80; Youth Chapl 75-80; V Cambridge St Jas 80-87; Chapl Mayday Univ Hosp Thornton Heath 87-94; Chapl Mayday Healthcare NHS Trust Thornton Heath 94-97; Staff Cllr Epsom and St Helier NHS Trust 97-02. *4 Station Road, Swaffham Bulbeck, Cambridge CB25 0NW* Tel (01223) 813122

WOODROW, Miss Alinda Victoria. b 60. Newnham Coll Cam BA82 MA86. Ripon Coll Cuddesdon 04. **d** 06 **p** 07. C Attleborough w Besthorpe *Nor* 06-08; C Sprowston w Beeston from 08. *6 Wroxham Road, Norwich NR7 8TZ* Tel (01603) 418296 E-mail alinda@sprowston.org.uk

WOODS, The Very Revd Alan Geoffrey. b 42. TD93. ACCA65 FCCA80. Sarum Th Coll 67. **d** 70 **p** 71. C Bedminster St Fran *Bris* 70-73; Youth Chapl 73-76; Warden Legge Ho Res Youth Cen 73-76; P-in-c Neston 76-79; TV Gtr Corsham 79-81; CF (TA) 80-94; P-in-c Charminster *Sarum* 81-83; V Charminster and Stinsford 83-90; RD Dorchester 85-90; Chapl Dorchester Hosps 86-87; V Calne and Blackland *Sarum* 90-96; RD Calne 90-96; Chapl St Mary's Sch Calne 90-96; Can and Preb Sarum Cathl 92-96; Sen Chapl Malta and Gozo *Eur* 96-03; Chan Malta Cathl 96-03; Dean Gib 03-08; V Gen to Bp Eur 03-05; Adn Gib 05-08; P-in-c Mlaga 06-07; rtd 08; Perm to Offic *Sarum* and *Eur* from 08. *6 Maumbury Square, Weymouth Avenue, Dorchester DT1 1TY* Tel (01305) 264877 E-mail abwoods@tiscali.co.uk

WOODS, Charles William. b 31. Lich Th Coll 55. **d** 58 **p** 59. C Hednesford *Lich* 58-62; V Wilnecote 62-67; V Basford 67-76; V Chasetown 76-81; P-in-c Donington 81-83; V 83-96; V Boningale 83-96; RD Shifnal 84-89; rtd 96; Perm to Offic *Lich* from 96. *17 Campion Drive, Telford TF2 7RH* Tel (01952) 677134

WOODS, Christopher Guy Alistair. b 35. Dur Univ BA60. Clifton Th Coll 60. **d** 62 **p** 63. C Rainham *Chelmsf* 62-65; C Edin St Thos 65-69; Sec Spanish and Portuguese Ch Aid Soc 69-79; C Willesborough w Hinxhill *Cant* 74-80; P-in-c Murston w Bapchild and Tonge 80-87; R 87-90; R Gt Horkesley *Chelmsf* 90-98; RD Dedham and Tey 91-98; rtd 98; P-in-c Tenerife Sur *Eur* 99-00; Perm to Offic *Chelmsf* from 00. *Bluebonnet, Mill Lane, Bradfield, Manningtree CO11 2UT* Tel (01255) 870411

WOODS, Christopher Morrison. b 77. St Andr Univ MA00 TCD BTh04. CITC 01. **d** 04 **p** 05. C Dundela St Mark *D & D* 04-07; Chapl Ch Coll Cam from 07. *Christ's College, Cambridge CB2 3BU* Tel (01223) 334922 E-mail cmw66@cam.ac.uk

WOODS, David Arthur. b 28. Bris Univ BA52. Tyndale Hall Bris 48. **d** 53 **p** 54. C Camborne *Truro* 53-56; C Bromley Ch Ch *Roch* 56-58; V Tewkesbury H Trin *Glouc* 58-62; V Stapleford *S'well* 66-70; Miss to Seamen 70-93; Hon Chapl Miss to Seamen 70-93; V Fowey *Truro* 70-93; RD St Austell 80-88; rtd 93; Perm to Offic *Truro* from 93. *Linden, 7 Richmond Road, Pelynt, Looe PL13 2NH* Tel (01503) 220374

WOODS, David Benjamin. b 42. Linc Th Coll 88. **d** 90 **p** 91. C Louth *Linc* 90-93; P-in-c Ingoldmells w Addlethorpe 93-97; R 97-01; P-in-c Sutton Bridge 01-08; rtd 08; Hon C Digby Gp *Linc* from 08. *The Rectory, 1 Thomas à Becket Close, Digby, Lincoln LN4 3GA* Tel (01526) 323794 E-mail revwoods@ukonline.co.uk

WOODS, David Edward. b 36. City Univ FBCO61 FSMC61. SW Minl Tr Course 83 S Dios Minl Tr Scheme 94. **d** 95 **p** 96. NSM Bemerton *Sarum* 95-98; NSM Salisbury St Martin 98-00; NSM Laverstock 98-00; NSM Salisbury St Martin and Laverstock 00-05; Perm to Offic *Truro* from 05. *8 Tower Meadows, St Buryan, Penzance TR19 6AJ* Tel (01736) 811253

WOODS, Edward Christopher John. b 44. NUI BA67. CITC 66. **d** 67 **p** 68. C Drumglass *Arm* 67-70; C Belfast St Mark *Conn* 70-73; I Kilcolman *L & K* 73-78; I Portarlington w Cloneyhurke and Lea *M & K* 78-84; Chan Kildare Cathl 81-84; I Killiney Ballybrack *D & G* 85-92; I Dublin Rathfarnham from 93; Dir of Ords (Dub) from 98. *Rathfarnham Rectory, Rathfarnham, Terenure, Dublin 6W, Republic of Ireland* Tel and fax (00353) (1) 490 5543 E-mail anneted@gofree.indigo.ie

WOODS, Canon Eric John. b 51. Magd Coll Ox BA72 MA77 Trin Coll Cam BA77 MA83 FRSA94. Westcott Ho Cam 75. **d** 78 **p** 79. C Bris St Mary Redcliffe w Temple etc 78-81; Hon C Clifton St Paul 81-83; Asst Chapl Bris Univ 81-83; V Wroughton 83-93; RD Wroughton 88-93; V Sherborne w Castleton, Lillington and Longburton *Sarum* from 93; Chapl Sherborne Sch for Girls 93-99; RD Sherborne *Sarum* 96-04; Can and Preb Sarum Cathl from 98; Chapl Dorset Community NHS Trust 93-00; Chapl SW Dorset Primary Care Trust from 01; Chapl St Antony's Leweston Sch Sherborne from 03. *The Vicarage, Abbey Close, Sherborne DT9 3LQ* Tel (01935) 812452 Fax 812206 E-mail vicar@sherborneabbey.com

WOODS, Frederick James. b 45. Southn Univ BA66 MPhil74 Fitzw Coll Cam BA76 MA79. Ridley Hall Cam 74. **d** 77 **p** 78. C Stratford-on-Avon w Bishopton *Cov* 77-81; V Warminster Ch Ch *Sarum* 81-96; RD Heytesbury 95-96; TR Woodley *Ox* 96-01; V Colchester St Pet and St Botolph *Chelmsf* from 01. *St Peter's Vicarage, Balkerne Close, Colchester CO1 1NZ* Tel (01206) 572641 E-mail fredjwoods@hotmail.com

WOODS, Geoffrey Edward. b 49. Lon Univ BD70 K Coll Lon MA94. Tyndale Hall Bris 67. **d** 73 **p** 74. C Gipsy Hill Ch Ch *S'wark* 73-76; C Uphill *B & W* 76-79; R Swainswick w Langridge and Woolley 79-84; Perm to Offic *Bris* 84-96; NSM Colerne w N Wraxall from 96; NSM By Brook from 06. *22 Watergates, Colerne, Chippenham SN14 8DR* Tel (01225) 743675

WOODS, John William Ashburnham. b 22. Reading Univ BSc50. NW Ord Course 73 St Jo Coll Lusaka 69. **d** 71 **p** 74. C Kitwe Zambia 71-72; C Goole *Sheff* 73-75; P-in-c Firbeck w Letwell 75-76; R 76-82; P-in-c Woodsetts 75-76; V 76-82; Bp's Rural Adv 80-92; R Barnburgh w Melton on the Hill 82-92; RD Wath 86-92; rtd 92; NSM Birdsall w Langton *York* 93-96; P-in-c Settrington w Scrampton, Birdsall w Langton 96-98; Perm to Offic from 00. *1 Smithson Court, Malton YO17 7BQ* Tel and fax (01653) 694613 E-mail revjwoods@btinternet.com

WOODS, Joseph Richard Vernon. b 31. Solicitor 57. Cuddesdon Coll 58. **d** 60 **p** 61. C Newc St Gabr 60-63; Trinidad and Tobago 63-67; Chapl Long Grove Hosp Epsom 67-76; P-in-c Ewell St Fran *Guildf* 76-79; V 79-87; V Englefield Green 87-96; rtd 96; Perm to Offic *Win* from 97. *8 Wren Close, Christchurch BH23 4BD* Tel (01425) 270799 E-mail trendi2@btinternet.com

WOODS, Michael. b 57. Ripon Coll Cuddesdon 99. **d** 01 **p** 02. C Bamber Bridge St Aid *Blackb* 01-06; P-in-c Rishton from 06. *The Vicarage, Somerset Road, Rishton, Blackburn BB1 4BP* Tel (01254) 886191 E-mail woodsfamily@cuddesdon.fsnet.co.uk

WOODS, Canon Michael Spencer. b 44. K Coll Lon BD66 AKC66 Sheff Univ MMinTheol99. **d** 67 **p** 68. C Sprowston *Nor* 67-70; C Malaysia 70-74; TV Hempnall *Nor* 74-79; TV Halesworth w Linstead, Chediston, Holton etc *St E* 79-85; TR Braunstone *Leic* 85-92; RD Sparkenhoe E 89-91; TR Gt Yarmouth *Nor* 92-09; Hon Can Nor Cathl 96-09; rtd 09. *4 Old Church Close, Caistor St Edmund, Norwich NR14 8QX* Tel (01508) 493650 E-mail michael.woods@rjt.co.uk

WOODS, Canon Norman Harman. b 35. K Coll Lon BD62 AKC62. **d** 63 **p** 64. C Poplar All SS w St Frideswide *Lon* 63-67; C-in-c W Leigh CD *Portsm* 68-76; V Hythe *Cant* 76-01; RD Elham 83-89; Hon Can Cant Cathl 90-01; rtd 01; Perm to Offic *Cant* from 01. *36 Abbey Gardens, Canterbury CT2 7EU* Tel (01227) 470957 E-mail normanwoods@v21.me.net

WOODS, Richard. See WOODS, Joseph Richard Vernon

WOODS, Richard Thomas Evelyn Brownrigg. b 51. St Steph Ho Ox 83. **d** 85 **p** 86. C Southgate Ch Ch *Lon* 85-88; C Northampton All SS w St Kath *Pet* 88-89; V Maybridge *Chich* 89-99; V E Dean 99-05; R Singleton 99-05; V W Dean 99-05; R E Dean, Singleton, and W Dean from 05. *The Rectory, Singleton, Chichester PO18 0EZ* Tel and fax (01243) 811213 E-mail rector_singleton@hotmail.com

WOODS, Roger Andrew. b 60. Southn Univ BSc81. Oak Hill Th Coll BA01. **d** 98 **p** 99. C Audley *Lich* 98-02; TV Leek and Meerbrook from 02. *St Luke's Vicarage, Novi Lane, Leek ST13 6NR* Tel (01538) 386109

WOODS, Tanya Joy. b 73. CITC 99. **d** 02 **p** 03. NSM Killesher *K, E & A* from 02. *Cornacrea, Cavan Town, Republic of Ireland* Tel (00353) (49) 433 2188 *or* (42) 966 9229 Mobile 87-233 4534 Fax (42) 966 9119 E-mail revtanyawoods@hotmail.com

WOODS, Theodore Frank Spreull. b 37. Cam Univ BA58 DipEd80. Wells Th Coll 60. **d** 62 **p** 63. C Stocking Farm CD *Leic* 62-67; Papua New Guinea 67-77; V Knighton St Jo *Leic* 77-80; Australia from 80; Chapl Angl Ch Gr Sch Brisbane 80-88; Chapl Hillbrook Angl Sch from 89; rtd 03. *44 Merle Street, Carina Qld 4152, Australia* Tel (0061) (7) 3398 4437 *or* 3354 3422 Fax 3354 1057

WOODS, Timothy James. b 52. Poly Cen Lon BA78 MSc79 Ex Univ MA96 ACIB75. Qu Coll Birm 81. **d** 83 **p** 84. C Brierley Hill *Lich* 83-86; C Stoneydelph St Martin CD 86-88; World Development Officer 86-88; Chr Aid Area Sec (SE Lon) 88-91; V Estover *Ex* 91-97; TR Brixham w Churston Ferrers and Kingswear 97-00; Dir Bd of Ch and Soc *Sarum* 00-05; RD Salisbury 05-07; Advocacy and Middle E Desk Officer USPG from 05. *USPG, 200 Great Dover Street, London SE1 4YB* Tel (020) 7378 5669 E-mail timw@uspg.org.uk

WOODS, Mrs Valerie Irene. b 44. Trin Coll Bris 82. **dss** 84 **d** 87 **p** 94. Coleford w Staunton *Glouc* 84-88; C 87-88; TD Bedminster *Bris* 88-96; V 96-97; Chapl HM Rem Cen Pucklechurch 95-96; Chapl HM Pris Eastwood Park 96-00; V Wood End *Cov* from 01; P-in-c Potters Green from 08. *St Chad's Vicarage, Hillmorton Road, Coventry CV2 1FY* Tel (024) 7661 2909 E-mail philipandchad@btinternet.com

WOODSFORD, Canon Andrew Norman. b 43. Nottm Univ BA65. Ridley Hall Cam 65. **d** 67 **p** 68. C Radcliffe-on-Trent *S'well* 67-70; P-in-c Ladybrook 70-73; P-in-c Barton in Fabis 73-81; P-in-c Thrumpton 73-81; R Gamston w Eaton and W Drayton 81-88; Chapl Bramcote Sch Notts 81-93; Warden of Readers *S'well* 88-08; Hon Can S'well Minster 93-08; RD Retford 93-00; rtd 08. *3 Clinton Rise, Gamston, Retford DN22 0QJ* Tel (01777) 838706 E-mail woodsford@.msn.com
WOODSFORD, Martyn Paul. b 64. Oak Hill Th Coll 01. **d** 03 **p** 04. C Southover *Chich* 03-07; P-in-c S Malling from 07. *The Vicarage, Church Lane, Lewes BN7 2JA* Tel (01273) 474387 Mobile 07904-239842 E-mail revwoody@macdream.net
WOODWARD, Andrew John. b 59. ACIB85. SEITE 96. **d** 99 **p** 00. NSM Weybridge *Guildf* 99-03; NSM St Botolph Aldgate w H Trin Minories *Lon* 03-07; Perm to Offic *Guildf* 03-07; P-in-c Kemp Town St Mary *Chich* from 07. *11 West Drive, Brighton BN2 0GD* Tel (01273) 698601 E-mail thewoodys1@tiscali.co.uk
WOODWARD, Anthony John. b 50. Salford Univ BSc78. St Jo Coll Nottm 79. **d** 81 **p** 82. C Deane *Man* 81-84; CF 84-87; R Norris Bank *Man* 87-90; V Lostock St Thos and St Jo 92-96; Perm to Offic 96-01; C Halliwell 01-02; TV 02-04; P-in-c Chard and Distr *B & W* 04-06; V Chard St Mary from 06; P-in-c Combe St Nicholas w Wambrook and Whitestaunton from 08. *The Vicarage, Forton Road, Chard TA20 2HJ* Tel (01460) 62320 *or* 67867 E-mail revtony.woodward@tesco.net
WOODWARD, Arthur Robert Harry (Bob). b 28. **d** 76 **p** 77. Rhodesia 76-80; Zimbabwe 80-87; Adn E Harare 82-87; R Wymington w Podington *St Alb* 87-97; RD Sharnbrook 89-97; rtd 97; Perm to Offic *Portsm* from 97. *9 Briarfield Gardens, Horndean, Waterlooville PO8 9HX* Tel (023) 9259 6983 E-mail woodward@bushinternet.com
WOODWARD, Clive Ian. b 49. City of Lon Poly BSc84. STETS 01. **d** 04 **p** 05. NSM Willingdon *Chich* 04-06; Chapl E Sussex Hosps NHS Trust from 06. *The Chaplaincy Office, The Conquest Hospital, The Ridge, St Leonards-on-Sea TN37 7RD* Tel (01424) 757088 E-mail clive.woodward@tiscali.co.uk *or* chaplain@esht.nhs.uk
WOODWARD, Canon Ian. b 44. OLM course 96. **d** 97 **p** 98. OLM Queen Thorne *Sarum* 97-99; Adv to Bd of Ch and Soc 97-00; NSM Wilton w Netherhampton and Fugglestone 00-02; R Bere Regis and Affpuddle w Turnerspuddle from 02; Can Res and Prec Sarum Cathl from 07. *The Vicarage, West Street, Bere Regis, Wareham BH20 7HQ* Tel (01929) 471262 Mobile 07973-318866 E-mail revianw@btinternet.com
WOODWARD, Canon James Welford. b 61. K Coll Lon BD82 AKC82 Lambeth STh85 Birm Univ MPhil91 Open Univ PhD99. Westcott Ho Cam 83. **d** 85 **p** 86. C Consett *Dur* 85-87; Bp's Dom Chapl *Ox* 87-90; Chapl Qu Eliz Hosp Birm 90-96; Distr Chapl Co-ord S Birm HA 90-96; Chapl Manager Univ Hosp Birm NHS Trust 92-96; P-in-c Middleton *Birm* 96-98; P-in-c Wishaw 96-98; Bp's Adv on Health and Soc Care 96-09; V Temple Balsall 98-09; Master Foundn and Hosp of Lady Katherine Leveson 98-09; Dir Leveson Cen for the Study of Ageing, Spirituality and Soc Policy 00-09; Can Windsor from 09. *Windsor Castle, Windsor SL4 1NJ* Tel (01753) 848888 E-mail james.w.woodward@btinternet.com
WOODWARD, Canon John Clive. b 35. Univ of Wales (Lamp) BA56. St Jo Coll Dur 56. **d** 58 **p** 59. C Risca *Mon* 58-63; C Chepstow 63-66; V Ynysddu 66-74; V Newport Ch Ch 74-82; Can St Woolos Cathl 82-00; TR Cyncoed 84-00; rtd 00. *17 Carisbrooke Way, Cyncoed, Cardiff CF23 9HS* Tel (029) 2048 4448
WOODWARD, Mrs Margaret Ruth. b 59. EMMTC 04. **d** 08 **p** 09. NSM E Bridgford and Kneeton *S'well* from 08; NSM Flintham from 08; NSM Car Colston w Screveton from 08. *12 First Avenue, Colwick, Nottingham NG4 2DX* Tel 0115-912 8013 E-mail maggie.woodward@ntlworld.com
WOODWARD, Mark Christian. b 73. Univ of Wales (Lamp) BA95 Trin Coll Carmarthen PGCE97. Trin Coll Bris MA02. **d** 02 **p** 03. C Egham *Guildf* 02-06; R Stoke-next-Guildf from 06; Chapl Guildf Coll of FE and HE from 06. *8 Brockway Close, Guildford GU1 2LW* Tel (01483) 301393 Mobile 07949-630031 E-mail mark@stjohnstoke.com
WOODWARD, Matthew Thomas. b 75. Brunel Univ BA97 K Coll Lon MA99 Anglia Poly Univ MA05. Westcott Ho Cam 99. **d** 01 **p** 02. C Hampstead St Jo *Lon* 01-05; P-in-c Pimlico St Sav from 05. *59 Aylesford Street, London SW1V 3RY* Tel (020) 7821 9865 Mobile 07971-573734 E-mail matthewwoodward@mac.com
WOODWARD (née HIGGINS), Mrs Natasha Caroline. b 76. Clare Coll Cam BA98 MA02. Westcott Ho Cam 03. **d** 06 **p** 07. C Crayford *Roch* 06-07; C Orpington All SS from 08. *99 Gillmans Road, Orpington BR5 4LD* Tel (01689) 836650 Mobile 07758-579369 E-mail natasha.c.woodward@gmail.com
WOODWARD, Canon Peter Cavell. b 36. St Cath Coll Cam BA58 MA62. Bps' Coll Cheshunt 58. **d** 60 **p** 61. C Chingford St Anne *Chelmsf* 60-63; Madagascar 63-75; V Weedon Bec *Pet*

75-76; P-in-c Everdon 75-76; V Weedon Bec w Everdon 76-81; RD Daventry 79-81; Can Pet Cathl 81-02; V Brackley St Pet w St Jas 81-02; Chapl Brackley Cottage Hosp 81-02; RD Brackley 82-88; rtd 02; Perm to Offic *Pet* from 02; Chapl to Retired Clergy and Clergy Widows' Officer from 08. *7 Glastonbury Road, Northampton NN4 8BB* Tel (01604) 660679 E-mail pcwoodward@lineone.net
WOODWARD, Richard Tharby. b 39. Man Univ BA60. Chich Th Coll 60. **d** 62 **p** 63. C Mansfield St Mark *S'well* 62-65; Chapl Liddon Ho Lon 65-69; C-in-c Beaconsfield St Mich CD *Ox* 69-76; TV Beaconsfield 76-94; rtd 94; Perm to Offic *Ox* 97-00. *10 Baring Crescent, Beaconsfield HP9 2NG* Tel (01494) 670690
WOODWARD, Robert. *See* WOODWARD, Arthur Robert Harry
WOODWARD, Roger David. b 38. WMMTC 87. **d** 90 **p** 91. C Castle Bromwich SS Mary and Marg *Birm* 90-93; C Kingstanding St Luke 93-04; C Kingstanding St Mark 93-04; rtd 04; Hon C Kingstanding St Mark *Birm* 04-07. *10 Baldwin Road, Bewdley DY12 2BP* Tel (01299) 401119
WOODWARDS, David George. b 36. K Coll Lon BD62 MTh73. Oak Hill Th Coll 62. **d** 64 **p** 65. C Heworth H Trin *York* 64-66; Chapl St Pet Coll Kaduna Nigeria 67-71; V Edwardstone w Groton *St E* 72-82; RD Sudbury 81-88; R Glemsford 82-88; P-in-c Hartest w Boxted, Somerton and Stanstead 85-88; Hon Can St E Cathl 87-94; R Thorndon w Rishangles, Stoke Ash, Thwaite etc 88-94; RD Hartismere 88-93; rtd 98; Perm to Offic *St E* from 99 and *Chelmsf* from 03. *4 Cricketers Close, Sudbury CO10 2AL* Tel (01787) 374160 Fax 883312 E-mail tradrev@aol.com
WOODWELL, Sister Anita Marie. b 42. Nottm Univ BA74 CertEd80. St Deiniol's Hawarden 85. **dss** 87 **d** 87 **p** 05. Mottram in Longdendale w Woodhead *Ches* 86-89; Par Dn 87-89; TD Birkenhead Priory 89; Perm to Offic *Ban* from 01 and *St D* from 04; P-in-c Llanfrechfa and Llanddewi Fach w Llandegfeth *Mon* from 05. *The Vicarage, Llanfrechfa, Cwmbran NP44 8DQ* Tel (01633) 482343 E-mail awoodwell@yahoo.com
WOOFF, Ms Erica Mielle. b 67. City Univ BSc90 Lon Inst of Educn MA95. SEITE 02. **d** 05 **p** 06. C Sydenham St Bart *S'wark* 05-08; P-in-c Charlton 08-09; R from 09. *St Thomas House, Maryon Road, London SE7 8DJ* Tel (020) 8855 1718 E-mail ericauk@aol.com
WOOKEY, Canon Frances Anne. b 52. ACII73. WEMTC 94. **d** 97 **p** 98. C Glouc St Jas and All SS 97-01; V Hanley Castle, Hanley Swan and Welland *Worc* from 01; RD Upton from 05; Hon Can Worc Cathl from 07. *The Vicarage, 5 Westmere, Hanley Swan, Worcester WR8 0DG* Tel (01684) 310321 E-mail fwookey@fides.demon.co.uk
WOOKEY, Stephen Mark. b 54. Em Coll Cam BA76 MA80. Wycliffe Hall Ox 77. **d** 80 **p** 81. C Enfield Ch Ch Trent Park *Lon* 80-84; Asst Chapl Paris St Mich *Eur* 84-87; C Langham Place All So *Lon* 87-96; R Moreton-in-Marsh w Batsford, Todenham etc *Glouc* from 96; RD Stow 99-04. *The Rectory, Bourton Road, Moreton-in-Marsh GL56 0BG* Tel (01608) 652680 E-mail stevewookey@mac.com
WOOLCOCK, Mrs Annette Elisabeth. b 56. Qu Coll Birm BTheol94. **d** 94 **p** 95. C Hethersett w Canteloff w Lt and Gt Melton *Nor* 94-96; C Stourport and Wilden *Worc* 96-00; P-in-c The Ampneys w Driffield and Poulton *Glouc* 00-07; R Ampney Crucis, Poulton, Ampney St Mary etc 07-08; TV Fairford Deanery from 09. *The Rectory, Ampney Crucis, Cirencester GL7 5RY* Tel (01285) 851240
WOOLCOCK, Christine Ann. *See* FROUDE, Canon Christine Ann
WOOLCOCK, John. b 47. Open Univ BA82 BA86. Wm Temple Coll Rugby 69 Sarum & Wells Th Coll 70. **d** 72 **p** 73. C Kells *Carl* 72-76; C Barrow St Matt 76-78; R Distington 78-86; V Staveley w Kentmere 86-93; Soc Resp Officer 89-93; Hon Can Carl Cathl 91-93; TR Egremont and Haile 93-08; P-in-c Seascale and Drigg from 08; RD Calder from 07. *The Vicarage, The Banks, Seascale CA20 1QT* Tel (01946) 728217
WOOLCOCK, Mrs Olwen Sylvia. b 57. Birm Univ BA78. WEMTC 02. **d** 05 **p** 06. C Claines St Jo *Worc* 05-08; TR Hugglescote w Donington, Ellistown and Snibston *Leic* from 08. *The Rectory, 12 Grange Road, Hugglescote, Coalville LE67 2BQ* Tel (01530) 832557 Mobile 07913-977579 E-mail olwen@woolcock.org
WOOLDRIDGE, Derek Robert. b 33. Nottm Univ BA57. Oak Hill Th Coll. **d** 59 **p** 60. C Chesterfield H Trin *Derby* 59-63; C Heworth w Peasholme St Cuth *York* 63-70; R York St Paul 70-00; rtd 01; Perm to Offic *York* from 01. *80 Grantham Drive, York YO26 4TZ* Tel (01904) 798393 E-mail drw@100york.freeserve.co.uk
WOOLDRIDGE, John Bellamy. b 27. Tyndale Hall Bris 54. **d** 56 **p** 57. C Norbury *Ches* 56-58; C Bramcote *S'well* 58-60; R Eccleston *Ches* 60-66; NW Area Sec CPAS 66-68; P-in-c Knutsford St Jo *Ches* 68-71; V Knutsford St Jo and Toft 71-79; V Gt Clacton *Chelmsf* 79-82; V Disley *Ches* 82-88; Min Buxton Trin Prop Chpl *Derby* 88-92; rtd 92; Perm to Offic *Derby* and

S'well from 92. *227 Bramcote Lane, Nottingham NG8 2QL* Tel 0115-928 8332

WOOLF, Ms Elizabeth Louise. b 73. Qu Coll Cam BA95 MA99. Wycliffe Hall Ox BA05. **d** 06 **p** 07. C Holborn St Geo w H Trin and St Bart *Lon* 06-08; C Hammersmith St Paul 08-09; C Leamington Priors St Paul *Cov* from 09. *Address temp unknown*

WOOLHOUSE, Kenneth. b 38. BNC Ox BA61 MA65. Cuddesdon Coll 61. **d** 64 **p** 65. C Old Brumby *Linc* 64-67; Pastor Michaelshoven Soc Work Village W Germany 67-68; Chapl Cov Cathl 68-75; C-in-c Hammersmith SS Mich and Geo White City Estate CD *Lon* 75-81; Dir Past Studies Chich Th Coll 81-86; P-in-c Birdham w W Itchenor *Chich* 81-86; Chapl W Sussex Inst of HE 86-95; TV N Lambeth *S'wark* 95-01; rtd 01; Perm to Offic *S'wark* from 01. *15 Tavistock Tower, Russell Place, London SE16 7PQ* Tel (020) 7237 8147

WOOLLARD, David John. b 39. Leic Univ BSc62. Trin Coll Bris 86. **d** 88 **p** 89. C Clifton *York* 88-91; C York St Luke 91-94; V Selby St Jas 94-07; V Wistow 94-96; rtd 07; Perm to Offic *York* from 07. *6 Town Street, Settrington, Malton YO17 8NR* Tel (01944) 768665 E-mail d.wool@virgin.net

WOOLLASTON, Brian. b 53. CertEd76. St Paul's Coll Grahamstown 81. **d** 83 **p** 84. C Kington w Huntington, Old Radnor, Kinnerton etc *Heref* 88-89; C Tupsley 89-91; V Newbridge-on-Wye and Llanfihangel Brynpabuan etc *S & B* 91-98; CF 98-03; V Whiteshill and Randwick *Glouc* from 03. *The Vicarage, 98 Farmhill Lane, Stroud GL5 4DD* Tel (01453) 764757

WOOLLCOMBE (*née* DEARMER), Mrs Juliet. b 38. St Mary's Coll Dur BA60 Hughes Hall Cam DipEd61. Gilmore Course 74. **dss** 77 **d** 87 **p** 94. St Marylebone Ch Ch *Lon* 77-80; Dean of Women's Min (Lon Area) 87-89; Dn-in-c Upton Snodsbury and Broughton Hackett etc *Worc* 89-94; NSM Pershore w Pinvin, Wick and Birlingham 94-98; rtd 98; Perm to Offic *Worc* from 98. *19 Ashdale Avenue, Pershore WR10 1PL* Tel (01386) 556550 E-mail julietatashdale@talk21.com

WOOLLEY, Canon Francis Bertram Hopkinson. b 43. Sarum & Wells Th Coll 75. **d** 78 **p** 79. C Halesowen *Worc* 78-81; TV Droitwich 81-86; TV Cambridge Ascension *Ely* 86-92; R Leverington 92-01; P-in-c Wisbech St Mary 92-98; P-in-c Southea w Murrow and Parson Drove 98-01; P-in-c Balsham 01-02; P-in-c W Wickham 01-02; P-in-c Weston Colville 01-02; P-in-c W Wratting 01-02; R Balsham, Weston Colville, W Wickham etc 02-08; P-in-c 08-09; Hon Can Ely Cathl 05-08. *The Rectory, 19 West Wratting Road, Balsham, Cambridge CB21 4DX* Tel (01223) 894010 E-mail francis.woolley@tesco.net

WOOLLEY, Justine Clare. See RICHARDS, Mrs Justine Clare

WOOLMER, Preb John Shirley Thursby. b 42. Wadh Coll Ox BA63 MA69. St Jo Coll Nottm 70. **d** 71 **p** 72. Asst Chapl Win Coll 72-75; C Ox St Aldate w H Trin 75-82; R Shepton Mallet w Doulting *B & W* 82-02; Chapl Bath and West Community NHS Trust 97-01; Preb Wells Cathl 00-02; NSM Leic H Trin w St Jo 02-07; Par Evang 02-07; Springboard Missr 02-04; rtd 07. *Fig Tree Cottage, Roecliffe Road, Cropston, Leicester LE7 7HQ* Tel 0116-235 5237

WOOLMER, Kelvin Frederick. b 55. EAMTC 98. **d** 01 **p** 02. NSM Squirrels Heath *Chelmsf* 01-05; NSM Harold Hill St Paul 05-06; P-in-c Stratford New Town St Paul from 06; Ind Chapl from 06. *St Paul's Vicarage, 65 Maryland Road, London E15 1JL* Tel (020) 8534 4243 E-mail kelvin.woolmer@ntlworld.com

WOOLNOUGH, Jeffrey Ralph. b 59. MCSD88. Coll of Resurr Mirfield 00. **d** 02 **p** 03. C Gt Ilford St Mary *Chelmsf* 02-05; V Hockley from 05. *6A Silvertree Close, Hockley SS5 4SP* Tel (01702) 203668 E-mail jeff76@btinternet.com

WOOLNOUGH, Murray Robert. Wycliffe Hall Ox 07. **d** 09. C Newbury *Ox* from 09. *10 Braunfels Walk, Newbury RG14 5NQ* Tel 07823-335653 (mobile) E-mail mrwoolnough@gmail.com

WOOLSTENHOLMES, Cyril Esmond. b 16. Bede Coll Dur BA37 MA41. **d** 39 **p** 40. C Leadgate *Dur* 39-44; C Darlington St Cuth 44-46; C W Hartlepool St Paul 46-50; V Tudhoe Grange 50-67; R Shadforth 67-82; rtd 82. *12 Wearside Drive, The Sands, Durham DH1 1LE* Tel 0191-384 3763

WOOLVEN, Ronald. b 36. Oak Hill Th Coll 60. **d** 63 **p** 64. C Romford Gd Shep *Chelmsf* 63-68; C Widford 68-73; P-in-c Barling w Lt Wakering 73-84; V 84-05; rtd 05; Perm to Offic *Chelmsf* from 05. *119 Ness Road, Shoeburyness, Southend-on-Sea SS3 9ES* Tel (01702) 294436 E-mail r.woolven@btopenworld.com

WOOLVERIDGE, Gordon Hubert. b 27. CCC Cam BA51 MA55 Barrister-at-Law 52. S Dios Minl Tr Scheme 81. **d** 84 **p** 85. NSM St Edm the King w St Nic Acons etc *Lon* 84-85; NSM Chich St Paul and St Pet 85-88; P-in-c Greatham w Empshott and Hawkley w Prior's Dean *Portsm* 88-92; rtd 92; Perm to Offic *Sarum* from 93. *21 Back Lane, Cerne Abbas, Dorchester DT2 7JW* Tel (01300) 341020

WOOLWAY, Joanne. See GRENFELL, Canon Joanne Woolway

WOOLWICH, Area Bishop of. See CHESSUN, The Rt Revd Christopher Thomas James

WOON, Canon Edward Charles. b 43. SWMTC 94. **d** 96 **p** 97. OLM Tuckingmill *Truro* 96-02; P-in-c from 02; TV Redruth w Lanner and Treleigh from 04; Hon Can Truro Cathl from 09. *All Saints' Vicarage, 35 Roskear, Camborne TR14 8DG* Tel (01209) 715910 Mobile 07974-431863 E-mail eddie.woon@btopenworld.com

WOOSTER, Patrick Charles Francis. b 38. Qu Coll Birm 63. **d** 65 **p** 66. C Chippenham St Andr w Tytherton Lucas *Bris* 65-70; C Cockington *Ex* 70-72; V Stone w Woodford *Glouc* 72-73; P-in-c Hill 72-73; V Stone w Woodford and Hill 73-99; rtd 99; Perm to Offic *Worc* from 99. *20 Hylton Road, Hampton, Evesham WR11 2QB* Tel (01386) 45907

WOOSTER, Mrs Ruth Mary. b 45. SAOMC 95. **d** 98 **p** 99. OLM High Wycombe *Ox* from 98. *2 Beechwood View, Wycombe Road, Saunderton, High Wycombe HP14 4HR* E-mail ruth@woosies.freeserve.co.uk

WOOTTON, Philip Charles. b 63. Hatf Coll Dur BA85 Dur Inst of Educn PGCE86. Cranmer Hall Dur 98. **d** 00 **p** 01. C Meopham w Nurstead *Roch* 00-04; TV S Chatham H Trin from 04. *29 Keefe Close, Chatham ME5 9AG* Tel (01634) 660087 E-mail philip.wootton@diocese-rochester.org

WORCESTER, Archdeacon of. See MORRIS, The Ven Roger Anthony Brett

WORCESTER, Bishop of. See INGE, The Rt Revd John Geoffrey

WORCESTER, Dean of. See ATKINSON, The Very Revd Peter Gordon

WORDSWORTH, Jeremy Nathaniel. b 30. Clare Coll Cam BA54 MA58. Ridley Hall Cam 54. **d** 56 **p** 57. C Gt Baddow *Chelmsf* 56-59; Chapl Felsted Sch 59-63; Chapl Sherborne Sch 63-71; PV and Succ S'wark Cathl 71-73; P-in-c Stone *Worc* 73-77; V Malvern St Andr 77-82; V Combe Down w Monkton Combe and S Stoke *B & W* 82-95; rtd 95; Perm to Offic *B & W* from 05. *4 The Glebe, Hinton Charterhouse, Bath BA2 7SB* Tel (01225) 722520 E-mail hintonwordys@ukonline.co.uk

WORDSWORTH, Paul. b 42. Birm Univ BA64. Wells Th Coll 64. **d** 66 **p** 67. C Anlaby St Pet *York* 66-71; C Marfleet 71-72; TV 72-77; V Sowerby 77-90; P-in-c Sessay 77-90; V York St Thos w St Maurice 90-01; Local Community Miss Project Ldr 90-96; Abp's Miss Adv 96-00; Miss Strategy Development Officer 01-07; Abp's Officer for Miss and Evang 01-07; rtd 07; Perm to Offic *York* from 07. *10 Burniston Grove, York YO10 3RP* Tel (01904) 426891 Mobile 07711-371046 E-mail paul.wordsworth@homecall.co.uk

WORGAN, Maurice William. b 40. Ely Th Coll 62 Sarum Th Coll 64. **d** 65 **p** 66. C Cranbrook *Cant* 65-69; C Maidstone St Martin 69-72; P-in-c Stanford w Postling and Radegund 72-73; R Lyminge w Paddlesworth 72-73; R Lyminge w Paddlesworth, Stanford w Postling etc 73-88; V Cant St Dunstan w H Cross from 88. *St Dunstan's Vicarage, 5 Harkness Drive, Canterbury CT2 7RW* Tel and fax (01227) 463654 E-mail maurice@maurice-worgan.co.uk

WORKMAN, John Lewis. b 26. St Deiniol's Hawarden 82. **d** 83 **p** 84. C Brecon St Mary and Battle w Llanddew *S & B* 83-86; Min Can Brecon Cathl 83-86; P-in-c Swansea St Luke 86-87; V 87-95; rtd 95. *12 Grove House, Clyne Close, Mayals, Swansea SA3 5HL* Tel (01792) 405674

WORKMAN, Michael. b 49. Univ Coll Lon BSc70 Reading Univ PhD75. WEMTC 03. **d** 06 **p** 07. NSM Cheltenham St Mary w St Matt *Glouc* from 06. *Owls Barn, Badgeworth Lane, Badgeworth, Cheltenham GL51 4UH* Tel (01242) 863360 Mobile 07762-545098 E-mail curate@stmattchelt.org.uk

WORLEDGE, Paul Robert. b 70. Hertf Coll Ox BA91 Lon Inst of Educn PGCE92. Oak Hill Th Coll BA00. **d** 00 **p** 01. C Boscombe St Jo *Win* 00-04; V Ramsgate St Luke *Cant* from 04. *St Luke's Vicarage, St Luke's Avenue, Ramsgate CT11 7JX* Tel (01843) 592562 E-mail worledge@bigfoot.com

WORLEY, William. b 37. TD89. Cranmer Hall Dur 69. **d** 72 **p** 73. C Consett *Dur* 72-76; V Seaton Carew 76-03; CF (TA) from 77; rtd 03; Perm to Offic *Dur* from 03. *5 Peakston Close, Hartlepool TS26 0PN*

WORMALD, Roy Henry. b 42. Chich Th Coll 64. **d** 67 **p** 68. C Walthamstow St Mich *Chelmsf* 67-69; C Cov St Thos 69-72; C Cov St Jo 69-72; C Wood Green St Mich *Lon* 72-77; P-in-c Hanwell St Mellitus 77-80; V Hanwell St Mellitus w St Mark 80-95; C Hillingdon St Jo 95-99; R Kirkley St Pet and St Jo *Nor* 99-09; rtd 09. *12 Coppleston Close, Worlingham, Beccles NR34 7SF* Tel (01502) 710800

WORN, Nigel John. b 56. Sarum & Wells Th Coll. **d** 84 **p** 85. C Walworth St Jo *S'wark* 84-88; Succ S'wark Cathl 88-92; V Mitcham Ascension 92-01; RD Merton 97; V Kew from 01. *The Vicarage, 278 Kew Road, Kew, Richmond TW9 3EE* Tel (020) 8940 4616 E-mail nigel.worn@which.net

WORRALL, Frederick Rowland. b 27. **d** 86 **p** 87. NSM Chellaston *Derby* 86-93; NSM Barrow-on-Trent w Twyford and Swarkestone 94-97; Perm to Offic from 97. *37 St Peter's Road, Chellaston, Derby DE73 6UU* Tel (01332) 701890

WORRALL, Peter Henry. b 62. CA Tr Coll 85 WMMTC 93. **d** 95 **p** 96. C Bromsgrove St Jo *Worc* 95-99; P-in-c Hartlebury 99-04;

Par Support Officer CA 06-07; TV Redditch H Trin *Worc* from 07. *1 Hennals Avenue, Redditch B97 5RX* Tel (01527) 879500

WORRALL, Suzanne. *See* SHERIFF, Canon Suzanne

WORSDALL, John Robin. b 33. Dur Univ BA57. Linc Th Coll 62. **d** 63 **p** 64. C Manthorpe w Londonthorpe *Linc* 63-66; C Folkingham w Laughton 66-68; V New Bolingbroke w Carrington 68-74; P-in-c S Somercotes 74-80; V N Somercotes 74-80; P-in-c Stickney 80-82; P-in-c E Ville w Mid Ville 80-82; P-in-c Stickford 80-82; R Stickney Gp 82-98; rtd 98. *2 Streathers Court, Raunds, Wellingborough NN9 6DR* Tel (01933) 460078

WORSFOLD, Ms Caroline Jayne. b 61. St Steph Ho Ox. **d** 88 **p** 94. Chapl Asst Leic R Infirmary 88-90; C Sunderland Pennywell St Thos *Dur* 90-91; Sunderland HA Chapl 90-94; Chapl Priority Healthcare Wearside NHS Trust from 94. *Cherry Knowle Hospital, Ryhope, Sunderland SR2 0NB* Tel 0191-565 6256 ext 43370 *or* 522 7347

WORSFOLD, John. b 24. Keble Coll Ox BA50 MA50. Cuddesdon Coll 50. **d** 51 **p** 52. C Clapham H Spirit *S'wark* 51-62; C Richmond St Mary w St Matthias and St Jo 62-63; C Shirley St Geo *Cant* 63-80; C Croydon H Sav 80-84; C Croydon H Sav *S'wark* 85-89; rtd 90; Perm to Offic *S'wark* from 90 and *Roch* from 03. *c/o Pumfrey & Lythaby Solicitors, 155-159 High Street, Orpington BR6 0LN* Tel (01689) 833657 Fax 825906

WORSFOLD, Richard Vernon. b 64. Ex Univ LLB86. Cranmer Hall Dur BA94. **d** 95 **p** 96. C Countesthorpe w Foston *Leic* 95-99; TV Bradgate Team 99-01; TR 01-09; V Leic Martyrs from 09. *49 Westcotes Drive, Leicester LE3 0QT* E-mail rworsfold@btconnect.com

WORSLEY, Mrs Christine Anne. b 52. Hull Univ BA73 Bris Univ CertEd74 Birm Univ MPhil94. WMMTC 82. **dss** 84 **d** 87 **p** 94. Smethwick St Mary *Birm* 84-87; Par Dn Smethwick H Trin w St Alb 87-89; Par Dn Coventry Caludon 89-91; Chapl Myton Hamlet Hospice 91-95; Tutor WMMTC 95-04; Minl and Adult Learning Officer *Ely* from 05. *8 Hertford Close, Ely CB6 3QS* Tel (01353) 666628 *or* 652733 E-mail christine.worsley@ely.anglican.org

WORSLEY, Howard John. b 61. Man Univ BA83 Leeds Univ PGCE85 Birm Univ PhD00. St Jo Coll Nottm MA93. **d** 93 **p** 94. C Huthwaite *S'well* 93-96; V Radford St Pet 96-01; Dir Studies St Jo Coll Nottm 02-04; Dir of Educn *S'well* from 04. *St Christopher's Vicarage, 180 Sneinton Boulevard, Nottingham NG2 4GL* Tel 0115-941 5294 E-mail hjworsley@aol.com *or* dde@southwell.anglican.org

WORSLEY, Malcolm. b 37. Carl Dioc Tr Inst 94. **d** 96 **p** 97. NSM Hawes Side *Blackb* 96-98 and 01-04; NSM Lt Thornton 98-01; rtd 04; Perm to Offic *Blackb* from 04. *14 Winslow Avenue, Carleton, Poulton-le-Fylde FY6 7PQ* Tel (01253) 882208 *or* 621859 Fax 751156 E-mail m_worsley@dial.pipex.com

WORSLEY, Richard John. b 52. Qu Coll Cam BA74 MA78 Univ of Wales CertEd76 Birm Univ MPhil91 Warwick Univ MA96. Qu Coll Birm. **d** 80 **p** 81. C Styvechale *Cov* 80-84; V Smethwick H Trin w St Alb *Birm* 84-89; TV Coventry Caludon 89-96; Hon C Binley 97-05; Perm to Offic *Ely* from 05. *8 Hertford Close, Ely CB6 3QS* Tel (01353) 666628

WORSLEY, Canon Ruth Elizabeth. b 62. **d** 96 **p** 97. C Basford w Hyson Green *S'well* 96-99; C Hyson Green and Forest Fields 99-01; P-in-c 01-08; AD Nottingham N 06-09; P-in-c Sneinton St Chris w St Phil from 08; Dean of Women's Min from 07; Hon Can S'well Minster from 07. *St Christopher's Vicarage, 180 Sneinton Boulevard, Nottingham NG2 4GL* Tel 0115-941 5294 E-mail ruthworsley@aol.com

WORSNIP, Harry. b 29. St Alb Minl Tr Scheme 89. **d** 92 **p** 93. NSM Arlesey w Astwick *St Alb* 92-96; NSM Goldington 96-99; Perm to Offic from 00. *28 Milburn Road, Bedford MK41 0NZ* Tel (01234) 266422

WORSSAM, Brother Nicholas Alan. b 65. Selw Coll Cam BA87 MA91. Qu Coll Birm MA04. **d** 06 **p** 07. SSF from 99. *Glasshampton Monastery, Shrawley, Worcester WR6 6TQ* Tel (01299) 896345 Fax 896083 E-mail nicholasalanssf@franciscans.org.uk

WORSSAM, Richard Mark. b 61. St Jo Coll Dur BA83 Selw Coll Cam BA92. Ridley Hall Cam 90. **d** 93 **p** 94. C Green Street Green and Pratts Bottom *Roch* 93-97; R Fawkham and Hartley 97-08; V Otford from 08. *The Vicarage, The Green, Otford, Sevenoaks TN14 5PD* Tel (01959) 525417 *or* 523185 E-mail richard.worssam@kl.ac.uk

WORT, Gavin. b 78. K Alfred's Coll Win BTh99. Westcott Ho Cam 00. **d** 02 **p** 03. C Eastleigh *Win* 02-06; Chapl Univ of Northumbria at Newc from 06. *282 Wingrove Road North, Newcastle upon Tyne NE4 9EE* Tel 0191-274 9761 *or* 227 3284 E-mail g.wort@btopenworld.com

WORTHEN, Canon Jeremy Frederick. b 65. Rob Coll Cam BA86 MPhil88 Toronto Univ PhD92. Ripon Coll Cuddesdon 92. **d** 94 **p** 95. C Bromley SS Pet and Paul *Roch* 94-97; Tutor SEITE 97-05; Prin from 05; Wiccamical Preb Chich Cathl from 09. *SEITE, Ground Floor Offices, Sun Pier House, Medway Street, Chatham ME4 4HF* Tel (01634) 832299 E-mail j.f.worthen@kent.ac.uk

WORTHINGTON, George. b 35. AKC60. **d** 61 **p** 62. C Stockton St Pet *Dur* 61-65; C Poulton-le-Fylde *Blackb* 65-67; V Trawden 67-76; P-in-c Gressingham 76-78; P-in-c Arkholme 76-78; P-in-c Whittington 77-78; V Whittington w Arkholme and Gressingham 78-91; V Warton St Paul 91-00; rtd 00; Perm to Offic *Blackb* from 00 and *Carl* from 02. *4 Cavendish Gardens, Kirby Lonsdale, Carnforth LA6 3BW* Tel (01524) 271699

WORTHINGTON, Mark. b 55. Solicitor 80 Leeds Poly BA77. Cranmer Hall Dur 93. **d** 93 **p** 94. C Monkwearmouth St Andr *Dur* 93-96; C Chester le Street 96-00; V Harlow Green and Lamesley from 00. *The Vicarage, Lamesley, Gateshead NE11 0EU* Tel 0191-487 6490 E-mail mark.worthington@durham.anglican.org

WORTLEY, Prof John Trevor. b 34. Dur Univ BA57 MA60 DD86 Lon Univ PhD69 FRHistS. Edin Th Coll 57. **d** 59 **p** 60. C Huddersfield St Jo *Wakef* 59-64; Canada from 64; Prof Medieval Hist Manitoba Univ 69-02; Visiting Prof Sorbonne Univ 99; rtd 02. *298 Yale Avenue, Winnipeg MB R3M 0M1, Canada or Manitoba University, Winnipeg MB R3T 2N2, Canada* Tel (001) (204) 284 7554 E-mail wortley@cc.umanitoba.ca

WORTLEY, Mrs Lyn Sharon. b 59. Open Univ BA94 Coll of Ripon & York St Jo MA98. NOC 95. **d** 98 **p** 99. C Greasbrough *Sheff* 98-01; P-in-c Bramley and Ravenfield w Hooton Roberts etc 01-04; V Bramley from 04. *The Vicarage, 88 Main Street, Bramley, Rotherham S66 2SQ* Tel (01709) 702828 E-mail lyn.wortley@btinternet.com

WORTON, David Reginald (Brother Paschal). b 56. St Steph Ho Ox 88. **d** 90 **p** 90. SSF from 77; NSM Anfield St Columba *Liv* 90-92; Zimbabwe 92-94; Asst P Harare Cathl 92-93; Asst P St Aug Miss Penhalonga 93-94; Lic to Offic *Newc* 94-08; Guardian Alnmouth Friary 01-08; Asst P Shrine of Our Lady of Walsingham from 08. *Our Lady of the Angels Friary, 8 Knight Street, Walsingham NR22 6DA* Tel (01328) 820762 E-mail walsinghamssf@franciscans.org.uk

WOSTENHOLM, David Kenneth. b 56. Edin Univ BSc77 MB, ChB80 Southn Univ BTh88. Chich Th Coll 82. **d** 85 **p** 86. C Leytonstone St Marg w St Columba *Chelmsf* 85-90; V Brighton Annunciation *Chich* 90-01; TR Hove 01-07; RD Hove 03-05; P-in-c Glas St Matt from 07. *104 Erradale Street, Glasgow G22 6PT* Tel 0141-336 7480 *or* 347 1726 Mobile 07908-537085 E-mail stmatthews@btclick.com *or* david.wostenholm@hotmail.co.uk

WOTHERSPOON, David Colin. b 36. Portsm Coll of Tech CEng65 MIMechE65. St Jo Coll Dur 76. **d** 78 **p** 79. C Bashall St Gabr 78-81; V Witton 81-90; Chapl Berne w Neuchâtel *Eur* 90-01; rtd 01; Perm to Offic *Blackb* from 01. *300 Pleckgate Road, Blackburn BB1 8QU* Tel (01254) 249743

WOTTON, David Ashley. b 44. Chich Th Coll 71. **d** 74 **p** 75. C Allington and Maidstone St Pet *Cant* 74-77; C Ham St Andr *S'wark* 78-79; Chapl HM Rem Cen Latchmere Ho 78-79; C Tattenham Corner and Burgh Heath *Guildf* 85-88; P-in-c E Molesey St Mary 88-93; R Headley w Box Hill 93-06; Offg Chapl RAF 93-06; rtd 06. *Lion House, 6 Copper Beeches, St Leonards-on-Sea TN37 7RR* Tel (01424) 757122

WRAGG, Christopher William. b 60. SEITE 97. **d** 00 **p** 01. C Gt Warley Ch Ch *Chelmsf* 00-01; C Warley Ch Ch and Gt Warley St Mary 01-04; TV Buckhurst Hill 04-08; V Squirrels Heath from 08. *30 Wakerfield Close, Hornchurch RM11 2TH* Tel (020) 8504 6698 Mobile 07714-507147 E-mail vicarchris@btinternet.com

WRAGG, Peter Robert. b 46. Lon Univ BSc68. Sarum & Wells Th Coll 71. **d** 74 **p** 75. C Feltham *Lon* 74-79; TV Hackney 79-85; P-in-c Isleworth St Mary 85-94; V Feltham from 94. *The Vicarage, Cardinal Road, Feltham TW13 5AL* Tel (020) 8890 6681 *or* 8890 2011 E-mail peter.wragg@tesco.net

WRAIGHT, John Radford. b 38. St Chad's Coll Dur BA62. **d** 64 **p** 65. C Shildon *Dur* 64-67; C Newton Aycliffe 67-70; C Darlington St Jo 70-75; P-in-c Livingston LEP *Edin* 75-80; TV Carl H Trin and St Barn 80-85; P-in-c Lindale w Field Broughton 85-95; R Middleton Tyas w Croft and Eryholme *Ripon* 95-03; rtd 03. *14 Colorado Grove, Darlington DL1 2YW* Tel (01325) 354613 E-mail j.r.wraight@amserve.net

WRAKE, John. b 28. RMA. Clifton Th Coll 56. **d** 59 **p** 60. C Gt Baddow *Chelmsf* 59-62; CF 62-66; V Tilton w Lowesby *Leic* 66-73; R Maresfield *Chich* 73-79; rtd 93. *Parkfield, Batts Ridge Road, Maresfield, Uckfield TN22 2HJ* Tel (01825) 762727

WRAPSON, Donald. b 36. St Aid Birkenhead 60. **d** 63 **p** 64. C Bacup St Sav *Man* 65-68; C Wolverhampton St Matt *Lich* 68-72; C Normanton *Derby* 72-78; V Dordon *Birm* 78-82; Chapl Birm Accident Hosp and Selly Oak Hosp 82-92; Chapl Trauma Unit Birm Gen Hosp 92-95; Chapl S Birm Community Health NHS Trust 95-01; rtd 01; Perm to Offic *Worc* from 03. *7 Glebe Road, Avelchurch, Birmingham B48 7PS* Tel 0121-445 6568 E-mail donaldwrapson@tiscali.co.uk

WRATTEN, Martyn Stephen. b 34. AKC58. St Boniface Warminster 58. **d** 59 **p** 60. C Wandsworth Common St Mary *S'wark* 59-62; C Putney St Mary 62-65; C Pembury *Roch* 65-70; R Stone 70-76; Chapl Joyce Green Hosp Dartford 70-73; Stone Ho Hosp Kent 73-76; Hillcrest Hosp and Netherne Hosp

Coulsdon 76-87; Hon C Netherne St Luke CD *S'wark* 76-87; V Gt Doddington *Pet* 87-88; V Gt Doddington and Wilby 88-95; Hon C N Petherton w Northmoor Green *B & W* 95-96; rtd 95; Perm to Offic *B & W* from 96. *1 Baymead Close, North Petherton, Bridgwater TA6 6QZ* Tel (01278) 662873

WRAW, The Ven John Michael. b 59. Linc Coll Ox BA81 Fitzw Ho Cam BA84. Ridley Hall Cam 82. **d** 85 **p** 86. C Bromyard *Heref* 85-88; TV Sheff Manor 88-92; V Clifton St Jas 92-01; P-in-c Wickersley 01-04; AD Rotherham 98-04; Hon Can Sheff Cathl 01-04; Adn Wilts *Sarum* from 04. *Southbroom House, London Road, Devizes SN10 1LT* Tel (01380) 729808 E-mail adwilts@salisbury.anglican.org

WRAY, Christopher. b 48. Hull Univ BA70. Cuddesdon Coll 70. **d** 73 **p** 74. C Brighouse *Wakef* 73-76; C Almondbury 76-78; C Tong *Bradf* 78-80; V Ingleton w Chapel le Dale 80-86; R Brompton Regis w Upton and Skilgate *B & W* 86-91; V Yoxford and Peasenhall w Sibton *St E* 91-94; Perm to Offic *Carl* 94-97; R Brough w Stainmore, Musgrave and Warcop 97-02; R Walkingham Hill *Ripon* 02-07; V Ripponden *Wakef* from 07; V Barkisland w W Scammonden from 07. *St Bartholomew's Vicarage, Ripponden, Sowerby Bridge HX6 4DF* Tel (01422) 822731

WRAY, Christopher Brownlow. b 46. Open Univ BA91. Oak Hill Th Coll 86. **d** 88 **p** 89. C Quidenham *Nor* 88-91; TV Chippenham St Paul w Hardenhuish etc *Bris* 91-97; P-in-c Chipping Sodbury and Old Sodbury *Glouc* 97-09; P-in-c Horton and Lt Sodbury 04-09; rtd 09. *52 Linden Park, Shaftesbury SP7 8RN* Tel (01747) 851961

WRAY, Karl. b 51. St And Coll Greystoke 72 Ian Ramsey Coll 74 Coll of Resurr Mirfield 75. **d** 78 **p** 79. C Salford St Phil w St Steph *Man* 78-83; CF 83-86 and 89-92; V Sculcoates St Paul w Ch Ch and St Silas *York* 86-89; V Carl St Luke Morton from 92. *St Luke's Vicarage, Brownrigg Drive, Carlisle CA2 6PA* Tel and fax (01228) 515693 E-mail opusdei@live.co.uk

WRAY, Kenneth Martin. b 43. Linc Th Coll 72. **d** 75 **p** 76. C Shipley St Paul *Bradf* 75-79; V Edlington *Sheff* 79-85; V Nether Hoyland St Pet 85-97; V Up Hatherley *Glouc* 97-04; rtd 07. *5 Benall Avenue, Cheltenham GL51 6AF* Tel (01242) 236966 E-mail kmartinw026@btinternet.com

WRAY, Martin John. b 51. St Steph Ho Ox 86. **d** 88 **p** 89. C E Boldon *Dur* 88-90; C Seaham w Seaham Harbour 90-92; P-in-c Chopwell 92-95; V 95-97; C Shildon 98-00; C Croxdale and Tudhoe 00-04; P-in-c 04-06; C Spennymoor, Whitworth and Merrington 04-06; V Horsley Hill St Lawr from 06. *St Lawrence Vicarage, 84 Centenary Avenue, South Shields NE34 6SF* Tel 0191-456 1747

WRAY, Michael. b 49. Univ of Wales (Cardiff) BSc(Econ)77 Keele Univ PGCE78 RGN87. Ripon Coll Cuddesdon 80. **d** 82 **p** 83. C Blackpool St Steph *Blackb* 82-83; C Torrisholme 83-84; NSM Headington Quarry *Ox* 93-95; C Kennington *Cant* 95-99; CF (TA) 95-99; P-in-c Isham w Pytchley *Pet* 99-04; Chapl Rockingham Forest NHS Trust 99-01; Chapl Northants Healthcare NHS Trust 01-04; R Potterspury w Furtho and Yardley Gobion etc *Pet* from 04. *The Vicarage, 11 Church Lane, Potterspury, Towcester NN12 7PU* Tel (01908) 542428 E-mail revwray@btinternet.com

WRAYFORD, Geoffrey John. b 38. Ex Coll Ox BA61 MA65. Linc Th Coll 61. **d** 63 **p** 64. C Cirencester *Glouc* 63-69; Chapl Chelmsf Cathl 69-74; V 70-74; V Canvey Is 74-76; TR 76-80; P-in-c Woodlands *B & W* 80-88; V 89-92; P-in-c Frome St Jo 80-88; P-in-c Frome Ch Ch 80-85; P-in-c Frome St Mary 85-88; V Frome St Jo and St Mary 89-92; V Minehead 92-03; Chapl Taunton and Somerset NHS Trust 92-03; rtd 03; Perm to Offic *B & W* from 07. *Little Garth, Longmeadow Road, Lympstone, Exmouth EX8 5LF* Tel (01395) 267838 E-mail geoffjanw@agila.wanadoo.co.uk

WREN, Ann. See WREN, Mrs Kathleen Ann

WREN, Christopher John. b 54. Dur Univ BEd76 MA85. St Steph Ho Ox 77. **d** 79 **p** 80. C Stockton St Pet *Dur* 79-82; C Newton Aycliffe 82-85; V Gateshead St Chad Bensham 85-91; TR Bensham 91-98; V Marton *Blackb* from 98. *St Paul's Vicarage, 55 Vicarage Lane, Marton, Blackpool FY4 4EF* Tel (01253) 762679 Fax 318791 E-mail wthenest@aol.com

WREN, Douglas Peter. b 59. Lanc Univ BA82. Trin Coll Bris BA88. **d** 88 **p** 89. C Nantwich *Ches* 88-91; C Chatham St Phil and St Jas *Roch* 91-94; R Kingsdown 94-02; R Speldhurst w Groombridge and Ashurst from 02. *The Rectory, Southfields, Speldhurst, Tunbridge Wells TN3 0PD* Tel (01892) 862821 E-mail douglas.wren@diocese-rochester.org

WREN, John Aubrey. b 46. St Chad's Coll Dur BA69 Sussex Univ MA92. Cuddesdon Coll 72. **d** 74 **p** 75. C Fenny Stratford and Water Eaton *Ox* 74-77; TV Brighton Resurr *Chich* 77-84; V Eastbourne St Andr 84-92; V Hove St Barn and St Agnes 92-96. *24 Marlborough Road, Lowestoft NR32 3BU* Tel (01502) 530243

WREN, Mrs Kathleen Ann. b 50. St Steph Ho Ox 83. dss 85 **d** 87. Gateshead St Cuth w St Paul *Dur* 85-86; Gateshead St Chad Bensham 86-91; Par Dn 87-91; Adv for Women's Min 90-98; Par Dn Bensham 91-94; C 94-98; Hon Can Dur Cathl 93-98; C Marton *Blackb* from 98. *St Paul's Vicarage, 55 Vicarage Lane,*

Marton, Blackpool FY4 4EF Tel (01253) 762679 Fax 318791 E-mail wthenest@aol.com

WREN, Comdr Richard. b 35. S Dios Minl Tr Scheme 88. **d** 90 **p** 91. NSM Tisbury *Sarum* 90-01; TV 95-01; TV Nadder Valley 01-05; rtd 05. *Gaston House, Tisbury, Salisbury SP3 6LG* Tel (01747) 870674 E-mail twowrens@tesco.net

WRENBURY, The Revd and Rt Hon Lord (John Burton Buckley). b 27. K Coll Cam BA48 MA48 Solicitor 52. S'wark Ord Course 87. **d** 90 **p** 91. NSM Brightling, Dallington, Mountfield etc *Chich* from 90. *Oldcastle, Dallington, Heathfield TN21 9JP* Tel (01435) 830400 E-mail john.wrenbury@btinternet.com

WRENN, Peter Henry. b 34. Lon Univ BA56. Qu Coll Birm 58. **d** 60 **p** 61. C Dronfield *Derby* 60-64; C Hessle *York* 64-65; V Loscoe *Derby* 65-70; Asst Chapl Solihull Sch 71-77; Chapl 77-97; rtd 97; Perm to Offic *Birm* from 97. *63 Shakespeare Drive, Shirley, Solihull B90 2AN* Tel 0121-744 3941

WREXHAM, Archdeacon of. See SQUIRES, The Ven Malcolm

WRIGHT, Alan James. b 38. Chich Th Coll 63. **d** 66 **p** 67. C Edgehill St Dunstan *Liv* 66-69; Swaziland 69-71; P-in-c Seaforth *Liv* 71-76; V Taunton All SS *B & W* 76-95; rtd 99. *Bethel, Langford Lane, Norton Fitzwarren, Taunton TA2 6NZ* Tel (01823) 326558

WRIGHT, Alan Richard. b 31. **d** 96 **p** 97. OLM Quidenham Gp *Nor* 96-04; Perm to Offic from 04. *Upgate Farm, Carleton Rode, Norwich NR16 1NJ* Tel (01953) 860300

WRIGHT, Alan William. b 44. Hull Univ BA66 Bris Univ PGCE67 AMusTCL71. **d** 95 **p** 96. OLM Barton upon Humber *Linc* from 95. *1 Birchdale, Barton-upon-Humber DN18 5ED* Tel (01652) 632364 E-mail wrightherewrightnow@hotmail.com

WRIGHT, Alfred John. b 22. Wycliffe Hall Ox 66. **d** 66 **p** 67. C Newbury St Jo *Ox* 66-71; V E Challow 71-91; Chapl Community of St Mary V Wantage 75-89; rtd 91; Perm to Offic *Ox* from 92. *Polperro, Hampstead Norreys Road, Hermitage, Thatcham RG18 9RS* Tel (01635) 202889 E-mail sheba@eggconnect.net

WRIGHT, Andrew David Gibson. b 58. St Andr Univ MTheol81. Ridley Hall Cam. **d** 83 **p** 84. C W Derby Gd Shep *Liv* 83-86; C Carl H Trin and St Barn 86-88; V Wigan St Jas w St Thos *Liv* 88-91; Chapl St Edw Sch Ox 91-97 and 06-07; Ho Master 97-07; Miss Chapl R Nat Miss to Deep Sea Fishermen from 07. *46 Yarborough Road, East Cowes PO32 6SH* Tel (01983) 291855 *or* (01489) 566910 E-mail andrew@rnmdsf.org.uk

WRIGHT, Anna Chang. b 55. **d** 02 **p** 03. OLM Blyth Valley *St E* from 02. *Rose End, Back Road, Wenhaston, Halesworth IP19 9DY* Tel (01502) 478411 E-mail awright@dircon.co.uk

WRIGHT, Miss Anne. b 39. Dalton Ho Bris 67. dss 76 **d** 87 **p** 94. BCMS Uganda 71-77; N Area Sec BCMS 78-88; Pudsey St Lawr and St Paul *Bradf* 82-88; Hon Par Dn 87-88; Par Dn Kingston upon Hull H Trin *York* 88-93; Hd of Min amongst Women CPAS 93-02; CPAS Consultant (W Midl) 96-02; Regional Consultant (Midl) 99-02; Perm to Offic *Cov* 93-04 and *York* from 04; rtd 02. *Oxenby, Whitby Road, Pickering YO18 7HL* Tel (01751) 472689 E-mail jacquelinewright@btopenworld.com

WRIGHT, Anthony. See WRIGHT, Derek Anthony

WRIGHT, Anthony John. b 47. Ex Univ MA98 ACA70 FCA77. Ripon Coll Cuddesdon 86. **d** 88 **p** 89. C Kidderminster St Mary and All SS w Trimpley etc *Worc* 88-91; P-in-c Offenham and Bretforton 91-96; R Backwell w Chelvey and Brockley *B & W* 96-02; RD Portishead 01-02; P-in-c Tetbury w Beverston *Glouc* 02-03; R 03-06; R Tetbury, Beverston and Long Newnton from 07; P-in-c Shipton Moyne w Westonbirt and Lasborough 02-03; V Shipton Moyne from 03. *The Vicarage, 6 The Green, Tetbury GL8 8DN* Tel (01666) 502333 Fax 500893 E-mail sheba.wright@virgin.net

WRIGHT, Canon Anthony Robert. b 49. Lanchester Poly Cov BA70. St Steph Ho Ox 70. **d** 73 **p** 74. C Amersham on the Hill *Ox* 73-76; C Reading St Giles 76-78; P-in-c Prestwood 78-84; P-in-c Wantage 84-87; V 87-92; RD Wantage 84-92; P-in-c W w E Hanney 88-91; V Portsea St Mary *Portsm* 92-98; Hon Can Portsm Cathl 96-98; R Westmr St Marg from 98; Chapl to Speaker of Ho of Commons from 98; Can Westmr Abbey from 98. *5 Little Cloister, London SW1P 3PL* Tel (020) 7654 4806 Fax 7654 4821 E-mail robert.wright@westminster-abbey.org

WRIGHT, Canon Barry Owen. b 38. S'wark Ord Course 66. **d** 69 **p** 70. C Plumstead Ascension *S'wark* 69-74; Hon C Welling 74-89; Hon Can S'wark Cathl 79-89; Sen Chapl W Midl Police *Birm* 89-93; Sen Chapl Metrop Police *Lon* from 93; V Mill Hill St Mich from 02. *St Michael's Vicarage, 9 Flower Lane, London NW7 2JA* Tel (020) 8959 1449 *or* 8358 1077 Fax 8906 1857 E-mail bwrg8@aol.com

WRIGHT, Caroline. **d** 09. NSM Pontesbury I and II *Heref* from 09. *1 Higher Netley, Netley, Dorrington, Shrewsbury SY5 7SY* Tel (01743) 718790 E-mail info@carosbandb.co.uk

WRIGHT, Preb Catherine Jane. b 62. Bris Univ BA84 MA92 PhD00 Selw Coll Cam BA96. Ridley Hall Cam 94. **d** 97 **p** 98. C Highworth w Sevenhampton and Inglesham etc *Bris* 97-00; Perm to Offic *Ex* 00-01; NSM Stoke St Gregory w Burrowbridge and Lyng *B & W* 01-05; Dioc Voc Adv from 02; Assoc Dir of Ords from 02; Dean of Women Clergy and Preb Wells Cathl from 05. *The Rectory, West Monkton, Taunton TA2 8QT*   Tel (01823) 413380 E-mail cjwright@onetel.com

WRIGHT, Charles Frederick Peter. b 16. Qu Coll Ox BA39 MA42. Westcott Ho Cam 40. **d** 41 **p** 42. C Stocksbridge *Sheff* 41-43; C Goole 43-47; C Ecclesall 47-50; R Brown and Chilton Candover w Northington etc *Win* 50-54; V Long Sutton 54-61; V Welton *Linc* 61-69; Lect Linc Th Coll 61-63; Lic to Offic *Linc* 69-99; rtd 81. *9 Bromley College, London Road, Bromley BR1 1PE*   Tel (020) 8460 9461

WRIGHT, Charles Kenneth. b 38. CEng73 MIMechE73 MBIM91. Sarum & Wells Th Coll 91. **d** 93 **p** 94. C Bridgwater St Mary, Chilton Trinity and Durleigh *B & W* 93-96; Chapl Workington *Carl* 96-03; C Camerton, Seaton and W Seaton 96-03; Chapl W Cumbria Health Care NHS Trust 96-01; Chapl N Cumbria Acute Hosps NHS Trust 01-03; rtd 03; Perm to Offic *Carl* from 03. *Naemair, 72 Ruskin Close, High Harrington, Workington CA14 4LS*   Tel (01946) 833536

WRIGHT, Christopher Joseph Herbert. b 47. St Cath Coll Cam BA69 MA73 PhD77. Ridley Hall Cam 75. **d** 77 **p** 78. C Tonbridge SS Pet and Paul *Roch* 77-81; Perm to Offic *St Alb* 82-01; BCMS India 83-88; Tutor and Dir Studies All Nations Chr Coll Ware 88-93; Prin 93-04. *Address temp unknown*

WRIGHT, Christopher Nigel. b 39. Kelham Th Coll 60. **d** 65 **p** 66. C Ellesmere Port *Ches* 65-69; C Latchford Ch Ch 69-72; C Gt Budworth 72-75; C Wigan St Andr *Liv* 75-76; V New Springs 77-82; C Dovecot 82-85; C Rainford 85-89; rtd 89; Perm to Offic *Liv* 89-01. *105 Ilfracombe Road, Sutton Leach, St Helens WA9 4NN*   Tel (01744) 821199

WRIGHT, Clifford. *See* WRIGHT, The Rt Revd Royston Clifford

WRIGHT, Canon Clifford Nelson. b 35. K Coll Lon BD59 AKC59. **d** 60 **p** 61. C Stevenage *St Alb* 60-67; V Camberwell St Luke *S'wark* 67-81; RD Camberwell 75-80; Hon Can S'wark Cathl 79-01; TR Basingstoke *Win* 81-93; RD Basingstoke 84-93; Hon Can Win Cathl 89-00; R Win St Matt 93-00; rtd 00; Perm to Offic *Win* from 01. *1 Valley Dene, Dibden Purlieu, Southampton SO45 4NJ*   Tel (023) 8084 5898 E-mail cliffwright@waitrose.com

WRIGHT, David Evan Cross. b 35. K Coll Lon BD64 AKC64. **d** 65 **p** 66. C Morpeth *Newc* 65-69; C Benwell St Jas 69-70; C Bushey *St Alb* 70-74; V High Wych 74-77; R High Wych and Gilston w Eastwick 77-80; V St Alb St Mary Marshalswick 80-89; P-in-c Sandridge 87-89; R Lenham w Boughton Malherbe *Cant* 89-00; rtd 00; P-in-c Fuengirola St Andr *Eur* 01-06; Perm to Offic *Chich* 01-06. *536 Urban, Cerros del Aguila, 29649 Mijas (Málaga), Spain*

WRIGHT, David Henry. b 23. Keble Coll Ox BA48. St Steph Ho Ox 52. **d** 54 **p** 55. C Penton Street St Silas w All SS *Lon* 54-57; V Barnsbury St Clem 57-66; V Wandsworth St Anne *S'wark* 66-73; P-in-c Stanley *St And* 73-75; R Dunkeld 73-92; R Strathtay 75-92; rtd 92; Hon C Aberdeen St Marg from 00. *28 Midstocket Mews, Aberdeen AB15 5FG*   Tel (01224) 636554

WRIGHT, David William. b 63. Barrister 86 Liv Univ LLB85 Fitzw Coll Cam BA92 Cam Univ MA96 Univ of Wales (Cardiff) LLM99. Westcott Ho Cam 90. **d** 93 **p** 94. C Chorlton-cum-Hardy St Clem *Man* 93-97; P-in-c Donnington Wood *Lich* 97-99; V 99-09; TR Cen Wolverhampton from 09. *St Peter's Rectory, 42 Park Road East, Wolverhampton WV1 4QA*   Tel (01902) 428491   Mobile 07977-543735 E-mail david.wright@lichfield.anglican.org

WRIGHT, Denise Ann. *See* WILLIAMS, Denise Ann

WRIGHT, Derek Anthony. b 35. ACP66 Lon Univ CertEd57. Cranmer Hall Dur 80. **d** 81 **p** 82. C Auckland St Andr and St Anne *Dur* 81-83; V Cornforth 83-87; P-in-c Thornley 87-88; R Gt and Lt Glemham, Blaxhall etc *St E* 88-90; V Evenwood *Dur* 90-93; P-in-c Satley and Tow Law *Dur* 95; V 95-99; rtd 99. *39 Hilltop Road, Bearpark, Durham DH7 7TA*

WRIGHT, Edward Maurice Alexanderson. b 54. Wycliffe Hall Ox. **d** 88 **p** 91. C Maidstone St Luke *Cant* 88-93; R Cliffe at Hoo w Cooling *Roch* from 93. *St Helen's Rectory, Church Street, Cliffe, Rochester ME3 7PY*   Tel (01634) 220220 E-mail edward.wright@diocese-rochester.org

WRIGHT, Edward Michael. b 37. St Cath Soc Ox BA61 MA65. Cuddesdon Coll. **d** 64 **p** 65. C Willesden St Andr *Lon* 64-68; Bahamas 68-71; V Lewisham St Steph and St Mark *S'wark* 72-80; V Ox St Barn and St Paul 80-07; rtd 07; Perm to Offic *Ox* from 08. *9 Binswood Avenue, Headington, Oxford OX3 8NY* E-mail emichaelwright@ntlworld.com

WRIGHT, Frank Albert. b 51. Portsm Univ MA02. Sarum & Wells Th Coll 80. **d** 83 **p** 84. C Buckingham *Ox* 83-86; C Newport Pagnell w Lathbury and Moulsoe 86-89; TV W Slough 89-95; TR 95-99; TR Fareham H Trin *Portsm* from 99; Dioc Interfaith Adv 01-06. *The Rectory, 9 Brook Meadow, Fareham PO15 5JH*   Tel and fax (01329) 280180 Fax 232688 E-mail admin@holytrinity-fareham.fsnet.co.uk

WRIGHT, Frederic Ian. b 64. City Univ BSc85. Wycliffe Hall Ox BTh94. **d** 94 **p** 95. C Carl St Jo 94-98; C Bassenthwaite, Isel and Setmurthy 98-02; TV Binsey 02-07. *Aden House, The Square, Allonby, Maryport CA15 6QA*   Tel (01900) 881095

WRIGHT, Frederick John. b 15. AKC42. **d** 42 **p** 43. C Brierley Hill *Lich* 42-45; C Walsall Pleck and Bescot 45-49; V W Bromwich Gd Shep 49-54; R Headless Cross *Worc* 54-67; R Romsley 67-80; rtd 80; Perm to Offic *Ely* from 97. *Rosevear, 3 Drury Lane, Colne, Huntingdon PE28 3NB*   Tel (01487) 840518

WRIGHT, Graham. b 50. Oak Hill Th Coll 73. **d** 76 **p** 77. C Northampton St Giles *Pet* 76-79; C Man Resurr 79-82; V Barkingside St Laur *Chelmsf* 82-88; Chapl K Geo V Hosp Ilford 82-88; P-in-c Yoxford and Chapl Suffolk Constabulary *St E* 88-90; Perm to Offic *Linc* 03-05; Lic Preacher 05-07; R Rockingham w Safety Bay Australia from 07. *PO Box 799, Rockingham WA 6968, Australia*   Tel (0061) (8) 9523 1430 *or* 9527 1417 Fax 9527 1483   Mobile 48-892 7141 E-mail therockingrev@bigpond.com

WRIGHT, Graham John Aston. b 57. Moorlands Th Coll 77 Wycliffe Hall Ox 05. **d** 06 **p** 07. NSM Marston w Elsfield *Ox* 06-08; Asst Chapl St Edw Sch Ox 06-08; Chapl Queenswood Sch Herts from 09. *Queenswood School, Shepherds Way, Brookmans Park, Hatfield AL9 6NX*   Tel (01707) 602500

WRIGHT, Mrs Heather Margaret. b 47. EAMTC 93. **d** 96 **p** 97. NSM Heigham St Thos *Nor* 96-99; Hon Asst Dioc Chapl among deaf and deaf-blind people from 99; NSM Sprowston w Beeston from 03. *133 Moore Avenue, Norwich NR6 7LQ*   Tel (01603) 301329 Fax and minicom as telephone E-mail rev@wrighth.freeserve.co.uk

WRIGHT, Mrs Hilary. **d** 08. OLM Parkstone St Pet and St Osmund w Branksea *Sarum* from 08. *18 Springfield Crescent, Poole BH14 0LL*   Tel (01202) 747369

WRIGHT, Howard John Douglas. b 64. BA85. Trin Coll Bris BA94. **d** 96 **p** 97. C Ipswich St Matt *St E* 96-00; V Four Marks *Win* from 00. *The Vicarage, 22 Lymington Bottom, Four Marks, Alton GU34 5AA*   Tel (01420) 563344 E-mail howardwright@xalt.co.uk

WRIGHT, Hugh Edward. b 57. BNC Ox BA79 MA87 Ex Univ CertEd81. Sarum & Wells Th Coll 85. **d** 87 **p** 88. C Hobs Moat *Birm* 87-90; C W Drayton *Lon* 90-92; V Oakfield St Jo *Portsm* from 92; RD E Wight 00-05. *St John's Vicarage, Victoria Crescent, Ryde PO33 1DQ*   Tel (01983) 562863 E-mail hewright@stjohnsryde.freeserve.co.uk

WRIGHT, Ian. *See* WRIGHT, Frederic Ian

WRIGHT, Ian. b 65. Coll of Resurr Mirfield 97. **d** 99 **p** 00. C S Lafford *Linc* 99-01; C Hawley H Trin *Guildf* 01-03; Chapl Bonn w Cologne *Eur* 03-06; P-in-c Armley w New Wortley *Ripon* from 06. *19 St Mary's Park Green, Armley, Leeds LS12 3UY*   Tel 0113-263 8620

WRIGHT, Mrs Jean. b 41. Man Univ BA63 CertEd64. Carl Dioc Tr Inst 88. **d** 91 **p** 94. NSM Kirkby Stephen w Mallerstang etc *Carl* from 91. *Mains View, Crosby Garrett, Kirkby Stephen CA17 4PR*   Tel (01768) 371457

WRIGHT, John. *See* WRIGHT, Nicholas John

WRIGHT, John. *See* WRIGHT, Alfred John

WRIGHT, John. *See* WRIGHT, Anthony John

WRIGHT, John Alastair. b 30. FRSA72. Cranmer Hall Dur 62. **d** 64 **p** 65. C Thornton-le-Fylde *Blackb* 64-67; Miss to Seamen 67-72; V Darlington St Luke *Dur* 72-78; Community Chapl Darlington 78-89; rtd 89. *4 Grasmere, Agar Nook, Coalville LE67 4SH*   Tel (01530) 837390

WRIGHT, John Douglas. b 42. Birm Univ BSc64 CertEd66. St Steph Ho Ox 69. **d** 69 **p** 70. C Swanley St Mary *Roch* 69-74; C Stockwell Green St Andr *S'wark* 74-79; V Leigh St Jo *Man* 79-82; P-in-c Whitehawk *Chich* from 82. *St Cuthman's Vicarage, 1 St Cuthman's Close, Whitehawk, Brighton BN2 5HW*   Tel (01273) 699424   Mobile 07944-419007 E-mail jonda9@gmail.com

WRIGHT, Canon John Harold. b 36. Dur Univ BA58 Ch Ch Coll Cant MA96 ATCL ACertCM. Ely Th Coll 58. **d** 61 **p** 62. C Boston *Linc* 61-64; C Willesborough w Hinxhill *Cant* 64-68; V Westwell 68-75; R Eastwell w Boughton Aluph 68-75; V Rolvenden 75-84; R Cheriton St Martin 84-01; Hon Can Cant Cathl 97-01; rtd 01; Perm to Offic *Cant* from 01. *1 Cliff Road, Hythe CT21 5XA*   Tel (01303) 265303

WRIGHT, Judith Mary. b 44. Ex Univ MSc98. SWMTC 05. **d** 07. NSM Silverton, Butterleigh, Bickleigh and Cadeleigh *Ex* from 07. *Fine Oak Cottage, Newton St Cyres, Exeter EX5 5AA*   Tel (01392) 851330

WRIGHT, Miss Julia Mary. b 64. Reading Univ BA88. Trin Coll Bris 96. **d** 98 **p** 99. C Woodley *Ox* 98-03; TV Aylesbury w Bierton and Hulcott 03-05; C Bernwode 05-07; Chapl Burrswood Chr Hosp from 08. *The Chaplaincy, Burrswood, Groombridge, Tunbridge Wells TN3 9PY*   Tel (01892) 863637 Fax 863623

WRIGHT, Ken. *See* WRIGHT, Charles Kenneth

WRIGHT, Canon Kenyon Edward. b 32. CBE99. Glas Univ MA53 Fitzw Coll Cam BA55 Serampore Coll MTh61 Edin Univ DLitt00. Wesley Ho Cam 53. **d** 71 **p** 71. In Meth Ch India 57-71; Dir Urban Min Cov Cathl 71-81; Dir of Internat Min and Can Res 72-81; Public Preacher 72-74; Gen Sec Scottish Chs Coun 81-90; Dir Scottish Chs Ho Dunblane 81-90; Dir Kairos Trust 90-92; Hon C Glas H Cross 91-92; rtd 92; P-in-c Glencarse *Bre* 94-00. *1 Churchill Close, Ettington, Stratford-upon-Avon*

CV37 7SP Tel and fax (01789) 740356 Mobile 07801-849941 E-mail kenyonwright@aol.com

WRIGHT, Lawrence Charles. b 57. Hull Univ MA94. EMMTC 93. **d** 96 **p** 96. C Heathridge and Joondalup Australia 96-98; C Penzance St Jo *Truro* 98-02; TV Penzance St Mary w St Paul and St Jo 02-04; Manager Relig Affairs Yarlswood Immigration and Detention Cen 04-06; Chapl W Lon YMCA 06-07; SSF from 07; R Birm St Geo from 09. *St George's Rectory, 100 Bridge Street West, Birmingham B19 2YX* Tel 07964-452417 (mobile) E-mail larryssf@googlemail.com

WRIGHT, Leslie Vandernoll. b 24. Trin Hall Cam MA50. Ridley Hall Cam 49. **d** 51 **p** 52. C Aldershot H Trin *Guildf* 51-53; C Cambridge H Trin *Ely* 53-57; V Marston *Ox* 57-59; Asst Master Castle Ct Sch Parkstone 59-61; Asst Chapl Stowe Sch 61-64; Hd Master St Mich Prep Sch Five Oaks Jersey 64-66; Chapl Windlesham Ho Sch Sussex 66-68; Chapl Vevey *Eur* 68-73; Hd St Geo Sch Clarens 73-89; rtd 89; Chapl Lugano *Eur* 89-92. *18 avenue Schubert, Domaine Château Tournon, 83440 Montauroux, France* Tel (0033) (4) 94 47 62 43 E-mail leslie.wright@orange.fr

WRIGHT, Mrs Louisa Mary (Lisa). b 33. S'wark Ord Course. **d** 87 **p** 94. NSM Streatham Hill St Marg *S'wark* 87-95; Hon C Streatham St Leon 95-02; rtd 02; Perm to Offic *S'wark* from 02. *19 Hillside Road, London SW2 3HL* Tel (020) 8671 8037

WRIGHT, Mrs Marion Jane. b 47. Whitelands Coll Lon CertEd69. Cranmer Hall Dur 73. **d** 00 **p** 02. NSM Scalby *York* from 00. *3 East Park Road, Scalby, Scarborough YO13 0PZ* Tel (01723) 350208

WRIGHT, Martin. b 48. Avery Hill Coll BEd81 K Alfred's Coll Win CertEd69 LRAM76. SAOMC 95. **d** 98 **p** 99. NSM St Alb St Mary Marshalswick *St Alb* 98-01; C Gt Berkhamsted 02-05; V Reigate St Mark *S'wark* from 05. *St Mark's Vicarage, 8 Alma Road, Reigate RH2 0DA* Tel (01737) 241161 Mobile 07774-923550 E-mail mwright@stmarksreigate.co.uk

WRIGHT, Canon Martin Neave. b 37. AKC61. Tel Boniface Warminster. **d** 62 **p** 63. C Corby St Columba *Pet* 62-65; Ind Chapl 65-71; Nigeria 71-75; P-in-c Honiley *Cov* 75-84; P-in-c Wroxall 75-84; Ind Chapl 75-84; Soc Resp Officer 84-96; Hon Can Cov Cathl 95-96; Bp's Chapl and Past Asst *B & W* 96-02; Preb Wells Cathl 96-02; Sub-Dean Wells 00-02; rtd 02; Perm to Offic *Cov* from 02. *2 Honiwell Close, Harbury, Leamington Spa CV33 9LY* Tel (01926) 613699

WRIGHT, Michael. *See* WRIGHT, Edward Michael

WRIGHT, Canon Michael. b 30. St Chad's Coll Dur BA55 De Montfort Univ MPhil04. **d** 56 **p** 57. C New Cleethorpes *Linc* 56-59; C Skegness 59-62; V Louth St Mich 62-73; R Stewton 62-73; R Warmsworth *Sheff* 73-86; Warden Dioc Readers' Assn 81-86; Hon Can Sheff Cathl 82-95; V Wath-upon-Dearne w Adwick-upon-Dearne 86-94; V Wath-upon-Dearne 94-95; RD Wath 92-95; rtd 95; Perm to Offic *Linc* from 95. *17 Ashfield Road, Sleaford NG34 7DZ* Tel (01529) 415698

WRIGHT, Michael Christopher. b 44. Leeds Univ BA65 CertEd67 MSc75 Sheff Univ PhD02 FRSA95. Wells Th Coll 65. **d** 67 **p** 68. C Dormanstown *York* 67-69; Perm to Offic *Linc* 69-88 and *Sheff* 71-95; Hd Master Eastmoor High Sch Wakef 84-87; Hd Master Carleton High Sch Pontefract 87-95; C-in-c St Edm Anchorage Lane CD *Sheff* 95-96; Chapl Doncaster R Infirmary and Montagu Hosp NHS Trust 95-01; Research Fell Sheff Univ 01-03; Sen Research Fell Lanc Univ from 03; Hon C Gt Snaith *Sheff* 01-07; Perm to Offic *Wakef* from 01; *Eur* from 06; *Sheff* from 07. *Orchard End, Finkle Street, Hensall, Goole DN14 0QY* Tel (01977) 661900 *or* (01524) 593152 E-mail mc.wright@btinternet.com *or* m.c.wright@lancaster.ac.uk

WRIGHT, Michael George. b 52. WEMTC 01. **d** 04 **p** 05. NSM Woodchester and Brimscombe *Glouc* from 04. *The Trumpet, West End, Minchinhampton, Stroud GL6 9JA* Tel (01453) 883027 Mobile 07974-303527 E-mail thetrumpet.antiques@virgin.net

WRIGHT, Michael John. b 38. Dur Univ MA91. Chich Th Coll 59. **d** 62 **p** 63. C Yate *Glouc* 62-65; C Kirby Moorside w Gillamoor *York* 65-68; V 68-72; V Bransdale cum Farndale 68-72; V Kirkbymoorside w Gillamoor, Farndale etc 72-73; Dioc Communications Officer 72-74; V Ormesby 74-80; P-in-c Middlesbrough St Cuth 81-88; Perm to Offic 88-99; NSM W Acklam 91-97; Chapl Butterwick Hospice Stockton-on-Tees 97-99; Chapl S Dur Hospice Bp Auckland 97-99; rtd 03. *25 Thornfield Road, Middlesbrough TS5 5DD* Tel (01642) 816247 E-mail mjw@careatwork.fsnet.co.uk

WRIGHT, Nicholas John. b 65. Liv Univ BA87. Wycliffe Hall Ox 89. **d** 92 **p** 93. C Burley *Ripon* 92-95; C Brightside w Wincobank *Sheff* 95-97; TV Sheff Manor 97-03; Perm to Offic from 03. *22 Norfolk Road, Sheffield S2 2SX*

WRIGHT, Nicholas Mark. b 59. Loughb Univ BSc80. Qu Coll Birm 82. **d** 85 **p** 86. C Coney Hill *Glouc* 85-89; C Rotherham *Sheff* 89-91; TV Worc SE 91-98; R Inkberrow w Cookhill and Kington w Dormston from 98. *The Vicarage, High Street, Inkberrow, Worcester WR7 4DU* Tel (01386) 792222 E-mail ncbjmswright@btinternet.com

✠**WRIGHT, The Rt Revd Nicholas Thomas.** b 48. Ex Coll Ox BA71 MA75 DPhil81 DD00. Wycliffe Hall Ox BA73. **d** 75 **p** 76 **c** 03. Fell Mert Coll Ox 75-78; Chapl 76-78; Chapl and Fell Down Coll Cam 78-81; Asst Prof NT Studies McGill Univ Montreal 81-86; Chapl and Fell Worc Coll Ox and Univ Lect Th 86-93; Dean Lich 93-99; Can Th Cov Cathl 92-99; Lector Theologiae and Can Westmr Abbey 00-03; Bp Dur from 03. *Auckland Castle, Bishop Auckland DL14 7NR* Tel (01388) 602576 Fax 605264 E-mail bishop.of.durham@durham.anglican.org

WRIGHT, Nigel Christopher James. b 67. FCCA99 Leeds Univ BA07. NOC 04. **d** 07 **p** 08. NSM Utley *Bradf* from 07. *High Hob Cote Farm, Hob Cote Lane, Oakworth, Keighley BD22 0RW* Tel (01535) 644855 Fax 613396 Mobile 07970-751670 E-mail nigel@nwaccounting.co.uk

WRIGHT, Ms Pamela Anne. b 45. Open Univ BSc00. St As Minl Tr Course 01. **d** 03 **p** 04. NSM Llanrhos *St As* from 03. *Brackenrigg, Bryn Pydew Road, Bryn Pydew, Llandudno Junction LL31 9JH* Tel (01492) 541552 Fax 541652 Mobile 07850-180420 E-mail pamscot45@aol.com

WRIGHT, Miss Pamela Jean. b 38. ALA63. NTMTC 02. **d** 03 **p** 04. NSM Harrow Trin St Mich *Lon* 03-05; NSM Harrow Weald St Mich 05-08. *Address temp unknown* E-mail pamelajwright@btinternet.com

WRIGHT, Ms Patricia. b 46. MBE02. SRN68. S'wark Ord Course 80. **dss** 85 **d** 89. Asst Chapl R Lon Hosp (Mile End) 83-85; Bethnal Green St Matt w St Jas the Gt *Lon* 85-88; Hon C St Botolph Aldgate w H Trin Minories 89-05; Cathl Dn and Dioc HIV/AIDS Co-ord Swaziland 00-04; Hon C St Geo-in-the-East St Mary from 06. *8 Royal Mint Street, London E1 8LG* Tel (020) 7265 1814 E-mail patw@patthedeacon.com

WRIGHT, The Ven Paul. b 54. K Coll Lon BD78 AKC78 Heythrop Coll Lon MTh90. Ripon Coll Cuddesdon 78. **d** 79 **p** 80. C Beckenham St Geo *Roch* 79-83; Chapl Ch Sch Richmond 83-85; C Richmond St Mary w St Matthias and St Jo *S'wark* 83-85; V Gillingham St Aug *Roch* 85-90; R Crayford 90-99; RD Erith 93-97; V Sidcup St Jo 99-03; Adn Bromley and Bexley from 03; Hon Can Roch Cathl from 98. *The Archdeaconry, The Glebe, Chislehurst BR7 5PX* Tel and fax (020) 8467 8743 Mobile 07811-147219 E-mail archdeacon.bromley@rochester.anglican.org

WRIGHT, Paul Stephen. b 66. Cen Lancs Univ BA88 Liv Univ MA96. Westcott Ho Cam 90. **d** 93 **p** 94. C Upholland *Liv* 93-96; CF 96-08; Chapl Sen CF from 08. *c/o MOD Chaplains (Army)* Tel (01980) 615804 Fax 615800

WRIGHT, Peter. *See* WRIGHT, Charles Frederick Peter

WRIGHT, Canon Peter. b 35. K Coll Lon AKC61 Hull Univ MA86. St Boniface Warminster 61. **d** 62 **p** 63. C Goole *Sheff* 62-67; V Norton Woodseats St Chad 67-80; R Aston cum Aughton 80-84; P-in-c Ulley 80-84; Chapl Rotherham Priority Health Services NHS Trust 80-84; R Aston cum Aughton and Ulley *Sheff* 84-93; TR Aston cum Aughton w Swallownest, Todwick etc 93-00; RD Laughton 85-93; Chapter Clerk and Hon Can Sheff Cathl 92-00; rtd 00; Perm to Offic *Sheff* from 01; Chapl to Rtd Clergy and Clergy Widows Officer from 09. *40 Chancet Wood Drive, Sheffield S8 7TR* Tel and fax 0114-274 7218 E-mail allsaints.pw@talk21.com

WRIGHT, Peter Reginald. b 34. St Chad's Coll Dur BA60. Linc Th Coll 60. **d** 62 **p** 63. C Lt Ilford St Mich *Chelmsf* 62-65; C Billingham St Aid *Dur* 65-68; TV 68-71; TR 71-76; Chapl Portsm Poly 76-87; Sec Chapls in HE Gen Syn Bd of Educn 88-95; rtd 95; Perm to Offic *Portsm* from 95. *6 Garden Lane, Southsea PO5 3DP* Tel (023) 9273 6651

WRIGHT, Peter Westrope. b 24. Kelham Th Coll 43. **d** 48 **p** 49. C Pimlico St Barn *Lon* 48-50; C Sidley *Chich* 50-59; R E Blatchington 59-73; P-in-c Lewes St Mich 73-75; TV Lewes All SS, St Anne, St Mich and St Thos 75-84; TR 84-87; rtd 89; Perm to Offic *Chich* from 89. *17 South Street, Lewes BN7 2BT* Tel (01273) 473332

WRIGHT, Philip. b 32. G&C Coll Cam BA53 MA57. Wells Th Coll 56. **d** 57 **p** 58. C Barnard Castle *Dur* 57-60; C Heworth St Mary 60-64; V Tow Law 64-70; V Tanfield 70-78; V Gateshead Ch Ch 78-02; rtd 02. *Meldon, High Heworth Lane, Gateshead NE10 0PB* Tel 0191-469 2161

WRIGHT, Phillip. b 35. Kelham Th Coll 57 St Aid Birkenhead 59. **d** 61 **p** 62. C Goldthorpe *Sheff* 61-65; V Doncaster St Jude 65-71; V Kettering All SS *Pet* 71-82; V S Kirkby *Wakef* 82-94; rtd 98. *2 The Grove, Wickersley, Rotherham S66 2BP* Tel (01709) 543922 E-mail thegrove@onetel.com

WRIGHT, Robert. *See* WRIGHT, Canon Anthony Robert

WRIGHT, Robert Charles. b 31. Roch Th Coll 65. **d** 67 **p** 68. C Manston *Ripon* 67-70; C Moor Allerton 70-74; P-in-c Terrington St John *Ely* 74-79; P-in-c Walpole St Andrew 74-75; V Terrington St John 80-91; V Tilney St Lawrence 80-91; V Tilney All Saints 80-91; R Stiffkey and Cockthorpe w Morston, Langham etc *Nor* 91-96; rtd 96; Perm to Offic *Nor* from 96. *Glenfinnan, 83 Childs Way, Sheringham NR26 8TX* Tel (01263) 822535

WRIGHT, Canon Robert Doogan. b 24. TCD BA46 MA. TCD Div Sch Div Test 47. **d** 47 **p** 48. C Carnmoney *Conn* 47-49; C Belfast St Jas 49-51; C Belfast St Matt 51-53; P-in-c Belfast Whiterock 53-57; I Magheragall 57-64; I Belfast St Mark 64-70; I Carrickfergus 70-82; Can Conn Cathl 79-86; I Killead w Gartree 82-86; Chan Conn Cathl 83-86; rtd 86. *15 Mount Pleasant Road, Newtownabbey BT37 0NQ* Tel (028) 9086 2779

WRIGHT, Robert John. b 47. St Jo Coll Dur BA70. SEITE 00. **d** 03 **p** 04. NSM Notting Hill St Jo *Lon* 03-06; NSM Notting Hill St Pet 03-06; NSM N Hammersmith St Kath 06-08; NSM Cheddington w Mentmore *Ox* from 08. *The Rectory, 29 Mentmore Road, Cheddington, Leighton Buzzard LU7 0SD* Tel (01296) 661358 Mobile 07988-978419
E-mail robert@robert-wright.com

✠**WRIGHT, The Rt Revd Royston Clifford.** b 22. Univ of Wales BA42. St Steph Ho Ox 43. **d** 45 **p** 46 **c** 86. C Bedwas *Mon* 45-47; C Newport St Jo Bapt 47-49; C Walton St Mary *Liv* 49-51; Chapl RNVR 50-51; Chapl RN 51-68; V Blaenavon w Capel Newydd *Mon* 68-74; RD Pontypool 73-74; TR Ebbw Vale 74-77; Can St Woolos Cathl 74-77; Adn Mon 77-88; Adn Newport 77-86; Bp Mon 86-91; rtd 91; Lic to Offic *Mon* from 91. *23 Rupert Brooke Drive, Newport NP20 3HP* Tel (01633) 250770

WRIGHT (née PRECIOUS), Sally Joanne. b 75. Hatf Coll Dur BA97 Anglia Poly Univ MA03. Westcott Ho Cam 00. **d** 02 **p** 03. C Chich St Paul and Westhampnett 02-05; Perm to Offic *S'wark* 05-06; Hon C Peckham St Jo w St Andr from 06; Chapl Guildhall Sch of Music and Drama *Lon* 06-09. *St John's Vicarage, 10A Meeting House Lane, London SE15 2UN* Tel (020) 7635 5576 or 7639 0084
E-mail sallywright29@yahoo.co.uk

WRIGHT, Samuel. See WRIGHT, Canon William Samuel

WRIGHT, Simon Christopher. b 44. AKC67. **d** 68 **p** 69. C Bitterne Park *Win* 68-72; C Kirkby *Liv* 72-74; V Wigan St Anne 74-79; Abp's Dom Chapl and Dioc Dir of Ords *York* 79-84; V W Acklam 84-00; RD Middlesbrough 87-98; Can and Preb York Minster 94-00; V Dartmouth and Dittisham *Ex* from 00. *The Vicarage, Northford Road, Dartmouth TQ6 9EP* Tel and fax (01803) 835543

WRIGHT, Stephen Irwin. b 58. Ex Coll Ox BA80 MA84 Selw Coll Cam BA85 MA90 Lanc Univ MA92 St Jo Coll Dur PhD97. Ridley Hall Cam 83. **d** 86 **p** 87. C Newbarns w Hawcoat *Carl* 86-90; C Burton and Holme 90-94; NSM Esh *Dur* 94-97; NSM Hamsteels 94-97; C Consett 97-98; Dir Coll of Preachers 98-06; Tutor Spurgeon's Coll from 06; Perm to Offic *S'wark* from 99. *Spurgeon's College, 189 South Norwood Hill, London SE25 6DJ* Tel (020) 8653 0850 or 8768 0878 ext 233 Fax 8711 0959
E-mail s.wright@spurgeons.ac.uk

WRIGHT, Canon Stephen Mark. b 60. Keele Univ BA83. Trin Coll Bris 86. **d** 89 **p** 90. C Thorne *Sheff* 89-92; CMS 92-05; Nigeria 93-98; Hon Can Asaba from 98; Chapl Ahmadi St Paul Kuwait 99-03; Chapl Dubai and Sharjah w N Emirates from 03. *PO Box 7415, Dubai, United Arab Emirates* Tel (00971) (4) 884 4904 E-mail stephenw@emirates.net.ae

WRIGHT, Stewart. See WRIGHT, William Charles Stewart

WRIGHT, Stuart Kendle. b 73. **d** 08 **p** 09. C Tollington *Lon* from 08. *Emmanuel Vicarage, 145 Hornsey Road, London N7 6DU* Tel (020) 7607 1737 Mobile 07867-888999
E-mail vegetablestu@blueyonder.co.uk

WRIGHT, Thomas. See WRIGHT, The Rt Revd Nicholas Thomas

WRIGHT, Thomas Stephen. b 31. Fitzw Ho Cam BA54 MA58. Bps' Coll Cheshunt 56. **d** 57 **p** 58. C Bishop's Stortford St Mich *St Alb* 57-61; C St E Cathl 61-64; R Hartest w Boxted 64-82; Chapl RAF 64-71; RD Sudbury *St E* 70-81; P-in-c Somerton 71-82; P-in-c Stansfield 82-91; V Denston w Stradishall and Stansfield 91-97; Min Can St E Cathl 82-97; rtd 98. *c/o Messrs Ashton Graham Solicitors, 81 Guildhall Street, Bury St Edmunds IP33 1PZ*

WRIGHT, Tim Stanley. b 63. Derby Coll of Educn BEd86. St Jo Coll Dur 89. **d** 92 **p** 93. C Eccleshill *Bradf* 92-96; TV Southend *Chelmsf* 96-00; V Boulton *Derby* from 00. *The Vicarage, 1 St Mary's Close, Alvaston, Derby DE24 0GF* Tel (01332) 572308
E-mail revboulton@tiscali.co.uk

WRIGHT, Timothy. b 63. NUU BSc85. Cranmer Hall Dur 86. **d** 89 **p** 90. C Bramcote *S'well* 89-93; I Glenavy w Tunny and Crumlin *Conn* 93-98; Chapl RAF from 98; Perm to Offic *Lich* 01-08. *Chaplaincy Services, Valiant Block, HQ Air Command, RAF High Wycombe HP14 4UE* Tel (01494) 496800 Fax 496343

WRIGHT, Timothy John. b 41. K Coll Lon BD63 AKC63. **d** 64 **p** 65. C Highfield *Ox* 64-68; Asst Chapl Worksop Coll Notts 68-71; Chapl Malvern Coll 71-77; Ho Master 77-86; Hd Master Jo Lyon Sch Harrow 86-01; rtd 01. *Beech House, Colwall Green, Malvern WR13 6DX* Tel (01684) 541102

WRIGHT, Timothy John. b 54. Nottm Univ BA76. Ripon Coll Cuddesdon 90. **d** 92 **p** 93. C Dawlish *Ex* 92-95; TV Teignmouth, Ideford w Luton, Ashcombe etc 95-01; Chapl Wycombe Abbey Sch 01-08; NSM Wycombe Deanery 08-09; P-in-c Petworth *Chich* from 09; P-in-c Egdean from 09. *The Rectory, Rectory Lane, Petworth GU28 0DB* Tel (01798) 342505

WRIGHT, Toby Christopher. b 75. New Coll Ox BA98 MA01 Leeds Univ MA01. Coll of Resurr Mirfield 99. **d** 01 **p** 02. C Petersfield *Portsm* 01-04; P-in-c Peckham St Jo w St Andr *S'wark* 04-06; V from 06; AD Camberwell from 06. *St John's Vicarage, 10A Meeting House Lane, London SE15 2UN* Tel (020) 7635 4214 or 7639 0084 E-mail priest@stjohnspeckham.org.uk

WRIGHT, Mrs Vyvienne Mary. b 35. S Dios Mini Tr Scheme 80. **dss** 83 **d** 87 **p** 94. Martock w Ash *B & W* 83-00; Hon C 87-00; Perm to Offic from 00. *36 Church Close, Martock TA12 6DS* Tel (01935) 823292

WRIGHT, William Charles Stewart. b 53. Ulster Poly BSc81. CITC BTh95. **d** 95 **p** 96. C Ballyholme *D & D* 95-98; I Conwal Union w Gartan *D & R* from 98. *Conwal Rectory, New Line Road, Letterkenny, Co Donegal, Republic of Ireland* Tel (00353) (74) 912 2573

WRIGHT, Canon William Samuel. b 59. TCD BTh89 MA90. **d** 87 **p** 88. C Belfast St Aid *Conn* 87-91; Sec Dioc Bd of Miss 90-91; I Cleenish w Mullaghdun *Clogh* 91-99; I Lisburn Ch Ch Cathl from 99; Can and Preb Conn Cathl from 01. *Cathedral Rectory, 2 Clonevin Park, Lisburn BT28 3BL* Tel (028) 9266 2865 or 9260 2400 E-mail sam.wright@lisburncathedral.org

WRIGHTSON, Bernard. b 25. CertEd50 ACP65. Linc Th Coll 83. **d** 83 **p** 84. NSM Alford w Rigsby *Linc* 83-86; Perm to Offic 86-89; NSM Mablethorpe w Trusthorpe 89-94; Perm to Offic 94-04. *Pipits Acre, 64 Church Lane, Mablethorpe LN12 2NU* Tel (01507) 472394

WRIGLEY, George Garnett. b 50. St Cath Coll Cam BA71 Loughb Coll of Educn PGCE72. NTMTC 02. **d** 04 **p** 05. NSM Hounslow H Trin w St Paul *Lon* 04-08; P-in-c Langdale *Carl* from 08. *The Vicarage, Chapel Stile, Ambleside LA22 9JG* Tel (015394) 37267 E-mail georgewrig@hotmail.com

WRISDALE, Jean May. b 40. **d** 90 **p** 94. OLM Fotherby *Linc* from 90. *The Meadows, Livesey Road, Ludborough, Grimsby DN36 5SQ* Tel (01472) 840474

WROE, Mark. b 69. Surrey Univ BA92. Ridley Hall Cam 94. **d** 96 **p** 97. C Chilvers Coton w Astley *Cov* 96-00; P-in-c Newarth St Alb *Dur* 00-03; V 03-07; V Jesmond H Trin *Newc* from 07; P-in-c Newc St Barn and St Jude from 07. *13 Glastonbury Grove, Newcastle upon Tyne NE2 2HA* Tel 0191-240 1017
E-mail mark.wroe@htjesmond.org.uk

WROE, Martin Daniel Edward. b 61. NTMTC. **d** 04 **p** 05. NSM Covent Garden St Paul *Lon* 04-07; NSM W Holloway St Luke from 07. *45 Penn Road, London N7 9RE* Tel (020) 7607 6086
E-mail martinwroe@blueyonder.co.uk

WYARD, Peter Joseph. b 54. Pemb Coll Cam MA76 Sussex Univ MSc80 Brunel Univ MSc88 Anglia Ruskin Univ MA07. EAMTC 99. **d** 02 **p** 03. C Framlingham w Saxtead *St E* 02-05; P-in-c Riverside *Ox* 05-08; V Colnbrook and Datchet from 08. *St Mary's Vicarage, London Road, Datchet, Slough SL3 9JW* Tel (01753) 580467 E-mail peter.wyard@btinternet.com

WYATT, Colin. b 27. Ex Coll Ox BA54 MA55 Lon Univ BD62. Tyndale Hall Bris 60. **d** 63 **p** 64. C Radipole *Sarum* 63-66; C Southborough St Pet *Roch* 66-67; V Tetsworth *Ox* 67-72; Lect Bible Tr Inst Glas 72-74; R Hurworth *Dur* 74-79; P-in-c Dinsdale w Sockburn 74-76; R 76-79; R Sadberge 79-84; R Bacton w Wyverstone and Cotton *St E* 84-92; rtd 92; Perm to Offic *Ripon* from 92. *20 Harrogate Road, Ripon HG4 1SR* Tel (01765) 606810

WYATT, Canon David Stanley Chadwick. b 36. Fitzw Ho Cam DA59 MA71. Ely Th Coll 59. **d** 61 **p** 62. C Rochdale *Man* 61-63; Bp's Dom Chapl 63-68; R Salford St Paul w Ch Ch from 68; P-in-c Salford Ordsall St Clem 91-96; P-in-c Lower Broughton Ascension from 05; AD Salford 97; Hon Can Man Cathl from 82. *St Paul's Church House, Broadwalk, Salford M6 5FX* Tel 0161-736 8868

WYATT, Peter Charles. b 62. Bris Univ BSc85 CEng MIEE92. St Jo Coll Nottm 05. **d** 07 **p** 08. C Becontree St Thos *Chelmsf* from 07. *29 Warrington Road, Dagenham RM8 3JH* Tel (020) 8252 4148 E-mail peter.michelle@gmail.com

WYATT, Peter John. b 38. Kelham Th Coll 58. **d** 64 **p** 65. C N Stoneham *Win* 64-68; C Brixham *Ex* 68-69; Dominica 69-75; Zambia 76-78; P-in-c Ettington *Cov* 78-79; V Butlers Marston and the Pillertons w Ettington 79-86; V Codnor and Loscoe *Derby* 86-91; Chapl for Deaf People 91-03; rtd 03; Perm to Offic *Heref* from 04. *16 Cae Melyn, Tregynon, Newtown SY16 3EF* Tel (01686) 650508

WYATT, Richard Norman. b 21. LVCM. **d** 84 **p** 85. C Puttenham and Wanborough *Guildf* 84-90; Perm to Offic *Chich* 91-93 and from 97; P-in-c Stedham w Iping 93-97; rtd 97; RD Midhurst *Chich* 98-99. *Trenethick, June Lane, Midhurst GU29 9EL* Tel (01730) 813447 E-mail norman.wyatt@homecall.co.uk

WYATT, Royston Dennis. b 36. FRICS67. Sarum & Wells Th Coll 74. **d** 77 **p** 78. NSM Canford Magna *Sarum* 77-82; V Abbotsbury, Portesham and Langton Herring 82-88; Dioc Missr *Linc* 88-95; R Welford w Weston *Glouc* 95-05; RD Campden 96-01; rtd 05; Perm to Offic *B & W* from 06. *78 Lower Meadow, Ilminster TA19 9DP* Tel (01460) 53996
E-mail revrdw@talktalk.net

WYATT (*née* **OWEN**), **Mrs Susan Elizabeth.** b 53. Bris Univ BSc75 Bath Univ PGCE78. EAMTC 97. **d** 00 **p** 01. Asst Dioc Adv in Miss and Evang *Ely* from 00; C Over 00-06; C Long Stanton w St Mich 02-06; V Cherry Hinton St Jo from 06. *St John's Vicarage, 9 Luard Road, Cambridge CB2 8PJ* Tel (01223) 247451 Mobile 07713-241261
E-mail sue.wyatt1@ntlworld.com *or* sue.wyatt@ely.anglican.org

WYATT, Trevor. b 60. Keele Univ BSc81. SEITE 97. **d** 00 **p** 01. NSM Wilmington *Roch* from 00. *216 Birchwood Road, Wilmington, Dartford DA2 7HA* Tel (01322) 666521 Mobile 07860-306746 E-mail trevor.wyatt@diocese-rochester.org *or* trevor.wyatt@bt.com

WYBER, Richard John. b 47. G&C Coll Cam BA69 MA72 FCA73. SEITE 03. **d** 06 **p** 07. NSM Wanstead St Mary w Ch Ch *Chelmsf* from 06. *7 Mornington Close, Woodford Green IG8 0TT* Tel (020) 8504 2447

WYBREW, Canon Hugh Malcolm. b 34. Qu Coll Ox BA58 MA. Linc Th Coll 59. **d** 60 **p** 61. C E Dulwich St Jo *S'wark* 60-64; Tutor St Steph Ho Ox 65-71; Chapl Bucharest *Eur* 71-73; V Pinner *Lon* 73-83; Sec Fellowship of SS Alb and Sergius 84-86; Dean Jerusalem 86-89; Hon Can Gib Cathl 89-04; V Ox St Mary Magd 89-04; Hon Can Ch 01-04; rtd 04. *96 Warwick Street, Oxford OX4 1SY* Tel (01865) 241355
E-mail hugh.wybrew@theology.ox.ac.uk

WYER, Mrs Janet Beatrice. b 58. UEA BA00. ERMC 04. **d** 07 **p** 08. C Loddon, Sisland, Chedgrave, Hardley and Langley *Nor* from 07. *42 Langley Road, Chedgrave, Norwich NR14 6HD* Tel (01508) 520354 Mobile 07990-576118
E-mail wyer@supanet.com

WYER, Keith George. b 45. St Paul's Cheltenham CertEd66 K Coll Lon BD71 AKC71. St Aug Coll Cant 71. **d** 72 **p** 73. C Moseley St Mary *Birm* 72-76; Chapl RNR 73-92; C Walsall *Lich* 76-77; Min Walsall St Martin 77-79; Chapl Colston's Sch Bris 79-86; Chapl Kelly Coll Tavistock 86-92; R Combe Martin and Berrynarbor *Ex* 92-95; TR Combe Martin, Berrynarbor, Lynton, Brendon etc from 96; RD Shirwell 95-01. *The Rectory, Rectory Road, Combe Martin, Ilfracombe EX34 0NS* Tel (01271) 883203 E-mail keith@wyer.org

WYKES, Peter. b 44. Lon Univ MB, BS68. Ban & St As Minl Tr Course 97. **d** 00 **p** 01. NSM Trefnant w Tremeirchion *St As* 00-01; NSM Cefn w Trefnant w Tremeirchion from 01. *Clattwm, 1 Plas Chambres Road, Denbigh LL16 5UP* Tel (01745) 730263

WYLAM, John. b 43. AKC66 FE TCert75. **d** 67 **p** 68. C Derby St Bart 67-70; SSF 70-73; C Seaton Hirst *Newc* 74-77; V Byker St Silas 77-83; V Alwinton w Holystone and Alnham 83-98; R Chollerton w Birtley and Thockrington 98-09; rtd 09. *Nether House, Garleigh Road, Rothbury, Morpeth NE65 7RG* Tel (01669) 622805 E-mail johnwylam@googlemail.com

WYLD, Kevin Andrew. b 58. St Cath Coll Cam BA79 MA85 Univ Coll Dur MSc83 Edin Univ BD85. Edin Th Coll 82. **d** 85 **p** 86. C Winlaton *Dur* 85-87; C Houghton le Spring 87-90; V Medomsley 90-95; V High Spen and Rowlands Gill 95-00; R Winter Park St Rich USA 00-04. *Address temp unknown*

WYLIE, Alan. b 47. Is of Man Tr Inst 88. **d** 92 **p** 93. NSM Douglas St Geo *S & M* 92-97; NSM Challoch *Glas* 97-00; P-in-c Motherwell from 00; P-in-c Wishaw from 00. *The Rectory, 14 Crawford Street, Motherwell ML1 3AD* Tel (01698) 249441
E-mail alan.rev@hotmail.com

WYLIE, Clive George. b 64. QUB BSc86 TCD BTh90 MA93. CITC 87. **d** 90 **p** 91. C Drumglass w Moygashel *Arm* 90-93; I Tynan, Aghavilly and Middletown 93-98; Hon V Choral Arm Cathl 93-98; Team P Glas E End 98-03; TR 03-08; Miss 21 Co-ord 98-03; Perm to Offic *Nor* from 09. *14 Bridewell Street, Walsingham NR22 6BJ* Tel (01328) 820291 Mobile 07970-875052 E-mail clive.wylie@benedictines.org.uk

WYLIE, David Victor. b 61. ACA86 LSE BSc(Econ)82 Leeds Univ BA91. Coll of Resurr Mirfield 89. **d** 92 **p** 93. C Kilburn St Aug w St Jo *Lon* 92-95; C Heston 95-98; Chapl RN from 98. *Royal Naval Chaplaincy Service, Mail Point 1-2, Leach Building, Whale Island, Portsmouth PO2 8BY* Tel (023) 9262 5055 Fax 9262 5134

WYLIE-SMITH, Ms Megan Judith. b 52. S'wark Ord Course 88. **d** 91 **p** 94. C Greenstead *Chelmsf* 91-94; C W Ham 94-97; TV Becontree S 97-01; rtd 01; Perm to Offic *Chelmsf* from 01. *67 Gordon Road, London E11 2RA* Tel (020) 8530 6434
E-mail megan@wylie-smith.freeserve.co.uk

WYNBURNE, John Paterson Barry. b 48. St Jo Coll Dur BA70. Wycliffe Coll Toronto MDiv72 Ridley Hall Cam 72. **d** 73 **p** 74. C Gt Stanmore *Lon* 73-76; Chapl Bucharest w Sofia *Eur* 76-77; C Dorking w Ranmore *Guildf* 77-80; V Send 80-88; V York Town St Mich 88-93; V Camberley St Mich Yorktown 93-95; TR Beaconsfield *Ox* 95-09; AD Amersham 04-09; V Long Crendon w Chearsley and Nether Winchendon from 09. *The Vicarage, 84A High Street, Long Crendon, Aylesbury HP18 9AL* Tel (01844) 208363 E-mail jwynburne@aol.com

WYNES, Michael John. b 33. AKC57. **d** 58 **p** 59. C Gt Berkhamsted *St Alb* 58-62; C Silverhill St Matt *Chich* 62-65; C Wilton *B & W* 65-68; R Berkley w Rodden 68-77; V Priddy 77-86; V Westbury sub Mendip w Easton 77-86; C Milton 86-93;

rtd 93; Perm to Offic *B & W* from 95. *23A Fairways, Wells BA5 2DF* Tel (01749) 673778

WYNFORD-HARRIS, Robert William. b 61. Anglia Ruskin Univ BA. Ridley Hall Cam 06. **d** 08 **p** 09. C Sawbridgeworth *St Alb* from 08. *St Mary's Lodge, Knight Street, Sawbridgeworth CM21 9AX* Tel (01279) 723398 E-mail wynhar@hotmail.com

WYNN, Edward Laurence. b 65. Leeds Metrop Univ BSc96 Leeds Univ MA02 RGN88. NOC 98. **d** 01 **p** 02. C Emley *Wakef* 01-04; C Flockton cum Denby Grange 01-04; Chapl RAF from 04. *Chaplaincy Services, Valiant Block, HQ Air Command, RAF High Wycombe HP14 4UE* Tel (01494) 496800 Fax 496343 Mobile 07714-062869 E-mail eddie@wynn41.freeserve.co.uk

WYNN, Richard David. b 44. Univ Coll of Rhodesia & Nyasaland Inst of Educn TCert65. St Paul's Coll Grahamstown 86. **d** 88 **p** 89. C Kirby-Hilton Ascension S Africa 88-91; R Ixopo St Jo 91-99; R Richmond-cum-Byrne St Mary 99-02; P-in-c Cinderford St Steph w Littledean *Glouc* from 02; P-in-c Cinderford St Jo from 06. *The Vicarage, St Annal's Road, Cinderford GL14 2AS* Tel and fax (01594) 822286
E-mail rswynn@cinderschurch.fsnet.co.uk

WYNN (*née* **ARMSTRONG**), **Rosemary.** b 40. **d** 06. OLM Sturminster Newton, Hinton St Mary and Lydlinch *Sarum* from 06. *2 Alder Close, Sturminster Newton DT10 1AJ* Tel (01258) 472656 E-mail rwsturminster@orangehome.co.uk

WYNN-EVANS, Canon James Naylor. b 34. Magd Coll Ox BA55 MA59. Linc Th Coll 57. **d** 59 **p** 60. C Goole *Sheff* 59-62; C Hatfield 62-63; Chapl HM Borstal Hatfield 62-67; C-in-c Dunscroft CD *Sheff* 63-67; Bp's Dom Chapl *Edin* 67-75; C Edin St Columba 67-69; R Edin St Marg 69-85; P-in-c Edin SS Phil and Jas 76-85; P-in-c Edin St Dav 85-97; Info Officer Scottish Episc Ch 97-99; Admin Chapl to Primus 97-01; Can St Mary's Cathl 86-95; Hon Can St Mary's Cathl from 98. *1 Gayfield Place, Edinburgh EH7 4AB* Tel 0131-556 1566
E-mail wynn-evans@supanet.com

WYNNE, Preb Alan John. b 46. St Luke's Coll Ex CertEd71. St Steph Ho Ox BA71 MA75. **d** 71 **p** 72. C Watford St Pet *St Alb* 71-74; Chapl Lindian Ho Lon 74-75; Chapl Abp Tenison's Sch Kennington 75-86; Hon C St Marylebone Annunciation Bryanston Street *Lon* 81-86; V Hoxton St Anne w St Columba 86-94; TR Poplar from 94; Preb St Paul's Cathl from 01; AD Tower Hamlets 01-06. *Poplar Rectory, Newby Place, London E14 0EY* Tel and fax (020) 7987 3133 *or* tel 7538 9198
E-mail alan@poplar22.fsnet.co.uk

WYNNE (*née* **GORTON**), **Mrs Angela Deborah.** b 60. Leeds Univ BSc82 CSci04. CBDTI 04. **d** 07 **p** 08. NSM Penwortham St Mary *Blackb* from 07. *11 Freeman's Lane, Charnock Richard, Chorley PR7 5ER* Tel (01257) 791760

WYNNE, The Very Revd Frederick John Gordon. b 44. Chu Coll Cam BA66 MA70. CITC 81. **d** 84 **p** 85. C Dublin St Patr Cathl Gp 84-86; C Romsey *Win* 86-89; R Broughton, Bossington, Houghton and Mottisfont 89-97; I Dunleckney w Nurney, Lorum and Kiltennel *C & O* 97-08; I Leighlin w Grange Sylvae, Shankill etc from 08; Chan Ossory Cathl from 00; Chan Leighlin Cathl 00-04; Dean Leighlin from 04. *The Deanery, Old Leighlin, Co Carlow, Republic of Ireland* Tel (00353) (59) 972 1570
E-mail dunstan@eircom.net

WYNNE, Preb Geoffrey. b 41. K Coll Lon BD64 AKC64 Lon Univ BSc(Soc)75 Heythrop Coll Lon MTh86. **d** 66 **p** 67. C Wolverhampton St Pet *Lich* 66-70; Chapl Wolv Poly 66-79; Sen Chapl 79-92; Sen Chapl Wolv Univ from 92; Dir of Ords 76-83; Preb Lich Cathl from 83; AD Wolverhampton from 03; Bp's Adv for Univ and HE Chapl from 04. *The Chaplain's House, 1 Compton Park, Wolverhampton WV3 9DU* Tel (01902) 712051 *or* 322904 E-mail g.wynne@wlv.ac.uk

WYNNE, Jean. **d** 02 **p** 03. NSM Mullingar, Portnashangan, Moylisar, Kilbixy etc *M & K* from 02. *3 Doctor's Court, Rathangan, Co Kildare, Republic of Ireland* Tel (00353) (45) 524057 Mobile 86-356 4590

WYNNE, Mrs Teresa Anne Jane. b 58. Anglia Poly Univ BEd94 Middx Univ BA07. NTMTC 04. **d** 07 **p** 08. C Takeley w Lt Canfield *Chelmsf* from 07. *5 Chestnut Way, Takeley, Bishop's Stortford CM22 6RW* Tel (01279) 870376
E-mail teresa.wynne@btinternet.com

WYNNE, Trefor. b 35. St Mich Coll Llan 72. **d** 74 **p** 75. C Llangynwyd w Maesteg 74-77; V Trealaw 77-83; R Llanbeulan w Llanfaelog and Tal-y-Llyn *Ban* 83-96; RD Llifon and Talybolion 93-96; rtd 96; Perm to Offic *Llan* from 96. *3 St John's Drive, Ton Pentre, Pentre CF41 7EU* Tel (01443) 433660

WYNNE-GREEN, Roy Rowland. b 36. Chich Th Coll 67. **d** 70 **p** 71. C Fleetwood St Pet *Blackb* 70-73; C Cen Torquay *Ex* 73-75; Chapl SW Hosp and Chapl Asst St Thos Hosp Lon 75-85; Chapl R Surrey Co Hosp Guildf 85-94; Chapl R Surrey Co Hosp NHS Trust 94-01; Chapl Heathlands Mental Health Trust Surrey 94-98; Chapl Surrey Hants Borders NHS Trust 98-01; rtd 01; Perm to Offic *Guildf* from 02. *St Benedict's House, 6 Lawn Road, Guildford GU2 5DE* Tel (01483) 574582

WYNNE-JONES, Nicholas Winder. b 45. Jes Coll Ox BA67 MA72 Selw Coll Cam 71. Oak Hill Th Coll 69. **d** 72 **p** 73. C St Marylebone All So w SS Pet and Jo *Lon* 72-75; Chapl Stowe

Sch 75-83; V Gt Clacton *Chelmsf* 83-95; V Beckenham Ch Ch *Roch* from 95; RD Beckenham 00-05. *Christ Church Vicarage, 18 Court Downs Road, Beckenham BR3 6LR* Tel (020) 8650 3847 Fax 8658 9532 E-mail nick.wynnejones@diocese-rochester.org *or* vicar@ccb.org.uk

WYNTER, Michael Pallant. b 48. Ripon Coll Cuddesdon 93. **d** 95 **p** 96. C Hughenden *Ox* 95-98; P-in-c Norton sub Hamdon, W Chinnock, Chiselborough etc *B & W* 98-01; R 01-05; RD Ivelchester 01-04; Perm to Offic *Ox* 05-08; C Hazlemere from 08. *Pipers Cottage, Pipers Lane, Great Kingshill, High Wycombe HP15 6LW* Tel (01494) 714758

Y

YABBACOME, David Wallace. b 55. Bp Otter Coll BEd. Linc Th Coll. **d** 83 **p** 84. C Egham Hythe *Guildf* 83-86; C Cen Telford *Lich* 86-87; TV 87-92; R Cheadle w Freehay 92-00; V Linc St Nic w St Jo Newport from 00. *St Nicholas' Vicarage, 103 Newport, Lincoln LN1 3EE* Tel (01522) 525653 Mobile 07779-557541 E-mail revyabb@ntlworld.com

YABSLEY, Mrs Janet. b 42. St Alb Minl Tr Scheme 81. **dss** 84 **d** 87 **p** 94. Luton St Andr *St Alb* 84-87; NSM Luton St Aug Limbury 87-00; NSM Luton All SS w St Pet 00-06; Perm to Offic from 06. *11 Dale Road, Dunstable LU5 4PY* Tel (01582) 661480

YACOMENI, Peter Frederick. b 34. Worc Coll Ox BA58 MA61. Wycliffe Hall Ox 58. **d** 60 **p** 61. C New Malden and Coombe *S'wark* 60-64; C Bethnal Green St Jas Less *Lon* 64-68; V Barton Hill St Luke w Ch Ch *Bris* 68-75; V Bishopsworth 75-86; RD Bedminster 84-86; P-in-c Wick w Doynton 86-87; V Wick w Doynton and Dyrham 87-98; RD Bitton 95-98; Chapl Wilts and Swindon Healthcare NHS Trust from 98; rtd 98; Perm to Offic *Bris* from 98. *15 Orwell Close, Malmesbury SN16 9UB* Tel (01666) 826628

YACOMENI, Thomas Peter Bruce. b 71. Ex Univ BEng94. Trin Coll Bris BA09. **d** 09. C Weston-super-Mare St Paul *B & W* from 09. *15 Clarence Road North, Weston-super-Mare BS23 4AT* Tel (01934) 643851 Mobile 07786-806640 E-mail tom.yacomeni@googlemail.com

YALLOP, John. b 47. BA79. Oak Hill Th Coll 79. **d** 79 **p** 80. C Brinsworth w Catcliffe *Sheff* 79-81; C Heeley 81-83; C Pitsmoor Ch 83-86; V Ellesmere St Pet 86-88; V Worksop St Jo *S'well* 90-94; P-in-c Cliftonville *Cant* 94-99. *Address temp unknown*

YAM, David Tong Kho. *See* HAOKIP, Canon David Tongkhoyam

YANDELL, Caroline Jane. b 63. St Hugh's Coll Ox BA85 MA92 Bris Univ MB, ChB97 LSHTM MSc05 Bris Univ PhD07 Wolfs Coll Cam BTh08 St Jo Coll Cam MPhil09 MRCGP01. Ridley Hall Cam 06. **d** 09. C Henleaze *Bris* from 09. *87 Sea Mills Lane, Stoke Bishop, Bristol BS9 1DX* E-mail cj236@cam.ac.uk

YANGON, Bishop of. *See* SAN SI HTAY, The Most Revd Samuel

YAP, Thomas Fook Piau. b 75. Leeds Univ BA98 MA99. St Jo Coll Nottm MTh02. **d** 03 **p** 04. C Starbeck *Ripon* 03-07; Chapl Essex Univ from 07. *Mariners, Rectory Hill, Wivenhoe, Colchester CO7 9LB* Tel (01206) 823430 E-mail revthomas@hotmail.co.uk

YATES, Alan John Richard. b 38. Lon Univ LDS62. **d** 99 **p** 00. OLM Cley Hill Warminster *Sarum* 99-07; OLM Cley Hill Villages 07-08. *212 Pottle Street, Horningsham, Warminster BA12 7LX* Tel and fax (01985) 844374 Mobile 07970-864714 E-mail revajry@googlemail.com

YATES, Andrew Martin. b 55. St Chad's Coll Dur BA77. Linc Th Coll 78. **d** 80 **p** 81. C Brightside St Thos and St Marg *Sheff* 80-83; TV Haverhill w Withersfield, the Wrattings etc *St E* 84-90; Ind Chapl 84-90; R Aylesham w Adisham *Cant* 90-96; P-in-c Dudley St Aug Holly Hall *Worc* 96-03; Chapl Merry Hill Shopping Cen 96-03; P-in-c Tresillian and Lamorran w Merther *Truro* from 03; P-in-c St Michael Penkevil from 03; Dioc Soc Resp Officer from 03. *The Rectory, 18 Fore Street, Tregony, Truro TR2 5RN* Tel (01872) 530507 E-mail yatesasb@aol.com

YATES, Canon Anthony Hugh. b 39. Univ of Wales BA62. Wycliffe Hall Ox 62. **d** 65 **p** 66. C Withington St Crispin *Man* 65-68; C Sheff St Cecilia Parson Cross 68-73; CMP from 69; V Middlesbrough St Thos *York* 73-82; V Fenton *Lich* 82-95; V Kilburn St Aug w St Jo *Lon* from 95; Hon Can Koforidua from 01. *St Augustine's House, Kilburn Park Road, London NW6 5XD* Tel (020) 7624 1637 E-mail saint@augustine93.freeserve.co.uk

YATES, Mrs Esther Christine. b 46. Moray Ho Coll of Educn DipEd67 Cartrefle Coll of Educn BEd80. St As Minl Tr Course 02. **d** 05 **p** 06. NSM Newtown w Llanllwchaiarn w Aberhafesp *St As* 05-07; NSM Llanllwchaiarn and Newtown w Aberhafesp

from 07. *Gwawr-y-Grug, 7 Mill Fields, Milford, Newtown SY16 3JP* Tel (01686) 625559

YATES, Francis Edmund. b 49. Ox Univ BEd72 Sheff Univ MEd88. Linc Th Coll 95. **d** 95 **p** 96. C Chesterfield St Mary and All SS *Derby* 95-98; P-in-c Newlyn St Newlyn *Truro* 98-03; Dioc Adv for Schs and RE 98-03; P-in-c Tideswell *Derby* from 03; C Wormhill, Peak Forest w Peak Dale and Dove Holes from 03. *The Vicarage, 6 Pursglove Drive, Tideswell, Buxton SK17 8PA* Tel (01298) 871317 E-mail fryates@msn.com

YATES, Miss Joanna Mary. b 49. St Anne's Coll Ox BA71 MA74 K Coll Lon PGCE72. S'wark Ord Course 89. **d** 91 **p** 94. Promotions and Publications Officer Nat Soc 85-95; Chapl Ch Ho Westmr 91-95; C Regent's Park St Mark *Lon* 91-95; C Finchley St Mary 95-01; TV Leeds City *Ripon* from 01. *St Peter's Vicarage, 15 Parkside Green, Leeds LS6 4NY* Tel 0113-278 7449 *or* 245 2036 Fax 243 9737 Mobile 07961-654430 E-mail precentor@leedsparishchurch.com

YATES, Keith Leonard. b 36. K Coll Lon BD AKC61 Nottm Univ MPhil79. Wells Th Coll. **d** 69 **p** 70. C Luton Ch Ch *St Alb* 69-73; Hon C Luton St Andr 73-76; R Grimoldby w Manby *Linc* 76-80; P-in-c Yarburgh 76-78; R 78-80; P-in-c Alvingham w N and S Cockerington 76-78; V 78-80; Lect Sarum & Wells Th Coll 80-87; R Upper Chelsea H Trin *Lon* 87-96; rtd 96; Perm to Offic *Sarum* from 97. *50 Culverhayes, Beaminster DT8 3DG* Tel (01308) 863409

YATES, Lindsay Anne. b 69. Selw Coll Cam BA91 MA95 Barrister 92. Ripon Coll Cuddesdon BTh99. **d** 99 **p** 00. C Bampton w Clanfield *Ox* 99-02; Chapl Pemb Coll Cam 02-06; Chapl Westcott Ho Cam from 07. *The Rectory, 42 Church Lane, Girton, Cambridge CB3 0JP* Tel and fax (01223) 276235 *or* tel 741000 E-mail laa26@cam.ac.uk

YATES, Michael Anthony. b 48. Oak Hill Th Coll. **d** 82 **p** 83. C Hebburn St Jo *Dur* 82-85; C Sheldon *Birm* 85-87; V Lea Hall 87-92; TV Old Brampton and Loundsley Green *Derby* 92-98; V Loundsley Green 98-01; V Riddings and Ironville 01-07; P-in-c Seale and Lullington w Coton in the Elms from 07. *The Rectory, 24 Church Street, Netherseal, Swadlincote DE12 9AF* Tel (01283) 761179 E-mail mikeanbike@tiscali.co.uk

YATES, Michael Peter. b 47. JP91. Leeds Univ BA69 MA70 MPhil85 Potchefstroom Univ PhD03. Coll of Resurr Mirfield 69. **d** 71 **p** 72. C Crewe St Andr *Ches* 71-76; V Wheelock 76-79; Chapl Rainhill Hosp *Liv* 79-89; Chapl Barnsley Distr Gen Hosp 89-94; Chapl Barnsley Distr Gen Hosp NHS Trust from 94; Chapl Barnsley Hosp NHS Foundn Trust from 05. *The Chaplain's Office, Barnsley Hospital, Gawber Road, Barnsley S75 2EP* Tel (01226) 730000 Fax 202859 E-mail m.yates@nhs.net

YATES, Paul David. b 47. Sussex Univ BA73 DPhil80. Sarum & Wells Th Coll 88. **d** 91 **p** 92. NSM Lewes All SS, St Anne, St Mich and St Thos *Chich* 91-00; NSM Lewes St Mich and St Thos at Cliffe w All SS from 00. *17 St Swithun's Terrace, Lewes BN7 1UJ* Tel (01273) 473463

YATES, Peter Francis. b 47. Sheff Univ BA69. Kelham Th Coll 69. **d** 74 **p** 75. C Mexborough *Sheff* 74-78; C Sevenoaks St Jo *Roch* 78-81; CSWG from 81; Lic to Offic *Chich* from 85. *The Monastery, Crawley Down, Crawley RH10 4LH* Tel (01342) 712074

YATES, Raymond Paul. b 55. Oak Hill Th Coll BA88. **d** 88 **p** 89. C Bootle St Mary w St Paul *Liv* 88-91; C Drypool *York* 91-92; TV 92-97; C Orpington All SS *Roch* 97-00; R Beeford w Frodingham and Foston *York* 00-06; RD N Holderness 02-06; Chapl HM Pris Hull 01-02; P-in-c Quinton Road W St Boniface *Birm* from 06. *St Boniface Vicarage, Quinton Road West, Birmingham B32 2QD* Tel 0121-427 8551 *or* 426 3166

YATES, Richard. *See* YATES, Alan John Richard

YATES, Ricky. *See* YATES, Warwick John

YATES, Canon Roger Alan. b 47. Trin Coll Cam BA68 MA72 MB, BChir71 Bris Univ PhD75 MRCP77 FFPM93. NOC 84. **d** 87 **p** 88. NSM Wilmslow *Ches* from 87; Bp's Officer for NSM from 93; Hon Can Ches Cathl from 99; RD Knutsford from 06. *3 Racecourse Park, Wilmslow SK9 5LU* Tel (01625) 520246 E-mail raycandoc@yahoo.co.uk

YATES, Mrs Rosamund. b 63. Rob Coll Cam BA84 MA88. Oak Hill Th Coll BA93. **d** 93. C Holloway St Mary Magd *Lon* 93-95; NSM Tervuren w Liège *Eur* 95-97; NSM W Ealing St Jo w St Jas *Lon* 01-05; Perm to Offic *Eur* 05-08; NSM E Acton St Dunstan w St Thos *Lon* from 08. *14 Rosemount Road, London W3 9LR* Tel (020) 8993 6614 E-mail rosyates@tiscali.co.uk

YATES, Mrs Sian. b 57. Univ of Wales (Ban) Westmr Coll Ox MTh91. Linc Th Coll 78. **d** 80 **p** 94. C Risca *Mon* 80-83; Chapl Ch Hosp Horsham 83-85; TD Haverhill w Withersfield, the Wrattings etc *St E* 85-90; Dioc Youth Chapl *Cant* 90-93; Assoc Min Cant St Martin and St Paul 93-96; Educn Chapl *Worc* 96-03; P-in-c Dudley St Jas 96-03; P-in-c Dudley St Barn 01-03; P-in-c Tregony w St Cuby and Cornelly *Truro* from 03; Dioc Adv in RE from 03. *The Rectory, 18 Fore Street, Tregony, Truro TR2 5RN* Tel (01872) 530507 E-mail yatesasb@aol.com

YATES, Canon Timothy Edward. b 35. Magd Coll Cam BA59 MA62 Uppsala Univ DTh78. Ridley Hall Cam 58. **d** 60 **p** 61. C

Tonbridge SS Pet and Paul *Roch* 60-63; Tutor St Jo Coll Dur 63-71; Warden Cranmer Hall Dur 71-79; P-in-c Darley w S Darley *Derby* 79-82; R Darley 82-90; Dioc Dir of Ords 85-95; Hon Can Derby Cathl 89-00; C Ashford w Sheldon and Longstone 90-00; rtd 00; Perm to Offic *Derby* from 01; Hon Fell St Jo Coll Dur from 04. *Holly House, South Church Street, Bakewell DE45 1FD* Tel (01629) 812686

YATES, Timothy John Sturgis. b 56. Bradf Univ BTech83 Univ Coll Lon PhD86. ERMC 05. **d** 07 **p** 08. NSM Gt Chesham *Ox* from 07. *16 Chapmans Crescent, Chesham HP5 2QU* Tel (01494) 772914 Mobile 07802-155072 E-mail timyates3@btinternet.com

YATES, Warwick John (Ricky). b 52. Univ of Wales (Lamp) BA78. Wycliffe Hall Ox 87. **d** 89 **p** 90. C Hoddesdon *St Alb* 89-93; R Finmere w Mixbury, Cottisford, Hardwick etc *Ox* 93-95; R Shelswell 95-08; P-in-c Prague *Eur* from 08. *Pat'anka 2614/11B, Flat 7, 160 00 Praha 6 - Dejvice, Czech Republic* Tel (00420) (2) 3331 0266 E-mail chaplain@anglican.cz

YATES, William Herbert. b 35. Man Univ BA59. Chich Th Coll 60. **d** 61 **p** 62. C Blackpool St Steph *Blackb* 61-65; C Wednesbury St Jo *Lich* 65-69; V Porthill 69-78; R Norton in the Moors 78-84; R Church Aston 84-00; rtd 00; Perm to Offic *Lich* from 01. *83 Stallington Road, Blythe Bridge, Stoke-on-Trent ST11 9PD* Tel (01782) 397182

YATES, Mrs Yvonne Louise. b 52. NEOC 01. **d** 04 **p** 05. NSM Kirkbymoorside w Gillamoor, Farndale etc *York* 04-07; Chapl Oakhill Secure Tr Cen 07-08; Co-ord Chapl HM Pris Kirklevington Grange from 08. *The Chaplaincy, HM Prison Kirklevington Grange, Yarm TS15 9PA* Tel (01642) 792600 Fax 792601 E-mail ylyates@btinternet.com

YATES-ROUND, Joseph Laurence John. b 25. S'wark Ord Course 75. **d** 76 **p** 77. NSM Tonbridge SS Pet and Paul *Roch* 76-83; Chapl Palma and Balearic Is w Ibiza etc *Eur* 83-90; rtd 90; Perm to Offic *Ches* from 90. *5 Willow Tree Grove, Rode Heath, Stoke-on-Trent ST7 3TE* Tel (01270) 883425

YAU, Timothy Sang. b 71. Ridley Hall Cam 06. **d** 08 **p** 09. C Farcet Hampton *Ely* from 08. *Church House, 40 Hargate Way, Hampton Hargate, Peterborough PE7 8DW* Tel 07974-587841 (mobile) E-mail tim.yau@ely.anglican.org

YEADON, Mrs Penelope Susan. b 60. NEOC 03. **d** 06 **p** 07. NSM Penhill *Ripon* from 06. *Dale Cottage, Aysgarth, Leyburn DL8 3AB* Tel (01969) 663505

YEADON, Ms Victoria Jane. b 69. Univ Coll Lon BSc91 MSc92 Anglia Ruskin Univ BA09. Ridley Hall Cam 07. **d** 09. C Deptford St Nic and St Luke *S'wark* from 09. *41 Creek Road, London SE8 3BU* Tel 07952-292113 (mobile) E-mail jane@deptfordchurch.com

YEARWOOD, Jean Cornilia. b 43. Heythrop Coll Lon MA05 RGN74 RM76. **d** 07 **p** 08. NSM Croydon Woodside *S'wark* from 07. *59 Bradley Road, London SE19 3NT* Tel (020) 8771 7743 E-mail j.yearwood@btopenworld.com

YEATS, Charles. b 56. Natal Univ BCom77 Witwatersrand Univ MBA79 Ball Coll Ox MA85 K Coll Lon MTh90 Dur Univ PhD99. Wycliffe Hall Ox 85. **d** 87 **p** 88. C Islington St Mary *Lon* 87-90; Research Fell Whitefield Inst Ox 90-92; Chapl and Fell Univ Coll Dur 92-00; Perm to Offic *Dur* 00-08. *58 Archery Rise, Durham DH1 4LA* Tel 0191-384 0606

YELDHAM, Anthony Paul Richard. *See* KYRIAKIDES-YELDHAM, Preb Anthony Paul Richard

YELDHAM, Denise. b 51. Leeds Univ BSc72 MB, ChB75 Univ of Wales (Lamp) MA08 MRCPsych80. Westcott Ho Cam 06. **d** 08. C Plymstock and Hooe *Ex* from 08. *19 Long Park Close, Plymouth PL9 9JQ* E-mail denise.yeldham@btinternet.com

YELLAND, Jeffrey Charles. b 46. CEng MIStructE72. STETS 98. **d** 01 **p** 02. NSM Effingham w Lt Bookham *Guildf* 01-04; NSM Dorking St Paul from 04. *32 Fishfield, Epsom KT19 8JG* Tel and fax (01372) 807096 Mobile 07918-030513 E-mail jeff@stpaulsdorking.org.uk

YENDALL, John Edward Thomas. b 52. St Jo Coll Dur BA88. Cranmer Hall Dur 84. **d** 88 **p** 89. C Bangor 88-90; C Botwnnog 90-91; R Trefdraeth w Aberffraw etc 91-01; RD Malltraeth 97-01; V Llanwddyn and Llanfihangel-yng-Nghwynfa etc *St As* 01-07; V Llanrhaeadr ym Mochnant etc from 07. *The Vicarage, Llanrhaeadr ym Mochnant, Oswestry SY10 0JZ* Tel (01691) 780660

✠**YEOMAN, The Rt Revd David.** b 44. St Mich Coll Llan 66. **d** 70 **p** 71 **c** 04. C Cardiff St Jo *Llan* 70-72; C Caerphilly 72-76; V Ystrad Rhondda w Ynyscynon 76-81; V Mountain Ash 81-96; R Coity w Nolton 96-04; Can Llan Cathl 00-09; Asst Bp Llan 04-09; Adn Morgannwg 04-06; rtd 09. *4 Llety Gwyn, Bridgend CF31 1RG* Tel (01656) 649919 Mobile 07971-926631

YEOMAN, Douglas. b 35. ACII63. **d** 77 **p** 78. NSM Edin St Martin 77-96; NSM Edin St Luke 79-90; Chapl Edinburgh Healthcare NHS Trust 95-99; Chapl Lothian Primary Healthcare NHS Trust 98-06; NSM Edin St Cuth 96-06; Lic to Offic from 06. *6 Craiglockhart Crescent, Edinburgh EH14 1EY* Tel 0131-443 5449 E-mail d.yeoman@tiscali.co.uk

YEOMAN, Miss Ruth Jane. b 60. Sheff Univ BSc82 MSc85 Dur Univ PGCE83. Ripon Coll Cuddesdon BA90 MA94. **d** 91 **p** 94.

C Coleshill *Birm* 91-95; C Hodge Hill 95-01; Bp's Adv for Children's Work 95-01; L'Arche Lambeth Community 01-03; Perm to Offic *S'wark* 01-03 and *Birm* 03; V Menston w Woodhead *Bradf* from 03. *The Vicarage, 12 Fairfax Gardens, Menston, Ilkley LS29 6ET* Tel (01943) 877739 *or* 872433 Mobile 07752-912646 E-mail ruthjyeoman@hotmail.com

YEOMANS, Robert John. b 44. AKC66. **d** 67 **p** 68. C Pontesbury I and II *Heref* 67-70; Asst Youth Officer *St Alb* 70-72; Project Officer (Dio St Alb) Gen Syn Bd of Educn 73-77; V Is of Dogs Ch Ch and St Jo w St Luke *Lon* 77-87; V Waterloo St Jo w St Andr *S'wark* 87-93; Chapl United Bris Healthcare NHS Trust 93-02; Chapl Ex Hospiscare 02-06; rtd 06; Perm to Offic *Truro* from 02. *The White Barn, Maxworthy, Launceston PL15 8LY* Tel (01566) 781570 E-mail r.yeomans@virgin.net

YERBURGH, Canon David Savile. b 34. Magd Coll Cam BA57 MA61. Wells Th Coll 57. **d** 59 **p** 60. C Cirencester *Glouc* 59-63; C Bitterne Park *Win* 63-67; V Churchdown St Jo *Glouc* 67-74; RD Glouc N 73-74; V Charlton Kings St Mary 74-85; R Minchinhampton 85-95; Hon Can Glouc Cathl 86-95; rtd 95; Perm to Offic *Sarum* from 95. *2 Mill Race Close, Mill Road, Salisbury SP2 7RX* Tel (01722) 320064

YERBURGH, Peter Charles. b 31. Magd Coll Cam BA53 MA57. Wells Th Coll 53. **d** 55 **p** 56. C Southbroom *Sarum* 55-58; Chapl Wells Cathl Sch 58-71; Chapl Durlston Court Sch 71-91; rtd 91. *2 Mill Race Close, Mill Road, Salisbury SP2 7RX* Tel (01722) 327796

YERBURY, Gregory Howard. b 67. Trin Coll Bris BA93. St Jo Coll Nottm 94. **d** 96 **p** 97. C Crofton *Portsm* 96-00; P-in-c Bolton St Jo *Man* 00-06; P-in-c Bolton Breightmet St Jas 05-06; TR Leverhulme from 06. *St John's Vicarage, 7 Alford Close, Bolton BL2 6NR* Tel (01204) 389044 E-mail greg@stjohns.arbonne.co.uk

YEWDALL, Mrs Mary Doreen. b 23. Nottm Univ DipEd71 BTh85. EMMTC 76. **dss** 79 **d** 87 **p** 94. Kirkby in Ashfield St Thos *S'well* 79-81; Daybrook 81-87; Par Dn 87-89; rtd 89; Hon Par Dn Bilsthorpe *S'well* 89-91; Hon Par Dn Eakring 89-91; Hon Par Dn Winkburn 89-91; Hon Par Dn Maplebeck 89-91; NSM Norton juxta Malton *York* 92-95; NSM Whitwell w Crambe, Flaxton, Foston etc 95-98; Perm to Offic from 98. *Flat 30, Dulverton Hall, Esplanade, Scarborough YO11 2AR* Tel (01723) 340130

YIEND, Paul Martin. b 57. UEA BA80. St Jo Coll Nottm MA96. **d** 92 **p** 94. C Bushbury *Lich* 92-95; Asst Chapl Brussels *Eur* 99-00; P-in-c Charleroi 00-03; P-in-c Liège from 00. *rue Basse des Canes 11, 5300 Andenne, Belgium* Tel and fax (0032) (85) 844482 E-mail paul.yiend@skynet.be

YILDIRIM, Engin. b 67. **d** 07 **p** 08. C Istanbul *Eur* from 07. *Swedish Chapel of Istanbul, Seraskerci Çikmazi, No 9, Beyoglu, Istanbul, Turkey* E-mail beyogluanglican@yahoo.com

YIN, Canon Roy Henry Bowyer. b 10. K Coll Cam BA32 MA36. Cuddesdon Coll 32. **d** 33 **p** 34. C Cambridge St Giles w St Pet *Ely* 33-37; Chapl K Coll Cam 33-37; Chapl Hurstpierpoint Coll 37-46; Chapl St Thos Coll Colombo Ceylon 46-62; Lect Univ of Malaya 64-69; V Katong Singapore 70-75; rtd 75; Lic to Offic from 75; Hon Can Singapore from 80. *528 East Coast Road, #12-01 Ocean Park, Singapore 458969, Republic of Singapore* Tel (0065) 6444 4880

YONGE, James Mohun (Brother Amos). b 47. Keele Univ BA71. WMMTC 91. **d** 94 **p** 95. SSF from 76. *The Friary, Hilfield, Dorchester DT2 7BE* Tel (01300) 341345 Fax 341244

✠**YOON, The Rt Revd Paul Hwan.** b 38. **d** 67 **c** 87. Bp Taejon 87-02; Presiding Bp Korea 00-02; rtd 02. *PO Box 22, Taejon 300-600, Republic of Korea* Tel (0082) (42) 256 9987 Fax 255 8918

YORK, Canon Humphrey Bowmar. b 28. St Chad's Coll Dur BA54 Univ of Wales (Lamp) MA04. **d** 55 **p** 56. C Beamish *Dur* 55-57; C Tettenhall Regis *Lich* 57-62; P-in-c Lansallos w Pelynt *Truro* 62-63; R Lanreath 62-67; V Pelynt 63-67; P-in-c Lanlivery 67-74; P-in-c Luxulyan 67-74; P-in-c Lanlivery w Luxulyan 74-83; RD Bodmin 76-82; R Antony w Sheviock 83-93; Hon Can Truro Cathl 90-93; rtd 93; Perm to Offic *Truro* and *Sarum* from 93. *8 Huntingdon Street, Bradford-on-Avon BA15 1RF* E-mail canonhumphrey@tinyworld.co.uk

YORK, Archbishop of. *See* SENTAMU, The Most Revd and Rt Hon John Tucker Mugabi

YORK, Archdeacon of. *See* SEED, The Ven Richard Murray Crosland

YORK, Dean of. *See* JONES, The Very Revd Keith Brynmor

YORKE, John Andrew. b 47. Cranmer Hall Dur 70. **d** 73 **p** 74. C Spitalfields Ch Ch w All SS *Lon* 73-78; R Tuktoyaktuk Canada 78-88; R Fort Mcpherson 89-92; V Totland Bay *Portsm* from 92; V Thorley from 95. *The Vicarage, Alum Bay New Road, Totland Bay PO39 0ES* Tel (01983) 752031 E-mail andy.yorke@lineone.net

YORKE, The Very Revd Michael Leslie. b 39. Magd Coll Cam BA62 MA66. Cuddesdon Coll 62. **d** 64 **p** 65. C Croydon St Jo *Cant* 64-68; Succ Chelmsf Cathl 68-69; Prec and Chapl 69-73; Dep Dir Cathl Cen for Research and Tr 72-74; P-in-c Ashdon w Hadstock 74-76; R 76-78; Can Res Chelmsf Cathl 78-88; Vice-

Provost 84-88; P-in-c N Lynn w St Marg and St Nic *Nor* 88-92; P-in-c King's Lynn St Marg w St Nic 92-94; Chmn Dioc Adv Bd for Min 90-94; Hon Can Nor Cathl 93-94; Provost Portsm 94-99; Dean Lich 99-04; rtd 04; Perm to Offic *Nor* from 04. *Westgate House, The Green, Burnham Market, King's Lynn PE31 8HD* Tel (01328) 738833

YORKSTONE, Peter. b 48. Lough Univ BTech72. Oak Hill Th Coll 79. **d** 81 **p** 82. C Blackpool St Thos *Blackb* 81-85; V Copp 85-00; P-in-c Giggleswick and Rathmell w Wigglesworth *Bradf* 00-07; V Kettlewell w Conistone, Hubberholme etc from 07. *The Vicarage, Westgate, Kettlewell, Skipton BD23 5QU* Tel (01756) 760237 E-mail peter.yorkstone@bradford.anglican.org

YOUATT, Jennifer Alison. *See* MONTGOMERY, Mrs Jennifer Alison

YOUDE, Paul Crosland. b 47. Birm Univ LLB86. WEMTC 93. **d** 96 **p** 97. NSM Cheltenham St Luke and St Jo *Glouc* 96-99; C Cirencester 99-03; P-in-c Lydney from 03. *5 Raglan Gardens, Lydney GL15 5GZ* Tel and fax (01594) 842321 E-mail paul@pyoude.freeserve.co.uk

YOUELL, Mrs Deborah Mary. b 57. STETS 01. **d** 04. NSM Cowplain *Portsm* 04-08; NSM Crookhorn from 08. *42 The Yews, Horndean, Waterlooville PO8 0BH* Tel (023) 9279 9946 E-mail deborah.youell@ntlworld.com

YOUENS, Edward. *See* MONTAGUE-YOUENS, Canon Hubert Edward

YOUINGS, Adrian. b 65. Ex Univ BSc86 Bath Univ PhD90. Wycliffe Hall Ox 93. **d** 96 **p** 97. C Dorking St Paul *Guildf* 96-99; C S Croydon Em *S'wark* 99-03; R Trull w Angersleigh *B & W* from 03. *The Rectory, Wild Oak Lane, Trull, Taunton TA3 7JT* Tel (01823) 253518

YOULD, Guy Martin. b 37. Keble Coll Ox BA61 MA65 Magd Coll Ox BD68 Hull Univ PhD80 Lambeth STh75 FSAScot75. St Steph Ho Ox 61. **d** 63 **p** 64. C Middlesbrough St Jo the Ev *York* 63-65; Chapl Magd Coll and C Cowley St Jo *Ox* 65-68; Asst Chapl Radley Coll 68-71; C W Kirby St Bridget *Ches* 71-74; Chapl Loretto Sch Musselburgh 74; V Liscard St Mary w St Columba *Ches* 74-78; St Barn Coll Belair Australia 78-80; C Doncaster St Leon and St Jude *Sheff* 80-81; V Brodsworth w Hooton Pagnell, Frickley etc 81-87; Chapl St Mary's Sch Wantage 87-93; R Chapel Chorlton, Maer and Whitmore *Lich* 93-98; P-in-c Altarnon w Bolventor, Laneast and St Clether *Truro* 98-02; P-in-c Lezant 98-02; rtd 03; C Gt and Lt Torrington and Frithelstock *Ex* 03-05; P-in-c Bishopstone *Chich* from 05. *The Vicarage, Bishopstone, Seaford BN25 2UD* Tel (01323) 892972

YOUNG, Andrew Charles. b 54. FIBMS83. NOC 98. **d** 01 **p** 02. C Heywood *Man* 01-05; TV Eccles from 05. *St Paul's Vicarage, Egerton Road, Eccles, Manchester M30 9LR* Tel 0161-789 2420 E-mail andrew.young66@ntlworld.com

YOUNG, Andrew John. b 50. St Jo Coll Dur BA73. Westcott Ho Cam 73. **d** 75 **p** 89. C Nailsworth *Glouc* 75-76; NSM Yeovil w Kingston Pitney *B & W* 89-93; NSM Tintinhull w Chilthorne Domer, Yeovil Marsh etc from 93. *15 Cook Avenue, Chard TA20 2JR* Tel (01460) 62182

YOUNG, Miss Anne Patricia. b 44. Cov Coll of Educn CertEd66 Leeds Univ BEd76 Sheff Univ MEd82 Liv Univ BTh05. NOC 01. **d** 05 **p** 06. NSM Middlestown *Wakef* from 05. *58 The Crofts, Emley, Huddersfield HD8 9RU* Tel and fax (01924) 840738 Mobile 07906-835309 E-mail anne@ayoung94.fsbusiness.co.uk

YOUNG, Arthur. b 65. Belf Bible Coll BTh92. CITC 99. **d** 01 **p** 02. C Donaghadee *D & D* 01-04; I Tullylish from 04. *Tullylish Rectory, 100 Banbridge Road, Gilford, Craigavon BT63 6DL* Tel and fax (028) 3883 1298

YOUNG, Canon Brian Thomas. b 42. Linc Th Coll 67. **d** 70 **p** 71. C Monkseaton St Mary *Newc* 70-73; C Berwick H Trin 73-77; P-in-c Gt Broughton *Carl* 77-80; V Gt Broughton and Broughton Moor 80-83; V Chorley *Ches* 83-90; V Alderley Edge 90-07; RD Knutsford 96-06; Hon Can Ches Cathl 97-07; rtd 07. *6 St Denys Avenue, Sleaford NG34 8AR* Tel (01529) 306332 E-mail byoung@alderley.fsworld.co.uk

YOUNG, Canon Charles John. b 24. Open Univ BA98. Qu Coll Birm 52. **d** 55 **p** 56. C Dudley St Thos *Worc* 55-58; C Beeston *S'well* 58-61; V Lady Bay 61-66; R Kirkby in Ashfield 66-75; V Balderton 75-92; RD Newark 82-90; Hon Can S'well Minster 84-92; rtd 92; Bp's Chapl for Rtd Clergy *S'well* 92-04; Perm to Offic from 04. *9 The Paddocks, Newark NG24 1SS* Tel (01636) 613445

YOUNG, Christopher Terence. b 53. Cape Town Univ BA76 UNISA BTh80. St Bede's Coll Umtata 79. **d** 80 **p** 81. S Africa 80-86 and from 88; C Rainham *Chelmsf* 86-88. *Riversong Cottage, 11 Church Street, Villiersdorp, 6848 South Africa* Tel and fax (0027) (28) 840 0841 Mobile 82-377 8401

YOUNG, The Rt Revd Clive. b 48. St Jo Coll Dur BA70. Ridley Hall Cam 70. **d** 72 **p** 73 **c** 99. C Neasden cum Kingsbury St Cath *Lon* 72-75; C Hammersmith St Paul 75-79; P-in-c Old Ford St Paul w St Steph 79-82; V Old Ford St Paul w St Steph and St Mark 82-92; AD Tower Hamlets 88-92; Adn Hackney 92-99; V St Andr Holborn 92-99; Suff Bp Dunwich *St E* from 99.

28 Westerfield Road, Ipswich IP4 2UJ Tel (01473) 222276 Fax 210303 E-mail bishop.clive@stedmundsbury.anglican.org

YOUNG, Daniel George Harding. b 52. New Coll Ox BA73 MA83. Cranmer Hall Dur 77. **d** 80 **p** 81. C Bushbury *Lich* 80-83; Chapl Dean Close Sch Cheltenham 83-99; Perm to Offic *Win* from 01. *6 Tyfield, Sherborne St John, Basingstoke RG24 9HZ* Tel (01256) 850397 E-mail dan-young@tiscali.co.uk

YOUNG, David. b 37. STh79 Open Univ PhD89. Ely Th Coll 61 Linc Th Coll 64. **d** 67 **p** 68. C Crofton *Wakef* 67-68; C Heckmondwike 68-71; V Stainland 71-76; R Patrington w Winestead *York* 76-80; Chapl Winestead Hosp 76-80; Gen Preacher *Linc* from 80; Chapl St Jo Hosp Linc 80-90; Chapl N Lincs Mental Health Unit 90-93; Chapl Linc Distr Healthcare NHS Trust 93-97; Dep Chapl 98-04; rtd 04. *Westview, Aisthorpe, Lincoln LN1 2SG* Tel (01522) 730912

YOUNG, David Charles. b 54. Open Univ BA95 PGCE97 CQSW82. SEITE 03. **d** 06 **p** 07. NSM Haywards Heath St Wilfrid *Chich* from 06. *4 Ashurst Place, Heath Road, Haywards Heath RH16 3EJ* Tel (01444) 416074 Mobile 07921-144480 E-mail youngshouse1@yahoo.co.uk

YOUNG, David John. b 43. Nottm Univ BA64 MPhil89 Lambeth STh87. Coll of Resurr Mirfield 64. **d** 66 **p** 67. C Warsop *S'well* 66-68; C Harworth 68-71; P-in-c Hackenthorpe Ch *Derby* 71-73; TV Thecville and Hackenthorpe 73-75; V Chaddesden St Phil 75-83; R Narborough and Huncote *Leic* 83-89; RD Guthlaxton I 87-90; Chapl Leic Univ 90-95; V Eyres Monsell 95-98; Perm to Offic 98-99; rtd 03. *57 Castle Fields, Leicester LE4 1AN* Tel 0116-236 5634

YOUNG, Derek John. b 42. St D Coll Lamp. **d** 73 **p** 74. C Griffithstown *Mon* 73-76; C Ebbw Vale 76-77; V Penmaen 77-81; V Penmaen and Crumlin 81-87; Chapl Oakdale Hosp Gwent 83-87; V New Tredegar *Mon* 87-99; V Llanfihangel Crucorney w Oldcastle etc from 99. *The Vicarage, Llanfihangel Crucorney, Abergavenny NP7 8DH* Tel (01873) 890349

YOUNG, George William. b 31. Lon Coll of Div ALCD55. **d** 56 **p** 57. C Everton Em *Liv* 56-58; C Halliwell St Pet *Man* 58-61; V Newburn *Newc* 61-67; P-in-c Tyler's Green *Ox* 67-69; V 69-80; Lic to Offic 80-84; Area Sec (W England) SAMS 80-84; Hon C Purley Ch Ch *S'wark* 84-87; V Beckenham St Jo *Roch* 87-92; rtd 92; Perm to Offic *S'wark* from 92. *9 Shortacres, High Street, Nutfield, Redhill RH1 4HJ* Tel (01737) 822363

YOUNG, Mrs Hilary Antoinette Francesca. b 57. **d** 01 **p** 02. NSM Thorne *Sheff* 01-03; C 03-05; V Wigan St Jas w St Thos *Liv* from 05. *97 Melrose Drive, Wigan WN3 6EG* Tel (01942) 225311 E-mail hyoung.youngvic@virgin.net

YOUNG, Hyacinth Loretta. b 49. NTMTC 95. **d** 98 **p** 99. NSM Harlesden All So *Lon* 98-00; TV Wembley Park from 00. *194 Windermere Avenue, Wembley HA9 8QT* Tel (020) 8908 2252 E-mail hyacinth512@aol.com

YOUNG, Iain Clavering. b 56. Newc Poly BA79. Coll of Resurr Mirfield 80. **d** 83 **p** 84. C Wallsend St Luke *Newc* 83-86; C Horton 86-87; V 87-92; V Friern Barnet St Pet le Poer *Lon* 92-95; C Holborn St Alb w Saffron Hill St Pet 96-97; P-in-c Hoxton H Trin w St Mary 97-02; V 02-09; Chapl Moorfields Eye Hosp NHS Trust 97-03; P-in-c Lavender Hill Ascension etc *S'wark* from 09. *The Clergy House, Pountney Road, London SW11 5TU* Tel (020) 7228 5340 E-mail iain.young@ifightpoverty.com

YOUNG, Jeremy Michael. b 54. Ch Coll Cam BA76 MA80 Lon Univ MTh94. Coll of Resurr Mirfield 78. **d** 80 **p** 81. C Whitworth w Spennymoor *Dur* 80-83; C Boxmoor St Jo *St Alb* 83-86; V Croxley Green St Oswald 86-94; Dir Past Studies CITC 94-99; Lic to Offic *D & G* 99-03; Perm to Offic *B & W* from 06. *Westerley House, Tellisford, Bath BA2 7RL* Tel (01373) 830920 E-mail jeremy_young@mac.com

YOUNG, John. *See* YOUNG, David John

YOUNG, Canon John David. b 37. Lon Univ BD65 Sussex Univ MA77. Clifton Th Coll 62. **d** 65 **p** 66. C Plymouth St Jude *Ex* 65-68; Hd of RE Northgate Sch Ipswich 68-71; Chapl and Sen Lect Bp Otter Coll Chich 71-81; Chapl and Sen Lect W Sussex Inst of HE 77-81; Chapl and Sen Lect York St Jo Coll 81-87; C York St Paul 87-88; Dioc Ev 88-02; Can and Preb York Minster 92-03; Miss Strategy Development Officer 00-02; rtd 02; Lic to Offic *York* from 02. *72 Middlethorpe Grove, York YO24 1JY* Tel (01904) 704195 E-mail john.young@yorkcourses.co.uk

YOUNG, John Kenneth. Edin Th Coll 62. **d** 64 **p** 65. C Gosforth All SS *Newc* 64-67; C Newc St Gabr 67-69; R Bowers Gifford *Chelmsf* 69-72; R Bowers Gifford w N Benfleet 72-75; P-in-c Kirkwhelpington *Newc* 75-79; P-in-c Kirkharle 77-79; P-in-c Kirkheaton 75-79; P-in-c Cambo 77-79; V Kirkwhelpington, Kirkharle, Kirkheaton and Cambo 79-82; V Gosforth St Nic 82-92; V Healey and Slaley 92-97; rtd 97; Perm to Offic *Newc* from 97. *20 Mitford Way, Dinnington, Newcastle upon Tyne NE13 7LW* Tel (01661) 821050

YOUNG, John Robert. b 43. SSM 63. **d** 68 **p** 69. C Ch Ch Cathl Darwin Australia 68-70; C Murrumbeena 70-72; C Stocking Farm *Leic* 72-74; P-in-c W Reservoir Australia 75-78; I Montmorency 78-85; I E Burwood 85-96; R Warracknabeal 96-00; R Port Fairy 00-05; R Yea from 05. *St Luke's Rectory,*

Pellisier Street, PO Box 60, Yea Vic 3717, Australia Tel (0061) (3) 5797 2281 Fax 5797 2082

YOUNG, Canon Jonathan Frederick. b 25. Univ of Wales (Lamp) BA51 Birm Univ MA81. St Mich Coll Llan 51. **d** 53 **p** 54. C Roath St Martin *Llan* 53-59; Lic to Offic *Ox* 59-74; SSJE 62-71; Bp's Chapl for Community Relns *Birm* 71-74; Chapl Coun for Soc Resp 74-85; Hon Can Birm Cathl 84-85; USA from 85; rtd 90. *1573 Cambridge Street, Apt 606, Cambridge MA 02138-4377, USA* Tel (001) (617) 945 1072 E-mail youngmj@aol.com

YOUNG, Canon Jonathan Priestland. b 44. AKC68. **d** 69 **p** 70. C Clapham H Trin *S'wark* 69-73; C Mitcham St Mark 73-74; V Godmanchester *Ely* 74-82; P-in-c Cambridge St Giles w St Pet 82; P-in-c Chesterton St Luke 82; TR Cambridge Ascension 82-01; Chapl St Jo Coll Sch Cam 88-93; P-in-c Ellington *Ely* 01-02; P-in-c Grafham 01-02; P-in-c Easton 01-02; P-in-c Spaldwick w Barham and Woolley 01-02; R E Leightonstone from 02; P-in-c Alconbury cum Weston from 04; P-in-c Buckworth from 04; Hon Can Ely Cathl from 07; RD Leightonstone 02-04. *The Rectory, Parson's Drive, Ellington, Huntingdon PE28 0AU* Tel and fax (01480) 891695

YOUNG, Karen Heather. *See* ROSS, Mrs Karen Heather

YOUNG, Kathleen Margaret. *See* BROWN, Mrs Kathleen Margaret

YOUNG, Kenneth. *See* YOUNG, John Kenneth

YOUNG, Leonard Thomas. b 55. Ches Coll of HE BTh04 Leeds Univ MA06. Coll of Resurr Mirfield 04. **d** 06 **p** 07. C Failsworth H Family *Man* 06-09; P-in-c Man Clayton St Cross w St Paul from 09. *St Cross Rectory, 54 Clayton Hall Road, Manchester M11 4WH* Tel 0161-223 0766
E-mail frleonardyoung@aol.com

YOUNG, Mark Gilbert Campbell. b 60. Mert Coll Ox BA88. Wycliffe Hall Ox 86. **d** 91 **p** 92. C Holborn St Geo w H Trin and St Bart *Lon* 91-95; C St Pancras w St Jas and Ch Ch 95-99; V W Hampstead Trin 99-06; P-in-c W Hampstead St Cuth 01-06. *Address temp unknown*

YOUNG, Martin Edward. b 20. Oriel Coll Ox BA41 MA45. Cuddesdon Coll 41. **d** 43 **p** 44. C Newbury *Ox* 43-45; C Wymondham *Nor* 45-49; C Gt Berkhamsted *St Alb* 49-51; V Littlemore *Ox* 51-64; R Wootton w Quinton *Pet* 64-72; R Wootton w Quinton and Preston Deanery 72-78; V Welford w Sibbertoft 78-82; V Welford w Sibbertoft and Marston Trussell 82-88; rtd 88; Perm to Offic *Pet* 88-98. *2 Knutsford Lane, Long Buckby, Northampton NN6 7RL* Tel (01327) 843929

YOUNG, Martin John. b 72. Univ Coll Lon BSc93. Oak Hill Th Coll BA01. **d** 01 **p** 02. C Heigham H Trin *Nor* 01-05; P-in-c Nor St Andr from 05. *24 Carnoustie, Norwich NR4 6AY* Tel (01603) 498821 E-mail martin@standrewsnorwich.org
or mjy@ntlworld.com

YOUNG, Mrs Maureen. b 47. SEITE 02. **d** 04. NSM Roughey *Chich* from 04. *29 Badgers Close, Horsham RH12 5RU* Tel (01403) 263119 E-mail deaconmaureen@googlemail.com

YOUNG, Maurice. *See* YOUNG, William Maurice

YOUNG, Max. b 44. **d** 06 **p** 07. NSM Filey *York* from 06. *15 Belle Vue Crescent, Filey YO14 9AD* Tel (01723) 513761

YOUNG, Norman Keith. b 35. EAMTC 85. **d** 87 **p** 88. C Burwell *Ely* 87-91; V Swaffham Bulbeck and Swaffham Prior w Reach 91-92; V Barnby Dun *Sheff* 92-05; Ind Chapl 92-05; AD Doncaster 98-04; rtd 05; P-in-c Aspull St Eliz *Liv* 05-06; P-in-c Haigh and Aspull from 06. *97 Melrose Drive, Wigan WN3 6EG* Tel (01942) 225311 E-mail norman@youngvic.u-net.com

YOUNG, Peter John. b 26. Pemb Coll Cam BA49 MA54. Ridley Hall Cam 49. **d** 51 **p** 52. C Cheadle *Ches* 51-54; Malaya 54-63; Malaysia from 63; rtd 92. *247 Jalan 5/48, 46000 Petaling Jaya, Selangor, Malaysia* Tel (0060) (3) 7782 9269 Fax 7783 0849

YOUNG, Philip Anderson. b 53. St Jo Coll Dur BA75 Fitzw Coll Cam BA78 MA89. Ridley Hall Cam 75. **d** 78 **p** 79. C Surbiton St Andr and St Mark *S'wark* 78-80; NSM Aylsham *Nor* 04-05; C Bressingham w N and S Lopham and Fersfield 05-07; C Roydon St Remigius 05-07; V Heigham St Thos from 07. *St Thomas's Vicarage, 77 Edinburgh Road, Norwich NR2 3RL* Tel (01603) 624390 Mobile 07890-588295
E-mail philipyoung@btinternet.com

YOUNG, Rachel Elizabeth. b 61. Man Univ MusB82 Leeds Univ MA09 Lon Inst of Educn PGCE84. NOC 06. **d** 09. NSM Beverley Minster *York* from 09. *Monument House, 4 King Street, Woodmansey, Beverley HU17 0TE* Tel (01482) 861883
E-mail rachel.e.young@tesco.net

YOUNG, Richard Christian. b 65. Southn Univ LLB87 Solicitor 91. St Jo Coll Nottm 02. **d** 04 **p** 05. C Alperton *Lon* 04-07; V Yiewsley from 07. *St Matthew's Vicarage, 93 High Street, Yiewsley, West Drayton UB7 7QH* Tel (01895) 442093 Mobile 07940-810390 E-mail richard@theyoungones.org.uk

YOUNG, Richard Michael. b 63. **d** 96 **p** 97. NSM Brunswick *Man* from 96. *2 Birch Grove, Rusholme, Manchester M14 5JY* Tel 0161-225 0884 Mobile 07778-817784
E-mail richard_young3@igroup.com

YOUNG, Stephen. b 33. St Edm Hall Ox MA61. St Jo Coll Nottm 75 ALCD77. **d** 77 **p** 78. C Crofton *Portsm* 77-81; C Rainham *Chelmsf* 81-87; V Ramsgate Ch Ch *Cant* 87-98; rtd 98; Perm to

Offic *Cant* from 98. *9 Egerton Drive, Cliftonville, Margate CT9 9YE* Tel (01843) 223071

YOUNG, Stephen Edward. b 52. K Coll Lon BD73 AKC73 Ch Ch Coll Cant CertEd74 Open Univ PhD04. **d** 75 **p** 76. C Walton St Mary *Liv* 75-79; C St Marylebone All SS *Lon* 83; C Pimlico St Gabr 83-85; Chapl Whitelands Coll of HE *S'wark* 85-88; Asst Chapl St Paul's Sch Barnes 88-91; Chapl 91-02; P in O from 91; Hon C Pimlico St Mary Bourne Street *Lon* from 94; Chapl Dulwich Coll from 02. *Dulwich College, Dulwich Common, London SE21 7LD* Tel (020) 8693 3601
E-mail presby@btopenworld.com

YOUNG, Steven Peter. b 81. Lon Inst BA02 Leeds Univ BA07 MA08. Coll of Resurr Mirfield 05. **d** 08 **p** 09. C W Hendon St Jo *Lon* from 08. *22 Mount Road, London NW4 3PU* Tel 07590-636912 (mobile) E-mail steven_young81@hotmail.com

YOUNG, Stuart Kincaid. b 59. **d** 95 **p** 96. C Letchworth St Paul w Willian *St Alb* 95-00; V Pucklechurch and Abson *Bris* from 00. *The Vicarage, Westerleigh Road, Pucklechurch, Bristol BS16 9RD* Tel 0117-937 2260
E-mail vicar@pucklechurchandabson.org.uk

YOUNG, William Maurice. b 32. St Jo Coll Nottm 80. **d** 81 **p** 82. C Harlescott *Lich* 81-84; V Hadley 84-94; rtd 94; Perm to Offic *Heref* from 94. *Old Chapel School, Newport Street, Clun, Craven Arms SY7 8JZ* Tel (01588) 640846

YOUNGER, Jeremy Andrew. b 46. Nottm Univ BA68 Bris Univ MA71. Wells Th Coll 68. **d** 70 **p** 71. C Basingstoke *Win* 70-74; C Harpenden St Nic *St Alb* 74-76; Dir Communications 77-81; Chapl Sarum & Wells Th Coll 77-81; V Clifton All SS w St Jo *Bris* 81-84; Relig Affairs Producer BBC Radio Nottm *S'well* 84-86; C Bow w Bromley St Leon *Lon* 86-88; Projects and Min Manager Westmr St Jas 89-93; Hon C St Marylebone All SS 89-93; New Zealand from 93. *1/102 Valley Road, Mount Eden, Auckland 1024, New Zealand* Tel (0064) (9) 630 7867
E-mail jeremyyounger@clear.net.nz

YOUNGS, Denise. WMMTC. **d** 09. NSM Lich St Mich w St Mary and Wall from 09. *10 Tame Avenue, Burntwood WS7 9JQ* Tel (01543) 672646

YOUNGS-DUNNETT, Elizabeth Nigella. b 43. **d** 05 **p** 06. OLM Alde River *St E* from 05. *The Cottage, Ship Corner, Blaxhall, Woodbridge IP12 2DY* Tel (01728) 688248

YOUNGSON, David Thoms. b 38. Cuddesdon Coll 71. **d** 73 **p** 74. C Norton St Mary *Dur* 73-76; C Hartlepool St Paul 76-79; P-in-c Stockton St Jo CD 79-84; V Stockton St Jo 84-86; V Owton Manor 86-90; rtd 90; Perm to Offic *Dur* 90-99. *35 Buxton Gardens, Billingham TS22 5AJ*

YULE, John David. b 49. G&C Coll Cam BA70 MA74 PhD76. Westcott Ho Cam 79. **d** 81 **p** 82. C Cherry Hinton St Andr *Ely* 81-84; C Almondbury w Farnley Tyas *Wakef* 84-87; V Swavesey *Ely* 87-95; V Fen Drayton w Conington 87-95; R Fen Drayton w Conington and Lolworth etc from 95. *The Vicarage, Honey Hill, Fen Drayton, Cambridge CB24 4SF* Tel (01954) 231903 Fax 202816 E-mail vicar@honeyhill.org

YULE, Robert White. b 49. FCMA81. St Jo Coll Nottm. **d** 88 **p** 89. C Wilford *S'well* 88-91; TV Bestwood 91-96; P-in-c Selston 96-98; V Watford St Pet St Alb from 00. *68 Tudor Avenue, Watford WD24 7NX* Tel (01923) 223510, 337002 *or* 337000 E-mail bob.yule@soulsurvivor.com

Z

ZAIDI-CROSSE, Philip Kenneth. b 63. **d** 05 **p** 06. NSM Erdington *Birm* from 05. *34 Watt Road, Birmingham B23 6ET* Tel 0121-624 4752

ZAIR, Richard George. b 52. Newc Univ BSc74. Trin Coll Bris 75 St Jo Coll Dur 79. **d** 80 **p** 81. C Bishopsworth *Bris* 80-83; C New Malden and Coombe *S'wark* 83-91; Dir of Evang CPAS 91-99; Regional Dir 99-09; P-in-c Marcham w Garford *Ox* from 09. *1 All Saints Close, Marcham, Abingdon OX13 6PE* Tel (01865) 391319 E-mail r_zair@yahoo.co.uk

ZAMMIT, Mark Timothy Paul. b 60. Ox Brookes Univ MA07. Aston Tr Scheme 90 Sarum & Wells Th Coll 94. **d** 94 **p** 95. C Bitterne Park *Win* 94-98; TV Shaston *Sarum* 98-03; TR 03-08; RD Blackmore Vale 01-08; Chapl Port Regis Prep Sch 99-08; P-in-c Durrington *Sarum* from 08; C Avon Valley from 08. *The Rectory, Church Street, Durrington, Salisbury SP4 8AL* Tel and fax (01980) 653953 E-mail zammitparish@yahoo.co.uk

ZANDSTRA-HOUGH, Wendy Lorraine. *See* HOUGH, Wendy Lorraine

ZANKER, Mrs Diana. b 39. Leeds Univ BA01 Edge Hill Coll of HE TCert59. NOC 04. **d** 05 **p** 06. NSM Leeds St Aid *Ripon* from

05. *10 Mount Gardens, Leeds LS17 7QN* Tel 0113-267 5893 E-mail diana@zanker.org

ZAPHIRIOU, Paul Victor. b 49. Hamilton Coll (NY) BA73 INSEAD MBA74. Wycliffe Hall Ox 00. **d** 02 **p** 03. C Holborn St Geo w H Trin and St Bart *Lon* 02-06; V Holloway St Mary Magd from 06; Bp's Adv for Corporate Soc Resp from 05. *108 Liverpool Road, London N1 0RE* Tel (020) 7226 0854 Mobile 07899-796409 E-mail paul.zaphiriou@n7parish.net

ZAREK, Jennifer Hilary. b 51. Newnham Coll Cam BA72 MA76 Southn Univ MSc73 PhD78 Ox Univ BTh98 Garnett Coll Lon CertEd83. St Steph Ho Ox 95. **d** 97 **p** 98. C Caterham *S'wark* 97-00; V Hutton Cranswick w Skerne, Watton and Beswick *York* 00-05; rtd 05. *Horsedale House, Silver Street, Huggate, York YO42 1YB* Tel (01377) 288525

ZASS-OGILVIE, Ian David. b 38. MRICS72 FRICS80. AKC65 St Boniface Warminster 65. **d** 66 **p** 67. C Washington *Dur* 66-70; Bp's Soc and Ind Adv for N Dur 70-73; Hon C Newc St Jo 73-75; V Tynemouth St Jo 75-78; Hon C St Marylebone St Mary *Lon* 78-81; V Bromley St Jo *Roch* 81-84; R Keith, Huntly and Aberchirder *Mor* 84-88; R Edin St Pet 88-00; Dir Churches' Regional Commn in the NE *Newc* and *Dur* 00-05; rtd 05. *12 St Giles Close, Gilesgate, Durham DH1 1XH* Tel 0191-383 0887 E-mail ianzassogilvie@tiscali.co.uk

ZEAL, Stanley Allan. b 33. Leeds Univ BA55. Coll of Resurr Mirfield. **d** 57 **p** 58. C Perry Hill St Geo *S'wark* 57-61; C Cobham *Guildf* 61-64; R Ash and V Ash Vale 64-69; V Aldershot St Mich 69-98; Chapl Northfield Hosp Aldershot 69-98; rtd 98. *4 Spencers Row, Cardiff CF5 2EP* Tel (029) 2056 0778

ZIETSMAN, Sheila. **d** 90 **p** 91. C Geashill w Killeigh and Ballycommon *M & K* 90-91; C Mullingar, Portnashangan, Moyliscar, Kilbixy etc 91-96; Chapl Wilson's Hosp Sch Multyfarnham 91-96; Chapl E Glendalough Sch from 96. *East Glendalough School, Station Road, Wicklow, Republic of Ireland* Tel (00353) (404) 69608 Fax 68180

ZIHNI, Andrew Stephen. b 77. Mert Coll Ox BA99 MA06. St Steph Ho Ox BA01. **d** 02 **p** 03. C Goldthorpe w Hickleton *Sheff*

02-06; Min Can Windsor from 06; Chapl St Geo Sch Windsor from 06. *24 The Cloisters, Windsor Castle, Windsor SL4 1NJ* Tel (01753) 848781 *or* 848710 Fax 620165 E-mail frazihni4277@aol.com

ZIPFEL, Marilyn Ellen. b 48. Open Univ BA94 MA98 Goldsmiths' Coll Lon TCert70 LTCL97. Dioc OLM tr scheme 01. **d** 03 **p** 04. OLM Oulton Broad *Nor* from 03. *Rozel, Station Road, Lowestoft NR32 4QF* Tel (01502) 583825 Mobile 07818-093133 E-mail marilynzipfel@talktalk.net

ZORAB, Mark Elston. b 53. FRICS77. Mon Dioc Tr Scheme 92. **d** 94. NSM St Arvans w Penterry, Itton, Devauden etc *Mon* from 94. *Oak Cottage, Itton Road, Chepstow NP16 6BQ* Tel (01291) 626222 *or* 672138 E-mail fr.mark@elstons.co.uk

ZOTOV, Mrs Carolyn Ann. b 47. Lady Mabel Coll CertEd68 Open Univ BA78. EMMTC 91. **d** 92 **p** 94. NSM Hykeham *Linc* 92-94; NSM Aisthorpe w Scampton w Thorpe le Fallows etc 94; C Ingham w Cammeringham w Fillingham 94-97; C Linc Minster Gp 97-01; rtd 01; Assoc P Nettleham *Linc* from 01. *Greenleaves, 1 The Drive, Church Lane, Lincoln LN2 1QR* Tel (01522) 525435 E-mail caz@greenleaves.fsnet.co.uk

ZUCCA, Peter Rennie. b 43. **d** 96 **p** 97. NSM Spotland *Man* 96-99; NSM Bamford 99-05; NSM Rochdale St Geo w St Alb 99-05; NSM Oakenrod and Bamford from 05. *19 Judith Street, Rochdale OL12 7HS* Tel (01706) 675830 *or* 346003

ZVIMBA, Josephat. b 60. SEITE. **d** 04 **p** 05. C W Norwood St Luke *S'wark* 04-07; V Dalston St Mark w St Bart *Lon* from 07. *St Mark's Vicarage, Sandringham Road, London E8 2LL* E-mail janjosh@tiscali.co.uk

ZWALF, Canon Willem Anthony Louis (Wim). b 46. AKC68. **d** 71 **p** 72. C Fulham St Etheldreda w St Clem *Lon* 71-74; Chapl City Univ 74-78; R Coalbrookdale, Iron-Bridge and Lt Wenlock *Heref* 78-90; V Wisbech SS Pet and Paul *Ely* 90-08; P-in-c Wisbech St Aug 03-04; C 04-08; RD Wisbech Lynn Marshland 02-08; Hon Can Ely Cathl 07-08; rtd 09. *1 The Dell, Oakham LE15 6JG* Tel (01572) 770082 E-mail wimzwalf@aol.com

DEACONESSES

BENNETT, Miss Doreen. b 29. St Mich Ho Ox 60. **dss** 79. Moreton *Ches* 79-80; Dewsbury Moor *Wakef* 80-86; Germany 86-91; rtd 89; Perm to Offic *Blackb* from 95. *27 Stuart Court, High Street, Kibworth, Leicester LE8 0LR* Tel 0116-279 3812

BRIERLY, Margaret Ann. b 32. Dalton Ho Bris 54. **dss** 85. Wreningham *Nor* 85-86; Tetsworth, Adwell w S Weston, Lewknor etc *Ox* 86-95; rtd 95; Perm to Offic *Blackb* from 03. *13 Pinewood Avenue, Brookhouse, Lancaster LA2 9NU*

BUTLER, Miss Ann. b 41. St Mich Ho Ox 67 Dalton Ho Bris IDC69. **dss** 82. Bucknall and Bagnall *Lich* 82-87; Leyton St Mary w St Edw and St Luke *Chelmsf* 89-02; rtd 02. *40 Lichfield Street, Stone ST15 8NB* Tel (01785) 818160

BYATT, Margaret Nelly. b 18. Bedf Coll Lon BA40. Gilmore Ho 59. **dss** 62. Chelsea St Luke *Lon* 60-63; St Helier *S'wark* 63-66; Lee Gd Shep w St Pet 66-78; rtd 78. *41 Woodlands, Overton, Basingstoke RG25 3HW* Tel (01256) 770347

CARTER, Miss Crystal Dawn. b 49. SRN77 RSCN77. Trin Coll Bris 79. **dss** 82. Hengrove *Bris* 82-86; Dagenham *Chelmsf* 86-88; Perm to Offic from 88; rtd 08. *41 Rusholme Avenue, Dagenham RM10 7ND* Tel (020) 8596 0451 Mobile 07762-849403

COOPER, Janet Pamela. b 46. Glos Coll of Educn TCert67 Ox Poly CETD79. Trin Coll Bris. **dss** 83. Patchway *Bris* 83-88; Perm to Offic *Glouc* 90-96. *Ephraim Cottage, Kington Mead Farm, Kington Road, Thornbury, Bristol BS35 1PQ* Tel (01454) 415280 E-mail jan.ephraimcottage@uhu.co.uk

DEE, Mary. b 21. St Chris Coll Blackheath 55. **dss** 64. Shottermill *Guildf* 63-66; Bishop's Waltham *Portsm* 66-72; Cumnor *Ox* 75-81; rtd 81. *Flat 4, 45 Oxford Avenue, Bournemouth BH6 5HT* Tel (01202) 424240

DOROTHY, Sister. *See* WARR, Sister Dorothy Lilian Patricia

ESSAM, Catherine. b 46. Southn Univ BA67 CertEd68. Linc Th Coll. **dss** 80. Pershore w Pinvin, Wick and Birlingham *Worc* 78-82; CMS Nigeria from 83. *Bishopscourt, PO Box 6283, Jos, Plateau State, Nigeria* Tel (00234) (806) 876 9443 E-mail susanessam@aol.com

EVANS (née CHERRETT), Mrs Diana. b 59. Somerville Coll Ox BA81 MA85 Warwick Univ CertEd96. St Steph Ho Ox 81. **dss** 84. Sherborne w Castleton and Lillington *Sarum* 84-88; Northampton St Paul *Pet* 93-98; Sec Dioc Adv Cttee 94-08; Hd Places of Worship Policy English Heritage from 08; Lic to Offic *Pet* from 98. *The Rectory, London Road, Uppingham, Oakham LE15 9TJ* Tel (01572) 822010 E-mail diana.evans@peterborough-diocese.org.uk

FINDER, Miss Patricia Constance. b 30. Dalton Ho Bris 63. **dss** 79. Clapham St Jas *S'wark* 79-90; rtd 90. *5 Castle Gate, Ilkley LS29 8DF* Tel (01943) 607023

GOUGH, Janet Ainley. b 46. SRN67 RSCN68 SCM70. Dalton Ho Bris 70. **dss** 76. Leic H Apostles 73-80; Kansas City All SS USA 80-81; Perm to Offic *Leic* 81-96 and from 05. *410 Hinckley Road, Leicester LE3 0WA* Tel 0116-285 4284 E-mail jangough@hotmail.co.uk

GRIERSON, Miss Janet. b 13. Westf Coll Lon BA34. Lambeth STh37 MA82 Greyladies Coll 34 K Coll Lon 34. **dss** 48. Vice-Prin Gilmore Ho 48-55; Prin 55-60; Lect Div St Mary's Coll Ban 62-63; Prin Lect RE Summerfield Coll Kidderminster 63-75; rtd 75; Perm to Offic *Worc* from 75. *Davenham, 148 Graham Road, Malvern WR14 2HY* Tel (01684) 569341

HAMILTON, Miss Pamela Moorhead. b 43. SRN64 SCM66. Trin Coll Bris 75. **dss** 77. Derby St Pet and Ch w H Trin 77-84; Bedworth *Cov* from 85; rtd 03. *10 William Street, Bedworth, Nuneaton CV12 9DS* Tel (024) 7649 1608

HARRISON, Mrs Ann. b 55. Ex Univ BSc77. Linc Th Coll 79. **dss** 82. Acomb H Redeemer *York* 82-83; Lic to Offic *Wakef* 83-91. *The Vicarage, Church Hill, Easingwold, York YO61 3JT* Tel (01347) 821394

HEWITT, Miss Joyce Evelyn. b 30. SRN51 SCM55. St Mich Ho Ox IDC61. **dss** 67. Spitalfields Ch w All SS *Lon* 67-70; CMJ 71-73; Canonbury St Steph *Lon* 73-75; Chorleywood RNIB Coll for Blind Girls 75-80; rtd 90. *38 Ashridge Court, Station Road, Newbury RG14 7LL* Tel (01635) 47829

HIDER, Ms Margaret Joyce Barbara. b 25. St Mich Ho Ox 52. **dss** 77. Bris H Cross Inns Court 77-84; Uphill *B & W* 84-89; rtd 89; Perm to Offic *B & W* 89-05. *15 Stuart Court, High Street, Kibworth, Leicester LE8 0LR* Tel 0116-279 6885

HINDE, Miss Mavis Mary. b 29. Lightfoot Ho Dur. **dss** 65. Hitchin St Mary *St Alb* 65-68; Ensbury *Sarum* 68-70; Portsea St Alb *Portsm* 70-76; Houghton Regis *St Alb* 77-85; Eaton Socon 85-94; rtd 94; Perm to Offic *Ely* from 94. *8 Burnt Close, Eynesbury, St Neots PE19 2LZ* Tel (01480) 218219

HORNBY-NORTHCOTE, Mrs Vivien Sheena. b 42. Birkbeck Coll Lon BA91 Warwick Univ MA96. Gilmore Course 74. **dss** 79. Mitcham St Olave *S'wark* 79-81; St Dunstan in the West *Lon* 82-86; St Marg Lothbury and St Steph Coleman Street etc 86; rtd 98. *3 Priory Mews, Sidney Street, Cheltenham GL52 6DJ* Tel (01242) 525659

HOWARD, Jean Elizabeth. b 37. Man Univ BA59 Univ of Wales (Cardiff) TDip61 Lon Univ BD86. St Mich Ho Ox 61. **dss** 82. Hanger Lane St Ann *Lon* 82-84; Dagenham *Chelmsf* 88-90; Perm to Offic from 90; rtd 97. *99 Kitchener Road, London E17 4LJ* Tel (020) 8527 0472

MacCORMACK, Mrs June Elizabeth. b 45. Ab Dioc Tr Course 82 St Jo Coll Nottm 85. **dss** 86. Bieldside *Ab* from 86. *5 Overton Park, Dyce, Aberdeen AB21 7FT* Tel (01224) 722691 E-mail june@maccormack.co.uk

MOORHOUSE, Olga Marian. b 28. Dalton Ho Bris 54. **dss** 63. Wolverhampton St Matt *Lich* 62-68; Fazakerley Em *Liv* 68-70; Huyton St Geo 70-76; Blurton *Lich* 76-88; rtd 88. *37 Rosalind Grove, Wolverhampton WV11 3RZ* Tel (01902) 630128

MORGAN, Beryl. b 19. Dalton Ho Bris 47. **dss** 77. Princess Marg Hosp Swindon 69-79; rtd 79. *Ty Clyd, 120 Beacons Park, Brecon LD3 9BP* Tel (01874) 622398

OBEE, Sister Monica May. b 37. **dss** 82. Radford *Cov* 82-97; rtd 97. *14 The Hill, Walsingham NR22 6DF* Tel (01328) 821033

OLIVER, Miss Kathleen Joyce. b 44. Man Univ BA65. NOC 80. **dss** 83. Littleborough *Man* from 83. *Littleborough Christian Centre, 43 Todmorden Road, Littleborough OL15 9EA* Tel (01706) 376477 Fax 375520

OLPHIN, Miss Maureen Rose. b 30. Lon Univ BSc Sheff Univ DipEd. **dss** 84. Sheff St Barn and St Mary 84-90; rtd 90. *41A Queen Street, Mosborough, Sheffield S20 5BP* Tel 0114-247 3009

PIERSON, Mrs Valerie Susan (Sue). b 44. TCert65. Trin Coll Bris 76. **dss** 79. Fulham St Matt *Lon* from 79. *48 Peterborough Road, London SW6 3EB* Tel (020) 7731 6544 Fax 7731 1858 E-mail sue@lancepierson.org

RAINEY, Miss Irene May. b 14. RSCN36 SCM38. Gilmore Ho 69. **dss** 72. Filton *Bris* 70-74; Crowthorne *Ox* 74-79; rtd 79; Perm to Offic *Ely* 80-03. *12 Stevens Close, Cottenham, Cambridge CB24 8TT* Tel (01954) 251634

SAMPSON, Miss Hazel. b 35. Lightfoot Ho Dur 58. **dss** 64. Fenton *Lich* 64-67; Gt Wyrley 67-69; Chapl Asst Manor Hosp Walsall 69-76; Lich St Mary w St Mich 76-95; rtd 95; Perm to Offic *Lich* 95-03. *107 Walsall Road, Lichfield WS13 8DD* Tel (01543) 419664

SCHMIEGELOW, Patricia Kate Lunn. b 37. St Mich Ho Ox IDC65. **dss** 86. The Hague *Eur* 86-89; Perm to Offic *Glouc* from 90; Gen Sec ICS 92-97; rtd 97. *Waterside, Coln St Aldwyns, Cirencester GL7 5AJ* Tel (01285) 750218 Fax as telephone

SELWOOD, Miss Eveline Mary. b 34. Gilmore Ho 76. Huddersfield St Jo *Wakef* 76-79; King Cross 79-85; rtd 94; Perm to Offic *Wakef* from 94. *27 Alverthorpe Road, Wakefield WF2 9NW* Tel (01924) 378364

SPROSON, Doreen. b 31. St Mich Ho Ox IDC58. **dss** 70. Wandsworth St Mich *S'wark* 68-71; Women's Sec CMS 71-74; Goole *Sheff* 74-76; Kirby Muxloe *Leic* 76-77; Perm to Offic *S'wark* 85-97; rtd 91. *20 Huggens' College, College Road, Northfleet, Gravesend DA11 9LL* Tel (01474) 325262

STOKES, Audrey Margaret. b 39. Dalton Ho Bris 68. **dss** 82. Collier Row St Jas *Chelmsf* 82-85; Woking St Mary *Guildf* 85-95; rtd 95. *1 Greet Park Close, Southwell NG25 0EE*

SYMES, Miss Annabel. b 41. AIMLS68. S Dios Minl Tr Scheme 79. **dss** 85. Chapl Asst Salisbury Health Care NHS Trust from 85; Barford St Martin, Dinton, Baverstock etc *Sarum* 89-01; Nadder Valley from 01. *7 Shaftesbury Road, Barford St Martin, Salisbury SP3 4BL* Tel (01722) 744110

TAYLOR, Muriel. b 28. CA Tr Coll 48. **dss** 76. Gateshead Fell *Dur* 76-86; Gateshead Harlow Green 86-88; rtd 88. *18 Beechwood Avenue, Gateshead NE9 6PP* Tel 0191-487 6902

THUMWOOD, Janet Elizabeth. b 30. STh60. Trin Coll Toronto 58. **dss** 62. Canada 62-63; Mile End Old Town H Trin *Lon* 63-65; CSF 66-77; rtd 90. *24 Ramsay Hall, 11-13 Byron Road, Worthing BN11 3HN* Tel (01903) 203586

WARR, Sister Dorothy Lilian Patricia. b 14. Selly Oak Coll 38. **dss** 53. St Etheldreda's Children's Home Bedf 51-59; CSA from 53; Goldington *St Alb* 54-59; S'wark St Sav w All Hallows 59-65; St Mich Convalescent Home Westgate-on-Sea 65-74; rtd 75. *St Mary's Convent and Nursing Home, Burlington Lane, London W4 2QE*

WEBB, Sybil Janet. b 20. SRN42 SCM43. Gilmore Course 69. **dss** 77. Worthing St Geo *Chich* 77-80; rtd 80; Perm to Offic *Chich* from 80. *42 Ham Road, Worthing BN11 2QX* Tel (01903) 202997

WRIGHT, Edith Mary. b 22. St Hugh's Coll Ox MA46 DipEd46. Gilmore Ho STh58. **dss** 61. St Marylebone St Mary *Lon* 58-71; Lect Linc Th Coll 71-73; Oatlands *Guildf* 73-76; Roehampton H Trin *S'wark* 76-82; rtd 82. *26 Hazelwood Close, Harrow HA2 6HD* Tel 0181-863 7320

WRIGHT, Gloria Mary. b 40. **dss** 83. Smethwick St Matt w St Chad *Birm* 83-84; Tottenham H Trin *Lon* 84-86; rtd 00. *76 Barnards Hill, Marlow SL7 2NZ*

DIOCESAN, AREA, SUFFRAGAN AND ASSISTANT BISHOPS AND PROVINCIAL EPISCOPAL VISITORS IN ENGLAND, WALES, SCOTLAND AND IRELAND

BATH AND WELLS
Bishop of Bath and Wells — P B PRICE
Honorary Assistant Bishops — P E BARBER
W M D PERSSON
B ROGERSON
R F SAINSBURY
R H M THIRD
Suffragan Bishop of Taunton — P D MAURICE

BIRMINGHAM
Bishop of Birmingham — D A URQUHART
Honorary Assistant Bishops — A P HALL
A C DUMPER
M W SINCLAIR
M H D WHINNEY
I K MOTTAHEDEH
Suffragan Bishop of Aston — A J WATSON

BLACKBURN
Bishop of Blackburn — N S READE
Honorary Assistant Bishops — M E VICKERS
LORD HOPE OF THORNES
A L WINSTANLEY
Suffragan Bishop of Burnley — J W GODDARD
Suffragan Bishop of Lancaster — G S PEARSON

BRADFORD
Bishop of Bradford — D C JAMES
Honorary Assistant Bishops — C O BUCHANAN
LORD HOPE OF THORNES
M W JARRETT

BRISTOL
Bishop of Bristol — M A HILL
Honorary Assistant Bishops — J R G NEALE
P ST G VAUGHAN
Suffragan Bishop of Swindon — L S RAYFIELD

CANTERBURY
Archbishop of Canterbury, Primate of All England and Metropolitan — R D WILLIAMS
Honorary Assistant Bishops — G A CRAY
M F GEAR
J R A LLEWELLIN
Suffragan Bishop of Dover — S S VENNER
Suffragan Bishop of Maidstone — *Vacant*
Suffragan Bishop of Ebbsfleet (Provincial Episcopal Visitor) — A BURNHAM
Suffragan Bishop of Richborough (Provincial Episcopal Visitor) — K NEWTON

CARLISLE
Bishop of Carlisle — J W S NEWCOME
Honorary Assistant Bishops — A A K GRAHAM
I M GRIGGS
G L HACKER
R M HARDY
J H RICHARDSON
J R SATTERTHWAITE
G H THOMPSON
Suffragan Bishop of Penrith — *Vacant*

CHELMSFORD
Bishop of Chelmsford — *Vacant*
Honorary Assistant Bishops — J M BALL
C D BOND
Area Bishop of Barking — D J L HAWKINS
Area Bishop of Bradwell — L A GREEN
Area Bishop of Colchester — C H MORGAN

CHESTER
Bishop of Chester — P R FORSTER
Honorary Assistant Bishops — C F BAZLEY
A D CHESTERS
G G DOW
J D HAYDEN
W A PWAISIHO
Suffragan Bishop of Birkenhead — G K SINCLAIR
Suffragan Bishop of Stockport — R R ATWELL

CHICHESTER
Bishop of Chichester — J W HIND
Honorary Assistant Bishops — M E ADIE
K L BARHAM
R D FARRER
R A JUPP
C C LUXMOORE
M R J MANKTELOW
M E MARSHALL
L G URWIN
D P WILCOX

Area Bishop of Horsham — M C R SOWERBY
Area Bishop of Lewes — W P BENN

COVENTRY
Bishop of Coventry — C J COCKSWORTH
Honorary Assistant Bishop — D R J EVANS
Suffragan Bishop of Warwick — J R A STROYAN

DERBY
Bishop of Derby — A L J REDFERN
Honorary Assistant Bishops — R M C BEAK
J NICHOLLS
Suffragan Bishop of Repton — H I J SOUTHERN

DURHAM
Bishop of Durham — N T WRIGHT
Honorary Assistant Bishops — S W SYKES
M W JARRETT
Suffragan Bishop of Jarrow — M W BRYANT

ELY
Bishop of Ely — A J RUSSELL
Honorary Assistant Bishops — S BARRINGTON-WARD
P S DAWES
J B TAYLOR
Suffragan Bishop of Huntingdon — D THOMSON

EXETER
Bishop of Exeter — M L LANGRISH
Honorary Assistant Bishops — I C DOCKER
R S HAWKINS
J P MASON
R D SILK
M R WESTALL
Suffragan Bishop of Crediton — R J S EVENS
Suffragan Bishop of Plymouth — J F FORD

GLOUCESTER
Bishop of Gloucester — M F PERHAM
Honorary Assistant Bishops — P J FIRTH
P B HARRIS
M A MANN
J R G NEALE
P ST G VAUGHAN
E ST Q WALL
Suffragan Bishop of Tewkesbury — J S WENT

GUILDFORD
Bishop of Guildford — C J HILL
Honorary Assistant Bishop — M A BAUGHEN
C J BENNETTS
C W HERBERT
Suffragan Bishop of Dorking — I J BRACKLEY

HEREFORD
Bishop of Hereford — A M PRIDDIS
Suffragan Bishop of Ludlow — A J MAGOWAN

LEICESTER
Bishop of Leicester — T J STEVENS
Assistant Bishop — C J BOYLE
Honorary Assistant Bishop — C J F SCOTT

LICHFIELD
Bishop of Lichfield — J M GLEDHILL
Honorary Assistant Bishops — D E BENTLEY
R O BOWLBY
I K MOTTAHEDEH
Area Bishop of Shrewsbury — M J RYLANDS
Area Bishop of Stafford — A G MURSELL
Area Bishop of Wolverhampton — C M GREGORY

LINCOLN
Bishop of Lincoln — J C SAXBEE
Honorary Assistant Bishops — J E BROWN
D G SNELGROVE
D TUSTIN
Suffragan Bishop of Grantham — T W ELLIS
Suffragan Bishop of Grimsby — D D J ROSSDALE

LIVERPOOL
Bishop of Liverpool — J S JONES
Honorary Assistant Bishops — M W JARRETT
I C STUART
Suffragan Bishop of Warrington — D W M JENNINGS

LONDON

Bishop of London	R J C CHARTRES
Honorary Assistant Bishops	D S ARDEN
	E HOLLAND
Area Bishop of Edmonton	P W WHEATLEY
Suffragan Bishop of Fulham	J C BROADHURST
Area Bishop of Kensington	P G WILLIAMS
Area Bishop of Stepney	S J OLIVER
Area Bishop of Willesden	P A BROADBENT

MANCHESTER

Bishop of Manchester	N S MCCULLOCH
Honorary Assistant Bishops	R W N HOARE
	M W JARRETT
Suffragan Bishop of Hulme	*Vacant*
Suffragan Bishop of Middleton	M DAVIES
Suffragan Bishop of Bolton	C P EDMONDSON

NEWCASTLE

Bishop of Newcastle	J M WHARTON
Assistant Bishops	P RICHARDSON
	K E GILL
	J H RICHARDSON

NORWICH

Bishop of Norwich	G R JAMES
Honorary Assistant Bishops	E N DEVENPORT
	A C FOOTTIT
	P J FOX
	R GARRARD
	D K GILLETT
	D LEAKE
	M J MENIN
	L G URWIN
Suffragan Bishop of Lynn	J H LANGSTAFF
Suffragan Bishop of Thetford	A P WINTON

OXFORD

Bishop of Oxford	J L PRITCHARD
Honorary Assistant Bishops	K A ARNOLD
	J F E BONE
	A K CRAGG
	W J D DOWN
	J H GARTON
	A R M GORDON
	J N JOHNSON
	P J NOTT
	F H A RICHMOND
	H W SCRIVEN
	S E VERNEY
Area Bishop of Buckingham	A T L WILSON
Area Bishop of Dorchester	C W FLETCHER
Area Bishop of Reading	S G COTTRELL

PETERBOROUGH

Bishop of Peterborough	*Vacant*
Suffragan Bishop of Brixworth	F WHITE

PORTSMOUTH

Bishop of Portsmouth	*Vacant*
Honorary Assistant Bishops	M E ADIE
	G W E C ASHBY
	P S M SELBY

RIPON AND LEEDS

Bishop of Ripon and Leeds	J R PACKER
Honorary Assistant Bishops	C O BUCHANAN
	G C HANDFORD
	D E JENKINS
	M W JARRETT
Suffragan Bishop of Knaresborough	J H BELL

ROCHESTER

Bishop of Rochester	*Vacant*
Honorary Assistant Bishops	M F GEAR
	D HAMID
Suffragan Bishop of Tonbridge	B C CASTLE

ST ALBANS

Bishop of St Albans	A G C SMITH
Honorary Assistant Bishops	D J FARMBROUGH
	R J N SMITH
Suffragan Bishop of Bedford	R N INWOOD
Suffragan Bishop of Hertford	C R J FOSTER

ST EDMUNDSBURY AND IPSWICH

Bishop of St Edmundsbury and Ipswich	W N STOCK
Honorary Assistant Bishops	K NEWTON
	G H REID
	J WAINE
	G D J WALSH
Suffragan Bishop of Dunwich	C YOUNG

SALISBURY

Bishop of Salisbury	D S STANCLIFFE
Honorary Assistant Bishops	J K CAVELL
	J D G KIRKHAM
Area Bishop of Ramsbury	S D CONWAY
Area Bishop of Sherborne	G R KINGS

SHEFFIELD

Bishop of Sheffield	S J L CROFT
Honorary Assistant Bishops	D M HALLATT
	K H PILLAR
	D C HAWTIN
	M W JARRETT
Suffragan Bishop of Doncaster	C G ASHTON

SODOR AND MAN

Bishop of Sodor and Man	R M E PATERSON

SOUTHWARK

Bishop of Southwark	T F BUTLER
Honorary Assistant Bishops	LORD HARRIES OF PENTREGARTH
	M D DOE
Area Bishop of Kingston-upon-Thames	R I CHEETHAM
Area Bishop of Woolwich	C T J CHESSUN
Area Bishop of Croydon	N BAINES

SOUTHWELL AND NOTTINGHAM

Bishop of Southwell and Nottingham	P R BUTLER
Honorary Assistant Bishops	J T FINNEY
	R J MILNER
	R K WILLIAMSON
	M W JARRETT
Suffragan Bishop of Sherwood	A PORTER

TRURO

Bishop of Truro	T M THORNTON
Suffragan Bishop of St Germans	R SCREECH

WAKEFIELD

Bishop of Wakefield	S G PLATTEN
Honorary Assistant Bishop	M W JARRETT
Suffragan Bishop of Pontefract	A W ROBINSON

WINCHESTER

Bishop of Winchester	M C SCOTT-JOYNT
Honorary Assistant Bishops	J A BAKER
	E R BARNES
	S H BURROWS
	J DENNIS
	C C W JAMES
	L L REES
Suffragan Bishop of Basingstoke	T WILLMOTT
Suffragan Bishop of Southampton	P R BUTLER

WORCESTER

Bishop of Worcester	J G INGE
Honorary Assistant Bishops	C J MAYFIELD
	J RUHUMULIZA
Suffragan Bishop of Dudley	D S WALKER

YORK

Archbishop of York, Primate of England and Metropolitan	J T M SENTAMU
Honorary Assistant Bishops	C C BARKER
	R G G FOLEY
	D G GALLIFORD
	M HENSHALL
	D R LUNN
	D J SMITH
Suffragan Bishop of Hull	R M C FRITH
Suffragan Bishop of Selby	M W WALLACE
Suffragan Bishop of Whitby	*Vacant*
Suffragan Bishop of Beverley (Provincial Episcopal Visitor)	M W JARRETT

GIBRALTAR IN EUROPE

Bishop of Gibraltar in Europe	D G ROWELL
Suffragan Bishop in Europe	D HAMID
Honorary Assistant Bishops	A D CHESTERS
	R GARRARD
	E HOLLAND
	LORD HOPE OF THORNES
	C LÓPEZ-LOZANO
	M R J MANKTELOW
	D J SMITH
	F L SOARES
	J B TAYLOR
	J G VOBBE
	A W M WEEKES
	P W WHALON

CHURCH IN WALES

ST ASAPH
Bishop of St Asaph   G K CAMERON

BANGOR
Bishop of Bangor   A T G JOHN

ST DAVIDS
Bishop of St Davids   J W EVANS

LLANDAFF
Bishop of Llandaff   B C MORGAN
Assistant Bishop   D J WILBOURNE

MONMOUTH
Bishop of Monmouth   E W M WALKER

SWANSEA AND BRECON
Bishop of Swansea and Brecon   J D E DAVIES
Honorary Assistant Bishop   J K OLIVER

SCOTTISH EPISCOPAL CHURCH

ABERDEEN AND ORKNEY
Bishop of Aberdeen and Orkney   R A GILLIES

ARGYLL AND THE ISLES
Bishop of Argyll and the Isles   A M SHAW

BRECHIN
Bishop of Brechin   J A C MANTLE

EDINBURGH
Bishop of Edinburgh   B A SMITH

GLASGOW AND GALLOWAY
Bishop of Glasgow and Galloway   *Vacant*
Honorary Assistant Bishops   J M TAYLOR

MORAY, ROSS AND CAITHNESS
Bishop of Moray, Ross and Caithness   M J STRANGE

ST ANDREWS, DUNKELD AND DUNBLANE
Bishop of St Andrews, Dunkeld and   D R CHILLINGWORTH
Dunblane

CHURCH OF IRELAND

ARMAGH
Archbishop of Armagh and Primate   A E T HARPER
of All Ireland and Metropolitan

CASHEL AND OSSORY
Bishop of Cashel and Ossory   M A J BURROWS

CLOGHER
Bishop of Clogher   M G ST A JACKSON

CONNOR
Bishop of Connor   A F ABERNETHY

CORK, CLOYNE AND ROSS
Bishop of Cork, Cloyne and Ross   W P COLTON

DERRY AND RAPHOE
Bishop of Derry and Raphoe   K R GOOD

DOWN AND DROMORE
Bishop of Down and Dromore   H C MILLER

DUBLIN AND GLENDALOUGH
Archbishop of Dublin, Bishop of   J R W NEILL
Glendalough, Primate of Ireland
and Metropolitan

KILMORE, ELPHIN AND ARDAGH
Bishop of Kilmore, Elphin and Ardagh   K H CLARKE

LIMERICK AND KILLALOE
Bishop of Limerick and Killaloe   T R WILLIAMS

MEATH AND KILDARE
Bishop of Meath and Kildare   R L CLARKE

TUAM, KILLALA AND ACHONRY
Bishop of Tuam, Killala and Achonry   R C A HENDERSON

BISHOPS IN THE HOUSE OF LORDS

The Archbishops of Canterbury and York, and the Bishops of London, Durham and Winchester always have seats in the House of Lords. Twenty-one of the remaining Diocesan Bishops also sit in the Upper House, and they do so according to their dates of seniority. When a vacancy arises, it is filled by the senior Diocesan Bishop without a seat, and the vacated See is placed at the foot of the list of those awaiting seats. Translation of a Bishop from one See to another does not affect his right to sit in the House of Lords.

The Bishop of Sodor and Man and the Bishop of Gibraltar in Europe are not eligible to sit in the House of Lords, but the former has a seat in the Upper House of the Tynwald, Isle of Man.

ARCHBISHOPS

	Enthroned	Entered House of Lords
CANTERBURY	2003	2003
YORK	2005	2006

BISHOPS SITTING IN THE HOUSE OF LORDS
(as at 1 December 2009)

	Became Diocesan Bishop	Entered House of Lords
LONDON	1995	1996
DURHAM	2003	2003
WINCHESTER	1995	1996
SOUTHWARK	1991	1997
MANCHESTER	1992	1997
SALISBURY	1993	1998
CHESTER	1996	2001
NEWCASTLE	1997	2003
LIVERPOOL	1998	2003
LEICESTER	1999	2003
NORWICH	1999	2004
EXETER	2000	2005
RIPON AND LEEDS	2000	2006
ELY	2000	2007
CHICHESTER	2001	2008
LINCOLN	2001	2008
BATH AND WELLS	2002	2008
BRADFORD	2002	2009
WAKEFIELD	2003	2009
BRISTOL	2003	2009
LICHFIELD	2003	*Awaiting introduction*
BLACKBURN	2004	*Awaiting introduction*
HEREFORD	2004	*Awaiting introduction*
GLOUCESTER	2004	*Awaiting introduction*

BISHOPS AWAITING SEATS IN THE HOUSE OF LORDS
(in order of seniority)

	Became Diocesan Bishop
GUILDFORD	2004
DERBY	2005
BIRMINGHAM	2006
OXFORD	2007
ST EDMUNDSBURY AND IPSWICH	2007
WORCESTER	2007
COVENTRY	2008
TRURO	2008
SHEFFIELD	2009
ST ALBANS	2009
CARLISLE	2009
SOUTHWELL AND NOTTINGHAM	2009
PETERBOROUGH	*vacant*
CHELMSFORD	*vacant*
ROCHESTER	*vacant*
PORTSMOUTH	*vacant*

HISTORICAL SUCCESSION OF ARCHBISHOPS AND BISHOPS

In a number of dioceses, especially for the mediaeval period, the dating of some episcopal appointments is not known for certain. For ease of reference, the date of consecration is given when known, or, in the case of more modern appointments, the date of confirmation of election. More information on the dates of individual bishops can be found in the Royal Historical Society's *Handbook of British Chronology*.

ENGLAND

PROVINCE OF CANTERBURY

Canterbury		London

	1229 Richard le Grant	
	1234 Edmund Rich	
	1245 Boniface of Savoy	
	1273 Robert Kilwardby	
	1279 John Pecham	
	1294 Robert Winchelsey	
	1313 Walter Reynolds	
	1328 Simon Mepham	
	1333 John Stratford	
	1349 Thomas Bradwardine	
	1349 Simon Islip	
	1366 Simon Langham	

Description of arms. Azure, an archiepiscopal cross in pale or surmounted by a pall proper charged with four crosses patée fitchée sable.

	1368 William Whittlesey	*Description of arms.* Gules, two swords
	1375 Simon Sudbury	in saltire argent hilts and pommels or.
	1381 William Courtenay	
	1396 Thomas Arundel[1]	
	1398 Roger Walden	Theanus

597	Augustine	1414 Henry Chichele	Eluanus
604	Laurentius	1443 John Stafford	Cadar
619	Mellitus	1452 John Kempe	Obinus
624	Justus	1454 Thomas Bourgchier	Conanus
627	Honorius	1486 John Morton	Palladius
655	Deusdedit	1501 Henry Deane	Stephanus
668	Theodorus	1503 William Warham	Iltutus
693	Berhtwald	1533 Thomas Cranmer	Theodwinus
731	Tatwine	1556 Reginald Pole	Theodredus
735	Nothelm	1559 Matthew Parker	Hilarius
740	Cuthbert	1576 Edmund Grindal	314 Restitutus
761	Bregowine	1583 John Whitgift	Guitelinus
765	Jaenberht	1604 Richard Bancroft	Fastidius
793	Æthelheard	1611 George Abbot	Vodinus
805	Wulfred	1633 William Laud	Theonus
832	Feologild	1660 William Juxon	c.604 Mellitus
833	Ceolnoth	1663 Gilbert Sheldon	664 Cedd[2]
870	Æthelred	1678 William Sancroft	666 Wini
890	Plegmund	1691 John Tillotson	675 Eorcenwald
914	Æthelhelm	1695 Thomas Tenison	693 Waldhere
923	Wulfhelm	1716 William Wake	716 Ingwald
942	Oda	1737 John Potter	745 Ecgwulf
959	Ælfsige	1747 Thomas Herring	772 Wigheah
959	Byrhthelm	1757 Matthew Hutton	782 Eadbeorht
960	Dunstan	1758 Thomas Secker	789 Eadgar
c.988	Athelgar	1768 Frederick Cornwallis	793 Coenwalh
990	Sigeric Serio	1783 John Moore	796 Eadbald
995	Ælfric	1805 Charles Manners Sutton	798 Heathoberht
1005	Ælfheah	1828 William Howley	803 Osmund
1013	Lyfing [Ælfstan]	1848 John Bird Sumner	c.811 Æthelnoth
1020	Æthelnoth	1862 Charles Thomas Longley	824 Ceolberht
1038	Eadsige	1868 Archibald Campbell Tait	862 Deorwulf
1051	Robert of Jumièges	1883 Edward White Benson	898 Swithwulf
1052	Stigand	1896 Frederick Temple	898 Heahstan
1070	Lanfranc	1903 Randall Thomas Davidson	900 Wulfsige
1093	Anselm	1928 Cosmo Gordon Lang	c.926 Æthelweard
1114	Ralph d'Escures	1942 William Temple	926 Leofstan
1123	William de Corbeil	1945 Geoffrey Francis Fisher	926 Theodred
1139	Theobald of Bec	1961 Arthur Michael Ramsey	— Wulfstan I
1162	Thomas Becket	1974 Frederick Donald Coggan	953 Brihthelm
1174	Richard [of Dover]	1980 Robert Alexander Kennedy	959 Dunstan
1184	Baldwin	Runcie	964 Ælfstan
1193	Hubert Walter	1991 George Leonard Carey	996 Wulfstan II
1207	Stephen Langton	2002 Rowan Douglas Williams	1004 Ælfhun
			1014 Ælfwig

[1] On 19 October 1399 Boniface IX annulled Arundel's translation to St Andrew and confirmed him in the See of Canterbury.
[2] See vacant for a term of years.

1035 Ælfweard
1044 Robert of Jumièges
1051 William
1075 Hugh of Orival
1086 Maurice
1108 Richard de Belmeis
1128 Gilbert [the Universal]
1141 Robert de Sigillo
1152 Richard de Belmeis II
1163 Gilbert Foliot
1189 Richard Fitz Neal
1199 William of Ste-Mere-Eglise
1221 Eustace de Fauconberg
1229 Roger Niger
1244 Fulk Basset
1260 Henry Wingham
1263 Henry of Sandwich
1274 John Chishull
1280 Richard Gravesend
1306 Ralph Baldock
1313 Gilbert Segrave
1317 Richard Newport
1319 Stephen Gravesend
1338 Richard Bintworth
1340 Ralph Stratford
1355 Michael Northburgh
1362 Simon Sudbury
1375 William Courtenay
1382 Robert Braybrooke
1404 Roger Walden
1406 Nicholas Bubwith
1407 Richard Clifford
1421 John Kempe
1426 William Gray
1431 Robert Fitz-Hugh
1436 Robert Gilbert
1450 Thomas Kempe
1489 Richard Hill
1496 Thomas Savage
1502 William Warham
1504 William Barons [Barnes]
1506 Richard Fitz-James
1522 Cuthbert Tunstall [Tonstall]
1530 John Stokesley
1540 Edmund Bonner
1550 Nicholas Ridley
1553 Edmund Bonner (restored)
1559 Edmund Grindal
1570 Edwin Sandys
1577 John Aylmer
1595 Richard Fletcher
1597 Richard Bancroft
1604 Richard Vaughan
1607 Thomas Ravis
1610 George Abbot
1611 John King
1621 George Monteigne
     [Mountain]
1628 William Laud
1633 William Juxon
1660 Gilbert Sheldon
1663 Humfrey Henchman
1676 Henry Compton
1714 John Robinson
1723 Edmund Gibson
1748 Thomas Sherlock
1761 Thomas Hayter
1762 Richard Osbaldeston
1764 Richard Terrick
1778 Robert Lowth
1787 Beilby Porteus
1809 John Randolph
1813 William Howley
1828 Charles James Blomfield
1856 Archibald Campbell Tait

1869 John Jackson
1885 Frederick Temple
1897 Mandell Creighton
1901 Arthur Foley Winnington-
     Ingram
1939 Geoffrey Francis Fisher
1945 John William Charles Wand
1956 Henry Colville Montgomery
     Campbell
1961 Robert Wright Stopford
1973 Gerald Alexander Ellison
1981 Graham Douglas Leonard
1991 David Michael Hope
1995 Richard John Carew Chartres

†Westminster

1540 Thomas Thirlby

Winchester

Description of arms. Gules, two keys
endorsed and conjoined at the bows in
bend, the upper or, the lower argent,
between which a sword in bend sinister
of the third, hilt and pommel gold.

BISHOPS OF THE WEST SAXONS
  634 Birinus
  650 Ægilberht

BISHOPS OF WINCHESTER
  660 Wine
  670 Leutherius
  676 Haedde
  705 Daniel
  744 Hunfrith
  756 Cyneheard
  778 Æthelheard
  778 Ecbald
  785 Dudd
c 785 Cyneberht
  803 Eahlmund
  814 Wigthegn
  825 Herefrith[2]
  838 Eadmund
*c.*838 Eadhun
  839 Helmstan
  852 Swithhun
  867 Ealhferth
  877 Tunberht
  879 Denewulf
  909 Frithestan
  931 Byrnstan
  934 Ælfheah I
  951 Ælfsige I
  960 Brihthelm
  963 Æthelwold I
  984 Ælfheah II
1006 Cenwulf
1006 Æthelwold II
*c.*1014 Ælfsige II
1032 Ælfwine

1043 Stigand
     Ælfsige III?
1070 Walkelin
1107 William Giffard
1129 Henry of Blois
1174 Richard of Ilchester (Toclyve)
1189 Godfrey de Lucy
1205 Peter des Roches
1244 Will. de Raleigh
1260 Aymer de Valance [of
     Lusignan]
1262 John Gervaise
1268 Nicholas of Ely
1282 John of Pontoise
1305 Henry Merewell [or
     Woodlock]
1316 John Sandale
1320 Rigaud of Assier
1323 John Stratford
1333 Adam Orleton
1346 William Edendon [Edington]
1367 William of Wykeham
1404 Henry Beaufort
1447 William of Waynflete
1487 Peter Courtenay
1493 Thomas Langton
1501 Richard Fox
1529 Thomas Wolsey
1531 Stephen Gardiner (deposed)
1551 John Ponet [Poynet]
1553 Stephen Gardiner (restored)
1556 John White (deposed)
1561 Robert Horne
1580 John Watson
1584 Thomas Cowper [Cooper]
1595 William Wickham
     [Wykeham]
1596 William Day
1597 Thomas Bilson
1616 James Montague
1619 Lancelot Andrewes
1628 Richard Neile
1632 Walter Curll
1660 Brian Duppa
1662 George Morley
1684 Peter Mews
1707 Jonathan Trelawney
1721 Charles Trimnell
1723 Richard Willis
1734 Benjamin Hoadly
1761 John Thomas
1781 Brownlow North
1820 George Pretyman Tomline
1827 Charles Richard Sumner
1869 Samuel Wilberforce
1873 Edward Harold Browne
1891 Anthony Wilson Thorold
1895 Randall Thomas Davidson
1903 Herbert Edward Ryle
1911 Edward Stuart Talbot
1923 Frank Theodore Woods
1932 Cyril Forster Garbett
1942 Mervyn George Haigh
1952 Alwyn Terrell Petre Williams
1961 Sherard Falkner Allison
1975 John Vernon Taylor
1985 Colin Clement Walter James
1995 Michael Charles Scott-Joynt

---

† Indicates a diocese no longer extant, or united with another diocese.
[2] Never signed without Wigthegn.

Bath and Wells

Description of arms. Azure, a saltire per saltire quarterly counterchanged or and argent.

BISHOPS OF WELLS

909 Athelm
925 Wulfhelm I
928 Ælfheah
938 Wulfhelm II
956 Byrhthelm
974 Cyneweard
979 Sigegar
997 Ælfwine
999 Lyfing
1013 Æthelwine (ejected)
1013 Beorhtwine (deposed)
Æthelwine (restored)
Beorhtwine (restored)
1024 Brihtwig [also Merehwit]
1033 Duduc
1061 Gisa
1088 John of Tours [de Villula]

BISHOPS OF BATH

1090 John of Tours [de Villula]
1123 Godfrey
1136 Robert
1174 Reg. Fitz Jocelin
1192 Savaric FitzGeldewin

BATH AND GLASTONBURY

1206 Jocelin of Wells

BATH AND WELLS

1244 Roger of Salisbury
1248 William Bitton I
1265 Walter Giffard
1267 William Bitton II
1275 Robert Burnell
1293 William of March
1302 Walter Hasleshaw
1309 John Droxford
1329 Ralph of Shrewsbury
1364 John Barnet
1367 John Harewell
1386 Walter Skirlaw
1388 Ralph Erghum
1401 Henry Bowet
1407 Nicholas Bubwith
1425 John Stafford
1443 Thomas Beckington
1466 Robert Stillington
1492 Richard Fox
1495 Oliver King
1504 Adriano de Castello [di Corneto]
1518 Thomas Wolsey
1523 John Clerk
1541 William Knight
1548 William Barlow
1554 Gilbert Bourne
1560 Gilbert Berkeley
1584 Thomas Godwin
1593 John Still
1608 James Montague
1616 Arthur Lake
1626 William Laud

1628 Leonard Mawe
1629 Walter Curll
1632 William Piers
1670 Robert Creighton
1673 Peter Mews
1685 Thomas Ken (deposed)
1691 Richard Kidder
1704 George Hooper
1727 John Wynne
1743 Edward Willes
1774 Charles Moss
1802 Richard Beadon
1824 George Henry Law
1845 Richard Bagot
1854 Robert John Eden, Lord Auckland
1869 Arthur Charles Hervey
1894 George Wyndham Kennion
1921 St John Basil Wynne Wilson
1937 Francis Underhill
1943 John William Charles Wand
1946 Harold William Bradfield
1960 Edward Barry Henderson
1975 John Monier Bickersteth
1987 George Leonard Carey
1991 James Lawton Thompson
2002 Peter Bryan Price

Birmingham

Description of arms. Per pale indented or and gules, five roundels, two, two, and one, and in chief two crosses patée all counterchanged.

1905 Charles Gore
1911 Henry Russell Wakefield
1924 Ernest William Barnes
1953 John Leonard Wilson
1969 Laurence Ambrose Brown
1978 Hugh William Montefiore
1987 Mark Santer
2002 John Mugabi Sentamu
2006 David Andrew Urquhart

Bristol

Description of arms. Sable, three ducal coronets in pale or.

1542 Paul Bush
1554 John Holyman
1562 Richard Cheyney
1581 John Bullingham (held Gloucester and Bristol 1586–9)
1589 Richard Fletcher
[See vacant for ten years]
1603 John Thornborough
1617 Nicholas Felton

1619 Rowland Searchfield
1623 Robert Wright
1633 George Coke
1637 Robert Skinner
1642 Thomas Westfield
1644 Thomas Howell
1661 Gilbert Ironside
1672 Guy Carleton
1679 William Gulston
1684 John Lake
1685 Jonathan Trelawney
1689 Gilbert Ironside
1691 John Hall
1710 John Robinson
1714 George Smalridge
1719 Hugh Boulter
1724 William Bradshaw
1733 Charles Cecil
1735 Thomas Secker
1737 Thomas Gooch
1738 Joseph Butler
1750 John Conybeare
1756 John Hume
1758 Philip Yonge
1761 Thomas Newton
1782 Lewis Bagot
1783 Christopher Wilson
1792 Spencer Madan
1794 Henry Reginald Courtenay
1797 Ffolliott Herbert Walker Cornewall
1803 George Pelham
1807 John Luxmoore
1808 William Lort Mansel
1820 John Kaye
1827 Robert Gray
1834 Joseph Allen
[1836 to 1897 united with Gloucester]
1897 George Forrest Browne
1914 George Nickson
1933 Clifford Salisbury Woodward
1946 Frederick Arthur Cockin
1959 Oliver Stratford Tomkins
1976 Ernest John Tinsley
1985 Barry Rogerson
2003 Michael Arthur Hill

Chelmsford

Description of arms. Or, on a saltire gules a pastoral staff of the first and a sword argent, hilt and pommel gold.

1914 John Edwin Watts-Ditchfield
1923 Frederic Sumpter Guy Warman
1929 Henry Albert Wilson
1951 Sherard Falkner Allison
1962 John Gerhard Tiarks
1971 Albert John Trillo
1986 John Waine
1996 John Freeman Perry
2003 John Warren Gladwin

Chichester

Description of arms. Azure, our blessed Lord in judgement seated in His throne, His dexter hand upraised or, His sinister hand holding an open book proper, and issuant from His mouth a two-edged sword point to the sinister gules.

BISHOPS OF SELSEY

681	Wilfrid
716	Eadberht
731	Eolla
733	Sigga [Sigeferth]
765	Aaluberht
*c.*765	Oswald [Osa]
780	Gislhere
786	Tota
*c.*789	Wihthun
*c.*811	Æthelwulf
824	Cynered
845	Guthheard
900	Wighelm
909	Beornheah
931	Wulfhun
943	Ælfred
955	Daniel
956	Brihthelm
963	Eadhelm
980	Æthelgar
990	Ordbriht
1009	Ælfmaer
1032	Æthelric I
1039	Grimketel
1047	Heca
1058	Æthelric II
1070	Stigand

BISHOPS OF CHICHESTER

1075	Stigand
1088	Godfrey
1091	Ralph Luffa
1125	Seffrid I [d'Escures Pelochin]
1147	Hilary
1174	John Greenford
1180	Seffrid II
1204	Simon FitzRobert
1215	Richard Poore
1218	Ranulf of Wareham
1224	Ralph Nevill
1245	Richard Wich
1254	John Climping
1262	Stephen Bersted [or Pagham]
1288	Gilbert de St Leofard
1305	John Langton
1337	Robert Stratford
1362	William Lenn
1369	William Reade
1386	Thomas Rushock
1390	Richard Mitford
1396	Robert Waldby
1397	Robert Reade
1417	Stephen Patrington
1418	Henry de la Ware

1421	John Kempe
1421	Thomas Polton
1426	John Rickingale
1431	Simon Sydenham
1438	Richard Praty
1446	Adam de Moleyns
1450	Reginald Pecock
1459	John Arundel
1478	Edward Story
1504	Richard Fitz-James
1508	Robert Sherburne
1536	Richard Sampson
1543	George Day (deposed)
1552	John Scory
1553	George Day (restored)
1557	John Christopherson
1559	William Barlow
1570	Richard Curtis
1586	Thomas Bickley
1596	Anthony Watson
1605	Lancelot Andrewes
1609	Samuel Harsnett
1619	George Carleton
1628	Richard Montague
1638	Brian Duppa
1642	Henry King
1670	Peter Gunning
1675	Ralph Brideoake
1679	Guy Carleton
1685	John Lake
1689	Simon Patrick
1691	Robert Grove
1696	John Williams
1709	Thomas Manningham
1722	Thomas Bowers
1724	Edward Waddington
1731	Francis Hare
1740	Matthias Mawson
1754	William Ashburnham
1798	John Buckner
1824	Robert James Carr
1831	Edward Maltby
1836	William Otter
1840	Philip Nicholas Shuttleworth
1842	Ashurst Turner Gilbert
1870	Richard Durnford
1896	Ernest Roland Wilberforce
1908	Charles John Ridgeway
1919	Winfrid Oldfield Burrows
1929	George Kennedy Allen Bell
1958	Roger Plumpton Wilson
1974	Eric Waldram Kemp
2001	John William Hind

Coventry

Description of arms. Gules, within a bordure argent charged with eight torteaux, a cross potent quadrate of the second.

1918	Huyshe Wolcott Yeatman-Biggs
1922	Charles Lisle Carr
1931	Mervyn George Haigh
1943	Neville Vincent Gorton

1956	Cuthbert Killick Norman Bardsley
1976	John Gibbs
1985	Simon Barrington-Ward
1998	Colin James Bennetts
2008	Christopher John Cocksworth

Derby

Description of arms. Purpure, a cross of St Chad argent beneath three fountains in chief.

1927	Edmund Courtenay Pearce
1936	Alfred Edward John Rawlinson
1959	Geoffrey Francis Allen
1969	Cyril William Johnston Bowles
1988	Peter Spencer Dawes
1995	Jonathan Sansbury Bailey
2005	Alastair Llewellyn John Redfern

Dorchester[1]

634	Birinus
650	Agilbert
*c.*660	Ætla
*c.*888	Ahlheard

Ely

Description of arms. Gules, three ducal coronets or.

1109	Hervey
1133	Nigel
1174	Geoffrey Ridel
1189	William Longchamp
1198	Eustace
1220	John of Fountains
1225	Geoffrey de Burgo
1229	Hugh of Northwold
1255	William of Kilkenny
1258	Hugh of Balsham
1286	John of Kirkby
1290	William of Louth
1299	Ralph Walpole
1303	Robert Orford
1310	John Ketton
1316	John Hotham
1337	Simon Montacute
1345	Thomas de Lisle
1362	Simon Langham
1367	John Barnet
1374	Thomas Arundel
1388	John Fordham

---

[1] Originally a West Saxon, after Ahlheard's time a Mercian, bishopric. See transferred to Lincoln 1077.

1426 Philip Morgan
1438 Lewis of Luxembourg
1444 Thomas Bourgchier
1454 William Grey
1479 John Morton
1486 John Alcock
1501 Richard Redman
1506 James Stanley
1515 Nicholas West
1534 Thomas Goodrich
1555 Thomas Thirlby
1559 Richard Cox
1600 Martin Heton
1609 Lancelot Andrewes
1619 Nicolas Felton
1628 John Buckeridge
1631 Francis White
1638 Matthew Wren
1667 Benjamin Laney
1675 Peter Gunning
1684 Francis Turner
1691 Simon Patrick
1707 John Moore
1714 William Fleetwood
1723 Thomas Greene
1738 Robert Butts
1748 Thomas Gooch
1754 Matthias Mawson
1771 Edmund Keene
1781 James Yorke
1808 Thomas Dampier
1812 Bowyer Edward Sparke
1836 Joseph Allen
1845 Thomas Turton
1864 Edward Harold Browne
1873 James Russell Woodford
1886 Alwyne Frederick Compton
1905 Frederick Henry Chase
1924 Leonard Jauncey White-
       Thomson
1934 Bernard Oliver Francis
       Heywood
1941 Harold Edward Wynn
1957 Noel Baring Hudson
1964 Edward James Keymer
       Roberts
1977 Peter Knight Walker
1990 Stephen Whitefield Sykes
2000 Anthony John Russell

Exeter

Description of arms. Gules, a sword erect in pale argent hilt or surmounted by two keys addorsed in saltire gold.

BISHOPS OF CORNWALL

870 Kenstec
893 Asser
931 Conan
950 Æthelge[ard]
c.955 Daniel
963 Wulfsige Comoere
990 Ealdred
1009 Æthelsige

1018 Buruhwold
1027 Lyfing, Bishop of
       Crediton, Cornwall
       and Worcester
1046 Leofric, Bishop of
       Crediton and
       Cornwall
[See transferred to Exeter 1050]

BISHOPS OF CREDITON

909 Eadwulf
934 Æthelgar
953 Ælfwold I
973 Sideman
979 Ælfric
987 Ælfwold II
1008 Ælfwold III
1015 Eadnoth
1027 Lyfing
1046 Leofric[1]

BISHOPS OF EXETER

1050 Leofric
1072 Osbern Fitz-Osbern
1107 Will. Warelwast
1138 Robert Warelwast
1155 Robert II of Chichester
1161 Bartholomew
1186 John the Chanter
1194 Henry Marshall
1214 Simon of Apulia
1224 William Brewer
1245 Richard Blund
1258 Walter Bronescombe
1280 Peter Quinel [Wyvill]
1292 Thomas Bitton
1308 Walter Stapeldon
1327 James Berkeley
1328 John Grandisson
1370 Thomas Brantingham
1395 Edmund Stafford
1419 John Catterick
1420 Edmund Lacy
1458 George Nevill
1465 John Booth
1478 Peter Courtenay
1487 Richard Fox
1493 Oliver King
1496 Richard Redman
1502 John Arundel
1505 Hugh Oldham
1519 John Veysey (resigned)
1551 Miles Coverdale
1553 John Veysey (restored)
1555 James Turberville
1560 William Alley [or Allei]
1571 William Bradbridge
1579 John Woolton
1595 Gervase Babington
1598 William Cotton
1621 Valentine Carey
1627 Joseph Hall
1642 Ralph Brownrigg
1660 John Gauden
1662 Seth Ward
1667 Anthony Sparrow
1676 Thomas Lamplugh
1689 Jonathan Trelawney
1708 Offspring Blackall
1717 Lancelot Blackburn
1724 Stephen Weston
1742 Nicholas Claget
1747 George Lavington
1762 Frederick Keppel
1778 John Ross

1792 William Buller
1797 Henry Reginald
       Courtenay
1803 John Fisher
1807 George Pelham
1820 William Carey
1830 Christopher Bethell
1831 Henry Phillpotts
1869 Frederick Temple
1885 Edward Henry
       Bickersteth
1901 Herbert Edward Ryle
1903 Archibald Robertson
1916 Rupert Ernest William
       Gascoyne Cecil
1936 Charles Edward Curzon
1949 Robert Cecil Mortimer
1973 Eric Arthur John Mercer
1985 Geoffrey Hewlett
       Thompson
1999 Michael Laurence
       Langrish

Gibraltar in Europe

Description of arms. Argent, in base rising out of the waves of the sea a rock proper, thereon a lion guardant or supporting a passion cross erect gules, on a chief engrailed of the last a crosier in bend dexter and a key in bend sinister or surmounted by a Maltese cross argent fimbriated gold.

BISHOPS OF GIBRALTAR

1842 George Tomlinson
1863 Walter John Trower
1868 Charles Amyand Harris
1874 Charles Waldegrave Sandford
1904 William Edward Collins
1911 Henry Joseph Corbett Knight
1921 John Harold Greig
1927 Frederick Cyril Nugent
       Hicks
1933 Harold Jocelyn Buxton
1947 Cecil Douglas Horsley
1953 Frederick William Thomas
       Craske
1960 Stanley Albert Hallam Eley
1970 John Richard Satterthwaite[2]

BISHOPS OF GIBRALTAR IN
EUROPE

1980 John Richard
       Satterthwaite
1993 John William Hind
2001 Douglas Geoffrey Rowell

---

[1] Removed See from Crediton.   [2] Bishop of Fulham and Gibraltar from 1970 to 1980.

Gloucester

Description of arms. Azure, two keys addorsed in saltire the wards upwards or.

1541	John Wakeman *alias* Wiche
1551	John Hooper
1554	James Brooks
1562	Richard Cheyney[1]
1581	John Bullingham[2]
1598	Godfrey Goldsborough
1605	Thomas Ravis
1607	Henry Parry
1611	Giles Thompson
1612	Miles Smith
1625	Godfrey Goodman
1661	William Nicolson
1672	John Pritchett
1681	Robert Frampton
1691	Edward Fowler
1715	Richard Willis
1721	Joseph Wilcocks
1731	Elias Sydall
1735	Martin Benson
1752	James Johnson
1760	William Warburton
1779	James Yorke
1781	Samuel Hallifax
1789	Richard Beadon
1802	George Isaac Huntingford
1815	Henry Ryder
1824	Christopher Bethell
1830	James Henry Monk
[1836 to 1897, united with Bristol]

BISHOPS OF GLOUCESTER AND BRISTOL

1836	James Henry Monk
1856	Charles Baring
1861	William Thomson
1863	Charles John Ellicott[3]

BISHOPS OF GLOUCESTER

1897	Charles John Ellicott
1905	Edgar Charles Sumner Gibson
1923	Arthur Cayley Headlam
1946	Clifford Salisbury Woodward
1954	Wilfred Marcus Askwith
1962	Basil Tudor Guy
1975	John Yates
1992	Peter John Ball
1993	David Edward Bentley
2004	Michael Francis Perham

Guildford

Description of arms. Gules, two keys conjoined wards outwards in bend, the uppermost or, the other argent, interposed between them in bend sinister a sword of the third, hilt and pommel gold, all within a bordure azure charged with ten wool-packs argent.

1927	John Harold Greig
1934	John Victor Macmillan
1949	Henry Colville Montgomery Campbell
1956	Ivor Stanley Watkins
1961	George Edmund Reindorp
1973	David Alan Brown
1983	Michael Edgar Adie
1994	John Warren Gladwin
2004	Christopher John Hill

Hereford

Description of arms. Gules, three leopards' faces jessant-de-lis reversed or.

676	Putta
688	Tyrhtel
710	Torhthere
*c.*731	Wahistod
736	Cuthberht
741	Podda
*c.*758	Acca
*c.*770	Headda
777	Aldberht
786	Esne
*c.*788	Ceolmund
*c.*798	Utel
801	Wulfheard
824	Beonna
*c.*832	Eadwulf
*c.*839	Cuthwulf
866	Mucel
*c.*866	Deorlaf
888	Cynemund
890	EadBar
*c.*931	Tidhelm
940	Wulfhelm
*c.*940	Ælfric
971	Æthelwulf
1016	Æthelstan
1056	Leofgar
1056	Ealdred, Bishop of Hereford and Worcester

1060	Walter
1079	Robert Losinga
1096	Gerard
1107	Reinhelm
1115	Geoffrey de Clive
1121	Richard de Capella
1131	Robert de Bethune
1148	Gilbert Foliot
1163	Robert of Melun
1174	Robert Foliot
1186	William de Vere
1200	Giles de Braose
1216	Hugh of Mapenore
1219	Hugh Foliot
1234	Ralph Maidstone
1240	Peter d'Aigueblanche
1269	John Breton
1275	Thomas Cantilupe
1283	Richard Swinfeld
1317	Adam Orleton
1327	Thomas Chariton
1344	John Trilleck
1361	Lewis Charleton
1370	William Courtenay
1375	John Gilbert
1389	John Trefnant
1404	Robert Mascall
1417	Edmund Lacy
1420	Thomas Polton
1422	Thomas Spofford
1449	Richard Beauchamp
1451	Reginald Boulers
1453	John Stanbury
1474	Thomas Milling
1492	Edmund Audley
1502	Adriano de Castello [di Corneto]
1504	Richard Mayeu
1516	Charles Booth
1535	Edward Fox
1539	John Skip
1553	John Harley
1554	Robert Parfew or Wharton
1559	John Scory
1586	Herbert Westfaling
1603	Robert Bennett
1617	Francis Godwin
1634	Augustine Lindsell
1635	Matthew Wren
1635	Theophilus Field
1636	George Coke
1661	Nicolas Monk
1662	Herbert Croft
1691	Gilbert Ironside
1701	Humphrey Humphries
1713	Philip Bisse
1721	Benjamin Hoadly
1724	Henry Egerton
1746	James Beauclerk
1787	John Harley
1788	John Butler
1803	Ffolliott Herbert Walker Cornewall
1808	John Luxmoore
1815	George Isaac Huntingford
1832	Edward Grey
1837	Thomas Musgrave
1848	Renn Dickson Hampden
1868	James Atlay
1895	John Percival
1918	Herbert Hensley Henson
1920	Martin Linton Smith
1931	Charles Lisle Carr
1941	Richard Godfrey Parsons
1949	Tom Longworth

[1] Also Bishop of Bristol.   [2] Held Gloucester and Bristol 1581-9.   [3] Gloucester only from 1897.

955

1961 Mark Allin Hodson
1974 John Richard Gordon
      Eastaugh
1990 John Keith Oliver
2004 Anthony Martin Priddis

Leicester

see also under Lincoln

Description of arms. Gules, a pierced cinquefoil ermine, in chief a lion passant guardant grasping in the dexter forepaw a cross crosslet fitchée or.

NEW FOUNDATION

1927 Cyril Charles Bowman
      Bardsley
1940 Guy Vernon Smith
1953 Ronald Ralph Williams
1979 Cecil Richard Rutt
1991 Thomas Frederick Butler
1999 Timothy John Stevens

Lichfield

Description of arms. Per pale gules and argent, a cross potent quadrate in the centre per pale argent and or between four crosses patée those to the dexter argent and those to the sinister gold.

BISHOPS OF MERCIA

656 Diuma[1]
658 Ceollach
659 Trumhere
662 Jaruman

BISHOPS OF LICHFIELD

669 Chad[2]
672 Winfrith
676 Seaxwulf
691 Headda[3]
731 Aldwine
737 Hwita

757 Hemele
765 Cuthfrith
769 Berhthun
779 Hygeberht[4]
801 Aldwulf
816 Herewine
818 Æthelwald
830 Hunberht
836 Cyneferth
845 Tunberht
869 Eadberht
883 Wulfred
900 Wigmund or Wilferth
915 Ælfwine
941 Wulfgar
949 Cynesige
964 Wynsige
975 Ælfheah
1004 Godwine
1020 Leofgar
1026 Brihtmaer
1039 Wulfsige
1053 Leofwine
1072 Peter

BISHOPS OF LICHFIELD, CHESTER, AND COVENTRY[5]

1075 Peter
1086 Robert de Limesey[5]
1121 Robert Peche
1129 Roger de Clinton
1149 Walter Durdent
1161 Richard Peche
1183 Gerard La Pucelle
1188 Hugh Nonant
1198 Geoffrey Muschamp
1215 William Cornhill
1224 Alex. Stavensby
1240 Hugh Pattishall
1246 Roger Weseham
1258 Roger Longespee
1296 Walter Langton
1322 Roger Northburgh
1360 Robert Stretton
1386 Walter Skirlaw
1386 Richard le Scrope
1398 John Burghill
1415 John Catterick
1420 William Heyworth
1447 William Booth
1452 Nicholas Close
1453 Reginald Boulers
1459 John Hales
1493 William Smith
1496 John Arundel
1503 Geoffrey Blyth
1534 Rowland Lee
1541 [Chester formed as a
        bishopric]
1543 Richard Sampson
1554 Ralph Baynes
1560 Thomas Bentham
1580 William Overton
1609 George Abbot
1610 Richard Neile
1614 John Overall
1619 Thomas Morton
1632 Robert Wright

1644 Accepted Frewen
1661 John Hackett
1671 Thomas Wood
1692 William Lloyd
1699 John Hough
1717 Edward Chandler
1731 Richard Smalbroke
1750 Fred. Cornwallis
1768 John Egerton
1771 Brownlow North
1775 Richard Hurd
1781 James Cornwallis [4th Earl
        Cornwallis]
1824 Henry Ryder
1836 [Coventry transferred to
        Worcester diocese]
1836 Samuel Butler
1840 James Bowstead
1843 John Lonsdale
1868 George Augustus Selwyn
1878 William Dalrymple
        Maclagan
1891 Augustus Legge
1913 John Augustine
        Kempthorne
1937 Edward Sydney Woods
1953 Arthur Stretton Reeve
1975 Kenneth John Fraser
        Skelton
1984 Keith Norman Sutton
2003 Jonathan Michael
        Gledhill

Lincoln

Description of arms. Gules, two lions passant guardant or, on a chief azure, the Virgin ducally crowned sitting on a throne issuant from the chief, on her dexter arm the infant Jesus, and in her sinister hand a sceptre all gold.

BISHOPS OF LINDSEY

634 Birinus
650 Agilbert
660 Aetlai
678 Eadhaed
680 Æthelwine
693 (?)Edgar
731 (?)Cyneberht
733 Alwig
750 Aldwulf
767 Ceolwulf
796 Eadwulf
839 Beorhtred
869 Burgheard
933 Ælfred
953 Leofwine
996 Sigefrith

---

[1] Archbishop of the Mercians, the Lindisfari, and the Middle Angles.
[2] Bishop of the Mercians and the Lindisfari.
[3] Bishop of Lichfield and Leicester.
[4] Archbishop of Lichfield after 787.
[5] 1102 Robert de Limesey, Bishop of Lichfield, moved the See to Coventry. Succeeding bishops are usually termed *of Coventry* until 1228. Then *Coventry and Lichfield* was the habitual title until the Reformation. *Chester* was used by some 12th-century bishops, and popularly afterwards. After the Reformation *Lichfield and Coventry* was used until 1846.

BISHOPS OF LEICESTER

664 Wilfrid, translated from York
679 Cuthwine
691 Headda[1] (founder of Lichfield
     Cathedral 705–37)
727 Aldwine
737 Torhthelm
764 Eadberht
785 Unwona
803 Wernberht
816 Raethhun
840 Ealdred
844 Ceolred
874 [See of Leicester removed to
     Dorchester]

BISHOPS OF DORCHESTER

(after it became a Mercian See)
c.888 Ahlheard
 900 Wigmund or Wilferth
 909 Cenwulf
 925 Wynsige
c.951 Osketel
 953 Leofwine
 975 Ælfnoth
 979 Æscwig
1002 ÆIfheln
1006 Eadnoth I
1016 Æthelric
1034 Eadnoth II
1049 Ulf
1053 Wulfwig
1067 Remigius

BISHOPS OF LINCOLN

1072 Remigius
1094 Robert Bloett
1123 Alexander
1148 Robert de Chesney
1183 Walter de Coutances
1186 Hugh of Avalon
1203 William of Blois
1209 Hugh of Wells
1235 Robert Grosseteste
1254 Henry Lexington [Sutton]
1258 Richard Gravesend
1280 Oliver Sutton [Lexington]
1300 John Dalderby
1320 Henry Burghersh
1342 Thomas Bek
1347 John Gynewell
1363 John Bokyngham
     [Buckingham]
1398 Henry Beaufort
1405 Philip Repingdon
1420 Richard Fleming
1431 William Gray
1436 William Alnwick
1450 Marmaduke Lumley
1452 John Chedworth
1472 Thomas Rotherham [Scott]
1480 John Russell
1495 William Smith
1514 Thomas Wolsey
1514 William Atwater
1521 John Longland
1547 Henry Holbeach [Rands]
1552 John Taylor
1554 John White
1557 Thomas Watson
1560 Nicholas Bullingham
1571 Thomas Cooper
1584 William Wickham
1595 William Chaderton

1608 William Barlow
1614 Richard Neile
1617 George Monteigne [Mountain]
1621 John Williams
1642 Thomas Winniffe
1660 Robt. Sanderson
1663 Benjamin Laney
1667 William Fuller
1675 Thomas Barlow
1692 Thomas Tenison
1695 James Gardiner
1705 William Wake
1716 Edmund Gibson
1723 Richard Reynolds
1744 John Thomas
1761 John Green
1779 Thomas Thurlow
1787 George Pretyman [Pretyman
     Tomline after June 1803]
1820 George Pelham
1827 John Kaye
1853 John Jackson
1869 Christopher Wordsworth
1885 Edward King
1910 Edward Lee Hicks
1920 William Shuckburgh Swayne
1933 Frederick Cyril Nugent Hicks
1942 Henry Aylmer Skelton
1946 Leslie Owen
1947 Maurice Henry Harland
1956 Kenneth Riches
1975 Simon Wilton Phipps
1987 Robert Maynard Hardy
2001 John Charles Saxbee

Norwich

Description of arms. Azure, three
labelled mitres or.

BISHOPS OF DUNWICH

 631 Felix
 648 Thomas
c.653 Berhtgils [Boniface]
c.670 Bisi
c.673 Æcce
 693 Alric (?)
 716 Eardred
 731 Aldbeorht I
 747 Æscwulf
 747 Eardwulf
 775 Cuthwine
 775 Aldbeorht II
 781 Ecglaf
 781 Heardred
 793 Ælfhun
 798 Tidferth
 824 Waermund[2]
 825 Wilred
 836 Husa
 870 Æthelwold

BISHOPS OF ELMHAM

 673 Beaduwine
 706 Nothberht

c.731 Heathulac
 736 Æthelfrith
 758 Eanfrith
c.781 Æthelwulf
c.785 Alhheard
 814 Sibba
 824 Hunferth
 824 Hunbeorht
 836 Cunda[3]
c.933 Ælfred[4]
c.945 Æthelweald
 956 Eadwulf
 970 Ælfric I
 974 Theodred I
 982 Theodred II
 997 Æthelstan
1001 Ælfgar
1021 Ælfwine
1038 Ælfric II
1039 Ælfric III
1043 Stigand[5]
1043 Grimketel[6]
1044 Stigand (restored)
1047 Æthelmaer

BISHOPS OF THETFORD

1070 Herfast
1086 William de Beaufai
1091 Herbert Losinga

BISHOPS OF NORWICH

1091 Herbert Losinga
1121 Everard of
     Montgomery
1146 William de Turbe
1175 John of Oxford
1200 John de Gray
1222 Pandulf Masca
1226 Thomas Blundeville
1239 William Raleigh
1245 Walter Suffield or
     Calthorp
1258 Simon Walton
1266 Roger Skerning
1278 William Middleton
1289 Ralph Walpole
1299 John Salmon
1325 [Robert de Baldock]
1325 William Ayermine
1337 Anthony Bek
1344 William of Norwich
     [Bateman]
1356 Thomas Percy
1370 Henry Spencer
     [Dispenser]
1407 Alexander Tottington
1413 Richard Courtenay
1416 John Wakeryng
1426 William Ainwick
1436 Thomas Brown
1446 Walter Lyhert
     [le Hart]
1472 James Goldwell
1499 Thomas Jane
1501 Richard Nykke
1536 William Reppes
     [Rugge]
1550 Thomas Thirlby
1554 John Hopton
1560 John Parkhurst
1575 Edmund Freke
1585 Edmund Scambler
1595 William Redman
1603 John Jegon
1618 John Overall

---

[1] Bishop of Leicester and Lichfield.   [2] Bishop of Dunwich or Elmham.   [3] Bishop of Elmham or Dunwich.
[4] Bishop of Elmham or Lindsey.   [5] Deposed before consecration.   [6] Bishop of Selsey and Elmham.

1619 Samuel Harsnett	1699 William Talbot	1956 Robert Wright Stopford
1629 Francis White	1715 John Potter	1961 Cyril Eastaugh
1632 Richard Corbet	1737 Thomas Secker	1972 Douglas Russell Feaver
1635 Matthew Wren	1758 John Hume	1984 William John Westwood
1638 Richard Montagu	1766 Robert Lowth	1996 Ian Patrick Martyn Cundy
1641 Joseph Hall	1777 John Butler	
1661 Edward Reynolds	1788 Edward Smallwell	

Portsmouth

1676 Antony Sparrow	1799 John Randolph
1685 William Lloyd	1807 Charles Moss
1691 John Moore	1812 William Jackson
1708 Charles Trimnell	1816 Edward Legge
1721 Thomas Green	1827 Charles Lloyd
1723 John Leng	1829 Richard Bagot
1727 William Baker	1845 Samuel Wilberforce
1733 Robert Butts	1870 John Fielder Mackarness
1738 Thomas Gooch	1889 William Stubbs
1748 Samuel Lisle	1901 Francis Paget
1749 Thomas Hayter	1911 Charles Gore

Description of arms. Per fess or and gules, in chief upon waves of the sea proper a lymphad sable, and in base two keys conjoined wards outwards in bend, the uppermost or, the other argent, interposed between them in bend sinister a sword also argent, hilt and pommel gold.

1761 Philip Yonge	1919 Hubert Murray Burge
1783 Lewis Bagot	1925 Thomas Banks Strong
1790 George Horne	1937 Kenneth Escott Kirk
1792 Charles Manners Sutton	1955 Harry James Carpenter
	1971 Kenneth John Woollcombe
1805 Henry Bathurst	1978 Patrick Campbell Rodger
1837 Edward Stanley	1987 Richard Douglas Harries
1849 Samuel Hinds	2007 John Lawrence Pritchard

1927	Ernest Neville Lovett
1936	Frank Partridge
1942	William Louis Anderson
1949	William Launcelot Scott Fleming
1960	John Henry Lawrence Phillips
1975	Archibald Ronald McDonald Gordon
1985	Timothy John Bavin
1995	Kenneth William Stevenson

1857 John Thomas Pelham	
1893 John Sheepshanks	
1910 Bertram Pollock	
1942 Percy Mark Herbert	
1959 William Launcelot Scott Fleming	
1971 Maurice Arthur Ponsonby Wood	
1985 Peter John Nott	
1999 Graham Richard James	

Peterborough

Description of arms. Gules, two keys in saltire the wards upwards between four cross crosslets fitchée or.

Oxford

Description of arms. Sable, a fess argent, in chief three demi-ladies couped at the waist heads affrontée proper crowned or arrayed and veiled of the second, in base an ox of the last, horned and hoofed gold, passing a ford barry wavy of six azure and argent.

1542 Robert King[1]	
1558 [Thomas Goldwell]	
1567 Hugh Curen [Curwen]	
1589 John Underhill	
1604 John Bridges	
1619 John Howson	
1628 Richard Corbet	
1632 John Bancroft	
1641 Robert Skinner	
1663 William Paul	
1665 Walter Blandford	
1671 Nathaniel Crewe [Lord Crewe]	
1674 Henry Compton	
1676 John Fell	
1686 Samuel Parker	
1688 Timothy Hall	
1690 John Hough	

1541	John Chamber
1557	David Pole
1561	Edmund Scambler
1585	Richard Howland
1601	Thomas Dove
1630	William Piers
1633	Augustine Lindsell
1634	Francis Dee
1639	John Towers
1660	Benjamin Laney
1663	Joseph Henshaw
1679	William Lloyd
1685	Thomas White
1691	Richard Cumberland
1718	White Kennett
1729	Robert Clavering
1747	John Thomas
1757	Richard Terrick
1764	Robert Lambe
1769	John Hinchliffe
1794	Spencer Madan
1813	John Parsons
1819	Herbert Marsh
1839	George Davys
1864	Francis Jeune
1868	William Connor Magee
1891	Mandell Creighton
1897	Edward Carr Glyn
1916	Frank Theodore Woods
1924	Cyril Charles Bowman Bardsley
1927	Claude Martin Blagden
1949	Spencer Stottisbury Gwatkin Leeson

Rochester

Description of arms. Argent, on a saltire gules an escallop or.

604	Justus
624	Romanus
633	Paulinus
644	Ithamar
664	Damianus
669	Putta
676	Cwichelm
678	Gebmund
716	Tobias
727	Aldwulf
741	Dunn
747	Eardwulf
772	Diora
785	Waermund I
805	Beornmod
844	Tatnoth
868	Badenoth
868	Waermund II
868	Cuthwulf
880	Swithwulf
900	Ceolmund
c.926	Cyneferth
c.934	Burhric
949	Beorhtsige

---

[1] Bishop Rheon. *in partibus.* Of Oseney 1542-5. See transferred to Oxford 1545.

955 [Daniel?] Rochester or Selsey
964 Ælfstan
995 Godwine I
1046 Godwine II
1058 Siward
1076 Arnost
1077 Gundulf
1108 Ralph d'Escures
1115 Ernulf
1125 John
1137 John II
1142 Ascelin
1148 Walter
1182 Waleran
1185 Gilbert Glanvill
1215 Benedict of Sausetun
     [Sawston]
1227 Henry Sandford
1238 Richard Wendene
1251 Lawrence of St Martin
1274 Walter Merton
1278 John Bradfield
1283 Thomas Ingoldsthorpe
1292 Thomas of Wouldham
1319 Hamo Hethe
1353 John Sheppey
1362 William of Whittlesey
1364 Thomas Trilleck
1373 Thomas Brinton
1389 William Bottlesham
     [Bottisham]
1400 John Bottlesham
1404 Richard Young
1419 John Kempe
1422 John Langdon
1435 Thomas Brouns
1437 William Wells
1444 John Low
1468 Thomas Rotherham
     [otherwise Scott]
1472 John Alcock
1476 John Russell
1480 Edmund Audley
1493 Thomas Savage
1497 Richard Fitz-James
1504 John Fisher
1535 John Hilsey [Hildesleigh]
1540 Nicolas Heath
1544 Henry Holbeach
1547 Nicholas Ridley
1550 John Ponet [Poynet]
1551 John Scory
1554 Maurice Griffith
1560 Edmund Gheast [Guest]
1572 Edmund Freke
1576 John Piers
1578 John Young
1605 William Barlow
1608 Richard Neile
1611 John Buckeridge
1628 Walter Curil
1630 John Bowle
1638 John Warner
1666 John Dolben
1683 Francis Turner
1684 Thomas Sprat
1713 Francis Atterbury
1723 Samuel Bradford
1731 Joseph Wilcocks
1756 Zachary Pearce
1774 John Thomas
1793 Samuel Horsley
1802 Thomas Dampier
1809 Walker King
1827 Hugh Percy
1827 George Murray
1860 Joseph Cotton Wigram

1867 Thomas Legh Claughton
1877 Anthony Wilson Thorold
1891 Randall Thomas Davidson
1895 Edward Stuart Talbot
1905 John Reginald Harmer
1930 Martin Linton Smith
1940 Christopher Maude Chavasse
1961 Richard David Say
1988 Anthony Michael Arnold
     Turnbull
1994 Michael James Nazir-Ali

St Albans

Description of arms. Azure, a saltire or, overall a sword erect in pale proper, hilt and pommel gold, in chief a celestial crown of the same.

1877 Thomas Legh Claughton
1890 John Wogan Festing
1903 Edgar Jacob
1920 Michael Bolton Furse
1944 Philip Henry Loyd
1950 Edward Michael Gresford
     Jones
1970 Robert Alexander Kennedy
     Runcie
1980 John Bernard Taylor
1995 Christopher William
     Herbert
2009 Alan Gregory Clayton Smith

St Edmundsbury
and Ipswich

Description of arms. Per pale gules and azure, between three ducal coronets a demi-lion passant guardant conjoined to the demi-hulk of an ancient ship or.

1914 Henry Bernard Hodgson
1921 Albert Augustus David
1923 Walter Godfrey Whittingham
1940 Richard Brook
1954 Arthur Harold Morris
1966 Leslie Wilfrid Brown
1978 John Waine
1986 John Dennis
1997 John Hubert Richard Lewis
2007 William Nigel Stock

Salisbury

Description of arms. Azure, our Lady crowned, holding in her dexter arm the infant Jesus, and in her sinister arm a sceptre all or, round both the heads circles of glory gold.

BISHOPS OF SHERBORNE

705 Ealdhelm
709 Forthhere
736 Hereweald
774 Æthelmod
793 Denefrith
801 Wigberht
825 Ealhstan
868 Heahmund
877 Æthelheah
889 Wulfsige I
900 Asser
*c.*909 Æthelweard
*c.*909 Waerstan
925 Æthelbald
925 Sigehelm
934 Ælfred
943 Wulfsige II
958 Ælfwold I
979 Æthelsige I
992 Wulfsige III
1002 Æthelric
1012 Æthelsige II
1017 Brihtwine I
1017 Ælfmaer
1023 Brihtwine II
1045 Ælfwold II
1058 Hereman, Bishop of
     Ramsbury

BISHOPS OF RAMSBURY

909 Æthelstan
927 Oda
949 Ælfric I
951 Osulf
970 Ælfstan
981 Wulfgar
986 Sigeric
993 Ælfric II
1005 Brihtwold
1045 Hereman[1]

BISHOPS OF SALISBURY

1078 Osmund Osmer
1107 Roger
1142 Jocelin de Bohun
1189 Hubert Walter
1194 Herbert Poore
1217 Richard Poore
1229 Robert Bingham
1247 William of York
1257 Giles of Bridport
1263 Walter de la Wyle
1274 Robert Wickhampton
1284 Walter Scammel
1287 Henry Brandeston

---

[1] Ramsbury was added to Sherbourne in 1058 when Hereman became Bishop of Sherbourne. The See was moved to Salisbury in 1078.

1289 William de la Corner	
1292 Nicholas Longespee	
1297 Simon of Ghent	
1315 Roger de Mortival	
1330 Robert Wyville	
1375 Ralph Erghum	
1388 John Waltham	
1395 Richard Mitford	
1407 Nicholas Bubwith	
1407 Robert Hallum	
1417 John Chaundler	
1427 Robert Nevill	
1438 William Aiscough	
1450 Richard Beauchamp	
1482 Lionel Woodville	
1485 Thomas Langton	
1494 John Blythe	
1500 Henry Deane	
1502 Edmund Audley	
1525 Lorenzo Campeggio	
1535 Nicholas Shaxton	
1539 John Salcot [Capon]	
1560 John Jewell	
1571 Edmund Gheast [Guest]	
1577 John Piers	
1591 John Coldwell	
1598 Henry Cotton	
1615 Robert Abbot	
1618 Martin Fotherby	
1620 Robert Townson [Toulson]	
1621 John Davenant	
1641 Brian Duppa	
1660 Humfrey Henchman	
1663 John Earle	
1665 Alexander Hyde	
1667 Seth Ward	
1689 Gilbert Burnet	
1715 William Talbot	
1721 Richard Wilis	
1723 Benjamin Hoadly	
1734 Thomas Sherlock	
1748 John Gilbert	
1757 John Thomas	
1761 Robert Hay Drummond	
1761 John Thomas	
1766 John Hume	
1782 Shute Barrington	
1791 John Douglas	
1807 John Fisher	
1825 Thomas Burgess	
1837 Edward Denison	
1854 Walter Kerr Hamilton	
1869 George Moberly	
1885 John Wordsworth	
1911 Frederic Edward Ridgeway	
1921 St Clair George Alfred Donaldson	
1936 Ernest Neville Lovett	
1946 Geoffrey Charles Lester Lunt	
1949 William Louis Anderson	
1963 Joseph Edward Fison	
1973 George Edmund Reindorp	
1982 John Austin Baker	
1993 David Staffurth Stancliffe	

Southwark

Description of arms. Argent, eleven fusils in cross conjoined, seven in pale fesswise, four in fess palewise, in the dexter chief a mitre all gules.

1905 Edward Stuart Talbot
1911 Hubert Murray Burge
1919 Cyril Forster Garbett
1932 Richard Godfrey Parsons
1942 Bertram Fitzgerald Simpson
1959 Arthur Mervyn Stockwood
1980 Ronald Oliver Bowlby
1991 Robert Kerr Williamson
1998 Thomas Frederick Butler

Truro

Description of arms. Argent, on a saltire gules a sword and key or and in base a fleur-de-lis sable all within a bordure of the last charged with fifteen besants.

1877 Edward White Benson
1883 George Howard Wilkinson
1891 John Gott
1906 Charles William Stubbs
1912 Winfrid Oldfield Burrows
1919 Frederic Sumpter Guy Warman
1923 Walter Howard Frere
1935 Joseph Wellington Hunkin
1951 Edmund Robert Morgan
1960 John Maurice Key
1973 Graham Douglas Leonard
1981 Peter Mumford
1990 Michael Thomas Ball
1997 William Ind
2008 Timothy Martin Thornton

Worcester

Description of arms. Argent, ten torteaux, four, three, two, and one.

680 Bosel
691 Oftfor
693 Ecgwine
718 Wilfrid I

745 Milred
775 Waermund
777 Tilhere
781 Heathured
798 Deneberht
822 Heahberht
845 Alhhun
873 Waerferth
915 Æthelhun
922 Wilferth II
929 Cenwald
957 Dunstan
961 Oswald
992 Ealdwulf
1002 Wulfstan I
1016 Leofsige
1027 Lyfing
1033 Brihtheah
1040 Æltric Puttoc, Bishop of York and Worcester
1041 Lyfing (restored)
1046 Ealdred Bishop of Hereford and Worcester 1056–60
1062 Wulfstan II
1096 Samson
1115 Theulf
1125 Simon
1151 John of Pagham
1158 Aldred
1164 Roger of Gloucester
1180 Baldwin
1186 William of Northolt
1191 Robert Fitz Ralph
1193 Henry de Sully
1196 John of Coutances
1200 Mauger
1214 Walter de Gray
1216 Silvester of Evesham
1218 William of Blois
1237 Walter Cantilupe
1266 Nicolas of Ely
1268 Godfrey Giffard
1302 William Gainsborough
1308 Walter Reynolds
1313 Walter Maidstone
1317 Thomas Cobham
1327 Adam Orleton
1334 Simon Montacute
1337 Thomas Hempnall
1339 Wulstan Bransford
1350 John Thoresby
1353 Reginald Brian
1362 John Barnet
1364 William of Whittlesey
1369 William Lenn
1375 Henry Wakefield
1396 Robert Tideman of Winchcomb
1401 Richard Clifford
1407 Thomas Peverel
1419 Philip Morgan
1426 Thomas Polton
1435 Thomas Bourgchier
1444 John Carpenter
1476 John Alcock
1487 Robert Morton
1497 Giovanni de' Gigli
1499 Silvestro de' Gigli
1521 Julius de Medici Guilio de Medici (administrator)
1523 Geronimo Ghinucci
1535 Hugh Latimer
1539 John Bell
1544 Nicholas Heath (deposed)
1552 John Hooper
1554 Nicholas Heath (restored)
1555 Richard Pates
1559 Edwin Sandys
1571 Nicholas Bullingham
1577 John Whitgift

1584 Edmund Freke	1699 William Lloyd	1919 Ernest Harold Pearce
1593 Richard Fletcher	1717 John Hough	1931 Arthur William Thomson
1596 Thomas Bilson	1743 Isaac Maddox	Perowne
1597 Gervase Babington	1759 James Johnson	1941 William Wilson Cash
1610 Henry Parry	1774 Brownlow North	1956 Lewis Mervyn Charles-
1617 John Thornborough	1781 Richard Hurd	Edwards
1641 John Prideaux	1808 Ffolliott Herbert Walker	1971 Robert Wylmer Woods
1660 George Morley	Cornewall	1982 Philip Harold Ernest
1662 John Gauden	1831 Robert James Carr	Goodrich
1662 John Earle	1841 Henry Pepys	1997 Peter Stephen Maurice
1663 Robert Skinner	1861 Henry Philpott	Selby
1671 Walter Blandford	1891 John James Stewart Perowne	2007 John Geoffrey Inge
1675 James Fleetwood	1902 Charles Gore	
1683 William Thomas	1905 Huyshe Wolcott Yeatman-	
1689 Edward Stillingfleet	Biggs	

PROVINCE OF YORK

York

Description of arms. Gules, two keys in saltire argent, in chief a regal crown proper.

BISHOPS

314 Eborius
625 Paulinus
    [Vacancy 633–64]
664 Cedda
664 Wilfrid I
678 Bosa (retired)
686 Bosa (restored)
691 Wilfrith (restored)
706 John of Beverley
718 Wilfrid II

ARCHBISHOPS

734 Egberht
767 Æthelberht
780 Eanbald I
796 Eanbald II
808 Wulfsige
837 Wigmund
854 Wulfhere
900 Æthelbald
c.928 Hrothweard
931 Wulfstan I
956 Osketel
971 Oswald
971 Edwald
992 Ealdwulf [1]
1003 Wulfstan II
1023 Ælfric Puttoc
1041 Æthelric
1051 Cynesige
1061 Ealdred
1070 Thomas I of Bayeux
1100 Gerard
1109 Thomas II
1119 Thurstan
1143 William Fitzherbert
1147 Henry Murdac

1153 William Fitzherbert
    (restored)
1154 Roger of Pont l'Eveque
1191 Geoffrey Plantagenet
1215 Walter de Gray
1256 Sewal de Bovill
1258 Godfrey Ludham
    [Kineton]
1266 Walter Giffard
1279 William Wickwane
1286 John Romanus [le
    Romeyn]
1298 Henry Newark
1300 Thomas Corbridge
1306 William Greenfield
1317 William Melton
1342 William de la Zouche
1352 John Thoresby
1374 Alexander Neville
1388 Thomas Arundel
1396 Robert Waldby
1398 Richard le Scrope
1407 Henry Bowet
1426 John Kempe
1452 William Booth
1464 George Nevill
1476 Lawrence Booth
1480 Thomas Rotherham
    [Scott]
1501 Thomas Savage
1508 Christopher Bainbridge
1514 Thomas Wolsey
1531 Edward Lee
1545 Robert Holgate
1555 Nicholas Heath
1561 Thomas Young
1570 Edmund Grindal
1577 Edwin Sandys
1589 John Piers
1595 Matthew Hutton
1606 Tobias Matthew
1628 George Monteigne
    [Mountain]
1629 Samuel Harsnett
1632 Richard Neile
1641 John Williams
1660 Accepted Frewen
1664 Richard Sterne
1683 John Dolben
1688 Thomas Lamplugh
1691 John Sharp
1714 William Dawes
1724 Lancelot Blackburn
1743 Thomas Herring
1747 Matthew Hutton

1757 John Gilben
1761 Roben Hay Drummond
1777 William Markham
1808 Edward Venables Vernon
    Harcourt
1847 Thomas Musgrave
1860 Charles Thomas Longley
1863 William Thomson
1891 William Connor Magee
1891 William Dalrymple
    Maclagan
1909 Cosmo Gordon Lang
1929 William Temple
1942 Cyril Forster Garbett
1956 Arthur Michael Ramsey
1961 Frederick Donald Coggan
1975 Stuart Yarworth Blanch
1983 John Stapylton Habgood
1995 David Michael Hope
2005 John Tucker Mugabi Sentamu

Durham

Description of arms. Azure, a cross or between four lions rampant argent.

BISHOPS OF LINDISFARNE [2]

635 Aidan
651 Finan
661 Colman
664 Tuda
    [Complications involving
    Wilfrid and Chad]
681 Eata
685 Cuthberht
    [Vacancy during which
    Wilfrid administered the
    See]
688 Eadberht
698 Eadfenh
731 Æthelweald
740 Cynewulf
781 Higbald
803 Ecgberht

---

[1] Ealdwulf and Wulfstan II held the Sees of York and Worcester together, Ælfric Puttoc held both 1040-41 and Eadred 1060-61.
[2] See transferred to Chester-le-Street 883.

821 Heathwred
830 Ecgred
845 Eanberht
854 Eardwulf

BISHOPS OF HEXHAM

664 Wilfrith
678 Eata
681 Tunberht
684 Cuthbert
685 Eata (restored)
687 John of Beverley
709 Acca
734 Frithoberht
767 Ahimund
781 Tilberht
789 Æthelberht
797 Heardred
800 Eanberht
813 Tidferth

BISHOPS OF CHESTER-LE-STREET[1]

899 Eardwulf
899 Cutheard
915 Tilred
925 Wigred
944 Uhtred
944 Seaxhelm
944 Ealdred
968 Ælfsige
990 Aldhun

BISHOPS OF DURHAM

990 Aldhun d. 1018
    [See vacant 1018–1020]
1020 Edmund
c.1040 Eadred
1041 Æthelric
1056 Æthelwine
1071 Walcher
1081 William of Saint Calais
1099 Ralph [Ranulf] Flambard
1133 Geoffrey Rufus
1143 William of Sainte-Barbe
1153 Hugh of le Puiset
1197 Philip of Poitiers
1217 Richard Marsh
1228 Richard Poore
1241 Nicholas Farnham
1249 Walter Kirkham
1261 Robert Stichill
1274 Robert of Holy Island
1284 Anthony Bek
1311 Richard Kellaw
1318 Lewis de Beaumont
1333 Richard of Bury
1345 Thomas Hatfield
1382 John Fordham
1388 Walter Skirlaw
1406 Thomas Langley
1438 Robert Nevill
1457 Lawrence Booth
1476 William Dudley
1485 John Shirwood
1494 Richard Fox
1502 William Senhouse
    [Sever]
1507 Christopher
    Bainbridge
1509 Thomas Ruthall
1523 Thomas Wolsey
1530 Cuthbert Tunstall
1561 James Pilkington
1577 Richard Barnes
1589 Matthew Hutton

1595 Tobias Matthew
1606 William James
1617 Richard Neile
1628 George Monteigne
    [Mountain]
1628 John Howson
1632 Thomas Morton
1660 John Cosin
1674 Nathaniel Crew
    [Lord Crew]
1721 William Talbot
1730 Edward Chandler
1750 Joseph Butler
1752 Richard Trevor
1771 John Egerton
1787 Thomas Thurlow
1791 Shute Barrington
1826 William Van Mildert
1836 Edward Maltby
1856 Charles Thomas Longley
1860 Henry Montagu Villiers
1861 Charles Baring
1879 Joseph Barber Lightfoot
1890 Brooke Foss Westcott
1901 Handley Carr Glyn
    Moule
1920 Herbert Hensley Henson
1939 Alwyn Terrell Petre
    Williams
1952 Arthur Michael Ramsey
1956 Maurice Henry Harland
1966 Ian Thomas Ramsey
1973 John Stapylton Habgood
1984 David Edward Jenkins
1994 Anthony Michael Arnold
    Turnbull
2003 Nicholas Thomas Wright

Blackburn

Description of arms. Per fess gules and
or, in chief two keys in saltire wards
downwards argent, in base a rose of
the first barbed and seeded proper.

1926 Percy Mark Herbert
1942 Wilfred Marcus Askwith
1954 Walter Hubert Baddeley
1960 Charles Robert Claxton
1972 Robert Arnold Schürhoff
    Martineau
1982 David Stewart Cross
1989 Alan David Chesters
2004 Nicholas Stewart Reade

Bradford

Description of arms. Azure, two keys in
saltire or, in chief a woolpack proper
corded gold.

1920 Arthur William Thomson
    Perowne
1931 Alfred Walter Frank Blunt
1956 Frederick Donald Coggan
1961 Clement George St Michael
    Parker
1972 Ross Sydney Hook
1981 Geoffrey John Paul
1984 Robert Kerr Williamson
1992 David James Smith
2002 David Charles James

Carlisle

Description of arms. Argent, on a
cross sable a labelled mitre or.

1133 Æthelwulf
1203 Bernard
1219 Hugh of Beaulieu
1224 Walter Mauclerc
1247 Silvester Everdon
1255 Thomas Vipont
1258 Robert de Chause
1280 Ralph Ireton
1292 John of Halton
1325 John Ross
1332 John Kirkby
1353 Gilbert Welton
1363 Thomas Appleby
1396 Robert Reade
1397 Thomas Merks
1400 William Strickland
1420 Roger Whelpdale
1424 William Barrow
1430 Marmaduke Lumley
1450 Nicholas Close
1452 William Percy
1462 John Kingscote
1464 Richard le Scrope
1468 Edward Story
1478 Richard Bell
1496 William Senhouse
    [Sever]
1504 Roger Layburne
1508 John Penny
1521 John Kite
1537 Robert Aldrich
1556 Owen Oglethorpe

---

[1] See transferred to Durham 995.

1561 John Best
1570 Richard Barnes
1577 John May
1598 Henry Robinson
1616 Robert Snowden
1621 Richard Milbourne
1624 Richard Senhouse
1626 Francis White
1629 Barnabas Potter
1642 James Ussher
1660 Richard Sterne
1664 Edward Rainbowe
1684 Thomas Smith
1702 William Nicolson
1718 Samuel Bradford
1723 John Waugh
1735 George Fleming
1747 Richard Osbaldeston
1762 Charles Lyttleton
1769 Edmund Law
1787 John Douglas
1791 Edward Venables Vernon
        [Harcourt]
1808 Samuel Goodenough
1827 Hugh Percy
1856 Henry Montagu Villiers
1860 Samuel Waldegrave
1869 Harvey Goodwin
1892 John Wareing Bardsley
1905 John William Diggle
1920 Henry Herbert Williams
1946 Thomas Bloomer
1966 Sydney Cyril Bulley
1972 Henry David Halsey
1989 Ian Harland
2000 Geoffrey Graham Dow
2009 James William Scobie
        Newcome

Chester

Description of arms. Gules, three labelled mitres or.

1541 John Bird
1554 George Cotes
1556 Cuthbert Scott
1561 William Downham
1579 William Chaderton
1595 Hugh Bellott
1597 Richard Vaughan
1604 George Lloyd
1616 Thomas Morton
1619 John Bridgeman
1660 Brian Walton
1662 Henry Ferne
1662 George Hall
1668 John Wilkins
1673 John Pearson
1686 Thomas Cartwright
1689 Nicolas Stratford
1708 William Dawes
1714 Francis Gastrell
1726 Samuel Peploe
1752 Edmund Keene
1771 William Markham
1777 Beilby Porteus
1788 William Cleaver
1800 Henry William Majendie

1810 Bowyer Edward Sparke
1812 George Henry Law
1824 Charles James Blomfield
1828 John Bird Sumner
1848 John Graham
1865 William Jacobson
1884 William Stubbs
1889 Francis John Jayne
1919 Henry Luke Paget
1932 Geoffrey Francis Fisher
1939 Douglas Henry Crick
1955 Gerald Alexander Ellison
1974 Hubert Victor Whitsey
1982 Michael Alfred Baughen
1996 Peter Robert Forster

Liverpool

Description of arms. Argent, an eagle with wings expanded sable, holding in its dexter claw an ancient inkhorn proper, around its head a nimbus or, a chief paly azure and gules, the dexter charged with an open book or, inscribed with the words 'Thy Word is Truth', the sinister charged with a lymphad gold.

1880 John Charles Ryle
1900 Francis James Chavasse
1923 Albert Augustus David
1944 Clifford Arthur Martin
1966 Stuart Yarworth Blanch
1975 David Stuart Sheppard
1998 James Stuart Jones

Manchester

Description of arms. Or, on a pale engrailed gules three mitres of the first, on a canton of the second three bendlets enhanced gold.

1848 James Prince Lee
1870 James Fraser
1886 James Moorhouse
1903 Edmund Arbuthnott Knox
1921 William Temple
1929 Frederic Sumpter Guy
        Warman
1947 William Derrick Lindsay
        Greer
1970 Patrick Campbell Rodger
1979 Stanley Eric Francis Booth-
        Clibborn
1993 Christopher John
        Mayfield
2002 Nigel Simeon McCulloch

Newcastle

Description of arms. Gules, a cross between four lions rampant or, on a chief gold three triple-towered castles of the first.

1882 Ernest Roland Wilberforce
1896 Edgar Jacob
1903 Arthur Thomas Lloyd
1907 Norman Dumenil John
        Straton
1915 Herbert Louis Wild
1927 Harold Ernest Bilbrough
1941 Noel Baring Hudson
1957 Hugh Edward Ashdown
1973 Ronald Oliver Bowlby
1981 Andrew Alexander Kenny
        Graham
1997 John Martin Wharton

Ripon and Leeds
(Ripon until 1999)

Description of arms. Argent, on a saltire gules two keys wards upwards or, on a chief of the second a Holy Lamb proper.

*c.*678 Eadheath

NEW FOUNDATION

1836 Charles Thomas Longley
1857 Robert Bickersteth
1884 William Boyd Carpenter
1912 Thomas Wortley Drury
1920 Thomas Banks Strong
1926 Edward Arthur Burroughs
1935 Geoffrey Charles Lester
        Lunt
1946 George Armitage Chase
1959 John Richard Humpidge
        Moorman
1975 Stuart Hetley Price
1977 David Nigel de Lorentz
        Young
2000 John Richard Packer

Sheffield

Description of arms. Azure, a crosier in
pale ensigned by a fleur-de-lis vert,
between in fess a key surmounted by a
sword in saltire to the dexter, and to the
sinister eight arrows interlaced and
banded saltirewise, all or.

1914 Leonard Hedley Burrows
1939 Leslie Stannard Hunter
1962 Francis John Taylor
1971 William Gordon Fallows
1980 David Ramsay Lunn
1997 John Nicholls
2009 Steven John Lindsey Croft

Sodor and Man[1]

Description of arms. Argent, upon a
pedestal between two coronetted
pillars the Virgin Mary with arms
extended, in her dexter hand a church
proper and in base upon an
escutcheon, surmounted by a mitre,
the arms of Man – viz. gules, three legs
in armour conjoined at the thigh and
flexed at the knee.

  447 Germanus
        Conindrius
        Romulus
        Machutus
        Conanus
        Contentus
        Baldus
        Malchus
        Torkinus
        Brendanus
[Before 1080 Roolwer]
        William
        Hamond
1113 Wimund
1151 John
1160 Gamaliel
        Ragnald
        Christian of Argyle
        Michael

1203 Nicholas de Meaux
        Nicholas II
1217 Reginald
1226 John
1229 Simon of Argyle
1252 Richard
1275 Mark of Galloway
1305 Alan
1321 Gilbert Maclelan
1329 Bernard de Linton
1334 Thomas
1348 William Russell
1387 John Donegan
1387 Michael
1392 John Sproten
1402 Conrad
1402 Theodore Bloc
1429 Richard Messing Andrew
1435 John Seyre
1455 Thomas Burton
1458 Thomas Kirklam
1472 Angus
1478 Richard Oldham
1487 Hugh Blackleach
1513 Hugh Hesketh
1523 John Howden
1546 Henry Man
1556 Thomas Stanley
1570 John Salisbury
1576 John Meyrick
1600 George Lloyd
1605 John Philips
1634 William Forster
1635 Richard Parr
1661 Samuel Rutter
1663 Isaac Barrow
1671 Henry Bridgman
1683 John Lake
1685 Baptist Levinz
1698 Thomas Wilson
1755 Mark Hildesley
1773 Richard Richmond
1780 George Mason
1784 Claudius Crigan
1814 George Murray
1828 William Ward
1838 James Bowstead
1840 Henry Pepys
1841 Thomas Vowler Short
1847 Walter Augustus Shirley
1847 Robert John Eden
1854 Horatio Powys
1877 Rowley Hill
1887 John Wareing Bardsley
1892 Norman Dumenil John
        Straton
1907 Thomas Wortley Drury
1912 James Denton Thompson
1925 Charles Leonard Thornton-
        Duesbery
1928 William Stanton Jones
1943 John Ralph Strickland
        Taylor
1954 Benjamin Pollard
1966 George Eric Gordon
1974 Vernon Sampson Nicholls
1983 Arthur Henry Attwell
1989 Noël Debroy Jones

2003 Graeme Paul Knowles
2008 Robert Mar Erskine Paterson

Southwell and Nottingham
(Southwell until 2005)

Description of arms. Sable, three
fountains proper, on a chief or a pale
azure, charged with a representation
of the Virgin Mary seated bearing the
Infant Christ or between a stag lodged
proper and two staves raguly crossed
vert.

1884 George Ridding
1904 Edwyn Hoskyns
1926 Bernard Oliver Francis
        Heywood
1928 Henry Mosley
1941 Frank Russell Barry
1964 Gordon David Savage
1970 John Denis Wakeling
1985 Michael Humphrey Dickens
        Whinney
1988 Patrick Burnet Harris
1999 George Henry Cassidy
2009 Paul Roger Butler

Wakefield

Description of arms. Or, a fleur-de-lis
azure, on a chief of the last three
celestial crowns gold.

1888 William Walsham How
1897 George Rodney Eden
1928 James Buchanan Seaton
1938 Campbell Richard Hone
1946 Henry McGowan
1949 Roger Plumpton Wilson
1958 John Alexander Ramsbotham
1968 Eric Treacy
1977 Colin Clement Walter James
1985 David Michael Hope
1992 Nigel Simeon McCulloch
2003 Stephen George Platten

---

[1] Included in the province of York by Act of Parliament 1542. Prior to Richard Oldham there is some uncertainty as to several names and
dates. From 1425 to 1553 there was an English and Scottish succession. It is not easy to say which claimant was Bishop either *de jure* or *de facto*.

BISHOPS SUFFRAGAN IN ENGLAND

Aston (Birmingham)

1954 Clement George St Michael
    Parker
1962 David Brownfield Porter
1972 Mark Green
1982 Michael Humphrey Dickens
    Whinney
1985 Colin Ogilvie Buchanan
1989–92 *no appointment*
1992 John Michael Austin
2005–2008 *no appointment*
2008 Andrew John Watson

Barking (Chelmsford)

[in St Albans diocese to 1914]

1901 Thomas Stevens
1919 James Theodore Inskip
1948 Hugh Rowlands Gough
1959 William Frank Percival
    Chadwick
1975 Albert James Adams
1983 James William Roxburgh
1991 Roger Frederick Sainsbury
2002 David John Leader Hawkins

Barrow-in-Furness (Carlisle)

1889 Henry Ware
1909 Campbell West-Watson
1926 Henry Sidney Pelham
1944 *in abeyance*

Basingstoke (Winchester)

1973 Colin Clement Walter
    James
1977 Michael Richard John
    Manktelow
1994 Douglas Geoffrey
    Rowell
2002 Trevor Willmott

Bedford (St Albans)

1537 John Hodgkins[1]
1560–1879 *in abeyance*
1879 William Walsham How[2]
1888 Robert Claudius Billing[3]
1898–1935 *in abeyance*
1935 James Lumsden Barkway
1939 Aylmer Skelton
1948 Claude Thomas Thellusson
    Wood
1953 Angus Campbell MacInnes
1957 Basil Tudor Guy
1963 Albert John Trillo
1968 John Tyrrell Holmes Hare
1977 Andrew Alexander Kenny
    Graham
1981 David John Farmbrough
1994 John Henry Richardson
2003 Richard Neil Inwood

Berwick (Durham)

1536 Thomas Sparke
1572 *in abeyance*

Beverley (York)

1889 Robert Jarratt Crosthwaite
1923–94 *in abeyance*
1994 John Scott Gaisford
2000 Martyn William Jarrett

Birkenhead (Chester)

1965 Eric Arthur John Mercer
1974 Ronald Brown
1993 Michael Laurence
    Langrish
2000 David Andrew Urquhart
2007 Gordon Keith Sinclair

Bolton (Manchester)

1984 David George Galliford
1991 David Bonser
1999 David Keith Gillett
2008 Christopher Paul Edmondson

Bradwell (Chelmsford)

1968 William Neville Welch
1973 John Gibbs
1976 Charles Derek Bond
1993 Laurence Alexander Green

Bristol (Worcester)

1538 Henry Holbeach [Rands]
1542 *became diocesan see*

Brixworth (Peterborough)

1989 Paul Everard Barber
2002 Francis White

Buckingham (Oxford)

1914 Edward Domett Shaw
1921 Philip Herbert Eliot
1944 Robert Milton Hay
1960 Gordon David Savage
1964 George Christopher Cutts
    Pepys
1974 Simon Hedley Burrows
1994 Colin James Bennetts
1998 Michael Arthur Hill
2003 Alan Thomas Lawrence
    Wilson

Burnley (Blackburn)

[in Manchester diocese to 1926]

1901 Edwyn Hoskyns
1905 Alfred Pearson
1909 Henry Henn
1931 Edgar Priestley Swain
1950 Charles Keith Kipling Prosser
1955 George Edward Holderness
1970 Richard Charles Challinor
    Watson
1988 Ronald James Milner
1994 Martyn William Jarrett
2000 John William Goddard

Colchester (Chelmsford)

[in London diocese to 1845
in Rochester diocese to 1877
in St Albans diocese 1877–1914]

1536 William More
1541–91 *in abeyance*
1592 John Sterne
1608–1882 *in abeyance*
1882 Alfred Blomfield
1894 Henry Frank Johnson
1909 Robert Henry Whitcombe
1922 Thomas Alfred Chapman

1933 Charles Henry Ridsdale
1946 Frederick Dudley Vaughan
    Narborough
1966 Roderic Norman Coote
1988 Michael Edwin Vickers
1995 Edward Holland
2001 Christopher Heudebourck
    Morgan

Coventry (Worcester)

see also under Lichfield

1891 Henry Bond Bowlby
1894 Edmund Arbuthnott Knox
1903–18 *no appointment*
1918 *became diocesan see*

Crediton (Exeter)

1897 Robert Edward Trefusis
1930 William Frederick Surtees
1954 Wilfred Arthur Edmund
    Westall
1974 Philip John Pasterfield
1984 Peter Everard Coleman
1996 Richard Stephen Hawkins
2004 Robert John Scott Evens

Croydon (Southwark)

(in Canterbury diocese to 1985)

1904 Henry Horace Pereira
1924–30 *no appointment*
1930 Edward Sydney Woods
1937 William Louis Anderson
1942 Maurice Henry Harland
1947 Cuthbert Killick Norman
    Bardsley
1957 John Taylor Hughes
1977 Geoffrey Stuart Snell
1985 Wilfred Denniston Wood
2003 Nicholas Baines

Derby (Southwell)

1889 Edward Ash Were
1909 Charles Thomas Abraham
1927 *became diocesan see*

Doncaster (Sheffield)

1972 Stuart Hetley Price
1976 David Stewart Cross
1982 William Michael Dermot
    Persson
1993 Michael Frederick Gear
2000 Cyril Guy Ashton

Dorchester (Oxford)

see also under Dorchester (*diocesan
see) and* Lincoln

1939 Gerald Burton Allen
1952 Kenneth Riches
1957 David Goodwin Loveday
1972 Peter Knight Walker
1979 Conrad John Eustace Meyer
1988 Anthony John Russell
2000 Colin William Fletcher

Dorking (Guildford)

[in Winchester diocese to 1927]

1905 Cecil Henry Boutflower
1909–68 *in abeyance*
1968 Kenneth Dawson Evans

---

[1] Appointed for the diocese of London.   [2] Appointed for the diocese of London.
[3] Appointed for the diocese of London, and retained title after resigning his suffragan duties in 1895.

1986 David Peter Wilcox
1996 Ian James Brackley

Dover (Canterbury)

1537 Richard Yngworth
1545 Richard Thornden
1557–69 *no appointment*
1569 Richard Rogers
1597–1870 *in abeyance*
1870 Edward Parry
1890 George Rodney Eden
1898 William Walsh
1916 Harold Ernest Bilbrough
1927 John Victor Macmillan
1935 Alfred Careywollaston Rose
1957 Lewis Evan Meredith
1964 Anthony Paul Tremlett
1980 Richard Henry McPhail
       Third
1992 John Richard Allan Llewellin
1999 Stephen Squires Venner

Dudley (Worcester)

1974 Michael Ashley Mann
1977 Anthony Charles Dumper
1993 Rupert William Noel Hoare
2000 David Stuart Walker

Dunwich (St Edmundsbury and Ipswich)

see also under Norwich

1934 Maxwell Homfray Maxwell-
       Gumbleton
1945 Clement Mallory Ricketts
1955 Thomas Herbert Cashmore
1967 David Rokeby Maddock
1977 William Johnston
1980 Eric Nash Devenport
1992 Jonathan Sansbury Bailey
1995 Timothy John Stevens
1999 Clive Young

Ebbsfleet (Canterbury)

1994 John Richards
1998 Michael Alan Houghton
2000 Andrew Burnham

Edmonton (London)

1970 Alan Francis Bright Rogers
1975 William John Westwood
1985 Brian John Masters
1999 Peter William Wheatley

Europe (Europe)

1980 Ambrose Walter Marcus
       Weekes
1986 Edward Holland
1995 Henry William Scriven
2002 David Hamid

Fulham (London)[1]

1926 Basil Staunton Batty
1947 William Marshall Selwyn
1949 George Ernest Ingle
1955 Robert Wright Stopford
1957 Roderic Norman Coote
1966 Alan Francis Bright Rogers

1970 John Richard Satterthwaite[2]
1980–1982 *no appointment*
1982 Brian John Masters
1985 Charles John Klyberg
1996 John Charles Broadhurst

Grantham (Lincoln)

1905 Welbore MacCarthy
1920 John Edward Hine
1930 Ernest Morell Blackie
1935 Arthur Ivan Greaves
1937 Algernon Augustus Markham
1949 Anthony Otter
1965 Ross Sydney Hook
1972 Dennis Gascoyne Hawker
1987 William Ind
1997 Alastair Lewellyn John Redfern
2006 Timothy William Ellis

Grimsby (Lincoln)

1935 Ernest Morell Blackie
1937 Anhur Ivan Greaves
1958 Kenneth Healey
1966 Gerald Fitzmaurice Colin
1979 David Tustin
2000 David Douglas James Rossdale

Guildford (Winchester)

1874 John Sutton Utterton
1888 George Henry Sumner
1909 John Hugh Granville
       Randolph
1927 *became diocesan see*

Hertford (St Albans)

1968 Albert John Trillo
1971 Hubert Victor Whitsey
1974 Peter Mumford
1982 Kenneth Harold Pillar
1990 Robin Jonathan Norman
       Smith
2001 Christopher Richard James
       Foster

Horsham (Chichester)

1968 Simon Wilton Phipps
1975 Ivor Colin Docker
1991 John William Hind
1993 Lindsay Goodall Urwin
2009 Mark Crispin Rake Sowerby

Hull (York)

1538 Robert Sylvester (Pursglove)
1579–1891 *in abeyance*
1891 Richard Frederick Lefevre
       Blunt
1910 John Augustus Kempthome
1913 Francis Gurdon
1929–31 *no appointment*
1931 Bemard Oliver Francis
       Heywood
1934 Henry Townsend Vodden
1957 George Fredenck Townley
1965 Hubert Laurence Higgs
1977 Geoffrey John Paul
1981 Donald George Snelgrove
1994 James Stuart Jones

1998 Richard Michael Cockayne
       Frith

Hulme (Manchester)

1924 John Charles Hill
1930 Thomas Sherwood Jones
1945 Hugh Leycester Homby
1953 Kenneth Venner Ramsey
1975 David George Galliford
1984 Colin John Fraser Scott
1999 Stephen Richard Lowe

Huntingdon (Ely)

1966 Robert Arnold Schürhoff
       Martineau
1972 Eric St Quintin Wall
1980 William Gordon Roe
1997 John Robert Flack
2003 John Geoffrey Inge
2008 David Thomson

Ipswich (Norwich)

1536 Thomas Manning[3]
?–1899 *in abeyance*[4]
1899 George Carnac Fisher
1906 Henry Luke Paget
1909 *no appointment*
1914 *became diocesan see with*
       St Edmundsbury

Islington (London)

1898 Charles Henry Turner
1923 *in abeyance*

Jarrow (Durham)

1906 George Nickson
1914 John Nathaniel Quirk
1924 Samuel Kirshbaum Knight
1932 James Geoffrey Gordon
1939 Leslie Owen
1944 David Colin Dunlop
1950 John Alexander Ramsbotham
1958 Mervyn Armstrong
1965 Alexander Kenneth
       Hamilton
1980 Michael Thomas Ball
1990 Alan Smithson
2002 John Lawrence Pritchard
2007 Mark Watts Bryant

Kensington (London)

1901 Frederic Edward Ridgeway
1911 John Primatt Maud
1932 Bertram Fitzgerald Simpson
1942 Henry Colville Montgomery
       Campbell
1949 Cyril Eastaugh
1962 Edward James Keymer
       Roberts
1964 Ronald Cedric Osbourne
       Goodchild
1981 Mark Santer
1987 John George Hughes
1994–96 *no appointment*
1996 Michael John Colclough
2009 Paul Gavin Williams

---

[1] From 1926 to 1980 exercised the Bishop of London's extra-diocesan jurisdiction over chaplaincies in Northern and Central Europe. Since 1996 has assisted the Diocesan Bishop in all matters not delegated to the Areas, and in pastoral care of parishes operating under the London Plan.
[2] Bishop of Fulham and Gibraltar.
[3] Manning does not appear to have acted as a suffragan bishop in the diocese of Norwich.
[4] The date of Manning's death is not known.

Kingston-upon-Thames (Southwark)

1905 Cecil Hook
1915 Samuel Mumford Taylor
1922 Percy Mark Herbert
1927 Frederick Ochterlony Taylor Hawkes
1952 William Percy Gilpin
1970 Hugh William Montefiore
1978 Keith Norman Sutton
1984 Peter Stephen Maurice Selby
1992 John Martin Wharton
1997 Peter Bryan Price
2002 Richard Ian Cheetham

Knaresborough (Ripon)

1905 Lucius Frederick Moses Bottomley Smith
1934 Paul Fulcrand Dalacour de Labilliere
1938 John Norman Bateman-Champain
1948 Henry Handley Vully de Candole
1965 John Howard Cruse
1972 Ralph Emmerson
1979 John Dennis
1986 Malcolm James Menin
1997 Frank Valentine Weston
2004 James Harold Bell

Lancaster (Blackburn)

1936 Benjamin Pollard
1955 Anthony Leigh Egerton Hoskyns-Abrahall
1975 Dennis Fountain Page
1985 Ian Harland
1990 John Nicholls
1998 Geoffrey Stephen Pedley
2006 Geoffrey Seagrave Pearson
2008 Mark Davies

Leicester (Peterborough)

see also under Lichfield *and* Lincoln

1888 Francis Henry Thicknesse
1903 Lewis Clayton
1913 Norman MacLeod Lang
1927 *became diocesan see*

Lewes (Chichester)

1909 Leonard Hedley Burrows
1914 Herbert Edward Jones
1920 Henry Kemble Southwell
1926 Thomas William Cook
1929 William Champion Streatfield
1929 Hugh Maudsley Hordern
1946 Geoffrey Hodgson Warde
1959 James Herbert Lloyd Morrell
1977 Peter John Ball
1992 Ian Patrick Martyn Cundy
1997 Wallace Parke Benn

Ludlow (Hereford)

1981 Stanley Mark Wood
1987 Ian Macdonald Griggs
1994 John Charles Saxbee
2002 Michael Wrenford Hooper
2009 Alistair James Magowan

Lynn (Norwich)

1963 William Somers Llewellyn
1972 William Aubrey Aitken
1986 David Edward Bentley
1994 David John Conner
1999 Anthony Charles Foottit
2004 James Henry Langstaff

Maidstone (Canterbury)

1944 Leslie Owen
1946–56 *no appointment*
1956 Stanley Woodley Betts
1966–69 *no appointment*
1969 Geoffrey Lewis Tiarks
1976 Richard Henry McPhail Third
1980 Robert Maynard Hardy
1987 David James Smith
1992 Gavin Hunter Reid
2001 Graham Alan Cray

Malmesbury (Bristol)

1927 Ronald Erskine Ramsay
1946 Ivor Stanley Watkins
1956 Edward James Keymer Roberts
1962 Clifford Leofric Purdy Bishop
1973 Frederick Stephen Temple
1983 Peter James Firth
1994 *renamed* Swindon

Marlborough

1537 Thomas Morley (Bickley)[1]
c1561–1888 *in abeyance*
1888 Alfred Earle[2]
1919 *in abeyance*

Middleton (Manchester)

1927 Richard Godfrey Parsons
1932 Cecil Wilfred Wilson
1938 Arthur Fawssett Alston
1943 Edward Worsfold Mowll
1952 Frank Woods
1958 Robert Nelson
1959 Edward Ralph Wickham
1982 Donald Alexander Tytler
1994 Stephen Squires Venner
1999 Michael Augustine Owen Lewis

Nottingham (Lincoln)

[in York diocese to 1837]

1567 Richard Barnes
1570–1870 *in abeyance*
1870 Henry Mackenzie
1877 Edward Trollope
1893 *in abeyance*

Penrith (Carlisle)

see also under Richmond

1537 John Bird[3]
1539–1888 *in abeyance*
1888 John James Pulleine[4]
1939 Grandage Edwards Powell
1944 Herbert Victor Turner
1959 Sydney Cyril Bulley
1967 Reginald Foskett

Plymouth (Exeter)

1923 John Howard Bertram Masterman
1934 Francis Whitfield Daukes
1950 Norman Harry Clarke
1962 Wilfred Guy Sanderson
1972 Richard Fox Cartwright
1982 Kenneth Albert Newing
1988 Richard Stephen Hawkins
1996 John Henry Garton
2005 John Frank Ford

Pontefract (Wakefield)

1931 Campbell Richard Hone
1939 Tom Longworth
1949 Arthur Harold Morris
1954 George William Clarkson
1961 Eric Treacy
1968 William Gordon Fallows
1971 Thomas Richard Hare
1993 John Thornley Finney
1998 David Charles James
2002 Anthony William Robinson

Ramsbury (Salisbury)

see also under Salisbury

1974 John Robert Geoffrey Neale
1989 Peter St George Vaughan
1999 Peter Fearnley Hullah
2006 Stephen David Conway

Reading (Oxford)

1889 James Leslie Randall
1909–42 *in abeyance*
1942 Arthur Groom Parham
1954 Eric Henry Knell
1972 Eric Wild
1982 Ronald Graham Gregory Foley
1989 John Frank Ewan Bone
1997 Edward William Murray Walker
2004 Stephen Geoffrey Cottrell

Repton (Derby)

1965 William Warren Hunt
1977 Stephen Edmund Verney
1986 Francis Henry Arthur Richmond
1999 David Christopher Hawtin
2007 Humphrey Ivo John Southern

Richborough (Canterbury)

1995 Edwin Ronald Barnes
2002 Keith Newton

Richmond (Ripon)

1889 John James Pulleine[5]
1913 Francis Charles Kilner
1921 *in abeyance*

Pugh, William Edward Augustus

1970 William Edward Augustus Pugh
1979 George Lanyon Hacker
1994 Richard Garrard
2002 James William Scobie Newcome

---

[1] Appointed for the diocese of London.
[2] Appointed for the diocese of London, but retained the title while Dean of Exeter 1900-18.
[3] Appointed for the diocese of Lichfield.
[4] Appointed for the diocese of Ripon.
[5] His suffragan title was changed from Penrith to Richmond by Royal Warrant.

St Germans (Truro)

1905 John Rundle Cornish
1918–74 *in abeyance*
1974 Cecil Richard Rutt
1979 Reginald Lindsay Fisher
1985 John Richard Allan Llewellin
1993 Graham Richard James
2000 Royden Screech

Selby (York)

1939 Henry St John Stirling
      Woollcombe
1941 Carey Frederick Knyvett
1962 Douglas Noel Sargent
1972 Morris Henry St John
      Maddocks
1983 Clifford Conder Barker
1991 Humphrey Vincent Taylor
2003 Martin William Wallace

Shaftesbury (Salisbury)

[in Bristol diocese 1542–1836]

1539 John Bradley
? *in abeyance*[1]

Sheffield (York)

1901 John Nathaniel Quirk
1914 *became diocesan see*

Sherborne (Salisbury)

1925 Robert Crowther Abbott
1928 Gerald Burton Allen
1936 Harold Nickinson Rodgers
1947 John Maurice Key
1960 Victor Joseph Pike
1976 John Dudley Galtrey Kirkham
2001 Timothy Martin Thornton
2009 Graham Ralph Kings

Sherwood (Southwell)

1965 Kenneth George Thompson
1975 Harold Richard Darby
1989 Alan Wyndham Morgan
2006 Anthony Porter

Shrewsbury (Lichfield)

1537 Lewis Thomas[2]
1561–1888 *in abeyance*
1888 Sir Lovelace Tomlinson
      Stamer
1905–40 *in abeyance*
1940 Eric Knightley Chetwode
      Hamilton
1944 Robert Leighton Hodson
1959 William Alonzo Parker
1970 Francis William Cocks
1980 Leslie Lloyd Rees
1987 John Dudley Davies
1994 David Marrison Hallatt
2001 Alan Gregory Clayton Smith
2009 Mark James Rylands

Southampton (Winchester)

1895 William Awdry
1896 George Carnac Fisher
1898 The Hon Arthur Temple
      Lyttelton
1903 James Macarthur
1921 Cecil Henry Boutflower
1933 Arthur Baillie Lumsdaine
      Karney

1943 Edmund Robert Morgan
1951 Kenneth Edward Norman
      Lamplugh
1972 John Kingsmill Cavell
1984 Edward David Cartwright
1989 John Freeman Perry
1996 Jonathan Michael Gledhill
2004 Paul Roger Butler

Southwark (Rochester)

1891 Huyshe Wolcott Yeatman-
      Biggs
1905 *became diocesan see*

Stafford (Lichfield)

1909 Edward Ash Were
1915 Lionel Payne Crawfurd
1934 Douglas Henry Crick
1938 Lemprière Durell Hammond
1958 Richard George Clitherow
1975 John Waine
1979 John Stevens Waller
1987 Michael Charles Scott-Joynt
1996 Christopher John Hill
2005 Alfred Gordon Mursell

Stepney (London)

1895 George Forrest Browne
1897 Arthur Foley Winnington-
      Ingram
1901 Cosmo Gordon Lang
1909 Henry Luke Paget
1919 Henry Mosley
1928 Charles Edward Curzon
1936 Robert Hamilton Moberly
1952 Joost de Blank
1957 Francis Evered Lunt
1968 Ernest Urban Trevor
      Huddleston
1978 James Lawton Thompson
1992 Richard John Carew Chartres
1996 John Mugabi Sentamu
2003 Stephen John Oliver

Stockport (Chester)

1949 Frank Jackson Okell
1951 David Henry Saunders
      Saunders-Davies
1965 Rupert Gordon Strutt
1984 Frank Pilkington Sargeant
1994 Geoffrey Martin Turner
2000 William Nigel Stock
2008 Robert Ronald Atwell

Swindon (Bristol)

1994 Michael David Doe
2005 Lee Stephen Rayfield

Taunton (Bath and Wells)

1538 William Finch
1559–1911 *in abeyance*
1911 Charles Fane de Salis
1931 George Arthur Hollis
1945 Harry Thomas
1955 Mark Allin Hodson
1962 Francis Horner West
1977 Peter John Nott
1986 Nigel Simeon McCulloch
1992 John Hubert Richard Lewis
1997 William Allen Stewart
1998 Andrew John Radford
2006 Peter David Maurice

Tewkesbury (Gloucester)

1938 Augustine John Hodson
1955 Edward Barry Henderson
1960 Forbes Trevor Horan
1973 Thomas Carlyle Joseph
      Robert Hamish Deakin
1986 Geoffrey David Jeremy
      Walsh
1996 John Stewart Went

Thetford (Norwich)

see also under Norwich

1536 John Salisbury
1570–1894 *in abeyance*
1894 Arthur Thomas Lloyd
1903 John Philips Alcott Bowers
1926–45 *no appointment*
1945 John Walker Woodhouse
1953 Manin Patrick Grainge
      Leonard
1963 Eric William Bradley
      Cordingly
1977 Hugh Charles Blackburne
1981 Timothy Dudley-Smith
1992 Hugo Ferdinand de Waal
2001 David John Atkinson
2009 Alan Peter Winton

Tonbridge (Rochester)

1959 Russell Berridge White
1968 Henry David Halsey
1973 Philip Harold Ernest
      Goodrich
1982 David Henry Bartleet
1993 Brian Arthur Smith
2002 Brian Colin Castle

Warrington (Liverpool)

1918 Martin Linton Smith
1920 Edwin Hone Kempson
1927 Herbert Gresford Jones
1946 Charles Robert Claxton
1960 Laurence Ambrose Brown
1970 John Monier Bickersteth
1976 Michael Henshall
1996 John Richard Packer
2000 David Wilfred Michael
      Jennings

Warwick (Coventry)

1980 Keith Appleby Arnold
1990 Clive Handford
1996 Anthony Martin Priddis
2005 John Ronald Angus Stroyan

Whalley (Blackburn)

[in Manchester diocese to 1926]

1909 Atherton Gwillym Rawstorne
1936 *in abeyance*

Whitby (York)

1923 Harry St John Stirling
      Woollcombe
1939 Harold Evelyn Hubbard
1947 Walter Hubert Baddeley
1954 Philip William Wheeldon
1961 George D'Oyly Snow
1972 John Yates
1976 Clifford Conder Barker
1983 Gordon Bates
1999 Robert Sidney Ladds

---

[1] The date of Bradley's death is not known.
[2] Not appointed for Lichfield, but probably for Llandaff.

Willesden (London)

1911 William Willcox Perrin
1929 Guy Vernon Smith
1940 Henry Colville Montgomery
Campbell
1942 Edward Michael Gresford
Jones
1950 Gerald Alexander Ellison
1955 George Ernest Ingle
1964 Graham Douglas Leonard
1974 Geoffrey Hewlett Thompson
1985 Thomas Frederick Butler

1992 Geoffrey Graham Dow
2001 Peter Alan Broadbent

Wolverhampton (Lichfield)

1979 Barry Rogerson
1985 Christopher John Mayfield
1994 Michael Gay Bourke
2007 Clive Malcolm Gregory

Woolwich (Southwark)

1905 John Cox Leeke

1918 William Woodcock
Hough
1932 Arthur Llewellyn Preston
1936 Leslie Hamilton Lang
1947 Robert William Stannard
1959 John Arthur Thomas
Robinson
1969 David Stuart Sheppard
1975 Michael Eric Marshall
1984 Albert Peter Hall
1996 Colin Ogilvie Buchanan
2005 Christopher Thomas James
Chessun

WALES

Archbishops of Wales

1920 Alfred George Edwards
(St Asaph 1889–1934)
1934 Charles Alfred Howell Green
(Bangor 1928–44)
1944 David Lewis Prosser
(St Davids 1927–50)
1949 John Morgan (Llandaff
1939–57)
1957 Alfred Edwin Morris
(Monmouth 1945–67)
1968 William Glyn Hughes Simon
(Llandaff 1957–71)
1971 Gwilym Owen Williams
(Bangor 1957–82)
1983 Derrick Greenslade
Childs (Monmouth
1972–87)
1987 George Noakes (St Davids
1982–91)
1991 Alwyn Rice Jones (St Asaph
1982–99)
1999 Rowan Douglas Williams
(Monmouth 1992–2002)
2003 Barry Cennydd Morgan
(Llandaff 1999–)

Bangor[1]

Description of arms. Gules, a bend or
guttée de poix between two mullets
pierced argent.

c.550 Deiniol [Daniel]
c.775 Elfod [Elbodugen]
1092 Herve
[*Vacancy* 1109–20]
1120 David the Scot
1140 Maurice (Meurig)
[*Vacancy* 1161–77]
1177 Guy Rufus [Gwion Goch]
[*Vacancy* c1190–95]

1195 Alan [Alban]
1197 Robert of Shrewsbury
[*Vacancy* 1212–15]
1215 Cadwgan
1237 Richard
1267 Anian [or Einion]
1307 Gruflydd ab Iowerth
1309 Anian [Einion] Sais
1328 Matthew de Englefield
1357 Thomas de Ringstead
1366 Gervase de Castro
1371 Hywel ap Gronwy
1372 John Gilbert
1376 John Swaffham
1400 Richard Young
[*Vacancy* c1404–8]
1408 Benedict Nicolls
1418 William Barrow
1425 John Cliderow
1436 Thomas Cheriton
1448 John Stanbury
1453 James Blakedon
1465 Richard Edenham
1495 Henry Dean
1500 Thomas Pigot
1505 Thomas Penny
1509 Thomas Skevington
1534 John Salcot [or Capon]
1539 John Bird
1542 Arthur Bulkeley
1555 William Glynn
1559 Rowland Meyrick
1566 Nicholas Robinson
1586 Hugh Bellot
1596 Richard Vaughan
1598 Henry Rowlands
1616 Lewis Bayly
1632 David Dolben
1634 Edmund Griffith
1637 William Roberts
1666 Robert Morgan
1673 Humphrey Lloyd
1689 Humphrey Humphreys
1702 John Evans
1716 Benjamin Hoadley
1721 Richard Reynolds
1723 William Baker
1728 Thomas Sherlock
1734 Charles Cecil
1738 Thomas Herring
1743 Matthew Hutton
1748 Zachary Pearce
1756 John Egerton
1769 John Ewer
1775 John Moore

1783 John Warren
1800 William Cleaver
1807 John Randolph
1809 Henry William Majendie
1830 Christopher Bethell
1859 James Colquhoun Campbell
1890 Daniel Lewis Lloyd
1899 Watkin Herbert Williams
1925 Daniel Davies
1928 Charles Alfred Howell Green
(Archbishop of Wales 1934)
1944 David Edwardes Davies
1949 John Charles Jones
1957 Gwilym Owen Williams
(Archbishop of Wales 1971)
1982 John Cledan Mears
1993 Barry Cennydd Morgan
1999 Francis James Saunders Davies
2004 Phillip Anthony Crockett
2008 Andrew Thomas Griffith John

Llandaff[2]

Description of arms. Sable, two
pastoral staves endorsed in saltire, the
dexter or, the sinister argent. On a
chief azure three labelled mitres or.

c.550 Teiliau
c.872 Cyfeiliag
c.880 Libiau
c.940 Marchlwys
982 Gwyzan
c.995 Bledri
1027 Joseph
1056 Herewald
1107 Urban
[*Vacancy of six years*]
1140 Uchtryd
1148 Nicolas ap Gwrgant
[*Vacancy of two years*]
1186 William Saltmarsh
1193 Henry of Abergavenny

---

[1] Very few of the names of the Celtic bishops have been preserved.
[2] The traditional list of bishops of the Celtic Church has little historical foundation. But the names of the following, prior to Urban, may
be regarded as fairly trustworthy, though the dates are very uncertain.

1219 William of Goldcliff
1230 Elias of Radnor
1245 William de Burgh
1254 John de Ware
1257 William of Radnor
1266 Willam de Breuse [or Brus]
1297 John of Monmouth
1323 John of Eaglescliffe
1344 John Paschal
1361 Roger Cradock
1383 Thomas Rushook
1386 William Bottesham
1389 Edmund Bromfield
1393 Tideman de Winchcomb
1395 Andrew Barret
1396 John Burghill
1398 Thomas Peverel
1408 John de la Zouch [Fulford]
1425 John Wells
1441 Nicholas Ashby
1458 John Hunden
1476 John Smith
1478 John Marshall
1496 John Ingleby
1500 Miles Salley
1517 George de Athequa
1537 Robert Holdgate
         [or Holgate]
1545 Anthony Kitchin
1567 Hugh Jones
1575 William Blethin
1591 Gervase Babington
1595 William Morgan
1601 Francis Godwin
1618 George Carleton
1619 Theophilus Field
1627 William Murray
1640 Morgan Owen
1660 Hugh Lloyd
1667 Francis Davies
1675 William Lloyd
1679 William Beaw
1706 John Tyler
1725 Robert Clavering
1729 John Harris
1739 Matthias Mawson
1740 John Gilbert
1749 Edward Cressett
1755 Richard Newcome
1761 John Ewer
1769 Jonathan Shipley
1769 Shute Barrington
1782 Richard Watson
1816 Herbert Marsh
1819 William Van Mildert
1826 Charles Richard Sumner
1828 Edward Copleston
1849 Alfred Ollivant
1883 Richard Lewis
1905 Joshua Pritchard Hughes
1931 Timothy Rees
1939 John Morgan (Archbishop of
         Wales 1949)
1957 William Glyn Hughes Simon
         (Archbishop of Wales 1968)
1971 Eryl Stephen Thomas
1975 John Richard Worthington
         Poole-Hughes
1985 Roy Thomas Davies
1999 Barry Cennydd Morgan
         (Archbishop of Wales 2003)

Monmouth

Description of arms. Per pale azure
and sable, two crosiers in satire or
between in chief a besant charged with
a lion passant guardant gules, in fess
two fleurs-de-lis and in base a fleur-de-
lis all of the third.

1921 Charles Alfred Howell Green
1928 Gilbert Cunningham Joyce
1940 Alfred Edwin Monahan
1945 Alfred Edwin Morris
         (Archbishop of Wales 1957)
1968 Eryl Stephen Thomas
1972 Derrick Greenslade Childs
         (Archbishop of Wales 1983)
1986 Royston Clifford Wright
1992 Rowan Douglas Williams
         (Archbishop of Wales 1999)
2003 Edward William Murray
         Walker

St Asaph[1]

Description of arms. Sable, two keys
endorsed in saltire the wards upwards
argent.

*c.*560 Kentigern
*c.*573 Asaph
1143 Gilbert
1152 Geoffrey of Monmouth
1154 Richard
1160 Godfrey
1175 Adam
1183 John I
1186 Reiner
1225 Abraham
1235 Hugh
1242 Hywel Ab Ednyfed
1249 Anian I [or Einion]
1267 John II
1268 Anian II
1293 Llywelyn de Bromfield
1315 Dafydd ap Bleddyn
1346 John Trevor I
1357 Llywelyn ap Madoc ab Ellis
1377 William de Spridlington
1382 Lawrence Child
1390 Alexander Bache
1395 John Trevor II
1411 Robert de Lancaster
1433 John Lowe

1444 Reginald Pecock
1451 Thomas Bird *alias* Knight
1471 Richard Redman
1496 Michael Deacon
1500 Dafydd ab Iorwerth
1504 Dafydd ab Owain
1513 Edmund Birkhead
1518 Henry Standish
1536 Robert Warton [or Parfew]
1555 Thomas Goldwell
1560 Richard Davies
1561 Thomas Davies
1573 William Hughes
1601 William Morgan
1604 Richard Parry
1624 John Hanmer
1629 John Owen
1660 George Griffith
1667 Henry Glemham
1670 Isaac Barrow
1680 William Lloyd
1692 Edward Jones
1703 George Hooper
1704 William Beveridge
1708 Will. Fleetwood
1715 John Wynne
1727 Francis Hare
1732 Thomas Tanner
1736 Isaac Maddox
1744 Samuel Lisle
1748 Robert Hay Drummond
1761 Richard Newcome
1769 Jonathan Shipley
1789 Samuel Hallifax
1790 Lewis Bagot
1802 Samuel Horsley
1806 William Cleaver
1815 John Luxmore
1830 William Carey
1846 Thomas Vowler Short
1870 Joshua Hughes
1889 Alfred George Edwards
         (Archbishop of Wales 1920)
1934 William Thomas Havard
1950 David Daniel Bartlett
1971 Harold John Charles
1982 Alwyn Rice Jones (Archbishop
         of Wales 1991)
1999 John Stewart Davies
2009 Gregory Kenneth Cameron

St Davids[2]

Description of arms. Sable, on a cross
or five cinquefoils of the first.

*c.*601 David
*c.*606 Cynog
   831 Sadyrnfyw
         Meurig
*c.*840 Novis
         ?Idwal
*c.*906 Asser
         Llunwerth
   944 Eneuris

---

[1] Prior to the Norman period there is considerable uncertainty as to names and dates.
[2] The following names occur in early records though the dates given cannot always be reconciled.

970

c.961 Rhydderch
c.999 Morgeneu
1023 Morgeneu
1023 Erwyn
1039 Tramerin
1061 Joseph
1061 Bleddud
1072 Sulien
1078 Abraham
1080 Sulien
1085 Wilfrid
1115 Bernard
1148 David Fitz-Gerald
1176 Peter de Leia
1203 Geoffrey de Henlaw
1215 Gervase [Iorwerth]
1231 Anselm le Gras
1248 Thomas le Waleys
1256 Richard de Carew
1280 Thomas Bek
1296 David Martin
1328 Henry Gower
1347 John Thoresby
1350 Reginald Brian
1352 Thomas Fastolf
1362 Adam Houghton
1389 John Gilbert
1397 Guy de Mohne
1408 Henry Chichele
1414 John Catterick
1415 Stephen Patrington
1418 Benedict Nichols
1434 Thomas Rodburn
[Rudborne]
1442 William Lindwood
1447 John Langton
1447 John de la Bere
1460 Robert Tully
1482 Richard Martin
1483 Thomas Langton
1485 Hugh Pavy
1496 John Morgan [Young]
1505 Robert Sherborn
1509 Edward Vaughan
1523 Richard Rawlins

1536 William Barlow
1548 Robert Ferrar
1554 Henry Morgan
1560 Thomas Young
1561 Richard Davies
1582 Marmaduke Middleton
1594 Anthony Rudd
1615 Richard Milbourne
1621 William Laud
1627 Theophilus Field
1636 Roger Mainwaring
1660 William Lucy
1678 William Thomas
1683 Laurence Womock
1686 John Lloyd
1687 Thomas Watson
[Vacancy 1699–1705]
1705 George Bull
1710 Philip Bisse
1713 Adam Ottley
1724 Richard Smallbrooke
1731 Elias Sydall
1732 Nicholas Claggett
1743 Edward Willes
1744 Richard Trevor
1753 Anthony Ellis
1761 Samuel Squire
1766 Robert Lowth
1766 Charles Moss
1774 James Yorke
1779 John Warren
1783 Edward Smallwell
1788 Samuel Horsley
1794 William Stewart
1801 George Murray
1803 Thomas Burgess
1825 John Banks Jenkinson
1840 Connop Thirlwall
1874 William Basil Tickell Jones
1897 John Owen
1927 David Lewis Prosser
(Archbishop of Wales 1944)
1950 William Thomas Havard
1956 John Richards Richards

1971 Eric Matthias Roberts
1982 George Noakes (Archbishop
of Wales 1987)
1991 John Ivor Rees
1996 David Huw Jones
2002 Carl Norman Cooper
2008 John Wyn Evans

Swansea and Brecon

Description of arms. Per fess azure and or, in chief surmounting a catherine wheel issuant an eagle rising regardant of the second and in base a fleur-de-lis of the first.

1923 Edward Latham Bevan
1934 John Morgan
1939 Edward William Williamson
1953 William Glyn Hughes Simon
1958 John James Absalom Thomas
1976 Benjamin Noel Young
Vaughan
1988 Dewi Morris Bridges
1999 Anthony Edward Pierce
2008 John David Edward Davies

Provincial Assistant Bishops

1996 David Thomas

SCOTLAND

Sources: Bp Dowden's *The Bishops of Scotland* (Glasgow 1912), for all the sees up to the Reformation, and for Aberdeen and Moray to the present time.

For bishops after the Reformation (and for a few of the earliest ones before Queen Margaret) – Grub, *Ecclesiastical History of Scotland* (Edinburgh 1861, 4 Vols.) and Bp Keith and Bp Russel, *Scottish Bishops* (2nd ed. Edinburgh 1824).

Scottish episcopal elections became subject immediately to Roman confirmation in 1192. The subordination of the Scottish Church to York became less direct in 1165, and its independence was recognized in a bill of Celestine III in 1192. St Andrews was raised to metropolitan rank on 17 August 1472 and the Archbishop became primate of all Scotland with the same legative rights as the Archbishop of Canterbury on 27 March 1487.

The dates in the margin are those of the consecration or translation to the particular see of the bishops named; or in the case of bishops elect, who are not known to have been consecrated, they are those of the election; or in the case of titular bishops, of the date of their appointment.

The date of the death has been given where there was a long interregnum, or where there is dislocation (as at the Reformation and at the Revolution), or for some special reason to make the history intelligible.

The extra information in the list of College Bishops is given for the reason just stated.

St Andrews

St Andrews, Dunkeld and Dunblane

Description of arms. Quarterly, 1st azure, a saltire argent (for the See of St Andrews); 2nd per fess sable and vert, an open book proper in base, fore-edges and binding or, a dove argent, her wings displayed in chief perching thereon and holding in her beak a spray of olive of the second (for the See of Dunkeld); 3rd chevronny or and gules, a saltire engrailed azure, charged at the fess point with a crescent inverted argent (for the See of Dunblane); 4th azure, a saltire argent supported in front of and by St Andrew enhaloed or and vested pupure with mantle vert, and in base a crescent inverted of the second (for the See of St Andrews).

906 Cellach I
915(?) Fothad I
955 Malisius I
963 Maelbridge
970 Cellach II
996(?) Malasius II
(?) Malmore
1025 Alwyn
1028 Maelduin
1055 Tuthald or Tuadal
1059 Fothad II
1077 Gregory (elect)
to   Catharas (elect)
1107 Edmarus (elect)
      Godricus (elect)
1109 Turgot
1120 Eadmer (elect)
1127 Robert
1159 Waldeve (elect)
1160 Ernald
1165 Richard
1178 Hugh
1180 John the Scot
1198 Roger de Beaumon
1202 William Malveisin
1238 Geoffrey (elect)
1240 David de Bernham
1253 Robert de Stuteville (elect)
1254 Abel de Golin

1255 Gamelin
1273 William Wischard
1280 William Fraser
1298 William de Lamberton
1328 James Bennet
1342 William de Laundels
1385 Stephen de Pay (elect)
1386(?) Walter Trayl
1388 Alexander de Neville
1398 Thomas de Arundel
1401 Thomas Stewart (elect)
1402 Walter de Danielston
    (elect)
1403(?) Gilbert Greenlaw
1403 Henry Wardlaw
1408 John Trevor
1440 James Kennedy

ARCHBISHOPS

1465 Patrick Graham
1478 William Scheves
1497 James Stewart (elect)
1504 Alexander Stewart (elect)
1513 John Hepburn (elect)
1513 Innocenzo Cibo (elect)
1514 Andrew Forman
1522 James Betoun
1538 David Betoun [coadjutor]
1547 John Hamilton
1551 Gavin Hamilton [coadjutor]
    died 1571
1572 John Douglas (titular)
1576 Patrick Adamson (titular) died
    1592
1611 George Gladstanes
1615 John Spottiswoode, died 1639
1661 James Sharp
1679 Alexander Burnet
1684 Arthur Rose, died 1704

BISHOPS OF FIFE

[1704–26 See vacant]
1726 James Rose
1733 Robert Keith
1743 Robert White
1761 Henry Edgar

BISHOPS OF ST ANDREWS

1842 Patrick Torry
1853 Charles Wordsworth
1893 George Howard Wilkinson
1908 Charles Edward Plumb
1931 Edward Thomas Scott Reid
1938 James Lumsden Barkway
1949 Arnold Brian Burrowes
1955 John William Alexander Howe
1969 Michael Geoffrey Hare Duke
1995 Michael Harry George Henley
2005 David Robert Chillingworth

†Dunkeld

849(?) Tuathal
865(?) Flaithbertach
1114 Cormac
1147 Gregory
1170 Richard I
1178 Walter de Bidun (elect)
1183(?) John I, the Scot
1203 Richard II, de Prebenda
1212(?) John II, de Leycester
1214(?) Hugh de Sigillo
1229 Matthew Scot (elect)
1229 Gilbert
1236(?) Geoffrey de Liberatione
1252 Richard III, of Inverkeithing
1273(?) Robert de Stuteville
1283(?) Hugh de Strivelin [Stirling]
    (elect)
1283 William
1288 Matthew de Crambeth
1309 John de Leek (elect)
1312 William Sinclair
1337 Malcolm de Innerpeffray
    (elect)
1344 Richard de Pilmor
1347 Robert de Den (elect)
1347(?) Duncan de Strathearn
1355 John Luce
1370 John de Carrick (elect)
1371(?) Michael de Monymusk
1377(?) Andrew Umfray (elect)
1379 John de Peblys [? of Peebles]
1379 Robert de Derling
1390(?) Nicholas Duffield
1391 Robert Sinclair
1398(?) Robert de Cardeny
1430 William Gunwardby
1437 Donald MacNaughton (elect)
1438 James Kennedy
1440(?) Thomas Livingston
1440 Alexander de Lawedre
    [Lauder] (elect)
1442 James de Brois [Brewhous]
1447 William Turnbull (elect)
1448 John Ralston
1452(?) Thomas Lauder
1476 James Livingston
1483 Alexander Inglis (elect)
1484 George Brown
1515 Andrew Stewart (elect)
1516 Gavin Dougias
1524 Robert Cockburn
1526(?) George Crichton
1546 John Hamilton
1552 Robert Crichton
1572 James Paton (titular)
1585 Peter Rollock (titular)
1607 James Nicolson (titular)
1611(?) Alexander Lindsay (deposed
    1638)
1662 George Haliburton

† Indicates a diocese no longer extant, or united with another diocese.

1665 Henry Guthrie
1677 William Lindsay
1679 Andrew Bruce
1686 John Hamilton
1717 Thomas Rattray
1743 John Alexander
1776(?) Charles Rose
1792 Jonathan Watson
1808 Patrick Torry
1842 Held with St Andrews

†Dunblane

1162 Laurence
c.1180 Symon
1196 W[illelmus]
1198 Jonathan
1215 Abraham
1225 Ralph (elect)
1227 Osbert
1233 Clement
1259 Robert de Prebenda
1284 William I
1296 Alpin
1301 Nicholas
1307 Nicholas de Balmyle
1318(?) Roger de Balnebrich (elect)
1322 Maurice
c.1347 William II
c.1361 Walter de Coventre
c.1372 Andrew
c.1380 Dougal
1403(?) Finlay or Dermoch
1419 William Stephen
1430 Michael Ochiltree
1447(?) Robert Lauder
1468 John Hepburn
1487 James Chisolm
1527 William Chisolm I
1561 William Chisom II
　　　[coadjutor]
1575 Andrew Graham (titular)
1611 George Graham
1616 Adam Bellenden
1636 James Wedderburn
1661 Robert Leighton
1673 James Ramsay
1684 Robert Douglas
[1716–31 See vacant]
1731 John Gillan
1735 Robert White
1744 Thomas Ogilvie (elect)
1774 Charles Rose, died 1791
1776 Held with Dunkeld

Edinburgh

Description of arms. Azure, a saltire
and, in chief, a labelled mitre argent.

1634 William Forbes
1634 David Lindsay
1662 George Wishart
1672 Alexander Young
1679 John Paterson
1687 Alexander Rose
1720 John Fullarton
1727 Arthur Millar
1727 Andrew Lumsden
1733 David Freebairn

[1739–76 See vacant]
1776 William Falconer
1787 William Abernethy
　　　Drummond
1806 Daniel Sandford
1830 James Walker
1841 Charles Hughes Terrot
1872 Henry Cotterill
1886 John Dowden
1910 George Henry Somerset
　　　Walpole
1929 Harry Seymour Reid
1939 Ernest Denny Logie Danson
1947 Kenneth Charles Harman
　　　Warner
1961 Kenneth Moir Carey
1975 Alastair Iain Macdonald
　　　Haggart
1986 Richard Frederick Holloway
2001 Brian Arthur Smith

Aberdeen
Aberdeen and Orkney

Description of arms. Azure, parted
per pale: dexter, a chevron round
embattled on its upper edge between
a fleur-de-lis argent ensigned of an
open crown or in dexter chief, and in
base a bishop proper, attired of the
second, mitred and holding in his
sinister hand a pastoral staff of the
third, his dexter hand raised in
benediction over three children gules
issuant from a cauldron of the third;
sinister, an open boat or, an anchor
argent pendant from its prow, issuant
therefrom a saint proper, attired of
the third, enhaloed and holding in
his sinister hand a pastoral staff of
the second; over all and issuant from
the chief a sunburst or, the central
ray projected along the palar line to
the base.

BISHOPS AT MURTHLAC

(?)　Beyn [Beanus]
(?)　Donort
(?)　Cormac

BISHOPS AT ABERDEEN

1132 Nechtan
c.1150 Edward
c.1172 Matthew
c.1201 John
c.1208 Adam de Kalder
1228 Matthew Scot (elect)
1230 Gilbert de Strivelyn
1240 Radulf de Lamley
1247 Peter de Ramsey
1258 Richard de Pottun
1272 Hugh de Bennum
1282 Henry le Chene
1329 Walter Herok (elect)
1329 Alexander I, de Kyninmund
1344 William de Deyn
1351 John de Rate
1356 Alexander II, de Kyninmund

1380 Adam de Tynyngham
1391 Gilbert de Grenlaw
1422 Henry de Lychton [Leighton]
c.1441 Ingram de Lindsay
1458 Thomas Spens
1480 Robert Blackadder (elect)
1488 William Elphinstone
1515 Robert Forman (elect)
1516 Alexander Gordon
1519 Gavin Dunbar
1529 George Learmonth [coadjutor]
1533 William Stewart
1547 William Gordon
1577 David Cunningham (elect)
1611 Peter Blackburn
1616 Alexander Forbes
1618 Patrick Forbes of Corse
1635 Adam Bellenden [Bannatyne]
1662 David Mitchell
1663 Alexander Burnet
1664 Patrick Scougal
1682 George Halyburton
[1715–21 See vacant]
1721 Archibald Campbell
1724 James Gadderar
1733 William Dunbar
1746 Andrew Gerard
1768 Robert Kilgour
1786 John Skinner
1816 William Skinner
1857 Thomas George Spink
　　　Suther
1883 Arthur Gascoigne Douglas
1906 Rowland Ellis
1912 Anthony Mitchell
1917 Frederic Llewellyn Deane
1943 Herbert William Hall
1956 Edward Frederick Easson
1973 Ian Forbes Begg
1978 Frederick Charles Darwent
1992 Andrew Bruce Cameron
2007 Robert Arthur Gillies

†Orkney

1035 Henry
1050 Turolf
1072 John I
1072 Adalbert
1073 Radulf
1102 William I, 'the Old'
1108 Roger
1114 Radulf Novell
1168(?) William II
1188(?) Bjarni
1224 Jofreyrr
1248 Henry I
1270 Peter
1286 Dolgfinn
1310 William III
c.1369 William IV
c.1384 Robert Sinclair
1384(?) John
1394 Henry II
1396(?) John Pak
1407 Alexander Vaus (elect)
1415 William Stephenson
1420 Thomas Tulloch
1461 William Tulloch
1477 Andrew Painter
1500 Edward Stewart
1524 John Benston [coadjutor]
1526(?) Robert Maxwell
1541 Robert Reid
1559 Adam Bothwell
1611 James Law
1615 George Graham
1639 Robert Barron (elect)
1661 Thomas Sydserf
1664 Andrew Honeyman

1677 Murdo Mackenzie
1688 Andrew Bruce, See afterwards
    administered with Caithness
1857 Held with Aberdeen

Brechin

Description of arms. Or, three piles in point purpure.

1153(?) Samson
1178 Turpin
1202 Radulf
1215 Hugh
1218 Gregory
1246 Albin
1269(?) William de Crachin
    (elect)
1275 William Comyn
1296 Nicholas
1298 John de Kyninmund
1328 Adam de Moravia
1350 Philip Wilde
1351 Patrick de Locrys
    [Leuchars]
1383 Stephen de Cellario
1411 Walter Forrester
1426 John de Crannach
1455 George Schoriswood
1464 Patrick Graham
1465 John Balfour
1489 William Meldrum
1523 John Hepburn
1557 Donald Campbell (elect)
1565(?) John Sinclair (elect)
1566 Alexander Campbell
    (titular)
1610 Andrew Lamb
1619 David Lindsay
1634 Thomas Sydserf
1635 Walter Whitford
1662 David Strachan
1672 Robert Laurie
1678 George Haliburton
1682 Robert Douglas
1684 Alexander Cairncross
1684 James Drummond
1695–1709 Held with Edinburgh
1709 John Falconar
1724 Robert Norrie
1726 John Ochterlonie
1742 James Rait
1778 George Innes
1787 William Abernethy
    Drummond
1788 John Strachan
1810 George Gleig
1840 David Moir
1847 Alexander Penrose Forbes
1876 Hugh Willoughby Jermyn
1904 Walter John Forbes Robberds
1935 Kenneth Donald Mackenzie
1944 Eric Graham
1959 John Chappell Sprott
1975 Lawrence Edward Luscombe
1990 Robert Taylor Halliday
1997 Neville Chamberlain
2005 John Ambrose Cyril Mantle

Moray

Moray, Ross and Caithness

Description of arms. Party per fess and in chief per pale: 1 or, two lions combatant gules, pulling at a cushion of the last issuant from a crescent azure, on a chief wavy of the third three mullets argent (for the See of Moray); 2 argent, a bishop standing in the sinister vested purpure, mitred and holding in his sinister hand a crosier or and pointing with the dexter hand to a saint affontée, his hands clasped on this breast proper, habited gules, above his head a halo of the third (for the See of Ross); 3 azure, issuant from an antique boat or, a demi-bishop proper vested argent, his mitre and pastoral staff in hand sinister of the second, accompanied by two demi-angels, one in the dexter and the other in the sinister chief holding open books proper, their wings addorsed, also of the second (for the See of Caithness).

1114 Gregory
1153(?) William
1164 Felix
1172 Simon de Tonei
1187 Richard de Lincoln
1203 Brice de Douglas
1224(?) Andrew de Moravia
1244(?) Simon
1251 Radulf de Leycester (elect)
1253 Archibald
1299 David de Moravia
1326 John de Pilmor
1363 Alexander Bur
1397 William de Spyny
1407 John de Innes
1415 Henry Leighton
1422 Columba de Dunbar
1437 John de Winchester
1460(?) James Stewart
1463 David Stewart
1477 William de Tulloch
1487 Andrew Stewart
1501(?) Andrew Forman
1516(?) James Hepburn
1525 Robert Shaw
1532(?) Alexander Stewart
1538(?) Patrick Hepburn
1574 George Douglas
1611 Alexander Douglas
1623 John Guthrie
1662 Murdo Mackenzie
1677 James Aitken
1680 Colin Falconer
1687 Alexander Rose
1688 William Hay
1707 Held with Edinburgh
1725 Held with Aberdeen
1727 William Dunbar
1737 George Hay (elect)
1742 William Falconer
1777 Arthur Petrie
1787 Andrew Macfarlane

1798 Alexander Jolly
1838 Held with Ross
1851 Robert Eden
1886 James Butler Knill Kelly
1904 Arthur John Maclean
1943 Piers Holt Wilson
1953 Duncan Macinnes
1970 George Minshull Sessford
1994 Gregor Macgregor
1999 John Michael Crook
2007 Mark Jeremy Strange

†Ross

1131(?) Macbeth
1150(?) Simon
1161 Gregory
1195 Reginald
1213 Andrew de Moravia (elect)
1215(?) Robert I
1250 Robert II
1272 Matthew
1275(?) Robert II de Fyvin
1295(?) Adam de Derlingtun (elect)
1297(?) Thomas de Dundee
1325 Roger
1351 Alexander Stewart
1372 Alexander de Kylwos
1398(?) Alexander de Waghorn
1418 Thomas Lyell (elect)
    Griffin Yonge (elect)
1420 John Bulloch
1441(?) Andrew de Munro (elect)
1441(?) Thomas Tulloch
1464(?) Henry Cockburn
1478 John Wodman
1481 William Elphinstone (elect)
1483 Thomas Hay
1492 John Guthrie
1498 John Frisel [Fraser]
c.1507 Robert Cockburn
1525 James Hay
c.1539 Robert Cairncross
1552 David Painter
1561(?) Henry Sinclair
1566 John Lesley
1575 Alexander Hepburn
1611 David Lindsay
1613 Patrick Lindsay
1633 John Maxwell
1662 John Paterson
1679 Alexander Young
1684 James Ramsay
1696 See vacant or held with
    Caithness until 1727
1727 Held with Moray
1742 Held with Caithness
1762 Robert Forbes
1777 Held with Moray
1819 David Low
1851 Held with Moray

†Caithness

c.1146 Andrew
c.1187 John
1214 Adam
1223(?) Gilbert de Moravia
1250(?) William
1263 Walter de Baltrodin
1273(?) Nicholas (elect)
1275 Archibald Herok
1278 Richard (elect)
1279(?) Hervey de Dundee (elect)
1282 Alan de St Edmund
1295 John or James (elect)
1296 Adam de Derlingtun
1297 Andrew
1306 Fercard Belegaumbe
1328(?) David
1341 Alan de Moravia

1343 Thomas de Fingask
1370 Malcolm de Dumbrek
1381 Alexander Man
1414 Alexander Vaus
1425 John de Crannach
1428 Robert Strabrok
1446 John Innes
1448 William Mudy
1478(?) Prospero Camogli de Medici
1484(?) John Sinclair (elect)
1502 Andrew Stewart I
1517(?) Andrew Stewart II
1542 Robert Stewart (elect)
1600 George Gledstanes (elect)
1611 Alexander Forbes
1616 John Abernethy
1662 Patrick Forbes
1680 Andrew Wood
[1695 See vacant]
1731 Robert Keith
1741 Wm. Falconas
1762 Held with Ross
[1742 See Vacant]
1777 Held with Moray

Glasgow

Glasgow and Galloway

Description of arms. Party per pale:
dexter, vert, a fess wavy argent charged
with a bar wavy azure between a
representation of St Mungo issuant
from the fess proper, habited or, his
dexter hand raised in benediction and
in his sinister hand a Celtic cross of
the same in chief, in nombril point a
salmon proper and in base an annulet
of the fourth; sinister, argent a
representation of St Ninian standing
full-faced proper, clothed in a
pontifical robe purpure, on his head
a mitre and in his dexter hand a crosier
or.

550(?) Kentigern or Mungo (no
         record of his successors)
1114(?) (Michael)
1118(?) John
1147 Herbert
1164 Ingram
1175 Jocelin
1199 Hugh de Roxburgh (elect)
1200 William Malveisin
1202 Florence (elect)
1208 Walter de St Albans
1233 William de Bondington
1259 Nicholas de Moffat (elect)
1259 John de Cheam
1268 Nicholas de Moffat (elect)
1271 William Wischard (elect)
1273 Robert Wischard
1317 Stephen de Donydouer (elect)
1318 John de Eglescliffe
1323 John de Lindsay
1337 John Wischard

1339 William Rae
1367 Walter Wardlaw
1388 Matthew de Glendonwyn
1391 John Framisden (titular)
1408 William Lauder
1427 John Cameron
1447 James de Brois [Brewhouse]
1448 William Turnbull
1456 Andrew de Durrisdeer
1475 John Laing
1483 George Carmichael (elect)

ARCHBISHOPS

1483 Robert Blackadder
         (Archbishop 9 Jan 1492)
1509 James Betoun I
1525 Gavin Dunbar
1551 Alexander Gordon
1552 James Betoun II (restored
         1587)
1571 John Porterfield (titular)
1573 James Boyd (titular)
1581 Robert Montgomery (titular)
1585 William Erskine (titular)
1610 John Spottiswoode
1615 James Law
1633 Patrick Lindsay
1661 Andrew Fairfoul
1664 Alexander Burnet (restored
         1674)
1671 Robert Leighton, died 1684
         (resigned 1674)
1679 Arthur Rose
1684 Alexander Cairncross, died
         1701
1687 John Paterson,[1] died 1708
[1708 Vacant]

BISHOPS

1731 Alexander Duncan, died 1733
[1733 Vacant]
1787 Held with Edinburgh
1805 William Abernethy
         Drummond
1809–37 Held with Edinburgh
1837 Michael Russell
1848 Walter John Trower
1859 William Scott Wilson
1888 William Thomas Harrison
1904 Archibald Ean Campbell
1921 Edward Thomas Scott Reid
1931 John Russell Darbyshire
1938 John Charles Halland How
1952 Francis Hamilton Moncreiff
1974 Frederick Goldie
1981 Derek Alec Rawcliffe
1991 John Mitchell Taylor
1998 Idris Jones

†Galloway or Candida Casa or Whithorn[2]

         Ninian, died 432(?)
(?) Octa
681 Trumwine
731 Penthelm, died 735(?)
735 Frithowald, died 764
763 Pehtwine, died 776
777 Ethelbert
791 Beadwulf
1140 Gilla-Aldan
1154 Christian
1189 John
1214 Walter
1235 Odo Ydonc (elect)

1235 Gilbert
1255 Henry
1294 Thomas de Kircudbright [de
         Daltoun]
1327 Simon de Wedale
1355 Michael Malconhalgh
1359(?) Thomas Macdowell (elect)
1359 Thomas
1364 Adam de Lanark
(?) David Douglas, died 1373
(?) James Carron (resigned 1373)
1378 Ingram de Kethnis (elect)
1379 Oswald
1380 Thomas de Rossy
(?) Francis Ramsay, died 1402
1406 Elisaeus Adougan
1414(?) Gilbert Cavan (elect)
1415 Thomas de Butil
1422 Alexander Vaus
1451 Thomas Spens
1457(?) Thomas Vaus (elect)
1459 Ninian Spot
1482(?) George Vaus
1508(?) James Betoun (elect)
1509(?) David Arnot
1526 Henry Wemyss
1541(?) Andrew Dury
1559(?) Alexander Gordon
1610 Gavin Hamilton
1612(?) William Couper
1619 Andrew Lamb
1635 Thomas Sydserf
1661 James Hamilton
1675 John Paterson
1679 Arthur Rose
1680 James Aitken
1688 John Gordon, died 1726
1697 Held with Edinburgh
1837 Held with Glasgow

Argyll or Lismore

Argyll and The Isles

Description of arms. Azure, two
crosiers in saltire and in chief a mitre
or.

1193 Harald
1240 William
1253 Alan
1268 Laurence de Erganis
1300 Andrew
1342 Angusde Ergadia (elect)
1344 Martinde Ergaill
1387 John Dugaldi
1397(?) Bean Johannis
1420(?) Finlay de Albany
1428 George Lauder
1476 Robert Colquhoun
1504 David Hamilton
1532 Robert Montgomery
1539(?) William Cunningham (elect)
1553(?) James Hamilton (elect)
1580 Neil Campbell (titular)
1611 John Campbell (titular)

[1] After the deposition of John Paterson at the Revolution the See ceased to be Archiepiscopal.
[2] The traditional founder of the See is St Ninian, but nothing authentic is known of the bishops prior to the accession of Gilla-Aldan
between 1133 and 1140.

1613 Andrew Boyd
1637 James Fairlie
1662 David Fletcher
1665 John Young (elect)
1666 William Scroggie
1675 Arthur Rose
1679 Colin Falconer
1680 Hector Maclean
1688 Alexander Monro (elect)
Held with Ross
1847 Alexander Ewing
1874 George Mackarness
1883 James Robert Alexander
    Chinnery-Haldane
1907 Kenneth Mackenzie
1942 Thomas Hannay
1963 Richard Knyvet Wimbush
1977 George Kennedy Buchanan
    Henderson
1993 Douglas MacLean
    Cameron
2004 Alexander Martin Shaw

†The Isles

 900 Patrick
1080 Roolwer
1080 William
1095 Hamundr
1138 Wimund
1152 John I
1152(?) Ragnald
1154 Gamaliel
1170 Christian
1194 Michael
1210 Nicholas I
1219 Nicholas II of Meaux
1226(?) Reginald
1226 Simon
1249 Laurence (elect)
1253 Richard
1275 Gilbert (elect)
1275 Mark
1305 Alan
1324 Gilbert Maclelan
1328 Bernard de Linton
1331 Thomas de Rossy
1349 William Russell
1374 John Donkan
1387 Michael
1392 John Sproten (Man)
    (titular)
1402(?) Conrad (Man) (titular)
1402(?) Theodore Bloc (Man)
    (titular)
1410 Richard Messing (Man)
1422 Michael Anchire
1425(?) John Burgherlinus (Man)
1428 Angus I
1441(?) John Hectoris [McCachane]
    Macgilleon
1472 Angus II
1487 John Campbell

1511 George Hepburn
1514 John Campbell (elect)
1530(?) Ferchar MacEachan
    (elect)
1550(?) Roderick Maclean
1553(?) Alexander Gordon
1567 John Carswell (titular)
1573 John Campbell
1605 Andrew Knox
1619 Thomas Knox
1628 John Leslie
1634 Neil Campbell
1662 Robert Wallace
1677 Andrew Wood
1680 Archibald Graham [or
    McIlvernock]
    Held with Orkney and
    Caithness
1819 Held with Argyll

College Bishops, Consecrated without Sees

1705 John Sage, died 1711
1705 John Fullarton (Edinburgh
    1720), died 1727
1709 Henry Christie, died 1718
1709 John Falconar (Fife 1720),
    died 1723
1711 Archibald Campbell
    (Aberdeen 1721), died 1744
1712 James Gadderar (Aberdeen
    1725, Moray 1725), died
    1733
1718 Arthur Millar (Edinburgh
    1727), died 1727
1718 William Irvine, died 1725
1722 Andrew Cant, died 1730
1722 David Freebairn (Edinburgh
    1733)
1726 John Ochterlonie (Brechin
    1731), died 1742
1726 James Ross (Fife 1731), died
    1733
1727 John Gillan (Dunblane 1731),
    died 1735
1727 David Ranken, died 1728

Bishops who have held the Office of Primus

1704 Alexander Rose (Edinburgh
    1704–20)
1720 John Fullarton (Edinburgh
    1720–27)
1727 Arthur Millar (Edinburgh
    1727)
1727 Andrew Lumsden (Edinburgh
    1727–33)
1731 David Freebairn (Edinburgh
    1733–39)
1738 Thomas Rattray (Dunkeld
    1727–43)

1743 Robert Keith (Caithness
    1731–41)
1757 Robert White (Dunblane
    1735–43, St Andrews
    1743–61)
1762 William Falconar (Orkney and
    Caithness 1741–62)
1782 Robert Kilgour (Aberdeen
    1768–86)
1788 John Skinner (Aberdeen
    1786–1816)
1816 George Gleig (Brechin
    1810–40)
1837 James Walker (Edinburgh
    1880–41)
1841 William Skinner (Aberdeen
    1816–57)
1857 Charles Hughes Terrot
    (Edinburgh 1841–72)
1862 Robert Eden (Moray, Ross,
    and Caithness 1851–86)
1886 Hugh Willoughby Jermyn
    (Brechin 1875–1903)
1901 James Butler Knill Kelly
    (Moray, Ross, and Caithness
    1886–1904)
1904 George Howard Wilkinson (St
    Andrews, Dunkeld, and
    Dunblane 1893–1907)
1908 Walter John Forbes Robberds
    (Brechin 1904–34)
1935 Arthur John Maclean (Moray,
    Ross, and Caithness
    1904–43)
1943 Ernest Denny Logie Danson
    (Edinburgh 1939–46)
1946 John Charles Halland How
    (Glasgow and Galloway
    1938–52)
1952 Thomas Hannay (Argyll and
    The Isles 1942–62)
1962 Francis Hamilton Moncreiff
    (Glasgow and Galloway
    1952–74)
1974 Richard Knyvet Wimbush
    (Argyll and The Isles
    1963–77)
1977 Alastair Iain Macdonald
    Haggart (Edinburgh
    1975–85)
1985 Lawrence Edward Luscombe
    (Brechin 1975–90)
1990 George Kennedy Buchanan
    Henderson (Argyll and The
    Isles 1977–92)
1992 Richard Frederick Holloway
    (Edinburgh 1986–2000)
2000 Andrew Bruce Cameron
    (Aberdeen 1992–2006)
2006 Idris Jones (Glasgow and
    Galloway 1998–2009)
2009 David Robert Chillingworth
    (St Andrews, Dunkeld, and
    Dunblane 2005–)

IRELAND

PROVINCE OF ARMAGH

†Achonry

BISHOPS

c.558 Cathfuidh
1152 Mael Ruanaid ua Ruadain
1159 Gille na Naehm O Ruadain
     [Gelasius]
1208 Clemens O Sniadaig
1220 Connmach O Torpaig [Carus]
1226 Gilla Isu O Cleirig [Gelasius]
1237 Tomas O Ruadhan
1238 Oengus O Clumain [Elias]
1251 Tomas O Maicin
1266 Tomas O Miadachain
     [Dionysus]
1286 Benedict O Bracain
1312 David of Kilheny
1348 David II
1348 Nicol Alias Muircheartach O
     hEadhra
1374 William Andrew
1385 Simon
c.1390 Tomas mac Muirgheasa
     MacDonn-chadha
1401 Brian mac Seaain O hEadhra
1410 Maghnus O h Eadhra
1424 Donatus
1424 Richard Belmer
1436 Tadhg O Dalaigh
1442 James Blakedon
1449 Cornelius O Mochain
1463 Brian O hEasdhra [Benedictus]
1470 Nicholas Forden
1475 Robert Wellys
1484 Thomas fitzRichard
1484 Tomas O Conghalain
1489 John Bustamente
1492 Thomas Ford
1508 Eugenius O Flannagain
1522 Cormac O Snighe
1547 Thomas O Fihilly
1562 Eugene O'Harte
1613 Miler Magrath (with Cashel)
     United to Killala 1622

†Annadown

BISHOPS

1189 Conn ua Mellaig [Concors]
1202 Murchad ua Flaithbertaig
1242 Tomas O Mellaig
1251 Conchobar [Concors]
1283 John de Ufford
1308 Gilbert O Tigernaig
1323 Jacobus O Cethernaig
1326 Robert Petit
1328 Albertus
1329 Tomas O Mellaig
1359 Dionysius
1393 Johannes
1394 Henry Trillow
1402 John Bryt
1408 John Wynn
1421 John Boner [Camere]
1425 Seean Mac Braddaigh
1428 Seamus O Lonnghargain
1431 Donatus O Madagain
1446 Thomas Salscot
1450 Redmund Bermingham
1458 Thomas Barrett

1496 Francis Brunand
1540 John Moore
United to Tuam c.1555

†Ardagh

454 Mel
c.670 Erard
874 Faelghus
    Cele 1048
1152 Mac Raith ua Morain
1172 Gilla Crist O hEothaig
     [Christianus]
     O'Tirlenain 1187
     ua hEislinnen
     Annud O Muiredaig 1216
1217 Robert
1224 M.
1228 Loseph mac Teichthechain
1229 Mac Raith Mac Serraig
1232 Gilla Isu mac in Scelaige O
     Tormaid [Gelasius]
1232 Iocelinus
1238 Brendan Mac Teichthechain
1256 Milo of Dunstable
1290 Matha O'h-Eothaig
     [Mattheus]
1323 Robert Wirsop (did not get
     possession)
1324 Mac Eoaighseoan
1347 Eoghan O Ferghail
     [Audovenus]
1368 William Mac Carmaic
1373 Cairbre O'Ferghail
     [Charles]
1373 John Aubrey
1392 Henry Nony (did not get
     possession)
1396 Comedinus Mac Bradaigh
     [Gilbert]
1400 Adam Leyns
1419 Conchobar O'Ferghail
     [Cornelius]
1425 Risdeard O'Ferghail
[1444 O'Murtry, not consecrated
     resigned]
1445 Cormac Mac
     Shamhradhain
1462 Seaan O'Ferghail
1467 Donatus O'Ferghail
1482 William O'Ferghail
1517 Ruaidri O'Maoileoin
1517 Rory O'Mallone [Roger O
     Melleine]
1541 Richard O'Ferrall
1553 Patrick MacMahon
[1572 John Garvey, not
     consecrated]
1583 Lysach O'Ferrall
1604 Robert Draper
1613 Thomas Moigne
1679 William Bedell
1633 John Richardson
1661 Robert Maxwell
1673 Francis Marsh
1682 William Sheridan
1692 Ulysses Burgh
1604–33, 1661–92 and 1692–1751
     Held by the Bishops of
     Kilmore

1751–1839 Held by the Archbishops
     of Tuam
United to Kilmore 1839

Armagh

Description of arms. Azure, an
archiepiscopal staff in pale argent
ensigned with a cross pattée or,
surmounted by a pall argent
fimbriated and fringed or, charged
with four crosses pattées-fitchées sable.

BISHOPS

444 Patrick
    Benignus 467
    Jarlath 481
    Cormac 497
    Dubthach 513
    Ailill I 526
    Ailill II 536
    David O'Faranan 551
    Carlaen 588
    MacLaisre 623
–640 Thomian MacRonan
    Segeni 688
    Suibhne 730
–732 Congusa
    Affinth 794
–811 Nundha
–818 Artri
835 Forannan
    Mael Patraic I 862
    Fethgna 875
    Cathasach MacRobartach 883
    Mochta 893
900 Maelaithghin
    Cellach
    Mael Ciarain 915
    Joseph 936
    Mael Patraic II 936
    Cathasach MacDolgen 966
    Maelmiure 994
    Airindach 1000
    Maeltuile 1032
1032 Hugh O'Ferris
    Mael Patraic III 1096
1099 Caincomrac O'Boyle

ARCHBISHOPS

1105 Cellach mac Aeda meic Mael
     Isu [Celsus]
1132 Mael maedoc Ua Morgair
     [Malachais]
1137 Gilla Meic Liac mac
     Diarmata meic Ruaidri
     [Gelasius]
1174 Conchobar O Conchaille
     [Concors]

† Indicates a diocese no longer extant, or united with another diocese.

1175 Gille in Coimhedh O Caran [Gilbertus]
1180 Tomaltach O Conchobair [Thomas]
1184 Mael Isu Ua Cerbaill [Malachias]
1202 Echdonn mac Gilla Uidir [Eugenius]
1217 Lucas Neterville
1227 Donatus O Fidabra
1240 Albert Suebeer of Cologne
1247 Reginald
1258 Abraham O'Conallain
1261 Mael Patraic O Scannail
1270 Nicol Mac Mael Isu
1303 Michael MacLochlainn (not confirmed)
1304 Dionysius (not confirmed)
1306 John Taaffe
1307 Walter Jorz
1311 Roland Jorz
1324 Stephen Segrave
1334 David Mag Oireachtaigh
1347 Richard FitzRalph
1362 Milo Sweetman
1383 John Colton
1404 Nicholas Fleming
1418 John Swayne
1439 John Prene
1444 John Mey
1457 John Bole [Bull]
1471 John Foxhalls or Foxholes
1475 Edmund Connesburgh
1480 Ottaviano Spinelli [de Palatio]
1513 John Kite
1521 George Cromer
1543 George Dowdall
1552 Hugh Goodacre
1553 George Dowdall (again)
[1560 Donat MacTeague, not recognized by the Crown, 1562]
1563 Adam Loftus
1568 Thomas Lancaster
1584 John Long
1589 John Garvey
1595 Henry Ussher
1613 Christopher Hampton
1625 James Ussher
[Interregnum 1656–61]
1661 John Bramhall
1663 James Margetson
1679 Michael Boyle
1703 Narcissus Marsh
1714 Thomas Lindsay
1724 Hugh Boulter
1742 John Hoadly
1747 George Stone
1765 Richard Robinson [afterwards Baron Rokeby]
1795 William Newcome
1800 William Stuart
1822 John George Beresford
United to Clogher 1850–86
1862 Marcus Gervais Beresford
1886 Robert Bentknox
1893 Robert Samuel Gregg
1896 William Alexander
1911 John Baptist Crozier
1920 Charles Frederick D'Arcy
1938 John Godfrey FitzMaurice Day
1939 John Allen Fitzgerald Gregg
1959 James McCann
1969 George Otto Simms
1980 John Ward Armstrong

1986 Robert Henry Alexander Eames
2007 Alan Edwin Thomas Harper

Clogher

Description of arms. Azure, a bishop seated in full pontificals proper, in the act of benediction, and holding his pastoral staff in the left hand.

*c.*493 MacCarthinn or Ferdachrioch Ailill 869
1135 Cinaeth O Baigill
1135 Gilla Crist O Morgair [Christianus] (moved his see to Louth)

BISHOPS OF LOUTH

1135 Gilla Crist O Morgair [Christianus]
1138 Aed O Ceallaide [Edanus]
1178 Mael Isu O Cerbaill [Malachias]
1187 Gilla Crist O Mucaran [Christinus]
1194 Mael Isu Ua Mael Chiarain
1197 Gilla Tigernaig Mac Gilla Ronain [Thomas]

BISHOPS OF CLOGHER

1218 Donatus O Fidabra
1228 Nehemias
1245 David O Bracain
1268 Michael Mac an tSair
1287 Matthew Mac Cathasaigh I
–1310 Henricus
1316 Gelasius O Banain
1320 Nicholas Mac Cathasaigh
1356 Brian Mac Cathmaoil [Bernard]
1362 Matthew Mac Cathasaigh II
— Aodh O hEothaigh [*alias* O Neill]
1373 John O Corcrain [Wurzburg]
1390 Art Mac Cathmhail
1433 Piaras Mag Uidhir [Petrus]
1450 Rossa mac Tomais Oig Mag Uidhir [Rogerius]
1475 Florence Woolley
[1484 Niall mac Seamuis Mac Mathghamna]
1484 John Edmund de Courci
1494 Seamus Mac Pilip Mac Mathghamna
1500 Andreas
1502 Nehemias O Cluainin
1504 Giolla Padraig O Conalaigh [Patrick]
1505 Eoghan Mac Cathmhail [Eugenius]
1517 Padraig O Cuilin
1535 Aodh O Cearbhalain [Odo]
1517 Patrick O'Cullen
1535 Hugh O'Carolan
1570 Miler Magrath
1605 George Montgomery

1621 James Spottiswood
1645 Henry Jones
1661 John Leslie
1671 Robert Leslie
1672 Roger Boyle
1691 Richard Tennison
1697 St George Ashe
1717 John Stearne
1745 Robert Clayton
1758 John Garnett
1782 John Hotham
1796 William Foster
1797 John Porter
1819 John George Beresford
1820 Percy Jocelyn
1822 Robert Ponsonby Tottenham Luftus
United to Armagh 1850–86
1886 Charles Maurice Stack
1903 Charles Frederick D'Arcy
1908 Maurice Day
1923 James MacManaway
1944 Richard Tyner
1958 Alan Alexander Buchanan
1970 Richard Patrick Crosland Hanson
1973 Robert William Heavener
1980 Gordon McMullan
1986 Brian Desmond Anthony Hannon
2002 Michael Geoffrey St Aubyn Jackson

Connor

Description of arms. Azure, a lamb passant supporting with the dexter foreleg a staff proper flying therefrom a pennant argent charged with a saltire gules between three cross crosslets or; on a chief of the last two crosiers in saltire of the first.

506 Oengus MacNessa 514 Lughadh 543
640 Dimma Dubh [the Black] Duchonna the Pious 725 Cunnen or Cuinden 1038 Flann O'Sculu 1117
1124 Mael Maedoc Ua Morgair [Malachias]
–1152 MaelPatraic O'Banain
1172 Nehemias
1178 Reginaldus
1226 Eustacius
1242 Adam
1245 Isaac de Newcastle-on-Tyne
1258 William de Portroyal
1261 William de Hay [or la Haye]
1263 Robert de Flanders
1275 Peter de Dunach
1293 Johannes
1320 Richard
1321 James de Couplith
1323 John de Eglecliff
1323 Robert Wirsop
1324 Jacabus O Cetharnaig
1353 William Mercier
1374 Paulus
1389 Johannes

[1420 Seaan O Luachrain, not
    consecrated]
1423 Eoghan O'Domhnaill
1429 Domhnall O'Meraich
1431 John Fossade [Festade]
1459 Patricius
1459 Simon Elvington
United to Down 1441
1945 Charles King Irwin
1956 Robert Cyril Hamilton Glover
    Elliott
1969 Arthur Hamilton Butler
1981 William John McCappin
1987 Samuel Greenfield Poyntz
1995 James Edward Moore
2002 Alan Edwin Thomas
    Harper
2007 Alan Francis Abernethy

Derry

Derry and Raphoe

Description of arms. Party per pale:
dexter gules, two swords in saltire
proper, the hilts in base or, and on a
chief azure a harp or stringed argent
(for the See of Derry); sinister ermine,
a chief per pale azure and or, the first
charged with a sun in splendour of the
last, the second with a cross pattée
gules (for the See of Raphoe).

    Caencomhrac 927
–937 Finachta MacKellach
–949 Mael Finnen

BISHOPS OF MAGHERA
(Where the See was in the twelfth
and the thirteenth centuries)
1107 Mael Coluim O Brolchain
  — Mael Brigte O Brolchain
1152 O Gormgaile Muiredach O
    Cobthaig [Mauricius]
1173 Amhlaim O Muirethaig
1185 Fogartach O Cerballain
    [Florentius]
c.1230 Gilla in Coimhded O
    Cerballain [Germanus]
c.1280 Fogartach O
    Cerballain II
    [Florentius]

BISHOPS OF DERRY
(Where the See was resettled)
1295 Enri Mac Airechtaig
    [O'Reghly] [of Ardagh]
1297 Gofraid MacLochlainn
    [Godfrey]
1316 Aed O Neill [Odo]
1319 Michael Mac Lochlainn
    [Maurice]
1349 Simon
1391 Johannes
1391 John Dongan
1394 Seoan O Mochain
1398 Aodh [Hugo]
1401 Seoan O Flannabhra
1415 Domhnall Mac Cathmhail
1419 Domhnall O Mearaich
1429 Eoghan O Domhnaill
    [Eugenius]

1433 John Oguguin
[1456 John Bole, appointment not
    completed, translated to
    Armagh]
1458 Bartholomew O Flannagain
c.1464 Johannes
1467 Nicholas Weston
1485 Domhnall O Fallamhain
1501 Seamus mac Pilip Mac
    Mathghamna [MacMahon]
1520 Ruaidhri O Domhnaill
1520 Rory O'Donnell
1554 Eugene O'Doherty
1568 F. [doubtful authority]
1569 Redmond O'Gallagher
[1603 Denis Campbell, not
    consecrated]
1605 George Montgomery
1610 Brutus Babington
[1611 Christopher Hampton,
    consecrated]
1613 John Tanner
1617 George Downham
1634 John Bramhall
1661 George Wild
1666 Robert Mossom
1680 Michael Ward
1681 Ezekiel Hopkins
1691 William King
1703 Charles Hickman
1714 John Hartstonge
1717 St George Ashe
1718 William Nicolson
1727 Henry Downes
1735 Thomas Rundle
1743 Carew Reynell
1745 George Stone
1747 William Barnard
1768 Frederick Augustus Hervey
    [afterwards Earl of
    Bristol]
1803 William Knox
1831 Richard Ponsonby
Raphoe united to Derry from 1834
1853 William Higgin
1867 William Alexander
1896 George Alexander Chadwick
    (resigned)
1916 Joseph Irvine Peacocke
1945 Robert M'Neil Boyd
1958 Charles John Tyndall
1970 Cuthbert Irvine Peacocke
1975 Robert Henry Alexander
    Eames
1980 James Mehaffey
2002 Kenneth Raymond Good

Down

Down and Dromore

Description of arms. Quarterly, 1 and 4
azure, two keys endorsed in saltire the
wards in chief or, surmounted in the
fess point by a lamb passant proper
(for the See of Down); 2 and 3 Argent,
two keys endorsed in saltire in chief
gules, surmounted by an open
book in fess proper between two
crosses pattées-fitchées in pale sable
(for the See of Dromore).

Fergus 584
Suibhne 825
Graithene 956
Finghin 964
Flaithbertach 1043
MaelKevin 1086
  — Mael Muire 1117
Oengus Ua Gormain 1123
  — [Anonymous]
c.1124 Mael Maedoc O Morgair
    [Malachias]
1152 Mael Isu mac in Chleirig
    Chuirr [Malachias]
1175 Gilla Domangairt Mac
    Cormaic
c.1176 Echmilid [Malachias]
c.1202 Radulfus
1224 Thomas
1251 Randulphus
1258 Reginaldus
1265 Thomas Lydel
1277 Nicholas le Blund
1305 Thomas Ketel
1314 Thomas Bright
1328 John of Baliconingham
1329 Ralph of Kilmessan
1353 Richard Calf I
1365 Robert of Aketon
1367 William White
1369 Richard Calf [II]
1386 John Ross
1394 John Dongan
1413 John Cely [or Sely]
1445 Ralph Alderle

BISHOPS OF DOWN AND CONNOR

1441 John Fossard
1447 Thomas Pollard
1451 Richard Wolsey
1456 Thomas Knight
1469 Tadhg O Muirgheasa
    [Thaddeus]
1489 Tiberio Ugolino
1520 Robert Blyth
1542 Eugene Magennis
1565 James MacCawell
1569 John Merriman
1572 Hugh Allen
1593 Edward Edgeworth
1596 John Charden
1602 Roben Humpston
1607 John Todd (resigned)
1612 James Dundas
1613 Robert Echlin
1635 Henry Leslie
1661 Jeremy Taylor
1667 Roger Boyle
1672 Thomas Hacket
1694 Samuel Foley
1695 Edward Walkington
1699 Edward Smyth
1721 Francis Hutchinson
1739 Carew Reynell
1743 John Ryder
1752 John Whitcombe
1752 Robert Downes
1753 Arthur Smyth
1765 James Traill
1784 William Dickson
1804 Nathaniel Alexander
1823 Richard Mant

BISHOPS OF DOWN, CONNOR AND
DROMORE

1849 Robert Bent Knox
1886 William Reeves
1892 Thomas James Welland
1907 John Baptist Crozier
1911 Charles Frederick D'Arcy

1919 Charles Thornton Primrose
      Grierson
1934 John Frederick McNeice
1942 Charles King Irwin

BISHOPS OF DOWN AND
DROMORE

1945 William Shaw Kerr
1955 Frederick Julian Mitchell
1970 George Alderson Quin
1980 Robert Henry Alexander
      Eames
1986 Gordon McMullan
1997 Harold Creeth Miller

†Dromore

Mael Brighde 974
Riagan 1101
1197 Ua Ruanada
1227 Geraldus
1245 Andreas
1284 Tigernach I
1290 Gervasius
—   Tigernach II
1309 Florentius Mac Donnocain
1351 Anonymous
1366 Milo
1369 Christophorus Cornelius 1382
1382 John O'Lannoy
1398 Thomas Orwell
1400 John Waltham
1402 Roger Appleby
1408 Richard Payl
1410 Marcus
1411 John Chourles
1414 Seaan O Ruanadha
1419 Nicholas Wartre
1429 Thomas Rackelf
1431 William
1431 David Chirbury
1450 Thomas Scrope [Bradley]
1450 Thomas Radcliff
1456 Donatus O h-Anluain
      [Ohendua]
1457 Richard Messing
1463 William Egremond
—   Aonghus [Aeneas] 1476
1476 Robert Kirke
1480 Yvo Guillen
1483 George Braua
1511 Tadhg O Raghallaigh
      [Thaddeus]
1536 Quintin O Quigley [Cogley]
1539 Roger McHugh
1540 Arthur Magennis
1607 John Todd
[1613 John Tanner, not
      consecrated]
1613 Theophilus Buckworth
1661 Robert Leslie
1661 Jeremy Taylor (administered
      the diocese)
1667 George Rust
1671 Essex Digby
1683 Capel Wiseman
1695 Tobias Pullein
1713 John Stearne
1717 Ralph Lambert
1727 Charles Cobbe
1732 Henry Maule
1744 Thomas Fletcher
1745 Jemmett Browne
1745 George Marlay
1763 John Oswald
1763 Edward Young
1765 Henry Maxwell
1766 William Newcome
1775 James Hawkins
1780 William de la Poer Beresford

1782 Thomas Percy
1811 George Hall
1812 John Leslie
1819 James Saurin
United to Down since 1842

†Elphin

Domnall mac Flannacain Ua
Dubhthaig 1136
Muiredach O Dubhthaig 1150
1152 Mael Isu O Connachtain
      Flannacan O Dubhthaig 1168
c.1177 Tomaltach mac Aeda
      Ua Conchobhair [Thomas]
c.1180 Florint Ua Riacain Ui
      Maelrvanaid
1206 Ardgar O Conchobhair
1226 Dionysius O Mordha
c.1230 Alanus
1231 Donnchad mac Fingein O
      Conchobhair [Dionysius
      Donatus]
1245 Eoin O Mugroin
1247 Tomaltach macToirrdelbaig O
      Conchobhair [Thomas]
1260 Mael Sechlainn O
      Conchobhair [Milo]
1262 Tomas mac Fergail mac
      Diarmata
1266 Muiris O Conchobhair
[1285 Amiaim O Tommaltaig, not
      consecrated]
1285 Gilla Isu mac in Liathana O
      Conchobhair
1297 Maelsechlainn mac Briain
      [Malachias]
1303 Donnchad O Flannacain,
      [Donatus]
1307 Cathal O Conchobhair
1310 Mael Sechlainn Mac Aedha
1313 Lurint O Lachtnain [Laurence]
1326 Sean O Finnachta
1355 Carolus
1357 Gregory O Mochain
1372 Thomas Barrett
1383 Seoan O Mochain
1407 Seaan O Grada
1405 Gerald Caneton
1412 Thomas Colby
1418 Robert Fosten
1421 Edmund Barrett
1427 Johannes
1429 Laurence O Beolain
1429 William O hEidighean
1448 Conchobhar O Maolalaidh
1458 Nicholas O Flanagan
1487 Hugo Arward
1492 Rlocard mac Briain O
      gCuanach
1499 George Brana
1501 Cornelius O Flannagain
1508 Christopher Fisher
1525 John Maxey
1539 William Maginn 1541(?)
1539 Gabriel de Sancto Serio
1541 Conach or Con O'Negall or
      O'Shyagall
1552 Roland Burke [de Burgo]
1582 Thomas Chester
1583 John Lynch
1611 Edward King
1639 Henry Tilson
1661 John Parker
1667 John Hodson
1691 Simon Digby
1720 Henry Downes
1724 Theophilus Bolton
1730 Robert Howard
1740 Edward Synge

1762 William Gore
1772 Jemmett Browne
1775 Charles Dodgson
1795 John Law
1810 Power le Poer Trench
1819 John Leslie 1854
United to Kilmore and Ardagh on
the death of Bishop Beresford in
1841, when Bishop Leslie became
Bishop of the united dioceses.

†Killala

Muiredach
Kellach
O Maolfogmair I 1137
O Maolfogmair II 1151
Imar O Ruaidhin 1176
1179 O Maolfogmair III
1199 Domnall Ua Becdha
1207 Cormac O'Tarpy
      O'Kelly 1214
1226 Aengus O Maolfogmair [Elias]
      Gille Cellaig O Ruaidhin
1253 Seoan O Laidlg
1281 Donnchad O Flaithbertaig
      [Donatus]
1307 John Tankard
      Sean O Flaithim 1343
1344 James Bermingham
1347 William O DusucBhda
1351 Robert Elyot
1381 Thomas Lodowys
1383 Conchobar O Coineoil
      [Cornelius]
1390 Thomas Horwell [Orwell]
1400 Thomas Barrett
1403 Muircheartach Cleirach mac
      Donnchadha O DusucBhda
      Connor O'Connell 1423
1427 Fergal Mac Martain
1431 Thaddeus Mac Creagh
1432 Brian O Coneoil
1447 Robert Barrett
1452 Ruaidhri Bairead [Barrett]
1453 Thomas
1459 Richard Viel
      Miler O'Connell
1461 Donatus O Conchobhair
1470 Tomas Bairead [Barrett]
1487 John de Tuderto [Seaan O
      Caissin]
1500 Thomas Clerke
1508 Malachias O Clumhain
1513 Risdeard Bairead
1545 Redmond O'Gallagher
1570 Donat O'Gallagher
1580 John O'Casey
1592 Owen O'Conor
1613 Miler Magrath
Achonry united to Killala 1622
1623 Archibald Hamilton
1630 Archibald Adair (deposed, but
      subsequently restored)
164? John Maxwell
1661 Henry Hall
1664 Thomas Bayly
1671 Thomas Otway
1680 John Smith
1681 William Smyth
1682 Richard Tennison
1691 William Lloyd
1717 Henry Downes
1720 Charles Cobbe
1727 Robert Howard
1730 Robert Clayton
173? Mordecai Cary
175? Richard Robinson
      [afterwards Baron Rokeby]
1759 Samuel Hutchinson

1781 William Cecil Pery
1784 William Preston
1787 John Law
1795 John Porter
1798 Joseph Stock
1810 James Verschoyle
United to Tuam since 1834

Kilmore

Kilmore, Elphin and Ardagh

Description of arms. Argent, on a cross
azure a pastoral staff enfiling a mitre,
all or (for the See of Kilmore). Sable,
two pastoral staves in saltire or, in base
a lamb couchant, argent (for the See of
Elphin). Or, a cross gules between four
trefoils slipped vert, on a chief sable, a
key erect of the first (for the See of
Ardagh).

—   Aed Ua Finn 1136
—   Muirchenach Ua
        Maelmoeherge 1149
1152 Tuathal Ua Connachtaig
        [Thadeus]
1202 Mi Ua Dobailen
—   Flann O Connachtaig
        [Florentius] 1231
1237 Congalach Mac Idneoil
1251 Simon O Ruairc
1286 Mauricius
—   Matha Mac Duibne 1314
1320 Padraig O Cridecain
—   Conchobhar Mac
        Conshnamha [Ford] 1355
1356 Richard O Raghilligh
1373 Johannes
1388 Thomas Rushook
1392 Sean O Raghilligh I [John]
1398 Nicol Mac Bradaigh
1401 Sean O'Raghilligh II
1407 John Stokes
1409 David O'Fairchellaigh
1422 Domhnall O Gabhann
1445 Aindrias Mac Bradaigh
1455 Fear Sithe Mag Dhuibhne
1465 Sean O Raghilligh II
1476 Cormac Mag Shamhradhain
1480 Tomas MacBradaigh
1512 Diarmaid O Raghilligh
1530 Edmund Nugent
1540 Sean Mac Bradaigh
1585 John Garvey
1604 Robert Draper
1613 Thomas Moigne
1629 William Bedell
1643 Robert Maxwell
1673 Francis Marsh
1682 William Sheridan
1693 William Smyth
1699 Edward Wetenhall
1715 Timothy Godwin
1727 Josiah Hott
1742 Joseph Story
1757 John Cradock
1772 Denison Cumberland
1775 George Lewis Jones
1790 William Foster

1796 Charles Broderick
1802 George de la Poer Beresford
Ardagh united to Kilmore 1839
Elphin united to Kilmore 1841
1841 John Leslie
1854 Marcus Gervais Beresford
1862 Hamilton Verschoyle
1870 Charles Leslie
1870 Thomas Carson
1874 John Richard Darley
1884 Samuel Shone
1897 Alfred George Elliott
1915 William Richard Moore
1930 Arthur William Barton
1939 Albert Edward Hughes
1950 Frederick Julian Mitchell
1956 Charles John Tyndall
1959 Edward Francis Butler Moore
1981 William Gilbert Wilson
1993 Michael Hugh Gunton Mayes
2001 Kenneth Harbert Clarke

†Mayo

Gerald 732
Muiredach [or Murray]
Mcinracht 732
Aidan 773
1172 Gilla Isu Ua Mailin
        Cele O Dubhthaig 1210
1210 ?Patricius
1428 William Prendergast
1430 Nicholas 'Wogmay'
1439 Odo O h-Uiginn
1432 Martin Campania
1457 Simon de Duren
1493 John Bel
1541 Eugenius Macan Brehon
United to Tuam 1559

†Raphoe

Sean O Gairedain
Donell O Garvan
Felemy O Syda
Oengus O'Lappin 959
1150 Muiredhach O'Cofley
1156 Gille in Coimhded Ua Carain
        [Gilbertus]
—   Anonymous
1204 Mael Isu Ua Doirig
—   Anonymous
1253 Mael Padraig O Scannail
        [Patricius]
1263 John de Alneto
1265 Cairpre O Scuapa
1275 Fergal O Firghil [Florentius]
1306 Enri Mac-in-Chrossain
        [Henricus]
1319 Tomas Mac Carmaic Ui
        Domhnaill
1363 Padraig Mac Maonghail
1367 Conchobar Mac Carmaic Ui
        Domhnaill [Cornelius]
1397 Seoan MacMenmain
1400 Eoin MacCarmaic [Johannes]
–1413 Anthony
–1414 Robert Rubire
1416 John McCormic
1420 Lochlainn O Gallchobhair I
        [Laurentius]
1440 Cornelius Mac Giolla Brighde
1443 Lochlainn O Gallchobhair II
        [Laurentius]
1479 John de Rogeriis
1482 Meanma Mac Carmail
        [Menclaus Mac Carmacain]
1514 Conn O Cathain [Cornelius]
1534 Eamonn O Gallchobhair
1547 Arthur o'Gallagher

1563 Donnell Magonigle [or
        McCongail]
[1603 Denis Campbell, not
        consecrated]
1605 George Montgomery
1611 Andrew Knox
1633 John Leslie
1661 Robert Leslie
1671 Ezekiel Hopkins
1682 William Smyth
1693 Alexander Cairncross
1701 Robert Huntington
1702 John Pooley
1713 Thomas Lindsay
1714 Edward Synge
1716 Nicholas Forster
1744 William Barnard
1747 Philip Twysden
1753 Robert Downes
1763 John Oswald
1780 James Hawkins
1807 John George Beresford
1819 William Magee
1822 William Bissett
United to Derry since 1834

Tuam

Tuam, Killala and Achonry

Description of arms. Azure beneath a
triple architectural canopy three
figures, in the centre the Blessed Virgin
Mary holding in her arms the Holy
Child, between, on the dexter the
figure of a bishop (St Jarlath) in
pontificalibus and in the act of
benediction, and, on the sinister St
John supporting with his left arm a
lamb argent, each in proper vestments
or, the hands, feet, and faces proper.

BISHOPS

        Murrough O'Nioc 1032
        Hugh O'Hessian 1085
        Cathusach Ua Conaill 1117
        O Clerig 1137
        Muiredach Ua Dubhthaig
          1150

ARCHBISHOPS

1152 Aed Ua h-Oisin [Edanus]
1167 Cadhla Ua Dubhthaig
        [Catholicus]
1202 Felix Ua Ruanada
1236 Mael Muire O Lachtain
        [Marianus]
1250 Flann Mac Flainn [Florentius]
[1256 James O'Laghtnan, not
        confirmed or consecrated]
1257 Walter de Salerno
1258 Tomaltach O Conchobair
        [Thomas]
1286 Stephen de Fulbourn
1289 William de Bermingham
1312 Mael Sechlainn Mac Aeda
1348 Tomas MacCerbhaill
        [MacCarwill]
1364 Eoin O Grada
1372 Gregory O Mochain I

981

1384 Gregory O Mochain II
1387 William O Cormacain
1393 Muirchertach mac Pilb O
      Cellaigh
1410 John Babingle
1411 Cornelius
1430 John Bermingham
      [Winfield]
1438 Tomas mac Muirchearthaigh
      O Cellaigh
1441 John de Burgo
1452 Donatus O Muiredaigh
1485 William Seoighe [Joyce]
1503 Philip Pinson
1506 Muiris O Fithcheallaigh
1514 Tomas O Maolalaidh
1537 Christopher Bodkin
1573 William O'Mullally [or Lealy]
Annadown united to Tuam c.1555
Mayo united to Tuam 1559

1595 Nehemiah Donnellan
1609 William O'Donnell [or
      Daniel]
1629 Randolph or Ralph
      Barlow
1638 Richard Boyle
1645 John Maxwell
1661 Samuel Pullen
1667 John Parker
1679 John Vesey
1716 Edward Synge
1742 Josiah Hort
1752 John Ryder
1775 Jemmett Browne
1782 Joseph Dean Bourke
      [afterwards Earl of
      Mayo]
1794 William Beresford [afterwards
      Baron Decies]
1819 Power le Poer Trench

Killala united to Tuam from
      1834

BISHOPS

1839 Thomas Plunket [afterwards
      Baron Plunket]
1867 Charles Brodrick Bernard
1890 James O'Sullivan
1913 Benjamin John Plunket
1920 Arthur Edwin Ross
1923 John Ort
1928 John Mason Harden
1932 William Hardy Holmes
1939 John Winthrop Crozier
1958 Arthur Hamilton Butler
1970 John Coote Duggan
1986 John Robert Winder Neill
1998 Richard Crosbie Aitken
      Henderson

PROVINCE OF DUBLIN

†Ardfert

BISHOPS

Anmchad O h-Anmchada
      1117
1152 Mael Brenain Ua Ronain
Gilla Mac Aiblen
      O'Anmehadha 1166
Domnall O Connairche
      1193
1200 David Ua Duibdithrib
Anonymous 1217
1218 John
1218 Gilbertus
1237 Brendan
1253 Christianus
1257 Philippus
1265 Johannes
1286 Nicolaus
1288 Nicol O Samradain
1336 Ailin O hEichthighirn
1331 Edmund of Caermarthen
1348 John de Valle
1372 Cornelius O Tigernach
1380 William Bull
1411 Nicholas FitzMaurice
1404 Nicholas Ball
1405 Tomas O Ceallaigh
1409 John Attilburgh
      [Artilburch]
1450 Maurice Stack
1452 Maurice O Conchobhair
1461 John Stack
1461 John Pigge
1473 Philip Stack
1495 John FitzGerald
[See vacant in 1534]
1536 James FitzMaurice
1588 Nicholas Kenan
1600 John Crosbie
1622 John Steere
1628 William Steere
1641 Thomas Fulwar
United to Limerick 1661

†Ardmore

1153 Eugenius
Incorporated with Lismore
      1192

Cashel

*Cashel, Waterford, Lismore, Ossory,
Ferns and Leighlin*

Description of arms. Gules, two keys
addorsed in saltire the wards in
chief, or.

BISHOPS

Cormac MacCuillenan 908
Donnell O'Heney 1096 *or* 1098

ARCHBISHOPS

c.1111 Mael los Ua h-Ainmire
Mael Iosa Ua Fogludha
      [Mauricius] 1131
Domnall Ua Conaing 1137
Gilla Naomh O'Marty 1149
−1152 Donat O'Lonergan I
−c.1160 M.
1172 Domnall O h-Ualla-chain
      [Donatus]
1186 Muirghes O h-Enna [Matheus]
c.1208 Donnchad Ua
      Longargain I [Donatus]
1216 Donnchad Ua Longargain II
      [Donatus]
1224 Mairin O Briain [Marianus]
1238 David mac Ceallaig [O'Kelly]
1254 David Mac Cearbaill [Mac
      Carwill]
1290 Stiamna O Bracain
1303 Maurice Mac Cearbaill
1317 William FitzJohn
1327 Seoan Mac Cerbaill
1329 Walter le Rede
1332 Eoin O Grada
1346 Radulphus O Cellaigh [Kelly]
1362 George Roche [de Rupe]

1365 Tomas Mac Cearbhaill
1374 Philip of Torrington
1382 Michael
1384 Peter Hackett
1406 Richard O Hedian
1442 John Cantwell I
1452 John Cantwell II
1484 David Creagh
1504 Maurice FitzGerald
1525 Edmund Butler
1553 Roland Baron or FitzGerald
1567 James MacCawell
Emly united to Cashel 1569
1571 Miler Magrath (Bishop of
      Cashel and Waterford from
      1582)
1623 Malcolm Hamilton
1630 Archibald Hamilton
1661 Thomas Fulwar
1667 Thomas Price
[See vacant 1685–91]
1691 Narcissus Marsh
1694 William Palliser
[1727 William Nicolson, not
      enthroned]
1727 Timothy Goodwin
1730 Theophilus Bolton
1744 Arthur Price
1752 John Whitcombe
1754 Michael Cox
1779 Charles Agar
1801 Charles Brodrick
1822 Richard Laurence
Waterford and Lismore united to
Cashel from 1833; on the death of
Abp Laurence in 1838 the province
was united to Dublin and the see
ceased to be an Archbishopric

BISHOPS

1839 Stephen Creagh Sandes
1843 Robert Daly
1872 Maurice FitzGerald
      Day
1900 Henry Stewart O'Hara
1919 Robert Miller
1931 John Frederick McNeice
1935 Thomas Arnold Harvey
1958 William Cecil De Pauley

1968 John Ward Armstrong
Ossory united to Cashel 1977
1980 Noel Vincent Willoughby
1997 John Robert Winder
    Neill
2003 Peter Francis Barrett
2006 Michael Andrew James
    Burrows

†Clonfert

Moena, or Moynean, or
    Moeinend 572
Cummin the Tall 662
Ceannfaeladh 807
Laithbheartach 822
Ruthnel or Ruthme 826
Cormac MacEdain 922
Ciaran O'Gabbla 953
Cathal 963
Eochu 1031
O'Corcoran 1095
Muiredach Ua h-Enlainge 1117
Gille Patraic Ua Ailcinned
    1149
c.1152 Petrus Ua Mordha
1172 Mail Isu mac in Baird
1179 Celechair Ua h-Armedaig
    Muirchertach Ua'Maeluidir
    1187
    Domnall Ua Finn 1195
    Muirchertach Ua Carmacain
    1204
1205 Mael Brigte Ua hErurain
1224 Cormac O Luimlin [Carus]
1248 Thomas
1259 Tomas mac Domnaill Moire O
    Cellaig
1266 Johannes de Alatre
1296 Robert
c.1302 John
1308 Gregorius O Brocaig
1320 Robert Le Petit
1322 Seoan O Leaain
1347 Tomas mac Gilbert O Cellaigh I
1378 Muircheartach mac Pilib O
    Cellaigh [Maurice]
1393 William O Cormacain
1398 David Corre
1398 Enri O Conmaigh
1405 Tomasi O Cellaigh II
1410 Cobhthach O Madagain
1438 Seaan O hEidin
1441 John White
1447 Conchobhar O Maolalaidh
1448 Cornelius O Cuinnlis
1463 Matthaeus Mag Raith
1508 David de Burgo
1509 Dionysius O'Mordha
1534 Roland de Burgo
1536 Richard Nangle
1580 Hugh
1582 Stephen Kirwan
1602 Roland Lynch
1627 Robert Dawson
1644 William Baily
1665 Edward Wolley
1691 William FitzGerald
1722 Theophilus Bolton
1724 Arthur Price
1730 Edward Synge
1732 Mordecai Cary
1716 John Whitcombe
1752 Arthur Smyth
1753 William Carmichael
1758 William Gote
1762 John Oswald
1763 Denison Cumberland
1772 Walter Cope
1782 John Law

1787 Richard Marlay
1795 Charles Broderick
1796 Hugh Hamilton
1798 Matthew Young
1801 George de la l'oer Beresford
1802 Nathaniel Alexander
1804 Christopher Butson
United to Killaloe since 1834

†Clonmacnoise

–663 Baitan O'Cormac
–839 Joseph [of Rossmore]
    Maclodhar 890
    Cairbre Crom 904
    Loingsech 919
–940 Donough I
–953 Donough II
–966 Cormae O Cillin
    Maenach 971
    Conaing O'Cosgraigh 998
    Male Poil 1001
    Flaithbertach 1038
    Celechar 1067
    O'Mallaen 1093
    Christian Aherne 1104
?1111 Domnall mac Flannacain Ua
    Dubthaig
1152 Muirchertach Ua Maeluidir
    Cathal Ua Maeileoin 1207
c.1207 Muirchertach Ua Muiricen
1214 Aed O Maeileoin I
1227 Aed O Maeileoin II [Elias]
1236 Thomas Fitzpatrick
1252 Tomas O Cuinn
1280 Anonymous
1282 Gilbert (not consecrated)
1290 William O Dubhthaig
1298 William O Finnein
1303 Domnall O Braein
1324 Lughaid O Dalaigh
1337 Henricus
1349 Simon
1369 Richard [Braybroke]
1371 Hugo
1388 Philippus O Maoil
1389 Milo Corr
1397 O'Gallagher
1397 Philip Nangle
1423 David Prendergast
1426 Cormac Mac Cochlain
    [Cornelius]
1444 Sean O Dalaigh
1449 Thomas
1458 Robertus
1458 William
1459 John
1487 Walter Blake
1509 Tomas O Maolalaidh
1516 Quintin O h-Uiginn
1539 Richard O'Hogan
1539 Florence Kirwan
1556 Peter Wall [Wale]
United to Meath 1569

†Cloyne

    Reachtaidh 887
1148 Gilla na Naem O Muirchertaig
    [Nehemias]
    Ua Dubcroin 1159
    Ua Flannacain 1167
1177 Matthaeus Ua Mongaig
1201 Laurence Ua Suilleabain
1205 C.
1281 Luke
c.1224 Florence
1226 Daniel
1237 David mac Cellaig [O'Kelly]
1240 Ailinn O Suilleabain

1247 Daniel
1265 Reginaldus
1275 Alan O Longain
1284 Nicholas of Effingham
1323 Maurice O Solchain
1333 John Brid
1351 John Whitekot
1363 John Swaffham
1376 Richard Wye
1394 Gerard Caneton
1413 Adam Payn
United to Cork 1418–1638
1638 George Synge
1661–78 Held by the Bishops of Cork
1679 Patrick Sheridan
1683 Edward Jones
1693 William Palliser
1694 Tobias Pullein
1695 St George Ashe
1697 John Pooley
1702 Charles Crow
1726 Henry Maule
1732 Edward Synge
1734 George Berkeley
1753 James Stopford
1759 Robert Johnson
1767 Frederick Augustus Hervery
1768 Charles Agar
1780 George Chinnery
1781 Richard Woodward
1794 William Bennett
1820 Charles Mongan Warhurton
1826 John Brinkley
United to Cork on the death of Bp
Brinkley in 1835

Cork
Cork, Cloyne and Ross

Description of arms. Argent, on a plain
cross, the ends pattée, gules, a pastoral
staff, surmounted on a mitre, or (for
the See of Cork). Azure, a mitre proper
labelled or, between three crosses
pattées-fitchées argent (for the See of
Cloyne). No arms are borne for the See
of Ross.

    Donnell 876
    Soer Bhreatach 892
    DusucBhdhurn O'Stefam 959
    Cathmogh 969
    Mugron O'Mutan 1057
1138 Gregory
? Ua Menngorain 1147
1148 Gilla Aedha Ua Maigin
1174 [Gregorius] O h-Aedha
    [O Hea]
c.1182 Reginaldus I
1187 Aicher
1192 Murchad Ua h-Aedha
    Anonymous 1214
1215 Mairin Ua Briain [Marianus]
1225 Gilbertus
1248 Laurentius
1265 William of Jerpoint
1267 Reginaldus
1277 Robert Mac Donnchada

1302 Seoan Mac Cearbaill [Mac
          Carwill]
1321 Philip of Slane
1327 Walter le Rede
1330 John of Ballyconingham
1347 John Roche
1359 Gerald de Barri
1396 Roger Ellesmere
1406 Richard Kynmoure
1409 Patrick Fox
1409 Milo fitzJohn
1425 John Paston
1418 Adam Payn
1429 Jordan Purcell
1463 Gerald FitzGerald
1472 William Roche (Coadjutor)
1490 Tadhg Mac Carthaigh
1499 John FitzEdmund
          FitzGerald
1499 Patrick Cant
1523 John Benet
1536 Dominic Tyrre [Tirrey]
1562 Roger Skiddy
1570 Richard Dyxon
1572 Matthew Sheyn
Ross united to Cork 1583
1583 William Lyon
1618 John Boyle
1620 Richard Boyle
1638 William Chappell
1661 Michael Boyle
1663 Edward Synge
1679 Edward Wetenhall
1699 Dive Downes
1710 Peter Browne
1735 Robert Clayton
1745 Jemmett Browne
1772 Isaac Mann
1789 Euseby Cleaver
1789 William Foster
1790 William Bennet
1794 Thomas Stopford
1805 John George Beresford
1807 Thomas St Laurence
1831 Samuel Kyle
Cloyne united to Cork from 1835
1848 James Wilson
1857 William FitzGerald
1862 John Gregg
1878 Robert Samuel Gregg
1894 William Edward Meade
1912 Charles Benjamin Dowse
1933 William Edward Flewett
1938 Robert Thomas Hearn
1952 George Otto Sims
1957 Richard Gordon Perdue
1978 Samuel Greenfield Poyntz
1988 Robert Alexander Warke
1999 William Paul Colton

Dublin

Dublin and Glendalough

Description of arms. Azure, an
episcopal staff argent, ensigned with a
cross pattée or, surmounted by a
pallium of the second edged and
fringed or, charged with five crosses
formée fitchée, sable.

BISHOPS

Sinhail 790
*c.*1028 Dunan [Donatus]
1074 Gilla Patraic
1085 Donngus
1096 Samuel Ua'h-Aingliu

ARCHBISHOPS

1121 Grene [Gregorius]
1162 Lorcan Ua'Tuathail
          [Laurentius]
1182 John Cumin
1213 Henry de Loundres
Glendalough united to Dublin
1230 Luke
125? Fulk de Sandford
1279 John de Derlington
1286 John de Sandford
1295 Thomas de Chadworth
1296 William de Hotham
1299 Richard de Ferings
[1307 Richard de Havering, not
          consecrated]
1311 John de Leche
1317 Alexander de Bicknor
1349 John de St Paul
1363 Thomas Minot
1376 Robert de Wikeford
1391 Robert Waldeby
1396 Richard Northalis
1397 Thomas Cranley
1418 Richard Talbot
1451 Michael Tregury
1472 John Walton
1484 Walter Fitzsimons
1512 William Rokeby
1521 Hugh Inge
1529 John Alan
1535 George Browne
1555 Hugh Curwin
1567 Adam Loftus
1605 Thomas Jones
1619 Lancelot Bulkeley
1661 James Margetson
1663 Michael Boyle
1679 John Parker
1682 Francis Marsh
1694 Narcissus Marsh
1703 William King
1730 John Hoadly
1743 Charles Cobbe
1765 William Carmichael
1766 Arthur Smyth
1772 John Cradock
1779 Robert Fowler
1801 Charles Agar [Earl of
          Normanton]
1809 Euseby Cleaver
1820 John George Beresford
1822 William Magee
1831 Richard Whately
Kildare united to Dublin 1846
1864 Richard Chenevix Trench
          (resigned)
1885 William Conyngham [Lord
          Plunket]
1897 Joseph Ferguson Peacocke
1915 John Henry Bernard
1919 Charles Frederick D'Arcy
1920 John Allen Fitzgerald Gregg
1939 Arthur William Barton
1956 George Otto Simms
1969 Alan Alexander Buchanan
1977 Henry Robert McAdoo
1985 Donald Arthur Richard Caird
1996 Walton Newcome Francis
          Empey
2002 John Robert Winder Neill

†Emly

Raidghil 881
Ua Ruaich 953
Faelan 980
MaelFinan 1030
Diarmait Ua Flainnchua 1114
Gilla in Choimhded Ua
     h-Ardmhail Mael Isu Ua
     Laigenain 1163
1172 Ua Meic Stia
1177 Charles O'Buacalla
1177 Isaac O'Hamery
1192 Ragnall Ua Flainnchua
1205 M.
1209 William
1212 Henry
1227 John Collingham
1238 Daniel
1238 Christianus
1251 Gilbert O'Doverty
1266 Florence or Laurence O'hAirt
1272 Matthew MacGormain
1275 David O Cossaig
1286 William de Clifford
1306 Thomas Cantock [Quantock]
1309 William Roughead
1335 Richard le Walleys
1353 John Esmond
1363 David Penlyn [Foynlyn]
1363 William
1405 Nicholas Ball
1421 John Rishberry
1422 Robert Windell
1428 Thomas de Burgo
1428 Robert Portland
1445 Cornelius O Cuinnlis
1444 Robert
1448 Cornelius O Maolalaidh
1449 William O Hetigan
1476 Pilib O Cathail
1494 Donatus Mac Briain
1498 Cinneidigh Mac Briain
1507 Tomas O hUrthaille
1543 Angus O'Hernan
1551 Raymond de Burgo
United to Cashel 1569
Transferred to Limerick 1976

†Ferns

–598 Edan [or Maedoc or Hugh]
Maeldogair 676
Coman 678
Diratus 693
Cillenius 715
Cairbre O'Kearney 1095
Ceallach Ua Colmain 1117
Mael Eoin Ua Dunacain 1125
Ua Cattain 1135
1178 Loseph Ua h-Aeda
1186 Ailbe Ua Maelmuaid [Albinus]
1224 John of St John
1254 Geoffrey of St John
1258 Hugh of Lamport
1283 Richard of Northampton
1304 Simon of Evesham
1305 Robert Walrand
1312 Adam of Northampton
1347 Hugh de Saltu [of Leixlip]
1347 Geoffrey Grandfeld
1349 John Esmond
1350 William Charnells
1363 Thomas Dene
1400 Patrick Barret
1418 Robert Whittey
1453 Tadhg O Beirn
1457 John Purcell I
1479 Laurence Nevill
1505 Edmund Comerford

1510 Nicholas Comyn
1519 John Purcell II
1539 Alexander Devereux
1566 John Devereux
1582 Hugh Allen
Leighlin united to Ferns 1597
1600 Robert Grave
1601 Nicholas Statford
1605 Thomas Ram
1635 George Andrews
1661 Robert Price
1667 Richard Boyle
1683 Narcissus Marsh
1691 Bartholomew Vigors
1722 Josiah Hort
1727 John Hoadly
1730 Arthur Price
1734 Edward Synge
1740 George Stone
1743 William Cottrell
1744 Robert Downes
1752 John Garnet
1758 William Carmichael
1758 Thomas Salmon
1759 Richard Robinson
1761 Charles Jackson
1765 Edward Young
1772 Joseph Deane Bourke
1782 Walter Cope
1787 William Preston
1789 Euseby Cleaver
1809 Percy Jocelyn
1820 Robert Ponsonby Tottenham
       Loftus
1822 Thomas Elrington
United to Ossory 1835

†Glendalough

Dairchell 678
Eterscel 814
Dungal 904
Cormac 927
Nuadha 920 [or Neva]
Gilda Na Naomh
        c.1080
Cormac O'Mail 1101
Aed Ua Modain 1126
1140 Anonymous
1152 Gilla na Naem
1157 Cinaed O Ronain [Celestinus]
1176 Maelcallann Ua Cleirchen
       [Malchus]
1186 Macrobius
1192 William Piro
1214 Robert de Bedford
United to Dublin
After the union with Dublin some
rival bishops appear
c.1216 Bricheus
1468 John
1475 Michael
1481 Denis White John 1494
1494 Ivo Ruffi
1495 John
1500 Francis Fitzjohn of Corduba

†Iniscattery (Scattery Island)

861 Aidan
959 Cinaeda O'Chommind
973 Scandlam O'Lenz
       O'Bruil 1069
       O'Bruil II 1081
       Dermot O Lennain 1119
       Aed Ua Bechain I 1188
       Cearbhal Ua'h-Enna
       [Carolus] 1193
1360 Tomas Mac Mathghamhna
1392 John Donkan

1414 Richard Belmer
       Dionysius 1447
1447 John Grene
Incorporated with Limerick

†Kells

Mael Finnen 968
c.1152 Tuathal Ua Connachtarg
1185 Anonymous
1202 M. Ua Dobailen
Incorporated with Meath

†Kildare

Conlaedh 520
Hugh [or Hed] the Black 639
Maeldoborcon 709
Eutigern 762
Lomthiull 787
Snedbran 787
Tuatchar 834
Orthanach 840
Aedgene Britt 864
Macnghal 870
Lachtnan 875
Suibhne 881
Scannal 885
Lergus 888
Mael Findan 950
Annchadh 981
Murrough McFlan 986
1030 MaelMartain
       MaelBrighde 1042
       Finn 1085
       MaelBrighde O Brolchan
       1097
Hugh [Heremon] 1100
Ferdomnach 1101
Cormac O Cathassaig 1146
Ua Duibhin 1148
1152 Finn mac Mael Muire Mac
       Cianain
       Fin mac Gussain Ua
       Gormain
1161 Malachias Ua Brain
1177 Nehemias
1206 Cornelius Mac Fealain
1223 Ralph of Bristol
1233 John of Taunton
1258 Simon of Kilkenny
1280 Nicholas Cusack
1300 Walter Calf [de Veel]
1333 Richard Houlot
1352 Thomas Giffard
1366 Robert of Aketon
       [Acton]
1404 John Madock
1431 William fitzEdward
1449 Geoffrey Hereford
1456 John Bole [Bull]
1464 Richard Lang
1474 David Cone
1475 James Wall
       William Barret
1480 Edward Lane
1526 Thomas Dillon
1529 Walter Wellesley
1540 William Miagh
1550 Thomas Lancaster
1555 Thomas Leverous
1560 Alexander Craik
1564 Robert Daly
1583 Daniel Neylan
1604 William Pilsworth
1636 Robert Ussher
1644 William Golborne
1661 Thomas Price
1667 Ambrose Jones
1679 Anthony Dopping

1682 William Moreton
1705 Welbore Ellis
1731 Charles Cobbe
1743 George Stone
1745 Thomas Fletcher
1761 Richard Robinson
1765 Charles Jackson
1790 George Lewis Jones
1804 Charles Lindsay
United to Dublin after the death of
       Bp Lindsay in 1846
1976 Separated from Dublin and
       united to Meath

†Kilfenora

1172 Anonymous
1205 F.
1224 Johannes
1254 Christianus
       Anonymous 1264
1266 Mauricius
1273 Florentius O Tigernaig
1281 Congalach [O Lochlainn]
1291 G.
1299 Simon O Cuirrin
1303 Maurice O Briain
1323 Risdeard O Lochlainn
c.1355 Dionysius
1372 Henricus
       Cornelius
1390 Patricius
1421 Feidhlimidh mac
       Mathghamhna O Lochlainn
       [Florentius]
1433 Fearghal
1434 Dionysius O Connmhaigh
1447 John Greni
1476 [? Denis] O Tombaigh
1491 Muircheartach mac
       Murchadha O Briain
       [Mauricius]
1514 Maurice O'Kelly
1541 John O'Neylan
–1585 Daniel, bishop-elect
1606 Bernard Adams [with
       Limerick q.v.]
1617 John Steere
1622 William Murray
[1628 Richard Betts, not
       consecrated]
1630 James Heygate
1638 Robert Sibthorp
1661–1741 Held by the Archbishops
       of Tuam
1742–52 Held by the Bishop of
       Clonfert
United to Killaloe 1752

†Killaloe

BISHOPS

       O'Gerruidher 1054
       Domnall Ua hEnna 1098
       Mael Muire O Dunain 1117
       Domnall Ua Conaing 1131
       Domnall Ua Longargain 1137
       Tadg Ua Longargain 1161
       Donnchad mac Diarmata Ua
       Briain 1164
1179 Constantin mac Toirrdelbaig
       Ua Briain
1194 Diarmait Ua Conaing
1201 Conchobhar Ua h-Enna
       [Cornelius]
1217 Robert Travers
1221 Domnall Ua h-Enna
       [Donatus]
1231 Domnall O Cenneitig
       [Donatus]

1253 Isoc O Cormacain [Isaac]	1957 Henry Arthur Stanistreet	1527 Matthew Sanders
1268 Mathgamain O h-Ocain [O Hogan]	1972 Edwin Owen	1550 Robert Travers
1281 Maurice O h-Ocain	1976 United to Limerick	1555 Thomas O'Fihelly
1299 David Mac Mathghamna [Mac Mahon]		1567 Donnell or Daniel Cavanagh
1317 Tomas O Cormacain I	**†Kilmacduagh**	1589 Richard Meredith

†Kilmacduagh

1253 Isoc O Cormacain [Isaac]
1268 Mathgamain O h-Ocain [O Hogan]
1281 Maurice O h-Ocain
1299 David Mac Mathghamna [Mac Mahon]
1317 Tomas O Cormacain I
1323 Brian O Cosgraig
1326 David Mac Briain [David of Emly]
?1326 Natus O Heime
1343 Tomas O h-Ogain
1355 Tomas O Cormacain II
1389 Mathghamain Mag Raith
1400 Donatus Mag Raith
1409 Robert Mulfield
1418 Eugenius O Faolain
1423 Thadeus Mag Raith I
1429 Seamus O Lonnghargain
1443 Donnchadh mac Toirdhealbhaigh O Briain
1460 Thadeus Mag Raith II
1463 Matthaeus O Griobhtha
1483 Toirdhealbhach mac Mathghamhna O Briain [Theodoricus]
1523 Thadeus
1526 Seamus O Cuirrin
1546 Cornelius O Dea
1554 Turlough [or Terence] O'Brien II
1570 Maurice [or Murtagh] O'Brien-Arra
1613 John Rider
1633 Lewis Jones
1647 Edward Parry
1661 Edward Worth
1669 Daniel Wytter
1675 John Roan
1693 Henry Ryder
1696 Thomas Lindsay
1713 Thomas Vesey
1714 Nicholas Forster
1716 Charles Carr
1740 Joseph Story
1742 John Ryder
1743 Jemmet Browne
1745 Richard Chenevix
1746 Nicholas Synge
Kilfenora united to Killaloe 1752
1771 Robert Fowler
1779 George Chinnery
1780 Thomas Barnard
1794 William Knox
1803 Charles Dalrymple Lindsay
1804 Nathaniel Alexander
1804 Robert Ponsonby Tottenham Loftus
1820 Richard Mant
1823 Alexander Arbuthnot
1828 Richard Ponsonby
1831 Edmund Knox [with Clonfert]
Clonfert united to Killaloe 1834
Kilmacduagh united to Killaloe 1834
1834 Christopher Butson
1836 Stephen Crengh Sandes
1839 Ludlow Tonson [afterwards Baron Riversdale]
1862 William FitzGerald
1884 William Bennet Chester
1893 Frederick Richards Wynne
1897 Mervyn Archdall
1912 Charles Benjamin Dowse
1913 Thomas Sterling Berry (resigned)
1924 Henry Edmund Patton
1943 Robert M'Neil Boyd
1945 Hedley Webster
1953 Richard Gordon Perdue

1957 Henry Arthur Stanistreet
1972 Edwin Owen
1976 United to Limerick

†Kilmacduagh

? Ua Cleirig 1137
Imar Ua Ruaidin 1176
Rugnad O'Rowan 1178
1179 Mac Gilla Cellaig Ua Ruaidin
1206 Ua Cellaig
Mael Muire O Connmaig 1224
1227 Aed [Odo]
Conchobhar O Muiredaig 1247
1248 Gilla Cellaig O Ruaidin [Gilbertus]
1249 David yFredrakern
1254 Mauricius O Leaain
1284 David O Setachain
1290 Luirint O Lachtnain [Laurentius]
1307 Lucas
1326 Johannes
1360 Nicol O Leaain
1394 Gregory O Leaain
1405 Enri O Connmhaigh
1409 Dionysius
1409 Eugene O Faolain
1418 Diarmaid O Donnchadha
1419 Nicol O Duibhghiolla
1419 Seaan O Connmhaigh
1441 Dionysius O Donnchadha
1479 Cornelius O Mullony
1503 Matthaeus O Briain
1533 Christopher Bodkin
1573 Stephen O'Kirwan
[1584 Thomas Burke, not consecrated]
1587 Roland Lynch
1627–1836 Held in commendam by the Bishops of Clonfert
United to Killaloe since 1834

†Leighlin

-633 Laserian or Molaise
-865 Mainchin
-940 Conella McDonegan Daniel
969 Cleitic O'Muinic 1050
c.1096 Ferdomnac
Mael Eoin Ua Dunacain 1125
Sluaigedach Ua Cathain 1145
1152 Dungal O Caellaide
1192 Johannes
1197 Johannes
1202 Herlewin
1217 Richard [Fleming]
1228 William le Chauniver
1252 Thomas
1275 Nicholas Chever
1309 Maurice de Blanchville
1321 Meiler le Poer
1344 Radulphus O Ceallaigh
1349 Thomas of Brakenberg
1360 Johannes
1362 William (not consecrated)
1363 John Young
1371 Philip FitzPeter
1385 John Griffin
1398 Thomas Peverell
1400 Richard Bocomb
1419 John Mulgan
1432 Thomas Fleming
— Diarmaid 1464
1464 Milo Roche
1490 Nicholas Magwyr
1513 Thomas Halsey
1524 Mauricius O Deoradhain

1527 Matthew Sanders
1550 Robert Travers
1555 Thomas O'Fihelly
1567 Donnell or Daniel Cavanagh
1589 Richard Meredith
United to Ferns since 1597 on the death of Bp Meredith

Limerick

Limerick, Ardfert, Aghadoe, Killaloe, Kilfenora, Clonfert, Kilmacduagh and Emly

Description of arms. Azure two keys addorsed in saltire the wards upwards; in the dexter chief a crosier paleways, in the sinister a mitre, all or.

-1106 Gilli alias Gilla Espaic
1140 Patricius
1150 Erolb [? = Harold]
1152 Torgesius
1179 Brictius
1203 Donnchad Ua'Briain [Donatus]
1207 Geoffrey
-1215 Edmund
1223 Hubert de Burgo
1252 Robert de Emly or Neil
1273 Gerald [or Miles] de Mareshall
1302 Robert de Dundonald
1312 Eustace de Aqua or de l'Eau
1336 Maurice de Rochfort
1354 Stephen Lawless
1360 Stephen Wall [de Valle]
1369 Peter Curragh
1399 Bernardus O Conchobhair
1400 Conchobhar O Deadhaidh
1426 John Mothel (resigned)
Iniscattery incorporated with Limerick
1456 Thomas Leger
1458 William Russel, *alias* Creagh
1463 Thomas Arthur
[1486 Richard Stakpoll, not consecrated]
1486 John Dunowe
1489 John O'Phelan [Folan]
1524 Sean O Cuinn
1551 William Casey
1557 Hugh de Lacey or Lees (deposed)
1571 William Casey
1594 John Thornburgh
1604 Bernard Adams
1626 Francis Gough
1634 George Webb
1643 Robert Sibthorp
Ardfert united to Limerick 1661
1661 Edward Synge
1664 William Fuller
1667 Francis Marsh
1673 John Vesey
1679 Simon Digby
1692 Nathaniel Wilson
1695 Thomas Smyth
1725 William Burscough
1755 James Leslie
1771 James Averill

1772 William Gore
1784 William Cecil Pery
1794 Thomas Barnard
1806 Charles Morgan Warburton
1820 Thomas Elrington
1823 John Jebb
1834 Edmund Knox
1849 William Higgin
1854 Henry Griffin
1866 Charles Graves
1899 Thomas Bunbury
1907 Raymond D'Audemra Orpen
1921 Harry Vere White
1934 Charles King Irwin
1942 Evelyn Charles Hodges
1961 Robert Wyse Jackson
1970 Donald Arthur Richard Caird
Killaloe united to Limerick 1976
Emly transferred to Limerick 1976
1976 Edwin Owen
1981 Walton Newcome Francis
      Empey
1985 Edward Flewett Darling
2000 Michael Hugh Gunton Mayes
2008 Trevor Russell Williams

†Lismore

Ronan 764
Cormac MacCuillenan 918
–999 Cinneda O'Chonmind
Niall mac Meic Aedacain
      1113
Ua Daightig 1119
1121 Mael Isu Ua h-Ainmere
Mael Muire Ua Loingsig 1150
1151 Gilla Crist Ua Connairche
      [Christianus]
1179 Felix
Ardmore incorporated with Lismore
      1192
1203 Malachias, O'Heda or
      O'Danus
1216 Thomas
1219 Robert of Bedford
1228 Griffin Christopher
1248 Ailinn O Suilleabain
1253 Thomas
1270 John Roche
1280 Richard Corre
1309 William Fleming
1310 R.
1322 John Leynagh
1356 Roger Cradock, provision
      annulled
1358 Thomas le Reve
United to Waterford 1363

Meath

Meath and Kildare

Description of arms. Sable three mitres
argent, two, and one.

BISHOPS OF THE SEE OF CLONARD

Senach 588
–640 Colman 654
DusucBhduin O'Phelan 718
Tole 738

–778 Fulartach 779
Clothcu 796
Clemens 826
Cormac MacSuibhne
Cumsuth 858
Suarlech 870
Ruman MacCathasaid 922
Colman MacAilild 926
Tuathal O'Dubhamaigh 1028

BISHOPS OF MEATH

1096 Mael Muire Ua Dunain
1128 Eochaid O Cellaig
1151 Etru Ua Miadacain
      [Eleuzerius]
1177 Echtigern mac Mael Chiarain
      [Eugenius]
1192 Simon Rochfort
(The See was transferred from
      Clonard to Newtown near
      Trim, 1202)
Kells incorporated with Meath
1224 Donan De [Deodatus] (not
      consecrated)
1227 Ralph Petit
1231 Richard de la Corner
1253 Geoffrey Cusack
1255 Hugo de Taghmon
1283 Walter de Fulburn
1287 Thomas St Leger
1322 Seoan Mac Cerbaill [John
      MacCarwill]
1327 William de Paul
1350 William St Leger
1353 Nicholas [Allen]
1369 Stephen de Valle [Wall]
1380 William Andrew
1385 Alexander Petit [or de Balscot]
1401 Robert Montayne
1412 Edward Dantesey
[1430 Thomas Scurlog, apparently
      not consecrated]
1430 William Hadsor
1435 William Silk
1450 Edmund Ouldhall
1460 William Shirwood
1483 John Payne
1507 William Rokeby
1512 Hugh Inge
1523 Richard Wilson
1529 Edward Staples
1554 William Walsh
1563 Hugh Brady
Clonmacnoise united to Meath
      1569
1584 Thomas Jones
1605 Roger Dod
1612 George Montgomery
1621 James Usher
1625 Anthony Martin
[Interregnum 1650–61]
1661 Henry Leslie
1661 Henry Jones
1682 Anthony Dopping
1697 Richard Tennison
1705 William Moreton
1716 John Evans
1724 Henry Downes
1727 Ralph Lambert
1732 Welbore Ellis
1734 Arthur Price
1744 Henry Maule
1758 William Carmichael
1765 Richard Pococke
1765 Arthur Smyth
1766 Henry Maxwell
1798 Thomas Lewis O'Beirne
1823 Nathaniel Alexander

1840 Charles Dickinson
1842 Edward Stopford
1850 Thomas Stewart Townsend
1852 James Henderson Singer
1866 Samuel Butcher
1876 William Conyngham [Lord
      Plunket]
1885 Charles Parsons Reichel
1894 Joseph Ferguson Peacocke
1897 James Bennett Keene
1919 Benjamin John Plunket
1926 Thomas Gibson George
      Collins
1927 John Orr
1938 William Hardy Holmes
1945 James McCann
1959 Robert Bonsall Pike
Kildare united to Meath 1976
1976 Donald Arthur Richard Caird
1985 Walton Newcome Francis
      Empey
1996 Richard Lionel Clarke

†Ossory

Dermot 973
1152 Domnall Ua Fogartaig
1180 Felix Ua Duib Slaine
1202 Hugo de Rous [Hugo Rufus]
1220 Peter Mauveisin
1231 William of Kilkenny
1233 Walter de Brackley
1245 Geoffrey de Turville
1251 Hugh de Mapilton
1260 Geoffrey St Leger
1287 Roger of Wexford
1289 Michael d'Exeter
1303 William FitzJohn
1317 Richard Ledred
1361 John de Tatenhale
1366 William
— John of Oxford
1371 Alexander Petit [de Balscot]
1387 Richard Northalis
1396 Thomas Peverell
1399 John Waltham
1400 John Griffin
1400 John
1401 Roger Appleby
1402 John Waltham
1407 Thomas Snell
1417 Patrick Foxe
1421 Dionysius O Deadhaidh
1427 Thomas Barry
1460 David Hacket
1479 Seaan O hEidigheain
1487 Oliver Cantwell
1528 Milo Baron [or FitzGerald]
1553 John Bale
1554 John Tonory
1567 Christopher Gaffney
1577 Nicholas Walsh
1586 John Horsfall
1610 Richard Deane
1613 Jonas Wheeler
1641 Griffith Williams
1672 John Parry
1678 Benjamin Parry
1678 Michael Ward
1680 Thomas Otway
1693 John Hartstonge
1714 Thomas Vesey
1731 Edward Tennison
1736 Charles Este
1741 Anthony Dopping
1743 Michael Cox
1754 Edward Maurice
1755 Richard Pococke
1765 Charles Dodgson
1775 William Newcome

1779 John Hotham
1782 William Heresford
1795 Thomas Lewis O'Beirne
1799 Hugh Hamilton
1806 John Kearney
1813 Robert Fowler
Ferns united to Ossory 1835
1842 James Thomas O'Brien
1874 Robert Samuel Gregg
1878 William Pakenham Walsh
1897 John Baptist Crozier
1907 Charles Frederick D'Arcy
1911 John Henry Bernard
1915 John Allen Fitzgerald Gregg
1920 John Godfrey FitzMaurice
     Day
1938 Ford Tichbourne
1940 John Percy Phair
1962 Henry Robert McAdoo
United to Cashel 1977

†Ross

Nechtan MacNechtain 1160
Isaac O'Cowen 1161
O'Carroll 1168
1177 Benedictus
1192 Mauricius
1198 Daniel
1224 Fineen O Clothna [Florentius]
c.1250 Malachy
1254 Mauricius
1269 Walter O Mithigein
1275 Peter O h-Uallachain
     [? Patrick]
1291 Laurentius
1310 Matthaeus O Finn
1331 Laurentius O h-Uallachain
1336 Dionysius
1379 Bernard O Conchobhair
1399 Peter Curragh
1400 Thadeus O Ceallaigh
1401 Mac Raith O hEidirsgeoil
     [Macrobius]
1402 Stephen Brown
1403 Matthew
1418 Walter Formay

1424 John Bloxworth
1426 Conchobhar Mac
     Fhaolchadha [Cornelius]
     Maurice Brown 1431
1431 Walter of Leicester
1434 Richard Clerk
1448 Domhnall O Donnobhain
     John 1460
1460 Robert Colynson
−1464 Thomas
1464 John Hornse *alias* Skipton
1473 Aodh O hEidirsgeoil [Odo]
1482 Tadhg Mac Carthaigh
1494 John Edmund Courci
1517 Seaan O Muirthile
1519 Tadgh O Raghallaigh
     [Thaddeus]
1523 Bonaventura
1526 Diarmaid Mac Carthaigh
1544 Dermot McDonnell
1551 John
1554 Maurice O'Fihelly
1559 Maurice O'Hea
1561 Thomas O'Herlihy
1582 William Lyon [with Cork and
     Cloyne after 1581]
United to Cork 1583

†Waterford

1096 Mael Ius Ua h-Ainmere
1152 Toistius
1175 Augustinus Ua Selbaig
     Anonymous 1199
1200 Robert I
1204 David the Welshman
1210 Robert II [Breathnach]
1223 William Wace
1227 Walter
1232 Stephen
1250 Henry
1252 Philip
1255 Walter de Southwell
1274 Stephen de Fulbourn
1286 Walter de Fulbourn
1308 Matthew
1323 Nicholas Welifed

1338 Richard Francis
1349 Robert Elyot
1350 Roger Cradock
Lismore united to Waterford
     1363
1363 Thomas le Reve
1394 Robert Read
1396 Thomas Sparklord
1397 John Deping
1400 Thomas Snell
1407 Roger of Appleby (*see under*
     Ossory)
1409 John Geese
1414 Thomas Colby
1421 John Geese
1426 Richard Cantwell
1446 Robert Poer
1473 Richard Martin
1475 John Bulcomb
1480 Nicol O hAonghusa
1483 Thomas Purcell
1519 Nicholas Comyn
1551 Patrick Walsh
1579 Marmaduke Middleton
1582 Miler Magrath (Bishop
     of Cashel and
     Waterford)
1589 Thomas Wetherhead [or
     Walley]
1592 Miler Magrath
1608 John Lancaster
1619 Michael Boyle
1636 John Atherton
1641 Archibald Adair
1661 George Baker
1666 Hugh Gore
1691 Nathaniel Foy
1708 Thomas Mills
1740 Charles Este
1746 Richard Chenevix
1779 William Newcome
1795 Richard Marlay
1802 Power le Poer Trench
1810 Joseph Stock
1813 Richard Bourke
United to Cashel under Church
     Temporalities Act 1833

CATHEDRALS

CHURCH OF ENGLAND

(BATH AND) WELLS (St Andrew) **Dean** J M CLARKE,
Cans Res P H F WOODHOUSE, R I BOWMAN-EADIE,
A FEATHERSTONE, THE VEN N A SULLIVAN
BIRMINGHAM (St Philip) **Dean** R A WILKES,
Can Res P HOWELL-JONES, N A HAND, J E CHAPMAN,
Y L RICHMOND
BLACKBURN (St Mary) **Dean** C J ARMSTRONG,
Cans Res A D HINDLEY, C M CHIVERS, S I PENFOLD
BRADFORD (St Peter) **Dean** D J ISON,
Can Res F E F WARD, A J WILLIAMS,
Can Th K N MEDHURST
BRISTOL (Holy Trinity) **Dean** R W GRIMLEY,
Cans Res A TREMLETT, D R HOLT, T J HIGGINS, W A WILBY
CANTERBURY (Christ) **Dean** R A WILLIS,
Cans Res C P IRVINE, THE VEN S A WATSON, E F CONDRY,
D C EDWARDS
CARLISLE (Holy Trinity) **Dean** M C BOYLING,
Cans Res B R MCCONNELL, M A MANLEY
CHELMSFORD (St Mary, St Peter and St Cedd)
Dean P S M JUDD, **Cans Res** A W A KNOWLES, W R KING,
S J POTHEN
CHESTER (Christ and Blessed Virgin Mary)
Dean G F MCPHATE, **Cans Res** T J DENNIS, C P BURKETT,
C W HUMPHRIES, **Can Th** L C A ALEXANDER
CHICHESTER (Holy Trinity) **Dean** N A FRAYLING,
Cans Res A W N S CANE, P C KEFFORD, N T SCHOFIELD,
I GIBSON **PV** D NASON
COVENTRY (St Michael) **Dean** J D IRVINE,
Cans Res A M DAFFERN, T J PULLEN
DERBY (All Saints) **Dean** J C CUTTELL,
Cans Res D PERKINS, E J JONES, **Can Th** A BROWN,
Chapl C J HODDER
DURHAM (Christ, Blessed Virgin Mary and St Cuthbert)
Dean M SADGROVE, **Cans Res** THE VEN I JAGGER,
D J KENNEDY, S A CHERRY, R BROWN, **Min Can** D J SUDRON,
Chapl D C COULING
ELY (Holy Trinity) **Dean** M J CHANDLER,
Cans Res J R GARRARD, A L HARGRAVE, D P PRITCHARD
EXETER (St Peter) **Dean** C J MEYRICK,
Cans Res A P GODSALL, T D HONEY, C F TURNER,
M J RYLANDS
GLOUCESTER (St Peter and Holy Trinity)
Dean N A S BURY, **Cans Res** N C HEAVISIDES, D M HOYLE,
G H SIDAWAY, C S M THOMSON, **Can Th** C M METHUEN
GUILDFORD (Holy Spirit) **Dean** V A STOCK,
Cans Res A M WEAVER, N J THISTLETHWAITE, J H FROST
HEREFORD (Blessed Virgin Mary and St Ethelbert)
Dean M E TAVINOR, **Cans Res** C PULLIN, A PIPER,
M J COLMER
LEICESTER (St Martin) **Dean** V F FAULL,
Cans Res J B NAYLOR, S A FOSTER, P C HACKWOOD,
D R M MONTEITH
LICHFIELD (Blessed Virgin Mary and St Chad)
Dean A J DORBER, **Cans Res** W W BELL, P J WILCOX,
C F LILEY, **Dean's V** P LOCKETT, **Chan's V** P L HOLLIDAY
LINCOLN (Blessed Virgin Mary) **Dean** P J W BUCKLER,
Cans Res A H NUGENT, G J KIRK
LIVERPOOL (Christ) **Dean** J P WELBY,
Cans Res A B HAWLEY, M C DAVIES, **Chapl** J C LYNN
LONDON (St Paul) **Dean** G P KNOWLES,
Cans Res M J COLCLOUGH, M C WARNER, L C WINKETT,
G A FRASER, **Min Can** C E ROBSON, L J BURGESS, J RENDELL
MANCHESTER (St Mary, St Denys and St George)
Dean R M GOVENDER, **Cans Res** G M MYERS,
R A G SHANKS, A E HOLLINGHURST, A W HARDY

NEWCASTLE (St Nicholas) **Dean** C C DALLISTON,
Cans Res P R STRANGE, THE VEN G V MILLER,
D J ELKINGTON, R E GAGE
NORWICH (Holy Trinity) **Dean** G C M SMITH,
Cans Res P M DOLL, R CAPPER, **Prec** J M HASELOCK
OXFORD (Christ Church) **Dean** C A LEWIS,
Cans Res N J BIGGAR, J S K WARD, M M PARRY, E J NEWELL,
G L PATTISON, THE VEN J R H HUBBARD
PETERBOROUGH (St Peter, St Paul and St Andrew)
Dean C W TAYLOR, **Cans Res** J W BAKER, D S PAINTER,
R B RUDDOCK
PORTSMOUTH (St Thomas of Canterbury)
Dean D C BRINDLEY, **Cans Res** D T ISAAC, M A TRISTRAM,
N J ASH
RIPON (AND LEEDS) (St Peter and St Wilfrid)
Dean K M JUKES, **Cans Res** P GREENWELL, K PUNSHON
ROCHESTER (Christ and Blessed Virgin Mary)
Dean A NEWMAN, **Cans Res** P H D´A LOCK, N H THOMPSON,
P J HESKETH
ST ALBANS (St Alban) **Dean** J P H JOHN,
Cans Res M C SANSOM, K A WALTON, S D LAKE,
R R WHEELER, D L STAMPS, **Min Cans** A R MATTHEWS,
D V COLLINS
ST EDMUNDSBURY (St James) **Dean** N COLLINGS,
Cans Res M J VERNON, M H J HAMPEL
SALISBURY (Blessed Virgin Mary) **Dean** J OSBORNE,
Cans Res D J C DAVIES, I WOODWARD, E C PROBERT,
M P J BONNEY
SHEFFIELD (St Peter and St Paul)
Dean P E BRADLEY, **Cans Res** A P SHACKERLEY, W R S LAMB,
J W GRENFELL, S C COWLING, **Can Th** M W PERCY
SODOR AND MAN (St German) **Dean** THE BISHOP
SOUTHWARK (St Saviour and St Mary Overie)
Dean C B SLEE, **Cans Res** B A SAUNDERS, A P NUNN, M A HART,
J E STEEN, R J TITLEY, **Succ** A J M MACHAM
SOUTHWELL (Blessed Virgin Mary)
Dean J A GUILLE, **Cans Res** J D JONES, N J COATES
TRURO (St Mary) **Dean** C G HARDWICK,
Cans Res P R GAY, P A A WALKER, R C BUSH, P C LAMBERT
WAKEFIELD (All Saints) **Dean** J D F GREENER,
Cans Res J A LAWSON, A W ROBINSON, M G RAWSON,
Prec A M HOFBAUER **Can Missr** A S MACPHERSON
WINCHESTER (Holy Trinity, St Peter, St Paul and
St Swithun) **Dean** J E ATWELL,
Cans Res M A M ST JOHN-CHANNELL, S C PITTIS, R G A RIEM
WORCESTER (Christ and Blessed Virgin Mary)
Dean P G ATKINSON, **Cans Res** A L PETTERSEN,
D J STANTON, **Min Cans** M R DORSETT, C M MANSHIP
YORK (St Peter) **Dean** K B JONES,
Cans Res G H WEBSTER, J L DRAPER, J J FLETCHER

Collegiate Churches
WESTMINSTER ABBEY
ST GEORGE'S CHAPEL, WINDSOR
See Royal Peculiars, p. 991.

Diocese in Europe
GIBRALTAR (Holy Trinity) **Dean** J A B PADDOCK
MALTA Valletta (St Paul) Pro-Cathedral
Chan S H M GODFREY
BRUSSELS (Holy Trinity) Pro-Cathedral **Chan** R N INNES

CHURCH IN WALES

BANGOR (St Deiniol) **Dean** A J HAWKINS,
  Min Cans J K R ELLIS, A WILLIAMS
LLANDAFF (St Peter and St Paul) **Dean** J T LEWIS,
  Can G W A HOLCOMBE
MONMOUTH Newport (St Woolos) **Dean** R D FENWICK,
  Can Res K M DENISON, **Min Cans** G P HOWELL, R F DENNIS

ST ASAPH (St Asaph) **Dean** C N L POTTER,
  Can Res M K R STALLARD, **Chapl** V R HANCOCK
ST DAVIDS (St David and St Andrew) **Dean** D J R LEAN,
  Min Can J S BENNETT, R J PATTINSON
(SWANSEA AND) BRECON (St John the Evangelist)
  Dean G O MARSHALL, **Min Can** D M JONES

SCOTTISH EPISCOPAL CHURCH

For the members of the chapter the *Scottish Episcopal Church Directory* should be consulted.

Aberdeen and Orkney
ABERDEEN (St Andrew) **Provost** R E KILGOUR

Argyll and The Isles
OBAN (St John) **Provost** N D MACCALLUM
CUMBRAE (Holy Spirit) Cathedral of The Isles
Provost A M SHAW *Bishop of Argyll and The Isles*

Brechin
DUNDEE (St Paul) **Provost** *vacant*

Edinburgh
EDINBURGH (St Mary) **Provost** G J T FORBES

Glasgow and Galloway
GLASGOW (St Mary) **Provost** K HOLDSWORTH

Moray, Ross and Caithness
INVERNESS (St Andrew) **Provost** A R GORDON

St Andrews, Dunkeld and Dunblane
PERTH (St Ninian) **Provost** H B FARQUHARSON

Church of Ireland

Most cathedrals are parish churches, and the dean is usually, but not always, the incumbent. For the members of the chapter the *Church of Ireland Directory* should be consulted. The name of the dean is given, together with those of other clergy holding full-time appointments.

NATIONAL CATHEDRAL OF ST PATRICK, Dublin
Dean R B MacCARTHY, **Dean's V** C W MULLEN

CATHEDRAL OF ST ANNE, Belfast R S J H MCKELVEY
(St Anne's is a cathedral of the dioceses of Down and Dromore and of Connor)

Province of Armagh

Armagh
ARMAGH (St Patrick) P W ROOKE

Clogher
CLOGHER (St Macartan) *vacant*
ENNISKILLEN (St Macartin) *vacant*

Derry and Raphoe
DERRY (St Columb) W W MORTON
RAPHOE (St Eunan) J HAY

Down and Dromore
DOWN (Holy and Undivided Trinity) T H HULL
DROMORE (Christ the Redeemer) S H LOWRY

Connor
LISBURN (Christ) *(Dean of Connor)* J F A BOND,
  I W S WRIGHT

Kilmore, Elphin and Ardagh
KILMORE (St Fethlimidh) W R FERGUSON
SLIGO (St Mary and St John the Baptist) A WILLIAMS

Tuam, Killala and Achonry
TUAM (St Mary) A J GRIMASON
KILLALA (St Patrick) S M PATTERSON

Province of Dublin

Dublin and Glendalough
DUBLIN (Holy Trinity) Christ Church D P M DUNNE

Meath and Kildare
TRIM (St Patrick) R W JONES *Dean of Clonmacnoise*
KILDARE (St Brigid) J J MARSDEN

Cashel and Ossory
CASHEL (St John the Baptist) P J KNOWLES
WATERFORD (Blessed Trinity) Christ Church
T R LESTER
LISMORE (St Carthage) P R DRAPER
KILKENNY (St Canice) N N LYNAS *Dean of Ossory*
LEIGHLIN (St Laserian) F J G WYNNE
FERNS (St Edan) L D A FORREST

Cork, Cloyne and Ross
CORK (St Fin Barre) N K DUNNE
CLOYNE (St Colman) A G MARLEY
ROSS (St Fachtna) C L PETERS

Limerick and Killaloe
LIMERICK (St Mary) J M G SIRR
KILLALOE (St Flannan) S R WHITE

ROYAL PECULIARS, CLERGY OF THE QUEEN'S HOUSEHOLD, ETC.

Royal Peculiars

Description of arms. Azure the reputed arms of Edward the Confessor, viz. a cross patonce between five martlets or, on a chief of the same, between two double roses of Lancaster and York, barbed and seeded proper, a pale charged with the Royal arms (viz. Quarterly of France and England).

Collegiate Church of St Peter Westminster
(Westminster Abbey) **Dean** J R HALL,
Cans A R WRIGHT, N SAGOVSKY, R P REISS, J B HEDGES
Min Cans G S P C NAPIER, M D MACEY
PVs P A BAGOTT, N L BIDDLE, A R BODDY,
P F BRADSHAW, P A E CHESTER, A C COLES, J W CROSSLEY,
B D FENTON, R C GODSALL, J M GOODALL, A G GYLE,
S E HARTLEY, E J LEWIS, C LOWSON, P MCGEARY,
D A PETERS, G D SWINTON, G J WILLIAMS

Description of arms. The arms of the Order of the Garter, viz. Argent, a St George's Cross gules. The shield is encircled by the blue Garter with its motto.

Queen's Free Chapel of St George Windsor Castle
(St George's Chapel) **Dean** THE RT REVD
D J CONNER, **Cans** J A WHITE, J A OVENDEN,
H E FINLAY, J W WOODWARD, **Min Cans** M J BOAG,
A S ZIHNI

The Queen's Household

Royal Almonry

High Almoner THE RT REVD N S MCCULLOCH (Bishop of Manchester)
Sub-Almoner W S SCOTT

The College of Chaplains

Clerk of the Closet THE RT REVD C J HILL (Bishop of Guildford)

Deputy Clerk of the Closet W S SCOTT

Chaplains to The Queen

G R P ASHENDEN	C M FARRINGTON	J A OVENDEN
P D L AVIS	R A J HILL	S C PALMER
H W BEARN	R J HUDSON-WILKIN	J B V RIVIERE
R V BRAZIER	G I KOVOOR	R B RUDDOCK
J V BYRNE	E J LEWIS	C W J SAMUELS
G M CALVER	W A MATTHEWS	C M SMITH
P N CALVERT	P MILLER	E G STEPHENSON
A CLITHEROW	G MOFFAT	P H J THORNEYCROFT
R T COOPER	J W R MOWLL	A D C WINGATE
A R EASTER	W A NOBLETT	A R WOODHOUSE

Extra Chaplains to The Queen

A D CAESAR	J G M W MURPHY	J R W STOTT
E A JAMES	J P ROBSON	

Chapels Royal

Dean of the Chapels Royal THE BISHOP OF LONDON
Sub-Dean of the Chapels Royal W S SCOTT
Priests in Ordinary R D E BOLTON, P R THOMAS, S E YOUNG
Deputy Priests in Ordinary R J HALL, A H MEAD,
D R MULLINER, M D OAKLEY
Domestic Chaplain, Buckingham Palace W S SCOTT
Domestic Chaplain, Windsor Castle THE DEAN OF WINDSOR
Domestic Chaplain, Sandringham J B V RIVIERE
Chaplain, Royal Chapel, Windsor Great Park
J A OVENDEN
Chaplain, Hampton Court Palace D R MULLINER
Chaplain, HM Tower of London R J HALL

The Queen's Chapel of the Savoy
Chaplain P J GALLOWAY

Royal Memorial Chapel, Sandhurst
Chaplain J R B GOUGH

Royal Foundation of St Katharine in Ratcliffe
Master J D M PATON

DIOCESAN OFFICES

CHURCH OF ENGLAND

BATH AND WELLS
Diocesan Office, The Old Deanery, Wells BA5 2UG
Tel (01749) 670777 Fax 674240 E-mail general@bathwells.anglican.org
Web www.bathwells.anglican.org

BIRMINGHAM
Diocesan Office, 175 Harborne Park Road, Birmingham B17 0BH
Tel 0121–426 0400 Fax 428 1114 E-mail j.d.drennan@birmingham.anglican.org
Web www.birmingham.anglican.org

BLACKBURN
Church House, Cathedral Close, Blackburn BB1 5AA
Tel (01254) 503070 Fax 667309 E-mail diocese@blackburn.anglican.org
Web www.blackburn.anglican.org

BRADFORD
Kadugli House, Elmsley Street, Steeton, Keighley BD20 6SE
Tel (01535) 650555 Fax 650550 E-mail office@kadugli.org.uk
Web www.bradford.anglican.org

BRISTOL
Diocesan Church House, 23 Great George Street, Bristol BS1 5QZ
Tel 0117–906 0100 Fax 925 0460 E-mail any.name@bristoldiocese.org
Web www.bristol.anglican.org

CANTERBURY
Diocesan House, Lady Wootton's Green, Canterbury CT1 1NQ
Tel (01227) 459401 Fax 450964 E-mail reception@diocant.org
Web www.canterbury.anglican.org

CARLISLE
Church House, West Walls, Carlisle CA3 8UE
Tel (01228) 522573 Fax 815400 E-mail enquiries@carlislediocese.org.uk
Web www.carlisle.anglican.org.uk

CHELMSFORD
Diocesan Office, 53 New Street, Chelmsford CM1 1AT
Tel (01245) 294400 Fax 294477 E-mail mail@chelmsford.anglican.org
Web www.chelmsford.anglican.org

CHESTER
Church House, Lower Lane, Aldford, Chester CH3 6HP
Tel (01244) 681973 Fax 620456 E-mail churchhouse@chester.anglican.org
Web www.chester.anglican.org

CHICHESTER
Diocesan Church House, 211 New Church Road, Hove BN3 4ED
Tel (01273) 421021 Fax 421041 E-mail admin@diochi.org.uk
Web www.diochi.org.uk

COVENTRY
1 Hill Top, Coventry CV1 5AB
Tel (024) 7652 1200 Fax 7652 1330 E-mail simon.lloyd@covcofe.org
Web www.coventry.anglican.org

DERBY
Derby Church House, Full Street, Derby DE1 3DR
Tel (01332) 388650 Fax 292969 E-mail finance@derby.anglican.org
Web www.derby.anglican.org

DURHAM
Diocesan Office, Auckland Castle, Market Place, Bishop Auckland DL14 7QJ
Tel (01388) 604515 Fax 603695 E-mail diocesan.office@durham.anglican.org
Web www.durham.anglican.org

ELY
Diocesan Office, Bishop Woodford House, Barton Road, Ely CB7 4DX
Tel (01353) 652701 Fax 652745 E-mail d.secretary@office.ely.anglican.org
Web www.ely.anglican.org

EUROPE
Diocesan Office, 14 Tufton Street, London SW1P 3QZ
Tel (020) 7898 1155 Fax 7898 1166 E-mail diocesan.office@europe.c-of-e.org.uk
Web www.europe.anglican.org

EXETER
The Old Deanery, The Cloisters, Cathedral Close, Exeter EX1 1HS
Tel (01392) 272686 Fax 499594 E-mail admin@exeter.anglican.org
Web www.exeter.anglican.org

GLOUCESTER
Church House, College Green, Gloucester GL1 2LY
Tel (01452) 410022 Fax 308324 E-mail church.house@glosdioc.org.uk
Web www.glosdioc.org.uk

GUILDFORD	Diocesan House, Quarry Street, Guildford GU1 3XG Tel (01483) 571826 Fax 790333 E-mail reception.diocese@cofeguildford.org.uk Web www.guildford.anglican.org
HEREFORD	Diocesan Office, The Palace, Hereford HR4 9BL Tel (01432) 373300 Fax 352952 E-mail diooffice@hereford.anglican.org Web www.hereford.anglican.org
LEICESTER	Church House, 3–5 St Martin's East, Leicester LE1 5FX Tel 0116–248 7400 Fax 253 2889 E-mail jane.easton@leccofe.org Web www.leicester.anglican.org
LICHFIELD	St Mary's House, The Close, Lichfield WS13 7LD Tel (01543) 306030 Fax 306039 E-mail info@lichfield.anglican.org Web www.lichfield.anglican.org
LINCOLN	Diocesan Office, The Old Palace, Lincoln LN2 1PU Tel (01522) 504050 E-mail administrator@lincoln.anglican.org Web www.lincoln.anglican.org
LIVERPOOL	St James's House, 20 St James Road, Liverpool L1 7BY Tel 0151–709 9722 Fax 709 2885 Web www.liverpool.anglican.org
LONDON	Diocesan House, 36 Causton Street, London SW1P 4AU Tel (020) 7932 1100 Fax 7932 1112 E-mail keith.robinson@london.anglican.org Web www.london.anglican.org
MANCHESTER	Diocesan Church House, 90 Deansgate, Manchester M3 2GH Tel 0161–828 1400 Fax 828 1480 E-mail manchesterdbf@manchester.anglican.org Web www.manchester.anglican.org
NEWCASTLE	Church House, St John's Terrace, North Shields NE29 6HS Tel 0191–270 4100 Fax 270 4101 E-mail church_house@newcastle.anglican.org Web www.newcastle.anglican.org
NORWICH	Diocesan House, 109 Dereham Road, Easton, Norwich NR9 5ES Tel (01603) 880853 Fax 881083 E-mail diocesanhouse@norwich.anglican.org Web www.norwich.anglican.org
OXFORD	Diocesan Church House, North Hinksey Lane, Botley, Oxford OX2 0NB Tel (01865) 208200 Fax 790470 E-mail diosec@oxford.anglican.org Web www.oxford.anglican.org
PETERBOROUGH	The Palace, Peterborough PE1 1YB Tel (01733) 887000 Fax 555271 E-mail office@peterborough-diocese.org.uk Web www.peterborough-diocese.org.uk
PORTSMOUTH	First Floor, Peninsular House, Wharf Road, Portsmouth PO2 8HB Tel (023) 9289 9650 Fax 9289 9651 E-mail admin@portsmouth.anglican.org Web www.portsmouth.anglican.org
RIPON AND LEEDS	Ripon and Leeds Diocesan Office, St Mary's Street, Leeds LS9 7DP Tel 0113–200 0540 Fax 249 1129 E-mail philipa@riponleeds-diocese.org.uk Web www.ripon.anglican.org
ROCHESTER	St Nicholas Church, Boley Hill, Rochester ME1 1SL Tel (01634) 560000 Fax 408942 E-mail enquiries@rochester.anglican.org Web www.rochester.anglican.org
ST ALBANS	Holywell Lodge, 41 Holywell Hill, St Albans AL1 1HE Tel (01727) 854532 Fax 844469 E-mail mail@stalbans.anglican.org Web www.stalbans.anglican.org
ST EDMUNDSBURY AND IPSWICH	St Nicholas Centre, 4 Cutler Street, Ipswich IP1 1UQ Tel (01473) 298500 Fax 298501 E-mail dbf@stedmundsbury.anglican.org Web www.stedmundsbury.anglican.org
SALISBURY	Church House, Crane Street, Salisbury SP1 2QB Tel (01722) 411922 Fax 411990 E-mail enquiries@salisbury.anglican.org Web www.salisbury.anglican.org
SHEFFIELD	Diocesan Church House, 95/99 Effingham Street, Rotherham S65 1BL Tel (01709) 309100 Fax 512550 E-mail reception@sheffield.anglican.org Web www.sheffield.anglican.org

SODOR AND MAN	2 North Shore Road, Ramsey, Isle of Man IM8 3DF Tel (01624) 816538 E-mail dsec-sodor@mcb.net Web www.sodorman.anglican.org
SOUTHWARK	Trinity House, 4 Chapel Court, Borough High Street, London SE1 1HW Tel (020) 7939 9400 Fax 7939 9468 E-mail trinity@southwark.anglican.org Web www.southwark.anglican.org
SOUTHWELL AND NOTTINGHAM	Dunham House, 8 Westgate, Southwell NG25 0JL Tel (01636) 814331 Fax 815084 E-mail mail@southwell.anglican.org Web www.southwell.anglican.org
TRURO	Diocesan House, Kenwyn, Truro TR1 1JQ Tel (01872) 274351 Fax 222510 E-mail info@truro.anglican.org Web www.truro.anglican.org
WAKEFIELD	Church House, 1 South Parade, Wakefield WF1 1LP Tel (01924) 371802 Fax 364834 E-mail church.house@wakefield.anglican.org
WINCHESTER	The Diocesan Office, Old Alresford Place, Old Alresford, Alresford SO24 9DH Tel (01962) 737300 Fax 7373585 E-mail reception@winchester.anglican.org Web www. winchester.anglican.org
WORCESTER	The Old Palace, Deansway, Worcester WR1 2JE Tel (01905) 20537 Fax 612302 Web www.cofe-worcester.org.uk
YORK	Diocesan House, Aviator Court, Clifton Moor, York YO30 4WJ Tel (01904) 699500 Fax 699501 E-mail yorkdbf@yorkdiocese.org Web www.dioceseofyork.org.uk

CHURCH IN WALES

BANGOR	Diocesan Office, Cathedral Close, Bangor LL57 1RL Tel (01248) 354999 Fax 353882 Web www. churchinwales.org.uk/bangor
LLANDAFF	Diocesan Office, The Court, Coychurch, Bridgend CF35 5EH Tel (01656) 868868 Fax 868869 Web www.churchinwales.org.uk/llandaff
MONMOUTH	Diocesan Office, 64 Caerau Road, Newport NP20 4HJ Tel (01633) 267490 Fax 265586 Web www.churchinwales.org.uk/monmouth
ST ASAPH	St Asaph Diocesan Board of Finance, High Street, St Asaph LL17 0RD Tel (01745) 582245 Fax 583556 Web www. churchinwales.org.uk/asaph
ST DAVIDS	Diocesan Office, Abergwili, Carmarthen SA31 2JG Tel (01267) 236145 Fax 223046 Web www.churchinwales.org.uk/david
SWANSEA AND BRECON	Swansea and Brecon Diocesan Centre, Cathedral Close, Brecon LD3 9DP Tel (01874) 623716 Fax 623716 Web www.churchinwales.org.uk/swanbrec

SCOTTISH EPISCOPAL CHURCH

ABERDEEN AND ORKNEY	St Clement's Church House, Mastrick Drive, Aberdeen AB16 6UF Tel (01224) 662247 Fax 662168 E-mail office@aberdeen.anglican.org Web www.aberdeen.anglican.org
ARGYLL AND THE ISLES	St Moluag's Diocesan Centre, Croft Avenue, Oban PA34 5JJ Tel (01631) 570870 Fax 570411 E-mail office@argyll.anglican.org Web www.argyll.anglican.org
BRECHIN	Diocesan Office, Unit 14 Prospect III, Technology Park, Gemini Crescent, Dundee DD2 1SW Tel (01382) 562244 E-mail office@brechin.anglican.org Web www.thedioceseofbrechin.org
EDINBURGH	Diocesan Centre, 21A Grosvenor Crescent, Edinburgh EH12 5EL Tel 0131–538 7033 Fax 538 7088 E-mail office@edinburgh.anglican.org Web www.edinburgh.anglican.org
GLASGOW AND GALLOWAY	Diocesan Office, 5 St Vincent Place, Glasgow G1 2DH Tel 0141–221 5720 or 221 2694 Fax 221 7014 E-mail office@glasgow.anglican.org Web www.episcopalglasgow.org.uk

MORAY, ROSS AND CAITHNESS	Fairview, 48 Saltburn, Invergordon IV18 0JY Tel (01349) 854984 (mornings only) E-mail office@moray.anglican.org Web www.morayrossandcaithness.co.uk
ST ANDREWS, DUNKELD AND DUNBLANE	Perth Diocesan Centre, 28A Balhousie Street, Perth PH1 5HJ Tel (01738) 443173 Fax 443174 E-mail office@standrews.anglican.org Web www.standrews.anglican.org

CHURCH OF IRELAND

PROVINCE OF ARMAGH

ARMAGH	Church House, 46 Abbey Street, Armagh BT61 7DZ Tel (028) 3752 2858 Fax 3751 0596 E-mail secretary@armagh.anglican.org Web armagh.anglican.org
CLOGHER	Diocesan Office, St Macartin's Cathedral Hall, Hall's Lane, Enniskillen BT74 7DR Tel and fax (028) 6634 7879 E-mail secretary@clogher.anglican.org Web clogher.anglican.org
CONNOR	Diocesan Office, Church of Ireland House, 61/67 Donegall Street, Belfast BT1 2QH Tel (028) 9032 2268 *or* 9032 3188 Fax 9032 1635 Web www.connor.anglican.org
DERRY AND RAPHOE	Diocesan Office, 24 London Street, Londonderry BT48 6RQ Tel (028) 7126 2440 Fax 7137 2100 E-mail office@derry.anglican.org Web www.derry.anglican.org
DOWN AND	Diocesan Office, Church of Ireland House, 61/67 Donegall Street, Belfast BT1 2QH
DROMORE	Tel (028) 9032 2268 *or* 9032 3188 Fax 9032 1635 E-mail office@diocoff-belfast.org Web www.down.anglican.org
KILMORE	Kilmore Diocesan Office, Whitestar Complex, Market Street, Cootehill, Co Cavan, Republic of Ireland Tel and fax (00353) (49) 555 9954 E-mail secretary@kilmore.anglican.org Web kilmore.anglican.org
ELPHIN AND ARDAGH	The Rectory, Riverstown, Co Sligo, Republic of Ireland Tel (00353) (71) 916 5368 E-mail diosecea@eirom.net
TUAM, KILLALA AND ACHONRY	Stonehall House, Ballisodare, Co Sligo, Republic of Ireland Tel (00353) (71) 916 7280 Fax 913 0264 E-mail hsherlock@iolfree.ie Web tuam.anglican.org

PROVINCE OF DUBLIN

CASHEL AND OSSORY	Diocesan Office, St Canice's Library, Kilkenny, Republic of Ireland Tel (00353) (56) 776 1910 *or* 772 27248 Fax 51813 E-mail office@cashel.anglican.org Web www.cashel.anglican.org
CORK, CLOYNE AND ROSS	St Nicholas' House, 14 Cove Street, Cork, Republic of Ireland Tel (00353) (21) 500 5080 Fax 432 0960 E-mail secretary@cork.anglican.org Web www.cork.anglican.org
DUBLIN AND GLENDALOUGH	Diocesan Office, Church of Ireland House, Church Avenue, Rathmines, Dublin 6, Republic of Ireland Tel (00353) (1) 496 6981 Fax 497 2865 E-mail office@dublin.anglican.org Web www.dublin.anglican.org
LIMERICK, KILLALOE AND ARDFERT	St John's Rectory, Ashe Street, Tralee, Co Kerry, Republic of Ireland Tel (00353) (66) 712 2245 Fax 712 9004 E-mail secretary@limerick.anglican.org Web limerick.anglican.org
MEATH AND KILDARE	Meath and Kildare Diocesan Centre, Moyglare, Maynooth, Co Kildare, Republic of Ireland Tel (00353) (1) 629 2163 E-mail diomeath@iol.ie *or* office@mcath.anglican.org Web www.meath.anglican.org

ARCHDEACONRIES, DEANERIES AND RURAL/AREA DEANS OF THE CHURCH OF ENGLAND AND THE CHURCH IN WALES

The numbers given to the deaneries below correspond to those given in the benefice entries in the combined benefice and church index for England (p. 1004) and for Wales (p. 1182). Where an archdeaconry comes within the jurisdiction of a suffragan or area bishop under an established scheme, the respective bishop is indicated.
Some dioceses use the title Area Dean.

CHURCH OF ENGLAND

BATH AND WELLS

ARCHDEACONRY OF WELLS

1. AXBRIDGE   T D HAWKINGS
2. BRUTON   H E ALLEN
3. CARY   H E ALLEN
4. FROME   D R BARGE
5. GLASTONBURY JURISDICTION   F J GREED
6. IVELCHESTER   P J THOMAS
7. YEOVIL   A PERRIS
8. SHEPTON MALLET   A L BIRBECK

ARCHDEACONRY OF BATH

9. BATH   P J WHITWORTH
10. CHEW MAGNA   J P KNOTT
11. LOCKING   R J TAYLOR
12. MIDSOMER NORTON   C S HARE
13. PORTISHEAD   I M HUBBARD

ARCHDEACONRY OF TAUNTON

14. SEDGEMOOR   W H H LANE
15. CREWKERNE AND ILMINSTER   A F TATHAM
16. EXMOOR   J M THOROGOOD
17. QUANTOCK   S L CAMPBELL
18. TAUNTON   S TUCKER
19. TONE   C F E ROWLEY

BIRMINGHAM

ARCHDEACONRY OF BIRMINGHAM

1. BIRMINGHAM CITY CENTRE
   A G LENOX-CONYNGHAM
2. EDGBASTON   C J S TURNER
3. HANDSWORTH   H HINGLEY
4. KINGS NORTON   C J CORKE
5. MOSELEY   P G BABINGTON
6. SHIRLEY   Q D WARBRICK
7. WARLEY   A H PERRY

ARCHDEACONRY OF ASTON

8. ASTON   A J JOLLEY
9. COLESHILL   B S CASTLE
10. POLESWORTH   M A HARRIS
11. SOLIHULL   M J PARKER
12. SUTTON COLDFIELD   M I RHODES
13. YARDLEY AND BORDESLEY   P H SMITH

BLACKBURN

ARCHDEACONRY OF BLACKBURN

1. ACCRINGTON   T R SMITH
2. BLACKBURN AND DARWEN   A RAYNES
3. BURNLEY   L LAYCOCK
4. CHORLEY   M J EVERITT
5. LEYLAND   C J NELSON
6. PENDLE   A W RINDL
7. WHALLEY   J W HARTLEY

ARCHDEACONRY OF LANCASTER

8. BLACKPOOL   S J COX
9. GARSTANG   A W WILKINSON
10. KIRKHAM *Vacant*
11. LANCASTER   P S HUDD
12. POULTON   M P KEIGHLEY
13. PRESTON   T W LIPSCOMB
14. TUNSTALL   P K WARREN

BRADFORD

ARCHDEACONRY OF BRADFORD

1. AIREDALE   D R JACKSON
2. BOWLING AND HORTON   P M BILTON
3. CALVERLEY   P G WALKER
4. OTLEY   C NORMAN

ARCHDEACONRY OF CRAVEN

5. BOWLAND   R G WOOD
6. EWECROSS   I F GREENHALGH
7. SKIPTON   P A TURNER
8. SOUTH CRAVEN   J P GREENWOOD

BRISTOL

ARCHDEACONRY OF BRISTOL

1. BRISTOL SOUTH   D G OWEN
2. BRISTOL WEST   C M PILGRIM
3. CITY DEANERY   D FRAZER

ARCHDEACONRY OF MALMESBURY

4. CHIPPENHAM   S J TYNDALL
5. KINGSWOOD AND SOUTH GLOUCESTERSHIRE
   D J A ADAMS
6. NORTH WILTSHIRE   A EVANS
7. SWINDON   R J BURLES

CANTERBURY

ARCHDEACONRY OF CANTERBURY

1. EAST BRIDGE   J SWEATMAN
2. WEST BRIDGE   M J WALKER
3. CANTERBURY   N M HALL
4. DOVER   D G RIDLEY
5. ELHAM   H C JONES
6. OSPRINGE   A C OEHRING
7. RECULVER   R L HAWKES
8. SANDWICH   D A DEER
9. THANET   D J ROPER

ARCHDEACONRY OF MAIDSTONE

10. ASHFORD   S E MCLACHLAN
11. WEALD   G M CALVER
12. ROMNEY   N R GALLAGHER
13. MAIDSTONE   A J HOUSTON
14. NORTH DOWNS   R M GILL
15. SITTINGBOURNE   J H G LEWIS
16. TENTERDEN   J T M DESROSIERS

CARLISLE

ARCHDEACONRY OF CARLISLE

1. APPLEBY   J A H CLEGG
2. BRAMPTON   G M CREGEEN
3. CARLISLE   J R LIBBY
4. PENRITH   R A MOATT

ARCHDEACONRY OF WEST CUMBERLAND

5. CALDER   J WOOLCOCK
6. DERWENT   B ROTHWELL
7. SOLWAY   M E DAY

ARCHDEACONRY OF WESTMORLAND AND FURNESS

8. BARROW   I K HOOK
9. FURNESS   G WEMYSS
10. KENDAL   T J HARMER
11. WINDERMERE   W R F COKE

CHELMSFORD

ARCHDEACONRY OF WEST HAM
(BISHOP OF BARKING)

1. BARKING AND DAGENHAM   R K GAYLER
2. HAVERING   R LOVE
3. NEWHAM   D P WADE
4. REDBRIDGE   R W SPRINGETT
5. WALTHAM FOREST   S M P SAXBY

ARCHDEACONRY OF SOUTHEND
(BISHOP OF BRADWELL)

6. BASILDON   P G KEARNS
7. BRENTWOOD   I H JORYSZ
8. CHELMSFORD NORTH   C I HAMPTON
9. CHELMSFORD SOUTH   A T GRIFFITHS
10. HADLEIGH   D ST C TUDOR
11. MALDON AND DENGIE   G S ANDERSON
12. ROCHFORD   M J LODGE
13. SOUTHEND-ON-SEA   R H WILLIAMS
14. THURROCK   E W HANSON

ARCHDEACONRY OF COLCHESTER
(BISHOP OF COLCHESTER)

15. BRAINTREE   P A NEED
16. COLCHESTER   I A HILTON
17. DEDHAM AND TEY   P C BANKS
18. DUNMOW AND STANSTED   L BOND
19. HINCKFORD   G B T BAYLISS
20. HARWICH   P E MANN
21. SAFFRON WALDEN   D R TOMLINSON
22. ST OSYTH   G D A THORBURN
23. WITHAM   J M SUDDARDS

ARCHDEACONRY OF HARLOW
(BISHOP OF BARKING)

24. EPPING FOREST   G CONNOR
25. HARLOW   M J HARRIS
26. ONGAR *Vacant*

CHESTER

ARCHDEACONRY OF CHESTER

1. BIRKENHEAD   I A DAVENPORT
2. CHESTER   M HART
3. FRODSHAM   S S WILKINS
4. GREAT BUDWORTH   E C HALL
5. MALPAS   L R THOMAS
6. MIDDLEWICH   I G BISHOP
7. WALLASEY   C F BAZLEY
8. WIRRAL NORTH   G A ROSSITER
9. WIRRAL SOUTH   G J WELCH

ARCHDEACONRY OF MACCLESFIELD

10. BOWDON   J SUTTON
11. CONGLETON   D TAYLOR
12. KNUTSFORD   R A YATES
13. MACCLESFIELD   E W L DAVIES
14. MOTTRAM   R J LAMEY
15. NANTWICH   W J BAKER
16. CHADKIRK   P J JENNER
17. CHEADLE   H B EALES
18. STOCKPORT   A J BELL

CHICHESTER

ARCHDEACONRY OF CHICHESTER

1. ARUNDEL AND BOGNOR   M J STANDEN
2. BRIGHTON   N E D MILMINE
3. CHICHESTER   R W HUNT
4. HOVE *Vacant*
5. WORTHING   J K GAVIGAN

ARCHDEACONRY OF HORSHAM

6. CUCKFIELD   C R BREEDS
7. EAST GRINSTEAD   C EVERETT-ALLEN
8. HORSHAM   R C JACKSON
9. HURST *Vacant*
10. MIDHURST *Vacant*
11. PETWORTH *Vacant*
12. STORRINGTON   P B WELCH
13. WESTBOURNE   K M L H BANTING

ARCHDEACONRY OF LEWES AND HASTINGS

14. BATTLE AND BEXHILL   D R FROST
15. DALLINGTON   S J E TOMALIN
16. EASTBOURNE   W R LOVATT
17. HASTINGS   C H KEY
18. LEWES AND SEAFORD   G M DAW
19. ROTHERFIELD   J R JAMES
20. RYE   H M MOSELEY
21. UCKFIELD   P A HODGINS

COVENTRY

ARCHDEACONRY OF COVENTRY

1. COVENTRY EAST   M TYLER
2. COVENTRY NORTH   R E WALKER
3. COVENTRY SOUTH *Vacant*
4. KENILWORTH   R W E AWRE
5. NUNEATON   P B ALLAN
6. RUGBY   M P SAXBY

ARCHDEACONRY OF WARWICK

7. ALCESTER   R W DEIMEL
8. FOSSE   G J BURRELL
9. SHIPSTON   J TUCKER
10. SOUTHAM   J E ARMSTRONG
11. WARWICK AND LEAMINGTON   M RODHAM

DERBY

ARCHDEACONRY OF CHESTERFIELD

1. ALFRETON   G M KNOX
2. BAKEWELL AND EYAM   A S MONTGOMERIE
3. BOLSOVER AND STAVELEY   W T HICKS
4. BUXTON   J O GOLDSMITH
5. CHESTERFIELD   N V JOHNSON
6. GLOSSOP   G C GRIFFITHS
7. WIRKSWORTH   D C TRUBY

ARCHDEACONRY OF DERBY

8. ASHBOURNE *Vacant*
9. DERBY NORTH   J M PAGE
10. DERBY SOUTH   P R SANDFORD
11. DUFFIELD *Vacant*
12. HEANOR   M G ALEXANDER
13. EREWASH   I E GOODING
14. LONGFORD   A G MURPHIE
15. MELBOURNE   A LUKE
16. REPTON   L A DE POMERAI

DURHAM

ARCHDEACONRY OF DURHAM

1. DURHAM   R D ALLON-SMITH
2. EASINGTON   A MILNE
3. HARTLEPOOL   M R GILBERTSON
4. LANCHESTER   R G BIRCHALL
5. SEDGEFIELD   K LUMSDON

ARCHDEACONRY OF AUCKLAND

6. AUCKLAND   N P VINE
7. BARNARD CASTLE   A J HARDING
8. DARLINGTON   J R DOBSON
9. STANHOPE   V T FENTON
10. STOCKTON   D M BROOKE

ARCHDEACONRY OF SUNDERLAND

11. CHESTER-LE-STREET   D C GLOVER
12. GATESHEAD   V SHEDDEN
13. GATESHEAD WEST   K TEASDALE
14. HOUGHTON LE SPRING *Vacant*
15. JARROW   W E BRAVINER
16. WEARMOUTH   R G E BRADSHAW

ARCHDEACONRIES, DEANERIES AND RURAL/AREA DEANS

ELY

ARCHDEACONRY OF CAMBRIDGE

1. BOURN   C A COLLINS
2. CAMBRIDGE NORTH   J R E BINNS
3. CAMBRIDGE SOUTH   R A H GREANY
4. FORDHAM AND QUY   S G F EARL
5. GRANTA   M R GOATER
6. NORTH STOWE   N J BLANDFORD-BAKER
7. SHINGAY   S F C WILLIAMS

ARCHDEACONRY OF HUNTINGDON AND WISBECH

8. ELY   P TAYLOR
9. FINCHAM AND FELTWELL   J W MATHER
10. HUNTINGDON   E B ATLING
11. MARCH *Vacant*
12. ST IVES   C S BARTER
13. ST NEOTS   A S REED
14. WISBECH LYNN MARSHLAND   E J PENNY
15. YAXLEY   P M GRIFFITH

EXETER

ARCHDEACONRY OF EXETER

1. AYLESBEARE   I C MORTER
2. CADBURY   S G C SMITH
3. CHRISTIANITY *Vacant*
4. CULLOMPTON   D L D ROBOTTOM
5. HONITON   S E ROBERTS
6. KENN   G K MAYER
7. OTTERY   D H JAMES
8. TIVERTON   D M FLETCHER

ARCHDEACONRY OF TOTNES

9. MORETON   P WIMSETT
10. NEWTON ABBOT AND IPPLEPEN   I C EGLIN
11. OKEHAMPTON   S W COOK
12. TORBAY   G H MAUDE
13. TOTNES *Vacant*
14. WOODLEIGH   N A BARKER

ARCHDEACONRY OF BARNSTAPLE

15. BARNSTAPLE   P H HOCKEY
16. HARTLAND   S C HENDERSON
17. HOLSWORTHY   R B DORRINGTON
18. SHIRWELL   P BOWERS
19. SOUTH MOLTON   P J ATTWOOD
20. TORRINGTON   K D MATHERS

ARCHDEACONRY OF PLYMOUTH

21. IVYBRIDGE   D ARNOTT
22. PLYMOUTH DEVONPORT   R M SIGRIST
23. PLYMOUTH MOORSIDE   D B M GILL
24. PLYMOUTH SUTTON   N H P MCKINNEL
25. TAVISTOCK   W G LLOYD

GLOUCESTER

ARCHDEACONRY OF GLOUCESTER

1. FOREST NORTH   R G STURMAN
2. FOREST SOUTH   P A BRUNT
3. GLOUCESTER CITY   R C SIMPSON
4. GLOUCESTER NORTH   R J A MITCHELL
5. STROUD   S A BOWEN
6. WOTTON   R H AXFORD

ARCHDEACONRY OF CHELTENHAM

7. CHELTENHAM   A J M DOW
8. CAMPDEN   C G MATTOCK
9. CIRENCESTER   J E JESSOP
10. FAIRFORD   B C ATKINSON
11. NORTHLEACH *Vacant*
12. STOW   D C FRANCIS
13. TEWKESBURY AND WINCHCOMBE   N M ARTHY

GUILDFORD

ARCHDEACONRY OF SURREY

1. ALDERSHOT   D G WILLEY
2. CRANLEIGH   J N E BUNDOCK
3. FARNHAM   J T L STILL
4. GODALMING   J M FELLOWS
5. GUILDFORD   B L MESSHAM
6. SURREY HEATH   A BODY

ARCHDEACONRY OF DORKING

7. DORKING   P D BRYER
8. EMLY   N J WHITEHEAD
9. EPSOM   S G THOMAS
10. LEATHERHEAD   E R JENKINS
11. RUNNYMEDE   T J HILLIER
12. WOKING   G P WILLIAMS

HEREFORD

ARCHDEACONRY OF HEREFORD

1. ABBEYDORE   A F EVANS
2. BROMYARD   C M SYKES
3. HEREFORD CITY   P TOWNER
4. HEREFORD RURAL   P TOWNER
5. KINGTON AND WEOBLEY   S HOLLINGHURST
6. LEDBURY   M D VOCKINS
7. LEOMINSTER *Vacant*
8. ROSS AND ARCHENFIELD   E C GODDARD

ARCHDEACONRY OF LUDLOW

9. BRIDGNORTH   S H CAWDELL
10. CLUN FOREST   R T SHAW
11. CONDOVER   S A LOWE
12. LUDLOW   M J STEWART
13. PONTESBURY   M G WHITTOCK
14. TELFORD SEVERN GORGE   M A KINNA

LEICESTER

ARCHDEACONRY OF LEICESTER

1. CITY OF LEICESTER   J C BURCH
2. FRAMLAND (Melton)   B A STARK
3. GARTREE FIRST DEANERY (Harborough)   M F RUSK
4. GARTREE SECOND DEANERY (Wigston)   M F RUSK
5. GOSCOTE   R M GLADSTONE

ARCHDEACONRY OF LOUGHBOROUGH

6. AKELEY EAST (Loughborough)   C M HEBDEN
7. GUTHLAXTON   K W BAKER
8. NORTH WEST LEICESTERSHIRE   B A ROBERTSON
9. SPARKENHOE EAST   J E SHARPE
10. SPARKENHOE WEST (Hinckley and Bosworth)   T H C MEYRICK

LICHFIELD

ARCHDEACONRY OF LICHFIELD

1. LICHFIELD   J W ALLAN
2. PENKRIDGE   I B COOK
3. RUGELEY   S C DAVIS
4. TAMWORTH   J W TROOD

ARCHDEACONRY OF STOKE-ON-TRENT

5. ALSTONFIELD *Vacant*
6. CHEADLE   S J OSBOURNE
7. ECCLESHALL   N A CLEMAS
8. LEEK   M J PARKER
9. NEWCASTLE   W G H GARDINER
10. STAFFORD   P W THOMAS
11. STOKE NORTH   P R CLARK
12. STOKE   D P LINGWOOD
13. STONE   P D DAKIN
14. TUTBURY   A J WOOD
15. UTTOXETER   E G WHITTAKER

ARCHDEACONRY OF SALOP

16. EDGMOND AND SHIFNAL R B BALKWILL
17. ELLESMERE L FOSTER
18. HODNET J M STAGG
19. OSWESTRY D R NORTH
20. SHREWSBURY C S SIMS
21. TELFORD V C SWEET
22. WEM AND WHITCHURCH R R HAARHOFF
23. WROCKWARDINE D F CHANTREY

ARCHDEACONRY OF WALSALL

24. TRYSULL M P HOBBS
25. WALSALL J C HILL
26. WEDNESBURY R E INGLESBY
27. WEST BROMWICH A J SMITH
28. WOLVERHAMPTON A J JONES

LINCOLN
ARCHDEACONRY OF STOW

1. AXHOLME, ISLE OF M P COONEY
2. CORRINGHAM R PROSSER
3. LAWRES P D GODDEN
4. MANLAKE M P COONEY
5. WEST WOLD I ROBINSON
6. YARBOROUGH *Vacant*

ARCHDEACONRY OF LINDSEY

7. BOLINGBROKE P F COATES
8. CALCEWAITHE AND CANDLESHOE T STEELE
9. GRIMSBY AND CLEETHORPES P M MULLINS
10. HAVERSTOE I R SHELTON
11. HORNCASTLE A J BOYD
12. LOUTHESK S D HOLDAWAY

ARCHDEACONRY OF LINCOLN

13. AVELAND AND NESS WITH
    STAMFORD R J MACKRILL
14. BELTISLOE A T HAWES
15. CHRISTIANITY D J OSBOURNE
16. ELLOE EAST *Vacant*
17. ELLOE WEST *Vacant*
18. GRAFFOE N J BUCK
19. GRANTHAM C P ANDREWS
20. HOLLAND EAST R L WHITEHEAD
21. HOLLAND WEST R L WHITEHEAD
22. LAFFORD J A PATRICK
23. LOVEDEN A J MEGAHEY

LIVERPOOL
ARCHDEACONRY OF LIVERPOOL

1. BOOTLE R J DRIVER
2. HUYTON J A TAYLOR
3. LIVERPOOL NORTH H CORBETT
4. LIVERPOOL SOUTH C J CROOKS
5. SEFTON *Vacant*
6. TOXTETH AND WAVERTREE M R STANFORD
7. WALTON R S BRIDSON
8. WEST DERBY S MCGANITY

ARCHDEACONRY OF WARRINGTON

9. NORTH MEOLS C POPE
10. ST HELENS M G COCKAYNE
11. ORMSKIRK G E GREENWOOD
12. WARRINGTON S P ATTWATER
13. WIDNES D J GAIT
14. WIGAN M J SHERWIN
15. WINWICK J M MATTHEWS

LONDON
ARCHDEACONRY OF LONDON

1. THE CITY O C M ROSS

ARCHDEACONRY OF CHARING CROSS

2. WESTMINSTER PADDINGTON A G THOM
3. WESTMINSTER ST MARGARET P A E CHESTER
4. WESTMINSTER ST MARYLEBONE L A MOSES

ARCHDEACONRY OF HACKNEY
(BISHOP OF STEPNEY)

5. HACKNEY J F PORTER-PRYCE
6. ISLINGTON M W LEARMOUTH
7. TOWER HAMLETS A J E GREEN

ARCHDEACONRY OF MIDDLESEX
(BISHOP OF KENSINGTON)

8. CHELSEA A R GILLION
9. HAMMERSMITH AND FULHAM G Q D PIPER
10. HAMPTON D N WINTERBURN
11. HOUNSLOW D J SIMPSON
12. KENSINGTON M K HARGREAVES
13. SPELTHORNE R J COSH

ARCHDEACONRY OF HAMPSTEAD
(BISHOP OF EDMONTON)

14. BARNET, CENTRAL N T W TAYLOR
15. BARNET, WEST J E I HAWKINS
16. CAMDEN, NORTH (Hampstead) A D CAIN
17. CAMDEN, SOUTH (Holborn and
    St Pancras) A J B MELDRUM
18. ENFIELD J M PAUL
19. HARINGEY, EAST L J MILLER
20. HARINGEY, WEST T D PIKE

ARCHDEACONRY OF NORTHOLT
(BISHOP OF WILLESDEN)

21. BRENT P W STONE
22. EALING A R CORSIE
23. HARROW R C BARTLETT
24. HILLINGDON S EVANS

MANCHESTER
ARCHDEACONRY OF MANCHESTER

1. ARDWICK I D GOMERSALL
2. ECCLES E A CROFTON
3. HEATON L S IRELAND
4. HULME S D A KILLWICK
5. MANCHESTER, NORTH *Vacant*
6. SALFORD A I SALMON
7. STRETFORD C C BROWN
8. WITHINGTON I MCVEETY

ARCHDEACONRY OF BOLTON

9. BOLTON C A BRACEGIRDLE
10. BURY S MILLINGTON
11. DEANE R C COOPER
12. FARNWORTH *Vacant*
13. LEIGH R W BUCKLEY
14. RADCLIFFE AND PRESTWICH D A PLUMMER
15. ROSSENDALE *Vacant*
16. WALMSLEY A J LINDOP

ARCHDEACONRY OF ROCHDALE

17. ASHTON-UNDER-LYNE R FARNWORTH
18. HEYWOOD AND MIDDLETON I E BUTTERWORTH
19. OLDHAM EAST A BUTLER
20. OLDHAM WEST D R PENNY
21. ROCHDALE *Vacant*

NEWCASTLE
ARCHDEACONRY OF NORTHUMBERLAND

1. BEDLINGTON P J BRYARS
2. NEWCASTLE CENTRAL P J CUNNINGHAM
3. NEWCASTLE EAST K HUNT
4. NEWCASTLE WEST J R SINCLAIR
5. TYNEMOUTH A J HUGHES

ARCHDEACONRY OF LINDISFARNE

6. ALNWICK J M BREARLEY
7. BAMBURGH AND GLENDALE B C HURST
8. BELLINGHAM S M RAMSARAN
9. CORBRIDGE D B HEWLETT
10. HEXHAM G B USHER
11. MORPETH C R GOUGH
12. NORHAM *Vacant*

NORWICH

ARCHDEACONRY OF NORWICH

1. NORWICH EAST   P L HOWARD
2. NORWICH NORTH   J D BENNETT
3. NORWICH SOUTH   E HUTCHEON

ARCHDEACONRY OF NORFOLK

4. BLOFIELD   P CUBITT
5. DEPWADE   D L P SOCHON
6. GREAT YARMOUTH   M I KNOWLES
7. HUMBLEYARD   C J DAVIES
8. LODDON   N W R EVANS
9. LOTHINGLAND   J B SIMPSON
10. REDENHALL   A C BILLETT
11. THETFORD AND ROCKLAND *Vacant*
12. ST BENET AT WAXHAM AND TUNSTEAD   W HILL

ARCHDEACONRY OF LYNN

13. BRECKLAND   S R NAIRN
14. BRISLEY AND ELMHAM *Vacant*
15. BURNHAM AND WALSINGHAM   N BANKS
16. HEACHAM AND RISING   M J BROCK
17. DEREHAM IN MITFORD   D K ALEXANDER
18. HOLT   H C STOKER
19. INGWORTH   R D BRANSON
20. LYNN   C J IVORY
21. REPPS   M L LANGAN
22. SPARHAM   L S TILLETT

OXFORD

ARCHDEACONRY OF OXFORD
(BISHOP OF DORCHESTER)

1. ASTON AND CUDDESDON   S E BOOYS
2. BICESTER AND ISLIP   P T C MASHEDER
3. CHIPPING NORTON   J K FRENCH
4. COWLEY   J B GILLINGHAM
5. DEDDINGTON   B L M PHILLIPS
6. HENLEY   G D FOULIS BROWN
7. OXFORD   J A ELLIS
8. WITNEY   W G BLAKEY
9. WOODSTOCK   S A M'CAW

ARCHDEACONRY OF BERKSHIRE
(BISHOP OF READING)

10. ABINGDON   P J MCKELLEN
11. BRACKNELL   N A PARISH
12. BRADFIELD   P G STEELE
13. MAIDENHEAD AND WINDSOR   J R G HYDE
14. NEWBURY   N T MOFFATT
15. READING   B SHENTON
16. SONNING   D P HODGSON
17. VALE OF WHITE HORSE   R M A HANCOCK
18. WALLINGFORD   E J CARTER
19. WANTAGE   J C ROBERTSON

ARCHDEACONRY OF BUCKINGHAM

20. AMERSHAM   D C CARR
21. AYLESBURY   C D STIRLING
22. BUCKINGHAM   D R HEMSLEY
23. BURNHAM AND SLOUGH   A R WALKER
24. CLAYDON   D A HISCOCK
25. MILTON KEYNES   T NORWOOD
26. MURSLEY   J WALLER
27. NEWPORT   C E PUMFREY
28. WENDOVER   M C DEARNLEY
29. WYCOMBE   D A PICKEN

PETERBOROUGH

ARCHDEACONRY OF NORTHAMPTON

1. BRACKLEY   M R H BELLAMY
2. BRIXWORTH   M Y GARBUTT
3. DAVENTRY   A SLATER
4. NORTHAMPTON, GREATER   D J WISEMAN
5. TOWCESTER   J T P HALL
6. WELLINGBOROUGH   A M LYNETT

ARCHDEACONRY OF OAKHAM

7. CORBY   R J LEE
8. HIGHAM   G L BROCKHOUSE
9. KETTERING   B J WITHINGTON
10. OUNDLE   R J ORMSTON
11. PETERBOROUGH   G J STEELE
12. RUTLAND   S J EVANS

PORTSMOUTH

ARCHDEACONRY OF THE MEON

1. BISHOP'S WALTHAM   S H HOLT
2. FAREHAM   S P GIRLING
3. GOSPORT   P A SUTTON
4. PETERSFIELD   R M E DEWING

ARCHDEACONRY OF PORTSDOWN

5. HAVANT   P H MOORE
6. PORTSMOUTH   M D B LEWIS

ARCHDEACONRY OF ISLE OF WIGHT

7. WIGHT, EAST   G E MORRIS
8. WIGHT, WEST   J HALL

RIPON AND LEEDS

ARCHDEACONRY OF RICHMOND

1. HARROGATE   N C SINCLAIR
2. RICHMOND   S R HAWORTH
3. RIPON   D J CLEEVES
4. WENSLEY   J NELSON

ARCHDEACONRY OF LEEDS

5. ALLERTON   A L TAYLOR
6. ARMLEY   K A P DOWLING
7. HEADINGLEY   S SMITH
8. WHITKIRK   J SYKES

ROCHESTER

ARCHDEACONRY OF ROCHESTER

1. COBHAM *Vacant*
2. DARTFORD   R ARDING
3. GILLINGHAM   A T VOUSDEN
4. GRAVESEND   R OATES
5. ROCHESTER   P T KERR
6. STROOD   J F SOUTHWARD

ARCHDEACONRY OF TONBRIDGE

7. MALLING   J D BROWN
8. PADDOCK WOOD   R C PAGET
9. SEVENOAKS   P E FRANCIS
10. SHOREHAM   B E HURD
11. TONBRIDGE   L W G KEVIS
12. TUNBRIDGE WELLS   B S SENIOR

ARCHDEACONRY OF BROMLEY AND BEXLEY

13. BECKENHAM   P MILLER
14. BROMLEY   M M CAMP
15. ERITH   F D JAKEMAN
16. ORPINGTON   A A MUSTOE
17. SIDCUP   S SEALY

ST ALBANS

ARCHDEACONRY OF ST ALBANS

1. ALDENHAM   G E W BUCKLER
2. BERKHAMSTED   D J ABBOTT
3. HEMEL HEMPSTEAD   D M LAWSON
4. HITCHIN   M A H RODEN
5. RICKMANSWORTH   G A COLLINS
6. ST ALBANS   D RIDGEWAY
7. WATFORD   G R WARREN
8. WHEATHAMPSTEAD   J F H GREEN

ARCHDEACONRY OF BEDFORD

9. AMPTHILL   M F J BRADLEY
10. BEDFORD   C M DENT
11. BIGGLESWADE   D G WILLIAMS
12. DUNSTABLE   R J ANDREWS
13. ELSTOW   S J LILEY
14. LUTON   S PURVIS
15. SHARNBROOK   D G MASON
16. SHEFFORD   J A HARPER

ARCHDEACONRY OF HERTFORD

17. BARNET   R F WATSON
18. BISHOP'S STORTFORD   C D BOULTON
19. BUNTINGFORD   COUNTESS OF KIMBERLEY
20. CHESHUNT   C J SELBY
21. WELWYN HATFIELD   C GARNER
22. HERTFORD AND WARE   D J PROUD
23. STEVENAGE   G J TICKNER

ST EDMUNDSBURY AND IPSWICH

ARCHDEACONRY OF IPSWICH

1. BOSMERE   D R WILLIAMS
2. COLNEYS   G L GRANT
3. HADLEIGH   M J A TILLETT
4. IPSWICH   I D J MORGAN
5. SAMFORD   C L WINGFIELD
6. STOWMARKET   B B BILSTON
7. WOODBRIDGE   P C E STENTIFORD

ARCHDEACONRY OF SUDBURY

8. CLARE   I M FINN
9. IXWORTH   J W FULTON
10. LAVENHAM   S G HILL
11. MILDENHALL   S J MITCHELL
12. SUDBURY   R L C KING
13. THINGOE   A R GATES

ARCHDEACONRY OF SUFFOLK

14. BECCLES AND SOUTH ELMHAM   P J NELSON
15. HALESWORTH Vacant
16. HARTISMERE Vacant
17. HOXNE   F O NEWTON
18. LOES   G W OWEN
19. SAXMUNDHAM   N J HARTLEY

SALISBURY

ARCHDEACONRY OF SHERBORNE

1. DORCHESTER   P J SMITH
2. LYME BAY   R A D´V THORN
3. SHERBORNE   H G PEARSON
4. WEYMOUTH AND PORTLAND   K I HOBBS

ARCHDEACONRY OF DORSET

5. BLACKMORE VALE   D R R SEYMOUR
6. MILTON AND BLANDFORD   S F EVERETT
7. POOLE   J H T DE GARIS
8. PURBECK   J S WOOD
9. WIMBORNE   J E HOLBROOK

ARCHDEACONRY OF SARUM

10. ALDERBURY   V S PERRETT
11. CHALKE   D E HENLEY
12. SALISBURY   D J J R LINAKER
13. STONEHENGE   S E WILKINSON

ARCHDEACONRY OF WILTS

14. BRADFORD   A E EVANS
15. CALNE   T M B WOODHOUSE
16. DEVIZES   S ATTWATER
17. HEYTESBURY   J H TOMLINSON
18. MARLBOROUGH   A G STUDDERT-KENNEDY
19. PEWSEY   N A LEIGH-HUNT

SHEFFIELD

ARCHDEACONRY OF SHEFFIELD AND ROTHERHAM

1. ATTERCLIFFE   A PATTERSON
2. ECCLESALL   P A INGRAM
3. ECCLESFIELD   M J SNOW
4. HALLAM   P R TOWNSEND
5. LAUGHTON   J E BOLTON
6. ROTHERHAM Vacant

ARCHDEACONRY OF DONCASTER

7. ADWICK-LE-STREET   M WIGGLESWORTH
8. DONCASTER   J I WILLETT
9. DONCASTER, WEST   B J INSTON
10. SNAITH AND HATFIELD   C ROBERTS
11. TANKERSLEY   K J E HALE
12. WATH   N H ELLIOTT

SODOR AND MAN

ARCHDEACONRY OF SODOR AND MAN

1. CASTLETOWN AND PEEL   P C ROBINSON
2. DOUGLAS   D WHITWORTH
3. RAMSEY   N D GREENWOOD

SOUTHWARK

ARCHDEACONRY OF LEWISHAM AND GREENWICH
(BISHOP OF WOOLWICH)

1. CHARLTON   K W HITCH
2. DEPTFORD   N D R NICHOLLS
3. ELTHAM AND MOTTINGHAM   E CRANMER
4. LEWISHAM, EAST   R D BAINBRIDGE
5. LEWISHAM, WEST   M J KINGSTON
6. PLUMSTEAD   H D OWEN

ARCHDEACONRY OF SOUTHWARK
(BISHOP OF WOOLWICH)

7. BERMONDSEY   M J STEADMAN
8. CAMBERWELL   T C WRIGHT
9. DULWICH   D L GWILLIAMS
10. SOUTHWARK AND NEWINGTON   A P DODD

ARCHDEACONRY OF LAMBETH
(BISHOP OF KINGSTON)

11. LAMBETH NORTH   P J ROSE-CASEMORE
12. LAMBETH SOUTH   S P GATES
13. MERTON Vacant

ARCHDEACONRY OF WANDSWORTH
(BISHOP OF KINGSTON)

14. BATTERSEA   G M VEVERS
15. KINGSTON   K W SCOTT
16. RICHMOND AND BARNES   C PALMER
17. TOOTING   K PARKES
18. WANDSWORTH   H D TOLLER

ARCHDEACONRY OF CROYDON

19. CROYDON ADDINGTON   M R MCKINNEY
20. CROYDON CENTRAL   P J BROWN
21. CROYDON NORTH   A L NICKSON
22. CROYDON SOUTH   C F SPURWAY
23. SUTTON   C WHEATON

ARCHDEACONRY OF REIGATE
(BISHOP OF CROYDON)

24. CATERHAM   A D MIDDLETON
25. GODSTONE   G PADDICK
26. REIGATE   G A BARBER

SOUTHWELL AND NOTTINGHAM

ARCHDEACONRY OF NEWARK

1. BAWTRY   R A SPRAY
2. MANSFIELD   G J BUTLER
3. NEWARK   A I TUCKER
4. NEWSTEAD   R KELLETT
5. RETFORD Vacant
6. WORKSOP Vacant

ARCHDEACONRY OF NOTTINGHAM

7. BEESTON *Vacant*
8. EAST BINGHAM   J F WELLINGTON
9. WEST BINGHAM   J W BENTHAM
10. GEDLING   P A WILLIAMS
12. NOTTINGHAM NORTH   J J LEPINE
13. NOTTINGHAM CENTRAL   R M CLARK
14. NOTTINGHAM WEST *Vacant*
15. SOUTHWELL   S SPENCER

TRURO

ARCHDEACONRY OF CORNWALL

1. ST AUSTELL   K P ARTHUR
2. CARNMARTH NORTH   O STEVENS
3. CARNMARTH SOUTH   J HARRIS
4. KERRIER   D J STEVENS
5. PENWITH   R H PESKETT
6. POWDER   A G BASHFORTH
7. PYDAR   C M MALKINSON

ARCHDEACONRY OF BODMIN

8. STRATTON   R C W DICKENSON
9. TRIGG MAJOR   G PENGELLY
10. TRIGG MINOR AND BODMIN   S L BRYAN
11. WIVELSHIRE, EAST   J A C WILSON
12. WIVELSHIRE, WEST   A R INGLEBY

WAKEFIELD

ARCHDEACONRY OF HALIFAX

1. ALMONDBURY   R J STEEL
2. BRIGHOUSE AND ELLAND   D BURROWS
3. CALDER VALLEY   J T ALLISON
4. HALIFAX   J S BRADBERRY
5. HUDDERSFIELD   C OGLE
6. KIRKBURTON   C E BULLIMORE

ARCHDEACONRY OF PONTEFRACT

7. BARNSLEY   S P RACE
8. BIRSTALL   S J PITCHER
9. DEWSBURY   P D MAYBURY
10. PONTEFRACT   R G COOPER
11. WAKEFIELD   P M MAGUIRE

WINCHESTER

ARCHDEACONRY OF WINCHESTER

1. ALRESFORD *Vacant*
2. ALTON *Vacant*
3. ANDOVER   J M BENTALL
4. BASINGSTOKE   A S BISHOP
5. ODIHAM   R A EWBANK
6. WHITCHURCH   C DALE
7. WINCHESTER   A W GORDON

ARCHDEACONRY OF BOURNEMOUTH

8. BOURNEMOUTH   A L MCPHERSON
9. CHRISTCHURCH   D M WEBSTER
10. EASTLEIGH *Vacant*

11. LYNDHURST   D J FURNESS
12. ROMSEY   R A CORNE
13. SOUTHAMPTON   G J PHILBRICK

ARCHDEACONRY OF THE CHANNEL ISLANDS

14. GUERNSEY   K P MELLOR
15. JERSEY   R F KEY

WORCESTER

ARCHDEACONRY OF WORCESTER

1. EVESHAM   T M MASON
2. MALVERN   W D NICHOL
3. MARTLEY AND WORCESTER WEST *Vacant*
4. PERSHORE   M T C BAYNES
5. UPTON   F A WOOKEY
6. WORCESTER EAST   K A BOYCE

ARCHDEACONRY OF DUDLEY

7. BROMSGROVE *Vacant*
8. DROITWICH   S P KERR
9. DUDLEY   H C HANKE
10. KINGSWINFORD *Vacant*
11. KIDDERMINSTER   K N JAMES
12. STOURBRIDGE   A L HAZLEWOOD
13. STOURPORT   L S GRACE

YORK

ARCHDEACONRY OF YORK
(BISHOP OF SELBY)

1. AINSTY, NEW   P E BRISTOW
2. DERWENT   R M KIRKMAN
3. EASINGWOLD   J HARRISON
4. SELBY   C WILTON
5. SOUTH WOLD   J C FINNEMORE
6. SOUTHERN RYEDALE   Q H WILSON
7. YORK, CITY OF   C W M BALDOCK

ARCHDEACONRY OF EAST RIDING
(BISHOP OF HULL)

8. BEVERLEY   A BAILEY
9. BRIDLINGTON   P J PIKE
10. HARTHILL   M R G SMITH
11. HOLDERNESS, NORTH   C J SIMMONS
12. HOLDERNESS, SOUTH   A J BURDON
13. HOWDEN   P G FAULKNER
14. HULL   D A WALKER
15. SCARBOROUGH   M P DUNNING

ARCHDEACONRY OF CLEVELAND
(BISHOP OF WHITBY)

16. GUISBOROUGH   J C WEETMAN
17. HELMSLEY   J D PURDY
18. MIDDLESBROUGH   E WILSON
19. MOWBRAY   R F ROWLING
20. PICKERING   P J MOTHERSDALE
21. STOKESLEY   W J FORD
22. WHITBY   D S COOK

CHURCH IN WALES

ST ASAPH

ARCHDEACONRY OF ST ASAPH

1. ST ASAPH   R W ROWLAND
2. DENBIGH   J P P WILLIAMS
3. DYFFRYN CLWYD   J B DAVIES
4. HOLYWELL   J D P LOMAS
5. LLANRWST   R H GRIFFITHS
6. RHOS   J P ATACK

ARCHDEACONRY OF MONTGOMERY

7. CEDEWAIN   A S GRIMWOOD
8. CAEREINION   D E B FRANCIS
9. LLANFYLLIN   M R BALKWILL
10. POOL   R A BIRD

ARCHDEACONRY OF WREXHAM

11. BANGOR ISYCOED   D T B LEWIS
12. GRESFORD   S M HUYTON
13. HAWARDEN   M K SNELLGROVE
14. LLANGOLLEN   J S EVANS
15. MINERA   N W CARTER
16. MOLD   C I DAY
17. PENLLYN AND EDEIRNION   S J ROBERTS
18. WREXHAM   M F WEST

BANGOR

ARCHDEACONRY OF BANGOR

1. ARFON   R F DONALDSON
2. ARLLECHWEDD   P R JONES
3. LLIFON AND TALYBOLION   M M BRADY
4. MALLTRAETH   P MCLEAN
5. OGWEN   S H JONES
6. TINDAETHWY AND MENAI   P HUGHES
7. TWRCELYN   G W EDWARDS

ARCHDEACONRY OF MEIRIONNYDD

8. ARDUDWY   R A BEACON
9. ARWYSTLI   R P PITCHER
10. CYFEILIOG AND MAWDDWY   E W ROWLANDS
11. LLYN AND EIFIONYDD   A JONES
12. YSTUMANER   N D ADAMS

ST DAVIDS

ARCHDEACONRY OF ST DAVIDS

1. CASTLEMARTIN   V F MILLGATE
2. DAUGLEDDAU   G D GWYTHER
3. DEWISLAND AND FISHGUARD   R GRIFFITHS
4. NARBERTH   M BUTLER
5. ROOSE   D M WIGHT

ARCHDEACONRY OF CARDIGAN

6. CEMAIS AND SUB-AERON   P R MACKNESS
7. EMLYN   E ROBERTS
8. GLYN AERON   C L BOLTON
9. LAMPETER AND ULTRA-AERON   *Vacant*
10. LLANBADARN FAWR   D B THOMAS

ARCHDEACONRY OF CARMARTHEN

11. CARMARTHEN   L L RICHARDSON
12. CYDWELI   P C JONES
13. DYFFRYN AMAN   M L REES
14. LLANGADOG AND LLANDEILO   W R HUGHES
15. ST CLEARS   J GAINER

LLANDAFF

ARCHDEACONRY OF LLANDAFF

1. CARDIFF   M R PREECE
2. LLANDAFF   V J PAYNE
3. PENARTH AND BARRY   J M HUGHES

ARCHDEACONRY OF MARGAM

4. BRIDGEND   M KOMOR
5. MARGAM   C J AMOS
6. NEATH   S J RYAN
7. VALE OF GLAMORGAN   D G BELCHER

ARCHDEACONRY OF MORGANNWG

8. CAERPHILLY   A H STEVENS
9. CYNON VALLEY   B L JONES
10. MERTHYR TYDFIL   M J DAVIES
11. PONTYPRIDD   V L PARKINSON
12. RHONDDA   C R LEWIS-JENKINS

MONMOUTH

ARCHDEACONRY OF MONMOUTH

1. ABERGAVENNY   J H WINSTON
2. MONMOUTH   S L GUEST
3. NETHERWENT   J E L WHITE
4. RAGLAN-USK   T G CLEMENT

ARCHDEACONRY OF NEWPORT

5. BASSALEG   J S WILLIAMS
6. BEDWELLTY   T MORGAN
7. BLAENAU GWENT   R L HEWETT
8. NEWPORT   A J EDWARDS
9. PONTYPOOL   J V MOLE

SWANSEA AND BRECON

ARCHDEACONRY OF BRECON

1. BRECON   B H JOHN
2. BUILTH   H D HALL
3. CRICKHOWELL   K RICHARDS
4. HAY   R T EDWARDS
5. MAELIENYDD   A G LOAT

ARCHDEACONRY OF GOWER

6. CLYNE   G E BENNETT
7. CWMTAWE   D I DAVIES
8. GOWER   D J WILKINSON
9. LLWCHWR   D H E MOSFORD
10. PENDERI   H M WILLIAMS
11. SWANSEA   H V PARSELL

ENGLISH BENEFICES AND CHURCHES

An index of benefices, conventional districts, local ecumenical projects, and proprietary chapels (shown in bold type), together with entries for churches and other licensed places of worship listed on the Parish Index of the Central Board of Finance. Where the church name is the same as that of the benefice (or as that of the place whose name forms the beginning of the benefice name), the church entry is omitted. Church dedications are indicated in brackets.

The benefice entry gives the full legal name, followed by the diocese, its deanery number (p. 976), the patron(s), and the name(s) and appointment(s) of clergy serving there (if there are none, the telephone number of the parsonage house is given). The following are the main abbreviations used; for others see the full list of abbreviations.

C	Curate	**P**	Patron(s)
C-in-c	Curate-in-charge	**P-in-c**	Priest-in-charge
Dn-in-c	Deacon-in-charge	**Par Dn**	Parish Deacon
Dss	Deaconess	**R**	Rector
Hon C	Honorary Curate	**TM**	Team Minister
Hon Par Dn	Honorary Parish Deacon	**TR**	Team Rector
Min	Minister	**TV**	Team Vicar
NSM	Non-stipendiary Minister	**V**	Vicar

Listed below are the elements in place names which are not normally treated as substantive in the index:

CENTRAL	HIGHER	MUCH	OVER
EAST	LITTLE	NETHER	SOUTH
GREAT	LOW	NEW	THE
GREATER	LOWER	NORTH	UPPER
HIGH	MIDDLE	OLD	WEST

Thus WEST WIMBLEDON (Christ Church) appears as **WIMBLEDON, WEST (Christ Church)** and CENTRAL TELFORD as **TELFORD, CENTRAL**. The only exception occurs where the second element of the place name is a common noun thus, NEW LANE remains as **NEW LANE**, and WEST TOWN as **WEST TOWN**.

AB KETTLEBY (St James) and Holwell w Asfordby *Leic 2*
  P *DBP, MMCET and V Rothley (jt)* **P-in-c** S A PATERSON
ABBAS and Templecombe, Henstridge and Horsington *B & W 2*
  P *Bp and Ch Trust Fund Trust* **R** P HALLETT
ABBERLEY (St Mary) *see Shrawley, Witley, Astley and Abberley Worc*
ABBERLEY (St Michael) *as above*
ABBERTON (St Andrew) *see Fingringhoe w E Donyland and Abberton etc Chelmsf*
ABBERTON (St Edburga), The Flyfords, Naunton Beauchamp and Bishampton w Throckmorton *Worc 4* **P** *Bp and Croome Estate Trustees (1 turn), and Ld Chan (1 turn)*
  R C A FAIRCLOUGH, **Hon C** S L BENNETT
ABBESS RODING (St Edmund King and Martyr) *see S Rodings Chelmsf*
ABBEY CHAPEL (St Mary) *see Annesley w Newstead S'well*
ABBEY HULTON (St John) *see Bucknall Lich*
ABBEY WOOD (St Michael and All Angels) *S'wark 6* **P** *Bp*
  V D A SHERRATT, **NSM** D C ROBINSON
ABBEY WOOD (William Temple) *see Thamesmead S'wark*
ABBEYDALE *see Sheff St Pet and St Oswald Sheff*
ABBEYDALE (St John the Evangelist) *Sheff 2*
  P *Mrs C Longworth, Sir Samuel Roberts Bt, K B Jones, and J A Goodwin Esq* **P-in-c** H C BLACKBURN
ABBEYDORE (St Mary) *see Ewyas Harold w Dulas, Kenderchurch etc Heref*
ABBEYSTEAD (Christ Church) *see Dolphinholme w Quernmore and Over Wyresdale Blackb*
ABBOTS BICKINGTON (St James) *see Bradworthy, Sutcombe, Putford etc Ex*
ABBOTS BROMLEY (St Nicholas) w Blithfield *Lich 3* **P** *Bp and D&C (jt)* **P-in-c** S C DAVIS, **NSM** L J FARRINGTON
ABBOTS LANGLEY (St Lawrence) *St Alb 7* **P** *Bp*
  V J M M SPREADBURY, **C** M A DAVIS
ABBOTS LEIGH (Holy Trinity) w Leigh Woods *Bris 2* **P** *Bp*
  P-in-c D J SMITH, **NSM** R C WILSON
ABBOTS MORTON (St Peter) *see Church Lench w Rous Lench and Abbots Morton etc Worc*
ABBOTS RIPTON (St Andrew) w Wood Walton *Ely 10* **P** *Lord de Ramsey (2 turns), D&C (1 turn)* **P-in-c** E B ATLING, **C** B A STEWART
ABBOTSBURY (St Mary) *see Highweek Ex*
ABBOTSBURY (St Nicholas), Portesham and Langton Herring *Sarum 4* **P** *The Hon C A Townshend and Bp (alt)* **P-in-c** R J PRESS, **NSM** A J WHITTOCK
ABBOTSHAM (St Helen) *see Parkham, Alwington, Buckland Brewer etc Ex*
ABBOTSKERSWELL (Blessed Virgin Mary) *Ex 10*
  P *Ld Chan* **P-in-c** J F LEONARD, **C** G STILL
ABBOTSLEY (St Margaret) *see Gt Gransden and Abbotsley and Lt Gransden etc Ely*

ABBOTSWOOD (St Nicholas Family Centre) *see Yate New Town Bris*
ABBOTTS ANN (St Mary) and Upper Clatford and Goodworth Clatford *Win 3* **P** *Exors T P de Paravicini Esq and Bp (jt)*
  R D N A BROAD, **NSM** N J JUDD
ABDON (St Margaret) *Heref 12* **P** *Bp* **R** I E GIBBS
ABENHALL (St Michael) w Mitcheldean *Glouc 1* **P** *DBP*
  R R G STURMAN
ABERFORD (St Ricarius) *see Aberford w Micklefield York*
ABERFORD (St Ricarius) w Micklefield *York 4* **P** *Abp and Oriel Coll Ox (jt)* **P-in-c** B H FRAY
ABINGDON (Christ Church) (St Helen) (St Michael and All Angels) (St Nicolas) *Ox 10* **P** *Patr Bd* **TR** E C MILLER, **TV** T C DAVIS, **C** R R BUSHYAGER, **NSM** T W HEWES, L HODGES, J A TAFT
ABINGER (St James) cum Coldharbour *Guildf 7* **P** *Ch Patr Trust and J P M H Evelyn Esq (alt)* **R** A N BERRY
ABINGTON (St Peter and St Paul) *Pet 4* **P** *Bp* **R** P J BALL
ABINGTON, GREAT (St Mary the Virgin) w LITTLE (St Mary) *Ely 5* **P** *MMCET* **P-in-c** J M NORRIS
ABINGTON PIGOTTS (St Michael and All Angels) *see Shingay Gp Ely*
ABNEY (Mission Room) *see Hope, Castleton and Bradwell Derby*
ABRAM (St John) *Liv 14* **P** *R Wigan* **V** J L STEVENTON
ABRIDGE (Holy Trinity) *see Lambourne w Abridge and Stapleford Abbotts Chelmsf*
ABSON (St James the Great) *see Pucklechurch and Abson Bris*
ABTHORPE (St John the Baptist) *see Silverstone and Abthorpe w Slapton etc Pet*
ACASTER MALBIS (Holy Trinity) *York 1*
  P *R A G Raimes Esq* **V** C I COATES, **NSM** P MACNAUGHTON
ACASTER SELBY (St John) *see Appleton Roebuck w Acaster Selby York*
ACCRINGTON Christ Church *Blackb 1* **P** *Bp and V S Shore H Trin (jt)* **V** *vacant* (01254) 235089
ACCRINGTON Christ the King (St James) (St Paul) (St Andrew) (St Peter) (St Clement) (St Mary Magdalen) *Blackb 1* **P** *Patr Bd* **TR** A D LYON, **TV** L W CARSON-FEATHAM
ACCRINGTON (St John) w Huncoat St Augustine *Blackb 1*
  P *Bp and V Accrington St Jas w St Paul (jt)* **NSM** A J BINKS
ACKLAM (St John the Baptist) *see W Buckrose York*
ACKLAM, WEST (St Mary) *York 18* **P** *Trustees*
  V J H HEARN, **C** D B COOKE
ACKLETON (Mission Room) *see Worfield Heref*
ACKLINGTON (St John the Divine) *see Warkworth and Acklington Newc*
ACKWORTH (All Saints) (St Cuthbert) *Wakef 10* **P** *Duchy of Lanc* **R** P HARTLEY, **NSM** J S MONTGOMERY
ACLE (St Edmund) w Fishley; North Burlingham; Beighton w Moulton *Nor 4* **P** *Bp and Ch Soc Trust (jt)* **R** M GREENLAND

ACOCKS GREEN (St Mary) *Birm 13*   **P** *Trustees*
  V A T BULLOCK,   **NSM** R ANETTS
ACOL (St Mildred)   *see* Birchington w Acol and Minnis Bay *Cant*
ACOMB (Holy Redeemer) *York 7*   **P** *The Crown*   **V** M A HAND
ACOMB (St Stephen) *York 7*   **P** *Trustees*   **V** D J ERRIDGE,
  C P G CARMAN,   **NSM** S M WALLACE
ACOMB MOOR (James the Deacon) *York 7*   **P** *Abp*
  V A A HORSMAN
ACRISE (St Martin)   *see* Hawkinge w Acrise and Swingfield *Cant*
ACTON (All Saints) w Great Waldingfield *St E 12*   **P** *Bp*
  V *vacant* (01787) 377287
ACTON (St Mary) *Lon 22*   **P** *Bp*   **R** D J BRAMMER,
  NSM M J SPREDBURY
ACTON (St Mary) and Worleston, Church Minshull and
  Wettenhall *Ches 15*   **P** *Bp, V Over St Chad, and*
  R C Roundell Esq (jt)   **V** A LILLICRAP
ACTON, EAST (St Dunstan w St Thomas) *Lon 22*   **P** *Bp*
  V J M WESTALL,   **NSM** R YATES
ACTON, NORTH (St Gabriel) *Lon 22*   **P** *Bp*   **V** K A ROBUS
ACTON, WEST (St Martin) *Lon 22*   **P** *Bp*   **V** N P HENDERSON,
  Hon C A GRIFFITHS
ACTON BEAUCHAMP (St Giles)   *see* Frome Valley *Heref*
ACTON BURNELL (St Mary)   *see* Condover w Frodesley,
  Acton Burnell etc *Heref*
ACTON GREEN (St Alban)   *see* Oak Tree Angl Fellowship *Lon*
ACTON GREEN (St Peter) (All Saints) *Lon 22*   **P** *Bp*
  V J M V WILLMINGTON,   **C** B E F PEARSON
ACTON ROUND (St Mary) *Heref 9*   **P** *DBP*
  P-in-c A A ROBERTS,   **Hon C** H J PATTERSON
ACTON SCOTT (St Margaret) *Heref 11*   **P** *DBP*
  P-in-c M L COPE,   **NSM** M G WILLIAMS
ACTON TRUSSELL (St James)   *see* Penkridge *Lich*
ACTON TURVILLE (St Mary)   *see* Boxwell, Leighterton,
  Didmarton, Oldbury etc *Glouc*
ADBASTON (St Michael and All Angels), High Offley,
  Knightley, Norbury and Woodseaves *Lich 7*   **P** *Bp*
  R P M FREEMAN,   **NSM** D HOLLINGS
ADDERBURY (St Mary) w Milton *Ox 5*   **P** *New Coll Ox*
  V S W FLETCHER,   **OLM** S NEWBY
ADDERLEY (St Peter), Ash, Calverhall, Ightfield and Moreton
  Say *Lich 18*   **P** *C C Corbet Esq, A E H Heber-Percy Esq,*
  T C Heywood-Lonsdale Esq, and R Whitchurch (jt)
  R R J ANDERS
ADDINGHAM (St Michael)   *see* Cross Fell Gp *Carl*
ADDINGHAM (St Peter) *Bradf 4*   **P** *J R Thompson-Ashby Esq*
  R A R TAWN,   **NSM** B CLARKE
ADDINGTON (St Margaret)   *see* Birling, Addington, Ryarsh
  and Trottiscliffe *Roch*
ADDINGTON (St Mary)   *see* Winslow w Gt Horwood and
  Addington *Ox*
ADDINGTON (St Mary) *S'wark 19*   **P** *Abp*   **V** J M MALES,
  C C L DOWLAND-PILLINGER
ADDINGTON, GREAT (All Saints) w LITTLE (St Mary the
  Virgin) and Woodford *Pet 8*   **P** *Bp and DBP (alt)*
  P-in-c P A M GOMPERTZ,   **NSM** P M TATE
ADDINGTON, NEW (St Edward) *S'wark 19*   **P** *Bp*
  V M POWELL,   **C** J B EASTON-CROUCH,   **NSM** E ILORI
ADDISCOMBE (St Mary Magdalene) *S'wark 20*   **P** *Trustees*
  V R L WILLIAMS,   **C** E L ELLIS
ADDISCOMBE (St Mildred) *S'wark 20*   **P** *Bp*   **OLM** M KING
ADDLESTONE (St Augustine) (St Paul) *Guildf 11*   **P** *Bp*
  V B H BEECROFT,   **C** S A BRASSIL
ADDLETHORPE (St Nicholas)   *see* Skegness Gp *Linc*
ADEL (St John the Baptist) *Ripon 7*   **P** *Brig R G Lewthwaite,*
  D R Lewthwaite Esq, and J V Lewthwaite Esq (jt)
  P-in-c I J WHITE
ADEYFIELD (St Barnabas)   *see* Hemel Hempstead *St Alb*
ADFORTON (St Andrew)   *see* Wigmore Abbey *Heref*
ADISHAM (Holy Innocents)   *see* Aylesham w Adisham *Cant*
ADLESTROP (St Mary Magdalene)   *see* Broadwell, Evenlode,
  Oddington, Adlestrop etc *Glouc*
ADLINGFLEET (All Saints)   *see* The Marshland *Sheff*
ADLINGTON (St John's Mission Church)   *see* Prestbury *Ches*
ADLINGTON (St Paul) *Blackb 4*   **P** *Bp*   **V** D F C MORGAN
ADSTOCK (St Cecilia)   *see* Lenborough *Ox*
ADSTONE (All Saints)   *see* Lambfold *Pet*
ADSWOOD (St Gabriel's Mission Church)   *see* Stockport St
  Geo *Ches*
ADVENT (St Adwena)   *see* Lanteglos by Camelford w Advent
  Truro
ADWELL (St Mary)   *see* Thame *Ox*
ADWICK-LE-STREET (St Laurence) w Skelbrooke *Sheff 7*
  P *Mrs P N Fullerton and Bp (alt)*   **R** A B WALTON

ADWICK-UPON-DEARNE (St John the Baptist)
  see Barnburgh w Melton on the Hill etc *Sheff*
AFFPUDDLE (St Lawrence)   *see* Bere Regis and Affpuddle w
  Turnerspuddle *Sarum*
AIGBURTH (St Anne) *Liv 4*   **P** *Trustees*   **V** G G AMEY
AIKTON (St Andrew)   *see* Barony of Burgh *Carl*
AINDERBY STEEPLE (St Helen)   *see* Lower Swale *Ripon*
AINSDALE (St John) *Liv 9*   **P** *R Walton, Bp, and Adn (jt)*
  V G J BIRCH
AINSTABLE (St Michael and All Angels)   *see* Inglewood Gp
  Carl
AINSWORTH (Christ Church) *Man 14*   **P** *Bp*   **V** *vacant*
  (01204) 398567
AINTREE (St Giles) w St Peter *Liv 7*   **P** *Bp*   **V** B A WALLES
AIREDALE (Holy Cross) w Fryston *Wakef 10*   **P** *Bp*
  V T A IBBOTSON
AIRMYN (St David), Hook and Rawcliffe *Sheff 10*   **P** *Bp and*
  Ch Soc Trust (jt)   **V** G HOLLINGSWORTH
AISHOLT (All Saints), Enmore, Goathurst, Nether Stowey, Over
  Stowey and Spaxton w Charlynch *B & W 17*   **P** *Bp, D&C*
  Windsor, MMCET, and Ch Trust Fund Trust (jt)
  R C L MARSHALL,   **C** H O WATKINS
AISLABY (St Margaret)   *see* Lower Esk *York*
AISTHORPE (St Peter)   *see* Spring Line Gp *Linc*
AKELEY (St James)   *see* N Buckingham *Ox*
AKEMAN *Ox 2*   **P** *New Coll and Ch Ch (1 turn), Qu Coll,*
  St Jo Coll, and Period and Country Houses Ltd (1 turn)
  R D F WALKER,   **NSM** J M HEMMINGS
ALBERBURY (St Michael and All Angels) w Cardeston *Heref 13*
  P *Bp and Sir Michael Leighton Bt (alt)*   **P-in-c** V J TAIT
ALBOURNE (St Bartholomew) w Sayers Common and
  Twineham *Chich 9*   **P** *Bp (2 turns), Ex Coll Ox (1 turn)*
  R D M SWYER
ALBRIGHTON (St John the Baptist)   *see* Leaton and
  Albrighton w Battlefield *Lich*
ALBRIGHTON (St Mary Magdalene), Boningale and Donington
  Lich 16   **P** *Haberdashers' Co and MMCET (jt)*
  V R B BALKWILL
ALBURGH (All Saints)   *see* Ditchingham, Hedenham, Broome,
  Earsham etc *Nor*
ALBURY (St Helen) Tiddington   *see* Wheatley *Ox*
ALBURY (St Mary), Braughing, Furneux Pelham, Lt Hadham,
  Much Hadham and Stocking Pelham *St Alb 18*   **P** *Patr Bd*
  TR C D BOULTON,   **TV** J M GOSNEY
ALBURY (St Peter and St Paul)   *see* Shere, Albury and
  Chilworth *Guildf*
ALBY (St Ethelbert)   *see* Erpingham w Calthorpe, Ingworth,
  Aldborough etc *Nor*
ALCESTER (St Nicholas) and Arrow w Oversley and Weethley
  Cov 7   **P** *Marquess of Hertf*   **R** D C CAPRON
ALCISTON (not known)   *see* Berwick w Selmeston and Alciston
  Chich
ALCOMBE (St Michael the Archangel) *B & W 16*   **P** *Bp*
  V S STUCKES,   **C** K J CROSS
ALCONBURY (St Peter and St Paul) cum Weston *Ely 10*
  P *D&C Westmr*   **P-in-c** J P YOUNG
ALDBOROUGH (St Andrew) w Boroughbridge and Roecliffe
  Ripon 3   **P** *D&C York and Bp (alt)*   **V** P J SMITH
ALDBOROUGH (St Mary)   *see* Erpingham w Calthorpe,
  Ingworth, Aldborough etc *Nor*
ALDBOROUGH HATCH (St Peter) *Chelmsf 4*   **P** *The Crown*
  V C NICHOLSON
ALDBOURNE (St Michael)   *see* Whitton *Sarum*
ALDBROUGH (St Bartholomew) and Mappleton w Goxhill and
  Withernwick *York 11*   **P** *Ld Chan, Abp, and Adn E Riding*
  (by turn)   **C** S J K RICE-OXLEY
ALDBROUGH (St Paul)   *see* Forcett and Aldbrough and
  Melsonby *Ripon*
ALDBURY (St John the Baptist)   *see* Tring *St Alb*
ALDE, UPPER *St E 18*   **P** *R C Rous Esq, DBP, and CPAS (jt)*
  R J P T OLANCZUK
ALDE RIVER Benefice, The *St E 19*   **P** *Earl of Guilford,*
  Major P W Hope-Cobbold, DBP, CPAS, Miss S F R Heycock-
  Holland, and Exors Mrs A C V Wentworth (jt)   **R** B J SLATTER,
  OLM E N YOUNGS-DUNNETT
ALDEBURGH (St Peter and St Paul) w Hazlewood *St E 19*
  P *Mrs A C V Wentworth*   **V** N J HARTLEY,   **OLM** N J WINTER
ALDEBY (St Mary)   *see* Raveningham Gp *Nor*
ALDENHAM (St John the Baptist), Radlett and Shenley *St Alb 1*
  P *Patr Bd*   **TR** W I HOGG,   **TV** R A FLETCHER, V C ORAM,
  NSM A G HOGG
ALDERBROOK (St Richard)   *see* Crowborough *Chich*
ALDERBURY (St Mary the Virgin)   *see* Clarendon *Sarum*
ALDERCAR (St John)   *see* Langley Mill *Derby*
ALDERFORD (St John the Baptist)   *see* Wensum Benefice *Nor*

ALDERHOLT (St James) *Sarum 9* **P** *DBP* **V** P J MARTIN, **OLM** D A DENNIS

ALDERLEY (St Kenelm) *see* Wotton-under-Edge w Ozleworth, N Nibley etc *Glouc*

ALDERLEY (St Mary) w Birtles *Ches 12* **P** *Trustees and Bp (alt)* **R** J C MILNES

ALDERLEY EDGE (St Philip) *Ches 12* **P** *Trustees* **V** P J PARRY, **NSM** L C A ALEXANDER

ALDERMASTON (St Mary the Virgin) and Woolhampton *Ox 12* **P** *Bp, Keble Coll Ox, CPAS, Lady Dugdale, Worc Coll Ox, and DBP (jt)* **R** P G STEELE, **NSM** D FOOTE, E M OKE

ALDERMINSTER (St Mary and Holy Cross) *see* Stourdene Gp *Cov*

ALDERNEY (St Anne) *Win 14* **P** *The Crown* **V** S M MASTERS

ALDERSBROOK (St Gabriel) *Chelmsf 4* **P** *DBP* **V** P H SMITH, **NSM** A KENNY

ALDERSHOT (Holy Trinity) *Guildf 1* **P** *CPAS* **V** G P H NEWTON, **NSM** C J B KELLAGHER

ALDERSHOT (St Augustine) *Guildf 1* **P** *Bp* **V** K M HODGES, **OLM** J W A HARVEY

ALDERSHOT (St Michael the Archangel) (Ascension) *Guildf 1* **P** *Bp* **V** J A MARTIN, **C** T S MOORE

ALDERSLEY (Christ the King) *see* Tettenhall Regis *Lich*

ALDERTON (St Andrew) *see* Wilford Peninsula *St E*

ALDERTON (St Giles) *see* Sherston Magna, Easton Grey, Luckington etc *Bris*

ALDERTON (St Margaret) *see* Blisworth and Stoke Bruerne w Grafton Regis etc *Pet*

ALDERTON (St Margaret of Antioch) *see* Winchcombe *Glouc*

ALDERWASLEY (All Saints) *see* Wirksworth *Derby*

ALDFIELD (St Lawrence) *see* Fountains Gp *Ripon*

ALDFORD (St John the Baptist) *see* Waverton w Aldford and Bruera *Ches*

ALDHAM (St Margaret and St Catherine) *see* Marks Tey and Aldham *Chelmsf*

ALDHAM (St Mary) *see* Elmsett w Aldham, Hintlesham, Chattisham etc *St E*

ALDINGBOURNE (St Mary the Virgin), Barnham and Eastergate *Chich 1* **P** *Bp and D&C (jt)* **R** S P HOLLAND, **NSM** C R S HARDING, A R BRANT

ALDINGHAM (St Cuthbert) and Dendron and Rampside and Urswick *Carl 9* **P** *Prime Min (1 turn), V Dalton-in-Furness and Resident Landowners of Urswick (1 turn)* **R** C R HONOUR

ALDINGTON (St Martin) w Bonnington and Bilsington and Lympne w West Hythe *Cant 12* **P** *Abp* **P-in-c** R A LOVE

ALDRIDGE (St Mary the Virgin) (St Thomas) *Lich 25* **P** *MMCET* **R** R J CORNFIELD, **C** A G BURNAGE, J FISHER, **OLM** S E QUIBELL

ALDRINGHAM (St Andrew) *see* Whinlands *St E*

ALDRINGTON (St Leonard) *Chich 4* **P** *Bp* **R** S J TERRY

ALDSWORTH (St Bartholomew) *see* Sherborne, Windrush, the Barringtons etc *Glouc*

ALDWARK (St Stephen) *see* Alne *York*

ALDWICK (St Richard) *Chich 1* **P** *Bp* **V** L C J NAGEL

ALDWINCLE (St Peter), Clopton, Pilton, Stoke Doyle, Thorpe Achurch, Titchmarsh and Wadenhoe *Pet 10* **P** *G C Capron Esq, Wadenhoe Trust, Soc Merchant Venturers Bris, and DBP (jt)* **R** J B MYNORS, **NSM** E A WALLER

ALDWORTH (St Mary the Virgin) *see* Basildon w Aldworth and Ashampstead *Ox*

ALEXANDRA PARK (St Andrew) *Lon 20* **P** *Bp* **V** A F PYBUS

ALFINGTON (St James and St Anne) *see* Ottery St Mary, Alfington, W Hill, Tipton etc *Ex*

ALFOLD (St Nicholas) and Loxwood *Guildf 2* **P** *Bp and CPAS (jt)* **P-in-c** J R J BURLEY

ALFORD (All Saints) *see* Six Pilgrims *B & W*

ALFORD (St Wilfrid) w Rigsby *Linc 8* **P** *Bp* **P-in-c** C E KEAY, **OLM** W A HORTON

ALFRED JEWEL *B & W 14* **P** *D&C Windsor (4 turns), Bp (2 turns), Sir Benjamin Slade Bt (1 turn)* **C** M H CLEMENTS

ALFRETON (St Martin) *Derby 1* **P** *Bp* **P-in-c** F J C MERCURIO, **NSM** S L MASON

ALFRICK (St Mary Magdalene) *see* Worcs W *Worc*

ALFRISTON (St Andrew) w Lullington, Litlington and West Dean *Chich 18* **P** *Ld Chan (3 turns), R A Brown Esq (1 turn), and Duke of Devonshire (1 turn)* **R** J E HOWSON, **NSM** M E SITWELL

ALGARKIRK (St Peter and St Paul) and Fosdyke *Linc 21* **P** *Prime Min and Bp (alt)* **V** vacant

ALHAMPTON (Mission Church) *see* Fosse Trinity *B & W*

ALKBOROUGH (St John the Baptist) *Linc 4* **P** *Em Coll Cam and Bp (alt)* **V** A F PLEDGER

ALKERTON (St Michael and All Angels) *see* Ironstone *Ox*

ALKHAM (St Anthony) w Capel le Ferne and Hougham *Cant 4* **P** *Abp* **P-in-c** S M WHITE

ALKMONTON (St John), Cubley and Marston Montgomery *Derby 14* **P** *Bp (3 turns), V Shirley (1 turn)* **C** J J VICKERSTAFF, **NSM** J M LEGH

ALL CANNINGS (All Saints) *see* Bishop's Cannings, All Cannings etc *Sarum*

ALL SAINTS *see* Highertown and Baldhu *Truro*

ALL SAINTS (All Saints) *see* Axminster, Chardstock, All Saints etc *Ex*

ALL STRETTON (St Michael and All Angels) *see* Church Stretton *Heref*

ALLENDALE (St Cuthbert) w Whitfield *Newc 10* **P** *Viscount Allendale and J C Blackett-Ord Esq (alt)* **R** J W RUSSELL

ALLENS CROSS (St Bartholomew) *Birm 4* **P** *Bp* **P-in-c** H J OSBORNE

ALLENS GREEN (Mission Church) *see* High Wych and Gilston w Eastwick *St Alb*

ALLEN'S ROUGH (Worship Centre) *see* Willenhall H Trin *Lich*

ALLENSMORE (St Andrew) *see* Kingstone w Clehonger, Eaton Bishop etc *Heref*

ALLENTON (St Edmund) and Shelton Lock *Derby 15* **P** *Bp* **V** vacant (01332) 701194

ALLER (St Andrew) *see* Langport Area *B & W*

ALLERSTON (St John) *see* Thornton Dale w Allerston, Ebberston etc *York*

ALLERTHORPE (St Botolph) *see* Barmby Moor Gp *York*

ALLERTON (All Hallows) *see* Mossley Hill *Liv*

ALLERTON (not known) *see* Mark w Allerton *B & W*

ALLERTON (St Peter) (St Francis of Assisi) *Bradf 1* **P** *Bp* **V** G O WILLIAMS

ALLERTON BYWATER (St Mary) *see* Kippax w Allerton Bywater *Ripon*

ALLESLEY (All Saints) *Cov 2* **P** *J R W Thomson-Bree Esq* **R** R N TREW

ALLESLEY PARK (St Christopher) and Whoberley *Cov 3* **P** *Bp* **V** G L PRINGLE, **C** K J FLANAGAN, **OLM** L J CLARKE

ALLESTREE (St Edmund King and Martyr) *Derby 11* **P** *Bp* **P-in-c** C A DYER, **NSM** P A MALLINSON

ALLESTREE (St Nicholas) *Derby 11* **P** *Bp* **V** W F BATES, **NSM** J M NEEDLE

ALLHALLOWS (All Saints) *see* Binsey *Carl*

ALLINGTON (St John the Baptist) *see* Bourne Valley *Sarum*

ALLINGTON (St Nicholas) and Maidstone St Peter *Cant 13* **P** *Abp* **P-in-c** M L BORLEY, **NSM** L E LUDLOW

ALLINGTON (St Swithin) *see* Bridport *Sarum*

ALLINGTON, EAST (St Andrew) *see* Modbury, Bigbury, Ringmore w Kingston etc *Ex*

ALLINGTON, WEST (Holy Trinity) *see* Saxonwell *Linc*

ALLITHWAITE (St Mary) *see* Cartmel Peninsula *Carl*

ALLONBY (Christ Church), Cross Canonby and Dearham *Carl 7* **P** *TR Solway Plain, D&C, and Bp (jt)* **V** M E DAY, **NSM** M FOGG

ALMELEY (St Mary) *see* Eardisley w Bollingham, Willersley, Brilley etc *Heref*

ALMER (St Mary) *see* Red Post *Sarum*

ALMONDBURY (St Michael and St Helen) (St Mary) (All Hallows) w Farnley Tyas *Wakef 1* **P** *DBP* **TR** D F HANDLEY, **TV** M L BROWELL, **C** C M WATKINS, **NSM** M J BUTTERWORTH, **OLM** G M GARSIDE

ALMONDSBURY (St Mary the Virgin) and Olveston *Bris 2* **P** *Bp and D&C (jt)* **V** P W ROWE, **Hon C** D R F BAIN, **OLM** D H BONE

ALNE (St Mary) *York 3* **P** *CPAS and MMCET (alt)* **P-in-c** C J PARK, **NSM** R WADSWORTH

ALNE, GREAT (St Mary Magdalene) *see* Kinwarton w Gt Alne and Haselor *Cov*

ALNHAM (St Michael and All Angels) *see* Upper Coquetdale *Newc*

ALNMOUTH (St John the Baptist) *see* Lesbury w Alnmouth *Newc*

ALNWICK (St Michael and St Paul) *Newc 6* **P** *Duke of Northd* **V** M J WEBB, **C** R L SQUIRES

ALPERTON (St James) *Lon 21* **P** *CPAS* **V** J B ROOT, **C** T N CROWE, **Hon C** D B WADLAND, **NSM** A S JACOB

ALPHAMSTONE (not known) *see* N Hinckford *Chelmsf*

ALPHETON (St Peter and St Paul) *see* Chadbrook *St E*

ALPHINGTON (St Michael and All Angels), Shillingford St George and Ide *Ex 3* **P** *DBP, D&C, and Mrs J M Michelmore (jt)* **P-in-c** S L BESSENT, **C** C M MASON, J J CLARK

ALRESFORD (St Andrew) *Chelmsf 22* **P** *Bp* **P-in-c** P C M SCOTT, **NSM** D A DEENY

ALRESFORD, NEW (St John the Baptist) *see* Arle Valley *Win*

ALRESFORD, OLD (St Mary) *as above*

ALREWAS (All Saints) *Lich 1* **P** *Bp* **V** J W ALLAN,
NSM P A L MADDOCK, V A WILKERSON
ALSAGER (Christ Church) *Ches 11* **P** *Bp* **V** T S MAY
ALSAGER (St Mary Magdalene) (St Patrick's Mission Church)
Ches 11 **P** *Bp* **V** R J ISHERWOOD
ALSAGERS BANK (St John) *Lich 9* **P** *Bp*
P-in-c P T W DAVIES
ALSOP-EN-LE-DALE (St Michael and All Angels) *see* Fenny
Bentley, Thorpe, Tissington, Parwich etc *Derby*
ALSTON MOOR (St Augustine) *Newc 10* **P** *Bp*
R J R GLOVER
ALSTONE (St Margaret) *see* Overbury w Teddington, Alstone
etc *Worc*
**ALSTONFIELD (St Peter), Butterton, Ilam, Warslow w
Elkstone and Wetton** *Lich 5* **P** *Bp, DBP, V Mayfield, and
Sir Peter Walker-Okeover Bt (jt)* **V** A C BALLARD,
NSM A J HACK
ALSWEAR (not known) *see* Bishopsnympton, Rose Ash,
Mariansleigh etc *Ex*
ALTARNON (St Nonna) w Bolventor, Laneast and St Clether
Truro 9 **P** *Bp, D&C, and SMF (jt)* **P-in-c** P J HIBBERT
ALTCAR (St Michael and All Angels) and Hightown *Liv 5* **P** *Bp*
V J C BAKER, **NSM** D C M TAYLOR
ALTHAM (St James) w Clayton le Moors *Blackb 1* **P** *DBP and
Trustees (alt)* **V** J TRANTER, **NSM** M RUSSELL
ALTHORNE (St Andrew) *see* Creeksea w Althorne,
Latchingdon and N Fambridge *Chelmsf*
ALTHORPE (St Oswald) *see* Belton Gp *Linc*
ALTOFTS (St Mary Magdalene) *Wakef 11* **P** *Meynall Ingram
Trustees* **P-in-c** S J HOTCHEN
ALTON (All Saints) *Win 2* **P** *Bp* **P-in-c** P A BARLOW,
NSM J L WALKER
ALTON (St Lawrence) *Win 2* **P** *D&C* **P-in-c** P G H DOORES,
C A M MICKLEFIELD, **NSM** I M TOOMBS, T C L HELLINGS
ALTON (St Peter) w Bradley-le-Moors and Oakamoor w Cotton
Lich 6 **P** *Earl of Shrewsbury and Talbot, DBP, and
R Cheadle (jt)* **C** R P OWEN, J RICHARDSON
ALTON BARNES (St Mary the Virgin) *see* Pewsey and
Swanborough *Sarum*
ALTON COMMON (Mission Room) *see* Alton w Bradley-le-
Moors and Oakamoor w Cotton *Lich*
ALTON PANCRAS (St Pancras) *see* Piddle Valley, Hilton,
Cheselbourne etc *Sarum*
ALTRINCHAM (St George) *Ches 10* **P** *V Bowdon*
V E J BETTS, **C** J O MCKERAN, M A JONES
ALTRINCHAM (St John the Evangelist) *Ches 10* **P** *Bp*
P-in-c E J BETTS, **C** J O MCKERAN, M A JONES
ALVANLEY (St John the Evangelist) *Ches 3* **P** *Bp* **V** *vacant*
(01928) 722012
ALVASTON (St Michael and All Angels) *Derby 15* **P** *PCC*
NSM J P MUNRO
ALVECHURCH (St Lawrence) *Worc 7* **P** *Bp* **R** D H MARTIN
ALVEDISTON (St Mary) *see* Chalke Valley *Sarum*
ALVELEY (St Mary the Virgin) and Quatt *Heref 9*
P J W H Thompson Esq and Lady Labouchere (jt)
R N P ARMSTRONG, **NSM** R M SIMS
ALVERDISCOTT (All Saints) *see* Newton Tracey, Horwood,
Alverdiscott etc *Ex*
ALVERSTOKE (St Faith) (St Francis) (St Mary) *Portsm 3*
P *Bp* **R** E A GOODYER, **C** P G HISCOCK, **NSM** R A FORSE,
N S TERRY
ALVERSTONE (Church Hall) *see* Brading w Yaverland *Portsm*
ALVERTHORPE (St Paul) *Wakef 11* **P** *Bp*
P-in-c G A SYKES, **NSM** K KIDD
ALVESCOT (St Peter) *see* Shill Valley and Broadshire *Ox*
ALVESTON (St Helen) and Littleton-cn-Severn w Elberton
Bris 2 **P** *Bp and D&C (jt)* **V** D J POLE
ALVESTON (St James) *Cov 8* **P** *R Hampton Lucy w Charlecote
and Loxley* **V** R E WILLIAMS, **NSM** M KENT
ALVINGHAM (St Adelwold) *see* Mid Marsh Gp *Linc*
ALVINGTON (St Andrew) *see* Woolaston w Alvington and
Aylburton *Glouc*
ALVINGTON, WEST (All Saints) *see* Thurlestone, S Milton, W
Alvington etc *Ex*
ALWALTON (St Andrew) *see* The Ortons, Alwalton and
Chesterton *Ely*
ALWINGTON (St Andrew) *see* Parkham, Alwington,
Buckland Brewer etc *Ex*
ALWINTON (St Michael and All Angels) *see* Upper
Coquetdale *Newc*
ALWOODLEY (St Barnabas) *see* Moor Allerton *Ripon*
AMBERGATE (St Anne) and Heage *Derby 11* **P** *V Duffield and
Exors M A T Johnson Esq* **R** *vacant* (01773) 852072
AMBERLEY (Holy Trinity) *Glouc 5* **P** *DBP*
NSM A V M MORRIS

AMBERLEY (no dedication) *see* Marden w Amberley and
Wisteston *Heref*
**AMBERLEY (St Michael) w North Stoke and Parham,
Wiggonholt and Greatham** *Chich 12* **P** *Bp and Parham Estate
Trustees (jt)* **P-in-c** D S FARRANT
AMBLE (St Cuthbert) *Newc 6* **P** *Bp*
P-in-c D R WESTMORELAND
AMBLECOTE (Holy Trinity) *Worc 12* **P** *Bp*
P-in-c A R N WILLIAMS
AMBLESIDE (St Mary) w Brathay *Carl 11* **P** *DBP*
V W R F COKE, **C** M P WOODCOCK, D WHITEHEAD,
NSM N F HALLAM
AMBROSDEN (St Mary the Virgin) *see* Ray Valley *Ox*
AMCOTTS (St Mark) *see* Belton Gp *Linc*
AMERSHAM (St Leonard) *see* Chesham Bois *Ox*
AMERSHAM (St Mary the Virgin) *Ox 20* **P** *Capt
F Tyrwhitt Drake* **R** T J L HARPER, **NSM** D C CARR
AMERSHAM ON THE HILL (St Michael and All Angels)
Ox 20 **P** *Bp* **V** D M GLOVER, **C** A J CRAWLEY,
NSM P R BINNS
AMESBURY (St Mary and St Melor) *Sarum 13*
P *D&C Windsor* **P-in-c** S E WILKINSON
AMINGTON (St Editha) *Birm 10* **P** *Bp* **V** M A HARRIS,
NSM W T KNUCKEY
AMOTHERBY (St Helen) *see* The Street Par *York*
AMPFIELD (St Mark) *Win 12* **P** *Lady Jean Mackenzie*
P-in-c P M GILKS, **NSM** J FOSTER, V J LAWRENCE
**AMPLEFORTH (St Hilda) w Oswaldkirk, Gilling East and
Stonegrave** *York 17* **P** *Abp, Trin Coll Cam, and Prime Min
(by turn)* **V** W M CARTWRIGHT
AMPNEY (St Mary) *see* Fairford Deanery *Glouc*
AMPNEY (St Peter) *as above*
AMPNEY CRUCIS (Holy Rood) *as above*
AMPORT (St Mary) *see* Portway and Danebury *Win*
AMPTHILL (St Andrew) w Millbrook and Steppingley *St Alb 9*
P *Ld Chan* **R** M J TRODDEN
AMPTON (St Peter) *see* Blackbourne *St E*
**AMWELL, GREAT (St John the Baptist) w St Margaret's and
Stanstead Abbots** *St Alb 22* **P** *Bp, Peache Trustees, and
Haileybury Coll (jt)* **V** E A DONALDSON, **Hon
C** M G H LACKEY
AMWELL, LITTLE (Holy Trinity) *see* Hertford *St Alb*
ANCASTER (St Martin) *see* Ancaster Wilsford Gp *Linc*
ANCASTER WILSFORD Group, The *Linc 23* **P** *Bp (2 turns),
DBP (1 turn), and Mrs G V Hoare (1 turn)*
P-in-c A J LITTLEWOOD
ANCHORSHOLME (All Saints) *Blackb 8* **P** *Bp, V Bispham,
and Ch Soc Trust (jt)* **P-in-c** S M DNISTRIANSKYJ
ANCOATS (All Souls) *see* Manchester Gd Shep and St Barn
Man
ANCROFT (St Anne) *see* Lowick and Kyloe w Ancroft *Newc*
ANDERBY (St Andrew) *see* Sutton, Huttoft and Anderby *Linc*
ANDOVER (St Mary the Virgin) *Win 3* **P** *St Mary's Coll Win*
P-in-c D G WILLIAMS
ANDOVER (St Thomas) *see* Pastrow *Win*
ANDOVER, WEST (St Michael and All Angels) *see* Portway
and Danebury *Win*
ANDREAS (St Andrew) *S & M 3* **P** *The Crown* **R** *vacant*
ANDREAS (St Jude Chapelry) *S & M 3* **P** *R Andreas*
V *vacant*
ANERLEY (Christ Church) (St Paul) *Roch 13* **P** *Patr Bd*
TV M M JONES
ANFIELD (St Columba) *Liv 7* **P** *Bp* **V** R S BRIDSON,
NSM K L MILLER
ANFIELD (St Margaret) *Liv 3* **P** *Bp* **P-in-c** P A WINN,
NSM J E WINN, S J LUCAS
ANGELL TOWN (St John the Evangelist) *S'wark 11* **P** *Bp*
P-in-c M R MALLETT, **NSM** P J MILLIGAN
ANGERSLEIGH (St Michael) *see* Trull w Angersleigh *B & W*
ANGLESEY Group, The *Ely 4* **P** *Trin Coll Cam, D&C, and
Bp (jt)* **V** D H LEWIS, **C** J R DOWMAN, **NSM** D J KETTLE
ANGMERING (St Margaret) *Chich 1* **P** *J F P Somerset Esq
and Ch Patr Trust (jt)* **R** M J STANDEN, **C** B J REDDING,
A R THOMAS
ANKER PARISHES *see* Wolvey w Burton Hastings, Copston
Magna etc *Cov*
ANLABY (St Peter) *York 14* **P** *Trustees* **V** N D BARNES,
NSM C R TETLEY
ANLABY COMMON (St Mark) Hull *York 14* **P** *Abp*
P-in-c D J W DATII
ANMER (St Mary) *see* Dersingham w Anmer and Shernborne
Nor
ANNESLEY (Our Lady and All Saints) w Newstead *S'well 4*
P *Exors Major R P Chaworth-Musters*
P-in-c E A TURNER-LOISEL, **NSM** P H JONES

ANNFIELD PLAIN (St Aidan) *see* Collierley w Annfield Plain *Dur*

ANNSCROFT (Christ Church) *see* Longden and Annscroft w Pulverbatch *Heref*

ANSFORD (St Andrew) *see* Castle Cary w Ansford *B & W*

ANSLEY (St Lawrence) and Arley *Cov 5* P Ch Patr Trust, *N W H Sylvester Esq, and A C D'O Ransom Esq (jt)* R P B ALLAN

ANSLOW (Holy Trinity) *Lich 14* P *MMCET* V I R WHITEHEAD

ANSTEY (St George) *see* Hormead, Wyddial, Anstey, Brent Pelham etc *St Alb*

ANSTEY (St Mary) and Thurcaston w Cropston *Leic 9* P *Bp and Em Coll Cam (jt)* R S J D FOSTER

ANSTEY, EAST (St Michael) *see* Bishopsnympton, Rose Ash, Mariansleigh etc *Ex*

ANSTEY, WEST (St Petrock) *as above*

ANSTON (St James) *Sheff 5* P *Bp* V M CAUNT, C C J BETSON

ANSTY (St James) *see* Nadder Valley *Sarum*

ANSTY (St James) and Shilton *Cov 2* P *Ld Chan* P-in-c P J MESSAM, NSM N W STEVENS

ANSTY (St John) *see* Cuckfield *Chich*

ANTINGHAM (St Mary) *see* Trunch *Nor*

ANTONY (St James the Great) w Sheviock *Truro 11* P *Bp and Col Sir John Carew-Pole Bt (alt)* P-in-c B A ANDERSON

ANTROBUS (St Mark), Aston by Sutton, Little Leigh and Lower Whitley *Ches 4* P *Bp, V Gt Budworth, Lord Daresbury, and B H Talbot Esq (jt)* V R J DIGGLE

ANWICK (St Edith) *see* Ruskington Gp *Linc*

APETHORPE (St Leonard) *see* Nassington w Yarwell and Woodnewton w Apethorpe *Pet*

APLEY (St Andrew) *see* Bardney *Linc*

APPERLEY (Holy Trinity) *see* Deerhurst and Apperley w Forthampton etc *Glouc*

APPLEBY (St Bartholomew) *see* Winterton Gp *Linc*

APPLEBY (St Lawrence) *see* Heart of Eden *Carl*

APPLEBY MAGNA (St Michael and All Angels) *see* Woodfield Team *Leic*

APPLEDORE (St Mary) *see* Bideford, Northam, Westward Ho!, Appledore etc *Ex*

APPLEDORE (St Peter and St Paul) w Brookland and Fairfield and Brenzett w Snargate *Cant 12* P *Abp* P-in-c N R GALLAGHER, C P J WHITE, NSM S J BODY, K FAZZANI

APPLEDRAM (St Mary the Virgin) *Chich 3* P *D&C* P-in-c C A ASHLEY

APPLEFORD (St Peter and St Paul) *see* Sutton Courtenay w Appleford *Ox*

APPLESHAW (St Peter) Kimpton, Thruxton, Fyfield and Shipton Bellinger *Win 3* P *Bp (1 turn), and Bp, D&C, and M H Routh Esq (1 turn)* R I J TOMLINSON, Hon C S C KERSLEY, NSM A E MCKENZIE

APPLETHWAITE (St Mary) *see* Windermere St Mary and Troutbeck *Carl*

APPLETON (All Saints) *see* The Street Par *York*

APPLETON (St Lawrence) *Ox 10* P *Magd Coll Ox* P-in-c L L SAPWELL

APPLETON (St Mary Magdalene) *see* Stockton Heath *Ches*

APPLETON-LE-MOORS (Christ Church) *see* Lastingham w Appleton-le-Moors, Rosedale etc *York*

APPLETON ROEBUCK (All Saints) w Acaster Selby *York 1* P *Abp* P-in-c C I COATES, NSM J MACNAUGHTON

APPLETON THORN (St Cross) *see* Stretton and Appleton Thorn *Ches*

APPLETON WISKE (St Mary) *see* E Richmond *Ripon*

APPLETREEWICK (St John the Baptist) *see* Burnsall w Rylstone *Bradf*

APPLEY BRIDGE (All Saints) *Blackb 4* P *Bp* P-in-c M J EVERITT, C S A GLYNN

APSLEY END (St Mary) *see* Chambersbury *St Alb*

APULDRAM (St Mary the Virgin) *see* Appledram *Chich*

ARBORFIELD (St Bartholomew) w Barkham *Ox 16* P *DBP* R E P BICKERSTETH, C J P BIDGOOD, L J O PARKER

ARBORY (St Columba) *S & M 1* P *The Crown* V P C ROBINSON, NSM C L BARRY

ARBOURTHORNE (St Paul) and Norfolk Park *Sheff 1* P *Bp and V Sheffield (jt)* V J T HODGES, NSM C C TURNER

ARBURY (Good Shepherd) *see* Chesterton Gd Shep *Ely*

ARDELEY (St Lawrence) *St Alb 19* P *D&C St Paul's* V vacant

ARDINGLY (St Peter) *Chich 6* P *MMCET* R J H CRUTCHLEY

ARDINGTON (Holy Trinity) *see* Wantage Downs *Ox*

ARDLEIGH (St Mary the Virgin) and Bromleys, The *Chelmsf 20*

P *Ld Chan (2 turns), CR (1 turn), Wadh Coll Ox (1 turn)* R R E FARRELL

ARDLEIGH GREEN (All Saints) *see* Squirrels Heath *Chelmsf*

ARDLEY (St Mary) *see* Cherwell Valley *Ox*

ARDSLEY (Christ Church) *Sheff 12* P *R Darfield* V vacant (01226) 203784 or 742149

ARDSLEY, EAST (St Gabriel) (St Michael) *Wakef 11* P E C S J G Brudenell Esq V G COGGINS

ARDSLEY, WEST (St Mary) *Wakef 8* P E C S J G Brudenell Esq V B A J BARRACLOUGH

ARDWICK (St Benedict) *see* Longsight St Luke *Man*

ARDWICK (St Jerome and St Silas) *see* Manchester Gd Shep and St Barn *Man*

ARELEY KINGS (St Bartholomew) *Worc 13* P *R Martley* R M TURNER

ARICONIUM: Aston Ingham, Hope Mansel, Linton, The Lea, Upton Bishop and Weston-under-Penyard *Heref 8* P *Bp (3 turns), St Jo Coll Ox (2 turns), Exors Preb H L Whatley (1 turn)* V N S PATTERSON

ARKENDALE (St Bartholomew) *see* Walkingham Hill *Ripon*

ARKENGARTHDALE (St Mary) *see* Swaledale *Ripon*

ARKESDEN (St Mary the Virgin) *see* Clavering and Langley w Arkesden etc *Chelmsf*

ARKHOLME (St John the Baptist) *see* Hornby w Claughton and Whittington etc *Blackb*

ARKLEY (St Peter) *see* Chipping Barnet *St Alb*

ARKSEY (All Saints) *see* New Bentley w Arksey *Sheff*

ARLE VALLEY Benefice, The *Win 1* P *Bp* R P H N COLLINS, NSM P A CLEGG, B C FLETCHER

ARLECDON (St Michael) *see* Crosslacon *Carl*

ARLESEY (St Andrew) (St Peter) w Astwick *St Alb 16* P *DBP* V S D EDWARDS

ARLEY (St Michael) *see* Ansley and Arley *Cov*

ARLEY (St Wilfrid) *as above*

ARLEY, UPPER (St Peter) *see* Kidderminster St Mary and All SS w Trimpley etc *Worc*

ARLINGHAM (St Mary the Virgin) *see* Frampton on Severn, Arlingham, Saul etc *Glouc*

ARLINGTON (St James) *see* Shirwell, Loxhore, Kentisbury, Arlington, etc *Ex*

ARLINGTON (St Pancras), Folkington and Wilmington *Chich 18* P *Bp Lon, Mrs S J Harcourt-Smith, and Duke of Devonshire (by turn)* P-in-c I E MORRISON

ARMATHWAITE (Christ and St Mary) *see* Inglewood Gp *Carl*

ARMINGHALL (St Mary) *see* Stoke H Cross w Dunston, Arminghall etc *Nor*

ARMITAGE (Holy Trinity) (St John the Baptist) *Lich 3* P *Bp* R D R H THOMAS

ARMITAGE BRIDGE (St Paul) *see* Em TM *Wakef*

ARMLEY (St Bartholomew) w New Wortley *Ripon 6* P *Bp, DBP, and Hyndman Trustees (jt)* P-in-c I WRIGHT, C G NEWTON

ARMLEY, UPPER (Christ Church) *Ripon 6* P *Ch Patr Trust* V A SEN

ARMLEY HEIGHTS (Church of the Ascension) *see* Upper Armley *Ripon*

ARMTHORPE (St Leonard and St Mary) *Sheff 8* P *Bp* R R LANDALL

ARNCLIFFE (St Oswald) *see* Kettlewell w Conistone, Hubberholme etc *Bradf*

ARNE (St Nicholas) *see* Wareham *Sarum*

ARNESBY (St Peter) *see* Hexagon *Leic*

ARNOLD (Emmanuel) *see* Bestwood Em w St Mark *S'well*

ARNOLD (St Mary) *S'well 10* P *Bp* V K L SHILL, C J L BLATHERWICK

ARNSIDE (St James) *Carl 10* P *Bp* P-in-c D P COOPER, OLM J S BROCKBANK

ARRETON (St George) *Portsm 7* P *Bp* P-in-c J F O'SHAUGHNESSY

ARRINGTON (St Nicholas) *see* Orwell Gp *Ely*

ARROW (Holy Trinity) *see* Alcester and Arrow w Oversley and Weethley *Cov*

ARTHINGTON (St Peter) *see* Lower Wharfedale *Ripon*

ARTHINGWORTH (St Andrew) and Harrington w Oxendon and East Farndon *Pet 2* P *St Jo Coll Ox (2 turns), Nugee Foundn (2 turns), and Bp (1 turn)* R M Y GARBUTT, NSM D SPENCELEY

ARTHURET (St Michael and All Angels) w Kirkandrews-on-Esk and Nicholforest *Carl 2* P *Sir James Graham Bt (2 turns), Bp (1 turn)* R R TAGUE

ARUNDEL (St Nicholas) w Tortington and South Stoke *Chich 1* P *Bp (2 turns), Duke of Norfolk (1 turn)* V R D FARRER

ASBY (St Peter) *see* Heart of Eden *Carl*

ASCENSION Team Ministry, The *Leic 1* P *Patr Bd* TR V J JUPP, NSM C M COLDICOTT

ASCOT, NORTH (St Mary and St John) *see* Ascot Heath *Ox*

ASCOT, SOUTH (All Souls)   *see* Sunninghill and S Ascot *Ox*
ASCOT HEATH (All Saints) *Ox 11*   **P** *Bp*   **R** D D HANNAH
ASCOTT UNDER WYCHWOOD (Holy Trinity)   *see* Chase *Ox*
ASFORDBY (All Saints)   *see* Ab Kettleby and Holwell w Asfordby *Leic*
ASGARBY (St Andrew)   *see* Heckington Gp *Linc*
ASH (Christ Church)   *see* Adderley, Ash, Calverhall, Ightfield etc *Lich*
ASH (Holy Trinity)   *see* Martock w Ash *B & W*
ASH (St Nicholas) w Westmarsh *Cant 1*   **P** *Abp*
  V J SWEATMAN
ASH (St Peter) *Guildf 1*   **P** *Win Coll*   **R** K R M BRISTOW
ASH (St Peter and St Paul) *Roch 1*   **P** *J R A B Scott Esq*
  R J A PEAL,   **Hon C** J PEAL
ASH (Thomas Chapel)   *see* Sampford Peverell, Uplowman, Holcombe Rogus etc *Ex*
ASH PRIORS (Holy Trinity)   *see* Lydeard St Lawrence w Brompton Ralph etc *B & W*
ASH VALE (St Mary) *Guildf 1*   **P** *Bp*   **V** N J LAMBERT
ASHAMPSTEAD (St Clement)   *see* Basildon w Aldworth and Ashampstead *Ox*
ASHBOCKING (All Saints)   *see* Clopton w Otley, Swilland and Ashbocking *St E*
ASHBOURNE (St John the Baptist) *Derby 8*   **P** *Wright Trustees*
  V *vacant*
ASHBOURNE (St Oswald) w Mapleton *Derby 8*   **P** *Bp*
  P-in-c G P POND,   **C** M C DOYLE
ASHBRITTLE (St John the Baptist)   *see* Wellington and Distr *B & W*
ASHBURNHAM (St Peter) w Penhurst *Chich 14*
  P *Ashburnham Chr Trust*   **P-in-c** F R CUMBERLEGE,
  NSM A D WOODING JONES, J H SYKES
ASHBURTON (St Andrew), Bickington, Buckland in the Moor, Holne, Huccaby, Leusdon, Princetown, Postbridge, and Widecombe-in-the-Moor *Ex 9*   **P** *Duchy of Cornwall (1 turn), Patr Bd (1 turn)*   **TR** P W DARBY,   **TV** C E COOPER,
  C G A C P SAWYER
ASHBURY (St Mary the Virgin)   *see* Shrivenham and Ashbury *Ox*
ASHBY (St Catherine)   *see* Bottesford w Ashby *Linc*
ASHBY (St Mary)   *see* Somerleyton, Ashby, Fritton, Herringfleet etc *Nor*
ASHBY (St Mary)   *see* Thurton *Nor*
ASHBY (St Paul)   *see* Bottesford w Ashby *Linc*
ASHBY, WEST (All Saints)   *see* Hemingby *Linc*
ASHBY-BY-PARTNEY (St Helen)   *see* Partney Gp *Linc*
ASHBY-CUM-FENBY (St Peter)   *see* Laceby and Ravendale Gp *Linc*
ASHBY DE LA LAUNDE (St Hibald)   *see* Digby Gp *Linc*
ASHBY-DE-LA-ZOUCH (Holy Trinity) (St Helen) and Breedon on the Hill *Leic 8*   **P** *Patr Bd*   **TR** B A ROBERTSON,
  TV T L PHILLIPS,   **C** P J HUGHES,   **NSM** J W A DAWSON,
  T R PARKERSON
ASHBY FOLVILLE (St Mary)   *see* S Croxton Gp *Leic*
ASHBY MAGNA (St Mary)   *see* Willoughby Waterleys, Peatling Magna etc *Leic*
ASHBY PARVA (St Mary)   *see* Upper Soar *Leic*
ASHBY PUERORUM (St Andrew)   *see* Horncastle Gp *Linc*
ASHBY ST LEDGERS (St Mary)   *see* Daventry, Ashby St Ledgers, Braunston etc *Pet*
ASHCHURCH (St Nicholas) and Kemerton *Glouc 13*   **P** *DBP and K Storey Esq (jt)*   **R** R E ROBERTS
ASHCOMBE (St Nectan)   *see* Teignmouth, Ideford w Luton, Ashcombe etc *Ex*
ASHCOTT (All Saints)   *see* Shapwick w Ashcott and Burtle *B & W*
ASHDON (All Saints)   *see* Saffron Walden w Wendens Ambo, Littlebury etc *Chelmsf*
ASHE (Holy Trinity and St Andrew)   *see* N Waltham and Steventon, Ashe and Deane *Win*
ASHEN (St Augustine)   *see* Ridgewell w Ashen, Birdbrook and Sturmer *Chelmsf*
ASHENDON (St Mary)   *see* Bernwode *Ox*
ASHFIELD, GREAT (All Saints)   *see* Badwell and Walsham *St E*
ASHFIELD CUM THORPE (St Mary)   *see* Mid Loes *St E*
ASHFORD (St Hilda) *Lon 13*   **P** *Bp*   **V** C A ROGERS
ASHFORD (St Mary the Virgin) *Cant 10*   **P** *Abp*
  P-in-c C G PREECE,   **C** E LANCHANTIN
ASHFORD (St Matthew) *Lon 13*   **P** *Ld Chan*   **V** R E HORTON
ASHFORD (St Peter)   *see* Barnstaple *Ex*
ASHFORD, SOUTH (Christ Church) *Cant 10*   **P** *Abp*
  P-in-c A M HIRST
ASHFORD, SOUTH (St Francis of Assisi) *Cant 10*   **P** *Abp*
  P-in-c A M HIRST

ASHFORD BOWDLER (St Andrew)   *see* Ludlow *Heref*
ASHFORD CARBONEL (St Mary)   *as above*
ASHFORD COMMON (St Benedict)   *see* Upper Sunbury St Sav *Lon*
ASHFORD HILL (St Paul)   *see* Kingsclere and Ashford Hill w Headley *Win*
ASHFORD IN THE WATER (Holy Trinity) w Sheldon and Great Longstone *Derby 2*   **P** *V Bakewell*   **C** A P KAUNHOVEN,
  C H BENSON
ASHILL (Blessed Virgin Mary)   *see* Ilminster and Distr *B & W*
ASHILL (St Nicholas), Carbrooke, Ovington and Saham Toney *Nor 13*   **P** *Bp, New Coll Ox, Cam Univ, and SMF (jt)*
  V J E ATKINS,   **C** J L ODDY,   **OLM** T B C WESTON
ASHILL (St Stephen)   *see* Cullompton, Willand, Uffculme, Kentisbeare etc *Ex*
ASHINGDON (St Andrew) w South Fambridge *Chelmsf 12*
  P *CCC Cam*   **P-in-c** T F CLAY
ASHINGTON (Holy Sepulchre) *Newc 11*   **P** *Bp*   **V** E A BLAND,
  NSM L BEADLE
ASHINGTON (St Matthew)   *see* Canford Magna *Sarum*
ASHINGTON (St Peter and St Paul), Washington and Wiston w Buncton *Chich 12*   **P** *Bp and R H Goring Esq (alt)*
  P-in-c C W MACLAY
ASHINGTON (St Vincent)   *see* Chilton Cantelo, Ashington, Mudford, Rimpton etc *B & W*
ASHLEWORTH (St Bartholomew)   *see* Hasfield w Tirley and Ashleworth *Glouc*
ASHLEY (St Elizabeth)   *see* Hale and Ashley *Ches*
ASHLEY (St James), Crudwell, Hankerton and Oaksey *Bris 6*
  P *Bp and Personal Reps W A Sole (3 turns), Duchy of Lancaster(1 turn)*   **R** B RAVEN
ASHLEY (St John the Baptist) and Mucklestone *Lich 7*
  P *Meynell Ch Trustees and Mrs F F Friend (jt)*
  P-in-c J P EADES
ASHLEY (St Mary the Virgin)   *see* Stoke Albany w Wilbarston and Ashley etc *Pet*
ASHLEY (St Mary) w Silverley *Ely 4*   **P** *Bp and DBP (alt)*
  P-in-c M A GURNER
ASHLEY (St Peter)   *see* Milton *Win*
ASHLEY (St Peter and St Paul)   *see* Somborne w Ashley *Win*
ASHLEY GREEN (St John the Evangelist)   *see* Gt Chesham *Ox*
ASHMANHAUGH (St Swithin), Barton Turf, Beeston St Laurence, Horning, Irstead and Neatishead *Nor 12*   **P** *Bp and Sir Ronald Preston Bt (jt)*   **R** S A ELLISON
ASHMANSWORTH (St James)   *see* Highclere and Ashmansworth w Crux Easton *Win*
ASHMORE (St Nicholas)   *see* Iwerne Valley *Sarum*
ASHMORE PARK (St Alban)   *see* Wednesfield *Lich*
ASHOVER (All Saints) and Brackenfield w Wessington *Derby 5*
  P *Exors Revd J J C Nodder, Duke of Devonshire, V Crich and S Wingfield, and DBF (jt)*   **R** R G LAWRENCE
ASHOW (Assumption of Our Lady)   *see* Stoneleigh w Ashow *Cov*
ASHPERTON (St Bartholomew)   *see* Ledbury *Heref*
ASHPRINGTON (St David)   *see* Totnes w Bridgetown, Berry Pomeroy etc *Ex*
ASHREIGNEY (St James) *Ex 20*   **P** *DBP*   **R** P J NORMAN
ASHTEAD (St George) (St Giles) *Guildf 10*   **P** *Bp*
  R R J KITELEY,   **C** M R SEARLE, J A LEVASIER, J M LEVASIER,
  OLM R M N HOOKER, J M WATTS
ASHTON (Annunciation)   *see* Breage w Godolphin and Germoe *Truro*
ASHTON (St John the Baptist)   *see* Christow, Ashton and Bridford *Ex*
ASHTON (St Michael and All Angels)   *see* Roade and Ashton w Hartwell *Pet*
ASHTON, WEST (St John)   *see* Trowbridge St Thos and W Ashton *Sarum*
ASHTON GATE (St Francis)   *see* Bedminster *Bris*
ASHTON HAYES (St John the Evangelist) *Ches 2*   **P** *Keble Coll Ox*   **P-in-c** B R K PERKES
ASHTON-IN-MAKERFIELD (Holy Trinity) *Liv 14*   **P** *Bp*
  R D R ABBOTT
ASHTON-IN-MAKERFIELD (St Thomas) *Liv 14*
  P *R Ashton-in-Makerfield H Trin*   **V** M E GREENWOOD,
  C D A HAYES
ASHTON KEYNES (Holy Cross), Leigh and Minety *Bris 6*
  P *Bp*   **P-in-c** B RAVEN,   **C** J A S ASHBY,   **NSM** S E DANBY
ASHTON-ON-RIBBLE (St Andrew)   *see* W Preston *Blackb*
ASHTON-ON-RIBBLE (St Michael and All Angels)   *as above*
ASHTON UNDER HILL (St Barbara)   *see* Overbury w Teddington, Alstone etc *Worc*
ASHTON-UNDER-LYNE (Christ Church) *Man 17*   **P** *Bp*
  V L P LONGDEN,   **OLM** A A HILLS
ASHTON-UNDER-LYNE Good Shepherd (Holy Trinity) (St James) (St Michael and All Angels) (St Gabriel) (St Peter)

Man 17   **P** *Patr Bd*   **TR** R FARNWORTH,
TV J H FARNWORTH,   **C** R W A REECE,   **NSM** R FOX,
M WADSWORTH,   **OLM** P E LODGE
ASHTON-UPON-MERSEY (St Martin) *Ches 10*   **P** *SMF*
R R J E CLACK,   **NSM** D R LAW
ASHTON-UPON-MERSEY (St Mary Magdalene) *Ches 10*
P *Trustees*   **V** S B RANKIN,   **C** G FOSTER, J BEAUMONT
ASHURST (St James) *Chich 12*   **P** *MMCET*   **R** P M RAMPTON
ASHURST (St Martin of Tours)   *see* Speldhurst w Groombridge
and Ashurst *Roch*
ASHURST WOOD (St Dunstan)   *see* Forest Row *Chich*
**ASHWATER (St Peter ad Vincula), Halwill, Beaworthy, Clawton
and Tetcott w Luffincott** *Ex 17*   **P** *Ld Chan (1 turn), Major
L J Melhuish, Lt-Col Sir John Molesworth-St Aubyn Bt, and
Bp (jt) (2 turns)*   **P-in-c** J E LUCAS
ASHWELL (St Mary)   *see* Cottesmore and Barrow w Ashwell
and Burley *Pet*
ASHWELL (St Mary the Virgin) w Hinxworth and Newnham
St Alb 19   **P** *Bp, R Smyth Esq, and N J A Farr Esq (jt)
(1 turn), Bp (3 turns)*   **P-in-c** S P CHAMBERS
**ASHWELLTHORPE (All Saints), Forncett, Fundenhall,
Hapton, Tacolneston and Wreningham** *Nor 7*   **P** *Bp, Keble Coll
Ox, Ch Coll Cam, and MMCET (by turn)*   **V** C W J STYLES,
OLM J A L COOPER
ASHWICK (St James) w Oakhill and Binegar *B & W 8*   **P** *Bp*
P-in-c R W WIDDOWSON
ASHWICKEN (All Saints)   *see* Gayton, Gayton Thorpe, E
Walton, E Winch etc *Nor*
ASHWORTH (St James)   *see* Norden w Ashworth *Man*
ASKAM (Church Centre)   *see* Dalton-in-Furness and Ireleth-
with-Askam *Carl*
ASKAM (St Peter)   *as above*
ASKERN (St Peter) *Sheff 7*   **P** *Bp*   **V** M WIGGLESWORTH,
C A DOREY
ASKERSWELL (St Michael), Loders and Powerstock *Sarum 2*
P *Ld Chan, Lady Laskey, Bp, and D&C (by turn)*
P-in-c M N A JONES,   **OLM** E D MARSH
ASKHAM (St Nicholas)   *see* E Markham w Askham, Headon w
Upton and Grove *S'well*
ASKHAM (St Peter)   *see* Lowther and Askham and Clifton and
Brougham *Carl*
ASKHAM BRYAN (St Nicholas) *York 1*   **P** *Abp*
P-in-c G R MUMFORD
ASKHAM RICHARD (St Mary)   *see* Healaugh w Wighill,
Bilbrough and Askham Richard *York*
ASKRIGG (St Oswald) w Stallingbusk *Ripon 4*   **P** V *Aysgarth*
P-in-c A B CHAPMAN,   **NSM** I M ROBINSON, M D BLANCH
ASLACKBY (St James)   *see* Billingborough Gp *Linc*
ASLACTON (St Michael)   *see* Bunwell, Carleton Rode,
Tibenham, Gt Moulton etc *Nor*
ASLOCKTON (St Thomas)   *see* Whatton w Aslockton,
Hawksworth, Scarrington etc *S'well*
ASPALL (St Mary of Grace)   *see* Debenham and Helmingham
St E
ASPATRIA (St Kentigern) w Hayton and Gilcrux *Carl 7*   **P** *Bp*
V C R SHAW
ASPENDEN (St Mary), Buntingford and Westmill *St Alb 19*
P *CPAS, MCET, and K Coll Lon (jt)*   **NSM** G HOWDLE
ASPLEY (St Margaret) *S'well 14*   **P** *Trustees*
P-in-c J G HUTCHINSON,   **C** R S COLDICOTT
**ASPLEY GUISE (St Botolph) w Husborne Crawley and
Ridgmont** *St Alb 9*   **P** *Ld Chan (1 turn), Trustees Bedf Estates
(1 turn), and Bp (2 turns)*   **R** G BRADLEY
ASPULL (St Elizabeth)   *see* Haigh and Aspull *Liv*
ASSINGTON (St Edmund)   *see* Bures w Assington and Lt
Cornard *St E*
ASTBURY (St Mary) and Smallwood *Ches 11*   **P** *Sir Richard
Baker Wilbraham Bt*   **R** J D SHARPLES
ASTERBY Group, The *Linc 11*   **P** *Bp, DBP, Exors
J N Heneage Esq, and F Smith Esq (jt)*   **R** J D MCGRATH
ASTHALL (St Nicholas)   *see* Burford w Fulbrook, Taynton,
Asthall etc *Ox*
ASTLEY (St Mary the Virgin)   *see* Chilvers Coton w Astley *Cov*
ASTLEY (St Mary), Clive, Grinshill and Hadnall *Lich 22*
P *D R B Thompson Esq*   **P-in-c** R R HAARHOFF
ASTLEY (St Peter)   *see* Shrawley, Witley, Astley and Abberley
Worc
ASTLEY (St Stephen), Tyldesley and Mosley Common *Man 13*
P *DBP and V Leigh*   **TR** R J CARMYLLIE,   **TV** J J HARTLEY,
C J STRATON,   **OLM** A J DAND
ASTLEY ABBOTTS (St Calixtus)   *see* Bridgnorth, Tasley,
Astley Abbotts, etc *Heref*
ASTLEY BRIDGE (St Paul) *Man 16*   **P** *The Crown*
V A J LINDOP,   **OLM** G P WATERSON
ASTON (St Giles)   *see* Wigmore Abbey *Heref*

ASTON (St James) (St Peter and St Paul) and Nechells *Birm 8*
P *Patr Bd*   **V** A J JOLLEY,   **C** F J ROBERTSON, J A ARNOLD,
B A WATSON
ASTON (St Mary)   *see* Woore and Norton in Hales *Lich*
ASTON (St Mary)   *see* Stevenage St Mary Shephall w Aston
St Alb
ASTON (St Peter)   *see* Antrobus, Aston by Sutton, Lt Leigh etc
Ches
ASTON (St Saviour)   *see* Stone St Mich and St Wulfad w Aston
St Sav *Lich*
ASTON, LITTLE (St Peter) *Lich 1*   **P** *Patr Bd*   **V** P MOON
ASTON, NORTH (St Mary the Virgin)   *see* Steeple Aston w N
Aston and Tackley *Ox*
ASTON ABBOTS (St James the Great)   *see* Wingrave w
Rowsham, Aston Abbotts and Cublington *Ox*
ASTON BOTTERELL (St Michael and All Angels)   *see* Ditton
Priors w Neenton, Burwarton etc *Heref*
**ASTON CANTLOW (St John the Baptist) and Wilmcote w
Billesley** *Cov 7*   **P** *SMF*   **P-in-c** R LIVINGSTON,   Hon
C P G WIGNALL
**ASTON CLINTON (St Michael and All Angels) w Buckland and
Drayton Beauchamp** *Ox 28*   **P** *Bp, A R Pegg Esq, and Jes Coll
Ox (jt)*   **R** E J MOXLEY
ASTON CUM AUGHTON (All Saints) w Swallownest and Ulley
Sheff 5   **P** *Bp*   **TR** I JENNINGS,   **C** L C BETSON
ASTON EYRE (not known)   *see* Morville w Aston Eyre *Heref*
ASTON FLAMVILLE (St Peter)   *see* Burbage w Aston
Flamville *Leic*
ASTON INGHAM (St John the Baptist)   *see* Ariconium *Heref*
ASTON LE WALLS (St Leonard)   *see* Byfield w Boddington
and Aston le Walls *Pet*
**ASTON ON TRENT (All Saints), Elvaston, Weston on Trent and
Shardlow** *Derby 15*   **P** *Bp, Earl of Harrington, and DBP
(by turn)*   **R** A LUKE,   **NSM** J M INGRAM
ASTON ROWANT (St Peter and St Paul)   *see* Chinnor,
Sydenham, Aston Rowant and Crowell *Ox*
ASTON SANDFORD (St Michael and All Angels)
see Haddenham w Cuddington, Kingsey etc *Ox*
ASTON SOMERVILLE (St Mary)   *see* Winchcombe *Glouc*
ASTON-SUB-EDGE (St Andrew)   *see* Mickleton, Willersey,
Saintbury etc *Glouc*
ASTON TIRROLD (St Michael)   *see* The Churn *Ox*
ASTON UPTHORPE (All Saints)   *as above*
ASTWELL Group of Parishes, The *Pet 1*   **P** *Bp, Worc Coll Ox,
Ox Univ, Mert Coll Ox, DBP, and Jes Coll Ox (jt)*
R W T ADAMS,   **C** C G SIMPSON,   **NSM** D E MICKLETHWAITE
ASTWICK (St Guthlac)   *see* Arlesey w Astwick *St Alb*
ASTWOOD (St Peter)   *see* Sherington w Chicheley, N Crawley,
Astwood etc *Ox*
ASTWOOD BANK (St Matthias and St George)   *see* Redditch
Ch the K *Worc*
ASWARBY (St Denys)   *see* S Lafford *Linc*
ASWARDBY (St Helen)   *see* Partney Gp *Linc*
ATCHAM (St Eata)   *see* Shrewsbury St Giles w Sutton and
Atcham *Lich*
ATHELINGTON (St Peter)   *see* Stradbroke, Horham,
Athelington and Redlingfield *St E*
ATHELNEY Benefice, The *B & W 14*   **P** *D&C*   **V** P A STAPLE
ATHERINGTON (St Mary)   *see* Newton Tracey, Horwood,
Alverdiscott etc *Ex*
ATHERSLEY (St Helen) *Wakef 7*   **P** *Bp*   **V** R H MARSHALL,
C P CARTWRIGHT
ATHERSTONE (St Mary) *Cov 5*   **P** V *Mancetter*
V P I HARRIS
**ATHERTON (St John the Baptist) (St George) (St Philip) and
Hindsford w Howe Bridge** *Man 13*   **P** *DBP*
TR R W BUCKLEY,   **TV** K BAINES,   **C** B C RANDALL,
OLM R W SINCLAIR
ATLOW (St Philip and St James)   *see* Hulland, Atlow, Kniveton,
Bradley and Hognaston *Derby*
ATTENBOROUGH (St Mary the Virgin) *S'well 7*   **P** *CPAS*
P-in-c S M HEMSLEY HALLS
ATTERCLIFFE (Hill Top Chapel)   *see* Nine o'Clock
Community *Sheff*
ATTERCLIFFE (St Alban) and Darnall *Sheff 1*   **P** *Bp, Dean
Sheff, and Sheff Ch Burgesses Trust (jt)*   **V** P WHITTINGHAM
**ATTLEBOROUGH (Assumption of the Blessed Virgin Mary) w
Besthorpe** *Nor 11*   **P** *CR and Mrs S P J Scully (jt)*
R M AISBITT
ATTLEBOROUGH (Holy Trinity) *Cov 5*   **P** V *Nuneaton*
V C JONES
ATTLEBRIDGE (St Andrew)   *see* Wensum Benefice *Nor*
ATWICK (St Lawrence)   *see* Hornsea w Atwick *York*
ATWORTH (St Michael and All Angels) w Shaw and Whitley
Sarum 14   **P** *D&C Bris and R Melksham (alt)*
P-in-c J PERRETT,   **C** A E EVANS, D G SMITH,

NSM J DARLING, **OLM** N G LOCK, E A FIELDEN,
A E WINTOUR
AUBOURN (St Peter)   *see* Bassingham Gp *Linc*
AUCKLAND (St Andrew) (St Anne) *Dur 6*   **P** *Bp*   **V** N P VINE
AUCKLAND (St Helen) *Dur 6*   **P** *Bp*   **V** R I MCTEER
AUCKLAND (St Peter) *Dur 6*   **P** *The Crown*   **V** *vacant* (01388)
661856
AUCKLEY (St Saviour)   *see* Finningley w Auckley *Sheff*
AUDENSHAW (St Hilda) *Man 17*   **P** *Bp*   **V** J H KERSHAW
AUDENSHAW (St Stephen) *Man 17*   **P** *Bp*   **V** P R DIXON
AUDLEM (St James the Great) *Ches 15*   **P** *Bp*
P-in-c H F CHANTRY
AUDLEY (St James the Great) *Lich 9*   **P** *Ch Soc Trust*
V P T W DAVIES
AUGHTON (All Saints)   *see* Bubwith w Skipwith *York*
AUGHTON (Christ Church) *Liv 11*   **P** *R Aughton St Mich*
V R MOUGHTIN,   **C** J P THOMAS
AUGHTON (St Michael) and Bickerstaffe *Liv 11*   **P** *Bp and Earl
of Derby (jt)*   **R** *vacant* (01695) 423204
AUGHTON (St Saviour)   *see* Slyne w Hest and Halton w
Aughton *Blackb*
AUKBOROUGH (St John the Baptist)   *see* Alkborough *Linc*
AUKBOROUGH (St John the Baptist)   *as above*
AULT HUCKNALL (St John the Baptist) and Scarcliffe *Derby 3*
P *Bp and Duke of Devonshire (alt)*   **V** A L BELL
AUNSBY (St Thomas of Canterbury)   *see* S Lafford *Linc*
AUST (not known)   *see* Almondsbury and Olveston *Bris*
AUSTERFIELD (St Helen)   *see* Bawtry w Austerfield and
Misson *S'well*
AUSTREY (St Nicholas)   *see* N Warks *Birm*
AUSTWICK (Epiphany)   *see* Clapham-with-Keasden and
Austwick *Bradf*
AVEBURY (St James)   *see* Upper Kennet *Sarum*
AVELEY (St Michael) and Purfleet *Chelmsf 14*   **P** *Bp*
P-in-c V J ROCKALL,   **C** A J HUDSON
AVENING (Holy Cross) w Cherington *Glouc 9*
P *E A Tarlton Esq (1 turn), D&C (2 turns)*   **NSM** C CARTER
AVERHAM (St Michael and All Angels) w Kelham *S'well 3*
P *DBP*   **R** *vacant*
AVETON GIFFORD (St Andrew)   *see* Modbury, Bigbury,
Ringmore w Kingston etc *Ex*
AVINGTON (St Mary)   *see* Itchen Valley *Win*
AVON DASSETT w Farnborough and Fenny Compton *Cov 8*
P *G V L Holbech Esq and Mrs A D Seyfried (jt), CCC Ox, and
Bp(alt)*   **P-in-c** P T FRANCIS
AVON-SWIFT Group   *see* Gilmorton, Peatling Parva, Kimcote
etc *Leic*
AVON VALLEY *Sarum 13*   **P** *Bp (3 turns), MOD (2 turns), and
Ch Hosp (1 turn)*   **P-in-c** C G FOX,   **C** M T P ZAMMIT,
NSM A A BUSSEY
AVON VALLEY PARTNERSHIP   *see* Fordingbridge and
Breamore and Hale etc *Win*
AVONMOUTH (St Andrew)   *see* Lawrence Weston and
Avonmouth *Bris*
AWBRIDGE (All Saints)   *see* Michelmersh and Awbridge and
Braishfield etc *Win*
AWLISCOMBE (St Michael and All Angels)   *see* Honiton,
Gittisham, Combe Raleigh, Monkton etc *Ex*
AWRE (St Andrew)   *see* Newnham w Awre and Blakeney *Glouc*
AWSWORTH (St Peter)   *see* Trowell, Awsworth and Cossall
S'well
AXBRIDGE (St John the Baptist) w Shipham and Rowberrow
B & W 1   **P** *Bp and D&C (alt)*   **P-in-c** T D HAWKINGS,
NSM P R ROGERS
AXFORD (St Michael)   *see* Whitton *Sarum*
**AXMINSTER (St Mary), Chardstock, All Saints, Combpyne w
Rousdon and Membury** *Ex 5*   **P** *Bp*   **C** J ROBERTS
AXMOUTH (St Michael)   *see* Uplyme w Axmouth *Ex*
AYCLIFFE (Church Centre)   *see* Dover St Mary *Cant*
AYCLIFFE, GREAT (St Andrew) (St Clare) *Dur 5*   **P** *Patr Bd*
TR L POTTER,   **TV** J WING
AYLBURTON (St Mary)   *see* Woolaston w Alvington and
Aylburton *Glouc*
AYLBURTON COMMON (Mission Church)   *see* Lydney *Glouc*
**AYLESBEARE (Blessed Virgin Mary), Rockbeare, Farringdon,
Clyst Honiton and Sowton** *Ex 1*   **P** *Bp and D&C (jt)*
P-in-c M J PARTRIDGE
AYLESBURY (Holy Trinity)   *see* Walton H Trin *Ox*
AYLESBURY (St Mary the Virgin) w Bierton and Hulcott *Ox 21*
P *Bp and Patr Bd (jt)*   **TR** S G I WOOD,   **TV** C M ACKFORD,
R I S RYCRAFT,   **C** D M CLOAKE, A D WILLIS,   **NSM** M WOOD
AYLESBY (St Lawrence)   *see* Keelby Gp *Linc*
AYLESFORD (St Peter and St Paul) *Roch 7*   **P** *D&C*
V C J VAN STRAATEN
AYLESHAM (St Peter) w Adisham *Cant 1*   **P** *Abp*
P-in-c J M B HONNOR,   **NSM** D N J HALE

AYLESTONE (St Andrew) w St James *Leic 1*   **P** *Bp*
R D APPLEBY
AYLESTONE PARK (Church of the Nativity)   *see* Emmaus Par
Team *Leic*
**AYLMERTON (St John the Baptist), Runton, Beeston Regis,
Gresham** *Nor 21*   **P** *Bp and Guild of All So (2 turns), Duchy of
Lanc (1 turn)*   **P** L DAVIS
AYLSHAM (St Michael) *Nor 19*   **P** *D&C Cant*
V R D BRANSON
AYLTON (not known)   *see* Ledbury *Heref*
AYMESTREY (St John the Baptist and St Alkmund)
see Kingsland w Eardisland, Aymestrey etc *Heref*
**AYNHO (St Michael) and Croughton w Evenley and Farthinghoe
and Hinton-in-the-Hedges w Steane** *Pet 1*   **P** *Bp (2 turns),
Mrs E A J Cartwright-Hignett (1 turn), Magd Coll Ox (1 turn),
and Ld Chan (1 turn)*   **R** G A BARKER,   **NSM** E G SMITH
AYOT ST LAWRENCE (St Lawrence)   *see* Kimpton w Ayot
St Lawrence *St Alb*
AYOT ST PETER (St Peter)   *see* Welwyn *St Alb*
AYSGARTH (St Andrew)   *see* Penhill *Ripon*
AYSTON (St Mary the Virgin)   *see* Uppingham w Ayston and
Wardley w Belton *Pet*
AYTHORPE RODING (St Mary)   *see* Gt Canfield w High
Roding and Aythorpe Roding *Chelmsf*
AYTON, EAST (St John the Baptist)   *see* Seamer w East Ayton
York
**AYTON, GREAT (All Saints) (Christ Church) w Easby and
Newton under Roseberry** *York 21*   **P** *Abp*   **V** P H PEVERELL,
NSM G S JAQUES, J C DEAN
BABBACOMBE (All Saints) *Ex 12*   **P** *V St Marychurch*
P-in-c P E JONES
BABCARY (Holy Cross)   *see* Six Pilgrims *B & W*
BABRAHAM (St Peter) *Ely 5*   **P** *H R T Adeane Esq*
P-in-c A C PARTRIDGE
**BABWORTH (All Saints) w Sutton-cum-Lound and Scofton w
Osberton** *S'well 5*   **P** *Bp, G M T Foljambe Esq, and Sir John
Whitaker Bt (jt)*   **R** *vacant* (01777) 710007 *or* 703253
BACKFORD (St Oswald) and Capenhurst *Ches 9*   **P** *Bp*
R S M SOUTHGATE
BACKWELL (St Andrew) w Chelvey and Brockley *B & W 13*
P *DBP*   **R** S J HILL
BACKWORTH (St John)   *see* Earsdon and Backworth *Newc*
BACONSTHORPE (St Mary)   *see* Barningham w Matlaske w
Baconsthorpe etc *Nor*
**BACTON (St Andrew), Happisburgh, Hempstead w Eccles and
Lessingham, Ridlington, Sea Palling w Waxham, Walcott, and
Witton** *Nor 12*   **P** *Bp, Earl of Kimberley, K Coll Cam, and
Sir Edward Evans-Lombe (jt)*   **R** P N WOOD
BACTON (St Faith)   *see* Ewyas Harold w Dulas, Kenderchurch
etc *Heref*
**BACTON (St Mary the Virgin) w Wyverstone, Cotton and Old
Newton, and Wickham Skeith** *St E 6*   **P** *Patr Bd (2 turns),
Ld Chan (1 turn)*   **R** E A VARLEY
**BACUP (Christ Church) (St John the Evangelist) St Saviour and
Stacksteads** *Man 15*   **P** *Patr Bd*   **TR** G WHITTAKER,
TV D P WOODALL,   **OLM** D ALLEN
**BADBY (St Mary) w Newnham and Charwelton w Fawsley and
Preston Capes** *Pet 3*   **P** *Bp*   **R** *vacant* (01327) 310239
BADDESLEY, NORTH (All Saints' Mission Church)
see Chilworth w N Baddesley *Win*
BADDESLEY, NORTH (St John the Baptist)   *as above*
BADDESLEY, SOUTH (St Mary the Virgin)   *see* Boldre w S
Baddesley *Win*
BADDESLEY CLINTON (St Michael) *Birm 6*   **P** *T W Ferrers-
Walker Esq*   **V** *vacant*
BADDESLEY ENSOR (St Nicholas) w Grendon *Birm 10*   **P** *Bp,
V Polesworth, and PCC (jt)*   **V** *vacant* (01827) 715327
BADDILEY (St Michael) and Wrenbury w Burleydam *Ches 15*
P *V Acton and Bp (alt)*   **V** D W WALTON,
NSM R M HARRISON
**BADDOW, GREAT (Meadgate Church Centre) (St Mary the
Virgin) (St Paul)** *Chelmsf 9*   **P** *Patr Bd*   **TR** A COMFORT,
TV M A FARAH, A S M COPELAND,   **C** G R HAMBORG,   **Hon
C** R C MATTHEWS,   **NSM** S M SOUTHEE
BADDOW, LITTLE (St Mary the Virgin) *Chelmsf 9*   **P** *Bp*
C G R HAMBORG
BADGER (St Giles)   *see* Beckbury, Badger, Kemberton, Ryton,
Stockton etc *Lich*
**BADGEWORTH (Holy Trinity), Shurdington and Witcombe w
Bentham** *Glouc 4*   **P** *Bp and F D Hicks Beach Esq (jt)*
R R J A MITCHELL,   **NSM** M A WILFSMITH, A CHAMPION
BADGWORTH (St Congar)   *see* Crook Peak *B & W*
BADLESMERE (St Leonard)   *see* Selling w Throwley,
Sheldwich w Badlesmere etc *Cant*
BADMINTON (St Michael and All Angels)   *see* Boxwell,
Leighterton, Didmarton, Oldbury etc *Glouc*

BADMINTON, LITTLE (St Michael and All Angels) *as above*

BADSEY (St James) w Aldington and Offenham and Bretforton *Worc 1* **P** *Bp and Ch Ch Ox (jt)* **V** R L COURT

BADSHOT LEA (St George) *see* Hale w Badshot Lea *Guildf*

BADSWORTH (St Mary the Virgin) *Wakef 10* **P** *DBP*
R D MATHERS

BADWELL (St Mary) and Walsham *St E 9* **P** *Bp, DBP, R M Martineau Esq, and Soc of the Faith (jt)* **R** M G CLARKE

BAG ENDERBY (St Margaret) *see* S Ormsby Gp *Linc*

BAGBOROUGH (St Pancras) *see* Bishops Lydeard w Bagborough and Cothelstone *B & W*

BAGBY (St Mary) *see* Thirkleby w Kilburn and Bagby *York*

BAGENDON (St Margaret) *see* Stratton, N Cerney, Baunton and Bagendon *Glouc*

BAGINTON (St John the Baptist) w Bubbenhall and Ryton-on-Dunsmore *Cov 6* **P** *D&C (2 turns), Bp (1 turn), Lord Leigh and Bp (1 turn)* **V** D R WINTLE

BAGNALL (St Chad) w Endon *Lich 8* **P** *R Leek and Meerbrook and A D Owen Esq (jt)* **V** A J BETTS

BAGSHOT (Good Shepherd) *see* Savernake *Sarum*

BAGSHOT (St Anne) *Guildf 6* **P** *Ld Chan* **V** D J CHILLMAN

BAGULEY (St John the Divine) Brooklands *Man 8* **P** *Bp and A W Hargreaves Esq (jt)* **V** I MCVEETY, **C** V L JOHNSON,
NSM E SHORT

BAGWORTH (The Holy Rood) *see* Markfield, Thornton, Bagworth and Stanton etc *Leic*

BAILDON (St John the Evangelist) (St Hugh Mission Church) (St James) *Bradf 1* **P** J P Baxter Esq **V** J D NOWELL,
C P DEO, **NSM** K N MEDHURST, S KENNEDY

BAIN VALLEY Group, The *Linc 11* **P** *Baroness Willoughby de Eresby, R H Spurrier Esq, and DBP (1 turn), Ld Chan (1 turn)* **R** J R MOORE, **OLM** M DONE

BAINTON (St Andrew) *see* Woldsburn *York*

BAINTON (St Mary) *see* Barnack w Ufford and Bainton *Pet*

BAKEWELL (All Saints) *Derby 2* **P** *D&C Lich*
P-in-c A P KAUNHOVEN, **C** J P HOSKINS

BALBY (St John the Evangelist) *Sheff 9* **P** *Bp* **V** B J INSTON

BALCOMBE (St Mary) *Chich 6* **P** *P A D Secretan Esq*
R *vacant* (01444) 811249

BALDERSBY (St James) *see* Topcliffe, Baldersby w Dishforth, Dalton etc *York*

BALDERSTONE (St Leonard) *Blackb 7* **P** *V Blackb*
V *vacant* (01254) 812232

BALDERSTONE (St Mary) *see* S Rochdale *Man*

BALDERTON (St Giles) and Barnby-in-the-Willows *S'well 3*
P *Bp and Ld Chan (alt)* **V** A I TUCKER

BALDOCK (St Mary the Virgin) w Bygrave and Weston
St Alb 19 **P** *Patr Bd* **TR** A P HOLFORD, **TV** S TETZLAFF,
NSM E BUNKER

BALDWIN (St Luke) *see* Marown *S & M*

BALE (All Saints) *see* Stiffkey and Bale *Nor*

BALHAM (St Mary and St John the Divine) *S'wark 17* **P** *Bp and Keble Coll Ox (jt)* **P-in-c** W ROEST, **OLM** R E SERBUTT

BALHAM HILL (Ascension) *S'wark 17* **P** *Bp* **V** S J HANCE,
C J F FOLEY, B GOODYEAR, K V SEAGRAVE,
NSM D V PENNIECOOKE, P J HOUGHTON

BALKWELL (St Peter) *Newc 5* **P** *Bp* **P-in-c** S D MASON

BALLAM (St Matthew) *see* Ribby cum Wrea and Weeton *Blackb*

BALLAUGH (St Mary) (St Mary Old Church) *S & M 3*
P *The Crown* **R** C D ROGERS

BALLIDON (All Saints) *see* Wirksworth *Derby*

BALLINGER (St Mary Mission Hall) *see* Gt Missenden w Ballinger and Lt Hampden *Ox*

BALLINGHAM (St Dubricius) *see* Heref S Wye *Heref*

BALSALL COMMON (St Peter) *Birm 11* **P** *Bp*
P-in-c P W THOMAS

BALSALL HEATH (St Barnabas) *see* Sparkbrook St Agatha w Balsall Heath St Barn *Birm*

BALSALL HEATH (St Paul) and Edgbaston *Birm 5* **P** *Bp and Sir Euan Anstruther-Gough-Calthorpe Bt (jt)* **V** C A GRYLLS,
NSM U H K LANDMANN

BALSCOTE (St Mary Magdalene) *see* Ironstone *Ox*

BALSHAM (Holy Trinity), Weston Colville, West Wickham and West Wratting *Ely 5* **P** *Bp, D&C, and Charterhouse (jt)*
Hon C K W T W JOHNSON

BALTERLEY (All Saints' Memorial Church) *see* Barthomley *Ches*

BALTONSBOROUGH (St Dunstan) w Butleigh, West Bradley and West Pennard *B & W 5* **P** *Bp* **V** *vacant* (01458) 850409

BAMBER BRIDGE (St Aidan) *Blackb 5* **P** *Bp*
P-in-c T R WEBBER

BAMBER BRIDGE (St Saviour) *Blackb 5* **P** *V Blackb*
P-in-c G HALSALL

BAMBURGH (St Aidan) *Newc 7* **P** *Exors Lady Armstrong*
V B C HURST

BAMFORD (St John the Baptist) *see* Hathersage w Bamford and Derwent and Grindleford *Derby*

BAMFORD (St Michael) *see* Oakenrod and Bamford *Man*

BAMFURLONG (Good Shepherd) *see* Abram *Liv*

BAMPTON (Holy Trinity) (St James) (St Mary) w Clanfield
Ox 8 **P** *Bp, DBP, St Jo Coll Ox, D&C Ex, and B Babington-Smith Esq (jt)* **V** D J LLOYD, **NSM** T H N KUIN LAWTON

BAMPTON (St Michael and All Angels), Morebath, Clayhanger and Petton *Ex 8* **P** *DBP and D&C (jt)* **P-in-c** A J STONE

BAMPTON (St Patrick) *see* Shap w Swindale and Bampton w Mardale *Carl*

BAMPTON ASTON (St James) *see* Bampton w Clanfield *Ox*

BAMPTON LEW (Holy Trinity) *as above*

BAMPTON PROPER (St Mary) *as above*

BANBURY (St Francis) *Ox 5* **P** *Bp* **V** D JACKSON,
C C T GAYNOR

BANBURY (St Hugh) *Ox 5* **P** *Bp* **P-in-c** P S DAVIES

BANBURY (St Leonard) *Ox 5* **P** *Bp* **P-in-c** M R CHARMLEY,
NSM E S BURCHELL

BANBURY (St Mary) *Ox 5* **P** *Bp* **P-in-c** L J GREEN,
NSM J J WEST

BANBURY (St Paul) *Ox 5* **P** *Bp* **P-in-c** E N COOMBS,
C D I HUSS

BANHAM (St Mary) *see* Quidenham Gp *Nor*

BANKFOOT (St Matthew) *Bradf 2* **P** *Bp* **V** *vacant* (01274) 726529

BANKS (St Stephen's Church within the School) Conventional District *Liv 9* **Min** R J GIBBS

BANNINGHAM (St Botolph) *see* King's Beck *Nor*

BANSFIELD *St E 8* **P** *DBP, Mrs G S M Slater, and Ld Chan (by turn)* **R** S J ABBOTT

BANSTEAD (All Saints) *Guildf 9* **P** *Bp* **V** D N CHANCE,
Hon C E P I WESTBROOK

BANWELL (St Andrew) *B & W 11* **P** *D&C Bris*
P-in-c J W FRANKS

BAPCHILD (St Lawrence) *see* Murston w Bapchild and Tonge *Cant*

BAR HILL (not known) *Ely 6* **P** *Bp* **P-in-c** R H ADAMS

BARBON (St Bartholomew) *see* Kirkby Lonsdale *Carl*

BARBOURNE (St Stephen) *Worc 6* **P** *Bp* **V** S W CURRIE,
NSM G D MORPHY, D A JONES

BARBROOK (St Bartholomew) *see* Combe Martin, Berrynarbor, Lynton, Brendon etc *Ex*

BARBY (St Mary) w Kilsby *Pet 3* **P** *Bp*
R P M DE LA P BERESFORD

BARCHESTON (St Martin) *see* S Warks Seven Gp *Cov*

BARCOMBE (St Francis) (St Mary the Virgin) *Chich 18*
P *Ld Chan* **R** J W HOLLINGSWORTH

BARDFIELD, GREAT (St Mary the Virgin) and LITTLE (St Katherine) *Chelmsf 18* **P** *Ch Union Trust*
P-in-c R W F BEAKEN

BARDFIELD SALING (St Peter and St Paul) *see* Stebbing and Lindsell w Gt and Lt Saling *Chelmsf*

BARDNEY (St Laurence) *Linc 11* **P** *DBP (1 turn), Bp (2 turns), and St Jo Coll Cam (1 turn)* **R** *vacant* (01526) 398595

BARDON HILL (St Peter) *see* Coalville and Bardon Hill *Leic*

BARDSEA (Holy Trinity) *see* Pennington and Lindal w Marton and Bardsea *Carl*

BARDSEY (All Hallows) *Ripon 5* **P** *G L Fox Esq* **V** *vacant* (01937) 572243

BARDSLEY (Holy Trinity) *Man 20* **P** *Wm Hulme Trustees*
V A D GRANT, **OLM** E M LOWE

BARDWELL (St Peter and St Paul) *see* Blackbourne *St E*

BARE (St Christopher) *Blackb 11* **P** *Bp* **V** D L HEAP

BARFORD (St Botolph) *see* Barnham Broom and Upper Yare *Nor*

BARFORD (St John) *see* Deddington w Barford, Clifton and Hempton *Ox*

BARFORD (St Martin) *see* Nadder Valley *Sarum*

BARFORD (St Michael) *see* Deddington w Barford, Clifton and Hempton *Ox*

BARFORD (St Peter) w Wasperton and Sherbourne *Cov 8*
P *Major J M Mills, R Hampton Lucy, and Lady Jeryl Smith-Ryland (jt)* **P-in-c** D C JESSETT, **NSM** C O S S DAVIES

BARFORD, GREAT (All Saints) *see* Riversmeet *St Alb*

BARFREYSTONE (St Nicholas) *see* Eythorne and Elvington w Waldershare etc *Cant*

BARHAM (St Giles) *see* E Leightonstone *Ely*

BARHAM (St John the Baptist) w Bishopsbourne and Kingston
Cant 1 **P** *Abp* **P-in-c** S J A HARDY,
NSM E R G HOPTHROW

BARHAM (St Mary) *see* Claydon and Barham *St E*

BARHAM DOWNS *see* Barham w Bishopsbourne and Kingston *Cant*

BARHOLME (St Martin) *see* Uffington Gp *Linc*
BARKBY (St Mary) *see* Syston *Leic*
BARKESTONE (St Peter and St Paul) *see* Vale of Belvoir Par *Leic*
BARKHAM (St James) *see* Arborfield w Barkham *Ox*
BARKING (St Erkenwald) *Chelmsf 1* **P** *Bp* **V** C N POOLEY
BARKING (St Margaret) (St Patrick) *Chelmsf 1* **P** *Patr Bd*
  TR G M TARRY, **TV** G M BARLEY, J D PEARSON,
  C D A O IBIAYO
BARKING (St Mary) *see* Ringshall w Battisford, Barking w Darmsden etc *St E*
BARKINGSIDE (Holy Trinity) *Chelmsf 4* **P** *V Gt Ilford*
  V E A J CARGILL THOMPSON
BARKINGSIDE (St Cedd) *Chelmsf 4* **P** *Bp*
  V S G O O OLUKANMI, **NSM** M FLINTOFT-CHAPMAN
BARKINGSIDE (St Francis of Assisi) *Chelmsf 4* **P** *Bp*
  V A R FENBY
BARKINGSIDE (St George) *Chelmsf 4* **P** *Bp* **V** B J WALLIS
BARKINGSIDE (St Laurence) *Chelmsf 4* **P** *Bp* **V** E A GUEST,
  NSM S M TAYLOR
BARKISLAND (Christ Church) w West Scammonden *Wakef 4*
  P *V Halifax* **V** C WRAY, **C** K A SHOESMITH,
  NSM C A HIRST
BARKSTON (St Nicholas) and Hough Group, The *Linc 23*
  P *Sir Oliver Thorold Bt; the Revd J R H Thorold and J R Thorold Esq; Lord Brownlow; and Sir Lyonel Tollemache Bt (by turn)* **NSM** S J HADLEY, L A HARDING
BARKSTON ASH (Holy Trinity) *see* Sherburn in Elmet w Saxton *York*
BARKWAY (St Mary Magdalene), Reed and Buckland w Barley *St Alb 19* **P** *The Crown and DBP (alt)* **P-in-c** S C HILLMAN
BARKWITH Group, The *Linc 5* **P** *D&C, J N Heneage Esq, K Coll Cam, and DBP (by turn)* **P-in-c** J C PATRICK
BARKWITH, EAST (St Mary) *see* Barkwith Gp *Linc*
BARLASTON (St John the Baptist) *Lich 13* **P** *Countess of Sutherland* **P-in-c** J Y TILLIER
BARLAVINGTON (St Mary), Burton w Coates and Sutton w Bignor *Chich 11* **P** *Lord Egremont and Miss J B Courtauld (jt)* **P-in-c** D C G BROWN
BARLBOROUGH (St James) and Renishaw *Derby 3*
  P *Prime Min and Sir Reresby Sitwell Bt (alt)* **R** J PINDER-
  ^ae ard, **C** H GUEST, **NSM** M GUEST
BARLBY (All Saints) w Riccall *York 2* **P** *Abp and V Hemingbrough (jt)* **NSM** F LOFTUS, A D ROBINSON
BARLESTONE (St Giles) *Leic 10* **P** *Bp*
  P-in-c T H C MEYRICK
BARLEY (St Margaret of Antioch) *see* Barkway, Reed and Buckland w Barley *St Alb*
BARLING (All Saints) w Little Wakering *Chelmsf 12* **P** *D&C St Paul's and Bp (alt)* **P-in-c** A J HURD
BARLING MAGNA (All Saints) *see* Barling w Lt Wakering *Chelmsf*
BARLINGS (St Edward) *Linc 3* **P** *DBP* **V** R G SPAIGHT
BARLOW (not known) *see* Brayton *York*
BARLOW, GREAT (St Lawrence) *see* Old Brampton and Great Barlow *Derby*
BARLOW MOOR (Emmanuel) *see* Didsbury St Jas and Em *Man*
BARMBY MOOR Group, The (St Catherine) *York 5* **P** *Abp (1 turn), Abp and Trustees Duke of Norfolk's Settlement Everingham Fund (2 turns)* **V** V P HEWETSON,
  NSM J H DAWKINS
BARMING (St Margaret of Antioch) w West Barming *Roch 7*
  P *Ld Chan* **R** N S MCGREGOR
BARMING HEATH (St Andrew) *Cant 13* **P** *Abp* **V** B REED
BARMSTON (All Saints) *see* Skipsea and Barmston w Fraisthorpe *York*
BARNACK (St John the Baptist) w Ufford and Bainton *Pet 11*
  P *Bp and St Jo Coll Cam (alt)* **P-in-c** M J VENABLES
BARNACRE (All Saints) *see* Scorton and Barnacre and Calder Vale *Blackb*
BARNARD CASTLE (St Mary) w Whorlton *Dur 7* **P** *Trin Coll Cam* **V** A J HARDING
BARNARDISTON (All Saints) *see* Stourhead *St E*
BARNBURGH (St Peter) w Melton on the Hill and Aldwick-upon-Dearne *Sheff 12* **P** *Ld Chan (2 turns), Bp (1 turn)* **P-in-c** V D CLARKE
BARNBY (St John the Baptist) *see* Worlingham w Barnby and N Cove *St E*
BARNBY, EAST (Mission Chapel) *see* Hinderwell, Roxby and Staithes etc *York*
BARNBY DUN (St Peter and St Paul) *Sheff 8* **P** *Bp*
  P-in-c J M FODEN
BARNBY IN THE WILLOWS (All Saints) *see* Balderton and Barnby-in-the-Willows *S'well*

BARNEHURST (St Martin) *Roch 15* **P** *Bp* **V** G J BOWEN
BARNES Team Ministry, The (St Mary) (Holy Trinity) (St Michael and All Angels) *S'wark 16* **P** *Patr Bd*
  TR R N F COLLINS, **TV** P W HOLLAND, J BOULTON-REYNOLDS,
  Hon C L R F COLLINS, J AYOK-LOEWENBERG,
  NSM A J ROBERTS, D A THOMAS
BARNET (Christ Church) *see* S Mimms Ch Ch *Lon*
BARNET (St John the Baptist) *see* Chipping Barnet *St Alb*
BARNET (St Stephen) *as above*
BARNET, EAST (St Mary the Virgin) *St Alb 17* **P** *The Crown*
  R R F WATSON, **C** R M LEACH
BARNET, NEW (St James) *St Alb 17* **P** *Ch Patr Trust*
  P-in-c B UNWIN
BARNET VALE (St Mark) *see* Chipping Barnet *St Alb*
BARNETBY LE WOLD (St Barnabas) *see* N Wolds Gp *Linc*
BARNEY (St Mary), Fulmodeston w Croxton, Hindringham, Thursford, Great and Little Snoring w Kettlestone and Pensthorpe *Nor 15* **P** *Lord Hastings, St Jo Coll Cam, D&C, DBP, and CCC Cam (by turn)* **R** J MUGGLETON
BARNHAM (St Gregory) *see* Blackbourne *St E*
BARNHAM (St Mary) *see* Aldingbourne, Barnham and Eastergate *Chich*
BARNHAM BROOM (St Peter and St Paul) and Upper Yare *Nor 17* **P** *Patr Bd* **TR** D K ALEXANDER, **C** D J PLATTIN,
  OLM R A JACKSON
BARNINGHAM (St Andrew) *see* Stanton, Hopton, Market Weston, Barningham etc *St E*
BARNINGHAM (St Mary the Virgin) w Matlaske w Baconsthorpe w Plumstead w Hempstead *Nor 18* **P** *Duchy of Lanc (1 turn), Lady Mott-Radclyffe, CPAS, and D&C (jt) (1 turn)* **R** vacant (01263) 577420
BARNINGHAM (St Michael and All Angels) w Hutton Magna and Wycliffe *Ripon 2* **P** *Bp and V Gilling and Kirkby Ravensworth (jt)* **R** C H COWPER
BARNINGHAM, LITTLE (St Andrew), Blickling, Edgefield, Itteringham w Mannington, Oulton w Irmingland, Saxthorpe w Corpusty and Wickmere w Wolterton *Nor 19* **P** *Bp, Lord Walpole, SMF, MMCET (2 turns), and Pemb Coll Cam (1 turn)*
  R J S MORGAN, **NSM** P J CHAPMAN
BARNINGHAM WINTER (St Mary the Virgin)
  see Barningham w Matlaske w Baconsthorpe etc *Nor*
BARNOLDBY LE BECK (St Helen) *Linc 10* **P** *Ld Chan*
  R I R SHELTON, **NSM** A HUNDLEBY
BARNOLDSWICK (Holy Trinity) (St Mary le Gill) w Bracewell *Bradf 7* **P** *Bp* **V** J R LANCASTER
BARNSBURY (St Andrew) *Lon 6* **P** *Patr Bd*
  TR M W LEARMOUTH, **TV** M L J SAUNDERS, **C** M FLETCHER,
  J S SWIFT
BARNSLEY (St Edward the Confessor) *Wakef 7* **P** *Bp*
  P-in-c M S POSKITT
BARNSLEY (St George's Parish Church Centre) *Wakef 7* **P** *Bp*
  V D P J MUNBY
BARNSLEY (St Mary) *see* Fairford Deanery *Glouc*
BARNSLEY (St Mary) *Wakef 7* **P** *Bp* **NSM** A J EARL
BARNSLEY (St Paul) Old Town *see* Barnsley St Mary Make*
BARNSLEY (St Peter and St John the Baptist) *Wakef 7* **P** *Bp*
  V A BRISCOE
BARNSTAPLE (St Peter and St Mary Magdalene) (Holy Trinity) *Ex 15* **P** *Patr Bd (4 turns), Ld Chan (1 turn)*
  TV S G MAY, G CHAVE-COX, P K NIEMIEC, A J GILBERT,
  C A DODWELL
BARNSTON (Christ Church) *Ches 8* **P** *Bp* **V** G P BENSON,
  C I G URQUHART
BARNSTON (St Andrew) *see* Gt Dunmow and Barnston *Chelmsf*
BARNSTONE (St Mary Mission Room) *see* Cropwell Bishop w Colston Bassett, Granby etc *S'well*
BARNT GREEN (St Andrew) *see* Cofton Hackett w Barnt Green *Birm*
BARNTON (Christ Church) *Ches 4* **P** *Bp* **V** P NEWMAN
BARNWELL (All Saints) (St Andrew), Hemington, Luddington in the Brook, Lutton, Polebrook and Thurning *Pet 10* **P** *Bp, MMCET, Em Coll Cam, DBP, and Sir Philip Naylor-Leyland Bt (jt)* **R** C R IEVINS
BARNWOOD (St Lawrence) *Glouc 3* **P** *D&C*
  P-in-c A MORRIS, **NSM** A D HAYMAN, L SPARKES
BARONY OF BURGH, The (St Michael) *Carl 3* **P** *Patr Bd*
  R G M HART, **C** S J FYFE
BARR, GREAT (St Margaret) *Lich 25* **P** M D S *Farnham*
  V M C RUTTER, **NSM** T W WARD
BARRINGTON (All Saints) *see* Orwell Gp *Ely*
BARRINGTON (Blessed Virgin Mary) *see* Ilminster and Distr *B & W*
BARRINGTON, GREAT (St Mary) *see* Sherborne, Windrush, the Barringtons etc *Glouc*

BARRINGTON, LITTLE (St Peter) *as above*
BARROW (All Saints) *St E 13* **P** *Ld Chan (1 turn), Mrs E C Gordon-Lennox, the Russell-Cooke Trust Co and Bp (1 turn), and St Jo Coll Cam (1 turn)* **V** P N MACLEOD-MILLER
BARROW and Goxhill *Linc 6* **P** *Ld Chan* **V** J C GIRTCHEN
BARROW (St Bartholomew) *Ches 2* **P** *D Okell Esq*
P-in-c C A RANDALL
BARROW (St Giles) *see* Broseley w Benthall, Jackfield, Linley etc *Heref*
BARROW, NORTH (St Nicholas) *see* Six Pilgrims *B & W*
BARROW, SOUTH (St Peter) *as above*
BARROW GURNEY (The Blessed Virgin Mary and St Edward King and Martyr) *see* Long Ashton w Barrow Gurney and Flax Bourton *B & W*
BARROW HILL (St Andrew) *see* Staveley and Barrow Hill *Derby*
BARROW-IN-FURNESS (St Aidan) *see* S Barrow *Carl*
BARROW-IN-FURNESS (St George) *as above*
BARROW-IN-FURNESS (St James the Great) *Carl 8* **P** *DBP*
P-in-c S A EVASON
BARROW-IN-FURNESS (St John the Evangelist) *Carl 8*
P *DBP* **P-in-c** S HUGHES
BARROW-IN-FURNESS (St Luke) *see* S Barrow *Carl*
BARROW-IN-FURNESS (St Mark) *Carl 8* **P** *Bp*
V I K HOOK, **C** L N CRONIN
BARROW-IN-FURNESS (St Mary the Virgin) *see* Walney Is *Carl*
BARROW-IN-FURNESS (St Matthew) *Carl 8* **P** *Patr Bd*
TR M PEAT
BARROW IN FURNESS (St Paul) *Carl 8* **P** *Simeon's Trustees*
R D H PRICE
BARROW-ON-HUMBER (Holy Trinity) *see* Barrow and Goxhill *Linc*
BARROW-ON-TRENT (St Wilfrid) *see* Ticknall, Smisby and Stanton by Bridge etc *Derby*
BARROW UPON SOAR (Holy Trinity) w Walton le Wolds
Leic 6 **P** *St Jo Coll Cam and DBP (jt)* **P-in-c** J WHITTAKER,
Hon C M R SAMUEL, **NSM** T E EDMONDS, N J MCGINTY
BARROWBY (All Saints) and Gonerby, Great *Linc 19*
P *R Grantham, and Duke of Devonshire (by turn)*
R P HOPKINS
BARROWDEN (St Peter) and Wakerley w South Luffenham and Morcott w Duddington and Tixover *Pet 12* **P** *Burghley Ho Preservation Trust, P W Rowley Esq, and Bp (3 turns), Ball Coll Ox (1 turn)* **P-in-c** G ANGELL
BARROWFORD (St Thomas) and Newchurch-in-Pendle
Blackb 6 **P** *Ld Chan and trustees (alt)* **V** J M HALLOWS
BARSHAM (Holy Trinity) *see* Wainford *St E*
BARSHAM, EAST (All Saints) *see* Walsingham, Houghton and Barsham *Nor*
BARSHAM, NORTH (All Saints) *as above*
BARSHAM, WEST (The Assumption of the Blessed Virgin Mary) *as above*
BARSTON (St Swithin) *Birm 11* **P** *MMCET*
P-in-c R D TURNER
BARTHOMLEY (St Bertoline) *Ches 11* **P** *Lord O'Neill*
P-in-c D C SPEEDY, **Hon C** A M SPEEDY
BARTLEY (Mission Church) *see* Copythorne *Win*
BARTLEY GREEN (St Michael and All Angels) *Birm 2* **P** *Bp*
NSM B M A ROBERTS, A PATERSON
BARTLOW (St Mary) *see* Linton *Ely*
BARTON (St Cuthbert w St Mary) *see* E Richmond *Ripon*
BARTON (St Lawrence) *see* Fellside Team *Blackb*
BARTON (St Mark's Chapel) w Peel Green (St Michael and All Angels) (St Catherine) *Man 2* **P** *Bp and TR Eccles*
P-in-c B LAMB
BARTON (St Martin) *see* Torquay St Martin Barton *Ex*
BARTON (St Michael), Pooley Bridge and Martindale *Carl 4*
P *Bp and Earl of Lonsdale (jt)* **P-in-c** D C WOOD
BARTON (St Paul) *Portsm 8* **P** *R Whippingham*
V P E PIMENTEL
BARTON (St Peter) *Ely 1* **P** *Ld Chan* **P-in-c** C A COLLINS
BARTON, GREAT (Holy Innocents) *St E 13* **P** *Sir Michael Bunbury Bt* **P-in-c** A R GATES
BARTON BENDISH (St Andrew) w Beachamwell and Shingham
Ely 9 **P** *Bp and DBP (alt)* **R** *vacant* (01366) 348063
BARTON HARTSHORN (St James) *see* The Claydons and Swan *Ox*
BARTON HILL (St Luke w Ch Ch) and Moorfields St Matthew
Bris 3 **P** *Bp, CPAS, and V Bris St Phil and St Jacob w Em (jt)*
P-in-c D FRAZER, **C** C L JONES
BARTON IN FABIS (St George) *S'well 9* **P** *Ld Chan*
P-in-c S W OSMAN
BARTON-LE-CLEY (St Nicholas) w Higham Gobion and Hexton *St Alb 9* **P** *The Crown (3 turns), Mrs F A A Cooper (1 turn)* **R** G H NEWTON

BARTON-LE-STREET (St Michael) *see* The Street Par *York*
BARTON MILLS (St Mary) *see* Mildenhall *St E*
BARTON-ON-THE-HEATH (St Lawrence) *see* S Warks Seven Gp *Cov*
BARTON SEAGRAVE (St Botolph) w Warkton *Pet 9* **P** *Ch Soc Trust (2 turns), Duke of Buccleuch (1 turn)* **R** J M PERRIS
BARTON ST DAVID (St David) *see* Wheathill Priory Gp *B & W*
BARTON STACEY (All Saints) *see* Lower Dever *Win*
BARTON TURF (St Michael) *see* Ashmanhaugh, Barton Turf etc *Nor*
BARTON UNDER NEEDWOOD (St James) w Dunstall and Tatenhill *Lich 14* **P** *Bp and Sir Rupert Hardy Bt (jt)*
V A J WOOD
BARTON UPON HUMBER (St Mary) *Linc 6* **P** *Bp*
P-in-c D P ROWETT, **C** K E COLWELL, **OLM** A W WRIGHT
BARTON UPON IRWELL (St Catherine) *see* Barton w Peel Green *Man*
BARWELL (St Mary) w Potters Marston and Stapleton *Leic 10*
P *R J W Titley Esq* **R** *vacant* (01455) 843866
BARWICK (St Mary Magdalene) *see* Yeovil H Trin w Barwick *B & W*
BARWICK IN ELMET (All Saints) *Ripon 8* **P** *Duchy of Lanc*
P-in-c A J NICHOLSON
BASCHURCH (All Saints) and Weston Lullingfield w Hordley
Lich 17 **P** *Ch Patr Trust and Bp (jt)* **R** J J WILSON
BASCOTE HEATH (Chapel) *see* Radford Semele *Cov*
BASEGREEN (St Peter) *see* Gleadless *Sheff*
BASFORD (St Aidan) *S'well 12* **P** *Bp* **P-in-c** R SHAW
BASFORD (St Leodegarius) *S'well 12* **P** *Bp*
P-in-c N J ROOMS
BASFORD (St Mark) *Lich 9* **P** *Bp* **P-in-c** T B BLOOR,
NSM F P DUNN
BASFORD, NEW (St Augustine) *see* Basford St Leodegarius *S'well*
BASHLEY (St John) *see* Milton *Win*
BASILDON (St Andrew) (Holy Cross) *Chelmsf 6* **P** *Bp*
TV M A SHAW
BASILDON (St Martin of Tours) *Chelmsf 6* **P** *Bp*
R E E MCCAFFERTY
BASILDON (St Stephen) w Aldworth and Ashampstead *Ox 12*
P *St Jo Coll Cam, Simeon's Trustees, and DBF (by turn)*
OLM A KIGGELL
BASING, OLD (St Mary) and Lychpit *Win 4* **P** *Magd Coll Ox*
V A S BISHOP, **C** M JONES
BASINGSTOKE (All Saints) (St Michael) *Win 4* **P** *Patr Bd*
TR J M STOKER, **TV** R E RUTHERFORD, S P HEATHER,
M A PHILLIPS, A BOTHAM, **C** M S QUAYLE, **NSM** P PALMER
BASINGSTOKE Brighton Hill (Christ the King)
  see Basingstoke *Win*
BASINGSTOKE Popley (Bethlehem Chapel) *as above*
BASINGSTOKE South Ham (St Peter) *as above*
BASLOW (St Anne) w Curbar and Stoney Middleton *Derby 2*
P *Duke of Devonshire and V Hathersage (jt)*
C A S MONTGOMERIE, C H BENSON
BASSENTHWAITE (St Bega) *see* Binsey *Carl*
BASSENTHWAITE (St John) *as above*
BASSETT (St Michael and All Angels) *see* N Stoneham *Win*
BASSETT GREEN (St Christopher) *as above*
BASSINGBOURN (St Peter and St Paul) *Ely 7*
P *D&C Westmr* **P-in-c** D C R MCFADYEN
BASSINGHAM Group, The (St Michael and All Angels) *Linc 18*
P *Lady Jean Nevile, CCC Ox, Lord Middleton, Bp, and W R S Brown Esq (jt)* **R** N J BUCK, **C** H A JONES,
NSM J J PARR
BASSINGTHORPE (St Thomas à Becket) *see* N Beltisloe Gp *Linc*
BASTON (St John the Baptist) *see* Ness Gp *Linc*
BASWICH or Berkswich (Holy Trinity) *Lich 10* **P** *Bp*
V P A GRAYSMITH, **NSM** E J BISHOP
BATCOMBE (Blessed Virgin Mary) *see* Bruton and Distr *B & W*
BATCOMBE (St Mary) *see* Wriggle Valley *Sarum*
BATH Abbey (St Peter and St Paul) w St James *B & W 9*
P *Simeon's Trustees* **R** T E MASON, **C** A J P GARROW,
A W MCCONNAUGHIE
BATH Bathwick (St John the Baptist) (Blessed Virgin Mary)
B & W 9 **P** *Bp* **R** D J PROTHERO
BATH (Christ Church) Proprietary Chapel *B & W 11*
P *R Walcot* **Min** A A J CLARIDGE, **NSM** C R BURROWS
BATH (Holy Trinity) *B & W 9* **P** *SMF* **Hon C** M S HART
BATH Odd Down (St Philip and St James) w Combe Hay
B & W 9 **P** *Simeon's Trustees* **V** A BAIN, **NSM** M JOYCE
BATH (St Barnabas) w Englishcombe *B & W 9* **P** *Bp*
V D J BURLEIGH

BATH (St Bartholomew) *B & W 9*   **P** *Simeon's Trustees*
V I R LEWIS
BATH (St Luke) *B & W 9*   **P** *Simeon's Trustees*
P-in-c M D H FRANKUM
BATH (St Mary Magdalene) Holloway, Extra-parochial
Chapelry *B & W 11*   **P** *Bath Municipal Charities for Ld Chan*
Min W G BURMAN
BATH (St Michael) w St Paul *B & W 9*   **P** *CPAS*
R M C LLOYD WILLIAMS,   **C** S P FAUX
BATH (St Saviour) w Swainswick and Woolley *B & W 9*
P *Ch Patr Trust and Or Coll Ox (jt)*   **R** M J NORMAN
BATH (St Stephen)   *see Charlcombe w Bath St Steph B & W*
BATH Twerton-on-Avon (Ascension) (St Michael) *B & W 9*
P *Patr Bd*   **TR** R G WILSON,   **TV** R J PIMM,   **C** G A TYTE
BATH Walcot (St Andrew) (St Swithin) *B & W 9*   **P** *Simeon's*
Trustees   **P-in-c** S G HOLLAND,   **C** M R WILKINS
BATH Weston (All Saints) w North Stoke and Langridge *B & W 9*
P *Ld Chan*   **P** J WHITWORTH,   **C** M A JONES,
NSM J N RAWLINSON, P J NORMAN
BATH Weston (St John the Evangelist) (Emmanuel) w Kelston
B & W 9   **P** *Ld Chan*   **R** C R GARRETT
BATH Widcombe (St Matthew) (St Thomas à Becket) *B & W 9*
P *Simeon's Trustees*   **V** *vacant (01225) 464918*
BATHAMPTON (St Nicholas) w Claverton *B & W 9*
P *D&C Bris and Personal Reps R L D Skrine Esq (jt)*
R P BURDEN,   **C** R G THOMAS
BATHEALTON (St Bartholomew)   *see Wellington and Distr*
B & W
BATHEASTON (St John the Baptist) (St Catherine) *B & W 9*
P *Ch Ch Ox*   **V** A J FRY
BATHFORD (St Swithun) *B & W 9*   **P** *D&C Bris*   **V** T C LING
BATHWICK (Blessed Virgin Mary)   *see Bath Bathwick B & W*
BATHWICK (St John the Baptist)   *as above*
BATLEY (All Saints) and Purlwell *Wakef 9*
P E C S J G Brudenell Esq, Trustees D Stubley Esq, and Bp (jt)*
V A P JOHNSON,   **OLM** B R ASQUITH
BATLEY (St Thomas) *Wakef 9*   **P** *V Batley*   **P-in-c** P A CRABB
BATLEY CARR (Holy Trinity)   *see Dewsbury Wakef*
BATSFORD (St Mary)   *see Moreton-in-Marsh w Batsford,*
Todenham etc *Glouc*
BATTERSEA (Christ Church and St Stephen) *S'wark 14*   **P** *Bp*
and V Battersea St Mary (alt)   **V** G N OWEN
BATTERSEA (St George)   *see Battersea Fields S'wark*
BATTERSEA (St Luke) *S'wark 14*   **P** *Bp*   **V** E A MORSE,
C R HOLY,   **NSM** K J SMITH
BATTERSEA (St Mary) *S'wark 14*   **P** *Earl Spencer*
V J P KENNINGTON,   **C** A C BOULTER,   **NSM** P B WINTGENS
BATTERSEA (St Michael) Wandsworth Common *S'wark 14*
P *V Battersea St Mary*   **V** A H STEVENS
BATTERSEA (St Peter) (St Paul) *S'wark 14*   **P** *V Battersea*
St Mary   **P-in-c** P J S PERKIN,   **C** R P MALONE
BATTERSEA FIELDS (St Saviour) (All Saints) (St George)
S'wark 14   **P** *Bp, CPAS, and Ch Patr Trust (jt)*
V G M VEVERS,   **C** S A A ANAND
BATTERSEA PARK (All Saints)   *see Battersea Fields S'wark*
BATTERSEA PARK (St Saviour)   *as above*
BATTERSEA RISE (St Mark) *S'wark 14*   **P** *V Battersea*
St Mary   **V** P J S PERKIN,   **T** J J MAYFIELD,
NSM D A LARLEE
BATTISFORD (St Mary)   *see Ringshall w Battisford, Barking w*
Darmsden etc *St E*
BATTLE (Church of the Ascension) (St Mary the Virgin)
Chich 14   **P** *The Crown*   **V** J J W EDMONDSON
BATTLE HILL (Good Shepherd)   *see Willington Newc*
BATTLESDEN (St Peter and All Saints)   *see Woburn w*
Eversholt, Milton Bryan, Battlesden etc *St Alb*
BATTYEFORD (Christ the King) *Wakef 9*   **P** *V Mirfield*
P-in-c M A MCLEAN,   **Hon C** R E WHITNALL,
NSM M E WOOD
BAUGHURST (St Stephen) and Ramsdell and Wolverton w
Ewhurst and Hannington *Win 4*   **P** *Ld Chan, Duke of*
Wellington, and Bp (by turn)   **P-in-c** D BARLOW
BAULKING (St Nicholas)   *see Uffington, Shellingford,*
Woolstone and Baulking *Ox*
BAUMBER (St Swithin)   *see Hemingby Linc*
BAUNTON (St Mary Magdalene)   *see Stratton, N Cerney,*
Baunton and Bagendon *Glouc*
BAVERSTOCK (St Editha)   *see Nadder Valley Sarum*
BAWBURGH (St Mary and St Walstan)   *see Easton, Colton,*
Marlingford and Bawburgh *Nor*
BAWDESWELL (All Saints)   *see Lyng, Sparham, Elsing,*
Bylaugh, Bawdeswell etc *Nor*
BAWDRIP (St Michael and All Angels)   *see Woolavington w*
Cossington and Bawdrip *B & W*
BAWDSEY (St Mary)   *see Wilford Peninsula St E*

BAWTRY (St Nicholas) w Austerfield and Misson *S'well 1*   **P** *Bp*
P-in-c J E T STRICKLAND
BAXENDEN (St John) *Blackb 1*   **P** *Bp*   **P-in-c** J N FIELDER
BAXTERGATE (St Ninian)   *see Whitby w Ruswarp York*
BAXTERLEY (not known) w Hurley and Wood End and
Merevale w Bentley *Birm 10*   **P** *Ld Chan (1 turn), Bp and*
Sir William Dugdale Bt (1 turn)   **R** J E GASPER
BAYDON (St Nicholas)   *see Whitton Sarum*
BAYFORD (Mission Room)   *see Charlton Musgrove,*
Cucklington and Stoke Trister *B & W*
BAYFORD (St Mary)   *see Lt Berkhamsted and Bayford,*
Essendon etc *St Alb*
BAYLHAM (St Peter)   *see Gt and Lt Blakenham w Baylham*
and Nettlestead *St E*
BAYSTON HILL (Christ Church) *Lich 20*   **P** *V Shrewsbury*
H Trin w St Julian   **V** R M GOLDENBERG,   **C** I PALLENT
BAYSWATER (St Matthew) *Lon 2*   **P** *Exors Dame Jewell*
Magnus-Allcroft   **V** G M EVANS
BAYTON (St Bartholomew)   *see Mamble w Bayton, Rock w*
Heightington etc *Worc*
BEACHAMPTON (Assumption of the Blessed Virgin Mary)
see Buckingham Ox
BEACHAMWELL (St Mary)   *see Barton Bendish w*
Beachamwell and Shingham *Ely*
BEACON Parishes   *see Painswick, Sheepscombe, Cranham, The*
Edge etc *Glouc*
BEACON Team Ministry, The *Carl 10*   **P** *Patr Bd*
V N L DAVIES,   **TV** M J SHEPHERD,   **Hon C** C V TAYLOR,
NSM M MASHITER,   **OLM** J F RADLEY,   **Hon Par**
Dn J L TYRER
BEACON, The *York 10*   **P** *Ld Chan (2 turns), Sir Charles*
Legard Bt (1 turn)   **P-in-c** J H ANDERSON
BEACONSFIELD (St Mary and All Saints) (St Michael and All
Angels) *Ox 20*   **P** *Patr Bd*   **TV** S N PAINTING, C I WALTON,
C R B TOBIN,   **NSM** C T T ROGERS, C E CROISDALE-APPLEBY
BEADLAM (St Hilda)   *see Kirkdale w Harome, Nunnington*
and Pockley *York*
BEADNELL (St Ebba) *Newc 7*   **P** *Newc Dioc Soc*
V E J WOOD,   **C** A ATKINSON
BEAFORD (All Saints)   *see Newton Tracey, Horwood,*
Alverdiscott etc *Ex*
BEALINGS, GREAT (St Mary) and LITTLE (All Saints) w
Playford and Culpho *St E 7*   **P** *Lord Cranworth (1 turn), Bp*
(3 turns)   **P-in-c** P C E STENTIFORD
BEAMINSTER AREA (St Mary of the Annunciation) *Sarum 2*
P *Patr Bd*   **TR** K L MASTERS,   **TV** S M SYMONS
BEAMISH (St Andrew)   *see Ch the K Dur*
BEARD (St James the Less)   *see New Mills Derby*
BEARLEY (St Mary the Virgin)   *see Snitterfield w Bearley Cov*
BEARPARK (St Edmund)   *see Dur N Dur*
BEARSTED (Holy Cross) w Thurnham *Cant 14*   **P** *Abp*
V J CORBYN,   **C** S J BRADFORD,   **OLM** J H E MANNERS
BEARWOOD (St Catherine) *Ox 16*   **P** *Bp*   **R** H D ETCHES
BEARWOOD (St Mary the Virgin) *Birm 7*   **P** *V Smethwick*
V A H PERRY
BEAUCHAMP RODING (St Botolph)   *see S Rodings Chelmsf*
BEAUDESERT (St Nicholas) and Henley-in-Arden w Ullenhall
Cov 7   **P** *MMCET, Bp, and High Bailiff of Henley-in-*
Arden (jt)   **R** J F GANJAVI
BEAULIEU (Blessed Virgin and Holy Child) and Exbury and
East Boldre *Win 11*   **P** *Bp and Lord Montagu of Beaulieu (jt)*
P-in-c C R SMITH
BEAUMONT CUM MOZE (St Leonard and St Mary)
see Tendring and Lt Bentley w Beaumont cum Moze Chelmsf
BEAUMONT LEYS (Christ the King) *Leic 1*   **P** *Bp*
V A K FORD,   **NSM** L B PADMORE
BEAUWORTH (St James)   *see Upper Itchen Win*
BEAUXFIELD (St Peter)   *see Whitfield w Guston Cant*
BEAWORTHY (St Alban)   *see Ashwater, Halwill, Beaworthy,*
Clawton etc *Ex*
BEBINGTON (St Andrew) *Ches 8*   **P** *M C Saunders-*
Griffiths Esq   **R** P R M VENABLES,   **C** D G B NEWSTEAD,
D W LABDON
BEBINGTON, HIGHER (Christ Church) *Ches 8*
P *C J C Saunders-Griffiths Esq*   **V** A E SAMUELS,
C M E WATSON
BECCLES (St Michael the Archangel) (St Luke's Church Centre)
St E 14   **P** *Simeon's Trustees*   **R** J N BEAUCHAMP,
C R HENDERSON
BECK ROW (St John)   *see Mildenhall St E*
BECKBURY (St Milburga), Badger, Kemberton, Ryton,
Stockton and Sutton Maddock *Lich 16*   **P** *Lord Hamilton of*
Dalzell, Or Coll Ox, and MMCET (2 turns), Ld Chan (1 turn)
R K HODSON

BECKENHAM (Christ Church) *Roch 13*   P *Ch Trust Fund Trust*   V N W WYNNE-JONES,   C M D FITTER,   Hon C J T ANSCOMBE
BECKENHAM (Holy Trinity)   *see Penge Lane H Trin Roch*
BECKENHAM (St Barnabas) *Roch 13*   P *Keble Coll Ox* V S J HEANS
BECKENHAM (St George) *Roch 13*   P *Bp*   R M J HANCOCK
BECKENHAM (St James) Elmers End *Roch 13*   P *Bp* V L C CARBERRY
BECKENHAM (St John the Baptist) Eden Park *Roch 13* P *Ch Trust Fund Trust, Bp and Adn Bromley (jt)*   V N LANG, NSM E A LANDER
BECKENHAM (St Michael and All Angels) w St Augustine *Roch 13*   P *SMF and Bp (jt)*   V C M SMITH
BECKENHAM, NEW (St Paul) *Roch 13*   P *Bp* V B W ROWLAND,   Hon C N E BAINES
BECKERMET (St Bridget) (St Bridget Old Church) (St John) w Ponsonby *Carl 5*   P *Bp, Adn W Cumberland, P Stanley Esq, and PCCs of Beckermet St Jo and St Bridget (jt)* P-in-c A E HART
BECKFORD (St John the Baptist)   *see Overbury w Teddington, Alstone etc Worc*
BECKHAM, WEST (St Helen and All Saints)   *see Weybourne Gp Nor*
BECKINGHAM (All Saints)   *see Brant Broughton and Beckingham Linc*
BECKINGHAM (All Saints) and Walkeringham and Misterton w West Stockwith *S'well 1*   P *Bp, Ld Chan, and D&C (by turn)* P-in-c J D HENSON
BECKINGTON (St George) w Standerwick, Berkley, Rodden, Lullington and Orchardleigh *B & W 4*   P *Bp (3 turns), Ch Soc Trust (1 turn), and Exors A Duckworth Esq* P-in-c A W G CHALKLEY
BECKLEY (All Saints) and Peasmarsh *Chich 20*   P *Univ Coll Ox and SS Coll Cam (alt)*   R C F HOPKINS, NSM W F G DOLMAN
BECKLEY (Assumption of the Blessed Virgin Mary) *see Wheatley Ox*
BECKTON (St Mark) *Chelmsf 3*   P *Bp*   V O J BALOGUN
BECKWITHSHAW (St Michael and All Angels)   *see Pannal w Beckwithshaw Ripon*
BECONTREE (St Cedd) *Chelmsf 1*   P *Bp*   V S A LAW
BECONTREE (St Elisabeth) *Chelmsf 1*   P *Bp*   V S J HANNA
BECONTREE (St George) *Chelmsf 1*   P *Bp* V S L SMALLWOOD
BECONTREE (St Mary) *Chelmsf 1*   P *CPAS*   V E J FLEMING, NSM C C ASINUGO
BECONTREE (St Thomas) *Chelmsf 1*   P *Bp*   V P J WOOD, C P C WYATT
BECONTREE SOUTH (St Alban) (St John the Divine) (St Martin) *Chelmsf 1*   P *Patr Bd*   TR G A CLARKE, NSM J D HALLIDAY
BEDALE (St Gregory) and Leeming and Thornton Watlass *Ripon 4*   P *Bp, Sir Henry Beresford-Peirse Bt, R Kirklington w Burnestonand Wath and Pickhill, and D S Dodsworth Esq (jt)* R S D RUDKIN,   C C M VICKERS
BEDDINGHAM (St Andrew)   *see Glynde, W Firle and Beddingham Chich*
BEDDINGTON (St Francis' Church Hall)   *see S Beddington and Roundshaw S'wark*
BEDDINGTON (St Mary) *S'wark 23*   P *D&C* R J MIDDLEMISS,   C P C GOODRIDGE
BEDDINGTON, SOUTH (St Michael and All Angels) and Roundshaw *S'wark 23*   P *Bp*   V A M A GBEBIKAN, NSM S L BILLIN, E J GOODRIDGE
BEDFIELD (St Nicholas)   *see Worlingworth, Southolt, Tannington, Bedfield etc St E*
BEDFONT, EAST (St Mary the Virgin) *Lon 11*   P *Ld Chan* V G D G PRICE
BEDFORD (All Saints) *St Alb 10*   P *Bp*   P-in-c J M MACLEOD
BEDFORD (Christ Church) *St Alb 10*   P *Bp*   V R C HIBBERT, C T E HORLOCK
BEDFORD (St Andrew) *St Alb 10*   P *Ld Chan*   V C M DENT, C C J BALL,   Hon C J A ROWLANDS,   NSM M D ROBINSON
BEDFORD (St John the Baptist) (St Leonard) *St Alb 10* P *MMCET*   R N COOPER,   C R C A HANKEY
BEDFORD (St Mark) *St Alb 10*   P *Bp*   V C ROYDEN, NSM G R CAPPLEMAN, P J LITTLEFORD
BEDFORD (St Martin) *St Alb 10*   P *Bp*   P-in-c R S STOKES
BEDFORD (St Michael and All Angels)   *see Elstow St Alb*
BEDFORD (St Paul) *St Alb 10*   P *Bp*   V J G PEDLAR
BEDFORD (St Peter de Merton) w St Cuthbert *St Alb 10* P *Ld Chan*   R M L FUDGER
BEDFORD LEIGH (St Thomas) (All Saints' Mission) *Man 13* P *V Leigh St Mary*   V vacant (01942) 673519

BEDFORD PARK (St Michael and All Angels) *Lon 11*   P *Bp* V K J MORRIS,   C S F STAVROU,   NSM G MORGAN
BEDGROVE (Holy Spirit) *Ox 21*   P *DBP*   P-in-c M G KUHRT
BEDHAMPTON (St Nicholas's Mission Church) (St Thomas) *Portsm 5*   P *Bp*   R J A RISDON,   NSM H V HAWKES, S K BEAVIS
BEDINGFIELD (St Mary)   *see Eye St E*
BEDINGHAM (St Andrew)   *see Hempnall Nor*
BEDLINGTON (St Cuthbert) *Newc 1*   P *D&C Dur* V J F TWOMEY
BEDMINSTER (St Aldhelm) (St Paul) *Bris 1*   P *Bp* TV M F JEFFERY,   C C L GARDINER
BEDMINSTER (St Michael and All Angels) *Bris 1*   P *Bp* V D S MOSS
BEDMINSTER DOWN (St Oswald)   *see Bishopsworth and Bedminster Down Bris*
BEDMONT (Ascension)   *see Abbots Langley St Alb*
BEDNALL (All Saints)   *see Penkridge Lich*
BEDSTONE (St Mary)   *see Clungunford w Clunbury and Clunton, Bedstone etc Heref*
BEDWORTH (All Saints) *Cov 5*   P *Patr Bd*   TR R W HARE, TV M J HAMMOND,   C P A P DEN HAAN,   Dss P M HAMILTON
BEDWYN, GREAT (St Mary)   *see Savernake Sarum*
BEDWYN, LITTLE (St Michael)   *as above*
BEECH (St Peter)   *see Alton St Lawr Win*
BEECH, HIGH (Holy Innocents)   *see Waltham H Cross Chelmsf*
BEECH HILL (St Anne)   *see Wigan St Anne Liv*
BEECH HILL (St Mary the Virgin)   *see Loddon Reach Ox*
BEECHDALE ESTATE (St Chad)   *see Blakenall Heath Lich*
BEECHINGSTOKE (St Stephen)   *see Pewsey and Swanborough Sarum*
BEEDING (St Peter) and Bramber w Botolphs *Chich 12*   P *Bp* R J W A CHALLIS
BEEDING, LOWER (Holy Trinity) (St John the Evangelist) *Chich 8*   P *Bp*   P-in-c S GALLAGHER
BEEDON (St Nicholas) and Peasemore w West Ilsley and Farnborough *Ox 14*   P *Bp*   P-in-c J P TOWNEND, C G J STACEY, K E STACEY,   NSM D F BROWN
BEEFORD (St Leonard) w Frodingham and Foston *York 11* P *Abp and Ch Soc Trust (jt)*   R J E GRAINGER-SMITH
BEELEY (St Anne) and Edensor *Derby 2*   P *Duke of Devonshire* P-in-c D C GARNETT
BEELSBY (St Andrew)   *see Laceby and Ravendale Gp Linc*
BEENHAM VALENCE (St Mary)   *see Aldermaston and Woolhampton Ox*
BEER (St Michael)   *see Seaton and Beer Ex*
BEER HACKETT (St Michael)   *see Bradford Abbas and Thornford w Beer Hackett Sarum*
BEERCROCOMBE (St James)   *see Beercrocombe w Curry Mallet, Hatch Beauchamp etc B & W*
BEERCROCOMBE (St James) w Curry Mallet, Hatch Beauchamp, Orchard Portman, Staple Fitzpaine, Stoke St Mary w Thurlbear and West Hatch *B & W 15*   P *Bp, Ch Trust Fund Trust, and D&C (4 turns), Duchy of Cornwall (1 turn)*   R P A REYNOLDS,   NSM J A PRICE
BEESANDS (St Andrew)   *see Stokenham, Slapton, Charleton w Buckland etc Ex*
BEESBY (St Andrew)   *see Saleby w Beesby and Maltby Linc*
BEESTON (St Andrew)   *see Sprowston w Beeston Nor*
BEESTON (St John the Baptist) *S'well 7*   P *Duke of Devonshire* V W R PLIMMER,   C C L TOWNS
BEESTON (St Mary the Virgin) *Ripon 6*   P *Patr Bd* TV R BROOKE,   P-in-c W A D BERRYMAN,   C J SMITH
BEESTON HILL (Holy Spirit) and Hunslet Moor St Peter w St Cuthbert *Ripon 6*   P *Bp and TR Leeds City (jt)* V R W SHAW
BEESTON NEXT MILEHAM (St Mary the Virgin) *see Litcham w Kempston, E and W Lexham, Mileham etc Nor*
BEESTON REGIS (All Saints)   *see Aylmerton, Runton, Beeston Regis and Gresham Nor*
BEESTON RYLANDS (St Mary)   *see Beeston S'well*
BEESTON ST LAURENCE (St Laurence)   *see Ashmanhaugh, Barton Turf etc Nor*
BEETHAM (St Michael and All Angels) *Carl 10*   P *Bp* P-in-c A T SCHOFIELD
BEETLEY (St Mary)   *see Dereham and Distr Nor*
BEGBROKE (St Michael)   *see Blenheim Ox*
BEIGHTON (All Saints)   *see Acle w Fishley, N Burlingham, Beighton w Moulton Nor*
BEIGHTON (St Mary the Virgin) *Sheff 1*   P *Bp* P-in-c M H E HEALEY
BEKESBOURNE (St Peter)   *see Bridge Cant*
BELAUGH (St Peter)   *see Wroxham w Hoveton and Belaugh Nor*
BELBROUGHTON (Holy Trinity) w Fairfield and Clent *Worc 12*   P *Ld Chan and St Jo Coll Ox (alt)*   R B J MAPLEY

BELCHALWELL (St Aldheim)   *see* Hazelbury Bryan and the
  Hillside Par *Sarum*
BELCHAMP (St Paul and St Andrew)   *see* N Hinckford *Chelmsf*
BELCHAMP OTTEN (St Ethelbert and All Saints)   *as above*
BELCHAMP WALTER (St Mary the Virgin)   *as above*
BELCHFORD (St Peter and St Paul) *Linc 11*   **P** *Ld Chan*
  R *vacant*
BELFIELD (St Ann) *Man 21*   **P** *Bp*   **P-in-c** G W LINDLEY
BELFORD (St Mary) and Lucker *Newc 7*   **P** *V Bamburgh and*
  Beadnell and Bp (alt)   **V** J J BECKWITH
BELGRAVE (St Gabriel)   *see* Leic Resurr *Leic*
BELGRAVE (St Michael and All Angels)   *as above*
BELGRAVE (St Paul)   *see* Wilnecote *Lich*
BELGRAVE (St Peter)   *see* Leic Resurr *Leic*
BELHUS PARK (All Saints)   *see* S Ockendon and Belhus Park
  Chelmsf
BELLE GREEN (Mission)   *see* Ince Ch Ch w Wigan St Cath *Liv*
BELLE ISLE (St John and St Barnabas)   *see* Leeds Belle Is St Jo
  and St Barn *Ripon*
BELLEAU (St John the Baptist)   *see* Legbourne and Wold
  Marsh *Linc*
BELLERBY (St John)   *see* Leyburn w Bellerby *Ripon*
BELLFIELD (St Mark)   *see* Sutton St Jas and Wawne *York*
BELLINGDON (St John the Evangelist)   *see* Gt Chesham *Ox*
BELLINGHAM (St Cuthbert)   *see* N Tyne and Redesdale *Newc*
BELLINGHAM (St Dunstan) *S'wark 4*   **P** *Bp*
  V K L A FARRELL,   **NSM** D L RILEY
BELMONT (St Anselm) *Lon 23*   **P** *Bp*   **V** I BRADY
BELMONT (St John) *S'wark 23*   **P** *R Cheam*
  V M R WILLIAMS,   **NSM** A E DOERR
BELMONT (St Mary Magdalene) and Pittington *Dur 1*
  P *Prime Min and D&C (alt)*   **V** D M JOHNSON,
  C J A ASHURST
BELMONT (St Peter)   *see* Turton Moorland Min *Man*
BELPER (Christ Church) (St Faith's Mission Church) w
  Turnditch *Derby 11*   **P** *Bp*   **V** A M V ROOME
BELPER (St Peter) *Derby 11*   **P** *V Duffield*
  NSM A TOMPKINS
BELSIZE PARK (St Peter) *Lon 16*   **P** *D&C Westmr*
  P-in-c P S NICHOLSON
BELSTEAD (St Mary the Virgin)   *see* Sproughton w Burstall,
  Copdock w Washbrook etc *St E*
BELSTONE (St Mary)   *see* S Tawton and Belstone *Ex*
BELTINGHAM (St Cuthbert)   *see* Haydon Bridge and
  Beltingham w Henshaw *Newc*
BELTISLOE, NORTH Group *Linc 14*   **P** *Ch Coll Cam,*
  Sir Lyonel Tollemache Bt, D&C, Bp, DBP, Sir Richard Welby Bt,
  and Baroness Willoughby de Eresby (jt)   **R** R H IRESON
BELTON (All Saints) and Burgh Castle *Nor 6*   **P** *Bp and*
  Ld Chan (alt)   **R** J J QUINN
BELTON Group, The (All Saints) *Linc 1*   **P** *Bp and Prime Min*
  (alt)   **V** T D BUCKLEY
BELTON (St John the Baptist)   *see* Kegworth, Hathern, Long
  Whatton, Diseworth etc *Leic*
BELTON (St Peter)   *see* Uppingham w Ayston and Wardley w
  Belton *Pet*
BELTON (St Peter and St Paul)   *see* Barkston and Hough Gp
  Linc
BELVEDERE (All Saints) *Roch 15*   **P** *DBP*   **V** C A TERRY
BELVEDERE (St Augustine) *Roch 15*   **P** *Bp*   **V** C W JONES
BEMBRIDGE (Holy Trinity) (St Luke's Mission Church)
  Portsm 7   **P** *V Brading*   **V** A P MENNISS,   **NSM** L M BUSHELL
BEMERTON (St Andrew) (St John the Evangelist) (St Michael
  and All Angels) *Sarum 12*   **P** *Prime Min (2 turns) and Bp*
  (1 turn)   **TR** S A WOODLEY,   **NSM** S J DREWETT
BEMPTON (St Michael) w Flamborough, Reighton w Speeton
  York 9   **P** *Patr Bd*   **V** P J PIKE,   **C** E C HASSALL
BEN RHYDDING (St John the Evangelist) *Bradf 4*   **V** *Ilkey*
  P-in-c P WILLOX
BENCHILL (St Luke the Physician)   *see* Wythenshawe *Man*
BENEFIELD (St Mary the Virgin)   *see* Oundle w Ashton and
  Benefield w Glapthorn *Pet*
BENENDEN (St George and St Margaret) *Cant 16*   **P** *Abp*
  P-in-c C B HILL,   **NSM** R M VAN WENGEN
BENFIELDSIDE (St Cuthbert) *Dur 4*   **P** *Bp*   **V** M JACKSON,
  NSM I W WAUGH
BENFLEET, SOUTH (St Mary the Virgin) *Chelmsf 10*
  P *D&C Westmr*   **V** L BENNETT
BENGEO (Holy Trinity)   *see* Hertford *St Alb*
BENGEO (St Leonard)   *as above*
BENGEWORTH (St Peter) *Worc 1*   **P** *Bp*   **V** B D COLLINS
BENHALL (St Mary)   *see* Alde River *St E*
BENHILTON (All Saints) *S'wark 23*   **P** *Bp*   **V** M A J OADES
BENINGTON (All Saints)   *see* Freiston, Butterwick w
  Bennington, and Leverton *Linc*

BENINGTON (St Peter) w Walkern *St Alb 23*   **P** *Trustees Ripon*
  Coll Ox and K Coll Cam (alt), and Bp   **R** *vacant* (01438) 861322
BENNETTS END (St Benedict)   *see* Chambersbury *St Alb*
BENNIWORTH (St Julian)   *see* Asterby Gp *Linc*
BENSHAM AND TEAMS (St Chad) *Dur 12*   **P** *Bp*
  V M R PALMER
BENSINGTON (St Helen)   *see* Benson *Ox*
BENSON (St Helen) *Ox 1*   **P** *Ch Ch Ox*   **V** A R HAWKEN,
  OLM J K TRAVIS
BENTHAM (St John the Baptist) (St Margaret) *Bradf 6*   **P** *Bp*
  R C B BURGESS,   **NSM** M A PARR
BENTILEE (St Stephen)   *see* Bucknall *Lich*
BENTLEY (Emmanuel) *Lich 28*   **P** *Bp, Mrs H G Jenkins, and*
  A D Owen Esq (jt)   **P-in-c** S L HOUGH
BENTLEY (St Mary)   *see* Sproughton w Burstall, Copdock w
  Washbrook etc *St E*
BENTLEY (St Mary) and Binsted *Win 2*   **P** *Adn Surrey and*
  D&C (jt)   **R** *vacant* (01420) 22174
BENTLEY (St Peter) *Sheff 7*   **P** *Bp*   **V** D R FOUNTAIN
BENTLEY (St Peter)   *see* Rowley w Skidby *York*
BENTLEY, GREAT (St Mary the Virgin) and Frating w
  Thorrington *Chelmsf 22*   **P** *St Jo Coll Cam and Bp (alt)*
  R W B METCALFE
BENTLEY, LITTLE (St Mary)   *see* Tendring and Lt Bentley w
  Beaumont cum Moze *Chelmsf*
BENTLEY, LOWER (St Mary)   *see* Redditch H Trin *Worc*
BENTLEY, NEW (St Philip and St James) w Arksey *Sheff 7*
  P *Bp and DBP (jt)*   **V** S P DICKINSON
BENTLEY COMMON (St Paul), Kelvedon Hatch and
  Navestock *Chelmsf 7*   **P** *Bp*   **R** M N JAMES,
  NSM E E GOLDSMITH
BENTLEY HEATH (St James)   *see* Dorridge *Birm*
BENTWORTH (St Mary), Lasham, Medstead and Shalden
  Win 2   **P** *J L Jervoise Esq and Ld Chan (alt)*
  R B R G FLENLEY
BENWELL Team, The (St James) (St John) (Venerable Bede)
  Newc 4   **P** *Bp*   **TR** C R PICKFORD,   **TV** T M FERGUSON,
  OLM P D WILSON
BEOLEY Church Hill (St Andrew's Church Centre)
  see Redditch H Trin *Worc*
BEOLEY (St Leonard)   *as above*
BEPTON (St Mary)   *see* Cocking, Bepton and W Lavington
  Chich
BERDEN (St Nicholas)   *see* Manuden w Berden and Quendon w
  Rickling *Chelmsf*
BERE ALSTON (Holy Trinity)   *see* Bere Ferrers *Ex*
BERE FERRERS (St Andrew) *Ex 25*   **P** *DBP*   **R** N C LAW
BERE REGIS (St John the Baptist) and Affpuddle w
  Turnerspuddle *Sarum 8*   **P** *Ball Coll Ox (2 turns), Bp (1 turn)*
  R I WOODWARD
BERECHURCH (St Margaret w St Michael) *Chelmsf 16*   **P** *Bp*
  V A I FORDYCE
BERGH APTON (St Peter and St Paul)   *see* Thurton *Nor*
BERGHOLT, EAST (St Mary the Virgin) and Brantham *St E 5*
  P *Em Coll Cam*   **R** S VAN DER TOORN,   **NSM** A J MORTIMER
BERGHOLT, WEST (St Mary the Virgin) and Great Horkesley
  Chelmsf 17   **P** *Bp and Ball Coll Ox (alt)*   **R** C HORSEMAN
BERINSFIELD (St Mary and St Berin)   *see* Dorchester *Ox*
BERKELEY (St Mary the Virgin) w Wick, Breadstone, Newport,
  Stone, Woodford and Hill *Glouc 6*   **P** *Bp, Berkeley Will*
  Trustees, and Mrs J D Jenner-Fust (jt)   **P-in-c** R J AVERY,
  NSM R P CHIDLAW, C J BIRKETT
BERKHAMSTED, GREAT (All Saints) (St Peter), Great
  Gaddesden, Little Gaddesden, Nettleden and Potten End
  St Alb 2   **P** *Patr Bd*   **TR** M N R BOWIE,   **TV** P E GIBSON,
  C J A PRITCHARD,   **Hon C** J B RUSSELL,
  NSM L GEOGHEGAN
BERKHAMSTED, LITTLE (St Andrew) and Bayford, Essendon
  and Ponsbourne *St Alb 22*   **P** *Marquess of Salisbury (2 turns),*
  CPAS (1 turn), and Bp (1 turn)   **R** P M HIGHAM,
  NSM J D COPE, R P O'NEILL
BERKHAMSYTCH (St Mary and St John)   *see* Ipstones w
  Berkhamsytch and Onecote w Bradnop *Lich*
BERKLEY (Blessed Virgin Mary)   *see* Beckington w
  Standerwick, Berkley, Rodden etc *B & W*
BERKSWELL (St John the Baptist) *Cov 4*   **P** *Trustees*
  Col C J H Wheatley   **P-in-c** M Q BRATTON
BERKSWICH (Holy Trinity)   *see* Baswich *Lich*
BERMONDSEY (St Anne) and St Augustine *S'wark 7*   **P** *Bp*
  and F W Smith Esq (alt)   **V** S I R HARTLEY,   **C** L C VINCER
BERMONDSEY (St Hugh) Charterhouse Mission Conventional
  District *S'wark 10*   **C-in-c** B A SAUNDERS,   **C** K J GRANT,
  NSM L SCOTT-GARNETT
BERMONDSEY (St James w Christ Church) and St Crispin
  S'wark 7   **P** *The Crown, Bp, and R Bermondsey St Mary*

(by turn) **V** S J R HARTLEY, **C** L C VINCER,
OLM S C CATTON
BERMONDSEY (St Katharine) w St Bartholomew *S'wark 7*
P *Bp and R Rotherhithe St Mary w All SS (jt)* **V** L M WANJIE
**BERMONDSEY (St Mary Magdalen w St Olave, St John and
St Luke)** *S'wark 7* **P** *Ch Patr Soc (2 turns), Ld Chan (1 turn),
and Bp (1 turn)* **R** C D MOORE, **C** O I AOKO
BERNEY, GREAT (St John) *see Langdon Hills Chelmsf*
BERNWODE *Ox 21* **P** *Bp, CPAS, Earl Temple of Stowe, and
Sir Henry Aubrey-Fletcher Bt (jt)* **R** C D STIRLING,
C L J FELLOWS, **OLM** J EDMANS
BERRICK SALOME (St Helen) *see Chalgrove w Berrick
Salome Ox*
BERRINGTON (All Saints) *see Wenlock Heref*
BERROW (Blessed Virgin Mary) and Breane *B & W 1* **P** *Adn
Wells* **R** S F LACY
**BERROW (St Faith) w Pendock, Eldersfield, Hollybush and
Birtsmorton** *Worc 5* **P** *Bp, D&C, and Exors Sir Berwick
Lechmere Bt (jt)* **R** M A ROGERS
BERRY POMEROY (St Mary) *see Totnes w Bridgetown, Berry
Pomeroy etc Ex*
BERRYNARBOR (St Peter) *see Combe Martin, Berrynarbor,
Lynton, Brendon etc Ex*
BERSTED, NORTH (Holy Cross) *Chich 1* **P** *Abp* **V** *vacant*
(01243) 823800
BERSTED, SOUTH (St Mary Magdalene) w NORTH *Chich 1*
P *Abp* **V** T M CROOK
BERWICK (Holy Trinity) (St Mary) *Newc 12* **P** *Bp (2 turns),
D&C Dur (1 turn)* **V** A HUGHES
BERWICK (St John) *see Chalke Valley Sarum*
BERWICK (St Michael and All Angels) w Selmeston and Alciston
Chich 18 **P** *Miss I M Newson and Mrs A Fitzherbert (1 turn),
D&C (1 turn)* **R** P M BLEE
BERWICK PARK (Good Shepherd) *see Wood Green St Mich
w Bounds Green St Gabr etc Lon*
BERWICK ST JAMES (St James) *see Wylye and Till Valley
Sarum*
BESFORD (St Peter's Chapelry) *see Defford w Besford Worc*
BESSACARR, WEST (St Francis of Assisi) *Sheff 8* **P** *Bp*
V C S W VAN D'ARQUE
BESSELSLEIGH (St Lawrence) *Ox 10* **P** *Ox Ch Trust*
P-in-c L L SAPWELL
BESSINGBY (St Magnus) (St Mark) *York 9* **P** *Patr Bd*
V *vacant*
BESSINGHAM (St Mary) *see Roughton and Felbrigg, Metton,
Sustead etc Nor*
BESTHORPE (All Saints) *see Attleborough w Besthorpe Nor*
BESTHORPE (Holy Trinity) *see Collingham w S Scarle and
Besthorpe and Girton S'well*
BESTWOOD (Emmanuel) (St Mark) *S'well 12* **P** *Bp and Ch
Patr Trust (jt)* **V** P A HUXTABLE, **C** T E HODGETT
BESTWOOD (St Matthew on the Hill) (St Philip) *S'well 12*
P *Bp and Ch Patr Trust (jt)* **V** E A MORRIS
BESTWOOD/RISE PARK Local Ecumenical Partnership
S'well 9 vacant
BESTWOOD PARK (no dedication) w Rise Park *S'well 12*
P *Bp and Ch Patr Trust (jt)* **NSM** B J NEILL
BESWICK (St Margaret) *see Hutton Cranswick w Skerne,
Watton and Beswick York*
BETCHWORTH (St Michael and All Angels) and Buckland
S'wark 26 **P** *D&C Windsor and All So Coll Ox (jt)*
R C A COSLETT
BETHERSDEN (St Margaret) w High Halden *Cant 16* **P** *Abp*
P-in-c S FOULKES
BETHESDA (Shared Church) *see Hallwood Ecum Par Ches*
BETHNAL GREEN (St Barnabas) *Lon 7* **P** *D&C Cant*
V B C RALPH
BETHNAL GREEN (St James the Less) *Lon 7* **P** *CPAS*
V A J LOGAN
BETHNAL GREEN (St John) *see St Jo on Bethnal Green Lon*
BETHNAL GREEN (St Matthew w St James the Great) *Lon 7*
P *Bp* **R** K J SCULLY, **Hon C** H LODER
BETHNAL GREEN (St Peter) (St Thomas) *Lon 7* **P** *City Corp*
P-in-c J E BLACKBURN
BETHUNE ROAD (St Andrew) *see Stoke Newington St Andr
Lon*
BETLEY (St Margaret) *Lich 9* **P** *DBP* **V** B F WILSON,
C M J MAXWELL, **OLM** P LANE, G A BAILEY
BETTISCOMBE (St Stephen) *see Golden Cap Team Sarum*
BETTON STRANGE (St Margaret) *see Wenlock Heref*
BETTWS-Y-CRWYN (St Mary) *see Clun w Bettws-y-Crwyn
and Newcastle Heref*
BEVENDEAN (Holy Nativity) *see Moulsecoomb Chich*
BEVERLEY (St Mary) *York 8* **P** *Abp* **V** D W HOSKIN
BEVERLEY (St Nicholas) *York 8* **P** *Abp* **V** J A EVANS,
C M MARTINSON, **NSM** R MERRYWEATHER

BEVERLEY MINSTER (St John and St Martin) *York 8*
P *Simeon's Trustees* **V** J J FLETCHER, **C** N J Q DRAYSON,
R C CAREW, **NSM** R E YOUNG
BEVERSTON (St Mary the Virgin) *see Tetbury, Beverston and
Long Newnton Glouc*
BEWBUSH (Community Centre) *see Ifield Chich*
**BEWCASTLE (St Cuthbert), Stapleton and Kirklinton w
Hethersgill** *Carl 2* **P** *Bp, D&C, and DBP (jt)*
R P A GREENHALGH
BEWDLEY (St Anne) *see Ribbesford w Bewdley and Dowles
Worc*
BEWERLEY GRANGE (Chapel) *see Upper Nidderdale Ripon*
BEWHOLME (St John the Baptist) *see Sigglesthorne w
Nunkeeling and Bewholme York*
BEWICK, OLD (Holy Trinity) *see Glendale Gp Newc*
BEXHILL (All Saints) *see Sidley Chich*
BEXHILL (St Augustine) *Chich 14* **P** *Bp* **V** R COATES, **Hon
C** P A FROSTICK
BEXHILL (St Barnabas) *Chich 14* **P** *Bp*
P-in-c G R CROSTHWAITE
BEXHILL (St Mark) *Chich 14* **P** *Bp* **R** J J FRAIS
BEXHILL (St Peter) (St Michael) (Good Shepherd) (St Andrew)
Chich 14 **P** *Bp* **TR** E F P BRYANT, **TV** S D HUGGINS,
C D B SMITH, **Hon C** G R CROSTHWAITE,
NSM O M WERRETT
BEXHILL (St Stephen) *Chich 14* **P** *Bp* **V** D R FROST
BEXLEY (St John the Evangelist) *Roch 17* **P** *The Crown*
V S I LAMB
BEXLEY (St Mary) *Roch 17* **P** *Bp* **V** P A SPREADBRIDGE
BEXLEYHEATH (Christ Church) *Roch 15* **P** *Bp*
V F D JAKEMAN, **C** C F MORRISON
BEXLEYHEATH (St Peter) *Roch 15* **P** *Bp*
P-in-c J R CHARLES
BEXWELL (St Mary) *see Denver and Ryston w Roxham and W
Dereham etc Ely*
BEYTON (All Saints) *see Rougham, Beyton w Hessett and
Rushbrooke St E*
BIBURY (St Mary) *see Fairford Deanery Glouc*
BICESTER (St Edburg) w Bucknell, Caversfield and Launton
Ox 2 **P** *Patr Bd* **TR** T A SCOTT, **TV** M MULLINS,
C E VAN BLERK, C A BOYCE, **NSM** R B ATKINS
BICKENHILL (St Peter) *Birm 11* **P** *Birm Dioc Trustees*
P-in-c K CLARINGBULL
BICKER (St Swithin) *Linc 21* **P** *D&C* **V** *vacant* (01775)
822355
BICKERSHAW (St James and St Elizabeth) *Liv 14* **P** *Bp*
V J L STEVENTON
BICKERSTAFFE Four Lane Ends (not known) *see Aughton
St Mich and Bickerstaffe Liv*
BICKERSTAFFE (Holy Trinity) *as above*
BICKERTON (Holy Trinity), Bickley, Harthill and Burwardsley
Ches 5 **P** *Bp, Adn Ches, DBP, Dowager Marchioness of
Cholmondeley, and A G Barbour Esq (jt)* **V** L R THOMAS
BICKINGTON (St Andrew) *see Fremington Ex*
BICKINGTON (St Mary the Virgin) *see Ashburton,
Bickington, Buckland in the Moor etc Ex*
BICKINGTON, HIGH (St Mary) *see Newton Tracey,
Horwood, Alverdiscott etc Ex*
BICKLEIGH Roborough (St Mary the Virgin) and Shaugh Prior
Ex 23 **P** *Patr Bd* **TR** R J CARLTON, **C** M B BROWN
BICKLEIGH (St Mary) *see Silverton, Butterleigh, Bickleigh
and Cadeleigh Ex*
BICKLEIGH DOWN (School) *see Bickleigh and Shaugh Prior
Ex*
BICKLEY (St George) *Roch 14* **P** *SMF* **Hon C** B W SHARPE
BICKLEY (St Wenefrede) *see Bickerton, Bickley, Harthill and
Burwardsley Ches*
BICKNACRE (St Andrew) *see Woodham Ferrers and
Bicknacre Chelmsf*
BICKNOLLER (St George) *see Quantock Towers B & W*
BICKNOR (St James) *see Bredgar w Bicknor and Frinsted w
Wormshill etc Cant*
BICTON (Holy Trinity), Montford w Shrawardine and Fitz
Lich 20 **P** *Earl of Powis, N E E Stephens Esq, and
J G O Wingfield Esq (jt)* **P-in-c** C H DEAKIN, **Hon
C** R M PARSONS
BICTON (St Mary) *see E Budleigh w Bicton and Otterton Ex*
BIDBOROUGH (St Lawrence) *see Southborough St Pet w Ch
Ch and St Matt etc Roch*
BIDDENDEN (All Saints) and Smarden *Cant 16* **P** *Abp*
P-in-c A BIENFAIT
BIDDENHAM (St James) *St Alb 10* **P** *Bp*
P-in-c S L HUCKLE, **C** J NASH
BIDDESTONE (St Nicholas) *see By Brook Bris*
BIDDISHAM (St John the Baptist) *see Crook Peak B & W*

BIDDLESDEN (St Margaret)   *see* W Buckingham *Ox*
BIDDULPH (St Lawrence) *Lich 8*   **P** *MMCET*
  V M S J CANNAM,   **C** M J BARNSLEY
BIDDULPH MOOR (Christ Church) *Lich 8*   **P** *MMCET*
  P-in-c J A DAWSWELL
BIDEFORD (St Mary) (St Peter East the Water), Northam,
  Westward Ho!, Appledore, Weare Giffard, Littleham,
  Landcross and Monkleigh *Ex 16*   **P** *Patr Bd*   **TR** M EDSON,
  TV P J DOBBIN, R J FROST, J EWINGTON,   **C** T H F BENSON,
  NSM A GLOVER
BIDFORD-ON-AVON (St Laurence) *Cov 7*   **P** *Bp*
  NSM S M HENWOOD
BIDSTON (St Oswald) *Ches 1*   **P** *Bp*   **V** R E IVESON
BIELBY (St Giles)   *see* Holme and Seaton Ross Gp *York*
BIERLEY (St John the Evangelist) *Bradf 2*   **P** *DBP*
  P-in-c D G KENNEDY
BIERLEY, EAST (St Luke)   *see* Birkenshaw w Hunsworth
  Wakef
BIERTON (St James the Great)   *see* Aylesbury w Bierton and
  Hulcott *Ox*
BIGBURY (St Lawrence)   *see* Modbury, Bigbury, Ringmore w
  Kingston etc *Ex*
BIGBY (All Saints)   *see* N Wolds Gp *Linc*
BIGGIN (St Thomas)   *see* Hartington, Biggin and Earl
  Sterndale *Derby*
BIGGIN HILL (St Mark) *Roch 14*   **P** *Bp*   **V** J M MCLAREN
BIGGLESWADE (St Andrew) *St Alb 11*   **P** *Bp*   **V** *vacant*
  (01767) 312243
BIGHTON (All Saints)   *see* Arle Valley *Win*
BIGNOR (Holy Cross)   *see* Barlavington, Burton w Coates,
  Sutton and Bignor *Chich*
BIGRIGG (St John)   *see* Egremont and Haile *Carl*
BILBOROUGH (St John the Baptist) *S'well 14*   **P** *Bp*
  P-in-c A J CARTWRIGHT,   **C** J E LAMB
BILBOROUGH (St Martin) w Strelley *S'well 14*   **P** *SMF*
  P-in-c A J CARTWRIGHT,   **C** J E LAMB
BILBROOK (Holy Cross) and Coven *Lich 2*   **P** *Bp*
  V D C BAKER
BILBROUGH (St James)   *see* Healaugh w Wighill, Bilbrough
  and Askham Richard *York*
BILDESTON (St Mary Magdalene) w Wattisham and Lindsey,
  Whatfield w Semer, Nedging and Naughton *St E 3*   **P** *Abp, Bp,*
  CPAS, Jes Coll Cam, and Reformation Ch Trust (jt)
  R B STANTON
BILHAM *Sheff 12*   **P** *Bp, Major W Warde-Aldam,*
  W G A Warde-Norbury Esq, and Mrs S Grant-Dalton (jt)
  P-in-c C D LETHBRIDGE
BILLERICAY (Christ Church) (Emmanuel) (St John the Divine)
  (St Mary Magdalen) and Little Burstead *Chelmsf 6*   **P** *Bp*
  TR P A CARR,   **TV** W M PIDGEON, E POW
BILLESDON (St John the Baptist)   *see* Church Langton cum
  Tur Langton etc *Leic*
BILLESLEY COMMON (Holy Cross) *Birm 5*   **P** *Bp*
  V P OGILVIE
BILLING, GREAT (St Andrew) w LITTLE (All Saints) *Pet 4*
  P *BNC Ox and Bp (alt)*   **R** S R PALMER,   **C** R MULFORD
BILLINGBOROUGH Group, The (St Andrew) *Linc 13*
  P *Prime Min (2 turns), Bp and St Jo Coll Dur (1 turn)*
  P-in-c A K E SORENSEN,   **OLM** J G SPREADBURY
BILLINGE (St Aidan) *Liv 14*   **P** *R Wigan*   **C** A OVEREND
BILLINGFORD (St Leonard)   *see* Scole, Brockdish, Billingford,
  Thorpe Abbots etc *Nor*
BILLINGFORD (St Peter)   *see* N Elmham, Billingford, Bintree,
  Guist etc *Nor*
BILLINGHAM (St Aidan) *Dur 10*   **P** *D&C*   **P-in-c** S J LIDDLE
BILLINGHAM (St Cuthbert) *Dur 10*   **P** *D&C*   **V** R I SMITH,
  NSM M A VIGOR
BILLINGHAM (St Luke) *Dur 10*   **P** *D&C*   **V** T P PARKER
BILLINGHAM (St Mary Magdalene) *Dur 10*   **P** *D&C*
  V *vacant*
BILLINGHAM (St Mary Magdalene)   *see* Grindon, Stillington
  and Wolviston *Dur*
BILLINGHAY (St Michael)   *see* Carr Dyke Gp *Linc*
BILLINGSHURST (St Mary the Virgin) *Chich 8*   **P** *Bp*
  V B J PRITCHARD
BILLINGSLEY (St Mary)   *see* Highley w Billingsley, Glazeley
  etc *Heref*
BILLINGTON (St Michael and All Angels)   *see* Ouzel Valley
  St Alb
BILLOCKBY (All Saints)   *see* S Trin Broads *Nor*
BILLY MILL (St Aidan) *Newc 5*   **P** *Bp*   **V** A J CAVANAGH
BILNEY, EAST (St Mary)   *see* Dereham and Distr *Nor*
BILSBORROW (St Hilda)   *see* Fellside Team *Blackb*
BILSBY (Holy Trinity) w Farlesthorpe *Linc 8*   **P** *Bp*   **V** *vacant*
BILSDALE MIDCABLE (St John)   *see* Upper Ryedale *York*

BILSDALE PRIORY (St Hilda)   *see* Ingleby Greenhow, Bilsdale
  Priory etc *York*
BILSINGTON (St Peter and St Paul)   *see* Aldington w
  Bonnington and Bilsington etc *Cant*
BILSON (Mission Church)   *see* Cinderford St Steph w
  Littledean *Glouc*
BILSTHORPE (St Margaret) *S'well 15*   **P** *DBP*
  NSM M A GROVES
BILSTON (St Leonard) (St Chad) (St Mary the Virgin) *Lich 28*
  P *Patr Bd*   **TV** J L WATERFIELD,   **C** G R HARPER,
  OLM C E DAVIES
BILTON (St John the Evangelist) and St Luke *Ripon 1*   **P** *Bp*
  TV D J MCCLINTOCK,   **C** C J FALKINGHAM,
  NSM G P CORNISH
BILTON (St Mark) *Cov 6*   **P** *N M Assheton Esq*
  R T D COCKELL,   **C** R A BURLEY,   **OLM** M J SHARPE
BILTON, NEW (St Oswald)   *see* Rugby W *Cov*
BILTON-IN-AINSTY (St Helen)   *see* Tockwith and Bilton w
  Bickerton *York*
BILTON IN HOLDERNESS (St Peter) *York 12*   **P** *Abp*
  V R J E MAJOR
BINBROOK Group, The (St Mary) *Linc 10*   **P** *Ld Chan, DBP*
  and G F Sleight Esq (alt)   **R** T J WALKER
BINCOMBE (Holy Trinity) w Broadwey, Upwey and Buckland
  Ripers *Sarum 4*   **P** *G&C Coll Cam (2 turns),*
  Miss M B F Frampton (1 turn), and Bp (1 turn)
  R R A C SIMMONS
BINEGAR (Holy Trinity)   *see* Ashwick w Oakhill and Binegar
  B & W
BINFIELD (All Saints) (St Mark) *Ox 11*   **P** *Ld Chan*
  R W J MEYER
BINGFIELD (St Mary)   *see* St Oswald in Lee w Bingfield *Newc*
BINGHAM (St Mary and All Saints) *S'well 8*   **P** *The Crown*
  R D L HARPER
BINGLEY (All Saints) *Bradf 1*   **P** *Bp*   **P-in-c** D R JACKSON,
  NSM C M LOW
BINGLEY (Holy Trinity) *Bradf 1*   **P** *Bp*   **V** A J CLARKE,
  NSM C M LOW
BINHAM (St Mary)   *see* Stiffkey and Bale *Nor*
BINLEY (St Bartholomew) *Cov 1*   **P** *Bp*   **V** E E JONES,
  NSM R W BROMLEY
BINLEY WOODS Local Ecumenical Partnership *Cov 1*
  Min J CHEVERTON
BINSEY (St Margaret)   *see* Ox St Frideswide w Binsey *Ox*
BINSEY Team Ministry *Carl 6*   **P** *Patr Bd*   **S** P WALKER,
  TV P M F STREATFEILD,   **NSM** C C FRYER-SPEDDING
BINSTEAD (Holy Cross) *Portsm 7*   **P** *Bp*   **R** N R WALLACE
BINSTED (Holy Cross)   *see* Bentley and Binsted *Win*
BINSTED (St Mary)   *see* Walberton w Binsted *Chich*
BINTON (St Peter)   *see* Temple Grafton w Binton *Cov*
BINTREE (St Swithin)   *see* N Elmham, Billingford, Bintree,
  Guist etc *Nor*
BIRCH (St James) w Fallowfield *Man 4*   **P** *Bp*   **R** W G RAINES
BIRCH (St Mary)   *see* Rhodes *Man*
BIRCH-IN-RUSHOLME (St Agnes) w Longsight St John w
  St Cyprian *Man 1*   **P** *Prime Min and Bp (alt)*
  P-in-c S M EDWARDS,   **C** L E DOSE
BIRCHAM, GREAT (St Mary the Virgin)   *see* Docking, the
  Birchams, Stanhoe and Sedgeford *Nor*
BIRCHAM NEWTON (All Saints)   *as above*
BIRCHANGER (St Mary the Virgin)   *see* Stansted Mountfitchet
  w Birchanger and Farnham *Chelmsf*
BIRCHENCLIFFE (St Philip the Apostle)   *see* Birkby and
  Birchencliffe *Wakef*
BIRCHES HEAD (St Matthew)   *see* Hanley H Ev *Lich*
BIRCHFIELD (Holy Trinity) *Birm 3*   **P** *Bp*
  NSM L M ARLIDGE
BIRCHILLS, THE (St Andrew)   *see* Walsall St Andr *Lich*
BIRCHIN COPPICE (St Peter)   *see* Kidderminster St Jo and H
  Innocents *Worc*
BIRCHINGTON (All Saints) w Acol and Minnis Bay *Cant 9*
  P *Abp*   **V** D R WITTS
BIRCHMOOR (St John)   *see* Polesworth *Birm*
BIRCHOVER (St Michael)   *see* Youlgreave, Middleton, Stanton-
  in-Peak etc *Derby*
BIRCHWOOD (Mission Church)   *see* Blackdown *B & W*
BIRCHWOOD (St Luke) *Linc 15*   **P** *Bp*   **V** J B PAVEY
BIRCHWOOD (Transfiguration) *Liv 12*   **P** *Bp, Adn, and*
  R Warrington (jt)   **P-in-c** D J PRESCOTT
BIRCLE (St John the Baptist) *Man 10*   **P** *R Middleton St Leon*
  V A R BROCKBANK,   **NSM** D ALTHAM
BIRDBROOK (St Augustine)   *see* Ridgewell w Ashen,
  Birdbrook and Sturmer *Chelmsf*
BIRDHAM (St James)   *see* W Wittering and Birdham w
  Itchenor *Chich*

BIRDINGBURY (St Leonards) *see* Leam Valley *Cov*
BIRDLIP (St Mary in Hamlet) *see* Brimpsfield w Birdlip, Syde, Daglingworth etc *Glouc*
BIRDSALL (St Mary) *see* W Buckrose *York*
BIRKBY (St Cuthbert) Huddersfield and Birchencliffe *Wakef 5* **P** *V Lindley and Bp (jt)* **V** M RAILTON-CROWDER, **NSM** M FOSSEY, **OLM** J SARGENT
BIRKBY (St John the Evangelist) Huddersfield and Woodhouse *Wakef 5* **P** *Bp and DBP (jt)* **V** S C CLARKE
BIRKBY (St Peter) *see* E Richmond *Ripon*
BIRKDALE (St James) *Liv 9* **P** *Trustees* **P-in-c** I G MAINEY
BIRKDALE (St John) *Liv 9* **P** *Trustees* **V** P C CATON
BIRKDALE (St Peter) *Liv 9* **P** *Trustees* **P-in-c** I G MAINEY, **NSM** S CALVELEY, **OLM** E LOXHAM
BIRKENHEAD (Christ Church) *Ches 1* **P** *Bp* **V** A J HASLAM
BIRKENHEAD (St James) w St Bede *Ches 1* **P** *Trustees* **V** *vacant* 0151-652 1016
BIRKENHEAD PRIORY (Christ the King) *Ches 1* **P** *Patr Bd* **R** D J AYLING
BIRKENSHAW (St Paul) w Hunsworth *Wakef 8* **P** *V Birstall* **V** M J LOWLES, **C** L A MATTACKS, **NSM** D S ANDREW, C WALKER, **OLM** R DAVIDSON
BIRKIN (St Mary) *see* Haddlesey w Hambleton and Birkin *York*
BIRLEY (St Peter) *see* Canon Pyon w King's Pyon, Birley and Wellington *Heref*
BIRLING (All Saints), Addington, Ryarsh and Trottiscliffe *Roch 7* **P** *Bp* **R** J B CROSS
BIRLING, LOWER (Christ Church) *see* Snodland All SS w Ch Ch *Roch*
BIRLINGHAM (St James the Great) *see* Pershore w Pinvin, Wick and Birlingham *Worc*
BIRMINGHAM (Bishop Latimer w All Saints) *Birm 3* **P** *St Martin's Trustees* **R** G F KIMBER
BIRMINGHAM (St George) *Birm 8* **P** *St Martin's Trustees* **R** L C WRIGHT, **NSM** C A B GEORGE
BIRMINGHAM (St George w St Michael) *see* Edgbaston St Geo *Birm*
BIRMINGHAM (St John the Evangelist) *see* Ladywood St Jo and St Pet *Birm*
BIRMINGHAM (St Luke) *Birm 1* **P** *Trustees* **V** A G LENOX-CONYNGHAM
BIRMINGHAM (St Martin-in-the-Bull-Ring) w Bordesley St Andrew *Birm 1* **P** *St Martin's Trustees* **R** S W JONES, **C** E C M SYKES, J E DOUGLAS, **NSM** E BLAIR-CHAPPELL
BIRMINGHAM (St Paul) *Birm 1* **P** *St Martin's Trustees* **V** M R GILBERT
BIRSTALL (St James the Great) and Wanlip *Leic 5* **P** *Bp and C A Palmer-Tomkinson Esq (jt)* **P-in-c** J D G SHAKESPEARE, **C** S A CROFTS
BIRSTALL (St Peter) *Wakef 8* **P** *Bp* **V** P J KNIGHT
BIRSTWITH (St James) *see* Hampsthwaite and Killinghall and Birstwith *Ripon*
BIRTLES (St Catherine) *see* Alderley w Birtles *Ches*
BIRTLEY (St Giles) *see* Chollerton w Birtley and Thockrington *Newc*
BIRTLEY (St John the Evangelist) *Dur 11* **P** *R Chester le Street* **V** E G LLOYD, **Hon C** B M C BROGGIO
BIRTSMORTON (St Peter and St Paul) *see* Berrow w Pendock, Eldersfield, Hollybush etc *Worc*
BISBROOKE (St John the Baptist) *see* Lyddington w Stoke Dry and Seaton etc *Pet*
BISCATHORPE (St Helen) *see* Asterby Gp *Linc*
BISCOT (Holy Trinity) *St Alb 14* **P** *Bp* **V** T B SINGH
BISHAM (All Saints) *see* Gt Marlow w Marlow Bottom, Lt Marlow and Bisham *Ox*
BISHAMPTON (St James) *see* Abberton, The Flyfords, Naunton Beauchamp etc *Worc*
BISHOP AUCKLAND (St Andrew) (St Anne) *see* Auckland St Andr and St Anne *Dur*
BISHOP AUCKLAND (St Peter) *see* Auckland St Pet *Dur*
BISHOP AUCKLAND Woodhouse Close Area of Ecumenical Experiment (Conventional District) *Dur 10* **C-in-c** B JONES, **OLM** L DODDS
BISHOP BURTON (All Saints) w Walkington *York 8* **P** *Abp and DBP (alt)* **R** *vacant* (01482) 868379
BISHOP CAUNDLE (not known) *see* Vale of White Hart *Sarum*
BISHOP MIDDLEHAM (St Michael) *see* Upper Skerne *Dur*
BISHOP MONKTON (St John the Baptist) *see* Ripon Cathl *Ripon*
BISHOP NORTON (St Peter), Waddingham and Snitterby *Linc 6* **P** *Bp and The Crown (alt)* **P-in-c** C H LILLEY, **C** P L COSTIN
BISHOP SUTTON (Holy Trinity) and Stanton Drew and Stowey *B & W 10* **P** *Bp and Adn Bath (alt)* **V** *vacant* (01275) 333385

BISHOP THORNTON (St John the Evangelist) *see* Markington w S Stainley and Bishop Thornton *Ripon*
BISHOP WILTON (St Edith) *see* Garrowby Hill *York*
BISHOPDALE (Mission Room) *see* Penhill *Ripon*
BISHOPHILL JUNIOR (St Mary) *see* York St Clem w St Mary Bishophill *York*
BISHOPHILL SENIOR (St Clement w St Mary) *as above*
BISHOP'S CANNINGS (St Mary the Virgin), All Cannings and Etchilhampton *Sarum 16* **P** *DBP* **P-in-c** S ATTWATER
BISHOP'S CASTLE (St John the Baptist) w Mainstone, Lydbury North and Edgton *Heref 10* **P** *Earl of Powis (3 turns), Ld Chan (1 turn), and Mrs R E Bell (1 turn)* **P-in-c** P D A COLLINS, **C** D C HOARE
BISHOP'S CLEEVE (St Michael and All Angels) and Woolstone w Gotherington and Oxenton *Glouc 13* **P** *Patr Bd* **TR** M ALLEN, **TV** M S HOLLOWAY, **NSM** J PHILLIPS
BISHOP'S FROME (St Mary the Virgin) *see* Frome Valley *Heref*
BISHOPS GREEN (Community Church) *see* Burghclere w Newtown and Ecchinswell w Sydmonton *Win*
BISHOP'S HATFIELD (St Etheldreda) (St Luke) (St John) (St Michael and All Angels), Lemsford and North Mymms *St Alb 21* **P** *Patr Bd* **TR** R E PYKE, **TV** E C CARDALE, S E DAVENPORT, P D SWINN, P L SEGRAVE-PRIDE, **C** M L MOORE, **NSM** S E MARSH
BISHOP'S HULL (St John the Evangelist) *see* Taunton St Jo *B & W*
BISHOPS HULL (St Peter and St Paul) *B & W 18* **P** *Adn Taunton* **V** S TUCKER
BISHOP'S ITCHINGTON (St Michael) *Cov 10* **P** *Bp* **P-in-c** M C GREEN
BISHOP'S LAVINGTON (All Saints) *see* The Lavingtons, Cheverells, and Easterton *Sarum*
BISHOPS LYDEARD (Blessed Virgin Mary) w Bagborough and Cothelstone *B & W 19* **P** *D&C (3 turns), Ms P M G Mitford (1 turn)* **R** M L WISHART
BISHOPS NORTON (St John the Evangelist) *see* Twigworth, Down Hatherley, Norton, The Leigh etc *Glouc*
BISHOP'S STORTFORD (Holy Trinity) *St Alb 18* **P** *Bp* **P-in-c** S MARTIN
BISHOP'S STORTFORD (St Michael) *St Alb 18* **P** *Bp* **V** R A V MARCHAND, **C** D M JORDAN, **NSM** D C HINGE, J E KNIGHT
BISHOP'S SUTTON (St Nicholas) and Ropley and West Tisted *Win 1* **P** *Peache Trustees* **R** R J SUCH
BISHOP'S TACHBROOK (St Chad) *Cov 11* **P** *Bp* **P-in-c** K M ROBERTS
BISHOPS TAWTON (St John the Baptist) *see* Barnstaple *Ex*
BISHOP'S WALTHAM (St Peter) *Portsm 1* **P** *Bp* **R** J C HUNT, **NSM** J BELOE
BISHOP'S WOOD (St Mary) *see* Hartlebury *Worc*
BISHOPSBOURNE (St Mary) *see* Barham w Bishopsbourne and Kingston *Cant*
BISHOPSNYMPTON (St Mary the Virgin), Rose Ash, Mariansleigh, Molland, Knowstone, East Anstey and West Anstey *Ex 19* **P** *DBP* **P-in-c** A C JONES
BISHOPSTEIGNTON (St John the Baptist) *see* Teignmouth, Ideford w Luton, Ashcombe etc *Ex*
BISHOPSTOKE (St Mary) (St Paul) *Win 10* **P** *Bp* **P-in-c** R E WISE
BISHOPSTON (Church of the Good Shepherd) *see* Bishopston and St Andrews *Bris*
BISHOPSTON (St Michael and All Angels) *as above*
BISHOPSTON (St Michael and All Angels) (Church of the Good Shepherd) and St Andrews *Bris 3* **P** *Patr Bd* **TV** R J BURBRIDGE, **NSM** B J PULLAN, V LEE, **OLM** S A TRUSCOTT
BISHOPSTONE (St Andrew) *see* E Blatchington and Bishopstone *Chich*
BISHOPSTONE (St John the Baptist) *see* Chalke Valley *Sarum*
BISHOPSTONE (St Lawrence) *see* Credenhill w Brinsop and Wormsley etc *Heref*
BISHOPSTONE (St Mary the Virgin) *see* Lyddington and Wanborough and Bishopstone etc *Bris*
BISHOPSTROW (St Aldhelm) and Boreham *Sarum 17* **P** *DBP* **R** D R A BRETT
BISHOPSWOOD (All Saints) *see* Dixton, Wyesham, Bishopswood, Whitchurch etc *Heref*
BISHOPSWOOD (St John the Evangelist) *Lich 2* **P** *V Brewood* **P-in-c** C A HOST, **NSM** M J COULTER
BISHOPSWORTH (St Peter) and Bedminster Down *Bris 1* **P** *Bp* **TR** T R J GODDEN, **TV** I L GARRETT, **NSM** E P WHERLOCK, R A LANE
BISHOPTHORPE (St Andrew) *York 1* **P** *Abp* **V** C I COATES, **NSM** P MACNAUGHTON

BISHOPTON (St Peter) w Great Stainton *Dur 10*　**P** *Ld Chan*
V D M BROOKE,　**NSM** P CLAYTON
BISHOPWEARMOUTH (Good Shepherd) *Dur 16*　**P** *Bp*
P-in-c B SKELTON,　**NSM** D RAINE
BISHOPWEARMOUTH (St Gabriel) *Dur 16*　**P** *V Sunderland*
P-in-c J R MCMANNERS,　**C** P ROBSON,　**NSM** J P TALBOT
BISHOPWEARMOUTH (St Luke Pallion) *see* Millfield St
Mark and Pallion St Luke *Dur*
BISHOPWEARMOUTH (St Mary) *see* Millfield St Mary *Dur*
BISHOPWEARMOUTH (St Nicholas) (Christ Church) *Dur 16*
P *Bp*　**V** N B WARNER
BISLEY (All Saints), Chalford, France Lynch, and Oakridge
Glouc 5　**P** *Bp and Adn Glouc (1 turn), and Ld Chan (1 turn)*
V S G RICHARDS,　**NSM** S J JARVIS, R M BRYANT
BISLEY (St John the Baptist) and West End (Holy Trinity)
Guildf 6　**P** *Bp*　**R** A J ARMITT,　**C** A S JOHNSON,
NSM D H ROBINSON,　**OLM** R ABBOTT
BISPHAM (All Hallows) *Blackb 8*　**P** *Ch Soc Trust*　**R** S J COX,
C M COOK
BISTERNE (St Paul) *see* Ringwood *Win*
BITCHFIELD (St Mary Magdalene) *see* N Beltisloe Gp *Linc*
BITTADON (St Peter) *see* Ilfracombe, Lee, Woolacombe,
Bittadon etc *Ex*
BITTERING PARVA (St Peter and St Paul) *see* Gressenhall w
Longham w Wendling etc *Nor*
BITTERLEY (St Mary) w Middleton, Stoke St Milborough w
The Heath and Hopton Cangeford, Clee St Margaret and Cold
Weston *Heref 12*　**P** *Bp, DBP, Walcott Trustees, and Miss*
M F Rouse-Boughton (jt)　**P-in-c** B L CURNEW
BITTERNE (Holy Saviour) *Win 13*　**P** *Bp*
P-in-c A M M PARKER,　**C** A G H GAY
BITTERNE PARK (All Hallows) (Ascension) *Win 13*　**P** *Bp*
V S J CHAPMAN,　**C** G I COLLINGRIDGE
BITTESWELL (St Mary) *see* Lutterworth w Cotesbach and
Bitteswell *Leic*
BITTON (St Mary) *see* Warmley, Syston and Bitton *Bris*
BIX (St James) *see* Nettlebed w Bix, Highmoor, Pishill etc *Ox*
BLABY (All Saints) *Leic 7*　**P** *Bp*　**P-in-c** J G GIBBINS
BLACK BOURTON (St Mary the Virgin) *see* Shill Valley and
Broadshire *Ox*
BLACK NOTLEY (St Peter and St Paul) *Chelmsf 15*
P *St Jo Coll Cam*　**R** *vacant* (01376) 349619
BLACK TORRINGTON (St Mary), Bradford w Cookbury,
Thornbury and Highampton *Ex 17*　**P** *DBP*
P-in-c K M ROBERTS
BLACKAWTON (St Michael) *see* Stoke Fleming, Blackawton
and Strete *Ex*
BLACKBIRD LEYS (Holy Family) *Ox 4*　**P** *Bp*
V D T N PARRY,　**NSM** S R BURNE, P D BAKER
BLACKBOURNE *St E 9*　**P** *Patr Bd*　**TR** P R GARBETT,
TV E A JUMP,　**NSM** A J REDMAN,　**OLM** D A NEUPERT,
S M NUTT, J F WALKER
BLACKBROOK (St Paul) *see* Parr *Liv*
BLACKBURN (Christ Church w St Matthew) *Blackb 2*　**P** *Bp*
V A RAYNES,　**NSM** J R TERRY
BLACKBURN Christ the King (St Luke) (St Mark) *Blackb 2*
P *Bp and V Blackb (jt)*　**V** F E GREEN
BLACKBURN (St Barnabas) *Blackb 2*　**P** *Bp*　**V** *vacant* (01254)
56587
BLACKBURN (St Francis) (St Aidan) *Blackb 2*　**P** *Bp*
P-in-c P V F CHEW
BLACKBURN (St Gabriel) *Blackb 2*　**P** *Bp*
P-in-c S P CORBETT
BLACKBURN (St James) *Blackb 2*　**P** *Bp*　**P-in-c** S TRANTER,
C C E BROOKS
BLACKBURN (St Luke) *see* Blackb Christ the King *Blackb*
BLACKBURN (St Michael and All Angels) (Holy Trinity
Worship Centre) w St John the Evangelist *Blackb 2*
P *V Blackb*　**C** P A KNOWLES
BLACKBURN (St Silas) *Blackb 2*　**P** *Trustees*
P-in-c A F RANSON
BLACKBURN (St Stephen) *Blackb 2*　**P** *Trustees*
P-in-c S TRANTER
BLACKBURN St Thomas (St Jude) *Blackb 2*　**P** *Bp and*
Trustees (alt)　**C** P A KNOWLES
BLACKBURN The Redeemer (St Bartholomew) (The Saviour)
Blackb 2　**P** *Bp and CPAS (jt)*　**V** R A H MARSHALL,
C S P WATKINSON
BLACKDOWN Benefice, The *B & W 15*　**P** *DBP (4 turns),*
Pitminster PCC and Corfe PCC (1 turn)　**R** S M GREEN
BLACKDOWN (Holy Trinity) *see* Beaminster Area *Sarum*
BLACKFEN (Good Shepherd) *see* Lamorbey H Redeemer
Roch
BLACKFORD (Holy Trinity) *see* Wedmore w Theale and
Blackford *B & W*

BLACKFORD (St John the Baptist) *see* Rockcliffe and
Blackford *Carl*
BLACKFORD (St Michael) *see* Camelot Par *B & W*
BLACKFORDBY (St Margaret) and Woodville *Leic 8*　**P** *Bp*
V T S G VALE
BLACKHALL (St Andrew), Castle Eden and Monkhesleden
Dur 2　**P** *Bp*　**R** G LIDDLE
BLACKHAM (All Saints) *see* Withyham St Mich *Chich*
BLACKHEATH (All Saints) *S'wark 4*　**P** *V Lewisham St Mary*
V N W S CRANFIELD,　**OLM** T W CHATTERTON
BLACKHEATH (Ascension) *see* Deptford St Jo w H Trin and
Ascension *S'wark*
BLACKHEATH (St John the Evangelist) *S'wark 1*　**P** *CPAS*
V P J FARLEY-MOORE,　**C** E J CHEVILL,
NSM A M BESWETHERICK
BLACKHEATH (St Martin) *see* Wonersh w Blackheath *Guildf*
BLACKHEATH (St Paul) *Birm 7*　**P** *Bp*　**V** M J SERMON,
C A SIMMONS,　**NSM** C G CHRISTENSEN
BLACKHEATH PARK (St Michael and All Angels) *S'wark 1*
P *Bp*　**V** A R CHRISTIE,　**NSM** A SCOTT, J E CROUCHER
BLACKLAND (St Peter) *see* Calne and Blackland *Sarum*
BLACKLANDS Hastings (Christchurch and St Andrew) *Chich 17*
P *Ch Patr Trust*　**V** I COOPER
BLACKLEY (Holy Trinity) *Man 5*　**P** *Bp*　**R** P A STAMP
BLACKLEY (St Andrew) *Man 5*　**P** *Bp*　**P-in-c** I C FELLOWS
BLACKLEY (St Mark) White Moss *Man 5*　**P** *D&C*　**R** *vacant*
0161-740 5558
BLACKLEY (St Paul) *Man 5*　**P** *Bp*　**P-in-c** J L CLEGG
BLACKLEY (St Peter) *Man 5*　**P** *D&C*　**OLM** G L CORNISH
BLACKMOOR (St Matthew) and Whitehill *Portsm 4*　**P** *Earl of*
Selborne　**V** W P M HUGHES,　**NSM** W N MALLAS, L C PAGE
BLACKMORE (St Laurence) and Stondon Massey *Chelmsf 26*
P *Bp*　**C** C A HILLS
BLACKPOOL (Christ Church w All Saints) (St Andrew)
Blackb 8　**P** *Bp and Trustees (jt)*　**V** P J WARREN
BLACKPOOL (Holy Cross) South Shore *Blackb 8*　**P** *Bp*
V S EDWARDS,　**NSM** K THORN
BLACKPOOL (Holy Trinity) *see* S Shore H Trin *Blackb*
BLACKPOOL (St John) *Blackb 8*　**P** *Trustees*
P-in-c D CONNOLLY,　**C** H HORNBY
BLACKPOOL (St Mark) *Blackb 8*　**P** *CPAS*　**V** S E BROOK
BLACKPOOL (St Mary) South Shore *Blackb 8*　**P** *Bp*
P-in-c G ROUSE
BLACKPOOL (St Michael and All Angels) *Blackb 8*　**P** *Bp*
V N J HEALE
BLACKPOOL (St Paul) Marton *see* Marton *Blackb*
BLACKPOOL (St Paul's Worship Centre) *Blackb 8*　**P** *Trustees*
V J E SHAW
BLACKPOOL (St Peter) *see* S Shore St Pet *Blackb*
BLACKPOOL (St Stephen on the Cliffs) *Blackb 8*　**P** *Bp,*
R Bispham All Hallows, and Ch Wardens (jt)　**V** A G SAGE,
C T H DAVIS
BLACKPOOL (St Thomas) *Blackb 8*　**P** *CPAS*
P-in-c R F T MURPHY
BLACKPOOL (St Wilfrid) Mereside *Blackb 8*　**P** *Bp*
V P H HUDSON
BLACKROD (St Catherine) (Scot Lane School) *Man 11*
P *V Bolton-le-Moors St Pet*　**V** R C COOPER,
OLM C MCCABE, H K SHARP
BLACKTOFT (Holy Trinity) *see* Howden *York*
BLACKWATER (St Barnabas) *see* Arreton *Portsm*
BLACKWELL (All Saints) and Salutation *Dur 8*　**P** *Bp*
V J R DOBSON
BLACKWELL (St Catherine) *see* The Lickey *Birm*
BLACKWELL (St Werburgh) w Tibshelf *Derby 1*　**P** *Bp and*
MMCET (jt)　**V** *vacant* (01773) 873305
BLACON (Holy Trinity) *see* Ches H Trin *Ches*
BLADON (St Martin) *see* Blenheim *Ox*
BLAGDON (St Andrew) w Compton Martin and Ubley *B & W 10*
P *Bp and Sir John Wills Bt (jt)*　**R** V E S GOODMAN,
NSM J L CHAMBERLAIN
BLAGREAVES (St Andrew) *Derby 10*　**P** *Bp, Churchwardens,*
and CPAS (jt)　**V** P G BYSOUTH
BLAISDON (St Michael and All Angels) *see* Westbury-on-
Severn w Flaxley, Blaisdon etc *Glouc*
BLAKEDOWN (St James the Great) *see* Churchill-in-Halfshire
w Blakedown and Broome *Worc*
BLAKEMERE (St Leonard) *see* Cusop w Blakemere,
Bredwardine w Brobury etc *Heref*
BLAKENALL HEATH (Christ Church) *Lich 25*　**P** *Patr Bd*
TR P H MYERS,　**TV** D A MURPHY, B D SIMS
BLAKENEY (All Saints) *see* Newnham w Awre and Blakeney
Glouc
BLAKENEY (St Nicholas w St Mary and St Thomas) w Cley,
Wiveton, Glandford and Letheringsett *Nor 18*　**P** *Bp and Keble*
Coll Ox (jt)　**P-in-c** N G BATCOCK,　**NSM** J M FAWCETT

BLAKENHALL (St Luke)   *see* Wolverhampton St Luke *Lich*
BLAKENHAM, GREAT (St Mary) and LITTLE (St Mary) w
Baylham and Nettlestead *St E 1*   P *Bp and MMCET (jt)*
C   P THORN
BLAKESLEY (St Mary)   *see* Lambfold *Pet*
BLANCHLAND (St Mary's Abbey) w Hunstanworth and
Edmundbyers and Muggleswick *Newc 9*   P *D E Scott-*
Harden Esq, Lord Crewe's Trustees and D&C (alt)
P-in-c   D J IRVINE,   NSM   J LYNCH
BLANDFORD FORUM (St Peter and St Paul) and Langton
Long *Sarum 6*   P *Bp*   R   T STOREY,   NSM   R A COLDWELL
BLANDFORD ST MARY (St Mary)   *see* Spetisbury w
Charlton Marshall etc *Sarum*
BLANKNEY (St Oswald)   *see* Metheringham w Blankney and
Dunston *Linc*
BLASTON (St Giles)   *see* Six Saints circa Holt *Leic*
BLATCHINGTON, EAST (St John the Evangelist) (St Peter)
and Bishopstone *Chich 18*   P *Bp and Bp Lon (alt)*
R   B R COOK,   NSM   R J WOODHAMS
BLATCHINGTON, WEST (St Peter) *Chich 4*   P *Bp*
R   R T A FARROW
BLAXHALL (St Peter)   *see* Alde River *St E*
BLAYDON (St Cuthbert) and Swalwell *Dur 13*   P *Bp*
R   A THORP,   C   M P TARLING,   NSM   H M THORP
BLEADON (St Peter and St Paul) *B & W 11*   P *Guild of All So*
R   *vacant* (01934) 812297
BLEAN (St Cosmus and St Damian) *Cant 3*   P *Master of*
Eastbridge Hosp   P-in-c   S C E LAIRD
BLEASBY (St Mary)   *see* Thurgarton w Hoveringham and
Bleasby etc *S'well*
BLEASDALE (St Eadmor)   *see* Fellside Team *Blackb*
BLEATARN (Chapel of Ease)   *see* Brough w Stainmore,
Musgrave and Warcop *Carl*
BLEDINGTON (St Leonard)   *see* Broadwell, Evenlode,
Oddington, Adlestrop etc *Glouc*
BLEDLOW (Holy Trinity)   *see* Risborough *Ox*
BLEDLOW RIDGE (St Paul)   *see* W Wycombe w Bledlow
Ridge, Bradenham and Radnage *Ox*
BLENDON (St James the Great) *Roch 17*   P *The Crown*
V   A F WEIGHTMAN
BLENDWORTH (Holy Trinity) w Chalton w Idsworth *Portsm 5*
P *Bp*   P-in-c   R A DONALD,   NSM   B R SMITH
BLENHEIM *Ox 9*   P *Patr Bd*   TR   R J HUMPHREYS,
TV   A PARKINSON,   C   S C HENSON,   NSM   C A W SANDERS,
B R WOOD
BLETCHINGDON (St Giles)   *see* Akeman *Ox*
BLETCHINGLEY (St Mary) and Nutfield *S'wark 25*   P *Em*
Coll Cam and Jes Coll Ox (jt)   R   P MOSELING,
C   C G THOMSON
BLETCHLEY (St Mary) (St John's District Church) *Ox 25*
P *DBP*   P-in-c   M J ARCHER,   C   T M BUSTIN, C BUTT
BLETCHLEY, NORTH (Whaddon Way Church) Conventional
District *Ox 25 vacant* (01908) 75370
BLETSOE (St Mary)   *see* Riseley w Bletsoe *St Alb*
BLEWBURY (St Michael and All Angels)   *see* The Churn *Ox*
BLICKLING (St Andrew)   *see* Lt Barningham, Blickling,
Edgefield etc *Nor*
BLIDWORTH (St Mary of the Purification) w Rainworth
S'well 2   P *DBP and Ld Chan (alt)*   P-in-c   H ROBINSON,
NSM   B A ALLSOP
BLIDWORTH, NEW (St Andrew)   *see* Blidworth w Rainworth
S'well
BLINDLEY HEATH (St John the Evangelist)   *see* Godstone
and Blindley Heath *S'wark*
BLISLAND (St Protus and St Hyacinth) w St Breward *Truro 10*
P *SMF and D&C (alt)*   P-in-c   S L BRYAN
BLISWORTH (St John the Baptist) and Stoke Bruerne w Grafton
Regis and Alderton *Pet 5*   P *BNC Ox and MMCET (2 turns),*
Ld Chan (1 turn)   R   R MELLOR
BLITHFIELD (St Leonard)   *see* Abbots Bromley w Blithfield
Lich
BLO' NORTON (St Andrew)   *see* Guiltcross *Nor*
BLOCKLEY (St Peter and St Paul) w Aston Magna and Bourton
on the Hill *Glouc 8*   P *Lord Dulverton and DBP (jt)*
P-in-c   G L HUMPHRIES
BLOFIELD (St Andrew) w Hemblington *Nor 4*   P *G&C Coll*
Cam   R   P CUBITT
BLOOMSBURY (St George) w Woburn Square (Christ Church)
Lon 17   P *Ld Chan*   R   P A BUTLER,   C   R I T JARRETT
BLORE RAY (St Bartholomew)   *see* Calton, Cauldon, Grindon,
Waterfall etc *Lich*
BLOXHAM (Our Lady of Bloxham) w Milcombe and South
Newington *Ox 5*   P *Ex Coll Ox and Eton Coll (jt)*
P-in-c   S L TILLETT
BLOXHOLME (St Mary)   *see* Digby Gp *Linc*

BLOXWICH (All Saints) (Holy Ascension) *Lich 25*   P *Patr Bd*
TR   R S WILLIAMS,   TV   K A LOWTHER
BLOXWORTH (St Andrew)   *see* Red Post *Sarum*
BLUBBERHOUSES (St Andrew)   *see* Washburn and Mid-
Wharfe *Bradf*
BLUCHER (St Cuthbert)   *see* Newburn *Newc*
BLUE BELL HILL (St Alban)   *see* S Chatham H Trin *Roch*
BLUNDELLSANDS (St Michael) *Liv 5*   P *Trustees*
P-in-c   M C FREEMAN
BLUNDELLSANDS (St Nicholas) *Liv 5*   P *Trustees*
V   C M M THORNBOROUGH
BLUNDESTON (St Mary)   *see* Somerleyton, Ashby, Fritton,
Herringfleet etc *Nor*
BLUNHAM (St Edmund King and Martyr and St James)
see Riversmeet *St Alb*
BLUNSDON (St Andrew)   *see* N Swindon St Andr *Bris*
BLUNTISHAM (St Mary) cum Earith w Colne and Woodhurst
Ely 12   P *Ch Ch Ox*   P-in-c   S M ANTHONY
BLURTON (St Bartholomew) (St Alban) *Lich 13*   P *Bp*
V   P J MOCKFORD,   C   B A A LAWAL,   OLM   H T ADAMS,
L J WALKER
BLYBOROUGH (St Alkmund)   *see* Glentworth Gp *Linc*
BLYFORD (All Saints)   *see* Blyth Valley *St E*
BLYMHILL (St Mary) w Weston-under-Lizard *Lich 2*
P *W H C Montgomery Esq, Sir Brooke Boothby Bt, and*
Viscount Boyne (jt)   P-in-c   G J THOMPSON,   NSM   L BEECH
BLYTH (St Cuthbert) *Newc 1*   P *Bp*   V   R D TAYLOR
BLYTH (St Mary) *Newc 1*   P *Bp*   V   A J ELDER
BLYTH (St Mary and St Martin) and Scrooby w Ranskill *S'well 1*
P *Bp and Trin Coll Cam (jt)*   V   R A SPRAY
BLYTH VALLEY Team Ministry, The *St E 15*   P *Patr Bd*
TR   E L RENNARD,   TV   E M CANNON,   OLM   A C WRIGHT
BLYTHBURGH (Holy Trinity)   *see* Sole Bay *St E*
BLYTON (St Martin)   *see* Corringham and Blyton Gp *Linc*
BOARHUNT (St Nicholas)   *see* Southwick w Boarhunt *Portsm*
BOARSTALL (St James)   *see* Bernwode *Ox*
BOBBING (St Bartholomew)   *see* Sittingbourne H Trin w
Bobbing *Cant*
BOBBINGTON (Holy Cross)   *see* Smestow Vale *Lich*
BOBBINGWORTH (St Germain)   *see* Fyfield, Moreton w
Bobbingworth etc *Chelmsf*
BOCKING (St Mary) *Chelmsf 15*   P *Abp Cant*   R   P A NEED,
C   T D CHAPMAN
BOCKING (St Peter) *Chelmsf 15*   P *Abp Cant*   V   T C DIAPER,
C   J S RIDGE
BOCKLETON (St Michael)   *see* Leominster *Heref*
BOCONNOC (not known)   *see* Lostwithiel, St Winnow w
St Nectan's Chpl etc *Truro*
BODDINGTON (St John the Baptist)   *see* Byfield w Boddington
and Aston le Walls *Pet*
BODDINGTON (St Mary Magdalene)   *see* Twigworth, Down
Hatherley, Norton, The Leigh etc *Glouc*
BODENHAM (St Michael and All Angels), Felton and Preston
Wynne *Heref 4*   P *Bp*   P-in-c   H M SHORT
BODHAM (All Saints)   *see* Weybourne Gp *Nor*
BODIAM (St Giles) *Chich 20*   P *All So Coll Ox*
V   G L WINCHESTER
BODICOTE (St John the Baptist) *Ox 5*   P *New Coll Ox*
V   B L M PHILLIPS,   OLM   B C GARDNER
BODINNICK (St John)   *see* Lanteglos by Fowey *Truro*
BODLE STREET GREEN (St John the Evangelist)
see Warbleton and Bodle Street Green *Chich*
BODMIN (St Petroc) (St Lawrence w St Leonard) w Lanhydrock
and Lanivet *Truro 10*   P *DBP*   TR   G G C MINORS,
TV   A B SHAW,   NSM   C F CLEMOW
BODNEY (St Mary)   *see* Hilborough w Bodney *Nor*
BOGNOR (St Wilfrid) *Chich 1*   P *Abp*   V   A J WADSWORTH
BOLAM (St Andrew)   *see* Heighington *Dur*
BOLAM (St Andrew) w Whalton and Hartburn w Meldon
Newc 11   P *Ld Chan (2 turns), J I K Walker Esq (1 turn), and*
D&C Dur (1 turn)   R   M A G BRYCE,   OLM   F J SAMPLE
BOLAS MAGNA (St John the Baptist)   *see* Tibberton w Bolas
Magna and Waters Upton *Lich*
BOLDMERE (St Michael) *Birm 12*   P *Birm Dioc Trustees*
V   P D RATTIGAN,   C   M E BRIGHTON
BOLDON (St Nicholas) *Dur 15*   P *Bp*   R   *vacant* 0191-536 7370
BOLDON, EAST (St George) *Dur 15*   P *Bp*   P-in-c   J S BAIN
NSM   M R DEVINE
BOLDRE (St John the Baptist) w South Baddesley *Win 11*   P *Bp*
and Lord Teynham (jt)   P-in-c   N R SMART
BOLDRE, EAST (St Paul)   *see* Beaulieu and Exbury and E
Boldre *Win*
BOLDRON (Mission Room)   *see* Startforth and Bowes and
Rokeby w Brignall *Ripon*
BOLE (St Martin)   *see* N Wheatley, W Burton, Bole, Saundby,
Sturton etc *S'well*

BOLINGBROKE (St Peter and St Paul)   *see* Marden Hill Gp *Linc*

BOLINGBROKE, NEW (St Peter)   *see* Sibsey w Frithville *Linc*

BOLLINGHAM (St Silas)   *see* Eardisley w Bollingham, Willersley, Brilley etc *Heref*

BOLLINGTON (Holy Trinity)   *see* Rostherne w Bollington *Ches*

BOLLINGTON (St Oswald) (Holy Trinity) *Ches 13*   **P** *V Prestbury*   **V** V W HYDON

BOLNEY (St Mary Magdalene) *Chich 6*   **P** *K Coll Lon*   **P-in-c** K D LITTLEJOHN

BOLNHURST (St Dunstan)   *see* Keysoe w Bolnhurst and Lt Staughton *St Alb*

BOLSOVER (St Mary and St Laurence) *Derby 3*   **P** *Bp*   **V** W T HICKS

BOLSTERSTONE (St Mary) *Sheff 3*   **P** *R B Rimington-Wilson Esq*   **V** K J BARNARD

BOLTBY (Holy Trinity)   *see* Felixkirk w Boltby *York*

BOLTON (All Saints)   *see* Binsey *Carl*

BOLTON (All Saints) *Carl 1*   **P** *V Morland w Thrimby etc*   **P-in-c** S D RUDKIN

BOLTON Breightmet (St James)   *see* Leverhulme *Man*

BOLTON Chapel (unknown)   *see* Whittingham and Edlingham w Bolton Chapel *Newc*

BOLTON (St Chad)   *see* Tonge Fold *Man*

BOLTON (St James w St Chrysostom) *Bradf 3*   **P** *Bp*   **NSM** H LEALMAN

BOLTON (St Matthew w St Barnabas)   *see* Halliwell *Man*

BOLTON (St Paul)   *see* Halliwell *Man*

BOLTON (St Thomas the Apostle)   *as above*

BOLTON Top o' th' Moss (St John the Evangelist)   *see* Leverhulme *Man*

BOLTON ABBEY (St Mary and St Cuthbert) *Bradf 7*   **P** *Duke of Devonshire*   **R** G MOFFAT,   **NSM** J D BENNETT

BOLTON BY BOWLAND (St Peter and St Paul) w Grindleton *Bradf 5*   **P** *Bp and V Hurst Green and Mitton (jt)*   **R** D W MEWIS,   **Hon C** J R BROCKLEHURST

BOLTON LE MOORS (St Bede) *Man 11*   **P** *Bp*   **P-in-c** V ASHWORTH,   **NSM** T ASHWORTH

BOLTON LE MOORS (St Paul) (Emmanuel) *Man 9*   **P** *Patr Bd*   **P-in-c** F ADMAN

BOLTON LE MOORS (St Peter) *Man 9*   **P** *Bp*   **P-in-c** M THOMPSON,   **NSM** K G C NEWPORT

BOLTON LE MOORS (St Philip) *Man 9*   **P** *Bp and Hulme Trustees (alt)*   **P-in-c** M THOMPSON,   **NSM** R E IDDON

BOLTON LE MOORS (St Simon and St Jude) *Man 9*   **P** *Trustees*   **P-in-c** G KENNEDY

BOLTON-LE-SANDS (Holy Trinity) *Blackb 14*   **P** *Bp*   **P-in-c** G H CAPON,   **NSM** B C JONES, L MACLUSKIE

BOLTON ON SWALE (St Mary)   *see* Easby w Skeeby and Brompton on Swale etc *Ripon*

BOLTON PERCY (All Saints) *York 1*   **P** *Abp*   **P-in-c** G R MUMFORD

BOLTON-UPON-DEARNE (St Andrew the Apostle) *Sheff 12*   **P** *Meynall Ch Trust*   **V** D G STAFFORD

BOLTONS, THE   *see* W Brompton St Mary w St Peter and St Jude *Lon*

BOLVENTOR (Holy Trinity)   *see* Altarnon w Bolventor, Laneast and St Clether *Truro*

BOMERE HEATH (Mission Room)   *see* Leaton and Albrighton w Battlefield *Lich*

BONBY (St Andrew) *Linc 6*   **P** *DBP*   **V** *vacant*

BONCHURCH (St Boniface) (St Boniface Old Church) *Portsm 7*   **P** *Ch Patr Trust*   **R** G E MORRIS

BONDLEIGH (St James the Apostle)   *see* N Tawton, Bondleigh, Sampford Courtenay etc *Ex*

BONEY HAY   *see* Chase Terrace *Lich*

BONINGALE (St Chad)   *see* Albrighton, Boningale and Donington *Lich*

BONNINGTON (St Rumwold)   *see* Aldington w Bonnington and Bilsington etc *Cant*

BONSALL (St James the Apostle)   *see* Wirksworth *Derby*

BOOKER (St Birinus' Mission Church)   *see* High Wycombe *Ox*

BOOKHAM, GREAT (St Nicolas) *Guildf 10*   **P** *Bp*   **R** A D JENKINS,   **C** C D BESSANT

BOOKHAM, LITTLE (not known)   *see* Effingham w Lt Bookham *Guildf*

BOONGATE (St Mary)   *see* Pet St Mary Boongate *Pet*

BOOSBECK (St Aidan) and Lingdale *York 16*   **P** *Abp*   **V** *vacant* (01287) 651728

BOOTHBY GRAFFOE (St Andrew)   *see* Graffoe Gp *Linc*

BOOTHBY PAGNELL (St Andrew)   *see* N Beltisloe Gp *Linc*

BOOTHSTOWN (St Andrew's Church Institute)   *see* Worsley *Man*

BOOTLE (Christ Church) *Liv 1*   **P** *Bp*   **V** T RICH,   **NSM** J WILLIAMS

BOOTLE (St Andrew) (St Leonard) (St Mary w St Paul) (St Matthew) (St Thomas) *Liv 1*   **P** *Patr Bd*   **TR** R J DRIVER,   **TV** J C M BISSEX, I A WHITAKER,   **Hon C** R J LEE

BOOTLE (St Michael and All Angels), Corney, Whicham and Whitbeck *Carl 5*   **P** *Earl of Lonsdale*   **P-in-c** G T WILSON

BORASTON (not known)   *see* Burford I *Heref*

BORDEN (St Peter and St Paul) *Cant 15*   **P** *SMF*   **V** J H G LEWIS

BORDER Group of Parishes   *see* Llanyblodwel, Llanymynech, Morton and Trefonen *Lich*

BORDERLINK PARISHES   *see* Cusop w Blakemere, Bredwardine w Brobury etc *Heref*

BORDESLEY (St Alban and St Patrick)   *see* Highgate *Birm*

BORDESLEY (St Benedict) *Birm 13*   **P** *Keble Coll Ox*   **V** N A C VON MALAISÉ,   **NSM** P L CADOGAN

BORDESLEY GREEN (St Paul)   *see* Ward End w Bordesley Green *Birm*

BORDON (St Mark) *Guildf 3*   **P** *Bp*   **V** D J SCOTT-BROMLEY,   **NSM** W N MALLAS

BOREHAM (St Andrew) *Chelmsf 9*   **P** *Bp*   **P-in-c** L P BATSON

BOREHAM (St John the Evangelist)   *see* Bishopstrow and Boreham *Sarum*

BOREHAMWOOD (All Saints)   *see* Elstree and Borehamwood *St Alb*

BOREHAMWOOD (Holy Cross)   *as above*

BOREHAMWOOD (St Michael and All Angels)   *as above*

BORLEY (not known)   *see* N Hinckford *Chelmsf*

BOROUGH GREEN (Good Shepherd) *Roch 10*   **P** *Bp*   **V** A J POWELL

BOROUGHBRIDGE (St James)   *see* Aldborough w Boroughbridge and Roecliffe *Ripon*

BORROWASH (St Stephen's Chapel)   *see* Ockbrook *Derby*

BORROWDALE (St Andrew)   *see* Upper Derwent *Carl*

BORSTAL (St Matthew) *Roch 5*   **P** *V Rochester St Marg*   **P-in-c** M T PRIOR

BORWICK (St Mary)   *see* Warton St Oswald w Yealand Conyers *Blackb*

BOSBURY (Holy Trinity)   *see* Ledbury *Heref*

BOSCASTLE w Davidstow *Truro 10*   **P** *Duchy of Cornwall (1 turn), DBP (2 turns)*   **P-in-c** R S THEWSEY,   **NSM** M PARSONS

BOSCOMBE (St Andrew)   *see* Bourne Valley *Sarum*

BOSCOMBE (St Andrew) *Win 8*   **P** *Bp*   **V** *vacant* (01202) 394575

BOSCOMBE (St John the Evangelist) *Win 8*   **P** *Peache Trustees*   **V** R P KHAKHRIA,   **C** P J TAYLOR

BOSCOPPA *Truro 1*   **P** *Prime Min*   **P-in-c** S D MICHAEL

BOSHAM (Holy Trinity) *Chich 3*   **P** *Bp*   **V** T J INMAN

BOSLEY (St Mary the Virgin) and North Rode (St Michael) w Wincle (St Michael) and Wildboarclough (St Saviour) *Ches 13*   **P** *Bp, V Prestbury, and Earl of Derby (jt)*   **V** V BREED

BOSSALL (St Botolph)   *see* Sand Hutton *York*

BOSSINGTON (St James)   *see* Broughton, Bossington, Houghton and Mottisfont *Win*

BOSTALL HEATH (St Andrew) *Roch 15*   **P** *DBP*   **V** *vacant* (020) 8303 9332 *or* 8301 6479

BOSTON (Holy Trinity)   *see* Skirbeck H Trin *Linc*

BOSTON (St Botolph) (St Christopher) *Linc 20*   **P** *Bp*   **TR** R L WHITEHEAD,   **TV** S A C FOUNTAIN,   **C** A P WICKENS

BOSTON (St Nicholas)   *see* Skirbeck St Nic *Linc*

BOSTON (St Thomas)   *see* Boston *Linc*

BOSTON SPA (St Mary) *York 1*   **P** *Ch Ch Ox*   **V** P E BRISTOW,   **C** P D WATSON,   **NSM** S H MENZIES

BOSWORTH (St Peter) and Sheepy Group *Leic 10*   **P** *Patr Bd (2 turns), Ld Chan (1 turn)*   **TR** J F PLANT,   **TV** A S G PIKE,   **NSM** A C HOLDSTOCK, G R JACKSON, A C THORP

BOTCHERBY (St Andrew)   *see* Carl St Aid and Ch Ch *Carl*

BOTESDALE (St Botolph)   *see* Redgrave cum Botesdale w Rickinghall *St E*

BOTHAL (St Andrew) and Pegswood w Longhirst *Newc 11*   **P** *Bp*   **R** J C PARK

BOTHAMSALL (Our Lady and St Peter)   *see* Elkesley w Bothamsall *S'well*

BOTHENHAMPTON (Holy Trinity)   *see* Bridport *Sarum*

BOTLEY (All Saints) *Portsm 1*   **P** *Bp*   **R** P J F GOODEY,   **NSM** R E SCHOFIELD

BOTLEY (St Peter and St Paul)   *see* N Hinksey and Wytham *Ox*

BOTLEYS AND LYNE (Holy Trinity)   *see* Chertsey, Lyne and Longcross *Guildf*

BOTOLPHS (St Botolph)   *see* Beeding and Bramber w Botolphs *Chich*

BOTTESFORD (St Mary the Virgin)   *see* Vale of Belvoir Par *Leic*

BOTTESFORD (St Peter) w Ashby *Linc 4*   **P** *Patr Bd*   **TR** P J LILEY,   **TV** G M LINES

BOTTISHAM (Holy Trinity)   *see* Anglesey Gp *Ely*
BOTUS FLEMING (St Mary)   *see* Landrake w St Erney and Botus Fleming *Truro*
BOUGHTON (All Saints) *Ely 9*   **P** *Bp*   **R** vacant
BOUGHTON (St John the Baptist)   *see* Pitsford w Boughton *Pet*
BOUGHTON (St Matthew)   *see* Ollerton w Boughton *S'well*
BOUGHTON ALUPH (All Saints)   *see* Wye w Brook and Hastingleigh etc *Cant*
BOUGHTON ALUPH (St Christopher)   *as above*
BOUGHTON MALHERBE (St Nicholas)   *see* Len Valley *Cant*
BOUGHTON MONCHELSEA (St Augustine) (St Peter) *Cant 14*   **P** *Abp*   **V** R G DAVIS,   **OLM** Y D SALMON
BOUGHTON UNDER BLEAN (St Barnabas) (St Peter and St Paul) w Dunkirk and Hernhill *Cant 6*   **P** *Abp*
P-in-c J BURROWS
BOULGE (St Michael) w Burgh, Grundisburgh and Hasketon *St E 7*   **P** *Bp and DBP* (jt)   **P-in-c** H C SANDERS
BOULMER (St Andrew)   *see* Longhoughton w Howick *Newc*
BOULTHAM (Holy Cross) (St Helen) *Linc 15*   **P** *DBP*
R D J OSBOURNE,   **C** C M THACKER
BOULTON (St Mary the Virgin) *Derby 15*   **P** *Bp*
V T S WRIGHT
BOUNDSTONE (Mission Church)   *see* Wrecclesham *Guildf*
BOURN (St Helena and St Mary)   *see* Papworth *Ely*
BOURNE (St Peter and St Paul) *Linc 13*   **P** *DBP*
V C J ATKINSON
BOURNE, The (St Thomas) and Tilford *Guildf 3*   **P** *Bp and Adn Surrey* (alt)   **V** J T L STILL,   **Hon C** J W BELL,
NSM M E JACKSON,   **OLM** E M POWELL
BOURNE, LOWER (St Martin)   *see* The Bourne and Tilford *Guildf*
BOURNE END (St John)   *see* Sunnyside w Bourne End *St Alb*
BOURNE END (St Mark)   *see* Hedsor and Bourne End *Ox*
BOURNE STREET (St Mary)   *see* Pimlico St Mary Bourne Street *Lon*
BOURNE VALLEY *Sarum 10*   **P** *Patr Bd*   **TR** V S PERRETT,
TV P A OSTLI-EAST,   **C** P F D TAYLOR, G A HUNT,
NSM T G MANN
BOURNEMOUTH (All Saints)   *see* Pokesdown All SS *Win*
BOURNEMOUTH (Christ Church)   *see* Westbourne Ch Ch Chpl *Win*
BOURNEMOUTH (Holy Epiphany) *Win 8*   **P** *Bp*
P-in-c R D PETERS,   **NSM** D S THOMPSON
BOURNEMOUTH (St Alban) *Win 8*   **P** *Bp*   **P-in-c** R L NASH
BOURNEMOUTH (St Ambrose) *Win 8*   **P** *Bp*   **V** vacant (01202) 764957
BOURNEMOUTH (St Andrew) Bennett Road *Win 8*
P *Trustees*   **V** G M ROBERTS,   **Hon C** J W DAVIES
BOURNEMOUTH (St Barnabas) Queen's Park
see Holdenhurst and Iford *Win*
BOURNEMOUTH (St Christopher)   *see* Southbourne St Chris *Win*
BOURNEMOUTH (St Clement) *Win 8*   **P** *DBP*
P-in-c K P ARKELL,   **C** J W E RODLEY
BOURNEMOUTH (St Francis) *Win 8*   **P** *CR*   **V** P G BERRETT
BOURNEMOUTH (St James)   *see* Pokesdown St Jas *Win*
BOURNEMOUTH (St John) (St Michael and All Angels) *Win 8*
P *Bp and S R Willcox Esq* (jt)   **P-in-c** R D BALDOCK
BOURNEMOUTH (St John the Evangelist)   *see* Boscombe St Jo *Win*
BOURNEMOUTH (St Luke) *Win 8*   **P** *Bp*   **V** S HOLMES
BOURNEMOUTH Town Centre (St Augustin) (St Stephen) w St Swithun and Holy Trinity *Win 8*   **P** *Patr Bd*
TR I A TERRY,   **TV** R C N HARGER,   **C** S W MILLER,
Hon C B G APPS
BOURNVILLE (St Andrew)   *see* Weston-super-Mare St Andr Bournville *B & W*
BOURNVILLE (St Francis) *Birm 5*   **P** *Bp*   **V** P G BABINGTON,
NSM J M ADAMS, E L BREUILLY
BOURTON (Holy Trinity)   *see* Wenlock *Heref*
BOURTON (St George)   *see* Upper Stour *Sarum*
BOURTON (St James)   *see* Shrivenham and Ashbury *Ox*
BOURTON (St Peter) w Frankton and Stretton on Dunsmore w Princethorpe *Cov 6*   **P** *Bp (2 turns), Simeon's Trustees (1 turn), and Mrs J H Shaw-Fox (1 turn)*   **P-in-c** B C CLUTTON
BOURTON, GREAT (All Saints)   *see* Shires' Edge *Ox*
BOURTON ON THE HILL (St Lawrence)   *see* Blockley w Aston Magna and Bourton on the Hill *Glouc*
BOURTON-ON-THE-WATER (St Lawrence) w Clapton and The Rissingtons *Glouc 12*   **P** *Wadh Coll Ox, DBP and C T R Wingfield Esq, and Ld Chan (by turn)*
R E N P TUFNELL,   **NSM** J Y CARMAN, S M COX
BOVEY, NORTH (St John the Baptist)   *see* Moretonhampstead, Manaton, N Bovey and Lustleigh *Ex*
BOVEY TRACEY (St John the Evangelist) w Heathfield *Ex 9*
P *Guild of All So*   **V** vacant (01626) 833451

BOVEY TRACEY (St Peter and St Paul and St Thomas of Canterbury) w Hennock *Ex 9*   **P** *Prime Min (2 turns), MMCET (1 turn)*   **V** W G HAMILTON,   **C** D J CARRINGTON,
Hon C J E SPENCER, R H TOTTERDELL
BOVINGDON (St Lawrence) *St Alb 5*   **P** *Ch Soc Trust*
V T J MARSHALL
BOW (All Hallows)   *see* Bromley by Bow All Hallows *Lon*
BOW (St Bartholomew) w Broad Nymet *Ex 2*   **P** *DBP*
R vacant (01363) 82566
BOW (St Mary) and Holy Trinity w Bromley St Leonard *Lon 7*
P *Bp and Grocers' Co (jt)*   **R** J M PEET,   **NSM** D F WAXHAM
BOW BRICKHILL (All Saints)   *see* Brickhills and Stoke Hammond *Ox*
BOW COMMON (St Paul) *Lon 7*   **P** *Bp*   **V** D G ROSS
BOWBROOK NORTH: Feckenham and Hanbury and Stock and Bradley *Worc 8*   **P** *Bp and D&C (jt)*   **P-in-c** J H GREEN
BOWBROOK SOUTH: Crowle w Bredicot and Hadzor w Oddingley and Tibberton and Himbleton and Huddington *Worc 8*   **P** *Bp, D&C, R J G Berkeley Esq, and J F Bennett Esq (jt)*   **P-in-c** J H GREEN
BOWBURN (Christ the King)   *see* Cassop cum Quarrington *Dur*
BOWDEN, GREAT (St Peter and St Paul)   *see* Market Harborough and The Transfiguration etc *Leic*
BOWDEN, LITTLE (St Hugh)   *as above*
BOWDEN, LITTLE (St Nicholas)   *as above*
BOWDEN HILL (St Anne)   *see* Gtr Corsham and Lacock *Bris*
BOWDON (St Luke) (St Mary the Virgin) *Ches 10*   **P** *Bp*
V R M H PREECE,   **NSM** S G TALBOT, G C JAQUISS
BOWERCHALKE (Holy Trinity)   *see* Chalke Valley *Sarum*
BOWERS GIFFORD (St John) (St Margaret) w North Benfleet *Chelmsf 6*   **P** *Em Coll Cam and Brig R H C Bryhers CBE (alt)*
P-in-c B C R JOHNSON
BOWES (St Giles)   *see* Startforth and Bowes and Rokeby w Brignall *Ripon*
BOWES PARK (St Michael-at-Bowes)   *see* Wood Green St Mich w Bounds Green St Gabr etc *Lon*
BOWLEE (St Thomas)   *see* Rhodes *Man*
BOWLING (St John) *Bradf 2*   **P** *V Bradford*   **V** H K ASTIN,
NSM C BARNES
BOWLING (St Stephen) *Bradf 2*   **P** *CPAS*
P-in-c J W HINTON,   **C** A S TREASURE
BOWNESS-ON-SOLWAY (St Michael), Kirkbride and Newton Arlosh *Carl 3*   **P** *Earl of Lonsdale (2 turns), V Holme Cultram (1 turn)*   **R** R P BLACKETT
BOWTHORPE (St Michael) *Nor 3*   **P** *Bp and CPAS (jt)*
P-in-c S C STOKES,   **C** T A P WEATHERSTONE
BOX (St Barnabas)   *see* Minchinhampton *Glouc*
BOX (St Thomas à Becket) w Hazlebury and Ditteridge *Bris 4*
P *Bp*   **P-in-c** J M ANDERSON-MACKENZIE,   **NSM** J AYERS
BOX HILL (St Andrew)   *see* Headley w Box Hill *Guildf*
BOX RIVER   *see* Boxford, Edwardstone, Groton etc *St E*
BOXFORD (St Andrew)   *see* Welford w Wickham and Gt Shefford, Boxford etc *Ox*
BOXFORD (St Mary), Edwardstone, Groton, Little Waldingfield and Newton *St E 12*   **P** *DBP and The Hon Thomas Lindsay (1 turn), Ld Chan (2 turns), Peterho Cam (1 turn)*
R D W MATTHEWS
BOXGROVE (St Mary and St Blaise) *Chich 3*   **P** *Duke of Richmond and Gordon*   **P-in-c** I M FORRESTER
BOXLEY (St Mary the Virgin and All Saints) w Detling *Cant 14*
P *Abp*   **P-in-c** P S HOLLINS,   **NSM** E A ATTAWAY
BOXMOOR (St John the Evangelist) *St Alb 3*   **P** *Bp*
V J S REVELEY,   **C** E M HOOD,   **NSM** G A J ADAM, R C GOATLY
BOXTED (Holy Trinity)   *see* Glemsford, Hartest w Boxted, Somerton etc *St E*
BOXTED (St Peter)   *see* Langham w Boxted *Chelmsf*
BOXWELL (St Mary the Virgin), Leighterton, Didmarton, Oldbury-on-the-Hill, Sopworth, Badminton w Little Badminton, Acton Turville, Hawkesbury, Westonbirt and Lasborough *Glouc 6*   **P** *Duke of Beaufort, J A Hutley Esq, and Westonbirt Sch (jt)*   **R** N C J MULHOLLAND,
NSM H K NICHOLS, E M NICHOLS
BOXWORTH (St Peter)   *see* Papworth *Ely*
BOYATT WOOD (St Peter) *Win 10*   **P** *Bp*   **P-in-c** B ROSTILL,
NSM V A CORCORAN
BOYLESTONE (St John the Baptist), Church Broughton, Dalbury, Longford, Long Lane, Radbourne, Sutton on the Hill and Trusley *Derby 14*   **P** *Patr Bd*   **R** P M BISHOP,
NSM J M LEGH
BOYNE HILL (All Saints) *Ox 13*   **P** *Bp*   **V** J M HARRIS
BOYNTON (St Andrew)   *see* Rudston w Boynton, Carnaby and Kilham *York*
BOYTHORPE (St Francis)   *see* Chesterfield St Aug *Derby*
BOYTON (Holy Name), North Tamerton, Werrington w St Giles-in-the-Heath and Virginstow *Truro 9*   **P** *Duke of Cornwall,*

M M CET, Ld Chan, and R Williams Esq (by turn)
R K WAKEFIELD
BOYTON (St Andrew)   *see* Wilford Peninsula *St E*
BOYTON (St Mary the Virgin)   *see* Upper Wylye Valley *Sarum*
BOZEAT (St Mary)   *see* Wollaston w Strixton and Bozeat etc *Pet*
BRABOURNE (St Mary the Blessed Virgin)   *see* Smeeth w
Monks Horton and Stowting and Brabourne *Cant*
BRACEBOROUGH (St Margaret)   *see* Uffington Gp *Linc*
BRACEBRIDGE (All Saints) *Linc 15*   **P** *Mrs B M Ellison-*
Lendrum   **P-in-c** H C MIDDLETON
BRACEBRIDGE HEATH (St John the Evangelist) *Linc 15*
P *Bp*   **V** H C MIDDLETON
BRACEBY (St Margaret)   *see* N Beltisloe Gp *Linc*
BRACEWELL (St Michael)   *see* Barnoldswick w Bracewell
Bradf
BRACKENFIELD (Holy Trinity)   *see* Ashover and
Brackenfield w Wessington *Derby*
BRACKLEY (St Peter w St James) *Pet 1*   **P** *Bp*   **V** N J GANDY,
C A R SHORTER,   **NSM** G D MOORE
BRACKNELL (Holy Trinity) *Ox 11*   **P** *Bp*   **TV** A R FREARSON,
P-in-c N A PARISH,   **C** J E MANLEY,   **Hon C** M G CLARKE
BRACON ASH (St Nicholas)   *see* Mulbarton w Bracon Ash,
Hethel and Flordon *Nor*
BRADBOURNE (All Saints)   *see* Wirksworth *Derby*
BRADDAN (St Brendan) *S & M 2*   **P** *Bp*   **V** P S FREAR
BRADDEN (St Michael)   *see* Towcester w Caldecote and Easton
Neston etc *Pet*
BRADELEY (St Mary and All Saints), Church Eaton,
Derrington and Haughton *Lich 10*   **P** *Bp and*
Mrs M N Nutt (jt)   **R** P G ASHBY
BRADENHAM (St Botolph)   *see* W Wycombe w Bledlow
Ridge, Bradenham and Radnage *Ox*
BRADENHAM, WEST (St Andrew)   *see* Shipdham w E and W
Bradenham *Nor*
BRADENSTOKE (St Mary)   *see* Lyneham w Bradenstoke
Sarum
BRADFIELD (St Andrew) and Stanford Dingley *Ox 12*
P *Ch Soc Trust*   **NSM** R C OBIN, L E BLISS,   **OLM** R S GREEN
BRADFIELD (St Giles)   *see* Trunch *Nor*
BRADFIELD (St Lawrence)   *see* Mistley w Manningtree and
Bradfield *Chelmsf*
BRADFIELD (St Nicholas) *Sheff 3*   **P** *V Ecclesfield*
R A T ISAACSON
BRADFIELD COMBUST (All Saints)   *see* St Edm Way *St E*
BRADFIELD ST CLARE (St Clare), Bradfield St George w
Little Whelnetham, Cockfield, Felsham and Gedding *St E 10*
P *St Jo Coll Cam (1 turn), Bp and Lt-Col J G Aldous (1 turn)*
R S G HILL
BRADFIELD ST GEORGE (St George)   *see* Bradfield St Clare,
Bradfield St George etc *St E*
BRADFORD (All Saints)   *see* Black Torrington, Bradford w
Cookbury etc *Ex*
BRADFORD (St Augustine) Undercliffe *Bradf 3*   **P** *V Bradf*
P-in-c D BARTON,   **C** D J MUGHAL,   **NSM** A CHALLENGER
BRADFORD (St Clement) *Bradf 3*   **P** *Bp (2 turns) and Trustees*
(1 turn)   **P-in-c** D BARTON,   **C** T A MILNE, D J MUGHAL,
NSM A CHALLENGER
BRADFORD (St Martin)   *see* Heaton St Martin *Bradf*
BRADFORD (St Oswald)   *see* Lt Horton *Bradf*
BRADFORD (St Saviour)   *see* Fairweather Green *Bradf*
BRADFORD (St Stephen)   *see* Bowling St Steph *Bradf*
BRADFORD (St Wilfrid) (St Columba w St Andrew) *Bradf 2*
P *Bp*   **V** P M BILTON,   **NSM** G A BRIGHOUSE
BRADFORD, SOUTH   *see* Oakenshaw, Wyke and Low Moor
Bradf
BRADFORD, WEST (St Catherine)   *see* Waddington *Bradf*
BRADFORD ABBAS (St Mary the Virgin) and Thornford w
Beer Hackett *Sarum 3*   **P** *J K Wingfield Digby Esq and Win*
Coll (alt)   **R** J A EVANS
BRADFORD-ON-AVON (Christ Church) *Sarum 14*   **P** *V Bradf*
H Trin   **P-in-c** R M LOWRIE,   **NSM** B F CHAPMAN
BRADFORD-ON-AVON (Holy Trinity) *Sarum 14*   **P** *D&C*
V vacant (01225) 864444
BRADFORD ON TONE (St Giles)   *see* Deane Vale *B & W*
BRADFORD PEVERELL (Church of the Assumption),
Stratton, Frampton and Sydling St Nicholas *Sarum 1*   **P** *Win*
Coll and Bp (alt)   **R** vacant (01300) 320429
BRADGATE TEAM, The - Ratby cum Groby w Newton Linford
Leic 9   **P** *Patr Bd*   **TV** L D CORKE,   **NSM** A M STRATTON
BRADING (St Mary the Virgin) w Yaverland *Portsm 7*
P *Hon Mrs I S T Monck and Trin Coll Cam (jt)*
R D J B ABINGTON
BRADLEY (All Saints)   *see* Hulland, Atlow, Kniveton, Bradley
and Hognaston *Derby*
BRADLEY (All Saints)   *see* The Candover Valley *Win*

BRADLEY (St George)   *see* Gt and Lt Coates w Bradley *Linc*
BRADLEY (St John the Baptist)   *see* Bowbrook N *Worc*
BRADLEY (St Martin) *Lich 28*   **P** *Baldwin Pugh Trustees*
V R T M J DUCKETT
BRADLEY (St Mary)   *see* Cononley w Bradley *Bradf*
BRADLEY (St Thomas) *Wakef 5*   **P** *Bp*   **V** D R WARD
BRADLEY, GREAT (St Mary the Virgin)   *see* Stourhead *St E*
BRADLEY, LITTLE (All Saints)   *as above*
BRADLEY, NORTH (St Nicholas), Southwick, Heywood and
Steeple Ashton *Sarum 14*   **P** *Win Coll and Magd Coll Cam (jt)*
V J R PARKER,   **OLM** L J DOVE, A R J LONGDON
BRADLEY, WEST (not known)   *see* Baltonsborough w
Butleigh, W Bradley etc *B & W*
BRADLEY-LE-MOORS (St Leonard)   *see* Alton w Bradley-le-
Moors and Oakamoor w Cotton *Lich*
BRADLEY STOKE (Christ the King)   *see* Stoke Gifford *Bris*
BRADLEY STOKE NORTH (Holy Trinity) Conventional
District *Bris 5*   **C-in-c** P J PETERSON
BRADMORE (Mission Room)   *see* Keyworth and Stanton-on-
the-Wolds and Bunny etc *S'well*
BRADNINCH (St Disen) and Clyst Hydon *Ex 4*   **P** *D&C and*
D&C Windsor (jt)   **R** D L D ROBOTTOM
BRADNOP (Mission Church)   *see* Ipstones w Berkhamsytch
and Onecote w Bradnop *Lich*
BRADOC (Blessed Virgin Mary)   *see* Lanreath, Pelynt and
Bradoc *Truro*
BRADPOLE (Holy Trinity)   *see* Bridport *Sarum*
BRADSHAW (St John the Evangelist) and Holmfield *Wakef 4*
P *Bp*   **V** A DICK
BRADSHAW (St Maxentius)   *see* Turton Moorland Min *Man*
BRADWELL (Holy Trinity)   *see* Cressing w Stisted and
Bradwell etc *Chelmsf*
BRADWELL (St Barnabas)   *see* Hope, Castleton and Bradwell
Derby
BRADWELL (St Barnabas)   *see* Wolstanton *Lich*
BRADWELL (St Lawrence and Methodist United)
see Stantonbury and Willen *Ox*
BRADWELL (St Nicholas) *Nor 6*   **P** *Bp*   **R** R J TUCK,
NSM S D UPTON, C M UPTON
BRADWELL, NEW (St James)   *see* Stantonbury and Willen *Ox*
BRADWELL ON SEA (St Thomas) (St Peter-on-the-Wall) and
St Lawrence *Chelmsf 11*   **P** *Bp*   **R** W L WHITFORD,
C M E WHITFORD
BRADWORTHY (St John the Baptist), Sutcombe, Putford,
Abbots Bickington and Bulkworthy *Ex 17*   **P** *Prime Min and*
Bp (alt)   **R** R B DORRINGTON
BRAFFERTON (St Peter) w Pilmoor, Myton-on-Swale and
Thormanby *York 3*   **P** *Abp and Prof Sir Anthony Milnes*
Coates Bt (jt)   **P-in-c** C J PARK
BRAFIELD ON THE GREEN (St Laurence)   *see* Cogenhoe
and Gt and Lt Houghton w Brafield *Pet*
BRAILES (St George) *Cov 9*   **P** *D&C*   **V** N J MORGAN,
NSM J W ROLFE
BRAILSFORD (All Saints) w Shirley, Osmaston w Edlaston and
Yeaveley *Derby 8*   **P** *Bp, Earl Ferrers, and Sir Peter Walker-*
Okeover Bt (by turn)   **P-in-c** P M TAYLOR,   **C** A B LARKIN
BRAINTREE (St Michael) *Chelmsf 15*   **P** *Ch Trust Fund Trust*
V C O MASON,   **C** J A K WIGMORE
BRAINTREE (St Paul) *Chelmsf 15*   **P** *Ch Trust Fund Trust*
V R W SEWELL
BRAISHFIELD (All Saints)   *see* Michelmersh and Awbridge
and Braishfield etc *Win*
BRAITHWAITE (St Herbert)   *see* Upper Derwent *Carl*
BRAITHWELL (St James)   *see* Ravenfield, Hooton Roberts and
Braithwell *Sheff*
BRAMBER (St Nicholas)   *see* Beeding and Bramber w Botolphs
Chich
BRAMBLETON (not known)   *see* The Bourne and Tilford
Guildf
BRAMCOTE (St Michael and All Angels) *S'well 7*   **P** *CPAS*
P-in-c P F REYNOLDS,   **C** J L STEPHENS
BRAMDEAN (St Simon and St Jude)   *see* Upper Itchen *Win*
BRAMDEAN COMMON (Church in the Wood)   *as above*
BRAMERTON (St Peter)   *see* Rockland St Mary w Hellington,
Bramerton etc *Nor*
BRAMFIELD (St Andrew)   *see* Blyth Valley *St E*
BRAMFIELD (St Andrew), Stapleford, Waterford and Watton-
at-Stone *St Alb 22*   **P** *R M A Smith Esq (3 turns), Grocers' Co*
(1 turn)   **R** B D S FAIRBANK
BRAMFORD (St Mary the Virgin) *St E 1*   **P** *D&C Cant*
P-in-c R J DEDMAN
BRAMHALL (St Michael and All Angels) (Hall Chapel) *Ches 17*
P *Trustees*   **V** S R MARSH,   **C** E R FOSS,   **NSM** A HYDE
BRAMHAM (All Saints) *York 1*   **P** *G Lane Fox Esq*
P-in-c P E BRISTOW

BRAMHOPE (St Giles) *Ripon 7* **P** *Trustees* **P-in-c** J L SMITH, **C** D S FORD

BRAMLEY (Holy Trinity) and Grafham *Guildf 2* **P** *Ld Chan* **V** J N E BUNDOCK, **NSM** C E Z WHITE, **OLM** R E L TER HAAR

BRAMLEY (St Francis) *Sheff 6* **P** *Bp and Sir Philip Naylor-Leyland Bt (jt)* **V** L S WORTLEY

BRAMLEY (St James) *Win 4* **P** *Qu Coll Ox* **V** R C TOOGOOD

BRAMLEY (St Peter) *Ripon 6* **P** *DBP* **TR** I T RODLEY, **TV** J UPTON

BRAMPFORD SPEKE (St Peter) *see* Thorverton, Cadbury, Upton Pyne etc *Ex*

BRAMPTON (St Mark) *Derby 5* **P** *Bp* **P-in-c** F E WILLETT

BRAMPTON (St Martin) *see* Eden, Gelt and Irthing *Carl*

BRAMPTON (St Mary Magdalene) *Ely 10* **P** *Bp* **R** M R GREENFIELD

BRAMPTON (St Michael) *Heref 8* **P** *Bp (7 turns), D&C (2 turns), Exors Brig A F L Clive (1 turn)* **V** A KNIGHT

BRAMPTON (St Peter) *see* Bure Valley *Nor*

BRAMPTON (St Peter) *see* Hundred River *St E*

BRAMPTON (St Thomas the Martyr) *Derby 5* **P** *Bp* **R** M J BARNES, **C** R C TURNER, **NSM** A SMITH

BRAMPTON, OLD (St Peter and St Paul) (Cutthorpe Institute) and Great Barlow *Derby 5* **P** *Bp and TR Staveley and Barrow Hill (jt)* **P-in-c** W S MONKHOUSE

BRAMPTON ABBOTTS (St Michael) *see* Brampton *Heref*

BRAMPTON ASH (St Mary) *see* Desborough, Brampton Ash, Dingley and Braybrooke *Pet*

BRAMPTON BIERLOW (Christ Church) *Sheff 12* **P** *V Wath-upon-Dearne* **V** P E BOLD

BRAMPTON BRYAN (St Barnabas) *see* Wigmore Abbey *Heref*

BRAMSHALL (St Laurence) *see* Uttoxeter Area *Lich*

BRAMSHAW (St Peter) *see* Forest and Avon *Sarum*

BRAMSHILL (Mission Church) *see* Darby Green and Eversley *Win*

BRAMSHOTT (St Mary the Virgin) and Liphook *Portsm 4* **P** *Qu Coll Ox* **R** S A WEEDEN, **C** A BENNETT

BRANCASTER (St Mary the Virgin) *see* Hunstanton St Mary w Ringstead Parva etc *Nor*

BRANCEPETH (St Brandon) *Dur 1* **P** *Bp* **P-in-c** R L SIMPSON

BRANCEPETH, NEW (St Catherine) *see* Brandon and Ushaw Moor *Dur*

BRANDESBURTON (St Mary) and Leven w Catwick *York 11* **P** *St Jo Coll Cam, Exors Sir Henry Strickland-Constable Bt, and Simeon's Trustees (jt)* **R** B S DIXON

BRANDESTON (All Saints) w Kettleburgh and Easton *St E 18* **P** *J Austin Esq, Capt J L Round-Turner, and MMCET (jt)* **P-in-c** H V EDWARDS, **NSM** R E R ALDERSON

BRANDLESHOLME (St Francis House Chapel) *see* Kirklees Valley *Man*

BRANDON (Chapel) *see* Barkston and Hough Gp *Linc*

BRANDON (St John the Evangelist) and Ushaw Moor *Dur 1* **P** *R Brancepeth* **V** P BROWN, **Hon C** D B GODSELL

BRANDON (St Peter) and Santon Downham w Elveden and Lakenheath *St E 11* **P** *Ld Chan (1 turn), Bp, M F Carter Esq, Earl of Iveagh, and D&C Ely (2 turns)* **R** R N LEACH, **NSM** P W TAMS

BRANDON PARVA (All Saints) *see* Barnham Broom and Upper Yare *Nor*

BRANDSBY (All Saints) *see* Crayke w Brandsby and Yearsley *York*

BRANDWOOD (St Bede) *Birm 5* **P** *Bp* **V** A M DELMEGE, **NSM** R J REYNOLDS

BRANKSEA ISLAND (St Mary) *see* Parkstone St Pet and St Osmund w Branksea *Sarum*

BRANKSOME (St Aldhelm) (St Francis) *Sarum 7* **P** *Bp* **V** S R BATTY, **C** S E BRYANT

BRANKSOME (St Clement) (St Barnabas) *Sarum 8* **P** *MMCET* **V** J G V FOSTER, **C** G E BURRETT

BRANKSOME PARK (All Saints) *Sarum 7* **P** *MMCET* **V** J V BYRNE, **C** N D JACKSON

BRANSCOMBE (St Winifred) *see* Colyton, Musbury, Southleigh and Branscombe *Ex*

BRANSDALE (St Nicholas) *see* Kirkbymoorside w Gillamoor, Farndale etc *York*

BRANSFORD (St John the Baptist) *see* Worcs W *Worc*

BRANSGORE (St Mary the Virgin) and Hinton Admiral *Win 9* **P** *Sir George Meyrick Bt and Exors P W Jesson (jt)* **P-in-c** P A RICKMAN

BRANSHOLME (St John) *see* Sutton St Jas and Wawne *York*

BRANSTON (All Saints) w Nocton and Potterhanworth *Linc 18* **P** *Stowe Sch (2 turns), Ld Chan (1 turn), and Nocton Ltd (1 turn)* **R** *vacant* (01522) 791296

BRANSTON (St Saviour) *Lich 14* **P** *Simeon's Trustees* **V** *vacant* (01283) 568926

BRANSTON BY BELVOIR (St Guthlac) *see* High Framland Par *Leic*

BRANT BROUGHTON (St Helen) and Beckingham *Linc 23* **P** *Bp and Sir Richard Sutton Bt (alt)* **R** A J MEGAHEY

BRANT ROAD (Church Centre) *see* Bracebridge *Linc*

BRANTHAM (St Michael and All Angels) *see* E Bergholt and Brantham *St E*

BRANTINGHAM (All Saints) *see* Elloughton and Brough w Brantingham *York*

BRANXTON (St Paul) *Newc 12* **P** *Abp* **P-in-c** M J GILLHAM, **NSM** L E GARDHAM

BRASSINGTON (St James) *see* Wirksworth *Derby*

BRASTED (St Martin) *Roch 9* **P** *Abp* **P-in-c** P C STEPHENS

BRATHAY (Holy Trinity) *see* Ambleside w Brathay *Carl*

BRATOFT (St Peter and St Paul) *see* Burgh Gp *Linc*

BRATTLEBY (St Cuthbert) *see* Spring Line Gp *Linc*

BRATTON (St James the Great) (Oratory), Edington and Imber, Erlestoke and Coulston *Sarum 16* **P** *Bp and V Westbury (jt)* **R** G SOUTHGATE, **OLM** M R WIECK

BRATTON CLOVELLY (St Mary the Virgin) *see* Okehampton w Inwardleigh, Bratton Clovelly etc *Ex*

BRATTON FLEMING (St Peter) *see* Shirwell, Loxhore, Kentisbury, Arlington, etc *Ex*

BRATTON ST MAUR (St Nicholas) *see* Bruton and Distr *B & W*

BRAUGHING (St Mary the Virgin) *see* Albury, Braughing, Furneux Pelham, Lt Hadham etc *St Alb*

BRAUNSTON (All Saints) *see* Daventry, Ashby St Ledgers, Braunston etc *Pet*

BRAUNSTON (All Saints) *see* Oakham, Hambleton, Egleton, Braunston and Brooke *Pet*

BRAUNSTONE PARK (St Peter) *Leic 1* **P** *Bp* **V** J C BURCH

BRAUNSTONE TOWN (St Crispin) *Leic 9* **P** *Bp* **P-in-c** A C DEEGAN

BRAUNTON (St Brannock) *Ex 15* **P** *Bp* **P-in-c** A THORNE, **Hon C** L A BUTTLE

BRAXTED, GREAT (All Saints) *see* Tolleshunt Knights w Tiptree and Gt Braxted *Chelmsf*

BRAXTED, LITTLE (St Nicholas) *see* Wickham Bishops w Lt Braxted *Chelmsf*

BRAY (St Michael) and Braywood *Ox 13* **P** *Bp* **V** R M COWLES

BRAY, HIGH (All Saints) *see* S Molton w Nymet St George, High Bray etc *Ex*

BRAYBROOKE (All Saints) *see* Desborough, Brampton Ash, Dingley and Braybrooke *Pet*

BRAYDESTON (St Michael) *see* Brundall w Braydeston and Postwick *Nor*

BRAYTON (St Wilfrid) *York 4* **P** *Abp* **R** D R MOORE

BREADSALL (All Saints) *Derby 9* **P** *Miss A I M Harpur-Crewe* **C** C G PEARSON, **NSM** D M MORRISON

BREADSTONE (St Michael and All Angels) *see* Berkeley w Wick, Breadstone, Newport, Stone etc *Glouc*

BREAGE (St Breaca) w Godolphin and Germoe *Truro 4* **P** *Bp and Ld Chan (alt)* **P-in-c** P A PRINCE

BREAM (St James) *Glouc 2* **P** *Bp* **P-in-c** G C A STOREY, **NSM** A J WILLIAMS

BREAMORE (St Mary) *see* Fordingbridge and Breamore and Hale etc *Win*

BREAN (St Bridget) *see* Berrow and Breane *B & W*

BREARTON (St John the Baptist) *see* Knaresborough *Ripon*

BREASTON (St Michael) *see* Wilne and Draycott w Breaston *Derby*

BRECKLES (St Margaret) *see* Caston, Griston, Merton, Thompson etc *Nor*

BREDBURY (St Barnabas) *Ches 16* **P** *V Bredbury St Mark* **P-in-c** B J SWORD

BREDBURY (St Mark) *Ches 16* **P** *Bp* **V** A R GARNER

BREDE (St George) w Udimore *Chich 20* **P** *Bp and Mrs M E Crook (alt)* **R** M N HARPER

BREDENBURY (St Andrew) *Heref 2* **P** *DBP, V Bromyard, and Lt-Col H H Barneby (jt)* **R** *vacant* (01885) 482236

BREDFIELD (St Andrew) *see* Woodbridge St Jo and Bredfield *St E*

BREDGAR (St John the Baptist) w Bicknor and Frinsted w Wormshill and Milsted *Cant 15* **P** *Abp, Lord Kingsdown, M Nightingale Esq, and S McCandlish Esq (jt)* **P-in-c** J L SMITH

BREDHURST (St Peter) *see* S Gillingham *Roch*

BREDICOT (St James the Less) *see* Bowbrook S *Worc*

BREDON (St Giles) w Bredon's Norton *Worc 4* **P** *Bp* **R** M T C BAYNES, **C** C L TURPIN

BREDON'S NORTON (not known) *see* Bredon w Bredon's Norton *Worc*

BREDWARDINE (St Andrew) *see* Cusop w Blakemere,
Bredwardine w Brobury etc *Heref*
BREDY, LITTLE (St Michael and All Angels) *see* Bride Valley
Sarum
BREEDON-ON-THE-HILL (St Mary and St Hardulph)
see Ashby-de-la-Zouch and Breedon on the Hill *Leic*
BREIGHTMET (St James) *see* Leverhulme *Man*
BREIGHTMET Top o' th' Moss (St John the Evangelist)
as above
BREINTON (Common Mission Hall) *see* W Heref *Heref*
BREINTON (St Michael) *as above*
BREMHILL (St Martin) *see* Derry Hill w Bremhill and Foxham
Sarum
BRENCHLEY (All Saints) *Roch 8* **P** *D&C Cant* **V** R C PAGET
BRENDON (St Brendon) *see* Combe Martin, Berrynarbor,
Lynton, Brendon etc *Ex*
BRENT, EAST (St The Blessed Virgin Mary) *see* Brent Knoll, E
Brent and Lympsham *B & W*
BRENT, SOUTH (St Petroc) and Rattery *Ex 13* **P** *Bp and*
Sir Rivers Carew Bt (jt) **V** D R WINNINGTON-INGRAM
BRENT ELEIGH (St Mary) *see* Monks Eleigh w Chelsworth
and Brent Eleigh etc *St E*
BRENT KNOLL (St Michael) and East Brent and Lympsham
B & W 1 **P** *Adn Wells (1 turn), Bp (2 turns)*
P-in-c S W LEWIS
BRENT PELHAM (St Mary the Virgin) *see* Hormead,
Wyddial, Anstey, Brent Pelham etc *St Alb*
BRENT TOR (Christ Church) *see* Peter Tavy, Mary Tavy,
Lydford and Brent Tor *Ex*
BRENT TOR (St Michael) *as above*
BRENTFORD (St Paul w St Lawrence and St George) (St Faith)
Lon 11 **P** *Bp* **TR** D J SIMPSON, **TV** D M DURKIN,
C N K GUNASEKERA
BRENTRY (St Mark) *see* Henbury *Bris*
BRENTS and Davington w Oare and Luddenham, The *Cant 6*
P *Abp and Ld Chan (alt)* **P-in-c** A A DUGUID,
NSM C B CLAPPERTON
BRENTWOOD (St George the Martyr) *Chelmsf 7* **P** *DBP*
V G F JENKINS
BRENTWOOD (St Thomas) *Chelmsf 7* **P** *DBP*
C M J BEMAND
BRENZETT (St Eanswith) *see* Appledore w Brookland,
Fairfield, Brenzett etc *Cant*
BRERETON (St Michael) and Rugeley *Lich 3* **P** *Patr Bd*
TR M J NEWMAN, **TV** W H HEATH, L M DOWNS,
C J M HARTWELL, **OLM** J L BRITTLE, B D TABERNOR
BRERETON (St Oswald) w Eaton and Hulme Walfield *Ches 11*
P *Bp, R Astbury and Smallwood, and DBP (jt)*
P-in-c C M KEMP
BRESSINGHAM (St John the Baptist) *see* Upper Waveney *Nor*
BRETBY (St Wystan) *see* Hartshorne and Bretby *Derby*
BRETFORTON (St Leonard) *see* Badsey w Aldington and
Offenham and Bretforton *Worc*
BRETHERTON (St John the Baptist) *see* Croston and
Bretherton *Blackb*
BRETTENHAM (St Andrew) *see* E w W Harling, Bridgham w
Roudham, Larling etc *Nor*
BRETTENHAM (St Mary) *see* Rattlesden w Thorpe Morieux,
Brettenham etc *St E*
BRETTON (Holy Spirit) *see* Pet H Spirit Bretton *Pet*
BRETTON PARK (St Bartholomew) *see* Woolley *Wakef*
BREWHAM, SOUTH (St John the Baptist) *see* Bruton and
Distr *B & W*
BREWOOD (St Mary and St Chad) *Lich 2* **P** *Bp*
P-in-c C A HOST, **NSM** M J COULTER
BRICETT, GREAT (St Mary and St Lawrence) *see* Ringshall w
Battisford, Barking w Darmsden etc *St E*
BRICKENDON (Holy Cross and St Alban) *see* Lt
Berkhamsted and Bayford, Essendon etc *St Alb*
BRICKET WOOD (St Luke) *St Alb 1* **P** *CPAS*
V M RAJKOVIC
BRICKHILL, GREAT (St Mary) *see* Brickhills and Stoke
Hammond *Ox*
BRICKHILL, LITTLE (St Mary Magdalene) *as above*
BRICKHILL, NORTH (St Mark) *see* Bedf St Mark *St Alb*
BRICKHILLS and Stoke Hammond, The *Ox 26* **P** *Bp, Major*
Sir Philip Pauncefort-Duncombe Bt, St Edw Sch Ox, and Cam
Univ (jt) **P-in-c** D N A THOMPSON
BRICKLEHAMPTON (St Michael) *see* Elmley Castle w
Bricklehampton and Combertons *Worc*
BRIDE (St Bridget) *see* Kirkbride *S & M*
BRIDE VALLEY *Sarum 2* **P** *Sir Robert Williams Bt and*
G A Lane-Fox Pitt-Rivers Esq (jt) **R** R A D'V THORN,
NSM R R ROGERS
BRIDEKIRK (St Bridget) *see* Cockermouth Area *Carl*

BRIDESTOWE (St Bridget) *see* Okehampton w Inwardleigh,
Bratton Clovelly etc *Ex*
BRIDFORD (St Thomas à Becket) *see* Christow, Ashton and
Bridford *Ex*
BRIDGE Parishes, The *Sarum 9* **P** *Eton Coll and Nat Trust*
(alt) **V** A C STEWART-SYKES
BRIDGE (St Peter) *Cant 1* **P** *Abp and St Jo Coll Ox (jt)*
V S D ROWLANDS
BRIDGE SOLLARS (St Andrew) *see* Credenhill w Brinsop and
Wormsley etc *Heref*
BRIDGEMARY (St Matthew) *Portsm 3* **P** *Bp*
P-in-c R J PRESTON
BRIDGERULE (St Bridget) *see* Pyworthy, Pancrasweek and
Bridgerule *Ex*
BRIDGETOWN (St John the Evangelist) *see* Totnes w
Bridgetown, Berry Pomeroy etc *Ex*
BRIDGFORD, EAST (St Peter) and Kneeton *S'well 8* **P** *Magd*
Coll Ox (2 turns), C G Neale Esq (1 turn)
P-in-c J R CHAMBERS, **NSM** M R WOODWARD
BRIDGFORD, WEST (St Giles) (St Luke) *S'well 9*
P *Waddington Trustees* **P-in-c** L J PROUDLOVE,
C S R BUTLER
BRIDGHAM (St Mary) *see* E w W Harling, Bridgham w
Roudham, Larling etc *Nor*
BRIDGNORTH (St Mary Magdalene) (St Leonard) (St James),
Tasley, Astley Abbotts, Oldbury and Quatford *Heref 9* **P** *DBP*
(3 turns) and Ld Chan (1 turn) **TR** A A ROBERTS,
TV D G JONES, **C** H T GREENHAM, **NSM** A ROGERS,
OLM T O'BRIEN
BRIDGWATER (Holy Trinity) and Durleigh St Hugh *B & W 14*
P *Bp (2 turns) and Ld Chan (1 turn)* **V** N W M LEGGETT
BRIDGWATER (St Francis of Assisi) *B & W 14* **P** *Bp*
V B D JOY, **C** R B HICKS
BRIDGWATER (St John the Baptist) *B & W 14* **P** *Bp*
P-in-c G M KIRK
BRIDGWATER (St Mary) and Chilton Trinity *B & W 14*
P *Ld Chan* **V** C J P CHADWICK, **C** J R HICKS
BRIDLINGTON (Emmanuel) *York 9* **P** *Trustees*
V C J MCCARTHY, **C** B J NORTON, **NSM** B E HODGSON
BRIDLINGTON (Holy Trinity) and Sewerby w Marton *York 9*
P *Abp* **V** D J MATHER
BRIDLINGTON (St Mary's Priory Church) *York 9* **P** *Simeon's*
Trustees **C** K F GODFREY, **NSM** J L OATES
BRIDLINGTON QUAY (Christ Church) *York 9*
P *R Bridlington Priory* **V** J G COUPER, **C** D N H CHISLETT
BRIDPORT (St Mary) *Sarum 2* **P** *Patr Bd (2 turns) and*
Ld Chan (1 turn) **TV** P R H EDWARDS, **OLM** J E MOORE,
R F PITTARD, G A HEBBERN
BRIDSTOW (St Bridget) *see* Brampton *Heref*
BRIERCLIFFE (St James) *Blackb 3* **P** *Hulme Trustees*
V R D WATTS
BRIERFIELD (St Luke) *Blackb 6* **P** *Bp* **P-in-c** E A SAVILLE
BRIERLEY (St Paul) *see* Grimethorpe w Brierley *Wakef*
BRIERLEY HILL (St Michael) (St Paul) *Worc 10* **P** *Ld Chan*
(2 turns), Patr Bd (1 turn) **TR** B GILBERT,
TV G E P NATHANIEL, **C** N A POPHAM, **NSM** B I PRITCHETT
BRIGG (St John the Evangelist), Wrawby and Cadney cum
Howsham *Linc 6* **P** *Bp* **V** G O MITCHELL, **C** D J EAMES
BRIGHAM (St Bridget), Great Broughton and Broughton Moor
Carl 7 **P** *Bp and Earl of Lonsdale (jt)* **V** P L BENSON
BRIGHOUSE (St Martin) (St Chad) and Clifton *Wakef 2* **P** *Bp*
TV S J LORD, **C** R J SHRISUNDER, **NSM** C FOX
BRIGHSTONE (St Mary the Virgin) and Brooke w Mottistone
Portsm 8 **P** *Bp (2 turns), D&C St Paul's (1 turn)*
P-in-c M C WILLIAMS, **Hon C** D L DENNIS
BRIGHTLING (St Thomas of Canterbury), Dallington,
Mountfield and Netherfield *Chich 15* **P** *Bp, Adn Lewes and*
Hastings, H C Grissell Esq, Mrs A Egerton, and
Mrs L A Fraser (jt) **R** S BAKER, **NSM** J B B WRENBURY
BRIGHTLINGSEA (All Saints) (St James) *Chelmsf 22*
P *Ld Chan* **P-in-c** P A BALDWIN
BRIGHTON (Annunciation) *Chich 2* **P** *Wagner Trustees*
P-in-c S F FOSTER, **Hon C** R L CLARKE
BRIGHTON (Chapel Royal) *Chich 2* **P** *Bp* **P-in-c** D J BIGGS,
NSM J NEWSON
BRIGHTON (Good Shepherd) Preston *Chich 2* **P** *Bp*
P-in-c F P A MASCARENHAS
BRIGHTON (St Bartholomew) *Chich 2* **P** *Wagner Trustees*
V V W HOUSE
BRIGHTON (St Cuthman) *see* Whitehawk *Chich*
BRIGHTON (St George w St Anne and St Mark) *Chich 2* **P** *Bp*
and V Brighton (jt) **V** A H MANSON-BRAILSFORD
BRIGHTON (St John) *see* Preston St Jo w Brighton St Aug and
St Sav *Chich*
BRIGHTON (St Luke) Queen's Park *Chich 2* **P** *Bp*
V C J WOODMAN

BRIGHTON (St Martin) w St Wilfrid and St Alban *Chich 2*
P *SMF* V B L BRANDIE
BRIGHTON (St Mary the Virgin) *see* Kemp Town St Mary
Chich
BRIGHTON (St Matthias) *Chich 2* P *V Preston*
P-in-c E J POLLARD
BRIGHTON (St Michael and All Angels) *Chich 2* P *V Brighton*
V R S FAYERS, C B A NORTH, G E J P JONES
BRIGHTON (St Nicholas) *Chich 2* P *Bp* P-in-c R CHAVNER
BRIGHTON (St Paul) *Chich 2* P *Wagner Trustees*
P-in-c R S FAYERS, NSM J N BALDRY
BRIGHTON (St Peter) *Chich 2* P *Bp and V Brompton*
H Trin (jt) C J P GUMBEL
BRIGHTON, NEW (All Saints) *see* Wallasey St Nic w All SS
Ches
BRIGHTON, NEW (St James) (Emmanuel) *Ches 7* P *Bp*
V F R CAIN, C K L FREEMAN
BRIGHTSIDE (St Thomas and St Margaret) w Wincobank
Sheff 3 P *The Crown and Sheff Ch Burgesses (alt)*
V P N WARMAN, NSM B M KIMARU
BRIGHTWALTON (All Saints) w Catmore, Leckhampstead,
Chaddleworth and Fawley *Ox 14* P *Bp, P L Wroughton Esq,*
and D&C Westmr (jt) P-in-c J P TOWNEND, C G J STACEY,
K E STACEY, NSM D F BROWN
BRIGHTWELL (St Agatha) *see* Wallingford *Ox*
BRIGHTWELL (St John the Baptist) *see* Martlesham w
Brightwell *St E*
BRIGHTWELL BALDWIN (St Bartholomew) *see* Ewelme,
Brightwell Baldwin, Cuxham w Easington *Ox*
BRIGNALL (St Mary) *see* Startforth and Bowes and Rokeby w
Brignall *Ripon*
BRIGSLEY (St Helen) *see* Laceby and Ravendale Gp *Linc*
BRIGSTOCK (St Andrew) w Stanion and Lowick and
Sudborough *Pet 7* P *Bp (2 turns), L G Stopford Sackville Esq*
(1 turn) P-in-c S J P FISHER
BRILL (All Saints) *see* Bernwode *Ox*
BRILLEY (St Mary) *see* Eardisley w Bollingham, Willersley,
Brilley etc *Heref*
BRIMFIELD (St Michael) *see* Leominster *Heref*
BRIMINGTON (St Michael) *Derby 3* P *V Chesterfield*
R M SHAW
BRIMPSFIELD (St Michael) w Birdlip, Syde, Daglingworth,
The Duntisbournes, Winstone, Miserden and Edgeworth *Glouc 9*
P *Ld Chan (1 turn), Bp, DBP, Major M N T H Wills and*
CCC Ox (1 turn) R J E JESSOP, NSM J R HOBBS,
R H GEORGE
BRIMPTON (St Peter) *see* Aldermaston and Woolhampton *Ox*
BRIMSCOMBE (Holy Trinity) *see* Woodchester and
Brimscombe *Glouc*
BRINDLE (St James) *Blackb 4* P *Trustees*
P-in-c M H CANNON
BRINGHURST (St Nicholas) *see* Six Saints circa Holt *Leic*
BRINGTON (All Saints) w Molesworth and Old Weston *Ely 10*
P *Bp* P-in-c J DUCK
BRINGTON (St Mary w St John) w Whilton and Norton and
Church Brampton w Chapel Brampton and Harlestone and East
Haddon and Holdenby *Pet 2* P *Patr Bd (5 turns), Prime Min*
(1 turn) Hon C A D RICHARDS
BRININGHAM (St Maurice) *see* Brinton, Briningham,
Hunworth, Stody etc *Nor*
BRINKBURN (St Peter and St Paul) *see* Longframlington w
Brinkburn *Newc*
BRINKHILL (St Philip) *see* S Ormsby Gp *Linc*
BRINKLEY (St Mary) *see* Raddesley Gp *Ely*
BRINKLOW (St John the Baptist) *Cov 6* P *Ld Chan*
P-in-c C A GARROD
BRINKWORTH (St Michael and All Angels) w Dauntsey *Bris 6*
P *Bp* R D ORMSTON
BRINNINGTON (St Luke) w Portwood St Paul *Ches 18* P *Bp*
V C A FURNESS, C L J HITCHEN
BRINSCALL (St Luke) *see* Heapey and Withnell *Blackb*
BRINSLEY (St James the Great) w Underwood *S'well 4* P *Bp*
P-in-c R B MURRAY
BRINSOP (St George) *see* Credenhill w Brinsop and Wormsley
etc *Heref*
BRINSWORTH (St Andrew) *see* Rivers Team *Sheff*
BRINTON (St Andrew), Briningham, Hunworth, Stody, Swanton
Novers and Thornage *Nor 18* P *J S Howlett Esq, Lord*
Hastings, and DBP (by turn) R *vacant* (01263) 860295
BRISLEY (St Bartholomew) *see* Upper Wensum Village Gp
Nor
BRISLINGTON (St Anne) *Bris 1* P *Bp* V *vacant* 0117-983
0283
BRISLINGTON (St Christopher) *Bris 1* P *Simeon's Trustees*
V N HAWKINS

BRISLINGTON (St Cuthbert) *Bris 1* P *Bp*
P-in-c I L GARRETT
BRISLINGTON (St Luke) *Bris 1* P *Bp* P-in-c D M DEWES
BRISTOL (Christ Church) w St Ewen, All SS and St George
Bris 3 P *J E Heal Esq* R *vacant*
BRISTOL (Christ the Servant) Stockwood *Bris 1* P *Bp*
V D G OWEN, C A W E SCHUMAN
BRISTOL Lockleaze (St Mary Magdalene w St Francis) *Bris 3*
P *Bp* V J J HASLER, NSM J MARKER, OLM E R MILLS
BRISTOL St Aidan w St George *Bris 3* P *Bp and SMF*
C N S ADAMS, NSM J F J GOODRIDGE, OLM T M DENLEY
BRISTOL (St Andrew) Hartcliffe *Bris 1* P *Bp* V R H MARTIN
BRISTOL (St Andrew w St Bartholomew) *see* Bishopston and
St Andrews *Bris*
BRISTOL (St Anne w St Mark and St Thomas) *see* Eastville St
Anne w St Mark and St Thos *Bris*
BRISTOL (St Leonard) Redfield *see* E Bris St Ambrose and St
Leon *Bris*
BRISTOL (St Mary the Virgin) Redcliffe w Temple and
Bedminster St John the Baptist *Bris 1* P *Bp*
P-in-c S J TAYLOR, C W L HOUGH, NSM S H E JONES
BRISTOL (St Matthew and St Nathanael) (St Katharine) *Bris 3*
P *Bp and CPAS (jt)* P-in-c M D INESON, C T M LORD,
NSM E G INESON, OLM J M CAITHNESS
BRISTOL St Paul's (St Agnes) *Bris 3* P *Ld Chan and Patr Bd*
(alt) P-in-c P BARTLE-JENKINS
BRISTOL (St Philip and St Jacob w Emmanuel) *Bris 3*
P *Trustees* V *vacant* 0117-924 3169
BRISTOL (St Stephen) w St James and St John the Baptist w
St Michael and St George *Bris 3* P *Ld Chan (1 turn), Bp, Bris*
Ch Trustees, and D&C (2 turns) P-in-c T J HIGGINS,
C E A KESTEVEN
BRISTOL, EAST (St Aidan) *see* Bristol St Aid w St Geo *Bris*
BRISTOL, EAST (St Ambrose) (St Leonard) *Bris 3* P *Bp*
V R D JAMES, C N S ADAMS, NSM J F J GOODRIDGE
BRISTOL, EAST (St George) *see* Bristol St Aid w St Geo *Bris*
BRISTON (All Saints), Burgh Parva, Hindolveston and Melton
Constable *Nor 18* P *Bp, Lord Hastings, and D&C (jt)*
P-in-c J G SYKES
BRITFORD (St Peter) *see* Chalke Valley *Sarum*
BRITWELL St George *Ox 23* P *Eton Coll*
V J S W CHORLTON, C S A L PIX, C A M STYLES
BRITWELL SALOME (St Nicholas) *see* Icknield *Ox*
BRIXHAM (St Mary) (All Saints) w Churston Ferrers and
Kingswear *Ex 12* P *The Crown* TR T R DEACON,
TV A M BURDEN, I H BLYDE
BRIXTON (St Mary) *see* Yealmpton and Brixton *Ex*
BRIXTON (St Matthew) (St Jude) *S'wark 11* P *Abp and Ch Soc*
Trust (jt) V S M SICHEL, NSM W W SHARPE
BRIXTON (St Paul) (St Saviour) *S'wark 11* P *Ch Soc Trust*
P-in-c B GOODYEAR
BRIXTON, NORTH (Christ Church) *see* Brixton Road Ch Ch
S'wark
BRIXTON DEVERILL (St Michael) *see* Cley Hill Villages
Sarum
BRIXTON ROAD (Christ Church) *S'wark 11* P *CPAS*
V T J JEFFREYS, NSM J CONNELL
BRIXWORTH (All Saints) w Holcot *Pet 2* P *Bp*
V A J WATKINS
BRIZE NORTON (St Britius) and Carterton *Ox 8* P *Patr Bd*
TR W G BLAKEY, TV J T MADDERN
BROAD BLUNSDON (St Leonard) *see* Broad Blunsdon *Bris*
BROAD BLUNSDON (St Leonard) *Bris 7* P *Bp*
P-in-c G D SOWDEN, NSM J N REES
BROAD CAMPDEN (St Michael and All Angels) *see* Chipping
Campden w Ebrington *Glouc*
BROAD HINTON (St Peter ad Vincula) *see* Upper Kennet
Sarum
BROAD LANE (Licensed Room) *see* Wybunbury w
Doddington *Ches*
BROAD OAK (St George) *see* Heathfield *Chich*
BROAD TOWN (Christ Church), Clyffe Pypard, Hilmarton and
Tockenham *Sarum 15* P *Ld Chan, DBP, and Prime Min*
(by turns) P-in-c A J WAY
BROADBOTTOM (St Mary Magdalene) *see* Mottram in
Longdendale *Ches*
BROADBRIDGE HEATH (St John) *see* Horsham *Chich*
BROADCHALKE (All Saints) *see* Chalke Valley *Sarum*
BROADCLYST (St John the Baptist) *see* Pinhoe and Broadclyst
Ex
BROADFIELD (Christ the Lord) *see* Southgate *Chich*
BROADHEATH (Christ Church) *see* Worc St Clem and Lower
Broadheath *Worc*
BROADHEATH (St Alban) *Ches 10* P *Bp* V H SCARISBRICK,
NSM T HODSON

BROADHEMBURY (St Andrew the Apostle and Martyr), Payhembury and Plymtree *Ex 7* **P** *W Drewe Esq, Ex Coll Ox, and Or Coll Ox (by turn)* **P-in-c** R S CRITTALL, **C** C E EDMONDS

BROADHEMPSTON (St Peter and St Paul), Woodland, Staverton w Landscove and Littlehempston *Ex 13* **P** *Prime Min (1 turn), D&C and Bp (1 turn)* **R** N R C PEARKES

BROADMAYNE (St Martin) *see* Watercombe *Sarum*

BROADOAK (St Paul) *see* Symondsbury *Sarum*

BROADSTAIRS (Holy Trinity) *Cant 9* **P** *V St Peter-in-Thanet* **P-in-c** D J ROPER

BROADSTAIRS (St Andrew) *see* St Peter-in-Thanet *Cant*

BROADSTONE (not known) *see* Diddlebury w Munslow, Holdgate and Tugford *Heref*

BROADSTONE (St John the Baptist) *Sarum 7* **P** *Bp* **V** M FREDRIKSEN

BROADWAS (St Mary Magdalene) *see* Worcs W *Worc*

BROADWATER (St Mary) (St Stephen) (Queen Street Church Centre) *Chich 5* **P** *Patr Bd* **TR** P E IRWIN-CLARK, **TV** W M TSANG, G R NEAL, E V QUIBELL, **C** M J LUFF

BROADWATER DOWN *see* Tunbridge Wells St Mark *Roch*

BROADWATERS (St Oswald) *see* Kidderminster St Mary and All SS w Trimpley etc *Worc*

BROADWAY (St Aldhem and St Eadburga) *see* Ilminster and Distr *B & W*

BROADWAY (St Eadburgha) (St Michael and All Angels) w Wickhamford *Worc 1* **P** *Peache Trustees and Ch Ch Ox (jt)* **V** T M MASON

BROADWELL (Good Shepherd) *see* Coleford, Staunton, Newland, Redbrook etc *Glouc*

BROADWELL (St Paul), Evenlode, Oddington, Adlestrop and Westcote w Icomb and Bledington *Glouc 12* **P** *Bp, Ch Soc Trust, Lord Leigh and DBP (1 turn), and Ch Ch Ox and D&C Worc (1 turn)* **R** R J RENDALL, **NSM** L WILSON

BROADWELL (St Peter and St Paul) *see* Shill Valley and Broadshire *Ox*

BROADWEY (St Nicholas) *see* Bincombe w Broadwey, Upwey and Buckland Ripers *Sarum*

BROADWINDSOR (St John the Baptist) *see* Beaminster Area *Sarum*

BROADWOODKELLY (All Saints) *Ex 20* **P** *DBP* **R** P J NORMAN

BROADWOODWIDGER (St Nicholas) *see* Lifton, Broadwoodwidger, Stowford etc *Ex*

BROCKDISH (St Peter and St Paul) *see* Scole, Brockdish, Billingford, Thorpe Abbots etc *Nor*

BROCKENHURST (St Nicholas) (St Saviour) *Win 11* **P** *E J F Morant Esq* **P-in-c** N R SMART, **Hon C** R DROWN

BROCKHALL (St Peter and St Paul) *see* Heyford w Stowe Nine Churches and Flore etc *Pet*

BROCKHAM GREEN (Christ Church) *S'wark 26* **P** *Hon R P Hamilton* **P-in-c** J M A WILLANS, **NSM** F G LEHANEY

BROCKHAMPTON (All Saints) *see* Fownhope w Mordiford, Brockhampton etc *Heref*

BROCKHAMPTON (Chapel) *see* Bromyard and Stoke Lacy *Heref*

BROCKHOLES (St George) *see* Honley *Wakef*

BROCKLESBY PARK (All Saints) *Linc 6* **P** *Earl of Yarborough* **NSM** F A COUCH

BROCKLEY (St Andrew) *see* Horringer *St E*

BROCKLEY (St Peter) *S'wark 2* **P** *Bp* **V** C M E G TOURNAY

BROCKLEY HILL (St Saviour) *S'wark 5* **P** *V Forest Hill Ch Ch* **V** A S PEBERDY, **NSM** S D LECK

BROCKMOOR (St John) *see* Brierley Hill *Worc*

BROCKWORTH (St George) *Glouc 4* **P** *DBP* **P-in-c** D A GILL

BROCTON (All Saints) *see* Baswich *Lich*

BRODSWORTH (St Michael and All Angels) *see* Bilham *Sheff*

BROKENBOROUGH (St John the Baptist) *see* Malmesbury w Westport and Brokenborough *Bris*

BROKERS WOOD (All Saints) *see* White Horse *Sarum*

BROMBOROUGH (St Barnabas) *Ches 9* **P** *D&C* **R** D WALKER

BROME (St Mary) *see* N Hartismere *St E*

BROMESWELL (St Edmund) *see* Wilford Peninsula *St E*

BROMFIELD (St Mary the Virgin) *see* Ludlow *Heref*

BROMFIELD (St Mungo) *see* Solway Plain *Carl*

BROMFORD FIRS (not Known) *see* Hodge Hill *Birm*

BROMHAM (St Nicholas) *see* Rowde and Bromham *Sarum*

BROMHAM (St Owen) w Oakley and Stagsden *St Alb 13* **P** *Bp* **P-in-c** L BOND, **NSM** D J HARPHAM, P A VENNELLS

BROMLEY (Christ Church) *Roch 14* **P** *CPAS* **V** I J BROOMFIELD, **C** N R T HISCOCKS, **Hon C** V G WILKINS

BROMLEY (Holy Trinity Mission Church) *see* Pensnett *Worc*

BROMLEY (St Andrew) *Roch 14* **P** *Bp* **V** H A ATHERTON, **NSM** E J DAVIS, A M KING

BROMLEY (St John the Evangelist) *Roch 14* **P** *Bp* **P-in-c** A D MCCLELLAN

BROMLEY (St Mark) *Roch 14* **P** *V Bromley SS Pet & Paul* **V** S C VARNEY

BROMLEY (St Mary) *see* Plaistow St Mary *Roch*

BROMLEY (St Peter and St Paul) *Roch 14* **P** *Bp* **V** M M CAMP, **C** P F PRENTICE

BROMLEY, GREAT (St George) *see* Ardleigh and The Bromleys *Chelmsf*

BROMLEY BY BOW (All Hallows) *Lon 7* **P** *Bp and Grocers' Co (jt)* **R** *vacant*

BROMLEY COMMON (Holy Trinity) *Roch 14* **P** *The Crown* **V** R BRISTOW, **NSM** G E COLLETT

BROMLEY COMMON (St Augustine) *Roch 14* **P** *Bp* **V** K C BARNES, **C** K J CABLE

BROMLEY COMMON (St Luke) *Roch 14* **P** *Bp* **V** M G P INSLEY

BROMLEY CROSS (St Andrew's Mission Church) *see* Turton Moorland Min *Man*

BROMPTON (Holy Trinity) w Onslow Square St Paul *Lon 8* **P** *Bp and MMCET (jt)* **V** N G P GUMBEL, **C** M R TOULMIN, R M COATES, P W COWLEY, N K LEE, T FLINT, J MARCH, T J MATTHEWS, J R HAITH, E Q HOBBS, M HOGG, D G WALKER, **Hon C** J A K MILLAR

BROMPTON (St Thomas) w Deighton *York 19* **P** *D&C Dur* **V** M S SNOWBALL

BROMPTON, NEW (St Luke) *Roch 3* **P** *Bp* **V** *vacant* (01634) 853060

BROMPTON, WEST (St Jude) (St Mary) St Peter *Lon 8* **P** *Bp and Sir Laurence Magnus Bt (jt)* **C** R M LAMPARD, **NSM** V J THOMAS

BROMPTON-BY-SAWDON (All Saints) *see* Upper Derwent *York*

BROMPTON ON SWALE (St Paul) *see* Easby w Skeeby and Brompton on Swale etc *Ripon*

BROMPTON RALPH (The Blessed Virgin Mary) *see* Lydeard St Lawrence w Brompton Ralph etc *B & W*

BROMPTON REGIS (Blessed Virgin Mary) w Upton and Skilgate *B & W 16* **P** *Bp, Em Coll Cam, and Keble Coll Ox (jt)* **P-in-c** J M THOROGOOD, **Hon C** J H GRAY

BROMSBERROW (St Mary the Virgin) *see* Redmarley D'Abitot, Bromesberrow, Pauntley etc *Glouc*

BROMSGROVE (All Saints) *Worc 7* **P** *V Bromsgrove St Jo* **NSM** F J MANT

BROMSGROVE (St John the Baptist) *Worc 7* **P** *D&C* **C** A G STAND, **NSM** M C T B JONES

BROMWICH, WEST (All Saints) (St Mary Magdalene) *Lich 27* **P** *Bp* **V** A J SMITH, **C** P J SELLICK, **OLM** A M BIRD

BROMWICH, WEST (Good Shepherd w St John) *Lich 27* **P** *Bp* **NSM** M BEDEAU

BROMWICH, WEST (Holy Trinity) *Lich 27* **P** *Peache Trustees* **V** J N ROBBIE

BROMWICH, WEST (St Andrew) (Christ Church) *Lich 27* **P** *Bp and V W Bromwich All SS (jt)* **V** M J CLARIDGE

BROMWICH, WEST (St Francis of Assisi) *Lich 27* **P** *Bp* **V** R A FARRELL, **C** A K W HUGHES

BROMWICH, WEST (St James) (St Paul) *Lich 27* **P** *Bp and V Tipton St Martin and St Paul* **V** D HART

BROMWICH, WEST (St Peter) *Lich 27* **P** *Bp* **V** I NEWTON

BROMWICH, WEST (St Philip) *Lich 27* **P** *Bp* **V** *vacant* 0121-525 1985

BROMYARD (St Peter) and Stoke Lacy *Heref 2* **P** *Bp (4 turns), Exors P H G Morgan Esq (1 turn)* **V** G T G SYKES, **NSM** C A STOKES, C M SYKES, D B HYETT

BROMYARD DOWNS (Mission Church) *see* Bromyard and Stoke Lacy *Heref*

BRONDESBURY (Christ Church) (St Laurence) *Lon 21* **P** *Ld Chan* **R** D E NENO, **C** N CRITCHLOW

BRONDESBURY St Anne w Kilburn (Holy Trinity) *Lon 21* **P** *Bp and Ch Patr Soc (alt)* **V** F B CAPIE, **NSM** L C F HILLEL

BROOK (St Mary) *see* Wye w Brook and Hastingleigh etc *Cant*

BROOKE (St Mary the Virgin) *see* Brighstone and Brooke w Mottistone *Portsm*

BROOKE (St Peter) *see* Oakham, Hambleton, Egleton, Braunston and Brooke *Pet*

BROOKE (St Peter), Kirstead, Mundham w Seething and Thwaite *Nor 5* **P** *G&C Coll Cam, Gt Hosp and Countess Ferrers, and Ld Chan (by turn)* **R** J H ROBSON

BROOKE STREET (St Alban the Martyr) *see* Holborn St Alb w Saffron Hill St Pet *Lon*

BROOKEND (Mission Room) *see* Sharpness, Purton, Brookend and Slimbridge *Glouc*

BROOKFIELD (St Anne), Highgate Rise *Lon 17* **P** *Bp* **V** A J B MELDRUM

BROOKFIELD (St Margaret) *York 21* **P** *Abp* **V** R W SMITH
BROOKFIELD (St Mary) *Lon 17* **P** *Bp* **V** C G POPE
BROOKHOUSE (St Paul) *see* Caton w Littledale *Blackb*
BROOKHURST (St Peter's Chapel) *see* Eastham *Ches*
BROOKING (St Barnabas) *see* Totnes w Bridgetown, Berry
Pomeroy etc *Ex*
BROOKLAND (St Augustine) *see* Appledore w Brookland,
Fairfield, Brenzett etc *Cant*
BROOKLANDS *see* Baguley *Man*
BROOKSBY (St Michael and All Angels) *see* Upper Wreake
Leic
BROOKSIDE (Pastoral Centre) *see* Cen Telford *Lich*
BROOKWOOD (St Saviour) *see* Knaphill w Brookwood *Guildf*
BROOM (St Matthew) *see* Bidford-on-Avon *Cov*
BROOM LEYS (St David) *Leic 8* **P** *Bp* **V** J W STEVENSON
BROOM VALLEY (St Barnabas) *see* Rotherham *Sheff*
BROOME (St Michael) *see* Ditchingham, Hedenham, Broome,
Earsham etc *Nor*
BROOME (St Peter) *see* Churchill-in-Halfshire w Blakedown
and Broome *Worc*
BROOMFIELD (St Margaret) *see* Hollingbourne and Hucking
w Leeds and Broomfield *Cant*
BROOMFIELD (St Mary and All Saints) *see* Kingston St Mary
w Broomfield etc *B & W*
BROOMFIELD (St Mary w St Leonard) *Chelmsf 8* **P** *Bp*
V P E BALL
BROOMFLEET (St Mary) *see* S Cave and Ellerker w
Broomfleet *York*
BROOMHILL (St Mark) *see* Sheff St Mark Broomhill *Sheff*
**BROSELEY (All Saints) w Benthall, Jackfield, Linley, Willey and
Barrow** *Heref 14* **P** *Patr Bd* **R** M A KINNA,
NSM B D SHINTON
**BROTHERTOFT Group, The (Christ Church) (St Gilbert of
Sempringham)** *Linc 21* **P** *Bp* (2 turns), V Algarkirk (1 turn)
V vacant (01205) 280856
BROTHERTON (St Edward the Confessor) *Wakef 10* **P** *D&C*
York **P-in-c** E M WOODCOCK
BROTTON PARVA (St Margaret) *York 16* **P** *Abp*
R G R DREWERY
BROUGH (All Saints) *see* Elloughton and Brough w
Brantingham *York*
BROUGH (St Michael) w Stainmore, Musgrave and Warcop
Carl 1 **P** *Bp* (2 turns) and Lord Hothfield (1 turn)
P-in-c B G MAGORRIAN
BROUGHAM (St Wilfrid Chapel) *see* Lowther and Askham
and Clifton and Brougham *Carl*
BROUGHTON (All Saints) *see* Warboys w Broughton and
Bury w Wistow *Ely*
BROUGHTON (All Saints), Marton and Thornton *Bradf 7*
P *Ch Ch Ox and Exors Dame Harriet Nelson* (jt)
R N A TURNER, **C** P A TURNER
BROUGHTON (no church) *Ox 21* **P** *Ch Patr Trust*
Hon C G M BUTTERWORTH
**BROUGHTON (St Andrew) w Loddington and Cransley and
Thorpe Malsor** *Pet 9* **P** *Ld Chan* (1 turn), Bp (2 turns), and
Keble Coll Ox (1 turn) **P-in-c** B J WITHINGTON,
C P S SEATON-BURN, R A PRIESTLEY, **NSM** A R G DUTTON,
C H DOBSON
BROUGHTON (St James) (St Clement and St Matthias)
St John the Baptist *Man 6* **P** *Patr Bd* **TR** H R F MARTIN,
C S D J COOK, **OLM** J S CORRIE
BROUGHTON (St John the Baptist) *Blackb 13* **P** *Trustees*
V S FOX, **C** N F E STARKEY
BROUGHTON (St Mary) *Lich 22* **P** *D R B Thompson Esq*
P-in-c P F BARNES, A EVANS
BROUGHTON (St Mary) *Linc 6* **P** *MMCET* **R** J W COTTON
**BROUGHTON (St Mary Magdalene) (Holy Innocents) and
Duddon** *Carl 9* **P** *V Millom, Lt-Col D A S Pennefather, and
Ch Patr Trust* (by turn) **P-in-c** A P ADAMS
BROUGHTON (St Mary the Virgin) *see* Wykeham *Ox*
**BROUGHTON (St Mary) w Bossington and Houghton and
Mottisfont** *Win 12* **P** *Ld Chan* (1 turn), Mr and Mrs
R G L Pugh, A Humbert Esq and Miss R A Humbert (jt)
(2 turns) **R** R A CORNE
BROUGHTON (St Peter) w Croxton and Cotes Heath w Standon
Lich 7 **P** *Bp, V Eccleshall, and T A J Hall Esq* (jt)
C J P EADES, S G MCKENZIE
BROUGHTON, GREAT (Christ Church) *see* Brigham, Gt
Broughton and Broughton Moor *Carl*
BROUGHTON, LOWER (Ascension) *Man 6* **P** *Trustees*
P-in-c D S C WYATT
BROUGHTON, NETHER (St Mary the Virgin) *see* Old Dalby,
Nether Broughton, Saxelbye etc *Leic*
BROUGHTON, UPPER (St Luke) *see* Hickling w Kinoulton
and Broughton Sulney *S'well*
BROUGHTON ASTLEY (St Mary) and Croft w Stoney Stanton
Leic 7 **P** *Patr Bd* **TR** D T SHAW

**BROUGHTON GIFFORD (St Mary the Virgin), Great
Chalfield and Holt St Katharine** *Sarum 14* **P** *D&C Bris*
(3 turns), Ld Chan (2 turns), and R C Floyd Esq (1 turn)
P-in-c A E EVANS, **C** J PERRETT, D G SMITH,
NSM J DARLING, **OLM** E A FIELDEN, N G LOCK,
A E WINTOUR
BROUGHTON HACKETT (St Leonard) *see* Peopleton and
White Ladies Aston w Churchill etc *Worc*
BROUGHTON IN FURNESS (St Mary Magdalene)
see Broughton and Duddon *Carl*
BROUGHTON MILLS (Holy Innocents) *as above*
BROUGHTON MOOR (St Columba) *see* Brigham, Gt
Broughton and Broughton Moor *Carl*
BROUGHTON POGGS (St Peter) *see* Shill Valley and
Broadshire *Ox*
BROWN CANDOVER (St Peter) *see* The Candover Valley *Win*
BROWN CLEE *see* Ditton Priors w Neenton, Burwarton etc
Heref
BROWN EDGE (St Anne) *Lich 8* **P** *Bp* **P-in-c** R J S GRIGSON
BROWNHILL (St Saviour) *Wakef 8* **P** *V Batley*
V P N A SENIOR
BROWNHILLS (St James) *see* Ogley Hay *Lich*
BROWNSOVER (Christ Church) *see* Clifton upon Dunsmore w
Newton and Brownsover *Cov*
BROWNSWOOD PARK (St John the Evangelist) *Lon 5* **P** *City
Corp* **P-in-c** J D CLARK, **C** M J HAWKES, L ASHDOWN
BROXBOURNE (St Augustine) w Wormley *St Alb 20* **P** *Bp and
Peache Trustees* (jt) **R** I J TOMKINS, **C** S J CHAPMAN,
NSM R A MARTIN
BROXHOLME (All Saints) *see* Saxilby Gp *Linc*
**BROXTED (St Mary the Virgin) w Chickney and Tilty and Great
and Little Easton** *Chelmsf 18* **P** *Mrs F Spurrier* (2 turns),
DBP (1 turn), and MMCET (1 turn) **P-in-c** I E CRAWFORD
BROXTOWE (St Martha) *S'well 14* **P** *Bp*
P-in-c J M KIRKHAM
BRUERA (St Mary) *see* Waverton w Aldford and Bruera *Ches*
BRUISYARD (St Peter) *see* Upper Alde *St E*
BRUMBY (St Hugh) (All Saints) *Linc 4* **P** *Bp*
TR C A B MARTIN, **OLM** A K PEAT
BRUNDALL (St Lawrence) w Braydeston and Postwick *Nor 4*
P *Bp and MMCET* (jt) **R** D L SMITH, **C** A J AVERY
BRUNDISH (St Lawrence) *see* Laxfield, Cratfield, Wilby and
Brundish *St E*
BRUNSWICK (Christ Church) *Man 4* **P** *Ch Soc Trust*
R S J T GATENBY, **C** J B EDSON, **NSM** R M YOUNG
BRUNSWICK (St Cuthbert) *see* The King *Newc*
BRUNTCLIFFE (St Andrew) *see* Morley *Wakef*
BRUNTINGTHORPE (St Mary) *see* Hexagon *Leic*
BRUNTON PARK (St Aidan) *see* The King *Newc*
BRUSHFORD (St Mary the Virgin) *Ex 20* **P** *D&C*
V P J NORMAN
BRUSHFORD (St Nicholas) *see* Dulverton and Brushford
B & W
BRUTON (Blessed Virgin Mary) and District *B & W 2*
P *Patr Bd* **P-in-c** J M BAILEY, **C** T G RAE SMITH
BRYANSTON SQUARE (St Mary) w St Marylebone (St Mark)
Lon 4 **P** *The Crown* **R** J P T PETERS, **C** A N KIRKE,
P HUGHES, G L DICKINSON, L A M W FLINT, **NSM** B J KISSELL
BRYANSTON STREET (Annunciation) *see* St Marylebone
Annunciation Bryanston Street *Lon*
BRYHER (All Saints) *see* Is of Scilly *Truro*
BRYMPTON (St Andrew) *see* Odcombe, Brympton, Lufton
and Montacute *B & W*
BRYN (St Chad) *see* Clun w Bettws-y-Crwyn and Newcastle
Heref
BRYN (St Peter) *Liv 14* **P** *Bp* **V** D J HOOTON
BUBBENHALL (St Giles) *see* Baginton w Bubbenhall and
Ryton-on-Dunsmore *Cov*
BUBWITH (All Saints) w Skipwith *York 2* **P** *Abp and D&C, and
Ld Chan* (alt) **P-in-c** J M OLIVER
BUCKDEN (St Mary) w the Offords *Ely 13* **P** *Bp and
Ld Chan* (alt) **R** A M BARRETT, **C** T D M HAYWARD
BUCKENHAM, NEW (St Martin) *see* Quidenham Gp *Nor*
BUCKENHAM, OLD (All Saints) *as above*
BUCKERELL (St Mary and St Giles) *see* Honiton, Gittisham,
Combe Raleigh, Monkton etc *Ex*
BUCKFAST SANCTUARY (not known) *see* Buckfastleigh w
Dean Prior *Ex*
**BUCKFASTLEIGH (Holy Trinity) (St Luke's Mission) w Dean
Prior** *Ex 13* **P** *D&C* (2 turns), DBP (1 turn)
V D J ROWLAND, **NSM** J N C IRWIN
BUCKHORN WESTON (St John the Baptist) *see* Stour Vale
Sarum

BUCKHURST HILL (St Elisabeth) (St John the Baptist) (St Stephen) *Chelmsf 24*   **P** *Patr Bd*   **TR** I D FARLEY, **C** C J BRIXTON

BUCKINGHAM (St Peter and St Paul) *Ox 22*   **P** *Bp, Adn Buckm, Mrs S A J Doulton, G&C Coll Cam, New Coll Ox, and Exors R J Dalziel Smith Esq (jt)*   **C** P D DERBYSHIRE, **NSM** J F KING

BUCKINGHAM, NORTH *Ox 22*   **P** *Ch Soc Trust, Mrs J M Williams, and D J Robarts Esq (by turn)*   **R** J A TALING

BUCKINGHAM, WEST *Ox 22*   **P** *Bp, D&C Westmr, G Purefoy Esq, and R L Randall Esq (1 turn), New Coll Ox (1 turn), and DBP (1 turn)*   **P-in-c** E A SIMPSON, **NSM** C P CARTER

BUCKLAND (All Saints)   *see* Aston Clinton w Buckland and Drayton Beauchamp *Ox*

BUCKLAND (St Mary the Virgin)   *see* Cherbury w Gainfield *Ox*

BUCKLAND (St Mary the Virgin)   *see* Betchworth and Buckland *S'wark*

BUCKLAND (St Michael)   *see* Winchcombe *Glouc*

BUCKLAND, EAST (St Michael)   *see* S Molton w Nymet St George, High Bray etc *Ex*

BUCKLAND, WEST (Blessed Virgin Mary)   *see* Wellington and Distr *B & W*

BUCKLAND, WEST (St Peter)   *see* Swimbridge w W Buckland and Landkey *Ex*

BUCKLAND BREWER (St Mary and St Benedict)   *see* Parkham, Alwington, Buckland Brewer etc *Ex*

BUCKLAND DINHAM (St Michael and All Angels)   *see* Mells w Buckland Dinham, Elm, Whatley etc *B & W*

BUCKLAND FILLEIGH (St Mary and Holy Trinity)   *see* Shebbear, Buckland Filleigh, Sheepwash etc *Ex*

BUCKLAND IN DOVER (St Andrew) w Buckland Valley (St Nicholas) *Cant 4*   **P** *Abp*   **R** T FOREMAN

BUCKLAND IN THE MOOR (St Peter)   *see* Ashburton, Bickington, Buckland in the Moor etc *Ex*

BUCKLAND MONACHORUM (St Andrew) *Ex 25*   **P** *Bp* **V** G M COTTER

BUCKLAND NEWTON (Holy Rood), Cerne Abbas, Godmanstone and Minterne Magna *Sarum 1*   **P** *Adn Sherborne, Lord Digby, D H C Batten Esq, G E H Gallia Esq, and Col J L Yeatman (jt)*   **V** K S CURNOCK, **NSM** K C GOODMAN

BUCKLAND RIPERS (St Nicholas)   *see* Bincombe w Broadwey, Upwey and Buckland Ripers *Sarum*

BUCKLAND ST MARY (Blessed Virgin Mary)   *see* Blackdown *B & W*

BUCKLAND TOUT SAINTS (St Peter)   *see* Stokenham, Slapton, Charleton w Buckland etc *Ex*

BUCKLAND VALLEY (St Nicholas)   *see* Buckland in Dover w Buckland Valley *Cant*

BUCKLEBURY (St Mary) w Marlston *Ox 12*   **P** *C J Pratt Esq* **P-in-c** J T D M GADSBY,   **C** D M CHATTELL,   **NSM** R C OBIN, L E BLISS

BUCKLEBURY, UPPER (All Saints)   *see* Bucklebury w Marlston *Ox*

BUCKLERS HARD (St Mary)   *see* Beaulieu and Exbury and E Boldre *Win*

BUCKLESHAM (St Mary)   *see* Nacton and Levington w Bucklesham etc *St E*

BUCKMINSTER (St John the Baptist)   *see* S Framland *Leic*

BUCKNALL (St Margaret)   *see* Woodhall Spa Gp *Linc*

BUCKNALL Team Ministry, The (St Mary the Virgin) *Lich 12* **P** *Patr Bd*   **TR** M K ELLOR,   **TV** M N STEPHENS, **C** D A FRASER,   **OLM** J MARSHALL

BUCKNELL (St Mary) w Chapel Lawn, Llanfair Waterdine and Stowe *Heref 10*   **P** *Earl of Powis, Grocers' Co, and J Coltman Rogers Esq (jt)*   **V** vacant (01547) 530340

BUCKNELL (St Peter)   *see* Bicester w Bucknell, Caversfield and Launton *Ox*

BUCKROSE, WEST *York 6*   **P** *Ld Chan (1 turn), Lord Middleton and Abp (3 turns)*   **R** vacant

BUCKROSE CARRS *York 6*   **P** *Prime Min, Major G R H Cholmley, Sir Philip Naylor-Leyland Bt, and D&C (by turn)*   **R** J M DUKE

BUCKS MILLS (St Anne)   *see* Parkham, Alwington, Buckland Brewer etc *Ex*

BUCKWORTH (All Saints) *Ely 10*   **P** *Bp*   **P-in-c** I P YOUNG

BUDBROOKE (St Michael) *Cov 11*   **P** *MMCET* **P-in-c** D A BROWN,   **OLM** M LODGE

BUDE HAVEN (St Michael and All Angels) and Marhamchurch *Truro 8*   **P** *Bp and PCC (jt)*   **P-in-c** D C STANDEN

BUDLEIGH, EAST (All Saints) w Bicton and Otterton *Ex 1* **P** *Lord Clinton*   **P-in-c** J S CACKETT

BUDLEIGH SALTERTON (St Peter) *Ex 1*   **P** *Lord Clinton* **V** R S J CHARLES

BUDOCK (St Budock) *Truro 3*   **P** *Bp*   **V** G K BENNETT, **C** R M PAUL

BUDWORTH, GREAT (St Mary and All Saints) *Ches 4* **P** *Ch Ch Ox*   **V** A G BROWN

BUDWORTH, LITTLE (St Peter)   *see* Whitegate w Lt Budworth *Ches*

BUGBROOKE (St Michael and All Angels) w Rothersthorpe *Pet 3*   **P** *Exors E W Harrison (2 turns), DBP (1 turn)* **P-in-c** S R J FRENCH

BUGLAWTON (St John the Evangelist)   *see* Congleton *Ches*

BUGTHORPE (St Andrew)   *see* Garrowby Hill *York*

BUILDWAS (Holy Trinity)   *see* Wrockwardine Deanery *Lich*

BULCOTE (Holy Trinity)   *see* Burton Joyce w Bulcote and Stoke Bardolph *S'well*

BULFORD (St Leonard)   *see* Avon Valley *Sarum*

BULKELEY (All Saints)   *see* Bickerton, Bickley, Harthill and Burwardsley *Ches*

BULKINGTON (Christ Church)   *see* Seend, Bulkington and Poulshot *Sarum*

BULKINGTON (St James) *Cov 5*   **P** *Ld Chan*   **V** vacant (024) 7631 8241

BULKWORTHY (St Michael)   *see* Bradworthy, Sutcombe, Putford etc *Ex*

BULLEY (St Michael and All Angels)   *see* Huntley and Longhope, Churcham and Bulley *Glouc*

BULLINGHOPE, UPPER (St Peter)   *see* Heref S Wye *Heref*

BULLINGTON (St Michael and All Angels)   *see* Lower Dever *Win*

BULMER (St Andrew)   *see* N Hinckford *Chelmsf*

BULMER (St Martin)   *see* Howardian Gp *York*

BULPHAN (St Mary the Virgin)   *see* Orsett and Bulphan and Horndon on the Hill *Chelmsf*

BULWELL (St John the Divine) *S'well 12*   **P** *Bp*   **V** D GRAY

BULWELL (St Mary the Virgin and All Souls) *S'well 12*   **P** *Bp* **P-in-c** A J NICOLLS

BULWICK (St Nicholas) and Blatherwycke w Harringworth and Laxton *Pet 10*   **P** *G T G Conant Esq (3 turns), F & A George Ltd (1 turn)*   **C** J E BAXTER, P J DAVIES

BUNBURY (St Boniface) and Tilstone Fearnall *Ches 5* **P** *Haberdashers' Co*   **V** R J GATES

BUNCTON (All Saints)   *see* Ashington, Washington and Wiston w Buncton *Chich*

BUNGAY (Holy Trinity) w St Mary *St E 14*   **P** *DBP* **P-in-c** I B BYRNE,   **NSM** L JACQUET,   **OLM** R C B ALLEN

BUNNY (St Mary the Virgin)   *see* Keyworth and Stanton-on-the-Wolds and Bunny etc *S'well*

BUNWELL (St Michael and All Angels), Carleton Rode, Tibenham, Great Moulton and Aslacton *Nor 5*   **P** *Bp and DBP (alt)*   **R** vacant (01953) 789218

BURBAGE (All Saints)   *see* Savernake *Sarum*

BURBAGE (Christ Church)   *see* Buxton w Burbage and King Sterndale *Derby*

BURBAGE (St Catherine) w Aston Flamville *Leic 10* **P** *Ball Coll Ox*   **R** F D JENNINGS,   **NSM** R STEPHEN

BURCHETTS GREEN *Ox 13*   **P** *DBP and Bp (jt)* **V** K B NICHOLLS,   **NSM** D M WOODMORE

BURE VALLEY Benefice, The *Nor 19*   **P** *Bp, Mercers' Co, and J M Roberts Esq (jt)*   **C** E C BAILEY

BURES (St Mary the Virgin) w Assington and Lt Cornard *St E 12* **P** *DBP and Bp (jt)*   **V** R L C KING,   **C** A J WOLTON, **NSM** K M KING, M J CANTACUZENE,   **OLM** J L GOYMOUR

BURFORD First Portion *Heref 12*   **P** *DBP, Bp Birm, Bp, and J J C Caldwell Esq (jt)*   **R** vacant

BURFORD Second Portion (St Mary) w Greete and Hope Bagot *Heref 12*   **P** *DBP*   **R** vacant

BURFORD (St John the Baptist) w Fulbrook, Taynton, Asthall, Swinbrook and Widford *Ox 8*   **P** *Bp and Capt D Mackinnon (jt)*   **V** R M COOMBS,   **C** T M GARRETT, **Hon C** N R GARRETT,   **OLM** C REAVLEY

BURFORD Third Portion (St Mary) w Little Hereford *Heref 12* **P** *DBP and Bp Birm (jt)*   **R** vacant

BURGATE (St Mary)   *see* N Hartismere *St E*

BURGESS HILL (St Andrew) *Chich 9*   **P** *Bp*   **V** I G PRIOR

BURGESS HILL (St Edward) *Chich 9*   **P** *Bp Chich, Bp Horsham, and R Clayton w Keymer (jt)*   **V** D M BRADSHAW, **NSM** S S MACCARTHY

BURGESS HILL (St John the Evangelist) *Chich 9*   **P** *Bp Chich, Bp Horsham, and R Clayton w Keymer (jt)*   **V** M C KNOWLES

BURGH Group, The *Linc 8*   **P** *Bp (2 turns), H J Montgomery-Massingberd Esq (1 turn), SMF (1 turn)*   **R** I STEELE

BURGH (St Botolph)   *see* Boulge w Burgh, Grundisburgh and Hasketon *St E*

BURGH (St Margaret and St Mary)   *see* S Trin Broads *Nor*

BURGH (St Peter)   *see* Raveningham Gp *Nor*
BURGH-BY-SANDS (St Michael)   *see* Barony of Burgh *Carl*
BURGH CASTLE (St Peter and St Paul)   *see* Belton and Burgh Castle *Nor*
BURGH HEATH (St Mary the Virgin)   *see* Howell Hill w Burgh Heath *Guildf*
BURGH LE MARSH (St Peter and St Paul)   *see* Burgh Gp *Linc*
BURGH-NEXT-AYLSHAM (St Mary)   *see* Bure Valley *Nor*
BURGH-ON-BAIN (St Helen)   *see* Asterby Gp *Linc*
BURGH PARVA (St Mary)   *see* Briston, Burgh Parva, Hindolveston etc *Nor*
BURGHCLERE (Ascension) (All Saints) w Newtown and Ecchinswell w Sydmonton *Win 6*   **P** *Earl of Carnarvon*
   R D G BARTHOLOMEW
BURGHFIELD (St Mary the Virgin) *Ox 12*   **P** *Earl of Shrewsbury*   **P-in-c** G J LOVELL,   **NSM** M A HARWOOD
BURGHILL (St Mary the Virgin) *Heref 4*   **P** *DBP*
   V J W R MORRISON,   **NSM** E S V VERWEY, P A LITTLEWOOD
BURGHWALLIS (St Helen) and Campsall *Sheff 7*   **P** *Bp* (2 turns), *Mrs E H I Ellison-Anne (1 turn)*   **R** M G JOHNSON
BURHAM (Methodist Church) and Wouldham *Roch 5*   **P** *Bp and Ld Chan (alt)*   **P-in-c** J M BRADSHAW
BURITON (St Mary the Virgin) *Portsm 4*   **P** *Bp*
   R W G HARRIS-EVANS,   **NSM** D C STICKLAND
BURLESCOMBE (St Mary)   *see* Sampford Peverell, Uplowman, Holcombe Rogus etc *Ex*
BURLEY (St Matthias) *Ripon 7*   **P** *G M Bedford Esq, J C Yeadon Esq, E Beety Esq, Mrs M E Dunham, and Mrs L M Rawse (jt)*   **V** K TROUT,   **NSM** M PLANT
BURLEY IN WHARFEDALE (St Mary the Virgin) *Bradf 4*
   P *Bp*   **V** M BURLEY,   **C** E A LENNON
BURLEY VILLE (St John the Baptist) *Win 9*   **P** *V Ringwood*
   P-in-c D M WEBSTER
BURLEYDAM (St Mary and St Michael)   *see* Baddiley and Wrenbury w Burleydam *Ches*
BURLINGHAM (St Andrew)   *see* Acle w Fishley, N Burlingham, Beighton w Moulton *Nor*
BURLINGHAM (St Edmund King and Martyr) w Lingwood, Strumpshaw w Hassingham and Buckenham *Nor 4*   **P** *Ch Soc Trust, MMCET, and Bp (jt)*   **R** D K WAKEFIELD
BURLTON (St Anne)   *see* Loppington w Newtown *Lich*
BURMANTOFTS (St Stephen and St Agnes) *Ripon 5*
   P *Ch Trust Fund Trust*   **NSM** I WILLIAMS
BURMARSH (All Saints)   *see* Dymchurch w Burmarsh and Newchurch *Cant*
BURMINGTON (St Nicholas and St Barnabas)   *see* S Warks Seven Gp *Cov*
BURNAGE (St Margaret) *Man 3*   **P** *Bp*   **R** I D THOMPSON
BURNAGE (St Nicholas) *Man 8*   **P** *Trustees*   **P-in-c** R MANN
BURNBY (St Giles) *York 5*   **P** *Trustees*   **NSM** S D JONES
BURNESIDE (St Oswald)   *see* Beacon *Carl*
BURNESTON (St Lambert)   *see* Kirklington w Burneston and Wath and Pickhill *Ripon*
BURNETT (St Michael)   *see* Keynsham *B & W*
BURNEY LANE (Christ Church)   *see* Ward End w Bordesley Green *Birm*
BURNHAM (St Andrew) *B & W 1*   **P** *D&C*   **V** G R WITTS
BURNHAM (St Mary the Virgin) *Chelmsf 11*
   P *N D Beckett Esq and Walsingham Coll Trust (jt)*   **V** *vacant* (01621) 782071
BURNHAM (St Peter) *Ox 23*   **P** *Eton Coll*   **V** W S JACKSON
BURNHAM DEEPDALE (St Mary)   *see* Hunstanton St Mary w Ringstead Parva etc *Nor*
BURNHAM NORTON (St Margaret)   *see* Burnham Gp of Par *Nor*
BURNHAM-ON-CROUCH (St Mary the Virgin)   *see* Burnham *Chelmsf*
BURNHAM-ON-SEA (St Andrew)   *as above*
BURNHAM OVERY (St Clement)   *see* Burnham Gp of Par *Nor*
BURNHAM THORPE (All Saints)   *as above*
BURNHAM ULPH (All Saints)   *as above*
BURNHAM WESTGATE (St Mary), Burnham Norton, Burnham Overy, Burnham Thorpe, and Burnham Sutton w Ulph (The Burnham Group of Parishes) *Nor 15*   **P** *Ch Coll Cam (1 turn), Ld Chan (2 turns), and DBP (1 turn)*   **R** *vacant* (01328) 738317
BURNLEY (St Andrew) w St Margaret and Burnley St James *Blackb 3*   **P** *Prime Min and R Burnley St Pet (alt)*
   V P R HAPGOOD-STRICKLAND
BURNLEY (St Catherine) (St Alban) and St Paul *Blackb 3*
   P *R Burnley*   **V** R T D PARKER
BURNLEY (St Cuthbert) *Blackb 3*   **P** *R Burnley*
   P-in-c I C WATTS
BURNLEY (St Mark) *Blackb 3*   **P** *Bp*   **P-in-c** C W HILL
BURNLEY (St Matthew the Apostle) Habergham Eaves w Holy Trinity *Blackb 3*   **P** *R Burnley*   **V** *vacant* (01282) 424839

BURNLEY (St Peter) *Blackb 3*   **P** *Bp*   **R** T A G BILL
BURNLEY (St Stephen) *Blackb 3*   **P** *R Burnley*
   P-in-c T A G BILL,   **Hon C** L LAYCOCK
BURNLEY, WEST (All Saints) *Blackb 3*   **P** *Bp and R Burnley (jt)*   **P-in-c** C W HILL,   **C** D J LLOYD
BURNMOOR (St Barnabas) *Dur 14*   **P** *Lord Lambton*
   P-in-c E M WILKINSON
BURNOPFIELD (St James) *Dur 4*   **P** *Bp*   **V** R G BIRCHALL,   **NSM** H MURRAY
BURNSALL (St Wilfrid) w Rylstone *Bradf 7*   **P** *Exors Earl of Craven and CPAS (jt)*   **P-in-c** A J CHRICH,   **C** F JENKINS,   **NSM** K M HAMMOND
BURNT OAK (St Alphage)   *see* Hendon St Alphage *Lon*
BURNT YATES (St Andrew)   *see* Ripley w Burnt Yates *Ripon*
BURNTWOOD (Christ Church) *Lich 1*   **P** *D&C*
   V M M MATTOCKS,   **OLM** C J LATIMER
BURPHAM (Holy Spirit) (St Luke) Guildford *Guildf 5*   **P** *Bp*
   V C J MATTHEWS,   **NSM** C E REDDIN, J C L RUNNACLES
BURPHAM (St Mary the Virgin) *Chich 1*   **P** *D&C*   **V** *vacant* (01903) 882948
BURRADON (Good Shepherd)   *see* Weetslade *Newc*
BURRILL (Mission Church)   *see* Bedale and Leeming and Thornton Watlass *Ripon*
BURRINGTON (Holy Trinity)   *see* Wrington w Butcombe and Burrington *B & W*
BURRINGTON (Holy Trinity), Chawleigh, Cheldon, Chulmleigh, Meshaw, Thelbridge, Wembworthy, Witheridge and the Worlingtons *Ex 19*   **P** *Patr Bd*   **TR** R D WITHNELL,
   TV J HANNA
BURRINGTON (St George)   *see* Wigmore Abbey *Heref*
BURROUGH GREEN (St Augustine of Canterbury)   *see* Raddesley Gp *Ely*
BURROUGH HILL Parishes, The: Burrough on the Hill, Great Dalby, Little Dalby, Pickwell and Somerby *Leic 2*   **P** *Bp, DBP, and Mrs M Burdett Fisher (jt)*   **P-in-c** M N DALE,
   C M W R COVINGTON
BURROUGH ON THE HILL (St Mary the Virgin)
   see Burrough Hill Pars *Leic*
BURROWBRIDGE (St Michael)   *see* Athelney *B & W*
BURRSVILLE (St Mark)   *see* Gt Clacton *Chelmsf*
BURSCOUGH BRIDGE (St John) (St Andrew) (St Cyprian) *Liv 11*   **P** *V Ormskirk*   **P-in-c** J R JONES,
   C I R GREENWOOD,   **OLM** B ABRAHAM
BURSDON MOOR (St Martin)   *see* Parkham, Alwington, Buckland Brewer etc *Ex*
BURSEA (Chapel)   *see* Holme and Seaton Ross Gp *York*
BURSLEDON Pilands Wood (St Paul)   *see* Bursledon *Win*
BURSLEDON (St Leonard) *Win 10*   **P** *Bp*   **V** P A VARGESON,
   C J E OGLEY,   **NSM** C A PARKES
BURSLEM (St John the Baptist) (St Paul) *Lich 11*   **P** *Bp and MMCET (jt)*   **R** C R JOHNSON
BURSLEM (St Werburgh) *Lich 11*   **P** *Bp*   **V** K L ROUND
BURSTALL (St Mary the Virgin)   *see* Sproughton w Burstall, Copdock w Washbrook etc *St E*
BURSTEAD, GREAT (St Mary Magdalene) *Chelmsf 6*   **P** *Bp*
   V S SWIFT
BURSTEAD, LITTLE (St Mary)   *see* Billericay and Lt Burstead *Chelmsf*
BURSTOCK (St Andrew)   *see* Beaminster Area *Sarum*
BURSTON (St Mary)   *see* Winfarthing w Shelfanger w Burston w Gissing etc *Nor*
BURSTON (St Rufin)   *see* Mid Trent *Lich*
BURSTOW (St Bartholomew) w Horne *S'wark 25*   **P** *Ld Chan and Bp (alt)*   **R** C E GALE
BURSTWICK (All Saints) w Thorngumbald *York 12*   **P** *Abp*
   V A J BURDON,   **Hon C** I J BLYTH,   **NSM** P M BURDON
BURTLE (St Philip and St James)   *see* Shapwick w Ashcott and Burtle *B & W*
BURTON (All Saints) w Christ Church *Lich 14*   **P** *CPAS and Ch Soc Trust (jt)*   **V** N R IRONS,   **C** S WILLETTS
BURTON (St Aidan) (St Paul) *Lich 14*   **P** *Bp and Lord Burton (jt)*   **V** P A FARTHING
BURTON (St James) and Holme *Carl 10*   **P** *Simeon's Trustees*
   P-in-c P G BAXENDALE
BURTON (St Luke) and Sopley *Win 9*   **P** *Bp and D&C Cant (alt)*   **P-in-c** M C SURMAN
BURTON (St Nicholas) and Shotwick *Ches 9*   **P** *D&C (1 turn) and St Jo Hosp Lich (2 turns)*   **V** C M HELM
BURTON w COATES (St Agatha)   *see* Barlavington, Burton w Coates, Sutton and Bignor *Chich*
BURTON AGNES (St Martin)   *see* The Beacon *York*
BURTON BRADSTOCK (St Mary)   *see* Bride Valley *Sarum*
BURTON BY LINCOLN (St Vincent)   *see* Spring Line Gp *Linc*
BURTON COGGLES (St Thomas à Becket)   *see* N Beltisloe Gp *Linc*

BURTON DASSETT (All Saints) *Cov 8* **P** *Bp* **V** P T FRANCIS
BURTON FLEMING (St Cuthbert) w Fordon, Grindale and Wold Newton *York 9* **P** *Abp and MMCET (jt)*
P-in-c G J OWEN, **Hon C** M H WAINWRIGHT
BURTON GREEN (Chapel of Ease) *see* Kenilworth St Nic *Cov*
BURTON HASTINGS (St Botolph) *see* Wolvey w Burton Hastings, Copston Magna etc *Cov*
BURTON IN LONSDALE (All Saints) *see* Thornton in Lonsdale w Burton in Lonsdale *Bradf*
BURTON JOYCE (St Helen) w Bulcote and Stoke Bardolph *S'well 10* **P** *MMCET* **V** J A FISHER
BURTON LATIMER (St Mary the Virgin) *Pet 9* **P** *Bp*
R Q D CHANDLER
BURTON LAZARS (St James) *see* Melton Mowbray *Leic*
BURTON LEONARD (St Leonard) *see* Ripon Cathl *Ripon*
BURTON-ON-TRENT (All Saints) *see* Burton All SS w Ch Ch *Lich*
BURTON-ON-TRENT (St Aidan) *see* Burton St Aid and St Paul *Lich*
BURTON-ON-TRENT (St Chad) *Lich 14* **P** *Bp*
P-in-c G J CROSSLEY, **OLM** P J ORTON
BURTON-ON-TRENT (St Modwen) *see* Burton St Modwen *Lich*
BURTON-ON-TRENT (St Paul) *see* Burton St Aid and St Paul *Lich*
BURTON OVERY (St Andrew) *see* Glen Magna cum Stretton Magna etc *Leic*
BURTON PEDWARDINE (St Andrew and the Blessed Virgin Mary and St Nicholas) *see* Helpringham w Hale *Linc*
BURTON PIDSEA (St Peter) and Humbleton w Elsternwick *York 12* **P** *Ld Chan and D&C (alt)* **V** J L CAMPBELL
BURTON UPON STATHER (St Andrew) *see* Flixborough w Burton upon Stather *Linc*
BURTON-UPON-TRENT (St Modwen) *Lich 14* **P** *Bp*
V *vacant* (01283) 544054
BURTONWOOD (St Michael) *Liv 15* **P** *R Warrington* **Hon C** A LITTON
BURWARDSLEY (St John) *see* Bickerton, Bickley, Harthill and Burwardsley *Ches*
BURWASH (St Bartholomew) *Chich 14* **P** *BNC Ox*
R S M FRANCE
BURWASH WEALD (St Philip) *Chich 15* **P** *Bp*
P-in-c J C HAWKINS
BURWELL (St Andrew) (St Mary) w Reach *Ely 4* **P** *DBP*
V S G F EARL
BURY (All Saints) *see* Kirklees Valley *Man*
BURY (Christ the King) *Man 10* **P** *Patr Bd*
P-in-c K M TRIVASSE
BURY (Holy Cross) *see* Warboys w Broughton and Bury w Wistow *Ely*
BURY (Holy Trinity) *Man 10* **P** *Patr Bd* **V** *vacant* 0161-764 2006
BURY (St John the Evangelist) w Houghton and Coldwaltham and Hardham *Chich 11* **P** *Pemb Coll Ox, D&C, and Col Sir Brian Barttelot Bt (jt)* **V** D A TWINLEY
BURY (St John w St Mark) *Man 10* **P** *R Bury St Mary*
V I J STAMP, **OLM** P SANDERSON, E A BINNS
BURY (St Mary the Virgin) *Man 10* **P** *Earl of Derby*
R J C FINDON, **C** G F JOYCE
BURY St Paul *Man 10* **P** *Trustees* **V** *vacant* 0161-761 6991
BURY (St Peter) *Man 10* **P** *R Bury St Mary*
P-in-c J F J O'DWYER, **NSM** J M SMITH, C T HAYDEN
BURY (St Stephen) *see* Elton St Steph *Man*
BURY, NEW (St Catherine) (St George) (St James) w Great Lever *Man 12* **P** *Bp* **TR** R J HORROCKS,
TV S M DNISTRIANSKYJ, **NSM** D F THOMSON,
OLM A COMBER, N A COWELL, E V LARKIN
BURY, NORTH *see* Bury St Edmunds All SS w St Jo and St Geo *St E*
BURY ST EDMUNDS (All Saints) (St John the Evangelist) (St George) *St E 13* **P** *Patr Bd* **TR** J PARR, **TV** J P WEBB,
OLM J C MANN
BURY ST EDMUNDS (Cathedral of St James) District *St E 13*
V *vacant*
BURY ST EDMUNDS (Christ Church) Moreton Hall *St E 13*
P *Bp, V Bury St Edm St Jas, and V Bury St Edm St Mary (jt)*
V J L ALDERTON-FORD, **C** D G GRANTHAM,
NSM N T CORWIN
BURY ST EDMUNDS (St Mary) (St Peter's District Church) *St E 13* **P** *Hyndman Trustees* **V** M D ROGERS,
C M D J HOLDAWAY, **OLM** D T CROFTS, T SAVEGE
BURYTHORPE (All Saints) *see* W Buckrose *York*
BUSBRIDGE (St John the Baptist) and Hambledon *Guildf 4*
P *Patr Bd* **R** C J TRICKEY, **C** S J COUVELA,
NSM M P W SPENCER, L J MASON, **OLM** A SPENCER

BUSCOT (St Mary) *see* Gt Coxwell w Buscot, Coleshill etc *Ox*
BUSH END (St John the Evangelist) *see* Hatfield Broad Oak and Bush End *Chelmsf*
BUSH HILL PARK (St Mark) *Lon 18* **P** *Bp*
V P C ATHERTON, **NSM** S E HEARD
BUSH HILL PARK (St Stephen) *Lon 18* **P** *V Edmonton All SS*
V R J ANNIS
BUSHBURY (St Mary) *Lich 28* **P** *Patr Bd* **TR** P A DOBSON,
TV I R M POOLE, G R SMITH
BUSHEY (Holy Trinity) (St James) (St Paul) *St Alb 1* **P** *Bp*
R G E W BUCKLER, **NSM** V M HARVEY, B R ADAMS
BUSHEY HEATH (St Peter) *St Alb 1* **P** *Bp* **V** A J BURTON
BUSHLEY (St Peter) *see* Longdon, Castlemorton, Bushley, Queenhill etc *Worc*
BUSHMEAD (Christ Church) *St Alb 14* **P** *Bp*
P-in-c M J BURRELL
BUSSAGE (St Michael and All Angels) *Glouc 5* **P** *Bp*
V H J VAN DER LINDE
BUTCOMBE (St Michael and All Angels) *see* Wrington w Butcombe and Burrington *B & W*
BUTLEIGH (St Leonard) *see* Baltonsborough w Butleigh, W Bradley etc *B & W*
BUTLERS MARSTON (St Peter and St Paul) *see* Stourdene Gp *Cov*
BUTLEY (St John the Baptist) *see* Wilford Peninsula *St E*
BUTTERCRAMBE (St John the Evangelist) *see* Sand Hutton *York*
BUTTERLEIGH (St Matthew) *see* Silverton, Butterleigh, Bickleigh and Cadeleigh *Ex*
BUTTERMERE (St James) *see* Lorton and Loweswater w Buttermere *Carl*
BUTTERMERE (St James the Great) *see* Savernake *Sarum*
BUTTERSHAW (St Aidan) *see* Shelf w Buttershaw St Aid *Bradf*
BUTTERSHAW (St Paul) *Bradf 2* **P** *Bp* **V** D J GRIFFITHS,
C R I TAYLOR, S A GRIFFITHS
BUTTERTON (St Bartholomew) *see* Alstonfield, Butterton, Ilam etc *Lich*
BUTTERTON (St Thomas) *see* Newcastle w Butterton *Lich*
BUTTERWICK (Mission Chapel) *see* The Street Par *York*
BUTTERWICK (St Andrew) *see* Freiston, Butterwick w Bennington, and Leverton *Linc*
BUTTERWICK (St Nicholas) *see* Langtoft w Foxholes, Butterwick, Cottam etc *York*
BUTTERWICK, EAST (St Andrew) *see* Messingham *Linc*
BUTTERWICK, WEST (St Mary the Virgin) *see* Epworth Gp *Linc*
BUTTSBURY (St Mary) *see* Margaretting w Mountnessing and Buttsbury *Chelmsf*
BUXHALL (St Mary) *see* Gt Finborough w Onehouse, Harleston, Buxhall etc *St E*
BUXTED (St Margaret the Queen) (St Mary) and Hadlow Down *Chich 21* **P** *Abp, Bp, and Wagner Trustees (jt)*
NSM D J BLACKDEN
BUXTON (St Andrew) *see* Bure Valley *Nor*
BUXTON (St Anne) (St John the Baptist) (St Mary the Virgin) w Burbage and King Sterndale *Derby 4* **P** *Patr Bd*
TR J F HUDGHTON, **C** C F EDWARDS
BUXTON (Trinity Chapel) Proprietary Chapel *Derby 4*
C-in-c R MARSDEN
BUXWORTH (St James) *see* Hayfield and Chinley w Buxworth *Derby*
BY BROOK *Bris 4* **P** *Patr Bd* **TR** A C ASHCROFT,
TV V I D F PLUMB, **Hon C** M E G WARCHUS,
NSM G E WOODS
BYERS GREEN (St Peter) *Dur 6* **P** *Bp* **P-in-c** W SCOTT
BYFIELD (Holy Cross) w Boddington and Aston le Walls *Pet 1*
P *Bp, CCC Ox, and Em Coll Cam (by turn)* **R** L L RANDALL
BYFLEET (St Mary) *Guildf 12* **P** *Ld Chan* **R** J H MCCABE,
Hon C P M S ROSS-MCCABE
BYFLEET, WEST (St John) *Guildf 12* **P** *Bp*
P-in-c A B ELKINS, **C** J K ELKINS
BYFORD (St John the Baptist) *see* Letton w Staunton, Byford, Mansel Gamage etc *Heref*
BYGRAVE (St Margaret of Antioch) *see* Baldock w Bygrave and Weston *St Alb*
BYKER (St Anthony) *Newc 3* **P** *Bp* **P-in-c** D M MADZIMURE
BYKER St Mark and Walkergate (St Oswald) *Newc 3* **P** *Bp and Ch Trust Fund Trust (jt)* **V** K MOULDER
BYKER (St Martin) Newcastle upon Tyne *Newc 3* **P** *Bp*
P-in-c S E HERBERT
BYKER (St Michael w St Lawrence) *Newc 3* **P** *Bp*
P-in-c S E HERBERT
BYKER (St Silas) *Newc 3* **P** *Bp* **P-in-c** S A FAULKNER,
NSM A F TAYLOR

BYLAND, OLD (All Saints)   *see* Upper Ryedale *York*

BYLAUGH (St Mary)   *see* Lyng, Sparham, Elsing, Bylaugh, Bawdeswell etc *Nor*

BYLEY CUM LEES (St John the Evangelist)   *see* Middlewich w Byley *Ches*

BYRNESS (St Francis)   *see* N Tyne and Redesdale *Newc*

BYTHAM, LITTLE (St Medardus)   *see* Castle Bytham w Creeton *Linc*

BYTHORN (St Lawrence)   *see* Keyston and Bythorn *Ely*

BYTON (St Mary)   *see* Pembridge w Moor Court, Shobdon, Staunton etc *Heref*

BYWELL (St Peter) and Mickley *Newc 9*   **P** *Bp and Adn Lindisfarne (jt)*   **V** W RIGBY

BYWORTH (St Francis)   *see* Farnham *Guildf*

CABLE STREET (St Mary)   *see* St Geo-in-the-East St Mary *Lon*

CABOURN (St Nicholas)   *see* Swallow *Linc*

CADBURY (St Michael and All Angels)   *see* Thorverton, Cadbury, Upton Pyne etc *Ex*

CADBURY, NORTH (St Michael the Archangel)   *see* Camelot Par *B & W*

CADBURY, SOUTH (St Thomas à Becket)   *as above*

CADDINGTON (All Saints) *St Alb 14*   **P** *D&C St Paul's*   **P-in-c** R C PYKE

CADEBY (All Saints)   *see* Bosworth and Sheepy Gp *Leic*

CADELEIGH (St Bartholomew)   *see* Silverton, Butterleigh, Bickleigh and Cadeleigh *Ex*

CADGWITH (St Mary)   *see* St Ruan w St Grade and Landewednack *Truro*

CADISHEAD (St Mary the Virgin) *Man 2*   **P** *Bp*   **V** J R R TALLON,   **OLM** J DODD, J STEPHENS

CADMORE END (St Mary le Moor)   *see* Lane End w Cadmore End *Ox*

CADNEY (All Saints)   *see* Brigg, Wrawby and Cadney cum Howsham *Linc*

CADOGAN SQUARE (St Simon Zelotes)   *see* Upper Chelsea *Lon*

CAERHAYS (St Michael)   *see* St Goran w Caerhays *Truro*

CAGE GREEN (St Philip)   *see* Tonbridge SS Pet and Paul *Roch*

CAINSCROSS (St Matthew) w Selsley *Glouc 5*   **P** *Bp and Sir Charles Marling Bt (alt)*   **P-in-c** K C FLEMING,   **NSM** B P LUDLOW, M J PAGE

CAISTER NEXT YARMOUTH (Holy Trinity) (St Edmund) *Nor 6*   **P** *SMF*   **R** T C THOMPSON

CAISTOR Group, The (St Peter and St Paul) *Linc 5*   **P** *Bp and D&C (jt)*   **V** I ROBINSON,   **Hon C** S W ANDREW,   **NSM** J MCMANN

CAISTOR ST EDMUNDS (St Edmund)   *see* Stoke H Cross w Dunston, Arminghall etc *Nor*

CALBOURNE (All Saints) w Newtown *Portsm 8*   **P** *Bp*   **V** D J BEVINGTON,   **NSM** M O´DONNELL, J C LEACH

CALCOT (St Birinus)   *see* Tilehurst St Cath and Calcot *Ox*

CALDBECK (St Mungo) (Fellside), Castle Sowerby and Sebergham *Carl 3*   **P** *Bp and D&C (alt)*   **NSM** K M ASHBRIDGE

CALDECOTE (All Saints), Northill and Old Warden *St Alb 11*   **P** *Grocers' Co (2 turns), R O Shuttleworth Remembrance Trust (1 turn)*   **V** F COLEMAN,   **NSM** J S HUMPHRIES

CALDECOTE (St Michael and All Angels)   *see* Toft w Caldecote and Childerley *Ely*

CALDECOTE (St Theobald and St Chad)   *see* Weddington and Caldecote *Cov*

CALDECOTT (St John the Evangelist)   *see* Lyddington w Stoke Dry and Seaton etc *Pet*

CALDER GROVE (St John the Divine)   *see* Chapelthorpe *Wakef*

CALDER VALE (Mission)   *see* Scorton and Barnacre and Calder Vale *Blackb*

CALDER VALE (St John the Evangelist)   *as above*

CALDERBROOK (St James the Great) *Man 21*   **P** *Bp*   **P-in-c** J MCGRATH,   **OLM** B WOODHEAD

CALDMORE (St Michael and All Angels) w All Saints Palfrey *Lich 25*   **P** *Bp*   **V** F R MILLER,   **C** T R H COYNE

CALDWELL (Chapel)   *see* Forcett and Aldbrough and Melsonby *Ripon*

CALDWELL (St Giles)   *see* Stapenhill w Cauldwell *Derby*

CALDY (Church of the Resurrection and All Saints)   *see* W Kirby St Bridget *Ches*

CALEDONIAN ROAD (All Saints Hall)   *see* Barnsbury *Lon*

CALIFORNIA (St Mary and St John) *Ox 16*   **P** *DBP*   **P-in-c** C R EDWARDS

CALLINGTON (St Mary)   *see* S Hill w Callington *Truro*

CALLOW END (St James)   *see* Powick and Guarlford and Madresfield w Newland *Worc*

CALMORE (St Anne)   *see* Totton *Win*

CALNE (Holy Trinity) (St Mary the Virgin) and Blackland *Sarum 15*   **P** *Bp*   **V** R A KENWAY,   **NSM** M KIRBY

CALOW (St Peter) and Sutton cum Duckmanton *Derby 3*   **P** *Bp and V Chesterfield (jt)*   **R** M H CHAMPNEYS

CALSHOT (St George)   *see* Fawley *Win*

CALSTOCK (St Andrew) *Truro 11*   **P** *Duchy of Cornwall*   **R** J A C WILSON,   **C** R OAKES,   **NSM** R MUNRO, L S SCOTT

CALSTONE WELLINGTON (St Mary the Virgin)   *see* Oldbury *Sarum*

CALTHORPE (Our Lady w St Margaret)   *see* Erpingham w Calthorpe, Ingworth, Aldborough etc *Nor*

CALTHWAITE (All Saints)   *see* Inglewood Gp *Carl*

CALTON (St Mary the Virgin), Cauldon, Grindon, Waterfall and Blore Ray w Okeover *Lich 5*   **P** *Bp and Sir Peter Walker-Okeover Bt (jt)*   **R** M P SKILLINGS

CALUDON   *see* Coventry Caludon *Cov*

CALVELEY CHURCH (not known)   *see* Bunbury and Tilstone Fearnall *Ches*

CALVERHALL or CORRA (Holy Trinity)   *see* Adderley, Ash, Calverhall, Ightfield etc *Lich*

CALVERLEIGH (St Mary the Virgin)   *see* Washfield, Stoodleigh, Withleigh etc *Ex*

CALVERLEY (St Wilfrid) *Bradf 3*   **P** *Bp*   **V** J H WALKER,   **C** S M KAYE

CALVERTON (All Saints) *Ox 25*   **P** *DBP*   **R** R NORTHING

CALVERTON (St Wilfrid) *S'well 15*   **P** *Bp*   **V** P HEMSTOCK,   **NSM** M N TAYLOR

CAM (St George) w Stinchcombe *Glouc 6*   **P** *Bp*   **V** J M DOORES,   **NSM** S J FISHER

CAM, LOWER (St Bartholomew) w Coaley *Glouc 6*   **P** *Bp*   **V** I A ROBB

CAM VALE *B & W 3*   **P** *Bp and DBP (2 turns), CPAS, MMCET and Revd G Bennett (1 turn)*   **R** M J M PERRY,   **NSM** R A HOSKINS

CAMBER (St Thomas)   *see* Rye *Chich*

CAMBERLEY (St Martin) Old Dean *Guildf 6*   **P** *Bp*   **V** R J PECK,   **NSM** M JAMES

CAMBERLEY (St Mary) *Guildf 6*   **P** *Bp*   **V** M J WAINWRIGHT,   **OLM** R WALKER

CAMBERLEY (St Michael) Yorktown *Guildf 6*   **P** *Bp*   **V** B NICOLE,   **NSM** M A GROUNDSELL,   **OLM** K M MURRAY

CAMBERLEY (St Paul) (St Mary) *Guildf 6*   **P** *Bp*   **V** M CHESTER,   **C** G L SHAW,   **OLM** S H STEPHENS

CAMBERLEY HEATHERSIDE (Community Centre) *Guildf 6*   **P** *Bp*   **P-in-c** L J W BAIN

CAMBERWELL (All Saints) Blenheim Grove *S'wark 8*   **P** *Ch Trust Fund Trust*   **V** I L ORR-EWING

CAMBERWELL (Christ Church) *S'wark 8*   **P** *Trustees*   **V** H R BALFOUR,   **Hon C** J A NICKOLS

CAMBERWELL (St George) *S'wark 8*   **P** *Bp and Trin Coll Cam (jt)*   **V** N J ELDER,   **C** J SAXTON,   **OLM** M JOHN

CAMBERWELL (St Giles) (St Matthew) *S'wark 8*   **P** *Bp*   **V** N P GEORGE,   **C** N P MORROW,   **OLM** I L RUSSELL

CAMBERWELL (St Luke) *S'wark 8*   **P** *Bp*   **V** J D JELLEY

CAMBERWELL (St Michael and All Angels w All Souls w Emmanuel) *S'wark 10*   **P** *DBP*   **V** E J OGLESBY,   **NSM** S L SAUNDERS

CAMBERWELL (St Philip) and St Mark *S'wark 7*   **P** *The Crown*   **P-in-c** M J STEADMAN,   **NSM** P A ALDEN

CAMBO (Holy Trinity)   *see* Kirkwhelpington, Kirkharle, Kirkheaton and Cambo *Newc*

CAMBOIS St Peter (St Andrew's Mission Church) and Sleekbur *n Newc 1*   **P** *D&C*   **V** J BLAKESLEY

CAMBORNE (St Martin and St Meriadoc) *Truro 2*   **P** *Ch Soc Trust*   **P-in-c** M J FIRBANK,   **C** O STEVENS,   **NSM** D E HARVEY, M CARVETH

CAMBOURNE *Ely 1*   **P** *Bp*   **NSM** A M MYERS

CAMBRIDGE Ascension (St Giles) (St Luke the Evangelist) (St Augustine of Canterbury) (All Souls Chapel) *Ely 2*   **P** *Bp*   **TR** P A KING,   **C** J C BUNKER,   **NSM** A C RIGELSFORD

CAMBRIDGE (Good Shepherd)   *see* Chesterton Gd Shep *Ely*

CAMBRIDGE (Holy Cross) *Ely 2*   **P** *Bp*   **V** R T WILLIAMS

CAMBRIDGE (Holy Sepulchre) (St Andrew the Great) *Ely 2*   **P** *PCC*   **V** M H ASHTON,   **C** G R WALTER, B R ELFICK, J C POOLE, N J BUTTERY

CAMBRIDGE (Holy Trinity) *Ely 3*   **P** *D&C and Peache Trustees (jt)*   **V** R A CHARKHAM,   **C** B J DE LA T DE BERRY,   **NSM** C M BENNETT-REES

CAMBRIDGE (St Andrew the Less) (Christ Church) *Ely 2*   **P** *Ch Trust Fund Trust*   **P-in-c** S N MIDGLEY,   **C** A C LOWE

CAMBRIDGE (St Barnabas) *Ely 3*   **P** *V Cam St Paul*   **C** J L SCAMMAN

CAMBRIDGE (St Benedict) *Ely 3*   **P** *CCC Cam*   **V** A C W TILBY,   **NSM** D P FORD, R M NICHOLLS

CAMBRIDGE (St Botolph) *Ely 3*   **P** *Qu Coll Cam*   **P-in-c** W HORBURY,   **NSM** M J WIDDESS

CAMBRIDGE (St Clement) *Ely 2*   **P** *Jes Coll Cam*   **V** *vacant*
CAMBRIDGE (St Edward King and Martyr) Proprietary Chapel
Ely 3, F N WATTS   **NSM** M J RAMSHAW
CAMBRIDGE (St James) *Ely 3*   **P** *Bp*   **P-in-c** J BRUECK
CAMBRIDGE (St John the Evangelist)   *see* Cherry Hinton St Jo
Ely
CAMBRIDGE (St Mark) *Ely 3*   **P** *DBP*   **P-in-c** M A GUITE,
Hon **C** M M G ROBERTS
CAMBRIDGE (St Martin) (St Thomas) *Ely 3*   **P** *V Cam St Paul*
V S O LEEKE,   **NSM** J PARSONS
CAMBRIDGE (St Mary the Great) w St Michael *Ely 2*   **P** *Trin*
Coll Cam   **V** J R E BINNS,   **C** P J HAYLER,   **Hon**
C A M SHILSON-THOMAS
CAMBRIDGE (St Mary the Less) *Ely 3*   **P** *Peterho Cam*
V R A H GREANY,   **NSM** M A BISHOP
CAMBRIDGE (St Matthew) *Ely 2*   **P** *V Cam St Andr the Less*
P-in-c F L PRICE
CAMBRIDGE (St Paul) *Ely 3*   **P** *Ch Trust Fund Trust*
V M S BECKETT
CAMBRIDGE (St Philip) (St Stephen) *Ely 3*   **P** *Ch Trust Fund*
Trust   **V** S TAYLOR,   **NSM** R A HIGGINSON
CAMDEN SQUARE (St Paul)   *see* Old St Pancras *Lon*
CAMDEN TOWN (St Michael)   *as above*
CAMEL, WEST (All Saints)   *see* Cam Vale *B & W*
CAMELFORD (St Julitta)   *see* Lanteglos by Camelford w
Advent *Truro*
CAMELFORD (St Thomas of Canterbury)   *as above*
CAMELOT Parishes, The *B & W 3*   **P** *Patr Bd*
R T G RAE SMITH
CAMELSDALE (St Paul)   *see* Lynchmere and Camelsdale
Chich
CAMERTON (St Peter) w Dunkerton, Foxcote and Shoscombe
B & W 12   **P** *Bp*   **P-in-c** K G X TINGAY
CAMERTON (St Peter), Seaton and West Seaton *Carl 7*
P *D&C and Ch Trust Fund Trust (jt)*   **V** I GRAINGER,
NSM I FEARON
CAMMERINGHAM (St Michael)   *see* Spring Line Gp *Linc*
CAMP HILL (St Mary and St John) *Cov 5*   **P** *Bp*
V S D SNEATH
CAMPBELL ROOMS (not known)   *see* Parr *Liv*
CAMPDEN HILL (St George)   *see* Holland Park *Lon*
CAMPSALL (St Mary Magdalene)   *see* Burghwallis and
Campsall *Sheff*
CAMPSEA ASHE (St John the Baptist) w Marlesford, Parham
and Hacheston *St E 18*   **P** *Prime Min, Ch Soc Trust, and*
J S Schreiber Esq (by turn)   **R** H V EDWARDS
CAMPTON (All Saints), Clophill and Haynes *St Alb 16*   **P** *Bp*
and Ball Coll Ox (alt)   **R** D HENLEY
CANALSIDE Benefice, The *Sarum 14*   **P** *Viscount Long, Magd*
Coll Cam, and R Trowbridge St Jas and Keevil (by turn)
P-in-c S A BALL,   **OLM** J M CLARK
CANDLESBY (St Benedict)   *see* Partney Gp *Linc*
CANDOVER VALLEY, The *Win 1*   **P** *D&C and Lord*
Ashburton (jt)   **R** *vacant* (01256) 389245
CANEWDON (St Nicholas) w Paglesham *Chelmsf 12*   **P** *D&C*
Westmr and Hyndman Trustees (jt)   **P-in-c** T F CLAY
CANFIELD, GREAT (St Mary) w High Roding and Aythorpe
Roding *Chelmsf 18*   **P** *A Sainthill Esq, Ch Soc Trust, and Bp*
(by turn)   **P-in-c** E C GARRETT
CANFIELD, LITTLE (All Saints)   *see* Takeley w Lt Canfield
Chelmsf
CANFORD CLIFFS (Transfiguration) and Sandbanks *Sarum 7*
P *Bp*   **V** J C OAKES
CANFORD HEATH (St Paul)   *see* N Poole Ecum Team *Sarum*
CANFORD MAGNA (no dedication) (Bearwood) (The Lantern)
Sarum 9   **P** *Patr Bd*   **TV** A M RIMMER, G BOLAND,
NSM A SIMPSON, H WALDSAX,   **OLM** C CLARK, A J CORKE,
B S PROBERT
CANLEY (St Stephen) *Cov 3*   **P** *Bp*   **P-in-c** P FINDLEY
CANNING TOWN (St Luke)   *see* Victoria Docks St Luke
Chelmsf
CANNING TOWN (St Matthias)   *see* Plaistow and N Canning
Town *Chelmsf*
CANNINGTON (Blessed Virgin Mary), Otterhampton,
Combwich and Stockland *B & W 17*   **P** *Bp*   **R** P MARTIN,
NSM R A SELLERS
CANNOCK (St Luke) *Lich 3*   **P** *Patr Bd*   **TV** K M BUCK,
L B VASEY-SAUNDERS, R I O'CONNOR, P O HART,
NSM S P REYNOLDS,   **OLM** D J SUNLEY, M E FRONDIGOUN
CANON FROME (St James)   *see* Ledbury *Heref*
CANON PYON (St Lawrence) w King's Pyon, Birley and
Wellington *Heref 7*   **P** *Bp, Ch Union, and D&C (jt)*
V M C CLUETT
CANONBURY (St Stephen) *Lon 6*   **P** *V Islington St Mary*
V N J GROARKE,   **NSM** M E EVANS

CANTERBURY (All Saints) *Cant 3*   **P** *Abp*   **P-in-c** M J STACE
CANTERBURY (St Dunstan w Holy Cross) *Cant 3*   **P** *Abp*
V M W WORGAN
CANTERBURY (St Martin) (St Paul) *Cant 3*   **P** *Abp*
R N M HALL,   **C** P R RATCLIFF
CANTERBURY (St Mary Bredin) *Cant 3*   **P** *Simeon's Trustees*
V A T C PEMBERTON,   **C** P WILLIAMS
CANTERBURY (St Peter w St Alphege) (St Mildred) and
St Margaret w St Mary de Castro *Cant 3*   **P** *The Crown*
P-in-c M F BALL,   **Hon C** P E S DAVIE,   **OLM** I W J TAYLOR
CANTERBURY (St Stephen)   *see* Hackington *Cant*
CANTLEY (St Margaret)   *see* Freethorpe, Wickhampton,
Halvergate etc *Nor*
CANTLEY (St Wilfrid) *Sheff 8*   **P** *Guild of All So*
V J I WILLETT
CANTLEY, NEW (St Hugh of Lincoln) *Sheff 8*   **P** *Guild of*
All So   **V** *vacant* (01302) 535739
CANTRIL FARM (St Jude)   *see* Stockbridge Village *Liv*
CANVEY ISLAND (St Anne) (St Katherine's Worship Centre)
(St Nicholas) *Chelmsf 10*   **P** *Bp and Patr Bd (jt)*
TR D ST C TUDOR,   **TV** T J HIDE,   **NSM** J M BARHAM,
M G WALFORD
CANWELL (St Mary, St Giles and All Saints) *Lich 4*   **P** *Bp*
V H J BAKER,   **Hon C** M R F MACLACHLAN,   **NSM** R G DAVIES
CANWICK (All Saints)   *see* Washingborough w Heighington
and Canwick *Linc*
CAPEL (St John the Baptist)   *see* Surrey Weald *Guildf*
CAPEL (St Thomas à Becket)   *see* Tudeley cum Capel w Five
Oak Green *Roch*
CAPEL LE FERNE (St Radigund)   *see* Alkham w Capel le
Ferne and Hougham *Cant*
CAPEL ST MARY (St Mary) w Little Wenham and Great
Wenham *St E 5*   **P** *Bp and SMF (jt)*   **R** D B SINGLETON
CAPENHURST (Holy Trinity)   *see* Backford and Capenhurst
Ches
CAPESTHORNE (Holy Trinity) w Siddington and Marton
Ches 13   **P** *W A B Davenport Esq*   **P-in-c** P O MOULTON
CAR COLSTON (St Mary) w Screveton *S'well 8*
P *H S Blagg Esq*   **P-in-c** J R CHAMBERS,
NSM M R WOODWARD
CARBIS BAY (St Anta and All Saints) w Lelant (St Uny) *Truro 5*
P *Bp*   **P-in-c** J S HOLLAND,   **NSM** C Z WILTON,
S A CHALCRAFT, J A SEYMOUR
CARBROOKE (St Peter and St Paul)   *see* Ashill, Carbrooke,
Ovington and Saham Toney *Nor*
CARBURTON (St Giles)   *see* Worksop Priory *S'well*
CARDESTON (St Michael)   *see* Alberbury w Cardeston *Heref*
CARDINGTON (St James) *Heref 11*   **P** *Rt Hon Sir Frederick*
Corfield   **P-in-c** J GROVES
CARDINGTON (St Mary)   *see* Elstow *St Alb*
CARDYNHAM (St Mewbud)   *see* St Neot and Warleggan w
Cardynham *Truro*
CAREBY (St Stephen)   *see* Castle Bytham w Creeton *Linc*
CARHAM (St Cuthbert)   *see* Cornhill w Carham *Newc*
CARHAMPTON (St John the Baptist)   *see* Dunster,
Carhampton, Withycombe w Rodhuish etc *B & W*
CARHARRACK (St Piran's Mission Church)   *see* Chacewater
w St Day and Carharrack *Truro*
CARISBROOKE (St John the Baptist)   *see* Newport St Jo
Portsm
CARISBROOKE (St Mary the Virgin) *Portsm 8*   **P** *Qu Coll Ox*
V M A J EXELL
CARISBROOKE St Nicholas in the Castle *Portsm 8*   **P** *Qu Coll*
Ox   **V** M A J EXELL
CARLBY (St Stephen)   *see* Ryhall w Essendine and Carlby *Pet*
CARLECOATES (St Anne)   *see* Penistone and Thurlstone
Wakef
CARLETON (St Chad)   *see* Poulton Carleton and Singleton
Blackb
CARLETON (St Mary the Virgin)   *see* Skipton Ch Ch w
Carleton *Bradf*
CARLETON (St Michael) and E Hardwick *Wakef 10*
P *V Pontefract and Cawood Trustees (jt)*   **V** S A STACEY
CARLETON (St Peter)   *see* Rockland St Mary w Hellington,
Bramerton etc *Nor*
CARLETON, EAST (St Mary)   *see* Swardeston w E Carleton,
Intwood, Keswick etc *Nor*
CARLETON IN CRAVEN   *see* Skipton Ch Ch w Carleton
Bradf
CARLETON RODE (All Saints)   *see* Bunwell, Carleton Rode,
Tibenham, Gt Moulton etc *Nor*
CARLIN HOW (St Helen)   *see* Loftus and Carlin How w
Skinningrove *York*
CARLINGHOW (St John the Evangelist)   *see* Staincliffe and
Carlinghow *Wakef*
CARLISLE Belah (St Mark)   *see* Stanwix *Carl*

CARLISLE (Holy Trinity) (St Barnabas) *Carl 3*   **P** *Patr Bd*
P-in-c E M C HANCOCK,   **C** J H POWLEY
CARLISLE (St Aidan) and Christ Church *Carl 3*   **P** *Bp*
V R J OAKLEY
CARLISLE (St Cuthbert) *Carl 3*   **P** *D&C*   **V** *vacant* (01228)
521982
CARLISLE (St Herbert) w St Stephen *Carl 3*   **P** *Bp*
V A JONES
CARLISLE (St James)   *see Denton Holme Carl*
CARLISLE (St John the Evangelist) *Carl 3*   **P** *CPAS*
V S DONALD,   **C** A V WEST
CARLISLE (St Luke) Morton *Carl 3*   **P** *Bp*   **V** K WRAY
CARLISLE (St Michael)   *see Stanwix Carl*
CARLISLE, SOUTH Team Ministry (St John the Baptist)
(St Elisabeth) *Carl 3*   **P** *Patr Bd*   **TR** T J HYSLOP,
TV S L WICKS,   **C** C G Y HYSLOP,   **NSM** P J IRWIN
CARLTON (St Aidan)   *see Helmsley York*
CARLTON (St Andrew)   *see Nailstone and Carlton w*
Shackerstone *Leic*
CARLTON (St Bartholomew)   *see Guiseley w Esholt Bradf*
CARLTON (St Botolph)   *see Whorlton w Carlton and Faceby*
York
CARLTON (St John the Baptist) *S'well 10*   **P** *Bp*
V A M LUCKCUCK
CARLTON (St John the Evangelist) *Wakef 7*   **P** *DBP*
V *vacant* (01226) 722086
CARLTON (St Mary)   *see Harrold and Carlton w Chellington*
St Alb
CARLTON (St Peter)   *see Raddesley Gp Ely*
CARLTON (St Peter)   *see Saxmundham w Kelsale cum Carlton*
St E
CARLTON, EAST (St Peter)   *see Gretton w Rockingham and*
Cottingham w E Carlton *Pet*
CARLTON, GREAT (St John the Baptist)   *see Mid Marsh Gp*
Linc
CARLTON, NORTH (St Luke)   *see Spring Line Gp Linc*
CARLTON, SOUTH (St John the Baptist)   *as above*
CARLTON BY SNAITH (St Mary) and Drax *York 4*   **P** *Abp*
and Ch Trust Fund Trust *(jt)*   **P-in-c** J H MDUMULLA
CARLTON COLVILLE (St Peter) and Mutford *Nor 9*
P *Simeon's Trustees and G&C Coll Cam (jt)*   **V** J S BISHOP
CARLTON CURLIEU (St Mary the Virgin)   *see Glen Magna*
cum Stretton Magna etc *Leic*
CARLTON FOREHOE (St Mary)   *see Barnham Broom and*
Upper Yare *Nor*
CARLTON HUSTHWAITE (St Mary)   *see Coxwold and*
Husthwaite *York*
CARLTON-IN-LINDRICK (St John the Evangelist) and
Langold w Oldcotes *S'well 6*   **P** *Bp and Ld Chan (alt)*
R *vacant* (01909) 730398
CARLTON-IN-THE-WILLOWS (St Paul) *S'well 10*
P *MMCET*   **R** B HALL,   **NSM** M A SKIDMORE
CARLTON-LE-MOORLAND (St Mary)   *see Bassingham Gp*
Linc
CARLTON MINIOTT (St Lawrence)   *see Thirsk York*
CARLTON-ON-TRENT (St Mary)   *see Sutton w Carlton and*
Normanton upon Trent etc *S'well*
CARLTON SCROOP (St Nicholas)   *see Caythorpe Linc*
CARNABY (St John the Baptist)   *see Rudston w Boynton,*
Carnaby and Kilham *York*
CARNFORTH (Christ Church) *Blackb 14*   **P** *Bp*   **V** S L JONES,
C C G HOLDEN
CARNFORTH (Holy Trinity)   *see Bolton-le-Sands Blackb*
CARPENTER'S ARMS, The   *see Deal, The Carpenter's Arms*
Cant
CARR CLOUGH (St Andrew)   *see Kersal Moor Man*
CARR DYKE GROUP, The *Linc 22*   **P** *Sir Philip Naylor-*
Leyland Bt and Ld Chan (alt)   **V** M K NICHOLAS,
NSM S C LAWRENCE
CARR MILL (St David) *Liv 10*   **P** *V St Helens St Mark and*
Bp (jt)   **V** T THOMAS
CARRINGTON (St John the Evangelist) *S'well 12*   **P** *Bp*
V J M MACGILLIVRAY,   **C** S F WALES
CARRINGTON (St Paul)   *see Sibsey w Frithville Linc*
CARSHALTON (All Saints) *S'wark 23*   **P** *Bp*   **R** J C THEWLIS,
NSM D R BILLIN
CARSHALTON BEECHES (Good Shepherd) *S'wark 23*   **P** *Bp*
V C WHEATON,   **OLM** P C M TURRELL
CARSINGTON (St Margaret)   *see Wirksworth Derby*
CARTERTON (St John the Evangelist)   *see Brize Norton and*
Carterton *Ox*
CARTMEL FELL (St Anthony) *Carl 10*   **P** *Bp*
P-in-c M D WOODCOCK
CARTMEL PENINSULA Team Ministry, The (St Mary and
St Michael) *Carl 11*   **P** *Patr Bd*   **TR** N J ASH,
TV J E CROSSLEY, R A LATHAM, R W BAILEY,   **NSM** D S SIMON

CASSINGTON (St Peter)   *see Eynsham and Cassington Ox*
CASSOP CUM QUARRINTON *Dur 5*   **P** *Bp*   **V** *vacant*
0191-377 0347
CASTERTON (Holy Trinity)   *see Kirkby Lonsdale Carl*
CASTERTON, GREAT (St Peter and St Paul) and LITTLE (All
Saints) w Pickworth and Tickencote *Pet 12*   **P** *Burghley Ho*
Preservation Trust (2 turns), Lord Chesham (1 turn), and Bp
(1 turn)   **P-in-c** J M SAUNDERS
CASTLE ACRE (St James)   *see Castleacre, Newton, Westacre*
and Southacre *Nor*
CASTLE ASHBY (St Mary Magdalene)   *see Yardley Hastings,*
Denton and Grendon etc *Pet*
CASTLE BOLTON (St Oswald)   *see Penhill Ripon*
CASTLE BROMWICH (St Clement) *Birm 9*   **P** *Bp*
V W J SANDS
CASTLE BROMWICH (St Mary and St Margaret) *Birm 9*
P *Earl of Bradf*   **R** G A DOUGLAS,   **NSM** A J BROWN
CASTLE BYTHAM (St James) w Creeton *Linc 14*   **P** *D&C, Bp,*
Ld Chan, and DBP (by turn)   **R** *vacant* (01780) 410166
CASTLE CAMPS (All Saints)   *see Linton Ely*
CASTLE CARROCK (St Peter)   *see Eden, Gelt and Irthing Carl*
CASTLE CARY (All Saints) w Ansford *B & W 3*   **P** *Bp*
V J G PESCOD
CASTLE CHURCH (St Mary) *Lich 10*   **P** *Bp*
V P J SOWERBUTTS,   **NSM** C V SYKES
CASTLE COMBE (St Andrew)   *see By Brook Bris*
CASTLE DONINGTON (St Edward the King and Martyr) and
Lockington cum Hemington *Leic 6*   **P** *Lady Gretton and*
C H C Coaker Esq (jt)   **V** A Q MICKLETHWAITE,
NSM M J BENNETT
CASTLE EATON (St Mary the Virgin)   *see Fairford Deanery*
Glouc
CASTLE EDEN (St James)   *see Blackhall, Castle Eden and*
Monkhesleden *Dur*
CASTLE FROME (St Michael)   *see Frome Valley Heref*
CASTLE HEDINGHAM (St Nicholas)   *see Sible Hedingham w*
Castle Hedingham *Chelmsf*
CASTLE HILL (St Philip)   *see Hindley All SS Liv*
CASTLE RISING (St Lawrence) *Nor 16*   **P** *G Howard Esq*
P-in-c J B V RIVIERE
CASTLE SOWERBY (St Kentigern)   *see Caldbeck, Castle*
Sowerby and Sebergham *Carl*
CASTLE TOWN (St Thomas and St Andrew) *Lich 10*
P *Hyndman Trustees*   **P-in-c** P W THOMAS
CASTLE VALE (St Cuthbert of Lindisfarne) w Minworth
Birm 12   **P** *Bp*   **V** J B A COPE
CASTLE VIEW ESTATE (St Francis)   *see Langley Marish Ox*
CASTLEACRE (St James), Newton-by-Castleacre, Westacre
and Southacre *Nor 13*   **P** *Bp, Earl of Leicester, and Capt*
H Birkbeck (jt)   **P-in-c** S R NAIRN
CASTLECROFT (The Good Shepherd)   *see Tettenhall Wood*
and Perton *Lich*
CASTLEFIELDS (All Saints and St Michael)   *see Shrewsbury*
All SS w St Mich *Lich*
CASTLEFORD (St Michael and All Angels)   *see Smawthorpe*
St Mich *Wakef*
CASTLEFORD Team Parish (All Saints) *Wakef 10*   **P** *Duchy of*
Lanc and Bp (alt)   **TR** M F WOOD,   **C** P W ATKINSON,
NSM M J MARSH
CASTLEMORTON (St Gregory)   *see Longdon, Castlemorton,*
Bushley, Queenhill etc *Worc*
CASTLESIDE (St John the Evangelist) *Dur 4*   **P** *Bp*
P-in-c S BENNETT
CASTLETHORPE (St Simon and St Jude)   *see Hanslope w*
Castlethorpe *Ox*
CASTLETON (St Edmund)   *see Hope, Castleton and Bradwell*
Derby
CASTLETON (St Mary Magdalene)   *see Sherborne w*
Castleton, Lillington and Longburton *Sarum*
CASTLETON (St Michael and St George)   *see Danby w*
Castleton and Commondale *York*
CASTLETON MOOR (St Martin) *Man 18*   **P** *Bp*
V I E BUTTERWORTH
CASTLETOWN (St Mary) *S & M 1*   **P** *Bp*   **V** P C ROBINSON
CASTON (St Cross), Griston, Merton, Thompson, Stow Bedon,
Breckles and Great Hockham *Nor 13*   **P** *Bp and DBP (jt)*
R R W NICHOLS
CASTOR (St Kyneburgha) w Sutton and Upton w Marholm
Pet 11   **P** *Sir Philip Naylor-Leyland Bt (2 turns),*
Mrs V S V Gunnery (1 turn)   **R** W S D BURKE,
NSM R HEMINGRAY
CATCLIFFE (St Mary)   *see Rivers Team Sheff*
CATCOTT (St Peter)   *see W Poldens B & W*
CATERHAM (St Mary the Virgin) (St Laurence) (St Paul)
(St John the Evangelist) *S'wark 24*   **P** *Bp*   **TR** D J SWAN,

TV G P REEVES, J GARTON, C A BRADSHAW,
NSM F M BALDWIN, A-M GARTON, R P WELDON
CATESBY (St Mary)   see Daventry, Ashby St Ledgers,
Braunston etc Pet
CATFIELD (All Saints)   see Ludham, Potter Heigham, Hickling
and Catfield Nor
CATFORD (St Andrew) S'wark 4   P Bp   V vacant (020) 8697
2600
CATFORD (St John) and Downham S'wark 4   P Bp
TR C A FRENCH,   TV P G JORDAN,   C S A JAMES
CATFORD (St Laurence) S'wark 4   P Bp   V C F PICKSTONE,
OLM I J FARQUHAR
CATHERINGTON (All Saints) and Clanfield Portsm 5   P Bp
V G B HILL,   C A COLLINSON,   NSM A M GOTHARD
CATHERSTON LEWESTON (St Mary)   see Golden Cap Team
Sarum
CATON (St Paul) w Littledale Blackb 14   P V Lanc
P-in-c G A POLLITT
CATSFIELD (St Laurence) and Crowhurst Chich 14   P Bp and
J P Papillon (alt)   R M A BRYDON
CATSHILL (Christ Church) and Dodford Worc 7   P Bp
V vacant (01527) 579619
CATTERICK (St Anne) Ripon 2   P Bp   V F M WILSON,
C P J MATTHEWS
CATTHORPE (St Thomas)   see Gilmorton, Peatling Parva,
Kimcote etc Leic
CATTISTOCK (St Peter and St Paul)   see Melbury Sarum
CATTON (All Saints)   see Stamford Bridge Gp York
CATTON (St Nicholas and the Blessed Virgin Mary)
see Walton-on-Trent w Croxall, Rosliston etc Derby
CATTON, NEW (Christ Church) Nor 2   P Bp
V K G CROCKER,   C M S WHITAKER,   OLM J EASTON
CATTON, NEW (St Luke) w St Augustine Nor 2   P Bp, D&C,
and CPAS (jt)   V N I VESEY
CATTON, OLD (St Margaret) Nor 2   P D&C   V A D PARSONS
CATWICK (St Michael)   see Brandesburton and Leven w
Catwick York
CATWORTH, GREAT   see Catworth Magna Ely
CATWORTH MAGNA (St Leonard) Ely 10   P BNC Ox
R vacant
CAULDON (St Mary and St Laurence)   see Calton, Cauldon,
Grindon, Waterfall etc Lich
CAUNDLE MARSH (St Peter and St Paul)   see Vale of White
Hart Sarum
CAUNTON (St Andrew)   see Norwell w Ossington, Cromwell
and Caunton S'well
CAUSEWAY HEAD (St Paul)   see Solway Plain Carl
CAUTLEY (St Mark)   see Sedbergh, Cautley and Garsdale
Bradf
CAVENDISH (St Mary)   see Stour Valley St E
CAVENHAM (St Andrew)   see Mildenhall St E
CAVERSFIELD (St Laurence)   see Bicester w Bucknell,
Caversfield and Launton Ox
CAVERSHAM (Park Church)   see Emmer Green w Caversham
Park Ox
CAVERSHAM (St Andrew) Ox 15   P Bp   V N D JONES,
NSM C S WILSON
CAVERSHAM (St John the Baptist) Ox 15   P Bp   V vacant
0118-947 1814
CAVERSHAM (St Peter) and Mapledurham Ox 15   P Eton Coll
and Ch Ch Ox (jt)   P-in-c D F TYNDALL,
NSM A F THORESEN,   OLM K F KNEE-ROBINSON
CAVERSHAM HEIGHTS (St Andrew)   see Caversham St Andr
Ox
CAVERSHAM PARK Local Ecumenical Partnership
Ox 15 vacant
CAVERSWALL (St Peter) and Weston Coyney w Dilhorne Lich 6
P D&C   V S J OSBOURNE
CAWOOD (All Saints) w Ryther and Wistow York 4   P Abp and
Ld Chan (alt)   P-in-c I M W ELLERY
CAWSAND (St Andrew's Mission Church)   see Maker w Rame
Truro
CAWSTON (St Agnes) w Booton and Brandiston, Haveringland
andHeydon Nor 19   P Pemb Coll Cam (3 turns), DBP (1 turn)
P-in-c T W HARRIS
CAWTHORNE (All Saints) Wakef 7   P S W Fraser Esq
P-in-c S A REYNOLDS,   NSM J E DAYKIN
CAXTON (St Andrew)   see Papworth Ely
CAYNHAM (St Mary)   see Ludlow Heref
CAYTHORPE (St Aidan)   see Lowdham w Caythorpe, and
Gunthorpe S'well
CAYTHORPE (St Vincent) Linc 23   P Bp, J F Fane Esq, and
S J Packe-Drury-Lowe Esq (by turn)   P-in-c J FRESHNEY
CAYTON (St John the Baptist) w Eastfield York 15   P Abp
V A CAMPBELL-WILSON
CENTRAL see under substantive place names

CERNE ABBAS (St Mary)   see Buckland Newton, Cerne
Abbas, Godmanstone etc Sarum
CERNEY, NORTH (All Saints)   see Stratton, N Cerney,
Baunton and Bagendon Glouc
CERNEY, SOUTH (All Hallows) w Cerney Wick, Siddington
and Preston Glouc 9   P Bp and Mrs P Chester-Master (1 turn),
Ld Chan (1 turn)   V D BOWERS
CERNEY WICK (Holy Trinity)   see S Cerney w Cerney Wick,
Siddington and Preston Glouc
CHACELEY (St John the Baptist)   see Deerhurst and Apperley
w Forthampton etc Glouc
CHACEWATER (St Paul) w St Day and Carharrack Truro 2
P D&C and R Kenwyn w St Allen (jt)   V A S GOUGH,
NSM I D T LITTLE
CHACOMBE (St Peter and St Paul)   see Chenderit Pet
CHADBROOK St E 12   P Bp and DBP (jt)   R I M G FRIARS
CHADDERTON (Christ Church) (St Saviour) Man 20
P Trustees   V J G SIMMONS,   C A FORD
CHADDERTON (Emmanuel) (St George) Man 20   P Trustees
V E D H LEAF
CHADDERTON (St Mark) Man 20   P The Crown
V A COOKE
CHADDERTON (St Matthew) St Luke Man 20   P Bp and
Prime Min (alt)   V D R PENNY,   NSM M A STIRZAKER
CHADDESDEN (St Mary) Derby 9   P MMCET
V W A STILLWELL
CHADDESDEN (St Philip) Derby 9   P Bp   V J M PAGE,
C C I LOWDON
CHADDESLEY CORBETT (St Cassian) and Stone Worc 11
P Ld Chan   V J A COX
CHADDLEWORTH (St Andrew)   see Brightwalton w Catmore,
Leckhampstead etc Ox
CHADKIRK (St Chad) Ches 16   P R Stockport St Mary
V T D BARLOW,   C J PIENAAR
CHADLINGTON (St Nicholas)   see Chase Ox
CHADSMOOR (St Aidan)   see Cannock Lich
CHADSMOOR (St Chad)   as above
CHADWELL (Emmanuel) (St Mary) Chelmsf 14
P Ch Soc Trust   R N T B DEANE
CHADWELL HEATH (St Chad) Chelmsf 1   P Vs Dagenham
and Ilford (alt)   V M J COURT
CHAFFCOMBE (St Michael and All Angels), Cricket Malherbie
w Knowle St Giles, Tatworth, Thorncombe and Winsham
B & W 15   P Bp and C G S Eyre Esq (jt)   V T F PRICE,
Hon C B WOOD,   NSM A T BOYLAND
CHAGFORD (St Michael), Drewsteignton, Hittisleigh, Spreyton,
Gidleigh, and Throwleigh Ex 11   P Bp, Guild of All So, Personal
reps Sir George Hayter-Hames, and Exors B Drew Esq
R A E GEERING,   C N WALTER
CHAILEY (St Peter) Chich 21   P J P B Tillard Esq
R R WARHURST
CHALBURY (All Saints)   see Horton, Chalbury, Hinton Martel
and Holt St Jas Sarum
CHALDON (St Peter and St Paul)   see Caterham S'wark
CHALDON HERRING (St Nicholas)   see The Lulworths,
Winfrith Newburgh and Chaldon Sarum
CHALE (St Andrew) Portsm 8   P Keble Coll Ox
P-in-c M C WILLIAMS,   Hon C D L DENNIS
CHALFIELD, GREAT (All Saints)   see Broughton Gifford, Gt
Chalfield and Holt Sarum
CHALFONT, LITTLE (St George)   see Chenies and Lt
Chalfont, Latimer and Flaunden Ox
CHALFONT ST GILES (St Giles) Ox 20   P Bp
R T A STACEY,   NSM A L J THOMPSON, M T BLEAKLEY
CHALFONT ST PETER (St Peter) Ox 20   P St Jo Coll Ox
R C H OVERTON,   NSM N RODE, J A KING,
OLM W GRAHAM
CHALFORD (Christ Church)   see Bisley, Chalford, France
Lynch, and Oakridge Glouc
CHALGRAVE (All Saints)   see Toddington and Chalgrave
St Alb
CHALGROVE (St Mary) w Berrick Salome Ox 1   P Ch Ch Ox
V I G H COHEN
CHALK (St Mary) Roch 4   P R Milton   V N I BOURNE,
C A L HAMMILL
CHALKE VALLEY (Team Ministry) Sarum 11   P Bp, DBP, and
K Coll Cam (by turn)   TR D E HENLEY,   TV R C REDDING,
A L WILLIAMS,   Hon C J C HATTON,   NSM S W T COLE,
J A TAYLOR
CHALLACOMBE (Holy Trinity)   see Shirwell, Loxhore,
Kentisbury, Arlington, etc Ex
CHALLOCK (St Cosmas and St Damian)   see Chilham w
Challock and Molash Cant
CHALLOW, EAST (St Nicholas)   see Hanney, Denchworth and E
Challow Ox

CHALLOW, WEST (St Laurence) *see* Ridgeway *Ox*
CHALTON (St Michael and All Angels) *see* Blendworth w Chalton w Idsworth *Portsm*
CHALVEY (St Peter) *see* Upton cum Chalvey *Ox*
CHALVINGTON (St Bartholomew) *see* Laughton w Ripe and Chalvington *Chich*
CHAMBERSBURY Hemel Hempstead (Holy Trinity) (St Mary) (St Benedict) *St Alb 3* **P** *DBP* **TR** D M LAWSON, **TV** S G CUTMORE, L J WILSON, **Hon C** D A BUTLER, **NSM** K L TURNER
CHANDLER'S FORD (St Boniface) (St Martin in the Wood) *Win 10* **P** *Bp* **C** I N BIRD, F C GIBBS, **NSM** L BUNTING
CHANTRY (Holy Trinity) *see* Mells w Buckland Dinham, Elm, Whatley etc *B & W*
CHAPEL ALLERTON (St Matthew) *Ripon 5* **P** *V Leeds St Pet* **V** D M ROBINSON, **C** M R COUTTS
CHAPEL CHORLTON (St Laurence), Maer and Whitmore *Lich 7* **P** *Bp and G Cavenagh-Mainwaring Esq (jt)* **R** N A CLEMAS
CHAPEL-EN-LE-FRITH (St Thomas à Becket) *Derby 4* **P** *PCC* **V** N R BRALESFORD
CHAPEL GREEN (St Oswald) *see* Lt Horton *Bradf*
CHAPEL HOUSE (Holy Nativity) *Newc 4* **P** *Bp* **P-in-c** P KENNEY, **NSM** A E MARR, **OLM** D P MARR, R AYRE
CHAPEL LAWN (St Mary) *see* Bucknell w Chapel Lawn, Llanfair Waterdine etc *Heref*
CHAPEL LE DALE (St Leonard) *see* Ingleton w Chapel le Dale *Bradf*
CHAPEL PLAISTER (not known) *see* Box w Hazlebury and Ditteridge *Bris*
CHAPEL ST LEONARDS (St Leonard) w Hogsthorpe *Linc 8* **P** *V Willoughby St Helen* **V** *vacant (01754) 871176*
CHAPELTHORPE (St James) *Wakef 11* **P** *V Sandal* **V** I M GASKELL
CHAPELTOWN (St John the Baptist) *Sheff 3* **P** *Bp* **V** R A STORDY
CHAPMANSLADE (St Philip and St James) *see* Cley Hill Villages *Sarum*
CHAPPEL (St Barnabas) *see* Gt and Lt Tey w Wakes Colne and Chappel *Chelmsf*
CHARBOROUGH (St Mary) *see* Red Post *Sarum*
CHARD (Blessed Virgin Mary) *B & W 15* **P** *Bp* **V** A J WOODWARD, **C** J T TYLER, **NSM** V M HOARE
CHARD (Good Shepherd) and Cricket St Thomas *B & W 15* **P** *Bp* **V** C FURNESS
CHARDSTOCK (All Saints) *see* Axminster, Chardstock, All Saints etc *Ex*
CHARDSTOCK (St Andrew) *as above*
CHARFIELD (St John) and Kingswood *Glouc 6* **P** *Bp, DBP and R W Neeld Esq (jt)* **NSM** V J KERNER
CHARFORD (St Andrew) *see* Bromsgrove St Jo *Worc*
CHARING (St Peter and St Paul) w Charing Heath (Holy Trinity) and Little Chart *Cant 10* **P** *Abp and D&C (jt)* **P-in-c** L J HAMMOND, **C** R D KING, S A WOMERSLEY, **OLM** P G COX
CHARLBURY (St Mary the Virgin) w Shorthampton *Ox 3* **P** *St Jo Coll Ox* **V** J K FRENCH, **NSM** J W FIELDEN
CHARLCOMBE (Blessed Virgin Mary) w Bath (St Stephen) *B & W 9* **P** *DBP and Simeon's Trustees (jt)* **P-in-c** J W LLOYD
CHARLECOTE (St Leonard) *see* Hampton Lucy w Charlecote and Loxley *Cov*
CHARLES (St John the Baptist) *see* S Molton w Nymet St George, High Bray etc *Ex*
CHARLES w Plymouth St Matthias *Ex 24* **P** *Ch Patr Trust* **V** *vacant (01752) 665640*
CHARLESTOWN (St George) *see* Salford All SS *Man*
CHARLESTOWN (St Paul) *Truro 1* **P** *The Crown* **V** J C GREATBATCH
CHARLESTOWN (St Thomas the Apostle) *see* Southowram and Claremount *Wakef*
CHARLESWORTH (St John the Evangelist) and Dinting Vale *Derby 6* **P** *The Crown (2 turns), Bp (1 turn)* **P-in-c** A J PRICE, **NSM** R G ALLARD, C A PRICE
CHARLETON (St Mary) *see* Stokenham, Slapton, Charleton w Buckland etc *Ex*
CHARLTON (All Saints) *see* Chalke Valley *Sarum*
CHARLTON (Holy Trinity) *see* Wantage *Ox*
CHARLTON (St John) *see* Fladbury w Wyre Piddle and Moor etc *Worc*
CHARLTON (St John the Baptist) *see* Garsdon, Lea and Cleverton and Charlton *Bris*
CHARLTON (St John the Baptist) *see* St Bartholomew *Sarum*
CHARLTON (St Luke w Holy Trinity) (St Richard) (St Thomas) *S'wark 1* **P** *Bp and Viscount Gough (jt)* **R** E M WOOFF,

Hon C J A CONALTY, **NSM** M R HOUSE, **OLM** B J SPONG, E A NEWMAN
CHARLTON (St Peter) *see* Upavon w Rushall and Charlton *Sarum*
CHARLTON (St Thomas the Apostle) *see* Pastrow *Win*
CHARLTON, SOUTH (St James) *see* Glendale Gp *Newc*
CHARLTON ABBOTS (St Martin) *see* Sevenhampton w Charlton Abbots, Hawling etc *Glouc*
CHARLTON ADAM (St Peter and St Paul) *see* Somerton w Compton Dundon, the Charltons etc *B & W*
CHARLTON HORETHORNE (St Peter and St Paul) *see* Milborne Port w Goathill etc *B & W*
CHARLTON-IN-DOVER (St Peter and St Paul) *Cant 4* **P** *Keble Coll Ox* **P-in-c** C S JOHNSON
CHARLTON KINGS (Holy Apostles) *Glouc 7* **P** *R Cheltenham* **P-in-c** R J PATERSON, **C** R ROSBOROUGH
CHARLTON KINGS (St Mary) *Glouc 7* **P** *Bp* **V** M GARLAND, **C** L A HILL
CHARLTON MACKRELL (Blessed Virgin Mary) *see* Somerton w Compton Dundon, the Charltons etc *B & W*
CHARLTON MARSHALL (St Mary the Virgin) *see* Spetisbury w Charlton Marshall etc *Sarum*
CHARLTON MUSGROVE (St John) (St Stephen), Cucklington and Stoke Trister *B & W 2* **P** *Bp* **P-in-c** H E ALLEN
CHARLTON ON OTMOOR (St Mary) *see* Ray Valley *Ox*
CHARLWOOD (St Nicholas) *S'wark 26* **P** *DBP* **R** W G CAMPEN
CHARMINSTER (St Mary the Virgin) and Stinsford *Sarum 1* **P** *The Hon C A Townshend and Bp (alt)* **V** P J SMITH, **OLM** W I FOBISTER
CHARMOUTH (St Andrew) *see* Golden Cap Team *Sarum*
CHARNEY BASSETT (St Peter) *see* Cherbury w Gainfield *Ox*
CHARNOCK RICHARD (Christ Church) *Blackb 4* **P** *DBF* **V** *vacant (01257) 791385*
CHARSFIELD W DEBACH (St Peter) *see* Mid Loes *St E*
CHART, GREAT (St Mary) *Cant 10* **P** *Abp* **P-in-c** T C WILSON
CHART, LITTLE (St Mary) *see* Charing w Charing Heath and Lt Chart *Cant*
CHART SUTTON (St Michael) *see* Sutton Valence w E Sutton and Chart Sutton *Cant*
CHARTERHOUSE-ON-MENDIP (St Hugh) *see* Blagdon w Compton Martin and Ubley *B & W*
CHARTHAM (St Mary) *Cant 2* **P** *Abp* **P-in-c** P A BROWN
CHARWELTON (Holy Trinity) *see* Badby w Newham and Charwelton w Fawsley etc *Pet*
CHASE *Ox 3* **P** *Bp and D&C Ch Ch (jt)* **V** M E J ABREY, **Hon C** M B CRAMERI
CHASE *Sarum 6* **P** *Bp, Adn Dorset, Ch Soc Trust, Pemb Coll Cam, Univ Coll Ox, J P C Bourke Esq (4 turns), Ld Chan (1 turn)* **R** M J FOSTER, **C** M R B DURRANT, **Hon C** W H G JOHNSTONE
CHASE TERRACE (St John) *Lich 1* **P** *Bp* **V** D B LEAKE, **NSM** L HOOD, **OLM** D POOLE
CHASETOWN (St Anne) *Lich 1* **P** *V Burntwood* **OLM** R V BAGLEY
CHASETOWN (St John) *see* Chase Terrace *Lich*
CHASTLETON (St Mary the Virgin) *see* Chipping Norton *Ox*
CHATBURN (Christ Church) and Downham *Blackb 7* **P** *Hulme Trustees and Lord Clitheroe (jt)* **P-in-c** R NICHOLSON
CHATHAM (Christ the King) *see* Prince's Park *Roch*
CHATHAM (St Mary and St John) *Roch 5* **P** *D&C* **P-in-c** B P ADAMS
CHATHAM (St Paul w All Saints) *Roch 5* **P** *Bp* **V** *vacant (01634) 845419*
CHATHAM (St Philip and St James) *Roch 5* **P** *Ch Soc Trust* **V** G J ACKERLEY, **C** D R J GREEN, **NSM** S C SPENCER
CHATHAM (St Stephen) *Roch 5* **P** *Bp* **V** A L SMITH
CHATHAM, SOUTH Holy Trinity (St William) (St Alban) (St David) *Roch 5* **P** *Bp* **TR** M ILYAS, **TV** J S CURRIE, P C WOOTTON
CHATTENDEN (Bishop Gundulph) *see* Frindsbury w Upnor and Chattenden *Roch*
CHATTERIS (St Peter and St Paul) *Ely 11* **P** *G&C Coll Cam* **V** J M THOMSON, **C** C W L THOMSON
CHATTISHAM (All Saints and St Margaret) *see* Elmsett w Aldham, Hintlesham, Chattisham etc *St E*
CHATTON (Holy Cross) *see* Glendale Gp *Newc*
CHAULDEN (St Stephen) *see* Hemel Hempstead *St Alb*
CHAVEY DOWN (St Martin) *see* Winkfield and Cranbourne *Ox*
CHAWLEIGH (St James) *see* Burrington, Chawleigh, Cheldon, Chulmleigh etc *Ex*
CHAWTON (St Nicholas) *see* Northanger *Win*
CHEADLE (All Hallows) (St Philip's Mission Church) *Ches 17* **P** *R Cheadle* **V** P W HIGHTON, **C** D A WALKER

CHEADLE (St Cuthbert) (St Mary) *Ches 17* **P** *Ch Soc Trust*
R R S MUNRO, **C** J E M NEWMAN, D G WHITEHOUSE,
G A LUCAS, **NSM** N C HALL
CHEADLE (St Giles) w Freehay *Lich 6* **P** *DBP*
R I C THURSTON
CHEADLE HULME (All Saints) *Ches 17* **P** *Bp* **V** H B EALES,
C D A PARKER
CHEADLE HULME (Emmanuel) Conventional District *Ches 17*
C-in-c R G IVESON
CHEADLE HULME (St Andrew) *Ches 17* **P** *R Cheadle*
V D W GUEST, **C** J D WARD
CHEAM (St Dunstan) (St Alban the Martyr) (St Oswald)
S'wark 23 **P** *Patr Bd* **TR** D N MILLER, **TV** Y FRANCIS,
C P T JOHNSON, **OLM** D W F BRICE
CHEAM COMMON (St Philip) *see* Worcester Park Ch Ch w St
Phil *S'wark*
CHEARSLEY (St Nicholas) *see* Long Crendon w Chearsley
and Nether Winchendon *Ox*
**CHEBSEY (All Saints), Creswell, Ellenhall, Ranton and
Seighford** *Lich 7* **P** *D&C, Qu Eliz Grant Trustees, Trustees Earl
of Lich, and J Eld Esq (jt)* **V** A HETHERINGTON
CHECKENDON (St Peter and St Paul) *see* Langtree *Ox*
CHECKLEY (Mission Room) *see* Fownhope w Mordiford,
Brockhampton etc *Heref*
CHECKLEY (St Mary and All Saints) *see* Uttoxeter Area *Lich*
CHEDBURGH (All Saints) *see* Chevington w Hargrave,
Chedburgh w Depden etc *St E*
CHEDDAR (St Andrew) *B & W 1* **P** *D&C* **P-in-c** S M ROSE,
NSM R D H BURSELL
CHEDDINGTON (St Giles) w Mentmore *Ox 26* **P** *Earl of
Rosebery* **P-in-c** D W F WITCHELL **NSM** R J WRIGHT
CHEDDLETON (St Edward the Confessor) *Lich 8* **P** *Bp*
P-in-c L R PRICE
CHEDDON FITZPAINE (The Blessed Virgin Mary)
see Kingston St Mary w Broomfield etc *B & W*
CHEDGRAVE (All Saints) *see* Loddon, Sisland, Chedgrave,
Hardley and Langley *Nor*
CHEDISTON (St Mary) *see* Blyth Valley *St E*
**CHEDWORTH (St Andrew), Yanworth and Stowell, Coln Rogers
and Coln St Denys** *Glouc 11* **P** *Ld Chan (2 turns), Qu Coll Ox
(1 turn)* **P-in-c** D G MITCHELL
CHEDZOY (The Blessed Virgin Mary) *see* Weston Zoyland w
Chedzoy *B & W*
CHEETHAM (St John the Evangelist) *Man 5* **P** *Patr Bd*
P-in-c D J A BURTON, **C** C H MCCULLOCH
CHEETHAM (St Mark) *see* Lower Crumpsall w Cheetham St
Mark *Man*
CHELBOROUGH, EAST (St James) *see* Melbury *Sarum*
CHELBOROUGH, WEST (St Andrew) *as above*
CHELDON (St Mary) *see* Burrington, Chawleigh, Cheldon,
Chulmleigh etc *Ex*
CHELFORD (St John the Evangelist) w Lower Withington
Ches 12 **P** *J M Dixon Esq* **P-in-c** J READER
CHELL (St Michael) *Lich 11* **P** *Ch Patr Trust and V Newchapel
St Jas (jt)* **V** S S PRATT, **C** J C TAYLOR
CHELL HEATH (Saviour) *see* Chell *Lich*
CHELLASTON (St Peter) *Derby 15* **P** *Bp* **V** P SWALES
CHELLS (St Hugh) *see* Stevenage St Hugh and St Jo *St Alb*
CHELLS (St John) *as above*
CHELMARSH (St Peter) *see* Highley w Billingsley, Glazeley etc
Heref
CHELMONDISTON (St Andrew) *see* Shoreline *St E*
CHELMORTON AND FLAGG (St John the Baptist)
see Taddington, Chelmorton and Flagg, and Monyash *Derby*
CHELMSFORD (All Saints) (St Michael's Church Centre)
Chelmsf 8 **P** *Bp* **V** M A HALL
CHELMSFORD (Ascension) *Chelmsf 8* **P** *Bp*
CHELMSFORD (St Andrew) *Chelmsf 8* **P** *Bp*
V P H GREENLAND, **C** L R MULLEN, **NSM** S E IVES
CHELMSLEY WOOD (St Andrew) *Birm 9* **P** *Bp*
R J M FATHERS, **NSM** C A CAMP
CHELSEA (All Saints) (Old Church) *Lon 8* **P** *R Chelsea
St Luke and Earl Cadogan (jt)* **V** D P E REINDORP
CHELSEA (St John w St Andrew) (St John) *Lon 8* **P** *CPAS and
Lon Coll of Div (jt)* **V** *vacant* (020) 7352 1675
CHELSEA (St Luke) (Christ Church) *Lon 8* **P** *Earl Cadogan*
R B LEATHARD, **C** J B MOFFATT, A R M CRAVEN
CHELSEA, UPPER (Holy Trinity) *Lon 8* **P** *Earl Cadogan*
R A R GILLION, **Hon C** N NASSAR, R G RAINFORD
CHELSEA, UPPER (St Saviour) (St Simon Zelotes) *Lon 8*
P *R Upper Chelsea H Trin w St Jude and Hyndman's
Trustees (jt)* **C** E J OLSWORTH-PETER
CHELSFIELD (St Martin of Tours) *Roch 16* **P** *All So Coll Ox*
R L G VIRGO
CHELSHAM (St Christopher) *see* Warlingham w Chelsham
and Farleigh *S'wark*

CHELSHAM (St Leonard) *as above*
CHELSTON (St Peter) *see* Cockington *Ex*
CHELSWORTH (All Saints) *see* Monks Eleigh w Chelsworth
and Brent Eleigh etc *St E*
CHELTENHAM (All Saints) *see* N Cheltenham *Glouc*
CHELTENHAM Benefice, The NORTH *Glouc 7* **P** *Patr Bd*
TR M G COZENS, **TV** S W ELDRIDGE, D J PAPWORTH,
P-in-c D R EADY, **C** D A GARDINER, **Hon C** P R ILES,
NSM P T BROWN, M J FRENCH, A J SWINBANK
CHELTENHAM (Christ Church) *Glouc 7* **P** *Simeon's Trustees*
V T J E MAYFIELD, **C** J FAULL
CHELTENHAM (Emmanuel) (St Stephen) *Glouc 7* **P** *Bp*
P-in-c P WILKINSON, **NSM** H R WOOD, B E TORODE,
J M RODWELL
CHELTENHAM (Holy Trinity) (St Paul) *Glouc 7* **P** *Patr Bd*
TR M R BAILEY, **TV** K J HITCHMAN, R J WIDDECOMBE,
NSM T R GREW, J R B STOTT
CHELTENHAM (St Luke and St John) *Glouc 7*
P *R Cheltenham and Simeon's Trustees (alt)*
P-in-c R C PESTELL, **NSM** R I MERCHANT, Y R BRAE
**CHELTENHAM (St Mark) (St Barnabas) (St Aidan)
(Emmanuel)** *Glouc 7* **P** *Patr Bd* **TR** P HARRIS,
TV P D SMITH, **C** J J H WARD, **NSM** A M OSMOND,
OLM B E HORNE, M L D HORNE
CHELTENHAM (St Mary) (St Matthew) *Glouc 7* **P** *Simeon's
Trustees* **R** A J M DOW, **C** M C BAKER,
NSM M WORKMAN, T CURTIS
CHELTENHAM (St Michael) *Glouc 7* **P** *Bp*
P-in-c R C PESTELL, **NSM** R I MERCHANT, Y R BRAE
CHELTENHAM, WEST Team Ministry *see* Cheltenham St
Mark *Glouc*
CHELVESTON (St John the Baptist) *see* Higham Ferrers w
Chelveston *Pet*
CHELVEY (St Bridget) *see* Backwell w Chelvey and Brockley
B & W
CHELWOOD (St Leonard) *see* Publow w Pensford, Compton
Dando and Chelwood *B & W*
CHELWOOD GATE (not known) *see* Danehill *Chich*
CHENDERIT *Pet 1* **P** *Bp and BNC Ox (2 turns), Ld Chan
(1 turn)* **R** D P RANDELL, **NSM** T D RICHARDS
**CHENIES (St Michael) and Little Chalfont, Latimer and
Flaunden** *Ox 20* **P** *Bedf Estates Trustees and Lord
Chesham (jt)* **R** D G ALLSOP, **C** P M COLLINS,
Hon C M F PAYNE, **OLM** R BOUGHTON
CHEQUERBENT (St Thomas) *see* Westhoughton and
Wingates *Man*
CHEQUERFIELD (St Mary) *see* Pontefract St Giles *Wakef*
CHERBURY w Gainfield *Ox 17* **P** *Bp, DBP, Jes Coll, Oriel Coll,
and Worc Coll Ox (jt)* **NSM** J HANCE
CHERHILL (St James the Great) *see* Oldbury *Sarum*
CHERINGTON (St John the Baptist) *see* S Warks Seven Gp
Cov
CHERINGTON (St Nicholas) *see* Avening w Cherington *Glouc*
CHERITON (All Souls) w Newington *Cant 5* **P** *Abp*
P-in-c H C JONES, **C** C M SIGRIST, **OLM** J THORNBY,
E M WEBB
CHERITON (St Martin) *Cant 5* **P** *Abp* **R** H C JONES,
C C M SIGRIST, **OLM** E M WEBB
CHERITON (St Michael and All Angels) *see* Upper Itchen *Win*
CHERITON, NORTH (St John the Baptist) *see* Camelot Par
B & W
CHERITON BISHOP (St Mary) *see* Tedburn St Mary,
Whitestone, Oldridge etc *Ex*
CHERITON FITZPAINE (St Matthew) *see* N Creedy *Ex*
CHERITON STREET *see* Cheriton All So w Newington *Cant*
CHERRY BURTON (St Michael) *York 8* **P** *Mrs P J Burton*
P-in-c M J WESTBY
CHERRY HINTON (St Andrew) *Ely 3* **P** *Peterho Cam*
V B J LINNEY
CHERRY HINTON (St John the Evangelist) *Ely 3* **P** *Bp*
V S E WYATT, **Hon C** P S HESLAM
CHERRY WILLINGHAM (St Peter and St Paul) *see* S Lawres
Gp *Linc*
CHERTSEY (St Peter w All Saints), Lyne and Longcross
Guildf 11 **P** *Bp and Haberdashers' Co (jt)* **V** T J HILLIER,
Hon C W K PUGH, **NSM** L W GAMLEN,
OLM C B PATTINSON
CHERWELL VALLEY *Ox 2* **P** *Patr Bd* **TR** P E HUNT,
TV E B GREEN, **C** I R BISCOE
CHESELBORNE (St Martin) *see* Piddle Valley, Hilton,
Cheselbourne etc *Sarum*
**CHESHAM, GREAT (Christ Church) (Emmanuel) (St Mary the
Virgin)** *Ox 20* **P** *Patr Bd* **TR** S J L CANSDALE,
TV R S HARRIS, J M SHEPHERD, **C** M S R COLES,
NSM T J S YATES, H A WILSON

CHESHAM BOIS (St Leonard) *Ox 20* **P** *Peache Trustees*
R P H DAVIES,   **C** J B MURRAY, R J BAKER,   **NSM** D J BUTLER,
C CLARE

CHESHUNT (St Mary the Virgin) *St Alb 20* **P** *Patr Bd*
TR J K WILLIAMS,   **TV** J E DICKER, C J SELBY,
C K I MITCHELL

CHESSINGTON (St Mary the Virgin) *Guildf 9* **P** *Mert Coll Ox*
V S M OAKLAND

CHESTER (Christ Church) *see* Plas Newton w Ches Ch Ch
Ches

CHESTER (Holy Trinity without the Walls) *Ches 2* **P** *Bp*
R J A STONE,   **NSM** M R NEEDHAM

CHESTER (St Barnabas) *see* Ches St Pet w St Jo *Ches*

CHESTER (St Mary on the Hill) *Ches 2* **P** *Duke of Westmr*
R P C O DAWSON,   **C** R P BURTON,   **NSM** M A PICKERING,
R H MOSLEY

CHESTER St Oswald (St Thomas of Canterbury) *Ches 2*
P *D&C*   **V** P WALSH

CHESTER (St Paul) *Ches 2* **P** *R Ches*   **V** S T PENDLEBURY

CHESTER (St Peter) (St John the Baptist) *Ches 2* **P** *Bp and
Duke of Westminster (jt)*   **V** D N CHESTERS

CHESTER GREEN (St Paul) *see* Derby St Paul *Derby*

CHESTER LE STREET (St Mary and St Cuthbert) *Dur 11*
P *St Jo Coll Dur*   R D J TULLY,   **C** P J W TYREUS, J ANDERSON

CHESTER SQUARE (St Michael) (St Philip) *Lon 3* **P** *Duke of
Westmr*   **V** C C MARNHAM,   **C** W P H COLERIDGE, E CLIFFORD

CHESTERBLADE (The Blessed Virgin Mary) *see* Evercreech w
Chesterblade and Milton Clevedon *B & W*

CHESTERFIELD (Holy Trinity) (Christ Church) *Derby 5*
P *CPAS*   **P-in-c** C J W JACKSON

CHESTERFIELD (St Augustine) *Derby 5* **P** *Bp*   **V** *vacant*
(01246) 273942

CHESTERFIELD (St Mary and All Saints) *Derby 5* **P** *Bp*
V M R KNIGHT

**CHESTERFORD, GREAT (All Saints) w LITTLE (St Mary the
Virgin)** *Chelmsf 21* **P** *Bp*   **P-in-c** C P WARREN

CHESTERTON (Good Shepherd) *Ely 2* **P** *Bp*   **V** D J MAHER,
C A J LEES-SMITH

CHESTERTON (Holy Trinity) (St Chad) *Lich 9* **P** *Prime Min*
V B R WILSON,   **C** K A RODDY,   **NSM** S SIDEBOTTOM

CHESTERTON (St Andrew) *Ely 2* **P** *Trin Coll Cam*
V N I MOIR,   **NSM** D H PEYTON JONES, A J COLES

CHESTERTON (St George) *Ely 2* **P** *Bp*   **V** S J BOWRING,
NSM S H M CAMERON

CHESTERTON (St Giles) *Cov 8* **P** *Lady Willoughby de Broke*
V G J BURRELL

CHESTERTON (St Lawrence) *see* Cirencester *Glouc*

CHESTERTON (St Michael) *see* The Ortons, Alwalton and
Chesterton *Ely*

CHESTERTON, GREAT (St Mary) *see* Akeman *Ox*

**CHESWARDINE (St Swithun), Childs Ercall, Hales, Hinstock,
Sambrook and Stoke on Tern** *Lich 18* **P** *Patr Bd*
TR J M STAGG,   **NSM** L CHAPMAN

CHET VALLEY, The *see* Loddon, Sisland, Chedgrave, Hardley
and Langley *Nor*

CHETNOLE (St Peter) *see* Wriggle Valley *Sarum*

CHETTISHAM (St Michael and All Angels) *see* Ely *Ely*

CHETTLE (St Mary) *see* Chase *Sarum*

CHETTON (St Giles) *see* Ditton Priors w Neenton, Burwarton
etc *Heref*

CHETWODE (St Mary and St Nicholas) *see* The Claydons and
Swan *Ox*

CHETWYND (St Michael and All Angels) *see* Newport w
Longford, Chetwynd and Forton *Lich*

CHEVELEY (St Mary) *Ely 4* **P** *DBP and Mrs D A Bowlby
(alt)*   **P-in-c** M A GURNER

CHEVENING (St Botolph) *Roch 9* **P** *Abp*   **R** *vacant* (01732)
453555

CHEVERELL, GREAT (St Peter) *see* The Lavingtons,
Cheverells, and Easterton *Sarum*

CHEVERELL, LITTLE (St Peter) *as above*

**CHEVINGTON (All Saints) w Hargrave, Chedburgh w Depden,
Rede and Hawkedon** *St E 8* **P** *Guild of All So (1 turn),
Ld Chan (2 turns), Bp and DBP (1 turn)*   **P-in-c** R J BROOKS

CHEVINGTON (St John the Divine) *Newc 6* **P** *Bp*
P-in-c W E AIRD,   **Hon C** F L BROOKS

CHEVITHORNE (St Thomas) *see* Tiverton St Pet and
Chevithorne w Cove *Ex*

CHEW MAGNA (St Andrew) w Dundry and Norton Malreward
B & W 10 **P** *Bp*   **R** C R M ROBERTS,   **NSM** S E LOVERN

CHEW STOKE (St Andrew) w Nempnett Thrubwell *B & W 10*
P *Bp and SMF (jt)*   **P-in-c** C R M ROBERTS,
NSM V L BARLEY

CHEWTON (Mission Church) *see* Keynsham *B & W*

CHEWTON MENDIP (St Mary Magdalene) w Ston Easton,

Litton and Emborough *B & W 8* **P** *Earl Waldegrave (2 turns),
Bp (1 turn)*   **P-in-c** J SMITH,   **NSM** H J LATTY

CHEYLESMORE (Christ Church) *Cov 3* **P** *Ch Trust Fund
Trust*   **V** F P SELDON,   **NSM** G J BARTLEM

CHICHELEY (St Laurence) *see* Sherington w Chicheley, N
Crawley, Astwood etc *Ox*

CHICHESTER (St Pancras and St John) *Chich 3* **P** *Simeon's
Trustees (2 turns), St Jo Chpl Trustees (1 turn)*
R R B M GRIFFITHS

CHICHESTER (St Paul) and Westhampnett St Peter *Chich 3*
P *Bp and D&C (jt)*   **R** R W HUNT,   **C** J W F THEODOSIUS,
P D C KANE, A E WAIZENEKER

CHICHESTER (St Wilfrid) *Chich 3* **P** *Bp*
P-in-c P M GILBERT

CHICKERELL (St Mary) w Fleet *Sarum 4* **P** *Bp*
R R J PRESS,   **OLM** M LEE

CHICKLADE (All Saints) *see* Nadder Valley *Sarum*

CHIDDINGFOLD (St Mary) *Guildf 4* **P** *Ld Chan*
R S A BROUGH,   **OLM** G M WELFORD

CHIDDINGLY (not known) w East Hoathly *Chich 21* **P** *Bp*
R P A HODGINS

CHIDDINGSTONE (St Mary) w Chiddingstone Causeway
Roch 11 **P** *Abp and Bp (jt)*   **P-in-c** I D HARRISON

CHIDDINGSTONE CAUSEWAY (St Luke)
see Chiddingstone w Chiddingstone Causeway *Roch*

CHIDEOCK (St Giles) *see* Golden Cap Team *Sarum*

CHIDHAM (St Mary) *Chich 13* **P** *Bp*   **P-in-c** D C PAIN

CHIEVELEY (St Mary the Virgin) w Winterbourne and Oare
Ox 14 **P** *Adn Berks*   **P-in-c** J P TOOGOOD

CHIGNAL SMEALEY (St Nicholas) *see* The Chignals w
Mashbury *Chelmsf*

CHIGNALS w Mashbury, The *Chelmsf 8* **P** *CPAS (2 turns), Bp
(1 turn)*   **R** *vacant*

CHIGWELL (St Mary) (St Winifred) and Chigwell Row
Chelmsf 24 **P** *The Crown and Patr Bd (alt)*   **TV** A J NEALE,
A SMITH

CHIGWELL ROW (All Saints) *see* Chigwell and Chigwell Row
Chelmsf

CHILBOLTON (St Mary) *see* Downs Benefice *Win*

CHILCOMB (St Andrew) *see* E Win *Win*

CHILCOMBE (not known) *see* Bride Valley *Sarum*

**CHILCOMPTON (St John the Baptist) w Downside and Stratton
on the Fosse** *B & W 12* **P** *Bp, MMCET, and V Midsomer
Norton (jt)*   **P-in-c** C D NORTH

CHILCOTE (St Matthew's Chapel) *see* Clifton Campville w
Edingale and Harlaston *Lich*

CHILDE OKEFORD (St Nicholas) *see* Okeford *Sarum*

CHILDERDITCH (All Saints and St Faith) *see* E and W
Horndon w Lt Warley and Childerditch *Chelmsf*

CHILDREY (St Mary the Virgin) *see* Ridgeway *Ox*

CHILDS ERCALL (St Michael and All Angels)
see Cheswardine, Childs Ercall, Hales, Hinstock etc *Lich*

CHILDS HILL (All Saints) *see* Hendon All SS Childs Hill *Lon*

CHILDSWYCKHAM (St Mary the Virgin) *see* Winchcombe
Glouc

CHILDWALL (All Saints) *Liv 4* **P** *Bp*   **V** G J RENISON,
C S L DAVIES,   **OLM** S J GILLIES

CHILDWALL (St David) *Liv 4* **P** *Bp*   **V** R WILLIAMS

CHILDWALL VALLEY (St Mark) *see* Gateacre *Liv*

CHILDWICK (St Mary) *see* St Alb St Mich *St Alb*

CHILFROME (Holy Trinity) *see* Melbury *Sarum*

CHILHAM (St Mary) w Challock and Molash *Cant 2* **P** *Abp
and Viscount Massereene and Ferrard (jt)*   **V** C R DUNCAN

CHILLENDEN (All Saints) *see* Nonington w Wymynswold
and Goodnestone etc *Cant*

CHILLESFORD (St Peter) *see* Wilford Peninsula *St E*

CHILLINGHAM (St Peter) *see* Glendale Gp *Newc*

CHILLINGTON (St James) *see* Ilminster and Distr *B & W*

CHILMARK (St Margaret of Antioch) *see* Nadder Valley
Sarum

CHILTHORNE DOMER (Blessed Virgin Mary) *see* Tintinhull
w Chilthorne Domer, Yeovil Marsh etc *B & W*

CHILTINGTON, EAST (not known) *see* Plumpton w E
Chiltington cum Novington *Chich*

CHILTINGTON, WEST (St Mary) *Chich 12* **P** *Bp*
R D M BEAL

CHILTON (All Saints) *see* Harwell w Chilton *Ox*

CHILTON (St Aidan) *Dur 5* **P** *Bp*   **P-in-c** C B LLOYD

CHILTON (St Mary) *see* Bernwode *Ox*

**CHILTON CANTELO (St James) w Ashington, Mudford,
Rimpton and Marston Magna** *B & W 7* **P** *DBP and D&C,
D&C Bris, and Bp Lon (by turn)*   **P-in-c** M G W HAYES

CHILTON FOLIAT (St Mary) *see* Whitton *Sarum*

CHILTON MOOR (St Andrew) *Dur 14* **P** *Bp*
P-in-c D NEWTON

CHILTON POLDEN (St Edward) *see* W Poldens *B & W*

CHILTON TRINITY (Holy Trinity) *see* Bridgwater St Mary and Chilton Trinity *B & W*

CHILVERS COTON (All Saints) w Astley *Cov 5* **P** *Viscount Daventry* **V** P BROWN, **NSM** D WATERTON

CHILWELL (Christ Church) *S'well 7* **P** *CPAS* **V** A R HOWE, **C** J M CORCORAN, **NSM** L HEPTINSTALL

CHILWORTH (St Denys) w North Baddesley *Win 12* **P** *Mrs P M A T Chamberlayne-Macdonald* **V** P M GILKS, **Hon C** A J WALKER, **NSM** J FOSTER, V J LAWRENCE

CHILWORTH (St Thomas) *see* Shere, Albury and Chilworth *Guildf*

CHINEHAM (Christ Church) *Win 4* **P** *Bp* **V** I R BENTLEY

CHINESE CONGREGATION *see* St Martin-in-the-Fields *Lon*

CHINGFORD (All Saints) (St Peter and St Paul) *Chelmsf 5* **P** *Bp* **R** T W PAGE, **C** C F WILSON, A W SUMMERS

CHINGFORD (St Anne) *Chelmsf 5* **P** *Bp* **V** J R BULLOCK

CHINGFORD (St Edmund) *Chelmsf 5* **P** *Bp* **V** L A GOLDSMITH

CHINLEY (St Mary) *see* Hayfield and Chinley w Buxworth *Derby*

CHINNOCK, EAST (Blessed Virgin Mary) *see* W Coker w Hardington Mandeville, E Chinnock etc *B & W*

CHINNOCK, MIDDLE (St Margaret) *see* Norton sub Hamdon, W Chinnock, Chiselborough etc *B & W*

CHINNOCK, WEST (Blessed Virgin Mary) *as above*

CHINNOR (St Andrew), Sydenham, Aston Rowant and Crowell *Ox 1* **P** *Bp, DBP, and Peache Trustees (jt)* **R** J M KINCHIN-SMITH, **C** H L O'SULLIVAN, **OLM** J M DEVAL, S Q HUTTON

CHIPPENHAM (St Andrew) w Tytherton Lucas *Bris 4* **P** *Ch Ch Ox* **V** S C TATTON-BROWN

CHIPPENHAM (St Margaret) *see* Three Rivers Gp *Ely*

CHIPPENHAM (St Paul) w Hardenhuish and Langley Burrell *Bris 4* **P** *Patr Bd* **TR** S J TYNDALL, **TV** M J WATKINS, **C** S J RUSHTON, **OLM** D J KILMISTER

CHIPPENHAM (St Peter) *Bris 4* **P** *Bp* **V** vacant (01249) 654835

CHIPPERFIELD (St Paul) *see* Sarratt and Chipperfield *St Alb*

CHIPPING (St Bartholomew) and Whitewell (St Michael) *Blackb 7* **P** *Bp and Hulme Trustees (jt)* **V** vacant (01995) 61252

CHIPPING BARNET (St John the Baptist) (St Mark) (St Stephen) *St Alb 17* **P** *Prime Min (2 turns) and Bp (1 turn)* **TR** S H SPEERS, **TV** M J WILLIAMS, **NSM** J KRAFT

CHIPPING CAMPDEN (St James) w Ebrington *Glouc 8* **P** *Peache Trustees (1 turn), Earl of Harrowby (2 turns)* **P-in-c** D C M COOK

CHIPPING NORTON (St Mary the Virgin) *Ox 3* **P** *Patr Bd* **TR** S J A WESTON, **TV** T A CANNON, **C** J M ALIDINA, **NSM** A J B KEITH

CHIPPING ONGAR (St Martin) w Shelley *Chelmsf 26* **P** *Guild of All So and Keble Coll Ox* **R** S M COOPER, **NSM** B L SURTEES

CHIPPING SODBURY (St John the Baptist) and Old Sodbury *Glouc 6* **P** *D&C Worc* **V** vacant (01454) 313159

CHIPPING WARDEN (St Peter and St Paul) *see* Culworth w Sulgrave and Thorpe Mandeville etc *Pet*

CHIPSTABLE (All Saints) *see* Wiveliscombe w Chipstable, Huish Champflower etc *B & W*

CHIPSTEAD (Good Shepherd) *see* Chevening *Roch*

CHIPSTEAD (St Margaret of Antioch) *S'wark 26* **P** *Abp* **P-in-c** P J BATEMAN, **OLM** J N WATES

CHIRBURY (St Michael) *Heref 13* **P** *Sir David Wakeman Bt and Bp (alt)* **V** vacant (01938) 561218

CHIRTON (St John the Baptist) *see* Redhorn *Sarum*

CHISELBOROUGH (St Peter and St Paul) *see* Norton sub Hamdon, W Chinnock, Chiselborough etc *B & W*

CHISHILL, GREAT (St Swithun) *see* Heydon, Gt and Lt Chishill, Chrishall etc *Chelmsf*

CHISHILL, LITTLE (St Nicholas) *as above*

CHISLEDON (Holy Cross) *see* Ridgeway *Sarum*

CHISLEHURST (Annunciation) *Roch 14* **P** *Keble Coll* **V** W B BEER

CHISLEHURST (Christ Church) *Roch 14* **P** *CPAS* **V** J M ADAMS, **C** A K VAUGHAN

CHISLEHURST (St Nicholas) *Roch 14* **P** *Bp* **R** S D BURTON-JONES, **C** E C KITCHENER, **NSM** J B HURN

CHISLET (St Mary the Virgin) *see* St Nicholas at Wade w Sarre and Chislet w Hoath *Cant*

CHISWICK (St Michael) *Lon 11* **P** *V St Martin-in-the-Fields* **P-in-c** N C FINCHAM

CHISWICK (St Michael and All Angels) *see* Bedford Park *Lon*

CHISWICK (St Nicholas w St Mary Magdalene) *Lon 11* **P** *D&C St Paul's* **V** S F BRANDES, **C** A M ALEXANDER

CHISWICK (St Paul) Grove Park *Lon 11* **P** *V Chiswick* **V** M C RILEY

CHITHURST (St Mary) *see* Rogate w Terwick and Trotton w Chithurst *Chich*

CHITTERNE (All Saints and St Mary) *see* Wylye and Till Valley *Sarum*

CHITTERNE (St Mary) *as above*

CHITTLEHAMHOLT (St John) *see* S Molton w Nymet St George, High Bray etc *Ex*

CHITTLEHAMPTON (St Hieritha) *as above*

CHITTS HILL (St Cuthbert) *Lon 19* **P** *CPAS* **V** D M DALEY

CHIVELSTONE (St Sylvester) *see* Stokenham, Slapton, Charleton w Buckland etc *Ex*

CHOBHAM (St Lawrence) w Valley End *Guildf 6* **P** *Bp and Brig R W Acworth (alt)* **V** A BODY, **OLM** C J BEDFORD

CHOLDERTON (St Nicholas) *see* Bourne Valley *Sarum*

CHOLESBURY (St Lawrence) *see* Hawridge w Cholesbury and St Leonard *Ox*

CHOLLERTON w Birtley and Thockrington *Newc 8* **P** *Mrs P I Enderby (2 turns), Newc Dioc Soc (1 turn)* **R** J WYLAM, **OLM** D I WILLIAMS

CHOLSEY (St Mary) and Moulsford *Ox 18* **P** *Ld Chan and Bp (alt)* **V** A M PETIT, **OLM** V M L GIBBONS

CHOPPARDS (Mission Room) *see* Upper Holme Valley *Wakef*

CHOPPINGTON (St Paul the Apostle) *Newc 1* **P** *D&C* **V** T MOAT

CHOPWELL (St John the Evangelist) *Dur 13* **P** *Bp* **P-in-c** P R MURRAY

CHORLEY (All Saints) *Blackb 4* **P** *Bp* **V** E N STRASZAK

CHORLEY (St George) *Blackb 4* **P** *R Chorley* **P-in-c** T D WILBY, **NSM** P MASON

CHORLEY (St James) *Blackb 4* **P** *R Chorley* **V** K HOWLES

CHORLEY (St Laurence) *Blackb 4* **P** *Bp* **C** H G SNOOK

CHORLEY (St Peter) *Blackb 4* **P** *R Chorley* **V** L T ATHERTON

CHORLEY (St Philip) *see* Alderley Edge *Ches*

CHORLEYWOOD (Christ Church) *St Alb 5* **P** *CPAS* **V** G A COLLINS, **C** R E JENKINSON

CHORLEYWOOD (St Andrew) *St Alb 5* **P** *Bp* **C** A T WILLIAMS

CHORLTON-CUM-HARDY (St Clement) (St Barnabas) *Man 4* **P** *D&C* **P-in-c** K FLOOD, **OLM** J KING

CHORLTON-CUM-HARDY (St Werburgh) *Man 4* **P** *Bp* **P-in-c** A F DAWTRY, **OLM** M J CLEALL-HILL

CHRISHALL (Holy Trinity) *see* Heydon, Gt and Lt Chishill, Chrishall etc *Chelmsf*

CHRIST THE KING comprising the parishes of Tanfield, Stanley and South Moor *Dur 4* **P** *Bp (4 turns), Prime Min (1 turn)* **TR** A JOHNSTON

CHRIST THE KING in the Diocese of Newcastle *Newc 2* **P** *Patr Bd* **TR** A J SHIPTON, **TV** I H FLINTOFT, M A EDWARDS

CHRISTCHURCH (Christ Church) and Manea and Welney *Ely 11* **P** *Bp and R T Townley Esq (jt)* **P-in-c** K P FITZGIBBON

CHRISTCHURCH (Holy Trinity) *Win 9* **P** *Bp* **V** H M WILLIAMS, **C** A HAWTHORNE, **NSM** A M SMITH, G A J SMITH

CHRISTCHURCH Stourvale (St George) *see* Christchurch *Win*

CHRISTIAN MALFORD (All Saints) *see* Draycot *Bris*

CHRISTLETON (St James) *Ches 2* **P** *Bp* **R** K P LEE

CHRISTON (Blessed Virgin Mary) *see* Crook Peak *B & W*

CHRISTOW (St James), Ashton and Bridford *Ex 6* **P** *SMF, MMCET, Viscount Exmouth, Bp, and E A Beard Esq (jt)* **P-in-c** G K MAYER

CHUDLEIGH (St Mary and St Martin) w Chudleigh Knighton and Trusham *Ex 9* **P** *Patr Bd* **V** P WIMSETT

CHUDLEIGH KNIGHTON (St Paul) *see* Chudleigh w Chudleigh Knighton and Trusham *Ex*

CHULMLEIGH (St Mary Magdalene) *see* Burrington, Chawleigh, Cheldon, Chulmleigh etc *Ex*

CHURCH ASTON (St Andrew) *Lich 16* **P** *R Edgmond* **P-in-c** L M WHEELER

CHURCH BRAMPTON (St Botolph) *see* Brington w Whilton and Norton etc *Pet*

CHURCH BROUGHTON (St Michael) *see* Boylestone, Church Broughton, Dalbury, etc *Derby*

CHURCH CONISTON (St Andrew) *Carl 9* **P** *Peache Trustees* **P-in-c** M R EAST

CHURCH EATON (St Editha) *see* Bradeley, Church Eaton, Derrington and Haughton *Lich*

CHURCH HONEYBOURNE (St Ecgwyn) *see* Pebworth, Dorsington, Honeybourne etc *Glouc*

CHURCH HULME (St Luke) *Ches 11* **P** *V Sandbach* **V** P MASON

CHURCH IN THE WOOD *see* Hollington St Leon *Chich*

CHURCH KIRK (St James) *Blackb 1* **P** *Hulme Trustees* **R** N A ASHTON

CHURCH KNOWLE (St Peter) *see* Corfe Castle, Church Knowle, Kimmeridge etc *Sarum*

CHURCH LANGLEY (Church and Community Centre) *Chelmsf 25*   **P** *V Harlow*   **V** T J VOLTZENLOGEL

CHURCH LANGTON (St Peter) cum Tur Langton, Thorpe Langton and Shangton, Billesdon cum Goadby and Rolleston and Skeffington *Leic 3*   **P** *Bp, E Brudenell Esq, and MMCET (jt)*   **P-in-c** G SPENCER,   **NSM** M B W COOK

CHURCH LAWFORD (St Peter) *see* Wolston and Church Lawford *Cov*

CHURCH LAWTON (All Saints) *Ches 11*   **P** *J Lawton Esq*   **R** G L JOYCE

CHURCH LENCH (All Saints) w Rous Lench and Abbots Morton and Harvington *Worc 1*   **P** *Bp and D&C (jt)*   **R** R J G THORNILEY,   **NSM** F M BATTIN

CHURCH MINSHULL (St Bartholomew) *see* Acton and Worleston, Church Minshull etc *Ches*

CHURCH OAKLEY (St Leonard) *see* Oakley w Wootton St Lawrence *Win*

CHURCH PREEN (St John the Baptist) *see* Wenlock *Heref*

CHURCH STRETTON (St Laurence) *Heref 11*   **P** *Ch Patr Trust*   **R** R H O HILL,   **Hon C** V R MORRIS,   **NSM** A J HUGHES, N CLEATON

CHURCHAM (St Andrew) *see* Huntley and Longhope, Churcham and Bulley *Glouc*

CHURCHDOWN (St Andrew) (St Bartholomew) *Glouc 4*   **P** *D&C*   **V** J G PERKIN,   **C** R E CROFTON,   **NSM** S A L JAMES

CHURCHDOWN (St John the Evangelist) and Innsworth *Glouc 4*   **P** *Bp*   **V** K I MORGAN,   **C** D J FORMAN,   **NSM** M D D WALKER

CHURCHILL (All Saints) *see* Chipping Norton *Ox*

CHURCHILL (St John the Baptist) and Langford *B & W 11*   **P** *D&C Bris*   **P-in-c** L D MACHELL

CHURCHILL-IN-HALFSHIRE (St James) w Blakedown and Broome *Worc 12*   **P** *Exors Viscount Cobham and N A Bourne Esq (alt)*   **P-in-c** P G HARRISON

CHURCHOVER (Holy Trinity) w Willey *Cov 6*   **P** *Bp*   **P-in-c** C A GARROD

CHURCHSTANTON (St Peter and St Paul) *see* Blackdown *B & W*

CHURCHSTOKE (St Nicholas) w Hyssington and Sarn *Heref 10*   **P** *The Crown (1 turn), Earl of Powis (2 turns)*   **NSM** I R BALL

CHURCHSTOW (St Mary) *see* Thurlestone, S Milton, W Alvington etc *Ex*

CHURCHTOWN (St Helen) *see* Garstang St Helen and St Michaels-on-Wyre *Blackb*

CHURN, The (Aston Tirrold w Aston Upthorpe, Blewbury, Hagbourne, North Moreton, South Moreton, and Upton) *Ox 18*   **P** *Bp and Magd Coll Ox (1 turn), Adn Berks and Hertf Coll Ox (1 turn)*   **R** J P ST JOHN NICOLLE,   **NSM** A P LURY,   **OLM** L G N BUTLER

CHURSTON FERRERS (St Mary the Virgin) *see* Brixham w Churston Ferrers and Kingswear *Ex*

CHURT (St John the Evangelist) and Hindhead *Guildf 3*   **P** *Adn Surrey*   **V** R T BODLE,   **C** S R JELLEY,   **NSM** J D STRAIN

CHURWELL (All Saints) *see* Morley *Wakef*

CHUTE (St Nicholas) *see* Savernake *Sarum*

CHYNGTON (St Luke) *see* Seaford w Sutton *Chich*

CINDERFORD (St John the Evangelist) *Glouc 2*   **P** *The Crown*   **P-in-c** R D WYNN,   **Hon C** G L BURN

CINDERFORD (St Stephen) w Littledean *Glouc 2*   **P** *Ch Patr Trust*   **P-in-c** R D WYNN

CINDERHILL (Christ Church) *S'well 14*   **P** *Bp*   **P-in-c** J WHYSALL

CINNAMON BROW (Resurrection) *Liv 12*   **P** *Bp, Adn, and R Warrington (jt)*   **P-in-c** D L WILLIAMS

CIPPENHAM (St Andrew) *Ox 23*   **P** *Eton Coll*   **V** S SMITH

CIRENCESTER (St John the Baptist) *Glouc 9*   **P** *Bp*   **V** L W DOOLAN,   **C** J K VAN DER LELY,   **Hon C** M J BETTIS,   **NSM** R M FRANKLIN, J P WILLIAMS, P A LIGHT

CLACTON, GREAT (St John the Baptist) *Chelmsf 22*   **P** *Ch Patr Trust*   **V** G D A THORBURN,   **C** T M MULRYNE

CLACTON, LITTLE (St James) *see* Weeley and Lt Clacton *Chelmsf*

CLACTON-ON-SEA (St Christopher) (St James) *Chelmsf 22*   **P** *Bp*   **V** A P D SPOONER

CLACTON-ON-SEA (St Paul) *Chelmsf 22*   **P** *Ch Patr Trust*   **V** D J TITLEY

CLAINES (St George w St Mary Magdalene) *see* Worc City *Worc*

CLAINES (St John the Baptist) *Worc 6*   **P** *Bp*   **V** S M AGNEW,   **C** N G KALENIUK

CLANDON, EAST (St Thomas of Canterbury) and WEST (St Peter and St Paul) *Guildf 5*   **P** *Earl of Onslow and Bp (alt)*   **R** B L PREECE,   **NSM** D M MACMILLAN

CLANFIELD (St James) *see* Catherington and Clanfield *Portsm*

CLANFIELD (St Stephen) *see* Bampton w Clanfield *Ox*

CLANNABOROUGH (St Petrock) *see* N Creedy *Ex*

CLAPHAM (Christ Church) (St John the Evangelist) *S'wark 11*   **P** *Bp*   **V** P J ROSE-CASEMORE,   **C** N J PEACOCK,   **NSM** S PEAKE

CLAPHAM (Holy Spirit) *S'wark 11*   **P** *Bp*   **V** J A BLUNDEN,   **Hon C** R F VICKERY,   **NSM** R A BURGE-THOMAS

CLAPHAM (Holy Trinity) (St Peter) *S'wark 11*   **P** *DBP*   **V** D O ISHERWOOD,   **NSM** C A CLARKE, R C B JONES

CLAPHAM (St James) *S'wark 12*   **P** *CPAS*   **Hon C** J MARSHALL,   **NSM** J OHEN

CLAPHAM (St Mary the Virgin) *see* Findon w Clapham and Patching *Chich*

CLAPHAM (St Paul) *S'wark 11*   **P** *Bp*   **V** D L MATTHEWS

CLAPHAM (St Thomas of Canterbury) *St Alb 13*   **P** *MMCET*   **V** S J LILEY

CLAPHAM COMMON (St Barnabas) *S'wark 14*   **P** *Ch Trust Fund Trust*   **V** R G TAYLOR,   **NSM** K W BISHOP

CLAPHAM PARK (All Saints) *S'wark 12*   **P** *CPAS*   **P-in-c** G W BRIGGS,   **C** J O ANI

CLAPHAM PARK (St Stephen) *see* Telford Park *S'wark*

CLAPHAM-WITH-KEASDEN (St James) and Austwick *Bradf 6*   **P** *Bp*   **V** I F GREENHALGH

CLAPTON (St James) *see* Bourton-on-the-Water w Clapton etc *Glouc*

CLAPTON (St James) *Lon 5*   **P** *Bp*   **V** R BROWN,   **NSM** H R GEORGE

CLAPTON (St Peter) *see* Aldwincle, Clopton, Pilton, Stoke Doyle etc *Pet*

CLAPTON, UPPER (St Matthew) *Lon 5*   **P** *D&C Cant*   **P-in-c** V A ROBERTS,   **Hon C** I E VIBERT

CLAPTON COMMON (St Thomas) *see* Stamford Hill St Thos *Lon*

CLARBOROUGH (St John the Baptist) w Hayton *S'well 5*   **P** *Bp*   **V** *vacant* (01777) 704781

CLARE (St Peter and St Paul) *see* Stour Valley *St E*

CLAREMOUNT (St Thomas the Apostle) *see* Southowram and Claremount *Wakef*

CLARENCE GATE GARDENS (St Cyprian) *see* St Marylebone St Cypr *Lon*

CLARENDON (Team Ministry) *Sarum 11*   **P** *Team Coun*   **TR** N H S BERSWEDEN,   **TV** E M MOORE-BICK,   **OLM** C M BUTTIMER

CLARENDON PARK (St John the Baptist) *see* Emmaus Par Team *Leic*

CLATFORD, UPPER (All Saints) *see* Abbotts Ann and Upper and Goodworth Clatford *Win*

CLATWORTHY (St Mary Magdalene) *see* Wiveliscombe w Chipstable, Huish Champflower etc *B & W*

CLAUGHTON VILLAGE (St Bede) *see* Birkenhead St Jas w St Bede *Ches*

CLAVERDON (St Michael and All Angels) w Preston Bagot *Cov 7*   **P** *Bp*   **P-in-c** L G MORTIMER

CLAVERHAM (St Barnabas) *see* Yatton Moor *B & W*

CLAVERING (St Mary and St Clement) and Langley w Arkesden and Wicken Bonhunt *Chelmsf 21*   **P** *Ch Hosp and Keble Coll Ox (jt)*   **V** D S MCGUFFIE

CLAVERLEY (All Saints) w Tuckhill *Heref 9*   **P** *Bp and E M A Thompson Esq (jt)*   **V** S H CAWDELL,   **Hon C** S H L CAWDELL

CLAVERTON (Blessed Virgin Mary) *see* Bathampton w Claverton *B & W*

CLAVERTON DOWN (St Hugh) *as above*

CLAWTON (St Leonard) *see* Ashwater, Halwill, Beaworthy, Clawton etc *Ex*

CLAXBY (St Mary) *see* Walesby *Linc*

CLAXTON (St Andrew) *see* Rockland St Mary w Hellington, Bramerton etc *Nor*

CLAY CROSS (St Bartholomew) *see* N Wingfield, Clay Cross and Pilsley *Derby*

CLAY HILL (St John the Baptist) (St Luke) *Lon 18*   **P** *V Enfield St Andr and Bp (jt)*   **NSM** R L MAUDSLEY

CLAYBROOKE (St Peter) *see* Upper Soar *Leic*

CLAYDON and Barham *St E 1*   **P** *G R Drury Esq*   **P-in-c** P THORN,   **OLM** C B AUSTIN, J V ABLETT

CLAYDON (St James the Great) *see* Shires' Edge *Ox*

CLAYDONS, The (St Mary) (All Saints) and Swan *Ox 24*   **P** *Patr Bd*   **TR** D A HISCOCK,   **TV** P M KNIGHT,   **NSM** K M PECK, A MANN

CLAYGATE (Holy Trinity) *Guildf 8*   **P** *Ch Patr Trust*   **V** P J J PLYMING,   **C** T J DARWENT,   **NSM** L M MORGAN

CLAYHANGER (Holy Trinity Worship Centre) *see* Ogley Hay *Lich*

CLAYHANGER (St Peter)   *see* Bampton, Morebath, Clayhanger and Petton *Ex*

CLAYHIDON (St Andrew)   *see* Hemyock w Culm Davy, Clayhidon and Culmstock *Ex*

CLAYPOLE (St Peter) *Linc 23*   **P** *DBP (2 turns), The Revd J R H Thorold and J R Thorold Esq (1 turn)*   **R** *vacant* (01636) 626224

CLAYTON (St Cross w St Paul)   *see* Man Clayton St Cross w St Paul *Man*

CLAYTON (St James the Great) *Lich 9*   **P** *Bp*
V N M EDWARDS

CLAYTON (St John the Baptist) *Bradf 2*   **P** *V Bradf*
V K O DUNNETT,   **C** S M STOBART,   **NSM** P COLES

CLAYTON (St John the Baptist) w Keymer *Chich 9*   **P** *BNC Ox*
P-in-c C J POWELL,   **NSM** M M SLATTERY

CLAYTON BROOK (Community Church)   *see* Whittle-le-Woods *Blackb*

CLAYTON LE MOORS (All Saints)   *see* Altham w Clayton le Moors *Blackb*

CLAYTON LE MOORS (St James)   *as above*

CLAYTON WEST w HIGH HOYLAND (All Saints)   *see* High Hoyland, Scissett and Clayton W *Wakef*

CLAYWORTH (St Peter)   *see* Everton, Mattersey, Clayworth and Gringley *S'well*

CLEADON (All Saints) *Dur 15*   **P** *R Whitburn*
P-in-c V J CUTHBERT

CLEADON PARK (St Mark and St Cuthbert) *Dur 15*   **P** *Bp*
V *vacant* 0191-456 2875

CLEARWELL (St Peter)   *see* Coleford, Staunton, Newland, Redbrook etc *Glouc*

CLEASBY (St Peter)   *see* E Richmond *Ripon*

CLEATOR (St Leonard)   *see* Crosslacon *Carl*

CLEATOR MOOR (St John)   *as above*

CLECKHEATON (St John the Evangelist) *Wakef 8*
P *V Birstall*   **C** A J RAGGETT

CLECKHEATON (St Luke) (Whitechapel) *Wakef 8*   **P** *Bp and Sir Martin Wilson (jt)*   **NSM** R M CAVE

CLEDFORD (Mission Room)   *see* Middlewich w Byley *Ches*

CLEE, NEW (St John the Evangelist) (St Stephen) *Linc 9*   **P** *Bp*
V J W ELLIS

CLEE, OLD (Holy Trinity and St Mary the Virgin) *Linc 9*   **P** *Bp*
P-in-c R G HOLDEN

CLEE HILL (St Peter) *Heref 12*   **P** *Bp*   **P-in-c** C A LORDING

CLEE ST MARGARET (St Margaret)   *see* Bitterley w Middleton, Stoke St Milborough etc *Heref*

CLEETHORPE (Christ Church)   *see* Clee *Linc*

CLEETHORPES St Aidan *Linc 9*   **P** *Bp*   **P-in-c** R G HOLDEN

CLEETHORPES (St Francis) Conventional District *Linc 9*
C-in-c T STOTT

CLEETHORPES (St Peter) *Linc 9*   **P** *Bp*   **R** P HUNTER,
NSM D H WEBSTER

CLEETON (St Mary)   *see* Stottesdon w Farlow, Cleeton St Mary etc *Heref*

CLEEVE (Holy Trinity)   *see* Yatton Moor *B & W*

CLEEVE, OLD (St Andrew), Leighland and Treborough
B & W 16   **P** *Selw Coll Cam (2 turns), Personal Reps G R Wolseley Esq (1 turn)*   **V** J HENNING

CLEEVE HILL (St Peter)   *see* Bishop's Cleeve and Woolstone w Gotherington etc *Glouc*

CLEEVE PRIOR (St Andrew) and The Littletons *Worc 1*
P *D&C and Ch Ch Ox (alt)*   **V** D R EVANS

CLEHONGER (All Saints)   *see* Kingstone w Clehonger, Eaton Bishop etc *Heref*

CLENCHWARTON (St Margaret) and West Lynn *Ely 14*
P *DBP*   **R** A J DAVEY

CLENT (St Leonard)   *see* Belbroughton w Fairfield and Clent *Worc*

CLEOBURY MORTIMER (St Mary the Virgin) w Hopton Wafers, Neen Sollars and Milson, Neen Savage w Kinlet
Heref 12   **P** *Patr Bd (2 turns), Ld Chan (1 turn)*
R W A BUCK,   **Hon C** R G SMITH,   **NSM** M H DABORN

CLEOBURY NORTH (St Peter and St Paul)   *see* Ditton Priors w Neenton, Burwarton etc *Heref*

CLERKENWELL (Our Most Holy Redeemer) *Lon 6*
P *Trustees*   **V** P A BAGOTT,   **C** M BRANDON,
NSM S J STOKES

CLERKENWELL (St James and St John) (St Peter) *Lon 6*
P *Ch Patr Trust and PCC (jt)*   **V** A J BAUGHEN

CLERKENWELL (St Mark) *Lon 6*   **P** *City Corp*
V P A BAGOTT

CLEVEDON (St Andrew) (Christ Church) (St Peter) *B & W 13*
P *Simeon's Trustees (1 turn), Ld Chan (2 turns)*
V T J BAILLIE,   **C** C J JENNINGS

CLEVEDON (St John the Evangelist) *B & W 13*   **P** *SMF*
V R JACKSON

CLEVEDON, EAST (All Saints) w Clapton in Gordano, Walton Clevedon, Walton in Gordano and Weston in Gordano *B & W 13*
P *Bp and SMF (jt)*   **R** N A HECTOR,   **Hon C** I D CORBETT,
NSM B L GUZEK

CLEVELEYS (St Andrew) *Blackb 12*   **P** *Trustees*
V D E REEVES

CLEWER (St Andrew) *Ox 13*   **P** *Eton Coll*   **P-in-c** L M BROWN

CLEWER (St Stephen)   *see* New Windsor *Ox*

CLEY (St Margaret)   *see* Blakeney w Cley, Wiveton, Glandford etc *Nor*

CLEY HILL Villages, The *Sarum 17*   **P** *Bp and DBP (jt)*
R N PAYNE,   **OLM** D J BRITTEN

CLIBURN (St Cuthbert)   *see* Morland, Thrimby, Gt Strickland and Cliburn *Carl*

CLIDDESDEN (St Leonard) and Ellisfield w Farleigh Wallop and Dummer *Win 1*   **P** *Earl of Portsm and DBP (jt)*
P-in-c C PARNELL-HOPKINSON

CLIFFE (St Andrew)   *see* Hemingbrough *York*

CLIFFE, SOUTH (St John)   *see* N Cave w Cliffe *York*

CLIFFE AT HOO (St Helen) w Cooling *Roch 6*   **P** *D&C*
R E M A WRIGHT

CLIFFORD (St Luke) *York 1*   **P** *G Lane-Fox Esq*
P-in-c K F A GABBADON

CLIFFORD (St Mary the Virgin)   *see* Cusop w Blakemere, Bredwardine w Brobury etc *Heref*

CLIFFORD CHAMBERS (St Helen)   *see* Stratford-upon-Avon, Luddington etc *Cov*

CLIFFORDS MESNE (St Peter)   *see* Newent and Gorsley w Cliffords Mesne *Glouc*

CLIFFSEND (St Mary the Virgin)   *see* St Laur in Thanet *Cant*

CLIFTON (All Saints) and Southill *St Alb 16*   **P** *Bp and C E S Whitbread Esq (jt)*   **P-in-c** M-A B TISDALE,
NSM C T TOPLEY

CLIFTON (All Saints w St John) *Bris 2*   **P** *Bp*
P-in-c R D HOYAL,   **Hon C** J H J PATRICK,   **NSM** R DURBIN

CLIFTON (Christ Church w Emmanuel) *Bris 2*   **P** *Simeon's Trustees*   **P-in-c** R A HIGGINS,   **C** M C CAIN, W P MASSEY,
D A CLARK

CLIFTON (Holy Trinity) *Derby 8*   **P** *Mrs M F Stanton, T W Clowes Esq, and V Ashbourne (by turn)*   **P-in-c** G P POND

CLIFTON (Holy Trinity) (St Francis) (St Mary the Virgin)
S'well 9   **P** *DBP*   **TR** S E CLARK,   **TV** C J COOKE,
L P B O'BOYLE,   **C** R H DAVEY

CLIFTON (Holy Trinity, St Andrew the Less and St Peter) *Bris 2*
P *Simeon's Trustees*   **NSM** I A BAILEY

CLIFTON (Mission Church)   *see* Conisbrough *Sheff*

CLIFTON (St Anne) (St Thomas) *Man 2*   **P** *Bp*
V J R BAXENDALE,   **OLM** M SOFIELD, A P GORDON

CLIFTON (St Cuthbert)   *see* Lowther and Askham and Clifton and Brougham *Carl*

CLIFTON (St James) *Sheff 6*   **P** *Bp*   **V** *vacant* (01709) 363082 or 836308

CLIFTON (St John the Evangelist)   *see* Lund *Blackb*

CLIFTON (St John the Evangelist)   *see* Brighouse and Clifton *Wakef*

CLIFTON (St Luke), Dean and Mosser *Carl 6*   **P** *Patr Bd*
R K KITCHIN

CLIFTON (St Paul)   *see* Cotham St Sav w St Mary and Clifton St Paul *Bris*

CLIFTON (St Philip and St James) *York 7*   **P** *Trustees*
V D O CASSWELL,   **C** E M MARSHMAN,   **NSM** C M A RUTT

CLIFTON, NORTH (St George)   *see* Harby w Thorney and N and S Clifton *S'well*

CLIFTON CAMPVILLE (St Andrew) w Edingale and Harlaston
Lich 4   **P** *Bp and Major F C Pipe-Wolferstan (jt)*
R S J LUMBY

CLIFTON HAMPDEN (St Michael and All Angels)
see Dorchester *Ox*

CLIFTON-ON-TEME (St Kenelm)   *see* Worcs W *Worc*

CLIFTON REYNES (St Mary the Virgin)   *see* Lavendon w Cold Brayfield, Clifton Reynes etc *Ox*

CLIFTON UPON DUNSMORE (St Mary) w Newton and Brownsover *Cov 6*   **P** *Bp and H A F W Boughton-Leigh Esq (jt)*   **V** E C LYONS,   **OLM** D J BUSSEY

CLIFTONVILLE (St Paul) *Cant 9*   **P** *Ch Patr Trust*
P-in-c P L S ELLISDON,   **C** H E HOBDAY

CLIPPESBY (St Peter)   *see* Martham and Repps with Bastwick, Thurne etc *Nor*

CLIPSHAM (St Mary)   *see* Greetham and Thistleton w Stretton and Clipsham *Pet*

CLIPSTON (All Saints) w Naseby and Haselbech w Kelmarsh
Pet 2   **P** *Ch Coll Cam, DBP, Mrs M F Harris, Exors Miss C V Lancaster (by turn)*   **R** D W FAULKS

CLIPSTONE (All Saints) *S'well 2*   **P** *Bp*   **P-in-c** M J GARRATT

CLITHEROE (St James) *Blackb 7*   **P** *Trustees*
R M W L PICKETT

CLITHEROE (St Mary Magdalene) *Blackb 7*   **P** *J R Peel Esq*
P-in-c A W FROUD,   **NSM** P W SHEPHERD
CLITHEROE (St Paul) Low Moor *Blackb 7*   **P** *Bp*
V R NICHOLSON
CLIVE (All Saints)   *see Astley, Clive, Grinshill and Hadnall Lich*
**CLODOCK (St Clydog) and Longtown w Craswall, Llanveynoe,
St Margaret's, Michaelchurch Escley and Newton** *Heref 1*
P *DBP (2 turns), MMCET (1 turn)*   **V** F E RODGERS
CLOFORD (St Mary)   *see Nunney and Witham Friary,
Marston Bigot etc B & W*
CLOPHILL (St Mary the Virgin)   *see Campton, Clophill and
Haynes St Alb*
CLOPTON (St Mary) w Otley, Swilland and Ashbocking *St E 7*
P *Ld Chan and Bp (alt)*   **P-in-c** G HEDGER,   **NSM** J D HALL,
OLM C G LA T BEAUMONT
CLOSWORTH (All Saints)   *see E Coker w Sutton Bingham and
Closworth B & W*
CLOTHALL (St Mary Virgin)   *see Sandon, Wallington and
Rushden w Clothall St Alb*
**CLOUGHTON (St Mary) and Burniston w Ravenscar and
Staintondale** *York 15*   **P** *Abp*   **P-in-c** E KITCHING
CLOVELLY (All Saints)   *see Parkham, Alwington, Buckland
Brewer etc Ex*
CLOVELLY (St Peter)   *as above*
CLOWNE (St John the Baptist) *Derby 3*   **P** *Ld Chan*
P-in-c J PINDER-PACKARD
CLOWS TOP (Mission Room)   *see Mamble w Bayton, Rock w
Heightington etc Worc*
CLUBMOOR (St Andrew) *Liv 8*   **P** *Bp*   **V** S MCGANITY,
C A C DOWSETT,   **OLM** S J JAMIESON
CLUMBER PARK (St Mary the Virgin)   *see Worksop Priory
S'well*
CLUN (St George) w Bettws-y-Crwyn and Newcastle *Heref 10*
P *Earl of Powis*   **V** R T SHAW,   **NSM** A OGRAM
CLUNBURY (St Swithin)   *see Clungunford w Clunbury and
Clunton, Bedstone etc Heref*
**CLUNGUNFORD (St Cuthbert) w Clunbury and Clunton,
Bedstone and Hopton Castle** *Heref 10*   **P** *Earl of Powis,
Mrs S B Rocke, M S C Brown Esq, and Sir Hugh Ripley Bt (jt)*
R S B BELL
CLUNTON (St Mary)   *see Clungunford w Clunbury and
Clunton, Bedstone etc Heref*
CLUTTON (St Augustine of Hippo) w Cameley *B & W 10*
P *Earl of Warw (2 turns), Exors J P Hippisley Esq (1 turn)*
P-in-c A D THORNE
CLYFFE PYPARD (St Peter)   *see Broad Town, Clyffe Pypard,
Hilmarton etc Sarum*
CLYMPING (St Mary the Virgin) and Yapton w Ford *Chich 1*
P *Bp (2 turns), Ld Chan (1 turn)*   **R** R H HAYES,
NSM P WALLIS
CLYST HEATH   *see Ex Trin CD Ex*
CLYST HONITON (St Michael and All Angels)   *see Aylesbeare,
Rockbeare, Farringdon etc Ex*
CLYST HYDON (St Andrew)   *see Bradninch and Clyst Hydon
Ex*
CLYST ST GEORGE (St George)   *see Clyst St Mary, Clyst
St George etc Ex*
CLYST ST LAWRENCE (St Lawrence)   *see Whimple, Talaton
and Clyst St Lawr Ex*
**CLYST ST MARY (St Mary), Clyst St George and Woodbury
Salterton** *Ex 1*   **P** *Lord Wraxall, D&C, and S Radcliffe (jt)*
R *vacant* (01392) 874363
**COALBROOKDALE (Holy Trinity), Iron-Bridge and Little
Wenlock** *Heref 14*   **P** *Bp, Lord Forester, V Madeley, and
V Much Wenlock (jt)*   **P-in-c** M A KINNA,
NSM J M EDWARDS, P M JORDAN
COALEY (St Bartholomew)   *see Lower Cam w Coaley Glouc*
COALPIT HEATH (St Saviour) *Bris 5*   **P** *Bp*   **V** C P LUNT
COALVILLE (Christ Church) and Bardon Hill *Leic 8*
P *Simeon's Trustees and R Hugglescote (jt)*   **P-in-c** M J T JOSS,
C V T GOODMAN
COASTAL Group, The   *see Bacton, Happisburgh, Hempstead w
Eccles etc Nor*
COATES (Holy Trinity)   *see Whittlesey, Pondersbridge and
Coates Ely*
COATES (St Edith)   *see Stow Gp Linc*
COATES (St Matthew)   *see Kemble, Poole Keynes, Somerford
Keynes etc Glouc*
**COATES, GREAT (St Nicholas) and LITTLE (Bishop Edward
King Church) (St Michael) w Bradley** *Linc 9*   **P** *Patr Bd*
TR P M MULLINS,   **C** S A ALLISON,   **Hon C** A I MCCORMICK
COATES, NORTH (St Nicholas)   *see Holton-le-Clay, Tetney
and N Cotes Linc*
COATHAM (Christ Church) and Dormanstown *York 16*
P *Trustees*   **V** *vacant* (01642) 482870

COBBOLD ROAD (St Saviour) (St Mary) *Lon 9*   **P** *Bp*
V D J WHEELER,   **NSM** P P Y MULLINGS
COBERLEY (St Giles), Cowley, Colesbourne and Elkstone
Glouc 9   **P** H W G *Elwes Esq (2 turns), Ld Chan (1 turn), and
W/Cdr H T Price (1 turn)*   **P-in-c** J W HOLDER
COBHAM Sole Street (St Mary's Church Room)   *see Cobham w
Luddesdowne and Dode Roch*
**COBHAM (St Andrew) (St John the Divine) and Stoke
D'Abernon** *Guildf 10*   **P** *D C H Combe Esq and K Coll
Cam (jt)*   **R** E R JENKINS,   **C** D R THORNTON,
OLM P G VICKERS, R PITTARIDES
COBHAM (St Mary Magdalene) w Luddesdowne and Dode
Roch 1   **P** *Earl of Darnley and CPAS (alt)*   **NSM** A E BEETY
COBO (St Matthew)   *see Guernsey St Matt Win*
COBRIDGE (Christ Church)   *see Hanley H Ev Lich*
COCKAYNE HATLEY (St John the Baptist)   *see Potton w
Sutton and Cockayne Hatley St Alb*
**COCKERHAM (St Michael) w Winmarleigh St Luke and
Glasson Christ Church** *Blackb 11*   **P** *Bp (2 turns), Trustees
(1 turn)*   **V** M B ROBERTS
COCKERINGTON, SOUTH (St Leonard)   *see Mid Marsh Gp
Linc*
**COCKERMOUTH AREA Team, The (All Saints) (Christ
Church)** *Carl 6*   **P** *Patr Bd*   **TR** W E SANDERS,
TV C GODDARD,   **C** P J PYE,   **NSM** M GODDARD, I J HALSALL
COCKERNHOE (St Hugh)   *see Luton St Fran St Alb*
COCKERTON (St Mary) *Dur 8*   **P** *Bp*   **V** R J WALLACE
COCKFIELD (St Mary) *Dur 7*   **P** *Bp*   **P-in-c** F J GRIEVE,
C E L JOHNSON
COCKFIELD (St Peter)   *see Bradfield St Clare, Bradfield St
George etc St E*
COCKFOSTERS (Christ Church) Trent Park   *see Enfield Ch Ch
Trent Park Lon*
COCKING (not known), Bepton and West Lavington *Chich 10*
P *Ld Chan, and Bp, Rathbone Trust Co and Cowdray Trust (alt)*
P-in-c C J BRADLEY
COCKINGTON (St George and St Mary) (St Matthew) *Ex 12*
P *Bp*   **V** A K F MACEY
COCKLEY CLEY (All Saints) w Gooderstone *Nor 13*   **P** *Bp*
P-in-c D J HANWELL
COCKSHUTT (St Simon and St Jude)   *see Petton w Cockshutt,
Welshampton and Lyneal etc Lich*
COCKYARD (Church Hall)   *see Chapel-en-le-Frith Derby*
**CODDENHAM (St Mary) w Gosbeck and Hemingstone w
Henley** *St E 1*   **P** *Pemb Coll Cam (2 turns), Lord de Saumarez
(1 turn)*   **P-in-c** T P HALL,   **OLM** H NORRIS, D L R MCLEOD
CODDINGTON (All Saints)   *see Colwall w Upper Colwall and
Coddington Heref*
**CODDINGTON (All Saints) and Winthorpe and Langford w
Holme** *S'well 3*   **P** *Keble Coll Ox and Bp (jt)*   **R** *vacant*
(01636) 704768
CODDINGTON (St Mary)   *see Farndon and Coddington Ches*
CODFORD (St Mary)   *see Upper Wylye Valley Sarum*
CODFORD (St Peter)   *as above*
CODICOTE (St Giles) *St Alb 21*   **P** *Abp*   **V** L J BIGGS
CODNOR (St James) *Derby 12*   **P** *The Crown*
V M M MOOKERJI,   **P-in-c** T J WILLIAMS
CODSALL (St Nicholas) *Lich 2*   **P** *Bp and Lady Wrottesley (jt)*
V S C WITCOMBE,   **NSM** M A O FOX
CODSALL WOOD (St Peter)   *see Codsall Lich*
COFFEEHALL (Community Church)   *see Woughton Ox*
COFFINSWELL (St Bartholomew)   *see Kingskerswell w
Coffinswell Ex*
COFTON (St Mary)   *see Kenton, Mamhead, Powderham,
Cofton and Starcross Ex*
COFTON HACKETT (St Michael) w Barnt Green *Birm 4*
P *Bp*   **V** R S FIELDSON
**COGENHOE (St Peter) and Great Houghton and Little
Houghton w Brafield on the Green** *Pet 6*
P *C G V Davidge Esq, Mrs A C Usher, Magd Coll Ox, and
DBP (jt)*   **R** R B STAINER
COGGES (St Mary) and South Leigh *Ox 8*   **P** *Bp and Payne
Trustees (jt)*   **V** A J SWEENEY,   **C** A J D PRITCHARD, M F KEEN,
NSM T P EDGE
COGGESHALL (St Peter ad Vincula) w Markshall *Chelmsf 17*
P *Bp (2 turns), SMF (1 turn)*   **V** P C BANKS,
C J SWEETMAN,   **NSM** W J L HOWES
COGGESHALL, LITTLE (St Nicholas)   *see Coggeshall w
Markshall Chelmsf*
**COKER, EAST (St Michael and All Angels) w Sutton Bingham
and Closworth** *B & W 7*   **P** *D&C Ex*   **P-in-c** R M BURT
**COKER, WEST (St Martin of Tours) w Hardington Mandeville,
East Chinnock and Pendomer** *B & W 7*   **P** *MMCET and
Ox Chs Trust, and DBP (alt)*   **R** *vacant* (01935) 862328
COLATON RALEIGH (St John the Baptist)   *see Ottery St
Mary, Alfington, W Hill, Tipton etc Ex*

COLBURN (St Cuthbert)   *see* Hipswell *Ripon*
COLBURY (Christ Church) *Win 11*   **P** *Mrs A V Barker-Mill*
V *vacant* (023) 8029 2132
COLBY (Belle Abbey Church)   *see* Arbory *S & M*
COLBY (St Giles)   *see* King's Beck *Nor*
COLCHESTER (Christ Church w St Mary at the Walls)
Chelmsf 16   **P** *Bp*   **R** P R NORRINGTON,   **NSM** R V SAMS
COLCHESTER (St Anne)   *see* Greenstead w Colchester St
Anne *Chelmsf*
COLCHESTER (St Barnabas) Old Heath *Chelmsf 16*   **P** *Bp*
V R E TILLBROOK
COLCHESTER (St James)   *see* Colchester St Jas and St Paul w
All SS etc *Chelmsf*
**COLCHESTER (St James) and St Paul w All Saints, St Nicholas
and St Runwald** *Chelmsf 16*   **P** *Bp*   **R** P S WALKER
COLCHESTER (St John the Evangelist) *Chelmsf 16*
P *Adn Colchester*   **V** R P FULLER,   **C** D TALKS, J A NOLES,
Hon C P H ADAMS
COLCHESTER (St Michael) Myland *Chelmsf 16*
P *Ball Coll Ox*   **P-in-c** R G GIBBS,   **NSM** J CHANDLER
COLCHESTER (St Peter) (St Botolph) *Chelmsf 16*   **P** *Bp and
Simeon's Trustees (jt)*   **V** F J WOODS,   **C** A FINCH
COLCHESTER (St Stephen)   *see* Colchester, New Town and
The Hythe *Chelmsf*
**COLCHESTER, New Town and The Hythe (St Stephen,
St Mary Magdalen and St Leonard)** *Chelmsf 16*
P *Ball Coll Ox (2 turns), Ld Chan (1 turn)*   **R** I A HILTON
COLD ASH (St Mark)   *see* Hermitage *Ox*
COLD ASHBY (St Denys)   *see* Guilsborough w Hollowell and
Cold Ashby *Pet*
COLD ASHTON (Holy Trinity)   *see* Marshfield w Cold Ashton
and Tormarton etc *Bris*
COLD ASTON (St Andrew)   *see* Northleach w Hampnett and
Farmington etc *Glouc*
COLD BRAYFIELD (St Mary)   *see* Lavendon w Cold
Brayfield, Clifton Reynes etc *Ox*
COLD HIGHAM (St Luke)   *see* Pattishall w Cold Higham and
Gayton w Tiffield *Pet*
COLD KIRBY (St Michael)   *see* Upper Ryedale *York*
COLD NORTON (St Stephen)   *see* Purleigh, Cold Norton and
Stow Maries *Chelmsf*
COLD OVERTON (St John the Baptist)   *see* Whatborough Gp
Leic
COLD SALPERTON (All Saints)   *see* Sevenhampton w
Charlton Abbots, Hawling etc *Glouc*
COLDEAN (St Mary Magdalene)   *see* Moulsecoomb *Chich*
COLDEN COMMON (Holy Trinity)   *see* Twyford and
Owslebury and Morestead etc *Win*
COLDHAM (St Etheldreda)   *see* Fen Orchards *Ely*
COLDHARBOUR (Christ Church)   *see* Abinger cum
Coldharbour *Guildf*
COLDHARBOUR (St Alban Mission Church)
see Mottingham St Andr *S'wark*
COLDHURST (Holy Trinity)   *see* Oldham *Man*
COLDRED (St Pancras)   *see* Eythorne and Elvington w
Waldershare etc *Cant*
COLDRIDGE (St Matthew)   *see* N Creedy *Ex*
COLDWALTHAM (St Giles)   *see* Bury w Houghton and
Coldwaltham and Hardham *Chich*
COLEBROOKE (St Andrew) *Ex 2*   **P** *D&C*   **V** *vacant*
COLEBY (All Saints)   *see* Graffoe Gp *Linc*
COLEFORD (Holy Trinity) w Holcombe *B & W 12*   **P** *Bp and
V Kilmersdon (jt)*   **P-in-c** V BONHAM,
NSM C R D CRIDLAND
**COLEFORD (St John the Evangelist), Staunton, Newland,
Redbrook and Clearwell** *Glouc 2*   **P** *Bp*   **V** D I LAWRENCE,
C S BICK,   **NSM** A W WEARMOUTH, M M HALE
COLEGATE (St George)   *see* Nor St Geo Colegate *Nor*
COLEHILL (St Michael and All Angels) *Sarum 9*   **P** *Wimborne
Minster Sch*   **V** J W GOODALL,   **OLM** L L MCGREGOR
COLEMAN'S HATCH (Holy Trinity)   *see* Hartfield w
Coleman's Hatch *Chich*
COLEORTON (St Mary the Virgin)   *see* Ashby-de-la-Zouch w
Breedon on the Hill *Leic*
COLERNE (St John the Baptist) w North Wraxall *Bris 4*
P *New Coll and Oriel Coll Ox (alt)*   **TV** V I D F PLUMB,
P-in-c A C ASHCROFT,   **NSM** G E WOODS
COLESBOURNE (St James)   *see* Coberley, Cowley,
Colesbourne and Elkstone *Glouc*
COLESHILL (All Saints)   *see* Amersham *Ox*
COLESHILL (All Saints)   *see* Gt Coxwell w Buscot, Coleshill etc
Ox
COLESHILL (St Peter and St Paul) *Birm 9*   **P** *J K Wingfield
Digby Esq*   **V** R N PARKER,   **C** K M LARKIN
COLEY Norwood Green (St George)   *see* Coley *Wakef*

COLEY (St John the Baptist) *Wakef 2*   **P** *V Halifax*
V M K MADELEY
COLGATE (St Saviour)   *see* Rusper w Colgate *Chich*
COLINDALE (St Matthias) *Lon 15*   **P** *Bp*
P-in-c J E I HAWKINS
COLKIRK (St Mary)   *see* Upper Wensum Village Gp *Nor*
COLLATON (St Mary the Virgin)   *see* Stoke Gabriel and
Collaton *Ex*
COLLIER ROW (Ascension)   *see* Romford Ascension Collier
Row *Chelmsf*
COLLIER ROW (Good Shepherd)   *see* Romford Gd Shep
Chelmsf
COLLIER ROW (St James) and Havering-atte-Bower *Chelmsf 2*
P *CPAS and Bp (jt)*   **P-in-c** D C MARSHALL,
Hon C A MARSHALL,   **NSM** A T POULTNEY
COLLIER STREET (St Margaret)   *see* Yalding w Collier Street
Roch
COLLIERLEY (St Thomas) w Annfield Plain *Dur 4*   **P** *Bp and
The Crown (alt)*   **V** *vacant* (01207) 236254
COLLIERS END (St Mary)   *see* High Cross *St Alb*
COLLIERS WOOD (Christ Church)   *see* Merton Priory *S'wark*
COLLINGBOURNE DUCIS (St Andrew)   *see* Savernake
Sarum
COLLINGBOURNE KINGSTON (St Mary)   *as above*
**COLLINGHAM (All Saints) (St John the Baptist) w South
Scarle and Besthorpe and Girton** *S'well 3*   **P** *Ld Chan and D&C
Pet (alt)*   **P-in-c** W D MILNER
COLLINGHAM (St Oswald) w Harewood *Ripon 1*   **P** *Earl of
Harewood and G H H Wheler Esq (jt)*   **P-in-c** M PALLIS
COLLINGTON (St Mary)   *see* Bredenbury *Heref*
**COLLINGTREE (St Columba) w Courteenhall and Milton
Malsor** *Pet 5*   **P** *H C Wake Esq, G Phipps-Walker Esq, and
Hyndman Trustees (by turn)*   **C** C H FF NOBBS, J SAFFORD
COLLYHURST (The Saviour) *Man 5*   **P** *Bp and Trustees (jt)*
P-in-c C FALLONE,   **OLM** M B ROGERS
COLLYWESTON (St Andrew)   *see* Ketton, Collyweston,
Easton-on-the-Hill etc *Pet*
COLMWORTH (St Denys)   *see* Wilden w Colmworth and
Ravensden *St Alb*
COLN ROGERS (St Andrew)   *see* Chedworth, Yanworth and
Stowell, Coln Rogers etc *Glouc*
COLN ST ALDWYN (St John the Baptist)   *see* Fairford
Deanery *Glouc*
COLN ST DENYS (St James the Great)   *see* Chedworth,
Yanworth and Stowell, Coln Rogers etc *Glouc*
COLNBROOK (St Thomas) and Datchet *Ox 23*   **P** *Bp and D&C
Windsor (jt)*   **V** P J WYARD
**COLNE (Christ Church) (Holy Trinity) (St Bartholomew) and
Villages** *Blackb 6*   **P** *Patr Bd*   **TR** A W RINDL,   **C** C STERRY,
NSM P BROOK, N J C KROUKAMP
COLNE (St Helen)   *see* Bluntisham cum Earith w Colne and
Woodhurst *Ely*
**COLNE, THE UPPER, Parishes of Great Yeldham, Little
Yeldham, Stambourne, Tilbury-juxta-Clare and Toppesfield**
Chelmsf 19   **P** *Prime Min, Ld Chan, Bp, Duchy of Lancaster,
and Trustees of the late Miss W M N Brett (by turn)*
R K G HOLLOWAY
COLNE ENGAINE (St Andrew)   *see* Halstead Area *Chelmsf*
COLNEY (St Andrew)   *see* Cringleford and Colney *Nor*
COLNEY (St Peter)   *see* London Colney St Pet *St Alb*
COLNEY HEATH (St Mark) *St Alb 21*   **P** *Trustees*
V H J SPANNER,   **NSM** J SUTTIE
COLSTERWORTH Group, The (St John the Baptist) *Linc 14*
P *Bp (2 turns), Mrs R S McCorquodale, The
Revd J R H Thorold and J R Thorold Esq (1 turn)*   **R** *vacant*
(01476) 861138
COLSTON BASSETT (St John the Divine)   *see* Cropwell Bishop
w Colston Bassett, Granby etc *S'well*
**COLTISHALL (St John the Baptist) w Great Hautbois,
Frettenham, Hainford, Horstead and Stratton Strawless** *Nor 19*
P *D&C, Bp, K Coll Cam, and Ch Soc Trust (jt)*
R C J ENGELSEN,   **OLM** K A DIGNUM
COLTON (Holy Trinity)   *see* Egton-cum-Newland and Lowick
and Colton *Carl*
COLTON (St Andrew)   *see* Easton, Colton, Marlingford and
Bawburgh *Nor*
COLTON (St Mary the Virgin)   *see* Colton, Colwich and Gt
Haywood *Lich*
**COLTON (St Michael and All Angels), Colwich and Great
Haywood** *Lich 3*   **P** *Bp and Earl of Lichfield's Trustees (jt)*
P-in-c S C DAVIS,   **C** J LEONARDI, G STATON,
NSM M A DAVYS
COLTON (St Paul)   *see* Bolton Percy *York*
**COLWALL (St Crispin's Chapel) (St James the Great) w Upper
Colwall (Good Shepherd) and Coddington** *Heref 6*   **P** *Bp*
R M J HORTON,   **NSM** A C LANYON-HOGG

COLWALL, UPPER (Good Shepherd) *see* Colwall w Upper Colwall and Coddington *Heref*

COLWICK (St John the Baptist) *S'well* 10   **P** *DBP* **P-in-c** R B CHAPMAN

COLYFORD (St Michael) *see* Colyton, Musbury, Southleigh and Branscombe *Ex*

COLYTON (St Andrew), Musbury, Southleigh and Branscombe *Ex* 5   **P** *D&C*   **R** N J EDWARDS

COMBE (St Swithin) *see* W Woodhay w Enborne, Hampstead Marshall etc *Ox*

COMBE DOWN (Holy Trinity) (St Andrew) w Monkton Combe and South Stoke *B & W* 9   **P** *R Bath, Ox Chs Trust, and Comdr H R Salmer (jt)*   **V** P J LANGHAM, **C** V W INGLIS-JONES

COMBE FLOREY (St Peter and St Paul) *see* Lydeard St Lawrence w Brompton Ralph etc *B & W*

COMBE HAY (not known) *see* Bath Odd Down w Combe Hay *B & W*

COMBE LONGA (St Laurence) *see* Stonesfield w Combe Longa *Ox*

COMBE MARTIN (St Peter ad Vincula), Berrynarbor, Lynton, Brendon, Countisbury, Parracombe, Martinhoe and Trentishoe *Ex* 18   **P** *Patr Bd*   **TR** K G WYER,   **TV** P A JARVIS, **NSM** S L GRAHAM

COMBE PYNE (St Mary the Virgin) *see* Axminster, Chardstock, All Saints etc *Ex*

COMBE RALEIGH (St Nicholas) *see* Honiton, Gittisham, Combe Raleigh, Monkton etc *Ex*

COMBE ST NICHOLAS (St Nicholas) w Wambrook *B & W* 15   **P** *Bp and T V D Eames Esq (jt)*   **P-in-c** A J WOODWARD, **C** J T TYLER

COMBEINTEIGNHEAD (All Saints) *see* Shaldon, Stokeinteignhead, Combeinteignhead etc *Ex*

COMBERFORD (St Mary and St George) *see* Wigginton *Lich*

COMBERTON (St Mary) *Ely* 1   **P** *Jes Coll Cam* **P-in-c** M P M BOOKER,   **C** M D WATTS

COMBERTON, GREAT (St Michael) *see* Elmley Castle w Bricklehampton and Combertons *Worc*

COMBERTON, LITTLE (St Peter) *as above*

COMBROKE (St Mary and St Margaret) w Compton Verney *Cov* 8   **P** *Bp*   **C** R J COOKE

COMBS (St Mary) and Little Finborough *St E* 6   **P** *Bp and Pemb Coll Ox (jt)*   **P-in-c** J C ROSS,   **OLM** A M LAY

COMBWICH (St Peter) *see* Cannington, Otterhampton, Combwich and Stockland *B & W*

COMER GARDENS (St David) *see* Worc St Clem and Lower Broadheath *Worc*

COMMONDALE (St Peter) *see* Danby w Castleton and Commondale *York*

COMPSTALL (St Paul) *see* Werneth *Ches*

COMPTON (All Saints), Hursley, and Otterbourne *Win* 7   **P** *Bp, Mrs P M A T Chamberlayne-Macdonald, and Lord Lifford (jt)*   **R** W A PRESCOTT

COMPTON (St Mary) *see* Farnham *Guildf*

COMPTON (St Mary and St Nicholas) *see* Hermitage *Ox*

COMPTON (St Mary), the Mardens, Stoughton and Racton *Chich* 13   **P** *Bp Lon (1 turn), Bp (2 turns)*   **V** *vacant* (023) 9263 1252

COMPTON (St Nicholas) w Shackleford and Peper Harow *Guildf* 4   **P** *Bp and Major J R More-Molyneux (jt)* **R** J M FELLOWS,   **NSM** J J SWANTON, J LEE

COMPTON, LITTLE (St Denys) *see* Chipping Norton *Ox*

COMPTON, NETHER (St Nicholas) *see* Queen Thorne *Sarum*

COMPTON, OVER (St Michael) *as above*

COMPTON ABBAS (St Mary the Virgin) *see* Shaston *Sarum*

COMPTON ABDALE (St Oswald) *see* Northleach w Hampnett and Farmington etc *Glouc*

COMPTON BASSETT (St Swithin) *see* Oldbury *Sarum*

COMPTON BEAUCHAMP (St Swithun) *see* Shrivenham and Ashbury *Ox*

COMPTON BISHOP (St Andrew) *see* Crook Peak *B & W*

COMPTON CHAMBERLAYNE (St Michael) *see* Fovant, Sutton Mandeville and Teffont Evias etc *Sarum*

COMPTON DANDO (Blessed Virgin Mary) *see* Publow w Pensford, Compton Dando and Chelwood *B & W*

COMPTON DUNDON (St Andrew) *see* Somerton w Compton Dundon, the Charltons etc *B & W*

COMPTON GREENFIELD (All Saints) *see* Pilning w Compton Greenfield *Bris*

COMPTON MARTIN (St Michael) *see* Blagdon w Compton Martin and Ubley *B & W*

COMPTON PAUNCEFOOT (Blessed Virgin Mary) *see* Camelot Par *B & W*

COMPTON VALENCE (St Thomas à Beckett) *see* The Winterbournes and Compton Valence *Sarum*

CONDICOTE (St Nicholas) *see* Stow on the Wold, Condicote and The Swells *Glouc*

CONDOVER (St Andrew and St Mary) w Frodesley, Acton Burnell and Pitchford *Heref* 11   **P** *Bp, Revd E W Serjeantson, and Mrs C R Colthurst (jt)*   **R** J C W ROSE, **NSM** M G GILLIONS

CONEY HILL (St Oswald) *Glouc* 3   **P** *The Crown* **V** L HOLLAND

CONEY WESTON (St Mary) *see* Stanton, Hopton, Market Weston, Barningham etc *St E*

CONEYSTHORPE (Chapel) *see* The Street Par *York*

CONGERSTONE (St Mary the Virgin) *see* Bosworth and Sheepy Gp *Leic*

CONGHAM (St Andrew) *see* Grimston, Congham and Roydon *Nor*

CONGLETON (St James) *Ches* 11   **P** *Bp*   **V** *vacant* (01260) 273722

CONGLETON (St John the Evangelist) (St Peter) (St Stephen) *Ches* 11   **P** *Patr Bd*   **TR** D TAYLOR,   **TV** M L EAMAN, P M WITHINGTON,   **C** A SHARPLES

CONGRESBURY (St Andrew) w Puxton and Hewish St Ann *B & W* 11   **P** *MMCET*   **V** M J THOMSON

CONINGSBY (St Michael) *see* Bain Valley Gp *Linc*

CONINGTON (St Mary) *see* Fen Drayton w Conington and Lolworth etc *Ely*

CONISBROUGH (St Peter) *Sheff* 9   **P** *Bp*   **V** A C GRIFFITHS

CONISCLIFFE (St Edwin) *Dur* 8   **P** *Bp*   **P-in-c** J R DOBSON

CONISHOLME (St Peter) *see* Somercotes and Grainthorpe w Conisholme *Linc*

CONISTON (St Andrew) *see* Church Coniston *Carl*

CONISTON COLD (St Peter) *see* Gargrave w Coniston Cold *Bradf*

CONISTONE (St Mary) *see* Kettlewell w Conistone, Hubberholme etc *Bradf*

CONONLEY (St John the Evangelist) w Bradley *Bradf* 8   **P** *Bp* **V** J C PEET

CONSETT (Christ Church) *Dur* 4   **P** *Bp*   **P-in-c** P SINCLAIR

CONSTABLE LEE (St Paul) *Man* 15   **P** *CPAS* **P-in-c** M R SHORT

CONSTANTINE (St Constantine) *Truro* 4   **P** *D&C* **P-in-c** D J STEVENS

COOKBURY (St John the Baptist and the Seven Maccabes) *see* Black Torrington, Bradford w Cookbury etc *Ex*

COOKHAMS, The (Holy Trinity) (St John the Baptist) *Ox* 13   **P** *Mrs E U Rogers*   **V** M D SMITH,   **Hon C** A W WELLING, **NSM** N PLANT

COOKHILL (St Paul) *see* Inkberrow w Cookhill and Kington w Dormston *Worc*

COOKLEY (St Michael and All Angels) *see* Heveningham *St E*

COOKLEY (St Peter) *see* Wolverley and Cookley *Worc*

COOKRIDGE (Holy Trinity) *Ripon* 7   **P** *R Adel* **V** J F HAMILTON

COOMBE (Christ Church) *see* New Malden and Coombe *S'wark*

COOMBE BISSET (St Michael and All Angels) *see* Chalke Valley *Sarum*

COOMBES (not known) *see* Lancing w Coombes *Chich*

COOMBS WOOD (St Ambrose) *see* Blackheath *Birm*

COOPERSALE (St Alban) *see* Epping Distr *Chelmsf*

COPDOCK (St Peter) *see* Sproughton w Burstall, Copdock w Washbrook etc *St E*

COPFORD (St Michael and All Angels) w Easthorpe and Messing w Inworth *Chelmsf* 23   **P** *Ld Chan, Duchy of Lanc, and DBP (by turn)*   **R** C J GARLAND

COPGROVE (St Michael) *see* Walkingham Hill *Ripon*

COPLE (All Saints), Moggerhanger and Willington *St Alb* 11   **P** *Bp (2 turns), Ch Ch Ox (1 turn)*   **V** L KLIMAS, **NSM** J R BUCK

COPLESTON CENTRE *see* Peckham St Sav *S'wark*

COPLEY *Wakef* 4   **P** *V Halifax*   **V** *vacant* (01422) 652964

COPMANTHORPE (St Giles) *York* 1   **P** *R York St Clement w St Mary Bishophill*   **P-in-c** G R MUMFORD

COPNOR (St Alban) *see* Portsea St Alb *Portsm*

COPNOR (St Cuthbert) *see* Portsea St Cuth *Portsm*

COPP (St Anne) w Inskip *Blackb* 9   **P** *V Garstang St Helen and St Michaels-on-Wyre*   **V** D GASKELL

COPPENHALL (All Saints and St Paul) *see* Crewe All SS and St Paul w St Pet *Ches*

COPPENHALL (St Laurence) *see* Penkridge *Lich*

COPPENHALL (St Michael) *Ches* 15   **P** *Bp*   **R** C H RAZZALL, **C** D J JOHNSON

COPPULL (not known) *Blackb* 4   **P** *R Standish*   **V** J HUDSON

COPPULL (St John) *Blackb* 4   **P** *R Standish* **P-in-c** A FISHWICK

COPSTON MAGNA (St John) *see* Wolvey w Burton Hastings, Copston Magna etc *Cov*

COPT HEWICK (Holy Innocents)   *see* Ripon Cathl *Ripon*

COPT OAK (St Peter)   *see* Markfield, Thornton, Bagworth and Stanton etc *Leic*

COPTHORNE (St John the Evangelist) *Chich 7*   **P** *Bp*
V A M CUTTING,   **NSM** P SMITH

COPYTHORNE (St Mary) *Win 11*   **P** *Bp Liv*
P-in-c N P JACOB

COQUETDALE, UPPER *Newc 6*   **P** *Duchy of Lanc (2 turns), Ld Chan (1 turn), and Duke of Northumberland (1 turn)*
NSM P M LEAR, S D JOYNER

CORBRIDGE (St Andrew) w Halton and Newton Hall *Newc 9*
P *D&C Carl*   **V** D B HEWLETT,   **NSM** J KINNAIRD

CORBY (Epiphany) (St John the Baptist) *Pet 7*
P *E Brudenell Esq*   **P-in-c** P S INMAN

CORBY (St Columba and the Northern Saints) *Pet 7*   **P** *Bp*
P-in-c R J LEE

CORBY (St Peter and St Andrew) (Kingswood Church) *Pet 7*
P *Bp*   **V** *vacant (01536) 267620 or 402442*

CORBY GLEN (St John the Evangelist) *Linc 14*   **P** *Ld Chan (2 turns), Sir Simon Benton Jones Bt (1 turn)*
P-in-c M A E BARTON

CORELEY (St Peter) and Doddington *Heref 12*   **P** *DBP and Mrs R C Woodward (jt)*   **R** *vacant (01584) 890129*

CORFE (St Nicholas)   *see* Blackdown *B & W*

CORFE CASTLE (St Edward the Martyr), Church Knowle, Kimmeridge Steeple w Tyneham *Sarum 8*   **P** *Major M J A Bond and Major J C Mansel (jt)*   **P-in-c** I JACKSON,
C A HAGENBUCH

CORFE MULLEN (St Hubert) *Sarum 9*   **P** *Bp*   **R** P S WALKER

CORHAMPTON (not known)   *see* Meonstoke w Corhampton cum Exton *Portsm*

CORLEY (not known)   *see* Fillongley and Corley *Cov*

CORNARD, GREAT (St Andrew) *St E 12*   **P** *Bp*
C J G BLEAZARD

CORNARD, LITTLE (All Saints)   *see* Bures w Assington and Lt Cornard *St E*

CORNELLY (St Cornelius)   *see* Tregony w St Cuby and Cornelly *Truro*

CORNEY (St John the Baptist)   *see* Bootle, Corney, Whicham and Whitbeck *Carl*

CORNFORTH (Holy Trinity) and Ferryhill *Dur 5*   **P** *D&C (2 turns), Bp (1 turn)*   **V** K LUMSDON,   **C** D GARRATT

CORNHILL (St Helen) w Carham *Newc 12*   **P** *Abp (2 turns), E M Straker-Smith Esq (1 turn)*   **P-in-c** M J GILLHAM,
NSM L E GARDHAM

CORNHOLME (St Michael and All Angels) and Walsden
Wakef 3   **P** *Bp and DBP (jt)*   **V** C SMITH,
OLM I M GREENMAN

CORNISH HALL END (St John the Evangelist)
  see Finchingfield and Cornish Hall End etc *Chelmsf*

CORNWELL (St Peter)   *see* Chipping Norton *Ox*

CORNWOOD (St Michael and All Angels) *Ex 21*   **P** *Bp*
P-in-c F G DENMAN

CORNWORTHY (St Peter)   *see* Totnes w Bridgetown, Berry Pomeroy etc *Ex*

CORONATION SQUARE (St Aidan)   *see* Cheltenham St Mark *Glouc*

CORRA (Holy Trinity)   *see* Adderley, Ash, Calverhall, Ightfield etc *Lich*

CORRINGHAM (St John the Evangelist) (St Mary the Virgin)
Chelmsf 14   **P** *SMF*   **P-in-c** D ROLLINS,   **C** C J MANN,
R D LANE

CORRINGHAM (St Lawrence) and Blyton Group, The *Linc 2*
P *Ld Chan (2 turns), Bp (1 turn), Meynell Ch Trustees (1 turn)*
V *vacant (01427) 628216*

CORSCOMBE (St Mary the Virgin)   *see* Melbury *Sarum*

CORSE (St Margaret)   *see* Hartpury w Corse and Staunton *Glouc*

CORSENSIDE (All Saints)   *see* N Tyne and Redesdale *Newc*

CORSENSIDE (St Cuthbert)   *as above*

CORSHAM, GREATER (St Bartholomew) and Lacock *Bris 4*
P *Patr Bd*   **TR** R G CLIFTON,   **TV** S A V WHEELER

CORSLEY (St Margaret of Antioch)   *see* Cley Hill Villages *Sarum*

CORSLEY (St Mary the Virgin)   *as above*

CORSTON (All Saints)   *see* Saltford w Corston and Newton St Loe *B & W*

CORSTON (All Saints)   *see* Gt Somerford, Lt Somerford, Seagry, Corston etc *Bris*

CORTON (St Bartholomew)   *see* Hopton w Corton *Nor*

CORTON (St Bartholomew)   *see* Abbotsbury, Portesham and Langton Herring *Sarum*

CORTON DENHAM (St Andrew)   *see* Cam Vale *B & W*

CORYTON (St Andrew)   *see* Milton Abbot, Dunterton, Lamerton etc *Ex*

COSBY (St Michael and All Angels) and Whetstone *Leic 7*
P *Bp*   **V** A PHILLIPSON,   **C** P L BAILEY

COSELEY (Christ Church) (St Cuthbert) *Worc 10*   **P** *Bp*
V H M HUMPHREY,   **NSM** R L ROWSON

COSELEY (St Chad) *Worc 10*   **P** *Bp*   **V** A HOWES

COSGROVE (St Peter and St Paul)   *see* Potterspury w Furtho and Yardley Gobion etc *Pet*

COSHAM (St Philip) *Portsm 6*   **P** *Bp*   **V** *vacant (023) 9232 6179*

COSSALL (St Catherine)   *see* Trowell, Awsworth and Cossall *S'well*

COSSINGTON (All Saints)   *see* Sileby, Cossington and Seagrave *Leic*

COSSINGTON (Blessed Virgin Mary)   *see* Woolavington w Cossington and Bawdrip *B & W*

COSTESSEY (St Edmund) *Nor 3*   **P** *Gt Hosp Nor*
V N J S PARRY

COSTESSEY, NEW (St Helen)   *see* Costessey *Nor*

COSTOCK (St Giles)   *see* E and W Leake, Stanford-on-Soar, Rempstone etc *S'well*

COSTON (St Andrew)   *see* S Framland *Leic*

COTEBROOKE (St John and Holy Cross)   *see* Tarporley *Ches*

COTEHELE HOUSE (Chapel)   *see* Calstock *Truro*

COTEHILL (St John the Evangelist)   *see* Scotby and Cotehill w Cumwhinton *Carl*

COTES HEATH (St James)   *see* Broughton w Croxton and Cotes Heath w Standon *Lich*

COTESBACH (St Mary)   *see* Lutterworth w Cotesbach and Bitteswell *Leic*

COTGRAVE (All Saints) *S'well 8*   **P** *DBP*   **R** P D S MASSEY

COTHAM (St Saviour w St Mary) and Clifton St Paul *Bris 3*
P *Bp*   **R** *vacant 0117-974 3198 or 973 3395*

COTHELSTONE (St Thomas of Canterbury)   *see* Bishops Lydeard w Bagborough and Cothelstone *B & W*

COTHERIDGE (St Leonard)   *see* Worcs W *Worc*

COTHERSTONE (St Cuthbert)   *see* Romaldkirk w Laithkirk *Ripon*

COTLEIGH (St Michael and All Angels)   *see* Offwell, Northleigh, Farway, Cotleigh etc *Ex*

COTMANHAY (Christ Church) *Derby 13*   **P** *Bp*   **V** P J DAVEY

COTON (St Peter) *Ely 1*   **P** *St Cath Coll Cam*
P-in-c C A COLLINS

COTON-IN-THE-ELMS (St Mary)   *see* Seale and Lullington w Coton in the Elms *Derby*

COTTENHAM (All Saints) *Ely 6*   **P** *Bp*   **P-in-c** K A HODGINS

COTTERED (St John the Baptist) w Broadfield and Throcking
St Alb 19   **P** *Bp*   **R** *vacant (01763) 281218*

COTTERIDGE (St Agnes) *Birm 4*   **P** *R Kings Norton*
V M W BLOOD,   **NSM** R R COLLINS

COTTERSTOCK (St Andrew)   *see* Warmington, Tansor and Cotterstock etc *Pet*

COTTESBROOKE (All Saints) w Great Creaton and Thornby
Pet 2   **P** *Bp (2 turns), MacDonald-Buchanan Trustees (1 turn)*
P-in-c M D PETITT,   **NSM** M R BATTISON

COTTESMORE (St Nicholas) and Barrow w Ashwell and Burley
Pet 12   **P** *E R Hanbury Esq, Viscount Downe, and DBP (by turn)*   **C** F B SOLMAN, L T FRANCIS-DEHQANI

COTTIMORE (St John)   *see* Walton-on-Thames *Guildf*

COTTINGHAM (St Mary) *York 14*   **P** *Abp*   **R** P A SMITH,
C O J COSS

COTTINGHAM (St Mary Magdalene)   *see* Gretton w Rockingham and Cottingham w E Carlton *Pet*

COTTINGLEY (St Michael and All Angels) *Bradf 1*   **P** *Bp*
C P MAYO-SMITH

COTTINGWITH, EAST (St Mary)   *see* Derwent Ings *York*

COTTISFORD (St Mary the Virgin)   *see* Shelswell *Ox*

COTTON (St Andrew)   *see* Bacton w Wyverstone, Cotton and Old Newton etc *St E*

COTTON (St John the Baptist)   *see* Alton w Bradley-le-Moors and Oakamoor w Cotton *Lich*

COTTON MILL (St Julian)   *see* St Alb St Steph *St Alb*

COTTONSTONES (St Mary)   *see* Sowerby *Wakef*

COUGHTON (St Peter) *Cov 7*   **P** *Bp*   **P-in-c** D C CAPRON

COULSDON (St Andrew) *S'wark 22*   **P** *Bp*   **P-in-c** V L SIMS,
NSM T F MUNRO

COULSDON (St John) *S'wark 22*   **P** *Abp*   **R** P C ROBERTS,
C L FLETCHER,   **NSM** S P STOCKS

COULSTON, EAST (St Thomas of Canterbury)   *see* Bratton, Edington and Imber, Erlestoke etc *Sarum*

COUND (St Peter)   *see* Wenlock *Heref*

COUNDON (St James) and Eldon *Dur 6*   **P** *Rp and Prime Min (alt)*   **P-in-c** G NICHOLSON

COUNTESS WEAR (St Luke) *Ex 3*   **P** *V Topsham*
V P J S CROCKETT

COUNTESTHORPE (St Andrew) w Foston *Leic 7*   **P** *DBP and*

Bp (alt)   **P-in-c** D E HEBBLEWHITE,   **C** A S W BOOKER, **NSM** M D GILLESPIE

COUNTISBURY (St John the Evangelist)   *see* Combe Martin, Berrynarbor, Lynton, Brendon etc *Ex*

COURTEENHALL (St Peter and St Paul)   *see* Collingtree w Courteenhall and Milton Malsor *Pet*

COVE (St John the Baptist) (St Christopher) *Guildf 1*   **P** *Bp* **TR** J H TYNDALL,   **TV** J HILLMAN, S J STEWART, **OLM** G H THOMAS

COVEHITHE (St Andrew)   *see* Wrentham, Covehithe w Benacre etc *St E*

COVEN (St Paul)   *see* Bilbrook and Coven *Lich*

COVEN HEATH (Mission Church)   *see* Bushbury *Lich*

COVENEY (St Peter ad Vincula) *Ely 8*   **P** *Bp*   **P-in-c** P TAYLOR

COVENHAM (Annunciation of the Blessed Virgin Mary)   *see* Fotherby *Linc*

COVENT GARDEN (St Paul) *Lon 3*   **P** *Bp*   **R** S J GRIGG

COVENTRY Caludon *Cov 1*   **P** *Bp and Ld Chan (alt)* **TR** W M SMITH,   **TV** A KAMBLE-HANSELL

COVENTRY Holbrooks (St Luke)   *see* Holbrooks *Cov*

COVENTRY (Holy Trinity) *Cov 2*   **P** *Ld Chan* **V** D F MAYHEW,   **NSM** J S HILL

COVENTRY (St Francis of Assisi) North Radford *Cov 2*   **P** *Bp* **P-in-c** J D IRVINE,   **NSM** M W HAYWARD

COVENTRY (St George) *Cov 2*   **P** *Bp*   **V** A J EVANS

COVENTRY (St John the Baptist) *Cov 2*   **P** *Trustees* **R** P N SUCH

COVENTRY (St Mary Magdalen) *Cov 3*   **P** *Bp* **P-in-c** D H ROBINSON

COVENTRY (St Nicholas)   *see* Radford *Cov*

COVENTRY EAST (St Anne and All Saints) (St Margaret) (St Peter) *Cov 1*   **P** *Patr Bd*   **TR** S W M HARTLEY, **TV** L D JOHNSON, L A HUMPHREYS,   **C** P BULLOCK

COVERACK (St Peter)   *see* St Keverne *Truro*

COVERDALE (St Botolph)   *see* Middleham w Coverdale and E Witton etc *Ripon*

COVINGHAM (St Paul)   *see* Swindon Dorcan *Bris*

COVINGTON (All Saints) *Ely 10*   **P** *Sir Philip Naylor-Leyland Bt*   **R** *vacant*

COWARNE, LITTLE (not known)   *see* Bredenbury *Heref*

COWARNE, MUCH (St Mary the Virgin)   *see* Frome Valley *Heref*

COWBIT (St Mary) *Linc 17*   **P** *Ld Chan and DBP (alt)* **V** *vacant* (01406) 373630

COWDEN (St Mary Magdalene) w Hammerwood *Chich 7* **P** *Ch Soc Trust*   **P-in-c** C W GIBBS

COWES (Holy Trinity) (St Mary the Virgin) *Portsm 8* **P** *Trustees and V Carisbrooke St Mary (jt)*   **V** R J EMBLIN, **C** D J HINKS,   **NSM** K H G MORRIS

COWES (St Faith) *Portsm 8*   **P** *Bp*   **V** L MCROSTIE, **NSM** K R ADLAM

COWES, EAST (St James)   *see* Whippingham w E Cowes *Portsm*

COWESBY (St Michael) *York 19*   **P** *Abp*   **R** I D HOUGHTON

COWFOLD (St Peter) *Chich 9*   **P** *Bp Lon* **P-in-c** K D LITTLEJOHN

COWGATE (St Peter) *Newc 4*   **P** *Bp*   **V** J B BABB

COWGILL (St John the Evangelist)   *see* Dent w Cowgill *Bradf*

COWICK (Holy Trinity)   *see* Gt Snaith *Sheff*

COWLAM (St Mary)   *see* Waggoners *York*

COWLEIGH (St Peter)   *see* Malvern Link w Cowleigh *Worc*

COWLEY (Holy Trinity)   *see* Headington Quarry *Ox*

COWLEY (St James) (St Francis) *Ox 4*   **P** *Patr Bd* **TR** H D THORNTON,   **TV** S L C REIDE

COWLEY (St John) (St Alban) (St Bartholomew) (St Mary and St John) *Ox 4*   **P** *St Steph Ho Ox*   **V** A J A ROMANIS, **NSM** S M ALKIRE

COWLEY (St Laurence) *Lon 24*   **P** *Bp*   **R** S M HARDWICKE

COWLEY (St Mary)   *see* Coberley, Cowley, Colesbourne and Elkstone *Glouc*

COWLEY CHAPEL (St Antony)   *see* Thorverton, Cadbury, Upton Pyne etc *Ex*

COWLING (Holy Trinity)   *see* Sutton w Cowling and Lothersdale *Bradf*

COWLINGE (St Margaret)   *see* Bansfield *St E*

COWPEN (St Benedict)   *see* Horton *Newc*

COWPLAIN (St Wilfrid) *Portsm 5*   **P** *Bp*   **V** P H MOORE, **C** R E N WILLIAMS,   **NSM** R LOVEMAN

COWTON, EAST (All Saints)   *see* E Richmond *Ripon*

COWTON, SOUTH (St Luke's Pastoral Centre)   *as above*

COX GREEN (Good Shepherd) *Ox 13*   **P** *Bp* **P-in-c** J R HICKS,   **NSM** M K BIRD

COXFORD Group, The   *see* E w W Rudham, Helhoughton etc *Nor*

COXHEATH (Holy Trinity), East Farleigh, Hunton, Linton and West Farleigh *Roch 7*   **P** *Ld Chan (1 turn), Abp, Lord*

Cornwallis, and D&C (1 turn)*   **R** P S C WALKER, **NSM** D W JONES

COXHOE (St Mary)   *see* Kelloe and Coxhoe *Dur*

COXLEY (Christ Church) w Godney, Henton and Wookey *B & W 8*   **P** *Bp*   **P-in-c** A SYER

COXWELL, GREAT (St Giles) w Buscot, Coleshill and Eaton Hastings *Ox 17*   **P** *Bp and Lord Faringdon (jt)* **P-in-c** J H NODDINGS

COXWELL, LITTLE (St Mary)   *see* Gt Faringdon w Lt Coxwell *Ox*

COXWOLD (St Michael) and Husthwaite *York 3*   **P** *Abp* **P-in-c** I B KITCHEN,   **NSM** N L CHAPMAN

CRABBS CROSS (St Peter)   *see* Redditch Ch the K *Worc*

CRADLEY (St James) w Mathon and Storridge *Heref 6*   **P** *Bp and D&C Westmr (jt)*   **R** R WARD,   **NSM** M D VOCKINS

CRADLEY (St Katherine's Mission Church)   *see* Halas *Worc*

CRADLEY (St Peter)   *as above*

CRADLEY HEATH (St Luke)   *see* Reddal Hill St Luke *Worc*

CRAGG VALE (St John the Baptist in the Wilderness)   *see* Erringden *Wakef*

CRAKEHALL (St Gregory) *Ripon 4*   **P** *Sir Henry Beresford-Peirse Bt*   **NSM** J T OLDFIELD

CRAMBE (St Michael)   *see* Whitwell w Crambe and Foston *York*

CRAMLINGTON (St Nicholas) *Newc 1*   **P** *Bp* **TR** S W HEWITT,   **TV** H L SAVAGE,   **NSM** D E BOWLER, **OLM** S M WARD

CRAMPMOOR (St Swithun)   *see* Romsey *Win*

CRANBORNE (St Mary and St Bartholomew) w Boveridge, Edmondsham, Wimborne St Giles and Woodlands *Sarum 9* **P** *Viscount Cranborne, Earl of Shaftesbury, and Mrs J E Smith (jt)*   **R** D J PASKINS

CRANBOURNE (St Peter)   *see* Winkfield and Cranbourne *Ox*

CRANBROOK (St Dunstan) *Cant 11*   **P** *Abp*   **Hon C** J A TAPPER

CRANFIELD (St Peter and St Paul) and Hulcote w Salford *St Alb 13*   **P** M M CET   **R** H K SYMES-THOMPSON

CRANFORD (Holy Angels) (St Dunstan) *Lon 11* **P** *R J G Berkeley Esq and Sir Hugo Huntington-Whiteley Bt (jt)*   **R** M J GILL

CRANFORD (St John the Baptist) w Grafton Underwood and Twywell *Pet 9*   **P** *Boughton Estates, DBP, and Sir John Robinson Bt (by turn)*   **R** D H P FOOT

CRANHAM (All Saints) *Chelmsf 2*   **P** *St Jo Coll Ox* **P-in-c** S J BREWSTER,   **NSM** G K W ARBER

CRANHAM (St James the Great)   *see* Painswick, Sheepscombe, Cranham, The Edge etc *Glouc*

CRANHAM PARK Moor Lane (not known)   *see* Cranham Park *Chelmsf*

CRANHAM PARK (St Luke) *Chelmsf 2*   **P** *Bp*   **V** M VICKERS

CRANLEIGH (St Nicolas) *Guildf 2*   **P** *Bp*   **R** N P NICHOLSON, **NSM** D C FRETT

CRANMER Group   *see* Whatton w Aslockton, Hawksworth, Scarrington etc *S'well*

CRANMORE, WEST (St Bartholomew)   *see* Shepton Mallet w Doulting *B & W*

CRANOE (St Michael)   *see* Welham, Glooston and Cranoe and Stonton Wyville *Leic*

CRANSFORD (St Peter)   *see* Upper Alde *St E*

CRANSLEY (St Andrew)   *see* Broughton w Loddington and Cransley etc *Pet*

CRANTOCK (St Carantoc) w Cubert *Truro 7*   **P** *DBP (1 turn) and SMF (2 turns)*   **P-in-c** J C E ANDREW,   **NSM** P M NIXON

CRANWELL (St Andrew) *Linc 22*   **P** *DBP*   **V** *vacant*

CRANWICH (St Mary) *Nor 13*   **P** *CPAS*   **R** *vacant*

CRANWORTH (St Mary the Virgin)   *see* Barnham Broom and Upper Yare *Nor*

CRASSWALL (St Mary)   *see* Clodock and Longtown w Craswall, Llanveynoe etc *Heref*

CRASTER (Mission Church)   *see* Embleton w Rennington and Rock *Newc*

CRATFIELD (St Mary)   *see* Laxfield, Cratfield, Wilby and Brundish *St E*

CRATHORNE (All Saints) *York 21*   **P** *Lord Crathorne, The Hon David Dugdale, and J Southern Esq (jt)* **P-in-c** P J SANDERS

CRAWCROOK (Church of the Holy Spirit)   *see* Greenside *Dur*

CRAWFORD (District Church)   *see* Upholland *Liv*

CRAWLEY (St John the Baptist) *Chich 7*   **P** *Bp* **TR** M D LILES,   **TV** F J M POLE, S J MURRAY,   **C** J M BALDWIN

CRAWLEY (St Mary)   *see* Downs Benefice *Win*

CRAWLEY, NORTH (St Firmin)   *see* Sherington w Chicheley, N Crawley, Astwood etc *Ox*

CRAWLEY DOWN (All Saints) *Chich 7*   **P** *R Worth* **V** A J HALE

CRAWSHAWBOOTH (St John)   *see* Goodshaw and Crawshawbooth *Man*

CRAY (St Barnabas)   *see* St Paul's Cray St Barn *Roch*
CRAY (St Mary and St Paulinus)   *see* St Mary Cray and St Paul's Cray *Roch*
CRAY, NORTH (St James)   *see* Footscray w N Cray *Roch*
CRAYFORD (St Paulinus) *Roch 15*   **P** *Bp*   **R** A K LANE, **C** J P WATTS,   **NSM** S CORRY
CRAYKE (St Cuthbert) w Brandsby and Yearsley *York 3*   **P** *The Crown and Abp (alt)*   **P-in-c** I B KITCHEN
CRAZIES HILL (Mission Room)   *see* Wargrave w Knowl Hill *Ox*
CREAKE, NORTH (St Mary) and SOUTH (St Mary) w Waterden, Syderstone w Barmer and Sculthorpe *Nor 15*   **P** *Bp, Earl Spencer, Earl of Leicester, Guild of All So, J Labouchere Esq, Major D J C Davenport and Bp (3 turns), Mrs M E Russell, and DBP (jt)*   **R** A M THOMSON
CREATON, GREAT (St Michael and All Angels)   *see* Cottesbrooke w Gt Creaton and Thornby *Pet*
CREDENHILL (St Mary) Brinsope and Wormsley, Mansel Lacy and Yazor, Kenchester, Bridge Sollers and Bishopstone *Heref 4*   **P** R M Ecroyd Esq, Major D J C Davenport and Bp (3 turns), Ld Chan (1 turn)   **P-in-c** A C E KNIGHT,   **NSM** A C DEANE
CREDITON (Holy Cross) (St Lawrence) Shobrooke and Sandford w Upton Hellions *Ex 2*   **P** *12 Govs of Crediton Ch*   **R** N GUTHRIE,   **C** C R CARLYON, C S RALPH
CREECH ST MICHAEL (St Michael) *B & W 18*   **P** *MMCET*   **P-in-c** I ALDERSLEY
CREED (St Crida)   *see* Probus, Ladock and Grampound w Creed and St Erme *Truro*
CREEDY, NORTH: Cheriton Fitzpaine, Woolfardisworthy, Kennerley, Washford Pyne, Puddington, Poughill, Stockleigh English, Morchard Bishop, Stockleigh Pomeroy, Down St Mary, Clannaborough, Lapford, Nymet Rowland, and Coldridge *Ex 2*   **P** *Ld Chan (1 turn), Patr Bd (5 turns)*   **TR** S G C SMITH,   **TV** L C STARRS, M A HALL,   **C** J C COPUS
CREEKMOOR (Christ Church)   *see* N Poole Ecum Team *Sarum*
CREEKSEA (All Saints) w Althorne and Latchingdon w North Fambridge *Chelmsf 11*   **P** *Bp, Abp and Ld Chan (by turn)*   **R** S E MANLEY,   **NSM** V M WADMAN
CREETING (St Peter)   *see* Creeting St Mary, Creeting St Peter etc *St E*
CREETING ST MARY (St Mary), Creeting St Peter and Earl Stonham w Stonham Parva *St E 1*   **P** *DBP (2 turns), Pemb Coll Cam (1 turn)*   **P-in-c** C M EVERETT,   **NSM** M G WAINWRIGHT,   **OLM** B J GALLAGHER
CREETON (St Peter)   *see* Castle Bytham w Creeton *Linc*
CREGNEISH (St Peter)   *see* Rushen *S & M*
CRESSAGE (Christ Church)   *see* Wenlock *Heref*
CRESSBROOK (St John the Evangelist)   *see* Tideswell *Derby*
CRESSING (All Saints) w Stisted and Bradwell-juxt-Coggeshall and Pattiswick *Chelmsf 15*   **P** *Bp, Exors Mrs D E G Keen, and Abp (by turn)*   **R** J R CORBYN
CRESSINGHAM, GREAT (St Michael) and LITTLE (St Andrew), w Threxton *Nor 13*   **P** *Bp and Sec of State for Defence*   **C** D J HANWELL
CRESSWELL (St Bartholomew) and Lynemouth *Newc 11*   **P** *Bp*   **V** A E SIMPSON
CRESWELL (St Mary Magdalene)   *see* Elmton *Derby*
CRETINGHAM (St Peter)   *see* Mid Loes *St E*
CREWE (All Saints and St Paul) (St Peter) *Ches 15*   **P** *Bp*   **V** S J CLAPHAM,   **C** J J WISE
CREWE (Christ Church) *Ches 15*   **P** *Bp*   **P-in-c** W J BAKER,   **NSM** H RUGMAN
CREWE (St Andrew w St John the Baptist) *Ches 15*   **P** *Bp*   **V** W J BAKER,   **C** A S JANES,   **NSM** H RUGMAN
CREWE (St Barnabas) *Ches 15*   **P** *Bp*   **V** R D POWELL
CREWE GREEN (St Michael and All Angels)   *see* Haslington w Crewe Green *Ches*
CREWKERNE (St Bartholomew)   *see* Wulfric Benefice *B & W*
CREWTON (St Peter)   *see* Boulton *Derby*
CRICH (St Mary) and South Wingfield *Derby 1*   **P** *Ch Trust Fund Trust and Duke of Devonshire (jt)*   **V** P D BROOKS,   **NSM** J W GRAY
CRICK (St Margaret) and Yelvertoft w Clay Coton and Lilbourne *Pet 2*   **P** *MMCET and St Jo Coll Ox (jt)*   **P-in-c** D M LAKE
CRICKET MALHERBIE (St Mary Magdalene)   *see* Chaffcombe, Cricket Malherbie etc *B & W*
CRICKET ST THOMAS (St Thomas)   *see* Chard Gd Shep and Cricket St Thomas *B & W*
CRICKLADE (St Sampson) w Latton *Bris 6*   **P** *D&C, Bp, and Hon P N Eliot (by turn)*   **P-in-c** J A J ASHBY,   **NSM** S E DANBY
CRICKLEWOOD (St Gabriel) and St Michael *Lon 21*   **P** *Bp*   **V** J E MORRIS,   **C** S W DOHERTY
CRICKLEWOOD (St Peter) *Lon 15*   **P** *Bp*   **V** *vacant* (020) 8450 9043

CRIFTINS (St Matthew) w Dudleston and Welsh Frankton *Lich 17*   **P** *Bp and V Ellesmere (by turn)*   **P-in-c** A C NETHERWOOD
CRIMPLESHAM (St Mary)   *see* Downham Market and Crimplesham w Stradsett *Ely*
CRINGLEFORD (St Peter) and Colney *Nor 7*   **P** *Exors E H Barclay Esq and Gt Hosp Nor (alt)*   **R** H D BUTCHER,   **NSM** G R EVEREST
CROCKENHILL (All Souls) *Roch 2*   **P** *Bp*   **P-in-c** L A GREEN
CROCKERNWELL (Holy Trinity)   *see* Tedburn St Mary, Whitestone, Oldridge etc *Ex*
CROCKHAM HILL (Holy Trinity) *Roch 11*   **P** J St A Warde Esq   **P-in-c** S A J MITCHELL,   **C** R JONES
CROFT (All Saints)   *see* The Wainfleet Gp *Linc*
CROFT (Christ Church)   *see* Newchurch w Croft *Liv*
CROFT (St Michael and All Angels)   *see* Leominster *Heref*
CROFT (St Michael and All Angels)   *see* Broughton Astley and Croft w Stoney Stanton *Leic*
CROFT (St Peter)   *see* E Richmond *Ripon*
CROFTON (All Saints) *Wakef 11*   **P** *Duchy of Lanc*   **P-in-c** L J COLLYER,   **OLM** A JORDAN
CROFTON (Holy Rood) (St Edmund) *Portsm 2*   **P** *Bp*   **V** S P GIRLING,   **NSM** C R PRESTIDGE, K A MACFARLANE
CROFTON (St Paul) *Roch 16*   **P** *V Orpington*   **V** B A ABAYOMI-COLE
CROFTON PARK (St Hilda w St Cyprian) *S'wark 5*   **P** *V Lewisham St Mary*   **V** S G BATES
CROGLIN (St John the Baptist) *Carl 2*   **P** *D&C*   **C** D A CRAVEN,   **NSM** A MAGUIRE
CROMER (St Peter and St Paul) *Nor 21*   **P** *CPAS*   **V** D E COURT,   **C** J R PORTER,   **OLM** P E NEALE
CROMFORD (St Mary)   *see* Matlock Bath and Cromford *Derby*
CROMHALL (St Andrew), Tortworth, Tytherington, Falfield and Rockhampton *Glouc 6*   **P** *Bp, R Thornbury and Oldbury etc, Adn, and J Leigh Esq (1 turn), Earl of Ducie, Oriel Coll Ox, and MMCET (1 turn)*   **R** P M LYES-WILSDON
CROMPTON, EAST (St James) *Man 19*   **P** *Bp*   **V** *vacant* (01706) 847454
CROMPTON, HIGH (St Mary) *Man 19*   **P** *Bp*   **P-in-c** A BUTLER,   **OLM** J M HURLSTON
CROMPTON FOLD (St Saviour)   *see* E Crompton *Man*
CROMWELL (St Giles)   *see* Norwell w Ossington, Cromwell and Caunton *S'well*
CRONDALL (All Saints) and Ewshot *Guildf 3*   **P** *Bp*   **V** K E HUTCHINSON,   **NSM** B D BURBIDGE, S M R CUMMING-LATTEY
CROOK (St Catherine) *Carl 10*   **P** *CPAS*   **V** *vacant*
CROOK (St Catherine) *Dur 9*   **P** *R Brancepeth*   **P-in-c** V T FENTON,   **NSM** A R M CROMARTY
CROOK PEAK *B & W 1*   **P** *Ld Chan, Bp, Bp Lon, and R M Dod Esq (by turn)*   **P-in-c** K R BROWN
CROOKES (St Thomas) *Sheff 4*   **P** *Patr Bd*   **TR** M WOODHEAD,   **C** T J FINNEMORE
CROOKES (St Timothy) *Sheff 4*   **P** *Sheff Ch Burgesses*   **V** P R TOWNSEND,   **NSM** S E WALSH
CROOKHAM (Christ Church) *Guildf 1*   **P** *V Crondall and Ewshot*   **V** M S NICHOLLS,   **NSM** D J MISTLIN
CROOKHORN (Good Shepherd) *Portsm 5*   **P** *Simeon's Trustees*   **V** J D NAUDE,   **NSM** D M YOUELL
CROPREDY (St Mary the Virgin)   *see* Shires' Edge *Ox*
CROPTHORNE (St Michael)   *see* Fladbury w Wyre Piddle and Moor etc *Worc*
CROPTON (St Gregory)   *see* Lastingham w Appleton-le-Moors, Rosedale etc *York*
CROPWELL BISHOP (St Giles) w Colston Bassett, Granby w Elton, Langar cum Barnstone and Tythby w Cropwell Butler *S'well 8*   **P** *CPAS and Bp, Ld Chan (alt)*   **P-in-c** R E B GAMBLE
CROSBY (St George) (St Michael) *Linc 4*   **P** *Sir Reginald Sheffield Bt*   **V** J W THACKER
CROSBY, GREAT (All Saints) *Liv 5*   **P** *R Sefton, Bp, V St Luke, and CPAS (jt)*   **P-in-c** M C FREEMAN
CROSBY, GREAT (St Faith) and Waterloo Park St Mary the Virgin *Liv 1*   **P** *St Chad's Coll Dur and Trustees (jt)*   **V** N G KELLEY,   **Hon C** D A SMITH,   **NSM** D A MCDOUGALL
CROSBY, GREAT (St Luke) *Liv 5*   **P** *R Sefton*   **P-in-c** P H SPIERS,   **C** S M ELLIOTT,   **OLM** B A CHAMBERS
CROSBY GARRETT (St Andrew)   *see* Kirkby Stephen w Mallerstang etc *Carl*
CROSBY-ON-EDEN (St John the Evangelist)   *see* Eden, Gelt and Irthing *Carl*
CROSBY RAVENSWORTH (St Lawrence) *Carl 1*   **P** *DBP*   **P-in-c** S D RUDKIN
CROSCOMBE (Blessed Virgin Mary)   *see* Pilton w Croscombe, N Wootton and Dinder *B & W*
CROSLAND, SOUTH (Holy Trinity)   *see* Em TM *Wakef*

CROSLAND MOOR (St Barnabas) and Linthwaite *Wakef 5*
P *Bp and R Almondbury (jt)*   **V** J J PERKINS,
C J M HONEYMAN
CROSS CANONBY (St John the Evangelist)   *see* Allonby, Cross
Canonby and Dearham *Carl*
CROSS FELL Group, The *Carl 4*   **P** *D&C (2 turns) and DBP*
(1 turn)   **V** R A MOATT,   **OLM** E M FROGGATT
CROSS GREEN (St Hilda)   *see* Hunslet w Cross Green *Ripon*
CROSS GREEN (St Saviour)   *see* Leeds Richmond Hill *Ripon*
CROSS HEATH (St Michael and All Angels) *Lich 9*   **P** *Bp*
V *vacant* (01782) 617241
CROSS IN HAND (St Bartholomew)   *see* Waldron *Chich*
CROSS ROADS cum Lees (St James) *Bradf 8*   **P** *Bp*
NSM P S WILSON
CROSS STONE (St Paul)   *see* Todmorden *Wakef*
CROSS TOWN (St Cross)   *see* Knutsford St Cross *Ches*
CROSSCRAKE (St Thomas) *Carl 10*   **P** *V Heversham and*
Milnthorpe   **NSM** T G WILCOCK, D A PRESTON
CROSSENS (St John)   *see* N Meols *Liv*
CROSSFLATTS (St Aidan)   *see* Bingley All SS *Bradf*
CROSSLACON Team Ministry *Carl 5*   **P** *Patr Bd*
TR J E CURTIS,   **TV** P F TURNBULL,   **Hon C** A–M L STUART,
NSM F A KEEGAN
CROSSPOOL (St Columba) *Sheff 4*   **P** *Bp*
P-in-c F M ECCLESTON,   **NSM** L A FURBEY
CROSTHWAITE (St Kentigern) Keswick *Carl 6*   **P** *Bp*
V A S E PENNY
CROSTHWAITE (St Mary) Kendal *Carl 10*   **P** *DBP*
P-in-c M D WOODCOCK
CROSTON (St Michael and All Angels) and Bretherton *Blackb 4*
P *M G Rawstorne Esq*   **P-in-c** D J REYNOLDS,
NSM W SLOAN
CROSTWICK (St Peter)   *see* Horsham St Faith, Spixworth and
Crostwick *Nor*
CROSTWIGHT (All Saints)   *see* Smallburgh w Dilham w
Honing and Crostwight *Nor*
CROUCH END HILL (Christ Church)   *see* Hornsey Ch Ch *Lon*
CROUGHTON (All Saints)   *see* Aynho and Croughton w
Evenley etc *Pet*
CROWAN (St Crewenna) and Treslothan *Truro 2*
P *D L C Roberts Esq and Mrs W A Pendarves (jt)*
V P DOUGLASS,   **C** M L PASCOE
CROWBOROUGH (All Saints) *Chich 19*   **P** *Ld Chan*
V A C J CORNES,   **C** J P FRITH, K R NEWMAN,
NSM J A HOBBS
CROWBOROUGH (St John the Evangelist) *Chich 19*   **P** *Guild*
of All So   **P-in-c** P A NAYLOR,   **NSM** R J NORBURY
CROWCOMBE (Holy Ghost)   *see* Quantock Towers *B & W*
CROWELL (Nativity of the Blessed Virgin Mary)   *see* Chinnor,
Sydenham, Aston Rowant and Crowell *Ox*
CROWFIELD (All Saints) w Stonham Aspal and Mickfield
St E 1   **P** *DBP, Bp, and Lord de Saumarez (alt)*
P-in-c T P HALL,   **OLM** H NORRIS, D L R MCLEOD
CROWHURST (St George)   *see* Catsfield and Crowhurst *Chich*
CROWHURST (St George)   *see* Lingfield and Crowhurst *S'wark*
CROWLAND (St Mary and St Bartholomew and St Guthlac)
Linc 17   **P** *Earl of Normanton*   **P-in-c** C H BROWN
CROWLE Group, The (St Oswald) *Linc 1*   **P** *Bp (2 turns),*
Prime Min (1 turn)   **P-in-c** T D BUCKLEY
CROWLE (St John the Baptist)   *see* Bowbrook S *Worc*
CROWMARSH GIFFORD (St Mary Magdalene)
see Wallingford *Ox*
CROWN EAST and RUSHWICK (St Thomas)   *see* Worc
Dines Green St Mich and Crown E, Rushwick *Worc*
CROWNHILL (Ascension)   *see* Plymouth Crownhill Ascension
Ex
CROWTHORNE (St John the Baptist) *Ox 16*   **P** *Bp*
V L M CORNWELL
CROWTON (Christ Church)   *see* Norley, Crowton and Kingsley
Ches
CROXALL-CUM-OAKLEY (St John the Baptist)   *see* Walton-
on-Trent w Croxall, Rosliston etc *Derby*
CROXBY (All Saints)   *see* Swallow *Linc*
CROXDALE (St Bartholomew) and Tudhoe *Dur 6*   **P** *D&C*
P-in-c G NORMAN
CROXDEN (St Giles)   *see* Rocester and Croxden w Hollington
Lich
CROXLEY GREEN (All Saints) *St Alb 5*   **P** *V Rickmansworth*
P-in-c M R MUGAN,   **NSM** M P L KINGSLEY
CROXLEY GREEN (St Oswald) *St Alb 5*   **P** *Bp*
P-in-c R J RILEY-BRALEY
CROXTETH (St Paul) *Liv 8*   **P** *R W Derby and Bp (jt)*
V I G BROOKS
CROXTETH PARK (St Cuthbert) *Liv 8*   **P** *Bp*   **V** *vacant*
0151-549 2202

CROXTON (All Saints)   *see* Thetford *Nor*
CROXTON Group, The SOUTH (St John the Baptist) *Leic 2*
P *DBP, Ch Soc Trust, and MMCET (jt)*   **TV** S LEIGHTON,
P-in-c M N DALE,   **NSM** A R LEIGHTON
CROXTON (St James)   *see* Papworth *Ely*
CROXTON (St John the Evangelist) *Linc 6*   **P** *Ld Chan*
NSM F A COUCH
CROXTON (St Paul)   *see* Broughton w Croxton and Cotes
Heath w Standon *Lich*
CROXTON KERRIAL (St Botolph and St John the Baptist)
see High Framland Par *Leic*
CROYDE (St Mary Magdalene)   *see* Georgeham *Ex*
CROYDON (All Saints)   *see* Orwell Gp *Ely*
CROYDON (Christ Church) Broad Green *S'wark 20*
P *Simeon's Trustees*   **V** W MUNCEY,   **OLM** K H VEEN
CROYDON (Holy Saviour) *S'wark 21*   **P** *Bp*
V X SOOSAINAYAGAM
CROYDON (St Andrew) *S'wark 20*   **P** *Trustees*
P-in-c K L W SYLVIA
CROYDON (St John the Baptist) *S'wark 20*   **P** *Abp*
V C J L BOSWELL,   **C** G P THOMPSON, T GOODE, K E ASTON,
Hon C E M HILL, S J H GOATCHER
CROYDON (St Mary Magdalene)   *see* Addiscombe St Mary
Magd w St Martin *S'wark*
CROYDON (St Matthew) *S'wark 20*   **P** *V Croydon*
V P J BROWN,   **NSM** R A HINDER
CROYDON (St Michael and All Angels w St James) *S'wark 20*
P *Trustees*   **V** D P MINCHEW,   **C** C J DICKSON
CROYDON Woodside (St Luke) *S'wark 21*   **P** *Bp*
V N C GOLDING,   **NSM** J C YEARWOOD
CROYDON, SOUTH (Emmanuel) *S'wark 20*   **P** *Ch Trust Fund*
Trust   **V** T A MAPSTONE,   **C** S L FENBY, B C SHEPHERD,
OLM J M WILSON
CROYDON, SOUTH (St Peter) (St Augustine) *S'wark 20*
P *V Croydon and Bp (jt)*   **V** W F WARREN,   **C** S C RAYNER,
NSM L M FOX
CROYLAND (St Mary and St Bartholomew and St Guthlac)
see Crowland *Linc*
CRUDGINGTON (St Mary Mission Church)
see Wrockwardine Deanery *Lich*
CRUDWELL (All Saints)   *see* Ashley, Crudwell, Hankerton and
Oaksey *Bris*
CRUMPSALL (St Matthew w St Mary) *Man 5*   **P** *Bp*
R *vacant* 0161-211 1483
CRUMPSALL, LOWER (St Thomas) w Cheetham St Mark
Man 5   **P** *Bp*   **P-in-c** N J ANDREWES
CRUNDALE (St Mary the Blessed Virgin) w Godmersham
Cant 2   **P** *Abp*   **P-in-c** I G CAMPBELL
CRUWYS MORCHARD (Holy Cross)   *see* Washfield,
Stoodleigh, Withleigh etc *Ex*
CRUX EASTON (St Michael and All Angels)   *see* Highclere and
Ashmansworth w Crux Easton *Win*
CUBBINGTON (St Mary) *Cov 11*   **P** *Bp*
P-in-c R C PANTLING
CUBERT (St Cubert)   *see* Crantock w Cubert *Truro*
CUBLEY (St Andrew)   *see* Alkmonton, Cubley and Marston
Montgomery *Derby*
CUBLINGTON (St Nicholas)   *see* Wingrave w Rowsham,
Aston Abbotts and Cublington *Ox*
CUCKFIELD (Holy Trinity) *Chich 6*   **P** *Bp*
V N G WETHERALL
CUCKLINGTON (St Lawrence)   *see* Charlton Musgrove,
Cucklington and Stoke Trister *B & W*
CUDDESDON (All Saints)   *see* Wheatley *Ox*
CUDDINGTON (St Mary) *Guildf 9*   **P** *Bp*   **V** A K SILLIS,
NSM S P AYLING,   **OLM** C M WHITE
CUDDINGTON (St Nicholas)   *see* Haddenham w Cuddington,
Kingsey etc *Ox*
CUDHAM (St Peter and St Paul) and Downe *Roch 16*
P *Ch Soc Trust and Bp (jt)*   **P-in-c** E H HESELWOOD
CUDWORTH (St John) *Wakef 7*   **P** *Bp*   **V** D NICHOLSON
CUDWORTH (St Michael)   *see* Ilminster and Distr *B & W*
CUFFLEY (St Andrew)   *see* Northaw and Cuffley *St Alb*
CULBONE (St Beuno)   *see* Oare w Culbone *B & W*
CULFORD (St Mary)   *see* Lark Valley *St E*
CULGAITH (All Saints)   *see* Cross Fell Gp *Carl*
CULHAM (St Paul)   *see* Dorchester *Ox*
CULLERCOATS (St George) *Newc 5*   **P** *Duke of*
Northumberland   **V** A J HUGHES,   **C** G M SHORT,
NSM J R A SERGEANT
CULLERCOATS (St Paul)   *see* Tynemouth Cullercoats St Paul
Newc
CULLINGWORTH (St John the Evangelist) *Bradf 8*   **P** *Bp*
V *vacant* (01535) 272434
CULLOMPTON (St Andrew) (Langford Chapel), Willand,
Uffculme, Kentisbeare, and Blackborough *Ex 4*   **P** *Patr Bd*

TV A E NORMAN-WALKER, **C** B L HARDING, S C GARNER,
Hon C P S THOMAS, **NSM** L M BARLEY
CULM DAVY (St Mary's Chapel)   *see* Hemyock w Culm Davy,
Clayhidon and Culmstock *Ex*
CULM VALLEY   *see* Cullompton, Willand, Uffculme,
Kentisbeare etc *Ex*
CULMINGTON (All Saints)   *see* Ludlow *Heref*
CULMSTOCK (All Saints)   *see* Hemyock w Culm Davy,
Clayhidon and Culmstock *Ex*
CULPHO (St Botolph)   *see* Gt and Lt Bealings w Playford and
Culpho *St E*
CULWORTH (St Mary the Virgin) w Sulgrave and Thorpe
Mandeville and Chipping Warden w Edgcote and Moreton
Pinkney *Pet 1*   **P** *T M Sergison-Brooke Esq, DBP,*
D L P Humfrey Esq, Ch Patr Trust, and Oriel Coll Ox (jt)
R C H R WHITEMAN
CUMBERWORTH (St Helen)   *see* Sutton, Huttoft and Anderby
Linc
CUMBERWORTH (St Nicholas), Denby and Denby Dale
Wakef 6   **P** *Bp and V Penistone (jt)*   **R** *vacant* (01484) 606225
CUMDIVOCK (St John)   *see* Dalston w Cumdivock, Raughton
Head and Wreay *Carl*
CUMMERSDALE (St James)   *see* Denton Holme *Carl*
CUMNOR (St Michael) *Ox 10*   **P** *St Pet Coll Ox*
V G N MAUGHAN,   **NSM** H A AZER
CUMREW (St Mary the Virgin)   *see* Eden, Gelt and Irthing *Carl*
CUMWHINTON (St John's Hall)   *see* Scotby and Cotehill w
Cumwhinton *Carl*
CUMWHITTON (St Mary the Virgin)   *see* Eden, Gelt and
Irthing *Carl*
CUNDALL (St Mary and All Saints)   *see* Kirby-on-the-Moor,
Cundall w Norton-le-Clay etc *Ripon*
CURBAR (All Saints)   *see* Baslow w Curbar and Stoney
Middleton *Derby*
CURBRIDGE (St Barnabas)   *see* Sarisbury *Portsm*
CURBRIDGE (St John the Baptist)   *see* Witney *Ox*
CURDRIDGE (St Peter) *Portsm 1*   **P** *D&C Win*
V P J F GOODEY,   **NSM** R E SCHOFIELD
CURDWORTH (St Nicholas and St Peter ad Vincula)
(St George), Middleton and Wishaw *Birm 12*   **P** *Bp*
R M I RHODES
CURRY, NORTH (St Peter and St Paul)   *see* Athelney *B & W*
CURRY MALLET (All Saints)   *see* Beercrocombe w Curry
Mallet, Hatch Beauchamp etc *B & W*
CURRY RIVEL (St Andrew) w Fivehead and Swell *B & W 15*
P *D&C Bris (1 turn), P G H Speke Esq (2 turns)*
R J M LANGDOWN
CURY (St Corentine) and Gunwalloe *Truro 4*   **P** *Bp*
P-in-c S O GRIFFITHS
CUSOP (St Mary) w Blakemere, Bredwardine w Brobury,
Clifford, Dorstone, Hardwicke, Moccas and Preston-on-Wye
Heref 1   **P** *Bp, D&C, CPAS, MMCET, P M I S Trumper Esq,*
S Penoyre Esq, and Mrs P Chester-Master (jt)
Hon C S F BARNES,   **OLM** R R DAVIES-JAMES
CUSTOM HOUSE (Ascension)   *see* Victoria Docks Ascension
Chelmsf
CUTCOMBE (St John the Evangelist)   *see* Exton and Winsford
and Cutcombe w Luxborough *B & W*
CUTSDEAN (St James)   *see* The Guitings, Cutsdean, Farmcote
etc *Glouc*
CUXHAM (Holy Rood)   *see* Ewelme, Brightwell Baldwin,
Cuxham w Easington *Ox*
CUXTON (St Michael and All Angels) and Halling *Roch 6*
P *Bp and D&C (jt)*   **R** R I KNIGHT
CUXWOLD (St Nicholas)   *see* Swallow *Linc*
CWM HEAD (St Michael)   *see* Wistanstow *Heref*
DACRE (Holy Trinity) w Hartwith and Darley w Thornthwaite
Ripon 3   **P** *Bp, D&C, V Masham and Healey, and*
Mrs K A Dunbar (jt)   **P-in-c** M S EVANS,   **NSM** A J COLLINS
DACRE (St Andrew) *Carl 4*   **P** *Trustees*   **P-in-c** R C PATTINSON
DADLINGTON (St James)   *see* Fenn Lanes Gp *Leic*
DAGENHAM (St Martin)   *see* Becontree S *Chelmsf*
DAGENHAM (St Peter and St Paul) *Chelmsf 1*   **P** *Ch Soc Trust*
V R M REITH,   **C** R J WOOD
DAGLINGWORTH (Holy Rood)   *see* Brimpsfield w Birdlip,
Syde, Daglingworth etc *Glouc*
DAGNALL (All Saints)   *see* Kensworth, Studham and
Whipsnade *St Alb*
DAISY HILL (St James) *Man 11*   **P** *Bp*   **P-in-c** J C BRADING
DALBURY (All Saints)   *see* Boylestone, Church Broughton,
Dalbury, etc *Derby*
DALBY (St James)   *see* Patrick *S & M*
DALBY (St Lawrence and Blessed Edward King)   *see* Partney
Gp *Linc*
DALBY (St Peter)   *see* Howardian Gp *York*

DALBY, GREAT (St Swithun)   *see* Burrough Hill Pars *Leic*
DALBY, LITTLE (St James)   *as above*
DALBY, OLD (St John the Baptist), Nether Broughton, Saxelbye
w Shoby, Grimston and Wartnaby *Leic 2*   **P** *Bp, MMCET,*
V Rothley, and Personal Reps K J M Madocks-Wright Esq (jt)
V J S HOPEWELL
DALE ABBEY (All Saints)   *see* Stanton-by-Dale w Dale Abbey
and Risley *Derby*
DALE HEAD (St James)   *see* Long Preston w Tosside *Bradf*
DALHAM (St Mary), Gazeley, Higham, Kentford and Moulton
St E 11   **P** *Bp (2 turns), Ch Coll Cam (1 turn),*
C E L Philipps Esq (1 turn), and D W Barclay Esq (1 turn)
V S J MITCHELL
DALLAM (St Mark) *Liv 12*   **P** *R Warrington and Bp (jt)*
V P J MARSHALL
DALLINGHOO (St Mary)   *see* Mid Loes *St E*
DALLINGTON (St Giles)   *see* Brightling, Dallington,
Mountfield etc *Chich*
DALLINGTON (St Mary) *Pet 4*   **P** *Earl Spencer*
P-in-c S N MOUSIR-HARRISON
DALLOWGILL (St Peter)   *see* Fountains Gp *Ripon*
DALSTON (Holy Trinity) w St Philip and Haggerston All Saints
Lon 5   **P** *Ld Chan and Bp (alt)*   **V** R J HUDSON-WILKIN
DALSTON (St Mark w St Bartholomew) *Lon 5*   **P** *Ch Patr*
Trust   **V** J ZVIMBA,   **NSM** A SHEERAN
DALSTON (St Michael) w Cumdivock, Raughton Head and
Wreay *Carl 3*   **P** *Bp, DBP, and D&C (jt)*   **V** S P CARTER,
C R J SANER-HAIGH,   **NSM** H R CARTER
DALTON (Holy Trinity)   *see* Newburn *Newc*
DALTON (Holy Trinity) *Sheff 6*   **P** *Bp*   **V** M INESON
DALTON (St James)   *see* Gilling and Kirkby Ravensworth *Ripon*
DALTON (St John the Evangelist)   *see* Topcliffe, Baldersby w
Dishforth, Dalton etc *York*
DALTON (St Michael and All Angels) *Liv 11*   **P** *Bp*
V T C BARTON
DALTON, NORTH (All Saints)   *see* Woldsburn *York*
DALTON, SOUTH   *see* Dalton le Dale and New Seaham *Dur*
DALTON HOLME (St Mary)   *see* Etton w Dalton Holme *York*
DALTON-IN-FURNESS (St Mary) and Ireleth-with-Askam
Carl 9   **P** *Bp*   **V** A MITCHELL,   **C** M COWAN
DALTON LE DALE (St Andrew) and New Seaham *Dur 2*   **P** *Bp*
and D&C (alt)   **V** P T HARRISON
DALWOOD (St Peter)   *see* Kilmington, Stockland, Dalwood,
Yarcombe etc *Ex*
DAMERHAM (St George)   *see* W Downland *Sarum*
DANBURY (St John the Baptist) *Chelmsf 9*   **P** *Lord Fitzwalter*
P-in-c M G BLYTH,   **C** C M BALL
DANBY (St Hilda) w Castleton and Commondale *York 22*
P *Viscountess Downe*   **V** M J HAZELTON
DANBY WISKE (not known)   *see* E Richmond *Ripon*
DANEHILL (All Saints) *Chich 21*   **P** *Ch Soc Trust*
V D M HALL,   **C** S G RAE
DANESMOOR (St Barnabas)   *see* N Wingfield, Clay Cross and
Pilsley *Derby*
DARBY END (St Peter) *Worc 9*   **P** *Bp*   **V** S H CARTER
DARBY GREEN (St Barnabas) and Eversley *Win 5*   **P** *Bp*
V M W SAUNDERS
DARENTH (St Margaret) *Roch 2*   **P** *D&C*   **P-in-c** J E G DASH
DARESBURY (All Saints) *Ches 4*   **P** *D G Greenhall Esq*
V D R FELIX
DARFIELD (All Saints) *Sheff 12*   **P** *MMCET*   **Hon**
C J M STRIDE
DARLASTON (All Saints) *Lich 26*   **P** *Simeon's Trustees*
P-in-c J R BARNETT,   **C** D WILLS, R E INGLESBY
DARLASTON (St Lawrence) *Lich 26*   **P** *Bp and Simeon's*
Trustees (jt)   **R** D WILLS,   **C** R E INGLESBY
DARLEY (Christ Church)   *see* Dacre w Hartwith and Darley w
Thornthwaite *Ripon*
DARLEY (St Helen) *Derby 7*   **P** *Bp*   **R** R E QUARTON
DARLEY, SOUTH (St Mary the Virgin), Elton and Winster
Derby 7   **P** *Bp and DBF (jt)*   **P-in-c** R E QUARTON,
Hon C J MARSHALL
DARLEY ABBEY (St Matthew) *Derby 11*   **P** *DBP*
P-in-c C A DYER,   **NSM** J CALDWELL, P A MALLINSON
DARLINGSCOTT (St George)   *see* Tredington and
Darlingscott *Cov*
DARLINGTON (All Saints)   *see* Blackwell All SS and
Salutation *Dur*
DARLINGTON (Holy Trinity) *Dur 8*   **P** *Adn Dur*
P-in-c N J W BARKER,   **C** E B SAVIGEAR
DARLINGTON (St Cuthbert) *Dur 8*   **P** *Lord Barnard*
V R J WILLIAMSON,   **NSM** P M SINCLAIR
DARLINGTON St Hilda and (St Columba) *Dur 8*   **P** *Bp*
P-in-c S C WILLIAMSON,   **NSM** D V ROBINSON
DARLINGTON (St James) *Dur 8*   **P** *The Crown*
V I L GRIEVES

DARLINGTON (St Mark) w St Paul *Dur 8*   **P** *Bp and St Jo Coll Dur*   **V** P A BAKER,   **C** K J BAGNALL
DARLINGTON (St Matthew) and St Luke *Dur 8*   **P** *Bp*
 V *vacant* (01325) 354669
DARLINGTON, EAST (St John) (St Herbert) *Dur 8*
 P *The Crown*   **TR** M L DENT,   **TV** C M BLAKESLEY,
 C L J ROGERS
DARNALL (Church of Christ)   *see* Attercliffe and Darnall *Sheff*
DARRINGTON (St Luke and All Saints)   *see* Went Valley
 Wakef
DARSHAM (All Saints)   *see* Yoxmere *St E*
DARTFORD (Christ Church) *Roch 2*   **P** *V Dartford H Trin*
 V *vacant* (01322) 220036
DARTFORD (Holy Trinity) *Roch 2*   **P** *Bp*   **V** M J HENWOOD,
 NSM N L WILLIAMS
DARTFORD (St Alban) *Roch 2*   **P** *V Dartford H Trin*
 V C F GILBERT
DARTFORD (St Edmund the King and Martyr) *Roch 2*   **P** *Bp*
 V R P CALLAGHAN,   **C** A M SPREADBRIDGE
DARTINGTON (Old St Mary's Church Tower)   *see* Totnes w
 Bridgetown, Berry Pomeroy etc *Ex*
DARTINGTON (St Mary)   *as above*
DARTMOUTH (St Petrox) (St Saviour) and Dittisham *Ex 13*
 P *Sir John Seale Bt, DBP, and Bp (jt)*   **V** S C WRIGHT
DARTMOUTH PARK (St Mary)   *see* Brookfield St Mary *Lon*
DARTON (All Saints) *Wakef 7*   **P** *Bp*   **P-in-c** S A REYNOLDS
DARWEN (St Barnabas) *Blackb 2*   **P** *Bp*   **V** L R COLLINSON
DARWEN (St Cuthbert) w Tockholes St Stephen *Blackb 2*   **P** *Bp*
 P-in-c D G MOORE
DARWEN (St Peter) w Hoddlesden St Paul *Blackb 2*
 P *V Blackburn and DBP (jt)*   **P-in-c** A HOLLIDAY,
 C J D JONES,   T N DYER
DARWEN, LOWER (St James) *Blackb 2*   **P** *V Blackb*
 P-in-c G M DYER,   **Hon C** F NAYLOR,   **NSM** J R H CRAWFORD
DARWEN, OVER (St James) *Blackb 2*   **P** *V Blackb*
 P-in-c T N DYER,   **NSM** M E CROOK
DASSETT MAGNA (All Saints)   *see* Burton Dassett *Cov*
DATCHET (St Mary the Virgin)   *see* Colnbrook and Datchet *Ox*
DATCHWORTH (All Saints)   *see* Welwyn *St Alb*
DAUBHILL (St George the Martyr) *Man 9*   **P** *Trustees*
 P-in-c F ADMAN
DAUNTSEY (St James Great)   *see* Brinkworth w Dauntsey *Bris*
DAVENHAM (St Wilfrid) *Ches 6*   **P** *Bp*   **R** M C R CRIPPS,
 Hon C M W WALTERS,   **NSM** R J HUGHES
DAVENTRY (Holy Cross), Ashby St Ledgers, Braunston,
 Catesby, Hellidon, Staverton and Welton *Pet 3*   **P** *Patr Bd*
 TV C P ROSE-CASEMORE, E M COWLEY,   **P-in-c** M C W WEBBER
DAVIDSTOW (St David)   *see* Boscastle w Davidstow *Truro*
DAVINGTON (St Mary Magdalene)   *see* The Brents and
 Davington w Oare and Luddenham *Cant*
DAVYHULME (Christ Church) *Man 7*   **P** *Bp*   **P-in-c** R J HILL
DAVYHULME (St Mary) *Man 7*   **P** *Bp*   **P-in-c** C S FORD
DAWLEY (Holy Trinity)   *see* Cen Telford *Lich*
DAWLEY (St Jerome)   *see* W Hayes *Lon*
DAWLISH (St Gregory) *Ex 6*   **P** *D&C*   **C** D A BURTON,
 NSM H M BAYS
DAWLISH WARREN (Church Hall)   *see* Kenton, Mamhead,
 Powderham, Cofton and Starcross *Ex*
DAYBROOK (St Paul) *S'well 12*   **P** *Bp*   **P-in-c** S A BAYLIS
DAYLESFORD (St Peter)   *see* Chipping Norton *Ox*
DE BEAUVOIR TOWN (St Peter) *Lon 5*   **P** *Bp*
 V J F PORTER-PRYCE,   **C** F C DYER,   **NSM** D GERRANS
DEAL (St Andrew) *Cant 8*   **P** *Abp*   **P-in-c** C M D LINDLAR
DEAL (St George the Martyr) *Cant 8*   **P** *Abp*   **V** C G SPENCER,
 C S PORTER
DEAL (St Leonard) (St Richard) and Sholden w Great
 Mongeham *Cant 8*   **P** *Abp*   **P-in-c** D W FLEWKER,   **Hon**
 C M H CLARK,   **NSM** P T KAVANAGH,   **OLM** P J HAMBROOK
DEAL The Carpenter's Arms (extra-parochial place)
 Cant 8 vacant
DEAN (All Hallows)   *see* The Stodden Churches *St Alb*
DEAN (St Oswald)   *see* Clifton, Dean and Mosser *Carl*
DEAN COURT (St Andrew)   *see* Cumnor *Ox*
DEAN FOREST (Christ Church)   *see* Forest of Dean Ch Ch w
 English Bicknor *Glouc*
DEAN FOREST (St Paul)   *see* Parkend and Viney Hill *Glouc*
DEAN PRIOR (St George the Martyr)   *see* Buckfastleigh w
 Dean Prior *Ex*
DEANE (All Saints)   *see* N Waltham and Steventon, Ashe and
 Deane *Win*
DEANE (St Mary the Virgin) *Man 11*   **P** *Patr Bd*
 TV J G ARMSTRONG,   **C** D J HOWARD,   **OLM** J M DAVIES,
 E B PLANT
DEANE VALE Benefice, The *B & W 19*   **P** *Bp and PCCs*
 Heathfield, Hillfarrance, and Oake (jt)   **P-in-c** A NORRIS

DEANSHANGER (Holy Trinity)   *see* Passenham *Pet*
DEARHAM (St Mungo)   *see* Allonby, Cross Canonby and
 Dearham *Carl*
DEARNLEY (St Andrew) *Man 21*   **P** *Bp*   **P-in-c** S A JONES,
 C K N BLAY,   **NSM** G D MANCO
DEBDEN (St Mary the Virgin) and Wimbish w Thunderley
 Chelmsf 21   **P** *Bp*   **P-in-c** H M DAVEY
DEBENHAM (St Mary Magdalene) and Helmingham *St E 18*
 P *Ld Chan, Lord Henniker, MMCET, Bp, and Lord Tollemache*
 (by turn)   **P-in-c** P A W COTTON,   **NSM** R J BARNES,
 OLM P A R WILKES
DEDDINGTON (St Peter and St Paul) Barford, Clifton and
 Hempton *Ox 5*   **P** *D&C Windsor and Bp (jt)*   **V** H R B WHITE
DEDHAM (St Mary the Virgin) *Chelmsf 17*   **P** *Duchy of Lanc*
 and Lectureship Trustees (alt)   **V** G G MOATE
DEDWORTH (All Saints) *Ox 13*   **P** *Bp*   **P-in-c** L M BROWN
DEEPCAR (St John the Evangelist) *Sheff 3*   **P** *Bp*
 P-in-c D B JEANS,   **C** H R ISAACSON
DEEPING, WEST (St Andrew)   *see* Uffington Gp *Linc*
DEEPING ST JAMES (St James) *Linc 13*   **P** *Burghley Ho*
 Preservation Trust   **NSM** S M C MARSHALL
DEEPING ST NICHOLAS (St Nicholas)   *see* Spalding St Jo w
 Deeping St Nicholas *Linc*
DEEPLISH (St Luke)   *see* S Rochdale *Man*
DEERHURST (St Mary) and Apperley w Forthampton,
 Chaceley, Tredington, Stoke Orchard and Hardwicke *Glouc 13*
 P *Bp, V Longdon, and J S Yorke Esq (jt)*   **P-in-c** T E CLAMMER
DEFFORD (St James) w Besford *Worc 4*   **P** *D&C Westmr*
 V S K RENSHAW
DEIGHTON (All Saints)   *see* Brompton w Deighton *York*
DELABOLE (St John the Evangelist)   *see* St Teath *Truro*
DELAMERE (St Peter) *Ches 6*   **P** *The Crown*
 P-in-c B R K PERKES
DELAVAL (Our Lady) *Newc 1*   **P** *Lord Hastings*
 V P J BRYARS,   **OLM** D R ORMESHER
DEMBLEBY (St Lucia)   *see* S Lafford *Linc*
DENABY, OLD (Mission Church)   *see* Mexborough *Sheff*
DENABY MAIN (All Saints) *Sheff 7*   **P** *Bp*   **V** R C DAVIES
DENBURY (St Mary the Virgin)   *see* Ipplepen, Torbryan and
 Denbury *Ex*
DENBY (St John the Evangelist)   *see* Cumberworth, Denby and
 Denby Dale *Wakef*
DENBY (St Mary the Virgin)   *see* Horsley and Denby *Derby*
DENBY DALE (Holy Trinity)   *see* Cumberworth, Denby and
 Denby Dale *Wakef*
DENCHWORTH (St James)   *see* Hanney, Denchworth and E
 Challow *Ox*
DENDRON (St Matthew)   *see* Aldingham, Dendron, Rampside
 and Urswick *Carl*
DENESIDE (All Saints)   *see* Seaham *Dur*
DENFORD (Holy Trinity)   *see* Thrapston, Denford and Islip
 Pet
DENGIE (St James) w Asheldham *Chelmsf 11*   **P** *Bp*   **R** *vacant*
DENHAM (St John the Baptist)   *see* Hoxne w Denham,
 Syleham and Wingfield *St E*
DENHAM (St Mark) (St Mary the Virgin) *Ox 20*
 P *L J Way Esq*   **R** J A HIRST
DENHAM (St Mary)   *see* Barrow *St E*
DENHAM, NEW (St Francis)   *see* Denham *Ox*
DENHOLME *Bradf 8*   **P** *Bp*   **P-in-c** R J BROOKS
DENMARK PARK (St Saviour)   *see* Peckham St Sav *S'wark*
DENMEAD (All Saints) *Portsm 5*   **P** *Ld Chan*
 V S M EDWARDS,   **NSM** A C L JOHNSON
DENNINGTON (St Mary)   *see* Upper Alde *St E*
DENSHAW (Christ Church) *Man 19*   **P** *Bp*   **V** *vacant* (01457)
 874575
DENSTON (St Nicholas)   *see* Bansfield *St E*
DENSTONE (All Saints) w Ellastone and Stanton *Lich 15*   **P** *Bp*
 and Col Sir Walter Bromley-Davenport (jt)   **C** R P OWEN,
 J RICHARDSON
DENT (St Andrew) w Cowgill *Bradf 6*   **P** *Bp and Sidesmen of*
 Dent (alt)   **V** P J BOYLES
DENTON (Christ Church) *Man 17*   **P** *Bp*
 P-in-c S A HARRISON
DENTON Dane Bank (St George)   *see* Denton Ch Ch *Man*
DENTON (Holy Spirit) *Newc 4*   **P** *Bp*   **V** J GOODE,
 NSM P H PEARSON
DENTON (St Andrew)   *see* Harlaxton Gp *Linc*
DENTON (St Helen)   *see* Washburn and Mid-Wharfe *Bradf*
DENTON (St Lawrence) *Man 17*   **P** *Earl of Wilton*
 P-in-c E M POPE
DENTON (St Leonard) w South Heighton and Tarring Neville
 Chich 18   **P** *MMCET and Bp (alt)*   **R** P J OWEN
DENTON (St Margaret)   *see* Yardley Hastings, Denton and
 Grendon etc *Pet*

DENTON (St Mary)   *see* Ditchingham, Hedenham, Broome, Earsham etc *Nor*

DENTON (St Mary Magdalene)   *see* Elham w Denton and Wootton *Cant*

DENTON, NETHER (St Cuthbert)   *see* Lanercost, Walton, Gilsland and Nether Denton *Carl*

DENTON HOLME (St James) *Carl 3*   **P** *Trustees*   **V** J R LIBBY,   **C** E F A L SCRASE-FIELD

DENVER (St Mary) and Ryston w Roxham and West Dereham and Bexwell *Ely 9*   **P** *G&C Coll Cam and Bp (jt)*   **R** J M T M GRUNDY

DENVILLE (Christchurch Centre)   *see* Havant *Portsm*

DEOPHAM (St Andrew)   *see* High Oak, Hingham and Scoulton w Wood Rising *Nor*

DEPDEN (St Mary the Virgin)   *see* Chevington w Hargrave, Chedburgh w Depden etc *St E*

DEPTFORD Brockley (St Peter)   *see* Brockley St Pet *S'wark*

DEPTFORD (St John) (Holy Trinity) (Ascension) *S'wark 2*   **P** *Patr Bd*   **TR** C S BAINBRIDGE,   **TV** T A DONNELLY,   **NSM** E R NEWNHAM,   **OLM** P K M SOER

DEPTFORD (St Nicholas) (St Luke) *S'wark 2*   **P** *MMCET, Peache Trustees, and CPAS (jt)*   **V** P S DOEL,   **C** V J YEADON

DEPTFORD (St Paul) *S'wark 2*   **P** *Bp*   **R** P D BUTLER,   **Hon C** P A PACKER,   **NSM** B E MCHENRY

DERBY (St Alkmund and St Werburgh) *Derby 9*   **P** *Simeon's Trustees*   **V** J M WHITE

DERBY (St Andrew w St Osmund) *Derby 10*   **P** *Bp*   **V** D C MACDONALD,   **NSM** R HOWORTH, V M HART, J M LYON

DERBY (St Anne) (St John the Evangelist) *Derby 9*   **P** *Bp*   **V** *vacant* (01332) 32681

DERBY (St Augustine)   *see* Walbrook Epiphany *Derby*

DERBY (St Barnabas) *Derby 9*   **P** *Bp*   **V** *vacant* (01332) 342553

DERBY (St Bartholomew) *Derby 10*   **P** *Bp*   **V** *vacant* (01332) 347709

DERBY (St Luke) *Derby 9*   **P** *Bp*   **V** G W SILLIS

DERBY (St Mark) *Derby 9*   **P** *Bp*   **P-in-c** J M PAGE,   **Hon C** M R FUTERS

DERBY (St Paul) *Derby 9*   **P** *Bp*   **NSM** G M WHITE

DERBY (St Peter and Christ Church w Holy Trinity) *Derby 10*   **P** *CPAS*   **P-in-c** P D MORRIS

DERBY (St Thomas)   *see* Walbrook Epiphany *Derby*

DERBY, WEST (Good Shepherd) *Liv 8*   **P** *Bp and R W Derby (jt)*   **V** J DAVIES,   **OLM** S TRAPNELL

DERBY, WEST (St James) (St Mary) *Liv 8*   **P** *Bp and Adn Liv (jt)*   **V** J M COLEMAN,   **C** P C WETHERELL,   **NSM** S C LEDBETTER, M A MONTROSE

DERBY, WEST (St John) *Liv 8*   **P** *Trustees*   **V** T P E NENER

DERBY, WEST (St Luke) *Liv 2*   **P** *Bp*   **P-in-c** A D STOTT

DERBYHAVEN (Chapel)   *see* Malew *S & M*

DERBYSHIRE HILL (St Philip)   *see* Parr *Liv*

DEREHAM (St Nicholas) and District *Nor 17*   **P** *Ld Chan (2 turns), Patr Bd (1 turn)*   **TR** S M THEAKSTON,   **Hon C** J M TAYLOR,   **NSM** K G PILGRIM,   **OLM** J L NURSEY

DEREHAM, WEST (St Andrew)   *see* Denver and Ryston w Roxham and W Dereham etc *Ely*

DERRINGHAM BANK (Ascension) (St Thomas) *York 14*   **P** *Abp*   **V** S J WHALEY

DERRINGTON (St Matthew)   *see* Bradeley, Church Eaton, Derrington and Haughton *Lich*

DERRY Hill (Christ Church) w Bremhill and Foxham *Sarum 15*   **P** *Prime Min and V Calne and Blackland*   **V** D C FROST

DERSINGHAM (St Nicholas) w Anmer and Shernborne *Nor 16*   **P** *Ld Chan*   **R** M J BROCK,   **NSM** A F AUBREY-JONES

DERWENT, UPPER *Carl 6*   **P** *V Keswick St Jo (1 turn), V Crosthwaite (2 turns)*   **P-in-c** P H VIVASH,   **NSM** G E PYE

DERWENT, UPPER *York 20*   **P** *Viscountess Downe (1 turn), Sir Philip Naylor-Leyland (Bt) (1 turn), Abp (2 turns)*   **V** S G HILL

DERWENT INGS *York 2*   **P** *Abp, Lt Col J Darlington, and Sir Mervyn Dunnington-Jefferson Bt (jt)*   **R** P A HORSLEY,   **C** C N B MORGAN,   **NSM** P A BURGESS

DESBOROUGH (St Giles), Brampton Ash, Dingley and Braybrooke *Pet 9*   **P** *Bp, Earl Spencer, and DBP (by turn)*   **P-in-c** P S SEATON-BURN,   **C** J P LEAVER,   **NSM** N M CLARKE

DESFORD (St Martin) and Peckleton w Tooley *Leic 9*   **P** *Ld Chan*   **R** R G SHARPE

DETHICK (St John the Baptist)   *see* Tansley, Dethick, Lea and Holloway *Derby*

DETLING (St Martin)   *see* Boxley w Detling *Cant*

DEVER, LOWER *Win 7*   **P** *Bp and D&C (jt)*   **R** M D BAILEY,   **NSM** K P KOUSSEFF

DEVER, UPPER *Win 7*   **P** *Lord Northbrook (3 turns), Bp (2 turns)*   **V** S A FOSTER

DEVIZES (St John) (St Mary) *Sarum 16*   **P** *Ld Chan*   **R** P RICHARDSON,   **C** J C E POTTINGER

DEVIZES (St Peter) *Sarum 16*   **P** *Bp*   **P-in-c** P J MOSS

DEVONPORT (St Aubyn)   *see* Stoke Damerel and Devonport St Aubyn *Ex*

DEVONPORT (St Bartholomew) and Ford St Mark *Ex 22*   **P** *Bp and Trustees (jt)*   **V** R M SIGRIST

DEVONPORT (St Boniface)   *see* Devonport St Boniface and St Phil *Ex*

DEVONPORT (St Boniface) (St Philip) *Ex 22*   **P** *Bp*   **TR** *vacant* (01752) 361137

DEVONPORT (St Budeaux) *Ex 22*   **P** *V Plymouth St Andr w St Paul and St Geo*   **V** S J BEACH,   **C** G R SHIRLEY

DEVONPORT St Michael (St Barnabas) *Ex 22*   **P** *Bp and Trustees Lord St Levan (jt)*   **P-in-c** T J BUCKLEY

DEVONPORT (St Thomas)   *see* Plymouth St Pet and H Apostles *Ex*

DEVONPORT, NORTH   *see* Devonport St Boniface and St Phil *Ex*

DEVORAN (St John the Evangelist and St Petroc) *Truro 6*   **P** *Bp*   **P-in-c** D R CARRIVICK

DEWCHURCH, LITTLE (St David)   *see* Heref S Wye *Heref*

DEWCHURCH, MUCH (St David)   *see* Wormelow Hundred *Heref*

DEWLISH (All Saints)   *see* Puddletown, Tolpuddle and Milborne w Dewlish *Sarum*

DEWSALL (St Michael)   *see* Heref S Wye *Heref*

DEWSBURY (All Saints) (St Mark) (St Matthew and St John the Baptist) *Wakef 10*   **P** *Bp, Adn Pontefract, RD Dewsbury, and Lay Chmn Dewsbury Deanery Syn (jt)*   **TR** K PARTINGTON,   **TV** K ROBERTSON,   **C** L E SENIOR

DEWSBURY (St Matthew and St John the Baptist)   *see* Dewsbury *Wakef*

DEWSBURY (All Saints)   *as above*

DEWSBURY (St Mark)   *as above*

DEWSBURY MOOR (St John the Evangelist)   *as above*

DHOON (Christ Church)   *see* Maughold *S & M*

DIBDEN (All Saints) *Win 11*   **P** *MMCET*   **R** J CURRIN,   **C** S HAYWARD

DIBDEN PURLIEU (St Andrew)   *see* Dibden *Win*

DICKER, UPPER (Holy Trinity)   *see* Hellingly and Upper Dicker *Chich*

DICKLEBURGH (All Saints) and The Pulhams *Nor 10*   **P** *Ld Chan (1 turn), Patr Bd (2 turns), Prime Min (1 turn)*   **R** J B SCOTT,   **NSM** N W STEER,   **OLM** P D SCHWIER, D J ADLAM

DIDBROOK (St George)   *see* Winchcombe *Glouc*

DIDCOT (All Saints) *Ox 18*   **P** *BNC Ox*   **P-in-c** K M BECK,   **C** H R BOORMAN,   **NSM** A J EDWARDS

DIDCOT (St Peter) *Ox 18*   **P** *Bp*   **P-in-c** E J CARTER,   **C** J R BAKER,   **OLM** J CARTER

DIDDINGTON (St Laurence)   *see* The Paxtons w Diddington *Ely*

DIDDLEBURY (St Peter) w Munslow, Holdgate and Tugford *Heref 12*   **P** *Bp (3 turns), D&C (1 turn)*   **R** I E GIBBS

DIDLINGTON (St Michael) *Nor 13*   **P** *CPAS*   **V** *vacant*

DIDMARTON (St Lawrence)   *see* Boxwell, Leighterton, Didmarton, Oldbury etc *Glouc*

DIDSBURY (St James) (Emmanuel) *Man 8*   **P** *Patr Bd*   **TV** N J BUNDOCK,   **C** N J MCKEE

DIDSBURY, WEST (Christ Church) and Withington St Christopher *Man 8*   **P** *Trustees and Prime Min (alt)*   **R** A PILKINGTON,   **C** A J J DEVADASON

DIGBY GROUP, The (St Thomas of Canterbury) *Linc 22*   **P** *Mrs H E Gillatt, Ld Chan, and DBP (by turn)*   **Hon C** D B WOODS

DIGMOOR (Christ the Servant)   *see* Upholland *Liv*

DIGSWELL (St John the Evangelist) (Christ the King) and Panshanger *St Alb 21*   **P** *Patr Bd*   **TR** C GARNER,   **TV** S SHAHZAD, S Q MOORE,   **NSM** K E SUCKLING, A E COUPER

DILHAM (St Nicholas)   *see* Smallburgh w Dilham w Honing and Crostwight *Nor*

DILHORNE (All Saints)   *see* Caverswall and Weston Coyney w Dilhorne *Lich*

DILSTON (St Mary Magdalene)   *see* Corbridge w Halton and Newton Hall *Newc*

DILTON or LEIGH (Holy Saviour)   *see* White Horse *Sarum*

DILTON MARSH (Holy Trinity)   *as above*

DILWYN AND STRETFORD (St Mary the Virgin)   *see* Leominster *Heref*

DINDER (St Michael and All Angels)   *see* Pilton w Croscombe, N Wootton and Dinder *B & W*

DINEDOR (St Andrew)   *see* Heref S Wye *Heref*

DINES GREEN (St Michael)   *see* Worc Dines Green St Mich and Crown E, Rushwick *Worc*

DINGLEY (All Saints)   *see* Desborough, Brampton Ash, Dingley and Braybrooke *Pet*

DINNINGTON (St Leonard) w Laughton-en-le-Morthen and Throapham *Sheff 5* **P** *Bp and J C Athorpe Esq (jt)* **R** J E BOLTON, **C** D F DEAN-REVILL

DINNINGTON (St Matthew) *see* Ch the King *Newc*

DINNINGTON (St Nicholas) *see* Merriott w Hinton, Dinnington and Lopen *B & W*

DINSDALE (St John the Baptist) w Sockburn *Dur 8* **P** *D&C and Sherburn Hosp (alt)* **R** M D M FERGUSON

DINTING VALE (Holy Trinity) *see* Charlesworth and Dinting Vale *Derby*

DINTON (St Mary) *see* Nadder Valley *Sarum*

DINTON (St Peter and St Paul) *see* Stone w Dinton and Hartwell *Ox*

DIPTFORD (St Mary the Virgin), North Huish, Harberton, Harbertonford, Halwell and Moreleigh *Ex 13* **P** *Bp and D&C (jt)* **R** J C OUGH, **C** C M S LUFF, **Hon C** J E SPENCE, B PETTY

DIPTON (St John the Evangelist) and Leadgate *Dur 4* **P** *Bp* **V** D G HERON

DISCOED (St Michael) *see* Presteigne w Discoed, Kinsham, Lingen and Knill *Heref*

DISEWORTH (St Michael and All Angels) *see* Kegworth, Hathern, Long Whatton, Diseworth etc *Leic*

DISHLEY (All Saints) *see* Thorpe Acre w Dishley *Leic*

DISLEY (St Mary the Virgin) *Ches 16* **P** *Lord Newton* **V** M J OWENS

DISS Heywood (St James the Great) *see* Diss *Nor*

DISS (St Mary) *Nor 10* **P** *Bp* **R** A C BILLETT

DISTINGTON (Holy Spirit) *Carl 7* **P** *Earl of Lonsdale* **P-in-c** K B RICHARDSON

DITCHINGHAM (St Mary), Hedenham, Broome, Earsham, Alburgh and Denton *Nor 10* **P** *Abp, Bp, Countess Ferrers, J M Meade Esq, and St Jo Coll Cam (jt)* **R** L BUTLER, **OLM** B L CRAMP, S L CRAMP, R A KIRKPATRICK

DITCHLING (St Margaret), Streat and Westmeston *Chich 9* **P** *Bp* **R** D P WALLIS

DITTERIDGE (St Christopher) *see* Box w Hazlebury and Ditteridge *Bris*

DITTISHAM (St George) *see* Dartmouth and Dittisham *Ex*

DITTON (St Basil and All Saints) *see* Hough Green St Basil and All SS *Liv*

DITTON (St Michael) (St Thomas) *Liv 13* **P** *Bp* **V** L RILEY-DAWKIN, **OLM** J I CLARKE, D STRATFORD, L MOSS

DITTON (St Peter ad Vincula) *Roch 7* **P** *Ch Trust Fund Trust* **R** J R TERRANOVA, **OLM** P M PAYNE

DITTON PRIORS (St John the Baptist) w Neenton, Burwarton, Cleobury North, Aston Botterell, Wheathill and Loughton and Chetton *Heref 9* **P** *Exors Josephine zu Loewenstein, and Exors Viscount Boyne (jt)* **P-in-c** J N ROWLAND

DIXTON (St Peter), Wyesham, Bishopswood, Whitchurch and Ganarew *Heref 8* **P** *Bp (5 turns), Ld Chan (1 turn)* **V** K V CECIL

DOBCROSS (Holy Trinity) *see* Saddleworth *Man*

DOBWALLS (St Peter) *see* Liskeard and St Keyne *Truro*

DOCCOMBE (Chapel) *see* Moretonhampstead, Manaton, N Bovey and Lustleigh *Ex*

DOCK (Mission Church) *see* Immingham *Linc*

DOCKENFIELD (Church of the Good Shepherd) *see* Rowledge and Frensham *Guildf*

DOCKING (St Mary), the Birchams, Stanhoe and Sedgeford *Nor 16* **P** *Bp, D&C, and Mrs A J Ralli (3 turns), The Crown (1 turn)* **V** P R COOK

DOCKLOW (St Bartholomew) *see* Leominster *Heref*

DODBROOKE (St Thomas à Beckett) *see* Kingsbridge and Dodbrooke *Ex*

DODDERHILL (St Augustine) *see* Droitwich Spa *Worc*

DODDINGHURST (All Saints) *Chelmsf 7* **P** *Bp* **P-in-c** G FRITH

DODDINGTON (All Saints) *see* Quantock Coast *B & W*

DODDINGTON (St John) *see* Wybunbury w Doddington *Ches*

DODDINGTON (St John the Baptist) *see* Coreley and Doddington *Heref*

DODDINGTON (St John the Baptist), Newnham and Wychling *Cant 6* **P** *Abp, Adn, and Exors Sir John Croft Bt (jt)* **NSM** R A BIRCH

DODDINGTON (St Mary and St Michael) *see* Glendale Gp *Newc*

DODDINGTON (St Mary) w Benwick and Wimblington *Ely 11* **P** *Bp, St Jo Coll Dur, and R Raynar Esq (jt)* **P-in-c** V A FERNANDEZ

DODDINGTON (St Peter) *see* Skellingthorpe w Doddington *Linc*

DODDINGTON, GREAT (St Nicholas) and Wilby *Pet 6* **P** *Exors Lt-Col H C M Stockdale and Ld Chan (alt)* **P-in-c** C J PEARSON

DODDISCOMBSLEIGH (St Michael) *see* Tedburn St Mary, Whitestone, Oldridge etc *Ex*

DODFORD (Holy Trinity and St Mary) *see* Catshill and Dodford *Worc*

DODFORD (St Mary the Virgin) *see* Weedon Bec w Everdon and Dodford *Pet*

DODLESTON (St Mary) *Ches 2* **P** *D&C* **P-in-c** E H CLARKE

DODWORTH (St John the Baptist) *Wakef 7* **P** *V Silkstone* **V** S P RACE

DOGMERSFIELD (All Saints) *see* Hartley Wintney, Elvetham, Winchfield etc *Win*

DOGSTHORPE (Christ the Carpenter) *see* Pet Ch Carpenter *Pet*

DOLPHINHOLME (St Mark) w Quernmore and Over Wyresdale *Blackb 11* **P** *Bp and V Lanc (jt)* **V** vacant (01524) 791300

DOLTON (St Edmund King and Martyr) *Ex 20* **P** *Ch Soc Trust* **P-in-c** C A BRODRIBB, **NSM** D J URSELL

DONCASTER Holy Trinity *Sheff 8* **P** *SMF* **V** vacant (01302) 349684

DONCASTER Intake (All Saints) *Sheff 8* **P** *Bp* **V** L M WELLS

DONCASTER (St George) (St Edmund's Church Centre) *Sheff 8* **P** *Bp* **V** C M SMITH, **C** M J ROWBERRY, **NSM** D D SIRCAR

DONCASTER (St James) *Sheff 9* **P** *Hyndman's Trustees* **V** A MURRAY

DONCASTER (St Jude) *Sheff 9* **P** *Bp* **V** vacant (01302) 852057

DONCASTER (St Leonard and St Jude) *Sheff 7* **P** *The Crown* **V** N J PAY

DONCASTER (St Mary) *Sheff 8* **P** *Hyndman's Trustees* **P-in-c** R B RADLEY

DONHEAD ST ANDREW (St Andrew) *see* St Bartholomew *Sarum*

DONHEAD ST MARY (St Mary the Virgin) *as above*

DONINGTON (St Cuthbert) *see* Albrighton, Boningale and Donington *Lich*

DONINGTON (St Mary and the Holy Rood) *Linc 21* **P** *Simeon's Trustees* **V** vacant (01775) 822355

DONINGTON-ON-BAIN (St Andrew) *see* Asterby Gp *Linc*

DONISTHORPE (St John) *see* Woodfield Team *Leic*

DONNINGTON (St George) *Chich 3* **P** *Bp* **P-in-c** C R BEARD

DONNINGTON WOOD (St Matthew) *Lich 21* **P** *Bp* **V** D W WRIGHT

DONYATT (The Blessed Virgin Mary) *see* Ilminster and Distr *B & W*

DONYLAND, EAST (St Lawrence) *see* Fingringhoe w E Donyland and Abberton etc *Chelmsf*

DORCHESTER (St George) (St Mary the Virgin) (St Peter, Holy Trinity and All Saints) *Sarum 1* **P** *Patr Bd (3 turns), Ld Chan (1 turn)* **TR** H W B STEPHENS, **TV** V A THURTELL, R A BETTS, **Hon C** J H GOOD, **NSM** C TURNOCK, J M CULLIFORD, R L BASSETT, **OLM** J LACY-SMITH

DORCHESTER (St Peter and St Paul) *Ox 1* **P** *Patr Bd* **TR** S E BOOYS, **TV** N A R HAWKES, R M LATHAM, **C** D R CLEUGH, H F CLEUGH, **NSM** R M GODFREY, A F ILSLEY, **OLM** D W HAYLETT

DORDON (St Leonard) *Birm 10* **P** *V Polesworth* **V** V J HICKS

DORE (Christ Church) *Sheff 2* **P** *Sir Philip Naylor-Leyland Bt* **V** M J HUNTER

DORKING (St Martin) w Ranmore *Guildf 7* **P** *Bp* **V** R M CATTLEY, **C** M J HAYES, **NSM** D J COWAN, **OLM** L J TROMBETTI, S V PEACE

DORKING (St Paul) *Guildf 7* **P** *Ch Patr Trust* **V** P D BRYER, **NSM** J C YELLAND, **OLM** J A FIRTH

DORMANSLAND (St John) *S'wark 25* **P** *Bp* **V** G PADDICK

DORMANSTOWN (All Saints) *see* Coatham and Dormanstown *York*

DORMINGTON (St Peter) *see* Fownhope w Mordiford, Brockhampton etc *Heref*

DORMSTON (St Nicholas) *see* Inkberrow w Cookhill and Kington w Dormston *Worc*

DORNEY (St James the Less) *see* Eton w Eton Wick, Boveney and Dorney *Ox*

DORRIDGE (St Philip) *Birm 6* **P** *Bp* **V** T D HILL-BROWN, **C** H E A JOHNSTON

DORRINGTON (St Edward) w Leebotwood, Longnor, Stapleton, Smethcote and Woolstaston *Heref 11* **P** *DBP and J J C Coldwell Esq (jt)* **R** R S PAYNE

DORRINGTON (St James) *see* Digby Gp *Linc*

DORSINGTON (St Peter) *see* Pebworth, Dorsington, Honeybourne etc *Glouc*

DORSTONE (St Faith) *see* Cusop w Blakemere, Bredwardine w Brobury etc *Heref*

DORTON (St John the Baptist) *see* Bernwode *Ox*

DOSTHILL (St Paul) *Birm 10* **P** *Bp* **V** J L C SHAW

DOTTERY (St Saviour)　*see* Askerswell, Loders and Powerstock *Sarum*

DOUGLAS (All Saints) (St Thomas the Apostle) *S & M 2*　**P** *Bp*　**P-in-c** M A M WOLVERSON, I BRADY,　**NSM** L BRADY, **OLM** S A FERRIS

DOUGLAS (Christ Church) *Blackb 4*　**P** *Bp*　**P-in-c** S A GLYNN

DOUGLAS (St George) *S & M 2*　**P** *Bp*　**V** B SMITH, **NSM** R HARPER

DOUGLAS (St Matthew the Apostle) *S & M 2*　**P** *Bp* **V** D WHITWORTH

DOUGLAS (St Ninian) *S & M 2*　**P** *CPAS*　**V** vacant (01624) 676310

DOUGLAS-IN-PARBOLD (Christ Church)　*see* Douglas *Blackb*

DOULTING (St Aldhelm)　*see* Shepton Mallet w Doulting *B & W*

DOVE HOLES (St Paul)　*see* Wormhill, Peak Forest w Peak Dale and Dove Holes *Derby*

DOVECOT (Holy Spirit) *Liv 2*　**P** *Bp*　**V** J R STOTT

DOVER Buckland Valley (St Nicholas)　*see* Buckland in Dover w Buckland Valley *Cant*

DOVER (St Martin) *Cant 4*　**P** *CPAS*　**V** K G GARRETT, **OLM** P M DAY

DOVER (St Mary the Virgin) *Cant 4*　**P** *Abp, Ld Warden of Cinque Ports, and Ld Lt of Kent (jt)*　**V** D G RIDLEY, **NSM** P A GODFREY, S J CAROLAN-EVANS

DOVER (St Peter and St Paul)　*see* Charlton-in-Dover *Cant*

DOVERCOURT (All Saints)　*see* Harwich Peninsula *Chelmsf*

DOVERDALE (St Mary)　*see* Ombersley w Doverdale *Worc*

DOVERIDGE (St Cuthbert), Scropton, Sudbury and Somersal Herbert *Derby 14*　**P** *Duke of Devonshire* **P-in-c** J J VICKERSTAFF,　**NSM** P R JONES, J M LEGH

DOVERSGREEN (St Peter)　*see* Reigate St Luke w Doversgreen *S'wark*

DOWDESWELL (St Michael)　*see* Sevenhampton w Charlton Abbots, Hawling etc *Glouc*

DOWLAND (St Peter)　*see* Iddesleigh w Dowland *Ex*

DOWLES Button Oak (St Andrew)　*see* Ribbesford w Bewdley and Dowles *Worc*

DOWLISHWAKE (St Andrew)　*see* Ilminster and Distr *B & W*

DOWN, East (St John the Baptist)　*see* Shirwell, Loxhore, Kentisbury, Arlington, etc *Ex*

DOWN AMPNEY (All Saints)　*see* Fairford Deanery *Glouc*

DOWN HATHERLEY (St Mary and Corpus Christi)　*see* Twigworth, Down Hatherley, Norton, The Leigh etc *Glouc*

DOWN ST MARY (St Mary the Virgin)　*see* N Creedy *Ex*

DOWNDERRY (St Nicholas)　*see* St Germans *Truro*

DOWNE (St Mary Magdalene)　*see* Cudham and Downe *Roch*

DOWNEND (Christ Church) (Church Centre) *Bris 5*　**P** *Peache Trustees*　**V** J L VICKERY,　**C** P J NASH, C J DOBSON

DOWNHAM (St Barnabas) *S'wark 4*　**P** *Bp*　**V** J D S FRENCH

DOWNHAM (St Leonard)　*see* Chatburn and Downham *Blackb*

DOWNHAM (St Leonard)　*see* Ely *Ely*

DOWNHAM (St Luke)　*see* Catford (Southend) and Downham *S'wark*

DOWNHAM (St Margaret) w South Hanningfield *Chelmsf 9* **P** *Bp*　**R** S A ROBERTSON

DOWNHAM, NORTH (St Mark)　*see* Catford (Southend) and Downham *S'wark*

DOWNHAM MARKET (St Edmund) and Crimplesham w Stradsett *Ely 9*　**P** *Bp*　**R** J W MATHER,　**C** C M MILLER

DOWNHEAD (All Saints)　*see* Leigh upon Mendip w Stoke St Michael *B & W*

DOWNHOLME (St Michael and All Angels)　*see* Richmond w Hudswell and Downholme and Marske *Ripon*

DOWNLEY (St James the Great)　*see* High Wycombe *Ox*

DOWNS Benefice, The *Win 3*　**P** *Ld Chan (1 turn), Bp and Marquess Camden (1 turn)*　**R** J MONTAGUE,　**C** S P RASON, **NSM** J A AUSSANT

DOWNS BARN and NEAT HILL (Community Church)　*see* Stantonbury and Willen *Ox*

DOWNSFOOT　*see* Selling w Throwley, Sheldwich w Badlesmere etc *Cant*

DOWNSHIRE HILL (St John)　*see* Hampstead St Jo Downshire Hill Prop Chpl *Lon*

DOWNSIDE (St Michael's Chapel)　*see* E Horsley and Ockham w Hatchford and Downside *Guildf*

DOWNSWAY (All Souls Worship Centre)　*see* Southwick *Chich*

DOWNTON (St Giles)　*see* Wigmore Abbey *Heref*

DOWNTON (St Lawrence)　*see* Forest and Avon *Sarum*

DOWSBY (St Andrew)　*see* Billingborough Gp *Linc*

DOXEY (St Thomas and St Andrew)　*see* Castle Town *Lich*

DOXFORD (St Wilfrid) *Dur 16*　**P** *Bp*　**P-in-c** J MORGAN

DOYNTON (Holy Trinity)　*see* Wick w Doynton and Dyrham *Bris*

DRAKES BROUGHTON (St Barnabas)　*see* Stoulton w Drake's Broughton and Pirton etc *Worc*

DRAUGHTON (St Augustine)　*see* Skipton H Trin *Bradf*

DRAUGHTON (St Catherine)　*see* Maidwell w Draughton, Lamport w Faxton *Pet*

DRAX (St Peter and St Paul)　*see* Carlton and Drax *York*

DRAYCOT *Bris 6*　**P** *Bp, D&C Sarum, and R W Neeld Esq (jt)* **P-in-c** G W HEWITT,　**NSM** E M BONE

DRAYCOTT (St Mary)　*see* Wilne and Draycott w Breaston *Derby*

DRAYCOTT (St Peter)　*see* Rodney Stoke w Draycott *B & W*

DRAYCOTT IN THE CLAY (St Augustine)　*see* Hanbury, Newborough, Rangemore and Tutbury *Lich*

DRAYCOTT-LE-MOORS (St Margaret) w Forsbrook *Lich 6* **P** *Bp*　**R** D C BICKERSTETH

DRAYTON (Iron Mission Room)　*see* Chaddesley Corbett and Stone *Worc*

DRAYTON (St Catherine)　*see* Langport Area *B & W*

DRAYTON (St Leonard and St Catherine)　*see* Dorchester *Ox*

DRAYTON (St Margaret) *Nor 2*　**P** *Bp*　**R** D WELLS

DRAYTON (St Peter)　*see* Ironstone *Ox*

DRAYTON (St Peter) Berks *Ox 10*　**P** *Bp* **P-in-c** J I MIDWINTER

DRAYTON, EAST (St Peter)　*see* Dunham w Darlton, Ragnall, Fledborough etc *S'well*

DRAYTON, LITTLE (Christ Church) *Lich 18*　**P** *V Drayton in Hales*　**P-in-c** H G SNOOK

DRAYTON, WEST (St Martin) *Lon 24*　**P** *Bp*　**V** O J FIELD

DRAYTON, WEST (St Paul)　*see* Gamston w Eaton and W Drayton *S'well*

DRAYTON BASSETT (St Peter) *Lich 4*　**P** *Bp*　**R** H J BAKER, Hon **C** M R F MACLACHLAN,　**NSM** R G DAVIES

DRAYTON-BEAUCHAMP (St Mary the Virgin)　*see* Aston Clinton w Buckland and Drayton Beauchamp *Ox*

DRAYTON IN HALES (St Mary) *Lich 18*　**P** *C C Corbet Esq* **P-in-c** M P TANNER,　**OLM** C SIMPSON

DRAYTON PARSLOW (Holy Trinity)　*see* Stewkley w Soulbury and Drayton Parslow *Ox*

DRESDEN (Resurrection) *Lich 12*　**P** *V Blurton* **P-in-c** P J MOCKFORD

DREWSTEIGNTON (Holy Trinity)　*see* Chagford, Drewsteignton, Hittisleigh etc *Ex*

DRIFFIELD (St Mary)　*see* Fairford Deanery *Glouc*

DRIFFIELD, GREAT (All Saints) and LITTLE (St Peter) *York 10*　**P** *Abp*　**V** M R G SMITH

DRIGG (St Peter)　*see* Seascale and Drigg *Carl*

DRIGHLINGTON (St Paul) *Wakef 8*　**P** *Bp*　**P-in-c** S M ASKEY

DRIMPTON (St Mary)　*see* Beaminster Area *Sarum*

DRINGHOUSES (St Edward the Confessor) *York 7*　**P** *Abp* **V** C W M BALDOCK,　**NSM** S M COLLIER

DRINKSTONE (All Saints)　*see* Woolpit w Drinkstone *St E*

DROITWICH SPA (St Andrew w St Mary de Witton) (St Nicholas) (St Peter) (St Richard) *Worc 8*　**P** *Bp* **TR** S K BANYARD,　**TV** D C OWEN, D A CHAPLIN, **NSM** R HOLDEN, S L BARRETT, A D MORRIS

DRONFIELD (St John the Baptist) w Holmesfield *Derby 5* **P** *Ld Chan*　**TR** B GREEN,　**TV** C D I REES, W R EARDLEY, **NSM** R DOVE

DROPMORE (St Anne)　*see* Taplow and Dropmore *Ox*

DROXFORD (St Mary and All Saints) *Portsm 1*　**P** *Bp* **P-in-c** S H HOLT

DROYLSDEN (St Andrew) *Man 17*　**P** *Bp* **OLM** J A HEMSWORTH

DROYLSDEN (St Martin) *Man 17*　**P** *Bp* **P-in-c** D A WILLIAMS

DROYLSDEN (St Mary) (St John) *Man 17*　**P** *Bp* **P-in-c** A M BAILIE,　**OLM** E M ROBERTS

DRY DODDINGTON (St James)　*see* Claypole *Linc*

DRY DRAYTON (St Peter and St Paul) *Ely 1*　**P** *MMCET* **P-in-c** C A COLLINS

DRY SANDFORD (St Helen)　*see* Wootton and Dry Sandford *Ox*

DRYBROOK (Holy Trinity), Lydbrook and Ruardean *Glouc 2* **P** *Prime Min and Bp (alt)*　**R** N R BROMFIELD,　**Hon C** F H LONG,　**OLM** W J CAMMELL

DRYPOOL (St Columba) (St John) *York 14*　**P** *Patr Bd* **TR** W B G MATHER,　**TV** C J GRUNDY, J V TAYLOR, **C** L A HILLIARD

DUCKLINGTON (St Bartholomew) *Ox 8*　**P** *DBP* **P-in-c** R J EDY

DUCKMANTON (St Peter and St Paul)　*see* Calow and Sutton cum Duckmanton *Derby*

DUDDENHOE END (The Hamlet Church)　*see* Heydon, Gt and Lt Chishill, Chrishall etc *Chelmsf*

DUDDESTON (St Matthew)　*see* Aston and Nechells *Birm*

DUDDINGTON (St Mary)   *see* Barrowden and Wakerley w S Luffenham etc *Pet*

DUDDON (St Peter)   *see* Tarvin *Ches*

DUDLESTON (St Mary)   *see* Criftins w Dudleston and Welsh Frankton *Lich*

DUDLEY (St Andrew)   *see* Netherton St Andr *Worc*

DUDLEY (St Augustine) (St Barnabas) (St Francis) (St James) (St Thomas and St Luke) *Worc* 9   **P** *Patr Bd*
TR A N ATTWOOD,   **TV** C M BROWNE, A ST L J WICKENS

DUDLEY (St Edmund King and Martyr) *Worc* 9   **P** *Bp*
V *vacant* (01384) 252532

DUDLEY (St John) Kate's Hill *Worc* 9   **P** *Bp*
P-in-c D GEORGE

DUDLEY (St Paul)   *see* Weetslade *Newc*

DUDLEY WOOD (St John) *Worc* 9   **P** *V Netherton*
V J A OLIVER,   **C** M RUTTER

DUFFIELD (St Alkmund) and Little Eaton *Derby* 11   **P** *Patr Bd*
V M A PICKLES,   **C** D E BARNSLEY

DUFTON (St Cuthbert)   *see* Heart of Eden *Carl*

DUKINFIELD (St John) (St Alban Mission Church) *Ches* 14
P *R Stockport St Mary*   **V** T J HAYES

DUKINFIELD (St Luke) *Ches* 14   **P** *Bp*
P-in-c D L SCHOFIELD

DUKINFIELD (St Mark) *Ches* 14   **P** *Bp*   **P-in-c** A C COX

DULCOTE (All Saints)   *see* Wells St Cuth w Wookey Hole *B & W*

DULLINGHAM (St Mary)   *see* Raddesley Gp *Ely*

DULOE (St Cuby), Herodsfoot, Morval and St Pinnock *Truro* 12
P *Ld Chan, Ch Soc Trust, and Ball Coll Ox (by turn)*
P-in-c A C HODGE

DULVERTON (All Saints) and Brushford *B & W* 16   **P** *D&C and Bp (jt)*   **R** J M THOROGOOD,   **C** J C RICHARDS,
Hon C J H GRAY

DULWICH (St Barnabas) *S'wark* 9   **P** *Bp*   **V** D L GWILLIAMS,
Hon C A G BUCKLEY

DULWICH (St Clement) St Peter *S'wark* 9   **P** *Bp*
V M E A COULTER

DULWICH, EAST (St John the Evangelist) *S'wark* 9   **P** *Ripon Coll Cuddesdon*   **V** C L J RICHARDSON,   **Hon C** R A SHAW,
J M W SEDGWICK,   **OLM** A CLARKE

DULWICH, NORTH (St Faith) *S'wark* 9   **P** *Bp*
V H W DAWES

DULWICH, SOUTH (St Stephen) *S'wark* 9   **P** *Dulwich Coll*
V B G SCHUNEMANN,   **C** N D DAVIES

DULWICH, WEST (All Saints) *S'wark* 12   **P** *Bp*
V D J STEPHENSON,   **C** M E BOWDEN

DULWICH, WEST (Emmanuel) *S'wark* 12   **P** *Bp*
V K G A ANSAH,   **Hon C** O O SOTONWA,   **OLM** H O KIMBER

DUMBLETON (St Peter)   *see* Winchcombe *Glouc*

DUMMER (All Saints)   *see* Cliddesden and Ellisfield w Farleigh Wallop etc *Win*

DUNCHIDEOCK (St Michael and All Angels) *Ex* 6
P *Mrs J M Michelmore*   **P-in-c** G K MAYER

DUNCHURCH (St Peter) *Cov* 6   **P** *Bp*   **V** *vacant* (01788) 810274

DUNCTON (Holy Trinity) *Chich* 11   **P** *Lord Egremont*
R *vacant*

DUNDRY (St Michael)   *see* Chew Magna w Dundry and Norton Malreward *B & W*

DUNHAM, GREAT (St Andrew) and LITTLE (St Margaret), w Great and Little Fransham and Sporle *Nor* 14   **P** *Hertf Coll Ox, Ch Soc Trust, Magd Coll Cam, and DBP (by turn)*
C S J SMITH, D W A RIDER

DUNHAM MASSEY (St Margaret) (St Mark) (All Saints)
Ches 10   **P** *J G Turnbull Esq*   **V** J J E SUTTON

DUNHAM-ON-THE-HILL (St Luke)   *see* Helsby and Dunham-on-the-Hill *Ches*

DUNHAM-ON-TRENT (St Oswald) w Darlton, Ragnall, Fledborough and East Drayton *S'well* 5   **P** *Bp (2 turns), D&C York (1 turn)*   **P-in-c** J M JESSON

DUNHOLME (St Chad)   *see* Welton and Dunholme w Scothern *Linc*

DUNKERTON (All Saints)   *see* Camerton w Dunkerton, Foxcote and Shoscombe *B & W*

DUNKESWELL (Holy Trinity) (St Nicholas), Luppitt, Sheldon and Upottery *Ex* 5   **P** *MMCET, Bp, and D&C (jt)*
V N J WALL

DUNMOW, GREAT (St Mary the Virgin) and Barnston
Chelmsf 18   **P** *Ld Chan (2 turns), CPAS (1 turn)*
R D S AINGE,   **NSM** R DREW

DUNMOW, LITTLE (St Mary the Virgin)   *see* Felsted and Lt Dunmow *Chelmsf*

DUNNINGTON (not known)   *see* Salford Priors *Cov*

DUNNINGTON (St Nicholas)   *see* Beeford w Frodingham and Foston *York*

DUNNINGTON (St Nicholas) *York* 2   **P** *Abp*
P-in-c N W R BIRD,   **NSM** L E LUDKIN

DUNS TEW (St Mary Magdalene)   *see* Westcote Barton w Steeple Barton, Duns Tew etc *Ox*

DUNSBY (All Saints)   *see* Ringstone in Aveland Gp *Linc*

DUNSCROFT (St Edwin) *Sheff* 10   **P** *Bp*   **V** A WATSON

DUNSDEN (All Saints)   *see* Shiplake w Dunsden and Harpsden *Ox*

DUNSFOLD (St Mary and All Saints) and Hascombe *Guildf* 2
P *Bp and SMF (jt)*   **P-in-c** P M JENKINS

DUNSFORD (St Mary)   *see* Tedburn St Mary, Whitestone, Oldridge etc *Ex*

DUNSFORTH (St Mary)   *see* Aldborough w Boroughbridge and Roecliffe *Ripon*

DUNSLAND (Mission Church)   *see* Ashwater, Halwill, Beaworthy, Clawton etc *Ex*

DUNSLEY (Mission Room)   *see* Whitby w Ruswarp *York*

DUNSMORE (Chapel of the Ressurection)   *see* Ellesborough, The Kimbles and Stoke Mandeville *Ox*

DUNSOP BRIDGE (St George)   *see* Slaidburn *Bradf*

DUNSTABLE (St Augustine of Canterbury) (St Fremund the Martyr) (St Peter) *St Alb* 12   **P** *Bp*   **TR** R J ANDREWS,
TV M C HATHAWAY, P M TRIMMER,   **C** V M GOODMAN

DUNSTALL (St Mary)   *see* Barton under Needwood w Dunstall and Tatenhill *Lich*

DUNSTAN (St Leonard)   *see* Penkridge *Lich*

DUNSTAN (St Peter)   *see* Metheringham w Blankney and Dunston *Linc*

DUNSTER (St George), Carhampton, Withycombe w Rodhuish, Timberscombe and Wootton Courtenay *B & W* 16   **P** *Bp*
R K L BRANT,   **NSM** M N ALLSO

DUNSTON (Church House)   *see* Newbold w Dunston *Derby*

DUNSTON (St Nicholas) w (Christ Church) *Dur* 13   **P** *Bp*
V K TEASDALE

DUNSTON (St Remigius)   *see* Stoke H Cross w Dunston, Arminghall etc *Nor*

DUNSWELL (St Faith's Mission Church)   *see* Hull St Jo Newland *York*

DUNTERTON (All Saints)   *see* Milton Abbot, Dunterton, Lamerton etc *Ex*

DUNTISBOURNE ABBOTS (St Peter)   *see* Brimpsfield w Birdlip, Syde, Daglingworth etc *Glouc*

DUNTISBOURNE ROUS (St Michael and All Angels)   *as above*

DUNTON (St Martin)   *see* Schorne *Ox*

DUNTON (St Mary Magdalene) w Wrestlingworth and Eyeworth *St Alb* 11   **P** *Ld Chan and DBP (alt)*   **P-in-c** L C DEW

DUNTON BASSETT (All Saints)   *see* Upper Soar *Leic*

DUNWICH (St James)   *see* Yoxmere *St E*

DURHAM (St Giles) *Dur* 1   **P** *D&C*   **V** A B BARTLETT,
NSM R A M THOMAS

DURHAM (St Margaret of Antioch) and Neville's Cross St John *Dur* 1   **P** *D&C*   **R** B T HUISH,   **NSM** N C CHATER

DURHAM (St Nicholas) *Dur* 1   **P** *CPAS*   **V** J S BELLAMY,
C S V MELLOR,   **NSM** D V DAY, P S JOHNSON, C H PATTERSON

DURHAM (St Oswald King and Martyr) and Shincliffe *Dur* 1
P *D&C*   **P-in-c** P Z KASHOURIS,   **C** P J REGAN

DURHAM NORTH (St Cuthbert) *Dur* 1   **P** *Patr Bd*
TR R W LAWRANCE,   **TV** J THORNS, C A DICK,
NSM O R OMOLE, E STRAFFORD

DURLEIGH (St Hugh)   *see* Bridgwater H Trin and Durleigh *B & W*

DURLEY (Holy Cross) *Portsm* 1   **P** *Ld Chan*   **R** P J F GOODEY,
NSM R E SCHOFIELD

DURNFORD (St Andrew)   *see* Woodford Valley *Sarum*

DURRINGTON (All Saints) *Sarum* 13   **P** *D&C Win*
P-in-c M T P ZAMMIT,   **C** C G FOX,   **NSM** R A BUSSEY

DURRINGTON (St Symphorian) *Chich* 5   **P** *Bp*
V N A TAYLOR

DURSLEY (St James the Great) *Glouc* 6   **P** *Bp*
R J C G BROMLEY,   **C** E K DENNO,   **NSM** I N GARDNER

DURSTON (St John the Baptist)   *see* Alfred Jewel *B & W*

DURWESTON (St Nicholas)   *see* Pimperne, Stourpaine, Durweston and Bryanston *Sarum*

DUSTON Team, The (St Francis) (St Luke) *Pet* 4   **P** *Bp*
TV A W BAINES,   **NSM** H C WILSON

DUSTON, NEW (Mission Church)   *see* Duston Team *Pet*

DUTTON (Licensed Room)   *see* Antrobus, Aston by Sutton, Lt Leigh etc *Ches*

DUXFORD (St Peter) w St John *Ely* 5   **P** *Bp*   **R** *vacant* (01223) 832137

DYMCHURCH (St Peter and St Paul) w Burmarsh and Newchurch *Cant* 12   **P** *Abp*   **R** *vacant* (01303) 872150

DYMOCK (St Mary the Virgin)   *see* Redmarley D'Abitot, Bromesberrow, Pauntley etc *Glouc*

DYRHAM (St Peter) *see* Wick w Doynton and Dyrham *Bris*
EAGLE (All Saints) *see* Swinderby *Linc*
EAKRING (St Andrew) *S'well 15* **P** *DBP* **R** *vacant*
EALING (All Saints) *Lon 22* **P** *Bp* **V** N P HENDERSON,
  Hon C A GRIFFITHS
EALING (Ascension) *see* Hanger Hill Ascension and W
  Twyford St Mary *Lon*
EALING (Christ the Saviour) *Lon 22* **P** *Bp* **V** A F DAVIS
EALING (St Barnabas) *Lon 22* **P** *Bp* **V** D G DEBOYS
EALING (St Mary) *Lon 22* **P** *Bp* **V** S D PAYNTER,
  C T J M READ-SMITH, **NSM** M P J DEL RIO
EALING (St Paul) *Lon 22* **P** *Bp* **V** M P MELLUISH,
  C B D HINGSTON, **NSM** T R SAIET
EALING (St Peter) Mount Park *Lon 22* **P** *Bp* **V** M POWELL,
  NSM M J JOACHIM, J O A CHOUFAR, N K STEPHENSON
EALING (St Stephen) Castle Hill *Lon 22* **P** *D&C St Paul's*
  V S M NEWBOLD
EALING, WEST (St John) w St James *Lon 22* **P** *Bp*
  V P S MACKENZIE, **C** C M DUNK, S F METRY, S A HITCHINER
EALING COMMON (St Matthew) *Lon 22* **P** *Bp*
  V P G WATKINS
EARBY (All Saints) w Kelbrook *Bradf 7* **P** *Bp* **V** H FIELDEN
EARDISLAND (St Mary the Virgin) *see* Kingsland w
  Eardisland, Aymestrey etc *Heref*
EARDISLEY (St Mary Magdalene) w Bollingham, Willersley,
  Brilley, Michaelchurch, Whitney, Winforton, Almeley and
  Kinnersley *Heref 5* **P** *Patr Bd* **R** M J SMALL
EARL SHILTON (St Simon and St Jude) w Elmesthorpe *Leic 10*
  P *Bp* **V** G GITTINGS
EARL SOHAM (St Mary) *see* Mid Loes *St E*
EARL STERNDALE (St Michael and All Angels)
  see Hartington, Biggin and Earl Sterndale *Derby*
EARL STONHAM (St Mary) *see* Creeting St Mary, Creeting
  St Peter etc *St E*
EARLESFIELD (The Epiphany) *see* Grantham, Earlesfield
  Linc
EARLESTOWN (St John the Baptist) *see* Newton *Liv*
EARLEY (St Nicolas) *Ox 15* **P** *DBP* **V** N M WARWICK
EARLEY (St Peter) *Ox 15* **P** *DBP* **R** R R D SPEARS,
  C M R C THORNE
EARLEY Trinity *Ox 15* **P** *DBP* **P-in-c** J SALMON
EARLEY, LOWER Trinity Church Local Ecumenical
  Partnership *Ox 15* vacant
EARLHAM (St Anne) (St Elizabeth) (St Mary) *Nor 3* **P** *Bp and*
  Trustees (jt) **R** E M CONSTANTINE, **C** D A COUSINS,
  OLM R M A HOUGHTON, K M BROWN
EARLS BARTON (All Saints) *Pet 6* **P** *DBP* **V** *vacant*
  (01604) 810447
EARLS COLNE (St Andrew) *see* Halstead Area *Chelmsf*
EARL'S COURT (St Cuthbert) (St Matthias) *Lon 12*
  P *Trustees* **V** J VINE
EARL'S COURT (St Philip) *see* Kensington St Mary Abbots w
  Ch Ch and St Phil *Lon*
EARLS CROOME (St Nicholas) *see* Upton-on-Severn, Ripple,
  Earls Croome etc *Worc*
EARL'S HEATON *see* Dewsbury *Wakef*
EARL'S HEATON (St Peter) *as above*
EARLSDON (St Barbara) *Cov 3* **P** *Bp* **V** H J WILD
EARLSFIELD (St Andrew) *S'wark 18* **P** *Bp* **V** J BROWN,
  Hon C R C PEERS, **NSM** V A HACKETT
EARLSFIELD (St John the Divine) *S'wark 18* **P** *Bp*
  V E C ROBERTS
EARLY (St Bartholomew) *see* Reading St Luke w St Bart *Ox*
EARNLEY (not known) and East Wittering *Chich 3* **P** *Bp*
  (2 turns), Bp Lon (1 turn) **R** S J DAVIES
EARNSHAW BRIDGE (St John) *see* Leyland St Jo *Blackb*
EARSDON (St Alban) and Backworth *Newc 5* **P** *Bp*
  V J A FRANCE
EARSHAM (All Saints) *see* Ditchingham, Hedenham, Broome,
  Earsham etc *Nor*
EARSWICK, NEW (St Andrew) *see* Huntington *York*
EARTHAM (St Margaret) *see* Slindon, Eartham and
  Madehurst *Chich*
EASBY (Chapel) *see* Gt Ayton w Easby and Newton under
  Roseberry *York*
EASBY (St Agatha) w Skeeby and Brompton on Swale and Bolton
  on Swale *Ripon 2* **P** *Bp* **V** L A CHEETHAM
EASEBOURNE (St Mary) *Chich 10* **P** *Rathbone Trust Co and*
  Cowdray Trust (jt) **V** D B WELSMAN, **NSM** A M HALLIWELL
EASINGTON (All Saints) *see* Withernsea w Owthorne and
  Easington etc *York*
EASINGTON (All Saints) w Liverton *York 16* **P** *Ld Chan*
  P-in-c M E GARDNER
EASINGTON (St Hugh) *see* Banbury St Hugh *Ox*
EASINGTON (St Mary), Easington Colliery and South Hetton
  Dur 2 **P** *Bp* **R** B E CLOSE, **Hon C** S R DYER

EASINGTON (St Peter) *see* Ewelme, Brightwell Baldwin,
  Cuxham w Easington *Ox*
EASINGTON COLLIERY (The Ascension) *see* Easington,
  Easington Colliery and S Hetton *Dur*
EASINGWOLD (St John the Baptist and All Saints) w Raskelf
  York 3 **P** *Abp* **V** J HARRISON
EAST *see also under substantive place name*
EAST DEAN (All Saints), Singleton, and West Dean *Chich 13*
  P *Bp (2 turns), D&C (1 turn)* **R** R T E B WOODS
EAST DEAN (St Simon and St Jude) w Friston and Jevington
  Chich 16 **P** *Duke of Devonshire (1 turn), D&C (2 turns)*
  R D A BAKER
EAST DEAN (St Winifred) *see* Lockerley and E Dean w E and
  W Tytherley *Win*
EAST FERRY (St Mary the Virgin) *see* Scotter w E Ferry *Linc*
EAST HAM (St Bartholomew) (St Mary Magdalene) w Upton
  Park *Chelmsf 3* **P** *Patr Bd* **TV** Q B D PEPPIATT, J FREEMAN,
  C F B QUIST
EAST HAM (St George and St Ethelbert) *Chelmsf 3* **P** *Bp*
  V D T HAOKIP
EAST HAM (St Paul) *Chelmsf 3* **P** *Ch Patr Trust*
  V M L PLAYLE
EAST LANE (St Mary) *see* W Horsley *Guildf*
EAST MARSHLAND *Ely 14* **P** *Bp and MMCET (1 turn),*
  Pemb Coll Cam (2 turns), Prime Min (1 turn), and Ld Chan
  (1 turn) **V** D E PENNY, **NSM** A M HALLIWELL
EAST ORCHARD (St Thomas) *see* Shaston *Sarum*
EAST WINCH (All Saints) *see* Gayton, Gayton Thorpe, E
  Walton, E Winch etc *Nor*
EASTBOURNE (All Saints) *Chich 16* **P** *Trustees*
  V W R LOVATT, **C** N S CORNELL
EASTBOURNE (All Souls) *Chich 16* **P** *Ch Soc Trust*
  V N H GREEN, **C** J G SCRIVENER
EASTBOURNE (Christ Church) (St Philip) *Chich 16* **P** *Bp and*
  V Eastbourne (jt) **V** N P CHATFIELD, **C** C R GORING
EASTBOURNE (Holy Trinity) *Chich 16* **P** *V Eastbourne*
  V J A CHEESEMAN, **C** M A LLOYD
EASTBOURNE (St Andrew) *Chich 16* **P** *Bp* **V** D J KING
EASTBOURNE (St Elisabeth) *Chich 16* **P** *Bp* **V** D J GILLARD
EASTBOURNE (St John) Meads *Chich 16* **P** *Trustees*
  V *vacant* (01323) 721105
EASTBOURNE (St Mary) *Chich 16* **P** *Bp* **V** T O MENDEL,
  C N P HAIGH
EASTBOURNE (St Michael and All Angels) Ocklynge *Chich 16*
  P *V Eastbourne* **V** *vacant* (01323) 645740
EASTBOURNE (St Richard of Chichester) *see* Langney *Chich*
EASTBOURNE (St Saviour and St Peter) *Chich 16* **P** *Keble*
  Coll Ox **V** J T GUNN
EASTBOURNE The Haven *see* The Haven CD *Chich*
EASTBURY (St James the Great) and East Garston *Ox 14*
  P *Bp and Ch Ch Ox (alt)* **P-in-c** A W CUMBERLIDGE
EASTCHURCH (All Saints) w Leysdown and Harty *Cant 15*
  P *Abp and Keble Coll Ox (jt)* **NSM** B BIRCH
EASTCOMBE (St Augustine) *see* Bussage *Glouc*
EASTCOTE (St Lawrence) *Lon 24* **P** *Bp* **V** S DANDO,
  C R S PHILLIPS
EASTER, HIGH (St Mary the Virgin) and Good Easter w
  Margaret Roding *Chelmsf 18* **P** *Bp Lon, Trustees*
  R K Shepherd Esq, and D&C St Paul's (by turn) **R** *vacant*
  (01245) 231429
EASTERGATE (St George) *see* Aldingbourne, Barnham and
  Eastergate *Chich*
EASTERN GREEN (St Andrew) *Cov 3* **P** *R Allesley*
  P-in-c G P SMITH, **C** M CATLEY
EASTERTON (St Barnabas) *see* The Lavingtons, Cheverells,
  and Easterton *Sarum*
EASTFIELD (Holy Nativity) *see* Cayton w Eastfield *York*
EASTGATE (All Saints) *see* Upper Weardale *Dur*
EASTHAM (St Mary the Blessed Virgin) (St Peter's Chapel)
  (Chapel of the Holy Spirit) *Ches 9* **P** *D&C* **V** E A GLOVER,
  C S E BURTON
EASTHAM (St Peter and St Paul) *see* Teme Valley S *Worc*
EASTHAMPSTEAD (St Michael and St Mary Magdalene)
  Ox 11 **P** *Ch Ch Ox* **R** G S COLE, **C** B WHITLEY,
  P M BESTLEY
EASTHOPE (St Peter) *see* Wenlock *Heref*
EASTHORPE (St Mary the Virgin) *see* Copford w Easthorpe
  and Messing w Inworth *Chelmsf*
EASTINGTON (St Michael and All Angels), Frocester,
  Haresfield, Moreton Valence, Standish and Whitminster
  Glouc 5 **P** *Bp and J F Bengough Esq (1 turn), DBP and Exors*
  Lady Mary Cooper (1 turn) **R** R J R AMYS
EASTLEACH (St Andrew) *see* Fairford Deanery *Glouc*
EASTLEIGH (All Saints) *Win 10* **P** *Bp* **V** R P DAVIES
EASTLEIGH Nightingale Avenue (St Francis) *see* Eastleigh
  Win

EASTLING (St Mary) w Ospringe and Stalisfield w Otterden
Cant 6 **P** *The Crown* **P-in-c** C R PINCHBECK,
OLM A M CHEESEMAN
EASTMOORS (St Mary Magdalene) *see* Helmsley *York*
EASTNEY (St Margaret) *Portsm 6* **P** *Bp* **V** R M SMITH
EASTNOR (St John the Baptist) *see* Ledbury *Heref*
EASTOFT (St Bartholomew) *see* The Marshland *Sheff*
EASTOKE (St Andrew) *see* Hayling Is St Andr *Portsm*
EASTON (All Hallows) *Bris 3* **P** R Bris St Steph
P-in-c R D HOYAL
EASTON (All Saints) *see* Brandeston w Kettleburgh and Easton
St E
**EASTON (Holy Trinity w St Gabriel and St Lawrence and
St Jude)** *Bris 3* **P** *Trustees* **P-in-c** P J NOTT,
NSM D J P MOORE
EASTON (St Mary) *see* Itchen Valley *Win*
EASTON (St Paul) *see* Westbury sub Mendip w Easton *B & W*
EASTON (St Peter) *see* E Leightonstone *Ely*
EASTON (St Peter), Colton, Marlingford and Bawburgh *Nor 17*
P *Bp, D&C, Adn, and Sir Edward Evans-Lombe (jt)*
P-in-c A H REYNOLDS
EASTON, GREAT (St Andrew) *see* Six Saints circa Holt *Leic*
EASTON, GREAT (St John and St Giles) *see* Broxted w
Chickney and Tilty etc *Chelmsf*
EASTON, LITTLE (not known) *as above*
EASTON GREY (not known) *see* Sherston Magna, Easton
Grey, Luckington etc *Bris*
EASTON IN GORDANO (St George) *see* Pill, Portbury and
Easton-in-Gordano *B & W*
EASTON MAUDIT (St Peter and St Paul) *see* Wollaston w
Strixton and Bozeat etc *Pet*
EASTON NESTON (St Mary) *see* Towcester w Caldecote and
Easton Neston etc *Pet*
EASTON ON THE HILL (All Saints) *see* Ketton, Collyweston,
Easton-on-the-Hill etc *Pet*
EASTON ROYAL (Holy Trinity) *see* Pewsey and Swanborough
Sarum
EASTOVER (St John the Baptist) *see* Bridgwater St Jo *B & W*
EASTRINGTON (St Michael) *see* Howden *York*
EASTROP (St Mary) *Win 4* **P** *CPAS* **R** C L HAWKINS,
C C J KEANE, **NSM** C E WEST
**EASTRY (St Mary Blessed Virgin) and Northbourne w
Tilmanstone and Betteshanger w Ham** *Cant 8* **P** *Abp and Lord
Northbourne (jt)* **P-in-c** D A DEER, **OLM** J A PILCHER
EASTTHORPE (St Paul) *see* Mirfield *Wakef*
EASTVILLE (St Anne w St Mark and St Thomas) *Bris 3* **P** *Bp*
V P J HAYWARD
EASTVILLE (St Paul) *see* Stickney Gp *Linc*
EASTWELL (St Michael) *see* Ironstone Villages *Leic*
EASTWICK (St Botolph) *see* High Wych and Gilston w
Eastwick *St Alb*
EASTWOOD (St David) *Chelmsf 10* **P** *Bp* **V** P D JOYCE
EASTWOOD (St Laurence and All Saints) *Chelmsf 10*
P *Ld Chan* **V** N L RANSOM
EASTWOOD (St Mary) *S'well 4* **P** J N Plumptre Esq
P-in-c D A STEVENSON
EATON (All Saints) *see* Gamston w Eaton and W Drayton
S'well
EATON (Christ Church) *see* Brereton w Eaton and Hulme
Walfield *Ches*
EATON (Christ Church) *Nor 3* **P** D&C **V** P H RICHMOND,
Hon C A TYLER
EATON (St Andrew) *Nor 3* **P** D&C **V** P R RODD
EATON (St Denys) *see* Ironstone Villages *Leic*
EATON (St Thomas) *see* Tarporley *Ches*
EATON, LITTLE (St Paul) *see* Duffield and Lt Eaton *Derby*
EATON BISHOP (St Michael and All Angels) *see* Kingstone w
Clehonger, Eaton Bishop *Heref*
EATON BRAY (St Mary the Virgin) w Edlesborough *St Alb 12*
P *DBP* **V** *vacant (01525) 220261*
EATON HASTINGS (St Michael and All Angels) *see* Gt
Coxwell w Buscot, Coleshill etc *Ox*
EATON SOCON (St Mary) *St Alb 11* **P** E W Harper Esq
V T S ROBB, **C** D R MILLER
EATON SQUARE (St Peter) *see* Pimlico St Pet w Westmr Ch
Ch *Lon*
EATON-UNDER-HEYWOOD (St Edith) *see* Hope Bowdler w
Eaton-under-Heywood *Heref*
EBBERSTON (St Mary) *see* Thornton Dale w Allerston,
Ebberston etc *York*
EBBESBOURNE WAKE (St John the Baptist) *see* Chalke
Valley *Sarum*
EBCHESTER (St Ebba) *Dur 4* **P** *Bp* **R** A D WHIPP
EBERNOE (Holy Trinity) *see* N Chapel w Ebernoe *Chich*
EBONY (St Mary the Virgin) *see* Wittersham w Stone-in-Oxney
and Ebony *Cant*

EBREY WOOD (Mission Chapel) *see* Wrockwardine Deanery
Lich
EBRINGTON (St Eadburgha) *see* Chipping Campden w
Ebrington *Glouc*
ECCHINSWELL (St Lawrence) *see* Burghclere w Newtown
and Ecchinswell w Sydmonton *Win*
ECCLES (St Mary the Virgin) *see* Quidenham Gp *Nor*
ECCLES (St Mary the Virgin) (St Andrew) *Man 2* **P** *Patr Bd
and Ld Chan (alt)* **TR** E A CROFTON, **TV** A-L CRITCHLOW,
A C YOUNG
ECCLESALL (St Gabriel) *see* Greystones *Sheff*
ECCLESALL BIERLOW (All Saints) *Sheff 2* **P** *Dean*
V S D BESSANT, **C** E H STEELE, **NSM** S A P HUNTER
ECCLESFIELD (St Mary the Virgin) *Sheff 3* **P** *DBF*
V P I IMPEY, **C** S HAMMERSLEY
ECCLESFIELD (St Paul) *see* Sheff St Paul *Sheff*
ECCLESHALL (Holy Trinity) *Lich 7* **P** *Bp* **V** J H GRAHAM
ECCLESHILL (St Luke) *Bradf 3* **P** V *Bradf* **V** J P HARTLEY
ECCLESTON (Christ Church) *see* Eccleston *Liv*
ECCLESTON (St Luke) *as above*
ECCLESTON (St Mary the Virgin) *Blackb 4* **P** *DBP*
P-in-c B J WARD
ECCLESTON (St Mary the Virgin) and Pulford *Ches 2* **P** *Duke
of Westmr* **R** I M THOMAS
ECCLESTON (St Thomas) *Liv 10* **P** *Bp* **V** *vacant (01744)*
22295
ECCLESTON Team, The *Liv 10* **P** *Patr Bd* **TR** J H WELCH,
TV P G DAY, W FORSTER
ECCLESTON, GREAT *see* Copp w Inskip *Blackb*
ECCLESTON PARK (St James) *see* Eccleston *Liv*
ECKINGTON (Holy Trinity) *Worc 4* **P** D&C *Westmr*
V S K RENSHAW
ECKINGTON (St Peter and St Paul) and Ridgeway *Derby 3*
P *The Crown and Patr Bd (alt)* **R** *vacant (01246) 432196*
ECKINGTON, UPPER (St Luke) *see* Eckington and Ridgeway
Derby
ECTON (St Mary Magdalene) *Pet 6* **P** *The Crown*
P-in-c C J PEARSON
EDALE (Holy and Undivided Trinity) *Derby 2* **P** *Rep
Landowners* **P-in-c** A J G MURRAY-LESLIE
EDBURTON (St Andrew) *see* Poynings w Edburton,
Newtimber and Pyecombe *Chich*
EDEN, Gelt and Irthing Team Ministry, The *Carl 2* **P** *Patr Bd*
TR A BRADBROOK, **TV** E GOUGH, E A JOHNSEN,
C N J H REEVES
EDEN PARK (St John the Baptist) *see* Beckenham St Jo *Roch*
EDENBRIDGE (St Peter and St Paul) *Roch 11* **P** *Bp*
V S A J MITCHELL, **C** R JONES
EDENFIELD (not known) *see* Ramsbottom and Edenfield
Man
EDENHALL (St Cuthbert) *see* Cross Fell Gp *Carl*
EDENHAM (St Michael) w Witham on the Hill and Swinstead
Linc 14 **P** *Baroness Willoughby de Eresby, Ld Chan, and Bp
(by turn)* **V** A T HAWES, **NSM** I K WILLIAMS
EDENSOR (St Paul) *see* Longton Hall *Lich*
EDENSOR (St Peter) *see* Beeley and Edensor *Derby*
EDGBASTON (St Augustine) *Birm 2* **P** *Bp*
V M R E TOMLINSON
EDGBASTON (St Bartholomew) *Birm 2* **P** *Sir Euan
Anstruther-Gough-Calthorpe Bt* **P-in-c** A J JOYCE
EDGBASTON (St George w St Michael) (St Michael's Hall)
Birm 2 **P** *Sir Euan Anstruther-Gough-Calthorpe Bt*
NSM J F KENNEDY
EDGBASTON (St Germain) *Birm 2* **P** *Trustees*
V H A SCRIVEN, **C** D E D'SOUZA
EDGBASTON (St Mary and St Ambrose) *see* Balsall Heath
and Edgbaston SS Mary and Ambrose *Birm*
EDGCOTE (St James) *see* Culworth w Sulgrave and Thorpe
Mandeville etc *Pet*
EDGCOTT (St Michael) *see* The Claydons and Swan *Ox*
EDGE, THE (St John the Baptist) *see* Painswick, Sheepscombe,
Cranham, The Edge etc *Glouc*
EDGE HILL (St Cyprian) (St Mary) *Liv 3* **P** *Simeon's Trustees
and Bp (jt)* **P-in-c** M D COATES
EDGE HILL (St Dunstan) *see* St Luke in the City *Liv*
EDGE HILL (St Mary) *see* Edge Hill St Cypr w St Mary *Liv*
EDGEFIELD (School Room) *see* Worsley *Man*
EDGEFIELD (St Peter and St Paul) *see* Lt Barningham,
Blickling, Edgefield etc *Nor*
EDGELEY (St Mark) (St Matthew) and Cheadle Heath *Ches 18*
P *Bp* **V** D T BREWSTER, **C** B E STATHAM,
NSM J M JOHNSON
EDGESIDE (St Anne) *see* Rossendale Middle Valley *Man*
EDGEWORTH (St Mary) *see* Brimpsfield w Birdlip, Syde,
Daglingworth etc *Glouc*

EDGMOND (St Peter) w Kynnersley and Preston Wealdmoors *Lich 16* **P** *Bp, Adn Salop, Chan Lich, MMCET, and Preston Trust Homes Trustees (jt)* **R** W E WARD, **NSM** D N H STOKES-HARRISON

EDGTON (St Michael the Archangel) *see* Bishop's Castle w Mainstone, Lydbury N etc *Heref*

EDGWARE (St Alphage) *see* Hendon St Alphage *Lon*

EDGWARE (St Andrew) (St Margaret) (St Peter) *Lon 15* **P** *MMCET* **TR** M D CLARK, **TV** P E BERRY, **C** S W J REA

EDINGALE (Holy Trinity) *see* Clifton Campville w Edingale and Harlaston *Lich*

EDINGLEY (St Giles) w Halam *S'well 14* **P** *Bp* **P-in-c** D MCCOULOUGH, **NSM** E C KIRK

EDINGTHORPE (All Saints) *see* N Walsham and Edingthorpe *Nor*

EDINGTON (St George) *see* W Poldens *B & W*

EDINGTON (St Mary, St Katharine and All Saints) *see* Bratton, Edington and Imber, Erlestoke etc *Sarum*

EDITH WESTON (St Mary) w North Luffenham and Lyndon w Manton *Pet 12* **P** *Baroness Willoughby de Eresby, Sir John Conant Bt, and Em Coll Cam (by turn)* **P-in-c** S MITCHELL, **Hon C** R A MASON

EDITHMEAD (Mission) *see* Burnham *B & W*

EDLASTON (St James) *see* Brailsford w Shirley, Osmaston w Edlaston etc *Derby*

EDLINGHAM (St John the Baptist w Bolton Chapel) *see* Whittingham and Edlingham w Bolton Chapel *Newc*

EDLINGTON (St Helen) *see* Hemingby *Linc*

EDLINGTON (St John the Baptist) *Sheff 9* **P** *Bp* **V** W J STOKOE

EDMONDSHAM (St Nicholas) *see* Cranborne w Boveridge, Edmondsham etc *Sarum*

EDMONTON (All Saints) (St Michael) *Lon 18* **P** *D&C St Paul's* **V** S J OWEN, **C** K M SALA

EDMONTON (St Aldhelm) *Lon 18* **P** *V Edmonton All SS* **V** D R BOLSTER

EDMONTON (St Alphege) *Lon 18* **P** *Bp* **V** R C KNOWLING, **C** A C NEWCOMBE, **NSM** N H ASBRIDGE

EDMONTON (St Mary w St John) (St Mary's Centre) *Lon 18* **P** *D&C St Paul's* **NSM** J A NOWAK

EDMONTON (St Matthew) *see* Ponders End St Matt *Lon*

EDMONTON (St Peter w St Martin) *Lon 18* **P** *Bp* **V** C D MITCHELL

EDMUNDBYERS (St Edmund) *see* Blanchland w Hunstanworth and Edmundbyers etc *Newc*

EDSTASTON (St Mary the Virgin), Fauls, Prees, Tilstock and Whixall *Lich 22* **P** *R Wem, R Whitchurch, and Bp (jt)* **V** D J POMERY, **OLM** S E ARMSTRONG

EDSTON (St Michael) *see* Kirby Misperton w Normanby, Edston and Salton *York*

EDVIN LOACH (St Mary) w Tedstone Delamere, Tedstone Wafer, Upper Sapey, Wolferlow and Whitbourne *Heref 2* **P** *Bp, BNC Ox, Sir Francis Winnington Bt, and D P Barneby Esq (jt)* **P-in-c** D P HOWELL

EDWALTON (Holy Rood) *S'well 8* **P** *Exors Major R P Chaworth-Musters* **P-in-c** P W WENHAM, **NSM** P A EDWARDS

EDWARDSTONE (St Mary the Virgin) *see* Boxford, Edwardstone, Groton etc *St E*

EDWINSTOWE (St Mary) *S'well 2* **P** *Earl Manvers' Trustees* **P-in-c** A D LITTLEWOOD, **C** A FLETCHER

EDWYN RALPH (St Michael) *see* Bredenbury *Heref*

EFFINGHAM (St Lawrence) w Little Bookham *Guildf 10* **P** *Keble Coll Ox* **V** A J K MACKENZIE

EFFORD (St Paul) *see* Plymouth Em, St Paul Efford and St Aug *Ex*

EGDEAN (St Bartholomew) *Chich 11* **P** *Bp* **P-in-c** T J WRIGHT

EGERTON (St James) w Pluckley *Cant 10* **P** *Abp* **R** *vacant* (01233) 756224

EGG BUCKLAND (St Edward) *Ex 23* **P** *Ld Chan* **V** T R J DICKENS

EGGESFORD (All Saints) *see* Burrington, Chawleigh, Cheldon, Chulmleigh etc *Ex*

EGGINTON (St Michael) *see* Ouzel Valley *St Alb*

EGGINTON (St Wilfrid) *see* Etwall w Egginton *Derby*

EGGLESCLIFFE (St John the Baptist) *Dur 10* **P** *Bp* **R** T J D OLLIER

EGGLESTON (Holy Trinity) *Dur 7* **P** *The Crown* **V** *vacant*

EGHAM (St John the Baptist) *Guildf 11* **P** *Ch Soc Trust* **V** J R WATTLEY, **C** C W HOLMES, **NSM** T M SUDWORTH

EGHAM HYTHE (St Paul) *Guildf 11* **P** *Bp* **P-in-c** M D A ROPER, **NSM** S M LOVEDAY

EGLETON (St Edmund) *see* Oakham, Hambleton, Egleton, Braunston and Brooke *Pet*

EGLINGHAM (St Maurice) *see* Glendale Gp *Newc*

EGLOSHAYLE (St Petroc) *see* St Breoke and Egloshayle *Truro*

EGLOSKERRY (St Petrock and St Keri), North Petherwin, Tremaine and Tresmere *Truro 9* **P** *Duchy of Cornwall and Bp (alt)* **V** G PENGELLY, **NSM** G DARBY

EGMANTON (Our Lady of Egmanton) *S'well 3* **P** *SMF* **V** C C LEVY

EGREMONT (St Mary and St Michael) and Haile *Carl 5* **P** *Patr Bd* **TR** T R LEE, **TV** L D GRAY, **NSM** B J JEAPES, L V FULKER

EGTON (St Hilda) *see* Middle Esk Moor *York*

EGTON-CUM-NEWLAND (St Mary the Virgin) and Lowick and Colton *Carl 9* **P** *Patr Bd* **V** G WEMYSS, **NSM** J HENSON

EIGHT ASH GREEN (All Saints) *see* Fordham *Chelmsf*

EIGHTON BANKS (St Thomas) *Dur 12* **P** *Bp* **P-in-c** D M SNOWBALL

ELBERTON (St John) *see* Alveston and Littleton-on-Severn w Elberton *Bris*

ELBURTON (St Matthew) *Ex 24* **P** *CPAS* **V** R C H THOMAS, **C** J J MARLOW

ELDENE (not known) *see* Swindon Dorcan *Bris*

ELDERSFIELD (St John the Baptist) *see* Berrow w Pendock, Eldersfield, Hollybush etc *Worc*

ELDON (St Mark) *see* Coundon and Eldon *Dur*

ELDWICK (St Lawrence) *see* Bingley All SS *Bradf*

ELFORD (St Peter) *Lich 4* **P** *Bp* **C-in-c** S J LUMBY, **NSM** D BURGESS

ELHAM (St Mary the Virgin) w Denton and Wootton *Cant 5* **P** *Abp and Mert Coll Ox (jt)* **P-in-c** D J ADLINGTON

ELING (St Mary) *see* Totton *Win*

ELING, NORTH (St Mary) *see* Copythorne *Win*

ELKESLEY (St Giles) w Bothamsall *S'well 5* **P** *SMF* **V** *vacant* (01777) 838293

ELKINGTON, SOUTH (All Saints) *see* Louth *Linc*

ELKSTONE (St John the Baptist) *see* Alstonfield, Butterton, Ilam etc *Lich*

ELKSTONE (St John the Evangelist) *see* Coberley, Cowley, Colesbourne and Elkstone *Glouc*

ELLACOMBE (Christ Church) *see* Torquay St Jo and Ellacombe *Ex*

ELLAND (All Saints) (St Mary the Virgin) *Wakef 2* **P** *Bp, Adn Halifax, and V Halifax (jt)* **TR** D BURROWS, **C** R A CHAPMAN, M ASKEY, **OLM** P E CHADWICK

ELLASTONE (St Peter) *see* Denstone w Ellastone and Stanton *Lich*

ELLEL (St John the Evangelist) w Shireshead *Blackb 11* **P** *V Cockerham w Winmarleigh and Glasson* **P-in-c** S J C CORLEY, **C** G S PEARSON

ELLENBROOK (St Mary's Chapel) *see* Worsley *Man*

ELLENHALL (St Mary) *see* Chebsey, Creswell, Ellenhall, Ranton etc *Lich*

ELLERBURN (St Hilda) *see* Thornton Dale w Allerston, Ebberston etc *York*

ELLERBY (St James) *see* Skirlaugh w Long Riston, Rise and Swine *York*

ELLERKER (not known) *see* S Cave and Ellerker w Broomfleet *York*

ELLESBOROUGH (St Peter and St Paul), The Kimbles and Stoke Mandeville *Ox 28* **P** *Chequers Trustees, The Hon I Hope-Morley, and D&C Linc (by turn)* **NSM** J E HENDERSON

ELLESMERE (St Mary) *Lich 17* **P** *Bp* **V** P J EDGE

ELLESMERE (St Peter) *Sheff 3* **P** *Bp* **V** *vacant* 0114-276 2555

ELLESMERE PORT *Ches 9* **P** *Bp* **R** G B MCGUINNESS, **NSM** G J WELCH, S N HUGHES

ELLINGHAM (St Mary) *see* Gillingham w Geldeston, Stockton, Ellingham etc *Nor*

ELLINGHAM (St Mary and All Saints) and Harbridge and Hyde w Ibsley *Win 9* **P** *Earl of Normanton and Keble Coll Ox (jt)* **V** M L RICHES

ELLINGHAM (St Maurice) *Newc 7* **P** *D&C Dur* **V** B C HURST

ELLINGHAM, GREAT (St James), LITTLE (St Peter), Rockland All Saints, Rockland St Peter and Shropham w Snetterton *Nor 11* **P** *Bp, Major E H C Garnier, and CCC Cam (jt)* **P-in-c** K J REEVE

ELLINGTON (All Saints) *see* E Leightonstone *Ely*

ELLISFIELD (St Martin) *see* Cliddesden and Ellisfield w Farleigh Wallop etc *Win*

ELLISTOWN (St Christopher) *see* Hugglescote w Donington, Ellistown and Snibston *Leic*

ELLOUGHTON (St Mary) and Brough w Brantingham *York 13* **P** *Abp and D&C Dur (jt)* **V** R J WALKER, **C** D T PHILLIPS

ELM (All Saints)   *see* Fen Orchards *Ely*
ELM (St Mary Magdalene)   *see* Mells w Buckland Dinham, Elm, Whatley etc *B & W*
ELM PARK (St Nicholas) Hornchurch *Chelmsf 2*   **P** *Bp*
V R W FINCH,   **NSM** R MORTON
ELMBRIDGE (St Mary)   *see* Elmley Lovett w Hampton Lovett and Elmbridge etc *Worc*
ELMDON (St Nicholas)   *see* Heydon, Gt and Lt Chishill, Chrishall etc *Chelmsf*
ELMDON (St Nicholas) (St Stephen's Church Centre) (Valley Church Centre) *Birm 11*   **P** *Ch Trust Fund Trust*
R P R CARTER,   **NSM** C L CARTER
ELMDON HEATH (St Francis of Assisi)   *see* Solihull *Birm*
ELMERS END (St James)   *see* Beckenham St Jas *Roch*
ELMESTHORPE (St Mary)   *see* Earl Shilton w Elmesthorpe *Leic*
ELMHAM, NORTH (St Mary), Billingford, Bintree, Guist, Twyford and Worthing *Nor 22*   **P** *Bp, Earl of Leicester, G & C Coll Cam, and DBP (jt)*   **R** N C H VARNON
ELMHAM, SOUTH (St Cross) (St James) (St Margaret) (St Peter) (St Michael and All Angels) and Ilketshall *St E 14*   **P** *Bp (3 turns), Ld Chan (1 turn), and Duke of Norfolk (1 turn)*
R R H P THORNBURGH,   **NSM** C S LEE
ELMHURST (Mission Room)   *see* Lich St Chad *Lich*
ELMLEY   *see* Emley *Wakef*
ELMLEY CASTLE (St Mary) w Bricklehampton and the Combertons *Worc 4*   **P** *Bp*   **R** T J HENDERSON
ELMLEY LOVETT (St Michael) w Hampton Lovett and Elmbridge w Rushdock *Worc 8*   **P** *Bp and Ch Coll Cam (alt)*
R *vacant* (01299) 251798
ELMORE (St John the Baptist)   *see* Hardwicke and Elmore w Longney *Glouc*
ELMSALL, NORTH (St Margaret)   *see* Badsworth *Wakef*
ELMSALL, SOUTH (St Mary the Virgin) *Wakef 10*   **P** *Bp*
V P M WITTS
ELMSETT (St Peter) w Aldham, Hintlesham, Chattisham and Kersey *St E 3*   **P** *Bp, MMCET, and St Chad's Coll Dur (jt)*
R T E FFRENCH,   **C** J P FFRENCH
ELMSTEAD (St Anne and St Laurence) *Chelmsf 20*   **P** *Jes Coll Cam*   **P-in-c** T C PLATTS
ELMSTED (St James the Great)   *see* Stone Street Gp *Cant*
ELMSTONE (not known)   *see* Wingham w Elmstone and Preston w Stourmouth *Cant*
ELMSTONE HARDWICKE (St Mary Magdalene)   *see* N Cheltenham *Glouc*
ELMSWELL (St John) *St E 10*   **P** *MMCET*
R M I MCNAMARA,   **C** D M RUDDICK
ELMTON (St Peter) *Derby 3*   **P** *Bp*   **V** D J HULL
ELSDON (St Cuthbert)   *see* N Tyne and Redesdale *Newc*
ELSECAR (Holy Trinity)   *see* Worsbrough w Elsecar *Sheff*
ELSENHAM (St Mary the Virgin)   *see* Henham and Elsenham w Ugley *Chelmsf*
ELSFIELD (St Thomas of Canterbury)   *see* Marston w Elsfield *Ox*
ELSHAM (All Saints)   *see* N Wolds Gp *Linc*
ELSING (St Mary)   *see* Lyng, Sparham, Elsing, Bylaugh, Bawdeswell etc *Nor*
ELSON (St Thomas) *Portsm 3*   **P** *DBP*   **P-in-c** S P RUNDELL,
NSM M A HAY
ELSTEAD (St James) *Guildf 4*   **P** *Adn Surrey*   **R** W D LANG,
OLM P R J MUIR
ELSTED (St Paul)   *see* Harting w Elsted and Treyford cum Didling *Chich*
ELSTERNWICK (St Laurence)   *see* Burton Pidsea and Humbleton w Elsternwick *York*
ELSTON (All Saints) w Elston Chapelry *S'well 3*
P J C S Darwin Esq   **P-in-c** D HOLLIS
ELSTOW (St Mary and St Helena) *St Alb 13*   **P** *Patr Bd*
TR J R CROCKER,   **TV** S T SMITH
ELSTREE (St Nicholas) and Borehamwood *St Alb 1*   **P** *Patr Bd (3 turns), Ld Chan (1 turn)*   **TR** T G WARR,
TV R C A LESLIE, A-M L RENSHAW, K J GARDINER
ELSWICK (St Stephen) (St Paul) *Newc 4*   **P** *Ch Soc Trust and Trustees (jt)*   **V** G R CURRY
ELSWICK, HIGH (St Philip)   *see* Newc St Phil and St Aug and St Matt w St Mary *Newc*
ELSWORTH (Holy Trinity)   *see* Papworth *Ely*
ELTHAM (Holy Trinity) *S'wark 3*   **P** *Bp*   **P-in-c** B E WARD,
NSM T N ALEXANDER-YATES, S J CHARLES
ELTHAM (St Barnabas) *S'wark 3*   **P** *Bp*   **P-in-c** S COOK,
Hon C G E STEVENSON,   **NSM** S E BLACKALL
ELTHAM (St John the Baptist) *S'wark 3*   **P** *DBP*   **V** J E NEAL
ELTHAM (St Saviour) *S'wark 3*   **P** *Bp*   **P-in-c** W J SAUNDERS
ELTHAM, NEW (All Saints) *S'wark 3*   **P** *Bp*   **P-in-c** A S ROSE
ELTHAM PARK (St Luke) *S'wark 3*   **P** *Bp*   **P-in-c** E CRANMER

ELTISLEY (St Pandionia and St John the Baptist)   *see* Papworth *Ely*
ELTON (All Saints)   *see* S Darley, Elton and Winster *Derby*
ELTON (All Saints)   *see* Kirklees Valley *Man*
ELTON (All Saints) w Stibbington and Water Newton *Ely 15*
P *Sir Peter Proby Bt, Sir Philip Naylor-Leyland Bt, and Keble Coll Ox (jt)*   **P-in-c** M J INGHAM
ELTON (St John) *Dur 10*   **P** *St Chad Coll Dur*   **V** *vacant* (01642) 586179
ELTON (St Mary the Virgin)   *see* Wigmore Abbey *Heref*
ELTON (St Stephen) *Man 10*   **P** *V Elton All SS*   **V** *vacant* 0161-764 9894
ELTON-ON-THE-HILL (St Michael)   *see* Cropwell Bishop w Colston Bassett, Granby etc *S'well*
ELVASTON (St Bartholomew)   *see* Aston on Trent, Elvaston, Weston on Trent etc *Derby*
ELVEDEN (St Andrew and St Patrick)   *see* Brandon and Santon Downham w Elveden etc *St E*
ELVETHAM HEATH Local Ecumenical Partnership *Guildf 1*
Min D G M PRICE
ELVINGTON (Holy Trinity)   *see* Derwent Ings *York*
ELWICK HALL (St Peter)   *see* Hart w Elwick Hall *Dur*
ELWORTH (St Peter) and Warmingham *Ches 11*
P *V Sandbach, Q H Crewe Esq and J C Crewe Esq (alt)*
R D J PAGE,   **C** J R L PRIOR
ELY (Holy Trinity w St Mary) (St Mary) (St Peter) *Ely 8*   **P** *Patr Bd*
TR A J HULME,   **TV** M HARPER,   **Hon C** M J M HUGHES,
NSM J I HULME
EMBERTON (All Saints)   *see* Lamp *Ox*
EMBLETON (Holy Trinity) w Rennington and Rock *Newc 6*
P *Mert Coll Ox*   **V** P D HARRATT
EMBLETON (St Cuthbert)   *see* Cockermouth Area *Carl*
EMBROOK (Community of St Nicholas)   *see* Wokingham St Paul *Ox*
EMBSAY (St Mary the Virgin) w Eastby *Bradf 7*   **P** *R Skipton H Trin*   **P-in-c** A P BOTWRIGHT,   **C** J W DANIELS,
NSM A L SPRAGGETT
EMERY DOWN (Christ Church)   *see* Lyndhurst and Emery Down and Minstead *Win*
EMLEY (St Michael the Archangel) *Wakef 6*   **P** *Lord Savile*
P-in-c C E BULLIMORE
EMMANUEL Team Ministry, The *Wakef 1*   **P** *Patr Bd*
TR S GOTT,   **TV** S J BUCHANAN,   **NSM** D KENT,
OLM C A SYKES
EMMAUS Parish Team, The *Leic 1*   **P** *Bp*   **R** J APPLEBY,
TV S KUMAR
EMMER GREEN (St Barnabas) w Caversham Park *Ox 15*
P *Bp and Ch Ox (jt)*   **R** D E CHANDLER,
OLM M L DIMMICK
EMNETH (St Edmund)   *see* Fen Orchards *Ely*
EMPINGHAM (St Peter) and Exton w Horn w Whitwell *Pet 12*
P *Bp and Earl of Gainsborough (alt)*   **C** F B SOLMAN,
S MITCHELL,   **Hon C** R A MASON
EMPSHOTT (Holy Rood)   *see* Greatham w Empshott and Hawkley w Prior's Dean *Portsm*
EMSCOTE (All Saints)   *see* Warwick *Cov*
EMSWORTH (St James)   *see* Warblington w Emsworth *Portsm*
ENBORNE (St Michael and All Angels)   *see* W Woodhay w Enborne, Hampstead Marshall etc *Ox*
ENDCLIFFE (St Augustine) *Sheff 2*   **P** *Ch Burgesses*
P-in-c I W DRAFFAN
ENDERBY (St John the Baptist) w Lubbesthorpe and Thurlaston *Leic 7*   **P** *Bp and F B Drummond Esq*   **P-in-c** S J DAVIES
ENDON (St Luke)   *see* Bagnall w Endon *Lich*
ENFIELD (Christ Church) Trent Park *Lon 18*   **P** *Ch Trust Fund Trust*   **V** R D JAMES,   **C** A J WADSWORTH, T W C LAKE
ENFIELD (St Andrew) *Lon 18*   **P** *Trin Coll Cam*   **V** M M EDGE,
C L P BEADLE
ENFIELD (St George) *Lon 18*   **P** *Bp*   **V** C J FULLER
ENFIELD (St James) (St Barnabas) *Lon 18*   **P** *V Enfield*
V S LEADER,   **NSM** M S LUNN
ENFIELD (St John the Baptist)   *see* Clay Hill St Jo and St Luke *Lon*
ENFIELD (St Luke)   *as above*
ENFIELD (St Mark)   *see* Bush Hill Park St Mark *Lon*
ENFIELD (St Matthew)   *see* Ponders End St Matt *Lon*
ENFIELD (St Michael and All Angels) *Lon 18*   **P** *V Enfield*
P-in-c S TAYLOR
ENFIELD (St Peter and St Paul) *Lon 18*   **P** *Bp*
V J C VAUGHAN
ENFIELD (St Stephen)   *see* Bush Hill Park St Steph *Lon*
ENFIELD CHASE (St Mary Magdalene) *Lon 18*   **P** *Bp*
V G J GILES,   **NSM** J W FISH
ENFORD (All Saints)   *see* Avon Valley *Sarum*
ENGLEFIELD (St Mark)   *see* Theale and Englefield *Ox*

ENGLEFIELD GREEN (St Jude) *Guildf 11*   **P** *Bp*
  V M R EWBANK
ENGLISH BICKNOR (St Mary)   *see* Forest of Dean Ch Ch w
  English Bicknor *Glouc*
ENGLISHCOMBE (St Peter)   *see* Bath St Barn w Englishcombe
  B & W
ENHAM ALAMEIN (St George)   *see* Knight's Enham and
  Smannell w Enham Alamein *Win*
ENMORE (St Michael)   *see* Aisholt, Enmore, Goathurst,
  Nether Stowey etc *B & W*
ENMORE GREEN (St John the Evangelist)   *see* Shaston *Sarum*
ENNERDALE (St Mary)   *see* Lamplugh w Ennerdale *Carl*
ENSBURY PARK (St Thomas) *Sarum 7*   **P** *Bp*   **V** S A EVANS
ENSTONE (St Kenelm)   *see* Chase *Ox*
ENVILLE (St Mary the Virgin)   *see* Kinver and Enville *Lich*
EPPERSTONE (Holy Cross) *S'well 15*   **P** *Bp, Ld Chan, and*
  C P L Francklin Esq (by turn)   **P-in-c** A R GILES,
  NSM M N TAYLOR
EPPING District (All Saints) (St John the Baptist) *Chelmsf 24*
  P *Patr Bd*   **TR** G CONNOR,   **TV** B C MORRISON
EPSOM (St Barnabas) *Guildf 9*   **P** *Bp*   **V** M C PRESTON
EPSOM (St Martin) (St Stephen on the Downs) *Guildf 9*   **P** *Bp*
  V S J TALBOTT,   **NSM** C A CASE
EPSOM COMMON (Christ Church) *Guildf 9*   **P** *Bp*
  V A J FACEY,   **C** P M DICKIN,   **OLM** S A CURTIS
EPWELL (St Anne)   *see* Wykeham *Ox*
EPWORTH Group, The (St Andrew) *Linc 1*   **P** *Prime Min*
  (2 turns), Ld Chan (1 turn)   **P-in-c** I R S WALKER
ERCALL, HIGH (St Michael and All Angels)
  see Wrockwardine Deanery *Lich*
ERDINGTON Christ the King *Birm 8*   **P** *Bp*   **V** R R SOUTER,
  C L M GASTON
ERDINGTON Team Ministry, The (St Barnabas) (St Chad)
  Birm 8   **P** *Patr Bd*   **TR** F C EVANS,   **TV** N M A TRAYNOR,
  NSM E BLAIR-CHAPPELL, J N WANYOIKE, P K ZAIDI-CROSSE
ERIDGE GREEN (Holy Trinity)   *see* Frant w Eridge *Chich*
ERISWELL (St Laurence and St Peter)   *see* Mildenhall *St E*
ERITH (Christ Church) *Roch 15*   **P** *Bp*   **V** J DRAYCOTT
ERITH (St John the Baptist) *Roch 15*   **P** *Bp*   **P-in-c** R J IRETON
ERITH (St Paul) Northumberland Heath *Roch 15*   **P** *CPAS*
  V G CLARKE
ERLESTOKE (Holy Saviour)   *see* Bratton, Edington and Imber,
  Erlestoke etc *Sarum*
ERMINE (St John)   *see* Linc St Jo *Linc*
ERMINGTON (St Peter and St Paul) and Ugborough *Ex 21*
  P *Prime Min (1 turn), Bp and Grocers' Co (3 turns)*
  V N M HUNT
ERNESETTLE (St Aidan) *Ex 22*   **P** *Bp*   **P-in-c** T THORP,
  C D R BAILEY
ERPINGHAM (St Mary) w Calthorpe, Ingworth, Aldborough,
  Thurgarton and Alby w Thwaite *Nor 19*   **P** *Bp, Lord Walpole,*
  Gt Hosp Nor, Mrs S M Lilly, and DBP (by turn)
  R B T FAULKNER
ERRINGDEN *Wakef 3*   **P** *Bp and V Halifax (jt)*
  V J T ALLISON,   **NSM** A MAUDE, N K WHITE
ERWARTON (St Mary the Virgin)   *see* Shoreline *St E*
ERYHOLME (St Mary)   *see* E Richmond *Ripon*
ESCOMB (no dedication) *Dur 6*   **P** *Bp*   **V** *vacant* (01388)
  602861
ESCOT (St Philip and St James)   *see* Feniton and Escot *Ex*
ESCRICK (St Helen) and Stillingfleet w Naburn *York 2*   **P** *Abp,*
  D&C, and N C Forbes Adam Esq (jt)   **R** R M KIRKMAN
ESH (St Michael and All Angels) *Dur 1*   **P** *Prime Min*
  V M J PEERS
ESHER (Christ Church) (St George) *Guildf 8*   **P** *Wadh Coll Ox*
  R W A J ALLBERRY,   **OLM** H E KEMPSTER
ESHOLT (St Paul)   *see* Guiseley w Esholt *Bradf*
ESK, LOWER *York 22*   **P** *Abp*   **V** D S COOK
ESK MOOR, MIDDLE *York 22*   **P** *Abp*
  V C M HADDON-REECE
ESKDALE (St Catherine) (St Bega's Mission), Irton, Muncaster
  and Waberthwaite *Carl 5*   **P** *Bp, Adn W Cumberland,*
  Mrs P Gordon-Duff-Pennington, and P Stanley Esq (jt)
  P-in-c A C BAKER
ESSENDINE (St Mary the Virgin)   *see* Ryhall w Essendine and
  Carlby *Pet*
ESSENDON (St Mary the Virgin)   *see* Lt Berkhamsted and
  Bayford, Essendon etc *St Alb*
ESSINGTON (St John the Evangelist) *Lich 2*   **P** *Bp,*
  R Bushbury, R Wednesfield, and Simeon's Trustees (jt)
  C J M THOMAS
ESTON (Christ Church) w Normanby *York 18*   **P** *Abp*
  TR J G BLAKELEY
ESTOVER (Christ Church) *Ex 23*   **P** *Bp*   **P-in-c** T R J DICKENS
ETAL (St Mary the Virgin)   *see* Ford and Etal *Newc*

ETCHILHAMPTON (St Andrew)   *see* Bishop's Cannings, All
  Cannings etc *Sarum*
ETCHING HILL (The Holy Spirit)   *see* Brereton and Rugeley
  Lich
ETCHINGHAM (Assumption and St Nicholas) *Chich 15*   **P** *Bp*
  R R DIXON
ETHERLEY (St Cuthbert) *Dur 6*   **P** *Bp*   **R** *vacant* (01388)
  832350
ETON (St John the Evangelist) w Eton Wick, Boveney and
  Dorney *Ox 23*   **P** *Eton Coll and Mrs J M Palmer (jt)*
  V L J HOLT
ETON WICK (St John the Baptist)   *see* Eton w Eton Wick,
  Boveney and Dorney *Ox*
ETTINGSHALL (Holy Trinity) *Lich 28*   **P** *Bp*   **V** A J JONES
ETTINGTON (Holy Trinity and St Thomas of Canterbury)
  see Stourdene Gp *Cov*
ETTON (St Mary) w Dalton Holme *York 8*   **P** *Lord Hotham*
  R *vacant* (01430) 810735
ETTON (St Stephen) w Helpston and Maxey *Pet 11*   **P** *Sir Philip*
  Naylor-Leyland Bt (2 turns), D&C (1 turn)
  P-in-c H P GEISOW
ETWALL (St Helen) w Egginton *Derby 14*   **P** *Bp, Sir Henry*
  Every Bt, Major J W Chandos-Pole, and DBP (by turn)
  NSM P A SHORT, K WOOD
EUSTON (St Genevieve)   *see* Blackbourne *St E*
EUXTON (not known) *Blackb 4*   **P** *Bp*   **V** J G RILEY
EVE HILL (St James the Great)   *see* Dudley TM *Worc*
EVEDON (St Mary)   *see* Ruskington Gp *Linc*
EVENLEY (St George)   *see* Aynho and Croughton w Evenley
  etc *Pet*
EVENLODE (St Edward King and Martyr)   *see* Broadwell,
  Evenlode, Oddington, Adlestrop etc *Glouc*
EVENWOOD (St Paul) *Dur 7*   **P** *Bp*   **P-in-c** K STEVENTON
EVERCREECH (St Peter) w Chesterblade and Milton Clevedon
  B & W 2   **P** *DBP*   **P-in-c** P N RAPSEY,   **NSM** R F REAKES
EVERDON (St Mary)   *see* Weedon Bec w Everdon and Dodford
  Pet
EVERINGHAM (St Everilda)   *see* Holme and Seaton Ross Gp
  York
EVERSDEN, GREAT (St Mary)   *see* Haslingfield w Harlton
  and Gt and Lt Eversden *Ely*
EVERSDEN, LITTLE (St Helen)   *as above*
EVERSHOLT (St John the Baptist)   *see* Woburn w Eversholt,
  Milton Bryan, Battlesden etc *St Alb*
EVERSHOT (St Osmund)   *see* Melbury *Sarum*
EVERSLEY (St Mary)   *see* Darby Green and Eversley *Win*
EVERTON (Holy Trinity), Mattersey, Clayworth and Gringley-
  on-the-Hill *S'well 1*   **P** *Bp and Ld Chan (alt)*
  P-in-c J P SMITHURST
EVERTON (St George) *Liv 3*   **P** *Bp*   **P-in-c** K E WHARTON,
  NSM I D CASSIDY
EVERTON (St Mary)   *see* Gamlingay and Everton *Ely*
EVERTON (St Mary)   *see* Milford *Win*
EVERTON (St Peter) (St John Chrysostom) (Emmanuel) *Liv 3*
  P *Patr Bd*   **R** H CORBETT,   **C** E F LOUDON
EVESBATCH (St Andrew)   *see* Frome Valley *Heref*
EVESHAM (All Saints w St Lawrence) w Norton and Lenchwick
  Worc 1   **P** *Bp and D&C (jt)*   **V** A SPURR
EVINGTON (St Denys) *Leic 1*   **P** *Bp*   **V** J G RILEY   [*sic*]   S B HEYGATE
EVINGTON (St Stephen)   *see* Twigworth, Down Hatherley,
  Norton, The Leigh etc *Glouc*
EVINGTON, NORTH (St Stephen) *Leic 1*   **P** *Bp*
  P-in-c P J BRINDLE,   **NSM** L M HUGHES
EWELL (St Francis of Assisi) Ruxley Lane *Guildf 9*   **P** *Bp*
  V S G THOMAS,   **NSM** E R RICHARDSON
EWELL (St Mary the Virgin) *Guildf 9*   **P** *Bp*   **V** *vacant* (020)
  8393 2643
EWELL, WEST (All Saints) *Guildf 9*   **P** *Bp*   **V** I S WHITHAM
EWELME (St Mary the Virgin), Brightwell Baldwin, Cuxham w
  Easington *Ox 1*   **P** *F D Wright Esq and Mert Coll Ox,*
  Prime Min (alt)   **P-in-c** J P MEYER
EWERBY (St Andrew)   *see* Kirkby Laythorpe *Linc*
EWHURST (St James the Great) *Chich 20*   **P** *K Coll Cam*
  R G L WINCHESTER
EWHURST (St Peter and St Paul) *Guildf 2*   **P** *Ld Chan*
  R D A MINNS,   **OLM** P E HISLOP, T J SELLER
EWOOD (St Bartholomew)   *see* Blackb Redeemer *Blackb*
EWSHOT (St Mary the Virgin)   *see* Crondall and Ewshot *Guildf*
EWYAS HAROLD (St Michael and All Angels) w Dulas,
  Kenderchurch, Abbeydore, Bacton, Kentchurch, Llangua,
  Rowlestone, Llancillo, Walterstone, Kilpeck, St Devereux and
  Wormbridge *Heref 1*   **P** *Patr Bd*   **P-in-c** A F EVANS
EXBOURNE (St Mary the Virgin)   *see* Hatherleigh, Meeth,
  Exbourne and Jacobstowe *Ex*
EXBURY (St Katherine)   *see* Beaulieu and Exbury and E Boldre
  Win

EXE, WEST (St Paul)   *see* Tiverton St Geo and St Paul *Ex*
EXE VALLEY   *see* Washfield, Stoodleigh, Withleigh etc *Ex*
EXETER (St David) (St Michael and All Angels) *Ex 3*   **P** *D&C*
   Hon C P A LEE,   **NSM** M C HEARL
EXETER (St James) *Ex 3*   **P** *D&C*   **R** H H D PRYSE,
   C J B B HUTCHINGS
EXETER (St Leonard w Holy Trinity) *Ex 3*   **P** *CPAS*
   R D R HARRIS,   **C** N S GOWERS, S J GOODBODY
EXETER (St Mark) (St Matthew) (St Sidwell) *Ex 3*   **P** *Bp and*
   D&C (jt)   **R** S CROFT,   **C** P J SOURBUT
EXETER (St Mary Steps)   *see* Heavitree and St Mary Steps *Ex*
EXETER (St Paul)   *as above*
EXETER (St Thomas the Apostle) (Emmanuel) (St Andrew)
   (St Philip) *Ex 3*   **P** *Bp*   **TV** M P SMITH
EXETER (Trinity) Conventional District *Ex 3*   **Min** J P A ELVIN
EXETER, CENTRAL (St Martin) (St Mary Arches) (St Olave)
   (St Pancras) (St Petrock) (St Stephen) *Ex 3*   **P** *Patr Bd*
   P-in-c C J MEYRICK,   **Hon C** S R SWARBRICK,
   NSM A A HALL
EXFORD (St Mary Magdalene), Exmoor, Hawkridge and
   Withypool *B & W 16*   **P** *Bp (1 turn), Peterho Cam (2 turns)*
   R *vacant* (01643) 831586
EXHALL (St Giles) *Cov 5*   **P** *Bp*   **V** *vacant* (024) 7636 2997
EXHALL (St Giles) w Wixford *Cov 7*   **P** *Bp*   **NSM** L E DAVIES,
   J HORTON
EXMINSTER (St Martin) and Kenn *Ex 6*   **P** *Mrs M P L Bate*
   and 12 Govs of Crediton Ch (jt)   **P-in-c** J D A WILLIAMS
EXMOOR (St Luke)   *see* Exford, Exmoor, Hawkridge and
   Withypool *B & W*
EXMOUTH (All Saints)   *see* Withycombe Raleigh *Ex*
EXMOUTH (Holy Trinity)   *see* Littleham w Exmouth *Ex*
EXMOUTH (St Andrew)   *as above*
EXMOUTH (St John in the Wilderness)   *see* Withycombe
   Raleigh *Ex*
EXMOUTH (St John the Evangelist)   *as above*
EXMOUTH (St Saviour)   *see* Littleham w Exmouth *Ex*
EXNING (St Agnes)   *see* Newmarket St Mary w Exning St
   Agnes *St E*
EXNING (St Martin) (St Philip) w Landwade *St E 11*   **P** *D&C*
   Cant   **V** K J WILLIAMS,   **NSM** C T MCCARTY, P S GILL
EXTON (St Andrew)   *see* Lympstone and Woodbury w Exton
   Ex
EXTON (St Peter and St Paul)   *see* Empingham and Exton w
   Horn w Whitwell *Pet*
EXTON (St Peter and St Paul)   *see* Meonstoke w Corhampton
   cum Exton *Portsm*
EXTON (St Peter) and Winsford and Cutcombe w Luxborough
   B & W 16   **P** *Ld Chan (2 turns), Em Coll Cam (1 turn), and*
   G A Warren Esq and D M Warren Esq (1 turn)   **R** T M STAPLES
EXWICK (St Andrew) *Ex 3*   **P** *Lord Wraxall*   **P-in-c** J P BIRD
EYAM (St Lawrence) *Derby 2*   **P** *Earl Temple*
   P-in-c A S MONTGOMERIE
EYDON (St Nicholas)   *see* Woodford Halse w Eydon *Pet*
EYE (St Matthew) *Pet 11*   **P** *Bp*   **P-in-c** C HURST
EYE (St Peter and St Paul)   *see* Leominster *Heref*
EYE (St Peter and St Paul) *St E 16*   **P** *Bp, SMF, and Lt Comdr*
   G C Marshall (jt)   **R** A M MITCHAM
EYEWORTH (All Saints)   *see* Dunton w Wrestlingworth and
   Eyeworth *St Alb*
EYKE (All Saints)   *see* Wilford Peninsula *St E*
EYNESBURY (St Mary) *Ely 13*   **P** *Bp*   **R** T J MCCABE
EYNSFORD (St Martin) w Farningham and Lullingstone
   Roch 10   **P** *D&C*   **NSM** C H SALMON
EYNSHAM (St Leonard) and Cassington *Ox 9*   **P** *Wycliffe Hall*
   Ox and Ch Ch Ox (alt)   **V** M A C ANDREWS,   **C** D W SALTER,
   NSM A C ATHERSTONE,   **OLM** J A UNDERWOOD, R ASTON
EYPE (St Peter)   *see* Symondsbury *Sarum*
EYRES MONSELL (St Hugh) *Leic 1*   **P** *Bp*   **V** A J JORDAN
EYTHORNE (St Peter and St Paul) and Elvington w
   Waldershare and Barfreystone w Sherdswell and Coldred *Cant 4*
   P *Abp, St Jo Coll Ox, and Earl of Guilford (jt)*   **R** A L WAY,
   OLM C M WILKINSON
EYTON (All Saints)   *see* Leominster *Heref*
EYTON (St Catherine)   *see* Wellington All SS w Eyton *Lich*
FACCOMBE (St Barnabas)   *see* Hurstbourne Tarrant,
   Faccombe, Vernham Dean etc *Win*
FACEBY (St Mary Magdalene)   *see* Whorlton w Carlton and
   Faceby *York*
FACIT (St John the Evangelist)   *see* Whitworth w Facit *Man*
FACIT (St Michael the Archangel)   *as above*
FAILAND (St Bartholomew)   *see* Wraxall *B & W*
FAILSWORTH (Holy Family) *Man 20*   **P** *Prime Min and*
   Bp (alt)   **R** *vacant* 0161-681 3644
FAILSWORTH (St John) (St John the Evangelist) *Man 20*
   P *Bp*   **R** A J MATTHEWS,   **OLM** M HOWARTH

FAIR OAK (St Thomas) *Win 10*   **P** *Bp*   **V** D S SNUGGS,
   C P DEVER, S P E MOURANT,   **NSM** R G NICHOLLS
FAIRBURN (St James)   *see* Ledsham w Fairburn *York*
FAIRFIELD (St John the Divine) *Liv 3*   **P** *MMCET*
   V A W PORTER,   **NSM** A MURRAY, C E PORTER
FAIRFIELD (St Mark)   *see* Belbroughton w Fairfield and Clent
   Worc
FAIRFIELD (St Peter) *Derby 4*   **P** *Ch Govs*
   P-in-c C F EDWARDS
FAIRFIELD (St Thomas à Becket)   *see* Appledore w Brookland,
   Fairfield, Brenzett etc *Cant*
FAIRFORD (St Mary the Virgin)   *see* Fairford Deanery *Glouc*
FAIRFORD DEANERY *Glouc 10*   **P** *Patr Bd*
   TR B C ATKINSON,   **TV** A E WOOLCOCK, C P BRYAN,
   S C BISHOP,   **NSM** T M HASTIE-SMITH, J H MAIS, C J FINLAY,
   J BROWN, A J ROBINSON,   **OLM** D HYDE
FAIRHAVEN (St Paul) *Blackb 10*   **P** *J C Hilton Esq*
   P-in-c D L CAREY
FAIRLIGHT, Guestling and Pett *Chich 20*   **P** *Patr Bd*
   R B E CROSBY,   **Hon C** H E PATTEN,   **NSM** J BURGESS
FAIRSEAT (Holy Innocents)   *see* Stansted w Fairseat and Vigo
   Roch
FAIRSTEAD (St Mary) w Terling and White Notley w
   Faulkbourne *Chelmsf 23*   **P** *Bp, Exors Lord Rayleigh, and*
   C W O Parker Esq (by turn)   **R** J M HALL
FAIRWARP (Christ Church) *Chich 21*   **P** *Bp*
   P-in-c D A TIDSWELL
FAIRWEATHER GREEN (St Saviour) *Bradf 1*   **P** *Bp*
   P-in-c A J GREIFF
FAKENHAM (St Peter and St Paul) w Alethorpe *Nor 15*
   P *Trin Coll Cam*   **R** A C BELL
FAKENHAM MAGNA (St Peter)   *see* Blackbourne *St E*
FALCONWOOD (Bishop Ridley Church) *Roch 15*   **P** *Bp*
   V T R HATWELL
FALDINGWORTH (All Saints)   *see* Middle Rasen Gp *Linc*
FALFIELD (St George)   *see* Cromhall, Tortworth,
   Tytherington, Falfield etc *Glouc*
FALKENHAM (St Ethelbert)   *see* Nacton and Levington w
   Bucklesham etc *St E*
FALLOWFIELD (St Crispin)   *see* Withington St Crispin *Man*
FALMER (St Laurence)   *see* Stanmer w Falmer *Chich*
FALMOUTH (All Saints) *Truro 3*   **P** *Bp*
   P-in-c S R F DRAKELEY,   **NSM** S G TURNER
FALMOUTH (King Charles the Martyr) *Truro 3*   **P** *Bp*
   P-in-c S J TUDGEY
FALSTONE (St Peter)   *see* N Tyne and Redesdale *Newc*
FAMBRIDGE, NORTH (Holy Trinity)   *see* Creeksea w
   Althorne, Latchingdon and N Fambridge *Chelmsf*
FAMBRIDGE, SOUTH (All Saints)   *see* Ashingdon w S
   Fambridge *Chelmsf*
FANGFOSS (St Martin)   *see* Barmby Moor Gp *York*
FAR FOREST (Holy Trinity)   *see* Mamble w Bayton, Rock w
   Heightington etc *Worc*
FAR HEADINGLEY St Chad (St Oswald) *Ripon 7*   **P** *Lord*
   Grimthorpe   **V** B M OVEREND,   **Hon C** M I KIMBALL
FARCET HAMPTON (St Mary) *Ely 17*   **P** *Bp and Em Coll*
   Cam (jt)   **P-in-c** J A RANDALL,   **C** N E DEVENISH, T S YAU
FAREHAM (Holy Trinity) (St Columba) *Portsm 2*   **P** *Bp*
   TR F A WRIGHT,   **TV** P A COCHRANE
FAREHAM (St John the Evangelist) *Portsm 2*   **P** *CPAS*
   V P D HALL,   **C** I R HILL,   **NSM** J M TERRY
FAREHAM (St Peter and St Paul) *Portsm 2*   **P** *Bp*   **V** *vacant*
   (01329) 280256 *or* 236003
FAREWELL (St Bartholomew) *Lich 1*   **P** *MMCET*
   P-in-c M J BUTT,   **NSM** M R AUSTIN,   **OLM** J R ANDREWS
FARFORTH (St Peter)   *see* S Ormsby Gp *Linc*
FARINGDON, GREAT (All Saints) w Little Coxwell *Ox 17*
   P *Simeon's Trustees*   **V** C J DRAPER,   **C** S J WEARN
FARINGDON, LITTLE (St Margaret of England)   *see* Shill
   Valley and Broadshire *Ox*
FARLAM (St Thomas à Becket)   *see* Eden, Gelt and Irthing *Carl*
FARLEIGH (St Mary)   *see* Warlingham w Chelsham and
   Farleigh *S'wark*
FARLEIGH, EAST (not known)   *see* Coxheath, E Farleigh,
   Hunton, Linton etc *Roch*
FARLEIGH, WEST (All Saints)   *as above*
FARLEIGH HUNGERFORD (St Leonard)   *see* Hardington
   Vale *B & W*
FARLEIGH WALLOP (St Andrew)   *see* Cliddesden and
   Ellisfield w Farleigh Wallop etc *Win*
FARLESTHORPE (St Andrew)   *see* Bilsby w Farlesthorpe *Linc*
FARLEY (All Saints)   *see* Clarendon *Sarum*
FARLEY CHAMBERLAYNE (St John)   *see* Michelmersh and
   Awbridge and Braishfield etc *Win*
FARLEY GREEN (St Michael)   *see* Shere, Albury and
   Chilworth *Guildf*

FARLEY HILL (St John the Baptist) *St Alb 14*   **P** *Bp*
  P-in-c D F SANDERS
FARLEY HILL (St John the Evangelist)   *see* Loddon Reach *Ox*
FARLINGTON (St Andrew) (Church of the Resurrection)
  Portsm 6   **P** *Mrs S J Wynter-Bee and E G Nugee Esq (jt)*
  R S B SUMMERS,   **NSM** T M FILTNESS
FARLINGTON (St Leonard)   *see* Forest of Galtres *York*
FARLOW (St Giles)   *see* Stottesdon w Farlow, Cleeton St Mary
  etc *Heref*
FARMBOROUGH (All Saints) and Marksbury and Stanton
  Prior *B & W 10*   **P** *MMCET (3 turns), Duchy of Cornwall*
  (1 turn), and DBF (1 turn)   **R** J P KNOTT,   **C** T NIXON
FARMCOTE (St Faith)   *see* The Guitings, Cutsdean, Farmcote
  etc *Glouc*
FARMINGTON (St Peter)   *see* Northleach w Hampnett and
  Farmington etc *Glouc*
FARMOOR (St Mary)   *see* Cumnor *Ox*
FARNBOROUGH (All Saints)   *see* Beedon and Peasemore w W
  Ilsley and Farnborough *Ox*
FARNBOROUGH (St Botolph)   *see* Avon Dassett w
  Farnborough and Fenny Compton *Cov*
FARNBOROUGH (St Giles) (St Nicholas) *Roch 16*   **P** *Em Coll*
  Cam   **R** M J HUGHES,   **C** A M NEWMAN,   **NSM** J DRIVER
FARNBOROUGH, NORTH (St Peter) (Good Shepherd)
  Guildf 1   **P** *Patr Bd*   **TR** D G WILLEY,   **TV** R M BENNETTS,
  C W W NORTH, C F HOLT
FARNBOROUGH, SOUTH (St Mark) *Guildf 1*   **P** *Bp*
  V I C HEDGES
FARNCOMBE (St John the Evangelist) *Guildf 4*   **P** *Bp*
  C M H DEAN
FARNDALE (St Mary)   *see* Kirkbymoorside w Gillamoor,
  Farndale etc *York*
FARNDON (St Chad) and Coddington *Ches 5*   **P** *Duke of*
  Westmr and D&C (jt)   **P-in-c** D SCURR
FARNDON (St Peter) w Thorpe, Hawton and Cotham *S'well 3*
  P *Ld Chan*   **R** *vacant* (01636) 705048
FARNDON, EAST (St John the Baptist)   *see* Arthingworth,
  Harrington w Oxendon and E Farndon *Pet*
FARNHAM (St Andrew) (St Francis) (St Mary) *Guildf 3*   **P** *Bp*
  R A K TUCK,   **C** T E F ROSE,   **NSM** J M LIEVESLEY
FARNHAM (St Laurence)   *see* Chase *Sarum*
FARNHAM (St Mary)   *see* Alde River *St E*
FARNHAM (St Mary the Virgin)   *see* Stansted Mountfitchet w
  Birchanger and Farnham *Chelmsf*
FARNHAM (St Oswald)   *see* Walkingham Hill *Ripon*
FARNHAM COMMON (St John the Evangelist)   *see* Farnham
  Royal w Hedgerley *Ox*
FARNHAM ROYAL (St Mary the Virgin) w Hedgerley *Ox 23*
  P *Bp and Eton Coll (jt)*   **R** G H SAUNDERS,   **OLM** G J BRIGGS
FARNHAM ROYAL SOUTH (St Michael)   *see* Manor Park
  and Whitby Road *Ox*
FARNINGHAM (St Peter and St Paul)   *see* Eynsford w
  Farningham and Lullingstone *Roch*
FARNLEY (All Saints)   *see* Washburn and Mid-Wharfe *Bradf*
FARNLEY (St Michael) *Ripon 6*   **P** *Bp*   **R** D GRASBY
FARNLEY, NEW (St James)   *see* Farnley *Ripon*
FARNLEY TYAS (St Lucias)   *see* Almondbury w Farnley Tyas
  Wakef
FARNSFIELD (St Michael) *S'well 15*   **P** *Bp*
  NSM M A GROVES
FARNWORTH (St George)   *see* New Bury w Gt Lever *Man*
FARNWORTH (St James)   *as above*
FARNWORTH (St Luke) (Bold Mission) (Cronton Mission)
  Liv 13   **P** *V Prescot St Mary*   **V** H M MORBY,   **C** P MAKIN
FARNWORTH, EAST (All Saints) (St John) (St Peter)
  (St Thomas) and Kearsley *Man 12*   **P** *Bp (2 turns), Ld Chan*
  (1 turn)   **P-in-c** C H PHARAOH,   **OLM** P S CASTLE
FARRINGDON (All Saints)   *see* Northanger *Win*
FARRINGDON (St Petrock and St Barnabas)   *see* Aylesbeare,
  Rockbeare, Farringdon etc *Ex*
FARRINGTON GURNEY (St John the Baptist)   *see* Paulton w
  Farrington Gurney and High Littleton *B & W*
FARSLEY (St John the Evangelist) *Bradf 3*   **P** *V Calverley*
  P-in-c P Q TUDGE,   **C** P R ARNOLD
FARTHINGHOE (St Michael and All Angels)   *see* Aynho and
  Croughton w Evenley etc *Pet*
FARTHINGSTONE (St Mary the Virgin)   *see* Lambfold *Pet*
FARWAY (St Michael and All Angels)   *see* Offwell, Northleigh,
  Farway, Cotleigh etc *Ex*
FATFIELD (St George) *Dur 11*   **P** *Lord Lambton*
  P-in-c B P S VALLIS,   **C** J A MIDDLETON
FAULKBOURNE (St Germanus)   *see* Fairstead w Terling and
  White Notley etc *Chelmsf*
FAULS (Holy Emmanuel)   *see* Edstaston, Fauls, Prees, Tilstock
  and Whixall *Lich*

FAVELL, WEST (Emmanuel)   *see* Northampton Em *Pet*
FAVERSHAM (St Mary of Charity) *Cant 6*   **P** *D&C*
  P-in-c A C OEHRING,   **C** J L PETTIT,   **Hon C** R V PARRETT,
  NSM N M ASH
FAWDON (St Mary the Virgin) *Newc 2*   **P** *Bp*
  P-in-c S MCCORMACK,   **OLM** M A ATKINSON
FAWKENHURST *Cant 10*   **P** *DBP*   **R** *vacant*
FAWKHAM (St Mary) and Hartley *Roch 1*   **P** *Bp and D&C (jt)*
  R J A FLETCHER,   **NSM** E M ROBERTSON
FAWLEY (All Saints) *Win 11*   **P** *Bp*   **R** B P JAMES,
  NSM M G WHITE, D WHITE
FAWLEY (St Mary)   *see* Brightwalton w Catmore,
  Leckhampstead etc *Ox*
FAWLEY (St Mary the Virgin)   *see* Hambleden Valley *Ox*
FAWSLEY (St Mary the Virgin)   *see* Badby w Newnham and
  Charwelton w Fawsley etc *Pet*
FAZAKERLEY (Emmanuel) (St Paul) *Liv 7*   **P** *Patr Bd*
  TR M SIMMONS,   **TV** M A HINDLEY,   **NSM** J A FLOOD
FAZAKERLEY (St Nathanael)   *see* Walton-on-the-Hill *Liv*
FAZELEY (St Paul) (St Barnabas) *Lich 4*   **P** *Bp*   **V** H J BAKER,
  NSM R G DAVIES,   **OLM** S ROWLEY
FEATHERSTONE (All Saints) (St Thomas) *Wakef 10*
  P *Ch Ch Ox and Bp (jt)*   **V** I GROSU
FEATHERSTONE (School Chapel)   *see* Haltwhistle and
  Greenhead *Newc*
FECKENHAM (St John the Baptist)   *see* Bowbrook N *Worc*
FEERING (All Saints)   *see* Kelvedon and Feering *Chelmsf*
FELBRIDGE (St John) *S'wark 25*   **P** *DBP*   **V** S G BOWEN
FELBRIGG (St Margaret)   *see* Roughton and Felbrigg, Metton,
  Sustead etc *Nor*
FELIXKIRK (St Felix) w Boltby *York 19*   **P** *Abp*
  V I D HOUGHTON
FELIXSTOWE (St John the Baptist) (St Edmund) *St E 2*   **P** *Bp*
  P-in-c R C HINSLEY
FELIXSTOWE (St Peter and St Paul) (St Andrew) (St Nicholas)
  St E 2   **P** *Ch Trust Fund Trust*   **P-in-c** J L ASTON,
  OLM H STALKER
FELKIRK (St Peter) *Wakef 10*   **P** *Bp*   **P-in-c** J HADJIOANNOU
FELLING (Christ Church) *Dur 12*   **P** *CPAS*   **V** T J DAVIDSON
FELLISCLIFFE (Mission Church)   *see* Hampsthwaite and
  Killinghall and Birstwith *Ripon*
FELLSIDE TEAM, The *Blackb 9*   **P** *Patr Bd*   **TR** J W FINCH,
  TV S P C COOPER,   **NSM** M A SHERDLEY
FELMERSHAM (St Mary)   *see* Sharnbrook, Felmersham and
  Knotting w Souldrop *St Alb*
FELMINGHAM (St Andrew)   *see* King's Beck *Nor*
FELPHAM (St Mary the Virgin) *Chich 1*   **P** *D&C*
  R T L PESKETT
FELSHAM (St Peter)   *see* Bradfield St Clare, Bradfield St
  George etc *St E*
FELSTED (Holy Cross) and Little Dunmow *Chelmsf 18*
  P *CPAS*   **V** C J TAYLOR,   **C** M J WINDSOR
FELTHAM (Christ Church) (St Dunstan) *Lon 11*   **P** *Bp*
  V P R WRAGG,   **NSM** D MAPES
FELTHORPE (St Margaret)   *see* Horsford, Felthorpe and
  Hevingham *Nor*
FELTON (St Katharine and the Noble Army of Martyrs)
  see Winford w Felton Common Hill *B & W*
FELTON (St Michael and All Angels) *Newc 6*   **P** *Bp*
  P-in-c S J H WHITE
FELTON (St Michael the Archangel)   *see* Bodenham, Felton
  and Preston Wynne *Heref*
FELTON, WEST (St Michael) *Lich 19*   **P** *Bp*
  P-in-c D R NORTH
FELTWELL (St Mary)   *see* Grimshoe *Ely*
FEN AND HILL Group, The *Linc 11*   **P** *Bp, DBP,*
  G J R Wiggins-Davies Esq, and Lt Col J L M Dymoke (jt)
  R A J BOYD,   **OLM** K A BUSH
FEN DITTON (St Mary the Virgin) *Ely 4*   **P** *Bp*
  P-in-c M C BOWERS
FEN DRAYTON (St Mary the Virgin) w Conington and Lolworth
  and Swavesey *Ely 6*   **P** *The Crown, Jes Coll Cam, SMF, and*
  Ch Coll Cam (by turn)   **R** J D YULE
FEN ORCHARDS, The *Ely 14*   **P** *Bp*   **V** D L MASON,
  C M HANCOCK
FENCE-IN-PENDLE (St Anne) and Higham *Blackb 6*   **P** *Bp*
  and Ld Chan (alt)   **V** R J ADAMS,   **NSM** P M SHOOTER
FENCOTE (St Andrew)   *see* Lower Swale *Ripon*
FENHAM (Holy Cross)   *see* Newc H Cross *Newc*
FENHAM (St James and St Basil) *Newc 4*   **P** *Bp*
  V N P DARBY,   **C** H E ARNOLD
FENISCLIFFE (St Francis)   *see* Blackb St Fran and St Aid
  Blackb
FENISCOWLES (Immanuel) *Blackb 2*   **P** *V Blackb*
  NSM A S HORSFALL

FENITON (St Andrew) and Escot *Ex 7*　**P** *DBP and J M Kennaway Esq (jt)*　**P-in-c** S G FRANKLIN

FENN LANES Group, The *Leic 10*　**P** *Bp, D&C, and Lord O'Neill (jt)*　**R** L J BLAY

FENNY BENTLEY (St Edmund King and Martyr), Thorpe, Tissington, Parwich and Alsop-en-le-Dale *Derby 8*　**P** *Bp, D A G Shields Esq, and Sir Richard FitzHerbert Bt (jt)*　**R** *vacant* (01335) 390226

FENNY COMPTON (St Peter and St Clare) *see* Avon Dassett w Farnborough and Fenny Compton *Cov*

FENNY DRAYTON (St Michael and All Angels) *see* Fenn Lanes Gp *Leic*

FENNY STRATFORD (St Martin) *Ox 25*　**P** *Bp*　**V** J A BULLOCK,　**NSM** I W THOMAS, J D HIBBARD

FENSTANTON (St Peter and St Paul) *Ely 10*　**P** *Bp*　**P-in-c** R P MCKENZIE

FENTON (All Saints) *see* Claypole *Linc*

FENTON (Christ Church) *Lich 12*　**P** *R Stoke-on-Trent*　**V** D A CAMERON

FENWICK and MOSS (St John) *see* Fishlake w Sykehouse and Kirk Bramwith etc *Sheff*

FEOCK (St Feock) *Truro 6*　**P** *Bp*　**P-in-c** P A A WALKER,　**NSM** B J HESELTINE

FERHAM PARK (St Paul) *see* Masbrough *Sheff*

FERNDOWN (St Mary) *see* Hampreston *Sarum*

FERNHAM (St John the Evangelist) *see* Shrivenham and Ashbury *Ox*

FERNHURST (St Margaret) *Chich 10*　**P** *Rathbone Trust Co and Cowdray Trust (jt)*　**P-in-c** A N ROCKEY

FERNILEE (Holy Trinity) *see* Whaley Bridge *Ches*

FERRIBY, NORTH (All Saints) *York 14*　**P** *H Trin Hull and Distr Ch Patr Soc Ltd*　**P-in-c** M C BRAILSFORD,　**NSM** J D GRIFFITH

FERRIBY, SOUTH (St Nicholas) *Linc 6*　**P** *Bp*　**R** *vacant* (01652) 635258

FERRING (St Andrew) *Chich 5*　**P** *D&C*　**P-in-c** G S INGRAM

FERRYBRIDGE (St Andrew) *Wakef 10*　**P** *D&C York*　**P-in-c** E M WOODCOCK

FERRYHILL (St Luke) *see* Cornforth and Ferryhill *Dur*

FERRYHILL (St Martha and St Mary) *as above*

FERSFIELD (St Andrew) *see* Upper Waveney *Nor*

FETCHAM (St Mary) *Guildf 10*　**P** *Bp*　**R** P H BOUGHTON,　**NSM** E M V BOUGHTON

FEWSTON (St Michael and St Lawrence) *see* Washburn and Mid-Wharfe *Bradf*

FIDDINGTON (St Martin) *see* Quantock Coast *B & W*

FIELD BROUGHTON (St Peter) *see* Cartmel Peninsula *Carl*

FIELD DALLING (St Andrew) *see* Stiffkey and Bale *Nor*

FIFEHEAD MAGDALEN (St Mary Magdalene) *see* Stour Vale *Sarum*

FIFEHEAD NEVILLE (All Saints) *see* Hazelbury Bryan and the Hillside *Par Sarum*

FIFIELD (St John the Baptist) *see* Shipton-under-Wychwood w Milton, Fifield etc *Ox*

FIFIELD BAVANT (St Martin) *see* Chalke Valley *Sarum*

FIGHELDEAN (St Michael and All Angels) *see* Avon Valley *Sarum*

FILBY (All Saints) *see* S Trin Broads *Nor*

FILEY (St John) (St Oswald) *York 15*　**P** *PCC*　**V** M E WILLIAMS,　**NSM** M J YOUNG

FILKINS (St Peter) *see* Shill Valley and Broadshire *Ox*

FILLEIGH (St Paul) *see* S Molton w Nymet St George, High Bray etc *Ex*

FILLINGHAM (St Andrew) *see* Spring Line Gp *Linc*

FILLONGLEY (St Mary and All Saints) and Corley *Cov 5*　**P** *Bp and Ch Soc Trust (jt)*　**P-in-c** I D KENNEDY

FILTON (St Gregory) *see* Horfield St Greg *Bris*

FILTON (St Peter) *Bris 5*　**P** *Bp*　**R** B R ARMAN,　**NSM** M E DESMOND

FILWOOD PARK *Bris 1*　**P** *Bp and Bris Ch Trustees (jt)*　**V** A G PALMER

FIMBER (St Mary) *see* Waggoners *York*

FINBOROUGH, GREAT (St Andrew) w Onehouse, Harleston, Buxhall and Shelland *St E 6*　**P** *Bp*　**P-in-c** L LLEWELLYN-MACDUFF,　**NSM** C CHILDS, T A J GRAY,　**OLM** A E H CRUICKSHANKS

FINBOROUGH, LITTLE (St Mary) *see* Combs and Lt Finborough *St E*

FINCHAM (St Martin) *Ely 9*　**P** *Bp*　**R** *vacant* (01366) 347491

FINCHAMPSTEAD (St James) *Ox 16*　**P** *DBP*　**P-in-c** R J WARDEN,　**NSM** J R EDWARDS

FINCHFIELD (St Thomas) *see* Tettenhall Wood and Perton *Lich*

FINCHINGFIELD (St John the Baptist) and Cornish Hall End and Wethersfield w Shalford *Chelmsf 15*　**P** *Mrs E M Bishop and Bp (alt)*　**P-in-c** C E WILSON

FINCHLEY (Christ Church) *Lon 14*　**P** *Ch Patr Trust*　**V** T D ATKINS

FINCHLEY (Holy Trinity) *Lon 16*　**P** *Bp*　**V** L B HILL

FINCHLEY (St Barnabas) *see* Woodside Park St Barn *Lon*

FINCHLEY (St Mary) *Lon 14*　**P** *Bp*　**R** P A DAVISON

FINCHLEY (St Paul) (St Luke) *Lon 14*　**P** *Simeon Trustees and Ch Patr Trust (jt)*　**V** N R PYE

FINCHLEY, EAST (All Saints) *Lon 14*　**P** *Bp*　**V** C R HARDY

FINDERN (All Saints) *Derby 16*　**P** *Bp*　**V** S A SIARKEY

FINDON (St John the Baptist) w Clapham and Patching *Chich 5*　**P** *Abp, Bp, and J E P Somerset Esq (jt)*　**V** *vacant* (01903) 873601

FINDON VALLEY (All Saints) *Chich 5*　**P** *Bp*　**V** G J WHITING,　**NSM** B A MILES

FINEDON (St Mary the Virgin) *Pet 8*　**P** *Bp*　**V** *vacant* (01933) 680285

FINGEST (St Bartholomew) *see* Hambleden Valley *Ox*

FINGHALL (St Andrew) *see* Spennithorne w Finghall and Hauxwell *Ripon*

FINGRINGHOE (St Andrew) w East Donyland and Abberton w Langenhoe *Chelmsf 16*　**P** *Bp (3 turns), Ld Chan (1 turn)*　**R** R J MARTIN

FINHAM (St Martin in the Fields) *Cov 3*　**P** *Bp*　**V** P WATKINS

FINMERE (St Michael) *see* Shelswell *Ox*

FINNINGHAM (St Bartholomew) *see* Badwell and Walsham *St E*

FINNINGLEY (Holy Trinity and St Oswald) w Auckley *Sheff 9*　**P** *Bp*　**P-in-c** N M REDEYOFF

FINSBURY (St Clement) (St Barnabas) (St Matthew) *Lon 5*　**P** *D&C St Paul's*　**V** D E ALLEN

FINSBURY PARK (St Thomas) *Lon 6*　**P** *Abp*　**V** S R COLES,　**NSM** V R ATTA-BAFFOE

FINSTALL (St Godwald) *Worc 7*　**P** *V Stoke Prior*　**C** S C WINTER,　**NSM** M WOODGATES

FINSTHWAITE (St Peter) *see* Leven Valley *Carl*

FINSTOCK (Holy Trinity) *see* Forest Edge *Ox*

FIR VALE (St Cuthbert) *see* Sheff St Cuth *Sheff*

FIRBANK (St John the Evangelist), Howgill and Killington *Bradf 6*　**P** *Ld Chan and V Sedbergh (alt)*　**P-in-c** A W FELL

FIRBECK (St Martin) w Letwell *Sheff 5*　**P** *Bp*　**R** *vacant* (01909) 730346

FIRLE, WEST (St Peter) *see* Glynde, W Firle and Beddingham *Chich*

FIRSBY (St Andrew) *see* Spilsby Gp *Linc*

FIRSWOOD (St Hilda) and Gorse Hill *Man 7*　**P** *Prime Min*　**P-in-c** T R MALKIN,　**C** D J CATTLE

FISHBOURNE, NEW (St Peter and St Mary) *Chich 3*　**P** *Ld Chan*　**R** C A ASHLEY

FISHBURN (St Catherine) *see* Upper Skerne *Dur*

FISHERMEAD (Trinity Church) *see* Woughton *Ox*

FISHERTON ANGER (St Paul) *Sarum 12*　**P** *Ch Patr Trust*　**R** A S W CULLIS,　**C** R T MORGAN,　**NSM** A B KEATING

FISHLAKE (St Cuthbert) w Sykehouse and Kirk Bramwith w Fenwick and Moss *Sheff 10*　**P** *Duchy of Lanc (1 turn), D&C Dur (2 turns), and Bp (1 turn)*　**R** E S ATHERFOLD

FISHLEY (St Mary) *see* Acle w Fishley, N Burlingham, Beighton w Moulton *Nor*

FISHPOND (St John the Baptist) *see* Golden Cap Team *Sarum*

FISHPONDS (All Saints) *Bris 3*　**P** *Bp*　**C** N S ADAMS,　**NSM** J F J GOODRIDGE

FISHPONDS (St John) *Bris 3*　**P** *Bp*　**C** N S ADAMS,　**NSM** J F J GOODRIDGE

FISHPONDS (St Mary) *Bris 3*　**P** *Bp*　**C** N S ADAMS,　**NSM** J F J GOODRIDGE

FISHTOFT (St Guthlac) *Linc 20*　**P** *DBP*　**R** M A R COOPER

FISKERTON (St Clement) *see* S Lawres Gp *Linc*

FITTLETON (All Saints) *see* Avon Valley *Sarum*

FITTLEWORTH (St Mary the Virgin) *see* Stopham and Fittleworth *Chich*

FITTON HILL (St Cuthbert) *see* Bardsley *Man*

FITZ (St Peter and St Paul) *see* Bicton, Montford w Shrawardine and Fitz *Lich*

FITZHEAD (St James) *see* Milverton w Halse and Fitzhead *B & W*

FITZWILLIAM (St Maurice) *see* Kinsley w Wragby *Wakef*

FIVE ASHES (Church of the Good Shepherd) *see* Mayfield *Chich*

FIVE OAK GREEN (St Luke) *see* Tudeley cum Capel w Five Oak Green *Roch*

FIVE SAINTS *see* New Bury w Gt Lever *Man*

FIVEHEAD (St Martin) *see* Curry Rivel w Fivehead and Swell *B & W*

FIXBY (St Francis) and Cowcliffe, Huddersfield *Wakef 5*　**P** *DBP*　**Hon C** G S HODGSON

FLACKWELL HEATH (Christ Church) *Ox 29*　**P** *DBP*　**V** C D BULL,　**NSM** G P HARTNELL,　**OLM** M H COURTNEY

FLADBURY (St John the Baptist) w Wyre Piddle and Moor and Cropthorne w Charlton *Worc 4* **P** *Bp and D&C (jt)*
P-in-c L M BUSFIELD

FLAGG (School Mission Room) *see* Taddington, Chelmorton and Flagg, and Monyash *Derby*

FLAMBOROUGH (St Oswald) *see* Bempton w Flamborough, Reighton w Speeton *York*

FLAMSTEAD (St Leonard) *St Alb 8* **P** *Univ Coll Ox*
P-in-c J F H GREEN

FLAUNDEN (St Mary Magdalene) *see* Chenies and Lt Chalfont, Latimer and Flaunden *Ox*

FLAX BOURTON (St Michael and All Angels) *see* Long Ashton w Barrow Gurney and Flax Bourton *B & W*

FLAXLEY (St Mary the Virgin) *see* Westbury-on-Severn w Flaxley, Blaisdon etc *Glouc*

FLAXTON (St Lawrence) *see* Sand Hutton *York*

FLECKNEY (St Nicholas) *see* Wistow *Leic*

FLECKNOE (St Mark) *see* Leam Valley *Cov*

FLEET (All Saints) (St Philip and St James) *Guildf 1* **P** *Bp*
V R O WOODHAMS,   **C** A SISTIG,   **NSM** J J SISTIG

FLEET (Holy Trinity) *see* Chickerell w Fleet *Sarum*

FLEET (Old Church) *as above*

FLEET (St Mary Magdalene) w Gedney *Linc 16* **P** *The Crown and DBP (alt)*   **P-in-c** R J GODDARD

FLEETWOOD (St David) *Blackb 12* **P** *Bp and Meynell Trustees (jt)*   **P-in-c** J M HALL

FLEETWOOD (St Nicholas) *Blackb 12* **P** *Bp and Meynell Trustees (jt)*   **V** P J BENFIELD

FLEETWOOD (St Peter) *Blackb 12* **P** *Meynell Trustees*
P-in-c J M HALL

FLEGG COASTAL Benefice, The: Hemsby, Winterton, East and West Somerton and Horsey *Nor 6* **P** *Bp, D&C, SMF, and Major R A Ferrier (jt)*   **R** A R LING,   **NSM** A T CADMORE

FLEMPTON (St Catherine of Alexandria) *see* Lark Valley *St E*

FLETCHAMSTEAD (St James) *Cov 3* **P** *Bp*   **V** S R BURCH,
C C D HOGGER

FLETCHING (St Mary and St Andrew) *Chich 21* **P** *Abp*
P-in-c H E HOWELL

FLETTON (St Margaret) *Ely 15* **P** *Sir Philip Naylor-Leyland Bt*   **P-in-c** W P L GAMMON

FLIMBY (St Nicholas) *see* Maryport, Netherton and Flimby *Carl*

FLIMWELL (St Augustine of Canterbury) *see* Ticehurst and Flimwell *Chich*

FLINTHAM (St Augustine of Canterbury) *S'well 8*
P R H T Hildyard Esq   **P-in-c** J R CHAMBERS,
NSM M R WOODWARD

FLITCHAM (St Mary the Virgin) *see* Sandringham w W Newton and Appleton etc *Nor*

FLITTON (St John the Baptist) *see* Silsoe, Pulloxhill and Flitton *St Alb*

FLITWICK (St Andrew) (St Peter and St Paul) *St Alb 9* **P** *DBP*
V M F J BRADLEY

FLIXBOROUGH (All Saints) w Burton upon Stather *Linc 4*
P *Sir Reginald Sheffield Bt*   **P-in-c** A F PLEDGER

FLIXTON (St John) *Man 7* **P** *Bp*   **V** K J MASSEY,
OLM R W GREEN, B R CORKE, J N EDGE

FLIXTON (St Mary) *see* S Elmham and Ilketshall *St E*

FLIXTON (St Michael) *Man 7* **P** *Bp*   **P-in-c** S J SMITH,
OLM A H CLEPHANE

FLOCKTON (St James the Great) cum Denby Grange *Wakef 6*
P *R Carter's Trustees*   **P-in-c** C E BULLIMORE

FLOOKBURGH (St John the Baptist) *see* Cartmel Peninsula *Carl*

FLORDON (St Michael) *see* Mulbarton w Bracon Ash, Hethel and Flordon *Nor*

FLORE (All Saints) *see* Heyford w Stowe Nine Churches and Flore etc *Pet*

FLOWTON (St Mary) *see* Somersham w Flowton and Offton w Willisham *St E*

FLUSHING (St Peter) *see* Mylor w Flushing *Truro*

FLYFORD FLAVELL (St Peter) *see* Abberton, The Flyfords, Naunton Beauchamp etc *Worc*

FOBBING (St Michael) *Chelmsf 14* **P** *The Crown*
P-in-c D ROLLINS

FOLESHILL (St Laurence) *Cov 2* **P** *Ld Chan*
V M R CLEVELAND

FOLESHILL (St Paul) *Cov 2* **P** *Ld Chan*   **V** A J CANNING

FOLEY PARK (Holy Innocents) *see* Kidderminster St Jo and H Innocents *Worc*

FOLKE (St Lawrence) *see* Vale of White Hart *Sarum*

FOLKESTONE (St Augustine) Conventional District
Cant 5 vacant (01303) 245807

FOLKESTONE (St Augustine) (St Mary and St Eanswythe)
Cant 5 **P** *Abp*   **NSM** B F WILLIAMS, R C SIEBERT

FOLKESTONE (St John the Baptist) *see* Foord St Jo *Cant*

FOLKESTONE (St Peter) *Cant 5* **P** *Trustees*
P-in-c S F BOULD

FOLKESTONE (St Saviour) *Cant 5* **P** *Abp*
NSM B F WILLIAMS

FOLKESTONE Trinity Benefice, The (Holy Trinity w Christ Church) (St George) *Cant 5* **P** *Abp and Ld Chan (alt)*
P-in-c M W HAYTON,   **C** S FITZGERALD, J A ROBERTSON,
NSM R O SMITH, K M MCNEICE

FOLKESWORTH (St Helen) *see* Stilton w Denton and Caldecote etc *Ely*

FOLKINGHAM (St Andrew) *see* S Lafford *Linc*

FOLKINGTON (St Peter ad Vincula) *see* Arlington, Folkington and Wilmington *Chich*

FOLKTON (St John) *see* Willerby w Ganton and Folkton *York*

FOLLIFOOT (St Joseph and St James) *see* Spofforth w Kirk Deighton *Ripon*

FONTHILL BISHOP (All Saints) *see* Nadder Valley *Sarum*

FONTHILL GIFFORD (Holy Trinity) *as above*

FONTMELL MAGNA (St Andrew) *see* Iwerne Valley *Sarum*

FOOLOW (St Hugh) *see* Eyam *Derby*

FOORD (St John the Baptist) *Cant 5* **P** *CPAS*   **V** J LEACH,
C K HARLOW

FOOTSCRAY (All Saints) w North Cray *Roch 17* **P** *Bp and Ld Chan (alt)*   **R** A C UPHILL,   **NSM** P A PERCIVAL

FORCETT (St Cuthbert) and Aldbrough and Melsonby *Ripon 2*
P *DBP and Univ Coll Ox (alt)*   **P-in-c** S R HAWORTH

FORD (St Andrew) *see* Clymping and Yapton w Ford *Chich*

FORD (St John of Jerusalem) *see* Leominster *Heref*

FORD (St John the Evangelist) *see* Colerne w N Wraxall *Bris*

FORD (St Mark) *see* Devonport St Bart and Ford St Mark *Ex*

FORD (St Michael) *Heref 13* **P** *Bp*   **P-in-c** V J TAIT

FORD (St Michael and All Angels) and Etal *Newc 12* **P** *Lord Joicey*   **R** V T DICKINSON

FORD END (St John the Evangelist) *see* Gt Waltham w Ford End *Chelmsf*

FORDCOMBE (St Peter) *see* Penshurst and Fordcombe *Roch*

FORDHAM (All Saints) *Chelmsf 17* **P** *Reformation Ch Trust, Ball Coll Ox (alt)*   **R** M R J NEVILLE,   **C** A SAVILLE

FORDHAM (St Peter and St Mary Magdalene) *see* Three Rivers Gp *Ely*

FORDHOUSES (St James) *see* Bushbury *Lich*

FORDINGBRIDGE (St Mary) and Breamore and Hale with the Charfords *Win 9* **P** *Patr Bd* **TR** M R GODSON,
C T ROBINSON,   **Hon C** P D ASHTON, P F MURPHY, J F TOWLER,
NSM S T HORNE

FORDON (St James) *see* Burton Fleming w Fordon, Grindale etc *York*

FOREBRIDGE (St Paul) *see* Stafford St Paul Forebridge *Lich*

FOREMARK (St Saviour) and Repton w Newton Solney *Derby 16* **P** *Bp and DBP (jt)*   **V** P S PAINE

FOREST (St Stephen) *see* Rainow w Saltersford and Forest *Ches*

FOREST AND AVON *Sarum 10* **P** *Patr Bd* **TR** F H GIMSON,
TV D G BACON,   **OLM** P J WHITMARSH

FOREST EDGE *Ox 3* **P** *Bp, V Charlbury, and Sir Mark Norman Bt (jt)*   **V** J F KNOWLES,   **NSM** B FORD, S C JONES

FOREST GATE (All Saints) (St Edmund) *Chelmsf 3* **P** *Bp*
P-in-c B K SHIPSIDES

FOREST GATE (Emmanuel w St Peter) Upton Cross *Chelmsf 3*
P *Bp*   **V** P J MOSSOP,   **C** D L MCINDOE

FOREST GATE (St James) *see* Stratford St Jo w Ch Ch and St Jas *Chelmsf*

FOREST GATE (St Mark) *Chelmsf 3* **P** *Ch Patr Trust*
V P J STOW

FOREST GATE (St Saviour) w West Ham St Matthew *Chelmsf 3*
P *Patr Bd* **TR** J H WILLIAMS,   **TV** M OKELLO

FOREST GREEN (Holy Trinity) *see* Ockley, Okewood and Forest Green *Guildf*

FOREST HILL (Christ Church) *see* Perry Hill St Geo w Ch Ch and St Paul *S'wark*

FOREST HILL (St Augustine) *see* Sydenham H Trin and St Aug *S'wark*

FOREST HILL (St Nicholas) *see* Wheatley *Ox*

FOREST HILL (St Paul) *see* Perry Hill St Geo w Ch Ch and St Paul *S'wark*

FOREST-IN-TEESDALE (St Mary the Virgin) *see* Middleton-in-Teesdale w Forest and Frith *Dur*

FOREST OF DEAN (Christ Church) w English Bicknor *Glouc 2*
P *The Crown (3 turns), SMF (1 turn)*   **P-in-c** V K TURNER,
NSM H RODWELL

FOREST OF DEAN (Holy Trinity) *see* Drybrook, Lydbrook and Ruardean *Glouc*

FOREST OF GALTRES (Farlington, Marton w Moxby, Sheriff Hutton, and Sutton-on-the-Forest) *York 3* **P** *Abp (2 turns), Ld Chan (1 turn)*   **V** C C ELLIS

FOREST ROW (Holy Trinity) *Chich 7*   **P** *V E Grinstead*
  V N H LAMB

FOREST TOWN (St Alban) *S'well 2*   **P** *Bp*   **P-in-c** P J STEAD

FORESTSIDE (Christ Church) *see* Stansted *Chich*

FORMBY (Holy Trinity) *Liv 5*   **P** *Trustees*   **V** K E JONES,
  C J HILL,   **NSM** K ROGERS

FORMBY (St Luke) *Liv 5*   **P** *Bp*   **V** H T NICOL,   **C** M A RIDGE

FORMBY (St Peter) *Liv 5*   **P** *R Walton*   **V** P W ORMROD,
  C R D FIELDING

FORNCETT (St Peter) *see* Ashwellthorpe, Forncett,
Fundenhall, Hapton etc *Nor*

FORNCETT END (St Edmund) *as above*

FORNHAM ALL SAINTS (All Saints) *see* Lark Valley *St E*

FORNHAM ST MARTIN (St Martin) *as above*

FORRABURY (St Symphorian) *see* Boscastle w Davidstow
Truro

FORSBROOK (St Peter) *see* Draycott-le-Moors w Forsbrook
Lich

FORTHAMPTON (St Mary) *see* Deerhurst and Apperley w
Forthampton etc *Glouc*

FORTON (All Saints) *see* Newport w Longford, Chetwynd and
Forton *Lich*

FORTON (St James) *see* Ellel w Shireshead *Blackb*

FORTON (St John the Evangelist) *Portsm 3*   **P** *DBP*
  V C J L J THOMPSON

FORTY HILL (Jesus Church) *Lon 18*   **P** *V Enfield*
  V I H CROFTS

FOSDYKE (All Saints) *see* Algarkirk and Fosdyke *Linc*

FOSSE TRINITY *B & W 8*   **P** *Bp and Canon D S Salter (jt)*
  P-in-c C M DONKERSLEY

FOSTON (All Saints) *see* Whitwell w Crambe and Foston *York*

FOSTON (St Bartholomew) *see* Countesthorpe w Foston *Leic*

FOSTON (St Peter) *see* Saxonwell *Linc*

FOSTON-ON-THE-WOLDS (St Andrew) *see* Beeford w
Frodingham and Foston *York*

FOTHERBY (St Mary) *Linc 12*   **P** *Ld Chan (1 turn), DBP,
MMCET and G F Sleight Esq (1 turn), and Bp (1 turn)*
  OLM J M WRISDALE

FOTHERINGHAY (St Mary and All Saints) *see* Warmington,
Tansor and Cotterstock etc *Pet*

FOULDEN (All Saints) *see* Oxborough w Foulden and
Caldecote *Nor*

FOULNESS (St Mary the Virgin) *see* Gt Wakering w Foulness
Chelmsf

FOULRIDGE (St Michael and All Angels) *see* Colne and
Villages *Blackb*

**FOULSHAM (Holy Innocents), Guestwick, Stibbard,
Themelthorpe and Wood Norton** *Nor 22*   **P** *Bp, DBP,
Mrs H M Cook, Lord Hastings, and B E Bulwer-Long Esq (jt)*
  V V M WILSON

FOUNTAINS Group, The *Ripon 3*   **P** *D&C*   **R** R SELLERS

FOUR ELMS (St Paul) *see* Hever, Four Elms and Mark Beech
Roch

FOUR MARKS (Good Shepherd) *Win 2*   **P** *Bp*
  V H J D WRIGHT,   **C** Y DUBREUIL

FOUR OAKS (All Saints) *Birm 12*   **P** *Bp*   **V** D A LEAHY,
  C J J BRIDGE,   **NSM** R M SHEPPARD

FOURSTONES (St Aidan) *see* Warden w Newbrough *Newc*

**FOVANT (St George), Sutton Mandeville and Teffont Evias w
Teffont Magna and Compton Chamberlayne** *Sarum 11*
  P *Reformation Ch Trust, Bp, and Ch Soc Trust (jt)*   **R** *vacant*
(01722) 714826

FOWEY (St Fimbarrus) *Truro 1*   **P** *Ch Soc Trust*
  P-in-c P DE GREY-WARTER

FOWLMERE (St Mary), Foxton, Shepreth and Thriplow *Ely 7*
  P *Bp*   **R** L A CHURCH

**FOWNHOPE (St Mary) w Mordiford, Brockhampton and
Fawley and Woolhope** *Heref 4*   **P** *D&C (4 turns), and
Major R J Hereford (1 turn)*   **R** W R PRIDIE,   **NSM** M M DEES

FOXCOTE (St James the Less) *see* Camerton w Dunkerton,
Foxcote and Shoscombe *B & W*

FOXDALE (St Paul) *S & M 1*   **P** *The Crown and Bp (alt)*
  V *vacant*

FOXEARTH (St Peter and St Paul) *see* N Hinckford *Chelmsf*

FOXHAM (St John the Baptist) *see* Derry Hill w Bremhill and
Foxham *Sarum*

FOXHILL (Chapel) *see* Frodsham *Ches*

FOXHOLE (St Boniface) *see* Paignton St Jo *Ex*

FOXHOLES (St Mary) *see* Langtoft w Foxholes, Butterwick,
Cottam etc *York*

FOXLEY (not known) *see* Sherston Magna, Easton Grey,
Luckington etc *Bris*

FOXLEY (St Thomas) *see* Lyng, Sparham, Elsing, Bylaugh,
Bawdeswell etc *Nor*

FOXT (St Mark the Evangelist) *see* Kingsley and Foxt-w-
Whiston *Lich*

FOXTON (St Andrew) w Gumley and Laughton *Leic 3*
  P *Bp Leic and D&C Linc (alt)*   **P-in-c** I L JOHNSON

FOXTON (St Laurence) *see* Fowlmere, Foxton, Shepreth and
Thriplow *Ely*

FOY (St Mary) *see* Brampton *Heref*

FRADLEY (St Stephen) *see* Alrewas *Lich*

FRADSWELL (St James the Less) *see* Mid Trent *Lich*

FRAISTHORPE (St Edmund King and Martyr) *see* Skipsea
and Barmston w Fraisthorpe *York*

FRAMFIELD (St Thomas à Becket) *Chich 21*   **P** *Mrs E R Wix*
  P-in-c C D LAWRENCE

FRAMILODE (St Peter) *see* Frampton on Severn, Arlingham,
Saul etc *Glouc*

FRAMINGHAM EARL (St Andrew) *see* Poringland *Nor*

FRAMINGHAM PIGOT (St Andrew) *see* Thurton *Nor*

FRAMLAND Parishes, The HIGH *Leic 2*   **P** *Duke of Rutland
and Sir Lyonel Tollemache Bt (jt)*   **P-in-c** P L BOTTING

FRAMLAND, SOUTH *Leic 2*   **P** *Ld Chan, Duke of Rutland,
Lady Gretton, and Sir Lyonel Tollemache Bt (by turn)*
  P-in-c R A KING

FRAMLINGHAM (St Michael) w Saxtead *St E 18*   **P** *Pemb
Coll Cam*   **P-in-c** G W OWEN,   **C** R P CLEMENT

FRAMPTON (St Mary) *see* Bradford Peverell, Stratton,
Frampton etc *Sarum*

FRAMPTON (St Mary) (St Michael) *Linc 21*   **P** *Trustees*
  P-in-c C W B SOWDEN

FRAMPTON COTTERELL (St Peter) and Iron Acton *Bris 5*
  P *SMF and Ch Ch Ox (jt)*   **C** D B HARREX, M A CLACKER

FRAMPTON MANSELL (St Luke) *see* Kemble, Poole Keynes,
Somerford Keynes etc *Glouc*

**FRAMPTON ON SEVERN (St Mary), Arlingham, Saul,
Fretherne and Framilode** *Glouc 5*   **P** *DBP, V Standish w
Haresfield etc, Brig Sir Jeffrey Darell Bt, and Bp (jt)*
  P-in-c J F HUBBARD,   **NSM** A E SPARGO

FRAMSDEN (St Mary) *see* Debenham and Helmingham *St E*

FRAMWELLGATE MOOR (St Aidan) *see* Dur N *Dur*

FRANCE LYNCH (St John the Baptist) *see* Bisley, Chalford,
France Lynch, and Oakridge *Glouc*

FRANCHE (St Barnabas) *see* Kidderminster St Mary and All
SS w Trimpley etc *Worc*

FRANKBY (St John the Divine) w Greasby St Nicholas *Ches 8*
  P *D&C*   **V** K P OWEN,   **C** G S FOSTER

FRANKLEY (St Leonard) *Birm 4*   **P** *Bp*   **P-in-c** R H TEBBS

FRANKTON (St Nicholas) *see* Bourton w Frankton and
Stretton on Dunsmore etc *Cov*

FRANSHAM, GREAT (All Saints) *see* Gt and Lt Dunham w
Gt and Lt Fransham and Sporle *Nor*

FRANSHAM, LITTLE (St Mary) *as above*

FRANT (St Alban) w Eridge *Chich 19*   **P** *Bp and Marquess of
Abergavenny (jt)*   **R** J M PACKMAN

FREASLEY (St Mary) *see* Dordon *Birm*

FRECHEVILLE (St Cyprian) *Sheff 2*   **P** *Bp*
  R M J GILLINGHAM

FRECKENHAM (St Andrew) *see* Mildenhall *St E*

FRECKLETON (Holy Trinity) *Blackb 10*   **P** *Bp*
  P-in-c J E C PERCIVAL,   **NSM** T B SCHOLZ

FREEBY (St Mary) *see* Melton Mowbray *Leic*

FREEHAY (St Chad) *see* Cheadle w Freehay *Lich*

FREELAND (St Mary the Virgin) *see* Hanborough and
Freeland *Ox*

FREEMANTLE (Christ Church) *Win 13*   **P** *Bp*
  P-in-c B L COX

**FREETHORPE (All Saints), Wickhampton, Halvergate w
Tunstall, Reedham, Cantley and Limpenhoe w Southwood** *Nor 4*
  P *Patr Bd*   **R** D ROGERS

FREEZYWATER (St George) *see* Enfield St Geo *Lon*

FREISTON (St James), Butterwick w Bennington, and Leverton
Linc 20   **P** *Ld Chan and Bp (alt)*   **P-in-c** A J HIGGINSON

FREMINGTON (St Peter) *Ex 15*   **P** *MMCET*
  V P H HOCKEY,   **C** A J RYAN

FRENCHAY (St John the Baptist) and Winterbourne Down
Bris 5   **P** *St Jo Coll Ox and SMF (jt)*   **C** S J PULLIN,
  M A CLACKER,   **OLM** J M LEE

FRENSHAM (St Mary the Virgin) *see* Rowledge and Frensham
Guildf

**FRESHFORD (St Peter) w Limpley Stoke and Hinton
Charterhouse** *B & W 9*   **P** *Simeon's Trustees and V Norton
St Phil (jt)*   **P-in-c** J M HOFFMANN

FRESHWATER (All Saints) (St Agnes) *Portsm 8*   **P** *St Jo Coll
Cam*   **R** M E C WHATSON,   **NSM** D K BELLAMY, G M HURT

**FRESSINGFIELD (St Peter and St Paul), Mendham, Metfield,
Weybread and Withersdale** *St E 17*   **P** *Bp, Em Coll Cam,
Ch Soc Trust, and SMF (jt)*   **P-in-c** S A LOXTON,
  NSM P A SCHWIER,   **OLM** R A WILLIS

FRESTON (St Peter) *see* Holbrook, Stutton, Freston,
Woolverstone etc *St E*

FRETHERNE (St Mary the Virgin)　*see* Frampton on Severn, Arlingham, Saul etc *Glouc*

FRETTENHAM (St Swithin)　*see* Coltishall w Gt Hautbois, Frettenham etc *Nor*

FRIAR PARK (St Francis of Assisi)　*see* W Bromwich St Fran *Lich*

FRIARMERE (St Thomas)　*see* Saddleworth *Man*

FRICKLEY (All Saints)　*see* Bilham *Sheff*

FRIDAY BRIDGE (St Mark)　*see* Fen Orchards *Ely*

FRIDAYTHORPE (St Mary)　*see* Waggoners *York*

FRIERN BARNET (All Saints) *Lon 14*　**P** *Bp*　**V** A V BENJAMIN

FRIERN BARNET (St James the Great) (St John the Evangelist) *Lon 14*　**P** *D&C St Paul's*　**R** P A WALMSLEY-MCLEOD

FRIERN BARNET (St Peter le Poer) *Lon 14*　**P** *D&C St Paul's*　**P-in-c** B W BRIDGEWOOD

FRIESTHORPE (St Peter)　*see* Middle Rasen Gp *Linc*

FRIETH (St John the Baptist)　*see* Hambleden Valley *Ox*

FRIEZLAND (Christ Church)　*see* Saddleworth *Man*

FRILSHAM (St Frideswide)　*see* Hermitage *Ox*

FRIMLEY (St Francis) (St Peter) *Guildf 6*　**P** *R Ash*　**R** M K WILSON,　**C** A H WALDEN,　**NSM** W H THOMAS

FRIMLEY GREEN (St Andrew) and Mytchett *Guildf 6*　**P** *Bp*　**V** S EDWARDS,　**OLM** C D COWELL

FRINDSBURY (All Saints) w Upnor and Chattenden *Roch 6*　**P** *Bp*　**V** I D BROWN,　**C** S A HERON

FRING (All Saints)　*see* Snettisham w Ingoldisthorpe and Fring *Nor*

FRINGFORD (St Michael)　*see* Shelswell *Ox*

FRINSTED (St Dunstan)　*see* Bredgar w Bicknor and Frinsted w Wormshill etc *Cant*

FRINTON (St Mary Magdalene) (St Mary the Virgin Old Church) *Chelmsf 22*　**P** *CPAS*　**R** D E SMITH

FRISBY-ON-THE-WREAKE (St Thomas of Canterbury)　*see* Upper Wreake *Leic*

FRISKNEY (All Saints) *Linc 20*　**P** *Bp*　**P-in-c** F J M COTTON-BETTERIDGE

FRISTON (St Mary Magdalene)　*see* Whinlands *St E*

FRISTON (St Mary the Virgin)　*see* E Dean w Friston and Jevington *Chich*

FRITCHLEY (Mission Room)　*see* Crich and S Wingfield *Derby*

FRITHELSTOCK (St Mary and St Gregory)　*see* Gt and Lt Torrington and Frithelstock *Ex*

FRITHVILLE (St Peter)　*see* Sibsey w Frithville *Linc*

FRITTENDEN (St Mary)　*see* Sissinghurst w Frittenden *Cant*

FRITTON (St Catherine)　*see* Hempnall *Nor*

FRITTON (St Edmund)　*see* Somerleyton, Ashby, Fritton, Herringfleet etc *Nor*

FRITWELL (St Olave)　*see* Cherwell Valley *Ox*

FRIZINGHALL (St Margaret) *Bradf 1*　**P** *Bp*　**P-in-c** S P HACKING,　**C** S D LEES

FRIZINGTON (St Paul)　*see* Crosslacon *Carl*

FROCESTER (St Andrew)　*see* Eastington, Frocester, Haresfield etc *Glouc*

FRODESLEY (St Mark)　*see* Condover w Frodesley, Acton Burnell etc *Heref*

FRODINGHAM (St Lawrence) *Linc 4*　**P** *Lord St Oswald*　**P-in-c** F CORE,　**C** G P THORNALLEY, E L WAKEHAM,　**NSM** M DUNFORD

FRODINGHAM, NORTH (St Elgin)　*see* Beeford w Frodingham and Foston *York*

FRODSHAM (St Lawrence) *Ches 3*　**P** *Ch Ch Ox*　**V** M H MILLS,　**NSM** K L WILLIAMSON

FROGMORE (Holy Trinity) *St Alb 1*　**P** *CPAS*　**V** D R HEATH-WHYTE,　**NSM** N A WARD

FROLESWORTH (St Nicholas)　*see* Upper Soar *Leic*

FROME (Christ Church) *B & W 4*　**P** *Bp*　**P-in-c** N A MAXTED

FROME (Holy Trinity) *B & W 4*　**P** *Bp*　**V** G A OWEN,　**C** J E BURGESS

FROME (St John the Baptist) *B & W 4*　**P** *DBP*　**V** C ALSBURY

FROME (St Mary the Virgin) *B & W 4*　**P** *Bp*　**V** D R BARGE

FROME ST QUINTON (St Mary)　*see* Melbury *Sarum*

FROME VALLEY Group of Parishes, The *Heref 2*　**P** *Bp (6 turns), MMCET (2 turns), D&C (1 turn)*　**V** J A DAVIES,　**NSM** C M SYKES

FROME VAUCHURCH (St Mary)　*see* Melbury *Sarum*

FROMES HILL (St Matthew)　*see* Frome Valley *Heref*

FROSTENDEN (All Saints)　*see* Wrentham, Covehithe w Benacre etc *St E*

FROSTERLEY (St Michael and All Angels)　*see* Upper Weardale *Dur*

FROXFIELD (All Saints)　*see* Whitton *Sarum*

FROXFIELD (St Peter)　*see* Steep and Froxfield w Privett *Portsm*

FROXFIELD (St Peter on the Green)　*as above*

FROYLE (Assumption of the Blessed Virgin Mary) and

Holybourne *Win 2*　**P** *Guild of All So and D&C (jt)*　**V** J S CROFT

FRYERNING (St Mary the Virgin)　*see* Ingatestone w Fryerning *Chelmsf*

FRYSTON (St Peter)　*see* Airedale w Fryston *Wakef*

FUGGLESTONE (St Peter)　*see* Wilton w Netherhampton and Fugglestone *Sarum*

FULBECK (St Nicholas)　*see* Caythorpe *Linc*

FULBOURN (St Vigor w All Saints) *Ely 4*　**P** *St Jo Coll Cam*　**R** R E JONES

FULBROOK (St Gabriel)　*see* Walsall St Gabr Fulbrook *Lich*

FULBROOK (St James the Great)　*see* Burford w Fulbrook, Taynton, Asthall etc *Ox*

FULFORD (St Oswald) *York 7*　**P** *Abp*　**V** S R TASH,　**NSM** A V BURR

FULFORD-IN-STONE (St Nicholas) w Hilderstone *Lich 13*　**P** *D&C*　**P-in-c** P D DAKIN,　**NSM** C E DAKIN

FULHAM (All Saints) *Lon 9*　**P** *Bp*　**V** J P HAWES,　**C** P A SEABROOK, J B HEARD

FULHAM (Christ Church) *Lon 9*　**P** *CPAS*　**V** S C R LEES,　**C** R L PENNYSTAN

FULHAM (St Alban) (St Augustine) *Lon 9*　**P** *Bp and City Corp (jt)*　**V** vacant (020) 7381 1500 *or* 7385 0724

FULHAM (St Andrew) Fulham Fields *Lon 9*　**P** *Bp*　**V** M R EASTWOOD,　**C** M J MCCARRON

FULHAM (St Dionis) Parson's Green *Lon 9*　**P** *Bp*　**V** T J STILWELL

FULHAM (St Etheldreda) (St Clement) *Lon 9*　**P** *Bp*　**P-in-c** J F H HENLEY

FULHAM (St Mary) North End *Lon 9*　**P** *Ch Soc Trust*　**V** R W CURL

FULHAM (St Matthew) *Lon 9*　**P** *Ch Patr Trust*　**V** G Q D PIPER,　**C** T J MCGOWAN,　**Dss** V S PIERSON

FULHAM (St Peter) *Lon 9*　**P** *Bp*　**P-in-c** J E JEPSON

FULKING (Good Shepherd)　*see* Poynings w Edburton, Newtimber and Pyecombe *Chich*

FULL SUTTON (St Mary)　*see* Garrowby Hill *York*

FULLETBY (St Andrew) *Linc 11*　**P** *Keble Coll Ox*　**V** vacant

FULMER (St James)　*see* Gerrards Cross and Fulmer *Ox*

FULMODESTON (Christ Church)　*see* Barney, Fulmodeston w Croxton, Hindringham etc *Nor*

FULSHAW (St Anne)　*see* Wilmslow *Ches*

FULSTOW (St Laurence)　*see* Fotherby *Linc*

FULWOOD (Christ Church) *Blackb 13*　**P** *V Lanc*　**V** B R MCCONKEY

FULWOOD (Christ Church) *Sheff 4*　**P** *CPAS*　**V** P A WILLIAMS,　**C** A R A REES, E F Q PENNINGTON

FULWOOD Lodge Moor (St Luke)　*see* Lodge Moor St Luke *Sheff*

FULWOOD (St Cuthbert)　*see* Preston St Cuth *Blackb*

FUNDENHALL (St Nicholas)　*see* Ashwellthorpe, Forncett, Fundenhall, Hapton etc *Nor*

FUNTINGTON (St Mary) and Sennicotts *Chich 13*　**P** *Bp*　**V** J J HOLLIMAN

FUNTLEY (St Francis)　*see* Fareham SS Pet and Paul *Portsm*

FURNACE GREEN (St Andrew)　*see* Southgate *Chich*

FURNESS VALE (St John)　*see* Disley *Ches*

FURNEUX PELHAM (St Mary the Virgin)　*see* Albury, Braughing, Furneux Pelham, Lt Hadham etc *St Alb*

FURNHAM (Good Shepherd)　*see* Chard Gd Shep and Cricket St Thomas *B & W*

FURTHO (St Bartholomew)　*see* Potterspury w Furtho and Yardley Gobion etc *Pet*

FURZE PLATT (St Peter) *Ox 13*　**P** *Bp*　**V** M A BALFOUR,　**C** E K HONEY,　**NSM** J R G HYDE

FURZEBANK (Worship Centre)　*see* Willenhall H Trin *Lich*

FURZEDOWN (St Paul)　*see* Streatham St Paul *S'wark*

FURZTON (not known)　*see* Watling Valley *Ox*

FYFIELD (St Nicholas)　*see* Upper Kennet *Sarum*

FYFIELD (St Nicholas)　*see* Appleshaw, Kimpton, Thruxton, Fyfield etc *Win*

FYFIELD (St Nicholas) w Tubney and Kingston Bagpuize *Ox 10*　**P** *St Jo Coll Ox*　**P-in-c** D A A PICKERING

FYFIELD (St Nicholas), Moreton w Bobbingworth and Willingale w Shellow and Berners Roding *Chelmsf 26*　**P** *Ld Chan, St Jo Coll Cam, MMCET, and Major G N Capel-Cure (by turn)*　**P-in-c** V ROSS

FYLINGDALES (St Stephen) and Hawsker cum Stainsacre *York 22*　**P** *Abp*　**V** vacant (01947) 880232

GADDESBY (St Luke)　*see* S Croxton Gp *Leic*

GADDESDEN, GREAT (St John the Baptist)　*see* Gt Berkhamsted, Gt and Lt Gaddesden etc *St Alb*

GADDESDEN, LITTLE (St Peter and St Paul)　*as above*

GADEBRIDGE (St Peter)　*see* Hemel Hempstead *St Alb*

GAINFORD (St Mary) *Dur 7*　**P** *Trin Coll Cam*　**P-in-c** M JACQUES

GAINSBOROUGH (All Saints) (St George) and Morton *Linc 2*
P *Bp*   **TR** N A THORNLEY,   **C** S R BENHAM,
OLM F A JEFFRIES
GALLEY COMMON (St Peter)   *see* Hartshill and Galley
Common *Cov*
GALLEYWOOD (Junior School Worship Centre)
see Galleywood Common *Chelmsf*
GALLEYWOOD COMMON (St Michael and All Angels)
Chelmsf 9   **P** *CPAS*   **V** A T GRIFFITHS,   **C** G E ANDERSON,
S R GILLINGHAM
GALMINGTON (St Michael) *B & W 18*   **P** *Bp*   **V** C SNELL
GALMPTON (Chapel of The Good Shepherd)   *see* Brixham w
Churston Ferrers and Kingswear *Ex*
GAMESLEY (Bishop Geoffrey Allen Church and County Centre)
see Charlesworth and Dinting Vale *Derby*
GAMLINGAY (St Mary the Virgin) and Everton *Ely 13*   **P** *Bp,
Clare Coll Cam, and Down Coll Cam (by turn)*   **R** S ROTHWELL
GAMLINGAY HEATH (St Sylvester)   *see* Gamlingay and
Everton *Ely*
GAMSTON and Bridgford *S'well 5*   **P** *DBP*
P-in-c M A FRASER
GAMSTON (St Peter) w Eaton and West Drayton *S'well 5*
P *D&C York and Bp (alt)*   **R** *vacant* (01777) 838706
GANAREW (St Swithin)   *see* Dixton, Wyesham, Bishopswood,
Whitchurch etc *Heref*
GANTON (St Nicholas)   *see* Willerby w Ganton and Folkton
York
GARBOLDISHAM (St John the Baptist)   *see* Guiltcross *Nor*
GARFORD (St Luke)   *see* Marcham w Garford *Ox*
GARFORTH (St Mary the Virgin) *Ripon 8*   **P** *DBP*
P-in-c G W COOPER,   **NSM** H BANKS
GARGRAVE (St Andrew) w Coniston Cold *Bradf 5*   **P** *Bp*
P-in-c R C GEDDES
GARRETTS GREEN (St Thomas) and Tile Cross *Birm 9*   **P** *Bp*
V B S CASTLE,   **NSM** M MACLACHLAN
GARRIGILL (St John)   *see* Alston Moor *Newc*
GARROWBY HILL *York 5*   **P** *Ld Chan (1 turn), Abp, D&C,
and Earl of Halifax (3 turns)*   **R** J C FINNEMORE
GARSDALE (St John the Baptist)   *see* Sedbergh, Cautley and
Garsdale *Bradf*
GARSDON (All Saints), Lea and Cleverton and Charlton *Bris 6*
P *Ch Soc Trust and Bp (jt)*   **R** R K EAST
GARSINGTON (St Mary)   *see* Wheatley *Ox*
GARSTANG (St Helen) Churchtown and St Michaels-on-Wyre
Blackb 9   **P** *Dr I R H Jackson and R P Hornby Esq (jt)*
V A W WILKINSON,   **NSM** C M WHALLEY
GARSTANG (St Thomas) *Blackb 9*   **P** *V Churchtown St Helen*
V M A GISBOURNE,   **NSM** A J ROBERTS
GARSTON (St Michael) *Liv 4*   **P** *Trustees*
P-in-c R L METCALF
GARSTON, EAST (All Saints)   *see* Eastbury and E Garston *Ox*
GARSWOOD (St Andrew)   *see* Ashton-in-Makerfield H Trin
Liv
GARTHORPE (St Mary)   *see* Crowle Gp *Linc*
GARTON IN HOLDERNESS (St Michael)   *see* Roos and
Garton w Tunstall, Grimston and Hilston *York*
GARTON-ON-THE-WOLDS (St Michael and All Angels)
see Woldsburn *York*
GARVESTON (St Margaret)   *see* Barnham Broom and Upper
Yare *Nor*
GARWAY (St Michael)   *see* St Weonards *Heref*
GASTARD (St John the Baptist)   *see* Gtr Corsham and Lacock
Bris
GATCOMBE (St Olave) *Portsm 8*   **P** *Qu Coll Ox*
P-in-c J F O'SHAUGHNESSY
GATE BURTON (St Helen)   *see* Lea Gp *Linc*
GATE HELMSLEY (St Mary)   *see* Sand Hutton *York*
GATEACRE (St Stephen) *Liv 4*   **P** *Bp*   **TR** P H JANVIER,
TV J L MCKELVEY,   **C** N H LEA-WILSON,   **NSM** K A CANTY
GATEFORTH (St Mary's Mission Room)   *see* Haddlesey w
Hambleton and Birkin *York*
GATELEY (St Helen)   *see* Upper Wensum Village Gp *Nor*
GATESHEAD Lobley Hill (All Saints)   *see* Hillside *Dur*
GATESHEAD (St Chad)   *see* Bensham and Teams *Dur*
**GATESHEAD (St Edmund's Chapel w Holy Trinity) (Venerable
Bede)** *Dur 12*   **P** *Bp and The Crown (alt)*   **TR** J C WILKINSON,
NSM E CARR, A PHILLIPS
GATESHEAD (St George) *Dur 12*   **P** *Trustees*
V E M T UNDERHILL
GATESHEAD (St Helen) *Dur 12*   **P** *Bp*   **V** B M HARRISON
GATESHEAD (St Ninian) Harlow Green   *see* Harlow Green
and Lamesley *Dur*
GATESHEAD FELL (St John) *Dur 12*   **P** *Bp*   **R** *vacant*
0191-440 2190
GATLEY (St James) *Ches 17*   **P** *R Stockport St Thos*
P-in-c R E READ,   **NSM** K M KIRBY

GATTEN (St Paul) *Portsm 7*   **P** *Ch Patr Trust*   **V** P G ALLEN
GATTON (St Andrew)   *see* Merstham and Gatton *S'wark*
GAULBY (St Peter) *Leic 4*   **P** *Ch Soc Trust*
V A F B CHEESMAN
GAUTBY (All Saints)   *see* Bardney *Linc*
GAWBER (St Thomas) *Wakef 7*   **P** *V Darton*
P-in-c M S POSKITT
GAWCOTT (Holy Trinity)   *see* Lenborough *Ox*
GAWSWORTH (St James) *Ches 13*   **P** *T R R Richards Esq*
R W A PWAISIHO
GAYDON (St Giles) w Chadshunt *Cov 8*   **P** *Bp*   **V** P T FRANCIS
**GAYHURST (St Peter) w Ravenstone, Stoke Goldington and
Weston Underwood** *Ox 27*   **P** *Bp and Lord Hesketh (jt)*
R C E PUMFREY,   **Hon C** J M LAWRENCE
GAYTON (St Mary)   *see* Pattishall w Cold Higham and Gayton
w Tiffield *Pet*
**GAYTON (St Nicholas), Gayton Thorpe, East Walton, East
Winch w West Bilney, Ashwicken w Leziate and Bawsey** *Nor 20*
P *Bp, Capt H Birkbeck, and W O Lancaster Esq (jt)*
R I C WHITTLE,   **NSM** S M MARTIN
GAYTON (St Peter)   *see* Mid Trent *Lich*
GAYTON LE WOLD (St Peter)   *see* Asterby Gp *Linc*
GAYTON THORPE (St Mary)   *see* Gayton, Gayton Thorpe, E
Walton, E Winch etc *Nor*
GAYWOOD (St Faith) King's Lynn *Nor 20*   **P** *Patr Bd*
TR S M THEAKSTON,   **TV** D R GINGRICH,
C L A HUMPHREYS, E A MARTIN,   **OLM** H E BERRY
GAZELEY (All Saints)   *see* Dalham, Gazeley, Higham,
Kentford and Moulton *St E*
GEDDING (St Mary the Virgin)   *see* Bradfield St Clare,
Bradfield St George etc *St E*
GEDDINGTON (St Mary Magdalene) w Weekley *Pet 9*
P *Boughton Estates*   **P-in-c** F G GODBER
GEDLING (All Hallows) *S'well 10*   **P** *DBP*   **R** M J TAYLOR,
NSM K D WILLIAMS
GEDNEY (St Mary Magdalene)   *see* Fleet w Gedney *Linc*
GEDNEY DROVE END (Christ Church)   *see* Lutton w Gedney
Drove End, Dawsmere *Linc*
GEDNEY HILL (Holy Trinity) (St Polycarp) *Linc 16*   **P** *Bp*
V R J MORRISON
GEE CROSS (Holy Trinity) (St Philip's Mission Room) *Ches 14*
P *V Werneth*   **V** M I BENNETT,   **C** J HALSTEAD
GELDESTON (St Michael)   *see* Gillingham w Geldeston,
Stockton, Ellingham etc *Nor*
GENTLESHAW (Christ Church) *Lich 1*   **P** *MMCET*
P-in-c M J BUTT,   **NSM** M R AUSTIN,   **OLM** L MCKEON
GEORGEHAM (St George) *Ex 15*   **P** *MMCET*
P-in-c B STRANGE
GERMAN (St German) *S & M 1*   **P** *Bp*   **V** N P GODFREY
GERMAN (St John the Baptist) *S & M 1*   **P** *Bp*   **V** *vacant*
GERMANSWEEK (St German)   *see* Okehampton w
Inwardleigh, Bratton Clovelly etc *Ex*
GERMOE (St Germoe)   *see* Breage w Godolphin and Germoe
Truro
GERRANS (St Gerran) w St Anthony-in-Roseland and Philleigh
Truro 6   **P** *Bp and MMCET (jt)*   **P-in-c** J K EDWARDS
GERRARDS CROSS (St James) and Fulmer *Ox 20*   **P** *Bp and
Simeon's Trustees (jt)*   **C** M J WILLIAMS, H A MONAGHAN,
J R LEACH,   **NSM** M R L BEEBEE
GESTINGTHORPE (St Mary)   *see* Knights and Hospitallers
Par *Chelmsf*
**GIDDING, GREAT (St Michael) w LITTLE (St John) and
Steeple Gidding** *Ely 10*   **P** *Sir Philip Naylor-Leyland Bt and Bp
(alt)*   **P-in-c** J DUCK
GIDEA PARK (St Michael) *Chelmsf 2*   **P** *Bp*   **V** M A H FINCH,
C C A TIBBOTT
GIDLEIGH (Holy Trinity)   *see* Chagford, Drewsteignton,
Hittisleigh etc *Ex*
GIGGETTY LANE (The Venerable Bede)   *see* Smestow Vale
Lich
GIGGLESWICK (St Alkelda) and Rathmell w Wigglesworth
Bradf 5   **P** *Bp and Ch Trust Fund Trust (jt)*
P-in-c N S KENDRA,   **NSM** A T HELM
GILCRUX (St Mary)   *see* Aspatria w Hayton and Gilcrux *Carl*
GILDERSOME (St Peter) *Wakef 8*   **P** *V Batley*
V A F LAWSON
GILLAMOOR (St Aidan)   *see* Kirkbymoorside w Gillamoor,
Farndale etc *York*
GILLING (St Agatha) and Kirkby Ravensworth *Ripon 2*   **P** *Bp
and A C P Wharton Esq (jt)*   **P-in-c** A GLEDHILL
GILLING EAST (Holy Cross)   *see* Ampleforth w Oswaldkirk,
Gilling E etc *York*
GILLINGHAM (Holy Trinity) *Roch 3*   **P** *Bp*   **V** G E TOVAR
GILLINGHAM (St Augustine) *Roch 3*   **P** *Bp*
P-in-c J P JENNINGS,   **NSM** P MATTHIAS

GILLINGHAM (St Barnabas) *Roch 3*   **P** *Bp*   **V** *vacant* (01634) 851010

GILLINGHAM (St Luke)   *see* New Brompton St Luke *Roch*

GILLINGHAM (St Mark) *Roch 3*   **P** *Hyndman Trustees*
C G E MCWATT

GILLINGHAM (St Mary Magdalene) *Roch 3*   **P** *DBP*
P-in-c S M PATTLE,   **NSM** E A CHAPMAN

GILLINGHAM (St Mary the Virgin) and Milton-on-Stour
Sarum 5   **P** *Bp*   **V** *vacant* (01747) 822435 *or* 821598

GILLINGHAM (St Mary) w Geldeston w Stockton w Ellingham
St Mary and Kirby Cane *Nor 8*   **P** *Ld Chan (1 turn), Bp,*
MMCET and Ch Trust Fund Trust (1 turn)   **P-in-c** J L ODDY

GILLINGHAM, SOUTH (St Matthew) *Roch 3*   **P** *Patr Bd*
TR C M BUTT,   **TV** S C FERRIS, P J BARNES,   **NSM** G R LEWIS

GILLOW HEATH (Mission Room)   *see* Biddulph *Lich*

GILMORTON (All Saints), Peatling Parva, Kimcote cum
Walton, North Kilworth, South Kilworth, Misterton, Swinford,
Catthorpe, Shawell and Stanford *Leic 7*   **P** *Patr Bd (5 turns),*
Ld Chan (1 turn)   **TR** K W BAKER,   **NSM** J R KENNEDY

GILSLAND (St Mary Magdalene)   *see* Lanercost, Walton,
Gilsland and Nether Denton *Carl*

GILSTEAD (St Wilfrid)   *see* Bingley H Trin *Bradf*

GILSTON (St Mary)   *see* High Wych and Gilston w Eastwick
St Alb

GIMINGHAM (All Saints)   *see* Trunch *Nor*

GIPPING (Chapel of St Nicholas)   *see* Haughley w Wetherden
and Stowupland *St E*

GIPSY HILL (Christ Church) *S'wark 12*   **P** *CPAS*
V A P RUMSEY

GIPTON (Church of the Epiphany)   *see* Leeds Gipton Epiphany
Ripon

GIRLINGTON (St Philip) *Bradf 1*   **P** *Simeon's Trustees*
V A A TOOBY

GIRTON (St Andrew) *Ely 6*   **P** *Ld Chan*   **R** W J ADAM,
NSM M C BARROW

GIRTON (St Cecilia)   *see* Collingham w S Scarle and Besthorpe
and Girton *S'well*

GISBURN (St Mary the Virgin) *Bradf 5*   **P** *Bp*
P-in-c E A KYTE,   **Hon C** K J PHILLIPS

GISLEHAM (Holy Trinity)   *see* Kessingland, Gisleham and
Rushmere *Nor*

GISLINGHAM (St Mary)   *see* S Hartismere *St E*

GISSING (St Mary the Virgin)   *see* Winfarthing w Shelfanger w
Burston w Gissing etc *Nor*

GITTISHAM (St Michael)   *see* Honiton, Gittisham, Combe
Raleigh, Monkton etc *Ex*

GIVENDALE, GREAT (St Ethelberga)   *see* Pocklington and
Owsthorpe and Kilnwick Percy etc *York*

GLAISDALE (St Thomas)   *see* Middle Esk Moor *York*

GLANDFORD (St Martin)   *see* Blakeney w Cley, Wiveton,
Glandford etc *Nor*

GLANTON (St Peter)   *see* Whittingham and Edlingham w
Bolton Chapel *Newc*

GLANVILLES WOOTTON (St Mary the Virgin)   *see* Vale of
White Hart *Sarum*

GLAPTHORN (St Leonard)   *see* Oundle w Ashton and
Benefield w Glapthorn *Pet*

GLAPWELL (St Andrew)   *see* Ault Hucknall and Scarcliffe
Derby

GLASCOTE (St George) and Stonydelph *Lich 4*   **P** *Patr Bd*
TR I H MURRAY,   **TV** J W TROOD, D S MCDONOUGH,
OLM M R LE-WORTHY, R J LOCKWOOD, P D FAULTLESS,
K R LINDSAY-SMITH

GLASCOTE HEATH (St Peter)   *see* Glascote and Stonydelph
Lich

GLASSHOUGHTON (St Paul)   *see* Castleford *Wakef*

GLASSON (Christ Church)   *see* Cockerham w Winmarleigh and
Glasson *Blackb*

GLASTON (St Andrew)   *see* Lyddington w Stoke Dry and
Seaton etc *Pet*

GLASTONBURY (St John the Baptist) (St Benedict) w Meare
B & W 5   **P** *Bp*   **P-in-c** D J L MACGEOCH,   **Hon C** M B MUDIE

GLATTON (St Nicholas)   *see* Sawtry and Glatton *Ely*

GLAZEBURY (All Saints) w Hollinfare *Liv 15*   **P** *Bp and*
R Warrington (jt)   **R** R G LEWIS,   **C** P L GRAY

GLAZELEY (St Bartholomew)   *see* Highley w Billingsley,
Glazeley etc *Heref*

GLEADLESS (Christ Church) *Sheff 1*   **P** *DBP*
TR H A JOWETT,   **NSM** S D HOLDAWAY

GLEADLESS VALLEY (Holy Cross)   *see* Heeley and Gleadless
Valley *Sheff*

GLEM VALLLEY United Benefice, The   *see* Glemsford, Hartest
w Boxted, Somerton etc *St E*

GLEMHAM, GREAT (All Saints)   *see* Alde River *St E*

GLEMHAM, LITTLE (St Andrew)   *as above*

GLEMSFORD (St Mary the Virgin), Hartest w Boxted,
Somerton and Stanstead (Glem Valley United Benefice) *St E 12*
P *Bp, Prime Min, and Ch Soc Trust (by turn)*   **R** P J PRIGG

GLEN AULDYN (Mission Church)   *see* Lezayre *S & M*

GLEN GROUP, The *Linc 17*   **P** *Bp*   **V** M A HARVEY,
C L PUGH,   **OLM** P E HARDINGHAM

GLEN MAGNA (St Cuthbert) cum Stretton Magna w Carlton
Curlieu and Burton Overy *Leic 4*   **P** *Bp, Dr A Llewelyn, and*
Sir Geoffrey Palmer Bt (jt)   **P-in-c** M J IRELAND

GLEN PARVA and South Wigston *Leic 4*   **P** *Bp*   **V** P DAY

GLENDALE Group, The *Newc 7*   **P** *Patr Bd (4 turns), Ld Chan*
(1 turn)   **TR** R B S BURSTON,   **TV** G R KELSEY

GLENEAGLES Conventional District *Pet 6*   **Min** M C PEREIRA

GLENFIELD (St Peter) *Leic 9*   **P** *Bp*   **R** J E SHARPE,
C K R THOMAS

GLENHOLT (St Anne)   *see* Bickleigh and Shaugh Prior *Ex*

GLENTHAM (St Peter)   *see* Owmby Gp *Linc*

GLENTWORTH Group, The (St Michael) *Linc 2*   **P** *Bp,*
MMCET, and Ch Soc Trust (jt)   **V** M DAWSON

GLINTON (St Benedict)   *see* Peakirk w Glinton and
Northborough *Pet*

GLODWICK (St Mark w Christ Church) *Man 19*   **P** *Bp*
V G HOLLOWOOD

GLOOSTON (St John the Baptist)   *see* Welham, Glooston and
Cranoe and Stonton Wyville *Leic*

GLOSSOP (All Saints) *Derby 6*   **P** *Patr Bd*   **V** *vacant* (01457)
852146

GLOUCESTER (St Aldate) Finlay Road *Glouc 3*   **P** *Bp*
P-in-c K C JONES

GLOUCESTER (St Barnabas)   *see* Tuffley *Glouc*

GLOUCESTER (St Catharine) *Glouc 3*   **P** *Bp*
V G D OSBORNE,   **C** A C SWIFT,   **NSM** M WILLIAMS

GLOUCESTER (St George) w Whaddon *Glouc 3*   **P** *Bp*
P-in-c D R SMITH

GLOUCESTER (St James and All Saints) *Glouc 3*   **P** *Bp*
P-in-c R C SIMPSON,   **NSM** J M HOWARD

GLOUCESTER (St Mark) (St Mary de Crypt) (St John the
Baptist) (Christ Church) (St Mary de Lode) (St Nicholas)
Glouc 3   **P** *D&C (1 turn), Bp (3 turns), Ld Chan (1 turn)*
R *vacant* (01452) 412679

GLOUCESTER (St Michael)   *see* Tuffley *Glouc*

GLOUCESTER (St Oswald)   *see* Coney Hill *Glouc*

GLOUCESTER (St Paul) *Glouc 3*   **P** *Bp*
P-in-c R J WITCOMBE,   **NSM** J R MURPHY, G HUBBARD

GLOUCESTER (St Stephen) *Glouc 3*   **P** *Bp*
P-in-c J A L B CATERER

GLOUCESTER DOCKS Mariners' Church Proprietary Chapel
Glouc 3   **P** *Ch Soc Trust vacant*

GLOUCESTER ROAD (St Stephen)   *see* S Kensington St Steph
Lon

GLUSBURN (All Saints)   *see* Sutton w Cowling and
Lothersdale *Bradf*

GLYMPTON (St Mary)   *see* Wootton w Glympton and
Kiddington *Ox*

GLYNDE (St Mary), West Firle and Beddingham *Chich 18*
P *Bp and D&C Windsor (alt)*   **P-in-c** P C OWEN-JONES

GNOSALL (St Lawrence) and Moreton *Lich 7*   **P** *Bp*
P-in-c M S BRIDGEN,   **OLM** E HAYCOCK

GOADBY (St John the Baptist)   *see* Church Langton cum Tur
Langton etc *Leic*

GOADBY MARWOOD (St Denys)   *see* Ironstone Villages *Leic*

GOATHILL (St Peter)   *see* Milborne Port w Goathill etc *B & W*

GOATHLAND (St Mary)   *see* Middle Esk Moor *York*

GOATHURST (St Edward the King and Martyr)   *see* Aisholt,
Enmore, Goathurst, Nether Stowey etc *B & W*

GOBOWEN (All Saints)   *see* Selattyn and Hengoed w Gobowen
Lich

GOBOWEN ROAD (Mission Room)   *see* Oswestry *Lich*

GODALMING (St Peter and St Paul) *Guildf 4*   **P** *Bp*
TV P F HARTOPP,   **C** C D WILLIAMS,   **NSM** T C P DEAN,
OLM R HARVIE

GODINGTON (Holy Trinity)   *see* Shelswell *Ox*

GODLEY cum Newton Green (St John the Baptist) *Ches 14*
P R Cheadle   **P-in-c** M D HARRIES

GODMANCHESTER (St Mary) *Ely 10*   **P** *D&C Westmr*
P-in-c D W BUSK,   **C** M P JEPP

GODMANSTONE (Holy Trinity)   *see* Buckland Newton, Cerne
Abbas, Godmanstone etc *Sarum*

GODMERSHAM (St Lawrence the Martyr)   *see* Crundale w
Godmersham *Cant*

GODREVY *Truro 5*   **P** *Patr Bd*   **TV** E V A FOOT,
NSM P C JOHNSON, P M MURLEY, M A TREMBATH

GODSHILL (All Saints) *Portsm 7*   **P** *Guild of All So*
V J M RYDER

GODSHILL (St Giles)   *see* Fordingbridge and Breamore and
Hale etc *Win*

GODSTONE (St Nicholas) and Blindley Heath *S'wark 25*   **P** *Bp and T Goad Esq (jt)*   **R** R E WATTS
GOFF'S OAK (St James) *see* Cheshunt *St Alb*
GOLBORNE (St Thomas) *Liv 15*   **P** *Bp*   **P-in-c** J W REED
GOLCAR (St John the Evangelist) *Wakef 5*   **P** *V Huddersfield*   **V** R M F CROMPTON,   **C** B M MITCHELL
GOLDEN CAP TEAM (Team Ministry) *Sarum 2*   **P** *Patr Bd*   **TR** S J SKINNER,   **TV** J A L HARRISSON,   **NSM** R E BRAGG, J M SKINNER
GOLDEN GREEN (Mission) *see* Hadlow *Roch*
GOLDEN VALLEY (St Matthias) *see* Riddings and Ironville *Derby*
GOLDENHILL (St John the Evangelist) *Lich 11*   **P** *Bp* **P-in-c** K P SCOTT
GOLDERS GREEN (St Alban the Martyr and St Michael) *Lon 15*   **P** *Bp*   **V** R G MORTON
GOLDHANGER (St Peter) *see* Gt Totham and Lt Totham w Goldhanger *Chelmsf*
GOLDINGTON (St Mary the Virgin) *St Alb 10*   **P** *Bp*   **V** R L HOWLETT,   **C** C N NJOKU,   **NSM** B JOHNSON
GOLDS HILL (St Paul) *see* W Bromwich St Jas w St Paul *Lich*
GOLDSBOROUGH (St Mary) *see* Knaresborough *Ripon*
GOLDSWORTH PARK (St Andrew) *Guildf 12*   **P** *Bp*   **V** R J N COOK,   **NSM** C A HARRISON,   **OLM** P R B DONAGHY
GOLDTHORPE (St John the Evangelist and St Mary Magdalene) w Hickleton *Sheff 12*   **P** *CR (2 turns), Earl of Halifax (1 turn)*   **V** C R SCHAEFER
GOMERSAL (St Mary) *Wakef 8*   **P** *Bp*   **C** A J RAGGETT
GONALSTON (St Laurence) *S'well 15*   **P** *C P L Francklin Esq, Bp, and Ld Chan (by turn)*   **P-in-c** A R GILES, **NSM** M N TAYLOR
GONERBY, GREAT (St Sebastian) *see* Barrowby and Gt Gonerby *Linc*
GOOD EASTER (St Andrew) *see* High and Gd Easter w Margaret Roding *Chelmsf*
GOOD SHEPHERD TEAM MINISTRY, The *Carl 4*   **P** *Patr Bd*   **TR** W J WHITE,   **TV** H M K BRETT YOUNG
GOODERSTONE (St George) *see* Cockley Cley w Gooderstone *Nor*
GOODLEIGH (St Gregory) *see* Barnstaple *Ex*
GOODMANHAM (All Saints) *York 5*   **P** *Abp*   **R** L C MUNT
GOODMAYES (All Saints) *Chelmsf 4*   **P** *Hyndman Trustees*   **V** P H NYATSANZA
GOODMAYES (St Paul) *Chelmsf 4*   **P** *Bp*   **V** B J RUTT-FIELD
GOODNESTONE (Holy Cross) *see* Nonington w Wymynswold and Goodnestone etc *Cant*
GOODRICH (St Giles), Marstow, Welsh Bicknor, Llangarron, Llangrove and Welsh Newton w Llanrothal *Heref 8*   **P** *Bp (2 turns), D&C and DBP (2 turns)*   **V** S C MONDON, **NSM** R J STEPHENS
GOODRINGTON (St George) *Ex 12*   **P** *Bp*   **V** G H MAUDE, **C** D A PARSONS
GOODSHAW (St Mary and All Saints) and Crawshawbooth *Man 15*   **P** *Bp and Wm Hulme Trustees (jt)*   **C** L E M WOODALL,   **OLM** D SMITH
GOODWORTH CLATFORD (St Peter) *see* Abbotts Ann and Upper and Goodworth Clatford *Win*
GOOLE (St John the Evangelist) (St Mary) (Mariners' Club and Chapel) *Sheff 10*   **P** *Bp*   **V** N A SOPHIANOU
GOOSE GREEN (St Paul) *Liv 14*   **P** *Bp*   **V** *vacant* (01942) 242984
GOOSEY (All Saints) *see* Stanford in the Vale w Goosey and Hatford *Ox*
GOOSNARGH (St Mary the Virgin) *see* Fellside Team *Blackb*
GOOSTREY (St Luke) w Swettenham *Ches 11*   **P** *V Sandbach and MMCET (jt)*   **V** D R OTTLEY,   **NSM** P E SOULT
GORAN HAVEN (St Just) *see* St Goran w Caerhays *Truro*
GORDON HILL (St Michael and All Angels) *see* Enfield St Mich *Lon*
GOREFIELD (St Paul) *see* Wisbech St Mary and Guyhirn w Ring's End etc *Ely*
GORING (St Thomas of Canterbury) and Streatley with South Stoke *Ox 6*   **P** *Ch Ch Ox and Bp (jt)*   **V** M K BLAMEY, **C** C M K HARGRAVES,   **NSM** E J DOWDING
GORING-BY-SEA (St Mary) (St Laurence) *Chich 4*   **P** *Bp* **P-in-c** C L WILSON,   **C** A M PATTENDEN,   **NSM** P MATTHEWS
GORLESTON (St Andrew) *Nor 6*   **P** *Ch Trust Fund Trust*   **V** A P WARD,   **C** M K SIMM, D R CURRIE,   **NSM** H F WARD, **OLM** D A N WAITE
GORLESTON (St Mary Magdalene) *Nor 6*   **P** *Bp and Ch Trust Fund Trust (jt)*   **V** L E RICKETTS
GORNAL (St Peter) and Sedgley *Worc 10*   **P** *Patr Bd* **TR** S R BUCKLEY
GORNAL, LOWER (St James the Great) *Worc 10*   **P** *Bp* **V** J W MOTT

GORSLEY (Christ Church) *see* Newent and Gorsley w Cliffords Mesne *Glouc*
GORTON (Emmanuel) (St James) (St Philip) and Abbey Hey *Man 1*   **P** *Patr Bd and Prime-Min (alt)*   **TR** J FARADAY, **OLM** D C GRAY
GOSBECK (St Mary) *see* Coddenham w Gosbeck and Hemingstone w Henley *St E*
GOSBERTON (St Peter and St Paul), Gosberton Clough and Quadring *Linc 17*   **P** *Bp and D&C (jt)*   **P-in-c** I R WALTERS, **OLM** P E HARDINGHAM
GOSBERTON CLOUGH (St Gilbert and St Hugh) *see* Gosberton, Gosberton Clough and Quadring *Linc*
GOSCOTE, EAST (St Hilda) *see* Syston *Leic*
GOSFIELD (St Katherine) *see* Halstead Area *Chelmsf*
GOSFORTH (All Saints) *Newc 2*   **P** *Bp*   **V** G L TUNBRIDGE, **C** A MAXWELL,   **NSM** R B BIRNIE
GOSFORTH (St Hugh) *Newc 2*   **P** *Bp*   **V** *vacant* 0191-285 8792
GOSFORTH (St Mary) w Nether Wasdale and Wasdale Head *Carl 5*   **P** *Bp, Earl of Lonsdale, V St Bees, and PCCs (jt)* **P-in-c** J M S FALKNER
GOSFORTH (St Nicholas) *Newc 2*   **P** *Bp*   **V** P J CUNNINGHAM,   **NSM** M C DOUGLASS
GOSFORTH, NORTH (St Columba) *see* Ch the King *Newc*
GOSFORTH VALLEY (St Andrew) *see* Dronfield w Holmesfield *Derby*
GOSPEL END (St Barnabas) *see* Gornal and Sedgley *Worc*
GOSPEL OAK (All Hallows) *see* Hampstead St Steph w All Hallows *Lon*
GOSPEL OAK (St Martin) *see* Kentish Town St Martin w St Andr *Lon*
GOSPORT (Christ Church) *Portsm 3*   **P** *Bp*   **V** A G DAVIS
GOSPORT (Holy Trinity) *Portsm 3*   **P** *DBP*   **V** A G DAVIS
GOSSOPS GREEN (St Alban) *see* Ifield *Chich*
GOTHAM (St Lawrence) *S'well 9*   **P** *Bp*   **P-in-c** S W OSMAN
GOUDHURST (St Mary the Virgin) w Kilndown *Cant 11*   **P** *Abp and Prime Min (alt)*   **V** J HORNSBY
GOULCEBY (All Saints) *see* Asterby Gp *Linc*
GOXHILL (All Saints) *see* Barrow and Goxhill *Linc*
GOXHILL (St Giles) *see* Aldbrough, Mappleton w Goxhill and Withernwick *York*
GRADE (St Grada and the Holy Cross) *see* St Ruan w St Grade and Landewednack *Truro*
GRAFFHAM (St Giles) w Woolavington *Chich 11*   **P** *Bp* **R** *vacant* (01798) 867247
GRAFFOE Group *Linc 18*   **P** *Ch Coll Cam, D&C and DBP, Viscountess Chaplin, Oriel Coll Ox, and Mrs P N Fullerton (by turn)*   **V** K A WINDSLOW,   **NSM** S G WILLIAMS
GRAFHAM (All Saints) *see* E Leightonstone *Ely*
GRAFHAM (St Andrew) *see* Bramley and Grafham *Guildf*
GRAFTON, EAST (St Nicholas) *see* Savernake *Sarum*
GRAFTON FLYFORD (St John the Baptist) *see* Abberton, The Flyfords, Naunton Beauchamp etc *Worc*
GRAFTON REGIS (St Mary) *see* Blisworth and Stoke Bruerne w Grafton Regis etc *Pet*
GRAFTON UNDERWOOD (St James the Apostle) *see* Cranford w Grafton Underwood and Twywell *Pet*
GRAHAME PARK (St Augustine) Conventional District *Lon 15* **C-in-c** D C BATLEY-GLADDEN
GRAIN (St James) w Stoke *Roch 6*   **P** *DBP* **P-in-c** G V HERBERT
GRAINSBY (St Nicholas) *see* The North-Chapel Parishes *Linc*
GRAINTHORPE (St Clement) *see* Somercotes and Grainthorpe w Conisholme *Linc*
GRAMPOUND (St Nun) *see* Probus, Ladock and Grampound w Creed and St Erme *Truro*
GRAMPOUND ROAD Mission Church *as above*
GRANBOROUGH (St John the Baptist) *see* Schorne *Ox*
GRANBY (All Saints) *see* Cropwell Bishop w Colston Bassett, Granby etc *S'well*
GRANDBOROUGH (St Peter) *see* Leam Valley *Cov*
GRANGE (Holy Trinity) *see* Upper Derwent *Carl*
GRANGE (St Andrew) *Ches 3*   **P** *Bp*   **P-in-c** U R ONUNWA
GRANGE FELL (not known) *see* Cartmel Peninsula *Carl*
GRANGE MOOR (St Bartholomew) *see* Kirkheaton *Wakef*
GRANGE-OVER-SANDS (St Paul) *see* Cartmel Peninsula *Carl*
GRANGE PARK (St Peter) *Lon 18*   **P** *Bp*   **V** E G GREER
GRANGE VILLA (St Columba) *see* Pelton and W Pelton *Dur*
GRANGETOWN (St Aidan) *Dur 16*   **P** *V Ryhope* **V** C COLLINS
GRANGETOWN (St Hilda of Whitby) *York 18*   **P** *Abp* **V** I M GRAHAM
GRANSDEN, GREAT (St Bartholomew) and Abbotsley and Lt Gransden and Waresley *Ely 13*   **P** *Pemb Coll Cam (1 turn), Clare Coll Cam (2 turns), and Ball Coll Ox (1 turn)* **P-in-c** C M FURLONG

GRANSDEN, LITTLE (St Peter and St Paul) *see* Gt Gransden and Abbotsley and Lt Gransden etc *Ely*

GRANTCHESTER (St Andrew and St Mary) *Ely 3* **P** *CCC Cam* **P-in-c** S P MEWS

GRANTHAM Earlesfield *Linc 19* **P** *Bp* **V** S G ROWLAND

GRANTHAM Harrowby w Londonthorpe *Linc 19* **P** *Bp* **P-in-c** C P BOLAND, **NSM** A P JABLONSKI

GRANTHAM Manthorpe *Linc 19* **P** *Bp* **NSM** J POTTS

GRANTHAM (St Anne) New Somerby and St John Spitalgate *Linc 19* **P** *Bp and R Grantham (jt)* **V** vacant (01476) 562822

GRANTHAM (St John the Evangelist) *see* Grantham, Manthorpe *Linc*

GRANTHAM (St Wulfram) *Linc 19* **P** *Bp* **R** C P ANDREWS, C A J JABLONSKI, **NSM** J T FARLEY, J M ROWLAND

GRANTHAM (The Ascension) *see* Grantham, Harrowby w Londonthorpe *Linc*

GRANTHAM (The Epiphany) *see* Grantham, Earlesfield *Linc*

GRAPPENHALL (St Wilfrid) *Ches 4* **P** *G Greenall Esq* **R** M B KELLY

GRASBY (All Saints) *see* Caistor Gp *Linc*

GRASMERE (St Oswald) *Carl 11* **P** *Qu Coll Ox* **R** C J BUTLAND

GRASSENDALE (St Mary) *Liv 4* **P** *Trustees* **P-in-c** P ELLIS

GRATELEY (St Leonard) *see* Portway and Danebury *Win*

GRATWICH (St Mary the Virgin) *see* Uttoxeter Area *Lich*

GRAVELEY (St Botolph) *see* Papworth *Ely*

GRAVELEY (St Mary) *see* Stevenage St Nic and Graveley *St Alb*

GRAVELLY HILL (All Saints) *Birm 8* **P** *Bp* **V** G R MENSINGH, **NSM** A R FRASER

GRAVENEY (All Saints) *see* Preston next Faversham, Goodnestone and Graveney *Cant*

GRAVENHURST, Shillington and Stondon *St Alb 16* **P** *Bp* **V** S J WHEATLEY

GRAVESEND (Holy Family) w Ifield *Roch 4* **P** *Bp and Lt-Col F B Edmeades (jt)* **R** vacant (01474) 356221 *or* 363038

GRAVESEND (St Aidan) *Roch 4* **P** *Bp* **V** P G RICH, C R A MARTIN, **NSM** J P LITTLEWOOD

GRAVESEND (St George) *Roch 4* **P** *Bp* **R** J C STONE

GRAVESEND (St Mary) *Roch 4* **P** *R Gravesend* **V** R OATES

GRAYINGHAM (St Radegunda) *Linc 6* **P** *Bp* **C** P L COSTIN, **OLM** J WILSON

GRAYRIGG (St John) *see* Beacon *Carl*

GRAYS NORTH (St John the Evangelist) *Chelmsf 14* **P** *Bp* **NSM** J C TOMLINSON

GRAYS THURROCK (St Peter and St Paul) *Chelmsf 14* **P** *DBP* **TR** D BARLOW, **TV** A J GOWING-CUMBER, M A REYNOLDS, **C** S E BRAZIER-GIBBS, S H GIBBS, **NSM** C M WILLIAMS, J G CHEGE

GRAYSHOTT (St Luke) *Guildf 3* **P** *Bp* **V** C M S R THOMAS, **Hon C** G E KNIFTON, **NSM** H J BENNET

GRAYSWOOD (All Saints) *see* Haslemere and Grayswood *Guildf*

GRAYTHWAITE (Mission Room) *see* Hawkshead and Low Wray w Sawrey and Rusland etc *Carl*

GREASBROUGH (St Mary) *Sheff 6* **P** *Sir Philip Naylor-Leyland Bt* **V** K E TONES

GREASBY (St Nicholas) *see* Frankby w Greasby *Ches*

GREASLEY (St Mary) *S'well 4* **P** *Bp* **P-in-c** D A MARVIN

GREAT *see also under substantive place name*

GREAT CAMBRIDGE ROAD (St John the Baptist and St James) *Lon 19* **P** *D&C St Paul's* **V** P B LYONS

GREAT GLEN (St Cuthbert) *see* Glen Magna cum Stretton Magna etc *Leic*

GREAT MOOR (St Saviour) *see* Stockport St Sav *Ches*

GREATER *see under substantive place name*

GREATFORD (St Thomas à Becket) *see* Uffington Gp *Linc*

GREATHAM (not known) *see* Amberley w N Stoke and Parham, Wiggonholt etc *Chich*

GREATHAM (St John the Baptist) *Dur 3* **P** *Trustees* **P-in-c** P T ALLINSON

GREATHAM (St John the Baptist) w Empshott and Hawkley w Prior's Dean *Portsm 4* **P** *DBP* **R** D H HEATLEY

GREATSTONE (St Peter) *see* Lydd *Cant*

GREATWORTH (St Peter) *see* Chenderit *Pet*

GREAVE FOLD (Holy Innocents) *see* Chadkirk *Ches*

GREEN HAMMERTON (St Thomas) *see* Gt and Lt Ouseburn w Marton cum Grafton etc *Ripon*

GREEN HAWORTH (St Clement) *see* Accrington Ch the King *Blackb*

GREEN HEATH (St Saviour) *see* Hednesford *Lich*

GREEN STREET GREEN (St Mary) and Pratts Bottom *Roch 16* **P** *Bp* **V** K A CARPANI, **C** P J AVANN

GREEN VALE (Holy Trinity) *see* Stockton Holy Trinity w St Mark *Dur*

GREENFIELD *see* Bridgwater H Trin and Durleigh *B & W*

GREENFIELD (St Mary) *see* Saddleworth *Man*

GREENFIELDS (United Church) *see* Shrewsbury St Geo w Greenfields *Lich*

GREENFORD (Holy Cross) (St Edward the Confessor) *Lon 22* **P** *K Coll Cam* **R** N RICHARDSON

GREENFORD, NORTH (All Hallows) *Lon 22* **P** *Bp* **V** P F HEAZELL, **Hon C** S J COLLIER, **NSM** D C DAVIS

GREENGATES (St John the Evangelist) *Bradf 3* **P** *D&C* **P-in-c** G S DARLISON, **C** P MAYO-SMITH

GREENHAM (St Mary the Virgin) *Ox 14* **P** *Bp* **V** J P H CLARKE, **NSM** B R JONES, J BRAMHALL

GREENHAM (St Peter) *see* Wellington and Distr *B & W*

GREENHEAD (St Cuthbert) *see* Haltwhistle and Greenhead *Newc*

GREENHILL (St John the Baptist) *Lon 23* **P** *Bp, Adn, and V Harrow St Mary (jt)* **V** R A WAKELING

GREENHILL (St Peter) *Sheff 2* **P** *Bp* **V** L C JENKINS

GREENHITHE (St Mary) *Roch 2* **P** *Ch Soc Trust and Personal Reps Canon T L Livermore (jt)* **R** R D BARRON

GREENHOW HILL (St Mary) *see* Upper Nidderdale *Ripon*

GREENLANDS (St Anne) *Blackb 8* **P** *Bp and V Blackpool St Steph (jt)* **V** A M BARTLETT

GREENLANDS (St John the Evangelist) *see* Ipsley *Worc*

GREEN'S NORTON (St Bartholomew) *see* Towcester w Caldecote and Easton Neston etc *Pet*

GREENSIDE (St John) *Dur 13* **P** *R Ryton w Hedgefield* **V** C W DEVONISH, **NSM** C A FRISWELL

GREENSTEAD (St Andrew) (St Edmund's Church Hall) (St Matthew) w Colchester St Anne *Chelmsf 16* **P** *Patr Bd and Ld Chan (alt)* **TR** M E WEST, **TV** J H LE SEVE, **C** T MCFADDEN, **NSM** A C BUSHELL

GREENSTEAD GREEN (St James Apostle) *see* Halstead Area *Chelmsf*

GREENSTED-JUXTA-ONGAR (St Andrew) w Stanford Rivers and Stapleford Tawney w Theydon Mount *Chelmsf 26* **P** *Bp Lon and DBP (1 turn), and Duchy of Lanc (1 turn)* **P-in-c** A A PETRINE

GREENWICH (St Alfege) *S'wark 1* **P** *The Crown* **V** C J E MOODY, **C** M K TWINING

GREENWICH, EAST (Christ Church) (St Andrew w St Michael) (St George) *S'wark 1* **P** *Patr Bd* **TR** M N A TORRY, **TV** D P CLACEY, **C** J S FRASER, **Hon C** J P LEE, **OLM** C A FINNERTY

GREETE (St James) *see* Burford II w Greete and Hope Bagot *Heref*

GREETHAM (All Saints) *see* Horncastle Gp *Linc*

GREETHAM (St Mary the Virgin) and Thistleton w Stretton and Clipsham *Pet 12* **P** *Bp and Sir David Davenport-Handley (alt)* **C** F B SOLMAN

GREETLAND (St Thomas) and West Vale *Wakef 2* **P** *V Halifax* **P-in-c** T L SWINHOE, **C** D BURROWS

GREETWELL (All Saints) *see* S Lawres Gp *Linc*

GREINTON (St Michael and All Angels) *B & W 5* **P** *Bp* **P-in-c** J K L POWELL

GRENDON (All Saints) *see* Baddesley Ensor w Grendon *Birm*

GRENDON (St Mary) *see* Yardley Hastings, Denton and Grendon etc *Pet*

GRENDON BISHOP (St John the Baptist) *see* Bredenbury *Heref*

GRENDON UNDERWOOD (St Leonard) *see* The Claydons and Swan *Ox*

GRENOSIDE (St Mark) *Sheff 3* **P** *Bp and V Ecclesfield (jt)* **V** J M KILNER

GRESHAM (All Saints) *see* Aylmerton, Runton, Beeston Regis and Gresham *Nor*

GRESLEY (St George and St Mary) *Derby 16* **P** *Simeon's Trustees* **P-in-c** D T PERRETT, **C** J A BURGESS

GRESSENHALL (Assumption of the Blessed Virgin Mary) w Longham w Wendling and Bittering Parva *Nor 14* **P** *Ld Chan (1 turn), CPAS (2 turns)* **P-in-c** R J MARSDEN, **NSM** K D BLOGG

GRESSINGHAM (St John the Evangelist) *see* Hornby w Claughton and Whittington etc *Blackb*

GRETTON (Christ Church) *see* Winchcombe *Glouc*

GRETTON (St James the Great) w Rockingham and Cottingham w East Carlton *Pet 7* **P** *Bp, Comdr L M M Saunders Watson, Sir Geoffrey Palmer Bt, and BNC Ox (jt)* **P-in-c** S J M READING

GREWELTHORPE (St James) *see* Fountains Gp *Ripon*

GREYSTOKE (St Andrew) *see* Gd Shep TM *Carl*

GREYSTONES (St Gabriel) *Sheff 2* **P** *Dean* **V** P W BECKLEY

GREYWELL (St Mary) *see* N Hants Downs *Win*

GRIMEHILLS (St Mary) *see* Darwen St Barn *Blackb*

GRIMETHORPE (St Luke) w Brierley *Wakef 7* **P** *Bp* **V** P D NEEDHAM

GRIMLEY (St Bartholomew) *see* Hallow and Grimley w Holt *Worc*

GRIMOLDBY (St Edith)   *see* Mid Marsh Gp *Linc*
GRIMSARGH (St Michael) *Blackb 13*   **P** *R Preston*
   V G R LOXHAM
GRIMSBURY (St Leonard)   *see* Banbury St Leon *Ox*
GRIMSBY (St Augustine of Hippo) *Linc 9*   **P** *TR Gt Grimsby*
   SS Mary and Jas   **V** S W JONES
GRIMSBY, GREAT (St Andrew w St Luke and All Saints) *Linc 9*
   P *Bp*   **P-in-c** T H ATKINSON
GRIMSBY, GREAT (St Mary and St James) (St Hugh)
   (St Mark) (St Martin) *Linc 9*   **P** *Bp*   **TR** M O HUNTER,
   TV T R BARDELL
GRIMSBY, LITTLE (St Edith)   *see* Fotherby *Linc*
GRIMSBY WEST   *see* Gt and Lt Coates w Bradley *Linc*
GRIMSHOE *Ely 9*   **P** *Bp, G&C Coll Cam, and Ld Chan (by*
   turn)   **R** *vacant* (01842) 828104
GRIMSTEAD, EAST (Holy Trinity)   *see* Clarendon *Sarum*
GRIMSTEAD, WEST (St John)   *as above*
GRIMSTON (St Botolph), Congham and Roydon *Nor 20*
   P *Qu Coll Cam, Bp, and G Howard Esq (jt)*   **R** W A HOWARD
GRIMSTON (St John the Baptist)   *see* Old Dalby, Nether
   Broughton, Saxelbye etc *Leic*
GRIMSTON, NORTH (St Nicholas)   *see* W Buckrose *York*
GRINDALE (St Nicholas)   *see* Burton Fleming w Fordon,
   Grindale etc *York*
GRINDLEFORD (St Helen)   *see* Hathersage w Bamford and
   Derwent and Grindleford *Derby*
GRINDLETON (St Ambrose)   *see* Bolton by Bowland w
   Grindleton *Bradf*
GRINDON (All Saints)   *see* Calton, Cauldon, Grindon,
   Waterfall etc *Lich*
GRINDON (St James), Stillington and Wolviston *Dur 10*   **P** *Bp*
   (2 turns), D&C (1 turn)   **R** D M BROOKE,   **NSM** P CLAYTON
GRINDON (St Oswald)   *see* Sunderland St Thos and St Oswald
   Dur
GRINGLEY-ON-THE-HILL (St Peter and St Paul)
   see Everton, Mattersey, Clayworth and Gringley *S'well*
GRINSDALE (St Kentigern)   *see* Barony of Burgh *Carl*
GRINSHILL (All Saints)   *see* Astley, Clive, Grinshill and
   Hadnall *Lich*
GRINSTEAD, EAST (St Mary the Virgin) *Chich 7*   **P** *Bp*
   V P R SEAMAN,   **NSM** J GAYFORD
GRINSTEAD, EAST (St Swithun) *Chich 7*   **P** *Bp*
   V C EVERETT-ALLEN,   **C** M F EMINSON,   **NSM** J K PEATY,
   G M W PARRY, D IVORSON
GRINSTEAD, WEST (St George) *Chich 8*   **P** *Bp*
   R W E M HARRIS
GRINTON (St Andrew)   *see* Swaledale *Ripon*
GRISTHORPE (St Thomas)   *see* Filey *York*
GRISTON (St Peter and St Paul)   *see* Caston, Griston, Merton,
   Thompson etc *Nor*
GRITTLETON (St Mary the Virgin)   *see* By Brook *Bris*
GRIZEBECK (The Good Shepherd)   *see* Kirkby Ireleth *Carl*
GROBY (St Philip and St James)   *see* Bradgate Team *Leic*
GROOMBRIDGE (St John the Evangelist)   *see* Speldhurst w
   Groombridge and Ashurst *Roch*
GROOMBRIDGE, NEW (St Thomas) *Chich 19*
   P *R Withyham*   **P-in-c** A B GREEN
GROSMONT (St Matthew)   *see* Middle Esk Moor *York*
GROSVENOR CHAPEL (no dedication) Chapel of Ease in the
   parish of Hanover Square St George w St Mark *Lon 3*
   P-in-c M D OAKLEY,   **Hon C** S D DEWEY
GROTON (St Bartholomew)   *see* Boxford, Edwardstone,
   Groton etc *St E*
GROVE (St Helen)   *see* E Markham w Askham, Headon w
   Upton and Grove *S'well*
GROVE (St John the Baptist) *Ox 19*   **P** *D&C Windsor*
   V J C ROBERTSON,   **C** P A EDDY,   **NSM** P D B GOODING
GROVE GREEN (St John) Local Ecumenical Partnership
   Cant 15 vacant (01622) 739294
GROVE PARK (St Augustine)   *see* Lee St Aug *S'wark*
GROVEHILL (Resurrection)   *see* Hemel Hempstead *St Alb*
GRUNDISBURGH (St Mary the Virgin)   *see* Boulge w Burgh,
   Grundisburgh and Hasketon *St E*
GUARLFORD (St Mary)   *see* Powick and Guarlford and
   Madresfield w Newland *Worc*
GUERNSEY (Holy Trinity) *Win 14*   **P** *Trustees*
   V J P HONOUR
GUERNSEY L'Islet (St Mary)   *see* Guernsey St Sampson *Win*
GUERNSEY (St Andrew de la Pommeraye) *Win 14*
   P *The Crown*   **P-in-c** J E IRONSIDE
GUERNSEY (St John the Evangelist) *Win 14*   **P** *Trustees*
   V A T SHARP
GUERNSEY (St Marguerite de la Foret) *Win 14*   **P** *The Crown*
   NSM L S LE VASSEUR
GUERNSEY (St Martin) *Win 14*   **P** *The Crown*
   R M R KEIRLE,   **NSM** R G BELLINGER

GUERNSEY (St Matthew) *Win 14*   **P** *R Ste Marie du Castel*
   V C E SELIM,   **NSM** J LE BILLON
GUERNSEY (St Michel du Valle) *Win 14*   **P** *The Crown*
   R K C NORTHOVER
GUERNSEY (St Peter Port) *Win 14*   **P** *The Crown*
   R K P MELLOR,   **NSM** J E D LUFF
GUERNSEY (St Philippe de Torteval) *Win 14*   **P** *The Crown*
   R M A STRIKE
GUERNSEY (St Pierre du Bois) *Win 14*   **P** *The Crown*
   R M A STRIKE
GUERNSEY (St Sampson) *Win 14*   **P** *The Crown*
   P-in-c P D BASKERVILLE
GUERNSEY (St Saviour) (Chapel of St Apolline) *Win 14*
   P *The Crown*   **NSM** L S LE VASSEUR
GUERNSEY (St Stephen) *Win 14*   **P** *R St Peter Port*
   V P J CARRINGTON
GUERNSEY (Ste Marie du Castel) *Win 14*   **P** *The Crown*
   R C E SELIM,   **NSM** J LE BILLON
GUESTLING (St Lawrence)   *see* Fairlight, Guestling and Pett
   Chich
GUESTWICK (St Peter)   *see* Foulsham, Guestwick, Stibbard,
   Themelthorpe etc *Nor*
GUILDEN MORDEN (St Mary)   *see* Shingay Gp *Ely*
GUILDEN SUTTON (St John the Baptist)   *see* Plemstall w
   Guilden Sutton *Ches*
GUILDFORD (All Saints) *Guildf 5*   **P** *Bp*   **V** B L MESSHAM
GUILDFORD (Christ Church) (St Martha-on-the-Hill) *Guildf 5*
   P *Simeon's Trustees and Duke Northd (jt)*   **V** S R SANDERS,
   C M G WALLACE,   **NSM** R D S SANDERS, B B MIRZANIA,
   B G MCNAIR SCOTT
GUILDFORD (Holy Spirit)   *see* Burpham *Guildf*
GUILDFORD (Holy Trinity) (St Mary the Virgin) (St Michael)
   Guildf 5   **P** *Bp*   **R** R L COTTON,   **OLM** B D ROBERTS,
   R M PIERCE, J J HEDGECOCK
GUILDFORD (St Clare)   *see* Westborough *Guildf*
GUILDFORD (St Francis)   *as above*
GUILDFORD (St Luke)   *see* Burpham *Guildf*
GUILDFORD (St Nicolas) *Guildf 5*   **P** *Bp*   **R** A H NORMAN
GUILDFORD (St Saviour) *Guildf 5*   **P** *Simeon's Trustees*
   R D J BRACEWELL,   **C** A C WHEELER,   **NSM** P J LEVELL,
   D M SELLIN, P D MANN
GUILSBOROUGH (St Ethelreda) w Hollowell and Cold Ashby
   Pet 2   **P** *J L Lowther Esq (2 turns) and Bp (1 turn)*
   P-in-c M D PETITT,   **NSM** M R BATTISON, C MOSS
GUILTCROSS *Nor 11*   **P** *Bp, Mrs C Noel, Exors*
   C P B Goldson, and DBP (jt)   **P-in-c** M J BULL,
   OLM D R A SHEPPARD
GUISBOROUGH (St Nicholas) *York 16*   **P** *Abp*   **R** G J PACEY
GUISELEY (St Oswald King and Martyr) w Esholt *Bradf 4*
   P *Patr Bd*   **TR** G B ATHERTON
GUIST (St Andrew)   *see* N Elmham, Billingford, Bintree, Guist
   etc *Nor*
GUITING POWER (St Michael)   *see* The Guitings, Cutsdean,
   Farmcote etc *Glouc*
GUITINGS, Cutsdean, Farmcote, Upper and Lower Slaughter w
   Eyford and Naunton, The *Glouc 12*   **P** *Bp, Ch Ch Ox, Guiting*
   Manor Amenity Trust, and F E B Witts Esq (jt)
   R G L SIMPSON,   **NSM** H J GARDNER
GULDEFORD, EAST (St Mary)   *see* Rye *Chich*
GULVAL (St Gulval) and Madron *Truro 5*   **P** *Ld Chan and*
   Bp (jt)   **P-in-c** T ST J HAWKINS,   **OLM** P A T HORDER
GULWORTHY (St Paul)   *see* Tavistock and Gulworthy *Ex*
GUMLEY (St Helen)   *see* Foxton w Gumley and Laughton *Leic*
GUNBY (St Nicholas)   *see* Witham Gp *Linc*
GUNBY (St Peter)   *see* Burgh Gp *Linc*
GUNHOUSE (St Barnabas)   *see* Trentside E *Linc*
GUNN CHAPEL (Holy Name)   *see* Swimbridge w W Buckland
   and Landkey *Ex*
GUNNERTON (St Christopher)   *see* Chollerton w Birtley and
   Thockrington *Newc*
GUNNESS (St Barnabas)   *see* Trentside E *Linc*
GUNNISLAKE (St Anne)   *see* Calstock *Truro*
GUNTHORPE (St John the Baptist)   *see* Lowdham w
   Caythorpe, and Gunthorpe *S'well*
GUNTHORPE (St Mary)   *see* Stiffkey and Bale *Nor*
GUNTON St Peter (St Benedict) *Nor 9*   **P** *CPAS*
   R J A FAIRBAIRN
GUNWALLOE (St Winwalloe)   *see* Cury and Gunwalloe
   Truro
GURNARD (All Saints) *Portsm 8*   **P** *Bp*   **V** L MCROSTIE,
   NSM D M NETHERWAY, K R ADLAM
GUSSAGE (St Andrew)   *see* Sixpenny Handley w Gussage St
   Andrew etc *Sarum*
GUSSAGE ALL SAINTS (All Saints)   *see* Chase *Sarum*
GUSSAGE ST MICHAEL (St Michael)   *as above*

GUSTARD WOOD (St Peter) *see* Wheathampstead *St Alb*
GUSTON (St Martin of Tours) *see* Whitfield w Guston *Cant*
GWEEK (Mission Church) *see* Constantine *Truro*
GWENNAP (St Weneppa) *see* St Stythians w Perranarworthal and Gwennap *Truro*
GWINEAR (St Winnear) *see* Godrevy *Truro*
GWITHIAN (St Gwithian) *as above*
HABBERLEY (St Mary) *Heref 13* **P** *Bp* **R** A N TOOP, **NSM** M-L TOOP
HABERGHAM (All Saints) *see* W Burnley All SS *Blackb*
HABERGHAM EAVES (St Matthew the Apostle) *see* Burnley St Matt w H Trin *Blackb*
HABROUGH Group, The (St Margaret) *Linc 10* **P** *DBP* **P-in-c** M W PAGE-CHESTNEY, **NSM** S V PAGE-CHESTNEY
HABTON, GREAT (St Chad) *see* Kirby Misperton w Normanby, Edston and Salton *York*
HACCOMBE (St Blaise) *see* Shaldon, Stokeinteignhead, Combeinteignhead etc *Ex*
HACCONBY (St Andrew) *see* Ringstone in Aveland Gp *Linc*
HACHESTON (St Andrew) *see* Campsea Ashe w Marlesford, Parham and Hacheston *St E*
HACKBRIDGE and Beddington Corner (All Saints) *S'wark 23* **P** *Bp* **V** A O ROLAND
HACKENTHORPE (Christ Church) *Sheff 2* **P** *Bp* **V** S J WILLETT, **C** R A HEARD
HACKFORD (St Mary the Virgin) *see* High Oak, Hingham and Scoulton w Wood Rising *Nor*
HACKINGTON (St Stephen) *Cant 3* **P** *Adn Cant* **R** J G LEWIS-ANTHONY, **Hon C** S C E LAIRD
HACKNESS (St Peter) w Harwood Dale *York 15* **P** *Lord Derwent* **V** *vacant* (01723) 882224
HACKNEY Mount Pleasant Lane (St Matthew) *see* Upper Clapton St Matt *Lon*
HACKNEY (St James) *see* Clapton St Jas *Lon*
HACKNEY (St John) *see* St John-at-Hackney *Lon*
HACKNEY (St Luke) Homerton Terrace *see* Homerton St Luke *Lon*
HACKNEY (St Thomas) *see* Stamford Hill St Thos *Lon*
HACKNEY, OVER (Mission Room) *see* Darley *Derby*
HACKNEY, SOUTH (St John of Jerusalem) (Christ Church) *Lon 5* **P** *Lord Amherst* **R** A M W WILSON
HACKNEY, SOUTH (St Michael and All Angels) London Fields w Haggerston (St Paul) *Lon 5* **P** R S Hackney St Jo w Ch Ch **V** A N EVERETT, **Hon C** A WINDROSS
HACKNEY, WEST St Barnabas (St Paul) *Lon 5* **P** *Bp* **R** W D N WEIR
HACKNEY MARSH (All Souls) *Lon 5* **P** *Patr Bd* **TR** D SILVESTER, **TV** A E MELANIPHY, **C** N NGURURI, **NSM** T A HALEY
HACKNEY WICK (St Mary of Eton) (St Augustine) *Lon 5* **P** *Eton Coll* **P-in-c** A R L PIGGOT
HACKTHORN (St Michael and All Angels) *see* Owmby Gp *Linc*
HADDENHAM (Holy Trinity) *Ely 8* **P** *Adn Ely* **V** F E G BRAMPTON, **NSM** E P ABRAHAM
HADDENHAM (St Mary the Virgin) w Cuddington, Kingsey and Aston Sandford *Ox 21* **P** *D&C Roch* **TR** M R HODSON
HADDESLEY (St John the Baptist) *see* Haddlesey w Hambleton and Birkin *York*
HADDISCOE (St Mary) *see* Raveningham Gp *Nor*
HADDLESEY w Hambleton and Birkin *York 4* **P** *Abp and Simeon's Trustees (jt)* **R** *vacant* (01757) 270245
HADDON (St Mary) *see* Stilton w Denton and Caldecote etc *Ely*
HADDON, EAST (St Mary the Virgin) *see* Brington w Whilton and Norton etc *Pet*
HADDON, OVER (St Anne) *see* Bakewell *Derby*
HADDON, WEST (All Saints) w Winwick and Ravensthorpe *Pet 2* **P** *DBP* **P-in-c** C R EVANS, **C** A J KNOWLES, M D PETITT
HADFIELD (St Andrew) *Derby 6* **P** *Bp* **V** G C GRIFFITHS, **NSM** J R ROSEDALE, R F HEELEY
HADHAM, LITTLE (St Cecilia) *see* Albury, Braughing, Furneux Pelham, Lt Hadham etc *St Alb*
HADHAM, MUCH (St Andrew) *as above*
HADLEIGH (St Barnabas) *Chelmsf 10* **P** *Bp* **P-in-c** M BROSNAN
HADLEIGH (St James the Less) *Chelmsf 10* · **P** *Dr P W M Copeman* **P-in-c** D R CHILDS
HADLEIGH (St Mary), Layham and Shelley *St E 3* **P** *St Jo Coll Cam and Abp (alt)* **V** M C THROWER
HADLEY (Holy Trinity) and Wellington Christ Church *Lich 21* **P** *Bp, Adn Salop, and V Wellington All SS w Eyton* **V** V C SWEET, **C** L M WHEELER, J E HOLMES, **Hon C** M F WALKER, **NSM** P R WALKER

HADLEY WOOD (St Paul) Proprietary Chapel *Lon 18* **Min** R MACKAY
HADLOW (St Mary) *Roch 8* **P** *Exors Miss I N King* **V** G A SMITH, **C** P R COOK
HADLOW DOWN (St Mark) *see* Buxted and Hadlow Down *Chich*
HADNALL (St Mary Magdalene) *see* Astley, Clive, Grinshill and Hadnall *Lich*
HADSTOCK (St Botolph) *see* Saffron Walden w Wendens Ambo, Littlebury etc *Chelmsf*
HADZOR w Oddingley (St James) *see* Bowbrook S *Worc*
HAGBOURNE (St Andrew) *see* The Churn *Ox*
HAGGERSTON (St Chad) *Lon 5* **P** *The Crown* **V** J J WESTCOTT
HAGLEY (St John the Baptist) *Worc 12* **P** *Exors Viscount Cobham* **R** R J C NEWTON
HAGLEY, WEST (St Saviour) *see* Hagley *Worc*
HAGNABY (St Andrew) *see* Marden Hill Gp *Linc*
HAGWORTHINGHAM (Holy Trinity) *as above*
HAIGH (St David) w Aspull *Liv 14* **P** *R Wigan* **V** S G PRITCHARD, **Hon C** N K YOUNG, **OLM** M L PERRIN
HAIL WESTON (St Nicholas) *see* Gt Staughton w Hail Weston w Southoe *Ely*
HAILE (not known) *see* Egremont and Haile *Carl*
HAILES (Chapel) *see* Winchcombe *Glouc*
HAILEY (St John the Evangelist) *see* Witney *Ox*
HAILSHAM (St Mary) *Chich 15* **P** *Ch Soc Trust* **V** D J BOURNE, **C** J B P BROOK
HAINAULT (St Paul) *Chelmsf 4* **P** *Bp* **V** C S T CANT, **NSM** S M HARTLEY
HAINFORD (All Saints) *see* Coltishall w Gt Hautbois, Frettenham etc *Nor*
HAINTON (St Mary) *see* Barkwith Gp *Linc*
HALA (St Paul's Centre) *see* Scotforth *Blackb*
HALAM (St Michael) *see* Edingley w Halam *S'well*
HALAS *Worc 9* **P** *Patr Bd* **TR** J C EVEREST, **TV** A D PETTIT, R S HALL, G A BYRNE, **C** M K LECLEZIO, **NSM** R M HEELEY
HALBERTON (St Andrew) *see* Sampford Peverell, Uplowman, Holcombe Rogus etc *Ex*
HALCON *see* Taunton All SS *B & W*
HALDEN, HIGH (St Mary the Virgin) *see* Bethersden w High Halden *Cant*
HALDENS (Christ the King) *see* Digswell and Panshanger *St Alb*
HALDON *see* Teignmouth, Ideford w Luton, Ashcombe etc *Ex*
HALE (St David) *see* Timperley *Ches*
HALE (St John the Evangelist) w Badshot Lea *Guildf 3* **P** *Patr Bd* **TR** J J PAGE, **TV** C A WILSON-BARKER
HALE (St Mary) *Liv 13* **P** *Trustees* **P-in-c** J M COLLIER
HALE (St Mary) *see* Fordingbridge and Breamore and Hale etc *Win*
HALE (St Peter) and Ashley *Ches 10* **P** *V Bowdon* **V** E J H LANE, **C** A D H DAWSON, **NSM** C E HOLMES
HALE, GREAT (St John the Baptist) *see* Helpringham w Hale *Linc*
HALE, UPPER (St Mark) *see* Hale w Badshot Lea *Guildf*
HALE BARNS (All Saints) w Ringway *Ches 10* **P** *Bp* **V** R M HINTON
HALEBANK (St Mary Mission) *see* Hale *Liv*
HALES (St Mary) *see* Cheswardine, Childs Ercall, Hales, Hinstock etc *Lich*
HALESOWEN (St John the Baptist) *see* Halas *Worc*
HALESWORTH (St Mary) *see* Blyth Valley *St E*
HALEWOOD (St Nicholas) (St Mary) *Liv 4* **P** *Bp* **TR** A D J JEWELL, **TV** S ERRINGTON
HALEY HILL (All Souls) *see* Halifax All So *Wakef*
HALFORD (Our Blessed Lady) *see* Stourdene Gp *Cov*
HALFORD (St Thomas) w Sibdon Carwood *Heref 11* **P** *Bp and R Holden (alt)* **P-in-c** M L COPE, **NSM** M G WILLIAMS
HALFWAY (St Peter) *see* Minster-in-Sheppey *Cant*
HALIFAX (All Saints) *Wakef 4* **P** *Ch Trust Fund Trust* **P-in-c** S LEES, **NSM** J C K FREEBORN
HALIFAX (All Souls) *Wakef 4* **P** *Simeon's Trustees and local trustees (jt)* **V** *vacant*
HALIFAX (Holy Trinity) (St Jude) *Wakef 4* **P** *Bp, V Halifax, and trustees (jt)* **V** M C RUSSELL, **NSM** M RUSSELL
HALIFAX (St Anne-in-the-Grove) *see* Southowram and Claremount *Wakef*
HALIFAX St Augustine (School Hall) and Mount Pellon *Wakef 4* **P** *Bp, Simeon's Trustees, and local trustees (jt)* **V** J HELLEWELL
HALIFAX (St Hilda) *Wakef 4* **P** *Bp* **P-in-c** P F MILLWARD
HALIFAX (St John the Baptist) *Wakef 4* **P** *The Crown* **V** H J BARBER, **C** R N FIRTH
HALL GREEN (Church of the Ascension) *Birm 6* **P** *Bp, V Yardley, and Vice-Chmn of PCC (jt)* **V** D J SENIOR

HALL GREEN (St Michael) *Birm 6*   **P** *Bp*   **V** *vacant* 0121-777 6132 *or* 777 8443

HALL GREEN (St Peter) *Birm 6*   **P** *Bp*   **V** M W STEPHENSON, **C** J LEWIS-GREGORY,   **NSM** S C HAYES

HALL STREET (St Andrew)   *see* Stockport St Mary *Ches*

HALLAM, WEST (St Wilfred) and Mapperley w Stanley *Derby 13*   **P** *Bp*   **R** S I D WHITE,   **NSM** P J OWEN-JONES, J FACEY

HALLATON (St Michael and All Angels) and Allexton, w Horninghold, Tugby, and East Norton, and Slawston *Leic 3*   **P** *Bp, DBP, and E Brudenell Esq (jt)*   **P-in-c** N MORGAN

HALLING (St John the Baptist)   *see* Cuxton and Halling *Roch*

HALLINGBURY, GREAT (St Giles) (St Andrew) and LITTLE (St Mary the Virgin) *Chelmsf 25*   **P** *Bp and Charterhouse (jt)*   **P-in-c** J A GREEN

HALLIWELL (St Luke) *Man 9*   **P** *MMCET*   **P-in-c** A S CORNES

HALLIWELL (St Margaret) *Man 9*   **P** *Trustees*   **P-in-c** D J FRENCH

HALLIWELL (St Matthew w St Barnabas) (St Paul) (St Thomas the Apostle) *Man 9*   **P** *Patr Bd*   **TV** D R PETCH, **P-in-c** A S CORNES,   **NSM** M A J TAYLOR,   **OLM** S FOSTER

HALLIWELL (St Peter) (Barrow Bridge Mission) (St Andrew's Mission Church) *Man 9*   **P** *Trustees*   **V** P D HARDINGHAM, **C** R F OLDFIELD, J A PENN,   **NSM** C WATSON

HALLOUGHTON (St James)   *see* Thurgarton w Hoveringham and Bleasby etc *S'well*

HALLOW (St Philip and St James) and Grimley w Holt *Worc 3*   **P** *Bp*   **R** R N LATHAM

HALLWOOD Ecumenical Parish (St Mark) *Ches 3*   **P** *DBP*   **V** S S WILKINS

HALSALL (St Cuthbert), Lydiate and Downholland *Liv 11*   **P** *Bp and Brig D H Blundell-Hollinshead-Blundell (jt)*   **R** P L ROBINSON,   **NSM** B C KEAL

HALSE (Mission Church)   *see* Brackley St Pet w St Jas *Pet*

HALSE (St James)   *see* Milverton w Halse and Fitzhead *B & W*

HALSETOWN (St John's in the Fields) *Truro 5*   **P** *D&C*   **C** M A J DAVIES,   **NSM** R G SELBY-BOOTHROYD

HALSHAM (All Saints)   *see* Keyingham w Ottringham, Halsham and Sunk Is *York*

HALSTEAD (St Margaret)   *see* Knockholt w Halstead *Roch*

HALSTEAD AREA Team Ministry, The (St Andrew) *Chelmsf 19*   **P** *Patr Bd*   **TR** J F BLORE,   **TV** V J BROOKS, G B T BAYLISS, **C** S N LODGE,   **NSM** M H M BURSELL

HALSTOCK (St Mary)   *see* Melbury *Sarum*

HALSTOW, HIGH (St Margaret) (All Hallows) and Hoo St Mary *Roch 6*   **P** *MMCET and Ch Soc Trust (jt)*   **R** S G GWILT

HALSTOW, LOWER (St Margaret)   *see* Upchurch w Lower Halstow *Cant*

HALTER DEVIL (Mission Room)   *see* Mugginton and Kedleston *Derby*

HALTON (St Mary) *Ches 3*   **P** *Bp*   **V** *vacant* (01928) 563636

HALTON (St Michael and All Angels)   *see* Wendover and Halton *Ox*

HALTON (St Oswald and St Cuthbert and King Alfwald)   *see* Corbridge w Halton and Newton Hall *Newc*

HALTON (St Wilfred)   *see* Slyne w Hest and Halton w Aughton *Blackb*

HALTON (St Wilfrid)   *see* Leeds Halton St Wilfrid *Ripon*

HALTON, EAST (St Peter)   *see* Habrough Gp *Linc*

HALTON, WEST (St Etheldreda)   *see* Alkborough *Linc*

HALTON HOLGATE (St Andrew)   *see* Spilsby Gp *Linc*

HALTON QUAY (St Indract's Chapel)   *see* St Dominic, Landulph and St Mellion w Pillaton *Truro*

HALTON WEST (Mission Church)   *see* Hellifield *Bradf*

HALTWHISTLE (Holy Cross) and Greenhead *Newc 10*   **P** *Bp*   **V** R BEST

HALVERGATE (St Peter and St Paul)   *see* Freethorpe, Wickhampton, Halvergate etc *Nor*

HALWELL (St Leonard)   *see* Diptford, N Huish, Harberton, Harbertonford etc *Ex*

HALWILL (St Peter and St James)   *see* Ashwater, Halwill, Beaworthy, Clawton etc *Ex*

HAM (All Saints)   *see* Savernake *Sarum*

HAM (St Andrew) *S'wark 15*   **P** *K Coll Cam*   **V** S BROCKLEHURST

HAM (St Barnabas Mission Church)   *see* Combe St Nicholas w Wambrook *B & W*

HAM (St James the Less)   *see* Plymouth St Pet and H Apostles *Ex*

HAM (St Richard) *S'wark 16*   **P** *Bp*   **V** P J H DUNN, **NSM** F M FORWARD

HAMBLE LE RICE (St Andrew) *Win 10*   **P** *St Mary's Coll Win*   **V** J W TRAVERS

HAMBLEDEN VALLEY (St Mary the Virgin) *Ox 29*   **P** *Bp, Viscount Hambleden, and Miss M Mackenzie (jt)*   **R** J M WIGRAM

HAMBLEDON (St Peter)   *see* Busbridge and Hambledon *Guildf*

HAMBLEDON (St Peter and St Paul) *Portsm 1*   **P** *Ld Chan*   **P-in-c** R I P COUTTS,   **NSM** J M BEE

HAMBLETON (St Andrew)   *see* Oakham, Hambleton, Egleton, Braunston and Brooke *Pet*

HAMBLETON (St Mary)   *see* Haddlesey w Hambleton and Birkin *York*

HAMBLETON (The Blessed Virgin Mary)   *see* Waterside Par *Blackb*

HAMBRIDGE (St James the Less)   *see* Kingsbury Episcopi w E Lambrook, Hambridge etc *B & W*

HAMER (All Saints) *Man 21*   **P** *Bp*   **V** K L SMEETON

HAMERINGHAM (All Saints)   *see* Fen and Hill Gp *Linc*

HAMERTON (All Saints) *Ely 10*   **P** *G R Petherick Esq*   **P-in-c** J DUCK

HAMILTON Conventional District *Leic 1*   **C-in-c** P C WHITE

HAMILTON TERRACE (St Mark)   *see* St Marylebone St Mark Hamilton Terrace *Lon*

HAMMER (St Michael)   *see* Lynchmere and Camelsdale *Chich*

HAMMERFIELD (St Francis of Assisi)   *see* Boxmoor St Jo *St Alb*

HAMMERSMITH (Holy Innocents) (St John the Evangelist) *Lon 9*   **P** *Bp*   **P-in-c** D W G MATTHEWS,   **NSM** A H MEAD, S R G MCDOWELL

HAMMERSMITH (St Luke) *Lon 9*   **P** *Bp*   **V** R D E JONES

HAMMERSMITH (St Matthew) *Lon 9*   **P** *Trustees*   **V** G H CHIPLIN

HAMMERSMITH (St Michael and St George)   *see* Shepherd's Bush St Steph w St Thos *Lon*

HAMMERSMITH St Paul *Lon 9*   **P** *Bp*   **V** S G DOWNHAM, **C** A J MEANEY, M T POWLEY,   **Hon C** R Q EDWARDS, **NSM** V I THOMAS

HAMMERSMITH (St Peter) *Lon 9*   **P** *Bp*   **V** J RECORD, **C** G M TREWEEK

HAMMERSMITH (St Saviour)   *see* Cobbold Road St Sav w St Mary *Lon*

HAMMERSMITH (St Simon) *Lon 9*   **P** *Simeon's Trustees*   **V** C J COLLINGTON

HAMMERSMITH, NORTH (St Katherine) *Lon 9*   **P** *Bp*   **P-in-c** J TATE

HAMMERWICH (St John the Baptist) *Lich 1*   **P** *Hammerwich Ch Lands Trustees*   **P-in-c** M J BUTT,   **NSM** M R AUSTIN

HAMMERWOOD (St Stephen)   *see* Cowden w Hammerwood *Chich*

HAMMOON (St Paul)   *see* Okeford *Sarum*

HAMNISH (St Dubricius and All Saints)   *see* Leominster *Heref*

HAMPDEN, GREAT (St Mary Magdalene)   *see* Prestwood and Gt Hampden *Ox*

HAMPDEN, LITTLE (not known)   *see* Gt Missenden w Ballinger and Lt Hampden *Ox*

HAMPDEN PARK (St Mary-in-the-Park) *Chich 16*   **P** *Bp*   **V** R L TREE

HAMPNETT (St George)   *see* Northleach w Hampnett and Farmington etc *Glouc*

HAMPRESTON (All Saints) *Sarum 9*   **P** *Patr Bd*   **TR** M J A HOWARD,   **TV** L S CLOW

HAMPSTEAD Belsize Park (St Peter)   *see* Belsize Park *Lon*

HAMPSTEAD (Christ Church) *Lon 16*   **P** *Trustees*   **V** P D CONRAD,   **Hon C** P J W BLACKBURN

HAMPSTEAD (Emmanuel) West End *Lon 16*   **P** *Trustees*   **P-in-c** J G F KESTER

HAMPSTEAD (St James)   *see* Kilburn St Mary w All So and W Hampstead St Jas *Lon*

HAMPSTEAD (St John) *Lon 16*   **P** *DBP*   **V** S R TUCKER, **C** J A WALTERS, S F L EYNSTONE

HAMPSTEAD (St John) Downshire Hill Proprietary Chapel *Lon 16*   **Min** J G L GOULD,   **NSM** J R LENTON

HAMPSTEAD St Stephen w (All Hallows) *Lon 16*   **P** *DBP and D&C Cant (jt)*   **V** D N C HOULDING

HAMPSTEAD, SOUTH (St Saviour) *Lon 16*   **P** *V Hampstead St Jo*   **P-in-c** P S NICHOLSON

HAMPSTEAD, WEST (Holy Trinity) *Lon 16*   **P** *MMCET*   **P-in-c** A K KEIGHLEY,   **C** G A SINGH

HAMPSTEAD, WEST (St Cuthbert) *Lon 16*   **P** *Ch Trust Fund Trust*   **NSM** D W JOHN

HAMPSTEAD, WEST (St Luke) *Lon 16*   **P** *CPAS*   **V** A C TRESIDDER

HAMPSTEAD GARDEN SUBURB (St Jude on the Hill) *Lon 15*   **P** *Bp*   **V** A R G WALKER

HAMPSTEAD NORREYS (St Mary)   *see* Hermitage *Ox*

HAMPSTHWAITE (St Thomas à Becket) and Killinghall and Birstwith *Ripon 1*   **P** *Mrs S J Finn, Sir James Aykroyd Bt, Sir Thomas Ingilby Bt, and Bp (jt)*   **V** G A F HINCHCLIFFE, **Hon C** R MCLEAN-REID

HAMPTON (All Saints) *Lon 10*   **P** *Ld Chan*   **V** J A GITTOES
HAMPTON (St Andrew)   *see* Herne Bay Ch Ch *Cant*
HAMPTON (St Andrew) w Sedgeberrow and Hinton-on-the-Green *Worc 1*   **P** *Ch Ch Ox, D&C Worc, and Laslett's Charity (jt)*   **P-in-c** A J BINNEY,   **NSM** C W PARR
HAMPTON (St Mary the Virgin) *Lon 10*   **P** *Ld Chan*
V D N WINTERBURN
HAMPTON, GREAT AND LITTLE (St Andrew)
see Hampton w Sedgeberrow and Hinton-on-the-Green *Worc*
HAMPTON BISHOP (St Andrew)   *see* Tupsley w Hampton Bishop *Heref*
HAMPTON GAY (St Giles)   *see* Akeman *Ox*
HAMPTON HILL (St James) *Lon 10*   **P** *V Hampton St Mary*
V P VANNOZZI,   **NSM** D G OADES
HAMPTON IN ARDEN (St Mary and St Bartholomew) *Birm 11*
P *Guild of All So*   **P-in-c** K CLARINGBULL
HAMPTON LOVETT (St Mary and All Saints)   *see* Elmley Lovett w Hampton Lovett and Elmbridge etc *Worc*
HAMPTON LUCY (St Peter ad Vincula) w Charlecote and Loxley *Cov 8*   **P** *Sir Edmund Fairfax-Lucy Bt (3 turns), Col A M H Gregory-Hood (1 turn)*   **P-in-c** D C JESSETT,   **NSM** C O S S DAVIES
HAMPTON POYLE (St Mary the Virgin)   *see* Kidlington w Hampton Poyle *Ox*
HAMPTON WICK (St John the Baptist)   *see* Teddington St Mark and Hampton Wick *Lon*
HAMSEY (St Peter) *Chich 18*   **P** *Bp*   **P-in-c** D BASTIDE
HAMSTALL RIDWARE (St Michael and All Angels)   *see* The Ridwares and Kings Bromley *Lich*
HAMSTEAD (St Bernard) *Birm 3*   **P** *Bp*   **P-in-c** H HINGLEY,   **Hon C** R C HINGLEY
HAMSTEAD (St Paul) *Birm 3*   **P** *Bp*   **V** M S PRASADAM,   **C** P A HARRISON
HAMSTEAD MARSHALL (St Mary)   *see* W Woodhay w Enborne, Hampstead Marshall etc *Ox*
HAMSTEELS (St John the Baptist) *Dur 1*   **P** *The Crown*
V M J PEERS
HAMSTERLEY (St James) and Witton-le-Wear *Dur 6*   **P** *Bp and The Crown (alt)*   **V** vacant (01388) 488418
HAMWORTHY (St Gabriel) (St Michael) *Sarum 7*
P M M C E T   **P-in-c** S D GODDARD,   **C** P G GODDARD
HANBOROUGH (St Peter and St Paul) and Freeland *Ox 9*
P *St Jo Coll Ox*   **P-in-c** D S TYLER,   **NSM** M S BRITT, J A GARDNER,   **OLM** P T BALL
HANBURY (St Mary the Virgin)   *see* Bowbrook N *Worc*
HANBURY (St Werburgh), Newborough, Rangemore and Tutbury *Lich 14*   **P** *Duchy of Lancaster (1 turn), DBP and Lord Burton (1 turn)*   **V** A E MANN,   **NSM** L REES,   **OLM** E A F SHEPPARD
HANCHURCH (Chapel of Ease)   *see* Trentham *Lich*
HANDBRIDGE (St Mary without the Walls)   *see* Ches St Mary *Ches*
HANDCROSS (All Saints)   *see* Slaugham *Chich*
HANDFORTH (St Chad) *Ches 17*   **P** *R Cheadle*
V S J BURMESTER
HANDLEY (All Saints)   *see* Tattenhall and Handley *Ches*
HANDLEY (St John the Baptist)   *see* Eckington and Ridgeway *Derby*
HANDLEY (St Mark)   *see* N Wingfield, Clay Cross and Pilsley *Derby*
HANDSACRE (St Luke)   *see* Armitage *Lich*
HANDSWORTH (St Andrew) *Birm 3*   **P** *Bp*   **V** E J NEWEY,   **C** J E HOUGHTON, J AUSTEN
HANDSWORTH (St James) *Birm 3*   **P** *Bp*   **V** D J P ISIORHO,   **NSM** M FARR
HANDSWORTH (St Mary) *Sheff 1*   **P** *DBP*
P-in-c K H JOHNSON
HANDSWORTH (St Mary) (Epiphany) *Birm 3*   **P** *Bp*
R B A HALL,   **C** R G MORTON
HANDSWORTH (St Michael) (St Peter) *Birm 3*   **P** *Bp*
P-in-c R F PAILING,   **NSM** J M CHAUDHARY
HANDSWORTH WOODHOUSE (St James)   *see* Woodhouse St Jas *Sheff*
HANFORD (St Matthias) *Lich 13*   **P** *Bp*
V N A DI CASTIGLIONE,   **C** R M D ORAM
HANGER HILL (Ascension) and West Twyford *Lon 22*   **P** *Bp and DBP (jt)*   **V** S J REED,   **Hon C** K F MCGARAHAN
HANGER LANE (St Ann)   *see* S Tottenham St Ann *Lon*
HANGING HEATON (St Paul) *Wakef 9*   **P** *R Dewsbury*
P-in-c P A CRADD
HANGLETON (St Helen) (St Richard) *Chich 4*   **P** *Bp*
V K G PERKINTON,   **C** M C C BARTER
HANHAM (Christ Church) (St George) *Bris 5*   **P** *Bp*
V P WILLIS
HANKERTON (Holy Cross)   *see* Ashley, Crudwell, Hankerton and Oaksey *Bris*

HANLEY (All Saints)   *see* Stoke-upon-Trent *Lich*
HANLEY Holy Evangelists (St Luke) *Lich 11*   **P** *Bp*
TR K R HAYWOOD,   **TV** P R CLARK,   **C** T S CARTER, I MAITIN
HANLEY (St Chad)   *see* Hanley H Ev *Lich*
HANLEY CASTLE (St Mary), Hanley Swan and Welland *Worc 5*   **P** *Ld Chan and Exors Sir Berwick Lechmere Bt (alt)*   **V** F A WOOKEY,   **NSM** L D BEDFORD
HANLEY CHILD (St Michael and All Angels)   *see* Teme Valley S *Worc*
HANLEY SWAN (St Gabriel)   *see* Hanley Castle, Hanley Swan and Welland *Worc*
HANLEY WILLIAM (All Saints)   *see* Teme Valley S *Worc*
HANNAH (St Andrew) cum Hagnaby w Markby *Linc 8*   **P** *Bp and Mrs A M Johnson (alt)*   **R** vacant
HANNEY (St James the Great), Denchworth and East Challow *Ox 19*   **P** *Bp (2 turns), Worc Coll Ox (1 turn)*   **V** A HOGG
HANNINGFIELD, EAST (All Saints) *Chelmsf 9*   **P** *CPAS*
P-in-c P PENNELL
HANNINGFIELD, WEST (St Mary and St Edward) *Chelmsf 9*
P *DBP*   **P-in-c** M J ASTON
HANNINGTON (All Saints)   *see* Baughurst, Ramsdell, Wolverton w Ewhurst etc *Win*
HANNINGTON (St John the Baptist)   *see* Highworth w Sevenhampton and Inglesham etc *Bris*
HANNINGTON (St Peter and St Paul)   *see* Walgrave w Hannington and Wold and Scaldwell *Pet*
HANOVER SQUARE (St George) *Lon 3*   **P** *Bp*
R R N S LEECE
HANSLOPE (St James the Great) w Castlethorpe *Ox 27*   **P** *Bp*
P-in-c G E ECCLESTONE
HANWELL (St Mary) (St Christopher) *Lon 22*   **P** *Bp*
R M R GRAYSHON,   **C** E J MOODY,   **NSM** H M V COSSTICK
HANWELL (St Mellitus w St Mark) *Lon 22*   **P** *Bp*
P-in-c J O HEREWARD
HANWELL (St Peter)   *see* Ironstone *Ox*
HANWELL (St Thomas) *Lon 22*   **P** *The Crown*
V P A ANDREWS
HANWOOD, GREAT (St Thomas) *Heref 13*   **P** *Lt-Col H de Grey-Warter*   **R** M G WHITTOCK
HANWORTH (All Saints) *Lon 11*   **P** *Bp*
P-in-c H C REYNOLDS
HANWORTH (St Bartholomew)   *see* Roughton and Felbrigg, Metton, Sustead etc *Nor*
HANWORTH (St George) *Lon 11*   **P** *Lee Abbey Movement*
P-in-c P S WILLIAMSON
HANWORTH (St Richard of Chichester) *Lon 11*   **P** *Bp*
V A JACKSON
HAPPISBURGH (St Mary)   *see* Bacton, Happisburgh, Hempstead w Eccles etc *Nor*
HAPTON (St Margaret)   *see* Padiham w Hapton and Padiham Green *Blackb*
HAPTON (St Margaret)   *see* Ashwellthorpe, Forncett, Fundenhall, Hapton etc *Nor*
HARBERTON (St Andrew)   *see* Diptford, N Huish, Harberton, Harbertonford etc *Ex*
HARBERTONFORD (St Peter)   *as above*
HARBLEDOWN (St Michael and All Angels) *Cant 3*   **P** *Abp*
R M A MORRIS
HARBORNE (St Faith and St Laurence) *Birm 2*   **P** *Bp*
P-in-c P A WHITE
HARBORNE (St Peter) *Birm 2*   **P** *Bp*   **V** vacant 0121-427 1949
HARBORNE HEATH (St John the Baptist) *Birm 2*   **P** *Ch Soc Trust*   **V** J P HUGHES,   **C** T J MEATHREL, R J BEWLEY,   A W SPENCER
HARBOROUGH MAGNA (All Saints) *Cov 6*   **P** A H F W *Boughton-Leigh Esq*   **P-in-c** C A GARROD
HARBRIDGE (All Saints)   *see* Ellingham and Harbridge and Hyde w Ibsley *Win*
HARBURY (All Saints) and Ladbroke *Cov 10*   **P** *Bp*
P-in-c C R GROOCOCK
HARBY (All Saints) w Thorney and North and South Clifton *S'well 3*   **P** *Ld Chan and Bp (alt)*   **P-in-c** K B POTTER
HARBY (St Mary the Virgin)   *see* Vale of Belvoir Par *Leic*
HARDEN (St Saviour) and Wilsden *Bradf 8*   **P** *Bp, Adn, V Bradf, and R Bingley Esq (jt)*   **P-in-c** R J BROOKS
HARDENHUISH (St Nicholas)   *see* Chippenham St Paul w Hardenhuish etc *Bris*
HARDHAM (St Botolph)   *see* Bury w Houghton and Coldwaltham and Hardham *Chich*
HARDINGHAM (St George)   *see* Barnham Broom and Upper Yare *Nor*
HARDINGSTONE (St Edmund) and Horton and Piddington *Pet 4*   **P** *Bp*   **V** B H STEVENS
HARDINGTON MANDEVILLE (Blessed Virgin Mary)
see W Coker w Hardington Mandeville, E Chinnock etc *B & W*

HARDINGTON VALE *B & W 4* **P** *Bp and J B Owen-Jones Esq (jt)* **R** N A DONE, **C** P A HAWTHORN

HARDLEY (St Margaret) *see* Loddon, Sisland, Chedgrave, Hardley and Langley *Nor*

HARDMEAD (St Mary) *see* Sherington w Chicheley, N Crawley, Astwood etc *Ox*

HARDRAW (St Mary and St John) *see* Hawes and Hardraw *Ripon*

HARDRES, LOWER (St Mary) *see* Bridge *Cant*

HARDRES, UPPER (St Peter and St Paul) *see* Stone Street Gp *Cant*

HARDSTOFT (St Peter) *see* Ault Hucknall and Scarcliffe *Derby*

HARDWICK (St James) *see* Stockton St Jas *Dur*

HARDWICK (St Leonard) *see* Mears Ashby and Hardwick and Sywell etc *Pet*

HARDWICK (St Margaret) *see* Hempnall *Nor*

HARDWICK (St Mary) *Ely 1* **P** *Bp* **P-in-c** K J BROWNING

HARDWICK, EAST (St Stephen) *see* Carleton and E Hardwick *Wakef*

HARDWICK-CUM-TUSMORE (St Mary) *see* Shelswell *Ox*

HARDWICKE (Holy Trinity) *see* Cusop w Blakemere, Bredwardine w Brobury etc *Heref*

HARDWICKE (St Mary the Virgin) *see* Schorne *Ox*

HARDWICKE (St Nicholas) and Elmore w Longney *Glouc 5* **P** *Adn Glouc and Ld Chan (alt)* **V** A N JAMES, **NSM** G R W PARFITT

HAREBY (St Peter and St Paul) *see* Marden Hill Gp *Linc*

HAREFIELD (St Mary the Virgin) *Lon 24* **P** *The Hon J E F Newdegate* **V** A J R GANDON

HAREHILLS (St Aidan) *see* Leeds St Aid *Ripon*

HAREHILLS (St Cyprian and St James) *see* Leeds St Cypr Harehills *Ripon*

HARESCOMBE (St John the Baptist) *see* Painswick, Sheepscombe, Cranham, The Edge etc *Glouc*

HARESFIELD (St Peter) *see* Eastington, Frocester, Haresfield etc *Glouc*

HAREWOOD (Methodist Chapel) *see* Collingham w Harewood *Ripon*

HARFORD (St Petroc) *see* Ivybridge w Harford *Ex*

HARGRAVE (All Saints) *see* Raunds, Hargrave, Ringstead and Stanwick *Pet*

HARGRAVE (St Edmund King and Martyr) *see* Chevington w Hargrave, Chedburgh w Depden etc *St E*

HARGRAVE (St Peter) *Ches 5* **P** *Bp* **P-in-c** P B BARROW

HARKSTEAD (St Mary) *see* Shoreline *St E*

HARLASTON (St Matthew) *see* Clifton Campville w Edingale and Harlaston *Lich*

HARLAXTON Group, The (St Mary and St Peter) *Linc 19* **P** *Bp, DBP, Sir Richard Welby Bt, D&C, and Duke of Rutland (jt)* **P-in-c** K HANSON

HARLESCOTT (Holy Spirit) (Emmanuel) *Lich 20* **P** *Bp* **V** M H SALMON, **C** E J FAIRLESS

HARLESDEN (All Souls) *Lon 21* **P** *The Crown* **V** M D MOORHEAD, **NSM** M D ENGLER

HARLESDEN (St Mark) *see* Kensal Rise St Mark and St Martin *Lon*

HARLESTON (St Augustine) *see* Gt Finborough w Onehouse, Harleston, Buxhall etc *St E*

HARLESTON (St John the Baptist) *see* Redenhall, Harleston, Wortwell and Needham *Nor*

HARLESTONE (St Andrew) *see* Brington w Whilton and Norton etc *Pet*

HARLEY (St Mary) *see* Wenlock *Heref*

HARLING, EAST (St Peter and St Paul) w West, Bridgham w Roudham, Larling, Brettenham and Rushford *Nor 11* **P** *Ld Chan (1 turn), DBP, Sir Robin Nugent Bt, C D F Musker Esq, Major E H C Garnier, and Exors Sir John Musker (3 turns)* **R** N P KINSELLA, **OLM** L J FRY

HARLINGTON (Christ Church) *see* W Hayes *Lon*

HARLINGTON (St Mary the Virgin) *St Alb 9* **P** *Bp* **V** S J WILLIAMS

HARLINGTON (St Peter and St Paul) *Lon 24* **P** *Bp* **R** M E SMITH

HARLOW (St Mary and St Hugh w St John the Baptist) *Chelmsf 25* **P** *Simeon's Trustees and Bp (alt)* **V** D J WELCH, **C** O FRANKLIN

HARLOW (St Mary Magdalene) *Chelmsf 25* **P** *V Harlow St Mary and St Hugh etc* **NSM** G R NEAVE

HARLOW Town Centre (St Paul) w Little Parndon *Chelmsf 25* **P** *Patr Bd* **TR** M J HARRIS, **TV** L G NORTON, **C** S J KNIGHT

HARLOW GREEN (St Ninian) and Lamesley *Dur 12* **P** *Bp* **V** M WORTHINGTON

HARLSEY, EAST (St Oswald) *see* Osmotherley w Harlsey and Ingleby Arncliffe *York*

HARLTON (Assumption of the Blessed Virgin Mary) *see* Haslingfield w Harlton and Gt and Lt Eversden *Ely*

HARMANSWATER (St Paul) *see* Bracknell *Ox*

HARMER HILL (St Andrew) *see* Myddle *Lich*

HARMONDSWORTH (St Mary the Virgin) *Lon 24* **P** *DBP* **NSM** A O CHRISTIAN-IWUAGWU

HARMSTON (All Saints) *see* Graffoe Gp *Linc*

HARNHAM (St George) (All Saints) *Sarum 12* **P** *Bp (1 turn), V Britford (2 turns)* **V** D P SCRACE, **NSM** J G POPPLETON

HARNHILL (St Michael and All Angels) *see* Fairford Deanery *Glouc*

HAROLD HILL (St George) *Chelmsf 2* **P** *Bp* **V** *vacant* (01708) 343415

HAROLD HILL (St Paul) *Chelmsf 2* **P** *Bp* **V** R D MOUL

HAROLD WOOD (St Peter) *Chelmsf 2* **P** *New Coll Ox* **V** D P BANTING, **C** A J GREY

HAROME (St Saviour) *see* Kirkdale w Harome, Nunnington and Pockley *York*

HARPENDEN (St John the Baptist) *St Alb 8* **P** *DBP* **NSM** J E H WHITE, C E BURCH

HARPENDEN (St Nicholas) (All Saints) *St Alb 8* **P** *Ld Chan* **R** C D FUTCHER, **C** E F INALL, J E PAVYER, G W A RUSSELL

HARPFORD (St Gregory the Great) *see* Ottery St Mary, Alfington, W Hill, Tipton etc *Ex*

HARPHAM (St John of Beverley) *see* The Beacon *York*

HARPLEY (St Lawrence) *see* Gt w Lt Massingham, Harpley, Rougham etc *Nor*

HARPOLE (All Saints) *see* Kislingbury and Harpole *Pet*

HARPSDEN (St Margaret) *see* Shiplake w Dunsden and Harpsden *Ox*

HARPSWELL (St Chad) *see* Glentworth Gp *Linc*

HARPTREE, EAST (St Laurence) w WEST (Blessed Virgin Mary) and Hinton Blewett *B & W 10* **P** *Duchy of Cornwall* **R** *vacant* (01761) 221239

HARPUR HILL (St James) *see* Buxton w Burbage and King Sterndale *Derby*

HARPURHEY (Christ Church) *Man 5* **P** *Bp and Trustees (jt)* **R** *vacant* 0161-205 4020

HARPURHEY (St Stephen) *see* Harpurhey Ch Ch *Man*

HARRABY (St Elisabeth) *see* S Carl *Carl*

HARRIETSHAM (St John the Baptist) *see* Len Valley *Cant*

HARRINGAY (St Paul) *Lon 19* **P** *Bp* **V** R P P MARTIN

HARRINGTON (St Mary) *Carl 7* **P** *Mrs E H S Thornely* **P-in-c** A H MCMICHAEL

HARRINGTON (St Mary) *see* S Ormsby Gp *Linc*

HARRINGTON (St Peter and St Paul) *see* Arthingworth, Harrington w Oxendon and E Farndon *Pet*

HARRINGWORTH (St John the Baptist) *see* Bulwick, Blatherwycke w Harringworth and Laxton *Pet*

HARROGATE (St Luke's Church Centre) *see* Bilton *Ripon*

HARROGATE (St Mark) *Ripon 1* **P** *Peache Trustees* **V** P D G HOOPER, **C** D J WATTS, P T ASKEW, J LOGAN, **NSM** A ARORA

HARROGATE (St Wilfrid) *Ripon 1* **P** *Bp* **TV** J A THOMPSON-VEAR, **NSM** T G BURRELL

HARROGATE, HIGH (Christ Church) *Ripon 1* **P** *Bp* **V** N J HENSHALL, **NSM** C M SEDGEWICK

HARROGATE, HIGH (St Peter) *Ripon 1* **P** *Ch Patr Trust* **V** A M SHEPHERD, **C** T J HURREN

HARROGATE, LOW St Mary *Ripon 4* **P** *Peache Trustees* **P-in-c** M J CAREY

HARROLD (St Peter and All Saints) and Carlton w Chellington *St Alb 15* **P** *Bp* **P-in-c** J FOX

HARROW (Church of the Holy Spirit) *see* Kenton *Lon*

HARROW (Holy Trinity) *see* Wealdstone H Trin *Lon*

HARROW (St John the Baptist) *see* Greenhill St Jo *Lon*

HARROW (St Peter) *see* Roxeth *Lon*

HARROW, NORTH (St Alban) *Lon 23* **P** *Bp* **V** J A FOSTER, **Hon C** D S ARDEN, D J TUCK, **NSM** P BAGULEY

HARROW, SOUTH (St Paul) *Lon 23* **P** *R St Bride Fleet Street w Bridewell and Trin Gough Square* **V** J P DOWSETT

HARROW GREEN (Holy Trinity and St Augustine of Hippo) *see* Leytonstone H Trin Harrow Green *Chelmsf*

HARROW ON THE HILL (St Mary) *Lon 23* **P** *Bp, Adn, and Hd Master Harrow Sch (jt)* **V** T J GOSDEN

HARROW WEALD (All Saints) *Lon 23* **P** *Bp, Adn, V Harrow St Mary, and R Bushey (jt)* **V** J J MERCER, **NSM** P M WARD

HARROW WEALD (St Michael and All Angels) *Lon 23* **P** *Bp* **V** G E HEWLETT

HARROWBARROW (All Saints) *see* Calstock *Truro*

HARROWBY (The Ascension) *see* Grantham, Harrowby w Londonthorpe *Linc*

HARROWDEN, GREAT (All Saints) w LITTLE (St Mary the Virgin) and Orlingbury and Isham w Pytchley *Pet 6* **P** *Bp and Sir Philip Naylor-Leyland Bt (jt)* **R** S P DOMMETT, **NSM** C A OSTLER

HARSTON (All Saints) w Hauxton and Newton *Ely 5* **P** *Bp* *(2 turns), D&C (1 turn)* **P-in-c** P A WAINWRIGHT, **NSM** R G HOWELLS

HARSTON (St Michael and All Angels) *see* High Framland Par *Leic*

HARSWELL (St Peter) *see* Holme and Seaton Ross Gp *York*

HART (St Mary Magdalene) w Elwick Hall *Dur 3* **P** *Bp and DBP (alt)* **V** J E LUND, **C** J BURBURY

HART COMMON (not known) *see* Westhoughton and Wingates *Man*

HARTBURN (All Saints) *see* Stockton St Pet *Dur*

HARTBURN (St Andrew) *see* Bolam w Whalton and Hartburn w Meldon *Newc*

HARTCLIFFE (St Andrew) *see* Bris St Andr Hartcliffe *Bris*

HARTEST (All Saints) *see* Glemsford, Hartest w Boxted, Somerton etc *St E*

HARTFIELD (St Mary) w Coleman's Hatch *Chich 19* **P** *Bp and Earl De la Warr (jt)* **R** P E P BRICE, **NSM** N T LEVISEUR

HARTFORD (All Saints) *see* Huntingdon w the Stukeleys *Ely*

HARTFORD (St John the Baptist) *Ches 6* **P** *Ch Soc Trust* **V** M I A SMITH, **C** G T CROWDER, J T HUGHES, **NSM** G AGAR

HARTFORD HUNDRED (WEST) Group *see* Lt Berkhamsted and Bayford, Essendon etc *St Alb*

HARTHILL (All Hallows) and Thorpe Salvin *Sheff 5* **P** *Bp* **P-in-c** G SCHOFIELD

HARTING (St Mary and St Gabriel) w Elsted and Treyford cum Didling *Chich 10* **P** *Bp* **P-in-c** M J LANE

HARTINGTON (St Giles), Biggin and Earl Sterndale *Derby 4* **P** *Duke of Devonshire* **P-in-c** J O GOLDSMITH

HARTISMERE, NORTH *St E 16* **P** *MMCET, K Coll Cam, Bp, and DBP (jt)* **R** M THOMPSON, **OLM** V A MANNING

HARTISMERE, SOUTH *St E 16* **P** *Bp, Comdr F P Brooke-Popham, MMCET, Ch Soc Trust, SMF, and Lord Henniker (jt)* **P-in-c** A S MASON, **C** C M S ROBINSON, **NSM** A HARDING

HARTLAND (St Nectan) *see* Parkham, Alwington, Buckland Brewer etc *Ex*

HARTLAND COAST *as above*

HARTLEBURY (St James) *Worc 13* **P** *Bp* **P-in-c** S P KERR

HARTLEPOOL (Holy Trinity) (St Mark's Centre) *Dur 3* **P** *Bp* **C** N J JARVIS

HARTLEPOOL (St Aidan) (St Columba) *Dur 3* **P** *Bp* **P-in-c** J P RHODES

HARTLEPOOL (St Hilda) *Dur 3* **P** *Bp* **R** *vacant (01429) 267030*

HARTLEPOOL (St Luke) *Dur 3* **P** *Bp* **V** M R JUDSON, **C** P W JUDSON, **NSM** D M WILSON

HARTLEPOOL (St Oswald) *Dur 3* **P** *Bp* **V** G BUTTERY

HARTLEPOOL (St Paul) *Dur 3* **P** *Bp* **R** A S MASSHEDAR

HARTLEY (All Saints) *see* Fawkham and Hartley *Roch*

HARTLEY, NEW (St Michael and All Angels) *see* Delaval *Newc*

HARTLEY BROOK (Mission Hall) *see* Becontree St Mary *Chelmsf*

HARTLEY MAUDITT (St Leonard) *see* Northanger *Win*

HARTLEY WESPALL (St Mary) *see* Sherfield-on-Loddon and Stratfield Saye etc *Win*

HARTLEY WINTNEY (St John the Evangelist), Elvetham, Winchfield and Dogmersfield *Win 5* **P** *Bp and Sir Euan Anstruther-Gough-Calthorpe Bt (jt)* **V** R A EWBANK, **C** D WARD

HARTLIP (St Michael and All Angels) *see* Newington w Hartlip and Stockbury *Cant*

HARTOFT (Mission Room) *see* Lastingham w Appleton-le-Moors, Rosedale etc *York*

HARTON (St Peter) (St Lawrence) *Dur 15* **P** *D&C* **V** R O DICK, **C** A Y BENNETT

HARTPLAIN (not known) *Portsm 5* **P** *DBP* **V** T E JESSIMAN

HARTPURY (St Mary the Virgin) w Corse and Staunton *Glouc 4* **P** *Bp (2 turns), DBP (1 turn)* **P-in-c** J G EVANS, **NSM** P A HAMER

HARTSHEAD (St Peter) *see* Roberttown w Hartshead *Wakef*

HARTSHILL (Holy Trinity) and Galley Common *Cov 5* **P** *Ch Patr Trust and Bp (jt)* **V** *vacant (024) 7639 2266*

HARTSHILL (Holy Trinity), Penkhull and Trent Vale *Lich 12* **P** *Patr Bd* **TR** A R OSBORNE, **TV** S R DUTTON

HARTSHORNE (St Peter) and Bretby *Derby 16* **P** *Bp and MMCET (jt)* **R** I R WILLIAMS-HUNTER

HARTWELL (St John the Baptist) *see* Roade and Ashton w Hartwell *Pet*

HARTWITH (St Jude) *see* Dacre w Hartwith and Darley w Thornthwaite *Ripon*

HARTY (St Thomas Apostle) *see* Eastchurch w Leysdown and Harty *Cant*

HARVINGTON (St James) *see* Church Lench w Rous Lench and Abbots Morton etc *Worc*

HARWELL (St Matthew) w Chilton *Ox 18* **P** *DBP and CPAS (jt)* **R** C J STOTT, **NSM** L B KEEBLE

HARWICH PENINSULA, The (St Nicholas) *Chelmsf 20* **P** *Patr Bd* **TR** P E MANN, **TV** E B E LAMMENS, **C** P S G WATKIN, **NSM** G M MOORE

HARWOOD (Christ Church) *Man 16* **P** *DBP* **V** W L OLIVER, **OLM** H MOLLOY, M J FROST

HARWOOD, GREAT (St Bartholomew) St John *Blackb 7* **P** *Patr Bd* **P-in-c** C R PENFOLD

HARWOOD DALE (St Margaret) *see* Hackness w Harwood Dale *York*

HARWORTH (All Saints) *S'well 1* **P** *Sir John Whitaker Bt* **P-in-c** J JOHNSON, **NSM** I F TISSINGTON

HASBURY (St Margaret) *see* Halas *Worc*

HASCOMBE (St Peter) *see* Dunsfold and Hascombe *Guildf*

HASELBECH (St Michael) *see* Clipston w Naseby and Haselbech w Kelmarsh *Pet*

HASELBURY PLUCKNETT (St Michael and All Saints) *see* Wulfric Benefice *B & W*

HASELEY (St Mary) *see* Hatton w Haseley, Rowington w Lowsonford etc *Cov*

HASELEY, GREAT (St Peter) *see* Gt w Lt Milton and Gt Haseley *Ox*

HASELOR (St Mary and All Saints) *see* Kinwarton w Gt Alne and Haselor *Cov*

HASELTON (St Andrew) *see* Northleach w Hampnett and Farmington etc *Glouc*

HASFIELD (St Mary) w Tirley and Ashleworth *Glouc 4* **P** *W G F Meath-Baker Esq, Ld Chan, and Bp (by turn)* **R** *vacant*

HASKETON (St Andrew) *see* Boulge w Burgh, Grundisburgh and Hasketon *St E*

HASLAND (St Paul) *Derby 5* **P** *V Chesterfield* **R** M R AINSCOUGH

HASLEMERE (St Bartholomew) (St Christopher) and Grayswood *Guildf 4* **P** *Ld Chan* **R** N JONES, **NSM** B A STEELE-PERKINS, D J ORME

HASLINGDEN (St James) w Grane and Stonefold *Blackb 1* **P** *Bp and Hulme Trustees (jt)* **V** T R SMITH, **NSM** R L MULLIGAN

HASLINGDEN (St Peter) *see* Laneside *Blackb*

HASLINGDEN (St Thomas) *see* Musbury *Blackb*

HASLINGFIELD (All Saints) w Harlton and Great and Little Eversden *Ely 1* **P** *Qu Coll Cam, Ld Chan, Jes Coll Cam (by turn)* **P-in-c** M R MATTHEWS

HASLINGTON (St Matthew) w Crewe Green St Michael *Ches 15* **P** *Bp* **V** S A LAWSON

HASSALL GREEN (St Philip) *see* Sandbach Heath w Wheelock *Ches*

HASSINGHAM (St Mary) *see* Burlingham St Edmund w Lingwood, Strumpshaw etc *Nor*

HASTINGLEIGH (St Mary the Virgin) *see* Wye w Brook and Hastingleigh etc *Cant*

HASTINGS (Christ Church and St Andrew) *see* Blacklands Hastings Ch Ch and St Andr *Chich*

HASTINGS (Emmanuel and St Mary in the Castle) *Chich 17* **P** *MMCET and Hyndman Trustees (alt)* **V** P J COLKIN

HASTINGS (Holy Trinity) *Chich 17* **P** *Bp* **C** C TOLWORTHY, **C** R J MORTIMER

HASTINGS (St Clement) (All Saints) *Chich 17* **P** *Bp* **P-in-c** R L FEATHERSTONE

HASTINGS (St Peter and St Paul) *see* Hollington St Jo *Chich*

HASWELL (St Paul), Shotton and Thornley *Dur 2* **P** *Bp* **V** D BODDY, **NSM** A STAINSBY

HATCH, WEST (St Andrew) *see* Beercrocombe w Curry Mallet, Hatch Beauchamp etc *B & W*

HATCH BEAUCHAMP (St John the Baptist) *as above*

HATCH END (St Anselm) *Lon 23* **P** *Bp* **V** C PEARCE

HATCH WARREN AND BEGGARWOOD (Immanuel) *Win 4* **P** *Bp* **P-in-c** L M HARRIS

HATCHAM (St Catherine) *S'wark 2* **P** *Haberdashers' Co* **V** F J MAKAMBWE, **NSM** J ELLIOTT, **OLM** A C OBIORA

HATCHAM (St James) (St George) (St Michael) *S'wark 2* **P** *Ch Patr Soc* **V** N D R NICHOLLS

HATCHAM PARK (All Saints) *S'wark 2* **P** *Hyndman Trustees (2 turns), Haberdashers' Co (1 turn)* **V** O J BEAMENT, **OLM** J FRANCIS

HATCLIFFE (St Mary) *see* Laceby and Ravendale Gp *Linc*

HATFIELD *see* Bp's Hatfield, Lemsford and N Mymms *St Alb*

HATFIELD (St Lawrence) *Sheff 10* **P** *Bp* **V** P D WILSON, **NSM** G BECKETT

HATFIELD (St Leonard) *see* Leominster *Heref*

HATFIELD BROAD OAK (St Mary the Virgin) and Bush End *Chelmsf 25* **P** *Bp* **P-in-c** N A WORMELL

HATFIELD HEATH (Holy Trinity) and Sheering *Chelmsf 25*
  P *Ch Ch Ox and V Hatfield Broad Oak (alt)*   **R** T J POTTER
HATFIELD HYDE (St Mary Magdalene) *St Alb 21*
  P *Marquess of Salisbury*   **P-in-c** D L MUNCHIN,
  C P E SEYMOUR,   **NSM** A C S WILLIS
HATFIELD PEVEREL (St Andrew) w Ulting *Chelmsf 23*   **P** *Bp*
  V S R NORTHFIELD
HATFIELD REGIS   *see* Hatfield Broad Oak and Bush End
  Chelmsf
HATHERDEN (Christ Church)   *see* Pastrow *Win*
**HATHERLEIGH (St John the Baptist) Meeth, Exbourne and
  Jacobstowe** *Ex 11*   **P** *CPAS, Lord Clinton, DBP, and Keble Coll
  Ox (jt)*   **P-in-c** R P HANSFORD
HATHERN (St Peter and St Paul)   *see* Kegworth, Hathern,
  Long Whatton, Diseworth etc *Leic*
HATHEROP (St Nicholas)   *see* Fairford Deanery *Glouc*
**HATHERSAGE (St Michael and All Angels) w Bamford and
  Derwent, and Grindleford** *Derby 2*   **P** *Duke of Devonshire,
  Earl Temple, and A C H Barnes Esq (jt)*   **P-in-c** C L TUPLING
HATHERTON (St Saviour) *Lich 3*   **P** *A R W Littleton Esq*
  V *vacant*
HATLEY ST GEORGE (St George)   *see* Gamlingay and
  Everton *Ely*
HATTERS LANE (St Andrew)   *see* High Wycombe *Ox*
HATTERSLEY (St Barnabas) *Ches 14*   **P** *Bp*   **V** *vacant*
  0161-368 2795
HATTON (All Saints) *Derby 14*   **P** *Bp and
  N J M Spurrier Esq (jt)*   **P-in-c** A L MARTIN
**HATTON (Holy Trinity) w Haseley, Rowington w Lowsonford
  and Honiley and Wroxall** *Cov 4*   **P** *Bp*   **R** K J MOBBERLEY,
  NSM S MOBBERLEY
HATTON (St Stephen)   *see* Hemingby *Linc*
HAUGH (St Leonard)   *see* S Ormsby Gp *Linc*
HAUGHLEY (St Mary the Virgin) w Wetherden and Stowupland
  St E 6   **P** *Ld Chan, Bp, and DBP (by turn)*   **V** D J SWALES,
  C K A VALENTINE,   **OLM** D WEBB
HAUGHTON (Mission Room)   *see* Bunbury and Tilstone
  Fearnall *Ches*
HAUGHTON (St Anne) *Man 17*   **P** *DBP*
  P-in-c A S MITCHELL
HAUGHTON (St Chad)   *see* W Felton *Lich*
HAUGHTON (St Giles)   *see* Bradeley, Church Eaton,
  Derrington and Haughton *Lich*
HAUGHTON (St Mary the Virgin) *Man 17*   **P** *Bp*
  R M J DOWLAND,   **C** M J MCGURK
HAUGHTON LE SKERNE (St Andrew) *Dur 8*   **P** *Bp*
  R D J BRYAN,   **OLM** S E BRUCE
HAUTBOIS, GREAT (Holy Trinity)   *see* Coltishall w Gt
  Hautbois, Frettenham etc *Nor*
HAUXTON (St Edmund)   *see* Harston w Hauxton and Newton
  Ely
HAUXWELL (St Oswald)   *see* Spennithorne w Finghall and
  Hauxwell *Ripon*
HAVANT (St Faith) *Portsm 5*   **P** *Bp*   **R** P A W JONES,
  NSM D I R WILLIAMS
HAVEN, THE Conventional District *Chich 16 vacant*
HAVENSTREET (St Peter) *Portsm 7*   **P** *SMF*
  V N R WALLACE
HAVERHILL (St Mary the Virgin) w Withersfield *St E 8*   **P** *Bp*
  V I M FINN,   **C** J A WARD
HAVERIGG (St Luke)   *see* Millom *Carl*
HAVERING-ATTE-BOWER (St John)   *see* Collier Row St Jas
  and Havering-atte-Bower *Chelmsf*
HAVERINGLAND (St Peter)   *see* Cawston w Booton and
  Brandiston etc *Nor*
HAVERSHAM (St Mary)   *see* Lamp *Ox*
HAVERSTOCK HILL (Holy Trinity)   *see* Kentish Town St Silas
  and H Trin w St Barn *Lon*
HAVERTHWAITE (St Anne)   *see* Leven Valley *Carl*
HAWBUSH (St Paul)   *see* Brierley Hill *Worc*
HAWES (St Margaret) and Hardraw *Ripon 4*   **P** *Bp, V Aysgarth
  and Bolton cum Redmire, Mrs R Metcalfe, and
  W H Willan Esq (jt)*   **V** *vacant* (01969) 667553
HAWES SIDE (St Christopher) and Marton Moss St Nicholas
  Blackb 8   **P** *Bp*   **V** G PIPER
HAWKCHURCH (St John the Baptist)   *see* Golden Cap Team
  Sarum
HAWKEDON (St Mary)   *see* Chevington w Hargrave,
  Chedburgh w Depden etc *St E*
HAWKESBURY (St Mary)   *see* Boxwell, Leighterton,
  Didmarton, Oldbury etc *Glouc*
HAWKHURST (St Laurance) *Cant 11*   **P** *Ch Ch Ox*
  V R G DREYER,   **OLM** A MCCALL
HAWKINGE (St Luke) w Acrise and Swingfield *Cant 5*   **P** *Abp*
  P-in-c R P GRINSELL

HAWKLEY (St Peter and St Paul)   *see* Greatham w Empshott
  and Hawkley w Prior's Dean *Portsm*
HAWKRIDGE (St Giles)   *see* Exford, Exmoor, Hawkridge and
  Withypool *B & W*
HAWKSHAW (St Mary)   *see* Holcombe and Hawkshaw *Man*
**HAWKSHEAD (St Michael and All Angels) and Low Wray w
  Sawrey and Rusland and Satterthwaite** *Carl 11*   **P** *Bp*
  V J S DIXON,   **NSM** N F HALLAM
HAWKSWOOD (Emmanuel) *Chich 15*   **P** *Ch Soc Trust*
  V S J E TOMALIN
HAWKSWORTH (St Mary and All Saints)   *see* Whatton w
  Aslockton, Hawksworth, Scarrington etc *S'well*
HAWKSWORTH WOOD (St Mary) *Ripon 7*   **P** *Patrons Leeds
  St Pet*   **P-in-c** L J ASHTON,   **NSM** B M HAWKINS
HAWKWELL (Emmanuel) (St Mary the Virgin) *Chelmsf 12*
  P *CPAS*   **R** P H SMITH
HAWKWOOD (St Francis)   *see* Chingford SS Pet and Paul
  Chelmsf
HAWLEY (Holy Trinity) *Guildf 1*   **P** *Keble Coll Ox*
  V M W NEALE
HAWLEY, SOUTH (All Saints)   *see* Hawley H Trin *Guildf*
HAWLING (St Edward)   *see* Sevenhampton w Charlton Abbots,
  Hawling etc *Glouc*
HAWNBY (All Saints)   *see* Upper Ryedale *York*
HAWORTH (St Michael and All Angels) *Bradf 8*   **P** *V Bradf
  and Haworth Ch Lands Trust (jt)*   **NSM** P S WILSON
HAWRIDGE (St Mary) w Cholesbury and St Leonard *Ox 28*
  P *Bp, Chpl Trust, and Neale's Charity (jt)*   **R** D J BURGESS,
  NSM I CORNISH
HAWSKER (All Saints)   *see* Fylingdales and Hawsker cum
  Stainsacre *York*
HAWSTEAD (All Saints)   *see* St Edm Way *St E*
HAWTHORN (St Michael and All Angels) and Murton *Dur 2*
  P *D&C and I Pemberton Esq (alt)*   **R** A MILNE
HAWTON (All Saints)   *see* Farndon w Thorpe, Hawton and
  Cotham *S'well*
HAXBY (St Mary) and Wigginton *York 7*   **P** *Abp and
  Ld Chan (alt)*   **P-in-c** S JARRATT,   **C** F M GRANDEY,
  NSM P A JACKSON
HAXEY (St Nicholas) *Linc 1*   **P** *Ld Chan*   **P-in-c** J N GREEN
HAY MILL (St Cyprian)   *see* Yardley St Cypr Hay Mill *Birm*
HAYDOCK (St James) *Liv 15*   **P** *R Ashton-in-Makerfield*
  V R MIDDLETON,   **C** A M OULTON,   **NSM** G J HARDMAN
HAYDOCK (St Mark) *Liv 10*   **P** *MMCET*   **V** M G COCKAYNE,
  C P POTTER, A J BRUCE, F HINDS
HAYDON BRIDGE (St Cuthbert) and Beltingham w Henshaw
  Newc 10   **P** *Bp and V Haltwhistle and Greenhead (jt)*
  V J E HAMPSON
HAYDON WICK (St John) *Bris 7*   **P** *CPAS*   **V** R W ADAMS
HAYES (St Anselm) *Lon 24*   **P** *Bp*   **NSM** D R H ELIZABETH
HAYES (St Edmund of Canterbury) *Lon 24*   **P** *Bp*
  V S M MORING,   **NSM** S J LAFFORD
HAYES (St Mary) *Lon 24*   **P** *Keble Coll Ox*
  R P L DE S HOMEWOOD
HAYES (St Mary the Virgin) *Roch 14*   **P** *D&C*
  R G D GRAHAM,   **NSM** M HALLAM
HAYES, NORTH (St Nicholas) *Lon 24*   **P** *Bp and Keble Coll
  Ox (jt)*   **V** J A EVANS
HAYES, WEST (Christ Church) (St Jerome) *Lon 24*   **P** *Bp and
  Hyndman Trustees (jt)*   **V** I W JONES,   **C** F A CALDECOURT
HAYFIELD (St Matthew) and Chinley w Buxworth *Derby 6*
  P *Bp and Resident Freeholders (jt)*   **V** H A EDGERTON,
  NSM S H COCKSEDGE
HAYLE (St Elwyn)   *see* Godrevy *Truro*
HAYLING, NORTH (St Peter) *Portsm 5*   **P** *DBP*
  V A C LEONARD,   **NSM** T R WOOD
HAYLING, SOUTH (St Mary) *Portsm 5*   **P** *DBP*
  V P M J GINEVER,   **NSM** P K PAYNE
HAYLING ISLAND (St Andrew) Eastoke *Portsm 5*   **P** *DBP*
  V A C LEONARD,   **NSM** T R WOOD
HAYNES (Mission Room)   *see* Campton, Clophill and Haynes
  St Alb
HAYNES (St Mary)   *as above*
HAYNES (St James)   *see* Aspatria w Hayton and Gilcrux *Carl*
HAYTON (St Martin)   *see* Shiptonthorpe and Hayton *York*
HAYTON (St Mary Magdalene)   *see* Eden, Gelt and Irthing *Carl*
HAYTON (St Peter)   *see* Clarborough w Hayton *S'well*
HAYWARDS HEATH (Church of the Ascension) *Chich 6*   **P** *Bp*
  V N TIPPLE
HAYWARDS HEATH (Church of the Presentation)
  see Haywards Heath St Wilfrid *Chich*
HAYWARDS HEATH (St Richard) *Chich 6*   **P** *Bp*
  V I N CHANDLER,   **Hon C** L D POODHUN, D F COOMBES
HAYWARDS HEATH (St Wilfrid) (Church of the Presentation)
  Chich 6   **P** *Bp*   **V** R C W SMITH,   **C** A C LETSCHKA,
  NSM J M ELLIOTT, D C YOUNG

HAYWOOD, GREAT (St Stephen)   *see* Colton, Colwich and Gt Haywood *Lich*

HAZELBURY BRYAN (St Mary and St James) and the Hillside Parishes *Sarum 5*   **P** *Duke of Northd (2 turns), M J Scott-Williams Esq, G A L-F Pitt-Rivers Esq, Exors F N Kent Esq, and Bp (1 turn each)*   **P-in-c** S A SMITH,   **C** W T RIDDING, R D G WEYMAN, D R R SEYMOUR,   **Hon C** T RAVEN

HAZELWELL (St Mary Magdalen) *Birm 5*   **P** *Bp* **V** A C PRIESTLEY

HAZELWOOD (St John the Evangelist), Holbrook and Milford *Derby 11*   **P** *Bp and DBP (jt)*   **V** R J HARRIS

HAZLEMERE (Holy Trinity) *Ox 29*   **P** *Peache Trustees* **V** P C COLLIER,   **C** M J MEARDON, M P WYNTER

HEACHAM (St Mary) *Nor 16*   **P** *Bp*   **V** S DAVIES

HEADBOURNE WORTHY (St Swithun) *Win 7*   **P** *Univ Coll Ox and Lord Northbrook (alt)*   **R** A W GORDON, **NSM** E CHASE

HEADCORN (St Peter and St Paul) *Cant 11*   **P** *Abp*   **V** *vacant* (01622) 890342

HEADINGLEY (St Chad)   *see* Far Headingley St Chad *Ripon*

HEADINGLEY (St Michael and All Angels) *Ripon 7* **P** *V Leeds St Pet*   **Hon C** C BARRETT,   **NSM** D W PEAT, K WARD

HEADINGLEY (St Oswald)   *see* Far Headingley St Chad *Ripon*

HEADINGTON (St Andrew) *Ox 4*   **P** *Keble Coll Ox* **V** W M BREWIN

HEADINGTON (St Mary) *Ox 4*   **P** *Bp*   **P-in-c** J W SEWELL, **Hon C** S C BULLOCK,   **NSM** R W CHAND

HEADINGTON QUARRY (Holy Trinity) *Ox 4*   **P** *Bp* **P-in-c** T J STEAD,   **NSM** R S S WEIR

HEADLESS CROSS (St Luke)   *see* Redditch Ch the K *Worc*

HEADLEY (All Saints) *Guildf 3*   **P** *Qu Coll Ox*   **R** H M SEMPLE

HEADLEY (St Mary the Virgin) w Box Hill (St Andrew) *Guildf 9* **P** *Bp*   **P-in-c** L HARKNETT,   **NSM** I A JACOBSON

HEADLEY (St Peter)   *see* Kingsclere and Ashford Hill w Headley *Win*

HEADON (St Peter)   *see* E Markham w Askham, Headon w Upton and Grove *S'well*

HEADSTONE (St George) *Lon 23*   **P** *Bp*   **V** S R KEEBLE

HEAGE (St Luke)   *see* Ambergate and Heage *Derby*

HEALAUGH (St John the Baptist) w Wighill, Bilbrough and Askham Richard *York 1*   **P** *Abp (3 turns), A G Wailes-Fairbairn Esq (1 turn)*   **P-in-c** P P ROBINSON, **NSM** M R SHAW

HEALD GREEN (St Catherine) *Ches 17*   **P** *Bp* **V** J F AMBROSE

HEALEY (Christ Church) *Man 21*   **P** *Bp*   **P-in-c** L O RUDEN

HEALEY (St John) *Newc 9*   **P** *V Bywell St Pet* **P-in-c** D J IRVINE,   **NSM** J LYNCH

HEALEY (St Paul)   *see* Masham and Healey *Ripon*

HEALEY (War Memorial Mission)   *see* S Ossett *Wakef*

HEALING (St Peter and St Paul)   *see* Keelby Gp *Linc*

HEAMOOR (St Thomas)   *see* Gulval and Madron *Truro*

HEANOR (St Laurence) *Derby 12*   **P** *Wright Trustees* **P-in-c** D J PATTIMORE,   **NSM** K PATTIMORE

HEANTON PUNCHARDON (St Augustine) w Marwood *Ex 15* **P** *CPAS (3 turns), St Jo Coll Cam (1 turn)*   **R** J S WOOD, **NSM** M E CRANSTON

HEAP BRIDGE (St Thomas and St George)   *see* Bury Ch King *Man*

HEAPEY (St Barnabas) and Withnell *Blackb 4*   **P** *V Leyland* **P-in-c** A F HOGARTH

HEAPHAM (All Saints)   *see* Lea Gp *Linc*

HEART OF EDEN *Carl 1*   **P** *Patr Bd*   **TR** J A H CLEGG, **TV** S A LUNN,   **C** S SARVANANTHAN,   **NSM** J COX

HEATH (All Saints) *Derby 5*   **P** *Duke of Devonshire and Simeon's Trustees (jt)*   **V** A LOVE

HEATH (Mission Church)   *see* Uttoxeter Area *Lich*

HEATH, LITTLE (Christ Church) *St Alb 17*   **P** *Ch Patr Trust* **P-in-c** S P REES,   **NSM** R H WIKNER

HEATH, THE (not known)   *see* Bitterley w Middleton, Stoke St Milborough etc *Heref*

HEATH AND REACH (St Leonard)   *see* Ouzel Valley *St Alb*

HEATH HAYES (St John)   *see* Cannock *Lich*

HEATH TOWN (Holy Trinity)   *see* Wednesfield Heath *Lich*

HEATHER (St John the Baptist)   *see* Ibstock w Heather *Leic*

HEATHERLANDS (St John) *Sarum 7*   **P** *MMCET* **C** P D HOMDEN, T F GOMM

HEATHERYCLEUGH (St Thomas)   *see* Upper Weardale *Dur*

HEATHFIELD (All Saints) *Chich 15*   **P** *Bp*   **V** *vacant* (01435) 862457

HEATHFIELD (St Catherine)   *see* Bovey Tracey St Jo w Heathfield *Ex*

HEATHFIELD (St John the Baptist)   *see* Deane Vale *B & W*

HEATHFIELD (St Richard) *Chich 15*   **P** *Bp*   **P-in-c** P M JONES

HEATON (Christ Church) *Man 9*   **P** *R Deane St Mary* **V** C A BRACEGIRDLE

HEATON (St Barnabas) *Bradf 1*   **P** *Trustees* **C** R S ANDERSON,   **NSM** M C FISHER

HEATON (St Gabriel)   *see* Newc St Gabr *Newc*

HEATON (St Martin) *Bradf 1*   **P** *Bp*   **V** *vacant* (01274) 543004

HEATON, HIGH (St Francis)   *see* Newc St Fran *Newc*

HEATON CHAPEL (St Thomas)   *see* Heatons *Man*

HEATON MERSEY (St John the Baptist)   *as above*

HEATON MOOR (St Paul)   *as above*

HEATON NORRIS (Christ w All Saints)   *as above*

HEATON REDDISH (St Mary) *Man 3*   **P** *Trustees* **P-in-c** S O'ROURKE,   **NSM** H T SCANLAN

HEATONS *Man 3*   **P** *Patr Bd (4 turns), Prime Min (1 turn)* **TR** M H MAXWELL,   **TV** M C MARSHALL, D BROWNHILL, **OLM** H J TATE, G H RICHARDS, D MACIVER

HEAVITREE (St Michael and All Angels) (St Lawrence) (St Loye) and St Mary Steps *Ex 3*   **P** *Patr Bd* **TV** J F SEWARD, P R MORRELL,   **P-in-c** R H S EASTOE

HEBBURN (St Cuthbert) (St Oswald) *Dur 15*   **P** *Prime Min and TR Jarrow (alt)*   **V** J B HUNT

HEBBURN (St John) *Dur 15*   **P** *Bp*   **P-in-c** D T OSMAN

HEBDEN (St Peter)   *see* Linton in Craven *Bradf*

HEBDEN BRIDGE (St James) and Heptonstall *Wakef 3* **P** *V Halifax*   **V** H PASK

HEBRON (St Cuthbert)   *see* Longhorsley and Hebron *Newc*

HECK (St John the Baptist)   *see* Gt Snaith *Sheff*

HECKFIELD (St Michael)   *see* Whitewater *Win*

HECKINGTON Group, The (St Andrew) *Linc 22*   **P** *Bp* **P-in-c** D F BOUTLE

HECKMONDWIKE (All Souls) (St James) *Wakef 8* **P** *V Birstall*   **P-in-c** S J PITCHER,   **C** T J-L GUILLEMIN, **NSM** P J DAWSON,   **OLM** J C LEE

HEDDINGTON (St Andrew)   *see* Oldbury *Sarum*

HEDDON-ON-THE-WALL (St Andrew) *Newc 9*   **P** *Ld Chan* **P-in-c** A D MCCARTAN

HEDENHAM (St Peter)   *see* Ditchingham, Hedenham, Broome, Earsham etc *Nor*

HEDGE END (St John the Evangelist) *Win 10*   **P** *Bp* **V** C J BANNISTER,   **NSM** S E LITJENS

HEDGE END (St Luke) *Win 10*   **P** *Bp*   **NSM** J WILLIAMS

HEDGERLEY (St Mary the Virgin)   *see* Farnham Royal w Hedgerley *Ox*

HEDNESFORD (St Peter) *Lich 3*   **P** *Bp*   **V** D A BUCK, **C** K M BUCK, L B VASEY-SAUNDERS

HEDON (St Augustine) w Paull *York 12*   **P** *Abp*   **V** *vacant* (01482) 897693

HEDSOR (St Nicholas) and Bourne End *Ox 29*   **P** *Bp* **R** A P TREW,   **NSM** R A PAYNE, M RODE

HEDWORTH (St Nicholas) *Dur 15*   **P** *The Crown* **P-in-c** J S BAIN,   **C** J A SKELLEY,   **Hon C** D M DUKE

HEELEY (Christ Church) and Gleadless Valley *Sheff 1*   **P** *DBP and Prime Min (alt)*   **TR** A PATTERSON,   **C** D W FRY

HEENE (St Botolph) *Chich 5*   **P** *D&C*   **R** P R ROBERTS

HEIGHAM (Holy Trinity) *Nor 3*   **P** *Ch Trust Fund Trust* **R** A M STRANGE,   **C** M G HUDDLESTON

HEIGHAM (St Barnabas) (St Bartholomew) *Nor 3*   **P** *Bp* **P-in-c** E HUTCHEON

HEIGHAM (St Thomas) *Nor 3*   **P** *Bp*   **V** P A YOUNG

HEIGHINGTON (not known)   *see* Washingborough w Heighington and Canwick *Linc*

HEIGHINGTON (St Michael) *Dur 8*   **P** *D&C* **V** P H E THOMAS

HEIGHTINGTON (St Giles)   *see* Mamble w Bayton, Rock w Heightington etc *Worc*

HELFORD (St Paul's Mission Church)   *see* Meneage *Truro*

HELHOUGHTON (All Saints)   *see* E w W Rudham, Helhoughton etc *Nor*

HELIDON (St John the Baptist)   *see* Daventry, Ashby St Ledgers, Braunston etc *Pet*

HELIONS BUMPSTEAD (St Andrew)   *see* Steeple Bumpstead and Helions Bumpstead *Chelmsf*

HELLAND (St Helena) *Truro 10*   **P** *MMCET* **P-in-c** S L BRYAN

HELLESDON (St Mary) (St Paul and St Michael) *Nor 2*   **P** *Bp* **V** P E GRIFFITHS,   **OLM** E O JONES-BLACKETT

HELLIFIELD (St Aidan) *Bradf 5*   **P** *Ch Ch Ox* **P-in-c** E A KYTE,   **Hon C** K J PHILLIPS

HELLINGLY (St Peter and St Paul) and Upper Dicker *Chich 15* **P** *Abp and Bp (jt)*   **V** C M HILL

HELMDON (St Mary Magdalene)   *see* Astwell Gp *Pet*

HELME (Christ Church)   *see* Meltham *Wakef*

HELMINGHAM (St Mary)   *see* Debenham and Helmingham *St E*

HELMSHORE (St Thomas)   *see* Musbury *Blackb*

HELMSLEY (All Saints) *York 17*   **P** *Lord Feversham*
NSM J B NICHOLSON, M D B SINCLAIR
HELMSLEY, UPPER (St Peter)   *see* Sand Hutton *York*
HELPERTHORPE (St Peter)   *see* Weaverthorpe w
Helperthorpe, Luttons Ambo etc *York*
HELPRINGHAM (St Andrew) w Hale *Linc 22*   **P** *Ld Chan*
(2 turns), D&C (1 turn), DBP (1 turn), and the Rt Revd A C
Foottit (1 turn)   **P-in-c** S SAMUEL
HELPSTON (St Botolph)   *see* Etton w Helpston and Maxey *Pet*
HELSBY (St Paul) and Dunham-on-the-Hill *Ches 3*   **P** *Bp*
P-in-c M SAVILLE
HELSINGTON (St John the Baptist) *Carl 10*   **P** *V Kendal*
H Trin   **P-in-c** T J HARMER
HELSTON (St Michael) and Wendron *Truro 4*   **P** *Patr Bd*
TR D G MILLER,   **OLM** D NOAKES
HEMBLINGTON (All Saints)   *see* Blofield w Hemblington *Nor*
HEMEL HEMPSTEAD (Holy Trinity) Leverstock Green
see Chambersbury *St Alb*
HEMEL HEMPSTEAD (St Benedict) Bennetts End   *as above*
HEMEL HEMPSTEAD (St Mary) *St Alb 3*   **P** *Ld Chan*
TV C K PERERA, P J STEVENSON, S R ALLEN, R W GRAHAM,
NSM T J BARTON, D SPINK, D A MACKRILL
HEMEL HEMPSTEAD (St Mary) Apsley End
see Chambersbury *St Alb*
HEMINGBROUGH (St Mary the Virgin) *York 2*   **P** *Abp*
NSM F LOFTUS
HEMINGBY (St Margaret) *Linc 11*   **P** *Bp (2 turns), Ld Chan*
(2 turns), and DBP (1 turn)   **R** *vacant*
HEMINGFORD ABBOTS (St Margaret of Antioch) *Ely 10*
P *Lord Hemingford*   **P-in-c** P H CUNLIFFE,   **C** J A RANDALL
HEMINGFORD GREY (St James) *Ely 10*   **P** *CPAS*
V P H CUNLIFFE,   **C** J A RANDALL
HEMINGSTONE (St Gregory)   *see* Coddenham w Gosbeck
and Hemingstone w Henley *St E*
HEMINGTON (Blessed Virgin Mary)   *see* Hardington Vale
B & W
HEMINGTON (St Peter and St Paul)   *see* Barnwell, Hemington,
Luddington in the Brook etc *Pet*
HEMLEY (All Saints)   *see* Waldringfield w Hemley and
Newbourn *St E*
HEMLINGTON (St Timothy) *York 21*   **P** *Abp*   **V** R A DESICS
HEMPNALL (St Margaret) *Nor 5*   **P** *Ld Chan (1 turn),*
Patr Bd (5 turns)   **TR** M M KINGSTON,   **TV** E N BILLETT
HEMPSTEAD (All Saints)   *see* Barningham w Matlaske w
Baconsthorpe etc *Nor*
HEMPSTEAD (All Saints)   *see* S Gillingham *Roch*
HEMPSTEAD (St Andrew)   *see* The Sampfords and Radwinter
w Hempstead *Chelmsf*
HEMPSTEAD (St Andrew)   *see* Bacton, Happisburgh,
Hempstead w Eccles etc *Nor*
HEMPSTED (St Swithun) *Glouc 3*   **P** *Bp*   **R** *vacant (01452)*
523025
HEMPTON (Holy Trinity) and Pudding Norton *Nor 15*
P *The Crown*   **P-in-c** A D BUIK
HEMPTON (St John the Evangelist)   *see* Deddington w Barford,
Clifton and Hempton *Ox*
HEMSBY (St Mary)   *see* Flegg Coastal Benefice *Nor*
HEMSWELL (All Saints)   *see* Glentworth Gp *Linc*
HEMSWORTH (St Helen) *Wakef 10*   **P**   **R** R W HART
HEMYOCK (St Mary) w Culm Davy, Clayhidon and Culmstock
Ex 4   **P** *DBP, SMF, and D&C (jt)*   **P-in-c** D C SHERWOOD
HENBURY (St Mary the Virgin) *Bris 2*   **P** *Lord Middleton*
(1 turn), Bp (3 turns)   **V** D P LLOYD,   **C** J C W STEVENSON
HENBURY (St Thomas) *Ches 13*   **P** *Bp*   **P-in-c** W G BOWNESS
HENDFORD (Holy Trinity)   *see* Yeovil H Trin w Barwick
B & W
HENDFORD (St Mary the Virgin and All Saints)   *as above*
HENDON (All Saints) Childs Hill *Lon 15*   **P** *Bp*
V J P WAINWRIGHT
HENDON (St Alphage) *Lon 15*   **P** *Bp*   **V** H D MOORE
HENDON (St Ignatius) *Dur 16*   **P** *Bp*   **R** A C JONES,
C S H J EDMONDS
HENDON (St Mary) (Christ Church) *Lon 15*   **P** *Bp*
V T G CLEMENT,   **C** D P SANDHAM,   **Hon C** R S LADDS
HENDON (St Paul) Mill Hill *Lon 15*   **P** *Bp*   **V** A J SHAW,
C J E LOWE
HENDON, WEST (St John) *Lon 15*   **P** *Bp*   **V** J E I HAWKINS,
C S P YOUNG,   **NSM** T J HALTON
HENDRED, EAST (St Augustine of Canterbury)   *see* Wantage
Downs *Ox*
HENDRED, WEST (Holy Trinity)   *as above*
HENFIELD (St Peter) w Shermanbury and Woodmancote
Chich 9   **P** *Bp*   **V** C J COLLISON,   **C** A F MARTIN,
NSM C M BENNETT
HENGROVE (Christ Church) *Bris 1*   **P** *Bp and Simeon's*
Trustees (alt)   **P-in-c** N HAWKINS

HENHAM (St Mary the Virgin) and Elsenham w Ugley
Chelmsf 21   **P** *Ch Hosp, Ch Soc Trust, and Bp (jt)*
P-in-c R W FARR,   **C** J P RICHARDSON
HENLEAZE (St Peter) *Bris 2*   **P** *Bp*   **V** C M PILGRIM,
C C J YANDELL
HENLEY (St Peter)   *see* Coddenham w Gosbeck and
Hemingstone w Henley *St E*
HENLEY IN ARDEN (St John the Baptist)   *see* Beaudesert and
Henley-in-Arden w Ullenhall *Cov*
HENLEY-ON-THAMES (Holy Trinity) *Ox 6*   **P** *R Rotherfield*
Greys St Nich   **V** D R B CARTER
HENLEY-ON-THAMES (St Mary the Virgin) w Remenham
Ox 6   **P** *Bp and Jes Coll Ox (jt)*   **R** M R GRIFFITHS
HENLOW (St Mary the Virgin) and Langford *St Alb 16*
P *Ld Chan*   **V** *vacant (01462) 700248*
HENNOCK (St Mary)   *see* Bovey Tracey SS Pet, Paul and Thos
w Hennock *Ex*
HENNY, GREAT (St Mary)   *see* N Hinckford *Chelmsf*
HENSALL (St Paul)   *see* Gt Snaith *Sheff*
HENSHAW (All Hallows)   *see* Haydon Bridge and Beltingham
w Henshaw *Newc*
HENSINGHAM (St John) (Keekle Mission) *Carl 5*   **P** *Trustees*
V F T PEARSON,   **C** T J PARSONS
HENSTEAD (St Mary)   *see* Wrentham, Covehithe w Benacre
etc *St E*
HENSTRIDGE (St Nicholas)   *see* Abbas and Templecombe,
Henstridge and Horsington *B & W*
HENTLAND (St Dubricius)   *see* St Weonards *Heref*
HENTON (Christ Church)   *see* Coxley w Godney, Henton and
Wookey *B & W*
HEPPLE (Christ Church)   *see* Upper Coquetdale *Newc*
HEPTONSTALL (St Thomas à Becket and St Thomas the
Apostle)   *see* Hebden Bridge and Heptonstall *Wakef*
HEPWORTH (Holy Trinity)   *see* Upper Holme Valley *Wakef*
HEPWORTH (St Peter) w Hinderclay, Wattisfield and
Thelnetham *St E 9*   **P** *Bp, K Coll Cam, MMCET, and P J Holt-*
Wilson Esq (jt)   **R** J W FULTON
HEREFORD (St Francis)   *see* Heref S Wye *Heref*
HEREFORD (St John the Baptist) *Heref 3*   **P** *D&C*   **V** *vacant*
HEREFORD (St Martin)   *see* Heref S Wye *Heref*
HEREFORD (St Paul)   *see* Tupsley w Hampton Bishop *Heref*
HEREFORD (St Peter w St Owen) (St James) *Heref 3*
P *Simeon's Trustees*   **P-in-c** P TOWNER,   **C** J COORE,
A J CLARK,   **NSM** P W MASSEY,   **OLM** S A ELSON
HEREFORD, LITTLE (St Mary Magdalene)   *see* Burford III w
Lt Heref *Heref*
HEREFORD, WEST Team Ministry (All Saints) (Holy Trinity)
(St Barnabas Church Centre) (St Nicholas) *Heref 3*   **P** *Patr Bd*
(3 turns) Ld Chan (1 turn)   **TR** R NORTH,   **TV** B P CHAVE,
C D A PRESCOTT
HEREFORD SOUTH WYE (St Francis) (St Martin) *Heref 3*
P *Patr Bd*   **TR** J D REESE,   **TV** M JOHNSON,   **C** I PRICE,
R C GREEN,   **NSM** P J BROWN,   **OLM** C R EVANS
HERMITAGE (Holy Trinity) *Ox 14*   **P** *Patr Bd*   **TR** R E BALL,
TV A H LYNN,   **NSM** M C CAWTE
HERMITAGE (St Mary)   *see* Wriggle Valley *Sarum*
HERNE (St Martin) *Cant 7*   **P** *Abp*   **V** E M RICHARDSON,
OLM J L HADLOW
HERNE BAY (Christ Church) (St Andrew's Church and Centre)
Cant 7   **P** *Simeon's Trustees*   **V** A W EVERETT,   **C** M G LANE,
OLM S PARRETT
HERNE BAY (St Bartholomew)   *see* Reculver and Herne Bay
St Bart *Cant*
HERNE HILL (St Paul) (St Saviour) *S'wark 9*   **P** *Bp and*
Simeon's Trustees (jt)   **V** C T BARKER,   **C** J M ITUMU,
NSM G S TAYLEUR
HERNER (Chapel)   *see* Barnstaple *Ex*
HERNHILL (St Michael)   *see* Boughton under Blean w
Dunkirk and Hernhill *Cant*
HERODSFOOT (All Saints)   *see* Duloe, Herodsfoot, Morval
and St Pinnock *Truro*
HERONSGATE (St John the Evangelist)   *see* Mill End and
Heronsgate w W Hyde *St Alb*
HERRIARD (St Mary)   *see* N Hants Downs *Win*
HERRINGFLEET (St Margaret)   *see* Somerleyton, Ashby,
Fritton, Herringfleet etc *Nor*
HERRINGSWELL (St Ethelbert)   *see* Mildenhall *St E*
HERRINGTHORPE (St Cuthbert) *Sheff 6*   **P** *Bp*
V J TRICKETT,   **C** M BAKER
HERRINGTON (St Aidan), Penshaw and Shiney Row *Dur 14*
P *Bp and Prime Min (alt)*   **NSM** M S GOURLEY
HERSHAM (St Peter) *Guildf 8*   **P** *Bp*   **V** N J WHITEHEAD,
NSM J W ANDREW,   **OLM** S H GRAY
HERSTMONCEUX (All Saints) and Wartling *Chich 15*   **P** *Bp*
R S L PANTER MARSHALL,   **NSM** J M MANNING

HERSTON (St Mark)   *see* Swanage and Studland *Sarum*

HERTFORD (All Saints) (St Andrew) *St Alb 22*   **P** *Ld Chan (1 turn), Duchy of Lanc (2 turns), Patr Bd (1 turn)*
   TR J M H LOVERIDGE,   **TV** R C THOMPSON, N L SHARP, H A STEWART,   **NSM** W J CHURCH, D R PEPPER

HERTFORD HEATH (Holy Trinity)   *see* Hertford *St Alb*

HERTINGFORDBURY (St Mary)   *as above*

HESKET-IN-THE-FOREST (St Mary the Virgin)   *see* Inglewood Gp *Carl*

HESKETH (All Saints) w Becconsall *Blackb 5*   **P** *Trustees*   **P-in-c** N E DAVIS,   **Hon C** J D BURNS

HESLERTON, EAST (St Andrew)   *see* Buckrose Carrs *York*

HESLERTON, WEST (All Saints)   *as above*

HESLINGTON (St Paul) *York 2*   **P** *Abp*   **V** N E ECKERSLEY

HESSAY (St John the Baptist)   *see* Rufforth w Moor Monkton and Hessay *York*

HESSENFORD (St Anne)   *see* St Germans *Truro*

HESSETT (St Ethelbert)   *see* Rougham, Beyton w Hessett and Rushbrooke *St E*

HESSLE (All Saints) *York 14*   **P** *Ld Chan*   **V** T M H BOYNS, C A C SIMPSON,   **Hon C** E ROSE

HESTER WAY LANE (St Silas)   *see* Cheltenham St Mark *Glouc*

HESTON (All Saints) (St Leonard) *Lon 11*   **P** *Bp*   **V** D COLEMAN

HESWALL (Church of the Good Shepherd) (St Peter) *Ches 8*   **P** *W A B Davenport Esq*   **R** J R GIBBS,   **C** S M MANSFIELD,   **NSM** A C G LEACH

HETHE (St Edmund King and Martyr and St George)   *see* Shelswell *Ox*

HETHEL (All Saints)   *see* Mulbarton w Bracon Ash, Hethel and Flordon *Nor*

HETHERSETT (St Remigius) w Canteloff w Little Melton and Great Melton *Nor 7*   **P** *G&C Coll Cam, E C Evans-Lombe Esq, and Em Coll Cam (by turn)*   **R** D B LAMMAS,   **NSM** J C MALLETT,   **OLM** M KERSLAKE

HETHERSGILL (St Mary)   *see* Bewcastle, Stapleton and Kirklinton etc *Carl*

HETTON, SOUTH (Holy Trinity)   *see* Easington, Easington Colliery and S Hetton *Dur*

HETTON-LYONS w Eppleton *Dur 14*   **P** *Bp (1 turn), Prime Min (2 turns)*   **R** A ANDERSON

HEVENINGHAM (St Margaret) w Ubbeston, Huntingfield and Cookley *St E 15*   **P** *Capt the Revd J S Peel*   **P-in-c** A B NORTON

HEVER (St Peter), Four Elms and Mark Beech *Roch 11*   **P** *Bp and C Talbot Esq (jt)*   **R** M G GRIBBLE,   **NSM** W J IZOD

HEVERSHAM (St Peter) and Milnthorpe *Carl 10*   **P** *Trin Coll Cam*   **P-in-c** S E WILSON,   **NSM** R RUTTER

HEVINGHAM (St Mary the Virgin and St Botolph)   *see* Horsford, Felthorpe and Hevingham *Nor*

HEWELSFIELD (St Mary Magdalene)   *see* St Briavels w Hewelsfield *Glouc*

HEWISH (Good Shepherd)   *see* Wulfric Benefice *B & W*

HEWORTH (Christ Church) *York 7*   **P** *Ch Trust Fund Trust*   **V** T MCDONOUGH

HEWORTH (Holy Trinity) (St Wulstan) *York 7*   **P** *Ch Trust Fund Trust*   **R** M B WOODMANSEY

HEWORTH (St Alban) *Dur 12*   **P** *V Heworth St Mary*   **V** R A LUMLEY,   **C** S M WHITE

HEWORTH (St Mary) *Dur 12*   **P** *Bp*   **V** V SHEDDEN,   **C** J M PERKINS

HEXAGON, THE: Arnesby w Shearsby, Bruntingthorpe, Husbands Bosworth, Mowsley and Knaptoft, and Theddingworth *Leic 7*   **P** *Bp and DBP (jt)*   **R** A J HAMPTON,   **C** A C RHOADES

HEXHAM (St Andrew) *Newc 10*   **P** *Mercers' Co and Viscount Allendale (alt)*   **R** G B USHER,   **C** J E ANDERSON,   **NSM** A R CURRIE

HEXTABLE (St Peter)   *see* Swanley St Paul *Roch*

HEXTHORPE (St Jude)   *see* Doncaster St Jude *Sheff*

HEXTON (St Faith)   *see* Barton-le-Cley w Higham Gobion and Hexton *St Alb*

HEY (St John the Baptist)   *see* Medlock Head *Man*

HEYBRIDGE (St Andrew) (St George) w Langford *Chelmsf 11*   **P** *D&C St Paul's and Lord Byron (alt)*   **V** P J LOW

HEYBROOK BAY (Holy Nativity)   *see* Wembury *Ex*

HEYDON (Holy Trinity), Great Chishill and Little Chishill, Chrishall, Elmdon w Wenden Lofts and Strethall *Chelmsf 21*   **P** *Patr Bd*   **R** A COLEBROOKE

HEYDON (St Peter and St Paul)   *see* Cawston w Booton and Brandiston etc *Nor*

HEYDOUR (St Michael and All Angels)   *see* Ancaster Wilsford Gp *Linc*

HEYFORD (St Peter and St Paul) w Stowe Nine Churches and Flore w Brockhall *Pet 3*   **P** *The Revd S Hope, Ch Ch Ox, DPB and Bp (by turn)*   **R** A SLATER,   **C** A L WATKINS

HEYFORD, LOWER (St Mary)   *see* Cherwell Valley *Ox*

HEYFORD, UPPER (St Mary)   *as above*

HEYHOUSES (St Nicholas)   *see* Sabden and Pendleton *Blackb*

HEYHOUSES ON SEA (St Anne)   *see* St Annes St Anne *Blackb*

HEYSHAM (St Peter) (St Andrew) (St James) *Blackb 11*   **P** *C E C Royds Esq*   **R** D A TICKNER

HEYSHOTT (St James) *Chich 10*   **P** *Bp*   **P-in-c** C BOXLEY

HEYSIDE (St Mark) *Man 20*   **P** *Trustees*   **V** R MORRIS,   **NSM** S E WARD

HEYTESBURY (St Peter and St Paul)   *see* Upper Wylye Valley *Sarum*

HEYTHROP (St Nicholas)   *see* Chase *Ox*

HEYWOOD (All Souls) (St Luke) (St Margaret) *Man 18*   **P** *Patr Bd*   **TV** S J BANKS, M D CARLISLE,   **OLM** I TAYLOR, I WARRINGTON, J M GEARY

HEYWOOD (St James) *Man 18*   **P** *Bp*   **P-in-c** L J READING

HIBALDSTOW (St Hibald)   *see* Scawby, Redbourne and Hibaldstow *Linc*

HICKLETON (St Wilfrid)   *see* Goldthorpe w Hickleton *Sheff*

HICKLING (St Luke) w Kinoulton and Broughton Sulney (Upper Broughton) *S'well 8*   **P** *Prime Min, Qu Coll Cam, and Bp (by turn)*   **R** S B FAHIE

HICKLING (St Mary)   *see* Ludham, Potter Heigham, Hickling and Catfield *Nor*

HIGH *see also under substantive name*

HIGH CROSS (St John the Evangelist) *St Alb 22*   **P** *DBP*   **V** H J SHARMAN

HIGH GREEN (St Saviour)   *see* Mortomley St Sav High Green *Sheff*

HIGH HAM (St Andrew)   *see* Langport Area *B & W*

HIGH LANE (St Thomas) *Ches 16*   **P** *R Stockport*   **V** *vacant* (01663) 762627

HIGH OAK, Hingham and Scoulton w Wood Rising *Nor 7*   **P** *Patr Bd*   **TV** M G KICHENSIDE,   **OLM** P J TRETT, S A HOLT

HIGHAM (St John the Evangelist)   *see* Fence-in-Pendle and Higham *Blackb*

HIGHAM (St John the Evangelist) and Merston *Roch 6*   **P** *St Jo Coll Cam*   **V** J F SOUTHWARD

HIGHAM (St Mary), Holton St Mary, Raydon and Stratford St Mary *St E 3*   **P** *Duchy of Lanc, Reformation Ch Trust, and Mrs S E F Holden*   **R** R M PAUL

HIGHAM FERRERS (St Mary the Virgin) w Chelveston *Pet 8*   **P** *Bp*   **V** G L BROCKHOUSE

HIGHAM GOBION (St Margaret)   *see* Barton-le-Cley w Higham Gobion and Hexton *St Alb*

HIGHAM GREEN (St Stephen)   *see* Dalham, Gazeley, Higham, Kentford and Moulton *St E*

HIGHAM HILL (St Andrew)   *see* Walthamstow St Andr *Chelmsf*

HIGHAM-ON-THE-HILL (St Peter)   *see* Fenn Lanes Gp *Leic*

HIGHAMPTON (Holy Cross)   *see* Black Torrington, Bradford w Cookbury etc *Ex*

HIGHAMS PARK (All Saints) Hale End *Chelmsf 5*   **P** *Bp*   **V** C A MCGHIE

HIGHBRIDGE (St John the Evangelist) *B & W 1*   **P** *Bp*   **V** R P LODGE,   **C** C A JUDSON

HIGHBROOK (All Saints) and West Hoathly *Chich 6*   **P** *Ld Chan*   **V** A C CARR

HIGHBURY (Christ Church) (St John) (St Saviour) *Lon 6*   **P** *Ch Trust Fund Trust and Islington Ch Trust (jt)*   **V** J D BREWSTER,   **C** T GOLDING

HIGHBURY NEW PARK (St Augustine) *Lon 6*   **P** *Trustees*   **V** C T MAIN

HIGHCLERE (St Michael and All Angels) and Ashmansworth w Crux Easton *Win 6*   **P** *Earl of Carnarvon*   **R** T F HORSINGTON

HIGHCLIFFE (St Mark) *Win 9*   **P** *Bp*   **V** G K TAYLOR

HIGHER *see also under substantive place name*

HIGHER FOLD Leigh (St Matthew)   *see* Bedford Leigh *Man*

HIGHERTOWN (All Saints) and Baldhu *Truro 6*   **P** *Bp and Viscount Falmouth (alt)*   **V** G W SMYTH

HIGHFIELD (All Saints) *Ox 4*   **P** *Bp*   **V** J E COCKE

HIGHFIELD (Christ Church)   *see* Portswood Ch Ch *Win*

HIGHFIELD (St Catherine)   *see* New Bury w Gt Lever *Man*

HIGHFIELD (St Mary)   *see* Sheff St Mary Bramall Lane *Sheff*

HIGHFIELD (St Matthew) *Liv 14*   **P** *Trustees*   **V** R L PEARSON

HIGHFIELD (St Paul)   *see* Hemel Hempstead *St Alb*

HIGHGATE (All Saints) *Lon 20*   **P** *Bp*   **P-in-c** J D TRIGG

HIGHGATE (St Alban and St Patrick) *Birm 13*   **P** *Keble Coll Ox*   **P-in-c** J A HERVE

HIGHGATE (St Augustine) *Lon 20*   **P** *Bp*   **P-in-c** P F M GOFF

HIGHGATE (St Michael) *Lon 20*   **P** *Bp*   **V** J D TRIGG,   **C** B WANDREY, C B STOLTZ, E M WEST

HIGHGATE CENTRE   *see* Bredbury St Barn *Ches*

HIGHGATE RISE (St Anne)   *see* Brookfield St Anne, Highgate Rise *Lon*

HIGHLEY (St Mary) w Billingsley, Glazeley and Deuxhill and Chelmarsh *Heref 9* **P** *MMCET* **V** C G WILLIAMS, **C** C E RESCH, **NSM** V R SMITH

HIGHMORE (St Paul) *see* Nettlebed w Bix, Highmoor, Pishill etc *Ox*

HIGHNAM (Holy Innocents), Lassington, Rudford, Tibberton and Taynton *Glouc 1* **P** *D&C, T J Fenton Esq, and A E Woolley (jt)* **R** P A KEMP, **NSM** S TAYLOR

HIGHTERS HEATH (Immanuel) *Birm 5* **P** *Bp* **V** E I PITTS

HIGHTOWN (All Saints) *see* Castleford *Wakef*

HIGHTOWN (St Barnabas) *see* Liversedge w Hightown *Wakef*

HIGHTOWN (St Stephen) *see* Altcar and Hightown *Liv*

HIGHWEEK (All Saints) (St Mary) *Ex 10* **P** *Bp* **P-in-c** M D THAYER

HIGHWORTH (St Michael) w Sevenhampton and Inglesham and Hannington *Bris 7* **P** *Bp (4 turns), Mrs M G Hussey-Freke (1 turn)* **V** G D SOWDEN, **C** A C WOO, **NSM** J N REES

HILBOROUGH (All Saints) w Bodney *Nor 13* **P** *DBP* **C** D J HANWELL

HILDENBOROUGH (St John the Evangelist) *Roch 11* **P** *V Tonbridge* **V** J C CHANDLER, **NSM** S BRAID

HILDERSHAM (Holy Trinity) *Ely 5* **P** *Trustees* **P-in-c** J M NORRIS

HILDERSTONE (Christ Church) *see* Fulford w Hilderstone *Lich*

HILFIELD (St Nicholas) *see* Wriggle Valley *Sarum*

HILGAY (All Saints) *Ely 9* **P** *Hertf Coll Ox* **R** D J EVANS

HILL (St James) *Birm 12* **P** *Bp* **V** A W MOORE, **C** A C REES, **NSM** A R PLATTS

HILL (St Michael) *see* Berkeley w Wick, Breadstone, Newport, Stone etc *Glouc*

HILL CROOME (St Mary) *see* Upton-on-Severn, Ripple, Earls Croome etc *Worc*

HILL TOP (Mission Room) *see* Greasley *S'well*

HILL TOP (St James) *see* W Bromwich St Jas w St Paul *Lich*

HILLESDEN (All Saints) *see* Lenborough *Ox*

HILLESLEY (St Giles) *see* Wickwar, Rangeworthy and Hillesley *Glouc*

HILLFARRANCE (Holy Cross) *see* Deane Vale *B & W*

HILLINGDON (All Saints) *Lon 24* **P** *Bp* **V** D P BANISTER

HILLINGDON (St John the Baptist) *Lon 24* **P** *Bp* **V** R W HARRISON, **NSM** G PINNELL

HILLINGTON (St Mary the Virgin) *Nor 16* **P** E W Dawnay Esq **P-in-c** J B V RIVIERE

HILLMORTON (St John the Baptist) *Cov 6* **P** *Bp and TR Rugby* **V** A P HAINES

HILLOCK (St Andrew) *Man 14* **P** *Bp and R Stand All SS* **V** *vacant* 0161-766 1635

HILLSBOROUGH and Wadsley Bridge (Christ Church) *Sheff 4* **P** *Ch Patr Trust* **P-in-c** K FARROW

HILLSIDE Lobley Hill and Marley Hill *Dur 13* **P** *Bp and Prime Min (alt)* **V** R K HOPPER, **OLM** N P HARDY

HILLTOP (Mission Room) *see* Bagnall w Endon *Lich*

HILMARTON (St Lawrence) *see* Broad Town, Clyffe Pypard, Hilmarton etc *Sarum*

HILPERTON MARSH (St Mary Magdalen) *see* Canalside Benefice *Sarum*

HILSTON (St Margaret) *see* Roos and Garton w Tunstall, Grimston and Hilston *York*

HILTON (All Saints) *see* Piddle Valley, Hilton, Cheselbourne etc *Sarum*

HILTON (St Mary Magdalene) *Ely 10* **P** *Bp* **P-in-c** R P MCKENZIE

HILTON (St Peter) *see* Stainton w Hilton *York*

HILTON w Marston-on-Dove *Derby 14* **P** *N J M Spurrier Esq* **V** A G MURPHIE, **C** J C CANT, **NSM** S K MATSON DE LAURIER

HIMBLETON (St Mary Magdalen) *see* Bowbrook S *Worc*

HIMLEY (St Michael and All Angels) *see* Smestow Vale *Lich*

HINCASTER (Mission Room) *see* Heversham and Milnthorpe *Carl*

HINCHLEY WOOD (St Christopher) *Guildf 8* **P** *Bp* **V** J S KRONENBERG

HINCKFORD, NORTH *Chelmsf 19* **P** *Patr Bd (4 turns), Ld Chan (1 turn)* **TR** E G BUCHANAN, **TV** M H KING

HINCKLEY (Assumption of St Mary the Virgin) (St Francis) (St Paul) *Leic 10* **P** *Bp* **V** B DAVIS, **NSM** J A GIBBS

HINCKLEY (Holy Trinity) (St John the Evangelist) *Leic 10* **P** *DBP* **TV** T J WARD, **P-in-c** G J WESTON, **C** A P CAIN, **NSM** A C WINTER

HINDERCLAY (St Mary) *see* Hepworth, Hinderclay, Wattisfield and Thelnetham *St E*

HINDERWELL (St Hilda), Roxby and Staithes w Lythe, Ugthorpe and Sandsend *York 22* **P** *Abp* **R** B J PYKE, **NSM** J EVETTS-SECKER

HINDHEAD (St Alban) *see* Churt and Hindhead *Guildf*

HINDLEY (All Saints) *Liv 14* **P** *R Wigan* **V** J TAYLOR

HINDLEY (St Peter) *Liv 14* **P** *St Pet Coll Ox* **V** S A MATHER

HINDLEY GREEN (St John) *Liv 14* **P** *Bp* **V** M J SHERWIN

HINDOLVESTON (St George) *see* Briston, Burgh Parva, Hindolveston etc *Nor*

HINDON (St John the Baptist) *see* Nadder Valley *Sarum*

HINDRINGHAM (St Martin) *see* Barney, Fulmodeston w Croxton, Hindringham etc *Nor*

HINGHAM (St Andrew) *see* High Oak, Hingham and Scoulton w Wood Rising *Nor*

HINKSEY, NEW (St John the Evangelist) *see* S Hinksey *Ox*

HINKSEY, NORTH (St Lawrence) and Wytham *Ox 7* **P** *Bp* **P-in-c** A C RUSTELL, **NSM** R M HILL, J M BROWN

HINKSEY, SOUTH (St Laurence) *Ox 7* **P** *Bp* **P-in-c** J D WILKINSON

HINSTOCK (St Oswald) *see* Cheswardine, Childs Ercall, Hales, Hinstock etc *Lich*

HINTLESHAM (St Nicholas) *see* Elmsett w Aldham, Hintlesham, Chattisham etc *St E*

HINTON ADMIRAL (St Michael and All Angels) *see* Bransgore and Hinton Admiral *Win*

HINTON AMPNER (All Saints) *see* Upper Itchen *Win*

HINTON BLEWETT (St Margaret) *see* E w W Harptree and Hinton Blewett *B & W*

HINTON CHARTERHOUSE (St John the Baptist) *see* Freshford, Limpley Stoke and Hinton Charterhouse *B & W*

HINTON-IN-THE-HEDGES (Holy Trinity) *see* Aynho and Croughton w Evenley etc *Pet*

HINTON MARTEL (St John the Evangelist) *see* Horton, Chalbury, Hinton Martel and Holt St Jas *Sarum*

HINTON-ON-THE-GREEN (St Peter) *see* Hampton w Sedgeberrow and Hinton-on-the-Green *Worc*

HINTON PARVA (St Swithun) *see* Lyddington and Wanborough and Bishopstone etc *Bris*

HINTON ST GEORGE (St George) *see* Merriott w Hinton, Dinnington and Lopen *B & W*

HINTON ST MARY (St Mary) *see* Sturminster Newton, Hinton St Mary and Lydlinch *Sarum*

HINTON WALDRIST (St Margaret) *see* Cherbury w Gainfield *Ox*

HINTS (St Bartholomew) *Lich 1* **P** *Personal Reps A E Jones Esq* **V** F A HASKETT, **Hon C** C M J IBALL

HINXHILL (St Mary) *see* Mersham w Hinxhill and Sellindge *Cant*

HINXTON (St Mary and St John) *Ely 5* **P** *Jes Coll Cam* **V** *vacant*

HINXWORTH (St Nicholas) *see* Ashwell w Hinxworth and Newnham *St Alb*

HIPSWELL (St John the Evangelist) *Ripon 2* **P** *Bp* **V** J E KEARTON

HISTON (St Andrew) *Ely 6* **P** *MMCET* **V** N J BLANDFORD-BAKER, **C** P H BUTLER, **NSM** J M GLOVER

HITCHAM (All Saints) *see* Rattlesden w Thorpe Morieux, Brettenham etc *St E*

HITCHAM (St Mary) *Ox 23* **P** *Eton Coll* **V** T R HEWSON, **NSM** R R HEWSON

HITCHIN (Holy Saviour) (St Faith) (St Mark) (St Mary) *St Alb 4* **P** *Patr Bd* **TR** M A H RODEN, **TV** I C TODD, J F MAINWARING, C C M SABEY-CORKINDALE, **C** O J LEARMONT, **NSM** S P WOOD

HITHER GREEN (St Swithun) *see* Lewisham St Swithun *S'wark*

HITTISLEIGH (St Andrew) *see* Chagford, Drewsteignton, Hittisleigh etc *Ex*

HIXON (St Peter) *see* Mid Trent *Lich*

HOAR CROSS (Holy Angels) w Newchurch *Lich 14* **P** *Bp and Meynell Ch Trustees* **P-in-c** P G GREEN

HOARWITHY (St Catherine) *see* St Weonards *Heref*

HOATH (Holy Cross) *see* St Nicholas at Wade w Sarre and Chislet w Hoath *Cant*

HOATHLY, EAST (not known) *see* Chiddingly w E Hoathly *Chich*

HOATHLY, WEST (St Margaret) *see* Highbrook and W Hoathly *Chich*

HOBS MOAT (St Mary) *Birm 11* **P** *Bp* **P-in-c** L GRANNER

HOBY (All Saints) *see* Upper Wreake *Leic*

HOCKERILL (All Saints) *St Alb 18* **P** *Bp Lon* **P-in-c** K I GOSS

HOCKERING (St Michael) *see* Mattishall and the Tudd Valley *Nor*

HOCKERTON (St Nicholas) *see* Kirklington w Hockerton *S'well*

HOCKHAM, GREAT (Holy Trinity) *see* Caston, Griston, Merton, Thompson etc *Nor*

HOCKLEY (St Matthew) *see* Wilnecote *Lich*

HOCKLEY (St Paul) *see* Birm St Paul *Birm*

HOCKLEY (St Peter and St Paul) *Chelmsf 12* **P** *Wadh Coll Ox*
V J R WOOLNOUGH

HOCKLIFFE (St Nicholas)   *see* Ouzel Valley *St Alb*

HOCKWOLD w WILTON (St James)   *see* Grimshoe *Ely*

HOCKWORTHY (St Simon and St Jude)   *see* Sampford
Peverell, Uplowman, Holcombe Rogus etc *Ex*

HODDESDON (St Catherine and St Paul) *St Alb 20*   **P** *Peache
Trustees*   **V** J P BROOKS,   **C** V C PARR,
NSM D A MOORE BROOKS

HODDESDON (St Cuthbert)   *see* Rye Park St Cuth *St Alb*

HODDLESDEN (St Paul)   *see* Darwen St Pet w Hoddlesden
Blackb

HODGE HILL (St Philip and St James) *Birm 9*   **P** *Bp*
TR *vacant* 0121-747 2094 *or* 747 9262

HODNET (St Luke) w Weston under Redcastle *Lich 18*
P *A E H Heber-Percy Esq*   **P-in-c** C P BEECH

HODTHORPE (St Martin)   *see* Whitwell *Derby*

HOE (St Andrew)   *see* Dereham and Distr *Nor*

HOE, WEST (St Michael)   *see* Plymouth St Andr and
Stonehouse *Ex*

HOE BENHAM (not known)   *see* Welford w Wickham and Gt
Shefford, Boxford etc *Ox*

HOGGESTON (Holy Cross)   *see* Schorne *Ox*

HOGHTON (Holy Trinity) *Blackb 5*   **P** *V Leyland*
P-in-c D C DICKINSON

HOGNASTON (St Bartholomew)   *see* Hulland, Atlow,
Kniveton, Bradley and Hognaston *Derby*

HOGSTHORPE (St Mary)   *see* Chapel St Leonards w
Hogsthorpe *Linc*

HOLBEACH (All Saints) *Linc 16*   **P** *Bp*   **V** G J WICKSTEAD,
C D C SWEETING

HOLBEACH FEN (St John) *Linc 16*   **P** *Bp*
OLM B A HUTCHINSON

HOLBEACH MARSH (St Luke) (St Mark) (St Martin) *Linc 16*
P *V Holbeach*   **P-in-c** R J GODDARD

HOLBECK (St Luke the Evangelist) *Ripon 6*   **P** *Bp, V Leeds
St Pet, and Meynell Ch Trust (jt)*   **P-in-c** C BUTLER,
C C PUCKRIN

HOLBETON (All Saints) *Ex 21*   **P** *The Crown*
P-in-c J G CRUICKSHANK

HOLBORN (St Alban the Martyr) w Saffron Hill St Peter
Lon 17   **P** *D&C St Paul's*   **V** H LEVETT,   **R** G CORP

**HOLBORN (St George the Martyr) Queen Square (Holy
Trinity) (St Bartholomew) Grays Inn Road** *Lon 17*
P *Ch Soc Trust*   **R** J H VALENTINE,   **C** D L INGALL

HOLBORN (St Giles-in-the-Fields)   *see* St Giles-in-the-Fields
Lon

**HOLBROOK (All Saints), Stutton, Freston, Woolverstone and
Wherstead** *St E 5*   **P** *Patr Bd*   **R** G P CLEMENT,
NSM J G PENDORF

HOLBROOK (St Michael)   *see* Hazelwood, Holbrook and
Milford *Derby*

HOLBROOK ROAD (St Swithin)   *see* Belper *Derby*

HOLBROOKS (St Luke) *Cov 2*   **P** *V Dunkley*

HOLBURY (Good Shepherd)   *see* Fawley *Win*

HOLCOMBE (Emmanuel) (Canon Lewis Hall) and Hawkshaw
Man 10   **P** *R Bury St Mary and F Whowell Esq (jt)*
R P H SUMSION,   **OLM** R W AIREY

HOLCOMBE (St Andrew)   *see* Coleford w Holcombe *B & W*

HOLCOMBE (St George)   *see* Dawlish *Ex*

HOLCOMBE BURNELL (St John the Baptist)   *see* Tedburn
St Mary, Whitestone, Oldridge etc *Ex*

HOLCOMBE ROGUS (All Saints)   *see* Sampford Peverell,
Uplowman, Holcombe Rogus etc *Ex*

HOLCOT (St Mary and All Saints)   *see* Brixworth w Holcot *Pet*

HOLDENHURST (St John the Evangelist) and Iford *Win 8*
P *Bp*   **V** A L MCPHERSON,   **C** J NIGHTINGALE,
NSM N M BENCE, J M SEARE, N S LEGRAND

HOLDGATE (Holy Trinity)   *see* Diddlebury w Munslow,
Holdgate and Tugford *Heref*

HOLFORD (St Mary the Virgin)   *see* Quantock Coast *B & W*

HOLGATE (St Paul)   *see* York St Paul *York*

**HOLKHAM (St Withiburga) w Egmere w Warham, Wells-next-
the-Sea and Wighton** *Nor 15*   **P** *Viscount Coke (2 turns),
M J Beddard Esq (2 turns), and D&C (1 turn)*
R A V DOUGLAS

HOLLACOMBE (St Petroc)   *see* Holsworthy w Hollacombe and
Milton Damerel *Ex*

HOLLAND, GREAT (All Saints)   *see* Kirby-le-Soken w Gt
Holland *Chelmsf*

HOLLAND, NEW (Christ Church)   *see* Barrow and Goxhill
Linc

HOLLAND FEN (All Saints)   *see* Brothertoft Gp *Linc*

HOLLAND-ON-SEA (St Bartholomew) *Chelmsf 22*   **P** *Ch Patr
Trust*   **P-in-c** P A JOHNSON

HOLLAND PARK (St George the Martyr) (St John the Baptist)
Lon 12   **P** *Trustees and Bp (jt)*   **V** M G FULLER,
Hon C R G THOMPSON

HOLLESLEY (All Saints)   *see* Wilford Peninsula *St E*

HOLLINFARE (St Helen)   *see* Glazebury w Hollinfare *Liv*

**HOLLINGBOURNE (All Saints) and Hucking w Leeds and
Broomfield** *Cant 14*   **P** *Abp*   **P-in-c** R M GILL,   **C** N FRY,
OLM N A DABBS

HOLLINGDEAN (St Richard)   *see* Brighton St Matthias *Chich*

HOLLINGTON (St John the Evangelist)   *see* Rocester and
Croxden w Hollington *Lich*

HOLLINGTON (St John the Evangelist) (St Peter and St Paul)
Chich 17   **P** *Ch Patr Trust*   **V** C D REDKNAP,
NSM M HINKLEY

HOLLINGTON (St Leonard) (St Anne) *Chich 17*
P *E G Brabazon Esq*   **R** D I CHARNOCK,   **C** V G DOIDGE

HOLLINGWOOD (St Francis)   *see* Staveley and Barrow Hill
Derby

HOLLINGWORTH (St Hilda)   *see* Milnrow *Man*

HOLLINGWORTH (St Mary) w Tintwistle *Ches 14*   **P** *Patr Bd*
V R A K LAW

HOLLINSWOOD (not known)   *see* Cen Telford *Lich*

HOLLINWOOD (St Margaret) and Limeside *Man 20*   **P** *Bp
and V Prestwich (jt)*   **V** D HAWTHORN

HOLLOWAY (Emmanuel)   *see* Tollington *Lon*

HOLLOWAY Hanley Road (St Saviour)   *as above*

HOLLOWAY (St Francis of Assisi)   *see* W Holloway St Luke
Lon

HOLLOWAY (St Mary Magdalene) (St David) *Lon 6*   **P** *Bp and
V Islington St Mary (jt)*   **V** P V ZAPHIRIOU,   **C** J K RUST,
G HUNTER

HOLLOWAY, UPPER (All Saints)   *see* Tufnell Park St Geo and
All SS *Lon*

**HOLLOWAY, UPPER (St Andrew) (St John) (St Mary)
(St Peter)** *Lon 6*   **P** *Patr Bd*   **TR** S J W COX,
TV R J POWELL, W K DORGU,   **C** B T ASMELASH,
NSM S PADDOCK, P M TAYLOR

HOLLOWAY, WEST (St Luke) *Lon 6*   **P** *Lon Coll Div Trustees*
V D W TOMLINSON,   **NSM** M D E WROE

HOLLOWELL (St James)   *see* Guilsborough w Hollowell and
Cold Ashby *Pet*

HOLLY HALL (St Augustine)   *see* Dudley TM *Worc*

HOLLY HILL (Church Centre)   *see* Frankley *Birm*

HOLLYBUSH (All Saints)   *see* Berrow w Pendock, Eldersfield,
Hollybush etc *Worc*

HOLLYM (St Nicholas)   *see* Patrington w Hollym, Welwick and
Winestead *York*

HOLMBRIDGE (St David)   *see* Upper Holme Valley *Wakef*

HOLMBURY ST MARY (St Mary the Virgin)   *see* Wotton and
Holmbury St Mary *Guildf*

HOLMCROFT (St Bertelin)   *see* Stafford *Lich*

HOLME (All Saints) and Seaton Ross Group, The *York 5*
P *St Jo Coll Cam and Ld Chan (alt)*   **R** N T B STRAFFORD

HOLME (Holy Trinity)   *see* Burton and Holme *Carl*

HOLME (St Giles)   *see* Yaxley and Holme w Conington *Ely*

HOLME (St Giles)   *see* Coddington and Winthorpe and
Langford w Holme *S'well*

HOLME, EAST (St John the Evangelist)   *see* Wareham *Sarum*

HOLME CULTRAM (St Cuthbert)   *see* Solway Plain *Carl*

HOLME CULTRAM (St Mary)   *as above*

HOLME EDEN (St Paul) and Wetheral w Warwick *Carl 2*
P *D&C and DBP (jt)*   **C** D A CRAVEN,   **NSM** P TIPLADY,
A MAGUIRE

HOLME HALE (St Andrew)   *see* Necton, Holme Hale w N and
S Pickenham *Nor*

HOLME-IN-CLIVIGER (St John) w Worsthorne *Blackb 3*
P *Patr Bd*   **V** *vacant* (01282) 428478 *or* 453728

HOLME-NEXT-THE-SEA (St Mary)   *see* Hunstanton St Mary
w Ringstead Parva etc *Nor*

HOLME-ON-SPALDING-MOOR (All Saints)   *see* Holme and
Seaton Ross Gp *York*

HOLME-ON-SPALDING-MOOR (Old School Mission Room)
as above

HOLME PIERREPONT (St Edmund King and Martyr)
see Lady Bay w Holme Pierrepont and Adbolton *S'well*

**HOLME RUNCTON (St James) w South Runcton and
Wallington** *Ely 9*   **P** *Bp*   **R** J C W NOLAN

HOLME VALLEY, The UPPER *Wakef 6*   **P** *Patr Bd*
TR J S ROBERTSHAW,   **TV** K GRIFFIN,   **NSM** M D ELLERTON,
S W DIXON,   **OLM** G B BAMFORD

HOLME WOOD (St Christopher)   *see* Tong *Bradf*

HOLMER (St Bartholomew) (St Mary) w Huntington *Heref 3*
P *D&C*   **V** P A WILLIAMS,   **C** B M JACOBS

HOLMER GREEN (Christ Church)   *see* Penn Street *Ox*

HOLMES CHAPEL (St Luke)   *see* Church Hulme *Ches*

HOLMESDALE (St Philip)   *see* Dronfield w Holmesfield *Derby*
HOLMESFIELD (St Swithin)   *as above*
HOLMEWOOD (St Alban Mission)   *see* Heath *Derby*
HOLMFIELD (St Andrew)   *see* Bradshaw and Holmfield *Wakef*
HOLMFIRTH (Holy Trinity)   *see* Upper Holme Valley *Wakef*
HOLMPTON (St Nicholas)   *see* Withernsea w Owthorne and
  Easington etc *York*
HOLMSIDE (St John the Evangelist) *Dur 4*   **P** *The Crown*
  P-in-c P WATERHOUSE
HOLMWOOD (St Mary Magdalene)   *see* Surrey Weald *Guildf*
HOLMWOOD, NORTH (St John the Evangelist) *Guildf 7*
  P *Bp*   **V** C A CORRY,   **NSM** N E COE
HOLNE (St Mary the Virgin)   *see* Ashburton, Bickington,
  Buckland in the Moor etc *Ex*
HOLNEST (Church of the Assumption)   *see* Vale of White Hart
  Sarum
HOLSWORTHY (St Peter and St Paul) w Hollacombe and
  Milton Damerel *Ex 17*   **P** *DBP and Mrs F M Palmer (jt)*
  R R M REYNOLDS
HOLT (St Andrew) w High Kelling *Nor 18*   **P** *St Jo Coll Cam*
  R H C STOKER,   **C** P A WELLS
HOLT (St James)   *see* Horton, Chalbury, Hinton Martel and
  Holt St Jas *Sarum*
HOLT (St Katharine)   *see* Broughton Gifford, Gt Chalfield and
  Holt *Sarum*
HOLT (St Martin)   *see* Hallow and Grimley w Holt *Worc*
HOLTBY (Holy Trinity)   *see* Stockton-on-the-Forest w Holtby
  and Warthill *York*
HOLTON (St Bartholomew)   *see* Wheatley *Ox*
HOLTON (St Nicholas)   *see* Camelot Par *B & W*
HOLTON (St Peter)   *see* Blyth Valley *St E*
HOLTON-CUM-BECKERING (All Saints)   *see* Wragby Gp
  Linc
HOLTON-LE-CLAY (St Peter), Tetney and North Cotes *Linc 10*
  P *Ld Chan, Bp, and Duchy of Lancaster (by turn)*
  V C M WOADDEN
HOLTON-LE-MOOR (St Luke)   *see* Kelsey Gp *Linc*
HOLTON ST MARY (St Mary)   *see* Higham, Holton St Mary,
  Raydon and Stratford *St E*
HOLTS (St Hugh) Conventional District *Man 18* vacant 0161-620
  1646
HOLTSPUR (St Thomas)   *see* Beaconsfield *Ox*
HOLWELL (St Laurence)   *see* Vale of White Hart *Sarum*
HOLWELL (St Leonard)   *see* Ab Kettleby and Holwell w
  Asfordby *Leic*
HOLWELL (St Mary the Virgin)   *see* Shill Valley and Broadshire
  Ox
HOLWELL (St Peter), Ickleford and Pirton *St Alb 4*   **P** *DBP
  and D&C Ely (jt)*   **R** J A S PAYNE COOK,   **NSM** M S HOLFORD
HOLWORTH (St Catherine by the Sea)   *see* Watercombe *Sarum*
HOLY ISLAND (St Mary the Virgin) *Newc 12*   **P** *Bp*
  V R J KIRKPATRICK
HOLYBOURNE (Holy Rood)   *see* Froyle and Holybourne *Win*
HOLYMOORSIDE (St Peter)   *see* Brampton St Thos *Derby*
HOLYSTONE (St Mary the Virgin)   *see* Upper Coquetdale
  Newc
HOLYWELL (St Cross)   *see* Ox St Mary V w St Cross and St
  Pet *Ox*
HOLYWELL (St John the Baptist) w Needingworth *Ely 12*
  P *Bp*   **P-in-c** S M ANTHONY
HOLYWELL (St Mary)   *see* Seghill *Newc*
HOMERSFIELD (St Mary)   *see* S Elmham and Ilketshall *St E*
HOMERTON (Christ Church on the Mead)   *see* Hackney
  Marsh *Lon*
HOMERTON (St Barnabas w St Paul)   *as above*
HOMERTON (St Luke) *Lon 5*   **P** *St Olave Hart Street Trustees*
  V I HARPER,   **C** E ADEKUNLE
HOMINGTON (St Mary the Virgin)   *see* Chalke Valley *Sarum*
HONEYCHURCH (St Mary)   *see* N Tawton, Bondleigh,
  Sampford Courtenay etc *Ex*
HONICKNOWLE (St Francis) *Ex 23*   **P** *Ld Chan*
  P-in-c D R BAILEY,   **C** T THORP
HONILEY (St John the Baptist)   *see* Hatton w Haseley,
  Rowington w Lowsonford etc *Cov*
HONING (St Peter and St Paul)   *see* Smallburgh w Dilham w
  Honing and Crostwight *Nor*
HONINGHAM (St Andrew) *Nor 17*   **P** *DBP*   **V** vacant
HONINGTON (All Saints)   *see* Shipston-on-Stour w
  Honington and Idlicote *Cov*
HONINGTON (All Saints)   *see* Blackbourne *St E*
HONINGTON (St Wilfred)   *see* Barkston and Hough Gp *Linc*
HONITON (St Michael) (St Paul), Gittisham, Combe Raleigh,
  Monkton, Awliscombe and Buckerell *Ex 5*   **P** *DBP*
  TR S E ROBERTS,   **TV** A P SHEATH,   **C** K P SPRAY,
  Hon C R C H SAUNDERS

HONLEY (St Mary) *Wakef 1*   **P** *R Almondbury*
  V D K BARNES
HONOR OAK PARK (St Augustine)   *see* Sydenham H Trin and
  St Aug *S'wark*
HOO (All Hallows)   *see* High Halstow w All Hallows and Hoo
  St Mary *Roch*
HOO (St Andrew and St Eustachius)   *see* Mid Loes *St E*
HOO (St Werburgh) *Roch 6*   **P** *D&C*   **V** A B HARDING
HOOBROOK (St Cecilia)   *see* Kidderminster St Geo *Worc*
HOOE (St John the Evangelist)   *see* Plymstock and Hooe *Ex*
HOOE (St Oswald) *Chich 14*   **P** *Bp*   **V** S R EARL
HOOK (St John the Evangelist)   *see* Whitewater *Win*
HOOK (St Mary the Virgin)   *see* Airmyn, Hook and Rawcliffe
  Sheff
HOOK (St Mary) w Warsash *Portsm 2*   **P** *Bp*   **V** A P NORRIS,
  NSM P J MILLS
HOOK (St Paul) *S'wark 15*   **P** *The Crown*
  V C P HOLLINGSHURST,   **OLM** D E HEATHER
HOOK COMMON (Good Shepherd)   *see* Upton-on-Severn,
  Ripple, Earls Croome etc *Worc*
HOOK NORTON (St Peter) w Great Rollright, Swerford and
  Wigginton *Ox 3*   **P** *Bp, DBP, BNC Ox, and Jes Coll Ox (jt)*
  R J ACREMAN,   **NSM** C G TURNER, W CUNNINGHAM
HOOKE (St Giles)   *see* Beaminster Area *Sarum*
HOOLE (All Saints) *Ches 2*   **P** *Simeon's Trustees*
  V R J KIRKLAND,   **NSM** R ACKROYD
HOOLE (St Michael) *Blackb 5*   **P** *Reps of Mrs E A Dunne and
  Mrs D Downes (jt)*   **R** vacant (01772) 612267
HOOLEY (Mission Hall)   *see* Redhill St Jo *S'wark*
HOOTON (St Paul) *Ches 9*   **P** *Trustees*   **V** K HOWARD
HOOTON PAGNELL (All Saints)   *see* Bilham *Sheff*
HOOTON ROBERTS (St John)   *see* Ravenfield, Hooton
  Roberts and Braithwell *Sheff*
HOPE (Holy Trinity) w Shelve *Heref 13*   **P** *New Coll Ox
  (3 turns), J J C Coldwell Esq (1 turn)*   **P-in-c** A N TOOP,
  NSM M-L TOOP
HOPE (St James)   *see* Eccles *Man*
HOPE (St Peter), Castleton and Bradwell *Derby 2*   **P** *Bp and
  D&C Lich (jt)*   **P-in-c** I A DAVIS
HOPE BAGOT (St John the Baptist)   *see* Burford II w Greete
  and Hope Bagot *Heref*
HOPE BOWDLER (St Andrew) w Eaton-under-Heywood
  Heref 11   **P** *DBP, Bp Birm, and Mrs R Bell (jt)*
  P-in-c J GROVES,   **NSM** J BELLAMY
HOPE COVE (St Clements)   *see* Salcombe and Malborough w S
  Huish *Ex*
HOPE MANSEL (St Michael)   *see* Ariconium *Heref*
HOPE-UNDER-DINMORE (St Mary the Virgin)
  see Leominster *Heref*
HOPESAY (St Mary the Virgin)   *see* Hopesay *Heref*
HOPESAY (St Mary the Virgin) *Heref 10*   **P** *Earl of Powis
  (3 turns), Mrs R E Bell (1 turn)*   **P-in-c** R T SHAW
HOPTON (All Saints)   *see* Stanton, Hopton, Market Weston,
  Barningham etc *St E*
HOPTON (St Peter)   *see* Mid Trent *Lich*
HOPTON w Corton *Nor 9*   **P** *Ld Chan and D&C (alt)*
  V R A KEY
HOPTON, UPPER (St John the Evangelist)   *see* Mirfield *Wakef*
HOPTON CASTLE (St Edward)   *see* Clungunford w Clunbury
  and Clunton, Bedstone etc *Heref*
HOPTON WAFERS (St Michael and All Angels)   *see* Cleobury
  Mortimer w Hopton Wafers etc *Heref*
HOPWAS (St Chad)   *see* Tamworth *Lich*
HOPWOOD (St John)   *see* Heywood *Man*
HORAM (Christ Church) (St James) *Chich 15*   **P** *Bp*
  V M D REDHOUSE
HORBLING (St Andrew)   *see* Billingborough Gp *Linc*
HORBURY (St Peter and St Leonard) w Horbury Bridge
  (St John) *Wakef 11*   **P** *Dean*   **V** B T B BELL,
  NSM J M PARTON
HORBURY JUNCTION (St Mary) *Wakef 11*   **P** *DBP*
  P-in-c K R M CAMPBELL,   **NSM** D M WALKER
HORDEN (St Mary) *Dur 2*   **P** *Bp*   **V** K SMITH,
  NSM D S CARR
HORDLE (All Saints) *Win 11*   **P** *Bp*   **V** P J TAYLOR,
  NSM A C PETTS, B J KENT
HORDLEY (St Mary the Virgin)   *see* Baschurch and Weston
  Lullingfield w Hordley *Lich*
HORFIELD (Holy Trinity) *Bris 3*   **P** *Bp*   **P-in-c** J S F HADLEY,
  NSM H BLANCHARDE,   **OLM** P L HINE
HORFIELD (St Gregory) *Bris 3*   **P** *Bp*   **P-in-c** J WILSON
HORHAM (St Mary)   *see* Stradbroke, Horham, Athelington
  and Redlingfield *St E*
HORKESLEY, GREAT (All Saints)   *see* W Bergholt and Gt
  Horkesley *Chelmsf*

HORKESLEY, GREAT (St John)   *as above*

HORKESLEY, LITTLE (St Peter and St Paul)
see Wormingford, Mt Bures and Lt Horkesley *Chelmsf*

HORKSTOW (St Maurice) *Linc 6*   **P** *DBP*   **V** vacant

HORLEY (St Bartholomew) (St Francis) (St Wilfrid) *S'wark 26*
P *Patr Bd*   **TR** S P DAVIE,   **TV** S A HOLLOWAY

HORLEY (St Etheldreda)   *see* Ironstone *Ox*

HORLEY ROW (St Wilfrid)   *see* Horley *S'wark*

**HORMEAD (St Nicholas), Wyddial, Anstey, Brent Pelham and
Meesden** *St Alb 19*   **P** *St Jo Coll Cam, Ch Coll Cam, and Bp
(by turn)*   **P-in-c** C L KIMBERLEY

HORN HILL (St Paul)   *see* Chalfont St Peter *Ox*

HORN PARK (St Francis)   *see* Eltham St Jo *S'wark*

HORNBLOTTON (St Peter)   *see* Six Pilgrims *B & W*

**HORNBY (St Margaret) w Claughton and Whittington w
Arkholme and Gressingham** *Blackb 14*   **P** *Patr Bd*
V I H RENNIE

HORNBY (St Mary) *Ripon 4*   **P** *D&C York*
NSM J T OLDFIELD

HORNCASTLE Group, The (St Mary the Virgin) *Linc 11*
P *Bp, Baroness Willoughby de Eresby and D&C (jt)*
P-in-c A C BUXTON,   **NSM** J F PARKIN, A C FORD

HORNCHURCH Elm Park (St Nicholas)   *see* Elm Park St Nic
Hornchurch *Chelmsf*

HORNCHURCH (Holy Cross) *Chelmsf 2*   **P** *Bp and
New Coll Ox (alt)*   **P-in-c** D A A PICKERING

**HORNCHURCH (St Andrew) (St George) (St Matthew and
St John)** *Chelmsf 2*   **P** *New Coll Ox*   **V** B R HOBSON,
C V N ARNOLD, C A HENRY

HORNCHURCH, SOUTH (St John and St Matthew) *Chelmsf 2*
P *MMCET*   **V** R LOVE,   **C** K S TURNER

HORNDALE (St Francis)   *see* Gt Aycliffe *Dur*

**HORNDON EAST (St Francis) and West Horndon w Little
Warley and Childerditch** *Chelmsf 7*   **P** *Sir Antony Browne's Sch
and Bp (by turn)*   **P-in-c** S C WILLIAMS,   **NSM** R WILLIAMS

HORNDON ON THE HILL (St Peter and St Paul)   *see* Orsett
and Bulphan and Horndon on the Hill *Chelmsf*

HORNE (St Mary)   *see* Burstow w Horne *S'wark*

HORNING (St Benedict)   *see* Ashmanhaugh, Barton Turf etc
Nor

HORNINGHOLD (St Peter)   *see* Hallaton and Allexton, w
Horninghold, Tugby etc *Leic*

HORNINGLOW (St John the Divine) *Lich 14*   **P** *Trustees*
V M R FREEMAN,   **C** G T READING

HORNINGSEA (St Peter) *Ely 4*   **P** *St Jo Coll Cam*
P-in-c M C BOWERS

HORNINGSHAM (St John the Baptist)   *see* Cley Hill Villages
Sarum

HORNINGTOFT (St Edmund)   *see* Upper Wensum Village Gp
Nor

HORNSEA (St Nicholas) w Atwick *York 11*   **P** *Ld Chan*
V P LAMB

HORNSEY (Christ Church) *Lon 20*   **P** *Bp*   **V** D O AGBELUSI

HORNSEY (Holy Innocents) *Lon 20*   **P** *Bp*   **V** T D PIKE
C P J HENDERSON,   **NSM** P G ATHERTON

HORNSEY (St Mary) (St George) *Lon 20*   **P** *Bp*
R G B SEABROOK

HORNSEY RISE (St Mary)   *see* Upper Holloway *Lon*

HORNTON (St John the Baptist)   *see* Ironstone *Ox*

HORRABRIDGE (St John the Baptist)   *see* Sampford Spiney w
Horrabridge *Ex*

HORRINGER (St Leonard) *St E 13*   **P** *Bp and DBP (jt)*
R S PETTITT

HORSEHEATH (All Saints)   *see* Linton *Ely*

HORSELL (St Mary the Virgin) *Guildf 12*   **P** *Bp*   **V** R JONES,
C A L BROWN

HORSENDON (St Michael and All Angels)   *see* Risborough *Ox*

HORSEY (All Saints)   *see* Flegg Coastal Benefice *Nor*

HORSFORD (All Saints), Felthorpe and Hevingham *Nor 2*
P *Sir Thomas Agnew Beevor Bt and Bp (jt)*   **R** S L GREEN

HORSFORTH (St Margaret) *Ripon 7*   **P** *Bp*   **V** R E HAYES,
C K L MARSHALL

**HORSHAM (Holy Trinity) (St Leonard) (St Mary the Virgin)
(St Mark)** *Chich 8*   **P** *Patr Bd*
TR G S BRIDGEWATER,   **TV** W E L SOUTER, M J BROADLEY,
D W BOUSKILL, P J APTED,   **C** P A FRANCIS,   **NSM** J ELVIDGE,
B SINTON

**HORSHAM ST FAITH (St Andrew and St Mary), Spixworth
and Crostwick** *Nor 2*   **P** *Bp and DBP (jt)*   **R** A M BEANE

HORSINGTON (All Saints)   *see* Woodhall Spa Gp *Linc*

HORSINGTON (St John the Baptist)   *see* Abbas and
Templecombe, Henstridge and Horsington *B & W*

HORSLEY (Holy Trinity)   *see* N Tyne and Redesdale *Newc*

HORSLEY (St Clement) and Denby *Derby 12*   **P** *Bp and
Mrs L B Palmer (jt)*   **V** K W HORLESTON,   **NSM** D C BEECH

HORSLEY (St Martin)   *see* Nailsworth w Shortwood, Horsley
etc *Glouc*

**HORSLEY, EAST (St Martin) and Ockham w Hatchford and
Downside** *Guildf 10*   **P** *D&C Cant and Bp (jt)*
NSM C J C KIRK, S C CONWAY,   **OLM** E A BURKE

HORSLEY, WEST (St Mary) *Guildf 10*   **P** *Col A R N Weston*
R J R PORTER

HORSLEY HILL (St Lawrence the Martyr) South Shields
Dur 15   **P** *D&C*   **V** M J WRAY

HORSLEY WOODHOUSE (St Susanna)   *see* Morley w
Smalley and Horsley Woodhouse *Derby*

HORSMONDEN (St Margaret) *Roch 8*   **P** *Bp*
P-in-c R J STEVEN

HORSPATH (St Giles)   *see* Wheatley *Ox*

HORSTEAD (All Saints)   *see* Coltishall w Gt Hautbois,
Frettenham etc *Nor*

HORSTED, LITTLE (St Michael and All Angels) *Chich 21*
P *Rt Revd P J Ball*   **R** B H WILCOX,   **NSM** C HOWARTH

HORSTED KEYNES (St Giles) *Chich 6*   **P** *Bp*
R J F TWISLETON

HORSTED PARVA (St Michael and All Angels)   *see* Lt Horsted
Chich

HORTON (St James the Elder) and Little Sodbury *Glouc 6*
P *Duke of Beaufort (1 turn), CPAS (2 turns)*   **R** vacant (01454)
313256

HORTON (St Mary Magdalene)   *see* Hardingstone and Horton
and Piddington *Pet*

HORTON (St Mary the Virgin) *Newc 1*   **P** *V Woodhorn w
Newbiggin*   **P-in-c** D W CARBERRY

HORTON (St Michael and All Angels) and Wraysbury *Ox 23*
P *Major J M Halford and D&C Windsor (jt)*
V C S P DOUGLAS LANE

HORTON (St Michael), Lonsdon and Rushton Spencer *Lich 8*
P *Bp and R Leek and Meerbrook (jt)*   **V** E J TOMLINSON,
OLM J A R LOVATT

HORTON (St Peter)   *see* Ilminster and Distr *B & W*

**HORTON (St Wolfrida), Chalbury, Hinton Martel and Holt
St James** *Sarum 9*   **P** *Earl of Shaftesbury and Qu Eliz Free
Gr Sch (jt)*   **P-in-c** J E HOLBROOK,   **NSM** A A GEE

HORTON, GREAT (St John the Evangelist) *Bradf 2*   **P** *V Bradf*
V N G JONES,   **NSM** I S SLATER

HORTON, LITTLE (All Saints) (St Oswald) *Bradf 2*   **P** *Bp and
J F Bardsley Esq (jt)*   **V** A S TREASURE,   **C** J W HINTON,
NSM M M MALEK

HORTON-CUM-STUDLEY (St Barnabas)   *see* Wheatley *Ox*

HORTON-IN-RIBBLESDALE (St Oswald)   *see* Langcliffe w
Stainforth and Horton *Bradf*

HORTON KIRBY (St Mary) and Sutton-at-Hone *Roch 2*   **P** *Bp
and D&C (jt)*   **V** F C PAPANTONIOU

**HORWICH (Holy Trinity) (St Catherine) (St Elizabeth) and
Rivington** *Man 11*   **P** *Patr Bd*   **TR** S FLETCHER,
TV G C BURROWS, M C BEHREND,   **C** M J DAY,
OLM T IMHERLAND, P D HARLEY

HORWOOD (St Michael)   *see* Newton Tracey, Horwood,
Alverdiscott etc *Ex*

HORWOOD, GREAT (St James)   *see* Winslow w Gt Horwood
and Addington *Ox*

HORWOOD, LITTLE (St Nicholas)   *see* Newton Longville and
Mursley w Swanbourne etc *Ox*

HOSE (St Michael)   *see* Vale of Belvoir Par *Leic*

HOTHAM (St Oswald) *York 13*   **P** *Ld Chan*
P-in-c P G FAULKNER,   **NSM** S J HUMPHRIES

HOTHFIELD (St Margaret)   *see* Westwell and Hothfield *Cant*

HOUGH GREEN (St Basil and All Saints) *Liv 13*   **P** *Bp*
V P W DAWKIN

HOUGH-ON-THE-HILL (All Saints)   *see* Barkston and Hough
Gp *Linc*

HOUGHAM (All Saints)   *as above*

HOUGHAM (St Laurence)   *see* Alkham w Capel le Ferne and
Hougham *Cant*

HOUGHTON (All Saints)   *see* Broughton, Bossington,
Houghton and Mottisfont *Win*

HOUGHTON (St Giles)   *see* Walsingham, Houghton and
Barsham *Nor*

HOUGHTON (St John the Evangelist) (St Peter) *Carl 3*
P *Trustees*   **V** S N AUSTEN,   **C** T A BODDAM-WHETHAM

HOUGHTON (St Martin)   *see* E w W Rudham, Helhoughton
etc *Nor*

HOUGHTON (St Mary) w Wyton *Ely 10*   **P** *Bp*
P-in-c E B ATLING,   **C** B A STEWART

HOUGHTON (St Nicholas)   *see* Bury w Houghton and
Coldwaltham and Hardham *Chich*

HOUGHTON, GREAT (St Mary)   *see* Cogenhoe and Gt and Lt
Houghton w Brafield *Pet*

**HOUGHTON, GREAT (St Michael and All Angels)
Conventional District** *Sheff 12* vacant

HOUGHTON, LITTLE (St Mary the Blessed Virgin)
see Cogenhoe and Gt and Lt Houghton w Brafield *Pet*
HOUGHTON, NEW (Christ Church) *see* E Scarsdale *Derby*
HOUGHTON CONQUEST (All Saints) *see* Wilshamstead and
Houghton Conquest *St Alb*
HOUGHTON LE SPRING (St Michael and All Angels) *Dur 14*
P *Bp*   R S J PINNINGTON,   NSM M LEE
HOUGHTON-ON-THE-HILL (St Catharine) Keyham and
Hungarton *Leic 4*   P *Bp*   P-in-c P M HOLLINGSWORTH
HOUGHTON REGIS (All Saints) (St Thomas) *St Alb 12*
P *DBP*   V B C D WHEELHOUSE
HOUND (St Edward the Confessor) (St Mary the Virgin) *Win 10*
P *St Mary's Coll Win*   P-in-c P A VARGESON,
C S F WARDELL
HOUNSLOW (Holy Trinity) (St Paul) *Lon 11*   P *Bp*
V M F HERBERT,   C S J SHAW, R L M ECKHARD,
NSM N LAWRENCE
HOUNSLOW (St Stephen) *Lon 11*   P *Bp*   V R L RAMSDEN
HOUNSLOW WEST (Good Shepherd) *Lon 11*   P *Bp*
V K A BUCKLER
HOVE (All Saints) (St Andrew Old Church) (St John the Baptist)
Holy Trinity *Chich 4*   P *Bp*   TV J R SWINDELLS, C G SPINKS,
P-in-c P S J RITCHIE,   C P S J DOICK,   NSM S UNDERDOWN,
D S G WEAVER
HOVE (Bishop Hannington Memorial Church) (Holy Cross)
Chich 4   P *Trustees*   V P R MOON,   C J B ERLEBACH,
J J MILSON, J S RADCLIFFE
HOVE (St Barnabas) and St Agnes *Chich 4*   P *Bp and V Hove*
(alt)   V A R REED
HOVE St Patrick *Chich 4*   P *Bp, V Hove, and V Brighton (jt)*
V *vacant* (01273) 327242
HOVE (St Philip) *see* Aldrington *Chich*
HOVERINGHAM (St Michael) *see* Thurgarton w
Hoveringham and Bleasby etc *S'well*
HOVETON (St John) *see* Wroxham w Hoveton and Belaugh
Nor
HOVETON (St Peter) *as above*
HOVINGHAM (All Saints) *see* The Street Par *York*
HOW CAPLE (St Andrew and St Mary) *see* Brampton *Heref*
HOWARDIAN GROUP, The *York 6*   P *Abp and Hon*
S B G Howard (jt)   R M C PARKIN
HOWDEN Team Ministry, The (St Peter) *York 13*   P *Abp*
(4 turns), Ld Chan (1 turn)   TR J H LITTLE,
TV K L BURGESS
HOWDEN-LE-WEAR St Mary the Virgin and Hunwick *Dur 9*
P *Bp and V Auckland St Andr (alt)*   V S IRWIN
HOWE (St Mary the Virgin) *see* Poringland *Nor*
HOWE BRIDGE (St Michael and All Angels) *see* Atherton and
Hindsford w Howe Bridge *Man*
HOWELL (St Oswald) *see* Heckington Gp *Linc*
HOWELL HILL (St Paul) w Burgh Heath *Guildf 9*   P *Bp*
C J L W HOOKWAY,   NSM B W RICHARDS
HOWGILL (Holy Trinity) *see* Firbank, Howgill and Killington
Bradf
HOWICK (St Michael and All Angels) *see* Longhoughton w
Howick *Newc*
HOWSHAM (St John) *see* Sand Hutton *York*
HOXNE (St Peter and St Paul) w Denham, Syleham and
Wingfield *St E 17*   P *Bp and DBP (jt)*   C F O NEWTON,
S A LOXTON, L DAWSON
HOXTON (Holy Trinity) (St Mary) *Lon 5*   P *Bp*   V *vacant*
(020) 7253 4796
HOXTON (St Anne) (St Columba) *Lon 5*   P *The Crown*
P-in-c I C CZERNIAWSKA EDGCUMBE,
Hon C W G CAMPBELL-TAYLOR
HOXTON (St John the Baptist) w Ch Ch *Lon 5*
P *Haberdashers' Co and Adn (jt)*   V A I KEECH,
NSM S C EJIAKU
HOYLAKE (Holy Trinity and St Hildeburgh) *Ches 8*   P *Bp*
V M J FLOWERDEW
HOYLAND (St Peter) (St Andrew) *Sheff 11*   P *Bp and Sir Philip*
Naylor-Leyland Bt (jt)   V R B PARKER
HOYLAND, HIGH (All Saints), Scissett and Clayton West
Wakef 6   P *Bp*   P-in-c J E COUSANS
HOYLANDSWAINE (St John the Evangelist) and Silkstone w
Stainborough *Wakef 7*   P *Bp*   V S A MOOR
HUBBERHOLME (St Michael and All Angels) *see* Kettlewell
w Conistone, Hubberholme etc *Bradf*
HUCCABY (St Raphael) *see* Ashburton, Bickington, Buckland
in the Moor etc *Ex*
HUCCLECOTE (St Philip and St James) *Glouc 3*   P *Bp*
C E C AMYES, G E AMYES
HUCKING (St Margaret) *see* Hollingbourne and Hucking w
Leeds and Broomfield *Cant*
HUCKLOW, GREAT (Mission Room) *see* Hope, Castleton
and Bradwell *Derby*

HUCKNALL TORKARD (St Mary Magdalene) (St Peter and
St Paul) (St John's Mission Church) *S'well 4*   P *Bp*
TR L A CHURCH,   TV D C NJUGUNA
HUDDERSFIELD All Saints (St Thomas) *Wakef 5*   P *DBP*
P-in-c L A PINFIELD
HUDDERSFIELD (Holy Trinity) *Wakef 5*   P *Simeon's Trustees*
V C C PRENTIS,   NSM R C SWINDELL, P T WILCOCK
HUDDERSFIELD (St Francis) Fixby   *see* Fixby and Cowcliffe
Wakef
HUDDERSFIELD (St Hilda) Cowcliffe   *as above*
HUDDERSFIELD (St John the Evangelist)   *see* Birkby and
Woodhouse *Wakef*
HUDDERSFIELD (St Peter) *Wakef 5*   P *DBP*   V C OGLE,
C A L WALLIS
HUDDERSFIELD, NORTH (St Cuthbert)   *see* Birkby and
Birchencliffe *Wakef*
HUDDINGTON (St James)   *see* Bowbrook S *Worc*
HUDSWELL (St Michael and All Angels)   *see* Richmond w
Hudswell and Downholme and Marske *Ripon*
HUGGATE (St Mary)   *see* Nunburnholme and Warter and
Huggate *York*
HUGGLESCOTE (St John the Baptist) w Donington, Ellistown
and Snibston *Leic 8*   P *Bp*   TR O S WOOLCOCK,
NSM R M PASSEY
HUGHENDEN (St Michael) *Ox 29*   P *DBP*   V S N CRONK,
NSM F J FRIEND
HUGHLEY (St John the Baptist)   *see* Wenlock *Heref*
HUISH (St James the Less)   *see* Shebbear, Buckland Filleigh,
Sheepwash etc *Ex*
HUISH (St Nicholas)   *see* Pewsey and Swanborough *Sarum*
HUISH, SOUTH (Holy Trinity)   *see* Salcombe and Malborough
w S Huish *Ex*
HUISH CHAMPFLOWER (St Peter)   *see* Wiveliscombe w
Chipstable, Huish Champflower etc *B & W*
HUISH EPISCOPI (Blessed Virgin Mary)   *see* Langport Area
B & W
HULCOTE (St Nicholas)   *see* Cranfield and Hulcote w Salford
St Alb
HULCOTT (All Saints)   *see* Aylesbury w Bierton and Hulcott
Ox
HULL (Ascension)   *see* Derringham Bank *York*
HULL (Holy Apostles)   *see* Kingston upon Hull H Trin *York*
HULL (Most Holy and Undivided Trinity)   *as above*
HULL (St Aidan) Southcoates   *see* Kingston upon Hull St Aid
Southcoates *York*
HULL (St Alban)   *see* Kingston upon Hull St Alb *York*
HULL (St Cuthbert) *York 14*   P *Abp*   V J C COWAN
HULL (St George)   *see* Marfleet *York*
HULL (St Giles)   *as above*
HULL (St Hilda)   *as above*
HULL (St John) Newland *York 14*   P *Abp*   V M TINKER,
C L J MCMUNN, M J PETERS
HULL (St John the Baptist)   *see* Newington w Dairycoates *York*
HULL (St Martin) w The Transfiguration *York 14*   P *Abp*
V S R J ELLIOTT
HULL (St Mary) Sculcoates *York 14*   P *V Sculcoates*
P-in-c J G LEEMAN
HULL (St Mary the Virgin) Lowgate   *see* Kingston upon Hull
St Mary *York*
HULL (St Matthew w St Barnabas)   *see* Kingston upon Hull St
Matt w St Barn *York*
HULL (St Nicholas)   *see* Kingston upon Hull St Nic *York*
HULL (St Paul)   *see* Sculcoates *York*
HULL (St Philip)   *see* Marfleet *York*
HULL (St Stephen)   *see* Sculcoates *York*
HULL (St Thomas)   *see* Derringham Bank *York*
HULL, NORTH (St Michael and All Angels) *York 14*   P *Abp*
V D A WALKER
HULLAND (Christ Church), Atlow, Kniveton, Bradley and
Hognaston *Derby 8*   P *Patr Bd*   R C A MITCHELL
HULLAVINGTON (St Mary Magdalene), Norton and Stanton
St Quintin *Bris 6*   P *Bp, Eton Coll, and R W Neeld Esq (jt)*
R A EVANS,   C E C PEGLER,   Hon C M M MASLEN,
NSM S R EVANS
HULLBRIDGE (St Thomas of Canterbury) *Chelmsf 12*   P *Bp*
V W H REED,   NSM S ADAMS
HULME (Ascension) *Man 4*   P *Trustees*   R A J SERVANT
HULME WALFIELD (St Michael)   *see* Brereton w Eaton and
Hulme Walfield *Ches*
HULTON, LITTLE (St John the Baptist)   *see* Walkden and Lt
Hulton *Man*
HULTON, OVER (St Andrew)   *see* Deane *Man*
HUMBER (St Mary the Virgin)   *see* Leominster *Heref*
HUMBERSTON (St Peter) *Linc 10*   P *Bp*   V B V EAST,
OLM P R SALMON

HUMBERSTONE (St Mary)   *see* Ascension TM *Leic*
HUMBERSTONE, NEW (St Barnabas)   *see* Leic Presentation *Leic*
HUMBLE, WEST (St Michael)   *see* Leatherhead and Mickleham *Guildf*
HUMBLETON (St Peter)   *see* Burton Pidsea and Humbleton w Elsternwick *York*
HUMPHREY PARK (St Clement)   *see* Urmston *Man*
HUMSHAUGH (St Peter) w Simonburn and Wark *Newc 8*
  P *Bp*   **R** J M THOMPSON
HUNCOAT (St Augustine)   *see* Accrington St Jo w Huncoat *Blackb*
HUNCOTE (St James the Greater)   *see* Narborough and Huncote *Leic*
HUNDLEBY (St Mary)   *see* Spilsby Gp *Linc*
HUNDON (All Saints)   *see* Stour Valley *St E*
HUNDRED RIVER Benefice, The *St E 14*   **P** *DBP, Shadingfield Properties Ltd, Bp, Miss to Seamen, and F D L Barnes Esq (by turn)*   **R** P J NELSON,   **OLM** J M LOFTUS
HUNGARTON (St John the Baptist)   *see* Houghton-on-the-Hill, Keyham and Hungarton *Leic*
HUNGERFORD (St Lawrence) and Denford *Ox 14*
  P *D&C Windsor*   **R** A W SAWYER
HUNMANBY (All Saints) w Muston *York 15*   **P** *MMCET*
  V J W R HATTAN
HUNNINGHAM (St Margaret) *Cov 10*   **P** *Ld Chan*
  P-in-c J T H BRITTON,   **C** D R PATTERSON
HUNSDON (St Dunstan) (St Francis) w Widford and Wareside *St Alb 22*   **P** *DBP*   **P-in-c** M P DUNSTAN
HUNSINGORE (St John the Baptist)   *see* Lower Nidderdale *Ripon*
HUNSLET (St Mary the Virgin) w Cross Green *Ripon 6*
  P *Keble Coll Ox, Bp and TR Leeds City (jt)*   **V** A J LANE
HUNSLET MOOR (St Peter's Christian Community Centre) *see* Beeston Hill and Hunslet Moor *Ripon*
HUNSLEY (St Peter)   *see* Rowley w Skidby *York*
HUNSTANTON (St Edmund) w Ringstead *Nor 16*
  P H Le Strange Esq   **V** J S BLOOMFIELD
HUNSTANTON (St Mary) w Ringstead Parva, Holme-next-the-Sea, Thornham, Brancaster, Burnham Deepdale and Titchwell *Nor 16*   **P** *Bp, Exors of the late H le Strange Esq, and Exors of the late H S N Simms-Adams Esq (jt)*   **R** C D WOOD
HUNSTANWORTH (St James)   *see* Blanchland w Hunstanworth and Edmundbyers etc *Newc*
HUNSTON (St Leodegar)   *see* N Mundham w Hunston and Merston *Chich*
HUNSTON (St Michael)   *see* Badwell and Walsham *St E*
HUNTINGDON (All Saints w St John the Baptist) (St Barnabas) (St Mary) w the Stukeleys *Ely 10*   **P** *Ld Chan (1 turn), Patr Bd (2 turns)*   **TR** A J MILTON,   **TV** J M SAVAGE,   **NSM** J J MARTIN
HUNTINGFIELD (St Mary)   *see* Heveningham *St E*
HUNTINGTON (All Saints) *York 7*   **P** *Patr Bd*
  TR I G BIRKINSHAW,   **TV** F R SCOTT
HUNTINGTON (St Luke) *Ches 2*   **P** *Bp*   **V** I J HUTCHINGS
HUNTINGTON (St Mary Magdalene)   *see* Holmer w Huntington *Heref*
HUNTINGTON (St Thomas)   *see* Cannock *Lich*
HUNTINGTON (St Thomas à Becket)   *see* Kington w Huntington, Old Radnor, Kinnerton etc *Heref*
HUNTLEY (St John the Baptist) and Longhope, Churcham and Bulley *Glouc 1*   **P** *Bp and D&C (jt)*   **P-in-c** F A WALTERS
HUNTON (St James)   *see* Upper Dever *Win*
HUNTON (St Mary)   *see* Coxheath, E Farleigh, Hunton, Linton etc *Roch*
HUNTS CROSS (St Hilda) *Liv 4*   **P** *Bp*   **P-in-c** E J DURHAM
HUNTSHAM (All Saints)   *see* Sampford Peverell, Uplowman, Holcombe Rogus etc *Ex*
HUNTSHAW (St Mary Magdalene)   *see* Newton Tracey, Horwood, Alverdiscott etc *Ex*
HUNTSPILL (St Peter and All Hallows) *B & W 1*   **P** *Ball Coll Ox*   **R** G M WALSH
HUNWICK (St Paul)   *see* Howden-le-Wear and Hunwick *Dur*
HUNWORTH (St Lawrence)   *see* Brinton, Briningham, Hunworth, Stody etc *Nor*
HURDSFIELD (Holy Trinity) *Ches 13*   **P** *Hyndman Trustees*
  V I M RUMSEY,   **C** J C ALLISTER
HURLEY (Resurrection)   *see* Baxterley w Hurley and Wood End and Merevale etc *Birm*
HURLEY (St Mary the Virgin)   *see* Burchetts Green *Ox*
HURSLEY (All Saints)   *see* Compton, Hursley, and Otterbourne *Win*
HURST   *see* Fawkenhurst *Cant*
HURST (St John the Evangelist) *Man 17*   **P** *The Crown*
  V A L OWENS,   **OLM** A G LEES, P C CARLIN

HURST (St Nicholas) *Ox 16*   **P** *Bp*   **P-in-c** J K COOMBS,   **Hon C** C SMITH
HURST GREEN (Holy Trinity) *Chich 15*   **P** *Bp*   **V** R DIXON
HURST GREEN (St John the Evangelist) *S'wark 25*   **P** *Bp*
  V D F G BUTLIN,   **NSM** M J SELLER, W M HARVEY
HURST GREEN (St John the Evangelist) and Mitton *Bradf 5*
  P *Bp and J E R Aspinall Esq (jt)*   **P-in-c** G F MACK,
  C D W MEWIS,   **Hon C** J R BROCKLEHURST,
  NSM G DEARDEN, J R GOODALL
HURSTBOURNE PRIORS (St Andrew), Longparish, St Mary Bourne and Woodcott *Win 6*   **P** *Bp and J C Woodcock Esq (jt)*
  V M A COPPEN,   **NSM** D M MARSDEN, T E HEMMING
HURSTBOURNE TARRANT (St Peter) and Faccombe and Vernham Dean and Linkenholt *Win 3*   **P** *Bp*
  P-in-c D J KEIGHLEY,   **NSM** P A MILLS
HURSTPIERPOINT (Holy Trinity) (St George) *Chich 9*
  P *Hurstpierpoint Coll*   **R** J B A JOYCE,   **C** W KEMP
HURSTWOOD, HIGH (Holy Trinity) *Chich 21*   **P** *Abp*
  P-in-c D A TIDSWELL
HURWORTH (All Saints) *Dur 8*   **P** *Ch Soc Trust*
  R M D M FERGUSON
HUSBANDS BOSWORTH (All Saints)   *see* Hexagon *Leic*
HUSBORNE CRAWLEY (St Mary Magdalene or St James) *see* Aspley Guise w Husborne Crawley and Ridgmont *St Alb*
HUSTHWAITE (St Nicholas)   *see* Coxwold and Husthwaite *York*
HUTHWAITE (All Saints) *S'well 4*   **P** *V Sutton-in-Ashfield*
  P-in-c C A K MAIDEN,   **C** A H DIGMAN
HUTTOFT (St Margaret)   *see* Sutton, Huttoft and Anderby *Linc*
HUTTON (All Saints) (St Peter) *Chelmsf 7*   **P** *D&C St Paul's*
  R R WALLACE,   **C** B C WALLACE,   **NSM** A BAXTER
HUTTON (Blessed Virgin Mary) and Locking *B & W 11*
  P *DBP and MMCET (jt)*   **C** R A LEE, A L LEE
HUTTON, OLD (St John the Baptist) and New Hutton (St Stephen) *Carl 10*   **P** *V Kendal*   **NSM** D A PRESTON,   T G WILCOCK
HUTTON BUSCEL (St Matthew)   *see* Upper Derwent *York*
HUTTON CRANSWICK (St Peter) w Skerne, Watton and Beswick *York 10*   **P** *Abp*   **V** R E HIND,   **NSM** B J LEES
HUTTON HENRY (St Francis)   *see* Wheatley Hill and Wingate w Hutton Henry *Dur*
HUTTON-IN-THE-FOREST (St James)   *see* Inglewood Gp *Carl*
HUTTON-LE-HOLE (St Chad)   *see* Lastingham w Appleton-le-Moors, Rosedale etc *York*
HUTTON MAGNA (St Mary)   *see* Barningham w Hutton Magna and Wycliffe *Ripon*
HUTTON ROOF (St John the Divine)   *see* Kirkby Lonsdale *Carl*
HUTTON RUDBY (All Saints)   *see* Rudby in Cleveland w Middleton *York*
HUTTONS AMBO (St Margaret)   *see* Howardian Gp *York*
HUXHAM (St Mary the Virgin)   *see* Stoke Canon, Poltimore w Huxham and Rewe etc *Ex*
HUXLEY (St Andrew)   *see* Hargrave *Ches*
HUYTON (St George) *Liv 2*   **P** *Bp*   **V** C DORAN
HUYTON (St Michael) *Liv 2*   **P** *Earl of Derby*   **V** J A STANLEY
HUYTON QUARRY (St Gabriel) *Liv 2*   **P** *V Huyton St Mich*
  V M K ROGERS,   **C** N J COOK
HYDE (Holy Ascension)   *see* Ellingham and Harbridge and Hyde w Ibsley *Win*
HYDE (Holy Trinity) Gee Cross   *see* Gee Cross *Ches*
HYDE (St George) *Ches 14*   **P** *R Stockport St Mary*
  V S J WILSON
HYDE (St John the Baptist) Godley cum Newton Green *see* Godley cum Newton Green *Ches*
HYDE (St Mary) Newton in Mottram   *see* Newton in Mottram *Ches*
HYDE (St Stephen) Newton Flowery Field   *see* Newton Flowery Field *Ches*
HYDE (St Thomas) *Ches 14*   **P** *Bp*   **P-in-c** P O BENNISON
HYDE, WEST (St Thomas of Canterbury)   *see* Mill End and Heronsgate w W Hyde *St Alb*
HYDE HEATH (Mission Church)   *see* Lt Missenden *Ox*
HYDE PARK CRESCENT (St John)   *see* Paddington St Jo w St Mich *Lon*
HYDNEYE, THE (St Peter) *Chich 16*   **P** *Bp*   **P-in-c** R L TREE,   **NSM** J MANN
HYKEHAM (All Saints) (St Hugh) (St Michael and All Angels) *Linc 18*   **P** *Ld Chan and Bp (alt)*   **TR** R S EYRE,
  C A J CHAPMAN,   **NSM** G F REID
HYLTON, SOUTH (St Mary) *Dur 16*   **P** *Bp*   **V** J E RUSCOE
HYSON GREEN (St Stephen) and Forest Fields *S'well 12*
  P *CPAS*   **C** K S F ROOMS

HYSSINGTON (St Etheldreda)   see Churchstoke w Hyssington and Sarn *Heref*

HYTHE Butts Ash (St Anne)   see Hythe *Win*

HYTHE (St John the Baptist) *Win 11*   **P** *Bp*   **V** E J WETHERELL

HYTHE (St Leonard) (St Michael and All Angels) *Cant 5*
   P *R Saltwood*   **V** A M WINDROSS,   **C** C N DATCHLER

HYTHE, WEST (St Mary)   see Aldington w Bonnington and Bilsington etc *Cant*

IBBERTON (St Eustace)   see Hazelbury Bryan and the Hillside Par *Sarum*

IBSTOCK (St Denys) w Heather *Leic 8*   **P** *Bp and MMCET (jt)*
   R R A WHITE

IBSTONE (St Nicholas)   see Stokenchurch and Ibstone *Ox*

ICKBURGH (St Peter) w Langford *Nor 13*   **P** *Bp*   **R** *vacant*

ICKENHAM (St Giles) *Lon 24*   **P** *Eton Coll*   **R** A M GUTHRIE,
   NSM K R TOMBS

ICKFORD (St Nicholas)   see Worminghall w Ickford, Oakley and Shabbington *Ox*

ICKHAM (St John the Evangelist)   see Littlebourne and Ickham w Wickhambreaux etc *Cant*

ICKLEFORD (St Katherine)   see Holwell, Ickleford and Pirton *St Alb*

ICKLESHAM (St Nicolas)   see Winchelsea and Icklesham *Chich*

ICKLETON (St Mary Magdalene) *Ely 5*   **P** *Ld Chan*   **V** *vacant*

ICKLINGHAM (All Saints w St James)   see Mildenhall *St E*

ICKNIELD *Ox 1*   **P** *Ld Chan (1 turn), Ch Ch Ox (1 turn), Bp and Earl of Macclesfield (1 turn)*   **R** C I EVANS,
   NSM A M PATERSON,   **OLM** A J B CLAYTON

ICOMB (St Mary)   see Broadwell, Evenlode, Oddington, Adlestrop etc *Glouc*

IDBURY (St Nicholas)   see Shipton-under-Wychwood w Milton, Fifield etc *Ox*

IDDESLEIGH (St James) w Dowland *Ex 20*   **P** *Bp*
   P-in-c C A BRODRIBB

IDE (St Ida)   see Alphington, Shillingford St George and Ide *Ex*

IDE HILL (St Mary the Virgin)   see Sundridge w Ide Hill and Toys Hill *Roch*

IDEFORD (St Mary the Virgin)   see Teignmouth, Ideford w Luton, Ashcombe etc *Ex*

IDEN (All Saints)   see Rye *Chich*

IDLE (Holy Trinity) *Bradf 3*   **P** *V Calverley*
   P-in-c R P GAMBLE,   **C** P MAYO-SMITH

IDLICOTE (St James the Great)   see Shipston-on-Stour w Honington and Idlicote *Cov*

IDRIDGEHAY (St James)   see Wirksworth *Derby*

IDSWORTH (St Hubert)   see Blendworth w Chalton w Idsworth *Portsm*

IFFLEY (St Mary the Virgin) *Ox 4*   **P** *Ch Ch Ox*
   V A R MCKEARNEY,   **C** G HANCOCK

IFIELD (St Margaret) *Chich 7*   **P** *Bp*   **TV** D G STANIFORD,
   NSM D M GOODWIN, M P HANSON

IFIELD (St Margaret)   see Gravesend H Family w Ifield *Roch*

IFORD (St Nicholas) w Kingston and Rodmell *Chich 18*   **P** *Bp*
   V G M DAW

IFORD (St Saviour)   see Holdenhurst and Iford *Win*

IGHTFIELD (St John the Baptist)   see Adderley, Ash, Calverhall, Ightfield etc *Lich*

IGHTHAM (St Peter) *Roch 10*   **P** C B Winnifrith Esq
   R S R JONES

IKEN (St Botolph)   see Wilford Peninsula *St E*

ILAM (Holy Cross)   see Alstonfield, Butterton, Ilam etc *Lich*

ILCHESTER (St Mary Major) w Northover, Limington, Yeovilton and Podimore *B & W 6*   **P** *Bp Lon (7 turns), Bp (1 turn), and Wadh Coll Ox (1 turn)*   **R** C F H SUTCLIFFE

ILDERTON (St Michael)   see Glendale Gp *Newc*

ILFORD, GREAT (St Alban) *Chelmsf 4*   **P** *Bp*   **V** D I MILNES

ILFORD, GREAT (St Andrew) *Chelmsf 4*   **P** *Bp*
   V R A D ENEVER,   **NSM** M SEGAL

ILFORD, GREAT (St John the Evangelist) *Chelmsf 4*   **P** *Bp*
   V J A H EVENS,   **C** G E EZE,   **NSM** A C OKWUOSA

ILFORD, GREAT (St Luke) *Chelmsf 4*   **P** *Bp*
   P-in-c J BROWN,   **Hon C** A W M RITCHIE,
   NSM B D D DE MELLO

ILFORD, GREAT (St Margaret of Antioch) (St Clement) *Chelmsf 4*   **P** *Patr Bd*   **V** S G PUGH

ILFORD, GREAT (St Mary) *Chelmsf 4*   **P** *V Gt Ilford*
   V *vacant* (020) 8478 0546

ILFORD, LITTLE (St Barnabas) *Chelmsf 3*   **P** *Bp*
   P-in-c J A RAMSAY

ILFORD, LITTLE (St Michael and All Angels) *Chelmsf 3*
   P *Hertf Coll Ox*   **R** B J LEWIS,   **C** N-A WALSH

ILFRACOMBE (Holy Trinity) (St Peter), Lee, Woolacombe, Bittadon and Mortehoe *Ex 15*   **P** *Patr Bd*
   TV G A B KING-SMITH

ILFRACOMBE (St Philip and St James) w West Down *Ex 15*
   P *Bp and Ch Trust Fund Trust (jt)*   **P-in-c** M H W ROGERS

ILKESTON (Holy Trinity) *Derby 13*   **P** *Bp*   **V** A M COLE

ILKESTON (St John the Evangelist) *Derby 13*   **P** *V Ilkeston St Mary*   **P-in-c** A J BROWN,   **NSM** C J GRAHAM

ILKESTON (St Mary the Virgin) *Derby 13*   **P** *Bp*
   V A J BROWN

ILKETSHALL ST ANDREW (St Andrew)   see Wainford *St E*

ILKETSHALL ST JOHN (St John the Baptist)   see S Elmham and Ilketshall *St E*

ILKETSHALL ST LAWRENCE (St Lawrence)   as above

ILKETSHALL ST MARGARET (St Margaret)   as above

ILKLEY (All Saints) *Bradf 4*   **P** *Hyndman Trustees*
   P-in-c L S TOWNEND,   **C** C A JOHNSON,   **NSM** R F WATSON

ILKLEY (St Margaret) *Bradf 4*   **P** *CR*   **P-in-c** P C GRAY,
   NSM A G BROWN, R G KELLETT

ILLINGWORTH (St Mary) *Wakef 4*   **P** *V Halifax*   **V** *vacant* (01422) 252557

ILLOGAN (St Illogan)   see St Illogan *Truro*

ILLSTON (St Michael and All Angels)   see Gaulby *Leic*

ILMER (St Peter)   see Risborough *Ox*

ILMINGTON (St Mary) and Stretton-on-Fosse and Ditchford w Preston-on-Stour w Whitchurch and Atherstone-on-Stour *Cov 9*
   P *Bp, MMCET, and Ms C A Alston-Roberts-West (jt)*
   P-in-c C GOBLE,   **Hon C** G W KUHRT

ILMINSTER (Blessed Virgin Mary) and District *B & W 15*
   P *Patr Bd*   **TR** A R WALLACE,   **TV** A F TATHAM, G A WADE

ILSINGTON (St Michael) *Ex 9*   **P** *D&C Windsor*
   P-in-c M T J SMITH

ILSLEY, EAST (St Mary)   see Hermitage *Ox*

ILSLEY, WEST (All Saints)   see Beedon and Peasemore w W Ilsley and Farnborough *Ox*

ILTON (St Peter)   see Ilminster and Distr *B & W*

IMMINGHAM (St Andrew) *Linc 10*   **P** *DBP*
   P-in-c M W PAGE-CHESTNEY,   **NSM** S V PAGE-CHESTNEY

IMPINGTON (St Andrew) *Ely 6*   **P** *Adn Ely*
   P-in-c N J BLANDFORD-BAKER,   **C** P H BUTLER,
   NSM J M GLOVER

INCE (St James)   see Thornton-le-Moors w Ince and Elton *Ches*

INCE IN MAKERFIELD (Christ Church) w Wigan St Catharine *Liv 14*   **P** *Bp, R Wigan and Simeon's Trustees (jt)*
   V S NICHOLSON

INCE IN MAKERFIELD (St Mary) *Liv 14*   **P** *Simeon's Trustees*   **V** D W LONG

INDIAN QUEEN (St Francis)   see St Enoder *Truro*

INGATESTONE (St Edmund and St Mary) w Fryerning *Chelmsf 7*   **P** *Bp and Wadh Coll Ox (jt)*   **V** P SHERRING,
   NSM S E CRUSE, M K SEAMAN

INGESTRE (St Mary the Virgin)   see Stafford St Jo and Tixall w Ingestre *Lich*

INGHAM (All Saints)   see Spring Line Gp *Linc*

INGHAM (Holy Trinity)   see Stalham, E Ruston, Brunstead, Sutton and Ingham *Nor*

INGHAM (St Bartholomew)   see Blackbourne *St E*

INGLEBY ARNCLIFFE (All Saints)   see Osmotherley w Harlsey and Ingleby Arncliffe *York*

INGLEBY BARWICK (St Francis) *York 21*   **P** *Abp*
   V J C ROUNDTREE,   **C** P A DOMINIAK

INGLEBY GREENHOW (St Andrew), Bilsdale Priory and Kildale w Kirkby-in-Cleveland *York 21*   **P** *Abp, Adn Cleveland, Bp Whitby, Viscount De L'Isle, R G Beckett Esq, and A H W Sutcliffe Esq (jt)*   **V** M A HEADING

INGLETON (St John the Evangelist) *Dur 8*   **P** *Lord Barnard*
   P-in-c K STEVENTON

INGLETON (St Mary the Virgin) w Chapel le Dale *Bradf 6*
   P *Bp*   **V** C H ELLIS

INGLEWOOD Group, The *Carl 4*   **P** *Bp, D&C, CCC Ox, and E P Ecroyd Esq (jt)*   **R** E M SMITH,   **C** J P COLDWELL,
   NSM J J H SMITH

INGOL (St Margaret) *Blackb 13*   **P** *Bp*   **V** M S HATTON

INGOLDISTHORPE (St Michael)   see Snettisham w Ingoldisthorpe and Fring *Nor*

INGOLDMELLS (St Peter and St Paul)   see Skegness Gp *Linc*

INGOLDSBY (St Bartholomew)   see N Beltisloe Gp *Linc*

INGRAM (St Michael)   see Glendale Gp *Newc*

INGRAVE (St Nicholas) (St Stephen) *Chelmsf 7*   **P** *Bp and Ch Patr Trust (jt)*   **V** P S HAMILTON

INGRAVE (St Stephen) Conventional District *Chelmsf 7*
   NSM J A SEDANO

INGROW (St John the Evangelist) cum Hainworth *Bradf 8*
   P *Bp*   **V** C H KIRKE

INGS (St Anne)   see Staveley, Ings and Kentmere *Carl*

INGWORTH (St Lawrence)   see Erpingham w Calthorpe, Ingworth, Aldborough etc *Nor*

INHAM NOOK (St Barnabas)   see Chilwell *S'well*

INKBERROW (St Peter) w Cookhill and Kington w Dormston
Worc 1   **P** *Bp*   **R** N M WRIGHT,   **NSM** D HAYWARD-WRIGHT
INKERSALL (St Columba)   *see* Staveley and Barrow Hill *Derby*
INKPEN (St Michael)   *see* W Woodhay w Enborne, Hampstead Marshall etc *Ox*
INNS COURT (Holy Cross)   *see* Filwood Park *Bris*
INSKIP (St Peter)   *see* Copp w Inskip *Blackb*
INSTOW (All Saints Chapel) (St John the Baptist) *Ex 16*
P *Christie Trustees*   **P-in-c** G CALWAY
INTAKE (All Saints)   *see* Doncaster Intake *Sheff*
INTWOOD (All Saints)   *see* Swardeston w E Carleton, Intwood, Keswick etc *Nor*
INWARDLEIGH (St Petroc)   *see* Okehampton w Inwardleigh, Bratton Clovelly etc *Ex*
INWORTH (All Saints)   *see* Copford w Easthorpe and Messing w Inworth *Chelmsf*
IPING (St Mary)   *see* Stedham w Iping *Chich*
IPPLEPEN (St Andrew), Torbryan and Denbury *Ex 10*
P *D&C Windsor and SMF (jt)*   **V** I C EGLIN
IPSDEN (St Mary the Virgin)   *see* Langtree *Ox*
IPSLEY (St Peter) *Worc 7*   **P** *Patr Bd*   **TR** W BROWN,
TV A J KELSO,   **C** K M JOHNSON,   **NSM** C WAUDBY
IPSTONES (St Leonard) w Berkhamsytch and Onecote w Bradnop *Lich 6*   **P** *Bp and R Leek and Meerbrook (jt)*
V C M SCARGILL,   **OLM** M J EVANS
IPSWICH (All Hallows) *St E 4*   **P** *Bp*   **V** R F TOBIN
IPSWICH (All Saints)   *see* Triangle, St Matt and All SS *St E*
IPSWICH (St Andrew) *St E 4*   **P** *Bp*   **V** S R LLOYD
IPSWICH (St Augustine of Hippo) *St E 4*   **P** *Bp*
V L F SIMPKINS
IPSWICH (St Bartholomew) *St E 4*   **P** *Bp*   **V** P J CARTER
IPSWICH (St Helen) (Holy Trinity) (St Clement w St Luke)
St E 4   **P** *Ch Patr Trust*   **OLM** S J POTTER
IPSWICH (St John the Baptist) *St E 4*   **P** *Simeon's Trustees*
V A C WILSON,   **NSM** M GREEN
IPSWICH (St Margaret) *St E 4*   **P** *Simeon's Trustees*
V D CUTTS,   **C** S G G TALBOT
IPSWICH (St Mary at Stoke) (St Peter) (St Francis) (St Clare's Church Centre) *St E 4*   **P** *Bp*   **TR** I D J MORGAN,
TV C G G EVERETT, M S G MORGAN,   **NSM** J FENNELL
IPSWICH (St Mary at the Elms) *St E 4*   **P** *Guild of All So*
P-in-c S J RAINE
IPSWICH (St Mary-le-Tower) (St Nicholas) *St E 4*   **P** *Bp*
(3 turns), Ch Patr Trust (1 turn)   **V** C A G JENKIN,
NSM D J WARNES
IPSWICH (St Matthew)   *see* Triangle, St Matt and All SS *St E*
IPSWICH (St Thomas) *St E 4*   **P** *Bp*   **V** P BOURNER
IPSWICH Triangle (Community Centre)   *see* Triangle, St Matt and All SS *St E*
IPSWICH, SOUTH WEST   *see* Ipswich St Mary at Stoke w St Pet and St Fran *St E*
IRBY (St Chad's Mission Church)   *see* Thurstaston *Ches*
IRBY-IN-THE-MARSH (All Saints)   *see* Burgh Gp *Linc*
IRBY ON HUMBER (St Andrew)   *see* Laceby and Ravendale Gp *Linc*
IRCHESTER (St Katharine) *Pet 8*   **P** *Bp*   **V** J SIMMONS
IRCHESTER, LITTLE (St John)   *see* Irchester *Pet*
IREBY (St James)   *see* Binsey *Carl*
IRELAND WOOD (St Paul) *Ripon 7*   **P** *R Adel*
P-in-c J L SMITH,   **C** S D FORD
IRLAM (St John the Baptist) *Man 2*   **P** *Trustees*
V D I WHEELER,   **OLM** J DODD, J STEPHENS
IRNHAM (St Andrew)   *see* Corby Glen *Linc*
IRON ACTON (St James the Less)   *see* Frampton Cotterell and Iron Acton *Bris*
IRON-BRIDGE (St Luke)   *see* Coalbrookdale, Iron-Bridge and Lt Wenlock *Heref*
IRONSTONE: Drayton, Hanwell, Horley, Hornton, Shenington w Alkerton, and Wroxton w Balscote *Ox 5*   **P** *Ld Chan (1 turn), Bp, Earl De la Warr, and DBP (1 turn)*
NSM P C SMITH
IRONSTONE VILLAGES Family of Churches, The *Leic 2*
P *Lady Gretton, Ld Chan, Duke of Rutland, Bp, and Sir Lyonel Tollemache Bt (by turn)*   **R** B A STARK,   **C** H G ORRIDGE,
NSM P C CONNELL
IRONVILLE (Christ Church)   *see* Riddings and Ironville *Derby*
IRSTEAD (St Michael)   *see* Ashmanhaugh, Barton Turf etc *Nor*
IRTHINGTON (St Kentigern)   *see* Eden, Gelt and Irthing *Carl*
IRTHLINGBOROUGH (St Peter) *Pet 8*   **P** *Sir Philip Naylor-Leyland Bt*   **R** J R WESTWOOD
IRTON (St Paul)   *see* Eskdale, Irton, Muncaster and Waberthwaite *Carl*
ISEL (St Michael)   *see* Binsey *Carl*
ISFIELD (St Margaret) *Chich 21*   **P** *Abp*   **R** B H WILCOX,
Hon C F J FOX-WILSON,   **NSM** C HOWARTH

ISHAM (St Peter)   *see* Gt w Lt Harrowden and Orlingbury and Isham etc *Pet*
ISLE ABBOTTS (Blessed Virgin Mary)   *see* Ilminster and Distr *B & W*
ISLE BREWERS (All Saints)   *as above*
ISLE OF DOGS (Christ Church and St John) (St Luke) *Lon 7*
P *Bp*   **V** T F PYKE,   **NSM** A J KEIGHLEY, T C KEIGHLEY
ISLEHAM (St Andrew)   *see* Three Rivers Gp *Ely*
ISLES OF SCILLY: St Mary's, St Agnes, St Martin's, Bryher and Tresco *Truro 5*   **P** *Duchy of Cornwall*   **R** G C SCOTT
ISLEWORTH (All Saints) *Lon 11*   **P** *D&C Windsor*
P-in-c A L BROOKER
ISLEWORTH (St Francis of Assisi) *Lon 11*   **P** *Bp*
NSM L P SMITH, A BURGESS
ISLEWORTH (St John the Baptist) *Lon 11*
P *V Isleworth All SS*   **V** *vacant* (020) 8560 4916
ISLEWORTH (St Luke)   *see* Spring Grove St Mary *Lon*
ISLEWORTH (St Mary) Osterley Road   *as above*
ISLEWORTH (St Mary the Virgin)   *see* Hounslow H Trin w St Paul *Lon*
ISLEY WALTON (All Saints)   *see* Ashby-de-la-Zouch and Breedon on the Hill *Leic*
ISLINGTON (St James the Apostle) (St Peter) *Lon 6*   **P** *Bp*
V A J BURNISTON
ISLINGTON (St Jude and St Paul)   *see* Mildmay Grove St Jude and St Paul *Lon*
ISLINGTON (St Mary) *Lon 6*   **P** *CPAS*   **C** T K HOLE,
M A OBORNE
ISLINGTON (St Mary Magdalene)   *see* Holloway St Mary Magd *Lon*
ISLIP (St Nicholas)   *see* Ray Valley *Ox*
ISLIP (St Nicholas)   *see* Thrapston, Denford and Islip *Pet*
ISTEAD RISE (St Barnabas) *Roch 4*   **P** *Bp*   **V** V C SHORT
ITCHEN, UPPER *Win 1*   **P** *Prime Min (2 turns), D&C (1 turn)*   **R** A N M CLARKE
ITCHEN ABBAS (St John the Baptist)   *see* Itchen Valley *Win*
ITCHEN VALLEY, The *Win 1*   **P** *Ld Chan*   **R** *vacant* (01962) 779832
ITCHENOR, WEST (St Nicholas)   *see* W Wittering and Birdham w Itchenor *Chich*
ITCHINGFIELD (St Nicholas) w Slinfold *Chich 7*   **P** *Bp*
R *vacant* (01403) 790197
ITTERINGHAM   *see* Lt Barningham, Blickling, Edgefield etc *Nor*
IVEGILL (Christ Church)   *see* Inglewood Gp *Carl*
IVER (St Peter) *Ox 23*   **P** *Trustees*   **V** T W EADY,
C G V R HOWARD,   **NSM** A M WILLIAMS,   **OLM** K WILSON,
B J GRIFFITHS
IVER HEATH (St Margaret) *Ox 23*   **P** *Trustees*
R W P G HAZLEWOOD
IVINGHOE (St Mary the Virgin) w Pitstone and Slapton and Marsworth *Ox 26*   **P** *Bp and Ch Ch Ox (jt)*   **V** T E DOYLE,
C C J PETERS
IVINGTON (St John)   *see* Leominster *Heref*
IVY HATCH (not known)   *see* Ightham *Roch*
IVY ROW (Mission Room)   *see* Roos and Garton w Tunstall, Grimston and Hilston *York*
IVYBRIDGE (St John the Evangelist) w Harford *Ex 21*   **P** *Bp*
V C H OSBORNE
IVYCHURCH (St George)   *see* St Mary's Bay w St Mary-in-the-Marsh etc *Cant*
IWADE (All Saints) *Cant 15*   **P** *Adn Maidstone*
P-in-c A J AMOS,   **C** H E NELSON
IWERNE COURTNEY (St Mary)   *see* Iwerne Valley *Sarum*
IWERNE MINSTER (St Mary)   *as above*
IWERNE VALLEY *Sarum 7*   **P** *D&C Windsor, DBP, G A L F Pitt-Rivers Esq, and A C L Sturge Esq (jt)*
V S F EVERETT,   **C** J MAW,   **NSM** J H SIMMONS,
OLM M A O MULLEY
IXWORTH (St Mary)   *see* Blackbourne *St E*
IXWORTH THORPE (All Saints)   *as above*
JACKFIELD (St Mary)   *see* Broseley w Benthall, Jackfield, Linley etc *Heref*
JACOBSTOW (St James)   *see* Week St Mary Circle of Par *Truro*
JACOBSTOWE (St James)   *see* Hatherleigh, Meeth, Exbourne and Jacobstowe *Ex*
JARROW (St John the Baptist) (St Mark) (St Paul) (St Peter)
Dur 15   **P** *Bp*   **TR** W E BRAVINER,   **TV** G W OPPERMAN,
J LANCASTER
JARROW GRANGE (Christ Church) *Dur 15*   **P** *Lord Northbourne*   **P-in-c** D T OSMAN
JARVIS BROOK (St Michael and All Angels) *Chich 19*   **P** *Bp*
V A W WEAVER
JERSEY (All Saints) *Win 15*   **P** *R St Helier, Bp, and The Crown (by turn)*   **NSM** G L BAUDAINS

JERSEY Gouray (St Martin) *Win 15* **P** *Bp and The Crown (alt)* **Hon C** C P WILLIAMS
JERSEY Greve d'Azette (St Nicholas) *see* Jersey St Clem *Win*
JERSEY (Holy Trinity) *Win 15* **P** *The Crown* **R** G J HOUGHTON
JERSEY Millbrook (St Matthew) *Win 15* **P** *The Crown* **V** P J WARREN
JERSEY (St Andrew) *Win 15* **P** *Dean of Jersey* **V** M S TAYLOR
JERSEY (St Brelade) (Communicare Chapel) (St Aubin) *Win 15* **P** *The Crown* **R** M F W BOND, **NSM** G GREEN, J A DAVY
JERSEY (St Clement) *Win 15* **P** *The Crown* **R** D M SHAW, **NSM** M J DRYDEN, T LE COUTEUR
JERSEY (St Helier) *Win 15* **P** *The Crown* **P-in-c** R F KEY, **NSM** A D WILLIAMS
JERSEY (St James) *Win 15* **P** *Bp* **V** D R D JONES, **NSM** A F PEARCE
JERSEY (St John) *Win 15* **P** *The Crown* **R** A J THEWLIS
JERSEY (St Lawrence) *Win 15* **P** *The Crown* **R** P J WARREN, **C** S M HUNTLEY
JERSEY (St Luke) *Win 15* **P** *Bp and The Crown (alt)* **V** D R D JONES, **NSM** A F PEARCE
JERSEY (St Mark) *Win 15* **P** *Bp* **P-in-c** M P L SHEA
JERSEY (St Martin) *Win 15* **P** *The Crown* **R** L J TURNER
JERSEY (St Mary) *Win 15* **P** *The Crown* **R** J NAYLOR, **NSM** A F PEARCE
JERSEY (St Ouen) (St George) *Win 15* **P** *The Crown* **R** J P HARKIN
JERSEY (St Paul) Proprietary Chapel *Win 15* **Min** P J BROOKS
JERSEY (St Peter) *Win 15* **P** *The Crown* **R** M R POOLTON
JERSEY (St Saviour) *Win 15* **P** *The Crown* **R** A C SWINDELL, **NSM** J J ILTON
JERSEY (St Simon) *Win 15* **P** *R St Helier, Bp, and The Crown (by turn)* **NSM** G L BAUDAINS
JERSEY DE GROUVILLE (St Martin) (St Peter la Roque) *Win 15* **P** *The Crown* **R** M L LANGE-MANS
JESMOND (Clayton Memorial Church) *Newc 2* **P** *Trustees* **V** D R J HOLLOWAY, **C** J J S PRYKE, **Hon C** A F MUNDEN
JESMOND (Holy Trinity) *Newc 2* **P** *Trustees* **V** M WROE, **C** T SANDERSON
JESMOND (St George) *see* Newc St Geo and St Hilda *Newc*
JESMOND (St Hilda) *as above*
JEVINGTON (St Andrew) *see* E Dean w Friston and Jevington *Chich*
JOYDENS WOOD (St Barnabas) *Roch 17* **P** *Bp* **V** G C DAY
JURBY (St Patrick) *S & M 3* **P** *Bp* **V** *vacant*
KATE'S HILL (St John) *see* Dudley St Jo *Worc*
KEA (All Hallows) (Old Church) *Truro 6* **P** *V St Clement* **P-in-c** C S PEER
KEAL, EAST (St Helen) *see* Marden Hill Gp *Linc*
KEAL, WEST (St Helen) *as above*
KEARSLEY MOOR (St Stephen) *Man 6* **P** *R E Farnworth and Kearsley* **V** K F WAINWRIGHT
KEASDEN (St Matthew) *see* Clapham-with-Keasden and Austwick *Bradf*
KEDINGTON (St Peter and St Paul) *see* Stourhead *St E*
KEEDWELL HILL (Ascension) *see* Long Ashton w Barrow Gurney and Flax Bourton *B & W*
KEELBY Group, The (St Bartholomew) *Linc 10* **P** J E Spilman Esq and DBP *(1 turn), Bp (1 turn)* **P-in-c** M W PAGE-CHESTNEY
KEELE (St John the Baptist) *Lich 9* **P** T H G Howard-Sneyd Esq **V** S A ANSELL, **C** M J MAXWELL
KEEVIL (St Leonard) *see* Trowbridge St Jas and Keevil *Sarum*
KEGWORTH (St Andrew), Hathern, Long Whatton, Diseworth, Belton and Osgathorpe *Leic 6* **P** *Patr Bd* **TR** G R TURNER-CALLIS, **TV** A M PRINCE
KEIGHLEY (All Saints) *Bradf 8* **P** *Bp and R Keighley St Andr* **P-in-c** J L PRITCHARD
KEIGHLEY (St Andrew) *Bradf 8* **P** *Bp* **P-in-c** P J MOTT, **NSM** E A CAISSIE
KEINTON MANDEVILLE (St Mary Magdalene) *see* Wheathill Priory Gp *B & W*
KELBROOK (St Mary) *see* Earby w Kelbrook *Bradf*
KELBY (St Andrew) *see* Ancaster Wilsford Gp *Linc*
KELHAM (St Wilfrid) *see* Averham w Kelham *S'well*
KELLAWAYS (St Giles) *see* Draycot *Bris*
KELLET, NETHER (St Mark) *see* Bolton-le-Sands *Blackb*
KELLET, OVER (St Cuthbert) *Blackb 14* **P** *Reformation Ch Trust* **V** K CLAPHAM
KELLING (St Mary) *see* Weybourne Gp *Nor*
KELLINGTON (St Edmund) *see* Knottingley and Kellington w Whitley *Wakef*
KELLOE (St Helen) and Coxhoe *Dur 5* **P** *Bp* **P-in-c** C B LLOYD
KELLS (St Peter) *Carl 5* **P** *Bp* **P-in-c** J A EVANS, **OLM** A J BANKS

KELLY (St Mary the Virgin) *see* Lifton, Broadwoodwidger, Stowford etc *Ex*
KELMARSH (St Denys) *see* Clipston w Naseby and Haselbech w Kelmarsh *Pet*
KELMSCOTT (St George) *see* Shill Valley and Broadshire *Ox*
KELSALE (St Peter) *see* Saxmundham w Kelsale cum Carlton *St E*
KELSALL (St Philip) *Ches 2* **P** *V Tarvin* **P-in-c** I P ENTICOTT
KELSEY Group, The *Linc 5* **P** *Bp (3 turns), J M B Young Esq and S B Young Esq (1 turn)* **R** *vacant and fax* (01652) 678924
KELSEY, NORTH (All Hallows) *see* Kelsey Gp *Linc*
KELSEY, SOUTH (St Mary) *as above*
KELSHALL (St Faith) *see* Therfield w Kelshall *St Alb*
KELSTERN (St Faith) *see* Binbrook Gp *Linc*
KELSTON (St Nicholas) *see* Bath Weston St Jo w Kelston *B & W*
KELVEDON (St Mary the Virgin) and Feering *Chelmsf 23* **P** *Bp* **V** D S REYNISH
KELVEDON HATCH (St Nicholas) *see* Bentley Common, Kelvedon Hatch and Navestock *Chelmsf*
KEMBERTON (St Andrew) *see* Beckbury, Badger, Kemberton, Ryton, Stockton etc *Lich*
KEMBLE (All Saints), Poole Keynes, Somerford Keynes w Shorncote, Coates, Rodmarton and Sapperton w Frampton Mansell *Glouc 9* **P** *Bp, Lord Bathurst, Mrs L R Rank, Guild of All So, and DBP (2 turns), Duchy of Lanc (1 turn)* **P-in-c** M B SANDERS, **OLM** P WALKER
KEMERTON (St Nicholas) *see* Ashchurch and Kemerton *Glouc*
KEMP TOWN (St Mary) *Chich 2* **P** *Bp, Mrs R A Hinton, A C R Elliott Esq, T J Elliott Esq, and the Revd Canon D H McKittrick (jt)* **P-in-c** A J WOODWARD
KEMPSEY (St Mary the Virgin) and Severn Stoke w Croome d'Abitot *Worc 5* **P** *D&C and Croome Estate Trustees (alt)* **R** P R HOLZAPFEL
KEMPSFORD (St Mary) *see* Fairford Deanery *Glouc*
KEMPSHOTT (St Mark) *Win 4* **P** *Bp* **V** K J TAYLOR, **C** C A GILLHAM, **NSM** R P BOWSKILL, A BOWSKILL
KEMPSTON (All Saints) *St Alb 10* **P** *Bp* **P-in-c** S L HUCKLE, **C** J NASH
KEMPSTON (Transfiguration) *St Alb 10* **P** *Bp* **V** D J P ISIORHO
KEMSING (St Mary the Virgin) w Woodlands *Roch 10* **P** *DBP* **P-in-c** J R OAKLEY
KENARDINGTON (St Mary) *see* Orlestone w Snave and Ruckinge w Warehorne etc *Cant*
KENCHESTER (St Michael) *see* Credenhill w Brinsop and Wormsley etc *Heref*
KENCOT (St George) *see* Shill Valley and Broadshire *Ox*
KENDAL (Holy Trinity) (All Hallows Chapel) *Carl 10* **P** *Trin Coll Cam* **P-in-c** E C ROBINSON, **C** S T MCCANN, **NSM** P SMITH, L C STOCK, P A HENDERSON
KENDAL (St Thomas) *Carl 10* **P** *CPAS* **V** T R MONTGOMERY, **NSM** S R WEATHERILL, W J HOLLIDAY
KENDAL (St George) *see* Beacon *Carl*
KENDERCHURCH (St Mary) *see* Ewyas Harold w Dulas, Kenderchurch etc *Heref*
KENDRAY (St Andrew) *Sheff 12* **P** *V Ardsley* **P-in-c** P C W JACKSON
KENILWORTH (St John) *Cov 4* **P** *Simeon's Trustees* **OLM** J M MULLANEY
KENILWORTH (St Nicholas) (St Barnabas) *Cov 4* **P** *Ld Chan* **V** R W E AWRE
KENLEY (All Saints) *S'wark 22* **P** *Abp* **V** R C HAGON, **NSM** D C HADLEY, L L P WILLIAMS
KENLEY (St John the Baptist) *see* Wenlock *Heref*
KENN (St Andrew) *see* Exminster and Kenn *Ex*
KENN (St John the Evangelist) *see* Yatton Moor *B & W*
KENN, NORTH *see* Tedburn St Mary, Whitestone, Oldridge etc *Ex*
KENNERLEIGH (St John the Baptist) *see* N Creedy *Ex*
KENNET, EAST (Christ Church) *see* Upper Kennet *Sarum*
KENNET, UPPER *Sarum 18* **P** *Bp* **P-in-c** K H LAMDIN, **C** P E BRADISH
KENNETT (St Nicholas) *see* Three Rivers Gp *Ely*
KENNINGHALL (St Mary) *see* Guiltcross *Nor*
KENNINGTON (St John the Divine w St James the Apostle) *S'wark 11* **P** *Ripon Coll Cuddesdon and Bp (jt)* **V** *vacant* (020) 7735 9340
KENNINGTON (St Mark) *S'wark 11* **P** *Abp* **V** M S STARKEY, **C** P O DANIEL
KENNINGTON (St Mary) *Cant 10* **P** *Abp* **V** *vacant* (01233) 620500
KENNINGTON (St Swithun) *Ox 10* **P** *Bp* **V** *vacant* (01865) 321504

KENNINGTON CROSS (St Anselm)　*see* N Lambeth *S'wark*
KENNINGTON PARK (St Agnes) *S'wark 10*　**P** *Trustees*
　V C I PEARSON
KENNY HILL (St James)　*see* Mildenhall *St E*
KENSAL GREEN (St John) *Lon 2*　**P** *Bp*　**V** A K DANGERFIELD
Kensal Rise Team Ministry, The (St Mark) (St Martin)
　Lon 21　**P** *Patr Bd*　**TR** P W STONE,　**TV** G P NOYCE,
　Hon C E J BARRATT, R L SMITH,　**NSM** T P GODDARD
KENSAL TOWN (St Thomas) (St Andrew) (St Philip) *Lon 12*
　P *Hyndman Trustees*　**P-in-c** M A MILLER
KENSINGTON (St Barnabas) *Lon 12*　**P** *V Kensington St Mary*
　Abbots w St Geo and Ch Ch　**V** T M HUMPHREY,
　C M C MACDONALD, S G D LARKIN,　**NSM** S K GREEN
KENSINGTON (St Clement)　*see* Notting Dale St Clem w St
　Mark and St Jas *Lon*
KENSINGTON (St George)　*see* Holland Park *Lon*
KENSINGTON (St Helen) (Holy Trinity) *Lon 12*　**P** *Bp*
　V S R DIVALL
KENSINGTON (St James)　*see* Notting Dale St Clem w St
　Mark and St Jas *Lon*
KENSINGTON (St Luke)　*see* S Kensington St Luke *Lon*
KENSINGTON (St Mary Abbots) (Christ Church) (St Philip)
　Lon 12　**P** *Bp*　**V** G W CRAIG,　**C** G K WARDELL, D C WALSH,
　Hon C R P MARSHALL,　**NSM** L A PERRY, R HAWES
KENSINGTON, NORTH (St Michael and All Angels)
　see Notting Hill St Mich and Ch Ch *Lon*
KENSINGTON, SOUTH (Holy Trinity w All Saints) *Lon 3*
　P *D&C Westmr*　**P-in-c** E M V RUSSELL
KENSINGTON, SOUTH (St Augustine) *Lon 12*　**P** *Keble Coll*
　Ox　**P-in-c** S M CAPLE
KENSINGTON, SOUTH (St Jude) Courtfield Gardens　*see* W
　Brompton St Mary w St Peter and St Jude *Lon*
KENSINGTON, SOUTH St Luke *Lon 8*　**P** *Ch Patr Trust*
　V A N BEAVIS
KENSINGTON, SOUTH (St Stephen) *Lon 12*　**P** *Guild of*
　All So　**V** R F BUSHAU
KENSINGTON, WEST (St Andrew)　*see* Fulham St Andr
　Fulham Fields *Lon*
KENSINGTON, WEST (St Mary)　*see* Fulham St Mary N End
　Lon
KENSINGTON, WEST (St Mary) The Boltons　*see* W
　Brompton St Mary w St Peter and St Jude *Lon*
KENSWORTH (St Mary the Virgin), Studham and Whipsnade
　St Alb 12　**P** *Ld Chan and D&C St Paul's (alt)*
　V N Y LENTHALL
KENT TOWN　*see* E Molesey *Guildf*
KENTCHURCH (St Mary)　*see* Ewyas Harold w Dulas,
　Kenderchurch etc *Heref*
KENTFORD (St Mary)　*see* Dalham, Gazeley, Higham,
　Kentford and Moulton *St E*
KENTISBEARE (St Mary)　*see* Cullompton, Willand,
　Uffculme, Kentisbeare etc *Ex*
KENTISBURY (St Thomas)　*see* Shirwell, Loxhore, Kentisbury,
　Arlington, etc *Ex*
KENTISH TOWN (St Benet and All Saints) (St Luke) *Lon 17*
　P *Prime Min and D&C St Paul's (alt)*　**V** R N ARNOLD
KENTISH TOWN (St Martin) (St Andrew) *Lon 17*　**P** *Exors*
　Dame Jewell Magnus-Allcroft　**P-in-c** C J BRICE
KENTISH TOWN (St Silas) and (Holy Trinity) w St Barnabas
　Lon 17　**P** *Bp and D&C St Paul's (jt)*　**V** G C ROWLANDS,
　NSM M G BURRIDGE
KENTMERE (St Cuthbert)　*see* Staveley, Ings and Kentmere
　Carl
KENTON (All Saints)　*see* Debenham and Helmingham *St E*
KENTON (All Saints), Mamhead, Powderham, Cofton and
　Starcross *Ex 6*　**P** *Earl of Devon, D&C Ex, D&C Sarum, and*
　SMF (jt)　**C** R M RANN, D A BURTON,　**Hon C** P DAWKES
KENTON (Ascension) *Newc 2*　**P** *Bp*　**P-in-c** L CHAPMAN
KENTON (St Mary the Virgin) *Lon 23*　**P** *Bp*　**V** G A PINNOCK
KENTON, SOUTH (Annunciation)　*see* Wembley Park *Lon*
KENWYN (St Keyne) w St Allen *Truro 6*　**P** *Bp*
　P-in-c C P PARSONS,　**OLM** R W HUMPHRIES
KERESLEY (St Thomas) and Coundon *Cov 2*　**P** *Bp*
　V P A WALKER,　**C** R E WALKER
KERESLEY END (Church of the Ascension)　*see* Keresley and
　Coundon *Cov*
KERRIDGE (Holy Trinity)　*see* Bollington *Ches*
KERSAL, LOWER (St Aidan)　*see* Salford All SS *Man*
KERSAL MOOR (St Paul) *Man 6*　**P** *Trustees*　**R** L K BATTYE
KERSEY (St Mary)　*see* Elmsett w Aldham, Hintlesham,
　Chattisham etc *St E*
KERSWELL GREEN (St John the Baptist)　*see* Kempsey and
　Severn Stoke w Croome d'Abitot *Worc*
KESGRAVE (All Saints) *St E 4*　**P** *Bp*　**V** R SPITTLE,
　NSM C J NUNN

KESSINGLAND (St Edmund), Gisleham and Rushmere *Nor 9*
　P *Ld Chan (1 turns) and Bp (2 turns)*　**R** L M DOMONEY
KESTON (not known) (St Audrey) *Roch 14*　**P** *D&C*
　R D F SPRINGTHORPE
KESWICK (All Saints)　*see* Swardeston w E Carleton, Intwood,
　Keswick etc *Nor*
KESWICK (St John) *Carl 6*　**P** *Trustees*　**V** A S PYE
KESWICK, EAST (St Mary Magdalene)　*see* Bardsey *Ripon*
KETLEY (St Mary the Virgin)　*see* Cen Telford *Lich*
KETTERING (All Saints) *Pet 9*　**P** *SMF*　**V** *vacant* (01536)
　513376
KETTERING (Christ the King) *Pet 9*　**P** *R Barton Seagrave w*
　Warkton　**V** S M BENOY,　**C** P W FROST
KETTERING (St Andrew) *Pet 9*　**P** *Bp*　**P-in-c** N R WILLS,
　NSM H M GOMPERTZ
KETTERING (St Mary the Virgin) (St John the Evangelist) *Pet 9*
　P *SMF*　**V** *vacant* (01536) 512736
KETTERING (St Peter and St Paul) (St Michael and All Angels)
　Pet 9　**P** *Comdr L M M Saunders Watson*
　P-in-c D M J BARRINGTON,　**NSM** J S SMITH, L S MCCORMACK
KETTERINGHAM (St Peter)　*see* Swardeston w E Carleton,
　Intwood, Keswick etc *Nor*
KETTLEBASTON (St Mary)　*see* Monks Eleigh w Chelsworth
　and Brent Eleigh etc *St E*
KETTLEBROOK (St Andrew)　*see* Tamworth *Lich*
KETTLEBURGH (St Andrew)　*see* Brandeston w Kettleburgh
　and Easton *St E*
KETTLENESS (St John the Baptist)　*see* Hinderwell, Roxby and
　Staithes etc *York*
KETTLESTONE (All Saints)　*see* Barney, Fulmodeston w
　Croxton, Hindringham etc *Nor*
KETTLETHORPE (St Peter and St Paul)　*see* Saxilby Gp *Linc*
KETTLEWELL (St Mary) w Conistone, Hubberholme and
　Arncliff w Halton Gill *Bradf 7*　**P** *Bp, Mrs J E Wright, and*
　W R G Bell Esq (jt)　**V** P YORKSTONE,　**C** F JENKINS
KETTON (St Mary the Virgin), Collyweston, Easton-on-the-Hill,
　Tinwell and Wittering *Pet 12*　**P** *Burghley Ho Preservation*
　Trust, Bp, and Ld Chan (by turn)　**R** D G EVERETT
KEW (St Anne) *S'wark 16*　**P** *The Crown*　**V** N J WORN
KEW (St Francis of Assisi) *Liv 9*　**P** *Bp, Adn Warrington, and*
　V Southport All SS and All So (jt)　**V** A P J GALBRAITH
KEW (St Philip and All Saints) (St Luke) *S'wark 16*　**P** *Bp*
　V P W HART
KEWSTOKE (St Paul) w Wick St Lawrence *B & W 11*
　P *Ld Chan*　**P-in-c** G P EALES
KEYHAM (All Saints)　*see* Houghton-on-the-Hill, Keyham and
　Hungarton *Leic*
KEYHAM, NORTH (St Thomas)　*see* Plymouth St Pet and H
　Apostles *Ex*
KEYINGHAM (St Nicholas) w Ottringham, Halsham and Sunk
　Island *York 12*　**P** *Abp (3 turns), DBP (1 turn)*　**R** *vacant*
　(01964) 622171
KEYMER (St Cosmas and St Damian)　*see* Clayton w Keymer
　Chich
KEYMER (St Francis of Assisi)　*as above*
KEYNSHAM (St Francis) (St John the Baptist) *B & W 10*
　P *Patr Bd*　**TR** J F SAMWAYS,　**TV** A D JUDGE, S G HOWELL
KEYSOE (St Mary the Virgin) w Bolnhurst and Little Staughton
　St Alb 15　**P** *CCC Ox (1 turn), Bp (2 turns)*　**V** *vacant*
　(01234) 708251
KEYSTON (St John the Baptist) and Bythorn *Ely 10*
　P *Sir Philip Naylor-Leyland Bt (2 turns), Bp (1 turn)*
　R *vacant*
KEYWORTH (St Mary Magdalene) and Stanton-on-the-Wolds
　and Bunny w Bradmore *S'well 8*　**P** *Bp and Ld Chan (alt)*
　R J F WELLINGTON,　**C** C FRENCH,　**NSM** T H KIRKMAN
KIBWORTH (St Wilfrid) and Smeeton Westerby and Saddington
　Leic 4　**P** *Mert Coll Ox and Bp (jt)*　**P-in-c** L FREMMER
KIDBROOKE (St James) (Holy Spirit) *S'wark 1*　**P** *Patr Bd*
　R K W HITCH,　**NSM** K F SITCH
KIDBROOKE (St Nicholas) *S'wark 1*　**P** *Bp and Simeon's*
　Trustees (jt)　**V** T M LINKENS
KIDDERMINSTER (St George) (St Chad) (St John the Baptist
　Church Hall) *Worc 11*　**P** *Patr Bd*　**P-in-c** H A BURTON
KIDDERMINSTER (St John the Baptist) (Holy Innocents)
　Worc 11　**P** *Patr Bd*　**TR** D J ARNOLD
KIDDERMINSTER (St Mary and All Saints) w Trimpley,
　Franche, Broadwaters and Upper Arley *Worc 11*　**P** *Bp*
　TR D O BELL,　**TV** R A LAWLEY,　**C** K M GREEN
KIDDERMINSTER WEST　*see* Kidderminster St Jo and H
　Innocents *Worc*
KIDDINGTON (St Nicholas)　*see* Wootton w Glympton and
　Kiddington *Ox*
KIDLINGTON (St Mary the Virgin) w Hampton Poyle *Ox 7*
　P *Patr Bd*　**TR** J A ELLIS,　**TV** H A CAMPBELL,
　C G K STRAINE,　**NSM** W H WHYTE

KIDLINGTON, SOUTH (St John the Baptist)   *see* Kidlington w Hampton Poyle *Ox*

KIDMORE END (St John the Baptist)   *see* Rotherfield Peppard and Kidmore End etc *Ox*

KIDSGROVE (St Thomas) *Lich 9*   **P** *MMCET*   **V** I BAKER

KILBURN (Mission Room)   *see* Horsley and Denby *Derby*

KILBURN (St Augustine) (St John) *Lon 2*   **P** *SMF*
V A H YATES,   **C** S HALSTEAD

KILBURN (St Mary)   *see* Thirkleby w Kilburn and Bagby *York*

KILBURN (St Mary w All Souls) Priory Road and W Hampstead St James *Lon 16*   **P** *Bp, Ch Patr Trust, and trustees (jt)*
V A D CAIN,   **NSM** M-E B R BRAGG

KILBURN, WEST (St Luke) (St Simon) (St Jude) *Lon 2*
P *CPAS*   **P-in-c** A G THOM,   **C** M R WALTON, J F BARRY,
NSM B A ENWUCHOLA

KILBY (St Mary Magdalene)   *see* Wistow *Leic*

KILDALE (St Cuthbert)   *see* Ingleby Greenhow, Bilsdale Priory etc *York*

KILDWICK (St Andrew) *Bradf 8*   **P** *Ch Ch Ox*   **V** R A R FIGG

KILHAM (All Saints)   *see* Rudston w Boynton, Carnaby and Kilham *York*

KILKHAMPTON (St James the Great) w Morwenstow *Truro 8*
P *DBP and Bp (jt)*   **R** P J ABELL

KILLAMARSH (St Giles) *Derby 3*   **P** *The Crown*
P-in-c H GUEST,   **NSM** M GUEST

KILLERTON (Holy Evangelist)   *see* Pinhoe and Broadclyst *Ex*

KILLINGHALL (St Thomas the Apostle)   *see* Hampsthwaite and Killinghall and Birstwith *Ripon*

KILLINGHOLME, NORTH AND SOUTH (St Denys)   *see* Habrough Gp *Linc*

KILLINGTON (All Saints)   *see* Firbank, Howgill and Killington *Bradf*

KILLINGWORTH (St John) *Newc 1*   **P** *V Longbenton St Bart*
V A PATTISON

KILMERSDON (St Peter and St Paul) w Babington *B & W 12*
P *Lord Hylton*   **R** S K GREATOREX,   **NSM** J A COLE

KILMESTON (St Andrew)   *see* Upper Itchen *Win*

KILMINGTON (St Giles)   *see* Kilmington, Stockland, Dalwood, Yarcombe etc *Ex*

KILMINGTON (St Giles), Stockland, Dalwood, Yarcombe and Shute *Ex 5*   **P** *Bp and D&C (2 turns), Prime Min (1 turn)*
V A C MCCOLLUM,   **NSM** L A MILLS

KILMINGTON (St Mary the Virgin)   *see* Upper Stour *Sarum*

KILNDOWN (Christ Church)   *see* Goudhurst w Kilndown *Cant*

KILNGREEN (Diggle Mission Church)   *see* Saddleworth *Man*

KILNHURST (St Thomas) *Sheff 12*   **P** *Ld Chan*
V A R BREWERTON

KILNWICK (All Saints)   *see* Woldsburn *York*

KILPECK (St Mary and St David)   *see* Ewyas Harold w Dulas, Kenderchurch etc *Heref*

KILSBY (St Faith)   *see* Barby w Kilsby *Pet*

KILVERSTONE (St Andrew)   *see* Thetford *Nor*

KILVINGTON (St Mary) *S'well 3*   **P** E G STAUNTON *Esq*
P-in-c D HOLLIS

KILVINGTON, SOUTH (St Wilfrid)   *see* Thirsk *York*

KILWORTH, NORTH (St Andrew)   *see* Gilmorton, Peatling Parva, Kimcote etc *Leic*

KILWORTH, SOUTH (St Nicholas)   *as above*

KIMBERLEY (Holy Trinity) *S'well 7*   **P** *Bp*
P-in-c B M HOLBROOK,   **C** H R BRIDGER

KIMBERLEY (St Peter)   *see* Barnham Broom and Upper Yare *Nor*

KIMBERWORTH (St Thomas) (St Mark) *Sheff 6*   **P** *Bp*
V A R WOOD

KIMBERWORTH PARK (St John) *Sheff 6*   **P** *Bp*   **V** *vacant* (01709) 552268

KIMBLE, GREAT (St Nicholas)   *see* Ellesborough, The Kimbles and Stoke Mandeville *Ox*

KIMBLE, LITTLE (All Saints)   *as above*

KIMBLESWORTH (St Philip and St James)   *see* Dur N *Dur*

KIMBOLTON (St Andrew) *Ely 10*   **P** *Trustees Duke of Manchester*   **R** A FROST

KIMBOLTON (St James the Great)   *see* Leominster *Heref*

KIMCOTE (All Saints)   *see* Gilmorton, Peatling Parva, Kimcote etc *Leic*

KIMMERIDGE (St Nicholas of Myra)   *see* Corfe Castle, Church Knowle, Kimmeridge etc *Sarum*

KIMPTON (St Peter and St Paul)   *see* Appleshaw, Kimpton, Thruxton, Fyfield etc *Win*

KIMPTON (St Peter and St Paul) w Ayot St Lawrence *St Alb 8*
P *Bp*   **P-in-c** L E SUMMERS

KINETON (St Peter) *Cov 8*   **P** *Lady Willoughby de Broke*
C R J COOKE

KING CROSS (St Paul) *Wakef 4*   **P** *Bp*   **V** J VICKERMAN

KING STERNDALE (Christ Church)   *see* Buxton w Burbage and King Sterndale *Derby*

KINGHAM (St Andrew)   *see* Chipping Norton *Ox*

KINGMOOR (St Peter)   *see* Houghton *Carl*

KING'S BECK *Nor 12*   **P** *Bp, D&C, P H C Barber Esq, and J T D Shaw Esq (jt)*   **R** S A SMITH

KINGS BROMLEY (All Saints)   *see* The Ridwares and Kings Bromley *Lich*

KING'S CAPLE (St John the Baptist)   *see* Wormelow Hundred *Heref*

KING'S CLIFFE (All Saints) *Pet 10*   **P** *Bp*   **P-in-c** P J DAVIES

KINGS HEATH (All Saints) *Birm 5*   **P** *V Moseley St Mary*
V *vacant* 0121-444 1207

KINGS HEATH (St Augustine) *Pet 4*   **P** *Bp*
P-in-c A J B SYMES

KING'S HILL (St Andrew)   *see* Wednesbury St Bart *Lich*

KINGS LANGLEY (All Saints) *St Alb 2*   **P** *Abp*   **V** *vacant* (01923) 262939

KING'S LYNN (All Saints)   *see* S Lynn *Nor*

KING'S LYNN (St John the Evangelist) *Nor 20*   **P** *Bp*
V C J CHILD

KING'S LYNN (St Margaret) (St Edmund) w St Nicholas *Nor 20*
P *D&C*   **R** C J IVORY,   **NSM** C COPSEY

KING'S LYNN (St Peter)   *see* Clenchwarton and W Lynn *Ely*

KING'S NORTON (St John the Baptist)   *see* Gaulby *Leic*

KINGS NORTON (St Nicolas) *Birm 4*   **P** *Patr Bd*
TR R J MORRIS,   **C** K J R PULLIN, J B CROOKS

KING'S PYON (St Mary the Virgin)   *see* Canon Pyon w King's Pyon, Birley and Wellington *Heref*

KINGS RIPTON (St Peter) *Ely 10*   **P** *Lord de Ramsey*
P-in-c E B ATLING,   **C** B A STEWART

KING'S SOMBORNE   *see* Somborne w Ashley *Win*

KING'S STANLEY (St George)   *see* The Stanleys *Glouc*

KING'S SUTTON (St Peter and St Paul) and Newbottle and Charlton *Pet 1*   **P** *SMF and Lady Townsend (jt)*
V M R H BELLAMY

KING'S WALDEN (St Mary) and Offley w Lilley *St Alb 4*
P *Sir Thomas Pilkington Bt (2 turns), St Jo Coll Cam (1 turn), D K C Salusbury-Hughes Esq and Mrs P A L McGrath (2 turns)*   **P-in-c** T J BELL,   **NSM** A J T HINKSMAN

KING'S WORTHY (St Mary) (St Mary's Chapel) *Win 7*
P *Univ Coll Ox and Lord Northbrook (alt)*   **R** A W GORDON,
NSM E CHASE

KINGSBRIDGE (St Edmund the King and Martyr) and Dodbrooke *Ex 14*   **P** *Bp*   **P-in-c** A P R KYRIAKIDES-YELDHAM

KINGSBURY (Holy Innocents) *Lon 21*   **P** *D&C St Paul's*
V C F MORTON,   **NSM** A J HOPKINS

KINGSBURY (St Andrew) *Lon 21*   **P** *The Crown*   **V** J T SMITH

KINGSBURY (St Peter and St Paul) *Birm 10*   **P** *Bp*
P-in-c J E GASPER

KINGSBURY EPISCOPI (St Martin) w East Lambrook, Hambridge and Earnshill *B & W 15*   **P** *Bp (2 turns), D&C (1 turn)*   **V** A R ELWOOD

KINGSCLERE (St Mary) and Ashford Hill w Headley *Win 6*
P *Bp*   **V** L R THIRTLE

KINGSCLERE WOODLANDS (St Paul)   *see* Kingsclere and Ashford Hill w Headley *Win*

KINGSCOTE (St John the Baptist)   *see* Nailsworth w Shortwood, Horsley etc *Glouc*

KINGSDON (All Saints)   *see* Somerton w Compton Dundon, the Charltons etc *B & W*

KINGSDOWN (St Edmund the King and Martyr) *Roch 10*
P *D&C*   **R** J M B THURLOW

KINGSDOWN (St John the Evangelist)   *see* Ringwould w Kingsdown and Ripple etc *Cant*

KINGSEY (St Nicholas)   *see* Haddenham w Cuddington, Kingsey etc *Ox*

KINGSHURST (St Barnabas) *Birm 9*   **P** *Bp*   **V** F J JOHNSON

KINGSKERSWELL (St Mary) w Coffinswell *Ex 10*
P *V St Marychurch*   **V** J F LEONARD

KINGSLAND (St Michael and All Angels) w Eardisland, Aymestrey and Leinthall Earles *Heref 7*   **P** *DBP (2 turns), Ld Chan (1 turn)*   **R** N J TYSON

KINGSLEY (All Saints)   *see* Northanger *Win*

KINGSLEY (St John the Evangelist)   *see* Norley, Crowton and Kingsley *Ches*

KINGSLEY (St Werburgh) and Foxt-with-Whiston *Lich 6*
P *Mrs N A Faulkner*   **P-in-c** A M HINDLE

KINGSLEY MOOR (St John the Baptist)   *see* Kingsley and Foxt-w-Whiston *Lich*

KINGSNORTH (St Michael and All Angels) and Shadoxhurst *Cant 10*   **P** *Abp*   **P-in-c** S E MCLACHLAN,   **C** I R PARRISH

KINGSNYMPTON (St James)   *see* S Molton w Nymet St George, High Bray etc *Ex*

KINGSTAG (not known)   *see* Sturminster Newton, Hinton St Mary and Lydlinch *Sarum*

KINGSTANDING (St Luke) *Birm 3*   **P** *Bp*   **C** L A COX

KINGSTANDING (St Mark) *Birm 3*   **P** *Bp*   **P-in-c** P CALVERT, **NSM** P GILLON

KINGSTEIGNTON (St Michael) and Teyngrace *Ex 10*   **P** *Bp* **NSM** R W BAMBERG, S J GILL

KINGSTHORPE (St John the Baptist) w Northampton St David *Pet 4*   **P** *Patr Bd*   **TV** M A TAYLOR, E M REW

KINGSTON (All Saints and St Andrew)   *see* Papworth *Ely*

KINGSTON (St Giles)   *see* Barham w Bishopsbourne and Kingston *Cant*

KINGSTON (St James)   *see* Modbury, Bigbury, Ringmore w Kingston etc *Ex*

KINGSTON (St James)   *see* Shorwell w Kingston *Portsm*

KINGSTON (St James), Langton Matravers and Worth Matravers *Sarum 8*   **P** *Bp, D E Scott Esq, and R Swanage and Studland (jt)*   **P-in-c** J MALINS

KINGSTON (St Pancras)   *see* Iford w Kingston and Rodmell *Chich*

KINGSTON (St Winifred) and Ratcliffe-on-Soar *S'well 9* **P** *D&C*   **P-in-c** S W OSMAN

KINGSTON BAGPUIZE (St John the Baptist)   *see* Fyfield w Tubney and Kingston Bagpuize *Ox*

KINGSTON BUCI (St Julian) *Chich 4*   **P** *Lord Egremont* **P-in-c** M WICKENS

KINGSTON DEVERILL (St Mary)   *see* Cley Hill Villages *Sarum*

KINGSTON HILL (St Paul) *S'wark 15*   **P** *DBP* **V** S C COUPLAND,   **C** S I A LIYANAGE,   **NSM** F M M DE QUIDT

KINGSTON LACY (St Stephen)   *see* Bridge Par *Sarum*

KINGSTON LISLE (St John the Baptist)   *see* Ridgeway *Ox*

KINGSTON PARK (not known) *Newc 2*   **P** *Bp*   **V** R C MILLS

KINGSTON SEYMOUR (All Saints)   *see* Yatton Moor *B & W*

KINGSTON ST MARY (Blessed Virgin Mary) Broomfield and Cheddon Fitzpaine *B & W 18*   **P** *D&C Bris and Bp (alt)* **R** R J EDWARDS,   **NSM** A E FULTON

KINGSTON UPON HULL (Ascension)   *see* Derringham Bank *York*

KINGSTON UPON HULL (Most Holy and Undivided Trinity) *York 14*   **P** *H Trin Hull & Distr Ch Patr Soc Ltd* **V** J O FORRESTER,   **C** M E BALL

KINGSTON UPON HULL (St Aidan) Southcoates *York 14* **P** *Simeon's Trustees*   **V** M A FRYER,   **C** M G CADWALLADER

KINGSTON UPON HULL (St Alban) *York 14*   **P** *Abp* **V** D JAGO

KINGSTON UPON HULL (St Cuthbert)   *see* Hull St Cuth *York*

KINGSTON UPON HULL (St John the Baptist) *see* Newington w Dairycoates *York*

KINGSTON UPON HULL (St Martin)   *see* Hull St Martin w Transfiguration *York*

KINGSTON UPON HULL (St Mary) Sculcoates   *see* Hull St Mary Sculcoates *York*

KINGSTON UPON HULL (St Mary the Virgin) *York 14* **P** *Abp*   **P-in-c** M R B HILLS

KINGSTON UPON HULL (St Matthew w St Barnabas) *York 14*   **P** *V Hull H Trin*   **V** J A BAGSHAWE

KINGSTON UPON HULL (St Nicholas) *York 14*   **P** *Abp* **P-in-c** P COPLEY,   **C** T A COTSON

KINGSTON UPON HULL (St Paul)   *see* Sculcoates *York*

KINGSTON UPON HULL (St Stephen)   *as above*

KINGSTON UPON HULL (St Thomas)   *see* Derringham Bank *York*

KINGSTON UPON THAMES (All Saints) (St John the Evangelist) *S'wark 15*   **P** *Patr Bd*   **TR** J P WILKES, **TV** V A MAUNDER,   **NSM** S A CRAGG, R P RITCHIE

KINGSTON UPON THAMES (St Luke) *S'wark 15*   **P** *Bp* **V** M G HISLOP

KINGSTON VALE (St John the Baptist) *S'wark 15*   **P** *Bp* **P-in-c** A R BECK

KINGSTONE (St John and All Saints)   *see* Ilminster and Distr *B & W*

KINGSTONE (St John the Baptist)   *see* Uttoxeter Area *Lich*

KINGSTONE (St Michael and All Angels) w Clehonger, Eaton Bishop, Allensmore and Thruxton *Heref 1*   **P** *Bp (2 turns), Prime Min (1 turn)*   **P-in-c** C L DYSON, **NSM** E A HITCHINER

KINGSWEAR (St Thomas of Canterbury)   *see* Brixham w Churston Ferrers and Kingswear *Ex*

KINGSWINFORD (St Mary) *Worc 10*   **P** *Patr Bd* **TV** D J HOSKIN,   **P-in-c** G KENDALL

KINGSWOOD (Church of the Ascension) (Holy Trinity) *Bris 5* **P** *Patr Bd*   **TR** P G HUZZEY,   **TV** A J MASON, **NSM** T M TAYLOR, L W CARR

KINGSWOOD (St Andrew) *S'wark 26*   **P** *Bp and R&S Ch Trust (jt)*   **P-in-c** G A BARBER, **NSM** A G F BOWYER

KINGSWOOD (St Mary the Virgin)   *see* Charfield and Kingswood *Glouc*

KINGSWOOD, LOWER (Wisdom of God)   *see* Kingswood *S'wark*

KINGTON (St James)   *see* Inkberrow w Cookhill and Kington w Dormston *Worc*

KINGTON (St Mary) w Huntington, Old Radnor, Kinnerton and Titley *Heref 5*   **P** *Patr Bd*   **R** N WESTON, **NSM** P J BUCKINGHAM

KINGTON, WEST (St Mary the Virgin)   *see* By Brook *Bris*

KINGTON LANGLEY (St Peter)   *see* Draycot *Bris*

KINGTON MAGNA (All Saints)   *see* Stour Vale *Sarum*

KINGTON ST MICHAEL (St Michael) *Bris 4*   **P** *Patr Bd* **V** S J TYNDALL,   **TV** M J WATKINS,   **C** S J RUSHTON, **OLM** D J KILMISTER

KINGWESTON (All Saints)   *see* Wheathill Priory Gp *B & W*

KINLET (St John the Baptist)   *see* Cleobury Mortimer w Hopton Wafers etc *Heref*

KINNERLEY (St Mary) w Melverley and Knockin w Maesbrook *Lich 19*   **P** *W H C Montgomery Esq, Sir Brooke Boothby Bt, and Viscount Boyne (jt)*   **P-in-c** R C BOWERS, **OLM** P L WEST, D K GOUGH

KINNERSLEY (St James)   *see* Eardisley w Bollingham, Willersley, Brilley etc *Heref*

KINNERTON (St Mary the Virgin)   *see* Kington w Huntington, Old Radnor, Kinnerton etc *Heref*

KINNERTON, HIGHER (All Saints)   *see* Dodleston *Ches*

KINNINVIE (Mission Room)   *see* Barnard Castle w Whorlton *Dur*

KINOULTON (St Luke)   *see* Hickling w Kinoulton and Broughton Sulney *S'well*

KINSBOURNE GREEN (St Mary)   *see* Harpenden St Nic *St Alb*

KINSHAM (All Saints)   *see* Presteigne w Discoed, Kinsham, Lingen and Knill *Heref*

KINSLEY (Resurrection) w Wragby *Wakef 10*   **P** *Bp and Lord St Oswald (jt)*   **V** J HADJIOANNOU,   **NSM** R H BAILEY, S HULME

KINSON (St Andrew) (St Philip) and West Howe *Sarum 7* **P** *Patr Bd*   **TR** R G SAUNDERS,   **TV** P J NESBITT, **NSM** D ROBERTS

KINTBURY (St Mary the Virgin) w Avington *Ox 14*   **P** *DBP (2 turns), Bp (1 turn)*   **P-in-c** J F RAMSBOTTOM, **NSM** C PYNN

KINVER (St Peter) and Enville *Lich 24*   **P** *Bp, Mrs A D Williams, and DBP (jt)*   **R** D J BLACKBURN,   **Hon C** M MORRIS

KINWARTON (St Mary the Virgin) w Great Alne and Haselor *Cov 7*   **P** *Bp*   **P-in-c** D C CAPRON

KIPPAX (St Mary the Virgin) w Allerton Bywater *Ripon 8*   **P** *Bp* **TR** W P B CARLIN,   **TV** J SYKES,   **C** A L RHODES

KIPPINGTON (St Mary) *Roch 9*   **P** *DBP*   **V** D B KITLEY, **NSM** L LEITHEAD

KIRBY, WEST (St Andrew) *Ches 8*   **P** *D&C*   **V** D M DIXON

KIRBY, WEST (St Bridget) *Ches 8*   **P** *D&C*   **R** R D CLARKE, **C** C P UPTON,   **NSM** D K CHESTER

KIRBY, WEST (St Michael and All Angels)   *see* Newton *Ches*

KIRBY BEDON (St Andrew)   *see* Rockland St Mary w Hellington, Bramerton etc *Nor*

KIRBY BELLARS (St Peter)   *see* Upper Wreake *Leic*

KIRBY CANE (All Saints)   *see* Gillingham w Geldeston, Stockton, Ellingham etc *Nor*

KIRBY GRINDALYTHE (St Andrew)   *see* Weaverthorpe w Helperthorpe, Luttons Ambo etc *York*

KIRBY KNOWLE (St Wilfrid) *York 19*   **P** *Abp* **V** I D HOUGHTON

KIRBY-LE-SOKEN (St Michael) w Great Holland *Chelmsf 22* **P** *Bp and CPAS (jt)*   **R** P L COLEY

KIRBY MISPERTON (St Laurence) w Normanby, Edston and Salton *York 20*   **P** *Lady Clarissa Collin, Abp, and St Jo Coll Cam (by turn)*   **R** J M E COOPER

KIRBY MUXLOE (St Bartholomew) *Leic 9*   **P** *Bp* **TR** T L RINGLAND,   **C** J WOOD

KIRBY-ON-THE-MOOR (All Saints), Cundall w Norton-le-Clay and Skelton-cum-Newby *Ripon 3*   **P** *Bp, Sir Arthur Collins, and R E J Compton Esq (jt)*   **V** J N O HORTON

KIRBY SIGSTON (St Lawrence)   *see* Northallerton w Kirby Sigston *York*

KIRBY UNDERDALE (All Saints)   *see* Garrowby Hill *York*

KIRBY WISKE (St John the Baptist)   *see* Lower Swale *Ripon*

KIRDFORD (St John the Baptist) *Chich 11*   **P** *Lord Egremont* **P-in-c** S MATTAPALLY

KIRK ARBORY (St Columba)   *see* Arbory *S & M*

KIRK BRAMWITH (St Mary)   *see* Fishlake w Sykehouse and Kirk Bramwith etc *Sheff*

KIRK DEIGHTON (All Saints) *see* Spofforth w Kirk Deighton *Ripon*

KIRK ELLA (St Andrew) and Willerby *York 14* **P** *Patr Bd* **TR** J S JUCKES, **TV** N J LITTLE, **C** S C F WILCOX

KIRK FENTON (St Mary) w Kirkby Wharfe and Ulleskelfe *York 1* **P** *Abp, J Fielden Esq, and T E Fielden Esq (jt)* **V** R A CLEGG

KIRK HALLAM (All Saints) *Derby 13* **P** *Bp* **P-in-c** D FERGUS

KIRK HAMMERTON (St John the Baptist) *see* Lower Nidderdale *Ripon*

KIRK IRETON (Holy Trinity) *see* Wirksworth *Derby*

KIRK LANGLEY (St Michael) *Derby 11* **P** *G Meynell Esq and J M Clark-Maxwell Esq (alt)* **P-in-c** S I MITCHELL

KIRK MAUGHOLD (St Maughold) *see* Maughold *S & M*

KIRK ONCHAN (St Peter) *see* Onchan *S & M*

KIRK PATRICK (Holy Trinity) *see* Patrick *S & M*

KIRK SANDALL and Edenthorpe (Good Shepherd) *Sheff 8* **P** *Ld Chan* **R** M E GREGORY

KIRK SANTON (St Sanctain) *see* Santan *S & M*

KIRK SMEATON (St Peter) *see* Went Valley *Wakef*

KIRKANDREWS ON EDEN (St Mary) *see* Barony of Burgh *Carl*

KIRKANDREWS ON ESK (St Andrew) *see* Arthuret w Kirkandrews-on-Esk and Nicholforest *Carl*

KIRKBAMPTON (St Peter) *see* Barony of Burgh *Carl*

KIRKBRIDE (St Bride) *see* Bowness-on-Solway, Kirkbride and Newton Arlosh *Carl*

KIRKBRIDE (St Bridget) *S & M 3* **P** *The Crown* **R** *vacant*

KIRKBURN (St Mary) *see* Woldsburn *York*

KIRKBURTON (All Hallows) *Wakef 6* **P** *Bp* **OLM** R A CHAMBERS

KIRKBY (St Andrew) *see* Kelsey Gp *Linc*

KIRKBY (St Chad) (St Mark) (St Martin) (St Andrew) *Liv 7* **P** *Patr Bd* **TR** T R STRATFORD, **TV** A J HEBER, J D FAGAN, **C** J DRUMMOND

KIRKBY, SOUTH (All Saints) *Wakef 10* **P** *Guild of All So* **V** T H KAYE

KIRKBY FLEETHAM (St Mary) *see* Lower Swale *Ripon*

KIRKBY GREEN (Holy Cross) *see* Digby Gp *Linc*

KIRKBY IN ASHFIELD (St Thomas) *S'well 4* **P** *Bp* **V** *vacant* (01623) 755131

KIRKBY IN ASHFIELD (St Wilfrid) *S'well 4* **P** *Bp* **P-in-c** G R PATCHELL, **NSM** A DEMPSTER

KIRKBY-IN-CLEVELAND (St Augustine) *see* Ingleby Greenhow, Bilsdale Priory etc *York*

KIRKBY-IN-MALHAMDALE (St Michael the Archangel) *Bradf 5* **P** *D&C* **P-in-c** H M BAKER

KIRKBY IRELETH (St Cuthbert) *Carl 9* **P** *D&C York* **P-in-c** M COWAN

KIRKBY KNOWLE (St Wilfrid) *see* Kirby Knowle *York*

KIRKBY LAYTHORPE (St Denys) *Linc 22* **P** *Bp and DBP (alt)* **R** *vacant* (01529) 304804

KIRKBY LONSDALE (St Mary the Virgin) Team Ministry *Carl 10* **P** *Patr Bd* **TR** R J SNOW, **TV** A WHITTAKER, **C** S H P THOMPSON, **NSM** P S ATKINSON, G BATES

KIRKBY MALHAM (St Michael the Archangel) *see* Kirkby-in-Malhamdale *Bradf*

KIRKBY MALLORY (All Saints) *see* Newbold de Verdun and Kirkby Mallory *Leic*

KIRKBY MALZEARD (St Andrew) *see* Fountains Gp *Ripon*

KIRKBY-ON-BAIN (St Mary) *see* Bain Valley Gp *Linc*

KIRKBY OVERBLOW (All Saints) *see* Lower Wharfedale *Ripon*

KIRKBY RAVENSWORTH (St Peter and St Felix) *see* Gilling and Kirkby Ravensworth *Ripon*

KIRKBY STEPHEN (not known) w Mallerstang and Crosby Garrett w Soulby *Carl 1* **P** *Bp, Earl of Lonsdale, and Lord Hothfield (jt)* **P-in-c** R A B HALL, **NSM** J WRIGHT, G D THOMPSON

KIRKBY THORE (St Michael) w Temple Sowerby and Newbiggin *Carl 1* **P** *Lord Hothfield (3 turns), Major and Mrs Sawrey-Cookson (1 turn)* **P-in-c** S MCMAHON

KIRKBY UNDERWOOD (St Mary and All Saints) *see* Ringstone in Aveland Gp *Linc*

KIRKBY WHARFE (St John the Baptist) *see* Kirk Fenton w Kirkby Wharfe and Ulleskelfe *York*

KIRKBY WOODHOUSE (St John the Evangelist) *S'well 4* **P** *Bp* **P-in-c** M R ESSEX

KIRKBYMOORSIDE (All Saints) w Gillamoor, Farndale and Bransdale *York 17* **P** *Countess Feversham* **V** J D PURDY

KIRKDALE (St Athanaseus with St Mary) *Liv 3* **P** *Simeon's Trustees* **V** *vacant* 0151-933 6860

KIRKDALE (St Gregory) w Harome, Nunnington and Pockley *York 17* **P** *Abp, Adn Cleveland, and Lady Clarissa Collin (2 turns), Ox Univ (1 turn)* **P-in-c** A C DE SMET

KIRKDALE (St Lawrence) *Liv 3* **P** *CPAS* **V** M GRIFFIN, **OLM** J D GARNER

KIRKDALE (St Paul) *see* Bootle *Liv*

KIRKHAM (St Michael) *Blackb 10* **P** *Ch Ch Ox* **V** *vacant* and fax (01772) 683644

KIRKHAUGH (Holy Paraclete) *see* Alston Moor *Newc*

KIRKHEATON (St Bartholomew) *see* Kirkwhelpington, Kirkharle, Kirkheaton and Cambo *Newc*

KIRKHEATON (St John the Baptist) *Wakef 1* **P** *Ch Trust Fund Trust* **R** R J STEEL, **OLM** B R SHORT

KIRKHOLT (St Thomas) *Man 21* **P** *Bp* **P-in-c** S D MORGAN, **NSM** C G GULLY

KIRKLAND (Mission Church) *see* Lamplugh w Ennerdale *Carl*

KIRKLAND (St Lawrence) *see* Cross Fell Gp *Carl*

KIRKLEATHAM (St Cuthbert) (St Hilda) *York 16* **P** *Abp* **V** M JACKSON

KIRKLEES VALLEY *Man 10* **P** *R Bury St Mary* **V** S MILLINGTON, **Hon C** P J BEDDINGTON

KIRKLEVINGTON (St Martin) w Picton, and High and Low Worsall *York 21* **P** *Abp (3 turns), V Northallerton w Kirby Sigston (1 turn)* **P-in-c** P J SANDERS

KIRKLEY (St Peter and St John) *Nor 9* **P** *Bp and DBP (jt)* **R** R H WORMALD

KIRKLINGTON (St Michael) w Burneston and Wath and Pickhill *Ripon 4* **P** *Ch Soc Trust, Mrs M St B Anderson, G W Prior-Wandesforde Esq, and DBP (jt)* **P-in-c** J NELSON, **C** L M SOUTHERN

KIRKLINGTON (St Swithin) w Hockerton *S'well 15* **P** *Bp* **V** *vacant*

KIRKLINTON (St Cuthbert) *see* Bewcastle, Stapleton and Kirklinton etc *Carl*

KIRKNEWTON (St Gregory) *see* Glendale Gp *Newc*

KIRKOSWALD (St Oswald), Renwick, Great Salkeld and Lazonby *Carl 4* **P** *Bp* **R** D M FOWLER

KIRKSTALL (St Stephen) *Ripon 7* **P** *Patrons Leeds St Pet* **P-in-c** R E HAYES, **NSM** B WOOD

KIRKSTEAD (St Leonard) *see* Woodhall Spa Gp *Linc*

KIRKTHORPE (St Peter) *see* Warmfield *Wakef*

KIRKWHELPINGTON (St Bartholomew) w Kirkharle, Kirkheaton and Cambo *Newc 11* **P** *Ld Chan (2 turns), J P P Anderson Esq (1 turn), and Bp (1 turn)* **P-in-c** D WINTER, **OLM** F H DOWER

KIRMINGTON (St Helen) *see* Brocklesby Park *Linc*

KIRMOND-LE-MIRE (St Martin) *see* Walesby *Linc*

KIRSTEAD (St Margaret) *see* Brooke, Kirstead, Mundham w Seething and Thwaite *Nor*

KIRTLING (All Saints) *Ely 4* **P** *Mrs D A Bowlby and Countess Ellesmere (alt)* **P-in-c** M A GURNER

KIRTLINGTON (St Mary the Virgin) *see* Akeman *Ox*

KIRTON (Holy Trinity) *S'well 3* **P** *SMF* **R** C C LEVY

KIRTON (St Mary and St Martin) *see* Nacton and Levington w Bucklesham etc *St E*

KIRTON HOLME (Christ Church) *see* Brothertoft Gp *Linc*

KIRTON IN HOLLAND (St Peter and St Paul) *Linc 21* **P** *Mercers' Co* **V** *vacant* (01205) 722380

KIRTON IN LINDSEY (St Andrew) w Manton *Linc 6* **P** *Bp* **P-in-c** C H LILLEY, **C** P L COSTIN, **OLM** J WILSON

KISLINGBURY (St Luke) and Harpole *Pet 3* **P** *Bp and Sir Philip Naylor-Leyland Bt (alt)* **P-in-c** S R J FRENCH

KITT GREEN (St Francis of Assisi) *see* Pemberton St Fran Kitt Green *Liv*

KITTISFORD (St Nicholas) *see* Wellington and Distr *B & W*

KLIVE (Blessed Virgin Mary) *see* Quantock Coast *B & W*

KNAITH (St Mary) *see* Lea Gp *Linc*

KNAPHILL (Holy Trinity) w Brookwood *Guildf 12* **P** *CPAS* **V** N D GREW, **NSM** B APPLETON

KNAPTON (St Peter) *see* Trunch *Nor*

KNAPWELL (All Saints) *see* Papworth *Ely*

KNARESBOROUGH (Holy Trinity) (St John the Baptist) *Ripon 1* **P** *Bp and Earl of Harewood (jt)* **TR** E J SEWELL, **C** D C HALL, **NSM** J R BULLAMORE

KNARESDALE (St Jude) *see* Alston Moor *Newc*

KNEBWORTH (St Martin) (St Mary the Virgin and St Thomas of Canterbury) *St Alb 23* **P** *Hon D A Fromanteel* **R** J T PYE

KNEESALL w Laxton and Wellow *S'well 3* **P** *DBP and Bp (jt)* **P-in-c** C C LEVY

KNEETON (St Helen) *see* E Bridgford and Kneeton *S'well*

KNIGHTLEY (Christ Church) *see* Adbaston, High Offley, Knightley, Norbury etc *Lich*

KNIGHTON (St Mary Magdalene) (St Guthlac) *Leic 1* **P** *Bp* **V** C D ALLEN, **C** C A M THOMAS, **NSM** R J BONNEY

KNIGHTON (Village Hall) *see* Ashley and Mucklestone *Lich*

KNIGHTON, WEST (St Peter) *see* Watercombe *Sarum*

KNIGHTON-ON-TEME (St Michael and All Angels) *see* Teme Valley N *Worc*

KNIGHTS AND HOSPITALLERS PARISHES, The *Chelmsf 19*   **P** *Hosp of St Jo of Jerusalem, Bp, and Earl of Verulam (jt)*   **V** J E DONALDSON

KNIGHT'S ENHAM (St Michael and All Angels) (St Paul's Church Centre) and Smannell w Enham Alamein *Win 3*   **P** *Patr Bd*   **TR** A W H ASHDOWN,   **TV** T G WHARTON

KNIGHTSBRIDGE (St Paul) Wilton Place   *see* Wilton Place St Paul *Lon*

KNILL (St Michael and All Angels)   *see* Presteigne w Discoed, Kinsham, Lingen and Knill *Heref*

KNIPTON (All Saints)   *see* High Framland Par *Leic*

KNOCKHOLT (St Katharine) w Halstead *Roch 9*   **P** *D&C*   **R** J P BENSON,   **NSM** H V THOMAS

KNOCKIN (St Mary)   *see* Kinnerley w Melverley and Knockin w Maesbrook *Lich*

KNODISHALL (St Lawrence)   *see* Whinlands *St E*

KNOOK (St Margaret)   *see* Upper Wylye Valley *Sarum*

KNOSSINGTON (St Peter)   *see* Whatborough Gp *Leic*

KNOTTINGLEY (St Botolph) and Kellington w Whitley *Wakef 10*   **P** *Patr Bd*   **TR** C A FLATTERS,   **TV** C D WHITE

KNOTTY ASH (St John) *Liv 2*   **P** *R W Derby*   **V** E R DORAN

KNOWBURY (St Paul)   *see* Ludlow *Heref*

KNOWL HILL (St Peter)   *see* Wargrave w Knowl Hill *Ox*

KNOWLE (Holy Nativity) *Bris 1*   **P** *Bp*   **V** J M BROWN

KNOWLE (Mission Room)   *see* Coreley and Doddington *Heref*

KNOWLE (St Barnabas)   *see* Filwood Park *Bris*

KNOWLE (St Boniface)   *see* Crediton, Shobrooke and Sandford etc *Ex*

KNOWLE (St John)   *see* E Budleigh w Bicton and Otterton *Ex*

KNOWLE (St John the Baptist) (St Lawrence and St Anne) *Birm 11*   **P** *Bp*   **V** M J PARKER,   **C** R J TRETHEWEY, R J HILL-BROWN

KNOWLE (St Martin) *Bris 1*   **P** *Bp*   **P-in-c** S A HAWKINS

KNOWLE, WEST (Holy Cross)   *see* Filwood Park *Bris*

KNOWSLEY (St Mary) *Liv 2*   **P** *Earl of Derby*   **V** C DOWDLE

KNOWSTONE (St Peter)   *see* Bishopsnympton, Rose Ash, Mariansleigh etc *Ex*

KNOYLE, EAST (St Mary the Virgin)   *see* St Bartholomew *Sarum*

KNOYLE, WEST (St Mary the Virgin)   *see* Mere w W Knoyle and Maiden Bradley *Sarum*

KNUTSFORD (St Cross) Cross Town *Ches 12*   **P** *Mrs J Singer*   **V** J E SHEPHERD

KNUTSFORD (St John the Baptist) and Toft *Ches 12*   **P** *Bp (3 turns), Mrs L M Anderson (1 turn)*   **V** N T ATKINSON, **C** M J LACY

KNUTTON (St Mary) *Lich 9*   **P** *Sir Beville Stanier Bt and T H G Howard-Sneyd Esq (alt)*   **V** W E J MASH

KNUZDEN (St Oswald) *Blackb 2*   **P** *Bp*   **V** M A MORRIS

KNYPERSLEY (St John the Evangelist) *Lich 8*   **P** *CPAS*   **V** J A DAWSWELL

KYME, NORTH (St Luke)   *see* Carr Dyke Gp *Linc*

KYME, SOUTH (St Mary and All Saints)   *see* Heckington Gp *Linc*

KYNNERSLEY (St Chad)   *see* Edgmond w Kynnersley and Preston Wealdmoors *Lich*

KYRE WYARD (St Mary)   *see* Teme Valley S *Worc*

LACEBY (St Margaret) and Ravendale Group, The *Linc 10*   **P** *D Parkinson Settled Estates, Ridley Hall Cam, and Earl of Yarborough (jt), Bp, and Ld Chan (by turn)*   **P-in-c** P M TOMPKINS

LACEY GREEN (Church Hall)   *see* Wilmslow *Ches*

LACEY GREEN (St John the Evangelist)   *see* Risborough *Ox*

LACH DENNIS (All Saints)   *see* Lostock Gralam *Ches*

LACHE (St Mark) cum Saltney *Ches 2*   **P** *Bp*   **V** T G N GREEN, **C** S CHESTERS,   **NSM** W A E STEADMAN

LACKFORD (St Lawrence)   *see* Lark Valley *St E*

LACOCK (St Cyriac)   *see* Gtr Corsham and Lacock *Bris*

LADBROKE (All Saints)   *see* Harbury and Ladbroke *Cov*

LADBROKE GROVE (St Michael and All Angels)   *see* Notting Hill St Mich and Ch Ch *Lon*

LADDINGFORD (St Mary)   *see* Yalding w Collier Street *Roch*

LADOCK (St Ladoca)   *see* Probus, Ladock and Grampound w Creed and St Erme *Truro*

LADY BAY (All Hallows) w Holme Pierrepont and Adbolton *S'well 9*   **P** *Bp and DBP (jt)*   **V** R W DRECKLES

LADYBARN (St Chad) *Man 8*   **P** *Bp*   **P-in-c** E J DAVIES

LADYBROOK (St Mary the Virgin) *S'well 2*   **P** *Bp*   **P-in-c** J M A ADAMS

LADYWOOD (St John the Evangelist) (St Peter) *Birm 2*   **P** *Trustees*   **V** *vacant* 0121-454 0973

LAFFORD, SOUTH *Linc 22*   **P** *G Heathcote Esq, Bp, J Wilson Esq, D&C, DBP, N Playne Esq, Sir Bruno Welby Bt, and Lady Willoughby de Eresby (by turn)*   **P-in-c** C P ROBERTSON

LAINDON (St Martin of Tours)   *see* Basildon St Martin *Chelmsf*

LAINDON (St Nicholas) w Dunton *Chelmsf 6*   **P** *Bp*   **R** D RICKETTS,   **NSM** H A BRYAN

LAIRA (St Augustine)   *see* Plymouth Em, St Paul Efford and St Aug *Ex*

LAIRA (St Mary the Virgin)   *see* Plymouth St Simon and St Mary *Ex*

LAISTERDYKE St Mary *Bradf 3*   **P** *Simeon's Trustees*   **C** J L TRENHOLME,   **NSM** M S BERNARD

LAITHKIRK (not known)   *see* Romaldkirk w Laithkirk *Ripon*

LAKE (Good Shepherd) *Portsm 7*   **P** *Bp*   **P-in-c** J H DAVIES

LAKENHAM (St Alban)   *see* Nor Lakenham St Alb and St Mark *Nor*

LAKENHAM (St John the Baptist and All Saints)   *see* Nor Lakenham St Jo and All SS and Tuckswood *Nor*

LAKENHAM (St Mark)   *see* Nor Lakenham St Alb and St Mark *Nor*

LAKENHEATH (St Mary)   *see* Brandon and Santon Downham w Elveden etc *St E*

LALEHAM (All Saints) *Lon 13*   **P** *Earl of Lucan*   **NSM** I C SMAILES

LAMARSH (Holy Innocents)   *see* N Hinckford *Chelmsf*

LAMBERHURST (St Mary) and Matfield *Roch 8*   **P** *D&C and V Brenchley (jt)*   **P-in-c** A H CARR,   **NSM** R J BISHOP

LAMBETH (St Andrew)   *see* Waterloo St Jo w St Andr *S'wark*

LAMBETH (St John the Evangelist)   *as above*

LAMBETH, NORTH (St Anselm) (St Mary's Mission) (St Peter) *S'wark 11*   **P** *The Crown (1 turn), Patr Bd (2 turns)*   **TR** A R AAGAARD,   **TV** A M KENNEDY,   **C** D J H LONGE, J E SPECK,   **NSM** M A K HILBORN

LAMBETH, SOUTH (St Anne and All Saints) *S'wark 11*   **P** *Abp and Bp*   **V** A B NEWBY,   **OLM** O O OGBEDE

LAMBETH, SOUTH (St Stephen) *S'wark 11*   **P** *CPAS*   **V** W A WILSON

LAMBFOLD Benefice, The *Pet 5*   **P** *Bp, Hertf Coll Ox, Sons of Clergy Corp, and S R de C Grant-Rennick Esq (alt)*   **R** J T P HALL,   **NSM** C J M OLEY

LAMBLEY (Holy Trinity) *S'well 10*   **P** *Revd W J Gull*   **P-in-c** K A PAYNE,   **NSM** A G MILBANK

LAMBLEY (St Mary and St Patrick)   *see* Alston Moor *Newc*

LAMBOURN (St Michael and All Angels) *Ox 14*   **P** *Bp*   **P-in-c** A W CUMBERLIDGE

LAMBOURNE (St Mary and All Saints) w Abridge and Stapleford Abbotts *Chelmsf 24*   **P** *CCC Cam and Ld Chan (alt)*   **P-in-c** G W ELLIS

LAMBROOK, EAST (St James)   *see* Kingsbury Episcopi w E Lambrook, Hambridge etc *B & W*

LAMERTON (St Peter)   *see* Milton Abbot, Dunterton, Lamerton etc *Ex*

LAMESLEY (St Andrew)   *see* Harlow Green and Lamesley *Dur*

LAMMAS (St Andrew)   *see* Bure Valley *Nor*

LAMORBEY (Holy Redeemer) *Roch 17*   **P** *Bp*   **V** N I KERR

LAMORBEY (Holy Trinity) *Roch 17*   **P** *Mrs H K L Whittow*   **V** G W DAVIES

LAMORRAN (St Moran)   *see* Tresillian and Lamorran w Merther *Truro*

LAMP *Ox 27*   **P** *CPAS*   **R** R A CADDELL,   **OLM** H J LOWNDES

LAMPLUGH (St Michael) w Ennerdale *Carl 5*   **P** *Trustees*   **NSM** J H MARSHALL

LAMPORT (All Saints)   *see* Maidwell w Draughton, Lamport w Faxton *Pet*

LAMYATT (St Mary and St John)   *see* Bruton and Distr *B & W*

LANCASTER (Christ Church) (Christ Church Worship Centre) *Blackb 11*   **P** *V Lanc and Trustees (alt)*   **V** P S HUDD,   **NSM** B K HARDING

LANCASTER (St Chad)   *see* Skerton St Chad *Blackb*

LANCASTER (St Luke)   *see* Skerton St Luke *Blackb*

LANCASTER (St Mary) w St John and St Anne *Blackb 11*   **P** *Trustees*   **C** H MATTHEWS

LANCASTER (St Paul)   *see* Scotforth *Blackb*

LANCASTER (St Thomas) *Blackb 11*   **P** *CPAS*   **V** P G GUINNESS,   **C** V M L MUTHALALY

LANCHESTER (All Saints) *Dur 4*   **P** *Ld Chan*   **V** P WATERHOUSE,   **Hon C** S J BAMBER

LANCING (St James the Less) w Coombes *Chich 5*   **P** *Bp Lon*   **R** R G RUSSELL,   **C** D C BERESFORD

LANCING (St Michael and All Angels) *Chich 5*   **P** *Bp*   **V** B G CARTER

LANDBEACH (All Saints) *Ely 6*   **P** *CCC Cam*   **P-in-c** L E CLELAND

LANDCROSS (Holy Trinity)   *see* Bideford, Northam, Westward Ho!, Appledore etc *Ex*

LANDEWEDNACK (St Wynwallow)   *see* St Ruan w St Grade and Landewednack *Truro*

LANDFORD (St Andrew)   *see* Forest and Avon *Sarum*

LANDKEY (St Paul)   *see* Swimbridge w W Buckland and Landkey *Ex*

LANDRAKE (St Michael) w St Erney and Botus Fleming *Truro 11*   **P** *Bp and MMCET (jt)*   **V** M GRIFFITHS, **OLM** P C WILLIAMS

LANDSCOVE (St Matthew)   *see* Broadhempston, Woodland, Staverton etc *Ex*

LANDULPH (St Leonard and St Dilpe)   *see* St Dominic, Landulph and St Mellion w Pillaton *Truro*

LANDYWOOD (St Andrew)   *see* Gt Wyrley *Lich*

LANE END (Holy Trinity) w Cadmore End *Ox 29*   **P** *Bp* **V** R H JENNINGS

LANEAST (St Sidwell and St Gulvat)   *see* Altarnon w Bolventor, Laneast and St Clether *Truro*

LANEHAM (St Peter)   *see* Rampton w Laneham, Treswell, Cottam and Stokeham *S'well*

LANERCOST (St Mary Magdalene), Walton, Gilsland and Nether Denton *Carl 2*   **P** *Bp, Adn, and the Hon P C W Howard (jt)*   **R** C J MORRIS, **Hon C** P J SWIFT

LANESIDE (St Peter) *Blackb 1*   **P** *V Haslingden St Jas* **V** S C BROWN

LANGAR (St Andrew)   *see* Cropwell Bishop w Colston Bassett, Granby etc *S'well*

LANGCLIFFE (St John the Evangelist) w Stainforth and Horton-in-Ribblesdale *Bradf 5*   **P** *Bp, Adn Craven, W R G Bell Esq, N Caton Esq, and Churchwardens of Horton-in-Ribblesdale (jt)* **V** R G WOOD

LANGDALE (Holy Trinity) (Mission Chapel) *Carl 11* **P** *R Grasmere*   **P-in-c** G G WRIGLEY

LANGDALE END (St Peter)   *see* Upper Derwent *York*

LANGDON, EAST (St Augustine)   *see* St Margarets-at-Cliffe w Westcliffe etc *Cant*

LANGDON, WEST (St Mary the Virgin)   *as above*

LANGDON HILLS (St Mary and All Saints) *Chelmsf 6* **P** *D&C St Paul's*   **R** C E HOPKINSON,   **C** S R SPENCER, **NSM** T G A BROWN

LANGFORD (Blessed Virgin Mary)   *see* Churchill and Langford *B & W*

LANGFORD (St Andrew)   *see* Henlow and Langford *St Alb*

LANGFORD (St Bartholomew)   *see* Coddington and Winthorpe and Langford w Holme *S'well*

LANGFORD (St Giles)   *see* Heybridge w Langford *Chelmsf*

LANGFORD (St Matthew)   *see* Shill Valley and Broadshire *Ox*

LANGFORD, LITTLE (St Nicholas of Mira)   *see* Wylye and Till Valley *Sarum*

LANGFORD BUDVILLE (St Peter)   *see* Wellington and Distr *B & W*

LANGHAM (St George)   *see* Stour Vale *Sarum*

LANGHAM (St Mary the Virgin)   *see* Badwell and Walsham *St E*

LANGHAM (St Mary the Virgin) w Boxted *Chelmsf 17*   **P** *Bp and Duchy of Lanc (alt)*   **P-in-c** T M BULL

LANGHAM (St Peter and St Paul) *Pet 12*   **P** *Bp* **P-in-c** L T FRANCIS-DEHQANI

LANGHAM EPISCOPI (St Andrew and St Mary)   *see* Stiffkey and Bale *Nor*

LANGHAM PLACE (All Souls) *Lon 4*   **P** *The Crown* **R** H PALMER,   **C** R J SALISBURY, M J H MEYNELL, M N PRENTICE, R I TICE,   **Hon C** J R W STOTT

LANGHO BILLINGTON (St Leonard) *Blackb 7*   **P** *V Blackb* **P-in-c** D NOBLET

LANGLEY (All Saints and Martyrs) and Parkfield *Man 18* **P** *Patr Bd*   **TR** P H MILLER

LANGLEY (St Francis)   *see* Fawley *Win*

LANGLEY (St John)   *see* Oldbury, Langley and Londonderry *Birm*

LANGLEY (St John the Evangelist)   *see* Clavering and Langley w Arkesden etc *Chelmsf*

LANGLEY (St Mary)   *see* Otham w Langley *Cant*

LANGLEY (St Mary the Virgin)   *see* Wolverton w Norton Lindsey and Langley *Cov*

LANGLEY (St Michael)   *see* Loddon, Sisland, Chedgrave, Hardley and Langley *Nor*

LANGLEY BURRELL (St Peter)   *see* Chippenham St Paul w Hardenhuish etc *Bris*

LANGLEY GREEN (St Leonard)   *see* Ifield *Chich*

LANGLEY MARISH (St Mary the Virgin) *Ox 23*   **P** *Patr Bd* **TR** R J GRAYSON,   **TV** C R HARTLEY, B H RUSSELL

LANGLEY MARSH (St Luke Mission Church)   *see* Wiveliscombe w Chipstable, Huish Champflower etc *B & W*

LANGLEY MILL (St Andrew) *Derby 12*   **P** *V Heanor* **V** *vacant* (01773) 712441

LANGLEY PARK (All Saints) *Dur 1*   **P** *Prime Min* **V** M J PEERS

LANGLEY PARK (St Peter's Church Hall)   *see* Beckenham St Barn *Roch*

LANGLEY STREET (Mission Room)   *see* Derby St Barn *Derby*

LANGLEYBURY (St Paul) *St Alb 7*   **P** *D W A Loyd Esq* **P-in-c** Y R PENTELOW

LANGNEY (St Richard of Chichester) *Chich 16*   **P** *Bp* **V** D ASHTON

LANGOLD (St Luke)   *see* Carlton-in-Lindrick and Langold w Oldcotes *S'well*

LANGPORT Area Churches, The *B & W 6*   **P** *Patr Bd* **TR** H W ELLIS,   **TV** R J TWITTY,   **NSM** J M CUMMINGS

LANGRICK (St Margaret of Scotland)   *see* Brothertoft Gp *Linc*

LANGRIDGE (St Mary Magdalene)   *see* Bath Weston All SS w N Stoke and Langridge *B & W*

LANGRISH (St John the Evangelist) *Portsm 4*   **P** *Bp* **V** T E LOUDEN

LANGSTONE (St Nicholas)   *see* Havant *Portsm*

LANGTOFT (St Michael)   *see* Ness Gp *Linc*

LANGTOFT (St Peter) w Foxholes, Butterwick, Cottam and Thwing *York 10*   **P** *Abp and Keble Coll Ox (2 turns), Ld Chan (1 turn)*   **P-in-c** A LINDSAY,   **NSM** C A ACONLEY

LANGTON (St Andrew)   *see* W Buckrose *York*

LANGTON (St Margaret)   *see* Woodhall Spa Gp *Linc*

LANGTON (St Peter)   *as above*

LANGTON, GREAT (St Wilfrid)   *see* Lower Swale *Ripon*

LANGTON, GREAT (The Good Shepherd)   *as above*

LANGTON BY PARTNEY (St Peter and St Paul)   *see* Partney Gp *Linc*

LANGTON-BY-WRAGBY (St Giles)   *see* Wragby Gp *Linc*

LANGTON GREEN (All Saints) *Roch 12*   **P** *R Speldhurst* **V** M J GENTRY,   **NSM** S E FRANCIS

LANGTON HERRING (St Peter)   *see* Abbotsbury, Portesham and Langton Herring *Sarum*

LANGTON LONG (All Saints)   *see* Blandford Forum and Langton Long *Sarum*

LANGTON MATRAVERS (St George)   *see* Kingston, Langton Matravers and Worth Matravers *Sarum*

LANGTON ON SWALE (St Wilfrid)   *see* Lower Swale *Ripon*

LANGTREE *Ox 6*   **P** *Patr Bd*   **TR** K G DAVIES, **TV** N E MOSS,   **NSM** A M LINTON, P J R STEDDON, D J F ADDISON

LANGTREE (All Saints)   *see* Shebbear, Buckland Filleigh, Sheepwash etc *Ex*

LANGWATHBY (St Peter)   *see* Cross Fell Gp *Carl*

LANGWITH, UPPER (Holy Cross)   *see* E Scarsdale *Derby*

LANGWORTH (St Hugh)   *see* Barlings *Linc*

LANHYDROCK (St Hydrock)   *see* Bodmin w Lanhydrock and Lanivet *Truro*

LANIVET (St Ia)   *as above*

LANLIVERY (St Brevita) *Truro 10*   **P** *Bp (1 turn), Adn Bodmin (1 turn), and DBP (2 turns)*   **P-in-c** P J CONWAY, **C** S DENYER

LANNER (Christ Church)   *see* Redruth w Lanner and Treleigh *Truro*

LANREATH (St Marnarck), Pelynt and Bradoc *Truro 12* **P** *A D G Fortescue Esq, J B Kitson Esq, and H M Parker Esq (jt)*   **C** L J SMITH, S DENYER

LANSALLOS (St Ildierna) *Truro 12*   **P** *DBP and W Gundry-Mills Esq (alt)*   **R** *vacant* (01503) 272028

LANSDOWN (St Stephen)   *see* Charlcombe w Bath St Steph *B & W*

LANSDOWNE ROAD (St Mary the Virgin)   *see* Tottenham St Mary *Lon*

LANTEGLOS BY CAMELFORD (St Julitta) w Advent *Truro 10*   **P** *Duchy of Cornwall*   **P-in-c** M J W BENTON-EVANS, **Hon C** J S THOROLD,   **NSM** D A ROBERTS

LANTEGLOS BY FOWEY (St Wyllow) *Truro 12*   **P** *D&C* **P-in-c** L A H COURTNEY

LAPAL (St Peter)   *see* Halas *Worc*

LAPFORD (St Thomas of Canterbury)   *see* N Creedy *Ex*

LAPLEY (All Saints) w Wheaton Aston *Lich 2*   **P** *Keble Coll Ox* **V** G J THOMPSON,   **NSM** L BEECH,   **OLM** G P ELLIS

LAPWORTH (St Mary the Virgin) *Birm 6*   **P** *Mert Coll Ox* **R** *vacant* (01564) 782098

LARCHFIELD (St George)   *see* Boyne Hill *Ox*

LARK VALLEY Benefice, The *St E 13*   **P** *R W Gough Esq (1 turn), Bp (2 turns)*   **R** D P BURRELL

LARKFIELD (Holy Trinity) *Roch 7*   **P** *DBP*   **V** D J WALKER

LARLING (St Ethelbert)   *see* E w W Harling, Bridgham w Roudham, Larling etc *Nor*

LASBOROUGH (St Mary)   *see* Boxwell, Leighterton, Didmarton, Oldbury etc *Glouc*

LASHAM (St Mary)   *see* Bentworth, Lasham, Medstead and Shalden *Win*

LASHBROOK (Mission Room)   *see* Shiplake w Dunsden and Harpsden *Ox*

LASTINGTON (St Mary) w Appleton-le-Moors, Rosedale and Cropton *York 17*   **P** *Abp (2 turns), Ld Chan (1 turn)*   **V** A S FERGUSON

LATCHFORD (Christ Church) *Ches 4*   **P** *R Grappenhall*   **V** J L GOODE

LATCHFORD (St James) (St Hilda) *Ches 4*   **P** *R Grappenhall*   **V** J T MCNAUGHTAN-OWEN,   **C** J E HARRIES

LATCHINGDON (Christ Church)   *see* Creeksea w Althorne, Latchingdon and N Fambridge *Chelmsf*

LATHBURY (All Saints)   *see* Newport Pagnell w Lathbury and Moulsoe *Ox*

LATHOM PARK (St John)   *see* Ormskirk *Liv*

LATIMER (St Mary Magdalene)   *see* Chenies and Lt Chalfont, Latimer and Flaunden *Ox*

LATTON (St John the Baptist)   *see* Cricklade w Latton *Bris*

LAUGHTON (All Saints)   *see* Corringham and Blyton Gp *Linc*

LAUGHTON (All Saints) w Ripe and Chalvington *Chich 18*   **P** *Bp (2 turns), Hertf Coll Ox (1 turn)*   **R** D M FAREY

LAUGHTON (St Luke)   *see* Foxton w Gumley and Laughton *Leic*

LAUGHTON-EN-LE-MORTHEN (All Saints)   *see* Dinnington w Laughton and Throapham *Sheff*

LAUNCELLS (St Andrew and St Swithin)   *see* Stratton and Launcells *Truro*

LAUNCESTON (St Mary Magdalene) (St Thomas the Apostle) (St Stephen) *Truro 9*   **P** *Patr Bd*   **P-in-c** D A E MICHAELS,   **NSM** M C WILLIAMSON

LAUNTON (Assumption of the Blessed Virgin Mary)   *see* Bicester w Bucknell, Caversfield and Launton *Ox*

LAVANT (St Mary) (St Nicholas) *Chich 3*   **P** *Earl of March and Kinrara*   **R** D L PARKER

LAVENDER HILL (The Ascension) and Battersea St Philip w St Bartholomew *S'wark 14*   **P** *Bp and Keble Coll Ox (jt)*   **P-in-c** I C YOUNG

LAVENDON (St Michael) w Cold Brayfield, Clifton Reynes and Newton Blossomville *Ox 27*   **P** T V Sutthery Esq, The Revd S F Hamill-Stewart, Exors M E Farrer Esq, and Bp (jt)   **R** C E PUMFREY

LAVENHAM (St Peter and St Paul) w Preston *St E 10*   **P** *G&C Coll Cam, and Em Coll Cam (by turn)*   **R** *vacant* (01787) 247244

LAVENHAM (St Peter and St Paul)   *see* Lavenham w Preston *St E*

LAVER, HIGH (All Saints) w Magdalen Laver and Little Laver and Matching *Chelmsf 26*   **P** *Bp*   **P-in-c** C L LAWS

LAVER, LITTLE (St Mary the Virgin)   *see* High Laver w Magdalen Laver and Lt Laver etc *Chelmsf*

LAVERSTOCK (St Andrew)   *see* Salisbury St Martin and Laverstock *Sarum*

LAVERSTOKE (St Mary)   *see* Overton w Laverstoke and Freefolk *Win*

LAVERTON (Blessed Virgin Mary)   *see* Hardington Vale *B & W*

LAVINGTONS, Cheverells, and Easterton, The *Sarum 16*   **P** *Bp and Ch Ch Ox (jt)*   **R** J M CAMPBELL,   **NSM** P A STROWGER,   **OLM** A L COCKING

LAWFORD (St Mary) *Chelmsf 20*   **P** *St Jo Coll Cam*   **R** P C M PRESTNEY,   **NSM** P W MANN

LAWHITTON (St Michael)   *see* Lezant w Lawhitton and S Petherwin w Trewen *Truro*

LAWLEY (St John the Evangelist)   *see* Cen Telford *Lich*

LAWRENCE WESTON (St Peter) and Avonmouth *Bris 2*   **P** *Bp*   **P-in-c** J A LOW

LAWRES Group, The SOUTH *Linc 3*   **P** *D&C Linc, D&C Pet, and Mercers' Co (jt)*   **C** P G COLLINS,   **OLM** S K BRADLEY

LAWSHALL (All Saints)   *see* St Edm Way *St E*

LAWTON (All Saints)   *see* Church Lawton *Ches*

LAWTON MOOR (St Michael and All Angels) *Man 8*   **P** *Bp*   **P-in-c** K L JUSTICE,   **OLM** I V SMITH

LAXEY (Christ Church) *S & M 2*   **P** *Bp*   **OLM** J E GUILFORD

LAXFIELD (All Saints), Cratfield, Wilby and Brundish *St E 17*   **P** *Patr Bd*   **R** F O NEWTON,   **C** L DAWSON,   **NSM** R T ORAMS

LAXTON (All Saints)   *see* Bulwick, Blatherwycke w Harringworth and Laxton *Pet*

LAXTON (St Michael)   *see* Kneesall w Laxton and Wellow *S'well*

LAXTON (St Peter)   *see* Howden *York*

LAYER BRETON (St Mary the Virgin)   *see* Layer de la Haye and Layer Breton w Birch etc *Chelmsf*

LAYER DE LA HAYE (St John the Baptist) and Layer Breton w Birch and Layer Marney *Chelmsf 23*   **P** *Bp, Col J G Round, and N S Charrington Esq (by turn)*   **R** M H CLARKE

LAYER MARNEY (St Mary the Virgin)   *see* Layer de la Haye and Layer Breton w Birch etc *Chelmsf*

LAYHAM (St Andrew)   *see* Hadleigh, Layham and Shelley *St E*

LAYSTON   *see* Aspenden, Buntingford and Westmill *St Alb*

LAYTON (St Mark)   *see* Blackpool St Mark *Blackb*

LAYTON, EAST (Christ Church)   *see* Forcett and Aldbrough and Melsonby *Ripon*

LAZONBY (St Nicholas)   *see* Kirkoswald, Renwick, Gt Salkeld and Lazonby *Carl*

LEA Group, The (St Helen) *Linc 2*   **P** *Bp, DBP, and Exors Lt Col J E W G Sandars (jt)*   **R** P WAIN,   **NSM** L Y LUCAS

LEA (St Christopher) (St Barnabas) *Blackb 13*   **P** *Bp*   **NSM** W I WALTERS

LEA (St Giles)   *see* Garsdon, Lea and Cleverton and Charlton *Bris*

LEA, THE (St John the Baptist)   *see* Ariconium *Heref*

LEA AND HOLLOWAY (Christ Church)   *see* Tansley, Dethick, Lea and Holloway *Derby*

LEA CROSS (St Anne)   *see* Pontesbury I and II *Heref*

LEA HALL (St Richard) *Birm 9*   **P** *Bp*   **V** P M BRACHER,   **NSM** M S WALTON

LEA MARSTON (St John the Baptist)   *see* The Whitacres and Shustoke *Birm*

LEADEN RODING (St Michael)   *see* S Rodings *Chelmsf*

LEADENHAM (St Swithin) *Linc 23*   **P** *P R Reeve Esq*   **R** A J MEGAHEY

LEADGATE (St Ives)   *see* Dipton and Leadgate *Dur*

LEAFIELD (St Michael and All Angels)   *see* Forest Edge *Ox*

LEAGRAVE (St Luke) *St Alb 14*   **P** *Bp*   **V** S PURVIS,   **C** A E A BICKLEY,   **NSM** L A JONES

LEAHOLM (St James's Chapel)   *see* Middle Esk Moor *York*

LEAKE (St Mary) w Over and Nether Silton and Kepwick *York 19*   **P** *Abp*   **V** I D HOUGHTON

LEAKE, EAST (St Mary), WEST (St Helena), Stanford-on-Soar, Rempstone and Costock *S'well 9*   **P** *Bp, DBP, Lord Belper, and SS Coll Cam (jt)*   **R** G C HETHERINGTON

LEAKE, NEW (St Jude)   *see* Stickney Gp *Linc*

LEAKE, OLD (St Mary) w Wrangle *Linc 20*   **P** *Bp and DBP (alt)*   **P-in-c** F J M COTTON-BETTERIDGE

LEAM LANE (St Andrew) *Dur 12*   **P** *Bp*   **V** A RAINE

LEAM VALLEY *Cov 6*   **P** *Bp (2 turns), Mrs H M O Lodder (1 turn)*   **P-in-c** J CLOSE,   **NSM** M I SIMMONS

LEAMINGTON, SOUTH (St John the Baptist) *Cov 11*   **P** *Bp*   **V** D W LAWSON

LEAMINGTON HASTINGS (All Saints)   *see* Leam Valley *Cov*

LEAMINGTON PRIORS (All Saints) *Cov 11*   **P** *Bp*   **P-in-c** C H WILSON,   **C** M R PITTAM,   **NSM** A MORRIS

LEAMINGTON PRIORS (St Mary) *Cov 11*   **P** *Ch Patr Trust*   **V** M RODHAM,   **C** A M ATTWOOD, B J JACKSON

LEAMINGTON PRIORS (St Paul) *Cov 11*   **P** *Ch Patr Trust*   **V** J N JEE,   **C** M P J KING, E L WOOLF

LEAMINGTON SPA (Holy Trinity) and Old Milverton *Cov 11*   **P** *Bp and M Heber-Percy Esq (jt)*   **C** C GALE, C H WILSON, M R PITTAM,   **NSM** F A SMITH, A MORRIS

LEAMINGTON SPA (St Mark New Milverton)   *see* New Milverton *Cov*

LEAMORE (St Aidan)   *see* Blakenall Heath *Lich*

LEASINGHAM (St Andrew) *Linc 22*   **P** *DBP*   **R** *vacant* (01529) 309239

LEASOWE (St Chad) *Ches 7*   **P** *Bp*   **P-in-c** A P WATTS,   **NSM** L R BANNON

LEATHERHEAD (All Saints) (St Mary and St Nicholas) and Mickleham *Guildf 10*   **P** *Bp Guildf and DBP and Ch Roch (jt)*   **NSM** D A IRELAND, V M CRUDDAS, C M STEWART

LEATHLEY (St Oswald)   *see* Washburn and Mid-Wharfe *Bradf*

LEATON (Holy Trinity) and Albrighton w Battlefield *Lich 20*   **P** *Mrs J M Jagger*   **P-in-c** C H DEAKIN,   **Hon C** R M PARSONS

LEAVELAND (St Laurence)   *see* Selling w Throwley, Sheldwich w Badlesmere etc *Cant*

LEAVENHEATH (St Matthew)   *see* Stoke by Nayland w Leavenheath and Polstead *St E*

LEAVENING (not known)   *see* W Buckrose *York*

LEAVESDEN (All Saints) *St Alb 7*   **P** *Bp*   **P-in-c** C M DAVEY,   **C** M M DU SAIRE, C N DRURY

LECHLADE (St Lawrence)   *see* Fairford Deanery *Glouc*

LECK (St Peter)   *see* E Lonsdale *Blackb*

LECKFORD (St Nicholas)   *see* Stockbridge and Longstock and Leckford *Win*

LECKHAMPSTEAD (Assumption of the Blessed Virgin Mary)   *see* N Buckingham *Ox*

LECKHAMPSTEAD (St James)   *see* Brightwalton w Catmore, Leckhampstead etc *Ox*

LECKHAMPTON (St Christopher) *see* Leckhampton SS Phil and Jas w Cheltenham St Jas *Glouc*
LECKHAMPTON (St Peter) *Glouc 7* **P** *Bp*
P-in-c P WILKINSON, **C** A M DOWDESWELL
LECKHAMPTON (St Philip and St James) w Cheltenham (St James) *Glouc 7* **P** *Bp* **P-in-c** I P BUSSELL, **Hon C** O C BARRACLOUGH, **NSM** J D HYDE
LECONFIELD (St Catherine) *see* Lockington and Lund and Scorborough w Leconfield *York*
LEDBURY Team Ministry, The (St Michael and All Angels) (St Katherine's Chapel) *Heref 6* **P** *Patr Bd*
TR P DUNTHORNE, **TV** H J MAYELL, S STRUTT, **C** F M ILIFFE, **NSM** E C REED, E N SEABRIGHT, J G WATKINS, **OLM** J L SCHOLEFIELD
LEDGEMOOR (Mission Room) *see* Canon Pyon w King's Pyon, Birley and Wellington *Heref*
LEDSHAM (All Saints) w Fairburn *York 4* **P** *Lady Elizabeth Hastings Estate Charity* **V** *vacant* (01977) 556946
LEDSTON LUCK (Mission Church) *see* Ledsham w Fairburn *York*
LEE (Good Shepherd) (St Peter) *S'wark 4* **P** *R Lee St Marg* **V** R D BAINBRIDGE, **C** A E HOAD, **NSM** B M KINGSTON
LEE (St Augustine) Grove Park *S'wark 4* **P** *Bp* **V** G A BERRIMAN
LEE (St Margaret) *S'wark 4* **P** *Ld Chan* **R** D S GATLIFFE, **NSM** J K BURKITT-GRAY
LEE (St Matthew) *see* Ilfracombe, Lee, Woolacombe, Bittadon etc *Ex*
LEE (St Mildred) Burnt Ash Hill *S'wark 4* **P** *Bp* **V** R J SHIMWELL, **NSM** S E KNIGHT, M BARBER
LEE (St Oswald) *see* St Oswald in Lee w Bingfield *Newc*
LEE, THE (St John the Baptist) *Ox 28* **P** *Bp* **V** D J BURGESS, **NSM** I CORNISH
LEE BROCKHURST (St Peter) *Lich 22* **P** *Lord Barnard* **P-in-c** C S COOKE, **NSM** T D SMITH
LEE MOOR (Mission Church) *see* Bickleigh and Shaugh Prior *Ex*
LEE-ON-THE-SOLENT (St Faith) *Portsm 3* **P** *Bp* **V** P A SUTTON, **C** S A THREADGILL, **NSM** B T WILLIAMS, W J J MATTHEWS
LEEBOTWOOD (St Mary) *see* Dorrington w Leebotwood, Longnor, Stapleton etc *Heref*
LEEDS (All Hallows) *Ripon 7* **P** *Bp and DBP (jt)* **V** S SMITH, **Hon C** D H RANDOLPH-HORN
LEEDS (All Saints) w Osmondthorpe *Ripon 8* **P** *Bp* **V** A M GUBBINS
LEEDS (All Souls) *Ripon 7* **P** *V Leeds St Pet, Simeon's Trustees, and DBP (jt)* **P-in-c** A I G SNOWDEN
LEEDS Belle Isle (St John and St Barnabas) *Ripon 6* **P** *Bp* **V** I W RUTHERFORD, **NSM** D T HAYES
LEEDS (Emmanuel) *see* Leeds St Geo *Ripon*
LEEDS Gipton (Church of the Epiphany) *Ripon 5* **P** *Bp* **P-in-c** P J PAYTON
LEEDS Halton (St Wilfrid) *Ripon 8* **P** *Bp* **V** M D G HEATHER
LEEDS (Parish Church) *see* Leeds City *Ripon*
LEEDS Richmond Hill (St Saviour) *Ripon 5* **P** *Bp and Keble Coll Ox (jt)* **V** A L TAYLOR
LEEDS (St Aidan) *Ripon 5* **P** *V Leeds St Pet* **V** A L TAYLOR, **NSM** C T RAWLINS, D ZANKER
LEEDS (St Cyprian and St James) Harehills *Ripon 5* **P** *Bp* **NSM** I WILLIAMS
LEEDS (St Edmund King and Martyr) *see* Roundhay St Edm *Ripon*
LEEDS (St George) *Ripon 7* **P** *Simeon's Trustees* **TR** J J CLARK, **TV** J A M BARNETT, **C** J R PEARSON
LEEDS (St John the Evangelist) *see* Roundhay St Jo *Ripon*
LEEDS (St Nicholas) *see* Hollingbourne and Hucking w Leeds and Broomfield *Cant*
LEEDS (St Paul) *see* Ireland Wood *Ripon*
LEEDS (St Wilfrid) *Ripon 5* **P** *Bp* **V** J HILTON
LEEDS CITY, The (St Peter) (Holy Trinity) *Ripon 5* **P** *DBP* **TR** A F BUNDOCK, **TV** J M YATES, **C** R I M COUTTS, **NSM** S J ROBINSON
LEEDSTOWN (St James's Mission Church) *see* Crowan and Treslothan *Truro*
LEEK (All Saints) (St Edward the Confessor) (St John the Evangelist) (St Luke) (St Paul) and Meerbrook *Lich 8* **P** *Patr Bd* **TR** M J PARKER, **TV** C R PETERS, R A WOODS, **C** L J DUCKERS
LEEK WOOTTON (All Saints) *Cov 4* **P** *Lord Leigh* **V** *vacant* (01926) 854832
LEEMING (St John the Baptist) *see* Bedale and Leeming and Thornton Watlass *Ripon*
LEEMING BAR (St Augustine) *as above*
LEES HILL (Mission Hall) *see* Lanercost, Walton, Gilsland and Nether Denton *Carl*

LEESFIELD Knoll's Lane (St Agnes) *see* Leesfield *Man*
LEESFIELD (St Thomas) *Man 19* **P** *Bp* **V** V T LEONARD, **NSM** D E LUKE, **OLM** R FARRAR
LEFTWICH (Farm of the Good Shepherd) *see* Davenham *Ches*
LEGBOURNE (All Saints) and Wold Marsh *Linc 12* **P** *Ld Chan (1 turn), Bp, Viscountess Chaplin, Ch Trust Fund Trust, D&C, and DBP (1 turn), Duchy of Lanc (1 turn)* **C** L E TURNER
LEGBURTHWAITE (Mission Church) *see* St John's-in-the-Vale, Threlkeld and Wythburn *Carl*
LEGH, HIGH (St John) *see* Over Tabley and High Legh *Ches*
LEGSBY (St Thomas) *Linc 5* **P** *Bp* **V** M J CARTWRIGHT
LEICESTER (All Saints) *see* Scraptoft *Leic*
LEICESTER (Church of the Nativity) *see* Emmaus Par Team *Leic*
LEICESTER Cornerstone *see* Leic St Leon CD *Leic*
LEICESTER (Holy Apostles) (St Oswald) *Leic 1* **P** *DBP and Ridley Hall Cam (jt)* **P-in-c** P R BERRY
LEICESTER (Holy Spirit) (St Andrew) (St Nicholas) *Leic 1* **P** *Bp* **TV** E MATTHEWS-LOYDALL, **P-in-c** J B NAYLOR
LEICESTER (Holy Trinity w St John the Divine) *Leic 1* **P** *Peache Trustees* **V** J C MCGINLEY
LEICESTER (Martyrs) *Leic 1* **P** *Bp* **V** R V WORSFOLD, **C** M R CASTLE
LEICESTER Presentation of Christ (St Barnabas) (St Peter) *Leic 1* **P** *Bp* **TR** P J BRINDLE, **TV** D H P BROWN, **NSM** A D BREAR
LEICESTER Resurrection (St Alban) *Leic 1* **P** *Bp* **TR** A A COSLETT, **TV** S P J BURNHAM, **C** B J EVANS-HILLS, T R MARTIN
LEICESTER (St Aidan) *Leic 1* **P** *Bp* **V** S LUMBY
LEICESTER (St Alban) *see* Leic Resurr *Leic*
LEICESTER (St Anne) St Paul and St Augustine *Leic 1* **P** *Bp* **V** C R OXLEY, **NSM** P J OXLEY, C A LACEY
LEICESTER (St Chad) *Leic 1* **P** *Bp* **P-in-c** M J COURT, **C** C M KING
LEICESTER St Christopher *Leic 1* **P** *MMCET* **V** A M ROCHE, **C** R J LING
LEICESTER (St James the Greater) *Leic 1* **P** *Bp* **V** G RICHERBY, **NSM** J M SHARP
LEICESTER (St John the Baptist) *see* Emmaus Par Team *Leic*
LEICESTER St Leonard Conventional District *Leic 1* **P-in-c** G W DUNSETH
LEICESTER (St Mary de Castro) *Leic 1* **P** *Bp* **V** D L CAWLEY, **NSM** S P WARD
LEICESTER (St Philip) *Leic 1* **P** *Adn Leic, V Evington, V Leic H Trin, G A Cooling Esq, and A S Price Esq (jt)* **P-in-c** A RACE
LEICESTER (St Stephen) *see* N Evington *Leic*
LEICESTER (St Theodore of Canterbury) *Leic 1* **P** *Bp* **V** *vacant* 0116-266 9956
LEICESTER, The Abbey (St Margaret and All Saints) *Leic 1* **P** *Bp* **P-in-c** J B NAYLOR, **NSM** F M KNIGHT
LEICESTER FOREST EAST (St Andrew) *see* Kirby Muxloe *Leic*
LEIGH (All Saints) *see* Ashton Keynes, Leigh and Minety *Bris*
LEIGH (All Saints) *see* Uttoxeter Area *Lich*
LEIGH (All Saints' Mission) *see* Bedford Leigh *Man*
LEIGH (Holy Saviour) *see* White Horse *Sarum*
LEIGH or WIMBORNE (St John the Evangelist) *see* New Borough and Leigh *Sarum*
LEIGH (St Andrew) *see* Wriggle Valley *Sarum*
LEIGH (St Bartholomew) *S'wark 26* **P** *N J Charrington Esq* **P-in-c** J M A WILLANS, **NSM** F G LEHANEY
LEIGH (St Catherine) *see* Twigworth, Down Hatherley, Norton, The Leigh etc *Glouc*
LEIGH (St Clement) *Chelmsf 10* **P** *Bp* **R** K R HAVEY, **NSM** D J COSTER
LEIGH (St Edburga) *see* Worcs W *Worc*
LEIGH (St Mary) *Roch 11* **P** *Ch Trust Fund Trust* **P-in-c** L W G KEVIS
LEIGH (St Mary the Virgin) *Man 13* **P** *Bp* **P-in-c** K D CRINKS
LEIGH, LITTLE (St Michael and All Angels) *see* Antrobus, Aston by Sutton, Lt Leigh etc *Ches*
LEIGH, NORTH (St Mary) *Ox 8* **P** *Ld Chan* **V** A J SWEENEY, **C** M F KEEN
LEIGH, SOUTH (St James the Great) *see* Cogges and S Leigh *Ox*
LEIGH, WEST (St Alban) *Portsm 5* **P** *Bp* **V** P A SMITH, **NSM** G A STEADMAN
LEIGH-ON-SEA (St Aidan) the Fairway *Chelmsf 10* **P** *Bp* **V** T BARNES, **NSM** P FURBY
LEIGH-ON-SEA (St James) *Chelmsf 10* **P** *Bp* **V** W G BULLOCH

LEIGH-ON-SEA (St Margaret of Antioch) *Chelmsf 10*   **P** *Bp*
  V I G BOOTH
LEIGH PARK (St Francis) *Portsm 5*   **P** *Bp*   **V** J G P JEFFERY,
  C E R JESSIMAN, S J TANCOCK
LEIGH UPON MENDIP (St Giles) w Stoke St Michael
  B & W 4   **P** *DBP and V Doulting (jt)*   **V** P D WINKS
LEIGH WOODS (St Mary the Virgin)   *see* Abbots Leigh w
  Leigh Woods *Bris*
LEIGHLAND (St Giles)   *see* Old Cleeve, Leighland and
  Treborough *B & W*
LEIGHS, GREAT (St Mary the Virgin) and LITTLE (St John)
  and Little Waltham *Chelmsf 8*   **P** *Linc Coll Ox, Reformation*
  Ch Trust, and Ex Coll Ox (jt)   **R** S J HOLMES,   **C** D P RITCHIE
LEIGHTERTON (St Andrew)   *see* Boxwell, Leighterton,
  Didmarton, Oldbury etc *Glouc*
LEIGHTON (Holy Trinity)   *see* Trelystan *Heref*
LEIGHTON (St Mary)   *see* Wrockwardine Deanery *Lich*
LEIGHTON BROMSWOLD (St Mary) *Ely 10*   **P** *Bp*
  P-in-c J DUCK
LEIGHTON BUZZARD (All Saints)   *see* Ouzel Valley *St Alb*
LEIGHTON-CUM-MINSHULL VERNON (St Peter) *Ches 15*
  P *Bp*   **P-in-c** P F DE J GOGGIN
LEIGHTONSTONE, EAST *Ely 10*   **P** *Bp (2 turns), Peterho*
  Cam (1 turn)   **R** J P YOUNG,   **Hon C** M D KETTLE
LEINTHALL EARLES (St Andrew)   *see* Kingsland w
  Eardisland, Aymestrey etc *Heref*
LEINTHALL STARKES (St Mary Magdalene)   *see* Wigmore
  Abbey *Heref*
LEINTWARDINE (St Andrew) Adforton   *as above*
LEINTWARDINE (St Mary Magdalene)   *as above*
LEIRE (St Peter)   *see* Upper Soar *Leic*
LEISTON (St Margaret) *St E 19*   **P** *Ch Hosp*
  P-in-c M E PERCIVAL,   **OLM** R ELLIS
LELANT (St Uny)   *see* Carbis Bay w Lelant *Truro*
LEMINGTON, LOWER (St Leonard)   *see* Moreton-in-Marsh
  w Batsford, Todenham etc *Glouc*
LEMSFORD (St John the Evangelist)   *see* Bp's Hatfield,
  Lemsford and N Mymms *St Alb*
LEN VALLEY, The *Cant 14*   **P** *Abp, All So Coll Ox, Viscount*
  Chilston, and Lord Cornwallis (jt)   **P-in-c** R F VENN,
  NSM M N H BOND
LENBOROUGH *Ox 22*   **P** *Ch Ch Ox, Cam Univ, and*
  New Coll Ox (2 turns), Ld Chan (1 turn)
  P-in-c R M ROBERTS,   **OLM** J J SHIELDS
LENHAM (St Mary)   *see* Len Valley *Cant*
LENTON (Holy Trinity) (Priory Church of St Anthony) *S'well 14*
  P *CPAS*   **V** M L KIRKBRIDE,   **C** E W KAMUYU
LENTON (St Peter)   *see* N Beltisloe Gp *Linc*
LENTON ABBEY (St Barnabas) *S'well 14*   **P** *CPAS*
  NSM A J FULFORD
LENWADE (All Saints)   *see* Wensum Benefice *Nor*
LEOMINSTER (St Peter and St Paul) *Heref 7*   **P** *Patr Bd*
  TV C E MUNDELL, J T MIDDLEMISS, M J KNEEN,
  NSM J H THEAKER,   **OLM** P C REES, P SMITH, C P REES
LEONARD STANLEY (St Swithun)   *see* The Stanleys *Glouc*
LEPTON (St John) *Wakef 6*   **P** R *Kirkheaton*   **V** *vacant*
  (01484) 602172
LESBURY (St Mary) w Alnmouth *Newc 6*   **P** *Dioc Soc*
  V P J SUTCLIFFE
LESNEWTH (St Michael and All Angels)   *see* Boscastle w
  Davidstow *Truro*
LESSINGHAM (All Saints)   *see* Bacton, Happisburgh,
  Hempstead w Eccles etc *Nor*
LETCHWORTH (St Mary the Virgin) (St Michael) *St Alb 4*
  P *Guild of All So*   **R** P BENNETT
LETCHWORTH (St Paul) w Willian *St Alb 4*   **P** *Bp*
  NSM M P DACK, A J FERRIS
LETCOMBE BASSETT (St Michael and All Angels)
  see Ridgeway *Ox*
LETCOMBE REGIS (St Andrew)   *as above*
LETHERINGHAM (St Mary)   *see* Mid Loes *St E*
LETHERINGSETT (St Andrew)   *see* Blakeney w Cley,
  Wiveton, Glandford etc *Nor*
LETTON (St John the Baptist) w Staunton, Byford, Mansel
  Gamage and Monnington *Heref 5*   **P** *Sir John Cotterell Bt*
  (2 turns), Exors Mrs Dew (1 turn), Ch Ch Ox (3 turns), and
  DBP (1 turn)   **R** R D KING,   **C** L A MONEY
LETWELL (St Peter)   *see* Firbeck w Letwell *Sheff*
LEUSDON (St John the Baptist)   *see* Ashburton, Bickington,
  Buckland in the Moor etc *Ex*
LEVEDALE (Mission Church)   *see* Penkridge *Lich*
LEVEN (Holy Trinity)   *see* Brandesburton and Leven w Catwick
  York
LEVEN VALLEY *Carl 11*   **P** *Mrs C M Chaplin, V Colton, and*
  Bp (jt)   **P-in-c** P N CALVERT

LEVENS (St John the Evangelist) *Carl 10*   **P** *Trustees*
  P-in-c R J CROSSLEY,   **Hon C** J C HANCOCK
LEVENSHULME (St Andrew) (St Mark) (St Peter) *Man 3*
  P *Bp and Trustees (jt)*   **R** L S IRELAND,   **C** L A IRELAND,
  OLM F G KERR
LEVER, GREAT (St Michael w St Bartholomew)   *see* New Bury
  w Gt Lever *Man*
LEVER, LITTLE (St Matthew) *Man 12*   **P** *V Bolton-le-Moors*
  St Pet   **V** J WISEMAN,   **NSM** I C ANTHONY
LEVER BRIDGE (St Stephen and All Martyrs)   *see* Leverhulme
  Man
LEVERHULME *Man 16*   **P** *Prime Min*   **TR** G H YERBURY,
  TV S EDWARDS,   **NSM** A PIERCE
LEVERINGTON (St Leonard), Newton and Tydd St Giles *Ely 14*
  P *Bp*   **R** S K GARDNER,   **Hon C** J E PHILLIPS,
  NSM R D PARKINSON
LEVERSTOCK GREEN (Holy Trinity)   *see* Chambersbury
  St Alb
LEVERTON (St Helena)   *see* Freiston, Butterwick w
  Bennington, and Leverton *Linc*
LEVERTON, NORTH and SOUTH (St Martin) (All Saints)
  S'well 5   **P** *Bp*   **NSM** I CARTER, F E M FERRITER
LEVINGTON (St Peter)   *see* Nacton and Levington w
  Bucklesham etc *St E*
LEVISHAM (St John the Baptist)   *see* Pickering w Lockton and
  Levisham *York*
LEWANNICK (St Martin)   *see* North Hill and Lewannick *Truro*
LEWES (St Anne) *Chich 18*   **P** *Bp and SMF (jt), and Ld Chan*
  R P R C HAMILTON-MANON
LEWES (St John sub Castro) *Chich 18*   **P** *Bp*   **R** M J SULLY
LEWES (St John the Baptist)   *see* Southover *Chich*
LEWES (St Mary)   *see* Lewes St Anne *Chich*
LEWES (St Michael) (St Thomas at Cliffe) w All Saints *Chich 18*
  P *Bp and SMF (jt), and Ld Chan*   **NSM** P D YATES
LEWISHAM (St Mary) *S'wark 4*   **P** *Earl of Dartmouth*
  V P S ANDERSON
LEWISHAM (St Stephen) and St Mark *S'wark 4*   **P** *Keble Coll*
  Ox   **V** G KIRK,   **Hon C** F D GARDOM,   **NSM** P J HUDSON
LEWISHAM (St Swithun) Hither Green *S'wark 4*
  P *V Lewisham St Mary*   **P-in-c** J L KUSTNER
LEWKNOR (St Margaret)   *see* Thame *Ox*
LEWSEY (St Hugh)   *see* Luton Lewsey St Hugh *St Alb*
LEWTRENCHARD (St Peter)   *see* Lifton, Broadwoodwidger,
  Stowford etc *Ex*
LEXDEN (St Leonard) *Chelmsf 16*   **P** *Bp*   **R** S CARTER,
  NSM R J ALLEN
LEXHAM, EAST (St Andrew)   *see* Litcham w Kempston, E and
  W Lexham, Mileham etc *Nor*
LEXHAM, WEST (St Nicholas)   *as above*
LEYBOURNE (St Peter and St Paul) *Roch 7*
  P *Major Sir David Hawley Bt*   **P-in-c** M A J BUCHAN
LEYBURN (St Matthew) w Bellerby *Ripon 4*   **P** *Lord Bolton and*
  Mrs M E Scragg (alt)   **P-in-c** C R HUGGETT
LEYFIELDS (St Francis)   *see* Tamworth *Lich*
LEYLAND (St Ambrose) *Blackb 5*   **P** *V Leyland*
  P-in-c D J E CLARKE
LEYLAND (St Andrew) *Blackb 5*   **P** *CPAS*   **V** D R A GIBB,
  C M L SIMPSON
LEYLAND (St James) *Blackb 5*   **P** *Sir Henry Farington Bt*
  P-in-c I S MOSSLEY,   **NSM** M H PENMAN, P A BELSHAW
LEYLAND (St John) *Blackb 5*   **P** *V Leyland St Andr and*
  CPAS (jt)   **V** A MCHAFFIE,   **NSM** B J WILSON, N J PROCTER
LEYSTERS (St Andrew)   *see* Leominster *Heref*
LEYTON (All Saints) *Chelmsf 5*   **P** *V St Mary's Leyton*
  V M I HOLMDEN
LEYTON (Christ Church) *Chelmsf 5*   **P** *Ch Trust Fund Trust*
  V M E BURKILL
LEYTON (Emmanuel) *Chelmsf 5*   **P** *Bp*   **V** A ADEMOLA,
  NSM S M FERNANDES
LEYTON (St Catherine) (St Paul) *Chelmsf 5*
  P *V Leyton St Mary w St Edw*   **V** P A REILY,
  C P W BOWTELL
LEYTON (St Mary w St Edward) and St Luke *Chelmsf 5*
  P *Simeon's Trustees*   **V** T A DAVIS,   **NSM** S C MOORE
LEYTONSTONE (Holy Trinity) Harrow Green *Chelmsf 5*
  P *Bp*   **V** I HARKER
LEYTONSTONE (St Andrew) *Chelmsf 5*   **P** *Bp*
  P-in-c D J DALAIS
LEYTONSTONE (St John the Baptist) *Chelmsf 5*   **P** *Bp*
  V R J DRAPER,   **NSM** R A WHITE, K E ROBINSON
LEYTONSTONE (St Margaret w St Columba) *Chelmsf 5*
  P *Bp*   **V** R W C PAGE
LEZANT (St Briochus)   *see* Stoke Climsland *Truro*
LEZANT (St Briochus) w Lawhitton and South Petherwin w
  Trewen *Truro 9*   **P** *Bp and Ox Univ (jt)*   **C** G PENGELLY,
  C J D PROBERT,   **NSM** G DARBY

LEZAYRE (Holy Trinity) *S & M 3* **P** *The Crown*
P-in-c B G EVANS-SMITH
LEZAYRE (St Olave) Ramsey *S & M 3* **P** *The Crown and Bp*
(alt) **V** *vacant*
LICHBOROUGH (St Martin) *see* Lambfold *Pet*
LICHFIELD (Christ Church) *Lich 1* **P** *Bp*
P-in-c A A LAUCKNER
LICHFIELD (St Chad) *Lich 1* **P** *D&C* **R** R D BULL,
C R J FARMER, J K B FOWLER, **NSM** E A WALL,
OLM J HEELEY
LICHFIELD (St John's Hospital) Proprietary Chapel *Lich 1*
P *Bp* **Master** J R WILLIAMS
LICHFIELD (St Michael) (St Mary) and Wall St John *Lich 1*
P *D&C* **R** D K BEEDON, **C** D A DYSON, **NSM** J ANKETELL,
C J BAKER, D YOUNGS
LICKEY, THE (Holy Trinity) *Birm 4* **P** *V Bromsgrove*
V P D SWAN
LIDEN (St Timothy) *see* Swindon Dorcan *Bris*
LIDGET GREEN (St Wilfrid) *see* Bradf St Wilfrid w St
Columba *Bradf*
LIFTON (St Mary), Broadwoodwidger, Stowford, Lewtrenchard,
Thrushelton and Kelly w Bradstone *Ex 25* **P** *Bp,*
Mrs A M Baring-Gould Almond, W F Kelly Esq, and
J B Wollocombe Esq (jt) **V** A S PAGETT, **C** T C CURRY
LIGHTBOWNE (St Luke) *Man 5* **P** *D&C* **P-in-c** P A STAMP,
Hon C J G O'CONNOR
LIGHTCLIFFE (St Matthew) *Wakef 2* **P** *V Halifax* **V** *vacant*
(01422) 202424
LIGHTHORNE (St Laurence) *Cov 8* **P** *Lady Willoughby*
de Broke **R** G J BURRELL
LIGHTWATER (All Saints) *Guildf 6* **P** *Ld Chan and Bp (alt)*
V M D SHELDON, **OLM** R D BROWNING
LILBOURNE (All Saints) *see* Crick and Yelvertoft w Clay
Coton and Lilbourne *Pet*
LILLESHALL (St Michael and All Angels) and Muxton *Lich 16*
P *Bp* **V** M C JONES, **OLM** J EVANS
LILLEY (St Peter) *see* King's Walden and Offley w Lilley *St Alb*
LILLINGSTONE DAYRELL (St Nicholas) *see* N Buckingham
Ox
LILLINGSTONE LOVELL (Assumption of the Blessed Virgin
Mary) *as above*
LILLINGTON (St Martin) *see* Sherborne w Castleton,
Lillington and Longburton *Sarum*
LILLINGTON (St Mary Magdalene) *Cov 11* **P** *Bp*
P-in-c C GALE, **C** G R COLES
LILLIPUT (Holy Angels) *Sarum 7* **P** *Bp* **C** C M LANGFORD
LIMBER, GREAT (St Peter) *see* Brocklesby Park *Linc*
LIMEHOUSE (St Anne) (St Peter) *Lon 7* **P** *BNC Ox*
R G L WARREN, **C** M C C NODDER
LIMESIDE (St Chad) *see* Hollinwood and Limeside *Man*
LIMINGTON (The Blessed Virgin Mary) *see* Ilchester w
Northover, Limington, Yeovilton etc *B & W*
LIMPENHOE (St Botolph) *see* Freethorpe, Wickhampton,
Halvergate etc *Nor*
LIMPLEY STOKE (St Mary) *see* Freshford, Limpley Stoke and
Hinton Charterhouse *B & W*
LIMPSFIELD (St Peter) and Titsey *S'wark 25* **P** *Bp*
OLM R P RAINBIRD
LIMPSFIELD CHART (St Andrew) Conventional District
S'wark 25 vacant
LINBY (St Michael) w Papplewick *S'well 4*
P T W A Cundy Esq **R** K H TURNER
LINCH (St Luke) *see* Lynch w Iping Marsh and Milland *Chich*
LINCHMERE (St Peter) *see* Lynchmere and Camelsdale *Chich*
LINCOLN (All Saints) *Linc 15* **P** *Bp* **P-in-c** D EDGAR,
Hon C R G WILKINSON
LINCOLN Minster Group, The (St Mary Magdalene)
(St Michael on the Mount) (St Peter in Eastgate) *Linc 15*
P *Adn Linc, D&C, and Bp (by turn)*
P-in-c E M C BOWES-SMITH, **C** N E ALEXANDER
LINCOLN (St Botolph by Bargate) *Linc 15* **P** *Bp*
Hon C N BURGESS
LINCOLN (St Faith) (St Martin) (St Peter-at-Arches) *Linc 15*
P *Bp* **P-in-c** A M PAVEY, **Hon C** N BURGESS
LINCOLN (St George) Swallowbeck *Linc 15* **P** *Bp and*
V Skellingthorpe (jt) **V** I G SILK, **NSM** D L FREEMAN,
OLM S A BROWN
LINCOLN (St Giles) *Linc 15* **P** *Bp* **V** M J O'CONNELL
LINCOLN (St John the Baptist) (St John the Evangelist) *Linc 15*
P *Bp* **V** S A HOY, **NSM** M J S JACKSON
LINCOLN (St Mary-le-Wigford) (St Benedict) (St Mark)
Linc 15 **P** *Bp* **Hon C** N BURGESS
LINCOLN (St Nicholas) (St John) Newport *Linc 15* **P** *Bp and*
D&C (alt) **V** D W YABBACOME, **C** M M ROSE
LINCOLN (St Peter-at-Gowts) (St Andrew) *Linc 15* **P** *Bp*
Hon C N BURGESS

LINCOLN (St Swithin) *Linc 15* **P** *Bp* **P-in-c** D EDGAR,
Hon C N BURGESS
LINDAL IN MARTON (St Peter) *see* Pennington and Lindal w
Marton and Bardsea *Carl*
LINDALE (St Paul) *see* Cartmel Peninsula *Carl*
LINDFIELD (All Saints) *Chich 6* **P** *Ch Soc Trust*
V D J CLARKE, **C** P-J GUY, S P DEAN
LINDLEY (St Stephen) *Wakef 5* **P** *V Huddersfield*
V J F WHITE, **C** K NICHOLL
LINDOW (St John) *Ches 12* **P** *Bp* **V** S R GALES
LINDRIDGE (St Lawrence) *see* Teme Valley N *Worc*
LINDSELL (St Mary the Virgin) *see* Stebbing and Lindsell w Gt
and Lt Saling *Chelmsf*
LINDSEY (St Peter) *see* Bildeston w Wattisham and Lindsey,
Whatfield etc *St E*
LINFORD (St Francis) *see* E and W Tilbury and Linford
Chelmsf
LINFORD, GREAT (St Andrew) *see* Stantonbury and Willen
Ox
LINFORD, LITTLE (St Leonard) *see* Lamp *Ox*
LINGDALE (Mission Room) *see* Boosbeck and Lingdale *York*
LINGEN (St Michael and All Angels) *see* Presteigne w Discoed,
Kinsham, Lingen and Knill *Heref*
LINGFIELD (St Peter and St Paul) and Crowhurst *S'wark 25*
P *Bp* **V** S M GENDALL, **NSM** J A ATTWOOD
LINGWOOD (St Peter) *see* Burlingham St Edmund w
Lingwood, Strumpshaw etc *Nor*
LINKENHOLT (St Peter) *see* Hurstbourne Tarrant, Faccombe,
Vernham Dean etc *Win*
LINKINHORNE (St Mellor) *Truro 12* **P** *DBP*
P-in-c W R STUART-WHITE, **C** M E ELLIOTT
LINSLADE (St Barnabas) *see* Ouzel Valley *St Alb*
LINSLADE (St Mary) *as above*
LINSTEAD PARVA (St Margaret) *see* Blyth Valley *St E*
LINTHORPE (St Barnabas) *York 18* **P** *Abp* **V** E WILSON,
C N J BARR-HAMILTON, **NSM** R A MORRIS
LINTHWAITE (Christ Church) *see* Crosland Moor and
Linthwaite *Wakef*
LINTON (Christ Church) *see* Walton-on-Trent w Croxall,
Rosliston etc *Derby*
LINTON (St Aidan) *see* Ashington *Newc*
LINTON (St Mary) *Ely 5* **P** *Patr Bd* **TR** S M GRIFFITHS,
TV J M NORRIS, **NSM** G E C RIDGWELL, M L GORE
LINTON (St Mary the Virgin) *see* Ariconium *Heref*
LINTON (St Nicholas) *see* Coxheath, E Farleigh, Hunton,
Linton etc *Roch*
LINTON IN CRAVEN (St Michael) *Bradf 7* **P** *D&C*
R A J CHRICH, **C** F JENKINS, **NSM** K M HAMMOND
LINWOOD (St Cornelius) *Linc 5* **P** *MMCET*
R M J CARTWRIGHT
LIPHOOK (Church Centre) *see* Bramshott and Liphook
Portsm
LISCARD Resurrection (St Mary w St Columba) *Ches 7* **P** *Bp*
V A J MANNINGS
LISCARD (St Thomas) *Ches 7* **P** *Bp* **P-in-c** R T NELSON
LISKEARD (St Martin) and St Keyne *Truro 12* **P** *Simeon's*
Trustees **P-in-c** A R INGLEBY, **C** P P C SHARP, M A TUBBS
LISS (St Mary) (St Peter) (St Saviour) *Portsm 4* **P** *Bp*
R *vacant* (01730) 890085
LISSET (St James of Compostella) *see* Beeford w Frodingham
and Foston *York*
LISSINGTON (St John the Baptist) *see* Lissington *Linc*
LISSINGTON (St John the Baptist) *Linc 5* **P** *D&C York*
V M J CARTWRIGHT
LISTON (not known) *see* N Hinckford *Chelmsf*
LITCHAM (All Saints) w Kempston, East and West Lexham,
Mileham, Beeston-next-Mileham, Stanfield, Tittleshall and
Godwick *Nor 14* **P** *Bp, Earl of Leic, Ch Soc Tr, DBP,*
Mrs E M Olesen, and N W D Foster Esq (jt) **C** D W A RIDER
LITCHFIELD (St James the Less) *see* Whitchurch w Tufton
and Litchfield *Win*
LITHERLAND (St Andrew) *see* Bootle *Liv*
LITHERLAND (St John and St James) *see* Orrell Hey St Jo and
St Jas *Liv*
LITHERLAND (St Paul) Hatton Hill *Liv 1* **P** *Bp*
V J W WHITLEY
LITHERLAND (St Philip) *Liv 1* **P** *Trustees* **V** *vacant*
0151-928 3902
LITLINGTON (St Catherine) *see* Shingay Gp *Ely*
LITLINGTON (St Michael the Archangel) *see* Alfriston w
Lullington, Litlington and W Dean *Chich*
LITTLE *see also under substantive place name*
LITTLE BIRCH (St Mary) *see* Wormelow Hundred *Heref*
LITTLE COMMON *see* Bexhill St Mark *Chich*
LITTLE DART Team Ministry *see* Burrington, Chawleigh,
Cheldon, Chulmleigh etc *Ex*

LITTLEBOROUGH (Holy Trinity) *Man 21* **P** *TR Rochdale*
P-in-c J MCGRATH, **Dss** K J OLIVER
LITTLEBOURNE (St Vincent) and Ickham w Wickhambreaux
and Stodmarsh *Cant 1* **P** *Abp, D&C, Ch Trust Fund Trust, and*
Adn Cant (jt) **R** A J ALLAN
LITTLEBURY (Holy Trinity) *see* Saffron Walden w Wendens
Ambo, Littlebury etc *Chelmsf*
LITTLEBURY GREEN (St Peter) *as above*
LITTLEDEAN (St Ethelbert) *see* Cinderford St Steph w
Littledean *Glouc*
LITTLEHAM (St Margaret) w Exmouth *Ex 1* **P** *Patr Bd*
TR I C MORTER, **TV** I W MACKENZIE, **C** G A VYE
LITTLEHAM (St Swithin) *see* Bideford, Northam, Westward
Ho!, Appledore etc *Ex*
LITTLEHAMPTON (St James) (St Mary) and Wick *Chich 1*
P *Bp* **TR** R J CASWELL, **TV** J S A HUDSON, S R MERRIMAN,
NSM E A CARVER, P P SEDLMAYR
LITTLEHEMPSTON (St John the Baptist)
see Broadhempston, Woodland, Staverton etc *Ex*
LITTLEMOOR (St Francis of Assisi) *see* Preston w Sutton
Poyntz and Osmington w Poxwell *Sarum*
LITTLEMORE (St Mary the Virgin and St Nicholas) *Ox 4*
P *Or Coll Ox* **P-in-c** M C M ARMITSTEAD,
NSM J B MUDDIMAN, T J MORGAN, H-A M HARTLEY
LITTLEOVER (St Peter) *Derby 10* **P** *PCC* **V** J A SEARLE
LITTLEPORT (St George) *Ely 8* **P** *Bp* **V** R H MASKELL
LITTLETHORPE (St Michael and All Angels) *see* Ripon Cathl
Ripon
LITTLETON (St Catherine of Alexandria) *see* Downs Benefice
Win
LITTLETON (St Mary Magdalene) *see* Shepperton and
Littleton *Lon*
LITTLETON, HIGH (Holy Trinity) *see* Paulton w Farrington
Gurney and High Littleton *B & W*
LITTLETON, NORTH (St Nicholas) *see* Cleeve Prior and The
Littletons *Worc*
LITTLETON, SOUTH (St Michael the Archangel) *as above*
LITTLETON, WEST (St James) *see* Marshfield w Cold Ashton
and Tormarton etc *Bris*
LITTLETON DREW (All Saints) *see* By Brook *Bris*
LITTLETON-ON-SEVERN (St Mary of Malmesbury)
see Alveston and Littleton-on-Severn w Elberton *Bris*
LITTLEWICK (St John the Evangelist) *see* Burchetts Green *Ox*
LITTLEWICK (St Thomas) *see* Horsell *Guildf*
LITTLEWORTH (Holy Ascension) *see* Cherbury w Gainfield
Ox
LITTON (Christ Church) *see* Tideswell *Derby*
LITTON (St Mary the Virgin) *see* Chewton Mendip w Ston
Easton, Litton etc *B & W*
LITTON CHENEY (St Mary) *see* Bride Valley *Sarum*
LIVERMERE, GREAT (St Peter) *see* Blackbourne *St E*
LIVERPOOL (All Souls) Springwood *Liv 4* **P** *The Crown*
P-in-c A J COLMER
LIVERPOOL (Christ Church) Norris Green *Liv 8* **P** *Bp*
V H A EDWARDS
LIVERPOOL (Our Lady and St Nicholas) *Liv 3* **P** *Sir William*
Gladstone Bt **R** S D BROOKES, **C** R M MACKLEY
LIVERPOOL (St Anne) *see* Stanley w Stoneycroft St Paul *Liv*
LIVERPOOL (St Christopher) Norris Green *Liv 8* **P** *Bp*
V P H BURMAN
LIVERPOOL (St Luke in the City) (St Bride w St Saviour)
(St Michael in the City) (St Stephen w St Catherine) *Liv 6*
P *Patr Bd* **TV** M J FRY, **P-in-c** G C ELSMORE
LIVERPOOL (St Philip w St David) *Liv 3* **P** *Bp*
P-in-c A W PORTER
LIVERPOOL Stoneycroft (St Paul) *see* Stanley w Stoneycroft St
Paul *Liv*
LIVERSEDGE (Christ Church) w Hightown *Wakef 8* **P** *Bp and*
V Birstall (jt) **C** T J-L GUILLEMIN, S J PITCHER,
NSM S M HOLT, P J DAWSON, **OLM** J C LEE
LIVERTON (St Michael) *see* Easington w Liverton *York*
LIVERTON MINES (St Hilda) *as above*
LIVESEY (St Andrew) *Blackb 2* **P** *Trustees*
P-in-c J P MILTON-THOMPSON
LLANCILLO (St Peter) *see* Ewyas Harold w Dulas,
Kenderchurch etc *Heref*
LLANDINABO (St Junabius) *see* Wormelow Hundred *Heref*
LLANFAIR WATERDINE (St Mary) *see* Bucknell w Chapel
Lawn, Llanfair Waterdine etc *Heref*
LLANGARRON (St Deinst) *see* Goodrich, Marstow, Welsh
Bicknor, Llangarron etc *Heref*
LLANGROVE (Christ Church) *as above*
LLANGUA (St James) *see* Ewyas Harold w Dulas,
Kenderchurch etc *Heref*
LLANVEYNOE (St Beuno and St Peter) *see* Clodock and
Longtown w Craswall, Llanveynoe etc *Heref*

LLANWARNE (Christ Church) *see* Wormelow Hundred *Heref*
LLANYBLODWEL (St Michael), Llanymynech, Morton and
Trefonen *Lich 19* **P** *Ld Chan (1 turn), Bp and Earl of Powis*
(2 turns) **R** C W PENN
LLANYMYNECH (St Agatha) *see* Llanyblodwel,
Llanymynech, Morton and Trefonen *Lich*
LOBLEY HILL (All Saints) *see* Hillside *Dur*
LOCKERLEY (St John) and East Dean w East and West
Tytherley *Win 12* **P** *DBP (1 turn), H B G Dalgety Esq*
(2 turns) **V** J M PITKIN
LOCKING (St Augustine) *see* Hutton and Locking *B & W*
LOCKING CASTLE (no church) Conventional District
B & W 11 vacant (01934) 516565
LOCKINGE (All Saints) *see* Wantage Downs *Ox*
LOCKINGE, WEST (All Souls) *as above*
LOCKINGTON (St Mary) and Lund and Scorborough w
Leconfield *York 8* **P** *Abp* **R** vacant (01430) 810604
LOCKINGTON (St Nicholas) *see* Castle Donington and
Lockington cum Hemington *Leic*
LOCKLEAZE (St Mary Magdalene w St Francis) *see* Bris
Lockleaze St Mary Magd w St Fran *Bris*
LOCKS HEATH (St John the Baptist) *Portsm 2* **P** *Bp*
V C E SUGDEN
LOCKTON (St Giles) *see* Pickering w Lockton and Levisham
York
LODDINGTON (St Leonard) *see* Broughton w Loddington
and Cransley etc *Pet*
LODDINGTON (St Michael and All Angels) *Leic 2* **P** *Bp*
P-in-c T J BLEWETT
LODDISWELL (St Michael and All Angels) *see* Modbury,
Bigbury, Ringmore w Kingston etc *Ex*
LODDON (Holy Trinity), Sisland, Chedgrave, Hardley and
Langley *Nor 8* **P** *Bp, E G Gilbert Esq, Gt Hosp, and*
Sir Christopher Beauchamp Bt (jt) **V** N W R EVANS,
C J B WYER, **NSM** R M SEEL
LODDON REACH *Ox 15* **P** *Patr Bd* **TR** M C STANTON-
SARINGER, **TV** B L PEARSON, **NSM** C J LESLIE
LODE (St James) *see* Anglesey Gp *Ely*
LODERS (St Mary Magdalene) *see* Askerswell, Loders and
Powerstock *Sarum*
LODGE, THE (St John) *see* St Martins and Weston Rhyn *Lich*
LODGE MOOR (St Luke) *Sheff 4* **P** *CPAS* **V** J D STRIDE
LODSWORTH (St Peter) *see* Lurgashall, Lodsworth and
Selham *Chich*
LOFTHOUSE (Christ Church) *Ripon 8* **P** *DBP*
V V G UTTLEY
LOFTUS-IN-CLEVELAND (St Leonard) and Carlin How w
Skinningrove *York 16* **P** *Ld Chan (2 turns), Abp (1 turn)*
R A GAUNT
LOLWORTH (All Saints) *see* Fen Drayton w Conington and
Lolworth etc *Ely*
LONAN (All Saints) *S & M 2* **P** *The Crown*
OLM J E GUILFORD
LONDESBOROUGH (All Saints) *York 5*
P *Mrs P R Rowlands* **NSM** S D JONES
LONDON, LITTLE (St Stephen) *see* Bramley *Win*
LONDON CITY CHURCHES:
All Hallows Berkynchirche by-the-Tower w St Dunstan-in-the-
East *Lon 1* **P** *Abp* **V** B M D OLIVER, **C** J HOGAN,
Hon C G R DE MELLO, **NSM** J M ROSENTHAL
St Andrew-by-the-Wardrobe w St Ann, Blackfriars *Lon 1*
P *PCC and Mercers' Co (jt)* **R** A H F GRIFFIN,
Hon C E R NORMAN
St Bartholomew the Great, Smithfield *Lon 1* **P** *D&C Westmr*
R M R DUDLEY, **Hon C** D W HIZA, P M FREEMAN,
NSM C T OLADUJI
St Bartholomew the Less, Smithfield Gate *Lon 1*
P *St Bart's Hosp* **V** P J COWELL, **NSM** N J GOULDING,
B RHODES
St Botolph Aldgate w Holy Trinity Minories *Lon 1* **P** *Bp*
NSM J PEIRCE, M W SPEEKS
St Botolph without Bishopgate *Lon 1* **P** *D&C St Paul's*
P-in-c A W MCCORMACK, **Hon C** H J M TURNER
St Bride Fleet Street w Bridewell and Trinity Gough Square *Lon 1*
P *D&C Westmr* **R** D G MEARA, **NSM** G M PITCHER
St Clement Eastcheap w St Martin Orgar *Lon 1*
P *D&C St Paul's* **P-in-c** J P WARNER
St Edmund the King and St Mary Woolnoth w St Nicholas Acons,
All Hallows Lombard Street, St Benet Gracechurch, St Leonard
Eastcheap, St Dionis Backchurch and St Mary Woolchurch,
Haw *Lon 1* **P** *The Crown (3 turns), D&C Cant (1 turn), Bp*
(1 turn), and Abp (1 turn) **R** A S WALKER
St Giles Cripplegate w St Bartholomew Moor Lane and
St Alphage London Wall and St Luke Old Street w St Mary
Charterhouse and St Paul Clerkenwell *Lon 1*
P *D&C St Paul's* **R** K M RUMENS

St Helen, Bishopsgate w St Andrew Undershaft and
St Ethelburga, Bishopsgate and St Martin Outwich and
St Mary Axe *Lon 1*   P *Merchant Taylors' Co*   R W T TAYLOR,
C A JONES, L GATISS, M R O´DONOGHUE, C W D SKRINE,
M J FULLER, C D FISHLOCK, P W CLARKE, A P J TOWNER, A SACH,
D M LLOYD, T J NASH, A GLYN

St James Garlickhythe w St Michael Queenhithe and Holy
Trinity-the-Less *Lon 1*   P *D&C St Paul's*   R A H F GRIFFIN,
Hon C E R NORMAN

St Magnus the Martyr w St Margaret New Fish Street and
St Michael Crooked Lane *Lon 1*   P *DBP*   P-in-c J P WARNER

St Margaret Lothbury and St Stephen Coleman Street w
St Christopher-le-Stocks, St Bartholomew-by-the-Exchange,
St Olave Old Jewry, St Martin Pomeroy, St Mildred Poultry
and St Mary Colechurch *Lon 1*   P *Simeon's Trustees*
R W J H CROSSLEY

St Mary at Hill w St Andrew Hubbard, St George Botolph Lane
and St Botolph by Billingsgate *Lon 1*   P *Ball Coll Ox (2 turns),
PCC (1 turn), and Abp (1 turn)*   P-in-c F J L WINFIELD

St Mary le Bow w St Pancras Soper Lane, All Hallows Honey
Lane, All Hallows Bread Street, St John the Evangelist Watling
Street, St Augustine w St Faith under St Paul's and St Mildred
Bread Street w St Margaret Moyses *Lon 1*   P *Grocers' Co
(1 turn), Abp (2 turns)*   R G R BUSH

St Michael Cornhill w St Peter le Poer and St Benet Fink *Lon 1*
P *Drapers' Co*   P-in-c P J MULLEN

St Olave Hart Street w All Hallows Staining and St Catherine
Coleman *Lon 1*   P *Trustees*   R O C M ROSS, C M BLACKLEY

St Peter Cornhill *Lon 1*   P *City Corp*   R W T TAYLOR

St Sepulchre w Christ Church Greyfriars and St Leonard Foster
Lane *Lon 1*   P *St Jo Coll Ox*   P-in-c P J MULLEN

St Stephen Walbrook and St Swithun London Stone w St Benet
Sherehog and St Mary Bothaw w St Laurence Pountney *Lon 1*
P *Grocers' Co and Magd Coll Cam (alt)*   P-in-c P A DELANEY

St Vedast w St Michael-le-Querne, St Matthew Friday Street,
St Peter Cheap, St Alban Wood Street, St Olave Silver Street,
St Michael Wood Street, St Mary Staining, St Anne and
St Agnes and St John Zachary Gresham Street *Lon 1*
P *D&C St Paul's*   P-in-c A W MCCORMACK

LONDON COLNEY (St Peter) *St Alb 1*   P *Bp*   V L FAWNS

LONDON DOCKS (St Peter) w Wapping St John *Lon 7*   P *Bp*
R T E JONES

LONDON GUILD CHURCHES:

All Hallows London Wall *Lon 1*   P *Ld Chan*   V G B HEWITT,
NSM C J ROSE, M C DONEY

St Andrew Holborn *Lon 1*   P *Bp*   V L DENNEN,   C M F LLOYD

St Benet Paul's Wharf *Lon 1*   P *Bp*   V *vacant* (020) 7723 3104 *or*
7489 8754

St Botolph without Aldersgate *Lon 1*   P *Bp*
P-in-c S M C DOWDY,   C R A BRAY

St Dunstan in the West *Lon 1*   P *Abp*   V W D F GULLIFORD

St Katharine Cree *Lon 1*   P *Bp*   P-in-c O C M ROSS,
C M BLACKLEY

St Lawrence Jewry *Lon 1*   P *City Corp*   V D W PARROTT

St Margaret Pattens *Lon 1*   P *Ld Chan*   V *vacant*

St Martin Ludgate *Lon 1*   P *D&C St Paul's*   P-in-c S E GENT,
NSM A J SMITH

St Mary Abchurch *Lon 1*   P *CCC Cam*   P-in-c J P WARNER

St Mary Aldermary *Lon 1*   P *The Crown and Ld Chan (alt)*
P-in-c J R MOTHERSOLE

St Michael Paternoster Royal *Lon 1*   P *Bp*   Hon C K PETERS

LONDONDERRY (St Mark)   *see* Oldbury, Langley and
Londonderry *Birm*

LONDONTHORPE (St John the Baptist)   *see* Grantham,
Harrowby w Londonthorpe *Linc*

LONG ASHTON (All Saints) w Barrow Gurney and Flax
Bourton *B & W 13*   P *Bp and Lady Virginia Gibbs (jt)*
R A SARGENT,   NSM R Q GREATREX

LONG BENNINGTON (St Swithin)   *see* Saxonwell *Linc*

LONG BENTON (St Bartholomew) *Newc 3*   P *Ball Coll Ox*
V M P LEE,   NSM A B BEESTON

LONG BENTON (St Mary Magdalene) *Newc 3*   P *Ball Coll Ox*
V D M GRAY,   Hon C P A JONES

LONG BREDY (St Peter)   *see* Bride Valley *Sarum*

LONG BUCKBY (St Lawrence) w Watford *Pet 2*   P *Bp and
Ld Chan (alt)*   V C R EVANS,   C A J KNOWLES

LONG BURTON (St James)   *see* Sherborne w Castleton,
Lillington and Longburton *Sarum*

LONG CLAWSON (St Remigius)   *see* Vale of Belvoir Par *Leic*

LONG COMPTON (St Peter and St Paul)   *see* S Warks Seven
Gp *Cov*

LONG CRENDON (St Mary the Virgin) w Chearsley and Nether
Winchendon *Ox 21*   P *Bp and R V Spencer-Bernard Esq (jt)*
V J P B WYNBURNE

LONG DITTON (St Mary) *Guildf 8*   P *Bp S'wark*
R V E BURROWS

LONG EATON (St John) *Derby 13*   P *Bp*   P-in-c P T WALLER,
C K E HAMBLIN

LONG EATON (St Laurence) *Derby 13*   P *Bp*   V S D ELLIS

LONG HANBOROUGH (Christ Church)   *see* Hanborough
and Freeland *Ox*

LONG ITCHINGTON (Holy Trinity) and Marton *Cov 10*
P *Bp*   P-in-c J T H BRITTON,   C D R PATTERSON

LONG LANE (Christ Church)   *see* Boylestone, Church
Broughton, Dalbury, etc *Derby*

LONG LOAD (Christ Church)   *see* Langport Area *B & W*

LONG MARSTON (All Saints)   *see* Tring *St Alb*

LONG MARSTON (All Saints) *York 1*   P *Col E C York*
P-in-c P P ROBINSON,   NSM M R SHAW

LONG MARTON (St Margaret and St James)   *see* Heart of
Eden *Carl*

LONG MELFORD (Holy Trinity)   *see* Chadbrook *St E*

LONG MELFORD (St Catherine)   *as above*

LONG NEWNTON (Holy Trinity)   *see* Tetbury, Beverston and
Long Newnton *Glouc*

LONG PRESTON (St Mary the Virgin) w Tosside *Bradf 5*
P *D&C Ch Ch Ox and V Gisburn (alt)*   P-in-c M R RUSSELL-
SMITH,   NSM R E WILSON

LONG RISTON (St Margaret)   *see* Skirlaugh w Long Riston,
Rise and Swine *York*

LONG STANTON (All Saints) w St Michael *Ely 6*   P *Magd
Coll Cam and Bp (alt)*   P-in-c M E RABY

LONG STANTON (St Michael and All Angels)   *see* Wenlock
Heref

LONG SUTTON (All Saints)   *see* N Hants Downs *Win*

LONG SUTTON (Holy Trinity)   *see* Langport Area *B & W*

LONG SUTTON (St Mary)   *see* Sutton St Mary *Linc*

LONG WHATTON (All Saints)   *see* Kegworth, Hathern, Long
Whatton, Diseworth etc *Leic*

LONG WITTENHAM (St Mary the Virgin)   *see* Dorchester *Ox*

LONGBOROUGH (St James)   *see* Moreton-in-Marsh w
Batsford, Todenham etc *Glouc*

LONGBRIDGE (St John the Baptist) *Birm 4*   P *Bp*
V C J CORKE

LONGBRIDGE DEVERILL (St Peter and St Paul)   *see* Cley
Hill Villages *Sarum*

LONGCOT (St Mary the Virgin)   *see* Shrivenham and Ashbury
Ox

LONGDEN (St Ruthen) and Annscroft w Pulverbatch *Heref 13*
P *Bp and MMCET (jt)*   R M G WHITTOCK,
OLM O S DAWSON-CAMPBELL

LONGDON (St James) *Lich 1*   P *Bp*   P-in-c R D BULL,
C R J FARMER

LONGDON (St Mary), Castlemorton, Bushley, Queenhill w
Holdfast *Worc 5*   P *Bp, D&C Westmr, and Soc of the Faith (jt)*
V C A MOSS

LONGDON-UPON-TERN (St Bartholomew)
see Wrockwardine Deanery *Lich*

LONGFIELD (Mission Room) (St Mary Magdalene) *Roch 1*
P *Ld Chan*   R D G S JOHNSTON

LONGFLEET (St Mary) *Sarum 7*   P *MMCET*   V A N PERRY

LONGFORD (St Chad)   *see* Boylestone, Church Broughton,
Dalbury, etc *Derby*

LONGFORD (St Thomas) *Cov 2*   P *Bp*   V P S BURCH

LONGFRAMLINGTON (St Mary the Virgin) w Brinkburn
Newc 6   P *Bp*   P-in-c S J H WHITE

LONGHAM (St Andrew and St Peter)   *see* Gressenhall w
Longham w Wendling etc *Nor*

LONGHILL (St Margaret)   *see* Sutton St Mich *York*

LONGHIRST (St John the Evangelist)   *see* Bothal and
Pegswood w Longhirst *Newc*

LONGHOPE (All Saints)   *see* Huntley and Longhope,
Churcham and Bulley *Glouc*

LONGHORSLEY (St Helen) and Hebron *Newc 11*   P *Ld Chan*
P-in-c P S MCCONNELL,   OLM J M QUINBY

LONGHOUGHTON (St Peter and St Paul) (including Boulmer)
w Howick *Newc 6*   P *Duke of Northd and Bp (alt)*
V P J SUTCLIFFE

LONGLEVENS (Holy Trinity)   *see* Wotton St Mary *Glouc*

LONGNEWTON (St Mary)   *see* Preston-on-Tees and
Longnewton *Dur*

LONGNEY (St Lawrence)   *see* Hardwicke and Elmore w
Longney *Glouc*

LONGNOR (St Bartholomew), Quarnford and Sheen *Lich 5*
P *Bp, V Alstonfield, and DBP (jt)*   V *vacant* (01298) 83742

LONGNOR (St Mary)   *see* Dorrington w Leebotwood,
Longnor, Stapleton etc *Heref*

LONGPARISH (St Nicholas)   *see* Hurstbourne Priors,
Longparish etc *Win*

LONGRIDGE (St Lawrence) (St Paul) *Blackb 13*   P *Trustees*
P-in-c D L ANDERSON

LONGSDON (St Chad)   *see* Horton, Lonsdon and Rushton Spencer *Lich*
LONGSIGHT (St Anne)   *see* Royton St Anne *Man*
LONGSIGHT (St Luke) *Man 1*   **P** *D&C and Trustees (jt)*
  R P N CLARK
LONGSLEDDALE (St Mary)   *see* Beacon *Carl*
LONGSOLE (Mission Room)   *see* Barming *Roch*
LONGSTOCK (St Mary)   *see* Stockbridge and Longstock and Leckford *Win*
LONGSTONE, GREAT (St Giles)   *see* Ashford w Sheldon and Longstone *Derby*
LONGSTOWE (St Mary)   *see* Papworth *Ely*
LONGTHORPE (St Botolph) *Pet 11*   **P** *Sir Philip Naylor-Leyland Bt*   **P-in-c** W S CROFT
LONGTON (St Andrew) *Blackb 5*   **P** *A F Rawstorne Esq*
  V A PARKINSON
LONGTON (St James and St John) *Lich 12*   **P** *Bp*   **R** S F JONES
LONGTON (St Mark)   *see* Longton Hall *Lich*
LONGTON (St Mary and St Chad) *Lich 12*   **P** *Bp*
  V P LOCKETT
LONGTON, NEW (All Saints) *Blackb 5*   **P** *Bp*   **V** D M ROGERS
LONGTON HALL *Lich 12*   **P** *Prime Min*
  P-in-c P J MOCKFORD
LONGWELL GREEN (All Saints) *Bris 5*   **P** *Bp*
  V D J A ADAMS,   **NSM** K E JONES
LONGWOOD (St Mark) *Wakef 5*   **P** *V Huddersfield*
  V J A HUNT
LONGWORTH (St Mary)   *see* Cherbury w Gainfield *Ox*
LONSDALE, EAST *Blackb 14*   **P** *Patr Bd*   **V** R N HAMBLIN,
  Hon C R HANNAFORD
LOOE, WEST (St Nicholas)   *see* St Martin w Looe *Truro*
LOOSE (All Saints) *Cant 13*   **P** *Abp*   **C** S A PRICE,
  NSM C H THOM
LOPEN (All Saints)   *see* Merriott w Hinton, Dinnington and Lopen *B & W*
LOPHAM NORTH (St Nicholas)   *see* Upper Waveney *Nor*
LOPHAM SOUTH (St Andrew)   *as above*
LOPPINGTON (St Michael and All Angels) w Newtown *Lich 22*
  P *Bp and R Wem (jt)*   **P-in-c** P F BARNES,   **OLM** J A EVANS
LORD'S HILL *Win 13*   **P** *Bp*   **V** vacant (023) 8073 1182
LORTON (St Cuthbert) and Loweswater w Buttermere *Carl 6*
  P *Bp and Earl of Lonsdale (alt)*   **P-in-c** S MCMAHON
LOSCOE (St Luke) *Derby 12*   **P** *Bp*   **P-in-c** M G ALEXANDER
LOSTOCK (St Thomas and St John) *Man 11*   **P** *Bp and TR Deane St Mary the Virgin (jt)*   **P-in-c** V ASHWORTH,
  NSM T ASHWORTH
LOSTOCK GRALAM (St John the Evangelist) *Ches 6*
  P *V Witton*   **P-in-c** B E SHARP
LOSTOCK HALL (St James) and Farington Moss *Blackb 5*
  P *Bp and V Penwortham (jt)*   **NSM** D A BAINES
LOSTWITHIEL (St Bartholomew), St Winnow w St Nectan's Chapel, St Veep and Boconnoc *Truro 10*   **P** *D&C and A D G Fortescue Esq (jt)*   **P-in-c** P J CONWAY,   **C** S DENYER,
  Hon C F E STUBBINGS
LOTHERSDALE (Christ Church)   *see* Sutton w Cowling and Lothersdale *Bradf*
LOTHERTON (St James)   *see* Aberford w Micklefield *York*
LOTTISHAM (The Blessed Virgin Mary)   *see* Baltonsborough w Butleigh, W Bradley etc *B & W*
LOUDWATER (St Peter) *Ox 21*   **P** *MMCET*   **V** T G BUTLIN
LOUGHBOROUGH (All Saints)   *see* Thorpe Acre w Dishley *Leic*
LOUGHBOROUGH (All Saints) w Holy Trinity *Leic 6*   **P** *Bp and Em Coll Cam (jt)*   **R** R A ROSS,   **C** S R GAMBLE
LOUGHBOROUGH (Emmanuel) (St Mary in Charnwood)
  Leic 6   **P** *Patr Bd*   **TR** D M F NEWMAN,   **TV** S E FIELD,
  NSM H M NEWMAN
LOUGHBOROUGH (Good Shepherd) *Leic 6*   **P** *Bp*
  V E K WHITLEY,   **NSM** R J WHITLEY
LOUGHTON (All Saints)   *see* Watling Valley *Ox*
LOUGHTON (not known)   *see* Ditton Priors w Neenton, Burwarton etc *Heref*
LOUGHTON (St John the Baptist) (St Gabriel) (St Nicholas)
  Chelmsf 24   **P** *Patr Bd*   **TR** G R SMITH,   **NSM** P M TRAIN,
  G A ANDERSON
LOUGHTON (St Mary the Virgin) *Chelmsf 24*   **P** *Bp*
  R M C MACDONALD,   **NSM** H N J TAYLOR
LOUGHTON (St Michael and All Angels) *Chelmsf 24*   **P** *Bp*
  V N M COULTHARD
LOUND (St Anne)   *see* Babworth w Sutton-cum-Lound and Scofton etc *S'well*
LOUND (St John the Baptist)   *see* Somerleyton, Ashby, Fritton, Herringfleet etc *Nor*
LOUNDSLEY GREEN (Church of the Ascension) *Derby 5*
  P *Bp*   **P-in-c** F E WILLETT

LOUTH (Holy Trinity) (St James) (St Michael) *Linc 12*
  P *Patr Bd*   **TR** S D HOLDAWAY,   **TV** S J OLIVER, L E TURNER,
  C A B BARTON,   **OLM** R W MANSFIELD
LOVERSALL (St Katherine)   *see* Wadworth w Loversall *Sheff*
LOVINGTON (St Thomas à Becket)   *see* Six Pilgrims *B & W*
LOW *see also under substantive place name*
LOW FELL (St Helen)   *see* Gateshead St Helen *Dur*
LOW HAM (Chapel)   *see* Langport Area *B & W*
LOW HILL (Good Shepherd)   *see* Bushbury *Lich*
LOW MOOR (Holy Trinity)   *see* Oakenshaw, Wyke and Low Moor *Bradf*
LOW VALLEY (St Matthew)   *see* Darfield *Sheff*
LOWDHAM (St Mary the Virgin) w Caythorpe, and Gunthorpe
  S'well 10   **P** V C A TAINTON
LOWER *see also under substantive place name*
LOWER MANOR (St Andrew)   *see* Sheff Manor *Sheff*
LOWER MOOR (St Stephen and All Martyrs)   *see* Oldham St Steph and All Martyrs *Man*
LOWESBY (All Saints)   *see* Whatborough Gp *Leic*
LOWESTOFT (Christ Church) *Nor 9*   **P** *CPAS*   **V** M C PAYNE,
  C N G T JEFFERS
LOWESTOFT (Good Shepherd)   *see* Lowestoft St Marg *Nor*
LOWESTOFT (St Andrew) *Nor 9*   **P** *Ch Patr Tr*
  V M A MCCAGHREY
LOWESTOFT (St Margaret) *Nor 9*   **P** *Patr Bd*
  TR J B SIMPSON,   **NSM** G WILSON
LOWESWATER (St Bartholomew)   *see* Lorton and Loweswater w Buttermere *Carl*
LOWGATE (St Mary)   *see* Hexham *Newc*
LOWGATE (St Mary the Virgin)   *see* Kingston upon Hull St Mary *York*
LOWICK (St John the Baptist) and Kyloe w Ancroft *Newc 12*
  P *D&C Dur (2 turns), Bp (1 turn)*   **V** V T DICKINSON
LOWICK (St Luke)   *see* Egton-cum-Newland and Lowick and Colton *Carl*
LOWICK (St Peter)   *see* Brigstock w Stanion and Lowick and Sudborough *Pet*
LOWSONFORD (St Luke)   *see* Hatton w Haseley, Rowington w Lowsonford etc *Cov*
LOWTHER (St Michael) and Askham and Clifton and Brougham
  Carl 1   **P** *Earl of Lonsdale*   **P-in-c** S MCMAHON
LOWTHORPE (St Martin)   *see* The Beacon *York*
LOWTON (St Luke) *Liv 15*   **P** *Bp*   **P-in-c** M A READ
LOWTON (St Mary) *Liv 15*   **P** *Bp*   **P-in-c** W J STALKER
LOXBEARE (St Michael and All Angels)   *see* Washfield, Stoodleigh, Withleigh etc *Ex*
LOXHORE (St Michael and All Angels)   *see* Shirwell, Loxhore, Kentisbury, Arlington, etc *Ex*
LOXLEY (St Nicholas)   *see* Hampton Lucy w Charlecote and Loxley *Cov*
LOXTON (St Andrew)   *see* Crook Peak *B & W*
LOXWOOD (St John the Baptist)   *see* Alfold and Loxwood *Guildf*
LOZELLS (St Paul and St Silas) *Birm 3*   **P** *Aston Patr Trust*
  V J PRASADAM
LUBENHAM (All Saints)   *see* Market Harborough and The Transfiguration etc *Leic*
LUCCOMBE (The Blessed Virgin Mary)   *see* Porlock and Porlock Weir w Stoke Pero etc *B & W*
LUCKER (St Hilda)   *see* Belford and Lucker *Newc*
LUCKINGTON (St Mary)   *see* Sherston Magna, Easton Grey, Luckington etc *Bris*
LUDBOROUGH (St Mary)   *see* Fotherby *Linc*
LUDDENDEN (St Mary) w Luddenden Foot *Wakef 3*   **P** *Bp and V Halifax (alt)*   **V** vacant (01422) 882127
LUDDESDOWN (St Peter and St Paul)   *see* Cobham w Luddesdowne and Dode *Roch*
LUDDINGTON (All Saints)   *see* Stratford-upon-Avon, Luddington etc *Cov*
LUDDINGTON (St Margaret)   *see* Barnwell, Hemington, Luddington in the Brook etc *Pet*
LUDDINGTON (St Oswald)   *see* Crowle Gp *Linc*
LUDFORD (St Giles)   *see* Ludlow *Heref*
LUDFORD MAGNA (St Mary)   *see* Binbrook Gp *Linc*
LUDGERSHALL (St James)   *see* Tidworth, Ludgershall and Faberstown *Sarum*
LUDGERSHALL (St Mary the Virgin)   *see* Bernwode *Ox*
LUDGVAN (St Ludgvan and St Paul), Marazion, St Hilary and Perranuthnoe *Truro 5*   **P** *D&C, Lord St Levan, and H M Parker Esq (jt)*   **R** N G MARNS,   **Hon C** F R N MICHELL,
  NSM L E M HALL, E A WHYTE
LUDHAM (St Catherine), Potter Heigham, Hickling and Catfield *Nor 12*   **P** *Bp and G M H Mills Esq (jt)*
  V N H KHAMBATTA,   **OLM** D M NICHOLSON
LUDLOW Team Ministry, The (St John) (St Laurence) *Heref 12*
  P *Patr Bd*   **TR** B L CURNEW,   **TV** R A GREEN, M J STEWART,
  NSM S R JARVIS, J S BEESLEY

LUFFENHAM, NORTH (St John the Baptist)   *see* Edith
Weston w N Luffenham and Lyndon w Manton *Pet*

LUFFENHAM, SOUTH (St Mary the Virgin)   *see* Barrowden
and Wakerley w S Luffenham etc *Pet*

LUFTON (St Peter and St Paul)   *see* Odcombe, Brympton,
Lufton and Montacute *B & W*

**LUGWARDINE (St Peter) w Bartestree, Weston Beggard and
Dormington** *Heref 4*   **P** *D&C (3 turns), and A T Foley Esq
(1 turn)*   **V** D J BOWEN

LULLINGSTONE (St Botolph)   *see* Eynsford w Farningham
and Lullingstone *Roch*

LULLINGTON (All Saints)   *see* Beckington w Standerwick,
Berkley, Rodden etc *B & W*

LULLINGTON (All Saints)   *see* Seale and Lullington w Coton
in the Elms *Derby*

LULLINGTON (not known)   *see* Alfriston w Lullington,
Litlington and W Dean *Chich*

**LULWORTHS, (St Andrew) (Holy Trinity) Winfrith Newburgh
and Chaldon, The** *Sarum 8*   **P** *Bp (3 turns), Col Sir Joseph
Weld (1 turn)*   **P-in-c** D F B BALDWIN

LUMLEY (Christ Church) *Dur 11*   **P** *Bp*   **P-in-c** R A COLLINS

LUND (All Saints)   *see* Lockington and Lund and Scorborough
w Leconfield *York*

LUND (St John the Evangelist) *Blackb 10*   **P** *Ch Ch Ox*
V G D ALLEN

LUNDWOOD (St Mary Magdalene) *Wakef 7*   **P** *Bp*
P-in-c J C MCCASKILL

LUNDY ISLAND (St Helen) Extra-Parochial Place
Ex 15 vacant

LUPPITT (St Mary)   *see* Dunkeswell, Luppitt, Sheldon and
Upottery *Ex*

LUPSET (St George) *Wakef 11*   **P** *Bp*   **P-in-c** P M MAGUIRE,
C J M WARE, R J BAILES

LUPTON (All Saints)   *see* Kirkby Lonsdale *Carl*

LURGASHALL (St Laurence), Lodsworth and Selham *Chich 11*
P *Rathbone Trust Co and Cowdray Trust, and Lord Egremont
(alt)*   **P-in-c** D B WELSMAN,   **C** D H HUMPHREY

LUSBY (St Peter)   *see* Marden Hill Gp *Linc*

LUSTLEIGH (St John the Baptist)   *see* Moretonhampstead,
Manaton, N Bovey and Lustleigh *Ex*

LUTON (All Saints) (St Peter) *St Alb 14*   **P** *Bp*
V R C H FRANKLIN

LUTON (Christ Church) *Roch 5*   **P** R Chatham   **R** D J SUTTON

LUTON (Christ Church)   *see* Bushmead *St Alb*

LUTON (Holy Cross)   *see* Marsh Farm *St Alb*

LUTON Lewsey (St Hugh) *St Alb 14*   **P** *Bp*   **V** P J LAW,
C H D BARNES, D E POULTNEY,   **NSM** C A PULLINGER

LUTON Limbury (St Augustine of Canterbury) *St Alb 14*   **P** *Bp*
V G R CALVERT,   **NSM** A M NEWTON

LUTON (St Andrew) *St Alb 14*   **P** *Bp*   **V** G A FINLAYSON

LUTON (St Anne) (St Christopher) Round Green *St Alb 14*
P *Bp, V Luton St Mary, and Peache Trustees*   **V** P C BUDGELL,
NSM G V FINLAYSON

LUTON (St Francis) *St Alb 14*   **P** *Peache Trustees, Bp, and
V Luton (jt)*   **V** M C NEWBON,   **C** M SWIRES-HENNESSY

LUTON (St John)   *see* Teignmouth, Ideford w Luton, Ashcombe
etc *Ex*

LUTON (St Mary) *St Alb 14*   **P** *Peache Trustees*   **V** N P J BELL,
NSM C A MOSS

LUTON (St Matthew) High Town *St Alb 14*   **P** *Ch Patr Trust*
V M J PRITCHARD

LUTON (St Paul) *St Alb 14*   **P** *Peache Trustees*   **V** A SELLERS

LUTON (St Saviour) *St Alb 14*   **P** *Bp*   **V** D H GOODBURN,
NSM D C ANDERSON

LUTTERWORTH (St Mary) w Cotesbach and Bitteswell *Leic 7*
P *Prime Min (3 turns), Ld Chan (1 turn), and Ch Hosp (1 turn)*
R M H W COUSSENS,   **Hon C** A W JOHNSON

LUTTON (St Nicholas) w Gedney Drove End, Dawsmere *Linc 16*
P *The Crown, Ld Chan, and V Long Sutton (by turn)*   **V** *vacant*
(01406) 364199

LUTTON (St Peter)   *see* Barnwell, Hemington, Luddington in
the Brook etc *Pet*

LUTTONS AMBO (St Mary)   *see* Weaverthorpe w
Helperthorpe, Luttons Ambo etc *York*

LUXBOROUGH (Blessed Virgin Mary)   *see* Exton and
Winsford and Cutcombe w Luxborough *B & W*

LUXULYAN (St Cyrus and St Julietta) *Truro 1*   **P** *Bp (1 turn),
Adn Cornwall (1 turn), and DBP (2 turns)*
P-in-c F M BOWERS,   **C** S K TANSWELL

LYDBROOK (Holy Jesus)   *see* Drybrook, Lydbrook and
Ruardean *Glouc*

LYDBURY NORTH (St Michael and All Angels)   *see* Bishop's
Castle w Mainstone, Lydbury N etc *Heref*

LYDD (All Saints) *Cant 12*   **P** *Abp*   **P-in-c** S R WILLIAMS,
OLM L P M TERRY

LYDDEN (St Mary the Virgin)   *see* Temple Ewell w Lydden
Cant

**LYDDINGTON (All Saints) and Wanborough and Bishopstone w
Hinton Parva** *Bris 7*   **P** *Bp and Ld Chan (alt)*
V J R CARDWELL

**LYDDINGTON (St Andrew) w Stoke Dry and Seaton w
Caldecott and Glaston and Blisbrooke** *Pet 12*   **P** *Bp, Burghley
Ho Preservation Trust, R E M Elborne Esq, and Peterho
Cam (jt)*   **P-in-c** J E BAXTER

**LYDEARD ST LAWRENCE (St Lawrence) w Brompton Ralph,
Combe Florey, Ash Priors and Tolland** *B & W 19*   **P** *Ld Chan
(2 turns), W H J Hancock Esq (2 turns), and MMCET (1 turn)*
P-in-c M B ARMSTRONG,   **Hon C** A C ARMSTRONG

LYDFORD (St Petrock)   *see* Peter Tavy, Mary Tavy, Lydford and
Brent Tor *Ex*

LYDFORD ON FOSSE (St Peter)   *see* Wheathill Priory Gp
B & W

LYDGATE (St Anne)   *see* Saddleworth *Man*

LYDGATE (St Mary)   *see* Bansfield *St E*

LYDHAM (Holy Trinity)   *see* Wentnor w Ratlinghope,
Myndtown, Norbury etc *Heref*

LYDIARD MILLICENT (All Saints)   *see* W Swindon and the
Lydiards *Bris*

LYDIARD TREGOZE (St Mary)   *as above*

LYDIATE (St Thomas)   *see* Halsall, Lydiate and Downholland
Liv

LYDLINCH (St Thomas à Beckett)   *see* Sturminster Newton,
Hinton St Mary and Lydlinch *Sarum*

LYDNEY (St Mary the Virgin) *Glouc 2*   **P** *Ld Chan*
P-in-c P C YOUDE,   **C** J M PHILPOTT,   **NSM** P J COX

LYE, THE (Christchurch) and Stambermill *Worc 12*   **P** *Bp and
CPAS (alt)*   **P-in-c** S M FALSHAW,   **NSM** C A KENT

LYFORD (St Mary)   *see* Cherbury w Gainfield *Ox*

LYME REGIS (St Michael the Archangel)   *see* Golden Cap
Team *Sarum*

**LYMINGE (St Mary and St Ethelburga) w Paddlesworth and
Stanford w Postling and Radegund** *Cant 5*   **P** *Abp*
R P N ASHMAN,   **NSM** V M ASHMAN,   **OLM** S G DOUGAL

LYMINGTON (St Thomas the Apostle) (All Saints) *Win 11*
P *Bp*   **V** P B C SALISBURY,   **C** A SMITH

LYMINSTER (St Mary Magdalene) *Chich 1*   **P** *Eton Coll on
nomination of BNC Ox*   **P-in-c** D A BURT

LYMM (St Mary the Virgin) *Ches 4*   **P** *Bp*   **R** K MAUDSLEY

LYMPNE (St Stephen)   *see* Aldington w Bonnington and
Bilsington etc *Cant*

LYMPSHAM (St Christopher)   *see* Brent Knoll, E Brent and
Lympsham *B & W*

**LYMPSTONE (Nativity of the Blessed Virgin Mary) and
Woodbury w Exton** *Ex 1*   **P** *SMF and D&C (jt)*   **R** *vacant*
(01395) 273343

LYNCH (St Luke) w Iping Marsh and Milland *Chich 10*
P *Rathbone Trust Co, Cowdray Trust and Bp (jt)*
P-in-c J A L HULBERT

LYNCHMERE (St Peter) and Camelsdale *Chich 10*   **P** *Prime
Min*   **V** W J MUSSON

LYNCOMBE (St Bartholomew)   *see* Bath St Bart *B & W*

LYNDHURST (St Michael) and Emery Down and Minstead
Win 11   **P** *Bp and P J P Green Esq (jt)*   **V** J H BRUCE

LYNDON (St Martin)   *see* Edith Weston w N Luffenham and
Lyndon w Manton *Pet*

LYNEAL (St John the Evangelist)   *see* Petton w Cockshutt,
Welshampton and Lyneal etc *Lich*

LYNEHAM (St Michael) w Bradenstoke *Sarum 15*   **P** *Ld Chan*
P-in-c J M S HOLLAND

LYNEMOUTH (St Aidan)   *see* Cresswell and Lynemouth *Newc*

LYNESACK (St John the Evangelist) *Dur 7*   **P** *Bp*
P-in-c F J GRIEVE,   **C** E L JOHNSON

LYNG (St Bartholomew)   *see* Athelney *B & W*

**LYNG (St Margaret), Sparham, Elsing, Bylaugh, Bawdeswell and
Foxley** *Nor 22*   **P** *DBP, Sir Edward Evans-Lombe, and Bp
(by turn)*   **R** D N HEAD

LYNGFORD (St Peter)   *see* Taunton Lyngford *B & W*

LYNMOUTH (St John the Baptist)   *see* Combe Martin,
Berrynarbor, Lynton, Brendon etc *Ex*

LYNN, NORTH (St Edmund)   *see* King's Lynn St Marg w
St Nic *Nor*

LYNN, SOUTH (All Saints) *Nor 20*   **P** *Bp*   **R** P KINSEY,
OLM P J NORWOOD

LYNN, WEST (St Peter)   *see* Clenchwarton and W Lynn *Ely*

LYNSTED (St Peter and St Paul)   *see* Teynham w Lynsted and
Kingsdown *Cant*

LYNTON (St Mary the Virgin)   *see* Combe Martin, Berrynarbor,
Lynton, Brendon etc *Ex*

LYONS (St Michael and All Angels)   *see* Hetton-Lyons w
Eppleton *Dur*

LYONSDOWN (Holy Trinity) *St Alb 17* **P** *Ch Patr Trust*
V C W G DOBBIE

LYONSHALL (St Michael and All Angels) *see* Pembridge w
Moor Court, Shobdon, Staunton etc *Heref*

LYSTON (not known) *see* N Hinckford *Chelmsf*

LYTCHETT MATRAVERS (St Mary the Virgin) *Sarum 6*
P *DBP* **R** vacant (01929) 459200

LYTCHETT MINSTER (not known) *Sarum 7* **P** *Bp*
P-in-c J H T DE GARIS, **C** A KERR, **NSM** J A ALEXANDER,
OLM H D PAGE-CLARK

LYTHAM (St Cuthbert) *Blackb 10* **P** *DBP*
P-in-c A CLITHEROW

LYTHAM (St John the Divine) *Blackb 10* **P** *J C Hilton Esq*
P-in-c A CLITHEROW, **Hon C** J WIXON

LYTHAM ST ANNE (St Margaret of Antioch) *see* St Annes St
Marg *Blackb*

LYTHAM ST ANNE (St Thomas) *see* St Annes St Thos *Blackb*

LYTHAM ST ANNES (St Anne) *see* St Annes St Anne *Blackb*

LYTHAM ST ANNES (St Paul) *see* Fairhaven *Blackb*

LYTHE (St Oswald) *see* Hinderwell, Roxby and Staithes etc
York

MABE (St Laudus) *Truro 3* **P** *Bp* **P-in-c** J SAVAGE

MABLETHORPE (St Mary) w Trusthorpe *Linc 8* **P** *Bp Lon
(2 turns), Bp Linc (1 turn)* **P-in-c** A C V HARVEY,
C A P SMITH

MACCLESFIELD (Holy Trinity) *see* Hurdsfield *Ches*

MACCLESFIELD (St John the Evangelist) *Ches 13* **P** *Bp*
P-in-c I SPARKS

MACCLESFIELD (St Paul) *Ches 13* **P** *Bp* **V** J C TEAR

MACCLESFIELD Team Parish, The (All Saints)
(Christ Church) (St Michael and All Angels) (St Peter)
(St Barnabas) *Ches 13* **P** *Patr Bd* **TR** G C TURNER,
TV D L MOCK, **C** A D BULL, **NSM** P J ROBINSON,
D W L WIGHTMAN

MACKWORTH (All Saints) *Derby 11* **P** *J M Clark-
Maxwell Esq* **P-in-c** S I MITCHELL

MACKWORTH (St Francis) *Derby 9* **P** *Bp*
P-in-c J R PHILLIPS

MADEHURST (St Mary Magdalene) *see* Slindon, Eartham
and Madehurst *Chich*

MADELEY (All Saints) *Lich 9* **P** *J C Crewe Esq*
V B F WILSON, **C** M J MAXWELL

MADELEY (St Michael) *Heref 14* **P** *Patr Bd* **TR** H J MORRIS,
TV M W LEFROY, **C** D I MOULDEN, **NSM** R FREEMAN

MADINGLEY (St Mary Magdalene) *Ely 6* **P** *Bp* **V** vacant

**MADLEY (Nativity of the Blessed Virgin Mary) w Tyberton,
Peterchurch, Vowchurch and Turnastone** *Heref 1* **P** *Bp and
D&C (jt)* **R** S D LOCKETT, **NSM** B A CHILLINGTON,
J M DINNEN

MADRESFIELD (St Mary) *see* Powick and Guarlford and
Madresfield w Newland *Worc*

MADRON (St Maddern) *see* Gulval and Madron *Truro*

MAER (St Peter) *see* Chapel Chorlton, Maer and Whitmore
Lich

MAESBROOK (St John) *see* Kinnerley w Melverley and
Knockin w Maesbrook *Lich*

MAESBURY (St John the Baptist) *Lich 19* **P** *Bp*
P-in-c R H MARTIN

MAGDALEN LAVER (St Mary Magdalen) *see* High Laver w
Magdalen Laver and Lt Laver etc *Chelmsf*

MAGHULL (St Andrew) (St James) (St Peter) and Melling
Liv 11 **P** *Patr Bd* **TR** N A WELLS, **TV** M S FOLLIN, S JONES

MAIDA VALE (St Peter) *see* Paddington St Pet *Lon*

MAIDA VALE (St Saviour) *see* Paddington St Sav *Lon*

MAIDEN BRADLEY (All Saints) *see* Mere w W Knoyle and
Maiden Bradley *Sarum*

MAIDEN NEWTON (St Mary) *see* Melbury *Sarum*

MAIDENHEAD (All Saints) *see* Boyne Hill *Ox*

MAIDENHEAD (St Andrew and St Mary Magdalene) *Ox 13*
P *Peache Trustees* **V** W M C STILEMAN, **C** A P KEARNS,
S ALLBERRY, **Hon C** R P TAYLOR

MAIDENHEAD (St Luke) *Ox 13* **P** *Bp* **P-in-c** J R HOLROYD,
NSM T J ROBINSON

MAIDENHEAD (St Peter) *see* Furze Platt *Ox*

MAIDFORD (St Peter and St Paul) *see* Lambfold *Pet*

MAIDS MORETON (St Edmund) *see* N Buckingham *Ox*

MAIDSTONE (All Saints) (St Philip) w St Stephen Tovil *Cant 13*
P *Abp* **C** J C MORGAN-JONES, **NSM** P S DOE

MAIDSTONE Barming Heath (St Andrew) *see* Barming Heath
Cant

MAIDSTONE (St Faith) *Cant 13* **P** *Abp* **P-in-c** J CRAY

MAIDSTONE (St Luke the Evangelist) *Cant 13* **P** *Trustees*
V E D DELVE, **Hon C** B H FIELD, **OLM** R H WILLIAMSON

MAIDSTONE (St Martin) *Cant 13* **P** *Abp*
P-in-c J R WALKER, **C** C E JAMES, **NSM** J E GREEN

MAIDSTONE (St Michael and All Angels) *Cant 13* **P** *Abp*
V P J GIBBONS

MAIDSTONE (St Paul) *Cant 13* **P** *Abp* **P-in-c** A J HOUSTON,
NSM J E MAYHEW, E S LANDER

MAIDWELL (St Mary) w Draughton and Lamport w Faxton
Pet 2 **P** *Bp (3 turns), Sir Ian Isham Bt (1 turn)*
R M Y GARBUTT, **NSM** D SPENCELEY

MAINSTONE (St John the Baptist) *see* Bishop's Castle w
Mainstone, Lydbury N etc *Heref*

MAISEMORE (St Giles) *Glouc 4* **P** *Bp* **P-in-c** J G EVANS

MAKER (St Mary and St Julian) w Rame *Truro 11*
P *The Crown and Earl of Mount Edgcumbe (jt)* **R** R A DOYLE

MALBOROUGH (All Saints) *see* Salcombe and Malborough w
S Huish *Ex*

MALDEN (St James) *S'wark 15* **P** *Bp* **V** L M M FERNANDEZ-
VICENTE, **OLM** C PIGGOTT

MALDEN (St John) *S'wark 15* **P** *Mert Coll Ox* **V** K W SCOTT,
NSM M D BROOME

**MALDEN, NEW (Christ Church) (St John the Divine) and
Coombe** *S'wark 15* **P** *CPAS* **P-in-c** S J KUHRT,
C H M DURANT-STEVENSEN, **NSM** I R L PRIOR,
H M HANCOCK, C G LUCAS

MALDON (All Saints w St Peter) *Chelmsf 11* **P** *Bp*
V D J ATKINS, **NSM** R J R HUMPHRIES

MALDON (St Mary) w Mundon *Chelmsf 11* **P** *D&C Westmr*
R L P DARRANT

MALEW Ballasalla (St Mary the Virgin) *see* Malew *S & M*

MALEW (St Lupus) (St Mark) *S & M 1* **P** *The Crown*
V M F ROBERTS

MALIN BRIDGE (St Polycarp) *Sheff 4* **P** *Bp* **V** P J COGHLAN

MALINS LEE (St Leonard) *see* Cen Telford *Lich*

MALLERSTANG (St Mary) *see* Kirkby Stephen w
Mallerstang etc *Carl*

MALLING, EAST (St James), Wateringbury and Teston *Roch 7*
P *D&C and Peache Trustees (jt)* **V** J D BROWN,
NSM A M SEARLE

MALLING, SOUTH (St Michael) *Chich 18* **P** *MMCET*
P-in-c M P WOODSFORD

MALLING, WEST (St Mary) w Offham *Roch 7* **P** *Ld Chan
and DBP (alt)* **V** R B STEVENSON

**MALMESBURY (St Peter and St Paul) w Westport and
Brokenborough** *Bris 6* **P** *Ch Trust Fund Trust*
P-in-c N J ARCHER, **C** L BARNES, **Hon C** C E WINDLE,
NSM M J NOAH

MALPAS (St Andrew) *see* Truro St Paul and St Clem *Truro*

MALPAS (St Oswald) and Threapwood *Ches 5* **P** *DBF*
R T ETHERIDGE

MALTBY (St Bartholomew) (Ascension) (Venerable Bede)
Sheff 5 **P** *Bp* **TR** P J CRAIG-WILD, **TV** D E CRAIG-WILD

MALTON, NEW (St Michael) *York 6* **P** *Sir Philip Naylor-
Leyland Bt* **P-in-c** P H BOWES

MALTON, OLD (St Mary the Virgin) *York 6* **P** *Sir Philip
Naylor-Leyland Bt* **V** J C MANCHESTER

MALVERN (Holy Trinity) (St James) *Worc 2* **P** *Bp and D&C
Westmr (jt)* **V** W D NICHOL, **C** A D DUCKWORTH,
NSM R HERBERT, A C LANYON-HOGG

MALVERN (St Andrew) and Malvern Wells and Wyche *Worc 2*
P *Bp* **V** P W FINCH, **C** S MARTIN

MALVERN, GREAT (Christchurch) *Worc 2* **P** *Bp*
C C E GRIFFITHS

MALVERN, GREAT (St Mary and St Michael) *Worc 2* **P** *Bp*
V M J A BARR, **NSM** M E BARR

MALVERN, LITTLE (St Giles) *Worc 2* **P** *Exors
T M Berington Esq* **P-in-c** E G KNOWLES

MALVERN, WEST (St James) *see* Malvern H Trin and St Jas
Worc

**MALVERN LINK (Church of the Ascension) (St Matthias) w
Cowleigh** *Worc 2* **P** *Patr Bd* **TR** P J KNIGHT,
NSM M J NOBLES

**MAMBLE (St John the Baptist) w Bayton, Rock w Heightington
w Far Forest** *Worc 4* **P** *Ld Chan and R Ribbesford w Bewdley
etc (alt)* **V** S G F OWENS

MAMHEAD (St Thomas the Apostle) *see* Kenton, Mamhead,
Powderham, Cofton and Starcross *Ex*

MANACCAN (St Manaccus and St Dunstan) *see* Meneage
Truro

MANATON (St Winifred) *see* Moretonhampstead, Manaton,
N Bovey and Lustleigh *Ex*

MANBY (St Mary) *see* Mid Marsh Gp *Linc*

MANCETTER (St Peter) *Cov 5* **P** *Ch Patr Trust* **V** vacant
(01827) 713266

MANCHESTER (Apostles) w Miles Platting *Man 1* **P** *DBP*
P-in-c P B ROUCH

MANCHESTER (Church of the Resurrection) *see* Manchester
Gd Shep and St Barn *Man*

MANCHESTER Clayton (St Cross w St Paul) *Man 1* **P** *Bp*
   P-in-c L T YOUNG
**MANCHESTER Good Shepherd (St Barnabas) (Church of the
   Resurrection)** *Man 1* **P** *Prime Min and Trustees (alt)*
   R T S R CHOW
MANCHESTER (St Ann) *Man 4* **P** *Bp* **R** J N ASHWORTH,
   C G R RAINES
MANCHESTER (St John Chrysostom) Victoria Park *Man 1*
   P *Bp* **P-in-c** I D GOMERSALL, **C** T CHARNOCK, **Hon**
   C J B F GRANT, K A C WASEY, **NSM** E J DISLEY
MANCHESTER (St Werburgh) *see* Chorlton-cum-Hardy St
   Werburgh *Man*
MANEA (St Nicholas) *see* Christchurch and Manea and
   Welney *Ely*
MANEY (St Peter) *Birm 12* **P** *Bp* **V** P T FISHER
MANFIELD (All Saints) *see* E Richmond *Ripon*
MANGOTSFIELD (St James) *Bris 5* **P** *Peache Trustees*
   P-in-c S A ABBOTT, **NSM** V A ABBOTT
MANLEY (St John the Evangelist) *see* Alvanley *Ches*
MANNINGFORD BRUCE (St Peter) *see* Pewsey and
   Swanborough *Sarum*
MANNINGHAM (St Paul and St Jude) *Bradf 1* **P** *Patr Bd*
   TV A A JOHN
MANNINGS HEATH (Church of the Good Shepherd)
   see Nuthurst and Mannings Heath *Chich*
MANOR PARK (St Barnabas) *see* Lt Ilford St Barn *Chelmsf*
MANOR PARK (St John the Baptist) and Whitby Road *Ox 23*
   P *Eton Coll* **V** J S G COTMAN
MANOR PARK (St John the Evangelist) *see* Lt Ilford St Mich
   Chelmsf
MANOR PARK (St Mary the Virgin) *as above*
MANOR PARK (St Michael and All Angels) *as above*
MANOR PARK (William Temple) *see* Sheff Manor *Sheff*
MANSEL LACY (St Michael) *see* Credenhill w Brinsop and
   Wormsley etc *Heref*
MANSERGH (St Peter) *see* Kirkby Lonsdale *Carl*
MANSFIELD Oak Tree Lane *S'well 2* **P** *DBP*
   P-in-c P J STEAD
MANSFIELD (St Augustine) *S'well 2* **P** *Bp*
   P-in-c G E HOLLOWAY
MANSFIELD (St John the Evangelist) *S'well 2* **P** *Bp*
   P-in-c J M A ADAMS
MANSFIELD (St Lawrence) *S'well 2* **P** *Bp* **V** *vacant* (01623)
   623698
MANSFIELD (St Mark) *S'well 2* **P** *Bp* **P-in-c** G J BUTLER
MANSFIELD (St Peter and St Paul) *S'well 2* **P** *Bp*
   P-in-c D J FUDGER
MANSFIELD WOODHOUSE (St Edmund King and Martyr)
   S'well 2 **P** *Bp* **V** R A SCRIVENER
MANSTON (St Catherine) *see* St Laur in Thanet *Cant*
MANSTON (St James) *Ripon 8* **P** *R Barwick in Elmet*
   V J ARENS, **NSM** K G ELLIOTT
MANSTON (St Nicholas) *see* Okeford *Sarum*
MANTHORPE (St John the Evangelist) *see* Grantham,
   Manthorpe *Linc*
MANTON (St Mary the Virgin) *see* Edith Weston w N
   Luffenham and Lyndon w Manton *Pet*
**MANUDEN (St Mary the Virgin) w Berden and Quendon w
   Rickling** *Chelmsf 21* **P** *Bp, DBP and Ch Hosp (jt)*
   P-in-c C BISHOP
MAPERTON (St Peter and St Paul) *see* Camelot Par *B & W*
MAPLEBECK (St Radegund) *S'well 15* **P** *Sir Philip Naylor-
   Leyland Bt* **V** *vacant*
MAPLEDURHAM (St Margaret) *see* Caversham St Pet and
   Mapledurham *Ox*
MAPLEDURWELL (St Mary) *see* N Hants Downs *Win*
MAPLESTEAD, GREAT (St Giles) *see* Knights and
   Hospitallers Par *Chelmsf*
MAPLESTEAD, LITTLE (St John) *as above*
MAPPERLEY (Holy Trinity) *see* W Hallam and Mapperley w
   Stanley *Derby*
MAPPERLEY (St Jude) *see* Nottingham St Jude *S'well*
MAPPLEBOROUGH GREEN (Holy Ascension) *see* Studley
   Cov
MAPPLETON (All Saints) *see* Aldbrough, Mappleton w
   Goxhill and Withernwick *York*
MAPPLETON (St Mary) *see* Ashbourne w Mapleton *Derby*
MAPPOWDER (St Peter and St Paul) *see* Hazelbury Bryan and
   the Hillside Par *Sarum*
MARAZION (All Saints) *see* Ludgvan, Marazion, St Hilary
   and Perranuthnoe *Truro*
MARBURY (St Michael) w Tushingham and Whitewell *Ches 5*
   P *MMCET and Bp (jt)* **R** S J WALTON
MARCH (St John) *Ely 11* **P** *Bp* **P-in-c** P BAXANDALL, **Hon**
   C D J ADDINGTON, **NSM** B L BURTON

MARCH (St Mary) *Ely 11* **P** *Bp* **R** A CHANDLER,
   NSM J R WEBB
MARCH (St Peter) *Ely 11* **P** *Bp* **R** A CHANDLER,
   NSM J R WEBB
MARCH (St Wendreda) *Ely 11* **P** *MMCET* **R** P BAXANDALL
MARCHAM (All Saints) w Garford *Ox 10* **P** *Ch Ch Ox*
   P-in-c R G ZAIR
MARCHINGTON (St Peter) *see* Uttoxeter Area *Lich*
MARCHINGTON WOODLANDS (St John) *as above*
MARCHWOOD (St John) *Win 11* **P** *Bp* **R** *vacant*
   (023) 8086 1496
MARCLE, LITTLE (St Michael and All Angels) *see* Ledbury
   Heref
MARCLE, MUCH (St Bartholomew) *as above*
MARDEN (All Saints) *see* Redhorn *Sarum*
MARDEN (St Hilda) w Preston Grange *Newc 5* **P** *Bp*
   V A J CAVANAGH
MARDEN (St Mary the Virgin) w Amberley and Wisteston
   Heref 4 **P** *D&C* **P-in-c** H M SHORT
MARDEN (St Michael and All Angels) *Cant 11* **P** *Abp*
   V J M ROBERTSON
MARDEN, EAST (St Peter) *see* Compton, the Mardens,
   Stoughton and Racton *Chich*
MARDEN, NORTH (St Mary) *as above*
MARDEN ASH (St James) *see* High Ongar w Norton
   Mandeville *Chelmsf*
MARDEN HILL Group, The *Linc 7* **P** *Various*
   R A M SULLIVAN
MAREHAM-LE-FEN (St Helen) *see* Fen and Hill Gp *Linc*
MAREHAM ON THE HILL (All Saints) *as above*
MARESFIELD (St Bartholomew) *Chich 21* **P** *Ch Trust Fund
   Trust* **R** J N A HOBBS
MARFLEET (St Giles) (St George) (St Hilda) (St Philip)
   York 14 **P** *Patr Bd* **TV** A R GILCHRIST, R J W LONG
MARGARET MARSH (St Margaret) *see* Shaston *Sarum*
MARGARET RODING (St Margaret) *see* High and Gd Easter
   w Margaret Roding *Chelmsf*
MARGARET STREET (All Saints) *see* St Marylebone All SS
   Lon
**MARGARETTING (St Margaret) w Mountnessing and
   Buttsbury** *Chelmsf 7* **P** *Bp* **V** *vacant* (01277) 355692
MARGATE (All Saints) *Cant 9* **P** *Abp* **Hon C** D L CAWLEY
MARGATE (Holy Trinity) *Cant 9* **P** *Ch Patr Trust*
   P-in-c J S RICHARDSON, **C** K M THORPE, H E HOBDAY
MARGATE (St John the Baptist in Thanet) *Cant 9* **P** *Abp*
   V B P SHARP
MARGATE (St Paul) *see* Cliftonville *Cant*
MARGATE (St Philip) Northdown Park *Cant 9* **P** *Ch Patr
   Trust* **V** S GAY
MARHAM (Holy Trinity) *Ely 9* **P** *St Jo Coll Cam* **V** *vacant*
MARHAMCHURCH (St Marwenne) *see* Bude Haven and
   Marhamchurch *Truro*
MARHOLM (St Mary the Virgin) *see* Castor w Sutton and
   Upton w Marholm *Pet*
MARIANSLEIGH (St Mary) *see* Bishopsnympton, Rose Ash,
   Mariansleigh etc *Ex*
MARISHES, THE (St Francis) *see* Pickering w Lockton and
   Levisham *York*
MARK (Holy Cross) w Allerton *B & W 1* **P** *Bp and D&C (jt)*
   P-in-c T D HAWKINGS, **C** G E C FENTON
MARK BEECH (Holy Trinity) *see* Hever, Four Elms and Mark
   Beech *Roch*
MARK CROSS (St Mark) *see* Rotherfield w Mark Cross *Chich*
MARKBY (St Peter) *see* Hannah cum Hagnaby w Markby *Linc*
MARKET BOSWORTH (St Peter) *see* Bosworth and Sheepy
   Gp *Leic*
MARKET DEEPING (St Guthlac) *Linc 13* **P** *Ld Chan*
   R P BRENT, **C** S I R HEARN
MARKET DRAYTON (St Mary) *see* Drayton in Hales *Lich*
MARKET HARBOROUGH (St Dionysius)
   **(The Transfiguration) - Little Bowden w Lubenham and Great
   Bowden** *Leic 3* **P** *Patr Bd* **TR** R H G BRAND,
   TV J S PARKIN, A QUIGLEY, **C** E L DAVIES,
   NSM J C DUDLEY
MARKET LAVINGTON (St Mary of the Assumption) *see* The
   Lavingtons, Cheverells, and Easterton *Sarum*
MARKET OVERTON (St Peter and St Paul) *see* Teigh w
   Whissendine and Market Overton *Pet*
MARKET RASEN (St Thomas the Apostle) *Linc 5* **P** *Ld Chan*
   V M J CARTWRIGHT
MARKET STAINTON (St Michael and All Angels)
   see Asterby Gp *Linc*
MARKET WEIGHTON (All Saints) *York 5* **P** *Abp*
   V L C MUNT, **NSM** A DAWSON
MARKET WESTON (St Mary) *see* Stanton, Hopton, Market
   Weston, Barningham etc *St E*

MARKFIELD (St Michael), Thornton, Bagworth and Stanton under Bardon, and Copt Oak *Leic 9* **P** *MMCET*
R S J NICHOLLS, **NSM** J A DOWNS
MARKHAM, EAST (St John the Baptist) w Askham, Headon w Upton and Grove *S'well 5* **P** *Grove Settled Estate Trustees and SMF (jt)* **P-in-c** J M JESSON
MARKHAM CLINTON (All Saints) *see* Tuxford w Weston and Markham Clinton *S'well*
MARKINGTON (St Michael) w South Stainley and Bishop Thornton *Ripon 3* **P** *Bp, D&C, Sir Thomas Ingilby Bt and N A Hudleston Esq (jt) (by turn)* **V** vacant (01765) 677123
MARKS GATE (St Mark) Chadwell Heath *Chelmsf 1* **P** *Bp*
V R K GAYLER
MARKS TEY (St Andrew) and Aldham *Chelmsf 17* **P** *CPAS and MMCET (jt)* **R** vacant (01206) 210396 *or* 213231
MARKSBURY (St Peter) *see* Farmborough, Marksbury and Stanton Prior *B & W*
MARKYATE STREET (St John the Baptist) *St Alb 8* **P** *Bp*
P-in-c J F H GREEN
MARLBOROUGH (St Mary the Virgin) *Sarum 18* **P** *Patr Bd*
TR A G STUDDERT-KENNEDY, **TV** I C COOPER, **C** T P SEAGO,
OLM D P MAURICE
MARLBROOK (St Luke) *see* Catshill and Dodford *Worc*
MARLBROOK Team Ministry, The *see* Bath Twerton-on-Avon *B & W*
MARLDON (St John the Baptist) *see* Totnes w Bridgetown, Berry Pomeroy etc *Ex*
MARLESFORD (St Andrew) *see* Campsea Ashe w Marlesford, Parham and Hacheston *St E*
MARLEY HILL (St Cuthbert) *see* Hillside *Dur*
MARLINGFORD (Assumption of the Blessed Virgin Mary) *see* Easton, Colton, Marlingford and Bawburgh *Nor*
MARLOW, GREAT (All Saints) w Marlow Bottom, Little Marlow and Bisham *Ox 29* **P** *Patr Bd* **TR** N J MOLONY,
TV D MUNOZ-TRIVINO, E C MACFARLANE, **NSM** G L C SMITH
MARLOW, LITTLE (St John the Baptist) *see* Gt Marlow w Marlow Bottom, Lt Marlow and Bisham *Ox*
MARLOW BOTTOM (St Mary the Virgin) *as above*
MARLPIT HILL (St Paulinus) *see* Edenbridge *Roch*
MARLPOOL (All Saints) *Derby 12* **P** *V Heanor* **V** K PADLEY
MARLSTON (St Mary) *see* Bucklebury w Marlston *Ox*
MARNHULL (St Gregory) *Sarum 5* **P** *DBF*
P-in-c R D G WEYMAN, **C** D A NEAUM, **NSM** S M W THOMAS
MAROWN (Old Parish Church) (St Runius) *S & M 2*
P *The Crown* **V** I DAVIES
MARPLE (All Saints) *Ches 16* **P** *R Stockport St Mary*
V I R PARKINSON, **C** B A PERRIN, **NSM** B J LOWE,
C M BLODWELL, E A SHERCLIFF
MARPLE, LOW (St Martin) *Ches 16* **P** *Keble Coll Ox*
P-in-c E P MCKENNA
MARR (St Helen) *see* Bilham *Sheff*
MARSDEN (St Bartholomew) *Wakef 5* **P** *R Almondbury*
P-in-c G CLAY
MARSDEN, GREAT (St John's Church Centre) w Nelson St Philip *Blackb 6* **P** *Prime Min and Bp (alt)* **V** vacant (01282) 697011
MARSDEN, LITTLE (St Paul) w Nelson St Mary and Nelson St Bede *Blackb 6* **P** *Bp* **V** A PIERCE-JONES
MARSH (St George) *see* Lancaster St Mary w St John and St Anne *Blackb*
MARSH (St James Chapel) *see* Huddersfield H Trin *Wakef*
MARSH BALDON (St Peter) *see* Dorchester *Ox*
MARSH FARM (Holy Cross) *St Alb 14* **P** *Bp*
P-in-c C R PERRY
MARSH GIBBON (St Mary the Virgin) *see* The Claydons and Swan *Ox*
MARSH GREEN (St Barnabas) w Newtown *Liv 14* **P** *Bp, Duke of Sutherland, and V Pemberton (jt)* **V** M J DUERDEN,
OLM S Y FULFORD, E TAULTY
MARSHALSWICK (St Mary) *see* St Alb St Mary Marshalswick *St Alb*
MARSHAM (All Saints) *see* Bure Valley *Nor*
MARSHCHAPEL (St Mary the Virgin) *see* The North-Chapel Parishes *Linc*
MARSHFIELD (St Mary the Virgin) w Cold Ashton and Tormarton w West Littleton *Bris 4* **P** *New Coll Ox and Bp (alt)* **V** S M DREW
MARSHLAND, The *Sheff 10* **P** *Ld Chan and Bp (alt)*
NSM K W SARGEANTSON
MARSHWOOD (St Mary) *see* Golden Cap Team *Sarum*
MARSKE (St Edmund King and Martyr) *see* Richmond w Hudswell and Downholme and Marske *Ripon*
MARSKE, NEW (St Thomas) *York 16* **P** *Abp*
V R E HARRISON
MARSKE IN CLEVELAND (St Mark) *York 16* **P** *Trustees*
V vacant (01642) 482896

MARSTON (St Alban) *see* Stafford *Lich*
MARSTON (St Leonard) *as above*
MARSTON (St Mary) *see* Barkston and Hough Gp *Linc*
MARSTON (St Nicholas) w Elsfield *Ox 4* **P** *Bp and D&C (jt)*
V A R PRICE, **NSM** A C HOLMES, A J PRICE
MARSTON, NEW (St Michael and All Angels) *Ox 4* **P** *Bp*
V E B BARDWELL
MARSTON, NORTH (Assumption of the Blessed Virgin Mary) *see* Schorne *Ox*
MARSTON, SOUTH (St Mary Magdalene) *see* Stratton St Margaret w S Marston etc *Bris*
MARSTON BIGOT (St Leonard) *see* Nunney and Witham Friary, Marston Bigot etc *B & W*
MARSTON GREEN (St Leonard) *Birm 9* **P** *Birm Dioc Trustees* **V** R V ALLEN
MARSTON MAGNA (Blessed Virgin Mary) *see* Chilton Cantelo, Ashington, Mudford, Rimpton etc *B & W*
MARSTON MEYSEY (St James) *see* Fairford Deanery *Glouc*
MARSTON MONTGOMERY (St Giles) *see* Alkmonton, Cubley and Marston Montgomery *Derby*
MARSTON MORTEYNE (St Mary the Virgin) w Lidlington *St Alb 13* **P** *Bp and St Jo Coll Cam (alt)* **P-in-c** G A WEBB
MARSTON ON DOVE (St Mary) *see* Hilton w Marston-on-Dove *Derby*
MARSTON SICCA (St James the Great) *see* Pebworth, Dorsington, Honeybourne etc *Glouc*
MARSTON ST LAWRENCE (St Lawrence) *see* Chenderit *Pet*
MARSTON TRUSSELL (St Nicholas) *see* Welford w Sibbertoft and Marston Trussell *Pet*
MARSTOW (St Matthew) *see* Goodrich, Marstow, Welsh Bicknor, Llangarron etc *Heref*
MARSWORTH (All Saints) *see* Ivinghoe w Pitstone and Slapton and Marsworth *Ox*
MARTHALL (All Saints) *Ches 12* **P** *DBP* **V** vacant (01625) 860981
MARTHAM (St Mary) and Repps with Bastwick, Thurne and Clippesby *Nor 6* **P** *Bp, D&C, DBP and K Edw VI Gr Sch (jt)* **V** J A CRAFER, **NSM** S H MITCHELL
MARTIN (All Saints) *see* W Downland *Sarum*
MARTIN (Holy Trinity) *see* Carr Dyke Gp *Linc*
MARTIN (St Michael) *see* Horncastle Gp *Linc*
MARTIN HUSSINGTREE (St Michael) *see* Salwarpe and Hindlip w Martin Hussingtree *Worc*
MARTINDALE (Old Church) *see* Barton, Pooley Bridge and Martindale *Carl*
MARTINDALE (St Peter) *as above*
MARTINHOE (St Martin) *see* Combe Martin, Berrynarbor, Lynton, Brendon etc *Ex*
MARTLESHAM (St Mary the Virgin) w Brightwell *St E 2*
P *Bp* **P-in-c** I S NAYLOR, **OLM** H L COOKE, E J CORKER
MARTLESHAM HEATH (St Michael and All Angels) *see* Martlesham w Brightwell *St E*
MARTLEY (St Peter) *see* Worcs W *Worc*
MARTOCK (All Saints) w Ash *B & W 6* **P** *Bp*
P-in-c D R GENT, **NSM** M I MACCORMACK
MARTON (Room) *see* Middleton, Newton and Sinnington *York*
MARTON (St Esprit) *see* Long Itchington and Marton *Cov*
MARTON (St James) *see* Capesthorne w Siddington and Marton *Ches*
MARTON (St Margaret of Antioch) *see* Lea Gp *Linc*
MARTON (St Mark) *Heref 13* **P** *V Chirbury* **V** vacant
MARTON (St Mary) *see* Forest of Galtres *York*
MARTON (St Paul) *Blackb 8* **P** *V Poulton-le-Fylde*
V C J WREN, **C** K A WREN
MARTON CUM GRAFTON (Christ Church) *see* Gt and Lt Ouseburn w Marton cum Grafton etc *Ripon*
MARTON-IN-CHIRBURY (St Mark) *see* Marton *Heref*
MARTON-IN-CLEVELAND (St Cuthbert) *York 18* **P** *Abp*
V M J PROCTOR, **C** N GREEN
MARTON IN CRAVEN (St Peter) *see* Broughton, Marton and Thornton *Bradf*
MARTON MOSS (St Nicholas) *see* Hawes Side and Marton Moss *Blackb*
MARTYR WORTHY (St Swithun) *see* Itchen Valley *Win*
MARWOOD (St Michael and All Angels) *see* Heanton Punchardon w Marwood *Ex*
MARY TAVY (St Mary) *see* Peter Tavy, Mary Tavy, Lydford and Brent Tor *Ex*
MARYFIELD (St Philip and St James) *see* Antony w Sheviock *Truro*
MARYLEBONE ROAD (St Marylebone) *see* St Marylebone w H Trin *Lon*
MARYPORT (St Mary) (Christ Church), Netherton and Flimby *Carl 7* **P** *Patr Bd* **TR** K S ELLIS, **TV** S M MCKENDREY

MARYSTOWE (St Mary the Virgin)   *see* Milton Abbot, Dunterton, Lamerton etc *Ex*

MASBROUGH (St Paul) *Sheff 6*   **P** *Bp and Ld Chan (alt)*   **V** T H CASWELL

MASHAM (St Mary the Virgin) and Healey *Ripon 3*   **P** *Trin Coll Cam*   **V** D J CLEEVES,   **NSM** M SAUNDERS, M A WARNER

MASSINGHAM, GREAT (St Mary) and LITTLE (St Andrew), Harpley, Rougham, Weasenham and Wellingham *Nor 14*   **P** *Bp, Earl of Leicester, Mrs P M Brereton, T F North Esq, and DBP (jt)*   **R** M E THORNE

MASTIN MOOR (St Paul)   *see* Staveley and Barrow Hill *Derby*

MATCHBOROUGH (Christ Church)   *see* Ipsley *Worc*

MATCHING (St Mary)   *see* High Laver w Magdalen Laver and Lt Laver etc *Chelmsf*

MATCHING GREEN (St Edmund)   *as above*

MATFEN (Holy Trinity)   *see* Stamfordham w Matfen *Newc*

MATFIELD (St Luke)   *see* Lamberhurst and Matfield *Roch*

MATHON (St John the Baptist)   *see* Cradley w Mathon and Storridge *Heref*

MATLASKE (St Peter)   *see* Barningham w Matlaske w Baconsthorpe etc *Nor*

MATLOCK (St Giles) (St John the Baptist) *Derby 7*   **P** *Bp*   **R** B M CROWTHER-ALWYN

MATLOCK BANK (All Saints) *Derby 7*   **P** *Bp*   **P-in-c** R B READE

MATLOCK BATH (Holy Trinity) and Cromford *Derby 7*   **P** *Ch Trust Fund Trust*   **P-in-c** P N W GRAYSHON, C D J BATTISON,   **J** E STANTON

MATSON (St Katharine) *Glouc 3*   **P** *D&C*   **R** J A PARSONS, C K O HEBDEN,   **NSM** A E SMITH

MATTERDALE (not known)   *see* Gd Shep TM *Carl*

MATTERSEY (All Saints)   *see* Everton, Mattersey, Clayworth and Gringley *S'well*

MATTINGLEY (not known)   *see* Whitewater *Win*

MATTISHALL (All Saints) and the Tudd Valley *Nor 17*   **P** *Bp, G&C Coll Cam, DBP, and J V Berney Esq (jt)*   **R** G R KEGG,   **NSM** G KEGG,   **OLM** S E THURGILL, G R ROOTHAM

MATTISHALL BURGH (St Peter)   *see* Mattishall and the Tudd Valley *Nor*

MAUGHOLD (St Maughold) *S & M 3*   **P** *The Crown*   **V** D J GREEN,   **NSM** I C FAULDS

MAULDEN (St Mary) *St Alb 9*   **P** *Bp*   **R** R C WINSLADE

MAUNBY (St Michael)   *see* Lower Swale *Ripon*

MAUTBY (St Peter and St Paul)   *see* S Trin Broads *Nor*

MAVESYN RIDWARE (St Nicholas)   *see* The Ridwares and Kings Bromley *Lich*

MAVIS ENDERBY (St Michael)   *see* Marden Hill Gp *Linc*

MAWDESLEY (St Peter) *Blackb 4*   **P** *R Croston*   **R** D J REYNOLDS

MAWNAN (St Mawnan) (St Michael) *Truro 3*   **P** *Bp*   **P-in-c** G K BENNETT,   **C** R M PAUL

MAXEY (St Peter)   *see* Etton w Helpston and Maxey *Pet*

MAXSTOKE (St Michael and All Angels) *Birm 9*   **P** *Lord Leigh*   **V** R N PARKER,   **C** K M LARKIN

MAY HILL (All Saints)   *see* Huntley and Longhope, Churcham and Bulley *Glouc*

MAYBRIDGE (St Richard) *Chich 5*   **P** *Bp*   **C** J K GAVIGAN

MAYBUSH Redbridge (All Saints)   *see* Maybush and Southampton St Jude *Win*

MAYBUSH (St Peter) and Southampton St Jude *Win 13*   **P** *Bp*   **V** R A HEMMINGS,   **C** S M PITKIN

MAYFAIR (Christ Church) extra-parochial place *Lon 3*   **P** *Bp vacant*

MAYFIELD (St Dunstan) *Chich 15*   **P** *Keble Coll Ox*   **V** N J PRIOR,   **Hon C** J P CAPERON

MAYFIELD (St John the Baptist) *Lich 15*   **P** *Ch Soc Trust*   **C** R P OWEN, J RICHARDSON

MAYFORD (Emmanuel)   *see* Woking St Jo *Guildf*

MAYLAND (St Barnabas) (St Barnabas Family Centre) *Chelmsf 11*   **P** *Bp*   **P-in-c** M R RYALL

MEANWOOD (Holy Trinity) *Ripon 7*   **P** *Bp*   **P-in-c** C M ORME

MEARE (Blessed Virgin Mary and All Saints)   *see* Glastonbury w Meare *B & W*

MEARS ASHBY (All Saints) and Hardwick and Sywell w Overstone *Pet 6*   **P** *Duchy of Cornwall (2 turns), Bracegirdle Trustees (1 turn), and Mrs C K Edmiston (1 turn)*   **P-in-c** D C BEET

MEASHAM (St Lawrence)   *see* Woodfield Team *Leic*

MEAVY (St Peter)   *see* Yelverton, Meavy, Sheepstor and Walkhampton *Ex*

MEDBOURNE (St Giles)   *see* Six Saints circa Holt *Leic*

MEDLOCK HEAD *Man 19*   **P** *Prime Min (2 turns), Patr Bd (1 turn)*   **TR** R W HAWKINS

MEDMENHAM (St Peter and St Paul)   *see* Hambleden Valley *Ox*

MEDOMSLEY (St Mary Magdalene) *Dur 4*   **P** *Bp*   **V** A D WHIPP

MEDSTEAD (St Andrew)   *see* Bentworth, Lasham, Medstead and Shalden *Win*

MEERBROOK (St Matthew)   *see* Leek and Meerbrook *Lich*

MEESDEN (St Mary)   *see* Hormead, Wyddial, Anstey, Brent Pelham etc *St Alb*

MEETH (St Michael and All Angels)   *see* Hatherleigh, Meeth, Exbourne and Jacobstowe *Ex*

MEIR (Holy Trinity) *Lich 6*   **P** *Bp*   **P-in-c** M M ALLBUTT

MEIR HEATH (St Francis of Assisi) and Normacot *Lich 12*   **P** *Bp and DBP (jt)*   **V** P F BLANCH

MEIR PARK (St Clare)   *see* Meir Heath and Normacot *Lich*

MELBECKS (Holy Trinity)   *see* Swaledale *Ripon*

MELBOURN (All Saints) *Ely 7*   **P** *D&C*   **V** A D O'BRIEN,   **NSM** M L PRICE

MELBOURNE (St Michael) *Derby 15*   **P** *Bp*   **V** J H DAVIES, C D J RAILTON,   **NSM** A J FLINTHAM

MELBOURNE (St Monica)   *see* Barmby Moor Gp *York*

MELBURY (St Mary the Virgin) (St Osmund) *Sarum 3*   **P** *Patr Bd*   **TR** G F PERRYMAN,   **TV** D P HARKNETT,   **NSM** J A RENNIE

MELBURY ABBAS (St Thomas)   *see* Shaston *Sarum*

MELBURY BUBB (St Mary the Virgin)   *see* Melbury *Sarum*

MELBURY OSMUND (St Osmund)   *as above*

MELCHBOURNE (St Mary Magdalene)   *see* The Stodden Churches *St Alb*

MELCOMBE HORSEY (St Andrew)   *see* Piddle Valley, Hilton, Cheselbourne etc *Sarum*

MELDON (St John the Evangelist)   *see* Bolam w Whalton and Hartburn w Meldon *Newc*

MELDRETH (Holy Trinity) *Ely 7*   **P** *D&C*   **V** A D O'BRIEN,   **NSM** M L PRICE

MELKSHAM (St Barnabas) (St Michael and All Angels) *Sarum 14*   **P** *DBP*   **TR** D G SMITH,   **C** A E EVANS, J PERRETT,   **NSM** J DARLING,   **OLM** A E WINTOUR, N G LOCK, E A FIELDEN

MELKSHAM FOREST (St Andrew)   *see* Melksham *Sarum*

MELLING (St Thomas)   *see* Maghull and Melling *Liv*

MELLING (St Wilfrid)   *see* E Lonsdale *Blackb*

MELLIS (St Mary the Virgin)   *see* S Hartismere *St E*

MELLOR (St Mary) *Blackb 7*   **P** *V Blackb*   **V** *vacant* (01254) 812324

MELLOR (St Thomas) *Ches 2*   **P** *Bp*   **V** P J JENNER

MELLS (St Andrew) w Buckland Dinham, Elm, Whatley, Vobster and Chantry *B & W 4*   **P** *DBP (2 turns), Bp (1 turns)*   **P-in-c** M E WEYMONT

MELMERBY (St John the Baptist)   *see* Cross Fell Gp *Carl*

MELPLASH (Christ Church)   *see* Beaminster Area *Sarum*

MELSONBY (St James the Great)   *see* Forcett and Aldbrough and Melsonby *Ripon*

MELTHAM Christ the King (St Bartholomew) (St James) *Wakef 1*   **P** *Simeon's Trustees, R Almondbury w Farnley Tyas, and Bp (jt)*   **V** M E READ,   **NSM** P ROLLS, D SHIELDS,   **OLM** J H HELLIWELL, J F RADCLIFFE

MELTHAM (St Bartholomew)   *see* Meltham *Wakef*

MELTHAM MILLS (St James)   *as above*

MELTON (St Andrew) and Ufford *St E 7*   **P** *D&C Ely (3 turns), and T R E Blois-Brooke Esq (1 turn)*   **R** M J HATCHETT,   **NSM** R M HATCHETT

MELTON, GREAT (All Saints)   *see* Hethersett w Canteloff w Lt and Gt Melton *Nor*

MELTON, HIGH (St James)   *see* Barnburgh w Melton on the Hill etc *Sheff*

MELTON, LITTLE (All Saints)   *see* Hethersett w Canteloff w Lt and Gt Melton *Nor*

MELTON, WEST (St Cuthbert)   *see* Brampton Bierlow *Sheff*

MELTON CONSTABLE (St Peter)   *see* Briston, Burgh Parva, Hindolveston etc *Nor*

MELTON MOWBRAY (St Mary) *Leic 2*   **P** *Patr Bd*   **TR** K P ASHBY,   **C** P G HOOPER

MELTON ROSS (Ascension)   *see* Brocklesby Park *Linc*

MELVERLEY (St Peter)   *see* Kinnerley w Melverley and Knockin w Maesbrook *Lich*

MEMBURY (St John the Baptist)   *see* Axminster, Chardstock, All Saints etc *Ex*

MENDHAM (All Saints)   *see* Fressingfield, Mendham etc *St E*

MENDLESHAM (St Mary) *St E 6*   **P** *SMF*   **V** P T GRAY

MENEAGE (St Anthony) (St Martin) (St Mawgan) *Truro 4*   **P** *Ld Chan and Bp (alt)*   **R** L A WALKER,   **NSM** M L JEPP

MENHENIOT (St Lalluwy and St Antoninus) *Truro 12*   **P** *Ex Coll Ox*   **V** *vacant* (01579) 342195

MENITH WOOD (Chapel)   *see* Teme Valley N *Worc*

MENSTON (St John the Divine) w Woodhead *Bradf 4*   **P** *Bp*   **V** R J YEOMAN

MENTMORE (St Mary the Virgin) *see* Cheddington w Mentmore *Ox*

MEOLE BRACE (Holy Trinity) *Lich 20* **P** *J K Bather Esq*
V P J CANSDALE, **C** C S MCBRIDE, **Hon C** J TILLER,
NSM L P WICKENS, **OLM** C RUXTON

MEOLS, GREAT (St John the Baptist) *Ches 8* **P** *Bp*
V G A ROSSITER, **NSM** J E BISSON

MEOLS, NORTH Team Ministry, The (St Cuthbert) *Liv 9*
P *Patr Bd* **TR** P C GREEN

MEON, EAST (All Saints) *Portsm 4* **P** *Ld Chan*
V T E LOUDEN

MEON, WEST (St John the Evangelist) and Warnford *Portsm 4*
P *Bp and DBP (alt)* **P-in-c** C E SACKLEY

MEONSTOKE (St Andrew) w Corhampton cum Exton *Portsm 1*
P *Bp* **P-in-c** S H HOLT

MEOPHAM (St John the Baptist) w Nurstead *Roch 1* **P** *D&C*
and Lt-Col F B Edmeades (jt) **NSM** C D FORMAN

MEPAL (St Mary) *see* Witcham w Mepal *Ely*

MEPPERSHALL (St Mary the Virgin) and Shefford *St Alb 16*
P *Bp and St Jo Coll Cam (alt)* **V** J A HARPER,
NSM P E CRITCHLEY

**MERE (St Michael the Archangel) w West Knoyle and Maiden
Bradley** *Sarum 17* **P** *Bp* **P-in-c** P N BARNES

MERESIDE (St Wilfrid) *see* Blackpool St Wilfrid *Blackb*

MEREVALE (St Mary the Virgin) *see* Baxterley w Hurley and
Wood End and Merevale etc *Birm*

MEREWORTH (St Lawrence) w West Peckham *Roch 7*
P *Viscount Falmouth and D&C (alt)* **R** R N MCCONACHIE

MERIDEN (St Laurence) *Cov 4* **P** *Chapter Cov Cathl*
R *vacant (01676) 522719*

MERRINGTON (St John the Evangelist) *Dur 6* **P** *D&C*
P-in-c G NORMAN

MERRIOTT (All Saints) w Hinton, Dinnington and Lopen
B & W 15 **P** *D&C Bris (2 turns), Bp (1 turn)* **R** V N JAMES

MERROW (St John the Evangelist) *Guildf 5* **P** *Earl of Onslow*
R C J LUCKRAFT, **C** E A M G BROWN,
OLM D E C MATTHEWS

MERRY HILL (St Joseph of Arimathea) *see* Penn Fields *Lich*

MERRYMEET (St Mary) *see* Menheniot *Truro*

MERSEA, WEST (St Peter and St Paul) w East (St Edmund)
Chelmsf 16 **P** *Bp and The Crown (alt)* **R** S C NORTON,
NSM J R PANTRY, A J ELMES

MERSHAM (St John the Baptist) w Hinxhill and Sellindge
Cant 10 **P** *Abp* **P-in-c** R L LE ROSSIGNOL,
NSM L C CLEVELAND, S M COX

MERSTHAM (St Katharine) (Epiphany) and Gatton *S'wark 26*
P *Abp* **P-in-c** J E SMITH, **NSM** S M WEAKLEY,
OLM V J WILLIAMS

MERSTHAM, SOUTH (All Saints) *S'wark 26* **P** *Bp*
C J P ASHTON

MERSTON (St Giles) *see* N Mundham w Hunston and
Merston *Chich*

MERTON (All Saints) *see* Shebbear, Buckland Filleigh,
Sheepwash etc *Ex*

MERTON (St James) *S'wark 13* **P** *Bp and V Merton
St Mary (jt)* **P-in-c** J B EASTON-CROUCH

MERTON (St John the Divine) *see* Merton Priory *S'wark*

MERTON (St Mary) *S'wark 13* **P** *Bp* **V** J A HAYWARD

MERTON (St Peter) *see* Caston, Griston, Merton, Thompson
etc *Nor*

MERTON (St Swithun) *see* Ray Valley *Ox*

MERTON PRIORY *S'wark 13* **P** *Patr Bd*
TR D R M MONTEITH, **TV** G M PAWSON, **C** D R THORNTON,
NSM H NEALE

MESHAW (St John) *see* Burrington, Chawleigh, Cheldon,
Chulmleigh etc *Ex*

MESSING (All Saints) *see* Copford w Easthorpe and Messing w
Inworth *Chelmsf*

MESSINGHAM (Holy Trinity) *Linc 4* **P** *Bp* **V** G D MASSEY

MESTY CROFT (St Luke) *see* Wednesbury St Paul Wood
Green *Lich*

METFIELD (St John the Baptist) *see* Fressingfield, Mendham
etc *St E*

METHERINGHAM (St Wilfred) w Blankney and Dunston
Linc 18 **P** *Bp (2 turns), Br Field Products Ltd (1 turn)*
V *vacant (01526) 321115*

METHLEY (St Oswald) w Mickletown *Ripon 8* **P** *Bp (3 turns),
Duchy of Lanc (1 turn)* **P-in-c** A J PEARSON, **Hon**
C M C E BOOTES

METHWOLD (St George) *see* Grimshoe *Ely*

METTINGHAM (All Saints) *see* Wainford *St E*

METTON (St Andrew) *see* Roughton and Felbrigg, Metton,
Sustead etc *Nor*

MEVAGISSEY (St Peter) *see* St Mewan w Mevagissey and St
Ewe *Truro*

MEXBOROUGH (St John the Baptist) *Sheff 12* **P** *Adn York*
V D R WISE

MEYSEY HAMPTON (St Mary) *see* Fairford Deanery *Glouc*

MICHAEL (St Michael and All Angels) *S & M 3* **P** *The Crown*
V *vacant*

MICHAELCHURCH ESCLEY (St Michael) *see* Clodock and
Longtown w Craswall, Llanveynoe etc *Heref*

MICHAELSTOW (St Michael) *see* St Tudy w St Mabyn and
Michaelstow *Truro*

MICHELDEVER (St Mary) *see* Upper Dever *Win*

**MICHELMERSH (Our Lady) and Awbridge and Braishfield and
Farley Chamberlayne and Timsbury** *Win 12* **P** *Bp*
R D B KINGTON

MICKLEGATE (Holy Trinity) *see* York H Trin Micklegate
York

MICKLEHAM (St Michael) *see* Leatherhead and Mickleham
Guildf

MICKLEHURST (All Saints Institute) *Ches 14* **P** *Bp*
V *vacant (01457) 837430*

MICKLEOVER (All Saints) *Derby 10* **P** *MMCET*
V A W WARD, **Hon C** M A PRIDDIN, **NSM** M P STAUNTON

MICKLEOVER (St John) *Derby 10* **P** *Bp*
P-in-c M A PRIDDIN, **C** A W WARD, **NSM** M P STAUNTON

**MICKLETON (St Lawrence), Willersey, Saintbury, Weston-sub-
Edge and Aston-sub-Edge** *Glouc 8* **P** *Bp, Lt Col J H Gibbon,
Viscount Sandon (1 turn), Ld Chan (1 turn)*
P-in-c F W DAWSON

MICKLEY (St George) *see* Bywell and Mickley *Newc*

MICKLEY (St John the Evangelist) *see* Fountains Gp *Ripon*

MID CHURNET *see* Kingsley and Foxt-w-Whiston *Lich*

MID LOES *St E 18* **P** *Ld Chan (1 turn), MMCET, CPAS, Bp,
and Wadh Coll Ox (1 turn)* **R** S F BRIAN,
OLM J M CHENERY

MID MARSH Group, The *Linc 12* **P** *A M D Hall Esq, Bp,
D&C, and Lord Deramore (by turn)* **P-in-c** C M TURNER,
OLM L W CARROLL, J R SELFE

MID TRENT *Lich 10* **P** *Patr Bd* **TR** P S DANIEL,
TV S J ABRAM, **NSM** J P PHILLIPS

MIDDLE *see also under substantive place name*

MIDDLE RASEN Group, The *Linc 5* **P** *Bp, Charterhouse, and
DBP (jt)* **P-in-c** P C PATRICK, **C** C R HARRINGTON

**MIDDLEHAM (St Mary and St Alkelda) w Coverdale and East
Witton and Thornton Steward** *Ripon 4* **P** *Bp, R Craven-Smith-
Milnes Esq, and W R Burdon Esq (jt)* **R** B A GIBLIN,
C Y S CALLAGHAN

MIDDLESBROUGH (All Saints) *York 18* **P** *Abp*
V G HOLLAND, **C** P B ARCHIBALD

MIDDLESBROUGH (Ascension) *York 18* **P** *Abp*
V D G HODGSON

MIDDLESBROUGH (Holy Trinity) *see* N Ormesby *York*

MIDDLESBROUGH (St Agnes) *York 18* **P** *Abp*
P-in-c A M GRANGE, **NSM** M EDWARDS

MIDDLESBROUGH (St Barnabas) *see* Linthorpe *York*

MIDDLESBROUGH (St Chad) *York 18* **P** *Abp* **V** *vacant*
(01642) 819854

MIDDLESBROUGH (St Columba w St Paul) *York 18* **P** *Abp*
V S COOPER, **C** A HOWARD, **NSM** P M KRONBERGS

MIDDLESBROUGH (St John the Evangelist) *York 18* **P** *Abp*
V S COOPER, **C** A HOWARD

MIDDLESBROUGH (St Martin of Tours) (St Cuthbert)
York 18 **P** *Abp* **V** D S WATSON, **NSM** J M COOK,
T A LEWIS

MIDDLESBROUGH (St Oswald) *York 18* **P** *Abp*
V S RICHARDSON

MIDDLESBROUGH (St Thomas) *York 18* **P** *Abp*
V T M LEATHLEY

MIDDLESMOOR (St Chad) *see* Upper Nidderdale *Ripon*

MIDDLESTOWN (St Luke) *Wakef 11* **P** *R Thornhill*
V H C BAKER, **NSM** A P YOUNG

MIDDLETON (All Saints) *see* N Hinckford *Chelmsf*

MIDDLETON (Holy Ghost) *see* Kirkby Lonsdale *Carl*

MIDDLETON (Holy Trinity) *see* Bitterley w Middleton, Stoke
St Milborough etc *Heref*

MIDDLETON (Holy Trinity) *Heref 13* **P** *V Chirbury*
V *vacant*

MIDDLETON (Holy Trinity) *see* Yoxmere *St E*

MIDDLETON (St Andrew), Newton and Sinnington *York 20*
P *Abp (2 turns), Simeon's Trustees (1 turn)* **R** A M F REED

MIDDLETON (St Cross) *Ripon 6* **P** *DBP*
P-in-c A T C MYERS, **NSM** J H TURNER

MIDDLETON (St John the Baptist) *see* Curdworth, Middleton
and Wishaw *Birm*

MIDDLETON (St Leonard) (St Margaret) w Thornham *Man 18*
P *Bp* **TR** N J FEIST, **OLM** F JACKSON, S L SPENCER,
D E BROOKS

MIDDLETON (St Mary) *see* W Winch w Setchey, N Runcton
and Middleton *Nor*

MIDDLETON (St Mary the Virgin) *Ripon 6*   **P** *V Rothwell*
P-in-c A T C MYERS
MIDDLETON (St Michael and All Angels)   *see* Youlgreave,
Middleton, Stanton-in-Peak etc *Derby*
MIDDLETON (St Nicholas) *Chich 1*   **P** *D&C*
V W T MARSTON
MIDDLETON-BY-WIRKSWORTH (Holy Trinity)
see Wirksworth *Derby*
MIDDLETON CHENEY (All Saints)   *see* Chenderit *Pet*
MIDDLETON-IN-CHIRBY (Holy Trinity)   *see* Middleton
Heref
**MIDDLETON-IN-TEESDALE (St Mary the Virgin) w Forest
and Frith** *Dur 7*   **P** *Lord Barnard and The Crown (alt)*
NSM A E FREESTONE
MIDDLETON JUNCTION (St Gabriel) *Man 18*   **P** *Bp*
V A E STARKIE
MIDDLETON ON LEVEN (St Cuthbert)   *see* Rudby in
Cleveland w Middleton *York*
MIDDLETON-ON-THE-HILL (St Mary the Virgin)
see Leominster *Heref*
MIDDLETON-ON-THE-WOLDS (St Andrew)   *see* Woldsburn
York
MIDDLETON SCRIVEN (St John the Baptist)   *see* Stottesdon
w Farlow, Cleeton St Mary etc *Heref*
MIDDLETON ST GEORGE (St George) (St Laurence) *Dur 8*
P *Bp*   **R** P S D NEVILLE,   **C** D TOLHURST
MIDDLETON STONEY (All Saints)   *see* Akeman *Ox*
MIDDLETON TYAS (St Michael and All Angels)   *see* E
Richmond *Ripon*
MIDDLETOWN (St John the Baptist)   *see* Gt Wollaston *Heref*
MIDDLEWICH (St Michael and All Angels) w Byley *Ches 6*
P *Bp*   **V** I G BISHOP,   **NSM** E WOODE
MIDDLEZOY (Holy Cross) and Othery and Moorlinch *B & W 5*
P *Bp Worc (1 turn), Bp (2 turns)*   **P-in-c** J K L POWELL
MIDGHAM (St Matthew)   *see* Aldermaston and Woolhampton
Ox
MIDHOPE (St James)   *see* Penistone and Thurlstone *Wakef*
MIDHURST (St Mary Magdalene and St Denis) *Chich 10*
P *Rathbone Trust Co and Cowdray Trust (jt)*
V Q M RONCHETTI
MIDSOMER NORTON (St John the Baptist) w Clandown
B & W 12   **P** *Ch Ch Ox*   **V** C G CHIPLIN
MIDVILLE (St Peter)   *see* Stickney Gp *Linc*
MILBER (St Luke) *Ex 10*   **P** *Bp*   **V** J E POTTER
MILBORNE (St Andrew)   *see* Puddletown, Tolpuddle and
Milborne w Dewlish *Sarum*
**MILBORNE PORT (St John the Evangelist) w Goathill and
Charlton Horethorne w Stowell** *B & W 12*   **P** *Bp and
J K Wingfield Digby Esq (jt)*   **V** J W B PERRY
MILBORNE WICK (Mission Church)   *see* Milborne Port w
Goathill etc *B & W*
MILBOURNE (Holy Saviour)   *see* Ponteland *Newc*
MILBURN (St Cuthbert)   *see* Heart of Eden *Carl*
MILCOMBE (St Laurence)   *see* Bloxham w Milcombe and S
Newington *Ox*
MILDEN (St Peter)   *see* Monks Eleigh w Chelsworth and Brent
Eleigh etc *St E*
MILDENHALL (St John the Baptist)   *see* Marlborough *Sarum*
MILDENHALL (St Mary) *St E 11*   **P** *Patr Bd (2 turns), Bp
(1 turn)*   **R** I MECHANIC, S M LEATHLEY,
OLM H B MULLIN, M E RUSTED
MILDMAY GROVE (St Jude and St Paul) *Lon 6*   **P** *Islington
Ch Trust*   **V** J A OMOYAJOWO
MILE CROSS (St Catherine) *Nor 2*   **P** *Dr J P English, Canon
G F Bridger, the Revd K W Habershon, and the Revd
H Palmer (jt)*   **V** P D MACKAY
MILE END Old Town (St Paul)   *see* Bow Common *Lon*
MILE OAK (The Good Shepherd)   *see* Portslade Gd Shep *Chich*
MILEHAM (St John the Baptist)   *see* Litcham w Kempston, E
and W Lexham, Mileham etc *Nor*
MILES PLATTING (St Cuthbert)   *see* Man Apostles w Miles
Platting *Man*
MILFORD (Holy Trinity)   *see* Hazelwood, Holbrook and
Milford *Derby*
MILFORD (St John the Evangelist) *Guildf 4*   **P** *V Witley*
V C G POTTER
MILFORD, SOUTH (St Mary the Virgin)   *see* Monk Fryston
and S Milford *York*
MILFORD-ON-SEA (All Saints) *Win 11*   **P** *Bp*
V D J FURNESS
MILL END (St Peter) and Heronsgate w West Hyde *St Alb 5*
P *Bp and V Rickmansworth*   **P-in-c** N P A PNEMATICATOS,
C D J BAVERSTOCK
MILL HILL (John Keble Church) *Lon 15*   **P** *Bp*
NSM I GODFREY

MILL HILL (St Michael and All Angels) *Lon 15*   **P** *Bp*
V B O WRIGHT
MILL HILL (St Paul)   *see* Hendon St Paul Mill Hill *Lon*
MILLAND (St Luke)   *see* Lynch w Iping Marsh and Milland
Chich
MILLBROOK (All Saints)   *see* St John w Millbrook *Truro*
MILLBROOK (Christ the King)   *see* Kettering Ch the King *Pet*
MILLBROOK (Holy Trinity) *Win 13*   **P** *Bp*
P-in-c W F P PERRY,   **NSM** W WHITFIELD
MILLBROOK Regents Park (St Clement)   *see* Millbrook *Win*
MILLBROOK (St James) *Ches 14*   **P** *Bp, V Stalybridge St Paul,
and Mrs E Bissill (jt)*   **P-in-c** A M DI CHIARA
MILLBROOK (St Michael and All Angels)   *see* Ampthill w
Millbrook and Steppingley *St Alb*
MILLERS DALE (St Anne)   *see* Tideswell *Derby*
MILLFIELD (St Mark) and Pallion St Luke *Dur 16*   **P** *Bp*
P-in-c O L ERIKSSON,   **C** K L WASSALL
MILLFIELD (St Mary) *Dur 16*   **P** *The Crown*   **V** B SKELTON,
NSM D RAINE
MILLHOUSES (Holy Trinity) *Sheff 2*   **P** *Bp*   **V** P A INGRAM,
C S A ST L HILLS
MILLHOUSES (St Oswald)   *see* Sheff St Pet and St Oswald
Sheff
MILLINGTON (St Margaret)   *see* Pocklington and Owsthorpe
and Kilnwick Percy etc *York*
MILLOM Holburn Hill (Mission)   *see* Millom *Carl*
MILLOM (Holy Trinity) (St George) *Carl 9*   **P** *Bp and
Trustees (jt)*   **V** R K S BRACEGIRDLE
MILNROW (St James) *Man 21*   **P** *TR Rochdale*   **V** R R USHER
MILNSHAW (St Mary Magdalen)   *see* Accrington Ch the King
Blackb
MILNTHORPE (St Thomas)   *see* Heversham and Milnthorpe
Carl
MILSON (St George)   *see* Cleobury Mortimer w Hopton Wafers
etc *Heref*
MILSTED (St Mary and the Holy Cross)   *see* Bredgar w Bicknor
and Frinsted w Wormshill etc *Cant*
MILSTON (St Mary)   *see* Avon Valley *Sarum*
MILTON (All Saints) *Ely 6*   **P** *K Coll Cam*
R D J CHAMBERLIN,   **NSM** E J WILLIAMS
MILTON (St Blaise)   *see* Steventon w Milton *Ox*
MILTON (St James) (St Andrew's Church Centre) (St Patrick)
Portsm 6   **P** *V Portsea St Mary*   **V** H O ALBY
MILTON (St John the Evangelist)   *see* Adderbury w Milton *Ox*
MILTON (St Mary Magdalene) *Win 9*   **P** *V Milford*
R A H BAILEY,   **C** H C JEVONS
MILTON (St Peter) w St Jude *B & W 11*   **P** *Ld Chan*
V G P EALES,   **NSM** G PUTNAM
MILTON (St Philip and St James) *Lich 8*   **P** *Bp*
V D W WATKIN
MILTON (St Simon and St Jude)   *see* Gillingham and Milton-
on-Stour *Sarum*
**MILTON, GREAT (St Mary the Virgin) w Little (St James) and
Great Haseley** *Ox 1*   **P** *Bp and D&C Windsor (jt)*
R V L STORY
MILTON, SOUTH (All Saints)   *see* Thurlestone, S Milton, W
Alvington etc *Ex*
MILTON ABBAS (St James the Great)   *see* Winterborne Valley
and Milton Abbas *Sarum*
**MILTON ABBOT (St Constantine), Dunterton, Lamerton,
Sydenham Damerel, Marystowe and Coryton** *Ex 25*   **P** *Bp,
Bedford Estates, J W Tremayne Esq, Mrs E J Bullock,
P T L Newman Esq (jt)*   **V** G J STANTON
MILTON BRYAN (St Peter)   *see* Woburn w Eversholt, Milton
Bryan, Battlesden etc *St Alb*
MILTON CLEVEDON (St James)   *see* Evercreech w
Chesterblade and Milton Clevedon *B & W*
MILTON COMBE (Holy Spirit)   *see* Buckland Monachorum
Ex
MILTON DAMEREL (Holy Trinity)   *see* Holsworthy w
Hollacombe and Milton Damerel *Ex*
MILTON ERNEST (All Saints), Pavenham and Thurleigh
St Alb 15   **P** *Bp (2 turns), Lord Luke (1 turn)*   **V** *vacant*
(01234) 822885
MILTON KEYNES (Christ the Cornerstone) *Ox 25*   **P** *Bp*
P-in-c E LOZADA-UZURIAGA
MILTON KEYNES VILLAGE (All Saints)   *see* Walton Milton
Keynes *Ox*
MILTON LILBOURNE (St Peter)   *see* Pewsey and
Swanborough *Sarum*
MILTON MALSOR (Holy Cross)   *see* Collingtree w
Courteenhall and Milton Malsor *Pet*
MILTON NEXT GRAVESEND (Christ Church) *Roch 4*   **P** *Bp*
V S C BREWER,   **Hon C** A P WIBROE
MILTON NEXT GRAVESEND (St Peter and St Paul) w Denton
Roch 4   **P** *Bp*   **R** *vacant* (01474) 533434

MILTON NEXT SITTINGBOURNE (Holy Trinity) *Cant 15*
P *D&C*   **P-in-c** L R DENNY

MILTON REGIS (Holy Trinity)   *see* Milton next Sittingbourne *Cant*

MILTON REGIS (St Mary)   *see* Sittingbourne St Mary and St Mich *Cant*

MILTON-UNDER-WYCHWOOD (St Simon and St Jude)   *see* Shipton-under-Wychwood w Milton, Fifield etc *Ox*

MILVERTON (St Michael) w Halse and Fitzhead *B & W 19*
P *Adn Taunton (4 turns), Bp and V Wiveliscombe (1 turn)*
P-in-c H L STAINER

MILVERTON, NEW (St Mark) *Cov 11*   **P** *CPAS*
P-in-c P MANUEL,   **C** E A J CLACK

MILVERTON, OLD (St James)   *see* Leamington Spa H Trin and Old Milverton *Cov*

MILWICH (All Saints)   *see* Mid Trent *Lich*

MIMMS *see also* MYMMS

MIMMS, SOUTH (Christ Church) *Lon 14*   **P** *Ch Patr Trust*
V N T W TAYLOR,   **C** K G M HILTON-TURVEY,
NSM P W LIDDELOW

MINCHINHAMPTON (Holy Trinity) *Glouc 5*   **P** *Bp*
P-in-c C P COLLINGWOOD,   **NSM** J WALDEN

MINEHEAD (St Andrew) (St Michael) (St Peter) *B & W 16*
P *Lt-Col G W F Luttrell and Bp (jt)*   **V** S D LLOYD,
C E A MORTIMER

MINETY (St Leonard)   *see* Ashton Keynes, Leigh and Minety *Bris*

MININGSBY WITH EAST KIRKBY (St Nicholas)   *see* Marden Hill Gp *Linc*

MINLEY (St Andrew) *Guildf 1*   **P** *Bp*   **V** M W NEALE

MINNIS BAY (St Thomas)   *see* Birchington w Acol and Minnis Bay *Cant*

MINSKIP (Mission Room)   *see* Aldborough w Boroughbridge and Roecliffe *Ripon*

MINSTEAD (All Saints)   *see* Lyndhurst and Emery Down and Minstead *Win*

MINSTER (St Mary the Virgin) w Monkton *Cant 9*   **P** *Abp*
P-in-c R R COLES,   **OLM** J A BAKER

MINSTER (St Merteriana)   *see* Boscastle w Davidstow *Truro*

MINSTER-IN-SHEPPEY (St Mary and St Sexburga) *Cant 15*
P *Ch Patr Trust*   **V** G H SPENCER,   **Hon C** C J SHIPLEY,
B I M DURKAN

MINSTER LOVELL (St Kenelm) *Ox 8*   **P** *Eton Coll and Ch Ch Ox (jt)*   **V** A W D GABB-JONES

MINSTERLEY (Holy Trinity) *Heref 13*   **P** *DBP and Bp (alt)*
V A N TOOP,   **NSM** M-L TOOP, P BICKLEY

MINSTERWORTH (St Peter)   *see* Westbury-on-Severn w Flaxley, Blaisdon etc *Glouc*

MINTERNE MAGNA (St Andrew)   *see* Buckland Newton, Cerne Abbas, Godmanstone etc *Sarum*

MINTING (St Andrew)   *see* Bardney *Linc*

MIREHOUSE (St Andrew) *Carl 5*   **P** *Bp*   **P-in-c** C N CASEY

MIRFIELD (St Mary) *Wakef 9*   **P** *Bp*   **C** G M JOHNSON,
W DALRYMPLE,   **NSM** H C BUTLER,   **OLM** A B POLLARD

MISERDEN (St Andrew)   *see* Brimpsfield w Birdlip, Syde, Daglingworth etc *Glouc*

MISSENDEN, GREAT (St Peter and St Paul) w Ballinger and Little Hampden *Ox 28*   **P** *Bp*   **V** R E HARPER,
NSM J-S S GALLANT

MISSENDEN, LITTLE (St John the Baptist) *Ox 28*
P *Earl Howe*   **P-in-c** J V SIMPSON

MISSION (St John the Baptist)   *see* Bawtry w Austerfield and Misson *S'well*

MISTERTON (All Saints)   *see* Beckingham and Walkeringham and Misterton etc *S'well*

MISTERTON (St Leonard)   *see* Wulfric Benefice *B & W*

MISTERTON (St Leonard)   *see* Gilmorton, Peatling Parva, Kimcote etc *Leic*

MISTLEY (St Mary and St Michael) w Manningtree and Bradfield *Chelmsf 20*   **P** *DBP and Bp (jt)*   **NSM** J R BRIEN

MITCHAM (Ascension) Pollards Hill *S'wark 13*   **P** *Bp*
V J M THOMAS,   **NSM** J E ROBERTS

MITCHAM (Christ Church)   *see* Merton Priory *S'wark*

MITCHAM (St Barnabas) *S'wark 13*   **P** *Bp*
V J G CAVALCANTI,   **Hon C** T PAYNE

MITCHAM (St Mark) *S'wark 13*   **P** *Bp*   **V** S H COULSON

MITCHAM (St Olave) *S'wark 13*   **P** *The Crown*   **V** P G ENSOR

MITCHAM (St Peter and St Paul) *S'wark 13*   **P** *Keble Coll Ox*
V J C ANSELL,   **NSM** M J COCKFIELD

MITCHELDEAN (St Michael and All Angels)   *see* Abenhall w Mitcheldean *Glouc*

MITFORD (St Mary Magdalene) *Newc 11*   **P** *Brig E C Mitford*
OLM J ROWLEY, J M QUINBY

MITHIAN (St Peter)   *see* St Agnes and Mount Hawke w Mithian *Truro*

MITTON (All Hallows)   *see* Hurst Green and Mitton *Bradf*

MIXBURY (All Saints)   *see* Shelswell *Ox*

MIXENDEN (Holy Nativity) *Wakef 4*   **P** *Bp*
P-in-c D E FLETCHER

MOBBERLEY (St Wilfrid) *Ches 12*   **P** *Bp*   **R** I BLAY

MOCCAS (St Michael and All Angels)   *see* Cusop w Blakemere, Bredwardine w Brobury etc *Heref*

MODBURY (St George), Bigbury, Ringmore w Kingston, Aveton Gifford, Woodleigh, Loddiswell and Allington, East *Ex 14*
P *Patr Bd*   **TR** N A BARKER,   **TV** M L JEFFERIES,
C J A ELLIOTT

MODDERSHALL (All Saints)   *see* Stone Ch Ch and Oulton *Lich*

MOGGERHANGER (St John the Evangelist)   *see* Cople, Moggerhanger and Willington *St Alb*

MOLASH (St Peter)   *see* Chilham w Challock and Molash *Cant*

MOLDGREEN (Christ Church) and Rawthorpe St James
Wakef 1   **P** *R Kirkheaton and DBP (jt)*
P-in-c H D ATKINSON

MOLESCROFT (St Leonard)   *see* Beverley Minster *York*

MOLESEY, EAST (St Mary) (St Paul) *Guildf 8*   **P** *Bp*
V A D MILTON,   **NSM** C S BOURNE, B C HUNT

MOLESEY, WEST (St Peter) *Guildf 8*   **P** *Canon W K Perry-Gore*   **V** P A TAILBY

MOLESWORTH (St Peter)   *see* Brington w Molesworth and Old Weston *Ely*

MOLLAND (St Mary)   *see* Bishopsnympton, Rose Ash, Mariansleigh etc *Ex*

MOLLINGTON (All Saints)   *see* Shires' Edge *Ox*

MOLTON, NORTH (All Saints)   *see* S Molton w Nymet St George, High Bray etc *Ex*

MOLTON, SOUTH (St Mary Magdalene) w Nymet St George, High Bray, Charles, Filleigh, East Buckland, Warkleigh, Satterleigh, Chittlehamholt, Kingsnympton, Romansleigh, North Molton, Twitchen and Chittlehampton *Ex 19*   **P** *DBP*
TV D W T RUDMAN, C A J DAVIS,   **C** C G ROBINSON,
P J ATTWOOD,   **NSM** C M G POUNCEY

MONEWDEN (St Mary)   *see* Mid Loes *St E*

MONGEHAM, GREAT (St Martin)   *see* Deal St Leon w St Rich and Sholden etc *Cant*

MONK BRETTON (St Paul) *Wakef 7*   **P** *V Royston*
OLM J M CROSSLAND

MONK FRYSTON (St Wilfrid of Ripon) and South Milford
York 4   **P** *Ld Chan and Abp (alt)*   **R** J C HETHERINGTON

MONK SHERBORNE (All Saints)   *see* The Sherbornes w Pamber *Win*

MONK SOHAM (St Peter)   *see* Worlingworth, Southolt, Tannington, Bedfield etc *St E*

MONKEN HADLEY (St Mary the Virgin) *Lon 14*   **P** *Bp*
R T J N L'ESTRANGE

MONKHOPTON (St Peter)   *see* Upton Cressett w Monk Hopton *Heref*

MONKLAND (All Saints)   *see* Leominster *Heref*

MONKLEIGH (St George)   *see* Bideford, Northam, Westward Ho!, Appledore etc *Ex*

MONKMOOR (St Peter)   *see* Shrewsbury H Cross *Lich*

MONKOKEHAMPTON (All Saints) *Ex 20*   **P** *Bp*
P-in-c C A BRODRIBB

MONKS COPPENHALL (Christ Church)   *see* Crewe Ch Ch *Ches*

MONKS ELEIGH (St Peter) w Chelsworth and Brent Eleigh w Milden and Kettlebaston *St E 10*   **P** *Bp, Guild of All So, Ld Chan (2 turns), and M J Hawkins Esq*   **R** B J FINDLAY

MONKS HILL (St Francis)   *see* Selsdon St Fran CD *S'wark*

MONKS HORTON (St Peter)   *see* Smeeth w Monks Horton and Stowting and Brabourne *Cant*

MONKS KIRBY (St Editha) w Pailton and Stretton-under-Fosse
Cov 6   **P** *Trin Coll Cam*   **P-in-c** C A GARROD

MONKS RISBOROUGH (St Dunstan)   *see* Risborough *Ox*

MONKSEATON (St Mary) *Newc 5*   **P** *Bp*
V R P GREENWOOD,   **Hon C** E J NOBLE,   **NSM** E LEWIS

MONKSEATON (St Peter) *Newc 5*   **P** *Bp*   **V** J A ROBERTSON,
C P A CRAIGHEAD

MONKSILVER (All Saints)   *see* Quantock Towers *B & W*

MONKTON (St Mary Magdalene)   *see* Minster w Monkton *Cant*

MONKTON, WEST (St Augustine) *B & W 18*   **P** *Bp*
P-in-c G J BOUCHER,   **NSM** S M HOUNSELL

MONKTON COMBE (St Michael)   *see* Combe Down w Monkton Combe and S Stoke *B & W*

MONKTON FARLEIGH (St Peter), South Wraxall and Winsley
Sarum 14   **P** *D&C Bris (2 turns), Bp (1 turn)*
P-in-c H K JAMESON

MONKTON WYLD (St Andrew)   *see* Golden Cap Team *Sarum*

MONKWEARMOUTH (All Saints) (St Andrew) (St Peter)
Dur 16   **P** *Bp*   **TR** I G STOCKTON,   **TV** L M GIBBONS,
T P GIBBONS,   **OLM** P G A SMITHSON

MONKWOOD (Mission Church) *see* Bishop's Sutton and Ropley and W Tisted *Win*

MONNINGTON-ON-WYE (St Mary) *see* Letton w Staunton, Byford, Mansel Gamage etc *Heref*

MONTACUTE (St Catherine of Alexandria) *see* Odcombe, Brympton, Lufton and Montacute *B & W*

MONTFORD (St Chad) *see* Bicton, Montford w Shrawardine and Fitz *Lich*

MONTON (St Paul) *see* Eccles *Man*

MONXTON (St Mary) *see* Portway and Danebury *Win*

MONYASH (St Leonard) *see* Taddington, Chelmorton and Flagg, and Monyash *Derby*

MOOR (St Thomas) *see* Fladbury w Wyre Piddle and Moor etc *Worc*

MOOR ALLERTON (St John the Evangelist) (St Stephen) *Ripon 5* **P** *Patr Bd* **TR** C P DOBBIN, **TV** N D BEER, P H AINSWORTH, **NSM** D J EVERETT

MOOR COURT (St Mary) *see* Pembridge w Moor Court, Shobdon, Staunton etc *Heref*

MOOR GRANGE (St Andrew) *see* Hawksworth Wood *Ripon*

MOOR MILNER (Church Institute) *see* Daresbury *Ches*

MOOR MONKTON (All Saints) *see* Rufforth w Moor Monkton and Hessay *York*

MOORBRIDGE LANE (St Luke) *see* Stapleford *S'well*

MOORCOURT (St Mary) *see* Pembridge w Moor Court, Shobdon, Staunton etc *Heref*

MOORDOWN (St John the Baptist) *Win 8* **P** *Bp* **NSM** J L WILLIAMS

MOORENDS (St Wilfrith) *Sheff 10* **P** *Bp* **V** *vacant* (01405) 741758

MOORHOUSE (Chantry Chapel) *see* Kneesall w Laxton and Wellow *S'well*

MOORHOUSES (St Lawrence) *see* Fen and Hill Gp *Linc*

MOORLAND TEAM *see* Ashburton, Bickington, Buckland in the Moor etc *Ex*

MOORLINCH (Blessed Virgin Mary) *see* Middlezoy and Othery and Moorlinch *B & W*

MOORSHOLM (St Mary) *York 22* **P** *Abp* **V** M J HAZELTON

MOORSIDE (St Thomas) *see* Oldham Moorside *Man*

MOORSIDE (St Wilfrid) *see* Doxford St Wilfrid *Dur*

MOORTOWN (St Stephen) *see* Moor Allerton *Ripon*

MORBORNE (All Saints) *see* Stilton w Denton and Caldecote etc *Ely*

MORCHARD BISHOP (St Mary) *see* N Creedy *Ex*

MORCOTT (St Mary the Virgin) *see* Barrowden and Wakerley w S Luffenham etc *Pet*

MORDEN (St Lawrence) (St George) (St Martin) (Emmanuel Church Hall) *S'wark 13* **P** *Patr Bd* **TR** R F SKINNER, **TV** D R H MCGOWAN, A L FLOWERDAY, **C** L J WELLS, **Hon C** P S OMUKU, **OLM** J D GODDARD

MORDEN (St Mary) *see* Red Post *Sarum*

MORDIFORD (Holy Rood) *see* Fownhope w Mordiford, Brockhampton etc *Heref*

MORE (St Peter) *see* Wentnor w Ratlinghope, Myndtown, Norbury etc *Heref*

MOREBATH (St George) *see* Bampton, Morebath, Clayhanger and Petton *Ex*

MORECAMBE (Holy Trinity) *see* Poulton-le-Sands w Morecambe St Laur *Blackb*

MORECAMBE (St Andrew) *see* Heysham *Blackb*

MORECAMBE (St Barnabas) *Blackb 11* **P** R *Poulton-le-Sands* **V** *vacant* (01524) 411283 *or* 401464

MORECAMBE (St Christopher) *see* Bare *Blackb*

MORECAMBE (St James) *see* Heysham *Blackb*

MORECAMBE (St John) *see* Sandylands *Blackb*

MORECAMBE (St Peter) *see* Heysham *Blackb*

MORECAMBE (The Ascension) *see* Torrisholme *Blackb*

MORELEIGH (All Saints) *see* Diptford, N Huish, Harberton, Harbertonford etc *Ex*

MORESBY (St Bridget) *Carl 5* **P** *Earl of Lonsdale* **P-in-c** S R GRIFFITHS

MORESBY PARKS (Mission Church) *see* Moresby *Carl*

MORESTEAD (not known) *see* Twyford and Owslebury and Morestead etc *Win*

MORETON (Christ Church) *Ches 8* **P** *Simeon's Trustees* **R** R G J COUSINS, **C** P C BOURKE

MORETON (St Mary) *see* Fyfield, Moreton w Bobbingworth etc *Chelmsf*

MORETON (St Mary) *see* Gnosall and Moreton *Lich*

MORETON (St Nicholas) and Woodsford w Tincleton *Sarum 1* **P** *Hon Mrs M A Bartenk and Miss M B F Frampton (alt)* **R** J A BIRDSEYE

MORETON, NORTH (All Saints) *see* The Churn *Ox*

MORETON, SOUTH (St John the Baptist) *as above*

MORETON CORBET (St Bartholomew) *Lich 22* **P** C C Corbet Esq **R** D J HUMPHRIES

MORETON HALL (Christ Church) *see* Bury St Edmunds Ch Ch *St E*

MORETON-IN-MARSH (St David) w Batsford, Todenham, Lower Lemington and Longborough w Sezincote *Glouc 12* **P** *Bp and Lord Dulverton (1 turn), and Bp, Lord Dulverton, Lord Leigh, and Mrs S Peake (1 turn)* **R** S M WOOKEY, **C** N P WELDON

MORETON JEFFRIES (St Peter and St Paul) *see* Bromyard and Stoke Lacy *Heref*

MORETON MORRELL (Holy Cross) *see* Newbold Pacey w Moreton Morrell *Cov*

MORETON-ON-LUGG (St Andrew) *see* Pipe-cum-Lyde and Moreton-on-Lugg *Heref*

MORETON PINKNEY (St Mary the Virgin) *see* Culworth w Sulgrave and Thorpe Mandeville etc *Pet*

MORETON SAY (St Margaret of Antioch) *see* Adderley, Ash, Calverhall, Ightfield etc *Lich*

MORETON VALENCE (St Stephen) *see* Eastington, Frocester, Haresfield etc *Glouc*

MORETONHAMPSTEAD (St Andrew), Manaton, North Bovey and Lustleigh *Ex 9* **P** *Bp and DBP (jt)* **R** I A HELLYER

MORGAN'S VALE (St Birinus) *see* Forest and Avon *Sarum*

MORLAND (St Lawrence), Thrimby, Gt Strickland and Cliburn *Carl 1* **P** *Lord Hothfield and D&C (jt)* **V** S D RUDKIN

MORLEY (St Botolph) *see* High Oak, Hingham and Scoulton w Wood Rising *Nor*

MORLEY (St Matthew) w Smalley and Horsley Woodhouse *Derby 12* **P** *Bp* **C** M G ALEXANDER

MORLEY (St Peter) *see* High Oak, Hingham and Scoulton w Wood Rising *Nor*

MORLEY (St Peter) (St Paul) *Wakef 8* **P** *Patr Bd* **TR** M M DYE, **TV** N M HEATON, **C** R SUTHERLAND, **OLM** K M DAVIS

MORNINGTHORPE (St John the Baptist) *see* Hempnall *Nor*

MORPETH (St Aidan) (St James) (St Mary the Virgin) *Newc 11* **P** *Bp* **R** R H MCLEAN, **NSM** M O CHESTER, **OLM** J L J COOPER

MORRIS GREEN (St Bede) *see* Bolton St Bede *Man*

MORSTON (All Saints) *see* Stiffkey and Bale *Nor*

MORTEHOE (St Mary Magdalene) *see* Ilfracombe, Lee, Woolacombe, Bittadon etc *Ex*

MORTIMER COMMON (St John) *see* Stratfield Mortimer and Mortimer W End etc *Ox*

MORTIMER WEST END (St Saviour) *as above*

MORTLAKE (St Mary) w East Sheen *S'wark 16* **P** *Patr Bd* **TV** W S GRIFFITH, C PALMER, **C** L A J CODRINGTON-MARSHALL, **Hon C** P D KING, **OLM** O J WILLIAMSON

MORTOMLEY (St Saviour) High Green *Sheff 3* **P** *Bp* **V** E MITCHELL

MORTON (Holy Cross) and Stonebroom w Shirland *Derby 1* **P** *Bp, St Jo Coll Cam, Adn Chesterfield, and trustees (by turn)* **P-in-c** M I JACQUES

MORTON (St Denis) *see* Rolleston w Fiskerton, Morton and Upton *S'well*

MORTON (St John the Baptist) *see* Ringstone in Aveland Gp *Linc*

MORTON (St Luke) *Bradf 8* **P** *Bp* **P-in-c** M C CANSDALE

MORTON (St Paul) *see* Gainsborough and Morton *Linc*

MORTON (St Philip and St James) *see* Llanyblodwel, Llanymynech, Morton and Trefonen *Lich*

MORTON, EAST *see* Morton St Luke *Bradf*

MORTON BAGOT (Holy Trinity) *see* Spernall, Morton Bagot and Oldberrow *Cov*

MORVAH (St Bridget of Sweden) *see* Pendeen w Morvah *Truro*

MORVAL (St Wenna) *see* Duloe, Herodsfoot, Morval and St Pinnock *Truro*

MORVILLE (St Gregory) w Aston Eyre *Heref 9* **P** *DBP* **P-in-c** A A ROBERTS, **Hon C** H J PATTERSON

MORWENSTOW (St John the Baptist) *see* Kilkhampton w Morwenstow *Truro*

MOSBROUGH (St Mark) *Sheff 1* **P** *Bp* **V** S T STEWART

MOSELEY (St Agnes) *Birm 5* **P** V *Moseley St Mary* **V** P H ANSELL

MOSELEY (St Anne) (St Mary) *Birm 5* **P** *Bp* **V** J N J C DUSSEK, **C** R A DONOVAN, **NSM** F J BERRY

MOSLEY COMMON (St John) *see* Astley, Tyldesley and Mosley Common *Man*

MOSS BANK (Mission Church) *see* Carr Mill *Liv*

MOSS SIDE (Christ Church) *Man 4* **P** *Trustees* **R** S D A KILLWICK

MOSS SIDE (St James w St Clement) *see* Whalley Range St Edm and Moss Side etc *Man*

MOSSER (St Michael's Chapel) *see* Clifton, Dean and Mosser *Carl*

MOSSER (St Philip) *as above*

MOSSLEY (Holy Trinity)   *see* Congleton *Ches*
MOSSLEY (St George) *Man 17*   **P** *R* Ashton-under-Lyne
St Mich   **V** R J LINDSAY,   **OLM** P PHILLIPS
MOSSLEY ESTATE (St Thomas Church)   *see* Bloxwich *Lich*
MOSSLEY HILL (St Barnabas) (St Matthew and St James)
Liv 4   **P** *Patr Bd*   **TR** G J BUTLAND,   **TV** A KENNEDY,
OLM C NICHOLSON
MOSSWOOD (St Barnabas)   *see* Cannock *Lich*
MOSTERTON (St Mary)   *see* Beaminster Area *Sarum*
MOSTON (St Chad) *Man 5*   **P** *Bp*   **P-in-c** I C J GORTON,
OLM I L SMITH
MOSTON (St John) Ashley Lane *Man 5*   **P** *Bp*
P-in-c I C J GORTON
MOSTON (St Luke)   *see* Lightbowne *Man*
MOSTON (St Mary) *Man 5*   **P** *D&C*
P-in-c M R M CALLADINE,   **OLM** J E GRAYSON
MOTCOMBE (St Mary)   *see* Shaston *Sarum*
MOTSPUR PARK (Holy Cross) *S'wark 13*   **P** *Bp*
V R S TAYLOR
MOTTINGHAM (St Andrew) (St Alban Mission Church)
S'wark 3   **P** *Bp*   **P-in-c** I M WELCH,   **NSM** S P WARNER
MOTTINGHAM (St Edward the Confessor) *S'wark 3*   **P** *Bp*
V M J JACKSON
MOTTISFONT (St Andrew)   *see* Broughton, Bossington,
Houghton and Mottisfont *Win*
MOTTISTONE (St Peter and St Paul)   *see* Brighstone and
Brooke w Mottistone *Portsm*
MOTTRAM IN LONGDENDALE (St Michael) *Ches 14*   **P** *Bp*
V P G BURROWS
MOULSECOOMB (St Andrew) *Chich 2*   **P** *Bp*   **TR** J C WALL,
C R C GOULDTHORPE, W J WESSON,   **NSM** J W M COLLINS
MOULSFORD (St John the Baptist)   *see* Cholsey and
Moulsford *Ox*
MOULSHAM (St John the Evangelist) *Chelmsf 9*   **P** *Dean*
V K R MAGEE
MOULSHAM (St Luke) *Chelmsf 9*   **P** *Bp*   **V** C SMITH,
C M L BISHOP
MOULSOE (The Assumption of the Blessed Virgin Mary)
see Newport Pagnell w Lathbury and Moulsoe *Ox*
MOULTON (All Saints) (St James) (Mission Room) *Linc 17*
P *DBP*   **P-in-c** R J SEAL
MOULTON (Mission Church)   *see* E Richmond *Ripon*
MOULTON (St Peter)   *see* Dalham, Gazeley, Higham, Kentford
and Moulton *St E*
MOULTON (St Peter and St Paul) *Pet 4*   **P** *Ch Soc Trust*
V P H BRECKWOLDT,   **C** R A MILES
MOULTON (St Stephen the Martyr) *Ches 6*   **P** *R Davenham*
P-in-c R W FORRESTER
MOULTON, GREAT (St Michael)   *see* Bunwell, Carleton Rode,
Tibenham, Gt Moulton etc *Nor*
MOUNT BURES (St John)   *see* Wormingford, Mt Bures and Lt
Horkesley *Chelmsf*
MOUNT GOULD (St Simon)   *see* Plymouth St Simon and St
Mary *Ex*
MOUNT HAWKE (St John the Baptist)   *see* St Agnes and
Mount Hawke w Mithian *Truro*
MOUNT PELLON (Christ Church)   *see* Halifax St Aug and
Mount Pellon *Wakef*
MOUNTFIELD (All Saints)   *see* Brightling, Dallington,
Mountfield etc *Chich*
MOUNTNESSING (St Giles)   *see* Margaretting w
Mountnessing and Buttsbury *Chelmsf*
MOUNTSORREL (Christ Church) (St Peter) *Leic 6*   **P** *CPAS*
and Bp   **P-in-c** K C EMMETT
MOW COP (St Luke's Mission Church)   *see* Odd Rode *Ches*
MOW COP (St Thomas) *Lich 11*   **P** *Prime Min*
P-in-c J C WATERS
MOWSLEY (St Nicholas)   *see* Hexagon *Leic*
MOXLEY (All Saints) *Lich 26*   **P** *Prime Min*   **V** R E INGLESBY,
OLM A J DUCKWORTH
MUCH *see also under substantive place name*
MUCH BIRCH (St Mary and St Thomas à Becket)
see Wormelow Hundred *Heref*
MUCHELNEY (St Peter and St Paul)   *see* Langport Area
B & W
MUCKLESTONE (St Mary)   *see* Ashley and Mucklestone *Lich*
MUDEFORD (All Saints) *Win 9*   **P** *Bp*   **P-in-c** H M GRIFFISS
MUDFORD (Blessed Virgin Mary)   *see* Chilton Cantelo,
Ashington, Mudford, Rimpton etc *B & W*
MUGGINTON (All Saints) and Kedleston *Derby 11*   **P** *Major*
J W Chandos-Pole   **P-in-c** S I MITCHELL
MUGGLESWICK (All Saints)   *see* Blanchland w
Hunstanworth and Edmundbyers etc *Newc*
MUKER (St Mary)   *see* Swaledale *Ripon*
**MULBARTON (St Mary Magdalene) w Bracon Ash, Hethel and
Flordon** *Nor 7*   **P** *R T Berney Esq (1 turn),*

*Mrs R M Watkinson (2 turns), DBP (1 turn), and Ld Chan
(1 turn)*   **R** J W STUBENBORD
MULLION (St Mellanus) *Truro 4*   **P** *Bp*   **P-in-c** S O GRIFFITHS
MUMBY (St Thomas of Canterbury)   *see* Willoughby *Linc*
MUNCASTER (St Michael)   *see* Eskdale, Irton, Muncaster and
Waberthwaite *Carl*
MUNDEN, LITTLE (All Saints)   *see* Standon and The
Mundens w Sacombe *St Alb*
MUNDESLEY (All Saints)   *see* Trunch *Nor*
MUNDFORD (St Leonard) w Lynford *Nor 13*   **P** *Ch Patr Trust*
R *vacant* (01842) 878220
MUNDHAM (St Peter)   *see* Brooke, Kirstead, Mundham w
Seething and Thwaite *Nor*
MUNDHAM, NORTH (St Stephen) w Hunston and Merston
Chich 3   **P** *St Jo Coll Cam*   **P-in-c** J A T RUSSELL
MUNGRISDALE (St Kentigern)   *see* Gd Shep TM *Carl*
MUNSLEY (St Bartholomew)   *see* Ledbury *Heref*
MUNSLOW (St Michael)   *see* Diddlebury w Munslow, Holdgate
and Tugford *Heref*
MUNSTER SQUARE (Christ Church) (St Mary Magdalene)
Lon 17   **P** *Bp*   **V** M R POOLE
MUNSTONE (Church Room)   *see* Holmer w Huntington *Heref*
MURCOTT (Mission Room)   *see* Ray Valley *Ox*
MURROW (Corpus Christi)   *see* Wisbech St Mary and Guyhirn
w Ring's End etc *Ely*
MURSLEY (St Mary the Virgin)   *see* Newton Longville and
Mursley w Swanbourne etc *Ox*
MURSTON (All Saints) w Bapchild and Tonge *Cant 15*   **P** *Abp*
and St Jo Coll Cam (jt)   **P-in-c** M MOSELEY
MURTON (Holy Trinity)   *see* Hawthorn and Murton *Dur*
MURTON (St James)   *see* Osbaldwick w Murton *York*
MURTON (St John the Baptist)   *see* Heart of Eden *Carl*
MUSBURY (St Michael)   *see* Colyton, Musbury, Southleigh and
Branscombe *Ex*
MUSBURY (St Thomas) *Blackb 1*   **P** *The Crown*
P-in-c T R SMITH
MUSGRAVE (St Theobald)   *see* Brough w Stainmore, Musgrave
and Warcop *Carl*
MUSKHAM, NORTH (St Wilfrid) and SOUTH (St Wilfrid)
S'well 3   **P** *Ld Chan*   **V** *vacant* (01636) 702655
MUSTON (All Saints)   *see* Hunmanby w Muston *York*
MUSTON (St John the Baptist)   *see* Vale of Belvoir Par *Leic*
MUSWELL HILL (St James) (St Matthew) *Lon 20*   **P** *Bp and
CPAS (jt)*   **V** K S SWITHINBANK,   **C** G J DALY,
W D HUNTER SMART,   **NSM** H C HENDRY
MUTFORD (St Andrew)   *see* Carlton Colville and Mutford *Nor*
MUXTON (St John the Evangelist)   *see* Lilleshall and Muxton
Lich
MYDDELTON SQUARE (St Mark)   *see* Clerkenwell St Mark
Lon
MYDDLE (St Peter) *Lich 22*   **P** *Bp*   **P-in-c** P F BARNES,
OLM A EVANS
MYLAND (St Michael)   *see* Colchester St Mich Myland
Chelmsf
MYLOR (St Mylor) w Flushing *Truro 3*   **P** *Bp*
P-in-c R F NICHOLLS,   **NSM** A J STEVENSON
MYLOR BRIDGE (All Saints)   *see* Mylor w Flushing *Truro*
MYMMS, NORTH (St Mary)   *see* Bp's Hatfield, Lemsford and
N Mymms *St Alb*
MYMMS, NORTH (St Michael)   *as above*
MYMMS, SOUTH (King Charles the Martyr)   *see* Potters Bar
K Chas *St Alb*
MYMMS, SOUTH (St Giles) and Ridge *St Alb 17*   **P** *DBP*
P-in-c B M TIPPING
MYNDTOWN (St John the Baptist)   *see* Wentnor w
Ratlinghope, Myndtown, Norbury etc *Heref*
MYTHOLMROYD (St Michael)   *see* Erringden *Wakef*
MYTON ON SWALE (St Mary)   *see* Brafferton w Pilmoor,
Myton-on-Swale etc *York*
NABB (Mission Church)   *see* Oakengates and Wrockwardine
Wood *Lich*
NABURN (St Matthew)   *see* Escrick and Stillingfleet w Naburn
York
NACKINGTON (St Mary)   *see* Bridge *Cant*
**NACTON (St Martin) and Levington w Bucklesham and Foxhall
w Kirton and Falkenham** *St E 2*   **P** *Ld Chan and DBP (alt)*
R G L GRANT,   **NSM** H M DAVY,   **OLM** D E N KING
NADDER VALLEY *Sarum 11*   **P** *Patr Bd (4 turns), Ld Chan
(1 turn)*   **TR** J C EADE,   **TV** J D TAILBY, A STALEY,
Dss A SYMES
NAFFERTON (All Saints) w Wansford *York 10*   **P** *Abp*
P-in-c P J ARTLEY
NAILSEA (Christ Church) w Tickenham *B & W 13*   **P** *CPAS
(3 turns), Ld Chan (1 turn)*   **R** A Q H WHEELER
NAILSEA (Holy Trinity) *B & W 13*   **P** *MMCET*
C J S TILLEY, M J PARKMAN

NAILSTONE (All Saints) and Carlton w Shackerstone *Leic 10*
P *The Crown and DBP (alt)*   **P-in-c** J F PLANT,   **C** A S G PIKE,
NSM A C HOLDSTOCK
NAILSWORTH (St George) w Shortwood, Horsley and
Newington Bagath w Kingscote *Glouc 5*   **P** *Bp*   **V** S J EARLEY
NANPANTAN (St Mary in Charnwood)   *see* Loughborough
Em and St Mary in Charnwood *Leic*
NANPEAN (St George)   *see* St Stephen in Brannel *Truro*
NANSTALLON (St Stephen's Mission Room)   *see* Bodmin w
Lanhydrock and Lanivet *Truro*
NANTWICH (St Mary) *Ches 15*   **P** *Q H Crewe Esq and*
J C Crewe Esq (jt)   **R** P T CHANTRY,   **C** T ROBINSON
NAPTON-ON-THE-HILL (St Lawrence), Lower Shuckburgh
and Stockton *Cov 10*   **P** *Ld Chan (2 turns), Sir Rupert*
Shuckburgh Bt (1 turn), and New Coll Ox (2 turns)
P-in-c M L D GREIG
NARBOROUGH (All Saints) and Huncote *Leic 7*   **P** *SMF*
R N J BURTON
NARBOROUGH (All Saints) w Narford and Pentney *Nor 13*
P *Bp*   **R** S R NAIRN
NARFORD (St Mary)   *see* Narborough w Narford and Pentney
Nor
NASEBY (All Saints)   *see* Clipston w Naseby and Haselbech w
Kelmarsh *Pet*
NASH (All Saints)   *see* Buckingham *Ox*
NASH (St John the Baptist)   *see* Burford I *Heref*
NASSINGTON (St Mary the Virgin and All Saints) w Yarwell
and Woodnewton w Apethorpe *Pet 10*   **P** *Bp and*
Lord Brassey (jt)   **P-in-c** J R FLACK
NATELY SCURES (St Swithun)   *see* N Hants Downs *Win*
NATLAND (St Mark) *Carl 10*   **P** *V Kendal H Trin*
NSM M P JAYNE
NAUGHTON (St Mary)   *see* Bildeston w Wattisham and
Lindsey, Whatfield etc *St E*
NAUNTON (St Andrew)   *see* The Guitings, Cutsdean, Farmcote
etc *Glouc*
NAUNTON BEAUCHAMP (St Bartholomew)   *see* Abberton,
The Flyfords, Naunton Beauchamp etc *Worc*
NAVENBY (St Peter)   *see* Graffoe Gp *Linc*
NAVESTOCK (St Thomas)   *see* Bentley Common, Kelvedon
Hatch and Navestock *Chelmsf*
NAWTON (St Hilda)   *see* Kirkdale w Harome, Nunnington and
Pockley *York*
NAYLAND (St James) w Wiston *St E 3*   **P** *Ld Chan (2 turns)*
and DBP (1 turn)   **P-in-c** C A GRAY
NAYLAND DRIVE (Church Centre)   *see* Clacton St Jas
Chelmsf
NAZEING (All Saints) (St Giles) *Chelmsf 25*   **P** *Ld Chan*
P-in-c C P PENNINGTON
NEASDEN (St Catherine w St Paul) *Lon 21*   **P** *Bp and*
D&C St Paul's (jt)   **V** E E GAUNT
NEATISHEAD (St Peter)   *see* Ashmanhaugh, Barton Turf etc
Nor
NECHELLS (St Matthew)   *see* Aston and Nechells *Birm*
NECTON (All Saints), Holme Hale w Pickenham, North and
South *Nor 13*   **P** *Major-Gen R S Broke, Ch Soc Trust,*
MMCET and S Pickenham Estate Co Ltd (jt)   **R** S L THORP
NEDGING (St Mary)   *see* Bildeston w Wattisham and Lindsey,
Whatfield etc *St E*
NEEDHAM (St Peter)   *see* Redenhall, Harleston, Wortwell and
Needham *Nor*
NEEDHAM MARKET (St John the Baptist) w Badley *St E 1*
P *PCC*   **P-in-c** D R WILLIAMS
NEEN SAVAGE (St Mary)   *see* Cleobury Mortimer w Hopton
Wafers etc *Heref*
NEEN SOLLARS (All Saints)   *as above*
NEENTON (All Saints)   *see* Ditton Priors w Neenton,
Burwarton etc *Heref*
NEITHROP (St Paul)   *see* Banbury St Paul *Ox*
NELSON (St Bede)   *see* Lt Marsden w Nelson St Mary and
Nelson St Bede *Blackb*
NELSON (St John the Evangelist)   *see* Gt Marsden w Nelson St
Phil *Blackb*
NELSON (St Mary)   *see* Lt Marsden w Nelson St Mary and
Nelson St Bede *Blackb*
NELSON (St Paul)   *as above*
NELSON (St Philip)   *see* Gt Marsden w Nelson St Phil *Blackb*
NEMPNETT THRUBWELL (The Blessed Virgin Mary)
see Chew Stoke w Nempnett Thrubwell *B & W*
NENTHEAD (St John)   *see* Alston Moor *Newc*
NESS Group, The *Linc 13*   **P** *Ld Chan (1 turn), Bp and DBP*
(2 turns)   **V** J M BEADLE,   **C** D M REES-JONES
NESS, GREAT (St Andrew)   *see* Ruyton XI Towns w Gt and Lt
Ness *Lich*
NESS, LITTLE (St Martin)   *as above*

NESTON (St Mary and St Helen) *Ches 9*   **P** *D&C*
V R H N ROBB,   **C** A A HARRIS
NESTON (St Phillip and St James)   *see* Gtr Corsham and
Lacock *Bris*
NESTON, LITTLE (St Michael and All Angels)   *see* Neston
Ches
NETHER *see also under subtantive place name*
NETHER HALL (St Elizabeth)   *see* Scraptoft *Leic*
NETHERAVON (All Saints)   *see* Avon Valley *Sarum*
NETHERBURY (St Mary)   *see* Beaminster Area *Sarum*
NETHEREXE (St John the Baptist)   *see* Stoke Canon,
Poltimore w Huxham and Rewe etc *Ex*
NETHERFIELD (St George) *S'well 10*   **P** *DBP*
P-in-c R B CHAPMAN
NETHERFIELD (St John the Baptist)   *see* Brightling,
Dallington, Mountfield etc *Chich*
NETHERHAMPTON (St Katherine)   *see* Wilton w
Netherhampton and Fugglestone *Sarum*
NETHERLEY (Christ Church)   *see* Gateacre *Liv*
NETHERNE (St Luke)   *see* Merstham and Gatton *S'wark*
NETHERSEAL (St Peter)   *see* Seale and Lullington w Coton in
the Elms *Derby*
NETHERTHONG (All Saints)   *see* Upper Holme Valley *Wakef*
NETHERTHORPE (St Bartholomew)   *see* Sheff St Bart *Sheff*
NETHERTHORPE (St Stephen) *Sheff 4*   **P** *Ch Patr Trust and*
Sheff Ch Burgesses Trust (jt)   **V** P J BATCHFORD,
C G L KALSI
NETHERTON (All Souls)   *see* Maryport, Netherton and
Flimby *Carl*
NETHERTON (St Andrew)   *see* Middlestown *Wakef*
NETHERTON (St Andrew) *Worc 9*   **P** *Bp*   **V** S H CARTER
NETHERTON (St Oswald) *Liv 1*   **P** *Bp*   **P-in-c** D H STATTER
NETHERWITTON (St Giles)   *see* Nether Witton *Newc*
NETLEY ABBEY   *see* Hound *Win*
NETLEY MARSH (St Matthew)   *see* Totton *Win*
NETTLEBED (St Bartholomew) w Bix, Highmoor, Pishill and
Rotherfield Greys *Ox 6*   **P** *DBP, Earl of Macclesfield, Ch Patr*
Trust, and Trin Coll Ox (jt)   **R** B J BAILEY,   **Hon**
C D J STOTER,   **OLM** E F LAKEY
NETTLECOMBE (Blessed Virgin Mary)   *see* Quantock Towers
B & W
NETTLEDEN (Ashridge Chapel)   *see* Gt Berkhamsted, Gt and
Lt Gaddesden etc *St Alb*
NETTLEDEN (St Lawrence)   *as above*
NETTLEHAM (All Saints) *Linc 3*   **P** *Bp*   **P-in-c** J J E ROWLEY,
C M J RUSHTON,   **NSM** C A ZOTOV, J L HART
NETTLESTEAD (St Mary)   *see* Gt and Lt Blakenham w
Baylham and Nettlestead *St E*
NETTLESTEAD (St Mary the Virgin)   *see* E Peckham and
Nettlestead *Roch*
NETTLETON (St John the Baptist)   *see* Swallow *Linc*
NETTLETON (St Mary)   *see* By Brook *Bris*
NEVENDON (St Peter)   *see* Pitsea w Nevendon *Chelmsf*
NEVILLE'S CROSS (St John)   *see* Dur St Marg and Neville's
Cross St Jo *Dur*
NEW *see also under substantive place name*
NEW BOROUGH and Leigh (St John the Evangelist) *Sarum 9*
P *Ch Soc Trust*   **V** R J A TULLOCH
NEW BUILDINGS (Beacon Church)   *see* Crediton, Shobrooke
and Sandford etc *Ex*
NEW CROSS   *see* Hatcham St Jas *S'wark*
NEW FERRY (St Mark) *Ches 8*   **P** *R Bebington*
V A Q GREENHOUGH,   **NSM** A D DRURY
NEW HAW (All Saints) *Guildf 11*   **P** *Bp*   **V** R J GOSTELOW
NEW MILL (Christ Church)   *see* Upper Holme Valley *Wakef*
NEW MILLS (St George) (St James the Less) *Derby 6*
P *V Glossop*   **P-in-c** J C BAINES
NEW PARKS (St Aidan)   *see* Leic St Aid *Leic*
NEW SPRINGS (St John the Baptist) and Whelley St Stephen
Liv 14   **P** *Bp*   **V** D J ROSCOE
NEWALL GREEN (St Francis of Assisi)   *see* Wythenshawe
Man
NEWARK-UPON-TRENT (St Mary Magdalene) (Christ
Church) (St Leonard) *S'well 3*   **P** *The Crown*   **TR** V J ENEVER,
TV S J TREDWELL, D E ANDERTON,   **C** T W POWNALL-JONES
NEWBALD (St Nicholas) *York 13*   **P** *Abp*   **P-in-c** M R BUSHBY
NEWBARNS (St Paul)   *see* Barrow St Paul *Carl*
NEWBIGGIN (St Edmund)   *see* Kirkby Thore w Temple
Sowerby and Newbiggin *Carl*
NEWBIGGIN-BY-THE-SEA (St Bartholomew)
see Woodhorn w Newbiggin *Newc*
NEWBIGGIN HALL (St Wilfrid) *Newc 4*   **P** *Bp*
V P D MCLEOD
NEWBOLD (St John the Evangelist) w Dunston *Derby 5*
P *R Chesterfield*   **V** N V JOHNSON,   **C** K COCKING
NEWBOLD (St Peter)   *see* S Rochdale *Man*

NEWBOLD DE VERDUN (St James) and Kirkby Mallory
Leic 10 **P** *Bp and Trin Coll Ox (jt)* **P-in-c** T H C MEYRICK
NEWBOLD ON AVON (St Botolph) *Cov 6*
P *H A F W Boughton Leigh Esq* **V** P M WILKINSON
NEWBOLD ON STOUR (St David) *see* Stourdene Gp *Cov*
NEWBOLD PACEY (St George) w Moreton Morrell *Cov 8*
P *Qu Coll Ox and Lt-Col J E Little (alt)* **V** G J BURRELL
NEWBOROUGH (All Saints) *see* Hanbury, Newborough, Rangemore and Tutbury *Lich*
NEWBOROUGH (St Bartholomew) *Pet 11* **P** *The Crown*
P-in-c C HURST
NEWBOTTLE (St James) *see* King's Sutton and Newbottle and Charlton *Pet*
NEWBOTTLE (St Matthew) *Dur 14* **P** *Bp* **V** E WILKINSON
NEWBOURN (St Mary) *see* Waldringfield w Hemley and Newbourn *St E*
NEWBROUGH (St Peter) *see* Warden w Newbrough *Newc*
NEWBURGH (Christ Church) w Westhead *Liv 11* **P** *Bp and V Ormskirk (jt)* **P-in-c** G A MILFORD, **NSM** D M BURROWS, **OLM** J SEPHTON, C DRAPER
NEWBURN (St Michael and All Angels) *Newc 4* **P** *MMCET* **V** J R SINCLAIR, **C** M S KNOX, **OLM** M P LEDGER
NEWBURY (St John the Evangelist) (St Nicholas and St Mary) *Ox 14* **P** *Bp* **TR** D A STONE, **TV** B DAGNALL, P H COWAN, **C** M R WOOLNOUGH, S L ALEXANDER, **NSM** J R COOK
NEWBY (St Mark) *York 15* **P** *Abp* **P-in-c** M J LEIGH
NEWCASTLE (Christ Church) (St Ann) *Newc 2* **P** *Bp*
P-in-c A W MARKS
NEWCASTLE (St Andrew) (St Luke) *Newc 2* **P** *Bp and V Newcastle (jt)* **P-in-c** G EVANS, **NSM** R C I WARD
NEWCASTLE (St John the Evangelist) *see* Clun w Bettws-y-Crwyn and Newcastle *Heref*
NEWCASTLE (St Philip) and St Augustine and (St Matthew w St Mary) *Newc 4* **P** *Bp* **V** R G S DEADMAN
NEWCASTLE UNDER LYME (St George) *Lich 9*
P *R Newcastle w Butterton* **V** W E J MASH
NEWCASTLE UNDER LYME (St Giles) w Butterton *Lich 9*
P *Simeon's Trustees* **R** S M LEE, **NSM** P NISBECK, **OLM** M A TAYLOR, J WARHAM
NEWCASTLE UNDER LYME (St Paul) *Lich 9* **P** *Trustees*
V *vacant* (01782) 617913
NEWCASTLE UPON TYNE (Christ Church) *see* Walker *Newc*
NEWCASTLE UPON TYNE Christ the King *see* Ch the King *Newc*
NEWCASTLE UPON TYNE (Clayton Memorial Church) *see* Jesmond Clayton Memorial *Newc*
NEWCASTLE UPON TYNE (Holy Cross) *Newc 4* **P** *Bp*
V A W MARKS, **C** J S PADDISON
NEWCASTLE UPON TYNE (Holy Trinity) *see* Jesmond H Trin *Newc*
NEWCASTLE UPON TYNE (St Anthony) *see* Byker St Ant *Newc*
NEWCASTLE UPON TYNE (St Barnabas and St Jude) *Newc 2*
P *V Jesmond Clayton Memorial and CPAS (alt)*
P-in-c M HUDSON, **C** T SAUNDERSON
NEWCASTLE UPON TYNE (St Francis) High Heaton *Newc 3*
P *Bp* **V** C J CLINCH, **C** J P HAGGER
NEWCASTLE UPON TYNE (St Gabriel) Heaton *Newc 3*
P *Bp* **V** S A WILSON
NEWCASTLE UPON TYNE (St George) (St Hilda) *Newc 2*
P *Bp* **V** N A CHAMBERLAIN, **C** A J FENTON, **OLM** C M CROMPTON
NEWCASTLE UPON TYNE (St James and St Basil) *see* Fenham St Jas and St Basil *Newc*
NEWCASTLE UPON TYNE (St John the Baptist) *Newc 2*
P *V Newc* **P-in-c** N WILSON
NEWCASTLE UPON TYNE (St Margaret) *see* Scotswood *Newc*
NEWCASTLE UPON TYNE (St Martin) *see* Byker St Martin *Newc*
NEWCASTLE UPON TYNE (St Michael w St Lawrence) *see* Byker St Mich w St Lawr *Newc*
NEWCASTLE UPON TYNE (St Oswald) *see* Byker St Mark and Walkergate St Oswald *Newc*
NEWCASTLE UPON TYNE (St Paul) *see* Elswick *Newc*
NEWCASTLE UPON TYNE (St Silas) *see* Byker St Silas *Newc*
NEWCASTLE UPON TYNE (St Stephen) *see* Elswick *Newc*
NEWCASTLE UPON TYNE (St Thomas) Proprietary Chapel
Newc 2 **P** *Trustees of St Thos Chpl Charity*
C-in-c C M LACK, **NSM** J SKINNER
NEWCASTLE UPON TYNE, WEST Benwell *see* Benwell *Newc*
NEWCHAPEL (St James the Apostle) *Lich 11* **P** *CPAS*
V W E SLATER, **C** C J BROAD
NEWCHURCH (All Saints) *Portsm 7* **P** *Bp*
P-in-c J F O'SHAUGHNESSY

NEWCHURCH (not known) w Croft *Liv 15* **P** *Bp*
R C J STAFFORD, **OLM** B SMART
NEWCHURCH (St Nicholas w St John) *see* Rossendale Middle Valley *Man*
NEWCHURCH (St Peter and St Paul) *see* Dymchurch w Burmarsh and Newchurch *Cant*
NEWCHURCH-IN-PENDLE (St Mary) *see* Barrowford and Newchurch-in-Pendle *Blackb*
NEWDIGATE (St Peter) *see* Surrey Weald *Guildf*
NEWENDEN (St Peter) *see* Sandhurst w Newenden *Cant*
NEWENT (St Mary the Virgin) and Gorsley w Cliffords Mesne
Glouc 1 **P** *Bp* **P-in-c** S I V MASON, **NSM** R G CHIVERS, K U MADDEN
NEWHALL (St John) *Derby 16* **P** *Bp* **V** R G HOLLINGS
NEWHAVEN (St Michael) *Chich 18* **P** *Ch Patr Trust*
R M M MILLER
NEWHEY (St Thomas) *Man 21* **P** *Bp* **P-in-c** G W LINDLEY
NEWICK (St Mary) *Chich 21* **P** *Ch Soc Trust* **R** P P FRANCIS
NEWINGTON (St Christopher) *see* St Laur in Thanet *Cant*
NEWINGTON (St Giles) *see* Dorchester *Ox*
NEWINGTON (St John the Baptist) w Dairycoates St Mary and St Peter *York 14* **P** *Abp* **P-in-c** P COPLEY, **C** T A COTSON
NEWINGTON (St Martin) *see* Hull St Martin w Transfiguration *York*
NEWINGTON (St Mary) *S'wark 10* **P** *Bp* **R** A P DODD, **C** R F HUNTE, **Hon C** M E TODD, **NSM** R HUTCHISON
NEWINGTON (St Mary the Virgin) w Hartlip and Stockbury
Cant 15 **P** *Abp* **P-in-c** A J AMOS, **C** H E NELSON, **NSM** E A COX
NEWINGTON (St Nicholas) *see* Cheriton All So w Newington *Cant*
NEWINGTON (St Paul) *S'wark 10* **P** *Bp* **V** G D SHAW, **NSM** E BOGLE
NEWINGTON, SOUTH (St Peter ad Vincula) *see* Bloxham w Milcombe and S Newington *Ox*
NEWLAND (All Saints) *see* Coleford, Staunton, Newland, Redbrook etc *Glouc*
NEWLAND (St John) *see* Hull St Jo Newland *York*
NEWLAND (St Lawrence) *see* Bradwell on Sea and St Lawrence *Chelmsf*
NEWLANDS (not known) *see* Upper Derwent *Carl*
NEWLAY LANE (St Margaret's Church Hall) *see* Bramley *Ripon*
NEWLYN (St Newlyn) *Truro 5* **P** *Bp* **P-in-c** H L SAMSON
NEWLYN (St Peter) *Truro 5* **P** *Bp* **V** R L STRANGE
NEWMARKET (All Saints) *St E 11* **P** *Bp* **V** M E OSBORNE
NEWMARKET (St Mary the Virgin) w Exning St Agnes *St E 11*
P *Bp and DBP (alt)* **R** J C HARDY
NEWNHAM (St Mark) *see* Cambridge St Mark *Ely*
NEWNHAM (St Michael and All Angels) *see* Badby w Newham and Charwelton w Fawsley etc *Pet*
NEWNHAM (St Nicholas) *see* N Hants Downs *Win*
NEWNHAM (St Peter and St Paul) *see* Doddington, Newnham and Wychling *Cant*
NEWNHAM (St Peter) w Awre and Blakeney *Glouc 2*
P *Haberdashers Co and Bp (alt)* **V** J STEPHENSON
NEWNHAM (St Vincent) *see* Ashwell w Hinxworth and Newnham *St Alb*
NEWNTON, NORTH (St James) *see* Pewsey and Swanborough *Sarum*
NEWPORT (St John the Baptist) *see* Barnstaple *Ex*
NEWPORT (St John the Baptist) *Portsm 8* **P** *Ch Patr Trust*
V S C PALMER, **NSM** R J WHATLEY, J K HALLAM
NEWPORT (St Mary the Virgin) and Widdington *Chelmsf 21*
P *Bp* **P-in-c** B L K SHERLOCK, **NSM** A P WANT
NEWPORT (St Nicholas) w Longford, Chetwynd and Forton
Lich 16 **P** *Bp* **R** S MITCHELL, **C** J H STOKES
NEWPORT (St Stephen) *see* Howden *York*
NEWPORT (St Thomas) *Portsm 8* **P** *Bp* **NSM** J K HALLAM
NEWPORT MINSTER *see* Newport St Thos *Portsm*
NEWPORT PAGNELL (St Luke) w Lathbury and Moulsoe
Ox 27 **P** *Bp, Ch Ch Ox, and Lord Carrington (jt)*
R M GODFREY, **OLM** G M BELL
NEWQUAY (St Michael) *Truro 7* **P** *Bp* **V** M J ADAMS, **C** S A BONE
NEWSHAM (St Bede) *Newc 1* **P** *Bp* **V** R J PRINGLE
NEWSHOLME (St John) *see* Oakworth *Bradf*
NEWSOME (St John the Evangelist) *see* Em TM *Wakef*
NEWSTEAD (St Mary the Virgin) *see* Annesley w Newstead *S'well*
NEWTIMBER (St John the Evangelist) *see* Poynings w Edburton, Newtimber and Pyecombe *Chich*
NEWTON (Church Hall) *see* Blackwell w Tibshelf *Derby*
NEWTON (Good Shepherd) *see* Clifton upon Dunsmore w Newton and Brownsover *Cov*
NEWTON (Mission Church) *see* Embleton w Rennington and Rock *Newc*

NEWTON (St Botolph) *see* S Lafford *Linc*

NEWTON (St John the Baptist) *see* Clodock and Longtown w Craswall, Llanveynoe etc *Heref*

NEWTON (St Luke) *see* Bp's Hatfield, Lemsford and N Mymms *St Alb*

NEWTON (St Margaret) *see* Harston w Hauxton and Newton *Ely*

NEWTON (St Michael and All Angels) *Ches 8* **P** *R W Kirby St Bridget* **V** C J COVERLEY

NEWTON (St Oswald) *see* Gt Ayton w Easby and Newton under Roseberry *York*

NEWTON (St Petrock) *see* Shebbear, Buckland Filleigh, Sheepwash etc *Ex*

NEWTON Team, The, (Emmanuel) (St Peter) *Liv 15* **P** *Patr Bd* **TR** J M MATTHEWS, **TV** V E HUGHES, **C** L A MONTGOMERY

NEWTON, NORTH (St Peter) *see* Alfred Jewel *B & W*

NEWTON, OLD (St Mary) *see* Bacton w Wyverstone, Cotton and Old Newton etc *St E*

NEWTON, SOUTH (St Andrew) *see* Wylye and Till Valley *Sarum*

NEWTON, WEST (St Matthew) *see* Solway Plain *Carl*

NEWTON, WEST (St Peter and St Paul) *see* Sandringham w W Newton and Appleton etc *Nor*

NEWTON ABBOT *see* Highweek *Ex*

NEWTON ABBOT (St Michael) *see* Wolborough and Ogwell *Ex*

NEWTON ABBOT (St Paul) *as above*

NEWTON ARLOSH (St John the Evangelist) *see* Bowness-on-Solway, Kirkbride and Newton Arlosh *Carl*

NEWTON AYCLIFFE (St Clare) *see* Gt Aycliffe *Dur*

NEWTON BLOSSOMVILLE (St Nicolas) *see* Lavendon w Cold Brayfield, Clifton Reynes etc *Ox*

NEWTON BROMSWOLD (St Peter) *see* Rushden St Mary w Newton Bromswold *Pet*

NEWTON-BY-CASTLE-ACRE (All Saints) *see* Castleacre, Newton, Westacre and Southacre *Nor*

NEWTON BY TOFT (St Michael) *see* Middle Rasen Gp *Linc*

NEWTON CAP (St Paul) *see* Auckland St Andr and St Anne *Dur*

NEWTON FERRERS (Holy Cross) w Revelstoke *Ex 21* **P** *Bp and Comdr P E Yonge* **P-in-c** J G CRUICKSHANK

NEWTON FLOTMAN (St Mary the Virgin), Swainsthorpe, Tasburgh, Tharston, Saxlingham Nethergate and Shotesham *Nor 5* **P** *Patr Bd* **TR** S A GAZE, **TV** A D MILLER, **C** C E MARTIN, **OLM** D L P SOCHON

NEWTON FLOWERY FIELD (St Stephen) *Ches 14* **P** *Bp* **P-in-c** P O BENNISON

NEWTON GREEN (All Saints) *see* Boxford, Edwardstone, Groton etc *St E*

NEWTON HALL (All Saints) *see* Dur N *Dur*

NEWTON HARCOURT (St Luke) *see* Wistow *Leic*

NEWTON HEATH (All Saints) *Man 5* **P** *Prime Min and D&C (alt)* **R** vacant 0161-681 3102

NEWTON IN MAKERFIELD (Emmanuel) *see* Newton *Liv*

NEWTON IN MAKERFIELD (St Peter) *as above*

NEWTON IN MOTTRAM (St Mary) *Ches 14* **P** *V Mottram* **P-in-c** R J LAMEY

NEWTON IN THE ISLE (St James) *see* Leverington, Newton and Tydd St Giles *Ely*

NEWTON-IN-WIRRAL (St Michael and All Angels) *see* Newton *Ches*

NEWTON KYME (St Andrew) *see* Tadcaster w Newton Kyme *York*

NEWTON-LE-WILLOWS (All Saints) *Liv 15* **P** *Bp* **V** D HALL

NEWTON LINFORD (All Saints) *see* Bradgate Team *Leic*

NEWTON LONGVILLE (St Faith) and Mursley w Swanbourne and Little Horwood *Ox 26* **P** *Ch Patr Trust, Lord Cottesloe, Ch Soc Trust, and New Coll Ox (jt)* **R** L P R MEERING, **Hon C** J M SAUNDERS, **NSM** J BROWN

NEWTON ON OUSE (All Saints) *see* Skelton w Shipton and Newton on Ouse *York*

NEWTON-ON-RAWCLIFFE (St John) *see* Middleton, Newton and Sinnington *York*

NEWTON-ON-TRENT (St Peter) *see* Saxilby Gp *Linc*

NEWTON POPPLEFORD (St Luke) *see* Ottery St Mary, Alfington, W Hill, Tipton etc *Ex*

NEWTON PURCELL (St Michael) *see* Shelswell *Ox*

NEWTON REGIS (St Mary) *see* N Warks *Birm*

NEWTON REIGNY (St John) *see* Penrith w Newton Reigny and Plumpton Wall *Carl*

NEWTON SOLNEY (St Mary the Virgin) *see* Foremark and Repton w Newton Solney *Derby*

NEWTON ST CYRES (St Cyr and St Julitta) *see* Thorverton, Cadbury, Upton Pyne etc *Ex*

NEWTON ST LOE (Holy Trinity) *see* Saltford w Corston and Newton St Loe *B & W*

NEWTON TONY (St Andrew) *see* Bourne Valley *Sarum*

NEWTON TRACEY (St Thomas à Becket), Horwood, Alverdiscott, Huntshaw, Yarnscombe, Tawstock, Atherington, High Bickington, Roborough, St Giles in the Wood and Beaford *Ex 20* **P** *Ld Chan (1 turn), Patr Bd (3 turns)* **TR** K D MATHERS, **TV** J C CARVOSSO, M J CLARK, **C** S R PATTERSON

NEWTON VALENCE (St Mary) *see* Northanger *Win*

NEWTOWN *see* Edgbaston St Geo *Birm*

NEWTOWN (Holy Spirit) *see* Calbourne w Newtown *Portsm*

NEWTOWN (Holy Trinity) *see* Soberton w Newtown *Portsm*

NEWTOWN (King Charles the Martyr) *see* Loppington w Newtown *Lich*

NEWTOWN (St George) *see* Birm St Geo *Birm*

NEWTOWN (St Mary) *see* Marsh Green w Newtown *Liv*

NEWTOWN (St Mary the Virgin) *see* Hungerford and Denford *Ox*

NEWTOWN (St Mary the Virgin and St John the Baptist) *see* Burghclere w Newtown and Ecchinswell w Sydmonton *Win*

NEWTOWN (St Paul) *see* Longnor, Quarnford and Sheen *Lich*

NIBLEY, NORTH (St Martin) *see* Wotton-under-Edge w Ozleworth, N Nibley etc *Glouc*

NICHOLFOREST (St Nicholas) *see* Arthuret w Kirkandrews-on-Esk and Nicholforest *Carl*

NIDD (St Paul and St Margaret) *Ripon 1* **P** *Viscount Mountgarret and R Knaresborough (alt)* **P-in-c** T J BUCKINGHAM

NIDDERDALE, LOWER *Ripon 3* **P** *Trustees K Bell Esq, DBP, and C J Dent Esq (jt)* **R** M P SPURGEON

NIDDERDALE, UPPER *Ripon 3* **P** *D&C and V Masham and Healey (jt)* **V** P L DUNBAR

NINE O'CLOCK COMMUNITY at Hill Top Chapel, The (extra-parochial place) *Sheff 1* vacant

NINEBANKS (St Mark) *see* Allendale w Whitfield *Newc*

NINEFIELDS (St Lawrence School Worship Centre) *see* Waltham H Cross *Chelmsf*

NINFIELD (St Mary the Virgin) *Chich 14* **P** *D&C Cant* **R** S R EARL

NITON (St John the Baptist) *Portsm 7* **P** *Qu Coll Ox* **R** S E LLOYD, **NSM** V M HEENAN

NOAK HILL (St Thomas) *see* Harold Hill St Geo *Chelmsf*

NOCTON (All Saints) *see* Branston w Nocton and Potterhanworth *Linc*

NOEL PARK (St Mark) *Lon 19* **P** *Bp* **P-in-c** S P J CLARK

NOKE (St Giles) *see* Ray Valley *Ox*

NONINGTON (St Mary the Virgin) w Wymynswold and Goodnestone w Chillenden and Knowlton *Cant 1* **P** *Abp and Lord Fitzwalter (jt)* **C** J SWEATMAN, **NSM** D N J HALE

NORBITON (St Peter) *S'wark 15* **P** *V Kingston All SS* **V** P A HOLMES, **OLM** C A GROVES

NORBURY (All Saints) *see* Wentnor w Ratlinghope, Myndtown, Norbury etc *Heref*

NORBURY (St Mary and St Barlok) w Snelston *Derby 8* **P** *Mrs M F Stanton, L A Clowes Esq, and V Ashbourne (by turn)* **P-in-c** G P POND

NORBURY (St Oswald) *S'wark 21* **P** *Bp* **V** C J MORGAN, **NSM** C MCARTHUR

NORBURY (St Peter) *see* Adbaston, High Offley, Knightley, Norbury etc *Lich*

NORBURY (St Philip) *S'wark 21* **P** *Bp* **V** P L WASHINGTON

NORBURY (St Stephen) and Thornton Heath *S'wark 21* **P** *Bp* **V** A L NICKSON, **OLM** J B FORBES

NORBURY (St Thomas) *Ches 16* **P** *Lord Newton* **V** R H LAWRY, **C** R H GREEN

NORDEN (St Paul) w Ashworth *Man 21* **P** *Bp* **V** S C A MAY

NORFOLK PARK (St Leonard) *see* Arbourthorne and Norfolk Park *Sheff*

NORHAM (St Cuthbert) and Duddo *Newc 12* **P** *D&C (1 turn), D&C Dur (2 turns)* **V** M J GILLHAM

NORK (St Paul) *Guildf 9* **P** *The Crown* **P-in-c** D S MILES

NORLAND (St Luke) *Wakef 4* **P** *Bp* **P-in-c** M C CRABTREE, **NSM** L ENNIS

NORLANDS (St James) *see* Notting Dale St Clem w St Mark and St Jas *Lon*

NORLEY (St John the Evangelist), Crowton and Kingsley *Ches 3* **P** *Bp, V Frodsham, and V Weaverham (jt)* **P-in-c** P RUGEN

NORMACOT (Holy Evangelists) *see* Meir Heath and Normacot *Lich*

NORMANBY (St Andrew) *see* Kirby Misperton w Normanby, Edston and Salton *York*

NORMANBY (St George) *see* Eston w Normanby *York*

NORMANBY-LE-WOLD (St Peter) *see* Walesby *Linc*

NORMANTON (All Saints) *Wakef 11* **P** *Trin Coll Cam* **V** D M GILKES, **OLM** D TEECE

NORMANTON (St Giles) *Derby 10* **P** *CPAS*
V N A A BARBER,   **C** A G P HUTCHINSON
NORMANTON, SOUTH (St Michael) *Derby 1* **P** *MMCET*
P-in-c S M POTTER
NORMANTON-LE-HEATH (Holy Trinity)   *see* Woodfield
Team *Leic*
NORMANTON-ON-SOAR (St James)   *see* Sutton Bonington
w Normanton-on-Soar *S'well*
NORMANTON-ON-TRENT (St Matthew)   *see* Sutton w
Carlton and Normanton upon Trent etc *S'well*
NORRIS BANK (St Martin)   *see* Heatons *Man*
NORRIS GREEN (Christ Church)   *see* Liv Ch Ch Norris Green
Liv
NORRIS GREEN (St Christopher)   *see* Liv St Chris Norris
Green *Liv*
NORRISTHORPE (All Souls)   *see* Heckmondwike *Wakef*
NORTH *see also under substantive place name*
NORTH BURY Team Ministry   *see* Bury St Edmunds All SS w
St Jo and St Geo *St E*
NORTH CAVE (All Saints) w Cliffe *York 13*
P C H J Carver Esq   **P-in-c** P G FAULKNER,
NSM S J HUMPHRIES
NORTH-CHAPEL Parishes, The *Linc 10*   **P** *The Revd*
J M Ashley, Mrs M F Davis, R H C Haigh Esq, and Trustees
(1 turn), and Duchy of Lanc (1 turn)   **R** R K EMM
NORTH CHAPEL (St Michael) w Ebernoe *Chich 11*   **P** *Lord*
Egremont   **R** *vacant* (01428) 707373
NORTH COVE (St Botolph)   *see* Worlingham w Barnby and N
Cove *St E*
NORTH DEVON COAST   *see* Combe Martin, Berrynarbor,
Lynton, Brendon etc *Ex*
NORTH END (Ascension)   *see* Portsea Ascension *Portsm*
NORTH END (Chapel of Ease)   *see* Burton Dassett *Cov*
NORTH END (St Francis)   *see* Portsea N End St Mark *Portsm*
NORTH END (St Mark)   *as above*
NORTH END (St Nicholas)   *as above*
NORTH HAMPSHIRE DOWNS Benefice, The *Win 5*   **P** *Bp,*
Qu Coll Ox, St Jo Coll Ox, N McNair Scott Esq, and
J L Jervoise Esq (jt)   **R** P W DYSON,   **C** S J KIPLING,
G M W KEITH,   **NSM** J E LEESE, K O´LOUGHLIN
NORTH HILL (St Torney) and Lewannick *Truro 9*   **P** *Ld Chan*
and DBP (alt)   **P-in-c** C J D PROBERT
NORTH SHIELDS (Christ Church)   *see* N Shields *Newc*
NORTH SHIELDS (St Augustine) (Christ Church) *Newc 2*
P *Patr Bd*   **TR** A D KIRKWOOD,   **C** C VAN DEN BOS
NORTH SHORE (St Paul's Worship Centre)   *see* Blackpool St
Paul *Blackb*
NORTH WEALD BASSETT (St Andrew) *Chelmsf 26*   **P** *Bp*
V T C THORPE
NORTHALLERTON (All Saints) w Kirby Sigston *York 19*
P *D&C Dur*   **V** H G SMITH,   **C** B T WALLET
NORTHAM (St Margaret)   *see* Bideford, Northam, Westward
Ho!, Appledore etc *Ex*
NORTHAMPTON (All Saints w St Katharine) (St Peter) *Pet 4*
P *Bp and R Foundn of St Kath (jt)*   **R** *vacant* (01604) 621854 or
632194
NORTHAMPTON (Christ Church) *Pet 4*   **P** *Bp*
P-in-c D J WISEMAN,   **NSM** A M MARCH
NORTHAMPTON (Emmanuel) *Pet 4*   **P** *DBP*
TR M A H JOHNSON,   **TV** H M JEFFERY,   **NSM** P J R KING
NORTHAMPTON (Holy Sepulchre w St Andrew and
St Lawrence) *Pet 4*   **P** *Bp*   **V** M W J HILLS,
NSM R M HETHERINGTON
NORTHAMPTON (Holy Trinity) (St Paul) *Pet 4*   **P** *Bp*
V A C MCGOWAN
NORTHAMPTON (St Alban the Martyr) (Glorious Ascension)
Pet 4   **P** *Bp*   **V** I R LOWELL
NORTHAMPTON (St Benedict) *Pet 4*   **P** *Bp*
P-in-c J R KIMBER,   **C** M J PURNELL,   **NSM** S M COLES
NORTHAMPTON (St David)   *see* Kingsthorpe w
Northampton St Dav *Pet*
NORTHAMPTON (St Giles) *Pet 4*   **P** *Simeon's Trustees*
V D R BIRD,   **C** N J HILL, A J B SYMES,   **NSM** G J WATERS
NORTHAMPTON (St James) *Pet 4*   **P** *Bp*   **P-in-c** P E NIXON
NORTHAMPTON (St Mary the Virgin) *Pet 4*   **P** *Bp*
V I S HOLDSWORTH
NORTHAMPTON (St Matthew) *Pet 4*   **P** *DBP*
V N M SETTERFIELD,   **C** P R ARMSTEAD,   **NSM** G C RUMBOLD
NORTHAMPTON (St Michael and All Angels w St Edmund)
Pet 4   **P** *Bp*   **V** M W J HILLS,   **NSM** P D MUNCH,
R M HETHERINGTON
NORTHAMPTON (St Peter)   *see* Northampton All SS w St
Kath and St Pet *Pet*
NORTHANGER Benefice, The *Win 2*   **P** *Bp (1 turn), D&C*
(1 turn), Bp, Earl of Selborne and Sir James Scott Bt (1 turn)
R A J PEARS,   **NSM** J ELLISON, L A LEON

NORTHAW (St Thomas of Canterbury) and Cuffley *St Alb 20*
P *Mrs S Peasley*   **V** M T BEER
NORTHBOROUGH (St Andrew)   *see* Peakirk w Glinton and
Northborough *Pet*
NORTHBOURNE (St Augustine)   *see* Eastry and Northbourne
w Tilmanstone etc *Cant*
NORTHCHURCH (St Mary) and Wigginton *St Alb 2*   **P** *Duchy*
of Cornwall and Bp (alt)   **R** J A GORDON,
NSM M J EGGLETON
NORTHCOURT (Christ Church)   *see* Abingdon *Ox*
NORTHDOWN PARK (St Philip)   *see* Margate St Phil *Cant*
NORTHENDEN (St Wilfrid) *Man 8*   **P** *Bp*   **R** G S FORSTER
NORTHFIELD (St Laurence) *Birm 4*   **P** *Keble Coll Ox*
R *vacant* 0121-477 3111 *or* 475 1558
NORTHFLEET (All Saints)   *see* Perry Street *Roch*
NORTHFLEET (St Botolph) and Rosherville *Roch 4*   **P** *Patr Bd*
and Prime Min (alt)   **TR** *vacant* (01474) 566400
NORTHGATE (St Elizabeth)   *see* Crawley *Chich*
NORTHIAM (St Mary) *Chich 20*   **P** *MMCET*   **R** R H WHITE
NORTHILL (St Mary the Virgin)   *see* Caldecote, Northill and
Old Warden *St Alb*
NORTHINGTON (St John the Evangelist)   *see* The Candover
Valley *Win*
NORTHLEACH (St Peter and St Paul) w Hampnett and
Farmington, Cold Aston w Notgrove and Turkdean, and
Compton Abdale w Haselton *Glouc 11*   **P** *Bp (2 turns),*
Ld Chan (1 turn)   **P-in-c** R W WOODGER,   **NSM** N FISHER
NORTHLEIGH (St Giles)   *see* Offwell, Northleigh, Farway,
Cotleigh etc *Ex*
NORTHLEW (St Thomas of Canterbury)   *see* Okehampton w
Inwardleigh, Bratton Clovelly etc *Ex*
NORTHMOOR (St Denys)   *see* Lower Windrush *Ox*
NORTHMOOR GREEN (St Peter and St John)   *see* Alfred
Jewel *B & W*
NORTHOLT (St Joseph the Worker) (St Hugh) West End *Lon 22*
P *DBP*   **V** S R WINN,   **C** D H CHAPMAN
NORTHOLT (St Mary) (St Richard) *Lon 22*   **P** *BNC Ox*
R G S THOMAS
NORTHOLT PARK (St Barnabas) *Lon 22*   **P** *Bp*
V P D HILLAS
NORTHORPE (St John the Baptist)   *see* Scotton w Northorpe
Linc
NORTHOWRAM (St Matthew) *Wakef 2*   **P** *Bp*
V P A HOLMES
NORTHREPPS (St Mary)   *see* Overstrand, Northrepps,
Sidestrand etc *Nor*
NORTHUMBERLAND HEATH (St Paul)   *see* Erith St Paul
Roch
NORTHWICH (St Helen)   *see* Witton *Ches*
NORTHWICH (St Luke) (Holy Trinity) *Ches 6*   **P** *Bp*
V C S SEDDON
NORTHWOLD (St Andrew)   *see* Grimshoe *Ely*
NORTHWOOD (Emmanuel) *Lon 23*   **P** *Ch Trust Fund Trust*
V D M TALBOT,   **C** H M WILKINSON, G H L WATTS, J E JAMES,
NSM P D O GREENE, S A L WATTS
NORTHWOOD (Holy Trinity)   *see* Hanley H Ev *Lich*
NORTHWOOD (Holy Trinity) *Lon 23*   **P** *Trustees*
V R C BARTLETT,   **C** E V DANDO
NORTHWOOD Pinner Road (St Edmund the King)
see Northwood Hills St Edm *Lon*
NORTHWOOD (St John the Baptist) *Portsm 8*   **P** *Bp*
R L MCROSTIE,   **NSM** D M NETHERWAY, K R ADLAM
NORTHWOOD (St Mark)   *see* Kirkby *Liv*
NORTHWOOD GREEN (Mission Church)   *see* Westbury-on-
Severn w Flaxley, Blaisdon etc *Glouc*
NORTHWOOD HILLS (St Edmund the King) *Lon 23*   **P** *Bp*
V P R BARNES
NORTON (All Saints)   *see* Hullavington, Norton and Stanton
St Quintin *Bris*
NORTON (All Saints)   *see* Brington w Whilton and Norton etc
Pet
NORTON (St Andrew)   *see* Pakenham w Norton and Tostock
St E
NORTON (St Berteline and St Christopher) *Ches 3*   **P** *DBP*
P-in-c J BEANEY
NORTON (St Egwin)   *see* Evesham w Norton and Lenchwick
Worc
NORTON (St George) (St Nicholas) *St Alb 4*   **P** *Bp*
V J N LUSCOMBE,   **C** R CHAPMAN
NORTON (St James) *Sheff 2*   **P** *CCC Cam*   **R** G B WHITE
NORTON (St James)   *see* Stoulton w Drake's Broughton and
Pirton etc *Worc*
NORTON (St Mary) *Cant 6*   **P** *Ld Chan*   **P-in-c** S H LILLICRAP
NORTON (St Mary)   *see* Twigworth, Down Hatherley, Norton,
The Leigh etc *Glouc*

NORTON (St Mary the Virgin) *Dur 10* **P** *Bp* **V** N R SHAVE,
C J NOBEL, C W PEARSON
NORTON (St Michael and All Angels) *Dur 10* **P** *V Norton
St Mary* **P-in-c** D J BAGE
NORTON (St Michael and All Angels) *see* Stourbridge St Mich
Norton *Worc*
NORTON (St Peter) *see* Norton juxta Malton *York*
NORTON, EAST (All Saints) *see* Hallaton and Allexton, w
Horninghold, Tugby etc *Leic*
NORTON, OVER (St James) *see* Chipping Norton *Ox*
NORTON BAVANT (All Saints) *see* Upper Wylye Valley *Sarum*
NORTON BRIDGE (St Luke) *see* Chebsey, Creswell, Ellenhall,
Ranton etc *Lich*
NORTON CANES (St James) *Lich 3* **P** *Bp* **R** N L HIBBINS
NORTON CANON (St Nicholas) *see* Weobley w Sarnesfield
and Norton Canon *Heref*
NORTON CUCKNEY (St Mary) *S'well 6* **P** *Lady Alexandra
Cavendish Bentinck* **P-in-c** S A CASH
NORTON DISNEY (St Peter) *see* Bassingham Gp *Linc*
NORTON FITZWARREN (All Saints) *see* Staplegrove w
Norton Fitzwarren *B & W*
NORTON IN HALES (St Chad) *see* Woore and Norton in
Hales *Lich*
NORTON IN THE MOORS (St Bartholomew) *Lich 8*
P *Walsingham Coll Trust Assn* **R** P W DAVEY,
NSM A BALLARD
NORTON JUXTA MALTON (St Peter) *York 6* **P** *Abp*
V C W ANKERS
NORTON JUXTA TWYCROSS (Holy Trinity) *see* Woodfield
Team *Leic*
NORTON LE MOORS *see* Norton in the Moors *Lich*
NORTON LEES (St Paul) *Sheff 2* **P** *R Norton* **V** P M BROWN
NORTON LINDSEY (Holy Trinity) *see* Wolverton w Norton
Lindsey and Langley *Cov*
NORTON MALREWARD (Holy Trinity) *see* Chew Magna w
Dundry and Norton Malreward *B & W*
NORTON MANDEVILLE (All Saints) *see* High Ongar w
Norton Mandeville *Chelmsf*
NORTON ST PHILIP (St Philip and St James) *see* Hardington
Vale *B & W*
**NORTON SUB HAMDON (Blessed Virgin Mary) w West
Chinnock, Chiselborough and Middle Chinnock** *B & W 6*
P *Bp* **P-in-c** P J THOMAS
NORTON SUBCOURSE (St Mary) *see* Raveningham Gp *Nor*
NORTON WOODSEATS (St Chad) *see* Woodseats St Chad
Sheff
NORTON WOODSEATS (St Paul) *see* Norton Lees St Paul
Sheff
NORWELL (St Laurence), w Ossington, Cromwell and Caunton
S'well 3 **P** *Bp, SMF, and Mrs P Goedhuis (jt)*
P-in-c S DIXON
NORWICH (Christ Church) *see* Eaton Ch Ch *Nor*
NORWICH (Christ Church) *see* New Catton Ch Ch *Nor*
NORWICH Heartsease (St Francis) *Nor 1* **P** *Bp*
P-in-c P L HOWARD
NORWICH (Holy Trinity) *see* Heigham H Trin *Nor*
NORWICH Lakenham (St Alban) (St Mark) *Nor 1* **P** *D&C*
V S E WEST-LINDELL, **OLM** M A HIDER
NORWICH (St Andrew) *see* Eaton St Andr *Nor*
NORWICH (St Andrew) *Nor 1* **P** *PCC* **P-in-c** M J YOUNG
NORWICH (St Anne) *see* Earlham *Nor*
NORWICH (St Barnabas) *see* Heigham St Barn w St Bart *Nor*
NORWICH (St Catherine) *see* Mile Cross *Nor*
NORWICH (St Elizabeth) *see* Earlham *Nor*
NORWICH (St Francis) *see* Nor Heartsease St Fran *Nor*
NORWICH (St George) Colegate *Nor 1* **P** *D&C*
P-in-c P MCFADYEN
NORWICH (St George) Tombland *Nor 1* **P** *Bp*
P-in-c J C MINNS, **OLM** M E DIFFEY
NORWICH (St Giles) *Nor 1* **P** *Ld Chan and Bp (alt)*
P-in-c D T THORNTON
NORWICH (St Helen) *Nor 1* **P** *Gt Hosp Nor* **V** *vacant*
NORWICH (St John the Baptist) Timberhill w Norwich St Julian
Nor 1 **P** *Bp, Guild of All So, and D&C (jt)* **R** M D SMITH,
C D E STEVENSON
NORWICH (St Julian) *see* St Jo w St Julian *Nor*
NORWICH (St Luke) *see* New Catton St Luke w St Aug *Nor*
NORWICH (St Mary) *see* Earlham *Nor*
NORWICH (St Mary in the Marsh) *Nor 1* **P** *D&C*
P-in-c R CAPPER
NORWICH (St Mary Magdalene) w St James *Nor 2* **P** *D&C*
NSM C J A BELCHER, **OLM** J SPENCER
NORWICH (St Matthew) *see* Thorpe St Matt *Nor*
NORWICH (St Michael) *see* Bowthorpe *Nor*
NORWICH (St Peter Mancroft) (St John Maddermarket) *Nor 1*
P *PCC* **R** P W NOKES

NORWICH (St Stephen) *Nor 1* **P** *D&C* **P-in-c** M M LIGHT
NORWICH (St Thomas) *see* Heigham St Thos *Nor*
**NORWICH, Lakenham (St John the Baptist and All Saints) and
Tuckswood St Paul** *Nor 1* **P** *Bp and D&C (jt)* **V** P J FOX
NORWOOD (St Leonard) *see* Sheff St Leon Norwood *Sheff*
NORWOOD (St Mary the Virgin) *Lon 22* **P** *SMF*
R L LAWRENCE
NORWOOD, SOUTH (Holy Innocents) *S'wark 21* **P** *Bp*
P-in-c N J COLEMAN, **C** A ELTRINGHAM
NORWOOD, SOUTH (St Alban the Martyr) *S'wark 21* **P** *Bp*
P-in-c R T LAWSON
NORWOOD, SOUTH (St Mark) *S'wark 21* **P** *Bp*
P-in-c T W HURCOMBE, **NSM** S E WHEELER-KILEY
NORWOOD, UPPER (All Saints) *S'wark 21* **P** *V Croydon*
V L S A MARSH
NORWOOD, UPPER (St John) *S'wark 21* **P** *Bp*
V B A MASON
NORWOOD, WEST (St Luke) *S'wark 12* **P** *Abp* **V** D R DAVIS
NOTGROVE (St Bartholomew) *see* Northleach w Hampnett
and Farmington etc *Glouc*
**NOTTING DALE (St Clement) (St Mark) and Norlands
St James** *Lon 12* **P** *Bp* **C** K G RIGLIN
NOTTING HILL (All Saints) (St Columb) *Lon 12* **P** *SMF*
V J K BROWNSELL
NOTTING HILL (St John) *Lon 12* **P** *Bp* **V** W H TAYLOR,
C S R S TELEN
**NOTTING HILL (St Michael and All Angels) (Christ Church)
(St Francis)** *Lon 12* **P** *Trustees* **V** A B ANDREWS
NOTTING HILL (St Peter) *Lon 12* **P** *Bp*
V M K HARGREAVES, **C** C ROBINSON
**NOTTINGHAM (All Saints) (St Mary the Virgin) (St Peter and
St James)** *S'well 13* **P** *Bp* **P-in-c** C D HARRISON,
C S F MORRIS, A J MADDOCKS, C LITTLE
NOTTINGHAM (St Andrew) *S'well 13* **P** *Peache Trustees*
V R M CLARK
NOTTINGHAM (St Ann w Emmanuel) *S'well 13* **P** *Trustees*
V *vacant* 0115-950 5471
NOTTINGHAM (St George w St John the Baptist) *S'well 13*
P *Bp* **P-in-c** A L WAUDE
NOTTINGHAM (St Jude) *S'well 13* **P** *CPAS*
P-in-c G F HADFIELD
NOTTINGHAM (St Nicholas) *S'well 13* **P** *CPAS*
P-in-c S D SILVESTER, **NSM** A R HASKEY
NOTTINGHAM (St Saviour) *S'well 13* **P** *CPAS*
P-in-c D G HAMMOND, **NSM** A R HASKEY
NOTTINGHAM (St Stephen) *see* Hyson Green and Forest
Fields *S'well*
NOWTON (St Peter) *see* St Edm Way *St E*
NUFFIELD (Holy Trinity) *Ox 6* **P** *MMCET*
P-in-c B J BAILEY
NUN MONKTON (St Mary) *see* Lower Nidderdale *Ripon*
NUNBURNHOLME (St James) and Warter and Huggate
York 5 **P** *Abp* **NSM** S D JONES
NUNEATON (St Mary) *Cov 5* **P** *V Nuneaton* **V** M LIDDELL
NUNEATON (St Nicolas) *Cov 5* **P** *The Crown* **V** D JONES
NUNHEAD (St Antony) (St Silas) *S'wark 8* **P** *Bp*
V C A M BRADDICK-SOUTHGATE
**NUNNEY (All Saints) and Witham Friary, Marston Bigot,
Wanstrow and Cloford** *B & W 4* **P** *Bp, SMF, and
C N Clarke Esq and Duke of Somerset (jt)* **R** J K HODDER
NUNNINGTON (All Saints) *see* Kirkdale w Harome,
Nunnington and Pockley *York*
NUNTHORPE (St Mary the Virgin) (St Mary's Church Hall)
York 21 **P** *Abp* **V** *vacant* (01642) 316570
NUNTON (St Andrew) *see* Chalke Valley *Sarum*
NURSLING (St Boniface) and Rownhams *Win 12* **P** *Bp*
R J T WILLIAMS
NURSTEAD (St Mildred) *see* Meopham w Nurstead *Roch*
NUTBOURNE (St Wilfrid) *see* Chidham *Chich*
NUTFIELD (St Peter and St Paul) *see* Bletchingley and
Nutfield *S'wark*
NUTFIELD, LOWER *see* S Nutfield w Outwood *S'wark*
NUTFIELD, SOUTH (Christ Church) w Outwood *S'wark 25*
P *Bp and Ch Patr Trust (jt)* **V** T G KEMP
NUTHALL (St Patrick) *S'well 7* **P** *Bp*
P-in-c B M HOLBROOK, **C** H R BRIDGER
NUTHURST (St Andrew) and Mannings Heath *Chich 8*
P *Bp Lon* **P-in-c** D EVANS
NUTHURST (St Thomas) *see* Packwood w Hockley Heath
Birm
NUTLEY (St James the Less) *Chich 21* **P** *R Maresfield*
V J N A HOBBS
NYMET (St George) *see* S Molton w Nymet St George, High
Bray etc *Ex*
NYMET ROWLAND (St Bartholomew) *see* N Creedy *Ex*

NYMET TRACEY (St Bartholomew)   *see* Bow w Broad Nymet *Ex*

NYMPSFIELD (St Bartholomew)   *see* Uley w Owlpen and Nympsfield *Glouc*

NYNEHEAD (All Saints)   *see* Wellington and Distr *B & W*

OADBY (St Paul) (St Peter) *Leic 4*   **P** *Bp*   **TR** M F RUSK, **TV** S J HARVEY,   **C** P CLEMENT

OAK TREE ANGLICAN FELLOWSHIP, The *Lon 22*   **Min** M R ALDRIDGE,   **C** M C BISHOP

OAKAMOOR (Holy Trinity)   *see* Alton w Bradley-le-Moors and Oakamoor w Cotton *Lich*

OAKDALE (St George)   *see* N Poole Ecum Team *Sarum*

OAKE (St Bartholomew)   *see* Deane Vale *B & W*

OAKENGATES (Holy Trinity) and Wrockwardine Wood *Lich 21*   **P** *Bp*   **R** M C STAFFORD,   **NSM** R J WALKER-HILL

OAKENROD (St George) and Bamford St Michael *Man 21*   **P** *Bp*   **R** P D GULLY,   C M Z WALL,   **NSM** P R ZUCCA

OAKENSHAW (Church of the Good Shepherd)   *see* Willington and Sunnybrow *Dur*

OAKENSHAW (St Andrew), Wyke and Low Moor (South Bradford Benefice) *Bradf 2*   **P** *Patr Bd*   **TR** S R EVANS, **TV** C E SHEDD, A D WOOD,   **Hon C** M R M LYONS, **NSM** D P ELLIS

OAKFIELD (St John the Baptist) *Portsm 7*   **P** *V St Helens* V H E WRIGHT,   **NSM** B M DOWNER

OAKFORD (St Peter)   *see* Washfield, Stoodleigh, Withleigh etc *Ex*

OAKHAM (All Saints) w Hambleton and Egleton and Braunston w Brooke *Pet 12*   **P** *Dr E R Hanbury (1 turn), D&C Linc (2 turns)*   **P-in-c** L T FRANCIS-DEHQANI,   **C** J RIDLEY, **NSM** H A CROWTHER, S C PARSONS

OAKHANGER (St Luke's Mission Church)   *see* Alsager Ch Ch *Ches*

OAKHANGER (St Mary Magdalene)   *see* Northanger *Win*

OAKHILL (All Saints)   *see* Ashwick w Oakhill and Binegar *B & W*

OAKHILL Eastwood View (shared church)   *see* Clifton St Jas *Sheff*

OAKINGTON (St Andrew) *Ely 6*   **P** *Qu Coll Cam* V J C ALEXANDER

OAKLEY (St Leonard) w Wootton St Lawrence *Win 4*   **P** *Qu Coll Ox and D&C (alt)*   **R** B W NICHOLSON, **NSM** C A VAUGHAN

OAKLEY (St Mary)   *see* Worminghall w Ickford, Oakley and Shabbington *Ox*

OAKLEY (St Mary)   *see* Bromham w Oakley and Stagsden *St Alb*

OAKLEY (St Nicholas)   *see* N Hartismere *St E*

OAKLEY, GREAT (All Saints) w Wix and Wrabness *Chelmsf 20*   **P** *Ld Chan, Ch Patr Trust, and St Jo Coll Cam (by turn)* **R** *vacant* (01255) 880230

OAKLEY, GREAT (St Michael) and LITTLE (St Peter) *Pet 7*   **P** *H W G de Capell Brooke Esq and Boughton Estates Ltd (alt)* **V** *vacant*

OAKLEY SQUARE (St Matthew)   *see* Old St Pancras *Lon*

OAKMOOR   *see* Bishopsnympton, Rose Ash, Mariansleigh etc *Ex*

OAKRIDGE (St Bartholomew)   *see* Bisley, Chalford, France Lynch, and Oakridge *Glouc*

OAKS IN CHARNWOOD (St James the Greater)   *see* Shepshed and Oaks in Charnwood *Leic*

OAKSEY (All Saints)   *see* Ashley, Crudwell, Hankerton and Oaksey *Bris*

OAKWOOD (no dedication) *Derby 9*   **P** *Bp and MMCET (jt)* **P-in-c** C L HUGHES,   **NSM** J L WHITEHEAD

OAKWOOD (St Thomas) *Lon 18*   **P** *Bp*   **V** C J P HOBBS

OAKWORTH (Christ Church) *Bradf 8*   **P** *Bp*   **V** J ROGERS, **NSM** J M MARKS

OARE (Blessed Virgin Mary) w Culbone *B & W 16*   **P** *Bp* **P-in-c** C D BURKE

OARE (Holy Trinity)   *see* Pewsey and Swanborough *Sarum*

OARE (St Bartholomew)   *see* Chieveley w Winterbourne and Oare *Ox*

OARE (St Peter)   *see* The Brents and Davington w Oare and Luddenham *Cant*

OATLANDS (St Mary) *Guildf 8*   **P** *Bp*   **OLM** L BOWDEN

OBORNE (St Cuthbert)   *see* Queen Thorne *Sarum*

OCCOLD (St Michael)   *see* Eye *St E*

OCKBROOK (All Saints) *Derby 13*   **P** *Lt-Col T H Pares* V T M SUMPTER,   **NSM** V A BILLINGS

OCKENDON, NORTH (St Mary Magdalene) *Chelmsf 2*   **P** *Bp* **P-in-c** G BAISLEY

OCKENDON, SOUTH (St Nicholas) and Belhus Park *Chelmsf 14*   **P** *Bp and Guild of All So (jt)* **R** B G DUCKWORTH,   **C** P D RABIN

OCKER HILL (St Mark) *Lich 26*   **P** *Bp*   **V** A J GWILLIM

OCKFORD RIDGE (St Mark)   *see* Godalming *Guildf*

OCKHAM (All Saints)   *see* E Horsley and Ockham w Hatchford and Downside *Guildf*

OCKLEY (St Margaret), Okewood and Forest Green *Guildf 7* **P** *Bp and J P M H Evelyn Esq (alt)* **P-in-c** N A KNIGHTS JOHNSON

OCLE PYCHARD (St James the Great)   *see* Frome Valley *Heref*

ODCOMBE (St Peter and St Paul), Brympton, Lufton and Montacute *B & W 7*   **P** *Ch Ch Ox (4 turns), C E B Clive-Ponsonby-Fane Esq (1 turn)*   **R** J F JENKINS

ODD DOWN (St Philip and St James)   *see* Bath Odd Down w Combe Hay *B & W*

ODD RODE (All Saints) *Ches 11*   **P** *R Astbury*   **R** T R EVANS

ODDINGLEY (St James)   *see* Bowbrook S *Worc*

ODDINGTON (Holy Ascension)   *see* Broadwell, Evenlode, Oddington, Adlestrop etc *Glouc*

ODDINGTON (St Andrew)   *see* Ray Valley *Ox*

ODDINGTON (St Nicholas)   *see* Broadwell, Evenlode, Oddington, Adlestrop etc *Glouc*

ODELL (All Saints) *St Alb 15*   **P** *Lord Luke* **P-in-c** C M CLARK

ODIHAM (All Saints)   *see* N Hants Downs *Win*

ODSTOCK (St Mary)   *see* Chalke Valley *Sarum*

OFFCHURCH (St Gregory) *Cov 10*   **P** *Bp* **P-in-c** J T H BRITTON,   **C** D R PATTERSON

OFFENHAM (St Mary and St Milburgh)   *see* Badsey w Aldington and Offenham and Bretforton *Worc*

OFFERTON (St Alban) (St John) *Ches 18*   **P** *Bp*   **V** J BATES, **NSM** G M SELLORS

OFFHAM (Old St Peter)   *see* Hamsey *Chich*

OFFHAM (St Michael)   *see* W Malling w Offham *Roch*

OFFLEY (St Mary Magdalene)   *see* King's Walden and Offley w Lilley *St Alb*

OFFLEY, HIGH (St Mary the Virgin)   *see* Adbaston, High Offley, Knightley, Norbury etc *Lich*

OFFLEY HAY (Mission Church)   *see* Eccleshall *Lich*

OFFORD D'ARCY w OFFORD CLUNY (All Saints)   *see* Buckden w the Offords *Ely*

OFFTON (St Mary)   *see* Somersham w Flowton and Offton w Willisham *St E*

OFFWELL (St Mary the Virgin), Northleigh, Farway, Cotleigh and Widworthy *Ex 5*   **P** *Trustees, R T Marker Esq, Cotleigh PCC, and Bp (jt)*   **P-in-c** J J WILSON

OGBOURNE (St Andrew)   *see* Ridgeway *Sarum*

OGBOURNE (St George)   *as above*

OGLEY HAY (St James) *Lich 1*   **P** *Bp*   **V** D BISHOP, **C** E SNOWDEN

OGWELL (St Bartholomew)   *see* Wolborough and Ogwell *Ex*

OKEFORD Benefice, The *Sarum 6*   **P** *G A L-F Pitt-Rivers Esq and DBP (alt)*   **P-in-c** S A SMITH,   **C** W T RIDDING, R D G WEYMAN, D R R SEYMOUR,   **NSM** S S MUFFETT, **OLM** D J MARL

OKEFORD FITZPAINE (St Andrew)   *see* Okeford *Sarum*

OKEHAMPTON (All Saints) (St James) w Inwardleigh; Bratton Clovelly w Germansweek; Northlew w Ashbury; and Bridestowe and Sourton *Ex 11*   **P** *Patr Bd*   **TR** S W COOK, **TV** S A WILSON,   **C** L BURGON, G D HARRIS

OKEWOOD (St John the Baptist)   *see* Ockley, Okewood and Forest Green *Guildf*

OLD   *see also under substantive place name*

OLD FORD (St Paul) (St Mark) *Lon 7*   **P** *Hyndman Trustees and CPAS (jt)*   **V** P J BOARDMAN,   **C** J F BRYSON

OLD HEATH (St Barnabas)   *see* Colchester St Barn *Chelmsf*

OLD HILL (Holy Trinity) *Worc 9*   **P** *Ch Soc Trust* V J M HANCOCK,   **C** R W HARDING

OLD LANE (Mission Church)   *see* Bloxwich *Lich*

OLD WIVES LEES (Mission Church)   *see* Chilham w Challock and Molash *Cant*

OLDBERROW (St Mary)   *see* Spernall, Morton Bagot and Oldberrow *Cov*

OLDBROOK (Community Church)   *see* Woughton *Ox*

OLDBURY *Sarum 15*   **P** *Bp, CPAS, Marquess of Lansdowne, and C E R Money-Kyrle Esq (jt)*   **R** P A BROMILEY

OLDBURY (Christ Church), Langley, and Londonderry *Birm 7* **P** *Prime Min (1 turn), Bp (3 turns)*   **C** A D BARRETT, **NSM** A E HANNY, P M EATON

OLDBURY (St Nicholas)   *see* Bridgnorth, Tasley, Astley Abbotts, etc *Heref*

OLDBURY-ON-SEVERN (St Arilda)   *see* Thornbury and Oldbury on Severn w Shepperdine *Glouc*

OLDCOTES (St Mark's Mission Church)   *see* Carlton-in-Lindrick and Langold w Oldcotes *S'well*

OLDHAM Moorside (St Thomas) *Man 19*   **P** *Trustees* **V** *vacant* 0161-652 6452

OLDHAM (St Andrew) (St Mary w St Peter) *Man 20*

P *Patr Bd* **TR** D J PALMER, **TV** N G SMEETON,
C P M S MONK

OLDHAM (St Barnabas) *see* Medlock Head *Man*

OLDHAM (St Chad) *see* Hollinwood and Limeside *Man*

OLDHAM (St James) (St Ambrose) *Man 19* **P** *Bp and R Prestwich (jt)* **V** P PLUMPTON

OLDHAM (St Paul) *Man 20* **P** *Bp* , **Hon C** D J QUARMBY

OLDHAM (St Stephen and All Martyrs) Lower Moor *Man 20*
P *Bp* **P-in-c** N G SMEETON

OLDHURST (St Peter) *see* Somersham w Pidley and Oldhurst *Ely*

OLDLAND (St Anne) *Bris 5* **P** *Bp* **V** A J M SPEAR

OLDRIDGE (St Thomas) *see* Tedburn St Mary, Whitestone, Oldridge etc *Ex*

OLDSWINFORD (St Mary) *see* Old Swinford Stourbridge *Worc*

OLIVER'S BATTERY (St Mark) *see* Stanmore *Win*

OLLERTON (St Giles) (St Paulinus) w Boughton *S'well 6*
P *Ld Chan and Bp (alt)* **P-in-c** R GOODHAND

OLNEY (St Peter and St Paul) *Ox 27* **P** *Bp* **R** C WOOD

OLTON (St Margaret) *Birm 11* **P** *Bp and V Bickenhill (jt)*
V J M KNAPP, **NSM** S M CHANDLER

OLVESTON (St Mary of Malmesbury) *see* Almondsbury and Olveston *Bris*

OMBERSLEY (St Andrew) w Doverdale *Worc 8* **P** *Bp and Lord Sandys (alt)* **P-in-c** S P KERR

ONCHAN (St Peter) *S & M 2* **P** *The Crown* **V** A M CONVERY

ONECOTE (St Luke) *see* Ipstones w Berkhamsytch and Onecote w Bradnop *Lich*

ONEHOUSE (St John the Baptist) *see* Gt Finborough w Onehouse, Harleston, Buxhall etc *St E*

ONGAR, HIGH (St Mary the Virgin) w Norton Mandeville *Chelmsf 26* **P** *Ch Soc Trust* **C** C P RUSSELL

ONIBURY (St Michael and All Angels) *see* Ludlow *Heref*

ONSLOW VILLAGE (All Saints) *see* Guildf All SS *Guildf*

OPENSHAW (St Barnabas) *see* Manchester Gd Shep and St Barn *Man*

OPENSHAW, HIGHER (St Clement) *Man 1* **P** *Trustees*
P-in-c C J R HOWITZ

OPENWOODGATE (St Mark) *see* Belper *Derby*

ORBY (All Saints) *see* Burgh Gp *Linc*

ORCHARD (Community Centre) *see* Egglescliffe *Dur*

ORCHARD PARK (St Michael and All Angels) *see* N Hull St Mich *York*

ORCHARD PORTMAN (St Michael) *see* Beercrocombe w Curry Mallet, Hatch Beauchamp etc *B & W*

ORCHARD WAY (St Barnabas) *see* Cheltenham St Mark *Glouc*

ORCHARDLEIGH (Blessed Virgin Mary) *see* Beckington w Standerwick, Berkley, Rodden etc *B & W*

ORCHESTON (St Mary) *see* Wylye and Till Valley *Sarum*

ORCOP (St John the Baptist) *see* St Weonards *Heref*

ORDSALL (All Hallows) *S'well 5* **P** *Bp* **R** *vacant* (01777) 702515

ORDSALL (St Clement) and Salford Quays *Man 6* **P** *Bp*
P-in-c S KEARNEY

ORE (Christ Church) *Chich 17* **P** *Simeon's Trustees*
V R P C ELVERSON

ORE (St Helen) (St Barnabas) *Chich 17* **P** *Simeon's Trustees*
R C H KEY, **C** A M HAWKINS, N G BURTON,
NSM A C WILLIAMS

ORESTON (Church of the Good Shepherd) *see* Plymstock and Hooe *Ex*

ORFORD (St Andrew) *Liv 12* **P** *Bp* **V** M RAYNOR

ORFORD (St Bartholomew) *see* Wilford Peninsula *St E*

ORFORD (St Margaret) *Liv 12* **P** *Bp* **P-in-c** S W BOYD

ORLESTONE (St Mary) w Snave and Ruckinge w Warehorne and Kenardington *Cant 12* **P** *Ld Chan and Abp (alt)*
R T R WHATELEY, **OLM** P L M FOGDEN

ORLETON (St George) *see* Leominster *Heref*

ORLINGBURY (St Mary) *see* Gt w Lt Harrowden and Orlingbury and Isham etc *Pet*

ORMESBY (St Cuthbert) *York 18* **P** *Abp* **V** R BROWN

ORMESBY, NORTH (Holy Trinity) *York 18* **P** *Abp*
V D P BLACK

ORMESBY ST MARGARET (St Margaret) w Scratby, Ormesby St Michael and Rollesby *Nor 6* **P** *Bp, D&C, DBP and R J H Tacon Esq (jt)* **V** N R SPENCER

ORMESBY ST MICHAEL (St Michael) *see* Ormesby St Marg w Scratby, Ormesby St Mich etc *Nor*

ORMSBY Group, The South (St Leonard) *Linc 7*
P *A J Massingberd-Mundy Esq, Sir Thomas Ingilby Bt, Mert Coll Ox, Bp, and DBP (jt)* **P-in-c** C HILLIAM

ORMSGILL (St Francis) *see* Barrow St Matt *Carl*

ORMSIDE (St James) *see* Heart of Eden *Carl*

ORMSKIRK (St Peter and St Paul) *Liv 11* **P** *Earl of Derby*
V C H JONES, **C** A E STEIN

ORPINGTON (All Saints) *Roch 16* **P** *D&C* **V** A A MUSTOE,
C N C WOODWARD

ORPINGTON (Christ Church) *Roch 16* **P** *Ch Trust Fund Trust, Bp, and V Orpington (jt)* **V** J P COLWILL

ORPINGTON (St Andrew) *Roch 16* **P** *Bp*
P-in-c M T SKINNER, **Hon C** D HAMID

ORRELL (St Luke) *Liv 14* **P** *Bp* **V** P G WHITTINGTON,
OLM F S FAIRBAIRN

ORRELL HEY (St John and St James) *Liv 1* **P** *CPAS*
V R J G PANTER, **C** C L DAWSON, **OLM** A J FINCH

ORSETT (St Giles and All Saints) and Bulphan and Horndon on the Hill *Chelmsf 14* **P** *Bp and D&C St Paul's (jt)*
R E W HANSON, **C** M J MARSHALL, **NSM** S R BLAKE

ORSTON (St Mary) *see* Whatton w Aslockton, Hawksworth, Scarrington etc *S'well*

ORTON (All Saints) and Tebay w Ravenstonedale and Newbiggin-on-Lune *Carl 1* **P** *Bp and Ravenstonedale Trustees (1 turn), Resident Landowners (1 turn)* **P-in-c** B LOCK

ORTON, GREAT (St Giles) *see* Barony of Burgh *Carl*

ORTON GOLDHAY (St John) *see* The Ortons, Alwalton and Chesterton *Ely*

ORTON LONGUEVILLE (Holy Trinity) *as above*

ORTON MALBORNE (not known) *as above*

ORTON-ON-THE-HILL (St Edith of Polesworth)
see Bosworth and Sheepy Gp *Leic*

ORTON WATERVILLE (St Mary) *see* The Ortons, Alwalton and Chesterton *Ely*

ORTONS, Alwalton and Chesterton, The *Ely 15* **P** *Patr Bd*
TV R A HAMILTON, M J INGHAM, I A PULLINGER,
P-in-c A J DUNNING

ORWELL Group, The (St Andrew) *Ely 7* **P** *Bp, DBP, and Trin Coll Cam (jt)* **R** N A BRICE

ORWELL Team Ministry *see* Walton and Trimley *St E*

OSBALDWICK (St Thomas) w Murton *York 2* **P** *Abp*
V A CLEMENTS

OSBOURNBY (St Peter and St Paul) *see* S Lafford *Linc*

OSCOTT, OLD (All Saints) *see* Kingstanding St Mark *Birm*

OSGATHORPE (St Mary the Virgin) *see* Kegworth, Hathern, Long Whatton, Diseworth etc *Leic*

OSMASTON (St Martin) *see* Brailsford w Shirley, Osmaston w Edlaston etc *Derby*

OSMINGTON (St Osmond) *see* Preston w Sutton Poyntz and Osmington w Poxwell *Sarum*

OSMONDTHORPE (St Philip) *see* Leeds All SS w Osmondthorpe *Ripon*

OSMOTHERLEY (St Peter) w Harlsey and Ingleby Arncliffe *York 19* **P** *J B Barnard Esq (1 turn), Ld Chan (2 turns)*
V I D HOUGHTON

OSMOTHERLY (St John) *see* Ulverston St Mary w H Trin *Carl*

OSPRINGE (St Peter and St Paul) *see* Eastling w Ospringe and Stalisfield w Otterden *Cant*

OSSETT (Holy and Undivided Trinity) and Gawthorpe *Wakef 9*
P *Bp and R Dewsbury (jt)* **V** P D MAYBURY,
C H M COLLINGS

OSSETT, SOUTH (Christ Church) *Wakef 9* **P** *Bp*
V J HARRIS

OSSINGTON (Holy Rood) *see* Norwell w Ossington, Cromwell and Caunton *S'well*

OSTERLEY ROAD (St Mary) *see* Spring Grove St Mary *Lon*

OSWALDKIRK (St Oswald) *see* Ampleforth w Oswaldkirk, Gilling E etc *York*

OSWALDTWISTLE (Immanuel) (All Saints) *Blackb 1*
P *Trustees* **V** *vacant* (01254) 233962

OSWALDTWISTLE (St Paul) *Blackb 1* **P** *Trustees*
V M D RATCLIFFE, **NSM** C WILLIAMS

OSWESTRY (Holy Trinity) *Lich 19* **P** *Bp*
P-in-c P T DARLINGTON

OSWESTRY (St Oswald) *Lich 19* **P** *Earl of Powis*
V S G THORBURN

OTFORD (St Bartholomew) *Roch 10* **P** *D&C Westmr*
V R M WORSSAM

OTFORD LANE (Mission Hall) *see* Knockholt w Halstead *Roch*

OTHAM (St Nicholas) w Langley *Cant 14* **P** *Abp and CPAS (jt)* **R** A W SEWELL, **C** M E BUSSMANN,
NSM D W BOND

OTHERY (St Michael) *see* Middlezoy and Othery and Moorlinch *B & W*

OTLEY (All Saints) *Bradf 4* **P** *Bp* **V** G C BUTTANSHAW,
NSM J A PARKIN

OTLEY (St Mary) *see* Clopton w Otley, Swilland and Ashbocking *St E*

OTTER VALE *see* Ottery St Mary, Alfington, W Hill, Tipton etc *Ex*

OTTERBOURNE (St Matthew) *see* Compton, Hursley, and Otterbourne *Win*

OTTERBURN (St John the Evangelist) *see* N Tyne and Redesdale *Newc*

OTTERFORD (St Leonard) *see* Blackdown *B & W*

OTTERHAM (St Denis) *see* Boscastle w Davidstow *Truro*

OTTERINGTON, NORTH (St Michael and All Angels) *see* The Thorntons and The Otteringtons *York*

OTTERINGTON, SOUTH (St Andrew) *as above*

OTTERSHAW (Christ Church) *Guildf 11* **P** *Bp*
P-in-c S C FACCINI, **OLM** J A M VICKERS, B A SEYMOUR

OTTERTON (St Michael) *see* E Budleigh w Bicton and Otterton *Ex*

OTTERY ST MARY (St Mary the Virgin), Alfington, West Hill, Tipton St John, Venn Ottery, Newton Poppleford, Harpford and Colaton Raleigh *Ex 7* **P** *Patr Bd* **TR** S G FRANKLIN,
TV C E EDMONDS, M WARD, **C** J S OLLIER, **Hon C** J G PANGBOURNE, A E H TURNER, **NSM** K J BRIMACOMBE, R J ALLEN

OTTRINGHAM (St Wilfrid) *see* Keyingham w Ottringham, Halsham and Sunk Is *York*

OUGHTIBRIDGE (Ascension) *Sheff 3* **P** *V Wadsley*
V J F E MANN

OUGHTRINGTON (St Peter) and Warburton *Ches 10* **P** *Bp and Viscount Ashbrook (jt)* **R** E M BURGESS

OULTON (St John the Evangelist) *see* Stone Ch Ch and Oulton *Lich*

OULTON (St John) w Woodlesford *Ripon 8* **P** *Bp*
P-in-c A J PEARSON

OULTON (St Michael) *Nor 9* **P** *Ch Soc Trust*
R A R PRITCHARD, **NSM** C S PRITCHARD

OULTON (St Peter and St Paul) *see* Lt Barningham, Blickling, Edgefield etc *Nor*

OULTON BROAD (St Mark) (St Luke the Evangelist) *Nor 9*
P *Simeon's Trustees* **V** I R BENTLEY, **C** H L JARY,
NSM G POWELL, **OLM** M E ZIPFEL

OUNDLE (St Peter) w Ashton and Benefield w Glapthorn *Pet 10*
P *Bp and Mrs G S Watts-Russell (jt)* **R** R J ORMSTON,
C S J WEBSTER

OUSBY (St Luke) *see* Cross Fell Gp *Carl*

OUSDEN (St Peter) *see* Bansfield *St E*

OUSEBURN, GREAT (St Mary) and LITTLE (Holy Trinity) w Marton cum Grafton and Whixley w Green Hammerton *Ripon 3*
P *Bp, R Knaresborough and DBP (3 turns), St Jo Coll Cam (1 turn)* **V** M RIMMER

OUT RAWCLIFFE (St John the Evangelist) *see* Waterside Par *Blackb*

OUTLANE (St Mary Magdalene) *see* Stainland w Outlane *Wakef*

OUTWELL (St Clement) *Ely 14* **P** *Bp* **R** A F JESSON

OUTWOOD (St John) *see* S Nutfield w Outwood *S'wark*

OUTWOOD (St Mary Magdalene) *Wakef 11* **P** *V Stanley*
V J W BUTTERWORTH, **Hon Par Dn** G BUTTERWORTH

OUTWOOD COMMON (St John the Divine) *see* Billericay and Lt Burstead *Chelmsf*

OUZEL VALLEY, The *St Alb 12* **P** *Patr Bd* **TR** G FELLOWS,
TV J M CARDLEMAN, J BOOTHBY, D J MINTON, **C** D G TEASDEL,
OLM W JONES

OVAL WAY (All Saints) *see* Chalfont St Peter *Ox*

OVENDEN (St George) *Wakef 4* **P** *V Halifax*
V D J ROBERTSON, **NSM** P A PICKARD, G ROPER

OVENDEN (St John the Evangelist) *see* Bradshaw and Holmfield *Wakef*

OVER *see also under substantive place name*

OVER (St Chad) *Ches 6* **P** *Bp* **V** A L D FRIEND

OVER (St John the Evangelist) *Ches 6* **P** *Lord Delamere and W R Cullimore Esq (jt)* **V** D M WILSON

OVER (St Mary) *Ely 6* **P** *Trin Coll Cam* P-in-c M E RABY

OVER WALLOP (St Peter) *see* Portway and Danebury *Win*

OVERBURY (St Faith) w Teddington, Alstone and Little Washbourne w Beckford and Ashton under Hill *Worc 4*
P *D&C and MMCET (jt)* **V** *vacant* (01386) 881349

OVERCHURCH (St Mary) *see* Upton (Overchurch) *Ches*

OVERPOOL (St Francis) *see* Ellesmere Port *Ches*

OVERSEAL (St Matthew) *see* Seale and Lullington w Coton in the Elms *Derby*

OVERSTONE (St Nicholas) *see* Mears Ashby and Hardwick and Sywell etc *Pet*

OVERSTRAND (St Martin), Northrepps, Sidestrand and Trimingham *Nor 21* **P** *Duchy of Lanc, DBP, and Bp (by turn)*
R M L LANGAN

OVERTON (St Helen) *Blackb 11* **P** *V Lanc*
P-in-c D E NEWTON

OVERTON (St Mary) w Laverstoke and Freefolk *Win 6* **P** *Bp*
P-in-c I K SMALE

OVERTON (St Michael and All Angels) *see* Upper Kennet *Sarum*

OVING (All Saints) *see* Schorne *Ox*

OVING (St Andrew) *see* Tangmere and Oving *Chich*

OVINGDEAN (St Wulfran) *Chich 2* **P** *SMF* **R** *vacant* (01273) 303633

OVINGHAM (St Mary the Virgin) *Newc 9* **P** *Bp*
P-in-c M NELSON

OVINGTON (St John the Evangelist) *see* Ashill, Carbrooke, Ovington and Saham Toney *Nor*

OVINGTON (St Mary) *see* N Hinckford *Chelmsf*

OVINGTON (St Peter) *see* Arle Valley *Win*

OWERMOIGNE (St Michael) *see* Watercombe *Sarum*

OWERSBY, NORTH (St Martin) *see* Kelsey Gp *Linc*

OWLERTON (St John the Baptist) *Sheff 4* **P** *Ch Patr Trust*
V N A DAWSON

OWLPEN (Holy Cross) *see* Uley w Owlpen and Nympsfield *Glouc*

OWLSMOOR (St George) *Ox 16* **P** *Bp* **V** R G BURGESS

OWLSWICK (Chapel) *see* Risborough *Ox*

OWMBY Group, The (St Peter and St Paul) *Linc 3* **P** *Duchy of Lanc, Bp and D&C, Bp and Mrs S Hutton, and Mrs B K Cracroft-Eley (by turn)* **R** P D GODDEN

OWSLEBURY (St Andrew) *see* Twyford and Owslebury and Morestead etc *Win*

OWSTON (All Saints) *Sheff 7* **P** *DBP* **V** M MOSSMAN

OWSTON (St Andrew) *see* Whatborough Gp *Leic*

OWSTON (St Martin) *Linc 1* **P** *The Crown* P-in-c J N GREEN

OWTHORNE (St Matthew) *see* Withernsea w Owthorne and Easington etc *York*

OWTHORPE (St Margaret) *S'well 8* **P** *Trustees Sir Rupert Bromley Bt* **P-in-c** P D S MASSEY

OWTON MANOR (St James) *Dur 3* **P** *Bp* **V** S J LOCKE,
C D G HUNTLEY

OXBOROUGH (St John the Evangelist) w Foulden and Caldecote *Nor 13* **P** *G&C Coll Cam* **C** D J HANWELL

OXCLOSE (not known) *Dur 11* **P** *R Washington, TR Usworth, and V Fatfield (jt)* **V** *vacant* 0191-415 9468

OXENDON (St Helen) *see* Arthingworth, Harrington w Oxendon and E Farndon *Pet*

OXENHALL (St Anne) *see* Redmarley D'Abitot, Bromesberrow, Pauntley etc *Glouc*

OXENHOPE (St Mary the Virgin) *Bradf 8* **P** *Bp*
P-in-c J MEDHURST

OXENTON (St John the Baptist) *see* Bishop's Cleeve and Woolstone w Gotherington etc *Glouc*

OXFORD Canning Crescent (St Luke) *see* Ox St Matt *Ox*

OXFORD (St Aldate) *Ox 7* **P** *Simeon's Trustees*
R C ST G CLEVERLY, **C** S C R PONSONBY, A E RAMSEY,
NSM G C F HICKSON

OXFORD (St Andrew) *Ox 7* **P** *Trustees*
V A R WINGFIELD DIGBY, **C** W O C PEARSON-GEE,
NSM R M CUNNINGHAM, J MOBEY

OXFORD (St Barnabas and St Paul) *Ox 7* **P** *Keble Coll Ox*
P-in-c J W BESWICK, **NSM** M E MAYLOR

OXFORD (St Clement) *Ox 4* **P** *Ox Ch Trust*
R J B GILLINGHAM

OXFORD (St Ebbe w Holy Trinity and St Peter-le-Bailey) *Ox 7*
P *Ox Ch Trust* **R** V E ROBERTS, **C** P D L WILKINSON,
P A JACK, **NSM** D G REID

OXFORD (St Frideswide) w Binsey *Ox 7* **P** *Ch Ch Ox*
P-in-c R J E DEWHURST

OXFORD (St Giles) St Philip and St James (St Margaret) *Ox 7*
P *St Jo Coll Ox* **V** A W H BUNCH, **C** S A WELCH,
Hon C B W SILVERMAN

OXFORD (St Mary Magdalene) *Ox 7* **P** *Ch Ch Ox*
P-in-c P J GROVES, **NSM** M E A MCALISTER

OXFORD (St Mary the Virgin) (St Cross *or* **Holywell) (St Peter in the East)** *Ox 7* **P** *Or Coll Ox and Mert Coll Ox (jt)*
V B W MOUNTFORD, **C** C W D'ALTON, **NSM** C BANNISTER-PARKER

OXFORD (St Matthew) *Ox 7* **P** *Ox Ch Trust*
P-in-c S J HELLYER, **Hon C** J A WILLIAMS,
NSM M J RAYNER, J SHERWOOD

OXFORD (St Michael at the North Gate w St Martin and All Saints) *Ox 7* **P** *Linc Coll Ox* P-in-c J C H M LEE,
Hon C G A D PLATTEN

OXFORD (St Thomas the Martyr) *Ox 7* **P** *Ch Ch Ox*
Hon C J W HUNWICKE, J M R BAKER

OXHEY (All Saints) *St Alb 7* **P** *Bp* **V** P M WISE,
C J M WILSON, A SOWTON

OXHEY (St Matthew) *St Alb 7* **P** *DBP* **V** D M SHEPHERD

OXHILL (St Lawrence) *see* Tysoe w Oxhill and Whatcote *Cov*

OXLEY (Epiphany) *Lich 28* **P** *Bp* **V** P S HAWKINS,
NSM R MAXFIELD

OXNEAD (St Michael & all Angels) *see* Bure Valley *Nor*

OXSHOTT (St Andrew) *Guildf 10* **P** *Bp* **V** J P CRESSWELL,
NSM V PITT, **OLM** M L L HAWRISH

OXSPRING (St Aidan)   *see* Penistone and Thurlstone *Wakef*
OXTED (St Mary) and Tandridge *S'wark 25*   **P** *Bp*
   R A J MAYER,   **OLM** D C WEIGHTMAN
OXTON (St Peter and St Paul) *S'well 15*   **P** *Ld Chan, Bp, and*
   C P L Francklin Esq (by turn)   **P-in-c** A R GILES,
   NSM M N TAYLOR
OXTON (St Saviour) *Ches 1*   **P** *DBP*   **V** I A DAVENPORT,
   C G V LAUTENBACH, D E WATSON
PACKINGTON (Holy Rood)   *see* Woodfield Team *Leic*
PACKWOOD (St Giles) w Hockley Heath *Birm 6*   **P** *Bp and*
   M R Parkes Esq (alt)   **V** Q D WARBRICK
PADBURY (St Mary the Virgin)   *see* Lenborough *Ox*
PADDINGTON (Emmanuel) Harrow Road *Lon 2*   **P** *Hyndman*
   Trustees   **P-in-c** A G THOM,   **C** J F BARRY
PADDINGTON (St David's Welsh Church) Extra-Parochial
   Place *Lon 2 vacant*
PADDINGTON (St James) *Lon 2*   **P** *Bp*   **V** W G WILSON,
   C G W MILLER,   **Hon C** W H BAYNES,   **NSM** R RAJ-SINGH
PADDINGTON (St John the Evangelist) (St Michael and All
   Angels) *Lon 2*   **P** *DBP*   **V** S D MASON,   **C** B Z GREEN,
   Hon C M S PUDGE,   **NSM** M LEGG
PADDINGTON (St Luke the Evangelist)   *see* W Kilburn
   St Luke w St Simon and St Jude *Lon*
PADDINGTON (St Mary) *Lon 2*   **P** *Bp*   **P-in-c** G S BRADLEY,
   NSM M GIBSON
PADDINGTON (St Mary Magdalene) (St Peter) *Lon 2*
   P *Keble Coll Ox and Ch Patr Trust*   **V** R H EVERETT,
   NSM F W WARD
PADDINGTON (St Saviour) *Lon 2*   **P** *Bp*   **V** G S BRADLEY,
   NSM F E BLACKMORE, M GIBSON
PADDINGTON (St Stephen w St Luke) *Lon 2*   **P** *Bp*
   V J R ALLCOCK
PADDINGTON GREEN (St Mary)   *see* Paddington St Mary
   Lon
PADDLESWORTH (St Oswald)   *see* Lyminge w Paddlesworth,
   Stanford w Postling etc *Cant*
PADDOCK WOOD (St Andrew) *Roch 8*   **P** *D&C Cant*
   V B T KNAPP,   **C** D J WATTS, P S CALLWAY
PADGATE (Christ Church) *Liv 12*   **P** *Bp, Adn, and*
   R Warrington (jt)   **V** S P ATTWATER
PADIHAM (St Leonard) w Hapton and Padiham Green *Blackb 3*
   P *Bp*   **V** M A JONES,   **C** D J T RUSSELL
PADSTOW (St Petroc) *Truro 7*   **P** *P J N Prideaux-Brune Esq*
   V C M MALKINSON
PADWORTH (St John the Baptist)   *see* Stratfield Mortimer and
   Mortimer W End etc *Ox*
PAGANHILL (Holy Spirit)   *see* Whiteshill and Randwick *Glouc*
PAGHAM (St Thomas à Becket) *Chich 1*   **P** *Abp*   **V** K SMITH
PAGLESHAM (St Peter)   *see* Canewdon w Paglesham *Chelmsf*
PAIGNTON (Christ Church) and Preston St Paul *Ex 12*   **P** *Bp*
   and Peache Trustees (jt)   **V** D W WITCHELL,   **C** P R BRYCE
PAIGNTON (St John the Baptist) (St Andrew) (St Boniface)
   Ex 12   **P** *DBP*   **V** B R TUBBS,   **C** R L BOYLE
PAILTON (St Denis)   *see* Monks Kirby w Pailton and Stretton-
   under-Fosse *Cov*
PAINSWICK (St Mary the Virgin), Sheepscombe, Cranham, The
   Edge, Pitchcombe, Harescombe and Brookthorpe *Glouc 5*
   P *Bp, D&C, Mrs N Owen (1 turn), and Ld Chan (1 turn)*
   V J LONGUET-HIGGINS,   **NSM** J A JAMES,
   OLM D W NEWELL, E J WARD
PAKEFIELD (All Saints and St Margaret) *Nor 9*   **P** *Ch Patr*
   Trust   **R** R J K BAKER,   **C** H Y WILCOX
PAKENHAM (St Mary) w Norton and Tostock *St E 9*   **P** *Bp and*
   Peterho Cam (jt)   **R** I HOOPER,   **NSM** S A LONG
PALGRAVE (St Peter)   *see* N Hartismere *St E*
PALLION (St Luke)   *see* Millfield St Mark and Pallion St Luke
   Dur
PALMARSH (Holy Cross)   *see* Hythe *Cant*
PALMERS GREEN (St John the Evangelist) *Lon 18*
   P *V Southgate Ch Ch*   **V** J A CULLEN
PALTERTON (St Luke's Mission Room)   *see* E Scarsdale *Derby*
PAMBER (St Mary and St John the Baptist)   *see* The Sherbornes
   w Pamber *Win*
PAMBER HEATH (St Luke)   *see* Tadley S and Silchester *Win*
PAMPISFORD (St John the Baptist) *Ely 5*
   P *Mrs B A Killander*   **V** *vacant*
PANCRASWEEK (St Pancras)   *see* Pyworthy, Pancrasweek and
   Bridgerule *Ex*
PANFIELD (St Mary the Virgin) and Rayne *Chelmsf 15*   **P** *Bp*
   and DBP (alt)   **R** *vacant* (01376) 320517
PANGBOURNE (St James the Less) w Tidmarsh and Sulham
   Ox 12   **P** *Bp, Ch Soc Trust, and Mrs I E Moon (jt)*
   P-in-c H C W PARBURY
PANNAL (St Robert of Knaresborough) w Beckwithshaw *Ripon 1*
   P *Bp and Peache Trustees (jt)*   **V** N C SINCLAIR,
   NSM S E PEARCE

PANSHANGER (United Church) Conventional District
   St Alb 7 vacant
PAPCASTLE (Mission Church)   *see* Cockermouth Area *Carl*
PAPPLEWICK (St James)   *see* Linby w Papplewick *S'well*
PAPWORTH (St Peter) *Ely 1*   **P** *Patr Bd*   **TR** J F WINDSOR,
   TV S M DAY,   **C** A N M CLARKE,   **NSM** P GILDERSLEVE,
   N H A PEARSON, S E JOHNSON
PAR (St Mary the Virgin) (Good Shepherd) *Truro 1*
   P *The Crown*   **P-in-c** I M TUCKER
PARHAM (St Mary the Virgin)   *see* Campsea Ashe w
   Marlesford, Parham and Hacheston *St E*
PARHAM (St Peter)   *see* Amberley w N Stoke and Parham,
   Wiggonholt etc *Chich*
PARK BARN (St Clare)   *see* Westborough *Guildf*
PARKEND (St Paul) and Viney Hill *Glouc 2*   **P** *Bp and Univ Coll*
   Ox (jt)   **V** P A BRUNT
PARKESTON (St Paul)   *see* Harwich Peninsula *Chelmsf*
PARKFIELD (Holy Trinity)   *see* Langley and Parkfield *Man*
PARKGATE (St Thomas)   *see* Neston *Ches*
PARKHAM (St James), Alwington, Buckland Brewer,
   Abbotsham, Hartland, Welcombe, Clovelly, Woolfardisworthy
   West and Buck Mills *Ex 16*   **P** *Patr Bd (4 turns), Crown*
   (1 turn)   **TV** A J RICHARDSON, M W MITCHELL,
   S C HENDERSON,   **C** F J R OTTO,   **Hon C** C W J HODGETTS,
   NSM D BAKER
PARKSTONE (Good Shepherd)   *see* Heatherlands St Jo *Sarum*
PARKSTONE (St Barnabas)   *see* Branksome St Clem *Sarum*
PARKSTONE (St Clement)   *as above*
PARKSTONE (St John)   *see* Heatherlands St Jo *Sarum*
PARKSTONE (St Luke) *Sarum 7*   **P** *Ch Trust Fund Trust*
   V C M STRAIN
PARKSTONE (St Peter) and St Osmund w Branksea St Mary
   Sarum 7   **P** *Patr Bd*   **R** N J C LLOYD,   **NSM** D J NEWMAN,
   J P M MARTIN,   **OLM** P SOUTHGATE, H S WRIGHT,
   Dss D J NEWMAN
PARKWOOD (Christ Church) Conventional District *Cant 15*
   C-in-c M A MCLAUGHLIN
PARKWOOD (St Paul)   *see* S Gillingham *Roch*
PARLAUNT ROAD (Christ the Worker)   *see* Langley Marish
   Ox
PARLEY, WEST (All Saints) (St Mark) *Sarum 9*
   P *P E E Prideaux-Brune Esq*   **R** E C BOOTH
PARNDON, GREAT (St Mary) *Chelmsf 25*   **P** *Patr Bd*
   TR M D BENNET,   **TV** N R TAYLOR,   **NSM** M J HILLIER
PARNDON, LITTLE (St Mary)   *see* Harlow Town Cen w Lt
   Parndon *Chelmsf*
PARR (St Peter) (St Paul) (St Philip) (Holy Trinity) *Liv 10*
   P *Patr Bd*   **TR** J L ROBERTS,   **TV** N MCCATHIE, J E DRAYCOTT,
   C V C WHITWORTH,   **OLM** A KIRKHAM, M E TAYLOR,
   H MCCANN
PARR MOUNT (Holy Trinity)   *see* Parr *Liv*
PARRACOMBE (Christ Church)   *see* Combe Martin,
   Berrynarbor, Lynton, Brendon etc *Ex*
PARSON CROSS (St Bernard)   *see* Southey Green St Bernard
   CD *Sheff*
PARSON CROSS (St Cecilia)   *see* Sheff St Cecilia Parson Cross
   Sheff
PARSON'S GREEN (St Dionis)   *see* Fulham St Dionis Parson's
   Green *Lon*
PARTINGTON (St Mary) and Carrington *Ches 10*   **P** *Bp and*
   V Bowdon (alt)   **V** P H GEDDES
PARTNEY Group, The (St Nicholas) *Linc 7*   **P** *Bp and DBP,*
   Baroness Willoughby de Eresby, Mrs E M V Drake, and
   Mrs D E P Douglas (by turn)   **R** R J BENSON
PARTRIDGE GREEN (St Michael and All Angels)   *see* W
   Grinstead *Chich*
PARWICH (St Peter)   *see* Fenny Bentley, Thorpe, Tissington,
   Parwich etc *Derby*
PASSENHAM (St Guthlac) *Pet 5*   **P** *MMCET*   **R** C J MURRAY
PASTON (All Saints) *Pet 11*   **P** *Bp*   **R** G M JESSOP,
   C C D DEVERELL,   **NSM** R F WATKINSON
PASTON (St Margaret)   *see* Trunch *Nor*
PASTROW *Win 3*   **P** *Bp, Qu Coll Ox, and St Mary's Coll*
   Win (jt)   **P-in-c** J M BENTALL,   **NSM** S HOBBINS
PATCHAM (All Saints) *Chich 2*   **P** *MMCET*
   V N E D MILMINE,   **C** A M BOUSFIELD, L H JACKSON,
   NSM M PHILIP
PATCHING (St John the Divine)   *see* Findon w Clapham and
   Patching *Chich*
PATCHWAY (St Chad) *Bris 5*   **P** *Trustees*   **V** D R BYRNE
PATELEY BRIDGE (St Cuthbert)   *see* Upper Nidderdale *Ripon*
PATRICK (Holy Trinity) *S & M 1*   **P** *Bp*   **V** *vacant* (01624)
   842637
PATRICK BROMPTON (St Patrick) and Hunton *Ripon 4*
   P *Bp*   **NSM** J T OLDFIELD

PATRICROFT (Christ Church)   *see* Eccles *Man*

PATRINGTON (St Patrick) w Hollym, Welwick and Winestead
York 12   **P** *DBP, Ld Chan, and CPAS (by turn)*
R D R HARRIS,   **Hon C** J A SHARP

PATRIXBOURNE (St Mary)   *see* Bridge *Cant*

PATTERDALE (St Patrick)   *see* Gd Shep TM *Carl*

PATTINGHAM (St Chad) w Patshull *Lich 24*   **P** *Bp and Lady
Kwiatkowska (jt)*   **P-in-c** M P HOBBS

**PATTISHALL (Holy Cross) w Cold Higham and Gayton w
Tiffield** *Pet 5*   **P** *Bp, SS Coll Cam, and SMF (jt)*
R P J BROADBENT

PAUL (St Pol de Lion) *Truro 5*   **P** *Ld Chan*   **P-in-c** T D HEANEY,
NSM Y M HOBSON

PAULERSPURY (St James the Apostle)   *see* Silverstone and
Abthorpe w Slapton etc *Pet*

PAULL (St Andrew and St Mary)   *see* Hedon w Paull *York*

PAULSGROVE (St Michael and All Angels) *Portsm 6*   **P** *Bp*
V G R WADDINGTON

**PAULTON (Holy Trinity) w Farrington Gurney and High
Littleton** *B & W 12*   **P** *Bp and Hyndman Trustees (jt)*
V J G EDWARDS

PAUNTLEY (St John the Evangelist)   *see* Redmarley D'Abitot,
Bromesberrow, Pauntley etc *Glouc*

PAVENHAM (St Peter)   *see* Milton Ernest, Pavenham and
Thurleigh *St Alb*

PAWLETT (St John the Baptist)   *see* Puriton and Pawlett *B & W*

PAXFORD (Mission Church)   *see* Blockley w Aston Magna and
Bourton on the Hill *Glouc*

PAXTONS, The (Holy Trinity) (St James) w Diddington *Ely 13*
P *D&C Linc (2 turns) and E G W Thornhill Esq (1 turn)*
V A S REED

PAYHEMBURY (St Mary the Virgin)   *see* Broadhembury,
Payhembury and Plymtree *Ex*

PEACEHAVEN (Ascension) and Telscombe Cliffs *Chich 18*
P *Bp*   **V** D A HIDER

PEAK DALE (Holy Trinity)   *see* Wormhill, Peak Forest w Peak
Dale and Dove Holes *Derby*

PEAK FOREST (St Charles the King and Martyr)   *as above*

PEAKIRK (St Pega) w Glinton and Northborough *Pet 11*
P *D&C*   **P-in-c** H P GEISOW

PEAR TREE (Jesus Chapel)   *see* Southampton St Mary Extra
Win

PEASE POTTAGE (Ascension)   *see* Slaugham *Chich*

PEASEDOWN ST JOHN (St John the Baptist) w Wellow
B & W 12   **P** *Bp and R H Horton-Fawkes Esq (jt)*
P-in-c M G STREET,   **Hon C** R P FOTHERGILL

PEASEMORE (St Barnabas)   *see* Beedon and Peasemore w W
Ilsley and Farnborough *Ox*

PEASENHALL (St Michael)   *see* Yoxmere *St E*

PEASE'S WEST (St George)   *see* Crook *Dur*

PEASLAKE (St Mark)   *see* Shere, Albury and Chilworth *Guildf*

PEASLEY CROSS (Mission Hall)   *see* Parr *Liv*

PEASMARSH (St Michael)   *see* Shalford *Guildf*

PEASMARSH (St Peter and St Paul)   *see* Beckley and
Peasmarsh *Chich*

PEATLING MAGNA (All Saints)   *see* Willoughby Waterleys,
Peatling Magna etc *Leic*

PEATLING PARVA (St Andrew)   *see* Gilmorton, Peatling
Parva, Kimcote etc *Leic*

PEBMARSH (St John the Baptist)   *see* Knights and Hospitallers
Par *Chelmsf*

**PEBWORTH (St Peter), Dorsington, Honeybourne and Marston
Sicca** *Glouc 8*   **P** *Bp*   **R** C G MATTOCK

PECKHAM (St John w St Andrew) *S'wark 8*   **P** *Bp*
V T C WRIGHT,   **C** S J HORNER,   **Hon C** S J WRIGHT

PECKHAM (St Luke)   *see* Camberwell St Luke *S'wark*

PECKHAM (St Mary Magdalene) (St Paul) *S'wark 8*
P *Ch Patr Soc*   **V** O A ADAMS

PECKHAM (St Saviour) *S'wark 9*   **P** *Bp*
P-in-c D L GWILLIAMS,   **C** J MUKUNGA

PECKHAM, EAST (Holy Trinity) and Nettlestead *Roch 8*
P *St Pet Coll Ox and D&C Cant (jt)*   **R** A H CARR,
NSM S M MORRELL

PECKHAM, WEST (St Dunstan)   *see* Mereworth w
W Peckham *Roch*

PECKLETON (St Mary Magdalene)   *see* Desford and Peckleton
w Tooley *Leic*

PEDLINGE (Estate Chapel)   *see* Saltwood *Cant*

PEDMORE (St Peter) *Worc 12*   **P** *Oldswinford Hosp*
R A L HAZLEWOOD,   **C** I R JENNINGS

PEEL (St Paul)   *see* Walkden and Lt Hulton *Man*

PEEL GREEN (St Catherine)   *see* Barton w Peel Green *Man*

PEEL GREEN (St Michael and All Angels)   *as above*

PEGSWOOD (St Margaret)   *see* Bothal and Pegswood w
Longhirst *Newc*

PELDON (St Mary) w Great and Little Wigborough *Chelmsf 16*
P *Ch Soc Trust and T Wheatley-Hubbard Esq*
P-in-c S C NORTON

PELSALL (St Michael and All Angels) *Lich 25*   **P** *Bp*
V C A ST A RAMSAY,   **NSM** A M MORRIS

PELTON (Holy Trinity) and West Pelton *Dur 11*   **P** *Bp*
V J LINTERN,   **C** D ATKINSON

PELTON, WEST (St Paul)   *see* Pelton and W Pelton *Dur*

PELYNT (St Nun)   *see* Lanreath, Pelynt and Bradoc *Truro*

PEMBERTON (St Francis of Assisi) Kitt Green *Liv 14*
P *R Wigan and Bp (jt)*   **P-in-c** H P HARVEY

PEMBERTON (St John) *Liv 14*   **P** *R Wigan*
V C B OXENFORTH

PEMBERTON (St Mark) Newtown   *see* Marsh Green w
Newtown *Liv*

**PEMBRIDGE (St Mary the Virgin) w Moor Court, Shobdon,
Staunton-on-Arrow, Byton and Lyonshall** *Heref 5*   **P** *Ld Chan
(1 turn), Patr Bd (4 turns)*   **R** J M READ

PEMBURY (St Peter) *Roch 8*   **P** *Ch Ch Ox*   **V** M C JACKSON,
NSM H A HUGHES

PEN SELWOOD (St Michael) *B & W 2*   **P** *Bp*
R N C M FEAVER

PENCOMBE (St John)   *see* Bredenbury *Heref*

PENCOYD (St Denys)   *see* St Weonards *Heref*

PENCOYS (St Andrew)   *see* Redruth w Lanner and Treleigh
Truro

PENDEEN (St John the Baptist) w Morvah *Truro 5*
P *R A H Aitken Esq and C W M Aitken Esq (jt)*   **V** A ROWELL

PENDEFORD (St Paul)   *see* Tettenhall Regis *Lich*

PENDLEBURY (St Augustine)   *see* Swinton and Pendlebury
Man

PENDLEBURY (St John) *Man 6*   **P** *Trustees*   **V** S K TIMMINS,
OLM V TYLDESLEY, J BRANDRETH

PENDLETON (All Saints)   *see* Sabden and Pendleton *Blackb*

PENDLETON Claremont (Holy Angels)   *see* Salford All SS
Man

PENDLETON (St Thomas)   *as above*

PENDOCK CROSS (Holy Redeemer)   *see* Berrow w Pendock,
Eldersfield, Hollybush etc *Worc*

PENDOMER (St Roch)   *see* W Coker w Hardington
Mandeville, E Chinnock etc *B & W*

PENGE (Christ Church w Holy Trinity)   *see* Anerley *Roch*

PENGE (St John the Evangelist) *Roch 13*   **P** *Simeon's Trustees*
V D MEDWAY

PENGE (St Paul)   *see* Anerley *Roch*

PENGE LANE (Holy Trinity) *Roch 13*   **P** *CPAS*
P-in-c N G READ,   **NSM** M A WILKINSON

PENHILL *Ripon 4*   **P** *Trin Coll Cam and Lord Bolton (jt)*
R S C WHITEHOUSE,   **C** J A WALKER-HUTCHINSON,
NSM P S YEADON

PENHILL (St Peter) *Bris 7*   **P** *Bp*   **P-in-c** C A STONE

PENHURST (St Michael the Archangel)   *see* Ashburnham w
Penhurst *Chich*

PENISTONE (St John the Baptist) and Thurlstone *Wakef 7*
P *Bp*   **TR** D J HOPKIN,   **OLM** A P PARR

PENKETH (St Paul) *Liv 12*   **P** *Bp*   **V** P W HOCKLEY

PENKEVIL (St Michael)   *see* St Michael Penkevil *Truro*

PENKHULL (St Thomas)   *see* Hartshill, Penkhull and Trent
Vale *Lich*

PENKRIDGE Team, The (St Michael and All Angels) *Lich 2*
P *Patr Bd*   **TR** M WILLIAMS,   **TV** C M PLANT,
C J M TAYLOR,   **OLM** I NICHOLLS

PENN (Holy Trinity) and Tylers Green *Ox 20*   **P** *Earl Howe*
V M D BISSET

PENN (St Bartholomew) (St Anne) *Lich 24*   **P** *Bp*
V B N WHITMORE,   **C** M HIRD

PENN FIELDS St Philip (St Aidan) *Lich 24*   **P** *Ch Trust Fund
Trust*   **V** J S OAKLEY,   **C** P J CANSDALE, T M LOMAX,
NSM K J LOMAX

PENN STREET (Holy Trinity) *Ox 20*   **P** *Earl Howe*
V W F MASON,   **NSM** C E L SMITH

PENNARD, EAST (All Saints)   *see* Fosse Trinity *B & W*

PENNARD, WEST (St Nicholas)   *see* Baltonsborough w
Butleigh, W Bradley etc *B & W*

PENNINGTON (Christ Church) *Man 13*   **P** *Trustees*
V A J BUTTERWORTH,   **C** C G ELMS,   **NSM** S G WILKINSON,
OLM E J WHITE

PENNINGTON (St Mark) *Win 11*   **P** *V Milford*
P-in-c A B RUSSELL

**PENNINGTON (St Michael and the Holy Angels) and Lindal w
Marton and Bardsea** *Carl 9*   **P** *Bp and DBP (jt)*
P-in-c G A TUBBS

PENNY LANE (St Barnabas)   *see* Mossley Hill *Liv*

PENNYCROSS (St Pancras) *Ex 22*   **P** *CPAS*
V A M M PARKER

PENNYWELL (St Thomas)   *see* Sunderland St Thos and St Oswald *Dur*

PENPONDS (Holy Trinity) *Truro 2*   **P** *The Crown*
P-in-c P DOUGLASS,   **C** M L PASCOE

PENRITH (Christ Church) (St Andrew) w Newton Reigny and Plumpton Wall *Carl 4*   **P** *Bp*   **TR** D G SARGENT,
TV A P HUTCHINSON, R C PATTINSON,   **C** A M WALSH,
A M E OSMASTON

PENRUDDOCK (All Saints)   *see* Gd Shep TM *Carl*

PENSAX (St James the Great)   *see* Teme Valley N *Worc*

PENSBY (St Michael and All Angels)   *see* Barnston *Ches*

PENSHAW (All Saints)   *see* Herrington, Penshaw and Shiney Row *Dur*

PENSHURST (St John the Baptist) and Fordcombe *Roch 12*
P *Viscount De L'Isle*   **R** T E HOLME

PENSILVA (St John)   *see* St Ive and Pensilva w Quethiock *Truro*

PENSNETT (St Mark) *Worc 10*   **P** *Bp*   **V** B M LEACH

PENTEWAN (All Saints)   *see* St Austell *Truro*

PENTLOW (St George and St Gregory)   *see* N Hinckford *Chelmsf*

PENTNEY (St Mary Magdalene)   *see* Narborough w Narford and Pentney *Nor*

PENTON MEWSEY (Holy Trinity)   *see* Pastrow *Win*

PENTONVILLE (St Silas w All Saints) (St James) *Lon 6*   **P** *Bp*
V S RICHARDS

PENTRICH (St Matthew)   *see* Swanwick and Pentrich *Derby*

PENTRIDGE (St Rumbold)   *see* Sixpenny Handley w Gussage St Andrew etc *Sarum*

PENWERRIS (St Michael and All Angels) (Holy Spirit) *Truro 3*
P *V St Gluvias*   **P-in-c** M T MESLEY

PENWORTHAM (St Leonard) *Blackb 5*   **P** *Bp*
V J N MANSFIELD,   **NSM** J V SCOTT, S J BAINES

PENWORTHAM (St Mary) *Blackb 5*   **P** *Miss A M Rawstorne*
V C J NELSON,   **NSM** A D WYNNE

PENZANCE (St Mary) (St Paul) (St John the Baptist) *Truro 5*
P *Bp*   **TR** K R OWEN,   **Hon C** R H PESKETT,
J K P S ROBERTSHAW,   **NSM** J COTTON

PEOPLETON (St Nicholas) and White Ladies Aston w Churchill and Spetchley and Upton Snodsbury and Broughton Hackett *Worc 4*   **P** *Bp, Croom Estate Trustees, and Major R J G Berkley (1 turn), and Ld Chan (1 turn)*   **R** S M EAST

PEOVER, OVER (St Lawrence) w Lower Peover (St Oswald) *Ches 12*   **P** *DBP and Man Univ (jt)*   **V** P J LLOYD

PEPER HAROW (St Nicholas)   *see* Compton w Shackleford and Peper Harow *Guildf*

PEPLOW (The Epiphany)   *see* Hodnet w Weston under Redcastle *Lich*

PERIVALE (St Mary w St Nicholas) *Lon 22*   **P** *Trustees*
R A R CORSIE,   **NSM** V A AITKEN

PERLETHORPE (St John the Evangelist) *S'well 2*   **P** *Earl Manvers' Trustees*   **P-in-c** A D LITTLEWOOD,   **C** A FLETCHER

PERRANARWORTHAL (St Piran)   *see* St Stythians w Perranarworthal and Gwennap *Truro*

PERRANPORTH (St Michael's Mission Church)
see Perranzabuloe *Truro*

PERRANUTHNOE (St Michael and St Piran)   *see* Ludgvan, Marazion, St Hilary and Perranuthnoe *Truro*

PERRANZABULOE (St Piran) *Truro 7*   **P** *D&C*
P-in-c J C E ANDREW,   **NSM** P M NIXON

PERROTT, NORTH (St Martin)   *see* Wulfric Benefice *B & W*

PERROTT, SOUTH (St Mary)   *see* Beaminster Area *Sarum*

PERRY BARR (St John the Evangelist) *Birm 3*   **P** *Bp and trustees (jt)*   **P-in-c** C A PAILING

PERRY BEECHES (St Matthew) *Birm 3*   **P** *St Martin's Trustees*   **V** S P M MACKENZIE

PERRY COMMON (St Martin)   *see* Erdington Ch the K *Birm*

PERRY GREEN (St Thomas)   *see* Albury, Braughing, Furneux Pelham, Lt Hadham etc *St Alb*

PERRY HILL (St George) (Christ Church) (St Paul) *S'wark 5*
P *D&C and Earl of Dartmouth (1 turn), Bp and Earl of Dartmouth (1 turn)*   **V** J R W ACKLAND,   **C** R S STANIER,
NSM A D W DUPUY

PERRY STREET (All Saints) *Roch 4*   **P** *Bp*
V J PERUMBALATH

PERSHORE (Holy Cross) w Pinvin, Wick and Birlingham *Worc 4*   **P** *Patr Bd*   **V** K I CRAWFORD,   **C** C J STUART

PERTENHALL (St Peter)   *see* The Stodden Churches *St Alb*

PETER TAVY (St Peter), Mary Tavy, Lydford and Brent Tor *Ex 25*   **P** *Guild of All So and Bp (1 turn), Duchy of Cornwall (1 turn)*   **Hon C** R D ORMSBY, I SYKES,   **NSM** J C HIGMAN

PETERBOROUGH (All Saints) *Pet 11*   **P** *Bp*   **V** *vacant* (01733) 554130

PETERBOROUGH (Christ the Carpenter) *Pet 11*   **P** *Bp*
V N E FRY,   **NSM** S M ROLFE

PETERBOROUGH (Holy Spirit) Bretton *Pet 11*   **P** *Bp*
P-in-c J M COLLINS

PETERBOROUGH (St John the Baptist) (Mission Church) *Pet 11*   **P** *Bp*   **V** G J STEELE

PETERBOROUGH (St Jude) *Pet 11*   **P** *Bp*   **V** G J KEATING

PETERBOROUGH (St Mark) and St Barnabas *Pet 11*   **P** *Bp*
P-in-c J J PRICE

PETERBOROUGH (St Mary) Boongate *Pet 11*   **P** *D&C*
P-in-c S A WALKER,   **C** M P J MOORE

PETERBOROUGH (St Paul) *Pet 11*   **P** *Bp*   **V** *vacant* (01733) 343746

PETERCHURCH (St Peter)   *see* Madley w Tyberton, Peterchurch, Vowchurch etc *Heref*

PETERLEE (St Cuthbert) *Dur 2*   **P** *Bp*   **V** P M TEMPLEMAN,
C R I COLEMAN,   **NSM** A J TEMPLEMAN

PETERSFIELD (St Peter) *Portsm 4*   **P** *Bp*   **V** W G HARRIS-EVANS,   **C** D J CLARKE

PETERSHAM (All Saints) (St Peter) *S'wark 16*   **P** *Bp*
P-in-c T J E MARWOOD,   **NSM** F M HOWARD

PETERSMARLAND (St Peter)   *see* Shebbear, Buckland Filleigh, Sheepwash etc *Ex*

PETERSTOW (St Peter)   *see* Brampton *Heref*

PETHAM (All Saints)   *see* Stone Street Gp *Cant*

PETHERTON, NORTH (St Mary the Virgin)   *see* Alfred Jewel *B & W*

PETHERTON, SOUTH (St Peter and St Paul) w the Seavingtons *B & W 15*   **P** *D&C*   **R** D J M JASPER,
NSM D B FYFE

PETHERWIN, NORTH (St Paternus)   *see* Egloskerry, N Petherwin, Tremaine and Tresmere *Truro*

PETROCKSTOWE (St Petrock)   *see* Shebbear, Buckland Filleigh, Sheepwash etc *Ex*

PETT (St Mary and St Peter)   *see* Fairlight, Guestling and Pett *Chich*

PETT LEVEL (St Nicholas)   *as above*

PETTAUGH (St Catherine)   *see* Debenham and Helmingham *St E*

PETTISTREE (St Peter and St Paul)   *see* Wickham Market w Pettistree *St E*

PETTON (not known) w Cockshutt, Welshampton and Lyneal w Colemere *Lich 17*   **P** *Bp and R K Mainwaring Esq (jt)*
P-in-c D N ASH

PETTON (St Petrock)   *see* Bampton, Morebath, Clayhanger and Petton *Ex*

PETTS WOOD (St Francis) *Roch 16*   **P** *Bp*   **V** O C G HIGGS

PETWORTH (St Mary) *Chich 11*   **P** *Lord Egremont*
P-in-c T J WRIGHT

PEVENSEY (St Nicholas) (St Wilfred) *Chich 16*   **P** *Bp*
V A C H CHRISTIAN

PEWSEY (St John the Baptist) and Swanborough Team Ministry, The *Sarum 19*   **P** *Patr Bd*   **TR** H G HOSKINS,
TV L J VALIANT, D F LARKEY,   **OLM** G E R OSBORNE

PHEASEY (St Chad) *Lich 25*   **P** *DBP*   **P-in-c** K S NJENGA

PHILADELPHIA (St Thomas) Extra-Parochial Place *Sheff 4*
Min A F MACLAURIN,   **NSM** R J G HOPKINS

PHILBEACH GARDENS (St Cuthbert)   *see* Earl's Court St Cuth w St Matthias *Lon*

PHILLACK (St Felicitas)   *see* Godrevy *Truro*

PHILLEIGH (St Philleigh)   *see* Gerrans w St Anthony-in-Roseland and Philleigh *Truro*

PICCADILLY (St James)   *see* Westmr St Jas *Lon*

PICKENHAM, NORTH (St Andrew)   *see* Necton, Holme Hale w N and S Pickenham *Nor*

PICKENHAM, SOUTH (All Saints)   *as above*

PICKERING (St Peter and St Paul) w Lockton and Levisham *York 20*   **P** *Abp*   **P-in-c** A M PRITCHET,   **NSM** L GROVE

PICKHILL (All Saints)   *see* Kirklington w Burneston and Wath and Pickhill *Ripon*

PICKWELL (All Saints)   *see* Burrough Hill Pars *Leic*

PICKWORTH (All Saints)   *see* Gt and Lt Casterton w Pickworth and Tickencote *Pet*

PICKWORTH (St Andrew)   *see* S Lafford *Linc*

PICTON (St Hilary)   *see* Kirklevington w Picton, and High and Low Worsall *York*

PIDDINGHOE (St John) *Chich 18*   **P** *Bp and Gorham Trustees (jt)*   **V** D A HIDER

PIDDINGTON (St John the Baptist)   *see* Hardingstone and Horton and Piddington *Pet*

PIDDINGTON (St Nicholas)   *see* Ray Valley *Ox*

PIDDLE, NORTH (St Michael)   *see* Abberton, The Flyfords, Naunton Beauchamp etc *Worc*

PIDDLE VALLEY, Hilton, Cheselbourne and Melcombe Horsey, The *Sarum 1*   **P** *Bp, Eton Coll, G A L F Pitt-Rivers Esq, D&C Sarum, and D&C Win (by turn)*   **V** A J B MONDS,
NSM H J P EXON

PIDDLEHINTON (St Mary the Virgin)   *see* Piddle Valley, Hilton, Cheselbourne etc *Sarum*

PIDDLETRENTHIDE (All Saints)   *as above*
PIDLEY CUM FENTON (All Saints)   *see* Somersham w Pidley and Oldhurst *Ely*
PIERCEBRIDGE (St Mary)   *see* Coniscliffe *Dur*
PILGRIM Benefice   *see* Bunwell, Carleton Rode, Tibenham, Gt Moulton etc *Nor*
PILHAM (All Saints)   *see* Corringham and Blyton Gp *Linc*
PILL (Christ Church), Portbury and Easton-in-Gordano *B & W 13*   **P** *Bp*   **R** H M LEGG,   **Hon C** J N O WILLIAMS
PILLATON (St Modwen)   *see* Penkridge *Lich*
PILLATON (St Odolph)   *see* St Dominic, Landulph and St Mellion w Pillaton *Truro*
PILLERTON HERSEY (St Mary)   *see* Stourdene Gp *Cov*
PILLEY (Mission Church)   *see* Tankersley, Thurgoland and Wortley *Sheff*
PILLEY (St Nicholas)   *see* Boldre w S Baddesley *Win*
PILLING (St John the Baptist)   *see* Stalmine w Pilling *Blackb*
PILNING (St Peter) w Compton Greenfield *Bris 2*   **P** *Bp*   **V** *vacant* (01454) 633409
PILSLEY (St Mary the Virgin)   *see* N Wingfield, Clay Cross and Pilsley *Derby*
PILTON (All Saints)   *see* Aldwincle, Clopton, Pilton, Stoke Doyle etc *Pet*
PILTON (St John the Baptist) w Croscombe, North Wootton and Dinder *B & W 8*   **P** *Bp and Peache Trustees (jt)*   **R** D R OSBORNE,   **C** L D A AVERY
PILTON (St Mary the Virgin)   *see* Barnstaple *Ex*
PILTON (St Nicholas)   *see* Preston and Ridlington w Wing and Pilton *Pet*
PIMLICO Bourne Street (St Mary)   *see* Pimlico St Mary Bourne Street *Lon*
PIMLICO (St Barnabas) *Lon 3*   **P** *Bp*   **V** A C COLES
PIMLICO (St Gabriel) *Lon 3*   **P** *Bp*   **V** L T IRVINE-CAPEL
PIMLICO (St James the Less)   *see* Westminster St Jas the Less *Lon*
PIMLICO (St Mary) Bourne Street *Lon 3*   **P** *Trustees*   **V** A C COLES,   **Hon C** S E YOUNG,   **NSM** S N LEAMY
PIMLICO (St Peter) w Westminster Christ Church *Lon 3*   **P** *Bp*   **V** N C PAPADOPULOS,   **C** J E A MUSTARD,   **Hon C** C L MADDOCK,   **NSM** P M LOWTHER
PIMLICO (St Saviour) *Lon 3*   **P** *Bp*   **P-in-c** M T WOODWARD
PIMPERNE (St Peter), Stourpaine, Durweston and Bryanston *Sarum 6*   **P** *DBP (2 turns), D&C (1 turn)*   **R** S P COULTER,   **NSM** J W WHITTLE
PIN GREEN (All Saints)   *see* Stevenage All SS Pin Green *St Alb*
PINCHBECK (St Mary)   *see* Glen Gp *Linc*
PINCHBECK, WEST (St Bartholomew)   *as above*
PINHOE (St Michael and All Angels) (Hall) and Broadclyst *Ex 1*   **P** *Patr Bd*   **TV** J E GRIER,   **P-in-c** M J PARTRIDGE
PINNER (St Anselm)   *see* Hatch End St Anselm *Lon*
PINNER (St John the Baptist) *Lon 23*   **P** *V Harrow*   **V** P C HULLYER
PINNER VIEW (St George)   *see* Headstone St Geo *Lon*
PINVIN (St Nicholas)   *see* Pershore w Pinvin, Wick and Birlingham *Worc*
PINXTON (St Helen) (Church Hall) *Derby 1*   **P** *Bp*   **R** L G C E HARRIS
PIPE-CUM-LYDE (St Peter) and Moreton-on-Lugg *Heref 4*   **P** *Bp, Soc of the Faith, and D&C (by turn)*   **P-in-c** J W R MORRISON,   **NSM** E S V VERWEY, P A LITTLEWOOD
PIPEWELL (St Mary)   *see* Rothwell w Orton, Rushton w Glendon and Pipewell *Pet*
PIRBRIGHT (St Michael and All Angels) *Guildf 12*   **P** *Ld Chan*   **P-in-c** C MUSSER
PIRNOUGH (All Hallows)   *see* Ditchingham, Hedenham, Broome, Earsham etc *Nor*
PIRTON (St Mary)   *see* Holwell, Ickleford and Pirton *St Alb*
PIRTON (St Peter)   *see* Stoulton w Drake's Broughton and Pirton etc *Worc*
PISHILL (not known)   *see* Nettlebed w Bix, Highmoor, Pishill etc *Ox*
PITCHCOMBE (St John the Baptist)   *see* Painswick, Sheepscombe, Cranham, The Edge etc *Glouc*
PITCHFORD (St Michael and All Angels)   *see* Condover w Frodesley, Acton Burnell etc *Heref*
PITCOMBE (St Leonard)   *see* Bruton and Distr *B & W*
PITMINSTER (St Mary and St Andrew)   *see* Blackdown *B & W*
PITNEY (St John the Baptist)   *see* Langport Area *B & W*
PITSEA (St Gabriel) w Nevendon *Chelmsf 6*   **P** *Bp*   **C** N CHUMU MUTUKU
PITSFORD (All Saints) w Boughton *Pet 2*   **P** *Bp*   **R** S TROTT
PITSMOOR (Christ Church) *Sheff 3*   **P** *Ch Patr Trust*   **V** M J SNOW,   **C** K R SKIDMORE

PITTINGTON (St Laurence)   *see* Belmont and Pittington *Dur*
PITTON (St Peter)   *see* Clarendon *Sarum*
PITTVILLE (All Saints)   *see* N Cheltenham *Glouc*
PIXHAM (St Mary the Virgin)   *see* Dorking w Ranmore *Guildf*
PIXLEY (St Andrew)   *see* Ledbury *Heref*
PLAISTOW (Holy Trinity)   *see* Kirdford *Chich*
PLAISTOW (St Martin) (St Mary) (St Philip and St James) and North Canning Town *Chelmsf 3*   **P** *Patr Bd*   **TV** E O ADOYO, R B REYNOLDS,   **Hon C** P B KENNEDY
PLAISTOW (St Mary) *Roch 14*   **P** *Bp*   **V** A KEELER
PLAISTOW The Divine Compassion   *see* Plaistow and N Canning Town *Chelmsf*
PLAITFORD (St Peter)   *see* Forest and Avon *Sarum*
PLAS NEWTON (St Michael) w Chester Christ Church *Ches 2*   **P** *Simeon's Trustees*   **C** A D BUCHANAN, A MITCHELL,   **NSM** R J KEMP
PLATT (Holy Trinity)   *see* Rusholme H Trin *Man*
PLATT (St Mary the Virgin) *Roch 10*   **P** *Bp*   **P-in-c** E M R WALKER
PLATT BRIDGE (St Nathaniel) *Liv 14*   **P** *Bp*   **V** *vacant* (01942) 866269
PLATT'S HEATH (St Edmund)   *see* Len Valley *Cant*
PLAXTOL (not known)   *see* Shipbourne w Plaxtol *Roch*
PLAYDEN (St Michael)   *see* Rye *Chich*
PLAYFORD (St Mary)   *see* Gt and Lt Bealings w Playford and Culpho *St E*
PLEASLEY (St Michael)   *see* E Scarsdale *Derby*
PLEASLEY HILL (St Barnabas) *S'well 2*   **P** *Bp*   **P-in-c** G E HOLLOWAY
PLEASLEY VALE (St Chad)   *see* Mansfield Woodhouse *S'well*
PLEMSTALL (St Peter) w Guilden Sutton *Ches 2*   **P** *Capt P Egerton Warburton*   **V** M HART
PLESHEY (Holy Trinity) *Chelmsf 8*   **P** *Bp*   **P-in-c** S F COUGHTREY,   **NSM** B M H MAIN
PLUCKLEY (St Mary)   *see* Egerton w Pluckley *Cant*
PLUCKLEY (St Nicholas)   *as above*
PLUMBLAND (St Cuthbert)   *see* Binsey *Carl*
PLUMPTON (All Saints) (St Michael and All Angels) w East Chiltington cum Novington *Chich 18*   **P** *Ld Chan*   **R** G D BROSTER
PLUMPTON (St John the Baptist)   *see* Astwell Gp *Pet*
PLUMPTON WALL (St John the Evangelist)   *see* Penrith w Newton Reigny and Plumpton Wall *Carl*
PLUMSTEAD (All Saints) Shooters Hill *S'wark 6*   **P** *CPAS*   **V** H D OWEN,   **NSM** D J OGUNYEMI
PLUMSTEAD (Ascension) *S'wark 6*   **P** *Bp*   **V** C R WELHAM
PLUMSTEAD (St John the Baptist) w St James and St Paul *S'wark 6*   **P** *Simeon's Trustees and CPAS (alt)*   **V** P J ROGERS
PLUMSTEAD (St Mark and St Margaret) *S'wark 6*   **P** *DBP*   **P-in-c** C R WELHAM
PLUMSTEAD (St Michael)   *see* Barningham w Matlaske w Baconsthorpe etc *Nor*
PLUMSTEAD (St Nicholas) *S'wark 6*   **P** *V Plumstead St Mark w St Marg*   **C** A G STEVENS
PLUMSTEAD, GREAT (St Mary) and LITTLE (St Gervase and Protase) w Thorpe End and Witton *Nor 4*   **P** *Bp and D&C (jt)*   **R** C A GARROD
PLUMTREE (St Mary) *S'well 8*   **P** *DBP*   **R** *vacant* 0115-937 6493
PLUNGAR (St Helen)   *see* Vale of Belvoir Par *Leic*
PLYMOUTH Crownhill (Ascension) *Ex 23*   **P** *Bp*   **V** *vacant* (01752) 783617
PLYMOUTH (Emmanuel), St Paul Efford and St Augustine *Ex 24*   **P** *Patr Bd*   **TR** K F FREEMAN,   **C** S M PAYNE, P R ANDREW
PLYMOUTH (St Andrew) and St Paul Stonehouse *Ex 24*   **P** *Patr Bd*   **TR** N H P MCKINNEL,   **TV** J C MONEY,   **C** A J DUNLOP, D M WELLS
PLYMOUTH (St Augustine)   *see* Plymouth Em, St Paul Efford and St Aug *Ex*
PLYMOUTH (St Gabriel) Peverell *Ex 24*   **P** *Bp*   **V** J J STARK
PLYMOUTH (St John the Evangelist)   *see* Sutton on Plym *Ex*
PLYMOUTH (St Jude) *Ex 24*   **P** *Trustees*   **P-in-c** T SMITH,   **C** I COOK
PLYMOUTH (St Mary the Virgin)   *see* Plymouth St Simon and St Mary *Ex*
PLYMOUTH (St Matthias)   *see* Charles w Plymouth St Matthias *Ex*
PLYMOUTH (St Pancras)   *see* Pennycross *Ex*
PLYMOUTH (St Peter) and the Holy Apostles *Ex 22*   **P** *Bp and Keble Coll Ox (jt)*   **V** S PHILPOTT,   **C** S A CHINERY
PLYMOUTH (St Simon) and St Mary Laira *Ex 24*   **P** *Bp and St Simon Trustees (jt)*   **P-in-c** P C B ALLEN,   **C** K F HAYDON
PLYMPTON (St Mary the Blessed Virgin) *Ex 23*   **P** *Bp*   **V** M M CAMERON,   **C** R W BECK,   **NSM** M BRIMICOMBE

PLYMPTON (St Maurice) *Ex 23*   **P** *D&C Windsor*
P-in-c J P MASON,   **NSM** J M FRENCH

PLYMSTOCK (St Mary and All Saints) and Hooe *Ex 24*
  P *Patr Bd*   **TR** D J WALLER,   **TV** I K PROVOST, J J SPEAR,
C D L YELDHAM,   **NSM** M P HINKS

PLYMTREE (St John the Baptist) *see* Broadhembury,
Payhembury and Plymtree *Ex*

POCKLEY (St John the Baptist) *see* Kirkdale w Harome,
Nunnington and Pockley *York*

**POCKLINGTON (All Saints) and Owsthorpe and Kilnwick
Percy w Great Givendale and Millington** *York 5*   **P** *Abp*
C J C PARKER,   **NSM** G M DALLEY

PODIMORE (St Peter) *see* Ilchester w Northover, Limington,
Yeovilton etc *B & W*

PODINGTON (St Mary the Virgin) *see* Wymington w
Podington *St Alb*

POINT CLEAR (Mission) *see* St Osyth *Chelmsf*

POINTON (Christ Church) *see* Billingborough Gp *Linc*

POKESDOWN (All Saints) *Win 8*   **P** *V Christchurch*
P-in-c K P ARKELL,   C J W E RODLEY

POKESDOWN (St James) *Win 8*   **P** *Bp*   **P-in-c** R L VERNON,
NSM P M SCHOLLAR, N J HOULTON

POLDENS, WEST *B & W 5*   **P** *Bp*   **P-in-c** P A OLLIVE

POLEBROOK (All Saints) *see* Barnwell, Hemington,
Luddington in the Brook etc *Pet*

POLEGATE (St John) *Chich 16*   **P** *Bp*   **V** M W LUCAS,
C G J BURROWS,   **NSM** R A HERKES

POLEGATE (St Wilfrid) *see* Lower Willingdon St Wilfrid CD
Chich

POLESWORTH (St Editha) *Birm 10*   **P** *Ld Chan*
V P A WELLS

POLING (St Nicholas) *Chich 1*   **P** *Bp*   **V** vacant

POLLINGTON (St John the Baptist) *see* Gt Snaith *Sheff*

POLPERRO (St John the Baptist) *see* Talland *Truro*

POLRUAN (St Saviour) *see* Lanteglos by Fowey *Truro*

POLSTEAD (St Mary) *see* Stoke by Nayland w Leavenheath
and Polstead *St E*

POLTIMORE (St Mary the Virgin) *see* Stoke Canon, Poltimore
w Huxham and Rewe etc *Ex*

PONDERS END (St Matthew) *Lon 18*   **P** *V Enfield*
P-in-c R C KNOWLING,   C A C NEWCOMBE,
NSM N H ASBRIDGE

PONDERSBRIDGE (St Thomas) *see* Whittlesey,
Pondersbridge and Coates *Ely*

PONSANOOTH (St Michael and All Angels) *see* Mabe *Truro*

PONSBOURNE (St Mary) *see* Lt Berkhamsted and Bayford,
Essendon etc *St Alb*

PONSONBY (not known) *see* Beckermet St Jo and St Bridget w
Ponsonby *Carl*

PONTEFRACT (All Saints) *Wakef 10*   **P** *Bp*
P-in-c V IWANUSCHAK

PONTEFRACT (St Giles) (St Mary) *Wakef 10*   **P** *Bp*
V R G COOPER,   C I BULLOCK

PONTELAND (St Mary the Virgin) *Newc 4*   **P** *Mert Coll Ox*
V P BARHAM,   C R B CROSS,   **NSM** C L BROWN,
B J CHANDLER

PONTESBURY First and Second Portions (St George) *Heref 13*
  P *St Chad's Coll Dur*   **P-in-c** S J TURNER,
NSM C A CHADWICK, S M SMALL, C WRIGHT

PONTON, GREAT (Holy Cross) *see* Colsterworth Gp *Linc*

PONTON, LITTLE (St Guthlac) *as above*

POOL (St Wilfrid) *see* Lower Wharfedale *Ripon*

POOLBROOK (St Andrew) *see* Malvern St Andr and Malvern
Wells and Wyche *Worc*

POOLE (St James w St Paul) *Sarum 7*   **P** *Ch Soc Trust and
J H Cordle Esq (jt)*   **R** R H G MASON

POOLE, NORTH Ecumenical Team *Sarum 7*   **P** *Bp*
TR A C MACROW-WOOD,   **TV** J E AUDIBERT, P W GIBBS,
C B D BLACKFORD, C BROOKS,   **OLM** T LOCK

POOLE KEYNES (St Michael and All Angels) *see* Kemble,
Poole Keynes, Somerford Keynes etc *Glouc*

POOLEY BRIDGE (St Paul) *see* Barton, Pooley Bridge and
Martindale *Carl*

POOLSBROOK (St Alban) *see* Staveley and Barrow Hill *Derby*

POORTON, NORTH (St Mary Magdalene) *see* Askerswell,
Loders and Powerstock *Sarum*

POPLAR (All Saints) *Lon 7*   **P** *Patr Bd*   **TR** A J WYNNE,
TV P W F MCBRIDE,   C J A C HODGES,   **NSM** T J DUNCAN,
J C SHELDON

POPPLETON, NETHER (St Everilda) w Upper (All Saints)
York 1   **P** *Abp*   **V** J C E SYLVESTER,   **NSM** M C S FOSSETT,
J O G HARDING

POPPLETON ROAD (Mission Room) *see* York St Paul *York*

PORCHESTER (St James) *S'well 10*   **P** *Bp*   **V** P A WILLIAMS,
C D K DODD,   **NSM** M A SKIDMORE

PORINGLAND (All Saints) *Nor 8*   **P** *Bp, BNC Ox,
J D Alston Esq, and G H Hastings Esq (3 turns) and DBP
(1 turn)*   **R** R H PARSONAGE

**PORLOCK (St Dubricius) w Porlock Weir w Stoke Pero,
Selworthy and Luccombe** *B & W 16*   **P** *Ld Chan*
R W H M LEMMEY,   C S R B HUMPHREYS

PORLOCK WEIR (St Nicholas) *see* Porlock and Porlock Weir
w Stoke Pero etc *B & W*

PORT ERIN (St Catherine) *see* Rushen *S & M*

PORT ISAAC (St Peter) *see* St Endellion w Port Isaac and
St Kew *Truro*

PORT ST MARY (St Mary) *see* Rushen *S & M*

PORTBURY (Blessed Virgin Mary) *see* Pill, Portbury and
Easton-in-Gordano *B & W*

PORTCHESTER (St Mary) *Portsm 2*   **P** *J R Thistlethwaite Esq*
V C ALLEN,   C C SHERMAN

PORTESHAM (St Peter) *see* Abbotsbury, Portesham and
Langton Herring *Sarum*

PORTHILL (St Andrew) *see* Wolstanton *Lich*

PORTHLEVEN (St Bartholomew) w Sithney *Truro 4*   **P** *Bp*
P-in-c H PUGH

PORTHPEAN (St Levan) *see* St Austell *Truro*

PORTINSCALE (Mission) *see* Crosthwaite Keswick *Carl*

PORTISHEAD (St Peter) *B & W 13*   **P** *Patr Bd*
TR A W BRYANT,   **TV** S M J CROSSMAN,   C D C WILLIAMSON

PORTKELLIS (St Christopher) *see* Helston and Wendron
Truro

PORTLAND (All Saints) (St Andrew) *Sarum 4*   **P** *Bp*
P-in-c N A MCKINTY

PORTLAND (St John) *Sarum 4*   **P** *Hyndman Trustees*
P-in-c D D BOTTERILL

PORTLEMOUTH, EAST (St Winwaloe Onocaus)
see Stokenham, Slapton, Charleton w Buckland etc *Ex*

PORTLOE (All Saints) *see* Veryan w Ruan Lanihorne *Truro*

PORTMAN SQUARE (St Paul) *see* Langham Place All So *Lon*

PORTON (St Nicholas) *see* Bourne Valley *Sarum*

PORTREATH (St Mary) *see* St Illogan *Truro*

PORTSDOWN (Christ Church) *Portsm 5*   **P** *Simeon's Trustees*
V A M WILSON,   **NSM** S G PHILLIPS

PORTSEA (All Saints) *Portsm 6*   **P** *V Portsea St Mary and
Bp (jt)*   **V** M F PYE,   C J A SWAINE,   **NSM** M E TILLMAN,
F M GATES

PORTSEA North End (St Mark) *Portsm 6*   **P** *V Portsea
St Mary*   **TR** T P KENNAR,   **TV** B A ROBERTSON,
NSM D R TOWNSEND

PORTSEA (St Alban) *Portsm 6*   **P** *Bp*   **V** R P CALDER,
NSM M C DORRELL

PORTSEA (St Cuthbert) *Portsm 6*   **P** *Bp*   **V** D M POWER,
NSM J POWER

PORTSEA (St George) *Portsm 6*   **P** *Bp*   **V** K B GREEN,
NSM F M GATES, S E WEST

PORTSEA (St Luke) *Portsm 6*   **P** *Ch Patr Trust*
P-in-c A J HUGHES,   C M N RODEL

PORTSEA (St Mary) (St Faith and St Barnabas) (St Wilfrid)
Portsm 6   **P** *Win Coll*   **V** R C WHITE,   C C E HETHERINGTON,
J D T HAWKEY,   **NSM** F M GATES, S K WHITELOCK,
E L A D'AETH

PORTSEA (St Saviour) *Portsm 6*   **P** *Bp*   **V** R P CALDER,
NSM M C DORRELL

PORTSEA (The Ascension) *Portsm 6*   **P** *Bp*   **V** R F ROBINSON

PORTSLADE (Good Shepherd) *Chich 4*   **P** *Bp*   **V** P D CLEGG

PORTSLADE (St Nicolas) (St Andrew) *Chich 4*   **P** *Bp*
V R H RUSHFORTH

PORTSWOOD (Christ Church) *Win 13*   **P** *Bp*   **V** G J ARCHER,
C P A ASHMAN,   **NSM** F M TYSON

PORTSWOOD (St Denys) *Win 13*   **P** *Bp*   C K J RANDALL

PORTWAY AND DANEBURY Benefice, The *Win 3*   **P** *Patr Bd*
TR C B RANKINE,   **TV** C F PETTET, V A COLE,
NSM J A TAYLOR, M J VICKERS

POSBURY (St Francis Proprietary Chapel) *see* Crediton,
Shobrooke and Sandford etc *Ex*

POSLINGFORD (St Mary) *see* Stour Valley *St E*

POSTBRIDGE (St Gabriel) *see* Ashburton, Bickington,
Buckland in the Moor etc *Ex*

POSTLEBURY *see* Nunney and Witham Friary, Marston Bigot
etc *B & W*

POSTLING (St Mary and St Radegund) *see* Lyminge w
Paddlesworth, Stanford w Postling etc *Cant*

POSTWICK (All Saints) *see* Brundall w Braydeston and
Postwick *Nor*

POTT SHRIGLEY (St Christopher) *Ches 13*   **P** *MMCET*
P-in-c J BUCKLEY

POTTEN END (Holy Trinity) *see* Gt Berkhamsted, Gt and Lt
Gaddesden etc *St Alb*

POTTER HEIGHAM (St Nicholas) *see* Ludham, Potter
Heigham, Hickling and Catfield *Nor*

POTTERHANWORTH (St Andrew) *see* Branston w Nocton and Potterhanworth *Linc*

POTTERNE (St Mary the Virgin) w Worton and Marston *Sarum 16* **P** *Bp* **V** D J HOWARD, **OLM** R Y COULSON

POTTERNEWTON (St Martin) *Ripon 5* **P** *Trustees* **P-in-c** D L STEVENS, **NSM** S J DE GAY

POTTERS BAR (King Charles the Martyr) *St Alb 17* **P** *Bp Lon* **P-in-c** M J BURNS

POTTERS BAR (St Mary and All Saints) *St Alb 17* **P** *Bp Lon* **V** P J BEVAN

POTTERS GREEN (St Philip Deacon) *Cov 1* **P** *Ld Chan* **P-in-c** V I WOODS

POTTERS MARSTON (St Mary) *see* Barwell w Potters Marston and Stapleton *Leic*

POTTERSPURY (St Nicholas) w Furtho and Yardley Gobion w Cosgrove and Wicken *Pet 5* **P** *D&C, Jes Coll Ox, and Soc Merchant Venturers Bris (jt)* **R** M WRAY

POTTO (St Mary) *see* Whorlton w Carlton and Faceby *York*

POTTON (St Mary the Virgin) w Sutton and Cockayne Hatley *St Alb 11* **P** *The Crown (3 turns), St Jo Coll Ox (1 turn)* **P-in-c** G SMITH

POUGHILL (St Michael and All Angels) *see* N Creedy *Ex*

POUGHILL (St Olaf King and Martyr) *Truro 8* **P** *Ch Soc Trust* **V** P A WHYBROW

POULNER (St John) *see* Ringwood *Win*

POULSHOT (St Peter) *see* Seend, Bulkington and Poulshot *Sarum*

POULTON (St Luke) *Ches 7* **P** *Bp* **P-in-c** I HUGHES

POULTON (St Michael and All Angels) *see* Fairford Deanery *Glouc*

POULTON CARLETON (St Chad) and Singleton *Blackb 12* **P** *DBP and Exors R Dumbreck Esq (jt)* **V** M P KEIGHLEY, **C** C J RIGNEY

POULTON LANCELYN (Holy Trinity) *Ches 8* **P** *R Bebington* **V** R K WILES

POULTON-LE-FYLDE (St Chad) *see* Poulton Carleton and Singleton *Blackb*

POULTON-LE-SANDS (Holy Trinity) w Morecambe St Laurence *Blackb 11* **P** *V Lanc* **P-in-c** M R PEATMAN, **NSM** A CUNLIFFE

POUND HILL (St Barnabas) *see* Worth, Pound Hill and Maidenbower *Chich*

POUNDSBRIDGE (Chapel) *see* Penshurst and Fordcombe *Roch*

POUNDSTOCK (St Winwaloe) *see* Week St Mary Circle of Par *Truro*

POWDERHAM (St Clement Bishop and Martyr) *see* Kenton, Mamhead, Powderham, Cofton and Starcross *Ex*

POWERSTOCK (St Mary the Virgin) *see* Askerswell, Loders and Powerstock *Sarum*

POWICK (St Peter) and Guarlford and Madresfield w Newland *Worc 2* **P** *Bp, Lady Rosalind Morrison, and Croome Estate Trustees (jt)* **R** S E IRWIN

POYNINGS (Holy Trinity) w Edburton, Newtimber and Pyecombe *Chich 9* **P** *Ld Chan (1 turn), Bp and Abp (1 turn)* **P-in-c** C M CURRER

POYNTINGTON (All Saints) *see* Queen Thorne *Sarum*

POYNTON (St George) *Ches 17* **P** *Bp* **V** R I MCLAREN, **C** G D FIRTH

POYNTON, HIGHER (St Martin) *see* Poynton *Ches*

PRADOE (extra-parochial place) *Lich 19* **C-in-c** O B PARRY

PRATTS BOTTOM (All Souls) *see* Green Street Green and Pratts Bottom *Roch*

PREES (St Chad) *see* Edstaston, Fauls, Prees, Tilstock and Whixall *Lich*

PREESALL (St Oswald) *see* Waterside Par *Blackb*

PRENTON (St Stephen) *Ches 1* **P** *Bp* **V** E W LAUTENBACH

PRENTON DELL (St Alban) *see* Prenton *Ches*

PRESCOT (St Mary) (St Paul) *Liv 2* **P** *K Coll Cam* **V** J A TAYLOR, **NSM** P COWLEY, **OLM** J D ROSE

PRESHUTE (St George) *see* Marlborough *Sarum*

PRESTBURY (St Mary) *see* N Cheltenham *Glouc*

PRESTBURY (St Nicholas) *as above*

PRESTBURY (St Peter) *Ches 13* **P** *Ms C J C B Legh* **V** P J M ANGIER, **NSM** P HARDMAN

PRESTEIGNE (St Andrew) w Discoed, Kinsham, Lingen and Knill *Heref 5* **P** *Patr Bd* **R** S HOLLINGHURST

PRESTLEIGH (St James Mission Church) *see* Shepton Mallet w Doulting *B & W*

PRESTOLEE (Holy Trinity) *see* Ringley w Prestolee *Man*

PRESTON Acregate Lane (Mission) *see* Preston Risen Lord *Blackb*

PRESTON (All Saints) *Blackb 13* **P** *Trustees* **V** D P A P G MEIRION-JONES, **Hon C** J D G NASH

PRESTON (All Saints) *see* S Cerney w Cerney Wick, Siddington and Preston *Glouc*

PRESTON (All Saints) and Sproatley in Holderness *York 12* **P** *Abp* **P-in-c** P M BURDON

PRESTON (Church of the Ascension) *see* Wembley Park *Lon*

PRESTON (Emmanuel) *Blackb 13* **P** *R Preston* **V** S JOHNSON

PRESTON (Good Shepherd) *see* Brighton Gd Shep Preston *Chich*

PRESTON (St Andrew) w Sutton Poyntz and Osmington w Poxwell *Sarum 4* **P** *Patr Bd* **TR** T R WEST, **TV** L S DOBBINS, **C** D M WILSHERE, **NSM** B E J ELLIS

PRESTON (St Cuthbert) *Blackb 13* **P** *Bp* **V** C E HALLIWELL

PRESTON (St John) (St George the Martyr) (Christ the King Chapel) *Blackb 13* **P** *DBP* **R** T W LIPSCOMB, **C** A J TEATHER, **Hon C** D M OVERTON

PRESTON (St John the Baptist) *see* Redmarley D'Abitot, Bromesberrow, Pauntley etc *Glouc*

PRESTON (St John) w Brighton St Augustine and St Saviour *Chich 2* **P** *Bp* **P-in-c** A V BOWMAN, **C** C M CHAMBERS

PRESTON (St Mark) *see* W Preston *Blackb*

PRESTON (St Martin) *see* King's Walden and Offley w Lilley *St Alb*

PRESTON (St Mary the Virgin) *see* Lavenham w Preston *St E*

PRESTON (St Matthias) *see* Brighton St Matthias *Chich*

PRESTON (St Mildred) *see* Wingham w Elmstone and Preston w Stourmouth *Cant*

PRESTON (St Oswald) St Jude *Blackb 13* **P** *Bp, Simeon's Trustees, and R Preston St Jo and St Geo (jt)* **P-in-c** G W NELSON

PRESTON (St Paul) *see* Paignton Ch Ch and Preston St Paul *Ex*

PRESTON (St Peter and St Paul) and Ridlington w Wing and Pilton *Pet 12* **P** *Bp, Baroness Willoughby de Eresby, and DBP (jt)* **P-in-c** S MITCHELL, **Hon C** R A MASON

PRESTON (St Stephen) *Blackb 13* **P** *Bp* **V** *vacant* (01772) 555762

PRESTON The Risen Lord (St Matthew) (St Hilda) (St James's church hall) *Blackb 13* **P** *Patr Bd* **P-in-c** P R NUNN, **C** J T RICHARDSON

PRESTON, EAST (St Mary) w Kingston *Chich 1* **P** *D&C* **V** J H LYON

PRESTON, WEST *Blackb 13* **P** *Patr Bd* **TR** R W BUNDAY, **TV** C J ENTWISTLE

PRESTON BAGOT (All Saints) *see* Claverdon w Preston Bagot *Cov*

PRESTON BISSET (St John the Baptist) *see* The Claydons and Swan *Ox*

PRESTON BROOK (St Faith) *see* Daresbury *Ches*

PRESTON CAPES (St Peter and St Paul) *see* Badby w Newnham and Charwelton w Fawsley etc *Pet*

PRESTON NEXT FAVERSHAM (St Catherine) w Goodnestone and Graveney *Cant 6* **P** *Abp* **V** S C WILSON, **C** A C OEHRING, **Hon C** D M OTTERSHEAD, **NSM** N M ASH

PRESTON ON STOUR (St Mary) *see* Ilmington w Stretton-on-Fosse etc *Cov*

PRESTON-ON-TEES (All Saints) and Longnewton *Dur 10* **P** *Bp* **V** A J FARISH, **C** J C LAMBERT, S R GREEN, **OLM** S WILSON

PRESTON-ON-WYE (St Lawrence) *see* Cusop w Blakemere, Bredwardine w Brobury etc *Heref*

PRESTON PATRICK (St Patrick) *see* Kirkby Lonsdale *Carl*

PRESTON PLUCKNETT (St James the Great) (St Peter) *B & W 7* **P** *Bp (2 turns), Mrs S W Rawlins (1 turn)* **V** A PERRIS, **C** D M KEEN

PRESTON UNDER SCARR (St Margaret) *see* Penhill *Ripon*

PRESTON WEALDMOORS (St Lawrence) *see* Edgmond w Kynnersley and Preston Wealdmoors *Lich*

PRESTON WYNNE (Holy Trinity) *see* Bodenham, Felton and Preston Wynne *Heref*

PRESTONVILLE (St Luke) *Chich 2* **P** *CPAS* **P-in-c** A W KILPATRICK

PRESTWICH (St Gabriel) *Man 14* **P** *Bp* **P-in-c** S S WILLIAMS, **NSM** M TRIVASSE

PRESTWICH (St Hilda) *Man 14* **P** *Trustees* **V** *vacant* 0161-773 1642

PRESTWICH (St Margaret) (St George) *Man 14* **P** *R Prestwich St Mary* **P-in-c** D A PLUMMER, **NSM** J D POSTON

PRESTWICH (St Mary the Virgin) *Man 14* **P** *Trustees* **P-in-c** B M HACKETT, **C** J M COOPER

PRESTWOLD (St Andrew) *see* Wymeswold and Prestwold w Hoton *Leic*

PRESTWOOD (Holy Trinity) and Great Hampden *Ox 28* **P** *Bp and Hon I H Hope-Morley (jt)* **R** D J O KEARLEY-HEYWOOD

PRICKWILLOW (St Peter) *see* Ely *Ely*

PRIDDY (St Lawrence) *B & W 1* **P** *Bp* **V** *vacant*

PRIESTWOOD (St Andrew)   *see* Bracknell *Ox*

PRIMROSE HILL (Holy Trinity)   *see* Lydney *Glouc*

**PRIMROSE HILL (St Mary the Virgin) w Avenue Road
(St Paul)** *Lon 16*   **P** *Trustees*   **V** M J BROWN,
NSM L L DEAN, M J WAKEFIELD

PRINCE ALBERT ROAD (St Mark)   *see* Regent's Park St
Mark *Lon*

PRINCE CONSORT ROAD (Holy Trinity)   *see* S Kensington H
Trin w All SS *Lon*

PRINCE'S PARK (Christ the King) *Roch 5*   **P** *Bp*   **V** K G FOOT

PRINCES RISBOROUGH (St Mary)   *see* Risborough *Ox*

PRINCETOWN (Church Hall)   *see* Ashburton, Bickington,
Buckland in the Moor etc *Ex*

PRIOR'S DEAN (not known)   *see* Greatham w Empshott and
Hawkley w Prior's Dean *Portsm*

**PRIORS HARDWICK (St Mary the Virgin) w Priors Marston
and Wormleighton** *Cov 10*   **P** *Earl Spencer*
P-in-c M L D GREIG

PRIORS LEE (St Peter) (St Georges) *Lich 21*   **P** *Bp and
V Shifnal (jt)*   **V** P G F LAWLEY

PRIORS MARSTON (St Leonard)   *see* Priors Hardwick, Priors
Marston and Wormleighton *Cov*

PRIORS PARK (Mission Hall)   *see* Tewkesbury w Walton
Cardiff and Twyning *Glouc*

PRISTON (St Luke)   *see* Timsbury and Priston *B & W*

PRITTLEWELL (All Saints)   *see* Southend *Chelmsf*

PRITTLEWELL (St Luke) *Chelmsf 13*   **P** *Bp*
V J T MCCLUSKEY

PRITTLEWELL (St Mary the Virgin) *Chelmsf 13*   **P** *Bp*
V S CONLON

**PRITTLEWELL (St Peter) w Westcliff St Cedd and the Saints of
Essex** *Chelmsf 13*   **P** *Bp*   **V** R H CADMAN,
NSM C ROBINSON

PRITTLEWELL (St Stephen) *Chelmsf 13*   **P** *Bp*
P-in-c C S BALDWIN

**PROBUS (St Probus and St Grace), Ladock and Grampound w
Creed and St Erme** *Truro 6*   **P** *DBP*   **TR** A J WADE,
C A E BROWN,   **Hon C** M E RICHARDS

PRUDHOE (St Mary Magdalene) *Newc 9*   **P** *Dioc Soc*
V C H HOPE

PSALTER LANE (St Andrew) *Sheff 2*   **P** *Trustees*
V N P A JOWETT

**PUBLOW (All Saints) w Pensford, Compton Dando and
Chelwood** *B & W 10*   **P** *Bp*   **NSM** S M E STEVENS

PUCKINGTON (St Andrew)   *see* Ilminster and Distr *B & W*

PUCKLECHURCH (St Thomas à Becket) and Abson *Bris 5*
P *D&C*   **V** S K YOUNG

PUDDINGTON (St Thomas à Becket)   *see* N Creedy *Ex*

**PUDDLETOWN (St Mary the Virgin), Tolpuddle and Milborne
w Dewlish** *Sarum 1*   **P** *Bp, Ch Ch Ox, Viscount Rothermere, and
trustees (jt)*   **R** D J B HAZLEHURST,   **NSM** S J GODFREY

PUDLESTON (St Peter)   *see* Leominster *Heref*

PUDSEY (St James the Great)   *see* Woodhall *Bradf*

PUDSEY (St Lawrence and St Paul) *Bradf 3*   **P** *Bp and
V Calverley (jt)*   **V** P N AYERS,   **C** P R ARNOLD

PULBOROUGH (St Mary) *Chich 12*   **P** *Lord Egremont*
R P B WELCH

PULFORD (St Mary the Virgin)   *see* Eccleston and Pulford *Ches*

PULHAM (St Thomas à Beckett)   *see* Vale of White Hart *Sarum*

PULHAM MARKET (St Mary Magdalene)   *see* Dickleburgh
and The Pulhams *Nor*

PULHAM ST MARY (St Mary the Virgin)   *as above*

PULLOXHILL (St James the Apostle)   *see* Silsoe, Pulloxhill and
Flitton *St Alb*

PULVERBATCH (St Edith)   *see* Longden and Annscroft w
Pulverbatch *Heref*

PUNCKNOWLE (St Mary the Blessed Virgin)   *see* Bride Valley
Sarum

PUNNETS TOWN (St Peter)   *see* Heathfield *Chich*

PURBROOK (St John the Baptist) *Portsm 5*   **P** *Bp*
Hon C C R ABBOTT

PUREWELL (St John)   *see* Christchurch *Win*

PURFLEET (St Stephen)   *see* Aveley and Purfleet *Chelmsf*

PURITON (St Michael and All Angels) and Pawlett *B & W 14*
P *Ld Chan (1 turn), D&C Windsor (2 turns)*
P-in-c D GODDARD

PURLEIGH (All Saints), Cold Norton and Stow Maries
Chelmsf 11   **P** *Charterhouse, Or Coll Ox, and Bp (jt)*
P-in-c S E MANLEY,   **NSM** G SWIFT

PURLEY (Christ Church) *S'wark 22*   **P** *Bp*   **V** C R TREFUSIS,
C L C J DUCKETT,   **OLM** S P BISHOP

PURLEY (St Barnabas) *S'wark 22*   **P** *Bp*   **P-in-c** R C HAGON,
NSM D C HADLEY

PURLEY (St Mark) Woodcote *S'wark 22*   **P** *Bp*
P-in-c F M LONG,   **NSM** N RICHES

PURLEY (St Mary the Virgin) *Ox 12*   **P** *Ld Chan*
R D J ARCHER,   **NSM** J ROTHERY,   **OLM** A MACKIE

PURLEY (St Swithun) *S'wark 22*   **P** *Bp*   **P-in-c** F M LONG,
NSM N RICHES

PURLWELL (St Andrew)   *see* Batley All SS and Purlwell *Wakef*

PURSE CAUNDLE (St Peter)   *see* Spire Hill *Sarum*

PURTON (St John)   *see* Sharpness, Purton, Brookend and
Slimbridge *Glouc*

PURTON (St Mary) *Bris 7*   **P** *Bp*   **P-in-c** J HASLAM

PUSEY (All Saints)   *see* Cherbury w Gainfield *Ox*

PUTFORD (St Stephen)   *see* Bradworthy, Sutcombe, Putford etc
Ex

PUTLEY (not known)   *see* Ledbury *Heref*

PUTNEY (St Margaret) *S'wark 18*   **P** *Bp*   **P-in-c** A BRODIE

PUTNEY (St Mary) (All Saints) *S'wark 18*   **P** *Patr Bd*
TR G A FRASER,   **TV** N L BIDDLE,   **C** C D EYDEN

PUTNOE HEIGHTS CHURCH CENTRE   *see* Bedf St Mark
St Alb

PUTTENHAM (St John the Baptist)   *see* Seale, Puttenham and
Wanborough *Guildf*

PUTTENHAM (St Mary)   *see* Tring *St Alb*

PYE NEST (St James)   *see* King Cross *Wakef*

PYECOMBE (Transfiguration)   *see* Poynings w Edburton,
Newtimber and Pyecombe *Chich*

PYLLE (St Thomas à Becket)   *see* Fosse Trinity *B & W*

PYPE HAYES (St Mary the Virgin)   *see* Erdington *Birm*

PYRFORD (Church of the Good Shepherd)   *see* Wisley w
Pyrford *Guildf*

PYRFORD (St Nicholas)   *as above*

PYRTON (St Mary)   *see* Icknield *Ox*

PYTCHLEY (All Saints)   *see* Gt w Lt Harrowden and
Orlingbury and Isham etc *Pet*

PYWORTHY (St Swithun), Pancrasweek and Bridgerule *Ex 17*
P *DBP*   **P-in-c** C J DAVIDSON

QUADRING (St Margaret)   *see* Gosberton, Gosberton Clough
and Quadring *Linc*

QUAINTON (Holy Cross and St Mary)   *see* Schorne *Ox*

QUANTOCK COAST Benefice, The *B & W 17*   **P** *Bp, DBP,
Eton Coll, and Lady Gass (jt)*   **R** P J RAHILLY,
NSM D D BRIMSON, S L CAMPBELL, P CUFF, M HANCE

QUANTOCK TOWERS, The *B & W 17*   **P** *Bp, D&C Windsor,
and D&C Wells (jt)*   **R** vacant (01984) 656262

QUANTOXHEAD, EAST (Blessed Virgin Mary)   *see* Quantock
Coast *B & W*

QUANTOXHEAD, WEST (St Ethelreda)   *as above*

QUARLEY (St Michael and All Angels)   *see* Portway and
Danebury *Win*

QUARNDON (St Paul) *Derby 11*   **P** *Exors Viscount Scarsdale*
P-in-c W F BATES,   **NSM** J M NEEDLE

QUARNFORD (St Paul)   *see* Longnor, Quarnford and Sheen
Lich

QUARRENDON ESTATE (St Peter)   *see* Aylesbury w Bierton
and Hulcott *Ox*

QUARRINGTON (St Botolph) w Old Sleaford *Linc 22*   **P** *Bp*
R vacant (01529) 306776

QUARRY BANK (Christ Church)   *see* Brierley Hill *Worc*

QUARRY HILL (St Mary)   *see* Leeds City *Ripon*

QUATFORD (St Mary Magdalene)   *see* Bridgnorth, Tasley,
Astley Abbotts, etc *Heref*

QUATT (St Andrew)   *see* Alveley and Quatt *Heref*

QUEDGELEY (St James) *Glouc 3*   **P** *Bp*   **V** G J B STICKLAND

QUEEN CAMEL (St Barnabas)   *see* Cam Vale *B & W*

QUEEN CHARLTON (St Margaret)   *see* Keynsham *B & W*

QUEEN THORNE *Sarum 3*   **P** *Bp, The Revd J M P Goodden,
J K Wingfield Digby Esq, and MMCET (jt)*   **R** H G PEARSON

QUEENBOROUGH (Holy Trinity) *Cant 15*   **P** *Abp*
P-in-c J W STREETING

QUEENHILL (St Nicholas)   *see* Longdon, Castlemorton,
Bushley, Queenhill etc *Worc*

QUEEN'S GATE (St Augustine)   *see* S Kensington St Aug *Lon*

QUEEN'S PARK (St Barnabas)   *see* Holdenhurst and Iford *Win*

QUEEN'S PARK (St Luke)   *see* Brighton St Luke Queen's Park
Chich

QUEENSBURY (All Saints) *Lon 23*   **P** *The Crown*
V I M STONE

QUEENSBURY (Holy Trinity) *Bradf 2*   **P** *Bp*   **V** P A HEDGE

QUENDON (St Simon and St Jude)   *see* Manuden w Berden and
Quendon w Rickling *Chelmsf*

QUENIBOROUGH (St Mary)   *see* Syston *Leic*

QUENINGTON (St Swithun)   *see* Fairford Deanery *Glouc*

QUERNMORE (St Peter)   *see* Dolphinholme w Quernmore and
Over Wyresdale *Blackb*

QUETHIOCK (St Hugh)   *see* St Ive and Pensilva w Quethiock
Truro

QUIDENHAM Group, The (St Andrew) *Nor 11*   **P** *Ld Chan
(1 turn), Bp, Sir Thomas Beevor Bt, Major E H C Garnier,*

Trustees, and New Buckenham PCC (3 turns)   **R** D R HILL,
OLM D R A SHEPPARD

QUINTET Group of Parishes   *see* Cranborne w Boveridge,
Edmondsham etc *Sarum*

QUINTON and PRESTON DEANERY (St John the Baptist)
see Wootton w Quinton and Preston Deanery *Pet*

QUINTON (St Swithin) and Welford w Weston *Glouc 8*   **P** *DBP
and D&C Worc (jt)*   **P-in-c** A M GRIGOR

QUINTON, THE (Christ Church) *Birm 2*   **P** *Bp*
P-in-c C J S TURNER,   **C** A J BOWNASS, S C CARTER

QUINTON ROAD WEST (St Boniface) *Birm 2*   **P** *Bp*
P-in-c R P YATES,   **NSM** J M PLATT

QUORN (St Bartholomew)   *see* Quorndon *Leic*

QUORNDON (St Bartholomew) *Leic 6*   **P** *Bp*   **V** D H BOWLER

QUY (St Mary)   *see* Anglesey Gp *Ely*

RACKENFORD (All Saints)   *see* Washfield, Stoodleigh,
Withleigh etc *Ex*

RACKHEATH (Holy Trinity) and Salhouse *Nor 4*   **P** *Bp*
P-in-c L G ALLIES

RACTON (St Peter)   *see* Compton, the Mardens, Stoughton and
Racton *Chich*

RADBOURNE (St Andrew)   *see* Boylestone, Church
Broughton, Dalbury, etc *Derby*

RADCLIFFE (St Andrew) Black Lane *Man 14*   **P** *R Radcliffe
St Mary*   **P-in-c** A B WILLIAMS,   **OLM** J VOST

**RADCLIFFE (St Mary) (St Thomas and St John) (St Philip
Mission Church)** *Man 14*   **P** *Patr Bd*   **C** F SHER

RADCLIFFE-ON-TRENT (St Mary) and Shelford *S'well 8*
P *DBP and Ld Chan (alt)*   **P-in-c** G E ANDERSON

RADCLIVE (St John the Evangelist)   *see* Buckingham *Ox*

RADDESLEY Group of Parishes, The *Ely 4*   **P** *E H Vestey Esq,
Mrs B O Killander, Mrs B A Taylor, F R Egerton Esq, Exors
C L Thomas (5 turns), St Jo Coll Cam (1 turn)*
P-in-c P A REID,   **NSM** K R BISHOP

RADDINGTON (St Michael)   *see* Wiveliscombe w Chipstable,
Huish Champflower etc *B & W*

RADDON   *see* Thorverton, Cadbury, Upton Pyne etc *Ex*

RADFORD (All Souls) w Christ Church and St Michael *S'well 13*
P *Bp*   **Hon C** M T PHILLIPS,   **NSM** J D LEEMING

RADFORD (St Nicholas) *Cov 2*   **P** *Bp*   **V** G J MARCER

RADFORD (St Peter) *S'well 13*   **P** *Bp*
P-in-c D EDINBOROUGH,   **Hon C** M T PHILLIPS,
NSM J D LEEMING

RADFORD, NORTH (St Francis of Assisi)   *see* Cov St Fran N
Radford *Cov*

RADFORD SEMELE (St Nicholas) *Cov 10*   **P** *Bp*
P-in-c M C GREEN

**RADIPOLE (Emmanuel) (St Adhelm) (St Ann) and Melcombe
Regis** *Sarum 4*   **P** *Patr Bd*   **TR** K I HOBBS,
TV T J GREENSLADE, P J SALMON,   **C** G R FOSTER,
NSM P E LEGG

RADLETT (Christ Church)   *see* Aldenham, Radlett and Shenley
St Alb

RADLETT (St John)   *as above*

RADLEY (St James the Great) and Sunningwell *Ox 10*
P *Radley Coll and DBP (by turn)*   **P-in-c** P J MCKELLEN

RADNAGE (St Mary)   *see* W Wycombe w Bledlow Ridge,
Bradenham and Radnage *Ox*

RADNOR, OLD (St Stephen)   *see* Kington w Huntington, Old
Radnor, Kinnerton etc *Heref*

RADSTOCK (St Nicholas) w Writhlington *B & W 12*   **P** *Bp*
R S K GREATOREX,   **NSM** J A COLE

RADSTONE (St Lawrence)   *see* Astwell Gp *Pet*

RADWAY (St Peter)   *see* Warmington w Shotteswell and
Radway w Ratley *Cov*

RADWELL (All Saints)   *see* Stotfold and Radwell *St Alb*

RADWINTER (St Mary the Virgin)   *see* The Sampfords and
Radwinter w Hempstead *Chelmsf*

RAGDALE (All Saints)   *see* Upper Wreake *Leic*

RAINBOW HILL (St Barnabas)   *see* Worc St Barn w Ch Ch
Worc

RAINFORD (All Saints) *Liv 11*   **P** *V Prescot*
P-in-c S W C GOUGH

RAINHAM (St Helen and St Giles) w Wennington *Chelmsf 2*
P *MMCET*   **R** H PRADELLA,   **C** G P DOWLING,
NSM K D NORRIS

RAINHAM (St Margaret) *Roch 3*   **P** *Bp*   **V** A T VOUSDEN,
C J E BATEMAN, R E L HARDING

RAINHILL (St Ann) *Liv 10*   **P** *Trustees*   **V** N P ANDERSON

RAINOW (Holy Trinity) w Saltersford and Forest *Ches 13*   **P** *Bp*
P-in-c S D RATHBONE

RAINTON (not known)   *see* Topcliffe, Baldersby w Dishforth,
Dalton etc *York*

RAINTON, EAST (St Cuthbert) *Dur 14*   **P** *D&C*
P-in-c M L BECK,   **NSM** G M BECK, J M JEWSBURY

RAINTON, WEST (St Mary) *Dur 14*   **P** *Bp*   **P-in-c** M L BECK,
NSM G M BECK, J M JEWSBURY

RAINWORTH (St Simon and St Jude)   *see* Blidworth w
Rainworth *S'well*

RAITHBY (Holy Trinity)   *see* Spilsby Gp *Linc*

RAITHBY (St Peter)   *see* Legbourne and Wold Marsh *Linc*

RAME (St Germanus)   *see* Maker w Rame *Truro*

RAMPISHAM (St Michael and All Angels)   *see* Melbury *Sarum*

RAMPSIDE (St Michael)   *see* Aldingham, Dendron, Rampside
and Urswick *Carl*

RAMPTON (All Saints) *Ely 6*   **P** *Bp*   **P-in-c** K A HODGINS

**RAMPTON (All Saints) w Laneham, Treswell, Cottam and
Stokeham** *S'well 5*   **P** *D&C York and The Crown (alt)*
R F E M FERRITER

RAMSBOTTOM (St Andrew) (St John) (St Paul) and Edenfield
Man 10   **P** *Patr Bd (3 turns), Prime Min (1 turn)*
TR I M ROGERSON,   **TV** A J BARNSHAW,   **NSM** J W DAVIES,
A E KAY,   **OLM** S J WOOD

RAMSBURY (Holy Cross)   *see* Whitton *Sarum*

RAMSDELL (Christ Church)   *see* Baughurst, Ramsdell,
Wolverton w Ewhurst etc *Win*

RAMSDEN (Church of Unity)   *see* Orpington All SS *Roch*

RAMSDEN (St James)   *see* Forest Edge *Ox*

RAMSDEN BELLHOUSE (St Mary the Virgin)   *see* Ramsden
Crays w Ramsden Bellhouse *Chelmsf*

RAMSDEN CRAYS w Ramsden Bellhouse *Chelmsf 6*
P *Reformation Ch Trust*   **R** *vacant* (01268) 521043

RAMSDEN HEATH (St John)   *see* Downham w S Hanningfield
Chelmsf

RAMSEY (St Michael)   *see* Harwich Peninsula *Chelmsf*

RAMSEY, NORTH (St Olave)   *see* Lezayre St Olave Ramsey
S & M

RAMSEY, SOUTH (St Paul) *S & M 3*   **P** *Bp*
V N D GREENWOOD

RAMSEY ST MARY'S (St Mary)   *see* The Ramseys and
Upwood *Ely*

RAMSEYS (St Thomas à Becket) (St Mary) and Upwood, The
Ely 12   **P** *Patr Bd*   **TR** R A DARMODY,   **C** G D BOND

RAMSGATE (Christ Church) *Cant 9*   **P** *Ch Patr Trust*
V P F TIZZARD

RAMSGATE (Holy Trinity) (St George) *Cant 9*   **P** *Abp*
R P A ADAMS

RAMSGATE (St Luke) *Cant 9*   **P** *CPAS*   **V** P R WORLEDGE

RAMSGATE (St Mark) *Cant 9*   **P** *CPAS*   **V** C G SKINGLEY

RAMSGILL (St Mary)   *see* Upper Nidderdale *Ripon*

RAMSHOLT (All Saints)   *see* Wilford Peninsula *St E*

RANBY (St German)   *see* Asterby Gp *Linc*

RANBY (St Martin)   *see* Babworth w Sutton-cum-Lound and
Scofton etc *S'well*

RAND (St Oswald)   *see* Wragby Gp *Linc*

RANDWICK (St John the Baptist)   *see* Whiteshill and
Randwick *Glouc*

RANGEMORE (All Saints)   *see* Hanbury, Newborough,
Rangemore and Tutbury *Lich*

RANGEWORTHY (Holy Trinity)   *see* Wickwar, Rangeworthy
and Hillesley *Glouc*

RANMOOR (St John the Evangelist) *Sheff 4*   **P** *Trustees*
P-in-c J C GRENFELL

RANMORE (St Barnabas)   *see* Dorking w Ranmore *Guildf*

RANSKILL (St Barnabas)   *see* Blyth and Scrooby w Ranskill
S'well

RANTON (All Saints)   *see* Chebsey, Creswell, Ellenhall, Ranton
etc *Lich*

**RANWORTH (St Helen) w Panxworth, Woodbastwick, South
Walsham and Upton** *Nor 4*   **P** *Bp, Qu Coll Cam, and
J Cator Esq (jt)*   **R** N J H GARRARD

RASEN, WEST (All Saints)   *see* Middle Rasen Gp *Linc*

RASHCLIFFE (St Stephen)   *see* Em TM *Wakef*

RASKELF (St Mary)   *see* Easingwold w Raskelf *York*

RASTRICK (St John the Divine) (St Matthew) *Wakef 2*   **P** *Bp
and V Halifax (jt)*   **V** M R POLLARD,   **NSM** R S HANNAM

RATBY (St Philip and St James)   *see* Bradgate Team *Leic*

RATCLIFFE CULEY (All Saints)   *see* Bosworth and Sheepy
Gp *Leic*

RATCLIFFE-ON-SOAR (Holy Trinity)   *see* Kingston and
Ratcliffe-on-Soar *S'well*

RATCLIFFE ON THE WREAKE (St Botolph)   *see* Syston
Leic

RATHMELL (Holy Trinity)   *see* Giggleswick and Rathmell w
Wigglesworth *Bradf*

RATLEY (St Peter ad Vincula)   *see* Warmington w Shotteswell
and Radway w Ratley *Cov*

RATLINGHOPE (St Margaret)   *see* Wentnor w Ratlinghope,
Myndtown, Norbury etc *Heref*

RATTERY (Blessed Virgin Mary)   *see* S Brent and Rattery *Ex*

RATTLESDEN (St Nicholas) w Thorpe Morieux, Brettenham and Hitcham *St E 10*　**P** *Bp (3 turns), Ld Chan (1 turn)*　**R** E A LAW

RAUCEBY, NORTH (St Peter)　*see* Ancaster Wilsford Gp *Linc*

RAUGHTON HEAD (All Saints)　*see* Dalston w Cumdivock, Raughton Head and Wreay *Carl*

RAUNDS (St Peter), Hargrave, Ringstead and Stanwick *Pet 8*　**P** *Ld Chan (1 turn), Bp and L G Stopford-Sackville Esq (2 turns)*　**R** S M BELL

RAVENDALE, EAST (St Martin)　*see* Laceby and Ravendale Gp *Linc*

RAVENFIELD (St James), Hooton Roberts and Braithwell *Sheff 6*　**P** *Bp and Sir Philip Naylor-Leyland Bt (jt)*　**V** *vacant* (01709) 812665

RAVENGLASS (Mission Room)　*see* Eskdale, Irton, Muncaster and Waberthwaite *Carl*

RAVENHEAD (St John)　*see* Parr *Liv*

RAVENHEAD (St John the Evangelist)　*see* Eccleston *Liv*

RAVENINGHAM Group, The (St Andrew) *Nor 8*　**P** *Bp, Adn Nor, Sir Nicholas Bacon Bt, Major C A Boycott, D&C, K Coll Cam, and DBP (jt)*　**R** N J WILL,　**Hon C** A M R HOUSMAN

RAVENSBOURNE　*see* Deptford St Jo w H Trin and Ascension *S'wark*

RAVENSCAR (St Hilda)　*see* Cloughton and Burniston w Ravenscar etc *York*

RAVENSDEN (All Saints)　*see* Wilden w Colmworth and Ravensden *St Alb*

RAVENSHEAD (St Peter) *S'well 4*　**P** *Bp*　**P-in-c** C J RATTENBERRY

RAVENSTHORPE (St Denys)　*see* W Haddon w Winwick and Ravensthorpe *Pet*

RAVENSTHORPE (St Saviour) and Thornhill Lees w Savile Town *Wakef 9*　**P** *Bp and V Mirfield (jt)*　**V** R A P WARD,　**OLM** A SHACKLETON

RAVENSTONE (All Saints)　*see* Gayhurst w Ravenstone, Stoke Goldington etc *Ox*

RAVENSTONE (St Michael and All Angels) and Swannington *Leic 8*　**P** *Ld Chan and V Whitwick (alt)*　**C** A J BURGESS, M J T JOSS, V T GOODMAN

RAVENSTONEDALE (St Oswald)　*see* Orton and Tebay w Ravenstonedale etc *Carl*

RAWCLIFFE (St James)　*see* Airmyn, Hook and Rawcliffe *Sheff*

RAWCLIFFE (St Mark)　*see* Clifton *York*

RAWCLIFFE BRIDGE (St Philip)　*see* Airmyn, Hook and Rawcliffe *Sheff*

RAWDON (St Peter) *Bradf 4*　**P** *Trustees*　**P-in-c** C NORMAN

RAWMARSH (St Mary the Virgin) w Parkgate *Sheff 6*　**P** *Ld Chan*　**R** J T BIRBECK

RAWMARSH (St Nicolas)　*see* Ryecroft St Nic *Sheff*

RAWNSLEY (St Michael)　*see* Hednesford *Lich*

RAWRETH (St Nicholas) w Rettendon *Chelmsf 12*　**P** *Ld Chan and Pemb Coll Cam (alt)*　**P-in-c** P K TRATHEN,　**C** W H REED,　**NSM** S ADAMS

RAWTENSTALL (St Mary) *Man 15*　**P** *CPAS*　**P-in-c** M R SHORT

RAWTHORPE (St James)　*see* Moldgreen and Rawthorpe *Wakef*

RAY VALLEY, The *Ox 2*　**P** *Canon E G A W Page-Turner, Ex Coll Ox, and Piddington PCC (1 Turn), D&C Westmr, Qu Coll Ox, and Walsingham Coll (1 turn)*　**R** P T C MASHEDER,　**NSM** D A R SODADASI, D S WIPPELL,　**OLM** A R MARSHALL

RAYDON (St Mary)　*see* Higham, Holton St Mary, Raydon and Stratford *St E*

RAYLEIGH (Holy Trinity) (St Michael) *Chelmsf 12*　**P** *Patr Bd*　**TR** M J LODGE,　**TV** J H E ROSKELLY,　**C** N E ROWAN, P HILLMAN

RAYNE (All Saints)　*see* Panfield and Rayne *Chelmsf*

RAYNES PARK (St Saviour) *S'wark 13*　**P** *Bp*　**P-in-c** M O BLACKMAN,　**NSM** C W NOKE

RAYNHAM, EAST (St Mary)　*see* E w W Rudham, Helhoughton etc *Nor*

RAYNHAM, SOUTH (St Martin)　*as above*

REACH (St Ethelreda and the Holy Trinity)　*see* Burwell w Reach *Ely*

READ IN WHALLEY (St John the Evangelist) *Blackb 7*　**P** *V Whalley*　**V** A SOWERBUTTS

READING (All Saints) *Ox 15*　**P** *Bp*　**V** N J CHEESEMAN

READING (Christ Church) *Ox 15*　**P** *Bp*　**V** D M WEST

READING Greyfriars (St James) *Ox 15*　**P** *Ch Trust Fund Trust*　**V** J A DE B WILMOT,　**C** C M MORRIS, M P DOLPHIN

READING (Holy Trinity) *Ox 15*　**P** *SMF*　**V** *vacant* 0118-957 2650

READING (St Agnes w St Paul) (St Barnabas) *Ox 15*　**P** *Bp*　**R** R V ORR,　**NSM** E J G ORME

READING (St Giles w St Saviour) *Ox 15*　**P** *Bp*　**R** *vacant* 0118-957 2831

READING (St John the Evangelist and St Stephen) *Ox 15*　**P** *Simeon's Trustees*　**V** V L GARDNER,　**NSM** S KNIGHT, A M MARSHALL, N H BENSON

READING (St Luke) (St Bartholomew) *Ox 15*　**P** *Bp and V Reading St Giles (alt)*　**V** N J HARDCASTLE,　**C** R CHRISTOPHER,　**NSM** C F BLACKMAN

READING (St Mark) *Ox 15*　**P** *Bp*　**V** *vacant* 0118-957 2650

READING (St Mary the Virgin) (St Laurence) *Ox 15*　**P** *Bp*　**R** B SHENTON,　**C** C I RUSSELL, M STEVENS

READING (St Matthew) *Ox 15*　**P** *Bp*　**P-in-c** J HUDSON

REAPSMOOR (St John)　*see* Longnor, Quarnford and Sheen *Lich*

REARSBY (St Michael and All Angels)　*see* Syston *Leic*

RECULVER (St Mary the Virgin) and Herne Bay St Bartholomew *Cant 7*　**P** *Abp*　**V** R L HAWKES,　**NSM** E A HAWKES,　**OLM** B R NICHOLSON, J L HADLOW

RED HOUSE (St Cuthbert)　*see* N Wearside *Dur*

RED POST *Sarum 6*　**P** *Mrs V M Chattey, H W Plunkett-Ernle-Erle-Drax Esq, and Bp (by turn)*　**P-in-c** J E WARING

REDBOURN (St Mary) *St Alb 8*　**P** *Earl of Verulam*　**V** W J M GIBBS

REDBROOK (St Saviour)　*see* Coleford, Staunton, Newland, Redbrook etc *Glouc*

REDCAR (St Peter) *York 16*　**P** *Trustees*　**V** J C WEETMAN,　**C** F J HARRISON-SMITH,　**NSM** J S WATSON

REDCLIFFE BAY (St Nicholas)　*see* Portishead *B & W*

REDCLIFFE GARDENS (St Luke)　*see* S Kensington St Luke *Lon*

REDCLIFFE WAY (St Mary the Virgin)　*see* Bris St Mary Redcliffe w Temple etc *Bris*

REDDAL HILL (St Luke) *Worc 9*　**P** *The Crown*　**V** H C HANKE

REDDISH (St Elisabeth) *Man 3*　**P** *Bp*　**P-in-c** A STANTON,　**OLM** H E EVANS

REDDISH (St Mary)　*see* Heaton Reddish *Man*

REDDISH, NORTH (St Agnes) *Man 3*　**P** *The Crown*　**P-in-c** C E LARSEN

REDDITCH Christ the King *Worc 7*　**P** *Patr Bd*　**TR** M F BARTLETT,　**TV** M DEW,　**C** J C MUSSON

REDDITCH Holy Trinity *Worc 7*　**P** *Patr Bd*　**TR** D ROGERS,　**TV** R M JOHNSON, P H WORRALL, M P DENT,　**C** J A HUMPHRIES

REDDITCH (St George)　*see* Redditch H Trin *Worc*

REDDITCH (St Stephen)　*as above*

REDE (All Saints)　*see* Chevington w Hargrave, Chedburgh w Depden etc *St E*

REDENHALL (Assumption of the Blessed Virgin Mary), Harleston, Wortwell and Needham *Nor 10*　**P** *Bp*　**R** D W JACKSON,　**OLM** C HUDSON

REDFIELD (St Leonard)　*see* E Bris St Ambrose and St Leon *Bris*

REDGRAVE cum Botesdale St Mary w Rickinghall *St E 16*　**P** *P J H Wilson Esq*　**R** C R NORBURN

REDHILL (Christ Church)　*see* Wrington w Butcombe and Burrington *B & W*

REDHILL (Holy Trinity) *S'wark 26*　**P** *Simeon's Trustees*　**V** G J JENKINS,　**C** C M GLASS, D M KING,　**OLM** H J COWAN

REDHILL (St John the Evangelist) (Meadvale Hall) *S'wark 26*　**P** *Bp*　**V** N J CALVER,　**NSM** P H BRADSHAW, D M WILLIAMS

REDHILL (St Matthew) *S'wark 26*　**P** *Bp*　**V** A T CUNNINGTON,　**OLM** C R W WEBB

REDHORN *Sarum 16*　**P** *Patr Bd*　**NSM** E P LORT-PHILLIPS

REDISHAM (St Peter)　*see* Wainford *St E*

REDLAND (not known) *Bris 3*　**P** *Ch Trust Fund Trust*　**P-in-c** R P SYMMONS,　**NSM** M K GOODMAN, A L PARKER,　**OLM** A M ROWLANDS

REDLINGFIELD (St Andrew)　*see* Stradbroke, Horham, Athelington and Redlingfield *St E*

REDLYNCH (St Mary)　*see* Forest and Avon *Sarum*

REDLYNCH (St Peter)　*see* Bruton and Distr *B & W*

REDMARLEY D'ABITOT (St Bartholomew), Bromesberrow, Pauntley, Upleadon, Oxenhall, Dymock, Donnington, Kempley and Preston *Glouc 1*　**P** *Pemb Coll Ox, Bp, R D Marcon Esq, and Miss C Daniel (jt)*　**R** P PHILLIPS,　**NSM** A W PERRY, P NEWING,　**OLM** V G CHESTER, J M BOND

REDMARSHALL (St Cuthbert) *Dur 10*　**P** *The Crown*　**R** D M BROOKE,　**NSM** P CLAYTON

REDMILE (St Peter)　*see* Vale of Belvoir Par *Leic*

REDMIRE (St Mary)　*see* Penhill *Ripon*

REDNAL (St Stephen the Martyr) *Birm 4*　**P** *Bp*　**P-in-c** M F SIBANDA

REDRUTH (St Andrew) (St Euny) w Lanner and Treleigh *Truro 2*　**P** *DBP*　**TR** S P V CADE,　**TV** E C WOON, P W FELLOWS,　**C** P DIXON

REED (St Mary)　*see* Barkway, Reed and Buckland w Barley *St Alb*

REEDHAM (St John the Baptist) *see* Freethorpe, Wickhampton, Halvergate etc *Nor*

REEPHAM (St Mary) and Hackford w Whitwell and Kerdiston, Thurning w Wood Dalling and Salle *Nor* 22 **P** *Bp, CCC Cam, Pemb Coll Cam, Trin Coll Cam, and Ch Soc Trust (jt)* **R** C MORGAN

REEPHAM (St Peter and St Paul) *see* S Lawres Gp *Linc*

REGENT'S PARK (Christ Church) *see* Munster Square Ch Ch and St Mary Magd *Lon*

REGENT'S PARK (St Mark) *Lon* 16 **P** *D&C St Paul's* **V** P G BAKER, **Hon C** R F MCLAREN

REGIL (St James Mission Church) *see* Winford w Felton Common Hill *B & W*

REIGATE (St Luke) w Doversgreen St Peter *S'wark* 26 **P** *Bp* **V** *vacant* (01737) 246302

REIGATE (St Mark) *S'wark* 26 **P** *Bp* **V** M WRIGHT, **NSM** S E SMITH

REIGATE (St Mary Magdalene) *S'wark* 26 **P** *Trustees* **V** P J ANDREW, **C** P M JACKSON, D T BULL, **Hon C** M J H FOX, **NSM** D G O ROBINSON

REIGATE (St Peter) Conventional District *S'wark* 24 *vacant*

REIGATE (St Philip) *S'wark* 26 **P** *Bp* **P-in-c** J P SCOTT, **OLM** E STANGHAN

REIGATE HEATH (not known) *see* Reigate St Mary *S'wark*

REIGHTON (St Peter) *see* Bempton w Flamborough, Reighton w Speeton *York*

REKENDYKE (St Jude) *Dur* 15 **P** *The Crown and D&C* **V** *vacant* 0191-455 2338

REMENHAM (St Nicholas) *see* Henley w Remenham *Ox*

REMPSTONE (All Saints) *see* E and W Leake, Stanford-on-Soar, Rempstone etc *S'well*

RENDCOMB (St Peter) *Glouc* 9 **P** *Major M T N H Wills* **R** *vacant* (01285) 831319

RENDHAM (St Michael) *see* Upper Alde *St E*

RENDLESHAM (St Gregory the Great) *see* Wilford Peninsula *St E*

RENHOLD (All Saints) *St Alb* 10 **P** *MMCET* **P-in-c** A S BURROW

RENISHAW (St Matthew) *see* Barlborough and Renishaw *Derby*

RENNINGTON (All Saints) *see* Embleton w Rennington and Rock *Newc*

RENWICK (All Saints) *see* Kirkoswald, Renwick, Gt Salkeld and Lazonby *Carl*

REPPS (St Peter) *see* Martham and Repps with Bastwick, Thurne etc *Nor*

REPTON (St Wystan) *see* Foremark and Repton w Newton Solney *Derby*

RESTON, NORTH (St Edith) *see* Legbourne and Wold Marsh *Linc*

RETFORD (St Michael the Archangel) (St Saviour) (St Swithin) *S'well* 5 **P** *Patr Bd* **TR** A C ST J WALKER, **TV** M J CANTRILL, **C** C M S MOLONEY

RETTENDON (All Saints) *see* Rawreth w Rettendon *Chelmsf*

REVELSTOKE (St Peter) *see* Newton Ferrers w Revelstoke *Ex*

REVESBY (St Lawrence) *see* Fen and Hill Gp *Linc*

REWE (St Mary the Virgin) *see* Stoke Canon, Poltimore w Huxham and Rewe etc *Ex*

REYDON (St Margaret) *see* Sole Bay *St E*

REYMERSTON (St Peter) *see* Barnham Broom and Upper Yare *Nor*

RHODES (All Saints) (St Thomas) *Man* 18 **P** *R Middleton* **OLM** A BROXTON

RHYDYCROESAU (Christ Church) *Lich* 19 **P** *Bp* **R** S G THORBURN

RIBBESFORD (St Leonard) w Bewdley and Dowles *Worc* 11 **P** *E J Winnington-Ingram Esq* **R** K N JAMES, **C** J A T HEATON

RIBBLETON (St Mary Magdalene) (St Anne's Church Centre) (Ascension) *Blackb* 13 **P** *Patr Bd* **TR** N L STIMPSON, **TV** K J FENTON, **Hon C** E A ALP

RIBBY CUM WREA (St Nicholas) and Weeton St Michael *Blackb* 10 **P** *V Kirkham* **P-in-c** R W MARKS

RIBCHESTER (St Wilfred) w Stidd *Blackb* 13 **P** *Bp* **R** J FRANCIS

RIBSTON, LITTLE (St Helen) *see* Spofforth w Kirk Deighton *Ripon*

RIBY (St Edmund) *see* Keelby Gp *Linc*

RICCALL (St Mary) *see* Barlby w Riccall *York*

RICHARDS CASTLE (All Saints) *see* Ludlow *Heref*

RICHMOND (Holy Trinity and Christ Church) *S'wark* 16 **P** *CPAS* **V** I H PATTERSON, **C** D M R COOKE

RICHMOND (St Luke) *see* Kew St Phil and All SS w St Luke *S'wark*

RICHMOND (St Mary Magdalene) (St Matthias) (St John the Divine) *S'wark* 16 **P** *K Coll Cam* **TR** M C J REINDORP,

TV C F IRVINE, P J ASHWIN-SIEJKOWSKI, **NSM** N T SUMMERS, A R SYKES

RICHMOND (St Mary w Holy Trinity) w Hudswell and Downholme and Marske *Ripon* 2 **P** *Bp* **R** R T COOPER

RICHMOND, EAST *Ripon* 2 **P** *Patr Bd* **TR** A L GLASBY, **TV** D T LEWIS, **Hon C** G O SPEDDING

RICHMOND HILL (All Saints) *see* Leeds All SS w Osmondthorpe *Ripon*

RICHMOND HILL (St Hilda) *see* Hunslet w Cross Green *Ripon*

RICHMOND HILL (St Saviour) *see* Leeds Richmond Hill *Ripon*

RICKERSCOTE (St Peter) *Lich* 10 **P** *Bp and V Stafford St Paul (jt)* **P-in-c** R M MCINTYRE, **NSM** G P BOTT

RICKINGHALL (St Mary) *see* Redgrave cum Botesdale w Rickinghall *St E*

RICKLING (All Saints) *see* Manuden w Berden and Quendon w Rickling *Chelmsf*

RICKMANSWORTH (St Mary the Virgin) *St Alb* 5 **P** *Bp* **P-in-c** D J SNOWBALL

RIDDINGS (Holy Spirit) *see* Bottesford w Ashby *Linc*

RIDDINGS (St James) and Ironville *Derby* 1 **P** *Wright Trustees and V Alfreton (jt)* **P-in-c** F J C MERCURIO, **C** J E MORRIS

RIDDLESDEN (St Mary the Virgin) *Bradf* 8 **P** *Bp* **P-in-c** M C CANSDALE

RIDDLESDOWN (St James) *S'wark* 22 **P** *Bp* **V** C F SPURWAY

RIDDLESWORTH (St Peter) *see* Guiltcross *Nor*

RIDGE (St Margaret) *see* S Mymms and Ridge *St Alb*

RIDGE, The *see* Redditch H Trin *Worc*

RIDGEWAY *Ox* 19 **P** *DBP, CCC Ox, and Qu Coll Ox (jt)* **R** A WADGE

RIDGEWAY *Sarum* 18 **P** *Patr Bd* **P-in-c** R R POWELL

RIDGEWAY (St John the Evangelist) *see* Eckington and Ridgeway *Derby*

RIDGEWELL (St Laurence) w Ashen, Birdbrook and Sturmer *Chelmsf* 19 **P** *Duchy of Lanc, Bp, and DBP (by turn)* **R** M D HEWITT

RIDGMONT (All Saints) *see* Aspley Guise w Husborne Crawley and Ridgmont *St Alb*

RIDING MILL (St James) *Newc* 9 **P** *Viscount Allendale* **P-in-c** G K HENWOOD

RIDLEY (St Peter) *Roch* 1 **P** *J R A B Scott Esq* **R** J A PEAL

RIDLINGTON (St Mary Magdalene and St Andrew) *see* Preston and Ridlington w Wing and Pilton *Pet*

RIDLINGTON (St Peter) *see* Bacton, Happisburgh, Hempstead w Eccles etc *Nor*

RIDWARES and Kings Bromley, The *Lich* 1 **P** *Bp, Lord Leigh, and D&C (jt)* **R** T J LEYLAND, **NSM** D J SHERIDAN

RIEVAULX (St Mary) *see* Helmsley *York*

RIGSBY (St James) *see* Alford w Rigsby *Linc*

RIGTON, NORTH (St John) *see* Lower Wharfedale *Ripon*

RILLINGTON (St Andrew) *see* Buckrose Carrs *York*

RIMPTON (The Blessed Virgin Mary) *see* Chilton Cantelo, Ashington, Mudford, Rimpton etc *B & W*

RINGLAND (St Peter) *see* Wensum Benefice *Nor*

RINGLEY (St Saviour) w Prestolee *Man* 12 **P** *R Prestwich St Mary* **P-in-c** D J THOMPSON

RINGMER (St Mary the Virgin) *Chich* 18 **P** *Abp* **V** W R PRATT

RINGMORE (All Hallows) *see* Modbury, Bigbury, Ringmore w Kingston etc *Ex*

RINGSFIELD (All Saints) *see* Wainford *St E*

RINGSHALL (St Catherine) w Battisford, Barking w Darmsden and Great Bricett *St E* 1 **P** *Bp, Ch Patr Trust, and J C W de la Bere Esq (jt)* **P-in-c** B F ROSE

RINGSTEAD (Nativity of the Blessed Virgin Mary) *see* Raunds, Hargrave, Ringstead and Stanwick *Pet*

RINGSTEAD (St Andrew) *see* Hunstanton St Edm w Ringstead *Nor*

RINGSTONE IN AVELAND Group, The *Linc* 13 **P** *Bp (2 turns), Baroness Willoughby de Eresby and Charterhouse (1 turn)* **P-in-c** G P WILLIAMS, **OLM** D J CREASEY

RINGWAY Hale Barns (All Saints) *see* Hale Barns w Ringway *Ches*

RINGWOOD (St Peter and St Paul) *Win* 9 **P** *K Coll Cam* **V** J R TURPIN, **C** J R EVANS

RINGWOULD (St Nicholas) w Kingsdown and Ripple w Sutton by Dover *Cant* 8 **P** *Abp, Ch Patr Trust, and R S C Monins Esq (jt)* **OLM** P J HAMBROOK, A J WINN

RIPE (St John the Baptist) *see* Laughton w Ripe and Chalvington *Chich*

RIPLEY (All Saints) *Derby* 12 **P** *Wright Trustees* **C** J R W BROOK

RIPLEY (All Saints) w Burnt Yates *Ripon* 3 **P** *Sir Thomas Ingilby Bt* **P-in-c** S J BROWN, **NSM** R HUDSPETH

RIPLEY (St Mary) *Guildf 12* **P** *Bp* **V** C J ELSON
RIPON (Holy Trinity) *Ripon 3* **P** *Simeon's Trustees*
V M S A TANNER, **C** I S LAWRENCE, **NSM** J A MONTGOMERY,
W H GOWING, J S RUTTER
RIPPINGALE (St Andrew) *see* Ringstone in Aveland Gp *Linc*
RIPPLE (St Mary) *see* Upton-on-Severn, Ripple, Earls Croome
etc *Worc*
RIPPLE (St Mary the Virgin) *see* Ringwould w Kingsdown and
Ripple etc *Cant*
RIPPONDEN (St Bartholomew) *Wakef 4* **P** *Bp and*
V Halifax (jt) **V** C WRAY, **C** K A SHOESMITH,
NSM M JAMES, C A HIRST
RISBOROUGH (St Mary) *Ox 21* **P** *Ld Chan (2 turns), Patr Bd (1 turn)*
TV J A TOMKINS, D E CRITCHELL, **NSM** D R DEWICK
RISBY (St Giles) *see* Barrow *St E*
RISE (All Saints) *see* Skirlaugh w Long Riston, Rise and Swine
York
RISE PARK *see* Bestwood Park w Rise Park *S'well*
RISEHOLME (St Mary) *see* Nettleham *Linc*
RISELEY (All Saints) w Bletsoe *St Alb 15* **P** *MMCET*
V M T BAILEY
RISHTON (St Peter and St Paul) *Blackb 7* **P** *Trustees*
P-in-c M WOODS
RISHWORTH (St John) *see* Ripponden *Wakef*
RISLEY (All Saints) *see* Stanton-by-Dale w Dale Abbey and
Risley *Derby*
RISSINGTON, GREAT (St John the Baptist) *see* Bourton-on-
the-Water w Clapton etc *Glouc*
RISSINGTON, LITTLE (St Peter) *as above*
RITCHINGS PARK (St Leonard) *see* Iver *Ox*
RIVENHALL (St Mary the Virgin and All Saints) *Chelmsf 23*
P *DBP* **P-in-c** S E A MILES
RIVER (St Peter and St Paul) *Cant 4* **P** *Abp*
P-in-c A J BAWTREE
RIVERHEAD (St Mary) w Dunton Green *Roch 9*
P *R Sevenoaks and Bp (jt)* **V** P E FRANCIS, **C** W J EDWARDS
RIVERS Team Ministry, The *Sheff 6* **P** *Patr Bd*
TR D M BENT, **TV** M J LUNT, J LEVERTON
RIVERSMEET Benefice, The *St Alb 11* **P** *Prime Min, Trin Coll*
Cam (2 turns), and Ball Coll Ox (by turn)
P-in-c M E MARSHALL
RIVINGTON (not known) *see* Horwich and Rivington *Man*
ROADE (St Mary the Virgin) and Ashton w Hartwell *Pet 5*
P *Ld Chan and Bp (alt)* **V** M J BURTON
ROADHEAD Kinkry Hill (Mission Room) *see* Bewcastle,
Stapleton and Kirklinton etc *Carl*
ROADWATER (St Luke) *see* Old Cleeve, Leighland and
Treborough *B & W*
ROBERTSBRIDGE (Mission Room) *see* Salehurst *Chich*
ROBERTTOWN (All Saints) w Hartshead *Wakef 8*
P *V Birstall and TR Dewsbury (jt)* **C** S J PITCHER,
NSM P J DAWSON, **OLM** J C LEE
ROBOROUGH *see* Bickleigh and Shaugh Prior *Ex*
ROBOROUGH (St Peter) *see* Newton Tracey, Horwood,
Alverdiscott etc *Ex*
ROBY (St Bartholomew) *Liv 2* **P** *Bp* **V** T C GILL,
C G P TRACEY
ROCESTER (St Michael) and Croxden w Hollington *Lich 15*
P *Bp and Trustees (jt)* **V** E G WHITTAKER, **C** K R GOVAN,
NSM B WARREN
ROCHDALE (St Aidan) Sudden *see* Sudden St Aidan *Man*
ROCHDALE (St Chad) St Edmund (St John the Divine)
(St Mary) *Man 21* **P** *Bp* **R** D B FOSS, **NSM** I G KAY
ROCHDALE (St George w St Alban) *see* Oakenrod and
Bamford *Man*
ROCHDALE, SOUTH (St Mary) (St Luke) (St Peter) *Man 21*
P *Patr Bd* **TV** P J MAGUMBA
ROCHE (St Gomonda of the Rock) and Withiel *Truro 1* **P** *Bp*
and DBP (jt) **P-in-c** J A COOMBS, **NSM** E C DEELEY
ROCHESTER (St Justus) *Roch 5* **P** *Bp* **V** P T KERR,
NSM P FOREMAN
ROCHESTER (St Margaret) (St Peter's Parish Centre) *Roch 5*
P *Bp and D&C (jt)* **V** G S COLVILLE, **C** D L ROBERTSON
ROCHESTER ROW (St Stephen) *see* Westmr St Steph w St Jo
Lon
ROCHFORD (St Andrew) *Chelmsf 12* **P** *Bp*
P-in-c C W COUSINS
ROCHFORD (St Michael) *see* Teme Valley S *Worc*
ROCK (St Peter and St Paul) *see* Mamble w Bayton, Rock w
Heightington etc *Worc*
ROCK (St Philip and St James) *see* Embleton w Rennington and
Rock *Newc*
ROCK FERRY (St Peter) *Ches 1* **P** *Bp* **V** P M FROGGATT,
C C R SLATER
ROCKBEARE (St Mary w St Andrew) *see* Aylesbeare,
Rockbeare, Farringdon etc *Ex*

ROCKBOURNE (St Andrew) *see* W Downland *Sarum*
ROCKCLIFFE (St Mary the Virgin) and Blackford *Carl 2*
P *D&C* **P-in-c** J J VAN DEN BERG
ROCKHAMPTON (St Oswald) *see* Cromhall, Tortworth,
Tytherington, Falfield etc *Glouc*
ROCKINGHAM (St Leonard) *see* Gretton w Rockingham and
Cottingham w E Carlton *Pet*
ROCKLAND (All Saints) *see* Gt and Lt Ellingham, Rockland
and Shropham etc *Nor*
ROCKLAND (St Peter) *as above*
**ROCKLAND ST MARY (St Mary) with Hellington, Bramerton,
Surlingham, Claxton, Carleton St Peter and Kirby Bedon w
Whitlingham** *Nor 8* **P** *Bp, Adn Nor, MMCET, and
BNC Ox (jt)* **R** J B SHAW, **NSM** G D SAUNDERS,
OLM M ANSELL
RODBOROUGH (St Mary Magdalene) *Glouc 5* **P** *Bp*
P-in-c M M LUDLOW
RODBOURNE (Holy Rood) *see* Gt Somerford, Lt Somerford,
Seagry, Corston etc *Bris*
RODBOURNE CHENEY (St Mary) *Bris 7* **P** *CPAS*
R N D J LINES
RODDEN (All Saints) *see* Beckington w Standerwick, Berkley,
Rodden etc *B & W*
RODE (St Lawrence) *see* Hardington Vale *B & W*
RODE, NORTH (St Michael) *see* Bosley and N Rode w Wincle
and Wildboarclough *Ches*
RODE HEATH (Good Shepherd) *see* Odd Rode *Ches*
RODHUISH (St Bartholomew) *see* Dunster, Carhampton,
Withycombe w Rodhuish etc *B & W*
RODING, HIGH (All Saints) *see* Gt Canfield w High Roding
and Aythorpe Roding *Chelmsf*
RODING, HIGH (Mission Hall) *as above*
RODINGS, SOUTH *Chelmsf 18* **P** *Ld Chan, Bp, and Viscount
Gough (by turn)* **P-in-c** M KITCHEN
RODINGTON (St George) *see* Wrockwardine Deanery *Lich*
RODLEY (Ecumenical Centre) *see* Bramley *Ripon*
RODLEY (Mission Church) *see* Westbury-on-Severn w Flaxley,
Blaisdon etc *Glouc*
RODMARTON (St Peter) Conventional District *Glouc 9 vacant*
RODMELL (St Peter) *see* Iford w Kingston and Rodmell *Chich*
RODMERSHAM (St Nicholas) *see* Tunstall w Rodmersham
Cant
RODNEY STOKE (St Leonard) w Draycott *B & W 1* **P** *Bp*
P-in-c S M ROSE
ROEHAMPTON (Holy Trinity) *S'wark 18* **P** *Bp*
V J A MCKINNEY
ROFFEY (All Saints) *see* Roughey *Chich*
ROGATE (St Bartholomew) w Terwick and Trotton w Chithurst
Chich 10 **P** *Ld Chan* **R** E M DOYLE
ROGERS LANE (St Andrew's Chapel) *see* Stoke Poges *Ox*
ROKER (St Aidan) *see* Monkwearmouth *Dur*
ROLLESBY (St George) *see* Ormesby St Marg w Scratby,
Ormesby St Mich etc *Nor*
ROLLESTON (Holy Trinity) w Fiskerton, Morton and Upton
S'well 15 **P** *Ld Chan* **P-in-c** S SPENCER
ROLLESTON (St John the Baptist) *see* Church Langton cum
Tur Langton etc *Leic*
ROLLESTON (St Mary) *Lich 14* **P** *MMCET*
R I R WHITEHEAD
ROLLRIGHT, GREAT (St Andrew) *see* Hook Norton w Gt
Rollright, Swerford etc *Ox*
ROLLRIGHT, LITTLE (St Phillip) *see* Chipping Norton *Ox*
ROLVENDEN (St Mary the Virgin) *Cant 16* **P** *Abp*
P-in-c J T M DESROSIERS
ROMALDKIRK (St Romald) w Laithkirk *Ripon 2* **P** *Bp and
Earl of Strathmore's Trustees (alt)* **P-in-c** S A ADESANYA
ROMANBY (St James) *see* Northallerton w Kirby Sigston *York*
ROMANSLEIGH (St Rumon) *see* S Molton w Nymet
St George, High Bray etc *Ex*
ROMFORD (Ascension) Collier Row *Chelmsf 2* **P** *Trustees*
P-in-c B M HULL
ROMFORD (Good Shepherd) Collier Row *Chelmsf 2* **P** *CPAS*
P-in-c D H HAGUE
ROMFORD (St Alban) *Chelmsf 2* **P** *Bp* **V** R S P HINGLEY
ROMFORD (St Andrew) (St Agnes) *Chelmsf 2* **P** *New Coll Ox*
R R G FRIENDSHIP
ROMFORD (St Augustine) Rush Green *see* Rush Green
Chelmsf
ROMFORD (St Edward the Confessor) *Chelmsf 2*
P *New Coll Ox* **V** S J WAINE, **C** S M LYNCH, B C DENNIS
ROMFORD (St John the Divine) *Chelmsf 2* **P** *Bp*
P-in-c S J WAINE
ROMILEY (St Chad) *see* Chadkirk *Ches*
ROMNEY, NEW (St Nicholas) w OLD (St Clement) and Midley
Cant 12 **P** *Abp* **P-in-c** J L FIELD

ROMSEY (St Mary and St Ethelflaeda) *Win 12*   **P** *Bp*
V T C K SLEDGE,   **NSM** D F WILLIAMS, B G TAPHOUSE
ROMSLEY (Mission Room)   *see* Halas *Worc*
ROMSLEY (St Kenelm)   *as above*
ROOKERY, THE (St Saviour)   *see* Mow Cop *Lich*
ROOKHOPE (St John the Evangelist)   *see* Upper Weardale *Dur*
ROOS (All Saints) and Garton in Holderness w Tunstall, Grimston and Hilston *York 12*   **P** *Abp (1 turn), SMF (2 turns)*
P-in-c A J BURDON,   **C** P M BURDON
ROOSE (St Perran)   *see* S Barrow *Carl*
ROPLEY (St Peter)   *see* Bishop's Sutton and Ropley and W Tisted *Win*
ROPSLEY (St Peter)   *see* N Beltisloe Gp *Linc*
ROSE ASH (St Peter)   *see* Bishopsnympton, Rose Ash, Mariansleigh etc *Ex*
ROSEDALE (St Lawrence)   *see* Lastingham w Appleton-le-Moors, Rosedale etc *York*
ROSHERVILLE (St Mark)   *see* Northfleet and Rosherville *Roch*
ROSLEY (Holy Trinity)   *see* Westward, Rosley-w-Woodside and Welton *Carl*
ROSLISTON (St Mary)   *see* Walton-on-Trent w Croxall, Rosliston etc *Derby*
ROSS (St Mary the Virgin) w Walford *Heref 8*   **P** *Bp (4 turns), Ld Chan (1 turn)*   **V** S J JONES
ROSSENDALE (St Anne) (St Nicholas w St John) Middle Valley *Man 15*   **P** *Patr Bd*   **TR** R BEVAN,   **TV** S A DAVIES,   **OLM** S LYNCH
ROSSENDALE (St Peter)   *see* Laneside *Blackb*
ROSSENDALE (St Thomas)   *see* Musbury *Blackb*
ROSSINGTON (St Michael) *Sheff 9*   **P** *Bp*   **R** N R RAO
ROSSINGTON, NEW (St Luke) *Sheff 9*   **P** *Bp*   **V** J P CARLISLE
ROSTHERNE (St Mary) w Bollington *Ches 12*   **P** C L K SLEDGE *Cornwall-Legh Esq*   **V** *vacant* (01565) 830595
ROTHBURY (All Saints)   *see* Upper Coquetdale *Newc*
ROTHERBY (All Saints)   *see* Upper Wreake *Leic*
ROTHERFIELD (St Denys) w Mark Cross *Chich 19*   **P** *Bp, Adn Lewes and Hastings, and Ch Patr Trust (jt)*   **R** N F MASON
ROTHERFIELD GREYS (Holy Trinity)   *see* Henley H Trin *Ox*
ROTHERFIELD GREYS (St Nicholas)   *see* Nettlebed w Bix, Highmoor, Pishill etc *Ox*
ROTHERFIELD PEPPARD (All Saints) and Kidmore End and Sonning Common *Ox 6*   **P** *Bp and Jes Coll Ox (jt)*   **R** G D FOULIS BROWN,   **Hon C** A B OLSEN
ROTHERHAM (All Saints) *Sheff 6*   **P** *Bp*   **V** D C BLISS,   **C** A NASCIMENTO COOK
ROTHERHAM (St Paul) Ferham Park   *see* Masbrough *Sheff*
ROTHERHITHE (Holy Trinity) *S'wark 7*   **P** R *Rotherhithe St Mary*   **V** A M DOYLE
ROTHERHITHE (St Katharine)   *see* Bermondsey St Kath w St Bart *S'wark*
ROTHERHITHE (St Mary) w All Saints *S'wark 7*   **P** *Clare Coll Cam*   **P-in-c** M R NICHOLLS
ROTHERSTHORPE (St Peter and St Paul)   *see* Bugbrooke w Rothersthorpe *Pet*
ROTHERWICK (not known)   *see* Whitewater *Win*
ROTHLEY (St Mary the Virgin and St John the Baptist) *Leic 5*   **P** MMCET   **V** R M GLADSTONE,   **C** L K SHUKER
ROTHWELL (Holy Trinity) *Ripon 8*   **P** *Bp*   **V** P R CRESSALL
ROTHWELL (Holy Trinity) w Orton and Rushton w Glendon and Pipewell *Pet 9*   **P** *Hosp of Jes (1 turn), Bp (2 turns), J Hipwell Esq (1 turn),and Mert Coll Ox (1 turn)*   **NSM** R W SMITH
ROTHWELL (St Mary the Virgin)   *see* Swallow *Linc*
ROTTINGDEAN (St Margaret) *Chich 2*   **P** *Bp*   **V** M P MORGAN
ROUGH CLOSE (St Matthew)   *see* Meir Heath and Normacot *Lich*
ROUGH COMMON (St Gabriel)   *see* Harbledown *Cant*
ROUGH HAY (St Christopher)   *see* Darlaston St Lawr *Lich*
ROUGH HILLS (St Martin) *Lich 28*   **P** *Bp*   **V** J C OAKES
ROUGHAM (St Mary)   *see* Gt w Lt Massingham, Harpley, Rougham etc *Nor*
ROUGHAM (St Mary), Beyton w Hessett and Rushbrooke *St E 10*   **P** *Bp, MMCET (2 turns), and Ld Chan*   **R** N CUTLER,   **OLM** G B RENDLE
ROUGHEY or Roffey (All Saints) *Chich 8*   **P** *Bp*   **V** K R C AGNEW,   **C** P R REDPARTH,   **NSM** M YOUNG
ROUGHTON (St Margaret)   *see* Bain Valley Gp *Linc*
ROUGHTON (St Mary) and Felbrigg, Metton, Sustead, Bessingham and Gunton w Hanworth *Nor 21*   **P** *Bp and Exors G Whately Esq (jt)*   **P-in-c** J W SMITH,   **NSM** J WISEMAN
ROUGHTOWN (St John the Baptist) *Man 17*   **P** *Bp*   **P-in-c** C NIGHTINGALE
ROUNDHAY (St Edmund King and Martyr) *Ripon 5*   **P** *Bp*   **V** D G PATON-WILLIAMS,   **C** D M FLYNN,   **NSM** S L LANCASTER

ROUNDHAY (St John the Evangelist) *Ripon 5*   **P** *DBF*   **P-in-c** C H CHEESEMAN
ROUNDS GREEN (St James) *Birm 7*   **P** V *Langley*   **V** *vacant* 0121-552 2822
ROUNDSHAW (St Paul)   *see* S Beddington and Roundshaw *S'wark*
ROUNDSWELL Conventional District *Ex 15 vacant*
ROUNTON, WEST (St Oswald) and East (St Laurence) w Welbury *York 19*   **P** *Ld Chan*   **R** *vacant* (01609) 882401
ROUS LENCH (St Peter)   *see* Church Lench w Rous Lench and Abbots Morton etc *Worc*
ROUSHAM (St Leonard and St James) *Ox 2*   **P** C *Cottrell-Dormer Esq*   **P-in-c** R C SMAIL
ROUTH (All Saints) *York 8*   **P** *Ch Soc Trust and Reformation Ch Trust (jt)*   **P-in-c** J J FLETCHER
ROWBARTON (St Andrew)   *see* Taunton St Andr *B & W*
ROWBERROW (St Michael and All Angels)   *see* Axbridge w Shipham and Rowberrow *B & W*
ROWDE (St Matthew) and Bromham *Sarum 16*   **P** *DBP and S Spicer Esq (jt)*   **R** J R J HISCOX
ROWENFIELD (Emmanuel)   *see* Cheltenham St Mark *Glouc*
ROWINGTON (St Lawrence)   *see* Hatton w Haseley, Rowington w Lowsonford etc *Cov*
ROWLAND LUBBOCK (Memorial Hall)   *see* E Horsley and Ockham w Hatchford and Downside *Guildf*
ROWLANDS CASTLE (St John the Baptist) *Portsm 5*   **P** *Bp*   **P-in-c** D J LLOYD
ROWLANDS GILL (St Barnabas)   *see* High Spen and Rowlands Gill *Dur*
ROWLEDGE (St James) and Frensham *Guildf 3*   **P** *Adn Surrey and Ld Chan (alt)*   **V** C J RICHARDSON,   **NSM** E HICKS,   S J CRABTREE
ROWLESTONE (St Peter)   *see* Ewyas Harold w Dulas, Kenderchurch etc *Heref*
ROWLEY (St Peter) w Skidby *York 8*   **P** *Abp and N A C Hildyard Esq (jt)*   **P-in-c** A BAILEY
ROWLEY REGIS (St Giles) *Birm 7*   **P** *Ld Chan*   **V** *vacant* 0121-559 1251
ROWNER (St Mary the Virgin) *Portsm 3*   **P** R J F *Prideaux-Brune Esq*   **R** J W DRAPER
ROWNEY GREEN (Mission Chapel)   *see* Alvechurch *Worc*
ROWNHAMS (St John the Evangelist)   *see* Nursling and Rownhams *Win*
ROWSLEY (St Katherine) *Derby 2*   **P** *Duke of Rutland*   **P-in-c** A P KAUNHOVEN
ROWSTON (St Clement)   *see* Digby Gp *Linc*
ROWTON (All Hallows)   *see* Wrockwardine Deanery *Lich*
ROXBOURNE (St Andrew) *Lon 23*   **P** *Bp*   **V** C M RABLEN,   **NSM** E J GARRISH
ROXBY (St Mary)   *see* Winterton Gp *Linc*
ROXBY (St Nicholas)   *see* Hinderwell, Roxby and Staithes etc *York*
ROXETH (Christ Church) *Lon 23*   **P** *Patr Bd*   **TR** M S PHILPS,   **TV** W R VAN DER HART,   **C** R A PETERS,   **NSM** R M ROGERS,   C I ROGERS
ROXHOLME   *see* Leasingham *Linc*
ROXTON (St Mary Magdalene)   *see* Riversmeet *St Alb*
ROXWELL (St Michael and All Angels) *Chelmsf 8*   **P** *New Coll Ox*   **P-in-c** K B BEST
ROYDON (All Saints)   *see* Grimston, Congham and Roydon *Nor*
ROYDON (St Peter) *Chelmsf 25*   **P** *Earl Cowley*   **P-in-c** C P PENNINGTON
ROYDON (St Remigius)   *see* Upper Waveney *Nor*
ROYSTON (St John the Baptist) *St Alb 19*   **P** *Bp*   **V** L D HARMAN,   **NSM** J H FIDLER, T R WEEKS
ROYSTON (St John the Baptist) *Wakef 7*   **P** *Bp*   **V** *vacant* (01226) 722410
ROYTON (St Anne) *Longsight* *Man 20*   **P** *Bp*   **P-in-c** J A READ,   **OLM** D J HALFORD, P A ROBINSON
ROYTON (St Paul) *Man 20*   **P** R *Prestwich St Mary*   **V** D BOOTH,   **C** P HUTCHINS
RUAN LANIHORNE (St Rumon)   *see* Veryan w Ruan Lanihorne *Truro*
RUAN MINOR (St Rumon)   *see* St Ruan w St Grade and Landewednack *Truro*
RUARDEAN (St John the Baptist)   *see* Drybrook, Lydbrook and Ruardean *Glouc*
RUBERY (St Chad) *Birm 4*   **P** *The Crown*   **P-in-c** D W JAMES,   **NSM** P A JOHNSTON
RUCKINGE (St Mary Magdalene)   *see* Orlestone w Snave and Ruckinge w Warehorne etc *Cant*
RUCKLAND (St Olave)   *see* S Ormsby Gp *Linc*
RUDBY IN CLEVELAND (All Saints) w Middleton *York 21*   **P** *Abp*   **P-in-c** P J SANDERS

RUDDINGTON (St Peter) *S'well 9*   **P** *Simeon's Trustees*
V A J AXON

RUDFORD (St Mary the Virgin)   *see* Highnam, Lassington, Rudford, Tibberton etc *Glouc*

RUDGWICK (Holy Trinity) *Chich 8*   **P** *Ld Chan*
V R C JACKSON

RUDHAM, EAST and WEST (St Mary), Helhoughton, Houghton-next-Harpley, The Raynhams, Tatterford, and Tattersett *Nor 15*   **P** *Bp, The Most Revd G D Hand, Marquess of Cholmondeley, and Marquess Townshend (jt)*
R E L BUNDOCK

RUDHEATH (Licensed Room)   *see* Witton *Ches*

RUDSTON (All Saints) w Boynton, Carnaby and Kilham *York 9*
P *Ld Chan (1 turn), Abp (3 turns)*   **V** G J OWEN

RUFFORD (St Mary the Virgin) *Blackb 5*   **P** *Bp*
P-in-c N E DAVIS,   **NSM** R J FISHER

RUFFORTH (All Saints) w Moor Monkton and Hessay *York 1*
P *MMCET and Abp (alt)*   **P-in-c** P P ROBINSON,
NSM M R SHAW

RUGBY (Christ Church)   *see* Clifton upon Dunsmore w Newton and Brownsover *Cov*

RUGBY (St Andrew) (St George) (St John) (St Peter) (St Philip)
Cov 6   **P** *Bp*   **TR** M H F BEACH,   **TV** J D PARKER, O SIMON,
C M I J DAFFERN,   **NSM** R C ROGERS, H G IREDALE

RUGBY WEST (St Matthew) (St Oswald) *Cov 6*   **P** *Dioc Trustees and Ch Trust Fund Trust (jt)*   **V** M P SAXBY,
C T NORMAN,   **OLM** A J CARTWRIGHT

RUGELEY (St Augustine)   *see* Brereton and Rugeley *Lich*

RUGELEY (The Good Shepherd)   *as above*

RUISHTON (St George) w Thornfalcon *B & W 18*   **P** *Bp and Dr W R Chisholm-Batten (alt)*   **P-in-c** I ALDERSLEY

RUISLIP (St Martin) *Lon 24*   **P** *D&C Windsor*   **V** S EVANS,
C R M BASTABLE,   **NSM** M A BEDFORD, S C SIMPKINS

RUISLIP (St Mary) *Lon 24*   **P** *Bp*   **V** N G T WHEELER

RUISLIP MANOR (St Paul) *Lon 24*   **P** *Bp*   **V** A C BALL,
NSM B C PINNELL

RUMBURGH (St Michael and All Angels and St Felix)   *see* S Elmham and Ilketshall *St E*

RUNCORN (All Saints) (Holy Trinity) *Ches 3*   **P** *Bp and Ch Ch Ox (jt)*   **V** J H A HAYES,   **NSM** M A HAYES

RUNCORN (St John the Evangelist) Weston *Ches 3*   **P** *Bp*
V E M GARDNER

RUNCORN (St Michael and All Angels) *Ches 3*   **P** *Bp*
V V L SCHOFIELD

RUNCTON, NORTH (All Saints)   *see* W Winch w Setchey, N Runcton and Middleton *Nor*

RUNCTON, SOUTH (St Andrew)   *see* Holme Runcton w S Runcton and Wallington *Ely*

RUNCTON HOLME (St James)   *as above*

RUNHALL (All Saints)   *see* Barnham Broom and Upper Yare *Nor*

RUNHAM (St Peter and St Paul)   *see* S Trin Broads *Nor*

RUNNINGTON (St Peter and St Paul)   *see* Wellington and Distr *B & W*

RUNNYMEDE (St Jude)   *see* Englefield Green *Guildf*

RUNTON (Holy Trinity)   *see* Aylmerton, Runton, Beeston Regis and Gresham *Nor*

RUNTON, EAST (St Andrew)   *as above*

RUNWELL (St Mary)   *see* Wickford and Runwell *Chelmsf*

RUSCOMBE (St James the Great) and Twyford *Ox 16*   **P** *Bp*
P-in-c S C HOWARD,   **Hon C** T J DAKIN,   **NSM** S DAKIN,
G W PUGH

RUSH GREEN (St Augustine) Romford *Chelmsf 2*   **P** *Bp*
V M D HOWSE

RUSHALL (Christ the King) (St Michael the Archangel) *Lich 25*
P *Sir Andrew Buchanan Bt and H C S Buchanan Esq (jt)*
V C R SUCH,   **NSM** S BOYCE

RUSHALL (St Mary)   *see* Dickleburgh and The Pulhams *Nor*

RUSHALL (St Matthew)   *see* Upavon w Rushall and Charlton *Sarum*

RUSHBROOKE (St Nicholas)   *see* Rougham, Beyton w Hessett and Rushbrooke *St E*

RUSHBURY (St Peter) *Heref 11*   **P** *Bp Birm*   **P-in-c** J GROVES

RUSHDEN (St Mary)   *see* Sandon, Wallington and Rushden w Clothall *St Alb*

RUSHDEN (St Mary) w Newton Bromswold *Pet 8*   **P** *CPAS*
R S K PRIOR

RUSHDEN (St Peter) *Pet 8*   **P** *CPAS*   **V** D J K WALLER

RUSHEN Christ Church (Holy Trinity) *S & M 1*   **P** *The Crown*
V N J COLE

RUSHEY MEAD (St Theodore of Canterbury)   *see* Leic St Theodore *Leic*

RUSHFORD (St John the Evangelist)   *see* E w W Harling, Bridgham w Roudham, Larling etc *Nor*

RUSHLAKE GREEN (Little St Mary)   *see* Warbleton and Bodle Street Green *Chich*

RUSHMERE (St Andrew) *St E 4*   **P** *Bp*   **V** B WAKELING,
C A J OAKEY-JONES

RUSHMERE (St Michael)   *see* Kessingland, Gisleham and Rushmere *Nor*

RUSHMOOR (St Francis)   *see* Churt and Hindhead *Guildf*

RUSHOCK (St Michael)   *see* Elmley Lovett w Hampton Lovett and Elmbridge etc *Worc*

RUSHOLME (Holy Trinity) *Man 4*   **P** *CPAS*   **R** S L JAMES,
C P G JUMP, P R HORLOCK,   **NSM** P J GASKELL

RUSHTON (All Saints)   *see* Rothwell w Orton, Rushton w Glendon and Pipewell *Pet*

RUSHTON SPENCER   *see* Horton, Lonsdon and Rushton Spencer *Lich*

RUSKIN PARK (St Saviour)   *see* Herne Hill *S'wark*

RUSKINGTON Group, The (All Saints) *Linc 22*   **P** *DBP*
P-in-c C PENNOCK,   **NSM** L M HUNTER

RUSLAND (St Paul)   *see* Hawkshead and Low Wray w Sawrey and Rusland etc *Carl*

RUSPER (St Mary Magdalene) w Colgate *Chich 8*
P *Mrs E C Calvert and Bp (alt)*   **R** N A FLINT

RUSTHALL (St Paul) (St Paul's Mission Church) *Roch 12*
P *R Speldhurst*   **V** *vacant* (01892) 521357

RUSTINGTON (St Peter and St Paul) *Chich 1*   **P** *Bp*
V Z E ALLEN

RUSTON, SOUTH   *see* Tunstead w Sco' Ruston *Nor*

RUSTON PARVA (St Nicholas)   *see* The Beacon *York*

RUSWARP (St Bartholomew)   *see* Whitby w Ruswarp *York*

RUYTON XI TOWNS (St John the Baptist) w Great Ness and Little Ness *Lich 17*   **P** *Bp and Guild of All So (jt) and Ld Chan (alt)*   **P-in-c** L FOSTER,   **OLM** J M BAKER

RYAL (All Saints)   *see* Stamfordham w Matfen *Newc*

RYARSH (St Martin)   *see* Birling, Addington, Ryarsh and Trottiscliffe *Roch*

RYBURGH, GREAT (St Andrew)   *see* Upper Wensum Village Gp *Nor*

RYDAL (St Mary) *Carl 11*   **P** *Bp*   **V** C J BUTLAND

RYDE (All Saints) *Portsm 7*   **P** *Bp*   **V** J F REDVERS HARRIS,
NSM E W BUTCHER

RYDE (Holy Trinity) *Portsm 7*   **P** *Bp*   **V** M F JONES

RYDE (St James) Proprietary Chapel *Portsm 7*   **P** *Ch Soc Trust*
C-in-c J H A LEGGETT

RYDE (St John the Baptist)   *see* Oakfield St Jo *Portsm*

RYE (St Mary the Virgin) *Chich 20*   **P** *Patr Bd*
TR H M MOSELEY,   **NSM** L E MURDOCH, J G DAVENPORT,
A J SARGEANT

RYE HARBOUR (Holy Spirit)   *see* Rye *Chich*

RYE PARK (St Cuthbert) *St Alb 20*   **P** *DBP*   **V** A F BURFORD

RYECROFT (St Nicolas) Rawmarsh *Sheff 6*   **P** *Bp*
V T A PARKINSON

RYEDALE, UPPER *York 17*   **P** *Abp, Adn Cleveland, Sir Richard Beckett Bt, and Sir George Wombwell Bt (jt)*
NSM J B NICHOLSON, M D B SINCLAIR

RYHALL (St John the Evangelist) w Essendine and Carlby *Pet 12*
P *Burghley Ho Preservation Trust*   **V** P J MCKEE

RYHILL (St James) *Wakef 11*   **P** *Bp*   **P-in-c** P A BOSTOCK

RYHOPE (St Paul) *Dur 16*   **P** *Bp*   **V** D E CHADWICK

RYLSTONE (St Peter)   *see* Burnsall w Rylstone *Bradf*

RYME INTRINSECA (St Hypolytus)   *see* Wriggle Valley *Sarum*

RYPE (St John the Baptist)   *see* Laughton w Ripe and Chalvington *Chich*

RYSTON (St Michael)   *see* Denver and Ryston w Roxham and W Dereham etc *Ely*

RYTHER (All Saints)   *see* Cawood w Ryther and Wistow *York*

RYTON (Holy Cross) *Dur 13*   **P** *Bp*   **R** T L JAMIESON,
C H T REYNOLDS

RYTON (Mission Chapel)   *see* Condover w Frodesley, Acton Burnell etc *Heref*

RYTON (St Andrew)   *see* Beckbury, Badger, Kemberton, Ryton, Stockton etc *Lich*

RYTON ON DUNSMORE (St Leonard)   *see* Baginton w Bubbenhall and Ryton-on-Dunsmore *Cov*

SABDEN (St Nicholas) and Pendleton-in-Whalley (All Saints)
Blackb 7   **P** *Bp and Trustees (jt)*   **V** *vacant* (01282) 771384

SACKLETON (St George the Martyr)   *see* The Street Par *York*

SACOMBE (St Catherine)   *see* Standon and The Mundens w Sacombe *St Alb*

SACRISTON (St Peter)   *see* Dur N *Dur*

SADBERGE (St Andrew) *Dur 8*   **P** *Bp*   **R** P S D NEVILLE

SADDINGTON (St Helen)   *see* Kibworth and Smeeton Westerby and Saddington *Leic*

SADDLEWORTH (St Chad) *Man 19*   **P** *Patr Bd*
TR C N R HALLIDAY,   **Hon C** G K TIBBO, H G SUTCLIFFE,
NSM A KERR, J M DEGG, J V BARTON,   **OLM** G B ADAMS,
B CHRISTOPHER

SAFFRON WALDEN (St Mary) w Wendens Ambo, Littlebury, Ashdon and Hadstock *Chelmsf 21* **P** *Patr Bd* **TR** D R TOMLINSON, **C** A M HOWSON, **NSM** J C TOMLINSON, W MOORE, P W L GRIFFITHS

SAHAM TONEY (St George) *see* Ashill, Carbrooke, Ovington and Saham Toney *Nor*

ST AGNES (St Agnes) *see* Is of Scilly *Truro*

ST AGNES (St Agnes) and Mount Hawke w Mithian *Truro 6* **P** *Bp and D&C (alt)* **V** A G BASHFORTH

ST ALBANS (Christ Church) *St Alb 6* **P** *Trustees* **V** J M FOLLETT

ST ALBANS (St Luke) *St Alb 6* **P** *DBP* **V** M A SLATER

ST ALBANS (St Mary) Marshalswick *St Alb 6* **P** *Bp* **NSM** M W BROWN

ST ALBANS (St Michael) *St Alb 6* **P** *Earl of Verulam* **V** B C GRAY, **NSM** J A HAYTON

ST ALBANS (St Paul) *St Alb 6* **P** *V St Alb St Pet* **V** A R HURLE, **C** J W D HASWELL, **Hon C** G M ABBOTT, **NSM** L M HURLE

ST ALBANS (St Peter) *St Alb 6* **P** *The Crown* **V** *vacant* (01727) 851464

ST ALBANS (St Saviour) *St Alb 6* **P** *Bp* **V** P R WADSWORTH, **NSM** A N FERRAR

ST ALBANS (St Stephen) *St Alb 6* **P** *J N W Dudley Esq* **V** D RIDGEWAY, **NSM** G I KEIR, P J MADGWICK, C BAYNES

ST ALLEN (St Alleyne) *see* Kenwyn w St Allen *Truro*

ST ANNES-ON-THE-SEA (St Anne) Heyhouses *Blackb 10* **P** *J C Hilton Esq* **C** S SMITH

ST ANNES-ON-THE-SEA (St Margaret of Antioch) *Blackb 10* **P** *Bp* **V** A R HODGSON

ST ANNES-ON-THE-SEA (St Thomas) *Blackb 10* **P** *J C Hilton Esq* **V** P D LAW-JONES, **C** N E GOODRICH

ST ANTHONY-IN-MENEAGE (St Anthony) *see* Meneage *Truro*

ST AUSTELL (Holy Trinity) *Truro 1* **P** *The Crown* **V** D P WHITE, **C** H M MEARS, **NSM** O H J MEARS

ST BEES (St Mary and St Bega) *Carl 5* **P** *Trustees* **P-in-c** L F NOWEN

ST BLAZEY (St Blaise) *Truro 1* **P** *Bp* **V** F M BOWERS, **C** S K TANSWELL

ST BREOKE (St Breoke) and Egloshayle in Wadebridge *Truro 10* **P** *Bp and DBP (jt)* **R** *vacant* (01208) 815526

ST BREWARD (St Breward) *see* Blisland w St Breward *Truro*

ST BRIAVELS (St Mary the Virgin) w Hewelsfield *Glouc 2* **P** *D&C Heref* **P-in-c** R J M GROSVENOR, **Hon C** F E BUXTON

ST BUDEAUX *see* Devonport St Budeaux *Ex*

ST BURYAN (St Buriana), St Levan and Sennen *Truro 5* **P** *Duchy of Cornwall* **P-in-c** B J BERRIMAN, **OLM** C M JAGO

ST CLEER (St Clarus) *Truro 12* **P** *Ld Chan* **P-in-c** K LANYON JONES

ST CLEMENT (St Clement) *see* Truro St Paul and St Clem *Truro*

ST CLEMENT DANES *see* St Mary le Strand w St Clem Danes *Lon*

ST CLETHER (St Clederus) *see* Altarnon w Bolventor, Laneast and St Clether *Truro*

ST COLAN (St Colan) *see* St Columb Minor and St Colan *Truro*

ST COLUMB MAJOR (St Columba) w St Wenn *Truro 7* **P** *Bp* **C** G F SHIELD, **NSM** E C DEELEY

ST COLUMB MINOR (St Columba) and St Colan *Truro 7* **P** *Bp* **P-in-c** C C MCQUILLEN-WRIGHT

ST DECUMANS (St Decuman) *B & W 17* **P** *Bp* **P-in-c** P J ALLEN, **C** F M B GUTTRIDGE

ST DENNIS (St Denys) *Truro 1* **P** *Bp* **P-in-c** K P ARTHUR

ST DEVEREUX (St Dubricius) *see* Ewyas Harold w Dulas, Kenderchurch etc *Heref*

ST DOMINIC (St Dominica), Landulph and St Mellion w Pillaton *Truro 11* **P** *D&C and Trustees Major J Coryton, Duchy of Cornwall, and SMF (by turn)* **R** P R J LAMB

ST EDMUND WAY *St E 10* **P** *Bp, Mrs J Oakes, and Lord de Saumarez* **C** A D SHANNON, **NSM** J R LONGE

ST EDMUNDS Anchorage Lane Conventional District *Sheff 7 vacant*

ST ENDELLION (St Endelienta) w Port Isaac and St Kew *Truro 10* **P** *Bp* **P-in-c** J A C MAY, **C** J R MOSEDALE, **NSM** J POLLINGER, A D E LEWIS

ST ENODER (St Enoder) *Truro 7* **P** *Bp* **P-in-c** H L SAMSON

ST ENODOC (St Enodoc) *see* St Minver *Truro*

ST ERME (St Hermes) *see* Probus, Ladock and Grampound w Creed and St Erme *Truro*

ST ERNEY (St Erney) *see* Landrake w St Erney and Botus Fleming *Truro*

ST ERTH (St Erth) *see* Godrevy *Truro*

ST ERVAN (St Ervan) *see* St Mawgan w St Ervan and St Eval *Truro*

ST EVAL (St Uvelas) *as above*

ST EWE (All Saints) *see* St Mewan w Mevagissey and St Ewe *Truro*

ST GENNYS (St Gennys) *see* Week St Mary Circle of Par *Truro*

ST GEORGE-IN-THE-EAST (St Mary) *Lon 7* **P** *Bp* **V** P MCGEARY, **Hon C** P WRIGHT

ST GEORGE-IN-THE-EAST w St Paul *Lon 7* **P** *Bp* **R** M R AINSWORTH

ST GEORGES (St George) *see* Priors Lee and St Georges *Lich*

ST GERMANS (St Germans of Auxerre) *Truro 11* **P** *D&C Windsor* **P-in-c** A I JOHNSTON, **OLM** J M LOBB

ST GILES-IN-THE-FIELDS *Lon 3* **P** *Bp* **R** W M JACOB

ST GILES-IN-THE-HEATH (St Giles) *see* Boyton, N Tamerton, Werrington etc *Truro*

ST GILES IN THE WOOD (St Giles) *see* Newton Tracey, Horwood, Alverdiscott etc *Ex*

ST GLUVIAS (St Gluvias) *Truro 3* **P** *Bp* **V** J HARRIS

ST GORAN (St Goranus) w Caerhays *Truro 1* **P** *Bp* **P-in-c** P A ROBSON, **NSM** R M MURFITT

ST HELENS (St Helen) (Barton Street Mission) (St Andrew) *Liv 10* **P** *Trustees* **TV** C R SMITH

ST HELENS (St Helen) (St Catherine by the Green) *Portsm 7* **P** *Bp* **V** M M STRANGE

ST HELENS (St Mark) *Liv 10* **P** *Trustees* **P-in-c** C R SMITH

ST HELIER (St Peter) (Bishop Andrewes Church) *S'wark 23* **P** *Bp* **P-in-c** H WONG, **C** K J LEWIS

ST HILARY (St Hilary) *see* Ludgvan, Marazion, St Hilary and Perranuthnoe *Truro*

ST ILLOGAN (St Illogan) *Truro 2* **P** *Ch Soc Trust* **R** M J KIPPAX, **C** S CLIFTON, **NSM** P I TREMELLING, P J KNIBBS

ST IPPOLYTS (St Ippolyts) *St Alb 4* **P** *Bp* **P-in-c** A E J POLLINGTON

ST ISSEY (St Issey) *see* St Merryn and St Issey w St Petroc Minor *Truro*

ST IVE (St Ive) and Pensilva w Quethiock *Truro 12* **P** *Bp (1 turn), The Crown (2 turns)* **C** P R SHARPE, K LANYON JONES

ST IVES (All Saints) *Ely 12* **P** *Guild of All So* **V** J S PULLEN

ST IVES (St Ia the Virgin) *Truro 5* **P** *V Lelant* **C** M A J DAVIES, **NSM** R G SELBY-BOOTHROYD

ST JOHN (St John the Baptist) w Millbrook *Truro 11* **P** *Bp and Col Sir John Carew-Pole Bt (alt)* **P-in-c** T E THOMAS

ST JOHN-AT-HACKNEY *Lon 5* **P** *Bp, Adn, and Lord Amherst of Hackney (jt)* **R** R J WICKHAM, **C** D J J EVANS, **NSM** J M KING, L HARVEY

ST JOHN IN BEDWARDINE (St John the Baptist) *Worc 3* **P** *D&C* **NSM** J M JAMES

ST JOHN IN WEARDALE (St John the Baptist) *see* Upper Weardale *Dur*

ST JOHN LEE (St John of Beverley) *Newc 10* **P** *Viscount Allendale* **R** J J T THOMPSON

ST JOHN ON BETHNAL GREEN *Lon 7* **P** *Patr Bd* **TR** A J E GREEN, **C** F J GREEN, **NSM** R R R O'CALLAGHAN, S M LEE

ST JOHN'S-IN-THE-VALE (St John), St Mary's Threlkeld and Wythburn *Carl 6* **P** *Bp, Adn, V Crosthwaite, and Earl of Lonsdale (jt)* **R** B ROTHWELL

ST JOHN'S WOOD (St John) *Lon 4* **P** *Bp* **V** A K BERGQUIST, **C** A C R HAMMOND

ST JOHN'S WOOD (St Mark) *see* St Marylebone St Mark Hamilton Terrace *Lon*

ST JULIOT (St Julitta) *see* Boscastle w Davidstow *Truro*

ST JUST IN PENWITH (St Just) *Truro 5* **P** *Ld Chan* **V** S W LEACH

ST JUST-IN-ROSELAND (St Just) and St Mawes *Truro 6* **P** *A M J Galsworthy Esq* **P-in-c** K J BOULLIER

ST KEVERNE (St Keverne) *Truro 4* **P** *CPAS* **P-in-c** A WHITAKER

ST KEW (St James the Great) *see* St Endellion w Port Isaac and St Kew *Truro*

ST KEYNE (St Keyna) *see* Liskeard and St Keyne *Truro*

ST LAURENCE in the Isle of Thanet (St Laurence) *Cant 9* **P** *Patr Bd* **TR** S IRELAND, **TV** G B GRIFFITHS, **C** L J W DEAN, **NSM** D VAN K VANNERLEY

ST LAWRENCE (Old Church) (St Lawrence) *Portsm 7* **P** *Bp* **P-in-c** A E FAULKNER

ST LAWRENCE (St Lawrence) *see* Bradwell on Sea and St Lawrence *Chelmsf*

ST LEONARD (St Leonard) *see* Hawridge w Cholesbury and St Leonard *Ox*

ST LEONARDS and St Ives (All Saints) *Win 9* **P** *Bp* **V** *vacant* (01425) 476198

ST LEONARDS (Christ Church and St Mary Magdalen) *Chich 17* **P** *Bp and Trustees (jt)* **R** R A JUPP, **C** T F TREGUNNO, **NSM** R G RALPH

ST LEONARDS, UPPER (St John the Evangelist) *Chich* 17
P *Trustees*   R A J PERRY,   NSM P J SAYER
ST LEONARDS-ON-SEA (St Ethelburga) *Chich* 17
P *Hyndman Trustees*   **P-in-c** M J MILLS,   **Hon C** E V WHEELER
ST LEONARDS-ON-SEA (St Leonard) *Chich* 17   P *Hyndman*
Trustees   **P-in-c** M J MILLS,   **Hon C** W D BOULTON,
E V WHEELER
ST LEONARDS-ON-SEA (St Matthew)   *see* Silverhill St Matt
Chich
ST LEONARDS-ON-SEA (St Peter and St Paul) *Chich* 17
P *Bp*   **V** A P-A BROWN
ST LEVAN (St Levan)   *see* St Buryan, St Levan and Sennen
Truro
ST MABYN (St Mabena)   *see* St Tudy w St Mabyn and
Michaelstow *Truro*
ST MARGARET'S (St Margaret)   *see* Clodock and Longtown
w Craswall, Llanveynoe etc *Heref*
ST MARGARETS-AT-CLIFFE (St Margaret of Antioch) w
Westcliffe and East Langdon w West Langdon *Cant* 4   P *Abp*
V *vacant* (01304) 852179
ST MARGARET'S-ON-THAMES (All Souls) *Lon* 11   P *Bp*
P-in-c R S FRANK,   **C** C E C HUDSON
ST MARTHA-ON-THE-HILL (St Martha)   *see* Guildf Ch Ch
w St Martha-on-the-Hill *Guildf*
ST MARTIN (St Martin) w Looe St Nicholas *Truro* 12   P *Bp*
and Revd W M M Picken (jt)   **R** B A MCQUILLEN
ST MARTIN-IN-MENEAGE (St Martin)   *see* Meneage *Truro*
ST MARTIN-IN-THE-FIELDS *Lon* 3   P *Bp*   **V** N R HOLTAM,
C K HEDDERLY, R A CARTER,   **Hon C** D R JACKSON,
NSM A HURST, W H MORRIS
ST MARTIN'S (St Martin)   *see* Is of Scilly *Truro*
ST MARTINS (St Martin) and Weston Rhyn *Lich* 19   P *Bp*
(2 turns), Bp and Lord Trevor (1 turn)   **V** S J JERMY
ST MARY ABBOTS   *see* Kensington St Mary Abbots w Ch Ch
and St Phil *Lon*
ST MARY-AT-LATTON Harlow *Chelmsf* 25
P *J L H Arkwright Esq*   **V** L S HURRY
ST MARY BOURNE (St Peter)   *see* Hurstbourne Priors,
Longparish etc *Win*
ST MARY CRAY and St Paul's (St Paulinus) Cray *Roch* 16
P *Bp*   **V** C W KITCHENER
ST MARY LE STRAND w St Clement Danes *Lon* 3   P *Ld Chan*
and Burley Ho Preservation Trust (alt)   **Hon C** J F A FARRANT
ST MARYCHURCH (St Mary the Virgin) *Ex* 12   P *D&C*
V D LASHBROOKE,   **C** D L BRACEY
ST MARYLEBONE (All Saints) *Lon* 4   P *Bp*   **V** L A MOSES,
C G C BEAUCHAMP
ST MARYLEBONE (All Souls)   *see* Langham Place All So *Lon*
ST MARYLEBONE (Annunciation) Bryanston Street *Lon* 4
P *Bp*   **V** *vacant* (020) 7262 4329
ST MARYLEBONE (St Cyprian) *Lon* 4   P *Bp*
NSM J BROWNING
ST MARYLEBONE (St Mark) Hamilton Terrace *Lon* 4
P *The Crown*   **V** J A BARRIE,   **NSM** R BARRIE
ST MARYLEBONE (St Mark w St Luke)   *see* Bryanston Square
St Mary w St Marylebone St Mark *Lon*
ST MARYLEBONE (St Marylebone) (Holy Trinity) *Lon* 4
P *The Crown*   **R** C R GOWER,   **C** P R THOMAS,
NSM R C D MACKENNA
ST MARYLEBONE (St Paul) *Lon* 4   P *Prime Min*
R G M BUCKLE,   **NSM** M J REDMAN
ST MARYLEBONE (St Peter)   *see* Langham Place All So *Lon*
ST MARY'S (St Mary)   *see* Is of Scilly *Truro*
ST MARY'S BAY (All Saints) w St Mary-in-the-Marsh (St Mary
the Virgin) and Ivychurch *Cant* 12   P *Abp*   **V** *vacant* (01797)
362308
ST MARY'S ISLAND   *see* Gillingham St Mark *Roch*
ST MAWES (St Mawes)   *see* St Just-in-Roseland and St Mawes
Truro
ST MAWGAN (St Mawgan) w St Ervan and St Eval *Truro* 7
P *D&C and Bp (alt)*   **P-in-c** G F SHIELD
ST MAWGAN-IN-MENEAGE (St Mawgan)   *see* Meneage
Truro
ST MELLION (St Melanus)   *see* St Dominic, Landulph and
St Mellion w Pillaton *Truro*
ST MERRYN (St Merryn) and St Issey w St Petroc Minor
Truro 7   P *Bp and Keble Coll Ox (jt)*   **R** J M WILKINSON,
NSM H P SHARP
ST MEWAN (St Mewan) w Mevagissey and St Ewe *Truro* 1
P *Bp, DBP, Penrice Ho (St Austell) Ltd, and*
A M J Galsworthy Esq (jt)   **R** M L BARRETT,   **C** J S HILL,
NSM R H GRIGG
ST MICHAEL PENKEVIL (St Michael) *Truro* 6   P *Viscount*
Falmouth   **P-in-c** A M YATES,   **NSM** A L BUTCHER
ST MICHAEL ROCK (St Michael)   *see* St Minver *Truro*

ST MICHAELCHURCH (St Michael)   *see* Alfred Jewel *B & W*
ST MICHAELS-ON-WYRE (St Michael)   *see* Garstang St
Helen and St Michaels-on-Wyre *Blackb*
ST MINVER (St Menefreda) *Truro* 10   P *DBP*
P-in-c J A C MAY,   **C** J R MOSEDALE,   **NSM** J POLLINGER,
A D E LEWIS
ST NECTAN (St Nectan)   *see* Lostwithiel, St Winnow w
St Nectan's Chpl etc *Truro*
ST NEOT (St Neot) and Warleggan w Cardynham *Truro* 12
P *R G Grylls Esq (2 turns), J Coode Esq (1 turn), and DBP*
(1 turn)   **R** A C R BALFOUR
ST NEOTS (St Mary) *Ely* 13   P *P W Rowley Esq*
P-in-c P D ANDREWS,   **C** S C GOWER
ST NEWLYN EAST (St Newlina)   *see* Newlyn St Newlyn *Truro*
ST NICHOLAS (St Nicholas)   *see* Shaldon, Stokeinteignhead,
Combeinteignhead etc *Ex*
ST NICHOLAS AT WADE (St Nicholas) w Sarre and Chislet w
Hoath *Cant* 7   P *Abp*   **P-in-c** R R COLES,   **Hon**
C P J RICHMOND,   **NSM** R D PLANT,   **OLM** J A BAKER
ST OSWALD IN LEE w Bingfield (St Mary) *Newc* 8   P *Bp*
P-in-c C F BULL
ST OSYTH (St Peter and St Paul) *Chelmsf* 22   P *Bp*   **V** *vacant*
(01255) 820348
ST PANCRAS (Holy Cross) (St Jude) (St Peter) *Lon* 17   P *Bp*
P-in-c C W CAWRSE,   **NSM** R W NORWOOD
ST PANCRAS (Holy Trinity)   *see* Kentish Town St Silas and H
Trin w St Barn *Lon*
ST PANCRAS (Old Church) *Lon* 17   P *Patr Bd*
TR P J NORTH,   **TV** B BATSTONE, J F CASTER,
NSM J I ELSTON, M R DUCKETT
ST PANCRAS (St Martin)   *see* Kentish Town St Martin w
St Andr *Lon*
ST PANCRAS (St Pancras) (St James) (Christ Church) *Lon* 17
P *D&C St Paul's*   **V** P H W HAWKINS,   **C** J L WELSH
ST PAUL'S CRAY (St Barnabas) *Roch* 16   P *CPAS*
V A E DAVIE,   **Hon C** J E RAWLING
ST PAUL'S WALDEN (All Saints) *St Alb* 4   P *D&C St Paul's*
V *vacant* (01438) 871658
ST PETER in the Isle of Thanet (St Peter the Apostle)
(St Andrew) *Cant* 9   P *Abp*   **P-in-c** J W RICHARDSON,
C P P HOBDAY,   **Hon C** M P M STEWART
ST PETER-UPON-CORNHILL   *see* St Pet Cornhill *Lon*
ST PETER'S HOUSE (extra-parochial place) *Man* 1 *vacant*
ST PETROC MINOR (St Petroc)   *see* St Merryn and St Issey w
St Petroc Minor *Truro*
ST PINNOCK (St Pinnock)   *see* Duloe, Herodsfoot, Morval and
St Pinnock *Truro*
ST RUAN w St Grade and Landewednack *Truro* 4   P *CPAS and*
A F Vyvyan-Robinson Esq (jt)   **P-in-c** W COLE
ST SAMPSON (St Sampson) *Truro* 1   P *Bp*
P-in-c P DE GREY-WARTER
ST STEPHEN IN BRANNEL (not known) *Truro* 1   P *Capt*
J D G Fortescue   **P-in-c** E J WESTERMANN-CHILDS
ST STEPHENS (St Stephen)   *see* Saltash *Truro*
ST STYTHIANS w Perranarworthal and Gwennap *Truro* 2
P *Viscount Falmouth (2 turns), D&C (1 turn)*   **V** E J M HOGAN,
NSM H V SPONG,   **OLM** L R T BARTER
ST TEATH (St Teatha) *Truro* 10   P *Bp*   **P-in-c** M J W BENTON-
EVANS,   **Hon C** J S THOROLD,   **NSM** D A ROBERTS
ST TUDY (St Tudy) w St Mabyn and Michaelstow *Truro* 10
P *Ch Ch Ox, Viscount Falmouth, and Duchy of Cornwall*
(by turn)   **P-in-c** M L MILLSON
ST VEEP (St Cyricius)   *see* Lostwithiel, St Winnow w
St Nectan's Chpl etc *Truro*
ST WENN (St Wenna)   *see* St Columb Major w St Wenn *Truro*
ST WEONARDS (St Weonard) *Heref* 8   P *Bp, D&C, and*
M M CET (jt)   **R** E C GODDARD
ST WINNOW (St Winnow)   *see* Lostwithiel, St Winnow w
St Nectan's Chpl etc *Truro*
SAINTBURY (St Nicholas)   *see* Mickleton, Willersey, Saintbury
etc *Glouc*
SALCOMBE (Holy Trinity) and Malborough w South Huish
Ex 14   P *Keble Coll Ox and D&C Sarum (jt)*   **V** D A FRENCH,
C A K HAYE,   **Hon C** E F CULLY
SALCOMBE REGIS (St Mary and St Peter)   *see* Sidmouth,
Woolbrook, Salcombe Regis, Sidbury etc *Ex*
SALCOT VIRLEY (St Mary the Virgin)   *see* Tollesbury w Salcot
Virley *Chelmsf*
SALE (St Anne) (St Francis's Church Hall) *Ches* 10   P *DBP*
V J R HEATON,   **C** J E PARKER
SALE (St Paul) *Ches* 10   P *Trustees*   **V** *vacant* 0161-973 1042
SALE, WEST   *see* Ashton-upon-Mersey St Mary Magd *Ches*
SALEBY (St Margaret) w Beesby and Maltby *Linc* 8   P *Bp and*
DBP (jt)   **R** *vacant*
SALEHURST (St Mary) *Chich* 15   P *Bp*   **V** J A LUSTED

SALESBURY (St Peter) *Blackb 7* **P** *V Blackb*
V J W HARTLEY, **NSM** A A MALCOLM

SALFORD All Saints *Man 6* **P** *Patr Bd* **TR** M N HAWORTH,
TV K M ARCHER, **Hon C** D J H KEYTE,
OLM J I WHITTINGHAM

SALFORD (Sacred Trinity) (St Philip) *Man 6* **P** *D&C Man
and Sir Josslyn Gore-Booth Bt (jt)* **P-in-c** A I SALMON,
NSM R C CRAVEN

SALFORD (St Clement) Ordsall *see* Ordsall and Salford Quays
Man

SALFORD (St Ignatius and Stowell Memorial) *as above*

SALFORD (St Mary) *see* Chipping Norton *Ox*

SALFORD (St Mary) *see* Cranfield and Hulcote w Salford
St Alb

SALFORD (St Paul w Christ Church) *Man 6* **P** *The Crown and
Trustees (alt)* **R** D S C WYATT

SALFORD PRIORS (St Matthew) *Cov 7* **P** *Peache Trustees*
NSM L E DAVIES

SALFORDS (Christ the King) *S'wark 26* **P** *Bp* **V** P KEOWN

SALHOUSE (All Saints) *see* Rackheath and Salhouse *Nor*

SALING, GREAT (St James) *see* Stebbing and Lindsell w Gt
and Lt Saling *Chelmsf*

SALING, LITTLE (St Peter and St Paul) *as above*

SALISBURY (St Francis) and St Lawrence Stratford sub Castle
Sarum 12 **P** *Bp (3 turns), D&C (1 turn)* **V** P F D TAYLOR,
C G A HUNT, V S PERRETT, P A OSTLI-EAST, **NSM** T G MANN

SALISBURY (St Mark) *Sarum 12* **P** *Bp* **P-in-c** J FINDLAY,
C M CASTLETON, **NSM** T A FISHER, D M COATES,
OLM J P OFFER

SALISBURY (St Martin) and Laverstock *Sarum 13* **P** *D&C
and Bp (alt)* **R** K ROBINSON

SALISBURY (St Paul) *see* Fisherton Anger *Sarum*

SALISBURY (St Thomas and St Edmund) *Sarum 12* **P** *Bp and
D&C (alt)* **P-in-c** D J J R LINAKER, **C** M T MCHUGH,
NSM J PLOWS

SALKELD, GREAT (St Cuthbert) *see* Kirkoswald, Renwick,
Gt Salkeld and Lazonby *Carl*

SALLE (St Peter and St Paul) *see* Reepham, Hackford w
Whitwell, Kerdiston etc *Nor*

SALT (St James the Great) *see* Mid Trent *Lich*

SALTASH (St Nicholas and St Faith) *Truro 11* **P** *Patr Bd*
TR A BUTLER, **NSM** P M SELLIX, D BURROWS

SALTBURN-BY-THE-SEA (Emmanuel) *York 16* **P** *Abp, Adn
Cleveland, Marquis of Zetland, Mrs M Brignall, and
Mrs S L Vernon (jt)* **V** G W DONEGAN-CROSS

SALTBY (St Peter) *see* High Framland Par *Leic*

SALTDEAN (St Nicholas) *Chich 2* **P** *Bp*
V G J BUTTERWORTH

SALTER STREET (St Patrick) and Shirley *Birm 6* **P** *Patr Bd*
TR M G B C CADDY, **TV** S J HEIGHT, I M ROBERTSON,
C K E STOWE

SALTERHEBBLE (All Saints) *see* Halifax All SS *Wakef*

SALTERSFORD (St John the Baptist) *see* Rainow w
Saltersford and Forest *Ches*

SALTFLEETBY (St Peter) *Linc 12* **P** *Or Coll Ox, Bp, and
MMCET (jt)* **P-in-c** C M TURNER

**SALTFORD (Blessed Virgin Mary) w Corston and Newton
St Loe** *B & W 10* **P** *DBP (2 turns), Duchy of Cornwall
(1 turn)* **R** G R W HALL, **C** C A SOURBUT

SALTHOUSE (St Nicholas) *see* Weybourne Gp *Nor*

SALTLEY (St Saviour) and Washwood Heath *Birm 13* **P** *Bp
and Trustees (jt)* **NSM** A THOMPSON

SALTNEY FERRY (St Matthew) *see* Lache cum Saltney *Ches*

SALTON (St John of Beverley) *see* Kirby Misperton w
Normanby, Edston and Salton *York*

SALTWOOD (St Peter and St Paul) *Cant 5* **P** *Abp*
P-in-c N COOPER

SALVINGTON (St Peter) *see* Durrington *Chich*

SALWARPE (St Michael) and Hindlip w Martin Hussingtree
Worc 8 **P** *Bp, D&C, and Exors Lady Hindlip (by turn)*
R *vacant* (01905) 778757

SALWAY ASH (Holy Trinity) *see* Beaminster Area *Sarum*

SAMBOURNE (Mission Church) *see* Coughton *Cov*

SAMBROOK (St Luke) *see* Cheswardine, Childs Ercall, Hales,
Hinstock etc *Lich*

SAMFORD, NORTH *see* Sproughton w Burstall, Copdock w
Washbrook etc *St E*

SAMLESBURY (St Leonard the Less) *see* Walton-le-Dale
St Leon w Samlesbury St Leon *Blackb*

SAMPFORD, GREAT (St Michael) *see* The Sampfords and
Radwinter w Hempstead *Chelmsf*

SAMPFORD, LITTLE (St Mary) *as above*

SAMPFORD ARUNDEL (Holy Cross) *see* Wellington and
Distr *B & W*

SAMPFORD BRETT (St George) *see* Quantock Towers *B & W*

SAMPFORD COURTENAY (St Andrew) *see* N Tawton,
Bondleigh, Sampford Courtenay etc *Ex*

**SAMPFORD PEVERELL (St John the Baptist), Uplowman,
Holcombe Rogus, Hockworthy, Burlescombe, Huntsham and
Halberton w Ash Thomas** *Ex 4* **P** *Patr Bd* **TV** K G GALE,
C R J CLOETE

SAMPFORD SPINEY (St Mary) w Horrabridge *Ex 25*
P *D&C Windsor* **P-in-c** W G LLOYD

**SAMPFORDS, The (St Michael) (St Mary) and Radwinter with
Hempstead** *Chelmsf 21* **P** *Guild of All So, New Coll Ox, and
Keble Coll Ox (jt)* **P-in-c** G M MANN

SANCREED (St Creden) *Truro 5* **P** *D&C* **V** S W LEACH

SANCTON (All Saints) *York 5* **P** *Abp* **V** L C MUNT

SAND HILL (Church of the Good Shepherd) *see* N
Farnborough *Guildf*

SAND HUTTON (St Leonard) *see* Thirsk *York*

SAND HUTTON (St Mary) *York 6* **P** *Abp and D&C Dur (jt)*
P-in-c I R HOWITT

SANDAL (St Catherine) *Wakef 11* **P** *V Sandal Magna*
V *vacant* (01924) 211176

SANDAL MAGNA (St Helen) *Wakef 11* **P** *Peache Trustees*
V R G MARTIN

SANDBACH (St Mary) *Ches 11* **P** *DBP* **V** T SHEPHERD

SANDBACH HEATH (St John the Evangelist) w Wheelock
Ches 11 **P** *V Sandbach* **V** J A BACON

SANDBANKS (St Nicolas) *see* Canford Cliffs and Sandbanks
Sarum

**SANDERSTEAD (All Saints) (St Antony) (St Edmund the King
and Martyr) (St Mary)** *S'wark 22* **P** *Bp* **TR** S BUTLER,
TV J F PERCIVAL, S F ATKINSON-JONES, **C** A M WATSON

SANDFORD (All Saints) *see* Winscombe and Sandford *B & W*

SANDFORD (St Martin) *see* Westcombe Barton w Steeple
Barton, Duns Tew etc *Ox*

SANDFORD (St Martin) *see* Wareham *Sarum*

SANDFORD (St Swithin) *see* Crediton, Shobrooke and
Sandford etc *Ex*

SANDFORD-ON-THAMES (St Andrew) *Ox 4* **P** *DBP*
P-in-c R C MORGAN

SANDFORD ORCAS (St Nicholas) *see* Queen Thorne *Sarum*

SANDGATE (St Paul) *see* Folkestone Trin *Cant*

SANDHURST (St Lawrence) *see* Twigworth, Down Hatherley,
Norton, The Leigh etc *Glouc*

SANDHURST (St Michael and All Angels) *Ox 16* **P** *Bp*
P-in-c J A CASTLE, **NSM** J W WHITE

SANDHURST (St Nicholas) (Mission Church) w Newenden
Cant 16 **P** *Abp* **P-in-c** C B HILL, **NSM** R M VAN WENGEN

SANDHURST, LOWER (St Mary) *see* Sandhurst *Ox*

SANDIACRE (St Giles) *Derby 13* **P** *Ld Chan*
R W B COONEY, **NSM** K W G JOHNSON

SANDIWAY (St John the Evangelist) *Ches 6* **P** *Bp* **V** M B COX

SANDLEHEATH (St Aldhelm) *see* Fordingbridge and
Breamore and Hale etc *Win*

SANDON (All Saints) *see* Mid Trent *Lich*

SANDON (All Saints), Wallington and Rushden w Clothall
St Alb 19 **P** *Duchy of Lanc (1 turn), Marquess of Salisbury
(1 turn), and Bp (2 turns)* **R** *vacant* (01763) 287256

SANDON (St Andrew) *Chelmsf 9* **P** *Qu Coll Cam*
P-in-c P PENNELL

SANDOWN (Christ Church) *Portsm 7* **P** *Ch Patr Trust*
P-in-c C M FEAK, **NSM** C C ETHERTON, T B RICHARDS

SANDOWN, LOWER (St John the Evangelist) *Portsm 7* **P** *Bp*
P-in-c C M FEAK, **NSM** C C ETHERTON, T B RICHARDS

SANDRIDGE (St Leonard) *St Alb 8* **P** *Earl Spencer*
P-in-c V G CATON, **NSM** J F HILLIER

**SANDRINGHAM (St Mary Magdalene) w West Newton and
Appleton, Wolferton w Babingley and Flitcham** *Nor 16*
P *The Crown* **R** J B V RIVIERE

SANDS (Church of the Good Shepherd) *see* Seale, Puttenham
and Wanborough *Guildf*

SANDS (St Mary and St George) *see* High Wycombe *Ox*

SANDSEND (St Mary) *see* Hinderwell, Roxby and Staithes etc
York

SANDSFIELD *see* Carl H Trin and St Barn *Carl*

SANDWELL (St Philip) *see* W Bromwich St Phil *Lich*

SANDWICH (St Clement) *Cant 8* **P** *Adn Cant*
R J M A ROBERTS, **NSM** J C ROBERTS, **OLM** H T PASHLEY

SANDY (St Swithun) *St Alb 11* **P** *Lord Pym* **R** D G WILLIAMS,
C J MACKENZIE

SANDY LANE (St Mary and St Nicholas) *see* Rowde and
Bromham *Sarum*

SANDYLANDS (St John) *Blackb 11* **P** *Bp* **V** *vacant* (01524)
411299

SANKEY, GREAT (St Mary) *Liv 12* **P** *Lord Lilford*
V M BUCKLEY

SANTAN (St Sanctain) *S & M 1* **P** *The Crown*
V P C ROBINSON

SANTON DOWNHAM (St Mary the Virgin) *see* Brandon and Santon Downham w Elveden etc *St E*

SAPCOTE (All Saints) and Sharnford w Wigston Parva *Leic 10* **P** *Ld Chan and DBP (alt)* **R** M J NORMAN

SAPEY, UPPER (St Michael) *see* Edvin Loach w Tedstone Delamere etc *Heref*

SAPPERTON (St Kenelm) *see* Kemble, Poole Keynes, Somerford Keynes etc *Glouc*

SAPPERTON (St Nicholas) *see* N Beltisloe Gp *Linc*

SARISBURY (St Paul) *Portsm 2* **P** *V Titchfield* **V** A J MATHESON

SARK (St Peter) *Win 14* **P** *Le Seigneur de Sercq* **P-in-c** K P MELLOR, **C** G L LEWORTHY

SARN (Holy Trinity) *see* Churchstoke w Hyssington and Sarn *Heref*

SARNESFIELD (St Mary) *see* Weobley w Sarnesfield and Norton Canon *Heref*

SARRATT (Holy Cross) and Chipperfield *St Alb 5* **P** *Churchwardens and DBP (jt)* **R** J A STEVENS

SATLEY (St Cuthbert), Stanley and Tow Law *Dur 9* **P** *Bp, Ld Chan, and R Brancepeth (by turn)* **P-in-c** J P L WHALLEY, **Hon C** G H LAWES

SATTERTHWAITE (All Saints) *see* Hawkshead and Low Wray w Sawrey and Rusland etc *Carl*

SAUGHALL, GREAT (All Saints) *Ches 9* **P** *Bp* **P-in-c** J B HARRIS

SAUL (St James the Great) *see* Frampton on Severn, Arlingham, Saul etc *Glouc*

SAUNDERTON (St Mary and St Nicholas) *see* Risborough *Ox*

SAUNTON (St Anne) *see* Braunton *Ex*

SAUSTHORPE (St Andrew) *see* Partney Gp *Linc*

SAVERNAKE (St Katharine) *Sarum 19* **P** *Patr Bd* **TR** N A LEIGH-HUNT, **TV** M EDWARDS, R L N HARRISON, **NSM** A J DEBOO

SAW MILLS (St Mary) *see* Ambergate and Heage *Derby*

SAWBRIDGEWORTH (Great St Mary) *St Alb 18* **P** *Bp* **V** R F SIBSON, **C** R W WYNFORD-HARRIS

SAWLEY (All Saints) (St Mary) *Derby 13* **P** *D&C Lich* **P-in-c** A C M PETTY, **C** C E MCDONALD

SAWLEY (St Michael) *see* Fountains Gp *Ripon*

SAWREY (St Peter) *see* Hawkshead and Low Wray w Sawrey and Rusland etc *Carl*

SAWSTON (St Mary) *Ely 5* **P** *SMF* **P-in-c** A C PARTRIDGE

SAWTRY (All Saints) and Glatton *Ely 15* **P** *Duke of Devonshire* **R** P M GRIFFITH, **NSM** S GRIFFITH

SAXBY (St Helen) *see* Owmby Gp *Linc*

SAXBY ALL SAINTS (All Saints) *Linc 6* **P** F C H H Barton Esq **R** vacant (01652) 618747

SAXELBYE (St Peter) *see* Old Dalby, Nether Broughton, Saxelbye etc *Leic*

SAXHAM, GREAT (St Andrew) *see* Barrow *St E*

SAXHAM, LITTLE (St Nicholas) *as above*

SAXILBY Group, The (St Botolph) *Linc 2* **P** *Bp and DBP (jt)* **R** R PROSSER, **C** M BRISCOE, **NSM** S PROSSER

SAXLINGHAM (St Margaret) *see* Stiffkey and Bale *Nor*

SAXLINGHAM NETHERGATE (St Mary) *see* Newton Flotman, Swainsthorpe, Tasburgh, etc *Nor*

SAXMUNDHAM (St John the Baptist) w Kelsale cum Carlton *St E 19* **P** *Patr Bd* **R** R F WEBB, **C** C J RAMSEY, **NSM** B L WEBB

SAXON SHORE *see* Hunstanton St Mary w Ringstead Parva etc *Nor*

SAXONWELL *Linc 23* **P** *Duchy of Lanc (2 turns), Ld Chan (1 turn)* **P-in-c** M E MASSEY

SAXTEAD (All Saints) *see* Framlingham w Saxtead *St E*

SAXTHORPE (St Andrew) *see* Lt Barningham, Blickling, Edgefield etc *Nor*

SAXTON (All Saints) *see* Sherburn in Elmet w Saxton *York*

SAYERS COMMON (Christ Church) *see* Albourne w Sayers Common and Twineham *Chich*

SCALBY (St Laurence) *York 15* **P** *Abp* **P-in-c** A J FERNELEY, **NSM** M J WRIGHT, D C PYNN

SCALDWELL (St Peter and St Paul) *see* Walgrave w Hannington and Wold and Scaldwell *Pet*

SCALEBY (All Saints) *see* Eden, Gelt and Irthing *Carl*

SCALFORD (St Egelwin) *see* Ironstone Villages *Leic*

SCAMMONDEN, WEST (St Bartholomew) *see* Barkisland w W Scammonden *Wakef*

SCAMPSTON (St Martin) *see* Buckrose Carrs *York*

SCAMPTON (St John the Baptist) *see* Spring Line Gp *Linc*

SCARBOROUGH (St Columba) *York 15* **P** *Abp* **P-in-c** K D JACKSON

SCARBOROUGH (St James w Holy Trinity) *York 15* **P** *Abp and CPAS (jt)* **P-in-c** P W WHITE, **NSM** L M HOLLIS

SCARBOROUGH (St Luke) *York 15* **P** *Abp* **P-in-c** A J FERNELEY, **NSM** D C PYNN

SCARBOROUGH (St Mark) *see* Newby *York*

SCARBOROUGH (St Martin) *York 15* **P** *Trustees* **V** A J MILLS, **C** R K DUERR, **NSM** R G C COSTIN

SCARBOROUGH (St Mary) w Christ Church and (Holy Apostles) *York 15* **P** *Abp* **V** M P DUNNING, **C** S WHITING, **NSM** P JENNINGS

SCARBOROUGH (St Saviour w All Saints) *York 15* **P** *Abp* **V** A J MILLS, **C** R K DUERR

SCARCLIFFE (St Leonard) *see* Ault Hucknall and Scarcliffe *Derby*

SCARISBRICK (St Mark) (Good Shepherd) *Liv 11* **P** *V Ormskirk* **V** vacant (01704) 880317

SCARLE, NORTH (All Saints) *see* Swinderby *Linc*

SCARLE, SOUTH (St Helena) *see* Collingham w S Scarle and Besthorpe and Girton *S'well*

SCARNING (St Peter and St Paul) *see* Dereham and Distr *Nor*

SCARRINGTON (St John of Beverley) *see* Whatton w Aslockton, Hawksworth, Scarrington etc *S'well*

SCARSDALE, EAST *Derby 3* **P** *Patr Bd* **TR** J W HARGREAVES, **TV** B DALE

SCARTHO (St Giles) St Matthew *Linc 9* **P** *Jes Coll Ox* **R** E J R MARTIN

SCAWBY (St Hibald), Redbourne and Hibaldstow *Linc 6* **P** *T M S Nelthorpe Esq (2 turns), Bp (1 turn), and Duke of St Alb (1 turn)* **V** C H LILLEY, **C** P L COSTIN

SCAWTHORPE (St Luke) *see* Doncaster St Leon and St Jude *Sheff*

SCAWTON (St Mary) *see* Upper Ryedale *York*

SCAYNES HILL (St Augustine) *Chich 6* **P** *Bp* **P-in-c** M J T PAYNE

SCHOLES (St Philip) *see* Barwick in Elmet *Ripon*

SCHOLES (St Philip and St James) *Wakef 8* **P** *Bp* **NSM** R M CAVE

SCHORNE *Ox 24* **P** *Patr Bd (2 turns), Ld Chan (1 turn)* **TV** A T BELL, **P-in-c** D J MEAKIN, **C** P J MANSELL, **Hon C** P D MEARS, **NSM** E A WELTERS, **OLM** J BAYLY

SCILLY *see* Is of Scilly *Truro*

SCISSETT (St Augustine) *see* High Hoyland, Scissett and Clayton W *Wakef*

SCOFTON (St John the Evangelist) *see* Babworth w Sutton-cum-Lound and Scofton etc *S'well*

SCOLE (St Andrew) w Brockdish, Billingford, Thorpe Abbots and Thorpe Parva *Nor 10* **P** *Bp, Ex Coll Ox, MMCET, Adn Norfolk, and Exors Lady Mann (jt)* **P-in-c** T W RIESS

SCOPWICK (Holy Cross) *see* Digby Gp *Linc*

SCORBOROUGH (St Leonard) *see* Lockington and Lund and Scorborough w Leconfield *York*

SCORTON (St Peter) and Barnacre All Saints and Calder Vale St John the Evangelist *Blackb 9* **P** *Bp, V Lanc St Mary w St Jo and St Anne, and Mrs V O Shepherd-Cross (jt)* **Hon C** D V A BROWN

SCOT WILLOUGHBY (St Andrew) *see* S Lafford *Linc*

SCOTBY (All Saints) and Cotehill w Cumwhinton *Carl 2* **P** *Trustees (2 turns), Prime Min (1 turn)* **V** G M CREGEEN, **C** T D HERBERT, **NSM** S HOLMES

SCOTFORTH (St Paul) *Blackb 11* **P** *The Rt Revd J Nicholls* **V** M G SMITH, **C** O TRELENBERG

SCOTHERN (St Germain) *see* Welton and Dunholme w Scothern *Linc*

SCOTSWOOD (St Margaret) *Newc 4* **P** *Bp* **P-in-c** C H KNIGHTS

SCOTTER (St Peter) w East Ferry *Linc 4* **P** *Bp* **R** vacant (01724) 762951

SCOTTON (St Genewys) w Northorpe *Linc 4* **P** *Ld Chan* **P-in-c** M E BURSON-THOMAS, **OLM** W KEAST, D L LANGFORD

SCOTTON (St Thomas) *see* Walkingham Hill *Ripon*

SCOTTOW (All Saints) *see* Worstead, Westwick, Sloley, Swanton Abbot etc *Nor*

SCOULTON (Holy Trinity) *see* High Oak, Hingham and Scoulton w Wood Rising *Nor*

SCRAMBLESBY (St Martin) *see* Asterby Gp *Linc*

SCRAPTOFT (All Saints) *Leic 1* **P** *Bp, Dr M J A Sharp, and DBP (jt)* **V** M J COURT, **NSM** A J POOLE

SCRAYINGHAM (St Peter and St Paul) *see* Stamford Bridge Gp *York*

SCREDINGTON (St Andrew) *see* Helpringham w Hale *Linc*

SCREMBY (St Peter and St Paul) *see* Partney Gp *Linc*

SCREMERSTON (St Peter) *Newc 12* **P** *Bp* **NSM** S J HARRISON

SCREVETON (St Wilfrid) *see* Car Colston w Screveton *S'well*

SCRIVELSBY (St Benedict) *see* Fen and Hill Gp *Linc*

SCROOBY (St Wilfrid) *see* Blyth and Scrooby w Ranskill *S'well*

SCROPTON (St Paul) *see* Doveridge, Scropton, Sudbury etc *Derby*

SCRUTON (St Radegund) *see* Lower Swale *Ripon*

SCULCOATES (St Mary)   *see* Hull St Mary Sculcoates *York*
SCULCOATES (St Paul) (St Stephen) *York* 14   **P** *Abp and V Hull H Trin (1 turn), Ld Chan (1 turn)*   **V** *vacant* (01482) 224370
SCULTHORPE (St Mary and All Saints)   *see* N and S Creake w Waterden, Syderstone etc *Nor*
SCUNTHORPE (All Saints)   *see* Brumby *Linc*
SCUNTHORPE (The Resurrection)   *see* Trentside E *Linc*
SEA MILLS (St Edyth) *Bris* 2   **P** *Bp*   **V** D A IZZARD, **NSM** E BEBB
SEA PALLING (St Margaret)   *see* Bacton, Happisburgh, Hempstead w Eccles etc *Nor*
SEA VIEW (St Peter) *Portsm* 7   **P** *Bp*   **V** M M STRANGE
SEABOROUGH (St John)   *see* Beaminster Area *Sarum*
SEABROOK (Mission Hall)   *see* Cheriton St Martin *Cant*
SEACOMBE (St Paul) *Ches* 7   **P** *Trustees*   **P-in-c** I HUGHES
SEACROFT (St James) (Church of the Ascension) (St Richard) *Ripon* 8   **P** *DBF*   **TR** M P BENWELL,   **TV** T M TUNLEY, C BANDAWE, C MACLAREN, R H JAMIESON,   **C** A J MARTIN
SEAFORD (St Leonard) w Sutton *Chich* 18   **P** *Ld Chan*   **V** C H ATHERSTONE,   **C** M E C TALBOT, M A BLEWETT, C DOHERTY
SEAFORTH (St Thomas)   *see* Bootle *Liv*
SEAGRAVE (All Saints)   *see* Sileby, Cossington and Seagrave *Leic*
SEAGRY (St Mary the Virgin)   *see* Gt Somerford, Lt Somerford, Seagry, Corston etc *Bris*
SEAHAM (St Mary the Virgin) *Dur* 2   **P** *Bp*   **V** *vacant* 0191-581 3385
SEAHAM, NEW (Christ Church)   *see* Dalton le Dale and New Seaham *Dur*
SEAHAM HARBOUR (St John) and Dawdon *Dur* 2   **P** *Bp*   **V** P TWISLETON
SEAL (St Lawrence) *Roch* 9   **P** *Bp*   **P-in-c** M D COOKE
SEAL (St Peter and St Paul) *Roch* 9   **P** *DBP*   **P-in-c** J A LE BAS
SEALE (St Lawrence), Puttenham and Wanborough *Guildf* 4   **P** *Adn Surrey, C R I Perkins Esq, and Ld Chan (by turn)*   **P-in-c** R E WOOD
SEALE (St Peter) (St Matthew) and Lullington w Coton in the Elms *Derby* 16   **P** *Bp, R D Nielson Esq, and C W Worthington Esq (jt)*   **P-in-c** M A YATES
SEAMER (St Martin) w East Ayton *York* 15   **P** *Abp*   **V** L J MCWILLIAMS,   **NSM** S R DRURY
SEAMER IN CLEVELAND (St Martin)   *see* Stokesley w Seamer *York*
SEARBY (St Nicholas)   *see* Caistor Gp *Linc*
SEASALTER (St Alphege)   *see* Whitstable *Cant*
SEASCALE (St Cuthbert) and Drigg *Carl* 5   **P** *DBP*   **P-in-c** J WOOLCOCK
SEATHWAITE (Holy Trinity)   *see* Broughton and Duddon *Carl*
SEATON (All Hallows)   *see* Lyddington w Stoke Dry and Seaton etc *Pet*
SEATON (St Gregory) and Beer *Ex* 5   **P** *Lord Clinton and D&C (jt)*   **V** J C TREW
SEATON (St Paul)   *see* Camerton, Seaton and W Seaton *Carl*
SEATON, WEST (Holy Trinity)   *as above*
SEATON CAREW (Holy Trinity) *Dur* 3   **P** *Bp*   **P-in-c** P T ALLINSON
SEATON HIRST (St John) (St Andrew) *Newc* 11   **P** *Bp*   **R** D P PALMER
SEATON ROSS (St Edmund)   *see* Holme and Seaton Ross Gp *York*
SEATON SLUICE (St Paul)   *see* Delaval *Newc*
SEAVIEW   *see* Sea View *Portsm*
SEAVINGTON (St Michael and St Mary)   *see* S Petherton w the Seavingtons *B & W*
SEBERGHAM (St Mary)   *see* Caldbeck, Castle Sowerby and Sebergham *Carl*
SECKINGTON (All Saints)   *see* N Warks *Birm*
SEDBERGH (St Andrew), Cautley and Garsdale *Bradf* 6   **P** *Trin Coll Cam*   **V** A W FELL,   **NSM** V J HOPKINS
SEDGEBERROW (St Mary the Virgin)   *see* Hampton w Sedgeberrow and Hinton-on-the-Green *Worc*
SEDGEBROOK (St Lawrence)   *see* Saxonwell *Linc*
SEDGEFIELD (St Edmund)   *see* Upper Skerne *Dur*
SEDGEHILL (St Katherine)   *see* St Bartholomew *Sarum*
SEDGEFORD (St Mary)   *see* Docking, the Birchams, Stanhoe and Sedgeford *Nor*
SEDGLEY (All Saints)   *see* Gornal and Sedgley *Worc*
SEDGLEY (St Mary the Virgin) *Worc* 10   **P** *Bp and V Sedgley All SS (jt)*   **T** WESTWOOD
SEDLESCOMBE (St John the Baptist) w Whatlington *Chich* 14   **P** *Ld Chan and Bp (alt)*   **P-in-c** A B SHARPE
SEEND (Holy Cross), Bulkington and Poulshot *Sarum* 16   **P** *D&C (2 turns), Bp (1 turn)*   **V** *vacant* (01380) 828615

SEER GREEN (Holy Trinity) and Jordans *Ox* 20   **P** *Bp*   **P-in-c** G M HOCKEY
SEETHING (St Margaret)   *see* Brooke, Kirstead, Mundham w Seething and Thwaite *Nor*
SEFTON (St Helen) and Thornton *Liv* 5   **P** *Bp*   **R** I C COWELL, **OLM** E M HALBERT
SEFTON PARK (Christ Church)   *see* Toxteth Park Ch Ch and St Mich w St Andr *Liv*
SEGHILL (Holy Trinity) *Newc* 1   **P** *The Crown*   **V** P G J HUGHES
SEIGHFORD (St Chad)   *see* Chebsey, Creswell, Ellenhall, Ranton etc *Lich*
SELATTYN (St Mary) and Hengoed w Gobowen *Lich* 19   **P** *Bp and Mrs A F Hamilton-Hill (jt)*   **P-in-c** A R BAILEY
SELBORNE (St Mary)   *see* Northanger *Win*
SELBY (St James the Apostle) *York* 4   **P** *Simeon's Trustees*   **V** C J REID
SELBY ABBEY (St Mary and St Germain) (St Richard) *York* 4   **P** *Abp*   **V** K D RICHARDS,   **NSM** R N WAINWRIGHT
SELHAM (St James)   *see* Lurgashall, Lodsworth and Selham *Chich*
SELLACK (St Tysilio)   *see* Wormelow Hundred *Heref*
SELLINDGE (St Mary the Virgin)   *see* Mersham w Hinxhill and Sellindge *Cant*
SELLING (St Mary the Virgin) w Throwley and Sheldwich w Badlesmere and Leaveland *Cant* 6   **P** *Abp and D&C (jt)*   **P-in-c** M G WEBB,   **NSM** M JOHNSON, D S WEBB
SELLY OAK (St Mary) *Birm* 2   **P** *Bp*   **NSM** S A IZZARD
SELLY PARK (Christ Church) *Birm* 5   **P** *Trustees*   **V** G P LANHAM
SELLY PARK (St Stephen) (St Wulstan) *Birm* 5   **P** *Trustees*   **V** C B HOBBS,   **C** A A UNDERWOOD
SELMESTON (St Mary)   *see* Berwick w Selmeston and Alciston *Chich*
SELSDON (St Francis) Conventional District *S'wark* 20   **Min** S L FENBY,   **NSM** A ONYEKWELU
SELSDON (St John) (St Francis) *S'wark* 19   **P** *Bp*   **R** I S BROTHWOOD,   **NSM** A M S DOVEY
SELSEY (St Peter) *Chich* 3   **P** *Bp*   **R** J C T HARRINGTON
SELSIDE (St Thomas)   *see* Beacon *Carl*
SELSLEY (All Saints)   *see* Cainscross w Selsley *Glouc*
SELSTON (St Helen) *S'well* 4   **P** *Wright Trustees*   **P-in-c** M F SHOULER
SELWORTHY (All Saints)   *see* Porlock and Porlock Weir w Stoke Pero etc *B & W*
SELWORTHY (Lynch Chapel)   *as above*
SEMER (All Saints)   *see* Bildeston w Wattisham and Lindsey, Whatfield etc *St E*
SEMINGTON (St George)   *see* Canalside Benefice *Sarum*
SEMLEY (St Leonard)   *see* St Bartholomew *Sarum*
SEMPRINGHAM (St Andrew)   *see* Billingborough Gp *Linc*
SEND (St Mary the Virgin) *Guildf* 12   **P** *Bp*   **P-in-c** A J SHUTT
SENNEN (St Sennen)   *see* St Buryan, St Levan and Sennen *Truro*
SENNICOTTS (St Mary)   *see* Funtington and Sennicotts *Chich*
SESSAY (St Cuthbert) *York* 19   **P** *Viscountess Downe*   **P-in-c** N J CARNALL
SETCHEY (St Mary)   *see* W Winch w Setchey, N Runcton and Middleton *Nor*
SETMURTHY (St Barnabas)   *see* Binsey *Carl*
SETTLE (Holy Ascension) *Bradf* 5   **P** *Trustees*   **P-in-c** N S KENDRA
SETTRINGTON (All Saints)   *see* W Buckrose *York*
SEVEN KINGS   *see* Gt Ilford St Jo *Chelmsf*
SEVENHAMPTON (St Andrew) w Charlton Abbots, Hawling and Whittington, Dowdeswell and Andoversford w The Shiptons and Cold Salperton, and Withington *Glouc* 11   **P** *Bp, MMCET, T W Bailey Esq, E M Bailey Esq, and Mrs J A Stringer (1 turn); Bp, MMCET, and Mrs L E Evans (1 turn)*   **P-in-c** J A BECKETT, **C** A D LOMAS
SEVENHAMPTON (St James)   *see* Highworth w Sevenhampton and Inglesham etc *Bris*
SEVENOAKS (St John the Baptist) *Roch* 9   **P** *Guild of All So*   **V** I D AQUILINA,   **C** M R NORTH
SEVENOAKS (St Luke) *Roch* 9   **P** *Bp*   **V** M R GRIFFIN
SEVENOAKS (St Nicholas) *Roch* 9   **P** *Trustees*   **R** A M MACLEAY,   **C** M ODEN, A D MCCLELLAN, **Hon C** N N HENSHAW, J M DENT
SEVENOAKS WEALD (St George) *Roch* 9   **P** *R Sevenoaks*   **P-in-c** S L WILLOUGHBY
SEVERN BEACH (St Nicholas)   *see* Pilning w Compton Greenfield *Bris*
SEVERN STOKE (St Dennis)   *see* Kempsey and Severn Stoke w Croome d'Abitot *Worc*
SEVERNSIDE Group of Parishes, The   *see* Frampton on Severn, Arlingham, Saul etc *Glouc*

SEVINGTON (St Mary) *Cant 10*   **P** *Ch Soc Trust*
P-in-c J C N MACKENZIE
SEWARDS END (not known)   *see* Saffron Walden w Wendens
Ambo, Littlebury etc *Chelmsf*
SEWERBY (St John)   *see* Bridlington H Trin and Sewerby w
Marton *York*
SEWSTERN (Holy Trinity)   *see* S Framland *Leic*
SHABBINGTON (St Mary Magdalene)   *see* Worminghall w
Ickford, Oakley and Shabbington *Ox*
SHACKERSTONE (St Peter)   *see* Nailstone and Carlton w
Shackerstone *Leic*
SHACKLEFORD (St Mary the Virgin)   *see* Compton w
Shackleford and Peper Harow *Guildf*
SHADFORTH (St Cuthbert)   *see* Shadforth and Sherburn *Dur*
SHADFORTH (St Cuthbert) and Sherburn *Dur 1*   **P** *D&C*
P-in-c A B BARTLETT,   **NSM** E TARREN, D J WILSON, M THRUSH
SHADINGFIELD (St John the Baptist)   *see* Hundred River
St E
SHADOXHURST (St Peter and St Paul)   *see* Kingsnorth and
Shadoxhurst *Cant*
SHADWELL (St Paul) *Ripon 5*   **P** *V Thorner*   **V** *vacant*
0113-273 7035
SHADWELL (St Paul) w Ratcliffe St James *Lon 7*   **P** *Bp*
P-in-c R C THORPE,   **C** A ATKINSON, E J DIX
SHAFTESBURY (St James)   *see* Shaston *Sarum*
SHAFTESBURY (St Peter)   *as above*
SHAFTON (St Hugh)   *see* Felkirk *Wakef*
SHALBOURNE (St Michael and All Angels)   *see* Savernake
Sarum
SHALDEN (St Peter and St Paul)   *see* Bentworth, Lasham,
Medstead and Shalden *Win*
SHALDON (St Nicholas) (St Peter), Stokeinteignhead,
Combeinteignhead and Haccombe *Ex 10*   **P** *SMF and*
Sir Rivers Carew Bt (jt)   **R** G S RICHARDSON,
C A N WOODASON
SHALFLEET (St Michael the Archangel) *Portsm 8*   **P** *Ld Chan*
V D J BEVINGTON,   **NSM** M O´DONNELL, J C LEACH
SHALFORD (St Andrew)   *see* Finchingfield and Cornish Hall
End etc *Chelmsf*
SHALFORD (St Mary the Virgin) *Guildf 5*   **P** *Ld Chan*
V J J CRUSE
SHALSTONE (St Edward the Confessor)   *see* W Buckingham
Ox
SHAMLEY GREEN (Christ Church) *Guildf 2*   **P** *Bp*
P-in-c S J DAVIES,   **NSM** R J HEYES
SHANGTON (St Nicholas)   *see* Church Langton cum Tur
Langton etc *Leic*
SHANKLIN (St Blasius) *Portsm 7*   **P** *Bp*
P-in-c A W SWANBOROUGH
SHANKLIN (St Paul)   *see* Gatten St Paul *Portsm*
SHANKLIN (St Saviour on the Cliff) *Portsm 7*   **P** *Bp*
P-in-c J H DAVIES
SHAP (St Michael) w Swindale and Bampton w Mardale *Carl 1*
P *Earl of Lonsdale*   **P-in-c** B LOCK,   **NSM** M J DEW
SHAPWICK (Blessed Virgin Mary) w Ashcott and Burtle
B & W 5   **P** *Lord Vestey (2 turns), Bp (1 turn)*
P-in-c P A OLLIVE
SHAPWICK (St Bartholomew)   *see* Bridge Par *Sarum*
SHARD END (All Saints) *Birm 9*   **P** *Keble Coll Ox*
P-in-c A J CLUCAS
SHARDLOW (St James)   *see* Aston on Trent, Elvaston, Weston
on Trent etc *Derby*
SHARESHILL (St Luke and St Mary the Virgin) *Lich 2*   **P** *Bp*
Hon C R J BELLAMY
SHARLSTON (St Luke) *Wakef 11*   **P** *Bp*   **P-in-c** P A BOSTOCK
SHARNBROOK (St Peter), Felmersham and Knotting w
Souldrop *St Alb 15*   **P** *Bp*   **R** R A EVENS,   **NSM** D G MASON
SHARNFORD (St Helen)   *see* Sapcote and Sharnford w
Wigston Parva *Leic*
SHAROW (St John the Evangelist)   *see* Ripon Cathl *Ripon*
SHARPNESS (St Andrew), Purton, Brookend and Slimbridge
Glouc 6   **P** *Magd Coll Ox and Bp (alt)*   **R** W J BOON,
NSM J A D´ESTERRE, G M TUCKER
SHARRINGTON (All Saints)   *see* Stiffkey and Bale *Nor*
SHARROW (St Andrew)   *see* Psalter Lane St Andr *Sheff*
SHASTON *Sarum 5*   **P** *Patr Bd*   **TV** A C HEYWOOD,
C A THOMAS,   **C** J MORTON,   **NSM** M E HARDING
SHAUGH PRIOR (St Edward)   *see* Bickleigh and Shaugh Prior
Ex
SHAVINGTON (St Mark)   *see* Weston *Ches*
SHAW (Christchurch)   *see* Atworth w Shaw and Whitley *Sarum*
SHAW (Holy Trinity)   *see* W Swindon and the Lydiards *Bris*
SHAW (Holy Trinity) *Man 20*   **P** *R Prestwich St Mary*
V *vacant* (01706) 847369
SHAW (St Mary) cum Donnington *Ox 14*   **P** *DBP*
R M DROBIG,   **NSM** E K FORBES STONE

SHAWBURY (St Mary the Virgin) *Lich 22*   **P** *C C Corbet Esq*
V D J HUMPHRIES
SHAWELL (All Saints)   *see* Gilmorton, Peatling Parva, Kimcote
etc *Leic*
SHEARSBY (St Mary Magdalene)   *see* Hexagon *Leic*
SHEBBEAR (St Michael), Buckland Filleigh, Sheepwash,
Langtree, Newton St Petrock, Petrockstowe, Petersmarland,
Merton and Huish *Ex 20*   **P** *Ld Chan (1 turn), Patr Bd*
(2 turns)   **P-in-c** M J WARREN
SHEDFIELD (St John the Baptist) and Wickham *Portsm 1*
P *DBP and Sir Richard Rashleigh Bt (jt)*   **R** B G DEANS,
NSM B R MCHUGH, E A GROVES
SHEEN (St Luke)   *see* Longnor, Quarnford and Sheen *Lich*
SHEEN, EAST (All Saints)   *see* Mortlake w E Sheen *S'wark*
SHEEN, EAST (Christ Church)   *as above*
SHEEPSCOMBE (St John the Evangelist)   *see* Painswick,
Sheepscombe, Cranham, The Edge etc *Glouc*
SHEEPSTOR (St Leonard)   *see* Yelverton, Meavy, Sheepstor
and Walkhampton *Ex*
SHEEPWASH (St Lawrence)   *see* Shebbear, Buckland Filleigh,
Sheepwash etc *Ex*
SHEEPY (All Saints)   *see* Bosworth and Sheepy Gp *Leic*
SHEERING (St Mary the Virgin)   *see* Hatfield Heath and
Sheering *Chelmsf*
SHEERNESS (Holy Trinity w St Paul) *Cant 15*   **P** *V Minster-*
in-Sheppey   **V** J W STREETING
SHEERWATER (St Michael and All Angels)   *see* Woodham
Guildf
SHEET (St Mary Magdalene) *Portsm 4*   **P** *Bp*
V R M E DEWING,   **NSM** A J MARSH
SHEFFIELD (St Aidan w St Luke)   *see* Sheff Manor *Sheff*
SHEFFIELD (St Andrew)   *see* Psalter Lane St Andr *Sheff*
SHEFFIELD (St Bartholomew) *Sheff 4*   **P** *Ch Patr Trust and*
Sheff Ch Burgesses Trust (jt)   **V** *vacant* 0114-233 6977
SHEFFIELD (St Catherine of Siena) Richmond Road *Sheff 1*
P *The Crown*   **V** H LOXLEY
SHEFFIELD (St Cecilia) Parson Cross *Sheff 3*   **P** *Bp*
V K RYDER-WEST
SHEFFIELD (St Cuthbert) *Sheff 3*   **P** *Ch Burgesses*
V L R COLLINS,   **NSM** M R SUTTON
SHEFFIELD (St John the Evangelist) *Sheff 1*   **P** *Ch Burgesses*
V C H STEBBING,   **C** D R GOUGH
SHEFFIELD (St Leonard) Norwood *Sheff 3*   **P** *Bp*
V I K DUFFIELD,   **NSM** J H DALEY
SHEFFIELD (St Mark) Broomhill *Sheff 4*   **P** *Ch Burgesses*
V I G WALLIS,   **C** S E HOBLEY
SHEFFIELD (St Mary) Bramall Lane *Sheff 2*   **P** *Ch Burgesses*
and Dean (alt)   **V** J C SULLIVAN,   **C** M J BAYLEY,
NSM G C D DUNCAN
SHEFFIELD (St Matthew) Carver Street *Sheff 2*   **P** *Bp and*
Sheff Ch Burgess Trust (jt)   **V** S M GRIFFITHS
SHEFFIELD (St Oswald) St Peter *Sheff 2*   **P** *Ch Burgesses*
C I N C LOTHIAN
SHEFFIELD (St Paul)   *see* Arbourthorne and Norfolk Park
Sheff
SHEFFIELD (St Paul) Wordsworth Avenue *Sheff 3*   **P** *DBP*
P-in-c I SMITH,   **NSM** K J CROOKES
SHEFFIELD MANOR (St Swithun) *Sheff 1*   **P** *Patr Bd*
C A L SMETHAM
SHEFFIELD PARK (St John the Evangelist)   *see* Sheff St Jo
Sheff
SHEFFORD (St Michael)   *see* Meppershall and Shefford *St Alb*
SHEFFORD, GREAT (St Mary)   *see* Welford w Wickham and
Gt Shefford, Boxford etc *Ox*
SHEINTON (St Peter and St Paul)   *see* Wenlock *Heref*
SHELDON (St Giles) *Birm 9*   **P** J K Wingfield Digby Esq
R B A L CAMP
SHELDON (St James the Greater)   *see* Dunkeswell, Luppitt,
Sheldon and Upottery *Ex*
SHELDON (St John)   *see* Shirley St Jo *S'wark*
SHELDON (St Michael and All Angels)   *see* Ashford w Sheldon
and Longstone *Derby*
SHELDWICH (St James)   *see* Selling w Throwley, Sheldwich w
Badlesmere etc *Cant*
SHELF (St Michael and All Angels) w Buttershaw St Aidan
Bradf 2   **P** *Bp*   **TR** M J GASKELL,   **TV** S E W SHRINE
SHELFANGER (All Saints)   *see* Winfarthing w Shelfanger w
Burston w Gissing etc *Nor*
SHELFIELD (St Mark) and High Heath *Lich 25*   **P** *R Walsall*
V J C HILL,   **NSM** C SILVESTER
SHELFORD (St Peter and St Paul)   *see* Radcliffe-on-Trent and
Shelford *S'well*
SHELFORD, GREAT (St Mary) *Ely 5*   **P** *Bp*
P-in-c M R GOATER,   **NSM** S G ANDERSON
SHELFORD, LITTLE (All Saints) *Ely 5*   **P** *Bp*   **R** S J SCOTT,
C R A HEYWOOD

SHELLAND (King Charles the Martyr)   *see* Gt Finborough w Onehouse, Harleston, Buxhall etc *St E*

SHELLEY (All Saints)   *see* Hadleigh, Layham and Shelley *St E*

SHELLEY (Emmanuel) and Shepley *Wakef 6*   **P** *V Kirkburton*   **P-in-c** J R JONES,   **OLM** J M CRAVEN

SHELLEY (St Peter)   *see* Chipping Ongar w Shelley *Chelmsf*

SHELLINGFORD (St Faith)   *see* Uffington, Shellingford, Woolstone and Baulking *Ox*

SHELSLEY BEAUCHAMP (All Saints)   *see* Worcs W *Worc*

SHELSLEY WALSH (St Andrew)   *as above*

SHELSWELL *Ox 2*   **P** *Ld Chan (1 turn) and Ch Ch Ox, CCC Ox, Baroness von Maltzahn, and R J Vallings Esq (1 turn)*   **R** C M K HARGRAVES,   **NSM** M REYNOLDS

SHELTHORPE (Good Shepherd)   *see* Loughb Gd Shep *Leic*

SHELTON (Christ Church) and Oxon *Lich 20*   **P** *V Shrewsbury St Chad w St Mary*   **P-in-c** S CADDY,   **OLM** M I FEARNSIDE

SHELTON (St Mark)   *see* Hanley H Ev *Lich*

SHELTON (St Mary)   *see* Hempnall *Nor*

SHELTON (St Mary)   *see* The Stodden Churches *St Alb*

SHELTON (St Mary and All Saints) *S'well 3*   **P** *Bp*   **P-in-c** D HOLLIS

SHELVE (All Saints)   *see* Hope w Shelve *Heref*

SHENFIELD (St Mary the Virgin) *Chelmsf 7*   **P** *Personal Reps R H Courage*   **R** D G THOMAS,   **NSM** E A LOCKHART

SHENINGTON (Holy Trinity)   *see* Ironstone *Ox*

SHENLEY (St Martin)   *see* Aldenham, Radlett and Shenley *St Alb*

SHENLEY (St Mary)   *see* Watling Valley *Ox*

SHENLEY GREEN (St David) *Birm 4*   **P** *Bp*   **V** N A P EVANS,   **NSM** A R BEVAN

SHENSTONE (St John the Baptist) *Lich 1*   **P** *MMCET*   **P-in-c** D F OLNEY

SHENTON (St John the Evangelist)   *see* Bosworth and Sheepy Gp *Leic*

SHEPHERD'S BUSH (St Luke) Uxbridge Road   *see* Hammersmith St Luke *Lon*

SHEPHERD'S BUSH (St Michael and St George) (St Stephen) (St Thomas) *Lon 9*   **P** *Bp*   **V** R W MAYO,   **C** B P HUMPHRIES,   **NSM** J A COWLEY

SHEPHERD'S BUSH (St Simon)   *see* Hammersmith St Simon *Lon*

SHEPLEY (St Paul)   *see* Shelley and Shepley *Wakef*

SHEPPERDINE (Chapel)   *see* Thornbury and Oldbury-on-Severn w Shepperdine *Glouc*

SHEPPERTON (St Nicholas) and Littleton *Lon 13*   **P** *Bp and C W L Barratt Esq (jt)*   **R** C J SWIFT,   **C** A J WATERS

SHEPRETH (All Saints)   *see* Fowlmere, Foxton, Shepreth and Thriplow *Ely*

SHEPSHED (St Botolph) and Oaks in Charnwood *Leic 6*   **P** *DBP and Lord Crawshaw (jt)*   **V** C M HEBDEN,   **C** C D TAYLOR,   **Hon C** M R DUNK

SHEPTON BEAUCHAMP (St Michael)   *see* Ilminster and Distr *B & W*

SHEPTON MALLET (St Peter and St Paul) w Doulting *B & W 8*   **P** *Duchy of Cornwall and Bp (alt)*   **R** E J SMITH,   **C** D J PARR, T HANDY

SHEPTON MONTAGUE (St Peter)   *see* Bruton and Distr *B & W*

SHEPWELL GREEN (St Matthias)   *see* Willenhall St Giles *Lich*

SHERBORNE (Abbey Church of St Mary) (All Souls) (St Paul) w Castleton, Lillington and Longburton *Sarum 3*   **P** *J K Wingfield Digby Esq*   **V** E J WOODS,   **C** J P TRIFFITT, G W HARTLEY,   **Hon C** J J RICHARDSON,   **OLM** B PHILLIPS

SHERBORNE (St Mary Magdalene), Windrush, the Barringtons and Aldsworth *Glouc 11*   **P** *C T R Wingfield Esq, Ch Ch Ox, and DBP (by turn)*   **P-in-c** D M ACKERMAN,   **C** R W WOODGER

SHERBORNES (St Andrew) (Vyne Chapel) w Pamber, The *Win 4*   **P** *Bp and Qu Coll Ox (jt)*   **R** J N HAMILTON

SHERBOURNE (All Saints)   *see* Barford w Wasperton and Sherbourne *Cov*

SHERBURN (St Mary)   *see* Shadforth and Sherburn *Dur*

SHERBURN (St Hilda)   *see* Buckrose Carrs *York*

SHERBURN IN ELMET (All Saints) w Saxton *York 4*   **P** *Abp*   **V** C WILTON

SHERE (St James), Albury and Chilworth *Guildf 2*   **P** *Bp, Mrs H Bray, Duke of Northd, W F P Hugonin Esq, and the Hon M W Ridley (jt)*   **R** C A E LAWRENCE,   **C** S M SOKOLOWSKI,   **NSM** K B HOBBS,   **OLM** A M PEARSON

SHEREFORD (St Nicholas)   *see* Upper Wensum Village Gp *Nor*

SHERFIELD ENGLISH (St Leonard)   *see* E w W Wellow and Sherfield English *Win*

SHERFIELD-ON-LODDON (St Leonard) and Stratfield Saye w Hartley Wespall w Stratfield Turgis *Win 4*   **P** *Bp, Duke of Wellington, and D&C Windsor (jt)*   **R** R W POLITT

SHERFORD (St Martin)   *see* Stokenham, Slapton, Charleton w Buckland etc *Ex*

SHERIFF HUTTON (St Helen and the Holy Cross)   *see* Forest of Galtres *York*

SHERIFFHALES (St Mary)   *see* Shifnal and Sheriffhales *Lich*

SHERINGHAM (St Peter) *Nor 21*   **P** *Bp*   **V** C J HEYCOCKS

SHERINGHAM, UPPER (All Saints)   *see* Weybourne Gp *Nor*

SHERINGTON (St Laud) w Chicheley, North Crawley, Astwood and Hardmead *Ox 27*   **P** *Bp (2 turns), MMCET (1 turn), and Major J G B Chester (1 turn)*   **R** A J MARRIOTT

SHERMANBURY (St Giles)   *see* Henfield w Shermanbury and Woodmancote *Chich*

SHERNBOURNE (St Peter and St Paul)   *see* Dersingham w Anmer and Shernborne *Nor*

SHERRARDS GREEN (St Mary the Virgin)   *see* Gt Malvern Ch Ch *Worc*

SHERRINGTON (St Cosmo and St Damian)   *see* Upper Wylye Valley *Sarum*

SHERSTON MAGNA (Holy Cross), Easton Grey, Luckington, Alderton and Foxley w Bremilham *Bris 6*   **P** *D&C, Bp, Adn Malmesbury and Lord Lilford (jt)*   **P-in-c** A EVANS,   **C** E C PEGLER,   **Hon C** M M MASLEN,   **NSM** S R EVANS

SHERWOOD (St Martin) *S'well 12*   **P** *Bp*   **V** S J GRIFFITHS

SHERWOOD PARK (St Philip)   *see* Tunbridge Wells St Phil *Roch*

SHEVINGTON (St Anne) *Blackb 4*   **P** *R Standish*   **V** P I DENNISON

SHEVIOCK (Blessed Virgin Mary)   *see* Antony w Sheviock *Truro*

SHIFFORD (St Mary)   *see* Bampton w Clanfield *Ox*

SHIFNAL (St Andrew) and Sheriffhales *Lich 16*   **P** *Bp and R I Legge Esq (jt)*   **V** C D C THORPE,   **OLM** S A DAY

SHILBOTEL (St James)   *see* Shilbottle *Newc*

SHILBOTTLE (St James) *Newc 6*   **P** *Dioc Soc*   **V** vacant (01665) 575800

SHILDON (St John) *Dur 6*   **P** *Bp*   **V** R KALUS,   **C** D R TOMLINSON

SHILL VALLEY and Broadshire *Ox 8*   **P** *J Heyworth Esq, Mrs P Allen, and Ch Ch Ox (1 turn), Ch Soc Tr, F R Goodenough Esq, and D F Goodenough Esq (1 turn)*   **R** H C MACINNES,   **C** P E WHEATON,   **Hon C** J M MOUNT,   **NSM** L N USHER-WILSON

SHILLING OKEFORD (Holy Rood)   *see* Okeford *Sarum*

SHILLINGFORD (St George)   *see* Alphington, Shillingford St George and Ide *Ex*

SHILLINGSTONE (Holy Rood)   *see* Okeford *Sarum*

SHILLINGTON (All Saints)   *see* Gravenhurst, Shillington and Stondon *St Alb*

SHILTON (Holy Rood)   *see* Shill Valley and Broadshire *Ox*

SHILTON (St Andrew)   *see* Ansty and Shilton *Cov*

SHIMPLINGTHORNE (St George)   *see* Chadbrook *St E*

SHINCLIFFE (St Mary the Virgin)   *see* Dur St Oswald and Shincliffe *Dur*

SHINEY ROW (St Oswald)   *see* Herrington, Penshaw and Shiney Row *Dur*

SHINFIELD (St Mary)   *see* Loddon Reach *Ox*

SHINGAY Group of Parishes, The *Ely 7*   **P** *Bp, Mrs E E Sclater, Ch Patr Trust, Down Coll Cam, New Coll Ox, and Jes Coll Cam (jt)*   **R** S F C WILLIAMS,   **NSM** P M SHARKEY

SHIPBOURNE (St Giles) w Plaxtol *Roch 10*   **P** *Bp and Sir Edward Cazalet*   **R** A D PROCTER

SHIPDHAM (All Saints) w East and West Bradenham *Nor 17*   **P** *Bp*   **P-in-c** A-L ALDER,   **OLM** D FOTHERBY

SHIPHAM (St Leonard)   *see* Axbridge w Shipham and Rowberrow *B & W*

SHIPHAY COLLATON (St John the Baptist) *Ex 12*   **P** *Bp*   **V** C E DEACON

SHIPLAKE (St Peter and St Paul) w Dunsden and Harpsden *Ox 6*   **P** *All So Coll Ox, D&C Windsor, and DBP (jt)*   **R** M R C PRICE,   **NSM** S M COUSINS,   **OLM** M D SEYMOUR-JONES

SHIPLEY (St Mary the Virgin) *Chich 8*   **P** *C R Burrell Esq*   **P-in-c** P A SINTON

SHIPLEY (St Paul) *Bradf 1*   **P** *Simeon's Trustees*   **P-in-c** S HOPE

SHIPLEY (St Peter) *Bradf 1*   **P** *V Shipley St Paul*   **V** J C RAINER,   **C** N MCCATHIE

SHIPPON (St Mary Magdalene) *Ox 10*   **P** *Bp*   **V** vacant

SHIPSTON-ON-STOUR (St Edmund) w Honington and Idlicote *Cov 9*   **P** *Jes Coll Ox, D&C Worc, Bp (jt)*   **R** D R THURBURN-HUELIN,   **NSM** J TUCKER

SHIPTON (Holy Evangelist)   *see* Skelton w Shipton and Newton on Ouse *York*

SHIPTON (St James)   *see* Wenlock *Heref*

SHIPTON BELLINGER (St Peter)   *see* Appleshaw, Kimpton, Thruxton, Fyfield etc *Win*

SHIPTON GORGE (St Martin)   *see* Bride Valley *Sarum*
SHIPTON MOYNE (St John the Baptist) *Glouc 9*   **P** *DBP*
   V A J WRIGHT
SHIPTON OLIFFE (St Oswald)   *see* Sevenhampton w Charlton
   Abbots, Hawling etc *Glouc*
SHIPTON ON CHERWELL (Holy Cross)   *see* Blenheim *Ox*
SHIPTON-UNDER-WYCHWOOD (St Mary) w Milton-under-
   Wychwood, Fifield and Idbury *Ox 3*   **P** *Bp*   **V** W M CALLAN,
   OLM A T HARTLEY
SHIPTONTHORPE (All Saints) and Hayton *York 5*   **P** *Abp*
   NSM S D JONES
SHIREBROOK (Holy Trinity)   *see* E Scarsdale *Derby*
SHIREGREEN (St James and St Christopher) *Sheff 3*   **P** *Bp*
   and Dean (alt)   **P-in-c** D F DEAN-REVILL
SHIREHAMPTON (St Mary) *Bris 2*   **P** *Bp*
   P-in-c C A FROUDE
SHIREMOOR (St Mark) *Newc 5*   **P** *Bp*   **V** P M SCOTT,
   C L OSBALDESTON
SHIREOAKS (St Luke) *S'well 6*   **P** *Bp*   **P-in-c** J L ALLEN
SHIRES' EDGE *Ox 5*   **P** *Bp*   **V** P FREETH,
   OLM L M ALCOCK
SHIRLAND (St Leonard)   *see* Morton and Stonebroom w
   Shirland *Derby*
SHIRLEY (Christ the King)   *see* Salter Street and Shirley *Birm*
SHIRLEY (St George) *S'wark 19*   **P** *Bp*   **V** D J FROST,
   Hon C H A FIFE,   **OLM** C JONES
SHIRLEY (St James) (St John) *Win 13*   **P** *Ch Patr Trust*
   V D P HAZLEWOOD,   **C** A D HARGREAVES
SHIRLEY (St James the Great)   *see* Salter Street and Shirley
   Birm
SHIRLEY (St John) *S'wark 19*   **P** *Bp*   **V** S J KNOWERS,
   Hon C A C COLLIER,   **NSM** B C GENTILELLA
SHIRLEY (St John the Divine)   *see* Salter Street and Shirley
   Birm
SHIRLEY (St Luke)   *as above*
SHIRLEY (St Mary Magdalene)   *as above*
SHIRLEY (St Michael)   *see* Brailsford w Shirley, Osmaston w
   Edlaston etc *Derby*
SHIRLEY WARREN (St Jude)   *see* Maybush and Southampton
   St Jude *Win*
SHIRWELL (St Peter), Loxhore, Kentisbury, Arlington, East
   Down, Bratton Fleming, Challacombe and Stoke Rivers *Ex 18*
   P *Patr Bd*   **TR** L E AUSTIN,   **TV** C J HUDSPITH
SHOBDON (St John the Evangelist)   *see* Pembridge w Moor
   Court, Shobdon, Staunton etc *Heref*
SHOBROOKE (St Swithin)   *see* Crediton, Shobrooke and
   Sandford etc *Ex*
SHOCKLACH (St Edith)   *see* Tilston and Shocklach *Ches*
SHOEBURY, NORTH (St Mary the Virgin) *Chelmsf 13*
   P *Ld Chan*   **V** I ST J FISHER
SHOEBURY, SOUTH (St Andrew) (St Peter) *Chelmsf 13*
   P *Hyndman Trustees*   **R** *vacant* (01702) 292778
SHOLDEN (St Nicholas)   *see* Deal St Leon w St Rich and
   Sholden etc *Cant*
SHOLING (St Francis of Assisi) (St Mary) *Win 13*   **P** *Bp*
   V G K BAKKER,   **NSM** J J BAKKER
SHOOTERS HILL (All Saints)   *see* Plumstead All SS *S'wark*
SHOOTERS HILL (Christ Church) *S'wark 3*   **P** *Bp*
   V N C WHITTLE,   **NSM** J N PHILPOTT-HOWARD, A S J HEALY
SHORE (St Barnabas) *Man 21*   **P** *D&C*   **P-in-c** J MCGRATH,
   OLM B WOODHEAD
SHOREDITCH (All Saints) Haggerston Road   *see* Dalston H
   Trin w St Phil and Haggerston All SS *Lon*
SHOREDITCH (St Anne) Hoxton Street   *see* Hoxton St Anne w
   St Columba *Lon*
SHOREDITCH (St Leonard) w St Michael *Lon 5*   **P** *Bp and*
   Adn (jt)   **V** P R TURP,   **C** G E FOUHY
SHOREHAM (St Giles)   *see* Kingston Buci *Chich*
SHOREHAM (St Peter and St Paul) *Roch 10*   **P** *D&C Westmr*
   P-in-c R A FREEMAN
SHOREHAM, NEW (St Mary de Haura) *Chich 4*   **P** *Bp*
   V V STANDING,   **C** T S STRATFORD
SHOREHAM, OLD (St Nicolas) *Chich 4*   **P** *Bp*
   V V STANDING,   **C** T S STRATFORD
SHOREHAM BEACH (Good Shepherd) *Chich 4*   **P** *Bp*
   P-in-c G C SOUPPOURIS
SHORELINE Benefice, The *St E 5*   **P** *Ld Chan (1 turn), Bp*
   (3 turns)   **R** L OOSTERHOF
SHORNE (St Peter and St Paul) *Roch 4*   **P** *D&C*
   V P E LONGBOTTOM
SHORT HEATH (Holy Trinity)   *see* Willenhall H Trin *Lich*
SHORT HEATH (St Margaret)   *see* Erdington Ch the K *Birm*
SHORTHAMPTON (All Saints)   *see* Charlbury w
   Shorthampton *Ox*
SHORTLANDS (All Saints' Community Church)   *see* Bromley
   SS Pet and Paul *Roch*

SHORTLANDS (St Mary) *Roch 13*   **P** *Bp*   **V** P MILLER,
   NSM J E PETERS
SHORTWOOD (All Saints)   *see* Nailsworth w Shortwood,
   Horsley etc *Glouc*
SHORWELL (St Peter) w Kingston *Portsm 8*   **P** *Bp*
   P-in-c M C WILLIAMS,   **Hon C** D L DENNIS
SHOSCOMBE (St Julian)   *see* Camerton w Dunkerton, Foxcote
   and Shoscombe *B & W*
SHOTESHAM (All Saints w St Mary)   *see* Newton Flotman,
   Swainsthorpe, Tasburgh, etc *Nor*
SHOTLEY (St John) *Newc 9*   **P** *Lord Crewe's Trustees*
   NSM D J WOOD
SHOTLEY (St Mary)   *see* Shoreline *St E*
SHOTTERMILL (St Stephen) *Guildf 4*   **P** *Adn Surrey*
   V D R P WIGNALL
SHOTTERY (St Andrew) *Cov 8*   **P** *Bp*   **V** J R WARREN
SHOTTESBROOKE (St John the Baptist)   *see* White Waltham
   w Shottesbrooke *Ox*
SHOTTESWELL (St Lawrence)   *see* Warmington w Shotteswell
   and Radway w Ratley *Cov*
SHOTTISHAM (St Margaret)   *see* Wilford Peninsula *St E*
SHOTTLE (St Lawrence)   *see* Hazelwood, Holbrook and
   Milford *Derby*
SHOTTON (St Saviour)   *see* Haswell, Shotton and Thornley *Dur*
SHOTWICK (St Michael)   *see* Burton and Shotwick *Ches*
SHOULDHAM (All Saints) *Ely 9*   **P** *Bp*   **V** *vacant*
SHOULDHAM THORPE (St Mary) *Ely 9*   **P** *Bp*   **V** *vacant*
SHRAWARDINE (St Mary)   *see* Bicton, Montford w
   Shrawardine and Fitz *Lich*
SHRAWLEY (St Mary), Witley, Astley and Abberley *Worc 13*
   P *Bp and Guild of All So (jt)*   **R** A NORKETT
SHRED (Mission Church)   *see* Slaithwaite w E Scammonden
   Wakef
SHREWSBURY (All Saints and St Michael) *Lich 20*   **P** *Bp*
   P-in-c M FISH
SHREWSBURY (Christ Church)   *see* Shelton and Oxon *Lich*
SHREWSBURY (Holy Cross) (St Peter) *Lich 20*   **P** *Bp*
   V C S SIMS,   **C** J E WILLIS
SHREWSBURY (Holy Trinity) (St Julian) *Lich 20*   **P** *Bp and*
   Ch Patr Trust (jt)   **P-in-c** R D SPENCER
SHREWSBURY (St Chad) St Mary (St Alkmund) *Lich 20*
   P *Bp*   **V** M W THOMAS,   **Hon C** C J D WALKER, R HAYES
SHREWSBURY (St George of Cappadocia) w Greenfields
   United Church *Lich 20*   **P** *V Shrewsbury St Chad*
   V M MCBRIDE
SHREWSBURY (St Giles) w Sutton and Atcham *Lich 20*   **P** *Bp*
   and R L Burton Esq (jt)   **R** P J WILLIAMS
SHREWTON (St Mary)   *see* Wylye and Till Valley *Sarum*
SHRIVENHAM (St Andrew) and Ashbury *Ox 17*   **P** *Ld Chan*
   V R M A HANCOCK,   **Hon C** E G CLEMENTS,   **NSM** A E BELL
SHROPHAM (St Peter)   *see* Gt and Lt Ellingham, Rockland and
   Shropham etc *Nor*
SHROTON (St Mary)   *see* Iwerne Valley *Sarum*
SHRUB END (All Saints) (St Cedd) *Chelmsf 16*   **P** *Bp*
   V N A W DAVIS,   **NSM** B HADFIELD
SHUCKBURGH, LOWER (St John the Baptist)   *see* Napton-
   on-the-Hill, Lower Shuckburgh etc *Cov*
SHUDY CAMPS (St Mary)   *see* Linton *Ely*
SHURDINGTON (St Paul)   *see* Badgeworth, Shurdington and
   Witcombe w Bentham *Glouc*
SHUSTOKE (St Cuthbert)   *see* The Whitacres and Shustoke
   Birm
SHUTE (St Michael)   *see* Kilmington, Stockland, Dalwood,
   Yarcombe etc *Ex*
SHUTFORD (St Martin)   *see* Wykeham *Ox*
SHUTTINGTON (St Matthew)   *see* N Warks *Birm*
SHUTTLEWOOD (St Laurence Mission Church)   *see* Bolsover
   Derby
SHUTTLEWORTH (St John)   *see* Ramsbottom and Edenfield
   Man
SIBBERTOFT (St Helen)   *see* Welford w Sibbertoft and Marston
   Trussell *Pet*
SIBERTSWOLD (St Andrew)   *see* Eythorne and Elvington w
   Waldershare etc *Cant*
SIBFORD (Holy Trinity)   *see* Wykeham *Ox*
SIBLE HEDINGHAM (St Peter) w Castle Hedingham
   Chelmsf 19   **P** *Bp, and Hon T R Lindsay (alt)*   **R** *vacant*
   (01787) 460274
SIBSEY (St Margaret) w Frithville *Linc 20*   **P** *Ld Chan*
   P-in-c R E TAYLOR,   **NSM** J M MORTON
SIBSON (St Botolph)   *see* Bosworth and Sheepy Gp *Leic*
SIBTHORPE (St Peter) *S'well 3*   **P** *Bp*   **P-in-c** D HOLLIS
SIBTON (St Peter)   *see* Yoxmere *St E*
SICKLINGHALL (St Peter)   *see* Lower Wharfedale *Ripon*
SID VALLEY   *see* Sidmouth, Woolbrook, Salcombe Regis,
   Sidbury etc *Ex*

SIDBURY (Holy Trinity) *see* Stottesdon w Farlow, Cleeton St Mary etc *Heref*

SIDBURY (St Giles and St Peter) *see* Sidmouth, Woolbrook, Salcombe Regis, Sidbury etc *Ex*

SIDCUP (Christ Church) Longden *Roch 17* **P** *Ch Trust Fund Trust* **V** A K WILSON

SIDCUP (St Andrew) *Roch 17* **P** *Bp* **V** D HILDRED

SIDCUP (St John the Evangelist) *Roch 17* **P** *D&C* **V** S SEALY, **NSM** S E TWYNAM

SIDDAL (St Mark) *Wakef 4* **P** *Ch Trust Fund Trust* **P-in-c** C MACDONALD

SIDDINGTON (All Saints) *see* Capesthorne w Siddington and Marton *Ches*

SIDDINGTON (St Peter) *see* S Cerney w Cerney Wick, Siddington and Preston *Glouc*

SIDESTRAND (St Michael) *see* Overstrand, Northrepps, Sidestrand etc *Nor*

SIDFORD (St Peter) *see* Sidmouth, Woolbrook, Salcombe Regis, Sidbury etc *Ex*

SIDLESHAM (St Mary the Virgin) *Chich 3* **P** *Bp* **P-in-c** S GUISE

SIDLEY (All Saints) *Chich 14* **P** *R Bexhill* **V** T G BUXTON

SIDLOW BRIDGE (Emmanuel) *S'wark 26* **P** *DBP* **R** W G CAMPEN

SIDMOUTH (St Nicholas w St Giles), Woolbrook, Salcombe Regis, Sidbury w Sidford, and All Saints Sidmouth *Ex 7* **P** *Patr Bd* **TR** D H JAMES, **TV** R G PECKHAM, R D TRUMPER, **C** D M BROWN

SIGGLESTHORNE (St Lawrence) w Nunkeeling and Bewholme *York 11* **P** *Prime Min* **R** vacant (01964) 533033

SILCHESTER (St Mary) *see* Tadley S and Silchester *Win*

SILCHESTER COMMON (Mission Church) *as above*

SILEBY (St Mary), Cossington and Seagrave *Leic 5* **P** *Patr Bd* **R** R C J HOPKINS

SILK WILLOUGHBY (St Denis) *Linc 22* **P** *Sir Lyonel Tollemache Bt* **R** vacant

SILKSTONE (All Saints) *see* Hoylandswaine and Silkstone w Stainborough *Wakef*

SILKSTONE COMMON (Mission Room) *as above*

SILKSWORTH (St Matthew) *Dur 16* **P** *Bp* **V** R G E BRADSHAW, **C** S CLARK, **Hon C** J A BRADSHAW

SILLOTH (Christ Church) *see* Solway Plain *Carl*

SILSDEN (St James) *Bradf 8* **P** *Bp, Adn Craven, and Trustees (jt)* **V** J P GREENWOOD

SILSOE (St James), Pulloxhill and Flitton *St Alb 9* **P** *Ball Coll Ox and Bp (alt)* **V** S C HOLROYD

SILTON (St Nicholas) *Sarum 5* **P** *DBP* **R** vacant

SILTON, NETHER (All Saints) *see* Leake w Over and Nether Silton and Kepwick *York*

SILTON, OVER (St Mary) *as above*

SILVER END (St Francis) *see* Rivenhall *Chelmsf*

SILVERDALE (St John) *Blackb 14* **P** *V Warton* **P-in-c** P K WARREN, **NSM** J NOVELL

SILVERDALE (St Luke) *Lich 9* **P** *T H G Howard-Sneyd Esq* **V** S A ANSELL, **C** M J MAXWELL

SILVERHILL (St Matthew) *Chich 17* **P** *Simeon's Trustees* **R** M S COE, **C** A D PICKERING

SILVERSTONE (St Michael) and Abthorpe w Slapton and Whittlebury and Paulerspury *Pet 5* **P** *T L Langton-Lockton Esq, Leeson's Trustees, and New Coll Ox (3 turns), Prime Min (2 turns)* **R** vacant (01327) 857996

SILVERTON (St Mary), Butterleigh, Bickleigh and Cadeleigh *Ex 8* **P** *Bp and Sir Rivers Carew Bt* **R** A H MACDONALD, **NSM** C JENKINS, J M WRIGHT

SILVINGTON (St Michael) *see* Stottesdon w Farlow, Cleeton St Mary etc *Heref*

SIMONBURN (St Mungo) *see* Humshaugh w Simonburn and Wark *Newc*

SIMONSTONE (St Peter) *see* Padiham w Hapton and Padiham Green *Blackb*

SIMPSON (St Thomas) *see* Woughton *Ox*

SINFIN (St Stephen) *Derby 10* **P** *CPAS* **P-in-c** P R SANDFORD

SINFIN MOOR (not known) *Derby 10* **P** *Bp* **V** vacant (01332) 760016

SINGLETON (Blessed Virgin Mary) *see* E Dean, Singleton, and W Dean *Chich*

SINGLETON (St Anne) *see* Poulton Carleton and Singleton *Blackb*

SINNINGTON (All Saints) *see* Middleton, Newton and Sinnington *York*

SISLAND (St Mary) *see* Loddon, Sisland, Chedgrave, Hardley and Langley *Nor*

SISSINGHURST (Holy Trinity) w Frittenden *Cant 11* **P** *CPAS* **V** A E NORRIS

SITHNEY (St Sithney) *see* Porthleven w Sithney *Truro*

SITTINGBOURNE (Holy Trinity) w Bobbing *Cant 15* **P** *Abp* **P-in-c** M J RESCH, **OLM** S M SAMSON

SITTINGBOURNE (St Mary) (St Michael) *Cant 15* **P** *Abp and D&C (jt)* **V** N FINLAY, **C** A C COLPUS

SITTINGBOURNE (St Peter and St Paul) *see* Borden *Cant*

SIX HILLS (Mission) *see* Old Dalby, Nether Broughton, Saxelbye etc *Leic*

SIX MILE BOTTOM (St George) *see* Lt Wilbraham *Ely*

SIX PILGRIMS, The *B & W 3* **P** *Ch Soc Trust, D&C, DBF, and Bp (by turn)* **P-in-c** P T CRAIG

SIX SAINTS circa Holt: Bringhurst, Great Easton, Medbourne cum Holt, Stockerston and Blaston *Leic 3* **P** *D&C Pet and Adn Leic (2 turns), St Jo Coll Cam (1 turn)* **R** S J BISHOP

SIXHILLS (All Saints) *see* Barkwith Gp *Linc*

SIXPENNY HANDLEY (St Mary) w Gussage St Andrew and Pentridge *Sarum 6* **P** *D&C Windsor and Earl of Shaftesbury (alt)* **P-in-c** M R B DURRANT, **C** M J FOSTER

SKEEBY (St Agatha's District Church) *see* Easby w Skeeby and Brompton on Swale etc *Ripon*

SKEFFINGTON (St Thomas à Beckett) *see* Church Langton cum Tur Langton etc *Leic*

SKEFFLING (St Helen) *see* Withernsea w Owthorne and Easington etc *York*

SKEGBY (St Andrew) w Teversal *S'well 4* **P** *DBP and Ld Chan (alt)* **R** R KELLETT, **C** K BOTTLEY

SKEGNESS Group, The (St Clement) (St Matthew) *Linc 8* **P** *Bp and DBP (2 turns), and Ld Chan (1 turn)* **R** C M FRANCE

SKELBROOKE (St Michael and All Angels) *see* Adwick-le-Street w Skelbrooke *Sheff*

SKELLINGTHORPE (St Lawrence) w Doddington *Linc 18* **P** *MMCET* **R** G BILLINGHURST

SKELLOW (St Michael and All Angels) *see* Owston *Sheff*

SKELMANTHORPE (St Aidan) *Wakef 6* **P** *Bp* **P-in-c** P D REYNOLDS

SKELMERSDALE (Church at the Centre) *Liv 11* **P** *Bp* **P-in-c** G E GREENWOOD

SKELMERSDALE (St Paul) *Liv 11* **P** *V Ormskirk* **V** G E GREENWOOD

SKELSMERGH (St John the Baptist) *see* Beacon *Carl*

SKELTON (All Saints) w Upleatham *York 16* **P** *Abp* **C** K M LAWRIE

SKELTON (St Giles) w Shipton and Newton on Ouse *York 3* **P** *Abp* **R** E W A CRAGG

SKELTON (St Michael) *see* Inglewood Gp *Carl*

SKELTON-CUM-NEWBY (St Helen's Old Church) *see* Kirby-on-the-Moor, Cundall w Norton-le-Clay etc *Ripon*

SKENDLEBY (St Peter and St Paul) *see* Partney Gp *Linc*

SKERNE (St Leonard) *see* Hutton Cranswick w Skerne, Watton and Beswick *York*

SKERNE, UPPER *Dur 5* **P** *Ld Chan (1 turn), Patr Bd (2 turns)* **TR** M G T GOBBETT, **TV** P L TAIT, **C** J WILLIAMS

SKERTON (St Chad) *Blackb 11* **P** *Bp* **V** vacant (01524) 63816

SKERTON (St Luke) *Blackb 11* **P** *Trustees* **V** G LEWIS

SKEYTON (All Saints) *see* King's Beck *Nor*

SKIDBY (St Michael) *see* Rowley w Skidby *York*

SKILGATE (St John the Baptist) *see* Brompton Regis w Upton and Skilgate *B & W*

SKILLINGTON (St James) *see* Colsterworth Gp *Linc*

SKIPSEA (All Saints) and Barmston w Fraisthorpe *York 9* **P** *Abp and The Hon S E Cunliffe-Lister (jt)* **V** vacant

SKIPTON (Christ Church) w Carleton St Mary *Bradf 7* **P** *Ch Ch Ox and R Skipton H Trin (jt)* **V** D N WILLIAMS, **C** L M TAYLOR-KENYON, **NSM** V A LOWE

SKIPTON (Holy Trinity) *Bradf 7* **P** *Ch Ch Ox* **R** A P BOTWRIGHT, **C** J W DANIELS, L M TAYLOR-KENYON

SKIPTON ON SWALE (St John) *see* Topcliffe, Baldersby w Dishforth, Dalton etc *York*

SKIPWITH (St Helen) *see* Bubwith w Skipwith *York*

SKIRBECK (Holy Trinity) *Linc 20* **P** *Trustees* **V** S P DOWSON, **C** D P GREEN

SKIRBECK (St Nicholas) *Linc 20* **P** *DBP* **R** P V NOBLE

SKIRBECK QUARTER (St Thomas) *see* Boston *Linc*

SKIRLAUGH (St Augustine) w Long Riston, Rise and Swine *York 11* **P** *Abp, Abp and Baroness de Stempel, and Ld Chan (by turn)* **P-in-c** C J SIMMONS

SKIRPENBECK (St Mary) *see* Garrowby Hill *York*

SKIRWITH (St John the Evangelist) *see* Cross Fell Gp *Carl*

SLAD (Holy Trinity) *see* Stroud and Uplands w Slad *Glouc*

SLADE GREEN (St Augustine) *Roch 15* **P** *Bp* **V** A J TARPER

SLAIDBURN (St Andrew) *Bradf 5* **P** *Ch Soc Trust* **P-in-c** M R RUSSELL-SMITH, **NSM** R E WILSON

SLAITHWAITE (St James) w East Scammonden *Wakef 5* **P** *V Huddersfield* **V** C R TOWNSEND

SLALEY (St Mary the Virgin) *Newc 9* **P** *Bp* **P-in-c** D J IRVINE, **NSM** J LYNCH

SLAPTON (Holy Cross)   *see* Ivinghoe w Pitstone and Slapton and Marsworth *Ox*

SLAPTON (St Botolph)   *see* Silverstone and Abthorpe w Slapton etc *Pet*

SLAPTON (St James the Great)   *see* Stokenham, Slapton, Charleton w Buckland etc *Ex*

SLAUGHAM (St Mary) *Chich 6*   **P** *Mrs D M Irwin-Clark*   **R** G D SIMMONS,   **C** J W B WADDELL,   **Hon C** K W HABERSHON

SLAUGHTER, LOWER (St Mary)   *see* The Guitings, Cutsdean, Farmcote etc *Glouc*

SLAUGHTER, UPPER (St Peter)   *as above*

SLAUGHTERFORD (St Nicholas)   *see* By Brook *Bris*

SLAWSTON (All Saints)   *see* Hallaton and Allexton, w Horninghold, Tugby etc *Leic*

SLEAFORD, NEW (St Denys) *Linc 22*   **P** *Bp*   **P-in-c** J A PATRICK,   **C** J S CULLIMORE

SLEDMERE (St Mary)   *see* Waggoners *York*

SLEEKBURN (St John)   *see* Cambois and Sleekburn *Newc*

SLEIGHTS (St John)   *see* Lower Esk *York*

SLIMBRIDGE (St John the Evangelist)   *see* Sharpness, Purton, Brookend and Slimbridge *Glouc*

SLINDON (St Chad)   *see* Eccleshall *Lich*

SLINDON (St Mary), Eartham and Madehurst *Chich 1*   **P** *Bp, D&C, and Mrs J Izard (jt)*   **R** vacant (01243) 814275

SLINFOLD (St Peter)   *see* Itchingfield w Slinfold *Chich*

SLINGSBY (All Saints)   *see* The Street Par *York*

SLIPTON (St John the Baptist) *Pet 9*   **P** *L G Stopford Sackville Esq*   **P-in-c** D H P FOOT

SLITTING MILL (St John the Baptist)   *see* Brereton and Rugeley *Lich*

SLOANE STREET (Holy Trinity)   *see* Upper Chelsea H Trin *Lon*

SLOLEY (St Bartholomew)   *see* Worstead, Westwick, Sloley, Swanton Abbot etc *Nor*

SLOUGH (St Paul) (Christ Church) *Ox 23*   **P** *Trustees*   **V** M C COTTERELL,   **C** J V BINNS

SLYNE W HEST (St Luke) and Halton St Wilfrid w Aughton St Saviour *Blackb 14*   **P** *Bp and Exors R T Sanderson (jt)*   **R** P A BICKNELL

SMALL HEATH (All Saints) *Birm 13*   **P** *Patr Bd*   **C** D J H G ELLIOTT

SMALLBRIDGE (St John the Baptist) and Wardle *Man 21*   **P** *Bp*   **P-in-c** A J HOWELL

SMALLBURGH (St Peter) w Dilham w Honing and Crostwight *Nor 12*   **P** *Bp, T R Cubitt Esq, and J C Wickman Esq (jt)*   **P-in-c** B K FURNESS

SMALLEY (St John the Baptist)   *see* Morley w Smalley and Horsley Woodhouse *Derby*

SMALLFIELD (Church Room)   *see* Burstow w Horne *S'wark*

SMALLHYTHE (St John the Baptist)   *see* Tenterden St Mildred w Smallhythe *Cant*

SMALLTHORNE (St Saviour) *Lich 11*   **P** *R Norton in the Moors*   **V** R J S GRIGSON

SMALLWOOD (St John the Baptist)   *see* Astbury and Smallwood *Ches*

SMANNELL (Christ Church)   *see* Knight's Enham and Smannell w Enham Alamein *Win*

SMARDEN (St Michael)   *see* Biddenden and Smarden *Cant*

SMAWTHORPE (St Michael and All Angels) *Wakef 10*   **P** *Bp*   **V** vacant (01977) 557079

SMEATON, GREAT (St Eloy)   *see* E Richmond *Ripon*

SMEETH (St Mary) w Monks Horton and Stowting and Brabourne *Cant 10*   **P** *Abp*   **P-in-c** R L LE ROSSIGNOL,   **NSM** S M COX

SMEETON WESTERBY (Christ Church)   *see* Kibworth and Smeeton Westerby and Saddington *Leic*

SMESTOW VALE TEAM *Lich 24*   **P** *Patr Bd*   **TR** A P BROWN,   **C** E I ANDERTON,   **OLM** R A M COOK

SMETHCOTT (St Michael)   *see* Dorrington w Leebotwood, Longnor, Stapleton etc *Heref*

SMETHWICK (Old Church) *Birm 7*   **P** *Dorothy Parkes Trustees*   **V** N J MASON

SMETHWICK (Resurrection) (St Stephen and St Michael) *Birm 7*   **P** *Bp*   **V** D R GOULD,   **NSM** H M WHEELER

SMETHWICK (St Mary the Virgin)   *see* Bearwood *Birm*

SMETHWICK (St Matthew w St Chad) *Birm 7*   **P** *Bp and V Smethwick (alt)*   **V** P E NICHOLSON

SMISBY (St James)   *see* Ticknall, Smisby and Stanton by Bridge etc *Derby*

SMITHILLS HALL (Chapel)   *see* Halliwell St Pet *Man*

SMORRALL LANE (St Andrew)   *see* Bedworth *Cov*

SNAILBEACH (St Luke)   *see* Minsterley *Heref*

SNAILWELL (St Peter)   *see* Three Rivers Gp *Ely*

SNAINTON (St Stephen)   *see* Upper Derwent *York*

SNAITH (St Laurence Priory)   *see* Gt Snaith *Sheff*

SNAITH, GREAT (Holy Trinity) (St John the Baptist) (St Paul) *Sheff 10*   **P** *Bp*   **TR** C ROBERTS,   **NSM** P W HIBBS

SNAPE (St John the Baptist)   *see* Alde River *St E*

SNAPE CASTLE (Chapel of St Mary)   *see* W Tanfield and Well w Snape and N Stainley *Ripon*

SNARESTONE (St Bartholomew)   *see* Woodfield Team *Leic*

SNARGATE (St Dunstan)   *see* Appledore w Brookland, Fairfield, Brenzett etc *Cant*

SNEAD (St Mary the Virgin)   *see* Wentnor w Ratlinghope, Myndtown, Norbury etc *Heref*

SNEATON (St Hilda)   *see* Lower Esk *York*

SNEINTON (St Christopher) w St Philip *S'well 13*   **P** *CPAS and Trustees (alt)*   **P-in-c** R E WORSLEY,   **NSM** A R HASKEY

SNEINTON (St Cyprian) *S'well 13*   **P** *Bp*   **P-in-c** A L WAUDE

SNEINTON (St Stephen) w St Matthias *S'well 13*   **P** *Bp and SMF (jt)*   **V** M G CROOK

SNELLAND (All Saints)   *see* Wragby Gp *Linc*

SNELSTON (St Peter)   *see* Norbury w Snelston *Derby*

SNETTISHAM (St Mary) w Ingoldisthorpe and Fring *Nor 16*   **P** *Bp, CPAS, and D&C (jt)*   **R** G H SUART

SNEYD (Holy Trinity) *Lich 11*   **P** *Bp*   **V** B L WILLIAMS

SNEYD GREEN (St Andrew) *Lich 11*   **P** *Bp*   **V** G R DAVIES

SNITTERBY (St Nicholas)   *see* Bishop Norton, Wadingham and Snitterby *Linc*

SNITTERFIELD (St James the Great) w Bearley *Cov 7*   **P** *Bp and V Wootton Wawen*   **P-in-c** R LIVINGSTON

SNODLAND (All Saints) (Christ Church) *Roch 1*   **P** *Bp and CPAS (jt)*   **R** vacant (01634) 240232

SNORING, GREAT (St Mary)   *see* Barney, Fulmodeston w Croxton, Hindringham etc *Nor*

SNORING, LITTLE (St Andrew)   *as above*

SNOWDEN HILL Chapel Farm (not known)   *see* Penistone and Thurlstone *Wakef*

SNOWSHILL (St Barnabas)   *see* Winchcombe *Glouc*

SOAR, UPPER *Leic 7*   **P** *Prime Min (1 turn), Mrs A M Finn, Adn Loughb, and Ball Coll Ox (1 turn)*   **R** C M BRENNAND,   **NSM** J G HARGREAVES

SOBERTON (St Peter) w Newtown *Portsm 1*   **P** *Bp*   **V** vacant (01489) 877400

SOCKBURN (All Saints)   *see* Dinsdale w Sockburn *Dur*

SODBURY, LITTLE (St Adeline)   *see* Horton and Lt Sodbury *Glouc*

SODBURY, OLD (St John the Baptist)   *see* Chipping Sodbury and Old Sodbury *Glouc*

SOHAM (St Andrew) and Wicken *Ely 4*   **P** *Pemb Coll Cam (1 turn), Pemb Coll Cam and Ch Patr Trust (jt) (1 turn)*   **V** M T ALBAN-JONES

SOHO (St Anne) (St Thomas) (St Peter) *Lon 3*   **P** *R Westmr St Jas*   **R** D S GILMORE,   **NSM** R S F BUCKLEY

SOLE BAY *St E 15*   **P** *Patr Bd*   **TV** D A EATON, R HENDERSON, J E EATON,   **C** C M HALLETT

SOLIHULL (Catherine de Barnes) (St Alphege) (St Helen) (St Michael) *Birm 11*   **P** *Patr Bd*   **TR** T W PILKINGTON,   **TV** P J TAYLOR, S H MARSHALL, M A JONES,   **C** P H GERARD

SOLLARS HOPE (St Michael)   *see* Brampton *Heref*

SOLWAY PLAIN *Carl 7*   **P** *Patr Bd*   **TR** S J SWAIN,   **TV** A BYROM,   **Hon C** P N HAYWARD,   **NSM** D TEMBEY, M I STUDHOLME

SOMBORNE w Ashley *Win 12*   **P** *Bp*   **P-in-c** R V STAPLETON

SOMERBY (All Saints)   *see* Burrough Hill Pars *Leic*

SOMERBY (St Margaret)   *see* N Wolds Gp *Linc*

SOMERBY, NEW (St Anne)   *see* Grantham St Anne New Somerby and Spitalgate *Linc*

SOMERBY, OLD (St Mary Magdalene)   *see* N Beltisloe Gp *Linc*

SOMERCOTES and Grainthorpe w Conisholme *Linc 12*   **P** *Duchy of Lanc (2 turns), Magd Coll Cam and Bp (1 turn)*   **R** vacant (01507) 358829

SOMERCOTES (St Thomas) *Derby 1*   **P** *Bp*   **V** G M KNOX,   **NSM** T J HOLMES

SOMERCOTES, NORTH (St Mary)   *see* Somercotes and Grainthorpe w Conisholme *Linc*

SOMERFORD (All Saints)   *see* Astbury and Smallwood *Ches*

SOMERFORD (St Mary)   *see* Christchurch *Win*

SOMERFORD, GREAT (St Peter and St Paul), Little Somerford, Seagry and Corston w Rodbourne *Bris 6*   **P** *Bp, MMCET, and Ex Coll Ox (jt) (3 turns), Ld Chan (2 turns)*   **C** L BARNES

SOMERFORD, LITTLE (St John the Baptist)   *see* Gt Somerford, Lt Somerford, Seagry, Corston etc *Bris*

SOMERFORD KEYNES (All Saints)   *see* Kemble, Poole Keynes, Somerford Keynes etc *Glouc*

SOMERLEYTON (St Mary), Ashby, Fritton, Herringfleet, Blundeston and Lound *Nor 9*   **P** *Lord Somerleyton and SMF (jt)*   **R** L R HOBBS

SOMERS TOWN (St Mary the Virgin) *see* Old St Pancras *Lon*
SOMERSAL HERBERT (St Peter) *see* Doveridge, Scropton, Sudbury etc *Derby*
SOMERSBY (St Margaret) *see* S Ormsby Gp *Linc*
SOMERSHAM (St John the Baptist) w Pidley and Oldhurst *Ely 12* **P** *Bp* **R** C S BARTER, **Hon C** F J KILNER, **NSM** A M PETERS-WOTHERSPOON
SOMERSHAM (St Mary) w Flowton and Offton w Willisham *St E 1* **P** *Bp and MMCET (jt)* **P-in-c** B F ROSE
SOMERTON (St James) *see* Cherwell Valley *Ox*
SOMERTON (St Margaret) *see* Glemsford, Hartest w Boxted, Somerton etc *St E*
SOMERTON (St Michael and All Angels) w Compton Dundon, the Charltons and Kingsdon *B & W 6* **P** *Bp Lon (1 turn), Bp (2 turns), and DBP (1 turn)* **P-in-c** A J SYMONDS, **C** B S FAULKNER, **NSM** W M GRIFFITH
SOMERTON, WEST (St Mary) *see* Flegg Coastal Benefice *Nor*
SOMPTING (St Mary the Virgin) (St Peter) *Chich 5* **P** *OStJ* **V** E K HOWARD
SONNING (St Andrew) (St Patrick) *Ox 16* **P** *Bp* **V** J A F TAYLOR, **Hon C** M D C FORRER
SONNING COMMON (Christ the King) *see* Rotherfield Peppard and Kidmore End etc *Ox*
SOOKHOLME (St Augustine) *see* Warsop *S'well*
SOOTHILL (St Luke) *see* Hanging Heaton *Wakef*
SOPLEY (St Michael and All Angels) *see* Burton and Sopley *Win*
SOPWORTH (St Mary the Virgin) *see* Boxwell, Leighterton, Didmarton, Oldbury etc *Glouc*
SOTHERTON (St Andrew) *see* Sole Bay *St E*
SOTTERLEY (St Margaret) *see* Hundred River *St E*
SOTWELL (St James) *see* Wallingford *Ox*
SOUDLEY (St Michael) *see* Cinderford St Jo *Glouc*
SOULBURY (All Saints) *see* Stewkley w Soulbury and Drayton Parslow *Ox*
SOULDERN (Annunciation of the Blessed Virgin Mary) *see* Cherwell Valley *Ox*
SOULDROP (All Saints) *see* Sharnbrook, Felmersham and Knotting w Souldrop *St Alb*
SOUNDWELL (St Stephen) *Bris 5* **P** *Bp* **V** I L WILLS, **NSM** A J G COOPER, E A PERRY
SOURTON (St Thomas of Canterbury) *see* Okehampton w Inwardleigh, Bratton Clovelly etc *Ex*
SOUTH *see also under substantive place name*
SOUTH BANK (St John) *York 18* **P** *Abp* **V** T M LEATHLEY
SOUTH BARROW Team Ministry, The *Carl 8* **P** *Bp* **TR** E J NATTRASS, **C** I M HARVEY, **NSM** H GRAINGER
SOUTH CAVE (All Saints) and Ellerker w Broomfleet *York 13* **P** *CPAS and D&C Dur (jt)* **V** P G FAULKNER, **NSM** P R DRAPER
SOUTH COVE (St Lawrence) *see* Sole Bay *St E*
SOUTH HILL (St Sampson) w Callington *Truro 11* **P** *PCC* **R** P R SHARPE, **NSM** L PARKER, **OLM** P A RAYNHAM
SOUTH MOOR (St George) *see* Ch the K *Dur*
SOUTH PARK (St Luke) *see* Reigate St Luke w Doversgreen *S'wark*
SOUTH POOL (St Nicholas and St Cyriac) *see* Stokenham, Slapton, Charleton w Buckland etc *Ex*
SOUTH SHIELDS (All Saints) (St Mary w St Martin) *Dur 15* **P** *Patr Bd* **TR** J D MILLER, **TV** D R D MASLEN, J C G POLLOCK
SOUTH SHIELDS St Aidan (St Stephen) The Lawe *Dur 15* **P** *Bp and D&C* **P-in-c** P G STANNARD
SOUTH SHIELDS (St Hilda) w St Thomas *Dur 15* **P** *D&C* **P-in-c** P G STANNARD
SOUTH SHIELDS (St Lawrence the Martyr) *see* Horsley Hill St Lawr *Dur*
SOUTH SHIELDS (St Simon) *Dur 15* **P** *The Crown* **V** *vacant* 0191-455 3164 *or* 424 0690
SOUTH SHORE (Holy Trinity) *Blackb 8* **P** J C Hilton Esq **P-in-c** G ROUSE, **C** D O'BRIEN
SOUTH SHORE (St Peter) *Blackb 8* **P** *Bp* **P-in-c** G ROUSE, **NSM** M H WARD
SOUTH TRINITY BROADS Benefice, The: Filby, Thrigby, Mautby, Stokesby, Runham and Burgh w Billockby *Nor 6* **P** *Bp, Adn Nor, DBP, Mrs Z K Cognetti, R T Daniel Esq, and I F M Lucas Esq (jt)* **R** G R STEEL
SOUTH WARWICKSHIRE SEVEN Group, The *Cov 9* **P** *Bp, Mert Coll Ox, Ch Ch Ox, and Trin Coll Ox (jt)* **R** R K SMITH, **Hon C** G EVANS
SOUTHACRE (St George) *see* Castleacre, Newton, Westacre and Southacre *Nor*
SOUTHALL (Christ the Redeemer) *Lon 22* **P** *Bp* **V** N J ORCHARD
SOUTHALL (Emmanuel) *Lon 22* **P** *Bp and Ch Patr Trust (jt)* **V** W E GILL

SOUTHALL (Holy Trinity) *Lon 22* **P** *Ch Patr Trust* **V** M F BOLLEY
SOUTHALL (St George) *Lon 22* **P** *D&C St Paul's* **V** C RAMSAY, **C** J M PAYNE
SOUTHALL GREEN (St John) *Lon 22* **P** *Ch Patr Trust* **V** M A POULSON, **Hon C** D J C BOOKLESS
SOUTHAM (Ascension) *see* Bishop's Cleeve and Woolstone w Gotherington etc *Glouc*
SOUTHAM (St James) *Cov 10* **P** *The Crown* **P-in-c** J E ARMSTRONG
SOUTHAMPTON (Christ Church) Portswood *see* Portswood Ch Ch *Win*
SOUTHAMPTON City Centre (St Mary) (St Michael) *Win 13* **P** *Bp* **TR** J E DAVIES, **TV** S P HALL, T E DAYKIN, **NSM** P R HAND
SOUTHAMPTON (Holy Trinity) *see* Weston *Win*
SOUTHAMPTON (St Alban) *see* Swaythling *Win*
SOUTHAMPTON (St Barnabas) *Win 13* **P** *Bp* **V** B J FRY
SOUTHAMPTON (St Denys) Portswood *see* Portswood St Denys *Win*
SOUTHAMPTON (St Jude) *see* Maybush and Southampton St Jude *Win*
SOUTHAMPTON (St Mark) *Win 13* **P** *Ch Patr Trust* **V** G MARCH
SOUTHAMPTON (St Mary Extra) *Win 13* **P** *Bp* **V** P G FIRMIN
SOUTHAMPTON Thornhill (St Christopher) *Win 13* **P** *Bp* **V** G P ANNAS, **C** D W JENNINGS, **NSM** J B WALTERS
SOUTHAMPTON Winkle Street (St Julian) *see* Southampton (City Cen) *Win*
SOUTHBERGH (St Andrew) *see* Barnham Broom and Upper Yare *Nor*
SOUTHBOROUGH (St Peter) (Christ Church) (St Matthew) and Bidborough *Roch 12* **P** *Patr Bd* **TR** G E HOVENDEN, **TV** C B WICKS, S A HILLS, **C** P M WHITE, **NSM** S G FAUCHON-JONES
SOUTHBOROUGH (St Thomas) *Roch 12* **P** *Bp* **P-in-c** J A WHEELER
SOUTHBOURNE (All Saints) *see* Pokesdown All SS *Win*
SOUTHBOURNE (St Christopher) *Win 8* **P** *Bp* **P-in-c** A L MCPHERSON, **NSM** N S LEGRAND
SOUTHBOURNE (St John the Evangelist) w West Thorney *Chich 13* **P** *Bp* **V** C R JENKINS
SOUTHBOURNE (St Katharine) (St Nicholas) *Win 8* **P** *Bp* **V** J C WHITE
SOUTHBROOM (St James) *Sarum 16* **P** *D&C* **V** C M TEBBUTT, **C** J R G BRADBURY, **NSM** S E TEBBUTT, S A IBBETSON, **OLM** J A HAYNES
SOUTHCHURCH (Christ Church) *Chelmsf 13* **P** *Bp* **V** S N ROSCOE
SOUTHCHURCH (Holy Trinity) *Chelmsf 13* **P** *Abp Cant* **R** M A BALLARD
SOUTHCOATES (St Aidan) *see* Kingston upon Hull St Aid Southcoates *York*
SOUTHCOURT (Good Shepherd) *see* Walton H Trin *Ox*
SOUTHDENE (St Martin) *see* Kirkby *Liv*
SOUTHEA (Emmanuel) *see* Wisbech St Mary and Guyhirn w Ring's End etc *Ely*
SOUTHEASE (St Peter) *Chich 18* **P** *Bp and Gorham Trustees (jt)* **V** D A HIDER
SOUTHEND (St John the Baptist) (St Mark) (All Saints) (St Alban) *Chelmsf 13* **P** *Patr Bd* **TR** S M BURDETT, **TV** W N PAXTON, P A ROBERTS, **NSM** S SAYERS, P E OWEN
SOUTHEND (St Peter) *see* Bradfield and Stanford Dingley *Ox*
SOUTHEND-ON-SEA (St Saviour) Westcliff *Chelmsf 13* **P** *Bp, Adn Southend, and Churchwardens (jt)* **V** R H WILLIAMS, **C** L M WILLIAMS
SOUTHERY (St Mary) *Ely 9* **P** *Guild of All So* **R** D J EVANS
SOUTHEY GREEN (St Bernard) Conventional District *Sheff 3* **C-in-c** R GOMERSALL
SOUTHFIELDS (St Barnabas) *S'wark 18* **P** *Bp* **P-in-c** I S TATTUM
SOUTHFIELDS (St Michael and All Angels) *see* Wandsworth St Mich w St Steph *S'wark*
SOUTHFLEET (St Nicholas) *Roch 4* **P** *CPAS* **R** D W J HOUSTON
SOUTHGATE (Christ Church) *Lon 18* **P** *V Edmonton All SS* **V** P J E JACKSON
SOUTHGATE Local Ecumenical Partnership *St E 13 vacant*
SOUTHGATE (Shared Church) *see* Grange St Andr *Ches*
SOUTHGATE (St Andrew) *Lon 18* **P** *Bp* **V** M C H JONES
SOUTHGATE (St Mary) *Chich 7* **P** *Patr Bd* **TR** T J WILSON, **TV** R E POOLE, S D K TAYLOR, R J EDWARDS, **NSM** G D M RICHARDS
SOUTHGATE, NEW (St Paul) *Lon 14* **P** *V Southgate Ch Ch* **V** M J S MCAULAY

SOUTHILL (All Saints)   *see* Clifton and Southill *St Alb*
SOUTHLAKE (St James) *Ox 15*   **P** *DBP*   **V** M A E ASTIN
SOUTHLAKE (St James's Church Centre)   *see* Woodley *Ox*
SOUTHLEIGH (St Lawrence)   *see* Colyton, Musbury, Southleigh and Branscombe *Ex*
SOUTHMEAD (St Stephen) *Bris 2*   **P** *Bp*   **V** J C HALL
SOUTHMINSTER (St Leonard) *Chelmsf 11*   **P** *Govs Charterhouse*   **V** G S ANDERSON
SOUTHOE (St Leonard)   *see* Gt Staughton w Hail Weston w Southoe *Ely*
SOUTHOVER (St John the Baptist) *Chich 18*   **P** *CPAS*
  R S J DAUGHTERY,   **C** D J GARRATT,   **NSM** J J BAMBER
SOUTHOWRAM (St Anne-in-the-Grove) and Claremount
  Wakef 4   **P** *V Halifax*   **V** G S JAMIESON
SOUTHPORT (All Saints) *Liv 9*   **P** *Trustees*   **C** A J EDWARDS,
  T P JARDINE
SOUTHPORT (Christ Church) *Liv 9*   **P** *Trustees*   **V** S T REID,
  NSM S T MARSHALL
SOUTHPORT (Emmanuel) *Liv 9*   **P** *PCC*   **V** C POPE,
  C B J STOBER
SOUTHPORT (Holy Trinity) *Liv 9*   **P** *Trustees*
  V R G GARNER
SOUTHPORT (St Luke) *Liv 9*   **P** *V Southport H Trin*
  P-in-c R WIFFEN,   **NSM** D H MARSTON
SOUTHPORT (St Philip) (St Paul) *Liv 9*   **P** *V Southport Ch Ch and Trustees (jt)*   **V** A J EDWARDS
SOUTHPORT (St Simon and St Jude) All Souls *Liv 9*
  P *Trustees*   **V** T P JARDINE
SOUTHREPPS (St James)   *see* Trunch *Nor*
SOUTHREY (St John the Divine)   *see* Bardney *Linc*
SOUTHROP (St Peter)   *see* Fairford Deanery *Glouc*
SOUTHSEA (Holy Spirit) *Portsm 6*   **P** *Bp*   **V** M D B LEWIS,
  C P M AMEY
SOUTHSEA (St Jude) *Portsm 6*   **P** *Trustees*   **V** M I DUFF
SOUTHSEA (St Luke)   *see* Portsea St Luke *Portsm*
SOUTHSEA (St Peter) *Portsm 6*   **P** *Bp*   **P-in-c** A J HUGHES
  V M F HOLLAND,   **NSM** P A O'GORMAN
SOUTHSEA (St Simon) *Portsm 6*   **P** *Ch Patr Trust*
SOUTHTOWN (St Mary)   *see* Gt Yarmouth *Nor*
SOUTHWARK (Christ Church) *S'wark 10*   **P** *Marshall's Charity*   **R** T C N SCOTT
SOUTHWARK (Holy Trinity w St Matthew) *S'wark 10*   **P** *Bp*
  R N A MCKINNON
SOUTHWARK (St George the Martyr) (St Alphege) (St Jude)
  S'wark 10   **P** *Lon Corp (1 turn), Ld Chan (4 turns), Walsingham Coll Trust Assn (1 turn)*   **P-in-c** R C ANDREWS,
  Hon C M DURRAN,   **NSM** D SWABY,   **OLM** D PAPE
SOUTHWARK (St Hugh)   *see* Bermondsey St Hugh CD *S'wark*
SOUTHWATER (Holy Innocents) *Chich 8*   **P** *V Horsham*
  V *vacant* (01403) 730229
SOUTHWAY (Holy Spirit) *Ex 23*   **P** *Ld Chan*
  P-in-c W P JACKSON,   **C** M L SIMMS, D B M GILL,
  NSM M J FAIRALL
SOUTHWELL (Holy Trinity) *S'well 15*   **P** *CPAS*
  V M S TANNER,   **NSM** D L ROBBINS
SOUTHWELL (St Andrew)   *see* Portland All SS w St Andr *Sarum*
SOUTHWICK (Holy Trinity)   *see* N Wearside *Dur*
SOUTHWICK (St Columba)   *as above*
SOUTHWICK (St James) w Boarhunt *Portsm 1*
  P *R Thistlewayte Esq*   **P-in-c** R L GREEN
SOUTHWICK (St Mary the Virgin)   *see* Warmington, Tansor and Cotterstock etc *Pet*
SOUTHWICK (St Michael and All Angels) (St Peter) *Chich 4*
  P *Bp and Ld Chan (alt)*   **R** R D HARRIS,   **C** D A GUEST,
  M J BETSON,   **NSM** B A WILSON
SOUTHWICK (St Thomas)   *see* N Bradley, Southwick, Heywood and Steeple Ashton *Sarum*
SOUTHWOLD (St Edmund King and Martyr)   *see* Sole Bay *St E*
SOUTHWOOD (Mission Church)   *see* Evercreech w Chesterblade and Milton Clevedon *B & W*
SOWERBY (St Mary) (St Peter) *Wakef 3*   **P** *DBP*
  P-in-c M C CRABTREE,   **NSM** C J WARDMAN, L ENNIS
SOWERBY (St Oswald) *York 19*   **P** *Abp*   **P-in-c** N J CARNALL
SOWERBY BRIDGE (Christ Church) *Wakef 4*   **P** *V Halifax*
  V *vacant* (01422) 831253
SOWTON (St Michael and All Angels)   *see* Aylesbeare, Rockbeare, Farringdon etc *Ex*
SPALDING (St John the Baptist) w Deeping St Nicholas *Linc 17*
  P *Bp*   **V** P S J GARLAND
SPALDING (St Mary and St Nicolas) *Linc 17*   **P** *Feoffees*
  C V POLLARD, D J CLUNE
SPALDING (St Paul) *Linc 17*   **P** *Bp and V Spalding (jt)*
  C V POLLARD

SPALDWICK (St James)   *see* E Leightonstone *Ely*
SPARHAM (St Mary)   *see* Lyng, Sparham, Elsing, Bylaugh, Bawdeswell etc *Nor*
SPARKBROOK (Christ Church) *Birm 13*   **P** *Aston Trustees*
  P-in-c S R SIMCOX
SPARKBROOK (St Agatha) w Balsall Heath St Barnabas
  Birm 13   **P** *Bp*   **V** J A HERVE
SPARKFORD (St Mary Magdalene)   *see* Cam Vale *B & W*
SPARKHILL (St John the Evangelist) *Birm 13*   **P** *Dioc Trustees and Aston Trustees (alt)*   **V** J A SELF,   **C** S G TAYLOR
SPARKWELL (All Saints) *Ex 21*   **P** *D&C Windsor*
  V F G DENMAN
SPARROW HALL (St George)   *see* Fazakerley Em *Liv*
SPARSHOLT (Holy Cross)   *see* Ridgeway *Ox*
SPARSHOLT (St Stephen)   *see* Downs Benefice *Win*
SPAXTON (St Margaret)   *see* Aisholt, Enmore, Goathurst, Nether Stowey etc *B & W*
SPEEN (St Mary the Virgin)   *see* Newbury *Ox*
SPEETON (St Leonard)   *see* Bempton w Flamborough, Reighton w Speeton *York*
SPEKE (St Aidan) (All Saints) *Liv 4*   **P** *Bp*   **TR** C I KIDD,
  TV G PINNINGTON
SPELDHURST (St Mary the Virgin) w Groombridge and Ashurst *Roch 12*   **P** *DBP*   **R** D P WREN,   **NSM** J E PERKINS
SPELSBURY (All Saints)   *see* Chase *Ox*
SPEN, HIGH (St Patrick) and Rowlands Gill *Dur 13*   **P** *Bp*
  V *vacant* (01207) 542815
SPENCER BENEFICE   *see* Brington w Whilton and Norton etc *Pet*
SPENCER PERCIVAL MEMORIAL CHURCH   *see* Ealing All SS *Lon*
SPENCERS WOOD (St Michael and All Angels)   *see* Loddon Reach *Ox*
SPENNITHORNE (St Michael) w Finghall and Hauxwell
  Ripon 4   **P** *R J Dalton Esq and M C AWyvill Esq (alt)*
  P-in-c W J HULSE
SPENNYMOOR (St Paul) and Whitworth *Dur 6*   **P** *D&C*
  V L E GOUGH,   **C** A M RICHARDSON, W SCOTT
SPERNALL, Morton Bagot and Oldberrow *Cov 7*   **P** *Mrs J M Pinney and Bp (alt)*   **P-in-c** R W DEIMEL,
  NSM M M DEIMEL
SPETISBURY (St John the Baptist) w Charlton Marshall and Blandford St Mary *Sarum 6*   **P** *Worc Coll Ox (1 turn), Bp (2 turns)*   **R** S F TREEBY
SPEXHALL (St Peter)   *see* Blyth Valley *St E*
SPILSBY Group, The (St James) *Linc 7*   **P** *Baroness Willoughby de Eresby (3 turns), Mrs J M Fox-Robinson (1 turn), and Bp (1 turn)*   **P-in-c** P F COATES,   **C** G MORGAN
SPIRE HILL *Sarum 5*   **P** *Bp, CCC Cam, and Mrs J C M Langmead (jt)*   **R** W T RIDDING
SPITAL (St Agnes)   *see* New Windsor *Ox*
SPITAL (St Leonard's Mission Room)   *see* Chesterfield St Mary and All SS *Derby*
SPITALFIELDS (Christ Church w All Saints) *Lon 7*
  P *MMCET*   **R** A RIDER,   **C** R GREEN
SPITALGATE (St John the Evangelist)   *see* Grantham St Anne New Somerby and Spitalgate *Linc*
SPITTAL (St John) *Newc 12*   **P** *Bp and Mercers' Co (alt)*
  NSM S J HARRISON
SPIXWORTH (St Peter)   *see* Horsham St Faith, Spixworth and Crostwick *Nor*
SPOFFORTH (All Saints) w Kirk Deighton *Ripon 1*   **P** *Bp*
  P-in-c M PALLIS,   **C** K COUCHMAN,   **Hon C** M L SHACKLEY
SPONDON (St Werburgh) *Derby 9*   **P** *Mrs L B Palmer*
  V J F HOLLYWELL,   **NSM** E S BERRY
SPORLE (St Mary)   *see* Gt and Lt Dunham w Gt and Lt Fransham and Sporle *Nor*
SPOTLAND (St Clement) *Man 21*   **P** *Bp*   **V** L CONNOLLY
SPRATTON (St Andrew) *Pet 2*   **P** *Bp*   **P-in-c** M D PETITT,
  NSM M R BATTISON
SPREYTON (St Michael)   *see* Chagford, Drewsteignton, Hittisleigh etc *Ex*
SPRIDLINGTON (St Hilary)   *see* Owmby Gp *Linc*
SPRIGG'S ALLEY (Mission Room)   *see* Chinnor, Sydenham, Aston Rowant and Crowell *Ox*
SPRING GROVE (St Mary) *Lon 11*   **P** *Ch Patr Trust*
  V R C HOAD,   **Hon C** M A WARMAN
SPRING LINE Group, The *Linc 3*   **P** *Lord Monson, Ball Coll Ox, J M Wright Esq, Bp, and DBP (jt)*   **P-in-c** P D GODDEN
SPRING PARK (All Saints) *S'wark 19*   **P** *Bp*   **V** Y V CLARKE
SPRINGFIELD (All Saints) *Chelmsf 8*   **P** *Air Cdre N S Paynter*
  R R J BROWN
SPRINGFIELD (Holy Trinity) *Chelmsf 8*   **P** *Simeon's Trustees*
  V T W BALL,   **C** D V CHESNEY
SPRINGFIELD (St Christopher) *Birm 13*   **P** *Trustees*
  P-in-c T M HOWARTH

SPRINGFIELD Wallington   *see* Wallington Springfield Ch *S'wark*

SPRINGFIELD, EAST (Church of Our Saviour) (not known) *Chelmsf 8*   **P** *Bp*   **P-in-c** A MACKENZIE,   **Hon C** C A KOSLA

SPRINGFIELD, NORTH (St Augustine of Canterbury) *Chelmsf 8*   **P** *Bp*   **P-in-c** J V ANDERSON

SPRINGFIELDS (St Stephen)   *see* Wolverhampton St Steph *Lich*

SPRINGTHORPE (St George and St Laurence)   *see* Corringham and Blyton Gp *Linc*

SPRINGWELL (St Mary the Virgin)   *see* Sunderland St Mary and St Pet *Dur*

SPRINGWOOD (All Souls)   *see* Liv All So Springwood *Liv*

SPROATLEY (St Swithin)   *see* Preston and Sproatley in Holderness *York*

SPROTBROUGH (St Mary the Virgin) *Sheff 7*   **P** *Bp* **R** J M RICHARDS,   **C** K J FRANCIS

SPROUGHTON (All Saints) w Burstall, Copdock w Washbrook and Belstead and Bentley w Tattingstone *St E 5*   **P** *Patr Bd* **R** C L WINGFIELD,   **NSM** R J NEEDLE,   **OLM** D W MEHEN

SPROWSTON (St Cuthbert) (St Mary and St Margaret) w Beeston *Nor 2*   **P** *D&C*   **R** J D BENNETT,   **C** A V WOODROW, D AKRILL,   **NSM** H M WRIGHT,   **OLM** P CHARLESWORTH

SPROXTON (St Bartholomew)   *see* High Framland Par *Leic*

SPROXTON (St Chad)   *see* Helmsley *York*

SQUIRRELS HEATH (All Saints) *Chelmsf 2*   **P** *Bp* **V** C W WRAGG

ST BARTHOLOMEW *Sarum 11*   **P** *Ch Ch Ox, New Coll Ox, and DBP (by turn)*   **R** S J MORGAN

STADHAMPTON (St John the Baptist)   *see* Dorchester *Ox*

STAFFHURST WOOD (St Silvan)   *see* Limpsfield and Titsey *S'wark*

STAFFORD (Christ Church) (St Chad) (St Mary) *Lich 10* **P** *Patr Bd*   **TR** G C FOWELL,   **TV** J E EVANS, **C** R M MCINTYRE, A F WALKER,   **NSM** M J FISHER, J J DAVIS, **OLM** B BUTTERY

STAFFORD (St John the Baptist) and Tixall w Ingestre *Lich 10* **P** *Bp and Earl of Shrewsbury and Talbot (jt)*   **V** A G STONE, **C** A C T KELLY

STAFFORD (St Paul) Forebridge *Lich 10*   **P** *V Castle Ch* **V** P KELLY

STAFFORD (St Thomas and St Andrew) Doxey   *see* Castle Town *Lich*

STAFFORD, WEST (St Andrew)   *see* Dorchester *Sarum*

STAGSDEN (St Leonard)   *see* Bromham w Oakley and Stagsden *St Alb*

STAGSHAW CHAPEL (St Aidan)   *see* St John Lee *Newc*

STAINBY (St Peter)   *see* Witham Gp *Linc*

STAINCLIFFE (Christ Church) and Carlinghow *Wakef 9* **P** *V Brownhill and V Batley (jt)*   **V** A G HOWE, **Hon C** M G INMAN

STAINCROSS (St John the Evangelist) *Wakef 7*   **P** *Bp* **V** J K BUTTERWORTH,   **OLM** J M CROSSLAND

STAINDROP (St Mary) *Dur 7*   **P** *Lord Barnard* **P-in-c** K STEVENTON

STAINES (Christ Church) (St Mary) (St Peter) *Lon 13*   **P** *Bp and Ld Chan (alt)*   **V** K J COSH,   **C** E R H BUSH, **NSM** J M TEED

STAINFIELD (St Andrew)   *see* Bardney *Linc*

STAINFORTH (St Mary) *Sheff 10*   **P** *Bp*   **V** A W ALLINGTON

STAINFORTH (St Peter)   *see* Langcliffe w Stainforth and Horton *Bradf*

STAINING (St Luke Mission Church)   *see* Blackpool St Mich *Blackb*

STAINLAND (St Andrew) w Outlane *Wakef 2*   **P** *V Halifax* **V** R A CHAPMAN,   **C** D BURROWS

STAINLEY, NORTH (St Mary the Virgin)   *see* W Tanfield and Well w Snape and N Stainley *Ripon*

STAINLEY, SOUTH (St Wilfrid)   *see* Markington w S Stainley and Bishop Thornton *Ripon*

STAINMORE (St Stephen)   *see* Brough w Stainmore, Musgrave and Warcop *Carl*

STAINTON (St Peter w St Paul) w Hilton *York 21*   **P** *Abp (2 turns), DBP (1 turn)*   **P-in-c** W J FORD, **NSM** W A DEWING

STAINTON (St Winifred)   *see* Tickhill w Stainton *Sheff*

STAINTON, GREAT (All Saints)   *see* Bishopton w Gt Stainton *Dur*

STAINTON BY LANGWORTH (St John the Baptist)   *see* Barlings *Linc*

STAINTON DALE (St John the Baptist)   *see* Cloughton and Burniston w Ravenscar etc *York*

STAINTON LE VALE (St Andrew)   *see* Walesby *Linc*

STAITHES (St Peter)   *see* Hinderwell, Roxby and Staithes etc *York*

STAKEFORD (Holy Family)   *see* Choppington *Newc*

STALBRIDGE (St Mary)   *see* Spire Hill *Sarum*

STALHAM (St Mary), East Ruston, Brunstead, Sutton and Ingham *Nor 12*   **P** *Bp, DBP and Mrs S F Baker (jt)* **R** S P LAWRENCE,   **NSM** R R F WASHFORD, **OLM** R H JACKSON

STALISFIELD (St Mary)   *see* Eastling w Ospringe and Stalisfield w Otterden *Cant*

STALLING BUSK (St Matthew)   *see* Askrigg w Stallingbusk *Ripon*

STALLINGBOROUGH (St Peter and St Paul)   *see* Keelby Gp *Linc*

STALMINE (St James) w Pilling St John the Baptist *Blackb 9* **P** *Bp, V Lanc St Mary, Mrs C B Mason-Hornby, and H D H Elletson Esq (jt)*   **V** G BILLINGTON, **NSM** D A DICKINSON, C PRITCHARD

STALYBRIDGE (Holy Trinity and Christ Church) *Ches 14* **P** *Trustees*   **P-in-c** T R PARKER

STALYBRIDGE (St George) *Man 17*   **P** *Lord Deramore and R Ashton-under-Lyne St Mich (jt)*   **V** I K STUBBS, **OLM** P BRIERLEY, K M M STEWART

STALYBRIDGE (St Paul) *Ches 14*   **P** *Trustees*   **V** *vacant* 0161-338 2514

STAMBOURNE (St Peter and St Thomas Becket)   *see* Upper Colne *Chelmsf*

STAMBRIDGE (St Mary and All Saints) *Chelmsf 12* **P** *Ld Chan (1 turn), Charterhouse (3 turns)* **P-in-c** C W COUSINS

STAMFORD (All Saints) w St John the Baptist *Linc 13* **P** *Ld Chan and Burghley Ho Preservation Trust (alt)* **P-in-c** M WARRICK,   **Hon C** D M BOND

STAMFORD (Christ Church) *Linc 13*   **P** *Bp* **P-in-c** R J MACKRILL,   **C** J M HOLMES

STAMFORD (St George) (St Paul) *Linc 13*   **P** *Burghley Ho Preservation Trust*   **R** M A N TAYLOR,   **D C** MAYLOR

STAMFORD (St Mary) (St Martin) *Linc 13*   **P** *Burghley Ho Preservation Trust*   **P-in-c** M R RUFF

STAMFORD BRIDGE Group of Parishes, The (St John the Baptist) *York 5*   **P** *Lord Egremont (2 turns), Prime Min (1 turn)*   **P-in-c** A F WAKEFIELD

STAMFORD HILL (St Bartholomew) *Lon 5*   **P** *The Crown* **V** C L CARD-REYNOLDS

STAMFORD HILL (St Thomas) *Lon 5*   **P** *R Hackney* **Hon C** I E VIBERT,   **NSM** M F E STEWART

STAMFORDHAM (St Mary the Virgin) w Matfen *Newc 9* **P** *Ld Chan*   **P-in-c** M C V NASH-WILLIAMS

STAMSHAW (St Saviour)   *see* Portsea St Sav *Portsm*

STANBRIDGE (St John the Baptist)   *see* Totternhoe, Stanbridge and Tilsworth *St Alb*

STANBURY (Mission Church)   *see* Haworth *Bradf*

STAND (All Saints) *Man 14*   **P** *Earl of Wilton*   **R** A J HARDY, **NSM** C D BINNS

STANDISH (St Nicholas)   *see* Eastington, Frocester, Haresfield etc *Glouc*

STANDISH (St Wilfrid) *Blackb 4*   **P** *Bp*   **R** M J EVERITT, **C** T B ENSOR, S MCCARTER,   **NSM** G E WATSON

STANDLAKE (St Giles)   *see* Lower Windrush *Ox*

STANDON (All Saints)   *see* Broughton w Croxton and Cotes Heath w Standon *Lich*

STANDON (St Mary) and The Mundens w Sacombe *St Alb 18* **P** *Ch Trust Fund Trust, K Coll Cam, and R Abel-Smith Esq (1 turn), Ch Trust Fund Trust (1 turn)*   **R** D C PAYNE, **C** L MOSS

STANFIELD (St Margaret)   *see* Litcham w Kempston, E and W Lexham, Mileham etc *Nor*

STANFORD (All Saints)   *see* Lyminge w Paddlesworth, Stanford w Postling etc *Cant*

STANFORD (All Saints) *Nor 13*   **P** *Bp*   **V** *vacant*

STANFORD (St Nicholas)   *see* Gilmorton, Peatling Parva, Kimcote etc *Leic*

STANFORD BISHOP (St James)   *see* Frome Valley *Heref*

STANFORD DINGLEY (St Denys)   *see* Bradfield and Stanford Dingley *Ox*

STANFORD IN THE VALE (St Denys) w Goosey and Hatford *Ox 17*   **P** *D&C Westmr (3 turns), Simeon's Trustees (2 turns)* **V** *vacant* (01367) 710267

STANFORD-LE-HOPE (St Margaret) w Mucking *Chelmsf 14* **P** *MMCET*   **R** J A K GUEST,   **C** J WHITE

STANFORD-ON-SOAR (St John the Baptist)   *see* E and W Leake, Stanford on Soar, Rempstone etc *S'well*

STANFORD-ON-TEME (St Mary)   *see* Teme Valley N *Worc*

STANFORD RIVERS (St Margaret)   *see* Greensted-juxta-Ongar w Stanford Rivers etc *Chelmsf*

STANGROUND (St John the Baptist) (St Michael and All Angels) *Ely 15*   **P** *Em Coll Cam*   **P-in-c** S BETSON

STANHOE (All Saints) *see* Docking, the Birchams, Stanhoe and Sedgeford *Nor*

STANHOPE (St Thomas) *see* Upper Weardale *Dur*

STANION (St Peter) *see* Brigstock w Stanion and Lowick and Sudborough *Pet*

STANLEY (All Saints) *see* W Hallam and Mapperley w Stanley *Derby*

STANLEY (St Agnes) *see* Bagnall w Endon *Lich*

STANLEY (St Andrew) *see* W Hallam and Mapperley w Stanley *Derby*

STANLEY (St Andrew) *see* Ch the K *Dur*

STANLEY (St Anne) w Stoneycroft St Paul *Liv 8* **P** *V W Derby St Mary and St Chad's Coll Dur (jt)* **V** M C DAVIES, **C** E L CALDERWOOD, **Hon C** C WARRILOW

STANLEY (St Peter) *Wakef 11* **P** *Dean* **V** W E HENDERSON, **NSM** J KILSBY

STANLEY (St Thomas) *see* Satley, Stanley and Tow Law *Dur*

STANLEY PONTLARGE (Chapel) *see* Winchcombe *Glouc*

STANLEYS, The *Glouc 5* **P** *Mrs L Y K Fisher and Jes Coll Cam (jt)* **P-in-c** S P PHILLIPSON-MASTERS

STANMER w Falmer *Chich 2* **P** *Bp* **P-in-c** A N ROBINSON

STANMORE (St Luke) *Win 7* **P** *Bp* **V** M R GARDNER, **C** M C BAGG

STANMORE, GREAT (St John the Evangelist) *Lon 23* **P** *R O Bernays Esq* **R** A J CHRISTIAN, **C** W T SMALLMAN

STANMORE, LITTLE (St Lawrence) *Lon 23* **P** *Bp* **R** P M REECE

STANNEY (St Andrew) *see* Ellesmere Port *Ches*

STANNINGFIELD (St Nicholas) *see* St Edm Way *St E*

STANNINGLEY (St Thomas) *Ripon 6* **P** *V Leeds St Pet* **R** *vacant* 0113-257 8966

STANNINGTON (Christ Church) *Sheff 4* **P** *Bp* **V** P W WEST

STANNINGTON (St Mary the Virgin) *Newc 11* **P** *Bp* **P-in-c** C R GOUGH

STANSFIELD (All Saints) *see* Bansfield *St E*

STANSTEAD (St James) *see* Glemsford, Hartest w Boxted, Somerton etc *St E*

STANSTEAD ABBOTS (St Andrew) *see* Gt Amwell w St Margaret's and Stanstead Abbots *St Alb*

STANSTEAD ST MARGARET (St Mary the Virgin) *as above*

STANSTED (St Mary) w Fairseat and Vigo *Roch 10* **P** *Bp* **R** C J L NOBLE

STANSTED (St Paul) (Christ Church) *Chich 13* **P** *Stansted Park Foundation* **V** *vacant*

STANSTED MOUNTFITCHET (St John) w Birchanger and Farnham *Chelmsf 18* **P** *Bp, New Coll Ox, and Mrs L A Murphy (jt)* **R** P J WILKIN, **C** G D TULK

STANTON (All Saints), Hopton, Market Weston, Barningham and Coney Weston *St E 9* **P** *Ld Chan (2 turns) and Bp (1 turn)* **R** D H MESSER

STANTON (St Gabriel) *see* Golden Cap Team *Sarum*

STANTON (St Mary) *see* Denstone w Ellastone and Stanton *Lich*

STANTON (St Mary and All Saints) *see* Markfield, Thornton, Bagworth and Stanton etc *Leic*

STANTON (St Michael and All Angels) *see* Winchcombe *Glouc*

STANTON BY BRIDGE (St Michael) *see* Ticknall, Smisby and Stanton by Bridge etc *Derby*

STANTON-BY-DALE (St Michael and All Angels) w Dale Abbey and Risley *Derby 13* **P** *Bp* **R** I E GOODING, **NSM** G W DUNDAS

STANTON DREW (Blessed Virgin Mary) *see* Bishop Sutton and Stanton Drew and Stowey *B & W*

STANTON FITZWARREN (St Leonard) *see* Stratton St Margaret w S Marston etc *Bris*

STANTON HARCOURT (St Michael) *see* Lower Windrush *Ox*

STANTON HILL (All Saints) *see* Skegby w Teversal *S'well*

STANTON-IN-PEAK (Holy Trinity) *see* Youlgreave, Middleton, Stanton-in-Peak etc *Derby*

STANTON LACY (Hayton Bent Hall) *see* Ludlow *Heref*

STANTON LACY (St Peter) *as above*

STANTON ON HINE HEATH (St Andrew) *Lich 22* **P** *Sir Beville Stanier Bt* **V** D J HUMPHRIES

STANTON-ON-THE-WOLDS (All Saints) *see* Keyworth and Stanton-on-the-Wolds and Bunny etc *S'well*

STANTON PRIOR (St Lawrence) *see* Farmborough, Marksbury and Stanton Prior *B & W*

STANTON ST BERNARD (All Saints) *see* Pewsey and Swanborough *Sarum*

STANTON ST JOHN (St John the Baptist) *see* Wheatley *Ox*

STANTON ST QUINTIN (St Giles) *see* Hullavington, Norton and Stanton St Quintin *Bris*

STANTONBURY (Christ Church) and Willen *Ox 25* **P** *Patr Bd* **TR** P A SMITH, **TV** A R B JOWITT, C E COLLINGE, P S BALLANTINE, **NSM** D B BELL, **OLM** J B ROSE

STANWAY (St Albright) (St Andrew) *Chelmsf 17* **P** *Magd Coll Ox* **R** P R MCLAREN-COOK

STANWAY (St Peter) *see* Winchcombe *Glouc*

STANWELL (St Mary the Virgin) *Lon 13* **P** *Ld Chan* **V** W P STAFFORD-WHITTAKER

STANWICK (St Laurence) *see* Raunds, Hargrave, Ringstead and Stanwick *Pet*

STANWIX (St Michael) *Carl 3* **P** *Bp* **V** B G PHILLIPS, **C** B W KING

STAPEHILL (All Saints) *see* Hampreston *Sarum*

STAPENHILL (Immanuel) *Derby 16* **P** *Ch Soc Trust* **V** B S P LEATHERS

STAPENHILL (St Peter) w Cauldwell *Derby 16* **P** *Ch Soc Trust* **V** M ANDREYEV

STAPLE (St James) *see* Woodnesborough w Worth and Staple *Cant*

STAPLE FITZPAINE (St Peter) *see* Beercrocombe w Curry Mallet, Hatch Beauchamp etc *B & W*

STAPLE TYE (St James) *see* Gt Parndon *Chelmsf*

STAPLECROSS (St Mark) *see* Ewhurst *Chich*

STAPLEFIELD COMMON (St Mark) *Chich 6* **P** *V Cuckfield* **P-in-c** G D SIMMONS

STAPLEFORD (All Saints) *see* Bassingham Gp *Linc*

STAPLEFORD (St Andrew) *Ely 5* **P** *D&C* **P-in-c** J R PINDER

STAPLEFORD (St Helen) (St Luke) *S'well 7* **P** *CPAS* **V** W N CRAFT, **C** D C CORCORAN

STAPLEFORD (St Mary) *see* Bramfield, Stapleford, Waterford etc *St Alb*

STAPLEFORD (St Mary) *see* Wylye and Till Valley *Sarum*

STAPLEFORD ABBOTTS (St Mary) *see* Lambourne w Abridge and Stapleford Abbotts *Chelmsf*

STAPLEFORD TAWNEY (St Mary the Virgin) *see* Greensted-juxta-Ongar w Stanford Rivers etc *Chelmsf*

STAPLEGROVE (St John) w Norton Fitzwarren *B & W 18* **P** *Bp and MMCET (jt)* **R** M S KIVETT

STAPLEHURST (All Saints) *Cant 11* **P** *St Jo Coll Cam* **R** G M CALVER, **C** L NSENGA-NGOY

STAPLETON (Holy Trinity) *Bris 3* **P** *Bp* **P-in-c** S J PULLIN

STAPLETON (St John) *see* Dorrington w Leebotwood, Longnor, Stapleton etc *Heref*

STAPLETON (St Martin) *see* Barwell w Potters Marston and Stapleton *Leic*

STAPLETON (St Mary) *see* Bewcastle, Stapleton and Kirklinton etc *Carl*

STARBECK (St Andrew) *Ripon 1* **P** *V Harrogate Ch Ch* **V** F S K WAINAINA, **NSM** S J REILLY

STARCROSS (St Paul) *see* Kenton, Mamhead, Powderham, Cofton and Starcross *Ex*

STARSTON (St Margaret) *see* Dickleburgh and The Pulhams *Nor*

STARTFORTH (Holy Trinity) and Bowes and Rokeby w Brignall *Ripon 2* **P** *Ld Chan (1 turn), Bp, Earl of Lonsdale and Lords of the Manor of Bowes (2 turns)* **P-in-c** S A ADESANYA

STATFOLD (St Matthew) *see* Clifton Campville w Edingale and Harlaston *Lich*

STATHERN (St Guthlac) *see* Vale of Belvoir Par *Leic*

STAUGHTON, GREAT (St Andrew) w Hail Weston w Southoe *Ely 13* **P** *Mert Coll Ox and St Jo Coll Ox (alt)* **R** J I CLARKE

STAUGHTON, LITTLE (All Saints) *see* Keysoe w Bolnhurst and Lt Staughton *St Alb*

STAUNTON (All Saints) *see* Coleford, Staunton, Newland, Redbrook etc *Glouc*

STAUNTON (St James) *see* Hartpury w Corse and Staunton *Glouc*

STAUNTON (St Mary) w Flawborough *S'well 3* **P** *E G Staunton Esq* **P-in-c** D HOLLIS

STAUNTON HAROLD (Holy Trinity) *see* Ashby-de-la-Zouch and Breedon on the Hill *Leic*

STAUNTON-ON-ARROW (St Peter) *see* Pembridge w Moor Court, Shobdon, Staunton etc *Heref*

STAUNTON-ON-WYE (St Mary the Virgin) *see* Letton w Staunton, Byford, Mansel Gamage etc *Heref*

STAVELEY (All Saints) *see* Walkingham Hill *Ripon*

STAVELEY (St James), Ings and Kentmere *Carl 11* **P** *V Kendal H Trin* **V** G WATSON

STAVELEY (St John the Baptist) and Barrow Hill *Derby 3* **P** *Bp, Adn Chesterfield, and Duke of Devonshire (jt)* **TR** W A BUTT, **TV** L M DANIELS

STAVELEY IN CARTMEL (St Mary) *see* Leven Valley *Carl*

STAVERTON (St Catherine) *see* Twigworth, Down Hatherley, Norton, The Leigh etc *Glouc*

STAVERTON (St Mary the Virgin) *see* Daventry, Ashby St Ledgers, Braunston etc *Pet*

STAVERTON (St Paul) *see* Canalside Benefice *Sarum*

STAVERTON (St Paul de Leon) *see* Broadhempston, Woodland, Staverton etc *Ex*

STAWELL (St Francis)   *see* Middlezoy and Othery and Moorlinch *B & W*

STAWLEY (St Michael and All Angels)   *see* Wellington and Distr *B & W*

STEANE (St Peter)   *see* Aynho and Croughton w Evenley etc *Pet*

STEART BAY (St Andrew)   *see* Cannington, Otterhampton, Combwich and Stockland *B & W*

STEBBING (St Mary the Virgin) and Lindsell w Great and Little (Bardfield) Saling *Chelmsf 18*   **P** *Bp*   **P-in-c** T E GOODBODY, **C** R V GOODBODY

STECHFORD (All Saints) (St Andrew) *Birm 13*   **P** *St Pet Coll Ox*   **V** G S GAKURU

STEDHAM (St James) w Iping *Chich 10*   **P** *Bp*   **P-in-c** R B WILLIAMSON

STEEP (All Saints) and Froxfield w Privett *Portsm 4*   **P** *Ld Chan and Magd Coll Cam (alt)*   **V** J E OWEN, **NSM** J S E FARRELL

STEEPING, GREAT (All Saints)   *see* Spilsby Gp *Linc*

STEEPING, LITTLE (St Andrew)   *as above*

STEEPLE (St Lawrence and All Saints) *Chelmsf 11*   **P** *Bp*   **P-in-c** G S ANDERSON

STEEPLE (St Michael and All Angels)   *see* Corfe Castle, Church Knowle, Kimmeridge etc *Sarum*

STEEPLE ASHTON (St Mary the Virgin)   *see* N Bradley, Southwick, Heywood and Steeple Ashton *Sarum*

STEEPLE ASTON (St Peter and St Paul) w North Aston and Tackley *Ox 9*   **P** *BNC Ox, St Jo Coll Ox, and Exors Lt-Col A D Taylor (jt)*   **R** S A M´CAW, **NSM** S K R PARKINSON

STEEPLE BARTON (St Mary)   *see* Westcote Barton w Steeple Barton, Duns Tew etc *Ox*

STEEPLE BUMPSTEAD (St Mary) and Helions Bumpstead *Chelmsf 19*   **P** *Ld Chan*   **P-in-c** J HART

STEEPLE CLAYDON (St Michael)   *see* The Claydons and Swan *Ox*

STEEPLE LANGFORD (All Saints)   *see* Wylye and Till Valley *Sarum*

STEEPLE MORDEN (St Peter and St Paul)   *see* Shingay Gp *Ely*

STEETLY (All Saints)   *see* Whitwell *Derby*

STEETON (St Stephen) *Bradf 8*   **P** *V Kildwick*   **P-in-c** M H NEVILL, **C** D B WEAVER

STELLA (St Cuthbert)   *see* Blaydon and Swalwell *Dur*

STELLING (St Mary)   *see* Stone Street Gp *Cant*

STENIGOT (St Nicholas)   *see* Asterby Gp *Linc*

STEPNEY (St Dunstan and All Saints) *Lon 7*   **P** *Bp*   **R** C M BURKE, **Hon C** G G WHITE, **NSM** C B HALL

STEPPINGLEY (St Lawrence)   *see* Ampthill w Millbrook and Steppingley *St Alb*

STERNFIELD (St Mary Magdalene)   *see* Alde River *St E*

STERT (St James)   *see* Redhorn *Sarum*

STETCHWORTH (St Peter)   *see* Raddesley Gp *Ely*

STEVENAGE (All Saints) Pin Green *St Alb 23*   **P** *Bp*   **P-in-c** M J LEVERTON, **NSM** E W FAURE WALKER

STEVENAGE (Holy Trinity) (Christ the King) *St Alb 23*   **P** *Bp*   **P-in-c** G J TICKNER, **C** S L UNDERWOOD, **NSM** A MARINER, A J GILES, A J THOMAS

STEVENAGE (St Andrew and St George) *St Alb 23*   **P** *Bp*   **R** M BARNSLEY

STEVENAGE (St Hugh) (St John) Chells *St Alb 23*   **P** *Bp*   **V** J D CAMPBELL, **C** F K WHEATLEY

STEVENAGE (St Mary) Shephall w Aston *St Alb 23*   **P** *Bp*   **P-in-c** V A HATHAWAY, **Hon C** V CAROLAN

STEVENAGE (St Nicholas) and Graveley *St Alb 23*   **P** *Bp*   **V** D E DOWLING, **C** C M HINA

STEVENAGE (St Peter) Broadwater *St Alb 23*   **P** *Bp*   **V** *vacant* (01438) 238236

STEVENTON (St Michael and All Angels) w Milton *Ox 10*   **P** *Ch Ch Ox and D&C Westmr (jt)*   **P-in-c** C J PATCHING

STEVENTON (St Nicholas)   *see* N Waltham and Steventon, Ashe and Deane *Win*

STEVINGTON (Church Room) (St Mary the Virgin) *St Alb 15*   **P** *Bp*   **V** *vacant*

STEWARDS LANE (St Thomas)   *see* Ditton St Mich w St Thos *Liv*

STEWKLEY (St Michael and All Angels) w Soulbury and Drayton Parslow *Ox 26*   **P** *Bp, Earl of Rosebery, and MMCET (jt)*   **P-in-c** M MORTON, **OLM** P LYMBERY

STEWTON (St Andrew)   *see* Louth *Linc*

STEYNING (St Andrew) *Chich 12*   **P** *MMCET*   **V** P M RAMPTON

STIBBARD (All Saints)   *see* Foulsham, Guestwick, Stibbard, Themelthorpe etc *Nor*

STIBBINGTON (St John the Baptist)   *see* Elton w Stibbington and Water Newton *Ely*

STICKER (St Mark's Mission Church)   *see* St Mewan w Mevagissey and St Ewe *Truro*

STICKFORD (St Helen)   *see* Stickney Gp *Linc*

STICKLEPATH (St Mary)   *see* S Tawton and Belstone *Ex*

STICKLEPATH (St Paul)   *see* Barnstaple *Ex*

STICKNEY Group, The (St Luke) *Linc 7*   **P** *DBP, Ld Chan, and Bp (by turn)*   **P-in-c** A M SULLIVAN, **OLM** J THORNETT

STIDD (St Saviour)   *see* Ribchester w Stidd *Blackb*

STIFFKEY (St John and St Mary) and Bale *Nor 18*   **P** *MMCET, Bp, DBP, Keble Coll Ox, and Sir Euan Hamilton Anstruther-Gough-Calthorpe Bt (jt)*   **R** *vacant* (01328) 830246

STIFFORD (St Cedd) (St Mary) *Chelmsf 14*   **P** *Bp*   **R** A R B HIGGS

STIFFORD, SOUTH (St Mary the Virgin)   *see* Grays Thurrock *Chelmsf*

STILLINGFLEET (St Helen)   *see* Escrick and Stillingfleet w Naburn *York*

STILLINGTON (St John)   *see* Grindon, Stillington and Wolviston *Dur*

STILLINGTON (St Nicholas)   *see* Forest of Galtres *York*

STILTON (St Mary Magdalene) w Denton and Caldecote and Folkesworth w Morborne and Haddon *Ely 15*   **P** *Mrs H R Horne and Bp, Ld Chan (alt)*   **R** R LONGFOOT

STINCHCOMBE (St Cyr)   *see* Cam w Stinchcombe *Glouc*

STINSFORD (St Michael)   *see* Charminster and Stinsford *Sarum*

STIRCHLEY (All Saints)   *see* Cen Telford *Lich*

STIRCHLEY (Ascension) *Birm 5*   **P** *R Kings Norton*   **P-in-c** P A KAYE

STISTED (All Saints)   *see* Cressing w Stisted and Bradwell etc *Chelmsf*

STITHIANS (St Stythians)   *see* St Stythians w Perranarworthal and Gwennap *Truro*

STIXWOULD (St Peter)   *see* Woodhall Spa Gp *Linc*

STOAK (St Lawrence)   *see* Ellesmere Port *Ches*

STOCK (St Barnabas)   *see* Spire Hill *Sarum*

STOCK HARVARD (All Saints) *Chelmsf 9*   **P** *Guild of All So*   **R** N D L DE KEYSER

STOCKBRIDGE (Old St Peter) (St Peter) and Longstock and Leckford *Win 12*   **P** *Bp and St Jo Coll Ox (jt)*   **R** *vacant* (01264) 810810

STOCKBRIDGE VILLAGE (St Jude) *Liv 2*   **P** *Bp and R W Derby (jt)*   **V** E D O´NEILL

STOCKBURY (St Mary Magdalene)   *see* Newington w Hartlip and Stockbury *Cant*

STOCKCROSS (St John)   *see* Welford w Wickham and Gt Shefford, Boxford etc *Ox*

STOCKERSTON (St Peter)   *see* Six Saints circa Holt *Leic*

STOCKING FARM (St Luke) *Leic 1*   **P** *Bp*   **V** P WATSON

STOCKING PELHAM (St Mary)   *see* Albury, Braughing, Furneux Pelham, Lt Hadham etc *St Alb*

STOCKINGFORD (St Paul) *Cov 5*   **P** *V Nuneaton*   **V** M F VINCENT

STOCKLAND (St Mary Magdalene)   *see* Cannington, Otterhampton, Combwich and Stockland *B & W*

STOCKLAND (St Michael and All Angels)   *see* Kilmington, Stockland, Dalwood, Yarcombe etc *Ex*

STOCKLAND GREEN (St Mark) *Birm 8*   **P** *The Crown*   **V** S W POWELL

STOCKLEIGH ENGLISH (St Mary the Virgin)   *see* N Creedy *Ex*

STOCKLEIGH POMEROY (St Mary the Virgin)   *as above*

STOCKLINCH (St Mary Magdalene)   *see* Ilminster and Distr *B & W*

STOCKPORT (St George) *Ches 18*   **P** *Trustees*   **V** A J BELL, **NSM** H GRIFFITHS

STOCKPORT (St Mark)   *see* Edgeley and Cheadle Heath *Ches*

STOCKPORT (St Martin)   *see* Heatons *Man*

STOCKPORT (St Mary) *Ches 18*   **P** *G&C Coll Cam*   **R** R P SCOONES

STOCKPORT (St Matthew)   *see* Edgeley and Cheadle Heath *Ches*

STOCKPORT (St Saviour) *Ches 18*   **P** *Trustees*   **V** D V COOKSON, **NSM** L BOYLE

STOCKPORT (St Thomas) (St Peter) *Ches 18*   **P** *Bp and Soc of the Faith (jt)*   **R** K D N KENRICK, **Hon C** K R BROOKES

STOCKSBRIDGE (St Matthias) *Sheff 3*   **P** *Bp*   **P-in-c** C E BARNARD

STOCKSFIELD (St John)   *see* Bywell and Mickley *Newc*

STOCKTON (St Andrew)   *see* Teme Valley N *Worc*

STOCKTON (St Chad) *Dur 10*   **P** *Bp*   **P-in-c** N R SHAVE, **C** J NOBEL, C W PEARSON, **NSM** E WALKER

STOCKTON (St Chad)   *see* Beckbury, Badger, Kemberton, Ryton, Stockton etc *Lich*

STOCKTON (St John the Baptist)   *see* Wylye and Till Valley *Sarum*

STOCKTON (St Michael and All Angels)   *see* Napton-on-the-Hill, Lower Shuckburgh etc *Cov*

STOCKTON (St Michael and All Angels) *see* Gillingham w Geldeston, Stockton, Ellingham etc *Nor*

STOCKTON HEATH (St Thomas) *Ches 4* **P** *P G Greenall Esq* **V** M L RIDLEY, **C** J E PROUDFOOT, **Hon C** H S HOUSTON, **NSM** M A THOMSON

STOCKTON ON TEES (Holy Trinity) (St Mark) *Dur 10* **P** *Bp* **V** *vacant* (01642) 586179

STOCKTON-ON-TEES (St Chad) *see* Stockton St Chad *Dur*

STOCKTON ON TEES (St James) *Dur 10* **P** *Bp* **P-in-c** D J BELL

STOCKTON-ON-TEES (St John the Baptist) *Dur 10* **P** *Bp* **P-in-c** D J BELL

STOCKTON-ON-TEES (St Paul) *Dur 10* **P** *The Crown* **P-in-c** D W ROSAMOND

STOCKTON-ON-TEES (St Peter) *Dur 10* **P** *Bp* **V** P D ASHDOWN

STOCKTON-ON-TEES (St Thomas) *Dur 10* **P** *Bp* **P-in-c** A J FARISH, **C** S R GREEN

STOCKTON-ON-THE-FOREST (Holy Trinity) w Holtby and Warthill *York 2* **P** *Abp* **P-in-c** N W R BIRD, **NSM** M F W WILLETTS

STOCKWELL (St Andrew) (St Michael) *S'wark 11* **P** *Bp* **OLM** I A BOWMAN

STOCKWITH, EAST (St Peter) *see* Corringham and Blyton Gp *Linc*

STOCKWITH, WEST (St Mary the Virgin) *see* Beckingham and Walkeringham and Misterton etc *S'well*

STOCKWOOD (Christ the Servant) *see* Bris Ch the Servant Stockwood *Bris*

STODDEN Churches, The *St Alb 15* **P** *MMCET and DBP (alt)* **R** J C BROOKSHAW

STODMARSH (St Mary) *see* Littlebourne and Ickham w Wickhambreaux etc *Cant*

STODY (St Mary) *see* Brinton, Briningham, Hunworth, Stody etc *Nor*

STOGUMBER (Blessed Virgin Mary) *see* Quantock Towers *B & W*

STOGURSEY (St Andrew) *see* Quantock Coast *B & W*

STOKE (St Mary and St Andrew) *see* Colsterworth Gp *Linc*

STOKE (St Michael) *see* Coventry Caludon *Cov*

STOKE (St Peter and St Paul) *see* Grain w Stoke *Roch*

STOKE, EAST (St Oswald) w Syerston *S'well 3* **P** *Bp* **P-in-c** D HOLLIS

STOKE, NORTH (St Martin) *see* Bath Weston All SS w N Stoke and Langridge *B & W*

STOKE, NORTH (St Mary the Virgin) *see* Langtree *Ox*

STOKE, SOUTH (St Andrew) *see* Goring and Streatley w S Stoke *Ox*

STOKE, SOUTH (St James the Great) *see* Combe Down w Monkton Combe and S Stoke *B & W*

STOKE, SOUTH (St Leonard) *see* Arundel w Tortington and S Stoke *Chich*

STOKE, WEST (St Andrew) *Chich 13* **P** *Bp* **R** J J HOLLIMAN

STOKE ABBOTT (St Mary) *see* Beaminster Area *Sarum*

STOKE ALBANY (St Botolph) w Wilbarston and Ashley w Weston-by-Welland and Sutton Bassett *Pet 7* **P** *Comdr L M M Saunders-Watson (2 turns), Bp (1 turn), DBP (1 turn)* **P-in-c** S L HUGHES

STOKE ALDERMOOR (St Catherine) *see* Coventry Caludon *Cov*

STOKE ASH (All Saints) *see* S Hartismere *St E*

STOKE BARDOLPH (St Luke) *see* Burton Joyce w Bulcote and Stoke Bardolph *S'well*

STOKE BISHOP (St Mary Magdalene) *Bris 2* **P** *Bp* **V** D J R RITCHIE, **NSM** A L FARMER

STOKE BLISS (St Peter) *see* Teme Valley S *Worc*

STOKE BRUERNE (St Mary the Virgin) *see* Blisworth and Stoke Bruerne w Grafton Regis etc *Pet*

STOKE BY CLARE (St John the Baptist) *see* Stour Valley *St E*

STOKE BY NAYLAND (St Mary) w Leavenheath and Polstead *St E 3* **P** *Mrs S E F Holden and St Jo Coll Ox (alt)* **R** M J A TILLETT, **NSM** J T FOWLER, **OLM** V ARMSTRONG

STOKE CANON (St Mary Magdalene), Poltimore w Huxham and Rewe w Netherexe *Ex 2* **P** *D&C, Lady Stucley, and Bp (by turn)* **P-in-c** D J DETTMER, **NSM** S SHEPPARD

STOKE CHARITY (St Mary and St Michael) *see* Upper Dever Win

STOKE CLIMSLAND (not known) *Truro 12* **P** *Bp and Duchy of Cornwall (alt)* **P-in-c** W R STUART-WHITE, **C** M E ELLIOTT

STOKE D'ABERNON (St Mary the Virgin) *see* Cobham and Stoke D'Abernon *Guildf*

STOKE DAMEREL (St Andrew w St Luke) and Devonport St Aubyn *Ex 22* **P** *Trustees Lord St Levan (2 turns), Prime Min (1 turn)* **R** D J NIXON

STOKE DOYLE (St Rumbold) *see* Aldwincle, Clopton, Pilton, Stoke Doyle etc *Pet*

STOKE DRY (St Andrew) *see* Lyddington w Stoke Dry and Seaton etc *Pet*

STOKE EDITH (St Mary) *see* Ledbury *Heref*

STOKE FLEMING (St Peter), Blackawton and Strete *Ex 14* **P** *Bp and BDP (jt)* **V** J H BELL

STOKE GABRIEL (St Gabriel) and Collaton *Ex 13* **P** *Bp* **V** D A TREBY

STOKE GIFFORD (St Michael) *Bris 5* **P** *Bp* **TR** S JONES, **TV** T G E WEBBER, **C** S D DUNN, **NSM** J C BRADLEY

STOKE GOLDING (St Margaret) *see* Fenn Lanes Gp *Leic*

STOKE GOLDINGTON (St Peter) *see* Gayhurst w Ravenstone, Stoke Goldington etc *Ox*

STOKE HAMMOND (St Luke) *see* Brickhills and Stoke Hammond *Ox*

STOKE HEATH (St Alban) *see* Cov E *Cov*

STOKE HILL (St Peter) *Guildf 5* **P** *Bp* **V** D G HONOUR, **OLM** B J RICH

STOKE HOLY CROSS (Holy Cross) w Dunston, Arminghall and Caistor St Edmunds w Markshall *Nor 8* **P** *D&C and Mrs D Pott (jt)* **R** R J BUNN, **C** K P B LOVESEY

STOKE LACY (St Peter and St Paul) *see* Bromyard and Stoke Lacy *Heref*

STOKE LYNE (St Peter) *see* Shelswell *Ox*

STOKE MANDEVILLE (St Mary the Virgin) *see* Ellesborough, The Kimbles and Stoke Mandeville *Ox*

STOKE NEWINGTON (St Andrew) *Lon 5* **P** *Bp* **P-in-c** V A ROBERTS

STOKE NEWINGTON St Faith (St Matthias) and All Saints *Lon 5* **P** *City Corp* **V** D J LAMBERT

STOKE NEWINGTON (St John the Evangelist) *see* Brownswood Park *Lon*

STOKE NEWINGTON (St Mary) (Old Parish Church) *Lon 5* **P** *Bp* **C** J D CLARK, **C** L ASHDOWN, M J HAWKES

STOKE NEWINGTON (St Olave) *Lon 5* **P** *Ld Chan* **V** V A ROBERTS

STOKE NEWINGTON COMMON (St Michael and All Angels) *Lon 5* **P** *Bp* **V** J B LAWSON

STOKE-NEXT-GUILDFORD (St John the Evangelist) *Guildf 5* **P** *Simeon's Trustees* **R** M C WOODWARD, **C** F E SIMON

STOKE-ON-TRENT *see* Stoke-upon-Trent *Lich*

STOKE ORCHARD (St James the Great) *see* Deerhurst and Apperley w Forthampton etc *Glouc*

STOKE PARK (St Peter) *see* Ipswich St Mary at Stoke w St Pet and St Fran *St E*

STOKE PERO (not known) *see* Porlock and Porlock Weir w Stoke Pero etc *B & W*

STOKE POGES (St Giles) *Ox 23* **P** *Ch Ch Ox* **V** H N L LATHAM, **C** M GRIFFITHS

STOKE PRIOR (St Luke) *see* Leominster *Heref*

STOKE PRIOR (St Michael), Wychbold and Upton Warren *Worc 8* **P** *Bp and D&C (alt)* **R** R H ANTELL

STOKE RIVERS (St Bartholomew) *see* Shirwell, Loxhore, Kentisbury, Arlington, etc *Ex*

STOKE ROW (St John the Evangelist) *see* Langtree *Ox*

STOKE ST GREGORY (St Gregory) *see* Athelney *B & W*

STOKE ST MARY (St Mary) *see* Beercrocombe w Curry Mallet, Hatch Beauchamp etc *B & W*

STOKE ST MICHAEL (St Michael) *see* Leigh upon Mendip w Stoke St Michael *B & W*

STOKE ST MILBOROUGH (St Milburgha) *see* Bitterley w Middleton, Stoke St Milborough etc *Heref*

STOKE SUB HAMDON (Blessed Virgin Mary) (All Saints Mission Church) *B & W 6* **P** *Ch Patr Trust* **P-in-c** P KERTON-JOHNSON

STOKE TALMAGE (St Mary Magdalene) *see* Thame *Ox*

STOKE TRISTER (St Andrew) *see* Charlton Musgrove, Cucklington and Stoke Trister *B & W*

STOKE UPON TERN (St Peter) *see* Cheswardine, Childs Ercall, Hales, Hinstock etc *Lich*

STOKE-UPON-TRENT (St Peter-ad-Vincula) (St Paul) *Lich 12* **P** *Bp* **TR** D P LINGWOOD, **TV** P R SEARLE, **NSM** L M A TIDESWELL, **OLM** P M LOCKLEY

STOKEHAM (St Peter) *see* Rampton w Laneham, Treswell, Cottam and Stokeham *S'well*

STOKEINTEIGNHEAD (St Andrew) *see* Shaldon, Stokeinteignhead, Combeinteignhead etc *Ex*

STOKENCHURCH (St Peter and St Paul) and Ibstone *Ox 29* **P** *Bp* **P-in-c** R A FRANCE

STOKENHAM (St Michael and All Angels), Slapton, Charleton w Buckland-Tout-Saints, East Portlemouth, South Pool, and Chivelstone *Ex 14* **P** *Prime Min (1 turn), Bp, DBP, N Tyler Esq, and Ms S Tyler (1 turn), and Ld Chan (1 turn)* **R** R M HARDING

STOKESAY (St Christopher) (St John the Baptist) *Heref 11*
  P *T P D La Touche Esq* **P-in-c** M L COPE,
  NSM M G WILLIAMS
STOKESBY (St Andrew)   *see* S Trin Broads *Nor*
STOKESLEY (St Peter and St Paul) w Seamer *York 21* **P** *Abp*
  R A P HUTCHINSON
STOLFORD (St Peter)   *see* Quantock Coast *B & W*
STON EASTON (Blessed Virgin Mary)   *see* Chewton Mendip w
  Ston Easton, Litton etc *B & W*
STONDON (All Saints)   *see* Gravenhurst, Shillington and
  Stondon *St Alb*
STONDON MASSEY (St Peter and St Paul)   *see* Blackmore and
  Stondon Massey *Chelmsf*
STONE (All Saints)   *see* Berkeley w Wick, Breadstone, Newport,
  Stone etc *Glouc*
STONE (Christ Church) and Oulton-with-Moddershall *Lich 13*
  P *Simeon's Trustees* **V** P H C KINGMAN, **C** T R VASBY-
  BURNIE
STONE near Dartford (St Mary) *Roch 2* **P** *Bp* **R** K W CLARK
STONE (St John the Baptist) w Dinton and Hartwell *Ox 21*
  P *Bp and Grocers' Co (jt)* **R** *vacant* (01296) 748215
STONE (St Mary the Virgin)   *see* Chaddesley Corbett and Stone
  Worc
STONE (St Michael and St Wulfad) w Aston (St Saviour) *Lich 13*
  P *Bp* **R** I R CARDINAL, **C** S A SMITH
STONE CROSS (St Luke) w Langney, North *Chich 16* **P** *Bp*
  V J D VINE, **NSM** S A SHERIDAN
STONE-IN-OXNEY (St Mary the Virgin)   *see* Wittersham w
  Stone-in-Oxney and Ebony *Cant*
STONE QUARRY (St Luke)   *see* E Grinstead St Swithun *Chich*
STONE STREET Group, The *Cant 2* **P** *Abp and Trustees Lord
  Tomlin (jt)* **NSM** M J WALKER
STONEBRIDGE (St Michael and All Angels) *Lon 21* **P** *Bp*
  V R HERBERT
STONEBROOM (St Peter)   *see* Morton and Stonebroom w
  Shirland *Derby*
STONEGATE (St Peter) *Chich 19* **P** *E J B Hardcastle Esq and
  Mrs C J J Reid (jt)* **P-in-c** J R JAMES, **NSM** R G ALFORD
STONEGRAVE (Holy Trinity)   *see* Ampleforth w Oswaldkirk,
  Gilling E etc *York*
STONEHAM, NORTH (St Nicholas) (All Saints) *Win 10*
  P *R H W Fleming Esq* **R** *vacant* (023) 8076 8123
STONEHAM, SOUTH (St Mary)   *see* Swaythling *Win*
STONEHOUSE (St Cyr) *Glouc 5* **P** *The Crown*
  P-in-c C S MINCHIN
STONEHOUSE (St Paul)   *see* Plymouth St Andr and
  Stonehouse *Ex*
STONELEIGH (St John the Baptist) *Guildf 9* **P** *Bp*
  V L M HELLMUTH
STONELEIGH (St Mary the Virgin) w Ashow *Cov 4* **P** *Lord
  Leigh and Bp (jt)* **P-in-c** J E PERRYMAN, **NSM** P E FRANK
STONESBY (St Peter)   *see* Ironstone Villages *Leic*
STONESFIELD (St James the Great) w Combe Longa *Ox 9*
  P *Duke of Marlborough* **P-in-c** A R TURNER
STONEY MIDDLETON (St Martin)   *see* Baslow w Curbar and
  Stoney Middleton *Derby*
STONEY STANTON (St Michael)   *see* Broughton Astley and
  Croft w Stoney Stanton *Leic*
STONEYCROFT (All Saints) *Liv 8* **P** *Bp* **V** R WILLIAMS
STONEYCROFT (St Paul)   *see* Stanley w Stoneycroft St Paul
  Liv
STONEYDELPH (St Martin in the Delph)   *see* Glascote and
  Stonydelph *Lich*
STONHAM ASPAL (St Mary and St Lambert)   *see* Crowfield w
  Stonham Aspal and Mickfield *St E*
STONHAM PARVA (St Mary)   *see* Creeting St Mary, Creeting
  St Peter etc *St E*
STONNALL (St Peter) *Lich 1* **P** *V Shenstone*
  P-in-c D F OLNEY
STONTON WYVILLE (St Denys)   *see* Welham, Glooston and
  Cranoe and Stonton Wyville *Leic*
STONY STRATFORD (St Mary and St Giles) *Ox 25* **P** *Bp*
  V R NORTHING
STOODLEIGH (St Margaret)   *see* Washfield, Stoodleigh,
  Withleigh etc *Ex*
STOPHAM (St Mary the Virgin) and Fittleworth *Chich 11*
  P *D&C and Col Sir Brian Barttelot Bt (jt)* **P-in-c** C A WATERS
STOPSLEY (St Thomas) *St Alb 14* **P** *Bp* **V** D G ALEXANDER
STORRIDGE (St John the Baptist)   *see* Cradley w Mathon and
  Storridge *Heref*
STORRINGTON (St Mary) *Chich 12* **P** *Keble Coll Ox*
  R J M ACHESON, **NSM** A R ROSS
STORTH (All Saints Mission)   *see* Arnside *Carl*
STOTFOLD (St Mary the Virgin) and Radwell *St Alb 4* **P** *Bp*
  V P M QUINT

**STOTTESDON (St Mary) w Farlow, Cleeton St Mary,
  Silvington, Sidbury and Middleton Scriven** *Heref 9* **P** *Bp*
  P-in-c C G WILLIAMS
STOUGHTON (Emmanuel) *Guildf 5* **P** *Simeon's Trustees*
  V F SCAMMELL, **C** D J MUSKETT
STOUGHTON (St Mary)   *see* Compton, the Mardens,
  Stoughton and Racton *Chich*
STOUGHTON (St Mary and All Saints)   *see* Thurnby w
  Stoughton *Leic*
**STOULTON (St Edmund) w Drake's Broughton and Pirton and
  Norton** *Worc 4* **P** *Croome Estate Trustees, D&C, and Bp (jt)*
  R D G SLOGGETT
STOUR, EAST (Christ Church)   *see* Stour Vale *Sarum*
STOUR, UPPER *Sarum 17* **P** *Exors H P R Hoare (1 turn), Bp
  (2 turns), and Bourton Chpl Trustees (1 turn)*
  R C A R MOORSOM, **NSM** T F HEATON
STOUR, WEST (St Mary)   *see* Stour Vale *Sarum*
STOUR PROVOST (St Michael and All Angels)   *as above*
STOUR ROW (All Saints)   *as above*
STOUR VALE *Sarum 5* **P** *Bp* **V** J E SALTER,
  NSM J B WEBB
STOUR VALLEY, The *St E 8* **P** *DBP, Jes Coll Cam, Lady
  Loch, and Duchy of Lanc (by turn)* **R** W J A RANKIN,
  C A R GEORGE, **NSM** G GREEN
STOURBRIDGE (St John the Evangelist)   *see* Old Swinford
  Stourbridge *Worc*
STOURBRIDGE (St Mary)   *as above*
STOURBRIDGE (St Michael and All Angels) Norton *Worc 12*
  P *Bp* **V** E BUTT
STOURBRIDGE (St Thomas) *Worc 12* **P** *Bp*
  P-in-c R V CURTIS
STOURDENE Group, The *Cov 9* **P** *SMF, Bp, Major and
  Mrs J E Shirley, Miss M L P Shirley, P E Shirley Esq, Ch Ch
  Ox, Jes Coll Ox, and Mr and Mrs G Howell* **R** A J ADAMS,
  Hon C D R J EVANS
STOURHEAD *St E 8* **P** *E H Vestey Esq, St Chad's Coll Dur,
  Ridley Hall Cam, and Walsingham Coll Trust (jt)* **V** J E ELEY
STOURPAINE (Holy Trinity)   *see* Pimperne, Stourpaine,
  Durweston and Bryanston *Sarum*
**STOURPORT-ON-SEVERN (St Michael and All Angels) and
  Wilden** *Worc 13* **P** *Earl Baldwin of Bewdley and
  V Kidderminster St Mary and All SS (jt)*
  V I E MCINTYRE DE ROMERO
STOURTON (St Peter)   *see* Kinver and Enville *Lich*
STOURTON (St Peter)   *see* Upper Stour *Sarum*
STOURTON CAUNDLE (St Peter)   *see* Spire Hill *Sarum*
STOVEN (St Margaret)   *see* Hundred River *St E*
STOW Group, The (St Mary the Virgin) *Linc 2* **P** *Bp and
  DBP (jt)* **OLM** P I ROSE
STOW, WEST (St Mary)   *see* Lark Valley *St E*
STOW BARDOLPH (Holy Trinity)   *see* Wimbotsham w Stow
  Bardolph and Stow Bridge etc *Ely*
STOW BEDON (St Botolph)   *see* Caston, Griston, Merton,
  Thompson etc *Nor*
STOW BRIDGE Mission (St Peter)   *see* Wimbotsham w Stow
  Bardolph and Stow Bridge etc *Ely*
STOW LONGA (St Botolph) *Ely 10* **P** *Bp* **V** R A FROST
STOW MARIES (St Mary and St Margaret)   *see* Purleigh, Cold
  Norton and Stow Maries *Chelmsf*
STOW ON THE WOLD (St Edward), Condicote and The Swells
  Glouc 12 **P** *DBP and Ch Ch Ox (jt)* **R** D C FRANCIS,
  NSM J A H FRANCIS
STOWE (Assumption of St Mary the Virgin) *Ox 22*
  P *Stowe Sch* **P-in-c** R M BUNDOCK
STOWE (St Michael and All Angels)   *see* Bucknell w Chapel
  Lawn, Llanfair Waterdine etc *Heref*
STOWE, UPPER (St James)   *see* Heyford w Stowe Nine
  Churches and Flore etc *Pet*
STOWE BY CHARTLEY (St John the Baptist)   *see* Mid Trent
  Lich
STOWE NINE CHURCHES (St Michael)   *see* Heyford w Stowe
  Nine Churches and Flore etc *Pet*
STOWELL (St Leonard)   *see* Chedworth, Yanworth and Stowell,
  Coln Rogers etc *Glouc*
STOWELL (St Mary Magdalene)   *see* Milborne Port w Goathill
  etc *B & W*
STOWEY (St Nicholas and Blessed Virgin Mary)   *see* Bishop
  Sutton and Stanton Drew and Stowey *B & W*
STOWEY, NETHER (Blessed Virgin Mary)   *see* Aisholt,
  Enmore, Goathurst, Nether Stowey etc *B & W*
STOWEY, OVER (St Peter and St Paul)   *as above*
STOWFORD (St John)   *see* Lifton, Broadwoodwidger, Stowford
  etc *Ex*
STOWLANGTOFT (St George)   *see* Badwell and Walsham *St E*
STOWMARKET (St Peter and St Mary) *St E 6* **P** *Ch Patr
  Trust* **P-in-c** M W EDEN, **OLM** R M STRETCH, R F GILBERT

STOWTING (St Mary the Virgin) *see* Smeeth w Monks Horton and Stowting and Brabourne *Cant*

STOWUPLAND (Holy Trinity) *see* Haughley w Wetherden and Stowupland *St E*

STRADBROKE (All Saints) w Horham, Athelington and Redlingfield *St E 17* **P** *Bp (3 turns), Lt-Comdr G C Marshall (1 turn), and Dr G I Soden (1 turn)* **R** D J STREETER

STRADISHALL (St Margaret) *see* Bansfield *St E*

STRADSETT (St Mary) *see* Downham Market and Crimplesham w Stradsett *Ely*

STRAGGLETHORPE (St Michael) *see* Brant Broughton and Beckingham *Linc*

STRAITS, The (St Andrew) *see* Gornal and Sedgley *Worc*

STRAMSHALL (St Michael and All Angels) *see* Uttoxeter Area *Lich*

STRANTON (All Saints) *Dur 3* **P** *St Jo Coll Dur* **V** M R GILBERTSON, **C** K M BROOKE, **NSM** A J CRAIG

STRATFIELD MORTIMER (St Mary) and Mortimer West End w Padworth *Ox 12* **P** *Eton Coll, Ld Chan, and Englefield Estate Trust Corp (by turn)* **V** P CHAPLIN, **NSM** J L STRAW

STRATFIELD SAYE (St Mary) *see* Sherfield-on-Loddon and Stratfield Saye etc *Win*

STRATFORD (St John the Evangelist w Christ Church) and St James *Chelmsf 3* **P** *V W Ham* **V** D A RICHARDS, **NSM** J V MEADWAY

STRATFORD NEW TOWN (St Paul) *Chelmsf 3* **P** *Ch Patr Trust* **P-in-c** K F WOOLMER, **Hon C** D M WEBB

STRATFORD ST MARY (St Mary) *see* Higham, Holton St Mary, Raydon and Stratford *St E*

STRATFORD SUB CASTLE (St Lawrence) *see* Salisbury St Fran and Stratford sub Castle *Sarum*

STRATFORD-UPON-AVON (Holy Trinity), Luddington and Clifford Chambers *Cov 8* **P** *Bp* **R** M C W GORICK, **C** D P BANBURY, S LABRAN, **NSM** M A SWEET

STRATTON (St Andrew) and Launcells *Truro 8* **P** *Duchy of Cornwall and CPAS (alt)* **P-in-c** D C STANDEN

STRATTON (St Mary) (St Michael) and Wacton *Nor 5* **P** *G&C Coll Cam, DBP, and New Coll Ox (by turn)* **R** J A NASH, **OLM** E R SPRY, G M OSBORNE

STRATTON (St Mary the Virgin) *see* Bradford Peverell, Stratton, Frampton etc *Sarum*

STRATTON (St Peter), North Cerney, Baunton and Bagendon *Glouc 9* **P** *Mrs P M Chester Master, Jes Coll Ox, Univ Coll Ox (jt)* **P-in-c** W G HEATHCOTE, **NSM** D H S LEESON

STRATTON, EAST (All Saints) *see* Upper Dever *Win*

STRATTON, UPPER (St Philip) *Bris 7* **P** *Bp* **V** C A STONE

STRATTON AUDLEY (St Mary and St Edburga) *see* Shelswell *Ox*

STRATTON ON THE FOSSE (St Vigor) *see* Chilcompton w Downside and Stratton on the Fosse *B & W*

STRATTON ST MARGARET (St Margaret) w South Marston and Stanton Fitzwarren *Bris 7* **P** *Patr Bd* **TV** V R FLEMING, **P-in-c** V J HOWLETT, **Hon C** R J BURSTON, **NSM** P C ASHBY

STRATTON STRAWLESS (St Margaret) *see* Coltishall w Gt Hautbois, Frettenham etc *Nor*

STREAT (not known) *see* Ditchling, Streat and Westmeston *Chich*

STREATHAM (Christ Church) (St Margaret the Queen) *S'wark 12* **P** *Bp and R Streatham St Leon (jt)* **V** S TRICKLEBANK, **NSM** J G BOYCE

STREATHAM (Immanuel) (St Andrew) *S'wark 12* **P** *Bp, Hyndman Trustees, and R Streatham St Leon (jt)* **V** E M SHEARCROFT

STREATHAM (St Leonard) *S'wark 12* **P** *Bp* **R** A J HODGSON, **NSM** M E HAWES

STREATHAM (St Paul) *S'wark 17* **P** *Bp* **NSM** J B BOYCE-TILLMAN

STREATHAM (St Peter) *S'wark 12* **P** *St Steph Ho Ox* **V** P D ANDREWS

STREATHAM (St Thomas) *see* Telford Park *S'wark*

STREATHAM, WEST (St James) *S'wark 17* **P** *CPAS* **V** G G HOWARD, **NSM** S E M CLARKE, J ALLEN

STREATHAM HILL (St Margaret the Queen) *see* Streatham Ch Ch w St Marg *S'wark*

STREATHAM PARK (St Alban) *S'wark 17* **P** *Ch Soc Trust* **V** M S RICHEUX

STREATHAM VALE (Holy Redeemer) *S'wark 12* **P** *CPAS* **V** I H GILMOUR

STREATLEY (St Margaret) *St Alb 14* **P** *Bp* **V** R W WOOD

STREATLEY (St Mary) *see* Goring and Streatley w S Stoke *Ox*

STREET (Holy Trinity) (Mission Church) w Walton *B & W 5* **P** *DBP* **R** F J GREED, **Hon C** D N HATREY

STREET Parishes, The *York 6* **P** *Patr Bd* **R** B S BOWES

STREETLY (All Saints) *Lich 25* **P** *Bp* **V** A T BARTLAM, **C** R E LIVESEY, **OLM** J W BLUNT

STRELLEY (All Saints) *see* Bilborough w Strelley *S'well*

STRENSALL (St Mary the Virgin) *York 3* **P** *Abp* **V** M HARRISON, **NSM** J A PALMER

STRETE (St Michael) *see* Stoke Fleming, Blackawton and Strete *Ex*

STRETFORD (All Saints) *Man 7* **P** *Bp* **P-in-c** M E SLACK, **OLM** H TOMLINSON

STRETFORD (St Bride) *see* Old Trafford St Bride *Man*

STRETFORD (St Matthew) *Man 7* **P** *D&C* **P-in-c** D T THOMAS

STRETFORD (St Peter) *see* Firswood and Gorse Hill *Man*

STRETHALL (St Mary the Virgin) *see* Heydon, Gt and Lt Chishill, Chrishall etc *Chelmsf*

STRETHAM (St James) *see* Ely *Ely*

STRETTON (St John) *see* Penkridge *Lich*

STRETTON (St Mary) w Claymills *Lich 14* **P** *Baroness Gretton* **V** K A THOMAS, **NSM** D V WARNER

STRETTON (St Matthew) and Appleton Thorn *Ches 4* **P** *Mrs P F du Bois Grantham and Dr S P L du Bois Davidson (jt)* **V** E C HALL, **C** G H BUCHAN

STRETTON (St Nicholas) *see* Greetham and Thistleton w Stretton and Clipsham *Pet*

STRETTON, LITTLE (All Saints) *see* Church Stretton *Heref*

STRETTON GRANDISON (St Laurence) *see* Ledbury *Heref*

STRETTON MAGNA (St Giles) *see* Glen Magna cum Stretton Magna etc *Leic*

STRETTON ON DUNSMORE (All Saints) *see* Bourton w Frankton and Stretton on Dunsmore etc *Cov*

STRETTON ON DUNSMORE (Mission Church) *as above*

STRETTON ON FOSSE (St Peter) *see* Ilmington w Stretton-on-Fosse etc *Cov*

STRETTON PARVA (St John the Baptist) *see* Gaulby *Leic*

STRETTON SUGWAS (St Mary Magdalene) *Heref 4* **P** *DBP* **R** J W R MORRISON, **NSM** E S V VERWEY, P A LITTLEWOOD

STRICKLAND, GREAT (St Barnabas) *see* Morland, Thrimby, Gt Strickland and Cliburn *Carl*

STRINES (St Paul) *see* Marple All SS *Ches*

STRINGSTON (St Mary the Virgin) *see* Quantock Coast *B & W*

STRIXTON (St Romwald) *see* Wollaston w Strixton and Bozeat etc *Pet*

STROOD (St Francis) *Roch 6* **P** *Bp* **V** H DAUBNEY

STROOD (St Nicholas) w St Mary *Roch 6* **P** *Bp and D&C (jt)* **V** D W GREEN, **C** D L TURNER

STROUD (Holy Trinity) (St Alban Mission Church) *Glouc 5* **P** *Bp* **V** M J WITHEY

STROUD (Mission Church) *see* Steep and Froxfield w Privett *Portsm*

STROUD (St Laurence) and Uplands w Slad *Glouc 5* **P** *Bp* **V** B C E COKER

STROUD GREEN (Holy Trinity) *Lon 20* **P** *Bp* **V** P J HENDERSON, **C** T D PIKE, **NSM** P G ATHERTON

STROXTON (All Saints) *see* Harlaxton Gp *Linc*

STRUBBY (St Oswald) *see* Legbourne and Wold Marsh *Linc*

STRUMPSHAW (St Peter) *see* Burlingham St Edmund w Lingwood, Strumpshaw etc *Nor*

STUBBINGS (St James the Less) *see* Burchetts Green *Ox*

STUBBINGTON (St Edmund) *see* Crofton *Portsm*

STUBBINS (St Philip) *see* Ramsbottom and Edenfield *Man*

STUBBS CROSS (St Francis) *see* Kingsnorth and Shadoxhurst *Cant*

STUBSHAW CROSS (St Luke) *see* Ashton-in-Makerfield St Thos *Liv*

STUBTON (St Martin) *see* Claypole *Linc*

STUDHAM (St Mary the Virgin) *see* Kensworth, Studham and Whipsnade *St Alb*

STUDLAND (St Nicholas) *see* Swanage and Studland *Sarum*

STUDLEY (Nativity of the Blessed Virgin Mary) *Cov 7* **P** *DBP* **V** R W DEIMEL, **NSM** M M DEIMEL, **OLM** J A STOTE

STUDLEY (St John the Evangelist) *Sarum 14* **P** *R Trowbridge St Jas* **P-in-c** S F DEACON, **NSM** E A GIFFORD

STUKELEY, GREAT (St Bartholomew) *see* Huntingdon w the Stukeleys *Ely*

STUKELEY, LITTLE (St Martin) *as above*

STUKELEY MEADOWS Local Ecumenical Partnership *Ely 12 vacant*

STUNTNEY (Holy Cross) *see* Ely *Ely*

STURMER (St Mary) *see* Ridgewell w Ashen, Birdbrook and Sturmer *Chelmsf*

STURMINSTER MARSHALL (St Mary) *see* Bridge Par *Sarum*

STURMINSTER NEWTON (St Mary), Hinton St Mary and Lydlinch *Sarum 5* **P** *Col J L Yeatman (1 turn), G A L F Pitt-Rivers Esq (3 turns), V Iwerne Valley (1 turn)* **V** D R R SEYMOUR, **C** R E GREENE, **OLM** R WYNN

STURRY (St Nicholas) w Fordwich and Westbere w Hersden
Cant 3 **P** *Abp, Ld Chan, and St Aug Foundn Cant (by turn)*
R P A CORNISH, **OLM** P C J FREEMAN
STURTON (St Hugh) *see* Stow Gp *Linc*
STURTON, GREAT (All Saints) *see* Hemingby *Linc*
STURTON-LE-STEEPLE (St Peter and St Paul)
see N Wheatley, W Burton, Bole, Saundby, Sturton etc *S'well*
STUSTON (All Saints) *see* N Hartismere *St E*
STUTTON (St Aidan) *see* Tadcaster w Newton Kyme *York*
STUTTON (St Peter) *see* Holbrook, Stutton, Freston,
Woolverstone etc *St E*
STYVECHALE (St James) *Cov 3* **P** *Col A M H Gregory-Hood*
V J K MILLS, **OLM** C M NEWBORN, A PRETT
SUCKLEY (St John the Baptist) *see* Worcs W *Worc*
SUDBOROUGH (All Saints) *see* Brigstock w Stanion and
Lowick and Sudborough *Pet*
SUDBOURNE (All Saints) *see* Wilford Peninsula *St E*
SUDBROOKE (St Edward) *see* Barlings *Linc*
SUDBURY (All Saints) *see* Doveridge, Scropton, Sudbury etc
Derby
SUDBURY (All Saints) w Ballingdon and Brundon *St E 12*
P *Simeon's Trustees* **P-in-c** S D GILL
SUDBURY (St Andrew) *Lon 21* **P** *Bp* **V** F M-L SCROGGIE,
NSM L P NORTH
SUDBURY (St Gregory) St Peter and Chilton *St E 12* **P** *Bp*
(3 turns), Ch Soc Trust (1 turn) **P-in-c** G J WEBB,
C J M SEGGAR
SUDDEN (St Aidan) *Man 21* **P** *Bp* **V** *vacant* (01706) 631812
SUDELEY MANOR (St Mary) *see* Winchcombe *Glouc*
SUFFIELD (St Margaret) *see* King's Beck *Nor*
SUFFIELD PARK (St Martin) *see* Cromer *Nor*
SUFFOLK HEIGHTS *see* Chevington w Hargrave, Chedburgh
w Depden etc *St E*
SUGLEY (Holy Saviour) *Newc 4* **P** *Bp* **V** S T ROBSON
SULBY (St Stephen's Chapel) *see* Lezayre *S & M*
SULGRAVE (St James the Less) *see* Culworth w Sulgrave and
Thorpe Mandeville etc *Pet*
SULHAM (St Nicholas) *see* Pangbourne w Tidmarsh and
Sulham *Ox*
SULHAMSTEAD ABBOTS (St Mary) and Bannister w Ufton
Nervet *Ox 12* **P** *Qu Coll Ox and Or Coll Ox (alt)*
P-in-c P L DEWEY, **NSM** A J PEABODY
SULLINGTON (St Mary) and Thakeham w Warminghurst
Chich 12 **P** *Bp and DBP (alt)* **P-in-c** D K SPENCER
SUMMERFIELD (Christ Church) (Cavendish Road Hall) *Birm 2*
P *R Birm St Martin w Bordesley* **V** P D SAINSBURY
SUMMERFIELD (St John's Chapel) *see* Hartlebury *Worc*
SUMMERSDALE (St Michael) *see* Chich St Paul and
Westhampnett *Chich*
SUMMERSTOWN (St Mary) *S'wark 17* **P** *Ch Soc Trust*
V R J RYAN
SUMMERTOWN (St Michael and All Angels) *Ox 7* **P** *St Jo*
Coll Ox **P-in-c** J M RUSHTON, **NSM** W L A PRYOR
SUNBURY, UPPER (St Saviour) *Lon 13* **P** *V Sunbury*
P-in-c D R MCDOUGALL, **C** P OXLEY
SUNBURY-ON-THAMES (St Mary) *Lon 13* **P** *D&C St Paul's*
V P S DAVIES
SUNDERLAND (St Bede) Town End Farm *see* N Wearside
Dur
SUNDERLAND (St Chad) *Dur 16* **P** *Bp* **V** J D CHADD,
NSM P THOMPSON
SUNDERLAND (St Cuthbert) Red House *see* N Wearside *Dur*
SUNDERLAND (St Ignatius) *see* Hendon *Dur*
SUNDERLAND (St Mary the Virgin) (St Peter) *Dur 16* **P** *Bp*
V *vacant* 0191-528 3754
SUNDERLAND (St Michael) *see* Sunderland Minster *Dur*
SUNDERLAND (St Thomas) (St Oswald) *Dur 16* **P** *Bp*
V D G JONES
SUNDERLAND, NORTH (St Paul) *Newc 7* **P** *Lord Crewe's*
Trustees **V** E J WOOD, **C** A ATKINSON
SUNDERLAND MINSTER Extra-Parochial Place *Dur 16*
C-in-c S R TAYLOR, **Min** M E ANDERSON, S D HAZLETT,
C S A A FAGBEMI, **NSM** J M M FRANCIS
SUNDERLAND POINT (Mission Church) *see* Overton *Blackb*
SUNDON (St Mary) *St Alb 14* **P** *Bp* **P-in-c** Y M SMEJKAL
SUNDRIDGE (St Mary) w Ide Hill and Toys Hill *Roch 9*
P *Abp* **R** D J E ATTWOOD, **NSM** A M BOYLE
SUNNINGDALE (Holy Trinity) *Ox 11* **P** *Bp*
V H D UFFINDELL
SUNNINGHILL (St Michael and All Angels) and South Ascot
Ox 11 **P** *St Jo Coll Cam* **V** S A JOHNSON,
NSM A B COOPER, S M VAN BEVEREN
SUNNINGWELL (St Leonard) *see* Radley and Sunningwell
Ox
SUNNYSIDE (St Barnabas) *see* E Grinstead St Swithun *Chich*

SUNNYSIDE (St Michael and All Angels) w Bourne End
St Alb 2 **P** *CPAS* **V** D J ABBOTT, **C** H E GARDNER,
NSM R CLARKSON
SURBITON (St Andrew) (St Mark) *S'wark 15* **P** *Bp*
P-in-c D J HOUGHTON, **C** I J NAY, **NSM** E D LONGFELLOW
SURBITON (St Matthew) *S'wark 15* **P** *Patr Bd*
TR S A HONES, **TV** C S LAKER, **OLM** V CUTHBERT
SURBITON HILL (Christ Church) *S'wark 15* **P** *Ch Soc Trust*
and Trustees (jt) **V** J D BIRCHALL, **NSM** A G FAIRBAIRN
SURFLEET (St Lawrence) *see* Glen Gp *Linc*
SURLINGHAM (St Mary) *see* Rockland St Mary w
Hellington, Bramerton etc *Nor*
SURREY WEALD *Guildf 7* **P** *Patr Bd (1 turn), Ld Chan*
(2 turns) **TR** A D J COE, **TV** B STEADMAN-ALLEN,
NSM J R BAXTER, V J SMITH, **OLM** S D EGERTON
SUSSEX GARDENS (St James) *see* Paddington St Jas *Lon*
SUSTEAD (St Peter and St Paul) *see* Roughton and Felbrigg,
Metton, Sustead etc *Nor*
SUTCOMBE (St Andrew) *see* Bradworthy, Sutcombe, Putford
etc *Ex*
SUTTERBY (not known) *see* Partney Gp *Linc*
SUTTERTON (St Mary) and Wigtoft *Linc 21* **P** *Prime Min*
and Bp (alt) **V** *vacant*
SUTTON (All Saints) *see* Potton w Sutton and Cockayne
Hatley *St Alb*
SUTTON (All Saints) *see* Wilford Peninsula *St E*
SUTTON (All Saints) w Shopland *Chelmsf 12* **P** *SMF*
P-in-c C W COUSINS
SUTTON (Christ Church) (St Barnabas) (St Nicholas) *S'wark 23*
P *Patr Bd* **TR** S E MULLALLY, **TV** P M PULLINGER,
C J S CRESSWELL, **NSM** M HARTLAND
SUTTON (Mission Room) *see* Felixkirk w Boltby *York*
SUTTON (St Andrew) *Ely 8* **P** *D&C* **V** J M AMEY
SUTTON (St Barnabas' Mission Church) *see* Macclesfield
Team *Ches*
SUTTON (St Clement), Huttoft and Anderby *Linc 8*
P *Bp (2 turns), Magd Coll Cam (1 turn)* **R** *vacant* (01507)
441169
SUTTON (St James) *Ches 13* **P** *Trustees* **V** E W L DAVIES,
NSM V B GISBY
SUTTON (St James) and Wawne *York 14* **P** *Patr Bd*
TV C FISHER-BAILEY, H H NESBITT, S G SANDHAM,
C R J GANNEY
SUTTON (St John the Baptist) *see* Barlavington, Burton w
Coates, Sutton and Bignor *Chich*
SUTTON (St Mary) *see* Calow and Sutton cum Duckmanton
Derby
SUTTON (St Michael) *see* Stalham, E Ruston, Brunstead,
Sutton and Ingham *Nor*
SUTTON (St Michael and All Angels) *see* Castor w Sutton and
Upton w Marholm *Pet*
SUTTON (St Nicholas) (All Saints) (St Michael and All Angels)
Liv 10 **P** *Patr Bd* **TR** C B SPITTLE, **TV** M J TAYLOR,
OLM M A HARRISON
SUTTON (St Thomas) w Cowling and Lothersdale *Bradf 8*
P *Ch Ch Ox and Bp (jt)* **V** M COWGILL, **Hon C** G L HALL
SUTTON w Carlton and Normanton upon Trent and Marnham
S'well 3 **P** *Bp* **P-in-c** S DIXON
SUTTON, EAST (St Peter and St Paul) *see* Sutton Valence w E
Sutton and Chart Sutton *Cant*
SUTTON, GREAT (St John the Evangelist) *Ches 9*
P *V Eastham* **V** D S FISHER
SUTTON, NORTH *see* Plymouth Em, St Paul Efford and
St Aug *Ex*
SUTTON AT HONE (St John the Baptist) *see* Horton Kirby
and Sutton-at-Hone *Roch*
SUTTON BASSETT (All Saints) *see* Stoke Albany w
Wilbarston and Ashley etc *Pet*
SUTTON BENGER (All Saints) *see* Draycot *Bris*
SUTTON BINGHAM (All Saints) *see* E Coker w Sutton
Bingham and Closworth *B & W*
SUTTON BONINGTON (St Michael) (St Anne) w Normanton-
on-Soar *S'well 9* **P** *Bp* **P-in-c** G MARTIN
SUTTON BRIDGE (St Matthew) *Linc 16* **P** *Bp* **V** *vacant*
(01406) 351503
SUTTON BY DOVER (St Peter and St Paul) *see* Ringwould w
Kingsdown and Ripple etc *Cant*
SUTTON CHENEY (St James) *see* Bosworth and Sheepy Gp
Leic
SUTTON COLDFIELD (Holy Trinity) *Birm 12* **P** *Bp*
P-in-c W J ROUTH, **NSM** P G DUCKERS
SUTTON COLDFIELD (St Chad) *Birm 12* **P** *Bp*
P-in-c W J ROUTH, **C** E M WALLACE
SUTTON COLDFIELD (St Columba) *Birm 12* **P** *Bp*
V R P TUCKER

SUTTON COURTENAY (All Saints) w Appleford *Ox 10*
P *D&C Windsor*   **P-in-c** H G KENDRICK
SUTTON-CUM-LOUND (St Bartholomew) *see* Babworth w
    Sutton-cum-Lound and Scofton etc *S'well*
SUTTON GREEN (All Souls)   *see* Woking St Pet *Guildf*
SUTTON HILL (Pastoral Centre)   *see* Madeley *Heref*
SUTTON IN ASHFIELD (St Mary Magdalene) *S'well 4*   **P** *Bp*
P-in-c J E PALMER,   **C** A H DIGMAN
SUTTON IN ASHFIELD St Michael and All Angels *S'well 4*
P *Bp*   **P-in-c** T MITCHELL
SUTTON IN HOLDERNESS (St Michael) *York 14*   **P** *Abp*
V M A JEAVONS,   **NSM** H M HOTCHIN
SUTTON LE MARSH (St Clement)   *see* Sutton, Huttoft and
    Anderby *Linc*
SUTTON MADDOCK (St Mary)   *see* Beckbury, Badger,
    Kemberton, Ryton, Stockton etc *Lich*
SUTTON MANDEVILLE (All Saints)   *see* Fovant, Sutton
    Mandeville and Teffont Evias etc *Sarum*
SUTTON MONTIS (Holy Trinity)   *see* Cam Vale *B & W*
SUTTON ON DERWENT (St Michael)   *see* Derwent Ings
    York
SUTTON ON PLYM (St John the Evangelist) *Ex 24*   **P** *Keble*
    Coll Ox   **P-in-c** P C B ALLEN,   **C** K F HAYDON
SUTTON-ON-SEA (St Clement)   *see* Sutton, Huttoft and
    Anderby *Linc*
SUTTON ON THE FOREST (All Hallows)   *see* Forest of
    Galtres *York*
SUTTON ON THE HILL (St Michael)   *see* Boylestone, Church
    Broughton, Dalbury, etc *Derby*
SUTTON-ON-TRENT (All Saints)   *see* Sutton w Carlton and
    Normanton upon Trent etc *S'well*
SUTTON PARK (St Andrew)   *see* Sutton St Jas and Wawne
    York
SUTTON ST EDMUND (St Edmund King and Martyr)
    see The Suttons w Tydd *Linc*
SUTTON ST JAMES (St James)   *as above*
SUTTON ST MARY (otherwise known as Long Sutton)
(St Mary) *Linc 16*   **P** *Bp*   **P-in-c** J P E SIBLEY
SUTTON ST MICHAEL (St Michael)   *see* Sutton St Nicholas w
    Sutton St Michael *Heref*
SUTTON ST NICHOLAS   *see* Lutton w Gedney Drove End,
    Dawsmere *Linc*
SUTTON ST NICHOLAS (St Nicholas) w Sutton St Michael
    Heref 4   **P** *Bp*   **P-in-c** H M SHORT
SUTTON UNDER BRAILES (St Thomas à Becket) *Cov 9*
    P *Bp*   **R** N J MORGAN,   **NSM** J W ROLFE
SUTTON VALENCE (St Mary the Virgin) w East Sutton and
Chart Sutton *Cant 14*   **P** *Abp York*   **V** vacant (01622) 843156
SUTTON VENY (St John the Evangelist)   *see* Upper Wylye
    Valley *Sarum*
SUTTON WALDRON (St Bartholomew)   *see* Iwerne Valley
    Sarum
SUTTONS w Tydd, The *Linc 16*   **P** *Ld Chan (1 turn), V Long*
    Sutton (2 turns)   **V** vacant (01945) 440457
SWABY (St Nicholas)   *see* Legbourne and Wold Marsh *Linc*
SWADLINCOTE (Emmanuel) *Derby 16*   **P** *V Gresley*
    V D J HORSFALL
SWAFFHAM (St Peter and St Paul) *Nor 13*   **P** *Bp*
    V S J SMITH
SWAFFHAM BULBECK (St Mary)   *see* Anglesey Gp *Ely*
SWAFFHAM PRIOR (St Mary)   *as above*
SWAFIELD (St Nicholas)   *see* Trunch *Nor*
SWAINSTHORPE (St Peter)   *see* Newton Flotman,
    Swainsthorpe, Tasburgh, etc *Nor*
SWAINSWICK (Blessed Virgin Mary)   *see* Bath St Sav w
    Swainswick and Woolley *B & W*
SWALCLIFFE (St Peter and St Paul)   *see* Wykeham *Ox*
SWALE, LOWER *Ripon 4*   **P** *D&C York, Duke of*
    Northumberland, and Bp (jt)   **R** R J GLOVER,
    Hon C W H THACKRAY,   **NSM** M TONGE
SWALECLIFFE (St John the Baptist)   *see* Whitstable *Cant*
SWALEDALE *Ripon 2*   **P** *Bp*   **V** C J HEWLETT
SWALLOW (Holy Trinity) *Linc 5*   **P** *The Revd J R H Thorold*
    and J R Thorold Esq (jt), DBP, Bp, and Earl of Yarborough
    (by turn)   **R** vacant (01472) 371560
SWALLOWBECK (St George)   *see* Linc St Geo Swallowbeck
    Linc
SWALLOWCLIFFE (St Peter)   *see* Nadder Valley *Sarum*
SWALLOWFIELD (All Saints)   *see* Loddon Reach *Ox*
SWALLOWNEST (Christ Church)   *see* Aston cum Aughton w
    Swallownest and Ulley *Sheff*
SWALWELL (Holy Trinity)   *see* Blaydon and Swalwell *Dur*
SWANAGE (All Saints) (St Mary the Virgin) and Studland
    Sarum 8   **P** *Patr Bd*   **TR** J S WOOD,   **TV** W H N WATTS,
    NSM W M FELLINGHAM,   **OLM** A C HIGGINS

SWANBOURNE (St Swithun)   *see* Newton Longville and
    Mursley w Swanbourne etc *Ox*
SWANLAND (St Barnabas) *York 14*   **P** *H Trin Hull and Distr*
    Ch Patr Soc Ltd   **NSM** D KITCHING
SWANLEY (St Mary) *Roch 2*   **P** *Guild of All So*
    V J E MOWBRAY
SWANLEY (St Paul) *Roch 2*   **P** *Merchant Taylors' Co*
    P-in-c R C SAMME
SWANMORE (St Barnabas) *Portsm 1*   **P** *DBP*   **V** P H KELLY,
    NSM M J MORFILL
SWANMORE (St Michael and All Angels) *Portsm 7*   **P** *SMF*
    V M F JONES
SWANNINGTON (St George)   *see* Ravenstone and
    Swannington *Leic*
SWANNINGTON (St Margaret)   *see* Wensum Benefice *Nor*
SWANSCOMBE (St Peter and St Paul) *Roch 4*   **P** *DBP*
    R D SCOTT
SWANTON ABBOT (St Michael)   *see* Worstead, Westwick,
    Sloley, Swanton Abbot etc *Nor*
SWANTON MORLEY (All Saints)   *see* Dereham and Distr *Nor*
SWANTON NOVERS (St Edmund)   *see* Brinton, Briningham,
    Hunworth, Stody etc *Nor*
SWANWICK (St Andrew) and Pentrich *Derby 1*   **P** *Wright*
    Trustees and Duke of Devonshire (alt)   **V** T B JOHNSON
SWANWICK (St Barnabas)   *see* Sarisbury *Portsm*
SWARBY (St Mary and All Saints)   *see* S Lafford *Linc*
SWARCLIFFE (St Luke)   *see* Seacroft *Ripon*
SWARDESTON (St Mary the Virgin) w East Carleton, Intwood,
    Keswick and Ketteringham *Nor 7*   **P** *Bp, DBP, and*
    Miss M B Unthank (jt)   **R** P D BURR
SWARKESTONE (St James)   *see* Ticknall, Smisby and Stanton
    by Bridge etc *Derby*
SWARTHMORE (Mission Church)   *see* Pennington and Lindal
    w Marton and Bardsea *Carl*
SWATON (St Michael)   *see* Helpringham w Hale *Linc*
SWAVESEY (St Andrew)   *see* Fen Drayton w Conington and
    Lolworth etc *Ely*
SWAY (St Luke) *Win 11*   **P** *Bp*   **P-in-c** J PAWSON,
    NSM R D C ELLIOTT
SWAYFIELD (St Nicholas)   *see* Corby Glen *Linc*
SWAYTHLING (St Mary South Stoneham w St Alban the
    Martyr) *Win 13*   **P** *Bp and TR Southn City Cen (jt)*
    V G J PHILBRICK,   **NSM** C A DAY
SWEFFLING (St Mary)   *see* Upper Alde *St E*
SWELL (St Catherine)   *see* Curry Rivel w Fivehead and Swell
    B & W
SWELL, LOWER (St Mary)   *see* Stow on the Wold, Condicote
    and The Swells *Glouc*
SWELL, UPPER (St Mary)   *as above*
SWEPSTONE (St Peter)   *see* Woodfield Team *Leic*
SWERFORD (St Mary)   *see* Hook Norton w Gt Rollright,
    Swerford etc *Ox*
SWETTENHAM (St Peter)   *see* Goostrey w Swettenham *Ches*
SWILLAND (St Mary)   *see* Clopton w Otley, Swilland and
    Ashbocking *St E*
SWILLINGTON (St Mary) *Ripon 8*   **P** *Bp*
    P-in-c L C PEARSON
SWIMBRIDGE (St James the Apostle) w West Buckland and
    Landkey *Ex 18*   **P** *Bp and Trustees Earl Fortescue (jt)*
    R P BOWERS,   **NSM** G F SQUIRE
SWINBROOK (St Mary)   *see* Burford w Fulbrook, Taynton,
    Asthall etc *Ox*
SWINDERBY (All Saints) *Linc 18*   **P** *Bp, Ld Chan,*
    E M K Kirk Esq, and D&C (by turn)   **V** G C GOALBY,
    NSM J T ROOKE
SWINDON (All Saints) (St Barnabas) *Bris 7*   **P** *Bp*
    V A R STEVENSON,   **C** A M OVERTON-BENGE
SWINDON (Christ Church) (St Mary) *Bris 7*   **P** *Ld Chan*
    V S M STEVENETTE,   **NSM** J E NORTHEY
SWINDON Dorcan *Bris 7*   **P** *Bp*   **TR** A B KNAPP
SWINDON New Town (St Mark) (St Adhelm) (St Luke)
    (St Saviour) *Bris 7*   **P** *Patr Bd*   **TR** D B MCCONKEY,
    TV C D KINCH
SWINDON (St Andrew) (St John the Baptist) *Bris 7*   **P** *Ld Chan*
    TR R J BURLES
SWINDON (St Augustine) *Bris 7*   **P** *Bp*   **C** A M OVERTON-
    BENGE
SWINDON (St John the Evangelist)   *see* Smestow Vale *Lich*
SWINDON (St Lawrence)   *see* N Cheltenham *Glouc*
SWINDON (St Peter)   *see* Penhill *Bris*
SWINDON, NORTH (St Andrew) *Bris 7*   **P** *Bp*
    P-in-c M H HASLAM,   **C** E C BROWN
SWINDON, WEST and the Lydiards *Bris 7*   **P** *Patr Bd*
    TV T V ROBERTS
SWINE (St Mary)   *see* Skirlaugh w Long Riston, Rise and Swine
    York

SWINEFLEET (St Margaret)   *see* The Marshland *Sheff*

SWINESHEAD (St Mary) *Linc 21*   **P** *Bp*   **V** *vacant* (01205) 820271

SWINESHEAD (St Nicholas)   *see* The Stodden Churches *St Alb*

SWINFORD (All Saints)   *see* Gilmorton, Peatling Parva, Kimcote etc *Leic*

SWINFORD, OLD Stourbridge (St Mary) *Worc 12*   **P** *Bp*   **R** G S CROSS,   **C** R I ATKINSON

SWINHOPE (St Helen)   *see* Binbrook Gp *Linc*

SWINNOW (Christ the Saviour)   *see* Stanningley St Thos *Ripon*

SWINSTEAD (St Mary)   *see* Edenham w Witham on the Hill and Swinstead *Linc*

SWINTON (Holy Rood) *Man 2*   **P** *TR Swinton and Pendlebury*   **P-in-c** C J C HEWITT

SWINTON (St Margaret) *Sheff 12*   **P** *Sir Philip Naylor-Leyland Bt*   **V** C J BARLEY

SWINTON (St Peter) and Pendlebury *Man 2*   **P** *Patr Bd*   **TR** J P SHEEHY,   **C** J LIVESLEY

SWISS COTTAGE (Holy Trinity)   *see* W Hampstead Trin *Lon*

SWITHLAND (St Leonard)   *see* Woodhouse, Woodhouse Eaves and Swithland *Leic*

SWYNCOMBE (St Botolph)   *see* Icknield *Ox*

SWYNNERTON (St Mary) and Tittensor *Lich 13*   **P** *Bp and Simeon's Trustees (jt)*   **P-in-c** S G MCKENZIE

SWYRE (Holy Trinity)   *see* Bride Valley *Sarum*

SYDE (St Mary)   *see* Brimpsfield w Birdlip, Syde, Daglingworth etc *Glouc*

SYDENHAM (All Saints) *S'wark 5*   **P** *V Sydenham St Bart*   **P-in-c** P H SMITH

SYDENHAM (Holy Trinity) (St Augustine) *S'wark 5*   **P** *Bp and Simeon's Trustees (jt)*   **V** S A LASKEY,   **NSM** S R SCOTT, M BROOKS,   **OLM** J J SHIRLEY

SYDENHAM (St Bartholomew) *S'wark 5*   **P** *Earl of Dartmouth*   **V** M J KINGSTON,   **C** H A HUNTLEY

SYDENHAM (St Mary)   *see* Chinnor, Sydenham, Aston Rowant and Crowell *Ox*

SYDENHAM (St Philip) *S'wark 5*   **P** *V Sydenham St Bart*   **V** P W TIERNAN

SYDENHAM, LOWER (St Michael and All Angels) Bell Green *S'wark 5*   **P** *Bp*   **V** *vacant* (020) 8778 7196

SYDENHAM DAMEREL (St Mary)   *see* Milton Abbot, Dunterton, Lamerton etc *Ex*

SYDERSTONE (St Mary)   *see* N and S Creake w Waterden, Syderstone etc *Nor*

SYDLING ST NICHOLAS (St Nicholas)   *see* Bradford Peverell, Stratton, Frampton etc *Sarum*

SYERSTON (All Saints)   *see* E Stoke w Syerston *S'well*

SYKEHOUSE (Holy Trinity)   *see* Fishlake w Sykehouse and Kirk Bramwith etc *Sheff*

SYLEHAM (St Mary)   *see* Hoxne w Denham, Syleham and Wingfield *St E*

SYMONDS GREEN (Christ the King)   *see* Stevenage H Trin *St Alb*

SYMONDSBURY (St John the Baptist) *Sarum 2*   **P** *Bp*   **P-in-c** M N A JONES,   **OLM** E D MARSH

SYRESHAM (St James)   *see* Astwell Gp *Pet*

SYSTON (St Mary)   *see* Barkston and Hough Gp *Linc*

SYSTON Team Ministry, The (St Peter and St Paul) *Leic 5*   **P** *Patr Bd*   **TR** D C WHITE,   **TV** L D BRABIN-SMITH, J IQBAL,   **C** E P ANGELL,   **NSM** I M HILL

SYSTON (St Anne)   *see* Warmley, Syston and Bitton *Bris*

SYSTONBY (not known)   *see* Melton Mowbray *Leic*

SYWELL (St Peter and St Paul)   *see* Mears Ashby and Hardwick and Sywell etc *Pet*

TABLEY, WEST (St Paul) and High Legh *Ches 12*   **P** *Bp and Mrs P H Langford-Brooke (1 turn), C L S Cornwall-Legh Esq (1 turn)*   **V** M R CAVANAGH

TACKLEY (St Nicholas)   *see* Steeple Aston w N Aston and Tackley *Ox*

TACOLNESTON (All Saints)   *see* Ashwellthorpe, Forncett, Fundenhall, Hapton etc *Nor*

TADCASTER (St Mary) w Newton Kyme *York 1*   **P** *Abp*   **V** S SHERIFF,   **C** C L CULLINGWORTH

TADDINGTON (St Michael), Chelmorton and Flagg, and Monyash *Derby 4*   **P** *V Bakewell*   **P-in-c** J O GOLDSMITH,   **NSM** M L GOLDSMITH, J S FOUNTAIN

TADDIPORT (St Mary Magdalene)   *see* Gt and Lt Torrington and Frithelstock *Ex*

TADLEY, NORTH (St Mary) *Win 4*   **P** *Bp*   **V** B J NORRIS

TADLEY SOUTH (St Peter) (St Paul) and Silchester *Win 4*   **P** *Duke of Wellington and Bp (alt)*   **R** P D COOPER,   **Hon C** K V BATT

TADLOW (St Giles)   *see* Shingay Gp *Ely*

TADMARTON (St Nicholas)   *see* Wykeham *Ox*

TADWORTH (Good Shepherd) *S'wark 26*   **P** *V Kingswood St Andr*   **P-in-c** M W ELFRED,   **OLM** A S BLAIN

TAKELEY (Holy Trinity) w Little Canfield *Chelmsf 18*   **P** *Bp and Ch Coll Cam*   **R** L BOND,   **C** T A J WYNNE,   **NSM** C M HAWKES

TALATON (St James the Apostle)   *see* Whimple, Talaton and Clyst St Lawr *Ex*

TALBOT VILLAGE (St Mark) *Sarum 7*   **P** *Trustees*   **V** C J F RUTLEDGE,   **C** J C GAFFIN,   **OLM** P G C JONES, J P T G SMITH

TALKE O' THE HILL (St Martin) *Lich 9*   **P** *V Audley*   **P-in-c** P D HOWARD

TALKIN (not known)   *see* Eden, Gelt and Irthing *Carl*

TALLAND (St Tallan) *Truro 12*   **P** *DBP and W Gundry-Mills Esq (alt)*   **P-in-c** L J SMITH

TALLINGTON (St Laurence)   *see* Uffington Gp *Linc*

TAMERTON, NORTH (St Denis)   *see* Boyton, N Tamerton, Werrington etc *Truro*

TAMERTON FOLIOT (St Mary) *Ex 23*   **P** *Ld Chan*   **P-in-c** D B M GILL,   **C** W P JACKSON

TAMWORTH (St Editha) *Lich 4*   **P** *Bp*   **V** A BARRETT,   **C** V M C VAN DEN BERGH,   **Hon C** A L WHEALE

TANDRIDGE (St Peter)   *see* Oxted and Tandridge *S'wark*

TANFIELD (St Margaret of Antioch)   *see* Ch the K *Dur*

TANFIELD, WEST (St Nicholas) and Well w Snape and North Stainley *Ripon 3*   **P** *Bp and Mrs M E Bourne-Arton (alt)*   **R** M DE LA P BERESFORD-PEIRSE

TANGLEY (St Thomas of Canterbury)   *see* Pastrow *Win*

TANGMERE (St Andrew) and Oving *Chich 3*   **P** *Bp and Duke of Richmond (jt)*   **P-in-c** I C ROGERS

TANHOUSE The Oaks (Conventional District) *Liv 11*   **Min** W D PETTY

TANKERSLEY (St Peter), Thurgoland and Wortley *Sheff 11*   **P** *Dowager Countess of Wharncliffe, Sir Philip Naylor-Leyland Bt, and V Silkstone (jt)*   **R** K J E HALE

TANNINGTON (St Ethelbert)   *see* Worlingworth, Southolt, Tannington, Bedfield etc *St E*

TANSLEY (Holy Trinity), Dethick, Lea and Holloway *Derby 7*   **P** *Bp, V Crich, and DBF (jt)*   **R** *vacant* (01629) 534275

TANSOR (St Mary)   *see* Warmington, Tansor and Cotterstock etc *Pet*

TANWORTH (St Mary Magdalene) *Birm 6*   **P** *F D Muntz Esq*   **V** P E F CUDBY

TAPLOW (St Nicolas) and Dropmore *Ox 23*   **P** *Eton Coll and DBP (jt)*   **V** A C DIBDEN

TARDEBIGGE (St Bartholomew)   *see* Redditch H Trin *Worc*

TARLETON (Holy Trinity) *Blackb 5*   **P** *St Pet Coll Ox*   **P-in-c** N E DAVIS,   **Hon C** T TAYLOR,   **NSM** R J FISHER

TARLTON (St Osmund)   *see* Rodmarton CD *Glouc*

TARPORLEY (St Helen) *Ches 5*   **P** *DBP (1 turn), D&C (1 turn), and Sir John Grey Regerton Bt (1 turn)*   **R** K E HINE,   **NSM** A J SANDERS

TARRANT GUNVILLE (St Mary)   *see* Chase *Sarum*

TARRANT HINTON (St Mary)   *as above*

TARRANT KEYNSTON (All Saints)   *as above*

TARRANT MONKTON (All Saints)   *as above*

TARRANT RUSHTON (St Mary)   *as above*

TARRING, WEST (St Andrew) *Chich 5*   **P** *Abp*   **R** W E JERVIS,   **NSM** G T SPENCER

TARRING NEVILLE (St Mary)   *see* Denton w S Heighton and Tarring Neville *Chich*

TARRINGTON (St Philip and St James)   *see* Ledbury *Heref*

TARVIN (St Andrew) *Ches 2*   **P** *Bp*   **NSM** M R MARR, R G TUCKWELL

TAS VALLEY   *see* Newton Flotman, Swainsthorpe, Tasburgh, etc *Nor*

TAS VALLEY, UPPER   *see* Ashwellthorpe, Forncett, Fundenhall, Hapton etc *Nor*

TASBURGH (St Mary)   *see* Newton Flotman, Swainsthorpe, Tasburgh, etc *Nor*

TASLEY (St Peter and St Paul)   *see* Bridgnorth, Tasley, Astley Abbotts, etc *Heref*

TATENHILL (St Michael and All Angels)   *see* Barton under Needwood w Dunstall and Tatenhill *Lich*

TATHAM (St James the Less)   *see* E Lonsdale *Blackb*

TATHAM FELLS (Good Shepherd)   *as above*

TATHWELL (St Vedast)   *see* Legbourne and Wold Marsh *Linc*

TATSFIELD (St Mary) *S'wark 25*   **P** *Bp*   **R** *vacant* (01959) 577289

TATTENHALL (St Alban) and Handley *Ches 5*   **P** *Bp and D&C (jt)*   **P-in-c** L MUTETE

TATTENHAM CORNER (St Mark) *Guildf 9*   **P** *Bp*   **V** R J WHITTLE

TATTENHOE (St Giles)   *see* Watling Valley *Ox*

TATTERFORD (St Margaret)   *see* E w W Rudham, Helhoughton etc *Nor*

TATTERSETT (All Saints and St Andrew)   *as above*

1155

TATTERSHALL (Holy Trinity)   *see* Bain Valley Gp *Linc*
TATTINGSTONE (St Mary)   *see* Sproughton w Burstall,
  Copdock w Washbrook etc *St E*
TATWORTH (St John the Evangelist)   *see* Chaffcombe, Cricket
  Malherbie etc *B & W*
TAUNTON (All Saints) *B & W 18*   **P** *Bp*   **V** D C W FAYLE
TAUNTON (Holy Trinity) *B & W 18*   **P** *Bp*
  V J B V LAURENCE,   **Hon C** J J STRATTON
TAUNTON (St Andrew) *B & W 18*   **P** *Bp*   **V** J D R COX
TAUNTON (St James) *B & W 18*   **P** *Simeon's Trustees*
  V T R N JONES,   **NSM** D G AGER
TAUNTON (St John the Evangelist) *B & W 18*   **P** *Bp*
  P-in-c D ROBERTS,   **Hon C** J R EASTELL
TAUNTON (St Mary Magdalene) *B & W 18*   **P** *Ch Patr Trust*
  V R G CORKE,   **C** P B TULLETT,   **Hon C** D E CAVAGHAN
TAUNTON (St Peter) Lyngford *B & W 18*   **P** *Bp*
  V I S MCFARLANE
TAVERHAM (St Edmund) *Nor 2*   **P** *Bp*   **R** P SEABROOK
TAVISTOCK (St Eustachius) and Gulworthy (St Paul) *Ex 25*
  P *Bp*   **P-in-c** M W BRIERLEY,   **C** T L V TREANOR,
  NSM P RENNIE
TAW VALLEY   *see* Barnstaple *Ex*
TAWSTOCK (St Peter)   *see* Newton Tracey, Horwood,
  Alverdiscott etc *Ex*
TAWTON, NORTH (St Peter), Bondleigh, Sampford Courtenay
  and Honeychurch *Ex 11*   **P** *MMCET, K Coll Cam, and*
  D&C (jt)   **R** R W B ARDILL
TAWTON, SOUTH (St Andrew) and Belstone *Ex 11*   **P** *D&C*
  Windsor and Bp (jt)   **R** *vacant* (01837) 849048
TAYNTON (St John the Evangelist)   *see* Burford w Fulbrook,
  Taynton, Asthall etc *Ox*
TAYNTON (St Laurence)   *see* Highnam, Lassington, Rudford,
  Tibberton etc *Glouc*
TEALBY (All Saints)   *see* Walesby *Linc*
TEAN, UPPER (Christ Church) *Lich 6*   **P** *R Checkley*
  P-in-c D C BICKERSTETH,   **Hon C** E C LAST,
  NSM P A BECKETT, C M RICHARDSON
TEBAY (St James)   *see* Orton and Tebay w Ravenstonedale etc
  Carl
TEDBURN ST MARY (St Mary), Whitestone, Oldridge,
  Holcombe Burnell, Dunsford, Doddiscombsleigh and Cheriton
  Bishop *Ex 6*   **P** *Patr Bd*   **P-in-c** M R WOOD
TEDDINGTON (St Mark) and Hampton Wick *Lon 11*   **P** *Bp*
  V D P LUND
TEDDINGTON (St Mary) (St Alban the Martyr) *Lon 10*   **P** *Bp*
  V *vacant* (020) 8977 2761
TEDDINGTON (St Nicholas)   *see* Overbury w Teddington,
  Alstone etc *Worc*
TEDDINGTON (St Peter and St Paul) and Fulwell St Michael
  and St George *Lon 10*   **P** *Bp*   **V** J W KNILL-JONES,
  Hon C P R TOPHAM
TEDSTONE DELAMERE (St James)   *see* Edvin Loach w
  Tedstone Delamere etc *Heref*
TEDSTONE WAFER (St Mary)   *as above*
TEFFONT EVIAS (St Michael)   *see* Fovant, Sutton Mandeville
  and Teffont Evias etc *Sarum*
TEFFONT MAGNA (St Edward)   *as above*
TEIGH (Holy Trinity) Whissendine and Market Overton *Pet 12*
  P *Bp and Lady Gretton (alt)*   **C** L T FRANCIS-DEHQANI
TEIGNGRACE (St Peter and St Paul)   *see* Kingsteignton and
  Teigngrace *Ex*
TEIGNMOUTH (St James) (St Michael the Archangel), Ideford
  w Luton, Ashcombe and Bishopsteignton *Ex 6*   **P** *Patr Bd*
  TR J G STONES,   **TV** S P WEST,   **C** S ASTBURY
TELFORD, CENTRAL: Dawley, Lawley, Malinslee, Stirchley,
  Brookside and Hollinswood *Lich 21*   **P** *Patr Bd (3 turns),*
  The Crown (1 turn)   **TR** M A PETERS,   **TV** G N CROWE,
  K S EVANS,   **C** S J MORRIS, S A KELLY,   **NSM** E C PHILLIPS
TELFORD PARK (St Stephen) (St Thomas) *S'wark 12*
  P *V Streatham and CPAS (jt)*   **V** S P GATES,   **C** E BLATCHLEY
TELLISFORD (All Saints)   *see* Hardington Vale *B & W*
TELSCOMBE VILLAGE (St Laurence) *Chich 18*   **P** *Bp and*
  Gorham Trustees (jt)   **V** D A HIDER
TEME VALLEY, LOWER   *see* Worcs W *Worc*
TEME VALLEY NORTH: Knighton-on-Teme, Lindridge,
  Pensax, Menith Wood, Stanford-on-Teme and Stockton
  Worc 13   **P** *Bp and D&C (alt)*   **R** L S GRACE,   **NSM** S JONES
TEME VALLEY SOUTH: Eastham, Rochford, Stoke Bliss,
  Hanley Child, Hanley William and Kyre Wyard *Worc 13*
  P *Ld Chan, Bp, and Mrs M M Miles (by turn)*   **R** A M SHARPE
TEMPLE (St Catherine)   *see* Blisland w St Breward *Truro*
TEMPLE BALSALL (St Mary) *Birm 11*   **P** *Lady Leveson Hosp*
  V K A M LLOYD ROBERTS
TEMPLE BRUER (St John the Baptist)   *see* Graffoe Gp *Linc*
TEMPLE CLOUD (St Barnabas)   *see* Clutton w Cameley
  B & W

TEMPLE EWELL (St Peter and St Paul) w Lydden *Cant 4*
  P *Abp*   **R** P CHRISTIAN
TEMPLE GRAFTON (St Andrew) w Binton *Cov 7*   **P** *Dioc*
  Trustees   **NSM** L E DAVIES
TEMPLE GUITING (St Mary)   *see* The Guitings, Cutsdean,
  Farmcote etc *Glouc*
TEMPLE HIRST (St John the Baptist)   *see* Haddlesey w
  Hambleton and Birkin *York*
TEMPLE NORMANTON (St James the Apostle) *Derby 5*
  P *Bp*   **V** M R AINSCOUGH
TEMPLE SOWERBY (St James)   *see* Kirkby Thore w Temple
  Sowerby and Newbiggin *Carl*
TEMPLECOMBE (Blessed Virgin Mary)   *see* Abbas and
  Templecombe, Henstridge and Horsington *B & W*
TEMPLETON (St Margaret)   *see* Washfield, Stoodleigh,
  Withleigh etc *Ex*
TEMPSFORD (St Peter)   *see* Riversmeet *St Alb*
TEN MILE BANK (St Mark)   *see* Hilgay *Ely*
TENBURY (St Mary) *Heref 12*   **P** *The Revd F J Evans*
  TR C A LORDING,   **TV** J M DUNKLING,   **C** C K W MOORE,
  NSM S FOSTER, H MORGAN
TENBURY (St Michael and All Angels) *Heref 12*   **P** *St Mich*
  Coll   **TV** *vacant* (01584) 810702
TENDRING (St Edmund King and Martyr) and Little Bentley w
  Beaufort cum Moze *Chelmsf 20*   **P** *Em Coll Cam, DBP, and*
  Ball Coll Ox (by turn)   **R** F R A MASON
TENTERDEN (St Michael and All Angels) *Cant 16*   **P** *Abp*
  P-in-c D G TRUSTRAM,   **C** N COOPER,   **NSM** M ROYLANCE
TENTERDEN (St Mildred) w Smallhythe *Cant 16*   **P** *D&C*
  V D G TRUSTRAM,   **C** N COOPER,   **NSM** M ROYLANCE
TERLING (All Saints)   *see* Fairstead w Terling and White
  Notley etc *Chelmsf*
TERRIERS (St Francis) *Ox 29*   **P** *V High Wycombe*
  V A W DICKINSON
TERRINGTON (All Saints)   *see* Howardian Gp *York*
TERRINGTON ST CLEMENT (St Clement) *Ely 14*
  P *The Crown*   **V** R J SLIPPER,   **NSM** C G TINKER
TERRINGTON ST JOHN (St John)   *see* E Marshland *Ely*
TERWICK (St Peter)   *see* Rogate w Terwick and Trotton w
  Chithurst *Chich*
TESTON (St Peter and St Paul)   *see* E Malling, Wateringbury
  and Teston *Roch*
TESTWOOD (St Winfrid)   *see* Totton *Win*
TETBURY (St Mary the Virgin and St Mary Magdalen),
  Beverston and Long Newnton *Glouc 9*   **P** *Mrs J C B Joynson*
  (5 turns), Prime Min (1 turn), DBP and R Boggis-Rolfe Esq
  (1 turn)   **R** A J WRIGHT,   **C** J A JACK
TETCOTT (Holy Cross)   *see* Ashwater, Halwill, Beaworthy,
  Clawton etc *Ex*
TETFORD (St Mary)   *see* S Ormsby Gp *Linc*
TETNEY (St Peter and St Paul)   *see* Holton-le-Clay, Tetney and
  N Cotes *Linc*
TETSWORTH (St Giles)   *see* Thame *Ox*
TETTENHALL REGIS (St Michael and All Angels) *Lich 24*
  P *Patr Bd*   **TR** R M REEVE,   **TV** J M PERRY, E RATHBONE,
  NSM A ROBERTS,   **OLM** J F LLOYD
TETTENHALL WOOD (Christ Church) and Perton *Lich 24*
  P *Patr Bd*   **TR** K M ELBOURNE,   **OLM** P A P SNAPE,
  C A HARLEY
TEVERSAL (St Katherine)   *see* Skegby w Teversal *S'well*
TEVERSHAM (All Saints) *Ely 4*   **P** *Bp*   **P-in-c** M C BOWERS
TEW, GREAT (St Michael and All Angels) w Little (St John the
  Evangelist) *Ox 3*   **P** *Bp and J M Johnston Esq (jt)*
  P-in-c B J RUMBOLD
TEWIN (St Peter)   *see* Welwyn *St Alb*
TEWKESBURY (Holy Trinity) *Glouc 13*   **P** *Ch Soc Trust*
  P-in-c S M M WALKER
TEWKESBURY (St Mary the Virgin) w Walton Cardiff and
  Twyning *Glouc 13*   **P** *Ld Chan (2 turns) and Ch Ch Ox*
  (1 turn)   **V** P R WILLIAMS,   **C** S L MILLER, S T SHORT,
  NSM C E WHITNEY, C F METHVEN, D COULTON
TEY, GREAT (St Barnabas) and LITTLE (St James the Less) w
  Wakes Colne and Chappel *Chelmsf 17*   **P** *Bp, DBP,*
  PCC Chappel and Ch Patr Trust (jt)   **R** J RICHARDSON
TEYNHAM (St Mary) (Primary School Worship Centre) w
  Lynsted and Kingsdown *Cant 6*   **P** *Adn Cant*
  P-in-c S H LILLICRAP
THAKEHAM (St Mary)   *see* Sullington and Thakeham w
  Warminghurst *Chich*
THAME (All Saints) (St Mary the Virgin) *Ox 1*   **P** *Patr Bd*
  TR A W GARRATT,   **TV** S F L BRIGNALL, I D MOUNTFORD,
  Hon C K A A WESTON, J H FIELDSEND, S H BAYNES, R COPPING
THAMES DITTON (St Nicholas) *Guildf 8*   **P** *K Coll Cam*
  V J A SILK,   **NSM** M J HUSSEY
THAMES VIEW (Christ Church)   *see* Barking St Marg w St
  Patr *Chelmsf*

THAMESMEAD (Church of the Cross) (St Paul's Ecumenical Centre) (William Temple) *S'wark 6* **P** *Bp*
TR C H CLEMENTS, **TV** P ORGAN, S R BOXALL
THANET (St Andrew) *see* St Peter-in-Thanet *Cant*
THANET (St Laurence) *see* St Laur in Thanet *Cant*
THANET (St Peter the Apostle) *see* St Peter-in-Thanet *Cant*
THANINGTON (St Nicholas) (St Faith's Mission Church)
Cant 3 **P** *Abp* **P-in-c** C TODD, **NSM** F E CANHAM
THARSTON (St Mary) *see* Newton Flotman, Swainsthorpe, Tasburgh, etc *Nor*
THATCHAM (St Mary) *Ox 14* **P** *Patr Bd* **TR** N T MOFFATT, **TV** P T JARVIS, **NSM** R A BEVAN, B HARLAND, **OLM** M E FONTAINE
THATTO HEATH (St Matthew) *see* Eccleston *Liv*
THAXTED (St John the Baptist, Our Lady and St Laurence)
Chelmsf 21 **P** *Bp* **V** R M TAYLOR
THE *see under substantive place name*
THEALE (Christ Church) *see* Wedmore w Theale and Blackford *B & W*
THEALE (Holy Trinity) and Englefield *Ox 12* **P** *Magd Coll Ox and Englefield Est Trust (jt)* **P-in-c** G N BORROWDALE, **Hon C** B R SPENCE
THEBERTON (St Peter) *see* Yoxmere *St E*
THEDDINGWORTH (All Saints) *see* Hexagon *Leic*
THEDDLETHORPE (St Helen) *Linc 12* **P** *Baroness Willoughby de Eresby (2 turns), Bp (1 turn)*
P-in-c C M TURNER
THELBRIDGE (St David) *see* Burrington, Chawleigh, Cheldon, Chulmleigh etc *Ex*
THELNETHAM (St Nicholas) *see* Hepworth, Hinderclay, Wattisfield and Thelnetham *St E*
THELVETON (St Andrew) *see* Dickleburgh and The Pulhams *Nor*
THELWALL (All Saints) *Ches 4* **P** *Keble Coll Ox*
V D J BLACK
THEMELTHORPE (St Andrew) *see* Foulsham, Guestwick, Stibbard, Themelthorpe etc *Nor*
THENFORD (St Mary the Virgin) *see* Chenderit *Pet*
THERFIELD (St Mary the Virgin) w Kelshall *St Alb 19*
P *Ld Chan and D&C St Paul's (alt)* **R** R M MORGAN
THETFORD (St Cuthbert) St Peter *Nor 11* **P** *Patr Bd*
TV S D GRIFFITHS, R M BAKER, **C** J M MURPHY, **Hon C** B R HOGWOOD
THETFORD, LITTLE (St George) *see* Ely *Ely*
THEYDON BOIS (St Mary) *Chelmsf 24*
P *M G E N Buxton Esq* **V** C J TRAVERS, **NSM** A M CANNELL
THEYDON GARNON (All Saints) *see* Epping Distr *Chelmsf*
THEYDON MOUNT (St Michael) *see* Greensted-juxta-Ongar w Stanford Rivers etc *Chelmsf*
THIMBLEBY (St Margaret) *see* Horncastle Gp *Linc*
THIRKLEBY (All Saints) w Kilburn and Bagby *York 19* **P** *Abp*
P-in-c R W DAVILL
THIRSK (St Mary) *York 19* **P** *Abp* **TR** R F ROWLING, **C** G P BOWKETT
THISTLETON (St Nicholas) *see* Greetham and Thistleton w Stretton and Clipsham *Pet*
THIXENDALE (St Mary) *see* Waggoners *York*
THOCKRINGTON (St Aidan) *see* Chollerton w Birtley and Thockrington *Newc*
THOMPSON (St Martin) *see* Caston, Griston, Merton, Thompson etc *Nor*
THONGSBRIDGE (St Andrew) *see* Upper Holme Valley *Wakef*
THORESBY, NORTH (St Helen) *see* The North-Chapel Parishes *Linc*
THORESBY, SOUTH (St Andrew) *see* Legbourne and Wold Marsh *Linc*
THORESWAY (St Mary) *see* Swallow *Linc*
THORGANBY (All Saints) *see* Binbrook Gp *Linc*
THORGANBY (St Helen) *see* Derwent Ings *York*
THORINGTON (St Peter) *see* Blyth Valley *St E*
THORLEY (St James the Great) *St Alb 18* **P** *Bp*
R R H V PAYNE, **NSM** A K H PLATT
THORLEY (St Swithun) *Portsm 8* **P** *Bp* **V** J A YORKE
THORMANBY (St Mary Magdalene) *see* Brafferton w Pilmoor, Myton-on-Swale etc *York*
THORNABY, NORTH (St Luke) (St Paul) *York 18* **P** *Abp*
V H C HOPKINS, **NSM** N PETTY
THORNABY, SOUTH (St Mark) (St Peter ad Vincula) *York 18*
P *Abp* **V** M L CATHERALL
THORNAGE (All Saints) *see* Brinton, Briningham, Hunworth, Stody etc *Nor*
THORNBOROUGH (St Mary) *see* Buckingham *Ox*
THORNBURY (St Anna) *see* Bredenbury *Heref*
THORNBURY (St Margaret) *Bradf 3* **P** *Vs Bradf, Calverley, and Laisterdyke (jt)* **P-in-c** N CLEWS, **C** D J MUGHAL

THORNBURY (St Mary) (St Paul) and Oldbury-on-Severn w Shepperdine *Glouc 6* **P** *Ch Ch Ox* **V** D E S PRIMROSE, **C** B W GOODWIN
THORNBURY (St Peter) *see* Black Torrington, Bradford w Cookbury etc *Ex*
THORNBY (St Helen) *see* Cottesbrooke w Gt Creaton and Thornby *Pet*
THORNCOMBE (The Blessed Virgin Mary) *see* Chaffcombe, Cricket Malherbie etc *B & W*
THORNDON (All Saints) *see* S Hartismere *St E*
THORNE (St Nicholas) *Sheff 10* **P** *Bp* **V** *vacant (01405) 814055*
THORNE COFFIN (St Andrew) *see* Tintinhull w Chilthorne Domer, Yeovil Marsh etc *B & W*
THORNE ST MARGARET (St Margaret) *see* Wellington and Distr *B & W*
THORNER (St Peter) *Ripon 8* **P** *Earl of Mexborough*
P-in-c A J NICHOLSON, **NSM** A B HAIGH
THORNES (St James) w Christ Church *Wakef 11* **P** *DBP*
P-in-c P M MAGUIRE, **C** J M WARE, R J BAILES
THORNEY (St Helen) *see* Harby w Thorney and N and S Clifton *S'well*
THORNEY, WEST (St Nicholas) *see* Southbourne w W Thorney *Chich*
THORNEY ABBEY (St Mary and St Botolph) *Ely 14* **P** *Bp*
P-in-c C HURST
THORNEY CLOSE (St Peter) *see* Sunderland St Mary and St Pet *Dur*
THORNEY HILL (All Saints) *see* Bransgore and Hinton Admiral *Win*
THORNEYBURN (St Aidan) *see* N Tyne and Redesdale *Newc*
THORNFALCON (Holy Cross) *see* Ruishton w Thornfalcon *B & W*
THORNFORD (St Mary Magdalene) *see* Bradford Abbas and Thornford w Beer Hackett *Sarum*
THORNGUMBALD (St Mary) *see* Burstwick w Thorngumbald *York*
THORNHAM (All Saints) *see* Hunstanton St Mary w Ringstead Parva etc *Nor*
THORNHAM (St James) *Man 20* **P** *Bp* **V** P N BARRATT
THORNHAM (St John) *see* Middleton w Thornham *Man*
THORNHAM MAGNA (St Mary Magdalene) *see* S Hartismere *St E*
THORNHAM PARVA (St Mary) *as above*
THORNHAUGH (St Andrew) and Wansford *Pet 10* **P** *Bp*
P-in-c T R CHRISTIE
THORNHILL (Mission Church) *see* Beckermet St Jo and St Bridget w Ponsonby *Carl*
THORNHILL (St Christopher) *see* Southampton Thornhill St Chris *Win*
THORNHILL (St Michael and All Angels) and Whitley Lower
Wakef 9 **P** *Lord Savile* **OLM** N F WEBB
THORNHILL LEES (Holy Innocents w St Mary)
see Ravensthorpe and Thornhill Lees w Savile Town *Wakef*
THORNLEY (St Bartholomew) *see* Wolsingham and Thornley *Dur*
THORNTHWAITE (St Mary the Virgin) *see* Upper Derwent *Carl*
THORNTHWAITE (St Saviour) *see* Dacre w Hartwith and Darley w Thornthwaite *Ripon*
THORNTON (St Frideswyde) *see* Sefton and Thornton *Liv*
THORNTON (St James) *Bradf 1* **P** *V Bradf*
P-in-c A J GREIFF
THORNTON (St Michael) *see* Barmby Moor Gp *York*
THORNTON (St Peter) *see* Markfield, Thornton, Bagworth and Stanton etc *Leic*
THORNTON (St Wilfrid) *see* Horncastle Gp *Linc*
THORNTON, LITTLE (St John) *Blackb 12* **P** *Bp*
V P R F CLEMENCE
THORNTON CURTIS (St Laurence) *see* Ulceby Gp *Linc*
THORNTON DALE (All Saints) w Allerston, Ebberston, Ellerburn and Wilton *York 20* **P** *A R Dudley-Smith Esq (1 turn), Abp (3 turns)* **R** P J MOTHERSDALE
THORNTON HEATH (St Jude w St Aidan) *S'wark 21* **P** *Bp*
V N K NTEGE
THORNTON HEATH (St Paul) *S'wark 21* **P** *The Crown*
V M P N JEWITT
THORNTON HOUGH (All Saints) *Ches 9* **P** *Simeon's Trustees* **V** *vacant 0151-336 3429 or 336 1654*
THORNTON IN CRAVEN (St Mary) *see* Broughton, Marton and Thornton *Bradf*
THORNTON IN LONSDALE (St Oswald) w Burton in Lonsdale *Bradf 6* **P** *Bp* **V** J A SAVAGE
THORNTON LE FEN (St Peter) *see* Brothertoft Gp *Linc*
THORNTON-LE-FYLDE (Christ Church) *Blackb 12*
P *Trustees* **V** N SALT

THORNTON-LE-MOOR (All Saints) *see* Kelsey Gp *Linc*
THORNTON-LE-MOORS (St Mary) w Ince and Elton *Ches 3*
P *Bp* **V** M FLETCHER
THORNTON LE STREET (St Leonard) *see* The Thorntons
and The Otteringtons *York*
THORNTON RUST (Mission Room) *see* Penhill *Ripon*
THORNTON STEWARD (St Oswald) *see* Middleham w
Coverdale and E Witton etc *Ripon*
THORNTON WATLASS (St Mary the Virgin) *see* Bedale and
Leeming and Thornton Watlass *Ripon*
THORNTONS and The Otteringtons, The *York 19* **P** *Ch Ch
Ox, Linc Coll Ox, and Abp (by turn)* **P-in-c** S N FISHER,
NSM A FISHER
THOROTON (St Helena) *see* Whatton w Aslockton,
Hawksworth, Scarrington etc *S'well*
THORP ARCH (All Saints) w Walton *York 1* **P** *Lady Elizabeth
Hastings Estate Charity and G Lane Fox Esq (alt)*
P-in-c P E BRISTOW, **C** P D WATSON
THORPE (St Andrew) (Good Shepherd) *Nor 1* **P** *Trustees
W J Birkbeck Esq* **R** B R OAKE, **C** J A HAWKINS, C D ELLIS,
NSM L WOOD
Thorpe (St Laurence) *see* Farndon w Thorpe, Hawton and
Cotham *S'well*
THORPE (St Leonard) *see* Fenny Bentley, Thorpe, Tissington,
Parwich etc *Derby*
THORPE (St Mary) *Guildf 11* **P** *Keble Coll Ox*
V M J HEREWARD-ROTHWELL
THORPE (St Matthew) *Nor 1* **P** *R Thorpe St Andr*
V G R DRAKE
THORPE (St Peter) *see* The Wainfleet Gp *Linc*
THORPE ABBOTS (All Saints) *see* Scole, Brockdish,
Billingford, Thorpe Abbots etc *Nor*
THORPE ACHURCH (St John the Baptist) *see* Aldwincle,
Clopton, Pilton, Stoke Doyle etc *Pet*
THORPE ACRE w Dishley (All Saints) *Leic 6* **P** *Bp*
V K A ELLIOTT, **NSM** E T SKINNER
THORPE ARNOLD (St Mary the Virgin) *see* Melton
Mowbray *Leic*
THORPE AUDIN (Mission Room) *see* Badsworth *Wakef*
THORPE BASSETT (All Saints) *see* Buckrose Carrs *York*
THORPE BAY (St Augustine) *Chelmsf 13* **P** *Bp* **V** J COLLIS
THORPE CONSTANTINE (St Constantine) *Lich 4*
P *Mrs E V G Inge-Innes* **P-in-c** S J LUMBY
THORPE EDGE (St John the Divine) *Bradf 3* **P** *Vs Bradf,
Calverley, and Idle (jt)* **P-in-c** G S DARLISON
THORPE END (St David) *see* Gt and Lt Plumstead w Thorpe
End and Witton *Nor*
THORPE EPISCOPI (St Andrew) *see* Thorpe St Andr *Nor*
THORPE HESLEY (Holy Trinity) *Sheff 6* **P** *Sir Philip Naylor-
Leyland Bt* **V** J F HARDY
THORPE LANGTON (St Leonard) *see* Church Langton cum
Tur Langton etc *Leic*
THORPE-LE-SOKEN (St Michael) *Chelmsf 22* **P** *Bp*
P-in-c J C DOWDING
THORPE MALSOR (All Saints) *see* Broughton w Loddington
and Cransley etc *Pet*
THORPE MANDEVILLE (St John the Baptist) *see* Culworth
w Sulgrave and Thorpe Mandeville etc *Pet*
THORPE MARKET (St Margaret) *see* Trunch *Nor*
THORPE MORIEUX (St Mary the Virgin) *see* Rattlesden w
Thorpe Morieux, Brettenham etc *St E*
THORPE-NEXT-HADDISCOE (St Matthias)
see Raveningham Gp *Nor*
THORPE-ON-THE-HILL (St Michael) *see* Swinderby *Linc*
THORPE SALVIN (St Peter) *see* Harthill and Thorpe Salvin
Sheff
THORPE SATCHVILLE (St Michael and All Angels)
see S Croxton Gp *Leic*
THORPE WILLOUGHBY (St Francis of Assisi) *see* Brayton
York
THORRINGTON (St Mary Magdalene) *see* Gt Bentley and
Frating w Thorrington *Chelmsf*
**THORVERTON (St Thomas of Canterbury), Cadbury, Upton
Pyne, Brampford Speke and Newton St Cyres** *Ex 2* **P** *Ld Chan
(1 turn), Patr Bd (3 turns)* **P-in-c** D J DETTMER,
C H DAWSON, **NSM** S SHEPPARD
THRANDESTON (St Margaret) *see* N Hartismere *St E*
THRAPSTON (St James), Denford and Islip *Pet 10* **P** *Ld Chan
(2 turns), L G Stopford-Sackville Esq (1 turn)*
R C D JEFFERSON
THREAPWOOD (St John) *see* Malpas and Threapwood *Ches*
THRECKINGHAM (St Peter) *see* S Lafford *Linc*
THREE LEGGED CROSS (All Saints) *see* Verwood *Sarum*
THREE RIVERS Group, The *Ely 4* **P** *Jes Coll Cam and
Mrs D A Crawley (2 turns), Ld Chan (1 turn)*

C K R PEACOCK, **NSM** P M DEBENHAM, M G BANYARD,
J A GAGE
THRELKELD (St Mary) *see* St John's-in-the-Vale, Threlkeld
and Wythburn *Carl*
THREXTON (All Saints) *see* Gt and Lt Cressingham w
Threxton *Nor*
THRIGBY (St Mary) *see* S Trin Broads *Nor*
THRIMBY (St Mary) *see* Morland, Thrimby, Gt Strickland
and Cliburn *Carl*
THRINGSTONE (St Andrew) *Leic 8* **P** *Duchy of Lanc*
P-in-c J A BURGESS, Hon **C** R J SEAMAN, **NSM** J A BIRD
THRIPLOW (St George) *see* Fowlmere, Foxton, Shepreth and
Thriplow *Ely*
THROCKING (Holy Trinity) *see* Cottered w Broadfield and
Throcking *St Alb*
THROCKLEY (St Mary the Virgin) *see* Newburn *Newc*
THROCKMORTON (Chapelry) *see* Abberton, The Flyfords,
Naunton Beauchamp etc *Worc*
THROOP (St Paul) *Win 8* **P** *Ch Soc Trust* **V** R D PETERS,
C M P R DIETZ, L P P JESUDASON
THROPTON (St Andrew) *see* Upper Coquetdale *Newc*
THROWLEIGH (St Mary the Virgin) *see* Chagford,
Drewsteignton, Hittisleigh etc *Ex*
THROWLEY (St Michael and All Angels) *see* Selling w
Throwley, Sheldwich w Badlesmere etc *Cant*
THRUMPTON (All Saints) *S'well 9* **P** *Mrs M Gottlieb*
P-in-c S W OSMAN
THRUSCROSS (no dedication) *see* Dacre w Hartwith and
Darley w Thornthwaite *Ripon*
THRUSHELTON (St George) *see* Lifton, Broadwoodwidger,
Stowford etc *Ex*
THRUSSINGTON (Holy Trinity) *see* Syston *Leic*
THRUXTON (St Bartholomew) *see* Kingstone w Clehonger,
Eaton Bishop etc *Heref*
THRUXTON (St Peter and St Paul) *see* Appleshaw, Kimpton,
Thruxton, Fyfield etc *Win*
THRYBERGH (St Leonard) *Sheff 6* **P** *Mrs P N Fullerton*
R J FRENCH
THUNDERSLEY (St Michael and All Angels) (St Peter)
Chelmsf 10 **P** *Bp* **R** M E STURROCK
THUNDERSLEY, NEW (St George) *Chelmsf 10* **P** *Bp*
V A J ROSE
THUNDRIDGE (St Mary) *St Alb 22* **P** *Bp* **V** H J SHARMAN
THURCASTON (All Saints) *see* Anstey and Thurcaston w
Cropston *Leic*
THURCROFT (St Simon and St Jude) *Sheff 5* **P** *Bp*
P-in-c P J CRAIG-WILD, **C** D E CRAIG-WILD
**THURGARTON (St Peter) w Hoveringham and Bleasby w
Halloughton** *S'well 15* **P** *Ld Chan and Trin Coll Cam (alt)*
V A P DE BERRY
THURGOLAND (Holy Trinity) *see* Tankersley, Thurgoland
and Wortley *Sheff*
THURLASTON (All Saints) *see* Enderby w Lubbesthorpe and
Thurlaston *Leic*
THURLASTON (St Edmund) *see* Dunchurch *Cov*
THURLBY (St Firmin) *see* Ness Gp *Linc*
THURLBY (St Germain) *see* Bassingham Gp *Linc*
THURLEIGH (St Peter) *see* Milton Ernest, Pavenham and
Thurleigh *St Alb*
**THURLESTON (All Saints), South Milton, West Alvington and
Churchstow** *Ex 14* **P** *Bp Ex and D&C Sarum (jt)*
P-in-c P OSLER
THURLOW, GREAT (All Saints) *see* Stourhead *St E*
THURLOW, LITTLE (St Peter) *as above*
THURLOXTON (St Giles) *see* Alfred Jewel *B & W*
THURLSTONE (St Saviour) *see* Penistone and Thurlstone
Wakef
THURLTON (All Saints) *see* Raveningham Gp *Nor*
THURMASTON (St Michael and All Angels) *see* Syston *Leic*
THURNBY (St Luke) w Stoughton *Leic 4* **P** MMCET
V J M BARRETT, **NSM** H M BENCE
THURNBY LODGE (Christ Church) *see* Ascension TM *Leic*
THURNE (St Edmund) *see* Martham and Repps with
Bastwick, Thurne etc *Nor*
THURNHAM (St Mary the Virgin) *see* Bearsted w Thurnham
Cant
THURNING (St Andrew) *see* Reepham, Hackford w Whitwell,
Kerdiston etc *Nor*
THURNING (St James the Great) *see* Barnwell, Hemington,
Luddington in the Brook etc *Pet*
THURNSCOE (St Helen) (St Hilda) *Sheff 12* **P** *Bp and
Sir Philip Naylor-Leyland Bt (jt)* **R** M P THOMPSON
THURROCK, LITTLE (St John the Evangelist) *see* Grays
North *Chelmsf*
THURROCK, LITTLE (St Mary the Virgin) *see* Grays
Thurrock *Chelmsf*

THURROCK, WEST (Church Centre)   *as above*
THURSBY (St Andrew) *Carl 3*   **P** *D&C*   **P-in-c** N L ROBINSON
THURSFORD (St Andrew)   *see* Barney, Fulmodeston w Croxton, Hindringham etc *Nor*
THURSLEY (St Michael and All Angels) *Guildf 4*   **P** *V Witley*   **V** W D LANG,   **OLM** P R J MUIR
THURSTASTON (St Bartholomew) *Ches 8*   **P** *D&C*   **R** E J TURNER
THURSTON (St Peter) *St E 9*   **P** *Bp*   **V** D M B MATHERS
THURSTONLAND (St Thomas)   *see* Upper Holme Valley *Wakef*
THURTON (St Ethelbert) w Ashby St Mary, Bergh Apton w Yelverton and Framingham Pigot *Nor 8*   **P** *Bp and Major J H Thursby, Bp and MMCET, and Ld Chan (by turn)*   **R** P M KNIGHT,   **NSM** R J M COLLIER
THUXTON (St Paul)   *see* Barnham Broom and Upper Yare *Nor*
THWAITE (All Saints)   *see* Erpingham w Calthorpe, Ingworth, Aldborough etc *Nor*
THWAITE (St Mary)   *see* Brooke, Kirstead, Mundham w Seething and Thwaite *Nor*
THWAITES (St Anne)   *see* Millom *Carl*
THWAITES BROW (St Barnabas) *Bradf 8*   **P** *DBP*   **P-in-c** J L PRITCHARD,   **NSM** K R B JONES
THWING (All Saints)   *see* Langtoft w Foxholes, Butterwick, Cottam etc *York*
TIBBERTON (All Saints) w Bolas Magna and Waters Upton *Lich 16*   **P** *R Edgmond w Kynnersley etc, MMCET, and A B Davies Esq (jt)*   **P-in-c** W E WARD,   **NSM** D N H STOKES-HARRISON
TIBBERTON (Holy Trinity)   *see* Highnam, Lassington, Rudford, Tibberton etc *Glouc*
TIBBERTON (St Peter ad Vincula)   *see* Bowbrook S *Worc*
TIBENHAM (All Saints)   *see* Bunwell, Carleton Rode, Tibenham, Gt Moulton etc *Nor*
TIBSHELF (St John the Baptist)   *see* Blackwell w Tibshelf *Derby*
TICEHURST (St Mary) and Flimwell *Chich 19*   **P** *Bp, J A Sellick Esq, and K M H Millar Esq (jt)*   **V** T J MILLS
TICHBORNE (St Andrew)   *see* Upper Itchen *Win*
TICHMARSH (St Mary the Virgin)   *see* Aldwincle, Clopton, Pilton, Stoke Doyle etc *Pet*
TICKENCOTE (St Peter)   *see* Gt and Lt Casterton w Pickworth and Tickencote *Pet*
TICKENHAM (St Quiricus and St Julietta)   *see* Nailsea Ch Ch w Tickenham *B & W*
TICKHILL (St Mary) w Stainton *Sheff 9*   **P** *Bp*   **V** G TAYLOR
TICKNALL (St George), Smisby and Stanton by Bridge, Barrow on Trent w Twyford and Swarkestone *Derby 15*   **P** *Bp, Exors Miss A I M Harpur-Crewe, and Repton Sch (jt)*   **C** A LUKE, J H DAVIES
TICKTON (St Paul)   *see* Beverley Minster *York*
TIDCOMBE (St Michael)   *see* Savernake *Sarum*
TIDDINGTON   *see* Wheatley *Ox*
TIDDINGTON (St Peter)   *see* Alveston *Cov*
TIDEBROOK (St John the Baptist) *Chich 19*   **P** *V Wadhurst and V Mayfield (alt)*   **V** J R JAMES
TIDEFORD (St Luke)   *see* St Germans *Truro*
TIDENHAM (St Mary) w Beachley and Lancaut *Glouc 2*   **P** *Bp*   **V** R J M GROSVENOR
TIDENHAM CHASE (St Michael and All Angels)   *see* Tidenham w Beachley and Lancaut *Glouc*
TIDESWELL (St John the Baptist) *Derby 4*   **P** *D&C Lich*   **P-in-c** F E YATES
TIDMARSH (St Laurence)   *see* Pangbourne w Tidmarsh and Sulham *Ox*
TIDMINGTON (not known)   *see* Shipston-on-Stour w Honington and Idlicote *Cov*
TIDWORTH (Holy Trinity), Ludgershall and Faberstown *Sarum 13*   **P** *Ld Chan and DBP (alt)*   **R** M R FREEMAN
TIFFIELD (St John the Baptist)   *see* Pattishall w Cold Higham and Gayton w Tiffield *Pet*
TILBROOK (All Saints) *Ely 10*   **P** *SMF*   **R** *vacant* (01480) 860147
TILBURY, EAST (St Katherine) and West Tilbury and Linford *Chelmsf 14*   **P** *Ld Chan*   **R** R J MAGOR
TILBURY DOCKS (St John the Baptist) *Chelmsf 14*   **P** *Bp*   **V** T M CODLING
TILBURY-JUXTA-CLARE (St Margaret)   *see* Upper Colne *Chelmsf*
TILE CROSS (St Peter)   *see* Garretts Green and Tile Cross *Birm*
TILE HILL (St Oswald) *Cov 3*   **P** *Bp*   **V** B REGAN
TILEHURST (St Catherine of Siena) and Calcot *Ox 15*   **P** *Magd Coll Ox*   **V** D R SMITH,   **OLM** L D COLAM
TILEHURST (St George) *Ox 15*   **P** *Bp*   **V** A J CARLILL, **NSM** M J OKE, P G GROSSE,   **OLM** D E WHITE
TILEHURST (St Mary Magdalen) *Ox 15*   **P** *Bp*

P-in-c A J CARLILL,   **NSM** M J OKE, P G GROSSE,   **OLM** D E WHITE
TILEHURST (St Michael) *Ox 15*   **P** *Magd Coll Ox*   **R** J A ROGERS
TILFORD (All Saints)   *see* The Bourne and Tilford *Guildf*
TILGATE (Holy Trinity)   *see* Southgate *Chich*
TILLINGHAM (St Nicholas) *Chelmsf 11*   **P** *D&C St Paul's*   **P-in-c** L R SMITH
TILLINGTON (All Hallows) *Chich 11*   **P** *Lord Egremont*   **P-in-c** R M MITCHELL
TILMANSTONE (St Andrew)   *see* Eastry and Northbourne w Tilmanstone etc *Cant*
TILNEY ALL SAINTS (All Saints)   *see* E Marshland *Ely*
TILNEY ST LAWRENCE (St Lawrence)   *as above*
TILSHEAD (St Thomas à Becket)   *see* Wylye and Till Valley *Sarum*
TILSTOCK (Christ Church)   *see* Edstaston, Fauls, Prees, Tilstock and Whixall *Lich*
TILSTON (St Mary) and Shocklach *Ches 5*   **P** *Bp*   **P-in-c** J E STEPHENSON
TILSTONE FEARNALL (St Jude)   *see* Bunbury and Tilstone Fearnall *Ches*
TILSWORTH (All Saints)   *see* Totternhoe, Stanbridge and Tilsworth *St Alb*
TILTON ON THE HILL (St Peter)   *see* Whatborough Gp *Leic*
TILTY (St Mary the Virgin)   *see* Broxted w Chickney and Tilty etc *Chelmsf*
TIMBERHILL (St John the Baptist)   *see* Nor St Jo w St Julian *Nor*
TIMBERLAND (St Andrew)   *see* Carr Dyke Gp *Linc*
TIMBERSCOMBE (St Petroc)   *see* Dunster, Carhampton, Withycombe w Rodhuish etc *B & W*
TIMPERLEY (Christ Church) (Holy Cross) *Ches 10*   **P** *Trustees*   **V** J SUTTON,   **C** J A KENDALL
TIMSBURY (Blessed Virgin Mary) and Priston *B & W 12*   **P** *Ball Coll Ox (3 turns), R W Lovegrove Esq (1 turn)*   **P-in-c** C S HARE,   **C** C A MARCUS
TIMSBURY (St Andrew)   *see* Michelmersh and Awbridge and Braishfield etc *Win*
TIMWORTH (St Andrew)   *see* Lark Valley *St E*
TINCLETON (St John the Evangelist)   *see* Moreton and Woodsford w Tincleton *Sarum*
TINDALE (Mission Church)   *see* Lanercost, Walton, Gilsland and Nether Denton *Carl*
TINGEWICK (St Mary Magdalene)   *see* W Buckingham *Ox*
TINGRITH (St Nicholas)   *see* Westoning w Tingrith *St Alb*
TINSLEY (St Lawrence)   *see* Rivers Team *Sheff*
TINTAGEL (St Materiana) *Truro 10*   **P** *D&C Windsor*   **NSM** J H BARFOOT
TINTINHULL (St Margaret) w Chilthorne Domer, Yeovil Marsh and Thorne Coffin *B & W 7*   **P** *Guild of All So*   **P-in-c** S J HARTREE,   **NSM** A J YOUNG
TINTWISTLE (Christ Church)   *see* Hollingworth w Tintwistle *Ches*
TINWELL (All Saints)   *see* Ketton, Collyweston, Easton-on-the-Hill etc *Pet*
TIPTOE (St Andrew)   *see* Hordle *Win*
TIPTON Great Bridge (St Luke)   *see* Tipton St Martin and St Paul *Lich*
TIPTON (St John)   *see* Ottery St Mary, Alfington, W Hill, Tipton etc *Ex*
TIPTON (St John the Evangelist) *Lich 26*   **P** *V W Bromwich St Jas*   **V** C R MARSHALL
TIPTON (St Mark)   *see* Ocker Hill *Lich*
TIPTON (St Martin) (St Paul) *Lich 26*   **P** *MMCET*   **V** J F DUNN
TIPTON (St Matthew) *Lich 26*   **P** *Simeon's Trustees*   **V** C E HOWARD
TIPTREE (St Luke)   *see* Tolleshunt Knights w Tiptree and Gt Braxted *Chelmsf*
TIRLEY (St Michael)   *see* Hasfield w Tirley and Ashleworth *Glouc*
TISBURY (St John the Baptist)   *see* Nadder Valley *Sarum*
TISMANS COMMON (St John the Baptist)   *see* Rudgwick *Chich*
TISSINGTON (St Mary)   *see* Fenny Bentley, Thorpe, Tissington, Parwich etc *Derby*
TISTED, EAST w Colemore (St James)   *see* Northanger *Win*
TISTED, WEST (St Mary Magdalene)   *see* Bishop's Sutton and Ropley and W Tisted *Win*
TITCHFIELD (St Peter) *Portsm 2*   **P** *D&C Win*   **V** W C DAY
TITCHWELL (St Mary)   *see* Hunstanton St Mary w Ringstead Parva etc *Nor*
TITLEY (St Peter)   *see* Kington w Huntington, Old Radnor, Kinnerton etc *Heref*
TITTENSOR (St Luke)   *see* Swynnerton and Tittensor *Lich*

TITTLESHALL (St Mary) *see* Litcham w Kempston, E and W Lexham, Mileham etc *Nor*

TIVERTON (St Andrew) *Ex 8* **P** *Bp* **P-in-c** D M FLETCHER

TIVERTON (St George) (St Paul) *Ex 8* **P** *MMCET and Peache Trustees (jt)* **P-in-c** B J DUGMORE, **C** C J ROUTLEDGE, **NSM** D A LYDDON

TIVERTON (St Peter) and Chevithorne w Cove *Ex 8* **P** *Peache Trustees (3 turns), Ld Chan (1 turn)* **P-in-c** R J GORDON

TIVETSHALL (St Mary and St Margaret) *see* Winfarthing w Shelfanger w Burston w Gissing etc *Nor*

TIVIDALE (St Michael the Archangel) (Holy Cross) (St Augustine) *Lich 26* **P** *Bp* **NSM** R C GILBERT

TIVINGTON (St Leonard) *see* Porlock and Porlock Weir w Stoke Pero etc *B & W*

TIXALL (St John the Baptist) *see* Stafford St Jo and Tixall w Ingestre *Lich*

TIXOVER (St Luke) *see* Barrowden and Wakerley w S Luffenham etc *Pet*

TOCKENHAM (St Giles) *see* Broad Town, Clyffe Pypard, Hilmarton etc *Sarum*

TOCKHOLES (St Stephen) *see* Darwen St Cuth w Tockholes St Steph *Blackb*

TOCKWITH (Epiphany) and Bilton w Bickerton *York 1* **P** *Abp and D&C (jt)* **P-in-c** P P ROBINSON, **NSM** M R SHAW

TODBER (St Andrew) *see* Stour Vale *Sarum*

TODDINGTON (St Andrew) *see* Winchcombe *Glouc*

TODDINGTON (St George of England) and Chalgrave *St Alb 12* **P** *Bp and DBP (jt)* **R** A E CRAWFORD

TODENHAM (St Thomas of Canterbury) *see* Moreton-in-Marsh w Batsford, Todenham etc *Glouc*

TODMORDEN (St Mary) (Christ Church) *Wakef 3* **P** *Bp* **V** O R PAGE, **C** J ROBERTS

TODWICK (St Peter and St Paul) *Sheff 5* **P** *Bp* **R** *vacant* (01909) 770283

TOFT (St Andrew) w Caldecote and Childerley *Ely 1* **P** *Ch Coll Cam* **P-in-c** M P M BOOKER, **C** M D WATTS, **NSM** M J REISS

TOFT (St John the Evangelist) *see* Knutsford St Jo and Toft *Ches*

TOFT MONKS (St Margaret) *see* Raveningham Gp *Nor*

TOFTREES (All Saints) *Nor 15* **P** *Marquess Townshend* **V** *vacant*

TOFTS, WEST and Buckenham Parva *Nor 13* **P** *Guild of All So* **R** *vacant*

TOKYNGTON (St Michael) *Lon 21* **P** *Bp* **V** P J HARNDEN

TOLLADINE (Christ Church) *see* Worc St Barn w Ch Ch *Worc*

TOLLAND (St John the Baptist) *see* Lydeard St Lawrence w Brompton Ralph etc *B & W*

TOLLARD ROYAL (St Peter ad Vincula) *see* Chase *Sarum*

TOLLER FRATRUM (St Basil) *see* Melbury *Sarum*

TOLLER LANE St Chad *Bradf 1* **P** *Keble Coll Ox* **V** S R CROWE

TOLLER PORCORUM (St Andrew) *see* Beaminster Area *Sarum*

TOLLERTON (St Michael) *see* Alne *York*

TOLLERTON (St Peter) *S'well 8* **P** *Ld Chan* **R** *vacant* 0115-937 2349

TOLLESBURY (St Mary) w Salcot Virley *Chelmsf 23* **P** *Bp (1 turn), Ex Coll Ox (3 turns)* **V** *vacant* (01621) 869393 *or* 868441

TOLLESHUNT D'ARCY (St Nicholas) and Tolleshunt Major *Chelmsf 23* **P** *Mrs E A Comerford and MMCET (jt)* **V** *vacant* (01621) 860521

TOLLESHUNT KNIGHTS w Tiptree and Great Braxted *Chelmsf 23* **P** *Bp (2 turns), Ld Chan (2 turns), and CCC Cam (1 turn)* **R** M FLETCHER, **NSM** J DUDLEY

TOLLESHUNT MAJOR (St Nicholas) *see* Tolleshunt D'Arcy and Tolleshunt Major *Chelmsf*

TOLLINGTON (St Mark) *Lon 6* **P** *Patr Bd* **P-in-c** J A K MILLAR, **C** S K WRIGHT, H W J CAHUSAC, O H D RYDER, **Hon C** E C M K JONES

TOLPUDDLE (St John the Evangelist) *see* Puddletown, Tolpuddle and Milborne w Dewlish *Sarum*

TOLWORTH (Emmanuel) *see* Surbiton Hill Ch Ch *S'wark*

TOLWORTH (St George) *see* Surbiton St Matt *S'wark*

TONBRIDGE (St Peter and St Paul) (St Andrew) (St Philip) (St Saviour) *Roch 11* **P** *Mabledon Trust* **P-in-c** M E BROWN, **C** P W GOODRIDGE, G TOWNSEND

TONBRIDGE (St Stephen) (St Eanswythe Mission Church) *Roch 11* **P** *CPAS* **V** M BARKER, **C** J G KENNEDY, **NSM** S B PERKINS

TONG (St Bartholomew) *Lich 16* **P** *Bp* **V** J B HALL

TONG (St James) *Bradf 3* **P** *CR* **TR** C G N DEY, **C** A J KIRK, J L TRENHOLME, **NSM** M S BERNARD

TONGE (St Giles) *see* Murston w Bapchild and Tonge *Cant*

TONGE (St Michael) w Alkrington *Man 18* **P** *R Middleton St Leon* **V** M S THORP, **C** D M H RICHARDS

TONGE FOLD (St Chad) *Man 9* **P** *Bp and Wm Hulme Trustees (alt)* **C** S M FORREST-REDFERN, **OLM** S P MCGREGOR

TONGE MOOR (St Augustine) (St Aidan) *Man 16* **P** *Keble Coll Ox* **V** D A DAVIES, **Hon C** J M DRUMMOND

TONGHAM (St Paul) *Guildf 1* **P** *Adn Surrey* **P-in-c** N J WILLIAMS

TOOT BALDON (St Lawrence) *see* Dorchester *Ox*

TOOTING (All Saints) *S'wark 17* **P** *Bp* **V** S D METZNER, **OLM** G R WALLER

TOOTING, UPPER (Holy Trinity) (St Augustine) *S'wark 17* **P** *Bp and R Streatham St Leon (jt)* **V** H M GREAR, **NSM** B E NICHOLS, M J HANCOCK

TOOTING GRAVENEY (St Nicholas) *S'wark 17* **P** *MMCET* **R** C J DAVIS, **C** J J G FLETCHER, **Hon C** S P ALLEN, **NSM** R A S THOMSON

TOP VALLEY (St Philip) *see* Bestwood St Matt w St Phil *S'well*

TOPCLIFFE (St Columba), Baldersby w Dishforth, Dalton and Skipton on Swale *York 19* **P** *Abp, Viscountess Downe, and D&C (jt)* **V** *vacant* (01845) 577939

TOPCROFT (St Margaret) *see* Hempnall *Nor*

TOPPESFIELD (St Margaret) *see* Upper Colne *Chelmsf*

TOPSHAM (St Margaret) *Ex 1* **P** *D&C* **V** R W C JEFFERY, **Hon C** M D A WILLIAMS

TORBRYAN (Holy Trinity) *see* Ipplepen, Torbryan and Denbury *Ex*

TORKSEY (St Peter) *see* Stow Gp *Linc*

TORMARTON (St Mary Magdalene) *see* Marshfield w Cold Ashton and Tormarton etc *Bris*

TORPENHOW (St Michael and all Angels) *see* Binsey *Carl*

TORPOINT (St James) *Truro 11* **P** *R Antony* **P-in-c** B A ANDERSON

TORQUAY (St John) and Ellacombe *Ex 12* **P** *Ch Patr Trust and Bp (jt)* **P-in-c** P IRETON, **C** R J MURRAY

TORQUAY (St Luke) *Ex 12* **P** *D&C* **P-in-c** M R WESTALL, **NSM** E P LEWIS

TORQUAY (St Martin) Barton *Ex 12* **P** *V St Marychurch* **V** G CHAPMAN, **Hon C** G R EVANS

TORQUAY (St Mary Magdalene) *see* Upton *Ex*

TORQUAY (St Matthias) (St Mark) (Holy Trinity) *Ex 12* **P** *Ch Patr Trust, Bp and Torwood Trustees (jt)* **R** G R PERCY, **NSM** G RIPLEY

TORRE (All Saints) *Ex 12* **P** *Bp* **P-in-c** R W SHAMBROOK

TORRIDGE ESTUARY *see* Bideford, Northam, Westward Ho!, Appledore etc *Ex*

TORRINGTON, EAST (St Michael) *see* Barkwith Gp *Linc*

TORRINGTON, GREAT (St Michael), Little Torrington and Frithelstock *Ex 20* **P** *Ch Ch Ox (8 turns), Lord Clinton (1 turn), J de C Stevens-Guille Esq (1 turn)* **V** J D HUMMERSTONE, **Hon C** J C ALLEN

TORRINGTON, LITTLE (St Giles) *see* Gt and Lt Torrington and Frithelstock *Ex*

TORRINGTON, WEST (St Michael) *see* Barkwith Gp *Linc*

TORRISHOLME (Ascension) *Blackb 11* **P** *Bp* **V** P ENNION

TORTWORTH (St Leonard) *see* Cromhall, Tortworth, Tytherington, Falfield etc *Glouc*

TORVER (St Luke) *Carl 9* **P** *Peache Trustees* **P-in-c** M R EAST

TOSELAND (St Michael) *see* Papworth *Ely*

TOSSIDE (St Bartholomew) *see* Long Preston w Tosside *Bradf*

TOSTOCK (St Andrew) *see* Pakenham w Norton and Tostock *St E*

TOTHAM, GREAT (St Peter) and Little Totham w Goldhanger *Chelmsf 23* **P** *Bp and Ld Chan (alt)* **R** J PEARCE

TOTHAM, LITTLE (All Saints) *see* Gt Totham and Lt Totham w Goldhanger *Chelmsf*

TOTLAND BAY (Christ Church) *Portsm 8* **P** *Ch Patr Trust* **V** J A YORKE

TOTLEY (All Saints) *Sheff 2* **P** *Bp* **V** D G RHODES

TOTNES (St Mary) w Bridgetown, Berry Pomeroy, Dartington, Marldon, Ashprington and Cornworthy *Ex 13* **P** *Patr Bd* **TR** J C OULD, **TV** J M ABECASSIS, P C BELLENES, **NSM** J E LANKESTER

TOTON (St Peter) *S'well 7* **P** *CPAS* **P-in-c** C D BOURNE

TOTTENHAM (All Hallows) *Lon 19* **P** *D&C St Paul's* **V** R B PEARSON

TOTTENHAM (Holy Trinity) *Lon 19* **P** *Bp* **V** O A FAGBEMI

TOTTENHAM (St Bartholomew) *see* Stamford Hill St Bart *Lon*

TOTTENHAM (St Benet Fink) *Lon 19* **P** *D&C St Paul's* **V** *vacant* (020) 8888 4541

TOTTENHAM (St Cuthbert) *see* Chitts Hill St Cuth *Lon*

TOTTENHAM (St Mary the Virgin) *Lon 19* **P** *Bp* **V** L J MILLER, **C** S J MORRIS

TOTTENHAM (St Paul) *Lon 19* **P** *V Tottenham All Hallows* **V** M C ELLIOTT SMITH, **C** J A H HILL

TOTTENHAM (St Philip the Apostle) *Lon 19*   **P** *Bp*
V K EVANS

TOTTENHAM, SOUTH (St Ann) *Lon 19*   **P** *D&C St Paul's*
V J M WOOD,   **Hon C** D A ROSS

TOTTENHILL (St Botolph) w Wormegay *Ely 9*   **P** *Bp*
V J C W NOLAN

TOTTERIDGE (St Andrew) *St Alb 17*   **P** *R Hatfield*
V C P HUITSON

TOTTERNHOE (St Giles), Stanbridge and Tilsworth *St Alb 12*
P *Bp*   **V** D J R SPICER

TOTTINGTON (St Ann) *Man 10*   **P** *R Bury St Mary*
V H W BEARN

TOTTON *Win 11*   **P** *Bp*   **TR** M N PREVETT,   **TV** J K OLIVER,
C M ROWBERRY, J R REEVE,   **NSM** L M ROBERTSON

TOVE Benefice   *see* Towcester w Caldecote and Easton Neston
etc *Pet*

TOW LAW (St Philip and St James)   *see* Satley, Stanley and Tow
Law *Dur*

**TOWCESTER (St Lawrence) w Caldecote and Easton Neston
and Greens Norton and Bradden (The Tove Benefice)** *Pet 5*
P *Prime Min (1 turn), Bp, Lord Hesketh, and J E Grant-Ives Esq
(1 turn)*   **V** A C BRYER,   **C** P J BOYLAND,   **NSM** E W PELLY

TOWEDNACK (St Tewinock) *Truro 5*   **P** *Bp*
P-in-c J S HOLLAND,   **NSM** S A CHALCRAFT

TOWER CHAPEL (St Nicholas)   *see* Whitehaven *Carl*

TOWERSEY (St Catherine)   *see* Thame *Ox*

TOWN END FARM (St Bede)   *see* N Wearside *Dur*

TOWNEND (St Paul)   *see* Morley *Wakef*

TOWNSTAL (St Clement)   *see* Dartmouth and Dittisham *Ex*

TOXTETH (St Bede) (St Clement) *Liv 6*   **P** *Simeon's Trustees
and Trustees (jt)*   **V** J E WARHURST

TOXTETH (St Margaret) *Liv 6*   **P** *St Chad's Coll Dur*
V R GALLAGHER,   **C** T WILSON

TOXTETH (St Philemon) (St Gabriel) St Cleopas *Liv 6*
P *Patr Bd*   **TR** D G GAVIN,   **TV** R V STOCK, M R STANFORD,
NSM J DUFF

**TOXTETH PARK (Christ Church) (St Michael-in-the-Hamlet)
(St Andrew)** *Liv 6*   **P** *Simeon's Trustees and Trustees (jt)*
V D A PARRY,   **C** A PRINCE,   **NSM** M WATERS

TOXTETH PARK (St Agnes and St Pancras) *Liv 6*   **P** *St Chad's
Coll Dur*   **V** J C D COOK

TOYNTON, HIGH (St John the Baptist)   *see* Horncastle Gp
Linc

TOYNTON ALL SAINTS (All Saints)   *see* Marden Hill Gp
Linc

TOYNTON ST PETER (St Peter)   *as above*

TOYS HILL (Hall)   *see* Hever, Four Elms and Mark Beech *Roch*

TRAFALGAR SQUARE (St Martin-in-the-Fields)
see St Martin-in-the-Fields *Lon*

TRAFFORD, OLD (St Bride) *Man 7*   **P** *Trustees*
R P J RAWLINGS,   **C** D A HOULTON,   **OLM** V M ECCLES,
O H SAMUEL

TRAFFORD, OLD (St Hilda)   *see* Firswood and Gorse Hill
Man

TRAFFORD, OLD (St John the Evangelist) *Man 7*
P *The Crown*   **P-in-c** J D HUGHES,   **C** E L TRIMBLE

TRANMERE (St Catherine) *Ches 1*   **P** *R Bebington*
V D L MOORE,   **C** C R SLATER

TRANMERE (St Paul w St Luke) *Ches 1*   **P** *Bp*
V J M CHESWORTH

TRANMERE PARK (St Peter's Hall)   *see* Guiseley w Esholt
Bradf

TRAWDEN (St Mary the Virgin)   *see* Colne and Villages *Blackb*

TREALES (Christ Church)   *see* Wesham and Treales *Blackb*

TREBOROUGH (St Peter)   *see* Old Cleeve, Leighland and
Treborough *B & W*

TREDINGTON (St Gregory) and Darlingscott *Cov 9*   **P** *Jes
Coll Ox*   **P-in-c** C GOBLE,   **Hon C** G W KUHRT

TREDINGTON (St John the Baptist)   *see* Deerhurst and
Apperley w Forthampton etc *Glouc*

TREETON (St Helen)   *see* Rivers Team *Sheff*

TREFONEN (All Saints)   *see* Llanyblodwel, Llanymynech,
Morton and Trefonen *Lich*

TREGADILLET (St Mary's Mission)   *see* Launceston *Truro*

TREGONY (not known) w St Cuby and Cornelly *Truro 6*   **P** *Bp*
P-in-c S YATES,   **NSM** A L BUTCHER

TREKNOW (Holy Family)   *see* Tintagel *Truro*

TRELEIGH (St Stephen)   *see* Redruth w Lanner and Treleigh
Truro

TRELYSTAN (St Mary the Virgin) *Heref 13*   **P** *Bp*   **V** *vacant*

TREMAINE (St Winwalo)   *see* Egloskerry, N Petherwin,
Tremaine and Tresmere *Truro*

TRENDLEWOOD   *see* Nailsea H Trin *B & W*

TRENEGLOS (St Gregory)   *see* Week St Mary Circle of Par
Truro

TRENT (St Andrew)   *see* Queen Thorne *Sarum*

TRENT PARK (Christ Church)   *see* Enfield Ch Ch Trent Park
Lon

TRENT VALE (St John the Evangelist)   *see* Hartshill, Penkhull
and Trent Vale *Lich*

TRENTHAM (St Mary and All Saints) *Lich 13*   **P** *CPAS*
V N A DI CASTIGLIONE,   **C** R M D ORAM

TRENTISHOE (St Peter)   *see* Combe Martin, Berrynarbor,
Lynton, Brendon etc *Ex*

TRENTSIDE EAST *Linc 4*   **P** *Bp Linc (2 turns), Bp Lon
(1 turn)*   **R** D J BEVERLEY

TRESCO (St Nicholas)   *see* Is of Scilly *Truro*

TRESHAM (not known)   *see* Wotton-under-Edge w Ozleworth,
N Nibley etc *Glouc*

TRESILLIAN (Holy Trinity) and Lamorran w Merther *Truro 6*
P *Viscount Falmouth*   **P-in-c** A M YATES,   **NSM** A L BUTCHER

TRESLOTHAN (St John the Evangelist)   *see* Crowan and
Treslothan *Truro*

TRESMERE (St Nicholas)   *see* Egloskerry, N Petherwin,
Tremaine and Tresmere *Truro*

TRESWELL (St John the Baptist)   *see* Rampton w Laneham,
Treswell, Cottam and Stokeham *S'well*

TRETHEVY (St Piran)   *see* Tintagel *Truro*

TRETIRE (St Mary)   *see* St Weonards *Heref*

TREVALGA (St Petroc)   *see* Boscastle w Davidstow *Truro*

TREVENSON (St Illogan)   *see* St Illogan *Truro*

TREVERBYN (St Peter) *Truro 1*   **P** *The Crown*
P-in-c S D MICHAEL,   **OLM** L N P HORE

TREVONE (St Saviour)   *see* Padstow *Truro*

TREWEN (St Michael)   *see* Lezant w Lawhitton and S
Petherwin w Trewen *Truro*

TREYFORD CUM DIDLING (St Andrew)   *see* Harting w
Elsted and Treyford cum Didling *Chich*

**TRIANGLE (All Saints) (St Matthew) (Community Centre)
Ipswich** *St E 4*   **P** *Bp and Ld Chan (alt)*   **R** N S ATKINS,
C M P FIRTH, J I SEARS,   **NSM** R H BEST, M J WALKER

TRIMDON (St Mary Magdalene)   *see* Upper Skerne *Dur*

TRIMDON GRANGE (St Alban)   *as above*

TRIMINGHAM (St John the Baptist)   *see* Overstrand,
Northrepps, Sidestrand etc *Nor*

TRIMLEY (St Martin)   *see* Walton and Trimley *St E*

TRIMLEY (St Mary the Virgin)   *as above*

TRIMPLEY (Holy Trinity)   *see* Kidderminster St Mary and All
SS w Trimpley etc *Worc*

TRING (St Martha) (St Peter and St Paul) (St Mary) *St Alb 2*
P *Bp*   **TR** H BELLIS,   **TV** J E J WETHERALL,
NSM J C BANISTER

TROSTON (St Mary the Virgin)   *see* Blackbourne *St E*

TROTTISCLIFFE (St Peter and St Paul)   *see* Birling,
Addington, Ryarsh and Trottiscliffe *Roch*

TROTTON (St George)   *see* Rogate w Terwick and Trotton w
Chithurst *Chich*

TROUTBECK (Jesus Church)   *see* Windermere St Mary and
Troutbeck *Carl*

TROWBRIDGE (Holy Trinity) *Sarum 14*   **P** *Patr Bd*
P-in-c S E HUTTON

TROWBRIDGE (St James) and Keevil *Sarum 14*   **P** *Ch Patr
Trust and D&C (jt)*   **R** *vacant* (01225) 755121

TROWBRIDGE (St Thomas) and West Ashton *Sarum 14*
P *CPAS*   **V** J A COUTTS

TROWELL (St Helen)   *see* Trowell, Awsworth and Cossall *S'well*

TROWELL (St Helen), Awsworth and Cossall *S'well 7*   **P** *Bp
and Lord Middleton (jt)*   **R** A M LORD,   **C** M G STRANG,
NSM P C WHITEHEAD

TROWSE (St Andrew) *Nor 1*   **P** *D&C*   **P-in-c** M D B LONG

TRULL (All Saints) w Angersleigh *B & W 18*   **P** *DBP and
M V Spurway Esq (jt)*   **R** A YOUINGS,   **C** S M GREEN,
M D WALLACE,   **Hon C** G C BOWYER

TRUMPINGTON (St Mary and St Michael) *Ely 3*   **P** *Trin Coll
Cam*   **V** A J CHRICH

TRUNCH (St Botolph) *Nor 21*   **P** *Duchy of Lanc (3 turns),
Patr Bd (1 turn)*   **TR** R C H KEY,   **TV** D W BARTLETT,
NSM R H MACPHEE, P A BAGGALEY

TRURO (St George the Martyr) (St John the Evangelist) *Truro 6*
P *Prime Min and V Kenwyn St Cuby (alt)*   **P-in-c** C D EPPS,
NSM A A HYDE

TRURO (St Mary's Cathedral and Parish Church) *Truro 6*
P *The Crown*   **R** C G HARDWICK

TRURO (St Paul) (St Clement) *Truro 6*   **P** *Bp*
P-in-c C D EPPS,   **NSM** A A HYDE

TRUSHAM (St Michael and All Angels)   *see* Chudleigh w
Chudleigh Knighton and Trusham *Ex*

TRUSLEY (All Saints)   *see* Boylestone, Church Broughton,
Dalbury, etc *Derby*

TRUSTHORPE (St Peter)   *see* Mablethorpe w Trusthorpe *Linc*

TRYSULL (All Saints) *see* Smestow Vale *Lich*

TRYTHALL (Mission Church) *see* Gulval and Madron *Truro*

TUBNEY (St Lawrence) *see* Fyfield w Tubney and Kingston Bagpuize *Ox*

TUCKHILL (Holy Innocents) *see* Claverley w Tuckhill *Heref*

TUCKINGMILL (All Saints) *Truro 2* **P** *Bp* **P-in-c** E C WOON

TUCKSWOOD (St Paul) *see* Nor Lakenham St Jo and All SS and Tuckswood *Nor*

TUDDENHAM (St Martin) *see* Westerfield and Tuddenham w Witnesham *St E*

TUDDENHAM (St Mary) *see* Mildenhall *St E*

TUDDENHAM, EAST (All Saints) *see* Mattishall and the Tudd Valley *Nor*

TUDDENHAM, NORTH (St Mary the Virgin) *as above*

TUDELEY (All Saints) cum Capel w Five Oak Green *Roch 11* **P** *Bp* **P-in-c** J G A IVE, **C** P F IVE

TUDHOE (St David) *see* Croxdale and Tudhoe *Dur*

TUDHOE GRANGE (St Andrew) *Dur 6* **P** *Bp* **V** *vacant* (01388) 814817

TUEBROOK (St John) *see* W Derby St Jo *Liv*

TUFFLEY (St Barnabas) *Glouc 3* **P** *Bp* **P-in-c** H M SAMMON, **NSM** R F JEWELL

TUFNELL PARK (St George and All Saints) *Lon 6* **P** *Trustees and CPAS (jt)* **V** M L TOOGOOD

TUFNELL PARK (St Mary) *see* Brookfield St Mary *Lon*

TUFTON (St Mary) *see* Whitchurch w Tufton and Litchfield *Win*

TUGBY (St Thomas à Becket) *see* Hallaton and Allexton, w Horninghold, Tugby etc *Leic*

TUGFORD (St Catherine) *see* Diddlebury w Munslow, Holdgate and Tugford *Heref*

TULSE HILL (Holy Trinity and St Matthias) *S'wark 12* **P** *Simeon's Trustees and Peache Trustees (jt)* **V** R P DORMANDY

TUNBRIDGE WELLS (Holy Trinity w Christ Church) *Roch 12* **P** *Mabledon Trust and CPAS (jt)* **V** H M FLINT

TUNBRIDGE WELLS (King Charles the Martyr) *Roch 12* **P** *Trustees* **V** R E AVERY, **NSM** S M PARTRIDGE

TUNBRIDGE WELLS (St Barnabas) *Roch 12* **P** *Guild of All So* **V** E J TOMLINSON

TUNBRIDGE WELLS (St James) *Roch 12* **P** *Ch Trust Fund Trust* **V** J P STEWART, **C** K L ROSSLYN-SMITH

TUNBRIDGE WELLS (St John) *Roch 12* **P** *CPAS and V Tunbridge Wells H Trin (jt)* **V** G R WALTER, **C** M W MASON, R W FARR

TUNBRIDGE WELLS (St Luke) *Roch 12* **P** *Five Trustees* **V** *vacant* (01892) 521374

TUNBRIDGE WELLS (St Mark) Broadwater Down *Roch 12* **P** *Bp* **V** B C H FORTNUM, **NSM** S J DIGGORY

TUNBRIDGE WELLS (St Peter) Windmill Fields *Roch 12* **P** *Trustees and CPAS (jt)* **V** M P WARREN

TUNBRIDGE WELLS (St Philip) *Roch 12* **P** *Ch Trust Fund Trust* **V** B S SENIOR

TUNSTALL (All Saints) *see* Roos and Garton w Tunstall, Grimston and Hilston *York*

TUNSTALL (Christ Church) *Lich 11* **P** *Bp* **P-in-c** T W J STATHER

TUNSTALL (Holy Trinity) *see* Catterick *Ripon*

TUNSTALL (St John the Baptist) *see* E Lonsdale *Blackb*

TUNSTALL (St John the Baptist) w Rodmersham *Cant 15* **P** *D&C and G L Doubleday Esq (jt)* **P-in-c** A K MCNICOL

TUNSTALL (St Michael and All Angels) *see* Wilford Peninsula *St E*

TUNSTEAD (Holy Trinity) *see* Bacup and Stacksteads *Man*

TUNSTEAD (St Mary) w Sco' Ruston *Nor 12* **P** *Bp* **P-in-c** A R LONG

TUNWORTH (All Saints) *see* N Hants Downs *Win*

TUPSLEY (St Paul) w Hampton Bishop *Heref 3* **P** *Bp* **V** J C WATSON

TUPTON (St John) *see* N Wingfield, Clay Cross and Pilsley *Derby*

TUR LANGTON (St Andrew) *see* Church Langton cum Tur Langton etc *Leic*

TURKDEAN (All Saints) *see* Northleach w Hampnett and Farmington etc *Glouc*

TURNASTONE (St Mary Magdalene) *see* Madley w Tyberton, Peterchurch, Vowchurch etc *Heref*

TURNDITCH (All Saints) *see* Belper Ch Ch w Turnditch *Derby*

TURNERS HILL (St Leonard) *Chich 7* **P** *Bp* **V** *vacant* (01342) 715278

TURNFORD (St Clement) *see* Cheshunt *St Alb*

TURNHAM GREEN (Christ Church) *Lon 11* **P** *Bp* **V** M J BOYES

TURNWORTH (St Mary) *see* Winterborne Valley and Milton Abbas *Sarum*

TURTON MOORLAND MINISTRY (St Anne) (St James) *Man 16* **P** *Patr Bd* **TR** D M DUNN, **TV** W BALDWIN, **NSM** D R JONES, K THOMAS, **OLM** L TAYLOR, A J HESLOP, A M BULCOCK

TURVEY (All Saints) *St Alb 15* **P** *Mrs P K C Hanbury* **P-in-c** J A SPRAY

TURVILLE (St Mary) *see* Hambleden Valley *Ox*

TURWESTON (Assumption of the Blessed Virgin Mary) *see* W Buckingham *Ox*

TUSHINGHAM (St Chad) *see* Marbury w Tushingham and Whitewell *Ches*

TUTBURY (St Mary the Virgin) *see* Hanbury, Newborough, Rangemore and Tutbury *Lich*

TUTSHILL (St Luke) *see* Tidenham w Beachley and Lancaut *Glouc*

TUTTINGTON (St Peter and St Paul) *see* King's Beck *Nor*

TUXFORD (St Nicholas) w Weston and Markham Clinton *S'well 3* **P** *Ld Chan and Bp (alt)* **P-in-c** C WALL

TWEEDMOUTH (St Bartholomew) *Newc 12* **P** *D&C Dur* **OLM** K R COULTER

TWERTON-ON-AVON *see* Bath Twerton-on-Avon *B & W*

TWICKENHAM (All Hallows) *Lon 10* **P** *D&C St Paul's* **V** N V STANLEY

TWICKENHAM (All Saints) *Lon 10* **P** *Bp* **V** P L BUSTIN

TWICKENHAM (St Mary the Virgin) *Lon 10* **P** *D&C Windsor* **V** R J H WILLIAMS, **C** A F G SAMUEL, K J SAMUEL, **Hon C** D J ELLIOTT

TWICKENHAM, EAST (St Stephen) (St Paul) *Lon 10* **P** *CPAS* **V** J P B BARNES, **C** E A ETHERINGTON, A J SACHS, L A J TAYLOR

TWICKENHAM COMMON (Holy Trinity) *Lon 10* **P** *Bp* **V** M S STARKEY

TWIGWORTH (St Matthew), Down Hatherley, Norton, The Leigh, Evington, Sandhurst and Staverton w Boddington *Glouc 4* **P** *Ld Chan (1 turn), Bp Glouc and D&C Bris (1 turn)* **V** J F WARD

TWINEHAM (St Peter) *see* Albourne w Sayers Common and Twineham *Chich*

TWINSTEAD (St John the Evangelist) *see* N Hinckford *Chelmsf*

TWITCHEN (St Peter) *see* S Molton w Nymet St George, High Bray etc *Ex*

TWO GATES (St Peter) *see* Wilnecote *Lich*

TWO MILE ASH (not known) *see* Watling Valley *Ox*

TWO MILE HILL (St Michael) *Bris 3* **P** *Prime Min* **C** N S ADAMS, **NSM** J F J GOODRIDGE

TWO RIVERS *see* Newton Tracey, Horwood, Alverdiscott etc *Ex*

TWO RIVERS *see* Holbrook, Stutton, Freston, Woolverstone etc *St E*

TWYCROSS (St James) *see* Bosworth and Sheepy Gp *Leic*

TWYFORD (Assumption of the Blessed Virgin Mary) *see* The Claydons and Swan *Ox*

TWYFORD (St Andrew) *see* Ticknall, Smisby and Stanton by Bridge etc *Derby*

TWYFORD (St Andrew) *see* S Croxton Gp *Leic*

TWYFORD (St Mary) and Owslebury and Morestead and Colden Common *Win 7* **P** *Bp and Em Coll Cam (jt)* **V** A C MILLAR, **NSM** M I JACKSON

TWYFORD (St Mary the Virgin) *see* Ruscombe and Twyford *Ox*

TWYFORD (St Nicholas) *see* N Elmham, Billingford, Bintree, Guist etc *Nor*

TWYNING (St Mary Magdalene) *see* Tewkesbury w Walton Cardiff and Twyning *Glouc*

TWYWELL (St Nicholas) *see* Cranford w Grafton Underwood and Twywell *Pet*

TYBERTON (St Mary) *see* Madley w Tyberton, Peterchurch, Vowchurch etc *Heref*

TYDD (St Mary) *see* The Suttons w Tydd *Linc*

TYDD ST GILES (St Giles) *see* Leverington, Newton and Tydd St Giles *Ely*

TYE GREEN (St Barnabas) *see* Fairstead w Terling and White Notley etc *Chelmsf*

TYE GREEN (St Stephen) w St Andrew Netteswell *Chelmsf 25* **P** *J L H Arkwright Esq* **R** A V WATSON, **NSM** B L SURTEES

TYLDESLEY (St George) *see* Astley, Tyldesley and Mosley Common *Man*

TYLER HILL (St Francis) *see* Hackington *Cant*

TYLERS GREEN (St Margaret) *see* Penn and Tylers Green *Ox*

TYLER'S HILL (St George) *see* Gt Chesham *Ox*

TYNE, NORTH and Redesdale Team *Newc 8* **P** *Patr Bd* **TR** S M RAMSARAN, **TV** M J PENFOLD, **OLM** A R VIRDEN

TYNEMOUTH Balkwell (St Peter) *see* Balkwell *Newc*

TYNEMOUTH Cullercoats (St Paul) *Newc 5* **P** *Dioc Soc* **V** G F GILCHRIST, **C** A R S FALUDY

TYNEMOUTH Shiremoor (St Mark)   *see* Shiremoor *Newc*
TYNEMOUTH (St John Percy) *Newc 5*   **P** *Dioc Soc*
  P-in-c H B GILL
TYNEMOUTH PRIORY (Holy Saviour) *Newc 5*   **P** *Dioc Soc*
  P-in-c G A LOWSON,   **NSM** D A ROBINSON
TYNINGS LANE (St Mary's Mission Church)   *see* Aldridge
  Lich
TYRINGHAM (St Peter)   *see* Lamp *Ox*
TYRLEY (Mission Room)   *see* Drayton in Hales *Lich*
TYSELEY (St Edmund) *Birm 13*   **P** *The Crown*
  P-in-c S R SIMCOX
TYSOE (Assumption of the Blessed Virgin Mary) w Oxhill and
  Whatcote *Cov 9*   **P** *Marquess of Northampton and DBP (jt)*
  P-in-c N J MORGAN,   **Hon C** M J LEATON
TYTHBY (Holy Trinity)   *see* Cropwell Bishop w Colston
  Bassett, Granby etc *S'well*
TYTHERINGTON (St James)   *see* Cromhall, Tortworth,
  Tytherington, Falfield etc *Glouc*
TYTHERINGTON (St James)   *see* Upper Wylye Valley *Sarum*
TYTHERLEY, EAST (St Peter)   *see* Lockerley and E Dean w E
  and W Tytherley *Win*
TYTHERLEY, WEST (St Peter)   *as above*
TYTHERTON KELLAWAYS (St Giles)   *see* Draycot *Bris*
TYTHERTON LUCAS (St Nicholas)   *see* Chippenham St Andr
  w Tytherton Lucas *Bris*
TYWARDREATH (St Andrew) w Tregaminion *Truro 1*   **P** *DBP*
  P-in-c F M BOWERS,   **C** S K TANSWELL
UBLEY (St Bartholomew)   *see* Blagdon w Compton Martin and
  Ubley *B & W*
UCKFIELD (Holy Cross) (St Saviour) *Chich 21*   **P** *Abp*
  R B H WILCOX,   **C** S J DATE,   **NSM** C HOWARTH
UDIMORE (St Mary)   *see* Brede w Udimore *Chich*
UFFCULME (St Mary the Virgin)   *see* Cullompton, Willand,
  Uffculme, Kentisbeare etc *Ex*
UFFINGTON Group, The (St Michael and All Angels) *Linc 13*
  P *Ld Chan (2 turns), Bp (2 turns), D&C (1 turn)*
  R C R KENNEDY
UFFINGTON (Holy Trinity)   *see* Wrockwardine Deanery *Lich*
UFFINGTON (St Mary), Shellingford, Woolstone and Baulking
  Ox 17   **P** *Bp (2 turns), J J Twynam Esq (1 turn)*
  P-in-c R S MARTIN
UFFORD (Assumption of the Blessed Virgin Mary)   *see* Melton
  and Ufford *St E*
UFFORD (St Andrew)   *see* Barnack w Ufford and Bainton *Pet*
UFTON (St Michael and All Angels) *Cov 10*   **P** *Bp*
  P-in-c J E ARMSTRONG
UGBOROUGH (St Peter)   *see* Ermington and Ugborough *Ex*
UGGESHALL (St Mary)   *see* Sole Bay *St E*
UGGLEBARNBY (All Saints)   *see* Lower Esk *York*
UGLEY (St Peter)   *see* Henham and Elsenham w Ugley *Chelmsf*
UGTHORPE (Christ Church)   *see* Hinderwell, Roxby and
  Staithes etc *York*
ULCEBY (All Saints)   *see* Willoughby *Linc*
ULCEBY Group, The (St Nicholas) *Linc 6*   **P** *Ld Chan*
  NSM F A COUCH
ULCOMBE (All Saints)   *see* Len Valley *Cant*
ULDALE (St James)   *see* Binsey *Carl*
ULEY (St Giles) w Owlpen and Nympsfield *Glouc 6*   **P** *Ld Chan*
  P-in-c D E CROOK
ULGHAM (St John the Baptist) *Newc 11*   **P** *Bp*
  V H M BARTON
ULLENHALL (St Mary the Virgin)   *see* Beaudesert and Henley-
  in-Arden w Ullenhall *Cov*
ULLESKELFE (St Saviour)   *see* Kirk Fenton w Kirkby Wharfe
  and Ulleskelfe *York*
ULLEY (Holy Trinity)   *see* Aston cum Aughton w Swallownest
  and Ulley *Sheff*
ULLINGSWICK (St Luke)   *see* Bredenbury *Heref*
ULPHA (St John)   *see* Broughton and Duddon *Carl*
ULROME (St Andrew)   *see* Bessingby *York*
ULTING (All Saints)   *see* Hatfield Peverel w Ulting *Chelmsf*
ULVERSTON (St Mary w Holy Trinity) (St Jude) *Carl 9*
  P *Peache Trustees*   **R** A C BING,   **C** P J DORLING,
  A G BATCHELOR
UMBERLEIGH (Church of the Good Shepherd)   *see* S Molton
  w Nymet St George, High Bray etc *Ex*
UNDERBARROW (All Saints) *Carl 10*   **P** *V Kendal H Trin*
  P-in-c T J HARMER
UNDERRIVER (St Margaret) *Roch 9*   **P** *Bp*
  P-in-c M D COOKE
UNDERSKIDDAW (Parish Room)   *see* Crosthwaite Keswick
  Carl
UNDERWOOD (St Michael and All Angels)   *see* Brinsley w
  Underwood *S'well*
UNSTONE (St Mary)   *see* Dronfield w Holmesfield *Derby*
UNSWORTH (St Andrew)   *see* Hillock *Man*

UNSWORTH (St George) *Man 14*   **P** *R Prestwich St Mary*
  V *vacant* 0161-766 2429
UP HATHERLEY (St Philip and St James) *Glouc 7*   **P** *Soc of*
  the Faith   **V** *vacant* (01242) 699846
UP MARDEN (St Michael)   *see* Compton, the Mardens,
  Stoughton and Racton *Chich*
UP NATELY (St Stephen)   *see* N Hants Downs *Win*
UP WALTHAM (St Mary the Virgin) *Chich 11*   **P** *Lord*
  Egremont   **R** *vacant*
UPAVON (St Mary the Virgin) w Rushall and Charlton *Sarum 19*
  P *Mert Coll Ox, Ld Chan, and Ch Ch Ox (by turn)*
  P-in-c H G HOSKINS
UPCHURCH (St Mary the Virgin) w Lower Halstow *Cant 15*
  P *D&C*   **P-in-c** A J AMOS,   **C** H E NELSON,
  NSM R W PARTRIDGE,   **OLM** J DAVIS
UPHAM (All Saints) (Blessed Mary of Upham) *Portsm 1*
  P *Ld Chan*   **R** J C HUNT,   **NSM** J BELOE
UPHILL (St Nicholas) (St Barnabas Mission Church) *B & W 11*
  P *Patr Bd*   **TR** E W MCLEOD
UPHOLLAND (St Thomas the Martyr) *Liv 11*   **P** *Patr Bd*
  TR P D D BRADLEY,   **TV** J E HEIGHTON,   **C** J A BALL
UPLANDS (All Saints)   *see* Stroud and Uplands w Slad *Glouc*
UPLEADON (St Mary the Virgin)   *see* Redmarley D'Abitot,
  Bromesberrow, Pauntley etc *Glouc*
UPLOWMAN (St Peter)   *see* Sampford Peverell, Uplowman,
  Holcombe Rogus etc *Ex*
UPLYME (St Peter and St Paul) w Axmouth *Ex 5*   **P** *CPAS and*
  Hyndman Trustees (jt)   **R** *vacant* (01297) 443256
UPMINSTER (St Laurence) *Chelmsf 2*   **P** *W R Holden Esq*
  R M J HORE
UPNOR (St Philip and St James)   *see* Frindsbury w Upnor and
  Chattenden *Roch*
UPOTTERY (St Mary the Virgin)   *see* Dunkeswell, Luppitt,
  Sheldon and Upottery *Ex*
UPPER *see under subantive place name*
UPPERBY (St John the Baptist)   *see* S Carl *Carl*
UPPERTHONG (St John the Evangelist)   *see* Upper Holme
  Valley *Wakef*
UPPINGHAM (St Peter and St Paul) w Ayston and Wardley w
  Belton *Pet 12*   **P** *Bp*   **R** S J EVANS,   **NSM** P R MORRELL
UPPINGTON (Holy Trinity)   *see* Wrockwardine Deanery *Lich*
UPSHIRE (St Thomas)   *see* Waltham H Cross *Chelmsf*
UPTON (All Saints)   *see* Lea Gp *Linc*
UPTON (Holy Ascension) *Ches 2*   **P** *Duke of Westmr*
  V P D SAYLE
UPTON (St Dunstan)   *see* Lytchett Minster *Sarum*
UPTON (St James)   *see* Brompton Regis w Upton and Skilgate
  B & W
UPTON (St John the Baptist)   *see* Castor w Sutton and Upton w
  Marholm *Pet*
UPTON (St Laurence)   *see* Upton cum Chalvey *Ox*
UPTON (St Margaret)   *see* Ranworth w Panxworth,
  Woodbastwick etc *Nor*
UPTON (St Margaret) and Copmanford *Ely 10*   **P** *Bp*
  V *vacant*
UPTON (St Mary) *Ches 8*   **P** *Simeon's Trustees*
  V G J SKINNER,   **C** M J DALY, K P ADDENBROOKE
UPTON (St Mary Magdalene) *Ex 12*   **P** *Simeon's Trustees and*
  Ch Patr Trust (alt)   **NSM** J H GARNER
UPTON (St Mary the Virgin)   *see* The Churn *Ox*
UPTON (St Peter and St Paul)   *see* Rolleston w Fiskerton,
  Morton and Upton *S'well*
UPTON BISHOP (St John the Baptist)   *see* Ariconium *Heref*
UPTON CRESSETT w Monk Hopton *Heref 9*   **P** *DBP and*
  Miss E A Bird (alt)   **P-in-c** A A ROBERTS,
  Hon C H J PATTERSON
UPTON CROSS (St Paul)   *see* Linkinhorne *Truro*
UPTON CUM CHALVEY (St Mary) *Ox 23*   **P** *Bp*
  TR A S ALLEN,   **TV** D E WEST
UPTON GREY (St Mary)   *see* N Hants Downs *Win*
UPTON HELLIONS (St Mary the Virgin)   *see* Crediton,
  Shobrooke and Sandford etc *Ex*
UPTON LOVELL (St Augustine of Canterbury)   *see* Upper
  Wylye Valley *Sarum*
UPTON MAGNA (St Lucia)   *see* Wrockwardine Deanery *Lich*
UPTON NOBLE (St Mary Magdalene)   *see* Bruton and Distr
  B & W
UPTON-ON-SEVERN (St Peter and St Paul), Ripple, Earls
  Croome w Hill Croome and Strensham *Worc 5*   **P** *Bp (2 turns),*
  Mrs A J Hyde-Smith and Mrs A L Wynne (1 turn)
  R D J RADCLIFFE,   **NSM** J A FRASER, G K MOORE,
  E R RADCLIFFE
UPTON PARK (St Alban)   *see* E Ham w Upton Park St Alb
  Chelmsf
UPTON PRIORY (Church of the Resurrection) *Ches 13*   **P** *Bp*
  V J H FIFE

UPTON PYNE (Our Lady) *see* Thorverton, Cadbury, Upton Pyne etc *Ex*

UPTON SCUDAMORE (St Mary the Virgin) *see* Warminster St Denys and Upton Scudamore *Sarum*

UPTON SNODSBURY (St Kenelm) *see* Peopleton and White Ladies Aston w Churchill etc *Worc*

UPTON ST LEONARDS (St Leonard) *Glouc 3* **P** *Bp* **P-in-c** P R LECKEY

UPTON WARREN (St Michael) *see* Stoke Prior, Wychbold and Upton Warren *Worc*

UPWELL (St Peter) *Ely 14* **P** R T Townley Esq **R** A F JESSON

UPWELL CHRISTCHURCH (Christ Church) *see* Christchurch and Manea and Welney *Ely*

UPWEY (St Laurence) *see* Bincombe w Broadwey, Upwey and Buckland Ripers *Sarum*

UPWOOD (St Peter) *see* The Ramseys and Upwood *Ely*

URCHFONT (St Michael and All Angels) *see* Redhorn *Sarum*

URMSTON (St Clement) *Man 7* **P** *Bp* **P-in-c** C C BROWN, **OLM** C E FAULKNER

URSWICK (St Mary the Virgin and St Michael) *see* Aldingham, Dendron, Rampside and Urswick *Carl*

USHAW MOOR (St Luke) *see* Dur N *Dur*

USSELBY (St Margaret) *see* Kelsey Gp *Linc*

USWORTH (Holy Trinity) (St Michael and All Angels) *Dur 11* **P** *Bp* **P-in-c** P GRUNDY

UTKINTON (St Paul) *see* Tarporley *Ches*

UTLEY (St Mark) *Bradf 8* **P** *Bp and R Keighley St Andr (jt)* **V** D WALMSLEY, **NSM** N C J WRIGHT

UTTERBY (St Andrew) *see* Fotherby *Linc*

UTTOXETER AREA (St Mary the Virgin) *Lich 15* **P** *Patr Bd* **TV** D C STONE, **P-in-c** E G WHITTAKER, **C** K R GOVAN, **NSM** B WARREN, **OLM** I M SMITH, C W DALE, C H BROWN, J S LANDER, E A ELLWOOD

UXBRIDGE (St Andrew) (St Margaret) (St Peter) *Lon 24* **P** *Bp* **TR** A F SHEARD, **TV** C W BOWMAN, **C** J A HUGHMAN, J K ATKINS

VALE OF BELVOIR Parishes *Leic 2* **P** *Patr Bd (2 turns), Ld Chan (1 turn)* **TV** F P R J CONNELL

VALE OF THE WHITE HART *Sarum 3* **P** *D&C, DBP, N G Halsey Esq, and J K Wingfield Digby Esq (jt)* **R** R G HART

VALLEY END (St Saviour) *see* Chobham w Valley End *Guildf*

VALLEY PARK (St Francis) *Win 10* **P** *Bp* **V** P F HUTCHINSON

VANGE (St Chad) *Chelmsf 6* **P** *MMCET* **R** B C R JOHNSON, **C** I J E SWIFT, **NSM** P CLARK

VAUXHALL (St Peter) *see* N Lambeth *S'wark*

VENN OTTERY (St Gregory) *see* Ottery St Mary, Alfington, W Hill, Tipton etc *Ex*

VENTA Group, The *see* Stoke H Cross w Dunston, Arminghall etc *Nor*

VENTNOR (Holy Trinity) *Portsm 7* **P** *Bp* **V** G E MORRIS

VENTNOR (St Alban) *see* Godshill *Portsm*

VENTNOR (St Catherine) *Portsm 7* **P** *Ch Patr Trust* **V** G E MORRIS

VERNHAM DEAN (St Mary the Virgin) *see* Hurstbourne Tarrant, Faccombe, Vernham Dean etc *Win*

VERWOOD (St Michael and All Angels) *Sarum 9* **P** *Bp* **V** A J M SINCLAIR, **NSM** P E MILES, **OLM** N F MOULAND

VERYAN w Ruan Lanihorne *Truro 6* **P** *D&C and DBP (jt)* **P-in-c** D G ROBINS

VICTORIA DOCKS (Ascension) *Chelmsf 3* **P** *Bp* **V** C HANSON

VICTORIA DOCKS (St Luke) *Chelmsf 3* **P** *Ld Chan* **V** D P WADE, **C** C CHIKE, **NSM** S M CHANDLER, **OLM** P E EJINKONYE

VICTORIA PARK (St John Chrysostom) *see* Man Victoria Park *Man*

VICTORIA PARK (St Mark) *see* Old Ford St Paul and St Mark *Lon*

VIGO (Village Hall) *see* Stansted w Fairseat and Vigo *Roch*

VINEY HILL (All Saints) *see* Parkend and Viney Hill *Glouc*

VIRGINIA WATER (Christ Church) *Guildf 11* **P** *Simeon's Trustees* **V** S R SIZER, **C** R K MODY, F C BLIGHT

VIRGINSTOW (St Bridget) *see* Boyton, N Tamerton, Werrington etc *Truro*

VOWCHURCH (St Bartholomew) *see* Madley w Tyberton, Peterchurch, Vowchurch etc *Heref*

WABERTHWAITE (St John) *see* Eskdale, Irton, Muncaster and Waberthwaite *Carl*

WACTON (All Saints) *see* Stratton St Mary w Stratton St Michael etc *Nor*

WADDESDON (St Michael and All Angels) *see* Schorne *Ox*

WADDINGHAM (St Mary and St Peter) *see* Bishop Norton, Wadingham and Snitterby *Linc*

WADDINGTON (St Helen) *Bradf 5* **P** E C Parker Esq **P-in-c** J R BROCKLEHURST, **C** D W MEWIS, **Hon C** G F MACK, **NSM** G DEARDEN

WADDINGTON (St Michael) *Linc 18* **P** *Linc Coll Ox* **R** R J G PARKER

WADDON (St George) *see* Croydon St Jo *S'wark*

WADEBRIDGE *see* St Breoke and Egloshayle *Truro*

WADENHOE (St Michael and All Angels) *see* Aldwincle, Clopton, Pilton, Stoke Doyle etc *Pet*

WADHURST (St Peter and St Paul) *Chich 19* **P** J M Hardcastle Esq and M R Toynbee Esq (jt) **V** J R JAMES, **C** I P HUGHES, **NSM** R G ALFORD

WADINGHAM (St Mary and St Peter) *see* Bishop Norton, Wadingham and Snitterby *Linc*

WADSHELF (Mission Room) *see* Old Brampton and Great Barlow *Derby*

WADSLEY (no dedication) *Sheff 4* **P** *Ch Patr Trust* **V** G J HUTCHISON

WADWORTH (St John the Baptist) w Loversall *Sheff 9* **P** V Doncaster and DBP (alt) **P-in-c** A PRICE

WAGGONERS *York 10* **P** *Abp and Sir Tatton Sykes Bt, and Ld Chan (alt)* **NSM** I D MACKARILL

WAINCLIFFE (St David) *see* Beeston *Ripon*

WAINFLEET (All Saints) *see* The Wainfleet Gp *Linc*

WAINFLEET Group, The (All Saints) (St Mary) (St Michael) *Linc 8* **P** *Ld Chan, Bp and T E Pitts Esq (alt)* **P-in-c** B C BECHTOLD

WAINFLEET (St Mary) *see* The Wainfleet Gp *Linc*

WAINFLEET (St Michael) *as above*

WAINFORD *St E 14* **P** *Bp, Mrs B I T Suckling, CPAS, Magd Coll Cam, and Ch Soc Trust (jt)* **C** P J NELSON, I B BYRNE, **OLM** N H SIMISTER

WAITHE (St Martin) *see* The North-Chapel Parishes *Linc*

WAKEFIELD (St Andrew and St Mary) (St Swithun) *Wakef 11* **P** *Peache Trustees* **P-in-c** D INGHAM

WAKEFIELD (St John the Baptist) *Wakef 11* **P** *Dean* **V** P M DOWLING, **Hon C** R B GRAINGER, **NSM** P ELLIS

WAKEFIELD (St Mary) Chantry Bridge *see* Wakef Cathl *Wakef*

WAKEFIELD (St Michael the Archangel) *see* Westgate Common *Wakef*

WAKERING, GREAT (St Nicholas) w Foulness *Chelmsf 13* **P** *Bp* **P-in-c** A J HURD

WAKERING, LITTLE (St Mary the Virgin) *see* Barling w Lt Wakering *Chelmsf*

WAKERLEY (St John the Baptist) *see* Barrowden and Wakerley w S Luffenham etc *Pet*

WAKES COLNE (All Saints) *see* Gt and Lt Tey w Wakes Colne and Chappel *Chelmsf*

WALBERSWICK (St Andrew) *see* Sole Bay *St E*

WALBERTON (St Mary) w Binsted *Chich 21* **P** *Bp* **V** T J C WARD

WALBROOK Epiphany *Derby 10* **P** *Patr Bd* **TV** A J WARD, **C** E RAWLINGS

WALCOT *see* Bath Walcot *B & W*

WALCOT (All Saints) *see* Bacton, Happisburgh, Hempstead w Eccles etc *Nor*

WALCOT (St Nicholas) *see* S Lafford *Linc*

WALCOT (St Oswald) *see* Carr Dyke Gp *Linc*

WALDEN, LITTLE (St John) *see* Saffron Walden w Wendens Ambo, Littlebury etc *Chelmsf*

WALDERSLADE (St William) *see* S Chatham H Trin *Roch*

WALDINGFIELD, GREAT (St Lawrence) *see* Acton w Gt Waldingfield *St E*

WALDINGFIELD, LITTLE (St Lawrence) *see* Boxford, Edwardstone, Groton etc *St E*

WALDITCH (St Mary) *see* Bridport *Sarum*

WALDRINGFIELD (All Saints) w Hemley and Newbourn *St E 2* **P** The Revd Canon T Waller and the Revd A H N Waller, Ld Chan, and Mrs S E F Holden (by turn) **R** J P WALLER

WALDRON (All Saints) *Chich 15* **P** *Ex Coll Ox* **P-in-c** J SHERWIN

WALES (St John the Baptist) *Sheff 5* **P** *Bp* **V** G SCHOFIELD, **NSM** J BACHU

WALESBY (St Edmund) *S'well 3* **P** *DBP* **V** C C LEVY

WALESBY (St Mary and All Saints) *Linc 5* **P** *Bp, DBP, and C Drakes Esq (jt)* **R** J H P CARR, **C** J H MACKAY, **OLM** E TURNER

WALFORD (St Michael and All Angels) *see* Ross w Walford *Heref*

WALGRAVE (St Peter) w Hannington and Wold and Scaldwell *Pet 2* **P** *Bp (2 turns), BNC Ox (1 turn)* **P-in-c** K A I JONGMAN

WALHAM GREEN (St John) (St James) *Lon 9* **P** *Bp* **P-in-c** M W OSBORNE

WALKDEN (St Paul) and Little Hulton *Man 12* **P** *Patr Bd*
TR S C EDWARDS, **TV** D A GREEN,
OLM K HOPWOOD OWEN, M SURREY

WALKER (Christ Church) *Newc 3* **P** *Bp* **V** K HUNT,
NSM K COCKBURN

WALKERGATE (St Oswald) *see* Byker St Mark and
Walkergate St Oswald *Newc*

WALKERINGHAM (St Mary Magdalene) *see* Beckingham
and Walkeringham and Misterton etc *S'well*

WALKERN (St Mary the Virgin) *see* Benington w Walkern
St Alb

WALKHAMPTON (St Mary the Virgin) *see* Yelverton, Meavy,
Sheepstor and Walkhampton *Ex*

WALKINGHAM HILL *Ripon 1* **P** *Bp, DBP, R Knaresborough,*
MMCET, and Major Sir Arthur Collins (jt) **R** P S MIDWOOD

WALKINGTON (All Hallows) *see* Bishop Burton w
Walkington *York*

WALKLEY (St Mary) *Sheff 4* **P** *Bp* **V** M A FITZGERALD

WALL (St George) *see* St Oswald in Lee w Bingfield *Newc*

WALL (St John the Baptist) *see* Lich St Mich w St Mary and
Wall *Lich*

WALL HEATH (Ascension) *see* Kingswinford St Mary *Worc*

WALLASEY (St Hilary) *Ches 7* **P** *Bp* **R** P L ROBINSON,
C J FARR

WALLASEY (St Nicholas) (All Saints) *Ches 7* **P** *Bp and*
DBP (jt) **V** J J STAPLES, **NSM** P A ROSSITER, D A LAMB

WALLINGFORD (St Mary le More w All Hallows) (St Leonard)
Ox 18 **P** *Bp* **TR** D RICE, **TV** J H GOULSTON,
Hon C J K SPENCE, **NSM** J CHILTON

WALLINGTON (Holy Trinity) (St Patrick) *S'wark 23*
P *Ch Soc Trust* **V** S D COE, **C** L A IJAZ, M C BREADMORE

WALLINGTON (Springfield Church) Extra-Parochial Place
S'wark 23 **Min** W COOKSON

WALLINGTON (St Mary) *see* Sandon, Wallington and
Rushden w Clothall *St Alb*

WALLINGTON (St Michael and All Angels) *see* S Beddington
and Roundshaw *S'wark*

WALLINGTON (St Paul) *as above*

WALLISDOWN (St Saviour) *see* Talbot Village *Sarum*

WALLOP, NETHER (St Andrew) *see* Portway and Danebury
Win

WALLSEND (St John the Evangelist) *Newc 5* **P** *Bp*
P-in-c C R BATES

WALLSEND (St Peter) (St Luke) *Newc 5* **P** *Bp* **R** M C VINE

WALMER (St Mary) (St Saviour) (Blessed Virgin Mary) *Cant 8*
P *Abp* **V** S W COOPER

WALMERSLEY (Christ Church) *Man 10* **P** *Trustees*
NSM D ALTHAM

WALMGATE (St Denys) *see* York St Denys *York*

WALMLEY (St John the Evangelist) *Birm 12* **P** *Trustees*
V S P CORBETT

WALMSLEY (Christ Church) *see* Turton Moorland Min *Man*

WALNEY ISLAND (St Mary the Virgin) *Carl 8* **P** *V Dalton-in-*
Furness **V** J D HODGKINSON

WALPOLE (St Mary the Virgin) *see* Blyth Valley *St E*

WALPOLE ST PETER (St Peter and St Paul) w Walpole
St Andrew *Ely 14* **P** *The Crown and DBP (alt)*
P-in-c M CHESHER

WALSALL (Annunciation of Our Lady) *see* Walsall St Gabr
Fulbrook *Lich*

WALSALL (St Andrew) *Lich 25* **P** *Bp* **V** I M TEMPLETON

WALSALL (St Gabriel) Fulbrook *Lich 25* **P** *Bp*
V T R H COYNE

WALSALL (St Matthew) (St Luke) (St Martin) *Lich 25*
P *Patr Bd* **TR** C T GIBSON, **TV** A P L SMITH,
S C BICKERSTETH, **C** P M SMITH, G S EVANS, M R KINDER,
Hon C G A FISHER, **NSM** L F SAMUEL, P E BALL

WALSALL (St Michael and All Angels) *see* Caldmore w Palfrey
Lich

WALSALL St Paul *Lich 25* **P** *R Walsall* **P-in-c** M R KINDER,
C G S EVANS, S M LEACH, A P L SMITH, C T GIBSON,
NSM P J W LEES

WALSALL (St Peter) *Lich 25* **P** *R Walsall* **P-in-c** C R SUCH

WALSALL THE PLECK (St John) and Bescot *Lich 25*
P *V Walsall* **V** G S EVANS, **C** A P L SMITH, C T GIBSON

WALSALL WOOD (St John) *Lich 25* **P** *R Walsall*
V N J CARTER

WALSDEN (St Peter) *see* Cornholme and Walsden *Wakef*

WALSGRAVE ON SOWE (St Mary) *Cov 1* **P** *Ld Chan*
V M TYLER, **C** S BAILEY, **NSM** F F TYLER

WALSHAM, NORTH (St Nicholas) and Edingthorpe *Nor 12*
P *Bp (3 turns), Duchy of Lancaster (1 turn)* **V** S D EARIS,
C K A F RENGERT, S M GUNNER, **NSM** V A WATTS,
OLM N J M PATERSON

WALSHAM, SOUTH (St Mary) *see* Ranworth w Panxworth,
Woodbastwick etc *Nor*

WALSHAM LE WILLOWS (St Mary) *see* Badwell and
Walsham *St E*

WALSHAW (Christ Church) *Man 10* **P** *Simeon's Trustees*
V S FOSTER

WALSINGHAM (St Mary and All Saints) (St Peter), Houghton
and Barsham *Nor 15* **P** *J Gurney Esq and Capt*
J D A Keith (jt) **V** N BANKS

WALSOKEN (All Saints) *Ely 14* **P** *DBP* **R** A R LANDALL

WALTERSTONE (St Mary) *see* Ewyas Harold w Dulas,
Kenderchurch etc *Heref*

WALTHAM (All Saints) *Linc 10* **P** *The Crown*
R I R SHELTON, **NSM** C E BUTLER

WALTHAM (Holy Cross) *Chelmsf 24* **P** *Patr Bd*
TV J M SMITH, **NSM** T I SCOTT

WALTHAM (St Bartholomew) *see* Stone Street Gp *Cant*

WALTHAM, GREAT (St Mary and St Lawrence) w Ford End
Chelmsf 8 **P** *Trin Coll Ox* **P-in-c** C I HAMPTON

WALTHAM, LITTLE (St Martin) *see* Gt and Lt Leighs and Lt
Waltham *Chelmsf*

WALTHAM, NEW (St Matthew) *Linc 10* **P** *The Crown*
V *vacant* (01472) 589998

WALTHAM, NORTH (St Michael) and Steventon, Ashe and
Deane *Win 6* **P** *DBP* **R** M S KENNING, **NSM** C S READER

WALTHAM ABBEY (Holy Cross) *see* Waltham H Cross
Chelmsf

WALTHAM CROSS (Christ Church) *see* Cheshunt *St Alb*

WALTHAM ON THE WOLDS (St Mary Magdalene)
see Ironstone Villages *Leic*

WALTHAM ST LAWRENCE (St Lawrence) *Ox 13* **P** *Lord*
Braybrooke **P-in-c** D N ANDREW, **NSM** A J HARTROPP

WALTHAMSTOW (St Andrew) *Chelmsf 5* **P** *Bp* **V** *vacant*
(020) 8527 3969

WALTHAMSTOW (St Barnabas and St James the Great)
Chelmsf 5 **P** *Bp* **P-in-c** S M P SAXBY

WALTHAMSTOW (St Gabriel) St Luke (St Mary) (St Stephen)
Chelmsf 5 **P** *Patr Bd* **TR** S D HEATHFIELD, **TV** N J ANSTEY,
A D CANT, **C** K ASHTON

WALTHAMSTOW (St John) *Chelmsf 5* **P** *TR Walthamstow*
V A J BISHOP

WALTHAMSTOW (St Michael and All Angels) *Chelmsf 5*
P *Bp* **V** J C RAVENSDALE

WALTHAMSTOW (St Peter-in-the-Forest) *Chelmsf 5* **P** *Bp*
Hon C E C M K JONES

WALTHAMSTOW (St Saviour) *Chelmsf 5* **P** *Bp*
V D A WALLER, **NSM** W OBEDOZA

WALTON (Holy Trinity) *see* Street w Walton *B & W*

WALTON (Holy Trinity) *Ox 21* **P** *Ch Patr Trust*
Hon C G M BUTTERWORTH, **NSM** J D HAWKINS

WALTON Milton Keynes *Ox 25* **P** *Patr Bd* **TR** D LUNN,
TV S JACKSON

WALTON (not known) *see* Gilmorton, Peatling Parva, Kimcote
etc *Leic*

WALTON (St John) *see* Brampton St Thos *Derby*

WALTON (St John) *Derby 5* **P** *Bp* **V** A C BROOM,
C L SHEMILT, D P MOUNCER

WALTON (St John the Evangelist) *Ches 4* **P** *P G Greenall Esq*
P-in-c J E HARRIES

WALTON (St Mary) *see* Lanercost, Walton, Gilsland and
Nether Denton *Carl*

WALTON (St Mary) (St Philip) and Trimley *St E 2* **P** *Patr Bd*
(2 turns), Ld Chan (1 turn) **TR** N JOHN, **TV** V J BUTLER,
OLM I W BARLEY

WALTON (St Paul) *see* Sandal St Helen *Wakef*

WALTON (St Peter) *see* Thorp Arch w Walton *York*

WALTON (St Thomas) *see* Baswich *Lich*

WALTON, EAST (St Mary) *see* Gayton, Gayton Thorpe, E
Walton, E Winch etc *Nor*

WALTON, HIGHER (All Saints) *Blackb 5* **P** *V Blackb*
V S J HUNT, **NSM** D G WARD

WALTON, WEST (St Mary) *Ely 14* **P** *Ld Chan*
P-in-c M CHESHER

WALTON BRECK (Christ Church) (Holy Trinity) *Liv 3*
P *Simeon's Trustees* **P-in-c** K BOLTON

WALTON CLEVEDON (St Mary) *see* E Clevedon w Clapton
in Gordano etc *B & W*

WALTON D'EIVILLE (St James) *Cov 8* **P** *Sir Richard*
Hamilton Bt **P-in-c** C E MIER

WALTON IN GORDANO (St Paul) *see* E Clevedon w Clapton
in Gordano etc *B & W*

WALTON-LE-DALE (St Leonard) w Samlesbury St Leonard the
Less *Blackb 5* **P** *V Blackb St Mary and St Paul*
V R MCCULLOUGH, **NSM** E BRIGGS

WALTON LE SOKEN (All Saints) (St George) *Chelmsf 22*
P *Bp* **V** T J FLETCHER

WALTON LE WOLDS (St Mary) *see* Barrow upon Soar w
Walton le Wolds *Leic*

WALTON-ON-THAMES (St Mary) *Guildf 8* **P** *Bp*
V C STEWART, **C** S A BAILEY, **OLM** L K KAYE-BESLEY
WALTON ON THE HILL (St John) *Liv 7* **P** *Bp, Adn, and*
R Walton (jt) **V** S L WILLIAMS
WALTON ON THE HILL (St Luke) *Liv 7* **P** *Bp* **V** H E ROSS
WALTON-ON-THE-HILL (St Mary) (St Aidan) *Liv 5* **P** *Bp*
TR T M LATHAM, **TV** J FLETCHER, C N PERRINS,
C I M GALLAGHER
WALTON-ON-THE-HILL (St Peter) *Guildf 9* **P** *Bp*
P-in-c M E MARSH
WALTON-ON-TRENT (St Lawrence) w Croxall, Rosliston w
Linton and Castle Gresley *Derby 16* **P** *Bp and*
R D Nielson Esq (jt) **R** L A DE POMERAI,
NSM D I M DE POMERAI
WALTON STREET (St Saviour) *see* Upper Chelsea *Lon*
WALWORTH (St Christopher) *S'wark 10* **P** *Bp and Pemb Coll*
Miss **V** M WILLIAMS, **C** A D P MOUGHTIN-MUMBY
WALWORTH (St John w the Lady Margaret) *S'wark 10* **P** *Bp*
V J F WALKER, **Hon C** G S ASKEY, **NSM** O S CROWN
WALWORTH (St Peter) *S'wark 10* **P** *Bp* **TR** G W GODDARD,
C S MOUGHTIN-MUMBY, **OLM** A J WILD
WAMBROOK (Blessed Virgin Mary) *see* Combe St Nicholas w
Wambrook *B & W*
WANBOROUGH (St Andrew) *see* Lyddington and
Wanborough and Bishopstone etc *Bris*
WANBOROUGH (St Bartholomew) *see* Seale, Puttenham and
Wanborough *Guildf*
WANDSWORTH (All Saints) (Holy Trinity) *S'wark 18*
P *Ch Soc Trust* **V** G S PRIOR, **C** A V CINNAMOND
WANDSWORTH (St Anne) (St Faith) *S'wark 18* **P** *Bp*
V G P JEANES, **NSM** L J BOULTON
WANDSWORTH (St Michael and All Angels) (St Stephen)
S'wark 18 **P** *CPAS and Ch Soc Trust (jt)* **V** S MELLUISH,
C D P J MELDRUM, **NSM** P A KURK, R J COLLINS
WANDSWORTH (St Paul) Wimbledon Park *S'wark 18* **P** *Bp*
V H D TOLLER, **Hon C** E M TOLLER, **NSM** C A MULLINS
WANDSWORTH COMMON (St Mary Magdalene) *S'wark 17*
P *Bp* **V** K PARKES, **NSM** C WILES
WANDSWORTH COMMON (St Michael) *see* Battersea
St Mich *S'wark*
WANGFORD (St Peter) *see* Sole Bay *St E*
WANLIP (Our Lady and St Nicholas) *see* Birstall and Wanlip
Leic
WANSFORD (St Mary) *see* Nafferton w Wansford *York*
WANSFORD (St Mary the Virgin) *see* Thornhaugh and
Wansford *Pet*
WANSTEAD (Holy Trinity) Hermon Hill *Chelmsf 4* **P** *Bp*
V R E HAMPSON
WANSTEAD (St Mary) (Christ Church) *Chelmsf 4* **P** *Bp*
R R W SPRINGETT, **C** E HORWELL, **NSM** R J WYBER
WANSTROW (Blessed Virgin Mary) *see* Nunney and Witham
Friary, Marston Bigot etc *B & W*
WANTAGE (St Peter and St Paul) *Ox 19* **P** *D&C Windsor*
V J L SALTER, **C** M M DIAZ BUTRON, **NSM** M V BERRETT
WANTAGE DOWNS *Ox 19* **P** *Bp, CCC Ox, and*
C L Loyd Esq (jt) **R** E A M BIRCH, **NSM** D J PAGE,
P A GORDON
WANTISDEN (St John the Baptist) *see* Wilford Peninsula *St E*
WANTSUM GROUP *see* St Nicholas at Wade w Sarre and
Chislet w Hoath *Cant*
WAPLEY (St Peter) *see* Yate New Town *Bris*
WAPPENBURY (St John the Baptist) w Weston under Wetherley
Cov 10 **P** *Bp* **P-in-c** J T H BRITTON, **C** D R PATTERSON
WAPPENHAM (St Mary the Virgin) *see* Astwell Gp *Pet*
WARBLETON (St Mary) and Bodle Street Green *Chich 15*
P *Revd E S Haviland* **R** *vacant* (01435) 830421
WARBLINGTON (St Thomas à Becket) w Emsworth *Portsm 5*
P *Bp and J H Norris Esq (alt)* **R** S P SAYERS,
C B C SARGENT
WARBOROUGH (St Lawrence) *Ox 1* **P** *CCC Ox*
V S E BOOYS
WARBOYS (St Mary Magdalene) w Broughton and Bury w
Wistow *Ely 12* **P** *Bp and Ch Soc Trust (jt)* **R** P R DOWMAN
WARBSTOW (St Werburgh) *see* Week St Mary Circle of Par
Truro
WARBURTON (St Werburgh) *see* Oughtrington and
Warburton *Ches*
WARCOP (St Columba) *see* Brough w Stainmore, Musgrave
and Warcop *Carl*
WARD END (Christ Church) *see* Ward End w Bordesley Green
Birm
WARD END Holy Trinity (St Margaret) w Bordesley Green
Birm 13 **P** *Prime Min (1 turn), Bp and Aston Patr Trust*
(1 turn) **V** P H SMITH, **C** S J CARTWRIGHT, S K BARTER
WARDEN (St Michael and All Angels) w Newbrough *Newc 10*
P *Bp* **V** J J T THOMPSON

WARDEN, OLD (St Leonard) *see* Caldecote, Northill and Old
Warden *St Alb*
WARDINGTON (St Mary Magdalene) *see* Shires' Edge *Ox*
WARDLEWORTH (St Mary w St James) *see* Rochdale *Man*
WARDLEY (All Saints) *see* Swinton and Pendlebury *Man*
WARDLEY (St Botolph) *see* Uppingham w Ayston and
Wardley w Belton *Pet*
WARDLOW (Good Shepherd) *see* Ashford w Sheldon and
Longstone *Derby*
WARE (Christ Church) *St Alb 22* **P** *CPAS* **V** D J PROUD,
C P OULD
WARE (St Mary the Virgin) *St Alb 22* **P** *Trin Coll Cam*
V D PEEL, **NSM** M S E M BEAZLEY
WAREHAM (Lady St Mary) (St Martin) *Sarum 8* **P** *Patr Bd*
P-in-c A M BOWERMAN
WAREHORNE (St Matthew) *see* Orlestone w Snave and
Ruckinge w Warehorne etc *Cant*
WARESIDE (Holy Trinity) *see* Hunsdon w Widford and
Wareside *St Alb*
WARESLEY (St James) *see* Gt Gransden and Abbotsley and Lt
Gransden etc *Ely*
WARFIELD (St Michael the Archangel) (All Saints) (St Peter)
Ox 11 **P** *DBP* **V** B H MEARDON, **C** A BRADFORD,
NSM C M HILL
WARGRAVE (St Mary the Virgin) w Knowl Hill *Ox 16* **P** *Lord*
Remnant **V** J R M COOK, **NSM** P A GORDON
WARHAM (All Saints) *see* Holkham w Egmere w Warham,
Wells and Wighton *Nor*
WARK (St Michael) *see* Humshaugh w Simonburn and Wark
Newc
WARKLEIGH (St John) *see* S Molton w Nymet St George,
High Bray etc *Ex*
WARKTON (St Edmund King and Martyr) *see* Barton
Seagrave w Warkton *Pet*
WARKWORTH (St Lawrence) and Acklington *Newc 6* **P** *Bp*
and Duke of Northd (alt) **V** J M BREARLEY,
NSM M E HOBROUGH
WARKWORTH (St Mary the Virgin) *see* Chenderit *Pet*
WARLEGGAN (St Bartholomew) *see* St Neot and Warleggan
w Cardynham *Truro*
WARLEY (Christ Church) and Gt Warley St Mary *Chelmsf 7*
P *Bp and Hon G C D Jeffreys (jt)* **V** C D GOLDSMITH,
C P A GAMBLING
WARLEY (St John the Evangelist) *Wakef 4* **P** *V Halifax*
V A J STREET, **NSM** J S BRADBERRY
WARLEY, GREAT (St Mary the Virgin) *see* Warley Ch Ch and
Gt Warley St Mary *Chelmsf*
WARLEY, LITTLE (St Peter) *see* E and W Horndon w Lt
Warley and Childerditch *Chelmsf*
WARLEY WOODS (St Hilda) *Birm 7* **P** *Bp* **V** P R G HINTON
WARLINGHAM (All Saints) w Chelsham and Farleigh *S'wark 24*
P *Patr Bd* **TR** A D MIDDLETON, **TV** M K EDMONDS,
Hon C J H STEVENS
WARMFIELD (St Peter) *Wakef 11* **P** *Oley Trustees Clare Coll*
Cam **P-in-c** L J COLLYER
WARMINGHAM (St Leonard) *see* Elworth and Warmingham
Ches
WARMINGTON (St Mary the Blessed Virgin), Tansor and
Cotterstock and Fotheringhay and Southwick *Pet 10* **P** *Bp and*
D&C Linc (alt) **V** B V ROGERS
WARMINGTON (St Michael) w Shotteswell and Radway w
Ratley *Cov 8* **P** *Bp* **C** R J COOKE
WARMINSTER (Christ Church) *Sarum 17* **P** *R Warminster*
St Denys etc **P-in-c** P W HUNTER, **C** A MEPHAM,
NSM P J FOY, **OLM** L A S MATHEW
WARMINSTER (St Denys) and Upton Scudamore *Sarum 17*
P *Bp and Qu Coll Ox (jt)* **R** H L GIBBONS, **C** N J W BROWN,
NSM C J OWEN
WARMLEY (St Barnabas), Syston and Bitton *Bris 5* **P** *Bp*
R P H DENYER, **C** M T SHEPHERDSON, **Hon C** J E NORMAN,
NSM C A COSTER
WARMSWORTH (St Peter) *Sheff 9* **P** *Bp* **R** S F BOND,
NSM R J WALTON
WARMWELL (Holy Trinity) *see* Watercombe *Sarum*
WARNBOROUGH, SOUTH (St Andrew) *see* N Hants Downs
Win
WARNDON (St Nicholas) *Worc 6* **P** *Bp* **P-in-c** D P RYAN,
NSM S E POLLARD
WARNDON (St Wulstan) *see* Worc St Wulstan *Worc*
WARNERS END (St Alban) *see* Hemel Hempstead *St Alb*
WARNFORD (Our Lady) *see* W Meon and Warnford *Portsm*
WARNHAM (St Margaret) *Chich 8* **P** *J C Lucas Esq*
V C H LOVELESS
WARNINGLID (St Andrew) *see* Slaugham *Chich*
WARREN PARK (St Clare) *Portsm 5* **P** *Bp* **V** J G P JEFFERY,
C S J TANCOCK

WARREN ROW (St Paul)   *see* Wargrave w Knowl Hill *Ox*
WARRINGTON (Holy Trinity) *Liv 12*   **P** *R Warrington*
   P-in-c S R PARISH,   **OLM** C E BATEY
WARRINGTON (St Ann)   *see* Warrington St Ann *Liv*
WARRINGTON (St Ann) *Liv 12*   **P** *Simeon's Trustees*
   V S R PARISH,   **OLM** P LOVATT, M M MCDONNELL, J M WEAVER
WARRINGTON (St Barnabas) Bank Quay *Liv 12*
   P *R Warrington and Bp (jt)*   **V** K L F TIMMIS
WARRINGTON (St Elphin) (St John) *Liv 12*   **P** *Lord Lilford*
   R M S FINLAY,   **C** A BEAHAN
WARSLOW (St Lawrence)   *see* Alstonfield, Butterton, Ilam etc
   Lich
WARSOP (St Peter and St Paul) *S'well 2*   **P** *Trustees*
   R K HERROD,   **C** P LAWLOR
WARTHILL (St Mary)   *see* Stockton-on-the-Forest w Holtby
   and Warthill *York*
WARTLING (St Mary Magdalene)   *see* Herstmonceux and
   Wartling *Chich*
WARTNABY (St Michael)   *see* Old Dalby, Nether Broughton,
   Saxelbye etc *Leic*
WARTON (Holy Trinity)   *see* N Warks *Birm*
WARTON (St Oswald or Holy Trinity) w Yealand Conyers
   Blackb 14   **P** *Bp*   **P-in-c** D M PORTER
WARTON (St Paul) *Blackb 10*   **P** *Ch Ch Ox*
   P-in-c M L HARTLEY
WARWICK (St Leonard)   *see* Holme Eden and Wetheral w
   Warwick *Carl*
WARWICK Team, The New (St Mary) (St Nicholas) (St Paul)
   Cov 11   **P** *Ld Chan and Patr Bd (alt)*   **TR** V S ROBERTS,
   TV A W J FITZMAURICE, J HEARN,   **C** S JONES
WARWICK SQUARE (St Gabriel)   *see* Pimlico St Gabr *Lon*
WARWICKSHIRE, NORTH All Souls *Birm 10*   **P** *Ld Chan
   (1 turn), V Polesworth, Birm Dioc Trustees and Mrs E V G Inge-
   Innes Lillington (1 turn)*   **R** S J BANKS
WASDALE, NETHER (St Michael)   *see* Gosforth w Nether
   Wasdale and Wasdale Head *Carl*
WASDALE HEAD (not known)   *as above*
WASH COMMON (St George)   *see* Newbury *Ox*
WASHBOURNE, GREAT (St Mary)   *see* Winchcombe *Glouc*
WASHBURN and Mid-Wharfe *Bradf 4*   **P** *Bp, G N le G Horton-
   Fawkes Esq, Lt Col H V Dawson and C Wyvill Esq (jt)*
   P-in-c S J WHARTON,   **NSM** T H BAXTER, M F CLEVERLEY
**WASHFIELD (St Mary the Virgin), Stoodleigh, Withleigh,
   Calverleigh, Oakford, Templeton, Loxbeare, Rackenford, and
   Cruwys Morchard** *Ex 8*   **P** *Patr Bd*   **TV** A D ROSE,
   NSM J C W ROBERTS
WASHFORD (St Mary)   *see* Old Cleeve, Leighland and
   Treborough *B & W*
WASHFORD PYNE (St Peter)   *see* N Creedy *Ex*
WASHINGBOROUGH (St John) w Heighington and Canwick
   Linc 18   **P** *DBP and Mercers' Co (jt)*   **R** S JONES-CRABTREE
WASHINGTON (Holy Trinity) *Dur 11*   **P** *Bp*   **R** D C GLOVER,
   C R HALL
WASHINGTON (St Mary)   *see* Ashington, Washington and
   Wiston w Buncton *Chich*
WASHWOOD HEATH (St Mark)   *see* Saltley and Washwood
   Heath *Birm*
WASING (St Nicholas)   *see* Aldermaston and Woolhampton *Ox*
WASKERLEY (St Andrew)   *see* Blanchland w Hunstanworth
   and Edmundbyers etc *Newc*
WASPERTON (St John the Baptist)   *see* Barford w Wasperton
   and Sherbourne *Cov*
WASS (St Thomas)   *see* Coxwold and Husthwaite *York*
WATCHET (Holy Cross Chapel)   *see* St Decumans *B & W*
WATCHET (St Decuman)   *as above*
WATCHFIELD (St Thomas's Chapel)   *see* Shrivenham and
   Ashbury *Ox*
WATER EATON (St Frideswide) *Ox 25*   **P** *Bp*   **V** *vacant
   (01908) 366710*
WATER NEWTON (St Remigius)   *see* Elton w Stibbington and
   Water Newton *Ely*
WATER ORTON (St Peter and St Paul) *Birm 9*   **P** *Patr Bd*
   V S T MAYES
WATER STRATFORD (St Giles)   *see* W Buckingham *Ox*
WATERBEACH (St John) *Ely 6*   **P** *Bp*   **P-in-c** L E CLELAND,
   NSM P M THORN
WATERCOMBE *Sarum 1*   **P** *M Cree Esq (1 turn), MMCET
   (2 turns), and Sir Robert Williams Bt (1 turn)*   **R** J M COATES,
   C M J HARRISON,   **OLM** W P A BUSH
WATERDEN (All Saints)   *see* N and S Creake w Waterden,
   Syderstone etc *Nor*
WATERFALL (St James and St Bartholomew)   *see* Calton,
   Cauldon, Grindon, Waterfall etc *Lich*
WATERFORD (St Michael and All Angels)   *see* Bramfield,
   Stapleford, Waterford etc *St Alb*

WATERHEAD (Holy Trinity)   *see* Medlock Head *Man*
WATERHOUSES (St Paul) *Dur 1*   **P** *R Brancepeth Esq*
   V M J PEERS
WATERINGBURY (St John the Baptist)   *see* E Malling,
   Wateringbury and Teston *Roch*
WATERLOO (Christ Church) St John *Liv 1*   **P** *Trustees and
   Simeon's Trustees (jt)*   **V** G J CUFF,   **OLM** A L BROOKS
WATERLOO (St John the Evangelist) (St Andrew) *S'wark 11*
   P *Abp and CPAS (jt)*   **P-in-c** G W GODDARD,
   NSM A M WARNER,   **OLM** D PAPE, G S N KAZIRO
WATERLOO PARK (St Mary the Virgin)   *see* Gt Crosby St
   Faith and Waterloo Park St Mary *Liv*
WATERLOOVILLE (St George the Martyr) *Portsm 5*   **P** *Bp*
   V M J SHEFFIELD,   **C** T B SINGH
WATERMILLOCK (All Saints)   *see* Gd Shep TM *Carl*
WATERMOOR (Holy Trinity)   *see* Cirencester *Glouc*
WATERPERRY (St Mary the Virgin)   *see* Wheatley *Ox*
WATERS UPTON (St Michael)   *see* Tibberton w Bolas Magna
   and Waters Upton *Lich*
**WATERSIDE PARISHES of Hambleton, Out Rawcliffe and
   Preesall** *Blackb 9*   **P** *Bp, V Kirkham, and V Garstang St Helen
   etc (jt)*   **V** S B GREY,   **NSM** D BANKS,   **OLM** J A SQUIRES
WATERSTOCK (St Leonard)   *see* Wheatley *Ox*
WATERTHORPE (Emmanuel)   *see* Mosbrough *Sheff*
WATFORD (Christ Church) (St Mark) *St Alb 7*   **P** *Bp,
   V Watford, and Churchwardens (jt)*
WATFORD (St Andrew) *St Alb 7*   **P** *Bp and Churchwardens (jt)*
   V G R WARREN,   **NSM** S M TALBOTT
WATFORD (St John) *St Alb 7*   **P** *Bp*   **V** *vacant (01923) 236174*
WATFORD (St Luke) *St Alb 7*   **P** *Bp, Adn St Alb, V Watford,
   and Ch Trust Fund Trust (jt)*   **P-in-c** D J MIDDLEBROOK,
   C I C PANKHURST,   **NSM** S W MASSEY
WATFORD (St Mary) *St Alb 7*   **P** *Ch Trust Fund Trust*
   P-in-c G K KNOTT
WATFORD (St Michael and All Angels) *St Alb 7*   **P** *Bp*
   NSM G O OCHOLA
WATFORD (St Peter) *St Alb 7*   **P** *Bp*   **V** C P COTTEE,
   C R W YULE,   **NSM** A D T GORTON, A P PRIOR
WATFORD (St Peter and St Paul)   *see* Long Buckby w Watford
   Pet
WATH (St Mary)   *see* Kirklington w Burneston and Wath and
   Pickhill *Ripon*
WATH BROW (Mission Church)   *see* Crosslacon *Carl*
WATH-UPON-DEARNE (All Saints) *Sheff 12*   **P** *Ch Ch Ox*
   V *vacant (01709) 872299*
WATLING VALLEY, Milton Keynes (not known) *Ox 25*
   P *Patr Bd*   **TV** M J MORRIS, T NORWOOD,
   NSM E M J M BAKER,   **OLM** T HADDEN
WATLINGTON (St Leonard)   *see* Icknield *Ox*
WATLINGTON (St Peter and St Paul) *Ely 9*   **P** *Bp*
   R J C W NOLAN
WATTISFIELD (St Margaret)   *see* Hepworth, Hinderclay,
   Wattisfield and Thelnetham *St E*
WATTLESBOROUGH (St Margaret)   *see* Alberbury w
   Cardeston *Heref*
WATTON (St Mary) *Nor 13*   **P** *Ld Chan*   **V** G D GARRETT
WATTON (St Mary)   *see* Hutton Cranswick w Skerne, Watton
   and Beswick *York*
WATTON AT STONE (St Mary and St Andrew)   *see* Bramfield,
   Stapleford, Waterford etc *St Alb*
WAVENDON (Assumption of the Blessed Virgin Mary)
   see Walton Milton Keynes *Ox*
WAVENEY Benefice, UPPER *Nor 10*   **P** *DBP, St Jo Coll Cam,
   MMCET, and R D A Woode Esq (jt)*   **R** R J MELLOWSHIP
WAVERTON (Christ Church)   *see* Solway Plain *Carl*
WAVERTON (St Peter) w Aldford and Bruera *Ches 5*   **P** *Bp,
   D&C, and Duke of Westmr (jt)*   **R** J T P BEAUCHAMP
WAVERTREE (Holy Trinity) *Liv 6*   **P** *Bp*   **R** J EASTWOOD,
   NSM J PHILLIPS
WAVERTREE (St Bridget) (St Thomas) *Liv 6*   **P** *Simeon's
   Trustees and R Wavertree H Trin (jt)*   **V** W J SANDERS
WAVERTREE (St Mary) *Liv 6*   **P** *Bp*
   P-in-c M L CHAMBERLAIN
WAWNE (St Peter)   *see* Sutton St Jas and Wawne *York*
WAXHAM, GREAT (St John)   *see* Bacton, Happisburgh,
   Hempstead w Eccles etc *Nor*
WAYFORD (St Michael and All Angels)   *see* Wulfric Benefice
   B & W
WAYLAND Group, The   *see* Caston, Griston, Merton,
   Thompson etc *Nor*
WEALD (St George)   *see* Sevenoaks Weald *Roch*
WEALD, SOUTH (St Peter) *Chelmsf 7*   **P** *Bp*   **V** I H JORYSZ
WEALDSTONE (Holy Trinity) *Lon 23*   **P** *Bp*
   V T M MALONEY,   **C** S J SWIFT,   **NSM** F E MALONEY
WEAR (St Luke)   *see* Countess Wear *Ex*

WEARDALE, UPPER *Dur 9*   **P** *Bp (5 turns), Duchy of Lancaster (1 turn), and Ld Chan (1 turn)*   **R** S E KENT, **NSM** B E BLOOMFIELD

WEARE (St Gregory)   *see Crook Peak B & W*

WEARE GIFFARD (Holy Trinity)   *see Bideford, Northam, Westward Ho!, Appledore etc Ex*

WEARSIDE, NORTH *Dur 16*   **P** *Patr Bd*   **TR** G DRIVER, **TV** S W ELSTOB

WEASENHAM (All Saints)   *see Gt w Lt Massingham, Harpley, Rougham etc Nor*

WEASENHAM (St Peter)   *as above*

WEASTE (St Luke w All Saints)   *see Salford All SS Man*

WEAVERHAM (St Mary the Virgin) *Ches 6*   **P** *Bp*   **V** A BROWN,   **C** J BROWN

WEAVERTHORPE (St Andrew) w Helperthorpe, Luttons Ambo and Kirby Grindalythe w Wharram *York 6*   **P** *Abp and D&C (jt)*   **V** *vacant* (01944) 738213

WEBHEATH (St Philip)   *see Redditch H Trin Worc*

WEDDINGTON (St James) and Caldecote *Cov 5*   **P** *Bp*   **R** *vacant* (024) 7635 3400

WEDMORE (St Mary) w Theale and Blackford *B & W 1*   **P** *Bp*   **V** R W NEILL

WEDNESBURY (St Bartholomew) *Lich 26*   **P** *Bp*   **V** *vacant* 0121-556 9378

WEDNESBURY (St James and St John) *Lich 26*   **P** *Trustees*   **R** K A PALMER,   **RC** R C GILBERT

WEDNESBURY (St Paul) Wood Green *Lich 26*   **P** *Bp*   **V** G WARREN,   **OLM** E A BROWN

WEDNESFIELD (St Gregory) *Lich 28*   **P** *Bp*   **P-in-c** S D MANSFIELD

WEDNESFIELD (St Thomas) (St Augustine and St Chad) (St Alban) *Lich 28*   **P** *Patr Bd*   **TR** N E WATSON, **TV** P PARKS, H L DUCKETT

WEDNESFIELD HEATH (Holy Trinity) *Lich 28*   **P** *CPAS*   **V** D A VESTERGAARD,   **C** V G HATTON

WEEDON (School Chapel)   *see Schorne Ox*

WEEDON BEC (St Peter and St Paul) w Everdon and Dodford *Pet 3*   **P** *Bp*   **V** H E RAYMENT

WEEDON LOIS (St Mary and St Peter)   *see Astwell Gp Pet*

WEEFORD (St Mary the Virgin)   *see Whittington w Weeford Lich*

WEEK ST MARY Circle of Parishes (St Mary the Virgin) *Truro 8*   **P** *Bp, Walsingham Coll, Guild of All So, SS Coll Cam, and Earl of St Germains (jt)*   **R** R C W DICKENSON,   **C** C J M RUGG,   **NSM** G W ROWE, R WARD-SMITH

WEEKE   *see Win St Matt Win*

WEEKLEY (St Mary the Virgin)   *see Geddington w Weekley Pet*

WEELEY (St Andrew) and Little Clacton *Chelmsf 22*   **P** *Bp and BNC Ox (alt)*   **R** D M NEWMAN

WEETHLEY (St James)   *see Alcester and Arrow w Oversley and Weethley Cov*

WEETING (St Mary)   *see Grimshoe Ely*

WEETON (St Barnabas)   *see Lower Wharfedale Ripon*

WEETON (St Michael)   *see Ribby cum Wrea and Weeton Blackb*

WEETSLADE (St Paul) *Newc 1*   **P** *Bp*   **V** A MAUGHAN

WELBORNE (All Saints)   *see Mattishall and the Tudd Valley Nor*

WELBOURN (St Chad) *Linc 23*   **P** *Hyndman Trustees*   **R** A J MEGAHEY

WELBURN (St John the Evangelist)   *see Howardian Gp York*

WELBURY (St Leonard)   *see Rounton w Welbury York*

WELBY (not known)   *see Melton Mowbray Leic*

WELBY (St Bartholemew)   *see Ancaster Wilsford Gp Linc*

WELCOMBE (St Nectan)   *see Parkham, Alwington, Buckland Brewer etc Ex*

WELDON (St Mary the Virgin) w Deene *Pet 7*   **P** *DBP and E Brudenell Esq (jt)*   **C** S J P FISHER

WELFORD (St Gregory) w Wickham and Great Shefford, Boxford and Stockcross *Ox 14*   **P** *Bp and BNC Ox (jt)*   **R** *vacant* (01488) 608244

WELFORD (St Mary the Virgin) w Sibbertoft and Marston Trussell *Pet 2*   **P** *Bp*   **P-in-c** I W Y GEMMELL, **NSM** S DENNER-BROWN

WELFORD (St Peter)   *see Quinton and Welford w Weston Glouc*

WELHAM (St Andrew), Glooston and Cranoe and Stonton Wyville *Leic 3*   **P** *Bp, E Brudenell Esq, and MMCET (jt)*   **P-in-c** J S PARKIN, R J P BARRIBAL

WELL (St Margaret) *Linc 8*   **P** *Bp*   **R** *vacant*

WELL (St Michael)   *see W Tanfield and Well w Snape and N Stainley Ripon*

WELL HILL (Mission)   *see Chelsfield Roch*

WELLAND (St James)   *see Hanley Castle, Hanley Swan and Welland Worc*

WELLESBOURNE (St Peter) *Cov 8*   **P** *Ld Chan*   **P-in-c** C E MIER,   **NSM** A W SHEARN, **OLM** W E BIDDINGTON

WELLING (St John the Evangelist) *Roch 15*   **P** *Bp*   **V** A J D FOOT,   **C** R M RADCLIFFE

WELLING (St Mary the Virgin) *S'wark 6*   **P** *Bp*   **NSM** S E GREENWOOD

WELLINGBOROUGH (All Hallows) *Pet 6*   **P** *Exors Major E C S Byng-Maddick*   **V** *vacant* (01933) 222002

WELLINGBOROUGH (All Saints) *Pet 6*   **P** *V Wellingborough*   **V** A M LYNETT

WELLINGBOROUGH (St Andrew) *Pet 6*   **P** *Bp*   **V** C M UPTON

WELLINGBOROUGH (St Barnabas) *Pet 6*   **P** *Bp*   **V** J P LEADER

WELLINGBOROUGH (St Mark) *Pet 6*   **P** *Bp*   **V** A CUTHBERTSON,   **NSM** G ALDERSON

WELLINGBOROUGH (St Mary the Virgin) *Pet 6*   **P** *Guild of All So*   **V** R J T FARMER

WELLINGHAM (St Andrew)   *see Gt w Lt Massingham, Harpley, Rougham etc Nor*

WELLINGORE (All Saints)   *see Graffoe Gp Linc*

WELLINGTON (All Saints) (St John the Baptist) and District *B & W 19*   **P** *Patr Bd*   **TR** C M S RANDALL, **TV** C F E ROWLEY, M R CAMPBELL,   **C** G H J CLAPHAM, C I BRIERLEY

WELLINGTON (All Saints) w Eyton (St Catherine) *Lich 21*   **P** *Ch Trust Fund Trust*   **V** M C IRELAND,   **C** G P RUTTER, **Hon C** M A SMALLMAN

WELLINGTON (Christ Church)   *see Hadley and Wellington Ch Ch Lich*

WELLINGTON (St Margaret of Antioch)   *see Canon Pyon w King's Pyon, Birley and Wellington Heref*

WELLINGTON HEATH (Christ Church)   *see Ledbury Heref*

WELLOW (St Julian the Hospitaller)   *see Peasedown St John w Wellow B & W*

WELLOW (St Swithin)   *see Kneesall w Laxton and Wellow S'well*

WELLOW, EAST w WEST (St Margaret) and Sherfield English *Win 12*   **P** *Bp and CPAS (jt)*   **V** G R BIGGS

WELLS (St Cuthbert) w Wookey Hole *B & W 8*   **P** *D&C*   **V** *vacant* (01749) 673136

WELLS (St Thomas) w Horrington *B & W 8*   **P** *D&C*   **P-in-c** J SMITH,   **NSM** A C HUNT, N T FRIDD

WELLS-NEXT-THE-SEA (St Nicholas)   *see Holkham w Egmere w Warham, Wells and Wighton Nor*

WELNEY (St Mary)   *see Christchurch and Manea and Welney Ely*

WELSH BICKNOR (St Margaret)   *see Goodrich, Marstow, Welsh Bicknor, Llangarron etc Heref*

WELSH FRANKTON (St Andrew)   *see Criftins w Dudleston and Welsh Frankton Lich*

WELSH NEWTON (St Mary the Virgin)   *see Goodrich, Marstow, Welsh Bicknor, Llangarron etc Heref*

WELSH NEWTON COMMON (St Faith)   *see St Weonards Heref*

WELSHAMPTON (St Michael)   *see Petton w Cockshutt, Welshampton and Lyneal etc Lich*

WELTON (St Helen) w Melton *York 14*   **P** *DBP*   **P-in-c** E E BIELBY,   **NSM** A A V SCHRIMSHAW

WELTON (St James)   *see Westward, Rosley-w-Woodside and Welton Carl*

WELTON (St Martin)   *see Daventry, Ashby St Ledgers, Braunston etc Pet*

WELTON (St Mary) and Dunholme w Scothern *Linc 3*   **P** *Bp and DBP (jt)*   **V** *vacant* (01673) 862820

WELTON-LE-MARSH (St Martin)   *see Burgh Gp Linc*

WELTON-LE-WOLD (St Martin)   *see Louth Linc*

WELWICK (St Mary)   *see Patrington w Hollym, Welwick and Winestead York*

WELWYN Team Ministry, The (St Mary the Virgin) (St Michael) *St Alb 21*   **P** *Patr Bd*   **TR** A P WINTON, **TV** C C MCCLUSKEY,   **C** D C WHITTAKER, **NSM** S L FIELDING

WELWYN GARDEN CITY (St Francis of Assisi) *St Alb 21*   **P** *Bp*   **C** J GRAY

WEM (St Peter and St Paul) *Lich 22*   **P** *Lord Barnard*   **P-in-c** C S COOKE,   **NSM** T D SMITH

WEMBDON (St George) *B & W 14*   **P** *Ch Soc Trust*   **V** C D E MOLL

WEMBLEY (St Augustine)   *see Wembley Park Lon*

WEMBLEY (St John the Evangelist) *Lon 21*   **P** *Ch Patr Trust*   **V** F ADU-BOACHIE,   **NSM** H M ASKWITH

WEMBLEY, NORTH (St Cuthbert) *Lon 21*   **P** *Bp*   **V** F G MCDERMOTT

WEMBLEY PARK (Church of the Ascension) (St Augustine) (Annunciation) *Lon 21*   **P** *Bp*   **TR** M J CATTERICK, **TV** T F CRITCHLOW, H L YOUNG, **Hon C** J M WARNER
WEMBURY (St Werburgh) *Ex 21*   **P** *D&C Windsor* **P-in-c** M J HARMAN
WEMBWORTHY (St Michael) *see* Burrington, Chawleigh, Cheldon, Chulmleigh etc *Ex*
WENDENS AMBO (St Mary the Virgin) *see* Saffron Walden w Wendens Ambo, Littlebury etc *Chelmsf*
WENDLEBURY (St Giles) *see* Akeman *Ox*
WENDLING (St Peter and St Paul) *see* Gressenhall w Longham w Wendling etc *Nor*
WENDOVER (St Agnes's Chapel) *see* Wendover and Halton *Ox*
WENDOVER (St Mary) *as above*
WENDOVER (St Mary) (St Agnes's Chapel) and Halton *Ox 28* **P** *Ld Chan*   **R** M C DEARNLEY, **NSM** B J ROBERTS
WENDRON(St Wendron) *see* Helston and Wendron *Truro*
WENDY (All Saints) *see* Shingay Gp *Ely*
WENHAM, GREAT (St John) *see* Capel St Mary w Lt and Gt Wenham *St E*
WENHASTON (St Peter) *see* Blyth Valley *St E*
WENLOCK *Heref 11*   **P** *Patr Bd*   **TR** S A LOWE, **TV** J DAVIES,   **C** J H H ASHTON
WENLOCK, LITTLE (St Lawrence) *see* Coalbrookdale, Iron-Bridge and Lt Wenlock *Heref*
WENLOCK, MUCH (Holy Trinity) *see* Wenlock *Heref*
WENNINGTON (St Mary and St Peter) *see* Rainham w Wennington *Chelmsf*
WENSUM Benefice, The *Nor 22*   **P** *New Coll Ox, Margaret Lady Prince-Smith, Bp, and D&C (jt)*   **R** L S TILLETT
WENSUM VILLAGE Group, UPPER *Nor 15* **P** *Marquess Townshend, the Revd C S P Douglas Lane, Ch Coll Cam, and DBP (jt)*   **R** R D STAPLEFORD
WENT VALLEY *Wakef 10*   **P** *Bp, Earl of Rosse, and Sir Philip Naylor-Leyland Bt (jt)*   **V** A T JUDD,   **OLM** H CRABTREE, M J TAYLOR
WENTBRIDGE (St John) *see* Went Valley *Wakef*
WENTNOR (St Michael and All Angels) w Ratlinghope, Myndtown, Norbury, More, Lydham and Snead *Heref 10* **P** *Ch Ch Ox (4 turns) and J J C Coldwell Esq (1 turn)* **R** N F M MORRIS
WENTWORTH (Harley Mission Church) (Holy Trinity) *Sheff 12*   **P** *Sir Philip Naylor-Leyland Bt*   **V** *vacant* (01226) 742274
WENTWORTH (St Peter) *see* Witchford w Wentworth *Ely*
WEOBLEY (St Peter and St Paul) w Sarnesfield and Norton Canon *Heref 5*   **P** *Bp (2 turns), R A Marshall Esq (1 turn)* **V** R D KING
WEOLEY CASTLE (St Gabriel) *Birm 2*   **P** *Bp*   **V** *vacant* 0121-475 1194
WEREHAM (St Margaret) *Ely 9*   **P** *Bp*   **V** *vacant*
WERNETH (St Paul) *Ches 16*   **P** *DBP*   **P-in-c** R J BROOKE, **NSM** J L C ATKINSON
WERNETH (St Thomas) *Man 20*   **P** *Bp* **P-in-c** F A O D DAWSON
WERRINGTON (St John the Baptist w Emmanuel) *Pet 11* **P** *Bp*   **V** G H ROGERS,   **C** S P KINDER
WERRINGTON (St Martin of Tours) *see* Boyton, N Tamerton, Werrington etc *Truro*
WERRINGTON (St Philip) and Wetley Rocks *Lich 6*   **P** *Bp and V Caverswall and Weston Coyney w Dilhorne (jt)* **V** S E GOODWIN,   **C** A MARCH,   **OLM** I T COPELAND
WESHAM (Christ Church) and Treales *Blackb 10* **P** *V Kirkham*   **V** *vacant* (01772) 682206
WESSINGTON (Christ Church) *see* Ashover and Brackenfield w Wessington *Derby*
WEST *see also under substantive place name*
WEST BAY (St John) *see* Bridport *Sarum*
WEST DEAN (All Saints) *see* Alfriston w Lullington, Litlington and W Dean *Chich*
WEST DEAN (St Andrew) *see* E Dean, Singleton, and W Dean *Chich*
WEST DEAN (St Mary) *see* Clarendon *Sarum*
WEST DOWN (St Calixtus) *see* Ilfracombe SS Phil and Jas w W Down *Ex*
WEST END *see* Northolt St Jos *Lon*
WEST END (Holy Trinity) *see* Bisley and W End *Guildf*
WEST END (St George) *see* Esher *Guildf*
WEST END (St James) *Win 10*   **P** *Bp*   **V** B L PICKETT, **NSM** J E PICKETT
WEST GREEN (Christ Church w St Peter) *Lon 19*   **P** *Bp* **Hon C** M A R HAYNES
WEST GREEN (St Peter) *see* Crawley *Chich*
WEST HAM (All Saints) *Chelmsf 3*   **P** *The Crown* **V** S R KIRBY,   **NSM** A R EASTER

WEST HAM (St Matthew) *see* Forest Gate St Sav w W Ham St Matt *Chelmsf*
WEST HEATH (St Anne) *Birm 4*   **P** *Bp*   **P-in-c** S C L DIMES, J G TSIPOURAS
WEST HILL (St Michael the Archangel) *see* Ottery St Mary, Alfington, W Hill, Tipton etc *Ex*
WEST HYDE (St Thomas of Canterbury) *see* Mill End and Heronsgate w W Hyde *St Alb*
WEST MOORS (St Mary the Virgin) *Sarum 9*   **P** *Bp* **V** A J W ROWLAND,   **C** E A CHARLTON
WEST ORCHARD (St Luke) *see* Shaston *Sarum*
WEST ROW (St Peter) *see* Mildenhall *St E*
WEST WINCH (St Mary) w Setchey, North Runcton and Middleton *Nor 20*   **P** *H N D Gurney Esq (1 turn) and Ld Chan (2 turns)*   **R** J F RYAN
WESTACRE (All Saints) *see* Castleacre, Newton, Westacre and Southacre *Nor*
WESTBERE (All Saints) *see* Sturry w Fordwich and Westbere w Hersden *Cant*
WESTBOROUGH (All Saints) *see* Claypole *Linc*
WESTBOROUGH (St Clare) (St Francis) *Guildf 5*   **P** *Bp* **TR** S M HODGES,   **TV** S POWNALL
WESTBOURNE (Christ Church) Chapel *Win 8* **Min** A D M PAINE
WESTBOURNE (St John the Baptist) *Chich 13*   **P** *Bp* **R** *vacant* (01243) 372867
WESTBROOK (All Saints) *see* Margate All SS *Cant*
WESTBROOK (St James) Hood Manor *Liv 12*   **P** *Bp, R Warrington, and V Gt Sankey (jt)*   **V** *vacant* (01925) 492631
WESTBROOK (St Philip) Old Hall and Callands *Liv 12*   **P** *Bp and R Warrington (jt)*   **V** M X THORPE,   **C** D D EASTWOOD
WESTBURY (All Saints) *see* White Horse *Sarum*
WESTBURY (St Augustine) *see* W Buckingham *Ox*
WESTBURY (St Mary) *Heref 13*   **P** *Bp*   **R** C B BULL
WESTBURY-ON-SEVERN (St Peter and St Paul) w Flaxley, Blaisdon and Minsterworth *Glouc 1*   **P** *Bp, D&C Heref, and Sir Thomas Crawley-Boevey Bt (jt)*   **P-in-c** I C GOBEY, **NSM** S L HOBBS
WESTBURY-ON-TRYM (Holy Trinity) *Bris 2*   **P** *SMF* **V** A H HART
WESTBURY-ON-TRYM (St Alban) *Bris 2*   **P** *Bp* **P-in-c** E L LANGLEY
WESTBURY PARK (Local Ecumenical Partnership) *Bris 2* **Min** E L LANGLEY,   **NSM** M H JAMES
WESTBURY PARK (St Alban) *see* Westbury-on-Trym St Alb *Bris*
WESTBURY SUB MENDIP (St Lawrence) w Easton *B & W 1* **P** *Bp*   **P-in-c** J A C SEWELL
WESTCLIFF (Church of Reconciliation) *see* Brumby *Linc*
WESTCLIFF (St Alban) *see* Southend *Chelmsf*
WESTCLIFF (St Andrew) *Chelmsf 13*   **P** *Bp*   **V** S F KIMBER
WESTCLIFF (St Cedd and the Saints of Essex) *see* Prittlewell St Pet w Westcliff St Cedd *Chelmsf*
WESTCLIFF (St Michael and All Angels) *Chelmsf 13*   **P** *Bp* **V** P C NICHOLSON
WESTCLIFF (St Saviour) *see* Southend St Sav Westcliff *Chelmsf*
WESTCLIFFE (St Peter) *see* St Margarets-at-Cliffe w Westcliffe etc *Cant*
WESTCOMBE PARK (St George) *see* E Greenwich *S'wark*
WESTCOTE (St Mary the Virgin) *see* Broadwell, Evenlode, Oddington, Adlestrop etc *Glouc*
WESTCOTE BARTON (St Edward the Confessor) w Steeple Barton, Duns Tew and Sandford St Martin *Ox 9*   **P** *Duke of Marlborough, Exors Mrs Rittson-Thomas, DBP, D C D Webb Esq, and Bp (jt)*   **R** G R ARTHUR
WESTCOTT (Holy Trinity) *Guildf 7*   **P** *Bp*   **P-in-c** A C JONAS
WESTCOTT (St Mary) *see* Schorne *Ox*
WESTDENE (The Ascension) *see* Patcham *Chich*
WESTERDALE (Christ Church) *York 22*   **P** *Abp* **V** M J HAZELTON
WESTERFIELD (St Mary Magdalene) and Tuddenham w Witnesham *St E 4*   **P** *Bp, Peterho Cam, and DBP (alt)* **P-in-c** S H COWLEY,   **NSM** A W FORSDIKE
WESTERHAM (St Mary the Virgin) *Roch 9* **P** *J St A Warde Esq*   **V** P S MCVEAGH
WESTERLEIGH (St James the Great) *see* Yate New Town *Bris*
WESTERN DOWNLAND *Sarum 11*   **P** *Hyndman Trustees, A N Hanbury Esq, and W J Purvis Esq (jt)*   **R** L M PLAYER
WESTFIELD (St Andrew) *see* Barnham Broom and Upper Yare *Nor*
WESTFIELD (St John the Baptist) *Chich 20*   **P** *Bp* **V** E N L FRANCE
WESTFIELD (St Mark) *see* Woking St Pet *Guildf*
WESTFIELD (St Mary) *Carl 7*   **P** *Bp*   **V** A M ARMSTRONG, **C** T COPELAND,   **NSM** M T STILWELL

WESTFIELD (St Peter) *B & W 12*   **P** *Bp*   **V** *vacant* (01761) 412105

WESTGATE (St Andrew)   *see* Upper Weardale *Dur*

WESTGATE (St James) *Cant 9*   **P** *Abp*   **V** R T BASHFORD

WESTGATE (St Martin of Tours)   *see* Torrisholme *Blackb*

WESTGATE COMMON (St Michael the Archangel) *Wakef 11*   **P** *V Alverthorpe*   **P-in-c** G A SYKES,   **NSM** C M FOGG

WESTGATE-ON-SEA (St Saviour) *Cant 9*   **P** *Abp*   **V** *vacant* (01843) 831869

WESTHALL (St Andrew)   *see* Hundred River *St E*

WESTHAM (St Mary the Virgin) *Chich 16*   **P** *Duke of Devonshire*   **V** G J BARRETT

WESTHAMPNETT (St Peter)   *see* Chich St Paul and Westhampnett *Chich*

WESTHEAD (St James)   *see* Newburgh w Westhead *Liv*

WESTHIDE (St Bartholomew)   *see* Withington w Westhide *Heref*

WESTHOPE (Mission Room)   *see* Canon Pyon w King's Pyon, Birley and Wellington *Heref*

WESTHORPE (St Margaret)   *see* Badwell and Walsham *St E*

WESTHOUGHTON (St Bartholomew) and Wingates *Man 11*   **P** *Patr Bd*   **TR** G A LAWSON,   **TV** R JACKSON,   **OLM** V A RADFORD

WESTHOUGHTON (St James)   *see* Daisy Hill *Man*

WESTHOUSES (St Saviour)   *see* Blackwell w Tibshelf *Derby*

WESTLANDS (St Andrew) *Lich 9*   **P** *Simeon's Trustees*   **V** W G H GARDINER,   **C** S A MORRIS

WESTLEIGH (St Paul) *Man 13*   **P** *V Leigh St Mary*   **P-in-c** S POLLARD,   **C** F C GUITE

WESTLEIGH (St Peter) *Ex 16*   **P** *D&C*   **P-in-c** G CALWAY

WESTLEIGH (St Peter) *Man 13*   **P** *Bp, Dioc Chan, and V Leigh St Mary (jt)*   **P-in-c** S POLLARD,   **C** F C GUITE,   **NSM** D VICKERS

WESTLETON (St Peter)   *see* Yoxmere *St E*

WESTLEY (St Mary)   *see* Horringer *St E*

WESTLEY WATERLESS (St Mary the less)   *see* Raddesley Gp *Ely*

WESTMEADS (St Michael and All Angels)   *see* Aldwick *Chich*

WESTMESTON (St Martin)   *see* Ditchling, Streat and Westmeston *Chich*

WESTMILL (St Mary the Virgin)   *see* Aspenden, Buntingford and Westmill *St Alb*

WESTMINSTER Hanover Square (St George)   *see* Hanover Square St Geo *Lon*

WESTMINSTER (St James) Piccadilly *Lon 3*   **P** *Bp (2 turns), Ld Chan (1 turn)*   **R** C J W HEDLEY,   **C** J L MEADER,   **NSM** H W J VALENTINE

WESTMINSTER (St James the Less) *Lon 3*   **P** *D&C Westmr*   **V** R P DORMANDY,   **NSM** W M CHOW

WESTMINSTER (St Mary le Strand)   *see* St Mary le Strand w St Clem Danes *Lon*

WESTMINSTER (St Matthew) *Lon 3*   **P** *D&C Westmr*   **V** P A E CHESTER,   **C** I J MOBSBY,   **Hon C** R CRAWFORD,   **NSM** P L HANAWAY

WESTMINSTER (St Michael)   *see* Ches Square St Mich w St Phil *Lon*

WESTMINSTER (St Saviour)   *see* Pimlico St Sav *Lon*

WESTMINSTER (St Stephen) w St John *Lon 3*   **P** *The Crown*   **V** P P WELSH,   **NSM** J M HICKS

WESTOE, SOUTH (St Michael and All Angels) *Dur 15*   **P** *Bp*   **P-in-c** P J A KENNEDY

WESTON (All Saints)   *see* Bath Weston All SS w N Stoke and Langridge *B & W*

WESTON (All Saints)   *see* Washburn and Mid-Wharfe *Bradf*

WESTON (All Saints) *Ches 15*   **P** *Bp*   **P-in-c** G M BREFFITT

WESTON (All Saints)   *see* Quinton and Welford w Weston *Glouc*

WESTON (All Saints) *Guildf 8*   **P** *Bp*   **V** P G MCAVOY

WESTON (All Saints)   *see* Tuxford w Weston and Markham Clinton *S'well*

WESTON (Emmanuel)   *see* Bath Weston St Jo w Kelston *B & W*

WESTON (Holy Trinity)   *see* Baldock w Bygrave and Weston *St Alb*

WESTON (Holy Trinity) *Win 13*   **P** *Bp*   **V** R A BURNINGHAM

WESTON (St John the Evangelist)   *see* Bath Weston St Jo w Kelston *B & W*

WESTON (St John the Evangelist)   *see* Runcorn St Jo Weston *Ches*

WESTON (St Mary)   *see* Cowbit *Linc*

WESTON (St Peter)   *see* Hundred River *St E*

WESTON, OLD (St Swithun)   *see* Brington w Molesworth and Old Weston *Ely*

WESTON, SOUTH (St Lawrence)   *see* Thame *Ox*

WESTON BAMPFYLDE (Holy Cross)   *see* Cam Vale *B & W*

WESTON BEGGARD (St John the Baptist)   *see* Lugwardine w Bartestree, Weston Beggard etc *Heref*

WESTON BY WELLAND (St Mary)   *see* Stoke Albany w Wilbarston and Ashley etc *Pet*

WESTON COLVILLE (St Mary)   *see* Balsham, Weston Colville, W Wickham etc *Ely*

WESTON COYNEY (St Andrew)   *see* Caverswall and Weston Coyney w Dilhorne *Lich*

WESTON ESTATE CHURCH (not known)   *see* Otley *Bradf*

WESTON FAVELL (St Peter) *Pet 4*   **P** *DBP*   **R** D G KIRBY

WESTON HILLS (St John the Evangelist)   *see* Cowbit *Linc*

WESTON IN GORDANO (St Peter and St Paul)   *see* E Clevedon w Clapton in Gordano etc *B & W*

WESTON LONGVILLE (All Saints)   *see* Wensum Benefice *Nor*

WESTON LULLINGFIELD (Holy Trinity)   *see* Baschurch and Weston Lullingfield w Hordley *Lich*

WESTON MILL (St Philip)   *see* Devonport St Boniface and St Phil *Ex*

WESTON-ON-THE-GREEN (St Mary)   *see* Akeman *Ox*

WESTON ON TRENT (St Mary the Virgin)   *see* Aston on Trent, Elvaston, Weston on Trent etc *Derby*

WESTON PATRICK (St Lawrence)   *see* N Hants Downs *Win*

WESTON POINT (Christ Church)   *see* Runcorn St Jo Weston *Ches*

WESTON RHYN (St John)   *see* St Martins and Weston Rhyn *Lich*

WESTON-SUB-EDGE (St Lawrence)   *see* Mickleton, Willersey, Saintbury etc *Glouc*

WESTON SUPER MARE (All Saints) and St Saviour *B & W 11*   **P** *Bp*   **V** P R S BOLTON

WESTON SUPER MARE (Christ Church) (Emmanuel) *B & W 11*   **P** *Trustees*   **V** G W HOBDEN,   **NSM** L J EVANS

WESTON-SUPER-MARE (St Andrew) Bournville *B & W 11*   **P** *Bp*   **V** *vacant* (01934) 627818

WESTON SUPER MARE (St John the Baptist) *B & W 11*   **P** *Bp and Trustees (jt)*   **R** R J TAYLOR

WESTON-SUPER-MARE (St Paul) *B & W 11*   **P** *Bp*   **V** A M ALDEN,   **C** T P B YACOMENI

WESTON TURVILLE (St Mary the Virgin) *Ox 28*   **P** *All So Coll Ox*   **R** D N WALES,   **NSM** S E FELLOWS

WESTON-UNDER-LIZARD (St Andrew)   *see* Blymhill w Weston-under-Lizard *Lich*

WESTON-UNDER-PENYARD (St Lawrence)   *see* Ariconium *Heref*

WESTON UNDER REDCASTLE (St Luke)   *see* Hodnet w Weston under Redcastle *Lich*

WESTON UNDER WETHERLEY (St Michael)   *see* Wappenbury w Weston under Wetherley *Cov*

WESTON UNDERWOOD (St Laurence)   *see* Gayhurst w Ravenstone, Stoke Goldington etc *Ox*

WESTON UPON TRENT (St Andrew)   *see* Mid Trent *Lich*

WESTON ZOYLAND (Blessed Virgin Mary) w Chedzoy *B & W 14*   **P** *Bp*   **P-in-c** J GREEN

WESTONING (St Mary Magdalene) w Tingrith *St Alb 9*   **P** *Ld Chan*   **P-in-c** N L WASHINGTON

WESTOW (St Mary)   *see* W Buckrose *York*

WESTWARD (St Hilda), Rosley-with-Woodside and Welton *Carl 3*   **P** *D&C*   **P-in-c** N L ROBINSON

WESTWARD HO! (Holy Trinity)   *see* Bideford, Northam, Westward Ho!, Appledore etc *Ex*

WESTWAY (St Katherine)   *see* N Hammersmith St Kath *Lon*

WESTWELL (St Mary)   *see* Shill Valley and Broadshire *Ox*

WESTWELL (St Mary) and Hothfield *Cant 10*   **P** *Abp and Lord Hothfield (jt)*   **P-in-c** L J HAMMOND

WESTWICK (St Botolph)   *see* Worstead, Westwick, Sloley, Swanton Abbot etc *Nor*

WESTWOOD (Mission Church)   *see* Golcar *Wakef*

WESTWOOD (St John the Baptist) *Cov 3*   **P** *Bp*   **V** P FINDLEY,   **C** A J DENNISS

WESTWOOD (St Mary) Jacksdale   *see* Selston *S'well*

WESTWOOD (St Mary the Virgin) and Wingfield *Sarum 14*   **P** *D&C Bris, CPAS, and Bp (jt)*   **R** R M LOWRIE

WESTWOOD, LOW (Christ Church)   *see* Ebchester *Dur*

WETHERAL (Holy Trinity and St Constantine)   *see* Holme Eden and Wetheral w Warwick *Carl*

WETHERBY (St James) *Ripon 1*   **P** *Bp*   **P-in-c** M A CROSS

WETHERDEN (St Mary the Virgin)   *see* Haughley w Wetherden and Stowupland *St E*

WETHERINGSETT (All Saints)   *see* S Hartismere *St E*

WETHERSFIELD (St Mary Magdalene)   *see* Finchingfield and Cornish Hall End etc *Chelmsf*

WETLEY ROCKS (St John the Baptist)   *see* Werrington and Wetley Rocks *Lich*

WETTENHALL (St David)   *see* Acton and Worleston, Church Minshull etc *Ches*

WETTON (St Margaret)   *see* Alstonfield, Butterton, Ilam etc *Lich*

WETWANG (St Nicholas)   see Waggoners York
WEXHAM (St Mary) Ox 23   **P** Ld Chan
  P-in-c R M DONOVAN,   **NSM** J M LOCKE
WEYBOURNE (All Saints), Upper Sheringham, Kelling,
  Salthouse, Bodham and East and West Beckham (The
  Weybourne Group) Nor 18   **P** Bp (2 turns), Sir Charles Mott-
  Radclyffe (1 turn), D&C (1 turn), and Lord Walpole (1 turn)
  P-in-c P G BLAMIRE,   **OLM** F A CLARKE
WEYBREAD (St Andrew)   see Fressingfield, Mendham etc St E
WEYBRIDGE (St James) Guildf 8   **P** Ld Chan
  R B D PROTHERO,   **C** J RATTUE, B HENGIST,
  NSM J L MULDER
WEYHILL (St Michael and All Angels)   see Pastrow Win
WEYMOUTH (Holy Trinity) (St Nicholas) Sarum 4   **P** Bp
  V R H FRANKLIN,   **C** D A'COURT,   **OLM** A DUNN
WEYMOUTH (St Edmund)   see Wyke Regis Sarum
WEYMOUTH (St John)   see Radipole and Melcombe Regis
  Sarum
WEYMOUTH (St Mary)   as above
WEYMOUTH (St Paul) Sarum 4   **P** Bp   **V** R M HARPER
WHADDON (St Margaret)   see Glouc St Geo w Whaddon
  Glouc
WHADDON (St Mary) Ely 7   **P** D&C Windsor
  P-in-c D C R MCFADYEN
WHADDON (St Mary)   see Buckingham Ox
WHADDON (St Mary)   see Clarendon Sarum
WHADDON (St Mary the Virgin)   see Canalside Benefice
  Sarum
WHALEY BRIDGE (St James) Ches 16   **P** Bp and Bp Derby
  (alt)   **R** vacant (01663) 719535
WHALEY THORNS (St Luke)   see E Scarsdale Derby
WHALLEY (St Mary and All Saints) Blackb 7   **P** Hulme
  Trustees   **NSM** J E HOLT
WHALLEY RANGE (St Edmund) and Moss Side St James w St
  Clement Man 4   **P** Bp and Simeon's Trustees (jt)
  R S R BULLOCK
WHALLEY RANGE (St Margaret) Man 4   **P** Trustees
  P-in-c R G BOULTER
WHALTON (St Mary Magdalene)   see Bolam w Whalton and
  Hartburn w Meldon Newc
WHAPLODE (St Mary) Linc 16   **P** Ld Chan   **V** vacant
  (01406) 370318
WHAPLODE DROVE (St John the Baptist) Linc 16   **P** Feoffees
  V R J MORRISON
WHARFEDALE, LOWER Ripon 1   **P** Bp, V Otley, and
  W G C Sheepshanks Esq (jt)   **R** S W LEWIS,
  Hon C J E BASSETT
WHARNCLIFFE SIDE (not known)   see Oughtibridge Sheff
WHARRAM (St Mary)   see Weaverthorpe w Helperthorpe,
  Luttons Ambo etc York
WHARTON (Christ Church) Ches 6   **P** R Davenham
  V T D HANSON,   **C** T A WATTS
WHATBOROUGH Group of Parishes, The Leic 3   **P** Bp
  V J D CURTIS
WHATCOTE (St Peter)   see Tysoe w Oxhill and Whatcote Cov
WHATFIELD (St Margaret)   see Bildeston w Wattisham and
  Lindsey, Whatfield etc St E
WHATLEY (St George)   see Mells w Buckland Dinham, Elm,
  Whatley etc B & W
WHATLINGTON (St Mary Magdalene)   see Sedlescombe w
  Whatlington Chich
WHATSTANDWELL (Mission Room)   see Crich and S
  Wingfield Derby
WHATTON (St John of Beverley) w Aslockton, Hawksworth,
  Scarrington, Orston and Thoroton S'well 8   **P** Trustees
  P-in-c K A PRZYWALA
WHEATACRE (All Saints)   see Raveningham Gp Nor
WHEATCROFT (St Michael and All Angels)   see Scarborough
  St Martin York
WHEATFIELD (St Andrew)   see Thame Ox
WHEATHAMPSTEAD (St Helen) St Alb 8   **P** Bp
  NSM M H KING
WHEATHILL (Holy Trinity)   see Ditton Priors w Neenton,
  Burwarton etc Heref
WHEATHILL PRIORY Group of Parishes, The B & W 3
  P Ch Soc Trust and J H Cordle Esq (1 turn), A J Whitehead Esq
  (2 turns), Bp (1 turn), and Mrs E J Burden (1 turn)
  P-in-c T R CRANSHAW
WHEATLEY (St Mary)   see Doncaster St Mary Sheff
WHEATLEY (St Mary the Virgin) Ox 1   **P** Patr Bd
  TR J V J G WATSON,   **TV** E L PENNINGTON, S CROSS,
  NSM J EDMONDS-SEAL, C N KING, M D CHAPMAN
WHEATLEY, NORTH (St Peter and St Paul) and West Burton w
  Bole and Saundby and Sturton w Littleborough S'well 5
  P Lord Middleton and G M T Foljambe Esq (alt)   **R** vacant
  (01427) 880293

WHEATLEY HILL (All Saints) and Wingate w Hutton Henry
  Dur 2   **P** Bp   **P-in-c** R C DAVIES
WHEATLEY HILLS (St Aidan) Sheff 8   **P** Bp   **V** D J GOSS
WHEATLEY PARK (St Paul) Sheff 8   **P** Bp
  P-in-c R B RADLEY
WHEATON ASTON (St Mary)   see Lapley w Wheaton Aston
  Lich
WHEELOCK (Christ Church)   see Sandbach Heath w
  Wheelock Ches
WHELDRAKE (St Helen)   see Derwent Ings York
WHELFORD (St Anne)   see Fairford Deanery Glouc
WHELLEY (St Stephen)   see New Springs and Whelley Liv
WHELNETHAM, GREAT (St Thomas à Becket)   see St Edm
  Way St E
WHELNETHAM, LITTLE (St Mary)   see Bradfield St Clare,
  Bradfield St George etc St E
WHELPLEY HILL (St Michael and All Angels)   see Gt
  Chesham Ox
WHENBY (St Martin)   see Howardian Gp York
WHEPSTEAD (St Petronilla)   see Horringer St E
WHERSTEAD (St Mary)   see Holbrook, Stutton, Freston,
  Woolverstone etc St E
WHERWELL (St Peter and Holy Cross)   see Downs Benefice
  Win
WHETSTONE (St John the Apostle) Lon 14   **P** Bp
  V K MITCHELL,   **NSM** C KENT
WHETSTONE (St Peter)   see Cosby and Whetstone Leic
WHICHAM (St Mary)   see Bootle, Corney, Whicham and
  Whitbeck Carl
WHICHFORD (St Michael)   see S Warks Seven Gp Cov
WHICKHAM (St Mary the Virgin) Dur 13   **P** Ld Chan
  R B J ABBOTT,   **C** J W BARRON
WHILTON (St Andrew)   see Brington w Whilton and Norton
  etc Pet
WHIMPLE (St Mary), Talaton and Clyst St Lawrence Ex 7
  P DBP, D&C and MMCET (jt)   **P-in-c** R S WILKINSON
WHINBURGH (St Mary)   see Barnham Broom and Upper Yare
  Nor
WHINLANDS Benefice, The St E 19   **P** Mrs A C V Wentworth,
  Ch Patr Trust, and Ch Soc Trust (by turn)   **R** C E BROOKS,
  NSM S E HART
WHINMOOR (St Paul)   see Seacroft Ripon
WHINNEY HILL (St Peter)   see Thrybergh Sheff
WHIPPINGHAM (St Mildred) w East Cowes Portsm 8
  P Ld Chan   **R** J HALL,   **NSM** V J HARDS
WHIPSNADE (St Mary Magdalene)   see Kensworth, Studham
  and Whipsnade St Alb
WHIPTON (St Boniface) Ex 3   **P** Bp   **P-in-c** J W BYATT
WHISSENDINE (St Andrew)   see Teigh w Whissendine and
  Market Overton Pet
WHISSONSETT (St Mary)   see Upper Wensum Village Gp Nor
WHISTON (St Mary Magdalene) Sheff 6   **P** Bp   **R** N BOWLER
WHISTON (St Mary the Virgin)   see Yardley Hastings, Denton
  and Grendon etc Pet
WHISTON (St Mildred)   see Kingsley and Foxt-w-Whiston Lich
WHISTON (St Nicholas) Liv 2   **P** V Prescot   **V** A J TELFER
WHITACRE, NETHER (St Giles)   see The Whitacres and
  Shustoke Birm
WHITACRE, OVER (St Leonard)   as above
WHITACRES and Shustoke, The Birm 9   **P** J K Wingfield
  Digby Esq (1 turn), Bp (2 turns), and Ld Chan (1 turn)
  R D COUTURE
WHITBECK (St Mary)   see Bootle, Corney, Whicham and
  Whitbeck Carl
WHITBOURNE (Bringsty Iron Church)   see Edvin Loach w
  Tedstone Delamere etc Heref
WHITBOURNE (St John the Baptist)   as above
WHITBURN (no dedication) Dur 16   **P** Bp   **R** K R SMITH
WHITBY (St Hilda) (St John) (St Mary) w Ruswarp York 22
  P Abp   **TR** D W SMITH,   **C** H N LAWRANCE
WHITBY (St Thomas)   see Ellesmere Port Ches
WHITBY ROAD (St Michael)   see Manor Park and Whitby
  Road Ox
WHITCHURCH (All Hallows) w Tufton and Litchfield Win 6
  P Bp   **V** K J INGLIS
WHITCHURCH (St Alkmund) Lich 22   **P** Bp   **R** A R RIDLEY
WHITCHURCH (St Andrew) Ex 25   **P** Bp   **NSM** M L DONNE
WHITCHURCH (St Augustine) (St Nicholas) Bris 1   **P** Bp
  V vacant (01275) 836505
WHITCHURCH (St Dubricius)   see Dixton, Wycsham,
  Bishopswood, Whitchurch etc Heref
WHITCHURCH (St John the Evangelist)   see Schorne Ox
WHITCHURCH (St Lawrence)   see Lt Stanmore St Lawr Lon
WHITCHURCH (St Mary the Virgin)   see Ilmington w Stretton-
  on-Fosse etc Cov

WHITCHURCH (St Mary the Virgin)　*see* Langtree *Ox*

WHITCHURCH CANONICORUM (St Candida and Holy Cross)　*see* Golden Cap Team *Sarum*

WHITCHURCH HILL (St John the Baptist)　*see* Langtree *Ox*

WHITE CITY ESTATE (St Michael and St George)　*see* Shepherd's Bush St Steph w St Thos *Lon*

WHITE COLNE (St Andrew)　*see* Halstead Area *Chelmsf*

WHITE HORSE, The *Sarum 17*　**P** *Bp*　**TR** J BURKE, **TV** M A DAVIES,　**C** J C TOTNEY,　**NSM** P J MCEUNE

WHITE LADIES ASTON (St John)　*see* Peopleton and White Ladies Aston w Churchill etc *Worc*

WHITE MOSS (St Mark)　*see* Blackley St Mark White Moss *Man*

WHITE NOTLEY (St Etheldreda)　*see* Fairstead w Terling and White Notley etc *Chelmsf*

WHITE RODING (St Martin)　*see* S Rodings *Chelmsf*

WHITE WALTHAM (St Mary the Virgin) w Shottesbrooke *Ox 13*　**P** *Sir John Smith*　**P-in-c** D N ANDREW, **NSM** A J HARTROPP

WHITE WELL (St Mary)　*see* St Paul's Walden *St Alb*

WHITECHAPEL (St James)　*see* Fellside Team *Blackb*

WHITEFIELD (St Andrew)　*see* Hillock *Man*

WHITEFRIARS (no dedication) Rushden *Pet 8*　**P** *CPAS* **V** P R EVANS

WHITEGATE (St Mary) w Little Budworth *Ches 6*　**P** *Bp, Lord Delamere and W R Cullimore Esq (alt)*　**V** L P EDEN

WHITEHALL (St Ambrose)　*see* E Bris St Ambrose and St Leon *Bris*

WHITEHALL PARK (St Andrew)　*see* Upper Holloway *Lon*

WHITEHAVEN (St James) *Carl 5*　**P** *Patr Bd* **TR** J L BANNISTER,　**Hon C** J D KELLY

WHITEHAWK (St Cuthman) *Chich 2*　**P** *Bp* **P-in-c** J D WRIGHT,　**NSM** D R S PORTER

WHITEHILLS (St Mark)　*see* Kingsthorpe w Northampton St Dav *Pet*

WHITELACKINGTON (The Blessed Virgin Mary)　*see* Ilminster and Distr *B & W*

WHITELEAS (St Mary w St Martin)　*see* S Shields All SS *Dur*

WHITELEY Conventional District *Portsm 2*　**C-in-c** L E SNAPE, **NSM** G J S SNAPE

WHITEPARISH (All Saints)　*see* Clarendon *Sarum*

WHITESHILL (St Paul) and Randwick *Glouc 5*　**P** *Bp* **V** B WOOLLASTON

WHITESTAUNTON (St Andrew) *B & W 15*　**P** *Personal Reps Gp Capt N W D Marwood-Elton*　**P-in-c** A J WOODWARD, **C** J T TYLER

WHITESTONE (St Catherine)　*see* Tedburn St Mary, Whitestone, Oldridge etc *Ex*

WHITESTONE PATHFINDER (St John the Evangelist)　*as above*

WHITEWATER Benefice, The *Win 5*　**P** *Bp and New Coll Ox (alt)*　**R** P F QUINNELL,　**C** M I ASHTON, **NSM** P B HEWLETT-SMITH

WHITEWELL (St Mary)　*see* Marbury w Tushingham and Whitewell *Ches*

WHITEWELL (St Michael)　*see* Chipping and Whitewell *Blackb*

WHITFIELD (Holy Trinity)　*see* Allendale w Whitfield *Newc*

WHITFIELD (St James) (St Luke) *Derby 6*　**P** *Bp* **V** C COOPER,　**C** T P CLARK, R A ENGLAND

WHITFIELD (St John)　*see* Allendale w Whitfield *Newc*

WHITFIELD (St John the Evangelist)　*see* Astwell Gp *Pet*

WHITFIELD (St Peter) w Guston *Cant 4*　**P** *Abp and D&C (alt)* **P-in-c** B E WAY

WHITFORD (St Mary at the Cross)　*see* Kilmington, Stockland, Dalwood, Yarcombe etc *Ex*

WHITGIFT (St Mary Magdalene)　*see* The Marshland *Sheff*

WHITGREAVE (St John the Evangelist)　*see* Stafford *Lich*

WHITKIRK (St Mary) *Ripon 8*　**P** *Meynell Trustees* **V** I C BLACK,　**C** S EARLE

WHITLEIGH St Chad *Ex 23*　**P** *Bp*　**P-in-c** T THORP, **C** D R BAILEY

WHITLEY (Christ Church)　*see* Reading Ch Ch *Ox*

WHITLEY (St Helen) *Newc 10*　**P** *Bp*　**V** A J PATTERSON

WHITLEY (St James) *Cov 1*　**P** *Bp*　**NSM** P A STOTE

WHITLEY, LOWER or NETHER (St Luke)　*see* Antrobus, Aston by Sutton, Lt Leigh etc *Ches*

WHITLEY BRIDGE (All Saints)　*see* Knottingley and Kellington w Whitley *Wakef*

WHITLEY LOWER (St Mary and St Michael)　*see* Thornhill and Whitley Lower *Wakef*

WHITMINSTER (St Andrew)　*see* Eastington, Frocester, Haresfield etc *Glouc*

WHITMORE (St Mary and All Saints)　*see* Chapel Chorlton, Maer and Whitmore *Lich*

WHITNASH (St Margaret) *Cov 11*　**P** *Lord Leigh* **R** R W S SUFFERN,　**OLM** S D BATE

WHITNEY (St Peter and St Paul)　*see* Eardisley w Bollingham, Willersley, Brilley etc *Heref*

WHITSBURY (St Leonard)　*see* W Downland *Sarum*

WHITSTABLE (All Saints) (St Alphage) (St Andrew) (St Peter) *Cant 7*　**P** *DBP*　**TR** S J CONEYS,　**TV** S C TILLOTSON, R C WEBBLEY,　**C** C N RUDD,　**Hon C** D A IRVINE, **OLM** A L MORETON

WHITSTONE (St Anne)　*see* Week St Mary Circle of Par *Truro*

WHITTINGHAM (St Bartholomew) and Edlingham w Bolton Chapel *Newc 6*　**P** *D&C Carl and D&C Dur (alt)* **V** M D CATLING

WHITTINGTON (Christ Church)　*see* Wretton w Stoke Ferry and Whittington *Ely*

WHITTINGTON (St Bartholomew) *Derby 5*　**P** *Bp*　**R** *vacant* (01246) 450651

WHITTINGTON (St Bartholomew)　*see* Sevenhampton w Charlton Abbots, Hawling etc *Glouc*

WHITTINGTON (St Giles) w Weeford *Lich 1*　**P** *Bp* **V** F A HASKETT,　**Hon C** C M J IBALL

WHITTINGTON (St John the Baptist) *Lich 19*　**P** *Mrs P Hamilton Hill*　**R** D R NORTH

WHITTINGTON (St Michael the Archangel)　*see* Hornby w Claughton and Whittington etc *Blackb*

WHITTINGTON (St Philip and St James)　*see* Worc SE *Worc*

WHITTINGTON, NEW (St Barnabas) *Derby 5*　**P** *Bp* **V** *vacant* (01246) 455830

WHITTLE-LE-WOODS (St John the Evangelist) *Blackb 4*　**P** *V Leyland*　**V** A L WINSTANLEY,　**C** T A DONAGHEY

WHITTLEBURY (St Mary)　*see* Silverstone and Abthorpe w Slapton etc *Pet*

WHITTLESEY (St Andrew) (St Mary), Pondersbridge and Coates *Ely 11*　**P** *Ld Chan (2 turns), Patr Bd (1 turn)* **TR** N A WHITEHOUSE,　**TV** G STEVENS,　**NSM** M B JONES

WHITTLESFORD Local Ecumenical Partnership *Ely 7 vacant*

WHITTLESFORD (St Mary and St Andrew) *Ely 5*　**P** *Jes Coll Cam*　**V** *vacant* (01223) 833382

WHITTON *Sarum 18*　**P** *Patr Bd*　**NSM** E A MASSEY

WHITTON (St Augustine of Canterbury) *Lon 10*　**P** *Bp* **NSM** A CLARRIDGE

WHITTON (St John the Baptist)　*see* Alkborough *Linc*

WHITTON (St Mary)　*see* Burford II w Greete and Hope Bagot *Heref*

WHITTON (St Mary and St Botolph) and Thurleston w Akenham *St E 4*　**P** *Bp (2 turns), Exors G K Drury Esq (1 turn)*　**R** A S DOTCHIN,　**NSM** M N C SOKANOVIC

WHITTON (St Philip and St James) *Lon 10*　**P** *V Twickenham St Mary*　**V** J V MOWBRAY,　**NSM** V F FRAY

WHITTONSTALL (St Philip and St James) *Newc 9*　**P** *D&C* **P-in-c** D J IRVINE,　**NSM** J LYNCH

WHITWELL (St John the Evangelist) w Crambe and Foston *York 6*　**P** *Abp*　**P-in-c** I R HOWITT

WHITWELL (St Lawrence) *Derby 3*　**P** *Bp*　**P-in-c** D J HULL

WHITWELL (St Mary)　*see* St Paul's Walden *St Alb*

WHITWELL (St Mary and St Rhadegunde) *Portsm 7*　**P** *Bp* **V** S E LLOYD,　**NSM** V M HEENAN

WHITWELL (St Michael and All Angels)　*see* Reepham, Hackford w Whitwell, Kerdiston etc *Nor*

WHITWELL (St Michael and All Angels)　*see* Empingham and Exton w Horn w Whitwell *Pet*

WHITWICK (St John the Baptist) *Leic 8*　**P** *Duchy of Lanc* **P-in-c** A J BURGESS,　**Hon C** R J SEAMAN

WHITWOOD (All Saints)　*see* Castleford *Wakef*

WHITWORTH (not known)　*see* Spennymoor and Whitworth *Dur*

WHITWORTH (not known)　*see* St Pet Ho *Man*

WHITWORTH (St Bartholomew) w Facit *Man 21*　**P** *Bp and Keble Coll Ox (jt)*　**OLM** A P WALLBANK

WHIXALL (St Mary)　*see* Edstaston, Fauls, Prees, Tilstock and Whixall *Lich*

WHIXLEY (Ascension)　*see* Gt and Lt Ouseburn w Marton cum Grafton etc *Ripon*

WHORLTON (Holy Cross Old Church) w Carlton and Faceby *York 21*　**P** *Mrs A P F Kynge*　**V** L M SHIPP, **NSM** P J JOHNSON

WHORLTON (St John the Evangelist) *Newc 4*　**P** *Bp* **V** A D BOWDEN,　**C** R M PADDISON

WHORLTON (St Mary)　*see* Barnard Castle w Whorlton *Dur*

WHYKE (St George) w Rumboldswhyke St Mary and Portfield All Saints *Chich 3*　**P** *Bp*　**R** S W CRADDUCK,　**Hon C** J RHODES-WRIGLEY

WHYTELEAFE (St Luke)　*see* Caterham *S'wark*

WIBTOFT (Assumption of Our Lady)　*see* Upper Soar *Leic*

WICHENFORD (St Lawrence)　*see* Worcs W *Worc*

WICK (All Saints)　*see* Littlehampton and Wick *Chich*

WICK (St Bartholomew) w Doynton and Dyrham *Bris 5*

P *Simeon's Trustees, Ld Chan, and M H W Blaythwayt Esq*
(by turn)   **P-in-c** T J K BELL

WICK (St Mary)   *see* Pershore w Pinvin, Wick and Birlingham
Worc

WICK ST LAWRENCE (St Lawrence)   *see* Kewstoke w Wick
St Lawrence *B & W*

WICKEN (St John the Evangelist)   *see* Potterspury w Furtho
and Yardley Gobion etc *Pet*

WICKEN (St Laurence)   *see* Soham and Wicken *Ely*

WICKEN BONHUNT (St Margaret)   *see* Clavering and
Langley w Arkesden etc *Chelmsf*

WICKENBY (St Peter and St Laurence)   *see* Wragby Gp *Linc*

WICKERSLEY (St Alban) *Sheff 6*   P *DBP*   **R** P J HUGHES

WICKFORD (St Andrew) (St Catherine) and Runwell *Chelmsf 6*
P *Patr Bd*   **TR** P G KEARNS,   **TV** J H DELFGOU,
A T FRANKLAND,   **C** G F HOPKINS

WICKHAM (St Nicholas)   *see* Shedfield and Wickham *Portsm*

WICKHAM (St Swithun)   *see* Welford w Wickham and Gt
Shefford, Boxford etc *Ox*

WICKHAM, EAST (St Michael the Archangel) *S'wark 6*
P *D&C*   **V** M HUME,   **OLM** I J THOMAS

WICKHAM, WEST (St Francis) (St Mary of Nazareth)
S'wark 19   P *Bp*   **V** M R MCKINNEY

WICKHAM, WEST (St John) *S'wark 19*   P *Bp*   **V** T D GILES,
OLM K J D GAVED

WICKHAM, WEST (St Mary)   *see* Balsham, Weston Colville,
W Wickham etc *Ely*

WICKHAM BISHOPS (St Bartholomew) w Little Braxted
Chelmsf 23   P *Bp (3 turns), CCC Cam (1 turn)*
P-in-c S W BATTEN,   **NSM** I R BENDREY

WICKHAM MARKET (All Saints) w Pettistree *St E 18*
P *Ch Trust Fund Trust and Ld Chan (alt)*   **V** J F ELDRIDGE

WICKHAM SKEITH (St Andrew)   *see* Bacton w Wyverstone,
Cotton and Old Newton etc *St E*

WICKHAM ST PAUL (St Paul and All Saints)   *see* N Hinckford
Chelmsf

WICKHAMBREAUX (St Andrew)   *see* Littlebourne and
Ickham w Wickhambreaux etc *Cant*

WICKHAMBROOK (All Saints)   *see* Bansfield *St E*

WICKHAMFORD (St John the Baptist)   *see* Broadway w
Wickhamford *Worc*

WICKHAMPTON (St Andrew)   *see* Freethorpe, Wickhampton,
Halvergate etc *Nor*

WICKLEWOOD (All Saints)   *see* High Oak, Hingham and
Scoulton w Wood Rising *Nor*

WICKMERE (St Andrew)   *see* Lt Barningham, Blickling,
Edgefield etc *Nor*

WICKWAR (Holy Trinity), Rangeworthy and Hillesley *Glouc 6*
P *Bp and Earl of Ducie (jt)*   **R** D J RUSSELL

WIDCOMBE   *see* Bath Widcombe *B & W*

WIDDINGTON (St Mary)   *see* Newport and Widdington
Chelmsf

WIDDRINGTON (Holy Trinity) *Newc 11*   P *Bp*
V H M BARTON

WIDDRINGTON STATION (St Mary)   *see* Ulgham *Newc*

WIDECOMBE-IN-THE-MOOR (St Pancras)   *see* Ashburton,
Bickington, Buckland in the Moor etc *Ex*

WIDEMOUTH BAY (Our Lady and St Anne)   *see* Week
St Mary Circle of Par *Truro*

WIDFORD (St John the Baptist)   *see* Hunsdon w Widford and
Wareside *St Alb*

WIDFORD (St Mary) (Holy Spirit) *Chelmsf 9*   P *CPAS*
R D R W ROBBINS

WIDFORD (St Oswald)   *see* Burford w Fulbrook, Taynton,
Asthall etc *Ox*

WIDMER END (Good Shepherd)   *see* Hazlemere *Ox*

WIDMERPOOL (St Peter)   *see* Willoughby-on-the-Wolds w
Wysall and Widmerpool *S'well*

WIDNES (St Ambrose) *Liv 13*   P *Trustees*   **V** J P LEFFLER

WIDNES (St John) *Liv 13*   P *Bp and V Farnworth (jt)*
V D J GAIT

WIDNES (St Mary) (St Paul) *Liv 13*   P *Bp*   **V** *vacant* 0151-424
2221

WIDWORTHY (St Cuthbert)   *see* Offwell, Northleigh, Farway,
Cotleigh etc *Ex*

WIELD (St James) *Win 2*   P *Ld Chan*   **R** *vacant* (01420)
562050

WIGAN (All Saints) (St George) *Liv 14*   P *Bp*
R R J HUTCHINSON,   **C** J E HAWORTH

WIGAN (St Andrew) *Liv 14*   P *R Wigan*   **V** C HURST

WIGAN (St Anne) *Liv 14*   P *Bp*   **P-in-c** D J BURY

WIGAN (St Barnabas) Marsh Green   *see* Marsh Green w
Newtown *Liv*

WIGAN (St Catharine)   *see* Ince Ch Ch w Wigan St Cath *Liv*

WIGAN (St James) (St Thomas) *Liv 14*   P *R Wigan and Bp (jt)*
V H A F YOUNG

WIGAN (St John the Baptist) New Springs   *see* New Springs and
Whelley *Liv*

WIGAN (St Michael and All Angels) *Liv 14*   P *R Wigan*
V L MCGREGOR,   **NSM** S HIGGINSON

WIGAN (St Stephen) Whelley   *see* New Springs and Whelley *Liv*

WIGBOROUGH, GREAT (St Stephen)   *see* Peldon w Gt and
Lt Wigborough *Chelmsf*

WIGBOROUGH, LITTLE (St Nicholas)   *as above*

WIGGATON (St Edward the Confessor)   *see* Ottery St Mary,
Alfington, W Hill, Tipton etc *Ex*

WIGGENHALL ST GERMANS (St Mary the Virgin)   *see* E
Marshland *Ely*

WIGGENHALL ST MARY (St Mary Magdalene)   *as above*

WIGGINTON (St Bartholomew)   *see* Northchurch and
Wigginton *St Alb*

WIGGINTON (St Giles)   *see* Hook Norton w Gt Rollright,
Swerford etc *Ox*

WIGGINTON (St Leonard) (St James) *Lich 4*   P *V Tamworth*
P-in-c M D GELDARD,   **NSM** R DAVIES

WIGGINTON (St Nicholas)   *see* Haxby and Wigginton *York*

WIGGLESWORTH (School)   *see* Giggleswick and Rathmell w
Wigglesworth *Bradf*

WIGGONHOLT (not known)   *see* Amberley w N Stoke and
Parham, Wiggonholt etc *Chich*

WIGHILL (All Saints)   *see* Healaugh w Wighill, Bilbrough and
Askham Richard *York*

WIGHTON (All Saints)   *see* Holkham w Egmere w Warham,
Wells and Wighton *Nor*

WIGMORE (St James the Apostle)   *see* Wigmore Abbey *Heref*

WIGMORE ABBEY *Heref 7*   P *Trustees*   **R** M D CATLING

WIGSLEY   *see* Harby w Thorney and N and S Clifton *S'well*

WIGSTON, SOUTH (St Thomas)   *see* Glen Parva and S
Wigston *Leic*

WIGSTON MAGNA (All Saints) (St Wistan) *Leic 4*
P *Haberdashers' Co*   **P-in-c** L R CURTIS,   **C** S D MONK

WIGSTON PARVA (St Mary the Virgin)   *see* Sapcote and
Sharnford w Wigston Parva *Leic*

WIGTOFT (St Peter and St Paul)   *see* Sutterton and Wigtoft
Linc

WIGTON (St Mary) *Carl 3*   P *Bp*   **V** G P RAVALDE

WIKE (School Room)   *see* Bardsey *Ripon*

WILBARSTON (All Saints)   *see* Stoke Albany w Wilbarston
and Ashley etc *Pet*

WILBERFOSS (St John the Baptist) w Kexby *York 5*
P *Viscount de Vesci and Lord Egremont (alt)*

WILBRAHAM, GREAT (St Nicholas) *Ely 4*   P *DBP*
V R E JONES

WILBRAHAM, LITTLE (St John) *Ely 4*   P *CCC Cam*
R R E JONES

WILBURTON (St Peter) *Ely 8*   P *Adn Ely*
V F E G BRAMPTON,   **NSM** E P ABRAHAM

WILBURY (St Thomas) *St Alb 4*   P *Bp*   **V** B E C PATE

WILBY (All Saints)   *see* Quidenham Gp *Nor*

WILBY (St Mary) *see* Laxfield, Cratfield, Wilby and Brundish
St E

WILBY (St Mary the Virgin)   *see* Gt Doddington and Wilby *Pet*

WILCOT (Holy Cross)   *see* Pewsey and Swanborough *Sarum*

WILCOTE (St Peter)   *see* Forest Edge *Ox*

WILDBOARCLOUGH (St Saviour)   *see* Bosley and N Rode w
Wincle and Wildboarclough *Ches*

WILDEN (All Saints)   *see* Stourport and Wilden *Worc*

WILDEN (St Nicholas) w Colmworth and Ravensden *St Alb 15*
P *Ld Chan, Bp, and DBP (by turn)*   **R** S MORTON

WILFORD (St Wilfrid) *S'well 9*   P *Lt Col Peter Clifton*
P-in-c P E MARSH,   **C** J E TREGALE, D R TREGALE,
NSM M R SMITH

WILFORD HILL (St Paul) *S'well 9*   P *DBP*   **V** *vacant*
0115-923 3492

WILFORD PENINSULA, The *St E 7*   P *Patr Bd*
TR D J MURDOCH,   **TV** J P LEAVER, J M ANDREWS

WILKSBY (All Saints)   *see* Fen and Hill Gp *Linc*

WILLAND (St Mary the Virgin)   *see* Cullompton, Willand,
Uffculme, Kentisbeare etc *Ex*

WILLASTON (Christ Church) *Ches 9*   P *DBF*   **V** R W DENT

WILLASTON (St Luke)   *see* Wistaston *Ches*

WILLEN (St Mary Magdalene)   *see* Stantonbury and Willen *Ox*

WILLENHALL (Holy Trinity) *Lich 28*   P *Patr Bd*
TR M S HATHORNE,   **TV** J D DEAKIN,   **NSM** C A HATHORNE

WILLENHALL (St Anne) *Lich 28*   P *Mrs L Grant-Wilson*
P-in-c L A W SWABY

WILLENHALL (St Giles) *Lich 28*   P *Trustees*   **V** *vacant*
(01902) 605722

WILLENHALL (St John the Divine) *Cov 1*   P *V Cov H Trin*
V K R SCOTT,   **NSM** N C A SCOTT, D HISCOX

WILLENHALL (St Stephen) *Lich 28*   P *Bp*   **V** G E T BENNETT

WILLERBY (St Luke) *see* Kirk Ella and Willerby *York*
WILLERBY (St Peter) w Ganton and Folkton *York 15*
  P *M H Wrigley Esq, MMCET, and the Revd C G Day (by turn)*
  P-in-c K G F HOLDING
WILLERSEY (St Peter) *see* Mickleton, Willersey, Saintbury etc
  Glouc
WILLESBOROUGH (St Mary the Virgin) *Cant 10* **P** *D&C*
  P-in-c J C N MACKENZIE, **NSM** L J SCHRYVER
WILLESDEN (St Mark) *see* Kensal Rise St Mark and St
  Martin *Lon*
WILLESDEN (St Martin) *as above*
WILLESDEN (St Mary) *Lon 21* **P** *D&C St Paul's*
  V D C CLUES, **NSM** H R F O'GARRO
WILLESDEN (St Matthew) *Lon 21* **P** *Bp* **V** D R HUMPHREYS
WILLESDEN (St Michael and All Angels) *see* Stonebridge St
  Mich *Lon*
WILLESDEN GREEN (St Andrew) (St Francis of Assisi)
  Lon 21 **P** *Bp* **V** C P M PATTERSON, **Hon C** J O KYEI-
  BAFFOUR
WILLEY (St Leonard) *see* Churchover w Willey *Cov*
WILLIAN (All Saints) *see* Letchworth St Paul w Willian *St Alb*
WILLINGALE (St Christopher) *see* Fyfield, Moreton w
  Bobbingworth etc *Chelmsf*
WILLINGDON (St Mary the Virgin) *Chich 16* **P** *D&C*
  V M G ONIONS, **C** D G CHARLES
WILLINGDON, LOWER (St Wilfrid) Conventional District
  Chich 16 **C-in-c** A M TUCKER
WILLINGHAM (St Mary and All Saints) *Ely 6* **P** *Bp*
  R *vacant* (01954) 261225
WILLINGHAM, NORTH (St Thomas) *see* Walesby *Linc*
WILLINGHAM, SOUTH (St Martin) *see* Barkwith Gp *Linc*
WILLINGHAM BY STOW (St Helen) *see* Stow Gp *Linc*
WILLINGTON (St Lawrence) *see* Cople, Moggerhanger and
  Willington *St Alb*
WILLINGTON (St Michael) *Derby 16* **P** *CPAS*
  V S A STARKEY
WILLINGTON (St Stephen) and Sunnybrow *Dur 9*
  P *R Brancepeth* **R** *vacant* (01388) 746242
WILLINGTON Team, The (Good Shepherd) (St Mary the
  Virgin) (St Paul) *Newc 5* **P** *Prime Min* **TR** R D HINDLEY,
  TV J E APPLEBY, **C** H C GREENWOOD
WILLINGTON QUAY (St Paul) *see* Willington *Newc*
WILLISHAM (St Mary) *see* Somersham w Flowton and Offton
  w Willisham *St E*
WILLITON (St Peter) *B & W 17* **P** *V Watchet* **V** R J ALLEN,
  C F M B GUTTRIDGE
WILLOUGHBY (St Helen) *Linc 8* **P** *Baroness Willoughby*
  de Eresby, Ball Coll Ox, and Bp (jt) **R** D C ROBINSON
WILLOUGHBY (St Nicholas) *see* Leam Valley *Cov*
WILLOUGHBY-ON-THE-WOLDS (St Mary and All Saints) w
  Wysall and Widerpool *S'well 8* **P** *MMCET*
  P-in-c S D HIPPISLEY-COX
WILLOUGHBY WATERLEYS (St Mary), Peatling Magna and
  Ashby Magna *Leic 7* **P** *Bp* **R** *vacant* (01455) 209406
WILLOUGHTON (St Andrew) *see* Glentworth Gp *Linc*
WILMCOTE (St Andrew) *see* Aston Cantlow and Wilmcote w
  Billesley *Cov*
WILMINGTON (St Mary and St Peter) *see* Arlington,
  Folkington and Wilmington *Chich*
WILMINGTON (St Michael) *Roch 2* **P** *D&C* **V** R ARDING,
  Hon C P J IVESON, **NSM** T WYATT
WILMSLOW (St Bartholomew) *Ches 12* **P** *Bp* **R** P A SMITH,
  C M M SMITH, **NSM** A A YATES, C J LEES
WILNE (St Chad) and Draycott w Breaston *Derby 13* **P** *Bp*
  R C J SMEDLEY, **NSM** R M THOMPSON
WILNECOTE (Holy Trinity) *Lich 4* **P** *V Tamworth*
  V O HARRISON, **NSM** S M ROSSETER, **OLM** C J ROBINSON
WILSDEN (St Matthew) *see* Harden and Wilsden *Bradf*
WILSFORD (St Mary) *see* Ancaster Wilsford Gp *Linc*
WILSFORD (St Michael) *see* Woodford Valley *Sarum*
WILSFORD (St Nicholas) *see* Redhorn *Sarum*
WILSHAMSTEAD (All Saints) and Houghton Conquest
  St Alb 13 **P** *St Jo Coll Cam and Bp (alt)* **V** S J TOZE,
  NSM R C WHITE
WILSHAW (St Mary) *see* Meltham *Wakef*
WILSILL (St Michael and All Angels) *see* Upper Nidderdale
  Ripon
WILSTHORPE (St Faith) *see* Uffington Gp *Linc*
WILSTONE (St Cross) *see* Tring *St Alb*
WILTON (St Cuthbert) *York 16* **P** *Abp* **V** R E HARRISON
WILTON (St George) *B & W 18* **P** *Mrs E C Cutbush*
  V N J TAYLOR, **C** J C N GAY, **NSM** J A JEFFERY
WILTON (St George) *see* Thornton Dale w Allerston,
  Ebberston etc *York*
WILTON (St Mary and St Nicholas) w Netherhampton and

Fugglestone *Sarum 12* **P** *Earl of Pembroke*
  P-in-c M R WOOD, **C** L J SWEET
WILTON PLACE (St Paul) *Lon 3* **P** *Bp* **V** A G GYLE,
  C R K R COLES, **Hon C** N S MERCER
WIMBISH (All Saints) *see* Debden and Wimbish w Thunderley
  Chelmsf
WIMBLEDON (Emmanuel) Ridgway Proprietary Chapel
  S'wark 13 **Min** J J M FLETCHER, **C** P R DAWSON,
  A T J BYFIELD, **NSM** R J COEKIN, J C NEWCOMBE
WIMBLEDON (St Luke) *see* Wimbledon Park St Luke *S'wark*
WIMBLEDON (St Mary) (St Matthew) (St Mark) (St John the
  Baptist) *S'wark 13* **P** *Patr Bd* **TR** M E BIDE, **TV** S G LEE,
  R M SEWELL, **C** M A BOOTH, **NSM** H A JOHNSON,
  C JACKSON, B W RICKARDS
WIMBLEDON, SOUTH (All Saints) *S'wark 13* **P** *Bp*
  P-in-c M O BLACKMAN, **NSM** C W NOKE
WIMBLEDON, SOUTH (Holy Trinity and St Peter)
  see Merton Priory *S'wark*
WIMBLEDON, SOUTH (St Andrew) *S'wark 13* **P** *Bp*
  V A D WAKEFIELD
WIMBLEDON, WEST (Christ Church) *S'wark 13*
  P *TR Wimbledon* **V** R P LANE
WIMBLEDON PARK (St Luke) *S'wark 13* **P** *Simeon's*
  Trustees **V** R J R PAICE, **Hon C** D J MIDDLETON
WIMBLEDON PARK (St Paul) *see* Wandsworth St Paul
  S'wark
WIMBLINGTON (St Peter) *see* Doddington w Benwick and
  Wimblington *Ely*
WIMBORNE (St John the Evangelist) *see* New Borough and
  Leigh *Sarum*
WIMBORNE MINSTER (St Cuthberga) *Sarum 9* **P** *Qu Eliz*
  Free Gr Sch **R** J E HOLBROOK, **C** D J TIGHE,
  NSM B GIBSON, T LOCKWOOD
WIMBORNE ST GILES (St Giles) *see* Cranborne w Boveridge,
  Edmondsham etc *Sarum*
WIMBOTSHAM (St Mary) w Stow Bardolph and Stow Bridge w
  Nordelph *Ely 9* **P** *Bp* **R** *vacant* (01366) 385713
WIMPOLE (St Andrew) *see* Orwell Gp *Ely*
WINCANTON (St Peter and St Paul) *B & W 2* **P** *D&C*
  R N C M FEAVER
WINCHAM (St Andrew) *see* Lostock Gralam *Ches*
WINCHCOMBE (St Peter) *Glouc 13* **P** *Patr Bd*
  TR P J PARTINGTON, **TV** J A NEWCOMBE, N M ARTHY,
  C J K WOODALL, **NSM** N A CARTER
WINCHELSEA (St Thomas) (St Richard) and Icklesham
  Chich 20 **P** *Bp and Guild of All So (jt)* **R** H A S COCKS,
  Hon C A H M COX
WINCHENDON, NETHER (St Nicholas) *see* Long Crendon
  w Chearsley and Nether Winchendon *Ox*
WINCHENDON, OVER (St Mary Magdalene) *see* Schorne *Ox*
WINCHESTER (All Saints) *see* E Win *Win*
WINCHESTER (Christ Church) *Win 7* **P** *Simeon's Trustees*
  V D G WILLIAMS, **NSM** B R WAKELIN, D F FENTON
WINCHESTER (Holy Trinity) *Win 7* **P** *Bp* **R** *vacant* (01962)
  863891
WINCHESTER (St Barnabas) *Win 7* **P** *Bp*
  P-in-c T H ROBERTS
WINCHESTER (St Cross Hospital w St Faith) *Win 7* **P** *Bp*,
  R C SWEET **P-in-c** M HARLEY, **Hon C** S S M DAVIES
WINCHESTER (St John the Baptist w St Martin Winnall) *see* E
  Win *Win*
WINCHESTER (St Lawrence) St Maurice (St Swithun-upon-
  Kingsgate) *Win 7* **P** *Ld Chan* **R** D V SCOTT
WINCHESTER (St Luke) *see* Stanmore *Win*
WINCHESTER St Matthew St Paul's Mission Church *Win 7*
  P *Bp* **P-in-c** N P SEAL, **NSM** N W BIRKETT
WINCHESTER, EAST *Win 7* **P** *Bp and Ld Chan (alt)*
  R P A KENNEDY, **C** S J COLLIER
WINCHESTER HYDE (St Bartholomew) *Win 7* **P** *Ld Chan*
  P-in-c C J BANNISTER, **NSM** A GOULDING
WINCHFIELD (St Mary the Virgin) *see* Hartley Wintney,
  Elvetham, Winchfield etc *Win*
WINCHMORE HILL (Holy Trinity) *Lon 18* **P** *V Winchmore*
  Hill St Paul **V** A J HOMER
WINCHMORE HILL (St Andrew) *see* Amersham *Ox*
WINCHMORE HILL (St Paul) *Lon 18* **P** *V Edmonton*
  V J M PAUL, **C** E N TURNER
WINCLE (St Michael) *see* Bosley and N Rode w Wincle and
  Wildboarclough *Ches*
WINCOBANK (St Thomas) *see* Brightside w Wincobank *Sheff*
WINDERMERE (St Martin) and St John *Carl 11* **P** *Bp and*
  Trustees (jt) **R** J J RICHARDS, **C** D J FRANKLIN
WINDERMERE (St Mary) Applethwaite and Troutbeck *Carl 11*
  P *Bp* **V** D M B WILMOT, **C** B T STREETER
WINDHILL (Christ Church) *Bradf 1* **P** *Bp*
  NSM M J ALLISON

WINDLESHAM (St John the Baptist) *Guildf 6* **P** *Ld Chan*
OLM J A LEWIS
WINDRUSH (St Peter) *see* Sherborne, Windrush, the
Barringtons etc *Glouc*
WINDRUSH, LOWER *Ox 8* **P** *Bp, DBP, St Jo Coll Ox,*
D&C Ex, and B Babington-Smith Esq (jt) **R** S E SHARP
WINDSOR, NEW (Holy Trinity) (St John the Baptist w All
Saints) *Ox 13* **P** *Ld Chan* **TV** M J BARNES,
P-in-c A L SWIFT, **Hon C** D I DADSWELL, **OLM** J M QUICK,
J FAULKNER
WINDSOR, OLD (St Luke's Mission Room) (St Peter and
St Andrew) *Ox 13* **P** *Ld Chan* **V** vacant (01753) 865778
WINDY NOOK (St Alban) *see* Heworth St Alb *Dur*
WINESTEAD (St German) *see* Patrington w Hollym, Welwick
and Winestead *York*
WINFARTHING (St Mary) w Shelfanger w Burston w Gissing
and Tivetshall *Nor 10* **P** *Ld Chan, Bp, and DBP (jt), Hertf*
Coll Ox (alt) **R** D F MILLS
WINFORD (Blessed Virgin Mary and St Peter) w Felton
Common Hill *B & W 10* **P** *Worc Coll Ox and*
Mrs H D Pullman (jt) **P-in-c** P STEPHENS
WINFORTON (St Michael and All Angels) *see* Eardisley w
Bollingham, Willersley, Brilley etc *Heref*
WINFRITH NEWBURGH (St Christopher) *see* The
Lulworths, Winfrith Newburgh and Chaldon *Sarum*
WING (St Peter and St Paul) *see* Preston and Ridlington w
Wing and Pilton *Pet*
WING w Grove (All Saints) *Ox 26* **P** *Bp*
P-in-c D W F WITCHELL, **OLM** S TUNNICLIFFE
WINGATE GRANGE (Holy Trinity) *see* Wheatley Hill and
Wingate w Hutton Henry *Dur*
WINGATES (St John the Evangelist) *see* Westhoughton and
Wingates *Man*
WINGERWORTH (All Saints) *Derby 5* **P** *Bp* **R** J M WHITE
WINGFIELD (St Andrew) *see* Hoxne w Denham, Syleham and
Wingfield *St E*
WINGFIELD (St Mary) *see* Westwood and Wingfield *Sarum*
WINGFIELD, NORTH (St Lawrence), Clay Cross and Pilsley
Derby 5 **P** *Bp* **TR** C E BERESFORD, **TV** L S LIVERSIDGE,
C C R BURROWS, R G LAWRENCE, M R BROOMHEAD
WINGFIELD, SOUTH (All Saints) *see* Crich and S Wingfield
Derby
WINGHAM (St Mary the Virgin) w Elmstone and Preston w
Stourmouth *Cant 1* **P** *Lord Fitzwalter and D&C (alt)*
V vacant (01227) 721530
WINGRAVE (St Peter and St Paul) w Rowsham, Aston Abbotts
and Cublington *Ox 26* **P** *Bp and Linc Coll Ox (jt)*
P-in-c D W F WITCHELL, **OLM** S TUNNICLIFFE
WINKBURN (St John of Jerusalem) *S'well 15* **P** *Bp* **V** vacant
WINKFIELD (St Mary the Virgin) and Cranbourne *Ox 11*
P *Bp* **V** C BLUNDELL, **NSM** I N JAMES
WINKLEBURY (Good Shepherd) and Worting *Win 4*
P *MMCET* **R** C J M VAUGHAN
WINKLEIGH (All Saints) *Ex 20* **P** *D&C* **V** P J NORMAN
WINKSLEY (St Cuthbert and St Oswald) *see* Fountains Gp
Ripon
WINLATON (St Paul) *Dur 13* **P** *Bp* **P-in-c** G W R HARPER
WINMARLEIGH (St Luke) *see* Cockerham w Winmarleigh
and Glasson *Blackb*
WINNERSH (St Mary the Virgin) *see* Hurst *Ox*
WINSCOMBE (St James) and Sandford *B & W 11* **P** *D&C*
V M J SLADE, **NSM** J M H SIMS
WINSFORD (St Mary Magdalene) *see* Exton and Winsford
and Cutcombe w Luxborough *B & W*
WINSHAM (St Stephen) *see* Chaffcombe, Cricket Malherbie
etc *B & W*
WINSHILL (St Mark) *Derby 16* **P** *Lady H M Gretton and*
Baroness Gretton (jt) **V** M M MOOKERJI
WINSLEY (St Nicholas) *see* Monkton Farleigh, S Wraxall and
Winsley *Sarum*
WINSLOW (St Laurence) w Great Horwood and Addington
Ox 24 **P** *Ld Chan (3 turns), New Coll Ox (2 turns), and DBP*
(1 turn) **R** B R SEARLE-BARNES, **C** A J HARWOOD,
NSM G E BALL
WINSON (St Michael) *see* Fairford Deanery *Glouc*
WINSTER (Holy Trinity) *Carl 10* **P** *V Kendal H Trin*
P-in-c M D WOODCOCK
WINSTER (St John the Baptist) *see* S Darley, Elton and Winster
Derby
WINSTON (St Andrew) *Dur 7* **P** *Bp* **P-in-c** M JACQUES
WINSTON (St Andrew) *see* Debenham and Helmingham *St E*
WINSTONE (St Bartholomew) *see* Brimpsfield w Birdlip, Syde,
Daglingworth etc *Glouc*
WINTERBORNE CLENSTON (St Nicholas) *see* Winterborne
Valley and Milton Abbas *Sarum*

WINTERBORNE HOUGHTON (St Andrew) *as above*
WINTERBORNE STICKLAND (St Mary) *as above*
WINTERBORNE VALLEY and Milton Abbas, The *Sarum 6*
P *Bp (3 turns) and P D H Chichester Esq (1 turn)*
V R N HUNGERFORD, **NSM** M C MILES, C M CHICHESTER
WINTERBORNE WHITECHURCH (St Mary)
see Winterborne Valley and Milton Abbas *Sarum*
WINTERBOURNE (St James) *see* Chieveley w Winterbourne
and Oare *Ox*
WINTERBOURNE (St Michael the Archangel) *Bris 5*
P *St Jo Coll Ox* **P-in-c** M A CLACKER
WINTERBOURNE ABBAS (St Mary) *see* The Winterbournes
and Compton Valence *Sarum*
WINTERBOURNE BASSETT (St Katharine) *see* Upper
Kennet *Sarum*
WINTERBOURNE DOWN (All Saints) *see* Frenchay and
Winterbourne Down *Bris*
WINTERBOURNE EARLS (St Michael and All Angels)
see Bourne Valley *Sarum*
WINTERBOURNE GUNNER (St Mary) *as above*
WINTERBOURNE KINGSTON (St Nicholas) *see* Red Post
Sarum
WINTERBOURNE MONKTON (St Mary Magdalene)
see Upper Kennet *Sarum*
WINTERBOURNE MONKTON (St Simon and St Jude)
see Dorchester *Sarum*
WINTERBOURNE ST MARTIN (St Martin) *see* The
Winterbournes and Compton Valence *Sarum*
WINTERBOURNE STEEPLETON (St Michael) *as above*
WINTERBOURNE STOKE (St Peter) *see* Wylye and Till
Valley *Sarum*
WINTERBOURNE ZELSTONE (St Mary) *see* Red Post
Sarum
WINTERBOURNES and Compton Valence, The *Sarum 1*
P *Adn Sherborne, Linc Coll Ox, and Sir Robert Williams Bt*
(by turn) **P-in-c** H W B STEPHENS, **Hon C** J H GOOD
WINTERBURN (Chapel of Ease) *see* Gargrave w Coniston
Cold *Bradf*
WINTERINGHAM (All Saints) *see* Alkborough *Linc*
WINTERSLOW (All Saints) *see* Clarendon *Sarum*
WINTERSLOW (St John) *as above*
WINTERTON Group, The (All Saints) *Linc 4* **P** *Lord*
St Oswald, Bp, and Exors Capt J G G P Elwes (jt)
V A C NUNN, **OLM** J J WHITEHEAD
WINTERTON (Holy Trinity and All Saints) *see* Flegg Coastal
Benefice *Nor*
WINTHORPE (All Saints) *see* Coddington and Winthorpe and
Langford w Holme *S'well*
WINTHORPE (St Mary) *see* Skegness Gp *Linc*
WINTON (St Mary Magdalene) *Man 2* **P** *Trustees*
P-in-c I A HALL
WINTRINGHAM (St Peter) *see* Buckrose Carrs *York*
WINWICK (All Saints) *Ely 10* **P** *Bp* **P-in-c** J DUCK
WINWICK (St Michael and All Angels) *see* W Haddon w
Winwick and Ravensthorpe *Pet*
WINWICK (St Oswald) *Liv 15* **P** *Bp* **R** R G LEWIS,
NSM M JONES
WIRKSWORTH (St Mary) *Derby 7* **P** *Bp* **TR** D C TRUBY,
TV G MANLEY, **C** A TAYLOR-COOK, **NSM** K J ORFORD
WISBECH (St Augustine) *Ely 14* **P** *Bp* **P-in-c** N K GARDNER
WISBECH (St Peter and St Paul) *Ely 14* **P** *Bp*
C N K GARDNER
WISBECH ST MARY (St Mary) and Guyhirn w Ring's End and
Gorefield and Southea w Murrow and Parson Drove *Ely 14*
P *Bp* **V** M L BRADBURY
WISBOROUGH GREEN (St Peter ad Vincula) *Chich 11*
P *Bp Lon* **V** S F E NEWHAM
WISHAW (St Chad) *see* Curdworth, Middleton and Wishaw
Birm
WISHFORD, GREAT (St Giles) *see* Wylye and Till Valley
Sarum
WISLEY (not known) w Pyrford *Guildf 12* **P** *Bp* **R** N J AIKEN,
C I M WALLACE, **OLM** C D GIBSON
WISSETT (St Andrew) *see* Blyth Valley *St E*
WISSINGTON (St Mary the Virgin) *see* Nayland w Wiston
St E
WISTANSTOW (Holy Trinity) *Heref 11* **P** *Bp*
P-in-c M L COPE
WISTASTON (St Mary) *Ches 15* **P** *Trustees*
R M F TURNBULL, **NSM** K H SAMBROOK
WISTOW (All Saints) *see* Cawood w Ryther and Wistow *York*
WISTOW (St John the Baptist) *see* Warboys w Broughton and
Bury w Wistow *Ely*
WISTOW (St Wistan) *Leic 4* **P** *Bp and The Hon Ann*
Brooks (jt) **V** P J O'REILLY

WITCHAM (St Martin) w Mepal *Ely 8* **P** *D&C* **R** J M AMEY

**WITCHAMPTON (St Mary and St Cuthberga and All Saints),
Stanbridge and Long Crichel w More Crichel** *Sarum 9* **P** *Hon
Mrs M A S E Marten* **P-in-c** J E HOLBROOK,
Hon C C L J FARMER

WITCHFORD (St Andrew) w Wentworth *Ely 8* **P** *D&C*
P-in-c F E G BRAMPTON, **NSM** T M DIXON, E P ABRAHAM

WITCHINGHAM GREAT (St Mary) *see* Wensum Benefice
Nor

WITCOMBE, GREAT (St Mary) *see* Badgeworth, Shurdington
and Witcombe w Bentham *Glouc*

WITHAM Group, The *Linc 14* **P** *Sir Lyonel Tollemache Bt, The
Revd J R H Thorold, J R Thorold Esq, and Bp (jt)*
P-in-c T W BROADBENT

WITHAM (St Nicholas) *Chelmsf 23* **P** *Patr Bd*
TR J M SUDDARDS, **TV** S F GARWOOD, **C** J E BENDREY

WITHAM, NORTH (St Mary) *see* Witham Gp *Linc*

WITHAM, SOUTH (St John the Baptist) *as above*

**WITHAM FRIARY (Blessed Virgin Mary and St John the Baptist
and All Saints)** *see* Nunney and Witham Friary, Marston
Bigot etc *B*

WITHAM-ON-THE-HILL (St Andrew) *see* Edenham w
Witham on the Hill and Swinstead *Linc*

WITHAMSIDE United Group *see* Bassingham Gp *Linc*

WITHCALL (St Martin) *see* Legbourne and Wold Marsh *Linc*

WITHERIDGE (St John the Baptist) *see* Burrington,
Chawleigh, Cheldon, Chulmleigh etc *Ex*

WITHERLEY (St Peter) *see* Fenn Lanes Gp *Leic*

**WITHERNSEA (St Nicholas) w Owthorne and Easington w
Skeffling and Holmpton** *York 12* **P** *Abp (1 turn), Ld Chan
(2 turns)* **R** S V COPE

WITHERNWICK (St Alban) *see* Aldbrough, Mappleton w
Goxhill and Withernwick *York*

WITHERSDALE (St Mary Magdalene) *see* Fressingfield,
Mendham etc *St E*

WITHERSFIELD (St Mary the Virgin) *see* Haverhill w
Withersfield *St E*

WITHERSLACK (St Paul) *Carl 10* **P** *DBP*
P-in-c M D WOODCOCK

WITHIEL (St Clement) *see* Roche and Withiel *Truro*

WITHIEL FLOREY (St Mary Magdalene) *see* Brompton Regis
w Upton and Skilgate *B & W*

WITHINGTON (St Christopher) *see* W Didsbury and
Withington St Chris *Man*

WITHINGTON (St Crispin) *Man 4* **P** *Bp* **P-in-c** P C S DAVIES

WITHINGTON (St John the Baptist) *see* Wrockwardine
Deanery *Lich*

WITHINGTON (St Michael and All Angels)
see Sevenhampton w Charlton Abbots, Hawling etc *Glouc*

WITHINGTON (St Paul) *Man 8* **P** *Trustees*
OLM R A W SMITH

WITHINGTON (St Peter) w Westhide *Heref 4* **P** *Bp*
P-in-c D J BOWEN

WITHINGTON, LOWER (St Peter) *see* Chelford w Lower
Withington *Ches*

WITHLEIGH (St Catherine) *see* Washfield, Stoodleigh,
Withleigh etc *Ex*

WITHNELL (St Paul) *see* Heapey and Withnell *Blackb*

WITHYBROOK (All Saints) *see* Wolvey w Burton Hastings,
Copston Magna etc *Cov*

WITHYCOMBE (St Nicholas) *see* Dunster, Carhampton,
Withycombe w Rodhuish etc *B & W*

**WITHYCOMBE RALEIGH (St John the Evangelist) (St John in
the Wilderness) (All Saints)** *Ex 1* **P** *Patr Bd* **TR** F A OSWIN,
TV S J HOYLE, T C SMYTH

WITHYHAM (St John the Evangelist) *see* Crowborough St Jo
Chich

WITHYHAM (St Michael and All Angels) *Chich 19* **P** *Earl
De la Warr* **P-in-c** A S LEAK

WITHYPOOL (St Andrew) *see* Exford, Exmoor, Hawkridge
and Withypool *B & W*

WITHYWOOD (shared church) *Bris 1* **P** *Bp*
V J M CARPENTER

WITLEY (All Saints) *Guildf 4* **P** *Bp* **V** B M SHAND,
OLM E A FRASER

WITLEY, GREAT (St Michael) *see* Shrawley, Witley, Astley
and Abberley *Worc*

WITLEY, LITTLE (St Michael) *as above*

WITNESHAM (St Mary) *see* Westerfield and Tuddenham w
Witnesham *St E*

WITNEY (St Mary the Virgin) (Holy Trinity) *Ox 8* **P** *Patr Bd*
TV E J THOMSON, **Hon C** J H COOK,
NSM J R COLLICUTT MCGRATH, **OLM** C TITCOMB

WITTENHAM, LITTLE (St Peter) *see* Dorchester *Ox*

WITTERING (All Saints) *see* Ketton, Collyweston, Easton-on-
the-Hill etc *Pet*

WITTERING, EAST (St Anne) *see* Earnley and E Wittering
Chich

**WITTERING, WEST (St Peter and St Paul) and Birdham w
Itchenor** *Chich 3* **P** *Bp* **R** J B WILLIAMS, **Hon
C** C J HANKINS, **NSM** B F HOLBEN, J M MOULD

**WITTERSHAM (St John the Baptist) w Stone-in-Oxney and
Ebony** *Cant 12* **P** *Abp* **P-in-c** S M HALMSHAW

WITTON (St Helen) *Ches 6* **P** *Bp* **V** M COWAN,
NSM B W JOBBER

WITTON (St Margaret) *see* Bacton, Happisburgh, Hempstead
w Eccles etc *Nor*

WITTON (St Margaret) *see* Gt and Lt Plumstead w Thorpe End
and Witton *Nor*

WITTON (St Mark) *see* Blackb Christ the King *Blackb*

WITTON, EAST (St John the Evangelist) *see* Middleham w
Coverdale and E Witton etc *Ripon*

WITTON, NETHER (St Giles) *Newc 11* **P** *Ld Chan*
V M A G BRYCE, **OLM** F J SAMPLE

WITTON, WEST (St Bartholomew) *see* Penhill *Ripon*

WITTON GILBERT (St Michael and All Angels) *see* Dur N
Dur

WITTON LE WEAR (St Philip and St James) *see* Hamsterley
and Witton-le-Wear *Dur*

WITTON PARK (St Paul) *Dur 6* **P** *Bp* **V** *vacant*

**WIVELISCOMBE (St Andrew) w Chipstable, Huish
Champflower and Clatworthy** *B & W 19* **P** *Bp and
A H Trollope-Bellew Esq (jt)* **R** *vacant (01984) 623309*

WIVELSFIELD (St Peter and St John the Baptist) *Chich 6*
P *DBP* **V** C R BREEDS

WIVENHOE (St Mary) *Chelmsf 16* **P** *Bp* **R** *vacant (01206)
825174*

WIVERTON GROUP *see* Cropwell Bishop w Colston Bassett,
Granby etc *S'well*

WIVETON (St Mary) *see* Blakeney w Cley, Wiveton, Glandford
etc *Nor*

WIX (St Mary the Virgin) *see* Gt Oakley w Wix and Wrabness
Chelmsf

WIXFORD (St Milburga) *see* Exhall w Wixford *Cov*

WIXOE (St Leonard) *see* Stour Valley *St E*

**WOBURN (St Mary) w Eversholt, Milton Bryan, Battlesden and
Pottesgrove** *St Alb 9* **P** *Bedf Estates Trustees* **V** S W NUTH,
NSM L J WASHINGTON

WOBURN SANDS (St Michael) *St Alb 9* **P** *Bp*
P-in-c C L D BEALES, **NSM** N J PARKINSON

WOBURN SQUARE (Christ Church) *see* Bloomsbury St Geo
w Woburn Square Ch Ch *Lon*

WOKING (Christ Church) *Guildf 12* **P** *Ridley Hall Cam*
V P J HARWOOD, **C** C J RYALLS, M F BALL, **NSM** M S SMITH,
P A SIMPSON

WOKING (St John the Baptist) *Guildf 12* **P** *V Woking St Pet*
V G P WILLIAMS, **C** P S ROBERTSON, **OLM** R G BENNETT

WOKING (St Mary of Bethany) *Guildf 12* **P** *V Woking Ch Ch*
V S R BEAK, **C** G HOLLAND, **OLM** D R MARKS

WOKING (St Paul) *Guildf 12* **P** *Ridley Hall Cam*
P-in-c J L BLAIR, **C** C J BLAIR

WOKING (St Peter) *Guildf 12* **P** *Patr Bd* **TR** B J GRIMSTER,
TV I D TWEEDIE-SMITH

WOKING, SOUTH Team Ministry *see* Woking St Pet *Guildf*

WOKINGHAM (All Saints) *Ox 16* **P** *Bp* **R** D P HODGSON,
C M R JOHNSON, E L ANTOINE, **NSM** C R JAMES

WOKINGHAM (St Paul) *Ox 16* **P** *DBP*
P-in-c J R CONNELL, **NSM** R G HOLMES, J E HARRISON,
A E KEMP

WOKINGHAM (St Sebastian) *Ox 16* **P** *Bp* **V** A P MARSDEN,
NSM E C FUDGE

WOLBOROUGH (St Mary) and Ogwell *Ex 10* **P** *Earl of
Devon and Bp (jt)* **R** R C CHAMBERLAIN, **C** A M WELLS,
NSM M J FLETCHER

WOLD (St Andrew) *see* Walgrave w Hannington and Wold and
Scaldwell *Pet*

WOLD NEWTON (All Saints) *see* Binbrook Gp *Linc*

WOLD NEWTON (All Saints) *see* Burton Fleming w Fordon,
Grindale etc *York*

WOLDINGHAM (St Agatha) *see* Caterham *S'wark*

WOLDINGHAM (St Paul) *as above*

WOLDS, NORTH Group *Linc 6* **P** *Bp, DBP, and D&C (jt)*
V M A BATTY

WOLDSBURN *York 10* **P** *Abp, St Jo Coll Ox, and
A J Page Esq (1 turn), and Ld Chan (1 turn)* **R** J TALLANT,
NSM R D WAITE

WOLFERTON (St Peter) *see* Sandringham w W Newton and
Appleton etc *Nor*

WOLFORD (St Michael) *see* S Warks Seven Gp *Cov*

WOLLASTON (St James) *Worc 12* **P** *Bp*
P-in-c A L HAZLEWOOD, **Hon C** D M FARMER

WOLLASTON (St Mary) w Strixton and Bozeat and Easton Maudit *Pet 6* **P** *Bp and Marquess of Northn (jt)*
V A I MORTON
WOLLASTON, GREAT (All Saints) (St John the Baptist) *Heref 13* **P** *Bp* **V** C B BULL, **P-in-c** V J TAIT
WOLLATON (St Leonard) *S'well 14* **P** *Lord Middleton*
R J J LEPINE, **C** A V NOBLE, M A C GAYNOR,
NSM P D C BROWN
WOLLATON PARK (St Mary) *S'well 14* **P** *CPAS*
P-in-c J H CURRAN
WOLLESCOTE (St Andrew) *Worc 12* **P** *Bp*
V R A BROADBENT
WOLSINGHAM (St Mary and St Stephen) and Thornley *Dur 9* **P** *Bp* **P-in-c** J P L WHALLEY
WOLSTANTON (St Margaret) *Lich 9* **P** *Bp* **C** A R KNIGHT, **Hon C** B E WARRILLOW
WOLSTON (St Margaret) and Church Lawford *Cov 6* **P** *DBP (2 turns), Bp (1 turn)* **Hon C** P A H SIMMONDS
WOLVERCOTE (St Peter) *Ox 7* **P** *Mert Coll Ox*
P-in-c M A BUTCHERS, **Hon C** J M CONEY,
NSM V P BRIDGES
WOLVERHAMPTON Pond Lane (Mission Hall)
see Wolverhampton St Luke *Lich*
WOLVERHAMPTON (St Andrew) *Lich 28* **P** *Bp*
V J L SMITH, **NSM** T B FYFFE
WOLVERHAMPTON (St Jude) *Lich 28* **P** *CPAS*
V R E CARTER, **C** N L MOY, **OLM** I J SAUNDERS
WOLVERHAMPTON (St Luke) Blakenhall *Lich 28*
P *Trustees* **V** R J ESPIN-BRADLEY
WOLVERHAMPTON (St Martin) *see Rough Hills* *Lich*
WOLVERHAMPTON (St Matthew) *Lich 28* **P** *Baldwin Pugh Trustees* **V** D GHOSH, **OLM** D G WATKIN, D G WATKIN
WOLVERHAMPTON (St Stephen) *Lich 28* **P** *Bp*
P-in-c J C OAKES
WOLVERHAMPTON, CENTRAL (All Saints) (St Chad and St Mark) (St John in the Square) (St Peter) *Lich 28* **P** *Patr Bd*
TR D W WRIGHT, **TV** M Y CLAYTON, S SCHOFIELD,
L K COLLINS, O SMITH, **C** P J L CODY, **OLM** E W BROOKES
WOLVERLEY (St John the Baptist) and Cookley *Worc 11*
P *D&C and Bp (jt)* **V** G SHILVOCK
WOLVERTON (Holy Trinity) (St George the Martyr) *Ox 25*
P *Bp* **R** J M TRIGG, **Hon C** M T HURLEY
WOLVERTON (St Katherine) *see Baughurst, Ramsdell, Wolverton w Ewhurst etc* *Win*
WOLVERTON (St Mary the Virgin) w Norton Lindsey and Langley *Cov 7* **P** *Bp* **P-in-c** R LIVINGSTON
WOLVEY (St John the Baptist) w Burton Hastings, Copston Magna and Withybrook *Cov 5* **P** *Bp* **V** T J COLLING
WOLVISTON (St Peter) *see Grindon, Stillington and Wolviston* *Dur*
WOMBOURNE (St Benedict) *see Smestow Vale* *Lich*
WOMBRIDGE (St Mary and St Leonard) *Lich 21*
P *W J Charlton Meyrick Esq* **P-in-c** K S EVANS
WOMBWELL (St Mary) (St George) *Sheff 12* **P** *Trin Coll Cam* **R** N H ELLIOTT
WOMERSLEY (St Martin) *see Went Valley* *Wakef*
WONERSH (St John the Baptist) w Blackheath *Guildf 2*
P *Selw Coll Cam* **V** I M SCOTT-THOMPSON,
OLM K N BATESON, J M COOKE, E A TILLEY
WONSTON (Holy Trinity) *see Upper Dever* *Win*
WONSTON, SOUTH (St Margaret) *see Lower Dever* *Win*
WOOBURN (St Paul) *Ox 29* **P** *Bp* **V** M J WALLINGTON
WOOD DALLING (St Andrew) *see Reepham, Hackford w Whitwell, Kerdiston etc* *Nor*
WOOD DITTON (St Mary) w Saxon Street *Ely 4* **P** *Duke of Sutherland* **P-in-c** M A GURNER
WOOD END (St Chad) *Cov 1* **P** *Ld Chan* **V** V I WOODS
WOOD END (St Michael and All Angels) *see Baxterley w Hurley and Wood End and Merevale etc* *Birm*
WOOD GREEN (St Michael) w Bounds Green (St Gabriel) (St Michael-at-Bowes) *Lon 19* **P** *Patr Bd* **TR** C W COPPEN,
TV R J WILKINSON, **NSM** D HARTLEY
WOOD GREEN (St Paul) *see Wednesbury St Paul Wood Green* *Lich*
WOOD NORTON (All Saints) *see Foulsham, Guestwick, Stibbard, Themelthorpe etc* *Nor*
WOOD STREET (St Alban) *see Worplesdon* *Guildf*
WOODBASTWICK (St Fabian and St Sebastian) *see Ranworth w Panxworth, Woodbastwick etc* *Nor*
WOODBERRY DOWN (St Olave) *see Stoke Newington St Olave* *Lon*
WOODBOROUGH (St Mary Magdalene) *see Pewsey and Swanborough* *Sarum*
WOODBOROUGH (St Swithun) *S'well 10* **P** *Bp*
P-in-c A R GILES, **NSM** M N TAYLOR

WOODBRIDGE (St John the Evangelist) and Bredfield *St E 7*
P *Ch Patr Trust (3 turns), and Ld Chan (1 turn)*
V D GARDNER, **C** P A M SHULER, **OLM** M M E ROBERTS,
L V WEBBER
WOODBRIDGE (St Mary the Virgin) *St E 7* **P** *Bp*
R K S MCCORMACK, **C** P G HAMBLING, **NSM** M J HARE
WOODBURY (Holy Cross) *see Axminster, Chardstock, All Saints etc* *Ex*
WOODBURY (St Swithun) *see Lympstone and Woodbury w Exton* *Ex*
WOODBURY SALTERTON (Holy Trinity) *see Clyst St Mary, Clyst St George etc* *Ex*
WOODCHESTER (St Mary) and Brimscombe *Glouc 5*
P *Simeon's Trustees* **R** S A BOWEN, **NSM** D E STODDART,
M G WRIGHT
WOODCHURCH (All Saints) *Cant 10* **P** *Abp*
P-in-c N R GALLAGHER, **C** P J WHITE
WOODCHURCH (Holy Cross) *Ches 1* **P** *DBP* **R** M A DAVIS,
NSM J CALVERT
WOODCOTE (St Leonard) *see Langtree* *Ox*
WOODCOTE (St Mark) *see Purley St Mark* *S'wark*
WOODCOTE (St Peter) *see Church Aston* *Lich*
WOODCOTT (St James) *see Hurstbourne Priors, Longparish etc* *Win*
WOODDITTON (St Mary) *see Wood Ditton w Saxon Street* *Ely*
WOODEATON (Holy Rood) *see Ray Valley* *Ox*
WOODFIELD Team Benefice, The *Leic 8* **P** *Patr Bd (6 turns), Prime Min (1 turn), Ld Chan (1 turn)* **TR** V M ELPHICK,
TV R L HUGHES, **C** H S WHITE, **NSM** L S BIRTWISTLE,
S C POLASHEK
WOODFORD (Christ Church) *Ches 12*
P *W A B Davenport Esq* **P-in-c** J G KNOWLES,
NSM F T COOKE
WOODFORD (St Barnabas) *Chelmsf 4* **P** *Bp* **V** *vacant* (020) 8504 4687
WOODFORD (St Mary the Virgin) *see Gt w Lt Addington and Woodford* *Pet*
WOODFORD (St Mary w St Philip and St James) *Chelmsf 4*
P *Bp* **R** I D TARRANT
WOODFORD, SOUTH (Holy Trinity) *see Wanstead H Trin Hermon Hill* *Chelmsf*
WOODFORD BRIDGE (St Paul) *Chelmsf 4* **P** *R Woodford*
V J H SPRINGBETT, **NSM** A F BOLDING
WOODFORD HALSE (St Mary the Virgin) w Eydon *Pet 1*
P *Ld Chan (2 turns), Bp (1 turn)* **V** T C OAKLEY
WOODFORD VALLEY (All Saints) *Sarum 13* **P** *Bp*
P-in-c A C PHILP, **NSM** P M POWELL, A P HAWKINS
WOODFORD WELLS (All Saints) (St Andrew) *Chelmsf 4*
P *Trustees* **V** P G HARCOURT, **C** S MARSHALL, S P CLARKE,
NSM D J BLACKLEDGE
WOODGATE VALLEY Conventional District *Birm 2 vacant*
WOODGATE VALLEY (St Francis) *see Bartley Green* *Birm*
WOODGREEN (St Boniface) *see Fordingbridge and Breamore and Hale etc* *Win*
WOODHALL (St James the Great) *Bradf 3* **P** *Bp*
P-in-c N CLEWS, **C** D J MUGHAL
WOODHALL, OLD *see Woodhall Spa Gp* *Linc*
WOODHALL SPA Group *Linc 11* **P** *Bp and DBP (jt)*
P-in-c A C SMITH
WOODHAM (All Saints) *Guildf 12* **P** *Bp* **V** I W FORBES,
C J A ROBINSON, **OLM** S V TASSELL
WOODHAM (St Elizabeth of Hungary) *see Gt Aycliffe* *Dur*
WOODHAM FERRERS (St Mary) and Bicknacre *Chelmsf 9*
P *Lord Fitzwalter* **P-in-c** M J COTTEE
WOODHAM FERRERS, SOUTH (Holy Trinity) (St Mary)
Chelmsf 9 **P** *Bp* **P-in-c** P HAWORTH, **NSM** S S STROEBEL
WOODHAM MORTIMER (St Margaret) w Hazeleigh
Chelmsf 11 **P** *Bp* **P-in-c** M L PUDNEY
WOODHAM WALTER (St Michael) *Chelmsf 11* **P** *Ch Soc Trust* **P-in-c** M L PUDNEY
WOODHAY, EAST (St Martin) and Woolton Hill *Win 6* **P** *Bp*
R C DALE
WOODHAY, WEST (St Laurence) w Enborne, Hampstead Marshall, Inkpen and Combe *Ox 14* **P** *Bp, D&C Windsor, and J R Henderson Esq (jt)* **R** J F RAMSBOTTOM, **NSM** C PYNN,
C F ROBINSON
WOODHORN w Newbiggin *Newc 11* **P** *Bp* **V** J M GRIEVE,
OLM F WALTON
WOODHOUSE (Christ Church) *see Birkby and Woodhouse* *Wakef*
WOODHOUSE (St James) *Sheff 1* **P** *Bp* **V** *vacant* 0114-269 4146
WOODHOUSE (St Mark) and Wrangthorn *Ripon 7* **P** *DBP*
V D A CALDER

WOODHOUSE (St Mary in the Elms), Woodhouse Eaves and Swithland *Leic 6* **P** *Ld Chan and DBP (alt)* **R** R A HORTON, **NSM** S R DELAFORCE

WOODHOUSE CLOSE (not known) *see* Bishop Auckland Woodhouse Close CD *Dur*

WOODHOUSE EAVES (St Paul) *see* Woodhouse, Woodhouse Eaves and Swithland *Leic*

WOODHOUSE MILL (St James) *see* Woodhouse St Jas *Sheff*

WOODHOUSE PARK (Wm Temple Church) *see* Wythenshawe Man

WOODHOUSES (not known) *see* Bardsley *Man*

WOODHOUSES (St John the Divine) *see* Dunham Massey St Marg and St Mark *Ches*

WOODHURST (St John the Baptist) *see* Bluntisham cum Earith w Colne and Woodhurst *Ely*

WOODINGDEAN (Holy Cross) *Chich 2* **P** *Bp* **V** R A BROMFIELD

WOODKIRK (St Mary) *see* W Ardsley *Wakef*

WOODLAND (St John the Baptist) *see* Broadhempston, Woodland, Staverton etc *Ex*

WOODLAND (St John the Evangelist) *see* Broughton and Duddon *Carl*

WOODLAND (St Mary) *see* Lynesack *Dur*

WOODLANDS (All Saints) *Sheff 7* **P** *Bp* **V** S J GARDNER

WOODLANDS (Ascension) *see* Cranborne w Boveridge, Edmondsham etc *Sarum*

WOODLANDS (Mission Chapel) *see* W Meon and Warnford *Portsm*

WOODLANDS (St Katherine) *B & W 4* **P** *DBP* **V** C ALSBURY

WOODLANDS (St Mary) *see* Kemsing w Woodlands *Roch*

WOODLANDS (St Stephen) *see* Welford w Wickham and Gt Shefford, Boxford etc *Ox*

WOODLEIGH (St Mary the Virgin) *see* Modbury, Bigbury, Ringmore w Kingston etc *Ex*

WOODLEY (St John the Evangelist) *Ox 15* **P** *DBP* **V** E MARQUEZ, **C** S C RIORDAN, **NSM** T R ASTIN

WOODMANCOTE (Mission Church) *see* Westbourne *Chich*

WOODMANCOTE (St James) *see* Upper Dever *Win*

WOODMANCOTE (St Mark) *see* Dursley *Glouc*

WOODMANCOTE (St Peter) *see* Henfield w Shermanbury and Woodmancote *Chich*

WOODMANSEY (St Peter) *see* Beverley Minster *York*

WOODMANSTERNE (St Peter) *S'wark 26* **P** *Ld Chan* **P-in-c** M J HOUGH, **NSM** A H BARRON

WOODNESBOROUGH (St Mary the Blessed Virgin) w Worth and Staple *Cant 8* **P** *Abp* **P-in-c** D D HARRISON, **C** J M A ROBERTS, **NSM** R STEVENSON

WOODNEWTON (St Mary) *see* Nassington w Yarwell and Woodnewton w Apethorpe *Pet*

WOODPLUMPTON (St Anne) *Blackb 9* **P** *V St Michael's-on-Wyre* **V** D P A FEENEY

WOODRISING (St Nicholas) *see* High Oak, Hingham and Scoulton w Wood Rising *Nor*

WOODSEATS (St Chad) *Sheff 2* **P** *Bp* **V** vacant 0114-274 5086

WOODSETTS (St George) *Sheff 5* **P** *Bp* **V** vacant

WOODSFORD (St John the Baptist) *see* Moreton and Woodsford w Tincleton *Sarum*

WOODSIDE (All Saints) *see* Lymington *Win*

WOODSIDE (St Andrew) *St Alb 14* **P** *D&C St Paul's* **P-in-c** J DANIEL

WOODSIDE (St James) *Ripon 7* **P** *Bp* **P-in-c** R J DIMERY

WOODSIDE (St Luke) *see* Croydon Woodside *S'wark*

WOODSIDE GREEN (St Andrew) *see* Gt Hallingbury and Lt Hallingbury *Chelmsf*

WOODSIDE PARK (St Barnabas) *Lon 14* **P** *Ch Patr Trust* **V** H D KENDAL, **C** C S BROOKES, J S H COLES, M PAVLOU

WOODSTOCK (St Mary Magdalene) *see* Blenheim *Ox*

WOODSTON (St Augustine of Canterbury) (Mission Church) *Ely 15* **P** *Bp* **R** W P L GAMMON

WOODTHORPE (St Mark) *S'well 10* **P** *Bp* **V** P J THOMAS, **NSM** M A SKIDMORE

WOODTHORPE (St Peter) *see* Staveley and Barrow Hill *Derby*

WOODTON (All Saints) *see* Hempnall *Nor*

WOODVILLE (St Stephen) *see* Blackfordby and Woodville *Leic*

WOOKEY (St Matthew) *see* Coxley w Godney, Henton and Wookey *B & W*

WOOKEY HOLE (St Mary Magdalene) *see* Wells St Cuth w Wookey Hole *B & W*

WOOL (Holy Rood) and East Stoke *Sarum 8* **P** *Bp (3 turns), Keble Coll Ox (1 turn)* **P-in-c** R C FLOATE, **C** D F B BALDWIN, **OLM** J A HILL

WOOLACOMBE (St Sabinus) *see* Ilfracombe, Lee, Woolacombe, Bittadon etc *Ex*

WOOLASTON (St Andrew) w Alvington and Aylburton *Glouc 2* **P** *DBP and Ld Chan (by turn)* **NSM** A JONES

WOOLAVINGTON (Blessed Virgin Mary) w Cossington and Bawdrip *B & W 14* **P** *D&C Windsor and J A Church Esq (alt)* **V** W H H LANE

WOOLBEDING (All Hallows) *Chich 10* **P** *Rathbone Trust Co and Cowdray Trust (jt)* **R** vacant

WOOLBROOK (St Francis of Assisi) *see* Sidmouth, Woolbrook, Salcombe Regis, Sidbury etc *Ex*

WOOLER (St Mary) *see* Glendale Gp *Newc*

WOOLFARDISWORTHY (Holy Trinity) *see* Parkham, Alwington, Buckland Brewer etc *Ex*

WOOLFARDISWORTHY EAST (St Mary) *see* N Creedy *Ex*

WOOLFOLD (St James) *see* Kirklees Valley *Man*

WOOLHAMPTON (St Peter) *see* Aldermaston and Woolhampton *Ox*

WOOLHOPE (St George) *see* Fownhope w Mordiford, Brockhampton etc *Heref*

WOOLLAND (not known) *see* Hazelbury Bryan and the Hillside Par *Sarum*

WOOLLEY (All Saints) *see* Bath St Sav w Swainswick and Woolley *B & W*

WOOLLEY (St Mary) *see* E Leightonstone *Ely*

WOOLLEY (St Peter) *Wakef 11* **P** *Bp* **P-in-c** S P KELLY

WOOLMER GREEN (St Michael) *see* Welwyn *St Alb*

WOOLPIT (Blessed Virgin Mary) w Drinkstone *St E 10* **P** *Bp and A Harvie-Clark Esq (alt)* **R** M R FARRELL

WOOLSTASTON (St Michael and All Angels) *see* Dorrington w Leebotwood, Longnor, Stapleton etc *Heref*

WOOLSTHORPE (St James) *see* Harlaxton Gp *Linc*

WOOLSTON (Ascension) *Liv 12* **P** *Bp, Adn, and R Warrington (jt)* **V** B F DRYDEN

WOOLSTON (St Mark) *Win 13* **P** *Bp* **V** M J A NEWTON, **NSM** A R BEVIS

WOOLSTONE (All Saints) *see* Uffington, Shellingford, Woolstone and Baulking *Ox*

WOOLSTONE (not known) *see* Woughton *Ox*

WOOLSTONE (St Martin) *see* Bishop's Cleeve and Woolstone w Gotherington etc *Glouc*

WOOLTON, MUCH (St Peter) *Liv 4* **P** *Bp* **R** C J CROOKS, **C** P ANDREWS, R J A GEDGE

WOOLTON HILL (St Thomas) *see* E Woodhay and Woolton Hill *Win*

WOOLVERSTONE (St Michael) *see* Holbrook, Stutton, Freston, Woolverstone etc *St E*

WOOLVERTON (St Lawrence) *see* Hardington Vale *B & W*

WOOLWICH (St Mary Magdalene and St Andrew) (St Michael and All Angels) *S'wark 1* **P** *Bp and Keble Coll Ox (jt)* **R** J VAN DER VALK

WOOLWICH (St Thomas) *see* Charlton *S'wark*

WOOLWICH, NORTH (St John) w Silvertown *Chelmsf 3* **P** *Bp and Lon Corp (alt)* **P-in-c** P M CAPRIELLO, **NSM** G J ANAN

WOONTON (Mission Room) *see* Eardisley w Bollingham, Willersley, Brilley etc *Heref*

WOORE (St Leonard) and Norton in Hales *Lich 18* **P** *Bp and CPAS (jt)* **V** vacant (01630) 647316

WOOSEHILL (Community Church) *see* Bearwood *Ox*

WOOTTON (St Andrew) *see* Ulceby Gp *Linc*

WOOTTON (St Edmund) *Portsm 8* **P** *DBP* **P-in-c** K F ABBOTT

WOOTTON (St George the Martyr) w Quinton and Preston Deanery *Pet 4* **P** *Ex Coll Ox and Bp (alt)* **P-in-c** J A PARKIN, **NSM** I E TEBBY

WOOTTON (St Martin) *see* Elham w Denton and Wootton *Cant*

WOOTTON (St Mary the Virgin) *St Alb 13* **P** *MMCET* **V** P M ACKROYD, **C** D E FELL

WOOTTON (St Mary) w Glympton and Kiddington *Ox 9* **P** *New Coll Ox (2 turns), Bp (1 turn), and Exors E W Towler Esq (1 turn)* **P-in-c** E E S JONES

WOOTTON (St Peter) and Dry Sandford *Ox 10* **P** *Bp and Ox Churches Trust (jt)* **V** J N COOPER, **C** P N TOVEY

WOOTTON, NORTH (All Saints) w SOUTH (St Mary) *Nor 20* **P** *Ld Chan and G Howard Esq (alt)* **C** N R MCLEOD, **OLM** D TATE, L ASHBY

WOOTTON, NORTH (St Peter) *see* Pilton w Croscombe, N Wootton and Dinder *B & W*

WOOTTON BASSETT (St Bartholomew and All Saints) *Sarum 15* **P** *DBP* **P-in-c** T M B WOODHOUSE, **C** J DELANEY, **Hon C** B W HORLOCK

WOOTTON BRIDGE (St Mark) *see* Wootton *Portsm*

WOOTTON COURTENAY (All Saints) *see* Dunster, Carhampton, Withycombe w Rodhuish etc *B & W*

WOOTTON FITZPAINE (not known) *see* Golden Cap Team *Sarum*

WOOTTON RIVERS (St Andrew)   *see* Pewsey and Swanborough *Sarum*

WOOTTON ST LAWRENCE (St Lawrence)   *see* Oakley w Wootton St Lawrence *Win*

WOOTTON WAWEN (St Peter) *Cov 7*   **P** *K Coll Cam*
P-in-c L G MORTIMER

WORCESTER Dines Green (St Michael), and Crown East, Rushwick *Worc 3*   **P** *Bp and D&C (jt)*   **V** R CHARLES

WORCESTER (St Barnabas) (Christ Church) *Worc 6*   **P** *Bp*
TR P G HADDLETON,   **C** P E JONES,   **NSM** A ORGAN

WORCESTER (St Clement) and Lower Broadheath *Worc 3*
P *Bp and D&C (jt)*   **V** S L BLOOMER

WORCESTER (St John in Bedwardine)   *see* St Jo in Bedwardine *Worc*

WORCESTER (St Martin in the Cornmarket)   *see* Worc City *Worc*

WORCESTER (St Nicholas)   *see* Warndon St Nic *Worc*

WORCESTER (St Stephen)   *see* Barbourne *Worc*

WORCESTER (St Wulstan) *Worc 6*   **P** *Bp*   **V** D MELVILLE

WORCESTER CITY (All Saints) (St George w St Mary Magdalene) (Old St Martin) *Worc 6*   **P** *V Claines (1 turn), Bp and D&C (2 turns), Bp (1 turn)*   **R** I PEARSON,
C A S COLLISHAW, P D J SWANN

WORCESTER PARK (Christ Church w St Philip) *S'wark 23*
P *R Cheam*   **V** C E ELVEY,   **NSM** C A ROWLES

WORCESTER SOUTH EAST (St Martin w St Peter) (St Mark in the Cherry Orchard) (Holy Trinity w St Matthew) *Worc 6*
P *Patr Bd*   **TR** K A BOYCE,   **TV** F M BINDING, D C J BALLARD,
C S ROSENTHAL, C A HOLZAPFEL,   **NSM** A M WHERRY

WORCESTERSHIRE WEST RURAL Team Ministry, The
Worc 3   **P** *Patr Bd (2 turns), Prime Min (1 turn)*
TR D R SHERWIN,   **TV** A B BULLOCK,   **C** S B THOMSON,
R M BARLOW,   **Hon C** J G SUMNER,   **NSM** J M WHITTAKER

WORDSLEY (Holy Trinity) *Worc 10*   **P** *Patr Bd*
TR C S JONES,   **TV** G W WARD, C WATKINS,
NSM G HODGSON

WORFIELD (St Peter) *Heref 9*   **P** *Trustees of the late J R S Greenshields Esq*   **V** M E THOMPSON

WORKINGTON (St John) *Carl 7*   **P** *R Workington*
V J M COOK

WORKINGTON (St Michael) *Carl 7*   **P** *Mrs E H S Thornely*
R B ROWE

WORKSOP (Christ Church) *S'well 6*   **P** *CPAS*
P-in-c M C ALVEY

WORKSOP (St Anne) *S'well 6*   **P** *Bp*   **P-in-c** S A CASH,
C P MACBAIN

WORKSOP (St John the Evangelist) *S'well 6*   **P** *CPAS*
V N R HOGG

WORKSOP (St Paul) *S'well 6*   **P** *Bp*   **V** B C B BROWN

WORKSOP PRIORY (St Mary and St Cuthbert) *S'well 6*
P *St Steph Ho Ox*   **P-in-c** N SPICER,   **C** P P CORBETT

WORLABY (St Clement) *Linc 6*   **P** *DBP*   **V** *vacant*

WORLDHAM, EAST (St Mary the Virgin)   *see* Northanger *Win*

WORLDHAM, WEST (St Nicholas)   *as above*

WORLE (St Martin) (St Mark's Church Centre) *B & W 11*
P *Ld Chan*   **TR** P R LARCOMBE,   **TV** C D BLAKE,
NSM G C BUNCE

WORLESTON (St Oswald)   *see* Acton and Worleston, Church Minshull etc *Ches*

WORLINGHAM (All Saints) w Barnby and North Cove *St E 14*
P *Ld Chan*   **R** S M ELLIS

WORLINGTON (All Saints)   *see* Mildenhall *St E*

WORLINGTON, EAST (St Mary)   *see* Burrington, Chawleigh, Cheldon, Chulmleigh etc *Ex*

WORLINGTON, WEST (St Mary)   *as above*

WORLINGWORTH (St Mary) w Southolt, Tannington, Bedfield and Monk Soham *St E 17*   **P** *Lord Henniker, R C Rous Esq and Bp, and DBP (by turn)*   **P-in-c** D G W GREEN

WORMBRIDGE (St Peter)   *see* Ewyas Harold w Dulas, Kenderchurch etc *Heref*

WORMEGAY (St Michael and All Angels and Holy Cross)
see Tottenhill w Wormegay *Ely*

WORMELOW HUNDRED *Heref 8*   **P** *A W Twiston-Davies Esq (1 turn), Bp (3 turns), and Ld Chan (1 turn)*
R *vacant* (01981) 540666

WORMHILL (St Margaret) and Peak Forest w Peak Dale and Dove Holes *Derby 4*   **P** *Bp and Duke of Devonshire (jt)*
C F E YATES

WORMINGFORD (St Andrew), Mount Bures and Little Horkesley *Chelmsf 17*   **P** *J J Tufnell Esq, Mrs F Reynolds, and Keble Coll Ox (jt)*   **P-in-c** H HEATH

WORMINGHALL (St Peter and St Paul) w Ickford, Oakley and Shabbington *Ox 21*   **P** *Bp and Guild of All So (jt)*
P-in-c D R KABOLEH

WORMINGTON (St Katharine)   *see* Winchcombe *Glouc*

WORMLEIGHTON (St Peter)   *see* Priors Hardwick, Priors Marston and Wormleighton *Cov*

WORMLEY (Church Room)   *see* Broxbourne w Wormley *St Alb*

WORMLEY (St Laurence)   *as above*

WORMSHILL (St Giles)   *see* Bredgar w Bicknor and Frinsted w Wormshill etc *Cant*

WORPLESDON (St Mary the Virgin) *Guildf 5*   **P** *Eton Coll*
OLM A J WELCH

WORSALL, HIGH AND LOW (All Saints)   *see* Kirklevington w Picton, and High and Low Worsall *York*

WORSBROUGH (St Mary) w Elsecar *Sheff 11*   **P** *DBP and Sir Philip Naylor-Leyland Bt (alt)*   **V** A LAMB

WORSBROUGH (St Thomas)   *see* Worsbrough Common w Worsbrough St Thos *Sheff*

WORSBROUGH COMMON (St Luke) w Worsbrough St Thomas and St James *Sheff 11*   **P** *Bp (2 turns), Prime Min (1 turn)*   **V** T C KEIGHTLEY

WORSLEY (St Mark) *Man 2*   **P** *Bp*   **TR** G TURNER,
TV K R CARMYLLIE

WORSLEY MESNES (not known)   *see* Wigan St Jas w St Thos *Liv*

WORSTEAD (St Mary), Westwick, Sloley, Swanton Abbot and Scottow *Nor 12*   **P** *DBP, J T D Shaw Esq, D&C, and Bp (by turn)*   **R** A R LONG

WORSTHORNE (St John the Evangelist)   *see* Holme-in-Cliviger w Worsthorne *Blackb*

WORTH (St Nicholas), Pound Hill and Maidenbower *Chich 7*
P *DBP*   **P-in-c** R A STIDOLPH,   **C** C J F BARBER

WORTH (St Peter and St Paul)   *see* Woodnesborough w Worth and Staple *Cant*

WORTH MATRAVERS (St Aldhelm)   *see* Kingston, Langton Matravers and Worth Matravers *Sarum*

WORTH MATRAVERS (St Nicholas)   *as above*

WORTHAM (St Mary the Virgin)   *see* N Hartismere *St E*

WORTHEN (All Saints) *Heref 13*   **P** *New Coll Ox (8 turns), J J C Coldwell Esq (1 turn), I Chirbury (1 turn)*
P-in-c C B BULL

WORTHING (Holy Trinity) (Christ Church) *Chich 5*
P *R Broadwater, Bp and Bp Horsham, Ch Soc Trust, and CPAS (jt)*   **V** L F WHATLEY,   **C** H W SCHNAAR

WORTHING (St Andrew) *Chich 5*   **P** *Keble Coll Ox*
P-in-c C G H KASSELL

WORTHING (St George) (Emmanuel) *Chich 5*   **P** *Ch Soc Trust*
V B R PENFOLD

WORTHING (St Margaret)   *see* N Elmham, Billingford, Bintree, Guist etc *Nor*

WORTHING (St Matthew) *Chich 5*   **P** *R Broadwater, Bp and Bp Horsham, Ch Soc Trust, and CPAS (jt)*   **V** E J CHITHAM,
NSM M E PARISH

WORTHING, WEST (St John the Divine) *Chich 5*   **P** *Bp*
V J K T ELDRIDGE

WORTHINGTON (St Matthew)   *see* Ashby-de-la-Zouch and Breedon on the Hill *Leic*

WORTING (St Thomas of Canterbury)   *see* Winklebury and Worting *Win*

WORTLEY (St Leonard)   *see* Tankersley, Thurgoland and Wortley *Sheff*

WORTLEY, NEW (St Mary's Parish Centre)   *see* Armley w New Wortley *Ripon*

WORTLEY DE LEEDS (St John the Evangelist) *Ripon 6*
P *Trustees*   **V** K A P DOWLING

WORTON (Christ Church)   *see* Potterne w Worton and Marston *Sarum*

WORTON, NETHER (St James)   *see* Over w Nether Worton *Ox*

WORTON, OVER (Holy Trinity) w Nether Worton *Ox 5*
P *Exors J B Schuster Esq*   **P-in-c** B J RUMBOLD

WOTTON (St John the Evangelist) and Holmbury St Mary
Guildf 7   **P** *Bp and J P M H Evelyn Esq (jt)*
NSM P J ROBSON

WOTTON ST MARY WITHOUT (Holy Trinity) *Glouc 3*
P *Bp*   **V** T J G NEWCOMBE,   **C** S SKEPPER,   **Hon C** M M ENNIS

WOTTON-UNDER-EDGE (St Mary the Virgin) w Ozleworth, N Nibley and Alderley *Glouc 6*   **P** *Ch Ch Ox and Bp (jt)*
P-in-c R H AXFORD,   **C** V J BEXON,   **NSM** P C E MARSH,
C R AXFORD

WOTTON UNDERWOOD (All Saints)   *see* Bernwode *Ox*

WOUGHTON *Ox 25*   **P** *Patr Bd*   **TV** C L WILLIAMS,
Hon C T P S GOODING,   **NSM** D J RUDIGER

WOUGHTON-ON-THE-GREEN (St Mary)   *see* Woughton *Ox*

WOULDHAM (All Saints)   *see* Burham and Wouldham *Roch*

WRABNESS (All Saints)   *see* Gt Oakley w Wix and Wrabness *Chelmsf*

WRAGBY Group, The (All Saints) *Linc 11* **P** *Bp, MMCET, and DBP (jt)* **R** M N HOLDEN

WRAGBY (St Michael and Our Lady) *see* Kinsley w Wragby *Wakef*

WRAMPLINGHAM (St Peter and St Paul) *see* Barnham Broom and Upper Yare *Nor*

WRANGBROOK (St Michael) *see* Badsworth *Wakef*

WRANGLE (St Mary and St Nicholas) *see* Old Leake w Wrangle *Linc*

WRANGTHORN (St Augustine of Hippo) *see* Woodhouse and Wrangthorn *Ripon*

WRATTING, GREAT (St Mary) *see* Stourhead *St E*

WRATTING, LITTLE (St Mary) *as above*

WRATTING, WEST (St Andrew) *see* Balsham, Weston Colville, W Wickham etc *Ely*

WRAWBY (St Mary the Virgin) *see* Brigg, Wrawby and Cadney cum Howsham *Linc*

WRAXALL (All Saints) *B & W 13* **P** *Trustees* **R** R C LUNN

WRAXALL (St Mary) *see* Melbury *Sarum*

WRAXALL, NORTH (St James) *see* Colerne w N Wraxall *Bris*

WRAXALL, SOUTH (St James) *see* Monkton Farleigh, S Wraxall and Winsley *Sarum*

WRAY (Holy Trinity) *see* E Lonsdale *Blackb*

WRAYSBURY (St Andrew) *see* Horton and Wraysbury *Ox*

WREAKE, UPPER *Leic 2* **P** *Bp and DBP (jt)* **P-in-c** M N DALE

WREAY (St Mary) *see* Dalston w Cumdivock, Raughton Head and Wreay *Carl*

WRECCLESHAM (St Peter) *Guildf 3* **P** *Bp* **V** A E GELL, **NSM** S J CAVALIER

WRENBURY (St Margaret) *see* Baddiley and Wrenbury w Burleydam *Ches*

WRENINGHAM (All Saints) *see* Ashwellthorpe, Forncett, Fundenhall, Hapton etc *Nor*

WRENTHAM (St Nicholas), Covehithe w Benacre, Henstead w Hulver and Frostenden *St E 15* **P** *Susan Lady Gooch* **P-in-c** L J PAYNE

WRENTHORPE (St Anne) *Wakef 11* **P** *Bp* **P-in-c** R HARRIS

WRESSLE (St John of Beverly) *see* Howden *York*

WRESTLINGWORTH (St Peter) *see* Dunton w Wrestlingworth and Eyeworth *St Alb*

WRETHAM (St Ethelbert) *see* Thetford *Nor*

WRETTON (All Saints) w Stoke Ferry and Whittington *Ely 9* **P** *Ld Chan and Ch Patr Trust (alt)* **V** *vacant (01366) 501075*

WRIBBENHALL (All Saints) *Worc 11* **P** *V Kidderminster* **P-in-c** H HUGHES

WRIGGLE VALLEY, The *Sarum 3* **P** *Duchy of Cornwall (1 turn), Bp (3 turns)* **P-in-c** G V BROWNING

WRIGHTINGTON (St James the Great) *Blackb 4* **P** *Bp* **V** R TOWNLEY

WRINGTON (All Saints) w Butcombe and Burrington *B & W 11* **P** *Patr Bd* **R** N R MADDOCK

WRITTLE (All Saints) w Highwood *Chelmsf 8* **P** *New Coll Ox* **V** D M JONES, **NSM** S M M ISKANDER

WROCKWARDINE, The Deanery of (St Peter) *Lich 23* **P** *Patr Bd* **TR** D F CHANTREY, **TV** P H CAWTHORNE, G S GOODWIN, **C** S E WILLIAMS

WROCKWARDINE WOOD (Holy Trinity) *see* Oakengates and Wrockwardine Wood *Lich*

WROOT (St Pancras) *see* Epworth Gp *Linc*

WROSE (St Cuthbert) *Bradf 3* **P** *The Crown* **V** P G WALKER

WROTHAM (St George) *Roch 10* **P** *D&C* **P-in-c** B E HURD

WROUGHTON (St John the Baptist and St Helen) *Bris 7* **P** *Bp* **V** M A JOHNSON, **C** R M BANHAM

WROXALL (St John the Evangelist) *Portsm 7* **P** *Bp* **P-in-c** A E FAULKNER

WROXETER (St Mary) *see* Wrockwardine Deanery *Lich*

WROXHAM (St Mary) w Hoveton St John w Hoveton St Peter and Belaugh *Nor 12* **P** *Bp* **R** M A SEARS

WROXTON (All Saints) *see* Ironstone *Ox*

WULFRIC Benefice, The *B & W 15* **P** *Ld Chan (4 turns), Bp and H W F Hoskyns Esq (1 turn)* **R** M C GALLAGHER, **C** J R MORRIS

WYBERTON (St Leodegar) *Linc 21* **P** *DBP* **P-in-c** C W B SOWDEN

WYBUNBURY (St Chad) w Doddington (St John) *Ches 15* **P** *Bp and Sir Evelyn Broughton Bt (jt)* **V** A A LONG

WYCH, HIGH (St James) and Gilston w Eastwick *St Alb 18* **P** *V Sawbridgeworth (2 turns), P T S Bowlby Esq (1 turn)* **P-in-c** W E G CARTER

WYCHBOLD (St Mary de Wyche) *see* Stoke Prior, Wychbold and Upton Warren *Worc*

WYCHE (All Saints) *see* Malvern St Andr and Malvern Wells and Wyche *Worc*

WYCHLING (St Margaret) *see* Doddington, Newnham and Wychling *Cant*

WYCHNOR (St Leonard) *Lich 1* **P** *Personal Reps W H Harrison Esq* **V** J W ALLAN, **NSM** P A L MADDOCK, V A WILKERSON

WYCK RISSINGTON (St Laurence) *see* Bourton-on-the-Water w Clapton etc *Glouc*

WYCLIFFE (St Mary) *see* Barningham w Hutton Magna and Wycliffe *Ripon*

WYCOMBE, HIGH (All Saints) (St Andrew) (St Anne and St Peter) (St Birinus) (St James) (St Mary and St George) *Ox 29* **P** *Patr Bd* **TR** D A PICKEN, **TV** M S GURR, S A WHITMORE, N R SKIPWORTH, Y L MURPHY, S P DUST, **C** P WILLIS, **NSM** P VINEY, **OLM** M A JACKSON, R M WOOSTER, J LOCK

WYCOMBE, WEST (St Laurence) (St Paul) w Bledlow Ridge, Bradenham and Radnage *Ox 29* **P** *Bp, DBP, Peache Trustees, and Sir Francis Dashwood Bt (jt)* **R** N J LACEY, **NSM** V J BEAUMONT, L J RICHARDSON

WYCOMBE AND CHADWELL (St Mary) *see* Ironstone Villages *Leic*

WYCOMBE LANE (St Mary) *see* Wooburn *Ox*

WYCOMBE MARSH (St Anne and St Peter) *see* High Wycombe *Ox*

WYDDIAL (St Giles) *see* Hormead, Wyddial, Anstey, Brent Pelham etc *St Alb*

WYE (St Gregory and St Martin) w Brook and Hastingleigh w Boughton Aluph and Eastwell *Cant 2* **P** *Abp* **NSM** L C CLEVELAND

WYE, SOUTH Team Ministry *see* Heref S Wye *Heref*

WYESHAM (St James) *see* Dixton, Wyesham, Bishopswood, Whitchurch etc *Heref*

WYFORDBY (St Mary) *see* S Framland *Leic*

WYKE *see* Win St Matt *Win*

WYKE (Holy Trinity) *see* Bruton and Distr *B & W*

WYKE (St Mark) *Guildf 5* **P** *Bp* **V** P A GODFREY, **OLM** M TAYLOR

WYKE (St Mary the Virgin) *see* Oakenshaw, Wyke and Low Moor *Bradf*

WYKE REGIS (All Saints) (St Edmund) *Sarum 4* **P** *D&C* **R** D J SMITH

WYKEHAM (All Saints) *see* Upper Derwent *York*

WYKEHAM: Broughton w North Newington, Epwell w Sibford, Shutford, Swalcliffe, and Tadmarton *Ox 5* **P** *New Coll, Worc Coll, and Lord Saye and Sele (jt)* **R** T WIMBUSH, **NSM** J H TATTERSALL

WYKEN (Church of Risen Christ) *see* Coventry Caludon *Cov*

WYKEN (Holy Cross) *as above*

WYKEN (St Mary Magdalene) *as above*

WYLAM (St Oswin) *Newc 9* **P** *Bp* **P-in-c** D E CANT

WYLDE GREEN (Emmanuel) *Birm 12* **P** *Bp* **V** R E CRANE

WYLYE (St Mary the Virgin) *see* Wylye and Till Valley *Sarum*

WYLYE AND TILL VALLEY *Sarum 13* **P** *Patr Bd (2 turns), Ld Chan (1 turn)* **TR** J H P HAMILTON, **TV** H R L BONSEY, S ARMITAGE, **NSM** L E HALLIDAY, **OLM** R D D HENDERSON, V M GARRARD

WYLYE VALLEY TEAM, UPPER *Sarum 17* **P** *Patr Bd (5 turns), Ld Chan (1 turn)* **TR** J H TOMLINSON, **NSM** H BEGLEY, **OLM** A E BENNETT-SHAW, D M HAMMOND

WYMERING (St Peter and St Paul) *Portsm 6* **P** *E G Nugee Esq* **V** *vacant (023) 9237 6307*

WYMESWOLD (St Mary) and Prestwold w Hoton *Leic 6* **P** *S J Packe-Drury-Lowe Esq and Bp (by turn)* **P-in-c** J WHITTAKER, **Hon C** M R SAMUEL, **NSM** J MCGINTY

WYMINGTON (St Lawrence) w Podington *St Alb 15* **P** *R M Orlebar Esq (1 turn), DBP (3 turns)* **R** *vacant (01933) 313069*

WYMONDHAM (St Mary and St Thomas) *Nor 7* **P** *Bp* **V** C J DAVIES, **C** E A SHIPP

WYMONDHAM (St Peter) *see* S Framland *Leic*

WYMONDLEY, GREAT (St Mary the Virgin) and LITTLE (St Mary the Virgin) *St Alb 4* **P** *Bp and MMCET (jt)* **P-in-c** A E J POLLINGTON

WYMYNSWOLD (St Margaret) *see* Nonington w Wymynswold and Goodnestone etc *Cant*

WYNYARD PARK (Chapel) *see* Grindon, Stillington and Wolviston *Dur*

WYRE PIDDLE (St Anne) *see* Fladbury w Wyre Piddle and Moor etc *Worc*

WYRESDALE, OVER (Christ Church) *see* Dolphinholme w Quernmore and Over Wyresdale *Blackb*

WYRLEY, GREAT (St Mark) *Lich 3* **P** *R Cannock* **V** G HORNER, **C** M J HEATH, R A WESTWOOD, **OLM** M J PRICE

WYSALL (Holy Trinity) *see* Willoughby-on-the-Wolds w Wysall and Widmerpool *S'well*

WYTHALL (no church) *Birm 6*   **P** *R Kings Norton*
  V M J GODFREY
WYTHAM (All Saints)   *see* N Hinksey and Wytham *Ox*
WYTHBURN (not known)   *see* St John's-in-the-Vale, Threlkeld
  and Wythburn *Carl*
WYTHENSHAWE Lawton Moor (St Michael and All Angels)
  see Lawton Moor *Man*
WYTHENSHAWE (St Francis of Assisi) (St Luke) (St Martin)
  (St Richard of Chichester) (William Temple Church) *Man 8*
  P *Patr Bd*   **TR** S E HERBERT,   **TV** K J STANTON, M J APPLEBY,
  J D DEVARAJ,   **C** J M A PARTRIDGE,   **OLM** G R MILLER
WYTHER (Venerable Bede) *Ripon 6*   **P** *Bp*   **V** B A A LAWAL
WYTHOP (St Margaret)   *see* Cockermouth Area *Carl*
WYVERSTONE (St George)   *see* Bacton w Wyverstone, Cotton
  and Old Newton etc *St E*
WYVILL (St Catherine)   *see* Harlaxton Gp *Linc*
YAFFORTH (All Saints)   *see* Lower Swale *Ripon*
YALDING (St Peter and St Paul) w Collier Street *Roch 8*
  P *Ld Chan*   **V** P J FILMER,   **NSM** T K ELSWORTH
YANWORTH (St Michael)   *see* Chedworth, Yanworth and
  Stowell, Coln Rogers etc *Glouc*
YAPHAM (St Martin)   *see* Barmby Moor Gp *York*
YAPTON (St Mary)   *see* Clymping and Yapton w Ford *Chich*
YARCOMBE (St John the Baptist)   *see* Kilmington, Stockland,
  Dalwood, Yarcombe etc *Ex*
YARDLEY (St Cyprian) Hay Mill *Birm 13*   **P** *Bp*
  V A P JOHNSON
YARDLEY (St Edburgha) *Birm 13*   **P** *St Pet Coll Ox*   **V** vacant
  0121-784 6556
YARDLEY (St Lawrence)   *see* Ardeley *St Alb*
YARDLEY, SOUTH (St Michael and All Angels) *Birm 13*
  P *Bp*   **V** D A J MADDOX
YARDLEY GOBION (St Leonard)   *see* Potterspury w Furtho
  and Yardley Gobion etc *Pet*
YARDLEY HASTINGS (St Andrew), Denton and Grendon w
  Castle Ashby and Whiston *Pet 6*   **P** *Marquess of Northampton*
  and Bp (alt)   **R** D L SPOKES,   **NSM** J H CRAIG PECK
YARDLEY WOOD (Christ Church) *Birm 5*   **P** *Bp*
  V J G RICHARDS
YARKHILL (St John the Baptist)   *see* Ledbury *Heref*
YARLINGTON (Blessed Virgin Mary)   *see* Camelot Par *B & W*
YARM (St Mary Magdalene) *York 21*   **P** *Abp*   **R** B C GURD
YARMOUTH (St James) *Portsm 8*   **P** *Keble Coll Ox*
  R M E C WHATSON,   **NSM** D K BELLAMY, G M HURT
YARMOUTH, GREAT (St John) (St Nicholas) (St Paul)
  (St Luke) (St Mary) *Nor 6*   **P** *Patr Bd*   **TV** M I KNOWLES,
  R J KNOWLES
YARNFIELD (Mission Room St Barnabas)   *see* Swynnerton
  and Tittensor *Lich*
YARNSCOMBE (St Andrew)   *see* Newton Tracey, Horwood,
  Alverdiscott etc *Ex*
YARNTON (St Bartholomew)   *see* Blenheim *Ox*
YARPOLE (St Leonard)   *see* Leominster *Heref*
YARWELL (St Mary Magdalene)   *see* Nassington w Yarwell
  and Woodnewton w Apethorpe *Pet*
YATE New Town (St Mary) *Bris 5*   **P** *Bp*   **TR** D B HARREX,
  TV I P MACFARLANE,   **NSM** C D VEREY
YATELEY (St Peter) *Win 5*   **P** *Bp*   **R** P F HINCKLEY,
  C B J DAVIES
YATESBURY (All Saints)   *see* Oldbury *Sarum*
YATTENDON (St Peter and St Paul)   *see* Hermitage *Ox*
YATTON (All Saints)   *see* Ledbury *Heref*
YATTON KEYNELL (St Margaret)   *see* By Brook *Bris*
YATTON MOOR (St Mary the Virgin) *B & W 13*   **P** *DBF*
  TR I M HUBBARD,   **TV** C J HORDER, J C ANDREWS,
  C C D STEED,   **NSM** C R LLEWELYN-EVANS
YAVERLAND (St John the Baptist)   *see* Brading w Yaverland
  Portsm
YAXHAM (St Peter)   *see* Mattishall and the Tudd Valley *Nor*
YAXLEY (St Mary the Virgin)   *see* S Hartismere *St E*
YAXLEY (St Peter) and Holme w Conington *Ely 15*   **P** *Ld Chan*
  (2 turns), J H B Heathcote Esq (1 turn)   **V** J A RANDALL
YEADON (St John the Evangelist) *Bradf 4*   **P** *Bp and R Guiseley*
  w Esholt (jt)   **V** R M WALKER,   **C** S V KAYE
YEALAND CONYERS (St John the Evangelist)   *see* Warton
  St Oswald w Yealand Conyers *Blackb*
YEALMPTON (St Bartholomew) and Brixton *Ex 21*
  P *D&C Windsor and Bp (jt)*   **V** D ARNOTT
YEARSLEY (Holy Trinity)   *see* Crayke w Brandsby and
  Yearsley *York*
YEAVELEY (Holy Trinity)   *see* Brailsford w Shirley, Osmaston
  w Edlaston etc *Derby*
YEDINGHAM (St John the Baptist)   *see* Buckrose Carrs *York*
YELDEN (St Mary)   *see* The Stodden Churches *St Alb*
YELDHAM, GREAT (St Andrew)   *see* Upper Colne *Chelmsf*
YELDHAM, LITTLE (St John the Baptist)   *as above*

YELFORD (St Nicholas and St Swithin)   *see* Lower Windrush
  Ox
YELLING (Holy Cross)   *see* Papworth *Ely*
YELVERTOFT (All Saints)   *see* Crick and Yelvertoft w Clay
  Coton and Lilbourne *Pet*
YELVERTON (St Mary)   *see* Thurton *Nor*
YELVERTON (St Paul), Meavy, Sheepstor and Walkhampton
  Ex 25   **P** *Patr Bd*   **NSM** J W M WEIR, M SALMON, N S SHUTT
YEOFORD CHAPEL (Holy Trinity)   *see* Crediton, Shobrooke
  and Sandford etc *Ex*
YEOVIL (Holy Trinity) w Barwick *B & W 7*   **P** *Ms Y L Bennett*
  and Ms R S Mullen (1 turn), The Crown (3 turns)
  R T J COOK,   **C** P T MEAD
YEOVIL (St Andrew) (St John the Baptist) w Kingston Pitney
  B & W 7   **P** *Mrs S W Rawlins (3 turns), DBP (1 turn)*
  R J DUDLEY-SMITH
YEOVIL (St James the Great)   *see* Preston Plucknett *B & W*
YEOVIL (St Michael and All Angels) *B & W 7*   **P** *Bp*
  V M D ELLIS,   **NSM** C Y JONES
YEOVIL (St Peter)   *see* Preston Plucknett *B & W*
YEOVIL MARSH (All Saints)   *see* Tintinhull w Chilthorne
  Domer, Yeovil Marsh etc *B & W*
YETMINSTER (St Andrew)   *see* Wriggle Valley *Sarum*
YIEWSLEY (St Matthew) *Lon 24*   **P** *V Hillingdon*
  V R C YOUNG
YOCKLETON (Holy Trinity) *Heref 13*   **P** *Bp*   **R** C B BULL
YORK Acomb (St Aidan)   *see* Acomb St Steph *York*
YORK (All Saints)   *see* Huntington *York*
YORK (All Saints) North Street *York 7*   **P** *D&C*
  P-in-c A A HORSMAN
YORK (All Saints) Pavement w St Crux and St Michael
  Spurriergate *York 7*   **P** *Abp*   **NSM** A P HUGHES
YORK (Christ Church)   *see* Heworth Ch Ch *York*
YORK (Holy Redeemer)   *see* Acomb H Redeemer *York*
YORK (Holy Trinity)   *see* Heworth H Trin and St Wulstan *York*
YORK (Holy Trinity) Micklegate *York 7*   **P** *D&C*
  R R M C SEED
YORK (James the Deacon)   *see* Acomb Moor *York*
YORK (St Barnabas) *York 7*   **P** *CPAS*   **P-in-c** K BURNETT-
  HALL
YORK (St Chad) *York 7*   **P** *Abp*   **P-in-c** S R STANLEY
YORK (St Clement w St Mary) Bishophill *York 7*   **P** *Abp and*
  D&C (jt)   **R** A STOKER,   **NSM** G J PETERS
YORK (St Denys) *York 7*   **P** *Abp*   **NSM** A P HUGHES
YORK (St Edward the Confessor)   *see* Dringhouses *York*
YORK (St Helen) Stonegate w (St Martin) Coney Street *York 7*
  P *Abp*   **NSM** S A WHITTINGTON, S A NORTON
YORK (St Hilda) *York 7*   **P** *Abp*   **P-in-c** T L JONES,
  NSM M FAIREY, M H ELLISON
YORK (St Lawrence w St Nicholas) *York 7*   **P** *D&C*
  P-in-c T L JONES,   **NSM** M H ELLISON
YORK (St Luke) *York 7*   **P** *Abp*   **P-in-c** S C BENFORD,
  NSM T M GANT, M E CARRINGTON
YORK (St Martin-cum-Gregory)   *see* York H Trin Micklegate
  York
YORK (St Michael-le-Belfrey) (St Cuthbert) *York 7*   **P** *Abp*
  V R W SIMPSON,   **C** M J PORTER, A J RYCROFT, A M LAMB,
  NSM W J ROBERTS, C N SELVARATNAM, A T LINDLEY
YORK (St Olave w St Giles) *York 7*   **P** *Abp*
  NSM S A WHITTINGTON, S A NORTON
YORK (St Oswald)   *see* Fulford *York*
YORK (St Paul) Holgate Road *York 7*   **P** *CPAS*   **R** J M A LEE,
  NSM U L SIMPSON
YORK (St Philip and St James)   *see* Clifton *York*
YORK (St Stephen)   *see* Acomb St Steph *York*
YORK (St Thomas w St Maurice) *York 7*   **P** *Abp*
  P-in-c P MOORE,   **OLM** E A RANSFORD
YORK (St Wulstan)   *see* Heworth H Trin and St Wulstan *York*
YORKLEY, LOWER (St Luke's Church Centre)   *see* Parkend
  and Viney Hill *Glouc*
YORKTOWN (St Michael)   *see* Camberley St Mich Yorktown
  Guildf
YOULGREAVE (All Saints), Middleton, Stanton-in-Peak and
  Birchover *Derby 2*   **P** *Duke of Devonshire and N B B Davie-*
  Thornhill Esq (jt)   **V** vacant (01629) 636285
YOXALL (St Peter) *Lich 1*   **P** *Bp*   **P-in-c** M H HAWKSWORTH,
  OLM M BINSLEY
YOXFORD (St Peter)   *see* Yoxmere *St E*
YOXMERE Benefice, The *St E 19*   **P** *Prime Min (1 turn),*
  Ch Patr Trust, Lady Penelope Gilbey, Shadingfield Property,
  J K A Brooke Esq, CPAS, and Bp (2 turns)   **V** R J GINN,
  OLM A B BAYMAN, S A WARNE, E M COLE
ZEAL, SOUTH (St Mary)   *see* S Tawton and Belstone *Ex*
ZEAL MONACHORUM (St Peter) *Ex 2*   **P** *DBP*   **R** vacant
ZEALS (St Martin)   *see* Upper Stour *Sarum*
ZENNOR (St Senera) *Truro 5*   **P** *Bp*   **P-in-c** J S HOLLAND,
  NSM S A CHALCRAFT

WELSH BENEFICES AND CHURCHES

An index of benefices of the Church in Wales (shown in bold type), together with entries for churches and other licensed places of worship. Where the church name is the same as the benefice (or the first place name in the benefice), the church entry is omitted. Church dedications are indicated in brackets.

The benefice entry gives the full legal name, followed by the diocese, its deanery number (p. 1003), and the name(s) and appointment(s) of the clergy serving there (if there are none, the telephone number of the parsonage house is given). The following are the main abbreviations used; for others see the full list of abbreviations.

C	Curate	P-in-c	Priest-in-charge
C-in-c	Curate-in-charge	Par Dn	Parish Deacon
Dn-in-c	Deacon-in-charge	R	Rector
Dss	Deaconess	TM	Team Minister
Hon C	Honorary Curate	TR	Team Rector
Hon Par Dn	Honorary Parish Deacon	TV	Team Vicar
NSM	Non-stipendiary Minister	V	Vicar

ABBEY CWMHIR (St Mary the Virgin) *see* Llanbadarn Fawr, Llandegley and Llanfihangel etc *S & B*
ABER (St Bodfan) *see* Llanfairfechan w Aber *Ban*
ABERAERON (Holy Trinity) *see* Henfynyw w Aberaeron and Llanddewi Aberarth etc *St D*
ABERAMAN (St Margaret) and Abercwmboi w Cwmaman *Llan 9* **V** D C WAY
ABERAVON (St Mary) (St Paul) (Holy Trinity) (St Agnes) *Llan 5* **TR** N CAHILL, **TV** A J COCKRAM, **C** J ELCOCK, **NSM** J A SLENNETT
ABERBARGOED (St Peter) *see* Bedwellty w New Tredegar *Mon*
ABERCANAID (St Peter) *Llan 10* **P-in-c** G G FOSTER
ABERCARN and Cwmcarn *Mon 6* **P-in-c** A M BAKER, **NSM** M REDWOOD
ABERCRAF (St David) *see* Cwmtawe Uchaf *S & B*
ABERCWMBOI *see* Aberaman and Abercwmboi w Cwmaman *Llan*
ABERCYNON (St Donat) (St Gwynno) *Llan 9* **P-in-c** P M WILLIAMS
ABERDARE (St Fagan) *Llan 9* **V** K W LAKE
ABERDARE (St John the Baptist) (St Elvan) (St Matthew) (St John the Evangelist) *Llan 9* **V** R E DAVIES
ABERDARON (St Hywyn) and Llanfaelrhys *Ban 11* **P-in-c** J E COTTER
ABERDYFI (St Peter) *see* Llanegryn w Aberdyfi w Tywyn *Ban*
ABEREDW (St Cewydd) w Llandeilo Graban and Llanbadarn-y-Garreg w Crickadarn and Gwenddwr *S & B 2* **V** T J WILLIAMS, **NSM** P J MORRIS
ABERERCH (St Cawrdaf) *see* Denio w Abererch *Ban*
ABERFFRAW (St Beuno) *see* Trefdraeth w Aberffraw, Llangadwaladr etc *Ban*
ABERGAVENNY (Holy Trinity) (Christ Church) *Mon 1* **C** B SIXTUS, **OLM** C R WALTERS
ABERGAVENNY (St Mary) (Christchurch) w Llanwenarth Citra *Mon 1* **V** J H WINSTON, **C** B SIXTUS, J K PLESSIS, **NSM** J L HUGHES
ABERGELE (St David) (St Michael) and St George *St As 6* **V** S T GRIFFITHS
ABERGORLECH (St David) *see* Brechfa w Abergorlech etc *St D*
ABERGWILI (St David) w Llanfihangel-uwch-Gwili and Capel-y-Groes *St D 11* **V** L L RICHARDSON
ABERGWYNFI (St Thomas) *see* Glyncorrwg and Upper Afan Valley *Llan*
ABERGWYNGREGYN (St Bodfan) *see* Llanfairfechan w Aber *Ban*
ABERGYNOLWYN *see* Llanegryn w Aberdyfi w Tywyn *Ban*
ABERHAFESP (St Gwynog) *see* Llanllwchaiarn and Newtown w Aberhafesp *St As*
ABERKENFIG (St John) *see* Llansantffraid, Bettws and Aberkenfig *Llan*
ABERNANT (St Lucia) *see* Abernant *St D*
ABERNANT (St Lucia) *St D 11* **P-in-c** J GAINER
ABERNANT (St Matthew) *see* Aberdare *Llan*
ABERPERGWM (St Cadoc) *see* Vale of Neath *Llan*
ABERPORTH (St Cynwyl) w Tremain w Blaenporth and Betws Ifan *St D 6* **V** J G MATTHEWS
ABERSYCHAN (St Thomas) and Garndiffaith *Mon 9* **P-in-c** J S BRAY
ABERTILLERY (St Michael) w Cwmtillery *Mon 7* **P-in-c** P F COLEMAN, **C** S K GILLARD-FAULKNER
ABERTYSSWG (St Paul) *see* Bedwellty w New Tredegar *Mon*
ABERYSKIR (St Mary and St Cynidr) *see* Trallwng w Bettws Penpont w Aberyskir etc *S & B*
ABERYSTWYTH (St Michael) (Holy Trinity) (St Mary) (St Anne) *St D 10* **TR** S R BELL, **TV** A F HERRICK,

H PORTER, I J GIRLING
AFAN VALE *see* Glyncorrwg and Upper Afan Valley *Llan*
ALLTMAWR (St Mauritius) *see* Builth and Llanddewi'r Cwm w Llangynog etc *S & B*
ALLTWEN (St John the Baptist) *see* Cilybebyll *Llan*
AMBLESTON (St Mary) *see* Spittal w Trefgarn and Ambleston w St Dogwells *St D*
AMLWCH (St Eleth) (St Peter) (St Gwenllwyfo) (St Eilian) *Ban 7* **R** D J WILLIAMS
AMMANFORD (All Saints) *see* Betws w Ammanford *St D*
AMMANFORD (St Michael) *as above*
AMROTH (St Elidyr) *see* St Issell's and Amroth *St D*
ANGLE (St Mary) *see* Monkton *St D*
ARTHOG (St Catherine) w Fairbourne w Llangelynnin w Rhoslefain *Ban 12* **P-in-c** P J CROOKS
BAGILLT (St Mary) (St Peter) *St As 4* **V** S F HILDRETH
BAGLAN (St Catherine) (St Baglan) *Llan 5* **V** D W LEWIS
BALA (Christ Church) *St As 17* **R** N W MORRIS
BANGOR (Cathedral of St Deiniol) *see* Ban Cathl *Ban*
BANGOR (St David) (Eglwys y Groes) (St Mary) (St Peter) *Ban 5* **TR** M L WILLIAMS, **TV** S H JONES, **NSM** C S B ROBERTS
BANGOR MONACHORUM (St Dunawd), Worthenbury and Marchwiel *St As 11* **R** A W A COPPING
BANGOR TEIFI (St David) *see* Llandysul w Bangor Teifi w Henllan etc *St D*
BARGOED (St Gwladys) and Deri w Brithdir *Llan 8* **V** A P BOOKLESS, **NSM** S A STEVENS
BARMOUTH *see* Llanaber w Caerdeon *Ban*
BARRY (All Saints) (St John w St Baruc) *Llan 3* **C** J A L BAKER
BARRY (St Paul) *see* Merthyr Dyfan *Llan*
BASSALEG (St Basil) *Mon 5* **TR** J S WILLIAMS, **TV** C M L STONE, **C** H J LONG, **NSM** R P MULCAHY
BATTLE (St Cynog) *see* Trallwng w Bettws Penpont w Aberyskir etc *S & B*
BEAUFORT (St Andrew) *see* Ebbw Vale *Mon*
BEAUFORT (St David) *as above*
BEAUMARIS (St Mary and St Nicholas) (St Catherine) (St Seiriol) (St Cawrdaf) (St Michael) *Ban 6* **R** N FAIRLAMB
BEDDGELERT (St Mary) *see* Penrhyndeudraeth and Llanfrothen w Maentwrog etc *Ban*
BEDLINOG (St Cadoc) *see* Treharris, Trelewis and Bedlinog *Llan*
BEDLINOG (St Mary) *as above*
BEDWAS (St Barrwg) w Machen w Rudry *Mon 5* **R** P D CROCKER, **Par Dn** D A WILLIAMS, **NSM** D E COLLINGBOURNE
BEDWELLTY (St Sannan) w New Tredegar *Mon 6* **V** R C DYMOND, **NSM** J EVANS
BEGELLY (St Mary) w Ludchurch and Crunwere *St D 4* **P-in-c** S J GEACH
BEGUILDY (St Michael and All Angels) (St Peter) and Heyope and Llangynllo and Bleddfa *S & B 5* **V** *vacant* (01547) 510252
BENLLECH (St Andrew) *see* Llanfair Mathafarn Eithaf w Llanbedrgoch *Ban*
BERRIEW (St Beuno) *St As 10* **V** J B THELWELL
BERSE (Parish Church) *see* Broughton and Berse Drelincourt *St As*
BERSHAM (St Mary) *see* Wrexham *St As*
BETTISFIELD (St John the Baptist) *see* Hanmer, Bronington, Bettisfield, Tallarn Green *St As*
BETTWS *see* Trallwng w Bettws Penpont w Aberyskir etc *S & B*
BETTWS (St David) *see* Llansantffraid, Bettws and Aberkenfig *Llan*
BETTWS (St David) *Mon 8* **R** *vacant* (01633) 855193
BETTWS CHAPEL *see* Llantilio Pertholey w Bettws Chpl etc *Mon*

BETTWS DISSERTH (St Mary)   *see* Colwyn *S & B*
BETTWS NEWYDD (not known) w Trostrey and Kemeys Commander and Llanfihangel Gobion w Llanfair Kilgeddin *Mon 4*   **R**   T G CLEMENT
BETWS (Holy Trinity)   *see* Glasbury and Llowes w Clyro and Betws *S & B*
BETWS (St David) w Ammanford *St D 13*   **V**   D BOWEN
BETWS BLEDRWS (St Bledrws or St Michael) *St D 9*   **R** *vacant*
BETWS CEDEWAIN (St Beuno) and Tregynon and Llanwyddelan *St As 7*   **Hon C**   W T BRYAN
BETWS GARMON (St Garmon)   *see* Llanbeblig w Caernarfon and Betws Garmon etc *Ban*
BETWS GWERFUL GOCH (St Mary) w Llangwm w Llawrybetws *St As 17*   **P-in-c**   S J ROBERTS
BETWS LEUCU (St Lucia)   *see* Bro Teifi Sarn Helen *St D*
BETWS-Y-COED (St Mary) and Capel Curig w Penmachno w Dolwyddelan *Ban 2*   **V**   C R HILLMAN
BETWS-YN-RHOS (St Michael) *St As 6*   **P-in-c**   J R MATTHIAS
BEULAH   *see* Blaenau Irfon *S & B*
BIRCHGROVE (St John)   *see* Llansamlet *S & B*
BISHOPSTON (St Teilo) w Penmaen and Nicholaston *S & B 8*   **V**   A J PEARCE
BISHTON (St Cadwaladr)   *see* Magor *Mon*
BISTRE (Emmanuel) (All Saints) (St Cecilia) *St As 13*   **V**   M J BATCHELOR,   **C**   A ANTHAPURUSHA,   **NSM**   S BAIRD
BLACKWOOD (St Margaret) *Mon 6*   **P-in-c**   M J TREGENZA
BLAENAU FFESTINIOG (St David)   *see* Llanffestiniog w Blaenau Ffestiniog etc *Ban*
BLAENAU IRFON *S & B 2*   **V**   C M HAYNES
BLAENAVON (St Peter) w Capel Newydd *Mon 9*   **V**   J S BRAY,   **C**   R A D LINDSAY
BLAENCELYN (St David)   *see* Llangrannog w Llandysiliogogo w Penbryn *St D*
BLAENGARW (St James)   *see* Llangeinor and the Garw Valley *Llan*
BLAENGWRACH (St Mary)   *see* Vale of Neath *Llan*
BLAENLLECHAU (St Thomas)   *see* Rhondda Fach Uchaf *Llan*
BLAENPENNAL (St David) *St D 9*   **V**   P W DAVIES
BLAENPENNAL (St David)   *see* Bro Teifi Sarn Helen *St D*
BLAENPORTH (St David)   *see* Aberporth w Tremain w Blaenporth and Betws Ifan *St D*
BLAINA (St Peter) and Nantyglo *Mon 7*   **R**   R L HEWETT,   **Par Dn**   C MORGAN
BLEDDFA (St Mary Magdalene)   *see* Beguildy and Heyope and Llangynllo and Bleddfa *S & B*
BLETHERSTON (St Mary)   *see* Llawhaden w Bletherston and Llanycefn *St D*
BODEDERN (St Edern) w Llanfaethlu *Ban 3*   **R** *vacant* (01407) 730142
BODELWYDDAN (St Margaret) *St As 1*   **V**   G B HUGHES,   **C**   P A RIMMER
BODEWRYD (St Mary)   *see* Llanfechell w Bodewryd w Rhosbeirio etc *Ban*
BODFARI (St Stephen)   *see* Caerwys and Bodfari *St As*
BODWROG (St Twrog)   *see* Llandrygarn w Bodwrog and Heneglwys etc *Ban*
BONTDDU   *see* Llanaber w Caerdeon *Ban*
BONVILSTON (St Mary)   *see* St Nicholas w Bonvilston and St George-super-Ely *Llan*
BONYMAEN (St Margaret)   *see* Glantawe *S & B*
BORTH (St Matthew) and Eglwys-fach w Llangynfelyn *St D 10*   **V** *vacant* (01970) 871594
BOSHERSTON (St Michael)   *see* Monkton *St D*
BOTWNNOG (St Beuno) w Bryncroes w Llangwnnadl w Penllech *Ban 11*   **P-in-c**   N M HAWKINS
BOUGHROOD (St Cynog)   *see* Llandefalle and Llyswen w Boughrood etc *S & B*
BOULSTON   *see* Slebech and Uzmaston w Boulston *St D*
BRAWDY (St David)   *see* Dewisland *St D*
BRECHFA (St Teilo) w Abergorlech and Llanfihangel Rhos-y-corn *St D 14*   **P-in-c**   L CHAMBERS
BRECON (Cathedral of St John the Evangelist) (St Mary) w Llanddew *S & B 1*   **V**   G O MARSHALL,   **P-in-c**   M R D THOMAS
BRECON (St David) w Llanspyddid and Llanilltyd *S & B 1*   **V** *vacant* (01874) 622707
BRIDELL (St David)   *see* Cilgerran w Bridell and Llantwyd and Eglwyswrw *St D*
BRIDGEND (St Illtud)   *see* Newcastle *Llan*
BRIDGEND (St Mary)   *see* Coity, Nolton and Brackla *Llan*
BRIGHTON, NEW (St James)   *see* Mold *St As*
BRITHDIR (St David)   *see* Bargoed and Deri w Brithdir *Llan*
BRITHDIR (St Mark)   *see* Dolgellau w Llanfachreth and Brithdir etc *Ban*

BRITHDIR (St Mary)   *see* Llanrhaeadr ym Mochnant etc *St As*
BRITON FERRY (St Clement)   *see* Llansawel, Briton Ferry *Llan*
BRO DDYFI UCHAF *Ban 10*   **NSM**   R P BARNES
BRO TEIFI SARN HELEN *St D 9*   **TR**   A W WILLIAMS,   **TV**   D C LLOYD,   **C**   S BALE,   **Hon C**   J C ROBBINS
BRONGWYN (St Mary)   *see* Newcastle Emlyn w Llandyfriog and Troedyraur etc *St D*
BRONINGTON (Holy Trinity)   *see* Hanmer, Bronington, Bettisfield, Tallarn Green *St As*
BRONLLYS (St Mary)   *see* Talgarth w Bronllys w Llanfilo *S & B*
BRONWYDD (St Celynnin)   *see* Llanpumsaint w Llanllawddog *St D*
BROUGHTON (St Mary)   *see* Hawarden *St As*
BROUGHTON (St Paul) (St Peter) and Berse Drelincourt *St As 15*   **V**   J G AYLWARD
BRYMBO (St Alban) (St Mary), Southsea and Tanyfron *St As 15*   **P-in-c**   N W CARTER
BRYN (St Tydfil)   *see* Llangynwyd w Maesteg *Llan*
BRYN Y MAEN (Christ Church)   *see* Brynymaen *St As*
BRYNAMAN (St Catherine) w Cwmllynfell *St D 13*   **V**   A TEALE
BRYNCETHIN   *see* Llansantffraid, Bettws and Aberkenfig *Llan*
BRYNCOEDIFOR (St Paul)   *see* Dolgellau w Llanfachreth and Brithdir etc *Ban*
BRYNCROES (St Mary)   *see* Botwnnog w Bryncroes w Llangwnnadl w Penllech *Ban*
BRYNEGLWYS (St Tysilio) *St As 17*   **P-in-c**   H FENTON
BRYNFORD (St Michael)   *see* Gorsedd w Brynford, Ysgeifiog and Whitford *St As*
BRYNGWRAN   *see* Valley w Llechylched and Caergeiliog *Ban*
BRYNGWYN (St Mary)   *see* Newcastle Emlyn w Llandyfriog and Troedyraur etc *St D*
BRYNGWYN (St Michael) and Newchurch and Llanbedr Painscastle and Llanddewi Fach *S & B 2*   **V** *vacant* (01497) 851260
BRYNGWYN (St Peter)   *see* Raglan w Llandenny and Bryngwyn *Mon*
BRYNMAWR (St Mary the Virgin) *S & B 3*   **V**   R T GREY
BRYNNA   *see* Llanharan w Peterston-super-Montem *Llan*
BRYNYMAEN (Christ Church) *St As*   **V** *vacant*
BUCKHOLT (St John the Baptist)   *see* Monmouth w Overmonnow etc *Mon*
BUCKLEY (St Matthew) (Good Shepherd) *St As 13*   **V**   A M TILTMAN,   **NSM**   P M OWENS
BUILTH (St Mary) and Llanddewi'r Cwm w Llangynog and Maesmynis and Llanynys and Alltmawr *S & B 2*   **V**   N D HALL,   **NSM**   C R HALL
BULWARK (St Christopher)   *see* Chepstow *Mon*
BURRY PORT (St Mary) and Pwll *St D 12*   **V**   R P DAVIES,   **NSM**   J E PHILLIPS
BURTON (St Mary) and Rosemarket *St D 5*   **P-in-c**   P BOYLE
BUTE TOWN (St Aidan)   *see* Pontlottyn w Fochriw *Llan*
BUTTINGTON (All Saints)   *see* Guilsfield w Buttington *St As*
BWLCH (All Saints)   *see* Llyn Safaddan *S & B*
BWLCHGWYN (Christ Church) and Minera *St As 15*   **V**   J P HARRIS
BWLCHYCIBAU (Christ Church)   *see* Llanfyllin and Bwlchycibau *St As*
BYLCHAU (St Thomas)   *see* Henllan and Llannefydd and Bylchau *St As*
CADOXTON-JUXTA-BARRY (St Cadoc) (St Mary) *Llan 3*   **R**   J M HUGHES
CADOXTON-JUXTA-NEATH (St Catwg) and Tonna *Llan 6*   **V**   C A OWEN
CAERAU (St Cynfelin) (St Peter) *Llan 5*   **V**   K ANDREWS
CAERAU w Ely (St David) (St Timothy) *Llan 2*   **V**   J L SMITH,   **NSM**   A M BEER
CAERDEON (St Philip)   *see* Llanaber w Caerdeon *Ban*
CAEREITHIN (St Teilo) *S & B 10*   **V**   P F M GALLAGHER
CAERFALLWCH (St Paul)   *see* Halkyn w Caerfallwch w Rhesycae *St As*
CAERGEILIOG   *see* Valley w Llechylched and Caergeiliog *Ban*
CAERGYBI   *see* Holyhead *Ban*
CAERHUN (St Mary) w Llangelynin w Llanbedr-y-Cennin *Ban 2*   **V**   T BONNET
CAERLEON (St Cadoc) w Llanhennock *Mon 8*   **V**   A J EDWARDS,   **C**   C A CAMPLING-DENTON,   **NSM**   E HILLS,   M R JARMAN
CAERLEON-ULTRA-PONTEM (Holy Spirit)   *see* Newport Ch Ch *Mon*
CAERNARFON (St Mary)   *see* Llanbeblig w Caernarfon and Betws Garmon etc *Ban*
CAERPHILLY (St Martin) (St Catherine) (St Andrew) *Llan 8*   **R**   R DONKIN,   **C**   S A ROGERS,   **NSM**   S G BROWN
CAERSWS (St Mary)   *see* Llanwnnog and Caersws w Carno *Ban*

CAERWENT (St Stephen and St Tathan) w Dinham and Llanfair Discoed and Shirenewton w Newchurch *Mon 3*
P-in-c W C INGLE-GILLIS, NSM E N M DAVIES
CAERWYS (St Michael) and Bodfari *St As 2*
NSM G L HUGHES
CALDICOT (St Mary) *Mon 3* TR L HARRISON,
TV D RICHARDS, C D C BOUTFLOWER, A M CHURCH
CALLWEN (St John the Baptist) *see* Cwmtawe Uchaf *S & B*
CAMROSE (St Ishmael) *St D 5* P-in-c C W BOWEN
CANTON Cardiff (St Luke) *Llan 1* TR M R PREECE,
TV M P COLTON
CANTON (St Catherine) *Llan 1* V vacant (029) 2038 2796
CANTON (St John) *Llan 1* R vacant
CANTREF (St Mary) *see* Llanfrynach and Cantref w Llanhamlach *S & B*
CAPEL (Dewi Sant) *see* Llansadwrn w Llanwrda and Manordeilo *St D*
CAPEL BANGOR (Church) *see* Elerch w Penrhyncoch w Capel Bangor and Goginan *St D*
CAPEL COELBREN (Capel Coelbren) *see* Cwmtawe Uchaf *S & B*
CAPEL COLMAN (St Colman) *see* Maenordeifi Gp *St D*
CAPEL CYNON (St Cynon) *see* Llanarth and Capel Cynon w Talgarreg etc *St D*
CAPEL DEWI (St David) *see* Llanfihangel-ar-arth w Capel Dewi *St D*
CAPEL GARMON *see* Llanrwst *St As*
CAPEL IFAN (St John the Baptist) *see* Cwm Gwendraeth *St D*
CAPEL LLANILLTERNE (St Ellteyrn) *see* Pentyrch w Capel Llanillterne *Llan*
CAPEL MAIR *see* Llangeler w Pen-Boyr *St D*
CAPEL NEWYDD (St Paul) *see* Blaenavon w Capel Newydd *Mon*
CAPEL TYGWYDD *see* Maenordeifi Gp *St D*
CAPEL-Y-FFIN (St Mary) *see* Hay w Llanigon and Capel-y-Ffin *S & B*
CAPEL-Y-GROES *see* Abergwili w Llanfihangel-uwch-Gwili etc *St D*
CARDIFF (Christ Church) Roath Park *Llan 1* V vacant (029) 2075 7940
CARDIFF (Dewi Sant) *Llan 1* P-in-c H J DAVIES
CARDIFF (St Andrew and St Teilo) *see* Cathays *Llan*
CARDIFF (St James the Great) *see* City Par St Jo *Llan*
CARDIFF (St John the Baptist) *as above*
CARDIFF (St Mary) (St Stephen) w Cardiff (St Dyfrig and St Samson) *Llan 1* V G J FRANCIS, C B ANDREWS
CARDIFF (St Michael and All Angels) *see* Cathays *Llan*
CARDIGAN (St Mary) w Mwnt and Y Ferwig w Llangoedmor *St D 6* V J POWELL
CAREW (St Mary) *St D 1* TR V F MILLGATE, N B THOMAS,
TV T N BARBER
CARMARTHEN (St David) (Christ Church) *St D 11*
V P H B THOMAS, NSM M K THORLEY
CARMARTHEN (St Peter) (St John the Evangelist) *St D 11*
C P G B RATCLIFFE
CARMEL (Eglwys Fair) *see* Gors-las *St D*
CARNHEDRYN *see* Dewisland *St D*
CARNO (St John) *see* Llanwnnog and Caersws w Carno *Ban*
CARROG (St Ffraid) *see* Corwen w Llangar, Glyndyfrdwy etc *St As*
CASCOB (St Michael) *see* Knighton, Norton, Whitton, Pilleth and Cascob *S & B*
CASTELL DWYRAN *see* Llanfallteg w Castell Dwyran *St D*
CASTELLAN *see* Maenordeifi Gp *St D*
CASTLE BYTHE *see* Letterston w Llanfair Nant-y-Gof etc *St D*
CASTLE CAEREINION (St Garmon) *see* Welshpool, Castle Caereinion and Pool Quay *St As*
CASTLEMARTIN (St Michael and All Angels) *see* Monkton *St D*
CATHAYS (St Andrew and St Teilo) (St Michael and All Angels) *Llan 1* P-in-c C R DOWNS
CATHEDINE (St Michael) *see* Llyn Safaddan *S & B*
CEFN (St Mary) (All Saints) w Trefnant w Tremeirchion *St As 2*
R C E MANSLEY, NSM P WYKES
CEFN COED (St John the Baptist) w Vaynor *S & B 1*
V B H JOHN
CEFN CRIBWR (St Colman) *see* Kenfig Hill *Llan*
CEFN FOREST (St Thomas) *see* Fleur-de-Lis *Mon*
CEFN HENGOED (St Anne) *see* Gelligaer *Llan*
CEFN PENNAR (St Illtyd) *see* Mountain Ash and Miskin *Llan*
CEFNLLYS (St Michael) *see* Llandrindod w Cefnllys and Disserth *S & B*
CEIRCHIOG (St David) *see* Valley w Llechylched and Caergeiliog *Ban*

CELLAN (All Saints) *see* Bro Teifi Sarn Helen *St D*
CEMAES *see* Llanfechell w Bodewryd w Rhosbeirio etc *Ban*
CEMAIS (St Tydecho) *see* Bro Ddyfi Uchaf *Ban*
CENARTH (St Llawddog) *see* Newcastle Emlyn w Llandyfriog and Troedyraur etc *St D*
CERRIGCEINWEN (St Ceinwen) *see* Trefdraeth w Aberffraw, Llangadwaladr etc *Ban*
CERRIGYDRUDION (St Mary Magdalene) w Llanfihangel Glyn Myfyr, Pentrefoelas and Ysbyty Ifan *St As 17*
P-in-c R J PEARCE
CHEPSTOW (St Mary) *Mon 3* V C J BLANCHARD
CHERITON *see* Monkton *St D*
CHERITON (St Cadoc) *see* Llangennith w Llanmadoc and Cheriton *S & B*
CHIRK (St Mary) *St As 14* V A J REES
CIL-Y-CWM (St Michael) and Ystrad-ffin w Rhandirmwyn Llanfair-ar-y-Bryn *St D 14* V vacant (01550) 21011
CILCAIN (St Mary) and Nannerch and Rhydymwyn *St As 16*
R vacant (01352) 740213
CILCENNIN (Holy Trinity) *see* Llanfihangel Ystrad and Cilcennin w Trefilan etc *St D*
CILFYNYDD (St Luke) *see* Pontypridd St Matt and Cilfynydd w Llanwynno *Llan*
CILGERRAN (St Llawddog) w Bridell and Llantwyd and Eglwyswrw *St D 6* R E L THOMAS
CILGWYN (St Mary) *see* Newport w Cilgwyn and Nevern and Y Beifil etc *St D*
CILIAU AERON (St Michael) *see* Llanerch Aeron w Ciliau Aeron and Dihewyd etc *St D*
CILYBEBYLL (St John the Evangelist) *Llan 6* R M PERRY
CITY Parish (St John the Baptist) *Llan 1* V J K KIMBER
CLARBESTON (St Martin of Tours) *see* Wiston w Walton E and Clarbeston *St D*
CLOCAENOG (St Foddhyd) *see* Llanfwrog and Clocaenog and Gyffylliog *St As*
CLUNDERWEN (St David) *see* Whitland w Cyffig and Henllan Amgoed etc *St D*
CLYDACH (St John the Evangelist) (St Mary) (St Michael) *S & B 7* V L J TAYLOR
CLYDACH VALE (St Thomas) *see* Tonypandy w Clydach Vale *Llan*
CLYDAU (St Clydai) *see* Crymych Gp *St D*
CLYNNOG FAWR (St Beuno) *see* Llanaelhaearn w Clynnog Fawr *Ban*
CLYRO (St Michael and All Angels) *see* Glasbury and Llowes w Clyro and Betws *S & B*
CLYTHA *see* Llanddewi Rhydderch w Llangattock-juxta-Usk etc *Mon*
COCKETT (St Peter) *see* Swansea St Pet *S & B*
COEDKERNEW *see* Marshfield and Peterstone Wentloog etc *Mon*
COEDYPAEN (Christchurch) *see* Llangybi and Coedypaen w Llanbadoc *Mon*
COETMOR *see* Glanogwen and Llanllechid w St Ann's and Pentir *Ban*
COITY (St Mary), Nolton and Brackla *Llan 4* R M KOMOR,
C C TREMHTHTHANMOR, S BOWIE, NSM S J BEVERLY
COLVA (St David) *see* New Radnor and Llanfihangel Nantmelan etc *S & B*
COLWINSTON (St Michael) *see* Colwinston, Llandow and Llysworney *Llan*
COLWINSTON (St Michael), Llandow and Llysworney *Llan 7*
R P M LEONARD
COLWYN *S & B 2* P-in-c J R F KIRLEW
COLWYN (St Catherine) (St John the Baptist) and Llanelian *St As 6* R J P ATACK
COLWYN BAY (St Paul) (St Andrew) (St David) w Brynymaen *St As 6* V N H WILLIAMS, C V A BURTON
COMINS COCH *see* Llanbadarn Fawr *St D*
CONNAH'S QUAY (St Mark) (St David's Mission Church) *St As 16* V P H VARAH, C R EVANS, NSM B P JONES
CONWY (St Mary and All Saints) w Gyffin *Ban 2* V P R JONES
CORRIS (Holy Trinity) *see* Pennal w Corris and Esgairgeiliog *Ban*
CORWEN (St Mael and St Sulien) w Llangar, Glyndyfrdwy and Llansantffraid Glyn Dyfrdwy *St As 17* V vacant
COSHESTON (St Michael) *see* Carew *St D*
COWBRIDGE (Holy Cross) *Llan 7* TR D G BELCHER,
TV J J JENKINS, C M J H TRICK
COYCHURCH (St Crallo), Llangan and St Mary Hill *Llan 4*
P-in-c V HAMER
COYTREAHEN (St Thomas) *see* Llansantffraid, Bettws and Aberkenfig *Llan*
CRAI (St Ilid) *see* Defynnog, Llandilo'r Fan, Llanulid, Llywel etc *S & B*

CREGRINA (St David)   *see* Colwyn *S & B*

CRIBYN (St Silin)   *see* Llanfihangel Ystrad and Cilcennin w Trefilan etc *St D*

CRICCIETH (St Catherine) and Treflys w Llanystumdwy w Llangybi and Llanarmon *Ban 11*   **R**   S WILLIAMS

CRICKADARN (St Mary)   *see* Aberedw w Llandeilo Graban and Llanbadarn etc *S & B*

CRICKHOWELL (St Edmund) w Cwmdu and Tretower *S & B 3*   **V**   B LETSON

CRIGGION (St Michael)   *see* Llandysilio and Penrhos and Llandrinio etc *St As*

CRINDAU (All Saints)   *see* Newport All SS *Mon*

CRINOW (St Teilo)   *see* Narberth w Mounton w Robeston Wathen and Crinow *St D*

CROESCEILIOG (St Mary)   *see* Cwmbran *Mon*

CROESERW (St Clare)   *see* Glyncorrwg and Upper Afan Valley *Llan*

CROSS HANDS (St Anne)   *see* Gors-las *St D*

CROSS INN (Holy Trinity)   *see* Llanllwchaearn and Llanina *St D*

CROSS KEYS (St Catherine)   *see* Risca *Mon*

CROSSGATES   *see* Llanbadarn Fawr, Llandegley and Llanfihangel etc *S & B*

CRUGYBYDDAR (St Peter)   *see* Beguildy and Heyope and Llangynllo and Bleddfa *S & B*

CRUNWERE (St Elidyr)   *see* Begelly w Ludchurch and Crunwere *St D*

CRYMYCH Group, The *St D 15*   **V**   J R THOMAS

CRYNANT (Chapel of Ease)   *see* Dulais Valley *Llan*

CRYNANT (St Margaret)   *as above*

CWM (St Mael and St Sulien)   *see* Dyserth and Trelawnyd and Cwm *St As*

CWM (St Paul)   *see* Ebbw Vale *Mon*

CWM-COCH (St Mark)   *see* Llandybie *St D*

CWM GWENDRAETH *St D 12*   **TV**   M A ROWLANDS

CWMAFAN (St Michael) *Llan 5*   **P-in-c**   H M O´SHEA, **NSM**   D J HARRIS

CWMAMAN (Christ Church) *St D 13*   **V**   A J MAUNDER

CWMAMAN (St Joseph)   *see* Aberaman and Abercwmboi w Cwmaman *Llan*

CWMANN (St James)   *see* Pencarreg and Llanycrwys *St D*

CWMAVON (St Michael)   *see* Cwmafan *Llan*

CWMBACH (St Mary Magdalene) *Llan 9*   **P-in-c**   C B W SMITH

CWMBACH LLECHRYD (St John the Divine)   *see* Upper Wye *S & B*

CWMBRAN (St Gabriel) *Mon 9*   **TR**   M J PHILLIPS, **TV**   A J TURNER, R LANGTON,   **OLM**   G M PROSSER

CWMBWRLA (St Luke)   *see* Manselton and Cwmbwrla *S & B*

CWMCARN (St John the Evangelist)   *see* Abercarn and Cwmcarn *Mon*

CWMCARVAN (St Clement)   *see* Rockfield and Dingestow Gp *Mon*

CWMDARE (St Luke)   *see* Aberdare St Fagan *Llan*

CWMDDAUDDWR (St Bride)   *see* Gwastedyn *S & B*

CWMDDAUDDWR (St Winifred)   *as above*

CWMDU (St Michael the Archangel)   *see* Crickhowell w Cwmdu and Tretower *S & B*

CWMDUAD (St Alban)   *see* Cynwyl Elfed w Newchurch and Trelech a'r Betws *St D*

CWMFFRWD (St Anne)   *see* Llangunnor w Cwmffrwd *St D*

CWMFFRWDOER (All Saints)   *see* Pontypool *Mon*

CWMLLYNFELL (St Margaret)   *see* Brynaman w Cwmllynfell *St D*

CWMPARC (St George)   *see* Pen Rhondda Fawr *Llan*

CWMTAWE UCHAF *S & B 7*   **P-in-c**   A J BROOKFIELD

CWMTILLERY (St Paul)   *see* Abertillery w Cwmtillery *Mon*

CWMYOY (St Martin)   *see* Llanfihangel Crucorney w Oldcastle etc *Mon*

CWRT-HENRI (St Mary)   *see* Llangathen w Llanfihangel Cilfargen etc *St D*

CYDWELI (St Mary) (St Teilo) and Llandyfaelog *St D 12*   **V**   J H A JAMES,   **NSM**   A R MORLEY-JONES

CYFFIG (St Cyffig)   *see* Whitland w Cyffig and Henllan Amgoed etc *St D*

CYMAU (All Saints)   *see* Llanfynydd *St As*

CYMMER (St John the Evangelist)   *see* Porth Newydd *Llan*

CYMMER AFAN (St John the Evangelist)   *see* Glyncorrwg and Upper Afan Valley *Llan*

CYNCOED (All Saints) (St Edeyrn) *Mon 5*   **TR**   S G WILLSON, **TV**   S G CARBY, S JENKYNS

CYNOG HONDDU *S & B 1*   **P-in-c**   N HOOK

CYNWYL ELFED (St Cynwyl) w Newchurch and Trelech a'r Betws *St D 11*   **V**   A W EVANS

CYNWYL GAEO (St Cynwyl) w Llansawel and Talley *St D 14*   **V**   J S PENBERTHY

DAFEN (St Michael and All Angels) *St D 12*   **V** *vacant*

DALE (St James) and St Brides w Marloes *St D 5*   **V**   D M WIGHT

DAROWEN (St Tudur)   *see* Bro Ddyfi Uchaf *Ban*

DEFYNNOG (St Cynog) and Llandilo'r Fan and Llanulid and Llywel and Traean-glas *S & B 1*   **V**   M P WILDING

DEGANWY (All Saints)   *see* Llanrhos *St As*

DENBIGH (St Mary) (St Marcella) (St David) *St As 2*   **R**   J P SMITH

DENIO (St Peter) w Abererch *Ban 11*   **V**   J E GOURDIE

DERI (St Peter)   *see* Bargoed and Deri w Brithdir *Llan*

DERWEN (St Mary)   *see* Llanfair DC, Derwen, Llanelidan and Efenechtyd *St As*

DEVAUDEN (St James)   *see* St Arvans w Penterry, Itton, Devauden etc *Mon*

DEWISLAND (Cathedral of St David and St Andrew) *St D 3*   **TR**   D J R LEAN,   **TV**   J S BENNETT, R J PATTINSON, **NSM**   M I PLANT

DIHEWYD (St Vitalis)   *see* Llanerch Aeron w Ciliau Aeron and Dihewyd etc *St D*

DINAS (Mission) and Penygraig w Williamstown *Llan 12*   **V**   C R LEWIS-JENKINS

DINAS (St Brynach)   *see* Newport w Cilgwyn and Nevern and Y Beifil etc *St D*

DINGESTOW (St Dingad)   *see* Rockfield and Dingestow Gp *Mon*

DINHAM   *see* Caerwent w Dinham and Llanfair Discoed etc *Mon*

DINMAEL (St Catherine)   *see* Betws Gwerful Goch w Llangwm w Llawrybetws *St As*

DISSERTH (St Cewydd)   *see* Llandrindod w Cefnllys and Disserth *S & B*

DOLBENMAEN (St Mary)   *see* Porthmadoc and Ynyscynhaearn and Dolbenmaen *Ban*

DOLFOR (St Paul)   *see* Kerry, Llanmerewig, Dolfor and Mochdre *St As*

DOLGARROG (St Mary)   *see* Caerhun w Llangelynin w Llanbedr-y-Cennin *Ban*

DOLGELLAU (St Mary) w Llanfachreth and Brithdir and Bryncoedifor and Llanelltud *Ban 12*   **R**   R B D REES, **C**   B BAILEY

DOLWYDDELAN (St Gwyddelan)   *see* Betws-y-Coed and Capel Curig w Penmachno etc *Ban*

DOWLAIS (St John the Baptist) (Christ Church) and Penydarren *Llan 10*   **R**   K J HARMAN

DULAIS VALLEY *Llan 6*   **V**   S BARNES

DWYGYFYLCHI or Penmaenmawr (St Gwynin) (St Seiriol) (St David) *Ban 2*   **V**   D M OUTRAM

DYFFRYN   *see* Llanenddwyn w Llanddwywe, Llanbedr w Llandanwg *Ban*

DYFFRYN (St Matthew) *Llan 6*   **V**   S J BODYCOMBE

DYFFRYN HONDDU (St Cynog)   *see* Cynog Honddu *S & B*

DYSERTH (St Bridget) (St Michael) (St Mael and St Sulien) and Trelawnyd and Cwm *St As 1*   **V**   R W ROWLAND

EBBW VALE (Christchurch) (St John the Baptist) *Mon 7*   **TR**   G J WAGGETT,   **TV**   P J ABBOTT, J A CARTER, **NSM**   P V GRIFFITHS, N C PERRY

EDERN (St Edern)   *see* Nefyn w Tudweiliog w Llandudwen w Edern *Ban*

EFENECHTYD (St Michael)   *see* Llanfair DC, Derwen, Llanelidan and Efenechtyd *St As*

EGLWYS-FACH (St Michael)   *see* Borth and Eglwys-fach w Llangynfelyn *St D*

EGLWYS FAIR GLYN-TAF   *see* Whitland w Cyffig and Henllan Amgoed etc *St D*

EGLWYS GYMYN (St Margaret)   *see* Pendine w Llanmiloe and Eglwys Gymyn w Marros *St D*

EGLWYS NEWYDD   *see* Grwp Bro Ystwyth a Mynach *St D*

EGLWYS OEN DUW   *see* Blaenau Irfon *S & B*

EGLWYSBREWIS (St Brewis)   *see* Llantwit Major *Llan*

EGLWYSFACH   *see* Llansantffraid Glan Conwy and Eglwysbach *St As*

EGLWYSILAN (St Ilan) *Llan 8*   **P-in-c**   S M REES

EGLWYSRHOS (St Eleri and St Mary)   *see* Llanrhos *St As*

EGLWYSWEN *St D 6*   **V** *vacant*

EGLWYSWRW (St Cristiolus)   *see* Cilgerran w Bridell and Llantwyd and Eglwyswrw *St D*

ELERCH (St Peter) w Penrhyncoch w Capel Bangor and Goginan *St D 10*   **V**   J P LIVINGSTONE,   **NSM**   P S NEIL

ELY (St David)   *see* Caerau w Ely *Llan*

ELY (St Timothy)   *as above*

ERBISTOCK (St Hilary)   *see* Overton and Erbistock and Penley *St As*

ESCLUSHAM (Holy Trinity)   *see* Wrexham *St As*

ESGAIRGEILIOG   *see* Pennal w Corris and Esgairgeiliog *Ban*

EVANCOYD (St Peter)   *see* New Radnor and Llanfihangel Nantmelan etc *S & B*

EWENNY (St Michael) w St Brides Major *Llan 4*
P-in-c P G MORRIS,   **NSM** M J SPENCE, C E A PASCOE

EYTON (St Deiniol)   *see* Bangor Monachorum, Worthenbury and Marchwiel *St As*

FAIRBOURNE (St Cynon)   *see* Arthog w Fairbourne w Llangelynnin w Rhoslefain *Ban*

FAIRHILL   *see* Cwmbran *Mon*

FAIRWATER (St Peter) *Llan 2*   **V** C P SUTTON

FAIRWATER (St Peter)   *see* Cwmbran *Mon*

FAWR   *see* Llandeilo Fawr and Taliaris *St D*

FELIN-FOEL (Holy Trinity)   *see* Llanelli *St D*

FELIN-GWM (St John)   *see* Llanegwad w Llanfynydd *St D*

FELINDRE (St Barnabas)   *see* Llangeler w Pen-Boyr *St D*

FERNDALE (St Dunstan)   *see* Rhondda Fach Uchaf *Llan*

FERRYSIDE (St Thomas)   *see* St Ishmael's w Llan-saint and Ferryside *St D*

FFESTINIOG (St Michael)   *see* Llanffestiniog w Blaenau Ffestiniog etc *Ban*

FFYNNONGROEW (All Saints) *St As 4*   **V** *vacant*

FISHGUARD (St Mary) w Llanychar and Pontfaen w Morfil and Llanychlwydog *St D 3*   **V** D A T MACGREGOR

FLEMINGSTON (St Michael)   *see* Cowbridge *Llan*

FLEUR-DE-LIS (St David) *Mon 6*   **P-in-c** T MORGAN

FLINT (St Mary) (St Thomas) (St David) *St As 4*   **R** B HARVEY

FOCHRIW (St Mary and St Andrew)   *see* Pontlottyn w Fochriw *Llan*

FORD (Church)   *see* Nolton w Roch and St Lawrence w Ford etc *St D*

FORDEN (St Michael)   *see* Montgomery and Forden and Llandyssil *St As*

FREYSTROP (St Justinian)   *see* Llangwm w Freystrop and Johnston *St D*

FRON (Mission Church)   *see* Berriew *St As*

FRONCYSYLLTE (St David)   *see* Chirk *St As*

FRONGOCH   *see* Bala *St As*

FURNACE (Mission Church)   *see* Llanelli *St D*

GABALFA (St Mark) (Highfields Centre and Mynachdy Institute) *Llan 1*   **V** R M CAPPER,   **C** J M WIDDESS,   **NSM** R H ALDIS

GAERWEN   *see* Llanfihangel Ysgeifiog w Llangristiolus etc *Ban*

GARNDIFFAITH (St John the Evangelist)   *see* Abersychan and Garndiffaith *Mon*

GARTHBEIBIO (St Tydecho) w Llanerfyl w Llangadfan w Llanfihangel yn Nghwynfa w Llwydiarth *St As 8*
V D E B FRANCIS

GARTHBRENGY (St David)   *see* Cynog Honddu *S & B*

GARTHELI (St Gartheli)   *see* Bro Teifi Sarn Helen *St D*

GAUFRON (St David)   *see* Gwastedyn *S & B*

GELLIGAER (St Catwg) (St Margaret) (St Anne) *Llan 8*
R A H STEVENS

GILESTON (St Giles)   *see* Llantwit Major *Llan*

GILFACH GOCH (St Barnabas)   *see* Tonyrefail w Gilfach Goch *Llan*

GILVACH (St Margaret)   *see* Gelligaer *Llan*

GLADWESTRY (St Mary)   *see* New Radnor and Llanfihangel Nantmelan etc *S & B*

GLAIS (St Paul)   *see* Llansamlet *S & B*

GLAN ELY (Resurrection) *Llan 2*   **P-in-c** J GOULD

GLANAMAN (St Margaret)   *see* Cwmaman *St D*

GLANGWRYNE (Mission Church)   *see* Llangenni and Llanbedr Ystrad Yw w Patricio *S & B*

GLANOGWEN (Christ Church) and Llanllechid w St Ann's and Pentir *Ban 5*   **V** N C WILLIAMS,   **NSM** C E MCCREA

GLANTAWE (St Margaret) (St Peter) *S & B 11*
V C P G DICKSON

GLASBURY (St Peter) (All Saints) and Llowes w Clyro and Betws *S & B 4*   **V** D E THOMAS

GLASCOED (St Michael)   *see* Mamhilad w Monkswood and Glascoed Chapel *Mon*

GLASCOMBE (St David)   *see* Colwyn *S & B*

GLYN   *see* Brecon St David w Llanspyddid and Llanilltyd *S & B*

GLYNCOCH (All Saints' Church Centre)   *see* Pontypridd St Matt and Cilfynydd w Llanwynno *Llan*

GLYNCORRWG (St John the Baptist) (St Clare) (St Thomas) and Upper Afan Valley *Llan 5*   **P-in-c** C E LASKEY

GLYNDYFRDWY (St Thomas)   *see* Corwen w Llangar, Glyndyfrdwy etc *St As*

GLYNTAFF (St Mary) *Llan 11*   **V** K D LERRY

GOETRE (St Peter) w Llanover *Mon 4*   **P-in-c** S N JAMES

GOGINAN (Church)   *see* Elerch w Penrhyncoch w Capel Bangor and Goginan *St D*

GOLDCLIFFE (St Mary Magdalen)   *see* Magor *Mon*

GOODWICK (St Peter)   *see* Llanwnda, Goodwick w Manorowen and Llanstinan *St D*

GORS-LAS (St Lleian) *St D 13*   **V** M L REES,   **NSM** J B JONES

GORSEDD (St Paul) w Brynford, Ysgeifiog and Whitford *St As 4*
V G BECKETT,   **Par Dn** S M MORIARTY

GORSEINON (St Catherine) *S & B 9*   **V** D H E MOSFORD,   **C** T D P ARDOUIN,   **NSM** W G G JAMES, A P DAVIES

GOVILON (Christchurch) w Llanfoist w Llanelen *Mon 1*
R A F PYE

GOWER, SOUTH WEST *S & B 8*   **V** J W GRIFFIN,   **Hon C** H M EVANS

GOWERTON (St John the Evangelist) *S & B 9*   **V** D ROBERTS

GRAIG (St John)   *see* Rhydyfelin w Graig *Llan*

GRANDSTON (St Catherine)   *see* Mathry w St Edren's and Grandston etc *St D*

GRANGETOWN (St Paul) *Llan 1*   **V** G J FRANCIS

GREENWAY (St Hilary)   *see* Rumney *Mon*

GRESFORD (All Saints) *St As 12*   **V** J T HUGHES,   **NSM** D F CHILD

GRIFFITHSTOWN (St Hilda) *Mon 9*   **V** P A GOLLEDGE,   **NSM** N J TAYLOR

GROESWEN (St David)   *see* Pentyrch w Capel Llanillterne *Llan*

GRONANT (St Winifred)   *see* Llanasa *St As*

GROSMONT (St Nicholas) and Skenfrith and Llangattock Lingoed and Llanfair Chapel *Mon 1*   **P-in-c** J PROSSER

GRWP BRO YSTWYTH A MYNACH: Llanfihangel-y-Creuddyn w Llanafan-y-Trawscoed w Llanwnnws w Ysbyty Ystwyth w Ysbyty Cynfyn w Lantrisant w Eglwys Newydd *St D 10*   **V** E HOWELLS,   **NSM** I E ROSE

GUILSFIELD (St Aelhaiarn) w Buttington *St As 10*
V R A BIRD

GUMFRESTON (St Lawrence)   *see* Tenby *St D*

GWAENYSGOR   *see* Meliden and Gwaenysgor *St As*

GWASTEDYN *S & B 5*   **P-in-c** P BROOKS

GWAUN-CAE-GURWEN *St D 13*   **V** *vacant* (01269) 822430

GWEHELOG   *see* Usk and Gwehelog w Llantrisant w Llanllowell *Mon*

GWENDDWR (St Dubricius)   *see* Aberedw w Llandeilo Graban and Llanbadarn etc *S & B*

GWENLLI (St Mark)   *see* Llanarth and Capel Cynon w Talgarreg etc *St D*

GWERNAFFIELD (Holy Trinity) and Llanferres *St As 16*
V *vacant* (01352) 740111

GWERNAMYNYDD (St Mark)   *see* Mold *St As*

GWERNESNEY (St Michael)   *see* Llangwm Uchaf and Llangwm Isaf w Gwernesney etc *Mon*

GWERNFFRWD (St David)   *see* Llanrhidian w Llanyrnewydd *S & B*

GWERSYLLT (Holy Trinity) *St As 12*   **V** S M HUYTON

GWYDDELWERN (St Beuno) *St As*   **P-in-c** H FENTON

GWYNFE (All Saints)   *see* Llangadog and Gwynfe w Llanddeusant *St D*

GWYTHERIN (St Winifred)   *see* Petryal *St As*

GYFFIN (St Benedict)   *see* Conwy w Gyffin *Ban*

GYFFYLLIOG (St Mary)   *see* Llanfwrog and Clocaenog and Gyffylliog *St As*

HAFOD (St John)   *see* Cen Swansea *S & B*

HAKIN (St Mary)   *see* Hubberston *St D*

HALKYN (St Mary the Virgin) w Caerfallwch w Rhesycae *St As 4*   **P-in-c** H N BURGESS

HANMER (St Chad) and Bronington and Bettisfield and Tallarn Green *St As 11*   **P-in-c** C HUGHES

HARLECH (St Tanwg) and Llanfair-juxta-Harlech w Llanfihangel-y-Traethau and Llandecwyn *Ban 8*
V R A BEACON

HAROLDSTON ST ISSELLS (St Issell)   *see* Haverfordwest St Mary and St Thos w Haroldston *St D*

HAROLDSTON WEST (St Madog)   *see* Walton W w Talbenny and Haroldston W *St D*

HAVERFORDWEST (St Martin) w Lambston *St D 5*
V C W BOWEN

HAVERFORDWEST (St Mary) and St Thomas w Haroldston St Issells *St D 5*   **R** *vacant* (01437) 763170

HAWARDEN (St Deiniol) (Holy Spirit) *St As 13*
TR T F L GRIFFITHS,   **TV** M W DOUGLAS, P R-M DE G GOWER,   **C** G CHIGUMIRA,   **NSM** J STEPHENS

HAY (St Mary) (St John) w Llanigon and Capel-y-Ffin *S & B 4*
V R D WILLIAMS

HAYSCASTLE (St Mary)   *see* Nolton w Roch and St Lawrence w Ford etc *St D*

HENDY (St David)   *see* Llangennech and Hendy *St D*

HENEGLWYS (St Llwydian)   *see* Llandrygarn w Bodwrog and Heneglwys etc *Ban*

HENFYNYW (St David) w Aberaeron and Llanddewi Aberarth w Llanbadarn Trefeglwys *St D 8*   **V** J P LEWIS,   **C** R S WOOD

HENLLAN (St David)   *see* Llandysul w Bangor Teifi w Henllan etc *St D*

HENLLAN (St Sadwrn) and Llannefydd and Bylchau *St As 2*
R J P P WILLIAMS
HENLLAN AMGOED (St David)   *see* Whitland w Cyffig and
Henllan Amgoed etc *St D*
HENLLYS (St Peter)   *see* Cwmbran *Mon*
HENRY'S MOAT (St Bernard)   *see* Maenclochog and New
Moat etc *St D*
HEOL-Y-CYW (St Paul)   *see* Llanilid w Pencoed *Llan*
HERBRANDSTON (St Mary) and Hasguard w St Ishmael's
St D 5   **P-in-c** S H WIGHT
HEYOPE (St David)   *see* Beguildy and Heyope and Llangynllo
and Bleddfa *S & B*
HIGH CROSS (St Anne)   *see* Bassaleg *Mon*
HIRWAUN (St Lleurwg) (St Winifred) *Llan 9*   **V** B L JONES
HODGESTON (Church)   *see* Monkton *St D*
HOLT (St Chad), Rossett and Isycoed *St As 12*   **V** R A SUTER,
NSM V C T TUCKER
HOLYHEAD (St Cybi) (Morawelon) (St Ffraid) (St Gwenfaen)
Ban 3   **R** C A LLEWELLYN,   **C** N B DILKES, H V JONES
HOLYWELL (St James) (Holy Trinity) *St As 4*
V J D P LOMAS,   **C** S ELLIOTT
HOPE (Parish Church) *St As 13*   **R** M K SNELLGROVE
HOWEY (St David)   *see* Llandrindod w Cefnllys and Disserth
S & B
HUBBERSTON (St David) (Holy Spirit) *St D 5*
R A M CHADWICK,   **C** P O JONES
HUNDLETON (St David)   *see* Monkton *St D*
ILSTON (St Illtyd) w Pennard *S & B 8*   **V** D J WILKINSON
IRFON VALLEY *S & B 2*   **R** C M HAYNES
ISYCOED (St Paul)   *see* Holt, Rossett and Isycoed *St As*
ITTON (St Deiniol)   *see* St Arvans w Penterry, Itton, Devauden
etc *Mon*
JAMESTON   *see* Carew *St D*
JEFFREYSTON (St Jeffrey) w Reynoldston and East
Williamston and Loveston *St D 4*   **R** N P DAVIES
JOHNSTON (St Peter)   *see* Llangwm w Freystrop and Johnston
St D
JORDANSTON (St Cawrda)   *see* Mathry w St Edren's and
Grandston etc *St D*
KEMEYS COMMANDER (All Saints)   *see* Bettws Newydd w
Trostrey etc *Mon*
KENFIG   *see* Pyle w Kenfig *Llan*
KENFIG HILL (St Theodore) (St Colman) *Llan 5*
P-in-c R H SPENCER
KERRY (St Michael), Llanmerewig, Dolfor and Mochdre *St As 7*
V M W A CHADWICK
KILGETTY   *see* Begelly w Ludchurch and Crunwere *St D*
KILGWRRWG (Holy Cross)   *see* St Arvans w Penterry, Itton,
Devauden etc *Mon*
KILLAY (St Hilary) (St Martin) *S & B 6*   **V** T J WILLIAMS
KILVEY (All Saints)   *see* Swansea St Thos and Kilvey *S & B*
KNELSTON   *see* SW Gower *S & B*
KNIGHTON (St Edward) and Norton and Whitton and Pilleth
and Cascob *S & B 5*   **V** C I BUCKLEY
LALEOTON (St David) and Merthyr Mawr *Llan 1*
V E J EVANS,   **NSM** J M LEWIS
LAMBSTON (St Ishmael)   *see* Haverfordwest St Martin w
Lambston *St D*
LAMPETER PONT STEFFAN (St Peter)   *see* Bro Teifi Sarn
Helen *St D*
LAMPETER VELFREY (St Peter) and Llanddewi Velfrey
St D 15   **R** *vacant*
LAMPHEY (St Faith and St Tyfei)   *see* Monkton *St D*
LANDORE (St Paul) *S & B 10*   **V** D JONES,   **NSM** N P DOYLE
LANGSTONE (not known)   *see* Magor *Mon*
LANKNANSH (St Mary)   *see* Llantwit Major *Llan*
LAUGHARNE (St Martin) w Llansadwrnen and Llandawke
St D 15   **V** D L R BROWNRIDGE
LAVERNOCK (St Lawrence)   *see* Penarth and Llandough *Llan*
LAWRENNY (St Caradog)   *see* Martletwy w Lawrenny and
Minwear etc *St D*
LECKWITH   *see* Penarth and Llandough *Llan*
LETTERSTON (St Giles) w Llanfair Nant-y-Gof and
Puncheston w Little Newcastle and Castle Bythe *St D 3*
R R GRIFFITHS,   **C** M C CHARLES
LISVANE (St Denys) *Llan 1*   **V** *vacant*
LISWERRY   *see* Newport St Andr *Mon*
LITTLE NEWCASTLE (St Peter)   *see* Letterston w Llanfair
Nant-y-Gof etc *St D*
LLAN-GAN   *see* Whitland w Cyffig and Henllan Amgoed etc
St D
LLAN-LLWCH (St Mary) w Llangain and Llangynog *St D 11*
V R I PROTHEROE
LLAN-NON (St Non)   *see* Cwm Gwendraeth *St D*
LLAN-SAINT (All Saints)   *see* St Ishmael's w Llan-saint and
Ferryside *St D*

LLAN-Y-BRI (Holy Trinity)   *see* Llansteffan and Llan-y-bri etc
St D
LLANABER (St Mary) (St John) (St David) w Caerdeon *Ban 8*
R K G HORSWELL,   **NSM** L R BAILY
LLANAELHAEARN (St Aelhaiarn) w Clynnog Fawr *Ban 1*
R I THOMAS
LLANAFAN FAWR (St Afan)   *see* Upper Wye *S & B*
LLANAFAN-Y-TRAWSCOED (St Afan)   *see* Grwp Bro
Ystwyth a Mynach *St D*
LLANALLGO (St Gallo)   *see* Llaneugrad w Llanallgo and
Penrhosllugwy etc *Ban*
LLANANNO (St Anno)   *see* Llanbister w Llanbadarn Fynydd
w Llananno etc *S & B*
LLANARMON (St Garmon)   *see* Criccieth and Treflys w
Llanystumdwy etc *Ban*
LLANARMON DYFFRYN CEIRIOG (St Garmon)
see Llansantffraid Glyn Ceirog and Llanarmon etc *St As*
LLANARMON MYNYD (St Garmon)   *see* Llanrhaeadr ym
Mochnant etc *St As*
LLANARMON YN IAL (St Garmon)   *see* Llanbedr DC w
Llangynhafal, Llanychan etc *St As*
LLANARTH (St David) (St Teilo) and Capel Cynon w Talgarreg
and (St Mark) *St D 8*   **C** L BOLTON
LLANARTH (St Teilo)   *see* Llanddewi Rhydderch w
Llangattock-juxta-Usk etc *Mon*
LLANARTHNE (St David) and Llanddarog *St D 11*   **V** *vacant*
LLANASA (St Asaph and St Cyndeyrn) (St Winifred) *St As 4*
V *vacant* (01745) 853512
LLANBABO (St Pabo)   *see* Valley w Llechylched and
Caergeiliog *Ban*
LLANBADARN FAWR (St Padarn) *St D 10*   **V** *vacant* (01970)
623368
LLANBADARN FAWR (St Padarn) and Llandegley and
Llanfihangel Rhydithon w Abbey Cwmhir *S & B 5*
C S E HARRIS
LLANBADARN FYNYDD (St Padarn)   *see* Llanbister w
Llanbadarn Fynydd w Llananno etc *S & B*
LLANBADARN ODWYN (St Padarn)   *see* Bro Teifi Sarn
Helen *St D*
LLANBADARN TREFEGLWYS (St Padarn)   *see* Henfynyw w
Aberaeron and Llanddewi Aberarth etc *St D*
LLANBADARN-Y-GARREG (St Padarn)   *see* Aberedw w
Llandeilo Graban and Llanbadarn etc *S & B*
LLANBADOC (St Madog)   *see* Llangybi and Coedypaen w
Llanbadoc *Mon*
LLANBADRIG (St Padrig)   *see* Llanfechell w Bodewryd w
Rhosbeirio etc *Ban*
LLANBEBLIG (St Peblig) w Caernarfon and Betws Garmon w
Waunfawr *Ban 1*   **TR** R F DONALDSON
LLANBEDR (St Peter)   *see* Llanenddwyn w Llanddwywe,
Llanbedr w Llandanwg *Ban*
LLANBEDR DYFFRYN CLWYD (St Peter) w Llangynhafal,
Llanychan, and Llanarmon yn Ial *St As 3*   **R** H BUTLER,
C R W CARTER
LLANBEDR PAINSCASTLE (St Peter)   *see* Bryngwyn and
Newchurch and Llanbedr etc *S & B*
LLANBEDR-Y-CENNIN (St Peter)   *see* Caerhun w
Llangelynin w Llanbedr-y-Cennin *Ban*
LLANBEDR YSTRAD YW (St Peter)   *see* Llangenni and
Llanbedr Ystrad Yw w Patricio *S & B*
LLANBEDRGOCH (St Peter)   *see* Llanfair Mathafarn Eithaf w
Llanbedrgoch *Ban*
LLANBEDROG (St Pedrog) w Llannor and Llangian *Ban 11*
R A JONES
LLANBERIS (St Padarn) (St Peris), Llanrug and Llandinorwig
Ban 1   **R** R W TOWNSEND
LLANBISTER (St Cynllo) w Llanbadarn Fynydd w Llananno
and Llanddewi Ystradenni *S & B 5*   **C** S E HARRIS
LLANBLETHIAN (St Blethian)   *see* Cowbridge *Llan*
LLANBOIDY (St Brynach)   *see* Meidrim and Llanboidy and
Merthyr *St D*
LLANBRADACH (All Saints)   *see* Ystrad Mynach w
Llanbradach *Llan*
LLANBRYN-MAIR (St Mary)   *see* Bro Ddyfi Uchaf *Ban*
LLANCARFAN (St Cadoc)   *see* Penmark w Llancarfan w
Llantrithyd *Llan*
LLANDAFF (Cathedral of St Peter and St Paul w St Dyfrig,
St Teilo and St Euddogwy) *Llan 2*   **V** J T LEWIS
LLANDAFF North (All Saints) *Llan 2*   **V** *vacant* (029) 2056 4096
LLANDANWG   *see* Llanenddwyn w Llanddwywe, Llanbedr w
Llandanwg *Ban*
LLANDAVENNY   *see* Penhow, St Brides Netherwent w
Llandavenny etc *Mon*
LLANDAWKE (St Odoceus)   *see* Laugharne w Llansadwrnen
and Llandawke *St D*

LLANDDANIEL-FAB (St Deiniolfab) *see* Llanfair-pwll and
Llanddaniel-fab etc *Ban*
LLANDDAROG (St Twrog) *see* Llanarthne and Llanddarog
St D
LLANDDEINIOL (St Deiniol) *see* Llansantffraed w
Llanrhystud and Llanddeiniol *St D*
**LLANDDEINIOLEN (St Deiniol) w Llanfair-is-gaer w Penisa'r-
waun** *Ban 1* **V** J L JONES
LLANDDERFEL (St Derfel) *see* Llandrillo and Llandderfel
St As
LLANDDEW (St David) *see* Brecon St Mary w Llanddew
S & B
LLANDDEWI *see* Blaenau Irfon *S & B*
LLANDDEWI (St David) *see* SW Gower *S & B*
LLANDDEWI ABERARTH (St David) *see* Henfynyw w
Aberaeron and Llanddewi Aberarth etc *St D*
LLANDDEWI FACH (St David) *see* Bryngwyn and
Newchurch and Llanbedr etc *S & B*
LLANDDEWI RHONDDA (St Barnabas) *see* Pwllgwaun and
Llanddewi Rhondda *Llan*
LLANDDEWI RHONDDA (St David) *as above*
**LLANDDEWI RHYDDERCH (St David) w Llangattock-juxta-
Usk and Llanarth w Clytha and Llansantffraed** *Mon 1*
V M S SADLER, **P-in-c** L J DEROSAIRE
LLANDDEWI YSTRADENNI (St David) *see* Llanbister w
Llanbadarn Fynydd w Llananno etc *S & B*
LLANDDEWIBREFI (St David) *see* Bro Teifi Sarn Helen *St D*
LLANDDEWI'R CWM (St David) *see* Builth and Llanddewi'r
Cwm w Llangynog etc *S & B*
LLANDDOGET (St Doged) *see* LLanrwst *St As*
LLANDDONA (St Dona) *see* Llansadwrn w Llanddona and
Llaniestyn etc *Ban*
LLANDDOWROR (St Teilo) *see* St Clears w Llangynin and
Llanddowror etc *St D*
LLANDDULAS (St Cynfryd) and Llysfaen *St As 6*
R M C PARRY
LLANDDWYWE (St Ddwywe) *see* Llanenddwyn w
Llanddwywe, Llanbedr w Llandanwg *Ban*
LLANDDYFNAN (St Ddyfnan) *see* Llansadwrn w Llanddona
and Llaniestyn etc *Ban*
LLANDDYFNAN (St Deiniol) *as above*
LLANDECWYN (St Tecwyn) *see* Harlech and Llanfair-juxta-
Harlech etc *Ban*
LLANDEFAELOG-FACH (St Maelog) *see* Cynog Honddu
S & B
**LLANDEFALLE (St Matthew) and Llyswen w Boughrood and
Llanstephen w Talachddu** *S & B 4* **R** I P CHARLESWORTH
LLANDEGFAN (St Tegfan) w Llandysilio *Ban 6*
V A WILLIAMS
LLANDEGLA (St Tecla) *St As 17* **R** M SQUIRES
LLANDEGLEY (St Tecla) *see* Llanbadarn Fawr, Llandegley
and Llanfihangel etc *S & B*
LLANDEGVETH (St Tegfeth) *see* Llanfrechfa and Llanddewi
Fach w Llandegfeth *Mon*
LLANDEILO *see* Maenclochog and New Moat etc *St D*
LLANDEILO ABERCYWYN *see* Llansteffan and Llan-y-bri
etc *St D*
LLANDEILO FAWR (St Teilo) and Taliaris *St D 14*
NSM P C A MANSEL LEWIS
LLANDEILO GRABAN (St Teilo) *see* Aberedw w Llandeilo
Graban and Llanbadarn etc *S & B*
LLANDEILO TAL-Y-BONT (St Teilo) (St Michael) *S & B 9*
V J P H WALTERS
LLANDELOY (St Teilo) *see* Dewisland *St D*
LLANDENNY (St John the Apostle) *see* Raglan w Llandenny
and Bryngwyn *Mon*
LLANDEUSSANT (St Simon and St Jude) *see* Llangadog and
Gwynfe w Llanddeusant *St D*
LLANDEVAUD (St Peter) *see* Penhow, St Brides Netherwent w
Llandavenny etc *Mon*
LLANDEWI FACH *see* Llanfrechfa and Llanddewi Fach w
Llandegfeth *Mon*
LLANDEWI SKIRRID (St David) *see* Llantilio Pertholey w
Bettws Chpl etc *Mon*
LLANDEWI VELFREY (St David) *see* Lampeter Velfrey and
Llanddewi Velfrey *St D*
LLANDILO'R FAN (St Teilo) *see* Defynnog, Llandilo'r Fan,
Llanulid, Llywel etc *S & B*
LLANDINAM (St Llonio) w Trefeglwys w Penstrowed *Ban 9*
P-in-c L B COWAN
LLANDINGAT (St Dingad) w Myddfai *St D 14* **V** I H AVESON,
NSM J M MCHALE
LLANDINORWIG (Christ Church) *see* Llanberis, Llanrug and
Llandinorwig *Ban*
LLANDINORWIG (St Mary) *as above*

LLANDOGO (St Oudoceus) w Whitebrook Chapel and Tintern
Parva *Mon 2* **NSM** J W DEARNLEY, N HILL
LLANDOUGH (St Dochdwy) *see* Penarth and Llandough *Llan*
LLANDOUGH (St Dochwy) *see* Cowbridge *Llan*
LLANDOVERY *see* Llandingat w Myddfai *St D*
LLANDOW (Holy Trinity) *see* Colwinston, Llandow and
Llysworney *Llan*
LLANDRILLO (St Trilio) (St Derfel) and Llandderfel *St As 17*
V S J ROBERTS, **NSM** M F WILKINSON
LLANDRILLO-YN-RHOS (St Trillo) (St George) *St As 6*
V D JACKS
**LLANDRINDOD (Holy Trinity) (Old Parish Church) w Cefnllys
and Disserth** *S & B 5* **R** A G LOAT, **NSM** A TWEED
LLANDRINIO (St Trinio, St Peter and St Paul) *see* Llandysilio
and Penrhos and Llandrinio etc *St As*
**LLANDRYGARN (St Trygarn) w Bodwrog, Heneglwys,
Trewalchmai and Llanerch-y-medd** *Ban 4* **NSM** E D JERMAN
**LLANDUDNO (St George) (St Tudno) (Holy Trinity)
(Our Saviour)** *Ban 2* **R** J E NICE, **TV** J R ALLEN
LLANDUDWEN (St Tudwen) *see* Nefyn w Tudweiliog w
Llandudwen w Edern *Ban*
LLANDULAIS IN TIR ABAD (St David) *see* Blaenau Irfon
S & B
LLANDWROG (St Twrog) and Llanwnda *Ban 1* **V** T ROBERTS
LLANDYBIE (St Tybie) *St D 13* **V** vacant (01269) 850337
LLANDYFAELOG (St Maelog) *see* Cydweli and Llandyfaelog
St D
LLANDYFAN (Church) *see* Llandybie *St D*
LLANDYFODWG (St Tyfodwg) and Cwm Ogwr *Llan 4*
P-in-c E F DOWLAND-OWEN
LLANDYFRIOG (St Tyfriog) *see* Newcastle Emlyn w
Llandyfriog and Troedyraur etc *St D*
LLANDYFRYDOG (St Tyfrydog) *see* Llandrygarn w Bodwrog
and Heneglwys etc *Ban*
LLANDYGAI (St Ann) *see* Glanogwen and Llanllechid w St
Ann's and Pentir *Ban*
LLANDYGAI (St Tegai) *see* Tregarth and Llandygai and Maes
y Groes *Ban*
LLANDYGWYDD (St Tygwydd) *see* Maenordeifi Gp *St D*
LLANDYRNOG (St Tyrnog) (St Cwyfan) and Llangwyfan
St As 2 **R** E B THOMAS
LLANDYRY (Church) *see* Pen-bre *St D*
LLANDYSILIO (St Tysilio) *see* Llandegfan w Llandysilio *Ban*
LLANDYSILIO (St Tysilio) *see* Whitland w Cyffig and Henllan
Amgoed etc *St D*
**LLANDYSILIO (St Tysilio) (St Mary) and Penrhos and
Llandrinio w Criggion** *St As 10* **R** A G ELLACOTT
LLANDYSILIOGOGO (St Tysilio) *see* Llangrannog w
Llandysiliogogo w Penbryn *St D*
LLANDYSSIL (St Tyssil) *see* Montgomery and Forden and
Llandyssil *St As*
**LLANDYSUL (St Tysul) w Bangor Teifi w Henllan and
Llanfairorllwyn w Llangynllo** *St D 7* **V** E ROBERTS
LLANEDEYRN (All Saints) *see* Cyncoed *Mon*
LLANEDI (St Edith) w Tycroes and Saron *St D 13*
P-in-c D A BAXTER
LLANEDWEN (St Edwen) *see* Llanfair-pwll and Llanddaniel-
fab etc *Ban*
LLANEGRYN (St Mary and St Egryn) w Aberdyfi w Tywyn
Ban 12 **C** A A WHITE, **NSM** C C TEN WOLDE
LLANEGWAD (St Egwad) w Llanfynydd *St D 14*
V P S JONES
LLANEILIAN (St Eilian) *see* Amlwch *Ban*
LLANELEN (St Helen) *see* Govilon w Llanfoist w Llanelen
Mon
LLANELIAN (St Elian) *see* Colwyn and Llanelian *St As*
LLANELIDAN (St Elidan) *see* Llanfair DC, Derwen,
Llanelidan and Efenechtyd *St As*
LLANELLI (St Elli) *S & B 3* **V** A FRANCIS
**LLANELLI (St Elli) (All Saints) (St Alban) (Christ Church)
(St David) (St John) (St Peter)** *St D 12* **TR** S E JONES,
TV D R PAYNE, C J DAVIES, **C** P DAVIES
LLANELLTUD (St Illtyd) *see* Dolgellau w Llanfachreth and
Brithdir etc *Ban*
LLANELWEDD (St Matthew) *see* Colwyn *S & B*
**LLANENDDWYN (St Enddwyn) w Llanddwywe and Llanbedr w
Llandanwg** *Ban 8* **S** K N BEACON
LLANENGAN (St Engan) *see* Llanbedrog w Llannor and
Llangian *Ban*
**LLANERCH AERON (St Non) w Ciliau Aeron and Dihewyd and
Mydroilyn** *St D 8* **P-in-c** R H E DAVIES
LLANERCH-Y-MEDD (Eglwys Crist) *see* Llandrygarn w
Bodwrog and Heneglwys etc *Ban*
LLANERCH-Y-MEDD (St Mair) *as above*
LLANERFYL (St Erfyl) *see* Garthbeibio w Llanerfyl w
Llangadfan etc *St As*

LLANEUGRAD (St Eugrad) w Llanallgo and Penrhosllugwy w Llanfihangel Tre'r Beirdd *Ban 7* **R** *vacant*

LLANFABON (St Mabon) (St John the Baptist) *Llan 8* **R** C T REANEY

LLANFACHRAETH (St Machraeth) *see* Bodedern w Llanfaethlu *Ban*

LLANFACHRETH (St Machreth) *see* Dolgellau w Llanfachreth and Brithdir etc *Ban*

LLANFAELOG (St Maelog) and Llangwyfan *Ban 3* **R** M M BRADY

LLANFAELRHYS (St Maelrhys) *see* Aberdaron and Llanfaelrhys *Ban*

LLANFAES *see* Brecon St David w Llanspyddid and Llanilltyd *S & B*

LLANFAETHLU (St Maethlu) *see* Bodedern w Llanfaethlu *Ban*

LLANFAGLAN (St Mary) *see* Llandwrog and Llanwnda *Ban*

LLANFAIR (Church) *see* Gwaun-cae-Gurwen *St D*

LLANFAIR (Church) *see* Llandingat w Myddfai *St D*

LLANFAIR (St Mary) *see* Grosmont and Skenfrith and Llangattock etc *Mon*

LLANFAIR-AR-Y-BRYN (St Mary) *see* Cil-y-Cwm and Ystrad-ffin w Rhandir-mwyn etc *St D*

LLANFAIR CAEREINION (St Mary), Llanllugan and Manafon *St As 8* **V** L E FLETCHER

LLANFAIR CLYDOGAU (St Mary) *see* Bro Teifi Sarn Helen *St D*

LLANFAIR DISCOED (St Mary) *see* Caerwent w Dinham and Llanfair Discoed etc *Mon*

LLANFAIR DYFFRYN CLWYD (St Cynfarch and St Mary) (Jesus Chapel) and Derwen and Llanelidan and Efenechtyd *St As 3* **V** *vacant* (01824) 704551

LLANFAIR-IS-GAER (Old Parish Church) *see* Llanddeiniolen w Llanfair-is-gaer etc *Ban*

LLANFAIR-IS-GAER (St Mary) *as above*

LLANFAIR-JUXTA-HARLECH (St Mary) *see* Harlech and Llanfair-juxta-Harlech etc *Ban*

LLANFAIR KILGEDDIN *see* Bettws Newydd w Trostrey etc *Mon*

LLANFAIR MATHAFARN EITHAF (St Mary) w Llanbedrgoch *Ban 6* **R** J E PEARCE

LLANFAIR NANT-GWYN (St Mary) *see* Maenordeifi Gp *St D*

LLANFAIR NANT-Y-GOF (St Mary) *see* Letterston w Llanfair Nant-y-Gof etc *St D*

LLANFAIR-PWLL (St Mary) and Llanddaniel-fab w Penmynydd w Llanedwen *Ban 6* **R** P HUGHES, **Hon C** L J FRANCIS

LLANFAIR TALHAEARN (St Mary) *see* Petryal *St As*

LLANFAIR-YN-NEUBWLL *see* Valley w Llechylched and Caergeiliog *Ban*

LLANFAIR-YN-Y-CWMWD (St Mary) *see* Newborough w Llanidan w Llangeinwen etc *Ban*

LLANFAIR-YNG-NGHORNWY (St Mary) *see* Bodedern w Llanfaethlu *Ban*

LLANFAIRFECHAN (St Mary) (Christ Church) w Aber *Ban 2* **R** C M EVANS

LLANFAIRORLLWYN (St Mary) *see* Llandysul w Bangor Teifi w Henllan etc *St D*

LLANFAIRPWLLGWYNGYLLGOGERYCHWYRND-ROBWLL-LLANTISILIOGOGOGOCH (St Mary) *see* Llanfair-pwll and Llanddaniel-fab etc *Ban*

LLANFALLTEG (St Mallteg) w Castell Dwyran *St D 15* **V** *vacant*

LLANFAREDD (St Mary) *see* Colwyn *S & B*

LLANFECHAIN (St Garmon) *see* Llansantffraid-ym-Mechain and Llanfechain *St As*

LLANFECHAN (St Afan) *see* Irfon Valley *S & B*

LLANFECHELL (St Mechell) w Bodewryd w Rhosbeirio w Llanfflewin and Llanbadrig *Ban 7* **R** G W EDWARDS

LLANFERRES (St Berres) *see* Gwernaffield and Llanferres *St As*

LLANFEUGAN (St Meugan) w Llanthetty w Llansantffraed-juxta-Usk *S & B 3* **P-in-c** A S ROBINSON

LLANFFESTINIOG (St Michael) w Blaenau Ffestiniog w Trawsfynydd *Ban 8* **R** A R M VAN DEN HOF

LLANFFINAN (St Ffinan) *see* Llanfihangel Ysgeifiog w Llangristiolus etc *Ban*

LLANFFLEWIN (St Fflewin) *see* Llanfechell w Bodewryd w Rhosbeirio etc *Ban*

LLANFIHANGEL (St Michael) *see* Llantwit Major *Llan*

LLANFIHANGEL ABERCYWYN (St Michael) *see* St Clears w Llangynin and Llanddowror etc *St D*

LLANFIHANGEL ABERGWESSIN *see* Blaenau Irfon *S & B*

LLANFIHANGEL ABERYTHYCH (St Michael) *see* Llangathen w Llanfihangel Cilfargen etc *St D*

LLANFIHANGEL-AR-ARTH (St Michael) w Capel Dewi *St D 7* **V** B D TIMOTHY

LLANFIHANGEL BRYNPABUAN (St Michael and All Angels) *see* Upper Wye *S & B*

LLANFIHANGEL CILFARGEN *see* Llangathen w Llanfihangel Cilfargen etc *St D*

LLANFIHANGEL CRUCORNEY (St Michael) w Oldcastle and Cwmyoy and Llanthony *Mon 1* **V** D J YOUNG, **Hon Par Dn** D A LEE

LLANFIHANGEL FECHAN (St Michael) *see* Cynog Honddu *S & B*

LLANFIHANGEL GENAU'R-GLYN (St Michael) and Llangorwen *St D 10* **V** D B THOMAS

LLANFIHANGEL GLYN MYFYR (St Michael) *see* Cerrigydrudion w Llanfihangel Glyn Myfyr etc *St As*

LLANFIHANGEL GOBION (St Michael) *see* Bettws Newydd w Trostrey etc *Mon*

LLANFIHANGEL HELYGEN (St Michael) *see* Upper Wye *S & B*

LLANFIHANGEL LLEDROD (St Michael) *see* Llanilar w Rhostie and Llangwyryfon etc *St D*

LLANFIHANGEL NANTBRAN (St Michael) *see* Trallwng w Bettws Penpont w Aberyskir etc *S & B*

LLANFIHANGEL NANTMELAN (St Michael) *see* New Radnor and Llanfihangel Nantmelan etc *S & B*

LLANFIHANGEL PENBEDW *see* Maenordeifi Gp *St D*

LLANFIHANGEL PONTYMOILE (St Michael) *see* Panteg w Llanfihangel Pontymoile *Mon*

LLANFIHANGEL RHOS-Y-CORN (St Michael) *see* Brechfa w Abergorlech etc *St D*

LLANFIHANGEL RHYDITHON (St Michael) *see* Llanbadarn Fawr, Llandegley and Llanfihangel etc *S & B*

LLANFIHANGEL ROGIET *see* Caldicot *Mon*

LLANFIHANGEL TALYLLYN (St Michael) *see* Llyn Safaddan *S & B*

LLANFIHANGEL-TOR-Y-MYNYDD (St Michael) *see* Llanishen w Trellech Grange and Llanfihangel etc *Mon*

LLANFIHANGEL TRE'R BEIRDD (St Michael) *see* Llaneugrad w Llanallgo and Penrhosllugwy etc *Ban*

LLANFIHANGEL-UWCH-GWILI (St Michael) *see* Abergwili w Llanfihangel-uwch-Gwili etc *St D*

LLANFIHANGEL-Y-CREUDDYN (St Michael) *see* Grwp Bro Ystwyth a Mynach *St D*

LLANFIHANGEL-Y-PENNANT (St Michael) *see* Llanegryn w Aberdyfi w Tywyn *Ban*

LLANFIHANGEL-Y-TRAETHAU (St Michael) *see* Harlech and Llanfair-juxta-Harlech etc *Ban*

LLANFIHANGEL-YN-NHYWYN *see* Valley w Llechylched and Caergeiliog *Ban*

LLANFIHANGEL-YNG-NGHWYNFA (St Michael) *see* Garthbeibio w Llanerfyl w Llangadfan etc *St As*

LLANFIHANGEL YSGEIFIOG (St Michael) w Llangristiolus w Llanffinan w Llangaffo *Ban 4* **R** E C WILLIAMS

LLANFIHANGEL-YSTERN-LLEWERN (St Michael) *see* Rockfield and Dingestow Gp *Mon*

LLANFIHANGEL YSTRAD (St Michael) and Cilcennin w Trefilan and Nantcwnlle *St D 8* **P-in-c** A R JOHNSON

LLANFILO (St Bilo) *see* Talgarth w Bronllys w Llanfilo *S & B*

LLANFOIST (St Ffwyst) *see* Govilon w Llanfoist w Llanelen *Mon*

LLANFOR (St Mor and St Deiniol) w Rhosygwaliau *St As 17* **R** *vacant*

LLANFRECHFA (All Saints) and Llanddewi Fach w Llandegfeth *Mon 9* **P-in-c** A M WOODWELL

LLANFROTHEN (St Brothen) *see* Penrhyndeudraeth and Llanfrothen w Maentwrog etc *Ban*

LLANFRYNACH (St Brynach) *see* Cowbridge *Llan*

LLANFRYNACH (St Brynach) and Cantref w Llanhamlach *S & B 3* **P-in-c** A J R THOMAS

LLANFUGAIL (St Migail) *see* Valley w Llechylched and Caergeiliog *Ban*

LLANFWROG (St Mwrog and St Mary) and Clocaenog and Gyffylliog *St As 3* **R** J B DAVIES

LLANFYLLIN (St Myllin) and Bwlchycibau *St As 9* **R** M R BALKWILL

LLANFYNYDD (St Egwad) *see* Llanegwad w Llanfynydd *St D*

LLANFYNYDD (St Michael) (All Saints) *St As 16* **P-in-c** A J POOLMAN

LLANFYRNACH (St Brynach) *see* Crymych Gp *St D*

LLANGADFAN (St Cadfan) *see* Garthbeibio w Llanerfyl w Llangadfan etc *St As*

LLANGADOG (St Cadog) and Gwynfe w Llanddeusant *St D 14* **V** K M D COTTAM

LLANGADWALADR (St Cadwaladr) *see* Llansilin w Llangadwaladr and Llangedwyn *St As*

LLANGADWALADR (St Cadwaladr) *see* Trefdraeth w Aberffraw, Llangadwaladr etc *Ban*

LLANGAFFO (St Caffo) *see* Llanfihangel Ysgeifiog w Llangristiolus etc *Ban*

LLANGAIN (St Cain) *see* Llan-llwch w Llangain and Llangynog *St D*

LLANGAMMARCH (St Cadmarch) *see* Irfon Valley *S & B*

LLANGAN (St Canna) *see* Coychurch, Llangan and St Mary Hill *Llan*

LLANGANTEN (St Cannen) *see* Irfon Valley *S & B*

LLANGAR (St John the Evangelist) *see* Corwen w Llangar, Glyndyfrdwy etc *St As*

LLANGASTY TALYLLYN (St Gastyn) *see* Llyn Safaddan *S & B*

LLANGATHEN (St Cathen) w Llanfihangel Cilfargen and Llanfihangel Aberythych *St D 14* **V** W R HUGHES

LLANGATTOCK (St Cattwg) and Llangyndir *S & B 3* **R** K RICHARDS

LLANGATTOCK-JUXTA-USK (St Cadoc) *see* Llanddewi Rhydderch w Llangattock-juxta-Usk etc *Mon*

LLANGATTOCK LINGOED (St Cadoc) *see* Grosmont and Skenfrith and Llangattock etc *Mon*

LLANGATTOCK-VIBON-AVEL (St Cadoc) *see* Rockfield and Dingestow Gp *Mon*

LLANGEDWYN (St Cedwyn) *see* Llansilin w Llangadwaladr and Llangedwyn *St As*

LLANGEFNI (St Cyngar) w Tregaean *Ban 4* **R** P MCLEAN

LLANGEINOR (St Ceinor) and the Garw Valley *Llan 4* **P-in-c** D J MORTIMORE

LLANGEINWEN (St Ceinwen) *see* Newborough w Llanidan w Llangeinwen etc *Ban*

LLANGEITHO (St Ceitho) *see* Bro Teifi Sarn Helen *St D*

LLANGELER (St Celer) w Pen-Boyr *St D 7* **P-in-c** J N GILLIBRAND

LLANGELYNIN (St Celynnin) *see* Caerhun w Llangelynin w Llanbedr-y-Cennin *Ban*

LLANGELYNNIN (St Celynin) *see* Arthog w Fairbourne w Llangelynnin w Rhoslefain *Ban*

LLANGENNECH (St Gwynog) and Hendy *St D 12* **V** P C JONES

LLANGENNI (St Cenau) and Llanbedr Ystrad Yw w Patricio *S & B 3* **NSM** R O MULLIS

LLANGENNITH (St Cenydd) w Llanmadoc and Cheriton *S & B 8* **R** P J WILLIAMS

LLANGERNYW (St Digain) *see* Petryal *St As*

LLANGEVIEW (St David) *see* Llangwm Uchaf and Llangwm Isaf w Gwernesney etc *Mon*

LLANGIAN (St Gian) *see* Llanbedrog w Llannor and Llangian *Ban*

LLANGIWG (St Ciwg) *S & B 7* **V** G H GREEN

LLANGLYDWEN (St Cledwyn) *see* Crymych Gp *St D*

LLANGOEDMOR (St Cynllo) *see* Cardigan w Mwnt and Y Ferwig w Llangoedmor *St D*

LLANGOLLEN (St Collen) (St John) w Trevor and Llantysilio *St As 14* **V** A C SULLY

LLANGOLMAN (St Colman) *see* Maenclochog and New Moat etc *St D*

LLANGORSE (St Paulinus) *see* Llyn Safaddan *S & B*

LLANGORWEN (All Saints) *see* Llanfihangel Genau'r-glyn and Llangorwen *St D*

LLANGOWER (St Cywair) *see* Bala *St As*

LLANGRANNOG (St Carannog) w Llandysiliogogo w Penbryn *St D 8* **V** I D FORSTER

LLANGRISTIOLUS (St Cristiolus) *see* Llanfihangel Ysgeifiog w Llangristiolus etc *Ban*

LLANGUNNOG *see* Llanishen w Trellech Grange and Llanfihangel etc *Mon*

LLANGUNNOR (St Ceinwr) w Cwmffrwd *St D 11* **V** W D A GRIFFITHS, **NSM** C M STEEL

LLANGURIG (St Curig) *see* Llanidloes w Llangurig *Ban*

LLANGWLLOG (St Cwyllog) *see* Llandyrygarn w Bodwrog and Heneglwys etc *Ban*

LLANGWLLONG (St Anau) *as above*

LLANGWM (St Catherine) *see* Betws Gwerful Goch w Llangwm w Llawrybetws *St As*

LLANGWM (St Jerome) w Freystrop and Johnston *St D 5* **R** J E GOUPILLON

LLANGWM ISAF (St John) *see* Llangwm Uchaf and Llangwm Isaf w Gwernesney etc *Mon*

LLANGWM UCHAF (St Jerome) and Llangwm Isaf w Gwernesney and Llangeview w Wolvesnewton *Mon 4* **NSM** K J HASLER

LLANGWNNADL (St Gwynhoedl) *see* Botwnnog w Bryncroes w Llangwnnadl w Penllech *Ban*

LLANGWYFAN *see* Llandyrnog and Llangwyfan *St As*

LLANGWYFAN (St Cwyfan) *see* Llanfaelog and Llangwyfan *Ban*

LLANGWYFAN (St Cwyfan Old Church) *as above*

LLANGWYRYFON (St Ursula) *see* Llanilar w Rhostie and Llangwyryfon etc *St D*

LLANGYBI (St Cybi) *see* Criccieth and Treflys w Llanystumdwy etc *Ban*

LLANGYBI (St Cybi) *see* Bro Teifi Sarn Helen *St D*

LLANGYBI (St Cybi) and Coedypaen w Llanbadoc *Mon 4* **R** A E MORTON

LLANGYFELACH (St David and St Cyfelach) (St Teilo-on-the-Clase) *S & B 7* **V** R J DAVIES-HANNEN

LLANGYNDEYRN (St Cyndeyrn) *see* Cwm Gwendraeth *St D*

LLANGYNDIR (St Cynidr and St Mary) *see* Llangattock and Llangyndir *S & B*

LLANGYNFELYN (St Cynfelyn) *see* Borth and Eglwys-fach w Llangynfelyn *St D*

LLANGYNHAFAL (St Cynhafal) *see* Llanbedr DC w Llangynhafal, Llanychan etc *St As*

LLANGYNIN (St Cynin) *see* St Clears w Llangynin and Llanddowror etc *St D*

LLANGYNLLO (St Cynllo) *see* Llandysul w Bangor Teifi w Henllan etc *St D*

LLANGYNLLO (St Cynllo) *see* Beguildy and Heyope and Llangynllo and Bleddfa *S & B*

LLANGYNOG *see* Builth and Llanddewi'r Cwm w Llangynog etc *S & B*

LLANGYNOG (St Cynog) *see* Llanrhaeadr ym Mochnant etc *St As*

LLANGYNOG (St Cynog) *see* Llan-llwch w Llangain and Llangynog *St D*

LLANGYNWYD (St Cynwyd) (St Stephen) (St Tydfil) w Maesteg *Llan 4* **V** G A BLYTH

LLANGYNYW (St Cynyw) *see* Meifod w Llangynyw w Pont Robert w Pont Dolanog *St As*

LLANGYSTENNIN (St Cystenin) (St Michael) (St Katherine) (St Mary) *St As 5* **NSM** R GREEN

LLANHAMLACH (St Peter and St Illtyd) *see* Llanfrynach and Cantref w Llanhamlach *S & B*

LLANHARAN (St Julius and St Aaron) w Peterston-super-Montem *Llan 4* **P-in-c** B A WOOD

LLANHARRY (St Illtud) *Llan 7* **P-in-c** R T PITMAN, **NSM** B J REANEY

LLANHENNOCK (St John) *see* Caerleon w Llanhennock *Mon*

LLANHILLETH (Christ Church) (St Mark) w Six Bells *Mon 7* **Hon C** M PARKER

LLANHYWEL (St Hywel) *see* Dewisland *St D*

LLANIDAN (St Nidan) *see* Newborough w Llanidan w Llangeinwen and Llangeinwen *Ban*

LLANIDLOES (St Idloes) w Llangurig *Ban 9* **V** R P PITCHER

LLANIESTYN (St Iestyn) *see* Llansadwrn w Llanddona and Llaniestyn etc *Ban*

LLANIESTYN (St Iestyn) *see* Botwnnog w Bryncroes w Llangwnnadl w Penllech *Ban*

LLANIGON (St Eigon) *see* Hay w Llanigon and Capel-y-Ffin *S & B*

LLANILAR (St Hilary) w Rhostie and Llangwyryfon w Llanfihangel Lledrod *St D 10* **V** E A HOWELLS

LLANILID (St Illid and St Curig) w Pencoed *Llan 4* **R** N P JONES

LLANILLTYD (St John) *see* Brecon St David w Llanspyddid and Llanilltyd *S & B*

LLANINA (St Ina) *see* Llanllwchaearn and Llanina *St D*

LLANISHEN (Christ Church) *see* Cardiff Ch Ch Roath Park *Llan*

LLANISHEN (St Dennis) w Trellech Grange and Llanfihangel Tor-y-Mynydd w Llangunnog and Llansoy *Mon 2* **P-in-c** D M OWEN

LLANISHEN (St Isan) (St Faith) *Llan 1* **V** M D WITCOMBE, **C** A P THOMAS

LLANLLAWDDOG (St Llawddog) *see* Llanpumsaint w Llanllawddog *St D*

LLANLLAWER *see* Newport w Cilgwyn and Nevern and Y Beifil etc *St D*

LLANLLECHID (St Cross) *see* Tregarth and Llandygai and Maes y Groes *Ban*

LLANLLECHID (St Llechid) *see* Glanogwen and Llanllechid w St Ann's and Pentir *Ban*

LLANLLEONFEL (Parish Church) *see* Irfon Valley *S & B*

LLANLLOWELL (St Llywel) *see* Usk and Gwehelog w Llantrisant w Llanllowell *Mon*

LLANLLUGAN (St Mary) *see* Llanfair Caereinion, Llanllugan and Manafon *St As*

LLANLLWCHAEARN (St Llwchaiarn) and Llanina *St D 8* **P-in-c** H Q GREGORY-SMITH

LLANLLWCHAIARN (All Saints) (St Llwchaiarn) and Newtown w Aberhafesp *St As 7*   **R** A S GRIMWOOD, **NSM** E C YATES

LLANLLWNI (St Luke or St Llonio)   *see* Llanybydder and Llanwenog w Llanllwni *St D*

LLANLLYFNI (St Rhedyw) (St John) (Christ Church) *Ban 1*   **R** A C N BUCKLEY

LLANLLYR-YN-RHOS (St Llyr)   *see* Upper Wye *S & B*

LLANMADOC (St Madoc)   *see* Llangennith w Llanmadoc and Cheriton *S & B*

LLANMAES (St Catwg)   *see* Llantwit Major *Llan*

LLANMARTIN (St Martin)   *see* Magor *Mon*

LLANMEREWIG (St Llwchaiarn)   *see* Kerry, Llanmerewig, Dolfor and Mochdre *St As*

LLANMILOE (St Barbara)   *see* Pendine w Llanmiloe and Eglwys Gymyn w Marros *St D*

LLANNEFYDD (St Nefydd and St Mary)   *see* Henllan and Llannefydd and Bylchau *St As*

LLANNOR (Holy Cross)   *see* Llanbedrog w Llannor and Llangian *Ban*

LLANOVER (St Bartholomew)   *see* Goetre w Llanover *Mon*

LLANPUMSAINT (Five Saints) w Llanllawddog *St D 11*   **V** *vacant* (01267) 253205

LLANRHAEADR YM MOCHNANT (St Dogfan) w Llanarmon Mynydd Mawr w Penybontfawr w Llanwddyn w Llangynog *St As 9*   **V** J E T YENDALL,   **C** L M EDWARDS, **NSM** J A PRUST

LLANRHAEADR-YNG-NGHINMEIRCH (St Dyfnog) w Prion and Nantglyn *St As 2*   **V** J M WILLIAMS

LLANRHEITHAN (St Rheithan)   *see* Dewisland *St D*

LLANRHIAN (St Rhian)   *as above*

LLANRHIDIAN (St Rhidian and St Illtyd) w Llanyrnewydd *S & B 8*   **V** D M T WALTERS

LLANRHOS (St Paul) *St As 5*   **V** R H GRIFFITHS, **C** J W JAUNDRILL,   **NSM** P A WRIGHT

LLANRHUDDLAD (St Rhuddlad)   *see* Bodedern w Llanfaethlu *Ban*

LLANRHWYDRUS   *as above*

LLANRHYCHWYN (St Rhychwyn)   *see* Caerhun w Llangelynin w Llanbedr-y-Cennin *Ban*

LLANRHYDD (St Meugan)   *see* Ruthin w Llanrhydd *St As*

LLANRHYSTUD (St Restitutis)   *see* Llansantffraed w Llanrhystud and Llanddeiniol *St D*

LLANRUG (St Gabriel)   *see* Llanberis, Llanrug and Llandinorwig *Ban*

LLANRUG (St Michael)   *as above*

LLANRUMNEY (St Dyfrig) *Mon 5*   **V** M I R DOWSETT, **NSM** A J JENKINS

LLANRWST (St Grwst) *St As 5*   **R** L D NORMAN

LLANSADWRN (St Sadwrn) w Llanddona and Llaniestyn w Pentraeth w Llanddyfnan *Ban 6*   **R** D PRYS

LLANSADWRN (St Sadwrn) w Llanwrda and Manordeilo *St D 14*   **V** A J LEGG

LLANSADWRNEN (St Sadwrnen)   *see* Laugharne w Llansadwrnen and Llandawke *St D*

LLANSAMLET (St Samlet) (St John) (St Paul) *S & B 7*   **V** C M DARVILL

LLANSANNAN (St Sannan)   *see* Petryal *St As*

LLANSANNOR (St Senwyr)   *see* Cowbridge *Llan*

LLANSANTFFRAED (St Bridget)   *see* Llanddewi Rhydderch w Llangattock-juxta-Usk etc *Mon*

LLANSANTFFRAED (St Bridget) w Llanrhystud and Llanddeiniol *St D 8*   **V** J W SMITH

LLANSANTFFRAED-IN-ELWELL (St Bridget)   *see* Colwyn *S & B*

LLANSANTFFRAED-JUXTA-USK (St Bride)   *see* Llanfeugan w Llanthetty etc *S & B*

LLANSANTFFRAID, Bettws and Aberkenfig *Llan 4* **P-in-c** S C PARE,   **C** G E DANIEL-LOWANS,   **NSM** O M PARRY

LLANSANTFFRAID GLAN CONWY (St Ffraid) (St Martin) and Eglwysbach *St As 5*   **R** C R OWEN

LLANSANTFFRAID GLYN CEIRIOG (St Ffraid) w Llanarmon Dyffryn Ceiriog and Pontfadog *St As 14* **V** P J CLARKE

LLANSANTFFRAID-YM-MECHAIN (St Ffraid) and Llanfechain *St As 9*   **V** P POWELL

LLANSANTFFRAID GLYN DYFRDWY (St Ffraid)   *see* Corwen w Llangar, Glyndyfrdwy etc *St As*

LLANSAWEL (St Mary), Briton Ferry *Llan 6*   **V** G C POWELL

LLANSAWEL (St Sawyl)   *see* Cynwyl Gaeo w Llansawel and Talley *St D*

LLANSILIN (St Silin) w Llangadwaladr and Llangedwyn *St As 9* **P-in-c** F M ROBARTS

LLANSOY (St Tysoi)   *see* Llanishen w Trellech Grange and Llanfihangel etc *Mon*

LLANSPYDDID (St Cattwg)   *see* Brecon St David w Llanspyddid and Llanilltyd *S & B*

LLANSTADWEL (St Tudwal) *St D 5*   **V** P W D FLAVELL

LLANSTEFFAN (St Ystyffan) and Llan-y-bri and Llandeilo Abercywyn *St D 11*   **P-in-c** P S JONES

LLANSTEPHEN (St Steffan)   *see* Llandefalle and Llyswen w Boughrood etc *S & B*

LLANSTINAN (St Justinian)   *see* Llanwnda, Goodwick w Manorowen and Llanstinan *St D*

LLANTARNAM (St Michael)   *see* Cwmbran *Mon*

LLANTHETTY (St Tetti)   *see* Llanfeugan w Llanthetty etc *S & B*

LLANTHONY (St David)   *see* Llanfihangel Crucorney w Oldcastle etc *Mon*

LLANTILIO CROSSENNY (St Teilo) and Penrhos w Llanvetherine and Llanvapley *Mon 1*   **P-in-c** D R OSBORN

LLANTILIO PERTHOLEY (St Teilo) w Bettws Chapel and Llanddewi Skirrid *Mon 1*   **P-in-c** P M WINCHESTER

LLANTOOD (St Illtud)   *see* Cilgerran w Bridell and Llantwyd and Eglwyswrw *St D*

LLANTRISANT (Church)   *see* Grwp Bro Ystwyth a Mynach *St D*

LLANTRISANT (St Afran, St Ieuan and St Sanan)   *see* Valley w Llechylched and Caergeiliog *Ban*

LLANTRISANT (St Illtyd, St Gwynno and St Dyfodwg) (St Michael) (St David) *Llan 11*   **V** V L PARKINSON, **C** I HODGES

LLANTRISANT (St Peter, St Paul and St John)   *see* Usk and Gwehelog w Llantrisant w Llanllowell *Mon*

LLANTRITHYD (St Illtyd)   *see* Penmark w Llancarfan w Llantrithyd *Llan*

LLANTWIT FARDRE (St Illtyd) (St Andrew) *Llan 11* **V** P M N GULLIDGE,   **NSM** K G SIMPSON

LLANTWIT MAJOR (St Illtud) (St Donat) *Llan 7* **TR** J A WEBBER,   **TV** M A PRINCE,   **NSM** D R BOULT

LLANTWYD (St Illtud)   *see* Cilgerran w Bridell and Llantwyd and Eglwyswrw *St D*

LLANTYSILIO (St Tysilio)   *see* Llangollen w Trevor and Llantysilio *St As*

LLANULID (St Ilid)   *see* Defynnog, Llandilo'r Fan, Llanulid, Llywel etc *S & B*

LLANUWCHLLYN (St Deiniol)   *see* Bala *St As*

LLANVACHES (St Dyfrig)   *see* Penhow, St Brides Netherwent w Llandavenny etc *Mon*

LLANVAPLEY (St Mable)   *see* Llantilio Crossenny w Penrhos, Llanvetherine etc *Mon*

LLANVETHERINE (St James the Elder)   *as above*

LLANWDDYN (St Wyddyn)   *see* Llanrhaeadr ym Mochnant etc *St As*

LLANWELLWYFO (St Gwenllwyfo)   *see* Amlwch *Ban*

LLANWENARTH CITRA (St Peter)   *see* Abergavenny St Mary w Llanwenarth Citra *Mon*

LLANWENOG (St Gwenog)   *see* Llanybydder and Llanwenog w Llanllwni *St D*

LLANWERN (St Mary)   *see* Magor *Mon*

LLANWINIO (St Gwynio)   *see* Crymych Gp *St D*

LLANWNDA (St Baglan Old Church)   *see* Llandwrog and Llanwnda *Ban*

LLANWNDA (St Gwyndaf)   *as above*

LLANWNDA (St Gwyndaf) and Goodwick (St Peter) w Manorowen and Llanstinan *St D 3*   **V** B BARNES

LLANWNNEN (St Lucia)   *see* Bro Teifi Sarn Helen *St D*

LLANWNNOG (St Gwynog) and Caersws w Carno *Ban 9* **P-in-c** C E BREWSTER,   **NSM** P N WARD

LLANWNNWS (St Gwnnws)   *see* Grwp Bro Ystwyth a Mynach *St D*

LLANWRDA (St Cwrdaf)   *see* Llansadwrn w Llanwrda and Manordeilo *St D*

LLANWRIN (St Ust and St Dyfrig)   *see* Machynlleth w Llanwrin and Penegoes *Ban*

LLANWRTHWL (St Gwrthwl)   *see* Gwastedyn *S & B*

LLANWRTYD (St David)   *see* Blaenau Irfon *S & B*

LLANWRTYD WELLS (St James)   *as above*

LLANWYDDELAN (St Gwyddelan)   *see* Betws Cedewain and Tregynon and Llanwyddelan *St As*

LLANWYNNO (Christ Church)   *see* Pontypridd St Matt and Cilfynydd w Llanwynno *Llan*

LLANWYNNO (St Gwynno)   *as above*

LLANYBYDDER (St Peter) and Llanwenog w Llanllwni *St D 9* **V** W R TILLERY

LLANYCEFN (Church)   *see* Llawhaden w Bletherston and Llanycefn *St D*

LLANYCHAEARN (St Llwchaiarn)   *see* Aberystwyth *St D*

LLANYCHAN (St Hychan)   *see* Llanbedr DC w Llangynhafal, Llanychan etc *St As*

LLANYCHAR (Church)   *see* Fishguard w Llanychar and
Pontfaen w Morfil etc *St D*
LLANYCHLWYDOG   *as above*
LLANYCIL (St Beuno)   *see* Bala *St As*
LLANYCRWYS (St David)   *see* Pencarreg and Llancrwys *St D*
LLANYMAWDDWY (St Tydecho)   *see* Bro Ddyfi Uchaf *Ban*
LLANYNGHENEDL VALLEY (St Michael)   *see* Valley w
Llechylched and Caergeiliog *Ban*
LLANYNYS   *see* Builth and Llanddewi'r Cwm w Llangynog etc
S & B
LLANYNYS (St Saeran) *St As 3*   **V** *vacant*
LLANYRE   *see* Upper Wye *S & B*
LLANYRNEWYDD (St Gwynour)   *see* Llanrhidian w
Llanyrnewydd *S & B*
LLANYSTYMDWY (St John the Baptist)   *see* Criccieth and
Treflys w Llanystumdwy etc *Ban*
LLANYWERN (St Mary the Virgin)   *see* Llyn Safaddan *S & B*
LLAWHADEN (St Aidan) w Bletherston and Llanycefn *St D 2*
P-in-c P H DAVIES,   **Hon C** J EVANS
LLAWRYBETWS (St James)   *see* Betws Gwerful Goch w
Llangwm w Llawrybetws *St As*
LLAY (St Martin) *St As 12*   **V** P A WALKER
LLECHGYNFARWY (St Cynfarwy)   *see* Bodedern w
Llanfaethlu *Ban*
LLECHRYD (St Tydfil)   *see* Maenordeifi Gp *St D*
LLECHYLCHED (Holy Trinity)   *see* Valley w Llechylched and
Caergeiliog *Ban*
LLISWERRY   *see* Newport St Andr *Mon*
LLOWES (St Meilig)   *see* Glasbury and Llowes w Clyro and
Betws *S & B*
LLWYDCOED (St James)   *see* Aberdare St Fagan *Llan*
LLWYDIARTH (St Mary)   *see* Garthbeibio w Llanerfyl w
Llangadfan etc *St As*
LLWYNCELLYN (St Luke)   *see* Porth Newydd *Llan*
LLWYNDERW (Holy Cross) (Clyne Chapel) *S & B 6*
V D B EVANS
LLWYNGWRIL   *see* Arthog w Fairbourne w Llangelynnin w
Rhoslefain *Ban*
LLWYNHENDY (St David) *St D 12*   **V** A M GRAY
LLWYNYPIA   *see* Pont Rhondda *Llan*
LLYN SAFADDAN *S & B 4*   **V** A N JEVONS
LLYS-Y-FRAN (St Meilyr)   *see* Maenclochog and New Moat
etc *St D*
LLYSFAEN (St Cynfran)   *see* Llanddulas and Llysfaen *St As*
LLYSWEN (St Gwendoline)   *see* Llandefalle and Llyswen w
Boughrood etc *S & B*
LLYSWORNEY (St Tydfil)   *see* Colwinston, Llandow and
Llysworney *Llan*
LLYWEL (St David)   *see* Defynnog, Llandilo'r Fan, Llanulid,
Llywel etc *S & B*
LOUGHOR (St Michael) (St David) (St Paul) *S & B 9*
V G J TURNER,   **NSM** K MORGAN
LOVESTON (St Leonard)   *see* Jeffreyston w Reynoldston and E
Williamston etc *St D*
LUDCHURCH (St Elidyr)   *see* Begelly w Ludchurch and
Crunwere *St D*
MACHEN (St John the Baptist)   *see* Bedwas w Machen w Rudry
Mon
MACHEN (St Michael)   *as above*
MACHYNLLETH (St Peter) w Llanwrin and Penegoes *Ban 10*
R E W ROWLANDS,   **C** K ROGERS
**MAENCLOCHOG (St Mary) and Llandeilo w Henry's Moat w
Mynachlogddu w Llanychlogddu w New Moat w Llys y Fran**
St D 2   **P-in-c** R J DAVIES
MAENORDEIFI Group, The (St David) *St D 6*
R P R MACKNESS
MAENORDEIFI (Old Parish Church)   *see* Maenordeifi Gp
St D
MAENTWROG (St Twrog)   *see* Penrhyndeudraeth and
Llanfrothen w Maentwrog etc *Ban*
MAERDY (All Saints)   *see* Rhondda Fach Uchaf *Llan*
MAESGLAS and Duffryn *Mon 8*   **P-in-c** L C HALL,
NSM S L COLLINGBOURNE
MAESMYNIS AND LLANYNYS (St David)   *see* Builth and
Llanddewi'r Cwm w Llangynog etc *S & B*
MAESTEG (St David)   *see* Llangynwyd w Maesteg *Llan*
MAESTEG (St Michael)   *as above*
MAESTEILO (St John)   *see* Llandeilo Fawr and Taliaris *St D*
MAESTIR (St Mary)   *see* Bro Teifi Sarn Helen *St D*
MAGOR (St Mary) *Mon 3*   **TR** C M LAWSON-JONES,   **Par
Dn** A M PRICE,   **NSM** N D HOWARD
**MAINDEE NEWPORT (St John the Evangelist) (St Mary)
(St Matthew)** *Mon 8*   **V** D NEALE,   **C** H C P M HALL,
NSM J K BEARDMORE, J A WELSH, C H HOCKEY
MALLYWD (St Tydecho)   *see* Bro Ddyfi Uchaf *Ban*

MALPAS (St Mary) *Mon 8*   **V** D G PARFITT,   **NSM** M E DUNN,
OLM F M A EVANS
MAMHILAD (St Illtud) w Monkswood and Glascoed Chapel
Mon 4   **P-in-c** R E PAIN
MANAFON (St Michael)   *see* Llanfair Caereinion, Llanllugan
and Manafon *St As*
MANCOT (St Michael)   *see* Hawarden *St As*
MANORBIER (St James)   *see* Carew *St D*
MANORDEILO (St Paul)   *see* Llansadwrn w Llanwrda and
Manordeilo *St D*
MANOROWEN (St Mary)   *see* Llanwnda, Goodwick w
Manorowen and Llanstinan *St D*
MANSELTON (St Michael and All Angels) and Cwmbwrla
S & B 10   **V** J B DAVIES
MARCHWIEL (St Marcella)   *see* Bangor Monachorum,
Worthenbury and Marchwiel *St As*
MARCROSS (Holy Trinity)   *see* Llantwit Major *Llan*
MARGAM (St Mary) (St David) *Llan 5*   **V** T A DOHERTY
MARLOES (St Peter)   *see* Dale and St Brides w Marloes *St D*
MARROS (St Lawrence)   *see* Pendine w Llanmiloe and Eglwys
Gymyn w Marros *St D*
**MARSHFIELD (St Mary) and Peterstone Wentloog and
Coedkernew w St Bride's Wentloog** *Mon 5*   **V** D C MATTHEWS
**MARTLETWY (St Marcellus) w Lawrenny and Minwear and
Yerbeston w Templeton** *St D 4*   **V** *vacant* (01834) 861017
MATHERN (St Tewdric) and Mounton w St Pierre *Mon 3*
V J E L WHITE
**MATHRY (Holy Martyrs) w St Edren's and Grandston w
St Nicholas and Jordanston** *St D 3*   **P-in-c** A C SALMON
MATTHEWSTOWN (All Saints)   *see* Penrhiwceiber,
Matthewstown and Ynysboeth *Llan*
MAUDLAM (St Mary Magdalene)   *see* Pyle w Kenfig *Llan*
MEIDRIM (St David) and Llanboidy and Merthyr *St D 15*
V J GAINER
**MEIFOD (St Tysilio and St Mary) w Llangynyw w Pont Robert w
Pont Dolanog** *St As 8*   **V** J L W WILLIAMS
MELIDEN (St Melyd) (St Mary Magdalene) and Gwaenysgor
St As 1   **V** J C HARVEY
MELINE (St Dogmael) *St D 6*   **V** *vacant*
MENAI BRIDGE (St Mary)   *see* Llandegfan w Llandysilio *Ban*
MERLIN'S BRIDGE (St Mark)   *see* Haverfordwest St Mary
and St Thos w Haroldston *St D*
MERTHYR (St Martin)   *see* Meidrim and Llanboidy and
Merthyr *St D*
MERTHYR CYNOG (St Cynog)   *see* Cynog Honddu *S & B*
MERTHYR DYFAN (St Dyfan and St Teilo) *Llan 3*
R R C PARRISH
MERTHYR MAWR (St Teilo)   *see* Laleston and Merthyr Mawr
Llan
MERTHYR TYDFIL (Christ Church) (St Luke) *Llan 10*
V S S MORGAN,   **C** J E PARKIN
MERTHYR TYDFIL (St David) (St Tydfil's Well) *Llan 10*
R M J DAVIES,   **C** D T MORRIS,   **NSM** W A DAVID
MERTHYR VALE (St Mary and Holy Innocents)
see Troedyrhiw w Merthyr Vale *Llan*
MICHAELSTON-LE-PIT (St Michael and All Angels)   *see* St
Andrews Major w Michaelston-le-Pit *Llan*
MICHAELSTON-SUPER-AVON   *see* Cwmafan *Llan*
MICHAELSTON-SUPER-ELY (St Michael)   *see* St Fagans w
Michaelston-super-Ely *Llan*
MICHAELSTON-Y-FEDW (St Michael) *Mon 5*
P-in-c M C G LANE
MICHEL TROY (St Michael)   *see* Monmouth w Overmonnow
etc *Mon*
**MILFORD HAVEN (St Katherine) (St Peter) (St Thomas
à Becket)** *St D 5*   **V** J H M DAVIES
MINERA (St Andrew)   *see* Bwlchgwyn and Minera *St As*
MINERA (St David)   *as above*
MINERA (St Mary)   *as above*
MINERA (St Tudfil)   *as above*
MINWEAR (St Womar)   *see* Martletwy w Lawrenny and
Minwear etc *St D*
MISKIN (St John the Baptist)   *see* Mountain Ash and Miskin
Llan
MOCHDRE (All Saints)   *see* Kerry, Llanmerewig, Dolfor and
Mochdre *St As*
MOLD (St Mary) *St As 16*   **V** C I DAY
MONINGTON (St Nicholas)   *see* St Dogmael's w Moylgrove
and Monington *St D*
MONKSWOOD (St Matthew)   *see* Mamhilad w Monkswood
and Glascoed Chapel *Mon*
MONKTON (St Nicholas and St John) *St D 1*   **TR** M L COX,
TV R JONES, M J DOBBS
**MONMOUTH (St Mary the Virgin) w Overmonnow w
Wonastow w Michel Troy** *Mon 2*   **V** D J MCGLADDERY,
C J D HARRIS,   **NSM** A M GREEN

PENMAEN (St John the Baptist) *see* Bishopston w Penmaen and Nicholaston *S & B*
PENMAENMAWR *see* Dwygyfylchi *Ban*
PENMARK (St Mary) w Llancarfan w Llantrithyd *Llan 3*
P-in-c F A JACKSON
PENMYNYDD (St Credifael) *see* Llanfair-pwll and Llanddaniel-fab etc *Ban*
PENNAL (St Peter ad Vincula) w Corris and Esgairgeiliog *Ban 10* **R** G AP IORWERTH
PENNANT (St Thomas) *see* Llanrhaeadr ym Mochnant etc *St As*
PENNANT MELANGELL (St Melangel) *as above*
PENNARD (St Mary) *see* Ilston w Pennard *S & B*
PENPONT (no dedication) *see* Trallwng w Bettws Penpont w Aberyskir etc *S & B*
PENRHIWCEIBER (St Winifred), Matthewstown and Ynysboeth *Llan 9* **V** A K HOLMES
PENRHOS (Holy Trinity) *see* Llandysilio and Penrhos and Llandrinio etc *St As*
PENRHOS (St Cadoc) *see* Llantilio Crossenny w Penrhos, Llanvetherine etc *Mon*
PENRHOSLLUGWY (St Michael) *see* Llaneugrad w Llanallgo and Penrhosllugwy etc *Ban*
PENRHYDD *see* Maenordeifi *Gp St D*
PENRHYN-COCH (St John) *see* Elerch w Penrhyncoch w Capel Bangor and Goginan *St D*
PENRHYNDEUDRAETH (Holy Trinity) and Llanfrothen w Maentwrog and Beddgelert *Ban 8* **NSM** J E BUCKLES
PENRHYNSIDE (St Sannan) *see* Llanrhos *St As*
PENRHYNSIDE BAY (St David) *as above*
PENRICE (St Andrew) *see* SW Gower *S & B*
PENSARN (St David) *see* Abergele and St George *St As*
PENSTROWED (St Gwrhai) *see* Llandinam w Trefeglwys w Penstrowed *Ban*
PENTERRY (St Mary) *see* St Arvans w Penterry, Itton, Devauden etc *Mon*
PENTIR (St Cedol) *see* Glanogwen and Llanllechid w St Ann's and Pentir *Ban*
PENTRAETH (St Mary) *see* Llansadwrn w Llanddona and Llaniestyn etc *Ban*
PENTRE (St Peter) *see* Ystradyfodwg *Llan*
PENTRECHWYTH (St Peter) *see* Glantawe *S & B*
PENTREFOELAS (Parish Church) *see* Cerrigydrudion w Llanfihangel Glyn Myfyr etc *St As*
PENTROBIN (St John) *see* Hawarden *St As*
PENTWYN (St David) *see* Cyncoed *Mon*
PENTYRCH (St Cadwg) w Capel Llanilterne *Llan 2* **V** J W BINNY
PENYBONTFAWR *see* Llanrhaeadr ym Mochnant etc *St As*
PENYCAE (St Thomas) *see* Rhosymedre w Penycae *St As*
PENYCLAWDD (St Martin) *see* Rockfield and Dingestow *Gp Mon*
PENYDARREN (St John the Baptist) *see* Dowlais and Penydarren *Llan*
PENYFAI (All Saints) *Llan 4* **P-in-c** E S HARRIS
PENYFFORDD (Emmanuel) *see* Hope *St As*
PENYGRAIG (St Barnabas) *see* Dinas and Penygraig w Williamstown *Llan*
PENYWAUN (St Winifred) *see* Hirwaun *Llan*
PETERSTON-SUPER-ELY (St Peter) w St Brides-super-Ely *Llan 7* **P-in-c** R V C LEWIS, **NSM** A B SWANN
PETERSTON-SUPER-MONTEM (St Peter) *see* Llanharan w Peterston-super-Montem *Llan*
PETERSTONE WENTLOOG (St Peter) *see* Marshfield and Peterstone Wentloog etc *Mon*
PETRYAL *St As 6* **V** J R MATTHIAS
PILLETH (Our Lady of Pilleth) *see* Knighton, Norton, Whitton, Pilleth and Cascob *S & B*
PISTYLL (St Beuno) *see* Nefyn w Tudweiliog w Llandudwen w Edern *Ban*
PONT AMAN (St Thomas) *see* Betws w Ammanford *St D*
PONT DOLANOG (St John the Evangelist) *see* Meifod w Llangynyw w Pont Robert w Pont Dolanog *St As*
PONT-IETS (St Mary) *see* Cwm Gwendraeth *St D*
PONT RHONDDA *Llan 12* **V** P S GALE
PONT ROBERT (St John the Evangelist) *see* Meifod w Llangynyw w Pont Robert w Pont Dolanog *St As*
PONTARDAWE (All Saints) *see* Llangiwg *S & B*
PONTARDAWE (St Peter) *as above*
PONTARDDULAIS *see* Llandeilo Tal-y-bont *S & B*
PONTARFYNACH *see* Grwp Bro Ystwyth a Mynach *St D*
PONTARGOTHI (Holy Trinity) *see* Llanegwad w Llanfynydd *St D*
PONTBLYDDYN (Christ Church) *St As 16* **P-in-c** C M POOLMAN

PONTERWYD *see* Grwp Bro Ystwyth a Mynach *St D*
PONTFADOG (St John) *see* Llansantffraid Glyn Ceirog and Llanarmon etc *St As*
PONTFAEN (St Brynach) *see* Fishguard w Llanychar and Pontfaen w Morfil etc *St D*
PONTLLANFRAITH (St Augustine) *see* Mynyddislwyn *Mon*
PONTLLIW (St Anne) *see* Penllergaer *S & B*
PONTLOTTYN (St Tyfaelog) (St Michael) (St Aidan) w Fochriw *Llan 8* **V** P A DEROY-JONES
PONTNEATHVAUGHAN (St John) *see* Penderyn Mellte *S & B*
PONTNEWYDD (Holy Trinity) *Mon 9* **V** D J DUNN, **Par Dn** H D THOMAS, **OLM** D L THOMAS
PONTNEWYNYDD (All Saints) *see* Pontypool *Mon*
PONTRHYDFENDIGAID (St David) *see* Tregaron w Ystrad Meurig and Strata Florida *St D*
PONTSIAN (St John) *see* Llandysul w Bangor Teifi w Henllan etc *St D*
PONTYATES (St Mary) *see* Cwm Gwendraeth *St D*
PONTYBEREM (St John) *as above*
PONTYCLUN (St Paul) w Talygarn *Llan 7* **V** G P KARAMURA
PONTYCYMMER (St David) *see* Llangeinor and the Garw Valley *Llan*
PONTYGWAITH (St Mary Magdalene) *see* Rhondda Fach Uchaf *Llan*
PONTYMISTER (St Margaret) *see* Risca *Mon*
PONTYPOOL (St James) (St Matthew) *Mon 9* **R** B R PIPPEN, **C** A TEMPLE-WILLIAMS
PONTYPRIDD (St Catherine) *Llan 11* **V** E M GREEN
PONTYPRIDD St Matthew and Cilfynydd w Llanwynno *Llan 11* **P-in-c** E EVANS
POOL QUAY (St John the Evangelist) *see* Welshpool, Castle Caereinion and Pool Quay *St As*
PORT EYNON (St Cattwg) *see* SW Gower *S & B*
PORT TALBOT (St Agnes) *see* Aberavon *Llan*
PORT TALBOT (St David) *see* Margam *Llan*
PORT TALBOT (St Theodore) (Holy Cross) (St Peter) *Llan 5* **V** C J AMOS, **C** W M T V COUGHLIN
PORTH NEWYDD (St Paul) *Llan 12* **P-in-c** C W COLES
PORTHCAWL (All Saints) *see* Newton Nottage *Llan*
PORTHKERRY (St Curig) and Rhoose *Llan 3* **P-in-c** D O TREHARNE
PORTHMADOC (St John) (St Cyngar) and Ynyscynhaearn and Dolbenmaen *Ban 11* **V** A J WILLIAMS
PORTSKEWETT (St Mary) *see* Caldicot *Mon*
PRENDERGAST (St David) w Rudbaxton *St D 2* **R** G D GWYTHY
PRESTATYN (Christ Church) (Church of Holy Spirit) *St As 1* **V** D Q BELLAMY, **C** K A JOHNSON
PRINCES GATE (St Catherine) *see* Lampeter Velfrey and Llanddewi Velfrey *St D*
PRION (St James) *see* Llanrhaeadr-yng-Nghinmeirch w Prion and Nantglyn *St As*
PUNCHESTON (St Mary) *see* Letterston w Llanfair Nant-y-Gof etc *St D*
PUNCHSTON *see* Fishguard w Llanychar and Pontfaen w Morfil etc *St D*
PWLL (Holy Trinity) *see* Burry Port and Pwll *St D*
PWLLCROCHAN *see* Monkton *St D*
PWLLGWAUN (St Mark) and Llanddewi Rhondda *Llan 11* **P-in-c** C E BURR
PWLLHELI *see* Denio w Abererch *Ban*
PYLE (St James) (St Mary Magdalene) w Kenfig *Llan 5* **P-in-c** I K REES
QUAR, THE (St Tydfil's Well) *see* Merthyr Tydfil St Dav *Llan*
QUEENSFERRY (St Andrew) *see* Shotton *St As*
RADNOR (St Mary) *see* New Radnor and Llanfihangel Nantmelan etc *S & B*
RADNOR, EAST *see* Knighton, Norton, Whitton, Pilleth and Cascob *S & B*
RADYR (St John the Baptist) (Christ Church) *Llan 2* **R** J WIGLEY, **NSM** C A COLTON
RAGLAN (St Cadoc) w Llandenny and Bryngwyn *Mon 4* **P-in-c** J WAKELING
REDBERTH (Church) *see* Carew *St D*
REDWICK (St Thomas) *see* Magor *Mon*
RESOLVEN (St David) *see* Vale of Neath *Llan*
REYNALSTON (Church) *see* Jeffreyston w Reynoldston and E Williamston etc *St D*
REYNOLDSTON (St George) *see* SW Gower *S & B*
RHANDIRMWYN (St Barnabas) *see* Cil-y-Cwm and Ystrad-ffin w Rhandir-mwyn etc *St D*
RHAYADER (St Clement) *see* Gwastedyn *S & B*
RHESYCAE (Christ Church) *see* Halkyn w Caerfallwch w Rhesycae *St As*

RHEWL (Church)   *see* Llanbedr DC w Llangynhafal,
  Llanychan etc *St As*
RHIWLAS (Mission Church)   *see* Llansilin w Llangadwaladr
  and Llangedwyn *St As*
RHONDDA FACH UCHAF *Llan 12*   **P-in-c** A J DAVIES
RHOOSE (St Peter)   *see* Porthkerry and Rhoose *Llan*
RHOS (St James)   *see* Llangeler w Pen-Boyr *St D*
RHOSBEIRIO   *see* Llanfechell w Bodewryd w Rhosbeirio etc
  Ban
RHOSCOLYN   *see* Holyhead *Ban*
RHOSCROWTHER (St Decumanus)   *see* Monkton *St D*
RHOSDDU   *see* Wrexham *St As*
RHOSESEMOR   *see* Halkyn w Caerfallwch w Rhesycae *St As*
RHOSILI (St Mary the Virgin)   *see* SW Gower *S & B*
RHOSLEFAIN (St Mary)   *see* Arthog w Fairbourne w
  Llangelynnin w Rhoslefain *Ban*
RHOSLLANNERCHRUGOG (St John the Evangelist)
  (St David) (St Mary) *St As 14*   **V** J S EVANS
RHOSTIE   *see* Llanilar w Rhostie and Llangwyryfon etc *St D*
RHOSYGWALIAU (Holy Trinity)   *see* Llanfor w Rhosygwaliau
  St As
RHOSYMEDRE (St John the Evangelist) w Penycae *St As 14*
  P-in-c A W COLEMAN
RHUDDLAN (St Mary) *St As 1*   **V** J G GRIFFITHS
RHULEN (St David)   *see* Colwyn *S & B*
RHYD-Y-MWYN (St John the Evangelist)   *see* Cilcain and
  Nannerch and Rhydymwyn *St As*
RHYDYBRIW (Capel Rhydybriw)   *see* Defynnog, Llandilo'r
  Fan, Llanulid, Llywel etc *S & B*
RHYDYFELIN (St Luke) w Graig *Llan 11*   **P-in-c** M D GABLE
RHYL (Holy Trinity) (St Thomas) (St John) (St Ann) *St As 1*
  V J GLOVER,   **C** P T ALLSWORTH
RHYMNEY (St David) *Mon 6*   **V** M OWEN
RISCA (St Mary) *Mon 5*   **V** J BLACKBURN,   **C** D G BATE
ROATH (St German) *Llan 1*   **V** R D DOXSEY
ROATH (St Margaret) (St Anne) (St Edward) (St Teilo's School)
  Llan 1   **V** S LISK,   **C** A M FLIPSE
ROATH (St Martin) *Llan 1*   **V** I D HAMER,   **NSM** T G WATKIN
ROATH (St Philip)   *see* Tremorfa St Phil CD *Llan*
ROATH (St Saviour) *Llan 1*   **P-in-c** D J ATKINS
ROATH PARK (Christ Church)   *see* Cardiff Ch Ch Roath Park
  Llan
ROBERTSTOWN (St John the Evangelist)   *see* Aberdare *Llan*
ROBESTON WATHEN (Church)   *see* Narberth w Mounton w
  Robeston Wathen and Crinow *St D*
ROBESTON WEST (St Andrew)   *see* Walwyn's Castle w
  Robeston W *St D*
ROCH (St Mary)   *see* Nolton w Roch and St Lawrence w Ford
  etc *St D*
ROCKFIELD (St Cenedlon) w St Maughans w Llangattock-
  vibon-Avel w LLanfihangel-ystern-LLewern w Dingestow w
  Llangovan and Penyclawdd w Tregaer w Cwmcarvan *Mon 2*
  V J L GUEST,   **NSM** I M ELLIS, J-J S AIDLEY
ROGERSTONE (St John the Baptist)   *see* Bassaleg *Mon*
ROGIET (St Mary)   *see* Caldicot *Mon*
ROSEMARKET (St Ishmael)   *see* Burton and Rosemarket *St D*
ROSSETT (Christ Church)   *see* Holt, Rossett and Isycoed *St As*
RUABON (St Mary) (All Saints) *St As 14*   **V** M A HARRISON
RUDBAXTON (St Michael)   *see* Prendergast w Rudbaxton
  St D
RUDRY (St James)   *see* Bedwas w Machen w Rudry *Mon*
RUMNEY (St Augustine) *Mon 5*   **V** D A G HATHAWAY
RUTHIN (St Peter) w Llanrhydd *St As 3*   **R** R BAYLEY
ST ANDREWS MAJOR (St Andrew) (St Peter) w Michaelston-
  le-Pit *Llan 3*   **R** D H RHYDDERCH
ST ARVANS (St Arvan) w Penterry, Itton, Devauden and
  Kilgwrrwg *Mon 3*   **V** M J GOLLOP,   **NSM** M E ZORAB
ST ASAPH (Cathedral of St Asaph and St Cyndeyrn) *St As 1*
  TR C N L POTTER,   **TV** V C ROWLANDS
ST ATHAN (St Tathan)   *see* Llantwit Major *Llan*
ST BRIDES (St Bridget)   *see* Dale and St Brides w Marloes *St D*
ST BRIDES MAJOR (St Bridget)   *see* Ewenny w St Brides
  Major *Llan*
ST BRIDES MINOR (St Bride)   *see* Llansantffraid, Bettws and
  Aberkenfig *Llan*
ST BRIDES NETHERWENT (St Bridget)   *see* Penhow, St
  Brides Netherwent w Llandavenny etc *Mon*
ST BRIDES-SUPER-ELY (St Bride)   *see* Peterston-super-Ely w
  St Brides-super-Ely *Llan*
ST BRIDES WENTLOOG   *see* Marshfield and Peterstone
  Wentloog etc *Mon*
ST CLEARS (St Mary Magdalene) w Llangynin and
  Llanddowror and Llanfihangel Abercywyn *St D 15*
  V B D WITT
ST DAVIDS (Cathedral of St David and St Andrew)
  see Dewisland *St D*

ST DOGMAEL'S (St Thomas) w Moylgrove and Monington
  St D 6   **V** D P DAVIES
ST DOGWELLS (St Dogfael)   *see* Spittal w Trefgarn and
  Ambleston w St Dogwells *St D*
ST EDREN'S   *see* Mathry w St Edren's and Grandston etc *St D*
ST ELVIS   *see* Dewisland *St D*
ST FAGANS (St Mary) w Michaelston-super-Ely *Llan 2*
  R A R WINTLE
ST FLORENCE (St Florentius)   *see* Carew *St D*
ST GEORGE (St George)   *see* Abergele and St George *St As*
ST GEORGE-SUPER-ELY (St George)   *see* St Nicholas w
  Bonvilston and St George-super-Ely *Llan*
ST HARMON (St Garmon)   *see* Gwastedyn *S & B*
ST HILARY (St Hilary)   *see* Cowbridge *Llan*
ST HILARY (St Hilary) Greenway   *see* Rumney *Mon*
ST ISHMAEL'S (St Ishmael)   *see* Herbrandston and Hasguard
  w St Ishmael's *St D*
ST ISHMAEL'S (St Ishmael) w Llan-saint and Ferryside *St D 12*
  V *vacant* (01267) 267288
ST ISSELL'S (St Issell) and Amroth *St D 4*   **V** M BUTLER
ST LAWRENCE (St Lawrence)   *see* Nolton w Roch and St
  Lawrence w Ford etc *St D*
ST LYTHANS (St Bleiddian)   *see* Wenvoe and St Lythans *Llan*
ST MARY CHURCH (St Mary)   *see* Cowbridge *Llan*
ST MARY HILL (St Mary)   *see* Coychurch, Llangan and St
  Mary Hill *Llan*
ST MAUGHEN'S (St Meugan)   *see* Rockfield and Dingestow
  Gp Mon
ST MELLONS (St Mellon) *Mon 5*   **V** D KELLEN
ST NICHOLAS (St Nicholas)   *see* Mathry w St Edren's and
  Grandston etc *St D*
ST NICHOLAS (St Nicholas) w Bonvilston and St George-super-
  Ely *Llan 7*   **P-in-c** R V C LEWIS
ST PETROX (St Pedrog)   *see* Monkton *St D*
ST PIERRE (St Peter)   *see* Mathern and Mounton w St Pierre
  Mon
ST THOMAS   *see* Haverfordwest St Mary and St Thos w
  Haroldston *St D*
ST TWYNNELLS (St Gwynog)   *see* Monkton *St D*
SANDFIELDS   *see* Aberavon *Llan*
SANDYCROFT (Holy Spirit)   *see* Hawarden *St As*
SANDYCROFT (St Francis)   *as above*
SARON (St David)   *see* Llanedi w Tycroes and Saron *St D*
SAUNDERSFOOT   *see* St Issell's and Amroth *St D*
SEALAND (St Barth)   *see* Hawarden *St As*
SEBASTOPOL (St Oswald)   *see* Griffithstown *Mon*
SENGHENYDD (St Peter)   *see* Eglwysilan *Llan*
SEVEN SISTERS (St David)   *see* Dulais Valley *Llan*
SEVEN SISTERS (St Mary)   *as above*
SHIRENEWTON (St Thomas à Becket)   *see* Caerwent w
  Dinham and Llanfair Discoed etc *Mon*
SHOTTON (St Ethelwold) *St As 13*   **V** S D GREEN
SILIAN (St Sulien)   *see* Bro Teifi Sarn Helen *St D*
SINAN (All Saints)   *see* Cefn w Trefnant w Tremeirchion *St As*
SIX BELLS (St John)   *see* Llanhilleth w Six Bells *Mon*
SKENFRITH (St Bride)   *see* Grosmont and Skenfrith and
  Llangattock etc *Mon*
SKETTY (St Paul) (Holy Trinity) *S & B 6*   **V** A J KNIGHT,
  C G D WATHAN
SKEWEN (St John) (All Saints) (St Mary) *Llan 6*
  V M WILLIAMS
SLEBECH (St John the Baptist Parish Centre) and Uzmaston w
  Boulston *St D 2*   **P-in-c** P H DAVIES,   **Hon C** J EVANS
SOLVA (St Aidan)   *see* Dewisland *St D*
SOUTHERNDOWN (All Saints)   *see* Ewenny w St Brides
  Major *Llan*
SOUTHSEA (All Saints)   *see* Brymbo, Southsea and Tanyfron
  St As
SPITTAL (St Mary) w Trefgarn and Ambleston w St Dogwells
  St D 2   **V** D R REES
STACKPOLE ELIDOR (St James and St Elidyr)   *see* Monkton
  St D
STEYNTON (St Cewydd and St Peter) *St D 5*
  V J I HOLDSWORTH,   **NSM** D G DAVIES
STRATA FLORIDA (St Mary)   *see* Tregaron w Ystrad Meurig
  and Strata Florida *St D*
SULLY (St John the Baptist) *Llan 3*   **R** E B DOWDING
SWANSEA (St Barnabas) *S & B 11*   **P-in-c** K SMALLDON
SWANSEA (St Gabriel) *S & B 6*   **V** D M GRIFFITHS
SWANSEA (St James) *S & B 11*   **V** D A WALKER
SWANSEA (St Jude) (St Nicholas-on-the-Hill) *S & B 11*
  V H V PARSELL
SWANSEA (St Luke)   *see* Manselton and Cwmbwrla *S & B*
SWANSEA (St Peter) *S & B 10*   **V** H M WILLIAMS
SWANSEA (St Thomas) (St Stephen) and Kilvey *S & B 11*
  V A J M MEREDITH,   **C** A W PULLEN,   **NSM** J W WEDGBURY

SWANSEA, CENTRAL (St Mary) (Holy Trinity) (Christ Church) (St Matthew) (St Mark) (St John) *S & B 11* TR A J VESSEY, TV C L WILLIAMS, S M KNIGHT, NSM I DREW-JONES

TAI'RGWAITH (St David) *see* Gwaun-cae-Gurwen *St D*

TAL-Y-LLYN (St David) *see* Llanegryn w Aberdyfi w Tywyn *Ban*

TALACHDDU (St Mary) *see* Llandefalle and Llyswen w Boughrood etc *S & B*

TALBENNY (St Mary) *see* Walton W w Talbenny and Haroldston W *St D*

TALGARREG (St David) *see* Llanarth and Capel Cynon w Talgarreg etc *St D*

TALGARTH (St Gwendoline) w Bronllys w Llanfilo *S & B 4* V R T EDWARDS

TALIARIS (Holy Trinity) *see* Llandeilo Fawr and Taliaris *St D*

TALLARN GREEN (St Mary Magdalene) *see* Hanmer, Bronington, Bettisfield, Tallarn Green *St As*

TALLEY (St Michael) *see* Cynwyl Gaeo w Llansawel and Talley *St D*

TALYBONT (St Cross) *see* Tregarth and Llandygai and Maes y Groes *Ban*

TALYBONT (St David) *see* Llanfihangel Genau'r-glyn and Llangorwen *St D*

TALYGARN (St Anne) *see* Pontyclun w Talygarn *Llan*

TALYLLYN (St David) *see* Pennal w Corris and Esgairgeiliog *Ban*

TALYLLYN (St Mary) *see* Llanegryn w Aberdyfi w Tywyn *Ban*

TEMPLETON (St John) *see* Martletwy w Lawrenny and Minwear etc *St D*

TENBY (St Mary) (St Julian's Chapel) *St D 4* TR A J DAVIES, TV S M JOHN, C M L OSBORNE

TINTERN (St Michael) *see* Llandogo w Whitebrook Chpl and Tintern Parva *Mon*

TIRABAD (St David) *see* Blaenau Irfon *S & B*

TIRTHIL (St Michael) *see* Pontlottyn w Fochriw *Llan*

TON PENTRE *see* Ystradyfodwg *Llan*

TON-YR-YWEN (School) *see* Llanishen *Llan*

TONDU (St John) *see* Llansantffraid, Bettws and Aberkenfig *Llan*

TONDU (St Thomas) *as above*

TONGWYNLAIS (St Michael) (St James) *Llan 2* V V J PAYNE

TONMAWR (St Teilo) *see* Neath *Llan*

TONNA (St Anne) *see* Cadoxton-juxta-Neath and Tonna *Llan*

TONYPANDY (St Andrew) w Clydach Vale *Llan 12* V P A LEYSHON

TONYREFAIL (St David) (St Alban) w Gilfach Goch *Llan 12* V R E MOVERLEY, NSM J SHAW

TOWNHILL *see* Swansea St Jude w St Nic *S & B*

TOWYN (St Mary) *St As 1* V M BURNS

TRAEAN-GLAS (St Mary) *see* Defynnog, Llandilo'r Fan, Llanulid, Llywel etc *S & B*

TRALLWNG (St David) w Bettws Penpont w Aberyskir w Llanfihangel Nantbran w Battle *S & B 1* P-in-c N HOOK

TRAWSFYNYDD (St Madryn) *see* Llanffestiniog w Blaenau Ffestiniog etc *Ban*

TRE-GROES (St Ffraid) *see* Llandysul w Bangor Teifi w Henllan etc *St D*

TRE-LECH A'R BETWS (St Teilo) *see* Cynwyl Elfed w Newchurch and Trelech a'r Betws *St D*

TREALAW (All Saints) *see* Pont Rhondda *Llan*

TREBANOS (St Michael) *see* Clydach *S & B*

TREBOETH (St Alban) (Penlan Church) *S & B 10* V D JONES, NSM N P DOYLE

TREDEGAR (St George) (St James) *Mon 6* V J G DAVIS, C V L ASHLEY

TREDUNNOC (St Andrew) *Mon 4* V vacant

TREFDRAETH (St Beuno) (Eglwys Crist y Brenin) w Aberffraw w Llangadwaladr w Cerrigceinwen *Ban 4* P-in-c J R BAILEY

TREFEGLWYS (St Michael) *see* Llandinam w Trefeglwys w Penstrowed *Ban*

TREFGARN (St Michael) *see* Spittal w Trefgarn and Ambleston w St Dogwells *St D*

TREFILAN (St Hilary) *see* Llanfihangel Ystrad and Cilcennin w Trefilan etc *St D*

TREFLYS (St Michael) *see* Criccieth and Treflys w Llanystumdwy etc *Ban*

TREFNANT (Holy Trinity) *see* Cefn w Trefnant w Tremeirchion *St As*

TREFOR (St George) *see* Llanaelhaearn w Clynnog Fawr *Ban*

TREFRIW (St Mary) *see* Caerhun w Llangelynin w Llanbedr-y-Cennin *Ban*

TREGAEAN (St Caian) *see* Llangefni w Tregaean *Ban*

TREGAER (St Mary) *see* Rockfield and Dingestow Gp *Mon*

TREGARON (St Caron) w Ystrad Meurig and Strata Florida *St D 9* V P W DAVIES

TREGARTH (St Mair) and Llandygai and Maes y Groes *Ban 5* V L J PERRY

TREGYNON (St Cynon) *see* Betws Cedewain and Tregynon and Llanwyddelan *St As*

TREHARRIS (St Matthias), Trelewis and Bedlinog *Llan 10* P-in-c M GIBBON

TREHERBERT (St Alban) *see* Pen Rhondda Fawr *Llan*

TREHERBERT (St Mary Communion Centre) *as above*

TRELAWNYD (St Michael) *see* Dyserth and Trelawnyd and Cwm *St As*

TRELLECH (St Nicholas) and Penallt *Mon 3* V S J HOWELLS, NSM J M BONE

TRELLECH GRANGE (not known) *see* Llanishen w Trellech Grange and Llanfihangel etc *Mon*

TREMAIN (St Michael) *see* Aberporth w Tremain w Blaenporth and Betws Ifan *St D*

TREMEIRCHION (Corpus Christi) *see* Cefn w Trefnant w Tremeirchion *St As*

TREMORFA (St Philip) Conventional District *Llan 3* P-in-c R M CAPPER

TREORCHY (St Matthew) *see* Pen Rhondda Fawr *Llan*

TRETHOMAS (St Thomas) *see* Bedwas w Machen w Rudry *Mon*

TRETOWER (St John the Evangelist) *see* Crickhowell w Cwmdu and Tretower *S & B*

TREUDDYN (St Mary) w Nercwys *St As 16* V J B JONES

TREVETHIN (St Cadoc) *see* Pontypool *Mon*

TREVETHIN (St John the Divine) *as above*

TREVOR (Church) *see* Llangollen w Trevor and Llantysilio *St As*

TREWALCHMAI (St Morhaiarn) *see* Llandrygarn w Bodwrog and Heneglwys etc *Ban*

TROED-YR-AUR (St Michael) *see* Newcastle Emlyn w Llandyfriog and Troedyraur etc *St D*

TROEDRHIWGARTH (St Mary the Virgin) *Llan 5* V D G MORRIS

TROEDYRHIW (St John) w Merthyr Vale *Llan 10* V S J BARNES

TROSTEY (St David) *see* Bettws Newydd w Trostrey etc *Mon*

TROWBRIDGE MAWR (St Hilary) *see* Rumney *Mon*

TUDWEILIOG (St Cwyfan) *see* Nefyn w Tudweiliog w Llandudwen w Edern *Ban*

TUMBLE (Dewi Sant) *see* Cwm Gwendraeth *St D*

TY SIGN (St David) *see* Risca *Mon*

TYCOCH (All Souls) *S & B 6* V P J GWYNN

TYCROES (St Edmund) *see* Llanedi w Tycroes and Saron *St D*

TYLORSTOWN (Holy Trinity) *see* Rhondda Fach Uchaf *Llan*

TYNANT (Mission Church) *see* Penrhyndeudraeth and Llanfrothen w Maentwrog etc *Ban*

TYWYN (St Cadfan) *see* Llanegryn w Aberdyfi w Tywyn *Ban*

TYWYN (St Matthew) *as above*

UNDY (St Mary) *see* Magor *Mon*

UPPER WYE, The *S & B 2* V B L T GRIFFITH

USK (St Mary) and Gwehelog w Llantrisant w Llanllowell *Mon 4* V J F GRAY

UZMASTON (St Ismael) *see* Slebech and Uzmaston w Boulston *St D*

VALE OF NEATH *Llan 6* V P A LEWIS

VALLEY (St Michael) w Llechylched and Caergeiliog *Ban 3* R N A RIDINGS

VAYNOR (St Gwynno) *see* Cefn Coed w Vaynor *S & B*

WALTON EAST (St Mary) *see* Wiston w Walton E and Clarbeston *St D*

WALTON WEST (All Saints) w Talbenny and Haroldston West *St D 5* R A P JOHNSON

WALWYN'S CASTLE (St James the Great) w Robeston West *St D 5* P-in-c R M M JOHNSON

WATERSTON *see* Llanstadwel *St D*

WATTSTOWN (St Thomas) *see* Ynyshir *Llan*

WAUNARLLWYDD (St Barnabas) *S & B 9* P-in-c I DAVIES

WAUNFAWR (St John the Evangelist) *see* Llanbeblig w Caernarfon and Betws Garmon etc *Ban*

WAUNFELIN (St John the Divine) *see* Pontypool *Mon*

WAUNWEN (St Mark) *see* Cen Swansea *S & B*

WELSH ST DONATS (St Donat) *see* Pendoylan w Welsh St Donats *Llan*

WELSHPOOL (St Mary), Castle Caereinion and Pool Quay *St As 10* R W K ROWELL, NSM E M POWELL

WENVOE (St Mary) and St Lythans *Llan 3* P-in-c A C BERRY

WHISTON (not known) *see* Magor *Mon*

WHITCHURCH (St David) *see* Dewisland *St D*

WHITCHURCH (St Mary) (St Thomas) (All Saints) *Llan 2* TR J H L ROWLANDS, TV A P JAMES, C T O HUGHES, Hon C H G LEWIS, NSM B A SMITH

WHITEBROOK (Holy Trinity) *see* Llandogo w Whitebrook Chpl and Tintern Parva *Mon*

WHITECHURCH IN KEMES   *see* Eglwyswen *St D*
WHITFORD (St Mary and St Beuno)   *see* Gorsedd w Brynford, Ysgeifiog and Whitford *St As*
WHITLAND (St Mary) w Cyffig and Henllan Amgoed and Llangan w Llandysilio and Clunderwen *St D 15*   **V** K G TAYLOR
WHITTON (St David)   *see* Knighton, Norton, Whitton, Pilleth and Cascob *S & B*
WICK (St James)   *see* Llantwit Major *Llan*
WILCRICK (St Mary)   *see* Magor *Mon*
WILLIAMSTON, EAST (Church)   *see* Jeffreyston w Reynoldston and E Williamston etc *St D*
WILLIAMSTOWN (St Illtud)   *see* Dinas and Penygraig w Williamstown *Llan*
WISTON (St Mary Magdalene) w Walton East and Clarbeston *St D 2*   **V** N CALE
WOLVESNEWTON (St Thomas à Becket)   *see* Llangwm Uchaf and Llangwm Isaf w Gwernesney etc *Mon*
WONASTOW (St Wonnow)   *see* Monmouth w Overmonnow etc *Mon*
WORTHENBURY (St Deiniol)   *see* Bangor Monachorum, Worthenbury and Marchwiel *St As*
WREXHAM (St Giles's Parish Church) (St David) (St Mark) (St Mary) (All Saints) (St Margaret) (St James) (St John) *St As 18*   **TR** M F WEST,   **TV** G J OWEN, S F WALKER, D R ANDERSON,   **P-in-c** G WINDON,   **C** M J G WILKINSON, R J HAINSWORTH
WYNDHAM (St David)   *see* Llandyfodwg and Cwm Ogwr *Llan*
Y BEIFIL (St Andrew)   *see* Newport w Cilgwyn and Nevern and Y Beifil etc *St D*
Y FERWIG (St Pedrog)   *see* Cardigan w Mwnt and Y Ferwig w Llangoedmor *St D*
YERBESTON   *see* Martletwy w Lawrenny and Minwear etc *St D*

YNYSBOETH   *see* Penrhiwceiber, Matthewstown and Ynysboeth *Llan*
YNYSCYHAEARN (Mission Church)   *see* Porthmadoc and Ynyscynhaearn and Dolbenmaen *Ban*
YNYSCYHAEARN (St Cynhaearn)   *as above*
YNYSCYNON (St Cynon)   *see* Pont Rhondda *Llan*
YNYSDDU (St Theodore)   *see* Mynyddislwyn *Mon*
YNYSHIR (St Anne) (St Thomas) *Llan 12*   **V** G P BIGMORE
YNYSMEUDW (St Mary)   *see* Llangiwg *S & B*
YSBYTY CYNFYN (St John the Baptist)   *see* Grwp Bro Ystwyth a Mynach *St D*
YSBYTY IFAN (St John the Baptist)   *see* Cerrigydrudion w Llanfihangel Glyn Myfyr etc *St As*
YSBYTY YSTWYTH (St John the Baptist)   *see* Grwp Bro Ystwyth a Mynach *St D*
YSFA (St Mark)   *see* Gwastedyn *S & B*
YSGEIFIOG (St Mary)   *see* Gorsedd w Brynford, Ysgeifiog and Whitford *St As*
YSTALYFERA (St David) *S & B 7*   **V** T J HEWITT
YSTRAD-FFIN (St Paulinus)   *see* Cil-y-Cwm and Ystrad-ffin w Rhandir-mwyn etc *St D*
YSTRAD MEURIG (St John the Baptist)   *see* Tregaron w Ystrad Meurig and Strata Florida *St D*
YSTRAD MYNACH (Holy Trinity) w Llanbradach *Llan 8*   **V** S P KIRK
YSTRAD RHONDDA (St Stephen)   *see* Pont Rhondda *Llan*
YSTRAD ROAD (St Illtyd)   *see* Swansea St Pet *S & B*
YSTRADFELLTE (St Mary)   *see* Penderyn Mellte *S & B*
YSTRADGYNLAIS (St Cynog) *S & B 7*   **R** D I DAVIES
YSTRADOWEN (St Owain)   *see* Cowbridge *Llan*
YSTRADYFODWG (St John the Baptist) *Llan 12*   **V** H H ENGLAND-SIMON

SCOTTISH INCUMBENCIES

An index of incumbencies of the Scottish Episcopal Church. The incumbency entry gives the full legal name, followed by the diocese and the name(s) and appointment(s) of the clergy serving there (if there are none, the telephone number of the parsonage house is given where known). Church dedications are indicated in brackets. The following are the main abbreviations used; for others see the full list of abbreviations.

C	Curate	**NSM**	Non-stipendiary Minister
Dss	Deaconess	**P-in-c**	Priest-in-charge
Hon C	Honorary Curate	**R**	Rector

ABERCHIRDER (St Marnan) *Mor*   **R** A J SIMPSON
ABERDEEN (Cathedral of St Andrew) *Ab*   **R** R E KILGOUR,
  NSM R FINNIE
ABERDEEN (St Clement) *Ab*   **NSM** N O EGBE
ABERDEEN (St James) *Ab*   **P-in-c** S M PATERSON,
  NSM R B EDWARDS
ABERDEEN (St John the Evangelist) *Ab*   **R** I M POOBALAN,
  C S J FERGUSON
ABERDEEN (St Margaret of Scotland) *Ab*   **R** A E NIMMO,
  Hon C D H WRIGHT
ABERDEEN (St Mary) *Ab*   **R** G S TAYLOR
ABERDEEN (St Ninian) *Ab*   **P-in-c** R E KILGOUR
ABERDEEN (St Peter) *Ab*   **P-in-c** I M POOBALAN,
  C S J FERGUSON
ABERDOUR (St Columba) - West Fife Team Ministry *St And*
  R V A NELLIST
ABERFOYLE (St Mary) *St And*   **R** R W GROSSE
ABERLOUR (St Margaret of Scotland) *Mor*   **NSM** N C MILNE
ABOYNE (St Peter) *Ab*   **R** J S CURRY
AIRDRIE (St Paul) *Glas*   **R** G B FYFE
ALEXANDRIA (St Mungo) *Glas*   **P-in-c** S H B GORTON
ALFORD (St Andrew) *Ab*   **P-in-c** A L JAMES,
  NSM J BURCHILL
ALLOA (St John the Evangelist) *St And*   **NSM** E FORGAN
ALYTH (St Ninian) *St And*   **R** K W RATHBAND,
  NSM D A CAMERON, M LEGGATT
ANNAN (St John the Evangelist) *Glas*   **P-in-c** M P CALLAGHAN,
  Hon C J L HIGGINS
APPIN   *see* W Highland Region *Arg*
ARBROATH (St Mary) *Bre*   **R** J CUTHBERT
ARDBRECKNISH (St James) *Arg*   **R** N D MACCALLUM
ARDCHATTAN (Holy Spirit) *Arg*   **R** N D MACCALLUM
ARDROSSAN (St Andrew) *Glas*   **P-in-c** S ROBERTSON,
  NSM A MONTGOMERIE
ARPAFEELIE (St John the Evangelist) *Mor*   **R** vacant
ARRAN, ISLE OF *Arg*   **R** vacant
AUCHENBLAE   *see* Drumtochty *Bre*
AUCHINDOIR (St Mary) *Ab*   **R** J WALKER,   **C** D ATKINSON,
  NSM J BURCHILL
AUCHMITHIE (St Peter) *Bre*   **R** J CUTHBERT
AUCHTERARDER (St Kessog) *St And*   **R** A E BARTON
AYR (Holy Trinity) *Glas*   **R** I MEREDITH
BAILLIESTON (St John)   *see* Glas E End *Glas*
BALERNO (St Mungo) *Edin*   **R** M J H ROUND
BALLACHULISH (St John) *Arg*   **R** vacant
BALLATER (St Kentigern) *Ab*   **R** J S CURRY
BANCHORY (St Ternan) *Ab*   **R** L K EUNSON
BANFF (St Andrew) *Ab*   **P-in-c** J M PAISEY
BARROWFIELD (St John the Baptist) *Glas*   **R** vacant
BATHGATE (St Columba) *Edin*   **P-in-c** P V P BLACKLEDGE,
  NSM P F KIRK
BEARSDEN (All Saints) w Milngavie *Glas*   **TR** vacant
BELLS WYND   *see* Douglas *Glas*
BIELDSIDE (St Devenick) *Ab*   **R** P R WATSON,
  Dss J E MACCORMACK
BIRNAM   *see* Dunkeld *St And*
BISHOPBRIGGS (St James-the-Less) *Glas*   **R** S A MARSH
BLAIR ATHOLL   *see* Kilmaveonaig *St And*
BLAIRGOWRIE (St Catherine) *St And*   **R** K W RATHBAND,
  NSM D A CAMERON, M LEGGATT
BO'NESS (St Catharine) *Edin*   **P-in-c** D R BUNYAN
BRAEMAR (St Margaret) *Ab*   **R** J S CURRY
BRECHIN (St Andrew) *Bre*   **R** D C MUMFORD,
  NSM U R SHONE, J NELSON
BRIDGE OF ALLAN (St Saviour) *St And*   **R** D M IND
BRIDGE OF WEIR (St Mary) *Glas*
  P-in-c P J C MCGRANAGHAN
BRIDGEND   *see* Islay *Arg*
BRORA (St Columba) *Mor*   **P-in-c** M O LANGILLE
BROUGHTY FERRY (St Mary) *Bre*   **R** J J BOWER,
  C W S H DOCHERTY
BUCKIE (All Saints) *Ab*   **P-in-c** J M PAISEY
BUCKSBURN (St Machar) *Ab*   **P-in-c** D HEDDLE
BUCKSTONE (St Fillan)   *see* Edin St Fillan *Edin*

BURNSIDE   *see* Moffat *Glas*
BURNTISLAND (St Serf) - West Fife Team Ministry *St And*
  R V A NELLIST
BURRAVOE (St Colman) *Ab*   **P-in-c** R K HENSHALL,
  NSM E H MCNAB
CALLANDER (St Andrew) *St And*   **R** R W GROSSE
CAMBUSLANG (St Cuthbert) *Glas*   **R** S L LILLIE,
  NSM M A DANSON
CAMPBELTOWN (St Kiaran) *Arg*   **R** vacant (01586) 53846
CARNOUSTIE (Holy Rood) *Bre*   **R** A M HUGHES,   **Hon**
  C J B HARDIE
CASTLE DOUGLAS (St Ninian) *Glas*   **P-in-c** D W BAYNE
CATHEDRAL OF THE ISLES   *see* Cumbrae (or Millport) *Arg*
CATTERLINE (St Philip) *Bre*   **P-in-c** M E JACKSON,
  NSM E H CAMPBELL
CENTRAL BUCHAN *Ab*   **R** vacant
CHALLOCH (All Saints) *Glas*   **P-in-c** C MYLNE
CHAPELHILL   *see* Cruden Bay *Ab*
CLARKSTON (St Aidan) *Glas*   **R** N H TAYLOR,
  NSM C CURTIS
CLERMISTON   *see* Edin Clermiston Em *Edin*
CLYDEBANK (St Columba) *Glas*   **R** vacant
COATBRIDGE (St John the Evangelist) *Glas*   **R** G B FYFE
COLDSTREAM (St Mary and All Souls) *Edin*
  P-in-c M LOCKEY,   **Hon C** J L EVANS
COLINTON   *see* Edin St Cuth *Edin*
COMRIE (St Serf) *St And*   **R** P LEWER ALLEN
COUPAR ANGUS (St Anne) *St And*   **R** K W RATHBAND,
  NSM D A CAMERON, M LEGGATT
COURTHILL Chapel   *see* Kishorn *Mor*
COVE BAY (St Mary) *Ab*   **R** vacant (01224) 895033
CRAIGHALL   *see* Ellon *Ab*
CRIEFF (St Columba) *St And*   **R** P LEWER ALLEN
CROACHY   *see* Strathnairn St Paul *Mor*
CROMARTY (St Regulus) *Mor*   **R** vacant
CRUDEN BAY (St James the Less) *Ab*   **R** P J MANDER,
  NSM G P WHALLEY
CULLODEN (St Mary-in-the-Fields) *Mor*
  P-in-c A A SINCLAIR
CUMBERNAULD (Holy Name) *Glas*   **P-in-c** B A OGUGUO
CUMBRAE (Cathedral of The Isles and Collegiate Church of the
  Holy Spirit) *Arg*   **R** vacant (01475) 530353
CUMINESTOWN (St Luke)   *see* Cen Buchan *Ab*
CUPAR (St James the Great) *St And*   **R** A HASELHURST,
  C J B BLACK
DALBEATTIE (Christ Church) *Glas*   **R** K G STEPHEN,   **Hon**
  C R W STEPHENS,   **NSM** B M SCOTT
DALKEITH (St Mary) *Edin*   **R** P S HARRIS,   **NSM** M E JONES,
  E S JONES, J O GODFREY
DALMAHOY (St Mary) *Edin*   **R** D L COLLINGWOOD,
  NSM J DYER
DALRY (St Peter) *Glas*   **P-in-c** S ROBERTSON
DENNISTOUN (St Kentigern)   *see* Glas E End *Glas*
DINGWALL (St James the Great) *Mor*   **P-in-c** I N PALLETT,
  NSM R FLOCKHART, V C SAUNDERS
DOLLAR (St James the Great) *St And*   **R** J R AULD,
  NSM F A M LAWRY, H I SOGA
DORNOCH (St Finnbarr) *Mor*   **P-in-c** M O LANGILLE
DOUGLAS (Sancta Sophia) *Glas*   **R** vacant (01555) 663065
DOUNE (St Modoc) *St And*   **NSM** S M COATES
DRUMLITHIE (St John the Baptist) *Bre*   **R** M J R TURNER
DRUMTOCHTY (St Palladius) *Bre*   **R** M J R TURNER
DUFFTOWN (St Michael and All Angels) *Mor*
  NSM N C MILNE
DUMBARTON (St Augustine) *Glas*   **R** K L MACAULAY
DUMFRIES (St John the Evangelist) *Glas*   **R** S R PAISLEY,
  Hon C A M SHUKMAN
DUNBAR (St Anne) *Edin*   **R** vacant
DUNBLANE (St Mary) *St And*   **R** K BOHAN
DUNDEE (Cathedral of St Paul) *Bre*   **R** vacant
DUNDEE (St John the Baptist) *Bre*   **NSM** J M PRIOR
DUNDEE (St Luke) *Bre*   **R** vacant (01382) 825165
DUNDEE (St Margaret) *Bre*   **Hon C** A WALLER
DUNDEE (St Martin) *Bre*   **P-in-c** D ELDER

DUNDEE (St Mary Magdalene) *Bre*   **R** D SHEPHERD
DUNDEE (St Ninian) *Bre*   **P-in-c** E M LAMONT,
NSM J M PRIOR
DUNDEE (St Salvador) *Bre*   **P-in-c** C H CLAPSON,   **Hon**
C G M GREIG
DUNFERMLINE (Holy Trinity) - West Fife Team Ministry
St And   **R** T P BENNISON,   **Hon C** R K KENNEDY
DUNKELD (St Mary) w Birnam *St And*   **R** D F BROOKE,
NSM I ATKINSON
DUNOON (Holy Trinity) *Arg*   **R** *vacant* (01369) 702444
DUNS (Christ Church) *Edin*   **P-in-c** K G WEBB
DUROR (St Adamnan)   *see* W Highland Region *Arg*
EAST END   *see* Glas E End *Glas*
EAST KILBRIDE (St Mark) *Glas*   **P-in-c** K H FREEMAN
EASTGATE (St Peter)   *see* Peebles *Edin*
EASTRIGGS (St John the Evangelist) *Glas*
P-in-c M P CALLAGHAN
EDINBURGH (Cathedral of St Mary) *Edin*   **R** G J T FORBES,
C N MCNELLY,   **NSM** G P FOSTER
EDINBURGH (Christ Church) *Edin*   **R** S E MACDONALD,
NSM J WILLIAMS, M H RAVEN
EDINBURGH (Emmanuel) *Edin*   **R** *vacant*
EDINBURGH (Good Shepherd) *Edin*   **R** D J B FOSTEKEW,
C N MOLL,   **NSM** B M JOHNSON
EDINBURGH (Holy Cross) *Edin*   **R** W D KORNAHRENS
EDINBURGH (Old St Paul) *Edin*   **R** I J PATON,   **C** S J TIBBS,
Hon C C S DAVIES-COLE,   **NSM** C NAISMITH
EDINBURGH (St Andrew and St Aidan) *Edin*   **R** *vacant*
EDINBURGH (St Barnabas) *Edin*   **P-in-c** P D DIXON,
NSM A C ANDERSON
EDINBURGH (St Columba) *Edin*   **R** A J FULLER,
TV R O GOULD, J S RICHARDSON, J D R WHITLEY,
C A C W WAGSTAFF
EDINBURGH (St Cuthbert) *Edin*   **R** S C PARSONS
EDINBURGH (St David of Scotland) *Edin*   **P-in-c** D J DURIE
EDINBURGH (St Fillan) *Edin*   **R** M D ROBSON,   **Hon**
C M C REED
EDINBURGH (St Hilda) *Edin*   **R** *vacant*
EDINBURGH (St James the Less) *Edin*   **R** D A S MACLAREN,
NSM M S NORTHCOTT, J P MITCHELL, J L MACLAREN
EDINBURGH (St John the Evangelist) *Edin*   **R** J A ARMES,
C D REID,   **NSM** P J BRAND, C A HUME, F E ALEXANDER
EDINBURGH (St Luke)   *see* Wester Hailes St Luke *Edin*
EDINBURGH (St Margaret of Scotland) *Edin*
P-in-c G R HART
EDINBURGH (St Mark) *Edin*   **P-in-c** R INNES
EDINBURGH (St Martin of Tours) *Edin*   **R** J A CONWAY,
C S B MARRIAGE,   **NSM** S KILBEY
EDINBURGH (St Michael and All Saints) *Edin*   **R** K PEARSON,
TV M C ALDCROFT,   **Hon C** M F CHATTERLEY
EDINBURGH (St Ninian) *Edin*   **P-in-c** A J BAIN
EDINBURGH (St Paul and St George) *Edin*   **R** D G RICHARDS
EDINBURGH (St Peter) *Edin*   **R** F W TOMLINSON,
C F S BURBERRY
EDINBURGH (St Philip and St James) *Edin*   **R** T N RONGONG
EDINBURGH (St Salvador) *Edin*   **C** N MOLL
EDINBURGH (St Thomas) Private Chapel *Edin*
R I R HOPKINS
EDINBURGH (St Vincent) Private Chapel *Edin*
P-in-c R A GRANT
ELGIN (Holy Trinity) w Lossiemouth (St Margaret) *Mor*
NSM R E TAIT, J SCLATER, N C MILNE
ELIE AND EARLSFERRY (St Michael and All Angels) *St And*
R *vacant* (01333) 330254
ELLON (St Mary on the Rock) *Ab*   **R** P J MANDER,
NSM G P WHALLEY, C A FOX
EORROPAIDH (St Moluag) *Arg*   **NSM** B A MORRISON,
C P A LOCKHART
ERSKINE   *see* Renfrew *Glas*
EYEMOUTH (St Ebba) *Edin*   **NSM** F D J SMOUT
FALKIRK (Christ Church) *Edin*   **R** J B PENMAN,   **Hon**
C T NJUGUNA,   **NSM** A V SMITH
FASQUE (St Andrew) *Bre*   **R** M J R TURNER
FETTERCAIRN   *see* Fasque *Bre*
FOCHABERS Gordon Chapel *Mor*   **P-in-c** A J SIMPSON
FORFAR (St John the Evangelist) *St And*   **R** W A MCCAFFERTY
FORRES (St John the Evangelist) *Mor*   **P-in-c** C J PIPER
FORT WILLIAM (St Andrew) *Arg*   **R** G A GUINNESS
FORTROSE (St Andrew) *Mor*   **R** *vacant*
FRASERBURGH (St Peter) *Ab*   **P-in-c** R A DANIEL,
NSM G G KELMAN
FYVIE (All Saints) *Ab*   **R** *vacant*
GALASHIELS (St Peter) *Edin*   **R** D I MCCOSH
GALLOWGATE   *see* Aberdeen St Marg *Ab*
GARTCOSH (St Andrew) *Glas*   **R** *vacant*

GATEHOUSE OF FLEET (St Mary) *Glas*   **R** R C CUTLER
GIRVAN (St John) *Glas*   **R** I MEREDITH
GLASGOW (All Saints) *Glas*   **R** A L CHESWORTH
GLASGOW (Cathedral of St Mary the Virgin) *Glas*
R K HOLDSWORTH,   **NSM** C A MCKILLOP
GLASGOW East End (St John) (St Kentigern) (St Serf) *Glas*
P-in-c A E J RICHARDSON
GLASGOW (Good Shepherd and Ascension) *Glas*
P-in-c C OKEKE
GLASGOW (Holy Cross) *Glas*   **P-in-c** A L CHESWORTH,
NSM D D KEEBLE
GLASGOW (St Bride) *Glas*   **R** J H MILNE,   **Hon**
C S M P MAITLAND,   **NSM** I T DRAPER
GLASGOW (St Gabriel) *Glas*   **R** *vacant*
GLASGOW (St George) *Glas*   **R** *vacant*
GLASGOW (St Margaret) *Glas*   **R** T C O MONTGOMERY,
NSM P ROMANO
GLASGOW (St Matthew) *Glas*   **P-in-c** D K WOSTENHOLM
GLASGOW (St Ninian) *Glas*   **R** G D DUNCAN,
NSM E J RODGERS
GLASGOW (St Oswald) *Glas*   **P-in-c** D A JUTE
GLASGOW (St Silas) Private Chapel *Glas*   **R** D W MCCARTHY
GLENCARSE (All Saints) *Bre*   **R** *vacant* (01738) 860386
GLENCOE (St Mary) *Arg*   **R** *vacant* (01855) 811335
GLENROTHES (St Luke the Evangelist) - Central Fife Team
Ministry *St And*   **TV** J D MARTIN
GLENURQUHART (St Ninian) *Mor*   **P-in-c** H B HUTCHENS
GOUROCK (St Bartholomew) *Glas*   **P-in-c** A R SHERIDAN
GOVAN   *see* Glas St Gabr *Glas*
GRANGEMOUTH (St Mary) *Edin*   **R** D R BUNYAN
GRANTOWN-ON-SPEY (St Columba) *Mor*
P-in-c P A THOMPSON
GREENOCK (St John the Evangelist) *Glas*   **R** A R SHERIDAN
GRETNA (All Saints) *Glas*   **P-in-c** M P CALLAGHAN
GREYFRIARS   *see* Kirkcudbright *Glas*
GRULINE (St Columba)   *see* W Highland Region *Arg*
GULLANE (St Adrian) *Edin*   **R** J C LINDSAY
HADDINGTON (Holy Trinity) *Edin*   **NSM** J WOOD
HAMILTON (St Mary the Virgin) *Glas*   **R** I D BARCROFT,
NSM J B M MACLEOD, D JASPER
HARRIS, ISLE OF   *see* Leverburgh *Arg*
HARRIS, ISLE OF (Christ Church) *Arg*   **P-in-c** J D L DAVIES
HAWICK (St Cuthbert) *Edin*   **R** *vacant* (01450) 372043
HAY DRIVE   *see* Edin St Andr and St Aid *Edin*
HELENSBURGH (St Michael and All Angels) *Glas*
P-in-c D A COOK
HUNTLY (Christ Church) *Mor*   **R** A J SIMPSON
HYNDLAND (St Bride)   *see* Glas St Bride *Glas*
INNERLEITHEN (St Andrew) *Edin*   **P-in-c** R D LEE,
NSM C B AITCHISON, C CHAPLIN
INSCH (St Drostan) *Ab*   **R** *vacant*
INVERARAY (All Saints) *Arg*   **P-in-c** R F F FLATT
INVERBERVIE (St David) *Bre*   **R** *vacant*
INVERGORDON (St Ninian) *Mor*   **R** *vacant* (01349) 852392
INVERGOWRIE (All Souls) *Bre*   **P-in-c** A W CUMMINS
INVERKEITHING (St Peter) - West Fife Team Ministry *St And*
R V A NELLIST
INVERNESS (Cathedral of St Andrew) *Mor*   **R** *vacant*
INVERNESS (St John the Evangelist) *Mor*
P-in-c A A SINCLAIR
INVERNESS (St Michael and All Angels) *Mor*   **R** L A BLACK,
C R F BURKITT
INVERURIE (St Mary) *Ab*   **R** J WALKER,   **C** D ATKINSON,
NSM J BURCHILL
IONA (St Columba) *Arg*   **R** *vacant*
IRVINE (St Andrew) Local Ecumenical Partnership *Glas*
P-in-c S ROBERTSON,   **NSM** A MONTGOMERIE
ISLAY (St Columba) *Arg*   **R** *vacant*
ISLE OF HARRIS   *see* Harris Ch Ch *Arg*
JEDBURGH (St John the Evangelist) *Edin*   **Hon C** W J GROVER
JOHNSTONE (St John) *Glas*   **P-in-c** D M ORR
JORDANHILL (All Saints)   *see* Glas All SS *Glas*
KEITH (Holy Trinity) *Mor*   **R** A J SIMPSON
KELSO (St Andrew) *Edin*   **R** M LOCKEY,   **Hon C** J L EVANS
KEMNAY (St Anne) *Ab*   **P-in-c** J WALKER,   **C** D ATKINSON,
NSM J BURCHILL
KENTALLEN (St Moluag)   *see* W Highland Region *Arg*
KESSOCK-TORE   *see* Arpafeelie *Mor*
KILLIN (St Fillan) *St And*   **Hon C** J L L FAGERSON
KILMACOLM (St Fillan) *Glas*   **P-in-c** P J C MCGRANAGHAN
KILMARNOCK (Holy Trinity) *Glas*   **P-in-c** P M DOUGLAS
KILMARTIN (St Columba) *Arg*   **R** R F F FLATT
KILMAVEONAIG (St Adamnan) *St And*   **R** *vacant*
KINCARDINE O'NEIL (Christ Church) *Ab*   **R** L K EUNSON
KINGHORN (St Mary and St Leonard) *St And*
NSM G N BENSON

KINLOCH RANNOCH (All Saints) *St And*   **R** *vacant*
KINLOCHLEVEN (St Paul)   *see* W Highland Region *Arg*
KINLOCHMOIDART (St Finian) *Arg*   **P-in-c** C G TONGUE
KINROSS (St Paul) *St And*   **P-in-c** M KESTON
KIRKCALDY (St Peter) *St And*   **NSM** G N BENSON
KIRKCUDBRIGHT (St Francis of Assisi) *Glas*   **R** R C CUTLER
KIRKWALL (St Olaf) *Ab*   **NSM** D DAWSON
KIRRIEMUIR (St Mary) *St And*   **R** R P HARLEY
KISHORN Chapel *Mor*   **NSM** H S WIDDOWS
KNIGHTSWOOD (Holy Cross)   *see* Glas H Cross *Glas*
LADYBANK (St Mary) *St And*   **R** A HASELHURST
LADYCROFT   *see* Balerno *Edin*
LANARK (Christ Church) *Glas*   **R** *vacant* (01555) 663065
LANGHOLM (All Saints) *Glas*   **R** *vacant* (01461) 38268
LARGS (St Columba) *Glas*   **R** *vacant*
LASSWADE (St Leonard) *Edin*   **R** P S HARRIS,
   NSM M E JONES, E S JONES, J O GODFREY
LAURENCEKIRK (St Laurence) *Bre*   **R** M J R TURNER
LEITH (St James the Less)   *see* Edin St Jas *Edin*
LENZIE (St Cyprian) *Glas*   **P-in-c** G E W SCOBIE,
   C M E JAMIESON
LERWICK (St Magnus) *Ab*   **P-in-c** R K HENSHALL,
   NSM E H MCNAB
LEVEN (St Margaret) - Central Fife Team Ministry *St And*
   TV J D MARTIN
LEVERBURGH *Arg*   **R** *vacant*
LEWIS, ISLE OF   *see* Stornoway *Arg*
LINLITHGOW (St Peter) *Edin*   **P-in-c** P V P BLACKLEDGE
LIVINGSTON Local Ecumenical Partnership *Edin*
   Min E C THOMPSON
LOCHALSH (St Donnan) *Mor*   **R** *vacant*
LOCHBUIE (St Kilda) *Arg*   **R** *vacant*
LOCHEARNHEAD (St Angus) *St And*   **R** P LEWER ALLEN
LOCHEE (St Margaret)   *see* Dundee St Marg *Bre*
LOCHGELLY (St Finnian) - Central Fife Team Ministry *St And*
   TV J D MARTIN
LOCHGILPHEAD (Christ Church) *Arg*   **R** R F F FLATT
LOCHINVER (St Gilbert) *Mor*   **R** *vacant*
LOCKERBIE (All Saints) *Glas*   **P-in-c** M P CALLAGHAN,
   C L M BANDS
LONGSIDE (St John)   *see* Cen Buchan *Ab*
LOSSIEMOUTH (St Margaret)   *see* Elgin w Lossiemouth *Mor*
LUNAN HEAD (St Margaret) *St And*   **R** W A MCCAFFERTY
MARYGATE   *see* Pittenweem *St And*
MAYBOLE (St Oswald) *Glas*   **R** I MEREDITH
MELROSE (Holy Trinity) *Edin*   **R** M I HOUSTON,
   NSM D W WOOD, D J DALGLISH
MILLPORT   *see* Cumbrae (or Millport) *Arg*
MILNGAVIE (St Andrew)   *see* Bearsden w Milngavie *Glas*
MOFFAT (St John the Evangelist) *Glas*
   P-in-c M P CALLAGHAN,   **C** L M BANDS
MONIFIETH (Holy Trinity) *Bre*   **R** A M HUGHES
MONKLANDS   *see* Airdrie *Glas*
MONKSTOWN   *see* Ladybank *St And*
MONTROSE (St Mary and St Peter) *Bre*   **R** *vacant*
MOTHERWELL (Holy Trinity) *Glas*   **P-in-c** A WYLIE
MUCHALLS (St Ternan) *Bre*   **P-in-c** M H SABELL
MULL, ISLE OF   *see* Lochbuie *Arg*
MULL, ISLE OF   *see* W Highland Region *Arg*
MURRAYFIELD (Good Shepherd)   *see* Edin Gd Shep *Edin*
MUSSELBURGH (St Peter) *Edin*   **Hon C** L A MORTIS,
   NSM D J S MUNRO
MUTHILL (St James) *St And*   **R** A E BARTON
NAIRN (St Columba) *Mor*   **R** *vacant*
NETHER LOCHABER (St Bride) *Arg*   **R** *vacant*
NEW GALLOWAY (St Margaret of Scotland) *Glas*
   P-in-c J R REPATH
NEW PITSLIGO (St John the Evangelist)   *see* Cen Buchan *Ab*
NEWBURGH (St Katherine) *St And*   **R** *vacant*
NEWLANDS (St Margaret)   *see* Glas St Marg *Glas*
NEWPORT-ON-TAY (St Mary) *St And*   **R** *vacant*
NEWTON STEWART   *see* Challoch *Glas*
NORTH BALLACHULISH   *see* Onich *Arg*
NORTH BERWICK (St Baldred) *Edin*   **R** J C LINDSAY
NORTH MEARNS   *see* Stonehaven *Bre*
OBAN (Cathedral of St John) *Arg*   **R** N D MACCALLUM
OLD DEER (St Drostan)   *see* Cen Buchan *Ab*
OLDMELDRUM (St Matthew) *Ab*   **P-in-c** R SPENCER
ONICH (St Bride) *Arg*   **R** *vacant*
OXGANGS (St Hilda)   *see* Edin St Hilda *Edin*
PAISLEY (Holy Trinity) *Glas*   **R** D W MCFARLAND,   **C** J PAGE
PAISLEY (St Barnabas) *Glas*   **R** D W MCFARLAND,   **C** J PAGE
PEEBLES (St Peter) *Edin*   **R** R D LEE,   **NSM** C B AITCHISON,
   C CHAPLIN
PENICUIK (St James the Less) *Edin*   **R** R J WARREN,
   Hon C G P C CROSFIELD,   **NSM** N F SUTTLE, T A BRAMLEY

PERTH (Cathedral of St Ninian) *St And*   **NSM** R F SAUNDERS
PERTH (St John the Baptist) *St And*   **R** P I D GRANT,
   Hon C R H DARROCH
PETERHEAD (St Peter) *Ab*   **P-in-c** R N O'SULLIVAN
PILTON (St David)   *see* Edin St Dav *Edin*
PINMORE *Glas* *vacant*
PITLOCHRY (Holy Trinity) *St And*   **R** *vacant* (01796) 472539
PITTENWEEM (St John the Evangelist) *St And*   **R** *vacant*
POLLOCKSHIELDS (St Ninian)   *see* Glas St Ninian *Glas*
POLTALLOCH   *see* Kilmartin *Arg*
POOLEWE (St Maelrubha) *Mor*   **NSM** H S WIDDOWS
PORT GLASGOW (St Mary the Virgin) *Glas*   **R** S D N BARRETT
PORTNACROIS (Holy Cross)   *see* W Highland Region *Arg*
PORTPATRICK (St Ninian) *Glas*   **P-in-c** E A TUGWELL
PORTREE (St Columba) *Arg*   **P-in-c** R W BREADEN
PORTSOY (St John the Baptist) *Ab*   **P-in-c** J M PAISEY
PRESTONPANS (St Andrew) *Edin*   **Hon C** L A MORTIS,
   NSM D J S MUNRO
PRESTWICK (St Ninian) *Glas*   **R** P D NOBLE
RENFREW (St Margaret) w Erskine *Glas*   **P-in-c** D M ORR
ROSLIN (Collegiate Church of St Matthew) *Edin*
   P-in-c J E ROULSTON,   **Hon C** W L F MOUNSEY
ROTHESAY (St Paul) *Arg*   **R** *vacant*
ROTHIEMURCHUS (St John the Baptist) *Mor*
   NSM P M LOCKHART
ST ANDREWS (All Saints) *St And*   **R** J P MASON,
   C M-L MOFFETT,   **Hon C** G D WHITE, D W DAY, M C ALDCROFT,
   NSM C A BARCLAY
ST ANDREWS (St Andrew) *St And*   **R** D WILSON,
   C P B ROBERTSON,   **NSM** D A BEADLE, R T EVANS, T A HART,
   N A WILKINS
ST FILLANS (Church of the Holy Spirit) *St And*   **R** *vacant*
SANDYLOAN   *see* Gullane *Edin*
SELKIRK (St John the Evangelist) *Edin*   **P-in-c** D D SCEATS
SHETTLESTON (St Serf)   *see* Glas E End *Glas*
SKYE, ISLE OF   *see* Portree *Arg*
SOUTH QUEENSFERRY (Priory Church St Mary of Mount
   Carmel) *Edin*   **P-in-c** T J HARKIN,   **NSM** I MACROBERT
STANLEY (St Columba) *St And*   **NSM** R F SAUNDERS
STIRLING (Holy Trinity) *St And*   **R** A M PEDEN
STONEHAVEN (St James) *Bre*   **R** M E JACKSON,
   NSM E H CAMPBELL
STORNOWAY (St Peter) *Arg*   **R** S J G BENNIE
STRANRAER (St John the Evangelist) *Glas*
   P-in-c E A TUGWELL
STRATHNAIRN (St Paul) *Mor*   **R** *vacant*
STRATHPEFFER (St Anne) *Mor*   **P-in-c** I N PALLETT,
   NSM R FLOCKHART, V C SAUNDERS
STRATHTAY (St Andrew) *St And*   **R** D F BROOKE
STRICHEN (All Saints)   *see* Cen Buchan *Ab*
STROMNESS (St Mary) *Ab*   **NSM** I ST C COSBY
STRONTIAN *Arg*   **P-in-c** C G TONGUE
TAIN (St Andrew) *Mor*   **R** *vacant*
TARFSIDE (St Drostan) *Bre*   **R** D C MUMFORD,
   NSM J NELSON
TAYPORT (St Margaret of Scotland) *St And*
   P-in-c R G SOMMERVILLE
TEINDHILLGREEN   *see* Duns *Edin*
THURSO (St Peter and Holy Rood) *Mor*   **P-in-c** W G KNOTT,
   Hon C F E DAVIES
TIGHNABRUAICH *Arg*   **R** *vacant*
TOFTS   *see* Dalry *Glas*
TORRY   *see* Aberdeen St Pet *Ab*
TROON (St Ninian) *Glas*   **R** D S MUNGAVIN
TURRIFF (St Congan) *Ab*   **Hon C** P J LEES,
   NSM R M HAINES
UDDINGSTON (St Andrew) *Glas*   **R** S L LILLIE,
   NSM M A DANSON
ULLAPOOL (St Mary the Virgin) *Mor*   **R** *vacant* (01854)
   612143
WEST FIFE Team Ministry - *see* ABERDOUR;
   BURNTISLAND; DUNFERMLINE; INVERKEITHING
   and LOCHGELLY *St And*   **TR** *vacant*
WEST HIGHLAND Region *Arg*   **R** S A FALLOWS,
   C D DAVIDSON
WEST LINTON (St Mungo) *Edin*   **P-in-c** R J WARREN,
   Hon C G P C CROSFIELD,   **NSM** T A BRAMLEY
WESTGATE   *see* Dunbar *Edin*
WESTHILL (Trinity) *Ab*   **R** I J FERGUSON
WHITERASHES (All Saints) *Ab*   **R** *vacant*
WHITING BAY   *see* Is of Arran *Arg*
WICK (St John the Evangelist) *Mor*   **R** W G KNOTT,
   Hon C F E DAVIES
WISHAW (St Andrew) *Glas*   **P-in-c** A WYLIE
WOODHEAD OF FETTERLETTER   *see* Fyvie *Ab*
YELL   *see* Burravoe *Ab*

IRISH BENEFICES AND CHURCHES

An index of benefices of the Church of Ireland (shown in bold type), together with entries for churches and other licensed places of worship. Where the church name is the same as that of the benefice (or the first place name in the benefice), the church entry is omitted. Church dedications are indicated in brackets.

The benefice entry gives the full legal name, together with the diocese and the name(s) and appointment(s) of clergy serving there (if there are none, the telephone number of the parsonage house is given). The following are the main abbreviations used; for others see the full list of abbreviations.

Bp's C	Bishop's Curate	**I**	Incumbent (includes Rector or Vicar)
C	Curate	**NSM**	Non-stipendiary Minister
C-in-c	Curate-in-charge	**P-in-c**	Priest-in-charge
Hon C	Honorary Curate		

AASLEAGH (St John the Baptist)   *see* Tuam w Cong and Aasleagh *T, K & A*

ABBEYLEIX (St Michael and All Angels) w Ballyroan, Ballinakill, Killermogh, Aughmacart, Durrow and Attanagh *C & O*   **I** P A HARVEY,   **NSM** A WALLACE

ABBEYSTREWRY (no dedication) w Creagh, Tullagh, Castlehaven and Caheragh *C, C & R*   **I** B J HAYES

ABINGDON (no dedication)   *see* Killaloe w Stradbally *L & K*

ACHILL (Holy Trinity)   *see* Aughaval w Achill, Knappagh, Dugort etc *T, K & A*

ACTON (no dedication) and Drumbanagher *Arm*   **I** vacant

ADARE (St Nicholas)   *see* Adare and Kilmallock w Kilpeacon, Croom etc *L & K*

ADARE (St Nicholas) and Kilmallock w Kilpeacon, Croom, Kilflynn, Kilfinane, Knockaney, Bruff and Caherconlish *L & K*   **I** A W MATCHETT

AGHABOG (no dedication)   *see* Ematris w Rockcorry, Aghabog and Aughnamullan *Clogh*

AGHADE (All Saints)   *see* Fenagh w Myshall, Aghade and Ardoyne *C & O*

AGHADERG (St Mellan) w Donaghmore and Scarva *D & D*   **I** P D THORNBURY

AGHADOE   *see* Killarney w Aghadoe and Muckross *L & K*

AGHADOWEY (St Guaire) w Kilrea *D & R*   **I** L D A CRAWFORD

AGHADOWN (Church Cross)   *see* Ballydehob w Aghadown *C, C & R*

AGHADOWN (St Matthew)   *as above*

AGHADRUMSEE (no dedication) w Clogh and Drumsnatt *Clogh*   **I** vacant

AGHALEE (Holy Trinity) *D & D*   **I** R C MCCARTNEY

AGHALURCHER (no dedication) w Tattykeeran, Cooneen and Mullaghfad *Clogh*   **I** R T GILLIAN

AGHANAGH (no dedication)   *see* Boyle and Elphin w Aghanagh, Kilbryan etc *K, E & A*

AGHANCON (no dedication)   *see* Shinrone w Aghancon etc *L & K*

AGHANLOO (St Lugha)   *see* Tamlaghtard w Aghanloo *D & R*

AGHAVEA (no dedication) *Clogh*   **I** D W ROBINSON

AGHAVILLY (St Mary)   *see* Tynan w Middletown and Aghavilly *Arm*

AGHAVOE (no dedication)   *see* Rathdowney w Castlefleming, Donaghmore etc *C & O*

AGHER (no dedication)   *see* Rathmolyon w Castlerickard, Rathcore and Agher *M & K*

AGHERTON (St John the Baptist) *Conn*   **I** S A FIELDING,   **C** J M NIBLOCK

AGHOLD (no dedication)   *see* Tullow w Shillelagh, Aghold and Mullinacuff *C & O*

AGHOUR (St Lachtan)   *see* Kilkenny w Aghour and Kilmanagh *C & O*

AHASCRAGH   *see* Aughrim w Ballinasloe etc *L & K*

AHERLA   *see* Moviddy Union *C, C & R*

AHOGHILL (St Colmanell) w Portglenone *Conn*   **I** M W J LONEY

ALDERGROVE   *see* Killead w Gartree *Conn*

ALMORITIA (St Nicholas)   *see* Mullingar, Portnashangan, Moyliscar, Kilbixy etc *M & K*

ALTEDESERT (no dedication)   *see* Kildress w Altedesert *Arm*

ANNACLONE (Christ Church)   *see* Magherally w Annaclone *D & D*

ANNADUFF (St Ann)   *see* Kiltoghart w Drumshambo, Annaduff and Kilronan *K, E & A*

ANNAGH (St Andrew) w Drumaloor, Cloverhill and Drumlane *K, E & A*   **I** S K CLARK,   **NSM** H R HICKS

ANNAGHMORE (St Francis) *Arm*   **I** D S MCVEIGH

ANNAHILT (Ascension) w Magherahamlet *D & D*   **I** J R HOWARD

ANNALONG (no dedication) *D & D*   **I** W J PRESS

ANNESTOWN   *see* Waterford w Killea, Drumcannon and Dunhill *C & O*

ANTRIM (All Saints) *Conn*   **I** S R MCBRIDE,   **NSM** D E FERGUSON

ANTRIM (St Patrick)   *see* Connor w Antrim St Patr *Conn*

ARBOE (no dedication)   *see* Ballinderry, Tamlaght and Arboe *Arm*

ARDAGH (St Patrick) w Tashinny, Shrule and Kilcommick *K, E & A*   **Bp's C** A W KINGSTON

ARDAMINE (St John the Evangelist) w Kiltennel, Glascarrig, Kilnamanagh, Kilmuckridge and Monamolin *C & O*   **I** R J GRAY,   **NSM** M SYKES

ARDARA (St Connall) w Glencolumbkille, Inniskeel, Glenties and Lettermacaward *D & R*   **Bp's C** J DEANE,   **NSM** M C CLASSON

ARDCARNE (no dedication)   *see* Boyle and Elphin w Aghanagh, Kilbryan etc *K, E & A*

ARDCLINIS (St Mary) and Tickmacrevan w Layde and Cushendun *Conn*   **P-in-c** M A HUTCHINSON

ARDCOLM (no dedication)   *see* Wexford w Ardcolm and Killurin *C & O*

ARDEE (St Mary)   *see* Drogheda w Ardee, Collon and Termonfeckin *Arm*

ARDGLASS (St Nicholas)   *see* Lecale Gp *D & D*

ARDKEEN (Christ Church)   *see* Ballyhalbert w Ardkeen *D & D*

ARDMORE (no dedication) w Craigavon *D & D*   **I** vacant (028) 3834 0357

ARDMORE (St Paul)   *see* Youghal Union *C, C & R*

ARDNAGEEHY (no dedication)   *see* Fermoy Union *C, C & R*

ARDOYNE (Holy Trinity)   *see* Fenagh w Myshall, Aghade and Ardoyne *C & O*

ARDOYNE (Immanuel)   *see* Belfast H Trin and St Silas *Conn*

ARDQUIN (no dedication)   *see* Ballyphilip w Ardquin *D & D*

ARDRAHAN   *see* Aughrim w Ballinasloe etc *L & K*

ARDSTRAW (St Eugene) w Baronscourt, Badoney Lower and Badoney Upper and Greenan *D & R*   **I** H HALL

ARDTREA (St Andrew) w Desertcreat *Arm*   **I** D J BELL

ARKLOW (St Saviour) w Inch and Kilbride *D & G*   **I** N J W SHERWOOD

ARMAGH (St Mark) *Arm*   **I** J W MCKEGNEY,   **C** J R MCLOUGHLIN

ARMAGHBREAGUE (no dedication)   *see* Keady w Armaghbreague and Derrynoose *Arm*

ARMOY (St Patrick) w Loughguile and Drumtullagh *Conn*   **I** F M BACH

ARVAGH (no dedication) w Carrigallen, Gowna and Columbkille *K, E & A*   **I** vacant

ASHFIELD (no dedication)   *see* Drumgoon *K, E & A*

ASKEATON (St Mary)   *see* Rathkeale w Askeaton, Kilcornan and Kilnaughtin *L & K*

ATHBOY (St James)   *see* Trim and Athboy Gp *M & K*

ATHLONE (St Mary) w Benown, Kiltoom and Forgney *M & K*   **I** G T DOYLE

ATHY (St Michael) w Kilberry, Fontstown and Kilkea *D & G*   **I** C P JEFFERS

AUGHANUNSHIN   *see* Conwal Union w Gartan *D & R*

AUGHAVAL (no dedication) w Achill, Knappagh, Dugort, Castlebar and Turlough *T, K & A*   **I** vacant

AUGHAVAS (no dedication)   *see* Mohill w Farnaught, Aughavas, Oughteragh etc *K, E & A*

AUGHER (no dedication) w Newtownsaville and Eskrahoole *Clogh*   **I** vacant

AUGHMACART (St Tighernagh)   *see* Abbeyleix w Ballyroan etc *C & O*

AUGHNACLIFFE   *see* Arvagh w Carrigallen, Gowna and Columbkille *K, E & A*

AUGHNACLOY   *see* Carnteel and Crilly *Arm*

AUGHNAMULLAN (Christ Church)   *see* Ematris w Rockcorry, Aghabog and Aughnamullan *Clogh*

AUGHRIM (Holy Trinity) w Ballinasloe, Clontuskert, Ahascragh, Woodlawn, Kilmacduagh and Ardrahan *L & K*
  I A V G FLYNN

AUGHRIM (St John the Evangelist)   *see* Castlemacadam w Ballinaclash, Aughrim etc *D & G*

BADONEY LOWER (St Patrick)   *see* Ardstraw w Baronscourt, Badoney Lower etc *D & R*

BADONEY UPPER (St Aichen)   *as above*

BAGENALSTOWN   *see* Dunleckney w Nurney, Lorum and Kiltennel *C & O*

BAILIEBOROUGH (no dedication) w Knockbride, Shercock and Mullagh *K, E & A*   I F E J RANKIN

BALBRIGGAN (St George)   *see* Holmpatrick w Balbriggan and Kenure *D & G*

BALGRIFFIN (St Doulagh)   *see* Malahide w Balgriffin *D & G*

BALLAGHTOBIN (no dedication)   *see* Kells Gp *C & O*

BALLEE (no dedication)   *see* Bright w Ballee and Killough *D & D*

BALLIGAN   *see* Ballywalter w Inishargie *D & D*

BALLINA   *see* Killala w Dunfeeny, Crossmolina, Kilmoremoy etc *T, K & A*

BALLINACLASH (no dedication)   *see* Castlemacadam w Ballinaclash, Aughrim etc *D & G*

BALLINADEE (no dedication)   *see* Bandon Union *C, C & R*

BALLINAFAD   *see* Boyle and Elphin w Aghanagh, Kilbryan etc *K, E & A*

BALLINAKILL (All Saints)   *see* Abbeyleix w Ballyroan etc *C & O*

BALLINALEA   *see* Mostrim w Granard, Clonbroney, Killoe etc *K, E & A*

BALLINALECK   *see* Cleenish w Mullaghdun *Clogh*

BALLINAMALLARD   *see* Magheracross *Clogh*

BALLINAMORE   *see* Mohill w Farnaught, Aughavas, Oughteragh etc *K, E & A*

BALLINASLOE (St John the Evangelist)   *see* Aughrim w Ballinasloe etc *L & K*

BALLINATONE   *see* Castlemacadam w Ballinaclash, Aughrim etc *D & G*

BALLINDERRY (no dedication) *Conn*   I E J HARRIS

BALLINDERRY (St John), Tamlaght and Arboe *Arm*   I *vacant*

BALLINEEN   *see* Kinneigh Union *C, C & R*

BALLINGARRY (no dedication)   *see* Cloughjordan w Borrisokane etc *L & K*

BALLINLOUGH   *see* Roscommon w Donamon, Rathcline, Kilkeevin etc *K, E & A*

BALLINROBE (St Mary)   *see* Tuam w Cong and Aasleagh *T, K & A*

BALLINTEMPLE (no dedication)   *see* Kilmore w Ballintemple *K, E & A*

BALLINTEMPLE (St Mary)   *see* Cashel w Magorban, Tipperary, Clonbeg etc *C & O*

BALLINTOGHER   *see* Taunagh w Kilmactranny, Ballysumaghan etc *K, E & A*

BALLINTOY (no dedication) w Rathlin and Dunseverick *Conn*
  I P M BARTON

BALLINTUBBERT (St Brigid)   *see* Stradbally w Ballintubbert, Coraclone etc *C & O*

BALLISODARE (Holy Trinity) w Collooney and Emlaghfad *T, K & A*   I *vacant*

BALLIVOR   *see* Trim and Athboy Gp *M & K*

BALLNACARGY   *see* Mullingar, Portnashangan, Moyliscar, Kilbixy etc *M & K*

BALLYBAY (Christ Church) w Mucknoe and Clontibret *Clogh*
  I J P HEYHOE

BALLYBEEN (St Mary) *D & D*   I J M HARVEY,
  NSM W M N JAMISON

BALLYBRACK (St Matthias)   *see* Killiney Ballybrack *D & G*

BALLYBUNNION   *see* Tralee w Kilmoyley, Ballymacelligott etc *L & K*

BALLYCANEW (no dedication)   *see* Gorey w Kilnahue, Leskinfere and Ballycanew *C & O*

BALLYCARNEY (no dedication)   *see* Ferns w Kilbride, Toombe, Kilcormack etc *C & O*

BALLYCARRY   *see* Kilroot and Templecorran *Conn*

BALLYCASTLE (Holy Trinity)   *see* Ramoan w Ballycastle and Culfeightrin *Conn*

BALLYCLARE   *see* Ballynure and Ballyeaston *Conn*

BALLYCLOG (St Patrick)   *see* Brackaville w Donaghendry and Ballyclog *Arm*

BALLYCLUG (St Patrick)   *see* Ballymena w Ballyclug *Conn*

BALLYCOMMON   *see* Geashill w Killeigh and Ballycommon *M & K*

BALLYCONNELL   *see* Kildallon and Swanlinbar *K, E & A*

BALLYCOTTON   *see* Youghal Union *C, C & R*

BALLYCULTER (Christ Church)   *see* Lecale Gp *D & D*

BALLYDEHOB (St Matthias) w Aghadown *C, C & R*   I *vacant*

BALLYEASTON (St John the Evangelist)   *see* Ballynure and Ballyeaston *Conn*

BALLYEGLISH (St Matthias)   *see* Desertlyn w Ballyeglish *Arm*

BALLYFIN (no dedication)   *see* Maryborough w Dysart Enos and Ballyfin *C & O*

BALLYGAWLEY (no dedication)   *see* Errigle Keerogue w Ballygawley and Killeshil *Arm*

BALLYHAISE   *see* Drung w Castleterra, Larah and Lavey etc *K, E & A*

BALLYHALBERT (St Andrew) w Ardkeen *D & D*
  I J J HEMPHILL

BALLYHOLME (St Columbanus) *D & D*   I S E DOOGAN,
  C W R S SMYTH

BALLYHOOLEY (no dedication)   *see* Fermoy Union *C, C & R*

BALLYJAMESDUFF (no dedication)   *see* Kildrumferton w Ballymachugh and Ballyjamesduff *K, E & A*

BALLYKELLY   *see* Tamlaghtfinlagan w Myroe *D & R*

BALLYLESSON   *see* Drumbo *D & D*

BALLYMACARRETT (St Patrick) (St Christopher) (St Martin) *D & D*   I C L HALL-THOMPSON, **NSM** I M FRAZER,
  S P HOOPER

BALLYMACASH (St Mark) *Conn*   I W G IRWIN,
  NSM K W GAMBLE

BALLYMACELLIGOTT (no dedication)   *see* Tralee w Kilmoyley, Ballymacelligott etc *L & K*

BALLYMACHUGH (St Paul)   *see* Kildrumferton w Ballymachugh and Ballyjamesduff *K, E & A*

BALLYMACKEY (St Michael)   *see* Nenagh *L & K*

BALLYMACORMACK (no dedication)   *see* Templemichael w Clongish, Clooncumber etc *K, E & A*

BALLYMAGLASSON   *see* Dunboyne Union *M & K*

BALLYMAHON   *see* Ardagh w Tashinny, Shrule and Kilcommick *K, E & A*

BALLYMARTLE (no dedication)   *see* Kinsale Union *C, C & R*

BALLYMASCANLAN (St Mary) w Creggan and Rathcor *Arm*
  I S A PRAGNELL, **NSM** R W R MOORE

BALLYMENA (St Patrick) w Ballyclug *Conn*   I S G E LLOYD,
  C D W R DUNN, A D IRWIN

BALLYMONEY   *see* Kinneigh Union *C, C & R*

BALLYMONEY (St Patrick) w Finvoy and Rasharkin *Conn*
  I J J CUNNINGHAM, **NSM** W J HOLMES

BALLYMORE   *see* Clondehorkey w Cashel *D & R*

BALLYMORE (St Mark) *Arm*   I T S FORSTER

BALLYMORE EUSTACE (St John)   *see* Blessington w Kilbride, Ballymore Eustace etc *D & G*

BALLYMOTE   *see* Ballisodare w Collooney and Emlaghfad *T, K & A*

BALLYMOYER (St Luke)   *see* Newtownhamilton w Ballymoyer and Belleck *Arm*

BALLYNAFEIGH (St Jude) *D & D*   I N JARDINE

BALLYNAHINCH   *see* Magheradroll *D & D*

BALLYNAKILL (St Thomas)   *see* Omey w Ballynakill, Errislannan and Roundstone *T, K & A*

BALLYNASCREEN   *see* Kilcronaghan w Draperstown and Sixtowns *D & R*

BALLYNURE (Ascension)   *see* Baltinglass w Ballynure etc *C & O*

BALLYNURE (Christ Church) and Ballyeaston *Conn*
  I R M MCCONNELL

BALLYPHILIP (no dedication) w Ardquin *D & D*   I *vacant*

BALLYRASHANE (St John the Baptist) w Kildollagh *Conn*
  I A E ADAMS

BALLYROAN (no dedication)   *see* Abbeyleix w Ballyroan etc *C & O*

BALLYSALLY (St Andrew)   *see* Coleraine *Conn*

BALLYSCULLION (no dedication)   *see* Drummaul w Duneane and Ballyscullion *Conn*

BALLYSCULLION (St Tida) *D & R*   **P-in-c** E R LAVERY

BALLYSEEDY (no dedication)   *see* Tralee w Kilmoyley, Ballymacelligott etc *L & K*

BALLYSHANNON   *see* Kilbarron w Rossnowlagh and Drumholm *D & R*

BALLYSILLAN   *see* Belfast St Mark *Conn*

BALLYSUMAGHAN (no dedication)   *see* Taunagh w Kilmactranny, Ballysumaghan etc *K, E & A*

BALLYWALTER (Holy Trinity) w Inishargie *D & D*
  I J R L BOWLEY

BALLYWARD   *see* Drumgath w Drumgooland and Clonduff *D & D*

BALLYWILLAN (Holy Trinity) *Conn*   I P K MCDOWELL,
  NSM J J STEELE, R J SIMPSON

BALRATHBOYNE   *see* Kells Union *M & K*

BALTEAGH (St Canice) w Carrick *D & R*   I I E DINSMORE

BALTIMORE   *see* Abbeystrewry Union *C, C & R*

BALTINGLASS (St Mary) w Ballynure, Stratford-on-Slaney and Rathvilly *C & O* **I** M A MCCULLAGH
BANAGHER (St Moresuis) *see* Cumber Lower w Banagher *D & R*
BANAGHER (St Paul) *see* Clonfert Gp *L & K*
BANBRIDGE *see* Seapatrick *D & D*
BANDON (St Peter) w Rathclaren, Innishannon, Ballinadee and Brinny *C, C & R* **I** W P HEWITT, **C** D G KEANE, **NSM** E C M FERGUSON
BANGOR Primacy (Christ Church) *D & D*
Bp's C F G RUTLEDGE
BANGOR (St Columbanus) *see* Ballyholme *D & D*
BANGOR (St Comgall) *D & D* **I** N H PARKER
BANGOR ABBEY (Bangor Abbey) *D & D* **I** R NESBITT, **C** A R MCLAUGHLIN
BANNOW (no dedication) *see* Taghmon w Horetown and Bannow *C & O*
BANTRY *see* Kilcomogue Union *C, C & R*
BARONSCOURT (no dedication) *see* Ardstraw w Baronscourt, Badoney Lower etc *D & R*
BARR (no dedication) *see* Donacavey w Barr *Clogh*
BEARA (St Peter) *C, C & R* **I** *vacant* (00353) (21) 63036
BECTIVE *see* Trim and Athboy Gp *M & K*
BELFAST (All Saints) *Conn* **I** B A FOLLIS
BELFAST (Cathedral of St Anne) *Conn* , S R MCBRIDE **C** J T P TWOMEY
BELFAST (Christ Church) *Conn* **I** *vacant*
BELFAST (Holy Trinity) (St Silas) *Conn* **I** R M M CREIGHTON, **NSM** D G BEATTIE
BELFAST Malone (St John) *Conn* **I** J O MANN, **C** A L STEWART
BELFAST (St Aidan) *Conn* **I** T P KERR
BELFAST (St Andrew) *Conn* **NSM** S K HOUSTON
BELFAST (St Bartholomew) *Conn* **I** R ELSDON
BELFAST (St Brendan) *D & D* **I** F MCCREA, **C** J HARRIS
BELFAST (St Christopher) *see* Ballymacarrett *D & D*
BELFAST (St Clement) *D & D* **I** S D LOGAN
BELFAST (St Donard) *D & D* **I** K H HIGGINS
BELFAST (St George) *Conn* **I** B STEWART
BELFAST (St Jude) *see* Ballynafeigh St Jude *D & D*
BELFAST (St Katharine) *Conn* **I** W J TAGGART
BELFAST (St Mark) *Conn* **I** R H MOORE
BELFAST (St Martin) *see* Ballymacarrett *D & D*
BELFAST (St Mary) (Holy Redeemer) *Conn* **I** J P WALKER
BELFAST (St Mary Magdalene) *Conn* **I** *vacant* (028) 9066 7516
BELFAST (St Matthew) *Conn* **I** G J O DUNSTAN
BELFAST (St Michael) *Conn* **I** N B DODDS, **NSM** J MCCLURE
BELFAST (St Nicholas) *Conn* **I** E HANNA
BELFAST (St Ninian) *Conn* **I** *vacant*
BELFAST (St Patrick) *see* Ballymacarrett *D & D*
BELFAST (St Paul) (St Barnabas) *Conn* **I** G MILLAR
BELFAST (St Peter) (St James) *Conn* **I** A T W DORRIAN
BELFAST (St Simon) (St Philip) *Conn* **I** P JACK
BELFAST (St Stephen) (St Luke) *Conn* **I** E QUIREY
BELFAST (St Thomas) *Conn* **I** W A LEWIS, **C** T MCROBERTS, **NSM** J M ELSDON
BELFAST Upper Falls (St John the Baptist) *Conn* **I** T CLELAND
BELFAST Upper Malone (Epiphany) *Conn* **I** E G BUNTING
BELFAST Whiterock (St Columba) *Conn* **P-in-c** C R A EASTON
BELLAGHY *see* Ballyscullion *D & D*
BELLEEK (no dedication) *see* Garrison w Slavin and Belleek *Clogh*
BELLEEK (St Luke) *see* Newtownhamilton w Ballymoyer and Belleck *Arm*
BELLERENA *see* Tamlaghtard w Aghanloo *D & R*
BELMONT (St Peter) *see* Londonderry Ch Ch, Culmore, Muff and Belmont *D & R*
BELTURBET *see* Annagh w Drumaloor, Cloverhill and Drumlane *K, E & A*
BELVOIR (Transfiguration) *D & D* **I** T KEIGHTLEY, **C** J MOULD, A A MCCARTNEY
BENOWN (no dedication) *see* Athlone w Benown, Kiltoom and Forgney *M & K*
BILBO (no dedication) *see* Castlecomer w Colliery Ch, Mothel and Bilbo *C & O*
BILLIS (no dedication) *see* Lurgan w Billis, Killinkere and Munterconnaught *K, E & A*
BILLY (no dedication) w Derrykeighan *Conn* **I** J R ANDERSON, **NSM** G H NEVIN
BIRR (St Brendan) w Eglish, Lorrha, Dorrha and Lockeen *L & K* **I** R W CARNEY, **NSM** R M GILL
BLACKLION *see* Killinagh w Kiltyclogher and Innismagrath *K, E & A*

BLACKROCK (All Saints) *see* Stillorgan w Blackrock *D & G*
BLACKROCK (St Michael) *see* Douglas Union w Frankfield *C, C & R*
BLARNEY *see* Carrigrohane Union *C, C & R*
BLESSINGTON (St Mary) w Kilbride, Ballymore Eustace and Holywood *D & G* **I** L W RUDDOCK
BOHO (no dedication) *see* Devenish w Boho *Clogh*
BOOTERSTOWN (St Philip and St James) *see* Dublin Booterstown *D & G*
BORNACOOLA *see* Templemichael w Clongish, Clooncumber etc *K, E & A*
BORRIS Clonagoose *see* Leighlin w Grange Sylvae, Shankill etc *C & O*
BORRIS Littleton *see* Kilcooley w Littleon, Crohane and Fertagh *C & O*
BORRIS-IN-OSSORY (no dedication) *see* Clonenagh w Offerlane, Borris-in-Ossory etc *C & O*
BORRISNAFARNEY (no dedication) *see* Cloughjordan w Borrisokane etc *L & K*
BORRISOKANE (no dedication) *as above*
BOURNEY (St Burchin) *see* Roscrea w Kyle, Bourney and Corbally *L & K*
BOVEVAGH (St Eugenius) *see* Dungiven w Bovevagh *D & R*
BOYLE (no dedication) and Elphin w Aghanagh, Kilbryan, Ardcarne and Croghan *K, E & A* **I** R S J BOURKE
BRACKAVILLE (Holy Trinity) w Donaghendry and Ballyclog *Arm* **I** K R J HALL
BRANTRY (Holy Trinity) *see* Caledon w Brantry *Arm*
BRAY (Christ Church) *D & G* **I** B T STANLEY, **C** A BARR
BRIGHT (no dedication) w Ballee and Killough *D & D* **I** J EWART
BRIGOWN (St George) *see* Fermoy Union *C, C & R*
BRINNY (no dedication) *see* Bandon Union *C, C & R*
BROOKEBOROUGH *see* Aghavea *Clogh*
BROOMHEDGE (St Matthew) *Conn* **I** P J GALBRAITH
BROUGHSHANE *see* Skerry w Rathcavan and Newtowncrommelin *Conn*
BRYANSFORD *see* Castlewellan w Kilcoo *D & D*
BUNBEG *see* Gweedore, Carrickfin and Templecrone *D & R*
BUNCLODY (St Mary) w Kildavin, Clonegal and Kilrush *C & O* **I** K L J HOMFRAY, **NSM** I DUNGAN
BUNCRANA *see* Fahan Lower and Upper *D & R*
BUNDORAN *see* Clooncare w Killasnett, Lurganboy and Drumlease *K, E & A*
BUSH *see* Ballymascanlan w Creggan and Rathcor *Arm*
BUSHMILLS *see* Dunluce *Conn*
CAHERAGH (St Mary) *see* Abbeystrewry Union *C, C & R*
CAHERCONLISH (St Ailbe) *see* Adare and Kilmallock w Kilpeacon, Croom etc *L & K*
CAHIR (St Paul) *see* Clonmel w Innislounagh, Tullaghmelan etc *C & O*
CAIRNCASTLE (St Patrick) *see* Kilwaughter w Cairncastle and Craigy Hill *Conn*
CALARY (no dedication) *see* Newcastle w Newtownmountkennedy and Calary *D & G*
CALEDON (St John) w Brantry *Arm* **I** D B WILSON
CALRY (no dedication) *K, E & A* **I** P H BAMBER
CAMLOUGH (Christ the Redeemer) w Mullaglass *Arm* **I** R G HOEY, **C** W J MCCRACKEN
CAMP *see* Dingle w Killiney and Kilgobbin *L & K*
CAMUS-JUXTA-BANN (St Mary) *D & R* **I** M P ROEMMELE
CAMUS-JUXTA-MOURNE (Christ Church) *D & R* **I** G S A WILSON
CAPPAGH (St Eugene) w Lislimnaghan *D & R* **I** D J QUINN
CAPPOQUIN (St Anne) *see* Lismore w Cappoquin, Kilwatermoy, Dungarvan etc *C & O*
CARBURY (no dedication) *see* Clonsast w Rathangan, Thomastown etc *M & K*
CARLOW (St Mary) w Urglin and Staplestown *C & O* **I** O H WILLIAMS
CARNALEA (St Gall) *D & D* **I** M A PARKER
CARNALWAY (St Patrick) *see* Newbridge w Carnalway and Kilcullen *M & K*
CARNDONAGH *see* Moville w Greencastle, Donagh, Cloncha etc *D & R*
CARNEW (All Saints) *see* Crosspatrick Gp *C & O*
CARNLOUGH *see* Ardclinis and Tickmacrevan w Layde and Cushendun *Conn*
CARNMONEY (Holy Evangelists) *Conn* **I** M A MALCOLM, **NSM** C R HARVEY
CARNTEEL (St James) and Crilly *Arm* **I** W T LONG
CARRICK (no dedication) *see* Balteagh w Carrick *D & R*
CARRICK-ON-SHANNON *see* Kiltoghart w Drumshambo, Annaduff and Kilronan *K, E & A*
CARRICKFERGUS (St Nicholas) *Conn* **I** G T W DAVISON

CARRICKFIN (St Andrew) *see* Gweedore, Carrickfin and Templecrone *D & R*

CARRICKMACROSS (St Fin Barre) w Magheracloone *Clogh*
   I R G KINGSTON

CARRIGALINE (St Mary) w Killanully and Monkstown
   C, C & R   **I** S D ARMSTRONG,   **NSM** H E A MINION

CARRIGALLEN (no dedication) *see* Arvagh w Carrigallen, Gowna and Columbkille *K, E & A*

CARRIGANS *see* Taughboyne, Craigadooish, Newtowncunningham etc *D & R*

CARRIGART *see* Mevagh w Glenalla *D & R*

CARRIGROHANE (St Peter) w Garrycloyne, Inniscarra and Magourney *C, C & R*   **I** I R JONAS,   **C** R E JACKSON

CARRIGTWOHILL (St David) *see* Rathcooney Union *C, C & R*

CARROWDORE (Christ Church) w Millisle *D & D*
   I T K D GRAHAM

CARRYDUFF (St Ignatius) *see* Killaney w Carryduff *D & D*

CASHEL (Cathedral of St John the Baptist) w Magorban, Tipperary, Clonbeg and Ballintemple *C & O*   **I** P J KNOWLES

CASHEL (no dedication) *see* Clondehorkey w Cashel *D & R*

CASTLEARCHDALE (St Patrick) *see* Derryvullen N w Castlearchdale *Clogh*

CASTLEBAR (Christ Church) *see* Aughaval w Achill, Knappagh, Dugort etc *T, K & A*

CASTLEBLAYNEY *see* Ballybay w Mucknoe and Clontibret *Clogh*

CASTLECOMER (St Mary) w the Colliery Church, Mothel and Bilbo *C & O*   **I** T A SHERLOCK

CASTLECONNELL *see* Killaloe w Stradbally *L & K*

CASTLECONNOR (no dedication) *see* Killala w Dunfeeny, Crossmolina, Kilmoremoy etc *T, K & A*

CASTLEDAWSON (Christ Church) *D & R*   **I** D S MCLEAN

CASTLEDERG *see* Derg w Termonamongan *D & R*

CASTLEDERMOT (St James) *see* Narraghmore and Timolin w Castledermot etc *D & G*

CASTLEFLEMING (no dedication) *see* Rathdowney w Castlefleming, Donaghmore etc *C & O*

CASTLEGREGORY *see* Dingle w Killiney and Kilgobbin *L & K*

CASTLEHAVEN (no dedication) *see* Abbeystrewry Union *C, C & R*

CASTLEKNOCK (St Brigid) and Mulhuddart w Clonsilla
   D & G   **C** E DUNNE

CASTLELOST *see* Mullingar, Portnashangan, Moyliscar, Kilbixy etc *M & K*

CASTLEMACADAM (Holy Trinity) w Ballinaclash, Aughrim and Macreddin *D & G*   **I** G W BUTLER

CASTLEMAINE *see* Kilcolman w Kiltallagh, Killorglin, Knockane etc *L & K*

CASTLEMARTYR (St Anne) *see* Youghal Union *C, C & R*

CASTLEPOLLARD (St Michael) and Oldcastle w Loughcrew, Mount Nugent, Mayne and Drumcree *M & K*
   I P M RUTHERFORD

CASTLEREA *see* Roscommon w Donamon, Rathcline, Kilkeevin etc *K, E & A*

CASTLERICKARD *see* Rathmolyon w Castlerickard, Rathcore and Agher *M & K*

CASTLEROCK (Christ Church) w Dunboe and Fermoyle *D & R*
   I D M MATCHETT,   **NSM** A QUIGLEY

CASTLETERRA (no dedication) *see* Drung w Castleterra, Larah and Lavey etc *K, E & A*

CASTLETOWN *see* Killeshin w Cloydagh and Killabban *C & O*

CASTLETOWN *see* Rathkeale w Askeaton, Kilcornan and Kilnaughtin *L & K*

CASTLETOWN *see* Kells Union *M & K*

CASTLETOWNBERE *see* Beara *C, C & R*

CASTLETOWNROCHE (no dedication) *see* Mallow Union *C, C & R*

CASTLETOWNSEND *see* Abbeystrewry Union *C, C & R*

CASTLEVENTRY (no dedication) *see* Ross Union *C, C & R*

CASTLEWELLAN (St Paul) w Kilcoo *D & D*   **I** B S CADDEN

CAVAN *see* Urney w Denn and Derryheen *K, E & A*

CELBRIDGE (Christ Church) w Straffan and Newcastle-Lyons
   D & G   **I** S L HALES,   **NSM** R W LAWSON

CHAPELIZOD (St Laurence) *see* Dublin Crumlin w Chapelizod *D & G*

CHARLEMONT (no dedication) *see* Moy w Charlemont *Arm*

CLABBY (St Margaret) *see* Tempo and Clabby *Clogh*

CLANABOGAN (no dedication) *see* Edenderry w Clanabogan *D & R*

CLANE (St Michael and All Angels) w Donadea and Coolcarrigan *M & K*   **Bp's C** K M RONNÉ,
   NSM D HUTTON-BURY

CLARA (St Brigid) w Liss, Moate and Clonmacnoise *M & K*
   I *vacant* (00353) (506) 31406

CLARE (no dedication) *see* Loughgilly w Clare *Arm*

CLAUDY *see* Cumber Upper w Learmount *D & R*

CLEENISH (no dedication) w Mullaghdun *Clogh*   **I** G P BRIDLE

CLIFDEN *see* Omey w Ballynakill, Errislannan and Roundstone *T, K & A*

CLOGH (Holy Trinity) *see* Aghadrumsee w Clogh and Drumsnatt *Clogh*

CLOGHER (Cathedral of St Macartan) w Errigal Portclare
   Clogh   **NSM** M B PRINGLE

CLOGHERNY (St Patrick) w Seskinore and Drumnakilly *Arm*
   R E O'BRIEN

CLONAGOOSE (St Moling) *see* Leighlin w Grange Sylvae, Shankill etc *C & O*

CLONAKILTY *see* Kilgariffe Union *C, C & R*

CLONALLON (no dedication) w Warrenpoint *D & D*   **I** *vacant*
   (028) 3077 2267

CLONARD *see* Mullingar, Portnashangan, Moyliscar, Kilbixy etc *M & K*

CLONASLEE *see* Mountmellick w Coolbanagher, Rosenallis etc *M & K*

CLONBEG (St Sedna) *see* Cashel w Magorban, Tipperary, Clonbeg etc *C & O*

CLONBRONEY (St John) *see* Mostrim w Granard, Clonbroney, Killoe etc *K, E & A*

CLONBULLOGUE *see* Clonsast w Rathangan, Thomastown etc *M & K*

CLONCHA (no dedication) *see* Moville w Greencastle, Donagh, Cloncha etc *D & R*

CLONDALKIN (St John) w Rathcoole *D & G*
   I W P HOUSTON,   **NSM** O BOOTHMAN, A A SHINE

CLONDEHORKEY (St John) w Cashel *D & R*   **I** *vacant*

CLONDEVADDOCK (Christ the Redeemer) w Portsalon and Leatbeg *D & R*   **I** *vacant* (00353) (74) 59020

CLONDUFF (St John) *see* Drumgath w Drumgooland and Clonduff *D & D*

CLONE (St Paul) *see* Enniscorthy w Clone, Clonmore, Monart etc *C & O*

CLONEGAL (no dedication) *see* Bunclody w Kildavin, Clonegal and Kilrush *C & O*

CLONEGAM (Holy Trinity) *see* Fiddown w Clonegam, Guilcagh and Kilmeaden *C & O*

CLONENAGH (no dedication) w Offerlane, Borris-in-Ossory, Seirkieran and Roskelton *C & O*   **I** S F JONES

CLONES (St Tighernach) w Killeevan *Clogh*   **I** H STEED

CLONEYHURKE (no dedication) *see* Portarlington w Cloneyhurke, Lea etc *M & K*

CLONFADFORAN *see* Tullamore w Durrow, Newtownfertullagh, Rahan etc *M & K*

CLONFEACLE (St Patrick) w Derrygortreavy *Arm*
   I A J PARKHILL

CLONFERT (Cathedral of St Brendan) w Donanaughta, Banagher and Lickmolassy *L & K*   **I** A J NEVIN

CLONGISH (St Paul) *see* Templemichael w Clongish, Clooncumber etc *K, E & A*

CLONLARA *see* Killaloe w Stradbally *L & K*

CLONLEIGH (St Lugadius) *see* Raphoe w Raymochy and Clonleigh *D & R*

CLONMACNOISE (St Kieran) *see* Clara w Liss, Moate and Clonmacnoise *M & K*

CLONMEL (St Mary) w Innislounagh, Tullaghmelan, Fethard, Kilvemnon and Cahir *C & O*   **I** B Y FRYDAY,   **C** A E CARTER,
   NSM J G MULHALL

CLONMEL UNION (Christ Church) *C, C & R*   **I** *vacant*
   (00353) (21) 811790

CLONMELLON (St John) *see* Trim and Athboy Gp *M & K*

CLONMORE (St John) *see* Enniscorthy w Clone, Clonmore, Monart etc *C & O*

CLONMORE (St John) *see* Kiltegan w Hacketstown, Clonmore and Moyne *C & O*

CLONOE (St Michael) *see* Tullaniskin w Clonoe *Arm*

CLONSAST (no dedication) w Rathangan, Thomastown, Monasteroris, Carbury and Rahan *M & K*   **I** L E A PEILOW

CLONSILLA (St Mary) *see* Castleknock and Mulhuddart w Clonsilla *D & G*

CLONTARF *see* Dublin Clontarf *D & G*

CLONTIBRET (St Colman) *see* Ballybay w Mucknoe and Clontibret *Clogh*

CLONTUSKERT (St Matthew) *see* Aughrim w Ballinasloe etc *L & K*

CLOONCLARE (no dedication) w Killasnett, Lurganboy and Drumlease *K, E & A*   **Bp's C** C J STEVENSON

CLOONCUMBER (no dedication) *see* Templemichael w Clongish, Clooncumber etc *K, E & A*

CLOONEY (All Saints) w Strathfoyle *D & R*   **I** M R K FERRY
CLOUGH   *see* Craigs w Dunaghy and Killagan *Conn*
CLOUGHFERN (Ascension) *Conn*   **I** D LOCKHART,
   C A E STEWART
CLOUGHJORDAN (St Kieran) w Borrisokane, Ballingary,
   Borrisnafarney and Templeharry *L & K*   **I** S M NEILL
CLOUGHMILLS   *see* Craigs w Dunaghy and Killagan *Conn*
CLOVERHILL (St John)   *see* Annagh w Drumaloor, Cloverhill
   and Drumlane *K, E & A*
CLOYDAGH (no dedication)   *see* Killeshin w Cloydagh and
   Killaban *C & O*
CLOYNE (Cathedral of St Colman) w Inch, Corkbeg, Midleton
   and Gurranekennefeake *C, C & R*   **I** A G MARLEY,
   NSM W H HILL
COACHFORD   *see* Carrigrohane Union *C, C & R*
COALISLAND   *see* Brackaville w Donaghendry and Ballyclog
   Arm
COBH   *see* Clonmel Union *C, C & R*
COLAGHTY   *see* Lack *Clogh*
COLEBROOK   *see* Aghalurcher w Tattykeeran, Cooneen etc
   Clogh
COLERAINE   *see* Killowen *D & R*
COLERAINE (St Patrick) *Conn*   **I** R COOKE,   **C** B G FORDE
COLIN (St Andrew)   *see* Derriaghy w Colin *Conn*
COLLIERY CHURCH, THE   *see* Castlecomer w Colliery Ch,
   Mothel and Bilbo *C & O*
COLLON (no dedication)   *see* Drogheda w Ardee, Collon and
   Termonfeckin *Arm*
COLLOONEY (St Paul)   *see* Ballisodare w Collooney and
   Emlaghfad *T, K & A*
COLPE (St Columba)   *see* Julianstown and Colpe w Drogheda
   and Duleek *M & K*
COLUMBKILLE (St Thomas)   *see* Arvagh w Carrigallen,
   Gowna and Columbkille *K, E & A*
COMBER (St Mary) *D & D*   **I** J P O BARRY,
   NSM R A B MOLLAN
COMERAGH   *see* Lismore w Cappoquin, Kilwatermoy,
   Dungarvan etc *C & O*
CONARY (St Bartholomew)   *see* Dunganstown w Redcross and
   Conary *D & G*
CONG (St Mary)   *see* Tuam w Cong and Aasleagh *T, K & A*
CONNOR (St Saviour) w Antrim St Patrick *Conn*
   I S GILCHRIST
CONVOY (St Ninian) w Monellan and Donaghmore *D & R*
   I D GRISCOME
CONWAL (no dedication) w Aughanunshin and Gartan *D & R*
   I W C S WRIGHT
COOKSTOWN   *see* Derryloran *Arm*
COOLBANAGHER (St John)   *see* Mountmellick w
   Coolbanagher, Rosenallis etc *M & K*
COOLCARRIGAN (no dedication)   *see* Clane w Donadea and
   Coolcarrigan *M & K*
COOLKELLURE (St Edmund)   *see* Fanlobbus Union *C, C & R*
COOLOCK (St John)   *see* Raheny w Coolock *D & G*
COONEEN (no dedication)   *see* Aghalurcher w Tattykeeran,
   Cooneen etc *Clogh*
COOTEHILL   *see* Drumgoon *K, E & A*
CORACLONE (St Peter)   *see* Stradbally w Ballintubbert,
   Coraclone etc *C & O*
CORBALLY (Christ Church)   *see* Roscrea w Kyle, Bourney and
   Corbally *L & K*
CORK (Cathedral of St Fin Barre) (St Nicholas) *C, C & R*
   I N K DUNNE,   **Dean's V** J K ARDIS,   **NSM** E W HUNTER
CORK (St Ann) Shandon w St Mary *C, C & R*
   I B J G O'ROURKE,   **NSM** A MORAN
CORKBEG (St Michael and All Angels)   *see* Cloyne Union
   C, C & R
CORRAWALLEN (no dedication)   *see* Kildallon and
   Swanlinbar *K, E & A*
COURTMACSHERRY (St John the Evangelist)   *see* Kilgariffe
   Union *C, C & R*
CRAIGADOOISH (no dedication)   *see* Taughboyne,
   Craigadooish, Newtowncunningham etc *D & R*
CRAIGAVAD   *see* Glencraig *D & D*
CRAIGAVON (St Saviour)   *see* Ardmore w Craigavon *D & D*
CRAIGS (no dedication) w Dunaghy and Killagan *Conn*
   I W R G WILLANS
CRAIGY HILL (All Saints)   *see* Kilwaughter w Cairncastle and
   Craigy Hill *Conn*
CREAGH   *see* Abbeystrewry Union *C, C & R*
CREAGH   *see* Aughrim w Ballinasloe etc *L & K*
CRECORA   *see* Adare and Kilmallock w Kilpeacon, Croom etc
   L & K
CREGAGH (St Finnian) *D & D*   **I** J D M PIERCE,
   C A W A MAYES

CREGGAN (no dedication)   *see* Ballymascanlan w Creggan and
   Rathcor *Arm*
CRILLY (St George)   *see* Carnteel and Crilly *Arm*
CRINKEN (St James) *D & G*   **I** E M VAUGHAN
CROGHAN (Holy Trinity)   *see* Boyle and Elphin w Aghanagh,
   Kilbryan etc *K, E & A*
CROHANE (no dedication)   *see* Kilcooley w Littleon, Crohane
   and Fertagh *C & O*
CROM (Holy Trinity)   *see* Kinawley w H Trin *K, E & A*
CROOKHAVEN (St Brendan)   *see* Kilmoe Union *C, C & R*
CROOM (no dedication)   *see* Adare and Kilmallock w
   Kilpeacon, Croom etc *L & K*
CROSSGAR   *see* Kilmore and Inch *D & D*
CROSSHAVEN   *see* Templebreedy w Tracton and Nohoval
   C, C & R
CROSSMOLINA (no dedication)   *see* Killala w Dunfeeny,
   Crossmolina, Kilmoremoy etc *T, K & A*
CROSSPATRICK Group (no dedication) w Kilcommon, Kilpipe,
   Preban and Carnew, The *C & O*   **I** A MINION
CRUMLIN   *see* Dublin Crumlin w Chapelizod *D & G*
CRUMLIN (St John)   *see* Glenavy w Tunny and Crumlin *Conn*
CRUMLIN ROAD   *see* Belfast St Mary w H Redeemer *Conn*
CULDAFF (no dedication)   *see* Moville w Greencastle, Donagh,
   Cloncha etc *D & R*
CULFEIGHTRIN (no dedication)   *see* Ramoan w Ballycastle
   and Culfeightrin *Conn*
CULLYBACKEY   *see* Craigs w Dunaghy and Killagan *Conn*
CULMORE (Holy Trinity)   *see* Londonderry Ch Ch, Culmore,
   Muff and Belmont *D & R*
CUMBER LOWER (Holy Trinity) w Banagher *D & R*   **I** *vacant*

CUMBER UPPER (no dedication) w Learmount *D & R*
   I J R D SLATER
CURRAGH (Garrison Church of St Paul)   *see* Kildare w
   Kilmeague and Curragh *M & K*
CURRIN (St Andrew) w Drum and Newbliss *Clogh*   **I** *vacant*
   (00353) (47) 56103
CUSHENDALL   *see* Ardclinis and Tickmacrevan w Layde and
   Cushendun *Conn*
CUSHENDUN (no dedication)   *as above*
DALKEY (St Patrick) *D & G*   **I** W B A NEILL
DARTREY   *see* Ematris w Rockcorry, Aghabog and
   Aughnamullan *Clogh*
DELGANY (Christ Church) *D & G*   **I** N J W WAUGH
DENN (no dedication)   *see* Urney w Denn and Derryheen
   K, E & A
DERG (no dedication) w Termonamongan *D & R*   **I** A N PEEK
DERNAKESH (Chapel of Ease)   *see* Drumgoon, K, E & A
DERRALOSSARY   *see* Rathdrum w Glenealy, Derralossary
   and Laragh *D & G*
DERRIAGHY (Christ Church) w Colin *Conn*   **I** J C BUDD,
   NSM H A MACARTHUR
DERRYBRUSK (St Michael)   *see* Maguiresbridge w
   Derrybrusk *Clogh*
DERRYGONNELLY   *see* Inishmacsaint *Clogh*
DERRYGORTREAVY (St Columba)   *see* Clonfeacle w
   Derrygortreavy *Arm*
DERRYHEEN (no dedication)   *see* Urney w Denn and
   Derryheen *K, E & A*
DERRYKIGHAN (St Colman)   *see* Billy w Derrykeighan *Conn*
DERRYLANE (no dedication)   *see* Killeshandra w Killegar and
   Derrylane *K, E & A*
DERRYLIN   *see* Kinawley w H Trin *K, E & A*
DERRYLORAN (St Luran) *Arm*   **I** R J N PORTEUS,
   NSM M H HAGAN
DERRYNOOSE (St John)   *see* Keady w Armaghbreague and
   Derrynoose *Arm*
DERRYVOLGIE (St Columba) *Conn*   **I** D M QUIGLEY
DERRYVULLEN NORTH (St Tighernach) w Castlearchdale
   Clogh   **I** E R G WEST
DERRYVULLEN SOUTH (St Tighernach) w Garvary *Clogh*
   I J W STEWART
DERVOCK   *see* Billy w Derrykeighan *Conn*
DESERTCREAT (no dedication)   *see* Ardtrea w Desertcreat
   Arm
DESERTLYN (St John) w Ballyeglish *Arm*   **I** A N STRINGER
DESERTMARTIN (St Conghall) w Termoneeny *D & R*
   I K R KINGSTON
DESERTOGHILL (no dedication)   *see* Errigal w Garvagh
   D & R
DESERTSERGES (no dedication)   *see* Kinneigh Union
   C, C & R
DEVENISH (St Molaise) w Boho *Clogh*   **I** *vacant*
DIAMOND (St Paul)   *see* Tartaraghan w Diamond *Arm*
DINGLE (St James) w Killiney and Kilgobbin *L & K*   **I** *vacant*

DOAGH   *see* Kilbride *Conn*

DOLLINGSTOWN (St Saviour)   *see* Magheralin w Dollingstown *D & D*

DONABATE (St Patrick)   *see* Swords w Donabate and Kilsallaghan *D & G*

DONACAVEY (no dedication) w Barr *Clogh*   **I** J E MARSBURG

DONADEA (St Peter)   *see* Clane w Donadea and Coolcarrigan *M & K*

DONAGH (no dedication)   *see* Moville w Greencastle, Donagh, Cloncha etc *D & R*

DONAGH (St Salvator) w Tyholland and Errigal Truagh *Clogh*   **I** *vacant* (00353) (47) 88277

DONAGHADEE (no dedication) *D & D*   **R** I R GAMBLE

DONAGHCLONEY (St Patrick) w Waringstown *D & D*   **I** T D ALLEN,   **C** C P E KAKURU,   **NSM** J R CORBETT

DONAGHEADY (St James) *D & R*   **I** D H J FERRY

DONAGHENDRY (St Patrick)   *see* Brackaville w Donaghendry and Ballyclog *Arm*

DONAGHMORE (no dedication)   *see* Rathdowney w Castlefleming, Donaghmore etc *C & O*

DONAGHMORE (St Bartholomew)   *see* Aghaderg w Donaghmore and Scarva *D & D*

DONAGHMORE (St Michael) w Upper Donaghmore *Arm*   **I** P A THOMPSON

DONAGHMORE (St Patrick)   *see* Convoy w Monellan and Donaghmore *D & R*

DONAGHMORE, UPPER (St Patrick)   *see* Donaghmore w Upper Donaghmore *Arm*

DONAGHPATRICK (St Patrick)   *see* Kells Union *M & K*

DONAMON (no dedication)   *see* Roscommon w Donamon, Rathcline, Kilkeevin etc *K, E & A*

DONANAUGHTA (St John the Baptist)   *see* Clonfert Gp *L & K*

DONARD (no dedication)   *see* Donoughmore and Donard w Dunlavin *D & G*

DONEGAL (no dedication) w Killymard, Lough Eske and Laghey *D & R*   **I** R FOX

DONEGORE (St John)   *see* Templepatrick w Donegore *Conn*

DONEMANA   *see* Donagheady *D & R*

DONERAILE (St Mary)   *see* Mallow Union *C, C & R*

DONNYBROOK (St Mary)   *see* Dublin Irishtown w Donnybrook *D & G*

DONOUGHMORE (no dedication) and Donard w Dunlavin *D & G*   **I** G D B SMITH

DORRHA (no dedication)   *see* Birr w Lorrha, Dorrha and Lockeen *L & K*

DOUGLAS (St Luke) w Blackrock, Frankfield and Marmullane *C, C & R*   **I** A M WILKINSON,   **C** P BURKE,   **NSM** P T HANNA

DOWN (Cathedral of the Holy and Undivided Trinity) *D & D*   **I** *vacant*

DOWN (St Margaret) w Hollymount *D & D*   **I** S S BURNS

DOWNPATRICK   *see* Down H Trin w Hollymount *D & D*

DOWNPATRICK   *see* Down Cathl *D & D*

DRAPERSTOWN (St Columb)   *see* Kilcronaghan w Draperstown and Sixtowns *D & R*

DREW MEMORIAL   *see* Belfast St Simon w St Phil *Conn*

DRIMOLEAGUE (St Matthew)   *see* Fanlobbus Union *C, C & R*

DRINAGH (Christ Church)   *as above*

DROGHEDA (St Mary)   *see* Julianstown and Colpe w Drogheda and Duleek *M & K*

DROGHEDA (St Peter) w Ardee, Collon and Termonfeckin *Arm*   **I** M GRAHAM,   **NSM** J MOORE

DROMAHAIR   *see* Cloonclare w Killasnett, Lurganboy and Drumlease *K, E & A*

DROMARA (St John) w Garvaghy *D & D*   **I** C B LEEKE

DROMARD (Christ Church)   *see* Skreen w Kilmacshalgan and Dromard *T, K & A*

DROMOD (St Michael and All Angels)   *see* Kenmare w Sneem, Waterville etc *L & K*

DROMORE (Cathedral of Christ the Redeemer) *D & D*   **I** S H LOWRY,   **NSM** T J MCKEOWN

DROMORE (Holy Trinity) *Clogh*   **I** B R MARTIN

DRUM (no dedication)   *see* Currin w Drum and Newbliss *Clogh*

DRUMACHOSE (Christ Church) *D & R*   **I** S MCVEIGH

DRUMALOOR (St Andrew)   *see* Annagh w Drumaloor, Cloverhill and Drumlane *K, E & A*

DRUMANY (Christ Church)   *see* Kinawley w H Trin *K, E & A*

DRUMBANAGHER (St Mary)   *see* Acton and Drumbanagher *Arm*

DRUMBEG (St Patrick) *D & D*   **I** R R W DEVENNEY

DRUMBO (Holy Trinity) *D & D*   **I** R C NEILL

DRUMCANNON (Christ Church)   *see* Waterford w Killea, Drumcannon and Dunhill *C & O*

DRUMCAR   *see* Kilsaran w Drumcar, Dunleer and Dunany *Arm*

DRUMCLAMPH (no dedication) w Lower Langfield and Upper Langfield *D & R*   **I** R G KEOGH

DRUMCLIFFE (St Columba) w Kilrush, Kilfenora, Kilfarboy, Kilnasoolagh, Shannon and Kilferagh *L & K*   **I** R C HANNA,   **NSM** P E HANNA

DRUMCLIFFE (St Columba) w Lissadell and Munninane *K, E & A*   **I** B I LINTON

DRUMCONDRA   *see* Dublin Drumcondra w N Strand *D & G*

DRUMCONRATH (St Peter)   *see* Kingscourt w Syddan *M & K*

DRUMCREE (Ascension) *Arm*   **I** G F GALWAY

DRUMCREE (St John)   *see* Castlepollard and Oldcastle w Loughcrew etc *M & K*

DRUMGATH (St John) w Drumgooland and Clonduff *D & D*   **I** D SOMERVILLE

DRUMGLASS (St Anne) w Moygashel *Arm*   **I** A J FORSTER,   **C** R S MCELHINNEY

DRUMGOOLAND (no dedication)   *see* Drumgath w Drumgooland and Clonduff *D & D*

DRUMGOON (All Saints)   *see* Drumgoon *K, E & A*

DRUMGOON (All Saints) w Ashfield, Killesherdoney and Dernakesh *K, E & A*   **P-in-c** R W STAFFORD

DRUMHOLM (no dedication)   *see* Kilbarron w Rossnowlagh and Drumholm *D & R*

DRUMINISKILL (Chapel of Ease)   *see* Killesher *K, E & A*

DRUMKEERAN   *see* Killinagh w Kiltyclogher and Innismagrath *K, E & A*

DRUMKEERAN (no dedication) w Templecarne and Muckross *Clogh*   **P-in-c** C T PRINGLE

DRUMLANE (no dedication)   *see* Annagh w Drumaloor, Cloverhill and Drumlane *K, E & A*

DRUMLEASE (no dedication)   *see* Cloonclare w Killasnett, Lurganboy and Drumlease *K, E & A*

DRUMMAUL (St Brigid) w Duneane and Ballyscullion *Conn*   **I** D P KERR

DRUMMULLY (no dedication)   *see* Galloon w Drummully and Sallaghy *Clogh*

DRUMNAKILLY (Holy Trinity)   *see* Clogherny w Seskinore and Drumnakilly *Arm*

DRUMQUIN   *see* Drumclamph w Lower and Upper Langfield *D & R*

DRUMRAGH (St Columba) w Mountfield *D & R*   **I** W A SEALE,   **C** A T E QUILL

DRUMREILLY (no dedication)   *see* Mohill w Farnaught, Aughavas, Oughteragh etc *K, E & A*

DRUMSHAMBO (St John)   *see* Kiltoghart w Drumshambo, Annaduff and Kilronan *K, E & A*

DRUMSNATT (St Molua)   *see* Aghadrumsee w Clogh and Drumsnatt *Clogh*

DRUMTALLAGH (no dedication)   *see* Armoy w Loughguile and Drumtullagh *Conn*

DRUNG (no dedication) w Castleterra, Larah and Lavey and Killoughter *K, E & A*   **P-in-c** R MOORE,   **NSM** R MOORE

DUBLIN Booterstown (St Philip and St James) *D & G*   **I** G V WHARTON,   **NSM** S S HARRIS

DUBLIN (Christ Church Cathedral) Group: (St Andrew) (St Werburgh) (St Michan) St Paul and Grangegorman *D & G*   **V** D A PIERPOINT,   **C** D MCDONNELL

DUBLIN Clontarf (St John the Baptist) *D & G*   **I** D C SARGENT

DUBLIN Crumlin (St Mary) w Chapelizod *D & G*   **I** A GALLIGAN

DUBLIN Drumcondra (no dedication) w North Strand *D & G*   **I** R H BYRNE

DUBLIN (Irish Church Missions) and St Thomas *D & G* ,   E J COULTER

DUBLIN Irishtown (St Matthew) w Donnybrook *D & G*   **I** E G ARDIS,   **NSM** J M GORDON

DUBLIN Mount Merrion (St Thomas) *D & G*   **I** G V WHARTON

DUBLIN Rathfarnham (no dedication) *D & G*   **I** E C J WOODS,   **C** A E TAYLOR

DUBLIN Rathmines (Holy Trinity) w Harold's Cross *D & G*   **I** N G MCENDOO

DUBLIN Sandford (no dedication) w Milltown *D & G*   **I** S O GYLES,   **NSM** A M O'FARRELL

DUBLIN Sandymount (St John the Evangelist) *D & G*   **C** S T IRVINE

DUBLIN Santry (St Pappan) w Glasnevin and Finglas *D & G*   **I** D W OXLEY

DUBLIN (St Ann) (St Stephen) *D & G*   **I** D I GILLESPIE,   **C** V R A FITZPATRICK

DUBLIN (St Bartholomew) w Leeson Park *D & G*   **I** A W MCCROSKERY

DUBLIN (St George and St Thomas) *D & G*   **Bp's C** K M POULTON

DUBLIN (St Patrick's Cathedral) Group: (St Catherine and St James) (St Audoen) *D & G*   **C** J M B KISSELL, R D JONES,   **NSM** C E BAKER

DUBLIN Whitechurch (no dedication) *D & G*
I A H N MCKINLEY, C O C ULOGWARA, **NSM** P COMERFORD
DUBLIN (Zion Church) *D & G* I W R J GOURLEY
DUGORT (St Thomas) *see* Aughaval w Achill, Knappagh,
Dugort etc *T, K & A*
DULEEK *see* Julianstown and Colpe w Drogheda and Duleek
M & K
DUN LAOGHAIRE (Christ Church) *D & G* I V G STACEY
DUNAGHY (St James) *see* Craigs w Dunaghy and Killagan
Conn
DUNANY *see* Kilsaran w Drumcar, Dunleer and Dunany *Arm*
DUNBOE (St Paul) *see* Castlerock w Dunboe and Fermoyle
D & R
**DUNBOYNE Union (St Peter and St Paul) w Kilcock, Maynooth,
Moyglare, Dunshaughlin and Ballymaglasson** *M & K*
I J H AITON, C W L STEACY, **NSM** A V STEWART
DUNDALK (St Nicholas) w Heynestown *Arm* I S A PRAGNELL,
NSM R W R MOORE
DUNDELA (St Mark) *D & D* I F J MCDOWELL
DUNDONALD (St Elizabeth) *D & D* I T G ANDERSON,
C G MCMURRAY
DUNDRUM *see* Cashel w Magorban, Tipperary, Clonbeg etc
C & O
DUNDRUM (St Donard) *see* Kilmegan w Maghera *D & D*
DUNEANE (no dedication) *see* Drummaul w Duneane and
Ballyscullion *Conn*
**DUNFANAGHY (Holy Trinity), Raymunterdoney and
Tullaghbegley** *D & R* I M S HARTE
DUNFEENY (no dedication) *see* Killala w Dunfeeny,
Crossmolina, Kilmoremoy etc *T, K & A*
DUNGANNON *see* Drumglass w Moygashel *Arm*
DUNGANSTOWN (St Kevin) w Redcross and Conary *D & G*
I J R HEANEY
DUNGARVAN (St Mary) *see* Lismore w Cappoquin,
Kilwatermoy, Dungarvan etc *C & O*
DUNGIVEN (no dedication) w Bovevagh *D & R*
Bp's C I J HANNA
DUNGLOE *see* Gweedore, Carrickfin and Templecrone *D & R*
DUNHILL (St John the Baptist) *see* Waterford w Killea,
Drumcannon and Dunhill *C & O*
DUNKERRIN (no dedication) *see* Shinrone w Aghancon etc
L & K
DUNLAVIN (St Nicholas) *see* Donoughmore and Donard w
Dunlavin *D & G*
DUNLECKNEY (St Mary) w Nurney, Lorum and Kiltennel
C & O I C J MCCOLLUM
DUNLEER (no dedication) *see* Kilsaran w Drumcar, Dunleer
and Dunany *Arm*
DUNLUCE (St John the Baptist) *Conn* I G E GRAHAM
DUNMANWAY *see* Fanlobbus Union *C, C & R*
DUNMORE EAST *see* Waterford w Killea, Drumcannon and
Dunhill *C & O*
DUNMURRY (St Colman) *Conn* I D M ACHESON
DUNNALONG (St John) *see* Leckpatrick w Dunnalong *D & R*
DUNSEVERICK (no dedication) *see* Ballintoy w Rathlin and
Dunseverick *Conn*
DUNSFORD (St Anne) *see* Lecale Gp *D & D*
DUNSHAUGHLIN (St Seachnal) *see* Dunboyne Union *M & K*
DURROW (St Columba) *see* Tullamore w Durrow,
Newtownfertullagh, Rahan etc *M & K*
DURROW (St Fintan) *see* Abbeyleix w Ballyroan etc *C & O*
DURRUS (St James the Apostle) *see* Kilmocomogue Union
C, C & R
DYSART ENOS (Holy Trinity) *see* Maryborough w Dysart
Enos and Ballyfin *C & O*
EASKEY (St Anne) *see* Killala w Dunfeeny, Crossmolina,
Kilmoremoy etc *T, K & A*
EDENDERRY *see* Clonsast w Rathangan, Thomastown etc
M & K
EDENDERRY (no dedication) w Clanabogan *D & R*
I R W CLARKE
EDGEWORTHSTOWN *see* Mostrim w Granard, Clonbroney,
Killoe etc *K, E & A*
EGLANTINE (All Saints) *Conn* I C W BELL
EGLINTON *see* Faughanvale *D & R*
EGLISH (Holy Trinity) w Killylea *Arm* I W QUIGLEY
ELPHIN (no dedication) *see* Boyle and Elphin w Aghanagh,
Kilbryan etc *K, E & A*
**EMATRIS (St John the Evangelist) w Rockcorry, Aghabog and
Aughnamullan** *Clogh* I vacant
EMLAGHFAD (no dedication) *see* Ballisodare w Collooney
and Emlaghfad *T, K & A*
ENNIS *see* Drumcliffe w Kilnasoolagh *L & K*
**ENNISCORTHY (St Mary) w Clone, Clonmore, Monart and
Templescobin** *C & O* I C W LONG

ENNISKEEN *see* Kingscourt w Syddan *M & K*
ENNISKERRY *see* Powerscourt w Kilbride *D & G*
ENNISKILLEN *see* Rossorry *Clogh*
ENNISKILLEN (Cathedral of St Macartin) *Clogh* I vacant
ENNISNAG (St Peter) *see* Kells Gp *C & O*
ERRIGAL (St Paul) w Garvagh *D & R* I K P WHITTAKER
ERRIGAL PORTCLARE (no dedication) *see* Clogh w Errigal
Portclare *Clogh*
ERRIGAL TRUAGH (St Muadhan) *see* Donagh w Tyholland
and Errigal Truagh *Clogh*
**ERRIGLE KEEROGUE (no dedication) w Ballygawley and
Killeshil** *Arm* I I A WILLIAMSON
ERRISLANNNAN (no dedication) *see* Omey w Ballynakill,
Errislannan and Roundstone *T, K & A*
ESKRAHOOLE (no dedication) *see* Augher w Newtownsaville
and Eskrahoole *Clogh*
EYRECOURT *see* Clonfert Gp *L & K*
FAHAN LOWER (Christ Church) and UPPER (St Mura)
D & R **Bp's C** S D BARTON
FALLS, LOWER (St Luke) *see* Belfast St Steph w St Luke *Conn*
FALLS, UPPER *see* Belfast Upper Falls *Conn*
**FANLOBBUS (St Mary) w Drimoleague, Drinagh and
Coolkellure** *C, C & R* I W NESBITT
FARNAUGHT (no dedication) *see* Mohill w Farnaught,
Aughavas, Oughteragh etc *K, E & A*
FAUGHANVALE (St Canice) *D & R* I J W BLAIR,
NSM B J HASSAN
FENAGH (All Saints) w Myshall, Aghade and Ardoyne *C & O*
I L D D SCOTT
**FERMOY (Christ Church) w Ballyhooley, Knockmourne,
Ardnageehy and Brigown** *C, C & R* I E V CREMIN
FERMOYLE (no dedication) *see* Castlerock w Dunboe and
Fermoyle *D & R*
**FERNS (Cathedral of St Edan) w Kilbride, Toombe, Kilcormack
and Ballycarney** *C & O* I L D A FORREST,
NSM R J STOTESBURY
FERRY, EAST *see* Cloyne Union *C, C & R*
FERTAGH (no dedication) *see* Kilcooley w Littleon, Crohane
and Fertagh *C & O*
FETHARD (Holy Trinity) *see* Clonmel w Innislounagh,
Tullaghmelan etc *C & O*
FETHARD (St Mogue) *see* New w Old Ross, Whitechurch,
Fethard etc *C & O*
**FIDDOWN (no dedication) w Clonegam, Guilcagh and
Kilmeaden** *C & O* I C G CLIFFE
FINAGHY (St Polycarp) *Conn* I E G BUNTING,
C E HENDERSON
FINGLAS (St Canice) *see* Dublin Santry w Glasnevin and
Finglas *D & G*
FINNER (Christ Church) *see* Killinagh w Kiltyclogher and
Innismagrath *K, E & A*
FINTONA *see* Donacavey w Barr *Clogh*
FINVOY (no dedication) *see* Ballymoney w Finvoy and
Rasharkin *Conn*
FIVEMILETOWN (St John) *Clogh* I T K HANLON
FLORENCECOURT *see* Killesher *K, E & A*
FONTSTOWN (St John the Evangelist) *see* Athy w Kilberry,
Fontstown and Kilkea *D & G*
FORGNEY (St Munis) *see* Athlone w Benown, Kiltoom and
Forgney *M & K*
FOUNTAINS *see* Lismore w Cappoquin, Kilwatermoy,
Dungarvan etc *C & O*
FOXFORD *see* Straid *T, K & A*
FOYNES *see* Rathkeale w Askeaton, Kilcornan and
Kilnaughtin *L & K*
FRANKFIELD (Holy Trinity) *see* Douglas Union w Frankfield
C, C & R
FRENCH CHURCH *see* Portarlington w Cloneyhurke, Lea etc
M & K
FRENCHPARK *see* Roscommon w Donamon, Rathcline,
Kilkeevin etc *K, E & A*
GALLOON (St Comgall) w Drummully and Sallaghy *Clogh*
I R D SEYMOUR-WHITELEY
GALWAY (St Nicholas) w Kilcummin *T, K & A* I G L HASTINGS
GARRISON (no dedication) w Slavin and Belleek *Clogh*
C N H L REGAN
GARRYCLOYNE (no dedication) *see* Carrigrohane Union
C, C & R
GARTAN (St Columba) *see* Conwal Union w Gartan *D & R*
GARTREE (no dedication) *see* Killead w Gartree *Conn*
GARVAGH *see* Errigal w Garvagh *D & R*
GARVAGHY (no dedication) *see* Dromara w Garvaghy *D & D*
GARVARY (Holy Trinity) *see* Derryvullen S w Garvary *Clogh*
GEASHILL (St Mary) w Killeigh and Ballycommon *M & K*
I vacant (00353) (506) 43242

KILCOOLEY (St Columba)   *see* Bangor Abbey *D & D*
KILCORMACK (St Cormac)   *see* Ferns w Kilbride, Toombe, Kilcormack etc *C & O*
KILCORNAN (no dedication)   *see* Rathkeale w Askeaton, Kilcornan and Kilnaughtin *L & K*
KILCROHANE   *see* Kenmare w Sneem, Waterville etc *L & K*
KILCRONAGHAN (no dedication) w Draperstown and Sixtowns *D & R*   **I** D MORROW
KILCULLEN (St John)   *see* Newbridge w Carnalway and Kilcullen *M & K*
KILCUMMIN (no dedication)   *see* Galway w Kilcummin *T, K & A*
KILDALLON (no dedication) w Newtowngore and Corrawallen and Swanlinbar w Kinawley, Templeport and Tomregan *K, E & A*   **I** *vacant*
KILDARE (Cathedral of St Brigid) w Kilmeague and Curragh Garrison Church *M & K*   **I** J J MARSDEN
KILDARTON (no dedication)   *see* Lisnadill w Kildarton *Arm*
KILDAVIN (St Paul)   *see* Bunclody w Kildavin, Clonegal and Kilrush *C & O*
KILDOLLAGH (St Paul)   *see* Ballyrashane w Kildollagh *Conn*
KILDRESS (St Patrick) w Altedesert *Arm*   **I** B J A CRUISE
KILDRUMFERTON (St Patrick) w Ballymachugh and Ballyjamesduff *K, E & A*   **I** *vacant*
KILFANE (no dedication)   *see* Kells Gp *C & O*
KILFARBOY (Christ Church)   *see* Drumcliffe w Kilnasoolagh *L & K*
KILFAUGHNABEG (Christ Church)   *see* Ross Union *C, C & R*
KILFENORA (Cathedral of St Fachan)   *see* Drumcliffe w Kilnasoolagh *L & K*
KILFERAGH (no dedication)   *as above*
KILFINANE (St Andrew)   *see* Adare and Kilmallock w Kilpeacon, Croom etc *L & K*
KILFITHMONE (no dedication)   *see* Templemore w Thurles and Kilfithmone *C & O*
KILFLYNN (no dedication)   *see* Adare and Kilmallock w Kilpeacon, Croom etc *L & K*
KILGARIFFE (no dedication) w Kilmalooda, Kilnagross, Timoleague and Courtmacsherry *C, C & R*   **I** *vacant* (00353) (23) 33357
KILGLASS (no dedication)   *see* Killala w Dunfeeny, Crossmolina, Kilmoremoy etc *T, K & A*
KILGLASS (St Anne)   *see* Mostrim w Granard, Clonbroney, Killoe etc *K, E & A*
KILGOBBIN (no dedication)   *see* Dingle w Killiney and Kilgobbin *L & K*
KILHORNE   *see* Annalong *D & D*
KILKEA (no dedication)   *see* Athy w Kilberry, Fontstown and Kilkea *D & G*
KILKEE   *see* Drumcliffe w Kilnasoolagh *L & K*
KILKEEL (Christ Church) *D & D*   **I** K D MCGRATH, **NSM** S J K TEGGARTY
KILKEEVIN (Holy Trinity)   *see* Roscommon w Donamon, Rathcline, Kilkeevin etc *K, E & A*
KILKENNY (Cathedral of St Canice) (St John), Aghour and Kilmanagh *C & O*   **I** N N JYNAS,   **C** E M E MURRAY
KILKENNY WEST   *see* Athlone w Benown, Kiltoom and Forgney *M & K*
KILL (no dedication) *D & G*   **I** S F GLENFIELD,   **C** T J SILK
KILL (St John)   *see* Naas w Kill and Rathmore *M & K*
KILL O' THE GRANGE   *see* Kill *D & G*
KILLABBAN (no dedication)   *see* Killeshin w Cloydagh and Killabban *C & O*
KILLADEAS (Priory Church)   *see* Trory w Killadeas *Clogh*
KILLAGAN (no dedication)   *see* Craigs w Dunaghy and Killagan *Conn*
KILLAGHTEE (St Peter)   *see* Inver w Mountcharles, Killaghtee and Killybegs *D & R*
KILLALA (Cathedral of St Patrick) w Dunfeeny, Crossmolina, Kilmoremoy, Castleconnor, Easkey and Kilglass *T, K & A*   **I** S M PATTERSON,   **Bp's** C N J O'RAW,   **NSM** D T S CLEMENTS
KILLALLON (St John)   *see* Trim and Athboy Gp *M & K*
KILLALOE (Cathedral of St Flannan) w Stradbally, Clonlara, Mountshannon, Abingdon and Tuomgraney *L & K*   **I** *vacant*
KILLANEY (St Andrew) w Carryduff *D & D*   **I** W S NIXON
KILLANNE (St Anne) w Killegney, Rossdroit and Templeshanbo *C & O*   **I** R J HARMSWORTH
KILLANULLY   *see* Carrigaline Union *C, C & R*
KILLARGUE (no dedication)   *see* Killinagh w Kiltyclogher and Innismagrath *K, E & A*
KILLARNEY (St Mary) w Aghadoe and Muckross *L & K*   **P-in-c** S M WATTERSON
KILLASHEE (St Paul)   *see* Templemichael w Clongish, Clooncumber etc *K, E & A*
KILLASNETT (no dedication)   *see* Clooncare w Killasnett, Lurganboy and Drumlease *K, E & A*

KILLCONNELL   *see* Aughrim w Ballinasloe etc *L & K*
KILLEA (St Andrew)   *see* Waterford w Killea, Drumcannon and Dunhill *C & O*
KILLEA (St Fiach)   *see* Taughboyne, Craigadooish, Newtowncunningham etc *D & R*
KILLEAD (St Catherine) w Gartree *Conn*   **I** W J C ORR, **NSM** W J FARR
KILLEDMOND   *see* Dunleckney w Nurney, Lorum and Kiltennel *C & O*
KILLEEVAN (no dedication)   *see* Clones w Killeevan *Clogh*
KILLEGAR (no dedication)   *see* Killeshandra w Killegar and Derrylane *K, E & A*
KILLEGNEY (no dedication)   *see* Killanne w Killegney, Rossdroit and Templeshanbo *C & O*
KILLEIGH (no dedication)   *see* Geashill w Killeigh and Ballycommon *M & K*
KILLELAGH (no dedication)   *see* Maghera w Killelagh *D & R*
KILLENAULE (no dedication)   *see* Kilcooley w Littleon, Crohane and Fertagh *C & O*
KILLERMOGH (no dedication)   *see* Abbeyleix w Ballyroan etc *C & O*
KILLERY   *see* Taunagh w Kilmactranny, Ballysumaghan etc *K, E & A*
KILLESHANDRA (no dedication) w Killegar and Derrylane *K, E & A*   **C** A CALVIN
KILLESHER (St John) *K, E & A*   **I** I J RUITERS, **NSM** T J WOODS
KILLESHERDONEY (St Mark)   *see* Drumgoon *K, E & A*
KILLESHIL (St Paul)   *see* Errigle Keerogue w Ballygawley and Killeshil *Arm*
KILLESHIN (no dedication) w Cloydagh and Killabban *C & O*   **I** O E HENDERSON
KILLESK (All Saints)   *see* New w Old Ross, Whitechurch, Fethard etc *C & O*
KILLETER   *see* Derg w Termonamongan *D & R*
KILLINAGH (no dedication) w Kiltyclogher and Innismagrath *K, E & A*   **I** *vacant*
KILLINCHY (no dedication) w Kilmood and Tullynakill *D & D*   **I** A S DELAMERE
KILLINEY Ballybrack (St Matthias) *D & G*   **I** I P POULTON, **NSM** N STRATFORD
KILLINEY (Holy Trinity) *D & G*   **I** H C MILLS
KILLINEY (St Brendan)   *see* Dingle w Killiney and Kilgobbin *L & K*
KILLINICK (no dedication)   *see* Kilscoran w Killinick and Mulrankin *C & O*
KILLINKERE (no dedication)   *see* Lurgan w Billis, Killinkere and Munterconnaught *K, E & A*
KILLISKEY (no dedication)   *see* Wicklow w Killiskey *D & G*
KILLODIERNAN (no dedication)   *see* Nenagh *L & K*
KILLOE (St Catherine)   *see* Mostrim w Granard, Clonbroney, Killoe etc *K, E & A*
KILLORAN (no dedication)   *see* Tubbercurry w Killoran *T, K & A*
KILLORGLIN (no dedication)   *see* Kilcolman W Kiltallagh, Killorglin, Knockane etc *L & K*
KILLOUGH (St Anne)   *see* Bright w Ballee and Killough *D & D*
KILLOUGHTER (no dedication)   *see* Drung w Castleterra, Larah and Lavey etc *K, E & A*
KILLOUGHY   *see* Tullamore w Durrow, Newtownfertullagh, Rahan etc *M & K*
KILLOWEN   *see* Kinneigh Union *C, C & R*
KILLOWEN (St John) *D & R*   **I** D M COLLINS, **C** S J CAMPBELL, I W MAGOWAN
KILLSALLAGHAN (St David)   *see* Swords w Donabate and Kilsallaghan *D & G*
KILLUCAN (St Etchen)   *see* Mullingar, Portnashangan, Moyliscar, Kilbixy etc *M & K*
KILLURIN (no dedication)   *see* Wexford w Ardcolm and Killurin *C & O*
KILLYBEGS (no dedication)   *see* Inver w Mountcharles, Killaghtee and Killybegs *D & R*
KILLYGARVAN (St Columb)   *see* Tullyaughnish w Kilmacrennan and Killygarvan *D & R*
KILLYLEA (St Mark)   *see* Eglish w Killylea *Arm*
KILLYLEAGH (St John the Evangelist) *D & D*   **I** J C MUNYANGAJU
KILLYMAN (St Andrew) *Arm*   **I** S R T BOYD
KILLYMARD (no dedication)   *see* Donegal w Killymard, Lough Eske and Laghey *D & R*
KILMACABEA (no dedication)   *see* Ross Union *C, C & R*
KILMACDUAGH (no dedication)   *see* Aughrim w Ballinasloe etc *L & K*
KILMACRENNAN (St Finnian and St Mark)   *see* Tullyaughnish w Kilmacrennan and Killygarvan *D & R*

KILMACSHALGAN (St Mary) *see* Skreen w Kilmacshalgan and Dromard *T, K & A*

KILMACTHOMAS (no dedication) *see* Lismore w Cappoquin, Kilwatermoy, Dungarvan etc *C & O*

KILMACTRANNY (no dedication) *see* Taunagh w Kilmactranny, Ballysumaghan etc *K, E & A*

KILMAINHAMWOOD *see* Kingscourt w Syddan *M & K*

KILMAKEE (St Hilda) *Conn*   **I** D H BOYLAND

KILMALLOCK (St Peter and St Paul) *see* Adare and Kilmallock w Kilpeacon, Croom etc *L & K*

KILMALOODA (All Saints) *see* Kilgariffe Union *C, C & R*

KILMANAGH (no dedication) *see* Kilkenny w Aghour and Kilmanagh *C & O*

KILMEADEN (St Mary) *see* Fiddown w Clonegam, Guilcagh and Kilmeaden *C & O*

KILMEAGUE (no dedication) *see* Kildare w Kilmeague and Curragh *M & K*

KILMEEN (Christ Church) *see* Kinneigh Union *C, C & R*

KILMEGAN (no dedication) w Maghera *D & D*   **I** C J CARSON

KILMOCOMOGUE Union (no dedication) *C, C & R*   **I** P M WILLOUGHBY

KILMOE (no dedication) w Teampol-na-mbocht, Schull and Crookhaven *C, C & R*   **I** E E M LYNCH

KILMOGANNY (St Matthew) *see* Kells Gp *C & O*

KILMOOD (St Mary) *see* Killinchy w Kilmood and Tullynakill *D & D*

KILMORE (Cathedral of St Fethlimidh) w Ballintemple *K, E & A*   **I** W R FERGUSON

KILMORE (Christ Church) and Inch *D & D*   **I** *vacant*

KILMORE (no dedication) *see* Monaghan w Tydavnet and Kilmore *Clogh*

KILMORE (no dedication) *see* Kiltoghart w Drumshambo, Annaduff and Kilronan *K, E & A*

KILMORE (St Aidan) (St Saviour) *Arm*   **I** M T KINGSTON

KILMOREMOY (St Michael) *see* Killala w Dunfeeny, Crossmolina, Kilmoremoy etc *T, K & A*

KILMOYLEY *see* Tralee w Kilmoyley, Ballymacelligott etc *L & K*

KILMUCKRIDGE (no dedication) *see* Ardamine w Kiltennel, Glascarrig etc *C & O*

KILMURRY (St Andrew) *see* Moviddy Union *C, C & R*

KILNAGROSS (no dedication) *see* Kilgariffe Union *C, C & R*

KILNAHUE (St John the Evangelist) *see* Gorey w Kilnahue, Leskinfere and Ballycanew *C & O*

KILNALECK *see* Kildrumferton w Ballymachugh and Ballyjamesduff *K, E & A*

KILNAMANAGH (St John) *see* Ardamine w Kiltennel, Glascarrig etc *C & O*

KILNASOOLAGH (no dedication) *see* Drumcliffe w Kilnasoolagh *L & K*

KILNAUGHTIN (St Brendan) *see* Rathkeale w Askeaton, Kilcornan and Kilnaughtin *L & K*

KILPEACON (St Beacon) *see* Adare and Kilmallock w Kilpeacon, Croom etc *L & K*

KILPIPE (no dedication) *see* Crosspatrick Gp *C & O*

KILREA (St Patrick) *see* Aghadowey w Kilrea *D & R*

KILRONAN (St Thomas) *see* Kiltoghart w Drumshambo, Annaduff and Kilronan *K, E & A*

KILROOT (St Colman) and Templecorran *Conn*   **I** M J MCCANN,   **NSM** W STEWART

KILROSSANTY (no dedication) *see* Lismore w Cappoquin, Kilwatermoy, Dungarvan etc *C & O*

KILRUSH *see* Drumcliffe w Kilnasoolagh *L & K*

KILRUSH (St Brigid) *see* Bunclody w Kildavin, Clonegal and Kilrush *C & O*

KILSARAN (St Mary) w Drumcar, Dunleer and Dunany *Arm*   **I** M GRAHAM

KILSCORAN (no dedication) w Killinick and Mulrankin *C & O*   **P-in-c** M P JANSSON

KILSKEERY (no dedication) w Trillick *Clogh*   **I** W J JOHNSTON

KILTALLAGH (St Carthage) *see* Kilcolman w Kiltallagh, Killorglin, Knockane etc *L & K*

KILTEEVOGUE (St John) *see* Stranorlar w Meenglas and Kilteevogue *D & R*

KILTEGAN (St Peter) w Hacketstown, Clonmore and Moyne *C & O*   **I** S E B DURAND

KILTENNEL (no dedication) *see* Ardamine w Kiltennel, Glascarrig etc *C & O*

KILTENNEL (St Peter) *see* Dunleckney w Nurney, Lorum and Kiltennel *C & O*

KILTERNAN (St Kiernan) *D & G*   **I** D G MOYNAN

KILTINANLEA (no dedication) *see* Killaloe w Stradbally *L & K*

KILTOGHART (St George) w Drumshambo, Anaduff and Kilronan *K, E & A*   **I** *vacant* (00353) (61) 20053

KILTOOM *see* Athlone w Benown, Kiltoom and Forgney *M & K*

KILTUBRIDE (St Brigid) *see* Mohill w Farnaught, Aughavas, Oughteragh etc *K, E & A*

KILTULLAGH (no dedication) *see* Roscommon w Donamon, Rathcline, Kilkeevin etc *K, E & A*

KILTYCLOGHER (no dedication) *see* Killinagh w Kiltyclogher and Innismagrath *K, E & A*

KILVEMNON (St Hugh) *see* Clonmel w Innislounagh, Tullaghmelan etc *C & O*

KILWARLIN UPPER (St John) w LOWER (St James) *D & D*   **I** T D B PIERCE

KILWATERMOY (St Mary) *see* Lismore w Cappoquin, Kilwatermoy, Dungarvan etc *C & O*

KILWAUGHTER (no dedication) w Cairncastle and Craigy Hill *Conn*   **I** R Q THOMPSON

KINAWLEY (no dedication) w Holy Trinity *K, E & A*   **I** *vacant*

KINAWLEY (St Paul) *see* Kildallon and Swanlinbar *K, E & A*

KINGSCOURT (St Ernan) w Drumconrath, Syddan and Moybologue *M & K*   **I** *vacant*

KINLOUGH *see* Killinagh w Kiltyclogher and Innismagrath *K, E & A*

KINNEAGH (no dedication) *see* Narraghmore and Timolin w Castledermot etc *D & G*

KINNEIGH (St Bartholomew) w Ballymoney, Kilmeen, Desertserges, Killowen and Murragh *C, C & R*   **I** *vacant* (00353) (73) 31043

KINNITTY (St Trinnian) *see* Shinrone w Aghancon etc *L & K*

KINSALE (St Multose) w Runcurran, Ballymartle and Templetrine *C, C & R*   **I** D WILLIAMS

KIRCONRIOLA *see* Ballymena w Ballyclug *Conn*

KIRCUBBIN (Holy Trinity) *see* Grey Abbey w Kircubbin *D & D*

KNAPPAGH (St Thomas) *see* Aughaval w Achill, Knappagh, Dugort etc *T, K & A*

KNOCK (St Columba) *D & D*   **I** J R AUCHMUTY,   **C** R J FERRIS

KNOCKANE (no dedication) *see* Kilcolman w Kiltallagh, Killorglin, Knockane etc *L & K*

KNOCKANEY (St John) *see* Adare and Kilmallock w Kilpeacon, Croom etc *L & K*

KNOCKBREDA (no dedication) *D & D*   **I** P F PATTERSON,   **C** S T R GAMBLE

KNOCKBRIDE (no dedication) *see* Bailieborough w Knockbride, Shercock and Mullagh *K, E & A*

KNOCKLOUGHRIM *see* Desertmartin w Termoneeny *D & R*

KNOCKMOURNE (no dedication) *see* Fermoy Union *C, C & R*

KNOCKNAGONEY (Annunciation) *D & D*   **Bp's C** D L BROWN

KNOCKNAMUCKLEY (St Matthias) *D & D*   **I** D J MCCARTNEY

KNOCKNAREA (St Anne) *see* Sligo w Knocknarea and Rosses Pt *K, E & A*

KYLE (no dedication) *see* Roscrea w Kyle, Bourney and Corbally *L & K*

LACK (no dedication) *Clogh*   **I** *vacant* (028) 6863 1360

LAGHEY (no dedication) *see* Donegal w Killymard, Lough Eske and Laghey *D & R*

LAMBEG (no dedication) *Conn*   **I** K A MCREYNOLDS

LANESBOROUGH *see* Roscommon w Donamon, Rathcline, Kilkeevin etc *K, E & A*

LANGFIELD, LOWER (no dedication) *see* Drumclamph w Lower and Upper Langfield *D & R*

LANGFIELD, UPPER (no dedication) *as above*

LARAGH (St John) *see* Rathdrum w Glenealy, Derralossary and Laragh *D & G*

LARAH and LAVEY (no dedication) *see* Drung w Castleterra, Larah and Lavey etc *K, E & A*

LARNE AND INVER (St Cedma) *Conn*   **I** S B FORDE,   **C** M HILLIARD,   **NSM** R A KER, H SHARP

LAVEY *see* Drung w Castleterra, Larah and Lavey etc *K, E & A*

LAYDE (no dedication) *see* Ardclinis and Tickmacrevan w Layde and Cushendun *Conn*

LEA (no dedication) *see* Portarlington w Cloneyhurke, Lea etc *M & K*

LEAP *see* Ross Union *C, C & R*

LEARMOUNT (no dedication) *see* Cumber Upper w Learmount *D & R*

LEATBEG (no dedication) *see* Clondevaddock w Portsalon and Leatbeg *D & R*

LECALE Group: Saul, Ardglass, Dunsford, Ballyculter and Kilclief *D & D*   **I** T H HULL,   **NSM** G J SAVAGE

LECKPATRICK (St Patrick) w Dunnalong *D & R*   **I** N I LYTTLE

LEESON PARK (Christ Church) *see* Dublin St Bart w Leeson Park *D & G*

LEIGHLIN (Cathedral of St Laserian) w Grange Sylvae, Shankill, Clonagoose and Gowran *C & O* **I** F J G WYNNE, **NSM** S G EVANS

LEIXLIP (St Mary) *see* Lucan w Leixlip *D & G*

LESKINFERE (no dedication) *see* Gorey w Kilnahue, Leskinfere and Ballycanew *C & O*

LETTERKENNY *see* Conwal Union w Gartan *D & R*

LETTERMACAWARD (no dedication) *see* Ardara w Glencolumbkille, Inniskeel etc *D & R*

LICKMOLASSY *see* Clonfert Gp *L & K*

LIFFORD *see* Raphoe w Raymochy and Clonleigh *D & R*

LIMAVADY *see* Drumachose *D & R*

LIMAVADY *see* Tamlaghtfinlagan w Myroe *D & R*

LIMERICK CITY (Cathedral of St Mary) (St Michael) *L & K* **I** J M G SIRR

LISBELLAW (no dedication) *Clogh* **I** B T KERR

LISBURN (Christ Church) *Conn* **I** E P DUNDAS

LISBURN (Christ Church Cathedral) *Conn* **I** W S WRIGHT, **C** S GENOE

LISBURN (St Paul) *Conn* **I** J I CARSON

LISLIMNAGHAN (Holy Trinity) *see* Cappagh w Lislimnaghan *D & R*

LISMORE (Cathedral of St Carthage) w Cappoquin, Kilwatermoy, Dungarvan, Kilrossanty, Stradbally and Kilmacthomas *C & O* **I** P R DRAPER, **C** I M JACKSON, **NSM** C O'DOWD SMYTH

LISNADILL (St John) w Kildarton *Arm* **I** M C KENNEDY

LISNASKEA (Holy Trinity) *Clogh* **I** W A CAPPER

LISS (no dedication) *see* Clara w Liss, Moate and Clonmacnoise *M & K*

LISSADELL (no dedication) *see* Drumcliffe w Lissadell and Munninane *K, E & A*

LISSAN (no dedication) *Arm* **I** T A CROSS

LISTOWEL *see* Tralee w Kilmoyley, Ballymacelligott etc *L & K*

LITTLE ISLAND (St Lappan) *see* Rathcooney Union *C, C & R*

LITTLETON (no dedication) *see* Kilcooley w Littleon, Crohane and Fertagh *C & O*

LOCKEEN (no dedication) *see* Birr w Lorrha, Dorrha and Lockeen *L & K*

LONDONDERRY *see* Templemore *D & R*

LONDONDERRY (Christ Church), Culmore, Muff and Belmont *D & R* **NSM** K M MCATEER

LONDONDERRY (St Augustine) *D & R* **I** P L STOREY

LONGFORD *see* Templemichael w Clongish, Clooncumber etc *K, E & A*

LORRHA (St Ruadhan) *see* Birr w Lorrha, Dorrha and Lockeen *L & K*

LORUM (no dedication) *see* Dunleckney w Nurney, Lorum and Kiltennel *C & O*

LOUGH ESKE (Christ Church) *see* Donegal w Killymard, Lough Eske and Laghey *D & R*

LOUGHBRICKLAND *see* Aghaderg w Donaghmore and Scarva *D & D*

LOUGHCREW *see* Castlepollard and Oldcastle w Loughcrew etc *M & K*

LOUGHGALL (St Luke) w Grange *Arm* **I** G P MCADAM

LOUGHGILLY (St Patrick) w Clare *Arm* **I** J L WILSON

LOUGHGUILE (All Saints) *see* Armoy w Loughguile and Drumtullagh *Conn*

LOUGHINISLAND (no dedication) *D & D* **I** *vacant*

LUCAN (St Andrew) w Leixlip *D & G* **I** J S PEOPLES

LUGGACURREN (Resurrection) *see* Stradbally w Ballintubbert, Coraclone etc *C & O*

LURGAN (Christ the Redeemer) (St Andrew) *D & D* **I** S G WILSON, **C** C S COONEY, **NSM** C E BAXTER

LURGAN (no dedication) w Billis, Killinkere and Munterconnaught *K, E & A* **I** C W L MCCAULEY

LURGAN (St John the Evangelist) *D & D* **I** J M WHITE

LURGANBOY (Chapel of Ease) *see* Cloonclare w Killasnett, Lurganboy and Drumlease *K, E & A*

MACOSQUIN *see* Camus-juxta-Bann *D & R*

MACREDDIN *see* Castlemacadam w Ballinaclash, Aughrim etc *D & G*

MACROOM *see* Moviddy Union *C, C & R*

MAGHERA *see* Kilmegan w Maghera *D & D*

MAGHERA (St Lurach) w Killelagh *D & R* **I** R S MILLER

MAGHERACLOONE (St Molua) *see* Carrickmacross w Magheracloone *Clogh*

MAGHERACROSS (no dedication) *Clogh* **I** C J MATCHETT, **NSM** C G EAMES

MAGHERACULMONEY (St Mary) *Clogh* **I** W E MCGIRR, **C** W H BLAIR

MAGHERADROLL (no dedication) *D & D* **I** W W RUSSELL

MAGHERAFELT (St Swithin) *Arm* **I** T SCOTT

MAGHERAGALL (no dedication) *Conn* **I** N J DARK

MAGHERAHAMLET (no dedication) *see* Annahilt w Magherahamlet *D & D*

MAGHERALIN (Holy and Undivided Trinity) w Dollingstown *D & D* **I** G A HARRON, **C** W J BOYD

MAGHERALLY (St John the Evangelist) w Annaclone *D & D* **I** *vacant*

MAGORBAN (no dedication) *see* Cashel w Magorban, Tipperary, Clonbeg etc *C & O*

MAGOURNEY *see* Carrigrohane Union *C, C & R*

MAGUIRESBRIDGE (Christ Church) w Derrybrusk *Clogh* **I** D SKUCE

MALAHIDE (St Andrew) w Balgriffin *D & G* **I** N E C GAMBLE, **NSM** K H SHERWOOD

MALIN *see* Moville w Greencastle, Donagh, Cloncha etc *D & R*

MALLOW (St James) w Doneraile and Castletownroche *C, C & R* **I** D F A MACCARTHY

MALLUSK (St Brigid) *Conn* **I** W A BOYCE

MALONE *see* Belfast Malone St Jo *Conn*

MALONE, UPPER *see* Belfast Upper Malone (Epiphany) *Conn*

MANORCUNNINGHAM *see* Raphoe w Raymochy and Clonleigh *D & R*

MANORHAMILTON *see* Cloonclare w Killasnett, Lurganboy and Drumlease *K, E & A*

MARKETHILL (no dedication) *see* Mullabrack w Markethill and Kilcluney *Arm*

MARMULLANE (St Mary) *see* Douglas Union w Frankfield *C, C & R*

MARYBOROUGH (St Peter) w Dysart Enos and Ballyfin *C & O* **I** H A DUNGAN

MAYNE *see* Castlepollard and Oldcastle w Loughcrew etc *M & K*

MAYNOOTH (St Mary) *see* Dunboyne Union *M & K*

MAYO (no dedication) *see* Killeshin w Cloydagh and Killabban *C & O*

MEALIFFE *see* Templemore w Thurles and Kilfithmone *C & O*

MEENGLASS (Ascension) *see* Stranorlar w Meenglass and Kilteevogue *D & R*

MEVAGH (Holy Trinity) w Glenalla *D & R* **I** *vacant*

MIDDLE CHURCH (no dedication) *see* Ballinderry *Conn*

MIDDLETOWN (St John) *see* Tynan w Middletown and Aghavilly *Arm*

MIDLETON (St John the Baptist) *see* Cloyne Union *C, C & R*

MILLISLE (St Patrick) *see* Carrowdore w Millisle *D & D*

MILLTOWN *see* Kilcolman w Kiltallagh, Killorglin, Knockane etc *L & K*

MILLTOWN (St Andrew) *Arm* **I** G W MACARTNEY

MILLTOWN (St Philip) *see* Dublin Sandford w Milltown *D & G*

MILLTOWN MALBAY *see* Drumcliffe w Kilnasoolagh *L & K*

MITCHELSTOWN *see* Fermoy Union *C, C & R*

MOATE (St Mary) *see* Clara w Liss, Moate and Clonmacnoise *M & K*

MOHILL (St Mary) w Farnaught, Aughavas, Oughteragh, Kiltubride and Drumreilly *K, E & A* **I** F W ATKINS

MOIRA (St John) *D & D* **I** T R WEST, **C** J M MEGARRELL

MONAGHAN (St Patrick) w Tydavnet and Kilmore *Clogh* **I** T H BERRY

MONAMOLIN (St Molig) *see* Ardamine w Kiltennel, Glascarrig etc *C & O*

MONART (St Peter) *see* Enniscorthy w Clone, Clonmore, Monart etc *C & O*

MONASTEREVAN (St John the Evangelist) *see* Portarlington w Cloneyhurke, Lea etc *M & K*

MONASTERORIS (no dedication) *see* Clonsast w Rathangan, Thomastown etc *M & K*

MONELLAN (St Anne) *see* Convoy w Monellan and Donaghmore *D & R*

MONEYMORE *see* Desertlyn w Ballyeglish *Arm*

MONEYREAGH (no dedication) *see* Orangefield w Moneyreagh *D & D*

MONKSTOWN (Good Shepherd) *Conn* **C** A MOORE

MONKSTOWN (no dedication) *D & G* **I** P H A LAWRENCE

MONKSTOWN (St John) *see* Carrigaline Union *C, C & R*

MOSSLEY (Holy Spirit) *Conn* **I** N R CUTCLIFFE

MOSTRIM (St John) w Granard, Clonbroney, Killoe, Rathaspeck and Streete *K, E & A* **P-in-c** J M CATTERALL

MOTHEL (no dedication) *see* Castlecomer w Colliery Ch, Mothel and Bilbo *C & O*

MOUNT MERRION (Pentecost) *D & D* **P-in-c** D A MCCLAY

MOUNT MERRION (St Thomas) *see* Dublin Mt Merrion *D & G*

MOUNT NUGENT (St Bride) *see* Castlepollard and Oldcastle w Loughcrew etc *M & K*

MOUNTCHARLES (Christ Church) *see* Inver w
Mountcharles, Killaghtee and Killybegs *D & R*

MOUNTFIELD (no dedication) *see* Drumragh w Mountfield
D & R

**MOUNTMELLICK (St Paul) w Coolbanagher, Rosenallis and
Clonaslee** *M & K* I O M R DONOHOE

MOUNTRATH *see* Clonenagh w Offerlane, Borris-in-Ossory
etc *C & O*

MOUNTSHANNON *see* Killaloe w Stradbally *L & K*

**MOVIDDY (no dedication), Kilbonane, Kilmurry, Templemartin
and Macroom** *C, C & R* I R E B WHITE, **NSM** P J GEARY

MOVILLA (no dedication) *D & D* I vacant

**MOVILLE (St Columb) w Greencastle, Donagh, Cloncha and
Culdaff** *D & R* I H GILMORE

MOY (St James) w Charlemont *Arm* I vacant

MOYBOLOGUE *see* Kingscourt w Syddan *M & K*

MOYDOW (no dedication) *see* Ardagh w Tashinny, Shrule and
Kilcommick *K, E & A*

MOYGASHEL (no dedication) *see* Drumglass w Moygashel
Arm

MOYGLARE (All Saints) *see* Dunboyne Union *M & K*

MOYLISCAR *see* Mullingar, Portnashangan, Moyliscar,
Kilbixy etc *M & K*

MOYNALTY (St Mary) *see* Kells Union *M & K*

MOYNE (St John) *see* Kiltegan w Hacketstown, Clonmore and
Moyne *C & O*

MOYNTAGHS *see* Ardmore w Craigavon *D & D*

MOYRUS *see* Omey w Ballynakill, Errislannan and
Roundstone *T, K & A*

MUCKAMORE (St Jude) (St Matthias) *Conn* I W J C ORR,
NSM W J FARR

MUCKNOE (St Maeldoid) *see* Ballybay w Mucknoe and
Clontibret *Clogh*

MUCKROSS (Holy Trinity) *see* Killarney w Aghadoe and
Muckross *L & K*

MUCKROSS (St John) *see* Drumkeeran w Templecarne and
Muckross *Clogh*

MUFF (no dedication) *see* Londonderry Ch Ch, Culmore, Muff
and Belmont *D & R*

MULHUDDART (St Thomas) *see* Castleknock and
Mulhuddart w Clonsilla *D & G*

MULLABRACK (no dedication) w Markethill and Kilcluney
Arm I N J HUGHES

MULLAGH (no dedication) *see* Bailieborough w Knockbride,
Shercock and Mullagh *K, E & A*

MULLAGHDUN (no dedication) *see* Cleenish w Mullaghdun
Clogh

MULLAGHFAD (All Saints) *see* Aghalurcher w Tattykeeran,
Cooneen etc *Clogh*

MULLAGLASS (St Luke) *see* Camlough w Mullaglass *Arm*

MULLAVILLY (no dedication) *Arm* I B J HARPER

MULLINACUFF (no dedication) *see* Tullow w Shillelagh,
Aghold and Mullinacuff *C & O*

**MULLINGAR (All Saints) w Portnashangan, Moyliscar, Kilbixy,
Almoritia, Killucan, Clonard and Castlelost** *M & K*
I M A GRAHAM, **NSM** J WYNNE

MULRANKIN (St David) *see* Kilscoran w Killinick and
Mulrankin *C & O*

MUNNINANE (St Kevin) *see* Drumcliffe w Lissadell and
Munninane *K, E & A*

MUNTERCONNAUGHT (no dedication) *see* Lurgan w Billis,
Killinkere and Munterconnaught *K, E & A*

MURRAGH (no dedication) *see* Kinneigh Union *C, C & R*

MYROE (St John) *see* Tamlaghtfinlagan w Myroe *D & R*

MYROSS *see* Ross Union *C, C & R*

MYSHALL (Christ the Redeemer) *see* Fenagh w Myshall,
Aghade and Ardoyne *C & O*

NAAS (St David) w Kill and Rathmore *M & K* I P G HEAK

**NARRAGHMORE (Holy Saviour) and Timolin w Castledermot
and Kinneagh** *D & G* I I G DELAMERE, **NSM** T ALCOCK

**NAVAN (St Mary) w Kentstown, Tara, Slane, Painestown and
Stackallen** *M & K* I J D M CLARKE

**NENAGH (St Mary) w Ballymackey, Templederry and
Killodiernan** *L & K* I M G ROWLEY-BROOKE,
NSM P E HANNA

NEWBLISS (no dedication) *see* Currin w Drum and Newbliss
Clogh

NEWBRIDGE (St Patrick) w Carnalway and Kilcullen *M & K*
I J J MARSDEN

**NEWCASTLE (no dedication) w Newtownmountkennedy and
Calary** *D & G* I W L BENNETT

NEWCASTLE (St John) *D & D* I I M ELLIS,
NSM M S WALSHE

NEWCASTLE-LYONS (no dedication) *see* Celbridge w
Straffan and Newcastle-Lyons *D & G*

NEWCESTOWN *see* Kinneigh Union *C, C & R*

NEWMARKET-ON-FERGUS *see* Drumcliffe w Kilnasoolagh
L & K

NEWRY (St Mary) (St Patrick) *D & D* I K E SUTTON

NEWTOWNARDS (St Mark) *D & D* I K J SMYTH

NEWTOWNBARRY *see* Bunclody w Kildavin, Clonegal and
Kilrush *C & O*

NEWTOWNBUTLER *see* Galloon w Drummully and Sallaghy
Clogh

NEWTOWNCROMMELIN (no dedication) *see* Skerry w
Rathcavan and Newtowncrommelin *Conn*

NEWTOWNCUNNINGHAM (All Saints) *see* Taughboyne,
Craigadooish, Newtowncunningham etc *D & R*

NEWTOWNFERTULLAGH *see* Tullamore w Durrow,
Newtownfertullagh, Rahan etc *M & K*

NEWTOWNFORBES *see* Templemichael w Clongish,
Clooncumber etc *K, E & A*

NEWTOWNGORE (no dedication) *see* Kildallon and
Swanlinbar *K, E & A*

NEWTOWNHAMILTON (St John) w Ballymoyer and Belleck
Arm I vacant

NEWTOWNMOUNTKENNEDY (St Matthew) *see* Newcastle
w Newtownmountkennedy and Calary *D & G*

NEWTOWNSAVILLE (no dedication) *see* Augher w
Newtownsaville and Eskrahoole *Clogh*

NEWTOWNSTEWART *see* Ardstraw w Baronscourt, Badoney
Lower etc *D & R*

NOHOVAL (no dedication) *see* Templebreedy w Tracton and
Nohoval *C, C & R*

NURNEY (no dedication) *see* Portarlington w Cloneyhurke,
Lea etc *M & K*

NURNEY (St John) *see* Dunleckney w Nurney, Lorum and
Kiltennel *C & O*

OFFERLANE (no dedication) *see* Clonenagh w Offerlane,
Borris-in-Ossory etc *C & O*

OLD LEIGHLIN *see* Leighlin w Grange Sylvae, Shankill etc
C & O

OLDCASTLE (St Bride) *see* Castlepollard and Oldcastle w
Loughcrew etc *M & K*

OMAGH *see* Drumragh w Mountfield *D & R*

**OMEY (Christ Church) w Ballynakill, Errislannan and
Roundstone** *T, K & A* I D L SANDES

ORANGEFIELD (St John the Evangelist) w Moneyreagh *D & D*
I W J R LAVERTY

OSSORY *see* Kilcooley w Littleon, Crohane and Fertagh *C & O*

OUGHTERAGH (no dedication) *see* Mohill w Farnaught,
Aughavas, Oughteragh etc *K, E & A*

OUGHTERARD *see* Galway w Kilcummin *T, K & A*

PACKANE *see* Nenagh *L & K*

PAINESTOWN *see* Navan w Kentstown, Tara, Slane,
Painestown etc *M & K*

PALLASKENRY *see* Rathkeale w Askeaton, Kilcornan and
Kilnaughtin *L & K*

PASSAGE WEST *see* Douglas Union w Frankfield *C, C & R*

PAULSTOWN *see* Leighlin w Grange Sylvae, Shankill etc
C & O

PETTIGO *see* Drumkeeran w Templecarne and Muckross
Clogh

PILTOWN *see* Fiddown w Clonegam, Guilcagh and Kilmeaden
C & O

POMEROY (no dedication) *Arm* **NSM** W J A DAWSON

PORT LAOIS *see* Maryborough w Dysart Enos and Ballyfin
C & O

PORTADOWN (St Columba) *Arm* I W M ADAIR,
C D E CAIRNS

PORTADOWN (St Mark) *Arm* I J N T CAMPBELL,
C C M HAYES

PORTAFERRY *see* Ballyphilip w Ardquin *D & D*

**PORTARLINGTON (St Paul) w Cloneyhurke, Lea,
Monasterevin, Nurney and Rathdaire** *M & K*
I L T C STEVENSON

PORTGLENONE (no dedication) *see* Ahoghill w Portglenone
Conn

PORTLAOISE *see* Maryborough w Dysart Enos and Ballyfin
C & O

PORTLAW *see* Fiddown w Clonegam, Guilcagh and
Kilmeaden *C & O*

PORTNASHANGAN *see* Mullingar, Portnashangan,
Moyliscar, Kilbixy etc *M & K*

PORTRUSH *see* Ballywillan *Conn*

PORTSALON (All Saints) *see* Clondevaddock w Portsalon and
Leatbeg *D & R*

PORTSTEWART *see* Agherton *Conn*

PORTUMNA (Christ Church) *see* Clonfert Gp *L & K*

POWERSCOURT (St Patrick) w Kilbride *D & G*
I R B ROUNTREE, **NSM** H E A LEW, J B MARCHANT

PREBAN (St John)   *see* Crosspatrick Gp *C & O*
RAHAN   *see* Clonsast w Rathangan, Thomastown etc *M & K*
RAHAN (St Carthach)   *see* Tullamore w Durrow, Newtownfertullagh, Rahan etc *M & K*
RAHENY (All Saints) w Coolock *D & G*   **I** J T CARROLL
RALOO (no dedication)   *see* Glynn w Raloo *Conn*
RAMELTON   *see* Tullyaughnish w Kilmacrennan and Killygarvan *D & R*
RAMOAN (St James) w Ballycastle and Culfeightrin *Conn*   **I** D M PALMER
RANDALSTOWN   *see* Drummaul w Duneane and Ballyscullion *Conn*
RAPHOE (Cathedral of St Eunan) w Raymochy and Clonleigh *D & R*   **I** J HAY,   **NSM** M T E PEOPLES
RASHARKIN (St Andrew)   *see* Ballymoney w Finvoy and Rasharkin *Conn*
RATHANGAN (no dedication)   *see* Clonsast w Rathangan, Thomastown etc *M & K*
RATHASPECK (St Thomas)   *see* Mostrim w Granard, Clonbroney, Killoe etc *K, E & A*
RATHBARRON   *see* Tubbercurry w Killoran *T, K & A*
RATHCAVAN (no dedication)   *see* Skerry w Rathcavan and Newtowncrommelin *Conn*
RATHCLAREN (Holy Trinity)   *see* Bandon Union *C, C & R*
RATHCLINE (no dedication)   *see* Roscommon w Donamon, Rathcline, Kilkeevin etc *K, E & A*
RATHCOOLE (no dedication)   *see* Clondalkin w Rathcoole *D & G*
RATHCOOLE (St Comgall) *Conn*   **I** A W MILLAR
RATHCOONEY (St Mary and All Saints) w Little Island and Carrigtwohill *C, C & R*   **I** D J OWEN
RATHCOR (no dedication)   *see* Ballymascanlan w Creggan and Rathcor *Arm*
RATHCORE (St Ultan)   *see* Rathmolyon w Castlerickard, Rathcore and Agher *M & K*
RATHDAIRE (Ascension)   *see* Portarlington w Cloneyhurke, Lea etc *M & K*
RATHDOWNEY (no dedication) w Castlefleming, Donaghmore, Rathsaran and Aghavoe *C & O*   **I** J G MURRAY
RATHDRUM (St Saviour) w Glenealy, Derralossary and Laragh *D & G*   **I** J E MCCULLAGH
RATHFARNHAM   *see* Dublin Rathfarnham *D & G*
RATHFRILAND   *see* Drumgath w Drumgooland and Clonduff *D & D*
RATHGAR   *see* Dublin Zion Ch *D & G*
RATHKEALE (Holy Trinity) w Askeaton, Foynes, Kilcornan and Kilnaughtin *L & K*   **I** *vacant* (00353) (61) 398269
RATHLIN (St Thomas)   *see* Ballintoy w Rathlin and Dunseverick *Conn*
RATHMICHAEL (no dedication) *D & G*   **I** F C APPELBE
RATHMINES   *see* Dublin Rathmines w Harold's Cross *D & G*
RATHMOLYON (St Michael and All Angels) w Castlerickard, Rathcore and Agher *M & K*   **NSM** A V STEWART
RATHMORE (St Columbkille)   *see* Naas w Kill and Rathmore *M & K*
RATHMULLAN   *see* Tullyaughnish w Kilmacrennan and Killygarvan *D & R*
RATHMULLAN (no dedication) w Tyrella *D & D*   **I** *vacant*
RATHOWEN   *see* Mostrim w Granard, Clonbroney, Killoe etc *K, E & A*
RATHSARAN (no dedication)   *see* Rathdowney w Castlefleming, Donaghmore etc *C & O*
RATHVILLY (St Mary)   *see* Baltinglass w Ballynure etc *C & O*
RAYMOCHY (no dedication)   *see* Raphoe w Raymochy and Clonleigh *D & R*
RAYMUNTERDONEY (St Paul)   *see* Dunfanaghy, Raymunterdoney and Tullaghbegley *D & R*
REDCROSS (Holy Trinity)   *see* Dunganstown w Redcross and Conary *D & G*
REDHILLS   *see* Drung w Castleterra, Larah and Lavey etc *K, E & A*
RICHHILL (St Matthew) *Arm*   **I** D COE
RIVERSTOWN   *see* Taunagh w Kilmactranny, Ballysumaghan etc *K, E & A*
ROCHFORT BRIDGE   *see* Mullingar, Portnashangan, Moylisear, Kilbixy etc *M & K*
ROCKCORRY (no dedication)   *see* Ematris w Rockcorry, Aghabog and Aughnamullan *Clogh*
ROSCOMMON (St Colman) w Donamon, Rathcline, Kilkeevin, Kiltullagh and Tybohine *K, E & A*   **NSM** A J LINDSAY
ROSCREA (St Cronan) w Kyle, Bourney and Corbally *L & K*   **NSM** E C L ROBINSON
ROSENALLIS (St Brigid)   *see* Mountmellick w Coolbanagher, Rosenallis etc *M & K*

ROSKELTON (no dedication)   *see* Clonenagh w Offerlane, Borris-in-Ossory etc *C & O*
ROSS (Cathedral of St Fachtna) w Kilmacabea, Myross, Kilfaughnabeg and Castleventry *C, C & R*   **I** C L PETERS
ROSS, NEW (St Mary) w OLD (St Mary), Whitechurch, Fethard, Killesk and Tintern *C & O*   **P-in-c** L R ROGERS,   **NSM** J E CROWLEY
ROSSCARBERY   *see* Ross Union *C, C & R*
ROSSDROIT (St Peter)   *see* Killanne w Killegney, Rossdroit and Templeshanbo *C & O*
ROSSES POINT (no dedication)   *see* Sligo w Knocknarea and Rosses Pt *K, E & A*
ROSSINVER (no dedication)   *see* Killinagh w Kiltyclogher and Innismagrath *K, E & A*
ROSSMIRE   *see* Lismore w Cappoquin, Kilwatermoy, Dungarvan etc *C & O*
ROSSNAKILL   *see* Clondevaddock w Portsalon and Leatbeg *D & R*
ROSSNOWLAGH (St John)   *see* Kilbarron w Rossnowlagh and Drumholm *D & R*
ROSSORRY (no dedication) *Clogh*   **I** K A L BARRETT,   **NSM** F I NIXON, E G MCM THOMPSON
ROSTREVOR   *see* Kilbroney *D & D*
ROUNDSTONE (no dedication)   *see* Omey w Ballynakill, Errislannan and Roundstone *T, K & A*
RUNCURRAN   *see* Kinsale Union *C, C & R*
RUSHBROOKE   *see* Clonmel Union *C, C & R*
RUTLAND   *see* Carlow w Urglin and Staplestown *C & O*
RYNAGH   *see* Clonfert Gp *L & K*
SAINTFIELD (no dedication) *D & D*   **I** C J POLLOCK
SALLAGHY (no dedication)   *see* Galloon w Drummully and Sallaghy *Clogh*
SANDFORD   *see* Dublin Sandford w Milltown *D & G*
SANDHILL   *see* Sligo w Knocknarea and Rosses Pt *K, E & A*
SANDYMOUNT   *see* Dublin Sandymount *D & G*
SANTRY   *see* Dublin Santry w Glasnevin and Finglas *D & G*
SAUL (St Patrick)   *see* Lecale Gp *D & D*
SCARVA (St Matthew)   *see* Aghaderg w Donaghmore and Scarva *D & D*
SCHULL (Holy Trinity)   *see* Kilmoe Union *C, C & R*
SCOTSHOUSE   *see* Currin w Drum and Newbliss *Clogh*
SEAFORDE   *see* Lecale Gp *D & D*
SEAGOE (St Gobhan) *D & D*   **I** T J CADDEN,   **C** B M O'REILLY
SEAPATRICK (Holy Trinity) (St Patrick) *D & D*   **I** W J SCOTT,   M G GREENSTREET
SEIRKIERAN (St Kieran)   *see* Clonenagh w Offerlane, Borris-in-Ossory etc *C & O*
SESKINORE (no dedication)   *see* Clogherny w Seskinore and Drumnakilly *Arm*
SEYMOUR HILL   *see* Kilmakee *Conn*
SHANDON (St Ann)   *see* Cork St Ann's Union *C, C & R*
SHANKILL   *see* Belfast St Matt *Conn*
SHANKILL   *see* Lurgan Ch the Redeemer *D & D*
SHANKILL (St John)   *see* Leighlin w Grange Sylvae, Shankill etc *C & O*
SHANNON (Christ Church)   *see* Drumcliffe w Kilnasoolagh *L & K*
SHERCOCK (no dedication)   *see* Bailieborough w Knockbride, Shercock and Mullagh *K, E & A*
SHILLELAGH (no dedication)   *see* Tullow w Shillelagh, Aghold and Mullinacuff *C & O*
SHINRONE (St Mary) w Aghancon, Dunkerrin and Kinnitty *L & K*   **I** M JOHNSTON,   **NSM** J J WHITE SPUNNER
SHRULE (no dedication)   *see* Ardagh w Tashinny, Shrule and Kilcommick *K, E & A*
SION MILLS (Good Shepherd)   *see* Urney w Sion Mills *D & R*
SIXMILECROSS (St Michael) w Termonmaguirke *Arm*   **I** *vacant*
SIXTOWNS (St Anne)   *see* Kilcronaghan w Draperstown and Sixtowns *D & R*
SKERRIES   *see* Holmpatrick w Balbriggan and Kenure *D & G*
SKERRY (St Patrick) w Rathcavan and Newtowncrommelin *Conn*   **I** J F A BOND,   **NSM** R E COTTER
SKIBBEREEN   *see* Abbeystrewry Union *C, C & R*
SKREEN (no dedication) w Kilmacshalgan and Dromard *T, K & A*   **I** A P S SYNNOTT
SLANE (St Patrick)   *see* Navan w Kentstown, Tara, Slane, Painestown etc *M & K*
SLAVIN (no dedication)   *see* Garrison w Slavin and Belleek *Clogh*
SLIGO (Cathedral of St Mary and St John the Baptist) w Knocknarea and Rosses Point *K, E & A*   **I** A WILLIAMS,   **NSM** A D C KERR
SNEEM (Transfiguration)   *see* Kenmare w Sneem, Waterville etc *L & K*

SPANISH POINT   *see* Drumcliffe w Kilnasoolagh *L & K*
STACKALLEN   *see* Navan w Kentstown, Tara, Slane,
  Painestown etc *M & K*
STAPLESTOWN (no dedication)   *see* Carlow w Urglin and
  Staplestown *C & O*
STEWARTSTOWN   *see* Brackaville w Donaghendry and
  Ballyclog *Arm*
STILLORGAN (St Brigid) w Blackrock *D & G*
  I I GALLAGHER, **C** R K ELMES, **NSM** R D MARSHALL
STONEYFORD (St John) *Conn*   **Bp's C** A MALLON
STORMONT (St Molua) *D & D*   **I** W D HUMPHRIES
STRABANE   *see* Camus-juxta-Mourne *D & R*
STRADBALLY (All Saints)   *see* Killaloe w Stradbally *L & K*
STRADBALLY (St James)   *see* Lismore w Cappoquin,
  Kilwatermoy, Dungarvan etc *C & O*
STRADBALLY (St Patrick) w Ballintubbert, Coraclone,
  Timogue and Luggacurren *C & O*   **I** *vacant*
STRAFFAN (no dedication)   *see* Celbridge w Straffan and
  Newcastle-Lyons *D & G*
STRAID (no dedication) *T, K & A*   **I** *vacant*
STRAND, NORTH (no dedication)   *see* Dublin Drumcondra w
  N Strand *D & G*
STRANGFORD   *see* Lecale Gp *D & D*
STRANORLAR (no dedication) w Meenglas and Kilteevogue
  D & R   **I** A S ADAMSON
STRATFORD-ON-SLANEY (St John the Baptist)
  see Baltinglass w Ballynure etc *C & O*
STRATHFOYLE (no dedication)   *see* Clooney w Strathfoyle
  D & R
STREETE (no dedication)   *see* Mostrim w Granard,
  Clonbroney, Killoe etc *K, E & A*
SUMMER COVE   *see* Kinsale Union *C, C & R*
SWANLINBAR (St Augustine)   *see* Kildallon and Swanlinbar
  K, E & A
SWATRAGH   *see* Maghera w Killelagh *D & R*
SWORDS (St Columba) w Donabate and Kilsallaghan *D & G*
  I R W DEANE, **NSM** K E LONG
SYDDAN (St David)   *see* Kingscourt w Syddan *M & K*
SYDENHAM   *see* Belfast St Brendan *D & D*
TAGHMON (St Munn) w Horetown and Bannow *C & O*
  I *vacant*
TALLAGHT (St Maelruain) *D & G*   **I** W R H DEVERELL,
  NSM A E J BENNETT
TAMLAGHT   *see* Derryvullen S w Garvary *Clogh*
TAMLAGHT (St Luke)   *see* Ballinderry, Tamlaght and Arboe
  Arm
TAMLAGHT O'CRILLY UPPER (no dedication) w LOWER
  (no dedication) *D & R*   **I** R J STEWART
TAMLAGHTARD (St Gedanus) w Aghanloo *D & R*
  I I E DINSMORE
TAMLAGHTFINLAGAN (St Findlunganus) w Myroe *D & R*
  I H R GIVEN
TANEY (Christ Church) (St Nahi) *D & G*   **I** W D SINNAMON,
  C N J SLOANE, S A FARRELL
TARA   *see* Navan w Kentstown, Tara, Slane, Painestown etc
  M & K
TARBERT   *see* Tralee w Kilmoyley, Ballymacelligott etc *L & K*
TARTARAGHAN (St Paul) w Diamond *Arm*   **I** D HILLIARD
TASHINNY (no dedication)   *see* Ardagh w Tashinny, Shrule and
  Kilcommick *K, E & A*
TATTYKEERAN (no dedication)   *see* Aghalurcher w
  Tattykeeran, Cooneen etc *Clogh*
TAUGHBOYNE (St Baithan) w Craigadooish,
  Newtowncunningham and Killea *D & R*   **I** D W T CROOKS
TAUNAGH (no dedication) w Kilmactranny, Ballysumaghan and
  Killery *K, E & A*   **I** *vacant* (00353) (71) 65368
TEAMPOL-NA-MBOCHT (Altar)   *see* Kilmoe Union
  C, C & R
TEMPLEBREEDY (Holy Trinity) w Tracton and Nohoval
  C, C & R   **I** *vacant*
TEMPLECARNE (no dedication)   *see* Drumkeeran w
  Templecarne and Muckross *Clogh*
TEMPLECORRAN (St John)   *see* Kilroot and Templecorran
  Conn
TEMPLECRONE (St Crone)   *see* Gweedore, Carrickfin and
  Templecrone *D & R*
TEMPLEDERRY (no dedication)   *see* Nenagh *L & K*
TEMPLEHARRY (no dedication)   *see* Cloughjordan w
  Borrisokane etc *L & K*
TEMPLEMARTIN (St Martin)   *see* Moviddy Union *C, C & R*
TEMPLEMICHAEL (St John) w Clongish, Clooncumber,
  Killashee and Ballymacormack *K, E & A*   **I** D A CATTERALL
TEMPLEMORE Londonderry (Cathedral of St Columb) *D & R*
  I W W MORTON
TEMPLEMORE (St Mary) w Thurles and Kilfithmone *C & O*
  I P M COLE-BAKER

TEMPLEPATRICK (St Patrick) w Donegore *Conn*   **I** J K BELL
TEMPLEPORT (St Peter)   *see* Kildallon and Swanlinbar
  K, E & A
TEMPLESCOBIN (St Paul)   *see* Enniscorthy w Clone,
  Clonmore, Monart etc *C & O*
TEMPLESHANBO (St Colman)   *see* Killanne w Killegney,
  Rossdroit and Templeshanbo *C & O*
TEMPLETRINE (no dedication)   *see* Kinsale Union *C, C & R*
TEMPO (no dedication) and Clabby *Clogh*   **I** M A ARMSTRONG
TERMONAMONGAN (St Bestius)   *see* Derg w
  Termonamongan *D & R*
TERMONEENY (no dedication)   *see* Desertmartin w
  Termoneeny *D & R*
TERMONFECKIN (St Feckin)   *see* Drogheda w Ardee, Collon
  and Termonfeckin *Arm*
TERMONMAGUIRKE (St Columbkille)   *see* Sixmilecross w
  Termonmaguirke *Arm*
THOMASTOWN (no dedication)   *see* Clonsast w Rathangan,
  Thomastown etc *M & K*
THURLES (no dedication)   *see* Templemore w Thurles and
  Kilfithmone *C & O*
TICKMACREVAN (St Patrick)   *see* Ardclinis and
  Tickmacrevan w Layde and Cushendun *Conn*
TIMOGUE (St Mogue)   *see* Stradbally w Ballintubbert,
  Coraclone etc *C & O*
TIMOLEAGUE (Ascension)   *see* Kilgariffe Union *C, C & R*
TIMOLIN (St Mullin)   *see* Narraghmore and Timolin w
  Castledermot etc *D & G*
TINTERN (St Mary)   *see* New w Old Ross, Whitechurch,
  Fethard etc *C & O*
TIPPERARY (St Mary)   *see* Cashel w Magorban, Tipperary,
  Clonbeg etc *C & O*
TOBERMORE   *see* Kilcronaghan w Draperstown and Sixtowns
  D & R
TOMREGAN (no dedication)   *see* Kildallon and Swanlinbar
  K, E & A
TOOMBE (St Catherine)   *see* Ferns w Kilbride, Toombe,
  Kilcormack etc *C & O*
TOOMNA (no dedication)   *see* Kiltoghart w Drumshambo,
  Annaduff and Kilronan *K, E & A*
TOORMORE   *see* Kilmoe Union *C, C & R*
TRACTON   *see* Templebreedy w Tracton and Nohoval
  C, C & R
TRALEE (St John the Evangelist) w Kilmoyley, Ballymacelligott,
  Ballyseedy, Listowel and Ballybunnion *L & K*   **I** R WARREN,
  C J HARDY, **NSM** M J HANLEY
TRAMORE   *see* Waterford w Killea, Drumcannon and Dunhill
  C & O
TRILLICK (Christ Church)   *see* Kilskeery w Trillick *Clogh*
TRIM (Cathedral of St Patrick) and Athboy Group, The *M & K*
  I R W JONES
TRORY (St Michael) w Killadeas *Clogh*   **I** G M S WATSON
TUAM (Cathedral of St Mary) w Cong and Aasleagh *T, K & A*
  I A J GRIMASON, **C** M RYAN
TUAMGRANEY (St Cronan)   *see* Killaloe w Stradbally *L & K*
TUBBERCURRY (St George) w Killoran *T, K & A*
  I K R TRIMBY
TUBRID   *see* Drumkeeran w Templecarne and Muckross *Clogh*
TULLAGH (no dedication)   *see* Abbeystrewry Union *C, C & R*
TULLAGHBEGLEY (St Ann)   *see* Dunfanaghy,
  Raymunterdoney and Tullaghbegley *D & R*
TULLAGHMELAN (no dedication)   *see* Clonmel w
  Innislounagh, Tullaghmelan etc *C & O*
TULLAMORE (St Catherine) w Durrow, Newtownfertullagh,
  Rahan, Tyrellspass and Killoughy *M & K*   **I** G G FIELD
TULLANISKIN (Holy Trinity) w Clonoe *Arm*
  I E M CULBERTSON
TULLOW (no dedication) *D & G*   **I** L J TANNER
TULLOW (St Columba) w Shillelagh, Aghold and Mullinacuff
  C & O   **I** A D H ORR
TULLYAUGHNISH (St Paul) w Kilmacrennan and Killygarvan
  D & R   **I** A E TILSON
TULLYLISH (All Saints) *D & D*   **I** A YOUNG
TULLYNAKILL (no dedication)   *see* Killinchy w Kilmood and
  Tullynakill *D & D*
TUNNY (St Andrew)   *see* Glenavy w Tunny and Crumlin *Conn*
TURLOUGH (no dedication)   *see* Aughaval w Achill,
  Knappagh, Dugort etc *T, K & A*
TYBOHINE (no dedication)   *see* Roscommon w Donamon,
  Rathcline, Kilkeevin etc *K, E & A*
TYDAVNET (St Davnet)   *see* Monaghan w Tydavnet and
  Kilmore *Clogh*
TYHOLLAND (St Sillian)   *see* Donagh w Tyholland and Errigal
  Truagh *Clogh*
TYNAN (St Vindic) w Middletown and Aghavilly *Arm*
  I W B PAINE

TYRELLA (St John) *see* Rathmullan w Tyrella *D & D*
TYRELLSPASS (St Sinian) *see* Tullamore w Durrow,
  Newtownfertullagh, Rahan etc *M & K*
UPPER DONAGHMORE (St Patrick) *see* Donaghmore w
  Upper Donaghmore *Arm*
URGLIN (no dedication) *see* Carlow w Urglin and Staplestown
  C & O
URNEY (Christ Church) w Sion Mills *D & R*
  I T R MCKNIGHT
URNEY (no dedication) w Denn and Derryheen *K, E & A*
  I M R LIDWILL
VALENTIA (St John the Baptist) *see* Kenmare w Sneem,
  Waterville etc *L & K*
VIRGINIA *see* Lurgan w Billis, Killinkere and
  Munterconnaught *K, E & A*
WARINGSTOWN (Holy Trinity) *see* Donaghcloney w
  Waringstown *D & D*
WARRENPOINT (no dedication) *see* Clonallon w Warrenpoint
  D & D
WATERFORD (Christ Church Cathedral) w Killea, Drumcannon
  and Dunhill *C & O* I T R LESTER, C R J WEST,
  NSM R F GREENE
WATERVILLE *see* Kenmare w Sneem, Waterville etc *L & K*

WESTPORT *see* Aughaval w Achill, Knappagh, Dugort etc
  T, K & A
WEXFORD (St Iberius) w Ardcolm and Killurin *C & O*
  I M P JANSSON, C G AQUILON-ELMQVIST, NSM P A NEILAND
WHITECHURCH *see* Dublin Whitechurch *D & G*
WHITECHURCH (no dedication) *see* New w Old Ross,
  Whitechurch, Fethard etc *C & O*
WHITEGATE *see* Cloyne Union *C, C & R*
WHITEHEAD (St Patrick) and Islandmagee *Conn*
  I M F TAYLOR
WHITEHOUSE (St John) *Conn*   I T A H FOSTER
WHITEROCK *see* Belfast Whiterock *Conn*
WICKLOW (no dedication) w Killiskey *D & G* I J P CLARKE,
  C P A TAYLOR
WILLOWFIELD (no dedication) *D & D* I D A MCCLAY,
  NSM A P GREEN
WOODBURN (Holy Trinity) *Conn*   I T A G MCCANN
WOODLAWN (no dedication) *see* Aughrim w Ballinasloe etc
  L & K
WOODSCHAPEL (St John) w Gracefield *Arm* I E R MURRAY
YOUGHAL (St Mary's Collegiate) w Ardmore, Castlemartyr
  and Ballycotton *C, C & R* I M J THOMPSON
ZION *see* Dublin Zion Ch *D & G*

THE DIOCESE IN EUROPE

Diocesan Office, 14 Tufton Street, London SW1P 3QZ
Tel (020) 7898 1155   Fax 7898 1166
E-mail diocesan.office@europe.c-of-e.org.uk
Web site www.europe.anglican.org

ARCHDEACONS
1. Eastern   P M S CURRAN
2. France   K J LETTS
3. Gibraltar   C D SUTCH
4. Italy and Malta   J BOARDMAN
5. North West Europe   J DE WIT
6. Germany and Northern Europe   J W LLOYD
7. Switzerland   P M POTTER

Further information may be obtained from the appropriate archdeacon (the archdeaconry number is given after the name of each country), and a detailed leaflet is obtainable from the diocesan office. Mission to Seafarers chaplaincies are listed separately at the end of the section.

Andorra 3
Served from Barcelona (Spain)

Armenia 1
YEREVAN   *vacant*

Austria 1
VIENNA (Christ Church)   Chapl P M S CURRAN, **Asst Chapl** A P HACKL

Azerbaijan 1
BAKU   *vacant*

Belgium 5
ANTWERP (St Boniface)   Chapl A R WAGSTAFF, **C** A E BABB
BRUSSELS (Pro-Cathedral of the Holy Trinity)
   Sen Chapl R N INNES, **Asst Chapl** G I WILTON, J M DAY, A U NWAEKWE
CHARLEROI   *vacant*
GHENT (St John)   P-in-c P R TILLEY
KNOKKE (St George)   P-in-c P R TILLEY
LEUVEN   *vacant*
LIÈGE   P-in-c P M YIEND
MONS   Served by Sen CF UK Support Unit Supreme Headquarters Allied Powers Europe
OSTEND   P-in-c P C OWEN
TERVUREN   Chapl C EDWARDS
YPRES (St George)   P-in-c R T JONES

Bosnia and Herzegovina 1
Served from Belgrade (Serbia and Montenegro)

Bulgaria 1
Served from Bucharest (Romania)

Croatia 1
Served from Vienna (Austria)

Czech Republic 1
PRAGUE   P-in-c W J YATES

Denmark 6
COPENHAGEN (St Alban) w Aarhus   Chapl J W LLOYD

Estonia 6
TALLINN (St Timothy and St Titus)   P-in-c G PIIR

Finland 6
HELSINKI w Tampere   Chapl R R J MORETON, **Asst Chapl** M K T PAJUNEN, **C** T MÄKIPÄÄ, A MANGA

France 2
AIX-EN-PROVENCE   *see* Marseille w Aix-en-Provence
AMBERNAC   *see* Poitou-Charentes
AQUITAINE (Bertric Burée, Bordeaux, Limeuil, Monteton, Périgueux-Chancelade, Sorges and Ste Nathalène)
   Chapl P D VROLIJK, **Asst Chapl** C GORDON-WALKER, C G L STRACHAN
ARRAS   *see* Pas de Calais
BARBEZIEUX ST HILAIRE   *see* Poitou-Charentes
BEAULIEU-SUR-MER (St Michael)   P-in-c R T GREENACRE
BEAULIEU-SUR-SONNETTE   *see* Poitou-Charentes
BIARRITZ   P-in-c P R DAWSON
BORDEAUX   *see* Aquitaine
BOULOGNE   *see* Poitou-Charentes
BOULOGNE-SUR-MER   *see* Pas de Calais
BRITTANY (Ploërmel, Huelgoat and Rostrene)
   P-in-c H L DOOR
CAEN   *see* Paris St George
CAHORS   *see* Midi-Pyrénés and Aude
CALAIS   *see* Pas de Calais
CANNES (Holy Trinity)   P J ANDERSON
CAYLUS   *see* Midi-Pyrénés and Aude
CHANTILLY (St Peter)   Chapl N J CLARKE
CHARENTE MARITIME   *see* Poitou-Charentes
CHASSENEUIL-SUR-BONNIEURE   *see* Poitou-Charentes
CHEVRY   *see* Versailles w Chevry
CIVRAY   *see* Poitou-Charentes
COGNAC (Charente)   *see* Poitou-Charentes
COUTANCES (Christ Church)   Chapl P J HALES
DINARD (St Bartholomew)   P-in-c G J RANDALL
FONTAINEBLEAU   Asst Chapl J A WILKINSON
GIF SUR YVETTE   *see* Versailles
GRENOBLE   Chapl S COFFIN
HESDIN   *see* Pas de Calais
HUELGOAT   *see* Brittany
LA MERLATIÈRE   *see* Poitou-Charentes
LE GARD   P-in-c J DEVERILL
LILLE (Christ Church)   P-in-c D M R FLACH
LIMEUIL   *see* Aquitaine
LIMOUX   *see* Midi-Pyrénés and Aude
LORGUES   *see* St Raphaël
LYON   Chapl C J MARTIN
MAGNÉ   *see* Poitou-Charentes
MAISONS-LAFFITTE (Holy Trinity)   Chapl T WHITFIELD
MARSEILLE (All Saints) w Aix-en-Provence
   P-in-c G J AMAT-TORREGROSA
MENTON (St John)   *vacant*
MIDI-PYRÉNÉS and Aude (Cahors, Caylus, Limoux, Tarn, Toulouse, and Valence d'Agen)   C J HUTCHINSON
MONTAUROUX   Served by the Community of the Glorious Ascension
MONTETON   *see* Aquitaine
NANTES   *see* Vendée
NICE (Holy Trinity) w Vence   Chapl K J LETTS
NORD PAS DE CALAIS (Arras, Boulogne-sur-Mer, Calais and Hesdin)   *vacant*
PARIS (St George)   Chapl M H HARRISON, **Asst Chapl** R M FERMER
PARIS (St Michael)   Chapl P I MOUNSTEPHEN, **C** J MOORE
PAU (St Andrew)   P-in-c I F NAYLOR
PÉRIGUEUX-CHANCELADE   *see* Aquitaine
PLOËRMEL   *see* Brittany

POITOU-CHARENTES (Ambernac, Barbezieux St Hilaire, Beaulieu-sur-Sonnette, Boulogne, Chasseneuil-sur-Bonnieure, Civray, Cognac (Charente), La Merlatière, Magné, Puy de Serre, Salles de Villefagnan, St Jean d'Angély, and St Léger de la Martinière) P-in-c C M A HEPPER
PORT GRIMAUD *see* St Raphaël
PUY DE SERRE *see* Poitou-Charentes
ROSTRENEN *see* Brittany
ST JEAN D'ANGÉLY *see* Poitou-Charentes
ST LÉGER DE LA MARTINIÈRE *see* Poitou-Charentes
ST RAPHAËL (St John the Evangelist) w Lorgues, Port Grimaud and Sellians P-in-c O B EATON
STE NATHALÈNE *see* Aquitaine
SALLES DE VILLEFAGNAN *see* Poitou-Charentes
SELLIANS *see* St Raphaël
SORGES *see* Aquitaine
STRASBOURG C C L BLOOMFIELD
TARN *see* Midi-Pyrénés and Aude
TOULOUSE *see* Midi-Pyrénés and Aude
VALENCE D'AGEN *see* Midi-Pyrénés and Aude
VENCE (St Hugh) *see* Nice w Vence
VENDÉE (All Saints) P-in-c A B DAVIES
VERSAILLES (St Mark) w Chevry Chapl P H KENCHINGTON, Asst Chapl E O LABOUREL

Georgia 1
TBILISI *vacant*

Germany 6
BERLIN (St George) Chapl C W JAGE-BOWLER, Asst Chapl I K E AHRENS
BONN w Cologne Chapl S J HOBBS
DRESDEN *see* Berlin
DÜSSELDORF (Christ Church) Chapl S J G SEAMER
FREIBURG-IM-BREISGAU P-in-c R P STOCKITT
HAMBURG (St Thomas à Becket) Chapl R I S WHITE, Asst Chapl E G ANDERS
HEIDELBERG *vacant*
LEIPZIG Chapl G M REAKES-WILLIAMS
STUTTGART P-in-c K R DIMMICK

Gibraltar 3
GIBRALTAR (Cathedral of the Holy Trinity) Chapl J A B PADDOCK (Dean), Asst Chapl W H D WATSON

Greece 1
ATHENS, GREATER Sen Chapl M M BRADSHAW, Hon C W J BURKE
CORFU (Holy Trinity) P-in-c J R GULLAND

Hungary 1
BUDAPEST Chapl D MOSS

Italy 4
AVIANO *see* Venice
BARI *see* Naples
BOLOGNA *see* Florence
BORDIGHERA *see* Genova
CADENABBIA *see* Milan and Varese
CAPRI *see* Naples
FLORENCE (St Mark) w Siena (St Peter) and Bologna Chapl L A C MACLEAN
GENOVA (The Holy Ghost) and Bordighera P-in-c N S D GIBSON
MACERATA *see* Rome
MILAN (All Saints) and Varese Chapl N S D GIBSON
NAPLES (Christ Church) w Sorrento, Capri and Bari Chapl K R JOYCE
PADOVA *see* Venice
PALERMO (Holy Cross) *see* Sicily
ROME (All Saints) w Macerata Chapl J BOARDMAN, C S MACVANE
SICILY *vacant*
SIENA *see* Florence
SORRENTO *see* Naples
TAORMINA (St George) *see* Sicily
TRIESTE *see* Venice

VARESE *see* Milan
VENICE (St George) w Trieste C S C AJUKA
VINCENZA Served by US Army Base

Latvia 6
RIGA (St Saviour) Chapl J CALITIS

Luxembourg 5
LUXEMBOURG Chapl C D LYON, Asst Chapl J B LYON

Malta and Gozo 4
VALLETTA (Pro-Cathedral of St Paul) w Sliema (Holy Trinity) Sen Chapl S H M GODFREY, Chapl J WILLIAMS

Monaco 2
MONTE CARLO (St Paul) Chapl W RAYMOND

Morocco 3
CASABLANCA (St John the Evangelist) P-in-c M CREGAN
TANGIER (St Andrew) *vacant*

The Netherlands 5
AMSTERDAM (Christ Church) w Heiloo Chapl M P C COLLINSON, Asst Chapl J R ALBERS, J R BALL, A R MACDONALD, C E FLORENTINUS
ARNHEM *see* East Netherlands
EAST NETHERLANDS Chapl S W VAN LEER, C A ROBINSON-MULLER
EINDHOVEN Chapl F P NOORDANUS
HAARLEM P-in-c C M P JONES
HAGUE, THE (St John and St Philip) Chapl A R G ROAKE, Asst Chapl R K PRICE, C B LONG
NIJMEGEN *see* East Netherlands
ROTTERDAM (St Mary) Chapl S G AXTELL
TWENTE (St Mary) *see* East Netherlands
UTRECHT (Holy Trinity) w Zwolle Chapl J DE WIT
VOORSCHOTEN Chapl A P ISON
ZWOLLE *see* Utrecht

Norway 6
OSLO (St Edmund) w Bergen, Trondheim , Stavanger, Drammen, Moss, Sandefjord, Tromsö and Kristiansand Chapl J HEIL, Asst Chapl P R HOGARTH, C M S MASEMOLA, NSM M STRØMMEN

Poland 1
WARSAW w Gdansk *vacant*

Portugal 3
ALGARVE (St Vincent) Sen Chapl H Q HUBBARD, Chapl R J BATES
ALMANCIL *see* Algarve
ESTORIL *see* Lisbon
GORJÔES *see* Algarve
LISBON (St George) w Estoril (St Paul) Chapl M BULLOCK
MADEIRA (Holy Trinity) P-in-c N DAWSON
PORTO (or OPORTO) (St James) P-in-c M SUMARES
PRAIA DA LUZ *see* Algarve

Romania 1
BUCHAREST (The Resurrection) *vacant*

Russian Federation 1
MOSCOW (St Andrew) w Vladivostock Chapl S E STEPHENS
ST PETERSBURG *vacant*

Serbia and Montenegro 1
BELGRADE Chapl J R FOX

Slovakia
Served from Vienna (Austria)

Slovenia
Served from Vienna (Austria)

Spain 3
ALCOCEBRE   *see* Costa Azahar
ALBOX   *see* Costa Almeria and Costa Calida
ALHAURÍN EL GRANDE   *see* Costa del Sol East
ALMUÑÉCAR   *see* Nerja and Almuñécar
BARCELONA (St George)   Chapl A C M TWEEDY
BENALMADENA COSTA   *see* Costa del Sol East
BENIDORM   *see* Costa Blanca
CALA BONA   *see* Palma de Mallorca
CALA D'OR   *see* Palma de Mallorca
CALAHONDA   *see* Costa del Sol East
CALPE   *see* Costa Blanca
CAMPOVERDE   *see* Torrevieja
CAYO SALVAJ   *see* Tenerife Sur
COIN   *see* Costa del Sol East
CÓMPETA   *see* Málaga
CORRALEJO   *see* Lanzarote
COSTA ALMERIA   P-in-c H D BROAD
COSTA AZAHAR   P-in-c P R NEEDLE
COSTA BLANCA   Sen Chapl P C EDWARDS,
   Chapl R CARTER
COSTA CALIDA   *see* Costa Almeria
COSTA DEL SOL EAST   Chapl C D SUTCH, C L JORDAN
COSTA DEL SOL WEST   P-in-c A MAUDE
COSTA TEGUISE   *see* Lanzarote
COSTACABANA   *see* Costa Almeria and Costa Calida
DENIA   *see* Costa Blanca
EL CAMPELLO   *see* Costa Blanca
FORMENTERA   *see* Ibiza
FUENGIROLA (St Andrew)   *see* Costa del Sol East
FUERTEVENTURA   *see* Lanzarote
GANDIA   *see* Costa Blanca
GOLF DEL SUR   *see* Tenerife Sur
IBIZA   P-in-c R L SHORT
JÁVEA   *see* Costa Blanca
LA GOMERA   *see* Tenerife Sur
LA MANGA   *see* Torrevieja
LA MARINA   *see* Torrevieja
LA PALMA   *see* Puerto de la Cruz
LA SIESTA   *see* Torrevieja
LAGO JARDIN   *see* Torrevieja
LANZAROTE   P-in-c I S VAUGHAN
LAS PALMAS (Holy Trinity)   P-in-c P FORD
LOS BALCONES   *see* Torrevieja
LOS GIGANTES   *see* Tenerife Sur
MADRID (St George)   Chapl I C HUTCHINSON CERVANTES
MÁLAGA (St George)   Chapl P G WOLFENDEN
MALLORCA   *see* Palma de Mallorca
MENORCA   Chapl M J BUNCE
MOJÁCAR   *see* Costa Almeria
MORALEDA DE ZAFAYONA   *see* Málaga
NAZARET   *see* Lanzarote
NERJA and Almuñécar   P-in-c G S JOHNSTON
ORBA   *see* Costa Blanca
PALMA DE MALLORCA (St Philip and St James)
   Chapl R A ELLIS, **Asst Chapl** M REDFEARN
PLAYA BLANCA   *see* Lanzarote
PLAYA DE LAS AMERICAS   *see* Tenerife Sur
PLAYA DEL INGLES   *see* Las Palmas
PUERTO DE LA CRUZ Tenerife (All Saints)   *vacant*
PUERTO DEL CARMEN   *see* Lanzarote

PUERTO POLLENSA   *see* Palma de Mallorca
PUERTO SOLLER   *see* Palma de Mallorca
ROQUETAS DE MAR   *see* Costa Almeria and Costa
   Calida
SAN ANTONIO   *see* Ibiza
SAN PEDRO   *see* Costa del Sol West
SAN RAFAEL   *see* Ibiza
SANTA EULALIA   *see* Ibiza
SOTOGRANDE   *see* Costa del Sol West
TENERIFE SUR (St Eugenio)   P-in-c K A GORDON
TEULADA   *see* Costa Blanca
TORRE DEL MAR   *see* Málaga
TORREMOLINOS   *see* Málaga
TORREVIEJA   Chapl C M SCARGILL
VILLENUEVA DE TAPIS   *see* Málaga
VINAROS   *see* Costa Azahar

Sweden 6
GOTHENBURG (St Andrew) w Halmstad, Jönköping and
   Uddevalla   Chapl B P MOSS
MALMÖ   Served from Copenhagen (Denmark)
STOCKHOLM (St Peter and St Sigfrid) w Gävle and
   Västerås   Chapl N S HOWE

Switzerland 7
ANZERE   *see* Montreux
BADEN   *see* Zürich
BASLE   Chapl G P READ, **Asst Chapl** R STOCKITT, R B
   HILLIARD, **NSM** A L LOWEN
BERNE (St Ursula) w Neuchâtel   Chapl P M POTTER,
   Asst Chapl L D BISIG
GENEVA (Holy Trinity)   Chapl R TAYLOR, C M E WILSON
GSTAAD   *see* Montreuz
LA CÔTE   P-in-c P R HOLLEY, C J CHAMBEYRON
LAUSANNE (Christ Church)   P-in-c A KELHAM
LUGANO (St Edward the Confessor)   P-in-c A J HORLOCK
MONTHEY   *see* Montreux
MONTREUX (St John) w Anzere, Gstaad and Monthey
   vacant
NEUCHÂTEL   *see* Berne
ST GALLEN   *see* Zürich
VEVEY (All Saints) w Château d'Oex   Chapl C J ATKINSON
VILLARS   *see* Montreux
ZUG   *see* Zürich
ZÜRICH (St Andrew) w Baden, St Gallen and Zug
   Chapl J K NEWSOME, **Asst Chapl** D R MORROW

Turkey 1
ANKARA (St Nicholas)   P-in-c G B EVANS
ISTANBUL (Christ Church) (Chapel of St Helena) w Moda
   (All Saints)   Chapl I W L SHERWOOD
IZMIR (SMYRNA) (St John the Evangelist) w Bornova
   (St Mary Magdalene)   Chapl R W EVANS

Turkmenistan 1
Served from Moscow (Russian Federation)

Ukraine 1
KIEV (Christ Church)   *vacant*

Uzbekistan 1
Served from Moscow (Russian Federation)

MISSION TO SEAFARERS CHAPLAINCIES

Belgium 5
ANTWERP   *Lay Chapl*
GHENT   Chapl P R TILLEY

France 2
DUNKERQUE   Chapl P W BENNETT

The Netherlands 5
ROTTERDAM and Schiedam   Chapl S G AXTELL
VLISSINGEN   Chapl J A VAN HANDENHOVEN

CHAPLAINS TO HER MAJESTY'S SERVICES

ROYAL NAVY

Chaplain of the Fleet and Archdeacon for the Royal Navy
Director General Naval Chaplaincy Service
The Ven J GREEN
Royal Naval Chaplaincy Service, Mail Point 1–2, Leach Building, Whale Island, Portsmouth PO2 8BY
Tel (023) 9262 5055   Fax 9262 5134

Chaplains RN

M D ALLSOPP	M L EVANS	A G PHILLIPS
J R BACKHOUSE	J S FRANCIS	M G POLL
R W BARBER	M J GOUGH	R L PYNE
N A BEARDSLEY	S P HALLAM	A RAWDING
S A R BEVERIDGE	J HILL	K A ROBUS
J M BRIDGES	A HILLIER	P J D S SCOTT
K C BROMAGE	M J HILLS	D J SIMPSON
M BROTHERTON	G E D HITCHINS	S P SPRINGETT
A M CALLON	M H JACKSON	J H TABOR
B R CLARKE	N J KELLY	M WAGSTAFF
A S CORNESS	A J F MANSFIELD	I J WHEATLEY
A J DUFF	J O MORRIS	D V WYLIE

ARMY

Chaplain-General HM Land Forces and Archdeacon for the Army
The Ven S ROBBINS QHC
Until June 2010: *Ministry of Defence, Chaplains (Army), Building 183, Trenchard Lines, Upavon, Pewsey SN9 6BE*
Tel (01980) 615801 Fax 615800

From July 2010: *Ministry of Defence, Chaplains (Army), Marlborough Lines, Andover SP11 8HJ*

Chaplains to the Forces

D J ADAMS	A J FELTHAM-WHITE	M P MORTON
W G ASHTON	S A FRANKLIN	F E MYATT
K G BARRY	L F GANDIYA	R OLLIFF
T J BATESON	J R B GOUGH	T R PLACE
A R F BATTEY	S E GRIFFITH	R PLUCK
C D BELL	C J GROOCOCK	R M PRIEST
K D BELL	L T J HILLARY	M E REYNOLDS
A S F BENNETT	G J HUMPHRYES	S A RICHARDS
S T BLOXAM ROSE	A W INGHAM	R J RICHARDSON
P R BOSHER	P A IRWIN	A ROACHE
C S T BRODDLE	M V JONES	G C SMITH
C S BUTLER	P W S KING	A C STEELE
M R CHRISTIAN	C M LANGSTON	M R N STEVENSON
J S CLARKE	A M LATIFA	S B THATCHER
T A R COLE	W B LISTER	A H THOMAS
D P CONNING	S H LODWICK	N S TODD
N L COOK	J M LOVEDAY	C A TOME DA SILVA
A J COOPER	S T J MCCAULAY	A J TOTTEN
D P CREES	J A MCWHIRTER	P VICKERS
A I DALTON	A C MARTLEW	D E VINCE
D W DAVIES	K D MENTZEL	J L VINCENT
R J DOWNES	D J MERCERON	B WALTON
S J H DUNWOODY	P J MILLS	H WANLISS
W J N DURANT	B D MILLSON	D C WEAVER
P A EAGLES	J S MOESEL	P S WRIGHT
H D EVANS	D T MORGAN	D C WEAVER

ROYAL AIR FORCE

Chaplain-in-Chief and Archdeacon for the RAF
The Ven R J PENTLAND QHC

Chaplaincy Services, Valiant Block, HQ Air Command, RAF High Wycombe HP14 4UE
Tel (01494) 496800   Fax 496343

Chaplains RAF

N B P BARRY	N P HERON	E J RANCE
J M BEACH	A D HEWETT	P A RENNIE
K S CAPELIN-JONES	J A HOBSON	D RICHARDSON
J P M CHAFFEY	I A JONES	L E SPICER
A T COATES	M P D KENNARD	J W K TAYLOR
G L COLLINGWOOD	S P LAMOND	P J M TOLLERSON
V R DUNSTAN-MEADOWS	C D LAWRENCE	A J TURNER
A L DYER	G L LEGOOD	A W WAKEHAM-DAWSON
M J ELLIOTT	A B MCMULLON	I S WARD
J R ELLIS	C A MITCHELL	G WILLIAMS
L FLEWKER-BARKER	D J NORFIELD	G E WITHERS
A C GATRILL	D T OSBORN	T WRIGHT
A J D GILBERT	S J RADLEY	E L WYNN
R V HAKE		

PRISON CHAPLAINS

HM PRISON SERVICE
(England and Wales)

Chaplain General to HM Prisons
The Ven W A NOBLETT
Anglican Adviser Canon M L KAVANAGH

Chaplaincy HQ, Room 310, Abell House, John Islip Street, London SW1P 4LH
Tel (020) 7217 8667 *or* 07807-509720   Fax 7217 8980

Prisons

Acklington   B K COOPER, M D TETLEY
Albany   S C LUCAS
Altcourse   K A CANTY
Ashfield   N J HAY
Ashwell   R J LUBKOWSKI
Askham Grange   R A CLEGG
Bedford   S M WHITE
Belmarsh   T G JACQUET
Birmingham   B J GRACIE, J R A SAMPSON
Blakenhurst   S A NALL
Blundeston   W J SALMON
Brinsford   L A W SWABY
Bristol   D J H POWE
Brixton   P T J CHADDER
Brockhill   M A SCHUTTE, P HAMMERSLEY
Bronzefield   M L HUNTER
Buckley Hall   R W A REECE
Bullingdon   A J FORAN
Bullwood Hall   A E DIXON
Camp Hill   T J MANN
Canterbury   C I HITCHENS
Cardiff   M C JOHN, M J UNDERDOWN
Channings Wood   N R MARTIN
Coldingley   C F HOLT
Coltishall   A V HEDGES
Dartmoor   W H BIRDWOOD
Doncaster   P IRESON
Dorchester   T A M SANKEY
Dovegate   R W BAILEY
Downview   R A DEEDES
Drake Hall   D J HOWARD
East Sutton Park   N FRY
Eastwood Park   J M PHILLIPS
Edmunds Hill   L R BELL
Elmley   M P M STEWART
Erlestoke   C F TODD
Everthorpe   C R DUXBURY
Exeter   C V CURD
Ford   P J WALKER
Forest Bank   S D HARROP
Foston Hall   H THAKE
Full Sutton   S JUKES
Gartree   I L JOHNSON
Gloucester   K A L DENNIS, C RAWLINSON
Grendon and Spring Hill   M B WHITAKER
Guys Marsh   M J RIDGEWELL
Haverigg   G JONES, R P SPRATT
Hewell Grange   M A SCHUTTE, P HAMMERSLEY
High Down   M E BRAIN
Hollesley Bay   J T PERRY, M R RENNARD
Holloway   K WILKIN
Holme House   T A MCCARTHY, J N GREENWOOD
Hull   N J WHETTON
Kennet   D W GOODWIN
Kingston (Portsmouth)   P A NEWMAN, R J PRESTON

Kirkham   D NOBLET
Kirklevington Grange   Y L YATES
Lancaster Castle   C WOODCOCK
Latchmere House   C R WOOD
Leeds   K F A GABBADON
Leicester   H E DEARNLEY
Lewes   G R HOCKEN
Leyhill   S BRACE
Lincoln   A J ROBERTS
Lindholme   N LEFROY-OWEN
Littlehey   D J KINDER
Liverpool   N G SHAW
Long Lartin   J K HAYWARD
Low Newton   C M PROUSE
Lowdham Grange   C KNIGHT
Maidstone   G L LONG
Manchester   D VICKERS
Moorland   C D LETHBRIDGE, G PITT
Morton Hall   C C MUNN
Mount, The   P J ABREY
New Hall   E J CLAY
North Sea Camp   P D STELL
Norwich   J A WILSON
Nottingham   L H COOPER
Onley   J A FOX
Parkhurst   L F HUMPHRYS
Pentonville   I G THOMPSON
Peterborough   T C HARLING
Preston   P C BROWNE
Ranby   D HIGGON
Reading   D J LITTLE
Risley   N D HAWLEY
Shrewsbury   D S FARLEY, R M WILTSHIRE, J J WADDINGTON-FEATHER
Stafford   J D BIRD
Standford Hill   R W HAYTER
Stocken   E GHINN
Styal   B A EATON, M THOMPSON
Sudbury   F V G BALLENTYNE
Swaleside   J H WAITE
Swansea   L HOPKINS
Swinfen Hall   A L FOWLER, R C PAYNE
Usk and Prescoed   N R SANDFORD
Wakefield   A R ROWE
Wandsworth   T A BRYAN
Warren Hill   J T PERRY
Wayland   S R TAN
Wealstun   T M BAYFORD
Whatton   J C HONOUR
Whitemoor   R B THOMPSON
Winchester   T LANE
Wolds, The   G F COOKE
Woodhill   A P HODGETTS, S C GRENHAM-TOZE
Wormwood Scrubs   H K DODHIA, W A WHITCOMBE
Wymott   P N TYERS

Young Offender Institutions

Castington E P BOSSWARD
Deerbolt D G HARTLEY, G KIRTLEY
Feltham P FOSTER
Glen Parva A M ADAMS
Huntercombe and Finnamore Wood I D THACKER
Isle of Man N D GREENWOOD
Lancaster Farms B J MAYNE
Northallerton C J TRUMAN

Northallerton C J TRUMAN
Portland P THOMPSON
Rochester S A SIMPSON
Stoke Heath M J NEWSOME
Thorn Cross S G VERHEY, M P MARTIN
Werrington House D E KENDRICK
Wetherby D E HERTH, S D JONES, K COUCHMAN

Immigration Centres

Campsfield House S K R PARKINSON

Haslar N G STARTIN

CHANNEL ISLANDS PRISON SERVICE

Guernsey K C NORTHOVER

Jersey P WILLCOX

SCOTTISH PRISON SERVICE

Scottish Prison Service, Calton House, 5 Redheughs Rigg, Edinburgh E12 9HW
Tel (0131) 556 8400   Fax 244 8774

Edinburgh M C REED

NORTHERN IRELAND PRISON SERVICE

Northern Ireland Office, Dundonald House, Upper Newtownards Road, Belfast BT4 3SU
Tel (028) 9052 0700   Fax 9052 5327

Belfast N B DODDS
Maghaberry J R HOWARD

Maze, The W A MURPHY

IRISH PRISON SERVICE

Department of Justice, 72–76 St Stephen's Green, Dublin 2, Republic of Ireland
Tel (00353) (1) 678 9711   Fax 676 4718

Limerick J M G SIRR

Midlands Portlaoise H A DUNGAN

HOSPITAL CHAPLAINS

An index of whole-time and part-time hospital chaplains

Secretary to the Hospital Chaplaincies Council
The Revd E J LEWIS
Church House, Great Smith Street, London SW1P 3AZ
Tel (020) 7898 1894   Fax 7898 1891

At institutions with more than one chaplain the names are listed in order of senority.

ABERDARE   *see* N Glam NHS Trust
ABERDEEN ROYAL INFIRMARY   *see* Grampian Univ Hosp NHS Trust
ABINGDON   *see* SW Oxon Primary Care Trust
ABRAHAM COWLEY UNIT Chertsey   *see* Surrey and Borders Partnership NHS Trust
ADDENBROOKE'S Cambridge   *see* Cam Univ Hosps NHS Foundn Trust
ADELAIDE AND MEATH Dublin   M A J WILSON
AINTREE HOSPITALS NHS TRUST Liverpool   I J LOVETT
AIREDALE GENERAL   *see* Airedale NHS Trust
AIREDALE NHS TRUST   B M WILKINSON, D J GRIFFITHS, J P SMITH
ALDEBURGH AND DISTRICT COMMUNITY   *see* Suffolk Coastal Primary Care Trust
ALDER HEY CHILDREN'S Liverpool   *see* R Liverpool Children's NHS Trust
ALEXANDRA Redditch   *see* Worcs Acute Hosps NHS Trust
ALL SAINTS Eastbourne   *see* E Sussex Hosps NHS Trust
ALNWICK INFIRMARY   *see* Northumbria Healthcare NHS Trust
ALPHA Woking   J A ROBINSON
ALTRINCHAM GENERAL   *see* Trafford Healthcare NHS Trust
AMBERSTONE Hailsham   *see* E Sussex Co Healthcare NHS Trust
AMERSHAM   *see* Bucks Hosps NHS Trust
ANDOVER DISTRICT COMMUNITY HEALTH CARE NHS TRUST   D F KING
ANDOVER WAR MEMORIAL COMMUNITY HOSPITAL *see* Andover District Community Health Care NHS Trust
ARCHERY HOUSE Dartford   *see* Kent & Medway NHS and Soc Care Partnership Trust
ARGYLL AND CLYDE   S H B GORTON
ARMAGH AND DUNGANNON HEALTH AND SOCIAL SERVICES TRUST   C W M ROLSTON
ASHFIELD COMMUNITY Kirkby-in-Ashfield   *see* Sherwood Forest Hosps NHS Trust
ASHFORD   *see* E Kent Hosps NHS Trust
ASHFORD   *see* Surrey and Borders Partnership NHS Trust
ASHINGTON   *see* Northumbria Healthcare NHS Trust
ASHWORTH Maghull   C J MOON
ATKINSON MORLEY   *see* SW Lon and St George's Mental Health NHS Trust
BARKING HAVERING AND REDBRIDGE HOSPITALS NHS TRUST   T COLEMAN, M R JUDGE
BARNES   *see* SW Lon and St George's Mental Health NHS Trust
BARNET   *see* Barnet and Chase Farm Hosps NHS Trust
BARNET, ENFIELD AND HARINGEY MENTAL HEALTH TRUST   T M BARON
BARNET AND CHASE FARM HOSPITALS NHS TRUST   T M BARON
BARNSLEY DISTRICT GENERAL HOSPITAL NHS TRUST   M P YATES
BARNSLEY HOSPITAL NHS FOUNDATION TRUST   M P YATES
BARTLET Felixstowe   *see* Suffolk Coastal Primary Care Trust
BARTS AND THE LONDON NHS TRUST   P J COWELL, B RHODES, M C DANKS-FLOWER
BASILDON   *see* S Essex Mental Health & Community Care NHS Trust
BASINGSTOKE AND NORTH HAMPSHIRE NHS FOUNDATION TRUST   D L GRACE, A J ASKEW
BASSETLAW DISTRICT GENERAL Worksop   *see* Doncaster and Bassetlaw Hosps NHS Trust
BATH AND WEST COMMUNITY NHS TRUST   H ANDREWE UTHWATT, M JOYCE
BATTLE Reading   *see* R Berks NHS Foundn Trust
BEBINGTON   M B KELLY
BECKENHAM   *see* S Lon Healthcare NHS Trust
BEDFORDSHIRE AND LUTON MENTAL HEALTH AND SOCIAL CARE NHS TRUST   P N MARSHALL
BEIGHTON HOSPITAL Sheffield   *see* Sheff Care Trust

BELFAST CITY   *see* Belfast Health and Soc Care Trust
BELFAST HEALTH AND SOCIAL CARE TRUST   J K BELL, A MOORE, D W GAMBLE
BENNION CENTRE Leicester   *see* Leics Partnership NHS Trust
BENSHAM Gateshead   *see* Gateshead Health NHS Trust
BERKSHIRE WEST PRIMARY CARE TRUST   B DAGNALL
BERWICK INFIRMARY   *see* Northumbria Healthcare NHS Trust
BETHLEM ROYAL Beckenham   *see* S Lon and Maudsley NHS Foundn Trust
BEXHILL   *see* E Sussex Co Healthcare NHS Trust
BIDEFORD   *see* N Devon Healthcare NHS Trust
BILLINGE   *see* Wrightington Wigan and Leigh NHS Trust
BIRCH HILL   *see* Pennine Acute Hosps NHS Trust
BIRMINGHAM AND SOLIHULL MENTAL HEALTH TRUST   R J FARMAN
BIRMINGHAM CHILDREN'S HOSPITAL NHS TRUST   N E BALL, E BLAIR-CHAPPELL, P NASH
BIRMINGHAM CITY   *see* Sandwell and W Birm Hosps NHS Trust
BIRMINGHAM HEARTLANDS AND SOLIHULL NHS TRUST   A M BOYD, N E BALL
BIRMINGHAM SKIN   *see* Sandwell and W Birm Hosps NHS Trust
BIRMINGHAM SPECIALIST COMMUNITY HEALTH NHS TRUST   L M MORRIS
BISHOP AUCKLAND GENERAL   *see* Co Durham and Darlington NHS Foundn Trust
BLACKBERRY HILL Bristol   *see* N Bris NHS Trust
BLACKBURN ROYAL INFIRMARY   *see* E Lancs Hosps NHS Trust
BLACKPOOL, FYLDE AND WYRE HOSPITALS NHS TRUST   C G LORD
BLYTH COMMUNITY   *see* Northumbria Healthcare NHS Trust
BODMIN   *see* Cornwall and Is of Scilly Primary Care Trust
BODMIN   *see* Cornwall Partnership NHS Trust
BOLTON GENERAL   *see* Bolton Hosps NHS Trust
BOLTON HOSPITALS NHS TRUST   N K GRAY, G F WEIR, S FOSTER
BOOTH HALL CHILDREN'S Manchester   *see* Cen Man/Man Children's Univ Hosp NHS Trust
BOOTHAM PARK   *see* York Hosps NHS Foundn Trust
BOURNE Lincs   *see* NW Anglia Healthcare NHS Trust
BOURNEMOUTH, ROYAL GENERAL   *see* R Bournemouth and Christchurch Hosps NHS Trust
BOWNESS UNIT Prestwich   *see* Gtr Man W Mental Health NHS Foundn Trust
BRADFORD HOSPITALS NHS TRUST   C P JOHNSON
BRADGATE MENTAL HEALTH UNIT Leicester   *see* Leics Partnership NHS Trust
BRADWELL Chesterton   *see* Newcastle-under-Lyme Primary Care Trust
BRAMCOTE Nuneaton   *see* N Warks NHS Trust
BRANDON MENTAL HEALTH UNIT Leicester   *see* Leics Partnership NHS Trust
BRIDGWATER COMMUNITY   *see* Somerset Primary Care Trust
BRIDLINGTON AND DISTRICT   *see* Scarborough and NE Yorks Healthcare NHS Trust
BRIDPORT COMMUNITY   *see* SW Dorset Primary Care Trust
BRIGHTON AND SUSSEX UNIVERSITY HOSPITALS NHS TRUST   R J ST C HARLOW-TRIGG, S UNDERDOWN, P R WELLS
BRIGHTON GENERAL   *see* Brighton and Sussex Univ Hosps NHS Trust
BRISTOL GENERAL   *see* Univ Hosps Bris NHS Foundn Trust
BRISTOL ROYAL HOSPITAL FOR CHILDREN   *as above*
BRISTOL ROYAL INFIRMARY   *as above*
BROADGREEN Liverpool   *see* R Liverpool and Broadgreen Univ Hosps NHS Trust
BROADMOOR Crowthorne   T W WALT

BROADMOOR Crowthorne   *see* W Lon Mental Health NHS Trust
BROOKLANDS Marston Green   *see* N Warks NHS Trust
BROOMFIELD Chelmsford   *see* Mid-Essex Hosp Services NHS Trust
BRYN Y NEUADD Llanfairfechan   *see* NW Wales NHS Trust
BUCKINGHAMSHIRE HOSPITALS NHS TRUST   J G C LAWRENCE
BUCKLAND Dover   *see* E Kent Hosps NHS Trust
BURNLEY GENERAL   *see* E Lancs Hosps NHS Trust
BURTON HOSPITALS NHS TRUST   C P BARRETT, G J CROSSLEY
CAERPHILLY DISTRICT MINERS'   *see* Gwent Healthcare NHS Trust
CALDERDALE AND HUDDERSFIELD NHS TRUST   M W PARROTT, S V BROOKS, M D ELLERTON
CAMBOURNE/REDRUTH COMMUNITY   *see* Cornwall and Is of Scilly Primary Care Trust
CAMBRIDGE UNIVERSITY HOSPITALS NHS FOUNDATION TRUST   D P FORD, A L ALDRIDGE, K C MORRISON
CAMBRIDGESHIRE AND PETERBOROUGH MENTAL HEALTH PARTNERSHIPS NHS TRUST   J P NICHOLSON
CAMDEN AND ISLINGTON COMMUNITY HEALTH SERVICES NHS TRUST   B BATSTONE
CANNOCK CHASE   *see* Mid Staffs NHS Foundn Trust
CANTERBURY St Martin's   *see* Kent & Medway NHS and Soc Care Partnership Trust
CARDIFF AND VALE NHS TRUST   D R LLOYD-RICHARDS, L E D CLARK, C ARGLES, E J BURKE
CARDIFF COMMUNITY HEALTHCARE NHS TRUST   J H L ROWLANDS
CARDIFF ROYAL INFIRMARY   *see* Cardiff and Vale NHS Trust
CASSEL Richmond   *see* W Lon Mental Health NHS Trust
CASTEL   *see* States of Guernsey Bd of Health
CASTLE Okehampton   *see* Mid Devon Primary Care Trust
CASTLE HILL Cottingham   *see* Hull and E Yorks Hosps NHS Trust
CASTLEFORD NORMANTON AND DISTRICT   *see* Mid Yorks Hosps NHS Trust
CATERHAM   *see* Surrey and Sussex Healthcare NHS Trust
CAWSTON PARK   T W HARRIS
CEFN COED Swansea   *see* Swansea NHS Trust
CENTRAL MANCHESTER/MANCHESTER CHILDREN'S UNIVERSITY HOSPITAL NHS TRUST   S TURNER, J S A LAW, M L T MCGONIGLE
CENTRAL MIDDLESEX NHS TRUST   M D MOORHEAD
CHAPEL ALLERTON Leeds   *see* Leeds Teaching Hosps NHS Trust
CHARING CROSS Pilot Wing   *see* W Lon Mental Health NHS Trust
CHARLTON LANE CENTRE Leckhampton   *see* Glos Hosps NHS Foundn Trust
CHASE FARM Enfield   *see* Barnet and Chase Farm Hosps NHS Trust
CHELMSFORD Broomfield   *see* Mid-Essex Hosp Services NHS Trust
CHELSEA AND WESTMINSTER HOSPITAL NHS FOUNDATION TRUST   S M CONNELL, C BEARDSLEY
CHELTENHAM GENERAL   *see* Glos Hosps NHS Foundn Trust
CHEPSTOW COMMUNITY   *see* Gwent Healthcare NHS Trust
CHERRY KNOWLE Sunderland   *see* Priority Healthcare Wearside NHS Trust
CHERRY TREE Stockport   *see* Stockport NHS Trust
CHESHIRE AND WIRRAL PARTNERSHIPS NHS TRUST   A SCAIFE, G L HODKINSON, D R NUGENT
CHESTERFIELD AND NORTH DERBYSHIRE NHS TRUST   J K BUTTERFIELD
CHESTERTON Cambridge   *see* Cam Univ Hosps NHS Foundn Trust
CHICHESTER St Richard's   *see* R W Sussex NHS Trust
CHIPPENHAM COMMUNITY   *see* Wilts and Swindon Healthcare NHS Trust
CHORLEY AND SOUTH RIBBLE DISTRICT GENERAL   *see* Lancs Teaching Hosps NHS Trust
CHRISTCHURCH   *see* R Bournemouth and Christchurch Hosps NHS Trust
CHRISTIE HOSPITAL NHS TRUST Manchester   K L DUNN
CHURCHILL, THE Oxford   *see* Ox Radcliffe Hosps NHS Trust
CIRENCESTER   *see* Glos Primary Care Trust
CIRENCESTER   *see* Glos Hosps NHS Foundn Trust
CITY Birmingham   *see* Sandwell and W Birm Hosps NHS Trust
CITY HOSPITAL York   *see* York Hosps NHS Foundn Trust

CITY HOSPITALS SUNDERLAND NHS TRUST   P H WEBB, M WARNER
CLACTON GENERAL   *see* Colchester Hosp Univ NHS Foundn Trust
CLATTERBRIDGE Wirral   *see* Cheshire and Wirral Partnerships NHS Trust
CLAYBURY Woodford Bridge   *see* Forest Healthcare NHS Trust Lon
CLAYTON Wakefield   *see* Mid Yorks Hosps NHS Trust
CLEVELAND, SOUTH Middlesbrough   *see* S Tees Hosps NHS Trust
CLIFTON Lytham St Annes   *see* Blackpool, Fylde and Wyre Hosps NHS Trust
COLCHESTER GENERAL   *see* Colchester Hosp Univ NHS Foundn Trust
COLCHESTER HOSPITAL UNIVERSITY NHS FOUNDATION TRUST   R SMITH, M W THOMPSON, J I SEARS, R J R HUMPHRIES, H A N PLATTS
COLCHESTER MATERNITY   *see* Colchester Hosp Univ NHS Foundn Trust
COLINDALE   *see* Enfield Primary Care Trust
CONQUEST St Leonards-on-Sea   *see* E Sussex Hosps NHS Trust
CONWY AND DENBIGHSHIRE NHS TRUST   J P ATACK
COOKRIDGE Leeds   *see* Leeds Teaching Hosps NHS Trust
CORK UNIVERSITY   D R NUZUM
CORNWALL AND ISLES OF SCILLY PRIMARY CARE TRUST   R OAKES
CORNWALL HEALTHCARE NHS TRUST, J T MCCABE
CORNWALL PARTNERSHIP NHS TRUST   C D NEWELL, E C DEELEY
COUNTESS MOUNTBATTEN HOSPICE Southampton   *see* Southn Univ Hosps NHS Trust
COUNTESS OF CHESTER HOSPITAL NHS FOUNDATION TRUST   G M HIBBERT, G L HODKINSON, E T DAVIES
COUNTY DURHAM AND DARLINGTON NHS FOUNDATION TRUST   B SELMES, K S TROMANS, L G PEALL, T P GIBBONS
COUNTY DURHAM AND DARLINGTON PRIORITY SERVICES NHS TRUST   C JAY
COVENTRY AND WARWICKSHIRE   *see* Univ Hosps Cov and Warks NHS Trust
CROMER   *see* Norfolk and Nor Univ Hosp NHS Trust
CROSSLANE Newby   *see* Tees and NE Yorks NHS Trust
CROWBOROUGH WAR MEMORIAL   *see* Sussex Downs and Weald Primary Care Trust
CROYDON MENTAL HEALTH SERVICES Warlingham   *see* S Lon and Maudsley NHS Foundn Trust
CUMBERLAND INFIRMARY   *see* N Cumbria Acute Hosps NHS Trust
DARLINGTON MEMORIAL   *see* Co Durham and Darlington NHS Foundn Trust
DARTFORD AND GRAVESHAM NHS TRUST   M H KELLY
DELANCEY Leckhampton   *see* Glos Hosps NHS Foundn Trust
DELLWOOD Reading   *see* R Berks NHS Foundn Trust
DERBY HOSPITALS NHS FOUNDATION TRUST   D W ASHTON, M HARGREAVES, H P JONES, P A SHORT
DERBYSHIRE CHILDREN'S   *see* Derby Hosps NHS Foundation Trust
DERBYSHIRE ROYAL INFIRMARY   *as above*
DEREHAM   *see* Norfolk Community Health and Care
DERRIFORD   *see* Plymouth Hosps NHS Trust
DEVIZES COMMUNITY   *see* Wilts and Swindon Healthcare NHS Trust
DEVONSHIRE ROAD Blackpool   *see* Blackpool, Fylde and Wyre Hosps NHS Trust
DEWI SANT Pontypridd   *see* Pontypridd and Rhondda NHS Trust
DEWSBURY AND DISTRICT   *see* Mid Yorks Hosps NHS Trust
DIANA, PRINCESS OF WALES Grimsby   *see* N Lincs and Goole Hosps NHS Trust
DILKE MEMORIAL Cinderford   *see* Glos Primary Care Trust
DODDINGTON COUNTY March   *see* NW Anglia Healthcare NHS Trust
DONCASTER AND BASSETLAW HOSPITALS NHS TRUST   C L SMITH
DONCASTER AND SOUTH HUMBER HEALTHCARE NHS TRUST   A I MCCORMICK
DONCASTER ROYAL INFIRMARY   *see* Doncaster and Bassetlaw Hosps NHS Trust
DONCASTER ROYAL INFIRMARY PSYCHIATRIC UNIT   *see* Doncaster and S Humber Healthcare NHS Trust
DORKING   *see* Surrey and Sussex Healthcare NHS Trust
DOWN LISBURN HEALTH AND SOCIAL SERVICES TRUST   E HENDERSON

DUCHESS OF KENT HOUSE St Andrews   *see* States of Guernsey Bd of Health

DUCHY Truro   H C T OLIVEY

DUNSTON HILL Gateshead   *see* Gateshead Health NHS Trust

DURHAM AND DARLINGTON NHS FOUNDATION TRUST   *see* Co Durham and Darlington NHS Foundn Trust

DURHAM AND DARLINGTON PRIORITY SERVICES NHS TRUST   *see* Co Dur & Darlington Priority Services NHS Trust

EALING HOSPITAL NHS TRUST   J L OSBORNE, M K DAVIDGE-SMITH, E J WALLER

EARLS HOUSE Durham   *see* Co Dur & Darlington Priority Services NHS Trust

EAST AND NORTH HERTFORDSHIRE NHS TRUST   F S E GIBBS, S J MANLEY-COOPER, A J FERRIS, J E HATTON, L E SUMMERS

EAST CHESHIRE NHS TRUST   J BUCKLEY

EAST HAM MEMORIAL   *see* E Lon NHS Foundation Trust

EAST HAMPSHIRE PRIMARY CARE TRUST   J E HAIR, C R PRESTIDGE

EAST KENT HOSPITALS NHS TRUST   P F HILL, P M KIRBY, K FAZZANI

EAST LANCASHIRE HOSPITALS NHS TRUST   A S HORSFALL, D ALTHAM

EAST LONDON NHS FOUNDATION TRUST   N J COPSEY

EAST SOMERSET NHS TRUST   E J ROTHWELL

EAST SURREY PRIORITY CARE NHS TRUST   N J COPSEY

EAST SUSSEX COUNTY HEALTHCARE NHS TRUST   M J ELWIS

EAST SUSSEX HOSPITALS NHS TRUST   G J A COOK, C I WOODWARD, C R GORING, J G DAVENPORT

EASTBOURNE GENERAL   *see* E Sussex Hosps NHS Trust

EASTBOURNE GENERAL   *see* E Sussex Co Healthcare NHS Trust

EASTBOURNE HOSPITALS NHS TRUST   D J JEFFREYS, N P CHATFIELD

EASTERN AND COASTAL KENT PRIMARY CARE TRUST   P M KIRBY

EDGWARE COMMUNITY   *see* Barnet and Chase Farm Hosps NHS Trust

EDITH CAVELL Peterborough   *see* Pet Hosps NHS Trust

ELIZABETH GARRETT ANDERSON OBSTETRIC London   *see* Univ Coll Lon Hosps NHS Foundn Trust

ELLESMERE PORT   *see* Cheshire and Wirral Partnerships NHS Trust

ELY Cardiff   *see* Cardiff and Vale NHS Trust

ELY Cardiff   *see* Cardiff Community Healthcare NHS Trust

ENFIELD PRIMARY CARE TRUST   T M BARON, T D ATKINS

EPSOM St Ebba's   *see* Surrey and Borders Partnership NHS Trust

EPSOM AND ST HELIER UNIVERSITY HOSPITALS NHS TRUST   S J ELLISON, S F SEWELL, D WALFORD

EPSOM GENERAL   *see* Epsom and St Helier Univ Hosps NHS Trust

ERITH AND DISTRICT   *see* S Lon Healthcare NHS Trust

ESSEX COUNTY   *see* Colchester Hosp Univ NHS Foundn Trust

EVESHAM COMMUNITY   *see* Worcs Community and Mental Health Trust

FAIRFIELD GENERAL   *see* Pennine Acute Hosps NHS Trust

FALMOUTH   *see* Cornwall and Is of Scilly Primary Care Trust

FARNHAM   *see* Surrey and Borders Partnership NHS Trust

FARNHAM ROAD Guildford   *as above*

FAZAKERLEY Liverpool   *see* Aintree Hosps NHS Trust Liv

FIELDHEAD Wakefield   *see* SW Yorks Mental Health NHS Trust

FINCHLEY MEMORIAL   *see* Enfield Primary Care Trust

FOREST HEALTHCARE NHS TRUST London   D J DALAIS

FOREST LODGE Sheffield   *see* Sheff Care Trust

FORSTER GREEN   *see* Belfast Health and Soc Care Trust

FORTH VALLEY NHS TRUST   T NJUGUNA

FREEMAN Newcastle   *see* Newcastle upon Tyne Hosps NHS Foundn Trust

FRENCHAY Bristol   *see* N Bris NHS Trust

FRIMLEY PARK HOSPITAL NHS FOUNDATION TRUST   B D BURBIDGE

FULBOURN Cambridge   *see* Cam Univ Hosps NHS Foundn Trust

FURNESS GENERAL Barrow-in-Furness   *see* Morecambe Bay Hosps NHS Trust

FURNESS GENERAL Barrow-in-Furness   *see* Morecambe Bay Primary Care Trust

GATESHEAD HEALTH NHS TRUST   J R PERRY

GEORGE ELIOT HOSPITAL NHS TRUST Nuneaton   E C POGMORE, S P MOULT, L A MUDD, P DODDS

GLENFIELD Bennion Centre   *see* Leics Partnership NHS Trust

GLENFIELD Bradgate Mental Health Unit   *as above*

GLENFIELD Leicester   *see* Univ Hosps Leic NHS Trust

GLENSIDE Bristol   R MEREDITH-JONES

GLOUCESTERSHIRE HOSPITALS NHS FOUNDATION TRUST   W B IRVINE, M S RILEY, C A MCCLURE

GLOUCESTERSHIRE PARTNERSHIP TRUST   M J WITHEY

GLOUCESTERSHIRE PRIMARY CARE TRUST   G L BURN, M J WITHEY

GLOUCESTERSHIRE ROYAL   *see* Glos Hosps NHS Foundn Trust

GOOD HOPE HOSPITAL NHS TRUST Sutton Coldfield   A T BALL

GOOLE AND DISTRICT   *see* N Lincs and Goole Hosps NHS Trust

GORSE HILL Leicester   *see* Leics Partnership NHS Trust

GOSPORT WAR MEMORIAL   *see* E Hants Primary Care Trust

GRAMPIAN HEALTHCARE NHS TRUST   J DUTHIE

GRAMPIAN UNIVERSITY HOSPITAL NHS TRUST   S SPENCER

GREAT ORMOND STREET HOSPITAL FOR CHILDREN NHS TRUST   J D LINTHICUM, J W ENEVER

GREATER MANCHESTER WEST MENTAL HEALTH NHS FOUNDATION TRUST   D R SUTTON

GREENACRES Dartford   *see* Kent & Medway NHS and Soc Care Partnership Trust

GRIMSBY   *see* N Lincs and Goole Hosps NHS Trust

GUILDFORD St Luke's   *see* R Surrey Co Hosp NHS Trust

GUY'S AND ST THOMAS' NHS FOUNDATION TRUST London   M A K HILBORN, N J K TEGALLY, A H BARRON, C B HALL, W W SHARPE, J M WATTS

GWENT COUNTY Griffithstown   *see* Gwent Healthcare NHS Trust

GWENT HEALTHCARE NHS TRUST   A W TYLER, M J MARSDEN, D C ROBERTS, M C G LANE

HALSTEAD COMMUNITY   *see* Colchester Hosp Univ NHS Foundn Trust

HALTON GENERAL   *see* N Cheshire Hosps NHS Trust

HAM GREEN Bristol   *see* N Bris NHS Trust

HAMPSHIRE PARTNERSHIP NHS TRUST   J E HAIR, D L GRACE, G M K MORGAN

HAROLD WOOD   *see* Barking Havering and Redbridge Hosps NHS Trust

HARTLEPOOL GENERAL   *see* N Tees and Hartlepool NHS Trust

HARTLEPOOL GENERAL   *see* Tees and NE Yorks NHS Trust

HARTSHILL ORTHOPAEDIC   *see* N Staffs Hosp NHS Trust

HARWICH COMMUNITY   *see* Colchester Hosp Univ NHS Foundn Trust

HASLAR   *see* Portsm Hosps NHS Trust

HEART HOSPITAL London   *see* Univ Coll Lon Hosps NHS Foundn Trust

HEART OF ENGLAND NHS FOUNDATION TRUST   M MACLACHLAN

HEATHERWOOD AND WEXHAM PARK HOSPITAL NHS TRUST   C E L SMITH, R A CHEEK

HELLESDON Norfolk   *see* Norfolk & Waveney Mental Health NHS Foundn Trust

HEMEL HEMPSTEAD GENERAL   *see* W Herts Hosps NHS Trust

HEREFORD HOSPITALS NHS TRUST   P A ROBERTS, L C RHODES

HERGEST UNIT Ysbyty Gwynedd   *see* NW Wales NHS Trust

HERTFORDSHIRE AND ESSEX COMMUNITY NHS TRUST   K I GOSS

HEXHAM   *see* Northumbria Healthcare NHS Trust

HIGHBURY Bulwell   *see* Notts Healthcare NHS Trust

HILL HOUSE Swansea   *see* Swansea NHS Trust

HILLINGDON HOSPITAL NHS TRUST   R CHRISTIAN

HINCHINGBROOKE HEALTH CARE NHS TRUST   P M DUFFETT-SMITH, S GRIFFITH, C M FURLONG

HITCHIN   *see* E and N Herts NHS Trust

HITHER GREEN London   *see* Lewisham Hosp NHS Trust

HOPE Salford   *see* Salford R Hosps NHS Foundn Trust

HORSHAM   *see* W Sussex Health and Soc Care NHS Trust

HUDDERSFIELD ROYAL INFIRMARY   *see* Calderdale and Huddersfield NHS Trust

HULL AND EAST YORKSHIRE HOSPITALS NHS TRUST   P J NELSON, J A SHARP, A M LAIRD, A R MARSDEN

HULL MATERNITY   *see* Hull and E Yorks Hosps NHS Trust

HULL ROYAL INFIRMARY   *as above*

HUMBER MENTAL HEALTH TEACHING NHS TRUST   E ROSE

HURSTWOOD PARK Haywards Heath   *see* Brighton and Sussex Univ Hosps NHS Trust

IDA DARWIN Cambridge *see* Cam Univ Hosps NHS Foundn Trust
IMPERIAL COLLEGE HEALTHCARE NHS TRUST
C P GUINNESS
INVICTA COMMUNITY CARE NHS TRUST
S A J MITCHELL
IPSWICH St Clements *see* Local Health Partnerships NHS Trust
IPSWICH HOSPITAL NHS TRUST G T MELVIN, S J RAINE, R A FINCH
ISLE OF MAN DEPARTMENT OF HEALTH AND SOCIAL SECURITY P S FREAR
ISLE OF WIGHT NHS PRIMARY CARE TRUST
G J CLIFTON-SMITH, D L DENNIS, M D H JOHNSTON, D M NETHERWAY
JAMES COOK UNIVERSITY Middlesbrough *see* S Tees Hosps NHS Trust
JAMES PAGET HEALTHCARE NHS TRUST V M STEADY
JERSEY GENERAL St Helier *see* Jersey Gp of Hosps
JERSEY GROUP M TURNER, G GREEN
JESSOP WOMEN'S Sheffield *see* Sheff Teaching Hosps NHS Foundn Trust
JOHN CONOLLY WING Southall *see* W Lon Mental Health NHS Trust
JOHN RADCLIFFE Oxford *see* Ox Radcliffe Hosps NHS Trust
KELLING *see* Norfolk Community Health and Care
KENT AND CANTERBURY *see* E Kent Hosps NHS Trust
KENT AND MEDWAY NHS AND SOCIAL CARE PARTNERSHIP TRUST P J RICHMOND, R A BIERBAUM, R P C PODGER, M CLEEVE
KENT AND SUSSEX Tunbridge Wells *see* Maidstone and Tunbridge Wells NHS Trust
KETTERING GENERAL HOSPITAL NHS TRUST
R G BROWN
KEYCOL Kent *see* Thames Gateway NHS Trust
KIDDERMINSTER *see* Worcs Acute Hosps NHS Trust
KIDDERMINSTER GENERAL *see* Worcs Community and Mental Health Trust
KING EDWARD VII Castel *see* States of Guernsey Bd of Health
KING EDWARD VII Midhurst D B WELSMAN
KING GEORGE Redbridge *see* Barking Havering and Redbridge Hosps NHS Trust
KING'S COLLEGE HOSPITAL NHS TRUST D W RUSHTON
KING'S LYNN AND WISBECH HOSPITALS NHS TRUST
A L HAIG
KINGS MILL Sutton-in-Ashfield *see* Sherwood Forest Hosps NHS Trust
KING'S WOOD CENTRE Colchester *see* N Essex Mental Health Partnership NHS Trust
KINGSTON HOSPITAL NHS TRUST Surrey G W HOLMES
KNEESWORTH HOUSE Royston N TAYLOR
LAGAN VALLEY *see* Down Lisburn Health and Soc Services Trust
LAKESIDE MENTAL HEALTH UNIT Isleworth *see* W Lon Mental Health NHS Trust
LANCASHIRE TEACHING HOSPITALS NHS TRUST
P TARLETON
LANSDOWNE *see* Cardiff and Vale NHS Trust
LEA CASTLE Wolverley *see* N Warks NHS Trust
LEEDS St Mary's *see* Leeds Mental Health Teaching NHS Trust
LEEDS GENERAL INFIRMARY *see* Leeds Teaching Hosps NHS Trust
LEEDS MENTAL HEALTH TEACHING NHS TRUST
M I KIMBALL
LEEDS TEACHING HOSPITALS NHS TRUST, The
C J SWIFT, G HANCOCKS, K S BURKE, C G WEDGE
LEICESTER GENERAL *see* Univ Hosps Leic NHS Trust
LEICESTER GENERAL Brandon Mental Health Unit *see* Leics Partnership NHS Trust
LEICESTER ROYAL INFIRMARY *see* Univ Hosps Leic NHS Trust
LEICESTERSHIRE PARTNERSHIP NHS TRUST
T H GIRLING
LEIGH INFIRMARY *see* Wrightington Wigan and Leigh NHS Trust
LEIGHTON Crewe *see* Cheshire and Wirral Partnerships NHS Trust
LEIGHTON Crewe *see* Mid Cheshire Hosps Trust
LEWISHAM HOSPITAL NHS TRUST A L SHAW
LIBERTON Edinburgh *see* Lothian Univ Hosps NHS Trust
LIFECARE Caterham *see* Surrey and Borders Partnership NHS Trust
LIMES, THE Southall *see* W Lon Mental Health NHS Trust

LINCOLN COUNTY *see* Lincs Partnership NHS Trust
LINCOLN COUNTY *see* United Lincs Hosps NHS Trust
LINCOLNSHIRE PARTNERSHIP NHS TRUST H G SMART, J K WILSON, A M PAVEY
LINCOLNSHIRE TEACHING PRIMARY CARE TRUST
P S J GARLAND
LINDEN CENTRE Broomfield *see* N Essex Mental Health Partnership NHS Trust
LISKEARD COMMUNITY *see* Cornwall and Is of Scilly Primary Care Trust
LISTER Stevenage *see* E and N Herts NHS Trust
LITTLE BROMWICH CENTRE FOR ELDERLY MENTAL HEALTH Small Heath *see* Birm and Solihull Mental Health Trust
LITTLE PLUMSTEAD *see* Norfolk Community Health and Care
LITTLEMORE Oxford *see* Oxon & Bucks Mental Health Partnership NHS Trust
LIVERPOOL CARDIOTHORACIC CENTRE *see* R Liverpool and Broadgreen Univ Hosps NHS Trust
LLANDOUGH *see* Cardiff and Vale NHS Trust
LLANDUDNO GENERAL *see* NW Wales NHS Trust
LLANFRECHFA GRANGE Cwmbran *see* Gwent Healthcare NHS Trust
LLANTRISANT Royal Glamorgan *see* Pontypridd and Rhondda NHS Trust
LLWYNYPIA *as above*
LOCAL HEALTH PARTNERSHIPS NHS TRUST Suffolk
G T MELVIN
LONDON AND SURREY *see* R Marsden NHS Foundn Trust
LONDON CHEST *see* Barts and The Lon NHS Trust
LONGLEY CENTRE Sheffield *see* Sheff Care Trust
LOTHIAN UNIVERSITY HOSPITALS NHS TRUST
C T UPTON
LOUTH COUNTY *see* United Lincs Hosps NHS Trust
LOVERSALL Doncaster *see* Doncaster and S Humber Healthcare NHS Trust
LOWESTOFT AND NORTH SUFFOLK *see* Jas Paget Healthcare NHS Trust
LUDLOW *see* Shropshire Co Primary Care Trust
LUTON AND DUNSTABLE HOSPITAL NHS TRUST
E A BRADLEY
MACCLESFIELD DISTRICT GENERAL *see* Cheshire and Wirral Partnerships NHS Trust
MACCLESFIELD DISTRICT GENERAL *see* E Cheshire NHS Trust
MAIDSTONE AND TUNBRIDGE WELLS NHS TRUST
N J MITRA
MAINDIFF COURT Abergavenny *see* Gwent Healthcare NHS Trust
MANCHESTER *see also* Greater Manchester
MANCHESTER AND SALFORD SKIN *see* Salford R Hosps NHS Foundn Trust
MANCHESTER ROYAL EYE *see* Cen Man/Man Children's Univ Hosp NHS Trust
MANCHESTER ROYAL INFIRMARY *as above*
MANOR Walsall *see* Walsall Hosps NHS Trust
MANSFIELD COMMUNITY *see* Sherwood Forest Hosps NHS Trust
MANSFIELD DISTRICT PRIMARY CARE TRUST
P BENTLEY
MATER *see* Belfast Health and Soc Care Trust
MAUDSLEY Denmark Hill *see* S Lon and Maudsley NHS Foundn Trust
MAYDAY HEALTHCARE NHS TRUST Thornton Heath
H A FIFE
MAYDAY UNIVERSITY *see* Mayday Healthcare NHS Trust Thornton Heath
MEADOWBROOK UNIT Salford *see* Gtr Man W Mental Health NHS Foundn Trust
MEADOWFIELD Worthing *see* W Sussex Health and Soc Care NHS Trust
MEANWOOD PARK Leeds *see* Leeds Mental Health Teaching NHS Trust
MEDWAY Gillingham *see* Thames Gateway NHS Trust
MEDWAY MARITIME Gillingham *see* Kent & Medway NHS and Soc Care Partnership Trust
MEDWAY NHS FOUNDATION TRUST D V GOWER, S C SPENCER
MELKSHAM COMMUNITY *see* Wilts and Swindon Healthcare NHS Trust
MERTHYR TYDFIL *see* N Glam NHS Trust
MICHAEL CARLISLE CENTRE Sheffield *see* Sheff Care Trust
MID CHESHIRE HOSPITALS TRUST G D GEDDES, D MARSH

MID DEVON PRIMARY CARE TRUST   D M FLETCHER
MID-ESSEX HOSPITAL SERVICES NHS TRUST
    J SHEFFIELD, S M SOUTHEE
MID STAFFORDSHIRE NHS FOUNDATION TRUST
    P J GRAYSMITH, M J COULTER
MID YORKSHIRE HOSPITALS NHS TRUST   M GASKELL,
    M J WINBOLT-LEWIS
MIDDLESBROUGH GENERAL   see S Tees Hosps NHS Trust
MIDDLESEX   see Univ Coll Lon Hosps NHS Foundn Trust
MILDMAY MISSION   M F SCHLEGER
MILLBROOK MENTAL HEALTH UNIT Sutton-in-Ashfield
    see Notts Healthcare NHS Trust
MILTON KEYNES HOSPITAL NHS FOUNDATION TRUST
    C E HOUGH, K S REEVES
MILTON KEYNES PRIMARY CARE TRUST   C E HOUGH
MONTAGU Mexborough   see Doncaster and Bassetlaw Hosps
    NHS Trust
MOORFIELDS EYE HOSPITAL NHS TRUST   D E ALLEN
MOORGREEN West End Southampton   see Chapl Hants
    Partnership NHS Trust
MORECAMBE BAY HOSPITALS NHS TRUST   J L TYRER,
    D V A BROWN
MORECAMBE BAY PRIMARY CARE TRUST
    D V A BROWN
MORPETH COTTAGE   see Northumbria Healthcare NHS
    Trust
MORRISTON Swansea   see Swansea NHS Trust
MOSELEY HALL Birmingham   see Birm Specialist
    Community Health Trust
MUSGRAVE PARK   see Belfast Health and Soc Care Trust
MUSGROVE PARK Taunton   see Taunton and Somerset NHS
    Trust
NAPSBURY St Albans   see Enfield Primary Care Trust
NATIONAL HOSPITAL FOR NEUROLOGY AND
    NEUROSURGERY London   see Univ Coll Lon Hosps NHS
    Foundn Trust
NEVILL HALL Abergavenny   see Gwent Healthcare NHS Trust
NEW CRAIGS Inverness   see NHS Highland
NEW CROSS Wolverhampton   see R Wolv Hosps NHS Trust
NEWARK   see Sherwood Forest Hosps NHS Trust
NEWCASTLE Freeman   see Newcastle upon Tyne Hosps NHS
    Foundn Trust
NEWCASTLE Royal Victoria Infirmary   as above
NEWCASTLE St Nicholas   see Newc City Health NHS Trust
NEWCASTLE CITY HEALTH NHS TRUST   F B ALLEN
NEWCASTLE GENERAL   see Newcastle upon Tyne Hosps
    NHS Foundn Trust
NEWCASTLE MENTAL HEALTH UNIT   A E MARR
NEWCASTLE-UNDER-LYME PRIMARY CARE TRUST
    P D HOWARD
NEWCASTLE UPON TYNE HOSPITALS NHS
    FOUNDATION TRUST   M J SHIPTON, K L JONES
NEWHAM PRIMARY CARE TRUST   N J COPSEY
NEWHAM UNIVERSITY HOSPITAL NHS TRUST
    R J OGSTON
NEWHAVEN DOWNS   see Sussex Downs and Weald Primary
    Care Trust
NEWTON ABBOT   see S Devon Healthcare NHS Foundn Trust
NEWTOWN Worcester   see Worcs Community and Mental
    Health Trust
NHS DUMFRIES AND GALLOWAY   S R PAISLEY
NHS HIGHLAND   M F HICKFORD
NORFOLK AND NORWICH UNIVERSITY HOSPITAL
    NHS TRUST   E S LANGAN, C B REED, P A ATKINSON,
    J M STEWART
NORFOLK AND WAVENEY MENTAL HEALTH NHS
    FOUNDATION TRUST   W F BAZELY, M I KNOWLES
NORFOLK COMMUNITY HEALTH AND CARE
    P A ATKINSON, R D BRANSON
NORTH BRISTOL NHS TRUST   S J ORAM, D C DAVIES,
    N A HECTOR, A J PARKER, C A G LEGGATE, A M BUCKNALL,
    A R GOOD
NORTH CAMBRIDGESHIRE Wisbech   see King's Lynn and
    Wisbech Hosps NHS Trust
NORTH CHESHIRE HOSPITALS NHS TRUST   J E DUFFIELD
NORTH CUMBRIA ACUTE HOSPITALS NHS TRUST
    J A EVANS
NORTH DEVON DISTRICT Barnstaple   see N Devon
    Healthcare NHS Trust
NORTH EAST LONDON MENTAL HEALTH TRUST
    M O PRITCHARD, G F JENKINS
NORTH EAST WALES NHS TRUST   K B COLLINS
NORTH ESSEX MENTAL HEALTH PARTNERSHIP NHS
    TRUST   R SMITH, C A HAWKINS
NORTH GLAMORGAN NHS TRUST   E A POWELL

NORTH MANCHESTER GENERAL   see Pennine Acute
    Hosps NHS Trust
NORTH MIDDLESEX HOSPITAL NHS TRUST
    B D FENTON, P C ATHERTON
NORTH STAFFORDSHIRE HOSPITAL NHS TRUST
    J M AUSTERBERRY, L B VARQUEZ, T B BLOOR
NORTH SURREY PRIMARY CARE TRUST   J M ALLFORD
NORTH TEES AND HARTLEPOOL NHS TRUST   L PURVIS
NORTH TEES GENERAL   see Tees and NE Yorks NHS Trust
NORTH TYNESIDE GENERAL North Shields   see
    Northumbria Healthcare NHS Trust
NORTH WARWICKSHIRE NHS TRUST   S P MOULT
NORTH WEST ANGLIA HEALTHCARE NHS TRUST
    S J SMITH
NORTH WEST WALES NHS TRUST   W ROBERTS,
    R H GRIFFITHS
NORTHAMPTON GENERAL HOSPITAL NHS TRUST
    G A SARMEZEY
NORTHAMPTONSHIRE HEALTHCARE NHS TRUST
    C R GOODLEY, R J T FARMER
NORTHCROFT Erdington   see Birm and Solihull Mental
    Health Trust
NORTHERN DEVON HEALTHCARE NHS TRUST
    K E W MATHERS, R M REYNOLDS
NORTHERN GENERAL Sheffield   see Sheff Teaching Hosps
    NHS Foundn Trust
NORTHERN LINCOLNSHIRE AND GOOLE HOSPITALS
    NHS TRUST   A R BARBER
NORTHGATE Great Yarmouth   see Jas Paget Healthcare NHS
    Trust
NORTHUMBERLAND MENTAL HEALTH NHS TRUST
    R H MCLEAN
NORTHUMBRIA HEALTHCARE NHS TRUST
    C F MEEHAN, D MACNAUGHTON, G HARWOOD, J WAIYAKI,
    R H MCLEAN
NORWICH, WEST   see Norfolk and Nor Univ Hosp NHS
    Trust
NOTTINGHAM CITY HOSPITAL NHS TRUST   Y E GLASS
NOTTINGHAMSHIRE COUNTY TEACHING PRIMARY
    CARE TRUST   J C B PEMBERTON
NOTTINGHAMSHIRE HEALTHCARE NHS TRUST
    C M J THODY, K R EVANS, C D WOOD, J L ALLEN
NUFFIELD Brighton   R A BROMFIELD
NUFFIELD ORTHOPAEDIC CENTRE NHS TRUST
    J E COCKE, T A WARD
NUNNERY FIELDS Canterbury   see E Kent Hosps NHS Trust
OKEHAMPTON AND DISTRICT   see Mid Devon Primary
    Care Trust
OLDCHURCH Romford   see Barking Havering and Redbridge
    Hosps NHS Trust
ORMSKIRK AND DISTRICT GENERAL   see W Lancashire
    NHS Trust
ORPINGTON   see S Lon Healthcare NHS Trust
OVERDALE St Helier   see Jersey Gp of Hosps
OXFORD RADCLIFFE HOSPITALS NHS TRUST
    J M TURNER, P F SUTTON, H L ADEY HUISH
OXFORDSHIRE AND BUCKINGHAMSHIRE MENTAL
    HEALTH PARTNERSHIP NHS TRUST   S L BUSHELL,
    A F RABLEN
OXLEAS NHS FOUNDATION TRUST   N C WHITTLE
OXTED   see Surrey and Sussex Healthcare NHS Trust
PAIGNTON   see S Devon Healthcare NHS Foundn Trust
PAPWORTH HOSPITAL NHS FOUNDATION TRUST
    G R ROWLANDS
PARKLANDS Basingstoke   see Chapl Hants Partnership NHS
    Trust
PEMBURY Tunbridge Wells   see Maidstone and Tunbridge
    Wells NHS Trust
PEMBURY Tunbridge Wells   see Kent & Medway NHS and Soc
    Care Partnership Trust
PENDERED CENTRE Northampton   see Northants
    Healthcare NHS Trust
PENDLE COMMUNITY Nelson   see E Lancs Hosps NHS
    Trust
PENNINE ACUTE HOSPITALS NHS TRUST, THE
    R R WATSON, S A PURVIS
PETERBOROUGH HOSPITALS NHS TRUST   R E HIGGINS
PETERSFIELD COMMUNITY   see E Hants Primary Care
    Trust
PIERREMONT UNIT Darlington   see Co Dur & Darlington
    Priority Services NHS Trust
PILGRIM Boston   see United Lincs Hosps NHS Trust
PINDERFIELDS GENERAL Wakefield   see Mid Yorks Hosps
    NHS Trust
PLAISTOW   see Newham Primary Care Trust

PLUMSTEAD, LITTLE *see* Norfolk Community Health and Care

PLYMOUTH HOSPITALS NHS TRUST R D BAXENDALE, S J PEARCE, M B BROWN

PONTEFRACT GENERAL INFIRMARY *see* Mid Yorks Hosps NHS Trust

PONTYPRIDD AND RHONDDA NHS TRUST R T PITMAN

POOLE HOSPITAL NHS TRUST E J LLOYD, I R PEARCE

PORTSMOUTH HOSPITALS NHS TRUST B R SMITH, N P FENNEMORE, C A SMITH, C J HEADLEY, B A MOSSE, J POWER, M J A LINDSAY

PRINCE CHARLES Merthyr Tydfil *see* N Glam NHS Trust

PRINCESS ALEXANDRA Harlow *see* N Essex Mental Health Partnership NHS Trust

PRINCESS ALEXANDRA HOSPITAL NHS TRUST Harlow T R WEEKS

PRINCESS ALICE Eastbourne *see* Eastbourne Hosps NHS Trust

PRINCESS ANNE Southampton *see* Southn Univ Hosps NHS Trust

PRINCESS ELIZABETH St Martin *see* States of Guernsey Bd of Health

PRINCESS MARGARET ROSE ORTHOPAEDIC Edinburgh *see* Lothian Univ Hosps NHS Trust

PRINCESS MARINA Northampton *see* Northants Healthcare NHS Trust

PRINCESS OF WALES COMMUNITY Bromsgrove *see* Worcs Community and Mental Health Trust

PRINCESS ROYAL Haywards Heath *see* Brighton and Sussex Univ Hosps NHS Trust

PRINCESS ROYAL Hull *see* Hull and E Yorks Hosps NHS Trust

PRINCESS ROYAL UNIVERSITY Farnborough *see* S Lon Healthcare NHS Trust

PRIORITY HEALTHCARE WEARSIDE NHS TRUST C J WORSFOLD

PRIORITY HOUSE Maidstone *see* Kent & Medway NHS and Soc Care Partnership Trust

PRIORY Birmingham J A GRIFFIN

PROSPECT PARK Reading R S WADEY

QUEEN ALEXANDRA Portsmouth *see* Portsm Hosps NHS Trust

QUEEN ELIZABETH Birmingham *see* Univ Hosp Birm NHS Foundn Trust

QUEEN ELIZABETH Gateshead *see* Gateshead Health NHS Trust

QUEEN ELIZABETH King's Lynn *see* King's Lynn and Wisbech Hosps NHS Trust

QUEEN ELIZABETH Woolwich *see* Qu Eliz Hosp NHS Trust

QUEEN ELIZABETH HOSPITAL NHS TRUST D M FLAGG, G M HESKINS, T N ALEXANDER-YATES

QUEEN ELIZABETH II Welwyn Garden City *see* E and N Herts NHS Trust

QUEEN ELIZABETH PSYCHIATRIC Birmingham *see* Birm and Solihull Mental Health Trust

QUEEN ELIZABETH THE QUEEN MOTHER Margate *see* E Kent Hosps NHS Trust

QUEEN MARY'S Sidcup *see* S Lon Healthcare NHS Trust

QUEEN MARY'S UNIVERSITY Roehampton Lane *see* Wandsworth Primary Care Trust

QUEEN VICTORIA Morecambe *see* Morecambe Bay Hosps NHS Trust

QUEEN VICTORIA HOSPITAL NHS TRUST East Grinstead C EVERETT-ALLEN

QUEEN VICTORIA MEMORIAL Welwyn *see* E and N Herts NHS Trust

QUEEN'S Burton-on-Trent *see* Burton Hosps NHS Trust

QUEEN'S Romford *see* Barking Havering and Redbridge Hosps NHS Trust

QUEEN'S MEDICAL CENTRE NOTTINGHAM UNIVERSITY HOSPITAL NHS TRUST W P WATERS, J HEMSTOCK, G SPENCER, C T DOLBY, A M BROOKS, P S WEEDING

QUEEN'S MEDICAL CENTRE UNIVERSITY HOSPITAL Nottingham, Department of Psychiatry and Psychiatric Medicine *see* Notts Healthcare NHS Trust

QUEEN'S PARK Blackburn *see* E Lancs Hosps NHS Trust

RADCLIFFE INFIRMARY Oxford *see* Ox Radcliffe Hosps NHS Trust

RAIGMORE HOSPITAL NHS TRUST Inverness A A SINCLAIR

RAMPTON Retford *see* Notts Healthcare NHS Trust

RAMSGATE GENERAL *see* E Kent Hosps NHS Trust

REASIDE CLINIC Rednal *see* Birm and Solihull Mental Health Trust

REDBRIDGE King George *see* Barking Havering and Redbridge Hosps NHS Trust

RICHMOND AND TWICKENHAM PRIMARY CARE TRUST J W KNILL-JONES

RIDGE LEA Lancaster *see* Morecambe Bay Primary Care Trust

RIDGEWOOD CENTRE Frimley *see* Surrey and Borders Partnership NHS Trust

ROBERT JONES/AGNES HUNT ORTHOPAEDIC HOSPITAL NHS TRUST Oswestry A R BAILEY

ROCHDALE INFIRMARY *see* Pennine Acute Hosps NHS Trust

ROCHFORD *see* S Essex Mental Health & Community Care NHS Trust

ROEHAMPTON LANE Queen Mary's University *see* Wandsworth Primary Care Trust

ROOKWOOD Llandaff *see* Cardiff and Vale NHS Trust

ROTHERAM NHS FOUNDATION TRUST H FERGUSON-STUART

ROTHERHAM GENERAL HOSPITALS NHS TRUST J E ASHTON

ROWLEY REGIS Warley *see* Sandwell and W Birm Hosps NHS Trust

ROYAL ALBERT EDWARD INFIRMARY *see* Wrightington Wigan and Leigh NHS Trust

ROYAL ALEXANDRA CHILDREN'S Brighton *see* Brighton and Sussex Univ Hosps NHS Trust

ROYAL BELFAST HOSPITAL FOR SICK CHILDREN *see* Belfast Health and Soc Care Trust

ROYAL BELFAST HOSPITAL FOR SICK CHILDREN *see* R Group of Hosps Health and Soc Services Trust

ROYAL BERKSHIRE NHS FOUNDATION TRUST M W SSERUNKUMA, F M G HALL

ROYAL BOURNEMOUTH AND CHRISTCHURCH HOSPITALS NHS TRUST B WILLIAMS, A SESSFORD, J R EVANS

ROYAL BROMPTON AND HAREFIELD NHS TRUST R G THOMPSON, N K LEE

ROYAL CHELSEA, R H WHITTINGTON

ROYAL CORNWALL HOSPITALS TRUST M A TREMBATH, A D WEST, R H GRIGG, J K P S ROBERTSHAW, J A MILLAR

ROYAL DERBY *see* Derby Hosps NHS Foundation Trust

ROYAL FREE HAMPSTEAD NHS TRUST R H MITCHELL, T HANDLEY MACMATH, C CARSON, P D CONRAD

ROYAL GLAMORGAN Llantrisant *see* Pontypridd and Rhondda NHS Trust

ROYAL GROUP OF HOSPITALS AND DENTAL HOSPITALS HEALTH AND SOCIAL SERVICES TRUST Belfast A MALLON

ROYAL GWENT Newport *see* Gwent Healthcare NHS Trust

ROYAL HALLAMSHIRE Sheffield *see* Sheff Teaching Hosps NHS Foundn Trust

ROYAL HOSPITAL FOR NEURO-DISABILITY J M FARMAN

ROYAL HOSPITAL FOR SICK CHILDREN Edinburgh *see* Lothian Univ Hosps NHS Trust

ROYAL HOSPITAL HASLAR *see* Portsm Hosps NHS Trust

ROYAL INFIRMARY OF EDINBURGH *see* Lothian Univ Hosps NHS Trust

ROYAL JUBILEE MATERNITY SERVICE *see* Belfast Health and Soc Care Trust

ROYAL LANCASTER INFIRMARY *see* Morecambe Bay Hosps NHS Trust

ROYAL LIVERPOOL AND BROADGREEN UNIVERSITY HOSPITALS NHS TRUST G A PERERA, C J PETER

ROYAL LIVERPOOL CHILDREN'S NHS TRUST D J WILLIAMS

ROYAL LONDON *see* Barts and The Lon NHS Trust

ROYAL MANCHESTER CHILDREN'S *see* Cen Man/Man Children's Univ Hosp NHS Trust

ROYAL MARSDEN NHS FOUNDATION TRUST London and Surrey A J MCCULLOCH, C E LATHAM

ROYAL MATERNITY Belfast *see* R Group of Hosps Health and Soc Services Trust

ROYAL NATIONAL ORTHOPAEDIC HOSPITAL NHS TRUST W A BROOKER, P M REECE

ROYAL OLDHAM *see* Pennine Acute Hosps NHS Trust

ROYAL PRESTON *see* Lancs Teaching Hosps NHS Trust

ROYAL SHREWSBURY *see* Shrewsbury and Telford NHS Trust

ROYAL SOUTH HAMPSHIRE *see* Southn Univ Hosps NHS Trust

ROYAL SURREY COUNTY HOSPITAL NHS TRUST D N HOBDEN, J S MCARTHUR-EDWARDS

ROYAL SUSSEX COUNTY Brighton *see* Brighton and Sussex Univ Hosps NHS Trust

ROYAL UNITED HOSPITAL BATH NHS TRUST A J DAVIES, S M E STEVENS

ROYAL VICTORIA Belfast   *see* Belfast Health and Soc Care Trust

ROYAL VICTORIA Belfast   *see* R Group of Hosps Health and Soc Services Trust

ROYAL VICTORIA Edinburgh   *see* Lothian Univ Hosps NHS Trust

ROYAL VICTORIA Folkestone   *see* E Kent Hosps NHS Trust

ROYAL VICTORIA INFIRMARY Newcastle   *see* Newcastle upon Tyne Hosps NHS Foundn Trust

ROYAL WEST SUSSEX NHS TRUST   J P COOPER, J V EMERSON

ROYAL WOLVERHAMPTON HOSPITALS NHS TRUST   C W FULLARD, C SILVESTER

RUNWELL   *see* S Essex Mental Health & Community Care NHS Trust

ST ALBANS Napsbury   *see* Enfield Primary Care Trust

ST ALBANS CITY   *see* W Herts Hosps NHS Trust

ST ANDREW'S Northampton   J M BOWERS, N PURVEY-TYRER, M R BASS

ST ANDREW'S HEALTHCARE BIRMINGHAM   D I A BRAZELL

ST ANNE'S CENTRE St Leonards-on-Sea   *see* E Sussex Co Healthcare NHS Trust

ST ANN'S Tottenham   *see* Barnet, Enfield and Haringey Mental Health Trust

ST AUSTELL COMMUNITY   *see* Cornwall and Is of Scilly Primary Care Trust

ST BARNABAS Saltash   *see* Cornwall Healthcare NHS Trust

ST BARTHOLOMEW'S London   *see* Barts and The Lon NHS Trust

ST BARTHOLOMEW'S Rochester   *see* Kent & Medway NHS and Soc Care Partnership Trust

ST BARTHOLOMEW'S Rochester   *see* Medway NHS Foundn Trust

ST CADOC'S Caerleon   *see* Gwent Healthcare NHS Trust

ST CATHERINE'S Doncaster   *see* Doncaster and S Humber Healthcare NHS Trust

ST CLEMENT'S London   *see* E Lon NHS Foundation Trust

ST CROSS Rugby   *see* Univ Hosps Cov and Warks NHS Trust

ST EBBA'S Epsom   *see* Surrey and Borders Partnership NHS Trust

ST EDMUND'S Northampton   *see* Northn Gen Hosp NHS Trust

ST GEORGE'S Morpeth   *see* Northd Mental Health NHS Trust

ST GEORGE'S Stafford   *see* S Staffs Healthcare NHS Trust

ST GEORGE'S HEALTHCARE NHS TRUST London   H A JOHNSON, R W WALL, J M FARMAN, C J CARTER

ST HELENS AND KNOWSLEY HOSPITALS NHS TRUST   M JONES

ST HELIER Carshalton   *see* Epsom and St Helier Univ Hosps NHS Trust

ST JAMES'S UNIVERSITY Leeds   *see* Leeds Mental Health Teaching NHS Trust

ST JAMES'S UNIVERSITY Leeds   *see* Leeds Teaching Hosps NHS Trust

ST LUKE'S Armagh   *see* Armagh and Dungannon Health and Soc Services

ST LUKE'S Bradford   *see* Bradf Hosps NHS Trust

ST LUKE'S Middlesbrough   *see* Tees and NE Yorks NHS Trust

ST MARTIN'S Bath   *see* Bath and West Community NHS Trust

ST MARTIN'S Canterbury   *see* Kent & Medway NHS and Soc Care Partnership Trust

ST MARY'S Armley   *see* Leeds Mental Health Teaching NHS Trust

ST MARY'S Kettering   *see* Northants Healthcare NHS Trust

ST MARY'S Portsmouth   *see* Portsm Hosps NHS Trust

ST MARY'S HOSPITAL FOR WOMEN AND CHILDREN Manchester   *see* Cen Man/Man Children's Univ Hosp NHS Trust

ST MARY'S NHS TRUST Paddington   S J FLATT

ST MICHAEL'S Aylsham   *see* Norfolk Community Health and Care

ST MICHAEL'S Bristol   *see* Univ Hosps Bris NHS Foundn Trust

ST MICHAEL'S Warwick   *see* S Warks Combined Care NHS Trust

ST NICHOLAS Canterbury   M A MORRIS

ST NICHOLAS Newcastle   *see* Newc City Health NHS Trust

ST PANCRAS   *see* Camden and Islington Community Health NHS Trust

ST PETER'S Chertsey   *see* N Surrey Primary Care Trust

ST RICHARD'S Chichester   *see* R W Sussex NHS Trust

ST SAVIOUR   *see* Jersey Gp of Hosps

ST THOMAS' London   *see* Guy's and St Thos' NHS Foundn Trust

ST THOMAS Stockport   *see* Stockport NHS Trust

ST TYDFIL'S Merthyr Tydfil   *see* N Glam NHS Trust

ST WOOLOS Newport   *see* Gwent Healthcare NHS Trust

SALFORD ROYAL HOSPITALS NHS FOUNDATION TRUST   I S CARTER, L H LEE

SALISBURY HEALTH CARE NHS TRUST   C RENYARD, M R CURTIS, K S M STEPHENS, A SYMES

SALKELD DAY Chepstow   *see* Gwent Healthcare NHS Trust

SALVINGTON LODGE Worthing   *see* W Sussex Health and Soc Care NHS Trust

SANDWELL AND WEST BIRMINGHAM HOSPITALS NHS TRUST   K A DUCKETT, D H GARNER, M FARR

SANDWELL GENERAL West Bromwich   *see* Sandwell and W Birm Hosps NHS Trust

SANDWELL MENTAL HEALTH NHS AND SOCIAL CARE TRUST   E C LOUIS

SAVERNAKE Marlborough   *see* Wilts and Swindon Healthcare NHS Trust

SCARBOROUGH AND NORTH EAST YORKSHIRE HEALTHCARE NHS TRUST   M C DOE, L M HOLLIS

SCARBOROUGH GENERAL   *see* Scarborough and NE Yorks Healthcare NHS Trust

SCUNTHORPE GENERAL   *see* N Lincs and Goole Hosps NHS Trust

SEACROFT Leeds   *see* Leeds Teaching Hosps NHS Trust

SELBY WAR MEMORIAL   *see* York Hosps NHS Foundn Trust

SELLY OAK   *see* Univ Hosp Birm NHS Foundn Trust

SEVENOAKS   *see* Invicta Community Care NHS Trust

SEVERALLS Colchester   *see* Colchester Hosp Univ NHS Foundn Trust

SEVERALLS HOUSE Colchester   *see* N Essex Mental Health Partnership NHS Trust

SHAROE GREEN Preston   *see* Lancs Teaching Hosps NHS Trust

SHEFFIELD CARE TRUST   S H ROSS, J P RAFFAY

SHEFFIELD CHILDREN'S NHS FOUNDATION TRUST   L A FURBEY, G L WILTON

SHEFFIELD TEACHING HOSPITALS NHS FOUNDATION TRUST   J H DALEY, M R COBB, K G LOWE, M J KERRY, N M JOHNSON, M J NEWITT

SHELTON Bicton Heath   *see* Shropshire Co Primary Care Trust

SHEPPEY COMMUNITY Minster-on-Sea   *see* Thames Gateway NHS Trust

SHEPTON MALLET COMMUNITY   *see* Somerset Primary Care Trust

SHERWOOD FOREST HOSPITALS NHS TRUST   J A S WOOD

SHOTLEY BRIDGE GENERAL Consett   *see* Co Durham and Darlington NHS Foundn Trust

SHREWSBURY AND TELFORD NHS TRUST   A W WARNER, P HRYZIUK, M I FEARNSIDE

SHREWSBURY ROYAL INFIRMARY   *see* Shrewsbury and Telford NHS Trust

SHROPSHIRE COUNTY PRIMARY CARE TRUST   M E POTTER, R A GREEN, E J FAIRLESS

SIMPSON MEMORIAL MATERNITY PAVILION Edinburgh   *see* Lothian Univ Hosps NHS Trust

SINGLETON Swansea   *see* Swansea NHS Trust

SIR ROBERT PEEL Tamworth   *see* S Staffs Healthcare NHS Trust

SOBELL HOUSE Oxford   *see* Ox Radcliffe Hosps NHS Trust

SOLIHULL   *see* Birm Heartlands and Solihull NHS Trust

SOMERSET PRIMARY CARE TRUST   R J ALLEN, G M KIRK, E J SMITH

SOUTH AND EAST DORSET PRIMARY CARE TRUST   J E HOLBROOK

SOUTH DEVON HEALTHCARE NHS FOUNDATION TRUST   M CHURCHER, J H GARNER, B R TUBBS

SOUTH DOWNS HEALTH NHS TRUST   D L I PERKS

SOUTH ESSEX MENTAL HEALTH AND COMMUNITY CARE NHS TRUST   J H DELFGOU

SOUTH LONDON AND MAUDSLEY NHS FOUNDATION TRUST   M R SUTHERLAND, I N FISHWICK, A A WILSON, R RATCLIFFE, J SAXTON

SOUTH LONDON HEALTHCARE NHS TRUST   D COUTTS, T J MERCER

SOUTH MANCHESTER UNIVERSITY HOSPITALS NHS TRUST   J F C PERRYMAN, S GROSSCURTH, P BUTLER

SOUTH SHORE Blackpool   *see* Blackpool, Fylde and Wyre Hosps NHS Trust

SOUTH STAFFORDSHIRE HEALTHCARE NHS TRUST   H J BAKER

SOUTH TEES HOSPITALS NHS TRUST   M MASTERMAN, A M GRANGE

SOUTH WARWICKSHIRE COMBINED CARE NHS TRUST
J A CARTWRIGHT
SOUTH WARWICKSHIRE GENERAL HOSPITALS NHS TRUST   F E TYLER, H F COCKELL
SOUTH WEST DORSET PRIMARY CARE TRUST
E J WOODS, D H BISHOP
SOUTH WEST LONDON AND ST GEORGE'S MENTAL HEALTH NHS TRUST   R J S ALLEN
SOUTH WEST OXFORDSHIRE PRIMARY CARE TRUST
L HODGES
SOUTH WEST YORKSHIRE MENTAL HEALTH NHS TRUST   C M GARTLAND, H WALKER
SOUTHAMPTON CITY PRIMARY CARE TRUST
A R BEVIS
SOUTHAMPTON GENERAL   *see* Southn Univ Hosps NHS Trust
SOUTHAMPTON UNIVERSITY HOSPITALS NHS TRUST
P A BOGGUST, R O L LOWNDES, J V PERCIVAL, K A MACKINNON
SOUTHEND HEALTH CARE NHS TRUST   G L CROOK, L M WILLIAMS
SOUTHLANDS Shoreham-by-Sea   *see* Worthing and Southlands Hosps NHS Trust
SOUTHMEAD Bristol   *see* N Bris NHS Trust
SOUTHPORT AND ORMSKIRK NHS TRUST
A P J GALBRAITH
SPRINGFIELD UNIVERSITY   *see* SW Lon and St George's Mental Health NHS Trust
STAFFORD DISTRICT GENERAL   *see* Mid Staffs NHS Foundn Trust
STAMFORD AND RUTLAND   *see* Pet Hosps NHS Trust
STANDISH Stonehouse   *see* Glos Hosps NHS Foundn Trust
STATES OF GUERNSEY BOARD OF HEALTH
P J CARRINGTON, J LE BILLON, J E D LUFF
STEPPING HILL Stockport   *see* Stockport NHS Trust
STOCKPORT NHS TRUST   B J LOWE
STOKE MANDEVILLE Aylesbury   *see* Bucks Hosps NHS Trust
STOKE MANDEVILLE HOSPITAL NHS TRUST
S BLAGDEN
STROUD GENERAL   *see* Severn NHS Trust
SUFFOLK COASTAL PRIMARY CARE TRUST   N J WINTER
SUNDERLAND DISTRICT GENERAL   *see* City Hosps Sunderland NHS Trust
SURREY AND BORDERS PARTNERSHIP NHS TRUST
S H BULL, J A ROBINSON, N J COPSEY, A K TUCK
SURREY AND SUSSEX HEALTHCARE NHS TRUST
J M GLASSPOOL, F G LEHANEY, D G O ROBINSON
SUSSEX DOWNS AND WEALD PRIMARY CARE TRUST
A C J CORNES
SUSSEX NUFFIELD   *see* Nuffield Hosp Brighton
SUSSEX PARTNERSHIP NHS TRUST   G S JOHNSON
SWAFFHAM COMMUNITY   *see* NW Anglia Healthcare NHS Trust
SWANSEA NHS TRUST   N R GRIFFIN, D M GRIFFITHS, P J GWYNN
TAMESIDE AND GLOSSOP ACUTE SERVICES NHS TRUST   J HILDITCH
TAMESIDE GENERAL   *see* Pennine Acute Hosps NHS Trust
TAUNTON AND SOMERSET NHS TRUST   M L GODIN, M D A WILLIAMS
TEES, ESK AND WEAR VALLEY NHS TRUST
R CUTHBERTSON
TEES AND NORTH EAST YORKSHIRE NHS TRUST
P L WALKER
TEIGNMOUTH   *see* S Devon Healthcare NHS Foundn Trust
TELFORD Princess Royal   *see* Shrewsbury and Telford NHS Trust
TEWKESBURY   *see* Glos Hosps NHS Foundn Trust
THAMES GATEWAY NHS TRUST   P R BECKINSALE, G H SPENCER, J PEAL
THANET MENTAL HEALTH UNIT Margate   *see* Kent & Medway NHS and Soc Care Partnership Trust
THETFORD COTTAGE DAY   *see* W Suffolk Hosps NHS Trust
THREE BRIDGES REGIONAL SECURE UNIT Southall   *see* W Lon Mental Health NHS Trust
THURROCK COMMUNITY   *see* S Essex Mental Health & Community Care NHS Trust
TICKHILL ROAD Doncaster   *see* Doncaster and S Humber Healthcare NHS Trust
TINDAL CENTRE Aylesbury   *see* Oxon & Bucks Mental Health Partnership NHS Trust
TIVERTON AND DISTRICT   *see* Mid Devon Primary Care Trust
TORBAY   *see* S Devon Healthcare NHS Foundn Trust
TRAFFORD HEALTHCARE NHS TRUST   C J BROWN

TRANWELL UNIT Gateshead   *see* Gateshead Health NHS Trust
TREDEGAR GENERAL   *see* Gwent Healthcare NHS Trust
TREORCHY Ysbyty George Thomas   *see* Pontypridd and Rhondda NHS Trust
TRINITY Retford   A J KERSWILL
TROPICAL DISEASES   *see* Camden and Islington Community Health NHS Trust
TROWBRIDGE COMMUNITY   *see* Wilts and Swindon Healthcare NHS Trust
ULVERSTON   *see* Morecambe Bay Hosps NHS Trust
UNITED LINCOLNSHIRE HOSPITALS NHS TRUST
C M BONNEYWELL, M R SAUNDERS, B M S CHAMBERS, A AMELIA, L E TURNER
UNIVERSITY Durham   *see* Co Durham and Darlington NHS Foundn Trust
UNIVERSITY Hartlepool   *see* N Tees and Hartlepool NHS Trust
UNIVERSITY Stockton-on-Tees   *as above*
UNIVERSITY COLLEGE LONDON HOSPITALS NHS FOUNDATION TRUST   P M FREEMAN
UNIVERSITY HOSPITAL BIRMINGHAM NHS FOUNDATION TRUST   R M WHARTON, R FARMAN, S H SHEWRING
UNIVERSITY HOSPITAL OF WALES   *see* Cardiff and Vale NHS Trust
UNIVERSITY HOSPITALS BRISTOL NHS FOUNDATION TRUST   D C DAVIES, J M TAYLOR, G S BROWN, M A SNOOK, J E NORMAN
UNIVERSITY HOSPITALS COVENTRY AND WARWICKSHIRE NHS TRUST   H PRIESTNER, S F BETTERIDGE
UNIVERSITY HOSPITALS OF LEICESTER NHS TRUST
M T SHARPE, I P BRENNAND, R C WILLIAMS, C R ROE, S C POLASHEK, M J MORRIS
VERRINGTON Wincanton   *see* E Somerset NHS Trust
VICTORIA Blackpool   *see* Blackpool, Fylde and Wyre Hosps NHS Trust
WALKERGATE Newcastle   *see* Newcastle upon Tyne Hosps NHS Foundn Trust
WALSALL HOSPITALS NHS TRUST   A E COLES
WALSGRAVE GENERAL Coventry   *see* Univ Hosps Cov and Warks NHS Trust
WALTON Liverpool   *see* Aintree Hosps NHS Trust Liv
WALTON COMMUNITY   *see* N Surrey Primary Care Trust
WANDSWORTH PRIMARY CARE TRUST   R J NORBURY
WANSBECK GENERAL Ashington   *see* Northumbria Healthcare NHS Trust
WAREHAM   *see* S and E Dorset Primary Care Trust
WARMINSTER COMMUNITY   *see* Wilts and Swindon Healthcare NHS Trust
WARNEFORD Leamington Spa   *see* S Warks Gen Hosps NHS Trust
WARNEFORD PARK Oxford   *see* Oxon & Bucks Mental Health Partnership NHS Trust
WARRINGTON   *see* N Cheshire Hosps NHS Trust
WARRINGTON COMMUNITY HEALTH CARE NHS TRUST   P LOVATT
WARWICKSHIRE, SOUTH   *see* S Warks Gen Hosps NHS Trust
WATFORD GENERAL   *see* W Herts Hosps NHS Trust
WAYLAND Attleborough   *see* Norfolk Community Health and Care
WELLS ROAD CENTRE Mapperley   *see* Notts Healthcare NHS Trust
WELWYN Queen Victoria Memorial   *see* E and N Herts NHS Trust
WELWYN GARDEN CITY Queen Elizabeth II   *as above*
WEST CHESHIRE   *see* Cheshire and Wirral Partnerships NHS Trust
WEST CORNWALL   *see* R Cornwall Hosps Trust
WEST CUMBERLAND   *see* N Cumbria Acute Hosps NHS Trust
WEST DORSET GENERAL HOSPITALS NHS TRUST
N D TOOTH
WEST HEATH Birmingham   *see* Birm Specialist Community Health NHS Trust
WEST HERTFORDSHIRE HOSPITALS NHS TRUST
G R COBB, D R ELLIOTT, D H LOVERIDGE
WEST HILL Dartford   *see* Dartford and Gravesham NHS Trust
WEST LANCASHIRE NHS TRUST   R MOUGHTIN, C H JONES
WEST LONDON MENTAL HEALTH NHS TRUST
D I BARNES, J L OSBORNE, G P HARRISON, R J SIMMONDS
WEST MIDDLESEX UNIVERSITY   *see* W Lon Mental Health NHS Trust

WEST MIDDLESEX UNIVERSITY HOSPITAL NHS TRUST
J L OSBORNE
WEST SUFFOLK HOSPITALS NHS TRUST   D CRAWLEY
WEST SUSSEX HEALTH AND SOCIAL CARE NHS TRUST
G REEVES
WESTERN COMMUNITY Southampton   *see* Chapl Hants Partnership NHS Trust
WESTERN GENERAL Edinburgh   *see* Lothian Univ Hosps NHS Trust
WESTMINSTER MEMORIAL Shaftesbury   M E HARDING
WESTMORLAND GENERAL   *see* Morecambe Bay Hosps NHS Trust
WESTMORLAND GENERAL   *see* Morecambe Bay Primary Care Trust
WESTON PARK Sheffield   *see* Sheff Teaching Hosps NHS Foundn Trust
WEXHAM PARK Slough   *see* Heatherwood and Wexham Park Hosp NHS Trust
WHARFEDALE GENERAL Otley   *see* Leeds Teaching Hosps NHS Trust
WHELLEY   *see* Wrightington Wigan and Leigh NHS Trust
WHIPPS CROSS   *see* Forest Healthcare NHS Trust Lon
WHISTON Prescot   *see* St Helens and Knowsley Hosps NHS Trust
WHITBY   *see* Scarborough and NE Yorks Healthcare NHS Trust
WHITCHURCH   *see* Cardiff and Vale NHS Trust
WHITCHURCH Cardiff   *see* Cardiff Community Healthcare NHS Trust
WHITCHURCH COMMUNITY   *see* Shropshire Co Primary Care Trust
WHITTINGTON HOSPITAL NHS TRUST   E C M K JONES
WILLIAM HARVEY Arundel Unit   *see* Kent & Medway NHS and Soc Care Partnership Trust
WILLIAM HARVEY Ashford   *see* E Kent Hosps NHS Trust
WILLITON   *see* Somerset Primary Care Trust
WILTSHIRE AND SWINDON HEALTHCARE NHS TRUST
P F YACOMENI, J A COUTTS
WIMBORNE   *see* S and E Dorset Primary Care Trust

WINWICK Warrington   *see* Warrington Community Health Care NHS Trust
WISBECH   *see* King's Lynn and Wisbech Hosps NHS Trust
WITHINGTON Manchester   *see* S Man Univ Hosps NHS Trust
WITNEY   *see* SW Oxon Primary Care Trust
WOKING COMMUNITY   *see* Surrey and Borders Partnership NHS Trust
WOODLANDS Worsley   *see* Gtr Man W Mental Health NHS Foundn Trust
WORCESTER ROYAL INFIRMARY   *see* Worcs Acute Hosps NHS Trust
WORCESTERSHIRE ACUTE HOSPITALS NHS TRUST
A J FISHER
WORCESTERSHIRE COMMUNITY AND MENTAL HEALTH TRUST, The   L L BURN, M E BARR, M E STANTON-HYDE
WORTHING AND SOUTHLANDS HOSPITALS NHS TRUST   R E BENNETT
WORTHING PRIORITY CARE NHS TRUST   R J CASWELL
WREXHAM MAELOR   *see* NE Wales NHS Trust
WRIGHTINGTON WIGAN AND LEIGH NHS TRUST
R J HUTCHINSON, A J HESLOP, R TOWNLEY, D J ROSCOE, A J EDWARDS
WYCOMBE   *see* Bucks Hosps NHS Trust
WYTHENSHAWE Manchester   *see* S Man Univ Hosps NHS Trust
YEOVIL DISTRICT   *see* E Somerset NHS Trust
YEOVIL DISTRICT HOSPITAL NHS FOUNDATION TRUST   J M CUMMINGS
YORK HOSPITALS NHS FOUNDATION TRUST   S PETTY, E W A CRAGG
YSBYTY GEORGE THOMAS Treorchy   *see* Pontypridd and Rhondda NHS Trust
YSBYTY GWYNEDD Penrhosgarnedd   *see* NW Wales NHS Trust
YSBYTY PENRHOS STANLEY Holyhead   *as above*
YSTRAD MYNACH Hengoed   *see* Gwent Healthcare NHS Trust

HOSPICE CHAPLAINS

BOLTON M O BRACKLEY
CHESTNUT TREE HOUSE Arundel S J GURR
CHILDREN'S SOUTH WEST Fremington G C PHILLIPS
COMPTON Wolverhampton B A I SMART
CRANSLEY L S MCCORMACK
DOROTHY HOUSE Winsley K M CROUCH
DOUGLAS MACMILLAN Blurton J Y TILLIER, S GOODWIN
EXETER HOSPISCARE, D J WALFORD
FARLEIGH Chelmsford K L HACKER HUGHES
GREENWICH AND BEXLEY COTTAGE A C WILLIAMSON
HEART OF KENT M J HAYES
HELEN AND DOUGLAS HOUSE Oxford M R BIRCH
ISABEL Welwyn Garden City D A MOORE BROOKS
JERSEY G J HOUGHTON
JOHN TAYLOR Birmingham N E D SCHIBILD
KATHARINE HOUSE Banbury P C SMITH
KATHARINE HOUSE Stafford P J GRAYSMITH
KIRKWOOD Huddersfield M E WOOD
MARIE CURIE Solihull D A KNIGHT, D R L WHITE
MARTLETS Hove C G SPINKS
MEADOW HOUSE London J L OSBORNE
MYTON HAMLET Warwick W S GRAHAM
NIGHTINGALE HOUSE Wrexham G WINDON
NORTH DEVON B P LUCK
OAKHAVEN TRUST J E L ALEXANDER
OVERGATE Elland D BURROWS
PILGRIMS Canterbury E R G HOPTHROW
PILGRIMS Thanet N H TAYLOR
PRIMROSE Bromsgrove D R L WHITE
ROWCROFT Torquay G STILL
ST ANDREW'S Airdrie M S PATERSON
ST ANDREW'S Grimsby T STOTT
ST ANN'S Manchester J A HORROCKS, J F AMBROSE
ST BARNABAS HOUSE Worthing S J GURR
ST CATHERINE'S Crawley J M NEVILL
ST CATHERINE'S Preston I J J DEWAR
ST CATHERINE'S Scarborough K D JACKSON
ST CHRISTOPHER'S London E M TOLLER, J K BURKITT-GRAY

ST CLARE Hastingwood C L LAWS
ST FRANCIS Berkhamsted E J HUGHES
ST GILES Lichfield D J SHERIDAN, P L HOLLIDAY
ST JOHN'S Moggerhanger S A WATTS
ST JOHN'S Wirral P B PRITCHARD
ST JOSEPH'S Hackney T C KEIGHLEY, S M HARTLEY
ST LEONARD'S York A G PEARSE, C W M BALDOCK
ST LUKE'S Cheshire A L D FRIEND
ST LUKE'S Plymouth T A SMITH
ST LUKE'S Sheffield J SANKEY, M W P REEDER
ST MARGARET'S Yeovil P KERTON-JOHNSON
ST MARY'S Birmingham R J FARMAN
ST MICHAEL'S Basingstoke A EDMEADS
ST MICHAEL'S Harrogate (Crimple House) C HENSON
ST MICHAEL'S St Leonards-on-Sea G L DRIVER
ST OSWALD'S Newcastle upon Tyne C L BROWN
ST PETER AND ST JAMES North Chailey G R HOCKEN,
    S C M MCLARNON
ST PETER'S Bristol W B M DOWIE
ST RICHARD'S Worcester D A KNIGHT
ST ROCCO'S Warrington H S HOUSTON
ST WILFRID'S Chichester B M WATERS
ST WILFRID'S Eastbourne C R BEARD
SAM BEARE Weybridge B D PROTHERO
SEVERN Shrewsbury E C PHILLIPS, H J EDWARDS
SHAKESPEARE Stratford-upon-Avon S L GOBLE
SPRINGHILL Rochdale M L T MCGONIGLE
STRATHCARRON Denny S M COATES
SUSSEX BEACON Brighton J K T ELDRIDGE
THORPE HALL Peterborough A-L K GARVIE
TRINITY London C A CLARKE
TRINITY IN THE FYLDE Blackpool J E DENNETT
WAKEFIELD G BUTTERWORTH
WHEATFIELDS Leeds T P LUSTY
WILLEN Milton Keynes S W BARNES
WISDOM Rochester J PEAL
WOKING P J HARWOOD

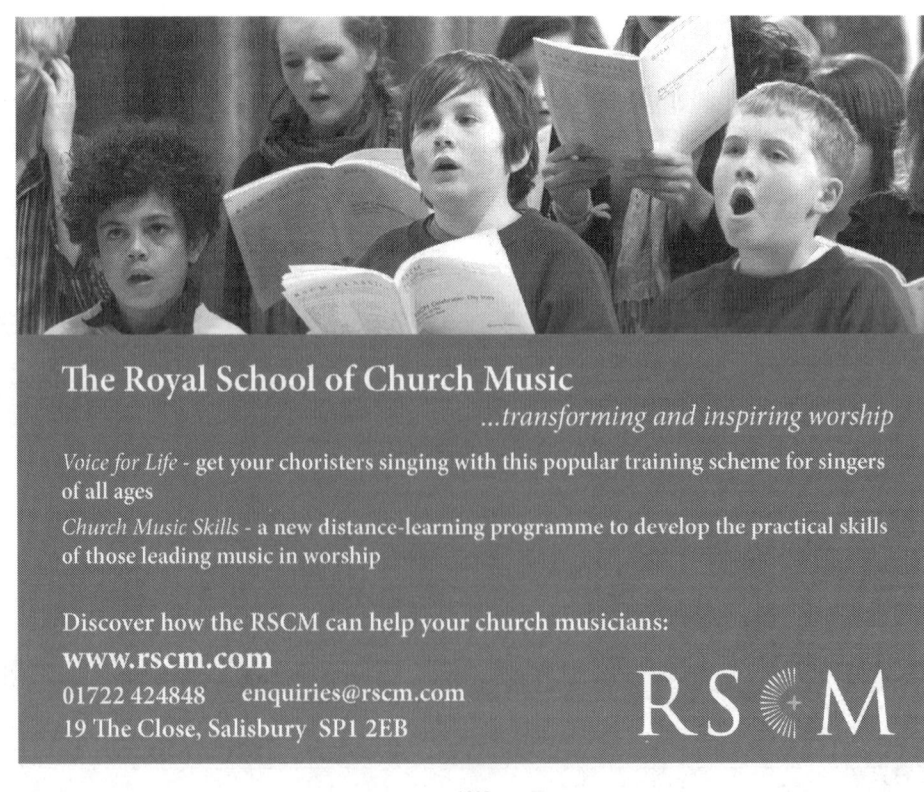

EDUCATIONAL CHAPLAINS

This index only lists deans and chaplains, and does not aim to provide a comprehensive list of clergy serving at educational institutions. Those institutions which do not currently have Anglican chaplains are not recorded.

UNIVERSITIES

ABERDEEN D HEDDLE
ABERTAY D SHEPHERD
ANGLIA RUSKIN N S COOPER, I R MOODY
BANGOR K P J PADLEY
BATH A V I BERNERS-WILSON, B F CHAPMAN
BATH SPA J P KNOTT
BEDFORDSHIRE A F M GOODMAN
BIRMINGHAM M A J JOYCE, N LO POLITO
BIRMINGHAM CITY C G GRAHAM
BOLTON P G EDWARDS
BOURNEMOUTH B MERRINGTON
BRIGHTON C R LAWLOR
BRISTOL E G A DAVIS
BRUNEL *Uxbridge Campus* C E SARGENT
BUCKINGHAMSHIRE NEW A W DICKINSON, T A STACEY
CAMBRIDGE
   Christ's C M WOODS
   Churchill J RAWLINSON
   Clare G J SEACH
   Corpus Christi J A D BUXTON
   Downing K J EYEONS
   Emmanuel J M MUNNS
   Fitzwilliam T J K CONLIN
   Girton A M GUITE
   Gonville and Caius C J-B HAMMOND
   Jesus J M D HUGHES
   King's R E LLOYD MORGAN
   Magdalene S BARRINGTON-WARD, P P HOBDAY
   Newnham H D SHILSON-THOMAS
   Pembroke J T D GARDOM
   Peterhouse S W P HAMPTON
   Queens' J M HOLMES
   Robinson M E DAWN
   Selwyn H D SHILSON-THOMAS
   Sidney Sussex P M WADDELL
   St Catharine's A M MOORE
   St John's G D BAYLISS, D J DORMAN
   Trinity A A GOODMAN, D G MACKENZIE MILLS
   Trinity Hall (Dean) J N MORRIS
CANTERBURY CHRIST CHURCH S J BLADE, J T LAW, D A STROUD
CENTRAL LANCASHIRE S JOHNSON
CHESTER I M ARCH, A D BUCHANAN, E M BURGESS, I M DELINGER
CHICHESTER J W DANE
CORK *University College* G P ST J HILLIARD
COVENTRY J S CROFT
CRANFIELD H K SYMES-THOMPSON
CREATIVE ARTS P J FILMER, S J TALBOTT
CUMBRIA A V WEST, M P WOODCOCK
DE MONTFORT P J LITTLEFORD
DERBY C J HODDER
DUBLIN CITY J B MARCHANT
DUBLIN *Trinity College* D M MCCALLIG
DUNDEE A WALLER
DURHAM
   Collingwood B J H DE LA MARE
   Grey S C AIREY
   Hatfield A BASH
   John Snow D J BAGE
   St Chad's A P WILSON
   St Cuthbert's Society D B GODSELL
   St Hild and St Bede J H LAWSON
   St John's K S BRUCE
   Trevelyan P J REGAN
   University M THRELFALL-HOLMES
   Van Mildert P J REGAN
EAST ANGLIA D I THORNTON
EAST LONDON J A RAMSAY, A W M RITCHIE
EDINBURGH F S BURBERRY, D P WILLIAMS
ESSEX T F P YAP
EXETER C A HADLEY, J W F THEODOSIUS
GLOUCESTERSHIRE T L R MERCHANT
GREENWICH C P BAKER, P J FILMER, J J FROST

HASTINGS R J MORTIMER
HUDDERSFIELD G S HODGSON
HULL D D S DE VERNY
KEELE C C CLAPHAM
KENT S C E LAIRD
KINGSTON D BUCKLEY
LANCASTER K J HUGGETT
LEEDS M A J WARD
LEEDS METROPOLITAN D A CALDER
LINCOLN L C ACKLAM
LIVERPOOL R G LEWIS
LIVERPOOL HOPE P G ANDERSON, S SHAKESPEARE, I C STUART
LIVERPOOL JOHN MOORES R G LEWIS
LONDON
   Central Chaplaincies S G WILLIAMS
   Goldsmiths' College P E COLLIER
   Imperial College of Science, Technology and Medicine A W WILLSON
   King's (Dean) R A BURRIDGE
   King's T F DITCHFIELD, A J M MACHAM, N P MORROW, J E SPECK
   London School of Economics and Political Science D T PEEBLES
   Queen Mary and Westfield J E PETERSEN
   Royal Free and University College Medical School P A TURNER
   Royal Holloway and Bedford New S J ROGERS
   Royal Veterinary College P A TURNER
   University J L WELSH
LONDON METROPOLITAN R M C LEIGH, F M WEAVER
LOUGHBOROUGH J O AJAEFOBI, S J RICHARDSON, R S TAYLOR
MANCHESTER T E BIDDINGTON
MANCHESTER METROPOLITAN T E BIDDINGTON, I D GOMERSALL
NEWCASTLE C M LACK
NORTHAMPTON S N MOUSIR-HARRISON
NORTHUMBRIA AT NEWCASTLE G WORT
NOTTINGHAM J W BENTHAM, J H CURRAN, I D TARRANT
NOTTINGHAM TRENT R H DAVEY
OXFORD
   All Souls J H DRURY
   Balliol J M BROWN, H D DUPREE
   Brasenose G J RICHARDSON
   Christ Church J A SHAW, R J WILLIAMSON
   Christ Church (Dean) C A LEWIS
   Corpus Christi J D MALTBY
   Exeter R J E DEWHURST, H C ORCHARD
   Hertford L K ROBERTS
   Jesus M I J DAFFERN
   Keble A K SHIN
   Lady Margaret Hall A G DOIG
   Lincoln G A D PLATTEN
   Magdalen S M ALKIRE, M J PIRET, A W M RITCHIE
   Mansfield J B MUDDIMAN
   Merton A P DAVISON, S M JONES
   New J A SHAW
   Oriel M J HARRIS
   Pembroke A R TEAL
   Queen's P J M SOUTHWELL
   St Edmund Hall G HEGARTY
   St Hilda's B W MOUNTFORD
   St Hugh's S C HENSON
   St John's E D H CARMICHAEL
   St Peter's M P WARD
   Trinity E M PERCY
   University A F GREGORY
   Wadham H A HARRIS
   Worcester J A ARNOLD
OXFORD BROOKES A J MARKEY
QUEEN'S *Belfast (Dean of Residence)* P G MCGLINCHEY
READING M D LAYNESMITH
ROYAL COLLEGE OF ART A W WILLSON
ST ANDREWS J P MASON
SALFORD D F MYERS
SHEFFIELD W R S LAMB
SOUTH BANK F Y-C HUNG
SOUTHAMPTON S M STEVENS

SOUTHAMPTON SOLENT A S MARSHALL
STAFFORDSHIRE B H CAMBRIDGE, W G MCNAMEE
STIRLING D M IND
STRATHCLYDE C OKEKE
SUNDERLAND S A A FAGBEMI
SURREY J H FROST
SURREY Roehampton D J ESHUN
SUSSEX G R P ASHENDEN, P OESTREICHER, A N ROBINSON
TEESSIDE A HOWARD
THAMES VALLEY *Ealing Campus* D M AYRES
ULSTER J E G BACH
ULSTER *Jordanstown and Belfast Campuses*
  T S JOHNSTON

UNIVERSITY CAMPUS SUFFOLK D L R MCLEOD
UNIVERSITY OF THE ARTS
  Chelsea College of Art and Design J HOGAN, A D NORWOOD
  London College of Fashion J E JEPSON
WALES
  Aberystwyth S R BELL
  Lampeter M A R HILL
  Swansea N JOHN
WESTMINSTER D W CHERRY
WINCHESTER P J DYKES
WOLVERHAMPTON G WYNNE
WORCESTER S L BLOOMER, F H HAWORTH
YORK ST JOHN J M S CLINES

COLLEGES OF HIGHER EDUCATION

This index only includes those establishments known to have Anglican chaplains. It is not intended to be comprehensive.

ASKHAM BRYAN *York* J H DAVIS
BISHOP GROSSETESTE *Lincoln* C A JAMES
COLEG GWENT *Usk* A E MORTON
HARPER ADAMS *Newport* W E WARD
MYERSCOUGH *Preston* M A SHERDLEY
NEWCASTLE W E J MASH
NORWICH CITY C J BLACKMAN

ROSE BRUFORD *Sidcup* G W DAVIES
ROYAL NAVAL *Greenwich* J J FROST
ST MARK AND ST JOHN *Plymouth* P N THOMPSON
TRINITY AND ALL SAINTS COLLEGE *Leeds* R G BOULTER
TRINITY COLLEGE OF MUSIC J J FROST
TRINITY *Carmarthen* J M A GRIFFITHS
WESLEY *Bristol* P M L PHILLIPS

COLLEGES OF FURTHER EDUCATION

This index only includes those establishments known to have Anglican chaplains. It is not intended to be comprehensive.

BISHOP BURTON COLLEGE OF AGRICULTURE *York*
  M J WESTBY
BOURNEMOUTH AND POOLE S W MILLER
BURY P H SUMSION
CANNINGTON P MARTIN
CITY OF BATH A R HAWKINS
FARNBOROUGH COLLEGE OF TECHNOLOGY
  G P H NEWTON
GUILDFORD M C WOODWARD
NEW *Swindon* D ORMSTON
NORTH EAST LONDON S P J CLARK

NORTH LINDSEY *Scunthorpe* S J WALKER
NORTH WARWICKSHIRE AND HINCKLEY N J NIXON
NORTH WEST LONDON F B CAPIE
NORTHUMBERLAND D P PALMER
PRESTON J T RICHARDSON
ROYAL ACADEMY OF MUSIC P R THOMAS
SOMERSET COLLEGE OF ARTS AND TECHNOLOGY
  D ROBERTS
SUFFOLK NEW *Ipswich* D L R MCLEOD
WORCESTER COLLEGE OF TECHNOLOGY
  P D J SWANN

SIXTH-FORM COLLEGES

This index only includes those colleges known to have Anglican chaplains. It is not intended to be comprehensive.

FARNBOROUGH R M BENNETTS
ROSSMORE COMMUNITY T F GOMM

ST VINCENT *Gosport* C J L J THOMPSON
STRODE'S *Egham* T M SUDWORTH

SCHOOLS

This index only includes those schools known to have Anglican chaplains. It is not intended to be comprehensive.

ABBEY GRANGE HIGH   D S FORD
ABBEY GRANGE HIGH *Leeds*   D L STEVENS
ABBOTS BROMLEY   P G GREEN
ABINGDON   H L KIRK
ALDENHAM *Hertfordshire*   D M BOND
ALLEYN'S *Dulwich*   A G BUCKLEY
ARCHBISHOP SENTAMU ACADEMY *Hull*   J V TAYLOR
ARDINGLY COLLEGE *Haywards Heath*
   D L LAWRENCE-MARCH
BACON'S COLLEGE *Rotherhithe*   R J HALL
BANCROFT'S *Woodford Green*   I MOORE
BARNARD CASTLE   S J RIDLEY
BEDFORD   A S ATKINS
BENNETT MEMORIAL DIOCESAN *Tunbridge Wells*
   R A KNAPP
BERKHAMSTED COLLEGIATE *Hertfordshire*   S GOLDING
BETHANY *Goudhurst*   P J BENTHAM
BISHOP BELL *Eastbourne*   V L FLANAGAN
BISHOP HENDERSON *Taunton*   J A JEFFERY
BISHOP JUSTUS CHURCH OF ENGLAND *Bromley*
   J A DONNELLY
BISHOP LUFFA *Chichester*   P M GILBERT
BISHOP OF LLANDAFF HIGH   G W WILLIAMS
BISHOP OF WINCHESTER COMPREHENSIVE
   Bournemouth   J NIGHTINGALE
BISHOP WAND *Sunbury-on-Thames*   S E LEESON
BISHOP WORDSWORTH *Salisbury*   J A BERSWEDEN
BISHOP'S BLUE COAT CHURCH OF ENGLAND HIGH
   Chester   I J HUTCHINGS
BISHOP'S STORTFORD COLLEGE   M D MARSHALL
BISHOPS' COLLEGE *Gloucester*   C J H BLOCKLEY
BLACKHEATH BLUECOAT CHURCH OF ENGLAND
   E T PRIOR
BLOXHAM   M G PRICE
BLUE COAT COMPREHENSIVE *Walsall*   A J DUCKWORTH
BLUE COAT *Reading*   D W MCHARDY
BLUECOAT *Nottingham*   K W G JOHNSON
BLUNDELL'S *Tiverton*   T C HUNT
BOX HILL   D A IRELAND
BRADFIELD COLLEGE *Berkshire*   R G HILLIARD
BRADFORD ACADEMY   R I TAYLOR
BRENTWOOD *Essex*   D J GILCHRIST
BRIDGEMARY COMMUNITY SPORTS COLLEGE
   R J PRESTON
BRIGHTON COLLEGE   R P S EASTON
BRISTOL CATHEDRAL   S B TAYLOR
BROMSGROVE   P S J HEDWORTH
BRYANSTON *Dorset*   A M J HAVILAND
CANFORD *Wimborne*   C JERVIS, K K SUGDEN
CASTERTON *Lancashire*   P S ATKINSON
CHARTERHOUSE *Godalming*   S J HARKER, R G LLOYD
CHELTENHAM COLLEGE   R DE LA BAT SMIT
CHELTENHAM LADIES' COLLEGE   D T MERRY, H R WOOD
CHRIST'S COLLEGE *Brecon*   R M LLEWELLYN
CHRIST'S HOSPITAL *Horsham*   I R COLSON
CITY OF LONDON FREEMEN'S *Ashtead*   D F P RUTHERFORD
CLAYESMORE *Blandford*   A J H EDWARDS
CLIFTON COLLEGE *Bristol*   K TAPLIN
COKETHORPE *Witney*   R J HUMPHREYS
COLFE'S *London*   A C COLLIER
COVENTRY BLUE COAT CHURCH OF ENGLAND
   P J MESSAM
CRANBROOK *Kent*   D COOK
CRANLEIGH *Surrey*   P V PARKER
CULFORD *Bury St Edmunds*   S C BATTERSBY
DAUNTSEY'S *Devizes*   D R JOHNSON
DEAN CLOSE *Cheltenham*   E L TALBOT
DEANERY CHURCH OF ENGLAND HIGH *Wigan*
   D J BURY
DENSTONE COLLEGE *Uttoxeter*   R C M JARVIS
DERBY HIGH   R J A BARRETT
DUKE OF YORK'S ROYAL MILITARY *Dover*
   A D T RICHARDS
DULWICH COLLEGE   S E YOUNG
EASTBOURNE COLLEGE   C K MACDONALD
ELIZABETH COLLEGE *Guernsey*   R G HARNISH
ELLESMERE COLLEGE *Shropshire*   D A SLIM
ELMHURST SCHOOL FOR DANCE *Birmingham*   A J JOYCE
EMANUEL *Wandsworth*   P M HUNT

EPSOM COLLEGE   P THOMPSON
ETON COLLEGE *Berkshire*   R E R DEMERY, P A HESS, C M JONES,
   K H WILKINSON
FELSTED *Essex*   J A W BRICE
FETTES COLLEGE *Edinburgh*   D CAMPBELL
GIGGLESWICK   J E BAVINGTON
GLENALMOND COLLEGE   G W DOVE
GODOLPHIN *Salisbury*   J BALL
GORDON'S *Woking*   D H ROBINSON
GOSDEN HOUSE   J N E BUNDOCK
GREIG CITY ACADEMY   P J HENDERSON
GRESHAM'S *Holt*   B R ROBERTS
GRYPHON *Sherborne*   J P TRIFFITT
HABERDASHERS' ASKE'S *Elstree*   J E MARKBY
HAILEYBURY COLLEGE *Hertfordshire*   C R BRIGGS
HARROGATE LADIES' COLLEGE   J CHEESEMAN
HARROW   J E POWER
HEATHFIELD ST MARY'S *Ascot*   M C ROBBINS
HEREFORD CATHEDRAL   P A ROW
HIGHGATE *London*   P J J KNIGHT
HURSTPIERPOINT COLLEGE *Hassocks*   M J LAWSON
IAN RAMSEY *Stockton*   S J GILES
IPSWICH   D J WARNES
KELLY COLLEGE *Tavistock*   K LANYON JONES
KING EDWARD VI *Southampton*   J G POPPLETON
KING EDWARD'S *Bath*   C L O'NEILL
KING EDWARD'S *Birmingham*   D H RAYNOR
KING EDWARD'S *Witley*   R W E MILLINGTON
KING HENRY VIII *Coventry*   R STEPHEN
KING WILLIAM'S COLLEGE *Isle of Man*   T H MORDECAI
KING'S *Bruton*   N H WILSON-BROWN
KING'S COLLEGE SCHOOL *Wimbledon*   L R F COLLINS,
   T J E MARWOOD
KING'S COLLEGE *Taunton*   M A SMITH
KING'S *Gloucester*   J B P J HADFIELD
KING'S HOSPITAL *Dublin*   P R CAMPION
KING'S *Rochester*   J A THACKRAY
KING'S *Tynemouth*   C J CLINCH
KING'S *Wolverhampton*   L K COLLINS
KING'S *Worcester*   M R DORSETT
KING'S, THE *Canterbury*   C F ARVIDSSON
KING'S, THE *Ely*   T P HUMPHRY
KINGHAM HILL *Oxfordshire*   A M SAVAGE
LANCING COLLEGE   R K HARRISON
LICHFIELD CATHEDRAL   T J WHITWELL
LLANDOVERY COLLEGE   J M MCHALE
LORD MAYOR TRELOAR COLLEGE *Alton*   E B PRUEN
LORD WANDSWORTH COLLEGE *Basingstoke*   S LEVSHON
LORETTO *Musselburgh*   A F C KEULEMANS
LOUGHBOROUGH GRAMMAR   A J S COX
MAGDALEN COLLEGE SCHOOL *Oxford*
   T H N KUIN LAWTON
MALVERN COLLEGE   R E M DOWLER, A P LAW
MANOR *York*   M A HAND
MARLBOROUGH COLLEGE   D J DALES, J G W DICKIE
MATTHEW HUMBERSTON *Grimsby*   T STOTT
MERCHANT TAYLORS' *Crosby*   D A SMITH
MERCHANT TAYLORS' *Northwood*   R D E BOLTON
MILL HILL *London*   A J KEEP
MILLFIELD *Somerset*   P C A HARBRIDGE
MILTON ABBEY *Dorset*   R W B THOMSON
MONKTON COMBE *Bath*   W P OLHAUSEN
MONMOUTH   J B HENCHER, G R KNIGHT, D J MCGLADDERY
MORETON HALL   A B STRATFORD
NORWICH   N TIVEY
OAKHAM   A C V ALDOUS, J P TAYLOR
OLD SWINFORD HOSPITAL *Stourbridge*   M W SOAR
OUNDLE *Peterborough*   I C BROWNE, D R H EDWARDSON,
   D M REES-JONES
PANGBOURNE COLLEGE *Berkshire*   B J CUNNINGHAM
PETER SYMONDS COLLEGE *Winchester*   N P SEAL
PETERBOROUGH HIGH   C D MASON
POCKLINGTON *York*   W J ROBERTS
PORTSMOUTH GRAMMAR   A K BURTT
PREBENDAL *Chichester*   T D NASON
PRIOR'S FIELD   J M FELLOWS
QUAINTON HALL *Harrow*   N V J ROPER
QUEEN ANNE'S *Caversham*   H C BENSON
QUEEN ELIZABETH'S *Mansfield*   A M SMYTHE

QUEEN MARGARET'S *York*   R L OWEN
QUEENSWOOD *Herts*   G J A WRIGHT
RADLEY COLLEGE *Oxfordshire*   T J E FERNYHOUGH,
   T D MULLINS
RANBY HOUSE *Retford*   D R MOORE
RATHDOWN *Dublin*   S T IRVINE
RAVENSCLIFFE HIGH *Halifax*   A MAUDE
REED'S *Cobham*   A J CLARKE
REPTON *Derby*   A J M WATKINSON
REPTON PREPARATORY *Foremarke Hall*   N A BAILEY
RIDDLESWORTH HALL *Norwich*   K A HAWKES
RIPLEY ST THOMAS CHURCH OF ENGLAND HIGH
   Lancaster   S IRVINE
RISHWORTH *Ripponden*   J S BRADBERRY
ROEDEAN *Brighton*   H J MATTHEWS, M E SITWELL
ROYAL MASONIC FOR GIRLS *Rickmansworth*   J H D JENKINS
ROYAL RUSSELL *Croydon*   S J PADFIELD
RUGBY   R M HORNER
RYDE *with Upper Chine*   A W SWANBOROUGH
ST AIDAN'S *Harrogate*   P T ASKEW
ST ALBANS   C D PINES
ST ALBANS HIGH SCHOOL FOR GIRLS
   D C FITZGERALD CLARK
ST BEDE'S ECUMENICAL *Reigate*   J P SCOTT
ST BEES *Cumbria*   L F NOWEN
ST CATHERINE'S *Bramley*   C DE F TICKNER
ST CECILIA'S WANDSWORTH CHURCH OF ENGLAND
   P A KURK
ST COLUMBA'S *Dublin*   N N CROSSEY
ST DAVID'S COLLEGE *Llandudno*   T R HALL
ST EDMUND'S *Canterbury*   R P PRANCE
ST EDWARD'S *Oxford*   R K F BUSHYAGER, E C KERR
ST FRANCIS XAVIER *Richmond*   P J MATTHEWS
ST GEORGE'S CHURCH OF ENGLAND *Blackpool*
   A W FROUD
ST GEORGE'S *Harpenden*   A P MANNING
ST GEORGE'S *Windsor*   A S ZIHNI
ST HELEN'S AND ST KATHARINE'S *Abingdon*
   J J HERAPATH
ST HILDA'S *Whitby*   M R STANFORD
ST JOHN'S *Leatherhead*   C A CASE
ST JOSEPH'S *Wrexham*   D R ANDERSON
ST LAWRENCE COLLEGE *Ramsgate*   P R RUSSELL
ST MARY'S *Calne*   P M O GILES
ST MARY'S HALL *Brighton*   D J BIGGS,
   A H MANSON-BRAILSFORD
ST MARY'S *Westbrook*   B D R WOOD
ST MARYLEBONE CHURCH OF ENGLAND   P R THOMAS
ST OLAVE'S GRAMMAR *Orpington*   A D MCCLELLAN
ST PAUL'S *Barnes*   P L F ALLSOP
ST PAUL'S GIRLS' *Hammersmith*   V L BARON

ST PETER'S CHURCH OF ENGLAND AIDED *Exeter*
   K D N CHANDRA
ST PETER'S COLLEGIATE *Wolverhampton*   L K COLLINS
ST PETER'S *York*   J DALY
ST SAVIOUR'S AND ST OLAVE'S *Newington*   K J GRANT
ST SWITHUN'S *Winchester*   K M DYKES
SEDBERGH   P L SWEETING
SEVENOAKS   N N HENSHAW
SHERBORNE   S J N GRAY
SHIPLAKE *Henley-on-Thames*   S M COUSINS
SHREWSBURY   G W DOBBIE
SIR THOMAS BOTELER HIGH *Warrington*   J E HARRIES
SMALLWOOD MANOR PREPARATORY *Uttoxeter*
   C J CANN
SOLIHULL   A C HUTCHINSON
STAMFORD   M A S GOODMAN
STOCKPORT GRAMMAR   L E J LEAVER
STOWE *Buckingham*   R B JACKSON
STRATHALLAN *Perth*   R A M T QUICK
ST MARY REDCLIFFE AND TEMPLE *Bristol*
   W L HOUGH
SUTTON VALENCE *Kent*   P A KISH
TALBOT HEATH *Bournemouth*   C M LANGFORD
TAVERHAM HALL *Norwich*   R W B MASSINGBERD-MUNDY
TONBRIDGE   S M BEAUMONT, T D PAGE, D A PETERS
TRENT COLLEGE *Nottingham*   T R HAGGIS
TRINITY *Belvedere*   R J IRETON
TRINITY *Teignmouth*   C M S LUFF
TUDOR HALL *Banbury*   J F JACKSON
UPPINGHAM *Leicestershire*   J B J SAUNDERS
WAKEFIELD CATHEDRAL   J M WARE
WARMINSTER   A G WATTS
WARWICK   A W GOUGH
WELLINGBOROUGH   M J WALKER
WELLINGTON COLLEGE *Berkshire*   T W G NOVIS
WELLINGTON *Somerset*   J P HELLIER
WELLS CATHEDRAL   J M HULME
WEST BUCKLAND *Barnstaple*   A M KETTLE
WEST OF ENGLAND *School for those with little or no sight*
   P J S CROCKETT
WESTMINSTER   J W CROSSLEY, G J WILLIAMS
WESTONBIRT   P DIXON
WINCHESTER COLLEGE   P A BURT, J M WHITE
WISPERS *Haslemere*   N JONES
WOODBRIDGE   I A WILSON
WORKSOP COLLEGE *Nottinghamshire*   P FINLINSON
WREN ACADEMY *London*   S T KIRBY
WYCLIFFE PREPARATORY   S P PHILLIPSON-MASTERS
WYCOMBE ABBEY *High Wycombe*   J F CHAFFEY
WYMONDHAM COLLEGE   I JONES

THEOLOGICAL COLLEGES AND COURSES

This index includes the name of the principal or warden and the names of staff members who are Anglican clergy and whose appointments are at least half-time.

Theological Colleges

Church of Ireland Theological College
Braemor Park, Dublin 14, Republic of Ireland
Tel (00353) (1) 492 3506 Fax 492 3082
E-mail admin@citc.ie
PRIN M J ELLIOTT TUTORS/LECTS T W GORDON, P COMERFORD

College of the Resurrection
Stocks Bank Road, Mirfield WF14 0BW
Tel (01924) 490441 Fax 492738
E-mail jkennedy@mirfield.org.uk
PRIN J KENNEDY VICE-PRIN P G ALLAN CR
TUTOR/LECT J GRIBBEN CR, B N GORDON-TAYLOR, J E COOPER

Cranmer Hall
St John's College, 3 South Bailey, Durham DH1 3RJ
Tel 0191–334 3500 Fax 334 3501
E-mail sj-cranmer-hall@durham.ac.uk
PRIN S D WILKINSON[1] WARDEN A C DYER
DIR MISS AND PIONEER MIN M J VOLLAND
DIR UNDERGRADUATE STUDIES G L MORLEY
DIR MINL PRACTICE D J GOODHEW

Oak Hill College
Chase Side, London N14 4PS
Tel (020) 8449 0467 Fax 8441 5996
E-mail mailbox@oakhill.ac.uk
PRIN M J OVEY VICE-PRIN C M GREEN
TUTORS/LECTS R J PORTER, G M N RAIKES, M T SLEEMAN

The Queen's College
Somerset Road, Edgbaston, Birmingham B15 2QH
Tel 0121–454 1527 Fax 454 8171
E-mail enquire@queens.ac.uk
PRIN D J P HEWLETT TUTOR/LECT M R EAREY

Ridley Hall
Ridley Hall Road, Cambridge CB3 9HG
Tel (01223) 741080 Fax 741081
E-mail ridley-pa@lists.cam.ac.uk
PRIN A R NORMAN VICE-PRIN M B THOMPSON
DIR PAST STUDIES R A HIGGINSON TUTORS/LECTS P P JENSON,
P S HESLAM, P D A WESTON, J E KEILLER, D C R MCFADYEN,
D E MALE, A C WALTON, A F CHATFIELD, G CHATFIELD

Ripon College
Cuddesdon, Oxford OX44 9EX
Tel (01865) 874404 Fax 875431
E-mail enquiries@ripon-cuddesdon.ac.uk
PRIN M W PERCY VICE-PRIN AND LECT M D CHAPMAN
DEAN STUDIES M J WHIPP
TUTORS/LECTS D S HEYWOOD, A R TEAL, P N TOVEY,
H-A M HARTLEY

St John's College
Chilwell Lane, Bramcote, Beeston, Nottingham NG9 3DS
Tel 0115–925 1114 Fax 943 6438
E-mail enquiries@stjohns-nottm.ac.uk
PRIN C BAXTER[2] DEAN N M LADD DEAN STUDIES I B PAUL
DIR EXT STUDIES E M TURNER
TUTORS/LECTS S D DYAS, P NASH, T D HULL, A P BOWSHER

St Michael and All Angels' College
54 Cardiff Road, Llandaff, Cardiff CF5 2YJ
Tel (029) 2056 3379 Fax 2083 8008
E-mail info@stmichaels.ac.uk
PRIN P H SEDGWICK VICE-PRIN S B ROBERTS
DEAN MIN STUDIES S P ADAMS DEAN NON-RES TR P J ROBERTS
DEAN CHAPL STUDIES A J TODD

St Stephen's House
16 Marston Street, Oxford OX4 1JX
Tel (01865) 613500 Fax 613513
E-mail enquiries@ssho.ox.ac.uk
PRIN R WARD VICE-PRIN D P A FEENEY
TUTOR A P DAVISON

Theological Institute of the Scottish Episcopal Church
21 Grosvenor Crescent, Edinburgh EH12 5EE
Tel 0131–225 6357 Fax 346 7247
E-mail tisec@scotland.anglican.org
PRIN M J FULLER

Trinity College
Stoke Hill, Bristol BS9 1JP
Tel 0117–968 2803 Fax 968 7470
E-mail principal@trinity-bris.ac.uk
PRIN G I KOVOOR VICE-PRIN AND SEN TUTOR D WENHAM
DIR PAST STUDIES W D MACDOUGALL
TUTORS/LECTS R P SYMMONS, J CORRIE, J SEARS, N A D SCOTLAND,
E G INESON, S M ARNOLD, J L NOLLAND

Westcott House
Jesus Lane, Cambridge CB5 8BP
Tel (01223) 741000 Fax 741002
E-mail general-enquiries@westcott.cam.ac.uk
PRIN M A SEELEY VICE-PRIN N M R BEASLEY
DIR STUDIES V E RAYMER TUTOR A C W TILBY

Wycliffe Hall
54 Banbury Road, Oxford OX2 6PW
Tel (01865) 274200 Fax 274215
E-mail enquiries@wycliffe.ox.ac.uk
PRIN R D TURNBULL VICE-PRIN S D N VIBERT
DIR CH LEADERSHIP W R DONALDSON
TUTORS P W L WALKER, J R WILLIAMS, E A HOARE,
A C ATHERSTONE, J E ROBSON

Regional Courses

Eastern Region Ministry Course
Wesley House, Jesus Lane, Cambridge CB5 8BJ
Tel (01223) 741026 Fax 741027
E-mail secretary@ermc.cam.ac.uk
PRIN I M MCINTOSH VICE-PRIN S A WOAN
CO-DIR PAST STUDIES E C CARDALE, E L GRIFFITHS
TUTOR R M MORGAN

East Midlands Ministry Training Course
Room C90, School of Continuing Education,
University of Nottingham, Jubilee Campus,
Wollaton Road, Nottingham NG8 1BB
Tel 0115–951 4854 Fax 951 4817
E-mail emmtc@nottingham.ac.uk
VICE-PRIN I MORTON

Lancashire and Cumbria Theological Partnership
Church House, West Walls, Carlisle CA3 8UE
Tel (01228) 522573 Fax 815400
E-mail admin@lctp.org.uk
PRIN T D HERBERT VICE- PRINS R A LATHAM, S J WILLIAMS

Lindisfarne Regional Training Partnership
Church House, St John's Terrace, North Shields NE29 6HS
Tel 0191 270 4100
E-mail enquiries@lindisfarnertp.org
PRIN C ROWLING DIR IME R L SIMPSON TUTORS M L BECK,
R K BRYANT,

North Thames Ministerial Training Course
The Crypt, St George-in-the-East, 16 Cannon Street Road,
London E1 0BH
Tel (020) 7481 9477 Fax 7481 8907
E-mail admin@ntmtc.org.uk
PRIN D H K HILBORN DIR LAY MIN STUDIES D P RITCHIE
TUTORS J F GANGA, A V COLEMAN

Oxford Ministry Course
Ripon College, Cuddesdon, Oxford OX44 9EX
Tel (01865) 208260 Fax 790470
PRIN M W PERCY VICE-PRIN G HEGARTY DIR STUDIES T J N NAISH

---

[1] Dr Wilkinson is a Methodist.   [2] Dr Baxter is a lay person.

St Paul's Theological Centre
Holy Trinity Brompton, Brompton Road, London SW7 1JA
Tel 08456–447533
E-mail sptc@htb.org.uk
PRIN G S TOMLIN   DIR A N EMERTON   TUTOR M F LLOYD

The South East Institute for Theological Education
Ground Floor, Sun Pier House, Medway Street,
Chatham ME4 4HF
Tel (01634) 846683 Fax 819347
E-mail principal@seite.fsnet.co.uk
PRIN J F WORTHEN   VICE-PRIN J P H ALLAIN CHAPMAN
TUTOR A R ANGEL

Southern North West Training Partnership
Aiken Hall, University of Chester, Crab Lane, Fernhead,
Warrington WA2 0BD
Tel (01925) 534373
E-mail snwtp@chester.ac.uk
PRIN THE VEN J APPLEGATE

Southern Theological Education and Training Scheme
19 The Close, Salisbury SP1 2EE
Tel (01722) 424820 Fax 424811
E-mail ayoung@stets.ac.uk
PRIN V P WHITE   VICE PRIN D A HOLGATE
DIR VOC STUDIES P J SEDDON   TUTORS K O'LOUGHLIN, P OVEREND,
S A GROOM

South West Ministry Training Course
Amory Building, University of Exeter, Rennes Drive, Exeter
EX4 4RJ
Tel (01392) 264403 E-mail
admin@swmtc.org.uk
PRIN D G MOSS   DIR READER TR J W F THEODOSIUS
TUTORS S SHEPPARD, P J SOUBUT

West Midlands Ministerial Training Course
The Queen's Foundation, Somerset Road, Edgbaston,
Birmingham B15 2QH
Tel 0121–454 1527
E-mail enquire@queens.ac.uk
PRIN D J P HEWLETT

West of England Ministerial Training Course
University of Gloucestershire, Francis Close Hall,
Swindon Road, Cheltenham GL50 4AZ
Tel and fax (01242) 714857 Fax 714641
E-mail office@wemtc.freeserve.co.uk
PRIN M W S PARSONS   VICE-PRIN R F DABORN   TUTOR H M BURN

Yorkshire Ministry Course
Mirfield Centre, Stocks Bank Road, Mirfield WF14 0BW
Tel (01924) 481925 Fax 481922
E-mail office@ymc.org.uk
PRIN C GORE   DIR PAST STUDIES T S EVANS   TUTOR S C SPENCER

Ordained Local Ministry Schemes

Canterbury OLM Scheme
Diocesan House, Lady Wootton's Green, Canterbury CT1 1NQ
Tel (01227) 459401 Fax 450964 E-mail ikhovacs@diocant.org
PRIN I KHOVACS

Gloucester OLM Scheme
4 College Green, Gloucester GL1 2LR
Tel (01452) 410022 ext 231 Fax 382905
E-mail dhoyle@glosdioc.org.uk
DIR D M HOYLE

Guildford Diocesan Ministry Course
Diocesan House, Quarry Street, Guildford GU1 3XG
Tel (01483) 790319
E-mail steve.summers@cofeguildford.org.uk
DIR S B SUMMERS

Hereford Local Ministry Scheme
The Cottage, Bishop Mascall Centre, Lower Galdeford, Ludlow
SY8 1RZ
Tel (01584) 872822 Fax 877945
E-mail a.holding@hereford.anglican.org
DIR G H EARNEY

Lichfield OLM Scheme
Backcester Lane, Lichfield WS13 6JJ
Tel (01543) 306225 Fax 306229
E-mail elizabeth.jordan@lichfield.anglican.org
DIR E A JORDAN

Manchester OLM Scheme
Church House, 90 Deansgate, Manchester M3 2GJ
Tel 0161–828 1455
E-mail preiss@manchester.anglican.org
DIR P H REISS

Newcastle OLM Scheme
Church House, St John's Terrace, North Shields NE29 6HS
Tel 0191–270 4150 Fax 270 4101
E-mail r.bryant@newcastle.anglican.org
PRIN R K BRYANT

Norwich OLM Scheme
Emmaus House, 65 The Close, Norwich NR1 4DH
Tel (01603) 611196 Fax 766476
E-mail suewoan@norwich.anglican.org
DIR S A WOAN

Oxford OLM Scheme
Oxford Ministry Course, Diocesan Church House,
North Hinksey Lane, Botley, Oxford OX2 0NB
Tel (01865) 208252
E-mail beren.hartless@oxford.anglican.org
PRIN B I DE LA T HARTLESS

St Edmundsbury and Ipswich Diocesan Ministry Course
Abbey House, Angel Hill, Bury St Edmunds IP33 1LS
Tel (01284) 749435
E-mail sheila@stedmundsbury.anglican.org
PRIN C AMJAD-ALI

Salisbury OLM Scheme
Board of Ministry, Church House, Crane Street,
Salisbury SP1 2QB
Tel (01722) 411944 Fax 411990
E-mail david.heslop@salisbury.anglican.org
PRIN D A HESLOP VICE-PRIN R BROWN

BISHOPS OF ANGLICAN DIOCESES OVERSEAS

AUSTRALIA

PROVINCE OF NEW SOUTH WALES

Armidale
Peter Robert Brain
Anglican Diocesan Registry, PO Box 198,
Armidale, NSW, Australia 2350
Tel (0061) (2) 6772 4491
Fax (0061) (2) 6772 9261
E-mail diocarm@northnet.com.au

Bathurst
Richard Warwick Hurford
PO Box 23, Bathurst, NSW, Australia 2795
Tel (0061) (2) 6331 1722
Fax (0061) (2) 6332 2772
E-mail
bishop.hurford@bathurstanglican.org.au

(Assistant)
Peter Thomas Danaher
PO Box 619, Dubbo, NSW, Australia 2830
Tel (0061) (2) 6882 2670
Fax (0061) (2) 6881 6740
E-mail peterdanaher@bigpond.com

Canberra and
Goulburn
Stuart Peter Robinson
GPO Box 1981, Canberra,
ACT, Australia 2601
Tel (0061) (2) 6248 0811
Fax (0061) (2) 6247 6829
E-mail Stuart.robinson@anglicancg.org.au

(Assistants)
Allan Bowers Ewing
GPO Box 1981, Canberra,
ACT, Australia 2601
Tel (0061) (2) 6248 0666
Fax (0061) (2) 6247 6829
E-mail allan.ewing@anglicancg.org.au

Trevor William Edwards
28 McBryde Crescent, Wanniassa, ACT 2903
Tel (0061) (2) 6231 7347
Fax (0061) (2) 6231 7500
E-mail trevor@stmattswanniassa.org.au

Grafton
Keith Francis Slater
Bishopsholme, PO Box 4,
Grafton, NSW, Australia 2460
Tel (0061) (2) 6643 4122
Fax (0061) (2) 6643 1814
E-mail angdiog@nor.com.au

Newcastle
Brian George Farran
The Bishop's Registry, PO Box 817,
Newcastle, NSW, Australia 2300
Tel (0061) (2) 4926 3733
Fax (0061) (2) 4936 1968 *or* 4925 2526
E-mail bishop@angdon.com

(Assistant)
Peter Derrick James Stuart
PO Box 817,
Newcastle, NSW, Australia 2300
Tel (0061) (2) 4926 3733
Fax (0061) (2) 4926 1968
E-mail bishoppeter@angdon.com

Riverina
Douglas Robert Stephens
PO Box 10, Narrandera,
NSW, Australia 2700
Tel (0061) (2) 6959 1648
Fax (0061) (2) 6959 2903
E-mail rivdio@dragnet.com.au

Sydney
(Archbishop
and
Metropolitan)
Peter Frederick Jensen
PO Box Q190, Queen Victoria Buildings,
Sydney, NSW, Australia 1230
Tel (0061) (2) 9265 1521
Fax (0061) (2) 9265 1504
E-mail res@sydney.anglican.asn.au

(Liverpool)
Peter John Tasker
address as above
Tel (0061) (2) 9265 1530
Fax (0061) (2) 9265 1543
E-mail ptasker@sydney.anglican.asn.au

(North
Sydney)
Glenn Naunton Davies
address as above
Tel (0061) (2) 9265 1533
Fax (0061) (2) 9265 1543
E-mail gdavies@sydney.anglican.asn.au

(Western
Sydney,
formerly
Parramatta)
Ivan Yin Lee
PO Box 129, Parramatta,
NSW, Australia 2124
Tel (0061) (2) 8023 6700
Fax (0061) (2) 9689 3636
E-mail ilee@westernsydney.anglican.asn.au

(South
Sydney)
Robert Charles Forsyth
PO Box Q190, Queen Victoria Buildings,
Sydney, NSW, Australia 1230
Tel (0061) (2) 9265 1501
Fax (0061) (2) 9265 1543
E-mail robforsyth@sydney.anglican.asn.au

(Wollongong)
Alan James Stewart
74 Church Street, Wollongong,
NSW, Australia 2500
Tel (0061) (2) 4201 1800
Fax (0061) (2) 4228 4296
E-mail astewart@wollongong.anglican.asn.au

PROVINCE OF QUEENSLAND

Brisbane
(Archbishop
and Primate)
Phillip John Aspinall
PO Box 421, Brisbane, Qld, Australia 4001
Tel (0061) (7) 3835 2222
Fax (0061) (7) 3832 5030
E-mail archbishop@anglicanbrisbane.org.au

(Northern
Region)
Jonathan Charles Holland
address as above
Tel (0061) (7) 3835 2213
Fax (0061) (7) 3832 5030
E-mail jholland@anglicanbrisbane.org.au

(Southern
Region)
Geoffrey Martyn Smith
address as above
Tel (0061) (7) 3420 6941
Fax (0061) (7) 3420 6216

(Western
Region)
Robert William Nolan
PO Box 2600, Toowoomba, Qld, Australia 4350
Tel (0061) (7) 4639 1875
Fax (0061) (7) 4632 6882
E-mail molan@anglicanbrisbane.org.au

North
Queensland
William James Ray
PO Box 1244, Townsville, Qld, Australia 4810
Tel (0061) (7) 4771 4175
Fax (0061) (7) 4721 1756
E-mail bishopnq@anglicannq.org

(Torres Strait
Islander
Bishop)
Saibo Mabo
PO Box 714, Thursday Island, Qld, Australia
1075
Tel (0061) (7) 4069 1960
E-mail bishopti@anglicannq.org

(National
Aboriginal
Bishop)
James Randolph Leftwich
14 Village Terrace, Redlynch, Qld, Australia 4870
Fax (0061) (7) 4058 1090
E-mail diocesecairns@bigpond.com

Northern
Territory, The
Gregory Edwin Thompson
PO Box 2950, Darwin, NT, Australia
0801
Tel (0061) (8) 8941 7440
Fax (0061) (8) 8941 7446 *or* 8941 7227
E-mail ntdiocese@internode.on.net

Rockhampton
Godfrey Charles Fryar
PO Box 6158, Central Queensland Mail Centre,
Rockhampton, Qld, Australia 4702
Tel (0061) (7) 4927 3188
Fax (0061) (7) 4922 4562
E-mail bishop@anglicanrock.org.au

PROVINCE OF SOUTH AUSTRALIA

Adelaide
(Archbishop
and
Metropolitan)
Jeffrey William Driver
26 King William Road,
North Adelaide, S Australia 5006
Tel (0061) (8) 8305 9350
Fax (0061) (8) 8305 9399
E-mail archbishop@adelaide.anglican.com.au

(Assistant)
Stephen Kim Pickard
address, tel and fax as above
E-mail spickard@adelaide.anglican.com.au

The Murray	Ross Owen Davies 23 Ellendale Avenue, PO Box 394, Murray Bridge, S Australia 5253 Tel (0061) (8) 8532 2270 Fax (0061) (8) 8532 5760 E-mail registry@murray.anglican.org
Willochra	Garry John Weatherill Bishop's House, Main North Road, Gladstone, S Australia 5473 Tel (0061) (8) 8662 2249 Fax (0061) (8) 8662 2070 E-mail bishop@diowillochra.org.au

PROVINCE OF VICTORIA

Ballarat	Michael George Hough PO Box 89, Ballarat, Vic, Australia 3350 Tel (0061) (3) 5331 1183 Fax (0061) (3) 5332 2982 E-mail bishop@ballaratanglican.au
Bendigo	Andrew William Curnow PO Box 2, Bendigo, Vic, Australia 3552 Tel (0061) (3) 5443 4711 Fax (0061) (3) 5441 2173 E-mail bishop@bendigoanglican.org.au
Gippsland	John Charles McIntyre PO Box 928, Sale, Vic, Australia 3853 Tel (0061) (3) 5144 2044 Fax (0061) (3) 5144 7183 E-mail bishop@gippsanglican.org.au
Melbourne (Archbishop)	Philip Leslie Freier The Anglican Centre, 209 Flinders Lane, Melbourne, Vic, Australia 3000 Tel (0061) (3) 9653 4220 Fax (0061) (3) 9650 2184 E-mail archbishopsoffice@melbourne.anglican.com.au
(Eastern Region)	Stephen John Hale *address, tel and fax as above* E-mail shale@melbourne.anglican.com.au
(North- western Region)	Philip James Huggins *address, tel and fax as above* E-mail phuggins@melbourne.anglican.com.au
(Southern Region)	Paul Raymond White *address and tel as above* Fax (0061) (3) 9653 4268 E-mail sthregbishop@melbourne.anglican.au
Wangaratta	Anthony John Parkes Bishop's Lodge, PO Box 457, Wangaratta, Vic, Australia 3676 Tel (0061) (3) 5721 3484 Fax (0061) (3) 5722 1427 E-mail bishop@wangaratta.anglican.org

PROVINCE OF WESTERN AUSTRALIA

Bunbury	William David Hair McCall Bishopscourt, PO Box 15, Bunbury, W Australia 6231 Tel (0061) (8) 9721 2100 Fax (0061) (8) 9791 2300 E-mail bishop@bunbury.org.au
North West Australia	David Gray Mulready PO Box 2783, Geraldton, W Australia 6531 Tel (0061) (8) 9921 7277 Fax (0061) (8) 9964 2220 E-mail bishop@anglicandnwa.org
Perth (Archbishop and Metropolitan)	Roger Adrian Herft GPO Box W2067, Perth, W Australia 6001 Tel (0061) (8) 9325 7455 Fax (0061) (8) 9325 6741 E-mail archbishop@perth.anglican.org
(Assistant Bishops)	Kay Maree Goldsworthy *address, tel and fax as above* E-mail kgoldsworthy@perth.anglican.org Tom Wilmot *address, tel and fax as above* E-mail twilmot@perth.anglican.org

EXTRA-PROVINCIAL DIOCESES

Defence Force (and Bishop Assistant to the Primate)	Leonard Sidney Eacott Department of Defence, DSG-Duntroon, ACT, Australia 2600 Tel (0061) (2) 9265 9935 Fax (0061) (2) 9265 9959 E-mail dfc@anglican.org.au
Tasmania	John Douglas Harrower GPO Box 748, Hobart, Tas, 7001 Tel (0061) (3) 6220 2015 Fax (0061) (3) 6223 8968 E-mail bishop@anglicantas.org.au

BRAZIL

Amazon	Saulo Mauricio de Barros Av. Sezerdelo Correia, 514, Batista Campos, 66025–240, Belem, PA, Brazil Tel: (0055) (91) 3241 9720 *fax as telephone* E-mail sbarros@ieab.org.br
Brasilia (Primate)	Maurício José Araújo de Andrade EQS 309/310, sala 1 – Asa Sul, Caixa Postal 093, 70.359–970, Brasilia, Brazil Tel (0055) (61) 443 4305 Fax (0055) (61) 443 4337 E-mail mandrade@ieab.org.br
Curitiba	Naudal Alves Gomes Rua Sete de Setembro, 3927 – Centro, 80250–010 Curitiba, PR, Brazil Tel (0055) (41) 3232 0917 E-mail ngomes@ieab.org.br
Pelotas	Renato da Cruz Raatz Rua Felix da Cunha, 425 – Centro, Caixa Postal Caixa Postal 791, 96001–970 Pelotas, RS, Brazil Tel (0055) (532) 277120 *fax as telephone* E-mail rcraatz@ieab.org.br
Recife	Sebastião Armando Gameleira Soares Rua Virgílio Mota, 70, Parnamirim, 52060–582, Recife, PE, Brazil Tel (0055) (81) 3441 6843 E-mail seags@terra.com.br
(Suffragan)	Filadelfo Oliveira Neto Av. Cons. Aguiar, 2178/602 Boa Viagem 51020–970 Recife, PE, Brazil Tel (0055) (81) 3326 8078 Fax (0055) (81) 3467 6508 E-mail foliveira@ieab.org.br
Rio de Janeiro	Filadelfo Oliveira Neto Rua Fonseca Guimarães, 12 Sta.Teresa, 20240–260, Rio de Janeiro, RJ, Brazil Tel (0055) (21) 2220 2148 Fax (0055) (21) 2252 9686 E-mail foliveira@ieab.org.br
São Paulo	Roger Douglas Bird Rua Borges Lagoa 172 Vila Clementino 04038–020, São Paulo, SP, Brazil Tel (0055) (11) 5549 9011 Fax (0055) (11) 5083 2619 E-mail dasp.br@dasp.org.br
South Western Brazil	Jubal Pereira Neves Av. Rio Branco, 880 / Sub-solo – Centro, Caixa Postal 116, Santa Maria, RS, Brazil Tel (0055) (55) 3223 4328 *fax as telephone* E-mail jneves@ieab.org.br
Southern Brazil	Orlando Santos de Oliveira Av. Eng. Ludolfo Boehl, 278, Teresópolis, 91720–150, Porto Alegre, RS, Brazil Tel (0055) (51) 318 6199 *fax as telephone* E-mail osoliveira@ieab.org.br

BURMA (MYANMAR)

Hpa-an
Saw Stylo
No (4) Block, Bishop Gone, Diocesan Office,
Hpa-an, Kayin State , Myanmar
Tel (0095) (58) 21696
Fax (0095) (1) 77512

Mandalay
Noel Nay Lin
Bishopscourt, 22nd Street, 'C' Road
(between 85–86 Road), Mandalay, Myanmar
Tel (0095) (2) 34110

Mytikyina
David Than Lwin
Diocesan Office, Tha Kin Nat Pe Road,
Thida Ya, Myitkyina, Kachin State, Myanmar
Tel (0095) (74) 23104

(Assistant)
Gam Dee
address etc as above

Sittwe
Barnabas Theaung Hawi
St John's Church, Paletwa,
Southern Chin State, via Sittwe, Myanmar

Toungoo
Saw John Wilme
Diocesan Office, Nat-shin-Naung Road,
Toungoo, Myanmar
Tel (0095) (54) 23519

Yangon
(Archbishop)
Stephen Than Myint Oo
PO Box 11191,
140 Pyidaungsu-Yeiktha Rd, Dagon,
Yangon, Myanmar
Tel (0095) (1) 395350
Fax (0095) (1) 251 405

(Assistant)
Samuel Htan Oak
44 Pyi Road, Dagon,
Yangon, Myanmar
Tel (0095) (1) 372 300

BURUNDI

Bujumbura
Pie Ntukamazina
BP 1300, Bujumbura, Burundi
Tel (00257) (22) 222 641
Fax (00257) (22) 227 495
E-mail mgrpie@cbinf.com *or*
bishoppie@yahoo.com

Buye
Sixbert Macumi
Eglise Episcopale du Burundi,
BP 94, Ngozi, Burundi
Tel (00257) (22) 302 210
Fax (00257) (22) 302 317
E-mail buyedioc@yahoo.fr

Gitega
Jean W Nduwayo
BP 23, Gitega, Burundi
Tel (00257) (22) 402 247
E-mail eebgitega@cbinf.com

Makamba
Martin Blaise Nyaboho
BP 96, Makamba, Burundi
Tel (00257) (22) 508 080
Fax (00257) (22) 229 129
E-mail eabdiocmak@yahoo.fr

Matana
(Archbishop)
Bernard Ntahoturi
BP 447, Bujumbura, Burundi
Tel (00257) (22) 924 595
Fax (00257) (22) 229 129
E-mail ntahober@cbinf.com

Muyinga
Eraste Bigirimana
BP 55, Muyinga, Burundi
Tel (00257) (22) 306 019
Fax (00257) (22) 306 152
E-mail bigirimanaerast@yahoo.fr

CANADA

Primate of
Canada
Fred J Hiltz
80 Hayden Street, Toronto ON,
Canada, M4Y 3G2
Tel (001) (416) 924 9192
Fax (001) (416) 924 0211
E-mail primate@national.anglican.ca *or*
glight@national.anglican.ca

PROVINCE OF BRITISH COLUMBIA AND YUKON

British Columbia
James A J Cowan
900 Vancouver Street,
Victoria BC, Canada, V8V 3V7
Tel (001) (250) 386 7781
Fax (001) (250) 386 4013
E-mail synod@bc.anglican.ca

Caledonia
William J Anderson
PO Box 278, Prince Rupert BC,
Canada, V8J 3P6
Tel (001) (250) 624 6013
Fax (001) (250) 624 4299
E-mail synodofc@citytel.net

Anglican
Parishes of the
Central Interior
Vacancy
c/o St. Paul's Cathedral, 360 Nicola
St, Kamloops, BC, Canada, V2C 2P5
Tel (001) (250) 819 5753
E-mail apcioffice@shawbiz.ca

Kootenay
John E Privett
1876 Richter Street,
Kelowna BC, Canada, V1Y 2M9
Tel (001) (250) 762 3306
Fax (001) (250) 762 4150
E-mail diocese_of_kootenay@telus.net

New
Westminster
Michael C Ingham
580, 401 W Georgia Street,
Vancouver BC, Canada, V6B 5A1
Tel (001) (604) 684 6306
Fax (001) (604) 684 7017
E-mail bishop@vancouver.anglican.ca

Yukon
(Archbishop
and
Metropolitan)
Terrence O Buckle
PO Box 31136, Whitehorse YT,
Canada, Y1A 3T3
Tel (001) (867) 667 7746
Fax (001) (867) 667 6125
E-mail synodoffice@klondiker.com

PROVINCE OF CANADA

Central
Newfoundland
F David Torraville
34 Fraser Road, Gander NL,
Canada, A1V 2E8
Tel (001) (709) 256 2372
Fax (001) (709) 256 2396
E-mail bishopcentral@nfld.net

Eastern
Newfoundland
and Labrador
Cyrus C J Pitman
19 King's Bridge Road,
St John's NL, Canada, A1C 3K4
Tel (001) (709) 576 6697
Fax (001) (709) 576 7122
E-mail cpitman@anglicanenl.nf.net

Fredericton
Claude E W Miller
115 Church Street,
Fredericton NB, Canada, E3B 4C8
Tel (001) (506) 459 1801
Fax (001) (506) 460 0520
E-mail diocese@anglican.nb.ca

Montreal
Barry B Clarke
1444 Union Avenue,
Montreal QC, Canada, H3A 2B8
Tel (001) (514) 843 6577
Fax (001) (514) 843 3221
E-mail bishops.office@montreal.anglican.org

Nova Scotia
and Prince
Edward Island
Susan Moxley
5732 College Street,
Halifax NS, Canada, B3H 1X3
Tel (001) (902) 420 0717
Fax (001) (902) 425 0717
E-mail office@nspeidiocese.ca

Quebec
Dennis P. Drainville
31 rue des Jardins,
Quebec QC, Canada, G1R 4L6
Tel (001) (418) 692 3858
Fax (001) (418) 692 3876
E-mail synodoffice@quebec.anglican.ca

Western
Newfoundland
Percy D Coffin
25 Main Street, Corner Brook NF,
Canada, A2H 1C2
Tel (001) (709) 639 8712
Fax (001) (709) 639 1636
E-mail dsown@nf.aibn.ca

PROVINCE OF ONTARIO

Algoma	Stephen Andrews, PO Box 1168, Sault Ste Marie ON, Canada, P6A 5N7 Tel (001) (705) 256 5061 Fax (001) (705) 946 1860 E-mail bishop@dioceseofalgoma.com
Huron	Robert F. Bennett, 190 Queens Avenue, London ON, Canada, N6A 6H7 Tel (001) (519) 434 6893 Fax (001) (519) 673 4151 E-mail bishops@huron.anglican.org
(Suffragan)	Terrance A. Dance *address etc as above*
Moosonee (Archbishop and Metropolitan)	Caleb James Lawrence Box 841, Schumacher ON, Canada, P0N 1G0 Tel (001) (705) 360 1129 Fax (001) (705) 360 1120 E-mail dmoose@domaa.ca
Niagara	Michael A Bird Cathedral Place, 252 James Street N, Hamilton ON, Canada, L8R 2L3 Tel (001) (905) 527 1316 Fax (001) (905) 527 1281 E-mail bishop@niagara.anglican.ca
Ontario	George L R Bruce 90 Johnson Street, Kingston ON, Canada, K7L 1X7 Tel (001) (613) 544 4774 Fax (001) (613) 547 3745 E-mail gbruce@ontario.anglican.ca
Ottawa	John H. Chapman 71 Bronson Avenue, Ottawa ON, Canada, K1R 6G6 Tel (001) (613) 232 7124 *or* 233 7741 ext 223 Fax (001) (613) 232 3955 E-mail ann-day@ottawa.anglican.ca
Toronto	Colin R Johnson 135 Adelaide Street East, Toronto ON, Canada, M5C 1L8 Tel (001) (416) 363 6021 Fax (001) (416) 363 3683 *or* 363 7678 E-mail cjohnson@toronto.anglican.ca *or* diocese@toronto.anglican.ca
(York-Simcoe)	George Elliott 2174 King Rd, Suite 2, King City ON, Canada, L7B 1L6 Tel (001) (905) 833 8327 Fax (001) (905) 833 8329 E-mail ysimcoe@neptune.on.ca
(York Credit Valley)	M Philip Poole 256 Sheldon Avenue, Etobicoke ON, Canada M8W 4X8 Tel (001) (416) 503 9903 Fax (001) (416) 503 8229 E-mail office@yorkcvalleyanglican.com
(Trent-Durham)	Linda Nicholls 965 Dundas St West, Suite 207, Whitby, ON, Canada L1P 1G8 Tel (001) (905) 668 1558 Fax (001) (905) 668 8216 E-mail lnicholls@toronto.anglican.ca
(York- Scarborough)	Patrick Yu Bishop's Room, St Paul's Church, 135 Adelaide St East, Scarborough ON, Canada, M1W 2R9 Tel (001) (416) 497 7750 Fax (001) (416) 497 4103 E-mail bys@bellnet.ca

PROVINCE OF RUPERT'S LAND

The Arctic	Andrew P. Atagotaaluk 4910 51st Street, PO Box 1454, Yellowknife NT, Canada, X1A 2P1 Tel (001) (867) 873 5432 Fax (001) (867) 837 8478 E-mail diocese@arcticnet.org
(Nunavik Region)	Benjamin T. Arreak Box 154, Kuujjuaqq, QC, Canada, J0M 1C0 Tel (001) (819) 964 2324 Fax (001) (819) 964 2113 E-mail btarreak@sympatico.ca
(Mackenzie and Kitikmeot Region)	Larry D Robertson Box 190, Yellowknife, NT, Canada, X1A 2N2 Tel (001) (867) 873 5432 Fax (001) (867) 873 8478 E-mail larryr@arcticnet.org
Athabasca	Vacant Box 6868, Peace River AB, Canada, T8S 1S6 Tel (001) (780) 624 2767 Fax (001) (780) 624 2365 E-mail dioath@telusplanet.net *or* bbpath@teleuplanet.net
Brandon	James D. Njegovan PO Box 21009, WEPO, Brandon MB, Canada, R7B 3W8 Tel (001) (204) 727 7550 Fax (001) (204) 727 4135 E-mail bishopbdn@mts.net
Calgary	Derek B E Hoskin 560 – 1207 11th Avenue SW Calgary AB, Canada, T3C 0M5 Tel (001) (403) 243 3673 Fax (001) (403) 243 2182 E-mail synod@calgary.anglican.ca
Edmonton	Jane Alexander 10035–103 Street, Edmonton AB, Canada, T5J 0X5 Tel (001) (403) 439 7344 Fax (001) (403) 439 6549 E-mail bishopv@edmonton.anglican.ca
Keewatin (Archbishop and Metropolitan)	David N Ashdown 915 Ottawa Street, Keewatin ON, Canada, P0X 1C0 Tel (001) (807) 547 3353 Fax (001) (807) 547 3356 E-mail dioceseofkeewatin@shaw.ca
Qu'Appelle	Gregory K. Kerr-Wilson 1501 College Avenue, Regina SK, Canada, S4P 1B8 Tel (001) (306) 522 1608 Fax (001) (306) 352 6808 E-mail quappelle@sasktel.net
Rupert's Land	Donald D Phillips 935 Nesbitt Bay, Winnipeg MB, Canada, R3T 1W6 Tel (001) (204) 922 4200 Fax (001) (204) 922 4219 E-mail general@rupertsland.ca
Saskatchewan	Michael W. Hawkins 1308 Fifth Avenue East, Prince Albert SK, Canada, S6V 2H7 Tel (001) (306) 763 2455 Fax (001) (306) 764 5172 E-mail synod@sasktel.net
Saskatoon	Rodney O. Andrews PO Box 1965, Saskatoon SK, Canada, S7K 3S5 Tel (001) (306) 244 5651 *or* 242 0837 Fax (001) (306) 933 4606 E-mail anglicansynod@sasktel.net

CENTRAL AFRICA

Botswana	Trevor Mwamba PO Box 679, Gaborone, Botswana Tel (00267) 395 3779 Fax (00267) 391 3015 E-mail angli_diocese@info.bw
Central Zambia	Derek Gary Kamukwanba PO Box 70172, Ndola, Zambia Tel (00260) (2) 612431 Fax (00260) (2) 615954 E-mail adcznla@zamnet.zm

Central Zimbabwe	Ishmael Mukuwanda PO Box 25, Gweru, Zimbabwe Tel (00263) (54) 21030 Fax (00263) (54) 21097 E-mail diocent@telconet.co.zw
Eastern Zambia	William Muchombo PO Box 510154, Chipata, Zambia Tel (00260) (62) 21294 *fax as telephone* E-mail dioeastzm@zamnet.zm
Harare	Chad Nicholas Gandiya Monmouth Road, Avondale, Harare, Zimbabwe Tel (00263) (4) 308042 E-mail diohrecpca@ecoweb.co.zw
Lake Malawi	Francis Kaulanda PO Box 30349, Lilongwe 3, Malawi Tel (00265) 797858 Fax (00265) 731966 *or* 731895
Luapula	Robert Mumbi PO Box 70210, Mansa, Luapula, Zambia
Lusaka	David Njovu Bishop's Lodge, PO Box 30183 Lusaka, Zambia Tel (00260) (1) 264515 Fax (00260) (1) 262379 E-mail dnjovu@zamnet.zm
Manicaland	Julius Makoni 115 Herbert Chitepo Street Mutare, Zimbabwe Tel (00263) (20) 64194 Fax (00262) (20) 63076 E-mail diomani@syscom.co.zw
Masvingo	Godfrey Tawonezvi PO 1421, Masvingo, Zambia Tel (00263) (39) 362 536 E-mail anglicandiomsv@comone.co.zw
Matabeleland	Wilson Sitshebo PO Box 2422, Bulawayo, Zimbabwe Tel (00263) (9) 61370 Fax (00263) (9) 68353 E-mail angdiomat@telconet.co.zw
Northern Malawi	Leslie Mtekateka PO Box 120, Mzuzu, Malawi Tel (00265) 331486 Fax (00265) 333805
Northern Zambia	Albert Chama PO Box 20798, Kitwe, Zambia Tel (00260) (2) 223 264 Fax (00260) (2) 224 778 E-mail dionorth@zamnet.zm
Southern Malawi	James Tengatenga PO Box 30220, Chichiri, Blantyre, 3, Malawi Tel (00265) (1) 641 218 Fax (00265) (1) 641 235 E-mail angsoma@sdnp.org.mw *or* jtengatenga@unima.wn.apc.org
Southern Malawi – Upper Shire (Archbishop)	Brighton Vitta Masala Private Bag 1, Chilema, Zomba, Malawi Tel (00260) (1) 539 514 *fax as telephone* E-mail dionorth@zamnet.zm

CENTRAL AMERICA

Costa Rica	Hector Monterroso Iglesia Episcopal Costarricense, Apt 10520, 1000 San Jose, Costa Rica Tel (00506) 225 0209 *or* 253 0790 Fax (00506) 253 8331 E-mail anglicancr@racsa.co.cr or iarca@amnet.co.cr
El Salvador (Primate)	Martin de Jesus Barahona 47 Avenida Sur, 723 Col Flor Blanca, Apt Postal (01), 274 San Salvador, El Salvador Tel (00503) 2 223 2252 Fax (00503) 2 223 7952 E-mail anglican.sal@integra.com.sv

Guatemala	Armando Roman Guerra-Soria Apartado 58A, Guatemala City, Guatemala Tel (00502) 2472 0852 Fax (00502) 2472 0764 E-mail diocesis@terra.com.gt *or* diocesis@infovia.com.gt
Nicaragua	Sturdie Downs Apartado 1207, Managua, Nicaragua Tel (00505) (2) 225174 Fax (00505) (2) 226701 E-mail episcnic@cablenet.com.ni *or* episcnic@tmx.com.ni
Panama	Julio Murray Box R, Balboa, Republic of Panama Tel (00507) 212 0062 Fax (00507) 262 2097 E-mail iepan@cwpanama.net *or* anglipan@sinfo.net

CEYLON (SRI LANKA)

Colombo	Duleep Kamil de Chickera 368/3A Bauddhaloka Mawatha, Colombo 7, Sri Lanka Tel (0094) (1) 684810 Fax (0094) (1) 684811 E-mail bishop@eureka.lk
Kurunegala	Kumara Bandara Samuel Illangasinghe Bishop's Office, Cathedral Close, Kurunegala, Sri Lanka Tel (0094) (37) 22191 Fax (0094) (37) 26806

CONGO (*formerly* ZAÏRE)

Aru	Georges Titre Ande PO Box 25586 Kampala, Uganda Tel (00256) (81) 393071 E-mail revdande@yahoo.co.uk
Boga	Henri Isingoma Kahwa PO Box 25586, Kampala, Uganda Tel (00256) (41) 273817 Mobile (00256) 77–647495 Fax (00256) (41) 343 497 (c/o Frédérick Ngadjole) E-mail peac_isingoma@yahoo.fr
Bukavu	Sylvestre Bahati Bali-Busane BP 134, Cyangugu, Rwanda Mobile (00243) 9861 1180 Fax (00256) (41) 343 497 (c/o Frédérick Ngadjole) E-mail anglicadiobkv@yahoo.co.uk
Katanga (formerly Shaba)	Corneille Kasima Muno PO Box 22037, Kitwe, Zambia Tel (00243) (97) 047 173 Fax (00243) (88) 46383
Kindu	Zacharie Masimango Katanda BP 5, Gisenyi, Rwanda Tel (243) 99 891 6258 Mobile (243) 813 286 255 E-mail angkindu@yahoo.fr *or* angkindu@antenna.nl
Kinshasa (Missionary diocese)	Vacancy 11 Ave. Basalakala, Quartier Immocongo Commune de Kalamu, Kinshasa 1, B.P. 16482, DR Congo Tel (00243) 998 611 180 E-mail dirokpa1@hotmail.com
(Assistants)	Jean Molanga Botola EAC Kinshasa, BP 16482, Kinshasa 1, DR Congo Mobile (00243) 908 623 508 E-mail molanga2k@yahoo.co.uk
	Abiodun Olaoye address as above Mobile (00243) 818 995 591 E-mail bishopolaoyeat@yahoo.com
Kisangani	Lambert Funga Botolome PO Box 25586, Kampala, Uganda Tel (00243) 9863 3545 Mobile (00243) 997 252 868 E-mail lambertfunga@hotmail.com

Nord Kivu	Vacancy PO Box 506, Bwera-Kasese, Uganda Mobile (00243) 983 85 509 Fax (00871) 166 1121 E-mail munzenda_eac@yahoo.fr
(Assistant)	Enoch Kayeeye *address as above*

HONG KONG

Eastern Kowloon	Louis Tsan-sang Tsui Diocesan Office, 4/F Holy Trinity Bradbury Centre, 139 Ma Tau Chung Road, Kowloon, Hong Kong, China Tel (00852) 2713 9983 Fax (00852) 2711 1609 E-mail ekoffice@ekhkskh.org.hk
Hong Kong Island (Archbishop)	Paul Kwong 25/F Wyndham Place, 40–44, Wyndham Street, Central Hong Kong SAR, China Tel (00852) 2526 5355 Fax (00852) 2525 3344 E-mail do.dhk@hkskh.org
Western Kowloon	Thomas Yee-po Soo 15/F Ultragrace Commercial Building, 5 Jordan Road, Kowloon, Hong Kong, China Tel (00852) 2783 0811 Fax (00852) 2783 0799 E-mail hkskhdwk@netvigator.com

INDIAN OCEAN

Antananarivo	Samoela Jaona Ranarivelo Evêché Anglican, Lot VK57 ter, Ambohimanoro, 101 Antananarivo, Madagascar Tel (00261) (20) 222 0827 Fax (00261) (20) 226 1331 E-mail eemdanta@dts.mg
(Assistant)	Todd McGregor *address as above*
Antsiranana	Roger Chung Po Chuen Evêché Anglican, BP 278, 201 Antsiranana, Madagascar Tel (00261) (20) 822 2650 *fax as telephone*
Fianarantsoa	Gilbert Rateloson Rakotondravelo Évêché Anglican, Manantsara, BP 1418, Madagascar
Mahajanga	Jean-Claude Andrianjafimanana BP 570, Mahajanga 401, Madagascar E-mail eemdmaha@dts.mg *or* revmctod@dts.mg
Mauritius (Archbishop)	Ian Ernest Bishop's House, Nallelamby Road, Phoenix, Mauritius Tel (00230) 686 5158 Fax (00230) 697 1096 E-mail dioang@intnet.mu
Seychelles	James Richard Wong Yin Song Bishop's House, PO Box 44, Victoria, Seychelles Tel (00248) 321 977 Fax (00248) 323 879 E-mail angdio@seychelles.net
Toamasina	Jean Paul Solo Evêché Anglican, Rue James Seth, BP 531, Toamasina 501, Madagascar Tel (00261) (20) 533 1663 Fax (00261) (20) 533 1689 E-mail eemtoam@wanadoo.mg

JAPAN

Chubu	Francis Toshiaki Mori 28–1 Meigetsu-cho, 2 chome, Showa-ku, Nagoya 466–0034, Japan Tel (0081) (52) 858 1007 Fax (0081) (52) 858 1008 E-mail office.chubu@nskk.org

Hokkaido (Primate)	Nathaniel Makoto Uematsu Kita 15 jo, Nishi 5–20, Kita-ku, Sapporo 001–0015, Japan Tel (0081) (11) 717 8181 Fax (0081) (11) 736 8377 E-mail hokkaido@nskk.org *or* bishop.hok@nskk.org
Kita Kanto	Zerubbabel Katsuichi Hirota 2–172 Sakuragi-cho, Omiya-ku, Saitama-shi, 331–0852, Japan Tel (0081) (48) 642 2680 Fax (0081) (48) 648 0358 *or* 476 7484 E-mail kitakanto@nskk.org
Kobe	Andrew Yutaka Nakamura, 5–11–1 Yamatedori, Chuo-ku, Kobe-shi 650–0011, Japan Tel (0081) (78) 351 5469 Fax (0081) (78) 382 1095 E-mail aao52850@syd.odn.ne.jp
Kyoto	Stephen Takashi Kochi 380 Okakuencho, Shimotachiuri-agaru, Karasumadori, Kamikyo-ku, Kyoto 602–8011, Japan Tel (0081) (75) 431 7204 Fax (0081) (75) 441 4238 *or* 432 6723 E-mail nskk-kyoto@mse.biglobe.ne.jp
Kyushu	Gabriel Shoji Igarashi 2–9–22 Kusakae, Chuo-ku, Fukuoka 810–0045, Japan Tel (0081) (92) 771 2050 Fax (0081) (92) 771 9857 E-mail d-kyushu@try-net.or.jp
Okinawa	David Shoji Tani 3–5–5 Meada, Urasoe-shi, Okinawa 910–2102, Japan Tel (0081) (98) 942 1101 Fax (0081) (98) 942 1102 E-mail office.okinawa@nskk.org
Osaka	Samuel Osamu Onishi 2–1–8 Matsuzaki-cho, Abeno-ku, Osaka 545–0053, Japan Tel (0081) (6) 621 2179 Fax (0081) (6) 621 3097 *or* 6219148 E-mail office.osaka@nskk.org
Tohoku	John Hiromichi Kato 2–13–15 Kokobun-cho, Aoba-ku, Sendai 980–0803, Japan Tel (0081) (22) 223 2349 Fax (0081) (22) 223 2387 E-mail hayashi.tohoku@nskk.org
Tokyo	Peter Jintaro Ueda 3–6–18 Shiba Koen, Minato-ku, Tokyo 105–0011, Japan Tel (0081) (3) 3433 0987 *or* 3433 2417 Fax (0081) (3) 3433 8678 E-mail office.tko@nskk.org
Yokohama	Laurence Yutaka Minabe 14–57 Mitsuzawa Shimo-cho, Kanagawa-ku, Yokohama 221–0852, Japan Tel (0081) (45) 321 4988 Fax (0081) (45) 321 4978 E-mail yokohama.kyouku@nskk.org

JERUSALEM AND THE MIDDLE EAST

Cyprus and the Gulf (Bishop *in*)	Michael Augustine Owen Lewis, PO Box 22075, CY 1517–Nicosia, Cyprus Tel (00357) (22) 671220 Fax (00357) (22) 674553 E-mail bishop@spidernet.com.cy *or* georgia@spidernet.com.cy
Egypt (Bishop *in*) (President)	Mouneer Hanna Anis Diocesan Office, PO Box 87, Zamalek Distribution, 11211, Cairo, Egypt Tel (0020) (2) 738 0829 Fax (0020) (2) 735 8941 E-mail bishopmouneer@gmail.com
(Suffragan) (Horn of Africa)	Andrew Proud *address etc as above*

(North Africa) Bill Musk
address etc as above
E-mail billamusk@googlemail.com

Iran (Episcopal Vicar General) Azad Marshall
St Thomas Center, Raiwind Road, PO Box 688, Lahore, Punjab, 54000, Pakistan
Tel (0092) (42) 542 0452
E-mail bishop@saintthomascenter.org

Jerusalem (Bishop *in*) Suheil Dawani
St George's Close, PO Box 9122, 20 Nablus Rd, Jerusalem 91 191, Israel
Tel (00972) (2) 627 1670
Fax (00972) (2) 627 3847
E-mail bishop@j-diocese.com

KENYA

All Saints Cathedral (Archbishop) Eliud Wabukala
PO Box 40502, 00100 Nairobi, Kenya
Tel (00254) (20) 714 755
Fax (00254) (20) 718 442/714 750
E-mail archoffice@swiftkenya.com

Bondo Johannes Otieno Angela
PO Box 240, 40601 Bondo, Kenya
Tel (00254) (335) 20415
E-mail ackbondo@swiftkenya.com

Bungoma Vacancy
PO Box 2392, 50200 Bungoma, Kenya
Tel (00254) (337) 30481
fax as telephone
E-mail ackbungoma@swiftkenya.com

Butere Michael Sande
PO Box 54, 50101 Butere, Kenya
Tel (00254) (56) 620 412
Fax (00254) (56) 620 038
E-mail ackbutere@swiftkenya.com

Eldoret Thomas Kogo
PO Box 3404, 30100 Eldoret, Kenya
Tel (00254) (321) 62785
E-mail ackeldoret@africaonline.co.ke

Embu Henry Tiras Nyaga Kathii,
PO Box 189, Embu, Kenya
Tel (00254) (68) 30614
Fax (00254) (68) 30468
E-mail ackembu@maf.org.ke *or* ackembu@swiftkenya.com

Kajiado Jeremiah John Mutua Taama
PO Box 203, 01100 Kajiado, Kenya
Tel (00254) (301) 21201
Fax (00254) (301) 21106
E-mail ackajiado@swiftkenya.com

Katakwa Zakayo Iteba Epusi
PO Box 68, 50244 Amagoro, Kenya
Tel (00254) (55) 54079
E-mail ackatakwa@swiftkenya.com

Kericho Jackson Ole Sapit

Kirinyaga Daniel Munene Ngoru
PO Box 95, 10304 Kutus, Kenya
Tel (00254) (163) 44221 *or* 44028
Fax (00254) (163) 44020
E-mail ackirinyaga@swiftkenya.com

Kitale Stephen Kewasis Nyorsok
PO Box 4176, 30200 Kitale, Kenya
Tel (00254) (325) 31631
Fax (00254) (325) 31387
E-mail ack.ktl@africaonline.co.ke

Kitui Josephat Mule
PO Box 1054, 90200 Kitui, Kenya
Tel (00254) (141) 22682
Fax (00254) (141) 22119
E-mail ackitui@swiftkenya.com

Machakos Joseph Mutie Kanuku
PO Box 282, 90100 Machakos, Kenya
Tel (00254) (145) 21379
Fax (00254) (145) 20178
E-mail ackmachakos@swiftkenya.com

Maseno North Simon Mutingole Oketch
PO Box 416, 50100 Kakamega, Kenya
Tel (00254) (331) 30729
Fax (00254) (331) 30752
E-mail ackmnorth@swiftkenya.com

Maseno South Francis Mwayi Abiero
PO Box 114, 40100 Kisumu, Kenya
Tel (00254) (35) 21297
Fax (00254) (35) 21009
E-mail ackmsouth@swiftkenya.com

Maseno West Joseph Otieno Wasonga
PO Box 793, 40600 Siaya, Kenya
Tel (00254) (334) 21483
Fax (00254) (334) 21483
E-mail ackmwest@swiftkenya.com

Mbeere Moses Masambe Nthuka
PO Box 122, 60104 Siakago, Kenya
Tel (00254) (162) 21261
Fax (00254) (162) 21083
E-mail ackmbeere@swiftkenya.com

Meru Charles Ndiga Mwendwa
PO Box 427, 60200 Meru, Kenya
Tel (00254) (64) 30719
E-mail ackmeru@swiftkenya.com *or* ackmeru@plansonline.net

Mombasa Julius Robert Katoi Kalu
Ukumbusho House, Nkrumah Road, PO Box 80072, 80100 Mombasa, Kenya
Tel (00254) (41) 231 1105
Fax (00254) (41) 231 6361
E-mail ackmsa@swiftmombasa.com

(Assistant) Lawrence Dena
address etc as above

Mt Kenya Central Isaac Maina Ng'ang'a
PO Box 121, 10200 Murang'a, Kenya
Tel (00254) (60) 30560 *or* 30559
Fax (00254) (60) 30148
E-mail ackmkcentral@wananchi.com

(Assistant) Allan Waithaka
address etc as above

Mt Kenya South Timothy Ranji
PO Box 886, 00900 Kiambu, Kenya
Tel (00254) (66) 22997 *or* 22521
Fax (00254) (66) 22408
E-mail ackmtksouth@swiftkenya.com

Mt Kenya West Joseph M Kagunda
PO Box 229, 10100 Nyeri, Kenya
Tel (00254) (61) 203 2281
E-mail ackmtkwest@africaonline.co.ke

Mumias Beneah Justin Okumu Salalah
PO Box 213, 50102 Mumias, Kenya
Tel: (00254) (333) 41476
Fax (00254) (333) 41232
E-mail ackmumias@swiftkenya.com

Nairobi Peter Njagi Njoka
PO Box 72846, 00200 Nairobi, Kenya
Tel (00254) (2) 714 755
Fax (00254) (2) 226 259
E-mail acknairobi@swiftkenya.com

Nakuru Stephen Njihia Mwangi
PO Box 56, (Moi Road), 20100 Nakuru, Kenya
Tel (00254) (37) 212155 *or* 212151
Fax (00254) (37) 44379
E-mail acknkudioc@net2000ke.com

Nambale Josiah Makhandia Were
PO Box 4, 50409 Nambale, Kenya
Tel (00254) (336) 24040
fax as telephone
E-mail acknambale@swiftkenya.com

Nyahururu Charles Gaikia Gaita
PO Box 926, 20300 Nyahururu, Kenya
Tel (00254) (365) 32179
E-mail nyahu_dc@africaonline.co.ke

Southern Nyanza James Kenneth Ochiel
PO Box 65, 40300 Homa Bay, Kenya
Tel (00254) (385) 22127
Fax (00254) (385) 22056
E-mail acksnyanza@swiftkenya.com

Taita Taveta Samson Mwakitawa Mwaluda
PO Box 75, 80300 Voi, Kenya
Tel (00254) (147) 30096
Fax (00254) (147) 30364 *or* 31387
E-mail acktaita@swiftmombasa.com

Thika Gideon Gichuhi Githiga
PO Box 214, 01000 Thika, Kenya
Tel (00254) (151) 21735 *or* 31654
Fax (00254) (151) 31544
E-mail ackthika@swiftkenya.com

KOREA

Pusan (Primate)	Solomon Jong Mo Yoon 18 Daechengdong-2ga, Chung-Ku, Pusan 600–092, Republic of Korea Tel (0082) (51) 463 5742 Fax (0082) (51) 463 5957 E-mail yoonsjm@hanmail.net
Seoul	Paul Keun Sang Kim 3 Chong-Dong, Chung-Ku, Seoul 100–120, Republic of Korea Tel (0082) (2) 735 6157 or 738 6597 Fax (0082) (2) 723 2640 E-mail 44kyung@hanmail.net
Taejon (Acting)	Michael Hi Yeon Kwon 87–6 Sunwha 2don, Chung-Ku, Taejon 302–823, Republic of Korea Tel (0082) (42) 256 9987 Fax (0082) (42) 255 8918 E-mail tdio@unitel.co.kr

MELANESIA

Banks and Torres (formerly North Vanuatu)	Nathan Tome c/o PO Box 19, Sola, Vanualava, Torba Province, Vanuatu Tel (00678) 38520 *fax as telephone*
Central Melanesia (Archbishop)	David Vunagi Church of Melanesia, PO Box 19, Honiara, Solomon Islands Tel (00677) 26601 Fax (00677) 21435 E-mail dvunagi@comphq.org.sb
Central Solomons	Charles Koete Church of Melanesia, PO Box 52, Tulagi, CIP, Solomon Islands Tel (00677) 32006 Fax (00677) 32119
Hanuato'o	Alfred Karibongi c/o Post Office, Kira Kira, Makira Province, Solomon Islands Tel (00677) 50012 E-mail ebiscobal@solomon.com.sb
Malaita	Samuel Sahu Bishop's House, PO Box 7, Auki Malaita, Solomon Islands Tel (0066) 11 4512 1071 Fax (00677) 40027 or (00872) (762) 822444 E-mail domauki@solomon.com.sb
Temotu	George Angus Takeli Bishop's House, Lluesalo, Lata, Santa Cruz, Temotu Province, Solomon Islands Tel (00677) 53080
Vanuatu	James Marvin Ligo Bishop's House, PO Box 238, Luganville, Santo, Vanuatu Tel (00678) 37065 or 36631 Fax (00678) 36631 E-mail diocese_of_vanuatu@ecunet.org
Ysabel	Richard Naramana PO Box 6, Buala, Jejevo, Ysabel Province, Solomon Islands Tel (00677) 35124 E-mail episcopal@solomon.com.sb

MEXICO

Cuernavaca	Ramiro Delgado Vera Calle Minerva No 1, Col. Delicas, CP 62330 Cuernavaca, Morelos, Mexico Tel (0052) (777) 315 2870 or 322 8035 *fax as telephone* E-mail adoc@cableonline.com.mx or diovca@edsa.net.mx
Mexico (Archbishop)	Carlos Touché-Porter Ave San Jeronimo 117, Col S Angel, Deleg A Obregon, 01000, Mexico Tel (0052) (55) 5616 3193 Tel (0052) (55) 5616 2205 E-mail diomex@netvoice.com.mx or diomex@adetel.net.mx

Northern Mexico	Marcelino Rivera Delgado Simón Bolivar 2005 Norte, Col. Mitras Centro CP 64460, Monterrey NL, Mexico Tel (0052) (81) 8333 0992 Fax (0052) (81) 8348 7362 E-mail diocesisdelnorte@att.net.mx
Southeastern Mexico	Benito Juárez-Martinez Avenida de Las Americas #73, Col Aguacatal 91130 Xalapa, Veracruz, Mexico Tel (0052) (228) 814 6951 Fax (0052) (228) 814 4387 E-mail dioste99@aol.com
Western Mexico	Lino Rodríguez-Amaro Fco. Javier Gamboa #255, Col. Sector Juarez 44100 Guadalajara, Jalisco, Mexico Tel (0052) (33) 3560 4726 Fax (0052) (33) 3616 4413 E-mail iamoccidente@prodigy.net.mx

MYANMAR *see* BURMA

NEW ZEALAND
(AOTEAROA, NEW ZEALAND AND POLYNESIA)

(Primate/ Archbishop and Co-Presiding Bishop)	Brown Turei P O Box 146, Rotorua, New Zealand Tel (0064) (7) 343 7280 Fax (0064) (7) 343 7281 E-mail pihopa.matamua@xtra.co.nz
Aotearoa (Bishop in Tai Rawhiti)	William Brown Turei PO Box 568, Gisborne, New Zealand Tel (0064) (6) 867 8856 Fax (0064) (6) 867 8859 E-mail browntmihi@xtra.co.nz
(Bishop in Te Manawa O Te Wheke)	Ngarahu Katene P O Box 146, Rotorua, New Zealand Tel (0064) (7) 348 4043 *fax as telephone* E-mail ngarahukatene@ihug.co.nz
(Bishop in Tai Tokerau)	Te Kitohi Wiremu Pikaahu PO Box 25, Paihia, Bay of Islands, New Zealand Tel (0064) (9) 402 6788 Fax (0064) (9) 402 6663 E-mail tkwp@xtra.co.nz
(Bishop in Te Waipounamu)	John Robert Kuru Gray PO Box 10086, Christchurch, New Zealand Tel (0064) (3) 389 1683 Fax (0064) (3) 389 0912 E-mail hawaipounamu@xtra.co.nz
(Bishop in Te Upoko O Te Ika)	Muru Walters 14 Amesbury Drive, Churton, Wellington, New Zealand Tel (0064) (4) 478 3549 Fax (0064) (4) 472 8863 E-mail muruwalters@xtra.co.nz
Auckland	John Campbell Paterson PO Box 37 242, Parnell, Auckland 1033, New Zealand Tel (0064) (9) 302 7202 Fax (0064) (9) 303 3321
Christchurch	Victoria Matthews PO Box 4438, Christchurch 8001, New Zealand Tel (0064) (3) 379 5950 Fax (0064) (3) 379 5954 E-mail bishop@chch.ang.org.nz
Dunedin	George Howard Douglas Connor PO Box 5445, Dunedin, New Zealand Tel (0064) (3) 477 4931 Fax (0064) (3) 477 4932 E-mail bishop@dn.anglican.org.nz
Nelson	Richard Ellena PO Box l00, Nelson, New Zealand Tel (0064) (3) 548 3124 Fax (0064) (3) 548 2125 or 548 8991 E-mail bpRichard@nelsonanglican.org.nz
Polynesia	Jabez Leslie Bryce Box 35, Suva, Fiji Tel (00679) 330 4716 Fax (00679) 330 2687 E-mail episcopus@connect.com.fj or diopolynesia@is.com.fj

(Diocese of Polynesia in Aotearoa New Zealand)	Winston Halapua St John's College, Private Bag 28–907, Remuera, Auckland, New Zealand Tel (0064) (9) 521 2725 Fax (0064) (9) 521 2420 E-mail winstonh@stjohns.auckland.ac.nz
(Vanua Levu and Taveuni)	Apimeleki Nadoki Qiliho Diocese of Polynesia, P O Box 35, Suva, Fiji Tel (00679) 330 8539 Fax (00679) 330 2152 E-mail minoff@connect.com.fj
(Viti Levu West)	Gabriel Mahesh Prasad Sharma P O Box 117, Lautoka, Fiji Tel (00679) 666 0124 *fax as telephone* E-mail gabsharma@yahoo.com
Waiapu	David Cappel Rice PO Box 227, Napier, New Zealand Tel (0064) (6) 835 8230 Fax (0064) (6) 835 0680
Waikato	David John Moxon PO Box 21, Hamilton 3240, New Zealand Tel (0064) (7) 838 2309 Fax (0064) (7) 838 0052 E-mail bishop@hn-ang.org.nz
(Taranaki)	Philip Richardson PO Box 547, Taranaki Mail Centre, New Plymouth, 4340, New Zealand Tel (0064) (6) 759 1178 Fax (0064) (6) 759 1180 E-mail philip.richardson@xtra.co.nz
Wellington	Thomas John Brown PO Box 12–046, Wellington, New Zealand Tel (0064) (4) 472 1057 Fax (0064) (4) 449 1360 E-mail bishoptom@paradise.net.nz

NIGERIA

A large number of new dioceses have been created in the Church of Nigeria. At the time of going to press, some details were unavailable, and so this list is incomplete.

PROVINCE OF ABUJA

Abuja (Archbishop and Primate)	Peter Jasper Akinola Archbishop's Palace, PO Box 212, ADCP, Abuja, Nigeria Tel (00234) (9) 524 0496 E-mail primate@anglican-nig.org
Bida	Jonah Kolo c/o PO Box 2469, Minna, Nigeria Tel (00234) (66) 460 178 E-mail bida@anglican-nig.org
Gwagwalada	Tanimu Samari Aduda Diocesan Headquarters, Secretariat Road, PO Box 287, Gwagwalada, FCT, Abuja, Nigeria Tel (00234) (9) 882 2083 E-mail gwagwalada@anglican-nig.org
Idah	Joseph N Musa Bishop's Lodge, PO Box 25, Idah, Kogi State, Nigeria Mobile (00234) 804 334 0189 E-mail idah@anglican-nig.org *or* jilmusa@yahoo.com
Kafanchan	William Weh Diya Bishopscourt, 5B Jemma'a Street, PO Box 29, Kafanchan, Kaduna State, Nigeria Tel (00234) (61) 20634
Kubwa	Duke Akamisoko Bishopscourt, PO Box 67, Kubwa FCT, Nigeria Tel (00234) (9) 6707094 E-mail kubwa@anglican-nig.org
Lafia	Miller Kangdim Maza PO Box 560, Lafia, Nasarawa State, Nigeria Tel (00234) (47) 221 329
Lokoja	Emmanuel Egbunu PO Box 11, Lokoja, Kogi State, Nigeria Tel (00234) (58) 220 588 Fax (00234) (58) 221 788 E-mail lokoja@anglican-nig.org

Makurdi	Nathaniel Nyitar Inyom Bishopscourt, PO Box 1, Makurdi, Benue State, Nigeria Tel (00234) (44) 533 349 E-mail makurdi@anglican-nig.org
Minna	Nathaniel Yisa Bishopscourt, Dutsen Kura, PO Box 2469, Minna, Niger State, Nigeria Tel (00234) (66) 220 035 (Office) *or* 220 514 (Home)
Otukpo	David K Bello St John's Cathedral, Sgt Ugbade Ave, PO Box 360, Otukpo, Benue State, Nigeria Tel (00234) (44) 662 212 E-mail otukpo@anglican-nig.org *or* bishopdkbello@yahoo.com
Zonkwa (Missionary diocese)	Praise Omole-Ekun Bishop's Residence, PO Box 21, Zonkwa, Kaduna State 802002, Nigeria E-mail zonkwa@anglican-nig.org

PROVINCE OF BENDEL

Asaba (Archbishop)	Nicholas D Okoh Bishopscourt, Cable Point, PO Box 216, Asaba, Delta State, Nigeria Tel (00234) (46) 280 682 or 280043 E-mail asaba@anglican-nig.org
Benin	P O J Imasuen Bishopscourt, PO Box 82, Benin City, Edo State, Nigeria Mobile (00234) 803 079 9560 E-mail benin@anglican-nig.org *or* petglad2002@yahoo.com
Esan	Friday John Imakhai Bishopscourt, Ujoelen, PO Box 921, Ekpoma, Edo State, Nigeria Tel (00234) (55) 981 29 E-mail bishopfriday@hotmail.com
Ika	Peter Onekpe Bishopscourt, c/o PO Box 5, Agbor, Delta State, Nigeria Tel (00234) (55) 25014 E-mail ika@anglican-nig.org *or* bishoppeter@yahoo.com
Oleh	Jonathan Francis Ekokotu Edewor PO Box 8, Oleh, Delta State, Nigeria Mobile (00234) 803 549 4215 E-mail oleh@anglican-nig.org *or* angoleh2000@yahoo.com
Sabongidda-Ora	John Akao Bishopscourt, PO Box 13, Sabongidda-Ora, Edo State, Nigeria Tel (00234) (57) 54049 E-mail akao@cashette.com
Ughelli	Vincent O Muoghereh Bishopscourt, Ovurodawanre, PO Box 760, Ughelli, Delta State, Nigeria Tel (00234) (53) 258 307 Fax (00234) (53) 250 091
Warri	Christian Ideh Bishopscourt, 17 Mabiaku Road, GRA, PO Box 4571, Warri, Nigeria Tel (00234) (53) 255 857 E-mail warri@anglican-nig.org
Western Izon (Missionary diocese)	Edafe Emamezi, Bishopscourt PO Box 56, Sagbama, River State, Nigeria Mobile (00234) 806 357 2263 E-mail anglizon@yahoo.co.uk

PROVINCE OF IBADAN

Ajayi Crowther	Olukemi Oduntan, Bishopscourt, Iseyin, PO Box 430, Iseyin, Oyo State Tel (00234) (837) 198 182 (Mobile) *email*: ajayicrowtherdiocese@yahoo.com
Ibadan (Archbishop)	Joseph Akinfenwa Bishopscourt, PO Box 3075, Mapo, Ibadan, Nigeria Tel (00234) (2) 810 1400 Fax (00234) (2) 810 1413 E-mail ibadan@anglican-nig.org *or* bishop@skannet.com

Ibadan North	Segun Okubadejo Bishopscourt, Moyede, PO Box 28961, Agodi, Ibadan, Nigeria Tel (00234) (2) 8107 482 E-mail angibn@skannet.com *or* segtal52@yahoo.co.uk
Ibadan South	Jacob Ademola Ajetunmobi Bishopscourt, PO Box 166, Dugbe, Ibadan, Nigeria Tel (00234) (2) 231 6464 *fax as telephone* E-mail ibadan-south@anglican-nig.org *or* jacajet@skannet.com
Ife	Oluranti Odubogun Bishopscourt, PO Box 312, Ife-Ife, Osun State, Nigeria Tel (00234) (36) 232 255 E-mail stphilipscathayetoroife@yahoo.com
Igbomina	Michael Oluwakayode Akinyemi Bishopscourt, Esie, PO Box 102, Oro P.A, Kwara State, Nigeria Tel (00234) (31) 700 0025
Ilesa	Olubayu Samuel Sowale Bishopscourt, Oke-Ooye, PO Box 237, Ilesa, Nigeria Tel (00234) (36) 461 153 E-mail ilesha@anglican-nig.org *or* bishop-solwale@yahoo.com
Kwara	Olusegun Adeyemi Bishopscourt, Fate Road, PO Box 1884, Ilorin, Kwara State, Nigeria Tel (00234) (31) 220879 E-mail kwara@anglican.skannet.com.ng
Offa	Gabriel Akinbolarin Akinbiyi PO Box 21, Offa, Kwara State, Nigeria Tel (00234) (31) 801011 E-mail offa@anglican-nig.org
Ogbomoso (Missionary diocese)	Matthew Osunade Bishop's House, PO Box 1909, Ogbomoso, Osun State, Nigeria Mobile (00234) 803 524 4606 E-mail ogbomoso@anglican-nig.org *or* maaosunade@yahoo.com
Oke-Osun	Nathaniel Fasogbon Bishopscourt, PO Box 251, Gbongan, Osun State, Nigeria Mobile: (00234) 803 356 9384
Osun	James Afolabi Popoola Bishopscourt, Isale-Aro, PO Box 285, Osogbo, Nigeria Tel (00234) (35) 240 036 Mobile (00234) 803 356 1628 E-mail osun@anglican-nig.org
Oyo	Jacob Ola Fasipe Bishopscourt, PO Box 23, Oyo, Nigeria Mobile (00234) 803 380 2530 E-mail oyo@anglican-nig.org

PROVINCE OF JOS

Bauchi	Musa Tula Bishop's House, 2 Hospital Road, PO Box 2450, Bauchi, Nigeria Tel (00234) (77) 543 460 E-mail bauchi@anglican-nig.org
Damaturu	Abiodun Ogunyemi PO Box 312, Damaturu, Yobe State, Nigeria Tel (00234) (74) 522 142 E-mail damaturu@anglican-nig.org
Gombe	Henry Chukwudum Ndukuba St Peter's Cathedral, PO Box 39, Gombe, Nigeria Tel (00234) (72) 220489 or 221212 Fax (00234) (72) 221141 E-mail gombe@anglican-nig.org *or* ndukuba@yahoo.com
Jalingo	Timothy Yahaya PO Box 4, Jalingo, Taraba State, Nigeria Tel (00234) (79) 23312 *fax as telephone* E-mail jalingo@anglican-nig.org

Jos (Archbishop)	Benjamin Argak Kwashi Bishopscourt, PO Box 6283, Jos, Plateau State, Nigeria Tel (00234) (73) 464 325 Mobile (00234) 803 701 7928 E-mail jos@anglican-nig.org
Maiduguri	Emmanuel K Mani Bishopscourt, Off Lagos Street, GRA PO Box 1693, Maiduguri, Borno State, Nigeria Tel (00234) (76) 234010 *fax as telephone* E-mail maiduguri@anglican-nig.org
Yola	Markus A Ibrahim PO Box 601, Jemeta-Yola, Adamawa State, Nigeria Tel (00234) (75) 624303 E-mail yola@anglican-nig.org

PROVINCE OF KADUNA

Dutse	Yusuf Ibrahim Lumu PO Box 15, Dutse, Jigawa State, Nigeria Tel (00234) (64) 721 379 E-mail dutse@anglican-nig.org
Gusau	John G Danbinta PO Box 64, Gusau, Zamfara State, Nigeria Tel (00234) (63) 204 747 E-mail gusau@anglican-nig.org
Kaduna	Josiah Idowu-Fearon PO Box 72, Kaduna, Nigeria Tel (00234) (62) 240 085 Fax (00234) (62) 244 408 E-mail kaduna@anglican-nig.org
Kano	Zakka Lalle Nyam Bishopscourt, PO Box 362, Kano, Nigeria Tel (00234) (64) 647 816 *fax as telephone* E-mail kano@anglican-nig.org *or* kano@anglican.skannet.com.ng
Katsina	Jonathan Bamaiyi Bishop's Lodge, PO Box 904, Katsina, Nigeria Tel (00234) (65) 432718 E-mail katsina@anglican-nig.org *or* bpjonathanbamaiyi@yahoo.co.uk
Kebbi (Archbishop)	Edmund Efoyikeye Akanya PO Box 701, Birnin Kebbi, Kebbi State, Nigeria Tel (00234) (68) 321 179 *fax as telephone* E-mail kebbi@anglican.skannet.com
Sokoto	Augustine Omole Bishop's Lodge, 68 Shuni Road, PO Box 3489, Sokoto, Nigeria Tel (00234) (60) 234 639 Fax (00234) (60) 232 323 E-mail sokoto@anglican-nig.org
Wusasa	Ali Buba Lamido Box 28, Wusasa Zaria, Nigeria Tel (00234) (69) 334 594 E-mail wusasa@anglican-nig.org *or* wusasa@anglican.skannet.com.ng

PROVINCE OF LAGOS

Badagry (Missionary diocese)	Babatunde J. Adeyemi Bishopscourt, PO Box 7, Badagry, Lagos State, Nigeria Tel (00234) (1) 773 5546 Mobile (00234) 803 306 4601 E-mail badagry@anglican-nig.org
Egba	Matthew Oluremi Owadayo Bishopscourt, Onikolobo, PO Box 267, Ibara, Abeokuta, Nigeria Tel (00234) (39) 240 933 *fax as telephone* E-mail egba@anglican-nig.org *or* mowadayo@yahoo.com
Ijebu	Ezekiel Awosoga Bishopscourt, Ejirin Road, PO Box 112, Ijebu-Ode, Nigeria Tel (00234) (37) 431 801 E-mail ijebu@anglican-nig.org *or* bishop@ang-ijebudiocese.com

Ijebu North	Solomon Kuponu Bishopscourt, PO Box 2, Ijebu-Igbo, Ogun State, Nigeria Mobile (00234) 803 741 9372 E-mail dioceseofijebunorth@yahoo.com
Lagos (Archbishop)	Ephraim Adebola Ademowo Archbishop's Palace, 29 Marina, PO Box 13, Lagos, Nigeria Tel and fax (00234) (1) 263 6026 Fax (00234) (1) 263 6536 E-mail lagos@anglican.skannet.com.ng *or* diocesan@dioceseoflagos.org
Lagos Mainland	Adebayo Akinde PO Box 45, Ebute-Metta, Lagos, Nigeria
Lagos West	Peter A Adebiyi Vining House (2nd Floor), Archbishop Vining Memorial Cathedral, Oba Akinjobi Road, G.R.A. Ikeja, Nigeria Tel (00234) (1) 493 7333 Fax (00234) (1) 493 7337 E-mail lagoswest@anglican-nig.org *or* dioceseoflagoswest@yahoo.com
On the Coast	Joshua Ogunele Bishopscourt, Ikoya Rd, P. M. B. 3, Ilutitun Osooro, Ondo State, Nigeria Mobile (00234) 8056 345 496
Remo	Michael O. Fape Bishopscourt, Ewusi Street, PO Box 522, Sagamu, Ogun State, Nigeria Tel (00234) (37) 640 598 E-mail remo@anglican-nig.org *or* mofape@skannet.com
Yewa	Simeon O M Adebola Bishopscourt, PO Box 484, Ilaro, Ogun State, Nigeria Tel (00234) (1) 792 696

PROVINCE OF THE NIGER

Abakaliki	Benson C B Onyeibor All Saints' Cathedral, PO Box 112, Abakaliki, Ebonyi State, Nigeria Tel (00234) (43) 220 762 Mobile (00234) 803 501 3083 E-mail abakaliki@anglican-nig.org
Aguata	Christian Ogochukwo Efobi Bishopscourt, PO Box 1128, Ekwulobia, Anambra State, Nigeria Mobile (00234) 803 750 1077
Awka (Archbishop)	Maxwell Samuel Chike Anikwenwa Bishopscourt, Ifite Road, PO Box 130, Awka, Anambra State, Nigeria Tel (00234) (48) 550 058 or 553 516 E-mail awka@anglican-nig.org *or* anglawka@infoweb.abs.net *or* provoftheniger@infoweb.abs.net
Enugu	Emmanuel O Chukwuma Bishop's House, PO Box 418, Enugu, Enugu State, Nigeria Tel (00234) (42) 435 804 Fax (00234) (42) 259 808 E-mail enugu@anglican-nig.org
Nnewi	Godwin Izundu Nmezinwa Okpala c/o Bishopscourt, PO Box 2630, Uruagu-Nnewi, Anambra State, Nigeria Mobile (00234) 803 348 5741 E-mail nnewi@anglican-nig.org
Nsukka	Alloysius Agbo PO Box 516, Nsukka, Enugu State, Nigeria E-mail nsukka@anglican-nig.org
Oji River	Amos Amankechinelo Madu PO Box 213, Oji River, Enugu State, Nigeria Tel (00234) (48) 882 219 Mobile (00234) 804 611 0117 E-mail ojiriver@anglican-nig.org
The Niger (Bishop *on*)	Ken Okeke PO Box 42, Onitsha, Anambra State, Nigeria Tel (00234) (46) 210 337 E-mail niger@anglican-nig.org *or* kengoziokeke@yahoo.com

PROVINCE OF THE NIGER DELTA

Aba (Archbishop)	Ugochukwu U. Ezuoke Bishopscourt, 70/72 St Michael's Road, PO Box 212, Aba, Nigeria Tel (00234) (82) 220 231 E-mail aba@anglican-nig.org
Aba Ngwa North	Nathan C. Kanu Bishopscourt, PO Box 43, Aba, Abia State Tel (00234) 803 822 4623 E-mail odinathnfe@sbcglobal.net
Ahoada	Clement Nathan Ekpeye Bishopscourt, St Paul's Cathedral, PO Box 4, Ahoada, Ahoada East L.G.A., Rivers State, Nigeria Mobile (00234) 803 542 2847 E-mail ahoada@anglican-nig.org
Arochukwu- Ohafia (Missionary diocese)	Johnson C. Onuoha, Bishopscourt, PO Box 193, Arochukwu, Abia State, Nigeria Mobile (00234) 802 538 6407 E-mail: aroohafia@anglican-nig.org *or* johnchiobishop@yahoo.com
Calabar	Tunde Adeleye Bishopscourt, PO Box 74, Calabar, Cross River State, Nigeria Tel (00234) (98) 232 812 Mobile (00234) 803 337 3120 E-mail calabar@anglican-nig.org *or* bishoptunde@yahoo.com
Etche	Okechukwu Precious Nwala Bishopscourt, PO Box 89, Okehi, Etche Rivers State Mobile (00234) 807 525 2842 E-mail etchediocese@yahoo.com *or* precious_model5@yahoo.com
Ikwerre	Blessing Enyindah Bishopscourt, PO Box 14229, Port Harcourt, Rivers State Mobile (00234) 802 321 2824 E-mail blessingenyindah@yahoo.com
Ikwuano (Missionary diocese)	Chigozirim Onyegbule Bishopscourt, PO Box 5, Oloko, Ikwuano, Abia State, Nigeria Mobile (00234) 803 085 9310 E-mail ikwuano@anglican-nig.org
Isiala Ngwa	Owen N. Azubuike Bishopscourt, St George's Cathedral Compound, Umuomainta Mbawsi P.M.B., Mbawsi, Abia State Mobile (00234) 805 467 0528 E-mail bpowenazubuike@yahoo.com
Isiala Ngwa South	Isaac Nwaobia St Peter's Cathedral, PO Box 15, Owerrinta, Abia State Mobile (00234_ 805 787 1100 E-mail bishopisaacnwaobia@priest.com
Isiukwuato (Missionary diocese)	Samuel C. Chukuka Bishop's House, PO Box 350, Ovim Abia State, Nigeria Mobile (00234) 803 338 6221 E-mail isiukwuato@anglican-nig.org *or* rootedword@yahoo.com
The Niger Delta	Gabriel H Pepple Bishopcourt, 4 Harley St, Old G.R.A./ Forces Ave, Port Harcourt, Rivers State, Nigeria Tel (00234) (84) 233308 E-mail nigerdelta@anglican-nig.org
Niger Delta North	Ignatius Kattey PO Box 53, Diobu, Port Harcourt, Rivers State, Nigeria Tel (00234) (84) 231 338 E-mail niger-delta-north@anglican-nig.org *or* bishopicokattey@yahoo.com
Niger Delta West	Adoluphus Amabebe Bishopscourt, PO Box 10, Yenagoa, Bayelsa, Nigeria Tel (00234) (84) 490 010 E-mail niger-delta-west@anglican-nig.org

Ogoni (Missionary diocese)
Solomon S Gberegbara
Bishopscourt, PO Box 73, Bori-Ogoni,
Rivers State, Nigeria
Mobile (00234) 803 339 2545
E-mail ogoni@anglican-nig.org *or*
ogoniangdiocese@yahoo.com

Okrika
Tubokosemie Abere
Bishopscourt, PO Box 11, Okrika, Rivers State,
Nigeria
Tel (00234) (84) 575 003
E-mail dioceseofokrika@yahoo.com

Ukwa
Samuel Kelechi Eze
PO Box 20468, Aba, Nigeria
Mobile (00234) 803 789 2431
E-mail ukwa@anglican-nig.org

Umuahia
Ikechi N Nwosu
St Stephen's Cathedral Church Compound,
PO Box 96, Umuahia, Abia State, Nigeria
Tel (00234) (88) 220 311
E-mail umuahia@anglican-nig.org

Uyo (Archbishop)
Isaac Orama
Bishopscourt, PO Box 70, Uyo,
Akwa Ibom State, Nigeria
Tel (00234) (85) 204142
E-mail uyo@anglican-nig.org

PROVINCE OF ONDO

Akoko
Gabriel Akinbiyi
PO Box 572, Ikare-Akoko,
Ondo State, Nigeria
Tel (00234) (50) 670 668
akoko@anglican.skannet.com.ng

Akure
Michael Ipinmoye
Bishopscourt, PO Box 1622, Akure, Nigeria
Tel (00234) (34) 241 572
fax as telephone
E-mail angdak@gannetcity.net

Ekiti (Archbishop)
Samuel Adedayo Abe
Bishopscourt, PO Box 12,
Okesa Street, Ado-Ekiti, Nigeria
Tel (00234) (30) 250 305
Mobile (00234) 802 225 9389
E-mail ekiti@anglican.skannet.com.ng *or*
ekiti@anglican-nig.org

Ekiti-Oke
Isaac Olatunde Olubowale
Bishopscourt, Temidire St, P.M.B. 207, Usi-
Ekiti, Ekiti State, Nigeria
Mobile (00234) 803 600 9582
E-mail ekitioke@anglican-nig.org

Ekiti West
Samuel Oludare Oke
Bishop's Residence, 6 Ifaki Street,
PO Box 477, Ijero-Ekiti, Nigeria
Tel (00234) (30) 850 314
Mobile (00234) 803 429 2823

Kabba
Samuel O Olayanju
Bishopscourt, Obaro Way, PO Box 62, Kabba,
Kogi State, Nigeria
Tel (00234) (58) 300 633
Mobile (00234) 803 653 0180

Ondo
George L Lasebikan
Bishopscourt, College Road,
PO Box 265, Ondo, Nigeria
Tel (00234) (34) 610 718
Mobile (00234) 803 472 1813
E-mail ondo@anglican-nig.org *or*
angondo@skannet.com

Owo
James Adedayo Oladunjoye
Bishopscourt, PO Box 472,
Owo, Ondo State, Nigeria
Tel (00234) (51) 241 463
Mobile (00234) 803 475 3291
E-mail owo@anglican-nig.org

PROVINCE OF OWERRI

Egbu
Emmanuel Uchechukwu Iheagwam
All Saints' Cathedral, Diocese of Egbu, PO Box
1967, Owerri, Imo State, Nigeria
Tel (00234) (83) 231 797
Mobile (00234) 803 491 1090
E-mail egbu@anglican-nig.org

Ideato
Caleb A Maduoma
Bishopscourt, PO Box 2, Arondizuogu, Ideato
North L.G.A., Imo State, Nigeria
Mobile (00234) 803 745 4503
E-mail ideato@anglican-nig.org *or*
bpomacal@hotmail.com

Mbaise
Bright Joseph Egemasi Ogu
Bishopscourt, PO Box 10, Ife,
Ezinihitte Mbaise, Imo State, Nigeria
Tel (00234) (83) 441 483
Mobile (00234) 803 553 4762
E-mail mbaise@anglican-nig.org *or*
bjeogu@yahoo.com

Okigwe North
Godson Ukanwa
PO Box 156, Okigwe,
Imo State, Nigeria
Tel (00234) (42) 420 124
Mobile (00234) 804 507 5592
E-mail okigwenorth@anglican-nig.org

Okigwe South
David Onuoha
Bishopscourt, Ezeoke Nsu,
PO Box 235, Nsu, Ehime Mbano LGA, Imo
State, Nigeria
Mobile (00234) 803 745 4510
E-mail okigwe-south@anglican-nig.org *or*
okisouth@yahoo.com

Orlu (Archbishop)
Bennett C I Okoro
Bishopscourt, PO Box 260,
Nkwerre, Imo State, Nigeria
Tel (00234) (82) 440 538
Mobile (00234) 803 671 1271

Owerri
Cyril Chukwunonyerem Okorocha
No. 1 Mission Crescent, PMB 1063,
Owerri, Imo State, Nigeria
Tel (00234) (83) 230 417
Mobile (00234) 803 338 9344
Fax (00234) (82) 440 183
E-mail owerri@anglican-nig.org *or*
adowe@phca.linkserve.com

PAPUA NEW GUINEA

Aipo Rongo (Archbishop)
James Simon Ayong
PO Box 893, Mount Hagen,
Western Highlands Province,
Papua New Guinea
Tel (00675) 542 1131 *or* 3727
Fax (00675) 542 1181
E-mail acpngair@global.net.pg *or*
archbishopjayong@hotmail.com

(Suffragans)
Nathan Ingen
address etc as above
Denys Ririka
PO Box 1178, Goroka, Eastern Highlands
Province, Papua New Guinea

Dogura
Clyde Igara
PO Box 19, Dogura, MBP,
Papua New Guinea
Tel (00675) 641 1530
Fax (00675) 641 1129

New Guinea Islands, The
Allan Migi
Bishop's House, PO Box 806,
Kimbe, Papua New Guinea
Tel (00675) 983 5120
fax as telephone
E-mail acpngngi@global.net.pg *or*
acpngngibishop@global.net.pg

Popondota
Joe Kopapa
Anglican Diocese of Popondota, PO Box 26,
Popondetta, Oro Province,
Papua New Guinea
Tel (00675) 329 7194
Fax (00675) 329 7476
E-mail acpngpop@online.net.pg

Port Moresby
Peter Ramsden
PO Box 6491, Boroko, NCD
Port Moresby, Papua New Guinea
Tel (00675) 323 2489
Fax (00675) 323 2493
E-mail acpngpom@global.net.pg *or*
psramsden.pomanglican@gmail.com

THE PHILIPPINES

Prime Bishop
Ignacio Capuyan Soliba
PO Box 10321, Broadway Centrum
1112 Quezon City, Philippines
or 275 E Rodriguez Sr Avenue
1102 Quezon City, Philippines
Tel (0063) (2) 722 8478, 722 8481 *or* 722 9459
Fax (0063) (2) 721 1923
E-mail isoliba@hotmail.com

Central
Philippines
Dixie C Taclobao
281 E. Rodriguez Sr. Avenue, 1102 Quezon City,
Philippines
Tel (0063) (2) 412 8561
Fax (0063) (2) 724 2143
E-mail central@i-next.net

North Central
Philippines
Joel A Pachao
358 Magsaysay Avenue,
Baguio City 2600, Philippines
Tel (0063) (74) 443 7705
Fax (0063) (74) 442 2432
E-mail edncp@digitelone.com

Northern Luzon
Renato M Abibico
Bulanao, 3800 Tabuk,
Kalinga, Philippines
Tel (0063) (74) 872 2295
Mobile (0063) 9921 687 1933
Fax (0063) (74) 872 2013

Northern
Philippines
Edward Pacyaya Malecdan
Diocesan Center, 2616 Bontoc,
Mountain Province, Philippines
Tel (0063) (74) 602 1026
fax as telephone
E-mail ednpvic@hotmail.com

Santiago
Alexander A Wandag Sr
Episcopal Diocese of Santiago, Divisoria,
3311 Santiago City, Isabela, Philippines
Tel (0063) (78) 682 3756
Fax (0063) (78) 682 1256
E-mail alexwandageds@yahoo.com

Southern
Philippines
Danilo Labacanacruz
186 Sinsuat Avenue, Rosario Heights,
Cotabato City 9600, Philippines
Tel (0063) (64) 421 2960
Fax (0063) (64) 421 1703
E-mail edsp_ecp@cotabato.mozcom.com

RWANDA

Butare
Nathan Gasatura
BP 255, Butare, Rwanda
Tel (00250) 530 504
fax as telephone
E-mail rusodilo@yahoo.fr

Byumba
Onesphore Rwaje
BP 17, Byumba, Rwanda
Tel (00250) 64242
fax as telephone
E-mail eer@rwanda1.com

Cyangugu
Geoffrey Rwubusisi
PO Box 52, Cyangugu, Rwanda
Tel (00250) 53 7878
fax as telephone
E-mail bishoprwubusisi@yahoo.co.uk

Gahini
Alexis Bilindabagabo
BP 22, Kigali, Rwanda
Tel (00250) 567 422

Kibungo
Josias Sendegaya
EER Kibungo Diocese,
BP 719, Kibungo, Rwanda
Tel (00250) 566 194
fax as telephone
E-mail bpjosias@yahoo.fr

Kigali
(Archbishop)
Emmanuel Musaba Kolini
EER/DK, BP 61, Kigali, Rwanda
Tel (00250) 573 213
fax as telephone
E-mail ek@terracom.rw

Kigeme
Augustin Mvunabandi
BP 67, Gikongoro, Rwanda
Tel (00250) 535 086 *or* 088 *or* 087
E-mail dkigeme@rwanda1.com

Kivu
Augustin Ahimana
BP 166 Gisenyi
Tel (00250) 788 350 119

Shyira
John Rucyahana Kabango
EER – Shyira Diocese, BP 26, Ruhengeri,
Rwanda
Tel (00250) 546 449
fax as telephone
E-mail bpjohnr@rwanda1.com

Shyogwe
Jéred Karimba
BP 27, Gitarama, Rwanda
Tel (00250) 562 469
fax as telephone
E-mail dsgwegit@yahoo.com

SOUTH EAST ASIA

Kuching
Bolly Anak Lapok
Bishop's House, PO Box 347,
93704 Kuching, Sarawak, Malaysia
Tel (0060) (82) 240 187 *or* 240188
Fax (0060) (82) 426 488
E-mail bishopk@streamyx.com

Sabah
Albert Vun Cheong Fui
PO Box 10811, 88809 Kota Kinabalu, Sabah,
Malaysia
Tel (0060) (88) 245 846
Fax (0060) (88) 245 942
E-mail dosabah@streamyx.com

Singapore
(Archbishop)
John Chew Hiang Chea
4 Bishopsgate, Singapore 249970
Tel (0065) 6288 7585
Fax (0065) 6288 5574
E-mail bpoffice@anglican.org.sg

(Assistant)
Rennis Poniah
St John's and St Margaret's Church, 30 Dover
Avenue, Singapore 139790, Singapore
Tel (0065) 6773 9415
Fax (0065) 6778 6264
E-mail rennis@sjsm.org.sg

West Malaysia
Ng Moon Hing
No.16 Jalan Pudu Lama, 50200 Kuala Lumpur,
Malaysia
Tel (0060) (3) 2031 2728
Fax (0060) (3) 2031 3225
E-mail anglican@streamyx.com

SOUTHERN AFRICA

Angola
(Missionary
diocese)
Andre Soares
Av Lenini, Travessa D Antonia,
Saldanha N 134, CP 10 1498, Angola
Tel (00244) (2) 395 792
Fax: (00244) (2) 396 794
E-mail anglicana@ebonet.net *or*
bispo-Soares@hotmail.com

Cape Town
(Archbishop)
Winston Hugh Njongonkulu Ndungane
16–20 Bishopscourt, Claremont 7708,
South Africa
Tel (0027) (21) 761 2531
Fax (0027) (21) 797 1298 *or* 761 4193
E-mail archpa@anglicanchurchsa.org.za

(Table Bay)
Garth Counsell
PO Box 1932, Cape Town 8000, South Africa
Tel (0027) (21) 465 1557
Fax (0027) (21) 465 1571
E-mail tablebay@ctdiocese.org.za

Christ the King
Peter John Lee
PO Box 1653, Rosettenville 2130, South Africa
Tel (0027) (11) 435 0097
Fax (0027) (11) 435 2868
E-mail dckpeter@corpdial.co.za

False Bay
Merwyn Edwin Castle
PO Box 2804, Somerset West 7129
South Africa
Tel (0027) (21) 852 5243
Fax (0027) (21) 852 9430
E-mail bishopm@falsebaydiocese.org.za

George
Donald Frederick Harker
PO Box 227, George 6530, South Africa
Tel (0027) (44) 873 5680
fax as telephone
E-mail dharker@intekom.co.za *or*
glynis@george.diocese.co.za

Grahamstown	Ebenezer St Mark Ntlali PO Box 181, Grahamstown 6140, South Africa Tel (0027) (46) 636 1996 Fax (0027) (46) 622 5231 E-mail bpgtn@intekom.co.za
Highveld	David Hugh Bannerman PO Box 17462, Benoni West 1503, South Africa Tel (0027) (11) 422 2231 Fax (0027) (11) 420 1336 E-mail bishophveld@iafrica.com
Johannesburg	Brian Charles Germond PO Box 1131, Johannesburg 2000, South Africa Tel (0027) (11) 336 8724 Fax (0027) (11) 333 3053 E-mail bgermond@cpsajoburg.org.za
Kimberley and Kuruman	Oswald Peter Patrick Swartz PO Box 45, Kimberley 8300, South Africa Tel (0027) (53) 833 2433 Fax (0027) (53) 831 2730 E-mail oppswartz@onetel.com
Lebombo	Dinis Salomâo Sengulane CP 120, Maputo, Mozambique Tel (00258) (1) 405 364 or 404 885 Fax (00258) (1) 401 093 E-mail bispo_sengulane@virconn.com
Lesotho	Adam Andrease Mallane Taaso PO Box 87, Maseru 100, Lesotho Tel (00266) (22) 311 974 Fax (00266) (22) 310 161 E-mail diocese@ilesotho.com
Matlosane	Stephen Molopi Diseko PO Box 11417, Klerksdorp, 2570 South Africa Tel (0027) (18) 462 5530 or 464 2260 Fax (0027) (18) 462 4939 E-mail diocesematlosane@telkomsa.net
Mpumalanga	Leslie Walker PO Box 4327, White River 1240, South Africa Tel (0027) (13) 751 1960 Fax (0027) (13) 751 3638 E-mail bishoples@telkomsa.net
Mthatha	Sitembele Tobela Mzamane PO Box 25, Umtata, Transkei 5100, South Africa Tel (0027) (47) 532 4450 Fax (0027) (47) 532 4191 E-mail anglicbspmthatha@intekom.co.za
Namibia	Nathaniel Ndxuma Nakwatumbah PO Box 57, Windhoek 9000, Namibia Tel (00264) (61) 238 920 Fax (00264) (61) 225 903 E-mail bishop@anglicanchurchnamibia.com
Natal	Rubin Phillip PO Box 47439, Greyville 4023, South Africa Tel (0027) (31) 309 2066 Fax (0027) (31) 308 9316 E-mail bishop@dionatal.org.za
(South)	Hummingfield Charles Nkosinathi Ndwandwe *address as above* Tel (0027) (33) 394 1560 E-mail bishopndwandwe@dionatal.org.za
(North-West)	Funginkosi Mbhele PO Box 123, Estcort 3310, South Africa Tel (0027) (36) 352 2893 Fax (0027) (36) 352 2810 E-mail bishopmbhele@dionatal.org.za
Niassa	Mark van Koevering Diocese do Niassa, CP 264, Lichinga, Niassa, Mozambique Tel (00258) 712 0735 *fax as telephone* E-mail bishop.niassa@gmail.com
Port Elizabeth	Nceba Bethlehem Nopece PO Box 7109, Newton Park 6055, South Africa Tel (0027) (41) 365 1387 Fax (0027) (41) 365 2049 E-mail pebishop@iafrica.com
Pretoria	Johannes T Seoka PO Box 1032, Pretoria, 0001 South Africa Tel (0027) (12) 322 2218 Fax (0027) (12) 322 9411 E-mail ptabish@cpsa.org.za

(Suffragan)	Mazwi Ernest Tisani 348 General Beyers St, PO Box 16425, Pretoria North 0116, South Africa Tel (00264) (12) 546 6253 E-mail bishopmazwi@mweb.co.za
Saldanha Bay	Raphael Bernard Viburt Hess PO Box 420, Malmesbury 7299, South Africa Tel (0027) (22) 487 3885 Fax (0027) (22) 487 3886 E-mail bishop@dioceseofsaldanhabay.org.za
St Helena	John William Salt Bishopsholme, PO Box 62, St Helena, South Atlantic Ocean Tel (00290) 4471 Fax (00290) 4728 E-mail bishop@helanta.sh
St Mark the Evangelist	Martin Andre Breytenbach PO Box 643, Polokwane 0700, South Africa Tel (0027) (15) 297 3297 Mobile (0027) 82 441 2568 Fax (0027) (15) 297 0408 E-mail martin@stmark.co.za
Swaziland	Meshack Boy Mabuza PO Box 118, Mbabane, Swaziland Tel (00268) 404 3624 Fax (00268) 404 6759 E-mail bishopmabuza@africaonline.co.sz
The Free State	Elistan Patrick Glover PO Box 411, Bloemfontein 9300, South Africa Tel (0027) (51) 447 6053 Fax (0027) (51) 447 5874 E-mail bishoppatrick@dsc.co.za
Umzimvubu	Mlibo Mteteleli Ngewu PO Box 644, Kokstad 4700, South Africa Tel (0027) (39) 727 4117 *fax as telephone* E-mail mzimvubu@futurenet.co.za
Zululand	Dino Gabriel PO Box 147, Eshowe, Zululand, 3815 South Africa Tel (0027) (354) 742047 *fax as telephone* E-mail bishopdino@netactive.co.za

SOUTHERN CONE OF AMERICA

Argentina (Presiding Bishop)	Gregory Venables Rioja 2995 (1636), Olivos, Provincia de Buenos Aires, Argentina Tel (0054) (11) 4342 4618 Fax (0054) (11) 4331 0234 E-mail bpgreg@ciudad.com.ar
Bolivia	Frank Lyons Iglesia Anglicana Episcopal de Bolivia, Casilla 848, Cochabamba, Bolivia Tel (00591) (4) 440 1168 *fax as telephone* E-mail BpFrank@sams-usa.org
Chile	Héctor Zavala Muñoz Casilla 50675, Correo Central, Santiago, Chile Tel (0056) (2) 638 3009 or 639 1509 Fax (0056) (2) 639 4581 E-mail tzavala@iach.cl
(Assistant)	Abelino Manuel Apeleo Casilla de Correo 26-D, Temuco, Chile Tel (0056) (45) 910 484 *fax as telephone* E-mail aapeleo@iach.cl
Northern Argentina	Gregory James Venables (Bishop of Argentina) *address etc as above*
(Assistant)	Nicholas Drayson Casilla 19, CP 3636 Ingeniero Juárez, FCNGB Formosa, Argentina Tel (0054) (387) 431 1718 Fal (0054) (387) 431 2622 E-mail diana.epi@salnet.com.ar

Paraguay	Peter Bartlett Iglesia Anglicana de Paraguya, Casilla de Correo 1124, Asunción, Paraguay Tel (00595) (21) 200 933 Fax (00595) (21) 214 328 E-mail jellison@pla.net.py
Peru	Harold William Godfrey Calle Alcalá 336, Urb. la Castellana, Santiago de Surco, Lima 33, Peru Tel (0051) (1) 422 9160 Fax (0051) (1) 440 8540 E-mail diocesisperu@anglicanperu.org *or* wgodfrey@amauta.rcp.net.pe
Uruguay	Miguel Tamayo Casilla de Correos 6108, 11000 Montevideo, Uruguay Tel (00598) (2) 915 9627 Fax (00598) (2) 916 2519 E-mail mtamayo@netgate.com.uy
(Suffragan)	Gilberto Obdulio Porcal Martinez Reconquista 522, CC 6108, 11000 Montevideo, Uruguay Tel (00598) (2) 915 9627 Fax (00598) (2) 916 2519 E-mail anglican@netgate.com.uy

SUDAN

A number of new dioceses have been created in the Church of the Province of Sudan. At the time of going to press, some details were unavailable, and so this list is incomplete.

Akot	Isaac Dhieu Ater c/o CMS Office, PO Box 40360, Nairobi, Kenya
Bor	Nathaniel Garang Anyieth c/o NSCC, PO Box 52802, Nairobi, Kenya Tel (00254) (733) 855 521 *or* 855 675 E-mail ecs_dioceseofbor@yahoo.co.uk
(Assistant)	Ezekel Diing Malaangdit c/o NSPCC, PO Box 52802, Nairobi, Kenya
Cueibet	Reuben Maciir Makoi c/o CEAS, PO Box 40870, Nairobi, Kenya Fax (00254) (2) 570807 E-mail eapo@cms-africa.org
El-Obeid	Ismail Abudigan Gibreil Kawo PO Box 211, El Obeid, Sudan Mobile (00249) 9122 53459 E-mail ecsprovince@hotmail.com
Ezo	John Zawo c/o ECS Support Office, PO Box 7576, Kampala, Uganda Tel (00256) (41) 343 497 E-mail kereborojohn@yahoo.com
Ibba	Wilson Elisa Kamani c/o ECS, PO Box 7576, Kampala, Uganda Tel (00256) (41) 343 497 *fax as telephone* E-mail ecs_ibbadiocese@hotmail.com *or* ecs-kpa@africaonline.co.ug
Juba (Archbishop)	Daniel Deng Bul PO Box 604, Khartoum, Sudan Tel (00249) (811) 820 065 E-mail dioceseofjuba@yahoo.com
(Assistant)	Joseph Makor Atot c/o CMS, PO Box 40360, Nairobi, Kenya
Kadugli and Nuba Mountains	Andudu Adam Elnail PO Box 35, Kadugli, Sudan Tel (00249) (631) 822898 E-mail bishandudu@yahoo.com *or* kadudiocese@hotmail.com
Kajo-Keji	Anthony Poggo c/o ECS Support Office, PO Box 7576, Kampala, Uganda Tel (00254) (41) 343 497 E-mail bishopkk@gmail.com
Khartoum	Ezekiel Kondo PO Box 65, Omdurman, 35 Khartoum, Sudan Tel (00249) (187) 556931 E-mail ecs_bishop_Khartoum@kastanet.org

Lainya	Peter Amidi c/o ECS Support Office, PO Box 7576, Kampala, Uganda Tel (00256) (77) 658 753 *fax as telephone* E-mail petamidi@yahoo.com
Lui	Bullen A Dolli PO Box 60837, Nairobi, Kenya Tel (00254) (2) 720 037 *or* 720 056 Fax (00249) (2) 714 420 E-mail bishop@luidiocese.org *or* cms-nbi@maf.org.ke
Malakal	Hilary Garang Aweer PO Box 604, Khartoum, Sudan E-mail ecsprovince@hotmail.com
Maridi	Justin Badi Arama c/o ECS, PO Box 7576, Kampala, Uganda Tel (00256) (41) 343 497 *fax as telephone* E-mail ecsmaridi@hotmail.com
Mundri	Bismark Monday Avokaya c/o ECS, PO Box 7576, Kampala, Uganda Tel (00256) (41) 343 497 *fax as telephone* E-mail ecsmundri@yahoo.com
Pacong	Joseph Maker E-mail ecs.pacongdiocese@yahoo.com
Port Sudan	Yousif Abdalla Kuku PO Box 278, Port Sudan, Sudan Tel (00249) (311) 821 224 E-mail ecsprovince@hotmail.com
Rejaf	Michael Sokiri Lugŏr PO Box 110, Juba, Sudan Tel (00249) 1290 76288 E-mail rejafdioceseecs@yahoo.com
Renk	Joseph Garang Atem PO Box 1532, Khartoum North, Sudan Mobile (00249) 122 99275 *fax as telephone* E-mail ecs_renk@hotmail.com
Rokon	Francis Loyo PO Box 6702, Nairobi 00100 APO, Kenya Tel (00254) (2) 568 541 *or* 568539 Fax (00254) (2) 560864 E-mail bployo@yahoo.co.uk
Rumbek	Alapayo Manyang Kuctiel c/o CMS Nairobi, PO Box 56, Nakuro, Kenya Tel (00254) (37) 43186 E-mail kuctiel@yahoo.com
(Assistants)	Isaac Dhieu Ater c/o CMS, PO Box 40360, Nairobi, Kenya Micah Dawidi, PO Box 111, Juba, Sudan
Terekeka	Micah Dawidi c/o CMS Nairobi, PO Box 56, Nakuro, Kenya
Torit	Bernard Oringa Balmoi c/o ECS Support Office, PO Box 7576, Kampala, Uganda Tel (00256) (41) 343 497 E-mail ecs_bishop_torit@kastanet.org
Wau	Henry Cuir Riak c/o CMS Nairobi, PO Box 56, Nakuru, Kenya Tel (00254) (37) 43186 E-mail riakcuir@yahoo.com *or* wauvtc@yahoo.com
Yambio	Peter Munde Yacoub c/o ECS, PO Box 7576, Kampala, Uganda Tel (00256) (41) 343 497 Mobile (00256) 77 622367 *fax as telephone* E-mail yambio2002@yahoo.com *or* ecs-kpa@africaonline.co.ug
Yei	Hilary Luate Adeba PO Box 588, Arua, Uganda Tel (00256) (756) 561 175 E-mail hill_sherpherd@yahoo.com *or* 72wca@techserve.org
Yirol	Benjamin Mangar Mamur c/o St Matthew's Church, PO Box 39, Eldoret, Kenya E-mail mamurmangar@yahoo.com *or* cms-nbi@maf.or.ke

TANZANIA

Central Tanganyika	Godfrey Mdimi Mhogolo Makay House, PO Box 15, Dodoma, Tanzania Tel (00255) (26) 232 1714 Fax (00255) (26) 232 4518 E-mail bishop@dct-tz.org *or* mhogolo@pnc.com.au
(Assistant)	Ainea Kusenha *address, tel and fax as above* E-mail ngombe2004@kicheko.com
Dar-es-Salaam (Archbishop)	Valentino Mokiwa PO Box 25016, Ilala, Dar-es-Salaam, Tanzania Tel (00255) (22) 286 4426 E-mail mokiwa_valentine@hotmail.com
Kagera	Aaron Kijanjali PO Box 18, Ngara, Tanzania Tel (00255) (28) 222 3624 Fax (00255) (28) 222 2518 E-mail act-kagera@africaonline.co.tz
Kiteto	Isaiah Chambala PO Box 74, Kibaya, Tanzania Tel (00255) (27) 255 2106 E-mail dkiteto@iwayafrica.com
Kondoa	Yohana Zakaria Mkavu PO Box 7, Kondoa, Tanzania Tel (00255) (26) 236 0312 Fax: (00255) (26) 236 0304 *or* 0324 E-mail d_kondoa@ do.ucc.co.tz
Lweru	Jackton Yeremiah Lugumira PO Box 12, Muleba, Tanzania Tel (00255) (713) 274 085 E-mail jlugumira2@juno.com
Mara	Hilkiah Deya Omindo Deya PO Box 131, Musoma, Tanzania Tel (00255) (28) 262 2376 Fax (00255) (28) 262 2414 E-mail actmara@juasun.net
Masasi	Patrick Mwachiko Private Bag, PO Masasi, Mtwara Region, Tanzania Tel (00255) (23) 251 0016 Fax (00255) (23) 251 0351 E-mail actmasasi@africaonline.co.tz
Morogoro	Dudley Mageni PO Box 320, Morogoro, Tanzania Tel (00255) (23) 260 4602 *fax as telephone* E-mail act-morogoro@africaonline.co.tz
Mount Kilimanjaro	Simon Elilekia Makundi PO Box 1057, Arusha, Tanzania Tel (00255) (27) 254 8396 Fax (00255) (27) 254 4187 E-mail dmk@habari.co.tz
Mpwapwa	Jacob Chimeledya PO Box 2, Mpwapwa, Tanzania Tel (00255) (26) 232 0017 *or* 0825 Fax (00255) (26) 232 0063 E-mail dmp@do.ucc.co.tz
Newala	Oscar Mnunga c/o Bishop of Masasi
Rift Valley	John Lupaa PO Box 16, Manyoni, Tanzania Tel (00255) (26) 254 0013 Fax (00255) (26) 250 3014 E-mail act-drv@maf.or.tz
Ruaha	Donald Leo Mtetemela Box 1028, Iringa, Tanzania Tel (00255) (26) 270 1211 Fax (00225) (26) 270 2479 E-mail ruaha@anglican.or.tz
Ruvuma	Maternus K Kapinga PO Box 1357, Songea, Ruvuma, Tanzania Tel (00255) (25) 260 0090 Fax (00255) (25) 260 2987 E-mail mkkapinga@yahoo.com
Shinyanga	Ngusa Charles Kija PO Box 421, Shinyanga, Tanzania Tel (00255) (28) 276 3584 E-mail ckngusa@yahoo.com
Southern Highlands	John Mwela PO Box 198, Mbeya, Tanzania Tel (00255) (25) 250 0216 E-mail dsh-dev@atma.co.tz
South West Tanganyika	*vacant* Bishop's House, PO Box 32, Njombe, Tanzania Tel (00255) (26) 278 2010 Fax (00255) (26) 278 2403 E-mail dswt@africaonline.co.tz
Tabora	Sadock Makaya PO Box 1408, Tabora, Tanzania Tel (00255) (26) 260 4124 Fax (00255) (26) 260 4899 E-mail dtdevtb@taboraonline.com *or* smakaya1@yahoo.co.uk
Tanga	Philip D Baji PO Box 35, Korogwe, Tanga, Tanzania Tel (00255) (27) 264 0522 Fax (00255) (27) 264 0631 E-mail bajipp@anglican.or.tz
Victoria Nyanza	Boniface Kwangu PO Box 278, Mwanza, Tanzania Tel (00255) (28) 250 0627 Fax (00255) (28) 250 0676 E-mail revkahene1@yahoo.com
Western Tanganyika	Gerard E Mpango PO Box 13, Kasulu, Tanzania Tel (00255) (28) 281 0321 Fax (00255) (28) 281 0706 E-mail askofugm@yahoo.com
(Lake Zone, Kigoma)	Naftali Bikaka PO Box 1378, Kigoma, Tanzania Tel (00255) (28) 280 3407 E-mail bpwbikaka@yahoo.co.uk
(Southern Zone, Rukwa in Sumbawanga)	Mark Badeleya PO Box 226, Sumbawanga, Tanzania Tel (00255) (25) 280 0287 E-mail bpbadeleya@yahoo.co.uk
Zanzibar	*vacant* PO Box 5, Mkunazini, Zanzibar, Tanzania Tel (00255) (24) 223 5348 Fax (00255) (24) 223 6772 E-mail secactznz@zanlink.com

UGANDA

Ankole	George Tibeesigwa PO Box 14, Mbarara, Ankole, Uganda Tel (00256) (485) 20290 Mobile (00256) 772 542 164
Bukedi	Nicodemus Engwalas-Okille PO Box 170, Tororo, Uganda Mobile (00256) 772 542 164
Bunyoro-Kitara	Nathan Kyamanywa PO Box 20, Hoima, Uganda Tel (00256) (465) 40128 Mobile (00256) 772 648 232 E-mail bkdioces@infocom.co.ug
Busoga	Michael Kyomya PO Box 1658, Jinja, Uganda Mobile (00256) 752 649 102
Central Buganda	Jackson Matovu PO Box 1200, Kinoni-Gomba, Mpigi, Uganda Mobile (00256) 772 475 640 E-mail bishopmatovu@yahoo.com
Kampala (Archbishop)	Henry Luke Orombi PO Box 335, Kampala, Uganda Tel (00256) (414) 279 218 Mobile (00256) 772 450 178 Fax (00256) (414) 251 925 E-mail kdcou@africaonline.co.ug
(Assistant)	Zac Niringiye PO Box 335, Kampala, Uganda Tel (00256) (414) 290 231 Fax (00256) (414) 342 601
Karamoja	Joseph Abura PO Box 44, Moroto, Uganda Tel (00256) 782 658 502

Kigezi George Katwesigye
PO Box 3, Kabale, Uganda
Tel (00256) (486) 22003
Mobile (00256) 772 446 954

Kinkizi John Ntegyereize
PO Box 77, Karuhinda, Rukungiri, Uganda
Tel (00873) (761) 604794 *or* 604795
Fax (00873) (761) 604796 *or* 604797
Mobile (00256) 772 507 163

Kitgum Benjamin Ojwang
PO Box 187, Kitgum, Uganda
Mobile (00256) 772 959 924
E-mail benojwang2004@yahoo.co.uk

Kumi Thomas Edison Irigei
PO Box 18, Kumi, Uganda
Mobile (00256) 772 659 460
E-mail coukumidiocese@yahoo.com

Lango John Charles Odurkami
PO Box 6, Lira, Uganda
Mobile (00256) 772 614 000
E-mail bishoplango@yahoo.com

Luwero Evans Mukasa Kisekka
PO Box 125, Luwero, Uganda
Tel (00256) (41) 610 070 *or* 610 048
Fax (00256) (41) 610 132 *or* 610 070
Mobile (00256) 772 421 220
E-mail kiromas@yahoo.co.uk

Madi and Joel Obetia
West Nile PO Box 370, Arua, Uganda
Mobile (00256) 752 625 414
E-mail jobetia@ucu.ac.ug

Masindi-Kitari Stanley Ntagali
PO Box 515, Masindi, Uganda
Tel (00256) (41) 270 218
Fax (00256) (41) 251 925
E-mail bishopntagali@yahoo.com

Mbale Samwiri Namakhetsa Khaemba Wabulakha
Bishop's House, PO Box 473, Mbale, Uganda
Tel (00256) (45) 33533
Mobile (00256) 772 512 051
E-mail wabulakhasa@yahoo.com

Mityana Stephen Samuel Kaziimba
PO Box 102, Mityana, Uganda
Tel (00256) (46) 2017
E-mail mtndiocese@hotmail.com

Muhabura Cranmer Mugisha
Church of Uganda, PO Box 22, Kisoro, Uganda
Tel (00256) (486) 30014 *or* 30058
Fax (00256) (486) 30059
Mobile (00256) 712 195 891

Mukono Elia Paul Luzinda
PO Box 39, Mukono, Uganda
Tel (00256) (41) 290 229
Mobile (00256) 772 603 348
E-mail mukodise@utlonline.co.ug

Namirembe Samuel Balagadde Ssekkadde
PO Box 14297, Kampala, Uganda
Tel (00256) (41) 271682 *or* 244347
Mobile (00256) 772 500 494
E-mail namid@infocom.co.ug

Nebbi Alphonse Watho-kudi
PO Box 27, Nebbi, Uganda
Mobile (00256) 772 650 032
E-mail bpalphonse@ekk.org

North Ankole John Muhanguzi
c/o PO Box 14, Rushere Mbarara, Ankole, Uganda
Mobile (00256) 772 369 947
E-mail northankole@gmail.com

North James Nasak
Karamoja PO Box 26, Kotido
Mobile (00256) 772 660 228

North Kigezi Edward Muhima
PO Box 23, Rukungiri, Uganda
Tel (00256) (486) 42433
Mobile (00256) 772 709 387
E-mail northkigezi@infocom.co.ug

North Mbale Daniel Gimadu
PO Box 1837, Mbale, Uganda
Fax (00256) (41) 254 576
E-mail northmbalediocese@yahoo.com *or* petgim2000@yahoo.com

Northern Nelson Onono-Onweng
Uganda PO Box 232, Gulu, Uganda
Mobile (00256) 772 838 193
E-mail ononobp@yahoo.co.uk

Ruwenzori Benezeri Kisembo
PO Box 37, Fort Portal, Uganda
Mobile (00256) 772 470 671
E-mail bishop@biznas.com

Sebei Augusto Arapyona Salimo
PO Box 23, Kapchorwa, Uganda
Tel (00256) (45) 51072 *or* 51008
Mobile (00256) 772 550 520
E-Mail augustinesalimo@yahoo.co.uk

Soroti Charles Bernard Obaikol-Ebitu
PO Box 107, Soroti, Uganda
Tel (00256) (45) 61795
Mobile (00256) 772 557 909
E-mail couteddo@infocom.co.ug

South Jackson T Nzerebende
Ruwenzori PO Box 42, Kasese, Uganda
Mobile (00256) 772 713 736
Fax (00256) (483) 44450
E-mail bpbende@yahoo.com

West Ankole Yonah Katoneene
PO Box 140, Bushenyi, Uganda
Tel (00256) 752 377 193
E-mail wad@westankolediocese.org

West Buganda Samuel Kefa Kamya
PO Box 242, Masaka, Uganda
Mobile (00256) 772 413 400
E-mail wesbug@infocom.co.ug

UNITED STATES OF AMERICA

The roman numerals indicate to which of the nine provinces of ECUSA the diocese belongs

Presiding Bishop Katharine Jefferts Schori
Episcopal Church Center,
815 Second Avenue,
New York, NY 10017, USA
Tel (001) (212) 716 6276
Fax (001) (212) 490 3298
E-mail stolley@episcopalchurch.org

(Office of Frank Clayton Matthews
Pastoral 8100 Three Chopt Road, Suite 102,
Development) Richmond, VA 23229, USA
Tel (001) (804) 282 6007
Fax (001) (804) 282 6008
E-mail cmatthews@episcopalchurch.org

(Bishop George Elden Packard
Suffragan for Episcopal Church Center,
Chaplaincies 815 Second Avenue,
and Bishop in New York, NY 10017, USA
Charge of Tel (001) (800) 334 7626 ext 6065
Micronesia) Fax (001) (212) 867 1654
E-mail gpackard@episcopalchurch.org

Alabama (IV) Henry Nutt Parsley
521 North 20th Street, Birmingham, AL 35203–2611, USA
Tel (001) (205) 715 2060
Fax (001) (205) 715 2066
E-mail Hparsley@dioala.org

(Suffragan) John McKee Sloan
address etc as above
Alaska (VIII) *vacant*
1205 Denali Way, Fairbanks, AK 99701–4137, USA
Tel (001) (907) 452 3040
Fax (001) (907) 456 6552

Albany (II) William Howard Love
68 South Swan Street, Albany, NY 12210, USA
Tel (001) (518) 465 4737
Fax (001) (518) 436 1182
E-mail *via* www.albanyepiscopaldiocese.org

Arizona (VIII)
Kirk Stevan Smith
114 West Roosevelt Street,
Phoenix, AZ 85003–1406, USA
Tel (001) (602) 254 0976
Fax (001) (602) 495 6603
Email bishop@azdiocese.org

Arkansas (VII)
Larry R Benfield
Cathedral House, PO Box 164668,
Little Rock, AR 72216–4668, USA
Tel (001) (501) 372 2168
Fax (001) (501) 372 2147
E-mail Lbenfield@arkansas.anglican.org

Atlanta (IV)
John Neil Alexander
2744 Peachtree Road NW,
Atlanta, GA 30363–0701, USA
Tel (001) (404) 601 5320
Fax (001) (404) 601 5330
E-mail bishop@episcopalatlanta.org

(Assistant)
Keith Bernard Whitmore
E-mail bishopkeith@episcopalatlanta.org

Bethlehem (III)
Paul Victor Marshall
333 Wyandotte Street,
Bethlehem, PA 18015–1527, USA
Tel (001) (610) 691 5655 or 691 5656
Fax (001) (610) 691 1682
E-mail bpoffice@diobeth.org

California (VIII)
Marc Handley Andrus
1055 Taylor Street,
San Francisco, CA 94108, USA
Tel (001) (415) 673 0606
Fax (001) (415) 673 1510
E-mail bishopmarc@diocal.org

Central
Ecuador (IX)
Wilfrido Ramos-Orench
Centro Diocesano de la ciudad de
Quito, calle Francisco Sarmiento No. 39–54 y
Portete, sector el Batán, Quito, Ecuador
Tel (00593) (2) 243 9183
E-mail wramos@ctdiocese.org

Central
Florida (IV)
John Wadsworth Howe
Diocesan Office, 1017 E Robinson
Street,
Orlando, FL 32801–2023, USA
Tel (001) (407) 423 3567
Fax (001) (407) 872 0006
E-mail jhowe@cfdiocese.net

Central Gulf
Coast (IV)
Philip Menzie Duncan II
201 Mo Baylen (BX13330),
Pensacola, FL 32591–3330, USA
Tel (001) (850) 434 7337
Fax (001) (850) 434 8577
E-mail bishopduncan@diocgc.org

Central
New York (II)
Gladstone Bailey Adams
310 Montgomery Street, Suite 200,
Syracuse, NY 13202–2093, USA
Tel (001) (315) 474 6596
Fax (001) (315) 478 1632
E-mail kmcdaniel@cny.anglican.org

Central
Pennsylvania
(III)
Nathan Dwight Baxter
Box 11937, Harrisburg, PA 17108–1937, USA
Tel (001) (717) 236 5959
Fax (001) (717) 236 6448
E-mail via www.diocesecpa.org

Chicago (V)
Jeffrey Dean Lee
65 East Huron Street,
Chicago, IL 60611, USA
Tel (001) (312) 751 4200 or 751 4217
E-mail bishop@episcopalchicago.org

(Assistant)
Victor Alfonso Scantlebury
Address and fax as above
Tel (001) (312) 751 4216
E-mail vscantlebury@episcopalchicago.org

Colombia (IX)
Francisco Jose Duque-Gómez
Apartado Aereo 52964, Bogotá 2, DC
Colombia
Tel (0057) (1) 288 3187 or 288 3167
Fax (0057) (1) 288 3248
E-mail iec@iglesiaepiscopal.org.co

Colorado (VI)
Robert John O'Neill
1300 Washington Street,
Denver, CO 80203–2008, USA
Tel (001) (303) 837 1173
Fax (001) (303) 837 1311
E-mail bishoponeill@coloradodiocese.org

Connecticut (I)
Andrew Donnan Smith
1335 Asylum Avenue, Hartford,
CT 06105–2295, USA
Tel (001) (860) 233 4481
E-mail adsmith@ctdiocese.org

(Suffragans)
James Elliott Curry
address etc as above
E-mail jcurry@ctdiocese.org

Laura Ahrens
address etc as above
E-mail lahrens@ctdiocese.org

Dallas (VII)
James Monte Stanton
1630 North Garrett Street, Dallas, TX 75206,
USA
Tel (001) (214) 826 8310
Fax (001) (214) 826 5968
E-mail jmsdallas@episcopal-dallas.org

Delaware (III)
Wayne Parker Wright
2020 Tatnall Street,
Wilmington, DE 19802, USA
Tel (001) (302) 656 5441
Fax (001) (302) 656 7342
E-mail waynewright@dioceseofdelaware.net

Dominican
Republic (IX)
Julio Cesar Holguin
Apartado 764, Calle Santiago No 114,
Santo Domingo, Dominican Republic
Tel (001) (809) 686 6014
Fax (001) (809) 686 6364
E-mail iglepidom@codetel.net.do

East Carolina
(IV)
Clifton Daniel
Box 1336, Kinston, NC 27803, USA
Tel (001) (252) 522 0885
Fax (001) (252) 523 5272
E-mail cdaniel@diocese-eastcarolina.org

East Tennessee
(IV)
Charles Glen vonRosenberg
401 Cumberland Avenue,
Knoxville, TN 37902–2302, USA
Tel (001) (865) 966 2110
Fax (001) (865) 966 2535
E-mail cgvonr@etdiocese.net

Eastern
Michigan (V)
Steven Todd Ousley
Diocesan Office, 924 N Niagara
Street, Saginaw, MI 48602, USA
Tel (001) (989) 752 6020
Fax (001) (989) 752 6120
E-mail bishop@eastmich.org

Eastern
Oregon (VIII)
vacant
PO Box 1548, The Dalles, OR 97058,
USA
Tel (001) (541) 298 4477
Fax (001) (541) 296 0939
E-mail diocese@episdioeo.org

(Assistant)
Bavi Edna Rivera
E-mail nrivera@episdioeo.org

Easton (III)
James Joseph Shand
314 North St, Easton, MD 21601–3684, USA
Tel (001) (410) 822 1919
E-mail bishopshand@dioceseofeaston.org

Eau Claire (V)
vacant
510 South Farwell Street,
Eau Claire, WI 54701, USA
Tel (001) (715) 835 3331
Fax (001) (715) 835 9212
E-mail deaconjeanne@dioceseofeauclaire.org

El Camino
Real (VIII)
Mary Gray-Reeves
PO Box 1903, Monterey, CA 93942, USA
Tel (001) (831) 394 4466
Fax (001) (831) 394 7133
E-mail Marygrayreeves@earthlink.net

Europe,
Convocation
of American
Churches in
(VII)
Pierre Welté Whalon
American Cathedral of the Holy Trinity,
23 Avenue George V, 75008 Paris, France
Tel (0033) (1) 53 23 84 00
Fax (0033) (1) 47 23 95 30
E-mail bishops@tec-europe.org

Florida (IV)
Samuel Johnson Howard
325 Market Street, Jacksonville,
FL 32202–2796, USA
Tel (001) (904) 356 1328
Fax (001) (904) 355 1934
E-mail jhoward@diocesefl.org

Fond du Lac (V) Russell Edward Jacobus
1047 N. Lynndale Dr., Suite 1B, Appleton, WI
54914, USA
Tel (001) (920) 830 8866
Fax (001) (920) 830 8761
E-mail diofdl@diofdl.org

Fort Worth (VII) Jack Leo Iker
2900 Alemeda Street, Fort Worth, TX 76116,
USA
Tel (001) (817) 244 2885
Fax (001) (817) 244 3363
E-mail jliker@fwepiscopal.org

Georgia (IV) Henry Irving Louttit
611 East Bay Street, Savannah, GA
31401–1296, USA
Tel (001) (912) 236 4279
Fax (001) (912) 236 2007
E-mail diocesega@att.net

Haiti (II) Jean Zache Duracin
Eglise Episcopale d'Haiti,
BP 1309, Port-au-Prince, Haiti
Tel (00509) 257 1624
Fax (00509) 257 3412
E-mail epihaiti@hotmail.com

Hawaii (VIII) Robert LeRoy Fitzpatrick
Diocesan Office, 229 Queen Emma Square,
Honolulu, HI 96813–2304, USA
Tel (001) (808) 536 7776
Fax (001) (808) 538 7194
E-mail rlfitzpatrick@episcopalhawaii.org

Honduras (IX) Lloyd Emmanuel Allen
23 Av 'C', 21 Calle Colonia, San Pedro Sula,
Cortés 21105, Honduras, Central America
Tel (00504) 566 6155 or 556 6268
Fax (00504) 556 6467
E-mail obispoallen@yahoo.com

Idaho (VIII) Brian James Thom
1858 W. Judith Lane, Boise, ID 83705, USA
Tel (001) (208) 345 4440
Fax (001) (208) 345 9735
E-mail bthom@idahodiocese.org

Indianapolis (V) Catherine Elizabeth Maples
Waynick
1100 West 42nd Street,
Indianapolis, IN 46208, USA
Tel (001) (317) 926 5454
Fax (001) (317) 926 5456
E-mail bishop@indydio.org

Iowa (VI) Alan Scarfe
225 37th Street, Des Moines,
IA 50312–4399, USA
Tel (001) (515) 277 6165
Fax (001) (515) 277 0273
E-mail Ascarfe@iowaepiscopal.org

Kansas (VII) Dean Elliott Wolfe
Bethany Place, 833–35 Polk Street,
Topeka, KS 66612, USA
Tel (001) (785) 235 9255
Fax (001) (785) 235 2449
E-mail Dwolfe@episcopal-ks.org

Kentucky (IV) Edwin Funsten Gulick
425 South Second Street,
Louisville, KY 40202–1417, USA
Tel (001) (502) 584 7148
Fax (001) (502) 587 8123
E-mail TedG@episcopalky.org

Lexington (IV) Stacy Fred Sauls
PO Box 610, Lexington, KY, 40586, USA
Tel (001) (859) 252 6527
Fax (001) (859) 231 9077
E-mail sfsauls@diolex.org

Litoral
Diocese of
Ecuador (IX) Alfredo Ulloa Morante España
Box 0901–5250,
Amarilis Fuentes entre V Trujillo,
y La 'D', Guayaquil, Ecuador
Tel (00593) (4) 443 050
Fax (00593) (4) 443 088
E-mail bishopmorante@hotmail.com or
iedl@gu.pro.ec

Long Island (II) Orris George Walker
36 Cathedral Avenue,
Garden City, NY 11530, USA
Tel (001) (516) 248 4800
Fax (001) (516) 248 1616
E-mail owalker@dioceseli.org

Los Angeles
(VIII) Joseph Jon Bruno
Box 512164, Los Angeles, CA 90051–0164,
USA
Tel (001) (213) 482 2040 ext 236
Fax (001) (213) 482 5304
E-mail bishop@ladiocese.org

(Suffragan) Chester Lovelle Talton
address etc as above
E-mail suffragan@ladiocese.org

Louisiana (IV) Charles Edward Jenkins
1623 Seventh Street, New Orleans,
LA 70115, USA
Tel (001) (504) 895 6634
Fax (001) (504) 895 6637
E-mail bishop@edola.org

Maine (I) Stephen Taylor Lane
Loring House, 143 State Street,
Portland, ME 04101, USA
Tel (001) (207) 772 1953
Fax (001) (207) 773 0095
E-mail slane@episcopalmaine.org

Maryland (III) Robert Wilkes Ihloff
4 East University Parkway,
Baltimore, MD 21218–2437, USA
Tel (001) (800) 443 1399 or (410) 467 1399
Fax (001) (410) 554 6387
E-mail +rihloff@ang-md.org

(Suffragan John Leslie Rabb
address etc as above
E-mail jrabb@ang-md.org

Massachusetts
(I) Marvil Thomas Shaw
Society of St John the Evangelist,
138 Tremont St, Boston, MA 02111, USA
Tel (001) (617) 482 5800
Fax (001) (617) 451 6446
E-mail chipbe@diomass.org

(Suffragans) Roy Frederick Cederholm
address etc as above
E-mail budc@diomass.org

Gayle Elizabeth Harris
address etc as above
E-mail SHP@diomass.org

Michigan (V) Wendell Nathaniel Gibbs
4800 Woodward Avenue,
Detroit, MI 48201, USA
Tel (001) (313) 832 4400
Fax (001) (313) 831 0259
E-mail Wgibbs@edomi.org

Milwaukee (V) Steven Andrew Miller
804 East Juneau Street,
Milwaukee, WI 53202, USA
Tel (001) (414) 272 3028
Fax (001) (414) 272 7790
E-mail bishop11@diomil.org

Minnesota (VI) James Louis Jelinek
1730 Clifton Place, Suite 201,
Minneapolis, MN 55403, USA
Tel (001) (612) 871 5311
Fax (001) (612) 871 0552
E-mail episcopal.centre@episcopalmn.org

Mississippi (IV) Duncan Montgomery Gray III
St Andrew's Cathedral, PO Box 23107,
Jackson, MS 39225–3107, USA
Tel (001) (601) 948 5954
Fax (001) (601) 354 3401
E-mail cjohns@dioms.org

Missouri (V) George Wayne Smith
1210 Locust Street,
St Louis, MO 63103, USA
Tel (001) (314) 231 1220
Fax (001) (314) 231 3373
E-mail pensmith@pensmith.net

Montana (VI)	Charles Franklin Brookhart, Jr 515 North Park Avenue, Helena, MT 59601, USA Tel (001) (406) 422 2230 Fax (001) (406) 442 2238 E-mail cfbmt@qwestoffice.net
Navajoland Area Mission (VIII)	Mark Lawrence MacDonald (Assisting Bishop) PO Box 720, Farmington, NM 87499–0720, USA Tel (001) (505) 327 7549 Fax (001) (505) 327 6904 E-mail mmacdonald@gci.net
Nebraska (VIII)	Joe Goodwin Burnett 109 North 18th Street, Omaha, NE 68102–4903, USA Tel (001) (402) 341 5373 Fax (001) (402) 341 8683 E-mail jburnett@episcopal-ne.org
Nevada (VIII)	Dan Thomas Edwards 6135 Harrison Drive, Suite 1, Las Vegas, NV 89120–4076, USA Tel (001) (702) 737 9190 Fax (001) (702) 737 6488 E-mail bishop@nvdiocese.org
New Hampshire (I)	Gene Robinson 63 Green Street, Concord, NH 03301, USA Tel (001) (603) 224 1914 Fax (001) (603) 225 7884 E-mail GRinNH@aol.com
New Jersey (II)	George Edward Councell 808 West State Street, Trenton, NJ 08618, USA Tel (001) (609) 394 5281 Fax (001) (609) 394 9546 E-mail gGCouncell@newjersey.anglican.org
New York (II)	Mark Sean Sisk Synod House, 1047 Amsterdam Avenue, Cathedral Heights, New York, NY 10025, USA Tel (001) (212) 316 7400 Fax (001) (212) 316 7405 E-mail bpsisk@dioceseny.org
(Suffragan)	Catherine Scimeca Roskam Region Two Office, 55 Cedar Street, Dobbs Ferry, NY 10522, USA Tel (001) (914) 693 3848 Fax (001) (914) 693 0407 E-mail bproskam@dioceseny.org
(Assistant)	Egbert Don Taylor Synod Office, 1047 Amsterdam Avenue, Cathedral Heights, New York, NY 10025, USA Tel (001) (212) 316 7400 Fax (001) (212) 316 7405 E-mail bptaylor@dioceseny.org
Newark (II)	Mark Beckwith 31 Mulberry Street, Newark, NJ 07102, USA Tel (001) (973) 622 4306 Fax (001) (973) 622 3503 E-mail mbeckwith@dioceseofnewark.org
North Carolina (IV)	Michael Bruce Curry 200 West Morgan St., Suite 300, Raleigh, NC 27601, USA Tel (001) (919) 834 7474 Fax (001) (919) 834 7546 E-mail via www.episdionc.org
North Dakota (VI)	Michael Gene Smith 3600 25th St S, Fargo, ND 58104–6861, USA Tel (001) (701) 235 6688 Fax (001) (701) 232 3077 E-mail BpNodak@aol.com
Northern California (VIII)	Barry Leigh Beisner Box 161268, Sacramento, CA 95816–5902, USA Tel (001) (916) 442 6918 Fax (001) (916) 442 6927 E-mail Bishopblb@dncweb.org
Northern Indiana (V)	Edward Stuart Little II 117 North Lafayette Boulevard, South Bend, IN 46601, USA Tel (001) (574) 233 6489 Fax (001) (574) 287 7914 E-mail bishop@ednin.org
Northern Michigan (V)	*vacant* 131 East Ridge Street, Marquette, MI 49855, USA Tel (001) (906) 228 7160 Fax (001) (906) 228 7171 E-mail diocese@upepiscopal.org
Northwest Texas (VII)	Charles Wallis Ohl Jr. The Hulsey Episcopal Church Center, 1802 Broadway, Lubbock, TX 79401, USA Tel (001) (806) 763 1370 Fax (001) (804) 472 0641 E-mail bishop@nwt.org
Northwestern Pennsylvania (III)	Sean W Rowe 145 West 6th Street, Erie, PA 16501, USA Tel (001) (814) 456 4203 *or* (800) 643 2351 Fax (001) (814) 454 8703 E-mail seanrowe@dionwpa.org
Ohio (V)	Mark Hollingsworth Jr. 2230 Euclid Avenue, Cleveland, OH 44115–2499, USA Tel (001) (216) 771 4815 Fax (001) (216) 623 0735 E-mail mh@dohio.org
Oklahoma (VII)	Edward Joseph Konieczny 924 North Robinson, Oklahoma City, OK 73102, USA Tel (001) (405) 232 4820 Fax (001) (405) 232 4912 E-mail bishopEd@episcopaloklahoma.org
Olympia (VIII)	Vincent Waydell Warner PO Box 12126, Seattle, WA 98102, USA Tel (001) (206) 325 4200 Fax (001) (206) 325 4631 E-mail grickel@ecww.org
(Suffragan)	Bavi Edna ('Nedi') Rivera *address etc as above* E-mail nrivera@ecww.org
Oregon (VIII)	*vacant* 11800 S.W. Military Lane, Portland, OR 97219, USA Tel (001) (503) 636 5613 Fax (001) (503) 636 5616 E-mail sandyh@diocese-oregon.org
(Assistant)	Sanford ('Sandy') Hampton *address etc as above*
Pennsylvania (III)	Charles Ellesworth Bennison 240 South Fourth Street, Philadelphia, PA 19106, USA Tel (001) (215) 627 6434 ext 112 *or* 131 Fax (001) (215) 627 7750 E-mail *via* www.diopa.org
Pittsburgh (III)	*vacant* 325 Oliver Avenue, Pittsburgh, PA 15222–2467, USA Tel (001) (412) 281 6131 Fax (001) (412) 471 5591 E-mail duncan@pgh.anglican.org
(Assistant)	Robert Hodges Johnson *address etc as above*
Puerto Rico	David Andres Alvarez PO Box 902, St Just, PR 00978, Puerto Rico Tel (001) (787) 761 9800 Fax (001) (787) 761 0320 E-mail obispoalvarez@spiderlink.net
Quincy (V)	Keith Lynn Ackerman 3601 N North Street, Peoria, IL 61604–1599, USA Tel (001) (309) 688 8221 Fax (001) (309) 688 8229 *or* 692 2421 E-mail bishop@dioceseofquincy.org
Rhode Island (I)	Geralyn Wolf 275 North Main Street, Providence, RI 02903–1298, USA Tel (001) (401) 274 4500 Fax (001) (401) 331 9430 E-mail bishop@episcopalri.org

Rio Grande (VII)
vacant
4304 Carlisle Boulevard North East,
Albuquerque, NM 87107–4811, USA
Tel (001) (505) 881 0636
Fax (001) (505) 883 9048
E-mail *via* www.riogrande.anglican.org

Rochester (II)
Jack Marston McKelvey
935 East Avenue, Rochester, NY 14607, USA
Tel (001) (585) 473 2977
E-mail BpJackM@aol.com

San Diego (VIII)
James Robert Mathes
2728 Sixth Avenue,
San Diego, CA 92103–6397, USA
Tel (001) (619) 291 5947
Fax (001) (619) 291 8362
E-mail bishopmathes@edsd.org

San Joaquin (VIII)
vacant
4159 East Dakota Avenue,
Fresno, CA 93726, USA
Tel (001) (559) 244 4828
Fax (001) (559) 244 4832

(Interim Bishop)
Jerry A Lamb
E-mail jerrylamb@diosanjoaquin.org

South Carolina (IV)
Edward Lloyd Salmon
Box 20127, Charleston,
SC 29413–0127, USA
Tel (001) (843) 722 4075
Fax (001) (843) 723 7628
E-mail elsalmon@dioceseofsc.org

South Dakota (VI)
Creighton Leland Robertson
500 South Main Street,
Sioux Falls, SD 57104–6814, USA
Tel (001) (605) 338 9751
Fax (001) (605) 336 6243
E-mail office.diocese@midconetwork.com *or*
creighton_robertson@ecunet.org

(Coadjutor)
John Thomas Tarrant
address etc as above

Southeast Florida (IV)
Leopold Frade
525 North East 15th Street,
Miami, FL 33132, USA
Tel (001) (305) 373 0881
Fax (001) (305) 375 8054
E-mail bishopfrade@aol.com

Southern Ohio (V)
Thomas Edward Breidenthal
412 Sycamore Street,
Cincinnati, OH 45202–4179, USA
Tel (001) (513) 421 0311
Fax (001) (513) 421 0315
E-mail bishop_breidenthal@episcopal-dso.org

Southern Virginia (III)
Herman 'Holly' Hollerith
600 Talbot Hall Road, Norfolk, VA
23505–4361, USA
Tel (001) (757) 423 8287
Fax (001) (757) 440 5354
E-mail 600@diosova.org

(Assistant)
John Clark Buchanan
address etc as above

Southwest Florida (IV)
John Bailey Liscomb
7313 Merchant Ct, Sarasota, FL
34240–8437, USA
Tel (001) (941) 556 0315
Fax (001) (941) 556 0321
E-mail jliscomb@dioceseswfla.org

Southwestern Virginia (III)
Frank Neff Powell
PO Box 2279, Roanoke,
VA 24009–2279, USA
Tel (001) (540) 342 6797
Fax (001) (540) 343 9114
E-mail npowell@dioswva.org

Spokane (VIII)
James Edward Waggoner
245 East 13th Avenue, Spokane,
WA 99202–1114, USA
Tel (001) (509) 624 3191
Fax (001) (509) 747 0049
E-mail jimw@spokanediocese.org

Springfield (VIII)
Peter Hess Beckwith
821 South 2nd Street, Springfield,
IL 62704–2694, USA
Tel (001) (217) 525 1876
Fax (001) (217) 525 1877
E-mail diocese@episcopalspringfield.org *or*
phbxebs@midwest.net

Taiwan (VIII)
David J H Lai
Friendship House, #7 Lane 105, Hangchow
South Rd, Sec. 1, Taipei, Taiwan 10044,
Republic of China
Tel (00886) (2) 2341 1265
Fax (00886) (2) 2396 2014
E-mail skh.tpe@msa.hinet.net

Tennessee (IV)
John Crawford Bauernschmidt
50 Vantage Way,
Suite 107, Nashville, TN 37228–1504, USA
Tel (001) (615) 251 3322
Fax (001) (615) 251 8010
E-mail info@episcopaldiocese tn.org

Texas (VII)
Charles Andrew Doyle
1225 Texas Ave, Houston, TX 77002, USA
Tel (001) (713) 353 2100
Fax (001) (713) 520 5723
E-mail dwimberly@epicenter.org

Upper South Carolina (IV)
Dorsey Felix Henderson
1115 Marion Street, Columbia, SC
29201, USA
Tel (001) (803) 771 7800
Fax (001) (803) 799 5119
E-mail jgoldsmith@edusc.org

Utah (VIII)
Carolyn Tanner Irish
80 South 300 East Street, PO Box 3090,
Salt Lake City, UT 84110–3090, USA
Tel (001) (801) 322 4131
Fax (001) (801) 322 5096
E-mail CIrish@episcopal-ut.org

Venezuela (IX)
Orlando Guerrero Torres
Apartado 49–143, Avenida Caroni 100, Colinas
de Bello Monte, Caracas 1042 A, Venezuela
Tel (0058) (212) 753 0723
Fax (0058) (212) 751 3180
E-mail obispoguerrero@iglesianglicanavzla.org

Vermont (I)
Thomas Clark Ely
Diocesan House, 5 Rock Point Road,
Burlington, VT 05401–2735, USA
Tel (001) (802) 863 3431
Fax (001) (802) 860 1562
E-mail tely@dioceseofvermont.org

Virgin Islands (II)
Edward Ambrose Gumbs
13 Commandant Gade, Charlotte Amalie, St
Thomas, VI 00801, USA
Tel (001) (340) 776 1797
Fax (001) (809) 777 8485
E-mail bishop@episcovi.org

Virginia (III)
Peter James Lee
110 West Franklin Street,
Richmond, VA 23220, USA
Tel (001) (804) 643 8451
Fax (001) (804) 644 6928
E-mail pjlee@thediocese.net

(Coadjutor)
Shannon Sherwood Johnston
address etc as above
E-mail kglasco@thediocese.net

(Suffragan)
David Colin Jones
Northern Virginia Office, Goodwin House,
4800 Fillmore Avenue, Alexandria, VA 22311,
USA
Tel (001) (703) 824 1325
Fax (001) (703) 824 1348
E-mail djones@thediocese.net

Washington (III)
John Bryson Chane
Episcopal Church House, Mount St Alban,
Washington, DC 20016, USA
Tel (001) (202) 537 6555
Tel (001) (202) 364 6605
E-mail jchane@edow.org

West Missouri (VII)
Barry Robert Howe
PO Box 413227, Kansas City,
MO 64141–3227, USA
Tel (001) (816) 471 6161
Fax (001) (816) 471 0379
E-mail bphowe@earthlink.net *or*
barryroberthowe@cs.com

West Tennessee (IV)
Don Edward Johnson
692 Poplar Avenue,
Memphis, TN 38105, USA
Tel (001) (901) 526 0023
Fax (001) (901) 526 1555
E-mail info@episwtn.org

West Texas (VII) Gary Richard Lillibridge
PO Box 6885, San Antonio, TX 78209, USA
Tel (001) (210) 824 5387
Fax (001) (210) 822 8779
E-mail gary.lillibridge@dwtx.org

(Suffragan) David Reed
address etc as above
E-mail david.reed@dwtx.org

West Virginia (III) William Michie Klusmeyer
PO Box 5400, Charleston,
WV 25361–5400, USA
Tel (001) (304) 344 3597
Fax (001) (304) 343 3295
E-mail mklusmeyer@wvdiocese.org

Western Kansas (VII) James Marshall Adams
Box 2507, Salina, KS 67401–2507, USA
Tel (001) (785) 825 1626
Fax (001) (785) 825 0974
E-mail myrnapeterson@sbcglobal.net

Western Louisiana (VII) David Bruce MacPherson
PO Box 2031, Alexandria, LA 71309, USA
Tel (001) (318) 442 1304
Fax (001) (318) 442 8712
E-mail dbm3wla@aol.com

Western Massachusetts (I) Gordon Paul Scruton
37 Chestnut Street,
Springfield, MA 01103, USA
Tel (001) (413) 737 4786
Fax (001) (413) 746 9873
E-mail JLewis@diocesewma.org

Western Michigan (V) Robert R Gepert
5220 Lovers Lane, LL100,
Portage, MI 49002–5653, USA
Tel (001) (616) 381 2710
Fax (001) (616) 381 7067
E-mail diowestmi@edwm.org *or*
edwmorg@edwm.org

Western New York (II) J Michael Garrison
1114 Delaware Avenue,
Buffalo, NY 14209, USA
Tel (001) (716) 881 0660
Fax (001) (716) 881 1724
E-mail jmgarrison@Episcopalwny.org *or*
michael.garrison4@gte.net

Western North Carolina (IV) Granville Porter Taylor
900B CenterPark Drive, Asheville,
NC 28805, USA
Tel (001) (828) 225 6656
Fax (001) (828) 225 6657
E-mail bishop@diocesewnc.org

Wyoming (VI) Bruce Edward Caldwell
104 South Fourth Street,
Laramie, WY 82070, USA
Tel (001) (307) 742 6606
Fax (001) (307) 742 2888
E-mail bruce@wydiocese.org

WEST AFRICA

Accra (Archbishop) Justice Ofei Akrofi
Bishopscourt, PO Box 8, Accra, Ghana
Tel (00233) (21) 662 292 *or* 663595
Fax (00233) (21) 668 822
E-mail adaccra@ghana.com *or*
bishopakrofi@ghana.com

Bo Emmanuel Josie Samuel Tucker
1 A MacRobert Street, PO Box 21, Bo,
Southern Province, Sierra Leone
Tel (00232) (32) 648
Fax (00233) (32) 605
Email bomission@justice.com

Cameroon Thomas-Babyngton Elango Dibo
BP 15705, Akwa, Duala, Cameroon
Tel (00237) 408 552
fax as telephone
E-mail camanglica-church@camnet.cm *or*
agneslabep@yahoo.com

Cape Coast Daniel S A Allotey
Bishopscourt, PO Box A233,
Adisadel Estates, Cape Coast, Ghana
Tel (00233) (42) 32 502
Fax (00233) (42) 32 637
E-mail danallotey@priest.com

(Suffragan) Edmund K. Dawson-Ahmoah
same address as above
Tel (233) 24 464 4764

Freetown Julius Olotu Prince Lynch
Bishop's Court, PO Box 537,
Freetown, Sierra Leone
Tel (00232) (22) 251 307
Mobile (00232) 76 620 690
E-mail bertajuls@yahoo.co.uk

The Gambia Solomon Tilewa E W Johnson
Bishopscourt, PO Box 51,
Banjul, The Gambia
Tel (00220) 228 405
Mobile (00220) 905 227
E-mail anglican@qanet.gm *or*
stilewaj@hotmail.com

Guinea Albert D Gomez
BP 187, Conakry, Guinea
Tel (00224) 451 323
E-mail agomezd@yahoo.fr

Ho Matthias K Mededues Badohu
Bishopslodge, PO Box MA 300, Ho, Volta
Region, Ghana
Tel (00233) (91) 26644 *or* 26806
Mobile (00233) 208 162 246
E-mail matthoda@ucomgh.com *or*
matthiaskwab@googlemail.com

Koforidua Francis B Quashie
PO Box 980, Koforidua, Ghana
Tel (00233) (81) 22 329
Fax (00233) (81) 22 060
E-mail cwpa_gh@yahoo.com

Kumasi Daniel Yinka Sarfo
St Cyprian's Avenue,
PO Box 144, Kumasi, Ghana
Tel (00233) (51) 24 117
Mobile (00233) 277 890 411
fax as telephone
E-mail anglicandioceseofkumasi@yahoo.com
or dysarfo2000@yahoo.co.uk

Liberia Jonathan B. B. Hart
PO Box 10–0277, 1000 Monrovia 10, Liberia
Tel (00231) 224 760
Mobile (00377) 47 516 440
Fax (00231) 227 519
E-mail jbbhart@yahoo.com *or*
bishopec112@yahoo.com

Sekondi John Kwamina Otoo
PO Box 85, Sekondi, Ghana
Tel (00233) (31) 4604
E-mail angdiosek@yahoo.com

Sunyani Festus Yeboah-Asuamah
PO Box 23, Sunyani, Ghana
Tel (00233) (61) 23213
Mobile (00233) 208 121 670
Fax (00233) (61) 712300
E-mail fyasuamah@yahoo.com

Tamale Emmanuel Anyindana Arongo
PO Box 110, Tamale NR, Ghana
Tel (00233) (71) 26639
Mobile (00233) 277 890 878
Fax (00233) (71) 22906
E-mail bishopea2000@yahoo.com

Wiawso Abraham Kobina Ackah
PO Box 4, Sefwi, Wiawso, Ghana
E-mail bishopackah@yahoo.com

WEST INDIES

The Bahamas and the Turks and Caicos Islands Laish Zane Bogd
Church House, PO Box N-7107,
Nassau, Bahamas
Tel (001242) 322 3015
Fax (001242) 322 7943

(New
Providence)
Gilbert Arthur Thompson
address etc as above

Barbados
John Walder Dunlop Holder
Mandeville House, Collymore Rock,
St Michael, Barbados
Tel (001246) 426 2762
Fax (001246) 426 0871
E-mail jwdh@sunbeach.net

Belize
Philip S. Wright
25 Bishopsthorpe, Southern Foreshore,
PO Box 535, Belize City, Belize
Tel (00501) (2) 73029
Fax (00501) (2) 76898
E-mail bzediocese@btl.net

Guyana
Cornell Moss
The Diocesan Office, PO Box 10949,
49 Barrack Street, Georgetown, Guyana
Tel (00592) (22) 64 775
Fax (00592) (22) 76 091
E-mail dioofguy@networksgy.com

Jamaica and
the Cayman
Islands
Alfred Charles Reid
2 Caledonia Avenue, Kingston 5, Jamaica
Tel (001876) 920 2712
Fax (001876) 960 1774
E-mail bishopja@anglicandiocese.com

(Kingston)
Robert McLean Thompson
14 Ottawa Avenue, Kingston 6, Jamaica
Tel (001876) 926 6692
Fax (001876) 960 8463
E-mail standrewch@cwjamaica.com

(Mandeville)
Harold Benjamin Daniel
Bishop's Residence, 3 Cotton Tree Road, PO
Box 84, Mandeville, Jamaica
Tel (001876) 625 6817
Fax (001876) 625 6819
E-mail hbdaniel@cwjamaica.com

(Montego Bay)
Howard Gregory
PO Box 346, Montego Bay, Jamaica
Tel (001876) 952 4963
Fax (001876) 971 8838
E-mail hkagregory@hotmail.com

North Eastern
Caribbean
and Aruba
Leroy Errol Brooks
St Mary's Rectory, PO Box 180,
The Valley, Anguilla

Tel (001264) 497 2235
Fax (001264) 497 8555
E-mail brookx@anguillanet.com

Trinidad and
Tobago
Calvin Wendell Bess
Hayes Court, 21 Maraval Road,
Port of Spain, Trinidad
Tel (001868) 622 7387
Fax (001868) 628 1319
E-mail bessc@tstt.net.tt

Windward
Islands
C. Leopold Friday,
Bishop's Court, Montrose, PO Box 502,
St Vincent and the Grenadines
Tel (001784) 456 1895
Fax (001784) 456 2591
E-mail diocesewi@vincysurf.com

EXTRA-PROVINCIAL DIOCESES

Bermuda
(Canterbury)
Vacant
Diocesan Office, PO Box HM 769,
Hamilton HM CX, Bermuda
Tel (001441) 293 1787
E-mail bishopratteray@ibl.bm *or*
diocoff@ibl.bm

§Cuba
Miguel Tamayo
Calle 6 No 273, Vedado,
Havana 4, 10400 Cuba
Tel (0053) (7) 35655, 38003, 321120 *or* 312436
Fax (0053) (7) 333293
E-mail episcopal@ip.etecsa.cu

Lusitanian
Church
(Canterbury)
Fernando da Luz Soares
Secretaria Diocesana, Apartado 392,
P-4430 Vila Nova de Gaia, Portugal
Tel (00351) (22) 375 4018
Fax (00351) (22) 375 2016
E-mail centrodiocesano@igreja-lusitana.org

Spanish
Reformed
Episcopal
Church
(Canterbury)
Carlos López Lozano
Calle Beneficencia 18, 28004 Madrid, Spain
Tel (0034) (91) 445 2560
Fax (0034) (91) 594 4572
E-mail eclesiae@arrakis.es

§ Under a Metropolitan Council of the Primate of Canada, the
Archbishop of the West Indies and the President-Bishop of the
Episcopal Church's Province IX.

BISHOPS OF CHURCHES WHERE ANGLICANS HAVE UNITED WITH CHRISTIANS OF OTHER TRADITIONS

NORTH INDIA

Agra
Samuel R Cutting
Bishop's House,
St Paul's Church Compound,
4/116-B Church Road, Civil Lines,
Agra, UP, 282 002, India
Tel (0091) (562) 285 4845
Fax (0091) (562) 252 0074
E-mail doacni@sancharnet.in

Amritsar
Pradeep Kumar Samantaroy
26 R B Prakash Chand Road, opp Police
Ground,
Amritsar, Punjab, 143 001, India
Tel (0091) (183) 222 2910
fax as telephone
E-mail bunu13@rediffmail.com

Andaman and
Car Nicobar
Islands
Christopher Paul
Bishop's House, 21 Church Lane, Goal Ghar,
Port Blair 744 101, Andaman and Nicobar
Islands, India
Tel (0091) (3192) 231 362
fax as telephone

Barrackpore
(Deputy
Moderator)
Brojen Malakar
Bishop's Lodge, 86 Middle Road,
Barrackpore, Kolkata 700120, West Bengal,
India
Tel (0091) (33) 2592 0147
Fax (0091) (33) 2561 1852

Bhopal
Laxman L Malda
Bishop's House, 57, Residency Area,
Behind Narmada Water Tank, Indore 452 001,
MP, India
Tel (0091) (731) 270 0232
Mobile (0091) 98270 34737
E-mail bhopal_diocese@rediffmail.com

Chandigarh
(Moderator)
Joel Vidyasagar Mal
Bishop's House, Mission Compound,
Brown Road, Ludhiana,
Punjab, 141 001, India
Tel (0091) (161) 222 5707
fax as telephone
E-mail bishopdoc@yahoo.com *or*
joelvmal@yahoo.com

Chotanagpur
B. B. Baskey
Bishop's Lodge, PO Box 1, Church Road,
Ranchi, Bihar, 834 001, India
Tel (0091) (651) 235 1184
Fax as telephone
E-mail rch_cndta@sancharnet.in

Cuttack
Samson Das
Bishop's House, Mission Road,
Cuttack, Orissa, 753 001, India
Tel (0091) (671) 230 0102
E-mail diocese@vsnl.net

Delhi	Sunil Singh Bishop's House, 1 Church Lane, off North Avenue, New Delhi, 110 001, India Tel (0091) (11) 2371 7471 E-mail stmartin@dels.vsnl.net.in
Durgapur	Probal Kanto Dutta St Michael's Church Compound, Aldrin Path, Bidhan Nagar, Dugapur 713 212, India Tel (0091) (343) 253 4552 E-mail probal_dutta@yahoo.com
Eastern Himalaya	Naresh Ambala Bishop's Lodge, PO Box 4, Darjeeling, West Bengal, 734 101, India Tel (0091) (354) 225 8183 E-mail bpambala@yahoo.com
Gujarat	Vinod Kumar Mathushellah Malaviya Bishop's House, Ellis Bridge, Ahmedabad, Gujarat State, 380 006, India Tel (0091) (79) 2656 1950 *fax as telephone* E-mail gujdio@yahoo.co.in
Jabalpur	Prem Chand Singh Bishop's House, 2131 Napier Town, Jabalpur, MP, 482 001, India Tel (0091) (761) 2622 109 E-mail bishoppcsingh@yahoo.co.in
Kolhapur	Bathuel Ramchandra Tiwade Bishop's House, EP School Compound, Kolhapur, Maharashtra, 416 001, India Tel (0091) (231) 2654 832 *fax as telephone* E-mail kdccni@vsnl.com
Kolkata	Ashok Biwas Bishop's House, 51 Chowringhee Road, Calcutta, WB, 700 071, India Tel (0091) (33) 6534 7770 Fax (0091) (33) 282 6340 E-mail samrajubh@vsnl.net
Lucknow	Anil R Stephen Bishop's House, 25 Mahatma Gandhi Marg, Allahabad, UP, 211 001, India Tel (0091) (532) 242 7053 Fax (0091) (532) 256 0713
Marathwada	M. U. Kasab, Bungalow 28/A, Mission Compound, Cantonment, Aurangabad 431 002, MS, India Tel (0091) (240) 237 3136 *fax as telephone*Email revmukasab@yahoo.co.in
Mumbai	Prakash Dinkar Patole 19 Hazarimal Somani Marg, Fort Mumbai 400 001, India Tel (0091) (22) 2206 0248 E-mail bishopbomcni@rediffmail.com
Nagpur	Paul Dupare Cathedral House, Sadar, Nagpur, MS, 440 001, India Tel (0091) (712) 562 1737 Fax (0091) (712) 309 7310 E-mail bishop@nagpur.dot.org.in
Nasik	Kamble Lemuel Pradip Bishop's House, Tarakur, 1 Outram Road, Ahmednagar, Maharashtra, 414 001, India Tel (0091) (241) 241 1806 Fax (0091) (241) 242 2314 E-mail bishopofnasik@rediffmail.com
North East India (Deputy Moderator)	Purely Lyngdoh Bishop's Kuti, Shillong 1, Meghalaya, 793 001, India Tel (0091) (364) 2223 155 Fax (0091) (364) 2501 178 E-mail bishopnei15@hotmail.com
Patna	Philip Phembuar Marandih Bishop's House, Christ Church Compound, Bhagalpur, Bihar, 812 001, India Tel (0091) (641) 2300 714 *fax as telephone* E-mail cnipatna@rediffmail.com

Phulbani	Bijay Kumar Nayak Bishop's House, Gudripori, Gudaigiri, Phulbani, Kandhamal, Orissa, 762 001, India Tel (0091) (6847) 260569 E-mail bp.bkn@rediffmail.com
Pune	Vijay Bapurao Sathe 1A Steveley Road (General Bhagat Marg), Pune, MS, 411 001, India Tel (0091) (20) 2633 4374 E-mail punediocese@yahoo.co.in
Rajasthan	Collin Theodore 2/10 CNI Social Centre, Civil Lines, Opp. Bus Stand, Jaipur Rd, Ajmer 305 001, India Tel (0091) (145) 2420 633 Fax (0091) (145) 2621 627
Sambalpur	Christ Kiron Das Mission Compound, Bolangir, Orissa, 767 001, India Tel (0091) (665) 2230 625 *fax as telephone* E-mail bishop–ckdas@rediffmail.com

SOUTH INDIA

Chennai	V Devasahayam Diocesan Office, PO Box 4914, Chennai, TN, 600 086, India Tel (0091) (44) 2811 3929 Fax (0091) (44) 2811 0608 Email bishopdeva@hotmail.com
Coimbatore	M Dorai Bishop's House, 256 Race Course Road, Coimbatore, TN1, 641018, India Tel (0091) (422) 213 605 Fax (0091) (442) 200 400 Email bishopdorai@presidency.com
Dornakal	B S Devamani Bishop's House, Cathedral Compound, Dornakal, Andhra Pradesh 506 381, India Tel (0091) (8719) 227 752 E-mail bshpindk@yahoo.co.in
East Kerala	K G Daniel Bishop's House, Melukavumattom, Kottayam, Kerala State, 686 652, India Tel (0091) (482) 291 044 *fax as telephone* Email bishopkgdaniel@rediffmail.com
Jaffna	Daniel S Thiagarajah Bishop's Office in Colombo, 36 5/2 Sinsapa Road, Colombo, Sri Lanka Tel (0094) (60) 21495 0795 Fax (0094) (11) 250 5805 Email dsthiagarajah@yahoo.com
Kanyakumari	G. Devakadasham CSI Diocesan Office, 71A Dennis Street, Nagercoil, 629 001, India Tel (0091) (4652) 231 539 Fax (0091) (4652) 226 560 Email csikkd@vsnl.in
Karimnagar	P Surya Prakas Bishop's House, PO Box 40, Mukarampura Post, Karimnagar, Andhra Pradesh, 505 001, India Tel (0091) (878) 226 2229 Email suryaprakash@yahoo.com
Karnataka Central	S Vasanthkumar Diocesan Office, 20 Third Cross, CSI Compound, Bangalore, Karnataka, 560 027, India Tel (0091) (80) 222 3766 Email csikcd@vsnl.com
Karnataka North	J Prabhakara Rao, Bishop's House, All Saints Church Compound, Dharwad, Karnataka State, 580 008, India Tel (0091) (836) 244 7733 Fax (0091) (836) 274 5461 Email bishopprabhakar@yahoo.co.in

Karnataka South	Devaraj Bangera Bishop's House, Balmatta, Mangalore, Karnataka, 575 001, India Tel (0091) (824) 243 2657 Fax (0091) (824) 242 1802 Email bishopbangera@rediffmail.com	

Krishna-
Godavari
G Dyvasirvadam
CSI St Andrew's Cathedral Campus, Main Rd,
Machilipatnam 521 002, AP, India
Tel (0091) (8672) 220 623
E-mail bishopkrishna@yahoo.com

Madhya
Kerala
Thomas Samuel
CSI Bishop's House, Cathedral Road,
Kottayam, Kerala State, 686 018, India
Tel (0091) (481) 2566 536
Fax (0091) (481) 2566 531
E-mail csimkdbishop@sancharnet.in

Madurai-
Ramnad
(Deputy
Moderator)
Christopher Asir
CSI Diocesan Office, 5 Bhulabai Desai Rd,
Chockikulam, Madurai District,
Tamil Nadu, 625 002, India
Tel (0091) (452) 732 0541
Fax (0091) (452) 256 0864
Email bishop@csidmr.net

Medak
Kanak Prasad
Bishop's Annexe, 145 MacIntyre Road,
Secunderabad, Andhra Pradesh, 500 003, India
Tel (0091) (40) 2783 3151
Fax (0091) (40) 2784 4215

Nandyal
P J Lawrence
Bishop's House, Nandyal RS, Kurnool District,
Andhra Pradesh, 518 502, India
Tel (0091) (8514) 222 477
Fax (0091) (8514) 242 255

North Kerala
K P Kuruvilla
PO Box 104, Shoranur,
Kerala State, 679 121, India
Tel (0091) (466) 222 4454
Fax (0091) (466) 222 2545
Email csinkd@md5.vsnl.net

Rayalaseema
K B Yesuvaraprasad
Bishop's House, CSI Compound,
Gooty, Ananthapur District,
Andhra Pradesh, 515 401, India
Tel (0091) (866) 232 5320
Fax (0091) (856) 227 5200

South Kerala
(Moderator)
John Wilson Gladstone
Bishop's House, LMS Compound,
Trivandrum 695 033, Kerala State, India
Tel (0091) (471) 231 5490
Fax (0091) (471) 231 6439
E-mail bishopgladstone@yahoo.com

Thoothukudi-
Nazareth
J A D Jebachdran
Bishop's House, 111/32T, Polpettai Extension,
State Bank Colony, Thoothukudi 628 002 TN,
India
Tel (0091) (461) 234 5430
Fax (0091) (431) 234 6911
Email bishoptnd@dataone.in

Tirunelveli
Jeyapaul David
Bishopstowe, PO Box 118, Tirunelveli, Tamil
Nadu, 627 002, India
Tel (0091) (462) 257 8744
Fax (0019) (462) 257 4525
E-mail bishop@csitirunelveli.org

Trichy-Tanjore
G P Vasanthakumar
PO Box 31, 17 VOC Road,
Tiruchirapalli, Tamil Nadu, 620 017, India
Tel (0091) (431) 771254
Fax (0091) (431) 418485
E-mail csittd@tr.net.in

Vellore
Yesurathnam William
CSI Diocesan Office, 1/A Officer's Lane,
Vellore, North Arcot District, 632 001, India

Tel (0091) (416) 2232 160
Fax (0091) (416) 2223 835
Email bishopwilliam@sify.com

BANGLADESH

Dhaka
Michael S Baroi
St Thomas's Church, 54 Johnson Road,
Dhaka-1100, Bangladesh
Tel (00880) (2) 711 6546
Fax (00880) (2) 712 1632
E-mail cbdacdio@bangla.net

Kushtia
(Moderator)
Paul S Sarkar
94 NS Road, Thanapara, Kushtia, Bangladesh
Tel (00880) (71) 61892
fax as telephone
E-mail cob@citechco.net

PAKISTAN

The Arabian
Gulf (Bishop
for) (Area
Bishop within
the Diocese
of Cyprus)
Azad Marshall
PO Box 688, Lahore,
Punjab, 54660, Pakistan
Tel (0092) (42) 542 0452
E-mail bishop@saintthomascenter.org

Faisalabad
John Samuel
Bishop's House, PO Box 27, Mission Road,
Gojra, Distt Toba Tek Sing, Faisalabad,
Pakistan
Tel (0092) (46) 351 4689
Mobile (0092) 300 655 0074
E-mail jsamuel@brain.net.pk

Hyderabad
Raffique Masih
27 Liaquat Road, Civil Lines,
Hyderabad, Sind, 71000, Pakistan
Tel (0092) (22) 2780 221
Fax (0092) (22) 2285 879
E-mail dohcop@yahoo.com

Karachi
(Deputy
Moderator)
Saddiq Daniel
Holy Trinity Cathedral, Fatima Jinnah Rd,
Karachi 75530, Pakistan
Tel (0092) (21) 521 6843
E-mail sadiqdaniel@hotmail.com

Lahore
(Moderator)
Alexander John Malik
Bishopsbourne, Cathedral Close,
The Mall, Lahore, 54000, Pakistan
Tel (0092) (42) 723 3560
Fax (0092) (42) 722 1270
E-mail bishop_Lahore@hotmail.com

Multan
vacant
113 Qasim Road, PO Box 204,
Multan Cantt, Pakistan
Tel (0092) (61) 458 8799
fax as telephone

Peshawar
Munawar Kenneth Rumalshah
Diocesan Centre, 1 Sir-Syed Road,
Peshawar, NWFP, 25000, Pakistan
Tel (0092) (91) 527 6519
E-mail bishopdop@hotmail.com

Raiwind
Samuel Azariah
17 Warris Road, PO Box 2319,
Lahore 54000, Pakistan
Tel (0092) (42) 758 8950
Fax (0092) (42) 757 7255
E-mail sammyazariah49@yahoo.com

Sialkot
Samuel Pervez
Lal Kothi, Barah Patthar,
Sialkot 2, Punjab, Pakistan
Tel (0092) (432) 264 895
Fax (0092) (432) 264 828
E-mail chs_sialkot@yahoo.com

English Clergy Association

www.clergyassoc.co.uk

Patron: The Rt. Rev'd and Rt. Hon. The Lord Bishop of London;
President:
Professor Sir Anthony Milnes Coates, Bt., B.Sc., M.D., F.R.C.P.

The Association seeks to be a Church of England mutual resource for clergy, patrons and churchwardens requiring information or insight.

2010 Annual Address in London:
The Rt. Hon.
The Baroness Cox, of Queensbury
Founder, HART international relief

Mon. 10th MAY 2010 2pm

**St. Giles-in-the-Fields, London
(St. Giles High St.; Tottenham Court Road tube)**

**12.45pm HOLY COMMUNION (B.C.P.)
Celebrant: The Rev'd John Masding (Chairman)**

Donations to the *Benefit Fund* provide Clergy Holidays: Gifts, Legacies, Church Collections much appreciated. Registered Charity No. 258559

Benoporto-eca@yahoo.co.uk for Membership enquiries.
The Old School House, Norton Hawkfield, Bristol BS39 4HB

The 2009 Annual Address by the Rt. Rev'd Dr. Michael Nazir-Ali entitled **Double Jeopardy: Secularism, Militant Islam and the Christian Faith** is fully reported in the new issue of the Members' journal *Parson & Parish*.

PROVINCIAL OFFICES

From which further information may be sought

Anglican Communion Office   St Andrew's House, 16 Tavistock Crescent, Westbourne Park, London W11 1AP, UK
Tel (020) 7313 3900   E-mail aco@anglicancommunion.org

Australia   Suite 2, Level 9, 51 Druitt Street, Sydney NSW 2000, Australia
Fax (0061) (2) 8267 2727   E-mail gsoffice@anglican.org.au

Bangladesh   St Thomas's Church, 54 Johnson Road, Dhaka 1100, Bangladesh
Fax (00880) (2) 712 1632   E-mail cbdacdio@bangla.net

Brazil   Caixa Postal 11510, Teresópolis, Cep 90841–970, Porto Alegre, RS, Brazil
Fax (0055) (51) 3318 6200   E-mail assis@ieab.org.br

Burma (Myanmar)   140 Pyidaungsu-Yeiktha Road, Dagon PO (11191), Yangon, Myanmar
Fax (0095) (1) 251 405   E-mail cpm.140@mptmail.net.mm

Burundi   BP 2098, Bujumbura, Burundi
Fax (00257) 22 229 129   E-mail peab@cbinf.com

Canada   80 Hayden Street, Toronto ON M4Y 3G2, Canada
Fax (001) (416) 924 0211   E-mail general.secretary@national.anglican.ca

Central Africa   Private Bag 1, Chilema, Malawi
E-mail esjopembamoyo@malawi.net

Central America   Iglesia Episcopal Costarricense, Apartado 2773–1000, San José, Costa Rica
Fax (00506) 253 8331   E-mail anglicancr@racsa.co.cr

Ceylon   Bishop's House, 368/3A Bauddhaloka Mawatha, Colombo 7, Sri Lanka
Fax (0094) (1) 684811   E-mail diocol@eureka.lk

Congo (formerly Zaïre)   PO Box 25586, Kampala, Uganda
Tel (00256) 7764 7495   E-mail eac-mags@infocom.co.ug

England   Church House, Great Smith Street, London SW1P 3NZ, UK
Tel (020) 7898 1000   Fax (020) 7898 1001   E-mail feedback@c-of-e.org.uk

Hong Kong   1 Lower Albert Road, Hong Kong, China
Fax (00852) 2521 2199   E-mail office1@hkskh.org

Indian Ocean   Evêché Anglican, 12 rue Rabezavana, Ambodifilao, 101TNR Antananarivo, Madagascar
Fax (00261) (20) 226 1331   E-mail eemdanta@dts.mg *or* eemtma@hotmail.com

Ireland   Church of Ireland House, Church Avenue, Rathmines, Dublin 6, Republic of Ireland
Fax (00353) (1) 497 8821   E-mail office@rcbdub.org

Japan   65–3 Yarai-cho, Shinjuku-ku,Tokyo 162–0805, Japan
Fax (0081) (3) 5228 3175   E-mail province@nskk.org

Jerusalem and the Middle East   PO Box 3, Doha, Qatar
Fax (00974) 442 4329   E-mail tianyoung@hotmail.com

Kenya   PO Box 40502, 00100 Nairobi, Kenya
Fax (00254) (2) 718 442   E-mail archoffice@swiftkenya.com

Korea   3 Chong-dong, Chung-ku, Seoul 100–120, Korea
Fax (0082) (2) 737 4210   E-mail abgwk@hanmail.net

Melanesia   Provincial Headquarters, PO Box 19, Honiara, Solomon Islands
Fax (0067) 21 890   E-mail kiriau_g@comphq.org.sb

Mexico   Calle La Otra Banda 40, Col. San Angel, Delegación Alvaro Obregón, 01000 México, DF, Mexico
Fax (0052) (55) 5616 4063   E-mail ofipam@att.net.mx *or* habacuc–mx@yahoo.es

New Zealand (Aotearoa, New Zealand and Polynesia)   PO Box 87188, Meadowbank, Auckland, New Zealand
Fax (0064) (9) 521 4490   E-mail gensec@ang.org.nz

Nigeria   Episcopal House, PO Box 212, AD CP, Abuja, Nigeria
E-mail abuja@anglican.skannet.com.ng

North India   CNI, 16 Pandit Pant Marg, New Delhi 110001, India
Fax (0091) (11) 2371 6901   E-mail gscni@ndb.vsnl.net.in

Pakistan   St John's Cathedral, 1 Sir Syed Road, Peshawar, Pakistan
Fax (0092) (91) 277 499

Papua New Guinea   Box 673, Lae, MP, Papua New Guinea
Fax (00675) 472 1852   E-mail acpnggensec@global.net.pg

Philippines   PO Box 10321, Broadway Centrum, 1112 Quezon City, Philippines
Fax (0063) (2) 721 1923   E-mail ecpnational@yahoo.com.ph

Rwanda   BP 2487, Kigali, Rwanda
Tel and fax (00250) 516 162   E-mail egapeer@yahoo.com

Scotland   21 Grosvenor Crescent, Edinburgh EH12 5EE, UK
   Tel 0131 255 6357   Fax 0131 346 7247   E-mail secgen@scotland.anglican.org

South East Asia   PO Box 347, Kuching, 93704 Sarawak, Malaysia
   Fax (0060) (82) 426488   E-mail denwee65@yahoo.com

South India   CSI Centre, 5 Whites Road, Royapettah, Chennai 600 041, India
   E-mail csi@vsnl.com

Southern Africa   20 Bishopscourt Drive, Bishopscourt, Claremont, 7708 South Africa
   Fax (0027) (21) 797 1329   E-mail peo@anglicanchurchsa.org.za

South America   A. Gallinal 1852, Montevideo, Uruguay
   E-mail lego@adinet.co.uy

Sudan   PO Box 604, Khartoum, Sudan
   E-mail ecsprovince@hotmail.com

Tanzania   PO Box 899, Dodoma, Tanzania
   Tel (00255) (26) 232 4565   E-mail akiri@anglican.or.tz

Uganda   PO Box 14123, Kampala, Uganda
   Fax (00256) (41) 251 925   E-mail provinceuganda@yahoo.com

USA   Episcopal Church Center, 815 Second Avenue, New York NY 10017, USA
   Fax (001) (212) 490 3298   E-mail pboffice@episcopalchurch.org

Wales   39 Cathedral Road, Cardiff CF11 9XF, UK
   Tel (029) 2034 8218   Fax (029) 2038 7835   E-mail: information@churchinwales.org.uk

West Africa   PO Box Lt 226, Lartebiokorshie, Accra, Ghana
   E-mail cpwa@ghana.com

West Indies   PO Box N-7107, Nassau, Bahamas
   Fax (001) (242) 322 7943   E-mail primate@bahamas.net.bs

DIRECTORIES OF THE ANGLICAN PROVINCES

Many provinces in the Anglican Communion now maintain online directories of their clergy. The website addresses given below are for the home pages of the provinces concerned. From the home page, follow links either to the online church or clergy directory, or to the pages for individual dioceses and, where available, to the information for individual parishes. The 'Tour' web page on the Anglican Communion Office website (www.anglicancommunion.org/tour/index.cfm) also lists information about Anglican provinces (bishops, provinicial secretary, provincial treasurer), and gives links to online provincial information where this is available.

Where a province is known to publish a printed directory, details are given below. For the provinces not listed here, information should be sought from the provincial secretary or from dioceses.

Australia   www.anglican.org.au

Canada   www.anglican.ca; *Anglican Church Directory*, published annually by Anglican Book Centre, 80 Hayden Street, Toronto ON M4Y 3G2, Canada, Tel (001) (416) 924 1332 Fax (001) (416) 924 2760 E-mail info@afcanada.com

Ireland   www.ireland.anglican.org;

Japan   www.nskk.org; *Seikokai Yearbook*, published annually (in Japanese) by Nippon Sei Ko Kai Provincial Office, 65 Yarai-cho, Shinijuku, Tokyo 162–0805, Japan

Jerusalem and the Middle East   *A Provincial Directory*, published by Provincial Office, Box 1248, 20 Nablus Road, Jerusalem

New Zealand   www.anglican.org.nz; *Clerical Directory*, published annually by General Synod Office, PO Box 11061, Ellerslie, New Zealand, Tel (0064) (9) 525 1380, Fax (0064) (9) 525 1664 E-mail sales@churchstores.co.nz

Nigeria   www.anglican-nig.org

Scotland   www.scotland.anglican.org

Southern Africa   www.anglicanchurchsa.org; *Clerical Directory*, published by CPSA, PO Box 61394, Marshalltown 2107, South Africa Tel (0027) (11) 836 5825 Fax (0027) (11) 836 5782 E-mail publish@mail.ngo.za

Southern Cone of America   *Directorio Provincial*, published every three years: Casilla 50675, Correo Central, Santiago, Chile

United States of America   www.episcopalchurch.org is the main website for ECUSA; the main online directory is to be found at www.redbook.org; *Episcopal Clerical Directory*, published every two years by Episcopal Books and Resources, 815 Second Avenue, NY 100017, USA Tel (001) (212) 716 6117 Fax (001) (212) 716 6206 E-mail bookstore@episcopalchurch.org

The Diocese of Jamaica (fax (001) (876) 968 0618) publishes a *Clerical Directory*.

Close links with many overseas provinces are maintained by the following missionary organizations:

Church Mission Society Watlington Road, Oxford OX4 6BZ Tel 0845-020 1799 or (01865) 787400 Fax (01865) 776375 E-mail info@cms-uk.org

Crosslinks (formerly the Bible Churchmen's Missionary Society)   251 Lewisham Way, London SE4 1XF Tel (020) 8691 6111 Fax (020) 8694 8023 E-mail *via website* www.crosslinks.org (link to Headquarters staff at the foot of the Contact page)

Mission to Seafarers (formerly The Missions to Seamen) St Michael Paternoster Royal, College Hill, London EC4R 2RL Tel (020) 7248 5202 Fax (020) 7248 4761 E-mail depsecgen@missiontoseafarers.org

Mothers' Union Mary Sumner House, 24 Tufton Street, London SW1P 3RB Tel (020) 7222 5533 Fax (020) 7222 1591 E-mail mu@themothersunion.org

Society for Promoting Christian Knowledge 36 Causton Street, London SW1P 4ST Tel (020) 7592 3900 Fax (020) 7592 3939 E-mail spck@spck.org.uk

South American Mission Society Allen Gardiner Cottage, Pembury Road, Tunbridge Wells, TN2 3QU Tel (01892) 538 647 Fax (01892) 525 797 E-mail finsec@samsgb.org

United Society for the Propagation of the Gospel 200 Great Dover Street, London SE1 4YB Tel 0845-273 1701 *or* (020) 7378 5678 Fax (020) 7378 5650 E-mail enquiries@uspg.org.uk

St Paul's Cathedral

SUNDAY SERVICES

0800   **Holy Communion**
(Book of Common Prayer)

1015   **Sung Mattins**

1130   **Sung Eucharist**

1515   **Sung Evensong**

1800   **Evening Service**

On other days of the week the Eucharist is celebrated at 0800 and 1230.

Evensong is usually sung at 1700.

On Feast Days and at other times service times may be subject to change.

Service and visitor information 020 7236 4128
www.stpauls.co.uk

ADDRESSES UNKNOWN

The following are clergy whose addresses are currently unknown. Fuller details are contained in the biographical section. We should be grateful for any information to help us complete our records in respect of these clergy.

ADENEKAN, Latiff Aremu. b 38. **d** 04. Perm to Offic *S'wark* 08-09

APPLEBY, Miss Janet Mohr. b 32. **d** 91. Perm to Offic *Ox* 02-07

ARNOLD, Adrian Paul. b 69. **d** 01. V New Cantley *Sheff* 04-08

ARTUS, Stephen James. b 60. **d** 95. V Norton *Ches* 05-07

ASHLEY, Ms Rosemary Clare. b 60. **d** 05. C Leyton St Cath and St Paul *Chelmsf* 05-09

AUSTIN, Ronald Glyn. b 52. **d** 90. V Llansantffraid, Bettws and Aberkenfig *Llan* 04-06

AVES, Peter Colin. b 57. **d** 88. TV Beaminster Area *Sarum* 03-07

BARNES, Duncan Christopher. b 64. **d** 93. TV Woughton *Ox* 00-08

BARNSLEY, Mrs Angela Vera. b 47. **d** 93. NSM Codicote *St Alb* 93-94

BARRON, Kurt Karl. b 60. **d** 92. P-in-c Mansfield St Lawr *S'well* 01-08

BIRD, Graham Desmond. b 44. **d** 02. NSM Stalham, E Ruston, Brunstead, Sutton and Ingham *Nor* 02-06

BLOCK, Robert Allen. b 62. **d** 88. P-in-c Hammersmith St Luke *Lon* 96-02

BRENTNALL, David John. b 53. **d** 86. V St Alb St Pet *St Alb* 96-09

BRUNN, Steven. b 67. **d** 05. C Chertsey, Lyne and Longcross *Guildf* 05-09

BURKE, Michael Robert. b 61. **d** 89. V Hucclecote *Glouc* 00-09

BUTLER, Betty. b 47. **d** 96. NSM Merthyr Dyfan *Llan* 98-07

BYRNE, David Patrick. b 48. **d** 77. Chapl NW Lon Hosp NHS Trust and Harrow and Hillingdon Healthcare NHS Trust 98-09

CALLAGHAN, Michael James. b 63. **d** 97. NSM Blackheath Park St Mich *S'wark* 94-09

CHRISTIE, David James. b 58. **d** 91. V Patrick Brompton and Hunton *Ripon* 95-09; V Hornby 95-09; V Crakehall 95-09

CLARK, Andrew James. b 50. **d** 94. NSM Walbrook Epiphany *Derby* 03-05

CLARK, Antony. b 61. **d** 88. C Bletchley *Ox* 98-00

CLARK, Brian John. b 48. **d** 00. Perm to Offic *Portsm* 02-06

CROSBY, David Edward. b 48. **d** 99. P-in-c Hurst Green and Mitton *Bradf* 04

DAVIES, Christopher. b 51. **d** 02. NSM Peckham St Sav *S'wark* 02-07

DAVIES, Neil Anthony Bowen. b 52. **d** 78. Perm to Offic *Ox* 99-02

DAVIS, Trevor Lorenzo. b 45. **d** 94. NSM Upper Norwood St Jo *S'wark* 94-00

DEUCHAR, Canon Andrew Gilchrist. b 55. **d** 84. Hon Prov Can Cant Cathl *Cant* from 95; Dioc Audit Officer *Mor* from 08

DINES, The Very Revd Philip Joseph (Griff). b 59. **d** 86. Lic to Offic *Glas* 05-08

DOWNES, Gregory Charles. b 69. **d** 96. Chapl Ox Pastorate 05-06

DOYE, Andrew Peter Charles. b 64. **d** 93. R Wheathampstead *St Alb* 00-09

EADES, David Julian John. b 74. **d** 00. Chapl Essex Univ *Chelmsf* 04-06

EATON, Mrs Margaret Anne. b 44. **d** 86. C Elgin w Lossiemouth *Mor* 06-09; C Aberlour 06-09; C Dufftown 06-09

ECHOLS, Mrs Janet Lyn Roberts. b 58. **d** 95. P-in-c Stapleford *Ely* 02-07

EDMUNDS, Andrew Charles. b 57. **d** 89. V Ripley *Derby* 97-09

ELMES, Sister Evelyn Sandra. b 61. **d** 97. rtd from 89

EMPEY, Clement Adrian. b 42. **d** 74. Hon Chapl Miss to Seafarers from 88; rtd 08

FISHER, Nicholas. **d** 08. NSM Northleach w Hampnett and Farmington etc *Glouc* from 08

FORMAN, Alastair Gordon. b 48. **d** 80. P-in-c Jersey Millbrook St Matt *Win* 95-01; P-in-c Jersey St Lawr 95-01

FOSTER-CLARK, Mrs Sarah Hazel. b 75. **d** 00. Perm to Offic *Man* from 07

FOULDS, John Stuart. b 64. **d** 91

GILLESPIE, Canon Nancy Gillian. b 41. **d** 97. rtd 09

GILPIN, Jeremy David. b 59. **d** 88. Chapl St Hugh's Coll Ox 97-07

GODFREY, Matthew Fenton. b 69. **d** 04. C Bodmin w Lanhydrock and Lanivet *Truro* 04-09

GOLLEDGE, Christopher John. b 66. **d** 92. Perm to Offic *Chich* 95-00

GOODHEW, Mrs Lindsey Jane Ellin. b 66. **d** 93. Hon C Fulford *York* 07-08

GRAHAM, Robert John. b 70. **d** 99. C Nailsea H Trin *B & W* 99-04

GREENE, Prof Colin John David. b 50. **d** 80. USA from 03

HAWORTH, Fiona. b 65. **d** 97. Chapl Worc Univ from 09

HAY, Miss Lesley Jean Hamilton. b 48. **d** 06. C Bethany USA 08; Asst R Hamden from 08

HAYES, Christopher John. b 64. **d** 96. C Heworth Ch Ch *York* 06-07

HEPPER, William Raymond. b 62. **d** 98. Perm to Offic *Lon* from 08

HINTON, Nigel Keith. b 49. **d** 92. Perm to Offic *Lon* from 03

HIRST, Malcolm. b 62. **d** 00. C Farnborough *Roch* 03-08

HOLDAWAY, Simon Douglas. b 47. **d** 81. NSM Gleadless *Sheff* from 81; Tutor Sheff Univ from 81

HOLDSWORTH, Michael Andrew. b 65. **d** 93. TV Sheff Manor *Sheff* 97-99; Tutor Ripon Coll Cuddesdon 97-99

HOLLIDAY, Arthur. b 22. **d** 81. Perm to Offic *Bradf* 91-01

HOLLINGTON, David Mark. b 61. **d** 94. C Cannock *Lich* 95-96

HOLMES, David Roy. b 34. **d** 84. Perm to Offic *St Alb* 00-06

HORTON, Andrew Charles. b 50. **d** 73. TR Selsdon St Jo w St Fran *S'wark* 98-03

HORTON, Cathy Lynne Bosworth. b 62. **d** 99. USA 03-07

HOUGHTON, Timothy John. b 56. **d** 97. C Normanton *Derby* 97-03

HULT, Mrs Anna Eva Hildegard. b 73. Sweden from 08

HUXLEY, Edward Jonathan. b 74. **d** 05. C Sea Mills *Bris* 05-08

HYETT, Derek Walter. b 79. **d** 05. C Edmonton St Alphege *Lon* 05-08; C Ponders End St Matt 05-08

JAMES, Robert William. b 79. **d** 05. C Bradfield St Clare, Bradfield St George etc *St E* 05-07

JEWELL, Mrs Maureen Ann. b 34. **d** 91. Perm to Offic *Chich* 97-09

JOHNSON, Douglas Leonard. b 45. **d** 73. Kenya from 08

JOHNSTON, Thomas David. b 52. **d** 98. P-in-c Daubhill *Man* 05-06

JOYCE, Miss Penelope Anne. b 53. **d** 00. C Cogges and S Leigh *Ox* 03-09

KASIBANTE, Amos Sebadduka. b 54. **d** 79. Chapl Leic Univ *Leic* 02-09

KELK, Michael Anthony. b 48. **d** 83. P-in-c Llangarron w Llangrove, Whitchurch and Ganarew *Heref* 02-08

KIMBERLEY, John Harry. b 49. **d** 76. Chapl Eastbourne Hosps NHS Trust 95-06

KING, David Charles. b 52. **d** 78. V Middle Esk Moor *York* 00-07

KOLOGARAS, Mrs Linda Audrey. b 48. **d** 95. Australia 03-07

LAMB, Graeme William. b 68. **d** 01. P-in-c Whaley Bridge *Ches* 06-09

LAWES, Timothy Stanley. b 57. **d** 88. Sweden from 96

LAWRENCE, Mrs Judith Patricia. b 53. **d** 04. C Glastonbury w Meare *B & W* 04-09

LEWIS, David Antony. b 48. **d** 83. rtd 08

LISTER (nee AISBITT), Mrs Joanne. b 69. **d** 93. NSM Mill End and Heronsgate w W Hyde *St Alb* 93-96

LISTON, Scott Carnie. b 62. **d** 88. rtd 06

LITTLE, Herbert Edwin Samuel. b 21. **d** 80. rtd 88

LLOYD JONES, Ieuan. b 31. **d** 83. Perm to Offic *Ox* 89-06

LOGUE, Mrs Rosemary Christine. **d** 93. Dn-in-c Cambuslang *Glas* 08; Dn-in-c Uddingston 08

LYALL, Richard Keith. b 70. **d** 02. Canada from 08

McBETH, David Ronald. **d** 06. C Glendermott *D & R* 06-09

McCAMMON, John Taylor. b 42. **d** 71. Kenya 98-07

McCARTHY, The Very Revd John Francis. b 38. **d** 62. USA from 94

McCLOSKEY, Robert Johnson. b 42. **d** 67. rtd 01

McDOUGALL, Sally-Anne. b 64. **d** 04. C Glas St Marg *Glas* 04-06

MacGILLIVRAY, Canon Alexander Buchan. b 33. **d** 57. rtd 07

MACKIE, Kenneth Johnston. b 20. **d** 47. Perm to Offic *Roch* 97-08

McLEOD, Ms Susan Margaret. b 48. **d** 95. NSM Charlesworth and Dinting Vale *Derby* 95-02; Chapl Asst S Man Univ Hosps NHS Trust 97-02

MANN, Lt Comdr Anthony James. b 34. **d** 88. rtd 01

MARQUIS-FAULKES, Edmund. b 62. **d** 91. R Bieldside *Ab* 02-07

MARTIN, Peter. b 66. **d** 92. Chapl Lancs Teaching Hosps NHS Trust 06-08

MAYBURY, Paul. b 31. **d** 88. Perm to Offic *Ches* 01-08

MEDHURST, Leslie John. b 56. **d** 85. I Helen's Bay *D & D* 97-05

MICKLETHWAITE, Peter William. b 62. **d** 90. R Windlesham *Guildf* 97-09

MILLER, John Forster. b 32. **d** 83. Perm to Offic *St Alb* 93-00 and *Sarum* 00-06

MILLER, Ronald Andrew John. b 46. d 96. NSM Heywood *Man* 96-09

MILLER, Stephen Michael. b 63. d 91. Miss to Seafarers from 99; Chapl Dubai and UAE from 02

MILLS-POWELL, Mark Oliver McLay. b 55. d 83. Warden Guild of St Jo and St Mary Magd from 08

MIR, Amene Rahman. b 58. d 83. Chapl R Marsden NHS Trust 96-04

MOORHOUSE, Christine Susan. b 49. d 87. Perm to Offic *Worc* 02-07

MORGANS, Paul Hywel. b 61. d 90. Hon C Roath St German *Llan* 99-00

MOYO, Edmore Illingworth. b 71. d 02. NSM Luton St Mary *St Alb* 06-08

MPUNZI, Nduna Ananias. b 46. d 71. TV Worc St Barn w Ch Ch *Worc* 04-08

MYNETT, John Alan. b 37. d 85. Perm to Offic *Ches* 01-05

NEWMAN, Alfred John Gordon. b 19. d 74. Perm to Offic *St E* 84-96 and *Chich* 96-07

NICHOLSON, Stephen Lee. b 65. d 00. Chapl York Univ *York* 05-08

ODEWOLE, Israel Oluwagbemiga Omoniyi. b 68. d 97. Perm to Offic *Man* 06-08

OKECHI, Patrick Otosio. b 62. d 95. V W Bromwich Gd Shep w St Jo *Lich* 02-08

OWEN-MOORE, Ms Petra Davine. b 65. d 98. TM N Wingfield, Clay Cross and Pilsley *Derby* 08-09

PAINE DAVEY, Nathan Paul. b 64. d 92. Perm to Offic *Lon* 01-05

PAINTER, Christopher Mark. b 65. d 00. TV Eccles *Man* 03-07

PARRY, Richard Neil. d 98. TV Canton Cardiff *Llan* 02-06

PATCH, Simon John. b 63. d 95. C Stepney St Dunstan and All SS *Lon* 03-06

PEARSON, Mrs Priscilla Dawn. b 45. d 90. Hon C Woking St Jo *Guildf* 03-05

PERRICONE, Vincent James. b 50. d 90. Asst Chapl Florence w Siena *Eur* 08-09

PETERS, Stephen Eric. b 45. d 77. Perm to Offic *Ex* from 93

PETZER, Garth Stephen. d 88. rtd 07

PHILLIPS, The Very Revd Christopher John. b 46. d 79. Perm to Offic *Ely* 04

PHILLIPSON, Hugh Brian. b 41. d 96. NSM Ox St Mary V w St Cross and St Pet *Ox* 06-08

PORTER, Malcolm Derek. b 53. d 05. C Woodford Wells *Chelmsf* 05-09

PRANCE, Jeremy Roy. b 64. d 99. Perm to Offic *S'well* 05-06

RANKIN, John Cooper. b 24. d 50. rtd 84

RAWLINGS, Gayle Ann Mary. b 53. d 03. Canada from 09

REED, Geoffrey Martin. b 51. d 76. R Teme Valley S *Worc* 01-04

REVELEY, Mrs Valerie Mary. b 39. d 99. NSM Olney *Ox* 99-05

RIGBY, Francis Michael. b 29. d 90. Perm to Offic *Heref* 00-07

ROBINSON, Mrs Gillian Dawn. b 69. d 96. P-in-c Roughtown *Man* 00-07

ROLFE, Paul Douglas. b 46. d 93. Costa Blanca *Eur* 07-08

ROMER, William Miller. b 35. d 60. rtd 08

ROSS (nee YOUNG), Mrs Karen Heather. b 66. d 05. Hon C Ravenshead *S'well* 07-09; Chapl Notts Healthcare NHS Trust 08-09

SANDERS, Diana Louise. b 59. d 98. NSM Clarendon *Sarum* 01-08

SAUNDERS, Moira Ruth Forbes. b 76. d 04. C Welling *Roch* 04-08

SCOTT, Mrs Erica Jane. b 58. d 02. Dn-in-c Whitchurch *Bris* 07-08

SEABROOK, Alistair William. b 78. d 06. Australia from 09

SIMS, Keith George. b 29. d 95. NSM Forest Hill St Aug *S'wark* 95-04

SIMS, Michael Graeme. b 37. d 98. rtd 07

SKILLEN, John Clifford Tainish. b 50. d 89. Asst Ed *The Church of Ireland Gazette* from 99; Bp's Sen Dom Chapl *Conn* from 08

SMAIL, Richard Charles. b 57. d 93. P-in-c Rousham *Ox* from 05

SMITH, Christopher James. b 72. d 02. USA 04-08

SMITH, Ms Gail Sampson. b 49. d 93. USA from 07

SMITH, Steven Barnes. b 60. d 87. Perm to Offic *Lon* from 07

SMITH, Ms Vivienne Ruth. b 57. d 00. TM Dewsbury *Wakef* 03-06

SPENCE, Beth Ann. b 65. d 05. Australia from 08

STAFFORD, Mark Anthony. b 64. d 98. TV Retford *S'well* 02-09; P-in-c Babworth w Sutton-cum-Lound and Scofton etc 08-09

STEVENS, David Norman. b 44. d 03. New Zealand from 06

STOKES, David Francis Robert. b 53. d 03. Perm to Offic *Sarum* from 08

STRATFORD, Niall. d 09. NSM Killiney Ballybrack *D & G* from 09

STUBBS, Canon Trevor Noel. b 48. d 74. Sudan from 09; Lic to Offic *Sarum* from 09; Can and Preb Sarum Cathl from 03

TAYLOR, Peter John. b 60. d 87. R Gatehouse of Fleet *Glas* 97-07

THOMAS, David William Wallace. b 51. d 75. Chapl RN 84-07

THOMAS, John Arun. b 47. d 88. India from 04

THOMPSON, Raymond Craigmile. b 42. d 84. rtd 09

TREASURE, Mrs Joy Elvira. b 23. d 87. rtd 92

TWOMEY, Jeremiah Thomas Paul. b 46. d 87. C Belfast St Anne *Conn* from 08

VIGERS, Neil Simon. b 62. d 90. R Hook *Win* 02-07

WALKER, Richard David. b 45. d 95. Hon C Cromhall, Tortworth, Tytherington, Falfield etc *Glouc* 04-07

WATKINS, Jonathan. b 58. d 92. Chapl Win Univ 99-08

WHATTON, Miss Joanna Nicola. b 72. d 01. C Chislehurst St Nic *Roch* 01-06

WHEATLEY, David Maurice. b 69. d 05. C Cheltenham H Trin and St Paul *Glouc* 07-08

WHEELER, Nicholas Paul. b 60. d 87. Brazil from 08

WICKS, Mrs Susan Joyce. b 51. d 00. R Fenn Lanes Gp *Leic* 04-07

WILKIE, Michael John David. b 65. d 00. NSM Combe Martin, Berrynarbor, Lynton, Brendon etc *Ex* 00-05

WILKINS, Nicki Anne. b 68. d 05. NSM St Andrews St Andr *St And* from 05

WILLIAMS, Bryan George. b 37. d 01. rtd 05

WILLIAMS, Canon David Gordon. b 43. d 68. rtd 08; Perm to Offic Perth from 08 and *Derby* from 09

WILLIAMS, Mary Elizabeth. b 72. d 06. C Birstall and Wanlip *Leic* 06-09

WILLIAMS, Paul Robert. b 66. d 99. Mongolia from 09

WILLIAMS, Robert Edward. b 50. d 74. Chapl Ellesmere Coll 05-08

WRIGHT, Christopher Joseph Herbert. b 47. d 77. Prin All Nations Chr Coll Ware 93-04

WRIGHT, Miss Pamela Jean. b 38. d 03. NSM Harrow Weald St Mich *Lon* 05-08

WYLD, Kevin Andrew. b 58. d 85. USA from 00

YALLOP, John. b 47. d 79. P-in-c Cliftonville *Cant* 94-99

CLERGY WHO HAVE DIED SINCE
THE LAST EDITION

A list of clergy who have died since 3 August 2007, when the compilation of the 2008/09 edition was completed. The month and year of death (if known) are recorded with each entry.

ABBOTT, Charles Peter 01/08
ACHESON, Russell Robert 04/08
ADAM, John Marshall William 09/07
ADDISON, Bernard Michael Bruce 11/07
ADDISON SMITH, Anthony Cecil 10/08
AKEHURST, Peter Russell 10/07
ALDERSON, Christopher Derek 05/08
ALLEN, Thomas Giles 09/08
ALLISTON, Cyril John 07/09
AMOS, Patrick Henry 02/09
ANDERSON, Francis Hindley 12/08
ANDERSON, Gordon Fleming 03/09
ANDERSON, John Michael 11/08
ANGWIN, Richard Paul 03/09
ANSELL, Howard 04/09
APPLETON, Timothy Charles 03/09
ARMFELT, Julian Roger 03/08
ARMITAGE, Bryan Ambrose 02/08
ARMSTRONG, John Hammond 10/07
ARNOTT, Eric William 10/08
ARRANDALE, Richard Paul Matthew 06/08
ARTHINGTON, Muriel 04/09
ARTHUR, Joan Diane 05/08
ASHE, Francis Patrick Bellesme 01/09
ASHWORTH, Edward James 12/07
ASKEW, Sydney Derek 05/08
ASQUITH, Eric Lees 11/08
ATTRILL, Norman Edmund Charles 01/08
AUST, Arthur John 06/09
BAGULEY, Henry 08/08
BAILEY, John Ernest 02/09
✠BAILEY, Jonathan Sansbury 12/08
BALDRY, Ralph Yorke 05/08
BALL, Frank 03/09
BALMFORTH, Anthony James 02/09
BANNISTER, Grattan Eric McGillycuddy Colm Brendon 02/09
BARD, Christopher Frederick Jesse 09/07
BARNES, Cyril Arthur 01/08
BARON, Noel Spencer Peter 02/08
BARR, John Gourlay Crichton 01/08
BATEMAN, Richard William 12/07
BATEMAN-CHAMPAIN, John Nicholas 03/09
BATES, Michael 07/09
BATSLEER, Albert 06/09
BAXTER, Peter James 02/08
BEACOM, Thomas Ernest 04/08
BEAMISH, Frank Edwin 05/08
BEAN, Alan Evison 06/09
BEARDSMORE, Alan 09/08
BEAUMONT, Timothy Wentworth 04/08
BECK, Stephen 12/08
BEDFORD, Christopher John Charles 06/08
BELL, Alan 03/09
BENIANS, Martin Ackland 10/08
BENNETT, Anthony 01/09
BENNETT, Richard Edward Stuart 06/09
BENTLEY, Edward John 01/09
BERG, Paul Michael 12/08
BEVAN, Noel Haden 04/08
BEVIS, Derek Harold 12/08

BIDDER, John 03/08
BILLS, Reginald 02/09
BINDOFF, Stanley 01/08
BIRCH, Arthur James Fleet 04/08
BIRCHMORE, Brian Leonard 03/09
BIRD, Maurice Pidding 06/08
BIRD, Rex Alan 04/08
BIRKET, Cyril 01/09
BISHOP, Michael George 11/07
BLACKMAN, James Bentley 11/07
BLACKMORE, Cuthbert 08/08
BLENNERHASSETT, Richard Noel Rowland 12/08
BOAR, Alan Bennett 01/08
BOLT, David Dingley 09/08
BONSEY, Thory Richmond 05/08
BOOTH, William James 06/09
BOTHAM, Norman 11/07
BOWN, John Frederick Olney 09/08
BOYD, Allan Newby 01/09
BRADFORD, Daphne Marcelle 09/08
BRADSHAW, Kenneth Allan 10/07
BRANNAGAN, Alan McKenzie 06/08
BRIERLEY, David James 08/09
BRISCOE, Gordon Michael 03/09
BROCK, Patrick Laurence 10/08
BROWN, Derek Frederick 07/09
BROWN, Henry 07/09
BROWN, Ivan James 11/07
BROWN, Stanley George 02/08
BROWNE, George William 12/07
BROWNING, Richard Geoffrey Claude 11/07
BROWNING, Thomas Clive 10/08
BRUNDLE, Michael Roy 12/07
BRYANT, Sidney John 01/08
BUCKLEY, Alan 01/08
BUDGE, Leonard Percival 01/09
BURCH, John Anthony 07/08
BURDON, William 06/09
BURGESS, Alfred George 06/09
BURRELL, Maurice Claude 06/08
BURY, Herbert John Malcolm 04/08
BUTTLE, Leslie Ronald Frank 01/09
BUTTREY, Anne Stella Ivy 12/08
CALDWELL, David Denzil 04/08
CANDLER, David Cecil 04/08
CANNING, John Graham 02/09
CARLOS, Francis John 10/08
CARNE-ROSS, Stewart Pattison 11/07
CARRICK, Ian Ross 02/09
CARRY, Edward Austin 03/09
CARTER, Charles Trevelyan Aubrey 12/08
✠CARTWRIGHT, Richard Fox 04/09
CARTWRIGHT, Roy Arthur 10/08
CAVE, Guy Newell 04/09
CAVE, Robert Philip 12/08
CAWLEY, Stephen 09/08
✠CHADWICK, Graham Charles 10/07
CHADWICK, Henry 06/08
CHALKLEY, Henry Roy 01/08
CHAPMAN, John 04/09
CHATHAM, Richard Henry 01/09
CHATTERJI DE MASSEY, Robert Arthur Sovan Lal 11/07
CHENNELL, Arthur John 03/08

CHETWYND, Edward Ivor 07/09
CLAPP, Nicholas Michel Edward 10/07
CLARK, Reginald Isaac 07/09
CLARKE, Maurice Fulford Lovell 11/08
CLARKE, Oswald Reeman 02/08
CLARKE, Vernon Douglas 02/09
CLEASBY, Thomas Wood Ingram 02/09
CLEGG, David Kneeshaw 06/09
CLIFF, Philip Basil 12/07
COBB, Douglas Arthur 11/08
COCKCROFT, Basil Stanley 06/09
CODRINGTON CLARKE, Harold Godfrey 09/08
COLE, Denise Helen 09/08
COLE, Donald Robertson 06/08
COLE, Henry Frederick Charles 10/07
COLTHURST, Reginald William Richard 03/09
COMBER, Keith Charles 08/08
COMMANDER, Reginald Arthur 09/08
COOK, Edward Rouse 11/07
COOK, Kenneth George Thomas 03/09
COOPER, David Jonathan 02/08
COPLEY, David Judd 02/09
COPPEN, Peter Euan 02/09
CORNWELL, Gertrude Florence 12/08
COTTER, John Beresford Dolmage 11/08
COX, George William 05/08
COX, Leonard James William 04/09
CRAVEN, Gordon Forster 03/08
CREERY-HILL, Anthony Thomas 01/08
✠CROCKETT, Phillip Anthony 06/08
CROFTS, Charles Arthur 01/08
CROOKS, Henry Cecil 11/08
CROSSLAND, Joyce 03/09
CROSSLEY, Hugh Vaughan 11/07
CROSSMAN, Charmian Jeanette 06/08
CULLIFORD, Michael 04/09
CUMMINGS, Richard Vivian Payn 08/07
CUMPSTY, John Sutherland 08/08
✠CUNDY, Ian Patrick Martyn 05/09
CURTIS, Frederick John 01/09
CUTHBERTSON, Christopher Martin 10/08
DAILEY, Arthur John Hugh 01/08
DAVENPORT, Michael Arthur 03/09
DAVIES, Stanley James 03/09
DAVIES, Thomas Derwent 12/07
DAVIES, William David 03/08
DAVIS, Christopher Eliot 11/07
DAVIS, William Henry 12/08
DAVISON, Thomas Alfred 01/08
DAWES, Peter Martin 05/08
DAY, John 11/08
DE MURALT, Robert Willem Gaston 02/09
✠de PINA CABRAL, Daniel Pereira dos Santos 06/08
DEAN, Archibald Charles 12/07
✠DEHQANI-TAFTI, Hassan Barnaba 04/08
DELL, Robert Sydney 01/08

DENING, John Cranmer 07/08
DENNIS, John Daniel 03/08
DERISLEY, Albert Donald 04/09
DEWHURST, George 05/08
DICK, Alexander Walter Henry 08/08
DICKER, David 04/08
DIXON, Clive Raylton 01/08
DOBBYN, Michael Newham 10/08
DOHERTY, Terence William 09/07
DOUGLAS, Alexander Joseph 11/08
DOUGLAS, Ian Alexander 01/08
DOUGLAS, John Howard Barclay 06/08
DOVE, Reginald George James Thomas 03/08
DOWDEN, Gordon Frederick 11/08
DRYDEN, Leonard 10/08
DUCKWORTH, Derek 10/08
D'YER, John Alan 07/08
EASTER, Brian James Bert 03/09
EASTER, Stephen Talbot 04/09
EBBITT, Francis Simon 11/07
EDMONDS, Sidney 01/09
EDWARDS, Geoffrey Lewis 09/07
EDWARDS, Gordon Henry 03/08
ELLEANOR, David John 04/08
ELLIOTT, Joseph William 12/07
ELLIOTT, Stanley Griffin 12/07
ELLIOTT, William Norman 07/08
ELLSLEY, Howard 09/08
ELMORE, Graeme Martin 05/09
EMBRY, Eileen Margaret 03/09
✠EMMERSON, Ralph 12/07
EMMETT, Thomas 05/09
EMSLEY, John Stobart 04/08
ENGLISH, Peter Redford 11/07
EVA, Owen Vyvyan 04/08
EVANS, Charles Wyndham 03/08
EVANS, Derek Courtenay 11/08
EVANS, Frank Owen 05/08
EVANS, Glyn 01/09
EVANS, Walter Tenniel 06/09
EVENS, Philip Alistair 12/07
EVEREST, Harold William 01/09
EYLES, David William 12/08
FARRANCE, William Kenneth 12/07
FARRER, Simon James Anthony 09/07
FATHERS, Derek Esmond 12/07
FENNELL, Alfred Charles Dennis 10/08
FENNING, John Edward 01/09
FENTON, John Charles 12/08
FINCH, Edward Alfred 02/09
FIRTH, Barry 03/08
FITZ, Lionel Alfred 12/08
✠FLAGG, John William Hawkins (Bill) 10/08
FLETCHER, George Henry Yorke 08/08
FLETCHER-CAMPBELL, Walter John Fletcher 11/08
FOLLAND, Mark Wilkins 04/09
FOOT, Leslie Robert James 09/07
FORD, John Albert 04/09
FORDER, Charles Robert 10/08
FORREST, Kenneth Malcolm 01/08
FOSKETT, Eric William 08/07
FOSTER, William Basil 10/07
FOX, Nigel Stephen 10/07
FROGGATT, Jeffrey 05/09
FRY, Joan Aileen 11/07
FRYER, Ida Doris 2008
FULLER, Frederick Walter Tom 12/07
FURNESS, Edward Peter Alexander 01/08
GANDON, Percy James 11/08
GARDNER, Clifton Gordon 03/09
GARLICK, Dennis 04/08

GARNER, Martin Wyatt 01/08
GEE, Norman 04/08
✠GENDERS, Roger Alban Marson (Anselm) 06/08
GEORGE, John Thomas 02/08
GERRARD, George Ernest 01/08
✠GIBBS, John 12/07
GILBERT, Frederick Herbert 12/08
GILBERT, Joseph 12/07
GILBERT, Roy Alan 07/08
GILES, Barry James 04/09
GILES, Robert Medwin 10/07
GILL, James Joseph 10/08
GILL, Mary 08/08
GILLHAM, Stephen John 04/08
GLEN, Robert Sawers 02/08
GLOVER, Henry Arthur 11/08
GOOD, William Thomas Raymond 01/09
GOODCHILD, Roy John 11/08
GOODMAN, Denys Charles 07/09
✠GOODRIDGE, Sehon Sylvester 12/07
GOTELEE, Peter Douglas 05/09
GRAHAM, Michael 08/08
GRANT, William James 05/09
GRAY, Frank Harold Castell 05/09
GRAY, Geoffrey Thomas 03/08
GRAYSON, Robert William 12/07
GREEN, Humphrey Christian (Benedict) 09/07
GREEN, John 09/07
GREEN, John Stanley 02/08
GREEN, Norman 02/08
GREEN, Sylvia 03/08
GREENE, David Arthur Kirsopp 11/08
GREENSLADE, Keith James Inglis 01/08
GREG, John Kennedy 03/08
GRELLIER, Brian Rodolph 01/09
GREWCOCK, Peter Joseph 02/08
✠GRINDROD, John Basil Rowland 01/09
GRITTEN, Desmond Digby 12/08
GUPPY, Kenneth Henry Stanley 06/08
HADLEY, Donald Thomas 01/09
HALE, Dennis Ernest (Jim) 06/08
HALL, Charles Bryan 03/09
HALL, Margaret Mercia 02/08
HALL, William Nawton Sinclair 03/08
HALL-CARPENTER, Leslie Thomas Frank 01/08
HALLIDIE SMITH, Andrew 02/08
✠HALSEY, Henry David 05/09
HANCOCK, David Richard 12/08
HANCOCK, Leonard George Edward 11/08
HANCOX, Granville Leonard 01/09
HANDS, Graeme 03/09
HANDSCOMBE, Richard John 05/08
HARDY, Daniel Wayne 11/07
HARGREAVES, Arthur Cecil Monsarrat 06/09
HARGREAVES, John Henry Monsarrat 02/08
✠HARLAND, Ian 12/08
HARMAN, Robert Desmond 12/07
HARRIES, Gwilym David 03/08
HARRIS, Robin Ramsey 01/09
HARRISON, Alan George 10/08
HARRISON, Ian Wetherby 06/09
HARVEY, Arthur Ernest 03/08
HARWOOD, Frederick Ronald 11/08
HASLAM-JONES, Christopher John 03/08
HATTER, David George 01/09

HAUGHAN, John Francis 03/08
HAWKSBEE, Derek John 08/08
HAYDON, Christine Mary 08/08
HAYES, Kenneth Richard 08/07
HAYLLAR, Bruce Sherwill 05/09
HAYTER, Ronald William Joseph 02/09
HAYTHORNTHWAITE, Robert Brendan 12/07
HEATLEY, Henry Daniel 01/08
HENDERSON, James 12/08
HENDEY, Clifford 10/07
HERBERT, Kenneth Cyril 02/09
HERYET, Dudley 06/09
HESKETH, Robin Adams Lempriere 02/09
HESS, John 12/08
HESTER, John Frear 02/08
HEWITT, Harold William 08/08
HICKEY, Francis Joseph (Tony) 12/08
HICKLING, Colin John Anderson 11/07
HIGDON, Lewis George 04/09
HIGGINSON, Gerald Scott 05/08
HILL, Bridget Ann 03/09
HILL, David 12/07
HILL, Geoffrey Dennison 09/07
HILL, Kenneth 11/08
HILL, Leslie Hugh 07/09
HILTON, John Read 07/09
HINTON, Terence 04/09
HOAR, George Stanley 11/07
HODGSON, John Derek 11/07
HOFFMAN, Stanley Harold 12/08
HOLLANDS, Albert William 05/08
HOLLEY, Graham Frank 02/08
HOLLIS, Howard Charles 03/08
HOLT, Harold 11/07
HOPKINS, Ernest 09/07
HOPLEY, William James Christopher 10/08
HOSKYNS, John Algernon Peyton 02/09
HOUGH, Sidney Stephen Valentine 10/07
HOUNSFIELD, Thomas Paul 10/07
HOWARD, Reginald James 10/08
HOWDEN, Frank Newton 08/07
HOWELL, Donald Martin 12/07
HUDSON, Mary Gertrude 03/08
HUGHES, Albert Ashbden 03/08
HUGHES, Arthur William Ronald 01/09
HUGHES, Eunice Nesta 01/08
HUGHES, Hywel Maldwyn 08/07
HUGHES, John Chester 10/08
HUMPHREYS, George Bernard 05/08
HUMPHREYS, John Elwyn Price 03/08
HURRELL, Lionel Rex 11/08
HUTCHINSON, Philip Sheldon 10/08
INGRAM, Michael 05/08
INKPEN, Richard John 11/08
IRWIN, Victor 02/08
ISRAEL, Martin Spencer 10/07
JACK, Robin Watson 08/07
JAMES, Dewi Hirwaun 12/07
JAMES, Idris Frank 12/08
JAMES, Noel Beddoe Walters 11/07
JAMIESON, Hugh Gollan 02/08
JAMIESON-HARVEY, Neil Benedict 12/08
JEFFERY, Norman 06/08
JELLEY, David 11/07
JENKINS, George Patrick 09/08
JENNINGS, Kenneth Neal 12/07
JIGNASU, Nallinkumar Hiralal 12/08
JOHN, Islwyn David 01/09

JOHNS, James Dudley 02/08
JOHNSON, Philip Martin 08/07
JOHNSON, Ronald 02/09
JONES, Edgar John 02/09
JONES, Edward Harries 08/07
JONES, Eric Alexander 12/08
JONES, Eric Wilfred 05/09
JONES, Hugh Owen 07/09
JONES, John Douglas Mathias 05/08
JONES, Kenneth Elwyn 09/07
JORDAN, Kenneth John 02/09
JOYCE, Norman 02/09
KELLY, John Rowe 01/08
KELLY, William Robert (Wilbert) 01/08
KENDRA, Kenneth Ernest 11/07
KENT, Roger Anthony Edward 02/09
KENYON, Stanley Robert 09/08
KEYES, Iris Doreen 01/09
KIDNER, Frank Derek 11/08
KING, Frederick William 02/09
KING, Maurice Charles Francis 11/07
KING, Stuart John Langley 12/07
KIRBY, Mary Elizabeth 11/08
KIRK, Gordon 08/08
KIRKPATRICK, Errol Francis 11/08
KITNEY, Joan Olive Lily 08/08
KNIGHT, Eric Frank Walter 08/08
KNIGHT, Kenneth William 05/08
KNOX, Thomas Anthony 10/07
LAKE, David Eurwyn 01/08
LAMB, John Romney 04/08
LANKEY, David 05/09
LAW, Bryan 01/08
LAW, Peter Leslie 09/07
LAWRENCE, John Shaw 07/08
LAWRENCE, Peter Halliday 02/09
LAWS, Edwin Kingsley 04/08
LEAMING, Ralph Desmond 10/07
LEE, Alan Charles 09/08
LEE, Christopher Garfield 09/07
LEE, William George 07/08
LEESE, Frederick Henry Brooke 12/07
LEGG, John Andrew Douglas 03/09
LEGG, Robert Richard 12/07
LEMPRIERE, Norman Everard 03/08
LENON, Philip John FitzMaurice 04/08
LEVICK, Frank Hemsley 07/08
LEWIS, Albert John Francis 11/08
LEWIS, Robert Charles 08/08
LILLINGTON, Brian Ray 01/08
LINDEN, Gregory 02/09
LINDLEY, Ralph Adrian 02/09
LINDSAY, Cecil 06/08
LLEWELYN, Robert Charles 02/08
LLOYD-JAMES, John Eifion 05/09
LOBLEY, Shirley Bruce Fenwick 03/09
LOCK, David Stephen 08/08
LONG, John Sanderson 06/08
LORD, John Fairbourne 11/07
LOWERSON, John Ridley 06/09
LUCAS, John Arthur 09/07
LUMLEY, William 11/07
LUTTON, Percy Theodore Bell Boyce 11/07
LYTLE, John Deaville 02/09
MacALISTER, Randal George Leslie 06/09
McALISTER, Thomas George 09/08
McCREERY, William Robert Desmond 06/08
MACDONALD, Stephen Calliss 11/08
McGEE, Peter John 09/08
McINTOSH, Andrew Malcolm Ashwell 10/07

McKEMEY, Robert 12/07
MACKENZIE, Alfred Arthur 04/08
MACLEAN, Dorothy 02/08
McLEAN, Frances Ellen 10/08
MACLEAN, John Raglan 04/08
MADDEX, Patrick John 09/07
MADDOCK, Francis James Wilson 11/07
✠MADDOCKS, Morris Henry St John 01/08
MAGAHY, Gerald Samuel 01/08
MAGEE, Patrick Connor 03/08
MAGILL, Waller Brian Brendan 01/09
MAKIN, Hubert 03/08
MALPASS, Clive William 03/09
MARKHAM, Gervase William 12/07
MARLOW, Walter Geoffrey 02/08
MARSHALL, Timothy James 10/08
MARTIN, John Tidswell 09/08
MASSINGBERD-MUNDY, John 09/07
MASTERS, Leslie 04/09
MATTHEWS, Gilbert Brian Reeves 02/08
MATTHEWS, John 11/08
MATTHEWS, Oswald John 10/08
MAYOH, Margaret Evelyn 10/07
MEADOWS, John Michael 11/07
MEADOWS, Stanley Percival 04/09
MELLISS, Laurence John Albert 10/08
MELROSE, Kenneth Mark Cecil 04/08
MELROSE, Michael James Gervase 07/09
MEMBERY, Donald Percy 01/09
MESSENGER, Reginald James 09/08
METCALFE, James 02/09
MILLINER, Llewelyn Douglas 02/09
MILTON, Derek Rees 05/08
MILTON-THOMPSON, David Gerald 01/08
MINHINNICK, Leslie 12/08
MITCHELL, Peter Derek 11/08
MOORE, David 09/08
MOORE, Dennis Charles 10/07
MOORE, Robert Denholm 05/08
MORECROFT, Michael William 03/08
MORGAN, Denis 11/07
MORGAN, Kenneth James 03/08
MORGAN, Thomas John Walford 04/08
MORRELL, Geoffrey Bernard 09/07
MORRIS, Alexander Dorner 02/09
MORRIS, Christopher Mangan 10/07
MORRIS, David Edmond 01/09
MORRIS, Joseph Woodstock 02/09
MORRISON, Alexander Grant 10/07
MORRISON, Dorothy Helen 09/08
MOSS, Victor Charles 11/08
MOULE, Charles Francis Digby 09/07
MOUNTFORD, John 07/09
MOWAT, Geoffrey Scott 05/08
MOYNAN, William John 01/09
MULLARD, George Edward 01/09
MULLENGER, Alan Edward Clement 02/08
MURRAY, Robert Blake 07/09
NATERS, Charles James Reginald 01/09
NELSON, Allen James 03/08
NESHAM, George Dove 12/07
NEVILLE, Graham 04/09
NEVIN, Ronald 02/09
NEWBON, Eric 12/07
NEWMAN, Graham Anthony 11/07
NEWTON, Roger James 03/09

NIBLETT, David John Morton 04/09
NICHOLAS, Arnold Frederick 07/08
NICHOLAS, Herbert Llewellyn 03/09
NICHOLLS, Alan Fryer 02/09
NICKSON, Patricia Jane 04/09
✠NOAKES, George 07/08
✠NORGATE, Cecil Richard 10/08
O'CONNOR, Nigel George 07/08
O'HANLON, William Douglas 11/08
ORMSBY, Diana Clare 02/08
OWEN, Lionel Edward Joseph 10/07
PAGE, Alan George 08/08
✠PAGE, Dennis Fountain 01/09
PAKENHAM, Stephen Walter 10/08
PALIN, John Edward 11/08
PARADISE, Bryan John 06/09
PARFITT, Neil 09/07
PARKER, David Arthur 11/07
PARKINSON, Raymond Neville 02/09
PARRY, William Daniel 09/07
PARSONS, David 04/09
PATERSON, Rita 09/07
PATTERSON, Ian Francis Riddell 04/08
PAXMAN, Denis James 04/09
PAYNE, Denis Alfred 12/08
PEAKE, Simon Jeremy Brinsley 06/09
PEARSON, Roderick Percy 09/07
PEATFIELD, Alfred Charles Henry 08/08
PEGG, Gerald Francis 05/09
PENN, Arthur William 02/08
PIKE, Horace Douglas 05/08
PILKINGTON, Christopher Frost 10/07
PLACE, Donald Lee Andrew 11/07
PLUMPTRE, John Basil 06/09
POLLARD, James Adrian Hunter 03/09
POOLE, Frederick Harold 09/07
POPPLE, Dennis 04/08
PORTER, Kenneth Wilfred 05/09
POTTS, William Gilbert 09/07
POUNDE, Nigel 04/08
POWELL, Raymond Leslie 11/08
POYNTING, Charles Robert Macvicar 09/07
PRATT, Benjamin John 06/08
PRICE, Frank Watkin 04/08
PRICE, William Haydn (Dai) 05/08
PRIESTLY, Thomas Herbert 08/07
PROPHET, John Roy Henderson 03/08
PROSSER, Malcolm George 03/09
PROUT, Hubert Douglas 12/08
PRUEN, Hugh Barrington 04/09
QUENNELL, Brian Michael 01/08
QUINN, Cecil Hugh 03/08
RAIKES, Myles Kenneth 07/08
RAMELL, John Edwin 04/08
READING, Laurence John 10/07
REDGRAVE, Cecil Goulden 02/09
REES, Brynley Mervyn 04/09
REES, Eric Vernon 05/09
REYNOLDS, Alfred Stanley 10/07
RHODES, David 08/08
RICE, Brian Keith 12/08
RICE, Brian Thomas 05/09
RICHARDS, John 05/09
RICHARDSON, Joseph Edmund 11/07
RICHARDSON, Maurice 11/08
RIDER, Kenneth 12/08
RIGBY, Michael John 07/08
RIPPINGALE, Denis Michael 12/07
ROBBINS, Richard Harry 09/08
ROBERTS, Elwyn 02/09
ROBERTS, James Arthur 06/08

ROBERTSON, Ernest Ian 12/08
ROE (*née* PROWSE), Elizabeth Helen 02/09
ROGERS, Alan David 12/07
ROGERS, Noel Desmond 10/08
ROGERSON, David George 11/07
ROOT, Howard Eugene 11/07
ROSE, Gordon Henry 12/08
ROSE, Judith Anne 10/07
ROSHEUVEL, Siegfried Winslow Patrick 02/09
ROTHERY, Cecil Ivor 12/07
ROWE, Antony Silvester Buckingham 11/07
✠ROXBURGH, James William 12/07
RUMBALL, Frank Thomas 05/08
RUNCORN, Dennis Brookes 10/07
RUSSELL, David Edward 10/08
RUTHERFORD, David Lesslie Calderwood 05/09
SAINT, Arthur James Maxwell 11/07
SALMON, Bernard Bryant 06/08
SALTER, Richard 12/08
SAMBELL, David John 03/09
SAMMONS, John Trevor 08/08
SANDFORD, (John Cyril Edmondson) 01/09
SARGEANT, Kenneth Stanley 03/08
SATTERFORD, Douglas Leigh 04/09
SCAMMELL, John Richard Lyn 07/08
SCOTT, Ian 07/09
SEAMAN, Brian Edward 01/08
SEGAL, Michael Bertram 03/08
SELMAN, Cyril Allen 06/09
SEMEONOFF, Robert 02/09
SHAFEE, Kenneth Harold 07/08
SHAW, Colin Martin 10/07
SHAW, Ernest Ronald 08/07
SHAW, Gary Robert 01/09
SHEASBY, Adrian 11/07
SHEPHERD, Peter James 12/07
SHERGOLD, William Frank 05/09
SHERLOCK, Desmond 01/09
SHONE, Raymond 07/09
SIMMONDS, William Hugh Cyril 10/08
SIMPSON, Thomas Eric 12/08
SINNICKSON, Charles 12/07
✠SITSHEBO, Wilson Timothy 09/08
SKIPPER, Lawrence Rainald 05/09
SLACK, Ellis Edward 03/08
SMALLEY, Kathleen 11/08
SMALLMAN, Sheila Maxine 07/09
SMETHURST, Gordon James 11/08
SMITH, Alfred Lawrence 02/09
SMITH, Douglas David Frederick 06/09
SMITH, Graham Francis 07/08
SMITH, John Eckersley 10/08
SMITH, Tony 01/09
SMYTHE, Ronald Ingoldsby Meade 10/08
SNAPE, Bernard Reginald Roy 02/08
SNELGAR, Douglas John 06/08
SPANNER, Douglas Clement 05/09
SPARKES, Colin Anthony 05/09
SPINNEY, Giles Martin 11/07
SQUIRE, John Brinsmead 09/08
STARR, Michael Reginald 11/08
STEAD, George Christopher 05/08
STEADMAN, Norman Neil 02/09
STEARN, Peter Reginald 09/08

STEELE, David Robert 03/09
STEPHENS, Ronald John 05/09
STEVENS, Frank Hayman 01/09
STEVENSON, Derick Neville 08/08
STEWART, Alexander Butler 09/08
STOCKLEY, Roland 09/08
STONE, Andrew Francis 03/08
STORR VENTER, Phillip 12/08
STRANACK, Fay Rosemary 09/08
STRANGE, Michael Paul 05/08
STRETTON, George Peter 03/09
STUBLEY, Peter Derek 05/09
SWABY, John Edwin 02/08
SWEET, John Philip McMurdo 07/09
SWEET-ESCOTT, Richard Mark 02/08
SYMONS, Fernley Rundle 06/08
TABERNACLE, Peter Aufrere 07/09
TABRAHAM, Albert John 06/08
TADMAN, John Christopher 12/07
TAMBLING, Peter Francis 12/08
TAYLOR, Gordon Clifford 06/09
TAYLOR, Janette Elizabeth 05/09
TAYLOR, Ronald Enfield Bisset 02/09
TEAGUE, Robert Hayden 07/09
TESTER, Francis Edward 04/08
THACKER, Kenneth Ray 11/07
THOM, Thomas Kennedy Dalziel 07/08
THOMAS, Arthur Norman 07/08
THOMAS, Geler Harries 02/09
THOMAS, Peter George Hartley 11/08
THOMPSON, David John 04/08
THOMPSON, George Harry Packwood 03/09
THORNTON, Cecil 10/07
THORPE, John Wellburn 11/07
TIDMARSH, Peter Edwin 09/08
TOON, Peter 04/09
TORRY, Alan Kendall 12/08
TRENCHARD, Hugh 11/07
TRINDER, John Derek 09/08
TROUNSON, Ronald Charles 05/09
TRUEMAN, Reginald 11/08
TULLOCH, Walter Harold 10/07
TURRALL, Albert Thomas George 03/08
TYLER, William Stanley 06/08
UDY, John Francis 06/08
UNDERWOOD, Jack Maurice 10/08
UPTON, Donald George Stanley 05/09
✠VERCOE, Whakahuihui 09/07
VINCENT, Noel Thomas 07/09
VYVYAN, John Philip 08/08
WADDLE, William 11/07
WADE-STUBBS, Edward Pomery Flood 12/07
WAINWRIGHT, Raymond Laycock 04/08
WALKER, Dennis Richard 04/09
WALKER, Douglas 02/08
WALKER, Graham 02/09
WALKER, Jill Dorothy Ann 05/09
WALKER, John Frederick 09/07
WALKER, John Michael 08/08
WALL, Martyn Philip Lucas 03/08
WALNE, John Clifford 12/08
WALSH, Bertram William Nicholas 03/08
WALTER, Christopher Stuart Radclyffe 09/08

WARD, Stanley Gordon 05/09
WARD-BODDINGTON, Douglas 03/09
WARREN, Clifford Frederick 04/09
WATKINS, Alfred Felix Maceroni 12/08
WATSON, John Derrick 02/09
WAY, Anthony Hilton 06/09
WEBB, Albert 04/08
WEBB, David Basil 04/08
WEBSTER, Alan Brunskill 09/07
WEBSTER, Peter 10/07
WELCH, Francis Hughan 06/08
WELLER, John Christopher 10/08
WEST, Arthur 09/08
WESTON, Christopher James 02/09
WHITE, Dudley William 10/07
WHITE, Trevor John 07/09
WHITING, Antony Gerald Stroud 12/08
WHITTAKER, John 07/08
WHITTAKER, John 10/07
WHYTE, Herbert Blayney 06/08
WIDDOWS, John Christopher (Kit) 12/07
WILKIE, Alan James 02/08
WILLIAMS, Anthony Riley 08/08
WILLIAMS, Cecil Augustus Baldwin 08/07
WILLIAMS, George Melvin (Kim) 02/08
WILLIAMS, Graham Ivor 06/09
WILLIAMS, Jack 12/08
WILLIAMS, John Francis Oliver 03/08
WILLIAMS, Joy Margaret 02/09
WILLIAMS, Mark Naylor 04/08
WILLIAMS, Richard Glyndwr 12/07
WILLIAMS, Tom David 03/08
WILLIAMS, William John 09/07
WILLIS, Marilyn Lesley 11/08
WILSON, John Christopher Heathcote 10/08
WILSON, John Hewitt 06/08
WILSON, Joseph William Sidney 01/08
WILSON, Paul Hugh 04/08
WINCH, Victor Edward 03/09
WINTER, Ernest Philip 05/08
WINTERBOURNE, George 08/08
WOLSTENHULME, Arthur James 09/07
WOOD, George Robert 04/09
WOOD, Peter Thomas 07/09
✠WOOD, Richard James 10/08
WOODS, Christopher Samuel 12/07
WOODS, John Mawhinney 06/09
WOODWARD, Reginald Charles Huphnill 07/09
✠WOOLLCOMBE, Kenneth John 03/08
WOOLLEY, John Alexander 10/08
WOOLLEY, Susan Margaret 12/07
WORSDELL, William Charles 09/07
WRIGHT, Antony John 12/08
WRIGHT, William Easton 02/08
WYNGARD, Ernest Clive 03/09
YATES, James Ainsworth 01/09
YATES, John 02/08
✠YOUNG, David Nigel de Lorentz 08/08
YOUNG, Desmond Terence 03/09
YOUNG, Raymond Grant 06/08
ZACHAU, Eric 04/08

ENGLAND AND WALES

Provincial Boundary
Diocesan Boundary
• Cathedral City

0 10 20 30 40 50miles
0 20 40 60 80km

SCOTLAND

IRELAND

NEWCASTLE

DURHAM

CARLISLE

YORK

RIPON
AND
LEEDS

BRADFORD

BLACKBURN

MANCHESTER

LIVERPOOL

CHESTER

WAKEFIELD

SHEFFIELD

SODOR
AND MAN

ST ASAPH

DERBY

SOUTHWELL
&
NOTTINGHAM

LINCOLN

The Channel Islands are annexed to the Diocese of Winchester

The Isles of Scilly are included in the Diocese of Truro

SCOTLAND

| 0 | 10 | 20 | 30 | 40 | 50miles |
| 0 | 20 | 40 | 60 | 80km |

〜〜〜 Provincial Boundary

〜 Diocesan Boundary

● Location of Cathedral

ABERDEEN AND ORKNEY

ABERDEEN AND ORKNEY

SHETLAND ISLANDS

MORAY, ROSS AND CAITHNESS

Inverness

ABERDEEN AND ORKNEY

Aberdeen ●

ARGYLL AND THE ISLES

● Oban

ST ANDREWS, DUNKELD AND DUNBLANE

BRECHIN

Perth ● Dundee ●

Glasgow ●

Edinburgh ●

GLASGOW AND GALLOWAY

EDINBURGH

IRELAND

ENGLAND

IRELAND

| 0 | 10 | 20 | 30 | 40 | 50miles |

| 0 | 20 | 40 | 60 | 80km |

━━ Provincial Boundary

── Diocesan Boundary

── National Boundary

● Location of Cathedral

CONNOR

● Londonderry

Raphoe
●

DERRY AND RAPHOE

Belfast
●
Lisburn

Dromore
●

ARMAGH

Clogher
●

Enniskillen
●

Armagh
●

CLOGHER

DOWN
AND
DROMORE

Downpatrick
●

Sligo
●

Killala
●

Kilmore
●

KILMORE, ELPHIN
AND ARDAGH

Trim
●

TUAM, KILLALA
AND ACHONRY

Tuam
●

MEATH AND KILDARE

Dublin
●

Clonfert
●

Kildare
●

DUBLIN AND
GLENDALOUGH

LIMERICK, ARDFERT, AGHADOE,
KILLALOE, KILFENORA, CLONFERT,
KILMACDUAGH AND EMLY

Leighlin
●

Kilkenny
●

Ferns
●

Killaloe
●

CASHEL, WATERFORD, LISMORE,
OSSORY, FERNS AND LEIGHLIN

Limerick
●

Cashel
●

Waterford
●

CORK, CLOYNE
AND ROSS

Lismore
●

Cork
●

Cloyne
●

Ross
●

1279